WITHDRAWN

DONATED TO THE
FOND DU LAC PUBLIC LIBRARY
BY
BERNICE AND ROBERT SEEFELD
TRUST

DIRECTORY OF

HISTORICAL

ORGANIZATIONS

IN THE UNITED STATES AND CANADA

Fifteenth Edition

DIRECTORY OF

HISTORICAL

ORGANIZATIONS

IN THE UNITED STATES
AND CANADA

Fifteenth Edition

American Association for State and Local History

A Division of
ROWMAN & LITTLEFIELD PUBLISHERS, INC.
Walnut Creek • Lanham • New York • Oxford

ALTAMIRA PRESS
A Division of Rowman & Littlefield Publishers, Inc.
1630 North Main Street, #367
Walnut Creek, CA 94596
www.altamirapress.com

Rowman & Littlefield Publishers, Inc.
4720 Boston Way
Lanham, MD 20706

12 Hid's Copse Road
Cumnor Hill, Oxford OX2 9JJ, England

ISBN 0-7591-0002-0
ISSN 1045-465X

Printed in the United States of America

The paper used in this publication meets the minimum requirements of American National Standard for Information Sciences—Permanence of Paper for Printed Library Materials, ANSI/NISO Z39.48–1992.

Contents

A Note from the Director of AASLH

AASLH and AltaMira Press are pleased to provide for you the fifteenth edition of the Directory of Historical Organizations in the United States and Canada. First published 1936 with 583 entries, the Directory's fifteenth edition now includes approximately 13,000 entries. The Directory is known in the United States and Canada as the most comprehensive list of state and local history organizations.

Even as this issue of the Directory goes to print in the year 2001, AASLH is busy pulling together a plan to comb grassroots communities in search of organizations we might have missed. For the first time in its sixty-five year history, the Directory has been put together using modern technology. The fourteenth edition published in 1990 and every previous issue was not able to take advantage of the technology available today for maintaining such a monster project. However, rest assured that AASLH and AltaMira Press have now put the Directory into the 21st century. And AASLH's relatively new partnership with AltaMira Press promises updates more often, utilizing new methods of discovery to search out history organizations in every community.

I hope you enjoy the fifteenth edition of the Directory of Historical Organizations in the United States and Canada. And please, let us know if you have changes to the information included in this directory or if you know of an institution that we've missed.

Terry Davis
Executive Director and CEO
American Association for State and Local History

Introduction

Creating A Directory

The creation of a new edition of the *Directory of Historical Organizations in the United States and Canada* had been a high priority both for AASLH and for AltaMira Press since the beginning of their publishing partnership in 1995. The project was begun in earnest in 1998 when the two organizations agreed to pool their resources to develop the book, assisted by a generous donation from *The History Channel.*

AASLH began to accumulate mailing lists to solicit information from the thousands of history organizations in North America. State, provincial, and regional historical associations, museum associations, state historic preservation offices, and historical agencies were solicited for their contacts. AASLH membership lists and AltaMira customer lists were added to the growing list. Other national organizations were also approached for their relevant member rolls. Both AASLH and AltaMira Press are deeply indebted to the directors and staff of these many organizations who provided us with the material necessary to find historical organizations in their states and provinces.

Simultaneously, the AASLH staff developed a four page questionnaire designed to elicit large amounts of valuable information from these organizations—a scale of information gathering far more extensive than that for previous editions of the *Directory.* The questionnaire was tested and reviewed by AASLH and AltaMira staff and by an AASLH committee consisting of Sandra Sageser Clark, Carey Caldwell, Debbie Kmetz, Gretchen Sullivan Sorin, Bryant Tolles, Terry Barnhart, and Michael Hammond. The final questionnaire was sent to well over 20,000 potential respondents, of which approximately 10,000 returned completed questionnaires. Follow-up questionnaires were sent to those who did not return the first one. State-level historians proffered their assistance in encouraging their state's organizations to respond to the information requests. Many additional organizations were added through phone and web research, as well as from informal contacts.

Other sources for accurate data on historical organizations were added to the general questionnaire mailings. An interim *Directory of Historic House Museums,* prepared for AltaMira and AASLH by Patricia Walker and the late Thomas Graham and published in 2000, was also incorporated in the final product. David Vanderstel of the National Council on Public History generously compiled a detailed list of public history programs in North America.

Organizations in the last edition of the directory, now over ten years old, were also solicited for updated information. But the world had changed since the publication of the 14th edition in 1990, and most of the organizations who had not already returned a questionnaire for the 15th edition either did not respond to this solicitation or mail to them was returned by the post office.

While the search process was designed to be inclusive, the selection criteria for what constituted an historical organization needed to be determined. Clearly, historical societies, historic houses, historical agencies, history museums of any sort, historic sites, historical gardens, archives, genealogical societies, tribal museums, and corporate history museums were designed to be included in this listing. While the bulk of the organizations were non-profit organizations, some for-profit historical organizations are also in the mix. General museums that maintained a historical collection and interpreted it were also deemed appropriate.

Excluded were some museums—natural science, art, botanical gardens—in which historical objects were not collected or for which historical interpretations were not attempted. Some for-profit organizations that claimed to be "historical" but whose primary mission was commercial were also deemed improper for listing here. We apologize in advance to any organization that was improperly left out because of misinterpretation of the material provided.

Once the thousands of questionnaires were received, they were processed by the staff at AltaMira Press, directed first by Pam Lucas, then by Susan Walters and Terry Cook. The directory staff entered this information into a specially-designed database and edited entries for consistency, appropriateness, and length. Entries were then sent back to the organizations to verify their accuracy before being finalized for publication. Final editing and page layout were done by Walters, Cook, and the rest of the directory staff. Cover illustrations and the house icon were created by Terry Cook.

Features of the Directory

The 15th edition differs from its predecessors in several ways. There are very few abbreviated entries in this edition. Every attempt was made to provide not only contact details for organizations but also some information on who they are and what they do, and wherever possible web and email addresses are included. New sections were added giving hours and admission fees.

University history departments are no longer included as this information is readily available in a more comprehensive fashion elsewhere. However, a special section was added to the Directory giving detailed information on history departments that offer formal Public History training.

Tales of the Directory

Any three-year long project involving a staff of more than twenty people and hundreds of contacts will have its moments. Scribbles on returned questionnaires provided some interesting translation challenges for the staff. Length limits were occasionally ignored by enthusiastic museum staff eager to show off their institution to the wider world. A flawed database design further tested the staff's ability to be flexible and patient and resulted in some lost data that could not be recovered for the final product. Not all organizations will find humorous the errors that inevitably remain in this document. We apologize in advance for them and hope to hear from these organizations so that we might correct the errors in future editions.

Still, we at AASLH and AltaMira Press were amazed at the extent and diversity of North American historical organizations. We each have our favorite ones and ones that we never knew existed before engaging in this project—the ones we'll visit on our next vacation. The sheer quantity of historical-based institutions in North America is impressive and gives hope for the future of the past in the United States and Canada.

What's Next, A New Edition?

For the first time, the entire corpus of information on these 10,000 historical organizations has been digitized to form the core of an ongoing database to be maintained by AASLH. The organization is proceeding with plans to create a history census to identify still thousands of other history institutions not ferreted out in the extensive research done for this directory. Updates to the Directory will be ongoing, so that the process of creating the next hard copy edition of the directory will be much easier. And the information will be available from AASLH in the interim for those who need it. An electronic edition of this directory is also contemplated. Certainly, it should not be another eleven years before the 16th edition of the *Directory of Historical Organizations in the United States and Canada* sees the light of day.

We encourage you to keep in touch so that the next edition can be even more complete and accurate than this one. To add an entry, or correct one that appears here, please contact history@aaslh.org or write to the AASLH at 1717 Church Street, Nashville, TN 37203.

Susan C. Walters
Terry A. Cook
AltaMira Press

Reading the Directory

The *Directory* is organized alphabetically by state and by city within each state. Occasionally a city may have two listings if its name begins with the word Fort or Saint, one listing beginning with the full word and one beginning with the abbreviation (Ft. or St.). If you are looking for an entry in one of these cities please check under both options. We apologize for this inconsistency, which will be corrected in future editions.

On page 9 is a sample entry with explanatory boxes detailing the material within each section of an entry. Not every entry will contain every section—sometimes this information was not provided or does not exist.

Each individual entry begins with a unique identifying number. This number is used as a locator device in the two indexes found in Part IV. The numbers move sequentially through the book and the range of numbers on each page appears at the top of the page. Once you know the number of the organization you are looking for you can quickly locate its entry by referring to the top of the page.

A word of caution regarding email and web addresses—these change often! As the web stabilizes and more organizations are able to create permanent sites under their own names changes will be reduced. In the meantime we realize some addresses provided here may not work and we ask that organizations advise AASLH of updates.

In formatting web and email addresses we have left off the http:// in all cases. Thus most addresses begin with "www," when they do not the "www" is not part of the address. We have made every attempt to break web and email addresses only at periods (.), slashes (/), and "at" signs (@). If a web or email address continues on to another line it should be typed exactly as it appears in the entry without introducing any additional spaces. If a hyphen appears in an address it is part of the official address.

In general, wording has been standardized in descriptive sections for consistency and space-saving. Don't be fooled by this standardization, there is a wealth of vibrant and active organizations represented here. Our goal here is to provide enough information to get you started on your project, whatever it may be, and facilitate future contact with these organizations.

Key to Abbreviations

We have tried to keep abbreviations to a minimum throughout the *Directory*, however, a few were necessary in order to conserve space and standardize information. They are identified below

In the Name and Address section of each entry the following abbreviations are used:

(p): phone number
(f): fax number
(c): county

In the Agency Details section the following are used:

(f): full time
(p): part time
(v): volunteer

In descriptive paragraphs a number followed by a lowercase "c" indicates a century, e.g., 18th c means eighteenth century. When needed for brevity we have used the US and Canadian postal service's two-letter state and province abbreviations.

In the HOURS section the following are used:

Yr: year around
Daily: Sunday-Saturday
Appt: appointment
Mbrs: members
Mem Day: Memorial Day

Days: M, T, W, Th, F, Sa, Su
Months: Jan, Feb, Mar, Apr, May, June, July, Aug, Sept, Oct, Nov, Dec

Sample Entry

State or Province

CALIFORNIA

City

LODI

Entry ID Number
(also used in indexes as item locator)

Name of organization

9846
San Joaquin County Historical
Society and Museum

11793 N Micke Grove Rd [PO Box 30,
95240-0030]; (p) (209) 331-2055; (f)
(209) 331-2057; info@sanjoaquinhistory.
org; www.sanjoaquinhistory.org; (c) San
Joaquin

Street address, zip or postal code
[mailing address, zip or postal code];
telephone; fax; e-mail; website; county

Type of agency/ year founded/ operates under authority of/ number of
staff: (f)full time; (p)part time; (v)volun-
teers/ number of dues-paying mem-
bers/ major publication title(s)

County/ 1966/ San Joaquin County Historical Society/ staff: 5 (f); 3 (p) 120 (v)/
members: 2000/ publication: *Historian*;
News and Notes

GARDEN; HISTORICAL SOCIETY; HIS-
TORY MUSEUM; LIBRARY AND/OR
ARCHIVES; LIVING HISTORY/OUT-
DOOR MUSEUM: Collects, preserves,
and interprets local San Joaquin history,
the county's evolution of agricultural
growth, social, cultural, and economic heritage; providing continuing education, enrichment, and knowledge of local history.

Type of organization: Description of
the organization and its operations

Major programs

PROGRAMS: Annual Meeting; Community Outreach; Concerts; Exhibits; Family
Programs; Festivals; Film/Video; Garden
Tours; Guided Tours; Interpretation; Lectures; Living History; Publication; Research Library/Archives; School-Based
Curriculum

COLLECTIONS: [1850-1950] Agricultural history, San Joaquin County history,
pioneers, archives, foot and hand-pow-
ered tools, photographs, county historic
buildings, and furnishings.

[Major period of collections]
Description of collections.

Hours/Days open to public

HOURS: Yr W-Su 1-4:45

Admission fees

ADMISSION: $2, Children $1, Seniors $1

9

Staff

Managing Editors
Terry A. Cook & Susan C. Walters
Pamela L. Winding

Contributing Staff
Mitch Allen
Buzz Brown
Molly Clarkson
Lora Collier
Kelly Cook
Nicolette Cook
Erin Dye
Grace Ebron
Nan Hara
Bronwyn Hoffpauir
Lise Marken
Sam Markham
Erica Mulkey
Kat Mulkey
Alex Nattkamper
Kathy Paparchontis
Detta Penna
Rosalie Robertson
Dennis Szelestey
Mary Tolstick

PART I

Historical Organizations in the United States

ALABAMA

ALICEVILLE

1
Aliceville Museum
104 Broad St, 35442; (p) (205) 373-2363; (f) (205) 373-3415; museum@pickens.net; www.pickens.net/~museum

Private non-profit/ 1993/ staff: 1(f); 2(p); 20(v)/ members: 305/publication: *Museum News*

HISTORY MUSEUM: Collects, preserves, and interprets artifacts from a WW II German POW camp (1942-1945) and from Pickens County's military and agricultural history.

PROGRAMS: Exhibits; Festivals; Guided Tours; Interpretation; Lectures; Publication; Reenactments

COLLECTIONS: [20th c] Art objects, photographs, publications, and manuscripts from and relating to Camp Aliceville; military artifacts from Pickens County, Alabama veterans, farm equipment, Coca-Cola assembly line equipment (1948-1978), and Coca-Cola memorabilia.

HOURS: Yr M-F 10-4, Sa 10-2

ADMISSION: $3, Student $2, Seniors $2

ANNISTON

2
Anniston Museum of Natural History
800 Museum Dr, 36202 [PO Box 1587, 36202]; (p) (256) 237-6766; (f) (256) 237-6776; info@ anniston museum.org; www.annistonmuseum. org; (c) Calhoun

1930/ Anniston Museum Board/ staff: 22(f); 7(p); 250(v)/ members: 1567

NATURAL HISTORY MUSEUM: Exhibits mounted animals in realistic displays combined with interpretive labels.

PROGRAMS: Community Outreach; Concerts; Exhibits; Facility Rental; Festivals; Garden Tours; Guided Tours; Lectures

COLLECTIONS: [Prehistory-present] Dinosaurs and fossils, mammals in open dioramas, four hundred specie bird collection, two Egyptian mummies, walk-through replica of an Alabama cave, nature trails and changing art exhibits.

HOURS: May-Sept M-Sa 10-5, Su 1-5: Sept-May T-Sa 10-5, Su 1-5

ADMISSION: $3.50, Children $2.50

3
Berman Museum of World History
840 Museum Dr, 36202 [PO Box 2245, 36202]; (p) (256) 237-6261; (f) (256) 238-9055; info@bermanmuseum.org; (c) Calhoun

Private non-profit/ 1996/ Farley L. Berman Foundation, Inc./ staff: 4(f); 18(v)/ members: 233

ART MUSEUM; HISTORY MUSEUM: Exhibits objects of historical significance and works of art. Preserves, manages, researches, collects, and utilizes objects for educational purposes.

PROGRAMS: Community Outreach; Exhibits; Facility Rental; Festivals; Guided Tours; Interpretation; Lectures; Living History

COLLECTIONS: [3000 BC-20th c] Guns of the

American West, W W I & II, Napoleon Bonaparte, and Jefferson Davis; swords; Adolf Hitler's silver; bronze sculptures by Frederic Remington; and medieval arms and armor.

HOURS: Yr M-Sa 10-5, Su 1-5 (Sept-May closed M)

ADMISSION: $3.50, Children $2.50

ASHLAND

4
Clay County Historical Society
The Wynn Bldg, 36251 [PO Box 998, 36251]; (p) (256) 396-2393; (c) Clay

Joint/ 1982/ County; Non-profit/ staff: 135(v)/ members: 135/publication: *Clay County History; Cemetery Survey*

HISTORIC PRESERVATION AGENCY; HISTORIC SITE; HISTORICAL SOCIETY; HISTORY MUSEUM; LIVING HISTORY/OUTDOOR MUSEUM: Collects printed material, designates historic sites, conducts cemetery surveys, publishes local histories, operates a pioneer museum.

PROGRAMS: Annual Meeting; Community Outreach; Exhibits; Family Programs; Festivals; Guided Tours; Interpretation; Lectures; Living History; Publication; Research Library/Archives; School-Based Curriculum

ATHENS

5
Houston Library and Museum
101 N Houston St, 35611; (p) (256) 233-8770; (c) Limestone

staff: 4(p)

GENEALOGICAL SOCIETY; HISTORIC SITE: Preserves former home of Governor & US Senator George S. Houston. Full-service public library.

PROGRAMS: Festivals; Living History; Reenactments

COLLECTIONS: [1835-present] Period furnishings and memorabilia.

HOURS: Yr M-F 10-5, Sa 9-12

6
Limestone County Archives
310 W Washington St, 35611; (p) (256) 233-6404; preyer@pclcable.com; (c) Limestone

County/ 1980/ Limestone County Commission/ staff: 1(f); 1(p); 2(v)

Official repository for county public records from 1818 and private papers pertaining to the county and its people.

COLLECTIONS: [1818-present] The public collections are probate court, circuit court, board of education, board of registrars, and county commission. The private collections include personal papers, church records, photographs, and various records from local organizations.

HOURS: Yr M-F 8-4:30

7
Limestone County Historical Society
[PO Box 82, 35612]; (p) (256) 233-2878; (c) Limestone

Private non-profit/ 1969/ staff: 12(v)/ members: 170/publication: *Limestone Legacy*

GENEALOGICAL SOCIETY; HISTORICAL SOCIETY; HISTORY MUSEUM: Records history and genealogy; operates museum.

PROGRAMS: Annual Meeting; Community Outreach; Exhibits; Interpretation; Lectures; Publication

COLLECTIONS: [1800-1950] Military weapons, agriculture, musical instruments, Native American

ATMORE

8
Atmore Historical Society
501 S Pensacola Ave, 36502; (p) (334) 368-3305; (c) Escambia

Private non-profit/ 1992/ staff: 25(v)/ members: 25

HISTORICAL SOCIETY: Collects, preserves, and publishes any materials, artifacts, and items of historical significance pertaining to the people and area of Atmore.

PROGRAMS: Annual Meeting;

AUBURN

9
Archives and Manuscripts Department, Auburn University
Auburn University Libraries, 36849; (p) (334) 844-1705; (f) (334) 844-4424; coxdway@lib.auburn.edu; www.lib.auburn.edu/archive/; (c) Lee

State/ 1963/ Auburn Univ/ staff: 7(f); 3(p); 1(v)

PROGRAMS: Community Outreach; Exhibits; Interpretation; Lectures; Research Library/Archives

COLLECTIONS: [19th-20th c]

HOURS: Yr

BESSEMER

10
Bessemer Hall of History Museum, Inc.
1905 Alabama Ave, 35020; (p) (205) 426-1633; (c) Jefferson

Private non-profit/ staff: 1(f); 30(v)/ members: 150

Maintains restored railroad station; focuses on local history, mining, railroads, and industry.

HOURS: Yr T-Sa 10-4

BIRMINGHAM

11
Alabama Civil War Roundtable
[PO Box 531305, 35253-1305]; (c) Jefferson

Private non-profit/ 1991/ members: 130/publication: *The Muster Roll*

Devoted to providing education to the public regarding history of the War Between the States and seeking to promote the preservation of Civil War sites.

PROGRAMS: Lectures; Publication.

12
Arlington
331 Cotton Ave SW, 35211; (p) (205) 780-5652; (f) (205) 788-0585

1850/ staff: 7(f); 1(p)

Home to General James Wilson, Daniel Pratt, and Henry Debardeleben.

COLLECTIONS: [1860-1900] 1838 life portrait of Osceola by William Laning; c. 1842 portrait of Henry Edward Dryton by M.S. Parker.

13
Arlington Historical Association
331 Cotton Ave SW, 35211 [PO Box 130237, 35213]; (p) (205) 780-5656; (f) (205) 788-0585; (c) Jefferson

City/ 1955/ staff: 7(f); 55(v)/ members: 688

GARDEN; HISTORIC PRESERVATION AGENCY; HISTORIC SITE; HOUSE MUSEUM: Promote and educate the public about Birmingham's only house museum.

PROGRAMS: Facility Rental; Festivals; Guided Tours; Lectures; School-Based Curriculum

COLLECTIONS: [1845-1900]

HOURS: Yr T-Sa 10-4, Su 1-4

ADMISSION: $3, Children $2.50

14
Birmingham Civil Rights Institute
520 16th St N, 35203; (p) (205) 328-9696; (f) (205) 323-5042; bcri.info@bcri.bham.al.us; bcri.bham.al.us; (c) Jefferson

Private non-profit/ 1992/ Board of Directors/ staff: 19(f); 1(p); 126(v)/ members: 900/publication: Visions

HISTORY MUSEUM: An institute for education on and discussion of civil and human rights issues.

PROGRAMS: Community Outreach; Exhibits; Facility Rental; Festivals; Guided Tours; Interpretation; Lectures; Living History; Publication; Research Library/Archives; School-Based Curriculum

COLLECTIONS: [1954-1970] Artifacts and archival collections from the Civil Rights Movement Era.

HOURS: Yr T-Sa 10-5, Su 1-5

ADMISSION: $6, Student $2, Seniors $3; Under 18 free

15
Birmingham Historical Society
One Sloss Quarters, 35222; (p) (205) 251-1880; (f) (215) 251-3260; mslwhite@aol.com; www.bhistorical.org; (c) Jefferson

Private non-profit/ 1942/ staff: 3(f); 1(p); 200(v)/ members: 1500

HISTORIC SITE: Conducts research and public programs to foster awareness of regional history and the preservation of significant sites.

PROGRAMS: Annual Meeting; Community Outreach; Exhibits; Guided Tours; Interpretation; Lectures; Publication; Research Library/ Archives; School-Based Curriculum

COLLECTIONS: [1871-present]

HOURS: Office: Daily 1-4

16
Birmingham Public Library, Department of Archives and Manuscripts
2100 Park Pl, 35203-2794; (p) (205) 226-3660; (f) (205) 226-3663; jbaggett@bham.lib.al.us; www.bham.lib.al.us; (c) Jefferson

City/ 1976/ staff: 3(f); 1(p); 2(v)

LIBRARY AND/OR ARCHIVES: Serves as the archives for the City of Birmingham and collects primary research material documenting the history and development of the Birmingham area.

PROGRAMS: Community Outreach; Exhibits; Guided Tours; Lectures; Research Library/ Archives

COLLECTIONS: [19th-20th c] 12,000 linear feet of archives and manuscript material and over 400,000 photographic images; Civil Rights Movement material.

HOURS: Yr M-F 9-6

17
Birmingham Public Library, Linn-Henley Research Library, Tutwiler Collection of Southern History
2100 Park Pl, 35203-2794; (p) (205) 226-3665; (f) (205) 226-3743; sou@bham.lib.al.us; www.bham.lib.al.us; (c) Jefferson

City/ 1927/ staff: 5(f); 4(p)

LIBRARY AND/OR ARCHIVES: Houses a collection of primarily Southern material.

PROGRAMS: Community Outreach; Lectures

COLLECTIONS: [1800-present] Over 150,000 printed volumes, 10,000 bound periodicals, and 18,000 reels of microfilm exclusive of newspaper and periodical holdings. Southern genealogy, state and local histories, Agee Map collection, and early American travel literature.

HOURS: Yr M-T 9-8, W-Sa 9-6, Su 2-6

18
Friends of Rickwood
2100 Morris Avenue, 35203; (p) (205) 458-8161; (f) (205) 252-1348; d.brewer@rickwood.com; (c) Jefferson

Private non-profit/ 1992/ staff: 1(f); 30(v)/ members: 150

HISTORIC SITE; LIVING HISTORY/OUTDOOR MUSEUM: Friends of Rickwood manages, markets, preserves and interprets Rickwood Field, America's oldest baseball park.

PROGRAMS: Exhibits; Facility Rental; Family Programs; Guided Tours; Interpretation; Lectures; Living History; School-Based Curriculum

COLLECTIONS: [1910-present] Birmingham, Alabama, and southern baseball history; social history

ADMISSION: No charge

19
Jefferson County Historical Commission
2027 1st Ave N Ste 801, 35203-4127; (p) (205) 324-0988; (c) Jefferson

County/ 1971/ staff: 1(p); 12(v)/publication: Historic Sites of Jefferson County Alabama; Images of America: Birmingham and Jefferson County, Alabama

HISTORIC PRESERVATION AGENCY; HISTORICAL SOCIETY: Directs historical preservation, restoration, and education efforts.

PROGRAMS: Annual Meeting; Film/Video; Publication; Research Library/Archives

20
Sloss Furnaces National Historic Landmark
20 32nd St, 35222; (p) (205) 324-1911; (f) (205) 324-5768; (c) Jefferson

City/ 1981/ staff: 10(f); 4(p); 30(v)/ members: 50/publication: The Iron Supplement

HISTORIC SITE: Preserves the only 20th c blast furnace in public hands in the world; maintains archives.

PROGRAMS: Annual Meeting; Community Outreach; Concerts; Exhibits; Facility Rental; Guided Tours; Interpretation; Publication; Research Library/Archives; School-Based Curriculum

COLLECTIONS: [1886-1971] Machinery, engines, molds, equipment, and archives.

HOURS: Yr T-Sa 10-4, Su 12-4

21
Southern Museum of Flight
4343 73rd St N, 35206; (p) (205) 833-8226; (f) (205) 833-8226; DrDonDodd@aol.com; www.bham.net/flight/museum.html; (c) Jefferson

1965/ City; Southern Museum of Flight Foundation/ staff: 7(f); 1(p); 125(v)/ members: 320/publication: Flight Lines

HISTORY MUSEUM: Preserves civilian, military, and experimental aircraft, including Alabama Aviation Hall of Fame exhibit.

PROGRAMS: Annual Meeting; Community Outreach; Exhibits; Facility Rental; Family Programs; Film/Video; Guided Tours; Publication; Research Library/Archives; School-Based Curriculum

COLLECTIONS: [20th c] Civilian and military flight artifacts; Tuskegee Airmen, aviatrix, WW II and Vietnam War memorabilia.

HOURS: Yr T-Sa 9:30-4:30, Su 1-4:30

ADMISSION: $3, Student $2, Seniors $2

22
State of Alabama Sports Hall of Fame and Museum
2150 Richard Arrington Blvd, 35202 [PO Box 10163, 35202-0163]; (p) (205) 323-6665; (f) (205) 252-2212; www.tech-comm.com/ashof/; (c) Jefferson

1967/ State; private non-profit/ staff: 4(f); 2(p)/ members: 67/publication: ASHOF Magazine

HISTORY MUSEUM: Preserves sports heritage and promotes athletic achievements.

PROGRAMS: Annual Meeting; Community Outreach; Exhibits; Facility Rental; Film/Video; Guided Tours; Publication; Research Library/Archives; School-Based Curriculum; Theatre

COLLECTIONS: [1890-present] Sporting memorabilia.

HOURS: Yr M-Sa 9-5, Su 1-5

ADMISSION: $5, Student $3, Seniors $4

23
University of Alabama at Birmingham Historical Collections
300 Lister Hill Library Bldg, 1700 University Blvd, 35294-0013; (p) (205) 934-4475; (f) (205) 975-8476; www.uab.edu/historical; (c) Jefferson

State/ 1958/ UAB/ staff: 4(f); 1(p)/publication: *Treasures*

HISTORY MUSEUM; RESEARCH CENTER: Preserves health science manuscripts, medical books, and university archives.

COLLECTIONS: University archives and oral history collection; photographs, incunabula, manuscripts, audio/videotapes, and instruments related to health sciences.

HOURS: Yr M-F 8:30-5

BREWTON

24
Thomas E. McMillan Museum
220 Alco Dr, 36427 [Jefferson Davis Comm College PO Box 958, 36427]; (p) (334) 867-4832; (f) (334) 867-7399; (c) Escambia

Joint/ 1978/ County; State/ staff: 1(f); 1(p)

HISTORY MUSEUM: Preserves and interprets material culture and history of southwest AL and northwest FL.

PROGRAMS: Community Outreach; Exhibits; Guided Tours; Interpretation; Lectures; Publication

COLLECTIONS: Prehistoric artifacts, colonial, Civil War artifacts, period household items, medical and dental instruments, and vintage

BRIDGEPORT

25
Russell Cave National Monument
3729 County Road 98, 35740; (p) (256) 495-2672; (f) (256) 495-9220; RUCA_Ranger_activities@nps.gov; www.nps.gov/RUCA; (c) Jackson

Federal/ 1961/ National Park Service/publication: *Life at Russell Cave; Investigations in Russell Cave*

LIVING HISTORY/OUTDOOR MUSEUM

PROGRAMS: Exhibits; Film/Video; Guided Tours; Interpretation; Publication

COLLECTIONS: [Prehistory] Prehistoric artifacts, stone and bone tools, pottery shards.

HOURS: Yr

BUTLER

26
Choctaw County Historical Museum
CR 14 & Hwy 17, 36904 [PO Box 758, 36904]; (p) (334) 843-2501, (205) 459-3383; (f) (205) 459-3000; chadv@mail.pinebelt.net; (c) Choctaw

Private non-profit/ 1987/ Board of Directors/ staff: 15(v)/ members: 250

HISTORY MUSEUM: Preserves local artifacts.

PROGRAMS: Annual Meeting; Community Outreach; Exhibits; Guided Tours

COLLECTIONS: [19th c-present] Agricultural, military, Native American, oil and gas production

CALERA

27
Heart of Dixie Railroad Museum, Inc.
1919 Ninth St, 35040 [PO Box 727, 35040-0727]; (p) (205) 668-3435, (800) 943-4490;

www.heartofdixierrmuseum.org; (c) Shelby

Private non-profit/ 1963/ staff: 1(f); 1(p); 40(v)/ members: 200/publication: *Cinders from the Smokestack*

HISTORY MUSEUM; LIVING HISTORY/OUTDOOR MUSEUM: A museum of the history of the railroad industry, particularly railroads of AL.

PROGRAMS: Exhibits; Festivals; Publication; Research Library/Archives

COLLECTIONS: [1887-1975] Steam and diesel engines, passenger cars, freight cars, and work equipment. Two railroad depots containing railroad artifacts.

HOURS: Jan 6-Dec 15 Sa 9-4; Apr 1-Dec 16 Su 1-4; Apr 3-Dec 18 T-F 10-3

CARROLTON

28
Tom Bevill Visitor Center
Rte 1, Box 352X, 35447; (p) (205) 373-8705; (c) Pickens

Federal/ 1985/ staff: 2(f); 1(p); 20(v)

Main visitor center for the Tennessee-Tombignes waterway.

COLLECTIONS: [1930-1960]

CENTRE

29
Cherokee County Historical Museum
101 E Main St, 35960 [PO Box 222, 35960]; (p) (256) 927-7835; (f) (256) 923-3633; bminnix@peop.tds.com; (c) Cherokee

County/ Cherokee County/ staff: 2(p)

HISTORIC PRESERVATION AGENCY; HISTORY MUSEUM

PROGRAMS: Exhibits; Guided Tours; Publication

COLLECTIONS: [1850s-present] Tools, farm implements, housewares, documents, and clothes.

HOURS: Yr T-Sa 8:30-4

ADMISSION: No charge

CHATHAM

30
Washington County Museum Association
403 Court St, 36518 [PO Box 549, 36518]; (p) (334) 847-2201, (334) 847-3156; basearch@millry.net; (c) Wahington

County; Private non-profit/ 1966/ Board of Directors

HISTORIC SITE; HISTORY MUSEUM: Preserves the history of Washington County.

PROGRAMS: Annual Meeting; Community Outreach; Guided Tours; Publication; School-Based Curriculum

COLLECTIONS: [1800-present] Artifacts related to early community life, country doctors, occupations, and a collection of china, cut glass, and egg art.

HOURS: Yr M-F 8-4:30

COLUMBIANA

31
Shelby County Historical Society
1854 Courthouse Main St, 35051 [PO Box 457, 35051]; (p) (205) 669-3912; www.rootsweb.com/~alshelby/schs.html

County/ 1974/ staff: 2(f)/ members: 280/publication: *Historical Quarterly*

HISTORICAL SOCIETY; HISTORY MUSEUM; RESEARCH CENTER

PROGRAMS: Annual Meeting; Community Outreach; Exhibits; Family Programs; Festivals; Interpretation; Lectures; Living History; Publication; Research Library/Archives; School-Based Curriculum

COLLECTIONS: [1800-present] Period artifacts.

HOURS: Yr M-F 8-3

CULLMAN

32
Ave Maria Grotto
St. Bernard Abbey, 35055 [1600 St. Bernard Dr, SE, 35055]; (p) (256) 737-8768; (f) (256) 734-2925; (c) Cullman

Private non-profit/ 1934/ Benedictine Society of Alabama, Inc/ staff: 4(f); 2(v)

Ave Maria Grotto is made up of one hundred twenty-five miniature stone and cement missions created by Brother Joseph, O.S.B.

HOURS: Apr-Sept Daily 7-7; Oct-Mar 7-5

ADMISSION: $5, Children $3.50, Seniors $4.50

33
Cullman County Archeological Society
1006 Brunner St NW, 35055; (p) (256) 734-4548; (f) (256) 737-8782; (c) Cullman

Private non-profit/ 1967/ members: 30

HISTORIC PRESERVATION AGENCY: Collection and preservation of Indian artifacts, programs, education, exhibits and lectures.

PROGRAMS: Community Outreach; Exhibits; Lectures

COLLECTIONS: Indian artifacts left behind as tribes migrated west in 1836-1839. Tribes include Cherokee, Creeks, and Choctow.

34
Cullman County Museum
211 2nd Ave NE, 35055; (p) (256) 739-1258; (f) (256) 737-8782; elaine.fuller@winserver.com; (c) Cullman

City/ 1973/ staff: 1(f); 3(p)

HISTORY MUSEUM; HOUSE MUSEUM: Museum housed in replica of founder's home.

PROGRAMS: Facility Rental; Festivals

COLLECTIONS: [1880s] Eight rooms containing artifacts relating to Cullman's history, archaeology, pioneer, dress shop, child's room, picture display, and Colonel Cullman's.

HOURS: Yr Su-F

ADMISSION: $2, Children $1; Group rates

DAUPHIN ISLAND

35
Fort Gaines Historic Site
51 Bienville Blvd, 36528; (p) (334) 861-6992;
(f) (334) 861-5092; dipbb@classic.msn.com;
www.dauphine.net/fortgaines/; (c) Mobile

Private for-profit/ 1954/ Dauphin Island Park
and Beach Board/ staff: 3(f); 2(p); 225(v)

HISTORIC SITE; HISTORICAL SOCIETY;
HISTORY MUSEUM; LIVING HISTORY/OUT-
DOOR MUSEUM: Built by U.S. Government
after Revolutionary War. Site of 1864 "Battle of
Mobile Bay."

COLLECTIONS: [Mid-Late 19th c] Civil War
fort and exhibits of post-Civil War photos of
Dauphin Island, uniforms, weapons, artillery
pieces, strategic maps, and ladies' outfits.

HOURS: Yr Daily 9-5; June-Aug 9-6

ADMISSION: Student $3, Children $1

DAVISTON

36
**Horseshoe Bend National Military
Park**
11288 Horseshoe Bend Rd, 36256; (p) (256)
234-7111; (f) (256) 329-9905;
HOBE_Administration@nps.gov;
www.nps.gov/hobe; (c) Tallapoosa

Federal/ 1959/ National Park Service/ staff:
8(f); 8(v)

HISTORIC SITE; HISTORY MUSEUM; LIV-
ING HISTORY/OUTDOOR MUSEUM: Inter-
prets the Civil War, War of 1812, and the
Creek Indian History.

PROGRAMS: Community Outreach; Exhibits;
Interpretation; Lectures; Living History; Publi-
cation; Research Library/Archives; School-
Based Curriculum

COLLECTIONS: [War of 1812, Creek War,
Federal Era] Creek War artifacts, materials relating to the life of native Creek or Muskogee,
and military combatants; library files on War of
1812, Creek War, and native life; correspondence and papers of Andrew Jackson.

HOURS: Visitor Center Daily 8-4:30; Road 8-5

ADMISSION: No charge

DECATUR

37
Morgan County Archives
624 Bank St, 35601; (p) (256) 351-4726; (f)
(256) 351-4738; mocoarch@ix.netcom.com;
www.netcom.com/~mocoarch/genealogy.html;
(c) Morgan

County/ 1995/ Morgan County Commission/
staff: 2(f); 2(p); 10(v)/publication: *Morgan
Memories*

HISTORY MUSEUM; LIBRARY AND/OR AR-
CHIVES: County archive, small museum area,
research library local genealogy and history.

PROGRAMS: Annual Meeting; Community Outreach; Elder's Programs; Facility Rental; Lectures; Publication; Research Library/ Archives

COLLECTIONS: [1819-1930] County records;
local and family history; photography collec-
tionincluding original photos from 1933-1934
"Scottsboro Trials."

HOURS: M-F 8-4:30

38
Old State Bank
925 Bank St NE, 35602 [PO Box 582, 35602];
(p) (256) 350-5060; (c) Morgan

Joint/ 1972/ City of Decatur; Old Bank Board
of Directors/ staff: 1(f); 1(p); 15(v)

HISTORIC SITE: Preserves historic site and
promotes bank's social role in local history.

PROGRAMS: Community Outreach; Concerts; Exhibits; Facility Rental; Family Programs; Garden Tours; Guided Tours; Interpretation; Lectures; Living History; School-Based
Curriculum

COLLECTIONS: [1833-1845] Banking memorabilia, period furnishings.

HOURS: Yr M-F 9:30-12/1:30-4:30

DEMOPOLIS

39
Bluff Hall
405 N Commissioner Ave, 36732 [PO Box 159,
36732]; (p) (334) 289-1666, (334) 289-0282

1853/ staff: 2(p)

COLLECTIONS: [1880s-1920s] Period antiques ca. 1840-1890s; 500 piece clothing collection

HOURS: Yr Jan-Feb T-Sa 10-4, Su 2-4; Mar-
Dec T-Sa 10-5; Su 2-5

40
Gaineswood
805 S Cedar Ave, 36732; (p) (334) 289-4846;
(f) (334) 289-1027; www.demopolis.com/
gaineswood/; (c) Marengo

State/ 1975/ AL Historical Commission/ staff:
2(f); 2(p); 30(v)

HISTORIC PRESERVATION AGENCY; HIS-
TORIC SITE; HISTORY MUSEUM; HOUSE
MUSEUM: Greek Revival mansion built during
the years 1843-1861 by skilled slaves, arti-
sans and laborers of owner-architect Nathan
Bryan Whitfield.

PROGRAMS: Facility Rental; Festivals; Guided Tours; Interpretation; Lectures; Living History; School-Based Curriculum

COLLECTIONS: [Mid-late 19th c]

HOURS: Yr M-Sa 9-5, Su 1-5

ADMISSION: $5, Student $3, Children $2

41
Marengo County Historical Society
311 N Walnut, 36732 [PO Box 159, 36732];
(p) (334) 289-0282; (c) Marengo

1967/ staff: 3(p); 100(v)/ members: 500

HISTORIC SITE; HOUSE MUSEUM: Commit-
ted to gathering, collecting, preserving, studying, and publicizing information and artifacts
related to the history of Marengo County.
Owns and operates two house museums.

PROGRAMS: Annual Meeting; Community
Outreach; Exhibits; Facility Rental; Family Programs; Festivals; Guided Tours

COLLECTIONS: [1832-1900] Two house museums with period furnishings and clothing-
Bluff Hall (1832), and Lyon Hall (1850-1853).

HOURS: Yr T-Su 10-5

ADMISSION: $5, Student $1

DOTHAN

42
Dothan Landmarks Foundation
4925 Reeves St, 36302 [PO Box 6362,
36302]; (p) (334) 794-3452; (f) (334) 677-
7229; (c) Houston

Private non-profit/ 1976/ staff: 6(f); 4(p); 50(v)/
members: 1500/publication: *The Lark*

LIVING HISTORY/OUTDOOR MUSEUM;
NATURAL HISTORY MUSEUM: Owns & operates Landmark Park, a 100-acre natural & cultural history museum. Official agricultural museum of AL.

PROGRAMS: Annual Meeting; Concerts; Exhibits; Facility Rental; Family Programs; Festivals; Guided Tours; Interpretation; Lectures;
Living History; Publication; School-Based Curriculum

COLLECTIONS: [1890-1930] 1890s rural
farmhouse with furnishings and outbuildings;
agricultural implements, local history, oral histories and photographs; natural history specimens.

HOURS: Yr M-Sa 9-5, Su 12-6

ADMISSION: $3, Children $2

43
Wiregrass Museum of Art
126 Museum Ave, 36302 [PO Box 1624,
36302]; (p) (334) 794-3871; (f) (334) 615-2217;
www.wiregrassmuseumoart.org; (c) Huston

Private non-profit/ 1989/ Board of Directors/
staff: 6(f); 4(p); 25(v)/ members: 800/publica-
tion: *Sketches*

ART MUSEUM: Collects, preserves, researches, and exhibits 19th and 20th c American Art.

PROGRAMS: Community Outreach; Exhibits;
Guided Tours; Lectures; Publication; Research
Library/Archives

COLLECTIONS: [16th-20th c] American art,
contemporary, regional paintings, 16th-20th c
European and American works on paper.

HOURS: Yr

ELBERTA

44
**Baldwin County Heritage Museum
Association, Inc.**
25521 US Hwy 98, 36530 [PO Box 356,
36530]; (p) (251) 986-8375; (c) Baldwin

1981/ Board of Directors/ staff: 38(v)/ members: 300

HISTORY MUSEUM: Maintains a barn-
shaped exhibition hall which houses a variety
of machinery and household goods.

PROGRAMS: Annual Meeting; Exhibits; Lectures; Publication

COLLECTIONS: [1900-1950] Displays of hand
tools, Josephine Post Office front, woodcarvings, pot mesil pottery, quilt hangings, 1908
church, picnic area, farm machinery, equipment and small engines, household goods.

HOURS: Yr May-Oct W-Sa 10-5; Nov-Apr, W-
Sa 10-4, Second Su 1-4

ADMISSION: $4, Student $2, Children $1

ENTERPRISE

45
Pea River Historical & Genealogical Society
108 S Main St, 36331 [PO Box 310628, 36331]; (p) (334) 393-2901; (c) Coffee

Private non-profit/ 1970/ staff: 53(v)/ members: 325/publication: *Pea River Trails*

GENEALOGICAL SOCIETY; HISTORICAL SOCIETY: Preserves genealogical records and maintains local historical artifacts.

PROGRAMS: Annual Meeting; Exhibits; Publication; Research Library/Archives

COLLECTIONS: [1850-present] Artifacts of local culture, fire-fighting, logging equipment, and personal effects.

HOURS: Library: Yr M-Sa 10-4; Museum: Yr Daily 10-12, 1-3

EUFAULA

46
Eufaula Heritage Association
340 N Eufaula Ave, 36027 [PO Box 486, 36027]; (p) (334) 687-3793; (f) (334) 687-1836; pilgrimage@zebra.net; www.zebra.net/~pilgramage; (c) Barbour

Private non-profit/ Heritage Board of Directors/ staff: 2(p)/ 12(v)/ members: 350

HISTORIC SITE; HISTORY MUSEUM

PROGRAMS: Annual Meeting; Exhibits; Facility Rental; Festivals; Garden Tours; Guided Tours

COLLECTIONS: [1880s-present] Regional memorabilia and antiques.

ADMISSION: $4, Children $1

47
Fendall Hall
917 W Barbour St, 36027; (p) (334) 687-8469; (f) (334) 687-8469; fendallhall@mindspring.com; www.preserveala.org; (c) Barbour

State/ 1973/ AL Historical Commission/ staff: 1(f); 20(v)

HOUSE MUSEUM: Preserves, restore, and interprets Fendall Hall (1860), according to the 1880-1916 time period.

PROGRAMS: Facility Rental; Guided Tours

COLLECTIONS: [1880-1916] Victorian Era murals, furnishings, and decorative arts pieces; furnishings, family photographs, and memorabilia.

HOURS: Yr M-Sa 10-4

ADMISSION: $4, Student $3, Children $2; Under 6 free

48
Historic Chattahoochee Commission
211 N Eufaula Ave, 36027 [PO Box 33, 36027-0033]; (p) (334) 687-9755; (f) (334) 687-6631; hcc1@zebra.net; www.hcc-al-ga.org; (c) Barbour

Joint; State/ 1970/ Board of Directors/ staff: 3(f); 28(v)/ members: 270

ALLIANCE OF HISTORICAL AGENCIES; HISTORIC PRESERVATION AGENCY; HISTORIC SITE: State agency of AL and GA that promotes historic preservation and tourism in the 18 county region.

PROGRAMS: Annual Meeting; Exhibits; Publication; School-Based Curriculum

FLORENCE

49
Florence Department of Arts and Museums
217 E Tuscaloosa St, 35630; (p) (256) 760-6379; (f) (256) 760-6382; bbroach@floweb.com; www.ci.florence.al.us; (c) Lauderdale

1976/ City of Florence/ staff: 3(f); 3(p); 150(v)/ members: 143

ART MUSEUM; HISTORY MUSEUM; HOUSE MUSEUM: The department operates four museums.

PROGRAMS: Exhibits; Family Programs; Festivals; Guided Tours; Interpretation; Lectures; Research Library/Archives

COLLECTIONS: [19th c] Kennedy-Douglass Center for the Arts: genealogical files and personal memorabilia of Hiram K. Douglass. Pope's Tavern: a former stagecoach stop and Civil War hospital, now houses 18th and 19th c antiques and memorabilia. W.C. Handy Museum: collection of W.C. Handy personal papers and artifacts in the world. Indian Mound & Museum: displays artifacts dating back 10,000 years, from the Paleo, Transitional, Archiac, Woodland and Mississippian Native American ages.

HOURS: Kennedy Douglass Center: M-F 9-4; Other museums: T-Sa 10-4

ADMISSION: Varies

50
W.C. Handy Birthplace, Museum, and Library
620 W College St, [PO Box 440, Tuscumbia, 35674]; (p) (334) 760-6434, (800) 344-0783; (f) (334) 383-2080; www.shoalsol.com/events/wchandy/handy.html

HISTORY MUSEUM; LIBRARY AND/OR ARCHIVES: Site where W.C. Handy was born.

PROGRAMS: Exhibits; Research Library/Archives

COLLECTIONS: [Late 19th and early 20th c] Hand-hewn log cabin, collection of W.C. Handy personal papers, artifacts, and memorabilia; Handy's trumpet, piano, handwritten sheet music, and photographs.

HOURS: T-Sa 10-4

FOLEY

51
Baldwin County Genealogical Society
319 E Laurel Ave, 36536 [PO Box 108, 36536]; (p) (334) 943-7665; (f) (334) 943-8637; library@gulftel.com; (c) Baldwin

Private non-profit; State/ 1988/ members: 90/publication: *Yore Lore*

GENEALOGICAL SOCIETY: Promotes genealogical research through programs, workshops and projects; educates and assists members in genealogical research.

PROGRAMS: Monthly Meeting; Publication; Research Library/Archives

COLLECTIONS: Foley Public Library: BCGS's research materials which include: 1,800 books, quarterlies, 2,000 microfiche, 300 microfilm, CDs, periodicals, and Alabama history and family history collections.

HOURS: Yr M,W 9-9, T,Th 1-9, F-Sa 9-6

FORT MCCLELLAN

52
United States Army Military Police Corps Regimental Museum
Building 3182, 36205; (p) (205) 848-3522; (f) (205) 848-6691; (c) Calhoun

Federal/ 1965/ U.S. Army Center of Military History/ staff: 3(f)

HISTORY MUSEUM: Preserves artifacts related to development of law enforcement in US Army.

PROGRAMS: Community Outreach; Exhibits; Guided Tours; Research Library/Archives

COLLECTIONS: [1776-present] Uniforms, weapons, and military

FORT PAYNE

53
Depot Museum, Inc.
105 5th Ave NE, 35968 [PO Box 681420, 35968]; (p) (256) 845-5714; (c) Dekalb

Private non-profit/ 1986/ Depot Museum Board of Directors/ staff: 1(f); 1(p); 15(v)

HISTORIC SITE; HISTORY MUSEUM: A museum is housed in the Richardsonian Romanesque-style southern railway building built in 1891. Displayed in the unique building are collections of Indian artifacts, local history, railroad memorabilia, dioramas.

PROGRAMS: Community Outreach; Exhibits; Festivals; Guided Tours; Lectures; School-Based Curriculum

COLLECTIONS: [19th c] Hundreds of Native American artifacts—Hopi, Seminole, Cherokee, Pueblo—turn of the century fashions, dioramas, railroad memorabilia, local history items and photographs, rock collections, early American history items and a fully equipped caboose.

HOURS: Yr M,W,F, Su, 10-4

ADMISSION: No charge

54
Landmarks of DeKalb County, Inc.
518 Gault Ave N, 35968 [PO Box 680518, 35968-0518]; (p) (256) 845-3137; (c) DeKalb

Private non-profit/ 1969/ staff: 15(v)/publication: *Landmark Bulletin; History of DeKalb Co*

HISTORIC PRESERVATION AGENCY; HISTORICAL SOCIETY; HISTORY MUSEUM: Preserves historical sites and local history.

PROGRAMS: Annual Meeting; Concerts; Exhibits; Facility Rental; Guided Tours; Lectures; Publication

GADSDEN

55
Center for Cultural Arts
501 Broad St, 35902 [PO Box 1507, 35902]; (p) (256) 543-2787; (f) (256) 546-7435; bob welch@cybrtyme.com; www.culturalarts.org; (c) Etowah

Private non-profit/ 1984/ Gadsden Cultural Arts Foundation, Inc/ staff: 8(f); 8(p); 100(v)/ members: 625/publication: *For Art's Sake*

ART MUSEUM; CULTURAL CENTER: Three changing visual art exhibit halls, Imagination Place Children's Museum, Etowah Youth Orchestra, model of 1950 Gadsden with working trains, and the Gadsden Community School for the Arts.

PROGRAMS: Annual Meeting; Community Outreach; Concerts; Elder's Programs; Exhibits; Facility Rental; Family Programs; Festivals; Guided Tours; Lectures; Publication

HOURS: Yr Daily 9-6

ADMISSION: $3, Children $2

GEORGIANA

56
Hank Williams, Sr. Boyhood Home and Museum
127 Rose St, 36033 [PO Box 310, 36033-0310]; (p) (334) 376-2396; (f) (334) 376-9850; georgian@alaweb.com; (c) Butler

City/ 1993/ Hank Williams Museum and Festival, Inc./ staff: 3(p)

HOUSE MUSEUM: To preserve and promote the life and music of Hank Williams, Sr.

PROGRAMS: Concerts; Exhibits; Festivals; Guided Tours

COLLECTIONS: [Mid 1900s] Thechildhood home Hank Williams, Sr., the only house he lived in still in existence. Recordings, pictures, period furniture, collections, and memorabilia.

HOURS: Yr M-Sa 10-5, Su 1-5

ADMISSION: $3, Children

GREENSBORO

57
Magnolia Grove Historic House Museum
1002 Hobson St, 36744; (p) (334) 624-8618; (f) (334) 624-8618; maggrove@westal.net; (c) Hale

State/ 1943/ Alabama Historical Commission/ staff: 1(f); 1(p)

HOUSE MUSEUM: Preserves the antebellum home of planters Isaac Croom and Spanish American war hero Richmond Pearson Hobson.

PROGRAMS: Interpretation; School-Based Curriculum

COLLECTIONS: [1830-1930] Period furnishings and personal effects.

HOURS: Yr T-Sa 10-4, Su 1-4

ADMISSION: $4

GROVE HILL

58
Clarke County Historical Society
116 Cobb St, 36451; (p) (334) 275-8684; (c) Clarke

Private non-profit/ 1972/ staff: 1(f); 2(p)/ members: 450/publication: *Clarke County Quarterly*

HISTORICAL SOCIETY; HISTORY MUSEUM: Operates a museum, publishes materials relating to the history of Clarke County and

erects signs and markers of historical interest for the public.

PROGRAMS: Exhibits; Facility Rental; Guided Tours; Publication

COLLECTIONS: [1813-present] Native American and military artifacts, tools, furnishings, documents, and photographs of Clarke County.

HOURS: Yr M-F 10-4

ADMISSION: No charge

HANCEVILLE

59
Family & Regional History Programs
5th fl, Library, 801 N Main St, Wallace State College, 35076 [Wallace State College, PO Box 2000, 35077-2000]; (p) (256) 352-8263; (f) (256) 352-8228; genws@hiwaay.net; (c) Cullman

State/ 1991/ staff: 2(f); 2(p); 15(v)

RESEARCH CENTER: Research center for the study of family history and genealogy focusing on southeastern United States.

PROGRAMS: Lectures; Publication; Research Library/Archives; School-Based Curriculum

COLLECTIONS: [1607-1920] Genealogy resources for the Native American, Civil War, and southeastern United States.

ADMISSION: No charge

HILLSBORO

60
Pond Spring
12280 Alabama Hwy 20, 35643; (p) (256) 637-8513; (f) (256) 637-8513; wheplan@hiwaay.net; www.wheelerplantation.org; (c) Lawrence

State/ 1994/ AL Historical Commission/ staff: 2(f); 1(p)/ members: 300/publication: *Friends of Pond Spring Newsletter*

HISTORIC SITE: Former home of Confederate Gen. Joseph Wheeler; 12 historic sites, 3 cemeteries, and gardens on 50 acres.

PROGRAMS: Annual Meeting; Exhibits; Facility Rental; Guided Tours; Interpretation; Living History; Publication

COLLECTIONS: [1830-1900] Civil war memorabilia, period furnishings, decorative arts, photographs, and personal effects.

HOURS: Yr T-Sa 9-4, Su 1-5

ADMISSION: $4, Student $3, Children $2

61
Wheeler Plantation
12280 Hwy 20, 35643 [12280 Highway 20, 35643]; (p) (256) 637-8513; (f) (256) 637-8513

1870/ Alabama Historical Commission/ staff: 2(f); 1(p)

COLLECTIONS: [Late 19th-early 20th c] Civil and Spanish-American Wars-uniforms and weapons; antique furniture, family portraits.; Newspapers 1800s through 1950s; books, magazines, gardening supply

HOURS: Yr

HUNTSVILLE

62
Alabama Constitution Hall Village
109 Gates Ave, 35801; (p) (256) 535-6564; (f) (256) 535-6019; TLeopld@ci.huntsville.al.us; http://hea–www.harvard.edu/hrc_art/huntsv/const.html; (c) Madison

1982

HISTORIC SITE; LIVING HISTORY/OUTDOOR MUSEUM: Site of AL's Constitutional Convention in 1819.

PROGRAMS: Exhibits; Living History

COLLECTIONS: [19th c] Historic buildings and structures.

63
American Indian Museum
2003 Poole Dr, 35810; (p) (256) 851-7241; (c) Madison

Private non-profit/ 1996/ staff: 10(v)/ members: 120

HISTORY MUSEUM: A mobile museum for northern AL and southern TN school systems that exhibits artifacts and holds classes on American Indian cultures.

PROGRAMS: Exhibits; Festivals; Interpretation; Monthly Meeting

COLLECTIONS: [15,000 years ago-present]

64
Burritt on the Mountain-A Living Museum
3101 Burritt Dr, 35801; (p) (256) 536-2882; (f) (256) 532-1784; bm–recep@ci.huntsville.al.us; (c) Madison

City/ 1955/ City of Huntsville/ staff: 7(f); 7(p); 125(v)/ members: 668

HISTORY MUSEUM; LIVING HISTORY/OUTDOOR MUSEUM; NATURAL HISTORY MUSEUM: Preserves, documents, and interprets everyday life within the Tennessee River Valley region as it relates to humankind's interrelationship with the land in the 19th and 20th c.

PROGRAMS: Community Outreach; Concerts; Exhibits; Facility Rental; Festivals; Guided Tours; Interpretation; Lectures; Living History; School-Based Curriculum

COLLECTIONS: [19th-early 20th c] Furnishings and decorative arts of Dr. William Henry Burritt, works by local artists, agricultural, domestic, medical and natural history artifacts. Southeast Native American artifacts.

HOURS: Mar-Dec T-Sa 10-4, Su 12-4

65
Early Works
404 Madison St, 35801; (p) (256) 564-8100; (f) (256) 564-8152; dbeaupre@ci.huntsville.al.us; www.earlyworks.com; (c) Madison

City/ 1978/ staff: 20(f); 50(p); 150(v)/ members: 7500

HISTORIC SITE; HISTORY MUSEUM; HOUSE MUSEUM; LIVING HISTORY/OUTDOOR MUSEUM: EarlyWorks encompasses four historical sites: EarlyWorks Children's Museum, Alabama Consitution Village, a living history museum, Historic Huntsville Depot, and the Humphrey Rodgers House, a restored Victorian house.

PROGRAMS: Community Outreach; Exhibits; Facility Rental; Family Programs; Festivals; Guided Tours; Interpretation; Lectures; Living History; Publication; Reenactments; School-Based Curriculum; Theatre

COLLECTIONS: [19th c] Southern, specifically Alabama artifacts: Andrew Jackson letter, Terrel Family papers, Alabama Doll, Southern Federal furniture, early cabinetmaking tools, train cars, Civil War letters, Native American artifacts.

HOURS: Yr M-Sa 9-5

ADMISSION: $10, Student $7.50, Seniors $9

66
Historic Huntsville Depot
320 Church St, 35801 [404 Madison St, 35801]; (p) (256) 564-8100; (f) (256) 564-8152; susan@ ci.hunstville.al.us; www.earlyworks.com; (c) Madison

City/ 1976/ staff: 2(f); 9(p)

HISTORIC PRESERVATION AGENCY; HISTORIC SITE; HISTORICAL SOCIETY; HISTORY MUSEUM: Old Memphis Charleston Corporate Headquarters, built in 1860. Civil War Site.

PROGRAMS: Community Outreach; Exhibits; Facility Rental; Family Programs; Festivals; Film/Video; Guided Tours; Reenactments; School-Based Curriculum; Theatre

COLLECTIONS: [1860-1920] Civil War letters, paintings, railroad cars, locomotives. Working reproduction of turntable; roundhouse used for rentals; railroad paraphernalia.

HOURS: Yr M-Sa 9-5

ADMISSION: $6, Children $3.50, Seniors $5

67
Huntsville-Madison County Historical Society
[PO Box 666, 35804]; (c) Madison

Private non-profit/ members: 238/publication: *Huntsville Historical Review*

HISTORICAL SOCIETY: Protects, preserves, and records the history of Huntsville and Madison County.

PROGRAMS: Annual Meeting; Lectures; Publication

COLLECTIONS: [19th c-present]

68
Oakwood College Archives and Museum
7000 Adventist Blvd, 35896; (p) (256) 726-7249; mdixon@oakwood.edu; (c) Madison

Private non-profit/ 1896/ staff: 1(f); 1(p); 5(v)

HISTORY MUSEUM: Preserves historic site and maintains archival documents.

PROGRAMS: Community Outreach; Concerts; Elder's Programs; Exhibits; Family Programs; Film/Video; Guided Tours; Lectures; Reenactments; Research Library/Archives

COLLECTIONS: [1920-present] Manuscripts, photographs, and archival documents.

HOURS: Yr M-Th

69
U.S. Space and Rocket Center
One Tranquility Base, 35805; (p) (256) 721-7167; (f) (256) 721-7180; davida@spacecamp.com; (c) Madison

Joint/ 1970/ AL Space Science Exhibit Commission; State/ staff: 190(f); 550(p); 76(v)/ members: 3600

AVIATION MUSEUM: Preserves and presents the past, present, and future of space exploration; home of U.S. SPACE CAMP.

PROGRAMS: Facility Rental; Family Programs; Film/Video; Guided Tours

COLLECTIONS: [1940-present] History of NASA and the American space program; 1,500 artifacts; Saturn V rocket; full-scale Space Shuttle exhibit; A-12 Blackbird jet.

HOURS: Yr Daily 9-5

ADMISSION: $14.95, Children $10.95

70
Weeden House Museum
300 Gates Ave, 35804 [PO Box 2239, 35804]; (p) (256) 536-7718; (f) (256) 536-7718; (c) Madison

Private non-profit/ 1981/ Twickenham Historic District Preservation Association/ staff: 1(f); 20(v)

HISTORIC PRESERVATION AGENCY; HISTORIC SITE; HISTORY MUSEUM; HOUSE MUSEUM: The home of Maria Howard Weeden, a renowned poet and artist (1846-1905).

PROGRAMS: Guided Tours

COLLECTIONS: [1819] Paintings and poetry of Maria Howard Weeden, and furnishings from the 1819-era.

HOURS: Yr M-F 11-5

ADMISSION: $4, Student $2, Children $2

JACKSON

71
Kimbell House
Mayton Drive, 36545 [PO Box 252, 36545]; (p) (334) 246-3251

1848/ City/ staff: 14(v)

HOUSE MUSEUM: Home of Isham Kimball and his family. Surviving pioneer dwellings.

COLLECTIONS: [19c] Furnishings and accessories.

HOURS: By appt

LAFAYETTE

72
Chambers County Museum, Inc.
111 First Ave SW, 36862 [PO Box 171, 36862]; (p) (334) 864-1727; (c) Chambers

County/ 1977/ Board of Directors/ staff: 14(p); 14(v)/ members: 104/publication: *Chambers County Museum, Inc.*

HISTORIC SITE; HISTORICAL SOCIETY; HISTORY MUSEUM; LIVING HISTORY/OUTDOOR MUSEUM: Operate and maintain museum. An educational tool for kids and adults motivating them to learn the history of their roots.

PROGRAMS: Annual Meeting; Exhibits; Facility Rental; Guided Tours; Lectures; Living History; Publication; Reenactments; Research Library/Archives

COLLECTIONS: [19th c-present] Artifacts relating to early Chambers County inhabitants.

HOURS: Yr W, Sa 9-12/1-5 and by appt

MARBURY

73
Confederate Memorial Park
437 County Rd 63, 36051; (p) (205) 755-1990; (f) (205) 755-8982; confedpk3@bellsouth.com; (c) Chilton

State/ 1975/ staff: 5(f)

HISTORIC SITE; HISTORY MUSEUM: Confederate veterans home in operation from 1902-1939. The park includes a museum, pavilions, nature trail and two cemeteries containing the graves of 313 Confederate veterans, wives, and widows.

PROGRAMS: Exhibits; Facility Rental; Guided Tours; Interpretation; Lectures; Living History

COLLECTIONS: [1860s] Uniforms, weapons, flags, accoutrements of the Civil War, artifacts from the Confederate Veterans Organization and United Daughters of the Confederacy, artifacts and documents from the soldiers home.

HOURS: Daily Park: 6-dusk; Museum: 9-5

ADMISSION: No charge

MARION

74
Perry County Historical and Preservation Society
204 W Monroe, 36756 [PO Box 257, 36756]; (p) (334) 683-6336; (c) Perry

Private non-profit/ 1948/ staff: 2(p)/ members: 124

HISTORIC SITE; HISTORICAL SOCIETY; HISTORY MUSEUM: Preserves historic site and collects local history.

PROGRAMS: Annual Meeting; Exhibits; Festivals; Guided Tours

COLLECTIONS: [1820-present] Local and county history housed in a female seminary built in 1839.

HOURS: By appt

ADMISSION: $2

MAXWELL AFB

75
Air Force Historical Research Agency
600 Chenault Circle, 36112-6424; (p) (334) 953-5342; (f) (334) 953-7428; afhranews@maxwell.af.mil; www.maxwell.af.mil/au/afhra; (c) Montgomery

Federal/ United States Air Force/ staff: 70(f)

LIBRARY AND/OR ARCHIVES; RESEARCH CENTER: Archive of Air Force Unit Histories and other special collections of US Air force documents.

COLLECTIONS: Archives of Air Force Unit Histories supplemented by other special collections of Air Force documents.

HOURS: Yr M-F 8:30-4

MCCALLA

76
Alabama Historic Ironworks Commission
12632 Confederate Pkwy, 35111; (p) (205) 477-5711; (f) (205) 477-9400; tannehil@dbtech.net; www.tannehill.org; (c) Bibb, Jefferson, and Tuscaloosa

State/ 1969/ staff: 22(f); 20(p)

HISTORIC SITE; HISTORY MUSEUM; LIVING HISTORY/OUTDOOR MUSEUM: Acquires and promotes historical resources of the Alabama iron, coal, and steel industries and interprets those resources through heritage programs.

PROGRAMS: Exhibits; Facility Rental; Festivals; Interpretation; Living History; Reenactments; Research Library/Archives

COLLECTIONS: [1830-1900] Collection of archaeological artifacts from Bibb and Tannehill furnace sites, library, photograph collection pertaining to local iron, coal, and steel industries.

HOURS: Yr Daily 7-dusk

ADMISSION: $2, Children $1, Seniors $1

77
Iron and Steel Museum of Alabama
Tannehill Ironworks Historical State Park, 35111 [12632 Confederate Pkwy, 35111]; (p) (205) 477-5711; (f) (205) 477-9400; Tannehil@dbtec.net; www.tanehill.org; (c) Jefferson, Tuscaloosa, & Bibb

1969/ AL Historic Ironworks Commission/ staff: 22(f); 20(p); 20(v)/publication: *Old Tannehill*

HISTORIC SITE; HISTORY MUSEUM; LIVING HISTORY/OUTDOOR MUSEUM: Park with museum and over 40 restored log homes. Preserves history of iron technology from the Native period through the Civil War.

PROGRAMS: Exhibits; Facility Rental; Family Programs; Festivals; Guided Tours; Interpretation; Living History; Publication; Reenactments; Research Library/Archives; School-Based Curriculum

COLLECTIONS: [1800-1900] Native and settler artifacts, Civil War memorabilia, Antebellum memorabilia, iron manufacturing history, cotton gin.

HOURS: Yr M-F

MIDLAND CITY

78
Howell House
Hilton Waters Ave, 36350 [PO Box 69, City Hall, 36350]; (p) (334) 983-3511; (f) (334) 983-5191

MOBILE

79
Bragg-Mitchell Mansion
1906 Springhill Ave, 36607; (p) (334) 471-6364; (f) (334) 478-3800; ginmckean@aol.com; www.braggmitchell.com; (c) Mobile

Private non-profit/ 1987/ staff: 2(f); 10(p)

HISTORIC SITE; HOUSE MUSEUM: 1855 antebellum mansion.

PROGRAMS: Community Outreach; Facility Rental; Guided Tours

COLLECTIONS: [1830-1890] Antiques and draperies, double parlors, and dining room.

HOURS: Yr T-F

80
Conde Charlotte Museum House
104 Theater St, 36600; (p) (334) 432-4722; (c) Mobile

Private non-profit/ 1822/ National Society of Colonial Dames of America in the State of Alabama/ staff: 9(p); 15(v)

HISTORIC SITE; HOUSE MUSEUM

PROGRAMS: Exhibits; Guided Tours

COLLECTIONS: [18th c] Periods and nationalities of Mobile's history, French Empire, 18th c English, American Federal, Confederate parlors; a walled 18th c Spanish Garden.

HOURS: Yr T-Sa 10-4

ADMISSION: $4, Student $2

81
Historic Mobile Preservation Society
300 Oakleigh Place, 36604; (p) (334) 432-6161; (f) (334) 432-8843; (c) Mobile

Private non-profit/ 1935/ Officers, Trustees & Board of Directors/ staff: 3(f); 6(p); 30(v)/ members: 900

HISTORIC PRESERVATION AGENCY; HISTORIC SITE; HISTORICAL SOCIETY; HISTORY MUSEUM; HOUSE MUSEUM; RESEARCH CENTER: Encourages study of history, promotes preservation and restoration of buildings, sites, and neighborhoods. Staffs and manages Mobile's Official Period House Museum, Oakleigh.

PROGRAMS: Annual Meeting; Community Outreach; Exhibits; Festivals; Film/Video; Guided Tours; Interpretation; Lectures; Publication; Reenactments; Research Library/ Archives

COLLECTIONS: [1895-1910] Mobile history, Mardi Gras, 2000 glass negatives of William E. Wilson photograph collection, scenes & people, 1895-1910, architecture books, library books, clippings, documents, maps.

HOURS: Yr M-Sa 10-4

ADMISSION: $5, Student $3, Children $2, Seniors $4.50

82
Mobile Historic Development Commission
205 Government St, 36633 [PO Box 1827, 36633-1827]; (p) (334) 208-7281; (f) (334) 208-7966; (c) Mobile

City/ 1962/ staff: 5(f)/ members: 60

HISTORIC PRESERVATION AGENCY: Oversees two architectural review boards that provide design assistance, small grants, and advocacy.

PROGRAMS: Guided Tours; Lectures

COLLECTIONS: Files on buildings in the city's eight historic districts.

84
Mobile Medical Museum
1504 Springhill Ave, 36616 [PO Box 160363, 36616-1363]; (p) (334) 434-5055; (f) (334) 434-3752; psofeh@aol.com; (c) Mobile

Private non-profit/ 1962/ Board of Directors/ Friends of Mobile Medical Museum/ staff: 1(f); 3(v)/ members: 180/publication: *Progress Notes*

HISTORIC SITE; HISTORY MUSEUM: Exhibits 300 years of medical history artifacts, documents, and photographs.

PROGRAMS: Community Outreach; Exhibits; Festivals; Guided Tours; Publication; Reenactments; School-Based Curriculum

COLLECTIONS: [1700-present] Three hundred years of medical history, especially in the southeastern region, are represented in artifacts, photos, and documents.

HOURS: Yr M-F 9-4

ADMISSION: No charge

83
Mobile Medical Museum
1504 Springhill Ave, 36616 [PO Box 160363, 36616]; (p) (334) 434-5055; (f) (334) 434-3752; PSofEH@aol.com; (c) Mobile

Private non-profit/ 1962/ Friends of Mobile Medical Museum/ staff: 1(p); 5(v)/ members: 180/publication: *Progress Notes*

HISTORIC SITE; HISTORY MUSEUM

PROGRAMS: Community Outreach; Exhibits; Festivals; Guided Tours; Publication; Reenactments; School-Based Curriculum

COLLECTIONS: [1859] Artifacts, photos, and papers.

HOURS: Yr M-F 9-4

85
Mobile Municipal Archives
457 Church St, 36633 [PO Box 1827, 36633]; (p) (334) 208-7740; (f) (334) 208-7428; archives@ci.mobile.us.al; (c) Mobile

City/ 1983/ City of Mobile/ staff: 6(f)/publication: *A Guide to the Mobile Municipal Archives*

LIBRARY AND/OR ARCHIVES: Collects and preserves public records of the city of Mobile since 1814, private manuscripts, and municipal agencies records.

PROGRAMS: Exhibits; Guided Tours; Publication; Research Library/Archives

COLLECTIONS: [1814-present] Contains all the city's public records, including a variety of resolutions, licenses, tax lists, and minutes. Maps, charts, and correspondence from various city departments.

ADMISSION: No Charge

86
Museum of Mobile
355 Government St, 36602; (p) (334) 208-7569; (f) (334) 208-7686; museum1@acan.net; www.ci.mobile.al.us/dept/museum/museum.htm (c) Mobile

1965/ City of Mobile/ staff: 12(f); 8(p); 35(v)/ members: 1

HISTORIC SITE; HISTORY MUSEUM; HOUSE MUSEUM: Records, collects, and exhibits local history artifacts and memorabilia in three historic structures: 19th c Gulf Coast Creole Cottage, 19th c rural farmhouse, period home.

PROGRAMS: Community Outreach; Exhibits; Facility Rental; Guided Tours; Interpretation; Lectures; Research Library/Archives; School-Based Curriculum

COLLECTIONS: [1702-present] Bernstein-Bush House: Tribal, colonial, and Civil War artifacts, horse carriages, Mardi Gras memorabilia; Phoenix House: steam engine, fire fighting equipment; Carlen House: period furnishings.

HOURS: T-Sa 10-5, Su 1-5

87
Richards-Daughters of the American Revolution House
256 N Joachim St, 36603; (p) (334) 208-7320; (c) Mobile

Joint/ 1972/ Richards-DAR House Governing Board/ staff: 4(p); 125(v)

HOUSE MUSEUM: Preserves historic house built in 1860.

PROGRAMS: Facility Rental; Festivals; Guided Tours

COLLECTIONS: [1800-1870] Period furnishings.

HOURS: Yr M-Sa 10-4, Su 1-4

ADMISSION: $4, Student $1

88
University of South Alabama Archives
1504 Springhill Ave, 36688 [USA Springhill, Rm 0722, 36688]; (p) (334) 434-3800; (f) (334) 434-3622; archives@jaguar1.usouthal.edu; www.southalabama.edu/archives; (c) Mobile

State/ 1978/ Univ of South Alabama/ staff: 1(f); 7(p); 1(v)/ members: 50

LIBRARY AND/OR ARCHIVES: Preserves social and cultural history of southern AL.

PROGRAMS: Exhibits; Research Library/Archives

COLLECTIONS: [Late 19th c- present] Maps, manuscripts, and photographic

89
USS Alabama Battleship Memorial Park
2703 Battleship Pkwy, 36601 [PO Box 65, 36601]; (p) (334) 433-2703; (f) (334) 433-2777; ussalbb60@aol.com; www.ussalabama.com; (c) Mobile

State/ 1963/ USS Alabama Battleship Commission/ staff: 43(f); 6(p)

HISTORIC SITE; LIVING HISTORY/OUTDOOR MUSEUM: Preserves AL and U.S. military history.

PROGRAMS: Concerts; Elder's Programs; Exhibits; Facility Rental; Family Programs; Festivals; Film/Video; Garden Tours; Guided Tours; Lectures; Living History; Reenactments; Research Library/Archives

COLLECTIONS: [1940-present] Military aircraft, ships, tanks, weapons, other artifacts related to WWII, Korea, Vietnam, and Persian Gulf War.

HOURS: Yr Daily 8-5

ADMISSION: $8, Student $4

MONROEVILLE

90
Monroe County Heritage Museums
Old Courthouse, 36461 [PO Box 1637, 36461]; (p) (334) 575-7433; (f) (334) 575-3974; (c) Monroe

County; Joint/ 1990/ staff: 5(f); 3(p); 50(v)/ members: 340/publication: *Legacy*

HISTORIC SITE; HISTORY MUSEUM; LIVING HISTORY/OUTDOOR MUSEUM: Manages four sites: a 1903 courthouse, historical park with working grist mill, a 1874 church and cemetery, and Riker Heritage Museum.

PROGRAMS: Annual Meeting; Community Outreach; Concerts; Exhibits; Facility Rental; Family Programs; Festivals; Guided Tours; Interpretation; Lectures; Living History; Publication; Reenactments; School-Based Curriculum; Theatre

COLLECTIONS: [1850s-1940s] 1900s domestic artifacts, prehistoric Native America, fossils, river-life artifacts, military artifacts from 1860 to present, literary artifact—archives for Harper Lee & Truman Capote.

ADMISSION: $3, Children $2; Mill (Courthouse no charge)

MONTGOMERY

91
Air Force Enlisted Heritage Hall
550 McDonald St, Maxwell AFB-Gunter Annex, 36114-3107; (p) (334) 416-3202; (f) (334) 416-5840; gakin@cepme.gunter.af.mil; www.airuniv.edu/au/crpme/heritage/homepage.htm; (c) Montgomery

1984/ Air Univ Foundation/ staff: 3(f); 2(p); 1(v)

HISTORY MUSEUM; RESEARCH CENTER: Part of the Air Force Enlisted Heritage Research Institute; center for enlisted heritage and history.

PROGRAMS: Community Outreach; Exhibits; Festivals; Guided Tours; Lectures; Research Library/Archives; School-Based Curriculum

COLLECTIONS: [18th-20th c] Collects and preserves enlisted-related items, photographs, documents, and other material from 1776 to the present.

HOURS: Yr T-Th 7-4, Sa 9-4

92
Alabama Department of Archives and History
624 Washington Ave, 36130 [PO Box 300100, 36130-0100]; (p) (334) 242-4363; (f) (334) 240-3433; ebridges@archives.state.al.us; www.archives.state.al.us/; (c) Montgomery

State/ 1901/ State of Alabama/ staff: 47(f); 24(p); 80(v)

HISTORY MUSEUM: Ensures the preservation of AL's historical records and artifacts and promotes a better understanding of AL history.

PROGRAMS: Exhibits; Guided Tours; Interpretation; Lectures; Research Library/Archives

COLLECTIONS: [18th-20th c] Private and state government records and artifacts. Includes rare books, maps, photographs, military regimental histories, regimental flags of the Civil War, and Southeastern Native American artifacts.

HOURS: Reference Room: Yr T-Sa; Museum: Yr M-F 8-5, Sa 9-5

93
Alabama Historical Association
[c/o Debbie Pendleton, PO Box 300100, 36130-0100]

Private non-profit/ 1947/ members: 1200/publication: *The Alabama Review*

HISTORICAL SOCIETY

PROGRAMS: Annual Meeting; Publication

94
Alabama Historical Commission
468 S Perry St, 36130-0900; (p) (334) 242-3184; (f) (334) 240-3477; preserveala.org; (c) Montgomery

State/ 1967/ staff: 78(f); 6(p); 45(v)

HISTORIC PRESERVATION AGENCY: Protects the state's historical and archaeological resources; operates fifteen historic sites and the State Capitol Building.

PROGRAMS: Annual Meeting; Community Outreach; Exhibits; Facility Rental; Guided Tours; Interpretation; Lectures; Living History; Reenactments

COLLECTIONS: [1400-1950]

HOURS: Yr M-F 8-5

95
Auburn University Montgomery Library
7300 University Dr, 36124 [PO Box 244023, 36124-4023]; (p) (334) 244-3200; (f) (334) 244-3720; coxdway@auburn.edu; www.lib.auburn.edu/sca; (c) Montgomery

State/ 1969/ staff: 6(f); 6(p)

LIBRARY AND/OR ARCHIVES: Collects, preserves, and makes accessible local, southern women's, and genealogical history.

PROGRAMS: Research Library/Archives

COLLECTIONS: Local histories, genealogical materials, and women's history materials.

HOURS: By appt

96
F. Scott and Zelda Fitzgerald Museum
919 Felder Ave, 36101 [PO Box 64, 36101]; (p) (334) 264-4222; (f) (334) 263-2321; jlmcp831@mindspring.com; www.communityal.com/cc/fitzgeraldmuseum; (c) Montgomery

Private non-profit/ 1995/ staff: 1(f); 5(v)/ members: 700

HISTORIC SITE: Promotes the lives and works of the Fitzgeralds and preserves historic site.

PROGRAMS: Community Outreach; Concerts; Exhibits; Festivals; Film/Video; Guided Tours; Lectures

COLLECTIONS: [1920-1970] Family photos, correspondence, memorabilia, rare editions of F. Scott and Zelda Fitzgerald's works.

HOURS: W-F 10-2, Sa-Su 1-5

ADMISSION: Donations accepted

97

First White House of the Confederacy, The

644 Washington St, 36102 [PO Box 1861, 36102-1861]; (p) (334) 242-1861; (c) Montgomery

Joint; Private non-profit; State/ 1900/ staff: 2(f); 61(v)/ members: 61/publication: *The First White House of the Confederacy; The Struggle to Preserve the First White House*

HISTORIC PRESERVATION AGENCY; HISTORIC SITE; HOUSE MUSEUM; PRESIDENTIAL SITE: The executive residence of provisional President Jefferson Davis and his family in 1861 while Montgomery was the capitol of the Confederacy.

PROGRAMS: Exhibits; Interpretation; Lectures; Publication

COLLECTIONS: [1861] Period furniture, paintings, decorative arts, clothing, textiles, manuscripts, photographs, Davis personal articles.

HOURS: M-F 8-4:30

ADMISSION: Donations accepted

98

Jasmine Hill Gardens and Outdoors Museum

US 231 N/Jasmine Hill Road Exit, 36121 [PO Box 210792, 36121]; jasminehill@mindspring.com; www.jasminehill.org; (c) Elmore

1928/ Jasmine Hill Foundation/ staff: 8(f); 2(p); 20(v)/ members: 180

GARDEN; HISTORIC SITE; LIVING HISTORY/OUTDOOR MUSEUM: Preserve gardens and promotes nature, art, and contributions of Ancient Greece.

PROGRAMS: Exhibits; Facility Rental; Family Programs; Festivals; Garden Tours; Guided Tours; Interpretation; School-Based Curriculum

COLLECTIONS: [400 BC-1800s] Reproductions of Greek statuary, Greek art, horticultural, and historical exhibits.

HOURS: T-Su 9-5

ADMISSION: $5, Children $3

99

Landmarks Foundation of Montgomery, Inc.

301 Columbus St, 36104; (p) (334) 240-4500; (f) (334) 240-4519; (c) Montgomery

Private non-profit/ 1968/ Exec. Committee, Landmarks Foundation of Montgomery, Inc./ staff: 10(f); 10(p)/ members: 1200/publication: *Old Alabama Town Gazette*

LIVING HISTORY/OUTDOOR MUSEUM: Develops and administers Old Alabama Town for City of Montgomery as preservation and educational site.

PROGRAMS: Community Outreach; Concerts; Exhibits; Facility Rental; Family

100

William Cook House

Wm Cook Pkwy, 36109 [929 Parkwood Dr, 36109]; (p) (334) 272-1972, (205) 697-5792; (c) Walker

Private for-profit/ 1989/ William Cook House/ staff: 1(f); 2(p); 15(v)

HISTORIC SITE; HOUSE MUSEUM: Promotes Scottish heritage. Preserves history of

coal mining, steel, iron industries.

PROGRAMS: Community Outreach; Concerts; Guided Tours; Theatre

COLLECTIONS: [1887-1840] Period furnishings.

HOURS: Yr by appt

ONEONTA

101

Blount County Memorial Museum

204 2nd St N, 35121 [PO Box 45, 35121]; (c) Blount

County/ Blount County Commission/ staff: 1(p)/ members: 80

HISTORICAL SOCIETY

PROGRAMS: Exhibits; Quarterly Meeting

COLLECTIONS: Folklore, Native American artifacts, genealogy reference books, and family histories.

HOURS: Yr Daily

OPELIKA

102

Museum of East Alabama

121 S 9th St, 36803 [PO Box 3085, 36803-3085]; (p) (334) 749-2751; (c) Lee

1989/ Board of Directors/ staff: 1(f); 1(p); 100(v)/ members: 500

HISTORY MUSEUM: Preserves local, state, and national history.

PROGRAMS: Community Outreach; Exhibits; Guided Tours

COLLECTIONS: [20th c] Alabama Roanoke dolls, WW II POW camp memorabilia, recording technology, fire trucks, agriculture implements.

HOURS: T-F 10-4, Sa 2-4

OPP

103

Opp Historical Society Inc.

208 Whaley St, 36467; (p) (334) 493-1125; ohsi@alaweb.com; (c) Covington

Private non-profit/ 1973/ staff: 50(v)/ members: 50/publication: *Covington County History 1821-1976*

HISTORICAL SOCIETY: Preserves and displays local history.

PROGRAMS: Annual Meeting; Community Outreach; Elder's Programs; Exhibits; Festivals; Guided Tours; Lectures; Publication

COLLECTIONS: [1800-present] Agricultural memorabilia and cotton mill.

HOURS: Yr M-Sa

OZARK

104

Mizell Mansion

409 E Broad St, 36360; (p) (334) 774-9323; (f) (334) 774-6450

HOUSE MUSEUM: Greek Revival home constructed by J.D. Holman, an aristocratic horse and mule trader, in 1912.

PRATTVILLE

105

Autauga County Heritage Association

102 E Main St, 36067; (p) (334) 361-0961; www.rootsweb/~alataug/; (c) Autauga

Private non-profit/ 1976/ Board of Directors/ staff: 1(f); 25(v)/ members: 323

GENEALOGICAL SOCIETY; HISTORIC PRESERVATION AGENCY; HISTORIC SITE; HISTORICAL SOCIETY; HISTORY MUSEUM; HOUSE MUSEUM; RESEARCH CENTER: Collects and preserves the history of Autauga County and makes historical information available.

PROGRAMS: Community Outreach; Exhibits; Guided Tours; Research Library/Archives

COLLECTIONS: [19th c] 400 local history paintings and period artifacts in a 19th c home.

HOURS: Yr M-F 10-4

106

Autauga Genealogical Society

102 E Main St, 36068 [PO Box 680668, 36068-0668]; (c) Autauga

Private non-profit/ 1991/ members: 200/publication: *Autauga Ancestry*

GENEALOGICAL SOCIETY: Promotes, collects, and preserves genealogical and historical data relating to Autauga County.

PROGRAMS: Lectures; Publication; Research Library/Archives

COLLECTIONS: Reference books, federal county censuses.

HOURS: Yr M-F 1st and 3rd Sa 10-4

ADMISSION: Donations accepted

107

Buena Vista Mansion

102 E Main St, 36067 [PO Box 178, 36067]; (p) (334) 365-3690 (Tuesdays only), (334) 361-0961

SELMA

108

Alabama Historical Commission-Old Cahawba

Old Cahawba Historic Park, 36701 [719 Tremont St, 36701]; (p) (334) 875-2529; (f) (334) 875-5168; cahawba@bellsouth.net; www.SelmaAlabama.com; (c) Dallas

State/ 1985/ Alabama Historical Commission/ staff: 6(f); 1(p); 25(v)/ members: 300

HISTORIC PRESERVATION AGENCY; HISTORIC SITE: Preserve, protect, and present history. Old Cahawba Park is the first state capitol site.

PROGRAMS: Annual Meeting; Community Outreach; Exhibits; Facility Rental; Family Programs; Festivals; Garden Tours; Guided Tours; Interpretation; Research Library/Archives; School-Based Curriculum

COLLECTIONS: [19th c] Artifacts recovered during archaeological study, documents, and genealogical research concerning the townsite.

HOURS: Yr M-Su 9-5

ADMISSION: $2

109
Joseph T. Smitherman Historic Building
109 Union St, 36701; (p) (334) 874-2174; (c) Dallas

City/ 1972/ staff: 2(f); 3(p)

HISTORIC SITE; HOUSE MUSEUM: Preserves historic building.

PROGRAMS: Exhibits; Facility Rental; Festivals; Guided Tours

COLLECTIONS: [Civil War and Victorian] 1847 building.

HOURS: Yr T-Sa 9-4

ADMISSION: $3

110
Old Cahawba Archaeological State Park
9518 Cahawba Rd, 36701 [719 Tremont St, 36701]; (p) (334) 875-2529; (f) (334) 875-5168; cahawba@zebra.net; (c) Dallas

1989/ Alabama Historical Commission/ staff: 5(f); 1(p); 26(v)

HISTORIC PRESERVATION AGENCY; HISTORIC SITE; LIVING HISTORY/OUTDOOR MUSEUM; RESEARCH CENTER: First state capitol site and thriving antebellum town; evolved into famous ghost town.

PROGRAMS: Community Outreach; Elder's Programs; Exhibits; Family Programs; Festivals; Guided Tours; Interpretation; Lectures; Living History; Research Library/Archives; School-Based Curriculum

COLLECTIONS: [19th c] Genealogical information from record stripping projects and town history from 1719-1900.

HOURS: Daily 9-5

ADMISSION: $2

111
Sturdivant Hall Museum
713 Mabry St, 36702 [PO Box 1205, 36702-1205]; (p) (334) 872-5626; (c) Dallas

Private non-profit/ 1957/ Sturdivant Museum Association/ staff: 2(f); 5(p); 24(v)/ members: 400

HISTORY MUSEUM; HOUSE MUSEUM: Preserves historic home and period furnishings.

PROGRAMS: Annual Meeting; Exhibits; Facility Rental; Festivals; Guided Tours

COLLECTIONS: [1850-present] Victorian furnishings.

HOURS: Yr T-Sa 9-4

ADMISSION: $5, Student $2; Group rates

SHEFFIELD

112
Tennessee Valley Historical Society
[PO Box 149, 35660]; (p) (256) 766-7521; KRJOHN@hiway.net; http://home.hiwaay.net/~krjohn/index.html; (c) Colbert

Private non-profit/ 1923/ staff: 2(v)/ members: 150/publication: *Journal of Muscle Shoal History*

HISTORICAL SOCIETY: Collects, preserves, and encourages the use of local historical materials.

COLLECTIONS: Collected materials are held in and administered by local public

STEVENSON

113
Stevenson Railroad Depot Museum
Main St, 35772 [Box 894, 35772]; (p) (256) 437-3012; (c) Jackson

City, non-profit/ 1982/ City of Stevenson/ staff: 1(f); 1(p)

HISTORIC SITE; HISTORY MUSEUM: Restored railroad depot.

PROGRAMS: Annual Meeting; Exhibits; Festivals; Reenactments

COLLECTIONS: [1800-present] Native American artifacts, Civil War memorabilia, and agricultural and railroad exhibits.

HOURS: Yr Nov-Apr 1 M-F 9-4:30, Apr 1-Nov M-Sa 9:00-4:30

TALLADEGA

114
International Motor Sports Hall of Fame
[PO Box 1018, 35161]; (p) (256) 362-5002; (f) (256) 362-5684; imhof@motorsportshalloffame.com; www.motorsportshalloffame.com; (c) Talladega

1982/ staff: 9(f); 75(v)

HISTORIC PRESERVATION AGENCY; HISTORY MUSEUM; RESEARCH CENTER: Promotes motor sports history.

PROGRAMS: Annual Meeting; Exhibits; Facility Rental; Festivals; Film/Video; Guided Tours; Living History; Research Library/Archives

COLLECTIONS: [1902-present] Autos and related memorabilia.

HOURS: Yr Daily 8:30-5

ADMISSION: $8, Student $7

TALLASSEE

115
Patterson Log Cabin/Tallassee Chamber of Commerce
Sims Ave, 36708 [301-A King St, 36708]; (p) (334) 283-5151; (f) (334) 283-2940

HOUSE MUSEUM: A circa1845 two-room log cabin; oldest dwelling in Tallassee and still on its original location. Renovated by the Carrville Historical Society, Inc. in the mid-1970s.

COLLECTIONS: [19th-20th c] Original 1845 log cabin with big stone chimneys and a "dog trot" hallway.

THEODORE

116
Bellingrath Gardens and Home
12401 Bellingrath Gardens Rd, 36587; (p) (334) 973-2217; (f) (334) 973-0540; bellingrath@juno.com; (c) Mobile

Private non-profit/ 1932/ Bellingrath-Morse Foundation/ staff: 64(f); 20(p); 120(v)/ members: 300/publication: *Vinelines*

GARDEN; HOUSE MUSEUM: Home of Walter and Bessie Bellingrath surrounded by gardens.

PROGRAMS: Facility Rental; Guided Tours; Publication

COLLECTIONS: [19th-20th c] Original furnishings, Meissen, Derby, Chelsea, and Bow porcelain, Georgian silver, china, and crystal.

HOURS: Summer and Spring: Daily 8-6; Winter: Daily 8-5; Dec: Daily 8-9

TUSCALOOSA

117
Battle-Friedman House
1010 Greensboro Ave, 35401 [1010 Greensboro Ave, 35401]; (p) (205) 758-6138, (205) 758-2238

1835/ City; Tuscaloosa County Preservation Society/ staff: 3(p)

HOUSE MUSEUM

COLLECTIONS: [Mid 19th c] Historic house with Renaissance Revival parlor suite, c.1878.

HOURS: Yr T-Sa 10-12/1-4; Su 1-4

118
Gorgas House
Capstone Dr, Univ of Alabama, 35487 [PO Box 870266, 35487-0266]; (p) (205) 348-5906; (f) (205) 348-9292; www.ua.edu/gorgasmain.html; (c) Tuscaloosa

State/ 1954/ Univ of AL Museums/ staff: 1(p); 10(v)

HISTORIC SITE; HOUSE MUSEUM: Built in 1829 and designed by William Nichols, the Gorgas House museum is one of four buildings that survived the burning of the University of Alabama campus during the Civil War.

PROGRAMS: Facility Rental; Guided Tours; Interpretation

COLLECTIONS: [1829-1900] Furniture and antiques that belonged to the Gorgas family.

HOURS: Yr

119
Jemison-Van de Graaff Mansion Foundation
1305 Greensboro Ave, 35403 [PO Box 1216, 35403]; (p) (205) 348-9538; (f) (205) 348-5383; gwolfe@english.as.ua.edu; (c) Tuscaloosa

1991/ Jemison-Van de Graaff Mansion Foundation/ staff: 1(p); 15(v)

HISTORIC SITE; HOUSE MUSEUM: Preserves antebellum Italianate villa.

COLLECTIONS: [Mid-19th c.]

HOURS: Yr M-F 10-4

120
Moundville Archaeological Park
1 Mound State Pkwy, 35487 [PO Box 870340, 35487]; (p) (205) 371-2234; (f) (205) 371-4180; www.ua.edu/mndville.htm; (c) Tuscaloosa/Hale

1933/ Univ of Alabama/ staff: 9(f); 20(p); 3(v)

ARCHAEOLOGICAL SITE/MUSEUM: Preserves and interprets prehistoric Native American mounds of Mississipian period.

PROGRAMS: Exhibits; Facility Rental; Family Programs; Festivals; Film/Video; Guided Tours; Interpretation; Living History; School-Based Curriculum

COLLECTIONS: [Mississippian period] Ceramic, lithic, and copper artifacts; excavation maps, and documentary photos.

HOURS: Yr Daily 9-5

ADMISSION: $4; Student $2

121
Paul W. Bryant Museum
300 Bryant Dr, 35487 [PO Box 870385, 35487-0385]; (p) (205) 348-4668; (f) (205) 348-8883; www.ua.edu/bryant.htm; (c) Tuscaloosa

State/ 1988/ University of Alabama Museums/ staff: 7(f); 5(p); 4(v)/ members: 300

RESEARCH CENTER: Preserves Univ of AL football history.

PROGRAMS: Community Outreach; Exhibits; Facility Rental; Family Programs; Film/Video; Guided Tours; Research Library/Archives; School-Based Curriculum; Theatre

COLLECTIONS: [1892-present] Archives, photographs, film, journals, and books related to AL football history.

HOURS: Yr Daily 9-4

ADMISSION: $2,

TUSCUMBIA

122
Alabama Music Hall of Fame
Hwy 72 W, 35674 [PO Box 740405, 35674]; (p) (256) 381-4417; (f) (256) 381-1031; alamhof@hiwaay.net; alamhof@hiwaay.org; (c) Colbert

State/ 1980/ Board of Directors/ staff: 11(f); 3(p); 10(v)

HISTORY MUSEUM: Honors Alabama's music performing and non-performing.

PROGRAMS: Concerts; Exhibits; Facility Rental; Festivals

COLLECTIONS: [1930s-present] Costumes, instruments, manuscripts, photographs, historical documents, and wax figures.

HOURS: Yr Su 1-5, M-Sa 9-5

ADMISSION: $6, Children $3, Seniors $5

TUSCUMBRIA

123
Belle Mont Mansion/Alabama Historical Society
Cooks Lane, S on Hwy 92 off Hwy 43, 35674 [468 S Perry St, Montgomery, 36130-0900]; (p) (256) 381-5052, (334) 242-3184

Alabama Historical Commission

HOUSE MUSEUM: Belle Mont Mansion (circa 1828) features brick neoclassical architecture of Jeffersonian-Palladian style.

HOURS: Mar-Oct T-Sa 10-2, Su 1-5 or by appt

124
Ivy Green, Birthplace of Helen Keller
300 W N Commons, 35674 [300 W N Commons, Tuscumbia, 35674]; (p) (205) 383-4066; http://www.helenkellerbirthplace.org/; (c) Tuscumbia

1820

HOUSE MUSEUM: Birthplace of Helen Keller; listed on the National Register of Historic Places, built in 1820.

PROGRAMS: Festivals; Guided Tours

ADMISSION: $3, Children $1

TUSKEGEE INSTITUTE

125
Tuskegee Institute National Historic Site, George Washington Carver Museum
Tuskegee Univ Campus, 36088 [1212 Old Montgomery Rd, 36088]; (p) (334) 727-6390, (334) 727-6391; (f) (334) 727-1448; (c) Macon

Joint/ 1975/ National Park Service; Tuskegee University/ staff: 14(f); 1(p); 8(v)

HISTORIC SITE; HOUSE MUSEUM: Promotes the lives of Booker T. Washington and George Washington Carver and the history of the Tuskegee Institute.

PROGRAMS: Exhibits; Family Programs; Festivals; Film/Video; Garden Tours; Interpretation; Reenactments; Research Library/Archives; School-Based Curriculum

COLLECTIONS: [19th-20th c] Personal effects of Booker T. Washington and George Washington Carver; artifacts of the Tuskegee Institute.

HOURS: Yr Daily 9-5

UNION SPRINGS

126
Bullock County Historical Society
[PO Box 563, 36089]; (p) (334) 474-3238; tghixon@ustconline.net; (c) Bullock

1975/ Executive Board/ members: 95

HISTORIC PRESERVATION AGENCY; HISTORIC SITE; HISTORICAL SOCIETY; HOUSE MUSEUM: Maintains log cabin and museum.

PROGRAMS: Exhibits; Festivals; Garden Tours; Guided Tours; Quarterly Meeting

COLLECTIONS: Artifacts of the area.

HOURS: Yr by appt

ADMISSION: Donations accepted

127
Log Cabin Museum
[PO Box 563, 36089]; (p) (334) 738-5411, (738) 738-5413; tghixon@ustconline.net; (c) Bullock

1851

HOUSE MUSEUM

COLLECTIONS: [1850s] 1851 log cabin authentically furnished-furniture, kitchen utensils, quilts; Pictures, books.

HOURS: By appt

VALLEY

128
Chattahoochee Valley Historical Society
3419 20th Avenue, 36854; (p) (334) 768-2050; (f) (334) 768-7272; (c) Chambers

Private non-profit/ 1953/ staff: 2(v)/ members: 65/publication: *The Voice; and others*

HISTORICAL SOCIETY: Collects, interprets, and publishes the local history of Chambers County, AL and West Point, GA.

PROGRAMS: Exhibits; Family Programs; Publication; Research Library/Archives

COLLECTIONS: [1825-present] Books, historic documents, papers, and genealogy of our local area, and the Southeast housed at Cobb Memorial Archives.

129
Cobb Memorial Archives
3419 20th Ave, 36854; (p) (334) 768-2050; (f) (334) 768-7272; (c) Chambers

Joint/ 1976/County; Private non-profit/ staff: 1(f); 1(p); 4(v)

LIBRARY AND/OR ARCHIVES: Collects and preserves local history through manuscripts, photographs, maps, scrapbooks, and clothing that document the history of the area for present and future generations.

PROGRAMS: Community Outreach; Exhibits; Research Library/Archives

COLLECTIONS: [1832 to present] Area maps, photographs, D.A.R. and U.D.C. records of local chapters, family histories, records of the building of West Point Dam, area newspapers from 1916 to present, and records of World War II servicemen and women.

HOURS: Yr M-F 10-6, Sa 10-5

ADMISSION: No charge

WATERLOO

130
Edith Newman Culver Memorial Museum
Main St, 35677 [PO Box 38, 35677]; (p) (205) 767-6081, (205) 764-3237; (f) (205) 764-3837

City/ 1870/ staff: 1(p); 4(v)

COLLECTIONS: Native American weapons and tools; also antique woodworking equipment, farm implements, buggies, wagons, 19th c papers, old Bibles,

WETUMPKA

131
Fort Toulouse/Jackson Park
2521 W Fort Toulouse Rd, 36093; (p) (334) 567-3002; (f) (334) 514-6625; (c) Elmore

State/ 1970/ AL Historical Commission/ staff: 7(f); 40(v)

HISTORIC SITE; LIVING HISTORY/OUTDOOR MUSEUM; RESEARCH CENTER: State Historic Site and National Historic Landmark in a rural setting.

PROGRAMS: Festivals; Interpretation; Living History; Reenactments

COLLECTIONS: [100 A.D.-1818] Excavated archaeological materials: Native American, French, British, American and War of 1812 artifacts.

HOURS: Visitor Center: Yr Daily 8-5;

ALASKA

AKUTAN

132
Akutan Traditional Council
[PO Box 89, 99553]; (p) (907) 698-2300; (f) (907) 698-2301; Qigiigun@aol.com

Private non-profit/ staff: 3(f)

HISTORY MUSEUM; TRIBAL MUSEUM: Informs tribal members on issues such as tribal monies and land.

PROGRAMS: Annual Meeting

HOURS: Yr M-F

ANAKTUVUK PASS

133
Simon Paneak Memorial Museum
North Slope Borough-Planning Dept.
341 Mekiana St, 99721 [PO Box 21085, 99721]; (p) (907) 661-3413; (f) (907) 661-3414; vweber@co.north-slope.ak.us; (c) North Slope Bourough

County/ 1986/ NSB Planning Dept/ staff: 2(p)

HISTORY MUSEUM

PROGRAMS: Community Outreach; Interpretation; Research Library/Archives; School-Based Curriculum

COLLECTIONS: [1940-1960] Collections of Nunamuit artifacts.

HOURS: Yr M-F 8:30-5

ADMISSION: $5

ANCHORAGE

134
Alaska Historical Society
1689 C St, #202, 99510 [PO Box 100299, 99510-0299]; (p) (907) 276-1596; (f) (907) 276-1596; ahs@alaska.net; www.alaska.net/~ahs

Private non-profit/ 1967/ staff: 2(v)/ members: 500/publication: *Alaska History News;*

HISTORICAL SOCIETY: Promotes, preserves, and interpretes Alaska's history.

PROGRAMS: Annual Meeting; Community Outreach; Publication

135
Alaska Office of History and
Archaeology
550 W 7th Ave, Ste 1310, 99501-3565; (p) (907) 269-8721; (f) (907) 269-8908; oha@alaska.net

State/ 1971/ staff: 14(f); 4(v)

HISTORIC PRESERVATION AGENCY: Promotes and facilitates preservation of Alaska's history and prehistory.

PROGRAMS: Community Outreach; Interpretation; Lectures

HOURS: Yr M-F 8-5

136
Alaska Support Office, National Park
Service
2525 Gambell St, Rm 107, 99503; (p) (907) 257-2656; (f) (907) 257-2510; bett-knight@nps.gov

Federal/ staff: 2(f)

LIBRARY AND/OR ARCHIVES: A collection repository for the National Park Service Alaska Region; exhibits at several off-site facilities.

PROGRAMS: Exhibits; Research Library/Archives

COLLECTIONS: Collections that document the cultural and natural history of park areas, administrative archives, and trends in development of Alaska federal lands.

HOURS: Yr M-F 8-4 by appt

137
Anchorage Historic Properties
645 W 3rd Ave, 99501; (p) (907) 274-3600; (f) (907) 274-3600; ahpi@customcpu.com; www.customcpu.com/np/ahpi

Private non-profit/ 1987/ Municipality of Anchorage/ staff: 1(f); 2(p); 30(v)/ members: 100

HISTORIC PRESERVATION AGENCY; HOUSE MUSEUM: Promotes preservation of the Oscar Anderson House Museum.

PROGRAMS: Annual Meeting; Concerts; Guided Tours; Interpretation; Lectures; Publication; School-Based Curriculum

COLLECTIONS: [1915-1920] Oscar Anderson House was one of the first permanent homes in Anchorage and is restored and furnished.

HOURS: June-Aug M-Sa 12-4 and 1st two wknds in Dec

ADMISSION: $3, Children $1, Seniors $2

138
Anchorage Museum of History and Art
121 W 7th Ave, 99501; (p) (907) 343-4326; (f) (907) 343-6149; museum@ci.anchorage.ak.us

City/ 1968/ staff: 20(f); 4(p); 182(v)/ members: 3000

ART MUSEUM; HISTORY MUSEUM: Dedicated to the collection, preservation, exhibition, and interpretation of Alaska art, history, and ethnography.

PROGRAMS: Annual Meeting; Community Outreach; Concerts; Exhibits; Facility Rental; Festivals; Guided Tours; Interpretation; Lectures; Research Library/Archives; School-Based Curriculum

COLLECTIONS: [Prehistory-present]

HOURS: May-Sept Daily 9-6; Oct-Apr T-Sa 10-6, Su 1-5

ADMISSION: $5, Seniors $4.50

139
Blacks in Alaska History Project, Inc.
418 S Bliss St, 99514 [PO Box 143507, 99514-3507]; (p) (907) 333-4719; (f) (907) 333-4238; akblkhist@bigfoot.com; www.big-foot.com/~akblkhist

Joint/ 1995/ State; Private non-profit/ staff: 1(v)/ members: 115

HISTORIC PRESERVATION AGENCY; RESEARCH CENTER: Maintains The George Harper Collection, collects, and publicizes the history of Black Alaskans.

PROGRAMS: Community Outreach; Exhibits; Lectures; Research Library/Archives

COLLECTIONS: [1867-present] Historical photographs, newspaper clippings, books, book references.

140
Cook Inlet Historical Society, Inc.
121 W 7th Ave, 99501-3696; (p) (907) 343-6172; (f) (907) 343-6149; (c) Anchorage

Private non-profit/ 1955/ Board of Directors/ staff: 22(v)/ members: 263

HISTORICAL SOCIETY: Preserves, interprets, gathers, and disseminates local and state history and supports the Anchorage Museum of History and Art.

PROGRAMS: Annual Meeting; Community Outreach; Guided Tours; Interpretation; Lectures; Research Library/Archives

COLLECTIONS: [20th c] Artifacts and photographs reflecting Alaskan development.

141
Heritage Library Museum
301 W Northern Lights Blvd, 99510 [PO Box 100600, 99510-0600]; (p) (907) 265-2834; (f) (907) 265-2002

Private non-profit/ 1968/ National Bank of AK/ staff: 1(f); 1(p)/publication: *Heritage of Alaska*

HISTORY MUSEUM: Promotes AK history and culture to local residents and visitors.

PROGRAMS: Exhibits; Guided Tours; Interpretation; Publication; Research Library/Archives; School-Based Curriculum

COLLECTIONS: [Prehistory] Archaeological collections representing the history and culture of AK's native people, artwork by AK's artists and a library of books on Alaskan subjects supporting the museum collection.

HOURS: Yr M-F 12-4

ADMISSION: No charge

142
Museums Alaska
[PO Box 242323, 99524]; (p) (907) 243-4714; (f) (907) 243-4714; www.museumsalaska.org

1983/ Museums Alaska Inc/ staff: 1(p)/ members: 160/publication: *Network*

ALLIANCE OF HISTORICAL AGENCIES: Disburses information about museums, cultural centers, and their activities; collects and shares professional opportunities.

PROGRAMS: Annual Meeting; Publication

143
Oscar Anderson House Museum
420 M St, 99501; (p) (907) 274-2336; (f) (907) 274-3600; www.customcpu.com/np/ahpi

Joint/ 1915/City; Anchorage Historic Properties, Inc./ staff: 1(p)

HOUSE MUSEUM: One of the first permanent family residences on the original Anchorage townsite.

COLLECTIONS: [1915-1925] Artifacts and memorabilia belonging to the Anderson family: Family photographs; photographs of early Anchorage; original writings and documents of the Anderson family.

HOURS: June-Sept, Dec

144
Inupiat Heritage Center
5421 N Star St, 99723 [PO Box 749, 99723];
(p) (907) 852-4594; (f) (907) 852-4594

1998/ Ilisagvik College/ staff: 3(f)

HISTORY MUSEUM; LIVING HISTORY/OUT-
DOOR MUSEUM; RESEARCH CENTER: Educational programs and exhibits on Inuit traditional knowledge, language, and culture.

PROGRAMS: Community Outreach; Elder's
Programs; Exhibits; Facility Rental; Film/Video;
Lectures; Living History; Research Library/
Archives; School-Based Curriculum

COLLECTIONS: [5000BC-present] Inuit/Inupi-
at artifacts.

HOURS: Daily

145
**North Slope Borough Commission on
Inupiat History, Language and Culture**
5421 N Star St, 99723 [PO Box 69, 99723]; (p)
(907) 852-0422; (f) (907) 852-1224; jharcharek
@co.north-slope.ak.us; www.co.north-slope. ak.
us/ihlc; (c) North Slope

County/ 1975/ Commission on Inupiat History,
Language and Culture/ staff: 5(f)

ALLIANCE OF HISTORICAL AGENCIES; GE-
NEALOGICAL SOCIETY; HISTORY MUSE-
UM: Documents, preserves, and perpetuates
the history, language, and culture of the North
Slope inhabitants

PROGRAMS: Community Outreach; Elder's
Programs; Exhibits; Facility Rental; Guided
Tours; Lectures; Living History; School-Based
Curriculum

COLLECTIONS: [Early to late prehistoric-
early history] Ethnographic material excavated
in the Utqiagvik Archaeological Site.

HOURS: Yr M-F 9-5

BETHEL

146
**Yupiit Piciryarait Cultural Center and
Museum**
420 State Hwy, 99559 [PO Box 219, 99559];
(p) (907) 543-1819; (f) (907) 543-1885;
joan_hamilton@avcp.org

Joint/ 1995/ Private non-profit; Association of
Village Council Presidents/ staff: 1(f); 1(p); 3(v)

RESEARCH CENTER: Three galleries: permanent exhibits of clothing, household, hunting and gathering implements used by the
people of the Yukon-Kuskokwim Delta in ancient and contemporary times. Two galleries
for short term exhibits.

PROGRAMS: Community Outreach; Elder's
Programs; Research Library/Archives; School-
Based Curriculum

COLLECTIONS: Collection of artifacts from
Yup'ik/Cup'ik Native Peoples, basket collection, hunting, and fishing materials.

HOURS: Yr T-Sa 12-5

ADMISSION: Donations requested

CENTRAL

147
Circle District Historical Society, Inc.
128 mile Steese Hwy, 99730 [PO Box 31893,
99730-0189]; (p) (907) 520-5312

Private non-profit/ staff: 20(v)/ members: 75

HISTORICAL SOCIETY; HISTORY MUSEUM

PROGRAMS: Annual Meeting; Exhibits; Research Library/Archives

COLLECTIONS: [1893-present]

HOURS: June-Aug Daily 12-5

ADMISSION: $1; Members free

CHICKALOON

148
Nay'dini'aa Na Tribal Cultural Center
[PO Box 1105, 99674]; (p) (907) 745-0707; (f)
(907) 745-7154; chickvill@akcache.com

Tribal/ Chickaloon Village Traditional Council/
staff: 2(v)

CULTURAL CENTER: Exhibits of Athabascan
People of Chickaloon Village. Programs that
teaches Athabascan tradition and heritage.

PROGRAMS: School-Based Curriculum

COLLECTIONS: [1800-present]

HOURS: M-F 9-5

ADMISSION: No charge

COOPER LANDING

149
K'Beg "Footprints" Interpretive Site
Mile 526 Starling Hwy, [PO Box 988, Kenai,
99611]; (p) (907) 283-3633; (f) (907) 283-
3052; (c) Kenai Peninsula Borough

Tribal/ 1971/ Kenaitze Indian Tribe, IRA/ staff:
2(f); 4(p); 4(v)

HISTORIC SITE; TRIBAL MUSEUM: Kenaitze
Indian tribal tradition and culture interpreted
and presented to visitors featuring archaeological sites, traditional plant use.

PROGRAMS: Exhibits; Family Programs;
Guided Tours; Interpretation; Lectures; Research Library/Archives; School-Based Curriculum

COLLECTIONS: [Denaina-Athabscan] Interpretive exhibits featuring Denaina-Athabasan
artifacts covering the last 1,500 years.

HOURS: May-Aug 31 Daily 10-6

ADMISSION: $5; Under 12 free

COPPER CENTER

150
Copper Valley Historical Society
Mile 101 Old Richardson Hwy, 99573 [PO
Box 84, 99573]; (p) (907) 822-5285

Private non-profit/ 1978/ staff: 10(v)/ members: 20

HISTORICAL SOCIETY; HISTORY MUSEUM:
Preserves and presents state and local history.

PROGRAMS: Annual Meeting; Exhibits; Guided Tours; Research Library/Archives

COLLECTIONS: [1898-early 1900s] Artifacts
from Gold Rush stampeders, Native Americans,
Russian traders, and the Kennicott Mines.

HOURS: June-Sept M-Sa 1-5

ADMISSION: Donations accepted

151
George Ashby Memorial Museum
Mile 101, Old Richardson Hwy, Copper Center
Loop Rd, 99573 [PO Box 84, 99573]; (p) (907)
822-5285; alaskan.com/docs/museums.html

HISTORY MUSEUM

CORDOVA

152
**Cordova Historical Society and
Museum**
622 First St, 99574 [PO Box 391, 99574-
0391]; (p) (907) 424-6665; (f) (907) 424-6666;
cdvmsm@ptialaska.net

Joint/ 1967/ City; Private non-profit/ staff: 2(p);
25(v)/ members: 147/publication: *Cordova to
Kennecott*

HISTORICAL SOCIETY; HISTORY MUSEUM:
Collects, preserves, interprets, and researches the history and cultural background of Cordova, Copper River, Kennecott, Katalla, Prince
William Sound and adjacent areas.

PROGRAMS: Annual Meeting; Community
Outreach; Exhibits; Facility Rental; Family Programs; Festivals; Film/Video; Guided Tours; Interpretation; Lectures; Publication; Research
Library/Archives; School-Based Curriculum

COLLECTIONS: [20th c] 2,500 artifacts relating to cultural and industrial history of the region, including photographs and complete
newspaper archives.

HOURS: Mey-Sept M-Sa 10-6, Su 2-4; Sept-
May T-F 1-5, Sa 2-4

ADMISSION: $1; Under 19 free

DELTA JUNCTION

153
Delta Historical Society
Museum in Big Delta State Historical Park,
99737 [PO Box 1089, 99737]; (p) (907) 895-4813

Private non-profit/ 1975/ staff: 1(v)/ members: 8

HISTORIC SITE; HISTORICAL SOCIETY;
HISTORY MUSEUM; HOUSE MUSEUM: 10-
acre state historical park, also Sullivan's
Roadhouse (1910), run by the Delta Junction
Chamber of Commerce as a museum.

PROGRAMS: Annual Meeting; Exhibits; Interpretation

COLLECTIONS: [1898-1940] Items from the
Gold Rush era, a Russian trading post, military
communication center/transportation hub and
first area farm, displayed in restored buildings.

HOURS: Park: Mid June-mid Sept Daily 6-9;
Roadhouse: Mid June-mid Sept Daily 9-6

ADMISSION: No charge

DILLINGHAM

154
**Dillingham Historic Preservation
Commission**
Main St, 99576 [PO Box 889, 99576]; (p)
(907) 842-5221

City/ 1984/ staff: 6(v)

HISTORIC PRESERVATION AGENCY: Preserves architectural, oral, written, and cultural history.

COLLECTIONS: Public and private buildings of historic significance, including the local Peter Pan cannery.

EAGLE CITY

155
Eagle Historical Society and Museums
Third & Chamberlain, 99738 [PO Box 23, 99738]; (p) (907) 547-2325; (f) (907) 547-2232; ehsmuseums@aol.com; www.alaska.net/~eagleak/index.htm

Private non-profit/ 1961/ staff: 1(f); 1(p); 24(v)/ members: 326/publication: *Jewel on the Yukon: Eagle City*

HISTORICAL SOCIETY: Discovers, collects, preserves, displays, and disseminates historical information about Eagle and the surrounding area.

PROGRAMS: Annual Meeting; Community Outreach; Exhibits; Facility Rental; Family Programs; Film/Video; Guided Tours; Interpretation; Lectures; Publication; Research Library/Archives

COLLECTIONS: [1898-1930] Five historic buildings, archives, and photograph collections.

HOURS: May-Sept Daily 9-12 by appt

ADMISSION: $5; Under 12/Mbrs free

EAGLE RIVER

156
Eklutna Historical Park, Inc.
Eklutna Village Rd, 99577 [16515 Centerfield Dr, Suite 201, 99577]; (p) (907) 688-6026, (907) 696-2828; (f) (907) 696-2845; ehp@alaska.net; www.alaskaone.com/eklutna

Private non-profit/ 1990/ staff: 1(f); 9(p)

HISTORIC SITE; HISTORY MUSEUM; HOUSE MUSEUM; LIVING HISTORY/OUTDOOR MUSEUM; TRIBAL MUSEUM: Preserves the heritage and traditions of the Dena'ina Athabaskan Indians.

PROGRAMS: Exhibits; Festivals; Guided Tours; Interpretation

COLLECTIONS: [Early 19th c-present] Russian Orthodox icons, crosses, birch bark baskets, medicine bags, drums, Alaska Native arts and crafts, photographs, and artifacts.

HOURS: Mid May-mid Sept Daily 8-6

ADMISSION: $3.50; Group rates

FAIRBANKS

157
Alaska and Polar Regions Department
P.O. Box 756808, 99775-6808; (p) (907) 474-7261; fyapr@uaf.edu; www.uaf.edu/library/collections/apr/

HISTORY MUSEUM; LIBRARY AND/OR ARCHIVES; RESEARCH CENTER: Acquires, preserves, and provides access to materials that document the past and present of Alaska and the polar regions, both Arctic and Antarctic including northern Canada, Greenland, northern Scandinavia, Iceland, and northern Russia (Siberia and the Russian Far East).

COLLECTIONS: Archives, manuscripts, historic photographs, rare books and maps, oral histories, and archival films on many subjects including: Russian-America, expeditions, politics, commerce, anthropology.

158
Alaskaland Pioneer Air Museum
Airport Way & Peger Rd, 99707 [PO Box 70437, 99707-0437]; (p) (907) 452-5609, (907) 451-0037; www.akpub.com/akttt/aviat.html; (c) Fairbanks

1990/ Interior and Arctic AK Aeronautical Foundation/ staff: 4(p); 7(v)/ members: 51

AVIATION MUSEUM: Chronicles a unique blend of unusual stories focusing on solo piloting adventures and pioneer aviation businesses operating in the arctic and interior bush areas.

PROGRAMS: Exhibits; Guided Tours

COLLECTIONS: [1900s] Antique aircraft and aviation memorabilia.

HOURS: May-Sept Daily 11-9

ADMISSION: $2; Under 12 free

159
Fairbanks Community Museum
410 Cushman St, 99701; (p) (907) 457-3669, (907) 452-8671

Private non-profit/ staff: 15(v)/ members: 38

HISTORY MUSEUM

PROGRAMS: Annual Meeting; Exhibits; Film/Video; Interpretation; Theatre

COLLECTIONS: [1896-present] Archival photos, period artifacts, and newspapers.

HOURS: Apr-Oct T-Sa 11-5

ADMISSION: Donations accepted

160
Joint Fairbanks North Star Borough/ City of Fairbanks Historic Preservation Commission
809 Pioneer Rd, 99707 [PO Box 71267, 99707-1267]; (p) (907) 459-1258; (f) (907) 459-1255; rpatten@co.fairbanks.ak.us; www.co.fairbanks.ak.us

Joint/ Borough; City

HISTORIC PRESERVATION AGENCY: Prepares and maintains an inventory of buildings and sites of historical, cultural, architectural, and archaeological significance, maintains the local historic preservation plan, reviews nominations to the National Register, and makes recommendations on local development projects.

161
Judge James Wickersham House, The
33 Alaskaland, 99701 [PO Box 71336, 99707-1336]; (p) (907) 455-8947, (907) 457-6165; (f) (907) 457-6165; (c) Fairbanks

1904/ staff: 4(p); 17(v)

HOUSE MUSEUM: Home of Judge James Wickersham, Alaska's delegate to Congress, who introduced the Alaska Statehood bill.

COLLECTIONS: [Early 20th c] Alaska Native basket collection.

162
Pioneer Memorial Park, Inc.
Airport Rd & Peger St, 99707 [PO Box 70176, 99707]; (p) (907) 456-8579; (f) (907) 456-3000; pioneer museum@mosquitonet.com; www.akpub.com/akttt/pione.html

Private non-profit/ 1961/ staff: 15(v)

HISTORICAL SOCIETY; HISTORY MUSEUM: Preserves and exhibits artifacts on the history of Fairbanks and the Alaskan interior.

PROGRAMS: Exhibits; Guided Tours; Theatre

COLLECTIONS: [1867-present] Gold prospecting/mining, vintage transportation artifacts, snowshoes, aircraft, agriculture, commerce, frontier life, communications, sports, entertainment, and professions; archives, photos, and publications. Collection of gold rush paintings by C.R. Heurlin.

HOURS: Daily

ADMISSION: Museum free

163
Tanana Yukon Historical Society
[PO Box 71336, 99707-1336]; (p) (907) 455-8947; www.polarnet.com/~tyhs/; (c) Fairbanks

Joint; Private non-profit/ 1958/ Board of Directors/ staff: 1(p); 25(v)/ members: 180/publication: *First Catch Your Moose: Fairbanks Cookbook, 1909*

HISTORICAL SOCIETY: Administers Wickersham House, an historic house museum, publishes local history, and advocates local historic preservation.

PROGRAMS: Annual Meeting; Guided Tours; Lectures; Publication

HOURS: June-Aug Daily 11-9

ADMISSION: Donations accepted

164
University of Alaska Museum
907 Yukon Dr, 99775 [PO Box 756960, 99775]; (p) (907) 474-7505; (f) (907) 474-5469; fyuamus@aurora.alaska.edu; www.zorba.uafadm.alaska.edu/museum

State/ 1929/ Univ of AK/ staff: 29(f); 40(p); 40(v)/ members: 176/publication: *Looking North*

ART MUSEUM; HISTORY MUSEUM; NATURAL HISTORY MUSEUM: Collects and preserve AK's natural, cultural, and art history; provides research material, specimens, and artifacts.

PROGRAMS: Community Outreach; Elder's Programs; Exhibits; Facility Rental; Family Programs; Guided Tours; Lectures; School-Based Curriculum; Theatre

COLLECTIONS: Alaska's natural, cultural, and art history; artworks, objects, mammal, herbarium, aquatic and bird specimens, frozen tissue samples, archaeological materials, earth science.

HOURS: Yr Daily

ADMISSION: $5, Student $3, Seniors $4.50

HAINES

165
Sheldon Museum and Cultural Center, Inc.
11 Main St, 99827 [PO Box 269, 99827]; (p) (907) 766-2366; (f) (907) 766-2368; curator@sheldonmuseum.org; www.sheldonmuseum.org; (c) Haines

Joint/ 1975/ County; Private non-profit/ staff: 1(f); 5(p); 200(v)/ members: 120

HISTORY MUSEUM: Pioneer history and Native Tlingit culture and art.

PROGRAMS: Community Outreach; Concerts; Elder's Programs; Exhibits; Facility Rental; Family Programs; Festivals; Film/Video; Guided Tours; Interpretation; Lectures; Publication; Research Library/Archives; School-Based Curriculum

COLLECTIONS: [1867-present] Military, mining, lighthouse lens, commercial fishing, household goods, unique items from local people, ethnographic collection: bentwood boxes, spruce root baskets, Chikat Blankets, totems, tools/utensils, camphorwood trunks, ivory; photographs, archival materials

HOURS: Yr mid May-mid Sept Daily 1-5, T-F 10-12, M-Th 7-9; Mid Sept-mid May M,W 1-4, T,Th, F 3-5

ADMISSION: $3; Under 12 free

HOPE

166
Hope and Sunrise Historical Society
[PO Box 88, 99605]; (p) (907) 782-3750; www.advenalaska.com/hope

Private non-profit/ 1970

HISTORICAL SOCIETY; HISTORY MUSEUM: Mining museum interprets Alaska's Turnagain Arm Gold Rush.

PROGRAMS: Annual Meeting; Exhibits; Research Library/Archives

COLLECTIONS: [1888-present]

HOURS: May-Sept M, F, Sa 12-4, Su 12-2

ADMISSION: Donations accepted

167
Kenai Peninsula Historical Association
[PO Box 41, 99605]; (p) (907) 782-3115; (c) Kenai Peninsula

Private non-profit

HISTORICAL SOCIETY: Represents five Alaskan historical societies.

PROGRAMS: Annual Meeting

JUNEAU

168
Alaska Historical Collection, Alaska State Library
333 Willoughby Ave, 99811 [PO Box 110571, 99811-0571]; (p) (907) 465-2925; (f) (907) 465-2990; www.library.state.ak.us/hist

State/ 1900/ Div. of Archives/ staff: 7(f)

LIBRARY AND/OR ARCHIVES: Alaskana collections and publications. Works withsister institutions, the AK State Museum and the AK State Archives, to document AK's history, cultures, and development.

PROGRAMS: Publication; Research Library/Archives

COLLECTIONS: [Prehistory-present] 65,000 artifacts and 1,000 manuscripts; photograph collections on all aspects of Alaska history, cultures, and development.

HOURS: M-F 1-5

169
Alaska State Museum
395 Whittier St, 99801; (p) (907) 465-2901; (f) (907) 465-2976; bruce_kato@educ.state.ak.us; www.educ.state.ak.us/lam/museum

State/ 1900/ staff: 12(f); 3(p); 175(v)/ members: 250/publication: *Bulletin/Concepts*

ART MUSEUM; HISTORY MUSEUM; RESEARCH CENTER: Collects and preserves human and natural history of AK.

PROGRAMS: Annual Meeting; Community Outreach; Exhibits; Guided Tours; Interpretation; Lectures; Publication

COLLECTIONS: [1700s-present] 20,000 catalogued objects, including ethnographic (Northwest Coast, Eskimo, Athabaskan, Aleut), and historical artifacts, works of art, and natural history specimens.

HOURS: May-Sept M-F 9-6, Sa-Su 10-6; Oct-Apr T-Sa 10-4

ADMISSION: $5

170
Gastineau Channel Historical Society
Last Chance Mining Museum, 1001 Basin Rd, 99801 [PO Box 21264, 99801]; (p) (907) 586-5338; (f) (907) 586-5820; glrrlg@alaska.net

Private non-profit/ 1956/ staff: 1(p); 100(v)/ members: 200/publication: *In the Miner's Footsteps; Old Gold; and others*

HISTORIC SITE; HISTORICAL SOCIETY; HISTORY MUSEUM: Collects, restores, preserves and interprets historic buildings. Fosters interest in history through the Last Chance Mining Museum and Sentinel Island Lighthouse.

PROGRAMS: Annual Meeting; Exhibits; Facility Rental; Guided Tours; Interpretation; Lectures; Publication

COLLECTIONS: [1880] 3-D glass maps of AJ Mine, tools and artifacts relating to the Gold Rush, and maritime history of Juneau and southeast Alaska.

HOURS: May-Sept Daily 9:30-12:30/3:30-6:30

ADMISSION: $3

171
Juneau-Douglas City Museum
155 S Seward, 99801; (p) (907) 856-3572; (f) (907) 586-3203; www.juneau.lib.ak.us/parksrec/museum/museum.htm; (c) Juneau

Joint/ 1976/ City; Borough/ staff: 3(p); 50(v)

ART MUSEUM; HISTORY MUSEUM: Collects, preserves, and interprets the human history of the Juneau-Douglas area.

INTERPRETATION: Community/State History; Mining; Native American Studies

PROGRAMS: Exhibits; Facility Rental; Family Programs; Film/Video; Interpretation; Lectures; Research Library/Archives; School-Based Curriculum

COLLECTIONS: [1880-present] Artifacts and archival materials focussing on mining and general history of Juneau-Douglas area.

HOURS: Yr Sept-Apr F-Sa 12-4 or by appt; May-Sept M-F 9-5, Sa-Su

KENAI

172
Kenai Visitors and Cultural Center
11471 Kenai Spur Hwy, 99611; (p) (907) 283-1991; (f) (907) 283-2230; kvcb@alaska.net; www.visitKenai.com

1991/ Kenai Visitors and Convention Bureau/ staff: 5(f); 2(p)/ members: 200

HISTORY MUSEUM: Museum and cultural center commemorates the city of Kenai's 200th anniversary.

PROGRAMS: Community Outreach; Concerts; Elder's Programs; Exhibits; Facility Rental; Family Programs; Festivals; Film/Video; Guided Tours; Interpretation; Lectures; Publication; School-Based Curriculum

COLLECTIONS: [Pre-history-present] Artifact collection; Athabaskan, Aleut, and Russian cultural exhibits; homesteading, mining, commercial fishing, oil industry history, and natural history exhibits.

HOURS: Summer M-Sa 9-7; Winter F 9-5 Sa 10-4

ADMISSION: Donations accepted

KETCHIKAN

173
Historic Ketchikan/Ketchikan Convention and Visitors Bureau
306 Main St, 99901-6413 [131 Front St, 99901-6413]; (p) (907) 225-5515; (f) (907) 225-5515

174
Tongass Historical Museum
629 Dock St, 99901; (p) (907) 225-5600; (f) (907) 225-5602; museumdir@city.ketchikan.ak.us; (c) Ketchikan Gateway

City/ 1961/ staff: 9(f); 7(p); 30(v)/publication: *Ketchikan Museums*

HISTORY MUSEUM: Collects, preserves, and interprets artifacts and information relating to Ketchikan and environs; Native Alaskan arts and culture.

PROGRAMS: Community Outreach; Exhibits; Family Programs; Interpretation; Lectures; Publication; Research Library/Archives; School-Based Curriculum

COLLECTIONS: [1830-present] Photographs, volumes, and artifacts related to the ethnogy and history of Ketchikan and environs; 19th c Tlingit and Haida totem poles, Native artifacts, carving, weaving, and ceremonial regalia.

HOURS: Yr May-Sept Daily 8-5; Oct-Apr Daily M-F 1-5

ADMISSION: $3; Under 12 free

175
Totem Heritage Center
601 Deermont St, 99901 [629 Dock St, 99901]; (p) (907) 225-5900; (f) (907) 225-5901; museumdir@city.ketchikan.ak.us; (c) Ketchikan Gateway

City/ 1976/ City of Ketchikan/ staff: 9(f); 7(p); 30(v)/publication: *Ketchikan Museums*

HISTORIC PRESERVATION AGENCY: Preserves and interprets a collection of 19th century totem poles retrieved from abandoned Native villages in the Ketchikan area;

PROGRAMS: Community Outreach; Exhibits; Guided Tours; Interpretation; Lectures; Publication; Research Library/Archives; School-Based Curriculum

COLLECTIONS: [1830-present]

HOURS: Yr May-Sept Daily 8-5; Oct-Apr M-F 1-5

ADMISSION: $4; Under 12 free

KODIAK

176
Alutiiq Museum and Archaeological Repository
215 Mission Rd, Ste 101, 99615; (p) (907) 486-7004; (f) (907) 486-7048; alutiiq2@ptialaska.net; (c) Kodiak Island Borough

Private non-profit/ 1995/ Alutiiq Heritage Foundation/ staff: 2(f); 3(p); 40(v)/ members: 200

HISTORY MUSEUM; RESEARCH CENTER; TRIBAL MUSEUM: Preserves the cultural tradition of the Alutiiq people in an archaeological repository.

PROGRAMS: Community Outreach; Exhibits; Guided Tours; Lectures; Research Library/Archives

COLLECTIONS: 100,000artifacts: archaeological collections, ethnographic specimens, historic photographs, film, audio, and paper archives, and natural history specimens.

HOURS: May-Sept M-F 9-5; Sa 10:30-4:30; Sept-May: T-F 9-5, Sa 10:30-4:30

ADMISSION: $2

177
Kodiak Historical Society
101 Marine Way, 99615; (p) (907) 486-5920; (f) (907) 486-3166

Private non-profit/ 1954/ staff: 2(f); 3(p); 14(v)/ members: 136

HISTORIC SITE; HISTORICAL SOCIETY; HISTORY MUSEUM; HOUSE MUSEUM: Operates the Baranov Museum and The Erskine House (Russian American Co. warehouse).

PROGRAMS: Annual Meeting; Community Outreach; Exhibits; Guided Tours; Interpretation; Living History; School-Based Curriculum

COLLECTIONS: [Prehistoric-present]

HOURS: Summer Daily 10-4; Winter 10-3

ADMISSION: $2; Under 12 free

178
St. Herman Theological Seminary
414 Mission Rd, 99615; (p) (907) 486-3524; (f) (907) 486-5935; stherman@ptialaska.net

1973/ OCA, Diocese of AK/ staff: 3(f); 2(p)

HISTORY MUSEUM; RESEARCH CENTER

PROGRAMS: Community Outreach; Exhibits; Guided Tours; Lectures; Research Library/Archives; School-Based Curriculum

COLLECTIONS: [1741-present] Archives of the Orthodox Church; rare books, journals, religious and secular literature.

HOURS: Yr Daily 10-5

ADMISSION: Donations accepted

METLAKATLA

179
Duncan Cottage Museum
110 Tait St, 99926 [PO Box 8, 99926]; (p) (907) 886-4441; (f) (907) 886-7997

City/ 1891/ Metlakatla Indian Community/ staff: 1(p)

HISTORIC PRESERVATION AGENCY; HISTORIC SITE; HISTORY MUSEUM; HOUSE MUSEUM; RESEARCH CENTER: A reserve founded in 1887 when the Tsimshian Indian tribe migrated from Canada. Maintains and operates this historic site.

PROGRAMS: Exhibits; Guided Tours; Interpretation; Lectures; Research Library/Archives

COLLECTIONS: [19th c] Photographs of migration, community building, historical documents and literature, artifacts, medical clinic, musical instruments, educational and legal books, furniture, clothing, and buildings.

HOURS: May-Sept Daily

ADMISSION: $2

180
Metlakatla Tribal Rights Committee
Milton St, 99926 [PO Box 8, 99926]; (p) (907) 886-4441; (f) (907) 886-7997; TSnoop@Metlakatla.net

Tribal/ staff: 4(f); 12(p)/publication: *Malshk*

HISTORIC PRESERVATION AGENCY; HISTORIC SITE; HISTORICAL SOCIETY; HOUSE MUSEUM; LIVING HISTORY/OUTDOOR MUSEUM: Oversees the tribe's historical, legal, and treaty rights re: the Federal Government and State of AK.

PROGRAMS: Publication

COLLECTIONS: Totem poles, cedar canoe, local tribal artifacts by local artists, and Native dance organizations.

HOURS: May-Sept Daily 8-4 or by appt

PALMER

181
Greater Palmer Chamber of Commerce
723 S Valley Way, 99645 [PO Box 45, 99645-0045]; (p) (907) 745-2880; (f) (907) 746-4164; palmerchambr@akcache.com; www.akcache.com/alaska/palmer; (c) Matanuska-Susitna Borough

City/ 1971/ staff: 1(f); 8(p)/ members: 195

GARDEN: Operates a visitor information center with an agricultural showcase demonstration garden and a small museum.

INTERPRETATION: Agriculture; Community/State History; Gardens

PROGRAMS: Exhibits; Festivals; Garden Tours

COLLECTIONS: [1935] New Deal relocation project artifacts, kitchen, tool room, and tack shop settings.

HOURS: Apr-Dec M-F 10-4; May-Sept Daily 8-7

ADMISSION: Donations accepted

182
Musk Ox Development Corporation
Archie Rd, 501 Glenn Hwy, 99645 [PO Box 587, 99645]; (p) (907) 745-4151; (f) (907) 746-4831; moxfarm@alaska.net; www.muskoxfarm.org

1985/ Musk Ox Dev Corp Board/ staff: 2(f); 17(p); 20(v)/ members: 450

LIVING HISTORY/OUTDOOR MUSEUM: Educational research facility that promotes the welfare of the musk ox and indigenous peoples advancing their economic and cultural objectives.

PROGRAMS: Community Outreach; Exhibits; Family Programs; Festivals; Guided Tours; Interpretation; Living History; School-Based Curriculum

COLLECTIONS: [Ice age-present] Hands on exhibits, archives, specimens, slides, and herd of 40 musk oxen.

HOURS: May-Sept M-Sa 10-6, Su 9-7; Nov-Apr Daily by appt

ADMISSION: $8, Student $6.50, Children $5, Seniors $6.50

PETERSBURG

183
Clausen Memorial Museum
203 Fram St, 99833 [PO Box 708, 99833]; (p) (907) 772-3598; cmm@alaska.net; www.alaska.net/~cmm

Private non-profit/ 1967/ staff: 1(f); 1(p); 1(v)/ members: 150/publication: *Petersburg: The Town That Fish Built; From Fish Camps to Cold Storages*

HISTORY MUSEUM: Collects, preserves, exhibits and interprets objects of historical, educational and artistic significance in order to promote the cultural heritage of Petersburg and the surrounding area.

PROGRAMS: Annual Meeting; Community Outreach; Exhibits; Family Programs; Film/Video; Guided Tours; Interpretation; Lectures; Publication

COLLECTIONS: [1897-present] Maritime and fishing equipment including a lighthouse lens, Tlingit canoe, cannery equipment, fish trap anchors, "Fisk" sculpture, 126 pound king salmon, and artifacts from local businesses and town life.

HOURS: Spring-Summer M-Sa 10-4:30; Fall-Winter W, Sa 12:30-4

ADMISSION: $2

SEWARD

184
Resurrection Bay Historical Society
336 3rd Ave, 99664 [PO Box 55, 99664-0055]; (p) (907) 224-3902

Private non-profit/ 1967/ Resurection Bay Historical Society, Inc/ staff: 1(f); 2(p); 10(v)/ members: 90

HISTORY MUSEUM: Operates the Seward Museum.

PROGRAMS: Annual Meeting; Community Outreach; Exhibits; Film/Video; Guided Tours

COLLECTIONS: [1903-present] Photographs and artifacts depicting the history of Seward.

HOURS: May-Oct Daily 9-5; Nov-Mar M-F 12-4

ADMISSION: $2, Children

SITKA

185
Friends of Sheldon Jackson Museum
104 College Dr, 99835; (p) (907) 747-6233; (f) (907) 747-3004; (c) Sitka

Private non-profit/ 1985/ staff: 2(p); 20(v)/ members: 145

HISTORIC SITE; HISTORY MUSEUM: Supports Sheldon Jackson Museum.

PROGRAMS: Annual Meeting; Community Outreach; Elder's Programs; Exhibits; Family Programs; Film/Video; Guided Tours; Interpretation; Lectures; Research Library/Archives; School-Based Curriculum

COLLECTIONS: [Mid 1800s-1930] Documents the art, technology, and culture of Eskimo Yup'ik, Inupiaq, Alieu, Alutiq, Athabaskan, and Pacific Northwest Coast Native Groups.

HOURS: Mid May-mid Sept Daily 8-5; Mid Sept-mid May T-Sa 10-4

ADMISSION: $3; Children free

186
Russian Bishop's House
Sitka National Historical Park, 99835 [PO Box 738, 99835]; (p) (907) 747-6281; (f) (907) 747-5938

1842/ National Park Service/ staff: 12(f); 1(v)

HOUSE MUSEUM: Russian Colonial building was home to Bishop Innocent, declared a saint by the Russian Orthodox Church.

COLLECTIONS: [1799-1867] Original furniture, Orthodox Chapel with icons; Library of AK history and Russian Orthodox Church.

187
Sheldon Jackson Museum
104 College Dr, 99835; (p) (907) 747-8981; (f) (907) 747-3004; rosemary_carlton@eed.state.ak.us; www.museums.state.ak.us

State/ 1888/ Div of Libraries, Archives, and Museum/ staff: 4(f); 2(p); 28(v)/ members: 130

HISTORIC SITE: Identifies, collects, preserves, and exhibits the material culture of Alaska's Native people.

PROGRAMS: Annual Meeting; Community Outreach; Exhibits; Film/Video; Interpretation; Lectures; Publication; Research Library/Archives; School-Based Curriculum

COLLECTIONS: [1870-1930] Alaska Native material culture, clothing, watercraft, basketry, utensils, tools, hunting equipment, toys, masks, sleds, jewelry, weapons; Aleut, Athabaskan, Eskimo, Northwest Coast Indian; Traditional and turn of the century market pieces.

HOURS: Yr Mid May-mid Sept Daily 9-5; Mid-Sept-mid May T-Sa 10- 4

ADMISSION: $4

188
Sitka Historical Society/Isabel Miller Museum
330 Harbor Dr, 99835 [PO Box 6181, 99835]; (p) (907) 747-6455; (f) (907) 747-6588; www.sitka.org

1957/ Sitka Historical Society/ staff: 2(p); 66(v)/ members: 148

HISTORICAL SOCIETY; HISTORY MUSEUM; RESEARCH CENTER: Collects, preserves, and interprets Sitka's past, Tlingit, Russian and early American settlers. Russian American transfer ceremony site 1867.

PROGRAMS: Annual Meeting; Elder's Programs; Exhibits; Guided Tours; Interpretation; Research Library/Archives; School-Based Curriculum

COLLECTIONS: [1799-1867] Tlingit culture, photographs, manuscripts, journals, cookbooks, Alexander Baranof's musical compositions, maps, rare journal of historic land transfer from Russia to Alaska, portraits and paintings.

HOURS: Yr May-Sept Daily 8-5; Sept-May T-Sa 10-4

ADMISSION: Donations accepted

189
Sitka National Historical Park
106 Metlakatla St, 99835; (p) (907) 747-6281; (f) (907) 747-5938; www.nps.gov

Federal/ 1890/ National Park Service/ staff: 9(f); 15(p); 5(v)

HISTORIC SITE: Federal reserve established in 1890; Site of the 1804 fort and battle site that marked the last major Tlingit resistance to Russian colonization.

PROGRAMS: Exhibits; Guided Tours; Interpretation; Living History; Publication; Research Library/Archives

COLLECTIONS: Historic collection of totem poles brought to the site in 1904 by Governor Brady.

HOURS: Yr May-Oct Daily 8-5; Oct-May 8-5

ADMISSION: $3

190
Southeast Alaska Indian Cultural Center, Inc.
106 Metlakatla St, 99835; (p) (907) 747-8061; (f) (907) 747-5938; SEAICC@PTIAlaska.net

Joint/ 1969/ SEAICC, Inc.; Private non-profit/ staff: 3(f); 300(p)/ members: 300

CULTURAL CENTER: To sustain and perpetuate the art and culture of the southeast Alaskan indigenous peoples in a manner that honors ancestral values.

PROGRAMS: Annual Meeting; Community Outreach; Elder's Programs; Exhibits; Family Programs; Interpretation; Living History

COLLECTIONS: Northwest Coast Indigenous art and regalia since 1969. Contemporary southeast Alaska Indian artwork.

HOURS: Yr May-Sept Daily 8-5; Oct-Apr Daily 8-12/1-4

ADMISSION: No charge

SKAGWAY

191
Klondike Gold Rush National Historical Park
2nd & Broadway, 99840 [PO Box 517, 99840]; (p) (907) 983-2921; (f) (907) 983-9249; www.nps.gov/klgo

Federal/ 1976/ National Park Service/ staff: 15(f); 20(p); 3(v)

HISTORIC SITE; HISTORY MUSEUM; LIVING HISTORY/OUTDOOR MUSEUM: Commemorates Klondike Gold Rush 1897-98. Chilkoot Trail: 33 miles jointly managed with Parks Canada.

PROGRAMS: Elder's Programs; Exhibits; Facility Rental; Film/Video; Guided Tours; Interpretation; Lectures; Research Library/Archives

COLLECTIONS: [1897-1900] Archeological artifacts from gold rush period. Archives, photographs, and dry mounted plant collection.

HOURS: May-Sept Daily 8-6

ADMISSION: Donations accepted

SUTTON

192
Alpine Historical Society
Mile 61.5 Glenn Hwy, 99674 [PO Box 266, 99674]; (p) (907) 745-7000; (c) Matanuska-Susitna Borough

Private non-profit/ 1982/ staff: 7(v)/ members: 7

HISTORIC SITE; HISTORICAL SOCIETY; HOUSE MUSEUM: Illustrates and interprets three eras of Alaska history: early Athabascan migration and Russian fur trading, the coal era, and the construction of the Glenn Highway.

PROGRAMS: Annual Meeting; Community Outreach; Exhibits; Festivals; Interpretation; Lectures; School-Based Curriculum

COLLECTIONS: [1900-1945] "Main Street" of historic buildings; Chickaloon Bunkhouse, Lucas House, and the original Sutton Post Office.

HOURS: May-Sept Daily 10-6

ADMISSION: No charge

TALKEETNA

193
Talkeetna Historical Society
Corner of First Alley & Village Airstrip, 99676 [PO Box 76, 99676]; (p) (907) 733-2487; (f) (907) 733-2484

1972/ Board of Directors/ staff: 3(p); 1(v)/ members: 110

HISTORIC SITE; HISTORICAL SOCIETY; HISTORY MUSEUM; HOUSE MUSEUM: Preservation of the history and historic artifacts of the northern Susitna Valley.

PROGRAMS: Annual Meeting; Community Outreach; Exhibits; Festivals; Interpretation; Lectures; Publication

COLLECTIONS: [1898-1965] Trading post materials, tools, mining and trapping equipment, papers and photographs, Alaskan art, Don Sheldon-Ray Genet memorial display, model of Denali, and depot building.

HOURS: Yr May-Sept Daily 10:30-5:30; Oct-Mar Sa-Su 11-5; Apr F-Su 11-6

ADMISSION: $2.50

TENAKEE SPRINGS

194
Tenakee Historical Collection
3/4 mile W Tenakee Trail, 99841 [PO Box 633, 99841]; (p) (907) 736-2243; (f) (907) 736-2243; wisentenakee@juno.com

Private non-profit/ 1984/ staff: 2(v)

LIBRARY AND/OR ARCHIVES: Collects local history photo, records, and papers.

COLLECTIONS: [1899-present] Collection of local newspapers, photos, permits, and old stores records, probate and criminal records.

HOURS: By appt

UNALASKA

195
Aleutian World War II National Battery
[PO Box 149, 99685]; (p) (907) 581-1276; Linda_Cook@nps.gov; www.nps.gov/aleu/index.htm

Federal/ 1996/ National Park Service

HISTORIC SITE; NATIONAL PARK: Interpret the history of the Aleut or Unangan people and the Aleutian Islands in the defense of the United States in WW II.

COLLECTIONS: [20th c] Bunkers and wooden remains of structures, gun mounts, lookouts, observation posts and command stations.

HOURS: Yr

VALDEZ

196
Valdez Museum and Historical Archive Association, Inc.
217 Egan Dr, 99686 [PO Box 8, 99686]; (p) (907) 835-2764; (f) (907) 835-5800; vldzmuse@alaska.net; www.alaska.net/~vldzmuse/index.html

Private non-profit/ 1977/ staff: 3(f); 6(p)/ members: 168

HISTORY MUSEUM: Interprets local and regional history, including the gold rush, founding of Valdez, exploration, 1964 Earthquake, oil pipeline and Exxon Valdez oil spill. Collections are focused on historical items related to the region.

PROGRAMS: Annual Meeting; Community Outreach; Exhibits; Facility Rental; Family Programs; Guided Tours; Interpretation; Publication; Research Library/Archives; School-Based Curriculum

COLLECTIONS: [1898-present] Artifacts and archival material to preserve and educate about Valdez, Prince William Sound and the Copper River Valley.

HOURS: Spring-Summer Daily; Fall-Winter M-Sa

ADMISSION: $3,

WASILLA

197
Dorothy Page Museum
323 Main St, 99654; (p) (907) 373-9071; (f) (907) 373-9072; museum@ci.wasilla.ak.us

Joint/ 1967/ City; Wasilla-Knik-Willow Creek Historical Society/ staff: 2(f); 50(v)/ members: 76

GARDEN; HISTORIC SITE; HISTORICAL SOCIETY; HISTORY MUSEUM: Natural and local history exhibits and dioramas of local mine shaft and mining district. Homesteader historic townsite. Alaska gardens and research library, visitors center, Iditarod dog mushing history.

PROGRAMS: Annual Meeting; Community Outreach; Exhibits; Family Programs; Festivals; Film/Video; Guided Tours; Lectures; Research Library/Archives; School-Based Curriculum

COLLECTIONS: [1900-1950s] Wasilla railroad and Knik history, Iditarod dog mushing history, homesteading, mining, trapping, natural history of area, historical townsite, archives, library, and farming.

HOURS: Fall-Winter T-Sa 9-5; Spring-Summer T-Sa 10-6

ADMISSION: $3, Seniors $2.50; Under 19 free

198
Herning-Teeland-Mead House
323 N Main St, 99654; (p) (907) 373-9071, (907) 373-9072

City/ 1937/ staff: 2(f); 2(v)

HISTORY MUSEUM: First store in Wasilla, including gold prospector, boat captain, and businessman O.G. Herning.

COLLECTIONS: [Early 1900]

HOURS: Yr

199
Museum of Alaska Transportation & Industry
Off mile 47 Parks Hwy next to Wasilla Airport, 99687 [PO Box 870646, 99687]; (p) (907) 376-1211; (f) (907) 376-3082; mati@mtaonline.net; www.alaska.net/rmorris/mati1.htm; (c) Matanuska-Susitna

1976/ Board of Directors/ staff: 3(f); 2(p); 26(v)/ members: 250/publication: *News and Views*

HISTORY MUSEUM: Collects, preserves, restores, and exhibits Alaskan transportation and industrial artifacts and social history.

PROGRAMS: Annual Meeting; Community Outreach; Exhibits; Facility Rental; Guided Tours; Interpretation; Research Library/Archives; School-Based Curriculum

COLLECTIONS: [1900-1970] Artifacts: dog sleds, cars, trucks, planes, jets, trains, boats, heavy equipment, mining, farming. Photos, ephemera, library, and archives.

HOURS: Yr May-Sept Daily 9-6; Oct-Apr T-Sat 9-5

ADMISSION: $5, Family $12, Student $4, Seniors $4; Group rates

200
Wasilla-Knik-Willow Creek Historical Society
300 W Boundary, 99654; (p) (907) 376-7005; wkwchistorical@hotmail.com; (c) Matanvska-Susitna

Private non-profit/ 1971/ staff: 10(v)/ members: 120

HISTORIC SITE; HISTORICAL SOCIETY; HISTORY MUSEUM: Dedicated to preservation of local historic buildings and artifacts.

PROGRAMS: Annual Meeting; Exhibits; Facili-

ty Rental; Guided Tours; Interpretation

COLLECTIONS: Local artifacts and memorabilia.

HOURS: Yr T-Sa 10-5

ADMISSION: $3

WRANGELL

201
Tribal House of the Bear
Foot of Shakes St, 99929 [PO Box 868, 99929]; (p) (907) 874-3747; (f) (907) 874-3747

Tribal/ staff: 2(p); 1(v)

HISTORIC SITE: Traditional tribal government recognized by Congress.

PROGRAMS: Guided Tours; Interpretation

COLLECTIONS: Photo display, clan house, Native made tools, totems.

HOURS: Yr By appt

ADMISSION: $2; Under 17 free

202
Wrangell Cooperative Association
321 Front St, 99929 [PO Box 868, 99929]; (p) (907) 874-3482; (f) (907) 874-2982

Tribal/ staff: 1(v)

HISTORIC SITE: Tribal government operating "the Tribal House of the Bear" on Shakes Island in Wrangell Harbor.

PROGRAMS: Interpretation; Reenactments

COLLECTIONS: Tribal house and photo display, totems, and native tools.

HOURS: April-Oct times vary and appt

ADMISSION: $2; Under 16 free

203
Wrangell Museum
318 Church St, 99929 [PO Box 1050, 99929]; (p) (907) 874-3770; (f) (907) 874-3785; museum@wrangell.com; www.wrangell.com

City/ 1967/ staff: 1(f); 2(p)/publication: *Authentic History of Chief Shakes Island*

HISTORY MUSEUM: Promotes and preserves local history.

PROGRAMS: Annual Meeting; Community Outreach; Exhibits; Guided Tours; Interpretation; Lectures; Research Library/Archives

COLLECTIONS: Artifacts, photographs, and memorabilia covering the prehistoric and historic Native Alaska, early exploration, gold rush, missionary period, communication, transpiration, fishing, and forest industry.

HOURS: Winter T-F 10-4; Summer M-Sa 10-5

ADMISSION: $3

ARIZONA

AJO

204
Ajo Historical Society Museum
Located in the old St. Catherine's Indian Mission, 85321 [PO Box 778, 85321]

HISTORY MUSEUM: Collects local history.

COLLECTIONS: Artifacts and memorabilia related to Ajo's history; blacksmith shop, a dentist's office, and an early print shop.

APACHE JUNCTION

205
Superstition Mountain Historical Society Inc.
4650 N Mammoth Mine Rd, 85217 [PO Box 3845, 85217-3845]; (p) (480) 983-4888; (f) (480) 983-3231; smgold@uswest.net; (c) Pinal

Private non-profit/ 1979/ staff: 1(f); 12(v)/ members: 200/publication: *Superstition Mountain Journal*

HISTORICAL SOCIETY

PROGRAMS: Annual Meeting; Community Outreach; Elder's Programs; Exhibits; Facility Rental; Festivals; Film/Video; Lectures; Publication

COLLECTIONS: [1800-present]

HOURS: Yr Daily 9-4

ADMISSION: $3, Children $1, Seniors $2

BENSON

206
San Pedro Arts and Historical Society
180 S San Pedro St, 85602 [PO Box 1090, 85602]; (p) (520)586-3070; (c) Cochise

Private non-profit/ 1975/ Board of Directors/ staff: 25(v)/ members: 100

ART MUSEUM; HISTORIC PRESERVATION AGENCY; HISTORIC SITE; HISTORICAL SOCIETY; HISTORY MUSEUM; LIBRARY AND/OR ARCHIVES: Operates a small museum.

PROGRAMS: Annual Meeting; Community Outreach; Exhibits; Festivals; Guided Tours; Research Library/Archives; School-Based Curriculum

COLLECTIONS: Artifacts and memerabilia relating to: art, household clothing, photos, oral histories, pioneers, farming, ranching, doctors, dentist, mining, music, railroad, Spanish and Indian culture, industry, businesses, medicine, newspapers, research library.

HOURS: Winter T-Sa 10-4; Summer T-Sa 10-2

ADMISSION: Donations accepted

BISBEE

207
Bisbee Mining and Historical Museum
5 Copper Queen Plaza, 85603 [PO Box 14, 85603]; (p) (520) 432-7071; (f) (520) 432-7800; bisbeemuseum@theriver.com; (c) Cochise

Private non-profit/ 1968/ Bisbee Council on the Arts and Humanities/ staff: 4(f); 1(p); 80(v)/ members: 480

HISTORIC SITE; HISTORY MUSEUM: Communicates the history of Bisbee beginning and its environs as a premier copper mining center.

PROGRAMS: Annual Meeting; Community Outreach; Exhibits; Guided Tours; Lectures; Research Library/Archives

COLLECTIONS: [1880-present] Artifacts relating to mining, minerals, Bisbe's social history; societal, economic, and business manuscripts, 25,000 historic photographs; and a research library.

HOURS: Yr Daily 10-4

ADMISSION: $4, Seniors $3.50; Under 16 free

208
Muheim Heritage House
207B Yougblood Hill, 85603 [PO Box 14, 85603]; (p) (520) 432-7071; (c) Cochise

Private non-profit/ 1975/ Bisbee Council on the Arts and Humanities/ staff: 1(f); 20(v)/ members: 400

HOUSE MUSEUM: 1898 house.

PROGRAMS: Annual Meeting; Community Outreach; Facility Rental; Guided Tours

COLLECTIONS: Muheim family Victorian furnishings, pioneer artifacts.

HOURS: Yr F-M

BUCKEYE

209
Buckeye Valley Historical and Archaeological Museum
116 E MC 85, 85326 [PO Box 292, 85326]; (p) (623) 386-4333; (c) Maricopa

Private non-profit/ 1954/ staff: 2(p); 4(v)/ members: 75

HISTORY MUSEUM: Collects, preserves, and interprets the prehistory and history of Buckeye Valley and the surrounding area.

PROGRAMS: Annual Meeting; Interpretation; Research Library/Archives; School-Based Curriculum

COLLECTIONS: 850 photographs, 200 documents, 400 prehistoric artifacts, 1,500 historic artifacts, pioneer association archives, and family histories.

HOURS: Oct-May W-F 1-4, Sa 10-4

CAMP VERDE

210
Fort Verde State Historic Park
125 E Hollamon, 86322 [PO Box 397, 86322]; (p) (520) 567-3275; (f) (520) 567-4036; ngraf@pr.state.az.us; www.pr.state.az.us

State/ 1871/ State Parks/ staff: 4(f); 1(p); 5(v)

HISTORIC SITE: Includes four of the remaining 10 Army buildings in AZ dating from the 1870s. Site where General George Crook accepted the surrender of one tribe of Yavapais Indians.

COLLECTIONS: [1870s-1880s] Military artifacts; furniture; medical equipment; clothing; textiles.; Microfilm (post returns) of all the forts in AZ; official records of activities at Fort Verde; biographies of approximately 350 soldiers, women, and pioneers that were on the site.

HOURS: Yr

CHANDLER

211
Arizona Railway Museum
399 N Delaware, 85224 [PO Box 842, 85224]; (p) (602) 821-1108; (c) Maricopa

Private non-profit/ 1984/ Board of Directors/ staff: 30(v)/ members: 300

HISTORY MUSEUM: The Arizona Railway Museum collects, preserves, and exhibits railroad-related artifacts and memorabilia from Arizona and the West, cars and locomotives.

PROGRAMS: Annual Meeting; Exhibits; Festivals; Interpretation; Research Library/Archives

COLLECTIONS: [1877-present] Freight and passenger cars, cabooses, locomotives, lanterns and railroad artifacts and memorabilia.

HOURS: Sept-May Sa-Su

COTTONWOOD

212
Verde Historical Society
1 N Willard, 86326 [PO Box 511, 86326]; (p) (520) 634-2868; (c) Yavapai

Private non-profit/ 1991/ Board of Trustees/ staff: 14(p); 80(v)/ members: 205

HISTORIC PRESERVATION AGENCY; HISTORICAL SOCIETY; HISTORY MUSEUM: Collects, preserves, and interprets materials associated with the explorers and settlers of the Verde Valley during the Territorial and Statehood eras.

PROGRAMS: Annual Meeting; Community Outreach; Exhibits; Guided Tours; Lectures; Research Library/Archives

COLLECTIONS: [1800s] Photos; ranching, farming, smelting, and railroad artifacts.

HOURS: Yr W 9-12, F-Su 11-3

ADMISSION: Donations accepted

DOUGLAS

213
Cochise County Historical Society
1001 North D Ave, 85608 [PO Box 818, 85608-0818]; (p) (520) 364-5226; (f) (520) 364- 5226; (c) Cochise

staff: 10(v)/ members: 300

HISTORICAL SOCIETY; LIBRARY AND/OR ARCHIVES; RESEARCH CENTER: Preserves the history of Cochise and Hidalgo Counties, New Mexico, Sonora, and Chihuahua states in Old Mexico.

PROGRAMS: Annual Meeting; Guided Tours; Research Library/Archives

COLLECTIONS: [1880-present] Books and photographs of the area and era which the public may use for reference.

HOURS: Yr T 1-4

ADMISSION: No charge

214
Slaughter Ranch Museum
6153 Geronimo Trail, 85608 [PO Box 438, 85608]; (p) (520) 558-2474; (f) (602) 933-3777; sranch@vtc.net; http://www.vtc.net/~sranch/index.html; (c) Cochise

Private non-profit/ 1979/ staff: 3(f); 3(p); 6(v)

HISTORIC SITE; HISTORY MUSEUM; HOUSE MUSEUM: Museum featuring a 19th c cattle ranch.

PROGRAMS: Exhibits

COLLECTIONS: [1800s] Artifacts and memorabilia; cattle ranch buildings.

HOURS: Yr, W-Su 10-3

ADMISSION, $3; Under 14 free

DRAGOON

215
Amerind Foundation, Inc., The
2100 N Amerind Rd, 85609 [PO Box 400, 85609]; (p) (520) 586-3666; (f) (520) 586-4679; amerind@amerind.org; www.amerind.org; (c) Cochise

Private non-profit/ 1937/ Board of Directors/ staff: 6(f); 4(p); 35(v)

ART MUSEUM; RESEARCH CENTER: Anthropological research facility and museum devoted to the study, preservation, and interpretation of prehistoric, historic, and contemporary Native American culture.

PROGRAMS: Exhibits; Guided Tours; Publication; Research Library/Archives

COLLECTIONS: Objects from all periods of Native American prehistory and history, Spanish retablos and bultos, paintings and furnishings, and a 30,000 volume archaeological research library, journals, unpublished manuscripts, and photographs.

HOURS: Sept-May Daily 10-4; June-Aug W-Su 10-4

ADMISSION: $3, Student $2, Seniors $2; Under 12 free

FLAGSTAFF

216
Arizona Historical Society - Northern Division
2340 N Fort Valley Rd, 86001; (p) (520) 774-6272; (f) (520) 774-1596; (c) Coconino

State/ 1960/ staff: 3(f); 6(v)/ members: 155/publication: *The Northerner*

HISTORICAL SOCIETY: A division of the statewide agency, the museum maintains a regular program of changing exhibits, school tours, special events, and archives.

PROGRAMS: Annual Meeting; Exhibits; Festivals; Guided Tours; Interpretation; Lectures; Living History; Publication; Reenactments; Research Library/Archives

COLLECTIONS: [19th-20th c] Items attributed to Anglo, Hispanic, and African American occupation of Northern Arizona, including those associated with logging, railroad, livestock, education, public health, commerce, social life, and the history of technology.

HOURS: Yr M-Sa

217
Museum of Northern Arizona
3101 N Fort Valley Rd, 86001; (p) (520) 774-5211; (f) (520) 779-1527; info@musnaz.org; www.musnaz.org; (c) Coconino

Private non-profit/ 1928/ staff: 35(f); 13(p); 150(v)/ members: 4249/publication: *MNA Bulletin; Plateau Magazine*

ART MUSEUM; HISTORY MUSEUM; RESEARCH CENTER: Provides leadership advancing multidisciplinary knowledge; social development, equality, and change; protects the Colorado Plateau's heritage and environment; provides a forum for the exchange of multicultural and societal issues.

PROGRAMS: Concerts; Elder's Programs; Exhibits; Facility Rental; Family Programs; Festivals; Guided Tours; Interpretation; Lectures; Publication; Research Library/Archives; School-Based Curriculum

COLLECTIONS: [Precambrian-present] Items related to the archaeology, ethnology, fine arts, botany, zoology, geology, and paleontology of the Colorado Plateau.

HOURS: Yr Daily 9-5

ADMISSION: $5, Student $3, Children $2, Seniors $4; $2 Native Americans

218
Northern Arizona University Cline Library Special Collections and Archives Department
Knoles Dr & Riordan Rd, 86011 [Box 6022, 86011-6022]; (p) (520) 523-5551; (f) (520) 523-3770; Special.Collections@nau.edu; www.nau.edu/library/speccoll/; (c) Coconino

Joint/ 1966/ Northern AZ Univ; State/ staff: 7(f); 1(p); 5(v)

LIBRARY AND/OR ARCHIVES: Collects, preserves, and makes available archival materials which document the history and development of the Colorado Plateau.

PROGRAMS: Community Outreach; Exhibits; Lectures; Publication; Research Library/ Archives

COLLECTIONS: [Late 19th c-present] 5 million manuscripts, 750,000 photographs, 2,000 maps, 900 oral histories,35,000 books, serials, subject files.

HOURS: Yr M-F 9-6, Fall/Spring Sa 1-4

219
Riordan Mansion State Historic Park
409 Riordan Rd, 86001; (p) (520) 779-4395; www.pr.state.az.us/parkhtml/riordan.html; (c) Coconino

1978/ Arizona State Parks/ staff: 4(f); 2(p); 6(v)

HISTORIC SITE; HOUSE MUSEUM: Collects, acquires, interprets, preserves, and exhibits artifacts pertaining to the history and mansion of the Riordan Family.

PROGRAMS: Facility Rental; Guided Tours; Interpretation; Research Library/Archives

COLLECTIONS: [1844-1940] Archival material; period furnishings, personal and household accessories, communication artifacts; tools, equipment, and recreational artifacts.

HOURS: May-Sept Daily 8-5; Oct-Apr 11-5

ADMISSION: $4; Children $2.50

FLORENCE

220
McFarland State Historic Park
Main & Ruggles St, 85232 [Box 109, 85232]; (p) (520) 868-5216; (f) (520) 868-5216; kmontano@pr.state.az.us; www.pr.state.az.us; (c) Pinal

State/ 1978/ State Parks Board/ staff: 2(f); 2(v)

HISTORIC SITE; HISTORY MUSEUM: Collects, acquires, interprets, preserves, and exhibits artifacts pertaining to the area; maintains archives/library; displays aspects of Ernest W. McFarland's life.

PROGRAMS: Exhibits; Interpretation; Publication; Research Library/Archives

COLLECTIONS: [1878-present] Personal archives and library of McFarland; photos, documents, maps, letters; period furnishings, clothing, and household/ personal accessories.

HOURS: Yr Th-M 8-5

ADMISSION: $2, Children $1

221
Pinal County Historical Society Museum
751 S Main St, 85232 [PO Box 851, 85232]; (p) (520) 868-4382; (c) Pinal

Private non-profit/ 1958/ staff: 1(p)/ members: 109/publication: *Our Heritage*

HISTORICAL SOCIETY; HISTORY MUSEUM; LIBRARY AND/OR ARCHIVES: Collects, preserves, interprets, disseminates, and exhibits historical archives and artifacts of Florence and the immediate area. Library and archives open to researchers.

PROGRAMS: Annual Meeting; Community Outreach; Exhibits; Film/Video; Guided Tours; Interpretation; Lectures; Publication; Research Library/Archives

COLLECTIONS: [1860s-1960s] Pioneer history, Native American artifacts, Arizona Territorial and State Prison collections, cactus furniture.

HOURS: Sept-mid July T-Sa 11-4, Su 12-4

ADMISSION: Donations

FORT APACHE

222
White Mountain Apache Heritage Program
W End of Historic Fort Apache, 85926 [PO Box 507, 85926]; (p) (520) 338-4625; (f) (520) 338-1716; (c) Navajo

Tribal/ 1969/ White Mountain Apache Tribe/ staff: 4(f); 5(p); 3(v)

HISTORIC SITE; TRIBAL MUSEUM: Includes: Historic Preservation Office, Noweke' Bagowa: Apache Culture Center and Museum, and the Cultural Resources Division.

PROGRAMS: Community Outreach; Exhibits; Film/Video; Guided Tours; Interpretation; Theatre

COLLECTIONS: [Prehistory-present] Historic materials related to the occupation of Fort Apache and the development of the Theodore Roosevelt Boarding School; small collections related to Pueblo, Apache, Colonial/military, BIA, and sovereignty eras.

HOURS: Yr M-Sa 8-5; Winter M-F

ADMISSION: $3, Children $2, Seniors $2; White Mtn. Apache Tribal Members Free

GANADO

223
Hubbell Trading Post National Historic Site
Hwy 264, 86505 [PO Box 150, 86505]; (p) (520) 755-3475, (520) 755-3477; (f) (520) 755-3405; e_chamberlin@nps.gov; www.nps.gov

1901/ National Park Service/ staff: 13(f)

HISTORIC SITE

COLLECTIONS: [1930s] 20th century fine arts collection, Native American baskets, weavings, jewelry, pottery. Business records covering 100 years of trading post operation.

HOURS: Yr

GLENDALE

224
American Museum of Nursing
7025 N 58th Ave, 85301; (p) (623) 842-4631; (c) Maricopa

Private non-profit/ 1993/ staff: 1(f); 20(v)

HISTORY MUSEUM: Collects, preserves, and documents materials of the nursing profession.

PROGRAMS: Exhibits; Guided Tours; Lectures; Research Library/Archives

COLLECTIONS: [19th c-present] Nursing memorabilia; uniforms, capes, caps, nursing school pins, nurse dolls, nursing equipment, books, stamps.

HOURS: Yr T-Sa 10-4

ADMISSION: No charge/Donations

225
Historic Sahuaro Ranch
9802 N 59th Ave, 85311 [PO Box 1824, 85311]; (p) (623) 939-5782; (f) (623) 939-0250; sahuarofdn@aol.com; www.ci.glendale.az.us; (c) Maricopa

Private non-profit/ 1993/ Sahuaro Ranch Foundation/ staff: 3(f); 1(p); 40(v)/ members: 75

HISTORIC SITE; HISTORY MUSEUM; HOUSE MUSEUM: Preserves and presents ranch and agricultural history of the west Salt River Valley on an 1885 homestead.

PROGRAMS: Annual Meeting; Concerts; Exhibits; Family Programs; Festivals; Guided Tours; Interpretation; Lectures; Living History

COLLECTIONS: [1885-1940] Historic buildings; agricultural and blacksmith equipment; dairy barn and milk house equipment; period furniture and clothing circa 1900-1930; site related photographs, newspapers, and archaeology.

HOURS: Exhibits: Sept-May, Grounds: Yr, W-F 10-2, Sa 10-4, Su 12-4

ADMISSION: $3

226
Manistee Ranch
5127 W Northern Ave, 85312-5606 [PO Box 5606, 85312-5606]; (p) (602) 931-8848, (602) 435-0072

1897/ staff: 12(v)

HOUSE MUSEUM: One of the oldest and best preserved ranches of the Salt River Valley of AZ; home of three generations of the Louis Marshall Sands family.

COLLECTIONS: [1925-1940] 3,000+ artifacts (furniture, clothing, photographs, party favors) of one family's occupancy of the home; artifacts of Glendale provenance; records of ranch business, 1930s-40s.

HOURS: Seasonal

GLOBE

227
Gila County Historical Museum
1330 N Broad St, 85501 [PO Box 2891, 85502]; (p) (520) 425-7385; (c) Gila

Private non-profit/ 1955/ staff: 12(p); 1(v)/ members: 140

HISTORIC SITE; HISTORICAL SOCIETY; HISTORY MUSEUM: To collect, preserve, display, and disseminate county history.

PROGRAMS: Annual Meeting; Exhibits; Guided Tours; Interpretation; Research Library/Archives

COLLECTIONS: [1875-1925] Artifacts from prehistoric people, Native Americans, mining, ranching, businesses, and daily life. Photo collection, small library.

HOURS: Yr M-Sa 10-4

ADMISSION: Donations accepted

GREEN VALLEY

228
Titan Missile Museum
1580 W Duval Mine Rd, 85614 [PO Box 150, 85622]; (p) (520) 625-7736; (f) (520) 625-9845; (c) Pima

Private non-profit/ 1986/ AZ Aerospace Foundation/ staff: 5(f); 3(p); 108(v)

HISTORIC SITE: Formerly active Titan II Missile Complex that has been preserved as a museum.

PROGRAMS: Annual Meeting; Community Outreach; Exhibits; Film/Video; Guided Tours; School-Based Curriculum

COLLECTIONS: [1963-1987] Titan II Missile Complex, Titan II Missile, support equipment, photos, technical data, construction plans, related artifacts.

HOURS: Yr Nov-Apr Daily; May-Oct W-Su

ADMISSION: $7.50, Children $4, Seniors $6.50; Under 6 free

JEROME

229
Jerome Historical Society
[PO Box 156, 86331]; (p) (520) 634-5477, (520) 634-7349; (c) Yavapai

Private non-profit/ 1953/ staff: 3(f); 3(p); 2(v)/ members: 375/publication: *They Came to Jerome; and others*

HISTORY MUSEUM: Maintains archives, museum, and several historic buildings, with emphasis on mining.

PROGRAMS: Annual Meeting; Exhibits; Facility Rental; Lectures; Living History; Publication; Research Library/Archives

COLLECTIONS: [1880-1950] Local mining artifacts; archives, photographs, and maps.

HOURS: Yr Daily 9-4:30

230
Jerome State Historic Park
Douglas Mansion Rd, 86331 [Box D, 86331]; (p) (520) 634-5381; (f) (520) 639-3132; www.pr.state.az.us/parkhtml/jerome.html; (c) Yavapai

State/ 1962/ State Parks/ staff: 4(f); 1(p); 4(v)

HISTORIC SITE; HISTORY MUSEUM; HOUSE MUSEUM: Collects, preserves, and interprets history of local mining and culture and the history of the James S. Douglas family. Includes the James S. Douglas Mansion.

PROGRAMS: Exhibits; Interpretation

COLLECTIONS: [1865-1953] Archival photographs, documents, maps, letters; period furnishings, household/personal accessories, and clothing; tools and equipment.

HOURS: Yr Daily

KINGMAN

231
Mohave Museum of History and Arts
400 W Beale St, 86401; (p) (520) 753-3195; (f) (520) 753-3195; mocohist@ctaz.com; www.ctaz.com/~mocohist/museum/index.htm; (c) Mohave

1960/ Board of Trustees/ staff: 1(f); 4(p); 163(v)/ members: 750/publication: *Mohave Museum Newsletter*

HISTORICAL SOCIETY; HISTORY MUSEUM: Preservation of pioneer and NW Arizona history and heritage.

PROGRAMS: Annual Meeting; Exhibits; Publication; Research Library/Archives

COLLECTIONS: [1863-present] 5,002 artifacts, 10,000 maps, Mohave County newspapers, 10,000 photos, and archives.

HOURS: Yr M-F 9-5, Sa-Su 1-5

ADMISSION: $3, Children $0.50-free w/adult

KYKOTSMOVI

232
Hopi Cultural Preservation Office
Main St, 86039 [PO Box 123, 86039]; (p) (520) 734-3750; (f) (520) 734-2331; www.nav.edu/~hcpo-pl; (c) Navajo

Tribal/ 1989/ Hopi Tribe/ staff: 15(f)

HISTORIC PRESERVATION AGENCY: Engages in research, consultation, and public efforts to preserve and protect Hopi culture, history, and language.

PROGRAMS: Community Outreach; Research Library/Archives

COLLECTIONS: [Prehistory-present] Educational materials, oral histories.

HOURS: M-F

MARICOPA

233
Ak-Chin Him-Dak EcoMuseum and Archives
47685 N EcoMuseum Rd, 85239; (p) (530) 568-9480; (f) (520) 568-9557; (c) Pinal

1991/ Tribal Council/ staff: 8(f)

TRIBAL MUSEUM: Promotes the sharing of the past, the present, and the future of the Ak-

Chin community and increases the awareness and perceptions of all members of the community to their evolving environment.

PROGRAMS: Exhibits; Guided Tours

COLLECTIONS: [History of Ak-Chin Indian Reservation] Archaeology collection, paintings produced by local tribal artists, photographic collection, tribal document collection, O'odham basket collection, and research collection materials.

HOURS: Yr M-F 9-5

MESA

234
Mesa Historical Museum
2345 N Horne, 85211 [PO Box 582, 85211]; (p) (280) 835-7358; (c) Maricopa

Private non-profit/ 1966/ Mesa Historical Society/ staff: 1(f); 4(p); 20(v)/ members: 280

HISTORIC PRESERVATION AGENCY; HISTORIC SITE; HISTORICAL SOCIETY: Create interest in the early history of the Mesa area; preservation of artifacts and maintenance of archives.

PROGRAMS: Annual Meeting; Community Outreach; Elder's Programs; Exhibits; Facility Rental; Family Programs; Festivals; Guided Tours; Interpretation; Lectures; Publication; Reenactments; Research Library/Archives

COLLECTIONS: [1890-1940s] Domestic and farm implements; archives, photos, family histories, murals, replicas of early structures.

HOURS: Yr T-Sa 10-4

235
Mesa Southwest Museum
53 N Macdonald St, 85201; (p) (602) 644-2169; (f) (602) 644-3424; mswmuseum@ infinet-is.com; www.ci.mesa.az.us/parksrec/ msm/index.htm; (c) Maricopa

City/ 1977/ staff: 13(f); 7(p); 250(v)/ members: 375/publication: *Southwest Quest*

HISTORY MUSEUM: Collects, exhibits, interprets, and preserves the cultural and natural history of the Mesa area.

PROGRAMS: Community Outreach; Exhibits; Facility Rental; Family Programs; Festivals; Guided Tours; Interpretation; Lectures; Publication; Research Library/Archives; School-Based Curriculum; Theatre

COLLECTIONS: [Prehistory-statehood] Paleontological research; gems and minerals; area photographs and artifacts; archaeological artifacts.

HOURS: Yr T-Sa 10-5, Su 1-5

ADMISSION: $4, Student $3.50, Children $2, Seniors $3.50

236
Sirrine House Museum
160 N Center St, 85201 [53 N Macdonald St, 85201]; (p) (602) 644-2760; (f) (602) 644-3424; mswmuseum@infinet-is.com; www.ci.mesa.az.us/parksrec/msm/index.html; (c) Maricopa

1986/ City of Mesa/ staff: 25(p); 1(v)

HOUSE MUSEUM: Preserves the house of Mesa's founding family.

PROGRAMS: Exhibits; Family Programs; Festivals; Guided Tours; Interpretation; Reenactments

COLLECTIONS: [1896-1905] Period furnishings, household items, and photographs.

HOURS: Oct-May Sa 10-5, Su 1-5

NOGALES

237
Pimeria Alta Historical Society
136 N Grand Ave, 85621 [PO Box 2281, 85621]; (p) (520) 287-4621; (c) Santa Cruz

Private non-profit/ 1948/ staff: 5(v)/ members: 400

HISTORICAL SOCIETY; HISTORY MUSEUM: Operates a museum, maintains archives, and preserves artifacts.

PROGRAMS: Annual Meeting; Community Outreach; Elder's Programs; Exhibits; Family Programs; Lectures; Research Library/ Archives; School-Based Curriculum

COLLECTIONS: [Prehistory; late 1800-present] Indigenous artifacts; personal and commercial artifacts.

HOURS: Yr

ORACLE

238
Oracle Historical Society, Inc.
825 E Mt. Lemmon Rd, 85623 [PO Box 10, 85623]; (p) (520) 896-9609; (c) Pinal

Private non-profit/ 1979/ Board of Directors/ staff: 2(p); 15(v)/ members: 175/publication: *Oracle Historian*

HISTORICAL SOCIETY; HISTORY MUSEUM: Maintains a museum and is dedicated to preservation of local history.

PROGRAMS: Annual Meeting; Community Outreach; Exhibits; Facility Rental; Guided Tours; Publication; Research Library/Archives

COLLECTIONS: [1870-present] Artifacts, photographs, documents, maps.

HOURS: Sept-July Sa-Su 1-5

ADMISSION: Donations accepted

PAGE

239
John Wesley Powell Memorial Museum, Historical and Archaeological Sociey, Inc.
#6 N Lake Powell Blvd, 86040 [PO Box 547, 86040]; (p) (520) 645-9496; (f) (520) 645-3412; director@powellmuseum.org; www.powellmuseum.org; (c) Coconino

Private non-profit/ 1969/ staff: 3(f); 2(p); 4(v)/ members: 120

HISTORY MUSEUM: Collects, preserves, and interprets local and Native culture and the explorations of Major John Wesley Powell.

PROGRAMS: Annual Meeting; Elder's Programs; Exhibits; Facility Rental; Film/Video; Guided Tours; Lectures; Research Library/ Archives

COLLECTIONS: [1869-1902/1956-present] Photographs, publications, and artifacts connected with Maj. Powell, City of Page, and local Native cultures.

HOURS: Feb-Apr, Oct-Dec M-F 9-5; May-Sept M-F 8:30-5:30

ADMISSION: $1, Children $0.50

PAYSON

240
Northern Gila County Historical Society, Inc.
700 Green Valley Pkwy, 85547 [PO Box 2532, 85547]; (p) (520) 474-3483; (f) (520) 474-1195; (c) Gila

Private non-profit/ 1986/ staff: 1(p)/ 45(v)/ members: 240/publication: *Rim Country Echos*

HISTORIC SITE; HISTORICAL SOCIETY; HISTORY MUSEUM: Collect, preserve, and interpret local prehistory and history.

PROGRAMS: Annual Meeting; Community Outreach; Exhibits; Facility Rental; Lectures; Publication; Research Library/Archives

COLLECTIONS: [1880-1930] Ancient Native peoples, cavalry, lumber, mining, ranching and agriculture; Zane Grey memorabilia; 1908 style household.

HOURS: Yr, W-Su 12-4

ADMISSION: $3, Student $2, Seniors $2.50

PHOENIX

241
Arizona Department of Library, Archives, and Public Records
1700 W Washington, 85007; (p) (602) 542-4035; (f) (602) 542-4972; services@dlapr.lib.az.us; www.dlapr.lib.az.us; (c) Maricopa

State/ 1863/ Library Board/ staff: 121(f); 200(v)

HISTORIC SITE; HISTORY MUSEUM; RESEARCH CENTER: Operation a research library, state archives, two historic buildings, and two museums of history.

PROGRAMS: Exhibits; Interpretation; Lectures; Research Library/Archives; School-Based Curriculum

242
Arizona Hall of Fame Museum
1101 W Washington, 85007; (p) (605) 255-2110; (f) (602) 255-3314; hofguide@dlapr.lib.az.us; dlapr.lib.az.us; (c) Maricopa

State/ 1987/ Museum Div, Dept. of Library, Archives, & Public Records/ staff: 4(f); 2(p)

HISTORY MUSEUM: Exhibits and educational programs are focused on people who have contributed to Arizona's development. Home of the Arizona Women's Hall of Fame.

PROGRAMS: Exhibits; Guided Tours; Interpretation; Lectures; School-Based Curriculum

COLLECTIONS: [1900-present] Material culture associated with the accomplishment of people who have made Arizona history.

HOURS: Yr M-F 8-5

ADMISSION: No charge

243
Arizona History and Archives Division, Arizona Department of Library, Archives, and Public Records
1700 W Washington, 85204; (p) (602) 542-4159; (f) (602) 542-4402; archive@dlapr.lib.az.us; www.dlapr.lib.az.us; (c) Maricopa

State/ 1937/ State Legislature/ staff: 9(f); 3(p)/publication: *Guide to Public Records in the Arizona State Archives*

LIBRARY AND/OR ARCHIVES: Statutory repository for AZ's permanently valuable state and local government records. The Division identifies, acquires, and provides access to records; provides assistance to organizations responsible for historical records; and promotes historical research.

PROGRAMS: Community Outreach; Exhibits; Guided Tours; Publication; Research Library/Archives

COLLECTIONS: [1863-present] Official records territorial, state, and local governments; AZ state and local history books and biographical and subject files; private manuscript collections; photograph collection; and Arizona newspapers.

HOURS: Yr M-F 8-5

244
Arizona Jewish Historical Society
4710 N 16th St, Ste 201, 85016; (p) (602) 241-7870; (f) (602) 264-9773; azjhs@aol.com; members.aol.com/azjhs/ajhshome.htm; (c) Maricopa

Private non-profit/ 1981/ Board of Directors/ staff: 3(p); 6(v)/ members: 300/publication: *Heritage*

HISTORIC SITE; HISTORICAL SOCIETY: Fosters appreciation and awareness of the AZ and Southwestern Jewish experience, collects, preserves, exhibits, and interprets archival materials.

PROGRAMS: Community Outreach; Exhibits; Lectures; Publication; Research Library/ Archives

COLLECTIONS: [1850-present] 30,000 pieces: photographs, letters, diaries, oral histories, scrapbooks, drawings, artifacts, paintings, newspapers, and maps.

HOURS: Yr M-F 9:30-3:30

245
Arizona State Capitol Museum
1700 W Washington, 85007; (p) (602) 542-4675; (f) (602) 542-4690; capmus@dlapr.lib.az.us; dlapr.lib.az.us; (c) Maricopa

State/ 1981/ Museum Div., Dept. of Library, Archives, and Public Records/ staff: 8(f); 7(p); 12(v)/ members: 74/publication: *Mermaid and Saguaros: The USS Arizona Silver*

HISTORY MUSEUM: Offers exhibits and programs on AZ territorial and state government history.

PROGRAMS: Exhibits; Festivals; Guided Tours; Interpretation; Lectures; Publication; Research Library/Archives; School-Based Curriculum

COLLECTIONS: [1863-1920] Building and office furnishings from Arizona territorial and state government period; a collection of 18 Lon Megargee paintings and 23 David Swing paintings depicting AZ sites and locations.

HOURS: Jan-May: M-F 8-5, Sa 10-3; June-Dec M-F 8-5

246
Arizona State Historic Preservation Office
1300 W Washington, 85007; (p) (602) 542-4009; (f) (602) 542-4180; (c) Maricopa

State/ staff: 9(f); 3(p)

HISTORIC PRESERVATION AGENCY: Assists private citizens, tribes, state, and federal agencies identify, evaluate, and protect historic and archaeological properties that have significance for local communities, the state of AZ, and the nation.

PROGRAMS: Community Outreach; Publication

COLLECTIONS: Several thousand archaeological reports, National Register of Historic Places documentation, and other materials on historic properties in AZ.

HOURS: Yr M-F 8-5

247
Mystery Castle
800 E Mineral Rd, 85066 [PO Box 8265, 85066]; (p) (602) 268-1581; (c) Maricopa

Private non-profit/ 1930/ staff: 3(p); 5(v)/publication: *My Mystery Castle*

HISTORIC SITE; HISTORICAL SOCIETY: Representation of organic architecture; houses Arizona historical artifacts.

PROGRAMS: Exhibits; Guided Tours; Lectures; Living History; Publication; Research Library/Archives

COLLECTIONS: [1900-present] Southwestern artifacts, antiques, and folk art

HOURS: Oct-June Th-Su 11-4

ADMISSION: $4; Children $2; Seniors $3

248
Phoenix Museum of History
105 N 5th St, 85004; (p) (602) 253-2734; (f) (602) 253-2348; (c) Maricopa

Private non-profit/ 1927/ staff: 7(f); 1(p); 100(v)/ members: 485

HISTORY MUSEUM: Interactive and educational exhibits showcasing Phoenix's history.

PROGRAMS: Annual Meeting; Community Outreach; Exhibits; Facility Rental; Family Programs; Guided Tours; Interpretation; Lectures; Research Library/Archives

COLLECTIONS: [1860-1940] Native American arts and crafts; artifacts from Hohokam prehistory and Victorian era Anglo settlements; photographs, Western art, textiles, archives.

HOURS: Yr M-Sa 10-5, Su 12-5

ADMISSION: $5, Student $3.50, Children $2.50, Seniors $3.50

249
Pueblo Grande Museum and Archaeological Park
4619 E Washington St, 85034-1909; (p) (602) 495-0901; (f) (602) 495-5645; prlpgstf@ci.phoenix.az.us; www.pueblogrande.com; (c) Maricopa

City/ 1929/ Parks & Recreation; Library Dept; Private non-profit/ staff: 10(f); 10(p); 30(v)/ members: 340

HISTORIC SITE: Educate the public about the archaeology and life of the Hohokam; preservation of the Hohokam ruin that includes a platform mound, ballcourt, and irrigation canals.

PROGRAMS: Community Outreach; Concerts; Elder's Programs; Exhibits; Facility Rental; Family Programs; Festivals; Guided Tours; Interpretation; Lectures; Publication; Research Library/Archives; School-Based Curriculum

COLLECTIONS: [500-1450] Archaeological artifacts from the Pueblo Grande and Phoenix area; historic and contemporary Native American material culture from the area.

HOURS: Yr M-Sa 9-4:45, Su 1-4:45

ADMISSION: $2, Children $1, Seniors $1.50; No charge Su

250
Rosson House-Heritage Square Foundation, Inc.
7th St & Monroe, 85004 [113 N 6th St, 85004]; (p) (602) 261-8948; (f) (602) 534-1786; (c) Maricopa

Private non-profit/ 1976/ staff: 4(p); 100(v)/ members: 250

HISTORIC SITE; HOUSE MUSEUM: Preserves Phoenix's Victorian history.

PROGRAMS: Exhibits; Facility Rental; Family Programs; Festivals; Guided Tours; Reenactments; School-Based Curriculum

COLLECTIONS: [1840-early 20th c] Restored buildings, period furnishings, and artifacts.

HOURS: Yr W-Sa 10-4, Su 12-4

ADMISSION: $4, Children $1, Seniors $3

PINE

251
Pine-Strawberry Archaeological and Historical Society, Inc.
Pine Community Center, 85544 [PO Box 564, 85544]; (p) (520) 476-4791; (f) (520) 476-5346; melevv@futureone.com; www.geocities.com/pinestrawhs; (c) Gila

Private non-profit/ 1978/ staff: 30(v)/ members: 250

HISTORICAL SOCIETY: Collects, preserves, and interprets the history of Pine and Strawberry.

PROGRAMS: Annual Meeting; Community Outreach; Exhibits; Lectures

COLLECTIONS: [1880-1945] Artifacts, photographs, and books.

HOURS: Museum: May-Oct M-Sa 10-4, Su 1-4; Nov-Apr M-Sa 10-2; Schoolhouse: May-Oct Sa 10-4, Su 12-4

ADMISSION: Donations accepted

PRESCOTT

252
Sharlot Hall Museum
415 W Gurley St, 86301; (p) (520) 445-3122; (f) (520) 776-9053; sharlot@sharlothall.lib.az.us; www.sharlot.org; (c) Yavapai

Private non-profit/ 1928/ staff: 23(f); 5(p); 325(v)/ members: 800

HISTORIC SITE; HISTORICAL SOCIETY; HISTORY MUSEUM; RESEARCH CENTER: Preservation of historic buildings and facilities.

PROGRAMS: Annual Meeting; Community Outreach; Concerts; Elder's Programs; Exhibits; Facility Rental; Family Programs; Festivals; Garden Tours; Guided Tours; Interpretation; Lectures; Living History; Publication; Research Library/Archives; School-Based Curriculum; Theatre

COLLECTIONS: [Prehistoric-present] Anthropology, prehistory, natural history, ethnographic, post-1863 Anglo history; Archives include photographs, documents, oral history, and genealogy.

HOURS: Yr Apr-Oct M-Sa 10-5, Su 1-5; Nov-Mar M-Sa 10-4, Su 1-5

ADMISSION: Donations requested

253
Yavapai Heritage Foundation
122 S Mt Vernon Ave, 86302 [PO Box 61, 86302-0061]; (p) (520) 445-5644; (f) (520) 778-5300; (c) Yavapai

Private non-profit/ 1974/ staff: 10(v)/ members: 50/publication: *Territorial Architecture of Prescott;The Tour Guide to the Forests and Grasslands*

HISTORICAL SOCIETY: Preservation, cultural history, natural history, and the environment.

PROGRAMS: Annual Meeting; Community Outreach; Lectures; Publication

COLLECTIONS: [20th c]

SAFFORD

254
Graham County Historical Society Museum
808 S 8th Ave, 85548 [PO Box 127, 85548]; (p) (520) 348-3212; (c) Graham

1962/ Graham County Historical Society/ staff: 1(p); 6(v)/ members: 200

HISTORICAL SOCIETY; HISTORY MUSEUM: Manages the museum; collects and preserves artifacts, photos, records, books, diaries, and other educational materials.

PROGRAMS: Annual Meeting; Community Outreach; Exhibits; Guided Tours; Interpretation; Lectures; Publication; Research Library Archives

COLLECTIONS: [1880-1950] Local manuscripts, diaries, photos, early books, farm and mining artifacts, clothing, and quilts.

SCOTTSDALE

255
Papago Trackers
PMB 155-11259 E Via Linda #100, 85259; (p) (480) 314-9139; (f) (480) 661-9986; (c) Maricopa

Private non-profit/ 1985/ staff: 28(v)/ members: 28/publication: *Papago Scout*

HISTORIC PRESERVATION AGENCY; HISTORIC SITE: Tracks the military usages of Papago Park.

PROGRAMS: Annual Meeting; Exhibits; Guided Tours; Lectures; Publication

COLLECTIONS: [1840s-present] Papago Park POW camp memorabilia, military archives.

HOURS: Yr

256
Scottsdale Corral of Westerners
7117 Main St, 85251 [c/o Guidon Book Store, Aaron Chohen, 85251]; (p) (480) 945-8811; (f) (480) 946-0521; bookmaster@guidon.com; www.guidon.com; (c) Maricopa

Private non-profit/ 1974/ staff: 15(v)/ members: 75

HISTORICAL SOCIETY: Monthly meetings with programs focusing on the American West.

PROGRAMS: Lectures; Monthly Meeting

SECOND MESA

257
Hopi Cultural Center, Inc.
Hwy 264, 86043 [PO Box 7, 86043]; (p) (520) 734-6650; (c) Navajo

Joint/ 1970/ Tribal; Private non-profit/ staff: 1(f); 2(v)

TRIBAL MUSEUM: Preserves, interpretes, and educates on Hopi culture.

PROGRAMS: Exhibits; Festivals; Lectures

COLLECTIONS: Photographs, Kachina dolls, overlay silver, weavings, pottery, and baskets.

HOURS: Mar-Oct M-F 8-5, Sa-Su 9-3

ADMISSION: $3, Children $1

SEDONA

258
Sedona Historical Society
735 Jordan Rd, 86339 [PO Box 10216, 86339]; (p) (520) 282-7038; (f) (520) 282-7038; www.sedona.net/SHS/; (c) Coconino

Private non-profit/ 1982/ staff: 80(v)/ members: 200/publication: *Journal of Sedona Historical Society*

HISTORICAL SOCIETY; HISTORY MUSEUM: Preserves and exhibits items and stories of homesteaders, pioneers, cowboys, and westerns filmed in Sedona.

PROGRAMS: Annual Meeting; Community Outreach; Concerts; Elder's Programs; Exhibits; Festivals; Film/Video; Guided Tours; Living History; Publication

COLLECTIONS: [1870-1960] Artifacts, documents, and photos of settlers; collection of films; fruit processing equipment and vehicles.

HOURS: Yr Sa-M 10-4

ADMISSION: Donations accepted

SHOW LOW

259
Show Low Historical Society
541 E Deuce of Clubs, 85902 [PO Box 3468, 85902]; (p) (520) 532-7115; (c) Navajo

Private non-profit/ 1992/ staff: 1(p); 10(v)/ members: 73

HISTORICAL SOCIETY; HISTORY MUSEUM: Preserving area history.

PROGRAMS: Annual Meeting; Exhibits; Guided Tours

COLLECTIONS: [1870-1950] Show Low artifacts and photos.

HOURS: Apr-Oct M-F 1-5

SPRINGERVILLE

260
Casa Malpais Restoration Project
318 E Main St, 85938 [PO Box 807, 85938]; (p) (520) 333-5375; (f) (520) 333-5690

261
White Mountain Historical Society
[PO Box 12, 85938]; (p) (520) 333-2671; (c) Apache

City/ 1976/ staff: 1(f); 1(p)

HISTORICAL SOCIETY: Researches, records, and preserves local history, including artifacts and structures.

SUPERIOR

262
Superior Historical Society, Inc.
300 Main, 85273 [PO Box 613, 85273]; (c) Pinal

Private non-profit/ 1987/ staff: 1(f); 30(v)/ members: 100

HISTORIC SITE; HISTORICAL SOCIETY; HISTORY MUSEUM: Collects, preserves, interprets, and disseminates mining and local history.

PROGRAMS: Annual Meeting; Exhibits; Guided Tours

COLLECTIONS: [1853-1996] Anthropological and geological artifacts; photos.

ADMISSION: Yr W,Th,Sa 10-2, Su 11-3

TEMPE

263
Arizona Historical Society Museum, Arizona Historical Society - Central Division
1300 N College, 85281; (p) (480) 929-0292; (f) (602) 861-3537; library.reference@ahs. maricopa.gov; (c) Maricopa

HISTORY MUSEUM; LIBRARY AND/OR ARCHIVES: Collect, preserve, interpret, and disseminate the history of AZ, in particular of 20th c Phoenix and Central AZ.

PROGRAMS: Exhibits; Guided Tours; Interpretation; School-Based Curriculum

COLLECTIONS: [20th c] Artifacts, objects, photographs, manuscripts, oral histories, archival materials, personal papers, books and periodicals, ephemera and art.

HOURS: Yr Library: T-Th 10-4, F 10-1; Museum: M-Sa 10-4, Su 12-4

ADMISSION: No charge

264
Arizona State University Museum of Anthropology
Arizona State University, 85287 [PO Box 872402, 85287-2402]; (p) (602) 965-6213; (f) (602) 965-7671; (c) Maricopa

1959/ staff: 1(f); 2(p)/publication: *Museum Studies Newsletter*

ANTHROPOLOGY MUSEUM: Features exhibits on archaeology, physical anthropology, and sociocultural anthropology.

PROGRAMS: Exhibits; Publication

COLLECTIONS: Ethnological collections, physical anthropological collections, and archaeological collections of more than two million specimens from the Southwest, primarily from Arizona, other areas of North America, Mesoamerica, and the near east.

HOURS: Yr M-F 10-4

265
Hackett House
95 W 4th St, 85281-2825; (p) (602) 350-8181

266
Tempe Historical Museum
809 E Southern Ave, 85282; (p) (480) 350-5100; (f) (480) 350-5150; www.tempe.gov/museum; (c) Maricopa

City/ 1972/ staff: 7(f); 6(p); 150(v)

HISTORIC SITE; HISTORY MUSEUM: Interprets local history.

PROGRAMS: Community Outreach; Exhibits; Family Programs; Festivals; Guided Tours; Lectures; Living History; Research Library/ Archives; School-Based Curriculum

COLLECTIONS: [1880-present] Period housewares, clothing, textiles, agricultural equip., business equip., toys; photos; archives.

HOURS: Yr M-Th 10-5, Sa 10-5, Su 1-5

TOMBSTONE

267
Tombstone Courthouse State Historic Park
Corner of Toughnut & 3rd St, 85638 [Box 216, 85638]; (p) (520) 457-3311; (f) (520) 457-2565; hcook@pr.state.az.us; www.pr.state.az.us; (c) Cochise

State/ 1960/ State Parks/ staff: 4(f); 1(p); 3(v)

HISTORIC SITE; HISTORY MUSEUM: Collects, acquires, interprets, preserves, and exhibits archives pertaining to the area's history.

PROGRAMS: Exhibits; Interpretation; Publication; Reenactments; Research Library/ Archives

COLLECTIONS: [1875-1929] Archaeological and Native American ethnological objects; archives; period furnishings.

HOURS: Yr Daily

TUBAC

268
Los Tubaquenos
Tubac Presidio State Historic Park, 85646 [PO Box 1296, 85646]; (p) (520) 398-2252; (f) (520) 398-2685; ckug@pr.state.az.us; (c) Santa Cruz

State/ 1993/ AZ State Parks/ staff: 32(v)

HISTORIC SITE; LIVING HISTORY/OUTDOOR MUSEUM: Costumed volunteers interpret, display, and demonstrate the life of the Spanish clergy, military, and settlers of Arizona's 1st European settlement.

PROGRAMS: Community Outreach; Exhibits; Interpretation; Living History; Reenactments

COLLECTIONS: [1752-1776] Original and reproduced carpentry, mining, and garden tools; household and weaving items; religious, medicinal, and agricultural implements.

HOURS: Oct-Mar, Su 1-4

ADMISSION: $2, Children $1

269
Tubac Presidio State Historic Park
1 Burrell St, 85646 [PO Box 1296, 85646]; (p) (520) 398-2252; (f) (520) 398-2685; Ckrug@ pr.state.az.us; www.pr.state.az.us; (c) Santa Cruz

State/ 1957/ AZ State Parks/ staff: 4(f); 37(v)

HISTORIC PRESERVATION AGENCY; HISTORIC SITE; HISTORY MUSEUM; LIVING HISTORY/OUTDOOR MUSEUM: Preserves and interpretes of the Spanish Colonial, Mexican Republic, and US Territorial periods of the Santa Cruz River Valley.

PROGRAMS: Community Outreach; Exhibits; Facility Rental; Family Programs; Festivals; Guided Tours; Interpretation; Lectures; Living History; Reenactments; School-Based Curriculum

COLLECTIONS: [1751-1950] Historic structures, ruins, and artifacts.

HOURS: Yr Daily 8-5

ADMISSION: $2, Children $1

TUCSON

270
390th Memorial Museum Foundation Inc.
6000 E Valencia Rd, 85706; (p) (520) 574-0287; (f) (520) 574-3030; the390th@aol.com; (c) Pima

Private non-profit/ 1985/ Foundation Board of Directors/ staff: 3(f); 2(p); 55(v)/ members: 855/publication: *J-Bulletin*

HISTORY MUSEUM: Preserves the history and heritage of the 390th Bomb Group, 390th Strategic Missile Wing, and any other future operational organizations designated with the 390th cardinal number.

PROGRAMS: Exhibits; Facility Rental; Guided Tours; Publication

COLLECTIONS: [1941-1945] WW II air crew equipment and artifacts, including a B-15G aircraft, bomb group mission and missing air crew reports, photographs, and veterans personnel records.

HOURS: Yr Daily 10-4:30

271
Arizona Archaeological and Historical Society
Arizona State Museum, University of Arizona, 85721; (p) (520) 621-3656; (f) (520) 621-2976; Jadams@Desert.com; w3fp.arizona.edu/asm/ aahs/aahs.html; (c) Pima

Private non-profit/ 1916/ staff: 3(p); 15(v)/ members: 960/publication: *KIVA, Glyphs*

HISTORICAL SOCIETY: Affiliated with the AZ State Museum, offers educational and research activities through lectures, classes, field trips, and the scholarly journal, KIVA.

PROGRAMS: Community Outreach; Exhibits; Guided Tours; Lectures; Monthly Meeting; Publication; Research Library/Archives

272
Arizona Historical Society - Southern Division
949 E 2nd St, 85719; (p) (520) 628-5774; (f) (520) 628-5695; azhist@azstarnet.com; www.azstarnet.com/~azhist/; (c) Pima

Joint/ 1884/ Private non-profit; State/ staff: 64(f); 26(p); 400(v)/ members: 2500/publication: *Journal of Arizona History*

HISTORICAL SOCIETY; HISTORY MUSEUM: Four museums in principal cities; certifies and contracts with local museums; and conducts a historical marker program.

PROGRAMS: Annual Meeting; Community Outreach; Exhibits; Facility Rental; Festivals; Guided Tours; Interpretation; Lectures; Living History; Publication; Research Library/ Archives; School-Based Curriculum

COLLECTIONS: [1540-1949] 65,000 artifacts, 56,000 books, 1000 periodical titles, 9000 reels of microfilm, 810,000 photographs, 1500 manuscripts, 600 maps, 12,000 biographical files, and 1200 oral history transcripts.

HOURS: Yr M-Sa 10-4

273
Arizona State Genealogical Society
[PO Box 42075, 85733-2075]; http://www.rootsweb.com/~asgs; (c) Pima

Private non-profit/ 1966/ members: 320

GENEALOGICAL SOCIETY: Provides classes, seminars, and research trips. Promotes the preservation of genealogical records and family research.

PROGRAMS: Annual Meeting; Community Outreach; Exhibits; Lectures; Publication; Research Library/Archives

274
Arizona State Museum
1013 University Blvd, 85721 [Univ of Arizona, PO Box 210026, 85721-0026]; (p) (520) 621-6281; (f) (520) 621-2976; www.arizona.edu/ ~asm; (c) Pima

State/ 1893/ AZ Board of Regents/ staff: 56(f); 60(p); 60(v)

HISTORY MUSEUM: Collects and conserves materials related to the Indian cultures of the Southwest.

PROGRAMS: Community Outreach; Exhibits; Festivals; Guided Tours; Lectures; Publication; Research Library/Archives

COLLECTIONS: Artifacts ranging from modern Kachina dolls to 12,000 year old spear points. Research library and archives and a photo archive of 200,000 images.

HOURS: Yr M-Sa 10-5, Su 12-5

275
Jewish Historical Society of Southern Arizona
[PO Box 57482, 85732-7482]; (p) (520) 299-4486; lipseya@prodigy.net; (c) Pima

Private non-profit/ 1982/ staff: 1(p); 20(v)/ members: 300/publication: *Chronicle*

HISTORICAL SOCIETY

PROGRAMS: Annual Meeting; Community Outreach; Exhibits; Lectures; Publication; Research

276
Otis H. Chidester Scout Museum of Southern Arizona, Inc., The
1937 E Blacklidge Dr, 85719; (p) (520) 326-7669; gruhl@azscoutmuseum.com; www.azscoutmuseum.com; (c) Pima

1986/ staff: 24(v)/ members: 110/publication: *The Messenger; Instagram*

HISTORY MUSEUM; LIBRARY AND/OR ARCHIVES; RESEARCH CENTER: Collects, preserves, and exhibits Boy Scout artifacts, memorabilia, and publications.

PROGRAMS: Annual Meeting; Community Outreach; Exhibits; Film/Video; Publication

COLLECTIONS: [1910-1970] Boy Scout memorabilia, artifacts, publications, uniforms, patches, oral histories, documents, photographs, histories, statues, and artwork.

HOURS: Yr T,Th 6-9, Sa 9-12

ADMISSION: No Charge

277
Pima Air and Space Museum
6000 E Valencia Rd, 85706; (p) (520) 574-0462; (f) (520) 574-9238; pimaair@azstarnet.com; www.pimaair.org; (c) Pima

Private non-profit/ 1976/ Arizona Aerospace Foundation/ staff: 65(f); 150(v)/ members: 1850/publication: *Skywriting*

HISTORY MUSEUM: Preserves and presents the history of flight for aerospace education.

PROGRAMS: Annual Meeting; Exhibits; Facility Rental; Film/Video; Guided Tours; Lectures; Publication; Research Library/Archives

COLLECTIONS: Archival materials, photographs, books, serial, aircraft manuals, govt. documents, clippings; artifacts.

HOURS: Yr Daily 9-5

ADMISSION: $7.50, Children $4, Seniors

278
Postal History Foundation, The
920 N 1st Ave, 85717 [PO Box 40725, 85717]; (p) (520) 623-6652; (f) (520) 623-6652; PHF@azstarnet.com; (c) Pima

Private non-profit/ 1960/ staff: 2(f); 35(v)/ members: 400/publication: *The Heliograph*

PROFESSIONAL ORGANIZATION: Postal history education and research.

PROGRAMS: Annual Meeting; Community Outreach; Lectures; Publication; Research Library/Archives; School-Based Curriculum

COLLECTIONS: [1800-present] Civil War library; US and Foreign stamps; postal artifacts and literature.

HOURS: Yr, 8-3

279
Society for Historical Archaeology, The
[PO Box 30446, 85751-0446]; (p) (520) 886-8006; (f) (520) 886-0182; sha@azstarnet.com; www.sha.org; (c) Pima

Private non-profit/ 1967/ Board of Directors/ staff: 250(v)/ members: 2300

PROFESSIONAL ORGANIZATION: Promotes scholarly research and the dissemination of knowledge concerning historical archaeology; emphasizes the archaeology of the New World.

PROGRAMS: Annual Meeting; Lectures; Publication

COLLECTIONS: History of the Society for Historical Archaeology.

280
Sosa-Carrillo-Fremont House
In Tuscon Conv Ctr Complex, 151 S Granada Ave, 85702 [PO Box 2588, 85702]; (p) (520) 622-0956; (f) (520) 628-5696; azhist@azstarnet.com

1880/ State; Arizona Historical Society/ staff: 1(f); 4(p); 10(v)

HOUSE MUSEUM: Maintains historic house.

COLLECTIONS: [1880s-1900] Late 19th c furniture, original furnishings, and personal items that belonged to residents and other area pioneers; local and oral histories, and photographs.

HOURS: Yr

281
Tucson Museum of Art and Historic Block
140 N Main Ave, 85701; (p) (520) 624-4333; (f) (520) 624-7202; info@tucsonarts.com; www.tucsonarts.com; (c) Pima

Private non-profit/ 1924/ staff: 16(f); 12(p); 484(v)/ members: 2500

ART MUSEUM; HISTORIC SITE; HISTORY MUSEUM: Collect, exhibits, conserves, and preserves art; art education.

PROGRAMS: Community Outreach; Exhibits; Facility Rental; Festivals; Guided Tours; Lectures

COLLECTIONS: [Pre-Columbian-present] Pre-Colombian, Spanish colonial, Western American, and 20th c paintings, sculptures, decorative and folk arts.

HOURS: Yr M-Sa 10-4, Su 12-4

ADMISSION: $5, Student $3, Seniors $4; Under 12 free; Families free Su

282
Tucson Rodeo Parade Commission and Museum
6th Ave & Irvington Rd, 85702 [PO Box 17788, 85702]; (p) (520) 294-1280; (c) Pima

Private non-profit/ 1925/ staff: 1(p); 36(v)

HISTORIC PRESERVATION AGENCY; HISTORIC SITE: Preserves pioneer history, an annual Feb parade of historic horse-drawn vehicles.

PROGRAMS: Exhibits; Festivals; Guided Tours

COLLECTIONS: [1850-1900] Historic wagons, buggies, stagecoaches, conistogas, freighters, and buckboards.

HOURS: Yr Daily

ADMISSION: Donations accepted

WICKENBURG

283
Desert Caballeros Western Museum
21 M Frontier St, 85390; (p) (520) 684-2272; (f) (520) 684-5794; info@westernmuseum.org; www.westernmuseum.org; (c) Maricopa

Private non-profit/ 1960/ staff: 3(f); 2(p)/ members: 600

ART MUSEUM: Preserve and exhibits the art and history of the rural Southwest and desert frontier.

PROGRAMS: Elder's Programs; Exhibits; Facility Rental; Family Programs; Guided Tours; Lectures

COLLECTIONS: Western art: Remington, Russell, Moran, Bierstadt, and J.H. Sharp; Western collection of cowboy gear: 500 artifacts, saddles, bits, spurs, chaps, lariats, guns; Native American Art and artifacts: Anasazi, Pueblo, Hopi, Navajo; Gems and minerals; mining, ranching, and local history.

HOURS: Yr Daily 10-5

ADMISSION: $5, Student $1, Seniors $4

WILLCOX

284
Rex Allen Arizona Cowboy Museum, The
150 N Railroad Ave, 85643; (p) (520) 384-4583; (c) Cochise

Private non-profit/ 1988/ staff: 10(v)/ members: 100

HISTORY MUSEUM: Documents the life of Rex Allen; preserves the history of local cowboys.

PROGRAMS: Annual Meeting; Community Outreach; Concerts; Exhibits; Film/Video; Guided Tours; Living History; Theatre

COLLECTIONS: [1940-1998] Memorabilia of Rex Allen, Western actor and narrator for Disney; Items related to the history of local ranchers and the AZ Coco Belles.

HOURS: Yr Daily 10-5

ADMISSION: $2, Family $5

285
Sulphur Springs Valley Historical Society/Chiricahua Regional Museum and Research Center
124 E Stewart St, 85643; (p) (520) 384-2272; (c) Cochise

Private non-profit/ 1972/ staff: 15(v)/ members: 75

HISTORICAL SOCIETY; HISTORY MUSEUM: Preserves the history of local pioneers and the Ciricahua Apaches; maintains a research center; preserves Historic District buildings.

PROGRAMS: Annual Meeting; Exhibits; Guided Tours; Interpretation; Lectures; Living History; Reenactments; Research Library/Archives

COLLECTIONS: [1800-present] Artifacts pertaining to the Chiricahua Apache, pioneer, miner, cattle, and agricultural histories.

HOURS: Yr Daily 1-4

ADMISSION: Donations accepted

WILLIAMS

286
Williams Historic Commission
113 S First St, 86046; (p) (520) 635-4451; (f) (520) 635-4495; (c) Coconino

City/ staff: 1(p); 7(v)

HISTORIC PRESERVATION AGENCY: The area historic preservation office is in the process of creating Route 66 memorabilia museum.

WINDOW ROCK

287
Navajo Nation Historic Preservation Department
Navajo Nation Inn Office Bldg Hwy 264, 86515 [PO Box 4950, 86515]; (p) (520) 871-7146; (f) (520) 871-7886; (c) Apache

Tribal/ 1988/ Navajo Nation Tribal Council/ staff: 70(f)

HISTORIC PRESERVATION AGENCY: Protects and preserves the Nation's cultural resources; including the Navajo Nation Museum, Repatriation/Traditional Program, Compliance, and Chaco Protection Sites Program; issue permits for site visitation and archaeological and ethnographic work on Navajo lands.

PROGRAMS: Community Outreach; Exhibits; Publication; Research Library/Archives

COLLECTIONS: [Historic Navajo/Anasazi] Navajo ethnographic materials: jewelry, rugs, dolls; archeological materials, historic photos of daily Navajo life, artwork, archives.

HOURS: M-F 8-5

288
Navajo Nation Museum
Hwy 264 & Post Office Loop Rd., 86515 [PO Box 900, 86515]; (p) (520) 871-7941; (f) (520) 871-7942; (c) Apache

Tribal/ 1961/ Historic Preservation Dept/ staff: 17(f); 2(p)

ART MUSEUM; HISTORY MUSEUM; LIBRARY AND/OR ARCHIVES; TRIBAL MUSEUM: Serves both the Navajo People and non-Navajo visitors and tourists through programs on Navajo history and culture.

PROGRAMS: Community Outreach; Exhibits; Facility Rental; Family Programs; Festivals; Lectures; Research Library/Archives

COLLECTIONS: [19-20th c] Navajo historical materials, textiles, art, and an archive of over 40,000 images from 1930s to present.

HOURS: Yr M, Sa 8-5, T-F 8-8

ADMISSION: No charge

WINSLOW

289
Homolovi Ruins State Park
Hwy 87 N, 86047 [HC 63 Box 5 (87N), 86047-9803]; (p) (520) 289-4106; (f) (520) 289-2021; homolovi@pr.state.az.us; www.pr.state.az.us

State/ 1986/ State Parks/ staff: 4(f); 3(p); 4(v)

HISTORY MUSEUM; STATE PARK: Eduates about archaeological site, preserves and interprets the prehistoric resources of the Little Colorado River Valley.

PROGRAMS: Exhibits; Festivals; Interpretation; School-Based Curriculum

COLLECTIONS: [Prehistory-present] Prehistoric and historic Native American objects associated with the Homolovi ruins archaeological sites; historic Hopi Indian artifacts.

HOURS: Yr Daily 8-5,

ADMISSION: $4/vehicle/4 people

290
Winslow Historical Society "Old Trails Museum"
212 Kinsley Ave, 86047 [Po Box 280, 86047]; (p) (520) 289-5861; oldtrails@Cybertrails.com; (c) Navajo

Private non-profit/ 1985/ staff: 2(f); 1(p); 4(v)/ members: 110

HISTORICAL SOCIETY; HISTORY MUSEUM: Containing exhibits related to the Santa Fe Railroad, Route 66, Harvey Houses, and community life.

PROGRAMS: Exhibits

COLLECTIONS: [Early 1900s] Anasazi artifacts, petrified mammoth bones, period drugstore and ranching items, "O" gauge model railroad, railroad memorabilia, period stage wardrobe, and photographs.

HOURS: Yr

YOUNGTOWN

291
Youngtown Historical Society, Inc., The
112th Ave at Alabama, 85363 [12030 Clubhouse Sq, 85363]; (p) (602) 977-6888; ythstsoc@yahoo.com; (c) Maricopa

Private non-profit/ 1988/ Board of Directors/ staff: 14(v)/ members: 86

HISTORICAL SOCIETY: Collects, preserves, and catalogs documents, and memorabilia related to the history of America's first retirement community.

PROGRAMS: Annual Meeting; Exhibits; Film/Video; Lectures; Living History; Research Library/Archives

COLLECTIONS: [1949-present] Items related to early retiree lifestyle period; scrapbooks, guest books, records, photographs, commemorative pins, and ribbons.

HOURS: Oct 1-May 31 T, W 9-11

YUMA

292
Arizona Historical Society - Rio Colorado Division
240 Madison Ave, 85364; (p) (520) 782-1841; (f) (520) 783-0680; (c) Yuma

State/ 1982/ staff: 3(f); 1(p); 80(v)

HISTORY MUSEUM: Housed in two 1870s adobe buildings. Exhibits portray Yuma, AZ, history.

PROGRAMS: Annual Meeting; Community Outreach; Exhibits; Festivals; Lectures; Living History; Research Library/Archives

COLLECTIONS: [1540s-present] Furniture, clothing, photographs, maps, archives, and tools and equipment relating to steamboats, railroads and agriculture.

HOURS: Yr T-Sa 10-4

293
Century House and Garden
240 Madison Ave, 85364 [240 Madison Ave, 85364]; (p) (520) 782-1841; (f) (520) 783-0689

1870/ State; AZ Historical Society/ staff: 3(f); 1(p); 80(v)

COLLECTIONS: [1540s-1940s] Mining, railroad, steamboat, farm artifacts, photographs and arial photos, historical archives.

HOURS: Yr T-Sa 10-4

294
Quechan Tribal Museum
350 Picado Rd, 85366 [PO Box 1899, 85366]; (p) (760) 572-0661; (f) (760) 572-2102; (c) Imperial

Private non-profit/ 1969/ staff: 2(f)

TRIBAL MUSEUM: Conserves artifacts, military, and Spanish era history.

PROGRAMS: Exhibits

COLLECTIONS: Tribal, Spanish, and military collections.

HOURS: Yr Daily

295
Yuma Crossing State Historic Park
201 N 4th Ave, 85366; (p) (520) 329-0471; (f) (520) 782-7124; keatherly@pr.state.az.us; www.pr.state.az.us; (c) Yuma

Joint/ 1986/ City; State/ staff: 3(f); 2(p); 2(v)

HISTORY MUSEUM; HOUSE MUSEUM: Collects, acquires, interprets, preserves, and exhibits artifacts pertaining to the history of Yuma Crossing.

PROGRAMS: Concerts; Exhibits; Facility Rental; Festivals; Interpretation; Living History; Reenactments; School-Based Curriculum

COLLECTIONS: [1540-1930] Horse drawn vehicles, period furnishings and household items, archival materials, railroad coach car, tools, and military objects.

HOURS: Oct-Apr Daily 8-5; May-Sept Th-M 8-5

ADMISSION: $3, Children $2; Under 6 free

296
Yuma Territorial Prison State Historic Park
1 Prison Hill Rd, 85364; (p) (520) 783-4771; (f) (520) 783-7442; jmasterson@pr.state.az.us; www.pr.state.az.us; (c) Yuma

State/ 1940/ State Parks/ staff: 5(f); 2(p); 4(v)

HISTORIC SITE; HISTORY MUSEUM: Collects, acquires, interprets, preserves, and exhibits artifacts pertaining to the history of the first Arizona Territorial Prison, including the prison cemetery.

PROGRAMS: Exhibits; Interpretation; Living History; Reenactments; School-Based Curriculum

COLLECTIONS: [1876-1909] Memorabilia, photographs, and manuscripts associated with the prison and area history.

HOURS: Yr Daily 8-5

ADMISSION: $3; Children $2

ARKANSAS

ALLEENE

297
Will Reed Log Home Museum
Corner of LR 133 & Hwy 234, 71820 [PO Box 4, 71820]; (p) (870) 542-6360; (c) Little River

County/ 1976/ staff: 6(v)

HISTORICAL SOCIETY

PROGRAMS: Community Outreach; Exhibits; Guided Tours; School-Based Curriculum

ARKADELPHIA

298
City of Arkadelphia
610 Caddo St, 71923; (p) (870) 246-9864; (f) (870) 246-1813; abby@hsu.edu; www.arkadelphia.org; (c) Clark

City/ 1857/ staff: 83(f); 60(p)

PROFESSIONAL ORGANIZATION: Houses records of the city since its inception.

PROGRAMS: Community Outreach; Research Library/Archives

COLLECTIONS: [20th c] Minutes from city council meetings, ordinances, historical documents, and contracts.

HOURS: Yr M-F 8-5

ADMISSION: No charge

299
Clark County Historical Association
Library, Ouachita Baptist Univ, 71923 [PO Box 516, 71923]; (p) (870) 245-5332; (f) (870) 245-5245; (c) Clark

Private non-profit/ 1972/ members: 300/publication: *Clark County Historical Journal*

GENEALOGICAL SOCIETY; HISTORICAL SOCIETY; LIBRARY AND/OR ARCHIVES; RESEARCH CENTER

PROGRAMS: Annual Meeting; Community Outreach; Exhibits; Festivals; Lectures; Publication; Research Library/Archives

HOURS: Yr M-F 8-4

ADMISSION: No charge

ASH FLAT

300
Sharp County Historical Society
[PO Box 185, 72513]; (p) (870) 257-2323; (c) Sharp

Private non-profit/ 1980/ Board of Trustees/ staff: 4(v)/ members: 76

HISTORICAL SOCIETY: Preserves county history.

PROGRAMS: Lectures; Publication

COLLECTIONS: [1890-1950] Archive library with county journals.

ASHDOWN

301
Little River County Historical Society
310 N 2nd St, 71822; (p) (870) 898-7242; (c) Little River

Private non-profit/ 1968/ Board of Directors/ staff: 1(p)/ 96(v)/ members: 55

HISTORICAL SOCIETY; HISTORY MUSEUM: Oversees 1918 Craftsman house.

PROGRAMS: Annual Meeting; Elder's Programs; Exhibits; Facility Rental; Family Programs; Guided Tours

COLLECTIONS: [Early 20th c] Farming tools, teachers' records, family records and photos, clothing exhibits, furniture.

HOURS: Yr by appt

ADMISSION: No charge

BATESVILLE

302
Old Independence Regional Museum
380 S 9th St, 72503 [PO Box 4506, 72503]; (p) (870) 793-2121; (c) Independence

Private non-profit/ 1993/ Board of Trustees/ staff: 1(f); 1(p); 45(v)/ members: 400

HISTORY MUSEUM; LIBRARY AND/OR ARCHIVES; RESEARCH CENTER: Preserves and interprets the history of Independence County from 1820.

PROGRAMS: Annual Meeting; Exhibits; Film/Video; Guided Tours; Interpretation; Lectures; Research Library/Archives; School-Based Curriculum

COLLECTIONS: [1820-present] Maps, photos, books, family files, archives, Shawnee room.

HOURS: Yr T-Sa 9-4:30, Su 1-4

ADMISSION: $3, Children $1, Seniors $2

BELLA VISTA

303
Bella Vista Historical Society/Museum
1885 Bella Vista Way, 72714; (p) (501) 855-2335; (c) Benton

Private non-profit/ 1975/ staff: 42(p)/ members: 235/publication: *Bella Vista Vision*

GENEALOGICAL SOCIETY; HISTORIC PRESERVATION AGENCY; HISTORIC SITE; HISTORICAL SOCIETY; HISTORY MUSEUM: Discovers, collects, preserves and displays historical material; disseminates historical information; marks sites, trails, and historic buildings.

PROGRAMS: Annual Meeting; Community Outreach; Exhibits; Facility Rental; Guided Tours; Interpretation; Lectures; Publication; Research Library/Archives; School-Based Curriculum

COLLECTIONS: [1912-present] Archaeological, geological, and historical artifacts and displayst, including audio-visuals, photographs, manuscripts, maps, newspapers, and cartoons.

HOURS: Mar-Nov Th-Su 1-4

BENTON

304
Gann Museum of Saline County, Inc.
218 S Market, 72015-4304; (p) (501) 778-5513; (c) Saline

Private non-profit/ 1980/ Board of Directors/ staff: 1(p)/ 6(v)/ members: 234/publication: *The Gann Legacy*

HISTORY MUSEUM: Presents historical chronicle of Saline County, the museum is building is made of bauxite.

PROGRAMS: Exhibits; Guided Tours; Publication

305
Saline County History and Heritage Society, Inc.
410 River St, 72018 [PO Box 1712, 72018]; (p) (501) 778-3770; (c) Saline

Private non-profit/ 1986/ staff: 1(p)/ 6(v)/publication: *Saline Journal*

HISTORICAL SOCIETY: Preserves history of Saline and its families.

PROGRAMS: Community Outreach; Elder's Programs; Exhibits; Family Programs; Publication; Research Library/Archives

HOURS: Yr T-W

BENTONVILLE

306
Benton County Historical Society
400 S Walton Blvd, 72712 [PO Box 1034, 72712]; (p) (501) 273-3890; BCHSArK@Juno.com; www.uark.edu/gmss/bchsark; (c) Benton

1954/ Board and members/ staff: 10(p)/ 10(v)/ members: 275/publication: *BC Pioneer*

LIBRARY AND/OR ARCHIVES; RESEARCH CENTER: Preserves history of Benton County and makes records available to the public.

PROGRAMS: Quarterly Meeting

COLLECTIONS: [1850-present] Quarterly issues of Pioneer, census, cemetery, obituaries from 1884-1933 and funeral home records.

HOURS: Summer T-Sa 10-4; Winter T-Sa 11-3

307
Peel Mansion Museum and Historic Gardens
400 S Walton Blvd, 72712; (p) (501) 273-9664; (f) (501) 273-9688; peel@IPA.net; biz.IPA.net/Peel; (c) Benton

Private non-profit/ 1992/ staff: 6(p)

GARDEN; HOUSE MUSEUM

PROGRAMS: Exhibits; Family Programs; Festivals; Garden Tours; Guided Tours; Lectures; Living History; Reenactments; Research Library/Archives

COLLECTIONS: [1850-1900] Historic cabin and house with furnishings, gardens.

HOURS: Mar-Nov T-Sa 10-4

ADMISSION: $3, Children $1; Under 18 Free w/adult

BERRYVILLE

308
Carroll County Historical & Genealogical Society, Inc.
401 Public Square, 72616 [PO Box 249, 72616]; (p) (870) 423-6312; history@cswnet.com; (c) Carroll

Private non-profit/ 1955/ staff: 1(f); 5(p)/ 5(v)/ members: 650/publication: *Carroll County Historical Quarterly*

GENEALOGICAL SOCIETY; HISTORIC SITE; HISTORICAL SOCIETY; HISTORY MUSEUM;

LIBRARY AND/OR ARCHIVES; RESEARCH CENTER: Operates the "Heritage Center" Pioneer Museum and Research Library, which is housed in an 1880 courthouse.

PROGRAMS: Annual Meeting; Community Outreach; Exhibits; Facility Rental; Festivals; Film/Video; Garden Tours; Guided Tours; Interpretation; Lectures; Publication; Reenactments; Research Library/Archives

COLLECTIONS: [19th-20th c] Working railroad, funeral parlor, pioneer kitchen, bedroom, country school room, barber shop, apothecary, post office, parlor, clocks, dishes, tools, family histories, and Mountain Meadows Massacre artifacts.

HOURS: Research: Yr M-F 9-4, Winter T-F; Museum: Apr-Oct M-F 9-4

ADMISSION: $2, Family $5, Children $0.50

BOONEVILLE

309
Logan County Historical Society
Depository: Booneville Public Library, [PO Box 40, Magazine, 72943]; (c) Logan

Private non-profit/ 1980/ staff: 10(v)/ members: 225/publication: *Wagon Wheels*

GENEALOGICAL SOCIETY; HISTORICAL SOCIETY; HISTORY MUSEUM: Collects and preserves historical and genealogical data of Logan County, publishes journal.

PROGRAMS: Annual Meeting; Exhibits; Publication

COLLECTIONS: [1870-present] General county history, compiled and published family histories, reference materials.

CAMDEN

310
Ouachita County Historical Society
926 Washington, 71701; (p) (870) 836-9243; (c) Ouachita

Private non-profit/ 1963/ staff: 1(f); 3(v)/ members: 500/publication: *Ouachita County Historical Quarterly*

HISTORICAL SOCIETY; HOUSE MUSEUM: Preserves, educates, and promotes interest in local history.

PROGRAMS: Guided Tours; Interpretation; Publication

COLLECTIONS: [1847-1865] Furniture, china, silver, photos, oil portraits, artifacts.

HOURS: Apr-Oct W-Sa 9-4

ADMISSION: $3, Student $1

CHERRY VALLEY

311
Mississippi Valley Educational Programs
55 CR 315, 72324; (p) (870) 588-4830; arkdepot@hotmail.com; www.mvep.org; (c) Cross

Private non-profit/ 1996/ staff: 1(f); 10(p)

LIVING HISTORY/OUTDOOR MUSEUM: Provides living history programs for parks, museums, schools, and other institutions.

PROGRAMS: Community Outreach; Exhibits; Festivals; Interpretation; Lectures; Living History; Reenactments; School-Based Curriculum; Theatre

CLINTON

312
Van Buren County Historical Society and Museum
3rd & Poplar St, 72031 [PO Box 1023, 72031]; (p) (501) 745-4066; (c) Van Buren

1976/ Board of Directors/ staff: 12(v)/ members: 300/publication: *Van Buren County Historical Journal*

HISTORICAL SOCIETY; HISTORY MUSEUM: Collects and displays artifacts relevant to the area's exploration, settlement, development, population, education, arts, science, agriculture, trade, and transportation.

PROGRAMS: Exhibits; Guided Tours; Publication; Research Library/Archives

COLLECTIONS: [Mid 1800s-early 1900s] Agricultural tools, household items, medical tools, office equipment, sports items, early schools, and early community photographs.

HOURS: Yr M-F 10-4

ADMISSION: Donations accepted

CONWAY

313
Faulkner County Museum
Courthouse Square, 72033 [PO Box 2442, 72033]; (p) (501) 329-5918; (c) Faulkner

Joint/ 1993/ County; Private non-profit/ staff: 1(f); 10(v)/publication: *Faulkner Facts and Fiddlings*

HISTORICAL SOCIETY; HISTORY MUSEUM: A 19th c log cabin and jail building house the permanent exhibits. Interpret Faulkner County history.

PROGRAMS: Exhibits; Publication; School-Based Curriculum

COLLECTIONS: [1873-present] Native American artifacts, photographs, maps and agrarian tools, period rooms.

HOURS: Yr T-Th 1-4, Su 2-4

ADMISSION: No charge

314
University of Central Arkansas Archives and Special Collections
201 Donaghey, 72035; (p) (501) 450-3418; (f) (501) 450-5208; JimmyB@mail.UCA.edu; Library.UCA.edu; (c) Faulkner

State/ 1986/ Torreyson Library/ staff: 1(f); 3(p)/publication: *Arkansas Researcher*

LIBRARY AND/OR ARCHIVES; RESEARCH CENTER: Collects and preserves information on AR and Arkansans.

PROGRAMS: Lectures; Publication; Research Library/Archives

COLLECTIONS: [1900-present] Archival collections related to education and politics.

HOURS: Yr M-F 8-5

CROSSETT

315
Wiggins Cabin and The Old Company House
Crossett City Park, 71635 [101 W 1St Ave, 71635]; (p) (870) 364-6591; crossett@cei.net; www.cei.net/~crossett; (c) Ashley

Private non-profit/ 1978/ staff: 25(v)/ members: 75

HOUSE MUSEUM: Preserves local pioneer history.

PROGRAMS: Exhibits; Festivals; Guided Tours; School-Based Curriculum

COLLECTIONS: [1830-1910] Restored cabin, furnishings.

HOURS: Yr by appt

ADMISSION: No charge

DARDANELLE

316
Yell County Historical and Genealogical Association
Box 622, 72834; (c) Yell

Private non-profit/ 1981/ members: 270/publication: *Yell Co. Historical and Genealogical Association Bulletin*

GENEALOGICAL SOCIETY: Collects historical information.

PROGRAMS: Publication; Research Library/Archives

DEQUEEN

317
Sevier County Historical Society Museum
717 N Maple, 71832; (p) (870) 642-6642; (f) (870) 642-6642; (c) Sevier

Private non-profit/ 1986/ staff: 1(f); 2(p); 4(v)/ members: 20/publication: *History of Sevier County*

HISTORICAL SOCIETY; HISTORY MUSEUM: Preserves the heritage of the county.

PROGRAMS: Community Outreach; Concerts; Elder's Programs; Exhibits; Facility Rental; Festivals; Garden Tours; Guided Tours; Publication; Reenactments

COLLECTIONS: [1850-present] Musical instruments, clothing, literature, archives, toys, furniture, and other artifacts.

HOURS: Yr T-Sa10-4, Su 2-4

DEWITT

318
Grand Prairie Historical Society
203 S Monroe, 72042; (c) Arkansas

Private non-profit/ 1952/ members: 250/publication: *Grand Prairie Historical Society Bulletin*

HISTORICAL SOCIETY

PROGRAMS: Publication

COLLECTIONS: [19th-20th c] Artifacts and memorabilia related to Arkansas, county, and surrounding area.

EL DORADO

319
Union County Genealogical Society
220 E Fifth, 71730; (c) Union

1976/ members: 200/publication: *Tracks and Traces*

GENEALOGICAL SOCIETY: Collects, preserves, and publishes genealogical materials.

PROGRAMS: Publication; Research Library/ Archives

COLLECTIONS: Census microfilm, family histories, and family tree maker CDs, Arkansas Death Index.

HOURS: Yr M,W,F 9:30-5:30, T,Th 1-9, Sa 1-5

EUREKA SPRINGS

320
Elna M. Smith Foundation
Passion Play Rd, 72632 [PO Box 471, 72632]; (p) (501) 253-8559, (800) 882-7529; (f) (501) 253-2302; drama@ipa.net; www.greatpassionplay.com; (c) Carroll

Private non-profit/ 1967/ staff: 50(f); 300(p)

ART MUSEUM; HISTORIC SITE; LIVING HISTORY/OUTDOOR MUSEUM: Preserves religious art, Biblical documents, manuscripts, and artifacts; monuments, shrines, galleries, museums, and theaters.

PROGRAMS: Concerts; Exhibits; Festivals; Guided Tours; Living History; Theatre

COLLECTIONS: [Biblical times-present] 6,000 rare Bibles, icons, marble and ivory sculptures, wood carvings, oil on canvas, tile, tin, and porcelain.

HOURS: Arts Center: May-Oct M-T, Th-Sa 10-8, W 10-4:30; Museum: M-T, Th-Sa 11-8, W 11-4:30

ADMISSION: Varies

321
Eureka Springs Historical Museum
95 S Main, 72632; (p) (501) 253-9417; oldognewt@arkansas.net; (c) Carroll

Private non-profit/ Board of Directors/ staff: 1(f); 1(p); 5(v)/ members: 130/publication: *Pioneer Tales; Bear Hunter*

HISTORY MUSEUM: Collects, preserves, documents and exhibits the cultural history of Eureka Springs and the surrounding area.

PROGRAMS: Annual Meeting; Exhibits; Film/Video; Living History; Publication; Research Library/Archives

COLLECTIONS: [1880s-present] Photographs, documents, genealogy, art work, research materials, and restored pioneer log cabins.

HOURS: Apr-Oct Daily 9:30-4; Nov-Mar T-Su 9:30-4

ADMISSION: $2.50; Children

322
Eureka Springs Parks and Recreation Commission
532 Spring St, 72632 [PO Box 325, 72632]; (p) (501) 253-2866; (f) (501) 253-2155; esparks@ipa.net; www.cityofeurekasprings.org; (c) Carroll

City/ 1981/ staff: 3(f); 7(p); 10(v)

GARDEN; HISTORIC SITE: Maintains, operates,and provides recreation programs and facilities.

PROGRAMS: Annual Meeting; Community Outreach; Concerts; Exhibits; Facility Rental; Family Programs; Festivals; Garden Tours; Guided Tours; Interpretation; Lectures; Reenactments

COLLECTIONS: [Early 20th c] Artifacts and research materials on the City of Eureka Springs, its origins and the parks.

HOURS: Yr Daily 7-sunset

ADMISSION: No charge

323
Eureka Springs Preservation Society
[PO Box 404, 72632]; (p) (501) 253-7416; williams@ipa.net; (c) Carroll

Private non-profit/ 1979/ staff: 1(p)/ members: 150/publication: *Six Walking Tours of Eureka Springs*

HISTORIC PRESERVATION AGENCY: Preserves the natural and architectural beauty of Eureka Springs.

PROGRAMS: Annual Meeting; Community Outreach; Guided Tours; Publication; School-Based Curriculum

324
Gables, The
44 Prospect Ave, 72632; (p) (501) 253-2428, (501) 253-9896; (f) (501) 253-9896; gables@ipa.net

1886/ Private/ staff: 2(f)

COLLECTIONS: [1850-1890] 16th-19th c paintings, porcelain, pottery, furniture.

HOURS: Yr

325
Lake Leatherwood City Park
1303 CR 204, 72632; (p) (501) 253-8624; (f) (501) 253-2155; lthrwood@ipa.net; www.eureka-springs-usa.com/leatherwood; (c) Carroll

City/ 1942/ Eureka Springs Parks and Recreation Commission/ staff: 2(f); 5(p); 25(v)

HISTORIC SITE

PROGRAMS: Community Outreach; Facility Rental; Family Programs; Festivals; Guided Tours; Interpretation

COLLECTIONS: [1941-1942] Park grounds, artifacts, arrowheads, typewriters.

HOURS: Yr Daily 7-10

326
Rosalie Tour Home
282 Spring St, 72632; (p) (501) 253-7377, (888) 374-7377; rosalie@arkansas.net; rosaliehouse.net; (c) Carroll

Private for-profit/ 1970/ staff: 1(f); 4(p); 4(v)

GARDEN; HOUSE MUSEUM: Preserves and exhibits a restored home and garden.

PROGRAMS: Exhibits; Facility Rental; Garden Tours; Guided Tours; Living History

COLLECTIONS: [1865-1900] European and American antiques including china, cookware, toys, telephone switchboard 1893, stoves.

HOURS: Mar-Apr Sa-Su 10-4, May-Dec Daily 10-4

ADMISSION: $5

FAYETTEVILLE

327
Arkansas Air Museum
4290 S School St, 72701; (p) (501) 521-4947; (f) (501) 521-4947; www.arkairmuseum.org; (c) Washington

Private non-profit/ 1986/ staff: 1(f); 3(p); 6(v)/ members: 100/publication: *Tailwinds*

AVIATION MUSEUM: Displays aviation artifacts and aircraft dating from 1928t in a W W II wooden arched truss hangar.

PROGRAMS: Exhibits; Festivals; Guided Tours; Lectures; Publication

COLLECTIONS: Uniforms, instruments, aircraft, and engines.

HOURS: Yr Daily 9:30-4:30

ADMISSION: $2

328
Arkansas Historical Association
Old Main 416, University of Arkansas, 72701; (p) (501) 575-5884; (f) (501) 575-2642; rhondak@comp.uark.edu; (c) Washington

1941/ staff: 3(f); 1(p)/ members: 1585/publication: *Arkansas Historical Quarterly*

PROFESSIONAL ORGANIZATION: Promotes the preservation, writing, publishing, teaching, and understanding of AR history.

PROGRAMS: Annual Meeting; Publication

329
Headquarters House Museum
118 E Dickson St, 72701; (p) (501) 521-2970

1853/ staff: 20(v)

COLLECTIONS: [Civil War] Authentic 1853 style furnishings.

HOURS: Yr

330
Teachers of Arkansas Studies Council
416 Old Main, 72701; (p) (501) 575-5884; (c) Washington

Private non-profit/ 1989/ staff: 20(v)/ members: 200/publication: *TASC Force*

PROFESSIONAL ORGANIZATION: Promotes Arkansas history.

PROGRAMS: Lectures; Living History; Publication; School-Based Curriculum

331
University Museum, University of Arkansas
Garland Ave Univ Campus, 72701 [202 Museum, 72701]; (p) (501) 575-3466; (f) (501) 575-8766; www.uark.edu/~muse.info/; (c) Washington

State/ 1873/ Univ of AR/ staff: 9(f); 2(p); 65(v)/ members: 235

HISTORY MUSEUM; NATURAL HISTORY MUSEUM: Exhibits natural history (zoology and geology), anthropological, ethnographic, and historical collections.

PROGRAMS: Community Outreach; Exhibits; Facility Rental; Family Programs; Guided Tours; Interpretation; Lectures

COLLECTIONS: Artifacts, specimens; records pertaining to the natural sciences, including zoology, archaeology, anthropology, and geology.

HOURS: Exhibit Hall: Sept-June M-Sa 9-4:30; Discovery Room: July-Aug M-Sa 9-12:30; Sa 10-3

ADMISSION: $2, Children $1; Group rates

FORDYCE

332

Dallas County Historical Museum
221 N Main St, 71742 [PO Box 703, 71742]; (p) (870) 352-5262; (c) Dallas

Private non-profit/ 1993/ staff: 1(f); 40(v)/ members: 250/publication: *The Historic Barns of Dallas County*

ART MUSEUM; HISTORIC SITE; HISTORY MUSEUM; LIVING HISTORY/OUTDOOR MUSEUM: Dedicated to the ongoing cultural and educational growth of the community.

PROGRAMS: Exhibits; Facility Rental; Guided Tours; Publication; Research Library/Archives; School-Based Curriculum

COLLECTIONS: [19th c-present] Maps, newspapers, pottery, Civil War artifacts.

HOURS: Yr T-Sa 10-5

ADMISSION: Donations accepted

FORREST CITY

333

Saint Francis County Museum
603 Front St, 72335; (p) (870) 261-1744; (f) (870) 630-1210; museum@lpa.net; (c) St. Francis

1995/ Board of Directors/ staff: 1(f); 1(p); 5(v)/ members: 150

HISTORY MUSEUM

PROGRAMS: Community Outreach; Exhibits; Facility Rental; Family Programs; Guided Tours; Lectures; Living History; Research Library/Archives; School-Based Curriculum

COLLECTIONS: [Prehistory-Early 20th c] Local historical, Native American, and ethnographic artifacts.

HOURS: Yr M-F 10-5, Sa 10-2

FORT SMITH

334

Bonneville House Association, The
318 N 7th St, 72913 [PO Box 5622, 72913]; (p) (501) 782-7854; (c) Sebastian

Private non-profit/ 1967/ Board of Directors/ staff: 1(f); 15(v)/ members: 250

HOUSE MUSEUM: Preserves, maintains the 1864 home of Susan Neis Bonneville, widow of General Benjamin Louis Eulalie de Bonneville.

PROGRAMS: Facility Rental; Guided Tours

COLLECTIONS: [Late 19th c]

HOURS: Yr by appt

ADMISSION: Donations accepted

335

Darby House: Museum and Heritage Center
311 General Darby St, 72902 [PO Box 1625, 72902]; (p) (501) 782-3388; (f) (501) 783-7590; darby1945@aol.com; (c) Sebastian

Private non-profit/ 1977/ William O. Darby Ranger Memorial Foundation, Inc./ staff: 1(f); 6(v)/ members: 500

HOUSE MUSEUM

PROGRAMS: Community Outreach; Family Programs

COLLECTIONS: [1939-present] General Darby's papers and WW II material.

HOURS: Yr M-F 8-1

ADMISSION: No charge

336

Fort Smith Historical Society
61 S 8th St, 72901; (p) (501) 783-1237, (501) 783-0229; (f) (501) 782-0649; amartin@ipa.net; (c) Sebastian

Private non-profit/ 1977/ members: 500/publication: *The Journal of the Fort Smith Historical Society*

HISTORICAL SOCIETY: Locates, collects, identifies, preserves and publishes written and oral history of the Fort Smith area.

PROGRAMS: Publication

COLLECTIONS: [1817-present] Newspapers, diaries, family histories, county and city records.

337

Fort Smith Museum of History
320 Rogers Ave, 72901; (p) (501) 783-7841; (f) (501) 783-3244; (c) Sebastian

Private non-profit/ 1910/ Board of Trustees/ staff: 2(f); 9(p)/ members: 360/publication: *Fort Smith: An Illustrated History*

HISTORY MUSEUM: Collects, preserves, exhibits, and interprets objects relevant to the founding and growth of Fort Smith and the region.

PROGRAMS: Exhibits; Facility Rental; Family Programs; Interpretation; Lectures; Publication

COLLECTIONS: [19th-20th c] Locally made furniture, photographs, documents, military artifacts relating to Camp Chaffee and Colonel William Darby, pharmacy collection, Niloak pottery, clothing, textiles, toys, industrial and commercial items.

HOURS: June-Aug T-Sa 9-5, Su 1-5; Sept-May T-Sa 10-5, Su 1-5

ADMISSION: $3, Children $1; Members free

338

Fort Smith National Historic Site
3rd & Parker, 72902 [PO Box 1406, 72902]; (p) (501) 783-3961; (f) (501) 783-5307; fosm_interpretation@nps.gov; www.nps. gov/fosm; (c) Sebastian

Federal/ 1961/ National Park Service/ staff: 15(f); 20(v)

HISTORIC SITE: Preserves the remains of two frontier forts and a federal court.

PROGRAMS: Exhibits; Festivals; Film/Video; Guided Tours; Interpretation; Living History; School-Based Curriculum

COLLECTIONS: [19th c] Archaeological artifacts.

HOURS: Yr Daily 9-5

339

Fort Smith Trolley Museum
100 S 4th St, 72901 [2121 Wolfe Lane, 72901]; (p) (501) 783-0205, (501) 783-1237; (f) (501) 782-0649; bmartin@ipa.net; www.fortsmith.com/trolley/; (c) Sebastian

Private non-profit/ 1979/ Board of Trustees/ staff: 40(v)/ members: 250/publication: *Trolley Report*

HISTORIC PRESERVATION AGENCY: Restores and operates Fort Smith electric streetcars and preserves rail equipment of all types.

GILLETT

340

Arkansas Post Museum State Park
5530 Hwy 165 S, 72055; (p) (870) 548-2634; arkpost@futura.net; www.state.ar.us; (c) Arkansas

State/ 1960/ Dept of Parks and Tourism/ staff: 3(f); 1(p); 16(v)

HISTORY MUSEUM: Operates first county museum established in AR.

PROGRAMS: Exhibits; Festivals; Guided Tours; Interpretation

COLLECTIONS: [1840-1940] Five buildings house artifacts, documents, and exhibits depicting AR history. Includes an 1877 log house, 1930s playhouse, "Summer Kitchen," and Quapaw Indian displays.

HOURS: Yr M-Sa 8-5, Su 1-5

ADMISSION: $2.25, Children $1.25

341

Refeld-Hinman House
5530 Hwy 1655, 72055; (p) (870) 548-2634; arkpost@futura.net; www.arkansas.com

1877/ Det. of Parks and Tourism/ staff: 3(f); 1(p)

COLLECTIONS: [1800s to present]

HOURS: Yr

GRAVETTE

342

Gravette Historical Museum
208 2nd Ave SE, 72736 [City Hall, 72736]; (c) Benton

City/ 1993/ staff: 7(v)

HISTORIC SITE; HISTORY MUSEUM; HOUSE MUSEUM: Collects, preserves, and displays artifacts of the City of Gravette.

PROGRAMS: Exhibits; School-Based Curriculum

COLLECTIONS: [1893-present] W W II, industrial and school items, train diorama, medical supplies, and photographs.

HOURS: Yr M-Sa 3:30-5:30

ADMISSION: No charge

GREENWOOD

343
South Sebastian County Historical Society
On the Square, 72936 [PO Box 523, 72936]; (c) Sebastian

Private non-profit/ 1966/ Board of Directors/ staff: 20(v)/ members: 166/publication: *The Key*

HISTORIC SITE

PROGRAMS: Community Outreach; Exhibits; Guided Tours; Publication

COLLECTIONS: [1851-1949] Artifacts relating to county and state history; 1892 stone jail; 1848 double log cabin.

HOURS: May-Oct Th-Sa 10-2

HARDY

344
Good Old Days Vintage Motorcar Museum, Inc.
302 W Main St, 72542 [PO Box 311, 72542]; (p) (870) 856-4884; (f) (870) 856-4885; (c) Sharp

Private for-profit/ 1996/ staff: 1(f); 2(p)

AUTOMOBILE MUSEUM: Exhibits 50 intriguing vehicles and automobile memorabilia.

PROGRAMS: Annual Meeting; Exhibits; Family Programs; Guided Tours

COLLECTIONS: [1920s-60s] Classic automobiles.

HOURS: Yr M-Sa 9-5, Su 12:30-5

ADMISSION: $5, Children

345
Veteran's Military Museum of Hardy, Inc.
78 Main St, 72542 [PO Box 1051, 72542]; (p) (870) 856-4133; (f) (870) 856-3833; (c) Sharp

Private non-profit/ 1992/ staff: 1(p); 5(v)

HISTORY MUSEUM: Collects and displays military items and vehicles.

PROGRAMS: Community Outreach; Exhibits; Guided Tours; School-Based Curriculum

COLLECTIONS: [1860-present] Military equipment, uniforms, pictures, personal items, vehicles.

HOURS: Dec-Mar Th-Su 11-3; Apr-Nov Daily 10-4

ADMISSION: Donations requested

HARRISON

346
Buffalo National River
Corner of Prospect & Erie, 72601 [402 N Walnut, Ste 136, 72601]; (p) (870) 741-5443; (f) (870) 741-7286; www.nps.gov/buff; (c) Boone, Newton, Searcy, Marion

Federal/ 1972/ National Park Service

HISTORIC PRESERVATION AGENCY; NATIONAL PARK: Conserves and interprets the scenic and scientific resources of Buffalo National River.

PROGRAMS: Exhibits; Interpretation; School-Based Curriculum

COLLECTIONS: [Prehistory] Archaeological, lithic, and organic material associated with bluff dwellers. Also pioneer materials, herbarium, and natural history specimens.

HOURS: Yr

HEBER SPRINGS

347
Cleburne County Historical Society
210 N Broadway, 72543 [PO Box 794, 72543]; (p) (501) 362-3992; (c) Cleburne

Private non-profit/ 1974/ staff: 20(v)/ members: 450/publication: *Cleburne County Historical Journal*

GENEALOGICAL SOCIETY; HISTORIC PRESERVATION AGENCY; HISTORICAL SOCIETY; HISTORY MUSEUM; HOUSE MUSEUM; RESEARCH CENTER: Maintains the museum displays.

PROGRAMS: Community Outreach; Exhibits; Film/Video; Guided Tours; Lectures; Publication; Research Library/Archives

COLLECTIONS: [19th-20th c] Genealogical research materials, including records, maps, books, microfilm and family histories. Also artifacts pertaining to early life in Cleburne County.

HOURS: Yr M-Sa 10-4

ADMISSION: No charge

348
Olmstead Funeral Museum
208 S 4th St, 72543 [PO Box 910, 72543]; (p) (501) 362-2422; (f) (501) 362-0200

Private non-profit/ 1896/ staff: 2(f)

HISTORY MUSEUM

COLLECTIONS: [1896-present]

349
William Carl Garner Visitor Center
700 Heber Springs Rd N, 72543; (p) (501) 362-9067; wcgvc@arkansas.net; www.swl.usace.army.mil/parks/greersferry; (c) Cleburne

Federal/ 1983/ US Army Corps of Engineers/ staff: 1(f); 3(p)

HISTORY MUSEUM: Promotes and educates about Greers Ferry Dam and Lake area by exposure to the geology, human history, natural environment, and recreational aspects.

PROGRAMS: Community Outreach; Concerts; Exhibits; Family Programs; Film/Video; Guided Tours; Interpretation; School-Based Curriculum; Theatre

COLLECTIONS: [Prehistory-present]

HOURS: Apr-Oct Daily 10-6; Mar and Nov Sa-Su 10-4

ADMISSION: No charge

HELENA

350
Delta Cultural Center
95 Missouri St, 72342 [PO Box 509, 72342]; (p) (870) 338-4350; (f) (870) 338-4367; (c) Phillips

State/ 1990/ Department of Arkansas Heritage/ staff: 10(f); 1(p)

HISTORY MUSEUM: Collects, preserves, interprets, and presents the historical and cultural heritage of the Arkansas Delta.

PROGRAMS: Community Outreach; Exhibits; Facility Rental; Family Programs; Garden Tours; Guided Tours; Lectures; Living History; Reenactments; Research Library/Archives

COLLECTIONS: [Prehistory-mid 20th c] Agricultural equipment, transportation, and music of the period.

HOURS: Yr M-Sa 10-5, Su 1-5

ADMISSION: No charge

351
Helena Library and Museum Association
623 Pecan St, 72342; (p) (870) 338-7790; (c) Phillips

Private non-profit/ 1888/ Board of Directors/ staff: 1(f); 15(v)/ members: 300

HISTORY MUSEUM: Documents, preserves, and displays historic artifacts.

PROGRAMS: Exhibits; Family Programs; Interpretation; Lectures; Research Library/Archives

COLLECTIONS: [19th c-present] Native American memorabilia, Mississippi River Delta life, firearms and military items emphasizing civil war history, Victoriana.

HOURS: Yr T-Sa

352
Phillips County Museum
623 Pecan St, 72342 [PO Box 38, 72342]; (p) (870) 338-7790; (c) Phillips

County, non-profit; Private non-profit/ 1929/ Board of Trustees/ staff: 1(f); 1(p); 15(v)/ members: 565

HISTORIC PRESERVATION AGENCY; HISTORY MUSEUM; LIBRARY AND/OR ARCHIVES: Houses artifacts and memorabilia of all periods of local history.

PROGRAMS: Community Outreach; Exhibits; Family Programs; Guided Tours; Interpretation; Lectures; Research Library/Archives

COLLECTIONS: [prehistory-present] War memorabilia, Native artifacts, art, clothing, archives including photos.

HOURS: Museum: Yr T-Sa 10-4; Library: M-Sa 9-5

ADMISSIONS: Donations accepted

HOPE

353
Clinton Birthplace Foundation
Hervey & 2nd St, 71801 [PO Box 1925, 71801]; (p) (870) 777-4455; (f) (870) 722-6929; clinton@arkansas.net; www.clintonbirthplace.com; (c) Hempstead

Private non-profit/ 1993/ staff: 1(f); 3(v)

HISTORIC PRESERVATION AGENCY; HISTORIC SITE; HISTORY MUSEUM; HOUSE MUSEUM; PRESIDENTIAL SITE: Focuses on the early years (1940-1957) of President Clinton. Operates the Clinton Center, replica of oval office rug, and computer/video room.

PROGRAMS: Community Outreach; Exhibits; Facility Rental; Film/Video; Garden Tours; Guided Tours; Living History; Research Library/Archives; School-Based Curriculum; Theatre

COLLECTIONS: [1940-1957] Period furniture, art, clothing, appliances, newspapers and magazines.

HOURS: Spring-Summer T-Sa 10-5, Su 1-5; Fall-Winter T-Sa 10-4:30

ADMISSION: $5, Family $12.50, Children $3, Seniors $4; Under 7 free

354
Hempstead County Historical Society
202 W Ave C, 71802 [PO Box 1257, 71802-1257]; (p) (501) 777-1278; (c) Hempstead

Private non-profit/ 1976/ members: 150/publication: *Journal of the Hempstead County Historical Society; Horace Jewell: Travelling Methodist Preacher;* and others

HISTORICAL SOCIETY: Preserves county history and holds monthly meetings in the 1903 Carrigan House.

HOT SPRINGS

355
Arkansas Genealogical Society
[PO Box 908, 71902]; Ags-l@rootsweb.com; www.rootsweb.com/~args

Private non-profit/ 1962/ Board of Directors/ staff: 1(p)/ members: 1000/publication: *The Arkansas Family Historian*

GENEALOGICAL SOCIETY: Preserves and shares AR genealogical material.

PROGRAMS: Annual Meeting; Publication

356
Garland County Historical Society
328 Quapaw Ave, 71913 [222 McMahan Dr, 71913]; (p) (501) 623-6766, (501) 321-2159; (f) (501) 623-6766; bjmclane@prodigy.net; (c) Garland

Private non-profit/ 1960/ staff: 5(v)/ members: 250

HISTORICAL SOCIETY: Collects and preserves the history of the local area.

PROGRAMS: Research Library/Archives

COLLECTIONS: Photographs, numerous newspapers, manuscripts, maps, and secondary sources.

HOURS: Yr T-Th 8-12

ADMISSION: No charge

HOXIE

357
Clover Bend Historic Preservation Association
S of Hoxie on Hwy 67, W at Minturn, 72433 [4679 Hwy 63, Black Rock, 72415]; (p) (870) 869-2708; (c) Lawrence

Private non-profit/ 1983/ Clover Bend Historic Preservation Board/ staff: 25(v)

HISTORIC PRESERVATION AGENCY: Preserves the school, community history, buildings, and research material.

PROGRAMS: Annual Meeting; Community Outreach; Exhibits; Family Programs; Guided Tours; Reenactments; Research Library/ Archives

COLLECTIONS: [Early 1800s-1983] Five restored buildings, museum, photographs, students and class rolls, trophies and sport memorabilia.

HOURS: Yr by appt and Mem Day Weekend

ADMISSION: Donations accepted

HUNTSVILLE

358
Madison County Genealogical and Historical Society
Hwy 74 & Mitchussen Park Rd, 72740 [PO Box 427, 72740]; (p) (501) 738-6408; (c) Madison

Private non-profit/ 1982/ staff: 20(v)/ members: 800/publication: *Madison County Musings*

GENEALOGICAL SOCIETY; HISTORICAL SOCIETY; LIBRARY AND/OR ARCHIVES

PROGRAMS: Community Outreach; Publication; Research Library/Archives

COLLECTIONS: [1830-1950] Archival materials, including photos, and newspapers.

HOURS: Mar-Oct M-F 10-3, Nov-Feb T-Th 10-3

JASPER

359
Newton County Historical Society/Bradley House Museum
403 W Clark St, 72641 [PO Box 360, 72641]; (p) (870) 446-6247; www.mcrush.com/history; (c) Newton

1967/ Newton County Historical Society Board of Directors/ staff: 1(p); 2(v)/publication: *Newton County Family History*

HISTORY MUSEUM: Collects, preserves, and displays the history of Newton County, interprets artifacts.

PROGRAMS: Community Outreach; Exhibits; Interpretation; Publication; Research Library/Archives

COLLECTIONS: [Circa 1900] Hand-built loom and rope bed (1850s), butter churns, old cook stoves, Jasper's telephone switchboard, early farming implements, clothing, Indian artifacts, natural history, old pictures, and documents.

HOURS: Apr-Oct T-Th 11-4, Nov-Mar T 11-4

ADMISSION: Donations requested

JONESBORO

360
Craighead County Historical Society
[PO Box 1011, 72403-1011]; (p) (870) 935-6838; (c) Craighead

1962/ staff: 12(p)/ members: 390/publication: *The Craighead County Historical Quarterly*

HISTORICAL SOCIETY: Publishes a quarterly journal.

PROGRAMS: Publication

COLLECTIONS: [1962-present] Booklets about Craighead County and local history.

LAKE VILLAGE

361
Lake Chicot State Park
2542 Hwy 257, 71653; (p) (870) 265-5480; (f) (870) 265-3162; chicotsp@ipa.com; (c) Chicot

State/ 1957/ Dept of Parks and Tourism/ staff: 15(f); 15(p)

HISTORY MUSEUM; LIVING HISTORY/OUTDOOR MUSEUM: Living history, reenactments, boat tours, and wildlife demonstrations.

PROGRAMS: Community Outreach; Concerts; Exhibits; Facility Rental; Family Programs; Festivals; Film/Video; Guided Tours; Interpretation; Lectures; Living History; Publication; Reenactments

COLLECTIONS: [1820-1865] County history, exhibits, and Civil War artifacts.

LEPANTO

362
Museum-Lepanto USA
Greenwood Ave, 72354; (p) (870) 475-2591, (870) 475-2438; (c) Poinsett

Private non-profit/ 1980/ staff: 10(v)

HISTORIC SITE: Preserves history of area since 1895.

PROGRAMS: Exhibits; Guided Tours

COLLECTIONS: [Circa 1895]

HOURS: Yr W, F 2-4 and by appt

LINCOLN

363
Arkansas Country Doctor Museum
107 N Starr Ave, 72744 [PO Box 1004, 72744]; (p) (501) 824-4307; (f) (501) 824-4307; acdm@pgtc.net; www.drmuseum.net; (c) Washington

Private non-profit/ 1994/ Board of Directors/ staff: 15(v)/ members: 15/publication: *Arkansas Country Doctor Museum Newsletter*

ALLIANCE OF HISTORICAL AGENCIES; HISTORY MUSEUM; HOUSE MUSEUM

PROGRAMS: Exhibits; Garden Tours; Guided Tours; Lectures; Publication; Research Library/ Archives

COLLECTIONS: [1900-1970] Medical instruments, dental and eyeglass displays, and medical text books. Private quarters contain original furnishings, hat and jewelry collection, salt and pepper collection, and quilt chest.

HOURS: By appt

ADMISSION: No charge

LITTLE ROCK

364
Aerospace Education Center
3301 E Roosevelt Rd, 72206; (p) (501) 376-4619; (f) (501) 372-4826; aerospace@aerospaced.org; www.aerospaced.org; (c) Pulaski

Private non-profit/ 1995/ staff: 10(f); 20(p); 7(v)

AVIATION MUSEUM: Creates an awareness of and an appreciation for advancing technologies in the aviation and aerospace industries.

PROGRAMS: Exhibits; Facility Rental; Lectures

COLLECTIONS: [Early 20th c] Aviation/ Arkansas collections of aircraft including the Command-aire, Curtiss Jenny, Sopwith Camel F-1, Wright flyer, and an Apollo command module replica.

HOURS: Yr

365
Arkansas Historic Preservation Program

1500 Tower Building, 323 Center St, 72201; (p) (501) 324-9880; (f) (501) 324-9184; info@dah.state.ar.us; www.heritage.state.ar.us; (c) Pulaski

State/ 1977/ staff: 22(f); 5(p)

HISTORIC PRESERVATION AGENCY: Initiates preservation projects, protecion, and technical assistance. Operates Main Street AR program.

COLLECTIONS: Maintains records of properties surveyed for nomination to the National and AR Register of Historic Places. Materials include photographic images of historic structures. 4,500 newspaper titles, 4,500 photographs, 165 volumes, 57 ledgers, 48 oral history tapes, 63 local directories, 500 slides, 550 local history topic files.

HOURS: Yr M-F 8-4

ADMISSION: No charge

366
Arkansas History Commission

One Capitol Mall, 72201; (p) (501) 682-6900; www.state.ar.us/ahc/; (c) Pulaski

State/ 1905/ State of Arkansas/ staff: 20(f); 2(p); 11(v)

LIBRARY AND/OR ARCHIVES: Collects, preserves and disseminates source materials of AR history.

PROGRAMS: Research Library/Archives

COLLECTIONS: [1541-present] US census records, manuscripts, newspaper files, state, county, military, church and cemetery records, photographs, maps, books, pamphlets and

367
Arkansas History Education Coalition

12 Normandy Rd, 72207; (p) (501) 918-3054; (c) Pulaski

Private non-profit/ 1987/ staff: 3(v)/ members: 100

PROFESSIONAL ORGANIZATION: Monitors the legal and regulatory situation as it pertains to Arkansas history education, including political advocacy.

PROGRAMS: Community Outreach; School-Based Curriculum

368
Arkansas Museums Association, Inc.

6900 Cantrell Rd #M27, 72207; mkbynum@amod.org; (c) Pulaski

Private non-profit/ staff: 9(v)/ members: 100/publication: AMA Directory, AMA Report

PROFESSIONAL ORGANIZATION: Offers support, education and encouragement for museums and related institutions. Promotes professional standards and public support for museums in the region.

369
Arkansas Territorial Restoration

200 E Third St, 72201 [200 E Third St, 72201]; (p) (501) 324-9351, (501) 324-9304; (f) (501) 324-9345; www.heritage.state.ar.us/atr/her_atr.html

Department of Arkansas Heritage/ staff: 20(f); 21(p); 20(v)

PROFESSIONAL ORGANIZATION: Maintains Arkansas Territorial Restoration complex: the 1840s Brownlee House built by a Scottish stone mason ; the 1850s McVicar House; the Woodruff Print Shop and the Hinderliter Grog Shop.

COLLECTIONS: Decorative, mechanical and fine arts of 19th century AR.

HOURS: Yr

370
Butler Center for Arkansas Studies

100 Rock St, 72201; (p) (501) 918-3056; (f) (501) 375-1451; arkinfo@cals.lib.ar.us; www.cals.lib.ar.us; (c) Pulaski

1997/ Central Arkansas Library System/ staff: 5(f); 3(p); 7(v)/publication: The Butler Banner

LIBRARY AND/OR ARCHIVES: Department of the Central Arkansas Library System that collects research materials on the state of AR.

COLLECTIONS: [1686-present] Books, periodicals, manuscripts, photographs and maps.

HOURS: Yr M-Sa 9-6, Su 1-5

371
Central High Museum and Visitor Center

2125 W 14th, 72202; (p) (501) 374-1957; (f) (501) 376-4728; chmuseum@swbell.net; www.home.swbell.net/chmuseum; (c) Pulaski

Private non-profit/ 1996/ Central High Museum, Inc./ staff: 3(f); 1(p); 15(v)

HISTORY MUSEUM: Documents, interprets, preserves and discovers the history of the 1957 desegregation crisis and its context.

PROGRAMS: Community Outreach; Guided Tours; Interpretation

COLLECTIONS: [Mid 20th c] Photographs, newspapers, yearbooks and scrapbooks relating to the 1957 Crisis, the history of Central High School and the desegregation of education in the United States.

HOURS: Yr M-Sa 10-4, Su 1-4

ADMISSION: No charge

372
Civil War Round Table of Arkansas

[PO Box 7281, 72217]; (p) (501) 225-3996; civilwarbuff@aristotlle.net; www.civilwarbuff.org; (c) Pulaski

Private non-profit/ 1968/ CWRT of Arkansas/ staff: 2(v)/ members: 95

HISTORICAL SOCIETY: Local Civil War study Group.

373
Decorative Arts Museum, Arkansas Arts Center

411 E 7th St, 72203 [MacArthur Park, Ninth St and Commerce St, 72203-2137]; (p) (501) 396-0358; (f) (501) 375-8053; center@arkars.org; (c) Pulaski

City/ 1937/ The Arkansas Arts Center/ staff: 3(f); 2(p); 18(v)/ members: 2300

ART MUSEUM; HOUSE MUSEUM: Specializes in contemporary craft media and decorative arts in historic Pike-Fletcher-Terry House.

PROGRAMS: Annual Meeting; Community Outreach; Concerts; Exhibits; Facility Rental; Guided Tours; Interpretation; Lectures

COLLECTIONS: [1950-present] American-made contemporary objects in craft media: clay, glass, fiber, metal and wood.

HOURS: Yr M-Sa 10-5, Su 12-5

ADMISSION: Donations accepted

374
Department of Arkansas Heritage

1500 Tower Building, 323 Center St, 72201; (p) (501) 324-9150; (f) (501) 324-9154; info@dah.state.ar.us; www.heritage.state.ar.us; (c) Pulaski

State/ 1975/ State of Arkansas/ staff: 155(f); 25(p)

ALLIANCE OF HISTORICAL AGENCIES; ART MUSEUM; HISTORIC SITE; HISTORY MUSEUM; HOUSE MUSEUM; LIVING HISTORY/OUTDOOR MUSEUM; NATURAL HISTORY MUSEUM; STATE AGENCY: Identifies, collects, preserves, protects, and interprets the cultural, natural and historic heritage of Arkansas.

PROGRAMS: Community Outreach; Concerts; Elder's Programs; Exhibits; Facility Rental; Family Programs; Guided Tours; Interpretation; Lectures; Living History; Publication; Reenactments; School-Based Curriculum

COLLECTIONS: [Prehistory-present]

HOURS: Museum: Yr Daily 9-5; Other Offices: Yr Daily 8-4:30

ADMISSION: Varies

375
EMOBA, The Museum of Black Arkansans and Performing Arts

1208 Louisana, 72201; (p) (501) 661-9903, (501) 372-0018; (c) Pulaski

Private non-profit/ 1993/ staff: 1(f); 1(p); 15(v)

HISTORIC SITE; HISTORY MUSEUM: Preserves the heritage and culture of African Americans in AR with exhibits and performing arts.

PROGRAMS: Annual Meeting; Community Outreach; Exhibits; Facility Rental; Festivals; Guided Tours; Living History; Theatre

COLLECTIONS: Clothing, artifacts, oral histories and photographs.

ADMISSION: $3

376
Historic Arkansas Museum (Arkansas Territorial Restoration)

Third & Scott St, 72201 [200 E Third St, 72201-1608]; (p) (501) 324-9351; (f) (501) 324-9345; info@dah.state.ar.us; www.heritage.state.ar.us/atr/her_atr.html; (c) Pulaski

State/ 1941/ Dept of Arkansas Heritage/ staff: 25(f); 10(p); 300(v)/ members: 600

HISTORY MUSEUM: Communicates early history of AR and its creative legacy through preserving, interpreting, and presenting stories and collections.

PROGRAMS: Community Outreach; Concerts; Exhibits; Facility Rental; Festivals; Guided Tours; Interpretation; Lectures; Living History; Reenactments; Research Library/Archives; School-Based Curriculum; Theatre

COLLECTIONS: [1819-1836] Decorative, mechanical and fine arts. Items from the frontier period are displayed in the historic homes.

HOURS: Yr M-Sa 9-5, Su 1-5

ADMISSION: $2, Children $0.50, Seniors $1

377
Historic Preservation Alliance of Arkansas
910 W 2nd, Ste 200, 72203 [PO Box 305, 72203]; (p) (501) 372-4757; (f) (501) 372-3845; thealliance@aristotle.net; (c) Pulaski

1983/ Board of Directors/ staff: 2(f); 28(v)/ members: 388/publication: *Arkansas Preservation Digest*

ALLIANCE OF HISTORICAL AGENCIES: Statewide organization of preservationists.

PROGRAMS: Annual Meeting; Community Outreach; Family Programs; Guided Tours; Interpretation; Lectures; Publication

HOURS: Yr M-F 8-5

378
Historical Resources and Museum Services
One Capitol Mall, 72201; (p) (501) 682-3603; (f) (501) 682-0081; patricia.murphy@mail.state.ar.us; www.arkansas.com; (c) Pulaski

State/ 1979/ staff: 4(f)

ALLIANCE OF HISTORICAL AGENCIES: Provides technical assistance to non-profit museums in Arkansas through consultations, grants, workshops and a lending library; administers four State Park museums.

HOURS: Yr M-F 8-5

379
Museum of Discovery: Arkansas Museum of Science and History
500 E Markham, Ste 150, 72201; (p) (501) 396-7050; (f) (501) 396-7054; mod@aristotle.net; www.amod.org; (c) Pulaski

Private non-profit/ 1927/ Museum Board/ staff: 20(f); 15(p); 476(v)/ members: 1700/publication: *Arkansas Indians*

HISTORY MUSEUM: Utilizes participatory and collections-based exhibits social sciences, sciences and technology.

PROGRAMS: Community Outreach; Exhibits; Facility Rental; Family Programs; Festivals; Interpretation; Publication; School-Based Curriculum; Theatre

COLLECTIONS: [Prehistoric—present] Anthropological, Historical and Life and Earth Science artifacts, including live animals, kewpie items, pottery, baskets, uniforms, toys, weapons, books, prints, maps, textiles, furniture, and machines.

HOURS: Yr M-Sa 9-5, Su 1-6

ADMISSION: $5.50, Children $5, Seniors $5; Under 3 Free

380
Old State House Museum
300 W Markham St, 72201; (p) (501) 324-9685; (f) (501) 324-9688; info@oldstatehouse.org; www.oldstatehouse.com; (c) Pulaski

State/ 1947/ Dept of Arkansas Heritage/ staff: 17(f); 4(p); 25(v)/publication: *The Arkansas News*

HISTORIC SITE; HISTORY MUSEUM: Interprets Arkansas' history and heritage from statehood (1836) onward.

PROGRAMS: Community Outreach; Exhibits; Interpretation; Lectures; Living History; Publication; Reenactments; Research Library/Archives

COLLECTIONS: [1836-1911] Political memorabilia, First Families of Arkansas, quilts by Black Arkansans, Confederate battle flags, Camark art pottery.

HOURS: Yr M-Sa 9-5, Su 1-5

ADMISSION: No charge

381
Pulaski County Historical Society
[PO Box 251903, 72225]; (c) Pulaski

Private non-profit/ 1951/ members: 243/publication: *Pulaski County Historical Review*

382
Riley-Luten Memorial Scout Museum
3220 Cantrell Rd, 72202; (p) (501) 664-4780; (f) (501) 664-4785; (c) Pulaski

Private non-profit/ 1993/ Quapaw Area Council and Boy Scouts of America/ staff: 9(v)

HISTORY MUSEUM: Preserves history of Boy Scouts, especially in AR.

COLLECTIONS: [1910-1990] Memorabilia such as uniforms, awards, equipment, and literature.

HOURS: Yr M-F 8:30-4:30

383
University History Institute
2801 S University Ave, 72204; (p) (501) 569-3235; (f) (501) 569-3059; lasmoller@ualr.edu; (c) Pulaski

Private non-profit/ 1987/ Board of Directors/ staff: 1(v)/ members: 65

HISTORICAL SOCIETY: Organization of private citizens who support regional history.

PROGRAMS: Lectures

COLLECTIONS: [Prehistory-present]

HOURS: Oct-Dec, Feb-Apr 1st T 8pm

LONOKE

384
Lonoke County Historical Society
Front Cat Stoplight, 72086 [PO Box 14, 72086]; (c) Lonoke

Private non-profit/ Lonoke County Historical Society Board/ staff: 14(v)/ members: 200

HISTORICAL SOCIETY; HISTORY MUSEUM

PROGRAMS: Annual Meeting; Community Outreach; Concerts; Exhibits; Facility Rental; Family Programs; Lectures; Living History; Publication; Research Library/Archives; School-Based Curriculum

COLLECTIONS: [1869-1960] Restored Rock Island depot, oral history tapes, memorabilia.

HOURS: Yr M-F 9-5 and Sa by appt

ADMISSION: No charge

MAGAZINE

385
Evans Museum, Inc.
6335 N State Hwy 109, 72943; (p) (501) 963-3987, (501) 963-8025; (f) (501) 963-3987; (c) Logan

1991/ staff: 1(f); 5(v)

HISTORY MUSEUM: Educates and promotes recognition and respect of patriotic obligations.

PROGRAMS: Annual Meeting; Exhibits; Film/Video; Guided Tours; Lectures

COLLECTIONS: [20th c] Military memorabilia, Bicentennial reminders in existence.

HOURS: Yr W, Sa-Su 1-5

ADMISSION: Donations accepted

MAGNOLIA

386
South West Arkansas Genealogical Society
220 E Main, 71754 [PO Box 375, 71754]; (p) (870) 234-1991; (f) (870) 234-5077; (c) Columbia

Private non-profit/ 1976/ members: 100/publication: *SO WE AR*

GENEALOGICAL SOCIETY: Facilitates discussions of genealogy and history, collects and preserves historical documents.

PROGRAMS: Family Programs; Lectures; Living History

MALVERN

387
Hot Spring County Museum-Boyle House
310 E Third St, 72104 [1220 Brownwood, 72104]; (p) (501) 337-4775; (c) Hot Spring

1981/ staff: 3(p); 10(v)/ members: 100

HISTORY MUSEUM; HOUSE MUSEUM: Preserves and presents county history.

PROGRAMS: Community Outreach; Exhibits; Facility Rental; Guided Tours

COLLECTIONS: [1850-1960] Furnishings, clothing, other historical artifacts, rocks and minerals.

HOURS: Yr M-F 12:30-4:30

388
Hot Spring County, Arkansas Historical Society
HSC Library, 301 S Main St, 72104 [PO Box 674, 72104]; (p) (501) 337-7488; (c) Hot Spring

County/ 1968/ members: 350

GENEALOGICAL SOCIETY; HISTORICAL SOCIETY: Publishes annual volume on county genealogy and history.

MAMMOTH SPRING

389
Mammoth Spring State Park
US Hwy 63 N & Hwy 9, 72554 [PO Box 36, 72554]; (p) (870) 625-7364; (f) (870) 625-3255; Mammoth@mail.oci-l.com; (c) Fulton

State/ 1957/ Dept of State Parks/ staff: 7(f); 6(p); 250(v)

GARDEN; HISTORIC SITE; HISTORY MUSEUM: Interprets community history and local natural resources.

INTERPRETATION: Community/State History; Education; Gardens; Historic Preservation; Natural History; Natural Resources; Railroading

PROGRAMS: Concerts; Exhibits; Facility Rental; Family Programs; Guided Tours; Interpretation; School-Based Curriculum

COLLECTIONS: [1885-present] Community and natural history, including railroading, 1886 depot museum, 1927 hydroplant, 1888 dam/spillway, 10th largest spring in the world.

HOURS: Park: Yr Daily 8-5; Museum Yr T-Su 8-5

ADMISSION: $2.25, Children $1.25; Park: Free

MARKED TREE

390
Marked Tree Delta Area Museum
308 Frisco St, 72365 [PO Box 72, 72365]; (p) (870) 358-4998, (870) 358-4272; (c) Poinsett

1992/ Tri-City Area Cultural Council, Inc./ staff: 42(v)

HISTORICAL SOCIETY; HISTORY MUSEUM; HOUSE MUSEUM; LIBRARY AND/OR ARCHIVES

PROGRAMS: Annual Meeting; Exhibits; Facility Rental; Guided Tours; Research Library/ Archives

COLLECTIONS: Medical and hospital equipment; local historical artifacts, northwest AR Delta area artifacts, early 1900 general store, replica of hospital.

HOURS: Yr W-F, Su 1-4, Sa 9:30-12:30

MAYNARD

391
Maynard Pioneer Museum and Park
516 Spring St, 72444 [PO Box 486, 72444]; (p) (870) 647-2701; (f) (870) 647-2701; (c) Randolph

City/ 1980/ Town of Maynard/ staff: 12(p); 25(v)

HISTORY MUSEUM: Depicts an original setting of local pioneers.

PROGRAMS: Festivals; Living History

COLLECTIONS: [Mid 1800s to late 1900s.] Restored log cabin with furniture, pictures, and other artifacts.

HOURS: May 1-Sep 30 T-Sa 10-4, Su 1-4

ADMISSION: Donations requested

MONTICELLO

392
Drew County Historical Museum
Cor of Main & College, 71655 [404 S Main, 71655]; (p) (870) 367-7446; (c) Drew

Joint/ 1970/ City; County/ staff: 4(p); 2(v)/ members: 120/publication: *Drew County Historical Journal*

HISTORIC PRESERVATION AGENCY; HISTORIC SITE; HISTORICAL SOCIETY; HISTORY MUSEUM; HOUSE MUSEUM; RESEARCH CENTER: Collects, preserves, displays and interprets county history.

PROGRAMS: Annual Meeting; Community Outreach; Exhibits; Festivals; Guided Tours; Lectures; Publication; Research Library/ Archives

COLLECTIONS: [1850-present] Victorian mansion furnished according to the period. Includes gun display, textiles, dolls and a history of medicine in Drew County.

HOURS: Yr F 1-5, Sa-Su 2-5

ADMISSION: Donations accepted

MORRILTON

393
Museum of Automobiles, The
8 Jones Lane, 72110; (p) (501) 727-5427; (f) (501) 727-6482; museumofautos@mev.net; www.museumofautos.com; (c) Conway

Private non-profit/ 1964/ Board of Directors/ staff: 2(f); 10(p)/ members: 150

AUTOMOBILE MUSEUM: Displays automobiles built at the turn of the century through the 1960s, interpreting the evolution of the automobile.

PROGRAMS: Exhibits; Festivals

COLLECTIONS: [1900-1970] Fifty cars including 1904 Oldsmobile, 1923 Arkansas built Climber, 1914 Cretors Popcorn Wagon, 1929 Model A Towncar.

HOURS: Yr Daily

394
Petit Jean State Park
1285 Petit Jean Mountain Rd, 72110; (p) (501) 727-5441, (501) 727-5431; (f) (501) 727-5458; pjsp@cswnet.com; (c) Conway

State/ 1923/ Dept of Parks and Tourism/ staff: 26(f)

HISTORIC PRESERVATION AGENCY: Protects habitats and cultural history.

PROGRAMS: Community Outreach; Concerts; Elder's Programs; Exhibits; Facility Rental; Family Programs; Festivals; Guided Tours; Interpretation; Lectures; Living History; Reenactments; School-Based Curriculum

COLLECTIONS: [prehistory-present] Native American artifacts, documents, park.

HOURS: Yr Daily 8-5

MOUNTAIN VIEW

395
Ozark Folk Center, The
Hwy 382, 72560 [PO Box 500, 72560]; (p) (870) 269-3851; (f) (870) 269-2909; ofc@mvtel.net; (c) Stone

State/ 1973/ staff: 20(f); 30(p); 15(v)

CULTURAL CENTER: Exhibits Ozark mountain cultural artifacts, presents outdoor events and concerts.

PROGRAMS: Community Outreach; Concerts; Elder's Programs; Exhibits; Facility Rental; Garden Tours; Interpretation; Lectures; Living History; Research Library/Archives; Theatre

COLLECTIONS: [1820-1940] Local historical artifacts.

HOURS: Apr-Oct Daily 10-6

NEWPORT

396
Jackson County Historical Society
7 Pickens St, 72112; (p) (870) 523-5150; (f) (870) 523-5196; waynboyce@aol.com; (c) Jackson

Joint/ 1961/ County; Private non-profit/ staff: 20(v)/ members: 330/publication: *The Stream*

of History; Fight and Survive; Reminiscences of a Private

GENEALOGICAL SOCIETY; HISTORICAL SOCIETY; HISTORY MUSEUM; HOUSE MUSEUM; RESEARCH CENTER: Presents programs and collects artifacts relevant to local history, maintains archive and sites.

PROGRAMS: Annual Meeting; Community Outreach; Exhibits; Facility Rental; Family Programs; Festivals; Guided Tours; Interpretation; Lectures; Living History; Publication; Research Library/Archives; School-Based Curriculum

COLLECTIONS: [Prehistory-1950] Pioneer artifacts, Civil War weapons, uniforms, Victorian artifacts, medical and office equipment, WWI weapons, photos, maps.

HOURS: Yr Daily 9-5

397
Jacksonport State Park
205 Avenue St, 72112; (p) (870) 523-2143; (f) (870) 523-4620; jacksonport@arkansas.com; www.arkansas.com; (c) Jackson

State/ 1965/ Parks Dept/ staff: 6(f); 4(p); 5(v)

HISTORIC SITE; HISTORY MUSEUM; STATE PARK: Collects, preserves, and interprets cultural and architectural history of area, and natural resources; recreation site.

PROGRAMS: Community Outreach; Exhibits; Facility Rental; Family Programs; Festivals; Guided Tours; Interpretation; Living History; School-Based Curriculum

COLLECTIONS: [1820-1967] 1872 courthouse/museum, 1931 steamboat, personal artifacts including clothing, weapons, photos, and maps.

HOURS: Courthouse Museum: Summer T-Sa 8-5, Su 1-5; Winter W-Sa 8-5, Su 1-5; Visitor Info Center: Summer Daily 8-5; Winter M-F 8-5, Sa, Su 1-5

ADMISSION: $2.25, Children $1.25

NORFOLK

398
Jacob Wolf House
Hwy 5, 72658 [PO Box 118, 72658]; (p) (870) 499-9653

1809/ City/ staff: 25(v)

COLLECTIONS: [1824-1835] 1800s furniture, cooking utensils, tools (medical and work), legal documents, store accounts, personal letters.

OSCEOLA

399
Mississippi County Historical and Genealogical Society
209 W Hale St, 72370 [PO Box 483, 72370]; (p) (870) 563-6161; (c) Mississippi

Joint/ 1988/ County; Private non-profit/ members: 110/publication: *Delta Review*

GENEALOGICAL SOCIETY; HISTORIC PRESERVATION AGENCY; HISTORIC SITE; HISTORICAL SOCIETY; HISTORY MUSEUM: Preserves the history of Mississippi County.

PROGRAMS: Exhibits; Guided Tours; Lectures; Publication

COLLECTIONS: Cut glass, military uniforms, old theatre seats, kitchen utensils, furniture, newspapers, books, old farming implements, photographs, receipts, letters, centennial items, and jewelry.

HOURS: Yr W, 1st Su 1-4

PARIS

400
Arkansas Historic Wine Museum
101 N Carbon City Rd, 72855; (p) (501) 963-3990; cowie@csnet.com; biz.opa.net/cowie-wine-cellars/; (c) Logan

1967/ members: 26

HISTORY MUSEUM: Preserves the history and artifacts of the wine-making tradition in AR.

PROGRAMS: Annual Meeting; Community Outreach; Exhibits; Festivals; Guided Tours; Lectures; Research Library/Archives

COLLECTIONS: [1840-present] Commercial and home wine-making equipment including wine presses, fermentation tanks, barrels, pumps, filters, testing instruments, bottles and labels, government records, correspondence, photographs, and newspapers.

HOURS: Yr M-Sa 10-6

ADMISSION: Donations accepted

PEA RIDGE

401
Pea Ridge National Military Park
15930 Hwy 62 E, 72756 [PO Box 700, 72756]; (p) (501) 451-8122; (f) (501) 451-0219; bill_corcoran@nps.gov; www.nps.gov/peri; (c) Benton

Federal/ 1957/ National Park Service/ staff: 11(f); 2(p); 12(v)

LIVING HISTORY/OUTDOOR MUSEUM: Preserves landscapes and resources of the Civil War battlefields of Leetown and Elkhorn Tavern

PROGRAMS: Community Outreach; Exhibits; Festivals; Film/Video; Guided Tours; Interpretation; Lectures; Living History; Reenactments; Research Library/Archives; School-Based Curriculum

COLLECTIONS: [1860-1865] Arms and equipment, personal items, art, photos, diaries, pertaining to the Civil War.

HOURS: Yr Daily 8-5

ADMISSION: $2, Family $4

PIGGOTT

402
Clay County Genealogical and Historical Society
Piggott Public Library, 316 W Main, 72454; (p) (870) 598-3666; (c) Clay

Private non-profit/ 1985/ members: 145

GENEALOGICAL SOCIETY; HISTORICAL SOCIETY: Preserves Clay County history.

PROGRAMS: Community Outreach; Film/Video; Lectures; Research Library/Archives

COLLECTIONS: [19th-20th c] Books, CDs, film, microfiche, obituaries, family folders, church records, newspapers, periodicals and pedigree charts.

HOURS: Yr M,T-Th 9-6, W,F 9-5

ADMISSION: No charge

403
Hemingway-Pfeiffer Museum and Educational Center
1021 W Cherry St, 72454; (p) (870) 598-3487; www.hemingway.astate.edu; (c) Clay

State/ 1999/ Arkansas State University/ staff: 4(f); 1(p); 25(v)

HOUSE MUSEUM; RESEARCH CENTER: Provides exhibits and educational programs related to the 1920s and 1930s eras in Northeast Arkansas. Primary focus is on the Pfeiffer family and their son-in-law Ernest Hemingway.

PROGRAMS: Community Outreach; Elder's Programs; Exhibits; Facility Rental; Family Programs; Festivals; Film/Video; Guided Tours; Interpretation; Lectures; Living History; Research Library/Archives; School-Based Curriculum

COLLECTIONS: [1920s-1930s] Furnishings original to the home, papers and memorabilia related to Ernest Hemingway and the Pfeiffer family.

HOURS: Yr M-F 9-3, Sa 12-3

ADMISSION: Donations accepted

PINE BLUFF

404
Band Museum, The
423 Main, 71601; (p) (870) 534-4676; (c) Jefferson

Private non-profit/ 1993/ staff: 2(f); 1(p); 1(v)/ members: 150

ART MUSEUM; HISTORY MUSEUM

PROGRAMS: Exhibits; Research Library/Archives

COLLECTIONS: [19th-20th c] 1,200 band instruments, 300 photographs, 1,000 phonograph records, books and newspaper articles.

HOURS: Yr M-F 10-4

405
Pine Bluff/Jefferson County Historical Museum
201 E 4th, 71601; (p) (870) 541-5402; (f) (870) 541-5405; (c) Jefferson

County/ 1980/ staff: 2(f); 1(p); 34(v)/ members: 270

HISTORY MUSEUM: Collects, preserves, interprets, and exhibits local historical artifacts in restored train station.

PROGRAMS: Community Outreach; Exhibits; Film/Video; Guided Tours

COLLECTIONS: [1840-1960] Native American artifacts, early agriculture tools; clothing from late Victorian era, Edwardian Period, flapper era; dolls, war artifacts, Black History artifacts.

HOURS: Yr M-F 9-5, Sa 10-2, and by appt

ADMISSION: No

PINE RIDGE

406
Lum and Abner Museum
4562 Hwy 88 W, 71966 [General Delivery, 71966]; (p) (870) 326-4442; (f) (870) 326-4442; nstucker@alltel.net; lum-abner.com; (c) Montgomery

Private for-profit/ 1971/ staff: 2(f)

HISTORIC SITE: Original general stores housing the Lum and Abner Radio memorabilia and history of Pine Ridge.

PROGRAMS: Exhibits; Guided Tours

COLLECTIONS: [1886-1950] General store fixtures, home and farm tools, photos, memorabilia, literature.

HOURS: Mar 1- Nov 1 T-Sa 9-5, Su 12-5

ADMISSION: $0.50, Children $0.25

POCAHONTAS

407
Good Earth Association, Inc./Living Farm Museum of the Ozarks
N-NW Pocahontas, Hwy 90 at Watts Trail, 72455 [203 E Church St, 72455-2899]; (p) (870) 892-9545; (f) (870) 892-8329; dwater@tcac.net; (c) Randolph

Joint/ 1984/ Private non-profit; State/ staff: 10(v)/ members: 50

GARDEN; LIVING HISTORY/OUTDOOR MUSEUM: Operates and displays historical farm equipment at a living farm museum.

PROGRAMS: Living History

COLLECTIONS: [20th c] Historical farm equipment such as tractors, plows and mowers.

HOURS: Apr-Nov M-Sa sunrise-sunset

ADMISSION: No charge

408
Old Davidson State Park
7953 Hwy 166 S, 72455; (p) (870) 892-4708; olddavid@tcac.net; (c) Randolph

State/ 1957/ AR State Parks/ staff: 5(f); 2(p)

STATE PARK: Preserves, protects, and interprets Western pioneer settlement in the township of Davidsonville.

PROGRAMS: Community Outreach; Elder's Programs; Exhibits; Facility Rental; Family Programs; Festivals; Film/Video; Interpretation; Lectures; Living History; School-Based Curriculum

COLLECTIONS: [1803-1836] Artifacts

POWHATAN

409
Ficklin-Imboden House
Hwy 25/Main St, 72458 [PO Box 93, 72458]; (p) (870) 878-6794

State/ 1833/ AR State Parks/ staff: 1(f); 1(p)

COLLECTIONS: [1840s] Antiques and reproductions; courthouse records from 1813-1920.

410
Powhatan Courthouse State Park
4414 Hwy 25, 72458 [PO Box 93, 72458]; (p) (870) 878-6794; (c) Lawrence

State/ 1974/ staff: 2(f); 4(p); 25(v)

HISTORIC SITE

PROGRAMS: Annual Meeting; Exhibits; Facility Rental; Living History; Reenactments; Research Library/Archives

COLLECTIONS: [1815-1945] Park, archives, historic buildings.

HOURS: Yr

ADMISSION: $2.39, Children $1.33

PRAIRIE GROVE

411
Latta House
Hwy 62, 72753 [PO Box 306, 72753]; (p) (501) 846-2990; (f) (501) 846-4035

1834/ State/ staff: 6(f)

COLLECTIONS: [1830s-1860s] Furniture

412
Prairie Grove Battlefield State Park
506 E Douglas, 72753 [PO Box 306, 72753]; (p) (501) 846-2990; (f) (501) 846-4035; prairiegrov@arkansas.com; (c) Washington

State/ 1973/ AR Dept of Parks and Tourism/ staff: 6(f); 4(p); 20(v)

HISTORY MUSEUM: Preserves site of 1862 Battle of Prairie Grove; interprets the Civil War in the Ozark region.

PROGRAMS: Concerts; Facility Rental; Film/Video; Guided Tours; Interpretation; Living History; Reenactments

COLLECTIONS: [1830-1870] Furniture, artillery, weapons, and other artifacts.

HOURS: Museum: Yr Daily 8-5, Park grounds: 8-sunset

ADMISSION: $2.25, Family $6,

ROGERS

413
Rogers Historical Museum
322 S Second St, 72756; (p) (501) 621-1154; (f) (501) 621-1155; museum@rogersarkansas.com; www.rogersarkansas.com/museum; (c) Benton

City/ 1976/ staff: 4(f); 5(p); 40(v)/ members: 278/publication: *The Friendly Note*

HISTORY MUSEUM; HOUSE MUSEUM; RESEARCH CENTER: Museum of local history, featuring the 1895 Hawkins House, exhibits with many hands-on components.

PROGRAMS: Annual Meeting; Community Outreach; Exhibits; Family Programs; Guided Tours; Interpretation; Lectures; Living History; Publication; Reenactments; Research Library/Archives; School-Based Curriculum

COLLECTIONS: [1880-1940] Photographic images, archival materials, household items, textiles, quilts, costumes, accessories, artworks, furniture.

HOURS: Yr T-Sa 10-4

ADMISSION: No charge

RUSSELLVILLE

414
Museum of Prehistory and History
Arkansas Tech University, 411 WN, 72801 [ATU Box 8526, Tucker Hall Ste 12, 72801]; (p) (501) 964-0826; (f) (501) 964-0872; tech.museum@mail.atu.edu; www.atu.edu/acad/museum; (c) Pope

1989/ Arkansas Tech University Board of Trustees/ staff: 1(f); 4(p); 2(v)/publication: *Discovery Handbook*

HISTORY MUSEUM: Collects, preserves, and interprets the people and events of the AR River Valley and the immediately adjacent Ozarks and Ouachitas.

PROGRAMS: Community Outreach; Exhibits; Guided Tours; Lectures; Publication; Research Library/Archives; School-Based Curriculum

COLLECTIONS: [Prehistory-present] Archeological and historical artifacts, archival papers, photos and art.

HOURS: Yr T-Th 9-4 and by appt; closed semester breaks and 1st wk Aug

ADMISSION: Donations requested

415
Pope County Historical Foundation, Inc.
124 Ash St, 72802 [1405 Lands End S, 72802]; (p) (501) 968-3339, (501) 968-8369; (c) Pope

County/ 1970/ Board of Directors/ staff: 2(f); 16(v)/ members: 16

HOUSE MUSEUM: Presents and preserves 1850 historical home with numerous artifacts.

PROGRAMS: Exhibits; Facility Rental; Guided Tours; Lectures; Living History; Theatre

COLLECTIONS: [1850-1900] Furnishings, hats and clothing, dolls in inauguration gowns of the First Ladies of AR and the US, stop of the Butterfield stage line.

HOURS: Feb-Nov W-Su 1-5

ADMISSION: $3, Children $1

SCOTT

416
Plantation Agriculture Museum
4815 Hwy 161, 72142 [PO Box 87, 72142]; (p) (501) 961-1409; (f) (501) 961-1579; plantationag@aristotle.net; www.arkansas.com; (c) Pulaski

State/ 1989/ AR Department of Parks and Tourism/ staff: 4(f); 2(p); 5(v)

HISTORY MUSEUM: Interprets history of cotton plantations and farms in AR from statehood to mechanization of farms.

PROGRAMS: Community Outreach; Exhibits; Family Programs; Guided Tours; Interpretation; Living History; Research Library/Archives; School-Based Curriculum

COLLECTIONS: [1836-1950] Cotton farming implements including gins, bales, mule-related items, literature, images, as well as cultural artifacts.

HOURS: Yr T-Sa 8-5, Su 1-5

ADMISSION: $2.25, Children $1.25; Group rates

417
Toltec Mounds Archeological State Park
490 Toltec Mounds Rd, 72142; (p) (501) 961-9442; (f) (501) 961-9221; toltecmounds@aristotle.net; (c) Lonoke

State/ 1975/ AR Dept of Parks and Tourism, AR Archeological Survey/ staff: 7(f); 2(p); 12(v)

HISTORIC SITE; RESEARCH CENTER: Educates about Native American mounds.

PROGRAMS: Exhibits; Facility Rental; Interpretation; Living History; School-Based Curriculum

COLLECTIONS: [650-1050 AD] Archaeological artifacts including pottery, flora and fauna, and lithics.

HOURS: Yr T-Sa 8-5, Su

SEARCY

418
White County Historical Society
[PO Box 537, 72145]; (c) White

Private non-profit/ 1961/ staff: 4(v)/ members: 140/publication: *White County Heritage*

HISTORIC SITE; HISTORICAL SOCIETY; HISTORY MUSEUM: Preserves community heritage.

PROGRAMS: Annual Meeting; Community Outreach; Exhibits; Guided Tours; Publication; Research

SILOAM SPRINGS

419
Siloam Springs Museum
112 N Maxwell, 72761 [PO Box 1164, 72761]; (p) (501) 524-4011; ssmuseum@ipa.net; (c) Benton

Private non-profit/ 1969/ Board of Directors/ staff: 1(f); 2(p); 10(v)/ members: 201/publication: *The Hummer*

HISTORY MUSEUM: Permanent and special exhibits on the history of Siloam Springs and vicinity.

PROGRAMS: Annual Meeting; Community Outreach; Exhibits; Guided Tours; Interpretation; Publication; Research Library/Archives

COLLECTIONS: [1880-1950]

HOURS: Yr T-F 10-5, Sa 12-5

ADMISSION: No Charge/Donations

SMACKOVER

420
Arkansas Museum of Natural Resources
St Hwy 7, 71762 [3853 Smackover Hwy, 71762]; (p) (870) 725-2877; (f) (870) 725-2161; amnr@cei.net; (c) Union

State/ 1984/ staff: 10(f); 5(p); 88(v)/ members: 786

HISTORY MUSEUM: Preserves, increases and disseminates knowledge of AR' natural resources with special reference to petroleum, timber and brine recovered for bromine extraction.

PROGRAMS: Community Outreach; Exhibits; Facility Rental; Festivals; Guided Tours; Interpretation; Lectures; Living History; Research Library/Archives; School-Based Curriculum

COLLECTIONS: [1920s South AR oil boom] Archival/research materials, oil field tools and equipment, oil company memorabilia, timber tools and equipment, geological and cultural artifacts, photographic prints, oral history tapes and corporate records.

HOURS: Yr M-Sa 8-5, Su 1-5

SPRINGDALE

421
Orphan Train Heritage Society of America

614 E Emma Ave #115, 72764; (p) (501) 756-2780; (f) (501) 756-0769; mej102339@aol.com; pda.republic.net/othsa; (c) Washington

Private non-profit/ 1987/ staff: 1(f); 1(v)/ members: 429/publication: *Crossroads*

HISTORIC PRESERVATION AGENCY; HISTORY MUSEUM; RESEARCH CENTER: Preserves the history of orphan train riders who traveled West.

PROGRAMS: Annual Meeting; Community Outreach; Exhibits; Film/Video; Lectures; Publication; Reenactments; Research Library/Archives

COLLECTIONS: [1854-1929] Photos, oral histories, videos and orphanage records.

HOURS: Yr M-F

422
Shiloh Museum of Ozark History

118 W Johnson Ave, 72764; (p) (501) 750-8165; (f) (501) 750-8171; shiloh@cavern.uark.edu; www.springdaleark.org/shiloh; (c) Washington

City/ 1968/ staff: 8(f); 5(p); 39(v)/ members: 886/publication: *Shiloh Scrapbook*

HISTORY MUSEUM; LIBRARY AND/OR ARCHIVES: Interprets history of the Ozarks.

PROGRAMS: Community Outreach; Elder's Programs; Exhibits; Family Programs; Festivals; Film/Video; Guided Tours; Interpretation; Lectures; Living History; Publication; Research Library/Archives

COLLECTIONS: Artifacts, archives, photos.

HOURS: Yr M-Sa 10-5

STATE UNIVERSITY

423
Arkansas State University Museum

110 Cooley Dr, 72467 [PO Box 490, 72467]; (p) (870) 972-2074; (f) (870) 972-2793; museum.astate.edu; (c) Craighead

State/ 1933/ Board of Trustees/ staff: 6(f); 2(p); 31(v)/ members: 248/publication: *A Different Drummer*

HISTORY MUSEUM: Preserves, increases, and disseminates knowledge of the natural and cultural history and prehistory of AR and the world.

PROGRAMS: Community Outreach; Concerts; Exhibits; Facility Rental; Guided Tours; Interpretation; Lectures; Living History; Publication; Reenactments; Research Library/Archives; School-Based Curriculum

COLLECTIONS: Specimens, artifacts, documents and photographs in categories of archives, art, library, natural history including earth science and life science, and social science.

HOURS: Yr M-F 9-4, Sa-Su 1-4

STUTTGART

424
Stuttgart Arkansas Agricultural Museum

921 E 4th St, 72160; (p) (870) 673-7001; (f) (870) 673-3959; (c) Arkansas

City/ 1974/ Board of Trustees/ staff: 4(f); 1(p); 30(v)/ members: 340/publication: *Sodbuster*

HISTORY MUSEUM: Preserves local pioneer history.

PROGRAMS: Community Outreach; Concerts; Elder's Programs; Exhibits; Facility Rental; Family Programs; Festivals; Film/Video; Guided Tours; Interpretation; Living History; Publication; Reenactments; School-Based Curriculum

COLLECTIONS: [1865-1940] Artifacts in village replica; farm equipment, tools, waterfowl, decoys, oral history tapes, native animals, early photographs, research library, toys, clothing, quilts, buggies, cars, early agricultural aviation equipment.

HOURS: Yr T-Sa 10-4:30, Su 1:30-430

ADMISSION: Donations accepted

TUCKER

425
Arkansas Prison Museum

[PO Box 240, 72168-2519]; (p) (870) 247-6344; (f) (870) 247-3700; (c) Jefferson

State/ 1994/ staff: 1(f)

HISTORY MUSEUM

PROGRAMS: Exhibits; Guided Tours

HOURS: Yr Daily

WASHINGTON

426
Old Washington Historic State Park

[PO Box 98, 72862]; (p) (870) 983-2684; (f) (870) 983-2736; owshp@usa.net; (c) Hempstead

State/ 1973/ AR Department of Parks and Tourism/ staff: 30(f); 10(p)

ALLIANCE OF HISTORICAL AGENCIES; HISTORIC SITE; HISTORY MUSEUM; HOUSE MUSEUM; LIBRARY AND/OR ARCHIVES; LIVING HISTORY/OUTDOOR MUSEUM: Interprets 19th c community during Territorial, Antebellum, Civil War, and Reconstruction eras of AR history.

PROGRAMS: Exhibits; Family Programs; Festivals; Guided Tours; Interpretation; Living History; Reenactments; Research Library/Archives; School-Based Curriculum; Theatre

COLLECTIONS: [1824-1875] Buildings, clothing, photographs, furniture, documents, tools, weapons, printing presses.

HOURS: Yr Daily 8-5

ADMISSION: $6.50

427
Southwest Arkansas Regional Archives

Hwy 195 W, 71862 [PO Box 134, 71862]; (p) (870) 983-2633; (c) Hempstead

Private non-profit/ 1978/ staff: 2(f); 5(v)

LIBRARY AND/OR ARCHIVES: Preserves local history.

PROGRAMS: Research Library/Archives

COLLECTIONS: [1819-present]

HOURS: Yr Daily

WEST FORK

428
Devil's Den State Park

11333 W AR Hwy 74, 72774; (p) (501) 761-3325; (f) (501) 761-3736; devden@arkansas.net; (c) Washington

State/ 1994/ AR Dept of Parks and Tourism

HISTORIC SITE; STATE PARK

PROGRAMS: Annual Meeting; Community Outreach; Elder's Programs; Exhibits; Facility Rental; Guided Tours; Interpretation; School-Based Curriculum

COLLECTIONS: [19th-20th c] Civilian Conservation Corps (CCC) photos, original CCC blueprints and memorabilia donated by CCC members and families, pioneer homesites.

HOURS: Visitor Center: Yr Daily 8-5

ADMISSION: No charge

WHITE HALL

429
White Hall Museum

9009 Dollarway Rd, 71602; (p) (870) 247-9406; whitec@bulldog.arsc.k12.ar.us; (c) Jefferson

City/ 1991/ staff: 1(f); 2(p); 10(v)/ members: 40

HISTORY MUSEUM: Collects, preserves, and displays historical artifacts.

PROGRAMS: Community Outreach; Exhibits; Guided Tours; Publication

COLLECTIONS: [1900-present] Military items, toys, collectibles, furniture, vehicles.

HOURS: Yr

WILSON

430
Hampson Museum State Park

#2 Lake Dr, 72395 [PO Box 156, 72395]; (p) (870) 655-8622; hampson@arkansas.net; (c) Mississippi

State/ 1961/ staff: 2(f)

ARCHAEOLOGICAL SITE/MUSEUM: Houses archaeological collections of Dr. J.K. Hampson.

PROGRAMS: Exhibits; Family Programs; Festivals; Guided Tours; Interpretation

COLLECTIONS: [1450-1650 AD] Ceramic, lithic, shell, and other artifacts primarily from Late Mississippian Moundbuilding culture, in Nadena Phase.

HOURS: Yr T-Sa 8-5, Su 1-5

ADMISSION: $2.25, Children $1.25; Group rates

CALIFORNIA

ALAMEDA

431
Aircraft Carrier Hornet Foundation
Pier 3 Alameda Pt, 94501 [PO Box 460, 94501]; (p) (510) 521-8448; (f) (510) 521-8327; hornetok@aol.com; uss_hornet.org; (c) Alameda

Private non-profit/ 1995/ Board of Trustees/ staff: 20(f); 10(p); 150(v)/ members: 2119

ART MUSEUM; HISTORIC SITE; HISTORY MUSEUM; LIVING HISTORY/OUTDOOR MUSEUM; RESEARCH CENTER: Dedicated to chronicling naval aviation and carrier operations in the Pacific from 1911 to the present.

PROGRAMS: Community Outreach; Concerts; Exhibits; Facility Rental; Guided Tours; Interpretation; Living History; Research Library/Archives; School-Based Curriculum; Theatre

COLLECTIONS: [1920s-1970] Artifacts and memorabilia relating to the Navy, naval aviation, and aircraft carriers. Major emphasis on Apollo Space program.

HOURS: Yr W-M 10-5

ADMISSION: $12, Children $5, Seniors $10

432
Alameda Architectural Preservation Society
[PO Box 1677, 94501]; (p) 510-986-9232; http://www.alameda-preservation.org/; (c) Alameda

Private non-profit/ 1972/ staff: 12(v)/ members: 150/publication: *AAPS News*

HISTORIC PRESERVATION AGENCY: Dedicated to preservation of Alameda's architectural heritage.

PROGRAMS: Community Outreach; Lectures; Publication; Quarterly Meeting; School-Based Curriculum

ALHAMBRA

433
Alhambra Historical Society, Inc.
1550 W Alhambra Rd, 91802 [PO Box 6687, 91802]; (p) (626) 300-8845; (c) Los Angeles

Private non-profit/ 1966/ staff: 4(p)/ members: 125/publication: *Alhambra Historical Society Bulletin*

HISTORICAL SOCIETY: Commemorates events and people in local history.

PROGRAMS: Exhibits; Guided Tours; Lectures; Publication

COLLECTIONS: [1870s-present] Memorabilia, period clothing, furnishings, books, and photographs.

HOURS: Yr W and two Su/mo 2-4

ADMISSION: Donations accepted

ALPINE

434
Alpine Historical Society
2116 Tavern Rd, 91903 [PO Box 382, 91903]; (p) (619) 445-5716; (f) (619) 445-4461; (c) San Diego

Private non-profit/ 1950/ staff: 12(v)/ members: 165

HISTORIC SITE; HISTORICAL SOCIETY; HOUSE MUSEUM: Collects and interprets documents and artifacts in two late nineteenth century homes.

PROGRAMS: Annual Meeting; Community Outreach; Exhibits; Festivals; Interpretation; Lectures; School-Based Curriculum

COLLECTIONS: [Prehistory-1920] Native American artifacts, Hispanic ranch documents, homesteader documents, and photos.

HOURS: Yr Sa 10-2, Su 12-4

ALTADENA

435
Altadena Historical Society
2246 N Lake Ave, 91003 [PO Box 144, 91003]; (p) (626) 794-4961; bettyherr@earthlink.net; (c) Los Angeles

Board of Directors/ staff: 6(p)/ 10(v)/ members: 225/publication: *The Echo*

HISTORICAL SOCIETY: Maintains archives of local persons, organizations, historical buildings.

PROGRAMS: Publication

COLLECTIONS: [1870-present] Records, photographs, and artifacts.

HOURS: Sept-July M-T 9-12 or by appt

ADMISSION: No charge

ALTURAS

436
Modoc County Historical Society
600 S Main St, 96101-4117; (p) (530) 233-2844; (c) Modoc

County/ 1978/ staff: 1(p)/ members: 560

HISTORICAL SOCIETY: To preserve and maintain the history of the area.

PROGRAMS: Annual Meeting; Family Programs; Guided Tours; Publication

ANAHEIM

437
Anaheim Museum, Inc.
241 S Anaheim Blvd, 92805; (p) (714) 778-3301; (f) (714) 778-6740; (c) Orange

Private non-profit/ 1987/ staff: 1(f); 2(p); 4(v)/ members: 350

ART MUSEUM; HISTORY MUSEUM: Explores history and diverse heritage of Anaheim.

PROGRAMS: Annual Meeting; Community Outreach; Exhibits; Guided Tours; Publication

COLLECTIONS: [1860-1960] Artifacts and photos related to Anaheim; general history items and artwork done by local artists.

HOURS: Yr W-Sa

ADMISSION: Donations requested

438
Historic Ramon Peralta Adobe
Fairmont & Santa Ana Canyon Rd, [625 W Bastonchury Rd, Placentia, 92870]; (p) (714) 528-4260

1871/ Harbors, Beaches & Parks

HISTORY MUSEUM: Late adobe built during the American period with traditional CA architecture of the Spanish and Mexican periods.

COLLECTIONS: [1880s] 1880 period room, archaeological artifact exhibits, structural exhibits, and historical photos.

HOURS: Yr

ANTIOCH

439
Haeger Pottery Collectors of America
5021 Toyon Way, 94509; (p) (925) 978-1368; (f) (925) 776-7784; lanettec@Colorspot.com; (c) Contra Costa

1997/ staff: 3(v)/ members: 65

HISTORIC PRESERVATION AGENCY: Collects, researches, and preserves original catalogs; documents numbers on molds and designs.

PROGRAMS: Annual Meeting; Community Outreach; Exhibits

COLLECTIONS: [1914-present] Pottery

ARCADIA

440
Arboretum of Los Angeles County
301 N Baldwin Ave, 91007; (p) (626) 821-3222; (f) (626) 445-1217; (c) Los Angeles

Joint/ 1947/ Los Angeles County/ staff: 25(f); 7(p); 290(v)/ members: 3000

GARDEN; HISTORIC SITE; HOUSE MUSEUM

PROGRAMS: Annual Meeting; Community Outreach; Concerts; Exhibits; Facility Rental; Festivals; Garden Tours; Guided Tours; Interpretation; Lectures; Publication; Research Library/Archives

COLLECTIONS: Four historic buildings furnished in period decor; archive with 5000 photographs and 3000 slides; and a 20,000 volume horticultural library.

HOURS: Yr Daily 9-4:30

ADMISSION: $5, Student $3, Children $1, Seniors $3

ARCATA

441
Phillips House Museum
7th & Union Sts, 95521 [PO Box 4521, 95518]; (p) (707) 822-4722, (707) 822-6466

1854/ Historical Sights of Arcata

HOUSE MUSEUM: Preserves local history.

COLLECTIONS: [1850-1900]

HOURS: Yr Su 1-4 and by appt

ATWATER

442
Atwater Historical Society, Inc.
1020 Cedar, 95301 [PO Box 111, 95301]; (p) (209) 357-6309; (c) Merced

Private non-profit/ 1972/ Board of Directors/ staff: 10(v)/ members: 60

HISTORIC SITE; HISTORICAL SOCIETY; HOUSE MUSEUM: Collects, maintains, protects, preserves, and researches items of historical significance to City and surrounding area.

PROGRAMS: Annual Meeting; Exhibits; Guided Tours

COLLECTIONS: Documents from pioneer John Mitchell, maps, photos dating from the founding period to the present, Bloss family bibles and documents, furniture, and Atwater family photos.

HOURS: Yr 1st and 3rd Su1-4

443
Castle Air Museum Foundation, Inc.
5050 Santa Fe, 95301; (p) (209) 723-2178; (f) (209) 723-0323; cam@elite.net; www.elite.net/castle.air; (c) Merced

Private non-profit/ 1981/ staff: 5(f); 15(p); 140(v)/ members: 500

AVIATION MUSEUM: Preserves and displays 46 military aircraft circa 1939 to present; indoor military display.

PROGRAMS: Community Outreach; Exhibits; Facility Rental; Family Programs; Guided Tours; Interpretation; Living History; Research Library/Archives

COLLECTIONS: [1939-present] 46 rare military aircraft including B-24, B-36, B18, B-2 Volcan, Sr-71 Blackbird, mash unit H-13 and period ambulance.

HOURS: Daily Summer 9-5; Winter 10-4

ADMISSION: $7,

AUBURN

444
Bernhard Museum Complex
291 Auburn-Folsom Rd, 95603 [101 Maple St, 95603]; (p) (530) 888-6891; www.placer.ca.gov/museum; (c) Placer

County/ 1982/ staff: 6(f); 3(p)

HISTORIC SITE; HISTORY MUSEUM; LIVING HISTORY/OUTDOOR MUSEUM

PROGRAMS: Community Outreach; Family Programs; Guided Tours; Interpretation; Living History; Research Library/Archives

COLLECTIONS: [1851-1900] The Bernhard Residence and Traveler's Rest Hotel furnished to reflect the lifestyle of a farm family in the 1890s; 1881 brick wine processing building; reconstructed carriage barn.

HOURS: Yr T-F 10:30-3, Sa, Su 12-4

445
Gold Country Museum
1273 High St, 95603 [101 Maple St, 95603]; (p) (530) 887-0690; www.placer.ca.gov/museums; (c) Placer

County/ 1949

HISTORY MUSEUM

PROGRAMS: Exhibits; Interpretation; School-Based Curriculum

COLLECTIONS: [1849-1900] Mining artifacts, tools, memorabilia; exhibits on the California Gold Rush and the history of gold mining; a reconstructed mine shaft, model of a stamp mill,

assay office, gold panning hands-on exhibit, gambling materials.

HOURS: Yr T-F 10-3:30, Sa, Su 11-4

ADMISSION: Donations accepted

446
Placer County Archives
11437 D Ave, 95603 [101 Maple St, 95603]; (p) (530) 889-7995; (f) (530) 889-7708; www.placer.ca.gov/museum; (c) Placer

County/ 1851/ staff: 1(f); 100(v)

LIBRARY AND/OR ARCHIVES; RESEARCH CENTER: Research facility and repository of volumes generated by county departments since 1851.

PROGRAMS: Research Library/Archives

COLLECTIONS: [1851-present] Mining records 1856-1947, court cases 1851-1924, assessment rolls and maps 1874-1963, Records of wills 1874-1963, Board of Supervisors 1852-1980, naturalization and citizenship 1852-1939, marks and brands 1855-1893, deed books 1851-1960, Great Register of Voters 1867-1918, water rights appropriations 1872-1940, Placer Herald 1852-1976.

HOURS: Yr M-T 9-4, Th 8-12 call for appt

447
Placer County Museum
101 Maple St, 95603; (p) (530) 889-6500; (f) (530) 889-6504; www.placer.ca.gov/museum; (c) Placer

County/ 1984/ staff: 6(f); 3(p)/publication: *Placer*

HISTORIC SITE; HISTORY MUSEUM

PROGRAMS: Annual Meeting; Community Outreach; Exhibits; Family Programs; Festivals; Film/Video; Guided Tours; Interpretation; Lectures; Publication; School-Based Curriculum

COLLECTIONS: [1849-present] Housed in the historic Placer Co Courthouse 1894; Gold Rush, stagecoach, documents, manuscripts, memorabilia, artifacts, photos, ephemera, gold ore samples.

HOURS: Yr

AVALON

448
Catalina Island Museum Society
One Casino Way, Casino Bldg, 90704 [PO Box 366, 90704]; (p) (310) 510-2414; (f) (310) 510-2780; museum@catalinas.net; www.catalina.com/museum; (c) Los Angeles

Joint/ 1953/ Board of Directors/ staff: 5(f); 3(p)/ members: 750

HISTORY MUSEUM: Collects, preserves, and interprets the cultural and historical heritage of Santa Catalina Island.

PROGRAMS: Community Outreach; Elder's Programs; Exhibits; Family Programs; Festivals; Film/Video; Guided Tours; Interpretation; Lectures; Publication; Research Library/Archives; School-Based Curriculum

COLLECTIONS: Archaeological collections of Island Gabrielino culture, maps, photos, ephemera, books, local newspapers. Historical collections including maritime, Catalina pottery and tile, souvenirs, and local industries.

HOURS: Jan-Mar Su-W, F-Sa 10-4; Apr-Dec Daily 10-4

ADMISSION: $2, Children $0.50, Seniors $1; Uunder 6 free

BAKERSFIELD

449
California Historical Resources Information System
Southern San Joaquin Valley Information Ctr, CSU, 93311 [CA State Univ, 9001 Stockdale Hwy, 93311-1099]; (p) (661) 664-2289; (f) (661) 664-2415; abaldwin@csubak.edu; www.csubak.edu/ssjvic; (c) Kern

State/ Dept of Parks and Recreation/ staff: 1(f); 3(p); 1(v)

PROFESSIONAL ORGANIZATION: Maintains cultural resource information and encourages cooperation among professional archaeologists, historians, architects, various government agencies, developers, landowners, and the general public.

PROGRAMS: Annual Meeting; Community Outreach; Research Library/Archives

COLLECTIONS: Site records, and historic maps, ethnographies, excavation reports that relate to known prehistoric and historic cultural resources.

HOURS: Yr 9-5

450
California Living Museum
10500 Alfred Harrell Hwy, 93306; (p) (661) 872-2256; (f) (661) 872-2205; calm@lightspeed.net; bizweb.lightspeed.net/~calm; (c) Kern

County/ 1981/ Superintendent of Schools/ staff: 12(f); 4(p)/ members: 950

GARDEN: CA-specific zoo, botanic garden, and natural history museum.

PROGRAMS: Community Outreach; Exhibits; Facility Rental; Guided Tours; School-Based Curriculum

COLLECTIONS: [Present and past California animals and plants] 200 animals and 2000 plants, Yokuts Indian artifacts, tar seep specimens from 10,000 years ago, and 20 million year old marine and terrestrial fossils.

HOURS: Yr T-Su 9-5

ADMISSION: $3.50, Student $2, Children $2, Seniors $2.50; Under 2 free

451
Kern County Museum
3801 Chester Ave, 93301; (p) (661) 852-5000; (f) (661) 322-6415; www.kcmuseum.org; (c) Kern

Joint/ 1945/ County Museum Authority/ staff: 16(f); 11(p); 200(v)/ members: 384/publication: *Nibbles, Nuggets, and Nostalgia; The Courier*

HISTORY MUSEUM; LIVING HISTORY/OUTDOOR MUSEUM: Focuses on local history.

PROGRAMS: Concerts; Elder's Programs; Exhibits; Facility Rental; Family Programs; Guided Tours; Interpretation; Lectures; Living History; Publication; Reenactments; Research Library/Archives; School-Based Curriculum

COLLECTIONS: [1860s-1950s] Over 250,000 historical photos; artifacts on Kern County history, including Native American basketry, textiles, and vehicles.

HOURS: Yr M-F 8-5, Sa 10-5, Su 12-5

ADMISSION: $5, Children $4, Seniors $4; Under 3 free

BALDWIN PARK

452
Historical Society of the City of Baldwin Park, The
4061 Sterling Way, 91706; (p) (626) 338-7130; (c) Los Angeles

City/ 1975/ staff: 4(f); 10(p); 5(v)/ members: 125/publication: *The Heritage of Baldwin Park*

HISTORICAL SOCIETY; HISTORY MUSEUM: Preserves city's history by publishing books and maintaining a museum.

PROGRAMS: Exhibits; Guided Tours; Publication

COLLECTIONS: [1850-1950] Artifacts, books, and newspaper clippings.

HOURS: T-Th 10-12/2-4

ADMISSION: No charge

BANNING

453
Malki Museum
11-795 Field Rd, 92220 [PO Box 578, 92220]; (p) (909) 849-7289; (c) Banning

Private non-profit/ 1965/ Board of Directors/ staff: 2(p); 20(v)/ members: 300

HISTORY MUSEUM: Promotes scholarship, cultural awareness and understanding of Southern CA Indian tribes; collects, displays, and explains the art and artifacts of the Indians of the San Gorgonio Pass.

PROGRAMS: Exhibits; Festivals; Garden Tours; Guided Tours; Lectures

COLLECTIONS: Cahuilla photos, books, archives, arts, and crafts.

HOURS: Yr W-Su 10-4

ADMISSION: Donations accepted

BARSTOW

454
Mojave River Valley Museum
Barstow Rd/Virginia Way, 92312 [PO Box 1282, 92312]; (p) (760) 256-5452; (c) San Bernardino

Private non-profit/ 1965/ staff: 1(p); 5(v)/ members: 400

HISTORICAL SOCIETY; HISTORY MUSEUM: Sponsors field trips in and around Mojave Desert to study plants, animals, fossils, rocks, history, railroads, space, mining.

PROGRAMS: Annual Meeting; Community Outreach; Exhibits; Family Programs; Guided Tours; Lectures; Living History; Research Library/Archives

COLLECTIONS: Fossils, minerals, and displays.

HOURS: Yr Daily 11-4

ADMISSION: No charge

BENICIA

455
Benicia Historical Museum and Cultural Foundation
2024 Camel Rd, 94510 [2060 Camel Rd, 94510]; (p) (707) 745-5435; (f) (707) 745-2135; (c) Solano

Private non-profit/ 1985/ staff: 1(p); 25(v)/ members: 250

HISTORIC SITE; HISTORY MUSEUM

PROGRAMS: Annual Meeting; Community Outreach; Concerts; Exhibits; Facility Rental; Festivals; Guided Tours; Interpretation; Research Library/Archives; School-Based Curriculum

COLLECTIONS: [1847-present] Artifacts pertaining to history of transportation, tools, and institutions, Benicia Arsenal, furniture, and over 4000 photos.

HOURS: Yr

ADMISSION: $2, Student $1, Seniors $1

456
Benicia Historical Society
[PO Box 773, 94510]; (p) (707) 745-1822; (c) Solano

Private non-profit/ 1973/ staff: 10(v)/ members: 86/publication: *Sentinel*

HISTORICAL SOCIETY: Preserves and publicizes the historical heritage of Benicia.

PROGRAMS: Annual Meeting; Exhibits; Guided Tours; Publication

COLLECTIONS: [1849-1990]

457
Fisher-Hanlon House
137 W "G" St, 94510 [115 W "G" St, 94510]; (p) (707) 745-3385; (f) (707) 745-8912

State/ 1864/ CA State Parks/ staff: 1(f)

COLLECTIONS: [1880-1902] Historic house with original artifacts.

HOURS: Yr

BERKELEY

458
Bancroft Library, The
University of California, 94720-6000; (p) (510) 642-3782; (f) (510) 642-7589; bancref@library.berkeley.edu; www://lib.berkeley.edu/BANC/; (c) Alameda

State/ 1860/ staff: 35(f); 35(p); 3(v)/ members: 1700/publication: *Bancroftiana*

RESEARCH CENTER

PROGRAMS: Annual Meeting; Community Outreach; Exhibits; Lectures; Publication; Research Library/Archives

COLLECTIONS: [2500 B.C.E-present] Rare books and manuscripts collections of all periods from ancient Egypt, Europe, and N America.

HOURS: Yr

459
Berkeley Architectural Heritage Association
2318 Durant Ave, 94701 [PO Box 1137, 94701]; (p) (510) 841-2242; (f) (510) 841-7421; baha@dnai.com; www.berkeleyheritage.com; (c) Alameda

Private non-profit/ 1974/ Board of Directors/ staff: 3(f); 1(v)/ members: 1500/publication: *BAHA Newsletter*

HISTORIC PRESERVATION AGENCY; HOUSE MUSEUM; RESEARCH CENTER: Promotes an awareness of the special architectural heritage of the city of Berkeley.

PROGRAMS: Annual Meeting; Concerts; Guided Tours; Lectures; Publication; Research Library/Archives; School-Based Curriculum

COLLECTIONS: [1860-present] Historical files on Berkeley buildings, real estate files, Sanborn atlases, block books, photographs, books, and city directories.

HOURS: Yr W-Th 2-5

460
Berkeley Historical Society
1931 Center St, 94701 [PO Box 1190, 94701-1190]; (p) (510) 848-0181; berkhist@concentric.net; www.ci.berkeley.ca.us; (c) Alameda

Private non-profit/ 1978/ Board of Directors/ staff: 5(v)/ members: 300/publication: *Exactly Opposite the Golden Gate*

HISTORICAL SOCIETY; HISTORY MUSEUM; RESEARCH CENTER: Focuses on City of Berkeley's history and preserves and communicates local history.

PROGRAMS: Annual Meeting; Community Outreach; Concerts; Exhibits; Guided Tours; Interpretation; Lectures; Publication; Research Library/Archives

COLLECTIONS: [1890-present] 10,000 photographs, 35,000 archives folders, 500 objects, and 1500 library volumes.

HOURS: Yr Th-Sa 1-4

461
Judah Magnes Museum
2911 Russell St, 94705; (p) (510) 549-6950; (f) (510) 849-3673; (c) Alameda

Private non-profit/ 1962/ staff: 6(f); 14(p); 13(v)/ members: 2200

ART MUSEUM; HISTORY MUSEUM: Collects, preserves, and exhibits works of Jewish art, culture, and history from around the world.

PROGRAMS: Community Outreach; Elder's Programs; Exhibits; Family Programs; Film/Video; Guided Tours; Interpretation; Lectures; Publication; Research Library/Archives

COLLECTIONS: [18th-20th c] Prints, drawings, paintings, sculpture; objects: Jewish ceremonial, folk, textile, art, collections; rare books and manuscripts; Western Jewish history collection, oral histories.

HOURS: Yr Su-Th 10-4

ADMISSION: No charge

462
Phoebe Hearst Museum of Anthropology
103 Kroeber Hall #3712, 94720; (p) (510) 642-3682; (f) (510) 642-6271; pahma@uclink. berkeley.edu; www.qal.berkeley.edu/~hearst

State/ 1901/ University of California, Berkeley/ staff: 21(f); 23(v)/ members: 300/publication: *Classics in California Anthropology*

ANTHROPOLOGY MUSEUM

PROGRAMS: Exhibits; Lectures; Publication; Research Library/Archives

COLLECTIONS: Includes 625,000 catalogued specimens, 3.8 million individual items on CA, North America, Middle and South America, Oceanic, Ancient Mediterranean, Ancient Egypt, Africa, human skeletal remains, photos negatives, prints, and slides.

HOURS: Yr W-Su 10-4:30

ADMISSION: $2, Student $0.50, Children $0.50, Seniors $1

463
Regional Oral History Office
486 Doe Library, University of California, 94720-6000; (p) (510) 642-7395; (f) (510) 642-7589; roho@library.berkeley.edu; library. berkeley.edu/BANC/ROHO; (c) Alameda

State/ 1954/ Regents of the Univ of California/ staff: 4(f); 28(p)

LIBRARY AND/OR ARCHIVES; RESEARCH CENTER: Conducts and makes available oral history interviews on CA history.

PROGRAMS: Publication

COLLECTIONS: [1900-1999] 1000 volumes of interviews.

HOURS: Yr M-F 9-5

ADMISSION: No charge

464
Western Jewish History Center
2911 Russell St, 94705; (p) (510) 549-6956; (f) (510) 849-3673; wjhc@magnesmuseum.org; (c) Alameda

Private non-profit/ 1967/ staff: 3(p); 6(v)

RESEARCH CENTER: Western Jewish is a department of the Judah Magnes Museum.

PROGRAMS: Research Library/Archives

COLLECTIONS: [1850-present] Personal collections and institutional records from Jewish communities in the western U.S.; correspondence, diaries, photographs, genealogical charts, minutes, by-laws and ephemera; books, oral histories, and unpublished material.

HOURS: Yr W-Th 10-4 and by appt

465
William R. Thorsen Residence
2307 Piedmont Ave, 94704; (p) (510) 929-3713, (510) 540-5158

1909

HOUSE MUSEUM

COLLECTIONS: [1880s-1915] All original furniture is housed in the Huntington Library, Pasadena, CA; 1912 Leroy Hulbert photos of the house; other documents in the Architecture School at UC Berkeley

HOURS: By appt

BIG BEAR CITY

466
Big Bear Valley Historical Society
Big Bear City Park, 92314 [PO Box 513, 92314]; (p) (909) 585-8100; (c) San Bernardino

Private non-profit/ 1971/ Board of Directors/ staff: 40(v)/ members: 200

HISTORICAL SOCIETY; HISTORY MUSEUM: Preserves Bear Valley history.

PROGRAMS: Exhibits; Guided Tours; Lectures; Monthly Meeting

COLLECTIONS: [1860-1930s] Artifacts relating to gold mining, stamp mill, lumbering, cattle ranching, fox farming, native animals, minerals, and motion picture history.

HOURS: May-Mid Oct

BISHOP

467
Bishop Museum and Historical Society
Laws Museum, Silver Canyon Rd, 93515 [PO Box 363, 93515]; (p) (760) 873-5950; www.mam-biz.com/lawsmuseum; (c) Inyo

Private non-profit/ 1966/ staff: 4(f); 12(p); 50(v)/ members: 750/publication: *News Bulletin*

HISTORIC SITE; HISTORICAL SOCIETY; HISTORY MUSEUM: Preserves Laws Railroad Depot 1883 train, agents house, 17 relocated buildings, and turntable for Carson and Colorado Narrow Gauge.

PROGRAMS: Annual Meeting; Exhibits; Facility Rental; Festivals; Publication; Research Library/Archives

COLLECTIONS: [19th-20th c] Print shop, general store, cameras, farm equipment, mining equipment, wagons, Native American artifacts, bottles, dolls, World War I and II artifacts, furniture, and books.

HOURS: Yr Daily 10-4

ADMISSION: $2

BLAIRSDEN

468
Plumas-Eureka State Park
310 Johnsville Rd, 96103; (p) (530) 836-2380; (f) (530) 836-0498; (c) Plumas

State/ 1959/ California State Parks/ staff: 2(f); 4(p); 6(v)/ members: 75

HISTORIC SITE; HISTORY MUSEUM: Focuses on High Sierra hard rock mining and blacksmithing, primitive skiing, and every day mining town life.

PROGRAMS: Exhibits; Facility Rental; Guided Tours; Interpretation; Living History

COLLECTIONS: [1860-1910] Mining and blacksmithing tools, domestic furnishing, skiing artifacts, carpentry tools.

HOURS: Daily

ADMISSION: $2, Children $1

BOLINAS

469
Bolinas Museum
48 Wharf Rd, 94924 [PO Box 450, 94924]; (p) (415) 868-0330; (f) (415) 868-0607; (c) Marin

Private non-profit/ 1983/ staff: 1(f); 3(p); 35(v)/ members: 480

ART MUSEUM; HISTORY MUSEUM: Collects and exhibits the art and history of coastal Marin and raises cultural awareness in the seven communities it serves.

COLLECTIONS: [1870-1970] Photos, tools, Miwok Indian relics, paintings, maps, baskets, clothing, furniture, and other objects of local historical interest.

HOURS: Yr F-Su 12-5

ADMISSION: Donations

BOONVILLE

470
Anderson Valley Historical Museum
[PO Box 676, 95415]; (p) (707) 895-3341; (c) Mendocino

1980/ Anderson Valley Historical Society/ staff: 30(v)/ members: 300

HISTORIC PRESERVATION AGENCY; HISTORIC SITE; HISTORICAL SOCIETY; HISTORY MUSEUM; HOUSE MUSEUM; LIVING HISTORY/OUTDOOR MUSEUM

PROGRAMS: Annual Meeting; Exhibits

COLLECTIONS: [19th-early 20th c]

ADMISSION: No charge

BREA

471
Brea Historical Society
652 S Brea Blvd, 92822 [PO Box 9764, 92822]; (p) (714) 256-2283; breahist@pacbell.net; www.ci.brea.ca/brea/depts/breahis/; (c) Orange

Federal/ 1971/ staff: 10(v)/ members: 233/publication: *Historical Happenings*

HISTORIC PRESERVATION AGENCY; HISTORICAL SOCIETY; HISTORY MUSEUM: Preserve Brea's past.

PROGRAMS: Exhibits; Publication; Research Library/Archives

COLLECTIONS: [1890-1950] Photographs of Brea and Olinda oilfields, early homes, businesses, and public structures; high school yearbooks; biographies and photographs of local pioneers; and The Brea Progress, the local newspaper.

HOURS: Yr Th, Sa 11-2

BRIDGEPORT

472
Bodie State Historic Park
Hwy 395 S of Bridgeport, 93517 [PO Box 515, 93517]; (p) (760) 647-6445; (f) (760) 647-6486; bodie@telis.org; (c) Mano

State/ 1962/ California State Parks/ staff: 5(f); 8(p); 8(v)

HISTORIC SITE: Ghost town site, formerly gold rush and hard rock mining boom town.

PROGRAMS: Interpretation; Research Library/Archives

COLLECTIONS: [1859-1932] Historic structures: residential, commercial, and industrial; domestic furnishings; mining tools and equipment; and commercial artifacts.

HOURS: Yr Summer Daily 8-7; Winter Daily

BURBANK

473
Burbank Historical Society
1015 W Olive Ave, 91506; (p) (818) 841-6333; (c) Los Angeles

Private non-profit/ 1973/ staff: 55(v)/ members: 370/publication: *About Times*

HISTORICAL SOCIETY; HISTORY MUSEUM: Operates the Gordon R. Howard Museum; collects and preserves artifacts and photographs of Burbank.

PROGRAMS: Annual Meeting; Community Outreach; Facility Rental; Guided Tours; Lectures; Publication; Research Library/Archives

COLLECTIONS: [1887-present] Three major build--ings; a restored and furnished 1887 house; photos; Lockheed, Disney, NBC, and Warner Brothers exhibits; antique cars, clothing, dolls, vignettes of an early store, hotel, and dentist's office.

HOURS: Yr Su 1-4

ADMISSION: Donations accepted

BURLINGAME

474
History and Heritage Committee/ American Society of Civil Engineers
708 Carolan Ave, 94010; (p) (650) 579-1944; (f) (650) 579-1960; (c) San Mateo

Private non-profit/ 1905/ staff: 1(f); 1(v)/ members: 6000/publication: *Civil Engineer Landmarks, Northern California 1977*

PROFESSIONAL ORGANIZATION: Maintains records of and celebrates anniversaries of major civil engineering projects such as Golden Gate Bridge, Bay Bridge, Hetch Hetchy, dams.

PROGRAMS: Exhibits; Publication

COLLECTIONS: [1900-1950] Historic ASCE publications and San Francisco section records to 1905, Civil Engineers Landmarks N California Salute to Bridge engineers.

HOURS: Yr

CALABASAS

475
Calabasas Historical Society
[PO Box 8067, 91372]; (p) (818) 347-0470; (c) Los Angeles

Private non-profit/ 1979/ members: 130

HISTORICAL SOCIETY: The Society seeks to promote and preserve the historical interest of Calabasas and surrounding environs and to maintain a local history library.

PROGRAMS: Annual Meeting; Community Outreach; Exhibits; Guided Tours; Lectures; Living History; Research Library/Archives

COLLECTIONS: [20th c] Photographs and oral history.

476
Leonis Adobe Museum
23537 Calabasas Rd, 91302; (p) (818) 222-6511; (f) (818) 222-0862; (c) Los Angeles

Private non-profit/ 1963/ Leonis Adobe Association/ staff: 3(f); 19(p)

HOUSE MUSEUM; LIVING HISTORY/OUTDOOR MUSEUM

PROGRAMS: Guided Tours; Living History; School-Based Curriculum

COLLECTIONS: [1880] 1880s early CA rancho with outbuildings and period furnishings; livestock, sheep, goats, and poultry.

HOURS: Yr W-Su 1-4

ADMISSION: Donations requested

CALISTOGA

477
Sharpsteen Museum
1311 Washington St, 94515 [PO Box 573, 94515]; (p) (707) 942-5911; (f) (707) 942-6325; www.napanet.net/vi/sharpsteen/; (c) Napa

Private non-profit/ 1978/ staff: 97(v)/ members: 450

HISTORY MUSEUM; HOUSE MUSEUM: Specializes in Napa Valley and surrounding area history.

PROGRAMS: Community Outreach; Exhibits; Guided Tours; Lectures

COLLECTIONS: [1850-1917] Scale model of dioramas, restored early cottages, interactive geo-thermal exhibit, original stage coach, re-created barn with implements.

HOURS: Yr Daily 10-4

ADMISSION: Yr Daily 10-4

CAMP ROBERTS

478
Camp Roberts Historical Museum and Museum Annex
Bldgs 114 & 6485, 93451-5000; (p) (805) 238-8418, (805) 238-3732; crmiltmus@tcsn.net; www.militarymuseum.org/CampRobertsMuseum.html; (c) San Luis Obispo/Monterey

State/ 1986/ staff: 4(f); 4(v)

HISTORY MUSEUM: Maintains museum of military related items and items specific to Camp Roberts.

PROGRAMS: Exhibits; Guided Tours; Living History

COLLECTIONS: [WWII-Present] Military uniforms, weapons, tracked and wheeled vehicles, library, and photos.

HOURS: Yr Th, Sa 9-4

ADMISSION: Donations accepted

CAMPBELL

479
Ainsley House
300 Grant St, 95008 [51 N Central Ave, 95008]; (p) (408) 866-2119; (f) (408) 866-2795; web.nvcom.com/chm/; (c) Santa Clara

City/ 1990/ City of Campbell/ staff: 2(f); 1(p); 125(v)/ members: 300/publication: *The Visitor*

HOUSE MUSEUM

PROGRAMS: Community Outreach; Exhibits; Facility Rental; Guided Tours; Interpretation; Lectures; School-Based Curriculum

COLLECTIONS: [20 c] Decorative Arts, furnishings 1925.

HOURS: Mar-Dec Th-Su 12-4

ADMISSION: $6, Student $2.50, Seniors $4; Under 7 free

480
Campbell Historical Museum
51 N Central Ave, 95008; (p) (408) 866-2119; (f) (408) 866-2795; web.nvcom.com/chm/; (c) Santa Clara

City/ 1963/ staff: 2(f); 1(p); 125(v)/ members: 300

HISTORY MUSEUM; HOUSE MUSEUM: Hands-on exhibits, material culture.

PROGRAMS: Community Outreach; Exhibits; Interpretation; Lectures

COLLECTIONS: Native American artifacts, 5,000 artifacts, 3,000 photographs, 4,000 archival reference material.

HOURS: Sept-July Th-Su

CARLSBAD

481
Friends of Carrillo Ranch, Inc.
2622 El Aguila Lane, 92009; (p) (760) 438-1666; ranch@email.com; www.carrillo-ranch.org; (c) San Diego

Private non-profit/ 1990/ staff: 200(v)/ members: 300/publication: *Carrillo Ranch Quarterly*

HISTORICAL SOCIETY: Preserves and restores an old CA style rancho recreated by actor and conservationist Leo Carrillo.

PROGRAMS: Community Outreach; Exhibits; Film/Video; Interpretation; Lectures; Publication; School-Based Curriculum

COLLECTIONS: [1879-1937] Artifacts, memorabilia, photos, documents, films, videos, oral histories.

HOURS: Yr Daily 10-5

ADMISSION: No charge

CARMEL

482
Henry Meade Williams Local History Department, Harrison Memorial Library
[PO Box 800, 93921]; (p) (831) 624-1615; (f) (831) 624-0407; dsallee@hm-lib.org; www.hm-lib.org; (c) Monterey

City/ 1928/ City of Carmel/ staff: 1(f); 2(p); 3(v)

LIBRARY AND/OR ARCHIVES: Focuses on the history of Carmel with information on surrouending areas such as Carmel Valley, Pebble Beach, and Big Sur.

PROGRAMS: Exhibits; Interpretation; Lectures; Research Library/Archives

COLLECTIONS: [20th c] Collected papers, manuscripts, photographs, pamphlets, posters, newspapers with special emphasis on Robinson Jefferson, George Sterling, Edward Wes Strong; focus on local theater, music, and art.

HOURS: Jan-Dec T-F 1-5

ADMISSION: No charge

483
Mission San Carlos Borromeo
3080 Rio Rd, 93923; (p) (831) 624-3600; (f) (831) 624-0658; (c) Monterey

Private non-profit/ 1770/ staff: 15(f)

HISTORIC SITE; HISTORY MUSEUM: Historic church and monument to Father Junipero Serra.

PROGRAMS: Exhibits; Festivals

COLLECTIONS: [Mid 18th c-present] Stone church and period artifacts.

HOURS: Yr Jan 1-May 31 and Sept 1-Dec 31 9:30-4:15; June 1-Aug 31 9:30-7:15

ADMISSION: $2, Children $1; Under 5 free

CARMEL POINT

484
Tor House
26304 Ocean View, [PO Box 2713, Carmel, 93921]; (p) (831) 624-1813, (408) 624-1840 Fri only; (f) (831) 624-3696; www.torhouse.org

CARPINTERIA

485
Carpinteria Valley Museum of History
956 Maple Ave, 93013; (p) (805) 684-3112; (f) (805) 684-4721; (c) Santa Barbara

Private non-profit/ 1959/ staff: 1(f); 85(v)/ members: 500/publication: *The Grapevine*

HISTORY MUSEUM: Native American through American pioneer period exhibits, early schools, agriculture, oil development.

PROGRAMS: Annual Meeting; Community Outreach; Exhibits; Festivals; Guided Tours; Publication; Research Library/Archives; School-Based Curriculum

COLLECTIONS: [Pre history-present] Furnishings, clothing, toys, tools, office, cameras, oil industry, schoolhouse and railroad, subject and photographs, archives, newspapers (local 1921-present) 200 oral histories.

HOURS: Yr T-Sa 1-4 and by appt

ADMISSION: Donations requested

CHEROKEE

486
Cherokee Museum
4226 Cherokee Rd, 95965; (p) (530) 533-1849; (c) Butte

Private non-profit/ 1969/ staff: 5(v)/ members: 25

HISTORY MUSEUM: Preserves items relating to the history of Cherokee and Table Mountain.

PROGRAMS: Exhibits; Festivals; Garden Tours; Guided Tours; Reenactments; Research Library/Archives

COLLECTIONS: [1849-1895] Photos, items, documents, artifacts.

HOURS: Yr by appt Su 11-2

ADMISSION: Donations requested

CHESTER

487
Chester County Historical Society Museum
107 McAliley St, 29706 [PO Box 811, 29706]; (p) (803) 385-2330; (c) Chester

Private non-profit/ 1971/ members: 211

HISTORY MUSEUM: Displays, interprets, and preserves artifacts on the history of Chester and Chester County.

PROGRAMS: Annual Meeting; Exhibits; Guided Tours

COLLECTIONS: [1750-present] Indian artifacts, rifles, and guns dating from 1850, genealogical materials, War Between the States artifacts, military medals, farm collections, 1800s clothing, Coca-Cola memorabilia.

HOURS: Yr W 11-3

ADMISSION: No charge

CHICO

488
Bidwell Mansion State Historic Park
525 The Esplanade, 95926; (p) (530) 895-6144; (f) (530) 895-6699; chiefmik@norcal. parks.state.ca.us; www.norcal.parks.state.ca. us/bidwellman.htm; (c) Butte

State/ 1964/ State Parks/ staff: 4(f); 8(p); 6(v)/ members: 380/publication: *Association Store*

ART MUSEUM; GARDEN; HISTORIC SITE; HISTORY MUSEUM; HOUSE MUSEUM; LIVING HISTORY/OUTDOOR MUSEUM; RESEARCH CENTER: Fosters preservation, restoration, and interpretation of the Bidwell home and the contributions of the Bidwells.

PROGRAMS: Annual Meeting; Exhibits; Guided Tours; Interpretation; Lectures; Living History; Publication; Reenactments; Research Library/Archives; School-Based Curriculum; Theatre

COLLECTIONS: [1865-1918] US, CA, and local history: 8000 museum artifacts, 1000 textiles, 150 paintings, 2500 photographs, 2500 library archives, 500 Native American artifacts, 1000 furniture wood artifacts, and local newspapers from 1898 to 1918.

HOURS: Yr M-F 12-5, Sa-Su 10-5, School programs M-F 10-12

ADMISSION: $3, Children $1.50; Under 6 free

489
Chico Museum Association
141 Salem St, 95928; (p) (530) 891-4336; (f) (530) 891-4336; (c) Butte

Private non-profit/ 1986/ staff: 2(f); 30(v)/ members: 300/publication: *Museum Notes*

HISTORY MUSEUM: Preserves, interprets, and researches the history and culture of Chico, Butte, and northern CA.

PROGRAMS: Annual Meeting; Community Outreach; Exhibits; Facility Rental; Family Programs; Guided Tours; Interpretation; Lectures; Publication; Research Library/Archives

COLLECTIONS: [1860-present] Artifacts and archives housed in a 1904 Carnegie Library; Chinese Taoist Temple.

HOURS: Yr W-Su 12-4

ADMISSION: Donations requested

490
Janet Turner Print Collection and Gallery
CSU, Chico, 95929 [400 W 1st St, 95929-0820]; (p) (530) 898-4476; (f) (530) 898-4082; csvullivan@exchange.csuchico.edu; www.csuchico.edu/hfa; (c) Butte

State/ 1981/ CSU-Chico/ staff: 4(p); 5(v)/ members: 40

ART MUSEUM: Educates in art and the fine art print through thematic exhibitions.

PROGRAMS: Community Outreach; Exhibits; Interpretation; Lectures; Research Library/ Archives; School-Based Curriculum

COLLECTIONS: [1400-present] Fine art prints; fine art printmaking throughout the centuries.

HOURS: Aug-May M-F 11-4 and by appt

ADMISSION: No charge

491
Museum of Anthropology
301 Langdon Hall, California State Univ, 95929 [California State University, Chico, 95929-0400]; (p) (530) 898-5397; (f) (530) 898-6143; anthromuseum@oavax.csuchico. edu/anth/museum; www.csuchico.edu/anth/ museum; (c) Butte

Joint/ 1970/ State; Trustees of CA State Univ/ staff: 3(p); 1(v)/ members: 40

HISTORIC PRESERVATION AGENCY; HISTORY MUSEUM: Showcases student-created exhibits, provides practical experience in museum operation, educational programming and services.

PROGRAMS: Community Outreach; Exhibits; Guided Tours; Interpretation; Lectures; Research Library/Archives

COLLECTIONS: [1900s] Ethnographic collection from historic and contemporary Africa, Alaska, the Pacific as well as CA; household objects.

HOURS: Sept-May T-Sa 11-3

ADMISSION: Donations accepted

492
Stansbury Home Preservation Association
307 W 5th St, 95928; (p) (530) 895-3848; (c) Butte

City/ 1976/ staff: 25(v)/ members: 150/publication: *The House at 5th and Salem*

GARDEN; HISTORIC PRESERVATION AGENCY; HISTORIC SITE; HISTORICAL SOCIETY; HISTORY MUSEUM; HOUSE MUSEUM; RESEARCH CENTER: Preserves and protects the Stansbury House Museum and educates on the 1880s West Coast Victorian era.

PROGRAMS: Annual Meeting; Community Outreach; Concerts; Elder's Programs; Exhibits; Facility Rental; Film/Video; Garden Tours; Guided Tours; Interpretation; Lectures; Publication; Research Library/Archives; School-Based Curriculum

COLLECTIONS: [1883-1974] 1883 Victorian (Italianate) two story house.

HOURS: Yr Sa-Su 1-4

ADMISSION: $2, Student $1

CHULA VISTA

493
Chula Vista Nature Center
1000 Gunpowder Point Dr, 91910; (p) (619) 409-5900; (f) (619) 409-5910; (c) San Diego

Joint/ 1987/ City; Private non-profit/ staff: 6(f); 3(p); 100(v)/ members: 278/publication: *Bayfront By-line*

NATURAL HISTORY MUSEUM: Living wetlands museum located within the Sweetwater Marsh National Wildlife Refuge.

PROGRAMS: Community Outreach; Elder's Programs; Exhibits; Facility Rental; Family Programs; Festivals; Garden Tours; Guided Tours; Interpretation; Lectures; Publication; School-Based Curriculum

COLLECTIONS: [Pre Spanish-present] Native plant, bird, fish, reptile, and invertebrates; jelly fish, Gyotaku art.

HOURS: Yr Summer Daily 10-5; School year T-Su

CITRUS HEIGHTS

494
Root Cellar - Sacramento Genealogical Society
1020 O St (in the CA State Archives), 95611 [PO Box 265, 95611-0265]; (p) (916) 481-4930; SAMIHUD@aol.com; www.rootcellar.com/~carsgs/rootcellar.html; (c) Sacramento

Private non-profit/ 1978/ Board of Directors/ staff: 30(p)/ members: 220/publication: *Root Cellar Preserves*

GENEALOGICAL SOCIETY: Provides education in genealogy.

PROGRAMS: Lectures; Publication; Research Library/Archives

COLLECTIONS: [Colonial U.S.-present, 1600 Europe-present] Genealogical books and publication from Europe and North America, and Revolutionary and Civil War books.

HOURS: Yr M-F 9:30-4

ADMISSION: No charge

CITY OF INDUSTRY

495
John Rowland House
16021 E Gale Ave, 91745 [PO Box 522, La Puente, 91747]; (p) (626) 369-7220, (626) 336-2382

1855/ staff: 6(f)

COLLECTIONS: [1850-1900] Furnishing, buggy, saddles, Indian baskets, toys, school items from East Coast.

HOURS: Seasonal

496
Workman and Temple Family Homestead Museum
15415 E Don Julian Rd, 91745; (p) (626) 968-8492; (f) (626) 968-2048; info@homesteadmuseum.org; www.homesteadmuseum.org; (c) Los Angeles

City/ 1981/ staff: 9(f); 66(v)

HISTORY MUSEUM: Documents southern California history from 1830-1930; Sites includes the Workman House (1842-1870), La Casa Nueva (1920), and a mid-19th century cemetery.

PROGRAMS: Community Outreach; Concerts; Exhibits; Facility Rental; Family Programs; Festivals; Film/Video; Guided Tours; Interpretation; Lectures; Living History; Publication; Research Library/Archives; School-Based Curriculum

COLLECTIONS: [1830s-1930s] Artifacts and memorabilia related to domestic life, architecture, interior design, home economics, clothing, history of San Gabriel Valley, the Workman and Temple families.

HOURS: Yr W-Su 1-4

CLAREMONT

497
Claremont Heritage, Inc.
590 W Bonita Ave, 91711 [PO Box 742, 91711]; (p) (909) 621-0848; (f) (909) 621-9995; (c) Los Angeles

Private non-profit/ 1979/ Board of Directors/ staff: 2(p); 150(v)/ members: 450/publication: *Heritage News*

HISTORIC PRESERVATION AGENCY; HISTORICAL SOCIETY

PROGRAMS: Annual Meeting; Community Outreach; Family Programs; Guided Tours; Interpretation; Lectures; Publication; School-Based Curriculum

COLLECTIONS: [20th c] Records of buildings and items for school programs

HOURS: Off hours M-F 9-12

COLOMA

498
Marshall Gold Discovery State Histioric Park
310 Back St, 95613 [PO Box 265, 95613]; (p) (530) 622-3470; (f) (530) 622-3472; (c) El Dorado

State/ 1948/ staff: 7(f); 12(p); 50(v)/ members: 200

STATE PARK: Site of James Marshall's discovery of gold at Sutter's Mill; replica of Sutter's Mill, Marshall's Monument, historic gold rush building museum.

PROGRAMS: Exhibits; Film/Video; Guided Tours; Interpretation; Lectures; Living History

COLLECTIONS: [1848-1900]

HOURS: Yr

COLUMBIA

499
Columbia State Historic Park
22708 Broadway, 95310; (p) (209) 532-0150; (f) (209) 532-5064; calavaras@gadsusa; www.sierra.parks.state.ca.us; (c) Tuolumne

State/ 1945/ staff: 6(f); 3(p); 90(v)

HISTORIC SITE; LIVING HISTORY/OUTDOOR MUSEUM: Restored Gold Rush town, mid 19th century buildings.

PROGRAMS: Guided Tours; Interpretation; Living History; Reenactments; School-Based Curriculum

COLLECTIONS: [1850-1900] Textiles, clothing, furniture, archives, photos of CA Gold Rush and Columbia.

HOURS: Yr Daily 9-4:30

ADMISSION: No

COLUSA

500
Colusa County Free Library
738 Market St, 95932; (p) (530) 458-7671; (f) (530) 458-7358; (c) Colusa

County/ staff: 5(f); 8(p); 15(v)

Provides local genealogy collection including local and regional history items.

INTERPRETATION: Community/State History; Genealogy

PROGRAMS: Exhibits; Family Programs

COLLECTIONS: [1850-present]

HOURS: Yr M, W 10-5, T, Th 10-8

ADMISSION: No charge

CONCORD

501
Concord Historical Society
1601 Sutter St, Ste E & F, 94522 [PO Box 404, 94522]; (p) (925) 827-3380; www.conhistsoc.org; (c) Contra Costa

Private non-profit/ 1971/ Board of Directors/ staff: 10(v)/ members: 299

HISTORICAL SOCIETY; HISTORY MUSEUM; RESEARCH CENTER

INTERPRETATION: Archaeology; Architecture; Aviation; Community/State History; Conservation of Artifacts; Dolls/Toys; Education; Genealogy; Historic Preservation; Literature; Medicine; Military; Native American Studies; Oral History; Photography; Pioneer; Railroading

PROGRAMS: Annual Meeting; Community Outreach; Exhibits; Film/Video; Guided Tours; Lectures; Research Library/Archives

COLLECTIONS: [1800s-present] Books, papers, documents, newspapers, yearbooks, letters, photographs.

HOURS: Yr T 1-4

CORONA

502
Corona Public Library-Heritage Room
650 S Main St, 91720; (p) (909) 736-2386; (f) (909) 736-2499; libgrp@ci.corona.ca.us; www.ci.corona.ca.us/library; (c) Riverside

City/ 1980/ staff: 1(f); 2(p); 14(v)/ members: 20/publication: *Corona: the Circle City*

LIBRARY AND/OR ARCHIVES: Collects, organizes, preserves, displays, primary and secondary materials relevant to the history of the City of Corona and surrounding environs.

INTERPRETATION: Agriculture; Community/State History; Genealogy; Historic Preservation; Oral History; Photography

PROGRAMS: Community Outreach; Exhibits; Family Programs; Publication

COLLECTIONS: [1886-present] Rare books on CA and Corona: Photos, maps, memorabilia, books, pamphlets, citrus labels, oral histories, videos, manuscript collections, art works and microforms.

HOURS: Yr M T 5-9, W Th Sa 1-5

ADMISSION: No charge

COSTA MESA

503
Costa Mesa Historical Society
1870 Anaheim Ave, 92628 [PO Box 1764, 92628]; (p) (949) 631-5918; cmhistory@lanset.com; www.lanset.com/cmhistory; (c) Orange

Private non-profit/ 1966/ Dave Gardner, Pres/ staff: 15(v)/ members: 1000

HISTORICAL SOCIETY; HISTORY MUSEUM; HOUSE MUSEUM: Maintains Diego Sepulveda Adobe, promotes, and preserves the history of Costa Mesa, CA and the Santa Ana Army Air Base.

PROGRAMS: Annual Meeting; Community Outreach; Exhibits; Family Programs; Guided Tours; Research Library/Archives

COLLECTIONS: [20th c] Manuscripts, oral histories, news clippings, photographs, and artifacts.

HOURS: Yr Museum Th-F 10-3, Historic site 12-4 M,W and Sa by appt

ADMISSION: Donations accepted

COULTERVILLE

504
Northern Mariposa County History Center
10301 Hwy 49, 95311; (p) (209) 878-3015; (f) (209) 878-0744; nmchc@inreach.com; (c) Mariposa

Private non-profit/ 1973/ Board of Directors/ staff: 1(f); 1(p); 30(v)/ members: 250/publication: *The Banderita*

HISTORY MUSEUM: Preserves the history of the founding of Coulterville in 1849 to the demise of minign after WWII.

PROGRAMS: Annual Meeting; Exhibits; Festivals; Publication; Research Library/Archives; School-Based Curriculum

COLLECTIONS: [1849-present] Toys, mining equipment, horse drawn vehicles, motor driven vehicles, and documents.

HOURS: Feb-Dec W-Su

CRESCENT CITY

505
Del Norte County Historical Society
577 H St, 95531; (p) (707) 464-9723; (c) Del Norte

Private non-profit/ 1951/ staff: 30(v)/ members: 300

HISTORICAL SOCIETY; HISTORY MUSEUM; RESEARCH CENTER

COLLECTIONS: [1800s-present] Artifacts; 1st order Fresnel lens from St George Reef Lighthouse - glass and brass.

HOURS: May-Sept M-Sa 10-4

ADMISSION: $2

506
Redwood National and State Parks
1111 Second St, 95531; (p) (707) 464-6101; (f) (707) 464-1813; REDW_Superintendent@nps.gov; WWW.NPS.GOV/REDW; (c) Del Norte

Joint/ 1968/ CA Parks & Recreation; Natl Park Service/ staff: 114(f); 98(v)

NATIONAL PARK: Preserves some of the remaining stands of world's tallest trees, and maintains scenic drive.

PROGRAMS: Community Outreach; Elder's Programs; Exhibits; Facility Rental; Festivals; Film/Video; Guided Tours; Interpretation; Lectures; Research Library/Archives; School-Based Curriculum

COLLECTIONS: Artifacts, archival materials, and natural history specimens related to Coast redwood and its coastal and watershed ecosystems; rehabilitation of previously logged lands; American Indian cultures; and modern history, including the 19th-20th century conservation movement, WW II, logging technologies, transportation, and mining.

HOURS: Yr Daily 9-5

CUPERTINO

507
California History Center and Foundation/De Anza College
21250 Stevens Creek Blvd, 95014; (p) (408) 864-8712; (f) (408) 864-5486; www.calhistory.org; (c) Santa Clara

Joint/ 1969/ Board of Trustees/ staff: 3(f); 8(v)/ members: 300/publication: *The Californian*

HOUSE MUSEUM; RESEARCH CENTER

PROGRAMS: Exhibits; Lectures; Publication; Research Library/Archives

COLLECTIONS: [Prehistory-present] Archival and published materials relating to California and Santa Clara County history, agriculture, the wine industry, labor history, ethnic groups, and public works.

HOURS: Sept-June M-Th 8:30-12/1-4:30

ADMISSION: $3

508
Cupertino Historical Society
10185 N Sterling Blvd, 95014; (p) (408) 973-1495; (f) (408) 973-8049; eworn@juno.com; (c) Santa Clara

Private non-profit/ 1966/ Board of Directories/ staff: 3(p); 40(v)/ members: 230/publication: *The Cornerstone*

HISTORICAL SOCIETY; HISTORY MUSEUM; RESEARCH CENTER: Preserves and interprets history of Cupertino and Silicon Valley area; operates satellite museum at Vallco Shopping Park.

PROGRAMS: Community Outreach; Exhibits; Family Programs; Guided Tours; School-Based Curriculum

COLLECTIONS: [1850-1960] Agricultural tools, textiles, household items, photographs, and documents.

HOURS: W-Sa 10-4

ADMISSION: Donation requested

DAGGETT

509
Augustan Society, Inc., The
36588 Santa Fe, 92327 [PO Box 75, 92327-0075]; (p) (760) 254-9223; (f) (760) 254-1953; ktberrant@earthlink.net; www.augustansociety.org; (c) San Bernardino

Private non-profit/ 1957/ Board of Directors/ staff: 2(f); 15(p)/ members: 500/publication: *The Augustan*

HISTORICAL SOCIETY; HISTORY MUSEUM; RESEARCH CENTER: Maintains historical, genealogical, heraldic, and Native American collections.

PROGRAMS: Exhibits; Guided Tours; Lectures; Publication; Research Library/Archives

COLLECTIONS: Genealogy, heraldry, chivalry, Egyptian and Roman history, Native American, Colonial United States, family histories, maps and atlases, ancient literature, Celtic studies, rock art philately, royal and noble genealogy, shamanism, Mojave Desert, and local history.

HOURS: Yr T-Sa 8-4

ADMISSION: Donations accepted

DANA POINT

510
Dana Point/Capistrano Beach Historical Society
34085 Pacific Coast Hwy, 92629 [PO Box 544, 92629-0544]; (p) (949) 248-8121; (f) (949) 248-5166; www.ocnow.com; (c) Orange

Private non-profit/ 1987/ staff: 23(v)/ members: 250

HISTORIC PRESERVATION AGENCY; HISTORICAL SOCIETY; HISTORY MUSEUM: Collects, preserves, and displays artifacts of the area's past and present.

PROGRAMS: Exhibits; Family Programs; Guided Tours; Lectures; Publication; Research Library/Archives

COLLECTIONS: [1800s-present] Pictures, books, models, and artifacts representing local history.

HOURS: Yr T-Sa 12:30-4

ADMISSION: No charge

DANVILLE

511
Blackhawk Automotive Museum
3750 Blackhawk Plaza Cr, 94506 [3700 Blackhawk Plaza Cr, 94506]; (p) (925) 736-2280; (f) (925) 736-4818; museum@blackhawkauto.org; www.blackhawkauto.org; (c) Contra Costa

Private non-profit/ 1983/ The Behring-Hofmann Educational Institute, Inc./ staff: 16(f); 13(p); 180(v)/ members: 825

AUTOMOBILE MUSEUM: Collects, exhibits, and interprets the art, design and social history of the automobile.

PROGRAMS: Community Outreach; Concerts; Exhibits; Facility Rental; Festivals; Guided Tours; Interpretation; Lectures; Research Library/Archives; School-Based Curriculum

COLLECTIONS: [1890s-present] 120 automobiles, 4000 piece collection of fine and decorative automotive art.

HOURS: Yr W-Su 10-5

ADMISSION: $8, Student $5, Seniors $5

512
Eugene O'Neill National Historic Site
1000 Kuss Road, 95426 [PO Box 280, 94526]; (p) (510) 838-0249; (f) (510) 838-9471

1937/ National Park Service/ staff: 5(f); 11(v)

COLLECTIONS: [1937-1944] Furnishings of Tao House, books, personal items, letters and historic photos

HOURS: Yr

DAVIS

513
Hattie Weber Museum of Davis, The
445 C St, 95616-4102; (p) (530) 758-5637; (f) (530) 758-0204; eppolito@dcn.davis.ca.us; www.dcn.davis.ca.ca/go/hattie; (c) Yolo

City/ 1992/ staff: 20(v)

HISTORY MUSEUM: Archives artifacts, conducts research, and presents exhibits on the history and heritage of the City of Davis and the surrounding area.

PROGRAMS: Exhibits; Facility Rental; Guided Tours; Lectures; Publication; Research Library/Archives

COLLECTIONS: [Prehistory-1950] 500 photos, 100 manuscripts, 150 artifacts, 100 maps, 30 oral histories.

HOURS: Yr W-Sa 10-4

ADMISSION: Donations accepted

514
Pence Gallery
212 D St, 95616; (p) (530) 758-3370; (f) (530) 758-4670; pencegallery@davis.com; (c) Yolo

Joint; Private non-profit/ 1975/ Pence Gallery Association/ staff: 2(p); 55(v)/ members: 300/publication: *Pence Events*

HISTORY MUSEUM: Provides programs in the visual and performing arts designed to enrich the understanding of the art, history, and culture of California.

PROGRAMS: Concerts; Exhibits; Garden Tours; Guided Tours; Lectures

HOURS: Sept-July T-Sa 12-4

ADMISSION: No charge

DEATH VALLEY

515
Death Valley National Park
[PO Box 579, 92328]; (p) (760) 786-2331; (f) (760) 786-3283; www.nps.gov/deva; (c) Inyo and San Bernadino

Federal/ 1933/ National Park Service/ staff: 80(f); 20(p); 20(v)

HISTORIC SITE; HISTORY MUSEUM; HOUSE MUSEUM; LIVING HISTORY/OUTDOOR MUSEUM; RESEARCH CENTER

PROGRAMS: Exhibits; Family Programs; Guided Tours; Interpretation; Lectures; Living History; Publication; Research Library

/Archives; School-Based Curriculum

COLLECTIONS: [1880s-present]

HOURS: Yr Daily

DESERT HOT SPRINGS

516
Cabot's Old Indian Pueblo Museum
67-616 E Desert View, 92240; (p) (760) 329-7610; (f) (760) 251-3523; www.cabotsmuseum.org; (c) Riverside

City/ 1980/ staff: 1(f); 20(v)

ART MUSEUM; GARDEN; HISTORIC SITE; HOUSE MUSEUM; LIVING HISTORY/OUTDOOR MUSEUM

PROGRAMS: Exhibits; Festivals; Garden Tours; Guided Tours

COLLECTIONS: Native American relics, photographs, and artwork.

HOURS: Sa-Su 9-4

DINUBA

517
Alta District Historical Society
289 S K St, 93618 [PO Box 254, 93618]; (p) (559) 591-2144; history@geocities.com; www.geocities.com/rainforest/andes/2210/; (c) Tulare

Private non-profit/ 1962/ Board of Trustees/ staff: 1(p)/ members: 270/publication: *Depot Dispatch*

HISTORICAL SOCIETY; HISTORY MUSEUM: Encourages and promotes the study of the history of the Alta District; collects, classifies, displays, and disseminate historical information, data, facts, and folklore of this area.

PROGRAMS: Annual Meeting; Exhibits; Facility Rental; Festivals; Publication

COLLECTIONS: [1800-present] Agricultural equipment, veteran and local family histories, school and church histories, and irrigation history.

HOURS: Yr T-Th 10-3

DOWNEY

518
Downey Historical Society
12540 Rives Ave, 90241 [PO Box 554, 90241]; (p) (562) 862-2777; (c) Los Angeles

Private non-profit/ 1965/ staff: 8(v)/ members: 211

HISTORICAL SOCIETY; HISTORY MUSEUM; HOUSE MUSEUM; RESEARCH CENTER: Collects, maintains, and exhibits examples of southeast Los Angeles County's past.

PROGRAMS: Annual Meeting; Community Outreach; Exhibits; Family Programs; Guided Tours; Interpretation; Lectures; Publication; Research Library/Archives

COLLECTIONS: [1700s-present] Artifacts, newspapers, maps, photographs, library, original records of Los Angeles County with particular emphasis on Governor Downey, pioneers, education, insurance, law, agriculture, and the aircraft industry.

HOURS: Yr W, Th 9-2, 3rd Sa 10-3

ADMISSION: No charge

DOWNIEVILLE

519
Sierra County Museum of Downieville
Main St, 95936 [PO Box 484, 95936]; (p) (530) 289-3423; (f) (530) 289-1501; arniekej@sccn.net; (c) Sierra

Private non-profit/ 1932/ Board of Trustees/Native Sons and Daughters of the Golden West/ staff: 3(p); 3(v)

HISTORIC SITE; HISTORY MUSEUM: Preserves historic buildings and sites in California and oversees the Downieville Museum.

PROGRAMS: Exhibits; Guided Tours

COLLECTIONS: [1849-1920] Documents, maps, schoolhouse, stamp mill, and other artifacts associated with Gold Rush

DUARTE

520
Duarte Historical Society and Friends of the Library, Inc.
777 Encanto Pkwy, 91009 [PO Box 263, 91009-0263]; (p) (626) 357-9419; (c) Los Angeles

Private non-profit/ 1963/ Board/ staff: 35(v)/ members: 60/publication: *Branding Iron*

HISTORICAL SOCIETY: Operates historical museum and supporting local library.

PROGRAMS: Community Outreach; Exhibits; Publication; Research Library/Archives

COLLECTIONS: [1840-present]

HOURS: Yr W 1-3, Sa

DUBLIN

521
Dublin Historical Preservation Association
[PO Box 2245, 94568]; tmccormclub@aol.com; (c) Alameda

Private non-profit/ 1976/ members: 148/publication: *Dublin Reflections*

HISTORICAL SOCIETY: Dedicated to education and the preservation of historical sites and artifacts of Dublin.

PROGRAMS: Annual Meeting; Exhibits; Festivals; Guided Tours; Lectures; Publication; School-Based Curriculum; Theatre

COLLECTIONS: [19th -20th c] Artifacts demonstrating life in Dublin in the 19th and early 20th century.

DUTCH FLAT

522
Golden Drift Historical Society
32820 Main St, 95714 [PO Box 253, 95714]; (p) (530) 389-2126; www.placer.ca.gov/museum/goldrift.htm; (c) Placer

Joint/ 1985/ County; Private non-profit/ staff: 35(v)/ members: 100

HISTORICAL SOCIETY: Operates a museum for Placer County Heritage of the North Mother Lode.

PROGRAMS: Annual Meeting; Exhibits; Family Programs; Guided Tours; Lectures

COLLECTIONS: [1851-present]

HOURS: May-Sept W,Sa,Su 12-4

ADMISSION: No charge

523
Golden Drift Museum
32820 Main St, 95714 [PO Box 253, 95714]; (p) (530) 389-2126; www.placer.ca.gov/museum; (c) Placer

County/ 1986/ staff: 6(f); 3(p); 25(v)

HISTORY MUSEUM: Chronicles glory days of hydraulic mining, laying of railroad lines, and history of region.

PROGRAMS: Annual Meeting; Community Outreach; Exhibits; Guided Tours; Interpretation; Research Library/Archives

COLLECTIONS: [1850-1880]

HOURS: May-Sept W, Sa, Su 12-4 and appt

ADMISSION: No charge

EARLIMART

524
Colonel Allensworth State Historic Park
4099 Douglas Ave, 93219 [Star Route 2, Box 148, 93219]; (p) (661) 849-3433; (f) (661) 849-3433; (c) Tulare

State/ 1978/ California Department of Parks and Recreation/ staff: 2(f); 1(p); 45(v)

HOUSE MUSEUM: Preserves eight reconstructed houses.

PROGRAMS: Annual Meeting; Community Outreach; Concerts; Exhibits; Guided Tours; Interpretation; Lectures; Living History; Reenactments

COLLECTIONS: [1908-1918] Furniture

EL CAJON

525
El Cajon Historical Society
280 N Magnolia, 92022 [PO Box 1973, 92022]; (p) (619) 444-3800; (c) San Diego

Private non-profit/ 1973/ staff: 30(v)/ members: 375/publication: *Heritage*

HISTORICAL SOCIETY; HOUSE MUSEUM: Preserves and promotes the history of El Cajon, including preservation of historic structures, artifacts, newspapers.

PROGRAMS: Annual Meeting; Exhibits; Guided Tours; Publication; Research Library/Archives

COLLECTIONS: [1870-1900] Furnishes a middle class 1900 home; kerosene heater, lighting fixtures, and wood/coal cooking range.

HOURS: Sept-July Th 12:30-3:30, Sa 12:30-3:30

ADMISSION: No charge

EL DORADO HILLS

526
California Foundry History Institute/Museum of California Foundry History
1011 St. Andrews Dr, Ste 1, 95762; (p) (916) 933-3062; (f) (916) 933-3072; cfhi@foundryccma.org; www.foundryccma.org/CFJI.html

Private non-profit/ 1997/ Board of Directors/ staff: 1(f); 4(p)

HISTORY MUSEUM; LIBRARY AND/OR ARCHIVES: Collects, exhibits, and preserves historical records and artifacts pertaining to the history of the foundry industry in CA.

PROGRAMS: Exhibits; Interpretation; Publication; Research Library/Archives; School-Based Curriculum

COLLECTIONS: [19th-20th c] Artifacts, photos, documents, letters, corporate histories, oral histories, ephemera.

HOURS: By appt

ADMISSION: No charge

EL TORO

527
Saddleback Area Historical Society
10950 S Valley View Ave, 92630 [PO Box 156, 92630]; (p) (562) 941-5059; (c) Orange

Joint/ 1974/ County, Private non-profit/ staff: 5(f); 7(p); 20(v)/ members: 195

HISTORIC SITE; HISTORICAL SOCIETY; HISTORY MUSEUM: Focuses on history of the Saddleback Valley, from the mountain to lands between Irvine and San Juan Capistrano.

PROGRAMS: Exhibits; Facility Rental; Family Programs; Lectures; Publication; School-Based Curriculum

COLLECTIONS: Photos, books, documents covering local history during the Native American, Spanish, Mexican rancho, and American rural period.

HOURS: W-Su 9-5

ADMISSION: No charge

ENCINITAS

528
San Dieguito Heritage Museum
561 S Vulcan Ave, 92023 [PO Box 230851, Encinitas, 92023]; (p) (760) 632-9711; (c) San Diego

Private non-profit/ 1988/ staff: 1(p); 45(v)/ members: 1200

HISTORY MUSEUM; LIVING HISTORY/OUTDOOR MUSEUM: Preserves and displays the multicultural heritage of the San Dieguito area.

PROGRAMS: Annual Meeting; Community Outreach; Exhibits; Festivals; Film/Video; Guided Tours; Lectures; Living History; School-Based Curriculum

COLLECTIONS: [1000 BC-Present] American Indian, Mexican, and white artifacts illustrating the history of the area.

HOURS: Yr Daily 12-4

ADMISSION: Donations accepted

ESCONDIDO

529
Escondido Historical Society and Heritage Walk Museum
321 N Broadway, 92033 [PO Box 263, 92033]; (p) (760) 743-8207; (f) (760) 743-8267; (c) San Diego

Private non-profit/ 1956/ Escondito Historical Society/ staff: 2(f); 1(p); 60(v)/ members: 300

HISTORICAL SOCIETY; HISTORY MUSEUM; HOUSE MUSEUM: Collects, preserves, and interprets Escondido's history; operates a museum, provides access to our archives, historical architecture survey and photo collection.

PROGRAMS: Annual Meeting; Community Outreach; Exhibits; Family Programs; Festivals; Guided Tours; Interpretation; Lectures; Publication; Research Library/Archives; School-Based Curriculum

COLLECTIONS: [1888-present] Residential, agricultural, business, transportation, and cultural materials; includes photographs, print mediums, oral histories, artifacts, textiles, tools, household items and memorabilia.

HOURS: Yr Th-Sa 1-4

ADMISSION: $3, Children $1

EUREKA

530
Clarke Memorial Museum
240 E St, 95501; (p) (707) 443-1947; (c) Homboldt

Private non-profit/ 1960/ staff: 2(f); 1(p); 6(v)/ members: 250

HISTORY MUSEUM

PROGRAMS: Annual Meeting; Community Outreach; Exhibits; Guided Tours; Interpretation; Lectures

COLLECTIONS: [1800-present] Significant collection of area Native American basketry and regalia; a large collection of local 19th century Euro-American apparel, weapons, and related artifacts.

HOURS: Feb-Dec T-Sa

531
Fort Humboldt State Historic Park
3431 Fort Ave, 95503; (p) (707) 445-6567; (f) (707) 441-5737; www.cal-parks.ca.gov; (c) Humboldt

State/ 1955/ State Parks/ staff: 2(f); 2(p); 2(v)

HISTORIC SITE; LIVING HISTORY/OUTDOOR MUSEUM

PROGRAMS: Exhibits; Festivals; Guided Tours; Interpretation; Reenactments

COLLECTIONS: [1850-1950] Historic fort, hospital, Native American artifacts, historical garden, materials and logging equipment, steam powered locomotives and "Steam Donkeys."

HOURS: Daily 9-5

ADMISSION: No charge

FAIRFIELD

532
Solano County Genealogical Society
Library in Old Town Hall, 620 E Main St, 94533 [POBox 2494, 94533]; (p) (707) 446-6869; nmorebeck@jps.net; www.scgsinc.org; (c) Solano

Private non-profit/ 1981/ Board of Directors/ staff: 15(v)/ members: 175/publication: *Root Digger*

GENEALOGICAL SOCIETY

PROGRAMS: Publication

COLLECTIONS: Solano county records, national and international material.

HOURS: M 10-2, 3rd Sa

ADMISSION: Donations accepted

FALL RIVER MILLS

533
Fort Crook Museum /Historical Society
Fort Crook Ave, 96028 [PO Box 417, 96028]; (p) (530) 336-5110; (c) Shasta

Private non-profit/ 1934/ staff: 1(f); 20(v)/ members: 100

HISTORIC PRESERVATION AGENCY; HISTORICAL SOCIETY; HISTORY MUSEUM: Collects and displays items owned and used by local pioneers.

PROGRAMS: Community Outreach; Guided Tours; Research Library/Archives

COLLECTIONS: [1930s-present] Replica of octagon barn; machinery barn, WPA jail house, Pittville one-room school, pony shed, pioneer cabin, period James building.

HOURS: May 1-Oct 31 T-Su 12-4

ADMISSION:

FALLBROOK

534
Fallbrook Historical Society
260 Rocky Crest Rd, 92088 [PO Box 1375, 92088]; (p) (760) 723-4125; Ly000@aol.com; sd.znet.com/~schester/fallbrook/historicals; (c) San Diego

Joint; Private non-profit/ 1978/ staff: 12(v)/ members: 200

HISTORICAL SOCIETY; HISTORY MUSEUM; HOUSE MUSEUM: Operates history museum, house, and mineral museum.

PROGRAMS: Annual Meeting; Community Outreach; Exhibits; Facility Rental; Guided Tours; Interpretation; Publication; Research Library/Archives

COLLECTIONS: [1700-1950] Indian, Spanish, Mexican, and homestead period artifacts, businesses (railroads), groves, fruit production, microfilm; early newspapers, census copies, homestead papers, business, private papers, photographs, antiques cars, farm machinery, clothing.

HOURS: Yr Th and one Su per month 1-5

ADMISSION: No charge

FERNDALE

535
Ferndale Museum, Inc.
Shaw & 3rd St, 95536 [Box 431, 95536]; (p) (707) 786-4466; (f) (707) 786-4466; (c) Humboldt

Private non-profit/ 1976/ staff: 2(p); 85(v)/ members: 340

HOUSE MUSEUM: Fosters an appreciation and understanding of the culture and heritage of Ferndale and the Eel River.

PROGRAMS: Annual Meeting; Guided Tours; Research Library/Archives

COLLECTIONS: [1860-1940] Local photos, textiles, Victoriana.

HOURS: Feb-Dec Winter W-Sa 11-4, Su 1-4; Summer T-Sa 11-4, Su

FILLMORE

536
Fillmore Historical Museum
350 Main St, 93016 [PO Box 314, 93016]; (p) (805) 524-0948; (f) (805) 524-0516; (c) Ventura

Private non-profit/ 1971/ staff: 1(p); 12(v)/ members: 200

HISTORICAL SOCIETY; HISTORY MUSEUM: Protects and preserves local history of Fillmore, and surrounding areas with emphasis on citrus oil and railroad.

PROGRAMS: Annual Meeting; Community Outreach; Exhibits; Facility Rental; Family Programs; Festivals; Guided Tours; Research Library/Archives

COLLECTIONS: [1900-present] Citrus oil, railroad, first families.

HOURS: Yr M-F 9-12

ADMISSION: No charge

FOLSOM

537
Folsom Historical Society
823 Sutter St, 95630; (p) (916) 985-2700; (f) (916) 985-7288; (c) Sacramento

Private non-profit/ 1960/ staff: 1(f); 70(v)/ members: 350/publication: *Tailings*

HISTORICAL SOCIETY; HISTORY MUSEUM: Collects, preserves, and makes accessible the heritage of Folsom and its surrounding area; identify and preserve places of historical interest.

PROGRAMS: Exhibits; Guided Tours; Lectures; Publication

COLLECTIONS: [Post 1860s-present] Quilts and vintage clothing; agriculture, gold-rush, the Pony Express, railroading, technology, photos.

HOURS: Yr W-Su 11-4

ADMISSION: $1; Under 12

538
Folsom Power House State Historical Park
Leidersdorf & Riley, 95630 [7806 Folsom-Auburn Rd, 95630]; (p) (916) 988-0205; (f) (916) 988-9062; rlee@parks.ca.gov; www.cal.parks.ca.gov; (c) Sacramento

State/ 1895/ staff: 2(p); 30(v)

HISTORICAL SOCIETY; HISTORY MUSEUM: Maintains Park as an example of early hydroelectric power generation.

PROGRAMS: Exhibits; Guided Tours; School-Based Curriculum

COLLECTIONS: [1895-1955] Original old brick structure with original generators, penstocks, and hydroelectric equipment; examples of first types of generators and equipment used to produce and transport electricity.

HOURS: Yr W-Su 11-4

ADMISSION: No charge

FORESTHILL

539
Foresthill Divide Museum
24601 Harrison St, 95631; (p) (530) 367-3988; www.foresthillhistory.org; (c) Placer

County/ staff: 6(f); 3(p)

HISTORY MUSEUM: Preserves history of Foresthill and Iowa Hill Divide.

PROGRAMS: Exhibits; Interpretation

COLLECTIONS: [1849-1880] Exhibits on mining a reconstructed livery stable/blacksmith shop, and the original Foresthill Jail.

HOURS: May-Oct W,Sa,Su 12-4 and by appt

ADMISSION: No charge

FORT BRAGG

540
Bo-Cah Ama Council
[PO Box 1144, 95437]; (p) (707) 964-2647; (c) Mendocino

Joint/ 1994/ staff: 8(v)/ members: 8

CULTURAL CENTER: Focuses on lives of the Coastal Pomo Indians.

PROGRAMS: Exhibits; Interpretation

541
Guest House Museum
343 N Main St, 95437 [416 N Franklin St, 95437]; (p) (707) 961-2840, (707) 961-2823; (f) (707) 961-2802; cindyvan@mcn.org; www.fortbragg.com; (c) Mendocino

City/ 1984/ staff: 3(p)

HISTORY MUSEUM; HOUSE MUSEUM: Victorian home built in 1892.

PROGRAMS: Exhibits

COLLECTIONS: [Early 1900s] Logging artifacts, photographs, photographs of shipping by sea and rail, miscellaneous household, business artifacts, photographs of 1906 earthquake.

HOURS: Apr-Oct T-Su 10:30-2:30; Dec-Feb F-Su

ADMISSION: $2, Student $1; Under 13 free

FORT JONES

542
Fort Jones Museum
11913 Main St, 96032 [PO Box 428, 96032]; (p) (530) 468-5568; (c) Siskiyou

City/ 1947/ staff: 20(v)

HISTORY MUSEUM: Collects, preserves, and interprets local history.

COLLECTIONS: [1850-1930s] Artifacts, memorabilia, and objects relating to indigenous people, trappers, miners, soldiers, and settlers; basket collection.

HOURS: June-Sept M-F 10-4, Sa 11-3 and by appt

ADMISSION: No charge

FORTUNA

543
Fortuna Depot Museum
3 Park, 95540; (p) (707) 725-7645; (c) Humboldt

City/ 1976/ staff: 1(p); 10(v)

HISTORY MUSEUM: Preserves history and artifacts of Fortuna and Eel River Valley.

PROGRAMS: Exhibits; Guided Tours

COLLECTIONS: Railroad, fishing, logging, barbwire.

HOURS: June-Aug Daily 10-4:30; Sept-May W-Su 12-4:30

ADMISSION: Donations accepted

FOUNTAIN VALLEY

544
Fountain Valley Historical Society
17841 Los Alamos, 92728 [PO Box 8592, 92728-8592]; (p) (714) 968-8149; (f) (714) 962-2239; Hoxsie@aol.com; (c) Orange

Private non-profit/ 1967/ staff: 20(v)/ members: 130

GARDEN; HISTORIC SITE; HISTORICAL SOCIETY; HOUSE MUSEUM: Collects and preserves the history of Fountain Valley.

PROGRAMS: Annual Meeting; Exhibits; Facility Rental

HOURS: Sa, Su 8:30-1:30 and by appt

ADMISSION:

FREMONT

545
Ardenwood Historic Farm
34600 Ardenwood Blvd, 94555; (p) (510) 796-0199; (f) (510) 796-0231; www.ebparks.org; (c) Alameda

County/ 1985/ East Bay Regional Park District/ staff: 11(f); 7(p); 80(v)

HISTORIC SITE: 205 acre site with historic home and buildings, farmfields, orchards, and livestock.

PROGRAMS: Festivals; Guided Tours; Interpretation; School-Based Curriculum

COLLECTIONS: [1850-present]

HOURS: Yr T-Su 10-4

ADMISSION: Varies

546
Mission Peak Heritage Foundation
1269 Peralta Blvd, 94539 [PO Box 3078, 94539]; (p) (510) 795-0891; (c) Alameda

Private non-profit/ 1972/ staff: 65(v)/ members: 65/publication: *Mission Peak Reporter*

HISTORY MUSEUM: Preserves Local History of Tri-city area; operates museum at Shinn House.

PROGRAMS: Annual Meeting; Guided Tours; Living History; Publication

COLLECTIONS: [1876] Photos, furnishings, and household materials of the Shinn Family.

HOURS: Yr 1st W and 3rd Su 1-3

ADMISSION: $4, Children $2

547
Old Mission San Jose and Museum
43300 Mission Blvd, 94539 [PO Box 3159, 94539]; (p) (510) 657-1797; (f) (510) 651-8332; (c) Alameda

Private non-profit/ 1797/ Diocese of Oakland/ staff: 2(f); 25(v)

HISTORIC SITE; HISTORY MUSEUM

PROGRAMS: Concerts; Exhibits; Festivals; Guided Tours; Lectures

COLLECTIONS: [1700s-1830s] Small collection of pre-Mission Ohlone Indian material, Mission period furniture, vestments, religious artifacts, artwork, 1809 adobe church.

HOURS: Yr Daily 10-5

ADMISSION: $2,

548
Washington Township Historical Society
190 Anza St, 94539 [PO Box 3045, 94539]; (p) (510) 656-9632; (c) Alameda

Private non-profit/ 1949/ staff: 5(v)/ members: 65

HISTORIC PRESERVATION AGENCY; HISTORICAL SOCIETY: The society preserves landmarks in the Washington Township area.

PROGRAMS: Annual Meeting; Community Outreach; Exhibits; Guided Tours; Lectures; Research Library/Archives

FRESNO

549
Fresno City and County Historical Society
7160 W Kearney Blvd, 93718 [PO Box 2029, 93718]; (p) (559) 441-0862; (f) (559) 441-1372; frhistsoc@aol.com; www.valleyhistory.org; (c) Fresno

Private non-profit/ 1919/ staff: 5(f); 5(p); 100(v)/ members: 1300/publication: *Fresno: past and Present*

HISTORIC SITE; HISTORICAL SOCIETY; HOUSE MUSEUM; LIVING HISTORY/OUTDOOR MUSEUM: Collects, preserves, and interprets history of central CA; administers the Kearney Mansion Museum.

PROGRAMS: Community Outreach; Exhibits; Family Programs; Guided Tours; Interpretation; Lectures; Living History; Publication; Reenactments; Research Library/Archives; School-Based Curriculum

COLLECTIONS: [1860-present] 1860s artifact collection; textiles, furniture, Native American pieces, agricultural equipment, and architectural remnants. Archives: photographs, manuscripts, newspapers, governmental, and business records, diaries, albums, maps, and ephemera.

HOURS: Feb-Dec F-Su1-4

ADMISSION: $4, Student $2, Children $2, Seniors $3

550
Fresno Metropolitan Museum
1515 Van Ness Ave, 93721-1200; (p) (559) 441-1444; (f) (559) 441-8607; marketing@fresnonet.org; www.fresnonet.org; (c) Fresno

Private non-profit/ 1978/ staff: 25(f); 5(p); 300(v)/ members: 4102

ART MUSEUM; HISTORIC SITE; HISTORY MUSEUM: Dedicated to furthering the educational opportunities available in central CA in the areas of art, history, and science.

PROGRAMS: Community Outreach; Concerts; Elder's Programs; Exhibits; Facility Rental; Family Programs; Festivals; Film/Video; Guided Tours; Lectures; School-Based Curriculum

COLLECTIONS: [17th-20th c] Salzer collection of European and American still life and Trompe L'Oeil paintings; Native American Cradleboards; puzzles; Asian art collection, Chinese snuff bottles.

HOURS: Yr T-Su 11-5

ADMISSION: $6, Children $3, Seniors $3

FULLERTON

551
Albert Launer Memorial Local History Room
353 W Commonwealth Ave, 92835; (p) (714) 738-6342; (f) (714) 447-3280; (c) Orange

City/ 1973/ staff: 1(p); 3(v)

LIBRARY AND/OR ARCHIVES: Serves as depository for materials on Fullerton and surrounding cities.

COLLECTIONS: [1880s-present] Books, city directories, scrapbooks, personal narratives written by early residents, manuscripts, program brochures, clippings, maps, speeches, photographs, Fullerton newspapers, videotapes, slides, posters, and memorabilia.

HOURS: Yr M-Th 2-5

552
Heritage Coordinating Council
c/o Fullerton Public Library, 353 W Commonwealth Ave, 92835; (p) (714) 738-6342; (f) (714) 447-3280; (c) Orange

members: 12

ALLIANCE OF HISTORICAL AGENCIES: Preserves Orange County heritage.

553
Heritage House, Fullerton Arboretum
1900 Associated Rd, 92834 [PO Box 6850, 92834-6850]; (p) (714) 278-4792; www.arboretum.fullerton.edu/house/house.asp; (c) Orange

1897/ Fullerton Arboretum/ staff: 9(f); 11(p); 600(v)/ members: 1400

HOUSE MUSEUM: Preserves Heritage House, an 1890 Eastlake-design Victorian doctor's home and office.

PROGRAMS: Community Outreach; Facility Rental; Family Programs; Garden Tours; Guided Tours; Lectures

COLLECTIONS: [Victorian Era] House, furniture (many Eastlake pieces), Clark memorabilia, and a collection of medical artifacts, 1895 pumphouse and windmill. Gardens and orchards.

HOURS: Yr Su

554
University Archives and Special Collection Unit, Pollak Library, CA State Univ, Fullerton
800 N State College Blvd, 92834 [PO Box 4150, 92634]; (p) (714) 278-3444; (f) (714) 278-7497; Sperry@fullerton.edu; www.library.fullerton.edu; (c) Orange

State/ 1967/ Board of Trustees/ staff: 1(f); 1(p)

LIBRARY AND/OR ARCHIVES: Collects rare books, manuscripts, documents, and non-circulating materials.

PROGRAMS: Exhibits; Guided Tours; Research Library/Archives; School-Based Curriculum

COLLECTIONS: [1900s] Rare books and maps, local history, and popular culture.

HOURS: Yr M-T 1-4, W-F 9-12

GARDEN GROVE

555
Garden Grove Historical Society
12174 Euclid Ave, 92842 [PO Box 4297, 92842-4297]; (p) (714) 530-8871; (c) Orange

Private non-profit/ 1966/ staff: 15(v)/ members: 200/publication: *Garden Grove Historical Society Newsletter*

HISTORIC PRESERVATION AGENCY; HISTORIC SITE; HISTORICAL SOCIETY; HOUSE MUSEUM: Preserves local history.

PROGRAMS: Facility Rental; Guided Tours; Publication

COLLECTIONS: [1870-present] Buildings: 1877-1920, Ware-Stanley Ranch House (1891) completely furnished; Garden Grove newspapers from early 1900s, photos and local historical materials.

HOURS: Yr 3rd Su 1:30-4

ADMISSION: Donations requested

GILROY

556
Gilroy Historical Museum
195 Fifth St, 95020; (p) (408) 848-0470; (c) Santa Clara

City/ 1968/ staff: 1(f); 2(p)/publication: *Short History of Gilroy*

HISTORY MUSEUM

PROGRAMS: Guided Tours; Publication

COLLECTIONS: Ohlone Indian materials, newspapers from 1868, city tax records, photographs, church histories, genealogies, farming dishware, tools, office equipment, clothing.

HOURS: Yr M,T,Th,F 10-5, 1st Sa 10-2

ADMISSION: No charge

GLEN ELLEN

557
Jack London State Historic Park
2400 London Ranch Road, 95442; (p) (707) 938-5216; (f) (707) 938-4827; (c) Sonoma

State/ 1960/ staff: 1(f); 6(p); 50(v)/publication: *Jack London Ranch Album*

HISTORIC SITE; HISTORY MUSEUM: Preserves history of famous author Jack London.

PROGRAMS: Exhibits; Guided Tours; Interpretation; Publication

COLLECTIONS: [1916] Artifacts from London's life, travels, and writings, including correspondence, manuscripts; farm implements.

HOURS: Yr Daily Winter 10-5 Summer 10-7

ADMISSION: $3/vehicle

GLENDALE

558
Forest Lawn Museum
1712 S Glendale Ave, 91205; (p) (323) 254-3131; (f) (323) 551-5329; (c) Los Angeles

Private non-profit/ 1951/ staff: 2(f); 2(p)

ART MUSEUM; HISTORY MUSEUM

PROGRAMS: Concerts; Exhibits; Family Programs; Film/Video; Living History

COLLECTIONS: American bronzes, 13th-14th century stained glass, coin collection, gem collection, paintings.

HOURS: Yr Daily 10-5

ADMISSION: Donations requested

559
Glendale Historical Society, The
[PO Box 4173, 91202]; (p) (818) 242-7447; (c) Los Angeles

Private non-profit/ 1980/ staff: 35(v)/ members: 250/publication: *TGHS Quarterly*

HISTORICAL SOCIETY: Advances study of local history, promotes preservation of historic resources, and operates the Doctors' House Museum.

PROGRAMS: Annual Meeting; Community Outreach; Exhibits; Guided Tours; Lectures; Publication

HOURS: Jan-June; Aug-Dec Su 2:00-4 and by appt

GOLETA

560
Goleta Valley Historical Society
304 N Los Carneros Rd, 93117; (p) (805) 964-4407; (f) (805) 681-4407; (c) Santa Barbara

Private non-profit/ 1966/ staff: 3(p); 100(v)/ members: 250/publication: *Goleta Valley*

HISTORICAL SOCIETY; HISTORY MUSEUM; HOUSE MUSEUM: Collects, preserves, and interprets the heritage of the Goleta Valley; operates the 1872 Stow House Museum, the Sexton Museum of Goleta History, and outdoor displays of farm equipment.

PROGRAMS: Annual Meeting; Community Outreach; Concerts; Exhibits; Facility Rental; Family Programs; Garden Tours; Guided Tours; Interpretation; Publication; Research Library/Archives

COLLECTIONS: [1880-1920] Victorian and post-Victorian furnishings and clothing, photographs, historical artifacts and materials: domestic items, farm equipment, maritime.

HOURS: Yr Daily Ground until sunset; House and Museum, Sa-Su 2-4

ADMISSION: Donations requested

561
South Coast Railroad Museum
300 N Los Carneros Rd, 93117; (p) (805) 964-3540; (f) (805) 964-3549; scrm@silcom.com; www.goletadepot.org; (c) Santa Barbara

Private non-profit/ 1982/ Institute for American Research/ staff: 1(f); 3(p); 50(v)/ members: 300

RAILROAD MUSEUM: Dedicated to history and adventure of railroading especially Southern Pacific Railroad, Santa Barbara South Coast.

PROGRAMS: Community Outreach; Exhibits; Facility Rental; Family Programs; Festivals; Film/Video; Guided Tours; Lectures; Research Library/Archives

COLLECTIONS: [1890-1970] Photos, artifacts, and printed materials.

HOURS: Yr

ADMISSION: Donations accepted

GRASS VALLEY

562
Empire Mine State Historic Park
10791 E Empire St, 95945; (p) (530) 273-8522; (f) (530) 273-0602; www.calparks.ca.gov; (c) Nevada

State/ 1850/ California State Parks/ staff: 8(f); 6(p); 170(v)/ members: 100

GARDEN; HISTORIC SITE; HISTORY MUSEUM; HOUSE MUSEUM; LIVING HISTORY/ OUTDOOR MUSEUM: Preserves historic gold mine in original, restored buildings and landscaped grounds.

PROGRAMS: Exhibits; Festivals; Garden Tours; Guided Tours; Interpretation; Living History; School-Based Curriculum

COLLECTIONS: [1850-1956] Artifacts, photos, and documents. Bourn Cottage, original mine yard buildings, deep pit mine diorama, core samples, gold nuggets, stamp mill, and mining equipment.

HOURS: Yr Sept-Apr Daily 10-5; May-Aug 9-6

ADMISSION: $1

HAWTHORNE

563
Historical Society of Centinela Valley
7634 Midfield Ave, 90250 [45513 W 138th St, 90250-6911]; (p) (310) 676-4363, (310) 649-6272; (c) Los Angeles

Private non-profit/ 1965/ staff: 10(p); 40(v)/ members: 400

HISTORIC SITE; HISTORICAL SOCIETY; HISTORY MUSEUM; HOUSE MUSEUM; RESEARCH CENTER: Preserves history of the Centennial Valley and the city of Inglewood.

PROGRAMS: Annual Meeting; Exhibits; Facility Rental; Festivals; Guided Tours; Publication

COLLECTIONS: [Early Indians-20th c] Memorabilia of Daniel Freeman, Adobe builder Machado, Inglewood and schools artifacts adobe on display with furniture.

HOURS: Yr W-Su 2-4

ADMISSION: Donations accepted

HAYWARD

564
Hayward Area Historical Society
22701 Main St, 94541; (p) (510) 581-0223; (f) (510) 581-0217; (c) Alameda

Private non-profit/ 1956/ Board of Directors/ staff: 2(f); 1(p); 65(v)/ members: 1300/publication: *Adobe Trails*

HISTORICAL SOCIETY: Preserves and disseminates knowledge about the history of the township of Eden.

PROGRAMS: Annual Meeting; Community Outreach; Exhibits; Guided Tours; Interpretation; Lectures; Publication; Research Library/Archives

COLLECTIONS: The collection consists of 10,000 objects, 13,000 photographic negatives, 6,000 photos, books, manuscripts, maps, and local records.

HOURS: Yr T-Sa 11-4, Su 1-4

ADMISSION: $1, Children $0.50

565
McConaghy House
18701 Hesperian Blvd, 94541 [22701 Main St, 94541]; (p) (510) 581-0223; (f) (510) 581-0217; (c) Alameda

Private non-profit/ 1984/ Hayward Area Historical Society/ staff: 2(f); 1(p); 40(v)/ members: 1300

HOUSE MUSEUM: Preserves 1886 farmhouse life of late Victorian businessman-farmer and his family.

PROGRAMS: Exhibits; Guided Tours; Interpretation

COLLECTIONS: [Victorian-Edwardian] 500-furnishings, 1,200 ceramics, 350 textiles, 1,250 decorative arts, 100 photos, and archival material.

HOURS: Feb-Dec Th-Su 1-4

ADMISSION: $4, Children $0.50, Seniors $3

HEALDSBURG

566
Healdsburg Museum and Historical Society
221 Matheson St, 95448 [PO Box 952, 95448]; (p) (707) 431-3325; (f) (707) 431-3325; museum@healdsburg.net; (c) Sonoma

City/ 1976/ staff: 1(f); 1(p); 100(v)/ members: 500/publication: *Russian River Recorder*

HISTORICAL SOCIETY; HISTORY MUSEUM: Records the history of the Healdsburg area through collection and preservation of historical materials and actively fosters appreciation of local history through programs, exhibits, activities, and research.

PROGRAMS: Annual Meeting; Community Outreach; Exhibits; Guided Tours; Interpretation; Publication; Research Library/Archives

COLLECTIONS: Artifacts and documents related to northern Sonoma County history; Pomo Indian basketry,19th century weapons, tools, textiles, crafts; extensive archival library including 8,000 photos and various documents.

HOURS: Yr T-Su 11-4

ADMISSION: No charge

567
Tile Heritage Foundation
[PO Box 1850, 95448]; (p) (707) 431-8453; (f) (707) 431-8455; foundation@tileheritage.org; www.tile.org; (c) Sonoma

Private non-profit/ 1987/ Board of Directors/ staff: 2(f); 1(p)/ members: 1100/publication: *Flash Point and Tile Heritage*

HISTORICAL SOCIETY: Promotes an awareness and appreciation of ceramic surfaces in the US.

PROGRAMS: Festivals; Guided Tours; Lectures; Publication; Research Library/Archives

COLLECTIONS: [1850-present] Rare and current books, magazines, bulletins, catalogs, slides, photographs, drawings, blueprints, and old tile company records.

HOURS: By appt only

ADMISSION: No charge

HOOPA

568
Hoopa Tribal Museum
Hoopa Shoping Center, 95546 [PO Box 1348, 95546]; (p) (530) 625-4110; (f) (530) 625-4694; (c) Humboldt

Joint/ 1974/ staff: 2(f); 1(p)

TRIBAL MUSEUM: Preserves Hoopa tribal heritage.

PROGRAMS: Exhibits; Guided Tours

COLLECTIONS: [1800-present] Native American artifacts: baskets, clothing, materials, regalia.

HOURS: Yr

HUNTINGTON BEACH

569
Newland House Museum
19820 Beach Blvd, 92648 [19820 Beach Blvd, 92647]; (p) (714) 962-5777

1897/ staff: 9(f)

COLLECTIONS: [1900-1930] Period furnishings; photo collection

HOURS: Yr

INDEPENDENCE

570
Eastern California Museum
155 N Grant St, 93526 [PO Box 206, 93526]; (p) (760) 878-0364; (f) (760) 872-2712; (c) Inyo

County/ 1928/ Inyo County/ staff: 2(f); 5(p)/ members: 350

HISTORY MUSEUM: Preserves and interprets the natural and cultural history of eastern CA.

PROGRAMS: Annual Meeting; Elder's Programs; Interpretation; Lectures; Research Library/Archives

COLLECTIONS: [1850-present] Oral histories, Paiute and Shoshone basketry, Manzanar Japanese American WW II Interment Camp, 18,000 historic photos, historic farming and mining equipment.

HOURS: Yr W-M

571
Manzanar National Historic Site
661 N Edwards St, 93526 [PO Box 426, 93526]; (p) (760) 878-2932; (f) (760) 878-2949; manz_superintendent@nps.gov; www.nps.gov/manz; (c) Inyo

Federal/ 1992/ National Park Service/ staff: 3(f); 1(p); 18(v)

HISTORIC SITE: Protects and interprets the historical, cultural, and natural resources associated with the relocation of 120,000 individuals of Japanese ancestry during WWII.

PROGRAMS: Annual Meeting; Elder's Programs; Festivals; Guided Tours; Interpretation

COLLECTIONS: [1942-1945]

HOURS: Yr Daily Dawn-Dusk

ADMISSION: No charge

INDIO

572
Coachella Valley Historical Society, Inc.
82616 Miles Ave, 92202 [PO Box 595, 92202]; (p) (760) 342-6651; (c) Riverside

Private non-profit/ 1965/ Board of Trustees/ staff: 100(v)/ members: 584/publication: *Periscope; Coachella Valley, California: Pictorial History*

GARDEN; HISTORIC SITE; HISTORICAL SOCIETY; HISTORY MUSEUM; HOUSE MUSEUM

PROGRAMS: Annual Meeting; Exhibits; Facility Rental; Guided Tours; Interpretation; Publication

COLLECTIONS: Early farm equipment, blacksmith shop.

HOURS: Sep 16-June15

ADMISSION: $2, Children

IRVINE

573
Irvine Historical Society
5 San Joaquin, 92612; (p) (949) 786-4112; (f) (949) 854-7994; www.irvine.awardgroup.com; (c) Orange

Private non-profit/ 1977/ Board of Directors/ staff: 8(v)/ members: 150

GARDEN; HISTORIC PRESERVATION AGENCY; HISTORIC SITE; HISTORICAL SOCIETY; HISTORY MUSEUM; RESEARCH CENTER: Collects and preserves local history; maintains 1877 agricultural ranch.

INTERPRETATION: Agriculture; Archaeology; Community/State History; Conservation of Artifacts; Education; Gardens; Historic Persons;

Historic Preservation; Railroading

PROGRAMS: Exhibits; Guided Tours; Lectures; Publication; Research Library/Archives

COLLECTIONS: [1900-1960] Artifacts from the Irvine Ranch, photos, paintings, salt works, citrus industry, Native American, and Mexican Rancheros.

HOURS: Yr T-Su 1-5 or by appt

ADMISSION: Donations requested

JACKSON

574
Amador County Archives
42 Summit St, 95642 [500 Argonaut Ln, 95642]; (p) (209) 223-6389; (f) (209) 223-6389; archives@amadorarchives.org; www.amadorarchives.org; (c) Amador

County/ 1981/ staff: 1(f); 1(p); 2(v)

HISTORIC PRESERVATION AGENCY; RESEARCH CENTER: Preserves county records from 1854 and acquires and preserves manuscripts and memorabilia of county residents.

PROGRAMS: Community Outreach; Lectures; Research Library/Archives

COLLECTIONS: [1854-present] Photos, manuscript, and document collection of county government and private citizens.

HOURS: Yr T-F 10-12/1-4

575
Amador County Historical Society
42 Summit, 95642 [PO Box 761, 95642]; (p) (209) 223-6389; (f) (209) 223-6389; (c) Amador

Private non-profit/ 1947/ members: 80

HISTORICAL SOCIETY

PROGRAMS: Community Outreach; Guided Tours; Interpretation; Lectures

JAMESTOWN

576
Railtown 1897 State Historic Park
[PO Box 1250, 95327]; (p) (209) 984-3953; (f) (209) 984-4936

Private non-profit/ 1897/ California State Railroad Museum/ staff: 4(f); 2(p); 50(v)

STATE PARK: Maintains 26 acre park, trains, and structures.

PROGRAMS: Community Outreach; Exhibits; Festivals; Guided Tours; Interpretation; Living History

COLLECTIONS: [1897-present] Roundhouse and turntable, working forge and belt-driven machine shop, Hollywood props, depot.

HOURS: Apr-Oct Sa,Su 9:30-4:30

JENNER

577
Fort Ross State Historic Park
19005 Coast Hwy 1, 95450; (p) (707) 847-3286, (707) 847-4777; (f) (707) 847-3601; frinterpamucn.org; (c) Sonoma

State/ 1906/ staff: 6(f); 8(p); 5(v)/ members: 300

HISTORIC SITE; HISTORY MUSEUM; LIV-ING HISTORY/OUTDOOR MUSEUM

PROGRAMS: Exhibits; Festivals; Guided Tours; Interpretation; Lectures; Living History; Publication; Research Library/Archives; School-Based Curriculum

COLLECTIONS: [16th-20th c] Restored fort, artifacts, and memorabilia from California Indian, Russian, and Ranch era.

HOURS: Yr Daily 10-4:30

ADMISSION: $2/car, Seniors $1/car

JULIAN

578
Julian Historical Society
[PO Box 513, 92036]; (p) (760) 765-0436; off@abac.com; (c) San Diego

Private non-profit/ 1963/ staff: 20(v)/publication: The History of Julian; The Julian Jail

HISTORIC PRESERVATION AGENCY; HISTORIC SITE; HISTORY MUSEUM; LIBRARY AND/OR ARCHIVES: Collects, preserves, and restores history related structures and materials.

PROGRAMS: Annual Meeting; Community Outreach; Elder's Programs; Exhibits; Family Programs; Guided Tours; Interpretation; Lectures; Living History; Publication; Research Library/Archives

COLLECTIONS: [1869-1913] Memorabilia.

579
Julian Pioneer Museum
2811 Washington St, 92036 [PO Box 511, 92036]; (p) (760) 765-0227; (c) San Diego

Private non-profit/ 1952/ Julian Women's Club/ staff: 1(f); 1(p)

HISTORIC SITE; HISTORY MUSEUM: Collects and preservesmemorabilia of Julian Township and environs in original 1876 wood and stone building.

PROGRAMS: Exhibits

COLLECTIONS: [1869-1913] Clothing, kitchen equipment, children's toys, dolls, photographs, musical equipment, mining equipment, buggy, and tools.

HOURS: Apr-Nov T-Su

KERNVILLE

580
Kern Valley Museum
49 Big Blue Rd, 93238 [PO Box 651, 93238]; (p) (760) 376-6683; (c) Kern

Private non-profit/ 1967/ Kern River Valley Historical Society/ staff: 150(p); 150(v)/ members: 850/publication: The Saddlebags

HISTORICAL SOCIETY; HISTORY MUSEUM: Promotes local history.

PROGRAMS: Community Outreach; Exhibits; Festivals; Film/Video; Guided Tours; Lectures; Publication; Reenactments; School-Based Curriculum

COLLECTIONS: [Prehistory-1930s] Milling and mining, gold mining methods, farming and ranching, local Indians, area movies, histories of pioneer families, restored miner's cabin.

HOURS: Yr Th-Su 10-4

ADMISSION: No charge

KING CITY

581
Monterey County Agricultural and Rural Life Museum
1160 Broadway, 93930 [PO Box 644, 93930]; (p) (831) 385-8020; (c) Monterey

Joint/ 1981/ County; Private non-profit/ staff: 3(p); 30(v)/ members: 85/publication: Antique Advocat

HISTORY MUSEUM; HOUSE MUSEUM; LIVING HISTORY/OUTDOOR MUSEUM: Agricultural museum interpreting heritage of Salinas Valley.

PROGRAMS: Community Outreach; Exhibits; Facility Rental; Family Programs; Festivals; Guided Tours; Interpretation; Lectures; Publication; Research Library/Archives; School-Based Curriculum

COLLECTIONS: [1860-1940] Schoolhouse, depot, farmhouse, working blacksmith, irrigation exhibit building, farm equipment.

HOURS: Yr Daily 10-4

LA CANADA

582
Lanterman Historical Museum Foundation
4420 Encinas Dr, 91011; (p) (818) 790-1421; (f) (818) 790-1421; www.lacanadaonline.com; (c) Los Angeles

Joint/ 1989/ City; Private non-profit/ staff: 2(p); 70(v)/ members: 256

HISTORICAL SOCIETY; HOUSE MUSEUM: Operates Lanterman historic house museum; local history archives; period gardens.

PROGRAMS: Community Outreach; Exhibits; Family Programs; Guided Tours; Lectures; Research Library/Archives; School-Based Curriculum

COLLECTIONS: [1914-1949] Furnishings and decorative arts; family papers; local history archives; photographs; Frank Lanterman political papers; sheet music.

HOURS: Sept-July T-TH and the 1st and 3rd Su 10-12 groups, 1-4 General Public

ADMISSION: $3, Student $1; Under 12 free

LA HABRA

583
La Habra Old Settler's Historical Society
600 Linden Lane, 90631; (p) (562) 697-1271; (c) Orange

Private non-profit/ staff: 20(v)/ members: 200/publication: Old Settlers

HISTORICAL SOCIETY; HISTORY MUSEUM: Preserves early La Habra Valley history..

PROGRAMS: Annual Meeting; Exhibits; Guided Tours; Interpretation

COLLECTIONS: [1890s-1940s]

HOURS: Yr Daily

ADMISSION: $3

LA JOLLA

584

James S. Copley Library, The
1134 Kline St, 92038 [PO Box 1530, 92038];
(p) (619) 484-0957; (f) (619) 454-5740;
carol.beales@copleypress.com; (c) San
Diego

Private non-profit/ 1966/ Copley Newspapers/
staff: 3(f)

LIBRARY AND/OR ARCHIVES: Maintains library and research facility.

PROGRAMS: Guided Tours; Lectures

COLLECTIONS: [1600-1700s] Rare books,
pamphlets, letters, documents, and manuscripts; artifacts and paintings; first printing of
the Declaration of Independence; American
Revolutionary War, the Southwest, presidential correspondence, limited edition books.

HOURS: Yr M-F 10-12/1-3

585

La Jolla Historical Society
7846 Eads Ave, 92038 [PO Box 2085,
92038]; (p) (619) 459-5335; (f) (619) 459-
0226; (c) San Diego

Private non-profit/ 1963/ staff: 2(p); 70(v)/
members: 800

HISTORICAL SOCIETY: Collects and preserves artifacts, memorabilia, sites, and structures pertaining to La Jolla.

PROGRAMS: Garden Tours

COLLECTIONS: [1890-2000] Collection of
local history:10,000 Photos, documents,

LA MESA

586

La Mesa Historical Society
8369 University Ave, 91941 [PO Box 882,
91941]; (p) (619) 466-0197; (c) San Diego

Private non-profit/ 1975/ Board of Directors/
staff: 40(v)/ members: 270

HISTORIC SITE; HISTORICAL SOCIETY;
HISTORY MUSEUM; HOUSE MUSEUM; LIV-
ING HISTORY/OUTDOOR MUSEUM: Col-
lects, preserves, and interprets history of La
Mesa area and operates 1908 Reverend
Henry A McKinney House.

PROGRAMS: Annual Meeting; Exhibits; Guided Tours; Interpretation; Lectures; Publication;
Research Library/Archives

COLLECTIONS: [1870-present] Photos,
maps, newspapers, "La Mesa Scout" 1916-
1985, oral interviews, artifacts, books,
brochures, manuscripts, and documents.

HOURS: Yr Sa 12-3 or by appt

ADMISSION: Free

LAFAYETTE

587

Museum of Vintage Fashion, Inc.
1712 Chapparal Ln, 94549-1712; (p) (925)
944-1896, (925) 938-3810; (c) Contra Costa

Private non-profit/ 1978/ Museum of Vintage
Fashion Board/ staff: 3(f); 3(p); 64(v)

GARDEN; HISTORY MUSEUM; RESEARCH
CENTER: Collect and preserve authentic gar-

ments and accessories.

PROGRAMS: Community Outreach; Elder's
Programs; Exhibits; Facility Rental; Family Pro-
grams; Film/Video; Garden Tours; Guided
Tours; Interpretation; Lectures; Publication;
Research Library/Archives; School-Based
Curriculum

COLLECTIONS: [1736-present] Vintage garments, 50 years of Vogue Magazines.

HOURS: By appt

LAGUNA HILLS

588

Leisure World Historical Society
Aragon, 92654 [PO Box 2220, 92654]; (p)
(949) 206-0150; (c) Orange

Private non-profit/ staff: 1(p); 20(v)/ members:
600/publication: *In the Past*

HISTORICAL SOCIETY: Documents history of
Leisure World.

PROGRAMS: Annual Meeting; Exhibits; Festivals; Film/Video; Guided Tours; Lectures; Publication; Research Library/Archives

COLLECTIONS: [1964-present]

HOURS: Yr M-F 9-4

ADMISSION: No charge

LAKE FOREST

589

Heritage Hill Historical Park
25151 Serrano Rd, 92630; (p) (949) 855-
2028; (f) (949) 855-6321; (c) Orange

County/ 1982/ County of Orange/Harbors,
Beaches, and Parks/Historical Facilities/ staff:
7(f); 75(v)/ members: 75

GARDEN; HISTORIC SITE; HISTORICAL SO-
CIETY; HISTORY MUSEUM; HOUSE MUSE-
UM; LIVING HISTORY/OUTDOOR MUSEUM

PROGRAMS: Elder's Programs; Exhibits; Facility Rental; Family Programs; Festivals; Guided Tours; Interpretation; Living History; Research Library/Archives; School-Based
Curriculum

COLLECTIONS: [1860-1908] Historical structures that contain period furnishings, Serrano
Adobe 1863, St. George's Episcopal Mission
1891, Bennett Ranch House 1908, El Toro
Grammar School 1890.

HOURS: Yr W-Su

LAKEPORT

590

Lake County Museum
255 N Forbes St, 95451; (p) (707) 263-4555;
(f) (707) 263-4555; (c) Lake

County/ 1936/ staff: 1(f); 6(p); 70(v)/ members:
600

GENEALOGICAL SOCIETY; HISTORIC SITE;
HISTORY MUSEUM; RESEARCH CENTER

PROGRAMS: Community Outreach; Exhibits;
Facility Rental; Family Programs; Festivals;
Guided Tours; Lectures; Living History; Reen-
actments; Research Library/Archives

COLLECTIONS: [1850-present] Pioneer and
Native American materials; Genealogical;

Lake County records, 1877 Schoolhouse, Indian baskets, milling slabs, arrowheads, mortars
and pestles.

HOURS: Yr W-Sa 11-4

ADMISSION: $2, Children $1

LAKESIDE

591

Lakeside Historical Society
9906 Maine Ave, 92040; (p) (619) 561-1886;
(c) San Diego

Private non-profit/ 1972/ Lakeside Historical
Society Membership/ staff: 40(v)/ members:
560

HISTORICAL SOCIETY; HISTORY MUSEUM;
HOUSE MUSEUM; LIVING HISTORY/OUT-
DOOR MUSEUM; RESEARCH CENTER

PROGRAMS: Annual Meeting; Community
Outreach; Elder's Programs; Exhibits; Facility
Rental; Guided Tours; Lectures; Publication

COLLECTIONS: [1880-present] Archives;
photos, collection of individual, family, business, club, church and local histories; artifacts
including clothing, jewelry, books, furniture,
farm implements, and tools.

HOURS: Yr T-Sa 10-2

ADMISSION: No charge

LANCASTER

592

Antelope Valley Indian Museum
15701 E Ave M, 93534 [Mojave Desert State
Parks, 43779 15th St West, 93534]; (p) (661)
946-3055; (c) Los Angeles

State/ 1928/ CA State Dept. of Parks and Rec/
staff: 1(f); 3(p); 100(v)/ members: 256

ANTHROPOLOGY MUSEUM; HISTORIC
SITE; HOUSE MUSEUM: Anthropological collections representing American Indian groups
(both prehistoric and ethnographic) from the
Southwest, CA, and Great Basin culture regions.

PROGRAMS: Annual Meeting; Community
Outreach; Exhibits; Festivals; Guided Tours; In-
terpretation; Lectures; Research
Library/Archives; School-Based Curriculum

COLLECTIONS: [11,000 B.C.- contemporary]
American Indian: Southwest, CA, and Great
Basin culture regions, some materials from
Northwest, Plains, eastern, and southeastern
US. Alaskan, African, and Latin American arti-
facts.

HOURS: Mid Sept-Mid June T-Th 10-12 guided tours, Sa-Su 11-4 general public

ADMISSION: $1, Children $1.50; Under 16
free

LEMON GROVE

593

Lemon Grove Historical Society, Inc.
7715 Church St, 91946 [PO Box 624, 91946];
(p) (619) 462-6494; (f) (619) 462-8266;
ofield@mail.sdsu.edu; (c) San Diego

Private non-profit/ 1979/ Exec Board/ staff:
18(v)/ members: 180

HISTORICAL SOCIETY: Dedicated to researching, preserving, and exhibiting the heritage of Lemon Grove.

PROGRAMS: Annual Meeting; Community Outreach; Exhibits; Guided Tours; Lectures; Publication; Reenactments; Research Library/Archives; School-Based Curriculum

COLLECTIONS: [1868-present] Bound newspapers, photographs, artifacts, books, paintings, furnishings, oral history tapes, genealogical records, diaries, letters, agricultural records, period clothing, and maps.

HOURS: Sept-July F-Sa 10-3; and by appt

ADMISSION: Donations accepted

LIVERMORE

594
Ravenswood Historic Site
2647 Arroyo Road, 94550 [71 Trevarno Road, 94550]; (p) (510) 373-5708, (510) 443-0238; (f) (510) 447-2754

City/ 1885/ Livermore Area Recreation and Park District/ staff: 12(v)

COLLECTIONS: [1890s] Furniture collection

HOURS: Yr

595
Ravenswood Progress League
2647 Arroyo Rd, 94550 [PMB 128, 1141 Catalina Dr, 94550]; (p) (925) 443-0238; (f) (925) 449-1159; maryalice_f@msn.com; www.larpd.dst.ca.us; (c) Alameda

Joint/ 1996/ Livermore Area Recreation and Park District

HOUSE MUSEUM: Acquires furnishings for the Cottage House Museum; furthers restoration of Ravenswood Historic Site; and supports public tours, historical programs, and community and cultural special events at Ravenswood.

PROGRAMS: Annual Meeting; Festivals; Garden Tours; Guided Tours; Publication

COLLECTIONS: [1885-1900] Late Victorian furnishings in house museum; small display of 1890s winemaking artifacts; antique and reproduction carriages.

HOURS: Yr 2nd Su of the month 11-4:30

ADMISSION: No charge

LODI

596
San Joaquin County Historical Society and Museum
11793 N Micke Grove Rd, 95240 [PO Box 30, 95240-0030]; (p) (209) 331-2055; (f) (209) 331-2057; info@sanjoaquinhistory.org; www.sanjoaquinhistory.org; (c) San Joaquin

County/ 1966/ San Joaquin County Historical Society/ staff: 5(f); 3(p); 120(v)/ members: 2000/publication: *Historian, News and Notes*

GARDEN; HISTORICAL SOCIETY; HISTORY MUSEUM; LIVING HISTORY/OUTDOOR MUSEUM: Collects, preserves, and interprets local San Joaquin history; county's evolution of agricultural growth, social, cultural and economic heritage.

PROGRAMS: Annual Meeting; Community Outreach; Concerts; Exhibits; Family Pro-

grams; Festivals; Film/Video; Garden Tours; Guided Tours; Interpretation; Lectures; Living History; Publication; Research Library/Archives; School-Based Curriculum

COLLECTIONS: [1850-1950] Agricultural history, San Joaquin County history, pioneers, archives, foot and hand powered tools, photographs, county historic buildings, and furnishings.

HOURS: Yr W-Su 1-4:45

ADMISSION: $2, Children $1, Seniors $1

LOMPOC

597
La Purisima Mission State Historic Park
2295 Purisima Rd, 93436; (p) (805) 733-3713; (f) (805) 733-2497; lapurmis@lapurisima.sbceo.k12.ca.us; (c) Santa Barbara

State/ 1941/ staff: 6(f); 4(p); 72(v)/ members: 148

HISTORIC SITE; HOUSE MUSEUM: Preserves and interprets the California mission period.

PROGRAMS: Community Outreach; Guided Tours; Interpretation; Living History

COLLECTIONS: [1787-1834] Room furnishings. These furnishings are all reproductions. The remaining objects in the collections are archeological artifacts found during the mission's reconstruction; documents from the reconstruction by the CCC.

HOURS: Yr Daily 9-5

ADMISSION: $2/vehcile

598
Lompoc Valley Historical Society, Inc. and Museum
207 N L St, 93438 [PO Box 88, 93438]; (p) (805) 735-4626; (c) Santa Barbara

Private non-profit/ 1964/ staff: 36(v)/ members: 675/publication: *Lompoc Legacy*

GENEALOGICAL SOCIETY; HISTORICAL SOCIETY; HISTORY MUSEUM; HOUSE MUSEUM; RESEARCH CENTER: Maintains Fabing-McKay-Spanne House

PROGRAMS: Community Outreach; Exhibits; Family Programs; Guided Tours; Publication; Research Library/Archives

COLLECTIONS: [1800-1950s] Victorian home, library, Lompoc family genealogies 1874-1940, family and town photos, shipwreck memorabilia, periodicals, books, blacksmith, carpenter's tools, buggies, farm equipment, exhibits, medical, kitchen, washhouse, Victorian children's items.

HOURS: 8:30-11

ADMISSION: No charge

LONG BEACH

599
California Folklore Society
[PO Box 3599, 90803]; (p) (562) 433-6855; ribbis@compuserve.com; (c) Los Angeles

Private non-profit/ 1941/ staff: 1(p); 8(v)/ members: 685/publication: *Western Folklore*

HISTORICAL SOCIETY: Studies folklore and

disseminates information on regional, national, and international folklore.

PROGRAMS: Annual Meeting; Publication

600
Historical Society of Long Beach
210 E Ocean Blvd, 90801 [PO Box 1869, 90801]; (p) (562) 495-1210; (f) (652) 495-1281; HSLB@thegrid.net; (c) Los Angeles

Private non-profit/ 1962/ Board of Directors/ staff: 2(f); 1(p); 35(v)/ members: 475

HISTORICAL SOCIETY: Promotes, develops, exhibits, and preserves local history.

PROGRAMS: Exhibits; Family Programs; Interpretation; Research Library/Archives; School-Based Curriculum

COLLECTIONS: [1880-1970] 11,000 photos, 16,000 negatives, 1,300 postcards 70 scrapbooks, society directories, maps, books, blueprints, artifacts, oral histories, films, and videos.

HOURS: Yr

601
Long Beach Heritage
[PO Box 92521, 90809-2521]; (p) (562) 493-7019; (f) (562) 493-7019; (c) Los Angeles

Private non-profit/ 1986/ staff: 1(f)/ members: 500

HISTORIC PRESERVATION AGENCY: Promotes the preserves of the neighborhood, architecture, and cultural heritage of Long Beach.

PROGRAMS: Annual Meeting; Garden Tours; Guided Tours; Lectures

602
Long Beach Public Library
101 Pacific Ave, 90823; (p) (562) 570-7500; www.lbpl.org/webpac-j; (c) Los Angeles

City/ 1896/ staff: 120(f); 20(p)

LIBRARY AND/OR ARCHIVES: Public Library

PROGRAMS: Community Outreach; Concerts; Elder's Programs; Exhibits; Facility Rental; Family Programs; Lectures; Research Library/Archives

COLLECTIONS: Long Beach History Collection.

HOURS: Yr Daily M 10-8, T-Sa 10-5:30, Su 1-5

603
Rancho Los Alamitos Historic Ranch and Gardens
6400 Bixby Hill Rd, 90815; (p) (562) 431-3541; (f) (562) 430-9694; (c) Los Angeles

Private non-profit/ 1984/ Board of Directors/ staff: 10(f); 6(p); 170(v)/ members: 800

HISTORIC SITE: Educates about history and relationship between people and place, from 500 A.D. to the present.

PROGRAMS: Community Outreach; Family Programs; Festivals; Garden Tours; Guided Tours; Interpretation; Lectures; School-Based Curriculum

COLLECTIONS: [1800-1950] Artwork, furnishings, agricultural equipment, heritage plant materials, plaques, garden furniture.

HOURS: Yr W-Su 1:-5

ADMISSION: No charge

604

Rancho Los Cerritos Historic Site
4600 Virginia Rd, 90807; (p) (562) 570-1755; (f) (652) 570-1893; www.ci.long-beach.ca.us/park/ranchlc.ht; (c) Los Angeles

City/ 1955/ staff: 3(f); 6(p); 80(v)/ members: 400

HOUSE MUSEUM: Interpreting Mexican and American CA history.

PROGRAMS: Exhibits; Garden Tours; Guided Tours; Interpretation; Lectures; Living History; Research Library/Archives; School-Based Curriculum

COLLECTIONS: [1844-1942] Adobe ranch house with furnishings emphasizing 1870s; western history research library; rancho archives; costume and textiles 1830-1930s; historic gardens of 1840 and 1930s.

HOURS: Yr

605

RMS Foundation, Inc./The Queen Mary
1126 Queen's Hwy, 90802; (p) (562) 435-3511; (f) (562) 437-4531; queenmry@gte.net; www.queenmary.com; (c) Los Angeles

Joint/ 1993/ City; Private non-profit/ staff: 700(f); 50(v)/ members: 400

ART MUSEUM; HISTORIC SITE; HISTORY MUSEUM

PROGRAMS: Exhibits; Facility Rental; Festivals; Guided Tours

COLLECTIONS: [1930-1960] Retired British ocean liner contains authentic 1930s decorative and industrial arts, architecture and mechanical installations.

HOURS: Yr Daily 10-6

ADMISSION: $15

LOS ALTOS

606

Association of the Los Altos Historical Museum, The
51 San Antonio Rd, 94022; (p) (650) 948-9427; (f) (650) 559-0268; www.losaltoshistory.org; (c) Santa Clara

Joint/ 1977/ City; Private non-profit/ staff: 1(f); 1(p); 100(v)/ members: 325

HISTORY MUSEUM; HOUSE MUSEUM

PROGRAMS: Community Outreach; Exhibits; Guided Tours; Lectures; Research Library/Archives; School-Based Curriculum

COLLECTIONS: [1930-1940]

HOURS: Yr W,Sa,Su 12-4

ADMISSION: $3

607

Historical Commission, City of Los Altos
1 N San Antonio Rd, 94022; (p) (650) 941-0950; (f) (650) 559-0268; madelyn.crawford@ci.los-altos.ca.us; www.losaltoshistory.org; (c) Santa Clara

City/ 1970/ staff: 10(p); 7(v)

HISTORIC PRESERVATION AGENCY: Preserves architectural and historical character of Los Altos.

PROGRAMS: Community Outreach; Guided Tours; Publication

608

Los Altos History House Museum
51 S San Antonio Rd, 94022 [51 S San Antonio Rd, 94022]; (p) (650) 948-9427

1901/ City/ staff: 1(p); 15(v)

COLLECTIONS: [1930s] 3-D objects typical of home & farm of depression; photos, clippings, books, manuscripts, ephemera on the history of Los Altos.

HOURS: Yr

LOS ALTOS HILLS

609

Los Altos Hills Historical Society
27200 Elena Rd, 94022; (c) Santa Clara

Private non-profit/ 1956/ members: 43

HISTORICAL SOCIETY: Collects historical objects, oral histories; marks historical sites.

PROGRAMS: Lectures

COLLECTIONS: Indian artifacts and old farm

LOS ANGELES

610

Amateur Athletic Foundation of Los Angeles
2141 W Adams Blvd, 90018-2040; (p) (323) 730-9600; (f) (323) 730-9637; library@aafla.org; www.aafla.org; (c) Los Angeles

Private non-profit/ 1985/ Board of Directors/ staff: 21(f); 1(p); 50(v)

HISTORY MUSEUM: Awards grants to youth sports organizations, initiates youth sports program, and manages Paul Ziffren Sports Resource Center Library.

PROGRAMS: Community Outreach; Exhibits; Guided Tours; Research Library/Archives

COLLECTIONS: [20th c] 9000 museum artifacts, 2000 original sports-related posters, 35,000 volumes, 90,000 photographs, 6000 video volumes, 400 magazines, and 100 oral histories.

HOURS: Yr M-T, Th-F 10-5, W 10-7:30, Sa

611

Autry Museum of Western Heritage
4700 Western Heritage Way, 90027; (p) (323) 667-2000; (f) (323) 660-5721; rroom@autry-museum.org; www.autry-museum.org/; (c) Los Angeles

Private non-profit/ 1984/ Board of Directors/ staff: 96(f); 4(p); 210(v)/ members: 5500/publication: Spur

HISTORY MUSEUM: Acquires, preserves, and interprets art, artifacts, archival materials, the history of the American West.

PROGRAMS: Annual Meeting; Community Outreach; Concerts; Exhibits; Facility Rental; Festivals; Guided Tours; Interpretation; Lectures; Publication; Research Library/Archives; School-Based Curriculum; Theatre

COLLECTIONS: [Prehistory-present] Material culture and fine arts materials to the present: Western shows, movies, television, and advertising.

HOURS: Yr T-Su 10-5, Th 10-8; 2nd T free

ADMISSION: $7.50, Student $5, Children $3, Seniors $5

612

California African American Museum
600 State Dr, 90037; (p) (213) 744-7432; (f) (213) 744-2050; www.caam.ca.gov; (c) Los Angeles

State/ 1977/ staff: 26(f); 2(p); 80(v)/ members: 300/publication: Museum Notes

ART MUSEUM; HISTORY MUSEUM: Documents the contributions of persons of African descent to world history and culture.

PROGRAMS: Community Outreach; Concerts; Exhibits; Facility Rental; Guided Tours; Interpretation; Lectures; Living History; Publication; Research Library/Archives; Theatre

COLLECTIONS: [19th-20th c] Historical documents, works by African-American artists.

HOURS: Yr T-Su 10-5

613

California Science Center
700 State Dr, 90037; (p) (213) 744-7400; (f) (213) 744-2134; www.casciencectr.org; (c) Los Angeles

Joint/ 1912/ State of California/ staff: 275(f); 150(p); 350(v)

HISTORY MUSEUM: Nurtures interest in science, mathematics, and technology within the science education community.

PROGRAMS: Community Outreach; Exhibits; Facility Rental; Lectures; School-Based Curriculum; Theatre

HOURS: Yr Daily 10-5

614

Chinese Historical Society of Southern California
411 Bernard St, 90012; (p) (323) 222-0856; (f) (323) 222-0856; www.chssc.org; (c) Los Angeles

Private non-profit/ 1975/ members: 363/publication: Gum Saan Journal, Linking Our Lives,

HISTORICAL SOCIETY; HOUSE MUSEUM: Recognizes the contributions of Chinese Americans; promotes cross cultural understanding.

PROGRAMS: Exhibits; Guided Tours; Publication

615

Edmund D. Edelman Hollywood Bowl Museum
2301 N Highland Ave, 90068; (p) (323) 850-2058; (f) (323) 850-2066; museum@laphil.org; www.hollywoodbowl.org; (c) Los Angeles

Private non-profit/ 1984/ Los Angeles Philharmonic Association/ staff: 2(f); 3(p); 35(v)

HISTORY MUSEUM: Preserves Hollywood Bowl history.

COLLECTIONS: [1920-present] Photographs, documents, programs, audio, video, and ephemera relating to Hollywood Bowl.

HOURS: Yr Sept 18-June 30 T-Sa 10-4; July-Sept 17 T-Sa 10-8:30

ADMISSION: No charge

616
El Pueblo de Los Angeles Historical Monument

125 Paseo de la Plaza, 400, 90012; (p) (213) 680-2525; (f) (213) 485-8238; www.cityofla.org/elp/; (c) Los Angeles

City/ 1781/ staff: 40(f); 30(p); 35(v)

HISTORIC PRESERVATION AGENCY; HISTORIC SITE; HOUSE MUSEUM

PROGRAMS: Guided Tours; Lectures; Publication

COLLECTIONS: [1818-1932] Photos slides, archeological artifacts, architectural drawings and blue prints, 19th century furnishings and fire fighting equipment.

HOURS: Yr Daily 10-3

ADMISSION: No charge

617
Historical Society of Southern California

200 E Ave 43, 90031; (p) (323) 222-0546; (f) (323) 222-0771; hssc@idt.net; www.socialhistory.org; (c) Los Angeles

Private non-profit/ 1883/ Board of Directors/ staff: 4(f); 2(p); 24(v)/ members: 850

HISTORICAL SOCIETY: Preserves the history of Southern CA.

PROGRAMS: Community Outreach; Family Programs; Lectures; Publication

618
Japanese American National Museum

369 E First St, 90012; (p) (213) 625-0414; (f) (213) 624-1770; www.janm.org; (c) Los Angeles

Private non-profit/ 1985/ staff: 74(f); 21(p); 350(v)/ members: 26000

ART MUSEUM; HISTORY MUSEUM; RESEARCH CENTER: Documents Japanese American experience as part of America's ethnic and cultural heritage.

PROGRAMS: Community Outreach; Concerts; Exhibits; Facility Rental; Family Programs; Film/Video; Guided Tours; Interpretation; Lectures; Research Library/Archives; School-Based Curriculum

COLLECTIONS: [1868-present] Artifacts, works of art, photographs, oral histories and films; archives, documents; resource center, reference books and periodicals.

HOURS: Yr T-Su 10-5; Th 10-8

ADMISSION: $6, Student $3, Children $3, Seniors $5; Under 5 free

619
Los Angeles Museum of the Holocaust-Martyrs Memorial

6006 Wilshire Blvd, 90036 [5700 Wilshire Blvd, 90036]; (p) (323) 761-8170; (f) (323) 761-8174; (c) Los Angeles

The Jewish Federation/ staff: 2(f)

HISTORY MUSEUM

PROGRAMS: Community Outreach; Concerts; Exhibits; Family Programs; Film/Video; Lectures; Research Library/Archives; School-Based Curriculum

COLLECTIONS: [1933-1948]

HOURS: Yr M, W, Th 10-4, T 10-8, F 10-2, Sa, Su 12-4

ADMISSION: No charge

620
Petersen Automotive Museum

6060 Wilshire Blvd, 90036; (p) (323) 964-6356; www.petersen.org; (c) Los Angeles

Private non-profit/ 1994/ staff: 20(f); 1(p); 80(v)/ members: 1500

AUTOMOBILE MUSEUM

COLLECTIONS: Collects and preserves automobiles history.

HOURS: Yr 10-6

ADMISSION: $7, Children $3, Seniors $5

621
Skirball Cultural Center

2701 N Sepulveda, 90049; (p) (310) 440-4600; (f) (310) 440-4695; www.skirball.com; (c) Los Angeles

Private non-profit/ 1990/ Board of Trustees/ staff: 44(f); 30(p); 300(v)/ members: 6700/publication: Oasis

ART MUSEUM; HISTORY MUSEUM: Promotes ties between American Jewish experience and American democratic values.

PROGRAMS: Community Outreach; Concerts; Elder's Programs; Exhibits; Facility Rental; Family Programs; Festivals; Film/Video; Guided Tours; Interpretation; Lectures; Publication; Research Library/Archives; School-Based Curriculum; Theatre

COLLECTIONS: [4000 years of Jewish history] Fine arts, prints, folk art, archaeological artifacts, ethnographic material.

HOURS: Yr T-Sa 12-5, Su 11-5

ADMISSION: $8, Children $6, Seniors $6; Under 12/Mbrs free

622
Southwest Museum

234 Museum Dr, 90065 [PO Box 41558, 90041-0558]; (p) (323) 221-2164; (f) (323) 224-8228; info@southwestmuseum.org; www.southwestmuseum.org; (c) Los Angeles

Private non-profit/ 1907/ Board of Trustees/ staff: 16(f); 8(p); 150(v)/ members: 2300

LIBRARY AND/OR ARCHIVES; RESEARCH CENTER: Preserves history and culture of Native Americans.

PROGRAMS: Annual Meeting; Community Outreach; Concerts; Exhibits; Facility Rental; Family Programs; Festivals; Film/Video; Garden Tours; Guided Tours; Interpretation; Lectures; Research Library/Archives; School-Based Curriculum

COLLECTIONS: [Prehistory-present]

HOURS: Yr T-Su 10-5

623
Travel Town Museum

5200 Zoo Dr, 90039 [3900 W Chevy Chase, 90039]; (p) (213) 485-5520; (f) (818) 243-0041; Traveltown@rap.lacity.org; www.lacity.org/RAP/grifmet/tt/index.htm; (c) Los Angeles

City/ 1952/ City of Los Angeles, Dept of Recreation and Parks/ staff: 3(f); 20(p); 150(v)/publication: Green Eye Newsletter

HISTORY MUSEUM: Promotes local and regional railroad history.

PROGRAMS: Community Outreach; Exhibits; Facility Rental; Family Programs; Festivals; Film/Video; Guided Tours; Interpretation; Lectures; Publication; Research Library/Archives; School-Based Curriculum

COLLECTIONS: [1880-1940s] Steam, diesel, and electric locomotives, freight and passenger, cars, wagon, trucks, automobiles, railroad documents, and ephemera.

HOURS: Yr Daily 10-4

ADMISSION: No charge

624
UCLA Fowler Museum of Cultural History

308 Charles E Young Dr, 90095 [PO Box 951549, 90095-1549]; (p) (310) 825-9672; (f) (310) 206-7007; www.fmch.ucla.edu; (c) Los Angeles

1963/ staff: 40(f); 37(p); 40(v)/ members: 490

HISTORY MUSEUM

PROGRAMS: Community Outreach; Facility Rental; Family Programs; Lectures; Publication; School-Based Curriculum

COLLECTIONS: [1900s] African, Oceanic, S.E. Asian, North, Middle, and South American art, archaeology, and material culture.

HOURS: Yr W-Su 12-5, Th 12-8

ADMISSION: $5, Student $1, Seniors $3; Under 17/Mbrs free; Th free

625
USC Archaeological Research Collection

School of Religion, 90089-0355; (p) (213) 740-0266; swartz@usc.edu; (c) Los Angeles

Private non-profit/ 1968/ Univ of Southern California/ staff: 1(f); 1(p); 2(v)

ART MUSEUM; RESEARCH CENTER: Preserves research collection focused on archaeology of the Middle East for undergraduates at USC.

PROGRAMS: Guided Tours; Lectures; Research Library/Archives; School-Based Curriculum

COLLECTIONS: [4000BCE-400CE] Material cultures of the Ancient

626
Wells Fargo Bank Museum

333 S Grand Ave, 90071; (p) (213) 253-7166

HISTORY MUSEUM: Museum focusing on the history of Wells Fargo Bank.

PROGRAMS: Exhibits; Guided Tours

COLLECTIONS: [19th-20 c] Concord stagecoach; Wells Fargo banking and express history; gold scales; mining; southern CA history.

LOS GATOS

627
Forbes Mill Regional History Museum and Los Gatos Museum of Art and Natural History

75 Church St & Tait Ave, 95031 [PO Box 1904, 95031]; (p) (408) 395-7375; (f) (408) 395-7386; LGMUSEUMS@aol.com; (c) Santa Clara

Joint; Private non-profit/ 1967/ Los Gatos Museum Association/ staff: 3(p); 50(v)/ members: 250

ART MUSEUM; HISTORIC SITE; HISTORICAL SOCIETY; HISTORY MUSEUM: Maintains collections in historic mountain retreat of Silicon Valley community.

PROGRAMS: Community Outreach; Concerts; Exhibits; Facility Rental; Family Programs; Film/Video; Garden Tours; Guided Tours; Interpretation; Lectures; Publication; Research Library/Archives; School-Based Curriculum

COLLECTIONS: [1700s-present] Memorabilia of Hemingway, Steinbeck, and their contemporaries, artists and intellectuals.

HOURS: Yr W-Su 12-4

ADMISSION: No charge

628
Los Gatos Historic Preservation Committee
101 E Main St, 95031 [PO Box 949, 95031]; (p) (408) 354-6872; (f) (408) 354-7593; (c) Santa Clara

City/ 1976/ staff: 1(p); 5(v)

LOWER LAKE

629
Lower Lake Schoolhouse Museum
16435 Morgan Valley Rd, 95457 [PO Box 1762, 95457]; (p) (707) 995-3565; (f) (707) 995-2618; llmuseum@jps.net; www.lakecounty.com; (c) Lake

Joint/ 1993/ Lower Lake Historical School Preservation Committee/County of Lake/ staff: 2(p); 15(v)/ members: 290/publication: *Lower Lake School-house Bulletin*

HISTORIC PRESERVATION AGENCY; HISTORIC SITE; HISTORY MUSEUM: Preserves 1877 schoolhouse.

PROGRAMS: Annual Meeting; Concerts; Exhibits; Facility Rental; Guided Tours; Publication; Research Library/Archives; Theatre

COLLECTIONS: [Late 18th-early 19th c] Pioneer artifacts.

HOURS: Yr W-Sa 11-4

ADMISSION: No charge/Donations

MADERA

630
Madera County Historical Society
210 Yosemite Ave, 93639 [PO Box 478, 93639]; (p) (559) 673-0291; (f) (559) 674-5114; (c) Madera

Private non-profit/ 1955/ staff: 14(v)/ members: 600

HISTORIC PRESERVATION AGENCY; HISTORICAL SOCIETY: Preserves Madera County history.

PROGRAMS: Annual Meeting; Exhibits; Facility Rental; Family Programs; Guided Tours; Publication; Reenactments

COLLECTIONS: [1800s-present] Clothing, farm equipment, MD equipment.

HOURS: Yr Sa-Su 1-4

ADMISSION: Donations accepted

MALIBU

631
Malibu Lagoon Museum-Adamson House
23200 Pacific Coast Hwy, 90265 [PO Box 291, 90265]; (p) (310) 456-8432; (c) Los Angeles

1982/ Parks and Recreation/ staff: 80(v)/ members: 400/publication: *Ceramic Art of the Malibu Potteries, and others*

GARDEN; HISTORIC SITE; HISTORY MUSEUM; HOUSE MUSEUM: Preserves historic home and gardens of the Adamson Family: Adohr Stock Farm and Chumash Indian site.

PROGRAMS: Annual Meeting; Community Outreach; Exhibits; Facility Rental; Festivals; Garden Tours; Guided Tours; Interpretation; Lectures

COLLECTIONS: [1900-1960] Home shows 1940s in Southern CA, Malibu pottery.

HOURS: W-Sa 11:00-3

ADMISSION: No charge

MARIPOSA

632
California State Mining and Mineral Museum
5005 Fairgrounds Rd, 95338 [PO Box 1192, 95338]; (p) (209) 742-7625; (f) (209) 966-3597; mineralmuseum@sierratel.com; (c) Mariposa

State/ 1882/ Dept of Parks & Recreation/ staff: 4(f); 6(p); 20(v)

HISTORY MUSEUM; STATE PARK: Collects, preserves, and displays the official state mineral collection originally established in 1880 and maintains museum.

PROGRAMS: Community Outreach; Exhibits; Family Programs; Festivals; School-Based Curriculum

COLLECTIONS: [Mid-late 1800s] 13,000 mineral specimens.

HOURS: May-Sept Daily 10-6 ; Oct-Apr W-M 10-4

ADMISSION: $1; Under 17 free

633
Mariposa Museum and History Center
5119 Jessie St, 95338 [PO Box 606, 95338]; (p) (209) 966-2924; (c) Mariposa

Private non-profit/ 1947/ Mariposa Historical Society/ staff: 1(f); 60(v)/ members: 500

HISTORY MUSEUM: Preserves and disseminates Mariposa County.

PROGRAMS: Annual Meeting; Community Outreach; Concerts; Elder's Programs; Exhibits; Guided Tours; Living History; Reenactments; Research Library/Archives; School-Based Curriculum

COLLECTIONS: [1850s] Recreated 1850s street, newspaper office, a sheriff's office, and assay office, saloon, drug store, classroom, wagons and carriages, stamp mill, hand operated printing press, and reconstructed Native American village, bark houses, and sweat lodge.

HOURS: Feb-Dec M-F 10-4:30

ADMISSION: Donations requested

MARKLEEVILLE

634
Alpine County Museum
School St, 96120 [PO Box 517, 96120]; (p) (530) 694-2317; (f) (530) 694-1087; alpinecountymuseum@gbis.com; (c) Alpine

Private non-profit/ 1963/ The Historical Society of Alpine County/ staff: 2(f); 6(v)/ members: 206/publication: *Alpine Heritage*

HISTORIC SITE; HISTORICAL SOCIETY; HISTORY MUSEUM: Preserves Native American, mining, and ranching heritage of Alpine County through preservation of photos, documents, buildings, and objects associated with everyday life.

PROGRAMS: Annual Meeting; Exhibits; Festivals; Interpretation; Lectures; Publication; Research Library/Archives

COLLECTIONS: [1870s-1930s] Washo basketry; photographs of Alpine County's people and environs; photos, documents, and equipment relating to ranching, mining, and commerce; original art by Sierra painter Walt Monroe; and county newspapers.

HOURS: May-Oct Th-M 11-4

ADMISSION: Donations accepted

MARTINEZ

635
John Muir National Historic Site
4202 Alhambra Ave, 94553; (p) (925) 228-8860; (f) (925) 228-8192; jomu_interpretation@nps.gov; www.nps.gov/jomu; (c) Contra Costa

Federal/ 1964/ National Park Service/ staff: 10(f); 2(p); 35(v)

HISTORIC SITE: Preserves John Muir's home.

PROGRAMS: Exhibits; Facility Rental; Family Programs; Film/Video; Guided Tours; Interpretation

COLLECTIONS: [1884-1914] Furnishings, decorative arts, textiles, period clothing, and material, letters, photographs, and artifacts relating to John Muir.

HOURS: Yr W-Su 10-4:30

ADMISSION: $2; Under 17 free

MARYSVILLE

636
Mary Aaron Memorial Museum
704 D St, 95901 [PO Box 1759, 95901]; (p) (530) 743-1004; (c) Yuba

Private non-profit/ 1953/ Mary Aaron Memorial Museum Association, Inc/ staff: 30(v)/ members: 50

HISTORY MUSEUM: Preserves historical heritage of Marysville and surrounding area.

PROGRAMS: Annual Meeting; Community Outreach; Exhibits; Facility Rental; Festivals; Guided Tours; Interpretation; Publication; School-Based Curriculum

COLLECTIONS: [1850-1920]

HOURS: Yr Th-Sa 1-4

ADMISSION: $2; Children $1

MENDOCINO

637
Ford House Museum
735 Main St, 95460 [PO Box 1387, Medoncino, 95460]; (p) (707) 937-5397

638
Mendocino Area Parks Association
735 Main St, 95460 [PO Box 1387, 95460]; (p) (707) 937-5397; (f) (707) 937-3845; mapa@mcn.org; (c) Mendocino

Private non-profit/ 1984/ Board of Directors/ staff: 2(p)/ 50(v)/ members: 400

HISTORIC SITE; HISTORY MUSEUM; HOUSE MUSEUM: Displays cultural and natural history in Ford House museums.

PROGRAMS: Exhibits; Family Programs; Festivals; Film/Video; Interpretation

COLLECTIONS: [1860-1890s] Historical photographs, old logging implements, personal articles of pioneers, Pomo Indian artifacts.

HOURS: Yr Daily

MERCED

639
Merced County Historical Society/Merced County Courthouse Museum
Courthouse Museum, 95340 [21st and N St, 95340]; (p) (209) 723-2401; (f) (209) 723-8029; museum@mercedmuseum.org; www.mercedmuseum.org; (c) Merced

Private non-profit/ 1982/ Merced County Historical Society/ staff: 1(f); 2(p); 80(v)/ members: 700/publication: For the Record

HISTORIC PRESERVATION AGENCY; HISTORIC SITE; HISTORICAL SOCIETY; HISTORY MUSEUM; LIVING HISTORY/OUTDOOR MUSEUM: Preserves local history.

PROGRAMS: Annual Meeting; Community Outreach; Exhibits; Family Programs; Guided Tours; Interpretation; Lectures; Publication; Research Library/Archives; School-Based Curriculum

COLLECTIONS: [Prehistory-present]

HOURS: Yr W-Su 1-4

ADMISSION: No charge

MISSION HILLS

640
Archival Center, Archdiocese of Los Angeles
15151 San Fernando Mission Blvd, 91345; (p) (818) 365-1501; (f) (818) 361-3276; (c) Los Angeles

Private non-profit/ 1962/ Archdiocese of Los Angeles/ staff: 3(f); 1(p); 20(v)/ members: 274/publication: Friends of the Archival Center

GENEALOGICAL SOCIETY; HISTORY MUSEUM; RESEARCH CENTER: Preserves history of Catholic Church in Southern CA.

PROGRAMS: Community Outreach; Exhibits; Facility Rental; Festivals; Guided Tours; Publication; Research Library/Archives

COLLECTIONS: [1840-1949] Sacramental records of mission period, correspondence, and files of Catholic presence in California.

HOURS: Yr Daily 9-4:30

ADMISSION: $4, Children $3, Seniors $3

641
San Fernando Valley Historical Society
10940 Sepulveda, 91346 [PO Box 7039, 91346-7039]; (p) (818) 365-7810; (c) Los Angeles

City/ 1943/ staff: 7(p); 7(v)/ members: 150/publication: The Valley

HISTORIC PRESERVATION AGENCY; HISTORIC SITE; HISTORICAL SOCIETY; HISTORY MUSEUM; RESEARCH CENTER: Collects, preserves, and interprets history of San Fernando Valley and provides tours for individuals and community organizations to view oldest house in Los Angeles.

PROGRAMS: Annual Meeting; Community Outreach; Exhibits; Facility Rental; Family Programs; Festivals; Guided Tours

COLLECTIONS: [1840-1940] Furniture from 1880s, maps, farm equipment, newspapers, clothing, paintings, artifacts from mission and Indian period.

HOURS: Yr

MODESTO

642
McHenry Mansion
906 15th St, 95353 [PO Box 642, 95353]; (p) (209) 577-5367; (f) (209) 491-4313; wmathes@modesto.ca.us; www.thevision.net/mchenry; (c) Stanislaus

City/ 1983/ staff: 2(f); 4(p); 170(v)/ members: 700/publication: About the House

HOUSE MUSEUM: Preserves 1883 High Victorian Italianate style house.

PROGRAMS: Annual Meeting; Exhibits; Facility Rental; Interpretation; Lectures; Publication; School-Based Curriculum

COLLECTIONS: [1870-1906] Furniture, household accessories, art, textiles, toys, clocks, silver hollowware.

HOURS: Yr Su-F 1-4

ADMISSION: No charge

MODJESKA CANYON

643
Arden, The Helena Modjeska Historic House and Gardens
29042 Modjeska Canyon Rd, 92630 [Heritage Hill Historical Park, 25151 Serrano Rd., Lake Forest, 92630]; (p) (949) 855-2028; (f) (949) 855-6321; (c) Orange

County/ 1888/ Harbors, Beaches, and Parks/Historical Facilities/ staff: 1(p); 20(v)

HOUSE MUSEUM: Maintains National Historic landmark and historical structures.

PROGRAMS: Guided Tours; Interpretation; School-Based Curriculum

COLLECTIONS: [1888-1906] Historic structures.

HOURS: By appt

ADMISSION: $5

MONTE SERENO

644
Heritage Preservation Committee/ City of Monte Serno
18041 Saratoga-Los Gatos Rd, 95030; (p) (408) 354-7635; (f) (408) 395-7653; (c) Santa Clara

City/ 1957/ staff: 5(v)

HISTORIC PRESERVATION AGENCY: Preserves heritage and collects oral and written community history.

COLLECTIONS: [1957-present] City records.

MONTEREY

645
Colton Hall Museum
Pacific St between Jefferson and Madison, 93940; (p) (408) 646-3851; (c) Monterey

City/ 1949/ staff: 2(f); 4(p); 24(v)

HISTORIC SITE; HISTORY MUSEUM; HOUSE MUSEUM; RESEARCH CENTER: Preserves and interprets city history and California's first Constitutional Convention.

PROGRAMS: Concerts; Exhibits; Festivals; Guided Tours; Living History; Reenactments; Research Library/Archives; School-Based Curriculum; Theatre

COLLECTIONS: [1850-present] Historic Colton Hall; Old Jail located nearby; artifacts, manuscripts, furnishing, and memorabilia.

HOURS: Yr Summer Daily 10-12 / 1-5; Winter Daily 10-12/1-4

ADMISSION: No charge

646
Cooper-Molera Adobe
525 Polk St, 93940; (p) (831) 649-7109

State/ 1828/ Monterey State Historic Park/ staff: 1(f); 2(p)

COLLECTIONS: [1820s-1850s] Furnishing from Spanish, Mexican and early Anglo periods.

HOURS: Winter 10-4; Summer 10-5

647
Monterey State Historic Park
#20 Custom House Plaza, 93940; (p) (831) 649-7118; (f) (831) 647-6236; ww.mbay.net/~mshp/; (c) Monterey

State/ staff: 12(f); 11(p); 110(v)

GARDEN; HISTORIC SITE; HISTORY MUSEUM; HOUSE MUSEUM; LIVING HISTORY/OUTDOOR MUSEUM: Collects, preserves, and interprets history of CA and Monterey through house museums, history museum, gardens.

PROGRAMS: Community Outreach; Exhibits; Facility Rental; Festivals; Film/Video; Garden Tours; Guided Tours; Interpretation; Lectures; Living History

COLLECTIONS: [1770-Early 20th c] Adobe structures, furnished with antiques.

HOURS: Yr Daily 10-5

ADMISSION: $5

648
Old Monterey Preservation Society
525 Polk St, 93940; (p) (831) 649-7111; (c) Monterey

Joint; State/ 1975/ California Charitable Trust/ staff: 4(p); 200(v)/ members: 150

HISTORIC SITE; HISTORICAL SOCIETY; HISTORY MUSEUM; HOUSE MUSEUM

PROGRAMS: Annual Meeting; Exhibits; Garden Tours; Guided Tours; Interpretation; Living History; Reenactments; School-Based Curriculum

COLLECTIONS: [19th century]

HOURS: Yr Daily

MONTEREY PARK

649
Historical Society of Monterey Park
709 S Orange Ave, 91754 [PO Box 272, 91754]; (p) (626) 307-1265; (c) Los Angeles

City/ 1970/ City of Monterey/ staff: 45(v)/ members: 250

HISTORIC SITE; HISTORICAL SOCIETY; HISTORY MUSEUM

PROGRAMS: Annual Meeting; Community Outreach; Exhibits; Film/Video; Guided Tours; Publication; School-Based Curriculum

COLLECTIONS: CA Mission models, murals, period clothes, tools, furniture, and other artifacts and memorabilia.

HOURS: Yr Sa-Su 2-4

ADMISSION: No charge

MORAGA

650
Moraga History Center
1500 St Mary's Rd, 94556; (p) (925) 377-8734; (f) (925) 376-3034; (c) Contra Costa

Private non-profit/ 1965/ Moraga Historical Society/ staff: 8(v)/ members: 300/publication: *Moraga's Pride-Rancho Laguna de los Palos Colorados*

HISTORICAL SOCIETY: Collects and preserves Spanish/Mexican Rancho history.

PROGRAMS: Annual Meeting; Community Outreach; Exhibits; Film/Video; Lectures; Publication; Research Library/Archives; School-Based Curriculum

COLLECTIONS: [1835-present] Artifacts; 1852 land case, books, oral histories, clippings, documents, letters, parish records, California Mission records, Moraga Rancho history books, Moraga Family tree.

HOURS: Yr M, W,F 1-3

ADMISSION: No charge

MORGAN HILL

651
Morgan Hill Historical Society
17860 Monterey, 95038 [PO Box 1258, 95038]; (p) (408) 782-9171, (408) 799-5755; (c) Santa Clara

Private non-profit/ 1971/ Board of Directors/ staff: 25(v)/ members: 200/publication: *Historically Speaking*

HISTORIC PRESERVATION AGENCY; HISTORIC SITE; HISTORICAL SOCIETY; HISTORY MUSEUM; HOUSE MUSEUM: Collects, conserves, interprets, and exhibits artifacts from history of Morgan Hill, at Morgan Hill Museum and Hiram Morgan Hill House (1884).

PROGRAMS: Annual Meeting; Community Outreach; Exhibits; Facility Rental; Festivals; Publication; Research Library/Archives

COLLECTIONS: [Late 1800-present] Local historic materials and artifacts. Poppy Jasper Rock collection.

HOURS: Museum: call for hours; MH House Sa 10-1

ADMISSION: No charge

MORRO BAY

652
Museum of Natural History, Morro Bay State Park
State Park Rd, 93442; (p) (805) 772-2694; (f) (805) 772-7129; www.mbspmuseum.org; (c) San Luis Obispo

State/ 1962/ California State Parks/ staff: 1(f); 1(p); 60(v)/ members: 1200

LIVING HISTORY/OUTDOOR MUSEUM: Interprets habitats around Moro Bay.

PROGRAMS: Annual Meeting; Community Outreach; Elder's Programs; Exhibits; Family Programs; Film/Video; Guided Tours; Interpretation; Lectures; School-Based Curriculum

COLLECTIONS: [Prehistoric-present] Mounts and study skins, skeletal pieces of local fauna, pressed plants, insects, eggs, and nests, Native American (Chumash)items.

HOURS: Yr Daily 10-5

ADMISSION: $2

MOUNTAIN VIEW

653
Friends of "R" House/Rengstorff House
3070 N Shoreline Blvd, 94043; (p) (650) 903-6073; (f) (650) 903-6099; (c) Santa Clara

City/ 1991/ staff: 20(v)/ members: 80

GARDEN; HOUSE MUSEUM: Preserves Rengstorff House

PROGRAMS: Facility Rental; Guided Tours; Publication

COLLECTIONS: [Victorian Era] Eastlake furniture.

HOURS: Yr Su,T,W 11-5

ADMISSION: No charge

654
Mountain View Historical Association
[PO Box 252, 94042-0252]; (c) Santa Clara

Private non-profit/ 1954/ Governing Board of Elected Office/ members: 278

HISTORICAL SOCIETY: Collects and preserves information and artifacts pertaining to history of Mountain View.

PROGRAMS: Exhibits; Publication; Research Library/Archives

COLLECTIONS: Maps, photos, and artifacts.

HOURS: Feb-May and Nov 1st S

NAPA

655
Napa County Historical Society
1219 First St, 94559; (p) (707) 224-1739; (f) (707) 224-5933; (c) Napa

Private non-profit/ 1948/ staff: 1(f); 2(p); 20(v)/ members: 400

HISTORICAL SOCIETY; HISTORY MUSEUM: Collects and disseminates information on pioneer heritage and history of Napa County.

PROGRAMS: Annual Meeting; Exhibits; Family Programs; Guided Tours; Publication; Research Library/Archives

COLLECTIONS: [1948-present] Indian artifacts, period clothing, books, architectural

NATIONAL CITY

656
National City Historical Society
1615 E 4th St, 91951 [PO Box 1251, 91951]; (p) (619) 477-3451; roseway@aol.com; (c) San Diego

Private non-profit/ 1960/ staff: 1(p); 6(v)/ members: 30/publication: *National*

HISTORICAL SOCIETY; HOUSE MUSEUM: Maintains Granger Music Hall, a Victorian music hall.

PROGRAMS: Concerts; Publication

HOURS: By appt

657
National City Public Library, Local History Room
200 E 12th St, 91950-3399; (p) (619) 336-4350; (f) (619) 336-4368; locoref@sdcoe.k12.ca.us; www.sdcoe.k12.ca.us/ncpl; (c) San Diego

Joint/ 1896/ City; Library Board of Trustees/ staff: 1(p); 3(v)

LIBRARY AND/OR ARCHIVES: Preserves the past and present accomplishments, history and heritage of National City.

PROGRAMS: Community Outreach; Exhibits; Guided Tours; Research Library/Archives

COLLECTIONS: [1868-present] Diaries 1854-1934, letters, newspapers 1882-present, 734 books, maps, photographs, paintings, artifacts, and Kimball family materials.

HOURS: Yr T-Th 2-6

ADMISSION: No charge

NEVADA CITY

658
Malakoff Diggins State Historic Park
23579 N Bloomfield Rd, 95959; (p) (530) 265-2740; (c) Nevada

State/ 1964/ staff: 2(f); 3(p)

HISTORIC SITE; HOUSE MUSEUM; LIVING HISTORY/OUTDOOR MUSEUM: Preserves history of hydraulic mining, town of North Bloomfield, and surrounding area.

PROGRAMS: Exhibits; Interpretation; Living History

COLLECTIONS: [1860-1911] Artifacts with special interest in hydraulic mining.

HOURS: Yr Daily

659
Nevada County Historical Society
214 Main St, 95959 [Box 1300, 95959]; (p) (530) 265-4606, (530) 265-5910; (c) Nevada

Private non-profit/ 1945/ Board of Directors/ staff: 1(p); 50(v)/ members: 600

HISTORICAL SOCIETY; HISTORY MUSEUM: Operates four museums on local cultural and mining history.

PROGRAMS: Annual Meeting; Exhibits; Guided Tours; Interpretation; Lectures; Publication; Research Library/Archives

COLLECTIONS: [1850-1950] Mining exhibit, old films made into videos, Narrow Gage Railroad rolling stock and artifacts, photos, Maidu baskets and other artifacts, Chinese altar and artifacts.

HOURS: Call

ADMISSION: Donations accepted

660
Searls Historical Library
214 Church St, 95959; (p) (530) 265-5910; (c) Nevada

Private non-profit/ 1972/ Nevade County Historical Society/ staff: 1(p); 8(v)/ members: 650

HISTORICAL SOCIETY: Collects, preserves, and interprets history of Nevada County from gold rush days.

COLLECTIONS: 1851-1950

HOURS: Yr 1-4

ADMISSION: No charge

NEWBURY PARK

661
Conejo Valley Historical Society/ Stagecoach Inn Museum Complex
51 S Ventu Park Rd, 91320; (p) (805) 498-9441; (f) (805) 498-6375; Stagecoach@toguide.com; www.toguide.com/stagecoach; (c) Ventura

Private non-profit/ 1964/ staff: 3(p); 150(v)/ members: 350

HISTORIC SITE; HISTORICAL SOCIETY: Preserves early house structures in Connejo Valley; Chumash Native People, early settlers, and Spanish Colonials.

PROGRAMS: Annual Meeting; Community Outreach; Elder's Programs; Exhibits; Facility Rental; Family Programs; Festivals; Garden Tours; Guided Tours; Interpretation; Lectures; Living History; Reenactments; Research Library/Archives; School-Based Curriculum

COLLECTIONS: [8,000 B.C.-1920s] Artifacts from the Chumash, Spanish/Mexican and pioneer eras in the Conejo Valley; archival materials, a library.

HOURS: Yr W-Su 1-4

ADMISSION: $3, Children $1, Seniors $2

NEWHALL

662
William S. Hart Museum
24151 San Fernando Rd, 91321; (p) (661) 254-4584; (f) (661) 254-6499; zstanley@nhm.org; NHM.org; (c) Los Angeles

County/ 1958/ staff: 2(f); 40(v)/ members: 120/publication: *Terra, The Naturalist*

HOUSE MUSEUM: Operates and interprets historical park.

PROGRAMS: Annual Meeting; Community Outreach; Concerts; Elder's Programs; Exhibits; Facility Rental; Family Programs; Festivals; Film/Video; Garden Tours; Guided Tours; Interpretation; Lectures; Living History; Publication; Reenactments; Research Library/Archives

COLLECTIONS: [1900-1950] Hart house museum, Navajo textures, Native American costumes, guns and other weaponry, sculptures, and Western paintings.

HOURS: Yr W-Sa 11-4

NEWPORT BEACH

663
Orange County Museum of Art
850 San Clemente Dr, 92660; (p) (949) 759-1122; (f) (949) 759-5623; ocma@pacbell.net; www.ocma.net; (c) Orange County

Private non-profit/ 1928/ Board of Trustees/ staff: 26(f); 10(p)/ members: 269

ART MUSEUM: Interprets visual arts in Orange County.

PROGRAMS: Community Outreach; Exhibits; Facility Rental; Family Programs; Film/Video; Garden Tours; Guided Tours; Lectures; Publication; Research Library/Archives; School-Based Curriculum

COLLECTIONS: [Mid 19th c-present] Paintings, sculptures, and mixed-media works.

HOURS: Yr T-Su 11-5

ADMISSION: $5, Student $4, Seniors $4; Under 16 free

NICE

664
Robinson Rancheria Band of Pomo Indians
1545 E Hwy 20, 95464 [PO Box 1580, 95464]; (p) (707) 275-0205; (f) (707) 275-0470; rquitiquit@hotmail.com; (c) Lake

1965/ Robinson Rancheria Citizens Business Council/ staff: 200(f); 30(p); 15(v)/ members: 476

TRIBAL MUSEUM: Promotes cultural resources and traditional values.

PROGRAMS: Annual Meeting; Community Outreach; Concerts; Elder's Programs; Exhibits; Facility Rental; Family Programs; Festivals; Film/Video; Garden Tours; Guided Tours; Interpretation; Lectures; Living History; Publication; Research Library/Archives

COLLECTIONS: [Pre-history-present] Tribal members' baskets and cultural artifacts.

NIPOMO

665
Dana Adobe
671 Oak Glenn, 93444-9009 [PO Box 1391, San Luis Obispo, 93406]; (p) (805) 929-2570, (805) 543-0638

1837/ staff: 6(p); 1(v)

COLLECTIONS: [1837-1900] Grease vat

HOURS: Yr

OAKHURST

666
Fresno Flats Historical Park
49777 School Rd, 93644 [PO Box 451, 93644]; (p) (209) 683-6570

staff: 2(p); 30(v)

HISTORIC SITE: Maintains research center and library.

COLLECTIONS: Journals, photos.

HOURS: Yr

OAKLAND

667
African American Museum and Library at Oakland
125 14th St, 94612; (p) (510) 238-7512; (c) Alameda

City/ Oakland Public Library/ staff: 3(f); 2(p); 10(v)/ members: 250/publication: *From the Archives*

HISTORY MUSEUM

PROGRAMS: Annual Meeting; Exhibits; Lectures; Living History; Publication; Reenactments; Research Library/Archives; School-Based Curriculum

COLLECTIONS: [1850-present]

HOURS: Yr

ADMISSION: No charge

668
Alameda County Historical Society
484 Lake Park Ave, PMB 307, 94610; (p) (510) 444-2187; (f) (510) 444-7120; (c) Alameda

Private non-profit/ 1966/ staff: 30(v)/ members: 250

HISTORICAL SOCIETY: Promotes Alameda-county history.

PROGRAMS: Annual Meeting; Guided Tours; Lectures; Publication; Quarterly Meeting

669
California Genealogical Society
1611 Telegraph Ave, Ste 200, 94612-2152; (p) (510) 663-1358; www.calgensoc.org; (c) Alameda

Private non-profit/ 1898/ Board of Directors/ staff: 2(p); 60(v)/ members: 900/publication: *Nugget*

GENEALOGICAL SOCIETY: Aids public in tracing and compiling family histories; gathers and preserves vital records, and provides education and research support.

PROGRAMS: Annual Meeting; Community Outreach; Lectures; Publication; Research Library/Archives

COLLECTIONS: [1700-present] Books, genealogical charts, maps, scrapbooks, and manuscripts about various families.

HOURS: Yr Th-Sa 9-4

ADMISSION: $5

670
California Preservation Foundation
1611 Telegraph Ave, Ste 820, 94612; (p) (510) 763-0972; (f) (510) 763-4724; cpf@slip.net; www.californiapreservation.org; (c) Alameda

Private non-profit/ 1975/ staff: 2(f); 1(p)/ members: 1000

HISTORIC PRESERVATION AGENCY

INTERPRETATION: Historic Preservation

PROGRAMS: Annual Meeting; Publication

671
Camron-Stanford House Preservation Association
1418 Lakeside Dr, 94612; (p) (510) 444-1876, (510) 874-7802; (f) (510) 874-7803; pelican@cshouse.org; (c) Alameda

1971/ staff: 3(p); 50(v)/ members: 100

HISTORIC PRESERVATION AGENCY; HISTORIC SITE; HOUSE MUSEUM: Preserves, and maintains architecture and lifestyle of the Victorian era of Oakland and CA.

PROGRAMS: Annual Meeting; Exhibits; Guided Tours; Interpretation; Research Library/Archives

COLLECTIONS: [1875-present] 1875-1885 Decorative arts, furnished period rooms, Pre-industrial Colonial and CA Indian life.

HOURS: Yr W 11-5, Su 1-5 and by appt

ADMISSION: $4, Student $2, Seniors $2; Under 13 free

672
Dunsmuir House and Gardens Historic Estate
2960 Peralta Oaks Ct, 94605; (p) (510) 615-5555; (f) (510) 562-8294; www.dunsmuir.org; (c) Alameda

Private non-profit/ 1972/ Dunsmuir House and Gardens, Inc/ staff: 5(f); 10(p); 175(v)/ members: 250/publication: *The Dunsmuir Times*

HISTORIC SITE; HOUSE MUSEUM; LIVING HISTORY/OUTDOOR MUSEUM: Manages and preserves historic mansion and farm buildings.

PROGRAMS: Community Outreach; Concerts; Exhibits; Facility Rental; Family Programs; Festivals; Garden Tours; Guided Tours; Interpretation; Lectures; Living History; Publication; School-Based Curriculum

COLLECTIONS: [1899-1920] Furnished Neoclassical Revival Mansion, farm buildings and a historic landscape of unique trees, ponds, and meadows.

HOURS: Feb-Oct T-F 10-4

673
Oakland Museum of California
1000 Oak St, 94607; (p) (510) 238-2200; (f) (510) 238-2258; www.museumca.org; (c) Alameda

Joint/ 1969/ staff: 55(f); 50(p); 1200(v)/ members: 10350/publication: *The Museum of California Magazine*

ART MUSEUM; GARDEN; HISTORY MUSEUM: Promotes CA's environment, history, and art.

PROGRAMS: Community Outreach; Concerts; Elder's Programs; Exhibits; Facility Rental; Family Programs; Film/Video; Guided Tours; Interpretation; Lectures; Living History; Research Library/Archives; School-Based Curriculum

COLLECTIONS: [1800-present] Art, historical

artifacts, ethnographic objects, natural specimens, photos, ephemera, and archival materials.

HOURS: Yr W, Th, Sa 10-5, F 10-9, Su 12-5

ADMISSION: $6, Student $4, Seniors $4

674
Pardee Home Museum
672 11th St, 94607-3651; (p) (510) 444-2187; (f) (510) 444-7120; nic@pacbell.net; www.pardeehome.org; (c) Alameda

Private non-profit/ 1981/ Pardee Home Foundation/ staff: 2(f); 5(v)/ members: 35/publication: *Pardee Home Newsletter*

HISTORIC SITE; HISTORY MUSEUM; HOUSE MUSEUM: Preserves 1868 Italianate Villa and its contents, carriage house, water tower, and gardens (home of two mayors of Oakland, a CA governor, and one collector of ethnographic Victorian in the U. S.)

PROGRAMS: Exhibits; Guided Tours; Interpretation; Publication; Research Library/Archives; Theatre

COLLECTIONS: [1868-1981] Original house furnishings, closets and drawers filled with family's personal possessions, Mrs. Pardee's diverse collections of perhaps 30,000 artifacts from around the world, extensive archival buildings.

HOURS: Yr by appt

ADMISSION: $5; Children 12 and under free

675
Victorian Preservation Center of Oakland
1440 29th Ave, 94618 [5337 College Ave, Ste 145, 94618]; (p) (510) 532-0704; (f) (510) 533-7384; cyqnet.wyo@worldnet.att.net; (c) Alameda

Private non-profit/ 1993/ staff: 1(p); 30(v)/ members: 125/publication: *Victorian Preservation Center News*

HISTORIC SITE; HOUSE MUSEUM; LIVING HISTORY/OUTDOOR MUSEUM: Preserves 1884 Cohen-Brau House; promotes commerce and culture of Bay area in late 19th and 20th centuries.

PROGRAMS: Community Outreach; Exhibits; Guided Tours; Interpretation; Lectures; Living History; Publication; Reenactments; Research Library/Archives

COLLECTIONS: [Late 19th and early 20th c] China, silver, carpets, decorative arts, furniture, wallpapers; paintings; library, personal correspondence, household accounts from 1884.

HOURS: Yr 4th Su or by appt

ADMISSION: $5

676
Western Aerospace Museum
8260 Boeing St, 94614 [PO Box 14264, 94614]; (p) (510) 638-7100; oakairmuseum@juno.com; www.aerospace.org; (c) Alameda

Private non-profit/ 1980/ staff: 2(f); 1(p); 30(v)/ members: 300

HISTORIC SITE; HISTORY MUSEUM; LIVING HISTORY/OUTDOOR MUSEUM; RESEARCH CENTER

PROGRAMS: Annual Meeting; Community Outreach; Exhibits; Facility Rental; Film/Video; Guided Tours; Interpretation; Lectures; Living History; Research Library/Archives; Theatre

COLLECTIONS: [1900-present] Collection consist of aircraft, artifacts, memorabilia.

HOURS: Yr W-Su 10-5

ADMISSION: $4; Under 12 free

677
Western Museum Association
655 Thirteenth St, Ste 301, 94612; (p) (510) 238-9700; (f) (510) 238-9701; director@westmuse.org; www.westmuse.org; (c) Alameda

1936/ staff: 1(f); 1(p)/ members: 900/publication: *Westmuse*

PROFESSIONAL ORGANIZATION: Serves members in museum and related fields; annual conference, quarterly newsletter, and job listing.

PROGRAMS: Annual Meeting; Publication

OCEANSIDE

678
Mission San Luis Rey de Francia
4050 Mission Ave, 92057; (p) (760) 757-3651; (f) (760) 775-4613; wwwsanluisrey.org; (c) San Diego

Private non-profit/ 1798/ Franciscan Friars of California, Inc/ staff: 25(f); 10(p); 25(v)

GARDEN; HISTORIC SITE; HISTORY MUSEUM: Maintains Native American and Spanish Colonial past as well as recent Franciscan history.

PROGRAMS: Exhibits; Facility Rental; Guided Tours

COLLECTIONS: [Spanish Colonial] Objects from Native American, Spanish Colonial, and CA Rancho periods, including Luiseno baskets; Spanish Colonial period arts and tools; decorative arts, paintings, sculptures, books, and photos.

HOURS: Yr Daily 10-4:30

ADMISSION: $4, Family $12, Student $3; Under 8 free

OJAI

679
Ojai Valley Historical Society and Museum
130 W Ojai Ave, 93024 [PO Box 204, 93024]; (p) (805) 640-1390; (f) (805) 640-1342; (c) Ventura

Private non-profit/ 1966/ Board of Directors/ staff: 1(f); 1(p); 60(v)/ members: 450

HISTORIC SITE; HISTORICAL SOCIETY; HISTORY MUSEUM

PROGRAMS: Annual Meeting; Community Outreach; Exhibits; Facility Rental; Family Programs; Guided Tours; Lectures; Research Library/Archives; School-Based Curriculum

COLLECTIONS: [20th c] Historic archives and objects, and local natural history and environmental education exhibits.

HOURS: Yr W-F 1-4,

ONTARIO

680
C.C. Graber Company
315 E 4th St, 91762 [PO Box 511, 91762]; (p) (909) 983-1761; (f) (909) 984-2180; www.graberolives.com; (c) San Bernardino

Private non-profit/ 1894/ Robert D. Garaber and Staff/ staff: 10(f); 100(p)

HISTORIC SITE; HISTORY MUSEUM: Preserves Graber Olive House, a historic canning facility.

PROGRAMS: Exhibits; Facility Rental; Guided Tours

COLLECTIONS: [1894] Early cultivator, antique olive grading machine and olive oil press, trivia of tools, chainless Bicycle and early CA pictures.

HOURS: Yr M-Sa 9-5:30, Su 9:30-6

ADMISSION: No charge

681
Museum of History and Art, Ontario
225 S Euclid Ave, 91762-3812; (p) (909) 983-3198; (f) (909) 983-8978; (c) San Bernardino

City/ 1979/ staff: 2(f); 3(p); 45(v)/ members: 258

ART MUSEUM; HISTORY MUSEUM: Documents history of Ontario, western San Bernardino County and inland Southern CA.

PROGRAMS: Annual Meeting; Community Outreach; Exhibits; Family Programs; Film/ Video; Guided Tours; Interpretation; Lectures; Research Library/Archives

COLLECTIONS: [1860-present] Agricultural implements and archives, personal and household items, mining tools.

HOURS: Yr W-Su 12-4

ADMISSION: No charge

ORANGE

682
Orange Community Historical Society
[PO Box 5484, 92863-5484]; (p) (714) 780-8701; (c) Orange

Private non-profit/ 1973/ staff: 25(v)/ members: 400/publication: *The Tribune*

HISTORICAL SOCIETY: Collects and shares information about the City of Orange and its surrounding communities.

PROGRAMS: Annual Meeting; Community Outreach; Guided Tours; Lectures; Publication; Research Library/Archives

COLLECTIONS: [Late 1800s-present] Books,

683
Orange County California Genealogical Society
7111 Talbert St, 92856 [PO Box 1587, 92856-0587]; www.occgs.com; (c) Orange

Private non-profit/ 1963/ staff: 85(v)/ members: 840/publication: *Saddleback Ancestors 1998*

Collects, and preserves family history and genealogy.

COLLECTIONS: 11,000 items of genealogical and family resources.

HOURS: Yr Daily

ADMISSION: No charge

ORLAND

684
Orland Historical and Cultural Society
936 4th St, 95963 [PO Box 183, 95963]; (p) (530) 865-5444; (c) Glenn

Private non-profit/ members: 100

HISTORIC PRESERVATION AGENCY; HISTORICAL SOCIETY; HISTORY MUSEUM; HOUSE MUSEUM: Preserves Orland area history.

PROGRAMS: Exhibits; Festivals; Guided Tours; School-Based Curriculum

COLLECTIONS: [1875-present] Artifacts of business, agriculture, lifestyle; historic buildings preserved at fairgrounds, railroad depot, blacksmith shop, service station, print shop, windmill, and tank house.

HOURS: May-Oct Su 2-5 and by

OROVILLE

685
Charles F. Lott Home
1067 Montgomery St, 95965; (p) (916) 538-2497, (916) 538-2415; (f) (916) 538-2426; www.oroville-ca.com

1856/ City/ staff: 1(f); 1(p); 38(v)

COLLECTIONS: [1849-1918] Glass, silver, ceramics, quilts, & needlework law books.

HOURS: Yr

686
Oroville Chinese Temple
1500 Broderick St, 95965; (p) (530) 538-2496; (c) Butte

City/ 1863/ staff: 1(f); 30(v)

ART MUSEUM; GARDEN; HISTORIC SITE; HISTORY MUSEUM: Preserves (mid-1800) temples: Taoist, Buddhist, and Confucianist.

PROGRAMS: Exhibits; Guided Tours

COLLECTIONS: [1800-1926] Folk art, Chinese artifacts, tapestries, clothing, memorabilia, and garden.

HOURS: Feb-Dec T-W 1-4, Th-M 11-4:30

ADMISSION: $2; Under 12 free

OXNARD

687
Ventura County Maritime Museum
2731 S Victoria Ave, 93035; (p) (805) 984-6260; (f) (805) 984-5970; VCMM@aol.com; (c) Ventura

Joint/ 1991/ Ventura County Maritime Museum, Inc./ staff: 2(f); 2(p); 80(v)/ members: 1100

ART MUSEUM; HISTORY MUSEUM: Presents and interprets maritime history of Channel Islands, Port of Hueneme, deep-water ports of Los Angeles and San Francisco.

PROGRAMS: Annual Meeting; Community Outreach; Concerts; Elder's Programs; Exhibits; Guided Tours; Interpretation; Lectures; Research Library/Archives; School-Based Curriculum

COLLECTIONS: [1500s-1800s] Maritime artifacts, artwork, boats, replicas, documents, whaling, sailor's art, local shipwrecks, navigation instruments.

HOURS: Yr Daily 11-5

ADMISSION: Donations accepted

PACIFIC GROVE

688
Point Pinos Lighthouse
Asilomar Blvd, 93950 [165 Forest Ave, 93950]; (p) (831) 648-5716; (f) (831) 372-3256; pgmuseum@mbay.net; www.pgmuseum. org; (c) Monterey

Joint/ 1855/ staff: 3(f); 3(p); 30(v)

HISTORIC SITE; HISTORY MUSEUM: Preserves and operates historic lighthouse.

PROGRAMS: Exhibits; Living History

COLLECTIONS: [1855-present] Lighthouse, period rooms with Victorian furnishings.

HOURS: Yr Th-Su 1-4

ADMISSION: No charge

PACIFIC PALISADES

689
Will Rogers State Historic Park
1501 Will Rogers State Park Rd, 90272 [1501 Will Rogers State Park Rd, 90272]; (p) (310) 454-8212; (f) (310) 459-2031

PACIFICA

690
Sanchez Adobe Historic Site
1000 Linda Mar Blvd, 94044-3534; (p) (650) 359-1462

County/ 1846/ staff: 4(p); 23(v)

HISTORIC SITE

COLLECTIONS: [1850] Native American artifacts

HOURS: Yr

PALA

691
Cupa Cultural Center
Pala Temecula Rd, 92059 [PO Box 445, 92059]; (p) (760) 742-1590; (f) (760) 742-4543; (c) San Diego

Federal/ 1974/ Pala Band of Mission Indians/ staff: 4(f)

TRIBAL MUSEUM: Preserves and interprets traditional and contemporary Native American cultures.

PROGRAMS: Elder's Programs; Exhibits; Festivals; Guided Tours; Interpretation; Lectures; Research Library/Archives

COLLECTIONS: [1903-present] Oral and written history of Cupeno Indians; photos.

HOURS: Yr

ADMISSION: No charge

PALM SPRINGS

692
Agua Caliente Cultural Museum
219 S Palm Canyon Dr, 92262; (p) (760) 323-0151; (f) (760) 320-0350; accmuseum@earthlink.net; www.prinet.com/accmuseum; (c) Riverside

Private non-profit/ 1990/ staff: 5(f); 2(p)/publication: *The Spirit*

TRIBAL MUSEUM: Collects, preserves, and studies historical and cultural resources of Agua Caliente Band of Cahuilla Indians, neighboring Cahuilla Indian tribes, nations, and other indigenous people.

PROGRAMS: Community Outreach; Exhibits; Festivals; Guided Tours; Interpretation; Lectures; Publication; Research Library/Archives; School-Based Curriculum

COLLECTIONS: [2000 BC-present] Historical photos and documents, Cahuilla Indian basketry and pottery, archaeological artifacts, traditional palm frond hut, and film of daily life of Cahuilla people circa 1850s.

HOURS: Sept-May T-Sa 10-4, Su 12-4; June-Aug F, Sa 10-4, Su 12-4

693
Palm Springs Desert Museum
101 Museum Dr, 92263 [PO Box 2310, 92263]; (p) (760) 325-7186; (f) (760) 327-5069; psmuseum@aol.com; www.psmuseum.org; (c) Riverside

Private non-profit/ 1938/ staff: 64(f); 32(p); 135(v)/ members: 4500

ART MUSEUM: Promotes a greater understanding of art, natural science, and performing arts.

PROGRAMS: Community Outreach; Concerts; Exhibits; Facility Rental; Family Programs; Guided Tours; Interpretation; Publication; Research Library/Archives; School-Based Curriculum; Theatre

COLLECTIONS: [19th and 20th c] Paintings, sculptures, graphics; ethnology, natural science, geology, and archaeology; contemporary American, CA, Western American and Native American, regional art; natural science.

HOURS: Yr T-Sa 10-5, Su 12-5

ADMISSION: $7.50, Student $3.50, Children $3.50, Seniors $6.50

694
Palm Springs Historical Society
221 S Palm Canyon Dr, 92263 [PO Box 1498, 92263]; (p) (760) 323-8297; (f) (760) 320-2561; (c) Riverside

1955/ staff: 1(f); 1(p); 16(v)/ members: 480/publication: *Whispering Palms*

HISTORICAL SOCIETY; HISTORY MUSEUM; RESEARCH CENTER: Maintains two 19th c pioneer homes.

PROGRAMS: Exhibits; Film/Video

COLLECTIONS: [1884-present] Photos, paintings, clothing tools, books, Indian ware, and the McCallum Adobe and Miss Cornelia's Little House.

HOURS: Oct-May W, Su 12-3, Th-Sa 10-4

ADMISSION: $1, Student $1;

PALO ALTO

695
Museum of American Heritage
351 Homer Ave, 94302 [PO Box 1731, 94302-1731]; (p) (650) 321-1004; (f) (650) 473-6950; mail@moah.org; www.moah.org; (c) Santa Clara

Private non-profit/ 1985/ staff: 3(f); 120(v)/ members: 568/publication: *Museum Update*

HISTORY MUSEUM: Presents 19th and 20th century electro-mechanical inventions and their role in shaping American culture.

PROGRAMS: Community Outreach; Elder's Programs; Exhibits; Facility Rental; Family Programs; Garden Tours; Guided Tours; Interpretation; Lectures; Publication; Research Library/Archives

COLLECTIONS: [Mid 19th-mid 20th c] American technology and inventions.

HOURS: Yr F-Su 11-4

ADMISSION: No charge/Donations

696
Palo Alto Historical Association
[PO Box 193, 94302]; (p) (650) 326-3355; (c) Santa Clara

Private non-profit/ 1948/ staff: 1(p)/ members: 550/publication: *Palo Alto: A Centennial History*

HISTORICAL SOCIETY: Collects, organizes, and preserves materials pertaining to history and heritage of Palo Alto; preserves historic sites and structures.

PROGRAMS: Annual Meeting; Exhibits; Lectures; Publication; Research Library/Archives

COLLECTIONS: [1894-present] Photos, clippings, and maps depicting Palo Alto region.

PARADISE

697
Gold Nugget Days, Inc.
502, 95967 [PO Box 949, 95967]; (p) (530) 872-8722; (f) (530) 872-1050; goldmuseum@aol.com; pardisedirect.com/goldnugget; (c) Butte

Private non-profit/ 1981/ staff: 3(p); 75(v)/ members: 150/publication: *Gold Dust*

HISTORY MUSEUM; LIVING HISTORY/OUTDOOR MUSEUM: Preserves and exhibits history of Paradise Ridge.

PROGRAMS: Annual Meeting; Community Outreach; Exhibits; Facility Rental; Festivals; Interpretation; Living History; Publication; School-Based Curriculum

COLLECTIONS: [1850s-present] Artifacts from mining, agriculture, recreation, education, toys, business, clothing, Native American crafts, tools.

HOURS: Yr 12-4

ADMISSION: No charge

698
Paradise Historical Society
[PO Box 1696, 95967-1696]; (p) (530) 873-6110; BEARFRM@aol.com; (c) Butte

Private non-profit/ 1960/ staff: 12(v)/ members: 230/publication: *Tales of the Paradise Ridge*

HISTORIC PRESERVATION AGENCY: Preserves and publishes local history.

PROGRAMS: Annual Meeting; Guided Tours; Publication

COLLECTIONS: [1850-present] Materials and photos.

PASADENA

699
Gamble House, The
4 Westmoreland Place, 91103-3593; (p) (626) 793-3334; (f) (626) 577-7547; gamblehs@usc.edu; www-gamblehouse.usc.edu; (c) Los Angeles

Joint/ 1966/ Univ of Southern CA/ staff: 6(f); 3(p); 170(v)/ members: 350

HOUSE MUSEUM

PROGRAMS: Community Outreach; Facility Rental; Guided Tours; Lectures; Research Library/Archives

COLLECTIONS: Gamble House and garage, decorative arts, furniture designed by Greene and Greene.

HOURS: Yr W-Su

ADMISSION: $8, Student $5, Seniors $5; Under 13 free

700
Heritage Square Museum
3800 Homer St, 91101 [225 S Lake Ave., Ste 1125, 91101]; (p) (626) 796-2898; (f) (626) 304-9652; www.heritagesquare.org; (c) Los Angeles

Private non-profit/ 1969/ The Cultural Heritage Foundation of Southern California, Inc/ staff: 4(f); 3(p); 56(v)/ members: 150/publication: *On the Square*

HISTORY MUSEUM; HOUSE MUSEUM; LIVING HISTORY/OUTDOOR MUSEUM: Preserves, restores, and interprets architectural and social history of Southern CA.

PROGRAMS: Exhibits; Family Programs; Guided Tours; Interpretation; Living History; Publication

COLLECTIONS: [1900s] Victorian/Edwardian era of Southern CA. Furniture, medical, communication, transportation, and business equipment.

HOURS: Yr F 10:30-3:30, Su 11:30-4:30

ADMISSION: $5, Student $4, Children $2, Seniors $4; Under 6 free

701
Ninth Judicial Circuit Historical Society
125 S Grand Ave, 91105; (p) (626) 795-0266; (f) (626) 229-7462; njchs@hotmail.com; (c) Los Angeles

Private non-profit/ 1985/ staff: 1(f); 3(p); 55(v)/ members: 2500

HISTORICAL SOCIETY: Educates on history of law in American West and judicial system.

INTERPRETATION: Legal Studies; U.S. Legal History

COLLECTIONS: [1840-present] Oral histories.

HOURS: By appt

702
Pasadena Historical Museum
470 W Walnut St, 91103; (p) (626) 577-1660; (f) (626) 577-1662; (c) Los Angeles

Private non-profit/ 1924/ staff: 4(f); 4(p); 200(v)/ members: 1000

HISTORICAL SOCIETY; HISTORY MUSEUM; HOUSE MUSEUM: Collects, preserves, and exhibits artifacts relating to Pasadena history and culture.

PROGRAMS: Exhibits; Family Programs; Guided Tours; Lectures; Living History; Research Library/Archives; School-Based Curriculum

COLLECTIONS: [1870s-1940s] Art and archival materials.

HOURS: Yr Th-Su 1-4

ADMISSION: $5, Student $4, Seniors $4; Under 12 free

PENRYN

703
Griffith Quarry Museum
Taylor Rd & Rock Spring Rd, 93663 [Taylor Rd, 93663]; (p) (916) 663-1837; www.placer.ca.gov/museum; (c) Placer

County/ staff: 6(f); 3(p)

HISTORIC SITE; HISTORY MUSEUM: Preserves ruins of polishing mill built in CA and quarry.

PROGRAMS: Exhibits

COLLECTIONS: [1864-1900] Original office furniture of Penryn Granite Works, the granite industry, and history of the Penryn-Loomis Basin area; 23 acre park; original office of Penryn Granite Works.

HOURS: Yr Sa, Su 12-4 and by appt

ADMISSION: No charge

PERRIS

704
Orange Empire Railway Museum
2201S A St, 92572 [PO Box 548, 92572]; (p) (909) 943-3020; (f) (909) 943-2676; OERM@juno.com; www.ocrm.mus.ca.us; (c) Riverside

Private non-profit/ 1956/ Board of Directors/ staff: 2(f); 250(v)/ members: 1300

RAILROAD MUSEUM: Operates railway museum.

PROGRAMS: Exhibits; Facility Rental; Festivals; Guided Tours

COLLECTIONS: [1880-1950] Diesel locomotives, steam engines, electric engines locomotives, trolley cars, street cars, passenger cars, cabooses, three gauges, standard 481/2", trolley gauge-42", and narrow gauge-36".

HOURS: Yr Daily 9-5

PETALUMA

705
Petaluma Adobe State Historic Park
3325 Old Adobe Rd, 94952; (p) (707) 762-4871

706
Petaluma Museum Association
20 Fourth St, 94952; (p) (707) 778-4398; (f) (707) 762-3923; (c) Sonoma

Private non-profit/ 1974/ staff: 2(p); 75(v)/ members: 600

HISTORIC SITE; HISTORY MUSEUM: Preserves and displays artifacts related to Petaluma's history.

PROGRAMS: Annual Meeting; Community

Outreach; Elder's Programs; Exhibits; Family Programs; Garden Tours; Guided Tours; Lectures; Living History; Research Library/Archives

COLLECTIONS: [1800s-present] Dairy/poultry artifacts, photos, Miwok Indians, Petaluma River, General Vallejo, textiles, clothing.

HOURS: Yr M, Th, F, Sa 10-4, Su 12-3

ADMISSION: No charge

PIEDMONT

707
Piedmont Historical Society
358 Hillside Ave, 94611; (p) (510) 547-3311; (c) Alameda

Private non-profit/ 1972/ Board of Directors/ staff: 40(v)/ members: 630/publication: *The Story of Piedmont Springs Park, The Attic Trunk*

HISTORICAL SOCIETY: Promotes Piedmont history.

PROGRAMS: Annual Meeting; Community Outreach; Exhibits; Publication; Research Library/Archives; School-Based Curriculum

COLLECTIONS: Memorabilia, photos, books, art, high school yearbooks, newspaper clippings, scrapbooks, decorative arts, clothing,

PINE GROVE

708
Indian Grinding Rock State Historic Park Chaw'se Regional Indian Museum
14881 Pine Grove-Volcano Rd, 95665; (p) (209) 296-7488; (f) (209) 296-7528; igr@goldrush. com; (c) Amador

State/ 1968/ Dept of Parks and Rec/ staff: 3(f); 3(p); 40(v)

HISTORIC SITE; HISTORY MUSEUM; LIVING HISTORY/OUTDOOR MUSEUM; TRIBAL MUSEUM: Preserves Sierra Nevada foothills where Native Americas gathered to grind acorns.

PROGRAMS: Elder's Programs; Exhibits; Festivals; Film/Video; Guided Tours; Interpretation; Lectures; Living History; Research Library/Archives; School-Based Curriculum

COLLECTIONS: [20,000 ago- present] Miwok, Maidu, Konkow, Monache, Nisenan, Tubatulabal, Washo, and Yokuts artifacts; basketry, feather regalia, jewelry, arrowpoints, and other tools; Native American structures.

HOURS: Yr M-F 11-3, Sa-Su 10-4

ADMISSION: $2/vehicle

PLACENTIA

709
City of Placentia Historical Committee
401 E Chapman Ave, 92870; (p) (714) 993-8124; (f) (714) 961-0283; (c) Orange

City/ 1985/ staff: 1(p); 9(v)

HISTORIC PRESERVATION AGENCY; RESEARCH CENTER: Advises city on matters of local history, preservation, and resources, evaluates and nominates local landmarks.

PROGRAMS: Community Outreach; Guided Tours; Research Library/Archives

COLLECTIONS: [1870-present] Documents and photos; oral interviews with prominent local residents; inventory of historic buildings.

HOURS: Library: Yr T-Th, Sa-Su Hours vary

ADMISSION: No charge

710
Historic George Key Ranch
625 W Bastonchury Rd, 92870 [625 W Bastonchury Rd, 92870]; (p) (714) 528-4260; (f) (714) 52408450

1898/ Harbors, Beaches and Parks/ staff: 3(f)

HISTORIC SITE; HISTORY MUSEUM: Preserves home of George Key, co-founder of Sunkist Growers and city of Placentia. Site is working citrus ranch and one of original Sunkist groves and ranch house.

COLLECTIONS: [1900] Citrus collection: tools and equipment of citrus production, agricultural catalogs, reference books, citrus publications.

HOURS: Yr

711
Placentia Founders Society, The Bradford House
136 Palm Circle, 92870; (p) (714) 993-6791; (f) (714) 528-7929; office@bradfordhouse. com; www.bradfordhouse.com; (c) Orange

Joint/ 1974/ Placentia Founders Society/ staff: 1(p)/ 30(v)/ members: 110

HISTORIC SITE: Maintains and preserves the A. S. Bradford House and related artifacts.

PROGRAMS: Annual Meeting; Community Outreach; Concerts; Facility Rental; Guided Tours; Publication; School-Based Curriculum

COLLECTIONS: [1860-1920] Period furniture, photographs, prints, interior design and decoration, and citrus tools.

HOURS: Yr 1st Su of month 2-4 and by appt

ADMISSION: $2, Children $1

PLACERVILLE

712
El Dorado County Historical Museum
104 Placerville Dr, 95667 [360 Fair Lane, 95667]; (p) (530) 621-5805; mcory@co.eldorado. ca.us; (c) El Dorado

County/ 1973/ Bd of Supervisors/ staff: 1(f); 50(v)

HISTORY MUSEUM; RESEARCH CENTER: Focuses on Gold Rush era.

PROGRAMS: Exhibits; Family Programs; Lectures; Research Library/Archives; School-Based Curriculum

COLLECTIONS: [1850-1940] Northern CA Native American baskets; gold rush, logging, transportation, clothing, agricultural, mining artifacts; railroad cars and locomotive.

HOURS: Yr Research only, T 10-4; Sa 10-4; Su 12-4

ADMISSION: No charge

713
Heritage Association of El Dorado County, The
[PO Box 62, 95667]; (p) (530) 622-0712; mfergie@jps.net; (c) El Dorado

Private non-profit/ 1973/ members: 20

HISTORICAL SOCIETY: Preserves and disseminates local history.

INTERPRETATION: Community/State History

PROGRAMS: Guided Tours; Publication; Research Library/Archives

COLLECTIONS: Deeds, probate, abstracts, photos, maps, births, marriages, deaths,

PLEASANT HILL

714
Contra Costa County Historical Society and History Center
1700 Oak Park Blved, 94523; (p) (925) 939-9180; (f) (925) 939-4832; cchistory@ix.netcom.com; www.ccnet.com/~xTom/ccchs; (c) Contra Costa

Private non-profit/ 1951/ staff: 35(v)/ members: 420/publication: Contra Costa County Bulletin

HISTORIC PRESERVATION AGENCY; HISTORICAL SOCIETY; RESEARCH CENTER: Collects, preserves local genealogy and history.

PROGRAMS: Annual Meeting; Community Outreach; Exhibits; Lectures; Publication; Research Library/Archives; School-Based Curriculum

COLLECTIONS: [1848-present] Photos, maps, court cases, tax records, marriage and death information, Biographies, oral histories, county history books, 3,900 photo and negatives, 3,000 slides, scrapbooks, daily news clippings, and ephemera.

HOURS: M-Th 9-3, F 9-1

PLEASANTON

715
Amador Livermore Valley Museum
603 Main St, 94566; (p) (925) 462-2766; (c) Alameda

Private non-profit/ 1963/ Amador Livermore Valley Historical Society

HISTORY MUSEUM: Collects, preserves, and interprets regional history ofTri-Valley area.

PROGRAMS: Annual Meeting; Community Outreach; Exhibits; Guided Tours; Lectures; Research Library/Archives; School-Based Curriculum

COLLECTIONS: [19th-20th c]

HOURS: Yr W-F 11-4, Sa-Su 1-4

ADMISSION: Donations accepted

POMONA

716
Historical Society of Pomona Valley, Inc., The
1569 N Park Ave, 91768; (p) (909) 623-2198; oqallivan@earthlink.net; www.osb.net; (c) Los Angeles

Private non-profit/ 1915/ Board of Directors/ staff: 30(v)/ members: 255/publication: News Notes

HISTORICAL SOCIETY: Preserves historical heritage of Pomona Valley.

PROGRAMS: Annual Meeting; Community Outreach; Facility Rental; Family Programs; Festivals; Guided Tours; Lectures; Publication; Research Library/Archives

COLLECTIONS: [1837-1880] Three historical homes with period furniture, art objects, paintings, decorative objects, linens, quilts, period clothing, cemetery.

HOURS: Yr Su

PORT HUENEME

717
Civil Engineer Corps/Seabee Museum
Bldg 99, 93043 [1000 23rd Ave, 93043]; (p) (805) 982-5165; (f) (805) 982-5595; langellierjp@slc.navfac.navy.mil; www.cbcph.navy.mil; (c) Ventura

Federal/ 1947/ staff: 6(f); 12(v)

HISTORY MUSEUM: History of U.S. Navy's Civil Engineer Corps in 19th century, and history of U.S. Navy Seabees.

PROGRAMS: Exhibits; Facility Rental; Film/Video; Guided Tours; Research Library/Archives

COLLECTIONS: [1867-present] Uniforms, insignia, weapons, construction equipment, art, photographs, films, archives, engineering materials, and models.

HOURS: Yr Daily M-Sa 10-4:30, Su

PORTERVILLE

718
Porterville Historical Museum
257 N "D" St, 93257; (p) (559) 784-2053; (c) Tulare

Private non-profit/ 1965/ Board of Directors/ staff: 1(f); 10(p); 15(v)/ members: 150

HISTORY MUSEUM: Maintains museum that focuses on local history.

PROGRAMS: Exhibits; Guided Tours; Lectures; Publication

COLLECTIONS: [1830-1930] Pioneer memorabilia, San Joaquin Valley Native American artifacts.

HOURS: Yr Th-Sa 10-4

ADMISSION: $1, Student $0.50; Members and under 6 free

719
Zalud House
393 N Hockett, 93257 [PO Box 432, 93257]; (p) (559) 782-7548; (f) (559) 782-4053; gmeacum@ci.porterville.ca.us; (c) Tulare

City/ 1977/ staff: 1(f); 2(p); 2(v)

GARDEN; HISTORY MUSEUM: Maintains 1891 period home; interprets local history.

PROGRAMS: Exhibits; Facility Rental; Family Programs; Film/Video; Garden Tours; Guided Tours

COLLECTIONS: [1891-1950] Historic house, garden; clothing, photos, memorabilia.

HOURS: Feb-Dec W-Sa

PORTOLA

720
Feather River Rail Society
700 Western Pacific Way, 96122 [PO Box 608, 96122-0608]; (p) (530) 832-4131; (f) (530) 832-1854; mywprr@compuserve.com; www.oz.net/-samh/frrs/; (c) Plumas

Private non-profit/ 1983/ Board of Directors/ staff: 4(p); 6(v)/ members: 1100/publication: Train Sheet

RAILROAD MUSEUM: Operates Portola Railroad Museum with history of Western Pacific Railroad.

PROGRAMS: Annual Meeting; Exhibits; Guided Tours; Publication

COLLECTIONS: [1940-1970] Diese, steam locomotives; freight, passenger cars; railroad artifacts.

HOURS: Yr Daily 10-5

ADMISSION: No charge/Donations requested

QUINCY

721
Plumas County Museum Association, Inc.
500 Jackson St, 95971; (p) (530) 283-6320; (f) (530) 283-6081; pcmuseum@psln.com; www.countyofplumas.com; (c) Plumas

Private non-profit/ 1964/ Plumas County Museum Association Trustees/ staff: 3(f); 2(p); 18(v)/ members: 578

HISTORICAL SOCIETY: Preserves and presents history and culture of Plumas County.

PROGRAMS: Annual Meeting; Elder's Programs; Exhibits; Guided Tours; Lectures; Living History; Publication; Research Library/Archives; School-Based Curriculum

COLLECTIONS: [1850-1920] Maidu Indian basketry, mining, logging, ranching, railroads, domestic life, firearms, Chinese artifacts, photos, diaries, histories, regional artifacts, maps.

HOURS: Yr M-F 8-5, May-Oct Sa-Su

ADMISSION: $1, Children $0.50; Under 12 free

RAMONA

722
Ramona Pioneer Historical Society and Guy B. Woodward Museum
645 Main St, 92065 [PO Box 625, 92065]; (p) (760) 789-7644; (c) San Diego

Private non-profit/ 1962/ staff: 2(f); 25(v)/ members: 500

HISTORIC SITE; HISTORICAL SOCIETY; HOUSE MUSEUM

PROGRAMS: Exhibits; Family Programs; Film/Video; Garden Tours; Guided Tours; Lectures; Living History

COLLECTIONS: [1640-1886] Historical buildings: adobe and French Provincial.

HOURS: Oct-Aug Daily

ADMISSION: $3

RANCHO CUCAMONGA

723
City of Rancho Cucamonga Historic Preservation Commission
10500 Civic Center Dr, 91729 [PO Box 807, 91729]; (p) (909) 477-2750; (f) (909) 477-2847; lhenders@rancho-cucmonga.ca.us; www.ci.rancho-cucamonga.ca.us/planning/histprog.ht; (c) San Bernardino

City/ 1977/ staff: 1(p)

HISTORIC PRESERVATION AGENCY; HISTORY MUSEUM: Preserves city's cultural and architectural heritage; reviews structures and sites for historic significance.

PROGRAMS: Community Outreach; Lectures; Living History; Research Library/Archives

COLLECTIONS: [1880s] City archives, photos, documents, and ephemera.

HOURS: Yr M-Th 7-6

ADMISSION: No charge

724
Rancho Cucamonga Historical Society
8810 Hemlock, 91729 [PO Box 401, 91729]; (p) (909) 989-4970; (c) San Bernardino

Private non-profit/ San Bernardino County Museum/ staff: 1(f); 39(v)/ members: 78

HISTORICAL SOCIETY: Maintains Casa de Rancho Cucamonga in conjunction with San Bernardino County Museum.

PROGRAMS: Exhibits; Festivals; Guided Tours

COLLECTIONS: [Mid 19th c] Period furnished historic house; clothing, books, kitchen utensils, farm equipment, personal effects.

HOURS: Yr

RED BLUFF

725
William B. Ide Adobe State Historic Park
21659 Adobe Rd, 96080 [21659 Adobe Rd, 96080]; (p) (530) 529-8599; (f) (530) 529-8599; www.ideadobe.tehama.k12.ca.us

REDDING

726
Shasta College Museum and Research Center
11555 Old Oregon Trail, 96001; (p) (530) 225-4754; (c) Shasta

Joint/ 1968/ College Board of Trustees/ staff: 1(f); 7(p)

HISTORY MUSEUM: Provides a depository for materials significant to history of area and operates as research center.

PROGRAMS: Annual Meeting; Community Outreach; Exhibits; Facility Rental; Guided Tours; Interpretation; Lectures

COLLECTIONS: [1849-present]

HOURS: M-F 10-4

ADMISSION: No charge

727
Turtle Bay Museums and Arboretum on the River
800 Auditorium Dr, 96099 [PO Box 992360, 96099-2360]; (p) (530) 243-8850; (f) (530) 243-8898; ahoveman@turtlebay.org; www.turtlebay.org; (c) Shasta

Private non-profit/ 1991/ staff: 35(f); 10(p); 150(v)/ members: 1

ART MUSEUM; GARDEN; HISTORY MUSEUM; LIVING HISTORY/OUTDOOR MUSEUM: Presents art history and natural science of Sacramento River watershed.

PROGRAMS: Community Outreach; Exhibits; Facility Rental; Family Programs; Festivals; Garden Tours; Guided Tours; Interpretation; Lectures; Living History; School-Based Curriculum

HOURS: Yr T-Su 10-5

ADMISSION: $4

REDLANDS

728
Kimberly-Shirk Association
1325 Prospect Dr, 92373 [PO Box 206, 92373]; (p) (909) 792-2111; (f) (909) 798-1716; kimcrest@empirenet.com; e2.empirenet.com/~kimcrest/; (c) San Bernardino

Private non-profit/ 1969/ staff: 3(f); 1(p); 80(v)/ members: 450/publication: *View from Kimberly Crest*

GARDEN; HISTORIC SITE; HOUSE MUSEUM: Preserves and interprets historic site of Kimberly Crest.

PROGRAMS: Exhibits; Facility Rental; Family Programs; Guided Tours; Interpretation; Publication; Research Library/Archives; School-Based Curriculum

COLLECTIONS: [1897-1970] Decorative arts objects, paintings, photos, slides, movies, manuscripts, and architectural drawings.

HOURS: Sept-July Th-Su 1-4

ADMISSION: $5, Student $4, Seniors $4; Donations requested; Under 12 free

729
Lincoln Memorial Shrine
125 W Vine St, 92373; (p) (909) 798-7636; (f) (909) 798-7566; archives@aksmiley.org; (c) San Bernardino

Joint/ 1932/ City; Private non-profit/ staff: 3(f); 3(p); 28(v)/ members: 200

HISTORY MUSEUM; PRESIDENTIAL SITE; RESEARCH CENTER: Maintains museum dedicated to Abraham Lincoln and American Civil War.

PROGRAMS: Lectures; Living History; Publication; Research Library/Archives

COLLECTIONS: [1800-1860s] 3,000 manuscripts of Civil War figures, uniforms, artwork, weaponry, newspapers, books, pamphlets.

HOURS: Yr T-Sa

730
San Bernardino County Museum
2024 Orange Tree Lane, 92374; (p) (909) 307-2669; (f) (909) 307-0539; adeegan@co.san-bernardino.ca.us; www.sbcountymuseum.org; (c) San Bernardino

County/ 1967/ Board of Supervisors/ staff: 66(f); 44(p); 100(v)/ members: 2030

HISTORY MUSEUM: Preserves and interprets prehistoric and historic cultural and natural heritage of San Bernardino.

PROGRAMS: Community Outreach; Exhibits; Facility Rental; Family Programs; Guided Tours; Interpretation; Lectures; Living History; Reenactments; School-Based Curriculum

COLLECTIONS: [1850-1950] Five structures: Yucaipa Adobe, Asistencia Mission, Agua Mansa Cemetery, John Rains House, and Yorba Slaughter Adobe.

HOURS: Yr T-Su 9-5

ADMISSION: $4, Student $3, Children $2, Seniors $3; Under 5 free

REDWOOD CITY

731
Lathrop House
627 Hamilton Ave, 94064 [Redwood City Heritage Assoc, PO Box 1273, 94064]; (p) (650) 365-5564; www.backinsf.com/attpen.html

732
San Mateo County Historical Association
777 Hamilton, 94063; (p) (650) 299-0104; (f) (650) 299-0141; (c) San Mateo

Private non-profit/ 1935/ Board of Directors/ staff: 6(f); 10(p); 125(v)/ members: 2431/publication: *La Peninsula*

HISTORIC SITE; HISTORICAL SOCIETY; HISTORY MUSEUM; HOUSE MUSEUM: Collects, preserves, and interprets history of San Mateo County.

PROGRAMS: Annual Meeting; Community Outreach; Exhibits; Facility Rental; Family Programs; Festivals; Guided Tours; Lectures; Living History; Publication; Research Library/Archives

COLLECTIONS: [Victorian Era] 15,000 pieces of archival and 3-D objects ranging from 6000 B.C. to present.

HOURS: Yr T-Su 10-4

ADMISSION: $2, Children $1, Seniors $1; Uunder 6 free

REEDLEY

733
Reedley Historical Society
1752 10th St, 93654 [PO Box 877, 93654]; (p) (559) 638-1913; dlbulls@uckac.edu; (c) Fresno

Private non-profit/ 1976/ Board of Directors/ staff: 20(v)/ members: 300

HISTORIC PRESERVATION AGENCY; HISTORICAL SOCIETY; HISTORY MUSEUM: Preserves, protects, and collects materials on Reedley history.

PROGRAMS: Annual Meeting; Community Outreach; Exhibits; Lectures

COLLECTIONS: Indian baskets, arrowhead collection, period furnishing, wagons, buggies, farm machinery, photos, books, videos.

HOURS: Yr M-F 9-1, Sa 10-1 and by appt

ADMISSION: $1, Student $0.50

RICHMOND

734
Richmond Museum of History
400 Nevin Ave, 84802 [PO Box 1267, 84802]; (p) (510) 235-7387; (f) (510) 235-4345; (c) Contra Costa

Joint/ 1954/ City; Richmond Museum Association/ staff: 5(p); 150(v)/ members: 460

HISTORIC SITE; HISTORY MUSEUM: Maintains local history museum housed in 1910 Carnegie Library building.

INTERPRETATION: Community/State History

PROGRAMS: Annual Meeting; Exhibits; Family Programs; Guided Tours; Interpretation

COLLECTIONS: [1900-present] Artifacts: household and decorative objects, farming and agricultural implements, tools, costume, local business, ephemeral materials, and photos, WWII Richmond-built Victory ship.

HOURS: Yr W-F, Su 1-4 and by appt

ADMISSION: No charge/Donations

RIDGECREST

735
Maturango Museum of the Indian Wells Valley
100 E Las Flores Ave, 93555; (p) (760) 375-6900; (f) (760) 375-0479; matmus1@ridgenet.net; www.maturango.org; (c) Kern

Private non-profit/ 1962/ Board of Trustees/ staff: 2(f); 9(p); 133(v)/ members: 968

HISTORY MUSEUM: Preserves and interprets natural and cultural history of Upper Mojave Desert region.

INTERPRETATION: Anthropology; Archaeology; Art; Community/State History; Education; Historic Persons; Historic Preservation; Military; Mining; Native American Studies; Natural History; Natural Resources; Paleontology; Photography; Pioneer; Science

PROGRAMS: Annual Meeting; Community Outreach; Concerts; Exhibits; Family Programs; Guided Tours; Interpretation; Lectures; Publication; Research Library/Archives; School-Based Curriculum

COLLECTIONS: [Paleo-Indian-present] Natural and physical sciences; cultural, social, and local history.

HOURS: Yr Daily 10-5

ADMISSION: $2, Student $1, Seniors $1

RIO VISTA

736
Rio Vista Museum
16 N Front St, 94571; (p) (707) 374-5169; (c) Solano

Private non-profit/ 1976/ Rio Vista Museum Association/ staff: 8(v)/ members: 190

HISTORY MUSEUM: Collects and preserves material on city of Rio Vista and surrounding area.

INTERPRETATION: Conservation of Artifacts; Dolls/Toys; Education; Folklore/Folklife; Photography; Pioneer

PROGRAMS: Annual Meeting; Community Outreach; Exhibits; Festivals; Research Library/Archives; School-Based Curriculum

COLLECTIONS: [1800-present] Farming materials, military, maps, newspapers, music, household items, clothing, photographs, and artifacts.

HOURS: Yr Sa-Su

ADMISSIONS: Donations requested

RIVERSIDE

737
Heritage House
8193 Magnolia Ave, 92504; (p) (909) 689-1333, (909) 732-5273; (f) (909) 369-4970

1891/ Riverside Municipal Museum/ staff: 2(f); 1(p); 67(v)

COLLECTIONS: [1890s] Furnishings, barn, and carriage house.

HOURS: Yr

738
Jurupa Mountains Cultural Center
7621 Granite Hill Dr, 92509; (p) (909) 685-5818; (f) (909) 685-1240; admin@the-jmcc.org; www.the-jmcc.org; (c) Riverside

Private non-profit/ 1964/ Board of Directors/ staff: 6(f); 4(p); 12(v)/ members: 518

RESEARCH CENTER: Maintains earth science museum and nature center;

PROGRAMS: Exhibits; Family Programs; Guided Tours; Research Library/Archives; School-Based Curriculum

COLLECTIONS: Rocks, minerals and fossils, Crestmore minerals.

HOURS: Yr T-Sa

739
March Field Museum
22550 Van Buren Blvd, 92518 [PO Box 6463, 92518]; (p) (909) 697-6602; (f) (909) 697-6605; marfldmu@pe.net; WWW.pe.net/~marfldmu; (c) Riverside

Private non-profit/ 1979/ staff: 5(f); 3(p); 125(v)/ members: 1200/publication: *Flightlines*

HISTORY MUSEUM: Collects, preserves, and exhibits the history, traditions, and technological developments of US Air Force and March Air Force Base.

PROGRAMS: Exhibits; Facility Rental; Guided Tours; Publication; Research Library/Archives

COLLECTIONS: [1918-present] 55 aircrafts, 4,800 photos, 2,000 clothing items, 1,300 prints/lithographs/paintings, 6,000 books/manuals/documents.

HOURS: Yr Daily 10-4

ADMISSION: $5, Family $10, Children $2; Donations requested

740
Riverside Local History Resource Center
Riverside Public Library, 3581 Mission Inn Ave, 92501; (p) (909) 826-5736; (f) (909) 788-1528; william_cld@riverside.lib.ca.us; www.vmoses@ci.riverside.ca.us; (c) Riverside

City/ 1888/ staff: 1(f); 3(p); 1(v)

RESEARCH CENTER: Preserves and interprets Riverside's past.

PROGRAMS: Community Outreach; Publication; Research Library/Archives; School-Based Curriculum

COLLECTIONS: [1870-present] 300 linear feet archival and manuscripts.

741
Riverside Municipal Museum
3580 Mission Inn Ave, 92501; (p) (909) 826-5273; (f) (909) 369-4970; www.ci.riverside.ca.us/museum

City/ 1924/ staff: 10(f); 5(p); 200(v)/ members: 700

HISTORY MUSEUM: Preserves natural and cultural history of Riverside and region.

PROGRAMS: Exhibits; Facility Rental; Family Programs; Festivals; Film/Video; Lectures; School-Based Curriculum

COLLECTIONS: Native American basketry and artifacts; citrus industry machinery, objects and label art; paleontology artifacts, decorative arts objects.

HOURS: Yr T-F 9-5, Sa 10-5, Su 11-5

ADMISSION: No charge

742
Sherman Indian Museum
9010 Magnolia Ave, 92503; (p) (909) 276-6719; (f) (909) 276-6336; laisquoc@bia.edu; (c) Riverside

Federal/ 1970/ Sherman Indian High School/ staff: 1(f)

HISTORIC SITE; TRIBAL MUSEUM: Maintains a museum on local North American tribes.

PROGRAMS: Exhibits; Festivals; Guided Tours; Interpretation; Lectures; Research Library/Archives

COLLECTIONS: [1892-present] Artwork, artifacts, crafts, baskets, pottery, photographs, and beads.

HOURS: Yr M-F By appt

ADMISSION: Donations requested

743
University of California Riverside/California Museum of Photography
3824 Main St, 92521 [University of California, 92521]; (p) (909) 787-4748; (f) (909) 787-4797; kbarber@ucrac1.ucr.edu; www.cmp.ucr.edu; (c) Riverside

Joint/ 1973/ University of California/ staff: 10(f); 10(p); 20(v)/ members: 500/publication: *FOTOTEXT*

ART MUSEUM; HISTORY MUSEUM: Promotes understanding of photography and related media through collection, research, exhibition, and instruction.

PROGRAMS: Community Outreach; Exhibits; Facility Rental; Family Programs; Lectures; Publication; Research Library/Archives

COLLECTIONS: [Late 19th and 20th c] Photographic arts, history, and technology; Keystone-Mast Collection: stereoscopic negatives and paper prints; Bingham Technology Collection: cameras, viewing devices, and photographic apparatus.

HOURS: Yr 12-5

ADMISSION: $2, Student $1, Seniors $1

ROHNERT PARK

744
Northwest Information Center of the California Historical Resources Information System
Sonoma State Univ Bldg 33, 94928 [1801 E Cotati Ave, Rohnert Park, 94928]; (p) (707) 664-2494; (f) (707) 664-3947; NWIC.center@ sonoma.edu; (c) Sonoma

Private non-profit/ Sonoma State University Academic Foundation, Inc/ staff: 2(f); 12(p); 5(v)

RESEARCH CENTER: Preserves and interprets archaeological and built-environment records for local, state, and federal agencies, and provides cultural resources information in 16-county service area.

PROGRAMS: Community Outreach; Guided Tours; Lectures

COLLECTIONS: [Prehistory-present] 20,000 site records; 23,000 reports;1,200 historic maps; selected local histories; 22,000 built environment records; ethnographic literature; and local reference materials.

HOURS: Yr M-F 9-4

ADMISSION: Call

ROSEVILLE

745
Maidu Interpretive Center
1960 Johnson Ranch Dr, 95661; (p) (916) 772-4242; (f) (916) 773-5595; kstevens@roseville.ca.us; (c) Placer

City/ 1999/ staff: 2(f); 6(p); 30(v)

HISTORIC SITE; HISTORY MUSEUM: Programs, classes, exhibits, and tours of the Maidu Historic Site interpret the daily life and culture of the Native Americans who lived on the site for nearly 10,000 years.

PROGRAMS: Community Outreach; Exhibits; Facility Rental; Family Programs; Festivals; Guided Tours; Interpretation; Lectures; Publication

COLLECTIONS: [1900 AD-3000 BC] Stone artifacts, Native cultural reproductions, ancient petroglyphs and bedrock mortars.

HOURS: Yr T-Sa

746
Roseville Historical Society
557 Lincoln St, 95678; (p) (916) 773-3003; (f) (916) 773-9691; carnegieli@jps.net; www.rosevillehistorical.org; (c) Placer

Private non-profit/ 1985/ staff: 1(f)/ members: 301

GENEALOGICAL SOCIETY; HISTORIC PRESERVATION AGENCY; HISTORIC SITE; HISTORICAL SOCIETY; HISTORY MUSEUM; RESEARCH CENTER: Operates railroad and music oriented museum.

PROGRAMS: Annual Meeting; Community Outreach; Elder's Programs; Exhibits; Facility Rental; Festivals; Film/Video; Lectures; Publication; Research Library/Archives

COLLECTIONS: [1860-1950] Railroad books, 700 movies videos, 400 cameras, 7,000 78 RPM records, 3,000 LPs, 2 scale model railroad displays.

HOURS: Yr Daily 12-5

ADMISSION: No charge

SACRAMENTO

747
California Council for the Promotion of History
6000 J St, 95819-6059; (p) (916) 278-4296; (f) (916) 278-6269; ccph@csus.edu; www.csus.edu/org/ccph; (c) Sacramento

Private non-profit/ 1977/ members: 300/publication: *California History Action*

HISTORICAL SOCIETY: Fosters, facilitates, and coordinates the preservation, interpretation, and management of CA's historical resources.

PROGRAMS: Annual Meeting; Publication

748
California Historical Resources Commission
[PO Box 942896, 94296-0001]; (p) (916) 653-6624; (f) (916) 653-9824; calshpo@quiknet.com; ohp.cal-parks.ca.gov

Joint/ Federal; State

HISTORIC PRESERVATION AGENCY: The nine member Commission carries out the goals and programs as mandated by the state and federal governments and preserves archaeological and historic sites.

PROGRAMS: Publication

749
California History Section, California State Library
900 N St Rm 200, 94237 [PO Box 942837, 94237-001]; (p) (916) 654-0176; (f) (916) 654-8777; cslcal@library.ca.gov; www.library.ca.gov; (c) Sacramento

State/ 1850/ staff: 17(f)/publication: *California State Library Foundation Bulletin*

LIBRARY AND/OR ARCHIVES: Collects, preserves, and disseminates information regarding history of state.

PROGRAMS: Exhibits; Lectures; Publication; Research Library/Archives

COLLECTIONS: [1540-present] 80,000 volumes; 6,000 periodical titles; 2,400 newspaper titles; 5,000 maps; 700 manuscript collections; 200,000 photographs; prints, posters, sheet music, menus, programs, brochures, and other ephemera.

HOURS: Yr M-F 9:30-4

ADMISSION: No charge

750
California Military Museum
1119 Second St, 95814; (p) (916) 442-2883; (f) (916) 442-7532; dir@militarymuseum.org; www.militarymuseum.org; (c) Sacramento

Private non-profit/ 1982/ California National Guard Historical Society/ staff: 4(p); 20(v)/publication: *The Bugle*

HISTORY MUSEUM; HOUSE MUSEUM: Collects, preserves, and interprets CA military history.

PROGRAMS: Community Outreach; Concerts; Exhibits; Guided Tours; Interpretation; Lectures; Living History; Publication; Reenact-

ments; Research Library/Archives; School-Based Curriculum

COLLECTIONS: [Pre-Statehood-present] 30,000 historic artifacts including mementos of individuals veterans.

HOURS: Yr T-Su 10-4

ADMISSION: $3, Children $1

751
California State Archives
1020 O St, 95814; (p) (916) 653-7715; (f) (916) 653-7363; ArchivesWeb@www.ss.ca.gov; www.ss.ca.gov/archives.htm; (c) Sacramento

State/ 1850/ Secretary of State/ staff: 32(f); 3(p); 2(v)

LIBRARY AND/OR ARCHIVES: Collects, preserves, and provides access to original records of CA government.

PROGRAMS: Exhibits; Facility Rental; Guided Tours; Lectures; Research Library/Archives

COLLECTIONS: [1849-present] CA's original Constitutions and working papers, artifacts, documents, Mexican land grants, election and political campaigns, legislative materials, court cases, CA Governors' records, Constitutional officers, state agencies, railroads, prison records, oral histories, maps, photographs, artifacts, genealogical materials, early CA military records, patent and trademark materials, incorporation papers, business, and election materials.

HOURS: Yr M-F 9:30-4, 1st Sa 10-4

ADMISSION: No charge

752
California State Capitol Museum
10th St & L St, 95814 [State Capitol, Rm B27, 95814]; (p) (916) 324-0312; (f) (916) 445-3628; stcapmus@cwo.com; (c) Sacramento

State/ 1981/ State Parks/ staff: 22(f); 15(p); 112(v)

HISTORIC SITE

PROGRAMS: Annual Meeting; Exhibits; Garden Tours; Guided Tours; Interpretation; Living History

COLLECTIONS: [1900-1910] Furniture, decorative arts, archives, photos, architectural drawings, and memorabilia that reflect CA's Government as it relates to the State Capitol.

HOURS: Yr Daily 9-5

ADMISSION: No charge

753
California State Indian Museum
2618 K St, 95816; (p) (916) 324-0971; (f) (916) 322-5231; (c) Sacramento

State/ 1940/ California Department of Parks/ staff: 1(f); 5(p); 50(v)/ members: 500

ANTHROPOLOGY MUSEUM; HISTORY MUSEUM: Preserves, collects, interprets, and exhibits Native American history.

INTERPRETATION: Anthropology; Native American Studies

PROGRAMS: Community Outreach; Exhibits; Festivals; Garden Tours; Guided Tours; Interpretation; Lectures; School-Based Curriculum

COLLECTIONS: [1900s] Native American Indian artifacts: baskets collection, canoe, mortar and pestle, bows and arrows, jewelry.

HOURS: Yr Daily 10-5

ADMISSION: Family $3, Children $1.50; Under 6 free

754
California State Railroad Museum
Second St & I St, 95814 [111 I St, 95814-2204]; (p) (916) 445-7387; (f) (916) 327-5655; csrmf@csrmf.org; www.scrmf.org; (c) Sacramento

State/ 1976/ Department of Parks and Recreation/ staff: 40(f); 20(p); 900(v)/ members: 9000/publication: *On Track!*

HISTORY MUSEUM; RAILROAD MUSEUM: Preserves railroad museum, theaters, and operating steam excursion trains.

PROGRAMS: Community Outreach; Exhibits; Facility Rental; Festivals; Guided Tours; Interpretation; Lectures; Living History; Publication; Research Library/Archives; Theatre

COLLECTIONS: [1830s-present] 214 locomotives and cars, 25,000 three-dimensional

755
California State University Sacramento/Department of Special Collections and University Archives
2000 State University Dr, East, 95819; (p) (916) 278-6144; (f) (916) 278-5469; pmacas@csus.edu; www.lib.csus.edu/services/dept/archives/; (c) Sacramento

State/ 1947/ staff: 3(f); 1(p); 5(v)

LIBRARY AND/OR ARCHIVES: Preserves history of CA State Univ and its role in the Sacramento region; history and culture of CA.

PROGRAMS: Community Outreach; Exhibits; Lectures

COLLECTIONS: [1900-present] Collection contains 5,300 linear feet of manuscripts, records, photographs, oral histories, audio video, microfilm and microfiche, prints and paintings; objects, clothing and artifacts associated with Japanese American history.

HOURS: Yr M-F 8:30-4:30

ADMISSION: No charge

756
Crocker Art Museum
216 O St, 95814; (p) (916) 264-5423; (f) (916) 264-7372; cam@cityofsacramento.org; www.crockerartmuseum.com; (c) Sacramento

Joint/ 1885/ City; Private non-profit/ staff: 34(f); 6(p); 600(v)

ART MUSEUM: Preserves and interprets 1885 historic Crocker Mansion.

PROGRAMS: Community Outreach; Concerts; Exhibits; Facility Rental; Family Programs; Guided Tours; Lectures

COLLECTIONS: Old Master drawing; 19th c CA art; Northern CA art since 1945; 19th c German paintings; European and American photo; 20th c international ceramics; Asian art.

HOURS: Yr T,W,F,Su 10-5, Th 10-9pm

ADMISSION: $6, Student $3, Seniors $4

757
Discovery Museum, The
101 I St, 95814; (p) (916) 264-7057; (f) (916) 264-5100; www.thediscovery.org; (c) Sacramento

Private non-profit/ 1985/ Board of Trustees/ staff: 15(f); 9(p); 120(v)/ members: 1000

HISTORY MUSEUM: Interprets regional history, science, and technology through exhibitions and educational programming.

PROGRAMS: Community Outreach; Concerts; Exhibits; Facility Rental; Family Programs; Festivals; Guided Tours; Interpretation; Lectures; Publication; Research Library/Archives; School-Based Curriculum

COLLECTIONS: [1849-present] Interprets collections of Sacramento Archives and Museum Collection Center.

HOURS: Yr June-Aug Daily 10-5; Sept-May T-Sa 10-5

ADMISSION: $5, Student $4, Children $3, Seniors $4; Under 5 free

758
E Clampus Vitus
1615 Markham Way, 95818; (p) (916) 448-0584; (c) Sacramento

Private non-profit/ 1852/ Board of Proctors

HISTORICAL SOCIETY: Promotes history of the Trans-Mississippi West by erecting plaques to commemorate the people, sites, and events of the Gold Rush era.

759
Golden State Museum
10th & O St, 95814 [1020 O St, 95814]; (f) (916) 653-0314; jdonovan@ss.ca.gov; www.ss.ca.gov/Museum/intro/htm; (c) Sacramento

Private non-profit/ 1998/ Golden State Museum-Public Benefit Corp/ staff: 7(f); 8(p); 90(v)

HISTORY MUSEUM: Collects, preserves, interprets, and exhibits materials related to CA history.

PROGRAMS: Community Outreach; Elder's Programs; Exhibits; Facility Rental; Family Programs; Festivals; Film/Video; Guided Tours; Interpretation; Lectures; School-Based Curriculum

COLLECTIONS: [1800s-present] Artifacts, memorabilia, and ephemera related to California's history; art, documents, manuscripts, maps, films, photographs, artifacts.

HOURS: Yr T-Sa 10-5, Su 12-5

ADMISSION: $6.50, Children $3.50, Seniors $5

760
Governor's Mansion State Historic Park
1526 H St, 95814; (p) (916) 323-3047; (c) Sacramento

State/ 1967/ Parks and Recreation/ staff: 1(f); 5(p); 40(v)/ members: 100

HISTORIC SITE; HOUSE MUSEUM; PRESIDENTIAL SITE: Preserves home of 13 CA governors and their families from 1903-1967.

PROGRAMS: Community Outreach; Concerts; Elder's Programs; Exhibits; Facility Rental; Family Programs; Film/Video; Living History; Publication; School-Based Curriculum

COLLECTIONS: [1877-1967] Household furnishings and decorations accumulated by 13 successive governors' families.

HOURS: Yr Daily 10-5

ADMISSION: $1

761
Leland Stanford Mansion State Historic Park
8th & N St, 95814 [802 N St, 95814]; (p) (916) 324-0575; (f) (916) 447-9318; (c) Sacramento

State/ Dept of Parks and Rec/ staff: 1(f); 15(v)

HISTORIC SITE; HOUSE MUSEUM: Manages and restores house museum.

COLLECTIONS: [1861-74] Historic structure, photos, furnishings.

762
Old City Cemetery Committee
1000 Broadway, 95818 [PO Box 255345, 95865-5345]; (p) (916) 448-0811, (916) 448-5665; (f) (916) 554-7508; (c) Sacramento

Private non-profit/ 1987/ Executive Board/ staff: 100(v)/ members: 25

HISTORICAL SOCIETY: Restores and preserves Sacramento historic City Cemetery.

PROGRAMS: Community Outreach; Concerts; Exhibits; Family Programs; Festivals; Garden Tours; Guided Tours; Lectures; Living History; Reenactments; Research Library/Archives; School-Based Curriculum

COLLECTIONS: [1849-present] Death and interments records, 1850-1927, Clark, Booth, and Yardley funeral records, 1903-1953, hand-carved marble tombstones.

HOURS: Yr Daily 7-5 Cemetery, M-F 10-3 Archives

763
Portuguese Historical and Cultural Society
12th & S St, 95816 [PO Box 161990, 95816]; (p) (916) 391-7356; portucal@aol.com; (c) Sacramento

Private non-profit/ 1979/ staff: 12(v)/ members: 400/publication: *O Pregresso*

HISTORICAL SOCIETY: Promotes and preserves Portuguese heritage and culture.

PROGRAMS: Exhibits; Festivals; Publication

COLLECTIONS: Historical photos of early Portuguese immigrants.

764
Sacramento Archives and Museum Collection Center
551 Sequoia Pacific Blvd, 95814; (p) (916) 264-7072; (f) (916) 264-7582; samcc@cityofsacramento.org; www.sacramentities.com/history/; (c) Sacramento

City/ 1953/ staff: 4(f); 2(p); 25(v)

RESEARCH CENTER: Maintains official City and County governmental records as well as private archives and manuscripts.

PROGRAMS: Community Outreach; Film/Video; Guided Tours; Interpretation; Lectures; Research Library/Archives

COLLECTIONS: [1849-present] 13,00 linear feet of archival records, 16,000 linear feet of artifacts, 100,000 maps, 3 million photos, 9 million feet of film from the NBC affiliate.

HOURS: Yr T 1-4:30, W 4-7:45, Th,F 8:15-12 By appt only

ADMISSION: No charge

765
Sacramento Room, Sacramento Public Library
828 I St, 95814; (p) (916) 264-2920; (f) (916) 264-2884; askus@sacramento.lib.ca.us; www.saclib.org; (c) Sacramento

Joint/ 1985/ City;County; Sacramento Public Library Authority/ staff: 2(f); 6(p); 20(v)

LIBRARY AND/OR ARCHIVES: Collects and preserves history of Sacramento and CA.

PROGRAMS: Community Outreach; Exhibits; Lectures; Research Library/Archives

COLLECTIONS: [1450-present] CDs, tapes, videos, maps, postcards, sheet music, prints, city directories, telephone books, ephemera, art works and book arts.

HOURS: Yr T, W 11-5, Th 11-9, Sa 11-3, Su 1-5

ADMISSION: No charge

766
Sutter's Fort State Historic Park
2701 L St, 95814; (p) (916) 445-4422; (f) (916) 442-8613; (c) Sacramento

State/ 1839/ CA Dept of Parks and Rec/ staff: 3(f); 20(p); 100(v)/ members: 110

HISTORIC SITE; LIVING HISTORY/OUTDOOR MUSEUM: Preserves historic fort from the 1840s.

PROGRAMS: Exhibits; Festivals; Interpretation; Living History; Publication; Reenactments; School-Based Curriculum

COLLECTIONS: [1839-1850] Artifacts, reproductions, graphics, photographs, documents and diaries pertaining to the pioneer and Gold Rush era in CA; canons and other firearms; fort; and archives.

HOURS: Yr Daily 10-5

ADMISSION: $6, Children $3; Under 6 free

767
Towe Auto Museum
2200 Front St, 95818; (p) (916) 442-6802; (f) (916) 442-2646; (c) Sacramento

Private non-profit/ 1982/ Board of Directors/ staff: 6(f); 5(p); 350(v)/ members: 900

HISTORY MUSEUM: Displays history of automobile in America.

PROGRAMS: Annual Meeting; Concerts; Exhibits; Facility Rental; Family Programs; Film/Video; Guided Tours; Interpretation; Lectures; Publication; Research Library/Archives; Theatre

COLLECTIONS: [1900s] Antique and classic American vehicles; bikes, motorcycles, cars, trucks, racing vehicles; additional period exhibits.

HOURS: Yr Daily 10-6

ADMISSION: $6

768
Wells Fargo Bank Museum
400 Capitol Mall, 95814; (p) (916) 440-4161; (c) Sacramento

HISTORY MUSEUM: Preserves history of Wells Fargo Bank.

PROGRAMS: Exhibits; Guided Tours

COLLECTIONS: [1800s-early 1900s] Concord stagecoach; Wells Fargo banking and express history; gold mining; gold specimens; original gold scales; Livingston Collection of Sacramento Postal; Wells Fargo express covers.

HOURS: M-F 9-5

769
Wells Fargo History Museum
1000 Second St, 95814; (p) (916) 396-3809; (f) (916) 498-0302; (c) Sacramento

1986/ Wells Fargo/ staff: 1(f); 5(p)

HISTORIC SITE; HISTORY MUSEUM: Displays and interprets artifacts, documents, and ephemera related to history of CA and Wells Fargo Company.

PROGRAMS: Exhibits; Guided Tours; Interpretation; Publication; School-Based Curriculum

COLLECTIONS: [1852-1900] Documents, photos, Wells Fargo banking, stage, and express history, Pony Express, gold scales, treasure box and safe, telegraph machine, and stage coach models.

HOURS: Yr M-F 9-5

ADMISSION: No charge

770
Westerners International, Sacramento Corral
2844 Honeysuckle Way, 95826; (p) (916) 388-0230; (f) (916) 388-9236; rwoodw1005@aol.com; (c) Sacramento

Private non-profit/ 1968/ Historical Society/ staff: 12(v)/ members: 50

HISTORICAL SOCIETY: Promotes interest in all phases of culture, history, and development of American West.

PROGRAMS: Annual Meeting; Monthly Meeting

HOURS: 1st W

SALINAS

771
Jose Eusibio Boronda Adobe
333 Baronda Drive, 93902 [PO Box 3576, 93912]; (p) (408) 757-8085

HISTORY MUSEUM; HOUSE MUSEUM

772
Monterey County Historical Society, Inc.
333 Boronda Rd, 93912 [PO Box 3576, 93912]; (p) (831) 757-8085; MCHS@dedot.com; www.dedot.com/mchs; (c) Monterey

Private non-profit/ 1933/ Board of Directors/ staff: 1(f); 8(v)/ members: 300

HISTORIC SITE; HISTORICAL SOCIETY; HISTORY MUSEUM; HOUSE MUSEUM; RESEARCH CENTER: Museum with 3 historic houses (Eusebio Boronda Adobe 1844, One room school house 1897, William Weeks Victorian 1844, Robert B. Johnston Archival Vault, and cultural resources.

PROGRAMS: Community Outreach; Exhibits; Facility Rental; Guided Tours; Interpretation; Research Library/Archives; School-Based Curriculum

COLLECTIONS: [1700-1945] Photos, negatives, Spanish and Mexican archives, assessor rolls, diaries, research papers on WW II, Monterey and Salinas Valley regional history and archaeology.

HOURS: Yr M-F 9-3

SAN ANDREAS

773
Calaveras County Historical Society
30 N Main St, 95249 [PO Box 721, 95249]; (p) (209) 754-1058; (f) (209) 754-1086; (c) Calaveras

County/ 1952/ staff: 2(f); 40(v)/ members: 865

HISTORICAL SOCIETY: Aids public with research.

PROGRAMS: Annual Meeting; Exhibits; Research Library/Archives

COLLECTIONS: [Late 1849-1850s] Gold Rush artifacts.

HOURS: Yr Daily 7-4

ADMISSION: $2, Children $0.50, Seniors $1

SAN BERNARDINO

774
San Bernardino County Archives
777 E Rialto Ave, 92415; (p) (909) 387-2030; (f) (909) 387-2232; (c) San Bernardino

County/ 1979/ Auditor-Controller-Recorder/ staff: 2(f); 4(v)

LIBRARY AND/OR ARCHIVES: Houses and maintains county records from 1853 to 1928; assists researchers in using records for historical, genealogical, and land title research; creates finding aids computer indexes.

PROGRAMS: Exhibits; Guided Tours; Research Library/Archives

COLLECTIONS: [1853-1920] Recorded documents: birth, death, marriage, deed, land patents, and homesteads. Court cases from 1853-1914, inquests, burials, mining records, Board of Supervisors minutes.

HOURS: Yr M-F 9-4

ADMISSION: No charge

SAN DIEGO

775
Cabrillo National Monument
1800 Cabrillo Memorial Dr, 92106-3601; (p) (619) 557-5450; (f) (619) 557-5469; www.nps.gov/cabr/; (c) San Diego

Federal/ 1913/ National Park Service/ staff: 22(f); 1(p); 33(v)

HISTORIC PRESERVATION AGENCY; HISTORIC SITE; LIVING HISTORY/OUTDOOR MUSEUM: Protects and preserves natural and cultural elements of San Diego and U.S. history.

PROGRAMS: Community Outreach; Exhibits; Festivals; Guided Tours; Interpretation; Lectures; Living History; Publication; Research Library/Archives; School-Based Curriculum; Theatre

COLLECTIONS: [16th c] 216,000 archival material and 1,600 historic objects relating to Old Point Loma Lighthouse.

HOURS: Yr July-Sept Daily 9-5:15

ADMISSION: $2; $5/vehicle

776
Conservation Corps State Museum Southern California Affiliate
5118 San Aquario Dr, 92109-1510; (p) (858) 270-5417; (f) (858) 270-5417; Budmarion@aol.com; (c) San Diego

Joint/ 1995/ Private non-profit; Conservation Corps State Museum/ staff: 1(f); 10(v)/ members: 2000

ALLIANCE OF HISTORICAL AGENCIES; HISTORIC PRESERVATION AGENCY; HISTORIC SITE; HISTORY MUSEUM; RESEARCH CENTER: Documents youth corps movement.

PROGRAMS: Community Outreach; Elder's Programs; Exhibits; Guided Tours; Interpretation; Living History; Quarterly Meeting; Research Library/Archives; School-Based Curriculum

COLLECTIONS: [1933-1942] 1933-1942 CCC Camp barracks, research library, legislative records, biographies and books.

HOURS: By appt

ADMISSION: No charge

777
Fort Guijarros Museum Foundation
US Naval Submarine Base, 140 Sylvester Rd Bldg, 92193 [PO Box 23130, 92193]; (p) (619) 229-9743; Tivella1@aol.com; (c) San Diego

Private non-profit/ 1981/ staff: 2(p); 3(v)/ members: 200/publication: *La Esplanada, Fort Guijarros Journal*

RESEARCH CENTER: Promotes local history through public outreach programs.

PROGRAMS: Annual Meeting; Community Outreach; Elder's Programs; Exhibits; Festivals; Guided Tours; Interpretation; Lectures; Publication; Research Library/Archives; Theatre

COLLECTIONS: [1796-1945] 262,000 objects; 9,000 image photo archives; 2 linear feet archives; the 262,000 artifacts are in 400 archival boxes in a HVAC bunker; science lab.

HOURS: Yr 10-4

ADMISSION: No charge

778
Gaslamp Quarter Historical Floundation
410 Island Ave, 92101; (p) (619) 233-4692; (f) (619) 233-4148; www.gqhf.com; (c) San Diego

Private non-profit/ 1982/ staff: 1(f); 100(v)/ members: 100/publication: *Quarternotes*

HISTORICAL SOCIETY: Operates William Heath Davis House Museum and provides tours of Gaslamp Quarter.

PROGRAMS: Facility Rental; Festivals; Guided Tours; Publication; Research Library/Archives

COLLECTIONS: [1850-1910] Local history, materials on William Heath Davis and Alonzo E. Horton, commercial and cultural materials.

HOURS: Yr Varies

ADMISSION: $3

779
Historical Shrine Foundation of San Diego County, The
2482 San Diego Ave, 92110; (p) (619) 298-2482; (c) San Diego

Private non-profit/ 1956/ staff: 2(f); 3(p); 2(v)/ members: 79

HISTORICAL SOCIETY: Operates and maintains the Whaley family house built in 1856.

PROGRAMS: Annual Meeting; Concerts; Festivals; Garden Tours; Guided Tours; Interpretation; Lectures

COLLECTIONS: [1849-1880] Historic house, period furniture, artifacts and memorabilia.

HOURS: Yr Oct-May M, W- Su; June-Sept M-Su

ADMISSION: $4, Student $2, Seniors $3

780
Maritime Museum of San Diego
1492 N Harbor Dr, 92101 [1306 N Harbor Dr, 92101]; (p) (619) 234-9153; (f) (619) 234-8345; info@sdmaritime.com; www.sdmaritime.com; (c) San Diego

Private non-profit/ 1948/ staff: 29(f); 20(p); 325(v)/ members: 2308

HISTORIC SITE; LIVING HISTORY/OUTDOOR MUSEUM: Preserves maritime history of San Diego.

PROGRAMS: Annual Meeting; Community Outreach; Concerts; Elder's Programs; Exhibits; Facility Rental; Family Programs; Festivals; Film/Video; Guided Tours; Interpretation; Lectures; Living History; Publication; Research Library/Archives; School-Based Curriculum; Thetre

COLLECTIONS: [1863] 1863 "Star of India", ferryboat "Berkeley", and 1904 steam yacht "Medea."

HOURS: Yr Daily 9-8

ADMISSION: $6, Children $2, Seniors $4

781
Mission Basilica San Diego de Alcal
10818 San Diego Mission Rd, 92108; (p) (619) 283-7319; (c) San Diego

Private non-profit/ 1769/ staff: 1(p); 50(v)/ members: 90

HISTORIC SITE: Preserves history of CA missions.

PROGRAMS: Concerts; Festivals; Guided Tours; Research Library/Archives

COLLECTIONS: [1769-1823] Books; birth, sacramental, and death records from 1776.

HOURS: Yr Daily 9-5

782
San Diego Aerospace Museum
2001 Pan American Plaza, 92101; (p) (619) 234-8291; (f) (619) 233-4526; www.aerospacemuseum.org; (c) San Diego

Private non-profit/ 1961/ Board of Directors/ staff: 16(f); 24(p); 273(v)/ members: 5200

HISTORIC SITE; HISTORY MUSEUM: Promotes air and space technology history through the display of historic collections.

PROGRAMS: Community Outreach; Elder's Programs; Exhibits; Facility Rental; Guided Tours; Lectures; Research Library/Archives

COLLECTIONS: [1900-present] 106 aircraft and spacecraft, 2,000,000 photos, 35,000 bound volumes, 12,000 supporting objects.

HOURS: Yr Daily 10-4:30

ADMISSION: $6,

783
San Diego Archaeological Center
334 11th Ave, 92101; (p) (619) 238-1868; (f) (619) 239-1869; (c) San Diego

Private non-profit/ 1993/ Board of Directors/ staff: 2(f); 2(p); 20(v)

ARCHAEOLOGICAL SITE/MUSEUM: Preserves and curates prehistoric and historic archaeological artifacts, and promotes educational, cultural, and scientific use of archaeological collections.

PROGRAMS: Community Outreach; Exhibits; Interpretation; Lectures

COLLECTIONS: [Prehistoric and historic] Prehistoric and historic archaeological artifacts, photos, monographs, and reports.

HOURS: Yr M-F 9-4, Sa 9-3

ADMISSION: No charge

784
San Diego Civil War Roundtable
[PO Box 22369, 92192]; (p) (619) 672-2593; djsj21643@aol.com; (c) San Diego

Private non-profit/ 1986/ members: 90

HISTORICAL SOCIETY: Promotes Civil War history.

PROGRAMS: Family Programs; Interpretation; Lectures; Living History

785
San Diego County Archaeological Society
[PO Box A-81106, 92138]; (p) (858) 538-0935; sdcas@email.com; www.groups.sdinsider.com/sdcas; (c) San Diego

Private non-profit/ staff: 220(v)/ members: 215

HISTORICAL SOCIETY: Preserves anthropological and archaeological heritage of San Diego County and environs.

PROGRAMS: Annual Meeting; Community Outreach; Exhibits; Guided Tours; Publication; Research Library/Archives

COLLECTIONS: Historic Johnson-Taylor adobe.

HOURS: Jan-Nov Sa 11-4

ADMISSION: Donations accepted

786
San Diego Hall of Champions Sports Museum
The Federal Building, 2133 Pan American Plaza, 92101; (p) (619) 234-2544; (f) (619) 234-4543; sdhoc@k-online.com; www.sandiegoinsider.com; (c) San Diego

Private non-profit/ 1946/ Board of Directors/ staff: 10(f); 5(p); 20(v)/ members: 553

HISTORIC SITE: Operates museum, library, and archives; preserves, studies, interprets, and exhibits significant materials and objects relating to athletes and athletics; provides related educational services for increasing public knowledge.

PROGRAMS: Community Outreach; Exhibits; Facility Rental; Family Programs; Film/Video; Guided Tours; Interpretation; Lectures; Publication; Research Library/Archives; School-Based Curriculum; Theatre

COLLECTIONS: [20th c] Objects and memorabilia, published works, manuscripts, periodicals, bulletins, and photos of local sports history.

HOURS: Yr

787
San Diego Historical Society
El Prado Blvd, 92138 [PO Box 81825, 92138]; (p) (619) 232-6203; (f) (619) 232-6297; htt://edweb.sdsu.edu/sdhs; (c) San Diego

Private non-profit/ staff: 30(f); 15(p); 40(v)/ members: 4000/publication: *Journal of San Diego History*

HISTORICAL SOCIETY; HISTORY MUSEUM; HOUSE MUSEUM: The Society operates four sites: Casa de Balboa - exhibits and research archives, Junipero Sera Museum - sit of the first presidio, Marston house - arts and crafts, Villa Montezuma - Victorian house.

PROGRAMS: Elder's Programs; Exhibits; Facility Rental; Family Programs; Festivals; Garden Tours; Guided Tours; Interpretation; Lectures; Publication; Research Library/Archives; School-Based Curriculum

COLLECTIONS: The collection includes 2 million photographs and archives collection; 10,000 artifacts and 3 historic sites representing San Diego Culture and history.

HOURS: Yr T-Su

788
San Diego Model Railroad Museum
1649 El Parado, 92101; (p) (619) 696-0199; (f) (619) 696-0239; SDModRailM@abac.com; www.sdmodelrailroadm.com; (c) San Diego

Private non-profit/ 1981/ Board of Directors/ staff: 2(f); 30(p); 300(v)/ members: 900

HISTORY MUSEUM

PROGRAMS: Community Outreach; Elder's Programs; Facility Rental; Family Programs; Film/Video; Guided Tours; Research Library/ Archives; School-Based Curriculum

COLLECTIONS: [1935-present] Scale model and toy train operation and historical rolling-stock; prototype artifacts; educational exhibits relating to trains; train model railroad related library.

HOURS: Yr

ADMISSION: $3; Under 15 free

789
San Diego Museum of Man, The
1350 El Prado, Balboa Park, 92101; (p) (619) 239-2001; (f) (619) 239-2749; www.museum ofman.org; (c) San Diego

Private non-profit/ 1915/ staff: 21(f); 14(p); 220(v)/ members: 1500

ANTHROPOLOGY MUSEUM: Focuses on diverse cultures of world, human biology, and human ecology through programs, exhibits, education, research, and publication.

PROGRAMS: Annual Meeting; Community Outreach; Exhibits; Facility Rental; Family Programs; Festivals; Guided Tours; Lectures; Research Library/Archives; School-Based Curriculum

COLLECTIONS: [4.4 million years of human history] 76,000 items primarily Southwest Americas; human origin collections, weapons collection, artifacts from the Egypt Exploration Society.

HOURS: Yr Daily 10-4:30

ADMISSION: $5, Children $3

790
San Diego Natural History Museum Library
1788 El Prado, 92112 [PO Box 121390, 92112-1390]; (p) (619) 232-3821; (f) (619) 232-0248; library@sdnhm.org; www.sdnhm.org; (c) San Diego

Private non-profit/ 1874/ Board of Trustees/ staff: 1(f); 13(v)

HISTORY MUSEUM: Contains information and documents on early San Diego history; the development of science and natural history explorations in the West, CA, and Baja CA.

PROGRAMS: Research Library/Archives

COLLECTIONS: [1800s-present] 92,000 volumes, 1,100 original watercolors, approximately 600 cubic feet of archives, 1,500 slides, 5,000 maps, 4,500 negatives and prints, and scrapbooks.

HOURS: Yr By appt only

ADMISSION: No charge

791
Save Our Heritage Organization
Senlis Cottage, 92163 [PO Box 3429, 92163-3429]; (p) (619) 297-9327; (f) (619) 238-1725; shohsd@aol.com; (c) San Diego

Joint/ 1969/ County; Private non-profit/ staff: 15(v)/ members: 700/publication: *Reflections*

HISTORIC PRESERVATION AGENCY: Promotes history of San Diego County.

PROGRAMS: Annual Meeting; Community Outreach; Guided Tours; Lectures

792
Wells Fargo Bank Museum
2733 San Diego Ave, 92110; (p) (619) 238-3929

HISTORY MUSEUM: Preserves history of Wells Fargo Bank.

PROGRAMS: Exhibits; Guided Tours

COLLECTIONS: [19th-20th c] Concord Stagecoach; Wells Fargo banking and express history; mining; staging.

HOURS: Daily 10-5

793
William Heath Davis House
410 Island Ave, 92101; (p) (619) 233-4692; (f) (619) 233-4148

1850/ staff: 10(v)

COLLECTIONS: [1850-1880]

HOURS: Yr

SAN FRANCISCO

794
AAA-California State Automobile Association Archives
150 Van Ness, 94102; (p) (415) 551-5466; (f) (415) 552-9269; alison_moore@csaa.com; (c) San Francisco

Private non-profit/ 1998/ staff: 1(f); 2(p)

LIBRARY AND/OR ARCHIVES: Collects, preserves, and exhibits CSAA's historic records, objects, and memorabilia.

PROGRAMS: Exhibits; Research Library/ Archives

COLLECTIONS: [20th c] Executive papers; employee publications; member magazine; insurance records and memorabilia; travel.

HOURS: Yr M-F 8:30-5:30

795
Alcatraz Island
Fort Mason, Building 20 - Alcatraz, 94123; (p) (415) 561-4900, (415) 705-5555; (f) (415) 561-4910; goga_alcatraz@nps.gov; www.nps.gov/alca/index.htm

Federal/ National Park Service

HISTORIC SITE; NATIONAL PARK: Preserves of former federal prison, early military fortification, and West Coast's first lighthouse.

PROGRAMS: Exhibits; Guided Tours; Interpretation

COLLECTIONS: [20th c] Artifacts, memorabilia.

HOURS: Yr

796
California Council for the Humanities
312 Sutter St, Ste 601, 94108; (p) (415) 391-1474; (f) (415) 391-1312; info@calhum.org; www.calhum.org; (c) San Francisco

Private non-profit/ 1975/ staff: 15(f); 3(p)/publication: *Humanities Network*

PROFESSIONAL ORGANIZATION: Creates and funds public humanities programs, many of a historical nature, for CA public.

PROGRAMS: Annual Meeting; Community Outreach; Exhibits; Lectures; Living History; Publication

797
California Exhibition Resources Alliance
312 Sutter St, Ste 601, 94108; (p) (415) 391-1474; (f) (415) 319-1312; leriksen@calhum.org; www.calhum.org; (c) San Francisco

Private non-profit/ 1988/ California Council for the Humanities/ staff: 1(f); 1(p)/publication: *Exhibition Guides*

ALLIANCE OF HISTORICAL AGENCIES: Presernts public programs and humanities exhibitions.

PROGRAMS: Community Outreach; Exhibits; Interpretation; Lectures; Publication; School-Based Curriculum

798
California Heritage Council
1088 Green St, 94133; (p) (415) 474-0780; (f) (415) 441-6338; (c) San Francisco

1959/ Board of Directors/ staff: 1(f); 10(v)/ members: 225

HISTORICAL SOCIETY: Promotes conservation of historical sites.

PROGRAMS: Annual Meeting; Community Outreach; Guided Tours; Lecures

799
California Historical Society
678 Mission St, 94105; (p) (415) 357-1848; (f) (415) 357-1850; info@calhist.org; www.calhist.org; (c) San Francisco

Private non-profit/ 1871/ staff: 15(f); 6(p); 35(v)/ members: 6500/publication: *California History*

ART MUSEUM; HISTORICAL SOCIETY; HISTORY MUSEUM; RESEARCH CENTER: Collects, preserves, exhibits, publishes, and interprets CA history.

PROGRAMS: Annual Meeting; Community Outreach; Exhibits; Guided Tours; Lectures; Publication; Research Library/Archives

COLLECTIONS: [Prehistory-present] 5000 works of fine art, 500,000 photographs; North Baker Research Library: 35,000 books and pamphlets, 3700 maps, posters, broadsides, 2500 periodicals, and 3800 manuscripts.

HOURS: Yr T-Sa 11-5

ADMISSION: $2, Student $1, Seniors $1

800
California Palace of the Legion of Honor
34th Ave and Clement St, 94121; (p) (415) 750-3600; (f) (415) 750-3696; www.legion of honor.org; (c) San Francisco

City/ 1924/ Board of Trustees/ staff: 170(f); 700(v)/ members: 56000

ART MUSEUM; HISTORY MUSEUM

PROGRAMS: Annual Meeting; Community Outreach; Exhibits; Festivals; Guided Tours; Interpretation

COLLECTIONS: [4,000 years of Ancient and European Art] Ancient Egyptian and Roman Art, Medieval Tapestries and sculpture, 15th to 20th century European paintings, decorative arts, porcelain works.

HOURS: Yr

801
Chinese Historical Society of America
644 Broadway St, 94123; (p) (415) 391-1188; (f) (415) 391-1150; www.chsa.org; (c) San Francisco

Private non-profit/ 1963/ staff: 1(f); 2(p); 5(v)/ members: 450/publication: *Chinese American History and Perspectives*

HISTORICAL SOCIETY: Preserves, documents, and disseminates Chinese American history.

PROGRAMS: Exhibits; Guided Tours; Lectures; Publication

COLLECTIONS: [1850s-1990s]

HOURS: Yr M 1-4, T-F 10:30-4

ADMISSION: No charge

802
Fort Point National Historic Site
Long Ave & Marina Dr/Presidio, 94129 [PO Box 29333, 94129-0333]; (p) (415) 556-1693; (f) (415) 556-8474; www.nps.gov/fopo; (c) San Francisco

Federal/ 1970/ National Park Service/ staff: 8(f); 85(v)/publication: *Fort Point: Sentry at the Golden Gate*

HISTORIC SITE; HISTORY MUSEUM; HOUSE MUSEUM; LIVING HISTORY/OUTDOOR MUSEUM: Preserves and interprets military, cultural, and natural histories.

PROGRAMS: Exhibits; Film/Video; Guided Tours; Interpretation; Publication; Reenactments; Research Library/Archives; School-Based Curriculum

COLLECTIONS: [Civil War-present] Civil War era fortification, 5 cannon accessories, 6 cannon, photographs, artifacts.

HOURS: Yr Daily 10-5

ADMISSION: No charge

803
Gay, Lesbian, Bisexual, Transgender Historical Society of Northern California
973 Market St #400, 94142 [PO Box 424280, 94142]; (p) (415) 777-5455; glhsnc@aol.com; www.glhs.org; (c) San Francisco

Private non-profit/ 1985/ staff: 4(p); 15(v)/ members: 500/publication: *Our Stories*

HISTORICAL SOCIETY; RESEARCH CENTER: Collects, preserves, and promotes history of sexual diversity in Northern CA.

PROGRAMS: Annual Meeting; Community Outreach; Exhibits; Interpretation; Lectures; Publication; Research Library/Archives

COLLECTIONS: [1945-present] 300 manuscripts, 300 oral histories, and 3,000 periodical files.

HOURS: Yr Sa, Su 2-5

ADMISSION: No charge

804
Haas-Lilienthal House
2007 Franklin St, 94109; (p) (415) 441-3000, (415) 441-3004; (f) (415) 441-3015; info@sfheritage.org; www.sfheritage.org

1886/ staff: 4(f); 1(p)

HOUSE MUSEUM

COLLECTIONS: [1890s-1906, 1970s] Home furnishings, appliances, art, and costumes from Haas and Lilienthal families; photos, deeds, public records, permits, blue prints, a reference library; survey work on San Francisco's neighborhoods, buildings; city history.

HOURS: Yr

805
International Museum of Women
[PO Box 642370, 94164-2370]; (p) (415) 775-1366; (f) (415) 775-6198; info@imow.org; www.imow.org; (c) San Francisco

Private non-profit

HISTORY MUSEUM: Documents lives of women worldwide.

ADMISSION: No charge

806
Levi Strauss and Company Archives
1155 Battery St, 94111; (p) (415) 501-6577; (f) (415) 501-6443; ldowney@levi.com; www.levistrauss.com; (c) San Francisco

Private non-profit/ 1853/ Levi Strauss Company/ staff: 1(f); 1(p)/ members: 1

CORPORATE ARCHIVES/MUSEUM: Collects, and preserves company's documentary, photographic, marketing, and textile collections; maintains corporate museum.

PROGRAMS: Guided Tours; Lectures; Publication

COLLECTIONS: [1853-present] Documents, photographs, marketing materials, and clothing regarding Levi's jeans and other clothing, corporate philanthropy, the life of Levi Strauss, the social history of clothing, and the history of the West.

HOURS: By appt only

807
M. H. deYoung Memorial Museum
Golden Gate Park, 94118; (p) (415) 750-3600; (f) (415) 750-7692; www.deyoungmuseum.org; (c) San Francisco

City/ 1894/ Board of Trustees/ staff: 170(f); 700(v)/ members: 56000

ART MUSEUM

PROGRAMS: Community Outreach; Exhibits; Guided Tours; Interpretation

COLLECTIONS: Artifacts, paintings, textiles, sculptures, furniture, and memorabilia.

ADMISSION: $7, Children $4, Seniors $5; Under 12

SAN FRANCISCO

808
Mission San Francisco de Asis (Mission Dolores)
3321 16th St, 94110; (p) (415) 621-8203; (f) (415) 621-2294; doloresssf@aol.com; (c) San Francisco

Private non-profit/ 1776/ Archdiocese of San Francisco

HISTORIC SITE; HISTORY MUSEUM: Preserves Spanish colonial and CA mission history.

PROGRAMS: Elder's Programs; Exhibits; Facility Rental; Garden Tours; School-Based Curriculum

COLLECTIONS: [18th-19th c] Church site and grounds; Mexican period artwork.

HOURS: Yr Daily 9-4

ADMISSION: $3, Children $2

809
Museum of Vision
655 Beach St, Ste 300, 94109-1336; (p) (415) 561-8500; (f) (415) 561-8533; www.aao.org; (c) San Francisco

Private non-profit/ 1980/ Foundation of the American Academy of Ophthalmology/ staff: 3(f); 18(v)

HISTORY MUSEUM: Collects, preserves, and interprets ophthalmic history.

PROGRAMS: Community Outreach; Interpretation; Research Library/Archives

COLLECTIONS: 10,000 artifacts: rare books, historical archives, memorabilia, art work, medals, coins, and stamps.

HOURS: Yr 9-4

ADMISSION: No charge

810

National Japanese American Historical Society

1684 Post, 94115; (p) (415) 921-5007; (f) (415) 921-5087; njahs@njahs.org; www.njahs.org; (c) San Francisco

Private non-profit/ 1981/ Board of Directors/ staff: 2(f); 3(p); 50(v)/ members: 2200/publication: *Reminiscing in Swingtime, Pacific War and Peace*

HISTORICAL SOCIETY: Preserves and promotes Japanese American history.

PROGRAMS: Annual Meeting; Community Outreach; Elder's Programs; Exhibits; Facility Rental; Family Programs; Garden Tours; Guided Tours; Interpretation; Lectures; Living History; Publication; Research Library/Archives; School-Based Curriculum

811

National Maritime Museum Association

900 Beach St, 94147 [PO Box 470310, 94147]; (p) (415) 561-6662; (f) (415) 561-6660; (c) San Francisco

Private non-profit/ 1950/ staff: 25(f); 35(p); 500(v)/ members: 1800/publication: *The Sea Letter*

ALLIANCE OF HISTORICAL AGENCIES; HISTORIC PRESERVATION AGENCY: Maintains Maritime Museum, Hyde St. Pier, and USS Pampanito.

PROGRAMS: Concerts; Exhibits; Facility Rental; Family Programs; Festivals; Guided Tours; Interpretation; Living History; Publication; School-Based Curriculum

COLLECTIONS: Artifacts, articles on maritime history, memorabilia, and restored ships and

812

National Society of the Colonial Dames of America in California, The

2645 Gough St, 94123; (p) (415) 441-7512; (c) San Francisco

Private non-profit/ 1895/ staff: 30(v)/ members: 463

HISTORICAL SOCIETY; HOUSE MUSEUM: Maintains museums and historic shrines across US.

PROGRAMS: Exhibits; Guided Tours; Publication

COLLECTIONS: [Colonial period-1830] Octagon House: museum of decorative arts and historic documents of Colonial and Federal periods of eastern US.

HOURS: Feb-Dec 2nd Su and 2nd and 4th Th 12-3

ADMISSION:

813

San Francisco Architectural Heritage

2007 Franklin St, 94109; (p) (415) 441-3000; (f) (415) 441-3015; info@sfheritage.org; www.sfheritage.org; (c) San Francisco

Private non-profit/ 1971/ staff: 6(f); 40(v)/ members: 1750/publication: *Heritage*

HISTORIC PRESERVATION AGENCY; HISTORIC SITE; HOUSE MUSEUM: Promotes conservation and adaptive reuse of architecturally and historically significant buildings in San Francisco; educates on City's architectural environment.

PROGRAMS: Annual Meeting; Community Outreach; Facility Rental; Guided Tours; Lectures; Publication; School-Based Curriculum

COLLECTIONS: Queen Anne Victorian house containing historical materials.

HOURS: Yr W-Sa 12-3, Su 11-4

ADMISSION: $5, Seniors $3

814

San Francisco Historical Society

[PO Box 420569, 94142]; (p) (415) 775-1111; (f) (415) 584-3984; www.sfhistory.org; (c) San Francisco

Private non-profit/ 1988/ staff: 1(p); 100(v)/ members: 1500/publication: *Argonaut*

HISTORICAL SOCIETY: Preserves, interprets, and presents historical data related to City and County of San Francisco.

PROGRAMS: Annual Meeting; Community Outreach; Exhibits; Festivals; Guided Tours; Interpretation; Lectures; Publication

COLLECTIONS: [1849-present]

815

San Francisco History Center/San Francisco Public Library

100 Larkin St, 94102 [Civic Center, 94102]; (p) (415) 557-4567; (f) (415) 437-4849; info@sfpl.org; www.sfpl.org; (c) San Francisco

Joint/ 1879/ City;County/ staff: 6(f); 7(p)

LIBRARY AND/OR ARCHIVES: Collects, preserves, and interprets the history of San Francisco.

PROGRAMS: Community Outreach; Exhibits; Facility Rental; Lectures; Research Library/Archives

COLLECTIONS: [1850-present] Primary and secondary materials in print, audiovisual and digital formats: books, pamphlets, newspapers, maps, videos, posters, manuscripts, diaries, scrapbooks, oral histories, artifacts, 250,000 photos, municipal records; gay and lesbian collection.

HOURS: Yr T-Th 10-6, F 12-6, Sa 10-6,

816

San Francisco Maritime National Historical Park

Bldg E Fort Mason Center, 94123; (p) (415) 556-1659; (f) (415) 556-1624; safr_adminis tration@nps.gov; www.nps.gov/safr; (c) San Francisco

1988/ National Park Service/ staff: 7(f); 300(v)/publication: *Sea Letter Magazine*

HISTORIC SITE: Preserves and interprets history of America's maritime heritage, especially of Pacific Coast.

PROGRAMS: Community Outreach; Concerts; Elder's Programs; Exhibits; Facility Rental; Family Programs; Festivals; Film/Video; Guided Tours; Interpretation; Lectures; Living History; Publication; Research Library/Archives; School-Based Curriculum; Theatre

COLLECTIONS: [Late 1800s-early 1900s] 1886 square-rigger,1895 schooner, 1890 fer-

ryboat, 1907 steam tugboat, 1915 steam schooner, 1914 tugboat, fine art, folk art, artifacts, photos, books, oral histories, periodicals, architectural drawings and textual records.

HOURS: Yr Daily 10-5

ADMISSION: $5, Children $2

817

Society of California Pioneers, The

300 Fourth St, 94107; (p) (415) 957-1849; (f) (415) 957-9858; pioneer@wenet.net; www.wenet.net/~pioneers; (c) San Francisco

Private non-profit/ 1850/ staff: 3(f); 3(p); 1(v)/ members: 1000

HISTORICAL SOCIETY: Preserves and promotes California heritage.

PROGRAMS: Exhibits; Research Library/ Archives; School-Based Curriculum

COLLECTIONS: [19th and 20th c] Paintings, artifacts, manuscripts, photos.

818

United States District Court for the Northern District of California Historical Society

450 Golden Gate Ave, 94102 [PO Box 36112, 94102]; (p) (415) 522-4620, (415) 522-2121; (c) San Francisco

Private non-profit/ 1977/ staff: 3(v)/ members: 300/publication: *Historical Reporter*

HISTORICAL SOCIETY: Preserves and interprets history of Court through oral histories, public programs, and publications.

PROGRAMS: Exhibits, lectures, publication.

819

Wells Fargo Historical Services

420 Montgomery St, 2nd Fl, 94163; (p) (415) 391-8644; (f) (415) 391-8644; smithb@wells fargo.com; www.wellsfargohistory.com; (c) San Francisco

Private for-profit/ 1852/ Wells Fargo and Company/ staff: 17(f); 29(p)/publication: *Wells Fargo Since 1852*

HISTORY MUSEUM: Collects and presents company history focusing on 19th century banking and express.

PROGRAMS: Exhibits; Guided Tours; Interpretation; Publication; Research Library/Archives

COLLECTIONS: [1849-1918] Original Concord stagecoaches, treasure boxes, Howard and Davis gold balance scales, Wiltsee and Livingston collection of western postal and express mail, Samuel Dorsey collection of gold ore, original Western art.

HOURS: Yr Daily 10-5

SAN GABRIEL

820

San Gabriel Mission Museum

428 S Mission, 91776; (p) (626) 457-3048; (f) (626) 282-5308; (c) Los Angeles

Private non-profit/ 1771/ Archdiocese of Los Angeles/ staff: 2(f); 3(p); 17(v)/ members: 1

ART MUSEUM; HISTORIC PRESERVATION AGENCY; HISTORIC SITE; HISTORY MUSEUM; LIVING HISTORY/OUTDOOR MUSEUM: The fourth oldest California Mission.

PROGRAMS: Community Outreach; Exhibits; Film/Video; Guided Tours; Lectures

COLLECTIONS: [1600s and 1700s] Crosses painted by Gabrielino Indian, 1623 bedroom set, original books from 1427 and 1588, original statues brought from Spain 1791.

HOURS: Yr Daily 9-4:30

ADMISSION: $4, Children

SAN JOSE

821
California Pioneers of Santa Clara County
[PO Box 8206, 95155]; (p) (408) 732-1946; (c) Santa Clara

County; Private non-profit/ 1875/ Board of Directors/ staff: 24(v)/ members: 700

HISTORICAL SOCIETY: Preserves and interprets history of CA pioneers.

PROGRAMS: Publication; Quarterly Meeting

COLLECTIONS: [18th -19th c]

822
Fallon House
175 W St John St, 95110; (p) (408) 993-8182; (f) (408) 993-8184; www.historysanjose.org

HOUSE MUSEUM

PROGRAMS: Exhibits

COLLECTIONS: 15 room Victorian with period furnishing.

823
Filipino American National History Society, Santa Clara Valley Chapter
1575 Amesbury Way, 95127-4604; (p) (408) 926-2039, (408) 726-1098; Rraymundo@ aol.com; www.fanhs-national.org; (c) Santa Clara

Private non-profit/ 1991/ members: 26/publication: *Filipino Journals*

HISTORICAL SOCIETY: Promotes history and culture of Filipino Americans in the US.

PROGRAMS: Annual Meeting; Community Outreach; Exhibits; Lectures; Publication; Research Library/Archives; Theatre

COLLECTIONS: Literature, artifacts, photos, media, maps, and decorative arts.

HOURS: Yr T-Su 12-5

ADMISSION: $6, Children $4, Seniors $5; Tu-F free

825
Japanese American Resource Center/Museum
535 N Fifth St, 95112; (p) (408) 294-3138; mail@jarc-m.org; www.jara-m.org; (c) Santa Clara

Private non-profit/ 1987/ State of California/ staff: 18(v)/ members: 470

HISTORY MUSEUM; LIVING HISTORY/OUTDOOR MUSEUM; RESEARCH CENTER: Collects, preserves, and disseminates arts, culture and history of Japanese Americans, with emphasis on Santa Clara County.

PROGRAMS: Community Outreach; Exhibits; Family Programs; Guided Tours; Lectures; Research Library/Archives; School-Based Curriculum

COLLECTIONS: [1865-1965] Photos and artifacts.

HOURS: Su 11-2, T-F 11-3

ADMISSION: No charge

826
Los Fundadores De Alta California
1509 Warburton Ave, 95127 [1053 S. White Rd, 95127]; (p) (408) 926-1165; EMartinz07@aol.com; (c) Santa Clara

Private non-profit/ 1987/ staff: 2(v)/ members: 100/publication: *Los Fundadores*

GENEALOGICAL SOCIETY; HISTORIC SITE; HOUSE MUSEUM; LIVING HISTORY/OUTDOOR MUSEUM; RESEARCH CENTER: Preserves history and heritage of founding families of California, early pioneers of Santa Clara County, and Native Americans.

PROGRAMS: Annual Meeting; Community Outreach; Exhibits; Festivals; Guided Tours; Publication; Research Library/Archives

COLLECTIONS: [1769-1852] Genealogical research materials; unpublished materials; early pioneer portraits.

HOURS: Jan-Nov Su 1-4 and by appt

827
Mount Diablo Surveyors Historical Society
5042 Amethyst Ct, 95136-2601; (p) (408) 265-9869; (f) (408) 265-9869; duncanma@ home.com; www.ca-surveyors.org/diablo; (c) Santa Clara

Private non-profit/ 1991/ Board of Directors/ staff: 74(v)/ members: 74/publication: *Mount Diablo Surveyors Historical Society*

Promotes history of land surveying.

COLLECTIONS: Land surveying instruments, books, maps, numerous

828
New Almaden Quicksilver County Park Association
21350 Almaden Rd, 95120; (p) (408) 323-1107; (f) (408) 323-0943; (c) Santa Clara

County/ 1981/ staff: 1(p); 55(v)/ members: 600/publication: *Quicksilver County Park News*

HISTORIC PRESERVATION AGENCY; HISTORIC SITE; HISTORY MUSEUM: Preserves history of mercury mining.

PROGRAMS: Community Outreach; Exhibits; Facility Rental; Family Programs; Film/Video; Guided Tours; Interpretation; Lectures; Living History; Publication; Reenactments; Research Library/Archives; Theatre

COLLECTIONS: [1845-1976] Ore samples, mining artifacts, historical papers, blacksmith tools, maps, drawings, household artifacts.

HOURS: Yr 10-4

ADMISSION: No charge

829
Sourisseau Academy for State and Local History
History Dept, San Jose State University, 95192; (p) (908) 924-6510; (c) Santa Clara

Private for-profit; Private non-profit/ 1970/ Board of Trustees/ staff: 2(p)

RESEARCH CENTER

PROGRAMS: Research Library/Archives

COLLECTIONS: [1850-1950] Photographs, newspapers, private papers, student papers, building permits, and books.

HOURS: By appt only

SAN JUAN BAUTISTA

830
Castro/Breen Adobe
19 Franklin St, 95045 [PO Box 787, 95045-0787]; (p) (408) 623-4526; (f) (408) 623-4312; sjbshp@pnet.

1840/ Dept of Parks & Recreation/ staff: 7(f); 3(p); 30(v)

HOUSE MUSEUM

PROGRAMS: Exhibits

COLLECTIONS: [1865-1870] Period furnished home, General Castro's office, early California artifacts.

HOURS: Yr

831
San Juan Bautista Historical Society
Monterey & Third Sts, 95045 [PO Box 1308, 95045-1308]; (p) (831) 623-4904; (f) (831) 623-4904; (c) San Benito

Private non-profit/ 1965/ staff: 3(v)/ members: 68/publication: *The Historian*

HISTORIC SITE; HISTORICAL SOCIETY; HISTORY MUSEUM; RESEARCH CENTER: Site for San Juan Bautista Mission and State Historic Park; encourages preservation of privately owned historic buildings and memorabilia of local citizens.

PROGRAMS: Annual Meeting; Exhibits; Film/Video; Interpretation; Publication; Research Library/Archives

COLLECTIONS: [1797-present] Photos, clippings, genealogy sources, artifacts, restored gas station, settler's cabin.

HOURS: Yr

824
History San Jose
1650 Senter Rd, 95112; (p) (408) 287-2290; (f) (408) 287-2291; dnowicki@historysj.org; www.historysanjose.org; (c) Santa Clara

Joint / 1971/ City; Private non-profit/ staff: 25(f); 200(v)/ members: 750

HISTORY MUSEUM: Manages two sites: History Park and Peralta Adobe and Fallon House; 500,000 historical artifacts from Santa Clara Valley.

PROGRAMS: Community Outreach; Exhibits; Facility Rental; Family Programs; Guided Tours; Lectures; Research Library/Archives; School-Based Curriculum

COLLECTIONS: 500,000 items: material culture artifacts, farm and medical equipment, wheeled vehicles, maps, private records, ephemera; 26 restored and reconstructed buildings; City and county archives, private manuscripts, corporate records, photos,

832

San Juan Bautista State Historic Park

19 Franklin St, 95045 [PO Box 787, 95045]; (p) (831) 623-4526; (f) (831) 623-4612; sjbshp@hollinet.com; (c) San Benito

State/ 1933/ State Parks/ staff: 7(f); 8(p); 35(v)

HISTORIC SITE; HOUSE MUSEUM: Maintains four historic house museums.

PROGRAMS: Exhibits; Facility Rental; Family Programs; Garden Tours; Guided Tours; Interpretation; Research Library/Archives; School-Based Curriculum

COLLECTIONS: [1830-1870] Period-furnished historic homes.

HOURS: Yr Daily 10-4:30

ADMISSION: $2, Children $1

SAN JUAN CAPISTRANO

833

Mission San Juan Capistrano

Corner of Ortega Hwy & Camino Capistrano, 92693 [PO Box 697, 92693]; (p) (949) 234-1300; (f) (949) 443-2061; museum@fea.net; www.missionsjc.com; (c) Orange

Joint; Private non-profit/ 1776/ Board of Directors/Mission Preservation Foundation/ staff: 30(f); 3(p); 100(v)

HISTORIC SITE; HISTORY MUSEUM; LIVING HISTORY/OUTDOOR MUSEUM; REENACTMENTS: Preserves history of CA missions.

PROGRAMS: Community Outreach; Concerts; Exhibits; Facility Rental; Family Programs; Festivals; Garden Tours; Guided Tours; Interpretation; Lectures; Living History; Reenactments; Research Library/Archives; School-Based Curriculum

COLLECTIONS: [Pre Spanish-present] Artifacts from Native American, Spanish, Mexican, and American cultures: stone tools, baskets, textiles, sculptures, religious statuary, mental implements, and furniture.

HOURS: Yr Daily 8:30-5

ADMISSION: $6, Children $4

834

San Juan Capistrano Historical Society

31831 Los Rios St, 92675; (p) (949) 493-8444; (f) (949) 493-0061; (c) Orange

Private non-profit/ 1963/ staff: 1(f); 30(v)/ members: 400

HISTORICAL SOCIETY: Preserves local history.

PROGRAMS: Annual Meeting; Exhibits; Guided Tours

COLLECTIONS: [Early 1900s] Photos, books, library, and artifacts.

HOURS: Yr T-F 9-12 1-4, Su 12-3

ADMISSION: Donations requested

SAN LUIS OBISPO

835

Conservation Corps State Museum

1536 Modoc St, 93401 [PO Box 13510, 93406]; (p) (805) 788-0517; (f) (805) 788-0819; cccmuseum@thegrind.net; (c) San Luis Obispo

Private non-profit/ 1995/ Conservation Corps Institute/ staff: 1(f)/ members: 700/publication: *The Courier*

PROGRAMS: Research Library/Archives

COLLECTIONS: [1930-present] Documents Youth Corps movement, and interprets Civilian Conservation Corps barracks.

HOURS: Yr by appt

ADMISSION: No charge

836

Dallidet Adobe and Gardens

1185 Pacific, 93401; (p) (805) 543-6762, (805) 543-0158

Private non-profit/ 1858/ San Luis Obispo Historical Society

HOUSE MUSEUM

PROGRAMS: Exhibits; Facility Rental; Garden Tours

COLLECTIONS: [1858-1959] Period-furnished home, Dallidet Family materials, periodicals.

HOURS: May-Sept Su 1-4 and by appt

837

San Luis Obispo County Historical Society and Museum

696 Monterey St, 93406 [PO Box 1391, 93406]; (p) (805) 543-0638; (f) (805) 543-6659; www.sponet.org/vv/ipsslochm/; (c) San Luis Obispo

Private non-profit/ 1955/ Board of Directors/ staff: 2(f); 3(p); 40(v)/ members: 500

HISTORICAL SOCIETY; HISTORY MUSEUM; HOUSE MUSEUM: Maintains house museum.

PROGRAMS: Annual Meeting; Community Outreach; Exhibits; Family Programs; Guided Tours; Interpretation; Lectures; Research Library/Archives; School-Based Curriculum

COLLECTIONS: [Late 19th-early 20th c] Period-furnished home; materials on SLO county; photos, and glass plate negatives.

HOURS: Yr W-Su 10-4

ADMISSION: Donations accepted

838

Shakespeare Press Printing Museum/Cal Poly State University

Bldg 26, 93407 [1 Grand Ave, 93407]; (p) (805) 756-1108; (f) (805) 756-7118; (c) San Luis Obispo

State/ 1966/ Graphic Communication Department/ staff: 1(p); 10(v)/ members: 10

HISTORY MUSEUM: Promotes and preserves California Gold Rush era newspaper types and presses.

PROGRAMS: Exhibits

COLLECTIONS: [1850-1900] 15 hand or foot presses, 700 type fonts, 3 cutters, 1 linograph.

HOURS: By appt

ADMISSION: No charge

SAN MARINO

839

Huntington Library, Art Collections, and Botanical Gardens, The

1151 Oxford Rd, 91108; (p) (626) 405-2147; (f) (626) 449-1987; (c) Los Angeles

Private non-profit/ 1919/ staff: 800(v)/ members: 15586

CULTURAL CENTER; GARDEN; LIBRARY AND/OR ARCHIVES

PROGRAMS: Concerts; Exhibits; Family Programs; Garden Tours; Publication; Research Library/Archives; School-Based Curriculum

COLLECTIONS: [18th-20th c] 18th-19th century British and French art; 18th-20th century American art; Library: 4 million manuscripts and 600,000 rare books on Anglo-American literature and culture.

HOURS: Yr June-Aug 10:30-4:30; Sept-May 12-4:30

ADMISSION:

840

Pacific Railroad Society, Inc.

[PO Box 80726, 91118-8726]; (p) (323) 283-0087; www.pacificrailroadsociety.org; (c) Los Angeles

Private non-profit/ 1936/ Board of Directors/ staff: 105(v)/ members: 613

HISTORY MUSEUM: Promotes interest in railroad operations and travel history.

PROGRAMS: Research Library/Archives

COLLECTIONS: [1935-present] Ten passenger cars, 1 locomotive, railroad equipment, railroad artifacts, books, documents, and ephemera.

HOURS: Yr W 5-8, Sa 10-4

ADMISSION: Donations accepted

SAN MARTIN

841

Wing of History

12777 Murphy Ave, 95046 [PO Box 495, 95046]; (p) (408) 683-2290; (f) (408) 683-2291; www@wingsofhistory.org; (c) Santa Clara

Private non-profit/ 1975/ staff: 2(f); 4(p); 50(v)/ members: 500

HISTORY MUSEUM: Preserves and restores aviation history.

PROGRAMS: Exhibits; Facility Rental; Festivals; Guided Tours; Interpretation; Research Library/Archives

COLLECTIONS: [1906-present] Restoration facility; two display buildings with aircraft, artifacts, and artwork; propeller shop.

HOURS: Yr T-Th 10-3; Sa-Su

SAN MIGUEL

842

Friends of the Adobes, Inc., The

700 S Mission St, 93451 [PO Box 326, 93451]; (p) (805) 467-3357; (c) San Luis Obispo

Private non-profit/ 1968/ Board of Directors/ staff: 2(p); 30(v)/ members: 187/publication: *Caledonia Enterprise*

HISTORICAL SOCIETY: Promotes interest in history of northern San Luis Obispo and southern Monterey counties, and maintains two state historical landmarks: Rios-Caledonia Adobe and Estrella Adobe Church.

PROGRAMS: Exhibits; Family Programs; Guided Tours; Interpretation; Publication; Quarterly Meeting; Reenactments; Research Library/Archives; School-Based Curriculum

COLLECTIONS: [1845-1920] Artifacts and furnishings from Mexican period through 1920s.

HOURS: Yr Daily 10-4

ADMISSION: No charge

843
Mission San Miguel Arcangel
775 Mission St, 93451 [PO Box 69, 93451]; (p) (805) 467-3256; (f) (805) 467-2448; (c) San Luis Obispo

Private non-profit/ 1797/ Diocese of Monterey/ staff: 3(f); 4(p)

HISTORIC SITE; HISTORY MUSEUM: California 17th Mission

PROGRAMS: Elder's Programs; Exhibits; Festivals; Guided Tours; Research Library/ Archives; School-Based Curriculum

COLLECTIONS: [1700s-present] Mission artifacts.

HOURS: Yr Daily 9:30-4:30

ADMISSION: Donations accepted

SAN PABLO

844
San Pablo Historical Society
One Alvarado Sq, 94806; (p) (510) 215-3046; (f) (510) 620-0329; (c) Contra Costa

Private non-profit/ 1969/ staff: 1(f); 1(p); 15(v)

HISTORICAL SOCIETY; HISTORY MUSEUM; LIBRARY AND/OR ARCHIVES: Operates two historic homes: Blume house and the Alvarado Adobe.

PROGRAMS: Annual Meeting; Community Outreach; Exhibits; Facility Rental; Family Programs; Interpretation

COLLECTIONS: [1830-1930] Historic houses, furnishings, photos, documents, artifacts, and archives.

HOURS: Yr Su

SAN PEDRO

845
Fort MacArthur Museum
3601 S Gaffey St, 90731; (p) (310) 548-2631; (f) (310) 241-0847; director@ftmac.org; www.ftmac.org; (c) Los Angeles

City/ 1986/ Los Angeles City Department of Recreation and Parks/ staff: 1(f); 2(p); 10(v)/ members: 200/publication: Alert and Observer

HISTORIC PRESERVATION AGENCY; HISTORIC SITE; HISTORY MUSEUM; LIVING HISTORY/OUTDOOR MUSEUM; RESEARCH CENTER

PROGRAMS: Exhibits; Guided Tours; Interpretation; Living History; Publication; Reenactments

COLLECTIONS: [1914-1945] Military memorabilia, photos.

HOURS: Yr 12-5

ADMISSION: Donations requested

846
Los Angeles Maritime Museum
Intersection of 6th St & Harbor Blvd, 90731 [Berth 84, Foot of 6th St, 90731]; (p) (310) 548-7618; (f) (310) 832-6537; www.lamaritimemuseum.org; (c) Los Angeles

City/ 1980/ City of Los Angeles/Rec & Parks/ staff: 8(f); 8(p); 600(v)/ members: 500

HISTORIC SITE: Collects and preserves materials documenting the maritime history of Southern CA.

PROGRAMS: Exhibits; Facility Rental; Guided Tours; Lectures; Research Library/Archives

COLLECTIONS: [Late 1800s- present] Maritime art, artifacts, photographic materials, books, periodicals, archival materials and watercraft.

HOURS: Yr T-Su 10-4:30

ADMISSION: $1

SAN RAFAEL

847
Marin History Museum
1125 B St, 94901; (p) (415) 454-8538; infomchs@pacbell.net; www.marinhistory.org; (c) Marin

Private non-profit/ 1935/ Board of Directors/ staff: 3(f); 2(p); 35(v)/ members: 500

GENEALOGICAL SOCIETY; HISTORIC SITE; HISTORY MUSEUM; HOUSE MUSEUM: Collects, preserves, and exhibits the history of Marin.

PROGRAMS: Annual Meeting; Community Outreach; Elder's Programs; Exhibits; Garden Tours; Guided Tours; Interpretation; Lectures; Research Library/Archives; School-Based Curriculum

COLLECTIONS: [1590-present] Marin artifacts, clothing, books, photos, maps, and ephemera, including Louise Boyd, San Quentin Prison.

HOURS: Yr Th-Sa 1-4

ADMISSION: No charge

848
Mission San Rafael Archangel
1102 5th Ave, 94901; (p) (415) 456-3016; www.missionreport.com; (c) Marin

Private non-profit/ 1817/ Roman Catholic Church/ staff: 6(f); 1(p)

HISTORIC SITE: California Mission.

PROGRAMS: Concerts; Guided Tours; School-Based Curriculum

COLLECTIONS: [1817-present] Native American artifacts, Hispanic history, church artifacts, and art.

HOURS: Yr Daily

SAN SIMEON

849
Hearst Castle-Hearst San Simeon State Historical Monument
750 Hearst Castle Rd, 93452; (p) (805) 927-2020; (f) (805) 927-2031; hfields@callamer.com; (c) San Luis Obispo

State/ 1957/ CA State Parks/ staff: 98(f); 250(p); 185(v)

ART MUSEUM; HOUSE MUSEUM

PROGRAMS: Family Programs; Film/Video; Garden Tours; Living History; Publication; Research Library/Archives; School-Based Curriculum

COLLECTIONS: [Gothic and Renaissance] Southern European architectural elements; silver, paintings, sculpture, antiquities, tapestries, textiles, Oriental rugs, 127 acres including gardens, pools, and guest houses.

HOURS: Yr Daily

SANTA ANA

850
California Association of Museums
2002 N Main St, 92706; (p) (714) 567-3645; (f) (714) 480-0053; cam@calmuseums.org; www.calmuseums.org; (c) Orange

Private non-profit/ 1979/ staff: 1(f); 1(p)/ members: 350/publication: Directory of California Museums

PROFESSIONAL ORGANIZATION: Serves as advocate for museum interests on state and federal level.

851
Discovery Museum of Orange County
3101 W Harvard St, 92704; (p) (714) 540-0404; (f) (714) 540-1932; www.discoverymuseumoc.com; (c) Orange

Private non-profit/ 1983/ staff: 4(f); 18(p); 250(v)/ members: 250

HISTORY MUSEUM; LIVING HISTORY/OUTDOOR MUSEUM

PROGRAMS: Community Outreach; Exhibits; Facility Rental; Family Programs; Festivals; Film/Video; Interpretation; Lectures; Living History; School-Based Curriculum

COLLECTIONS: [19th-20th c] Games, toys, instruments and household furnishings from Victorian era; native plants, rose garden and citrus grove; blacksmith.

HOURS: Yr W-F 1-5, Su 11-3

ADMISSION: $4, Children $3

852
Federation of Orange County Historical Organization/Historical Commission
211 W Santa Ana Blvd, 92702 [PO Box 4048, 92702-4048]; (p) (714) 834-5560; (f) (714) 834-2280; caversd@pfrd.co.orange.ca.us; (c) Orange

County/ County of Orange/ staff: 2(f); 15(v)

ALLIANCE OF HISTORICAL AGENCIES

PROGRAMS: Annual Meeting; Community Outreach; Exhibits; Facility Rental; Family Programs; Garden Tours; Guided Tours; Interpretation; Living History; Research Library/Archives

HOURS: Yr M-F 8-5

ADMISSION: No charge

853
Heritage Orange County, Inc.
515 N Main St, Ste 208, 92701; (p) (714) 835-7287; (c) Orange

Private non-profit/ 1974/ Board of Directors/ staff: 1(p)

HISTORIC PRESERVATION AGENCY: Preserves cultural environment of Orange County.

PROGRAMS: Annual Meeting; Community Outreach; Research Library/Archives

COLLECTIONS: Historic resource surveys

HOURS: By appt only M 10-2

854
Old Courthouse Museum

211 W Santa Ana Blvd, 92702 [PO Box 4048, 92702]; (p) (714) 834-3703; (f) (714) 834-2280; duellm@pfrd.co.orange.ca.us; (c) Orange

Joint/ 1988/ County;State/ staff: 2(f); 1(p); 15(v)/ members: 250

HISTORIC SITE; HISTORY MUSEUM: Displays and interprets local and regional history. includinghistory of the Old County Courthouse.

PROGRAMS: Annual Meeting; Community Outreach; Exhibits; Facility Rental; Guided Tours; Interpretation; Lectures; Living History; Research Library/Archives; School-Based Curriculum

COLLECTIONS: [1889-1960] Old Orange County Courthouse, law, photographs, natural history, pre-history, and aviation artifacts.

HOURS: Yr M-F 9-5

ADMISSION: No charge

855
Orange County Historical Commission

211 W Santa Ana Blvd, 92702 [PO Box 4048, 92702-4048]; (p) (714) 834-5560; (f) (714) 834-2280; (c) Orange

County/ 1973/ Board of Supervisors/ staff: 2(f); 25(v)/publication: *Federation of OC Historical Organizations*

HISTORIC PRESERVATION AGENCY: Reviews and advises on matters related to historical places and records.

PROGRAMS: Concerts; Exhibits; Facility Rental; Festivals; Guided Tours; Interpretation; Lectures; Living History; Publication; Research Library/Archives;

856
Orange County Historical Society

120 W Civic Center Dr, 92711 [PO Box 10984, 92711]; (p) (714) 543-8282; (c) Orange

Private non-profit/ 1919/ staff: 6(v)/ members: 250/publication: *County Courier*

HISTORICAL SOCIETY: Collects and preserves Orange County history.

PROGRAMS: Annual Meeting; Guided Tours; Lectures; Publication; Research Library/Archives

COLLECTIONS: [1890-present] Ephemera, books, and photos.

HOURS: Yr by appt only

ADMISSION: No charge

SANTA BARBARA

857
Casa del Herrero

1387 E Valley Rd, 93108; (p) (805) 565-5655; (f) (805) 969-2371; casa@silcom.com; www.casadelherrero.com

1993/ Board of Directors/ staff: 3(f); 3(p)

HOUSE MUSEUM: Maintains, preserves, and restores the house, furnishings, and gardens of the estate.

COLLECTIONS: Original furnishings purchased in Spain, 13-16 c.

HOURS: W-Sa 10-2; Spring & Fall W-Sa 10-2

ADMISSION: $10

858
Central Coast Archaeological Information Center

Rm #2211, Humanities & Social Sci Bldg, UCSB, 93106 [Dept of Anthropology, Univ of CA, Santa Barbara, 93106-3210]; (p) (805) 893-2474; (f) (805) 893-8707; (c) Santa Barbara

Joint/ CA State Office of Historic Preservation / Univ of CA, Santa Barbara/ staff: 1(p)

HISTORIC PRESERVATION AGENCY; RESEARCH CENTER: Manages archaeological and historical information for Santa Barbara and San Luis Obispo Counties.

PROGRAMS: Research Library/Archives

COLLECTIONS: [Prehistoric and historic California] Archaeological site reports; cultural resource survey reports.

HOURS: Yr by appt

859
Historic Landmarks Commission/City of Santa Barbara

630 Garden St, 93102 [PO Box 1990, 93102]; (p) (805) 564-5470; (f) (805) 897-1904; cpalmer@ci.santa-barbara.ca.us; www.ci.santa-barbara; (c) Santa Barbara

City/ 1978/ staff: 1(f)/ members: 9/publication: *El Pueblo Viejo Historic District Design Guidelines*

HISTORIC PRESERVATION AGENCY: Promotes and preserves historic sites.

PROGRAMS: Publication

COLLECTIONS: [1782-present]

HOURS: Weekdays

ADMISSION: No charge

860
History Committee of the Montecito Association, The

1469 E Valley Rd, 93108 [PO Box 5278, 93150]; (p) (805) 969-1597; (f) (805) 969-4043; (c) Santa Barbara

Private non-profit/ 1975/ Montecito Association/ staff: 4(p); 2(v)

HISTORICAL SOCIETY; LIBRARY AND/OR ARCHIVES: Collects local history material.

PROGRAMS: Guided Tours; Interpretation

COLLECTIONS: [1875-present] Artifacts, letters, oral history, photos, paintings, maps, city directories, books.

HOURS: Yr T-Th 10-12/2-4

ADMISSION: No charge

861
Karpeles Manuscript Library Museum

21 W Anapamu St, 93101; (p) (805) 962-5322; (f) (805) 564-1686; kmuseumba@aol.com; www.karpeles.com; (c) Santa Barbara

Private non-profit/ 1986/ David Karpeles/ staff: 6(p)

HISTORIC PRESERVATION AGENCY; HISTORY MUSEUM: Preserves original writings of authors, scientists, philosophers, statesmen, sovereigns, and leaders from all periods of world history.

PROGRAMS: Community Outreach; Concerts; Elder's Programs; Exhibits; Film/Video; Guided Tours; Lectures; Living History; Publication; Reenactments; Research Library/Archives; School-Based Curriculum; Theatre

COLLECTIONS: [All periods of world history] Manuscripts.

HOURS: Yr Daily 10-4

ADMISSION: No charge

862
La Casa de la Guerra

15 E de la Guerra St, 93102 [PO Box 388, 93102]; (p) (805) 966-9179, (805) 965-0093; (f) (805) 568-1999; sbthp@rain.org; www.rain.org/~sbthp

1820/ staff: 1(f); 1(p)

HOUSE MUSEUM: Home of Jose de la Guerra, last comandante of Royal Santa Barbara Presidio, and family.

COLLECTIONS: [1820s] Period furnishings; archeological artifacts; archives.

HOURS: Yr

863
Santa Barbara Historical Society

136 E De la Guerra St, 93102-0578; (p) (805) 966-1601; (f) (805) 966-1603; (c) Santa Barbara

Private non-profit/ 1932/ Board of Trustees/ staff: 7(f); 12(p); 65(v)/ members: 1600/publication: *Noticias*

HISTORICAL SOCIETY; HISTORY MUSEUM; HOUSE MUSEUM: Collects and interprets artifacts related to history of Santa Barbara.

PROGRAMS: Annual Meeting; Exhibits; Facility Rental; Guided Tours; Lectures; Publication; Research Library/Archives

COLLECTIONS: Books, pamphlets, photos, oral histories, maps government records, family papers, newspapers, artworks decorative art, toys, and costumes and accessories.

HOURS: Yr T-Sa 10-5, Su 12-5

ADMISSION: Donations accepted

864
Santa Barbara Maritime Museum

113 Harbor Way, 93109; (p) (805) 962-8404; (f) (805) 962-7634; museum@sbmm.org; www.sbmm.org; (c) Santa Barbara

Private non-profit/ 1994/ Santa Barbara Maritime Museum Board/ staff: 6(f); 10(p); 350(v)/publication: *Currents*

MARITIME MUSEUM: Preserves and presents to the public the maritime heritage of CA's central coast and human interaction with the marine environment.

PROGRAMS: Exhibits; Facility Rental; Film/Video; Guided Tours; Interpretation; Lectures; Publication; Research Library/Archives; School-Based Curriculum; Theatre

COLLECTIONS: [1800-present] Collection consists of maritime artifacts, cultural resources, photographs, archives, and research library.

865
Santa Barbara Mission Museum
2201 Laguna St, 93105; (p) (805) 682-4713; (f) (805) 682-6067; (c) Santa Barbara

Private non-profit/ 1786/ Franciscan Friars of CA

HISTORIC SITE; HISTORY MUSEUM; HOUSE MUSEUM: Provides interpretive displays of historical art and artifacts of California Mission.

PROGRAMS: Exhibits; Facility Rental; Festivals; Research Library/Archives

COLLECTIONS: [1786-1840s] Spanish Colonial religious art produced mainly in late 18th c Mexico, artifacts, tools, textiles, furnishings.

HOURS: Yr Daily

866
Santa Barbara Trust for Historic Preservation
123 Canon Perdido St, 93102 [PO Box 388, 93102-0388]; (p) (805) 965-0093; (f) (805) 568-1999; SBTHP@rain.org; www.rain.org/~sbthp; (c) Santa Barbara

1963/ Board of Trustees/ staff: 10(f); 4(p); 100(v)/ members: 400

HISTORIC PRESERVATION AGENCY: Preserves and interprets historic buildings and sites in Santa Barbara County; operates El Presidio State Historic Park; owns Casa de la Guerra Adobe and Santa Ines Mission Mills site.

PROGRAMS: Annual Meeting; Concerts; Exhibits; Facility Rental; Family Programs; Film/Video; Guided Tours; Interpretation; Lectures; Living History; Publication; Research Library/Archives

COLLECTIONS: [1500s-late 1800s] Archaeological artifacts from site and period furnishings; books, periodicals, maps, documents, and structures.

HOURS: Yr Daily 10:30-4:30

ADMISSION: Donations accepted

867
Vietnam Veterans Memorial Museum
476 El Sueno, 93110; (p) (805) 683-4301; (f) (805) 683-1223; (c) Santa Barbara

Federal; Private non-profit; State/ 1988/ staff: 1(f)

HISTORY MUSEUM: Collects, preserves and promotes Vietnam War history.

PROGRAMS: Annual Meeting; Exhibits; Lectures

COLLECTIONS: [1957-1975] Restored UH-1H helicopter, trailer modified for mobile displays.

HOURS: Sat 10-4 or by

SANTA CLARA

868
de Saisset Museum
Santa Clara Univ, 95053 [500 El Camino Real, 95053-0550]; (p) (408) 554-4528; (f) (408) 554-7840; www.scu.edu/deSaisset/; (c) Santa Clara

Private non-profit/ 1955/ Santa Clara Univ/ staff: 5(f); 21(p); 50(v)/ members: 250

ART MUSEUM; HISTORY MUSEUM: Resource for historical and cultural enrichment of university population and surrounding communities.

PROGRAMS: Concerts; Exhibits; Family Programs; Film/Video; Garden Tours; Guided Tours; Publication

COLLECTIONS: Fine art, decorative art, and historic artifacts from Santa Clara Mission de Asis; early Santa Clara College; early Native American inhabitants; 7,000 fine art objects, 700 decorative arts, 1,800 anthropological and archeological.

HOURS: Yr T-Su 11-4;00

ADMISSION: No

869
Harris Lass Historic Museum
1889 Market St, 95055 [PO Box 3311, 95055]; (p) (408) 249-7905; (c) Santa Clara

Private non-profit/ Historic Preservation Society of Santa Clara/ staff: 30(v)/ members: 200/publication: *The Meteor*

HOUSE MUSEUM: Preserves and interprets Harris Lass House, last remaining farm site in city.

PROGRAMS: Community Outreach; Facility Rental; Family Programs; Guided Tours; Publication; School-Based Curriculum

COLLECTIONS: [1865-1960s] Furnishings, clothing, artifacts.

HOURS: Yr

870
Intel Museum
Intel Corporation, 2200 Mission College Blvd, 95052; (p) (408) 765-0889; (f) (408) 765-1217; becky.r.raisch@intel.com; www.intel.com/intel/intelis/museum; (c) Santa Clara

Private non-profit/ 1992/ Robert Singer, Senior Mgr/ staff: 4(f); 3(p); 30(v)

CORPORATE ARCHIVES/MUSEUM: Collects, preserves, and exhibits Intel corporate history.

PROGRAMS: Community Outreach; Exhibits; Guided Tours; Research Library/Archives; School-Based Curriculum

COLLECTIONS: [1968-present] Artifacts, archives, documents, and photographs related to the high tech industry.

HOURS: Yr M-F 8-5

871
Santa Clara County Historical and Genealogical Society
N Wing of Santa Clara Central Library, 95051 [2635 Homestead Rd, 95051-5387]; (p) (408) 615-5387; www.katpher.com/SCCHGS/; (c) Santa Clara

Private non-profit/ 1957/ staff: 36(v)/ members: 258

GENEALOGICAL SOCIETY; RESEARCH CENTER

PROGRAMS: Research Library/Archives

COLLECTIONS: [1800s-present] U.S. and international materials; census indexes, local histories, period collection, maps, atlases, land records, vital statistics, Civil War and other military materials.

HOURS: Yr Daily M-Th 9-9, Sa 9-6, Sun 1-5

ADMISSION: No charge

SANTA CRUZ

872
Museum of Art and History at the McPherson Center
705 Front St, 95060; (p) (831) 429-1964; (f) (831) 429-1954; mah@cruzio.com; www.santacruzmah.org; (c) Santa Cruz

Private non-profit/ 1996/ staff: 8(f); 6(p); 150(v)/ members: 1200

ART MUSEUM; HISTORY MUSEUM: Presents visual and cultural experience focused on regional history.

PROGRAMS: Community Outreach; Exhibits; Facility Rental; Family Programs; Film/Video; Guided Tours; Interpretation; Lectures; Living History; Research Library/Archives

COLLECTIONS: [Post WWII-present] Modern art; historical artifacts.

HOURS: Yr T-Su 11-5, Th 11-7

ADMISSION: $4, Student $2, Seniors $2; Under 18

873
Santa Cruz City Museum of Natural History
1305 E Cliff Dr, 95062; (p) (831) 420-6115; (f) (831) 420-6451; citymnh@cruzio.com; (c) Santa Cruz

City/ 1905/ staff: 4(f); 6(p); 179(v)/ members: 550

HISTORY MUSEUM: Collects and preserves cultural and natural history of Monterey Bay region.

PROGRAMS: Annual Meeting; Community Outreach; Exhibits; Facility Rental; Family Programs; Festivals; Film/Video; Garden Tours; Guided Tours; Interpretation; Lectures; School-Based Curriculum

COLLECTIONS: [1800s-present] Natural history specimens, California Native American, surfing artifacts, regional history objects, and regional art

874
Santa Cruz Mission State Historic Park
144 School St, 95060 [600 Ocean St, 95060]; (p) (831) 425-5849; (f) (831) 429-2876; (c) Santa Cruz

State/ 1792/ California State Parks/ staff: 2(p)

HISTORIC SITE; HISTORY MUSEUM; HOUSE MUSEUM: State historic park containing only remaining structure from original mission: 1824 dormitory for mission neophytes.

PROGRAMS: Exhibits; Festivals; Guided Tours; Interpretation; Living History

COLLECTIONS: [1790-1900] Native American and Mission Period artifact; Victorian artifacts.

HOURS: Yr

875
Wilder Ranch State Park
Hwy 1, 2 mi N of Santa Cruz, 95060 [600 Ocean St, 95060]; (p) (831) 426-0505; (f) (831) 429-2876; wilder_ranch@juno.com; (c) Santa Cruz

State/ 1988/ California State Parks/ staff: 2(f); 3(p); 40(v)/publication: *Park Brochures*

GARDEN; HISTORIC SITE; HISTORY MUSEUM; LIVING HISTORY/OUTDOOR MUSEUM: 30 acre cultural preserve ranch complex interpreting California ranch life and agricultural and dairy history.

PROGRAMS: Exhibits; Facility Rental; Festivals; Garden Tours; Guided Tours; Interpretation; Living History; Publication; School-Based Curriculum

COLLECTIONS: [1870-1940] Furnished 1898 Victorian home uses original and period artifacts from 1898-1940; 1890s restored and furnished blacksmith, machine and carpentry shop.

HOURS: Yr Th-Su 10-4

ADMISSION: $2/vehicle

SANTA FE SPRINGS

876
Hathaway Ranch Museum
11901 E Florence Ave, 90670 [11901 E Florence Ave, 90670]; (p) (562) 944-7372

877
Heritage Park
12100 Mora Dr, 90670; (p) (562) 946-6476; (f) (562) 946-8593; heritage_park@santafe springs.org; www.santafesprings.org/ hpark.htm; (c) Los Angeles

City/ 1986/ staff: 4(f); 8(p); 35(v)

GARDEN; HISTORIC SITE; HISTORY MUSEUM; LIVING HISTORY/OUTDOOR MUSEUM; RAILROAD MUSEUM; RESEARCH CENTER: Reconstructed Victorian ranch and gardens; railroad exhibit with tankhouse/windmill, depot, steam locomotive, and rolling stock; carriage barn; Tongva Indian exhibit with dwelling and related structures; preserved foundation of adobe home and trash pit.

PROGRAMS: Community Outreach; Concerts; Facility Rental; Family Programs; Festivals; Guided Tours; Interpretation; Publication; Research Library/Archives; School-Based Curriculum

COLLECTIONS: [1880-1920] Horse drawn and steam driven vehicle, clothing, inventions, and technology; railroad history, agricultural artifacts, toys, tools, and furniture.

HOURS: Yr Daily T-Su 12-4, Park open 7-10

ADMISSION: No charge

SANTA MARIA

878
Santa Maria Valley Historical Society and Museum
616 S Broadway, 93454; (p) (805) 922-3130; (c) Santa Barbara

Private non-profit/ 1955/ staff: 1(f); 10(v)/ members: 500

HISTORICAL SOCIETY; HISTORY MUSEUM: Promotes Santa Maria Valley history.

PROGRAMS: Annual Meeting; Community Outreach; Exhibits

COLLECTIONS: [1850-1999]

HOURS: Yr T-Sa 12-5

ADMISSION: No charge

SANTA MONICA

879
California Heritage Museum
2612 Main St, 90405; (p) (610) 392-8537; (f) (310) 396-0547; (c) Los Angeles

Private non-profit/ 1976/ Board of Directors/ staff: 2(f); 2(p); 31(v)/ members: 350/publication: *Exhibition Catalogues*

ART MUSEUM; HISTORIC SITE; HISTORY MUSEUM; HOUSE MUSEUM; RESEARCH CENTER: Presents exhibitions, lectures, concerts, and workshops that promote history and cultures of California.

PROGRAMS: Community Outreach; Concerts; Exhibits; Facility Rental; Festivals; Guided Tours; Lectures; Publication; Research Library/Archives; School-Based Curriculum

COLLECTIONS: [1860-1960] Over 8000 photos and documents of Santa Monica Bay area.

HOURS: Yr W-Su 11-4

ADMISSION: $3, Student $2, Seniors $2

SANTA PAULA

880
Santa Paula Union Oil Museum
1001 E Main St, 93061 [PO Box 40, 93061]; (p) (805) 933-0076; (f) (805) 933-0096; info@oilmuseum.net; www.oilmuseum.net; (c) Ventura

City/ staff: 1(f); 3(p)

HISTORIC SITE; HISTORY MUSEUM: Preserves and presents the history of oil use, technology, and development in region.

PROGRAMS: Community Outreach; Exhibits; Facility Rental; Guided Tours; Lectures; Research Library/Archives; School-Based Curriculum

COLLECTIONS: [1890-1990] Printed material, artifacts, photos, paintings

HOURS: Yr W-Su 10-4

ADMISSION: $2, Children $1

SANTA ROSA

881
Luther Burbank Home and Gardens
Santa Rosa Ave & Sonoma Ave, 95402 [PO Box 1678, 95402]; (p) (707) 524-5445; (f) (707) 524-5827; burbankhome@flash.net

dex.com; ci.santa-rosa.ca.us/rp/burbank/; (c) Sonoma

City/ 1979/ staff: 2(f); 3(p); 200(v)/ members: 200

GARDEN; HISTORIC SITE; HOUSE MUSEUM; LIVING HISTORY/OUTDOOR MUSEUM: Historic site where famed horticulturist Luther Burbank lived, and worked.

PROGRAMS: Community Outreach; Exhibits; Festivals; Garden Tours; Guided Tours; Interpretation; Research Library/Archives; School-Based Curriculum

COLLECTIONS: [Late 1800s-early 1900s] Documents, photos, decorative arts, furnishings, tools relating to life and work of Luther Burbank; historic greenhouse, carriage house, and Greek Revival

882
Sonoma County Historical Society
[PO Box 1373, 95402]; (p) (707) 539-1786, (707) 528-3489; (c) Sonoma

Private non-profit/ 1962/ staff: 2(p); 15(v)/ members: 475/publication: *Sonoma County Atlas 1897*

HISTORIC PRESERVATION AGENCY; HISTORIC SITE; HISTORICAL SOCIETY

PROGRAMS: Annual Meeting; Interpretation; Lectures

COLLECTIONS: [1850-present] County histories, voter registrations.

883
Sonoma County Museum
425 7th St, 95401; (p) (707) 579-1500; (f) (707) 579-4849; scm@pon.net; www.pressde mo.com/scmuseum; (c) Sonoma

Private non-profit/ 1985/ staff: 4(f); 2(p); 100(v)/ members: 940/publication: *The Muse*

HISTORY MUSEUM: Collects and preserves artifacts, documents, photos.

PROGRAMS: Annual Meeting; Community Outreach; Facility Rental; Family Programs; Guided Tours; Interpretation; Lectures; Living History; Publication; Research Library/ Archives; School-Based Curriculum

COLLECTIONS: [Pre-European-present] 30,000 objects, including photos, documents, paintings, textiles, and artifacts.

HOURS: Yr W-Su 11-4

ADMISSION: $2, Student $1, Seniors $1; Under 13/Mbrs free

SARATOGA

884
Saratoga Heritage Preservation Commission
13777 Fruitvale Ave, 95070; (p) (408) 868-1230; (f) (408) 868-1280; (c) Santa Clara

City/ 1986/ staff: 1(p)/publication: *Saratoga's Heritage*

HISTORIC PRESERVATION AGENCY: Advises city council and planning commission on city heritage preservation.

PROGRAMS: Facility Rental; Guided Tours

885
Saratoga Historical Society
20450 Saratoga-Los Gatos Rd, 95071 [PO Box 172, 95071]; (p) (408) 867-4311; (c) Santa Clara

Private non-profit/ 1960/ Saratoga Historical Foundation/ staff: 30(v)/ members: 180

HISTORICAL SOCIETY; HISTORY MUSEUM: Preserves and promotes Saratoga's historical heritage.

PROGRAMS: Annual Meeting; Exhibits; Guided Tours; Lectures; Publication

COLLECTIONS: [Mid 1800s-present] Photos, maps, vintage clothing, household artifacts, agriculture implements; Civil War, WW I, and WW II memorabilia; books, documents, letters; Native American baskets.

HOURS: Yr F-Su 1-4

ADMISSION: No charge

SAUSALITO

886
Bay Area Discovery Museum
Fort Baker, 94965 [557 McReynolds Rd, 94965]; (p) (415) 289-7268; (f) (415) 332-9671; info@badm.org; www.badm.org; (c) Marin

Private non-profit/ 1987/ staff: 30(f); 40(p); 50(v)/ members: 5200

HISTORIC SITE; HISTORY MUSEUM: Provides exhibits on San Francisco Bay and architecture for children age 0 to 10.

PROGRAMS: Community Outreach; Concerts; Exhibits; Facility Rental; Festivals; Guided Tours; Interpretation; Living History; School-Based Curriculum; Theatre

COLLECTIONS: [1901-1910]

ADMISSION: $7, Children $6

SCOTIA

887
Pacific Lumber Company, The
126 Main St, 95565 [PO Box 37, 95565]; (p) (707) 764-2222; www.palco.com; (c) Humboldt

Private non-profit/ 1869/ staff: 5(v)

HISTORY MUSEUM: Self-guided tour of sawmill and historic logging museum in Scotia.

PROGRAMS: Exhibits; Film/Video

COLLECTIONS: [1869-1990] Photo, exhibits, examples of redwood products, logging equipment, and locomotive.

HOURS: June-Sept M-F

SEBASTOPOL

888
West County Museum
261 S Main, 95472; (p) (707) 829-6711; (c) Sonoma

Private non-profit/ 1993/ Western Sonoma County Historical Society/ staff: 15(v)/ members: 150/publication: *Apple Press*

HISTORIC SITE; HISTORY MUSEUM: Exhibits interpreting local history.

PROGRAMS: Community Outreach; Exhibits; Lectures; Publication; Research Library/ Archives

COLLECTIONS: [1855-1980] Photos and artifacts.

HOURS: Yr Th-Su 1-4

ADMISSION: No charge/Donations

SHAFTER

889
Minter Field Air Museum
401 Vultee, 93263 [PO Box 445, 93263]; (p) (661) 393-0291; (f) (661) 393-3296; (c) Kern

Private non-profit/ 1984/ staff: 1(f); 5(p); 10(v)/ members: 125/publication: *SNAP Roll II*

HISTORIC SITE: Preserves history of aviation training, focusing on WWII.

PROGRAMS: Annual Meeting; Exhibits; Guided Tours; Interpretation; Lectures; Publication; School-Based Curriculum

COLLECTIONS: [1941-1945] Artifacts, exhibits, aircraft books, personnel items, photos.

HOURS: Yr Sa 9-2

ADMISSION: No charge

890
Shafter Historical Society, Inc.
150 Central Valley Hwy, 93263 [PO Box 1088, 93263]; (p) (661) 746-1557; (f) (661) 746-1620; (c) Kern

Private non-profit/ 1979/ Board of Directors/ staff: 10(v)/ members: 200

HISTORIC SITE; HISTORY MUSEUM: Operates local history museum in old railroad depot and exhibit hall, and restored hotel.

PROGRAMS: Annual Meeting; Concerts; Exhibits; Facility Rental

COLLECTIONS: [1900-1940]

HOURS: 1st Sat of month 10-2 and by appt

ADMISSION: No charge

SHASTA

891
Shasta State Historic Park
[PO Box 2430, 96087]; (p) (530) 243-8194; (f) (530) 225-2038; shastahp@snowcrest.net; www.cal-parks.cagov/travel/regions/ shasta/shasta; (c) Shasta

State/ 1950/ CA State Parks/ staff: 2(f); 4(p); 15(v)/publication: *Shasta State Historic Park Brief History and Tour Guide*

ART MUSEUM; HISTORIC SITE; HISTORY MUSEUM; HOUSE MUSEUM; RESEARCH CENTER: Protects, preserves, and interprets Shasta's history.

PROGRAMS: Exhibits; Facility Rental; Festivals; Interpretation; Living History; Publication; Research Library/Archives; School-Based Curriculum

COLLECTIONS: [1840-1890] Paintings, prints, and drawings depicting early regional history; Native American artifacts; artifacts: fire arms, gold rush; pioneer family: furniture, clothing, tools, gold mining and agricultural tools.

HOURS: Yr W-Su 10-5

ADMISSION: $2, Children $1; Under 5 free

SHINGLETOWN

892
Shingletown Historical Society
[PO Box 291, 96088]; (p) (530) 474-3422; (c) Shasta

Private non-profit/ 1967/ Board

HISTORIC SITE; HISTORICAL SOCIETY

PROGRAMS: Exhibits; Guided Tours; School-Based Curriculum

COLLECTIONS: [1800s-present] Early settlers artifacts, Indian baskets, early trails and stops, early school sites, historic photos.

ADMISSION: No charge

SIERRA CITY

893
Kentucky Mine Museum
Hwy 49, 96125 [PO Box 260, 96125]; (p) (530) 862-1310; (f) (530) 862-1310; (c) Sierra

Private non-profit/ 1974/ staff: 1(f); 20(v)/ members: 250/publication: *The Sierra*

HISTORICAL SOCIETY: Preserves and displays artifacts relating to local history; operates Kentucky Mine Museum and Stamp mill.

PROGRAMS: Annual Meeting; Concerts; Exhibits; Facility Rental; Guided Tours; Interpretation; Living History; Publication; Research Library/Archives

COLLECTIONS: [1850-1940] Artifacts and exhibits from the California Gold Rush, ranching, logging, Native American, and Chinese.

HOURS: May-Sept W-Su

SIERRAVILLE

894
Sierra County Historical Society
507 S Lincoln, 96126 [PO Box 141, 96126]; (p) (530) 994-3480; (f) (530) 862-1310; (c) Sierra

Private non-profit/ 1968/ staff: 10(v)/ members: 257/publication: *The Sierran*

HISTORIC SITE; HISTORICAL SOCIETY; HISTORY MUSEUM: Operates Kentucky Mine Museum in Sierra City, and provides tours of Stamp Mill.

PROGRAMS: Annual Meeting; Community Outreach; Concerts; Exhibits; Facility Rental; Guided Tours

COLLECTIONS: [1849-present] Mining artifacts and pictures; materials on ranching, Chinese, Maidu Indians, and local history.

HOURS: June-Sept 10-5

ADMISSION: $1

SIMI VALLEY

895
Ronald Reagan Library
40 Presidential Dr, 93065-0666; (p) (805) 522-8444; (f) (805) 522-9621; library@rea gan.nara.gov; www.nara.gov; (c) Ventura

896
Simi Valley Historical Society
137 Strathearn Place, 93094 [PO Box 940461, 93094]; (p) (805) 526-6453; (f) (805) 526-6462; (c) Ventura

1965/ staff: 2(p); 55(v)/ members: 400/publication: *The Mailcart*

HISTORIC SITE; HISTORICAL SOCIETY: Collects artifacts of historical significance.

PROGRAMS: Annual Meeting; Facility Rental; Publication

COLLECTIONS: [1800-1950]

HOURS: Yr W, Sa, Su 1-4

ADMISSION: Donations

897
Strathearn Historical Park and Museum
137 Strathearn Place, 93065 [PO Box 351, 93062]; (p) (805) 526-6453; (f) (805) 526-6452

Simi Valley Historical Society; Rancho Simi Recreation and Park District/ staff: 2(p); 70(v)

COLLECTIONS: [1888 to 1950s] Early CA furniture and artifacts, farm implements; letters and photos.

SOLVANG

898
Elverhoj Museum of History and Art
1624 Elverhoy Way, 93464 [PO Box 769, 93464]; (p) (805) 686-1211; (f) (805) 686-1822; (c) Santa Barbara

Private non-profit/ 1988/ Solvang Heritage Associates/ staff: 2(p); 40(v)/ members: 232

HISTORY MUSEUM: Collects, preserves, and exhibits artifacts relating to Solvang history and Danish heritage; fine art gallery exhibits rotating art and craft displays.

PROGRAMS: Community Outreach; Concerts; Elder's Programs; Exhibits; Facility Rental; Family Programs; Festivals; Guided Tours; Interpretation; Lectures; Living History; Research Library/Archives

COLLECTIONS: [Early 20th c] Household artifacts, 500 tools, 200 photographs, 400 books, 300 prints and paintings, 75 sculpture, 150 news articles.

SONOMA

899
Sonoma League for Historic Preservation
El Paso at the Plaza, 95476 [PO Box 766, 95476]; (c) Sonoma

Private non-profit/ 1969/ Board of Directors/ staff: 80(v)/ members: 318

Survey of all property over 50 years old, landmarking.

COLLECTIONS: Local history, photos, articles, art.

HOURS: Yr Sa-M

SONORA

900
Tuolumne County Historical Society
158 W Bradford Ave, 95370 [PO Box 695, 95370-0695]; (p) (209) 532-1317; www.tchistory.org; (c) Tuolumne

County/ 1956/ TC Board of Supervisors/ staff: 40(v)/ members: 400/publication: *Historian*

GENEALOGICAL SOCIETY; HISTORIC PRESERVATION AGENCY; HISTORICAL SOCIETY; HISTORY MUSEUM: Preserves and promotes history of Tuolumne County.

PROGRAMS: Annual Meeting; Exhibits; Facility Rental; Guided Tours; Lectures; Publication; Research Library/Archives

COLLECTIONS: [1849-present] Photos, newspapers, oral history tapes, history books, personal, business, industry, period artifacts, and pioneer firearms.

HOURS: Yr Daily 10-4

ADMISSION: No charge

SOUTH LAKE TAHOE

901
Lake Tahoe Historical Society
3058 Lake Tahoe Blvd, 96156 [PO Box 383, 96156]; (p) (530) 541-5458; (c) El Dorado

Private non-profit/ 1970/ Lake Tahoe Historical Society/ staff: 1(p); 10(v)/ members: 200

HISTORICAL SOCIETY: Preserves artifacts and information on the Lake Tahoe area.

PROGRAMS: Annual Meeting; Exhibits; Festivals; Film/Video; Publication

COLLECTIONS: [1850-present] Artifacts, documents, and photos.

HOURS: June-Sept

ADMISSION: $1, Children $0.50

902
Tahoe Heritage Foundation
2435 Venice Dr East, Ste 108, 96158 [PO Box 8586, 96158]; (p) (530) 544-7383; (f) (530) 544-7778; www.tahoeheritage.org; (c) El Dorado

Private non-profit/ 1996/ Tahoe Heritage Foundation/ staff: 2(p); 10(v)

HISTORIC PRESERVATION AGENCY; HISTORIC SITE; HISTORY MUSEUM; HOUSE MUSEUM: Raises funds for preservation, restoration, and interpretation of diverse heritage resources in Lake Tahoe Basin.

PROGRAMS: Community Outreach; Exhibits; Family Programs; Festivals; Garden Tours; Guided Tours; Interpretation; Living History; Publication; Research Library/Archives

COLLECTIONS: [1880-1940] Collects and solicits materials for U.S. Forest Service's Tallac Historic Site.

HOURS: June-Sept call for hours

903
Tallac Historic Site
Hwy 89, 96150 [870 Emerald Box Rd, Ste # 1, 96150]; (p) (530) 541-5227; (f) (530) 573-2693; lcole/r5_ltbmu@fs.fed.us; (c) Eldorado

Federal/ 1978/ USDA Forest Service/ staff: 1(f); 2(p); 60(v)/publication: *Tallac Historic Site*

GARDEN; HISTORIC SITE; HOUSE MUSEUM: Preserves three summer estates and archaeological remains of located in oldest grove of ancient trees in Tahoe Basin.

PROGRAMS: Concerts; Elder's Programs; Exhibits; Facility Rental; Family Programs; Festivals; Garden Tours; Guided Tours; Interpretation; Living History; Publication

COLLECTIONS: [1880-1940] Structures and artifacts from period and photo.

HOURS: May-Sep Daily Dawn to Dusk

ADMISSION: No charge

SOUTH SAN FRANCISCO

904
South San Francisco History Room
306 Walnut Ave, 94080; (p) (650) 877-8533; (f) (650) 829-6615; kayk@pls.lib.ca.us; (c) San Mateo

City/ 1967/ staff: 2(p); 1(v)

LIBRARY AND/OR ARCHIVES: Preserves history of South San Francisco.

PROGRAMS: Exhibits; Lectures; Research Library/Archives

COLLECTIONS: [19th-20th c] Books, photos, newspapers, oral histories, and manuscripts.

HOURS: Yr M,W 1-7, T, Th 1-4, F

SPRING VALLEY

905
Bancroft Ranch House Museum
9050 Memory Lane, 91977-2152; (p) (619) 469-1480

1863

COLLECTIONS: Early Kumeyaay, pioneer artifacts, photographs of region; Clothes, furniture, books.

HOURS: Yr

ST. HELENA

906
Robert Louis Stevenson Silverado Museum
1409 Library Ln, 94574 [PO Box 409, 94574]; (p) (707) 963-3757; rlsnhs@calicom.net; (c) Napa

Private non-profit/ 1969/ Edmond J. Reynolds/ staff: 2(f)

HISTORY MUSEUM: Promotes life and works of author Robert Louis Stevenson.

PROGRAMS: Community Outreach; Exhibits; Film/Video; Interpretation; Research Library/Archives; Theatre

COLLECTIONS: [1850-1894] Manuscripts, documents, photos, books, memorabilia, letters, paintings, and sculptures.

HOURS: Yr T-Su 12-4

STINSON BEACH

907
Audubon Canyon Ranch
4900 Hwy 1, 94970; (p) (415) 868-9244; (f) (415) 868-1699

STOCKTON

908
Conference of California Historical Societies
University of the Pacific, 95211; (p) (209) 946-2169; (f) (209) 946-2578; cchs@uop.edu; www.uop.edu/organizations/CCHSBROC.html (c) San Joaquin

Private non-profit/ 1953/ staff: 1(p); 50(v)/ members: 1700/publication: *California Historian*

ALLIANCE OF HISTORICAL AGENCIES: Member organizations share information; join in preserving records, artifacts, sites; help form local societies; aid small museums with management, preservation, restoration; link to influence legislation and preservation efforts.

PROGRAMS: Annual Meeting; Community Outreach; Publication

HOURS: Yr M-F 8:30-12:30

909
Jedediah Smith Society
John Muir Center, University of the Pacific, 95211; (p) (209) 946-2169; (f) (209) 946-2578; hesppress@aol.com; www.upo.edu/organization/JSS96.html; (c) San Joaquin

Private non-profit/ 1957/ Board of Directors/ staff: 2(p); 4(v)/ members: 230

RESEARCH CENTER: Promotes works and exploits of Jedediah Strong Smith and Fur Trade Era especially focusing on CA.

PROGRAMS: Annual Meeting; Interpretation; Lectures; Living History; Publication

COLLECTIONS: [1600-1700s] Personal artifacts of Jedediah Strong Smith, papers, journals; Papers of Maurice Sullivan, Dr. Raymund Wood and others.

910
Stockton Corral of Westerners, The
[PO Box 1315, 95201-1314]; (c) San Joaquin

Private non-profit/ 1959/ Westerners International/ staff: 9(v)/ members: 37

Preserves and disseminates Western American history and local history of Stockton, San Joaquin County and Great Central Valley.

PROGRAMS: Lectures

COLLECTIONS: [Prehistory to present]

SUISUN

911
Bay Area Electric Railroad Association
5848 State Hwy 12, 94585; (p) (707) 374-2978; (f) (707) 374-6742; www.wrm.org

Private non-profit/ 1946/ staff: 100(v)/ members: 1000

HISTORIC SITE; HISTORICAL SOCIETY; LIVING HISTORY/OUTDOOR MUSEUM

PROGRAMS: Interpretation; Living History

COLLECTIONS: [1888-1970] Historical electric equipment.

HOURS: Yr 11-5

ADMISSION: $7, Children $4, Seniors $6

SUNNYVALE

912
Iron Man Museum, The
401 E Hendy Ave, 94088 [PO Box 3499, 94088-3499]; (p) (408) 735-2020; (f) (408) 735-5260; (c) Santa Clara

Private non-profit/ 1984/ Iron Man Museum Board/ staff: 2(p); 12(v)/ members: 150

CORPORATE ARCHIVES/MUSEUM: Preserves and documents history, memorabilia, and artifacts associated with Joshua Hendy Iron Works and Westinghouse Marina Division.

PROGRAMS: Community Outreach; Exhibits; Guided Tours; Interpretation; Lectures; Research Library/Archives

COLLECTIONS: [1906-1996] Artifacts and memorabilia; appliances made by Westinghouse; machinery.

HOURS: Jan-Nov 2nd M 11:30-1, and by appt

ADMISSION: Donations

913
Lace Museum, The
552 S Murphy Ave, 94086; (p) (408) 730-4695; www.thelacemuseum.org; (c) Santa Clara

Private non-profit/ 1981/ Board of Directors/ staff: 50(v)

HISTORY MUSEUM: Teaches lace making, preserves and exhibits lace collection.

PROGRAMS: Exhibits; Lectures; Research Library/Archives; School-Based Curriculum

COLLECTIONS: Lace and lace clothing; artifacts.

HOURS: Yr T-Sa 11-4 and by appt

ADMISSION: No charge

914
Sunnyvale Historical Society and Museum Association, Inc.
235 E California, 94088 [PO Box 61301, 94088]; (p) (408) 749-0220; (f) (408) 732-4726; (c) Sant Clara

Private non-profit/ 1957/ staff: 25(v)/ members: 270

PROGRAMS: Exhibits; Guided Tours; Lectures

HOURS: Yr T,Th 12-3:30, Su 1-4

ADMISSION: No charge

SUSANVILLE

915
Lassen County Historical Society
75 N Weatherlow, 96130 [PO Box 321, 96130]; (p) (530) 257-3292; (c) Lassen

Private non-profit/ 1958/ staff: 15(v)/ members: 200/publication: *Fairfield's History of Lassen County*

HISTORIC PRESERVATION AGENCY; HISTORIC SITE; HISTORICAL SOCIETY; HISTORY MUSEUM: Protects and preserves regional historical artifacts.

PROGRAMS: Annual Meeting; Community Outreach; Exhibits; Living History; Publication; Research Library/Archives

COLLECTIONS: [1860-1940] Native American baskets, clothing, and other artifacts; cameras, school memorabilia, logging items; old toys.

HOURS: May-Oct M-F 10-4, Sa 11-3

SYLMAR

916
Nethercutt Collection, The
15200 Bledsoe St, 91342; (p) (818) 364-6464; (f) (818) 367-4842; (c) Los Angeles

Private non-profit/ 1995/ staff: 25(f)

ART MUSEUM; HISTORY MUSEUM: Exhibits and restores "functional fine art."

PROGRAMS: Concerts; Exhibits; Guided Tours; Lectures; Research Library/Archives

COLLECTIONS: [1750-1970] Classic and antique automobiles, Louis XV furniture, and other decorative arts, mechanical musical instruments, concert pipe organ, research archive/library, Edwardian clothing, 1912 private railroad car.

HOURS: Yr T-Sa 10-1:30 and by appt

ADMISSION: No charge

TAHOE CITY

917
North Lake Tahoe Historical Society
130 W Lake Blvd, 96145 [PO Box 6141, 96145]; (p) (530) 583-1762; (f) (530) 583-8992; (c) Placer

Private non-profit/ 1969/ North Lake Tahoe Historical Society/ staff: 2(f); 1(p); 10(v)/ members: 700

HISTORIC SITE; HISTORICAL SOCIETY; HISTORY MUSEUM; HOUSE MUSEUM: Preserves, studies, and presents Lake Tahoe history and Native American culture.

PROGRAMS: Annual Meeting; Elder's Programs; Exhibits; Facility Rental; Guided Tours; Research Library/Archives; School-Based Curriculum

COLLECTIONS: [1844-1990] 1,000 Native American baskets, oral histories, pioneer history, photos, newspapers, environmental interpretive displays.

HOURS: May 1 - June 14 W-Su 11-5; June 15 - Sept 30, Daily

918
Watson Cabin
560 N Lake Blvd, 96145 [PO Box 6141, 96145]; (p) (916) 583-8717, (916) 583-1762; (f) (916) 583-8992

1908/ staff: 1(p); 10(v)

HISTORY MUSEUM: Maintains Gatekeeper's Cabin Museum and Marion Steinbach Indian Basket Museum.

PROGRAMS: Exhibits

COLLECTIONS: [1909-1929] Oral histories, newspapers, photos. Prehistoric and Washo tools, baskets; early logging, skiing, boating.

HOURS: Seasonal

TAHOMA

919
Ehrman Mansion
Hwy 89, 96142 [PO Box 266, 96142]; (p) (530) 525-0138; (f) (530) 525-6730; (c) El Dorado

State/ California State Parks/ staff: 2(p)

HOUSE MUSEUM; LIVING HISTORY/OUTDOOR MUSEUM: Historic California 1901 shingle style resort home with non-primary domestic furnishings, natural history programs.

PROGRAMS: Exhibits; Guided Tours; Interpretation; Living History

COLLECTIONS: [1901-1960] Domestic furnishings and natural history specimens.

HOURS: July-Sept 11-4

ADMISSION: $1

920
Vikingsholm
Emerald Bay State Park, 96142 [PO Box 266, 96142]; (p) (530) 525-7232; (f) (530) 525-6730; (c) El Dorado

State/ 1953/ California State Parks/ staff: 5(f); 5(p)

HISTORIC SITE; HOUSE MUSEUM: 1929 Scandinavian style resort house with primary historic domestic furniture.

PROGRAMS: Exhibits; Guided Tours

COLLECTIONS: [1929] Scandinavian antique folk furniture and 1929 reproductions from original antiques.

HOURS: Mid-June-Sept Daily 10-4

ADMISSION: $3, Children $2

TEHAMA

921
Tehama County Museum Foundation, Inc.
NE Corner of 3rd & C Sts, 96090 [PO Box 275, 96090]; (p) (530) 384-2595, (530) 384-2420; (f) (530) 529-4325; tcmuse@tco.net; www.tco.net/tehama/museum; (c) Tehama

Private non-profit/ 1980/ Tehama County Museum Board/ staff: 5(p); 35(v)/ members: 222

HISTORIC SITE; HISTORY MUSEUM; RESEARCH CENTER: Collects and exhibits artifacts and material from Tehama County.

PROGRAMS: Community Outreach; Concerts; Exhibits; Facility Rental; Family Programs; Guided Tours; Interpretation; Publication; Reenactments; Research Library/Archives; School-Based Curriculum

COLLECTIONS: [1840s-1980s] Preserves, and maintains artifacts and materials that reflect county history and displays; Native American

TEMPLETON

922
Templeton Historical Museum Society
309 Main St, 93465 [PO Box 788, 93465]; (p) (805) 434-0807; (f) (805) 434-1633; (c) San Luis Obispo

Private non-profit/ 1989/ staff: 35(v)/ members: 135/publication: *Templeton Times*

Collects, preserves, and displays local history.

PROGRAMS: Annual Meeting; Community Outreach; Exhibits; Guided Tours; Living History; Publication

COLLECTIONS: [1886-present] Furniture, books, clothes, farm equipment, personal items, and photos.

HOURS: Yr F-Su 1-4

ADMISSION: Donations

TIBURON

923
Angel Island Association
Angel Island State Park, 94920 [PO Box 866, 94920]; (p) (415) 435-3522; (f) (415) 435-2950; val.sherer@angelisland.org; www.angelisland.org; (c) Marin

Private non-profit/ 1986/ staff: 1(f); 2(p); 200(v)/ members: 150

HISTORIC SITE; LIVING HISTORY/OUTDOOR MUSEUM: Provides interpretive services at Angel Island State Park.

PROGRAMS: Concerts; Exhibits; Guided Tours; Interpretation; Living History; Reenactments; School-Based Curriculum

COLLECTIONS: [Civil War-1940] A Quarantine Station, a Civil War camp, WWII debarkation center; Immigration Station, a National Historic Monument, which detained Asian immigrants from 1910 to 1940.

HOURS: Yr Ferry services available Apr-Oct, weekends Nov-Mar

924
Belvedere-Tiburon Landmarks Society
1920 Paradise Dr, 94920 [PO Box 1073, 94920]; (p) (415) 435-1853; (c) Marin

Private non-profit/ 1959/ staff: 4(p); 90(v)/ members: 975

ART MUSEUM; GARDEN; HISTORIC PRESERVATION AGENCY; HISTORIC SITE; HISTORICAL SOCIETY; HOUSE MUSEUM: Acquires and preserves property and structures of local conservation and historical significance.

PROGRAMS: Annual Meeting; Community Outreach; Concerts; Exhibits; Facility Rental; Garden Tours; Guided Tours; Lectures; Publication; Research Library/Archives; School-Based Curriculum

COLLECTIONS: [19th-20th c] Photos, fine art, maps, documents, oral histories, newspapers, artifacts, ephemera focusing on San Francisco Bay area identified by Mexican land grant.

HOURS: Apr-Oct Sa, W 1-4 or by appt

ADMISSION: Donations accepted

TOMALES

925
Tomales Regional History Center, Inc.
26701 Hwy 1, 94971 [PO Box 262, 94971]; (p) (707) 878-9443; (c) Marin

Private non-profit/ 1978/ Mary Zimmerman, Pres/ staff: 30(v)/ members: 400

HISTORICAL SOCIETY; HISTORY MUSEUM: Preserves local history and provides educational resources.

PROGRAMS: Annual Meeting; Community Outreach; Exhibits; Guided Tours; Living History; Publication; Research Library/Archives; School-Based Curriculum

COLLECTIONS: [1825-1999] Artifacts from Marin and Sonoma counties coastal areas.

HOURS: Yr F-Su 1-4

ADMISSION: No charge

TORRANCE

926
Salvation Army Western Territorial Museum, The
2780 Lomita Blvd, 90505; (p) (310) 377-0481, (310) 534-6097; (f) (310) 534-7157; (c) Los Angeles

Private non-profit/ 1980/ staff: 1(f)

Preserves and displays Salvation Army history.

PROGRAMS: Interpretation; Lectures; Research Library/Archives

COLLECTIONS: [1883-present] Uniforms, photos, newspapers, books. musical instruments, posters.

TRAVIS AFB

927
Travis Air Museum
Bldg 80, Burgam Blvd, 94535 [400 Breman Circle, 94535]; (p) (707) 424-5605; (f) (707) 424-4451; www.Travis.of.mil

Federal/ US Air Force/ staff: 4(f); 12(v)/ members: 300

HISTORY MUSEUM: Portrays history of Travis Air Force Base and military airlift in the Pacific.

PROGRAMS: Exhibits; Guided Tours

COLLECTIONS: [1950-present] Collection of US military aircraft: bombers, fighters, trainers, cargo, and rescue aircraft.

HOURS: M-Sa 9-4

ADMISSION: No charge

TRONA

928
Searles Valley Historical Society, Inc.
13193 Main St, 93562 [PO Box 630, 93562]; (p) (760) 372-5222; rhartley@iwvisp.com; www.iwvisp.com/SVHS; (c) San Bernardino

Joint; Private non-profit/ 1979/ Board of Directors/ staff: 15(v)/ members: 150

HISTORICAL SOCIETY; HISTORY MUSEUM; HOUSE MUSEUM; RESEARCH CENTER: Collects and preserves material related to regional history.

PROGRAMS: Annual Meeting; Exhibits; Lectures; Publication; Research Library/Archives

COLLECTIONS: [1860-present] Manuscripts, maps, magazines, artifacts, books, newspapers, research materials, photos, and negatives.

HOURS: Yr M- W,F- Sa 10-1, and by appt.

TRUCKEE

929
Donner Memorial State Park and Emigrant Trail Museum
12593 Donner Pass Rd, 96161; (p) (530) 582-7892; (f) (530) 582-7893; smichel@jps.net; (c) Nevada

State/ 1962/ California State Parks/ staff: 6(f); 3(p)

HISTORIC SITE; HISTORY MUSEUM: Promotes CA Emigrant Trail and Truckee Route history; Secondary focus on Donner Party history, Central Pacific Railroad, and lumbering.

PROGRAMS: Exhibits; Living History; Reenactments; Research Library/Archives; Theatre

COLLECTIONS: [1840-1900] Weapons, photographs, Native American culture, and local history artifacts.

HOURS: Yr Daily

ADMISSION: $2, Children $1

930
Truckee-Donner Historical Society
Corner of Spring & Jibbom St, 96160 [PO Box 893, 96160]; (c) Nevada

Private non-profit/ 1968/ staff: 20(v)/ members: 320/publication: *Fire and Ice*

HISTORICAL SOCIETY; HISTORY MUSEUM; RESEARCH CENTER: Collects and catalogs photos and regional artifacts; maintains 1875 jail as museum.

PROGRAMS: Community Outreach; Exhibits; Film/Video; Guided Tours; Monthly Meeting

COLLECTIONS: [late 1800s-early 1900s] Photos illustrating local lumber mills and ice harvesting; ice harvesting and logging tools, clothing, jail logs, Chinese and Indian artifacts.

HOURS: May-Sept Sa-Su 11-4

ADMISSION: Donations accepted

TUJUNGA

931
Little Landers Historical Society
10110 Commerce Ave, Tujunga, 91043 [PO Box 2034, 91043]; (p) (818) 352-3420; (c) Los Angeles

Private non-profit/ 1959/ staff: 20(v)/ members: 110

HISTORIC SITE; HISTORICAL SOCIETY; HISTORY MUSEUM: Preserves and maintains Bolton Hall Museum.

PROGRAMS: Annual Meeting; Community Outreach; Exhibits; Facility Rental; Guided Tours; Research Library/Archives

COLLECTIONS: [Late 19th-20th c] Artifacts and records of Rancho Tujunga area; local newspapers, 1920-1980; local cemetery records; school yearbooks, telephone directories 1923-present; large collection of historical photos; pioneer artifacts; early maps; records of Little Landers settlement, 1913-1920.

HOURS: Yr T-Su 1-4

ADMISSION: No charge

TULARE

932
Tulare Historical Museum
444 W Tulare Ave, 93275 [PO Box 248, 93275]; (p) (559) 686-2074; (f) (559) 686-9295; tularehm@lightspeed.net; (c) Tulare

Private non-profit/ 1985/ Tulare City Historical Society/ staff: 3(p); 140(v)/ members: 1200/publication: *Then and Now*

HISTORICAL SOCIETY; HISTORY MUSEUM: Preserves and showcases the history of the city of Tulare and serves as a cultural center for the community.

PROGRAMS: Exhibits; Facility Rental; Family Programs; Film/Video; Guided Tours; Lectures; Publication; Research Library/Archives;

School-Based Curriculum

COLLECTIONS: [1800s-presents] Military artifacts, Olympic gold medallist Bob Mathias collection; archives; antique glass and furniture collection.

HOURS: Yr Th-Sa 10-4, Su

TULELAKE

933
Lava Beds National Monuments
#1 Indian Well Headquarters, 96134 [PO Box 867, 96134]; (p) (530) 667-2282; (f) (530) 667-2737; www.nps.gov/labe/; (c) Siskiyou

Federal/ 1925/ U.S. National Park Service/ staff: 2(f); 3(p); 4(v)

HISTORIC SITE: Preserves 46,000 acres of volcanic wilderness, including numerous sites associated with the Modoc War of 1872-73.

PROGRAMS: Community Outreach; Exhibits; Family Programs; Festivals; Film/Video; Guided Tours; Interpretation; Living History; Research Library/Archives; School-Based Curriculum

COLLECTIONS: [Pre-contact to 1945] Lava beds artifacts; archeological specimens.

HOURS: Yr Winter Daily 8-5; Summer 8-6

ADMISSION: $4 vehicle

TURLOCK

934
Central California Information Center/CA Historical Resource Information System
Rm C-205A, CSU, Stanislaus Campus, 95382 [801 W Monte Vista Ave, 95382]; (p) (209) 667-3307; (f) (209) 667-3324; egreatho@toto.csustan.edu; (c) Stanislaus

Joint/ 1976/ CSUS Foundation and CA Dept of Parks and Rec office of Hist. Preserv./ staff: 5(p); 5(v)

Collects and distributes prehistoric and historic archaeological and historical information to local, state and federal agencies.

PROGRAMS: Annual Meeting; Community Outreach; Research Library/Archives

COLLECTIONS: Data pertaining to archaeological sites and historic properties in Alpine, Calaveras, Mariposa, Merced, San Joaquin, Stanislaus, and Tuolumne Counties.

HOURS: By appt only

TUSTIN

935
Tustin Area Historical Society
395 El Camino Real, 92781 [PO Box 185, 92781]; (p) (714) 731-5701; TAHS@juno.com; (c) Orange

Private non-profit/ 1975/ Board of Directors/ staff: 1(p)/ 45(v)/ members: 275/publication: *Heritage*

HISTORICAL SOCIETY; HISTORY MUSEUM; RESEARCH CENTER: Collects, preserves, and interprets local history.

PROGRAMS: Exhibits; Garden Tours; Lectures; Publication; Research Library/Archives

COLLECTIONS: [Late 1800s-present] Books, ledgers, catalogs, school yearbooks, farm tools, business tools, home furnishings, maps, newspapers, photos and negatives.

HOURS: Yr T-Th 9-2; 1st & 3rd Sa

TWENTYNINE PALMS

936
Twentynine Palms Historical Society
6760 National Park Drive, 92277 [PO Box 1926, 92277]; (p) (760) 367-2366; (c) San Bernardino

1982/ Board of Directors/ staff: 50(v)/ members: 240/publication: *News and Notes*

HISTORIC PRESERVATION AGENCY; HISTORIC SITE; HISTORICAL SOCIETY; HISTORY MUSEUM; LIVING HISTORY/OUTDOOR MUSEUM; RESEARCH CENTER: Collects, preserves, and displays artifacts of local early inhabitants; provides regional historical and cultural research materials.

PROGRAMS: Annual Meeting; Community Outreach; Exhibits; Family Programs; Guided Tours; Interpretation; Lectures; Publication; Research Library/Archives

COLLECTIONS: [1800 and 1900s] Native American artifacts, early mining displays, early cattleman and ranching, homesteaders' artifacts, military history, maps, photographs, family histories, original school artifacts and local art.

HOURS: Yr Sept-May W-Su 1-4; June-Aug Sa-Su 1-4

UKIAH

937
Grace Hudson Museum and Sun House
431 S Main St, 95482; (p) (707) 467-2836; (f) (707) 467-2835; ghmuseum@jps.net; www.gracehudsonmuseum.org; (c) Mendocino

City/ 1986/ staff: 3(f); 2(p); 60(v)/ members: 640/publication: *The Painter Lady, Remember Your Relations*

ART MUSEUM; HISTORIC SITE; HISTORY MUSEUM: Preserves and interprets work of artist Grace Hudson and her husband, ethnologist Dr John Hudson.

PROGRAMS: Community Outreach; Exhibits; Facility Rental; Family Programs; Film/Video; Guided Tours; Interpretation; Lectures; Publication; Research Library/Archives; School-Based Curriculum

COLLECTIONS: [1850-1937] 1,000 ethnographic artifacts, 50 unpublished field notebooks, manuscripts and correspondence (41 linear feet), 6,000 historic photographs/glass plate negatives, 700 works of art, 1,300 volumes and 5,000 family articles.

HOURS: Yr W-Sa 10-4:30, Su 12-4:30

ADMISSION: Donations requested

938
Held Poage Memorial Home and Research Library
603 W Perkins St, 95482-4726; (p) (707) 462-6969; (c) Mendocino

Private non-profit/ 1970/ Mendocino County Historical Society/ staff: 12(v)

HOUSE MUSEUM; LIBRARY AND/OR ARCHIVES: Focuses on Mendocino County and surrounding county histories.

PROGRAMS: Exhibits; Research Library/ Archives

COLLECTIONS: [Early 20th c]

HOURS: Yr T-Sa 1-4 and by appt

939
Mendocino County Historical Society, Inc.
603 W Perkins St, 95482; (p) (707) 462-6969; (c) Mendocino

Private non-profit/ 1956/ Exective Board/ staff: 20(v)/ members: 340

GENEALOGICAL SOCIETY; HISTORIC SITE; RESEARCH CENTER: Maintains Held Poage Memorial Home and Research Library.

PROGRAMS: Annual Meeting; Research Library/Archives

COLLECTIONS: [Early 1900s]

HOURS: Yr T,Th,Sa 1:30-5 and by appt

ADMISSION: Donations accepted

UPLAND

940
Cooper Regional History Museum
217 E A St, 91785 [PO Box 772, 91785-0772]; (p) (909) 982-8010; (f) (909) 920-9292; info@culturalcenter.org; www.culturalcenter. org; (c) San Bernardino

Private non-profit/ 1965/ Chaffey Communities Cultural Center/ staff: 15(v)/ members: 200

HISTORY MUSEUM: History and culture of Upland, Ontario, Montclair, Mt. Baldy, and Rancho Cucamonga.

PROGRAMS: Annual Meeting; Concerts; Exhibits; Facility Rental; Family Programs; Festivals; Guided Tours; Interpretation; Lectures; Research Library/Archives; School-Based Curriculum; Theatre

COLLECTIONS: [1880-1950] 20,000 artifacts, 2,500 photographs, 60 linear feet of archives, 2 historic buildings, 2-acre citrus grove, 10 historic vehicles.

HOURS: Sa

VACAVILLE

941
Vacaville Museum
213 Buck Ave, 95688; (p) (707) 447-4513; (f) (707) 447-2661; vacmuseum@aol.com; www.vacavillemuseum.org; (c) Solano

Private non-profit/ 1981/ Vacaville Museum Foundation Board of Trustees/ staff: 2(f); 5(p); 100(v)/ members: 485/publication: *Vacaville News and Notes*

HOUSE MUSEUM: Preserves history and culture of Solano County.

PROGRAMS: Community Outreach; Concerts; Exhibits; Facility Rental; Family Programs; Film/Video; Garden Tours; Guided Tours; Interpretation; Lectures; Living History; Publication; Research Library/Archives; School-Based Curriculum

COLLECTIONS: [1885-2000] Photos and negatives; orchard industry artifacts.

HOURS: Yr

ADMISSION: $1, Student $0.50

VALLEJO

942
Solano County Historical Society
[PO Box 922, 94590]; (p) (707) 426-2081; (c) Solano

County; Private non-profit/ 1956/ Directors/ staff: 8(f); 10(v)/ members: 450/publication: *The Solano Historian*

HISTORICAL SOCIETY: Promotes local history.

PROGRAMS: Annual Meeting; Exhibits; Family Programs; Guided Tours; Lectures; Publication; Research Library/Archives

943
USDA Forest Service
1323 Club Dr, 94592; (p) (707) 562-8855; llux/r@fs.fed.us; (c) Solano

Federal/ 1986/ USDA/ staff: 1(f)

LIBRARY AND/OR ARCHIVES: Archive of material relevant to Forest Service history in CA.

PROGRAMS: Research Library/Archives

COLLECTIONS: [1900-present] Photos, documents, brochures, maps, documenting Forest Service history in CA.

HOURS: By appt

944
Vallejo Naval and Historical Museum
734 Martin St, 94590; (p) (707) 643-0077; (f) (707) 643-2443; valmuse@pacbell.net; www.vallejomuseum.org; (c) Solano

1974/ Board of Directors/ staff: 1(f); 2(p); 85(v)/ members: 500/publication: *Newsletter*

Interprets Vallejo community history and history of U.S. Navy in San Francisco Bay Area.

PROGRAMS: Annual Meeting; Community Outreach; Concerts; Exhibits; Facility Rental; Family Programs; Festivals; Film/Video; Guided Tours; Interpretation; Lectures; Publication; Research Library/Archives; School-Based Curriculum

COLLECTIONS: [1850-present] Mare Island Naval Shipyard and city artifacts.

HOURS: Yr T-Sa 10-4:30

ADMISSION: $2, Student $1, Seniors $1; Under 12/Mbrs free

VENTURA

945
Olivas Adobe Historical Park
4200 Olivas Park Dr, 93002 [PO Box 99, 93002-0099]; (p) (805) 658-4728; (f) (805) 698-1030; (c) Ventura

City/ 1972/ staff: 3(p); 42(v)/ members: 42

HISTORY MUSEUM: Maintains 1847 Rancho Adobe built by Raymundo Olivas, local Latino pioneer, rancher, and businessman.

PROGRAMS: Concerts; Facility Rental; Festivals; Film/Video; Guided Tours; Publication; Reenactments

COLLECTIONS: [1847-1890] Artifacts of late 19th century ranching society.

HOURS: Yr Sa-Su 10-4

ADMISSION: No charge

946
Ortega Adobe Historic Residence
213 W Main St, 93002 [PO Box 99, 93002-0099]; (p) (805) 658-4728; (f) (805) 648-1030; (c) Ventura

City/ 1969/ staff: 1(p); 14(v)

HOUSE MUSEUM: Historic 1857 Adobe of Ortega Chili Company.

COLLECTIONS: House furniture

HOURS: Yr Daily 10-3

947
San Buenaventura Mission
211 E Main St, 93001; (p) (805) 643-4318; (f) (805) 643-7831; mission @anacapa.net; www.anacapa.net/~mission; (c) Ventura

Private non-profit/ 1782/ staff: 1(f); 4(p)

HISTORIC SITE: Maintains 9th California mission, built in 1782.

PROGRAMS: Community Outreach

COLLECTIONS: Vestments, altar vessels, books, Indian baskets, and period pieces.

HOURS: Yr Daily

948
Ventura County Museum of History and Art
100 E Main St, 93001; (p) (805) 653-0323; (f) (805) 653-5267; director@vcmha.org; www.vcmha.org; (c) Ventura

Private non-profit/ 1913/ Board of Directors/ staff: 4(f); 8(p); 173(v)/ members: 2177/publication: *The Ventura County Historical Society Quarterly*

ART MUSEUM; HISTORICAL SOCIETY; HISTORY MUSEUM: Promotes history and art relating to Ventura County.

PROGRAMS: Annual Meeting; Community Outreach; Elder's Programs; Exhibits; Facility Rental; Family Programs; Interpretation; Lectures; Publication; Research Library/Archives; School-Based Curriculum

COLLECTIONS: [1700s-present] Books, articles of incorporation, architectural plans, oral histories, maps, photographs, farm implements, regional history artifacts, and works of art.

HOURS: Yr T-Su 10-5

ADMISSION: $4, Children $1, Seniors $3

VICTORVILLE

949
Roy Rogers-Dale Evans Museum, The
15650 Seneca Rd, 92392; (p) (760) 243-4548; (f) (760) 245-2009; www.royrogers.com

Private non-profit/ 1966/ Board of Director/ staff: 4(f); 10(p)/ members: 736

PROGRAMS: Concerts; Exhibits; Facility Rental; Festivals; Film/Video; School-Based Curriculum

COLLECTIONS: [1911-present] Roy Rogers and Dale Evans memorabilia; family pictures, costumes, gun collection, documentaries.

HOURS: Yr Daily 9-5

ADMISSION: $7, Children $5, Seniors $6

VISALIA

950
Tulare County Museum
27000 S Mooney Blvd, 93277; (p) (559) 733-6616; (f) (559) 737-4582; (c) Tulare

County/ 1948/ Tulare County Museum Board/ staff: 1(f); 6(p); 8(v)

HISTORIC SITE; HISTORICAL SOCIETY; HISTORY MUSEUM; HOUSE MUSEUM; LIVING HISTORY/OUTDOOR MUSEUM

PROGRAMS: Community Outreach; Exhibits; Facility Rental; Guided Tours; Interpretation; Reenactments; Research Library/Archives; School-Based Curriculum

COLLECTIONS: Extensive Native American (Yokes) baskets and artifacts collection; antique saddle and gun collection; vintage clothing; antique farm equipment; five acre grounds with historical buildings on site.

HOURS: Yr Th-M (Summer W-M)

ADMISSION: $4/vehicle

VISTA

951
Antique Gas and Steam Engine Museum, Inc.
2040 N Santa Fe Ave, 92083; (p) (760) 941-1791; (f) (760) 941-0690; www.agsem.com; (c) San Diego

Private non-profit/ 1986/ staff: 1(f); 1(p); 700(v)/ members: 700

HISTORY MUSEUM; LIVING HISTORY/OUTDOOR MUSEUM

PROGRAMS: Annual Meeting; Exhibits; Facility Rental; Festivals; Guided Tours; Living History; Research Library/Archives

COLLECTIONS: [1850-1950] Agricultural machinery and artifacts, including a large number of steam and gas-powered tractors.

HOURS: Yr Daily

952
Rancho Buena Vista Adobe
651 E Vista Way, 92084 [640 Alta Vista Dr, 92084]; (p) (760) 639-6164; (f) (760) 639-6152; www.ci.vista.ca.us/adobe; (c) San Diego

City/ 1990/ staff: 6(p); 40(v)/ members: 85

HISTORIC SITE: Preserves historic adobe and provides interpretive tours and programs.

PROGRAMS: Annual Meeting; Exhibits; Facility Rental; Festivals; Guided Tours; Interpretation; Living History; School-Based Curriculum

COLLECTIONS: [1850-1930] Adobe structure, antique furnishings.

HOURS: Yr W-Sa 10-3

ADMISSION: $3

953
Vista Historical Society
651 E Vista Way, 92085 [PO Box 1032, 92085]; (p) (760) 630-0444; (c) San Diego

Private non-profit/ 1967/ Board of Directors/ staff: 4(f); 8(p); 25(v)/ members: 250

HISTORICAL SOCIETY; HISTORY MUSEUM: Collects, preserve, and interprets Vista and regional history.

PROGRAMS: Annual Meeting; Community Outreach; Exhibits; Family Programs; Film/Video; Interpretation; Lectures; Research Library/Archives; School-Based Curriculum

COLLECTIONS: [1850-1963] Collects documents, maps, photos, natural history, and artifacts.

HOURS: Yr W-Sa 10-3

WALNUT

954
W.R. Rowland Adobe Ranch House
130 Avenida Alipaz, 91789 [PO Box 682, 91789]; (p) (909) 598-5605; (f) (909) 598-2160

1883/ City/ staff: 1(p)

COLLECTIONS: [1883] Beds; kitchen utensils; furniture.

HOURS: By appt

WALNUT CREEK

955
AltaMira Historical Society
1840 San Miguel No. 207, 94596; (p) (925) 938-7243; explore@altamirapress.com; www.altamirapress.com; (c) Contra Costa

1995/ Board of Directors/ staff: 5(f); 4(p); 25(v)/ members: 100/publication: *The Natural Superiority of Women; Inuit, Whaling, and Sustainability; and others*

HISTORICAL SOCIETY; RESEARCH CENTER: Collects, preserves, interprets, and exhibits publishing history.

PROGRAMS: Annual Meeting; Community Outreach; Exhibits; Festivals; Interpretation; Lectures; Publication; Reenactments; Research Library/Archives; School-Based Curriculum

COLLECTIONS: Artifacts, documents, manuscripts, photographs, rare books, ephemera, music, plastic animals, and art.

HOURS: Yr M-F 8-5

ADMISSION: No charge

956
Walnut Creek Historical Society
2660 Ygnacio Valley Rd, 94598; (p) (925) 935-7871; (f) (925) 935-7885; wch@jps.net; www.jps.net/wch/; (c) Contra Costa

Private non-profit/ 1969/ staff: 2(p); 100(v)/ members: 400

Preserve and interprets local history of Walnut Creek.

PROGRAMS: Annual Meeting; Community Outreach; Concerts; Exhibits; Facility Rental; Family Programs; Festivals; Film/Video; Interpretation; Living History

COLLECTIONS: [1852-1940] Artifacts and original materials of Penniman family, Albert Johnson, Shadelands Ranch, and Walnut Creek.

HOURS: Feb-Nov W, Th, Su 1-4

ADMISSION: $2, Children $1, Seniors $1

WEAVERVILLE

957
Trinity County Historical Society
508 Main St, 96093 [PO Box 333, 96093-33]; (p) (530) 623-5211; (c) Trinity

Private non-profit/ 1954/ Board of Directors/ staff: 5(p); 15(v)/ members: 350

HISTORICAL SOCIETY; HISTORY MUSEUM; RESEARCH CENTER: Operates Jake Jackson Museum, emphasizing pioneering life.

PROGRAMS: Annual Meeting; Exhibits; Interpretation; Publication; Research Library/Archives

COLLECTIONS: [1850-early -1900s]

HOURS: Yr May-Oct Daily 10-5; April, Nov Daily 12-4; Dec-Mar T-Sa 12-4

958
Weaverville Joss House State Historic Park
Main & Oregon St, 96093 [PO Box 1217, 96093]; (p) (530) 623-5284; (f) (530) 623-5284; htt//cal-parks.ca.gov/travel/regions/shasta/shast; (c) Trinity

State/ 1956/ CA State Parks/ staff: 1(f); 3(p); 2(v)/publication: *The History of Weaverville Joss House*

HISTORIC SITE; HISTORY MUSEUM; HOUSE MUSEUM: Maintains fully restored 1874 Chinese Taoist temple.

PROGRAMS: Exhibits; Guided Tours; Interpretation; Living History; Publication; School-Based Curriculum

COLLECTIONS: [1874-1900] Chinese objects: decorative arts, wood carvings, painted clay figures, textiles, furniture, candle holders, musical instruments, painted glass, offerings, castle lanterns, kitchen, and bedding objects.

HOURS: Yr June-Aug Daily

WEST HOLLYWOOD

959
Pacific Asia Museum
46 N Los Robles Ave, 91101; (p) (626) 449-2742; (f) (626) 449-2754; PacAsiaMus@aol.com; www.westmuse.org/pacasiamuseum; (c) Los Angeles

Private non-profit/ 1960/ staff: 19(f); 8(p); 300(v)/ members: 1300

ART MUSEUM: Collects, preserves, and exhibits art of Asia and Pacific Islands.

PROGRAMS: Community Outreach; Concerts; Exhibits; Facility Rental; Family Programs; Film/Video; Garden Tours; Guided Tours; Interpretation; Lectures; Publication; Research Library/Archives

COLLECTIONS: Ceramics, sculpture, screens, woodblock prints, textiles, folk art, ethnographic material, photos, jewelry, furniture.

HOURS: Yr W-Su 10-5

ADMISSION: $5, Student $3, Children $3, Seniors $3

960
Schindler House
835 N Kings Road, 90069 [835 N Kings Road, 90069]; (p) (213) 651-1510;

(f) (213) 651-2340; makcenter@earthlink.net

1921/ Mak Center for Art and Architecure LA; Friends of the Schindler House/ staff: 2(f); 15(v)

ART MUSEUM; HOUSE MUSEUM: Exhibits architecture and contemporary art programs in Schindler-designed home.

COLLECTIONS: [1920] Original furniture.

HOURS: Yr W-Su 11-6

WEST SACRAMENTO

961
California State Parks Photographic Archives
2517 Port St, 95691; (p) (916) 324-7001; (f) (916) 371-0301; photoarc@pacbell.net; (c) Yolo

State/ 1991/ staff: 2(f); 4(p)

LIBRARY AND/OR ARCHIVES: Collects and preserves photographic images in all formats relating to CA's natural and cultural resources and history.

PROGRAMS: Community Outreach; Exhibits; Interpretation; Reenactments; Research Library/Archives; School-Based Curriculum

COLLECTIONS: [1930-1970] Over 30,000 slides and 100,000 prints of CA's 265 Park units, including historical parks, recreation units, wilderness preserves, and beaches; 30,000 digital format records.

HOURS: Yr

WHITTIER

962
Pio Pico State Historic Park
6003 S Pioneer Blvd, 90606; (p) (562) 695-1217; (f) (562) 699-6916

State/ 1849/ California Parks & Recreation/ staff: 2(f); 10(v)

COLLECTIONS: [1880s-1920s] Adobe structure illustrating evolution of historic revival styles; interior decor and other social and cultural

963
Whittier Historical Society and Museum
6755 Newlin Ave, 90601; (p) (562) 945-3871; (f) (562) 945-9106; whittiermuseum@sol.com; www.whittiermuseum.org; (c) Los Angeles

Private non-profit/ 1972/ Board of Directors/ staff: 2(f); 2(p); 75(v)/ members: 475/publication: *Gazette*

HISTORICAL SOCIETY; HISTORY MUSEUM: Collects, preserves, and displays history of Whittier.

PROGRAMS: Annual Meeting; Exhibits; Facility Rental; Family Programs; Publication; Research Library/Archives; School-Based Curriculum

COLLECTIONS: [1887-present] Historic documents, textiles, photos, artifacts, archives.

HOURS: Sept-July; research T-Su, tours

WILLIAMS

964
Sacramento Valley Museum
1495 E St, 95987 [PO Box 1437, 95987]; (p) (530) 473-2798; (f) (530) 458-5769; (c) Colusa

City/ 1963/ staff: 1(f); 10(v)/ members: 110

HISTORY MUSEUM: The museum located in the old high school focuses on local history.

PROGRAMS: Facility Rental; Guided Tours

COLLECTIONS: [Early 1800s-Late 1900s] The collection includes antiques and artifacts depicting Sacramento Valley history.

HOURS: Yr

WILLITS

965
Mendocino County Museum
400 E Commercial St, 95490; (p) (707) 459-2736; (f) (707) 459-7836; museum@zap com.net; www.co.mendoncino.ca.us/muse um/index.html; (c) Mendocino

County/ 1972/ staff: 4(f); 1(p); 40(v)/publication: *Grassroots History Publication Program*

HISTORY MUSEUM: Promotes local history.

PROGRAMS: Community Outreach; Exhibits; Interpretation; Publication; Research Library/ Archives; School-Based Curriculum

COLLECTIONS: [20th c] Objects, photographs, and oral histories.

HOURS: Yr W-Su

WILLOW CREEK

966
Willow Creek-China Flat Museum
Corner Hwy 299 & Hwy 96, 95573 [PO Box 102, 95573]; mwooden@juno.com; (c) Humboldt

Private non-profit/ 1987/ Board of Directors/ staff: 30(v)/ members: 210

HISTORICAL SOCIETY: Collects and preserves mining, farming, and local Indian Tribe materials.

PROGRAMS: Annual Meeting; Community Outreach; Exhibits; Festivals; Lectures; Research Library/Archives; School-Based Curriculum

COLLECTIONS: [1850-1930] Photos; mining company records; WW II uniforms; Hoopa, Yurok, and Karok baskets; Chinese artifacts; blacksmith shop; mining equipment; Bigfoot literature.

HOURS: May-mid Oct F-Su

WILMINGTON

967
General Phineas Banning Residence Museum
401 E M St, 90748 [PO Box 397, 90748]; (p) (310) 548-7777; (f) (310) 548-2644; jah@hot mail.com; www.banning.org; (c) Los Angeles

City/ 1974/ staff: 4(f); 4(p); 150(v)/ members: 1100/publication: *Banning and Company*

HISTORIC SITE: Interprets 13-room Victorian

Greek revival mansion built by Phineas Banning in 1864.

PROGRAMS: Community Outreach; Exhibits; Guided Tours; Living History; Publication; Research Library/Archives

COLLECTIONS: [1864-1900] American Victorian decorative arts and textiles, period photos, and archival material related to Banning Family and Southern CA.

HOURS: Yr

WOODLAND

968
Yolo County Historical Museum
512 Gibson Rd, 95695; (p) (530) 666-1045; (c) Yolo

Private non-profit/ 1979/ Board of Directors/ staff: 1(p); 68(v)/ members: 420

HISTORIC SITE; HOUSE MUSEUM: Collects, exhibits, and interprets local history.

PROGRAMS: Annual Meeting; Community Outreach; Exhibits; Facility Rental; Festivals; Garden Tours; Guided Tours; Interpretation; Lectures; Living History; Publication; Research Library/Archives; School-Based Curriculum

COLLECTIONS: [1850-1940] Artifacts, art, photos, documents, manuscripts, books, farm equipment, buildings.

HOURS: Yr M,T 9-5, Sa-Su 12-4

969
Yolo County Historical Society
[PO Box 1447, 95776]; (p) (530) 662-2212; bjford@pacbell.net; (c) Yolo

Private non-profit/ 1963/ staff: 18(v)/ members: 350

HISTORICAL SOCIETY: Collects, preserves, educates and promotes local history.

WOODSIDE

970
Filoli
86 Canada Rd, 94062; (p) (605) 364-8300; (f) (605) 366-7836; filolifriend@earthlink.net; www.filoli.org; (c) San Mateo

Private non-profit/ 1975/ Filoli Center/ staff: 30(f); 8(p); 1046(v)/ members: 12261

GARDEN; HOUSE MUSEUM

PROGRAMS: Facility Rental; Festivals; Garden Tours; Guided Tours; Lectures; Research Library/Archives; School-Based Curriculum

COLLECTIONS: [1918-1970]

HOURS: Feb 15 - Nov 1 T-Sa 10-3

ADMISSION: $10

YORBA LINDA

971
Richard Nixon Presidential Library and Birthplace
18001 Yorba Linda Blvd, 92886; (p) (714) 993-5075; (f) (714) 528-0544; stedman@nixonfoundation.org; www.nixon foundation.org; (c) Orange

Private non-profit/ 1990/ staff: 30(f); 200(v)/ members: 6000

GARDEN; HISTORIC SITE; HISTORY MUSEUM; HOUSE MUSEUM; PRESIDENTIAL

SITE; RESEARCH CENTER: Operates a museum, birthplace, memorials, and archives dedicated to life and legacy of former President Richard Nixon.

PROGRAMS: Community Outreach; Concerts; Elder's Programs; Exhibits; Facility Rental; Family Programs; Film/Video; Garden Tours; Lectures; Living History; Publication; Reenactments; Research Library/Archives; School-Based Curriculum; Theatre

COLLECTIONS: [1912-1994] Materials on Nixon's life; Nixon's birthplace; Nixons' graves.

HOURS: Yr Daily M-Sa 10-5, Su 11-5

YOUNTVILLE

972
Napa Valley Museum
55 Presidents Circle, 94599 [PO Box 3567, 94599]; (p) (707) 944-0500; (f) (707) 945-0500; info@napavalleymuseum.org; www.napavalleymuseum.org; (c) Napa

Private non-profit/ 1972/ Board of Trustees/ staff: 7(f); 100(v)/ members: 700

ART MUSEUM; HISTORY MUSEUM

PROGRAMS: Community Outreach; Exhibits; Facility Rental; Family Programs; Guided Tours; Lectures; Publication; Reenactments; School-Based Curriculum

COLLECTIONS: [Prehistoric-present] Art: painting, sculpture, prints, drawings, photos; Human history: Native American, pioneer, ethnic; Natural Science: geology, paleontology, biology; Industry: agriculture, viticulture, mining, transportation; Archival: maps, letters, and photos.

HOURS: Yr W-M 10-5

ADMISSION: $4.50

YREKA

973
Siskiyou County Museum
910 S Main St, 96097; (p) (530) 842-3836; (f) (530) 842-3166; www.siskiyoucounty.com/museum; (c) Siskiyou

County/ 1945/ staff: 1(f); 2(p); 55(v)/ members: 950/publication: *Siskiyou Pioneer; Museum Series; and others*

HISTORY MUSEUM: Exhibits material associated with Siskiyou County and maintains outdoor museum.

PROGRAMS: Concerts; Exhibits; Facility Rental; Family Programs; Festivals; Film/Video; Guided Tours; Interpretation; Lectures; Living History; Publication; Research Library/Archives; School-Based Curriculum

COLLECTIONS: [1825-present] Ethnographic Indian and Chinese artifacts; trapping materials; gold mining; settlement, agricultural and lumbering artifacts; transportation, turn-of-century, Depression Era and other 20th century objects.

HOURS: Yr T-F 9-5, Sa 9-4

ADMISSION: $10, Children $0.75

YUBA CITY

974
Community Memorial Museum of Sutter
1333 Butte House Rd, 95992 [PO Box 1555, 95992]; (p) (530) 822-7141, (530) 822-7291; (c) Sutter

County/ 1975/ staff: 2(f); 3(p); 35(v)/ members: 500/publication: *Worth Keeping, Coping with Disaster*

HISTORY MUSEUM: Collects and interprets history of Sutter County, with emphasis on agriculture, Sutter Buttes, Maidu Indians.

PROGRAMS: Community Outreach; Exhibits; Family Programs; Publication; Research Library/Archives

COLLECTIONS: [1840-1940] Maidu Indian artifacts, baskets, photos, agricultural tools and artifacts, domestic artifacts, children's toys.

HOURS: Yr T-F 9-5, Sa-Su

975
Sutter County Historical Society
[PO Box 1004, 95992]; (p) (530) 674-8106; (f) (530) 822-7291; leone@jps.net; (c) Sutter

Private non-profit/ 1954/ Same/ members: 400

Preserve history of Sutter County through quarterly meeting and publications.

YUCAIPA

976
Los Rios Ranch
39610 Oak Glen Road, 92399; (p) (909) 797-1005

977
Yucaipa Adobe
32183 Kentucky St, 92399; (p) (909) 795-3485; (c) San Bernardino

County/ 1955/ staff: 1(f)

HISTORIC SITE; HISTORY MUSEUM: Provides tours and living history programs.

PROGRAMS: Exhibits; Facility Rental; Festivals; Guided Tours; Interpretation; Living History; Reenactments

COLLECTIONS: [1840-1880] Artifacts and other materials from Spanish, Mormon, and American eras.

HOURS: Yr W-Sa 10-5, Su 1-5

ADMISSION: Donations requested

COLORADO

AKRON

978
Washington County Museum Association
175 W 4th St, 80720; (p) (970) 345-6446; (c) Washington

County; Private non-profit/ 1958/ staff: 10(v)

HISTORIC SITE; HISTORY MUSEUM: Maintains and protects buildings and other collections donated by town and county.

PROGRAMS: Annual Meeting; Community Outreach; Guided Tours; Publication; School-Based Curriculum

COLLECTIONS: Four buildings, including Rock Building, a country schoolhouse, Burlington Northern Dorm and rail depot.

HOURS: June, July, Aug

ALAMOSA

979
Adams State College Luther Bean Museum
208 Edgemont Blvd, 81102; (p) (719) 587-7122; (f) (719) 587-7522; (c) Alamosa

1968/ staff: 1(p)

HISTORY MUSEUM

PROGRAMS: Exhibits

COLLECTIONS: Navajo weavings, Spanish general culture, santos, Spanish history primarily San Luis Valley and Southwest, and Woodard Antique Collection.

HOURS: Yr M-F 1-4:30

ANTONIO

980
Cumbres and Toltec Scenic Railroad Commission
5250 State Hwy 285, 81120 [PO Box 561, 81120]; (p) (719) 376-5488; (f) (719) 376-2545; ctsrrcom@fone.net; (c) Conejos

1970

HISTORIC SITE; LIVING HISTORY/OUTDOOR MUSEUM: Bi-state agency responsible for overseeing Cumbres and Toltec Scenic Railroad.

PROGRAMS: Annual Meeting; Exhibits; Interpretation; Living History

COLLECTIONS: 120 pieces of narrow gauge rolling stock, numerous historic buildings, equipment and tooling.

HOURS: May-Oct M-Su, 8-6

ADMISSION: Varies

ASPEN

981
Aspen Historical Society
620 W Bleeker, 81611; (p) (970) 925-3721; (f) (970) 925-5347; ahistory@rof.net; (c) Pitkin

Private non-profit/ 1963/ staff: 5(f); 2(p); 150(v)/ members: 600

HISTORICAL SOCIETY: Preserves and communicates history of Aspen area.

PROGRAMS: Annual Meeting; Community Outreach; Exhibits; Facility Rental; Guided Tours; Interpretation; Lectures; Living History

COLLECTIONS: [1879-present] 8,000 artifacts: ski collection, 20,000 photographic images, library and written material files, video and recorded history collection, and 104 years of Aspen Times newspapers.

AURORA

982
Aurora History Museum
15001 E Alameda Dr, 80012; (p) (303) 739-6660; (f) (303) 739-6657; www.ci.aurora.co.us; (c) Arapahoe

City/ 1979/ staff: 5(f); 6(p); 38(v)/ members: 180/publication: *Aurora: Gateway to the Rockies*

HISTORY MUSEUM: Collects, preserves, interprets and documents history of Aurora.

PROGRAMS: Annual Meeting; Community Outreach; Concerts; Exhibits; Facility Rental; Guided Tours; Interpretation; Lectures; Living History; Publication; Research Library/Archives; School-Based Curriculum

COLLECTIONS: [20th c] Local history collections reflecting rural Great Plains agricultural and nineteenth and twentieth century urban development.

HOURS: Yr T-Su 11-4

ADMISSION: $2, Children $1

BERTHOUD

983
Little Thompson Valley Pioneer Museum
228 Mountain Ave, 80513 [PO Box 225, 80513]; (p) (970) 532-2147

1928/ staff: 1(f); 100(v)/ members: 150

HISTORICAL SOCIETY; HISTORY MUSEUM: Preserves and interprets history of Berthoud.

PROGRAMS: Annual Meeting; Community Outreach; Exhibits; Festivals; Guided Tours; Interpretation; Lectures; Reenactments; Research Library/Archives; School-Based Curriculum

BOULDER

984
Archives, University of Colorado at Boulder Libraries
Norlin Library, University of Colorado at Boulder, 80309 [Campus Box 184, 80309-0184]; (p) (303) 492-7242; (f) (303) 492-3960; arv@colorado.edu; www.libraries.colorado.edu/ps/arv/; (c) Boulder

State/ 1917/ Board of Regents/ staff: 3(f); 10(p); 2(v)

LIBRARY AND/OR ARCHIVES: Collects, organizes and preserves primary sources for researchers in the following areas: Western Americana, Colorado politics, labor, environment, peace and justice, and University of Colorado.

PROGRAMS: Exhibits; Guided Tours; Lectures; Research Library/Archives

COLLECTIONS: [1859-present] Early CO (1859-1960) business, mining and settlement materials, CO Congressional collections (1930-1992), labor union material (1880s-1980s), environmental activist groups (1957-1980s), and peace and justice activists and groups (1960s-present).

HOURS: Yr M, W, F, 11-5, or by appt

985
Boulder Historical Society and Museum
1206 Euclid Ave, 80302; (p) (303) 449-3464; (f) (303) 938-8322; wgordon444@aol.com; bcn.boulder.co.us/; (c) Boulder

Private non-profit/ 1944/ staff: 2(f); 1(p); 50(v)/ members: 450

HISTORY MUSEUM: Preserves historical artifacts.

PROGRAMS: Annual Meeting; Community Outreach; Exhibits; Festivals; Guided Tours; Lectures; Living History

COLLECTIONS: [1858-present] 20,000 artifacts including agricultural tools, toys, costumes, and mining equipment; 111,000 photographs and 486,000 documents.

HOURS: Yr T-F 10-4, Sa-Su 12-4

ADMISSION: $3, Children $1, Seniors $2

986
Historic Boulder, Inc.
646 Pearl St, 80302; (p) (303) 444-5192; (f) (309) 444-5309; (c) Boulder

Private non-profit/ 1972/ staff: 4(p); 45(v)/ members: 375/publication: *Historic Boulder News*

HISTORIC PRESERVATION AGENCY: Promotes preservation efforts of historic sites and landmarks.

PROGRAMS: Annual Meeting; Community Outreach; Family Programs; Guided Tours; Lectures; Publication; Research Library/Archives; School-Based Curriculum

COLLECTIONS: [1859-present]

HOURS: Yr M-F 9-4

987
University of Colorado Museum of Natural History
CU Campus, Henderson Bldg, 15th & Broadway, 80309 [Campus Box 218, 80309]; (p) (303) 492-6892; (f) (303) 492-4095; www.colorado.edu/cumuseum; (c) Boulder

State/ 1902/ Univ of CO/ staff: 30(f); 10(p); 35(v)/ members: 150/publication: *Museum Insights*

NATURAL HISTORY MUSEUM: Major regional resource for research and formal and informal education on natural history of CO and Southwestern US; fosters multi-disciplinary graduate program in museum studies.

PROGRAMS: Community Outreach; Exhibits; Facility Rental; Family Programs; Guided Tours; Interpretation; Lectures; Publication; Research Library/Archives; School-Based Curriculum

COLLECTIONS: [Prehistory-present] Paleontology, geology, entomology, botany, zoology and anthropology.

HOURS: Yr M-F 9-5, Sa, 9-4, Sun, 10-4

ADMISSION: $3, Children $2

BRECKENRIDGE

988
Summit Historical Society
309 N Main St, 80424 [PO Box 745, 80424]; (p) (970) 453-9022; (f) (970) 453-8135; CELang@aol.com; www.usnet1.com/Historical_Society/index.html; (c) Summit

Private non-profit/ 1966/ staff: 1(f); 1(p); 35(v)/ members: 650

HISTORIC SITE; HISTORICAL SOCIETY; HISTORY MUSEUM; HOUSE MUSEUM: Coordinates restoration programs; operates Edwin Carter Museum, Dillon Museum, Milne Park House, Lomax Placer Gulch, and Washington Mine.

PROGRAMS: Annual Meeting; Community Outreach; Exhibits; Guided Tours; Interpretation; Lectures; Publication; Research Library/Archives

COLLECTIONS: [1860-1910] Period furnishing, mining and ranching artifacts, Victoriana, maps, archives housed in historical sites -- school house, log cabin, Victorian house.

BRIGHTON

989
Adams County Historical Society
9601 Henderson Rd, 80601-8100; (p) (303) 659-7103; (f) (303) 659-7103; (c) Adams

Private non-profit/ 1974/ staff: 1(f); 80(v)/ members: 212

HISTORICAL SOCIETY; HISTORY MUSEUM

PROGRAMS: Annual Meeting; Community Outreach; Exhibits; Festivals; Guided Tours; Lectures; Monthly Meeting; Publication; Research Library/Archives; School-Based Curriculum

COLLECTIONS: 1930s era Conoco Station, a one-room country schoolhouse, an operational blacksmith shop, and earth science area for hands-on activities.

HOURS: Yr T-Sa 10-4

ADMISSION: Donations accepted

BROOMFIELD

990
Broomfield Depot Museum
2201 W 10th Ave, 80020 [212 Agate Way, 80020]; (p) (303) 466-9014; (c) Boulder

City/ 1980/ staff: 4(f); 14(v)

HISTORY MUSEUM: Operates a small railroad depot museum.

PROGRAMS: Guided Tours

COLLECTIONS: Area genealogy and photos.

HOURS: Yr Su 2-4

BUENA VISTA

991
Buena Vista Heritage
506 E Main St, 81211 [PO Box 1414, 81211]; (p) (719) 345-8458; TempE-mailCo Buckshot@hotmail.com; (c) Chafee

Private non-profit/ 1974/ Buena Vista Heritage/ staff: 2(p); 20(v)

HISTORIC SITE; HISTORICAL SOCIETY; HISTORY MUSEUM; HOUSE MUSEUM; LIVING HISTORY/OUTDOOR MUSEUM; RESEARCH CENTER: Operates Buena Vista Heritage Museum, and Turner Living History Farm.

PROGRAMS: Annual Meeting; Community Outreach; Concerts; Exhibits; Facility Rental; Family Programs; Festivals; Garden Tours; Guided Tours; Interpretation; Living History; Research Library/Archives

COLLECTIONS: [1880-1940s] Mining, railroad, agriculture, medical, photos and textiles.

HOURS: Late May-Early Sept M-Su, 9-5

ADMISSION: Varies

BURLINGTON

992
Old Town Museum
420 S 14th St, 80807; (p) (719) 346-7382; (f)
(719) 346-7169; oldtown@ria.net;
www.burlingtoncolo.com; (c) Kit Carson

City/ 1988/ staff: 4(f); 3(p); 30(v)/ members: 1

HISTORY MUSEUM; LIVING HISTORY/OUT-
DOOR MUSEUM

PROGRAMS: Annual Meeting; Concerts; Exhibits; Facility Rental; Lectures; Living History;
School-Based Curriculum

COLLECTIONS: Native American.

CANON CITY

993
Fremont/Custer Historical Society
400 Elm St, 81212 [PO Box 965, 81212]; (p)
(719) 275-5876; (c) Fremont

Private non-profit/ 1971/ Executive Commit-
tee/ members: 110/publication: *Trapper to
Tourist; If Walls Could Speak; and others*

HISTORICAL SOCIETY: Maintains local history center and library, hardscrabble interpretive
sign, Galena Cemetery, and Prospect Heights
Jail.

PROGRAMS: Annual Meeting; Publication

994
Deweese-Rudd Museum Group, Inc.
612 Royal Gorge Blvd, 81215 [PO Box 1460,
81215-1460]; (p) (719) 276-5279; (f) (719)
269-9017

Private non-profit/ 1923/ Municipal Museum/
staff: 4(p); .3(v)/ members: 100/publication:
Canon City Municipal Museum News

HISTORIC SITE; HISTORY MUSEUM;
HOUSE MUSEUM: Manages Canon City Municipal Museum.

PROGRAMS: Annual Meeting; Exhibits; Guided Tours; Publication; Reenactments

COLLECTIONS: [1820-1900]

HOURS: Summer Tu-Su, Winter Tu-Sa 11-4

ADMISSION: $1.50, Children $1

995
Florence Pioneer Museum
Front St & Pikes Peak Ave, 81212 [1250 S
11th, 81212]; (p) (719) 275-9561; (c) Fremont

1964/ Florence Museum Board/ staff: 1(f);
15(v)

HISTORY MUSEUM: Preserves local history.

PROGRAMS: Exhibits; Guided Tours

COLLECTIONS: [19th c-present] Mining, agriculture, medicine, electricity, railroad, newspapers, western; period furnishings, clothing

HOURS: May 15-Sept 15 Su-Sa 1-4

996
Museum of Colorado Prisons
201 N 1st St, 81215 [PO Box 1229, 81215-
1229]; (p) (719) 269-3015; (f) (719) 269-9148;
CTPM@jprodiguy.net; www.prisonmuseum.
org; (c) Fremont

Private non-profit/ 1981/ Board of Directors/
staff: 3(f); 3(p); 10(v)/ members: 180

HISTORY MUSEUM: Collects, preserves, and
interprets history of Colorado prisons.

PROGRAMS: Annual Meeting; Community
Outreach; Exhibits; Family Programs;
Film/Video; Guided Tours; Interpretation; Lectures; Living History; Publication; Research Li-
brary/Archives; School-Based Curriculum

COLLECTIONS: [1871-present] Prison artifacts including uniforms, weapons, contra-
band, furniture, fixtures, arts and crafts, glass
negatives, photos, prison records.

HOURS: Summer Daily 8:30-6; Winter F-Su

CARBONDALE

997
Mount Sopris Historical Society
499 Weant Blvd, 81623 [PO Box 2, 81623];
(p) (970) 963-1890; (c) Garfield

Private non-profit/ 1973/ Mount Sopris Historical Society/ members: 42

HISTORICAL SOCIETY; HOUSE MUSEUM:
Collects and preserves local history.

PROGRAMS: Community Outreach; Exhibits

COLLECTIONS: [1880-present] Native American artifacts.

HOURS: 10-4

CEDAREDGE

998
**Surface Creek Valley Historical
Society**
Hwy 65, 81413 [PO Box 906, 81413]; (p)
(970) 856-7554; cedarfil@co.tds.net; pioneer-
town@mail.tds.net; (c) Delta

1981/ Board of Directors/ staff: 180(v)/ members: 368

HISTORICAL SOCIETY; HISTORY MUSEUM:
Preserves local history through 21 original, restored, and replica structures with period artifacts.

PROGRAMS: Annual Meeting; Community
Outreach; Concerts; Exhibits; Facility Rental;
Festivals; Guided Tours; Interpretation; Lec-
tures; Publication; Research Library/Archives

COLLECTIONS: [1882-1920] Period furnishing, agricultural, domestic artifacts, photos and
cultural memorabilia.

HOURS: June-Sept M-Sa 9-4, Su 1-4

ADMISSION: $3, Children $1.50, Seniors $2

CENTRAL CITY

999
**Gilpin County Historical Society and
Museum**
228 E High St, 80427 [PO Box 247, 80427-
0247]; (p) (303) 582-5283; (f) (303) 582-5283;
gchs@ecentral.cpm; www.culuradomuseums.
org/gilpin.htm; (c) Gilpin

Private non-profit/ 1973/ staff: 1(p); 5(v)/ members: 135/publication: *Central City: Mining
Gold to Wallets*

Collects, preserves, and interprets Gilpin
County history.

COLLECTIONS: [1860-present] Victoriana; artifacts and photos related to history of gold in
Colorado.

HOURS: June-Sept Su-Sa 11-4

ADMISSION: $3

CHEYENNE WELLS

1000
Eastern Colorado Historical Society
84 W 2nd N, 80810 [Box 582, 80810]; (p)
(719) 767-8842; (c) Cheyenne

Private non-profit/ 1962/ staff: 30(v)

HISTORIC PRESERVATION AGENCY; HIS-
TORIC SITE; RESEARCH CENTER: Promotes local history through preservation efforts, and research center.

PROGRAMS: Annual Meeting; Concerts; Exhibits; Festivals; Living History

HOURS: May-Aug Su 2-5, M-F 1-4

ADMISSION: Donation

COLORADO SPRINGS

1001
American Numismatic Association
818 N Cascade Ave, 80903; (p) (719) 632-
2646; (f) (719) 634-4085; anamus@money.
org; www.money.org; (c) El Paso

Private non-profit/ 1891/ staff: 30(f); 2(p); 5(v)/
members: 28000/publication: *The Numismatist*

ART MUSEUM; HISTORICAL SOCIETY; HIS-
TORY MUSEUM: Studies, collects, and preserves coins, medals, tokens, paper money
and related materials.

PROGRAMS: Annual Meeting; Community
Outreach; Exhibits; Interpretation; Lectures;
Publication; Research Library/Archives

COLLECTIONS: [700 BC-present] Coins,
medals, tokens and paper money; numismatic
reference library and photo archive of two million images.

1002
Colorado Springs Museum
215 S Tejon, 80903; (p) (719) 578-6650; cos-
museum@ci.colospgs.co.us; www.cspm.org;
(c) El Paso

City/ 1937/ staff: 12(f); 3(p); 250(v)/ members:
750

ART MUSEUM; HISTORY MUSEUM: Collects, preserves, and interprets history and
culture of Pikes Peak Region.

PROGRAMS: Annual Meeting; Community
Outreach; Concerts; Exhibits; Festivals;
Film/Video; Guided Tours; Interpretation; Lec-
tures; Publication; Research Library/Archives;
School-Based Curriculum

COLLECTIONS: [1870-present] Artifacts,
ethnographic materials, decorative arts, textiles, manuscripts, photos.

HOURS: Yr Tu-Sa

1003
McAllister House
423 N Cascade Ave, 80903; (p) (719) 635-
7925; (f) (719) 528-5869; patric@oldcolo.
com; oldcolo.com/~mcallister/; (c) El Paso

Private non-profit/ 1860/ staff: 2(p); 10(v)

HOUSE MUSEUM: First substantial brick
home built in Colorado Springs.

PROGRAMS: Facility Rental; Guided Tours

COLLECTIONS: [1870s-1880s] Furnishings typical of Victorian period.

HOURS: Yr May-Aug W-Sa 10-4, Su 12-4; Sept-Apr Th-Sa 10-4

ADMISSION: $4, Children $1, Seniors $2; Under 6 free

1004
Pikes Peak Ghost Town, Inc.
400 S 21st St, 80904; (p) (719) 634-2435; (c) El Paso

Private for-profit/ 1953/ staff: 5(f); 3(p)

HISTORY MUSEUM: Promotes history of old West with reproduction of 'Ghost Town' inside former Colorado midland railroad site.

PROGRAMS: Exhibits; Facility Rental; School-Based Curriculum

COLLECTIONS: [1880-1920] Old West artifacts.

HOURS: Yr

ADMISSION: $5, Children $2.50

1005
Rock Ledge Ranch Historic Site
E entrance to Garden of Gods State Pk at 30th St, 80905 [1401 Recreation Way, 80905]; (p) (719) 578-6777; (f) (719) 578-6965; ckennis@ci.colospgs.co.us; (c) El Paso

City/ 1978/ Colorado Springs Parks, Rec and Cultural Services/ staff: 2(f); 9(p); 100(v)/ members: 500

HISTORIC SITE; HOUSE MUSEUM; LIVING HISTORY/OUTDOOR MUSEUM: Nestled at foot of Pikes Peak, site illustrates four district settlements in a living history setting: American Indian life 1755-1835, 1860s Galloway Homestead, 1880s Chambers farm, and 1907 Palmer Estate.

PROGRAMS: Annual Meeting; Exhibits; Family Programs; Festivals; Guided Tours; Interpretation; Lectures; Living History

COLLECTIONS: [1755-early 20th c] Agricultural, arts and crafts and colonial revival artifacts.

HOURS: June-Aug W-Su 10-5, Weekends in fall

ADMISSION: $5, Student $3, Seniors $3

1006
Western Museum of Mining and Industry
1025 N Gate Rd, 80921; (p) (719) 488-0880; (f) (719) 488-9261; westernmuseum@aol.com; www.wmmi.org; (c) El Paso

Private non-profit/ 1970/ Board of Trustees/ staff: 5(f); 5(p); 13(v)/ members: 288

HISTORY MUSEUM: Preserves and interprets America's western mining heritage; restores mining equipment.

PROGRAMS: Annual Meeting; Community Outreach; Elder's Programs; Exhibits; Family Programs; Festivals; Garden Tours; Guided Tours; Interpretation; Lectures; Publication; Research Library/Archives; School-Based Curriculum

COLLECTIONS: [1850-present] Artifacts, library, and archival materials pertaining to history of mining metallurgy and support industries in American west.

HOURS: Yr M-Sa 9-4, June-Sept, Su 12-4

ADMISSION: $6, Student $5, Children $3, Seniors $5

1007
World Figure Skating Museum and Hall of Fame
20 First St, 80906; (p) (719) 228-3424; (f) (719) 228-3478; www.worldskatingmuseum.org; (c) El Paso

Private non-profit/ 1965/ United States Figure Skating Association/ staff: 3(f); 2(p)/publication: The Official Guide to Figure Skating; Skating in America

HISTORY MUSEUM; RESEARCH CENTER: Preserves all aspects of figure skating.

PROGRAMS: Community Outreach; Exhibits; Film/Video; Guided Tours; Publication; Research Library/Archives

COLLECTIONS: [18th c-present] Skating costumes, rare medals, trophies, photographic posters, magazines, programs, pins, paintings, porcelain figurines, silver, crystal, bronze and ivory pieces, carved bone skates, videos, films and rare books.

HOURS: Yr M-F, 1st Sa, 10-4; June-Aug Sa

ADMISSION: $3, Children $2, Seniors $2; Under 6/USFSA members free

CRAIG

1008
Museum of Northwest Colorado
590 Yampa Ave, 81625; (p) (970) 824-6360; (f) (970) 824-7175; musnwco@cmn.net; www.museumnwco.org; (c) Moffat

1964/ Moffat County Commissioners/ staff: 1(p)/ members: 700

HISTORY MUSEUM

PROGRAMS: Community Outreach; Exhibits; Interpretation; Lectures

COLLECTIONS: [1880-present]

HOURS: Yr M-Sa 10-5

1009
Wyman Historical Museum
3895 Routt Rd #29, 81626 [Box 278, 81626]; (p) (970) 824-6431; (f) (970) 824-6431; (c) Routt

Private non-profit/ 1975/ staff: 1(f); 2(p)

HISTORY MUSEUM: Promotes history of pioneer farming.

PROGRAMS: Guided Tours

COLLECTIONS: [1880s-1940] Farm implements, 1880s-1940 (horse-drawn, steam, gasoline), millitary and railroad, automobiles, Native American material.

HOURS: Yr M-Su By appt

ADMISSION: $5; Under 12 free

CRIPPLE CREEK

1010
Cripple Creek and Victor Narrow Gauge Railroad
520 E Carr St, 80813 [PO Box 459, 80813]; (p) (719) 689-2640; (f) (719) 689-3256; CCVNGRRr@aol.com; (c) Teller

Private for-profit/ 1967/ staff: 12(f)

HISTORIC SITE: Provides a train ride into historic gold mining district.

PROGRAMS: Guided Tours

HOURS: May-Oct Daily 9:30-5:30

ADMISSION: $8.75, Children $4.75, Seniors $7.56

1011
Cripple Creek District Museum
5th & Bennett St, 80813 [PO Box 1210, 80813]; (p) (719) 689-2634; (f) (719) 689-9540

Private non-profit/ 1953/ Board of Trustees/ staff: 5(f); 4(p)

Promotes local history through preservation of historic buildings and archives.

PROGRAMS: Exhibits; Festivals; Guided Tours; Interpretation; Research Library/Archives

COLLECTIONS: [1647-present] Period costumes, photos, mining equipment, ore exhibits, railroad memorabilia.

HOURS: Summer Daily 10-5; Winter Sa-Su 12-5

ADMISSION: $2.50, Children

1012
Old Homestead House Museum
353 E Myers, 80813 [PO Box 268, 80813]; (p) (719) 689-3090; (c) Teller

Private non-profit/ 1958/ Old Homestead House Museum, Inc./ staff: 3(f)/ members: 15

HISTORIC SITE: Preserves historical site.

PROGRAMS: Annual Meeting; Community Outreach; Guided Tours

COLLECTIONS: [1896-1916] Period furnishings.

HOURS: May-Oct 11-5 Daily

ADMISSION: $3

CROOK

1013
Crook Historical Society
401 4th St, 80726; (c) Logan

Private non-profit/ 1975/ staff: 25(v)

HISTORICAL SOCIETY; HISTORY MUSEUM: Preserves local history.

PROGRAMS: Annual Meeting; Exhibits; Family Programs; Film/Video

COLLECTIONS: Tools, cowboy memorabilia, newspapers.

HOURS: Summer, Su 2-4

DEER TRAIL

1014
Deer Trail Pioneer Historical Society
Second & Fur St, 80105 [PO Box 176, 80105]; (p) (303) 769-4542; (f) (303) 769-4542; seldring@aol.com; (c) Arapahoe

Private non-profit/ 1969/ staff: 6(v)/ members: 60/publication: Treasured Memories

HISTORICAL SOCIETY; HISTORY MUSEUM: Preserves local history.

PROGRAMS: Exhibits; Guided Tours; Publication

COLLECTIONS: Pioneer exhibits, tools, household items, clothing, photos, cowboy and rodeo memorabilia.

HOURS: By appt

DEL NORTE

1015
Rio Grande County Museum and Cultural Center

580 Oak St, 81132; (p) (719) 657-2847; (f) (719) 657-2627; rgcm@amigo.net; www.museumtrail.org; (c) Rio Grande

County/ 1986/ Rio Grande County/ staff: 1(f); 1(p); 7(v)/ members: 120

HISTORY MUSEUM: Maintains and interprets artifacts relevant to cultural and natural history of Rio Grande County and surrounding area.

PROGRAMS: Annual Meeting; Exhibits; Family Programs; Guided Tours; Interpretation; Lectures; Living History; Research Library/ Archives

COLLECTIONS: [Prehistoric; 1850s-1920s] Prehistoric artifacts and data of the local rock art, geological and palentological specimens and items, photos, and painted material about the Euro-American exploration, settlement and use of area.

HOURS: Yr Oct-Apr T-Sa 12-5 May-Sept T-Sa 10-5

ADMISSION: $1, Family $2.50, Children $0.50; Members free

DELTA

1016
Delta County Historical Society

251 Meeker St, 81416; (p) (970) 874-8721; deltamuseum@aol.com; (c) Delta

Private non-profit/ 1964/ Board of Trustees/ staff: 1(p); 35(v)/ members: 275

HISTORICAL SOCIETY; HISTORY MUSEUM: Preserves local history.

PROGRAMS: Annual Meeting; Exhibits; Guided Tours; Research Library/Archives

COLLECTIONS: [1880-1960] Pioneer artifacts, archives with newspapers from 1883 forward, manuscripts, photos, yearbooks, clipping files, obituaries, etc.

HOURS: Yr May-Sept T-Sa 10-4, Oct-Apr W, Sa 10-4

ADMISSION: $2, Seniors $1; Under 12 free

1017
Fort Uncompahagre Living History Museum

205 Gunnison River Dr, 81416 [530 Gunnison River Dr, 81416]; (p) (970) 874-8349; (f) (970) 874-8776; (c) Delta

City/ 1990/ staff: 2(f); 2(p); 20(v)

LIVING HISTORY/OUTDOOR MUSEUM: Promotes fur tade history.

PROGRAMS: Guided Tours; Interpretation; Living History; School-Based Curriculum

COLLECTIONS: [1828-1844] Artifacts, firearms, traps.

HOURS: March-Dec Tu-Sa 10-4

ADMISSION: $3.50, Seniors $2.50

DENVER

1018
Black American West Museum and Heritage Center

3091 California St, 80205; (p) (303) 292-2566; (f) (303) 382-1981; bawmhc@aol.com; www.coax.net/people/lwf/bawm.us.htm; (c) Denver

Private non-profit/ 1971/ staff: 2(f); 30(v)/ members: 300/publication: Westward Soul Chronicle; Black Cowboys; and others

HISTORY MUSEUM: Collects, houses, displays, exhibits and interprets role and contributions of Black Americans in settlement and development of American West.

PROGRAMS: Community Outreach; Concerts; Exhibits; Facility Rental; Guided Tours; Interpretation; Lectures; Publication

COLLECTIONS: [19th c] Ranching, mining, cowboy, homesteader, pioneer, and military artifacts and stories.

HOURS: Winter W-F 10-2, Sa-Su 10-5; Summer Daily 10-5

ADMISSION: $6, Children $4, Seniors $5.50

1019
Byers-Evans House Museum

1310 Bannock St, 80204; (p) (303) 620-4933; byer@rmi.net; (c) Denver

State/ 1989/ Colorado Historical Society/ staff: 1(f); 2(p); 40(v)/ members: 1

HOUSE MUSEUM: Preserves local history, and provides guided tours of historic homes.

PROGRAMS: Community Outreach; Concerts; Exhibits; Facility Rental; Garden Tours; Guided Tours; Interpretation; Lectures; Theatre

COLLECTIONS: [1912-1924] William Evans family collections: 1,700 books, 500 decorative and fine arts, 400 household objects, 245 clothing and textiles, 200 pieces of furniture, 160 ephemera, 120 pieces of glassware, and 100 toys and recreational objects.

HOURS: Yr T-Su 11-3

ADMISSION: $3, Student $1.50, Seniors $2.50; Under 6 free

1020
Central City Opera House Association

621 17th St Ste 1601, 80293; (p) (303) 292-6500; (f) (303) 292-4958; ccopera@mha.net; www.centralcityopera.org; (c) Gilpin

Private non-profit/ 1932/ staff: 15(f)/ members: 800

HISTORIC SITE: Preserves historic properties in Colorado mining town, including Teller House, a restored Victorian opera house.

PROGRAMS: Community Outreach; Family Programs; Festivals; Guided Tours

COLLECTIONS: [1870-1880] Victorian opera house and related memorabilia, antique furniture.

HOURS: Varied

1021
Colorado Historical Society

1300 Broadway, 80203; (p) (303) 866-3682; (f) (303) 866-5739; webmaster@chs.state.co.us, library@state.co.us; www.coloradohistory.org; (c) Denver

State/ 1879/ Dept of Higher Education, State of Colorado/ staff: 105(f); 25(p); 750(v)/ members: 8000/publication: Colorado History Now, Colorado History, Colorado Heritage

HISTORIC PRESERVATION AGENCY; HISTORIC SITE; HISTORICAL SOCIETY; HISTORY MUSEUM; HOUSE MUSEUM; RESEARCH CENTER; TRIBAL MUSEUM: Preserves history of Colorado and mountain west.

PROGRAMS: Annual Meeting; Community Outreach; Corporate History; Exhibits; Facility Rental; Family Programs; Festivals; Guided Tours; Interpretation; Lectures; Living History; Publication; Research Library/Archives; School-Based Curriculum

COLLECTIONS: [Prehistory-present]

HOURS: Yr M-Sa 10-4:30, Su 12-4:30

ADMISSION: $5, Student $4.50, Children $3.50, Seniors $4.50; CO Historical Museum

1022
Denver Firefighters Museum

1326 Tremont Place, 80204-2120; (p) (303) 892-1436; (f) (303) 892-1436; info@firedenver.org; www.firedenver.org; (c) Denver

Private non-profit/ 1979/ Board of Directors/ staff: 8(p); 20(v)/ members: 886

HISTORIC SITE; HISTORY MUSEUM: Promotes and interprets history of Denver Fire Department.

PROGRAMS: Exhibits; Facility Rental; Guided Tours; Interpretation; Research Library/ Archives; School-Based Curriculum

COLLECTIONS: [1800-present] Photos, archives, firefighting equipment.

HOURS: Yr M-Sa

1023
Denver Museum of Miniatures, Dolls, and Toys

1880 Gaylord, 80206; (p) (303) 322-1053; (f) (303) 322-3704; ldsbc@aol.com; www.sni.com/start/dmmdt; (c) Denver

Private non-profit/ 1981/ staff: 2(f); 4(p); 150(v)/ members: 400/publication: Museum Manager

HISTORIC SITE; HOUSE MUSEUM: Features exhibits on miniatures, dolls, doll houses and toys, housed in historic Pearce-McAllister cottage.

PROGRAMS: Community Outreach; Concerts; Elder's Programs; Exhibits; Facility Rental; Family Programs; Festivals; Garden Tours; Guided Tours; Interpretation; Publication; Research Library/Archives; School-Based Curriculum

COLLECTIONS: [18th c-present] Native American, African-American, Asian, German dolls, doll houses, miniatures, toys.

HOURS: Yr Su

1024
Denver Museum of Natural History

2001 Colorado Blvd, 80205; (p) (303) 370-8381; (f) (303) 331-6492; www.dmnh.org; (c) Denver

Private non-profit/ 1900/ Board of Trustees/ staff: 240(f); 250(p); 1400(v)/ members: 46000

HISTORY MUSEUM: Promotes natural history, biodiversity and cultures of Rocky Mountain region and beyond.

PROGRAMS: Community Outreach; Elder's Programs; Exhibits; Facility Rental; Family Programs; Guided Tours; Interpretation; Lectures; Publication; Research Library/Archives; School-Based Curriculum

COLLECTIONS: [Prehistory-present] Anthropological, biological, mineralogical, paleontological objects.

HOURS: Yr Daily Winter 9-5, Summer 9-7

ADMISSION: $6, Student $2, Seniors $4

1025
Four Mile Historic Park
715 S Forest St, 80246; (p) (303) 399-1859; (f) (303) 393-0788; (c) Denver

Private non-profit/ 1978/ Four Mile Historic Park, Inc/ staff: 4(f); 6(p); 80(v)/ members: 50

LIVING HISTORY/OUTDOOR MUSEUM: Preserves western rural heritage and traditions.

PROGRAMS: Exhibits; Family Programs; Festivals; Garden Tours; Guided Tours; Interpretation; Living History; Reenactments; School-Based Curriculum

COLLECTIONS: [1860-1924] Period furnishings, household items, decorative arts, agricultural tools, photos.

HOURS: Apr-Sept W-Su, Oct-Mar weekends

ADMISSION: $3.50, Children $2, Seniors $2

1026
Grant-Humphreys Mansion
770 Pennsylvania St, 80203; (p) (303) 894-2506; (f) (303) 894-2508; (c) Denver

State/ staff: 1(f); 3(p); 10(v)

HISTORIC SITE; HOUSE MUSEUM: Beaux-Arts home built in 1902 by James B. Grant, Colorado's 3rd governor.

PROGRAMS: Facility Rental; Family Programs; Lectures; Theatre

COLLECTIONS: [1930] Mansion furnished with period reproductions.

HOURS: Yr M-F 8:30-5

1027
Mining History Association
[PO Box 150300, 80215]; www.sni.net/~co; (c) Jefferson

Private non-profit/ 1989/ Mining History Association Board of Officers/ staff: 15(v)/ members: 390/publication: *Mining History News and the Mining History Journal*

HISTORICAL SOCIETY: Promotes US mining history.

PROGRAMS: Annual Meeting; Lectures; Publication

1028
Mizel Museum of Judaica
560 S Monaco Pkwy, 80224; (p) (303) 333-4156; (f) (303) 331-8477; (c) Denver

Private non-profit/ 1982/ staff: 4(f); 2(p); 50(v)/ members: 1500/publication: *Artifacts*

Presents continuum of Jewish experience

within multicultural context through the arts.

PROGRAMS: Community Outreach; Concerts; Elder's Programs; Exhibits; Facility Rental; Family Programs; Festivals; Film/Video; Guided Tours; Interpretation; Lectures; Living History; Publication; School-Based Curriculum

COLLECTIONS: Religious objects, artifacts related to Colorado Pioneer Jews, decorative arts.

HOURS: Yr M-F 10-4, Sa 11-1, Su 12-4

ADMISSION: Donations accepted

1029
Molly Brown House Museum
1340 Pennsylvania St, 80203; (p) (303) 832-4092; (f) (303) 832-2340; admin@molly brown.org; www.mollybrown.org; (c) Denver

Private non-profit/ 1970/ Historic Denver Inc./ staff: 6(f); 6(p); 150(v)/ members: 1124

HISTORIC PRESERVATION AGENCY; HISTORIC SITE; HISTORY MUSEUM; HOUSE MUSEUM: Preserves and interprets Margaret Brown's life in Denver.

PROGRAMS: Community Outreach; Exhibits; Facility Rental; Guided Tours; Interpretation; Lectures; Publication

COLLECTIONS: [1894-1912] Victorian period furnishings, decorative arts, textiles, household items.

HOURS: Sept-May Tu-Su 10-3:30, June-Aug Daily

1030
Museo de las Americas
861 Santa Fe Dr, 80204; (p) (303) 571-4401; (f) (303) 607-9761; jose.aguayo@cwix.com; www.museo.org; (c) Denver

Private non-profit/ 1991/ Board of Trustees/ staff: 3(f); 1(p); 130(v)/ members: 1050/publication: *Notitas*

ART MUSEUM; HISTORY MUSEUM: Collects, preserves, and interprets Latin American art and history.

PROGRAMS: Community Outreach; Exhibits; Facility Rental; Family Programs; Festivals; Interpretation; Lectures; Publication

COLLECTIONS: [Pre-Columbian to present] Paintings, retablos, manuscripts, textiles, and artifacts related to Latin America.

HOURS: Yr Tu-Sa 10-5

ADMISSION: $3, Student $1, Seniors $2

1031
Rocky Mountain Jewish Historical Society and Beck Archives
Penrose Library, Univ of Denver, 80208 [2199 S Univ Blvd, 80208]; (p) (303) 871-3016; (f) (303) 871-3037; jabrams@du.edu; (c) Denver

Private non-profit/ 1976/ staff: 1(f); 1(p); 10(v)/ members: 750/publication: *Rocky Mountain Jewish Historical Notes*

HISTORICAL SOCIETY: Preserves Jewish historical experience in CO and Rocky Mountain region.

PROGRAMS: Annual Meeting; Community Outreach; Exhibits; Family Programs; Festivals; Guided Tours; Interpretation; Lectures; Publication; Research Library/Archives;

School-Based Curriculum

COLLECTIONS: [1859-1960] Jewish artifacts, photographs, manuscripts, textiles.

HOURS: Yr M-F 8:30-4:30

1032
University of Denver Museum of Anthropology
Sturm Hall S-146, 80208 [Univ of Denver, 2000 Asbury, 80208-2406]; (p) (303) 871-2406; (f) (303) 871-2437; ckrep@du.edu; www.du.edu/duma; (c) Denver

1922/ University of Denver, Board of Trustees/ staff: 2(f); 10(p); 10(v)

HISTORY MUSEUM; RESEARCH CENTER: Teaching, research, and informational center for professional care and use of anthropological collections held for public in trust by museums and universities.

PROGRAMS: Exhibits; Lectures

COLLECTIONS: 165,000 items (archaeology and ethnography) Western states archeology, Puebloan pottery, textiles.

HOURS: Yr M-F 9-5

ADMISSION: No charge

1033
Western History/Genealogy Department, Denver Public Library
10 W Fourteenth Ave Pkwy, 80204; (p) (720) 865-1821; (f) (720) 865-1880; jkroll@denver.lib.co.us; www.denver.lib.co.us; (c) Denver

City/ 1910/ City and County of Denver/ staff: 32(f); 13(p); 40(v)

LIBRARY AND/OR ARCHIVES

PROGRAMS: Community Outreach; Exhibits; Publication; Research Library/Archives

COLLECTIONS: [17th/19th c-present] History of trans-Mississippi west with emphasis on Rocky Mountain region, US Genealogy collection.

HOURS: Yr M-W 10-9, Th-Sa 10-5:30, Su, 1-5

1034
Women of the West Museum
1536 Wynkoop St, Ste 400B, 80202; (p) (303) 446-9378; (f) (303) 446-9378; www.wowmuseum. org/

HISTORICAL SOCIETY: Discover, explore, and communicate the continuing roles of women in shaping the American West.

PROGRAMS: Community Outreach

DOLORES

1035
Anasazi Heritage Center
27501 Hwy 184, 81323; (p) (970) 882-4811; (f) (970) 882-7035; meastin@co.blm.gov; www.co.blm.gov/ahc/hmep; (c) Montezuma

Federal/ 1988/ Bureau of Land Management, Dept of the Interior/ staff: 10(f); 75(v)

ARCHAEOLOGICAL SITE/MUSEUM: Interprets history and culture of Four Corners region's archaeology, local history and the Pueblo, Ute and Navajo lifeways.

PROGRAMS: Community Outreach; Exhibits; Facility Rental; Interpretation; Lectures;

Research Library/Archives

COLLECTIONS: [Prehistory] Ancestral Puebloan artifacts, related site/excavation records and photographs.

HOURS: Yr Daily 9-5

ADMISSION: $3

DURANGO

1036
Center of Southwest Studies, Fort Lewis College

1000 Rim Dr, 81301-3999; (p) (970) 247-7456; (f) (970) 247-7422; Gulliford_A@fortlewis.edu; swcenter.fortlewis.edu; (c) La Plata

State/ 1964/ Fort Lewis College/ staff: 4(f); 12(p); 12(v)/publication: *Timelines*

RESEARCH CENTER: Identifies, acquires, organizes, and preserves historical, archaeological, ethnographic, administrative, legal, fiscal and informational materials pertaining to Fort Lewis College and Southwest US

PROGRAMS: Community Outreach; Exhibits; Facility Rental; Guided Tours; Interpretation; Lectures; Publication

COLLECTIONS: [Prehistory-present] 10,000 linear shelf feet. Volumes, periodicals, archival and manuscripts including Fort Lewis College Archives, papers of U.S. Senator Ben Nighthorse Campbell, printed materials, artifacts, microfilm, oral histories, photos, Southwestern weaving.

HOURS: Late Aug-mid Dec and Jan-Apr M-F 9-4:30; Library: May-Oct M-F 10-3

ADMISSION: No charge

1037
Durango and Silverton Narrow Gauge Railroad and Museum

479 Main Ave, 81301; (p) (970) 247-2733; (f) (970) 259-3570; www.durangotrain.com; (c) La Plata

Private for-profit/ 1881/ staff: 65(f)

HISTORIC SITE; HISTORY MUSEUM: Preserves railroad history of southwest CO.

PROGRAMS: Exhibits; Facility Rental; Guided Tours

COLLECTIONS: Coal fired, steam-powered narrow gauge railroad, railroad lamps, locks, photos, books, art, full size locomotive, vintage railroad cars.

HOURS: Yr

ADMISSION: $5, Children $2.50

1038
La Plata County Historical Society, Inc.

3065 W 2nd Ave, 81302 [PO Box 3384, 81302]; (p) (970) 259-2402; (f) (970) 259-4749; animasmuseum@frontier.net; www.frontier.net; (c) La Plata

Private non-profit/ 1972/ La Plata County Historical Society/ staff: 2(f); 1(p); 23(v)/ members: 325/publication: *Historic Durango, Artifacts*

HISTORIC SITE; HISTORICAL SOCIETY; HISTORY MUSEUM: Owns and operates Animas Museum, a history museum dedicated to

history of San Juan Basin.

PROGRAMS: Annual Meeting; Community Outreach; Elder's Programs; Exhibits; Family Programs; Festivals; Guided Tours; Interpretation; Lectures; Living History; Publication; Research Library/Archives

COLLECTIONS: [1850-present] Cultural material from Caucasian, Native American and Hispanic cultures present in Southwestern Colorado, including pre-historic, Pre-Puebloean materials, and photo archives.

HOURS: Yr Summer M-Sa 10-6, Winter, W-Sa 10-4

ADMISSION: $2.50; Under 12/Mbrs free

EADS

1039
Kiowa County Museum

1313 Maine St, 81036 [Box 787, 81036]; (p) (719) 438-2250; ruthannaj@ria.net; (c) Kiowa

Joint/ 1975/ Kiowa County Historical Society/ staff: 15(v)/ members: 20

HISTORICAL SOCIETY; RESEARCH CENTER: Preserves local area history, with emphasis on ranching and farming life.

PROGRAMS: Annual Meeting; Community Outreach; Exhibits; Guided Tours; Publication

COLLECTIONS: [1889-present] Native American artifacts, cowboy memorabilia, archives.

HOURS: May-Sept M-Sa

EAGLE

1040
Eagle County Historical Society, Inc.

[PO Box 192, 81531]; (p) (970) 328-7719; jepanim@juno.com; (c) Eagle

Private non-profit/ 1973/ staff: 5(p); 10(v)

HISTORIC PRESERVATION AGENCY; HISTORICAL SOCIETY; HISTORY MUSEUM

PROGRAMS: Annual Meeting; Exhibits; Guided Tours; Lectures; Research Library/Archives

COLLECTIONS: [1882-present] Over 4,000 obituaries; stories, letters, newspaper clippings and maps of Eagle County history.

HOURS: June-Sept M-Su 10-4

ADMISSION: Donations accepted

ENGLEWOOD

1041
Lincoln Forum, The

7285 E Fremont Plaza, 80112; (f) (303) 721-6682; anetwest@vswest.net; www.thelincoln forum.org

Private non-profit/ 1996/ staff: 5(v)/publication: *The Lincoln Forum Bulletin*

HISTORICAL SOCIETY: Preserves legacy of Abraham Lincoln.

PROGRAMS: Annual Meeting; Guided Tours; Interpretation; Lectures; Publication; Research Library/Archives

ESTES PARK

1042
Enos Mills Cabin

6760 Highway 7, 80517-6404; (p) (970) 586-4706; enosmillscbn@earthlink.net; www.home.earthlink.net/~enosmillscbn/index.htm; (c) Larimer

Private for-profit/ 1968/ Mills Family/ staff: 2(f)

GARDEN; HISTORIC SITE; HISTORY MUSEUM: Preserves original homestead cabin built by Enos Mills, 'Father of Rocky Mountain National Park.'

PROGRAMS: Guided Tours; Interpretation; Publication

COLLECTIONS: [1885-1925] Documents, photos, letters, personal effects of Enos Mills.

HOURS: Summer

1043
Estes Park Area Historical Museum

200 Fourth St, 80517 [PO Box 1691, 80517]; (p) (970) 586-6256; (f) (970) 586-2816; Bkilsdonk@estes.org; www.estes.on-line.com/epmuseum; (c) Larimer

1962/ Town of Estes Park/ staff: 2(f); 1(p); 50(v)/ members: 400

HISTORY MUSEUM: Collects, preserves, interprets and exhibits local history.

PROGRAMS: Annual Meeting; Community Outreach; Family Programs; Guided Tours; Interpretation; Lectures; Publication

COLLECTIONS: [1850-1950] Period furnishings of homestead, documents, textiles, local art, photos, books.

HOURS: May-Oct M-Sa 10-5, Su 1-5; Nov-Apr F-Sa 10-5, Su 1-5

ADMISSION: $2.50, Family $10, Children $1, Seniors $2

1044
Lula W. Dorsey Museum

2515 Tunnel Rd, 80511 [PO Box 20550, 80511]; (p) (970) 586-3341; (c) Larimer

Private non-profit/ 1979/ staff: 1(f); 3(p); 5(v)/ members: 800

PROGRAMS: Community Outreach; Elder's Programs; Exhibits; Family Programs; Guided Tours; Interpretation; Lectures

COLLECTIONS: [1900-1950]

HOURS: Yr Summer M-Sa 9-5, Su 12-5 Winter M-F 9-4, Sa, 10-12

ADMISSION: $1

1045
Muriel L. MacGregor Charitable Trust

1301 Clara Dr, 80517 [MacGregor Ranch, PO Box 4675, 80517]; (p) (970) 586-3749; (f) (970) 586-1092; macgtrst@frii.com; (c) Larimer

Private non-profit/ 1973/ Muriel L. MacGregor Charitable Trust Board of Trustees/ staff: 5(f); 20(v)

HISTORIC SITE; HOUSE MUSEUM; LIVING HISTORY/OUTDOOR MUSEUM: Working cattle ranch and youth education center promoting turn of the century homesteading.

PROGRAMS: Elder's Programs; Garden Tours; Guided Tours; Living History; School-

Based Curriculum

COLLECTIONS: [1870-1970] Period furnishings, household accessories, personal effects belonging to three generations of MacGregor Family who operated ranch.

HOURS: June-Aug Tu-F 10-4

EVANS

1046
Evans Historical Museum
3720 Golden St, 80620; (p) (970) 506-2721; (c) Weld

City/ 1984/ staff: 1(p); 7(v)

HISTORY MUSEUM; HOUSE MUSEUM: Preserves local history.

PROGRAMS: Guided Tours

COLLECTIONS: [1859-1990] Period furnishings, household items, tools, school memorabilia.

HOURS: Yr Su-F

EVERGREEN

1047
Hiwan Homestead Museum
4208 S Timbervale Dr, 80439; (p) (303) 674-6262; (f) (303) 670-7746; www.co.jefferson.co.us; (c) Jefferson

County/ 1975/ staff: 4(f); 12(p); 250(v)

HISTORIC SITE; HISTORY MUSEUM; HOUSE MUSEUM: Preserves local history and period 17-room log mansion through exhibits and education programs.

PROGRAMS: Community Outreach; Exhibits; Facility Rental; Festivals; Guided Tours; Living History; Research Library/Archives; School-Based Curriculum

COLLECTIONS: [1880-1973] Dolls, Plains beadwork, decorative arts, Southwestern Indian pots, rugs, weavings, photos.

HOURS: Daily Sept-May 12-5, June-Aug 11-5

FAIRPLAY

1048
South Park City Museum
4th & Front Sts, 80440 [PO Box 634, 80440]; (p) (719) 836-2387; www.southparkcity.org; (c) Park

Private non-profit/ 1957/ South Park Historical Foundation, Inc./ staff: 1(f); 9(p); 12(v)/ members: 125/publication: *A Town is Born*

HISTORIC PRESERVATION AGENCY; HISTORIC SITE; HISTORY MUSEUM; LIVING HISTORY/OUTDOOR MUSEUM: Collects, renovates, interprets and exhibits buildings and artifacts from the South Park and Colorado early mining boom period.

PROGRAMS: Exhibits; Film/Video; Guided Tours; Interpretation; Publication

COLLECTIONS: [Mid-late 19th c] 36 historic buildings and over 10,000 artifacts depict economic and social endeavors of boom-town life.

HOURS: May 15-Oct 15 M-Su 9-5

ADMISSION: $5, Children $2, Seniors $4

FLORENCE

1049
Price Pioneer Museum
305 Loma, 81226; (c) Tremont

City, non-profit; Private non-profit

GENEALOGICAL SOCIETY; HISTORIC PRESERVATION AGENCY; HISTORIC SITE; HISTORY MUSEUM: Preserves town mining and pioneer history.

PROGRAMS: Community Outreach; Exhibits

COLLECTIONS: [1860-1920] Mining and pioneer artifacts.

HOURS: May-Sept Su-Sa 1-4

FLORISSANT

1050
Florissant Fossil Beds National Monument
15807 Teller County #1, 80816 [PO Box 185, 80816]; (p) (719) 748-3253; (f) (719) 748-3164; www.nps.gov/flfo; (c) Teller

Federal/ 1969/ U.S. National Park Service/ staff: 1(p); 6(v)

HISTORIC SITE; HOUSE MUSEUM: Preserves, researches, and exhibits insect and plant fossils found on historic homestead.

PROGRAMS: Exhibits; Guided Tours; Interpretation; Living History

COLLECTIONS: [1870] Log homestead with period furnishing, farm implements, wagons.

HOURS: Yr Daily

FORT CARSON

1051
Third Cavalry Museum
Bldg 2160 Barkeley Rd, 80913 [ATTN: AFZC-DT-MM, 80913-5000]; (p) (719) 526-1404; (f) (719) 526-6573; martinp@carson-cav3.army.mil

Federal/ 1963/ Department of the Army/ staff: 2(f); 5(v)/publication: *Tracs, Turrets, and Tail Rotors: A Guide to the Armored Vehicle Park of the Third Cavalry Museum*

HISTORY MUSEUM: Collects, preserves, and interprets history of Third Armored Cavalry Regiment and related organizations.

PROGRAMS: Community Outreach; Film/Video; Guided Tours; Publication

COLLECTIONS: [1846-present] Uniforms, firearms, vehicles and equipment fielded by Regiment; photo, documentary

FORT COLLINS

1052
Fort Collins Museum
200 Mathews, 80524; (p) (970) 221-6738; (f) (970) 416-2236; (c) Larimer

1941/ City of Fort Collins/ staff: 5(f); 60(v)

HISTORY MUSEUM: Preserves history of Cachela Poudre Valley.

PROGRAMS: Community Outreach; Exhibits; Facility Rental; Family Programs; Festivals; Guided Tours; Interpretation; Lectures; Living History; Publication; School-Based Curriculum

COLLECTIONS: [1860-present] Textiles, household furnishings, personal effects, farm

tools, lithics, pottery, basketry.

HOURS: Yr Tu-Sa 10-5,

1053
Fort Collins Public Library, Local History Archive
201 Peterson, 80524; (p) (970) 221-6688; massey@libsys.ci.fort-collins.co.us; www.library.ci.fort-collins.co.us; (c) Larimer

City/ 1976/ staff: 1(f); 20(v)

LIBRARY AND/OR ARCHIVES: Collects and interprets information on Fort Collins and Larimer County history.

PROGRAMS: Community Outreach; Lectures; Research Library/Archives

COLLECTIONS: [1860-present] Manuscripts, rare books, slides, photos.

HOURS: Yr M 12-9, Tu-Th 9:30-5, F 10-5

1054
Historic Costume and Textiles Collection
316/318 Gifford, CSU, 80523 [314 Gifford, CSU, 80523]; (p) (970) 491-1983; (f) (970) 491-4376; carlson@cahs.colostate.edu; (c) Larimer

State/ 1950/ Colorado State Univ/ staff: 2(p); 12(v)/ members: 135

HISTORY MUSEUM: Collects, preserves, and interprets historic costume and textiles.

PROGRAMS: Annual Meeting; Community Outreach; Exhibits; Interpretation; Lectures; Research Library/Archives

COLLECTIONS: [19th-20th c] Clothing, apparel accessories, African textiles, Chinese clothing, Kimonos, designer collections, quilts, domestic linens.

HOURS: Mid Aug-mid May M-F 9-5

1055
Poudre Landmarks Foundation
328 W Mountain Ave, 80521; (p) (970) 221-0533; www.fortnet.org/plf; (c) Larimer

Private non-profit/ 1972/ Board of Directors/ staff: 45(v)/ members: 250

HISTORIC SITE; HOUSE MUSEUM: Preserves, restores, protects, and interprets architectural and cultural heritage of Fort Collins area. Manages Avery House Historic District and historic Fort Collins Water Works.

PROGRAMS: Community Outreach; Exhibits; Facility Rental; Guided Tours; Interpretation

COLLECTIONS: Victorian furnishings and artifacts, 1882 Water Works exhibit.

HOURS: Yr W, Su 1-3

FORT GARLAND

1056
Fort Garland Museum
29477 Hwy 159, 81133 [PO Box 368, 81133]; (p) (719) 379-3512; (f) (719) 379-4720; (c) Costilla

State/ 1945/ staff: 2(f); 3(p); 50(v)

HISTORIC SITE; HISTORY MUSEUM: Promotes local history through restored 1858 military adobe fort with military, Hispano, Buffalo soldier and Civil War interpretive exhibits.

PROGRAMS: Community Outreach; Exhibits; Facility Rental; Family Programs; Festivals; Guided Tours; Interpretation; Lectures; Living History

COLLECTIONS: [1850-1900] Indo Hispano traditional arts, 19th century transportation and military life, Kit Carson memorabilia, historic dioramas.

HOURS: Summer Daily

FORT MORGAN

1057
Fort Morgan Museum
414 Main St, 80701 [PO Box 184, 80701]; (p) (970) 867-6331; (f) (970) 542-3008; ftmormus@ftmorganmus.org; ftmorganmus.org; (c) Morgan

City; Private non-profit/ 1975/ staff: 3(f); 2(p); 31(v)/ members: 250

HISTORY MUSEUM: Promotes local history.

PROGRAMS: Community Outreach; Exhibits; Guided Tours; Interpretation; Lectures; Research Library/Archives; School-Based Curriculum

HOURS: Yr M-F 10-5, Sa

FRISCO

1058
Town of Frisco Historical Society
120 Main St, 80443 [PO Box 820, 80443]; (p) (970) 668-1969; (f) (970) 668-1969; (c) Summit

Private non-profit/ 1983

HISTORIC SITE; HISTORY MUSEUM; HOUSE MUSEUM: Preserves local history in ten historical buildings, including Schoolhouse Museum

PROGRAMS: Community Outreach; Concerts; Exhibits; Facility Rental; Family Programs; Festivals; Interpretation; Lectures; Living History

COLLECTIONS: [19th-20th] Exhibits related to Frisco and Summit County history.

HOURS: Fall, Spring, Winter Tu-Sa; Summer Tu-Su 11-4

ADMISSION: Donations accepted

GEORGETOWN

1059
Georgetown Energy Museum
600 Griffith St, 80444 [PO Box 398, 80444]; (p) (303) 569-3557; (f) (303) 569-3557; gtnem@juno.com; (c) Clear Creek

Private non-profit/ 1992/ Georgetown Energy Museum Foundation/ staff: 1(f); 20(v)/ members: 40/publication: Dynamo

HISTORY MUSEUM: Preserves history of hydroelectric industry.

PROGRAMS: Annual Meeting; Community Outreach; Exhibits; Guided Tours; Interpretation; Lectures; Publication; Research Library/Archives

COLLECTIONS: [1890-1950] Artifacts related to electrical, and plant generation housed in hydroelectric plant built in 1900.

HOURS: Summer Daily 10-4; Winter M-F 10-4

1060
Hamill House Museum
305 Argentine, 80444 [PO Box 667, 80444]; (p) (303) 569-2840, (303) 674-2625;

(f) (303) 674-2625; histgtwn@sprynet.com; home.sprynet.com/sprynet/histgwn

1867/ staff: 3(f); 5(p); 15(v)

COLLECTIONS: [1879-1885] Original 1879 fixtures and wall finishes, some original furnishings remain, conservatory and plant collection.; Historic photos, manuscripts; documents; local newspapers.

HOURS: Seasonal

1061
Historic Georgetown, Inc.
305 Argentine St, 80444 [Box 667, 80444]; (p) (303) 569-2840; preservation@historicgeorgetown.org; www.historicgeorgetown.org; (c) Clear Creek

Private non-profit/ 1971/ Board of Directors/ staff: 4(f); 2(p); 50(v)/ members: 510

HISTORIC PRESERVATION AGENCY: Preserves the cultural and architectural history of Georgetown.

PROGRAMS: Annual Meeting; Community Outreach; Facility Rental; Guided Tours; Interpretation; Lectures; Publication; Research Library/Archives

HOURS: Yr May-Oct 10-4; Nov-Dec Sa-Su 12-4

ADMISSION: $5, Student $4, Seniors $4

1062
Hotel de Paris Museum
409 Sixth St, 80444 [PO Box 746, 80444-0746]; (p) (303) 569-2311; (c) Clear Creek

Private non-profit/ 1954/ National Society of the Colonial Dames of America in the State of Colorado/ staff: 3(p); 25(v)/ members: 120

HISTORIC SITE; HOUSE MUSEUM: Preserves history of hotel through conservation efforts.

PROGRAMS: Community Outreach; Exhibits; Festivals; Guided Tours; Interpretation; Publication

COLLECTIONS: [1875-1900] Period furnishings, original plumbing and electrical fixtures, household goods, and library.

HOURS: Oct-May Sa-Su 12-4, June-Sept Daily 11-4:30; Sept-mid Nov M-F 12-4

ADMISSION: $4, Student $3, Children $2, Seniors $3

GLENWOOD SPRINGS

1063
Frontier Historical Society Museum
1001 Colorado Ave, 81601; (p) (970) 945-4448; (f) (970) 384-2477; history@rof.net; www.glenwoodguide.com/museum; (c) Garfield

Private non-profit/ 1963/ Frontier Historical Society/ staff: 1(f); 2(p); 25(v)/ members: 279/publication: Frontier Times

HISTORICAL SOCIETY; HISTORY MUSEUM: Collects, preserves, and interprets local history.

PROGRAMS: Annual Meeting; Community Outreach; Exhibits; Family Programs; Guided Tours; Lectures; Publication; Research Library/Archives; School-Based Curriculum

COLLECTIONS: [1880-1920] Artifacts, manuscripts, newspapers, maps, photos.

HOURS: May-Sept M-Sa 11-4; Oct-Apr M, Th-Sa 1-4

ADMISSION: $3, Seniors $2; Under 13/Mbrs free

GOLDEN

1064
Astor House Museum
822 12th St, 80401; (p) (303) 278-3557; (f) (303) 278-8916; ahmuseum@aol.com; www.AstorHouseMuseum.org; (c) Jefferson

Private non-profit/ 1972/ Friends of the Astor House Museum and Clear Creek History Park/ staff: 2(f); 3(p); 50(v)/ members: 200/publication: Dear Friends

HOUSE MUSEUM: Built in 1867 by Seth Lake as hotel to accommodate legislators when Golden was capital of Colorado Territory.

PROGRAMS: Annual Meeting; Community Outreach; Concerts; Exhibits; Facility Rental; Family Programs; Festivals; Garden Tours; Guided Tours; Interpretation; Lectures; Living History; Publication; Reenactments; School-Based Curriculum

COLLECTIONS: [1867-1908] Hotel/boarding house interior furnishings.

HOURS: Yr T-Sa 10-4:30

ADMISSION: $3; Children $1

1065
Buffalo Bill Memorial Museum
987 1/2 Lookout Mountain Rd, 80401; (p) (303) 526-0744; (f) (303) 526-0197; www.buffalobill.org; (c) Jefferson

City/ 1921/ City and County of Denver/ staff: 5(f); 1(p); 40(v)

HISTORY MUSEUM: Preserves and interprets life and times of William F. "Buffalo Bill" Cody.

PROGRAMS: Concerts; Exhibits; Festivals; Research Library/Archives

COLLECTIONS: [1840-1920] Artifacts from Buffalo Bill's life, Native American materials, Wild West Show posters and memorabilia, firearms and other western artifacts; extensive photo collection and small manuscript archives.

HOURS: Yr Summer M-Su 9-5, Winter: T-Su. 9-4

ADMISSION: $3, Children $1, Seniors $2

1066
Clear Creek History Park
11th & Arapahoe St, 80401 [822 12th St, 80401]; (p) (303) 278-3557; (f) (303) 278-8916; cchpark@aol.com; www.clearcreekhistorypark.org; (c) Jefferson

Private non-profit/ 1994/ Friends of the Astor House Museum and Clear Creek History Park/ staff: 2(f); 1(p)/ members: 200

LIVING HISTORY/OUTDOOR MUSEUM: Promotes 1800s Golden lifestyle through hands-on educational facility through preservation of historic buildings.

PROGRAMS: Annual Meeting; Community Outreach; Concerts; Exhibits; Facility Rental; Family Programs; Festivals; Guided Tours; Interpretation; Lectures; Living History; Publication; Reenactments; School-Based Curriculum

COLLECTIONS: [1843-1900]

ADMISSION: $3, Children $2

1067
Colorado Railroad Museum
17155 W 44th Ave, 80402 [PO Box 10, 80402-0010]; (p) (303) 279-4591; (f) (303) 279-4229; www.crrm.org; (c) Jefferson

Private non-profit/ 1958/ Colorado Railroad Historical Foundation, Inc./ staff: 8(f); 2(p); 60(v)/ members: 2541/publication: *Colorado Rail Annual*

HISTORY MUSEUM; LIVING HISTORY/OUT-DOOR MUSEUM: Preserves and interprets railroad history of the Rocky Mountain West through museum displays, research library, and educational programs.

PROGRAMS: Community Outreach; Elder's Programs; Exhibits; Interpretation; Publication; Research Library/Archives

COLLECTIONS: [1870-present] Locomotives, cars, artifacts, books, photos, corporate documents, ephemera from railroads of Rocky Mountain West.

HOURS: Yr Su-Sa 9-5

ADMISSION: $4, Family $9.50, Children $2, Seniors $3.50

1068
Golden Pioneer Museum
923 10th St, 80401; (p) (303) 278-7151; (f) (303) 278-2755; goldenpm@henge.com; www.henge.com/~goldenpm; (c) Jefferson

City, non-profit/ 1938/ City of Golden/ staff: 2(f); 1(p); 20(v)/ members: 190/publication: *History of Golden's Schools*

HISTORY MUSEUM: Collects, preserves, and interprets artifacts and photos of the City of Golden and Jefferson County.

PROGRAMS: Community Outreach; Exhibits; Facility Rental; Family Programs; Garden Tours; Guided Tours; Interpretation; Lectures; Publication; Research Library/Archives; School-Based Curriculum

COLLECTIONS: [1859-1930] Period furnishings, clothing, household goods, books, musical instruments, photos, mining implements, farming and ranching items, firearms.

HOURS: Yr M-Sa 10-4:30

ADMISSION: No charge

1069
Jefferson County Historical Commission
100 Jefferson County Pkwy #1500, 80419-1500; (p) (303) 271-8446; (f) (303) 271-8452; dmcollu@co.jefferson.co.us; co.jefferson.co.us/dpt/archives/histcomm.htm; (c) Jefferson

City; County/ 1974/ staff: 2(p); 23(v)/publication: *Historically-Jeffco Magazine*

HISTORIC PRESERVATION AGENCY; HISTORICAL SOCIETY: The Commission promotes, encourages, and coordinates awareness and preservation of the material and cultural history of Jefferson County.

PROGRAMS: Annual Meeting; Film/Video; Publication; Research Library/Archives

COLLECTIONS: [1859-present]

1070
Rocky Mountain Quilt Museum
1111 Washington Ave, 80401; (p) (303) 277-0377; (f) (303) 215-1636; rmgm@att.net;

www.rmqm.org; (c) Jefferson

Private non-profit/ 1990/ staff: 5(p); 50(v)/ members: 465

ART MUSEUM: Dedicated to preservation, interpretation of art of American quilting.

PROGRAMS: Annual Meeting; Community Outreach; Exhibits; Guided Tours; Interpretation; Lectures; Research Library/Archives; School-Based Curriculum

COLLECTIONS: [1840-present] 240 American quilts, focusing on quilts from Rocky Mountain region.

HOURS: Yr M-Sa 10-4

ADMISSION: $3, Seniors $2.50

GRAND LAKE

1071
Grand Lake Area Historical Society
[PO Box 656, 80447-0656]; (c) Grand

Private non-profit/ 1973/ Board of Directors/ staff: 15(p); 25(v)

HISTORIC SITE; HISTORICAL SOCIETY: Preserves local history and maintains the Kauffman House, a 19th century solid log private residence and hotel.

PROGRAMS: Annual Meeting; Exhibits; Publication

COLLECTIONS: [19th c-present] Artifacts, memorabilia, period furnishings, photos, clothing.

HOURS: June-Aug Daily 11-5

GRANITE

1072
Clear Creek Canyon Historical Society of Chaffee County, Inc.
[PO Box 2181, 81228]; (c) Chaffee

Private non-profit/ 1924/ Board of Directors/ staff: 20(v)/ members: 37

HISTORIC PRESERVATION AGENCY; HISTORIC SITE; HISTORICAL SOCIETY; HISTORY MUSEUM: Organized to restore and preserve the history and sites of Clear Creek Canyon.

PROGRAMS: Annual Meeting; Exhibits; Guided Tours

COLLECTIONS: [1881-20th c] Four log cabins with furnishings: home, livery, school and miner's cabin.

HOURS: May 30-Labor Day Sa, Su, Holidays, 9-5

GREELEY

1073
City of Greeley Museums
919 7th St, 80631; (p) (970) 350-9220; (f) (970) 350-9475; dillc@ci.greeley.co.us; (c) Weld

City/ 1929/ City of Greeley/ staff: 7(f); 10(p); 475(v)

HISTORIC PRESERVATION AGENCY; HISTORIC SITE; HISTORY MUSEUM; HOUSE MUSEUM; LIVING HISTORY/OUTDOOR MUSEUM; RESEARCH CENTER: Promotes local history through preservation of municipal archives and historic homes, including home of Nathan Cook Meeker, founder of Greeley,

and his family.

PROGRAMS: Annual Meeting; Community Outreach; Concerts; Elder's Programs; Exhibits; Facility Rental; Family Programs; Festivals; Film/Video; Garden Tours; Guided Tours; Interpretation; Lectures; Living History; Research Library/Archives; School-Based Curriculum

COLLECTIONS: [1860-1930] Archives, period furnishing, agriculture equipment, historic buildings, decorative arts, clothing, tools.

HOURS: Apr-Oct T-Su 10-5; Archives: Yr M-F 10-5

ADMISSION: $3.50, Children $2, Seniors $3

GUNNISON

1074
Black Canyon of the Gunnison National Monument/Curecanti National Recreation Area
102 Elk Creek, 81230; (p) (970) 641-2337; (f) (970) 641-3127; www.nps.gov/cure; (c) Gunnison and Montrose

Federal/ 1933/ National Park Service

Preserves natural and cultural features and objects within park.

PROGRAMS: Community Outreach; Concerts; Exhibits; Guided Tours; Interpretation; Research Library/Archives; School-Based Curriculum

COLLECTIONS: [Prehistoric/1880-1975] Prehistoric, lithic and domestic objects, railroad, pioneer and explorations objects, including photographs and archival records.

HOURS: Center: May-Sept Daily 9-4; Rail Cars:Yr

1075
Gunnison County Pioneer and Historical Society
110 S Adams, 81230 [304 S Colorado, 81230]; (p) (970) 641-4530; (c) Gunnison

Private non-profit/ 1972/ Gunnison County Pioneer Society/ staff: 50(v)/ members: 250

HISTORIC PRESERVATION AGENCY; HISTORICAL SOCIETY; HISTORY MUSEUM; LIVING HISTORY/OUTDOOR MUSEUM: Reflects cultural history of Gunnison County.

PROGRAMS: Exhibits; Living History; School-Based Curriculum

COLLECTIONS: [1870s-1930s] Gunnison's first post office, narrow gauge train, rural school house, house with period furnishings, antique cars and wagons, farm implement displays, ranch machinery, and arrowhead and mineral collections

HOURS: May-Sept M-Sa 9-5, Su 1-5

ADMISSION: $7

HAYDEN

1076
Hayden Heritage Center
300 W Pearl, 81639 [PO Box 543, 81639]; (p) (970) 276-4380; (c) Routt

Private non-profit/ 1968/ Hayden Heritage Center Board/ staff: 2(p); 9(v)/ members: 30

GENEALOGICAL SOCIETY; HISTORIC

PRESERVATION AGENCY; HISTORIC SITE; HISTORICAL SOCIETY; HISTORY MUSEUM: Collects, preserves, and interprets artifacts and memorabilia related to the history of Hayden and West Routt County.

PROGRAMS: Exhibits; Festivals; Guided Tours; Publication; Research Library/Archives

COLLECTIONS: [1870-present] Artifacts and photos.

HOURS: Summer F-M 11-5

HOT SULPHUR SPRINGS

1077
Grand County Historical Association
110 E Byers Ave, 80451 [PO Box 165, 80451]; (p) (970) 725-3939; (f) (970) 725-0129; gcha@rkymtnhi.com; grandcountymuseum.com

Private non-profit/ 1974/ staff: 2(f); 1(p); 25(v)/ members: 500/publication: *Annual Journals I-XIII*

HISTORIC SITE; HISTORICAL SOCIETY; HISTORY MUSEUM; HOUSE MUSEUM: Operates the Cozens Ranch Museum, an 1874 ranch house and stage stop and Grand County Museum.

PROGRAMS: Annual Meeting; Community Outreach; Exhibits; Facility Rental; Interpretation; Lectures; Publication; Research Library/Archives

COLLECTIONS: [1875-1950] Agricultural tools, clothing, household items, photos, archives.

HOURS: Sept-May W-Sa 11-4; June-Aug Su 12-5, Mo-Sa 10-5

ADMISSION: $4, Student $2, Seniors

HOTCHKISS

1078
Hotchkiss Crawford Historical Society
180 Second St, 81419 [PO Box 724, 81419]; (p) (970) 872-3780; (c) Delta

Private non-profit/ 1974/ Board of Directors/ staff: 3(f); 5(p); 5(v)/ members: 60

HISTORY MUSEUM: Preserves pioneer history of Hotchkiss and Crawford.

PROGRAMS: Annual Meeting; Exhibits

COLLECTIONS: [1880-present] Artifacts, tools, household items, Native American, archives, log cabin.

HOURS: May-Sept F-Sa 1-4

ADMISSION: $1

HUGO

1079
Lincoln County Historical Society
617 Third Ave, 80821 [PO Box 115, 80821]; (p) (719) 743-2233; (f) (719) 743-2447; twbndee@yahoo.com; (c) Lincoln

County; Private non-profit/ 1973/ staff: 5(v)/ members: 30/publication: *Where the Wagons Rolled, Lincoln County: The Beginning to 1920*

GARDEN; HISTORIC PRESERVATION AGENCY; HISTORIC SITE; HISTORICAL SOCIETY; HISTORY MUSEUM; HOUSE MUSEUM; LIVING HISTORY/OUTDOOR MUSEUM: Preserves history of Lincoln County.

PROGRAMS: Annual Meeting; Community Outreach; Elder's Programs; Exhibits; Family Programs; Festivals; Garden Tours; Guided Tours; Interpretation; Lectures; Living History; Publication; Reenactments; Research Library/Archives; School-Based Curriculum

COLLECTIONS: [1895-1945] Early ranching and railroad days, homestead era.

HOURS: By appt only

ADMISSION: Donations accepted

IDAHO SPRINGS

1080
Historical Society of Idaho Springs
2060 Miner St, 80452 [PO Box 1318, 80452]; (p) (303) 567-4709; (c) Clear Creek

Private non-profit/ 1963/ staff: 1(p); 15(v)/ members: 175

HISTORICAL SOCIETY; HISTORY MUSEUM; HOUSE MUSEUM: Preserves historic artifacts and buildings of Idaho Springs.

PROGRAMS: Annual Meeting; Exhibits; Facility Rental; Guided Tours; Interpretation

COLLECTIONS: [1860-present]

HOURS: Yr Daily 8-5

ADMISSION: Donations accepted

IGNACIO

1081
Southern Ute Cultural Center Museum
Hwy 172 N, 81137 [PO Box 737, 81137]; (p) (970) 563-9583; (f) (970) 563-4641; (c) La Plata

Private non-profit/ 1972/ Southern Ute Cultural Center Board of Directors/ staff: 7(f); 1(p)/ members: 20

TRIBAL MUSEUM

PROGRAMS: Annual Meeting; Community Outreach; Elder's Programs; Exhibits; Facility Rental; Film/Video; Interpretation

HOURS: Yr Daily

KIOWA

1082
Elbert County Historical Society and Museum
515 Comanche St Hwy 86, 80117 [PO Box 43, 80117]; (p) (303) 621-2229; ecmusuem@bewellnet.com; www.bewellnet.com/ecmuseum; (c) Elbert

Joint; Private non-profit/ 1956/ Elbert County Historical Society/ staff: 6(v)/ members: 80

HISTORICAL SOCIETY; HISTORY MUSEUM: Preserves and maintains original manuscripts, documents, and photographs of Elbert County.

PROGRAMS: Annual Meeting; Family Programs; Film/Video; Guided Tours; Lectures; Publication; Research Library/Archives; School-Based Curriculum

COLLECTIONS: [1870-present] Artifacts of pioneer life, homestead, cowboy.

HOURS: May-Sept Th 11-2, Sa 12-4, Su 2-4

KREMMLING

1083
Log Cabin Heritage Museum
Park Center, 80459 [PO Box 204, 80459-0204]

City; County; Private non-profit/ 1954/ Grand County Historical Association/ staff: 50(v)

HISTORIC SITE; HISTORICAL SOCIETY; HOUSE MUSEUM

PROGRAMS: Annual Meeting; Community Outreach; Elder's Programs; Exhibits; Garden Tours; Guided Tours; Interpretation; Living History; Reenactments

LA JUNTA

1084
Bent's Old Fort National Historic Site
35110 Hwy 194 East, 81050; (p) (719) 383-5010; (f) (719) 383-5031; www.nps.gov; (c) Otero

Federal/ 1960/ National Park Service/ staff: 13(f); 13(p); 165(v)

HISTORIC SITE; LIVING HISTORY/OUTDOOR MUSEUM: Reconstructed adobe trading fort on Mountain Route of the Santa Fe Trail.

PROGRAMS: Exhibits; Guided Tours; Interpretation; Living History; Publication; Reenactments

COLLECTIONS: [1833-1849] 200,000 archaeological artifacts from original fort, 5,000 historic and reproduction fort furnishings, 45,000 archival documents and photos and 170 herbarium specimens.

HOURS: June-Aug

1085
Koshare Indian Museum
115 W 18th St, 81050; (p) (719) 384-4411; (f) (179) 384-8836; www.koshare.org; (c) Otero

Private non-profit/ 1949/ staff: 3(f); 8(p); 100(v)/publication: *Koshare News*

HISTORY MUSEUM; TRIBAL MUSEUM: Collects, preserves, and interprets artifacts and arts and crafts of Southwest and Pueblo/Plains Native Americans.

PROGRAMS: Exhibits; Facility Rental; Family Programs; Guided Tours; Lectures; Publication; Theatre

COLLECTIONS: [19th c] Artifacts from Southwest, Pueblo/Plains Indian area; Kachinas, beadwork, paintings,

HOURS: Yr Su-Sa 10-5

ADMISSION: $2, Children $1

LAFAYETTE

1086
Lafayette Historical Society, Inc.
108 E Simpson St, 80026-2322; (p) (303) 665-7030, (303) 666-6686; (c) Boulder

Private non-profit/ 1975/ staff: 22(v)/ members: 130

HISTORY MUSEUM: Collects, preserves, and exhibits local and coal mining history.

PROGRAMS: Annual Meeting; Community Outreach; Elder's Programs; Exhibits; Guided

Tours; Research Library/Archives

COLLECTIONS: [1890-1920] Coal mining tools and equipment for the "hand loading" era. Household artifacts, vintage clothing, textiles and photographs from the homes of coal miners from the era. Printed material and manuscripts, mine union records and family

LAKEWOOD

1087
Lakewood's Heritage Center
797 S Wadsworth Blvd, 80226; (p) (303) 987-7850; (f) (303) 987-7851; (c) Jefferson

City/ 1976/ City of Lakewood/ staff: 7(f); 5(p)/ members: 60

HISTORY MUSEUM; LIVING HISTORY/OUTDOOR MUSEUM; RESEARCH CENTER: Preserves local history through outdoor exhibits.

PROGRAMS: Community Outreach; Exhibits; Facility Rental; Family Programs; Festivals; Garden Tours; Guided Tours; Interpretation; Lectures; Living History; Publication; Research Library/Archives; School-Based Curriculum

COLLECTIONS: [19th-20th c] Agricultural, archaelogical artifacts, household items.

HOURS: Yr

ADMISSION: $2, Children $1

LEADVILLE

1088
Healy House and Dexter Cabin Museum
912 Harrison Ave, 80461; (p) (719) 486-0487; (c) Lake

State/ 1948/ Colorado Historical Society/ staff: 1(f); 6(p); 1(v)

HOUSE MUSEUM: Preserves Leadville's silver mining history.

PROGRAMS: Concerts; Theatre

COLLECTIONS: Victorian furnishings, pioneer household items.

HOURS: Yr Daily 10-4:30

ADMISSION: $3.50, Children $2, Seniors $3

1089
Leadville Historical Society
123 W 4th St, 80461 [PO Box 911, 80461]; (p) (719) 486-3934; (c) Lake

County/ 1936/ members: 35

1090
Matchless Mine Museum
7th St East, 80461 [3940 Hwy 91, 80461]; (p) (719) 486-1899; (c) Lake

Private non-profit/ 1954/ Leadville Assembly/ staff: 6(f)

Promotes local mining history and preserves cabin of local figure Baby Doe Tabor.

PROGRAMS: Guided Tours

COLLECTIONS: Period furnishings, mining artifacts, tools.

HOURS: June-Aug Daily

ADMISSION: $3.50, Children $1

1091
National Mining Hall of Fame and Museum, The
120 W 9th St, 80461 [PO Box 981, 80461]; (p) (719) 486-1229; (f) (719) 486-3927; nationalmuseum@bemail.com; www.leadville. com/miningmuseum; (c) Lake

Private non-profit/ 1987/ staff: 2(f); 6(p); 2(v)/ members: 800/publication: The Hi-Grade

Promotes mining history.

PROGRAMS: Elder's Programs; Exhibits; Facility Rental; Lectures; Publication

COLLECTIONS: [19th c] Photos, mining artifacts, replicas, housed in Victorian school building.

HOURS: May-Oct Su-Sa 9-5; Nov-Apr M-F 9-3

ADMISSION: $3.50, Children $2, Seniors $3

LIMON

1092
Limon Heritage Society
899 1st, 80828 [Box 341, 80828]; (p) (719) 775-2373; (c) Lincoln

Private non-profit/ 1990/ Limon Heritage Society Board of Trustees/ staff: 1(p); 30(v)/ members: 85/publication: Windbreaker Newsletter; Hub City of the High Plains, 1888-1952

HISTORICAL SOCIETY; HISTORY MUSEUM: Preserves and interprets history of Colorado Eastern Plains, and supports Limon Heritage Museum.

PROGRAMS: Annual Meeting; Community Outreach; Exhibits; Festivals; Guided Tours; Lectures; Publication

COLLECTIONS: [1900-1940] Native American artifacts, railroads, homesteaders, Pioneer School House, 1914 Rail Lunch Counter-Diner, Steel Union Pacific Caboose, Prairie garden and memory rose garden.

HOURS: June-Aug, M-Sa 1-8

ADMISSION: No charge

LITTLETON

1093
Littleton Historical Museum
6029 S Gallup St, 80120; (p) (303) 795-3950; (f) (303) 730-9818; www.littleton.org; (c) Arapahoe

City/ 1969/ City of Littleton/ staff: 12(f); 9(p); 30(v)

HISTORY MUSEUM; LIVING HISTORY/OUTDOOR MUSEUM; RESEARCH CENTER: Preserves and interprets local history through outdoor exhibits of homestead farm.

PROGRAMS: Community Outreach; Concerts; Exhibits; Family Programs; Festivals; Interpretation; Living History; Reenactments; Research Library/Archives

COLLECTIONS: [1860-present]

HOURS: Yr Tu-F 8-5, Sa 10-5, Su 1-5

ADMISSION: Donations accepted

LONGMONT

1094
Longmont Museum
375 Kimbark St, 80501; (p) (303) 651-8374;

(f) (303) 651-8590; ci.longmont.co.us/ museum.htm; (c) Boulder

City/ 1936/ City of Longmont/ staff: 5(f); 3(p); 67(v)/ members: 120

HISTORY MUSEUM: Collects and exhibits materials from history of Northern CO and Longmont area.

PROGRAMS: Community Outreach; Concerts; Exhibits; Family Programs; Guided Tours; Interpretation; Lectures; Research Library/Archives; School-Based Curriculum

COLLECTIONS: [1871-present] Approximately 20,000 objects from a variety of households and businesses in the Longmont area; archival holdings include 400 linear feet of documents and 8,000 historic photographs.

HOURS: Yr M-F 9-5, Sa 10-4

ADMISSION: No charge

1095
Saint Vrain Historical Society, Inc., The
312 Terry St, 80502 [PO Box 705, 80502-7005]; (p) (303) 776-1870; (f) (303) 776-5778; svshstaff@peakpeak.com; www .stvrainhistoricalsociety.org; (c) Boulder

Private non-profit/ 1967/ Board of Directors/ staff: 3(p); 200(v)/ members: 210

HISTORIC SITE; HISTORICAL SOCIETY; HOUSE MUSEUM; LIVING HISTORY/OUTDOOR MUSEUM: Owns and operates Old Mill Park, Historic Hoverhome and farmstead.

PROGRAMS: Annual Meeting; Community Outreach; Facility Rental; Festivals; Garden Tours; Guided Tours; Living History

COLLECTIONS: [1860-1960] Old Mill Park: Artifacts and buildings from Colorado c. 1860-1875 for interpretation of pioneer farmers. Hoverhome: Original furnishings and paintings displayed in 1913 Tudor revival home.

HOURS: Vary

LOUISVILLE

1096
Louisville Historical Commission
1001 Main St, 80027 [749 Main St, 80027]; (p) (303) 665-9049; (c) Boulder

City/ 1979/ City of Louisville/ staff: 1(p); 12(v)/ members: 130

HISTORIC SITE; HISTORICAL SOCIETY; HISTORY MUSEUM; HOUSE MUSEUM: Preserves history of town and its mining past.

PROGRAMS: Annual Meeting; Exhibits; Guided Tours

COLLECTIONS: [1890-present] Western US household goods and coal mining equipment.

HOURS: Jan-Nov Th 3-5, and by appt

LOVELAND

1097
Loveland Museum and Gallery
503 N Lincoln Ave, 80537; (p) (970) 962-2410; (f) (970) 962-2910; isons@ci. loveland.co.us; (c) Larimer

City/ 1945/ City of Loveland/ staff: 7(f); 1(p); 75(v)/ members: 300

Collects, preserves and interprets Loveland history through art and history exhibits.

PROGRAMS: Facility Rental; Family Programs; Festivals; Publication; School-Based Curriculum

COLLECTIONS: [19th c-present] Social, natural, and cultural history artifacts.

HOURS: Yr T,W,F 10-5, Th 10-9, Sa-Su 10-4

ADMISSION: No charge

LYONS

1098
Lyons Historical Society
340 High, 80540 [PO Box 9, 80540]; (p) (303) 823-6692; (f) (303) 823-8257; (c) Boulder

Joint/ 1973/ Private non-profit; Town of Lyons; St Vrain School Dist/ staff: 2(p); 8(v)/ members: 50

HISTORIC SITE; HISTORY MUSEUM: Collects local history and operates Lyons Redstone Museum, a former schoolhouse.

PROGRAMS: Annual Meeting; Exhibits; Festivals; Living History; Publication

COLLECTIONS: [1880-present] Photos, archive, and cultural artifacts.

HOURS: June-Sept Su 12:30-4:30, M-Sa

ADMISSION: No charge/Donations

MANASSA

1099
Jack Dempsey Museum
[PO Box 130, 81141]; (p) (719) 842-5207; (f) (719) 842-5202; (c) Conejos

City/ 1966/ staff: 2(p); 1(v)

HISTORY MUSEUM: Promotes history of heavyweight boxer Jack Dempsey.

PROGRAMS: Exhibits; Film/Video

HOURS: Mem Day-end of Sept M-Sa 9-5

MANITOU SPRINGS

1100
Manitou Springs Historical Society/Miramont Castle
9 Capitol Hill Ave, 80829; (p) (719) 685-1011; (f) (719) 685-1985; (c) El Paso

Joint/ 1971/ Manitou Springs Historical Society/ staff: 4(f); 12(v)/ members: 114

HISTORIC SITE; HISTORICAL SOCIETY; HISTORY MUSEUM: Preserves Miramont Castle, a 48-room former residence.

PROGRAMS: Annual Meeting; Exhibits; Facility Rental; Guided Tours

COLLECTIONS: [1890-1920] Period furnishings, antique toys and dolls.

HOURS: Yr Tu-Su Winter 12-3; Fall/Spring 11-4, Summer 10-5

ADMISSION: $4,

1101
Pikes Peak Hill Climb Educational Museum
135 Manitou Ave, 80829; (p) (719) 685-4400; (f) (719) 685-5885; ppihc@ppihc.com; www.ppihc.com; (c) El Paso

1989

Promotes history of Pikes Peak Hill Climb.

COLLECTIONS: [1916-present] Vintage autos, motorcycles, photos, race memorabilia.

ADMISSION: $5, Children $2, Seniors $3

MEEKER

1102
White River Historical Society
555 Park St, 81641 [PO Box 413, 81641]; (p) (970) 879-2214; (f) (970) 879-6109; sbsmarty@juno.com; (c) Rio Blanco

Private non-profit/ 1948/ Tread of Pioneers Historical Commission/ staff: 1(f); 2(p); 20(v)/ members: 300

HISTORY MUSEUM; HOUSE MUSEUM; RESEARCH CENTER: Collects and preserves local history.

PROGRAMS: Annual Meeting; Community Outreach; Exhibits; Facility Rental; Family Programs; Festivals; Film/Video; Guided Tours; Interpretation; Lectures; Research Library/Archives; School-Based Curriculum

COLLECTIONS: [1840-1945] Native American, pioneer, ranching, mining, and skiing artifacts. Stagecoach, snowcat.

HOURS: Yr 11-5 Days vary

ADMISSION: $3, Children $1, Seniors $2

MONTROSE

1103
Ute Indian Museum
17253 Chipeta Rd, 81401; (p) (970) 249-3098; (c) Montrose

State/ 1956/ Colorado Historical Society/ staff: 1(f); 1(p); 3(v)

HISTORICAL SOCIETY: Preserves history of Ute people of Colorado, and operated by Colorado Historical Society.

PROGRAMS: Exhibits; Facility Rental; Festivals; Guided Tours; Interpretation; Lectures

COLLECTIONS: Memorabilia related to Chief Ouray, Ignacio, Colorow, Buckskin Charlie; Native plants garden, Dominguez-Escalante Expedition exhibit.

HOURS: May 15-Nov 15 Su-Sa 9-5; Nov 16-May 14 Tu-Sa 9-4

ADMISSION: $2.50, Student $1.50, Seniors $2

NEW CASTLE

1104
New Castle Historical Society, Inc.
116 N 4th, 81647 [PO Box 883, 81647]

1982/ staff: 6(v)/ members: 75

HISTORY MUSEUM: Promotes local history through preservation efforts.

PROGRAMS: Annual Meeting; Exhibits; Festivals; Research Library/Archives

COLLECTIONS: [1888-present] Mining tools, memorabilia, period clothing, blacksmith accessories.

HOURS: April-Sept W-Sa 1-4

ADMISSION: Donations accepted

OURAY

1105
Ouray County Historical Society
420 6th Ave, 81427 [PO Box 151, 81427]; (p) (970) 325-4576; anneil@rmi.net; (c) Ouray

Private non-profit/ 1971/ Board of Directors/ staff: 1(f); 1(p); 125(v)/ members: 458

HISTORIC PRESERVATION AGENCY; HISTORIC SITE; HISTORICAL SOCIETY; HISTORY MUSEUM; RESEARCH CENTER: Devoted to history of Ouray Count and historic preservation.

PROGRAMS: Annual Meeting; Community Outreach; Elder's Programs; Exhibits; Guided Tours; Interpretation; Lectures; Research Library/Archives; School-Based Curriculum

COLLECTIONS: [1875-1964] Mining, minerals, mineral library, transportation, Ute Indians, hospital and historical artifacts and memorabilia.

HOURS: Yr Summer Sa-Su 9-4 Winter Sa, Su, M 1-4

ADMISSION: $3, Children

PAGOSA SPRINGS

1106
Chimney Rock Archaeological Area
3 mi S of Hwy 160 on Hwy 151, 81147 [PO Box 310, 81147]; (p) (970) 264-2268, (970) 883-5359; (f) (970) 264-1538; chimneyrock@chimneyrockco.org; www.chimneyrocko.org

San Juan Mountains Assn. Chimney Rock Interpretive Program/ staff: 4(p); 60(v)

HISTORIC SITE: Preserves history of Pueblo Natives through interpretive programs and exhibits.

PROGRAMS: Concerts; Family Programs; Festivals; Guided Tours; Interpretation; Living History; School-Based Curriculum

COLLECTIONS: [925-1125] Native inhabitant artifacts and fossils.

HOURS: May 15-Sept 30 Daily 9-4

ADMISSION: $5, Children $2

PALMER LAKE

1107
Lucretia Vaile Museum
66 Valley Crescent, 80133 [PO Box 662, 80133]; (p) (719) 481-3772; plhis@aol.com; www.ci.palmer-lake.co.us/plhs/index.html; (c) El Paso

Private non-profit/ 1964/ Palmer Lake Historical Society/ staff: 14(v)

HISTORY MUSEUM: Preserves local history.

PROGRAMS: Community Outreach; Exhibits; Guided Tours; Research Library/Archives

COLLECTIONS: [1800-present] Photos, newspaper clippings, period clothing and research archives.

HOURS: Yr Sa 10-2; June-Aug Sa 10-2, W 1-4

PETERSON AFB

1108
Peterson Air and Space Museum
150 E Ent Ave, 80914-1303; (p) (719) 556-8278; (f) (719) 556-8509; Pasmuseum@aol.com; (c) El Paso

Federal/ 1981/ United States Air Force/ staff: 2(f); 1(p); 5(v)

HISTORIC SITE; HISTORY MUSEUM: Preserves aviation and aerospace heritage of Colorado Springs and Peterson AFB.

PROGRAMS: Publication

COLLECTIONS: [1926-present] Photos, uniforms, memorabilia and archives related to history of Colorado Springs Municipal Airport, Peterson AFB, Air Defense Command, NORAD, Air Force Space

PLATTEVILLE

1109
Fort Vasquez Museum
13412 US 85, 80651; (p) (970) 785-2832; (f) (970) 785-9193; (c) Weld

State/ 1964/ Colorado Historical Society/ staff: 1(f); 1(p); 10(v)

HISTORIC SITE; HISTORY MUSEUM: Preserves Native American culture through interpretive exhibits and Fort Vasquez Trading Post site.

PROGRAMS: Community Outreach; Exhibits; Interpretation; School-Based Curriculum

COLLECTIONS: [1935-1936] WPA reconstructed adobe fort, fur-trade and Native American objects.

HOURS: Summer Daily 9:30-4:30; Winter Su 1-4:30, W-Sa 9:30-4:30

ADMISSION: No charge

PUEBLO

1110
El Pueblo Museum
324 W First St, 81003; (p) (719) 583-0453; (f) (719) 583-8214; (c) Pueblo

State/ 195/ Colorado Historical Society/ staff: 1(f); 2(p); 40(v)/ members: 100/publication: Between Friends

HISTORIC SITE; HISTORY MUSEUM

PROGRAMS: Annual Meeting; Community Outreach; Exhibits; Facility Rental; Family Programs; Festivals; Guided Tours; Interpretation; Lectures; Living History; Publication; School-Based Curriculum

HOURS: Yr M-Sa 10-4:30, Su 12-3

ADMISSION: $3, Children $2.50, Seniors $2.50

1111
Pueblo City-County Library Distirct
100 E Abriendo Ave, 81004; (p) (719) 562-5626; www.Pueblolibrary.org; (c) Pueblo

City; County/ 1891/ staff: 1(f); 6(v)

Special collections western research department collects the history of Southern CO.

PROGRAMS: Research Library/Archives

1112
Pueblo County Historical Society Museum and Edward Broadhead Library
217 S Grand Ave, 81003; (p) (719) 543-6772; (c) Pueblo

Private non-profit/ 1986/ Board of Directors/ staff: 21(v)/ members: 304/publication: Lore

HISTORICAL SOCIETY: Promotes local history.

PROGRAMS: Annual Meeting; Community Outreach; Exhibits; Interpretation; Lectures; Publication; Research Library/Archives; School-Based Curriculum

COLLECTIONS: [19th-20th c] Western artifacts, historic photos, baseball history, pioneer and railroad artifacts.

HOURS: Yr T-Sa, 1-4

1113
Pueblo Dr. Martin Luther King Jr. Holiday Commission and Cultural Center
2713-15 N Grand, 81005 [PO Box 2297, 81005]; (p) (719) 253-1015; (f) (719) 253-1016; (c) Pueblo

Private non-profit/ 1993/ Pueblo Dr. Martin Luther King Jr. Holiday Commission/ staff: 20(v)/ members: 20

CULTURAL CENTER; HOUSE MUSEUM: Interprets local Afro-American culture through preservation of Lincoln Home, formerly the Pueblo Colored Orphanage and Old Folks Home.

PROGRAMS: Annual Meeting; Community Outreach; Exhibits; Family Programs; Film/Video; Guided Tours; Interpretation; Research Library/Archives; School-Based Curriculum

COLLECTIONS: [1925-1963] Archives, domestic items, film related to orphanage.

HOURS: Yr Th-F 10-3

ADMISSION: $5, Student $2.50, Seniors $4; Group

1114
Pueblo Weisbrod Aircraft Museum
31001 Magnuson Ave, 81001; (p) (719) 948-9219; (f) (719) 948-2437; pwam@iex.net; www.co.pueblo.co.us/pwam; (c) Pueblo

Private non-profit/ 1987/ Pueblo Historical Aircraft Society/ staff: 250(v)/ members: 200/publication: B-24 Air Scoop

AVIATION MUSEUM; HISTORIC PRESERVATION AGENCY; HISTORY MUSEUM; LIVING HISTORY/OUTDOOR MUSEUM: Collects and preserves US military and aviation history.

PROGRAMS: Exhibits; Family Programs; Festivals; Film/Video; Guided Tours; Interpretation; Lectures

COLLECTIONS: Outdoor display of military aircraft from World War II and post WW II aircraft.

HOURS: Yr M-F 10-4, Sa 10-2, Su 1-4

ADMISSION: Donations requested; Under 12 free

1115
Rosemount Museum
419 W 14th St, 81002 [PO Box 5259, 81002]; (p) (719) 545-5290; (f) (719) 545-5291; Rosemount@usa.net; www.rosemount.org; (c) Pueblo

Private non-profit/ 1968/ staff: 7(f); 2(p); 50(v)/ members: 700/publication: The Tidings

HOUSE MUSEUM: Maintains Victorian historic house, built between 1891-93 by Pueblo's prominent John A. Thacher family.

PROGRAMS: Annual Meeting; Exhibits; Facility Rental; Guided Tours; Interpretation; Lectures; Publication; Research Library/Archives

COLLECTIONS: [Late 19th-early 20th c] Antique furniture, decorative arts, paintings, prints, sculpture, stained glass. Tiffany

1116
Summit Brick and Tile Company Museum
13th & Erie, 81002 [PO Box 533, 81002-0533]; (p) (719) 542-8278; (f) (719) 542-5243; summit@summitbrick.com; (c) Pueblo

Private for-profit/ 1902/ staff: 1(v)

HISTORY MUSEUM: Preserves history of brick production.

PROGRAMS: Exhibits; Guided Tours; Lectures

COLLECTIONS: [19th-20th c]

HOURS: Yr M-F 9-4:30

ADMISSION: No charge

RIFLE

1117
Rifle Creek Museum
337 E Ave, 81650; (p) (970) 625-4862; (c) Garfield

Private non-profit/ 1967/ Board of Directors/ staff: 1(f); 15(v)/ members: 60

HISTORY MUSEUM; RESEARCH CENTER: Collects, preserves, displays and interprets western slope of CO history.

PROGRAMS: Annual Meeting; Exhibits; Guided Tours; Interpretation; Research Library/Archives; School-Based Curriculum

COLLECTIONS: [1880s-1980s] Native American artifacts, modern oil shale history.

HOURS: May-Oct M-F 10-4

ADMISSION: $2, Children $1, Seniors $1.50

ROCKY FORD

1118
Rocky Ford Museum
1005 Sycamore Ave, 81067 [PO Box 835, 81067]; (p) (719) 254-6737; curmudgeon@curmudgeon.org; www.curmudgeon.org/rfmuseum; (c) Otero

City/ 1941/ City of Rocky Ford/ staff: 1(p); 10(v)

HISTORY MUSEUM: Preserves archaeology and local cultural history.

PROGRAMS: Guided Tours; Lectures; Publication

COLLECTIONS: Archaeological artifacts and memorabilia.

HOURS: May-Sept Tu-Sa 10-4

ADMISSION: Donations accepted

SALIDA

1119
Salida Museum
Rainbow Blvd, 81201 [406 1/2 Rainbow, 81201]; (c) Chaffee

City/ 1954/ staff: 8(v)/ members: 30

HISTORIC SITE; HISTORICAL SOCIETY; HISTORY MUSEUM: Promotes local history.

PROGRAMS: Annual Meeting; Exhibits; Guided Tours; Interpretation; Living History; School-Based Curriculum

COLLECTIONS: [19th-20th c] Mining, farming and ranching, Indians, pioneer tools, schools, general store, WWI and WWII, Korea, local events, railroading, minerals, kitchens, living quarters, and old west doctors equipment.

HOURS: 30 May-2nd wk in Sept M-Sa 9-5

ADMISSION: $0.50

SAN LUIS

1120
San Luis Museum and Cultural Center
401 Church Pl, 81152 [PO Box 657, 81152]; (p) (719) 672-3611; morada@amigo.net; (c) Costilla

City/ 1980/ Town of San Luis/ staff: 1(f); 1(p)/publication: *La Cultura Constante: Penitente in Fantasy and Fact*

ART MUSEUM; HISTORY MUSEUM; RESEARCH CENTER: Houses colonial and post-colonial artifacts of Hispanic cultural tradition.

PROGRAMS: Concerts; Exhibits; Facility Rental; Festivals; Film/Video; Guided Tours; Lectures; Publication; Theatre

COLLECTIONS: [Late 19th c-present] Historical mural, pictorial exhibit, diorama of San Luis, art objects, colcha embroidery.

HOURS: May-Sept M-Su 9-4:30,

SILT

1121
Silt Historical Society
Orchard & 8th, 81652 [Box 401, 81652]; (p) (970) 876-5801, (970) 876-2668; (c) Garfield

Private non-profit/ 1982/ staff: 9(v)/ members: 65

HISTORIC PRESERVATION AGENCY; HISTORICAL SOCIETY; HISTORY MUSEUM: Preserves local history.

PROGRAMS: Annual Meeting; Exhibits; Film/Video; Lectures; Living History; Reenactments; Research Library/Archives

COLLECTIONS: [1881-1934] Nine period buildings; household furnishings, school desks, books, etc., wheelwright tools, store and office equipment with displays of each, Approx. 80,000 artifacts.

HOURS: May 1- Oct 1 T-Sa 10-3

ADMISSION: Donations accepted

SILVER CLIFF

1122
Silver Cliff Museum
610 Main St, 81249 [PO Box 154, 81249]; (p) (719) 783-2615; (f) (719) 783-2615; (c) Custer

City/ 1959/ staff: 1(p)

HISTORY MUSEUM; HOUSE MUSEUM

COLLECTIONS: [1880] Mining and pioneer memorabilia, firehouse equipment.

HOURS: May-Sep F-Sa 11-4, Su-M 12-4

ADMISSION: $2, Children $1

SILVER PLUME

1123
People for Silver Plume, Inc.
905 Main St, 80476 [PO Box 935, 80476]; (p) (303) 569-2562; (c) Clear Creek

Private non-profit/ 1974/ staff: 2(p)/ 50(v)/ members: 95

HISTORIC PRESERVATION AGENCY; HISTORIC SITE; HISTORY MUSEUM: Preserves and maintains buildings, records, artifacts in historic district.

PROGRAMS: Annual Meeting; Facility Rental; Family Programs; Publication; Theatre

COLLECTIONS: [1860-1960] Original 19th century school room, an exhibit from Georgetown Loop Railroad, home life exhibits, mining exhibits and fire department artifacts.

HOURS: May-Oct M-Su 10-4

ADMISSION: $2.50, Children $0.50, Seniors

SILVERTON

1124
San Juan County Historical Society, Inc.
1553 Greene St, 81433 [PO Box 154, 81433]; (p) (970) 387-5488; www.Silverton.org; (c) San Juan

Private non-profit/ 1965/ staff: 3(p)/ 10(v)/ members: 250/publication: *Hillside Cemetery Study, San Juan Courrier Newspaper Index*

HISTORIC PRESERVATION AGENCY; HISTORIC SITE; HISTORICAL SOCIETY; HISTORY MUSEUM: Maintains museum housed in 1903 county jail, and National Historic Landmark Mayflower Gold Mill.

PROGRAMS: Exhibits; Guided Tours; Interpretation; Publication

COLLECTIONS: [1870-present] Family artifacts, train, office, printing artifacts.

HOURS: End of May-mid-Oct M-Su 9-5

ADMISSION: $2.50

STEAMBOAT SPRINGS

1125
National Association for Cemetery Preservation
345 E View Dr, 80477 [PO Box 772922, 80477]; (p) (970) 276-3691; (c) Routt

Private non-profit/ 1990/ National Assoc for Cemetery Preservation/ staff: 20(v)/ members: 35

HISTORIC PRESERVATION AGENCY: Identifies documents, restores and preserves cemeteries and grave sites.

PROGRAMS: Annual Meeting; Lectures; Publication; Research Library/Archives

COLLECTIONS: [mid-1800] Cemetery inscriptions, burial and funeral records; computerized database for cemeteries and

1126
Tread of Pioneers Museum
800 Oak St, 80477 [PO Box 772372, 80477]; (p) (970) 879-2214; (f) (970) 879-6109; sbsmarty@juno.com; (c) Routt

Private non-profit/ 1959/ Tread of Pioneers Historical Commission/ staff: 1(f); 2(p); 20(v)/ members: 300

HISTORY MUSEUM; HOUSE MUSEUM; RESEARCH CENTER: Collects, preserves and exhibits objects and documents related to Routt County.

PROGRAMS: Annual Meeting; Community Outreach; Exhibits; Facility Rental; Family Programs; Festivals; Film/Video; Guided Tours; Interpretation; Lectures; Publication; Research Library/Archives; School-Based Curriculum

COLLECTIONS: [1840-1945] Historic photographs, Native American artifacts, paintings, pioneer artifacts and clothing, ranching, mining and skiing items, stagecoach and snowcat.

HOURS: Dec-Mar Mon-Sa; Kune-Aug Su-Sa Apr, May, Sept, Oct, Nov: Tu-Sa, 11-5

ADMISSION: $3, Children $1, Seniors $2; Under 6/Mbrs free

STIRLING

1127
Overland Trail Museum
21053 County Rd 26 5/10, 80751 [Box 4000, 80751]; (p) (970) 522-3895; (f) (970) 521-0632; (c) Logan

City/ 1936/ City of Stirling/ staff: 1(f); 4(p); 14(v)

HISTORICAL SOCIETY; HISTORY MUSEUM: Promotes history of early settlers and Native Americans in area.

PROGRAMS: Annual Meeting; Community Outreach; Exhibits; Festivals; Guided Tours; Lectures; Living History; Publication

COLLECTIONS: [1870s-1900s] Village buildings, tin-type pictures, dolls, wedding dresses, sunbonnets, and household items, Native American artifacts of stone metates and arrowheads. Furniture, and fireplace made of petrified wood.

HOURS: Nov 1-Mar 31 T-Sa 10-4 April 1-Oct 31 Su-Sa 9-5

ADMISSION: Donations accepted

STRASBURG

1128
Comanche Crossing Historical Society
56060 E Colfax Ave, 80136 [PO Box 647, 80136]; (p) (303) 622-4322

Private non-profit/ 1969/ Board of Directors/ staff: 5(p); 45(v)/ members: 168

HISTORICAL SOCIETY; HISTORY MUSEUM: Promotes local history.

PROGRAMS: Annual Meeting; Exhibits; Festivals; Guided Tours

COLLECTIONS: [1875-1930] Railroad artifacts, caboose, ranching equipment.

HOURS: June-Aug M-Su 12-4

TELLURIDE

1129
Telluride Historical Museum
317 N First St, 81435 [PO Box 1597, 81435];
(p) (970) 728-3344; museum@rmi.net;
www.telluridemuseum.com; (c) San Miguel

1966/ Board of Directors/ staff: 1(f); 5(p); 50(v)/
members: 700

HISTORIC SITE; HISTORICAL SOCIETY;
HISTORY MUSEUM: Preserves and interprets
regional cultural history.

PROGRAMS: Elder's Programs; Exhibits; Festivals; Guided Tours; Interpretation; Lectures

COLLECTIONS: [1880-1950] Anasazi textiles,
Ute Indian, mining, Victoriana, photos.

HOURS: Yr W-M 10-4

TRINIDAD

1130
Louden-Henritze Archaeology Museum
Trinidad State Junior College, 81082; (p)
(719) 846-5508; Loretta.Martin@tsjc.
cccoes.edu; (c) Las Animas

State/ 1950/ staff: 1(f); 2(v)

RESEARCH CENTER

PROGRAMS: Community Outreach; Exhibits;
Guided Tours; Lectures; Research Library/
Archives; School-Based Curriculum

COLLECTIONS: [Prehistoric] Geology, fossils,
and archaeological material from surrounding
area.

HOURS: Jan-Nov M-F 10-4

1131
Trinidad Historical Museum of the Colorado Historical Society
300 E Main St, 81082; (p) (719) 846-7217; (c)
Las Animas

State/ 1955/ Colorado Historical Society/ staff:
2(f); 6(p); 25(v)

GARDEN; HISTORIC PRESERVATION
AGENCY; HISTORIC SITE; HISTORICAL SOCIETY; HISTORY MUSEUM; HOUSE MUSEUM: Maintains Baca House, Bloom Mansion,
Santa Fe Trail Museum, and Historic Gardens.

PROGRAMS: Community Outreach; Concerts; Elder's Programs; Exhibits; Facility
Rental; Family Programs; Festivals; Garden
Tours; Guided Tours; Interpretation; Lectures;
Living History; Reenactments; Research Library/Archives; School-Based Curriculum;
Theatre

COLLECTIONS: [1870-1930] Victorian, Hispanic and Western collections.

HOURS: May-Sept Sa-Su

VAIL

1132
Colorado Ski Museum Hall of Fame
231 S Frontage Rd, 81658 [PO Box 1976,
81658]; (p) (970) 476-1876; (f) (970) 476-
1879; skimuse@vail.net; www.vailsoft.
com/ museum/; (c) Eagle

Private non-profit/ 1976/ staff: 4(f); 50(v)/
members: 500

HISTORY MUSEUM: Interprets history of skiing in CO.

PROGRAMS: Annual Meeting; Community
Outreach; Exhibits; Facility Rental; Family Programs; Festivals; Garden Tours; Guided Tours;
Interpretation; Lectures; Living History; Research Library/Archives; Theatre

COLLECTIONS: [1859-1998] Photos, ski
equipment, clothing and other memorabilia
from former champions.

HOURS: Nov-Apr, June-Sept Tu-Su

WESTMINSTER

1133
Westminster Area Historical Society
W 72nd Ave, 80030 [PO Box 492, 80030]; (p)
(303) 430-7929; (c) Adams

Private non-profit

HISTORICAL SOCIETY; HISTORY MUSEUM;
HOUSE MUSEUM: Preserves history of pioneer settlers.

PROGRAMS: Annual Meeting; Exhibits; Garden Tours; Guided Tours; Interpretation

COLLECTIONS: [1870-1940] Period furnishings, accessories, photos and archives.

HOURS: Yr Jan-Mar

WHEAT RIDGE

1134
Wheat Ridge Historical Society
4650 Oak, 80034 [PO Box 1853, 80034]; (p)
(303) 421-9111; (f) (303) 467-2539; (c)
Jefferson

Private non-profit/ 1973/ staff: 1(p)/ members:
200/publication: *The Woodbine*

GARDEN; HISTORIC PRESERVATION
AGENCY; HISTORIC SITE; HISTORICAL SOCIETY; HISTORY MUSEUM; HOUSE MUSEUM; LIVING HISTORY/OUTDOOR MUSEUM;
RESEARCH CENTER: Promotes local history
through preservation efforts.

PROGRAMS: Annual Meeting; Community
Outreach; Exhibits; Facility Rental; Festivals;
Guided Tours; Interpretation; Publication; Research Library/Archives

COLLECTIONS: [1860-1950] Furnishings, sod
house, 1910 brick museum, 1860s log cabin,
1913 post office, tool shed.

HOURS: Jan-Nov W-Sa, 10-3

ADMISSION: $2

WOODLAND PARK

1135
Ute Pass Historical Society-Pikes Peak Museum
210 E Midland Ave, 80866 [PO Box 6875,
80866]; (p) (719) 686-1125; uphs@aol.com;
(c) Teller

Private non-profit/ 1976/ staff: 20(v)/ members:
350/publication: *Pikes Peak's Shadow: Teller
County Centennial Local Legacies (video)*

HISTORICAL SOCIETY; HISTORY MUSEUM:
Preserves Ute Pass and Pikes Peak region
history and cultural heritage.

PROGRAMS: Community Outreach; Exhibits;
Family Programs; Film/Video; Lectures; Research Library/Archives

COLLECTIONS: [1850-present] Ute indian
collection, Midland and Midland Terminal Railroading artifacts and materials.

HOURS: Yr M-Th 9-12:30, F, 9-4

ADMISSION: Donations accepted

CONNECTICUT

ANSONIA

1136
Derby Historical Society
37 Elm St, 06401 [PO Box 331, Derby,
06418]; (p) (203) 735-1908;
Derbyhistoricalsoc@juno.com; derbyhistorical.org/; (c) New Haven

Private non-profit/ 1946/ Board of Directors/
staff: 9(p); 40(v)/ members: 350

HISTORIC SITE; HISTORICAL SOCIETY;
HISTORY MUSEUM; HOUSE MUSEUM; LIBRARY AND/OR ARCHIVES: Preserves, protects, identifies, and educates about the history and culture of Derby and the area. Located
in the historic Gen. David Humphreys house
(Ansonia Historical District). Owns Dr. John
Ireland Howe House (1848) and Rev. Richard
Mansfield House (c. 1700).

PROGRAMS: Annual Meeting; Exhibits; Guided Tours; Reenactments

COLLECTIONS: [17th-20th c] Historic house
and furnishings, special displays dating from
Pre-Colonial to Industrial Era. Large collection
of Civil War books.

HOURS: Yr M-F 1-4

ADMISSION: Donations requested

AVON

1137
Avon Historical Society, Inc., The
8 E Main St, 06001 [PO Box 448, 06001]; (p)
(860) 678-1043; www.avonct.com; (c)
Hartford

Private non-profit/ 1974/ staff: 1(p); 12(v)/
members: 250

HISTORIC SITE; HISTORICAL SOCIETY;
HISTORY MUSEUM; HOUSE MUSEUM; RESEARCH CENTER: Maintains historic museum, schoolhouse and house museum covering the years of 1830-1900; Maintains
extensive library of printed matter for genealogical research.

PROGRAMS: Annual Meeting; Community
Outreach; Exhibits; Lectures; Research Library/Archives; School-Based Curriculum

COLLECTIONS: [1830-1900] Farmington
Canal Period.

HOURS: May-Oct Su 2-4, or by appt

BETHLEHEM

1138
Bellamy-Ferriday House and Garden
9 Main St, 06751 [PO Box 181, 06751]; (p)
(203) 266-7596; (f) (203) 266-6253;
ferriday@wtco.net

1754/ staff: 1(f); 3(p); 3(v)

COLLECTIONS: [1912-1990] American 18th c. antiques; English & Dutch Delft.

HOURS: Seasonal

BRIDGEPORT

1139
Barnum Museum, The
820 Main St, 06604; (p) (203) 331-1104; (f) (203) 339-4341; www.barnum-museum.org

Private non-profit/ 1893/ The Barnum Museum Foundation, Inc/ staff: 7(f); 3(p); 30(v)/ members: 250

HISTORY MUSEUM: Celebrates life and times of world-famous showman and entrepreneur, P.T. Barnum.

PROGRAMS: Community Outreach; Exhibits; Facility Rental; Interpretation; Lectures; School-Based Curriculum

COLLECTIONS: [19th c] Art and artifacts owned by Phineas Taylor Barnum, circus-related memorabilia, and artifacts representative of 19th century Bridgeport.

HOURS: Yr T-Sa 10-4:30, Su 12-4:30

ADMISSION: $5,

1140
Bridgeport Public Library Historical Collections
Exit 27, I-95, Corner of State St & Broad St, 06604 [925 Broad St, 06604]; (p) (203) 576-7417; (f) (203) 576-8255; mwitkowski@ brdgprtpl.lib.ct.us; www.brdgprtpl.lib.ct.us; (c) Fairfield

City/ 1936/ staff: 5(f); 2(p); 2(v)

LIBRARY AND/OR ARCHIVES: Maintains public library system.

PROGRAMS: Research Library/Archives

COLLECTIONS: [1700-present emphasizing 19th and 20th centuries] Genealogy sources with local, national, and international focus, including Connecticut Census and LDS Family Search Program.

HOURS: Sept-June: T-W 10-8, Th-Sa 9-5; Mid June-Sept M 9-5, T-W 10-8, Th-F

1141
Discovery Museum
4450 Park Ave, 06604; (p) (203) 372-3521; (f) (203) 374-1929; www.discoverymuseum.org; (c) Fairfield

Private non-profit/ 1958/ staff: 17(f); 4(p); 60(v)/ members: 1500

Presents art and science and their interrelationship, primarily through participatory exhibits and programs.

PROGRAMS: Community Outreach; Concerts; Exhibits; Facility Rental; Family Programs; Festivals; Guided Tours; Interpretation; Lectures; Publication; Research Library/ Archives; School-Based Curriculum

COLLECTIONS: [18th-20th c] Non Exhibited: industrial murals, PT Barnum artifacts and photos, silhouettes, mourning pictures.

HOURS: Yr T-Sa 10-5, Su 12-5; July-Aug M 10-5

BRIDGEWATER

1142
Bridgewater Historical Society
42 Main St, 06752; (c) Litchfield

Private non-profit/ 1928/ staff: 10(v)/ members: 89

GENEALOGICAL SOCIETY; HISTORIC PRESERVATION AGENCY; HISTORICAL SOCIETY; HOUSE MUSEUM; RESEARCH CENTER: Promotes local history.

PROGRAMS: Annual Meeting; Exhibits; Festivals; Guided Tours; Lectures; Research Library/Archives

COLLECTIONS: [1850-present] Historic house and furnishings.

HOURS: May-Oct Sa 9-1 and by appt

ADMISSION: No charge

BRISTOL

1143
American Clock and Watch Museum
100 Maple St, 06010; (p) (860) 583-6070; (f) (860) 583-1862; (c) Hartford

Private non-profit/ 1952/ Board of Directors/ staff: 3(f); 4(p); 30(v)/ members: 930/publication: *Timepiece Journal*

GARDEN; HISTORY MUSEUM; RESEARCH CENTER: Maintains permanent exhibit about CTt clockmaking and the Industrial Revolution, housed in 1801 mansion with period garden.

PROGRAMS: Annual Meeting; Community Outreach; Exhibits; Facility Rental; Guided Tours; Lectures; Publication; Research Library/Archives

COLLECTIONS: [1600-1950] American clocks, watches and other timepieces of scientific and historical interest, equipment and machinery used in the manufacture of clocks and watches, books, catalogues, and other literature.

HOURS: Apr-Nov Daily 10-5

ADMISSION: $5, Children $2, Seniors $4; Under 8 free

1144
New England Carousel Museum, The
95 Riverside Ave, 06010; (p) (860) 585-5411; (f) (860) 585-5411; www.carousels.com; (c) Hartford

1990/ staff: 2(f); 6(p); 8(v)/ members: 650/publication: *The Carousel*

HISTORY MUSEUM: Acquires, restores, and preserves carousel memorabilia.

PROGRAMS: Annual Meeting; Community Outreach; Concerts; Exhibits; Facility Rental; Family Programs; Guided Tours; Interpretation; Lectures; Publication; Research Library/ Archives; School-Based Curriculum

COLLECTIONS: Antique wooden and modern carousel pieces representing three schools of carousel art created in US, including horses, menagerie figures, chariots, band organ, and trim pieces.

HOURS: Apr-Dec M-F 10-5, Sa-Su 12-5

ADMISSION: $4, Children $2, Seniors $3.50

BROOKFIELD

1145
Brookfield Museum and Historical Society, Inc.
165 Whisconier Rd, 06804 [PO Box 5231, 06804]; (p) (203) 740-8140; brookfieldhist-soc@sngt.net; www.brookfieldcthistory.org; (c) Fairfield

Private non-profit/ 1968/ Board of Directors/Pres/ staff: 50(v)/ members: 300

HISTORICAL SOCIETY; HISTORY MUSEUM: Collects, preserves, and documents materials related to local history.

PROGRAMS: Annual Meeting; Community Outreach; Concerts; Exhibits; Family Programs; Festivals; Garden Tours; Lectures; Living History; School-Based Curriculum

COLLECTIONS: Artifacts, maps, books, photographs, videos, genealogical records.

HOURS: May-Nov Sa

CANTERBURY

1146
Prudence Crandall Museum, The
Rt 14 & Rt 169 Junction, 06331 [PO Box 58, 06331]; (p) (860) 564-9916; (f) (860) 546-9916; (c) Windham

State/ 1984/ Connecticut Historical Commission/ staff: 2(f); 12(v)

Interprets the life and times of Prudence Crandall, who opened the first private academy in New England to educate young black women.

PROGRAMS: Community Outreach; Exhibits; Family Programs; Guided Tours; Interpretation; Lectures; Research Library/Archives

COLLECTIONS: [Early 19th c.] Period furnishings, decorative arts, books, and periodicals.

HOURS: Feb-Dec W-Su 10-4:30

ADMISSION: $2, Children $1, Seniors $1

CHESHIRE

1147
Cheshire Historical Society
43 Church St, 06410 [PO Box 281, 06410]; (p) (203) 272-2574

1785/ Private non-profit/ staff: 4(v)

COLLECTIONS: Antique tool room, children's room, and 12 other furnished rooms

HOURS: Yr

CLINTON

1148
Stanton House
63 E Main St, 06413 [Clinton Historical Society, PO Box 172, 06413]; (p) (860) 669-2132

HISTORIC HOUSE

COS COB

1149
Historical Society of the Town of Greenwich, The
39 Strickland Rd, 06807; (p) (203) 869-6899; (f) (203) 861-9720; admin@hstg.org; www.hstg.org/; (c) Fairfield

Private non-profit/ 1931/ staff: 8(f); 12(p); 90(v)/ members: 2000/publication: *Greenwich History Journal; Greenwich Before 2000; and others*

HISTORICAL SOCIETY; HOUSE MUSEUM; LIBRARY AND/OR ARCHIVES: Collects, preserves and disseminates the history of Greenwich, Connecticut, includes the William E. Finch, Jr. Archives and the National Historic Bush-Holley House, home of Connecticut's first art colony.

PROGRAMS: Annual Meeting; Community Outreach; Exhibits; Facility Rental; Family Programs; Festivals; Guided Tours; Interpretation; Lectures; Publication; Research Library/Archives; School-Based Curriculum

COLLECTIONS: [18th-20th c] Items and archival material documenting local history and the Cos Cob Impressionist art colony.

HOURS: Historic Site/House/Visitor Ctr: Jan-Feb Sa-Su 12-4: Mar-Dec W-Su 12-4; Archives: T/Th 10-4 & by appt: Office: M-F 9-5

ADMISSION: $6, Student $4, Seniors $4; Under 13 free; Visitor Ctr free

COVENTRY

1150
Coventry Historical Society
2382 South St, 06238 [PO Box 534, 06238]; coventrycthistory@yahoo.com; geocities.com/coventrycthistory/; (c) Tolland

Private non-profit/ Executive Board/ staff: 1(p); 20(v)/ members: 148/publication: *The Brick Schoolhouse*

HISTORICAL SOCIETY: Discovers, collects, and preserves history of town of Coventry, birthplace of Revolutionary War, Nathan Hale.

PROGRAMS: Annual Meeting; Community Outreach; Concerts; Exhibits; Family Programs; Guided Tours; School-Based Curriculum

COLLECTIONS: [18th-19th c] Two 18th c farmhouses, and a 19th c schoolhouse, artifacts, documents,

1151
Nathan Hale Homestead Museum
2299 S St, 06238 [66 Forest St, Hartford, 06105]; (p) (860) 742-6917, (860) 247-8996; (f) (860) 249-4907

1776/ staff: 11(p); 4(v)

COLLECTIONS: [1776-1832] Provenanced family items; Seymour collection on Hale & local history

HOURS: Seasonal

CROMWELL

1152
Cromwell Historical Society
395 Main St, 06416 [PO Box 146, 06416]; (p) (860) 635-0501; (c) Middlesex

Private non-profit/ 1964/ Board of Directors/ staff: 50(v)/ members: 300

Maintains Italianate house with local artifacts.

PROGRAMS: Exhibits; Guided Tours; Interpretation; Lectures; Monthly Meeting; Publication; Research Library/Archives

COLLECTIONS: [Colonial/Victorian Eras] Period household items and furniture; vintage clothing, toys, town records, genealogies, Native American artifacts.

HOURS: Yr 1st Su

DANBURY

1153
Danbury Scott-Fanton Museum
43 Main St, 06810 [43 Main St, 06810]; (p) (203) 743-5200; (f) (203) 743-1131

1154
Military Museum of Southern New England
125 Park Ave, 06810; (p) (203) 790-9277; (f) (203) 790-0420; mmsne@juno.com; www.danbury.org/org/military; (c) Fairfield

Private non-profit/ 1985/ staff: 1(f); 30(v)/ members: 225

HISTORY MUSEUM: Collects, preserves, and displays military vehicles, uniforms, artifacts, and related materials.

PROGRAMS: Exhibits; Guided Tours; Interpretation

COLLECTIONS: [20th c] Tanks and other military vehicles; life-size dioramas; WW II exhibit.

HOURS: Yr T-Sa 10-5, Su 12-5

ADMISSION: $4,

DANIELSON

1155
Killingly Historical Center and Museum
196 Main St, 06239 [PO Box 6000, 06239]; (p) (860) 779-7250; www.comnet.edu/QVCTC/brian/KHS/kilz1.html; (c) Windham

Private non-profit/ 1972/ Killingly Historical Society, Inc./ staff: 20(v)/ members: 354/publication: *Killingly Historical Journal*

HISTORICAL SOCIETY; HISTORY MUSEUM; RESEARCH CENTER: Promotes research in history of Killingly and Windham County; preserves historical and genealogical artifacts and information.

PROGRAMS: Annual Meeting; Community Outreach; Exhibits; Facility Rental; Family Programs; Lectures; Publication

COLLECTIONS: Genealogical research aids: microfilms, CD-ROM—census, IGI, local newspapers, vital records, family files.

HOURS: Yr M F 9-12, W Sa 10-4; Call for Jan-Apr Hours

ADMISSION: Museum Free; Research $5/Day-non-members

DARIEN

1156
Darien Historical Society, Inc., The
45 Old King's Hwy N, 06820; (p) (203) 655-9233; www.darien.lib.ct.us/historical/default.htm; (c) Fairfield

Private non-profit/ 1954/ staff: 3(p); 50(v)/ members: 700

HISTORICAL SOCIETY; HOUSE MUSEUM: Collects, preserves, publishes, and exhibits local historical material; operates a resource library; maintains the Bates-Scofield Homestead (c. 1736) and 18th c herb garden.

PROGRAMS: Annual Meeting; Community Outreach; Exhibits; Facility Rental; Family Programs; Festivals; Garden Tours; Guided Tours; Interpretation; Lectures; Living History; Publication; Reenactments; Research Library/Archives; School-Based Curriculum

COLLECTIONS: [18th-19th c] Regional furniture and decorative arts; maps photos, diaries, deeds, directories, letters, manuscripts; costume and quilt.

HOURS: Yr Society/Library: T,F 9-2; W-Th 9-4; Museum: Th, Su 2-4

ADMISSION: $2.50

DERBY

1157
Osborne Homestead Museum
500 Hawthorne Ave, 06418 [PO Box 435, 06418]; (p) (203) 922-7832; (f) (203) 922-7833; www.invalley/derby/rec/kellogg.html; (c) New Haven

State/ 1986/ Sate of Connecticut Department of Environmental Protection/ staff: 1(f); 1(p); 6(v)

GARDEN; HISTORIC SITE; HOUSE MUSEUM: Celebrates life of Frances Osborne Kellogg, entrepreneur and environmentalist; preserves Kellogg home, gardens, and antiques.

PROGRAMS: Exhibits; Garden Tours; Guided Tours

COLLECTIONS: [18th-20th c.] Porcelain, fine China, first edition books, Japanese Art books, sheet music, paintings, furniture.

HOURS: Apr-Dec Su T Th Sa 10-3

ADMISSION: Donations accepted

EAST HADDAM

1158
East Haddam Historical Society and Museum
264 Town St, 06423 [PO Box 27, 06423-0027]; (p) (860) 873-3944; (f) (860) 873-3341; (c) Middlesex

Private non-profit/ 1963/ staff: 60(v)/ members: 450

Collects, displays, and preserves artifacts, structures, relics, and records related to local history.

1159
Gillette Castle State Park
67 River Rd, 06423; (p) (860) 526-2336; (f) (860) 526-2336

State/ 1944/ staff: 5(f); 51(p); 130(v)/ members: 65

HOUSE MUSEUM; LIVING HISTORY/OUTDOOR MUSEUM: Maintains turn-of-the-century actor's residence and park grounds.

PROGRAMS: Exhibits; Interpretation

COLLECTIONS: [1900-1937] Artwork, china, period furniture.

ADMISSION: $4, Children $2

EAST HARTFORD

1160
Vintage Radio and Communications Museum of Connecticut

711 Main St, 06108; (p) (860) 675-9916; (f) (860) 675-9916; (c) Hartford

Private non-profit/ 1990/ staff: 12(v)/ members: 152/publication: *Connecticut Wireless Gazette*

Preserves and disseminates electronic communications history.

PROGRAMS: Exhibits; Film/Video; Guided Tours; Lectures; Publication; Research Library/Archives

COLLECTIONS: [1900-1970s] Displays include wireless telegraphy, spark gap transmitters, teletype, motion picture projectors, hearing aids, microphones, wire recorders, reel to reel tape players, tesla coils, sound effects equipment, and record players.

HOURS: Yr Th-F 10-2, Sa 11-4, Su 1-4

ADMISSION: $4, Student $1.50, Seniors $2

EAST HAVEN

1161
Branford Electric Railway Association, Inc.

17 River St, 06512-2519; (p) (203) 467-6927; (f) (203) 467-7635; berasltm@aol.com; bera.org; (c) New Haven

Private non-profit/ 1945/ staff: 1(f); 2(p); 80(v)/ members: 929/publication: *BERA Journal*

Operates oldest suburban trolley line in the US and restores antique streetcars.

PROGRAMS: Annual Meeting; Exhibits; Facility Rental; Guided Tours; Interpretation; Publication; Research Library/Archives

COLLECTIONS: [1878-1948] Streetcars and rapid transit cars from Northeastern US and Canada.

HOURS: Apr, Nov Su 10-5; May, Sept-Oct, Dec Sa-Su 10-5; May-Sept Daily

1162
East Haven Historical Society

200 Tyler St, 06512; (p) (203) 467-1766; annmcbre@aol.com; (c) New Haven

Private non-profit/ staff: 11(v)/ members: 110

HISTORIC PRESERVATION AGENCY; HISTORICAL SOCIETY; HOUSE MUSEUM; LIBRARY AND/OR ARCHIVES: Collects and preserves local history.

PROGRAMS: Annual Meeting; Community Outreach; Exhibits; Film/Video; Lectures; Research Library/Archives

COLLECTIONS: [19th c-present] Slides, pictures, and books on town's history; documents pertaining to genealogy, town abstracts, yearbooks, artifacts, tools furniture, stoneware.

HOURS: Yr W 11-2

EAST WINDSOR

1163
Connecticut Antique Fire Apparatus Assn.

Route 140 @ the Trolley Museum, 06088 [PO Box 297, 06088]; (p) (860) 623-4732; (f) (860) 623-4732; (c) Hartford

Private non-profit/ 1968/ staff: 4(v)/ members: 68

Preservation and appreciation of antique motor fire apparatus and associated equipment.

PROGRAMS: Exhibits; Research Library/Archives

COLLECTIONS: [1894-1967] Period fire apparatuses; airport crash truck; fire alarm equipment; fire truck models.

HOURS: Mem Day-Labor Day W-Sa 10-5, Sun 12-5; Labor Day-Oct Sa-Su 12-5

ADMISSION: $6, Children $4, Seniors $5

1164
Connecticut Electric Railway Assoc. Inc. dba:The Connecticut Trolley Museum, The

58 N Rd (Rte 140), 06088 [PO Box 360, 06088-0360]; (p) (860) 627-6540; (f) (860) 627-6510; office@ceraonline.org; (c) Hartford

Private non-profit/ 1940/ staff: 3(f); 3(p); 35(v)/ members: 500

Collects, restores, preserves, and operates street cars; provides educational information of the evolution of the trolley car and trolley rides.

PROGRAMS: Annual Meeting; Exhibits; Guided Tours

COLLECTIONS: [1875-1949] Trolley era documents and memorabilia.

HOURS: Labor Day-Dec 31 April-Mem Day Sa 10-5, Su 12-5; Mem Day-Labor Day W-Sa 10-5, Su 12-5

HOURS; $6; Children $3; Seniors $5

ENFIELD

1165
Martha A. Parsons Memorial Trust

1387 Enfield St, 06082; (p) (860) 745-3034; MKM-OF-ENFCT@worldnet.att.net; www.home.attnet/~MKM-OF-ENFCT/; (c) Hartford

1965/ Enfield Historical Society/ staff: 2(f)

HOUSE MUSEUM: Preserves historic home and furnishings of Parsons family and develops outdoor historical programs.

PROGRAMS: Concerts; Guided Tours; Living History; Reenactments

COLLECTIONS: [Late colonial, Victorian] Colonial keeping-room with fireplace and beehive oven; period furnishings; George Washington Memorial wallpaper.

HOURS: May-Oct Su 2-4:30, also 1st Su in Dec

ADMISSION: Donations accepted

ESSEX

1166
Essex Historical Society

Pratt House, W Ave, 06426 [PO Box 123, 06426]; (p) (860) 767-0681; (c) Middlesex

Private non-profit/ 1982/ staff: 40(v)/ members: 300

HISTORICAL SOCIETY: Maintain and operate two historic properties (Pratt House, Hills Academy); preserve area history and memorabilia.

PROGRAMS: Exhibits; Family Programs; Guided Tours; Interpretation; Lectures

COLLECTIONS: [Colonial] Paintings, furnishings, clothing, tools publications, signs, toys, and memorabilia related to the the history of Essex.

HOURS: June-Sept Sa-Su 1-4

ADMISSION: Donations accepted

FAIRFIELD

1167
Connecticut Audubon Birdcraft Museum

314 Unquowa Rd, 06430-5018; (p) (203) 259-0416; (f) (203) 259-1344; www.ctaudubon.org; (c) Fairfield

Private non-profit/ 1914/ Connecticut Audubon Society/ staff: 2(f); 3(p); 100(v)/ members: 10000

GARDEN; HISTORIC SITE: Collects and interprets the origins of the American Conservation Movement; maintains museum and country's oldest private songbird sanctuary.

PROGRAMS: Community Outreach; Exhibits; Facility Rental; Family Programs; Festivals; Guided Tours; Interpretation; Lectures; Research Library/Archives; School-Based Curriculum

COLLECTIONS: [1870s-present] Bird mounts and skins; archives and library relating to life of Mabel Osgood Wright.

HOURS: Yr T-F 10-5, Sa-Su 12-5

ADMISSION: $2, Children $1

1168
Fairfield Historical Society; David Ogden House

636 Old Post Rd, 06430; (p) (203) 259-1598; (f) (203) 255-2716; (c) Fairfield

Private non-profit/ 1903/ staff: 5(f); 1(p); 135(v)/ members: 900

HISTORICAL SOCIETY; HISTORY MUSEUM; HOUSE MUSEUM: Operates a museum and the Ogden House and Gardens; collect, preserve, and interpret local history and heritage.

PROGRAMS: Community Outreach; Exhibits; Facility Rental; Family Programs; Festivals; Guided Tours; Lectures; Living History; Publication; Reenactments; Research Library/Archives

COLLECTIONS: [1700-present] Native American artifacts; fine and decorative arts; agricultural and industrial artifacts; costumes, textiles and maritime items; books, manuscripts, maps, photos, journals, diaries, directories, deeds.

HOURS: Yr Museum: T-Sa 10-4:30, Su 1-4:30; Ogden House: May-Oct Sa-Su 1-4:30

ADMISSION: $3, Children $1

FALLS VILLAGE

1169
Falls Village-Canaan Historical Society

Main St, 06031 [PO Box 206, 06031]; (p) (860) 824-0707; (c) Litchfield

Private non-profit/ 1955/ Board of Directors/ staff: 18(v)/ members: 150

HISTORICAL SOCIETY: Records, preserves, and displas historical materials of area; maintains genealogical records.

PROGRAMS: Annual Meeting; Community Outreach; Concerts; Exhibits; Facility Rental; Guided Tours; Lectures; Research

FARMINGTON

1170
Hill-Stead Museum
35 Mountain Rd, 06032; (p) (860) 677-4787; (f) (860) 677-0174; www.hillstead.org; (c) Hartford

Private non-profit/ 1947/ Board of Trustees/Board of Govenors/ staff: 8(f); 3(p); 50(v)/ members: 900

ART MUSEUM; HISTORIC SITE; HOUSE MUSEUM; RESEARCH CENTER: Maintains a 1901 Colonial revival home and sunken garden.

PROGRAMS: Community Outreach; Concerts; Facility Rental; Family Programs; Festivals; Garden Tours; Guided Tours; Interpretation; Lectures; Research Library/Archives

COLLECTIONS: [1880-1940] Impressionist art work by Monet, Manet, Degas, Whistler, and Cassatt.

HOURS: May-Oct T-Su 10-4, Nov-Apr T-Su 11-4

ADMISSION: $7, Student $6, Children $4, Seniors $6; Under 6/Mbrs free

1171
Stanley-Whitman House
37 High St, 06032; (p) (860) 677-9222; (f) (860) 677-7758; (c) Hartford

Private non-profit/ 1935/ Farmington Village Green and Library Assoc/ staff: 1(f); 4(p); 35(v)/ members: 225

HISTORIC SITE; HISTORY MUSEUM; HOUSE MUSEUM: Maintains historic house and museum focused on 18th c. Connecticut history.

PROGRAMS: Community Outreach; Exhibits; Facility Rental; Family Programs; Festivals; Garden Tours; Guided Tours; Interpretation; Living History; Research Library/Archives; School-Based Curriculum

COLLECTIONS: [18th c] Period furniture and decorative arts; historic house and herb garden; archives and library.

HOURS: May-Oct W-Su 12-4; Nov-Apr Sa-Su 12-4

ADMISSION: $5, Children $2, Seniors $4

GALES FERRY

1172
Nathan Lester House
153 Vinegar Hill Rd, 06335 [153 Vinegar Hill Rd, 06335]; (p) (860) 464-8662

1793/ City/ staff: 2(v)

COLLECTIONS: [Early 1800s] Colonial tools; period furniture; clothing; linens.

HOURS: Jun-Aug

GAYLORDSVILLE

1173
Gaylordsville Historical Society
60 Gaylord Rd, 06755 [PO Box 25, 06755]; (p) (860) 350-0300; (f) (860) 354-1715; webmaster@gaylordsville; www.gaylordsville. org; (c) Litchfield

Private non-profit/ 1975/ staff: 26(v)/ members: 200

HISTORIC SITE; HISTORICAL SOCIETY; HISTORY MUSEUM: Maintains historic one room schoolhouse, forge, and fully equipped blacksmith shop.

PROGRAMS: Annual Meeting; Exhibits; Guided Tours; Publication

COLLECTIONS: [1725-present] Documents, letters, photos, burial records.

HOURS: July-Aug Su 2-5

ADMISSION: Donations accepted

GLATSTONBURY

1174
Historical Society of Glastonbury
1944 Main St, 06033 [PO Box 46, Glastonbury, 06033]; (p) (860) 633-6890; (f) (860) 633-6890; (c) Hartford

Private non-profit/ 1936/ staff: 1(f); 2(p)/ members: 385

HISTORIC SITE; HISTORICAL SOCIETY; HISTORY MUSEUM; HOUSE MUSEUM: Promotes community activity and interest in Glastonbury's heritage through publications, exhibits, and programs; acquires, maintains, and preserves historical properties and materials.

PROGRAMS: Annual Meeting; Elder's Programs; Exhibits; Festivals; Guided Tours; Interpretation; Lectures; Publication; Reenactments; Research Library/Archives

COLLECTIONS: [18th-19th c] Account Books, documents, letters, ephemera, genealogical material, cemetery records, costumes, vehicles, early industry artifacts, domestic items.

HOURS: Museum: Yr M-Th 10-4; Wells-Shipman-Ward House: May-June, Sept-Oct Su 2-4

ADMISSION: $2

GOSHEN

1175
Goshen Historical Society
21 Old Middle Rd, 06756 [27 Kimberly Rd, 06756]; (p) (860) 491-2665; (c) Litchfield

Private non-profit/ 1955/ staff: 5(v)/ members: 270

HISTORIC SITE; HISTORICAL SOCIETY: Collection of items and information concerning local history.

PROGRAMS: Annual Meeting; Family Programs; Guided Tours; Lectures; Publication

COLLECTIONS: [1800s]

HOURS: T 10-12

GRANBY

1176
Salmon Brook Historical Society, Inc.
208 Salmon Brook St, 06035; (p) (860) 653-9713; www.salmonbrookhistorical.org; (c) Hartford

Private non-profit/ 1959/ Board of Directors/ staff: 25(v)/ members: 300

HISTORICAL SOCIETY; HISTORY MUSEUM; HOUSE MUSEUM: Collects, preserves, interprets, and disseminates local history.

PROGRAMS: Annual Meeting; Exhibits; Guided Tours; Lectures; Research Library/ Archives; School-Based Curriculum

COLLECTIONS: [19th c.] Genealogy, documents, manuscripts; period furnishings; period barn and schoolhouse

HOURS: May-Oct Su 2-4

ADMISSION: $2, Children $1, Seniors $1

GREENWICH

1177
Bruce Museum of Arts and Science
1 Museum Dr, 06830; (p) (203) 869-0376; (f) (203) 869-0963; brucemus@netaxis.com; www.brucemuseum.org; (c) Fairfield

Joint/ 1912/ staff: 29(f); 12(p); 350(v)/ members: 3000

ART MUSEUM: Exhibits fine and decorative arts and artifacts; develops hands on activities.

PROGRAMS: Community Outreach; Concerts; Exhibits; Facility Rental; Family Programs; Festivals; Film/Video; Guided Tours; Lectures; Publication; School-Based Curriculum; Theatre

COLLECTIONS: American painting, sculpture, and decorative art; Native American art and artifacts; mounted mammals and birds; wildlife diorama; fossils; geology.

HOURS: Yr T-Sa 10-5, Su 1-5

ADMISSION: $3.50, Children $2.50, Seniors $2.50

1178
Putnam Hill Chapter, Daughters of the American Revolution
243 E Putnam Ave, 06830; (p) (203) 869-9697; (c) Fairfield

Private non-profit/ 1898/ Daughters of the American Revolution/ staff: 50(v)/ members: 175

GENEALOGICAL SOCIETY; HISTORIC SITE; HISTORICAL SOCIETY: Maintain historic Revolutionary tavern.

PROGRAMS: Facility Rental; Guided Tours; Reenactments

COLLECTIONS: [Mid 1700s] Antiques from the tavern/meeting house; genealogy.

HOURS: Apr-Dec Su W F 1-4

ADMISSION: $4

GROTON

1179
Avery Memorial Association
Fort Griswold, 06340 [PO Box 7245, 06340]; (p) (860) 446-9257; (c) New London

Private non-profit/ staff: 1(p); 5(v)/ members: 500

HOUSE MUSEUM: The Association maintains a tie between the descendants of James Avery.

COLLECTIONS: [1700-1900] Furniture, photographs, and artifacts contributed by members.

HOURS: May-Sept Sa-Su 1-5

1180
Historic Ship Nautilus and Submarine Force Museum
Naval Submarine Base New London, 06349 [1 Crystal Lake Rd, 06349]; (p) (860) 694-3558; (f) (860) 694-4150; nauitulus@subasenlon.navy.mil; www.ussnautilus.org

Federal; Private non-profit/ 1986/ US Navy/ staff: 29(f); 3(p); 1(v)/ members: 700/publication: *Klaxon*

HISTORIC SITE; HISTORY MUSEUM; RESEARCH CENTER: Preservation of the world's 1st nuclear powered submarine and 1st ship to go to the North Pole; creates and maintains museum exhibits concerned with naval history.

PROGRAMS: Annual Meeting; Community Outreach; Exhibits; Interpretation; Publication; Research Library/Archives

COLLECTIONS: [Revolutionary War-present] Artifacts, photos, documents, books, battleflags; drawings/blueprints of submarine inventors; submarine paintings; WW II war patrol reports.

HOURS: Yr Daily 9-5

ADMISSION: No charge

1181
U.S. Submarine Veterans of World War II
[PO Box 952, 06340]; (c) New London

Federal/ 1955/ staff: 8(f)/ members: 8500/publication: *Polaris Magazine*

HISTORIC SITE; HISTORY MUSEUM; LIVING HISTORY/OUTDOOR MUSEUM: Preserves the memory of those who served in submarine warfare and WW II.

PROGRAMS: Exhibits; Lectures; Publication; Reenactments

COLLECTIONS: Memorial consisting of a conning tower from a WW II type submarine; a "Wall of Honor" listing the names of those lost in submarines in WW II.

HOURS: Yr Daily 24 hrs

GUILFORD

1182
Dorothy Whitfield Historic Society
84 Boston St, 06437 [PO Box 229, 06437]; (p) (203) 453-9477; (c) New Haven

Private non-profit/ 1915/ staff: 5(p); 30(v)/ members: 300/publication: *Hyland House Times*

HISTORICAL SOCIETY; HOUSE MUSEUM: Preserves and interprets the Hyland House as significant example of early colonial architecture and living environment.

PROGRAMS: Annual Meeting; Community Outreach; Concerts; Elder's Programs; Exhibits; Family Programs; Guided Tours; Interpretation; Lectures; Living History; Publication; School-Based Curriculum

COLLECTIONS: [17th c-1850] Two over two saltbox house with lean-to kitchen; period furniture and decorative arts; hearth cooking utensils, slipware; quilts and early textiles.

HOURS: June-Aug T-Su 10-4:30, Sept-Oct Sa-Su 10-4:30

ADMISSION: $2

1183
Dudley Foundation, Inc., The
2351 Durham Rd, 06437; (p) (203) 457-0770; www.dudleyfarm.org; (c) New Haven

Private non-profit/ 1995/ staff: 1(p); 35(v)/ members: 400/publication: *Farm News*

Maintains a late 19th c. farm for educational purposes.

PROGRAMS: Annual Meeting; Concerts; Exhibits; Facility Rental; Family Programs; Guided Tours; Interpretation; Lectures; Living History; Publication; Reenactments; Research Library/Archives; School-Based Curriculum

COLLECTIONS: [18th-20th c] Period farm artifacts; woodworking artifacts; household items.

HOURS: Mar-Nov M-F 10-1, Sa-Su 10-2

ADMISSION: $3

1184
Henry Whitfield State Museum
248 Old Whitfield St, 06437 [PO Box 210, 06437]; (p) (203) 453-2457; (f) (203) 453-7544; (c) New Haven

State/ 1899/ Connecticut Historical Commission/ staff: 2(f); 1(p); 12(v)

HISTORIC SITE; HISTORY MUSEUM; HOUSE MUSEUM: A National Historic Landmark, CT's oldest house, and New England's oldest stone house.

PROGRAMS: Community Outreach; Exhibits; Family Programs; Garden Tours; Guided Tours; Interpretation; Lectures; Research Library/Archives; School-Based Curriculum

COLLECTIONS: [17th-19th c] Period furnishings; manuscript collection; weaving and textile equip; 1st clock tower in the colonies.

HOURS: Feb-Dec 15th W-Su 10-4:30

ADMISSION: $3.50, Student $2.50, Children $2, Seniors $2.50

1185
Thomas Griswold House
171 Boston St, 06437 [PO Box 363, 06437]; (p) (203) 453-3176, (203) 453-4666

1774/ staff: 2(p)

COLLECTIONS: [1800] Guilford crafted chairs, quilts and coverlets, clothing, and working large fireplace, double back ovens and cooking pots;

HOURS: Nov-May by appt;; Nov-May by appt

HADDAM

1186
Haddam Historical Society
14 Hayden Hill Rd, 06438 [PO Box 97, 06438]; (p) (860) 345-2400; thankfularnold@juno.com; (c) Middlesex

Private non-profit/ 1955/ Haddam Historical Society/ staff: 1(f); 1(p)/ members: 271

HISTORICAL SOCIETY; HOUSE MUSEUM: Preserves, collects, and interprets and promotes area history and heritage.

PROGRAMS: Annual Meeting; Community Outreach; Concerts; Elder's Programs; Exhibits; Family Programs; Garden Tours; Guided Tours; Lectures; Reenactments; Research Library/Archives; School-Based Curriculum

COLLECTIONS: [Early 1800s] Period furniture and decorative arts; local archival and genealogical materials.

HOURS: Yr Jan-Dec M-W

ADMISSION: Donations accepted

HAMDEN

1187
Connecticut League of History Organizations
940 Whitney Ave, 06517-4002; (p) (203) 624-9186; (f) (203) 793-0107; (c) New Haven

Private non-profit/ Connecticut League of History Organizations/ staff: 1(p); 25(v)/ members: 350

ALLIANCE OF HISTORICAL AGENCIES: Encourages and supports the activities of state historical organizations; enhances knowledge of state history; promotes professional standards; serves as a network for the exchange of information.

PROGRAMS: Annual Meeting, Community Outreach, lectures

HOURS: Yr Days Vary 9-4

1188
Hamden Historical Society Inc.
105 Mt Carmel Ave, 06518 [PO Box 5512, 06518]; (c) New Haven

Private non-profit/ 1945/ staff: 10(v)/ members: 180

HOUSE MUSEUM; RESEARCH CENTER: Restoration of 1792 Jonathan Dickerman farmhouse, herb garden, and Cider Mill; operates historical society library.

PROGRAMS: Annual Meeting; Guided Tours; Publication; Research Library/Archives

COLLECTIONS: [1790-1820] Period furnishings, tools, and toys.

HOURS: July-Aug Sa-Su 1-4

HARTFORD

1189
Antiquarian and Landmarks Society
66 Forest St, 06105; (p) (860) 247-8996; (f) (860) 249-4907; www.hartnet.org/als

Private non-profit/ 1936/ staff: 7(f); 1(p); 20(v)/ members: 800

GARDEN; HISTORIC PRESERVATION AGENCY; HISTORIC SITE; HISTORICAL SOCIETY; HISTORY MUSEUM; HOUSE MUSEUM: Preserves, interprets, and promotes interest in state's heritage through preservation of 13 historic properties and site programming.

PROGRAMS: Annual Meeting; Community Outreach; Concerts; Exhibits; Facility Rental; Festivals; Garden Tours; Guided Tours; Interpretation; Lectures; Living History; Reenactments; Research Library/Archives; School-Based Curriculum

COLLECTIONS: [Late 17th c-1950s] Domestic architecture and furnishings reflecting home; Victorian toys, weathervanes, and Japanese samurai accoutrements.

HOURS: May-Oct

ADMISSION: Varies

1190

Butler-McCook Homestead

396 Main St, 06103 [66 Forrest St, 06105]; (p) (860) 247-8996, (860) 522-1806; (f) (860) 249-4907

1782/ staff: 2(p); 1(v)

COLLECTIONS: [1900-1910] Victorian toys, Japanese bronzes including Samurai armor; Extensive family papers and photos

HOURS: Seasonal

1191

Connecticut Historical Society, The

1 Elizabeth St, 06105; (p) (860) 236-5621; (f) (860) 236-2664; www.chs.org; (c) Hartford

Private non-profit/ 1825/ staff: 36(f); 14(p); 11(v)/ members: 1700/publicatio

HISTORICAL SOCIETY: Collects, preserves, and interprets state history.

PROGRAMS: Annual Meeting; Community Outreach; Concerts; Exhibits; Facility Rental; Family Programs; Guided Tours; Interpretation; Lectures; Publication; Research Library/ Archives; School-Based Curriculum

COLLECTIONS: [17th c- 19th c] Manuscripts, paintings, furniture, graphics materials, textiles; state-related silver, pewter, tavern signs, and genealogy materials.

HOURS: Yr Library: T-Sa 10-5; Museum: T-Su 12-5

ADMISSION: $5; Student $3; Children $1; Seniors $3

1192

First Church of Christ in Hartford

675 Main St, 06103 [60 Gold St, 06103]; (p) (860) 249-5631; (f) (860) 246-3915; (c) Hartford

Private non-profit/ 1632/ staff: 5(f); 4(p); 2(v)/ members: 307

HISTORIC SITE: Maintain historic church.

PROGRAMS: Annual Meeting; Community Outreach; Concerts; Elder's Programs; Family Programs; Guided Tours; Research Library/ Archives; School-Based Curriculum

COLLECTIONS: [1880-1915] Stained glass windows including Tiffany's glass; ancient cemetery.

HOURS: Apr-Dec W-F

1193

Harriet Beecher Stowe Center

77 Forest St, 06105; (p) (860) 522-9258; (f) (860) 522-9259; stowelib@hartnet.org; www.hartnet.org/~stowe; (c) Hartford

Private non-profit/ 1942/ Board of Trustees/ staff: 8(f); 18(p); 20(v)/ members: 150/publication: The Journal

HISTORIC SITE; HOUSE MUSEUM; RESEARCH CENTER: Museum, library, and program center highlighting social justice and impact of Stowe's life and work.

PROGRAMS: Community Outreach; Concerts; Exhibits; Facility Rental; Family Programs; Festivals; Film/Video; Garden Tours; Guided Tours; Interpretation; Lectures; Publication; Research Library/Archives

COLLECTIONS: [19th c-early 20th c] Period furnishings; decorative and fine arts; rare books, manuscripts, and archives pertaining to

African American and women's history.

HOURS: Yr T-Sa 9:30-4:30, Su 12-4:30; June-May, Dec also M 9:30-4:30

ADMISSION: $6.50, Children $2.75, Seniors $6

1194

Mark Twain Home Foundation

351 Farmington Ave, 06105; (p) (860) 247-0998; (f) (860) 278-8148; lgregor@ursa. hartnet.org; www.MarkTwainHouse.org; (c) Hartford

Private non-profit/ 1929/ The Mark Twain Memorial/ staff: 21(f); 14(p)/ members: 800/publication: The Mark Twain News

Museum and research center dedicated to the study of Mark Twain, his works, and his time period, located in Twain's family house.

PROGRAMS: Annual Meeting; Concerts; Exhibits; Family Programs; Guided Tours; Interpretation; Lectures; Publication; Research Library/Archives; School-Based Curriculum

COLLECTIONS: [1874-1891] Primarily focused on Mark Twain/Samuel Clemens; elements of the historic site; fine and domestic arts and artifacts; library and archival material.

HOURS: Oct-May M W-Sa 9:30-5, Su 12-5; June-Oct M-Sa 9:30-5, Su 12-5

ADMISSION: $9, Children $5, Seniors $8

1195

Menczer Museum of Medicine and Dentistry

230 Scarborough St, 06105; (p) (860) 236-5613; (f) (860) 236-8401; (c) Hartford

1975/ Hartford Medical Society and Hartford Dental Society/ staff: 1(f); 1(p); 4(v)

HISTORY MUSEUM: Preserves history of medical and dental professions; exhibits development of instruments.

PROGRAMS: Exhibits; Facility Rental; Lectures; Research Library/Archives

COLLECTIONS: [1800-1950] Collection on anesthesia featuring information on Horace Wells who discovered the use of nitrous oxide, books, manuscripts, portraits, and instruments.

HOURS: Yr M-F 9:30-4:30

ADMISSION: $2

1196

Museum of Connecticut History

231 Capitol Ave, 06106; (p) (860) 757-6535; (f) (860) 757-6533; dnelson@cslib.org; www.cslib.org; (c) Hartford

State/ 1909/ staff: 3(f)

HISTORY MUSEUM; LIBRARY AND/OR ARCHIVES: Collects, preserves, and exhibits materials related to CT government, industrial, and military history; conducts research.

PROGRAMS: Exhibits; Lectures

COLLECTIONS: [1850-present] CT industrial machinery, factory goods, trade catalogs, photographs, American firearms, uniforms, equipment's, advertising, patented items, political memorabilia, Governor's portraits, US coins.

HOURS: Yr M-F 9-4, Sa 10-4, Su 12-4

ADMISSION: No charge

1197

Old New-Gate Prison and Copper Mine

115 Newgate Rd, 06106 [59 South Prospect St, 06106]; (p) (860) 566-3005, (860) 653-3563; (f) (860) 566-5078; (c) Hartford

State/ 1969/ Connecticut Historical Commission/ staff: 4(p)

HISTORIC SITE: Preserves and interprets history of early mining operation, colonial and state prisons, and American Revolution; maintains exhibits, trails and picnic areas.

PROGRAMS: Exhibits; Guided Tours; Lectures; Reenactments

COLLECTIONS: [17th-19th c]

HOURS: May-Oct W-Su and M Holidays 10-4:30

ADMISSION: $3, Children $1.50

1198

Old State House

800 Main St, 06106; (p) (860) 522-6766; (f) (860) 522-2812; whfaude@snet.net; (c) Hartford

Private non-profit/ staff: 6(f); 11(p)/ members: 850

HISTORIC SITE; HISTORY MUSEUM; LIVING HISTORY/OUTDOOR MUSEUM: Preservation and education about the Old State House, designed by Charles Bulfinch and a landmark of American political history.

PROGRAMS: Concerts; Exhibits; Family Programs; Guided Tours; Interpretation; Lectures; Living History; Reenactments; School-Based Curriculum

COLLECTIONS: [17th c.-present] Victorian architecture; Gilbert Stuart portrait of George Washington.

HOURS: Yr M-Su 10-4

ADMISSION: No charge

1199

Wadsworth Atheneum

600 Main St, 06103-2990; (p) (860) 278-2670; (f) (860) 527-0803; info@ wadsworthatheneum.org; www. wadsworthatheneum.org; (c) Hartford

Private non-profit/ 1842/ staff: 90(f); 47(p); 160(v)/ members: 7000

ART MUSEUM: Collects and preserves American and European arts and textiles.

PROGRAMS: Community Outreach; Concerts; Elder's Programs; Exhibits; Facility Rental; Family Programs; Festivals; Film/Video; Guided Tours; Interpretation; Lectures; Research Library/Archives; Theatre

COLLECTIONS: Mediterranean antiquities, European renaissance, Baroque paintings, Hudson-River -school landscapes, Impressionist paintings; period furniture; African-American art and history.

HOURS: Yr T-Su 11-5

ADMISSION: $7, Student $5,

IVORYTON

1200

Company of Fifers and Drummers, The

62 N Main St, 06442 [PO Box 525, 06442]; (p) (860) 767-2237; thecompanyoffd@juno.

com; www.fifedrum.com/the company; (c) Middlesex

Private non-profit/ 1965/ staff: 4(f); 10(p); 20(v)/ members: 1000/publication: *The Ancient Times*

Preserve and promote early American martial music.

PROGRAMS: Annual Meeting; Concerts; Exhibits; Facility Rental; Family Programs; Guided Tours; Interpretation; Lectures; Living History; Publication; Research Library/Archives

COLLECTIONS: [1750-present] Documents, artifacts, photographs, accoutrements, uniforms, and instruments relating to musical history of fife and drum in the US, England, France, Germany, and Switzerland.

HOURS: June-Sept Sa-Su 1-5

ADMISSION: Donations

LEBANON

1201
Doctor William Beaumont House
169 W Town St, 06249 [806 Trumbull Hwy, 06249]; (p) (860) 642-7247

1760

Birthplace of Dr. William Beaumont, father of gastric physiology.

COLLECTIONS: Medical instruments and related items.

HOURS: Jun-Sept

1202
Jonathan Trumbull, Junior, House Museum
780 Trumbull Hwy (Rte 87), 06249 [c/o First Selectman, 579 Exeter Rd, 06249]; (p) (860) 642-6100; (f) (860) 642-7716; (c) New London

City/ 1978/ Town Lebanon/ staff: 1(p); 7(v)

HOUSE MUSEUM: Preserves home of Trumbull, Military Sec to Gen George Washington during the Revolutionary War and governor of CT 1797-1809; Interprets architectural and social history of house through all owners.

PROGRAMS: Community Outreach; Family Programs; Festivals; Guided Tours

HOURS: May-Oct Sa 1-5, Yr by

LISBON

1203
John Bishop House and Museum
Rts 169 & 138, 06351 [Lisbon Town Hall, 1 Newent Rd, 06351]; (p) (860) 376-2708

LITCHFIELD

1204
Litchfield Historical Society
7 S St, 06759 [PO Box 385, 06759]; (p) (860) 567-4501; (f) (860) 567-3565; lhsoc@snet. net; (c) Litchfield

Private non-profit/ 1896/ staff: 4(f); 4(p); 60(v)/ members: 500

HISTORIC PRESERVATION AGENCY; HISTORIC SITE; HISTORICAL SOCIETY; HISTORY MUSEUM: Maintains local history museum, exhibits, and research library.

PROGRAMS: Annual Meeting; Community Outreach; Concerts; Elder's Programs; Exhibits; Facility Rental; Family Programs; Festivals; Garden Tours; Guided Tours; Interpretation; Lectures; Publication; Research Library/Archives; School-Based Curriculum; Theatre

COLLECTIONS: [18th c-present] Collections related to the Litchfield Female Academy and Litchfield Law School; local furniture and decorative arts.

HOURS: Museum: Apr-Nov T-Sa 11-5, Su 1-5; Library: Yr T-F 10-12, 1-4

ADMISSION: $5

MADISON

1205
Madison Historical Society
853 Boston Post Rd, 06443 [PO Box 17, 06443]; (p) (203) 245-4567; (c) New Haven

Private non-profit/ 1917/ Board of Directors/ staff: 3(p); 25(v)/ members: 500

HISTORICAL SOCIETY; HISTORY MUSEUM; HOUSE MUSEUM: Preserves local history by collecting artifacts, information, documents, and oral histories; maintains the Allis-Bushnell House.

PROGRAMS: Annual Meeting; Community Outreach; Exhibits; Guided Tours; Lectures; Research Library/Archives; School-Based Curriculum

COLLECTIONS: [1700-present] Home furnishings; farming, fishing, and shipbuilding equip. reflecting local history.

HOURS: May-Oct W, F-Sa 1-4

ADMISSION: Donations accepted

MANCHESTER

1206
Cheney Homestead
106 Hartford Rd, 06040; (p) (860) 643-5588; ManchesterHistory@juno.com; www.ci.manchester.ct.us/cheney/historic.htm; (c) Hartford

1965/ Manchester Historical Society/ staff: 1(f); 7(v)

HOUSE MUSEUM: Maintains the Cheney Homestead, birthplace of both the founders of the Cheney Brothers Silk business and 19th c. artists and engravers.

PROGRAMS: Guided Tours

COLLECTIONS: [1785-1860] CT River Valley and Philadelphia furniture; original sketches and oil paintings.

HOURS: Yr F-Su 10-3

ADMISSION: $2

1207
Connecticut Firemen's Historical Society
230 Pine St, 06040; (p) (860) 649-9436; (f) (860) 667-4975; (c) Hartford

Private non-profit/ 1971/ staff: 17(v)/ members: 285

HISTORIC SITE; HISTORICAL SOCIETY; HISTORY MUSEUM: Preservation of the history of the fire service in CT and the collection, conservation, interpretation, and display of its artifacts.

PROGRAMS: Annual Meeting; Community Outreach; Exhibits; Guided Tours; Publication; Research Library/Archives; School-Based Curriculum

COLLECTIONS: [1700-1950] Fire department memorabilia; manual horse-drawn, steam powered, and early motorized fire apparatus; leather hoses; fire buckets and helmets.

HOURS: Apr-Nov F-Sa 10-5, Su 12-5

ADMISSION: Donations accepted

1208
Manchester Historical Society, Inc.
126 Cedar St, 06040 [106 Hartford Rd, 06040]; (p) (860) 647-9983; manchesterhistory@juno.com; (c) Hartford

Private non-profit/ 1965/ staff: 1(f); 6(p); 20(v)/ members: 600/publication: *The Courier*

HISTORICAL SOCIETY; HISTORY MUSEUM: Created to preserve local history including buildings, objects, and artifacts.

PROGRAMS: Annual Meeting; Exhibits; Guided Tours; Lectures; Publication; Research Library/Archives

COLLECTIONS: Items from local manufacturers (Cheney Bros. Silk, Bon Ami soap, Pitkin Glass bottles); photos, local maps, genealogies, local newspapers.

HOURS: Cheney Homestead: Yr F-Su 10-3; History Museum: Yr Su 1-4, M 9-12

ADMISSION: $2

MASHANTUCKET

1209
Mashantucket Pequot Museum and Research Center
110 Pequot Trail, 06339-3180; (p) (800) 411-9671; (f) (860) 396-7013; dholahan@mptn. org; www.mashantucket.com; (c) New London

1998/ Mashantucket Pequot Tribal Nation/ staff: 145(f)/ members: 5000

HISTORY MUSEUM; TRIBAL MUSEUM: Focuses on public education of Native and natural history of S. New England from time of Wisconsin Glacier (18,000 yr. ago) to present.

PROGRAMS: Exhibits; Facility Rental; Family Programs; Film/Video; Guided Tours; Lectures; Research Library/Archives; Theatre

COLLECTIONS: [16th-20th c.] Print and electronic archives; ethnographic and archaeological collections.

HOURS: Sept-May W-M 10-6; June-Aug Daily 10-7

ADMISSION: $12, Children $8, Seniors

MERIDEN

1210
1711 Solomon Goffe House
677 N Colony St, 06450 [513 High Hill Rd, 06450]; (p) (203) 634-9088; SGOFFE@juno.com; (c) New Haven

City/ 1711/ City of Meriden/ staff: 25(v)/ members: 35

HISTORIC SITE; HISTORY MUSEUM; HOUSE MUSEUM; LIVING HISTORY/OUTDOOR MUSEUM: Early 18th and 19th c New England architecture.

PROGRAMS: Annual Meeting; Community Outreach; Exhibits; Guided Tours; Interpretation; Living History; Reenactments; School-Based Curriculum

COLLECTIONS: [18th-19th c] Furniture reproductions.

HOURS: Apr-Nov 1st Su 1:30-4:30

ADMISSION: $2

MIDDLETOWN

1211
Middlesex County Historical Society
151 Main St, 06457; (p) (860) 346-0746; (f) (860) 346-0746; (c) Middlesex

Private non-profit/ 1901/ staff: 1(f); 25(v)/ members: 275

HISTORICAL SOCIETY; HISTORY MUSEUM: Maintains archives of local history; operates a museum featuring local history.

PROGRAMS: Annual Meeting; Exhibits; Family Programs; Guided Tours; Lectures; Reenactments; Research Library/Archives

COLLECTIONS: [18th-19th c] Decorative arts, military, textiles, photos.

HOURS: Yr M 1-4, Su 2-4:30; Research: T-Th by appt

MILFORD

1212
Milford Historical Society Wharf Lane Museum Complex
34 High St, 06460 [PO Box 337, 06460]; (p) (203) 874-2664, (203) 874-5789; (f) (203) 874-5789
HOURS: Seasonal

MOODUS

1213
Amasa Day House
Plains Rd on the Green, 06469 [66 Forest St, Hartford, 06105]; (p) (860) 247-8996, (860) 247-8996; (f) (860) 249-4907

1816

COLLECTIONS: [1840s] early 20th photographic collection

HOURS: Seasonal

MYSTIC

1214
Denison Homestead Museum
120 Pequotsepos Rd, 06355 [PO Box 42, 06355]; (p) (860) 536-9248; (f) (860) 536-9248; www.visitmystic.com/ denisonhomestead:htm; (c) New London

Private non-profit/ 1930/ Denison Society, Inc./ staff: 3(p); 30(v)/ members: 600

GENEALOGICAL SOCIETY; HISTORIC SITE; HISTORY MUSEUM: Preserves Denison family history; maintains historic house museum.

PROGRAMS: Annual Meeting; Community Outreach; Guided Tours; Interpretation; Publication; Research Library/Archives; School-Based Curriculum

COLLECTIONS: [1654-1941] Period household furnishings; family records, photos, genealogy.

HOURS: May-Oct F-M 10-4

ADMISSION: $4, Student $3, Children $1, Seniors $3

1215
Mystic River Historical Society
74/76 High St, 06355 [PO Box 245, 06355-0245]; (p) (860) 536-4779; mrhs5@juno.com; (c) New London

Private non-profit/ 1973/ staff: 1(p); 25(v)/ members: 700

HISTORICAL SOCIETY: Collects, preserves, exhibit and interprets the regional history post-European settlement.

PROGRAMS: Exhibits; Lectures; Publication; Research Library/Archives; School-Based Curriculum

COLLECTIONS: [1654-present] Photos, manuscripts, volumes, artifacts, and maps.

HOURS: Yr T 9-12,

1216
Mystic Seaport Museum, Inc.
75 Greenmanville, 06355 [PO Box 6000, 06355-0990]; (p) (860) 572-0711; (f) (860) 572-5328; www.mysticseaport.org; (c) New London

Private non-profit/ 1929/ staff: 545(f); 74(p); 800(v)/ members: 24000/publication: *The Log of Mystic Seaport*

HISTORY MUSEUM: Creates broad, public understanding of the relationship of America and the sea through preservation and exhibition of historic watercraft and other maritime objects; development of innovative educational and interpretive programming; maintains maritime library.

PROGRAMS: Community Outreach; Concerts; Elder's Programs; Exhibits; Facility Rental; Family Programs; Film/Video; Garden Tours; Interpretation; Lectures; Living History; Publication; Research Library/Archives; School-Based Curriculum

COLLECTIONS: [1830-1929] Historic watercraft, marine paintings and prints, figureheads and wood carvings, ship models, nautical instruments, manuscripts, ship's logs and plans, photos video archives.

HOURS: Yr Daily 9-5

ADMISSION: $16, Children $8

NAUGATUCK

1217
Naugatuck Historical Society
87 Church St, 06770 [PO Box 317, 06770]; (c) New Haven

Private non-profit/ 1959/ staff: 5(v)/ members: 300

HISTORICAL SOCIETY; HISTORY MUSEUM: Operates museum focused on local history and environment with emphasis on the industrial age, promoting the interest and education of all age groups.

PROGRAMS: Annual Meeting; Community Outreach; School-Based Curriculum

COLLECTIONS: [1800-1970] Period knives

and buttons; rubber footwear; reference books, and clocks.

HOURS: Yr W 12-3, Th 2-5

NEW BRITAIN

1218
Local History Room of the New Britain Public Library
20 High St, 06051; (p) (860) 224-3155; (f) (860) 223-6729; www.nbpl.lib.ct.us; (c) Hartford

Private non-profit/ 1977/ New Britain Institute/ staff: 1(p)

Paper/print repository for the city of New Britain.

PROGRAMS: Elder's Programs

COLLECTIONS: [Mid 1800s-present] Industrial histories; catalogs; ephemera in addition to genealogies; Elihu Burritt collection; photos, slides, maps; city directories.

HOURS: Yr M 9-2, W 9-2

1219
New Britain Industrial Museum
185 Main St, 06051; (p) (860) 832-8654; odieinch@aol.com; (c) Hartford

Private non-profit/ 1995/ New Britain Institute/ staff: 25(v)/ members: 250

HISTORIC PRESERVATION AGENCY: Maintains collection of New Britain products representing "the Hardware City of the World."

PROGRAMS: Annual Meeting; Community Outreach; Exhibits; Guided Tours; Living History; Publication

COLLECTIONS: [1800-present] Period products by the Stanley Works, Landers, Frary and Clark, Fafnir Bearing Co., American Hardware, North and Judd.

HOURS: Yr M-F 1-5

ADMISSION: No charge

1220
New Britain Youth Museum
30 High St, 06051; (p) (860) 225-3020; (f) (860) 229-4982; NBYMDWTN@PortOne.com; (c) Hartford

Private non-profit/ 1956/ New Britain Institiute/ staff: 8(f); 8(p); 20(v)/ members: 300/publication: *Ramblings*

HISTORY MUSEUM: Encourages children and their families to explore the history and cultures of CT and the world through changing exhibits.

PROGRAMS: Annual Meeting; Community Outreach; Exhibits; Family Programs; Festivals; Guided Tours; Lectures; Publication; School-Based Curriculum

COLLECTIONS: [Late 18th c-present] Historical, international/cultural, ethnographic, and children's material culture; natural

NEW CANAAN

1221
Hanford-Silliman House
33 Oenoke Ridge, 06840 [13 Oenoke Ridge, 06840]; (p) (203) 966-1776; (f) (203) 972-5917; nchs@snet.net; danen.and.new-canaan.com/nchistory

1764/ staff: 3(f); 1(p); 152(v)

COLLECTIONS: [18th c] Early American furniture, pewter, samplers, quilts; Genealogical and local history. Extensive research library located in Town House at same location.

HOURS: Seasonal

1222
New Canaan Historical Society, The
13 Oenoke Ridge, 06840; (p) (203) 966-1776; (f) (203) 972-5917; newcanaan.historical@ snet.net; www.nchistory.org; (c) Fairfield

Private non-profit/ 1889/ staff: 3(f); 1(p); 102(v)/ members: 760

Collects local artifacts, genealogy, and history for the purposes of publication, education, exhibition, and preservation of the past.

PROGRAMS: Annual Meeting; Exhibits; Facility Rental; Family Programs; Festivals; Guided Tours; Lectures; Living History; Research Library/Archives

COLLECTIONS: [19th c.] Archives; costumes; drugstore furnishings; tools; doll collection; JohnRogers sculptures; historic printing office.

HOURS: Yr varies

ADIMISSION: Donations requested

NEW HAVEN

1223
Beinecke Rare Book and Manuscript Library
121 Wall St, 06520 [PO Box 208240, 06520-8240]; (p) (203) 432-2977; (f) (203) 432-4047; ellen.cordes@yale.edu; www.library.yale.edu/beinecke/; (c) New Haven

Private non-profit/ 1963/ Yale University/ staff: 42(f)/publication: *Yale University Library Gazette*

Collects early and important works in all fields of history and literature with particular emphasis on European and American literature and history, including African American, Native American, and western American history.

PROGRAMS: Exhibits; Lectures; Publication; Research Library/Archives

COLLECTIONS: [1200-2000] Manuscripts from papyri to contemporary archives; early printed books through the end of the eighteenth century and rare titles in history and literature after 1800; original art, prints, and photos.

HOURS: Yr M-F 8:30-5; Exhibition viewing: M-F 8:30-5, Sa 10-5 when Yale is in session

1224
Fort Nathan Hale Restoration Projects, Inc.
Woodward Ave, 06533 [PO Box 9244, 06533]; (p) (203) 946-6970; (c) New Haven

City; Private non-profit/ 1969/ staff: 3(f); 1(p); 25(v)/ members: 105

HISTORIC SITE; LIVING HISTORY/OUTDOOR MUSEUM: Preserve, maintain and restore two historic forts; historical education.

PROGRAMS: Annual Meeting; Film/Video; Guided Tours; Living History; Publication; Reenactments

COLLECTIONS: [1860-early 1900s] Rem-

nants of Civil War fort; spikes, bottles, clay pipes, household items.

HOURS: May-Sept M-Sa 10-4, Sun 12-4

ADMISSION: No charge

1225
Knights of Columbus Headquarters Museum-Archives
1 State St, 06511; (p) (203) 772-2130; www.kofc-supreme-council-org; (c) New Haven

Private non-profit/ 1982/ Knights of Columbus Charities, Inc./ staff: 4(f)

Preserves artifacts and a library focused on the history of the Knights of Columbus, the Catholic Church, and Christopher Columbus.

PROGRAMS: Exhibits; Film/Video; Publication; Research Library/Archives

COLLECTIONS: [1882-present] Fine and decorative paintings, prints, and sculpture; photos; costumes; manuscripts and library.

HOURS: Yr M-F 8-4:30

1226
New Haven Colony Historical Society
114 Whitney Ave, 06510; (p) (203) 562-4183; (f) (203) 562-4183; (c) New Haven

Private non-profit/ 1862/ staff: 5(f); 4(p); 20(v)/ members: 950/publication: *Journal of the New Haven Historical Society*

ART MUSEUM; GENEALOGICAL SOCIETY; HISTORY MUSEUM; HOUSE MUSEUM: Preservation of the Pardee-Morris House and collections documenting regional history; education through public programs.

PROGRAMS: Annual Meeting; Community Outreach; Exhibits; Family Programs; Guided Tours; Lectures; Publication; Research Library/Archives; School-Based Curriculum

COLLECTIONS: [18th-19th c] Printed titles and manuscripts on regional history; local fine and decorative arts; photos.

HOURS: Museum: Yr T-F 10-5, Sa 2-5, Sept-June Su 2-5; Library: Yr T-F 1-5

ADMISSION: $2, Student $1.50, Children $1, Seniors $1.50

1227
Pardee-Morris House
325 Lighthouse Rd, 06512; (p) (203) 562-4183
HOUSE MUSEUM

NEW LONDON

1228
Joshua Hempstead House
11 Hempstead St, 06320; (p) (860) 443-7749, (860) 247-8996

1678

COLLECTIONS: [1700-1730] Excellent furniture, early 18th c. many family artifacts; Hempsted family papers: mostly 19th c.

HOURS: Seasonal

1229
Monte Cristo Cottage Museum
325 Pequot Ave, 06355; (p) (860) 443-0051; (f) (860) 443-9653; (c) New London

Private non-profit/ 1974/ Eugene O'Neil The-

ater Center/ staff: 2(p)/ members: 250

HISTORIC SITE; HOUSE MUSEUM: Preservation of Nobel Prize Dramatist Eugene O'Neil's boyhood home.

PROGRAMS: Annual Meeting; Community Outreach; Exhibits; Facility Rental; Guided Tours; Interpretation; Lectures

COLLECTIONS: [1885-1920] Memorabilia concerning the playwright, his family, and his works.

HOURS:June-Sept T-Sa 10-5, Sun 1-5

ADIMISSION: $4

1230
New London County Historical Society, Inc.
11 Blinman St, 06320; (p) (860) 443-1209; (f) (860) 443-1209; (c) New London

Private non-profit/ 1870/ staff: 1(f); 2(p); 1(v)/ members: 250

HISTORIC SITE; HISTORICAL SOCIETY; RESEARCH CENTER: Collects and preserves material related to regional history.

PROGRAMS: Exhibits; Family Programs; Garden Tours; Guided Tours; Interpretation; Lectures

COLLECTIONS: [18th-early 20th c] Manuscripts, maps, newspaper volumes, and rare books; period furnishings and paintings; Ralph Earl family portraits; museum artifacts; photos.

HOURS: Yr W-F 1-4, Sa 10-4; Research: by appt

ADMISSION: $5, Student $2, Children $1, Seniors $4; Research Fee $15

NEW MILFORD

1231
Milford Historical Society and Museum
6 Aspetuck Ave, 06776 [PO Box 359, 06776-0359]; (p) (860) 354-3069; DJPD@ Freewwweb.com; www.nmhistorical.org; (c) Litchfield

Private non-profit/ 1915/ staff: 3(p); 75(v)/ members: 150

ART MUSEUM; HISTORIC PRESERVATION AGENCY; HISTORY MUSEUM; HOUSE MUSEUM; RESEARCH CENTER: Collects, preserves, and presents local history; interprets the past for educational purposes.

PROGRAMS: Annual Meeting; Community Outreach; Exhibits; Family Programs; Festivals; Guided Tours; Interpretation; Lectures; Publication; Research Library/Archives

COLLECTIONS: [18th-19th c] Portraits by Ralph Earl and Richard Jeneys; furniture, paintings, glass, silver, textiles, toys, tools, vegetable ivory buttons; genealogy; regional pottery; Merwin-Wilson pewter.

HOURS: May-Oct Th F Su, 1-4

ADMISSION: $3, Student $2, Seniors $2

NEWINGTON

1232
Kellogg-Eddy House & Museum
679 Willard Ave, 06111-2615; (p) (860) 666-7118

NIANTIC

1233
Thomas Lee House
226 W Main St, 06357 [PO Box 112, East Lyme, 06333]; (p) (860) 739-6070

1660

HISTORIC HOUSE:Built by Thomas Lee, early settler and large land owner, who served as Justice of the Peace in the late 17th century.

COLLECTIONS: [Early colonial]

NORWALK

1234
Lockwood-Mathews Mansion Museum
295 West Ave, 06850; (p) (203) 838-9799; (f) (203) 838-1434; (c) Fairfield

Private non-profit/ 1966/ staff: 2(f); 4(p); 150(v)/ members: 650

HOUSE MUSEUM: Preserves and interprets Civil War-era mansion; collects and exhibits furnishings and decorative arts associated with the original owners; sponsors educational events and programs.

PROGRAMS: Annual Meeting; Community Outreach; Concerts; Elder's Programs; Exhibits; Facility Rental; Family Programs; Festivals; Guided Tours; Interpretation; Lectures; Research Library/Archives; School-Based Curriculum

COLLECTIONS: [Victorian Era] Original artifacts belonging to Lockwood and Mathews families; high-style Victorian era furnishings, textiles, and decorative arts.

1235
Norwalk Historical Society, Inc.
2 E Wall St, 06852 [PO Box 335, 06852]; (p) (203) 846-0525; (c) Fairfield

Private non-profit/ 1899/ members: 80/publication: *Norwalk*

HISTORIC SITE; HISTORICAL SOCIETY; HISTORY MUSEUM: To preserve, promote, and exhibit the history of Norwalk; Its historical records, sites, and genealogical.

PROGRAMS: Annual Meeting; Exhibits; Family Programs; Guided Tours; Interpretation; Lectures; Publication; School-Based Curriculum

COLLECTIONS: [1640-1860] Documents, antiques, and artifacts related to Norwalk.

HOURS: May-Sept Su 1-4 and by appt

ADMISSION: Donations accepted

NORWICH

1236
Society of the Founders of Norwich, The
348 Washington St, 06360 [PO Box 13, 06360]; (p) (860) 889-9440; (c) New London

Private non-profit/ 1901/ Board of Managers/ staff: 2(p); 18(v)/ members: 400

Preserves the history of the original 35 settlers of Norwich; encourages the publication and study of local history; preserves documents, relics, and buildings pertaining to local history.

PROGRAMS: Annual Meeting; Community Outreach; Exhibits; Guided Tours; Interpretation

COLLECTIONS: Regional clocks, silver, books, and documents.

HOURS: Apr 1-Dec 1 T-Su 1-4

ADMISSION: $5, Children $2, Seniors $3

OLD LYME

1237
Lyme Historical Society; Florence Griswold Museum
96 Lyme St, 06371; (p) (860) 434-5542; (f) (860) 434-6259; flogris@connix.com; www.flogris.org; (c) New London

Private non-profit/ 1946/ staff: 8(f); 3(p); 200(v)/ members: 1856

ART MUSEUM; HISTORIC SITE; HISTORY MUSEUM: Home of an Impressionist art colony; houses new Hartman Education Center with recreated historic gardens.

PROGRAMS: Community Outreach; Concerts; Exhibits; Facility Rental; Family Programs; Festivals; Guided Tours; Interpretation; Lectures; Research Library/Archives

COLLECTIONS: [Early settlement- 1940] Fine art; artist studio material; decorative arts; historic toys, dolls, textiles, costumes, accessories, furniture; archival material.

HOURS: Apr-Dec T-Sa 10-5 Su

OLD MYSTIC

1238
Indian and Colonial Research Center, Inc.
37 Main St, 06372 [PO Box 525, 06372]; (p) (860) 536-6512

Private non-profit/ 1965/ staff: 3(p); 10(v)/ members: 225/publication: *Woodland Indian*

Preserves local history by collecting, and creating public access to, artifacts and research information.

PROGRAMS: Annual Meeting; Community Outreach; Film/Video; Guided Tours; Publication; Research Library/Archives

COLLECTIONS: [Colonial-present] Photos, period postcards, manuscripts, and rare old school books, and maps; printed genealogies, court records, land records, research archives, and oral history.

OLD SAYBROOK

1239
Old Saybrook Historical Society
350 Main St, 06475 [PO Box 4, 06475]; (p) (280) 395-1635; oldsaybrook.histrcl@snet.net; (c) Middlesex

Private non-profit/ 1959/ staff: 15(p); 127(v)/ members: 408

GENEALOGICAL SOCIETY; HISTORIC PRESERVATION AGENCY; HISTORIC SITE; HOUSE MUSEUM: Encourages the preservation of New England cultural and historical heritage by serving the public through exhibits, education, and research.

PROGRAMS: Annual Meeting; Exhibits; Facility Rental; Garden Tours; Guided Tours; Interpretation; Lectures; Research Library/Archives; School-Based Curriculum

COLLECTIONS: [1631-1900] A 1767 example of early Georgian Architecture; period fireplaces, furniture, portraits, and artifacts.

HOURS: May-Sept Research: M-Th

ORANGE

1240
Orange Historical Society, Inc.
605 Orange Center Rd, 06477 [PO Box 784, 06477-0784]; (p) (203) 795-3106; (f) (203) 795-3106; www.orangehistory.org; (c) New Haven

Private non-profit/ 1964/ staff: 20(v)/ members: 380

HISTORICAL SOCIETY; HOUSE MUSEUM: Collects and preserves historical material related to early settlement and subsequent history of Orange and its surrounding area; Maintains three historical sites.

PROGRAMS: Annual Meeting; Community Outreach; Exhibits; Festivals; Guided Tours; Living History; Reenactments; School-Based Curriculum

COLLECTIONS: [1840-1960] Restored 1740 farmhouse, 1878 former Town Hall, 1740 house.

HOURS: Apr-Oct Su 1-4 and by appt

ADMISSION: No charge

PLAINVILLE

1241
Plainville Historical Society, Inc.
29 Pierce St, 06062; (p) (860) 747-6577; (c) Hartford

Private non-profit/ 1969/ staff: 1(p); 30(v)/ members: 110

HISTORICAL SOCIETY; HISTORY MUSEUM: Preserves local history.

PROGRAMS: Community Outreach; Concerts; Exhibits; Family Programs; Film/Video; Guided Tours; Lectures; Research Library/Archives; School-Based Curriculum

COLLECTIONS: Paintings; Farmington Canal diorama; Victorian parlor; nature room; period toys and tools.

HOURS: May-Dec W-Sa 12-3

ADMISSION: Donations

RIDGEFIELD

1242
Keeler Tavern Preservation Society, Inc.
132 Main St, 06877 [PO Box 204, 06877]; (p) (203) 438-5485; (f) (203) 438-9953; (c) Fairfield

Private non-profit/ 1965/ staff: 1(f); 75(v)/ members: 400/publication: *Tavern Times*

GARDEN; HISTORIC PRESERVATION AGENCY; HISTORIC SITE; HOUSE MUSEUM: Preserves and protects historic Keeler Tavern; promotes appreciation of local history and heritage by providing educational and cultural programs.

PROGRAMS: Concerts; Exhibits; Facility Rental; Festivals; Guided Tours; Living History; Publication; Research Library/Archives

COLLECTIONS: [18th-early 20th c.] 19th c. tavern; period British cannonball; period furnishings, cookware; archival material; Cass Gilbert designed garden house and barn; costumes; glass photographic plates; tavern signs; artwork.

HOURS: Feb-Dec W Sa-Su 1-4

ADMISSION: $4, Children $1, Seniors $2

ROCKY HILL

1243
Dinosaur State Park
400 W St, 06067; (p) (860) 529-5816; (f) (860) 257-1405; www.dinosaurstatepark.org; (c) Hartford

State/ 1968/ staff: 5(f); 5(p); 35(v)/ members: 250/publication: *Tracks and Trails*

Protects and interprets dinosaur tracks on site; depicts the geology, paleontology, and climate of CT Valley 200 mill. years ago; maintenance of ancient plant arboretum.

PROGRAMS: Exhibits; Family Programs; Film/Video; Garden Tours; Guided Tours; Interpretation; Lectures; Publication; Research Library/Archives

COLLECTIONS: [Triassic, Jurassic] In site dinosaur tracks; local fossils, rocks and minerals; ancient trees and plants.

HOURS: Yr T-Su 9-4:30

ADMISSION: $2, Children $1

1244
Rocky Hill Historical Society, Inc.
785 Old Main St, 06067 [PO Box 185, 06067-0185]; (p) (860) 563-6704; (c) Hartford

Private non-profit/ 1962/ staff: 10(v)/ members: 144

HISTORICAL SOCIETY: Collects and catalogs items pertaining to local history; operates a historical library.

PROGRAMS: Annual Meeting; Exhibits; Research Library/Archives

COLLECTIONS: [1843-present]

HOURS: June-Nov T 10-12, Sa 2-4, Su

SALISBURY

1245
Holley-Williams House Museum and The Salisbury Cannon Museum
15 Millerton Rd/ Rte 44, 06068 [PO Box 553, 06068]; (p) (860) 435-2878; (f) (860) 435-6469; kakeser@discovernet.net; www.salisburyassociation.org; (c) Litchfield

Private non-profit/ 1971/ Salisbury Association, Inc./ staff: 1(f); 15(p); 10(v)/ members: 220

Operates family museums representing 18th and 19th c life.

PROGRAMS: Community Outreach; Concerts; Elder's Programs; Exhibits; Family Programs; Guided Tours; Interpretation; Living History; Reenactments; Theatre

COLLECTIONS: [18th-19th c] Family furnishings; portraits; pocketknife exhibits from the 1876 Centennial Exhibition; period kitchen implements.

HOURS: Mid June-Aug Sa-Su 12-5 and Yr by appt.

1246
Salisbury Association History Room
Scoville Memorial Library, Main St, 06068 [Box 553, 06068]; (p) (860) 435-1287; (f) (860) 435-6127; nsills01@snet.net; www.salisburyassociation.org; (c) Litchfield

Private non-profit/ 1902/ staff: 1(p)/ members: 900

HISTORICAL SOCIETY; HISTORY MUSEUM; HOUSE MUSEUM; LIBRARY AND/OR ARCHIVES: The Salisbury Association is the blanket organization for history, land trust, and the 19th Century House Museum, a community organization promoting best interest of the area.

PROGRAMS: Annual Meeting; Community Outreach; Exhibits; Reenactments

COLLECTIONS: [1741-present] Books on local history, iron mining, manufacturing, and railroads, oral histories, genealogy.

HOURS: Yr T-Sa varies

ADMISSION: No charge

SHARON

1247
Gay-Hoyt House
18 Main St, 06069 [PO Box 511, 06069]; (p) (860) 364-5688

1775/ staff: 1(p); 3(v)

HISTORIC HOUSE

COLLECTIONS: [1775-1950] Vernacular collection of furniture, decorative arts, textiles. Highlights include 3 Ammi Philips portraits, Silver Tea Set by Silversmith John McMullin, Philadelphia.

1248
Sharon Historical Society, Inc.
18 Main St, 06069 [PO Box 511, 06069]; (p) (860) 364-5688; www.sharonhist.org; (c) Litchfield

Private non-profit/ 1911/ staff: 1(p); 30(v)/ members: 302

HISTORICAL SOCIETY; HISTORY MUSEUM: Preserves, promotes, and disseminates regional history and culture through changing exhibits, hands-on children's programs, and publications.

PROGRAMS: Annual Meeting; Community Outreach; Exhibits; Family Programs; Festivals; Garden Tours; Guided Tours; Interpretation; Lectures; Publication; Research Library/Archives

COLLECTIONS: [1750-present] Decorative arts, furniture, folk art, tools, textiles, and photos; archival collection and library.

HOURS: Mid June-mid Oct F-Su 12-5; mid Oct-mid June T 2-5, W-F

SHELTON

1249
Shelton Historical Society
70 Ripton Rd, 06484 [PO Box 2155, 06484]; (p) (203) 925-1803; (f) (203) 925-1803; shltn.hst.soc@snet.net; (c) Fairfield

Private non-profit/ 1969/ Board of Directors/ staff: 2(p); 30(v)/ members: 150

HISTORICAL SOCIETY: Discovers, collects, and preserves historic pieces to record and illustrate the history of the community;

PROGRAMS: Annual Meeting; Community Outreach; Elder's Programs; Exhibits; Family Programs; Festivals; Guided Tours; Interpretation; Lectures; Living History; Research Library/Archives; School-Based Curriculum

COLLECTIONS: [Late 1800s] Household items and farming implements; textiles, tools, and image collections.

HOURS: Mar-Nov Su 1-4 and by appt

ADMISSION: $2, Student $1, Seniors

1250
Tree Farm Archives
272 Israel Hill Rd, 06484; (p) (203) 929-0126; (c) Fairfield

Private non-profit/ 1960/ staff: 1(v)

RESEARCH CENTER: Collecting and cataloging historic letters, records, and manuscripts.

PROGRAMS: Elder's Programs; Family Programs; Lectures; Research Library/Archives

COLLECTIONS: [1750-1950] Period letters and documents.

HOURS: By Appt

SHERMAN

1251
Sherman Historical Society, Inc.
10 Rte 37 Center, 06784; (p) (860) 354-3083; (f) (860) 350-1187; shermanhistsoc@aol.com; www.shermanhistorical.org; (c) Fairfield

Private non-profit/ 1975/ Board of Directors/ staff: 33(v)/ members: 346/publication: *S.H.S. Newsletter, and others*

HISTORICAL SOCIETY; HISTORY MUSEUM; HOUSE MUSEUM: Preservation of historic buildings and businesses.

PROGRAMS: Annual Meeting; Exhibits; Facility Rental; Family Programs; Guided Tours; Interpretation; Lectures; Living History; Publication; Reenactments; Research Library/Archives

COLLECTIONS: [1802-present] Regional furniture in an 1829 Federal house; photos; archives and library for state and local history.

HOURS: House Museum: May-Oct Sa-Su 11-5; The Old Store Mar-Dec W-Sa 11-5

ADMISSION: No charge

SIMSBURY

1252
Captain Elisha Phelps House
800 Hopmeadow St, 06070 [c/o Simsbury Historical Society, PO Box 2, 06070]; (p)

(860) 658-2500; (f) (860) 651-4354; simsbury historical@juno.com

1771/ staff: 2(p); 110(v)

HOUSE MUSEUM: Home of Captain Elisha Phelps, Revolutionary War soldier and brother of Major General Noah Phelps. The house served as a tavern during the canal period, 1827-1848. The museum complex includes ten other buildings.

COLLECTIONS: [1827-1848] Domestic life, textiles, farm implements. Houses the Ensign-Bickford safety fuse manufacturing equipment on site.; Published works, photos, and manuscript collection pertaining to Simsbury

SOMERS

1253
Somers Mountain Museum of Natural History and Primitive Technology
332 Turnpike Rd, 06071 [PO Box 55, 06071-0055]; (p) (860) 749-4129; (f) (860) 749-1634; somersmtn@aol.com; www.somersmountain.org; (c) Tolland

Private non-profit/ 1936/ staff: 5(p); 10(v)/ members: 30

HISTORY MUSEUM; LIVING HISTORY/OUTDOOR MUSEUM: Offers educational and interpretive programs to schools and youth groups; teaches workshops in primitive living skills and Native American arts and crafts; maintains a museum.

PROGRAMS: Community Outreach; Exhibits; Family Programs; Guided Tours; Interpretation; Lectures; School-Based Curriculum

COLLECTIONS: [Prehistory-present] Native American artifacts from across the Americas; interpretive displays.

HOURS: Apr-Dec Su

SOUTH GLASTONBURY

1254
Welles Shipman Ward House
972 Main St, 06073; (p) (860) 633-6890

SOUTH MERIDEN

1255
Meriden Historical Society
1090 Hanover St, 06451 [PO Box 3005, 06451]; (p) (203) 639-1913; (c) New Haven

1892/ Board/ staff: 5(v)

HISTORICAL SOCIETY; HOUSE MUSEUM; RESEARCH CENTER: Museum and research center featuring silver catalogs and local history.

PROGRAMS: Research Library/Archives

COLLECTIONS: [1850-1950] Products of local manufacturing (International Silver, Charles Parker Miller Co., Manning-Bowman, Handel, C.F. Monroe)

HOURS: Research Center: Yr W 2-4:30

ADMISSION: No charge

SOUTHINGTON

1256
Barnes Museum
85 N Main St, 06489; (p) (860) 628-5426; (c)

Hartford

City/ 1973/ Southington Public Library Board of Trustees/ staff: 1(f); 1(p); 20(v)/ members: 50

HOUSE MUSEUM: Interprets home of prominent local family during period of 1836 to 1973.

PROGRAMS: Community Outreach; Exhibits; Facility Rental; Guided Tours

COLLECTIONS: [1880-1940] Extensive glassware collection featuring 1100 goblets, 52 diaries, clothing, Victorian toys, books, games, and local genealogy.

HOURS: Yr M,T,W,F 1-5, Th 1-7

1257
Southington Historical Society
239 Main St, 06489 [PO Box 726, 06489]; (p) (860) 621-4811; southingtonhistory@yahoo.com; www.southington-history.org; (c) Hartford

Private non-profit/ staff: 15(v)/ members: 130

HISTORICAL SOCIETY; HISTORY MUSEUM: Preserves local history.

PROGRAMS: Annual Meeting; Exhibits; Family Programs

COLLECTIONS: [1800s] Photographs, artifacts, and relics from Southington; facade of the county's first bolt factory.

HOURS: 1st Sa of month 12-3

ADMISSION: No charge

STAMFORD

1258
Hoyt-Barnum House
733 Bedford St, 06902 [1508 High Ridge Rd, 06903]; (p) (203) 329-1183, (203) 322-1565; (f) (203) 322-1607; ebaulsir@ix.netcom.com; www.cslnet.ctstfteu.edu/stamford/index/html

1699/ staff: 3(f); 2(p); 42(v)

COLLECTIONS: [1699 and 1813] Furniture, tools; manuscripts, land records, genealogical records, diaries.

HOURS: Seasonal

1259
Stamford Historical Society
1508 High Ridge Rd, 06903; (p) (203) 329-1183; (f) (203) 322-1607; www.stamfordhistory.org; (c) Fairfield

Private non-profit/ 1901/ staff: 3(f); 2(p); 40(v)/ members: 400

HISTORIC SITE; HISTORY MUSEUM: Collects, preserves, conserves, interprets, and exhibits materials related to regional history.

PROGRAMS: Annual Meeting; Exhibits; Facility Rental; Family Programs; Lectures; Publication; Research Library/Archives; School-Based Curriculum

COLLECTIONS: [1641-present] Manuscripts, photos, maps, books, and periodicals; decorative arts, textiles, fine arts, and tools; Hoyt Barnum House built in 1699.

HOURS: Yr T-Sa

STONINGTON

1260
Captain Nathaniel B. Palmer House, The
40 Palmer St, 06378 [PO Box 103, 06378]; (p) (860) 535-8445

1852/ staff: 1(f); 22(v)

COLLECTIONS: [1850-1895] Portraits & Photos of Capt. N. B. Palmer & Family; memorabilia of shipping career: ship's Bible for Oriental scale model of Hero, hand carved ditty box from Hero; Palmer papers.

HOURS: Seasonal

STORRS

1261
Thomas J. Dodd Research Center
405 Babbadge Rd Box U-205, 06269-1205; (p) (860) 486-4500; (f) (860) 486-4521; doddref@lib.uconn.edu; www.lib.uconn.edu/DoddCenter; (c) Windham

1963/ University of Connecticut/ staff: 8(f); 21(p); 7(v)

RESEARCH CENTER: Collects, preserves, and makes accessible rare books, archives, and special collections to researchers, students, faculty, and the general public.

PROGRAMS: Exhibits; Facility Rental; Lectures; Research Library/Archives; School-Based Curriculum

COLLECTIONS: [1900-present] Archives, books, and manuscripts on alternative politics and culture, American and English literature, children's literature, CT business, politics, and labor, and Hispanic history.

HOURS: Yr M-F 8:30-4:30

STRATFORD

1262
Boothe Memorial Park and Museum
Main St Putney, 06615 [PO Box 902, 06615]; (p) (203) 381-2046; www.connix.com/~csl; (c) Fairfield

Joint/ 1955/ staff: 40(v)/ members: 350/publication: *Boothe Memorial Park and Museum Newsletter*

GARDEN; HISTORIC SITE

PROGRAMS: Concerts; Exhibits; Facility Rental; Festivals; Garden Tours; Guided Tours; Publication; School-Based Curriculum

COLLECTIONS: [1890] Americana emphasizing trades such as farming, ice harvesting, and blacksmithing; early tools; Victorian exhibits; and miniature lighthouse, windmill, and basilica.

HOURS: June-Oct T-F 11-1, Sa-Su 1-4

1263
Judson House
967 Academy Hill Rd, 06497 [967 Academy Hill Rd, 06497]; (p) (203) 378-0630

1264
Stratford Historical Society
967 Academy Hill, 06615 [Pox 382, 06615]; (p) (203) 378-0630; (c) Fairfield

Private non-profit/ 1925/ staff: 3(p); 20(v)/ members: 400

HISTORICAL SOCIETY; HISTORY MUSEUM; HOUSE MUSEUM

PROGRAMS: Annual Meeting; Community Outreach; Exhibits; Festivals; Guided Tours; Interpretation; Research Library/Archives

COLLECTIONS: [17th-19th c] Furniture, photos, glass, china, art, toys, and ephemera; tools and farm items.

HOURS: May-Oct W, Sa-Su 11-4

ADMISSION: $2

SUFFIELD

1265
Hatheway House
55 S Main St, 06078 [66 Forest St, Hartford, 06105]; (p) (860) 668-0055, (860) 247-8996; (f) (860) 249-4907

1761/ staff: 5(p); 10(v)

COLLECTIONS: [1760s and 1790s] Tin-glazed earthenwares

HOURS: Seasonal

TERRYVILLE

1266
Lock Museum of America, Inc.
230 Main St, 06786; (p) (860) 589-6359; (f) (860) 589-6359; www.lockmuseum.com; (c) Litchfield

Private non-profit/ 1972/ staff: 1(f); 4(p); 4(v)/ members: 450

HISTORY MUSEUM: Collects locks, keys, and ornate hardware; compiles information on locks, hardware and people in the industry.

PROGRAMS: Guided Tours

COLLECTIONS: [1500-1940] Period locks, keys, doorknobs, and ornate hardware.

HOURS: May-Oct T-Su 1:30-4:30

ADMISSION: $3

TOLLAND

1267
Hicks-Stearns Family Museum
42 Tolland Green, 06084 [PO Box 278, 06084]; (p) (860) 875-7552; (c) Tolland

Private non-profit/ 1978/ Board of Trustees/ staff: 3(p); 20(v)

HOUSE MUSEUM: Preserves buildings and grounds and offers programs and educational activities in order to foster an appreciation of history.

PROGRAMS: Community Outreach; Concerts; Elder's Programs; Exhibits; Facility Rental; Family Programs; Guided Tours; Interpretation; Living History; School-Based Curriculum

COLLECTIONS: [Victorian-mid 20th c] Family heirlooms, cloth tea balls, Victrola, faux bamboo furniture.

HOURS: Apr-Dec by appt

ADMISSION: $2

TORRINGTON

1268
Hotchkiss-Fyler House
192 Main St, 06790; (p) (860) 482-8260

1900/ staff: 2(f); 2(p)

HOUSE MUSEUM

COLLECTIONS: [1956] Impressive collection of art glass and porcelain (European, American, Chinese) Oriental carpets; paintings by Ammi Phillips, Winfield Scott Clime and George Laurence Nelson; French Provincial style furnishings; stenciled walls; photos.

HOURS: Seasonal

1269
Torrington Historical Society, Inc.
192 Main St, 06790; (p) (860) 482-8260; (c) Litchfield

Private non-profit/ 1944/ staff: 2(f); 2(p); 10(v)/ members: 450

HISTORICAL SOCIETY; HISTORY MUSEUM; HOUSE MUSEUM: Preserves and interprets local history; operates Hotchkiss-Fyler House Museum.

PROGRAMS: Community Outreach; Concerts; Exhibits; Facility Rental; Family Programs; Publication; Research Library/Archives; School-Based Curriculum

COLLECTIONS: [Pre-Columbian-present] Furnishings, photos, and archives pertaining to the Hotchkiss-Fyler family and house; local history collection of artifacts.

HOURS: Apr-Oct, Dec T-F 10-4, Sa-Su

UNIONVILLE

1270
Unionville Museum
15 School St, 06085; (c) Hartford

Private non-profit/ 1984/ staff: 30(v)/ members: 650

Collects and exhibits pictures and artifacts of local historical interest, located in a 1917 Andrew Carnegie Library Building.

PROGRAMS: Concerts; Exhibits; Guided Tours

COLLECTIONS: [1840-1960] Photos, books, tools, costumes, and other artifacts of local interest.

HOURS: Yr W, Sa-Su 2-4

ADMISSION: No charge

VERNON

1271
New England Civil War Museum
Park Place, 06066 [62 Hanson Dr, 06066]; (p) (860) 871-1552; rsdent@snet.net; (c) Hartford

Private non-profit/ 1993/ Alden Skinner Camp/SUV/ staff: 6(v)

HISTORIC SITE; HISTORY MUSEUM: Preservation of Civil War artifacts, GAR collection, and US history library.

PROGRAMS: Community Outreach; Exhibits; Facility Rental; Lectures; Research Library/Archives

COLLECTIONS: [Civil War] Civil War artifacts, photos, print, and books; GAR collection.

HOURS: Yr Su 12-4

ADMISSION: Donations accepted

WASHINGTON

1272
Gunn Memorial Library Inc.
5 Wykeham Rd, 06793 [PO Box 1273, 06793]; (p) (860) 868-7756; (f) (860) 868-7586; gunnmus@biblio.org; www.biblio.org/gunn; (c) Litchfield

Private non-profit/ 1908/ staff: 4(f); 7(p); 56(v)/ members: 1032

Maintains public library and historical museum with a focus on local history.

PROGRAMS: Annual Meeting; Community Outreach; Exhibits; Family Programs; Interpretation; Lectures; Publication; Research Library/Archives

COLLECTIONS: [19th- early 20th c] Period clothing textiles, decorative arts, photos, tools; genealogical, state, and local history materials.

HOURS: Yr Th-Su 12-4

ADMISSION: Donations accepted

WATERBURY

1273
Mattatuck Historical Society, Inc.
144 W Main St, 06702; (p) (203) 753-0381; (f) (203) 756-6283; info@mattatuckmuseum.org; www.mattatuckmuseum.org; (c) New Haven

Private non-profit/ 1902/ staff: 6(f); 12(p); 150(v)/ members: 900

ART MUSEUM; HISTORICAL SOCIETY; HISTORY MUSEUM: Exhibits works of CT artists; offers public programs, school programs, and professional development for teachers.

PROGRAMS: Annual Meeting; Community Outreach; Concerts; Exhibits; Facility Rental; Family Programs; Guided Tours; Lectures; Research Library/Archives; School-Based Curriculum; Theatre

COLLECTIONS: [Colonial-present] Local history collections; art works by regional artists.

HOURS: Yr T-Sa 10-5; Sept-June Su 12-5

ADMISSION: $4

WATERFORD

1274
Beebe-Phillips House
Jordan Green, Route 156, 06385 [Waterford Historical Society, PO Box 117, 06385]; (p) (860) 442-2707

WEST HARTFORD

1275
Museum of American Political Life, University of Hartford
200 Bloomfield Ave, 06117; (p) (860) 768-4090; (f) (860) 768-5159; Zdavis@mail.hartford.edu; (c) Hartford

Private non-profit/ 1989/ staff: 2(f); 2(p); 8(v)

HISTORY MUSEUM: Presents history of presidential politics.

PROGRAMS: Community Outreach; Exhibits; Lectures

COLLECTIONS: [Late 18th c-present] Political memorabilia.

HOURS: Yr T-F 11-4, Sa-Su 12-4

ADMISSION: Donations accepted

1276
Noah Webster House/Museum of West Hartford History
227 S Main St, 06107; (p) (860) 521-5362; (f) (860) 521-4036; www.ctstateu.edu/~noahweb/noahwebster.html; (c) Hartford

Private non-profit/ 1965/ Board of Trustees/ staff: 4(f); 19(p); 82(v)/ members: 450

HISTORICAL SOCIETY; HISTORY MUSEUM; HOUSE MUSEUM: Cultivates an interest in history by telling the stories of West Hartford and its residents.

PROGRAMS: Exhibits; Family Programs; Garden Tours; Guided Tours; Interpretation; Lectures; Living History; Research Library/Archives; School-Based Curriculum

COLLECTIONS: [Mid 18th c-present] Decorative art objects, period furniture, local artifacts, manuscripts and documents, memorabilia, textiles, and pottery.

HOURS: Sept-June M,Th, F, Sa, Su 1-4; July-Aug M,Th,F 11-4, Sa-Su 1-4

ADMISSION: $5, Student $3, Children $1, Seniors $4

WESTPORT

1277
Westport Historical Society
25 Avery Pl, 06880; (p) (203) 222-1424; (f) (203) 221-0981; www.whsoc.org; (c) Fairfield

Private non-profit/ 1899/ staff: 1(f); 1(p); 100(v)/ members: 1200

HISTORIC SITE; HISTORICAL SOCIETY; HOUSE MUSEUM: Preserves Victorian house museum and 19th c. barn.

PROGRAMS: Annual Meeting; Community Outreach; Exhibits; Facility Rental; Garden Tours; Guided Tours; Lectures; Publication; Research Library/Archives

COLLECTIONS: [19th c.] Costumes, photos, archives.

HOURS: Yr T-Sa 10-4

ADMISSION: Donations accepted

1278
Wheeler House
25 Avery Place, 06880; (p) (203) 222-1424; (f) (203) 221-0981

1795/ staff: 1(f); 1(p); 35(v)

HOUSE MUSEUM

COLLECTIONS: [1860-1900] Victorian period living room, kitchen & parlor. Decorations, costumes, furnishings; Business records, ship's manifests, photo collection, house histories, famous artists, local authors.

WETHERSFIELD

1279
Buttolph-Williams House
249 Broad St, 06109 [66 Forest St, Hartford,

06105]; (p) (860) 247-8996, (860) 529-0612; (f) (860) 249-4907

1710/ staff: 6(p)

COLLECTIONS: [1710-1720] Extensive kitchenware; fine vernacular furniture

HOURS: Seasonal

1280
Webb-Deane-Stevens Museum
211 Main St, 06109; (p) (860) 529-0612; (f) (860) 571-8636; wdsmusem@aol.com; www.webb-deane-stevens.org; (c) Hartford

Private non-profit/ 1919/ National Society of Colonial Dames of America, Connecticut/ staff: 4(f); 17(p); 2(v)/ members: 164

GARDEN; HISTORIC SITE; HOUSE MUSEUM: Preserves, interprets, and presents the buildings, collections, and grounds that comprise the museum; increases public understanding of the history of the CT River Valley.

PROGRAMS: Concerts; Exhibits; Facility Rental; Family Programs; Garden Tours; Guided Tours; Interpretation; Lectures; Research Library/Archives; School-Based Curriculum

COLLECTIONS: [Colonial-colonial revival] Colonial houses and privies; decorative arts; furniture, silver, textiles, ceramics, and glass; colonial manuscripts and institutional records.

HOURS: May-Oct W-M 10-4; Nov-Apr Sa-Su 10-4

ADMISSION: $8, Student $4, Children $4, Seniors $7

1281
Wethersfield Historical Society
200 Main St, 06109 [150 Main St, 06109]; (p) (860) 529-7656; (f) (860) 529-1905; director@wethhist.org; www.wethhist.org; (c) Hartford

Private non-profit/ 1932/ staff: 2(f); 5(p); 145(v)/ members: 1034

HISTORICAL SOCIETY; HISTORY MUSEUM; HOUSE MUSEUM: Operates two museums, two historic houses, and a research library; interprets regional history through exhibitions and programs.

PROGRAMS: Annual Meeting; Concerts; Exhibits; Facility Rental; Family Programs; Festivals; Guided Tours; Interpretation; Lectures; Publication; Research Library/Archives; School-Based Curriculum

COLLECTIONS: [19th c.] Utilitarian object, furniture, paintings, tools and textiles; manuscripts and genealogies.

HOURS: Yr

WILLIMANTIC

1282
Windham Textile and History Museum
157 Union and Main St, 06226; (p) (860) 456-2178; (c) Windham

Private non-profit/ 1989/ Board of Directors/ staff: 1(f); 1(p); 30(v)/ members: 600

HISTORIC SITE; HISTORY MUSEUM; HOUSE MUSEUM: Collects, preserves, and interprets social history related to the water powered textile production.

PROGRAMS: Community Outreach; Concerts; Elder's Programs; Exhibits; Facility Rental; Family Programs; Festivals; Guided

Tours; Interpretation; Lectures; Living History; Publication; Reenactments; Research Library/Archives; School-Based Curriculum; Theatre

COLLECTIONS: [1870-1940] Machinery and accessories related to producing cotton thread; household furnishings; clothing; blueprints of mills.

HOURS: Yr F-Su 1-4, and by appt.

WILTON

1283
Weir Farm National Historic Site
735 Nod Hill Rd, 06897; (p) (203) 834-1896; (f) (203) 834-2421; wefa_interpretation@nps.gov; www.nps.gov/wefa; (c) Fairfield

Federal/ 1990/ National Park Service/ staff: 8(f); 2(p); 70(v)/ members: 150/publication: *Weir Farm News*

HISTORIC SITE: Preserves and interprets the summer home and workplace of Julian Alden Weir, a leading figure in American art and the development of American Impressionism.

PROGRAMS: Annual Meeting; Community Outreach; Concerts; Exhibits; Garden Tours; Guided Tours; Interpretation; Lectures; Publication; Research Library/Archives; School-Based Curriculum

COLLECTIONS: [1882-1919] Furnishings, garden implements, art supplies, artwork, photos, diaries and letters associated with Weir

WINCHESTER CENTER

1284
Winchester Center Historical Assoc.
1 Chapel Rd, 06094 [PO Box 112, 06094]; (p) (860) 379-4442; (c) Litchfield

Private non-profit/ 1971/ staff: 4(f); 8(v)/ members: 100/publication: *WCHA Newsletter*

GARDEN; HISTORICAL SOCIETY; HISTORY MUSEUM: Devoted to early local history.

PROGRAMS: Annual Meeting; Exhibits; Family Programs; Festivals; Guided Tours; Lectures; Living History; Publication; Reenactments

COLLECTIONS: [18th c.]

HOURS: June-Oct Su 2-4

ADMISSION: Donations accepted

WINDSOR

1285
Connecticut Valley Tobacco Historical Society, Inc.; Luddy/ Taylor Connecticut Valley Tobacco Museum,
135 Lang Rd, NW Park, 06095 [PO Box 241, 06095]; (p) (860) 285-1888; (c) Hartford

Private non-profit/ 1989/ staff: 1(p)/ members: 51

HISTORY MUSEUM, HISTORICAL SOCIETY: Preserves history and artifacts of cigar tobacco growing in the CT River Valley.

PROGRAMS: Annual Meeting; Elder's Programs; Exhibits; Film/Video; Research Library/Archives

COLLECTIONS: [1900-1950] Photos, scrap book; shade tobacco growing literature; period farm equip and shade cloth.

HOURS: Mar-May, Oct-Dec T-Th, Sa 12-4; June-Sept M-Sa 10-4

ADMISSION: No charge

1286
Doctor Hezekiah Chaffee House
96 Palisado Ave, 06095 [96 Palisado Ave, 06095]; (p) (860) 688-3813

1765/ staff: 1(f); 3(p); 12(v)

HOUSE MUSEUM

COLLECTIONS: [Late 18th-early 19th c] Period furnishings, medical instruments, pharmaceutical receipes and doctor's journals.; History of Windsor doctors, 1635-1968; doctor's journals from 18th & 19th c.

HOURS: Yr

1287
Windsor Historical Society, The
96 Palisado Ave, 06095; (p) (860) 688-3813; (f) (860) 687-1633; (c) Hartford

Private non-profit/ 1921/ staff: 1(f); 1(p); 20(v)/ members: 1010/publication: *Windsor Historical Society NEWS*

HISTORICAL SOCIETY: Represents the oldest English settlement in CT; operates a museum with four exhibit galleries and two historic homes and a research library.

PROGRAMS: Annual Meeting; Community Outreach; Exhibits; Guided Tours; Publication

HOURS: Yr T-Sa 10-4

ADMISSION: $3

WINDSOR LOCKS

1288
New England Air Museum
N end of Bradley Int'l Airport, 06096 [Bradley Int'l Airport, 06096]; (p) (860) 623-3305; (f) (860) 627-2820; debbie@neam.org; www.neam.org; (c) Hartford

Private non-profit/ 1959/ staff: 3(f); 8(p); 100(v)/ members: 1068/publication: *NEAM-News*

HISTORY MUSEUM: Aviation museum and research library.

PROGRAMS: Annual Meeting; Elder's Programs; Exhibits; Facility Rental; Family Programs; Guided Tours; Publication; Research Library/Archives; School-Based Curriculum; Theatre

COLLECTIONS: [1860-Desert Storm] Aircraft and aircraft components; personal memorabilia; books and periodicals.

HOURS: Yr Daily 10-5

ADMISSION: $6.75, Children $3.50, Seniors $6

1289
Windsor Locks Historical Society, Inc.
58 W St, 06096 [PO Box 733, 06096]; (p) (860) 627-9212; (c) Hartford

Private non-profit/ 1974/ staff: 6(v)/ members: 70

HISTORICAL SOCIETY: Operates an estate museum, a house and barn containing articles of local history.

PROGRAMS: Guided Tours; Research Library/Archives

COLLECTIONS: Back issues of the Windsor Locks Journal since 1880; furniture, clothing, Native American artifacts relating to local history.

HOURS: May-Oct Su 1-5

ADMISSION: No charge

WINSTED

1290
Winchester Historical Society, The
225 Prospect St, 06098 [PO Box 206, 06098]; (p) (860) 379-8433; (c) Litchfield

Private non-profit/ 1905/ staff: 40(v)/ members: 300

HISTORICAL SOCIETY: Preserves historical information relating to local, state, and national heritage.

PROGRAMS: Annual Meeting; Community Outreach; Exhibits; Guided Tours; Research Library/Archives

COLLECTIONS: [Late 18th c.-early 19th c.] Period furniture; Fire Dept. Museum; furnished Victorian dollhouse; local manufacturing exhibits; period clothing; Civil War exhibit; china and pewter dishware.

HOURS: June-Oct Su 1-4, Yr by appt

ADMISSION: Donations accepted

WOODBURY

1291
Glebe House Museum and Gertrude Jekyll Garden
Hollow Rd, 06798 [PO Box 241, 06798]; (p) (203) 263-2855; (f) (203) 263-6726; (c) Litchfield

Private non-profit/ 1925/ staff: 1(f); 3(p); 200(v)/ members: 500

GARDEN; HISTORIC SITE; HISTORICAL SOCIETY; HISTORY MUSEUM: Preserving the birthplace of the Episcopal Church in America and maintaining the Jekyll gardens.

PROGRAMS: Annual Meeting; Concerts; Exhibits; Festivals; Garden Tours; Guided Tours; Lectures; Living History; Reenactments; School-Based Curriculum

COLLECTIONS: [1771-1790] Period household furnishings.

HOURS: Apr-Dec W-Su 1-4

ADMISSION: $5,

WOODSTOCK

1292
Bowen House, Roseland Cottage
Rte 169, 06281 [PO Box 186, 06281]; (p) (860) 928-4074, (617) 227-3956; (f) (860) 963-2208; www.spnea.org

1846/ SPNEA

HOUSE MUSEUM

COLLECTIONS: [1880] Gothic Revival furnishings & Lincrusta Walton wall coverings

HOURS: Seasonal

1293
Woodstock Historical Society, Inc.
Rt 169, 06281; (p) (860) 928-1035; (c) Windham

Private non-profit/ 1967/ staff: 10(v)/ members: 200

HISTORICAL SOCIETY

PROGRAMS: Annual Meeting; Community Outreach; Exhibits; Guided Tours; Lectures; Research Library/Archives

COLLECTIONS: [1686-present] Photos, glassplate negatives, prints, slides; regional maps.

HOURS: Yr

DELAWARE

CLAYMONT

1294
Robinson House
Naamans Rd & Philadelphia Pike, 19703 [#1 Naamans Rd, 19703]; (p) (302) 792-0285

HOUSE MUSEUM

DELAWARE CITY

1295
Fort Delaware Society
108 Old Ready Point Bridge Rd, 19706 [PO Box 553, 19706]; (p) (302) 834-1630; www.del.net/org/fort; (c) New Castle

Private non-profit/ 1950/ staff: 1(f); 100(v)/ members: 400/publication: *Fort Delaware Notes*

HISTORIC SITE; HISTORY MUSEUM: Preserves history of Fort Delaware.

PROGRAMS: Annual Meeting; Community Outreach; Exhibits; Publication; Research Library/Archives

COLLECTIONS: [1860-1943] Letters, memoirs, armaments, prints and photos.

HOURS: Jun-Sep W-Su

DOVER

1296
Delaware Agricultural Museum and Village
866 N DuPont Hwy, 19901; (p) (302) 734-1618; damv@dol.net; www.agriculturalmuseum.org; (c) Kent

Private non-profit/ 1974/ staff: 7(f); 3(p); 250(v)/ members: 1100

HISTORY MUSEUM; LIVING HISTORY/OUTDOOR MUSEUM: Collects, preserves and interprets the agricultural heritage and rural culture of Delaware and the Delmarva Peninsula, offering public education programs and services related to aspects of the same.

PROGRAMS: Annual Meeting; Community Outreach; Concerts; Exhibits; Facility Rental; Family Programs; Festivals; Guided Tours; Interpretation; Lectures; Living History; Publication; Research Library/Archives; School-Based Curriculum

COLLECTIONS: [19th-20th c] Folk art, archives, photos, agriculture.

HOURS: Jan-Mar M-F 10-4; Apr-Dec Tu-Sa 10-4, Su 1-4

ADMISSION: $3, Family $9, Seniors $2

1297
Delaware Public Archives
121 Duke of York St, 19901; (p) (302) 739-5318; (f) (302) 739-2578; archives@state.de.us; www.archives.lib.de.us; (c) Kent

1905

LIBRARY AND/OR ARCHIVE: Serves as repository for all permanent public records of the State of Delaware, its counties, and municipalities.

PROGRAMS: Publication

COLLECTIONS: [1680-present] State and local governments of Delaware records, printed Delawareana, manuscripts, genealogical materials and photos.

HOURS: Yr M-F 8:30-4:15

1298
Delaware State Museums
102 S State St, 19901; (p) (302) 739-5316; (f) (302) 739-6712; www.destatemuseums.org; (c) Kent

State/ 1949/ State of Delaware/ staff: 34(f); 47(p)

HISTORIC SITE; HOUSE MUSEUM; LIVING HISTORY/OUTDOOR MUSEUM: Collects, preserves and interprets Delaware history.

PROGRAMS: Exhibits; Facility Rental; Guided Tours; Interpretation; Lectures; School-Based Curriculum

COLLECTIONS: Archaeology, portraits, victrola, phonographs.

HOURS: Yr

1299
Sewell Biggs Museum of American Art
406 Federal St, 19903 [PO Box 711, 19903]; (p) (302) 674-2111; (f) (302) 674-5133; www.biggsmuseum.org; (c) Kent

Private non-profit/ 1989/ staff: 4(f); 10(v)/ members: 130/publication: *150 Years of Philadelphia Painters and Painting*

ART MUSEUM: Collects, preserves, and interprets American fine and decorative arts.

PROGRAMS: Concerts; Exhibits; Family Programs; Guided Tours; Interpretation; Lectures; Publication; School-Based Curriculum

COLLECTIONS: [1740-1970] Period furniture, silver, American fine and decorative arts from mid-18th through mid-20th century with a focus on works from Delaware and Delaware Valley.

HOURS: Yr W-F 10-4, Su 1:30-4:30

ADMISSION: No charge

DOVER AFB

1300
Air Mobility Command Museum
1301 Heritage Rd, 19902-5301; (p) (302) 677-5938; (f) (302) 677-5940; museum@dover.af.mil; www.amcmuseum.org; (c) Kent

Federal/ 1986/ US Air Force/ staff: 4(f); 2(p); 25(v)/ members: 180/publication: *Hangar Digest*

HISTORIC SITE; HISTORY MUSEUM: Collects, preserves and displays artifacts relating to the history of Air Force airlift and tanker operations, as well as the history of Dover AFB.

PROGRAMS: Community Outreach; Exhibits; Guided Tours; Interpretation; Lectures; Publication; Research Library/Archives

COLLECTIONS: [World War I-present] 21 aircraft, 6 engines,and approximately 1,400 items consisting of uniforms, insignia, documents, memorabilia, aircraft-related artifacts, survival gear and aviationartwork.

FREDERICA

1301
Barratt's Chapel and Museum
6362 Bay Rd, 19946; (p) (302) 335-5544; barratts@aol.com; users.aol.com/barratts/home.html; (c) Kent

Private non-profit/ 1964/ Peninsula-Delaware Annual Conference of the United Methodist Church, Inc./ staff: 4(p); 2(v)/publication: *New Light on Old Barratt's; Cultivating the Methodist Garden*

HISTORIC SITE; HISTORY MUSEUM: Museum and archives that concentrates upon the history of Methodism on Delmarva Peninsula.

PROGRAMS: Exhibits; Facility Rental; Guided Tours; Publication; Research Library/Archives

COLLECTIONS: [18th-20th c] Artifacts, books, 1780 church building, photographs and letters dealing with the Methodist movement on Delmarva Peninsula.

HOURS: Yr Sa-Su 1:30-4:30

GEORGETOWN

1302
Treasures of the Sea Exhibit
Rt 18, 19947 [PO Box 610, 19947-0610]; (p) (302) 856-5700; (f) (302) 858-5462; www.Treasureofthesea.org; (c) Sussex

1988/ Delaware Technical and Community College Education Foundation/Board of Trustees/ staff: 4(p)

HISTORY MUSEUM: Displays and interprets artifacts from Spanish shipwreck, Nuestra Senora de Atocha.

PROGRAMS: Elder's Programs; Facility Rental; Guided Tours

COLLECTIONS: [1500-1622] Artifacts include silver ingots, silver and gold coins, religious articles, precious stones from Spanish shipwreck Nuestra Senora de Atocha.

HOURS: Feb-Dec M-Tu 10-4, F 12-4, Sa

LEWES

1303
Lewes Historical Society Complex
110 Shipcarpenter St, 19958 [110 Shipcarpenter St, 19958]; (p) (302) 645-7670; www.leweschamber.com

1740/ staff: 20(v)

COLLECTIONS: [Colonial/Victorian] Few Civil War documents/photos/memorabilia; geneaology books.

HOURS: Seasonal

MILFORD

1304
Parson Thorne Mansion
501 NW Front St, 19963 [PO Box 352, 19963]; (p) (302) 422-3115

HOUSE MUSEUM

MILLSBORO

1305
Nanticoke Indian Museum
John Williams Rd Rt 24 & 5 Oak Orchard, 19966 [Rt 4 Box 107A, 19966]; (p) (302) 945-7022; nanticoke@bellatlantic.net; www.longdeckpage.com/nia; (c) Sussex

Private non-profit/ Nanticoke Indian Association/ staff: 1(f); 2(v)

HISTORIC SITE; HISTORY MUSEUM; TRIBAL MUSEUM: Preserves Native American cultural history.

PROGRAMS: Exhibits; Family Programs; Festivals; Film/Video; Guided Tours; Interpretation; Lectures; Living History; Research Library/Archives; School-Based Curriculum

COLLECTIONS: [Prehistory-present] Tools, weapons, baskets, pottery, quill work, beadwork.

HOURS: Yr Winter Tu-Th 9-4, Sa 12-4;

NEW CASTLE

1306
New Castle Historical Society
2 E Fourth St, 19720; (p) (302) 322-2794; (f) (302) 322-9823

HOUSE MUSEUM: Operates two house museums.

HOURS: Yr

NEWARK

1307
Delaware Academy of Science/ Iron Hill Museum
1355 Old Baltimore Pike, 19702; (p) (302) 368-5703; (f) (302) 369-4287; ironhill@magpage.com; (c) New Castle

1962/ Delaware Academy of Science

HISTORIC SITE; HISTORY MUSEUM: Collects and preserves cultural and natural history of Iron Hill region.

PROGRAMS: Annual Meeting; Community Outreach; Exhibits; Family Programs; Guided Tours; Interpretation; Publication; Reenactments; School-Based Curriculum

COLLECTIONS: Taxidermy, geology and paleontology specimens, Native American artifacts.

HOURS: Yr W-F 12-4, Sa 10-4

ADMISSION: $1

1308
Hale-Byrnes House
606 Stanton-Christina Road, 19713-2109; (p) (302) 998-3792

HOUSE MUSEUM

ODESSA

1309
Historic Houses of Odessa
Main & Second Sts, 19730 [PO Box 507, 19730]; (p) (302) 378-4069, (302) 378-4021; (f) (302) 378-4050

staff: 3(f); 21(p); 118(v)

HOUSE MUSEUM

COLLECTIONS: [1770-1830] 135 decorative arts pieces made, owned in Odessa, DE to families signed/dated Janvier pieces (premier DE cabinet maker); Family letters, tannery, dry goods store.

HOURS: Seasonal

SEAFORD

1310
Governor Ross Mansion
Pine St Ext, 19973 [Rt 1, Box 393, 19973]; (p) (302) 628-9500; (f) (302) 628-9501

1860/ staff: 1(p); 15(v)

HOUSE MUSEUM: Home of Delaware governor William H. Ross.

COLLECTIONS: [1860] Furnishings belonging to the Ross family.

HOURS: Yr

SMYRNA

1311
Allee House
Dutch Neck Rd (DE 9), in the Bombay Hook Wildlife, 19977 [PO Box 576, Dover, 19903]; (p) (302) 736-4266, (302) 653-6872; www.dmv.com/btob/dover/kentsights.html

HOUSE MUSEUM

WILFORD

1312
Commission of Landmarks and Museum
121S Walnut St, 19963; (p) (302) 424-1080; (c) Sussex

City/ 1983/ City of Milford/ staff: 1(p); 20(v)

HISTORY MUSEUM

PROGRAMS: Annual Meeting; Community Outreach; Exhibits; Guided Tours; Lectures; Research Library/Archives

COLLECTIONS: [19th and 20th c] Dolls, doll houses, ship building, medical equipment, silver artifacts.

HOURS: Sept-July, Sa-Su 2-4 and by appt

WILMINGTON

1313
Delaware Heritage Foundation
820 N French St, 19801; (p) (302) 577-5044; (f) (302) 577-5045; dhaskell@state.de.us; (c) New Castle

State/ 1971/ staff: 1(f); 2(p)

HISTORICAL SOCIETY: Promotes Delaware history and heritage through summer youth programs, and publishing.

PROGRAMS: Community Outreach; Festivals; Lectures; Publication

1314
Eleutherian Mills Residence
[PO Box 3630, 19807]; (p) (302) 658-2400; (f) (302) 658-0568; danmuir@udel.edu; www.hagley.lib.de.us; (c) New Castle

1802/ staff: 79(f); 99(p); 425(v)

HOUSE MUSEUM

COLLECTIONS: [19th and 20th c] 35,000 collection items, majority decorative arts; business and technology.

HOURS: Yr

1315
Hagley Museum and Library
[PO Box 3630, 19807]; (p) (302) 658-2400; (f) (302) 658-0568; danmuir@udel.edu; www.hagley.lib.de.us; (c) New Castle

Private non-profit/ 1952/ staff: 80(f); 96(p); 450(v)/ members: 1800

HISTORIC SITE: Preserves 19th century American working life at black powder works.

PROGRAMS: Concerts; Exhibits; Facility Rental; Family Programs; Festivals; Guided Tours; Interpretation; Lectures; Publication; Research Library/Archives

COLLECTIONS: [1802-1920] Artifacts related to the DuPont Company, industry, technology, and settler lifestyle.

HOURS: Yr Su-Sa Jan-March 14 1:30; March 15-Dec 31 9:30-4:30

ADMISSION: $9.75, Student $7.50, Children $3.50, Seniors $7.50

1316
Historical Society of Delaware
505 Market St, 19801; (p) (302) 655-7161; (f) (302) 655-7844; hsd@dca.net; www.hsd.org; (c) New Castle

1864/ staff: 15(f); 24(p); 10(v)/ members: 1549/publication: *Delaware Collections*

HISTORIC SITE; HISTORICAL SOCIETY; HOUSE MUSEUM: Collects, preserves and interprets local history through Delaware History Center, Wilmington Cold Town Hall, Willington Square, History Museum, Research Library, and the Reed House and Gardens.

PROGRAMS: Community Outreach; Concerts; Elder's Programs; Exhibits; Facility Rental; Family Programs; Festivals; Film/Video; Garden Tours; Guided Tours; Interpretation; Lectures; Living History; Publication; Reenactments; Research Library/Archives; School-Based Curriculum

1317
Holy Trinity Church Foundation, Inc.
606 Church St, 19801; (p) (302) 652-5629; (f) (302) 652-8615; oldswedes@aol.com; www.oldswedes.org; (c) New Castle

Private non-profit/ 1947/ Board of Managers/ staff: 1(f); 2(p); 12(v)/ members: 200

HISTORIC SITE, HISTORY MUSEUM: Preserves history of Delaware Valley colonial life; maintains Old Swedes Church Yard, library, and Henderson Museum.

PROGRAMS: Exhibits; Festivals; Guided Tours; Research Library/Archives

COLLECTIONS: [17th c-present] Period artifacts housed in Hendrickson House, a 1690

Swedish Blue Brandywine granite farmhouse, historical and genealogical book collection.

HOURS: Yr M-Sa 10-4

ADMISSION: $2;

1318
Lombardy Hall Foundation
1611 Concord Pike, 19803 [PO Box 7036, 19803]; (p) (302) 655-5454; (c) New Castle

Private non-profit/ 1975/ staff: 2(v)

HISTORY MUSEUM: Restores and maintains historic Lombardy Hall.

PROGRAMS: Exhibits

COLLECTIONS: Masonic and Delaware books and magazines.

HOURS: By appt, open house 1st Sa/Su Dec

1319
Nemours Mansion and Gardens
1600 Rockland Rd, 19899 [PO Box 109, 19899]; (p) (302) 651-6912; (f) (302) 651-6933; (c) New Castle

Private non-profit/ 1909/ Newmours Foundation/ staff: 4(f); 30(p)

GARDEN; HOUSE MUSEUM: Former residence of Alfred I. DuPont built 1909-1910. Modified Louix XVI French chateau containing 102 rooms. Formal French-style gardens with statuary, colonnade and temple of love.

PROGRAMS: Guided Tours

COLLECTIONS: [17th-19th c] Period furnishings, oriental rugs and fine arts.

HOURS: May-Nov T-Su

1320
Rockwood Museum
610 Shipley Rd, 19809; (p) (302) 761-4340; (f) (302) 764-4570; info@rockwood.org; www.rockwood.org; (c) New Castle

County/ 1976/ New Castle/ staff: 6(f); 10(p); 50(v)/ members: 415/publication: *Romantic Rockwood*

HISTORIC SITE: Preserves history of mid-19th century Gothic manor house.

PROGRAMS: Annual Meeting; Community Outreach; Concerts; Exhibits; Facility Rental; Family Programs; Festivals; Garden Tours; Guided Tours; Interpretation; Publication; Research Library/Archives; School-Based Curriculum

COLLECTIONS: [Victorian] English, Continental and American decorative arts, period furnishing.

HOURS: Yr Tu-Sa 11-4

ADMISSION: $5, Children $1, Seniors $4

WINTERTHUR

1321
Winterthur Museum, Garden and Library
Rt 52, 19735; (p) (800) 448-3883; (f) (302) 888-4700; www.udel.edu/winterthur; www.winterthur.org; (c) New Castle

Private non-profit/ 1951/ staff: 242(f); 143(p); 120(v)/ members: 22650

ALLIANCE OF HISTORICAL AGENCIES; ART MUSEUM; GARDEN; HISTORIC SITE; HISTORY MUSEUM; HOUSE MUSEUM; RE-

SEARCH CENTER: Collects, preserves and interprets American decorative arts before 1860; maintains research library.

PROGRAMS: Community Outreach; Concerts; Elder's Programs; Exhibits; Facility Rental; Family Programs; Festivals; Garden Tours; Guided Tours; Interpretation; Lectures; Living History; Publication; Reenactments; Research Library/Archives; School-Based Curriculum

COLLECTIONS: [1640-1860] Empire, Pennsylvania, German, Shaker period arts and crafts.

HOURS: Yr M-Sa 9-5, Su 12-5

ADMISSION: $8

DISTRICT OF COLUMBIA

WASHINGTON

1322
Advisory Council on Historic Preservation
Old Post Office, 20004 [1100 Pennsylvania Ave NW, Ste 809, 20004]; (p) (202) 606-8503; (f) (202) 606-8672; achp@achp.gov; www.achp.gov

Federal/ 1966/ staff: 32(f)

HISTORIC PRESERVATION AGENCY: Promotes protection and enhancement of nation's historic resources.

PROGRAMS: Publication

1323
American Association of Museums
1575 Eye St NW, 20005-1105; (p) (202) 289-1818; (f) (202) 289-6578; www.aam-us.org

Private non-profit/ 1906/ staff: 52(f)/ members: 16000/publication: *Museum News; AVISO*

PROFESSIONAL ORGANIZATION: Foremost representative of the national museum community. Helps museums and museum professionals across the country provide society with cultural and educational experiences through advocacy, professional education,

1324
American Catholic Historical Association
Mullen Library, Rm 318, Catholic Univ of America, 20064; (p) (202) 319-5079; (f) (202) 319-5079; cua-chraha@cua.edu; research.cua.edu/ACHA

Private non-profit/ 1919/ Executive Council/ staff: 1(f)/ members: 1100/publication: *Catholic Historical Review*

HISTORICAL SOCIETY: Promotes history of the Catholic Church from the first century to present in all parts of the world.

1325
American Institute for Conservation of Historic and Artistic Works
1717 K St NW, Ste 200, 20006; (p) (202) 452-9545; (f) (202) 452-9328; Infoaic@aol.com; aic.stanford.edu

Private non-profit/ 1972/ Board of Directors/ staff: 6(f); 60(v)/ members: 3200/publication: *AIC News and Journal of American Institute for Conservation*

PROFESSIONAL ORGANIZATION: Provides educational programs, annual meetings and publications for conservators; outreach programs and publications for the general public.

PROGRAMS: Annual Meeting; Community Outreach; Publication

1326
American Red Cross Museum
1730 E St NW, 20006; (p) (202) 639-3300; (f) (202) 628-1362; museum@usa.redcross.org; www.redcross.org/hec/index.html; (c) District of Columbia

Private non-profit/ 1995/ American Red Cross/ staff: 9(f); 15(v)

HISTORY MUSEUM: Educates people about the rich history and ongoing humanitarian actions of the American Red Cross through educational programs and exhibits.

PROGRAMS: Community Outreach; Exhibits; Guided Tours; Lectures

COLLECTIONS: [1881-present] Art, artifacts and photographs that capture the humanitarian work performed by the American Red Cross throughout the world.

HOURS: Yr M-F 8:30-4

1327
American Studies Association
1120 19th St NW, Ste 301, 20036; (p) (202) 467-4783; (f) (202) 467-4786; asastaff@erols.com; www.press.jhu/ associations/asa; (c) District of Columbia

Private non-profit/ 1951/ Council/ staff: 2(f); 6(p)/ members: 5500/publication: *American Quarterly; Guide to American Studies Resources; Directory of Graduate Programs in American Studies; and others*

PROFESSIONAL ORGANIZATION

PROGRAMS: Annual Meeting; Publication

HOURS: Yr M-F 8-5

1328
Anacostia Museum and Center for African American History and Culture
1901 Fort Pl SE, 20560 [900 Jefferson Dr SW, Ste 1130, 20560-0431]; (p) (202) 357-4500; (f) (202) 357-2636; www.si.edu

1967/ Smithsonian Institution/ staff: 30(f)

ART MUSEUM; HISTORY MUSEUM: One of the nation's first federally funded community-based neighborhood museums. Since its 1995 merger with the Smithsonian Institution, the museum has become a national resource that offers exhibitions, educational programs, publications and special events to serve local, nation and international constituencies.

PROGRAMS: Community Outreach; Exhibits; Lectures

COLLECTIONS: [Early 19th-20th c] Books, documents, photographs, household items and a wide array of archival object that shed light on the details of life in African American communities.

HOURS: Yr Daily 10-5:30

1329
Anderson House
2118 Massachusetts Ave, NW, 20008-2810; (p) (202) 785-2040

1902/ staff: 2(f); 3(p); 18(v)

HOUSE MUSEUM

COLLECTIONS: [1905-1937] Original furnishings, Larz and Isabel Anderson art collection, 17th century Belgian tapestries, Japanese lacquer and porcelain, Cincinnati china, paintings, and portraits; 42,000 titles dealing with the Art of War in 18th century and American Revolution.

HOURS: Yr

1330
Archives of American Art, Smithsonian Institution
750 9th St, NW Ste 2200, 20560 [Archives of American Art, Smithsonian Institution, 20560-9037]; (p) (202) 275-2156; www.aaa.si.edu/askus.htm; www.aaa.si.edu

Federal/ 1954/ Smithsonian Institution/ staff: 30(f); 4(p); 3(v)/ members: 1000/publication: *Archives of American Art Journal*

LIBRARY AND/OR ARCHIVES: Collects and preserves source materials pertaining to American visual arts and makes them available to researchers.

PROGRAMS: Publication; Research Library/ Archives

COLLECTIONS: [19th-20th c] 14.6 million items including manuscripts, printed material and documents related to lives and careers of artists, craftspeople, designers, historians, dealers, critics, museum personnel and collectors as well as records of art-related organizations and institutions.

1331
Archivists for Congregations of Women Religious (ACWR)
125 Michigan Ave NE, 20017 [ACWR National Office, Trinity College, 20017]; (p) (202) 884-9441; (f) (202) 884-9229; acwr@aol.com

Private non-profit/ 1992/ Board of Directors/ staff: 1(p)/ members: 300

LIBRARY AND/OR ARCHIVES: Maintains and organizes archives.

COLLECTIONS: [1790-present]

1332
B'nai B'rith Klutznick National Jewish Museum
1640 Rhode Island Ave, NW, 20036-3278; (p) (202) 857-6783; (f) (202) 857-1099; www.bnaibrith.com/museum

Private non-profit/ 1957/ B'nai B'rith International/ staff: 3(f); 1(v)

ART MUSEUM; HISTORY MUSEUM: Preserves and promotes history, culture and art of Jewish people.

PROGRAMS: Exhibits; Family Programs; Guided Tours

COLLECTIONS: [Biblical-present] Art, ethnographic and archaeological holdings.

HOURS: Yr Su-F 10-5

1333

Charles Sumner School Museum and Archives

17th & M Sts NW, 20036 [1201 17th St NW, 20036]; (p) (202) 727-3419; (f) (202) 727-6812; www.k12.dc.us

Federal; Private non-profit/ 1872/ DC Public Schools/ staff: 4(f); 1(p)

LIBRARY AND/OR ARCHIVES: Serves as archives and research library for District of Columbia public schools.

PROGRAMS: Community Outreach; Concerts; Exhibits; Facility Rental; Family Programs; Guided Tours; Lectures; Research Library/Archives

COLLECTIONS: [1804-present] Photos, yearbooks and other memorabilia related to public schools in the DC area. Minutes of Board of Education.

HOURS: Museum: Sept-June M-Sa 10-5; Archives: Yr

1334

Civil War Preservation Trust

1331 H St, NW, Ste 1001, 20005; (p) (202) 367-1861; (f) (202) 367-1865; civilwartrust@civilwar.org; www.civilwar.org

Private non-profit/ 1999/ staff: 2(p); 13(v)/ members: 35000/publication: Hallowed Ground

HISTORIC PRESERVATION AGENCY: Preserves America's Civil War battlefields.

PROGRAMS: Annual Meeting; Community Outreach; Interpretation; Publication; School-Based Curriculum

COLLECTIONS: [1861-1865] 3,500 acres of battlefield land, mostly in Virginia.

1335

Cleveland Park Historical Society

2938 Newark St NW, 20008 [PO Box 4862, 20008]; (p) (202) 363-6358; (f) (202) 966-3230

Private non-profit/ 1985/ staff: 1(p); 38(v)/ members: 600

HISTORICAL SOCIETY: Promotes history and architecture of Cleveland Park

PROGRAMS: Annual Meeting; Community Outreach; Exhibits; Festivals; Garden Tours; Guided Tours; Lectures

1336

Daughters of the American Revolution Museum

1776 D St NW, 20006; (p) (202) 879-3241; (f) (202) 628-0820; museum@dar.org; www.dar.org/museum/index.html

Private non-profit/ 1890/ National Society Daughters of the American Revolution/ staff: 13(f); 2(p); 50(v)

HISTORY MUSEUM

PROGRAMS: Exhibits; Facility Rental; Family Programs; Guided Tours; Interpretation; Lectures; Publication; Research Library/Archives; School-Based Curriculum

COLLECTIONS: [1700-1860] Decorative and fine arts, including furnishings, silver, paintings, ceramics and textiles made or used prior to the Industrial Revolution.

HOURS: Yr Su 1-5, M-F 8:30-4

1337

Decatur House

748 Jackson Pl NW, 20006; (p) (202) 842-0920; (f) (202) 842-0030; www.decaturhouse.org

Private non-profit/ 1956/ National Trust for Historic Preservation/ staff: 7(f); 5(p); 20(v)

HISTORIC SITE: Interprets periods of two 19th-century residents, Decaturs and the Beales, both prominent Washingtonians of national significance.

PROGRAMS: Community Outreach; Concerts; Exhibits; Facility Rental; Family Programs; Guided Tours; Interpretation; Lectures; Research Library/Archives

COLLECTIONS: [1818-1956] Archives, decorative arts, period furnishings.

HOURS: Yr T-F 10-3, Sa-Su 12-4

ADMISSION: $4, Student $2.50,

1338

Federick Douglass National Historic Site

1411 W St SE, 20020; (p) (202) 426-5961, (202) 426-1452; (f) (202) 426-0880; NACE_Frederick_Douglass_NHS@nps.gov; www.cr.nps.gov/csa/exhibit/douglass; (c) District of Columbia

Federal/ 1916/ Department of the Interior, National Park Service/ staff: 9(f); 2(v)

HISTORIC SITE: Collects, preserves and protects cultural and natural resources for the education and enjoyment of present and future generations.

PROGRAMS: Exhibits; Film/Video; Guided Tours; Interpretation; School-Based Curriculum

COLLECTIONS: [19th c] Books, fine arts, photographs, furniture, sheet music and archeological artifacts.

HOURS: Yr Daily Oct-Apr 9-4; Apr-Oct 9-5

ADMISSION: $3; School groups free

1339

Ford's Theatre National Historic Site

517 10th St, NW, 20004; (p) (202) 426-6924; (f) (202) 426-1845; Ford's_theatre@nps.gov; www.nps.gov/foth

Federal/ National Park Service/ staff: 25(f); 1(p); 25(v)

HISTORIC SITE; HOUSE MUSEUM: Preserves place of President Lincoln's assassination.

PROGRAMS: Exhibits; Family Programs; Interpretation; Lectures; Living History; Research Library/Archives; School-Based Curriculum; Theatre

COLLECTIONS: [1865] Collections focus on Lincoln's assassination and the time he lived in, including political artifacts, funerary objects, along with assassination objects and three furnished period rooms.

1340

Gallaudet University Archives

800 Florida Ave, NE, 20002; (p) (202) 651-5209; (f) (202) 651-5213; archives@gallaudet.edu; www.gallaudet.edu/arch

Private non-profit/ 1967/ Gallaudet University/ staff: 2(f); 5(p); 1(v)

LIBRARY AND/OR ARCHIVES: Preservation materials related to the deaf community.

COLLECTIONS: Deaf history and culture including archival manuscripts, rare books, architectural drawings, photographs, films, reports and objects.

1341

Georgetown Heritage Trust

1623 28th St NW, 20007; (p) (202) 338-6222; (f) (202) 333-6733; argonet@aol.com

Private non-profit/ 1989/ staff: 2(f); 50(v)

HISTORICAL SOCIETY; LIVING HISTORY/ OUTDOOR MUSEUM; RESEARCH CENTER: Provides general public with broad educational experience on history of Georgetown. Presents its historic, architectural and archeological landmarks; enhances, preserves and interprets legacy of Georgetown Historic District.

PROGRAMS: Community Outreach; Exhibits; Family Programs; Interpretation; Lectures; Publication; Reenactments; Research Library/Archives; School-Based Curriculum

COLLECTIONS: [1700-1950] Historical and archaeological inventory records of all 4,000 houses within Georgetown Historic District; maps and photographs.

1342

Hillwood Museum and Gardens

4155 Linnean Ave NW, 20008; (p) (202) 686-8500; (f) (202) 966-7846; hwdadmin@erols.com; www.hillwoodmuseum.org

1977/ Marjorie Merriweather Post Foundation of DC Board/ staff: 48(f); 20(p); 80(v)/ members: 500

ART MUSEUM; GARDEN; HOUSE MUSEUM: Preserves and interprets former residence of Marjorie Merriweather Post.

PROGRAMS: Concerts; Elder's Programs; Exhibits; Festivals; Film/Video; Garden Tours; Guided Tours; Interpretation; Lectures; Publication; Research Library/Archives

COLLECTIONS: [18th-19th c] Imperial Russian objects, plants, archives.

HOURS: Mar-Dec Tu-Sa 9:30, 10:45, 12:30, 1:45, 3

1343

Historical Society of Washington DC

1307 New Hampshire Ave NW, 20036; (p) (202) 785-2068; (f) (202) 887-5785; heurich@ibm.net; www.hswdc.org

Private non-profit/ 1897/ Historical Society of Washington, DC/ staff: 10(f); 15(p); 157(v)/ members: 1500/publication: Washington History

HISTORICAL SOCIETY: Preserves, collects and interprets artifacts related to family, community, social life, business, politics, art and architecture of the Wasington, DC area.

PROGRAMS: Annual Meeting; Community Outreach; Exhibits; Facility Rental; Family Programs; Lectures; Publication; Research Library/Archives; School-Based Curriculum

COLLECTIONS: [19th-present]

HOURS: Yr M-Sa 10-4

ADMISSION: $3, Children $1.50

1344
Institute of Museum and Library Services

1100 Pennsylvania Ave NW, 20506; (p) (202) 606-8536; (f) (202) 606-8591; imlsinfo@imls.fed.us; www.imls.fed.us

Federal/ staff: 30(f); 5(p)

Promotes leadership, innovation and educational initiatives to museums and libraries.

PROGRAMS: Publication

1345
Jewish Historical Society of Greater Washington

701 Third St NW, 20001; (p) (202) 789-0900; (f) (202) 789-0485

Private non-profit/ 1960/ Board of Directors/ staff: 2(f); 3(p); 15(v)/ members: 700/publication: *The Record*

HISTORIC SITE; HISTORICAL SOCIETY; HISTORY MUSEUM: Preserves and interprets historic presence of Jewish life in the greater Washington DC metropolitan area; operates the Lillian and Albert Small Jewish Museum.

PROGRAMS: Annual Meeting; Community Outreach; Exhibits; Facility Rental; Family Programs; Guided Tours; Lectures; Living History; Publication; School-Based Curriculum; Theatre

COLLECTIONS: [1850-present] Photos, manuscripts, religious artifacts, and memorabilia.

HOURS: Yr S-Th 12-4

ADMISSION: Donations requested

1346
Mt. Zion United Methodist Church

1334-29th St NW, 20011; (p) (202) 234-0148; (f) (202) 337-0428

Private non-profit/ 1816/ United Methodist Church/ staff: 2(f); 4(p); 12(v)/ members: 250

HISTORIC SITE: Oldest African-American church in the District, served as a stop on the Underground railroad; interprets the Mt. Zion/Female Union Band Cemeteries.

PROGRAMS: Guided Tours; Lectures

COLLECTIONS: [1834-present] Various 19th century records, including marriages, birth, death and church.

HOURS: Yr 10-4 by appt

1347
Museum Management Program, National Park Service

1849 C St NW, Room NC 230, 20240; (p) (202) 343-8142; (f) (202) 343-1767; www.cr.nps.gov/csd

Federal/ 1916/ National Park Service, Dept of Interior/ staff: 14(f); 3(p); 1(v)/publication: *Conserve O Gram; Museum Handbook*

ALLIANCE OF HISTORICAL AGENCIES: Coordinates strategies, policies and procedures for management of museum collections in over 300 national park areas.

PROGRAMS: Publication

1348
Museum Reference Center, Smithsonian Institution Libraries

900 Jefferson Dr SW, 20560 [A & I Building, Rm 2235, 20560-0427]; (p) (202) 786-2271;

(f) (202) 357-2311; www.sil.si.edu/mrchp.htm

Federal/ 1974/ staff: 1(f); 1(p); 1(v)

LIBRARY AND/OR ARCHIVE: Serves as information center on museum operations.

PROGRAMS: Research Library/Archives

COLLECTIONS: Books, periodicals, microfiche, slides, audio and videos.

HOURS: Yr M-F 10-5

1349
National Building Museum

401 F St NW, 20001; (p) (202) 272-2448; (f) (202) 272-2564; www.nbm.org

Private non-profit/ 1973/ staff: 20(f)/ members: 220/publication: *Blueprints*

HISTORY MUSEUM: Preserves and interprets history of American architecture and building through exhibits and publication.

PROGRAMS: Community Outreach; Concerts; Exhibits; Facility Rental; Family Programs; Festivals; Film/Video; Guided Tours; Lectures; Publication; Research Library/ Archives; School-Based Curriculum

COLLECTIONS: Photos, architectural prints and drawings, architectural fragments, material samples, memorabilia, archives.

1350
National Conference of State Historic Preservation Officers

444 N Capitol St NW Ste 342, 20001-1512; (p) (202) 624-5465; (f) (202) 624-5419; www.sso.org/ncshpo

Private non-profit/ 1969/ Board of Directors/ staff: 52(f); 8(p)/ members: 59

Represents the State Historic Preservation officers in the US and its territories.

1351
National Coordinating Committee for the Promotion of History

400 A St SE, 20003; (p) (202) 544-2422; (f) (202) 544-8307; Rbcrag3@juno.com; www.h-net-msu.edu/~ncc

Federal; Private non-profit/ 1976/ National Coordinating Committee for the Promotion of History/ staff: 1(f)/ members: 62/publication: *NCC Washington Update, Testimony on Capitol Hill*

Serves as national advocacy office for the historical and archival professions focusing on federal funding and policy issues.

1352
National Endowment for the Humanities Museums Program

1100 Pennsylvania Ave NW, 20506; (p) (202) 606-8267

1353
National Guard Educational Foundation

1 Massachusetts Ave NW, 20001; (p) (202) 789-0031; (f) (202) 682-9358

Private non-profit/ 1975/ The National Guard Association of the United States/ staff: 1(f); 2(p)

HISTORICAL SOCIETY: Maintaining the only national establishment for collecting and preserving National Guard archives and operating the galleries of the National Guard Memorial to

display the history and achievements of the National Guard.

PROGRAMS: Exhibits; Facility Rental; Guided Tours; Research Library/Archives

COLLECTIONS: [1878-present]

HOURS: Yr M-F 9-5

1354
National Historical Publications and Records Commission

700 Pennsylvania Ave NW Rm 111, 20408-0001; (p) (202) 501-5600; (f) (202) 501-5601; nhprc@arch1.nara.gov; www.nara.gov/nara/nhr

Federal/ 1934/ National Archives and Records Administration/ staff: 12(f); 5(v)

LIBRARY AND/OR ARCHIVE: Preserves and publishes documents on US history.

PROGRAMS: Publication; Research Library/ Archives

1355
National Museum of American History, Smithsonian Institution

14th St & Constitution Ave NW, 20560 [Smithsonian Institution, 20560-0627]; (p) (202) 357-2700; americanhistory.si.edu

1964/ Smithsonian Institution/ staff: 397(f); 100(v)

HISTORY MUSEUM: Traces American heritage through exhibits of social, cultural, scientific, and technological history. Collections are displayed in settings that recapture and interpret the American experience from Colonial times to the present.

PROGRAMS: Community Outreach; Concerts; Exhibits; Facility Rental; Family Programs; Film/Video; Guided Tours; Interpretation; Lectures; Research Library/Archives

COLLECTIONS: Americana memorabilia, including Star-Spangled Banner, First Ladies' gowns and cultural icons including Dorothy's ruby slippers; national treasures from America's presidents: George Washington's military uniform, the writing desk on which Thomas Jefferson drafted the Declaration of Independence, Abraham Lincoln's top hat and 3 million other objects representing nation's heritage.

HOURS: Yr Daily 10-5:30

1356
National Museum of American Jewish Military History

1811 R St NW, 20009; (p) (202) 265-6280; (f) (202) 462-3192; nmajmh@erols.com; www.penfed.org/jwu/museum.htm

Private non-profit/ 1958/ National Museum of American Jewish Military History/ staff: 23(f); 3(p); 25(v)/ members: 47000

HISTORY MUSEUM: Documents the contributions of Jewish Americans in the armed forces.

PROGRAMS: Annual Meeting; Community Outreach; Exhibits; Facility Rental; Guided Tours; Lectures; Research Library/Archives

COLLECTIONS: [1700-present] Archives, photos, military artifacts including guns, swords, patches, manuals, uniforms and medals.

1357
National Museum of the American Indian, Smithsonian Institution
470 L'Enfant Plaza SW, Ste 7102, 20560-0935; (p) (202) 287-2523; (f) (202) 287-2538; nmai.west@ic.si.edu; www.si.edu/nmai

Board of Trustees/ staff: 184(f); 4(p); 137(v)/ members: 52357

RESEARCH CENTER: Dedicated to the preservation, study and exhibition of the life, languages, literature, history and arts of the Native Peoples of the Western Hemisphere.

PROGRAMS: Community Outreach; Concerts; Elder's Programs; Exhibits; Facility Rental; Family Programs; Festivals; Film/Video; Guided Tours; Interpretation; Lectures; Publication; Research Library/Archives; School-Based Curriculum; Theatre

COLLECTIONS: [Paleo-Indian-present] Native American ethnographic and archaeological objects from North, Central, and South America; Native American life prints and negatives; film, video, multi-media collection; archives.

HOURS: Yr F-W 10-5, Th 10-8

ADMISSION: No charge

1358
National Register of Historic Places, National Park Service
800 N Capitol St, NW Ste 400, 20240 [1849 C St NW, NC-400, 20240]; (p) (202) 343-9536; (f) (202) 343-1836; nr_info@nps.gov; www.cr.nps.gov/nr

Federal/ 1966/ National Park Service, Dept of the Interior/ staff: 20(f)

HISTORIC PRESERVATION AGENCY; RESEARCH CENTER: Established under the National Historic Preservation Act of 1966. Identifies and documents more than 70,000 districts, sites buildings, structures and objects that are significant in American history, architecture, archaeology, engineering and culture.

PROGRAMS: Publication

HOURS: Yr M-F 9-5

1359
National Society of The Colonial Dames of America, The
Dumbarton House, 2715 Q St, NW, 20007; (p) (202) 337-2288; (f) (202) 337-0348; www.dumbartonhouse.org

Private non-profit/ 1891/ Acts in Council/ staff: 7(f); 2(p); 120(v)/ members: 15000

GENEALOGICAL SOCIETY; HISTORIC SITE; HISTORY MUSEUM: Preserves significant artifacts pertaining to the nation's early history, especially colonial history.

PROGRAMS: Community Outreach; Concerts; Exhibits; Facility Rental; Family Programs; Guided Tours; Interpretation; Lectures; Living History; School-Based Curriculum

COLLECTIONS: [1790-1830] Federal style furniture and decorative arts, including paintings, textiles, silver and ceramics.

HOURS: Sept-July T-Sa 10-12:30

ADMISSION: $3

1360
National Trust for Historic Preservation
1785 Massachusetts Ave NW, 20036; (p) (202) 588-6000; (f) (202) 588-6032; www.nationaltrust.org

Private non-profit/ 1949/ National Trust for Historic Preservation/ staff: 279(f); 24(p); 3000(v)/ members: 250000/publication: *Preservation Magazine; Forum News; Forum Journal*

HISTORIC PRESERVATION AGENCY: Promotes and advocates preservation of historic buildings and neighborhoods.

PROGRAMS: Annual Meeting; Community Outreach; Concerts; Elder's Programs; Facility Rental; Family Programs; Film/Video; Garden Tours; Guided Tours; Interpretation; Lectures; Living History; Publication; Reenactments; Research Library/Archives; School-Based Curriculum

COLLECTIONS: [18th-20th c] Fine and decorative arts, memorabilia, archaeological remains, local historical artifacts, and archival materials.

1361
National Woman's Party/Sewall Belmont House
144 Constitution Ave NE, 20002

Private non-profit/ 1913/ National Woman's Party/ staff: 2(f); 8(p); 6(v)/ members: 400

Serves as headquarters for the National Woman's Party.

COLLECTIONS: [1840-1920] Portraits and sculptures of suffrage leaders, antique furniture, china, and feminist library.

HOURS: Yr T-F 11-3, Sa 12-4

ADMISSION: Donations requested

1362
Navy Museum, The
Washington Navy Yard, 805 Kidder Breese SE, 20374-5060; (p) (202) 433-6897; (f) (202) 433-8200; www.history.navy.mil

Federal/ 1963/ US Navy/ staff: 13(f); 20(v)

HISTORY MUSEUM: Collects, preserves, and interprets historic naval artifacts and artwork to inform, educate and inspire naval personnel and the general public.

PROGRAMS: Community Outreach; Concerts; Exhibits; Family Programs; Festivals; Guided Tours; Interpretation; Lectures; Living History; Reenactments; Research Library/ Archives; School-Based Curriculum

COLLECTIONS: [Revolutionary War-Space Age] Paintings, weapons, photos, medals, naval memorabilia, ship models, ordinances, maps, prints, flags, scientific instruments.

HOURS: Yr M-F 9-4, Sa-Su 10-5

ADMISSION: No charge

1363
Octagon, The/Museum of the American Architectural Foundation, The
1799 New York Ave NW, 20006; (p) (202) 638-3221; (f) (202) 879-7764; octagon@aia.org; www.arhfoundation.org

Private non-profit/ 1942/ The American Architectural Foundation/ staff: 7(f); 2(p); 40(v)/ members: 952

HISTORY MUSEUM: Museum of architecture and design seeking to educate the public about the built environment and history of the early republic; promotes stewardship of America's architectural heritage.

PROGRAMS: Community Outreach; Exhibits; Family Programs; Guided Tours; Interpretation; Lectures; School-Based Curriculum

COLLECTIONS: [1800-1828] Decorative arts furnish house; archaeological and architectural artifacts from site; prints, drawings and architectural records.

HOURS: Yr T-Su

1364
Potomac Heritage Partnership
1623 28th St, NW, 20007; (p) (202) 338-1118; (f) (202) 333-6733; php623@aol.com

Private non-profit/ 1995/ Board Of Directors/ staff: 1(f); 50(v)

ALLIANCE OF HISTORICAL AGENCIES; LIVING HISTORY/OUTDOOR MUSEUM: Promotes positive resources of heritage tourism's impact upon commerce, culture and conservation throughout the Potomac River watershed.

PROGRAMS: Annual Meeting; Community Outreach; Exhibits; Facility Rental; Family Programs; Interpretation; Lectures; Living History; Publication; School-Based Curriculum

1365
Sheridan Kalorama Historical Association, Inc.
2144 California St NW, 20008; (p) (202) 483-4866

Private non-profit/ 1987/ staff: 20(v)/ members: 250/publication: *Views*

HISTORICAL SOCIETY: Preserves the history and architecture of the Sheridan-Kalorama neighborhood.

PROGRAMS: Annual Meeting; Publication; Research

1366
Smithsonian Institution Traveling Exhibition
1100 Jefferson Dr SW Ste 3146, 20560-0706; (p) (202) 357-3168; (f) (202) 357-4324; www.si.edu/sites

Federal; Private non-profit/ 1952/ staff: 60(f); 5(v)

PROGRAMS: Exhibits; Publication

1367
Society of the Cincinnati Museum at Anderson House, The
2118 Massachusetts Ave NW, 20008; (p) (202) 785-2040; (f) (202) 293-3350

Private non-profit/ 1783/ Society of the Cincinnati/ staff: 2(f); 4(p); 29(v)

Preserves the Late Renaissance Revival-style mansion of Ambassador Larz Anderson.

PROGRAMS: Concerts; Exhibits; Guided Tours; Research Library/Archives; School-Based Curriculum

COLLECTIONS: [American Revolutionary War] 19th century grand historic home and period furnishing.

HOURS: Yr Tu-Sa 1-4

1368
Textile Museum, The
2320 S St NW, 20008; (p) (202) 667-0441; (f) (202) 483-0994; info@textilemuseum.org; www.textilemuseum.org

Private non-profit/ 1925/ Board of Trustees/ staff: 30(f); 5(p); 50(v)/ members: 4000/publication: *The Textile Museum Journal*

HISTORY MUSEUM: Promotes creative efforts in the textile arts.

PROGRAMS: Exhibits; Facility Rental; Festivals; Film/Video; Guided Tours; Lectures; Publication; Research Library/Archives

COLLECTIONS: [Pre-historic-present] Oriental carpets, Islamic, Coptic, Indian, Chinese, African and pre-Columbian Native American; books and journals.

HOURS: Yr Su 1-5, M-Sa 10-5

ADMISSION: Donations

1369
Tudor Place Foundation, Inc.
1644 31st St NW, 20007 [1605 32nd St NW, 20007]; (p) (202) 965-0400; (f) (202) 965-0164; www.tudorplace.org

Private non-profit/ 1966/ staff: 6(f); 4(p); 40(v)/ members: 180

GARDEN; HISTORIC SITE; HOUSE MUSEUM: Operates historic house and garden owned by Martha Custis-Peter, granddaughter of Martha Washington

PROGRAMS: Exhibits; Facility Rental; Family Programs; Festivals; Garden Tours; Guided Tours; Interpretation; Lectures; Research Library/Archives; School-Based Curriculum

COLLECTIONS: [18th-20th c] Artifacts from Mt. Vernon.

HOURS: Feb-Dec T-Su 10-4

ADMISSION: $6, Student $3, Seniors $5

1370
U.S. Army Center of Military History Museum
Fort McNair, 20319 [103 Third Avenue Bldg 35, 20319-5058]; (p) (202) 685-2453; (f) (202) 685-2113; benneje@hqda.army.mil; www.army/mil/cmh-pg

Federal/ 1949/ staff: 28(f)

HISTORY MUSEUM: Preserves Army material culture.

PROGRAMS: Annual Meeting; Community Outreach; Exhibits; Guided Tours; Lectures; Research Library/Archives; School-Based Curriculum

COLLECTIONS: Military memorabilia, books and journals, uniforms, equipment and ephemeral items from the colonial period to the present. Also represented are items of allies and adversaries, a collection of historic flags and colors, and the official Army art collection.

HOURS: M-F by appt only

ADMISSION: No charge

1371
U.S. Navy Memorial Foundation
701 Pennsylvania NW, 20004-2608; (p) (202) 737-2300; (f) (202) 737-2308; ahoy@lone-sailor.org; www.lonesailor.org

Private non-profit/ 1987/ staff: 15(f); 8(p); 25(v)

Promotes US naval history.

PROGRAMS: Annual Meeting; Concerts; Exhibits; Family Programs; Film/Video

COLLECTIONS: [WWII] Sailor memorabilia and archives.

HOURS: Yr Summer M-Sa; Winter Tu-Sa 9:30-5

1372
United States Capitol Historic Society
200 Maryland Ave NE, 20002; (p) (202) 543-8919; (f) (202) 544-8244; uschs@uschs.org

Private non-profit/ 1962/ staff: 29(f); 50(v)/ members: 2500/publication: *The Capitol Dome*

HISTORICAL SOCIETY: Promotes the history and heritage of the US Congress and the Capitol building through tours, publications, scholarly conferences, and educational outreach programs.

PROGRAMS: Community Outreach; Exhibits; Film/Video; Guided Tours; Lectures; Publication

1373
Washington Dolls' House and Toy Museum
5236 44th St NW, 20015; (p) (202) 244-0024

1975/ staff: 1(f); 21(p)

HISTORY MUSEUM: Preserves dolls' houses and miniature decorative arts.

PROGRAMS: Exhibits; Facility Rental

COLLECTIONS: [Victorian] Victorian dolls' houses, toys and games.

HOURS: Yr Su 12-5, T-Sa 10-5

ADMISSION: $4, Children $2, Seniors $3

1374
Washington National Cathedral
Massachusetts and Wisconsin Aves NW, 20016; (p) (202) 537-6200; (f) (202) 364-6000; www.cathedral.org/cathedral

Private non-profit/ 1907/ Protestant Episcopal Cathedral Foundation/ staff: 492(f); 246(p); 1200(v)/ members: 14000

GARDEN; HISTORIC SITE: Serves as nation's "house of prayer for all people" welcoming visitors from all faith traditions to its educational programs, art and musical offerings.

PROGRAMS: Community Outreach; Concerts; Exhibits; Facility Rental; Family Programs; Festivals; Film/Video; Garden Tours; Guided Tours; Interpretation; Lectures; Publication; Reenactments; School-Based Curriculum

COLLECTIONS: [Gothic; 20th c] Administrative and policy records, service registers and leaflets, iconography and furnishings records, correspondence files of deans/canons and photos of major events.

HOURS: Yr M-Sa 10-5, Su 7:30-7:30

ADMISSION: $3, Children $1; Donations requested

1375
White House Historical Association
740 Jackson Pl NW, 20503; (p) (202) 737-8292; (f) (202) 682-0001; nhorstman@bhha.org; www.whitehousehistory.org

Private non-profit/ Board of Directors/publication: *White House History Journal*

HISTORICAL SOCIETY: Preserves White House history through research, educational programs, and publications.

PROGRAMS: Lectures; Publication; School-Based Curriculum

1376
White House, The
1600 Pennsylvania Ave NW, 20502; (p) (202) 456-2550; (f) (202) 456-6820; www.whitehousehistory.org

Federal/ 1792/ staff: 4(f)

HOUSE MUSEUM; PRESIDENTIAL SITE: Preserves and interprets historic and artistic contents of the president's home.

PROGRAMS: Concerts; Exhibits; Garden Tours; Interpretation; Lectures; Research Library/Archives

COLLECTIONS: [19th-20th c] Late 18th-20th century American and European decorative arts, paintings and prints; presidential porcelain, silver and glassware; manuscripts and archives on White House history; portraits of presidents, first ladies and American notables.

HOURS: Yr T-Sa

1377
Woodrow Wilson House
2340 S St NW, 20008; (p) (202) 387-4062; (f) (202) 483-1466; wilson@woodrowwilson house.org; www.woodrowwilsonhouse.org

Private non-profit/ 1964/ National Trust for Historic Preservation/ staff: 7(f); 25(p)/ members: 250

HOUSE MUSEUM; PRESIDENTIAL SITE: Promotes the legacy of President Woodrow Wilson as educator, statesman, and world leader through preservation of his home as presidential museum.

PROGRAMS: Community Outreach; Exhibits; Facility Rental; Guided Tours; Interpretation; Lectures

COLLECTIONS: [1912-1924] Furnishings, memorabilia and personal effects owned by President and Mrs. Wilson.

HOURS: Yr T-Su 10-4

ADMISSION: $5; Seniors $4

FLORIDA

ANNA MARIA

1378
Anna Maria Island Historical Society Inc.
402 Pine Ave, 34216 [PO Box 4315, 34216]; (p) (941) 778-0492; (c) Manatee

Private non-profit/ 1990/ Board of Directors/ staff: 1(p); 53(v)/ members: 160

HISTORICAL SOCIETY: Collects, researches, preserves, and exhibits artifacts from early days of Anna Maria Island.

PROGRAMS: Exhibits; Festivals; Lectures; Reenactments; School-Based Curriculum

COLLECTIONS: [Settlement-present] Rare photos, maps, charts, records, books, videos, clippings on island life, a fishing collection, fossils, shells, shark teeth and jaws, rattlesnake skin, household items, and quilts.

HOURS: Oct-May T-Th, Sa 10-3; June-Sept T-Th, Sa 10-1

APALACHICOLA

1379
Apalachicola Maritime Museum, Inc.
71 Market St, 32329 [PO Box 625, 32329]; (p) (850) 653-8700; (f) (850) 653-3714; (c) Franklin

Private non-profit/ staff: 2(f); 1(p); 12(v)/ members: 500

HISTORY MUSEUM: Preserves and interprets FL's Gulf Coast maritime history and historical coastal industries through permanent and changing exhibits.

PROGRAMS: Community Outreach; Exhibits; Family Programs; Interpretation; Research Library/Archives; School-Based Curriculum

COLLECTIONS: [1830-1950] Gulf Coast Schooner, and the Governor Stone; navigational artifacts, photos, oystering and fishing artifacts; vessels.

HOURS: Yr

1380
John Gorrie State Museum
46 Sixth St, 32329 [PO Box 267, 32329-0267]; (p) (850) 653-9347; (c) Franklin

State/ 1955/ staff: 1(f); 3(v)

HISTORY MUSEUM: Preserves the history of Dr John Gorrie, refrigeration pioneer.

COLLECTIONS: [1820-1855] Cotton trade items, Dr Gorrie's work.

HOURS: Yr Th-M 9-5

ADMISSION: $1; Under 6 free

BARTOW

1381
Polk County Historical Museum
100 E Main St, 33830; (p) (941) 634-4385; (c) Polk

County/ 1982/ Board of County Commissioners, Polk County/ staff: 2(f); 15(v)/ members: 1

HISTORY MUSEUM: Educates the public in the cultural, economics, political, and social history of Polk County and Central FL, in the state and national context.

PROGRAMS: Community Outreach; Elder's Programs; Exhibits; Facility Rental; Family Programs; Festivals; Guided Tours; Interpretation; Lectures; Publication; Research Library/Archives

COLLECTIONS: Artifacts related to Native Americans, African Americans, European, and white pioneers, agriculture, education, railroads, industry, tourism, sports, banking, medical, judicial, religious, and social history.

BOCA RATON

1382
Boca Raton Historical Society
71 N Federal Hwy, 33432; (p) (561) 395-6766; (f) (561) 395-4049; bocahist@aol.com; cbocahistory.org; (c) Palm Beach

Private non-profit/ 1972/ staff: 2(f); 2(p); 100(v)/ members: 800

HISTORICAL SOCIETY; HISTORY MUSEUM: Collects, preserves, and presents history of Boca Raton.

PROGRAMS: Exhibits; Facility Rental; Festivals; Garden Tours; Guided Tours; Lectures; Research Library/Archives; School-Based Curriculum

COLLECTIONS: [Late 19th-20th c] Photos and personal papers; period furniture and artifacts in Spanish-Moorish style of architect Addison Mizner.

HOURS: M-F 10-4

BOKEELIA

1383
Useppa Island Historical Society
Useppa Island, 33922 [PO Box 640, 33922]; (p) (941) 283-9600; (f) (841) 283-0290; useppamuse@aol.com; www.useppaisland.com; (c) Lee

Private non-profit/ 1994/ staff: 1(f); 1(p); 2(v)/ members: 205

HISTORICAL SOCIETY; HISTORY MUSEUM: Presents 10,000 years of Useppa's history; operates as a field station for the Univ of FL.

PROGRAMS: Annual Meeting; Exhibits; Guided Tours; Lectures

COLLECTIONS: Forensic restorations of Calusa man and woman; art work, maps, pictures, and exhibits, including Bay of Pigs/CIA occupation.

HOURS: Yr T-F 12-2, Sa-Su 1-2

ADMISSION: $2.50

BRADENTON

1384
De Soto National Memorial
75th St NW, 34280 [PO Box 15390, 34280]; (p) (941) 792-0458; (f) (941) 792-5094; DESO_interp_rangers@nps.gov; www.nps.gov/deso; (c) Manatee

Federal/ 1948/ National Park Service/ staff: 6(f); 4(p); 14(v)

HISTORIC SITE; HISTORY MUSEUM; LIVING HISTORY/OUTDOOR MUSEUM: Commemorates the expedition of Hernando de Soto from 1539-1543.

PROGRAMS: Exhibits; Film/Video; Interpretation; Living History; School-Based Curriculum

COLLECTIONS: [Early 16th c]

HOURS: Yr Daily 9-5

ADMISSION: No charge

1385
Eaton Florida History Room, Manatee County Central Library
1301 Barcarrota Blvd, 34205; (p) (941) 748-5555; (f) (941) 749-7155; (c) Manatee

County/ 1978/ Manatee County/ staff: 1(f)

LIBRARY AND/OR ARCHIVE: Maintains a special state and county reference collection and archives.

PROGRAMS: Research Library/Archives

COLLECTIONS: [1842-present] 5,500 history books, 12 drawers of maps, 20 plat books, 800 manuscripts, oral histories, census and newspaper microfilm, pamphlets and clippings, and over 28,000 local area negatives.

HOURS: Yr M-Th 9-9, F-Sa

1386
Manatee County Historical Commission
604 15th St E, 34208; (p) (941) 749-7465; (c) Manatee

Private non-profit/ 1974/ staff: 3(f); 1(p); 75(v)/publication: *Village Voice*

HISTORIC SITE: Protects and preserves county history; maintains 9 restored pioneer buildings.

PROGRAMS: Community Outreach; Concerts; Exhibits; Facility Rental; Family Programs; Festivals; Guided Tours; Interpretation; Lectures; Living History; Publication; Reenactments; School-Based Curriculum

COLLECTIONS: [1840-1914] Pioneer buildings with period furnishings.

HOURS: Yr M-F 9-4:30, Su 1:30-4:30

ADMISSION: No charge

1387
Manatee County Historical Records Library
1405 4th Ave W, 34205; (p) (941) 741-4070; cslusser@clerkofcourts.com; (c) Manatee

County/ 1977/ Manatee County Clerk of Circuit Court/ staff: 2(f)

LIBRARY AND/OR ARCHIVES: Houses records from county, beginning in 1855.

PROGRAMS: Community Outreach; Research Library/Archives

COLLECTIONS: [1855-present] Deed books, marriage licenses, probate files, court minute books, school attendance records, voter registration books, abstracts, marks and brands books, and soldier and sailor discharge books.

BRISTOL

1388
Torreya State Park
County Rd 1641 W of SR 12, 32321 [HC 2 Box 70, 32321]; (p) (850) 643-2674; (f) (850) 643-2987; torreya@nettally.com; www.dep state.fl.us; (c) Liberty

State/ 1935/ Dept of Environmental Protection/ staff: 3(f); 1(p); 2(v)

HISTORIC SITE; HOUSE MUSEUM: Provides resource-based recreation while preserving, interpreting, and restoring natural and cultural resources; preserves the Gregory House.

PROGRAMS: Facility Rental; Festivals; Guided Tours; Interpretation; Lectures

COLLECTIONS: [Mid 1800s] Furniture, textiles, books, and blueprints.

HOURS: Yr Daily

ADMISSION: $2/Vehicle

BUSHNELL

1389
Dade Battlefield State Historic Site
7200 CR 603, 33513; (p) (352) 793-4781; (f) (352) 793-4230; dbshs@sum.net; www.dep.state.fl.us/parks; (c) Sumter

Joint/ 1921/ State Park Service; Dade Battlefield Society, Inc/ staff: 3(f); 1(p); 15(v)

HISTORIC SITE; HISTORY MUSEUM: Interprets the battle between the US Army and Seminole Warriors; preservation of the battlefield trail and surrounding grounds.

PROGRAMS: Exhibits; Facility Rental; Interpretation; Reenactments

COLLECTIONS: [1835, Second Seminole War] Battle memorabilia, paintings, period clothing, and other period artifacts.

HOURS: Yr Park: Daily 8-Sunset; Visitor

CANTONMENT

1390
Roy L. Hyatt Environmental Center
1300 Tobias Rd, 32533; (p) (850) 937-2250; (f) (850) 937-2251; mwil2120@aol.com; (c) Escambia

County/ 1968/ School District of Escambia County/Board of Escambia Co./ staff: 4(f); 71(v)/publication: The Web Newsletter

GARDEN; HOUSE MUSEUM: Operates an environmental education center, pollution/recycling museum, gardens, and a natural history museum; maintains a one room school house and an 1890s dog trot farm house.

PROGRAMS: Community Outreach; Exhibits; Festivals; Garden Tours; Guided Tours; Interpretation; Publication

COLLECTIONS: [1890s] Farm house with antique furnishings, utensils, and other artifacts; one room school house with desks, books, pictures, and a bell; farm implements, pioneer garden and inventions of women and African Americans.

HOURS: Yr M-F 8:30-4:30

ADMISSION: No charge/Donations

CAPE CORAL

1391
Cape Coral Historical Society
544 Cultural Park Blvd, 33915 [PO Box 150637, 33990]; cchist@Juno.com; (c) Lee

Private non-profit/ 1987/ Board of Directors/ staff: 1(p); 20(v)/ members: 100/publication: Other Side of the River

HISTORY MUSEUM

PROGRAMS: Annual Meeting; Exhibits; Facility Rental; Festivals; Garden Tours; Guided Tours; Interpretation; Lectures; Living History; Publication; Research Library/Archives

COLLECTIONS: [1958-1998] Memorabilia and artifacts explaining the meteoric growth of Cape Coral.

CASSELBERRY

1392
Bahamas American Junkanoo Cultural and Goombay Festival Association of Florida, Inc., The
60 Carriage Hill Cr, 32718 [PO Box 181763, 32718-1763]; (p) (407) 260-1751; (f) (407) 265-0313; (c) Seminole

Private non-profit/ 1989/ staff: 25(f); 20(p); 30(v)

ART MUSEUM; LIVING HISTORY/OUTDOOR MUSEUM

PROGRAMS: Annual Meeting; Community Outreach; Concerts; Exhibits; Festivals; Living History

HOURS: Yr

CEDAR KEY

1393
Cedar Key State Museum
12231 SW 166 CT, 32625; (p) (352) 543-5350; cksm@svic.net; (c) Levy

State/ 1962/ staff: 1(f); 5(v)/ members: 5

HISTORY MUSEUM: Preserves local and state history.

PROGRAMS: Annual Meeting; Exhibits

COLLECTIONS: Shell and bottle collections; pre-Columbian artifacts; exhibits on local history on fishing, penal industry, railroads, Civil War, and early settlement of the region.

CHRISTMAS

1394
Fort Christmas Historical Park
1300 Fort Christmas Rd, 32709; (p) (407) 568-4149; (f) (407) 568-6629; (c) Orange

County/ 1931/ Orange Co. Parks and Recreation/ staff: 4(f); 4(p); 50(v)/ members: 65

HISTORY MUSEUM; HOUSE MUSEUM; LIVING HISTORY/OUTDOOR MUSEUM: Preserves Fort Christmas; operates tours and programs related to site; interprets cattle, citrus, and homesteading lifeways of region.

PROGRAMS: Exhibits; Festivals; Guided Tours; Interpretation; Living History; Reenactments

COLLECTIONS: [1835-1937] Military, Seminole Indian, and pioneer artifacts.

HOURS: Yr T-Sa 10-5, Su 1-5

ADMISSION: No charge/Donations

CLEARWATER

1395
Napoleonic Society of America
1115 Ponce De Leon Blvd, 33756; (p) (727) 586-1779; (f) (727) 581-2578; Napoleonicl@juno.com; www.napoleonic-society.com; (c) Pinellas

Private non-profit/ 1983/ staff: 2(f); 2(p)/ members: 1500

HISTORICAL SOCIETY: Provides people interested in Napoleon and his era with a means of communicating with each other and learn more about him.

PROGRAMS: Annual Meeting; Guided Tours

COLLECTIONS: Weapons, books, prints, porcelain, medals, paintings, marbles, and miniature soldiers.

CLEWISTON

1396
Ah-Tah-Thi-Ki Museum, Seminole Tribe of Florida
Big Cypress Indian Reservation, 33440 [HC-61, Box 21-A, 33440-9768]; (p) (863) 902-1113; (f) (863) 902-1117; museum@semtribe.com; www.seminoletribe.com/museum; (c) Hendry

1997/ Seminole Tribe of Florida/ staff: 21(f)/ members: 138/publication: Museum News: News from the Museum of the Seminole Tribe of Florida

TRIBAL MUSEUM: Collects, preserves, and exhibits material relating to the culture and history of the Seminole Indians of Florida.

PROGRAMS: Community Outreach; Exhibits; Guided Tours; Interpretation; Living History; Publication; Reenactments; Research Library/Archives; School-Based Curriculum

COLLECTIONS: [1800-present] Tribal artifacts, Seminole war militaria, paintings, monographs, serials, newspapers, photographs, maps, manuscripts, government documents, videos and microfilm.

HOURS: Yr T-Su 9-5

ADMISSION: $6, Student $4, Seniors $4

1397
Clewiston Museum
112 Commercio St, 33440; (p) (941) 983-2870; (c) Hendry

Private non-profit/ 1984/ staff: 2(p); 1(v)/ members: 110

HISTORY MUSEUM: Collects and preserves local history.

PROGRAMS: Annual Meeting; Exhibits; Film/Video

COLLECTIONS: [1920-1940] Period items and photos; two exhibits describing the process of sugarcane production and flight training of British flyers during WWII.

COCOA

1398
Brevard Museum of History and Science
2201 Michigan Ave, 32926; (p) (407) 632-1830; (f) (407) 631-7551; brevardmuseum@palmnet.net; www5.palmnet.net/~brevardmuseum; (c) Brevard

Private non-profit/ 1969/ Board of Trustees/ staff: 2(f); 1(p); 120(v)/ members: 490

HISTORY MUSEUM: Operates and maintains a museum for the education of the public about the regional cultural heritage and to preserve historic artifacts and natural history specimens.

PROGRAMS: Exhibits; Facility Rental; Guided Tours; Lectures; School-Based Curriculum

COLLECTIONS: 1000 volume research library; 2,000 historic photographs, maps, and documents; and over 1,000 artifacts, including furnishings.

HOURS: Yr T-Sa 10-4, Su 1-4

ADMISSION: $4, Children $2.50

CORAL GABLES

1399
Coral Gables Merrick House
907 Coral Way, 33134 [City of Coral Gables, 405 Biltmore Way, 33134]; (p) (305) 460-5361; (f) (305) 460-5317; (c) Dade

City/ 1978/ City of Coral Gables/ staff: 1(f); 25(v)

HISTORIC SITE; HOUSE MUSEUM: Preservation of the home of George E. Merrick, city founder; preserves and interprets early local history.

PROGRAMS: Exhibits; Facility Rental; Garden Tours; Guided Tours; Interpretation; Lectures; Research Library/Archives

COLLECTIONS: [Late 19th-early 20th c] Original artwork, furnishings, and memorabilia of the Merrick family and the region.

HOURS: Yr W, Su 1-4

ADMISSION: $2, Children $0.50

CRESTVIEW

1400
Carver-Hill Memorial and Historical Society, Inc.
901 McClelland St, Fairview Park, 32536 [649 McClelland St, 32536-3949]; (c) Okaloosa

Private non-profit/ 1969/ staff: 2(p); 2(v)

HISTORICAL SOCIETY; RESEARCH CENTER: Operates the Carver-Hill Museum and a School Center; presents cultural enrichment and awareness programs; emphasizes historical preservation, research, education, sports, music, and Black Heritage.

PROGRAMS: Annual Meeting; Community Outreach; Concerts; Elder's Programs; Exhibits; Facility Rental; Family Programs; Festivals; Lectures; Living History; Research Library/Archives; Theatre

COLLECTIONS: [1900-present] Books, magazine, newspapers, music, photos, clothing, school trophies, yearbooks, and school documents; local, state, national, and international Gov. materials; historical scenes, obituaries.

HOURS: Yr M-F 9-5, 1st and 3rd Sa 12-4

ADMISSION: No charge

CROSS CREEK

1401
Marjorie Kinnan Rawlings State Historic Site
S CR 325, [Rte 3 Box 92, Hawthorne, 32640]; (p) (352) 466-3672; (f) (352) 466-4743; (c) Alachua

State/ 1970/ staff: 2(f); 5(p); 20(v)/publication: News From the Creek

HISTORIC SITE; HOUSE MUSEUM; LIVING HISTORY/OUTDOOR MUSEUM: Preserves and interprets the Cross Creek farm that inspired Rawlings, the Pulitzer Prize Winning author of "The Yearling."

PROGRAMS: Annual Meeting; Guided Tours; Interpretation; Living History; Publication

COLLECTIONS: [1928-1941] Rawlings' possessions, furniture, and literature; original house and farmyard items.

HOURS: Oct-July Th-Su 10-4; Gounds: Yr Daily

ADMISSION: $3, Children $2; Grounds free

CRYSTAL RIVER

1402
Crystal River State Archaeological Site
3400 N Museum Pointe, 34428; (p) (352) 795-3817; (f) (352) 795-6061; crsas@sunco.com; (c) Citrus

State/ 1965/ Department of Environmental Protection/ staff: 3(f); 20(v)

HISTORIC SITE; HISTORY MUSEUM; TRIBAL MUSEUM: Preserves and interprets Pre-Columbian Native American ceremonial center and Mound Complex.

PROGRAMS: Community Outreach; Exhibits; Guided Tours; Interpretation; Lectures; School-Based Curriculum

COLLECTIONS: [500 BC-pre-European Contact] Site artifacts that interpret technologies, trade networks, and comparisons with other parts of the country and the world at various times in prehistory.

HOURS: Yr M-Su Grounds: 8-Sundown; Visitors Center: 9-5

ADMISSION: Varies

1403
Yulee Sugar Mill Ruins State Historic Site
CR 490, 34428 [3400 N Museum Pointe, Cystal River, 34428]; (p) (352) 795-3817; (f) (352) 795-6061; crsas@sunco.com; (c) Citrus

State/ 1955/ Department of Environmental Protection, Florida Park Service/ staff: 10(v)

HISTORIC SITE: Preserves history and site of the last remnants of FL's first US Senator's sugar plantation and Yulee's mill.

PROGRAMS: Community Outreach; Exhibits; Guided Tours; Interpretation

COLLECTIONS: [1851-1864] Sugar mill ruins; the masonry structure, iron cane crushing machinery, and remnants of a kettle train.

HOURS: Yr M-Su 8-Sunset

DADE CITY

1404
Pioneer Florida Museum Association, Inc.
15602 Pioneer Museum Rd, 33526 [PO Box 335, 33526]; (p) (352) 567-0262; (f) (352) 567-1262; www.dadecity.com/museum; (c) Pasco

Private non-profit/ 1961/ Board of Trustees/ staff: 4(p); 100(v)/ members: 400

HISTORY MUSEUM: Promotes, fosters, educates, and encourages public interest in pioneer FL life by collecting, preserving, restoring, arranging, and displaying articles of historical significance.

PROGRAMS: Annual Meeting; Community Outreach; Concerts; Exhibits; Facility Rental; Family Programs; Festivals; Guided Tours; Interpretation; Lectures; Living History; Reenactments; Research Library/Archives; School-Based Curriculum

COLLECTIONS: [Pioneer] 13 Star flag, doll collection of governor's wife, rose pottery collection, a 1913 steam engine, and a picture display of Cumner Sons Sawmill Co.

HOURS: Yr T, Th, F 1-5

ADMISSION: $5, Children $2, Seniors $4

DAVIE

1405
Flamingo Gardens
3750 Flamingo Rd, 33330; (p) (954) 473-2955; (c) Broward

Private non-profit/ 1927/ staff: 30(f); 18(p); 130(v)/ members: 2200

GARDEN; HOUSE MUSEUM

PROGRAMS: Community Outreach; Exhibits; Facility Rental; Family Programs; Festivals; Garden Tours; Guided Tours; Lectures

COLLECTIONS: [1930s] Historical home of pioneers Floyd and Jane Wray, depicting lifestyle typical of the era.

HOURS: Nov-May Daily 9:30-5:30, June-Oct T-Su 9:30-5:30

ADMISSION: $10, Children $5.50

DAYTONA BEACH

1406
Halifax Historical Museum
252 S Beach St, 32114; (p) (904) 255-6976; mail@halifaxhistorical.org; www.halifaxhistorical.org; (c) Volusia

Private non-profit/ 1949/ staff: 2(f); 3(p); 10(v)/ members: 450/publication: Daytona Bch and the Halifax River Area

HISTORICAL SOCIETY; HISTORY MUSEUM: Collects, preserves, and interprets the history of the Halifax River area for educational purposes.

PROGRAMS: Annual Meeting; Community Outreach; Concerts; Elder's Programs; Exhibits; Facility Rental; Family Programs; Festivals; Film/Video; Guided Tours; Lectures; Living History; Publication; Research Library/Archives; School-Based Curriculum

COLLECTIONS: [1500-1945] Maps, photos, museum artifacts, books, and newspaper archives.

1407
Mary Mcleod Bethune Foundation
640 Mary Mcleod Bethune Blvd, 32115; (p) (904) 255-1401 x 372

1408
Southeast Museum of Photography at Daytona Beach
1200 W International Speedway Blvd, 32114; (p) (904) 254-4475; (f) (904) 254-4487; nordsta@dbcc.cc.fl.us; (c) Volusia

1992/ staff: 3(f); 35(p)/ members: 140/publication: *Mangrove Coast- Fifty Years on the Mangrove Coast, and others*

ART MUSEUM; HISTORY MUSEUM: Dedicated to presentation and interpretation of photos as aesthetic and social objects.

PROGRAMS: Community Outreach; Exhibits; Family Programs; Film/Video; Guided Tours; Interpretation; Publication

COLLECTIONS: [20th c] Photos and periodicals from the US and elsewhere, with strengths in contemporary Cuba and American documentary and contemporary art.

HOURS: Yr M, W-F 9:30-4:30, T 9:30-7, Sa-Su 12-4

ADMISSION: No charge

DEERFIELD BEACH

1409
Deerfield Beach Historical Society
380 E Hillsboro Blvd, 33443 [PO Box 755, 33443]; (p) (954) 429-0378; (f) (954) 429-0378; (c) Broward

Private non-profit/ 1973/ staff: 1(f); 2(p); 30(v)/ members: 200/publication: *Images of America Deerfield Beach*

HISTORIC SITE; HISTORICAL SOCIETY; HOUSE MUSEUM: Collects and archives local historical information; preserves community's historic sites and structures.

PROGRAMS: Annual Meeting; Community Outreach; Exhibits; Facility Rental; Family Programs; Festivals; Guided Tours; Interpretation; Lectures; Living History; Publication; Research Library/Archives; School-Based Curriculum

COLLECTIONS: [1890s-1920s] Historic costumes, photos, documents, furnishings, and artifacts.

DELRAY BEACH

1410
Cason Cottage and Museum
5 NE 1st St, 33444 [5 NE First St, 33436]; (p) (561) 243-0223; (f) (561) 243-1062; tdwatdbhs@aol.com

1915/ staff: 1(f); 1(p)

HOUSE MUSEUM

COLLECTIONS: [1920s] Archives room with historic photos and research materials.

HOURS: Seasonal

1411
Cornell Museum at Old School Square
51 N Swinton Ave, 33444; (p) (561) 243-7922; (f) (561) 243-7018; (c) Palm Beach

Private non-profit/ 1989/ staff: 2(f); 60(p)/ members: 900

ART MUSEUM; HISTORIC SITE; HISTORY MUSEUM: Preserves historic site and local history.

PROGRAMS: Annual Meeting; Community Outreach; Concerts; Elder's Programs; Exhibits; Facility Rental; Family Programs; Guided Tours; Lectures; Research Library/Archives; Theatre

COLLECTIONS: [1800-1960s] Collection of art and sculpture; Rembrandt etchings.

HOURS: Yr T-Sa 11-4, Oct-May Su 1-4

ADMISSION: $3, Children $1; Under 6 free

1412
Delray Beach Historical Society, Inc.
200 NE First St, 33444; (p) (561) 243-0223, (561) 243-9578; (f) (561) 243-1062; (c) Palm Beach

Private non-profit/ 1965/ staff: 1(f); 1(p); 15(v)/ members: 500

HISTORICAL SOCIETY: Promotes local and state history with exhibits and educational programs; raises funds to maintain an archives room, restored house museum, and railway station historic site.

PROGRAMS: Annual Meeting; Community Outreach; Exhibits; Guided Tours; Lectures; Research Library/Archives

COLLECTIONS: [1895-present] Paper archives documenting local history; photos, original cartoons, railroad memorabilia, and period furnishings and accessories.

1413
Morikami Museum and Japanese Gardens, The
4000 Morikami Park Rd, 33446; (p) (561) 495-0233; (f) (561) 499-2557; morikami@co.palm-beach.fl.us; www.morikami.org; (c) Palm Beach

County; Private non-profit/ 1977/ staff: 25(f); 10(p); 230(v)/ members: 2100

HISTORY MUSEUM; GARDENS: Dedicated to interpreting Japanese culture and the Japanese heritage of FL through its collections, innovative programs, and Japanese gardens.

PROGRAMS: Annual Meeting; Community Outreach; Concerts; Elder's Programs; Exhibits; Facility Rental; Family Programs; Festivals; Film/Video; Garden Tours; Guided Tours; Interpretation; Lectures; Publication; Research Library/Archives; School-Based Curriculum

COLLECTIONS: [1868-present] 4,000 documents and photos of Japanese immigrants to Florida; folk crafts, paintings, prints, textiles, and decorative arts; tea ceremony utensils.

HOURS: Yr T-Su 10-5

ADMISSION: $7, Children $4, Seniors $6

EGLIN AFB

1414
U.S. Air Force Armament Museum
100 Museum Dr, 32542-1497; (p) (850) 882-4062; (f) (850) 882-3990; sneddon@eglin.af.mil; www.wg53.eglin.af.mil/armmus; (c) Okaloosa

Federal/ 1985/ US Air Force/ staff: 5(f); 1(p); 25(v)

HISTORY MUSEUM: Collects and preserves Air Force historical property.

PROGRAMS: Exhibits; Festivals; Film/Video

COLLECTIONS: [World War II-present] Artifacts related to aviation armament.

HOURS: Yr Daily 9:30-4:30

ADMISSION: No charge

ELLENTON

1415
Gamble Plantation State Historic Site
3708 Patten Ave, 34222; (p) (941) 723-4536; (f) (941) 723-4538; gpsh1@Juno.com

1844/ State/ staff: 4(f); 20(v)

HISTORIC SITE

COLLECTIONS: [1840-1860]

HOURS: Yr

ESTERO

1416
Koreshan State Historic Site
US Hwy 41 @ Corkscrew Rd, 33928 [PO Box 7, 33928]; (p) (941) 992-0311; (f) (941) 992-1607; B.J.Koresh@juno.com; www.dep.state.fl.us/parks; (c) Lee

State/ 1967/ Dept of Environmental Protection/Div of Rec and Parks/ staff: 11(f); 1(p); 85(v)/ members: 1

ART MUSEUM; HISTORIC SITE: Preserves the turn-of-the-century community compound, including buildings and artifacts.

PROGRAMS: Concerts; Exhibits; Facility Rental; Family Programs; Festivals; Guided Tours; Interpretation; Living History; Reenactments; Research Library/Archives; School-Based Curriculum

COLLECTIONS: [1894-1977] Buildings, paintings, tools, and machinery relating to a communal group known as the Koreshans.

HOURS: Yr Daily 8-Sunset

1417
Mound Key State Archaeological Site
Mouth of the Estero River near Big Carlos Pass, 33928 [PO Box 7, 33928]; (p) (941) 992-0311; (f) (941) 992-1607; J_Parks.KSHS@juno.com; www.dep.state.fl.us; (c) Lee

State/ Dept of Environmental Protection, Division of Recreation and Parks, FL State Parks/ staff: 11(f); 25(v)

HISTORIC SITE: Preserves the believed site of Calos, the capital of the Calusa Indians and the possible location of the Jesuit mission San Antonio de Carlos; also maintains an offshore island that has two shell mounds.

PROGRAMS: Exhibits; Guided Tours

COLLECTIONS: [100-1940] Archaeological site and materials along with two 30 ft. tall shell mounds.

HOURS: Yr Daily 8-Sundown

ADMISSION: No charge

EVERGLADES

1418
Museum of the Everglades
105 W Broadway, 34139 [PO Box 8, 34139]; (p) (941) 695-0008; (f) (941) 695-0036; donnaridewood@colliergov.net; www.collier museum.com; (c) Collier

1998/ Collier County Government/ staff: 1(f); 1(p); 40(v)/ members: 200

HISTORIC SITE; HISTORY MUSEUM: Showcases the history of the southwest Everglades region through exhibits, lectures, and programs; maintains a restored 1927 commercial laundry.

PROGRAMS: Community Outreach; Exhibits; Facility Rental; Interpretation; Lectures

COLLECTIONS: [1900-present] Photos and artifacts associated with European settlement of SW Florida, Seminole and Calusa settlements; artifacts from the founding of the city and the construction of the Tamiami Trail.

HOURS: Yr T-Sa

FERNANDINA BEACH

1419
Amelia Island Museum of History
233 S Third St, 32034; (p) (904) 261-7378; (f) (904) 261-9701; (c) Nassau

Private non-profit/ 1986/ Board of Trustees/ staff: 4(f); 2(p); 130(v)/ members: 600/publication: *Jailhouse Muse*

HISTORY MUSEUM: Focuses on historical education of Nassau County, Amelia Island, and Fernandina Beach.

PROGRAMS: Annual Meeting; Community Outreach; Exhibits; Guided Tours; Interpretation; Lectures; Publication; Research Library/Archives; School-Based Curriculum

COLLECTIONS: [Prehistory-1930] Photos, newspapers, books, and artifacts.

HOURS: Yr M-F 10-5, Sa 10-4

ADMISSION: $4

1420
Fort Clinch State Park
2601 Atlantic Ave, 32034; (p) (904) 277-7274; (f) (904) 277-7225; (c) Nassau

State/ State of FL/Dept of Environmental Protection/Division of Rec and Parks/ staff: 14(f); 2(p); 14(v)

HISTORIC SITE; LIVING HISTORY/OUTDOOR MUSEUM: Maintains historic Fort Clinch.

PROGRAMS: Exhibits; Festivals; Film/Video; Guided Tours; Interpretation; Living History

COLLECTIONS: [1864, Civil War] Seacoast Fort including drawbridge, guardhouse, blacksmith shop and kitchen; construction artifacts.

HOURS: Yr Daily

FORT LAUDERDALE

1421
Bonnet House
900 N Birch Rd, 33304; (p) (954) 563-5393; (f) (954) 561-4174; www.bonnethouse.com; (c) Broward

Private non-profit/ 1983/ Bonnet House, Inc/ staff: 10(f); 5(p); 125(v)/ members: 700/publication: *Reflections of a Legacy*

HISTORIC SITE; HOUSE MUSEUM: Thirty-five acre historic site and house museum that was once the residence of artists Fredric and Evelyn Bartlett.

PROGRAMS: Annual Meeting; Community Outreach; Concerts; Facility Rental; Garden Tours; Guided Tours; Lectures; Publication

COLLECTIONS: [1921-1995] Goods and decorative art collected byoriginal owners, including carousel animals, china, shells, and paintings.

HOURS: Yr W-F 10-3, Sa-Su 12-4

ADMISSION: $9

1422
Fort Lauderdale Historical Society, Inc.
219 SW 2nd Ave, 33301; (p) (954) 463-4451; (f) (954) 523-6228; ftlaud_hist_soc@ hotmail.com; www.oldfortlauderdale.org; (c) Broward

Private non-profit/ 1962/ Board of Trustees/ staff: 5(f); 4(p); 65(v)/publication: *New River Innsider*

HISTORIC PRESERVATION AGENCY; HISTORIC SITE; HISTORY MUSEUM; LIBRARY AND/OR ARCHIVES; RESEARCH CENTER: Collects, preserves, and disseminates history of Fort Lauderdale and its environs.

PROGRAMS: Annual Meeting; Community Outreach; Exhibits; Facility Rental; Film/Video; Guided Tours; Interpretation; Publication; Research Library/Archives; School-Based Curriculum

COLLECTIONS: [19th-20th c] Artifacts, manuscripts, maps, architectural drawings, oral histories, and 250,000 photo images.

HOURS: Yr T-SA 12-5

ADMISSION: $5, Children $2, Seniors $4; Under 6 free

1423
International Game Fish Assn., Fishing Hall of Fame and Museum
300 Gulf Stream Way, 33004; (p) (954) 922-4212; (f) (954) 954-4220; CMcDonald@ igfa.org; www.gfa.org; (c) Broward

Private non-profit/ 1998/ staff: 41(f); 8(p); 50(v)/ members: 21000/publication: *International Angler; World Record Game Fishes*

ART MUSEUM; RESEARCH CENTER: Maintains museum exhibits portraying history of IGFA, its founders, and sport of fishing.

PROGRAMS: Annual Meeting; Community Outreach; Exhibits; Facility Rental; Family Programs; Festivals; Film/Video; Garden Tours; Publication; Research Library/Archives; School-Based Curriculum

COLLECTIONS: [1900-present] Archival material on organization and sport of fishing.

HOURS: Yr Daily

ADMISSION: $4.99

1424
Old Dillard Museum
1009 NW Fourth St, 33311; (p) (954) 765-6952; (f) (954) 765-8899; (c) Broward

County/ 1995/ School Board of Broward County, Florida/ staff: 3(f); 2(p)

HISTORIC PRESERVATION AGENCY; HISTORIC SITE: Maintains exhibitions and develops programs, with an emphasis on African American history.

PROGRAMS: Community Outreach; Elder's Programs; Exhibits; Family Programs; Festivals; Film/Video; Guided Tours; Interpretation; Lectures; Research Library/Archives

COLLECTIONS: Artifacts and documents that represent examples of a rich African American Heritage as well as that of other peoples of color.

HOURS: Yr M-F

1425
Stranahan House, Inc.
335 SE 6th Ave, 33303 [PO Box 30207, 33303-0207]; (p) (954) 524-4736; (f) (954) 525-2838; stranahan1@aol.com; (c) Broward

Private non-profit/ 1981/ staff: 2(f); 4(p); 50(v)/ members: 450

HISTORIC SITE: Preserves, promotes, and interprets the 1901 Victorian Stranahan House and its collection.

PROGRAMS: Annual Meeting; Community Outreach; Exhibits; Facility Rental; Family Programs; Guided Tours; Interpretation; Lectures; Living History; School-Based Curriculum

COLLECTIONS: [1913-1915] Victorian era household items.

HOURS: Sept-June M-Sa 10-4, Su 1-4

ADMISSION: $5, Student $2

FORT MYERS

1426
Fort Myers Historical Museum
2300 Peck St, 33901; (p) (941) 332-5955; (f) (941) 332-6637; MSantiago@cityftmyers.com; (c) Lee

City/ 1982/ City of Fort Myers/ staff: 3(f); 1(p); 15(v)/ members: 180/publication: *The Fort Historian*

HISTORY MUSEUM: Housed in the former Atlantic Coastline Railroad depot, the museum focuses on regional history, including exhibits on the Caulsa and Seminole Indians, Spanish explorers, and early settlers.

PROGRAMS: Community Outreach; Elder's Programs; Exhibits; Facility Rental; Guided Tours; Interpretation; Lectures; Publication; Research Library/Archives; School-Based Curriculum

COLLECTIONS: [800 BC-1940] Artifacts covering all periods of Fort Myers History.

HOURS: Yr T-Sa 9-4

ADMISSION: $6, Children $3, Senior $5.50

1427
Burroughs Home
2505 First St, 33902 [PO Box 2217, 33902];
(p) (941) 332-6125; (f) (941) 332-6806; (c)
Lee

City/ 1901/ City of Ft. Myers/ staff: 1(f); 2(p)

HISTORIC SITE

PROGRAMS: Facility Rental; Garden Tours;
Living History

HOURS: Yr 11-4

ADMISSION: $6, Children $3

1428
Edison-Ford Winter Estates
2350 McGregor Blvd, 33901; (p) (941) 334-
3614, (941) 334-7419; (f) (941) 332-6684;
www.edison-ford-estate.com; (c) Lee

City/ 1947/ City of Fort Myers/ staff: 27(f);
60(p); 58(v)

GARDEN; HISTORIC SITE; LIVING HISTO-
RY/OUTDOOR MUSEUM: Collects, preserves, and exhibits artifacts relating to the
lives and works of Thomas Edison and Henry
Ford.

PROGRAMS: Community Outreach; Exhibits;
Family Programs; Film/Video; Garden Tours;
Guided Tours; Lectures; Living History; Reen-
actments; Research Library/Archives; School-
Based Curriculum

COLLECTIONS: [1865-1947] Edison Phonographs; a 1908 Cadillac Opera Coupe, a prototype Model T, and a 1936 Brewster limou-
sine; manuscripts; memorabilia related to
Edison's life and an assortment of his inventions.

HOURS: Yr M-Sa 9-4, Su 12-4

ADMISSION: $12, Children $5.50

1429
**Railroad Museum of Southern
Florida, Inc.**
2787 N Tamiami Trail, Unit 109, 33911 [PO
Box 7372, 33911-7372]; (p) (941) 997-2457;
(f) (941) 997-7673; (c) Lee

Private non-profit/ 1992/ Board of Directors/
staff: 3(p); 2(v)/ members: 153

HISTORY MUSEUM: Preserves, collects, documents, and interprets railroad history, with
emphasis on FL railroad history.

PROGRAMS: Exhibits; Guided Tours; Interpretation

COLLECTIONS: [1920-1970] Railroad
lanterns, tools, and artifacts from the steam
era; postcards, photos, maps, and baggage
carts; artifacts from the Atlantic Coast Line,
Seaboard Air Line, and Florida East Coast
Railway.

FORT PIERCE

1430
**Harbor Branch Oceanographic
Institution, Inc.**
5600 US-1 N, 34946; (p) (561) 465-2400; (f)
(561) 468-6910; tours@hboi.edu;
www.hboi.edu; (c) St. Lucie

Private non-profit/ 1971/ staff: 250(v)/ members: 1200

NATURAL HISTORY MUSEUM: Explores the

world's oceans; performs ocean engineering
and ship/sub operations; conducts aquacul-
ture, biomedical research.

PROGRAMS: Community Outreach; Concerts;
Exhibits; Facility Rental; Family Programs; Festivals; Film/Video; Guided Tours; Lectures

COLLECTIONS: Marine natural history specimens, predominantly from waters off the coast
of FL and Caribbean; research collection.

HOURS: Yr Daily

ADMISSION: $6, Children $4

1431
St. Lucie County Historical Museum
414 Seaway Dr, 34949; (p) (561) 462-1795;
(f) (561) 462-1877; (c) St Lucie

County/ 1967/ St Lucie County/ staff: 3(f); 4(p); 65(v)

HISTORY MUSEUM; HOUSE MUSEUM: Collects, interprets, and preserves county and
Treasure Coast history.

PROGRAMS: Community Outreach; Exhibits;
Family Programs; Guided Tours; Research Li-
brary/Archives; School-Based Curriculum

COLLECTIONS: [Turn of 19th c] Museum artifacts, artifacts, paintings, bound copies of local
newspapers, Seminole artifacts.

HOURS: Yr 10-4

ADMISSION: $3, Student $1.50

1432
UDT-Seal Museum Association, Inc.
3300 N State Rd AIA, 34949-8520; (p) (561)
595-5845; (f) (561) 595-5847; www.udt-seal.org;
(c) St Lucie

Private non-profit/ 1985/ staff: 2(f); 1(p); 18(v)/
members: 2400/publication: *Fire in the Hole*

HISTORY MUSEUM: Preserves the heritage
and equipment of naval special warfare teams
(NCDU, UDT, Scouts and Raiders, SEALS).

PROGRAMS: Community Outreach; Exhibits;
Guided Tours; Lectures; Publication; Reenactments

COLLECTIONS: [1943-present] Boats, swim-
mer delivery vehicles, Apollo training modules,
helicopter, photos, team histories, weapons,
and naval special warfare equipment.

HOURS: Yr

FORT WALTON BEACH

1433
Camp Walton Schoolhouse Museum
107 First St, 32549 [PO Box 4009, 32549];
(p) (850) 833-9596; (f) (850) 833-9675;
www.fwb.org; (c) Okaloosa

City/ 1976/ City of Fort Walton Beach/ staff:
4(f); 4(p)

HISTORY MUSEUM: Collects, preserves, and
interprets early school days and Camp Walton's early history.

PROGRAMS: Community Outreach; Exhibits;
Guided Tours; Interpretation; Living History;
School-Based Curriculum

COLLECTIONS: [1912-1950] Adaptively restored
one-room school with furnishings of the period.
Collection includes school furniture, books, photos, and memorabilia of the early 1900s.

HOURS: Sept-May

1434
Indian Temple Mound Museum
139 Miracle Strip Pkwy SE, 32549 [PO Box
4009, 32549]; (p) (850) 833-9595; (f) (850)
833-9675; www.fwb.org; (c) Okaloosa

City/ 1962/ City of Fort Walton Beach/ staff:
5(f); 3(p)/ members: 25

HISTORIC SITE; HISTORY MUSEUM: Collects, preserves, and interprets archaeological
artifacts of the prehistoric cultural traditions of
the SE US; preserves the Temple Mound.

PROGRAMS: Community Outreach; Exhibits;
Guided Tours; Interpretation; Lectures; Research Library/Archives; School-Based Curriculum

COLLECTIONS: [Prehistoric-1900s] Prehistoric Native American artifacts of stone, bone,
wood, and clay; artifacts from explorers, the
Civil War, and local settlers.

HOURS: June-Aug M-Sa 9-4:30, Su 12:30-
4:30;

FORTMYERS

1435
Koreshan Unity Alliance
2449 First St, 33902 [PO Box 2061, Fort
Myers, 33902]; (p) (941) 992-0311; (f) (941)
334-7799; Bill_Grace@msn.com; (c) Lee

Private non-profit/ staff: 4(v)/ members: 50

HISTORICAL SOCIETY: Support group for the
Koreshan State Historic Site and Mound Key
State Archaeological site; raises monies and
administers grants used for restoration, rehabilitation, and stabilization of cultural resources.

GAINESVILLE

1436
**Alachua County Historic Trust;
Matheson Museum, Inc.**
513 E University Ave, 32601; (p) (352) 378-
2280; (f) (352) 378-1246; matheson
museum@usa.net; (c) Alachua

Private non-profit/ 1994/ Board of Directors/
staff: 4(p); 10(v)/ members: 800

HISTORICAL SOCIETY; HISTORY MUSEUM;
HOUSE MUSEUM: Collects, preserves, and
interprets the history of Alachua County.

PROGRAMS: Annual Meeting; Exhibits; Family Programs; Guided Tours; Interpretation; Lectures; Publication

COLLECTIONS: [20th c] 10,000 historic photos, 3,000 books, ephemera, and records of
civic groups.

HOURS: Yr T-F 9:30-1:30, Su 1-5, 2nd and 4th
Sa 10-4

1437
Historic Thomas Center, The
302 NE Sixth Ave, 32602 [Station 30, PO Box
490, 32602]; (p) (352) 334-5064; (f) (352)
334-2314; fossreda@ci.gainesville.fl.us;
www.state.fl.us/gvl/; (c) Alachua

City/ 1910/ City of Gainesville/ staff: 13(f); 4(p)

A cultural center located in a 1910 hotel; maintains local history exhibits and art galleries.

PROGRAMS: Annual Meeting; Concerts; Exhibits; Facility Rental; Festivals; Garden Tours;

Guided Tours; Interpretation; Lectures; Theatre

COLLECTIONS: [1920s] Period antiques and artifacts from the hotel; historic dioramas; photos.

HOURS: Yr M-F 8-5

GRANT

1438
Grant Historical House
5795 S US Hwy 1, 32949 [PO Box 55, 32949]; (p) (407) 723-8543, (407) 723-2260

HOUSE MUSEUM

GREEN COVE SPRINGS

1439
Clay County Historical Society
403 Forris St, 32043 [PO Box 1202, 32043]; (p) (904) 284-9644; (c) Clay

County, non-profit; Private non-profit/ 1966/ staff: 70(v)/ members: 137/publication: *Parade of Memories*

HISTORIC PRESERVATION AGENCY; HISTORIC SITE; HISTORICAL SOCIETY; HISTORY MUSEUM; LIVING HISTORY/OUTDOOR MUSEUM: Maintains museum located in the old historic courthouse, along with a railroad depot and a caboose with railroad artifacts.

PROGRAMS: Annual Meeting; Community Outreach; Exhibits; Family Programs; Festivals; Guided Tours; Interpretation; Lectures; Living History; Publication; Research Library/Archives; School-Based Curriculum

COLLECTIONS: [Civil War-WWII] Period kitchen, stoves, and furniture; railroad collection with caboose and work car; pictures and records of area communities.

HOURS: Yr Su 2-5

ADMISSION: Donations requested

GULF BREEZE

1440
Gulf Islands National Seashore
1801 Gulf Breeze Pkwy, 32561; (p) (850) 934-2600; (f) (850) 932-9654; GUIS_Interpretation@nps.gov; www.nps.gov/guis/; (c) Escambia/Santa Rosa/Okaloosa

Federal/ 1971/ staff: 80(f); 50(p); 100(v)

HISTORY MUSEUM; LIVING HISTORY/OUTDOOR MUSEUM: Preserves cultural and natural resources with historical focus on the evolution of US Seacoast Defenses.

PROGRAMS: Community Outreach; Exhibits; Facility Rental; Family Programs; Guided Tours; Interpretation; Living History; Publication; Reenactments; Research Library/Archives; School-Based Curriculum

COLLECTIONS: Coastal defense collections from 1820-1940s; other items related to archaeology, US Quarantines, the lighthouse, the life-saving station, and barrier island natural history.

HOMELAND

1441
Homeland Heritage Park
578 2nd St, 33847 [Drawer CS07, PO Box 9005, Bartow, 33831]; (p) (941) 534-3766; (f) (941) 534-3766; (c) Polk

County/ 1985/ Polk County BoCC/ staff: 1(f); 1(p); 3(v)

HOUSE MUSEUM; LIVING HISTORY/OUTDOOR MUSEUM: Maintains a collection of buildings dating back to the 1880s; develops programs for school groups and seniors.

PROGRAMS: Exhibits; Facility Rental; Festivals; Guided Tours; Interpretation

COLLECTIONS: [1880-1912] Artifacts, farm equip, and household items; a historic church, school, farmhouse, pole barn, and log cabin.

HOURS: Yr M-F 9-4

ADMISSION: No charge

HOMESTEAD

1442
Everglades/Dry Tortugas National Parks
40001 State Rd 9336, 33034; (p) (305) 242-7700; (f) (305) 242-7711; www.nps.gov/ever; (c) Dade/Monroe/Collier

Federal/ 1935/ National Park Service/ staff: 230(f); 100(p); 200(v)

HISTORIC SITE; LIVING HISTORY/OUTDOOR MUSEUM: Preserves Ft. Jefferson, related artifacts, and the surrounding environment.

PROGRAMS: Community Outreach; Exhibits; Guided Tours; Interpretation; Lectures; Living History; School-Based Curriculum

COLLECTIONS: [Pre-Columbian-present] Natural history specimens, art/literature on Everglades, shipwrecks, and military artifacts.

HOURS: Yr Everglades: Daily, Tortugas: 24

ISLAMORADA

1443
Indian Key State Historic
[PO Box 1052, 33036]; (p) (305) 664-2560; (f) (305) 664-0713; PatWells@terranova.net; (c) Monroe

State/ 1972/ Florida State Parks/ staff: 6(f)

HISTORIC SITE: Preserves historic Indian Key Island, site of the First Dade County Seat, a village that was destroyed in an Indian attack in 1840.

PROGRAMS: Guided Tours; Interpretation

COLLECTIONS: [1830-Aug 7 1840] Streets and ruins of 1830s structures.

HOURS: Yr Th-M 8-5

ADMISSION: $1

1444
Lignumvitae State Botanical Site
[PO Box 1052, 33036]; (p) (305) 664-2540; (f) (305) 664-0713; PatWells@terranova.net; (c) Monroe

State/ 1972/ Florida Park Service/ staff: 6(f)/publication: *Charlotte's Story*

HOUSE MUSEUM; LIVING HISTORY/OUTDOOR MUSEUM: Maintains historical botanical site and the Matheson House, which dates to 1919.

PROGRAMS: Guided Tours; Interpretation; Publication

COLLECTIONS: [1880s-1960s] Native American artifacts, period furniture, and West Indies type hardwood hammock.

HOURS: Yr Th-M

1445
San Pedro Underwater Archaeological Preserve
1.25 Nautical mi SW of Indian Key, 33036 [Box 1052, 33036]; (p) (305) 664-2540; (f) (305) 664-0713; patwells@terranova.net; (c) Monroe

State/ 1989/ Florida Park Service/ staff: 6(f)

HISTORIC SITE: Maintains underwater wreckage site of a 1733 Spanish treasure ship.

PROGRAMS: Guided Tours

COLLECTIONS: [1733] Wreckage site, replica canoes, ballast stones, and mooring buoys.

HOURS: Yr

1446
Windlay Key Fossil Reef State Geological Site
Mile Marker 85.5, 33036 [PO Box 1052, 33036]; (p) (305) 664-2540; (f) (305) 664-0713; PatWells@terranova.net; (c) Monroe

State/ 1985/ Florida Park Service/ staff: 6(f)

HISTORY MUSEUM; LIVING HISTORY/OUTDOOR MUSEUM: Preserves geological site situated on a fossilized coral reef, which was also a quarry site.

PROGRAMS: Guided Tours; Interpretation

COLLECTIONS: [1908-1912] West Indies style hammock; fossilized coral and marine life.

HOURS: Yr Th-M 8-5

ADMISSION: $1.50

JACKSONVILLE

1447
Jacksonville Maritime Museum
1015 Museum Circle, Unit 2, 32207-9006; (p) (904) 398-9011; (f) (904) 398-7248; www.Jaxmarmus.com; (c) Duval

Private non-profit/ Board of Trustees/ staff: 2(p); 20(v)/ members: 250

MARITIME MUSEUM: Maintains two maritime history-related exhibits.

PROGRAMS: Annual Meeting; Community Outreach; Exhibits; Lectures; Research Library/Archives; School-Based Curriculum

COLLECTIONS: [1800s-1900s] Models of ships, dioramas, and photographic displays.

HOURS: Yr Daily

1448
Karpeles Manuscript Library
101 W 1st St, 33206; (p) (904) 356-2992; (f) (904) 356-4338; KmuseumJax@aol.com; www.rain.org/~karpeles/; (c) Duval

Private non-profit/ staff: 6(p); 20(v)/publication: *Karpeles Happenings*

HISTORY MUSEUM: Preserves original writings of authors, scientists, composers, philosophers, statesmen, sovereigns and leaders from all periods of world history.

PROGRAMS: Concerts; Facility Rental; Family Programs; Lectures; Living History; Publication; Reenactments

COLLECTIONS: [Renaissance-present] Artifacts, manuscripts, and documents.

HOURS: Yr M-Sa 10-3

1449
Kingsley Plantation (Timucuan Preserve)
11676 Palmetto Ave, 32226; (p) (904) 251-3537; (f) (904) 251-3477; www.nps.gov; (c) Duval

Federal/ 1991/ National Park Service/ staff: 5(f); 3(p); 2(v)

HISTORIC SITE; HOUSE MUSEUM: Maintains 19th c Sea Island cotton plantation; interprets history of slavery.

PROGRAMS: Exhibits; Interpretation; Research Library/Archives; School-Based Curriculum

COLLECTIONS: [Antebellum Florida] Personal artifacts from plantation owners and archaeological artifacts from the slave quarters.

1450
Museum of Science and History of Jacksonville, Inc.
1025 Museum Circle, 32207; (p) (904) 396-6674; (f) (904) 396-5799; (c) Duval

Private non-profit/ 1941/ staff: 35(f); 10(p); 400(v)/ members: 2035/publication: *MOSH Musings*

HISTORY MUSEUM: Collects, preserves, and exhibits collections relating to astronomy, physical science, and the history and natural science of NE Florida.

PROGRAMS: Annual Meeting; Community Outreach; Exhibits; Facility Rental; Family Programs; Interpretation; Lectures; Publication; School-Based Curriculum

COLLECTIONS: 5,000 archival records, 500 photography and motion picture pieces, 8,000 pre-Columbian pottery and stone artifacts, 10,300 non-living specimens, 80 living animals and 300 Native American artifacts.

HOURS: Yr M-F 10-5, Sa 10-6, Su 1-6

ADMISSION: $6, Children $4, Seniors $4.50; Military $4.50

1451
Museum of Southern History, The
4304 Herschel St, 37710; (p) (904) 388-3574; fladepot@aol.com; (c) Duval

Private non-profit/ staff: 1(f); 22(v)/ members: 401

HISTORY MUSEUM: Presents the lifestyle and culture of the Antebellum South.

PROGRAMS: Annual Meeting; Community Outreach; Exhibits; Guided Tours; Interpretation; Lectures; Living History; Reenactments; Research Library/Archives; School-Based Curriculum

COLLECTIONS: [1840-1870] Period memorabilia, uniforms, weapons, flags, and personal

items; research library includes genealogies.

HOURS: Yr T-Sa 10-5

ADMISSION: $1

JUPITER

1452
Florida History Center and Museum
Burt Reynolds Park, 33455 [805 N US Hwy One, 33455]; (p) (561) 747-6639; (f) (561) 575-3292; fhcm@bellsouth.net; (c) Palm Beach

Private non-profit/ 1972/ staff: 4(f); 1(p); 85(v)/ members: 450

HISTORIC SITE; HISTORY MUSEUM; HOUSE MUSEUM: Oversees the Jupiter Inlet Lighthouse and the DuBois Pioneer Home in addition to the museum; collects, preserves, and interprets the history of Florida.

PROGRAMS: Exhibits; Facility Rental; Festivals; Guided Tours; Lectures; Research Library/Archives

COLLECTIONS: [Late 1800s-early 1900s] Prehistoric archaeological artifacts; regional pioneer artifacts; state historical archives.

HOURS: Yr T-F 10-5, Sa-Su 12-5

ADMISSION: $5, Children $3, Seniors $4

KENNEDY SPACE CENTER

1453
Kennedy Space Center Visitor Complex
SR 405, 32899 [Mail Code DNPS, 32899]; (p) (321) 449-4444; (f) (321) 452-3043; www.kennedyspacecenter.com; (c) Brevard

Federal/ 1966/ NASA/ staff: 100(f); 500(p)

Offers tours of restricted Kennedy Space Center areas; educates the public about the space center and technology. Presents NASA history.

PROGRAMS: Annual Meeting; Exhibits; Guided Tours; Living History

COLLECTIONS: [1950s-present] Saturn V moon rocket, components of the International Space Station, and Space Shuttle Launch Pads, rocket garden, moon and Mars rocks, Mercury and Gemini artifacts.

HOURS: Yr Daily

KEY BISCAYNE

1454
Bill Baggs Cape Florida State Recreation Area
1200 S Crandon Blvd, 33149; (p) (305) 361-8779; (f) (305) 365-0003; capefla@gate.net; www.dep.state.fl.us/parks/; (c) Dade

State/ 1967/ State of FL Dept of Environmental Protection/ staff: 18(f); 2(p); 15(v)

HISTORIC SITE: Provides resource-based recreation while preserving, interpreting, and restoring natural and cultural resources.

PROGRAMS: Exhibits; Facility Rental; Guided Tours; Interpretation

COLLECTIONS: [1855] The newly renovated lightkeeper's cottage displays period furnishings supplemented by the interior and exterior interpretive museum panels which depict the history and lives of the earliest settlers through the time of the lightkeepers.

HOURS: Yr Th-M 10

ADMISSION: $4

KEY LARGO

1455
John Pennekamp Coral Reef State Park
Mile Marker 102.5 Overseas Hwy, 33037 [PO Box 487, 33037]; (p) (305) 451-1202; (f) (305) 853-3555; jpcrsp@reefnet.com; (c) Monroe

State/ 1961/ Department of Environmental Protection/ staff: 21(f); 2(p)

LIVING HISTORY/OUTDOOR MUSEUM: Maintains natural history exhibits interpreting park's unique marine environment.

PROGRAMS: Exhibits; Film/Video; Guided Tours; Interpretation; Lectures

COLLECTIONS: Tropical vegetation, shore birds, marine life, mangrove swamps, tropical hammocks, and extensive coral reefs.

HOURS: Yr M-F 8-Sunset

ADMISSION: $3.25/vehicle plus $0.50/person Monroe County Surcharge

KEY WEST

1456
Audubon House and Tropical Gardens
205 Whitehead, 33040; (p) (305) 294-2116; (f) (305) 294-4513; audubon@flakeysol.com; audubonhouse.com; (c) Monroe

Private non-profit/ 1960/ Mitchell Wolfson Family Foundation/ staff: 4(f); 5(p)

HOUSE MUSEUM: Preserves historic home and furnishings of John James Audubon.

PROGRAMS: Community Outreach; Exhibits; Garden Tours; Guided Tours

COLLECTIONS: [19th c] Furnishings; original John James Audubon artwork.

HOURS: Yr Daily 9:30-5

ADMISSION: $7.50, Children $3.50, Seniors $6.50

1457
Donkey Milk House, Historic Home
613 Eaton St, 33040; (p) (305) 296-1866; (f) (305) 296-0922; (c) Monroe

Private for-profit/ staff: 2(f)

HISTORIC SITE; HOUSE MUSEUM

PROGRAMS: Elder's Programs; Facility Rental; Garden Tours; Guided Tours; Living History

COLLECTIONS: [1830-1930] Wealthy businessman's home, representing four generations of collections/adaptations to house; tropical gardens.

1458
Ernest Hemingway Home and Museum
907 Whitehead St, 33040; (p) (350) 294-1136; (f) (305) 294-2755; hemingway-home@prodigy.net; www.hemingwayhome.com; (c) Monroe

1962/ Board of Directors/ staff: 20(f); 3(p)

GARDEN; HISTORIC SITE; HOUSE MUSEUM; LIVING HISTORY/OUTDOOR MUSEUM: Preserves and interprets material site, memorabilia, and artifacts of Ernest Hemingway.

PROGRAMS: Guided Tours; Living History

COLLECTIONS: Historic house, furnishings, artwork, gardens, ephemera, photos, literature, and artifacts.

HOURS: Yr Daily 9-5

ADMISSION: $8, Children $5

1459
Fort Zachary Taylor State Historic Site
End of Southard St & Truman Annex, 33041 [PO Box 6560, 33041]; (p) (305) 292-6713; (f) (305) 292-6881; fttaylor1@flakeysol.com; (c) Monroe

State/ 1976/ staff: 10(f); 1(p); 6(v)

HISTORIC SITE: Maintains historic fort and surrounding grounds.

PROGRAMS: Community Outreach; Concerts; Facility Rental; Family Programs; Festivals; Film/Video; Interpretation; Living History; Reenactments

COLLECTIONS: Cannons, projectiles, photos, maps, and artillery; models of the Civil War fort and other artifacts.

1460
Harry S. Truman Little White House Museum
111 Front St, 33041 [PO Box 6443, 33041]; (p) (305) 294-9911; (f) (305) 294-9988; bwolz@historictours.com; www.trumanlittle whitehouse.com; (c) Monroe

1991/ Historic Tours of America/ staff: 1(f); 10(p)

GARDEN; HISTORY MUSEUM; HOUSE MUSEUM; PRESIDENTIAL SITE: Restored presidential vacation home of Harry Truman.

PROGRAMS: Exhibits; Facility Rental; Film/Video; Garden Tours; Guided Tours; Interpretation

COLLECTIONS: [1940-1950s] Original furnishings, including official desk, piano, and poker table.

HOURS: Yr Daily 9-5

ADMISSION: $8, Children $4

1461
Jessie Porters Heritage House and Robert Frost Cottage, Inc.
410 Caroline St, 33040; (p) (305) 296-3573; (f) (305) 292-5723; (c) Monroe

Private non-profit/ 1992/ staff: 1(f); 4(p); 4(v)/ members: 20/publication: *Key West: Conch Smiles*

HOUSE MUSEUM: Showcases Key West's extraordinary literary and maritime history with exhibits of original furnishings of 6 generations of a notable local family.

PROGRAMS: Festivals; Garden Tours; Guided Tours; Lectures; Publication

COLLECTIONS: [1870-1950] Paintings, antiques, and mementos collected by the Porter family since 1840; Gifts given by Henry Flagler, Robert Frost , and Dr. Samuel Mudd.

1462
Key West Art and Historical Society, Inc.
3501 S Roosevelt Blvd, 33040; (p) (305) 296-3913; (f) (305) 296-6206; maine1898@aol.com; (c) Monroe

Private non-profit/ 1949/ staff: 8(f); 8(p); 75(v)/ members: 1050

ART MUSEUM; HISTORIC PRESERVATION AGENCY; HISTORIC SITE; HISTORICAL SOCIETY; HISTORY MUSEUM: Operates and maintains 3 National Register Historic Sites: the Key West Light House and Keepers Quarters (1847), the East Martello Museum (1862), and the Custom House Museum (1891).

PROGRAMS: Annual Meeting; Community Outreach; Concerts; Exhibits; Facility Rental; Family Programs; Interpretation; Lectures; Research Library/Archives

COLLECTIONS: [1800s-1900s] Repository of local history, culture, and art; WPA works and Hemingway books and memorabilia; wide military collection with specialization in the US Battleship Maine and Spanish American War maritime history.

HOURS: Yr Daily 9:30-4:30

ADMISSION: $6, Children $3

1463
Key West Shipwreck Historeum dba Historic Tours of America
1 Whitehead St - Mallory Sq, 33041 [Box 1237, 33041-1237]; (p) (305) 292-8990; www.historictours.com; (c) Monroe

Private for-profit/ 1994/ staff: 6(f)

HISTORY MUSEUM: Operates an interactive nautical museum; preserves shipwreck artifacts; develops programs to educate the public about local maritime history.

PROGRAMS: Community Outreach; Elder's Programs; Exhibits; Festivals; Film/Video; Guided Tours; Interpretation; Living History

COLLECTIONS: [1820-1870s] Household articles and personal accessories; part of the salvage of the 1850 ship Isaac Allerton; tools used in shipwreck salvage; a recreated wreckers warehouse.

HOURS: Yr Daily 9:45-4:45

ADMISSION: $8, Children $4

1464
Mel Fisher Maritime Heritage Society
200 Greene St, 33040; (p) (605) 294-2633; shipline@aol.com; (c) Monroe

Private non-profit/ 1982/ staff: 21(f); 9(p); 5(v)/ members: 460/publication: *The Navigator*

HISTORY MUSEUM: Preserves history of Spanish galleons, Colonial era, and transatlantic slave trade.

PROGRAMS: Community Outreach; Elder's Programs; Exhibits; Facility Rental; Family Programs; Festivals; Film/Video; Guided Tours; Interpretation; Lectures; Publication; Reenactments; Research Library/Archives; School-Based Curriculum

COLLECTIONS: [1550-1750] Shipwreck materials, primarily English and Spanish; slave trade artifacts, Spanish treasure, trade goods, and ship parts.

HOURS: Yr Daily 9:30-5:30

ADMISSION: $6.50, Children

1465
Old Island Restoration Foundation
#10 Mallory Sq, 33040 [Box 689, 33040]; (p) (305) 294-9501; (c) Monroe

Private non-profit/ 1960/ staff: 1(f); 5(p); 30(v)/ members: 850

HISTORIC PRESERVATION AGENCY; HOUSE MUSEUM: Protects and preserves architectural heritage of Key West.

PROGRAMS: Garden Tours; Guided Tours; Lectures

COLLECTIONS: [1850-1890] Home furnishings of a wreck captain and family; documents.

HOURS: Yr Daily 10-4

ADMISSION: $5, Children $1

KISSIMMEE

1466
Osceola County Historical Society, Inc.
750 N Bass Rd, 34746; (p) (407) 396-8644; oschist@kua.net; (c) Osceola

County/ 1949/ Osceola Co. Historical Society/ staff: 25(v)/ members: 100

GENEALOGICAL SOCIETY; HISTORICAL SOCIETY; HISTORY MUSEUM: Maintains buildings and grounds which represent the lifestyle, food production, and agriculture of the pioneer era.

PROGRAMS: Annual Meeting; Exhibits; Facility Rental; Guided Tours; Lectures; Reenactments

COLLECTIONS: [Pioneer era] Rare books, genealogies, cemetery and obituary records, pictures, postcards, maps, old courthouse records; quilts, clothing, and accessories; agricultural artifacts, veterans memorabilia, and artifacts from a 1910 soda fountain.

HOURS: Yr Th-Sa 10-4, Su

LABELLE

1467
LaBelle Heritage Museum, Inc.
150 Lee St, 33975 [PO Box 2846, 33975]; (p) (941) 674-0034; (f) (941) 675-2059; tsargent@gulfcoast.net; (c) Hendry

Private non-profit/ 1990/ Board of Directors/ staff: 20(v)/ members: 65/publication: *LaBelle Heritage Museum Newsletter*

HISTORICAL SOCIETY: Preserves LaBelle heritage and history.

PROGRAMS: Exhibits; Publication; Research Library/Archives

COLLECTIONS: [Early 1900s-present] Artifacts related to LaBelle history; household items and tools.

HOURS: Yr Th 9-12/2-4, Sa

LAKE CITY

1468
Columbia County Historical Museum
105 S Hernardo, 32056 [PO Box 3276, 32056-3276]; (p) (904) 755-9096; (c) Columbia

Private non-profit/ 1983/ staff: 10(v)/ members: 10

HISTORIC SITE; HISTORY MUSEUM; HOUSE MUSEUM: Maintains collection reflecting the history of N Central Florida, including Civil War history and genealogies.

PROGRAMS: Exhibits; Facility Rental; Guided Tours; Interpretation; Research Library/Archives

COLLECTIONS: [1860-1920] Civil War rifles and guns; diaries, antique furniture, tools, and kitchenware.

HOURS: Yr W, F, Sa 2-5

ADMISSION: Donations accepted

1469
Florida Sports Hall of Fame and Museum of Florida Sports History
601 Hall of Fame Dr, 32055 [PO Box 1630, 32055]; (p) (800) 352-3263, (904) 752-9566; Flafame@floridasports.org; www.floridasports.org; (c) Columbia

Private non-profit/ 1958/ staff: 2(f); 5(p)/ members: 170

HISTORY MUSEUM: Preserves, honors, and promotes knowledge of the tradition of excellence manifested through the individuals inducted into the Hall of Fame, and through the history and conduct of sports in Florida.

PROGRAMS: Exhibits; Facility Rental; Film/Video; School-Based Curriculum

HOURS: Yr M-Sa 9-4

ADMISSION: $3, Seniors $2

LAKE WALES

1470
Bok Tower Gardens
1151 Tower Blvd, 33853; (p) (863) 676-1408; (f) (863) 676-6770; www.boktower.org; (c) Polk

Private non-profit/ 1929/ Bok Tower Gardens Foundation, Inc/ staff: 471(f); 37(p); 386(v)

GARDEN; HISTORIC SITE; HOUSE MUSEUM: Provides educational, charitable, literary, and scientific activities to perpetuate the legacy of Edward Bok.

PROGRAMS: Concerts; Exhibits; Facility Rental; Festivals; Garden Tours; Guided Tours; Lectures; Research Library/Archives

HOURS: Yr Daily 8-5

ADMISSION: $6, Children $2; Under 5 free

1471
Lake Wales Depot Museum
325 S Scenic Hwy, 33853; (p) (941) 678-4209; (f) (941) 678-4299; lwdepot@digital.net; www.cityoflakewales.com; (c) Polk

Joint/ 1976/ City; Historic Lake Wales Society/ staff: 2(f); 1(p); 20(v)/ members: 200

Protects and preserves cultural and historical heritage of area.

PROGRAMS: Community Outreach; Exhibits; Facility Rental; Guided Tours; Lectures; Publication; Reenactments; Research Library/Archives

COLLECTIONS: [1900-present] Artifacts, photos, and documentary archives related to early industry and railroads; quilts; dugout canoes, vintage railcars, and model railroad exhibits.

HOURS: Yr M-F 9-5, Sa 10-4

LAKE WORTH

1472
Museum of the City of Lake Worth
414 Lake Ave, 33460; (p) (561) 586-1700; (f) (561) 586-1651; (c) Palm Beach

City/ 1982/ City of Lake Worth/ staff: 1(f); 4(v)

HISTORIC PRESERVATION AGENCY; HISTORIC SITE; HISTORY MUSEUM; RESEARCH CENTER: Exhibits, preserves, and collects artifacts related to city history.

PROGRAMS: Community Outreach; Exhibits; Facility Rental; Festivals; Guided Tours; Lectures; Research Library/Archives

COLLECTIONS: [1900s-1950s] Period costumes, jewelry, musical instruments, household implements and furnishings; Polish, Lithuanian, and Finnish cultural exhibits; photos, tools, and machinery.

HOURS: Yr M-F

LAKELAND

1473
Florida United Methodist Archives
Florida Southern College, 33802 [PO Box 3767, 33802]; (p) (941) 688-9276; (c) Polk

Private non-profit/ staff: 1(p)

LIBRARY AND/OR ARCHIVES: Collects and preserves record of the FL Conferences of the United Methodist Church; provides research services.

PROGRAMS: Exhibits; Research Library/Archives

COLLECTIONS: [1822-present] Archival material, publications, local church histories and records.

1474
International Sport Aviation Museum
4175 Medulla Rd, 33807 [PO Box 6795, 33807]; (p) (941) 644-0741; (f) (941) 648-9264; museum@airmuseum.org; www.airmuseum.org; (c) Polk

Private non-profit/ 1993/ Sun 'n Fun Fly-In, Inc/ staff: 2(f); 120(v)/ members: 1500

HISTORY MUSEUM

PROGRAMS: Community Outreach; Exhibits; Family Programs; Festivals; Film/Video; Guided Tours; Interpretation; Lectures; Research Library/Archives; Theatre

COLLECTIONS: 70 experimental, homebuilt, antique and classic aircraft; Howard R. Hughes personal aviation memorabilia collection and research library.

HOURS: Yr Daily M-F 9-5, Sa 10-4, Su 12-4

ADMISSION: $7, Children $4; Members free

LARGO

1475
Heritage Village-Pinellas County Historical Museum
11909 125th St N, 33774; (p) (727) 582-2123; (f) (727) 582-2455; www.co.pinellas.fl.us/bcc/heritag.htm; (c) Pinellas

County/ 1961/ Pinellas County/ staff: 10(f); 2(p); 275(v)/publication: Punta Pinal

HISTORY MUSEUM; HOUSE MUSEUM; LIVING HISTORY/OUTDOOR MUSEUM: 21 acre open air historical village and museum serving as resource center for exhibition and study of history of Pinellas county.

PROGRAMS: Annual Meeting; Community Outreach; Concerts; Exhibits; Family Programs; Festivals; Garden Tours; Guided Tours; Interpretation; Lectures; Living History; Publication; Reenactments; Research Library/Archives; School-Based Curriculum

COLLECTIONS: [1840-1930] Period buildings, furnishings, and textiles; photos, audio-visual materials, special books and ledgers, maps and atlases, newspapers, scrapbooks, census records, and other materials related to regional history.

HOURS: Yr T-Sa 10-4, Su 1-4

ADMISSION: No charge/Donations

1476
Pinellas Genealogy Society, Inc.
[PO Box 1614, 33779-1614]; www.geocities.com/heartland/Plains/8283; (c) Pinellas

Private non-profit/ 1977/ staff: 20(v)/ members: 208/publication: The Pinellas Genealogist

GENEALOGICAL SOCIETY: Maintains genealogical records.

PROGRAMS: Community Outreach; Publication; Research Library/Archives

COLLECTIONS: Genealogical and historical tittles.

HOURS: Yr M-Th 9:30-9, F 9:30-5:50

ADMISSION: No charge

LIVE OAK

1477
Suwannee County Historical Museum
208 N Ohio Ave, 32060; (p) (904) 362-1776; (c) Suwannee

County/ 1981/ Suwannee County Museum Association/ staff: 15(v)

HISTORIC SITE; HISTORY MUSEUM: Collects, interprets, and exhibits artifacts associated with natural and human regional history in a National Register railroad freight depot.

PROGRAMS: Annual Meeting; Community Outreach; Elder's Programs; Exhibits; Facility Rental; Interpretation; Lectures; Research Library/Archives; School-Based Curriculum

COLLECTIONS: [Prehistory-present] Fossils, Native American artifacts, photo archives, and items related to African American and pioneer business life.

MAITLAND

1478
Holocaust Memorial Resource and Education Center, Inc. of Central Florida
851 N Maitland Ave, 32751; (p) (407) 628-0555; (f) (407) 628-1079; execdir@holocaust edu.org; www.holocaustedu.org; (c) Orange

Private non-profit/ 1983/ staff: 5(f); 1(p); 150(v)/ members: 700

HISTORY MUSEUM; RESEARCH CENTER: Maintains a memorial; focuses on education and research;

PROGRAMS: Annual Meeting; Community Outreach; Concerts; Exhibits; Film/Video; Lectures; Research Library/Archives; School-Based Curriculum; Theatre

COLLECTIONS: [World War II] 5,500 books, 550 films and video, 200 posters, 50 oral histories; artifacts, memorabilia, published bibliographies, and newsletters.

HOURS: Yr M-Th 9-4, F 9-1, Su 1-4

ADMISSION: No charge

1479
Maitland Historical Society

840 Lake Lily Dr, 32751 [PO Box 941001, 32794-101]; (p) (407) 644-2451; (f) (407) 644-0057; www.ourfrontporch.com/osi/mhs; (c) Orange

Private non-profit/ 1970/ Board of Directors/ staff: 3(f); 7(p); 60(v)/ members: 253/publication: *Early Houses of Maitland; Maitland Milestones; and others*

HISTORIC SITE; HISTORICAL SOCIETY; HOUSE MUSEUM: Collects, preserves, interprets, and exhibits artifacts and records pertaining to the history of the Maitland area.

PROGRAMS: Annual Meeting; Community Outreach; Elder's Programs; Exhibits; Family Programs; Festivals; Film/Video; Guided Tours; Interpretation; Lectures; Research Library/Archives; School-Based Curriculum

COLLECTIONS: [Early 19th c-present] Museum focuses on Maitland's first telephone company. 1,500 paper and photographic items, 800 photo images, documents, recollections and oral histories; 3,000 artifacts, ceramics, glass, industrial machinery, telephones, and textiles.

HOURS: Yr Th-Su 12-4

ADMISSION: Donations requested

MELBOURNE BEACH

1480
Sebastian Fishing Museum

9700 S A1A, 32951-4116; (p) (561) 388-2750; (f) (321) 984-4852; (c) Indian River

State/ 1998/ Sebastian Inlet State Recreation Area/ staff: 60(v)/ members: 20

HISTORY MUSEUM: Exhibits history of commercial fishing industry around Sebastian area.

PROGRAMS: Exhibits; Interpretation

COLLECTIONS: [20th c] Artifacts and photos relating to commercial fishing industry.

HOURS: Yr

MIAMI

1481
American Police Hall of Fame

3801 Biscayne Blvd, 33137; (p) (305) 573-0070; (f) (305) 573-9819; policeinfo@ aphf.org; aphf.org; (c) Miami-Dade

Private non-profit/ 1960/ staff: 23(f); 10(p); 7(v)/publication: *The Chief of Police Magazine*

HISTORY MUSEUM: Commemorates law enforcement service through memorial, museum, and chapel.

PROGRAMS: Annual Meeting; Exhibits; Publication; Research Library/Archives

COLLECTIONS: [1700-present] Police pursuit vehicles, an electric chair, gas chamber, and jail cells.

HOURS: Yr Daily 10-5:30

ADMISSION: $6, Children $3, Seniors $4

1482
Barnacle Society, Barnacle State Historic Site

3485 Main Hwy, 33133; (p) (305) 448-9445; (f) (305) 448-7484; barnacle@gate.net; www.funandsun.com/parks; (c) Dade

State/ 1973/ State of Florida/ staff: 2(f); 2(p); 20(v)/ members: 200

HISTORIC SITE; HOUSE MUSEUM: Preserves historic home of Coconut Grove pioneer, Ralph Munroe.

PROGRAMS: Community Outreach; Concerts; Exhibits; Facility Rental; Festivals; Guided Tours; Interpretation; Reenactments; School-Based Curriculum

COLLECTIONS: [1890-1940] Heirloom of three generations of the Munroe family including photographs and artifacts of maritime interest.

HOURS: Yr Daily

ADMISSION: $1

1483
Black Heritage Museum, Inc.

20900 SW 97 Ave, 33157 [15801 SW 102 Ave, 33157]; (p) (305) 252-3535; (f) (305) 252-3535; blkhermu@bellsouth.net; (c) Dade

Private non-profit/ 1987/ staff: 1(f); 8(v)/ members: 28

ART MUSEUM; HISTORY MUSEUM

PROGRAMS: Annual Meeting; Community Outreach; Exhibits; Guided Tours; Lectures; Living History

COLLECTIONS: Furniture, paintings, textiles, books, carvings, chess sets, statues, dolls, and figurines.

HOURS: Yr M-F 9-4

1484
Fairchild Tropical Garden

10901 Old Cutler Rd, 33156; (p) (305) 667-1651; (f) (305) 661-8953; skores@ftg.org; www.ftg.org; (c) Miami-Dade

Private non-profit/ 1938/ staff: 59(f); 8(p); 235(v)/ members: 12000/publication: *Garden News*

GARDEN: Operates museum of living plants and places emphasis on horticulture, education, research, and conservation.

PROGRAMS: Annual Meeting; Community Outreach; Concerts; Exhibits; Facility Rental; Family Programs; Festivals; Garden Tours; Guided Tours; Interpretation; Lectures; Publication; Research Library/Archives; School-Based Curriculum

COLLECTIONS: Houses a museum of plant exploration and a scientific library, along with a sizable botanical collection.

HOURS: Yr Daily 9:30-4:30

ADMISSION: $8

1485
Gold Coast Railroad Museum, Inc.

12450 SW 152nd St, 33177-1402; (p) (605) 253-0063; (f) (305) 233-4641; lclltd@gate.net; www.elink.net/goldcoast; (c) Dade

Private non-profit/ 1957/ staff: 1(f); 15(v)/ members: 250

HISTORIC SITE; HISTORICAL SOCIETY: Maintains museum and national historic landmarks located on NAS Richmond airship base.

PROGRAMS: Community Outreach; Exhibits; Facility Rental; School-Based Curriculum

COLLECTIONS: [1920-present] Steam Locomotive #153 landmark; steam, diesel, freight, and passenger equipment.

HOURS: Yr M-F 11-3, Sa-Su 11-4

ADMISSION: $5, Children $3

1486
Historical Museum of Southern Florida

101 W Flagler St, 33130; (p) (305) 375-1492; (f) (305) 375-1609; hasf@historical-museum.org; www.historical-museum.org; (c) Dade

Private non-profit/ 1940/ Historical Association of Southern Florida/ staff: 21(f); 20(p)/ members: 2527/publication: *South Florida History and Tequesta*

HISTORICAL SOCIETY; HISTORY MUSEUM; RESEARCH CENTER: Preserves and interprets regional and Caribbean history through object and archival collections, historical publications, a research center and educational programming.

PROGRAMS: Annual Meeting; Community Outreach; Concerts; Exhibits; Facility Rental; Family Programs; Festivals; Film/Video; Guided Tours; Interpretation; Lectures; Living History; Publication; Reenactments; Research Library/Archives; School-Based Curriculum

COLLECTIONS: [Prehistory-present] Artifactual and archaeological holdings: maritime, aviation, and folklife; historic prints, photos, publications, manuscripts, maps, ephemera.

HOURS: Yr M-W, F, Sa 10-5, Th 10-9, Su 12-5

ADMISSION: $5, Student $4, Children $2, Seniors $4

1487
Miami Memorabilia Collector's Club, The

330 NE 96 St, 33138; (p) (305) 757-1016; (f) (305) 895-8178; mbramson@cwtel.com; (c) Dade

1992/ staff: 12(v)/ members: 72/publication: *Looking Back*

Collects and preserves memorabilia relating to the Miami, Dade County, and S. Florida areas.

PROGRAMS: Community Outreach; Exhibits; Lectures; Publication; Research Library/Archives

COLLECTIONS: [1890-1990] Region-related memorabilia.

HOURS: Yr By appt

1488
Vizcaya Museum and Gardens

3251 S Miami Ave, 33129 [3251 S Miami Ave, 33129]; (p) (305) 250-9133; (f) (305) 285-2004; (c) Dade

County/ 1914/ staff: 34(f); 10(p); 168(v)

HISTORIC SITE: Site of the Summit of the Americas in December of 1994.

COLLECTIONS: [1916-1925] European decorative arts of the 16th-19th centuries.; Photographs, blueprints and correspondence about the construction of Vizcaya.

HOURS: Yr

1489
Weeks Air Museum
14710 SW 128th St, 33196; (p) (305) 233-5197; (f) (205) 232-4134; www.weeks airmuseum.com; (c) Dade

Private non-profit/ 1986/ staff: 2(f); 7(p); 15(v)/ members: 450

HISTORY MUSEUM: Preserves and restores World War II aircraft.

PROGRAMS: Community Outreach; Exhibits; Facility Rental; Festivals; Guided Tours; Publication

COLLECTIONS: WWII aircraft and aviation artifacts.

HOURS: Yr Daily 10-5

ADMISSION: $9.95, Children $5.95, Seniors $6.95

MIAMI BEACH

1490
Jewish Museum of Florida
301 Washington Ave, 33139; (p) (305) 672-5044; (f) (305) 672-5933; mzerivitz@aol.com; www.jewishmuseum.com; (c) Dade

Private non-profit/ 1989/ Mosaic Inc. DBA Ziff Jewish Museum of Florida/ staff: 8(f); 3(p); 60(v)/ members: 1600/publication: *Tiles*

HISTORIC SITE; HISTORY MUSEUM: Retrieves, documents, and preserves FL Jewish experience since 1763, housed in restored Art Deco synagogue.

PROGRAMS: Annual Meeting; Community Outreach; Concerts; Elder's Programs; Exhibits; Facility Rental; Family Programs; Festivals; Film/Video; Guided Tours; Interpretation; Lectures; Living History; Publication; Research Library/Archives; School-Based Curriculum

COLLECTIONS: [1763-present] Oral histories, photos, documents, and ephemera of FL Jewish experience.

HOURS: Yr 10-5

ADMISSION: $5, Family $10, Student $4, Seniors $4

1491
Miami Design Preservation League
1001 Ocean Dr, 33119 [PO Box 190180, 33119-0180]; (p) (305) 672-2014; (f) (350) 672-4319; mdpl@shadow.net; (c) Dade

Private non-profit/ 1976/ Board of Directors/ staff: 3(f); 1(p)/ members: 350/publication: *HSPBC News*

HISTORIC PRESERVATION AGENCY; LIVING HISTORY/OUTDOOR MUSEUM: Preserves, protects, and promotes cultural, social, economic, environmental, and architectural integrity of Miami Beach Architectural Historic District.

PROGRAMS: Annual Meeting; Community

Outreach; Concerts; Festivals; Film/Video; Garden Tours; Guided Tours; Interpretation; Lectures; Living History; Publication; Research Library/Archives

COLLECTIONS: [1925-1945] Documents and related material on history and background of preservation and Art Deco period.

HOURS: Yr Daily 10-10

1492
Wolfsonian-Florida International University, The
1001 Washington Ave, 33139; (p) (305) 531-1001; (f) (305) 531-2133; (c) Miami-Dade

State/ 1986/ Florida International Univ/ staff: 29(f); 11(p); 60(v)/ members: 950/publication: *Journal of Decorative and Propaganda Arts*

HISTORY MUSEUM; RESEARCH CENTER: Preserves decorative and propaganda arts of period 1885-1945.

PROGRAMS: Community Outreach; Exhibits; Facility Rental; Family Programs; Film/Video; Guided Tours; Interpretation; Lectures; Publication; Research Library/Archives; School-Based Curriculum

COLLECTIONS: [1885-1945] More than 70,000 North American and European artifacts encompassing furniture, glass, ceramic, metalwork, books, works on paper, paintings, and sculpture; artifacts demonstraing relationship between design and socio-cultural experience.

HOURS: Yr M-T, F-Sa 11-6, Th 11-9, Su 12-5

ADMISSION: $5, Student $3.50, Children $3.50, Seniors $3.50

MIAMI LAKES

1493
Jay I. Kislak Foundation, Inc.
7900 Miami Lakes Dr W, 33016-5897; (p) (305) 364-4208; (f) (305) 821-1267; adunkelman@kislak.com; www.jayikislakfoundation.org; (c) Dade

Private non-profit/ 1984/ staff: 2(f); 4(p)/publication: *Columbus to Catherwood*

HISTORY MUSEUM; RESEARCH CENTER: Collects, conserves, interprets, and researches Pre-Columbian art and rare books, manuscripts, and maps with emphasis on FL, the Caribbean, and Mesoamerica.

PROGRAMS: Community Outreach; Exhibits; Publication; Research Library/Archives; School-Based Curriculum

COLLECTIONS: [Pre-Columbian]

HOURS: By Appt

ADMISSION: No charge

NAPLES

1494
Collier County Museum
3301 Tamiami Trail East, 34112; (p) (941) 774-8476; (f) (941) 774-8580; nfn14127@naples.net; www.colliermuseum.com; (c) Collier

County/ 1977/ Collier County Board of County Commissioners/ staff: 4(f); 2(p); 60(v)/ members: 160/publication: *Timelines*

GARDEN; HISTORY MUSEUM: Collects, preserves, and interprets the history, archaeology, and cultural development of Collier County and SW Florida.

PROGRAMS: Annual Meeting; Community Outreach; Exhibits; Family Programs; Festivals; Garden Tours; Guided Tours; Interpretation; Lectures; Living History; Publication; Reenactments; Research Library/Archives; School-Based Curriculum

COLLECTIONS: Artifacts, photos, and regional maps; archival newspapers and

1495
Collier-Seminole State Park
20200 Tamiami Trail E, 34114; (p) (941) 394-3397; (f) (941) 394-5113; (c) Collier

State/ 1947/ staff: 9(f); 30(v)

LIVING HISTORY/OUTDOOR MUSEUM: Maintains State Park and operates visitor's center featuring exhibits and nature trails.

PROGRAMS: Community Outreach; Exhibits; Festivals; Guided Tours; Interpretation; Living History

HOURS: Yr Daily 8-Sunset

ADMISSION: $3.25/vehicle

NEW PORT RICHEY

1496
West Pasco Historical Society
6431 Circle Blvd, 34652; (p) (727) 847-0680; (c) Pasco

Private non-profit/ 1973/ staff: 30(v)/ members: 220/publication: *West Pasco Heritage*

HISTORICAL SOCIETY; HISTORY MUSEUM; RESEARCH CENTER: Preserves and educates public about regional and state history.

PROGRAMS: Annual Meeting; Exhibits; Film/Video; Guided Tours; Lectures; Publication

COLLECTIONS: [1890s-present] Vignettes of local establishments; Seminole and early regional Native American artifacts.

HOURS: Yr F-Sa

ADMISSION: Donations accepted

NORTH MIAMI

1497
Holocaust Documentation and Education Center, Inc.
Florida International Univ, 3000 NE 151 St, 33181; (p) (305) 919-5690; (f) (305) 919-5691; xholocau@fiu.edu; www.holocaust.fiu.edu; (c) Dade

Private non-profit/ 1979/ staff: 5(f); 2(p); 60(v)

LIBRARY AND/OR ARCHIVES: Collects and preserves eyewitness testimonies of Holocaust survivors, rescuers, and liberators; conducts educational prejudice reduction programs for students and educators.

PROGRAMS: Annual Meeting; Research Library/Archives; School-Based Curriculum

COLLECTIONS: [1933-1945] 1,600 audio and video interviews; related books, manuscripts, newspaper

NORTH PALM BEACH

1498
John D. MacArthur Beach State Park
10900 State Rd 703, 33408; (p) (561) 624-6952; (f) (561) 624-6954; mac_ann@hotmail.com; (c) Palm Beach

1981/ Florida Park Service - Dept of Environmental Protection/ staff: 12(f); 2(p); 80(v)

LIVING HISTORY/OUTDOOR MUSEUM: Preserves natural and cultural resources.

PROGRAMS: Annual Meeting; Community Outreach; Exhibits; Facility Rental; Family Programs; Festivals; Film/Video; Guided Tours; Interpretation; Lectures; School-Based Curriculum

COLLECTIONS: Exhibits and aquariums providing information on the plants and animals found within the park.

HOURS: Yr M-S 8-Sunset

ADMISSION:

ORLANDO

1499
Orange County Regional History Center
65 E Central Blvd, 32801; (p) (321) 449-4444, (800) 965-2030; (f) (321) 836-8550; (c) Orange

County/ 1971/ staff: 25(f); 10(p); 150(v)/ members: 2000/publication: *Historic Quarterly*

HISTORICAL SOCIETY; HISTORY MUSEUM: Preserves Central FL history through exhibits, artifacts, and educational programs.

PROGRAMS: Community Outreach; Exhibits; Facility Rental; Festivals; Interpretation; Lectures; Publication; Research Library/Archives; School-Based Curriculum

COLLECTIONS: [1850-present] Photos, archives, and artifacts; Walt Disney World and popular culture.

HOURS: Yr M-Sa 9-5, Su 11-5

ADMISSION: $7, Senior $5, Children $4

OSPREY

1500
Gulf Coast Heritage Association, Inc.
337 N Tamiami Trail, 34229 [PO Box 856, 34229]; (p) (941) 966-5214; (f) (941) 966-1355; gchaz@gte.net; (c) Sarasota

Private non-profit/ 1975/ staff: 7(f); 4(p); 140(v)/ members: 750/publication: *Vision*

GARDEN; HISTORIC SITE; HISTORY MUSEUM: Preserves, interprets, and promotes Historic Spanish Point, a 30 acre environmental, archaeological, and historic site.

PROGRAMS: Annual Meeting; Community Outreach; Exhibits; Facility Rental; Family Programs; Garden Tours; Guided Tours; Interpretation; Lectures; Living History; Publication; School-Based Curriculum

COLLECTIONS: [Prehistoric and 19th-20th c] Archaeological materials of area prehistoric peoples; pioneer tools, textiles, furnishings and period buildings; maritime related artifacts; early 20th c gardens.

HOURS: Yr M-Sa 9-5, Su 12-5

ADMISSION: $7, Children $3

1501
Historic Spanish Point, Guptill House
337 N Tamiami Tr, 34229 [PO Box 846, 34229]; (p) (941) 966-5214; (f) (941) 966-1355; GCHA2@GTE.org

1901/ staff: 7(f); 4(p); 120(v)

HOUSE MUSEUM: Estate of Mrs. Potter (Bertha) Palmer, a leader of Chicago society and major Florida developer of early 1900s; pre-historic shell midden.

COLLECTIONS: [1910-1918; 1867-1910] Site/period specific; Letters of Eliza Webb, who pioneered Spanish Point, 1867-1885.

PALM BEACH

1502
Henry Morrison Flagler Museum
One Whitehall Way, 33480 [PO Box 969, 33480]; (p) (561) 655-2833; (f) (561) 655-2826; flagler@emi.net; www.flagler.org; (c) Palm Beach

Private non-profit/ 1959/ staff: 29(f); 10(p); 120(v)/ members: 950

HOUSE MUSEUM: Preserves, researches, and interprets Henry Flagler Gilded Age estate.

PROGRAMS: Community Outreach; Concerts; Exhibits; Family Programs; Guided Tours; Lectures; School-Based Curriculum

COLLECTIONS: [1865-1929] Original furnishings and other period objects and associated collections and materials related to life of Henry Flagler.

HOURS: Yr T-Sa 10-5, Su 12-5

ADMISSION: $8

1503
Palm Beach Maritime Museum
4512 Poinsettia Ave, 33480 [PO Drawer 2317, 33480]; (p) (561) 842-8202; (f) (561) 844-1636; (c) Palm Beach

Private non-profit/ 1974/ staff: 1(f); 5(p); 4(v)

HISTORIC SITE; HISTORY MUSEUM: Preserves maritime history; maintains an office/classroom facility, an environmental education center, a ferryboat embarkation, historic former Coast Guard station, and Pres. John Kennedy bunker.

PROGRAMS: Exhibits; Facility Rental; Guided Tours

COLLECTIONS: [20th c] Artifacts and items relating to maritime history, environment, science, technology, commerce, and recreation.

HOURS: Yr F-Su

1504
Preservation Foundation of Palm Beach
356 S County Rd, 33480; (p) (561) 832-0731; (f) (561) 832-7174; (c) Palm Beach

Private non-profit/ 1982/ Board of Trustees/ staff: 5(f); 7(p); 20(v)/ members: 1200/publication: *Landmark Architecture of Palm Beach*

HISTORIC PRESERVATION AGENCY; LIVING HISTORY/OUTDOOR MUSEUM; RESEARCH CENTER: Dedicated to preservation of local environment and heritage of Palm Beach.

PROGRAMS: Community Outreach; Concerts; Exhibits; Facility Rental; Garden Tours; Guided Tours; Lectures; Living History; Publication; Research Library/Archives; School-Based Curriculum

COLLECTIONS: [1886-present] 42,000 architectural drawings, 500 books, 1,000 newspaper titles, 5,000 photos/slides, 200 artifacts.

HOURS: M-F 9-5

PALM COAST

1505
Florida Agricultural Museum
1850 Princess Place Rd, 32137; (p) (904) 446-7630; (f) (904) 446-7631; famuseum@pcfl.net; (c) Flagler

Joint; Private non-profit/ 1983/ Dept of Agriculture/State of FL/ staff: 2(f); 40(v)/ members: 300

LIVING HISTORY/OUTDOOR MUSEUM

PROGRAMS: Exhibits; Festivals

COLLECTIONS: [1500-present] Farm equipment and artifacts; photos, films, and equipment from FL Dept of Agriculture.

HOURS: Yr

1506
Washington Oaks State Gardens
6400 N Oceanshore Blvd, 32137; (p) (904) 446-6780; (f) (904) 446-6781; matgeo@mail.state.fl.us; (c) Flagler

State/ 1964/ staff: 10(f); 1(p); 10(v)

GARDEN; HISTORIC SITE: Maintains ornamental gardens and exhibits at an Interpretive Center.

PROGRAMS: Exhibits; Facility Rental; Family Programs; Festivals; Garden Tours; Guided Tours; Interpretation; Living History

COLLECTIONS: [1700s-present]

HOURS: Yr Daily 8-Sundown

ADMISSION: $3.25/Vehicle

PANAMA CITY

1507
Junior Museum of Bay County, Inc.
1731 Jenks Ave, 32405; (p) (850) 769-6128; (f) (850) 769-6129; Jnanek@cityoflakewales.com; www.jrmuseum.org; (c) Bay

Private non-profit/ 1967/ staff: 3(f); 3(p); 50(v)/ members: 320/publication: *The Cracker Barrel*

HISTORY MUSEUM: Preserves and collects artifacts and materials from Lake Wales history.

PROGRAMS: Exhibits; Facility Rental; Family Programs; Festivals; Guided Tours; Publication

COLLECTIONS: [1890] Natural history: mollusks, echinoderms, minerals, lepidptera; cultural artifacts; pioneer state artifacts: tools, farming, and industrial implements, household items.

HOURS: Yr M-F

PANAMA CITY BEACH

1508
Museum of Man in the Sea, Inc., The

17314 Panama City Beach Pkwy, 32413; (p) (850) 235-4101; (f) (850) 235-4101; (c) Bay

Private non-profit/ 1982/ staff: 2(f); 1(p); 20(v)/ members: 500

Collects, preserves, and interprets the history of subsea technology and exploration.

PROGRAMS: Community Outreach; Elder's Programs; Exhibits; Film/Video; Guided Tours; Lectures; Research Library/Archives

COLLECTIONS: [1590-present] Diving equip, small submarine, underwater habitat, and decompression chambers; research library of related books, tapes, and photos.

HOURS: Yr Daily 9-5

ADMISSION: $5, Student $2.50, Seniors $4.50

PATRICK AIR FORCE BASE

1509
Air Force Space and Missile Museum

Cape Canaveral Air Station, 32925 [191 Museum Circle, 32925-2535]; (p) (407) 853-9171; (f) (407) 853-9172

Federal/ 1962/ US Air Force/ staff: 2(f); 1(p); 55(v)

HISTORIC SITE; HISTORY MUSEUM: Collects, restores, and exhibits items that relate to the development and heritage of US Air Force space launch activities.

PROGRAMS: Exhibits; Festivals; Guided Tours; Interpretation; Research Library/Archives

COLLECTIONS: [1957-present] Rockets, missiles, and related aerospace hardware on display in outdoor Rocket Garden; Launch Complex 26 Blockhouse with original consoles.

HOURS: Yr Sa-Su

PENSACOLA

1510
Civil War Soldiers Museum

108 S Palafox Pl, 32501; (p) (850) 469-1900; (f) (850) 469-9328; info@cwmuseum.org; www.cwmuseum.org; (c) Escambia

Private non-profit/ 1991/ staff: 1(f); 6(v)/ members: 125

HISTORY MUSEUM: Maintains Civil War collection and exhibits.

PROGRAMS: Guided Tours

COLLECTIONS: [Civil War Era] Civil War medical collection, life sized camp scenes, and hand crafted figurines; period artifacts, music and art.

HOURS: T-Sa 10-4:30

ADMISSION: $5, Children $2.50; Under 6 free

1511
Historic Pensacola Preservation Board

330 S Jefferson St, 32576 [PO Box 12866, 32576-2866]; (p) (850) 595-5985; (f) (850) 595-5989; penshpb@mail.dos.state.fl.us; www.flheritage.com; (c) Escambia

State/ 1967/ Florida Department of State/ staff: 14(f); 6(p); 50(v)/ members: 300

HISTORIC PRESERVATION AGENCY; HISTORIC SITE; HISTORY MUSEUM: Operates Historic Pensacola Village and T.T. Wentworth, Jr. Florida State Museum; collects and interprets the heritage of W Florida; maintains historic monuments, sites, and structures.

PROGRAMS: Annual Meeting; Community Outreach; Elder's Programs; Exhibits; Facility Rental; Festivals; Guided Tours; Interpretation; Lectures; Living History; Research Library/ Archives; School-Based Curriculum

COLLECTIONS: [18th-20th c] Artifacts representing the heritage of the region; furnishings, tools, equipment, costumes, art, and archaeology items.

HOURS: Yr T-Sa 10-4

ADMISSION: $6, Children $2.50, Seniors $5

1512
National Museum of Naval Aviation

1750 Radford Blvd, Ste C, 32508-5402; (p) (850) 452-3604; (f) (850) 452-3296; naval.museum@smtp.cnet.navy.mil; (c) Escambia

Federal/ 1962/ staff: 35(f); 341(v)

HISTORY MUSEUM; RESEARCH CENTER: Collects, preserves, and exhibits memorabilia significant to history and mission of Naval Aviation through appropriate displays and educational programs.

PROGRAMS: Concerts; Exhibits; Lectures; Research Library/Archives; School-Based Curriculum; Theatre

COLLECTIONS: Historic aircraft's; flight memorabilia, personal momentos from historic battles, flight logs, clothing, uniforms, carrier island and flight deck, cockpit trainers, and flight simulators.

1513
Pensacola Historical Society

117 E Government St, 32501; (p) (850) 434-5455; phstaff@pcola.gulf.net; www.pensacola history.org; (c) Escambia

Private non-profit/ 1933/ Board of Directors/ staff: 3(f); 1(p); 26(v)

Preserves the history of Pensacola through publicly accessible research and exhibition facilities.

PROGRAMS: Exhibits; Guided Tours; Interpretation; Research Library/Archives

COLLECTIONS: Manuscripts, maps, vertical files, photos, textiles, clothing, museum exhibit.

HOURS: Yr Museum: M-Sa 10-4:30; Resouce Center: T-Th, Sa 10-3

ADMISSION: Museum $1; Resource Center $5

PERRY

1514
Forest Capital State Museum

204 Forest Park Dr, 32347; (p) (850) 584-3227; (f) (850) 584-3488; forestcapital@perry.gulfnet.com; (c) Taylor

State/ 1973/ Dept. of Environmental Protection/ staff: 1(f); 2(p)

HISTORIC SITE; HISTORY MUSEUM; HOUSE MUSEUM: Preserves late 1800s Cracker homestead and maintains the forestry museum.

PROGRAMS: Exhibits; Facility Rental; Festivals; Film/Video; Guided Tours

COLLECTIONS: [Late 1800s] Items related to the historic homestead, period furnishings, cooking supplies, tools, and farming items.

HOURS: Yr Th-M 9-12, 1-5

ADMISSION: $1

PLANT CITY

1515
East Hillsborough Historical Society

605 N Collins St, 33566; (p) (813) 757-9226; (c) Hillsborough

Private non-profit/ 1974/ staff: 1(p); 15(v)/ members: 360/publication: *Pen and Quill Newsletter*

GENEALOGICAL SOCIETY; HISTORIC SITE; HISTORY MUSEUM: Preserves historical and cultural heritage of region.

PROGRAMS: Annual Meeting; Community Outreach; Facility Rental; Festivals; Guided Tours; Publication; Research Library/Archives

HOURS: Yr M-F 12:30-5

ADMISSION: Donations accepted

PLANTATION

1516
Plantation Historical Society

511 N Fig Tree Ln, 33317; (p) (954) 797-2722; (f) (954) 797-2717; phistorica@aol.com; (c) Broward

Joint/ 1974/ City of Plantation/Plantation Historical Society/ staff: 2(p); 15(v)/ members: 106

HISTORICAL SOCIETY; HISTORY MUSEUM: Promotes preservation of city's history and historical landmarks.

PROGRAMS: Annual Meeting; Exhibits; Guided Tours; Lectures

COLLECTIONS: [1940s-present] Artifacts, documents, photos, books, and newspaper clippings.

HOURS: Yr T-Sa 9-12, 1-4:30

POLK CITY

1517
American Water Ski Educational Foundation

1251 Holy Cow Rd, 33868; (p) (941) 324-2472; (f) (941) 324-3996; 102726,2751@compuserve.com; www.usawaterski.org; (c) Polk

1968/ Board of Trustees/ staff: 1(f); 2(p)/ members: 450/publication: *Water Ski Hall of Fame*

HISTORY MUSEUM: Preserves and educates on history of water skiing.

PROGRAMS: Annual Meeting; Exhibits; Publication; Research Library/Archives

COLLECTIONS: [1922-present] Evolution of water skis, newspaper articles, books, magazines, photos, film, video.

PONCE INLET

1518
Ponce de Leon Inlet Lighthouse Preservation Association, Inc.
4931 S Peninsula Dr, 32127; (p) (904) 761-1821; (f) (904) 761-1821; lighthouse@ponceinlet.org; www.ponceinlet.org; (c) Volusia

Private non-profit/ 1972/ staff: 7(f); 12(p); 15(v)/ members: 1500/publication: *Newsletter*

HISTORIC PRESERVATION AGENCY; HISTORIC SITE; HISTORICAL SOCIETY; HISTORY MUSEUM: Preserves history of Ponce Inlet lighthouse, the US Lighthouse Service, FL's maritime history, and local history.

PROGRAMS: Annual Meeting; Community Outreach; Exhibits; Festivals; Guided Tours; Interpretation; Lectures; Publication; Research Library/Archives

COLLECTIONS: [1882-1972] 175 foot lighthouse tower, three keeper's houses, and their outbuildings, and oil storage

PORT ST. JOE

1519
Constitution Convention State Museum
200 Allen Memorial Way, 32456 [8899 Cape San Blas Rd, 32456]; (p) (850) 229-8029, (850) 227-1327; (f) (850) 227-1488; sjpsp@juno.com; www.dep.state.fl.us/parks/st.joseph/st.joseph.html; (c) Gulf

State/ 1955/ Department of Environmental Protection/ staff: 1(f)

HISTORIC SITE; HISTORY MUSEUM: Preserves FL's 1st state constitutional convention and vanished city of St. Joe.

PROGRAMS: Exhibits; Family Programs; Guided Tours; Interpretation; Living History; Reenactments; School-Based Curriculum

COLLECTIONS: [1835-1845] Replica room of convention hall and its delegates and related artifacts.

HOURS: Yr Th-M 9-12, 1-5

ADMISSION: $1

PUNTA GORDA

1520
Florida Adventure Museum
260 W Retta Esplanade, 33950; (p) (941) 639-3777; (f) (941) 639-3505; museum@sun-line.net; (c) Charlotte

Private non-profit/ 1969/ Museum Society, Inc./ staff: 2(f); 3(p); 250(v)/ members: 59/publication: *The Adventurer; Punta Gorda Historic Walking Tour*

HISTORY MUSEUM: Offers programs on local and state history, FL natural history, and science.

PROGRAMS: Community Outreach; Exhibits; Family Programs; Festivals; Lectures; Publication

COLLECTIONS: [1800s-present] Artifacts pertaining to local/state history/natural history.

HOURS: Yr M-F 10-5, Sa 10-3

ADMISSION: $2, Children $1

SAFETY HARBOR

1521
Safety Harbor Museum of Regional History
329 S Bayshore Blvd, 34695; (p) (727) 726-1668; (f) (727) 725-9938; shmuseum@ij.net; www.safety-harbor-museum.org; (c) Pinellas

Private non-profit/ 1970/ Board of Trustees/ staff: 2(f); 1(p); 100(v)/ members: 200

HISTORY MUSEUM: A state history and archaeology museum that uses its collection to preserve and exhibit regional history.

PROGRAMS: Annual Meeting; Community Outreach; Elder's Programs; Exhibits; Facility Rental; Family Programs; Guided Tours; Lectures; School-Based Curriculum

COLLECTIONS: [Pre-history-early 20th c] FL Native American artifacts and turn of the century pioneer

SAINT AUGUSTINE

1522
Castillo de San Marcos National Monument/Fort Matanzas National Monument/ National Park Service
1 S Castillo Dr, 32086; (p) (904) 929-6506; (f) (904) 823-9388; Casa_historian@nps.gov; www.nps.gov/casa; (c) St. Johns

Federal/ 1924/ Department of the Interior/ staff: 27(f); 3(p); 150(v)

HISTORIC SITE: Preserves Spanish colonial stone fortifications.

PROGRAMS: Exhibits; Festivals; Guided Tours; Interpretation; Living History; Reenactments; School-Based Curriculum

COLLECTIONS: [Spanish colonial, British colonial, and American colonial] Spanish colonial stone fortifications; military artifacts from all periods.

1523
Museum of Weapons and Early American History
81C King St, 32084; (p) (904) 829-3727; (c) Saint Johns

Private for-profit/ 1986/ staff: 1(f); 2(p)

HISTORY MUSEUM: Collects and exhibits weapons, relics, and items related to early American history.

PROGRAMS: Guided Tours

COLLECTIONS: [1500-1900] Period weapons, Civil War items, President Tyler's Piano, Native American artifacts, and battlefield finds; newspapers spanning 3 centuries.

HOURS: Yr Daily 9:30-5

ADMISSION: $4, Children $1

1524
Oldest House, The/Gonzalez-Alvarez House
14 Saint Francis St, 32084 [271 Charlotte St, 32084]; (p) (904) 824-2872; (f) (904) 824-2569; oldhouse@aug.com; www.oldcity.com/oldhouse

1727/ St Augustine Historical Society/ staff: 8(f); 4(p)

COLLECTIONS: [1727-present] 5,000 items related to Fl. history. 4 original Spanish Colonial buildings with related artifacts; weapons,

Spanish coins, badges, and souvenirs.; 2,000 linear ft. of documents, personal papers, public records, 10,000 volumes, 5,000 photos and oral history.

HOURS: Yr

1525
Pena-Peck House/The Women's Exchange of St Augustine
143 Saint George St, 32084 [143 St George St, 32084]; (p) (904) 829-5064; (c) Saint Johns

1740/ City; the Women's Exchange/ staff: 1(f)

COLLECTIONS: [1832-1932] 18th century and early 19th century furnishings brought by the Peck family from New England; Family papers in the St. Augustine Historical Library

HOURS: Yr

1526
Saint Augustine Historical Society
271 Charlotte St, 32084; (p) (904) 824-2872; (f) (904) 824-2569; oldhouse@aug.com; www.oldcity.com/oldhouse; (c) Saint Johns

Private non-profit/ 1883/ staff: 8(f); 10(p); 31(v)/ members: 700/publication: *El Escribano*

HISTORICAL SOCIETY; HISTORY MUSEUM; HOUSE MUSEUM: Collects and catalogs materials documenting NE Florida history for public access.

PROGRAMS: Annual Meeting; Community Outreach; Elder's Programs; Exhibits; Facility Rental; Family Programs; Garden Tours; Guided Tours; Interpretation; Lectures; Publication; Research Library/Archives; School-Based Curriculum

COLLECTIONS: [Prehistory-present] 1720-1880 Spanish and American territorial items, paintings ca 1800-1920 by visiting artists, photos, and maps.

HOURS: Yr Daily 9-5

ADMISSION: $5, Family $12, Student $3, Seniors $4.50

SAINT PETERSBURG

1527
Florida Holocaust Museum
55 Fifth St, 33701; (p) (727) 820-0100; (f) (727) 821-8435; www.flholocaustmuseum.org; (c) Hillsborough

Private non-profit/ 1990/ staff: 20(f); 2(p); 270(v)/ members: 750/publication: *Clinging to Humanity: Search of Hope*

ART MUSEUM; HISTORY MUSEUM

PROGRAMS: Community Outreach; Concerts; Exhibits; Facility Rental; Family Programs; Film/Video; Guided Tours; Interpretation; Lectures; Living History; Publication; Research Library/Archives; School-Based Curriculum

COLLECTIONS: [1933-1948]

HOURS: Yr Daily M-F 10-5, Sa-Su 12-5

ADMISSION: $6, Student $5, Children $2, Seniors $5; Members

SANFORD

1528
Museum of Seminole County History
300 Bush Blvd, 32771 [1101 E First St, 32771]; (p) (407) 321-2489; (f) (407) 321-2489; rjocobs@co.seminole.fl.us; www.co.seminole.fl.us; (c) Seminole

County/ 1983/ Seminole County Board of County Commissioners/ staff: 1(f); 1(p); 10(v)

HISTORY MUSEUM: Provides preservation for and education about local history.

PROGRAMS: Community Outreach; Exhibits; Guided Tours; Interpretation

COLLECTIONS: [1830-1940] Artifacts, photos, and vertical files interpreting the development of local culture, agriculture, industry, and government.

HOURS: Yr T-F 9-12/1-4, Sa 1-4

ADMISSION: No charge

1529
Sanford Museum
520 E First St, 32772 [PO Box 1788, 32772-1788]; (p) (407) 302-1000; (f) (407) 330-5666; (c) Seminole

City/ 1957/ City of Sanford/ staff: 2(f); 3(p); 9(v)

HISTORY MUSEUM: Collects, preserves, and exhibits information and artifacts relating to the development of the city and to the life and times of city founder, Henry S. Sanford.

PROGRAMS: Exhibits; Guided Tours; Lectures

COLLECTIONS: [1840-1970] Maps, photos, and ephemera related to city history; 55,000 item manuscript collection and library of Henry Sanford; collection of Native American (Timucuan) objects.

HOURS: Yr T-F 11-4, Sa 1-4

ADMISSION: No charge

1530
School Board of Seminole County Student Museum and Center for the Social Studies
301 W Seventh St, 32771-2505; (p) (407) 320-0520; (f) (407) 320-0522; www.scps.k12.fl.us; (c) Seminole

County/ 1984/ Seminole County Public Schools/ staff: 4(f); 20(v)

GARDEN; HISTORY MUSEUM; LIVING HISTORY/OUTDOOR MUSEUM: Interpretive center and teaching museum.

PROGRAMS: Community Outreach; Exhibits; Festivals; Garden Tours; Guided Tours; Living History; Research Library/Archives; School-Based Curriculum

COLLECTIONS: Native American room, a pioneer room, a turn of the century classroom, "grandma's attic" with period clothing, tools, technology, and artifacts.

HOURS: Yr M-F 1:30-4

ADMISSION: Donations/student fees

SARASOTA

1531
Sarasota Classic Car Museum
5500 N Tamiami Trail, 34243; (p) (941) 355-6228; (f) (941) 358-8065; (c) Sarasota

Private non-profit/ 1953/ staff: 5(f); 12(p); 6(v)/ members: 16

HISTORY MUSEUM: Preserves, restores, and educates public about automobile history and its impact on American culture and lifestyles.

PROGRAMS: Annual Meeting; Community Outreach; Exhibits; Facility Rental; Family Programs; Festivals; Film/Video; Guided Tours; Interpretation; Living History; Research Library/Archives; School-Based Curriculum

COLLECTIONS: [1905-present] Over 75 antique, classic, and rare automobiles from around the world; collection of music machines and boxes from 17th and 18th c.

HOURS: Yr Daily 9-6

ADMISSION: $8.50, Student $5,

SEBRING

1532
Highlands Hammock State Park
5931 Hammock Rd, 33872; (p) (941) 386-6099; (f) (941) 386-6095; hammock@strato.net; (c) Highlands

State/ 1935/ DEP/Division of Recreation and Parks/ staff: 12(f); 3(p); 15(v)

LIVING HISTORY/OUTDOOR MUSEUM: Preserves Florida's natural and cultural resources.

PROGRAMS: Community Outreach; Exhibits; Facility Rental; Family Programs; Festivals; Guided Tours; Interpretation; Publication

COLLECTIONS: Civilian Conservation Corp memorabilia, tools, photos, and documents.

HOURS: Yr Daily

SILVER SPRINGS

1533
Marion County Museum of History
307 SE 26th Terrace, 34488 [PO Box 306, 34488]; (p) (352) 629-2773, (352) 694-2529; www.geocities.com/collegepark/stadium/1528/; (c) Marion

Private non-profit/ 1994/ staff: 1(f); 2(p); 36(v)/ members: 100

HISTORIC SITE; HISTORY MUSEUM; LIVING HISTORY/OUTDOOR MUSEUM: Collects and preserves artifacts and memorabilia related to county and state history; provides educational programs.

PROGRAMS: Annual Meeting; Community Outreach; Elder's Programs; Exhibits; Family Programs; Festivals; Film/Video; Guided Tours; Interpretation; Lectures; Living History; Publication; Research Library/Archives; School-Based Curriculum

COLLECTIONS: [Prehistory-1930] Seminole clothing, canoe, historic photos, pioneer homestead model, documents, loom, a round ladder, tools, wood washing machine, and carriage.

HOURS: Yr F-Sa 10-2

ADMISSION: $2

SOUTH GULFPORT

1534
Gulfport Historical Society
5301 28th Ave, 33707 [2625 58 St, 33707]; (p) (727) 321-2121; (f) (727) 864-4386; (c) Pinellas

Private non-profit/ 1980/ staff: 1(f); 5(p); 5(v)/ members: 60

HISTORIC SITE; HISTORICAL SOCIETY; HISTORY MUSEUM: Researches local family histories and maintains historical museum.

PROGRAMS: Annual Meeting; Community Outreach; Exhibits; Facility Rental; Family Programs; Festivals; Guided Tours; Living History; Reenactments

COLLECTIONS: [1865-present] Reference library; musical instruments, period clothing and toys; business and medical equip; tools.

HOURS: Yr M-F 2-4, Sa 10-12

ST. AUGUSTINE

1535
City of St. Augustine, Department of Historic Preservation and Heritage Tourism
29 St George St, 32085 [PO Box 210, St. Augustine, 32085]; (p) (904) 825-5033; (f) (904) 825-5096; (c) St. Johns

City/ 1965/ staff: 21(f); 8(p); 60(v)/ members: 200

HISTORIC PRESERVATION AGENCY; HISTORY MUSEUM; LIVING HISTORY/OUTDOOR MUSEUM: Operates two museum sites, the Spanish Quarter Museum and Government House Museum; manages 30+ historic structures and an education program.

PROGRAMS: Community Outreach; Family Programs; Festivals; Garden Tours; Guided Tours; Interpretation; Lectures; Living History; Reenactments; School-Based Curriculum

COLLECTIONS: [Mid 18th c] Decorative arts, period reproductions, and archaeological pieces from Spain, Latin America and Northern FL area.

1536
Lightner Museum, The
75 King St, 32085 [PO Box 334, St. Augustine, 32085]; (p) (904) 824-2874; (f) (904) 824-2712; (c) St Johns

Private non-profit/ 1948/ staff: 5(f); 5(p); 50(v)

Collects, preserves, and interprets 19th c fine and decorative arts through education and exhibits.

PROGRAMS: Community Outreach; Concerts; Exhibits; Facility Rental; Guided Tours; Lectures; Research Library/Archives; School-Based Curriculum

COLLECTIONS: [19th c] Fine and decorative arts.

HOURS: Yr Daily 9-5

ADMISSION: $6, Children $2

1537
St. Photios Greek Orthodox National Shrine
41 St George St, 32085 [PO Box 1960, St. Augustine, 32085]; (p) (904) 829-8205; (f) (904) 829-8707; (c) St John

Private non-profit/ 1981/ staff: 3(f); 4(p)

HISTORIC SITE: Preserves religious shrine with chapel representing the Greek Orthodox Christian religion; maintains historical display depicting the first Greek immigrants to come to the New World in the 1700s.

PROGRAMS: Exhibits; Festivals; Guided Tours

COLLECTIONS: Archaeological artifacts, religious icons, and reliquary.

1538
St. Augustine Lighthouse and Museum, Inc.
81 Lighthouse Ave, 32084; (p) (904) 829-0745; (f) (904) 829-0745; stauglh@aug.com; www.staugustinelighthouse.com/; (c) St Johns

Private non-profit/ 1988/ Board of Trustees/ staff: 12(f); 6(p); 57(v)/ members: 712

A working lighthouse and museum that preserves and interprets the history of the light station and its associated maritime, coastal, and social history.

PROGRAMS: Annual Meeting; Community Outreach; Exhibits; Facility Rental; Festivals; Guided Tours; Interpretation; Living History; School-Based Curriculum

COLLECTIONS: [1880s-1930s] 3,500 slides, 376 photos, 7,900 archival documents, personal items from keepers' families, USCG artifacts, 281 archaeological items, and 86 household items.

1539
World Golf Hall of Fame
One World Golf Pl, 32092; (p) (904) 940-4000; (f) (904) 940-4394; www.wgr.com; (c) St Johns

Private non-profit/ 1998/ World Golf Foundation, Inc./ staff: 65(f); 10(p); 150(v)

HISTORY MUSEUM: Maintains and creates exhibits that capture traditions, values, and historical attributes of golf through interactive displays.

PROGRAMS: Concerts; Exhibits; Facility Rental; Festivals; Film/Video; Research Library/Archives; School-Based Curriculum

COLLECTIONS: [1457-present] Golf memorabilia and artifacts including clubs, ball, tees, paintings, prints, photos, ceramics, glassware, sculpture, trophies, metal, and jewelry.

ST. JAMES CITY

1540
Museum of the Islands Society, Inc.
5728 Sesame Dr, 33956 [PO Box 305, 33956]; (p) (941) 293-1525; (c) Lee

Private non-profit/ 1990/ staff: 80(v)/ members: 250

HISTORICAL SOCIETY; HISTORY MUSEUM: Preserves history of Calusa Indian and Pioneer settlements on Pine Island through museum exhibits and maintenance of native landscape.

PROGRAMS: Annual Meeting; Community Outreach; Exhibits; Family Programs; Film/Video; Guided Tours; Research Library/Archives

COLLECTIONS: [Prehistory-present] Archaeological artifacts, fossils, and tools related to Calusa settlement, Spanish exploration, and European settlement.

HOURS: Yr May-Oct Th-Sa 11-3; Nov-Apr M 1-4, T-Sa 11-4, Su 1-4

ADMISSION: $1, Children $0.50

ST. PETERSBURG

1541
St. Petersburg Historical Society/St. Petersburg Museum of History
335 2nd Ave NE, 33701; (p) (727) 894-1052; (f) (727) 823-7276; spmh@ij.net; (c) Pinellas

Private non-profit/ 1920/ staff: 5(f); 4(p); 85(v)/ members: 600

HISTORICAL SOCIETY; HISTORY MUSEUM; RESEARCH CENTER: Collects, preserves, and interprets local, regional, and state history through exhibits, public programs, and research.

PROGRAMS: Annual Meeting; Community Outreach; Concerts; Elder's Programs; Exhibits; Facility Rental; Family Programs; Festivals; Film/Video; Guided Tours; Interpretation; Lectures; Research Library/Archives; School-Based Curriculum

COLLECTIONS: [19th and 20th c] Artifacts and archival material.

HOURS: Yr Daily 10-5

STARKE

1542
Camp Blanding Museum and Memorial Park
Bldg #3040, Tallahassee St, Camp Blanding, 32091 [Route 1, Box 465, 32091-9703]; (p) (904) 533-3196; (f) (904) 533-3276; parsonsg@gl-arng.ngb.army.mil; (c) Clay

State/ 1989/ State of Florida, Dept of Military Affairs/ staff: 1(f); 1(p); 12(v)/ members: 608/publication: Camp Blanding Echo

HISTORY MUSEUM: Dedicated to individuals and units of the U.S. Army in memory of their World War II service.

PROGRAMS: Annual Meeting; Exhibits; Guided Tours; Interpretation; Lectures; Living History; Publication; Research Library/Archives; School-Based Curriculum

COLLECTIONS: [World War II] Weapons, uniforms, and other accoutrements dealing with the World War II solider including tanks, jeeps, trucks and artillery pieces; materials relating to Korea, Vietnam and Desert Storm.

HOURS: Yr Daily 12-4; group tours available

ADMISSION: No charge

STUART

1543
Gilbert's Bar House of Refuge
301 SE MacArthur Blvd, 34996 [825 NE Ocean Blvd, 34996]; (p) (561) 225-1961; (f) (561) 225-2333; elliott.museum@mci2000.com; www.classicar.com

1875/ County; Historical Society of Martin County/ staff: 2(f); 1(p); 12(v)

HISTORY MUSEUM: Houses of Refuge were built along the coast of Florida to provide shelter and food for victims of shipwreck; Gilbert's Bar House of Refuge is the only surviving one.

COLLECTIONS: [1875-1914] Lifesaving equipment; Lyle gun; breeches buoy; navigation tools; bear trap; boatbuilding tools; homemaking utensils.; photos; original log books; US Lifesaving Service manuals for operations; maps; personal memoirs.

HOURS: Yr

1544
Historical Society of Martin County/ The Elliot Museum
825 NE Ocean Blvd, 34996; (p) (561) 225-1961; (f) (561) 225-2333; hsmc@bellsouth.net; www.goodnature.org/elliotmuseum; (c) Martin

Private non-profit/ 1955/ staff: 10(f); 2(p); 150(v)/ members: 600/publication: The History of Marin County

HISTORICAL SOCIETY; HISTORY MUSEUM: Founded by Harmon Elliott, American inventor, to showcase American ingenuity, art, and creativity; preserves county archives; maintains historic maritime site.

PROGRAMS: Annual Meeting; Community Outreach; Exhibits; Facility Rental; Guided Tours; Interpretation; Lectures; Publication; Research Library/Archives; School-Based Curriculum

COLLECTIONS: [1895-1940] Costumes, porcelains, glass, toys, paintings, baseball Hall of Fame collectibles, inventions, bicycles, vintage cars and motorcycles.

HOURS: Yr Daily 10-4

ADMISSION: $6, Children $2

1545
Stuart Heritage Inc.
161 SW Flagler Ave, 34994; (p) (561) 220-4600; (c) Martin

Private non-profit/ 1988/ Stuart Heritage Board/ staff: 1(p); 50(v)/ members: 150/publication: Martin Count, Our Heritage

HISTORIC PRESERVATION AGENCY; HISTORIC SITE; HISTORY MUSEUM; RESEARCH CENTER: Preserves local county history.

PROGRAMS: Annual Meeting; Exhibits; Guided Tours; Interpretation; Lectures; Publication; Research Library/Archives; School-Based Curriculum

COLLECTIONS: [1890-1940] Artifacts from a hardware store, a department store, a country store, and the charter fishing industry; author Earnest Lyons collection of papers and photos.

HOURS: Yr M-S 10-3

ADMISSION: Donations accepted

TALLAHASSEE

1546
Alfred B. Maclay State Gardens
3540 Thomasville Rd, 32308; (p) (850) 487-4115; (f) (850) 487-8808; (c) Leon

State/ 1953/ Department of Environmental Protection/ staff: 12(f); 4(p); 50(v)/ members: 200

GARDEN; HISTORIC SITE; HOUSE MUSEUM; STATE PARK: Historic gardens designed by Alfred B. Maclay between 1923-1944 on banks of Lake Hall.

PROGRAMS: Concerts; Facility Rental; Garden Tours; Interpretation; Lectures; School-Based Curriculum

COLLECTIONS: [1940-1950] Gardens represent a living collection of 160 species of winter and early spring blooming plants.

HOURS: Yr Daily 8-sunset

ADMISSION: $3, Children $1.50; $3/vehicle

1547
Florida Association of Museums, Inc.
1018 Thomasville Rd, Ste 103, 32302 [PO Box 10951, 32302-2951]; (p) (850) 222-6028; (f) (850) 222-6112; fam@flamuseums.org; www.flamuseums.org; (c) Leon

Private non-profit/ 1986/ staff: 1(f); 2(p)/ members: 700/publication: *FAM News*

PROFESSIONAL ORGANIZATION: Represents and addresses the needs of Florida's museum community.

1548
Florida Bureau of Natural and Cultural Resources
578A S Appleyard Dr, 32304; (p) (850) 488-5090; (f) (850) 922-4088; (c) Leon

State/ 1990/ Department of Environmental Protection Division of Recreation and Parks/ staff: 5(f); 2(p)

HISTORIC PRESERVATION AGENCY

PROGRAMS: Exhibits; Interpretation; Living History; Reenactments

COLLECTIONS: [Paleo-Indian- World War II] Material culture from Paleo-Indian through World War II and early state park history.

HOURS: Yr M-F 8-5

1549
Goodwood Plantation
1600 Miccosukee Rd, 32308 [1600 Miccosukee Road, 32308]; (p) (850) 877-4202; (f) (850) 877-3090

1837/ staff: 8(f); 1(p); 40(v)

HOUSE MUSEUM

COLLECTIONS: [1910s-1920s] Mid 19th century furniture, porcelain, dresses & garments; Papers of William C. Hodges, sheet music collection.

HOURS: Yr

1550
Knott House Museum, The
301 E Park, 32301; (p) (850) 922-2459; (f) (850) 413-7261; (c) Leon

State/ 1992/ Dept. of State/ staff: 2(f); 15(v)/ members: 500

HOUSE MUSEUM: Restoration and preservation of the 1843 Knott House and Victorian Era antiques.

PROGRAMS: Exhibits; Facility Rental; Family Programs; Interpretation

COLLECTIONS: [Victorian Era] Original furnishings and memorabilia used by the Knott Family, including decorative arts, textiles, and glass.

HOURS: Yr W-F 1-4, Sa 10-4

ADMISSION: No charge

1551
Mission San Luis Archaeological and Historic Site
2021 W Mission Rd, 32304; (p) (850) 487-3711; (f) (850) 488-8015; (c) Leon

State/ 1983/ FL Dept. of State/ staff: 15(f); 5(p); 40(v)/publication: *The Quarterly; The El Correo*

HISTORIC SITE; HISTORY MUSEUM; LIVING HISTORY/OUTDOOR MUSEUM: 17th c Spanish Mission and Apalachee Indian Village historical reconstruction.

PROGRAMS: Exhibits; Living History

COLLECTIONS: [Spanish Colonial/Apalachee Indians] Period/archaeological artifacts.

HOURS: Yr M-F 9-4:30, Sa 10-4:30, Su 12-4:30

ADMISSION: No charge

1552
Museum of Florida History
500 S Bronough, 32399-0350; (p) (850) 488-1484; (f) (850) 921-2503; wrichey@mail.dos.state.fl.us; www.dhr.dos.state.fl.us/museum; (c) Leon

State/ 1977/ Dept. of State/ staff: 25(f); 8(p); 28(v)/ members: 500/publication: *The Associate*

HISTORY MUSEUM: Collects, preserves, exhibits, and interprets the material record of human culture in FL; promotes and encourages knowledge and appreciation of FL history.

PROGRAMS: Community Outreach; Concerts; Exhibits; Facility Rental; Family Programs; Festivals; Film/Video; Lectures; Publication; School-Based Curriculum; Theatre

COLLECTIONS: [Paleo period-present] Artifacts which focus on FL's social, economic, cultural, and political history.

HOURS: Yr M-F

1553
Old Capitol Museum, The
400 S Monroe St, 32301; (p) (850) 487-1902; (f) (850) 921-2540; jbrightbill@mail.dos.state.fl.us; www.dhr.dos.state.fl.us/museum; (c) Leon

State/ 1845/ staff: 6(f); 20(v)/ members: 500

Preserves restored Capitol buildings.

PROGRAMS: Exhibits; Facility Rental; Family Programs; Lectures

COLLECTIONS: [Turn-of-the-Century] State artifacts and original furnishings of the Capitol; political history exhibits.

HOURS: Yr M-F 9-4:30, Sa 10-4:30, Su 12-4:30

ADMISSION: No charge

1554
Riley Museum of African American History and Culture
419 E Jefferson St, 32311; (p) (850) 681-7881; (f) (850) 386-4368; (c) Leon

Private non-profit/ 1996/ staff: 1(f); 2(p); 18(v)/ members: 260

HISTORY MUSEUM: Identifies, preserves, interprets, and protects the history and culture of African Americans and their influence on local and state development from the Reconstruction Era through the Civil Rights Movement.

PROGRAMS: Annual Meeting; Community Outreach; Exhibits; Guided Tours; Lectures

COLLECTIONS: [1865-1968] Photos, artifacts, and documents from reunions, churches, and schools; period furniture.

HOURS: M, W, F 10-4

1555
Tallahassee Museum of History and Natural Science
3945 Museum Dr, 32310; (p) (850) 575-8684; (f) (850) 574-8243; rdaws@tallahasseemuseum.org; www.tallahasseemuseum.org; (c) Leon

1957/ Board of Trustees/ staff: 21(f); 28(p); 260(v)/ members: 5000/publication: *Tallahssee Museum News*

HISTORY MUSEUM; LIVING HISTORY/OUTDOOR MUSEUM: Collects, preserves, and exhibits artifacts and historic buildings; maintains native animals in natural habitats; operates a 19th c farmstead to educate the public about natural and cultural history.

PROGRAMS: Annual Meeting; Community Outreach; Concerts; Exhibits; Facility Rental; Family Programs; Festivals; Guided Tours; Interpretation; Living History; Publication

COLLECTIONS: [Late 19th-20th c] 18,000 historical and natural history objects, 73 cubic feet of archival records, 100 native live animals, 14 historic structures (1840-1937).

HOURS: Yr M-Sa 9-5, Su 12:30-5

ADMISSION: $7, Children $5

TAMPA

1556
Henry B. Plant Museum
401 W Kennedy Blvd, 33606; (p) (813) 254-1891; (f) (813) 258-7272; jtwachtmann@alpha.utampa.edu; www.plantmuseum.com; (c) Hillsborough

Joint/ 1933/ The University of Tampa, The City of Tampa/ staff: 7(f); 48(v)

HISTORIC SITE; HOUSE MUSEUM: Interprets the history of the turn-of-the-century Tampa Bay Hotel and the lifestyles of America's Gilded Age.

PROGRAMS: Community Outreach; Exhibits; Facility Rental; Family Programs; Interpretation; Living History; Publication

COLLECTIONS: [1890-1920s] Antique furnishings and decorative arts.

HOURS: Yr T-Sa 10-4, Su 12-4

ADMISSION: $5

1557
History and Genealogy Department
900 N Ashley Dr, 33602; (p) (813) 273-3652; (f) (813) 273-3641; www.thpl.org; (c) Hillsborough

County/ Hillsborough County Public Library/ staff: 6(f); 4(p); 3(v)

LIBRARY AND/OR ARCHIVES: Resource center for in-depth use of genealogy and history material in print, microform, electronic format.

PROGRAMS: Community Outreach; Exhibits; Guided Tours; Research Library/Archives

COLLECTIONS: Genealogy materials, maps, atlases, books, 15,000 local photos.

HOURS: Yr Daily M-Th 9-9, F 9-6, Sa 9-5, Su 11-7

ADMISSION: No charge

1558
Museum of Science and Industry
4801 E Fowler Ave, 33617; (p) (813) 987-6300; (f) (813) 987-6310; blittlej@mosi.org; www.mosi.org; (c) Hillsborough

Private non-profit/ 1962/ Museum of Science and Industry Foundation, Inc./ staff: 74(f); 74(p); 345(v)/ members: 9000/publication: *MOSI Magazine*

HISTORY MUSEUM: Maintains public exhibits on science, technology, and natural history.

PROGRAMS: Annual Meeting; Community Outreach; Elder's Programs; Exhibits; Facility Rental; Family Programs; Film/Video; Lectures; Living History; Publication; Research Library/Archives; School-Based Curriculum; Theatre

COLLECTIONS: Small collection of science, technology, and natural history.

HOURS: Yr Daily

ADMISSION: $13, Children $9, Seniors $11

1559
Tampa Bay History Center
225 S Franklin St, 33602 [PO Box 948, 33602]; (p) (813) 228-0097; (f) (813) 223-7021; ebl47a@juno.com; www.home1.gte.net/thistory; (c) Hillsborough

Private non-profit/ 1989/ staff: 7(f); 3(p); 3(v)/ members: 440/publication: *Pastimes*

HISTORY MUSEUM: Serves and educates community of historic Hillsborough through discovery, preservation, and interpretation of people's heritage.

PROGRAMS: Annual Meeting; Community Outreach; Elder's Programs; Exhibits; Facility Rental; Family Programs; Lectures; Publication; Research Library/Archives; School-Based Curriculum

COLLECTIONS: Period artifacts and furniture; maps, documents, books, microfilm, and photos.

HOURS: Yr T-Sa 10-5, Su 1-5

ADMISSION: No charge

1560
Tampa Police Museum
411 N Franklin, 33672 [PO Box 172995, 33672]; (p) (813) 276-3392; (f) (813) 276-3701; (c) Hillborough

Private non-profit/ 1997/ Tampa Police Memorial Fund, Inc/ staff: 20(v)

HISTORY MUSEUM: Maintains artifacts and photos of the Tampa Police Dept; educates the public and students of our historical past.

PROGRAMS: Exhibits; Guided Tours

COLLECTIONS: [1890-present] Tampa Police photos, badges, equipment (police vehicles,

helicopter, motorcycle, radios), firearms, and uniforms; also police items from other agencies, local and international.

HOURS: Yr M-F 10-3

ADMISSION: No charge

1561
Ybor City Museum Society
2009 N 18th St, 33675 [PO Box 5421, 33675]; (p) (813) 247-1434; (f) (813) 242-4010; mnchavez@gte.net; (c) Hillsborough

Private non-profit/ 1982/ Ybor City Museum Society/ staff: 1(f); 1(p); 65(v)/ members: 250

HISTORY MUSEUM: Focuses on immigrants of Ybor City and maintains exhibits on cigar industry of Tampa.

PROGRAMS: Annual Meeting; Exhibits; Facility Rental; Family Programs; Festivals; Guided Tours; Interpretation; Lectures

COLLECTIONS: [1886-present] Artifacts and images related to the Tampa cigar industry and Ybor city's economy, social clubs and family life.

HOURS: Yr Daily 9-5

ADMISSION: $2

TAMPA BAY

1562
Egmont Key Alliance
Egmont Key, [4905 34th St S, PMB 5000, St Petersburg, 33711]; (p) (727) 893-2627; (f) (727) 893-1292; egmontkey@juno.com; www.dep.state.fl.us/parks; (c) Hillsborough

Private non-profit; State/ 1991/ staff: 325(v)/ members: 150/publication: *Key Notes*

HISTORIC SITE: Preserves, protects, and restores natural and cultural resources on Egmont Key, including lighthouse and coastal fortification.

PROGRAMS: Guided Tours; Interpretation; Publication

HOURS: Yr Daily 8-Sunset

TARPON SPRINGS

1563
Safford House/Tarpon Springs Cultural Center
23 Park Court, 34689 [101 S Pinellas Ave, 34689]; (p) (727) 942-5605; (f) (727) 938-2429; (c) Pinellas

City/ 1994/ City of Tarpon Springs

CULTURAL CENTER; HOUSE MUSEUM: Preserves late 19th c vernacular architecture style Safford House, the oldest surviving house in city.

PROGRAMS: Exhibits; Facility Rental; Guided Tours; Interpretation; Lectures; Living History; Reenactments; School-Based Curriculum

COLLECTIONS: Period furniture, decorative arts, and furnishings.

TAVARES

1564
Lake County Historical Museum
317 W Main St, 32778 [PO Box 7800, 32778-7800]; (p) (352) 343-9600; (f) (352) 343-9696; (c) Lake

County/ 1960/ Lake County Board of County Commissioners/ staff: 1(f); 1(p); 20(v)

HISTORY MUSEUM: Offers an informative view of history of Lake County.

PROGRAMS: Community Outreach; Elder's Programs; Exhibits; Family Programs; Festivals; Interpretation; Lectures; Living History; School-Based Curriculum

COLLECTIONS: [Victorian era-present] Artifacts related to the Native Americans, pioneers, and residents of Lake County.

HOURS: Yr M-F 8:30-5

ADMISSION: No charge

TITUSVILLE

1565
Astronaut Hall of Fame
W of Kennedy Space Center on SR 405, 32780 [6225 Vectorspace Blvd, 32780-8040]; (p) (407) 269-6100; (f) (407) 267-3970; ahof@spacecamp.com; www.astronauts.org; (c) Brevard

Private non-profit/ 1990/ U.S. Space Camp Foundation

HISTORY MUSEUM

PROGRAMS: Exhibits; Facility Rental; Festivals; Guided Tours

COLLECTIONS: Astronauts' personal artifacts and memorabilia.

HOURS: Yr Daily 9-5

ADMISSION: $13.95, Children $9.95; Under 6 free

1566
Valiant Air Command Warbird Museum
6600 Tico Rd, 32780; (p) (407) 268-1941; (f) (407) 268-5969; vacinfo1@aol.com; www.vacwarbirds.org; (c) Brevard

County, non-profit/ 1977/ Valiant Air Command Board of Directors/ staff: 3(p); 200(v)/ members: 780

HISTORY MUSEUM: Perpetuates history of aviation, encourages Warbird research and restoration, and serves as an educational resource.

PROGRAMS: Annual Meeting; Community Outreach; Exhibits; Facility Rental; Family Programs; Festivals; Guided Tours; Living History; Publication; Reenactments

COLLECTIONS: [World War II-present] Memorabilia and artifacts from WWII to Desert Storm; a hanger, a C-47 aircraft from the D-Day invasion, vintage flying gear, and uniforms.

HOURS: Yr Daily 10-6

ADMISSION: $9,

VALPARAISO

1567
Heritage Museum Association, Inc.
115 Westview Ave, 32580 [PO Box 488, 32580]; (p) (850) 678-2615; (f) (850) 678-2615; (c) Okaloosa

Private non-profit/ 1971/ staff: 1(f); 1(p); 25(v)/ members: 120/publication: *Heritage*

HISTORY MUSEUM: Preserves and interprets evidences of Okaloosa's past though exhibits and library collection.

PROGRAMS: Annual Meeting; Community Outreach; Elder's Programs; Exhibits; Family Programs; Festivals; Garden Tours; Guided Tours; Interpretation; Lectures; Publication; Reenactments; Research Library/Archives; School-Based Curriculum

COLLECTIONS: [Prehistory-1940] Native American artifacts; pioneer kitchen utensils, farm tools, industrial tools, and period costumes;one-room schoolhouse and a beauty shop; maps,photos and reference books.

VENICE

1568
Venice Archives & Area Historical Collection
351 S Nassau St, 34285; (p) (941) 486-2487; (f) (941) 480-3031; dkorwek@ci.venice.fl.us; www.venice.florida.com/community/archive.htm; (c) Sarasota

City/ 1991/ staff: 1(p); 12(v)

HISTORIC SITE; HISTORY MUSEUM; LIBRARY AND/OR ARCHIVES: To collect and preserve historical and archeological material relating to Venice and the communities of Nokmis, Laurel, and Osprey.

PROGRAMS: Exhibits; Research Library/Archives

COLLECTIONS: [20th c] Local history of individuals and organizations.

HOURS: Yr M-W 10-4

ADMISSION: No charge

VERO BEACH

1569
Indian River Citrus Museum/HeritageCenter
2140 14th Ave, 32961 [PO Box 758, 32961]; (p) (561) 770-2263; (f) (561) 770-2131; vbheritage@cs.com; (c) Indian River

Private non-profit/ 1992/ Vero Heritage, Inc/ staff: 1(f); 1(p); 35(v)/ members: 215

HISTORY MUSEUM: Promotes local and citrus industry.

PROGRAMS: Exhibits; Facility Rental; Guided Tours; Lectures

COLLECTIONS: [1800s-present] Historic photos, old farm tools, antique citrus labels, industry archive, original harvesting equipment, and early shipping containers.

1570
McKee Botanical Garden
350 US Hwy 1, 32962; (p) (561) 794-0601; (f) (561) 794-0602; info@mckeegarden.org; www.mckeegarden.org; (c) Indian River

Private non-profit/ 1994/ staff: 5(f); 1(p); 75(v)/ members: 850

GARDEN: Restored the garden to William Lyman Phillips' original historic design of the 1930s; operates the garden as a community and educational resource.

PROGRAMS: Community Outreach; Garden Tours

COLLECTIONS: [1930-present] Plant collection including ferns, palms, and orchids.

1571
McLarty Treasure Museum
13180 N A1A, 32963; (p) (561) 589-9656; (f) (407) 984-4854; (c) Indian River

State/ 1971/ Sebastian Inlet State Recreation Area/ staff: 1(f); 20(v)/ members: 20

HISTORIC SITE; HISTORY MUSEUM: Preserves the history of the Spanish Treasure Fleet that sunk along the coast.

PROGRAMS: Exhibits; Film/Video; Guided Tours; Interpretation; Lectures

COLLECTIONS: [1715] Items related to the Spanish Treasure Fleet that sunk, the survivors camp, and the recovery of the lost treasure.

HOURS: Yr Daily 10-4:30

ADMISSION: $1

WAKULLA SPRINGS

1572
Wakulla Springs State Park and Lodge
550 Wakulla Park Dr, 32305; (p) (850) 224-5950; (f) (850) 561-7282; www.floridadep.org/parks/district_1/wakulla/index.html; (c) Wakulla

State/ 1937/ Department of Environmental Protection/ staff: 40(f); 40(p); 10(v)

LIVING HISTORY/OUTDOOR MUSEUM: Maintains natural lands and historic lodge.

PROGRAMS: Facility Rental; Guided Tours; Interpretation

COLLECTIONS: Native American historical items and a lodge from 1937.

HOURS: Yr Daily 8-Sunset

ADMISSION: $3.25/Vehicle

WEST PALM BEACH

1573
Ann Norton Sculpture Gardens
253 Barcelona, 33401; (p) (561) 832-5328; (f) (561) 835-9305; annorton@Bellsouth.net; (c) Palm Beach

Federal; Private non-profit; State/ 1979/ staff: 2(f); 40(v)/ members: 400

GARDEN; HISTORIC SITE: Botanical gardens with a twenty-foot high brick sculpture by Ann Weaver Norton.

PROGRAMS: Annual Meeting; Exhibits; Facility Rental; Garden Tours; Guided Tours

COLLECTIONS: [1930s-1980s]

HOURS: Oct-May, W-Su 11-4

ADMISSION: $5

1574
Historic Preservation Division, City of West Palm Beach
200 2nd St, 33402 [PO Box 3366, 33402]; (p) (561) 659-8031; (f) (561) 653-2603; (c) Palm Beach

City/ staff: 2(f)

HISTORIC PRESERVATION AGENCY: Identifies and evaluates local historic resources; protects resources against adverse impact; promotes awareness of preserving historic resources.

HOURS: Yr M-F 8-5

1575
Historical Society of Palm Beach County
400 N Dixie Hwy, 33401; (p) (561) 832-4164; (f) (561) 832-7965; (c) Palm Beach

Private non-profit/ 1937/ staff: 3(f); 1(p); 80(v)/ members: 600/publication: *Palm Beach Past Times*

HISTORICAL SOCIETY; RESEARCH CENTER: Maintains a historical repository.

PROGRAMS: Annual Meeting; Community Outreach; Exhibits; Lectures; Publication

COLLECTIONS: [1850-present] Books, photos, periodicals, architectural drawings, maps, furniture, and artifacts.

HOURS: Yr 10-4

1576
Palm Beach County Genealogical Society
100 Clematis St, 33402 [PO Box 1746, 33402-1746]; (p) (561) 832-3279; pbcgenlib@juno.com; community.gopbi.com/pbc-gensoc; (c) Palm Beach

Private non-profit/ 1964/ Palm Beach County Genealogical Society/ staff: 25(v)/ members: 280

GENEALOGICAL SOCIETY

PROGRAMS: Annual Meeting; Community Outreach; Lectures; Publication; Research Library/Archives

COLLECTIONS: [Colonial-present] 11,000 books, mostly Eastern US.

HOURS: Yr M-S 10-4

ADMISSION: No charge

1577
Yesteryear Village at the South Florida Fairgrounds
9067 Southern Blvd, 33416 [PO Box 15915, 33416]; (p) (561) 795-6402; (f) (561) 753-2124; angela@southfloridafair.org; (c) Palm Beach

Private non-profit/ 1991/ South Florida Fair Board of Trustees/ staff: 3(f); 3(p); 325(v)

HISTORIC PRESERVATION AGENCY; HISTORY MUSEUM; HOUSE MUSEUM; LIVING HISTORY/OUTDOOR MUSEUM: Collects, preserves, and interprets general FL history, architecture, and historical objects.

PROGRAMS: Community Outreach; Elder's Programs; Exhibits; Facility Rental; Festivals; Guided Tours; Living History; Reenactments; School-Based Curriculum

COLLECTIONS: [1890s-1940s] 20 historic buildings, 15 antique vehicles, 50 historic implements, 250 furniture pieces, and 5,000 museum artifacts.

WHITE SPRINGS

1578
Stephen Foster State Folk Culture Center
US 41 N, 92096 [PO Drawer G, 92096]; (p) (904) 397-2733; (f) (904) 397-4262; (c) Hamilton

State/ 1950/ Florida Park Service/ staff: 16(f); 3(p); 95(v)

HERITAGE AREA; HISTORY MUSEUM: Interprets FL's natural and cultural heritage through craft demonstrations, concerts, tours, and outdoor activities.

PROGRAMS: Annual Meeting; Community Outreach; Concerts; Elder's Programs; Exhibits; Facility Rental; Family Programs; Festivals; Garden Tours; Guided Tours; Interpretation; Lectures

COLLECTIONS: Collection focuses on the folklife of Suwannee Valley, American music, and composer Stephen Foster; manuscripts.

HOURS: Yr Daily 8-Sundown

ADMISSION: $3.25/Vehicle

WINTER PARK

1579
Winter Park Historical Association
200 W New England Ave, 32790 [PO Box 51, 32790]; (p) (407) 647-2330, (407) 647-8180; WPHistory@aol.com; (c) Orange

Private non-profit/ 1995/ Board of Directors/ staff: 1(f); 45(v)/ members: 360/publication: *Winter Park Portrait*

HISTORICAL SOCIETY; HISTORY MUSEUM: Collects and shares historical data and artifacts of region.

PROGRAMS: Annual Meeting; Community Outreach; Exhibits; Guided Tours; Interpretation; Lectures; Publication

COLLECTIONS: [1850s-present] Artifacts of prominent regional families; photos of the area.

HOURS: Yr Th 11-3, F 11-3, Sa 9-1, Su 1-4

GEORGIA

ACWORTH

1580
Acworth Society for Historic Preservation
[PO Box 851, 30101]; (p) (770) 975-1930; (c) Cobb

Private non-profit/ 1996/ staff: 10(v)/ members: 40

HISTORICAL SOCIETY: Enhances and increases historic awareness; facilitates designation of historic districts; preserves historic structures, sites, documents and relics.

PROGRAMS: Annual Meeting; Interpretation; Lectures

ALBANY

1581
Southwest Georgia Genealogical Society
300 Pine Ave, 31706 [PO Box 4672, 31706]; (c) Dougherty

Private non-profit/ members: 285/publication: *Southwest GA Genealogical Gazette*

GENEALOGICAL SOCIETY: Supports genealogical research.

PROGRAMS: Publication; Research Library/ Archives

COLLECTIONS: [1600-present] Census records; military artifacts; county histories; marriage, cemetery, and DAR records; newspapers on film; land records and family histories.

HOURS: Yr M-W 10-9, Th-Sa 10-6

ADMISSION: No charge

1582
Thronateeska Heritage Center
100 Roosevelt Ave, 31701; (p) (912) 432-6955; heritagecenter.org; (c) Dougherty

Private non-profit/ 1974/ Thronateeska Heritage Foundation, Inc./ staff: 2(f); 5(p); 20(v)/ members: 253/publication: *Journal of Southwest Georgia History*

HISTORIC SITE; HISTORY MUSEUM: Preserves local history and Albany's historical railroad complex.

PROGRAMS: Annual Meeting; Community Outreach; Exhibits; Facility Rental; Festivals; Interpretation; Lectures; Publication; School-Based Curriculum

COLLECTIONS: [1880-1945] Personal artifacts, including clothing; machinery, photographs, and

ALPHARETTA

1583
Alpharetta Historical Society, Inc.
1835 Old Milton Pkwy, 30009-1386; (p) (770) 475-4663; (c) Fulton

Private non-profit/ staff: 15(v)/ members: 120

ALLIANCE OF HISTORICAL AGENCIES; GENEALOGICAL SOCIETY; HISTORIC PRESERVATION AGENCY; HISTORICAL SOCIETY; HOUSE MUSEUM: Preserves the history of Alpharetta and Old Milton County region.

PROGRAMS: Annual Meeting; Community Outreach; Facility Rental; Living History; Monthly Meeting

COLLECTIONS: [1857-1932] Photos of Alpharetta and Old Milton County.

HOURS: Yr M-F 10-4

ADMISSION: Donations accepted

ANDERSONVILLE

1584
Andersonville National Historic Site
Hwy 49 N, 31711 [Route 1, Box 800, 31711]; (p) (912) 924-0343; (f) (912) 928-9640; www.nps.ande.gov; (c) Macon and Sumter

Federal/ 1970/ National Park Service/ staff: 15(f); 1(p)

HISTORIC SITE: Provides an understanding of prisoner of war experience during the Civil War; interprets role of prisoner of war camps in history and commemorates sacrifice of Americans who lost their lives in such camps.

PROGRAMS: Community Outreach; Exhibits; Guided Tours; Interpretation; Living History; Reenactments; Research Library/Archives

COLLECTIONS: [19th-20th c] Archival and curatorial collection; exhibits items primarily used

or made by POWs; over 800 oral history interviews of POWs.

HOURS: Yr Daily 8-5

1585
Andersonville Oldtime Farm Area and Museum
114 Church St, 31711 [PO Box 6, 31711]; (p) (912) 924-2558; (f) (912) 924-2558; (c) Sumter

Private non-profit/ 1974/ Andersonville Guild/ staff: 3(f); 3(p); 10(v)/ members: 130

HISTORIC PRESERVATION AGENCY; HISTORICAL SOCIETY; HISTORY MUSEUM; LIVING HISTORY/OUTDOOR MUSEUM: Preserves the Civil War Village of Andersonville.

PROGRAMS: Festivals; Guided Tours; Lectures; Living History; Reenactments

COLLECTIONS: [Mid-late 19th c] Five acre outdoor living history museum depicts life on yeoman farm.

HOURS: Yr Daily 9-5

ADMISSION: No charge

ASHBURN

1586
Ashburn Historic Preservation Commission
121 E Madison Ave, 31714 [PO Box 766, 31714]; (p) (912) 567-3431; (f) (912) 567-9284; ashburn@plantel.net; (c) Turner

City/ 1984/ staff: 6(v)

HISTORIC PRESERVATION AGENCY: Preserves character of city's Historic Preservation Ordinance of 1984.

ATHENS

1587
Athens Historical Society, Inc.
[PO Box 7745, 30604-7745]; (p) (706) 425-9833; (f) (706) 425-9833; athens-historical-society@mailexcel.com; (c) Clarke

Private non-profit/ 1959/ Board of Directors/ staff: 1(p); 60(v)/ members: 298/publication: *Athens Historian*

HISTORICAL SOCIETY: Encourages interest in history of Athens and Clarke County; sponsors publication of cemetery surveys, an 1874 county map, reminiscences, and other topics. Contributes to programs at local library and University of GA.

PROGRAMS: Exhibits; Lectures; Publication; Quarterly Meeting

COLLECTIONS: [1800-present]

1588
Athens-Clarke County Library Heritage Room
2025 Baxter St, 30606; (p) (706) 613-3650; (f) (706) 613-3660; www.clarke.public.lib.ga.us/departments/; (c) Clarke

County/ 1992/ Athens Regional Library System/ staff: 2(f); 1(p); 2(v)

RESEARCH CENTER: Collects and preserves materials on the history and culture of Georgia, with major focus on genealogy.

PROGRAMS: Exhibits; Lectures; Research Library/Archives

COLLECTIONS: [18th-20th c] Books, maps, periodicals, records, vertical files, county histories, microform and surname

1589
Church-Waddel-Brumby House Museum

280 E Dougherty St, 30601; (p) (706) 353-1820; (f) (706) 353-1770; athenswc@negia. net; (c) Clarke

1972/ Athens-Clarke Heritage Foundation/ staff: 1(f); 2(p); 12(v)/publication: *Athens Welcome Center Rock Card*

HOUSE MUSEUM

PROGRAMS: Facility Rental; Guided Tours; Living History; School-Based Curriculum

COLLECTIONS: [1820-1840] Decorative arts.

HOURS: Yr M-Sa 10-6, Su 12-6

ADMISSION: No charge

1590
National Alliance of Preservation Commissions

[PO Box 1605, 30603]; (p) (706) 542-4731; (f) (706) 542-4485; pcassity@arches.uga.edu; (c) Clarke

Private non-profit/ 1983/ staff: 2(f); 1(p)/ members: 2000

HISTORIC PRESERVATION AGENCY; LIBRARY AND/OR ARCHIVES: 2,000 landmark, historical commission, and architectural review boards.

PROGRAMS: Community Outreach; Lectures; Publication

1591
Richard B. Russell Library for Political Research and Studies

320 S Jackson St, 30602 [Univ of Georgia Libraries, 30602-1641]; (p) (706) 542-0618; (f) (706) 542-4144; sbvogt@arches.uga.edu; www.libs.uga.edu/russell; (c) Clarke

State/ 1974/ Board of Regents, Univ System of GA/ staff: 7(f); 6(p)

LIBRARY AND/OR ARCHIVES: Repository for acquisition, arrangement and preservation; reference service for modern political and public policy collections.

PROGRAMS: Exhibits; Facility Rental; Interpretation; Lectures; Research Library/Archives

COLLECTIONS: [1900-present] Papers and records of congressional delegation, elected

1592
Southern Historical Association

Dept of History, Univ of Georgia, 30602-1602; (p) (706) 542-8848; (f) (706) 542-2455; gsdavis@arches.uga.edu; www.uga.edu/~sha; (c) Clarke

1934/ staff: 3(f)/ members: 4500/publication: *Journal of Southern History*

Encourages study of history in South.

1593
State Botanical Garden of Georgia, The

2450 S Milledge Ave, 30605; (p) (706) 542-1244; (f) (706) 542-3091; garden@arches.uga.edu; www.uga.edu/botgarden; (c) Clarke

State/ 1968/ The University of Georgia/ staff: 26(f); 8(p); 150(v)/ members: 1800/publication: *Garden News*

GARDEN; NATURAL HISTORY MUSEUM

PROGRAMS: Annual Meeting; Community Outreach; Concerts; Exhibits; Facility Rental; Family Programs; Festivals; Garden Tours; Guided Tours; Lectures; Publication

COLLECTIONS: [Prehistory-present] Native plants of Georgia and the Southeast; tropical plants; herb garden; other theme gardens and collections, nature trails.

HOURS: Yr Daily Oct-Mar 8-6; Apr-Sept 8-8

ADMISSION: No charge

1594
Taylor-Grady House

634 Prince Ave, 30601; (p) (706) 549-8688; (f) (706) 613-0860; jlathens@aol.com; (c) Clarke

County, non-profit/ 1968/ Junior League of Athens/ staff: 3(f); 200(v)/ members: 450

HISTORIC SITE; HOUSE MUSEUM: A National Historic Landmark, built in the 1840s as a Greek revival home by General Robert Taylor.

PROGRAMS: Guided Tours; Interpretation

COLLECTIONS: [1820-1950]

HOURS: Yr M-F 19-1/2:30-5

ADMISSION: $3

1595
United States Navy Supply Corps Museum

1425 Prince Ave, 30606-2205; (p) (706) 354-7349; (f) (706) 354-7239; (c) Clarke

Federal/ 1975/ US Government-Dept of the Navy/ staff: 1(f)

Collects, preserves, and presents to the public artifacts and documentary materials which relate to growth and development of Supply Corps.

PROGRAMS: Guided Tours; Interpretation; Research Library/Archives

COLLECTIONS: Ship models, uniforms, galley gear and mess equipment, disbursing materials, and personal memorabilia; archives includes manuals, directories, cookbooks, photos, newsletters, scrapbooks, yearbooks, command histories, and curriculum materials.

HOURS: Yr M-F 9-5:15

ADMISSION: No charge

ATLANTA

1596
Alpha Delta Pi Sorority Archives

1386 Ponce de Leon Ave NE, 30306; (p) (404) 378-3164; khenzl@alphadeltapi.com; (c) Dekalb

Private non-profit/ 1983/ Alpha Delta Pi Sorority/ staff: 1(p)

COLLECTIONS: [1851-present] Documents, artifacts and memorabilia pertinent to Alpha Delta Pi history; publications by Alpha Delta Pi authors and the Adelphean quarterly publication, 1907-present.

1597
Atlanta Cyclorama

800 Cherokee Ave SE, 30315; (p) (404) 658-7625; (f) (404) 658-7045; atlcyclora@mind spring.com; www.bcaatlanta.org; (c) Fulton

1898/ City of Atlanta/ staff: 15(f)

ART MUSEUM; HISTORIC SITE; HISTORY MUSEUM: Self-sustaining enterprise that seeks to educate, entertain and welcome guests to Atlanta.

PROGRAMS: Community Outreach; Exhibits; Facility Rental; Festivals; Guided Tours; Interpretation; Lectures; Living History; Reenactments; Theatre

COLLECTIONS: [1850-1890] Features painting-in-the-round, "The Battle of Atlanta." Many other Civil War exhibits, including the locomotive "Texas," weapons and photos.

HOURS: Yr Daily 9:30-4:30; June-Sept Daily 9:30-5:30

ADMISSION: Donations requested

1598
Atlanta Historical Society

130 W Paces Ferry Rd NW, 30305; (p) (404) 814-4000; (f) (404) 814-4186; webmaster@ atlhist.org; www.atlhist.org; (c) Fulton

Private non-profit/ 1926/ staff: 76(f); 54(p); 450(v)/ members: 5600/publication: *Atlanta History: A Journal of Georgia and the South*

GARDEN; HISTORIC SITE; HISTORICAL SOCIETY; HISTORY MUSEUM; HOUSE MUSEUM; LIVING HISTORY/OUTDOOR MUSEUM; RESEARCH CENTER: Maintains library/ archives and museum promoting history of Atlanta, Civil War, and southern folk arts

PROGRAMS: Community Outreach; Concerts; Exhibits; Facility Rental; Festivals; Garden Tours; Guided Tours; Interpretation; Lectures; Publication; Reenactments; Research Library/Archives; School-Based Curriculum

COLLECTIONS: [18th-20th c] Two historic houses: 1845 Tullie Smith Farm and 1928 Swan House; thirty-three acres of gardens.

HOURS: Yr M-Sa 10-5:30, Su 12-5:30

ADMISSION: $10, Student $8, Children $5, Seniors $8; Under 5/Mbrs free

1599
Atlanta History Center

130 W Paces Ferry Rd NW, 30305; (p) (404) 814-4000; (f) (404) 814-4029; www.atlantahis torycenter.com; (c) Fulton

Private non-profit/ 1926/ Atlanta Historical Society, Inc./ staff: 85(f); 75(p); 375(v)/ members: 5700/publication: *Atlanta History*

HISTORICAL SOCIETY; HISTORY MUSEUM; HOUSE MUSEUM: History museum, two National Register houses, period gardens, and a research library/archives.

PROGRAMS: Community Outreach; Concerts; Exhibits; Facility Rental; Festivals; Garden Tours; Guided Tours; Interpretation; Lectures; Living History; Publication; Reenactments; Research Library/Archives; School-Based Curriculum

COLLECTIONS: [1800-present] Library, archival, and visual arts holdings, heirloom plants and specimen collections.

HOURS: Yr M-Sa 10-5:30, Su 12-5:30

ADMISSION: $10, Student $8, Children $5, Seniors $8

1600
Atlanta Preservation Center
537 Peachtree St NE, 30308; (p) (404) 876-2041; (f) (404) 876-2618; www.preserveatlanta.com; (c) Fulton

Private non-profit/ 1980/ Board of Trustees/ staff: 4(f); 1(p); 150(v)/ members: 1000/publication: *Preservation Times*

HISTORIC PRESERVATION AGENCY: Preserves Atlanta's historically, architecturally and culturally significant buildings, neighborhoods and districts.

PROGRAMS: Community Outreach; Guided Tours; Lectures; Publication; School-Based Curriculum

HOURS: Yr

1601
Auburn Avenue Research Library on African American Culture and History
101 Auburn Ave NE, 30303-2503; (p) (404) 730-4001; (f) (404) 730-5879; www.aarl.af.public.lib.ga.us; (c) Fulton

County/ 1994/ Atlanta-Fulton Public Library System/ staff: 23(f); 1(p); 3(v)/publication: *Monograph Series; Research Guides*

Offers specialized reference and archival collections for the study and research of Black culture.

PROGRAMS: Community Outreach; Concerts; Exhibits; Guided Tours; Interpretation; Lectures; Publication; Research Library/Archives

COLLECTIONS: General reference items, microforms, audiovisuals, vertical files, photographs, artworks, archives, manuscripts and ephemera.

HOURS: Yr M-Th 10-8, F-Su 12-6

1602
Eleventh Circuit Historical Society, The
56 Forsyth St NW, 30301 [PO Box 1556, 30301]; (p) (404) 335-6395; (c) Fulton

Private non-profit/ 1983/ Board of Trustees/ staff: 1(p)/ members: 600

HISTORICAL SOCIETY: Maintains records of the history of the federal courts and judges within the Eleventh Circuit Court of Appeals.

PROGRAMS: Annual Meeting

COLLECTIONS: [1981-present] Portraits, photos, documents, videotaped oral histories, documents, news articles, books, and personal memorabilia.

1603
Fox Theatre
660 Peachtree St NE, 30365; (p) (404) 881-2100; (f) (404) 872-2972; molly@foxtheatre.org; www.foxtheatre.org; (c) Fulton

Private non-profit/ 1929/ Atlanta Landmarks, Inc./ staff: 60(f); 40(p); 100(v)/publication: *Framing the Cinema: Brenograph Slide Images from the Fox Theatre Collection*

HISTORIC SITE: 1929 art deco movie theatre.

PROGRAMS: Community Outreach; Con-

certs; Facility Rental; Film/Video; Guided Tours; Publication; Research Library/Archives; Theatre

COLLECTIONS: [1929] 1929 furniture collection; Brenograph/lantern slide; historic lighting collection; archives: theatre operation documents, photographs, architectural drawings; building artifacts.

HOURS: Yr hours vary

ADMISSION: No charge

1604
Georgia Capitol Museum
Washington St, 30334 [431 Capitol, 30334]; (p) (404) 651-6996; (f) (404) 657-3801; dolson@sos.state.ga.us; sos.state.ga.us/museum; (c) Fulton

State/ 1895/ staff: 4(f); 1(p)/publication: *Georgia's Capitol*

HISTORIC SITE; HISTORY MUSEUM: Preserves and interprets history of Georgia Capitol in Atlanta.

PROGRAMS: Exhibits; Publication

COLLECTIONS: [20th c] Artifacts significant to Georgia's capitol and its history.

HOURS: Yr M-F 8-5

1605
Georgia Department of Archives and History
330 Capitol Ave, 30334; (p) (404) 656-7365; www.sos.state.ga.us; (c) Fulton

State/ 1918/ staff: 45(f); 15(p)

LIBRARY AND/OR ARCHIVES: Repository for state government records.

COLLECTIONS: [19th c -20th c] Georgia state and county records.

HOURS: Yr M-F 8-4:45.

1606
Georgia State Parks and Historic Sites Division
205 Butler St, 30334; (p) (404) 656-2770; (f) (404) 651-5871; mail.dnr.state.ga.us; www.gastateparks.org/; (c) Fulton

State/ 1925/ Georgia Dept of Natural Resources/ staff: 915(f); 200(p); 150(v)

Operates and manages 61 state parks and historic sites

1607
Georgia Trust for Historic Preservation, The
1516 Peachtree St NW, s30309; (p) (404) 881-9980; infor@georgiatrust.org; www.georgiatrust.org; (c) Fulton

Private non-profit/ 1973/ staff: 22(f)/publication: *Neel Reid, Architect*

HISTORIC PRESERVATION AGENCY; HOUSE MUSEUM

PROGRAMS: Annual Meeting; Community Outreach; Exhibits; Facility Rental; Garden Tours; Guided Tours; Publication

COLLECTIONS: [1860-1940] Three house museums with furnishings, art, personal effects; Hay House, Macon, 1855; Rhodes Hall, Atlanta, 1904; McDaniel-Tichenor House, Monroe, 1887; 2 National Historic Landmark sites.

HOURS: M-F 9-5

1608
Governor's Mansion
391 W Paces Ferry Rd NW, 30305; (p) (404) 261-1776; (f) (404) 233-5843; moe@gov.state.ga.us; www.gagovernor.org; (c) Fulton

State/ 1967/ GA Building Authority/ staff: 6(f); 200(v)

GARDEN; HISTORY MUSEUM; LIBRARY AND/OR ARCHIVES; LIVING HISTORY/OUTDOOR MUSEUM: Residence of first family of GA.

PROGRAMS: Exhibits; Garden Tours; Guided Tours; Living History

COLLECTIONS: [1790-1840] American Federal Period artifacts.

HOURS: Yr T-Th 10am-11:30am

ADMISSION: No charge

1609
Herndon Home, The
587 University Pl, 30314; (p) (404) 581-9813; (f) (404) 588-0239; herndonhome@isaus.com; (c) Fulton

Private non-profit/ 1983/ Alonzo F. and Norris B. Herndon Foundation/ staff: 3(f); 1(p); 12(v)/publication: *Atlanta Life Insurance Company Guardian of Black Economic Dignity*

Beaux Arts Classical mansion constructed in 1910 by Black craftsmen; historic residence of Alonzo Herndon, a slave-born Georgian and founder of the Atlanta Life Insurance Company.

PROGRAMS: Concerts; Exhibits; Family Programs; Guided Tours; Lectures; Living History; Publication; School-Based Curriculum

COLLECTIONS: [19th-20th c] Furniture; Roman and Venetian glass; Persian rugs; antique silver and china; late 19th - early 20th c textiles; photos; decorative arts; jewelry; rare books; vintage records; toys; manuscripts; and letters.

HOURS: Yr T-Sa 10-4

ADMISSION: $5, Student $3; Donations requested

1610
Historic Oakland Foundation, Inc.
248 Oakland Ave SE, 30312; (p) (404) 688-2107; (f) (404) 658-6092; oaklandcemetery@mindspring.com; www.oaklandcemetery.com; (c) Fulton

City/ 1976/ staff: 3(f); 42(v)/ members: 811/publication: *Historic Oakland News*

Preserves and restores Historic Oakland Cemetery.

PROGRAMS: Community Outreach; Family Programs; Festivals; Garden Tours; Guided Tours; Lectures; Publication; Research Library/Archives

COLLECTIONS: [1850-present] Funerary sculpture; architecture; gardens; burial records of over 50,000 people including Confederate, Jewish, and African American people.

HOURS: Yr Daily Winter 8-6; Summer 8-7

ADMISSION: No charge

1611
Historic Preservation Division of the Department of Natural Resources
156 Trinity Ave, SW, Ste 101, 30303-3600; (p) (404) 656-2840; (f) (404) 651-8739; www.gashpo.org; (c) Fulton

State/ 1969/ GA Dept of Natural Resources/ staff: 36(f)

HISTORIC PRESERVATION AGENCY: State historic preservation office.

PROGRAMS: Annual Meeting; Community Outreach

COLLECTIONS: Preservation studies, reports, and technical material; National Register nominations; inventories of archaeological sites and historic structures.

1612
Home Depot Legacy, The
2455 Paces Ferry Rd NW Bldg C-6, 30339; (p) (770) 384-2219; (f) (770) 384-3538; Dan_Dmytrykiw@homedepot.com; (c) Cobb

Private for-profit/ 1998/ The Home Depot/ staff: 2(f)

Preserves and documents the history of The Home Depot.

COLLECTIONS: [1975-present] Clippings and articles, photos, slides, company publications, store catalogs, memorabilia from the Olympic and Paraolympic sponsorships, biographical files, annual reports; video and audio recordings.

1613
Inman Park Neighborhood Association
The Trolley Barn, Edgewood Ave, 30307 [PO Box 5958, 30307]; (p) (404) 588-0202; www.inmanpark.org; (c) Fulton

Private non-profit/ 1970/ staff: 35(v)/ members: 400/publication: The Advocator

LIBRARY AND/OR ARCHIVES: Association for preservation of Inman Park, listed on Historic Register.

PROGRAMS: Annual Meeting; Community Outreach; Facility Rental; Family Programs; Festivals; Guided Tours; Lectures; Publication; Research Library/Archives

COLLECTIONS: [1895-present] Photos, newspapers, policy papers, Civil War documents, architecture, historical landscape.

HOURS: 3rd wknd Apr F-Su

1614
Ivan Allen Jr. Braves Hall of Fame
755 Hank Aaron Dr, 30315; (p) (404) 614-2310; (f) (404) 614-1423; bravesmuseum@ mindspring.com; (c) Fulton

Private non-profit/ 1997/ Atlanta History Center/ staff: 3(f); 20(p)/ members: 20/publication: Touching Base

HISTORY MUSEUM: Promotes Braves History; offers tours of Turner Field.

PROGRAMS: Exhibits; Facility Rental; Family Programs; Guided Tours; Publication; School-Based Curriculum

COLLECTIONS: [1871-present] Over 200 artifacts representing important events and players in Braves history.

HOURS: Yr Apr-Oct Daily, Nov-Mar M-Sa, hours vary

ADMISSION: $7, Children $4; Group rates

1615
Jimmy Carter Library
441 Freedom Pkwy, 30307-1498; (p) (404) 331-3942; (f) (404) 730-2215; library@carter. nara.gov; www.nara.gov; (c) Fulton

Federal

HISTORY MUSEUM; LIBRARY AND/OR ARCHIVES; PRESIDENTIAL SITE

PROGRAMS: Community Outreach; Concerts; Exhibits; Family Programs; Film/Video; Guided Tours; Lectures; Publication; Research Library/Archives; School-Based Curriculum

1616
Margaret Mitchell House and Museum
990 Peachtree St, 30309 [999 Peachtree St, Ste 775, 30309]; (p) (404) 249-7012; (f) (404) 249-9388; alisont@gwtw.org; gwtw.org; (c) Fulton

Private non-profit/ 1985/ Margaret Mitchell House, Inc./ staff: 11(f); 4(p); 50(v)

HISTORIC SITE; HOUSE MUSEUM: Operates as landmark and cultural center.

PROGRAMS: Exhibits; Facility Rental; Family Programs; Guided Tours; Interpretation; Lectures

COLLECTIONS: [1899-1949] Archives; photos depicting historic Atlanta; "Gone With the Wind" memorabilia; restored apartment with period furnishings.

HOURS: Yr Daily 9-4

ADMISSION: $7, Student $6, Seniors $6

1617
Martin Luther King, Jr. National Historic Site and Preservation District
450 Auburn Ave NE, 30312; (p) (404) 331-6922; (f) (404) 730-3112; dean_rowley@nps. gov; www.nps.gov/malu; (c) Fulton

Federal/ 1980/ Department of the Interior/ staff: 35(f); 5(p); 100(v)

HISTORIC SITE; LIBRARY AND/OR ARCHIVES: Preserves, protects, and interprets places where Dr. King was born, preached, and was buried; interprets his life and the Civil Rights Movement.

PROGRAMS: Community Outreach; Exhibits; Family Programs; Film/Video; Guided Tours; Interpretation; Research Library/Archives; School-Based Curriculum

COLLECTIONS: [1929-1968] Recorded background studies for rehabilitation, interpretation, and adaptive reuse of historic structures; 760 artifacts, 50 linear ft. of unprocessed archives; 10 linear ft. unprocessed photographic archives; and 100 unprocessed video tapes.

HOURS: Yr Daily 9-5

ADMISSION: No charge

1618
Michael C. Carlos Museum
Emory Univ, 571 S Kilgo St, 30322; (p) (404) 727-4282; (f) (404) 727-4292; jbell@emory. edu; www.emory.edu/carlos; (c) DeKalb

Private non-profit/ 1919/ Emory Univ Board of Trustees/ staff: 26(f); 5(p); 176(v)/ members: 1475

ART MUSEUM: Collects, preserves, and exhibits art and artifacts of world cultures from antiquity to present .

PROGRAMS: Community Outreach; Concerts; Exhibits; Facility Rental; Family Programs; Festivals; Film/Video; Guided Tours; Lectures; School-Based Curriculum

COLLECTIONS: [Prehistory] Art and historical artifacts from Mediterranean, Asia, ancient Americas, Sub-Saharan Africa and Oceania, and works on paper from middle ages to present.

HOURS: Yr M-Sa 10-5, Su

1619
National Park Service, Southeast Regional Office
Atlanta Federal Center, 100 Alabama St, 30303; (p) (404) 562-3117; (f) (404) 562-3202; www.nps.gov/sero/crs; (c) Fulton

Federal/ 1916/ US Dept of the Interior/ staff: 28(f); 2(p)

Provides assistance to Southeastern National Parks in areas of history, historic architecture and landscapes, museum management, and general management of cultural resources.

COLLECTIONS: 3,000 volumes related to 64 National Parks and their associated themes.

HOURS: By appt

1620
Outdoor Activity Center
1442 Richland Rd, 30310; (p) (404) 752-5385; (f) (404) 756-7806; oac@mindspring. com; efg.org; (c) Fulton

Private non-profit/ 1975/ staff: 2(p); 15(v)/ members: 100

HISTORY MUSEUM; NATURAL HISTORY MUSEUM: Twenty-six acre mature old growth forest preserve and environmental education center.

PROGRAMS: Elder's Programs; Exhibits; Facility Rental; Guided Tours; School-Based Curriculum

COLLECTIONS: [Prehistory-present] Original Smokey Bear posters; numerous varied natural science exhibits and live animals.

HOURS: Yr M-Sa 9-4

ADMISSION: No charge

1621
Pitts Theology Library Archives Department
505 Kilgo Circle, 30322 [Emory University, 30322]; (p) (404) 727-4166; (f) (404) 727-1219; www.pitts.emory.edu/archives.html; (c) DeKalb

Private for-profit/ 1982/ Emory Univ/ staff: 2(f)

LIBRARY AND/OR ARCHIVES: Collects material documenting the history of religion in Great Britain with an emphasis on the 19th century: Christianity in South Africa and the history of Methodism in the Southeast and Georgia.

PROGRAMS: Concerts; Exhibits; Research Library/Archives

COLLECTIONS: [1420-present] Processed archives and manuscripts.

HOURS: Yr M-F 8-4:30

1622
Rhodes Hall
1516 Peachtree St NW, 30309; (p) (404) 885-7800; (f) (404) 875-2205; mteall@georgiatrust.org; www.georgiatrust.org; (c) Fulton

Private non-profit/ 1983/ The Georgia Trust/ staff: 2(f); 9(p); 30(v)

HOUSE MUSEUM

PROGRAMS: Facility Rental; Family Programs; Guided Tours; Interpretation; Lectures; School-Based Curriculum

COLLECTIONS: [Early 20th c] 1904 Romanesque Revival mansion constructed for furniture magnate Amos Rhodes. The interior features fine woodwork, mosaic tile fireplaces, decorative wall and ceiling finishes and stained glass windows.

HOURS: Yr M-F 11-5, Su 12-3

ADMISSION: $5, Children $4, Seniors

1623
Robert C. Williams American Museum of Papermaking
500 10th St NW, 30318; (p) (404) 894-6663; (f) (404) 894-4778; melanie.lynch@ipst.edu; www.ipst.edu/amp; (c) Fulton

Private non-profit/ 1934/ Institute of Paper Science and Technology/ staff: 3(f); 1(p); 10(v)/ members: 2

ART MUSEUM; HISTORY MUSEUM: Trace history of papermaking from ancient times; exhibits related art and information.

PROGRAMS: Community Outreach; Elder's Programs; Exhibits; Facility Rental; Festivals; Guided Tours; Lectures

COLLECTIONS: [6,000 BP-present] Artifacts related to early papermaking from various areas, cultures, and historic periods; paper samples, moulds, watermarks, art, prints, bark papers, and books.

HOURS: Yr M-F 9-5

ADMISSION: Tour fee

1624
Robert W. Woodruff Library, Archives and Special Collections
111 James P Brawley Dr SW, 30314; (p) (404) 522-8980; (f) (404) 577-5158; www.auctr.edu; (c) Fulton

Private non-profit/ 1982/ Atlanta University Center, Inc./ staff: 8(f); 1(p)

LIBRARY AND/OR ARCHIVES; RESEARCH CENTER: Serves the research needs of the faculty and students of Atlanta University Center schools.

PROGRAMS: Research Library/Archives

COLLECTIONS: [19th-20th c] Documentation on African American history and culture. Books, photographs, personal papers, organizational records of civil rights groups, community groups and professional

1625
Special Collections Department, Pullen Library, Georgia State University
8th Flr, 100 Decatur St, 30303; (p) (404) 651-2477; (f) (404) 651-4314; libsc@longate.gsu.edu; www.library.gsu.edu/spcoll/; (c) Fulton

State/ 1969/ GA State Univ; Board of Regents of the State of GA/ staff: 9(f); 1(p)

HISTORIC PRESERVATION AGENCY: Collects, preserves, and manages historical materials in selected subject areas; promotes their use by the university community, scholars, and the public.

PROGRAMS: Exhibits; Guided Tours; Research Library/Archives; School-Based Curriculum

COLLECTIONS: [20th c] Labor union records and trade unionist collections (primarily Southern), 20th century Atlanta photographs, political oral histories, popular music collections, university archives, women's collections (primarily ERA related).

HOURS: Yr M-F 8:30-5:15

ADMISSION: No charge

1626
Special Collections, Robert W. Woodruff Library, Emory University
540 Asbury Circle, 30322 [Emory Univ, 30322]; (p) (404) 727-6887; (f) (404) 727-0360; speccoll@emory.edu; info.library.emory.edu/special/; (c) DeKalb

Private non-profit/ Emory University Board of Trustees/ staff: 10(f); 3(p)

LIBRARY AND/OR ARCHIVES; RESEARCH CENTER: Houses and Provides access to the Library's collection of rare books, manuscripts, University Archives, and other special materials.

PROGRAMS: Exhibits; Guided Tours; Interpretation; Lectures; Publication; Research Library/Archives

COLLECTIONS: [1830-present] Over 30,000 rare volumes, numerous manuscripts of individuals and organizations, University Archives, and exhibits.

HOURS: Yr M-F

1627
Spelman College Archives
350 Spelman Lane SW, 30310 [PO Box 115, 30310]; (p) (404) 215-7875; (f) (404) 223-7665; www.spelman.edu; (c) Fulton

Private non-profit/ 1976/ Spelman College/ staff: 2(f); 1(p); 2(v)

LIBRARY AND/OR ARCHIVES: Preserves and organizes archival materials related to the college and education in general; provides access to these materials for research.

PROGRAMS: Exhibits; Lectures; Research Library/Archives

COLLECTIONS: [1881-present] Administrative records, departmental and program records, publications, and photos; personal papers of faculty, staff, alumni, and noted African Americans; publications from other Atlanta University Center institutions; periodicals and monographs.

HOURS: Yr

1628
William Berman Jewish Heritage Museum, The
1440 Spring St NW, 30068; (p) (404) 873-1661; (f) (404) 881-4009; Sberman@atljf.org; (c) Fulton

Private non-profit/ 1996/ staff: 5(f); 2(p)

HISTORY MUSEUM: Repository and resource for Jewish and other communities in Georgia, and visitors.

PROGRAMS: Community Outreach; Concerts; Exhibits; Facility Rental; Family Programs; Film/Video; Guided Tours; Interpretation; Lectures; Living History; Publication; Research Library/Archives; School-Based Curriculum

COLLECTIONS: [1845-present] Manuscripts, 10,000 photos, 250 oral histories, textiles and other artifacts relating to Jewish life in Georgia, including Holocaust survivors' personal histories.

HOURS: Yr M-Th 10-5, F 10-3, Su 1-3

ADMISSION: $5, Student

1629
Wren's Nest House Museum, The
1050 Ralph David Abernathy Blvd, 30310; (p) (404) 753-7735; (f) (404) 753-8535; wrensnest@mindspring.com; accessatlanta.com/community/groups/wrens/; (c) Fulton

Private non-profit/ 1909/ Joel Chandler Harris Association, Inc/ staff: 1(f); 6(p); 30(v)/ members: 156/publication: *Joel Chandler Harris' Booklist*

HOUSE MUSEUM: Interprets the life, writings, and times of Joel Chandler Harris.

PROGRAMS: Annual Meeting; Community Outreach; Concerts; Elder's Programs; Exhibits; Facility Rental; Family Programs; Festivals; Garden Tours; Guided Tours; Interpretation; Lectures; Living History; Publication; Research Library/Archives; School-Based Curriculum

COLLECTIONS: [1881-1913] Newly restored house and grounds of the Wren's Nest, filled with original artifacts an memorabilia.

HOURS: Yr 10-4

ADMISSION: $6, Student $4, Children $3, Seniors $4

AUGUSTA

1630
Augusta Museum of History
560 Reynolds St, 30901; (p) (706) 722-8454; (f) (706) 724-5192; amhe@CSRA.net; wwwaugustamuseum.org; (c) Richmond

Private non-profit/ 1937/ Board of Trustees/ staff: 10(f); 4(p); 30(v)/ members: 1425/publication: *Archive; Twentieth-Century Memories*

HISTORY MUSEUM: Collects, preserves, and interprets the history of Augusta and surrounding area for the education and enrichment of present and future generations.

PROGRAMS: Community Outreach; Concerts; Exhibits; Facility Rental; Guided Tours; Interpretation; Lectures; Publication; Research Library/Archives; School-Based Curriculum

COLLECTIONS: [18th-20th c] Local/regional historical artifacts and images, natural history specimens, manuscripts/diaries and monographs/reference books.

HOURS: Yr T-Sa 10-5, Su 1-5

ADMISSION: $4, Children $2, Seniors $3

1631
Historic Augusta, Inc.
111 Tenth St, 30903 [PO Box 37, 30903]; (p) (706) 724-0436; (f) (706) 724-3083; HistAug Inc@aol.com; (c) Richmond

Private non-profit/ 1965/ staff: 3(f); 75(v)/ members: 1500

HISTORIC PRESERVATION AGENCY; HISTORY MUSEUM; HOUSE MUSEUM: Facilitates preservation of historic buildings and neighborhoods; interprets cultural heritage. Preserves Ezekiel Harris House Museum and the Boyhood Home of President Woodrow Wilson House Museum.

PROGRAMS: Annual Meeting; Guided Tours; Lectures; Living History

COLLECTIONS: Photographs and files on historic properties.

HOURS: Yr M-F 9-5

1632
Historic Cotton Exchange Welcome Center and Museum
32 Eighth St, 30901; (p) (706) 724-4067; d.king@augustaga.org; www.augustaga.org; (c) Richmond

Private non-profit/ 1886/ Augusta Metropolitan Convention and Visitors Bureau/ staff: 2(f); 2(p)

HISTORIC SITE; HISTORY MUSEUM: Offers information on Augusta, runs history museum with cotton exhibits.

PROGRAMS: Exhibits; Guided Tours

COLLECTIONS: [Late 1800s-early 1900s] Original items including 45 ft wooden blackboard still chalked with cotton, currency, and commodity prices from early 1900s; other cotton-related artifacts.

HOURS: Yr M-Sa 9-5, Su 1-5

ADMISSION: No charge

1633
Lucy Craft Laney Museum
1116 Phillips St, 30901; (f) (706) 724-3576; (c) Richmond

Private non-profit/ 1986/ staff: 1(f); 1(p); 12(v)/ members: 50

HISTORIC SITE; HOUSE MUSEUM: Preserves history of Lucy Craft Laney.

PROGRAMS: Community Outreach; Exhibits; Facility Rental; Family Programs; Guided Tours; Lectures; Living History

HOURS: Yr M-F 9-1

ADMISSION: $2, Children $0.75

1634
Meadow Garden
1320 Independence Dr, 30901; (p) (706) 724-4174; (c) Richmond

Private non-profit/ 1901/ Daughters of the American Revolution, Georgia/ staff: 1(f); 25(v)

HISTORIC SITE; HOUSE MUSEUM: Preserves house owned by a signer of the Declaration of Independence.

PROGRAMS: Garden Tours; Guided Tours; Interpretation; School-Based Curriculum

COLLECTIONS: [1780-1850] Furnishings reflecting Revolutionary and early Victorian periods.

HOURS: Yr M-F 10-4, Sa-Su by appt

ADMISSION: $3, Student $2, Children $1

1635
Robert B. Greenblatt, MD Library, Special Collections
Medical College of GA, 1120 15th St, 30912-4400; (p) (706) 721-3444; (f) (706) 721-2018; suweaver@mail.mcg.edu; www.mcg.edu/history/specol.htm; (c) Richmond

State/ 1972/ Medical College of GA/ staff: 1(f)

LIBRARY AND/OR ARCHIVES: Acquires, organizes, preserves, and makes available historical collections related to the Medical College of Georgia and the history of the health sciences.

PROGRAMS: Exhibits; Research Library/Archives

COLLECTIONS: [late 18th c-early 19th c] Medical and health sciences artifacts, original MCG 19th c library, landmarks in modern medicine collection, various medical museum items and artifacts, Robert Greenblatt archive, and various MCG institutional publications.

HOURS: Yr M-F 8:30-5 by appt

ADMISSION: No charge

BAINBRIDGE

1636
Decatur County Historical Society
119 Water St, 31718 [PO Box 682, 31718]; (p) (912) 248-1719; (c) Decatur

Private non-profit/ 1972/ staff: 1(p); 3(v)/ members: 170/publication: *Decatur County Past and Present 1823-1991*

HISTORICAL SOCIETY; HISTORY MUSEUM; HOUSE MUSEUM: Records, preserves, and promotes local history.

PROGRAMS: Annual Meeting; Community Outreach; Exhibits; Facility Rental; Guided Tours; Interpretation; Lectures; Publication; Research Library/Archives

COLLECTIONS: [Late 19th-early 20th c] Artifacts of lives of different cultural groups that have lived in the area.

HOURS: Yr Sa-Su 1-5 and by appt

ADMISSION: No charge

BAXLEY

1637
Appling County Heritage Center
209 Thomas St, 31515 [PO Box 87, 31515]; (p) (912) 367-8133; (c) Appling

County/ 1995/ Board of Directors/ staff: 1(p); 8(v)/ members: 68

GENEALOGICAL SOCIETY; HISTORIC PRESERVATION AGENCY; HISTORICAL SOCIETY; HISTORY MUSEUM; RESEARCH CENTER: Original five-room school building restored for museum archival records and artifacts.

PROGRAMS: Annual Meeting; Community Outreach; Exhibits; Festivals; Guided Tours; Lectures; Living History; Reenactments; Research Library/Archives

COLLECTIONS: [1820-early 20th c] Written records and exhibits relating to wars, industry, agriculture and early life in Appling County; genealogical research including county records, census and family histories.

HOURS: Yr T,Th-F 12-5, Sa

BLAIRESVILLE

1638
Union County Historical Society
Town Square, 30514 [PO Box 35, 30514]; (p) (706) 745-5493; (c) Union

Private non-profit/ 1976/ staff: 25(p); 10(v)/ members: 200

GENEALOGICAL SOCIETY; HISTORICAL SOCIETY; HISTORY MUSEUM; RESEARCH CENTER: Preserves, displays, and interprets the history and culture of the county through the museum and cultural center.

PROGRAMS: Annual Meeting; Community Outreach; Concerts; Exhibits; Facility Rental; Family Programs; Festivals; Guided Tours; Interpretation; Lectures; Living History; Publication; Research Library/Archives; School-Based Curriculum

COLLECTIONS: [1830-present] Memorabilia; three large, fully furnished doll houses.

HOURS: Jun-Nov 1 W-Sa 10-4 and by appt

ADMISSION: $2

BLAKELY

1639
Kolomoki Mounds State Historic Park
Indian Mounds Rd, 31723 [Rt 1 Box 114, 31723]; (p) (912) 723-5296; (f) (912) 723-5338; kolomoki@sowega.net; www.gastateparks.org; (c) Early

State/ 1938/ Georgia Dept of Natural Resources/ staff: 6(f)

HISTORIC SITE; HISTORY MUSEUM; RESEARCH CENTER: Displays prehistoric Indian Mounds and many different forms of burial pottery.

PROGRAMS: Exhibits; Facility Rental; Family Programs; Festivals; Guided Tours; Interpretation; School-Based Curriculum; Theatre

COLLECTIONS: [250BC-AD900] Effigy Burial Pottery, shell beads, copper ear ornaments; one Temple Mound and two Burial Mounds; agricultural and archaeological displays.

HOURS: Yr T-Sa 9-5, Su 2-5:30

ADMISSION: $2, Children $1

BOWDON

1640
Bowdon Area Historical Society
College View St, 30103 [PO Box 112, 30103]; (p) (770) 258-2176; janicew527@aol.com; (c) Carroll

Private non-profit/ 1983/ Board of Directors/ members: 80

Preserves heritage of the area. Currently restoring oldest structure in town for use as a history museum.

BRUNSWICK

1641
Hofwyl-Broadfield Plantation
5556 US Hwy 17N, 31525; (p) (912) 264-7333

1642
Mary Miller Doll Museum
1532 Glynn Ave, 31520; (p) (912) 267-7569; (c) Glynn

Private non-profit/ 1976/ Board of Directors/ staff: 1(f); 1(p); 4(v)

HISTORY MUSEUM: Collects, preserves, and interprets historic dolls and toys, emphasizing educational and cultural information.

PROGRAMS: Exhibits; Lectures

COLLECTIONS: [1850-present] Doll houses from five countries; memorabilia from over 90 countries; and 3,000 dolls of varying media and construction.

HOURS: Yr M-F 11-4:30; Sa, Su by appt

ADMISSION: $2, Children $1.50

1643
Old Town Brunswick Preservation Association
1327 Union St, 31520; (p) (912) 264-0442; (c) Glynn

Private non-profit/ 1975/ Old Town Brunswick Preservation Association/ members: 100/publication: *Old Town Driving Tour Book*

HISTORIC PRESERVATION AGENCY; HISTORY MUSEUM; HOUSE MUSEUM: Preserves and enhances historic Brunswick; operates the Brunswick History Museum in the 1907 Queen Anne Lissner Home.

PROGRAMS: Annual Meeting; Exhibits; Facility Rental; Family Programs; Lectures; Publication

COLLECTIONS: [1700-present] Historical newspapers, photos, and artifacts from Brunswick's past.

HOURS: Yr M-F 8-3, Sa 11-2

ADMISSION: $1

BUCHANAN

1644
Haralson County Historical Society
Van Wart St, 30113 [PO Box 585, 30113]; (p) (770) 646-3509; (c) Haralson

Private non-profit/ 1973/ staff: 12(v)/ members: 80

HISTORICAL SOCIETY: Preserves historical sites, Buildings, documents, and artifacts.

PROGRAMS: Festivals; Guided Tours; School-Based Curriculum

HOURS: Yr 8:30-3:30 M, by appt

BYRON

1645
Byron Area Historical Society
[PO Box 755, 31008]; (p) (912) 956-5637; (c) Peach

Private non-profit/ 1987/ staff: 20(p)/ members: 60/publication: *Historical Sketches of Byron and the Railroad*

HISTORIC SITE; HISTORICAL SOCIETY; HISTORY MUSEUM

PROGRAMS: Annual Meeting; Community Outreach; Exhibits; Facility Rental; Festivals; Guided Tours; Lectures; Publication; Reenactments; School-Based Curriculum

COLLECTIONS: [1918-1955] Photographic history, railroad memorabilia and personal family histories.

CALHOUN

1646
Gordon County Historical Society
335 S Wall St, 30706 [PO Box 342, 30706]; (p) (706) 629-1515; (f) (706) 629-4570; (c) Gordon

City; County/ 1974/ staff: 1(f)/ members: 275

HISTORICAL SOCIETY

PROGRAMS: Annual Meeting; Community Outreach; Exhibits; Guided Tours

HOURS: Yr M-F 10-4, Sa by appt

1647
New Echota State Historic Site
1211 Chatsworth Hwy NE, 30701; (p) (706) 624-1321; (f) (706) 624-1323; n_echota@ innerx.net; www.gastateparks.org; (c) Gordon

State/ 1962/ staff: 4(f); 3(p)

HISTORIC SITE: Location of the last capitol of the Cherokee Nation prior to the removal of Cherokees West of the Mississippi; site of the signing of the Treaty of New Echota; site of first Native American journalism and Republican government.

PROGRAMS: Exhibits; Family Programs; Film/Video; Guided Tours; Interpretation; Research Library/Archives

COLLECTIONS: [1750-1850] Historic and re-constructed dwellings and public buildings with original and reproduction furnishings; tools and equipment.

HOURS: Yr T-Sa 9-5, Su 2-5:30

ADMISSION: $2.50, Children

CANTON

1648
Cherokee County Historical Society
100 N St, 3rd floor, 30114 [PO Box 1287, 30114]; (p) (770) 345-3288; (f) (770) 345-3289; info@rockbarn.org; www.rockbarn.org; (c) Cherokee

Private non-profit/ 1975/ Board of Directors/ members: 540

GENEALOGICAL SOCIETY; HISTORIC PRESERVATION AGENCY; HISTORICAL SOCIETY; LIBRARY AND/OR ARCHIVES: Preserves the history of Cherokee County.

PROGRAMS: Annual Meeting; Exhibits; Facility Rental; Film/Video; Guided Tours; Interpretation; Research Library/Archives

COLLECTIONS: Mill artifacts and documents.

HOURS: Yr W 1-5 or by appt

ADMISSION: No charge

CARROLLTON

1649
Carroll County Genealogical Society
805 Rome St, 30117 [PO Box 576, 30117]; (p) (770) 832-7746; mfword@aol.com; members.aol.com/carrollgen; (c) Carroll

Private non-profit/ 1980/ staff: 5(v)/ members: 221

GENEALOGICAL SOCIETY; HISTORIC PRESERVATION AGENCY: Publishes quarterly newsletter and other Carroll County resource guides; offers various programs of genealogical interest.

PROGRAMS: Lectures; Research Library/ Archives

COLLECTIONS: Genealogical records housed at Neva Lomason Library Special Collections, Carrollton, GA.

HOURS: Yr Daily

1650
Carroll County Historical Society
West Ave, 30117 [Box 1308, 30117]; (p) (770) 836-6494; jruskell@westga.edu; (c) Carroll

Joint/ 1976/ County; Private non-profit/ members: 100/publication: *At Home in Carrollton*

HISTORICAL SOCIETY: Promotes local history.

PROGRAMS: Annual Meeting; Community Outreach; Exhibits; Facility Rental; Family Programs; Festivals; Film/Video; Guided Tours; Lectures; Living History; Publication; Research Library/Archives

ADMISSION: No charge

1651
West Georgia Regional Library
710 W Rome St, 30135; (p) (770) 836-6711; (f) (770) 836-4787; willisr@mail.carroll.public.lib.ga.us; (c) Carroll

1944/ West Georgia Regional Library Board/ staff: 10(f); 6(p)

LIBRARY AND/OR ARCHIVES: Houses local, state, and regional histories.

PROGRAMS: Exhibits; Lectures; Research Library/Archives

COLLECTIONS: [1700-1900] Archives and other historical materials related to the American South.

HOURS: Yr M-Th 9-8, F 9-5:30, Sa 9-4:30, Su 2-6

CARTERSVILLE

1652
Etowah Foundation's History Center, The
13 N Wall St, 30120 [PO Box 1239, 30120]; (p) (770) 382-3818; (f) (770) 382-0288; (c) Bartow

Private non-profit/ 1987/ Etowah Foundation/ staff: 2(f); 1(p); 10(v)

HISTORY MUSEUM: Collects. preserves, and interprets local history.

PROGRAMS: Community Outreach; Elder's Programs; Exhibits; Family Programs; Guided Tours; Interpretation; Lectures; Living History; Research Library/Archives; School-Based Curriculum

COLLECTIONS: [19th c-early 20th c] Manuscripts, maps, photos, newspapers, volumes, and museum artifacts.

HOURS: Yr T-Sa 10-4

ADMISSION: $1

1653
Roselawn Museum
224 Cherokee Ave W, 30120 [PO Box 97, 30120]; (p) (770) 387-5162

CEDARTOWN

1654
Polk County Historical Society
205 College St, 30125 [PO Box 203, 30125]; (p) (770) 749-0073; (c) Polk

Joint/ 1974/ City; Private non-profit/ staff: 50(v)/ members: 200/publication: *Polk County, Georgia*

HISTORICAL SOCIETY: Collects artifacts of local historical significance; offers numerous programs and activities.

PROGRAMS: Annual Meeting; Community Outreach; Exhibits; Facility Rental; Family Programs; Festivals; Film/Video; Garden Tours; Guided Tours; Interpretation; Lectures; Publication; Research Library/Archives

COLLECTIONS: [1830-present] Newspapers, family histories, business histories, cemetery index, maps, photos, flags, furniture, household items, textiles, toys, ceramics, weapons, metalwork, coins, glass, ceramics, and Native American artifacts.

HOURS: Yr W, 4th Su 2-4

ADMISSION: Donations accepted

CHATSWORTH

1655
Chief Vann House Historic Site
82 Hwy 225 N, 30705; (p) (706) 695-2598; (f) (706) 517-4255; vannhouse@alltel.net; www.ganet.org/dnr/parks; (c) Murray

State/ 1958/ Georgia Department of Natural Resources/ staff: 2(f); 4(p)/ members: 150

HISTORIC SITE; HISTORY MUSEUM: Restored 1804 home of James Vann, Cherokee plantation owner.

PROGRAMS: Annual Meeting; Exhibits; Family Programs; Festivals; Film/Video; Guided Tours; Interpretation; Lectures; Living History; School-Based Curriculum

COLLECTIONS: [1804-1838] Various research material relating to the Cherokee Nation. Plantation relics include china, silverware and ironware in a two-story brick mansion.

HOURS: Yr T-Sa 9-5, Su 2-5:30

ADMISSION: $2.50, Children $1.50

CLARKESVILLE

1656
Northeast Georgia Regional Library, Cherokee Headquarters Branch
178 E Green St, 30523 [PO Box 2020, 30523]; (p) (706) 754-4413; (f) (706) 754-3479; richardm@mail.habersham.public.lib.ga.us; (c) Habersham

Joint/ staff: 9(f); 2(p)/publication: *1850 Habersham County Census Transcribed and Augmented*

LIBRARY AND/OR ARCHIVES; RESEARCH CENTER: Public libretto with records from Habersham and surrounding counties.

PROGRAMS: Publication; Research Library/Archives

COLLECTIONS: [1850-present] Locals histories and genealogy, especially of Habersham County.

HOURS: Yr M 9-8, T-F 9-6, Sa 9-1

CLAYTON

1657
Rabun County Historical Society
81 N Church St, 30525 [PO Box 921, 30525]; (p) (706) 746-2508; (c) Rabun

Private non-profit/ 1978/ staff: 13(v)/ members: 75/publication: *Sketches of Rabun County, Rabun County, GA and its People*

HISTORICAL SOCIETY; HOUSE MUSEUM; LIBRARY AND/OR ARCHIVES: Collects, preserves, and maintains county history through artifacts, newspapers, books, and family histories.

PROGRAMS: Community Outreach; Elder's Programs; Exhibits; Festivals; Film/Video; Guided Tours; Lectures; Living History; Publication; Research Library/Archives

COLLECTIONS: [1820-1950] Newspapers, books, pictures, marriage, census and cemetery records, household items, various surveys.

HOURS: Yr W 1-5, and by appt

COLUMBUS

1658
Historic Columbus Foundation Inc.
700 Broadway, 31906 [PO Box 5312, 31906]; (p) (706) 322-0756; (f) (706) 576-4760; hcf.inc@mindspring.com; (c) Muscogee

Private non-profit/ 1966/ staff: 5(f); 2(p); 100(v)/ members: 2500/publication: *Our Town Series*

PROGRAMS: Annual Meeting; Exhibits; Facility Rental; Festivals; Guided Tours; Lectures; Publication; School-Based Curriculum

COLLECTIONS: [1820-1870] Six house museums, with original or period furnishings.

HOURS: Yr Tours M-F 11 and 2; Sa-Su 2

ADMISSION: $5,

1659
Muscogee Genealogical Society
[PO Box 761, 31902]; (c) Muscogee

Private non-profit/ 1976/ members: 200/publication: *Muscogiana*

GENEALOGICAL SOCIETY

PROGRAMS: Publication; Research Library/Archives

1660
Port Columbus National Civil War Naval Museum
1000 Victory Dr, 31902 [PO Box 1022, 31902]; (p) (706) 324-7334; (f) (706) 324-2070; cwnavy@portcolumbus.org; www.portcolumbus.org; (c) Muscogee

Joint/ 1970/ staff: 5(f); 5(v)/ members: 155

HISTORY MUSEUM: Tells the comprehensive story of Naval operations during the Civil War.

PROGRAMS: Community Outreach; Exhibits; Guided Tours; Interpretation; Living History; Reenactments; School-Based Curriculum

COLLECTIONS: [1861-1865] Civil War Naval uniforms, photos, documents, weapons, and equipment; hulls of two Confederate warships, including a gunboat and a huge ironclad.

1661
Springer Opera House
103 10th St, 31902 [PO Box 1626, 31902]; (p) (706) 324-5714; (f) (706) 324-4681; www.springeroperahouse.org; (c) Muscogee

Private non-profit/ 1871/ staff: 12(f); 35(p); 225(v)/ members: 400

HISTORIC SITE; LIBRARY AND/OR ARCHIVES: A producing theatre; a historic part of the Theatre Education and Museum Complex; official state theatre of Georgia.

PROGRAMS: Concerts; Exhibits; Facility Rental; Family Programs; Guided Tours; Research Library/Archives; Theatre

HOURS: Yr 9-5

ADMISSION: $3

CORDELE

1662
Georgia Veterans State Park
2459 Hwy 280 West, 31015; (p) (912) 276-2371; (f) (912) 276-2372; gavets@sowega.net; (c) Crisp

State/ 1946/ Georgia Dept of Natural Resources/ staff: 11(f); 7(p); 2(v)

HISTORY MUSEUM; LIVING HISTORY/OUTDOOR MUSEUM: State park, museum, with outdoor exhibits; collects, preserves, and interprets military history of Georgia and nature; offers programs.

PROGRAMS: Exhibits; Facility Rental; Family Programs; Festivals; Film/Video; Guided Tours; Interpretation; Living History

COLLECTIONS: War related weaponry, personal items, clothing, photos, documents, memorabilia; transportation and communication

CRAWFORDVILLE

1663
A.H. Stephens State Historic Park
456 Alexander St N, 30631 [PO Box 310, 30631]; (p) (706) 456-2602; (f) (706) 456-2396; ahssp@g-net.net; (c) Taliaferro

State/ 1932/ Department of Natural Resources/ staff: 8(f); 9(p); 4(v)

HISTORIC SITE; HISTORY MUSEUM; HOUSE MUSEUM; STATE PARK: Over 1,100 acres dedicated to interpretation and conservation of CCC and WPA projects. Operates as both a state park and a historic site. Home of Alexander H. Stephens is the focal point of the operation.

PROGRAMS: Exhibits; Facility Rental; Guided Tours; Interpretation; School-Based Curriculum

COLLECTIONS: [Late 19th-early 20th c] Confederate Museum houses one of the best artifact collections in the state. Home of A.H. Stephens furnished in 1875 period. Park is Georgia's third oldest with many CCC and WPA structures still in use.

HOURS: Yr

ADMISSION: $2.50, Children $1.50; Group rates

CUMMING

1664
Forsyth County Public Library
585 Dahlonega Rd, 30040; (p) (770) 781-9840; (f) (770) 781-8089; (c) Forsyth

1996/ staff: 18(f); 36(p); 8(v)

Public library with local history collection of Forsyth and surrounding counties.

COLLECTIONS: [1830-present] Cemetery records, narrative histories, and census reels.

HOURS: Yr M-Th 10-8:30, F-Sa 10-5:30

1665
Historical Society of Forsyth County, Inc.
[PO Box 1334, 30028]; (p) (770) 887-8464; (c) Forsyth

Private non-profit/ 1994/ Exec Council, Historical Soc of Forsyth Co, Inc/ members: 130/publication: Stroll Around the Square in Cumming, Forsyth County: An Album from the Garland Bagley Collection

HISTORICAL SOCIETY: Preserves the county's history through structures, genealogies, historical publications, programs, community participation, and educational assistance.

PROGRAMS: Annual Meeting; Exhibits; Family Programs; Festivals; Lectures; Publication; School-Based Curriculum

COLLECTIONS: [1832-present] Photos, historical data, artifacts, genealogies, other donated material.

HOURS: 1st Tuesday (Mtg In Library)

CUTHBERT

1666
Andrew College Archives
413 College St, 31740; (p) (912) 732-5957; (f) (912) 732-2176; karanpittman@andrewcollege.edu; (c) Randolph

Private non-profit/ Andrew College/ staff: 1(p); 1(v)

LIBRARY AND/OR ARCHIVES: Collects and maintains the history of Andrew College, Cuthbert, Georgia, and Randolph County.

PROGRAMS: Research Library/Archives

COLLECTIONS: [1854-present]

HOURS: By appt

DAHLONEGA

1667
Dahlonega Club, Inc., The
W Main St & Vickery Dr, 30533 [PO Box 141, 30533]; (p) (706) 864-3365; (c) Lumpkin

Private non-profit/ 1941/ staff: 5(v)/ members: 100

HOUSE MUSEUM: Maintains and restores the Vickery House, the first house in Dahlonega to be listed on the National Register of Historic Places.

PROGRAMS: Annual Meeting; Community Outreach; Exhibits; Festivals

COLLECTIONS: [1941-present] Art (crafts and paintings), period furnishings, antique organ, period glassware, brumby rockers, iron beds, and Vickery family furnishings.

HOURS: 4th of July celebration, two weeks in December, and by appt

ADMISSION: $1

1668
Dahlonega Courthouse Gold Museum
9 Public Sq, 30533; (p) (706) 864-2257; (f) (706) 864-8730; dgmgold@stc.net; www.gastateparks.org; (c) Lumpkin

State/ 1967/ Dept of Natural Resources/ staff: 6(f); 1(p)

HISTORIC SITE: Interprets the history of America's first major gold rush and the historic County Courthouse, which houses its collection.

PROGRAMS: Exhibits; Film/Video; Guided Tours; Interpretation; Research Library/ Archives; School-Based Curriculum

COLLECTIONS: Examples of mined gold, rare gold coins, Native American artifacts, gold mining and processing artifacts; various research materials, including genealogy files, photos, and newspapers.

HOURS: Yr M-Sa 9-5, Su 10-5

ADMISSION: $2.50, Children $1.50

1669
Lumpkin County Historical Society, Inc.
[PO Box 894, 30533]; (c) Lumpkin

Private non-profit/ 1998/ staff: 10(v)/ members: 50

HISTORICAL SOCIETY: Sponsors numerous programs related to county history.

PROGRAMS: Annual Meeting; Community Outreach; Lectures; Publication

COLLECTIONS: [Late 19th c-early 20th c] Museum in Old Jail: Artifacts, photos and memorabilia; oral history cassettes.

HOURS: By appt

ADMISSION: No charge

DALLAS

1670
Paulding County Historical Society, Inc.
295 N Johnson St, 30132 [PO Box 333, 30132]; (p) (770) 505-3485; (c) Paulding

Private non-profit/ 1978/ Board of Directors/ staff: 5(v)/ members: 66/publication: Cemeteries of Paulding County, Heritage Book

Discovers, collects, and preserves historical materials of local significance, especially original and source materials.

COLLECTIONS: [1700-present]

HOURS: Yr T, Th, Sa 12-4

DALTON

1671
Blunt House
506 S Thornton Ave, 30720 [715 Chattanooga Ave, 30720]; (p) (706) 278-0217

1848/ staff: 5(v)

COLLECTIONS: [1848-1978] Furniture, linens, a water color portfolio painted by the four sisters, kitchen utensils, decorative objects, clothing, Olson rugs, Valentines, china, teapots, costume jewelry, Christmas decorations, toys, dolls from pre 1848 up to 1978. Mr. Blunt's diary, begun in 1827 telling of his trip from Amherst, NH to Brainard Mission in Tennessee and life at the mission into the 1830s. Family letters, writings, and photographs.

HOURS: Yr by appt only

1672
Whitfield-Murray Historical Society
715 Chatanooga Ave, 30720; (p) (706) 278-0217; (c) Whitfield

Private non-profit/ 1976/ staff: 1(f)/ members: 550

HISTORICAL SOCIETY; HISTORY MUSEUM; LIBRARY AND/OR ARCHIVES: Genealogical library, two house museums, church museum, hotel museum, two Civil War sites.

PROGRAMS: Annual Meeting; Exhibits; Facility Rental; Film/Video; Guided Tours; Interpretation; Lectures; Living History; Publication; Reenactments

COLLECTIONS: [1840-present]

HOURS: Yr T-F 10-5, Sa 9-1

ADMISSION: $3.00

DARIEN

1673
Lower Altamaha Historical Society
US Hwy 17, 31305 [PO Box 1405, 31305]; (p) (912) 485-2251; (f) (912) 485-2141; (c) McIntosh

Private non-profit/ 1979/ staff: 6(v)/ members: 225/publication: Altamaha Echoes

HISTORICAL SOCIETY: Gathers, preserves, and disseminates local historical artifacts.

PROGRAMS: Annual Meeting; Community Outreach; Guided Tours; Interpretation; Lectures; Publication; Research Library/Archives

COLLECTIONS: [1793-1950] Original and facsimile documents genealogical materials and local history source materials.

DAWSON

1674
Terrell County Historical Preservation Society
[PO Box 63, 31742]; (p) (229) 995-2125; (f) (229) 995-4000; scpa@surfsouth.com; (c) Terrell

1980/ Board of Directors/ members: 73

ADMISSION: No charge

DAWSONVILLE

1675
Dawson County Historical and Genealogical Society
Old Courthouse, 30534 [PO Box 1074, 30534]; (p) (706) 216-3439; (c) Dawson

Private non-profit/ 1987/ Dawson County Historical and Genealogical Society/ staff: 20(v)/ members: 75/publication: *Dawson County, GA Heritage 1857-1996*

HISTORICAL SOCIETY: Preserves local history.

COLLECTIONS: [Prehistory-present] Miscellaneous books on history and some genealogies.

HOURS: Yr

DECATUR

1676
DeKalb Historical Society
101 E Court Sq, 30030; (p) (404) 373-1088; (f) (404) 373-8287; dhs@dekalbhistory.org; www.dekalbhistory.org; (c) DeKalb

Private non-profit/ 1947/ Board of Directors/ staff: 2(f); 2(p); 53(v)/ members: 1000/publication: *Times of DeKalb; History of DeKalb; and others*

HISTORIC SITE; HISTORICAL SOCIETY; HISTORY MUSEUM; RESEARCH CENTER: Collects and preserves documents about the history of the area.

PROGRAMS: Annual Meeting; Community Outreach; Exhibits; Facility Rental; Family Programs; Guided Tours; Publication; Research Library/Archives

COLLECTIONS: Oral History, photographs, genealogy files, maps.

HOURS: Yr M-F 9-4

ADMISSION: Donation

DOUGLAS

1677
Genealogy and Local History Library
201 S Coffee Ave, 31533; (p) (912) 384-4667; (c) Coffee

County/ 1978/ Satilla Regional Library/ staff: 1(p); 2(v)/publication: *Coffe County, GA Cemeteries, Coffee Co. Marriages*

LIBRARY AND/OR ARCHIVES; RESEARCH CENTER: Preserves local and family histories.

PROGRAMS: Film/Video; Publication; Research Library/Archives

COLLECTIONS: [1853-present] GA Census film 1820-1999; archives; 5,000 books.

HOURS: Yr M-Th 8-6, F 8-300, Sa 10-3

ADMISSION: No charge

1678
Watkins Family History Society
[PO Box 1698, 31534]; (p) (912) 384-8428; watkinsfmh@alltel.net; www.iinet.net.au/~davwat/wfhs; (c) Coffee

Private non-profit/ 1995/ staff: 1(f); 3(v)/ members: 80

GENEALOGICAL SOCIETY; HISTORICAL SOCIETY: Publishes internet site, quarterly magazine, and an electronic mailing list.

PROGRAMS: Lectures; Publication

COLLECTIONS: [1200-present] Member submissions.

DUBLIN

1679
Laurens County Historical Society
311 Academy Ave, 31040 [PO Box 1461, 31040]; (p) (912) 272-9242; history@nlamerica.com; (c) Laurens

Private non-profit/ 1969/ Board of Directors/ staff: 1(p); 10(v)/ members: 425

HISTORICAL SOCIETY: Preserving the past, to interpret the present, to guide the future.

PROGRAMS: Annual Meeting; Exhibits; Guided Tours; Lectures

COLLECTIONS: [1850s-present] Local historical artifacts, genealogical records, memorabilia.

HOURS: Jan-Dec 15 T-F 1-4:30 and by appt

ADMISSION: No charge

DULUTH

1680
Atlanta Chapter, National Railway Historical Society
3595 Peachtree St, 30096 [PO Box 1267, 30096]; (p) (770) 476-2013; (f) (770) 908-8322; admin@srmduluth.org; www.srmduluth.org; (c) Gwinett

Private non-profit/ 1959/ staff: 44(v)/publication: *Milepost 613*

HISTORICAL SOCIETY; HISTORY MUSEUM; LIBRARY AND/OR ARCHIVES: Library and museum with exhibit hall, outdoor displays, and on-site train ride.

PROGRAMS: Exhibits; Facility Rental; Family Programs; Guided Tours; Interpretation; Publication

COLLECTIONS: [1910-1960] Retired rail cars and memorabilia include 90 pieces of railroad rolling stock, business records, blueprints, maps, books, trade journals, and house organs.

HOURS: Yr Sa 10-4, add'l days/hrs in Summer

ADMISSION: $6,Children $4, Seniors $4

1681
Southeastern Railway Museum
3595 S Old Peachtree Rd, 30096 [PO Box 1267, 30096]; (p) (770) 476-2013; (f) (770) 908-8322; 71045.2202@compuserve.com; www.srmduluth.org; (c) Gwinnettt

Private non-profit/ 1970/ Atlanta Chapter, National Railway Historical Society, Inc./ staff: 40(v)/ members: 385/publication: *Milepost 73*

HISTORY MUSEUM: Displays railway rolling stock in order to tell the story of local economic and social development.

PROGRAMS: Community Outreach; Elder's Programs; Exhibits; Facility Rental; Family Programs; Guided Tours; Interpretation; Publication; Research Library/Archives; School-Based Curriculum

COLLECTIONS: [1876-present] Eighty-nine pieces of railway equip including 1920s streetcar, 1940s trolley, 1906 "Steam Pumper" fire engine, 1911 private rail car "Superb" used by President Harding; 1941 troop kitchen.

HOURS: Yr Sa 9-5, 3rd Su 12-5

ADMISSION: $5, Children $3, Seniors $3

EAST POINT

1682
Friends of the National Archives, Southeast Division
1557 St Joseph Ave, 30344; (p) (404) 763-7477; (f) (404) 763-7033; fnasatl@aol.com; (c) Fulton

Private non-profit/ 1986/ staff: 10(v)/ members: 450

GENEALOGICAL SOCIETY; LIBRARY AND/OR ARCHIVES: Group of genealogists researching, training, and working in preservation at the National Archives.

PROGRAMS: Annual Meeting; Community Outreach; Exhibits; Festivals; Guided Tours; Lectures; Publication; Research Library/Archives

EATONTON

1683
Eatonton-Putnam County Historical Society, Inc.orporation
114 N Madison Ave, 31024 [104 Church St, 31024]; (p) (706) 485-4532; (c) Putnam

Private non-profit/ 1975/ staff: 30(v)/ members: 250

COLLECTIONS: [1817-1915] Period furnishings and accessories.

HOURS: Yr Daily 10-5, groups of 12 or more by appt only

ADMISSION: Varies

ELBERTON

1684
Elbert County Historical Society
Box 1033, 30635; (c) Elbert

Private non-profit/ 1975/ members: 103

HISTORICAL SOCIETY: Preserves local history and presents monthly historical programs.

FARGO

1685
Stephen C. Foster State Park
Rt 1, 31631 [Rt 1 Box 131, 31631]; (p) (912) 637-5274; (f) (912) 637-5587; scfost@surfsouth.com; (c) Charlton

State/ 1954/ GA Dept of Natural Resources/ staff: 14(f); 4(v)

HISTORY MUSEUM; NATURAL HISTORY MUSEUM: Provides access to the Okefenokee National Wildlife Refuge, interprets natural and cultural history of the area.

PROGRAMS: Elder's Programs; Exhibits; Facility Rental; Family Programs; Festivals; Film/Video; Guided Tours; Interpretation; Lectures; Living History; School-Based Curriculum

COLLECTIONS: [1850-present] Natural history displays; exhibits of artifacts recovered from site within the swamp.

HOURS: Sep 16-Feb 28 7-7; Mar 1-Sep 14 6:30-8:30

ADMISSION: $5 Gate fee

FITZGERALD

1686
Blue and Gray Memorial Association, The
116 N Johnston St, 31750 [PO Box 1285, 31750]; (p) (912) 426-5069; (c) Ben Hill

Private non-profit/ 1961/ City of Fitzgerald/ staff: 2(p)/ members: 200

HOUSE MUSEUM: Preserves Fitzgerald's unique history as a Union soldiers' colony city and is an educational tool for local citizens and visitors from around the nation.

COLLECTIONS: [Late 19th-early 20th c] Civil War Battle weapons, ammunition, medals, household items, tools, historic newspaper articles, period photographs, paintings, and flags from all fifty states.

HOURS: Yr M-F 1-4

ADMISSION: $2, Children $1

FLOVILLA

1687
Indian Springs State Park
618 Lake Clark Rd, 30216; (p) (770) 504-2277; (c) Butts

State/ 1926/ Georgia Dept of Natural Resources/ staff: 10(f); 5(p)

HISTORIC SITE; HISTORY MUSEUM

PROGRAMS: Facility Rental

HOURS: Yr Daily 7am-10pm

ADMISSION: $2 Parking

FOLKSTON

1688
Charlton County Historical Society
100 Cypress St, 31537 [PO Box 575, 31537]; (p) (912) 496-4578; (c) Charlton

County, non-profit/ 1975/ staff: 3(v)/ members: 20

GENEALOGICAL SOCIETY; HISTORICAL SOCIETY; LIBRARY AND/OR ARCHIVES: Collection of information on early Charlton Co history and history of Okefenokee Swamp; helps those researching family history; participates in annual Okefenokee festival.

PROGRAMS: Annual Meeting; Community Outreach; Interpretation; Research Library/ Archives

COLLECTIONS: [1850-present] Microfilm of county newspapers 1908-present; books of family history, artifacts of early life in Charlton county.

HOURS: Yr Daily by appt

ADMISSION: No charge

FORT GORDON

1689
United States Army Signal Corps Museum
Building 29807, 30905; (p) (706) 791-2818, (706) 791-3856; (f) (706) 791-6069; wiget@gordon.army; www.gordon.army.mil/ museum; (c) Richmond

Federal/ 1965/ US Government/ staff: 3(f); 2(p)/publication: *Signal Corps Camp of Instructions, Signaling Souls, "Hello Girls"*

HISTORY MUSEUM: Collects and preserves history of Fort Gordon and the US Army Signal Corps.

PROGRAMS: Community Outreach; Exhibits; Interpretation; Lectures; Living History; Publication; Reenactments; Research Library/ Archives

COLLECTIONS: [1860-present] Communication devices for military purposes.

HOURS: Yr T-F 8-5, Sa

FORT OGLETHORPE

1690
Chickamauga and Chattanooga National Military Park
LaFayette Rd, 30742 [PO Box 2128, 30742]; (p) (706) 866-9241; (f) (706) 752-5213; www.nps.gov/chch/; (c) Catoosa

Federal/ 1890/ National Park Service/ staff: 30(f); 15(p); 10(v)

BATTLEFIELD; HISTORIC SITE: Commemorates battles fought for control of Chattanooga in late summer and fall of 1863; nation's first military park.

PROGRAMS: Community Outreach; Concerts; Exhibits; Guided Tours; Interpretation; Living History; Research Library/Archives; School-Based Curriculum

COLLECTIONS: [1861-1865] Civil War artifacts (weapons, bullets, bayonets) and items from park's dedication ceremonies in 1895.

HOURS: Yr Daily 8-4:45

ADMISSION: $2

FORT STEWART

1691
Fort Steward Museum
2022 Frank Cochran Dr, 31314; (p) (912) 767-7885; (f) (912) 767-7885; meeksw@ emh5.steward.army.mail; (c) Liberty

Federal/ 1977/ US Army/ staff: 3(f); 1(p)

HISTORY MUSEUM: Interprets military history of Fort Steward and the Third Infantry Division.

PROGRAMS: Exhibits; Family Programs; Guided Tours; Interpretation; Lectures; Living History

COLLECTIONS: [1940-present] Military artifacts, photos, and documents of both US and Iraqi armies.

HOURS: Yr T-Su 10-4

ADMISSION: No charge

FORT VALLEY

1692
American Camellia Society
100 Massee Lane, 31030; (p) (912) 967-2358; (f) (912) 967-2083; (c) Peach

Private non-profit/ 1945/ staff: 8(f); 1(p); 2(v)/ members: 2500

ART MUSEUM; GARDEN

PROGRAMS: Exhibits; Facility Rental; Festivals; Garden Tours; Guided Tours; Publication; Research Library/Archives

HOURS: Yr T-Sa 10-5

ADMISSION: $3

FRANKLIN

1693
Heard County Historical Society
161 Shady St, 30217 [PO Box 990, 30217]; (p) (706) 675-6507; (f) (706) 675-0819; (c) Heard

Private non-profit/ 1979/ members: 104/publication: *Heard and Scene*

HISTORICAL SOCIETY: Collects, researches, and preserves all available historical material connected to the history of Heard County.

PROGRAMS: Exhibits; Guided Tours; Interpretation; Publication

COLLECTIONS: [1830-early 1900s] Genealogies; photos of early places and people; reference materials; archives.

HOURS: Yr T, Th8:30-12, 1-5

ADMISSION: No charge

GAINESVILLE

1694
Georgia Mountains History Museum at Brenau University
311 Green St SE, 30501; (p) (770) 536-0889; (f) (770) 534-9488; www.gamountains.arts host.com; (c) Hall

Private non-profit/ 1984/ Board of Directors/ staff: 2(f); 1(p); 30(v)/ members: 342

HISTORY MUSEUM: Promotes understanding of the NE GA mountains area, its settlers, geography, folklore, and the development of its cultural, social, economic, and political history.

PROGRAMS: Annual Meeting; Community Outreach; Elder's Programs; Exhibits; Guided Tours; Interpretation; School-Based Curriculum

COLLECTIONS: [mainly 20th c] Rooms include agriculture, textiles, poultry, fire-fighting, medicine, Cherokee, African-American, arts & crafts, Ed Dodd/Mark Trail, tools, and country store. Other locations include Indian log cabin, blacksmith shop, train engine and cars.

HOURS: Yr T-F 10-4, Sa-Su by appt

ADMISSION: $5, Family $10, Children $4, Seniors $4

GLENNVILLE

1695
Glennville-Tattnall Museum
Tillmanand Howard St, 30427 [PO Box 607, 30427]; (p) (912) 654-3375; (c) Tattnall

City/ 1994/ City of Glennville/ staff: 4(p); 8(v)

HISTORY MUSEUM: Sponsors history fairs and celebrations for young people.

PROGRAMS: Community Outreach; Exhibits; Festivals; Film/Video; School-Based Curriculum

COLLECTIONS: [1800-1915] Tattnall County history; Indian artifacts; logging and turpentine exhibits; Civil War artifacts; historic maps; cotton exhibit; wall mural of the city by local artists.

HOURS: Yr Sa-Su 1-3

ADMISSION: Donations accepted

GRAY

1696
Old Clinton Historical Society, Inc.
154 Randolph, 31032; (p) (478) 986-3384; (c) Jones

Private non-profit/ 1974/ Board of Directors/ staff: 20(v)/ members: 215

HISTORICAL SOCIETY: Preserves historical, archaeological, and cultural sites, structures, and objects in Clinton and Jones County.

PROGRAMS: Annual Meeting; Exhibits; Living History; Reenactments

HOURS: Yr

ADMISSION: No charge

GRIFFIN

1697
Bailey-Tebault House
633 Meriwether St, 30223; (p) (770) 229-2432; (f) (770) 227-5586

HAMILTON

1698
Harris County Trust for Historic Preservation
[PO Box 16, 31811]; (p) (706) 663-2815; (f) (706) 663-2815; (c) Harris

Private non-profit/ 1993/ Board of Directors

HISTORIC PRESERVATION AGENCY; HISTORICAL SOCIETY: Identifies and preserves historic resources in Harris Co.

PROGRAMS: Guided Tours;Interpretation

HAPEVILLE

1699
Hapeville Depot Museum
620 S Central Ave, 30354; (p) (404) 669-2175; (f) (404) 757-0809; zooman@mind spring.com; (c) Fulton

Private non-profit/ 1980/ staff: 75(v)/ members: 150/publication: A History of Hapeville

HISTORICAL SOCIETY; HISTORY MUSEUM

PROGRAMS: Exhibits; Guided Tours; Publication; Research Library/Archives

COLLECTIONS: [1895-present] Artifacts pertaining to transportation (rail, air, auto); 1900s home appliances; oral histories of citizens; old photo exhibit; radio and phonograph artifacts.

HOURS: Yr T-F 11-3, Su 1-4

ADMISSION: No charge

HARTWELL

1700
Hart County Historical Society and Museum
31 E Howell St, 30643 [PO Box 96, 30643]; (p) (706) 376-6330; sbohill@aol.com; (c) Hart

Private non-profit/ 1989/ Board of Directors/ staff: 55(v)

HISTORIC PRESERVATION AGENCY; HISTORICAL SOCIETY; HISTORY MUSEUM; HOUSE MUSEUM: Maintains a museum, collects and displays information concerning Hart County, and promotes interest in and study of Hart County history.

PROGRAMS: Annual Meeting; Exhibits; Lectures

COLLECTIONS: [1860-1920] Documents, artifacts, and photos of Hart county people and their history.

HOURS: Yr M-F 8:30-4:30

ADMISSION: Donations accepted

HINESVILLE

1701
Liberty County Historical Society
[PO Box 982, 31310]; (p) (912) 368-7002; (c) Liberty

Private non-profit/ 1965/ Board of Trustees/ staff: 4(v)/ members: 102

HISTORICAL SOCIETY: Preserves and interprets Liberty County History; has records housed in Midway Museum.

PROGRAMS: Annual Meeting; Lectures

COLLECTIONS: [1752-1865]

HOMERVILLE

1702
Huxford Genealogical Society
101 College Ave, 31634 [PO Box 595, 31634]; (p) (912) 487-2310; (f) (912) 487-3881; hux@planttel.net; www.planttel.net1~hux; (c) Clinch

Private non-profit/ 1972/ Board of Directors/ staff: 2(f); 1(p)/ members: 2000/publication: Pioneers of Winegrass Georgia

GENEALOGICAL SOCIETY; LIBRARY AND/OR ARCHIVES: Maintain library of genealogical and other written materials; publish books of historical interest.

PROGRAMS: Annual Meeting; Lectures; Publication; Research Library/Archives

COLLECTIONS: [1700-1920] Over 20,000 artifacts related to Southeastern history.

HOURS: Yr M-F 9-5, Sa 10-4

ADMISSION: $8, Members Free

JACKSON

1703
Butts County Historical Society
1813 S Hwy 42, 30233 [PO Box 215, 30233]; (p) (770) 775-2493; (f) (770) 775-2493; deryle1@juno.com; www.geocities.com; (c) Butts

Private non-profit/ 1979/ staff: 10(v)/ members: 300

GARDEN; HISTORIC SITE; HISTORICAL SOCIETY; HOUSE MUSEUM: Organized to satisfy the interest of citizen in the history of the region.

PROGRAMS: Annual Meeting; Festivals; Garden Tours; Guided Tours; Publication; Reenactments

COLLECTIONS: [1820s-1830s] Furniture, plants, and blacksmith tools.

HOURS: June, Sept-Oct by appt

JASPER

1704
Marble Valley Historical Society, The
[PO Box 815, 30143]; (p) (706) 268-3129; mvhs@marblevalleylorgm; www.marblevalley.org; (c) Pickens

Private non-profit/ 1981/ staff: 8(v)/ members: 78/publication: A Photographic History of Pickens County, History of Picken County

HISTORICAL SOCIETY: Maintains and provides tours through two county buildings: the Old Pickens County Jail and the Kirby-Quinton Log Cabin.

PROGRAMS: Exhibits; Facility Rental; Family Programs; Guided Tours; Lectures; Publication

COLLECTIONS: [1860-1930] Photographs and documents.

HOURS: Yr Sa, Su 2-5 (Tours)

ADMISSION: $2

JEFFERSON

1705
Jackson County Historical Society
28 College St, 30549; (p) (706) 367-5307; (f) (706) 367-5307; (c) Jackson

Private non-profit/ 1965/ staff: 8(v)/ members: 150

HISTORICAL SOCIETY; LIBRARY AND/OR ARCHIVES: Preserves genealogical library and historic photographs.

PROGRAMS: Annual Meeting; Family Programs; Publication

COLLECTIONS: [1786-1990] Family and Community historical artifacts.

HOURS: Yr T-Sa 10-4

1706
Shields-Ethridge Heritage Farm, Inc.
2355 Ethridge Rd, 30549 [PO Box 662, 30549]; (p) (706) 367-8693; (f) (706) 367-1994; secsusan@aol.com; www.shieldseth ridgefarm.org; (c) Jackson

Private non-profit/ 1994/ Board of Directors/ staff: 20(p); 7(v)

HISTORIC PRESERVATION AGENCY: Educational and interpretive outdoor museum that uses historic preservation and environmental displays and offers programs.

PROGRAMS: Community Outreach; Exhibits; Family Programs; Guided Tours; Interpretation; Living History

COLLECTIONS: [1865-1945] Agricultural buildings and equipment, restored to original condition.

HOURS: Apr 1-Oct 15 by appt

ADMISSION: $5, Children $3

JEKYLL ISLAND

1707
Jekyll Island Museum
381 Riverview Dr, 31522; (p) (912) 635-2119; (f) (912) 635-4420; (c) Glynn

State/ 1982/ staff: 16(f); 8(p); 40(v)/ members: 250

HISTORIC SITE; HOUSE MUSEUM: Preserves and interprets the history of Jekyll Island, especially the Jekyll Island Club National Historic Landmark.

PROGRAMS: Annual Meeting; Community Outreach; Elder's Programs; Exhibits; Facility Rental; Guided Tours; Interpretation; Lectures; Publication

COLLECTIONS: [1886-1947] Memorabilia and records pertaining to the Jekyll Island club and its members; furniture and decorative arts from 1830-1930.

HOURS: Yr Daily 9-5

ADMISSION: $10, Children $6

JONESBORO

1708
Ashley Oaks Mansion
144 College St, 30236; (p) (770) 478-8986; (f) (770) 478-0459; (c) Clayton

1879/ Private/ staff: 2(f)

Built and lived in by the first sheriff of Clayton County.

COLLECTIONS: [1879] Civil War and 17th, 18th, & 19th century antiques; art; porcelains; crysal; silver.

HOURS: Yr

1709
Historical Jonesboro/Clayton County, Inc.
100 Carriage Dr, 30237 [PO Box 922, 30237]; (p) (770) 473-0197; (f) (770) 473-9855; (c) Clayton

Private non-profit/ 1968/ staff: 2(f); 30(v)/ members: 275

PROGRAMS: Annual Meeting; Exhibits; Facility Rental; Festivals; Guided Tours; Living History; Reenactments

COLLECTIONS: [1839-1910] Local historical artifacts; Native American artifacts; antebellum clothing; buildings.

HOURS: Yr M-Sa 10:30-3:30

ADMISSION: $5, Children $2.50, Seniors $4.50

JULIETTE

1710
Jarrell Plantation State Historic Site
711 Jarrell Plantation Rd, 31046; (p) (912) 986-5172; (f) (912) 986-5919; jarrell@mylink.net; (c) Jones

State/ 1974/ staff: 4(f); 1(p); 120(v)/publication: *Come Explore Jarrell Plantation Activity Book*

HISTORIC SITE: Representation of a middle class plantation in Central Georgia.

PROGRAMS: Festivals; Film/Video; Interpretation; Living History; Publication

COLLECTIONS: [1830-1930] Over 20 original buildings with handmade furniture and crafts; farm tools; cotton, saw, grist, and shingle mills; cane press, clothing, houseware, paper artifacts, books, and oral history.

HOURS: Yr T-Sa 9-5, Su 2-5:30

ADMISSION: $3, Children $1.50

KENNESAW

1711
Friends of Kennesaw Mt. National Battlefield Park
900 Kennesaw Mt Dr, 30152; (p) (770) 422-3646; (f) (770) 422-3646; hayesjn@aol.com; (c) Cobb

Private non-profit/ 1972/ Board of Trustees/ staff: 1(v)

Supports projects such as entertainment and exhibits for the park.

COLLECTIONS: [1860-1865] Civil War artifacts.

HOURS: Yr Daily 8:30-5

ADMISSION: No charge

1712
Kennesaw Civil War Museum
2829 Cherokee St, 30144; (p) (770) 427-2117; (f) (770) 429-4538; kcwm@juno.com; www.thegeneral.org; (c) Cobb

City/ 1972/ City of Kennesaw/ staff: 2(f); 2(p)/ members: 75

HISTORY MUSEUM: Collects, preserves, and interprets the events, people, and history of The Great Locomotive Chase.

PROGRAMS: Community Outreach; Festivals; Film/Video; Lectures; Living History; School-Based Curriculum

COLLECTIONS: [1860s] The 1855 steam locomotive General; artifacts; thematic displays.

HOURS: Yr M-Sa 9:30-5:30, Su 12-5:30

ADMISSION: $3, Children $1.50, Seniors $2.50

1713
Kennesaw Historical Society, Inc.
2829 Cherokee St, 30144; (p) (770) 975-0877; robertcjones@mindspring.com; www.mindspring.com/~robertcjones/khs/khs.htm; (c) Cobb

Private non-profit/ 1993/ Board of Directors/ members: 25/publication: *Retracing the Route of the General, Kennesaw (Big Shanty) in 19th Century*

HISTORICAL SOCIETY: Preserves local history and Civil War locomotive "General," history.

PROGRAMS: Concerts; Family Programs; Guided Tours; Lectures; Publication

1714
Kennesaw Mountain National Battlefield Park
900 Kennesaw Mt Dr, 30152; (p) (770) 427-4686; (f) (770) 528-8398; (c) Cobb

Federal/ National Park Service/ staff: 15(f)

PROGRAMS: Exhibits; Film/Video; Interpretation; Lectures; Living History

COLLECTIONS: [1861-1865]

HOURS: Yr Daily

LAGRANGE

1715
Bellevue/LaGrange Woman's Club Charitable Trust
204 Ben Hill St, 30240-2668; (p) (706) 884-1832; (c) Troup

Private non-profit/ staff: 15(v)/ members: 90

HISTORIC PRESERVATION AGENCY; HIS-

TORY MUSEUM; HOUSE MUSEUM: Preserves and maintains the home of Ben Hill.

PROGRAMS: Facility Rental; Guided Tours

COLLECTIONS: [1850-1860] Greek revival temple-style plantation home of Ben Hill, period furnishings, portraits of Mr. and Mrs. Hill, and correspondence.

ADMISSION: $4, Student $2

1716
LaGrange Women's Club Charitable Trust
204 Ben Hill St, 30240; (p) (706) 884-1832; (c) Troup

Private non-profit/ 1972/ LaGrange Women's Club/ staff: 1(f); 10(v)/ members: 90

HISTORIC SITE: Preserves the Bellevue, the former home of the late Confederate and US senator Benjamin Harvey Hill.

PROGRAMS: Concerts; Facility Rental; Guided Tours; Interpretation

COLLECTIONS: [1820-1890] Artifacts; rooms furnished with period furniture.

HOURS: Yr

ADMISSION: $4, Student $2

1717
Troup County Historical Society and Archives
136 Main St, 30241 [PO Box 1051, 30241]; (p) (706) 884-1828; (f) (706) 884-1840; Info@trouparchives.org; www.trouparchives.org; (c) Troup

Private non-profit/ 1972/ Troup County Historical Society/ staff: 2(f); 4(p); 20(v)/ members: 700

HISTORICAL SOCIETY; LIBRARY AND/OR ARCHIVES: Provides central location for the permanent preservation of local historical records and offers numerous programs.

PROGRAMS: Annual Meeting; Community Outreach; Exhibits; Guided Tours; Lectures; Publication; Research Library/Archives

COLLECTIONS: [1826-present] Documents, photos, and artifacts; genealogy library covering family histories.

HOURS: Yr M, W, Th, F 9-5, T 9-8, Sa 9-1

ADMISSION: No charge

LAKE PARK

1718
Lake Park Area Historical Society
300 N Railroad Ave, 31636 [PO Box 803, 31636]; (p) (912) 559-7470; (c) Lowndes

Private non-profit/ 1991/ members: 175

HISTORICAL SOCIETY; HISTORY MUSEUM: Preserves history of the area.

PROGRAMS: Annual Meeting; Community Outreach; Exhibits; Guided Tours; School-Based Curriculum

COLLECTIONS: [1890-present] Early pictorial history of Lake Park and its families and sites; 1906 landowner's map; furniture; textiles; books; research materials; agricultural and medical instruments; original items from mercantile store.

HOURS: Yr T 3-5 and by appt

LAWRENCEVILLE

1719
Gwinnett Historical Society, Inc.
185 Crogan St, 30046 [PO Box 261, 30046]; (p) (770) 822-5174; GWHISSOC@bellsouth .net; www.adsd.com/ghs/; (c) Gwinnett

Private non-profit/ 1966/ Board of Trustees/ staff: 14(v)/ members: 600/publication: *Heritage*

PROGRAMS: Exhibits; Festivals; Lectures; Publication

COLLECTIONS: [1860-1940] Records of early settlers, of Gwinnett County families, and of county institutions.

HOURS: Yr M-F 9:30-1:30

ADMISSION: No charge

1720
Gwinnett History Museum
455 S Perry St, 30045; (p) (770) 822-5178; (f) (770) 237-5612; arnoldsa@co.gwinnett.ga.us; www.gogwinnett.com; (c) Gwinnett

County/ 1974/ staff: 1(f); 2(p); 2(v)/ members: 200/publication: *Gwinnett Muse*

HISTORIC PRESERVATION AGENCY; HISTO-RY MUSEUM: Houses Gwinnett Co.artifacts.

PROGRAMS: Concerts; Exhibits; Facility Rental; Family Programs; Festivals; Guided Tours; Interpretation; Lectures; Living History; Publication; Reenactments; Research Library/Archives; School-Based Curriculum

COLLECTIONS: [Victorian period] Artifacts from county establishment in 1818 to mid 1960s.

HOURS: Yr M-Th 10-4, Sa 12-5

ADMISSION: No charge

LEXINGTON

1721
Historic Oglethorpe County, Inc.
[PO Box 1793, 30648]; (c) Oglethorpe

Private non-profit/ 1977/ Board of Trustees/ members: 80/publication: *The Historical Marker*

Promotes historic preservation, holds monthly meetings, offers programs, and distributes materials related to Oglethorpe County.

PROGRAMS: Guided Tours; Lectures; Publication

LINCOLNTON

1722
Doctor's House Groves/May House/Lincoln County Historical Park
147 Lumber St, 30817-4201; (p) (706) 359-7970, (706) 359-1031; (f) (706) 359-5477

LITHIA SPRINGS

1723
Sweetwater Creek State Conservation Park
Mt Vernon Rd, 1/2 mi S of I-20W, 30122 [PO Box 816, 30122]; (p) (770) 732-5871; (f) (770) 732-5874; sweeth20@innerx.net; www.georgiastateparks.org; (c) Douglas

State/ 1975/ GA Dept of Natural Resources/ staff: 10(f); 1(p); 100(v)/ members: 100

HISTORIC SITE: Contains ruins of 19th c tex-tile mill and mill town destroyed by Union troops in 1864.

PROGRAMS: Exhibits; Guided Tours; Living History; School-Based Curriculum

COLLECTIONS: [1830s-present] Limited files of non-original documents, letters and photo-graphs relating to New Manchester Mfg. Co. mill and property.

HOURS: Yr Daily 7am-sundown

ADMISSION: $2 parking

LOOKOUT MOUNTAIN

1724
Cravens House
C&C NMP, 110 Point Park Rd, 37350 [PO Box 2128, Fort Oglethorpe, GA, 30742]; (p) (423) 821-7786, (706) 866-9241

Federal/ 1866/ National Park Service/ staff: 2(f); 3(p); 2(v)

COLLECTIONS: [1850s-1880s] Mostly time-pe-riod furniture and pieces from the Victorian era.

HOURS: Summer:Daily 9-5; Winter Sa-Su 9-4

LUMPKIN

1725
Providence Canyon State Park
7 mi W of Lumpkin on Hwy 39 C, 31815 [Rt 1 Box 158, 31815]; (p) (229) 838-6202; (f) (229) 838-6735; pcscdnr@sowega.net; (c) Stewart

State/ 1971/ Georgia Dept of Natural Re-sources/ staff: 5(f); 2(p); 20(v)

HISTORY MUSEUM: Protects natural re-sources of the canyon.

PROGRAMS: Elder's Programs; Exhibits; Fa-cility Rental; Family Programs; Festivals; Film/Video; Guided Tours; Interpretation

COLLECTIONS: [Jurassic Period-present] Fossils include primitive oysters, petrified wood, sea urchin, and primitive clam.

HOURS: Yr Daily Apr 15-Sep 14 7-9; Sept 15-Apr 14 7-6

ADMISSION: Park fee/Group rates

1726
Westville Historic Handicrafts, Inc.
1000 S MLK, Jr Dr, 31815 [PO Box 1850, 31815]; (p) (912) 838-6310; (f) (912) 838-4000; www.westville.org; (c) Stewart

Private non-profit/ 1966/ staff: 16(f); 14(p); 200(v)/ members: 725/publication: *Westville Mirror*

LIVING HISTORY/OUTDOOR MUSEUM: Recreates the atmosphere of life in pre-indus-trial West-Central Georgia.

PROGRAMS: Annual Meeting; Community Outreach; Concerts; Exhibits; Facility Rental; Family Programs; Festivals; Interpretation; Liv-ing History; Publication; Reenactments; Re-search Library/Archives; School-Based Cur-riculum

COLLECTIONS: [1825-1860] Artifacts of Ante-bellum West Georgia, including those pertain-ing to architecture, decorative arts, tools, and horticulture.

HOURS: Yr T-Sa 1000-5, Su 1-5

ADMISSION: $8, Student $7, Children $4, Se-niors $7; $7 Military

MACON

1727
Cannonball House, The
856 Mulberry St, 31201; (p) (478) 745-5982; www.cannonballhouse.org; (c) Bibb

Private non-profit/ 1853/ Friends of the Can-nonball House, Inc./ staff: 2(f); 4(p)/ members: 322

HISTORIC PRESERVATION AGENCY; HIS-TORIC SITE; HISTORICAL SOCIETY; HISTO-RY MUSEUM; HOUSE MUSEUM: Only struc-ture in Macon damaged in the Civil War.

PROGRAMS: Exhibits; Facility Rental; Garden Tours; Guided Tours

COLLECTIONS: [Mid-late 19th c] House con-tains period furnishings and two museum rooms. Museum with Civil War and period arti-facts.

HOURS: Yr M-Sa 10-4, Su by appt

ADMISSION: $4, Student $1, Seniors $3

1728
Georgia Sports Hall of Fame
301 Cherry St 31201, 31208 [PO Box 4644, 31208]; (p) (912) 752-1585; (f) (912) 752-1587; www.gshf.org; (c) Bibb

State/ 1956/ staff: 14(f); 10(p)/ members: 298

HISTORY MUSEUM; LIBRARY AND/OR ARCHIVES: Collects preserves, and interprets artifacts and records that documents Geor-gia's sports history.

PROGRAMS: Community Outreach; Exhibits; Facility Rental; Family Programs; Festivals; Film/Video; Guided Tours; Lectures; Publica-tion; Research Library/Archives; School-Based Curriculum

COLLECTIONS: [1900-present] Sports equip-ment, uniforms, trophies, medals; archives in-cluding photos, programs, and other docu-mentation; oral history interviews and video tapes of athletic events.

HOURS: Yr M-Sa 9-5, Su

1729
Hay House, The
934 Georgia Ave, 31201; (p) (478) 742-8155; (f) (478) 745-4277; hayhouse@mylink.net; www.georgiatrust.org; (c) Bibb

Private non-profit/ 1977/ The Georgia Trust for Historic Preservation/ staff: 4(f); 13(p); 10(v)/ members: 200

HOUSE MUSEUM: Hay House is a National Historic Landmark and one of the finest sur-viving examples of America's antebellum ar-chitecture.

PROGRAMS: Concerts; Exhibits; Facility Rental; Family Programs; Guided Tours; Lec-tures; School-Based Curriculum

COLLECTIONS: [Late 19th-mid 20 c] Hay House 1855 Italian Renaissance Revival, Fine art, porcelains, antiques, decorative arts, paintings, portraits, family letters, photo-graphs. William Butler-Johnston collection, Hay family collection.

HOURS: Yr M-Sa 10-4:30, Su 1-4:30

ADMISSION: $7, Children $2, Seniors $6; Children 6 and under free, GA Trust Members free

1730

Middle Georgia Historical Society, Inc.
935 High St, 31208 [PO Box 13358, 31208]; (p) (912) 743-3851; (f) (912) 745-3132; (c) Bibb

Private non-profit/ 1964/ Board of Trustees/ staff: 3(f); 4(p); 100(v)/ members: 1060

HISTORICAL SOCIETY; HOUSE MUSEUM: Operates a museum house; provides educational and historical information and programs to schools and citizens.

PROGRAMS: Annual Meeting; Facility Rental; Film/Video; Guided Tours; Lectures; Publication; Research Library/Archives; School-Based Curriculum

COLLECTIONS: [1823-present] Pictures and historical artifacts of the area and of Sidney Lanier.

HOURS: Yr M-F 9-1, 2-4; Sa 9:30-12:30

ADMISSION: $3, Student $1, Seniors $2.50

1731

Ocmulgee National Monument
1207 Emery Hwy, 31217; (p) (912) 752-8257; (f) (912) 752-8259; ocmu_interpretation@nps.gov; www.nps.gov/ocmu; (c) Bibb

Federal/ 1936/ National Park Service/ staff: 8(f); 6(p)

HISTORIC SITE; HISTORY MUSEUM; LIBRARY AND/OR ARCHIVES: Protects, preserves, and interprets the cultures that have left evidence of their presence on the Ocmulgee fields located at the Georgia Fall Lines.

PROGRAMS: Community Outreach; Exhibits; Festivals; Film/Video; Guided Tours; Interpretation; Lectures; Research Library/Archives; School-Based Curriculum

COLLECTIONS: [Mississippian-Historic Muscogee (Creek)] Third largest artifact collection in the National Park system; primarily housed at the NPS Southeastern Archaeology center in Tallahassee, FL.

HOURS: Yr Daily 9-5

ADMISSION: No charge

MADISON

1732

Morgan County Historical Society, Inc., The
277 S Main St, 30650; (p) (706) 342-9627; (c) Morgan

Private non-profit/ staff: 7(p)/ members: 145

PROGRAMS: Annual Meeting; Facility Rental; Guided Tours

COLLECTIONS: [1830-1860] Period furnishings and decorative accessories in an 1833 Greek revival home.

HOURS: Yr M-Sa 10-4:30, Su 1:30-4:30

ADMISSION: $5

MARIETTA

1733

Cobb County Genealogical Society, Inc.
[PO Box 1413, 30061-1413]; ccgs@mindspring.com; www.rootsweb.com/~gaccgs/; (c) Cobb

Private non-profit/ 1978/ staff: 25(v)/ members: 200

GENEALOGICAL SOCIETY: Offers support to members in researching their families.

PROGRAMS: Annual Meeting; Community Outreach; Lectures

COLLECTIONS: Books donated to CCGS are donated the Georgia Room of the Cobb County Main Library.

1734

Cobb County Historic Preservation Commission
191 Lawrence St, 30060; (p) (770) 528-2010; (f) (770) 528-2161; (c) Cobb

County/ 1984/ Cobb County/ staff: 1(f); 5(v)

HISTORIC PRESERVATION AGENCY: Recommends landmarks and historic designations, reviews certificates of appropriateness, seeks out grant monies, and carries out historic preservation functions.

1735

Marietta Museum of History, Inc.
1 Depot St, Ste 200, 30060; (p) (770) 528-0431, (770) 528-0432; (f) (770) 528-0450; dcox@city.marietta.ga.us; (c) Cobb

City/ 1994/ staff: 2(f); 2(p); 12(v)

HISTORY MUSEUM: General history museum, from the time of the Cherokee to the present.

PROGRAMS: Exhibits

HOURS: Yr M-Sa 11-4

ADMISSION: $3, Children $1, Seniors $2

1736

William Root House
Cor of Polk St & the N Marietta Pkwy, 30060 [145 Denmead St, 30060]; (p) (770) 426-4982; (f) (770) 499-9540

1844/ staff: 2(p); 41(v)

COLLECTIONS: [1850s] Shards from archaeological dig; wallpaper, china, furnishings, books.; Letters, maps, inventories, probate records, photographs.

HOURS: Yr

MCDONOUGH

1737

Genealogical Society of Henry and Clayton Counties, Inc.
71 Macon St, 30253 [PO Box 1296, 30253]; (p) (770) 954-1456; GenSoc@aol.com; (c) Henry

Private non-profit/ members: 300/publication: *Ancestor Update*

GENEALOGICAL SOCIETY; HOUSE MUSEUM: Preserves local history and genealogy; located at the Brown House, built by a Revolutionary soldier in the 1820s.

PROGRAMS: Annual Meeting; Family Programs; Lectures; Publication; Research Library/Archives

COLLECTIONS: Books on local families, census records, military source records, periodicals, courthouse records, newspaper records.

HOURS: Yr M, W, F 10-3 (Brown House)

ADMISSION: No charge

MIDWAY

1738

Fort Morris State Historic Site
2559 Fort Morris Rd, 31320; (p) (912) 884-5999; (f) (912) 884-5285; ftmorris@clds.net; (c) Liberty

State/ 1979/ GA Dept of Natural Resources/ staff: 3(f); 1(p)

HISTORIC SITE; HISTORY MUSEUM; LIVING HISTORY/OUTDOOR MUSEUM: An historic site that interprets the Colonial period, Revolutionary War, War of 1812, the Civil War, and the colonial seaport town of Sunbury, which it was originally built to protect.

PROGRAMS: Annual Meeting; Elder's Programs; Exhibits; Family Programs; Festivals; Film/Video; Guided Tours; Interpretation; Lectures; Living History; Reenactments; Research Library/Archives; School-Based Curriculum

COLLECTIONS: [1700-1870] Artifacts ranging from colonial tableware to mini, balls from the Civil War, including original equipment from the war of 1812 and Revolutionary War artillery.

HOURS: Yr T-Sa 9-5, Su 9:30-5:30

ADMISSION: $2.50, Student $1.50, Seniors $2; Under 5 free; group rates

1739

Midway Museum
Rt 17, 31320 [PO Box 126, 31320]; (p) (912) 884-5837; (c) Liberty

Private non-profit/ 1957/ Midway Museum, Inc. Board of Governors/ staff: 1(f); 3(v)/ members: 200

HISTORIC SITE; HOUSE MUSEUM: Colonial Museum.

PROGRAMS: Annual Meeting; Community Outreach; Concerts; Exhibits; Family Programs; Festivals; Guided Tours; Interpretation; Living History; Reenactments

COLLECTIONS: [1790-1900] Eighteenth c furniture; banquet table, rope beds, kitchen with original furnishings, music boxes.

HOURS: Yr T-Sa 10-4, Su 2-4

ADMISSION: $3, Children $1

MILLEDGEVILLE

1740

Georgia's Antebellum Capitol Society
109 E Hancock St, 31061 [PO Box 1177, 31061]; (c) Baldwin

Joint/ Board of Directors

HISTORIC SITE; HOUSE MUSEUM: Maintains regional museum which preserves local historical artifacts of local interest.

1741

Ina Dillard Russel Library Special Collections
Ina Dillard Russel Library, Georgia College, 31061; (p) (912) 445-0988; (f) (912) 445-6847; scinfo@mail.gcsu.edu; library.gcsu.edu; (c) Baldwin

State/ Ina Dillard Russel Library, Georgia College & State University/ staff: 2(f); 1(p)

LIBRARY AND/OR ARCHIVES: Administers the Flannery O'Connell Memorial Room, the

Museum and Archives of Georgia Education, the Georgia College and State University Archives, and Rare Books and Manuscripts; preserves and provides access to these materials.

PROGRAMS: Community Outreach; Exhibits; Family Programs; Lectures; Research Library/Archives

COLLECTIONS: [Late 19th c-present] Approx. 5,000 volumes; 1,000 maps; 250,000 manuscripts; 500

1742
Museum and Archives of Georgia Education
131 S Clarke St, 31061 [CPO 95 Georgia College and State University, 31061]; (p) (912) 445-4391; (f) (912) 445-6795; mhargaden@mail.gcsu.edu; (c) Baldwin

State/ 1975/ Georgia College and State University/ staff: 4(p)

HISTORY MUSEUM

PROGRAMS: Community Outreach; Elder's Programs; Exhibits; Facility Rental; Family Programs; Lectures

COLLECTIONS: [Late 19th c-present] Paper, period classroom, old desks, other furnishings.

HOURS: Yr M-F 12-5

1743
Old Governor's Mansion
120 S Clarke St, 31061; (p) (912) 445-4545; (f) (912) 445-3045; jcturner@mail.gac.peachnet.edu; ww.gcsu.edu/acd_affairs/ce_ps/mansion/default.html; (c) Baldwin

State/ 1839/ GA College and State Univ/ staff: 1(f); 4(p)

GARDEN; HISTORIC SITE; HISTORY MUSEUM: Public education center and academic center for the university.

PROGRAMS: Community Outreach; Elder's Programs; Exhibits; Facility Rental; Family Programs; Film/Video; Guided Tours; Interpretation; Lectures; Living History; Reenactments; School-Based Curriculum

COLLECTIONS: [1800-1870] Period furnishings and related decorative pieces.

HOURS: Yr T-Sa 10-4, Su

MONROE

1744
McDaniel-Tichenor House
319 McDaniel St, 30052; (p) (770) 267-5602; (f) (770) 267-2678; Tichenorhouse@aol.com; www.georgiatrust.org; (c) Walton

Private non-profit/ 1887/ The Georgia Trust/ staff: 2(p); 25(v)/ members: 85

HISTORIC SITE; HISTORY MUSEUM: Historic house museum plays important part in Walton County as a source of civic pride, gathering place for community and significant education facility. Former Governors Henry McDaniel.

PROGRAMS: Community Outreach; Concerts; Facility Rental; Family Programs; Guided Tours

COLLECTIONS: [1887-1987] McDaniel-Tichenor House1887, decorative objects, furnishings from 1887-1987, antiques, books,

portraits, library.

HOURS: Yr T-F 10-4, and Sa by appt

ADMISSION: $3, Student $2, Children $2

MONTEZUMA

1745
Macon County Historical Society
109 N Dooly St, 31063 [PO Box732, 31063]; (p) (912) 472-5038; 2052218@mcimail.com; (c) Macon

Private non-profit/ 1979/ Board of Directors/ staff: 1(p)/ members: 79/publication: *Macon County History, Macon County Life*

GENEALOGICAL SOCIETY; HISTORIC PRESERVATION AGENCY; HISTORIC SITE; HISTORICAL SOCIETY; HISTORY MUSEUM: Facilitates meetings on historical topics; encourages understanding of history.

PROGRAMS: Annual Meeting; Community Outreach; Concerts; Festivals; Film/Video; Interpretation; Lectures; Living History; Publication; Research Library/Archives

MORELAND

1746
Erskine Caldwell Birthplace and Museum, The
E Camp St, 30259 [PO Box 207, 30259]; (p) (770) 251-4438, (770) 254-8657; (f) (770) 253-2538; winston@newnan.com; www.newnan.com/ec/

1879/ staff: 15(v)

COLLECTIONS: [1903-1987] Items belonging to Erskine Caldwell—wedding ring, hat, jacket; items belonging to Caldwell's parents; large book collection by and about Caldwell.; Unpublished screenplay; photographs; movie

MOULTRIE

1747
Ellen Payne Odom Genealogical Library
204 5th St SE, 31776 [PO Box 2828, 31776]; (p) (229) 985-6540; (f) (229) 985-0936; (c) Colquitt

Private non-profit/ 1981/ staff: 1(f); 3(p)

LIBRARY AND/OR ARCHIVES: Genealogical library. Archival and genealogical repository for 115 Scottish clans.

COLLECTIONS: East Coast of US and migration routes west. Archival and genealogical records for 115 Scottish clans.

MOUNT BERRY

1748
Oak Hill and the Martha Berry Museum
2277 Martha Berry Hwy, 30149 [PO Box 490189, 30149]; (p) (706) 291-1883; (f) (706) 802-0902; oakhill@roman.net; www.berry.edu/oakhill; (c) Floyd

Private non-profit/ 1972/ Berry College/ staff: 6(f); 50(p)

ART MUSEUM; GARDEN; HISTORIC SITE; HISTORY MUSEUM; HOUSE MUSEUM: Educates public through programs, exhibits, and educational opportunities about the history

and impact of Martha Berry and Berry College. Also preserves Martha Berry's home, Oak Hill.

PROGRAMS: Exhibits; Facility Rental; Garden Tours; Guided Tours; School-Based Curriculum

COLLECTIONS: [1930s] Objects representative of Martha Berry, Berry Schools, the schools' benefactors, and Berry College, including institutional artifacts, Martha Berry's personal belongings, and the art collection of major benefactors.

HOURS: Yr M-Sa 10-5, Su 1-5

ADMISSION: $5, Children $3

MOUNTAIN CITY

1749
Foxfire Fund, Inc., The
2837 Hwy 4415, 30562 [PO Box 541, 30562]; (p) (706) 746-5828; (f) (706) 746-5829; foxfire@foxfire.org; www.foxfire.org; (c) Rabun

Private non-profit/ 1966/ staff: 9(f); 10(v)/ members: 75/publication: *The Active Learner: A Journal for Teachers; The Foxfire Magazine; and others*

HISTORY MUSEUM: Houses museum of artifacts related to the Foxfire Magazine and Appalachia; Offers a variety of handmade traditional crafts for sale.

PROGRAMS: Community Outreach; Exhibits; Facility Rental; Festivals; Film/Video; Garden Tours; Guided Tours; Interpretation; Publication

COLLECTIONS: Artifacts related to Appalachian life and Foxfire Magazine and books series; artifacts and crafted objects.

HOURS: Yr M-Sa

NEWNAN

1750
Newnan-Coweta Historical Society, Male Academy Museum
College Ave & Temple Ave, 30263 [PO Box 1001, 30263]; (p) (770) 251-0207; (f) (770) 683-0208; nchs@west.ga.net; www.newnan.com; (c) Coweta

Private non-profit/ 1972/ Board of Directors/ staff: 1(f); 2(p); 15(v)/ members: 300

HISTORY MUSEUM: Collects, preserves, and interprets artifacts at the Male Academy Museum; offers programs.

PROGRAMS: Annual Meeting; Exhibits; Guided Tours; Lectures; Publication

COLLECTIONS: [1850-1950] City/county historical artifacts including furniture, clothing, decorative arts, and work and home implements; Civil War armament and medical collection.

HOURS: Yr T-Th 10-12, 1-3; Sa, Su 2-5

ADMISSION: $2; Students/NCHS mbrs free

1751
Oak Grove Plantation and Gardens
4537 N Hwy 29, 30265; (p) (770) 463-3010, (770) 463-0135; (f) (770) 463-0541

1830/ Private/ staff: 2(f); 5(v)

COLLECTIONS: Southern antiques, Chinese and English porcelains.

HOURS: Seasonal

NICHOLSON

1752
Crawford W. Long Museum Association
28 College St, 30549; (p) (706) 367-5307; (f) (706) 367-5307; crawfordlong@mindspring.com; crawfordlong.org; (c) Jackson

Private non-profit/ 1957/ Board of Directors/ staff: 1(f); 8(v)/ members: 150/publication: *Jackson County Historical Society News*

HISTORY MUSEUM: Preserves, interprets, and promotes the life and times of Crawford Long and the history of the people of Jackson Co. GA.

PROGRAMS: Annual Meeting; Community Outreach; Exhibits; Facility Rental; Family Programs; Festivals; Film/Video; Garden Tours; Guided Tours; Interpretation; Lectures; Publication; Research Library/Archives; School-Based Curriculum

COLLECTIONS: [1840-1900] Medical instruments and books for a country doctor's office 1840-1878, anesthesia machines and apparatus, Jackson Co artifacts and genealogy materials.

HOURS: Yr T-Sa 10-4

ADMISSION: $2

OCHLOCKNEE

1753
Southeastern Cherokee Council
25580 US 19 N, 31773 [PO Box 367, 31773]; (p) (912) 574-5497; secci@surfsouth.com; members.seurfsouth.com/~secci; (c) Thomas

Tribal/ 1976/ Tribal Council/ staff: 4(f); 1700(v)/publication: *Secci Talking Leaves*

HISTORY MUSEUM; TRIBAL MUSEUM: American Indian descendents dedicated to preserving culture, religion, and language of the Cherokees.

PROGRAMS: Annual Meeting; Community Outreach; Elder's Programs; Exhibits; Family Programs; Festivals; Lectures; Publication; Research Library/Archives

COLLECTIONS: [1500-present] American Indian literature genealogy, records, and language of the Cherokees.

HOURS: Yr

ADMISSION: No charge

OXFORD

1754
Oxford Historical Shrine Society
Wesley & Fletcher, 30045 [PO Box 245, 30045]; (c) Newton

Private non-profit/ 1974/ staff: 15(v)/ members: 75

HISTORIC SITE; HISTORICAL SOCIETY: Preserves local culture and history; restores and preserves historic buildings.

PROGRAMS: Annual Meeting; Concerts; Facility Rental; Guided Tours; Lectures

COLLECTIONS: [1834-1900] Written histories; transcribed sermon by Bishop Hagood.

HOURS: Yr by appt

ADMISSION: Donations accepted

PINE MOUNTAIN

1755
Chipley Historical Center
146 McDougal Ave, 31822 [PO Box 1055, 31822]; (p) (706) 663-4044; www.pinemtn.org/page13.html; (c) Harris

Private non-profit/ 1985/ staff: 10(v)/ members: 100

HISTORICAL SOCIETY; HISTORY MUSEUM; LIBRARY AND/OR ARCHIVES: Non-profit organization with collection of historical artifacts.

PROGRAMS: Annual Meeting; Exhibits; Film/Video

COLLECTIONS: Photos, books, periodicals, city records, family histories, and church and cemetery records.

HOURS: Yr M, T, Th, F, Sa 10-12

PLAINS

1756
Jimmy Carter National Historic Site
300 Bond St, 31780 [Rt 1, Box 800, Andersonville, 31711]; (p) (912) 824-4104; (f) (912) 824-3441; www.nps.gov/jica; (c) Sumter

Federal/ 1987/ National Park Service/ staff: 8(f); 1(p)

HISTORIC SITE; PRESIDENTIAL SITE: Interprets the life of Jimmy Carter, life in Plains, and how community shaped a future president.

PROGRAMS: Community Outreach; Exhibits; Film/Video; Guided Tours; Interpretation; School-Based Curriculum

COLLECTIONS: [20th c] Memorabilia of Jimmy Carter's boyhood, 1976 and 1980 presidential campaigns; local historical artifacts.

HOURS: Yr M-Sa 9-5

ADMISSION: No charge

1757
Plains Preservation Historical Trust
[PO Box 17, 31780]; (c) Sumter

Private non-profit/ 1987/ staff: 20(v)/ members: 140/publication: *History of Plains*

POWDER SPRINGS

1758
Seven Springs Historical and Genealogical Museum
3901 Brownsville Rd, 30127 [PO Box 4, 30127]; (p) (770) 943-7949; (c) Cobb

City/ 1985/ City of Powder Springs/ staff: 8(v)/ members: 150/publication: *Annotated Census Books From 1920*

GENEALOGICAL SOCIETY; HISTORY MUSEUM: A small town museum operating in a restored home in a city park with collections and family histories.

PROGRAMS: Community Outreach; Exhibits; Facility Rental; Festivals; Garden Tours; Guided Tours; Lectures; Publication; Research Library/Archives

COLLECTIONS: Native American, Civil War, and Railroad artifacts; taxidermy and farm tools, loom, kitchen items; genealogical records of local families, house furnishings, children's library, photos.

HOURS: Yr

RINCON

1759
Georgia Salzburger Society
2980 Ebenezer Rd, 31326; (p) (912) 754-7001; (f) (912) 754-7001; bgriner@Pineland.net; www.msstate.edu/archives/history/salzb/index/html ; (c) Effingham

Private non-profit/ 1925/ staff: 1(p); 9(v)/ members: 1800

ALLIANCE OF HISTORICAL AGENCIES; HISTORIC SITE; HISTORY MUSEUM: Preserves genealogies, records, and histories of Georgia Salzburgers.

PROGRAMS: Annual Meeting; Community Outreach; Elder's Programs; Exhibits; Facility Rental; Family Programs; Festivals; Guided Tours; Interpretation; Lectures; Publication

COLLECTIONS: [1700s and 1800s] Pioneer personal items such as tools, guns, clothing, bibles, spinning wheels, beds and household furnishings, and various outdoor items; syrup mill, old house.

HOURS: Yr W, Sa, Su 1-5

ADMISSION: Donations accepted

ROBERTA

1760
Crawford County Historical Society
[PO Box 394, 31078]; (p) (912) 836-5753; (c) Crawford

Private non-profit/ 1986/ staff: 10(v)/ members: 30

HISTORICAL SOCIETY; HISTORY MUSEUM

PROGRAMS: Annual Meeting; Community Outreach; Concerts; Exhibits; Facility Rental; Family Programs; Guided Tours; Lectures; Publication; School-Based Curriculum

COLLECTIONS: Books, guns, quilts, miscellaneous artifacts.

HOURS: Mar-Nov, 1st wknd: Sa 10-12, Su 3-5

ADMISSION: No charge

ROME

1761
Chieftains Museum, Inc.
505 Riverside Pkwy, 30162 [PO Box 373, 30162]; (p) (706) 291-9494; (f) (706) 291-9494; (c) Floyd

Private non-profit/ 1971/ Board of Directors/ staff: 1(f); 2(p); 12(v)/ members: 400/publication: *Ridge Notes*

HISTORY MUSEUM: House containing log structure that once belonged to a Cherokee leader, Major Ridge.

PROGRAMS: Annual Meeting; Community Outreach; Exhibits; Facility Rental; Family Programs; Guided Tours; Interpretation; Lectures; Living History; Publication; Reenactments; School-Based Curriculum

COLLECTIONS: [1790-1840] Artifacts from excavations on property pertaining to Ridge family occupation; furniture and art.

HOURS: Yr T-Sa 10-4

ADMISSION: $3, Children $1, Seniors $2

1762
Rome Area Heritage Foundation
[PO Box 6181, 30162]; (c) Floyd

Private non-profit/ 1973/ Board of Directors/ members: 214

HISTORIC PRESERVATION AGENCY: Provides support for restoration and preservation projects, publishes educational materials on local history.

1763
Rome Area History Museum
305 Broad St, 30161; (p) (706) 235-8051; (f) (706) 235-6631; sbnoble@gateway.net; (c) Floyd

Private non-profit/ 1995/ staff: 2(f); 1(p); 3(v)/ members: 350

HISTORY MUSEUM: Museum organized in chronological order, with various exhibits on historical times an events.

PROGRAMS: Annual Meeting; Concerts; Exhibits; Family Programs; Guided Tours; Lectures; Research Library/Archives; School-Based Curriculum

COLLECTIONS: [Late 1700-1970s] Exhibits relating to Floyd county and its inhabitants archives; genealogies.

HOURS: Yr T-Sa 10-5

ADMISSION: $3, Children $1.50, Seniors $2

1764
Shorter College Museum and Archives
315 Shorter Ave, 30165; (p) (706) 233-7258; (f) (706) 236-1515; (c) Floyd

Private non-profit/ 1968/ Shorter College/ staff: 1(p)

HISTORY MUSEUM; LIBRARY AND/OR ARCHIVES: Preserves documents and artifacts related to the history of the college and makes them available for research.

PROGRAMS: Exhibits; Guided Tours; Research Library/Archives

COLLECTIONS: [1873-present] Papers, books, photos, and artifacts related to the college.

HOURS: By appt

ROOPVILLE

1765
Roopville Archive and Historical Society
Old US 27, 30170 [PO Box, 30170]; (p) (770) 845-4170; (f) (770) 854-4170; (c) Carroll

City/ 1985/ Town of Roopville/ staff: 3(v)/ members: 12

HISTORICAL SOCIETY; HISTORY MUSEUM: Compiles and preserves artifacts and information of local historical significance.

PROGRAMS: Exhibits; Festivals

COLLECTIONS: [1883-present] Agricultural and medical equipment; household artifacts; photos; archives in a restored bank building.

HOURS: By appt

ROSSVILLE

1766
Delta Genealogical Society
504 McFarland Ave, 30741; (c) Walker

Private non-profit/ 1985/ Delta Genealogical Society/ members: 185/publication: *Southern Roots and Shoots*

GENEALOGICAL SOCIETY: Performs genealogical research and supports the public library with genealogical materials.

PROGRAMS: Annual Meeting; Community Outreach; Lectures; Publication; Research Library/Archives

HOURS: Yr M-W 9-5, Th 1-8, F, Sa

ROSWELL

1767
Archibald Smith Plantation Home Preservationists, Inc.
935 Alpharetta St, 30075; (p) (770) 641-3978; (f) (770) 641-3974; (c) Fulton

Joint/ 1993/ City; Private non-profit/ City of Roswell/ staff: 1(f); 1(p); 50(v)/publication: *Death of a Confederate (Newsletter)*

GARDEN; HISTORIC PRESERVATION AGENCY; HOUSE MUSEUM; LIVING HISTORY/OUTDOOR MUSEUM: Preserves and interprets the history of the Archibald Smith family for the education and enjoyment of today's society.

PROGRAMS: Exhibits; Guided Tours; Interpretation; Living History; Publication; School-Based Curriculum

COLLECTIONS: [1840-1880] Plantation home, 13 outbuildings, 14,000 historic artifacts belonging to the James L. Skinner family; Smith family clothing dating to the 1850s.

HOURS: Yr M-F 11-2, Sa 11/12/1 tours

ADMISSION: $5, Children $3

1768
Bulloch Hall
180 Bulloch Ave, 30075; (p) (770) 992-1731; (f) (770) 587-1840; (c) Fulton

Joint/ 1978/ City; Private non-profit/ Friends of Bulloch, Inc./ staff: 1(f); 4(p); 27(v)/ members: 170

HISTORIC SITE; HOUSE MUSEUM: 1840 home of Major and Mrs. James S. Bulloch, grandparents of Teddy Roosevelt.

PROGRAMS: Exhibits; Festivals; Garden Tours; Guided Tours; Interpretation; Lectures; Living History; Reenactments; School-Based Curriculum

COLLECTIONS: [1840-1856] Original Bulloch china, Theodore Roosevelt's daughter's tea set, original Roosevelt letters and local artifacts of the Roswell railroad.

HOURS: Yr M-Sa 10-3, Su 1-3

ADMISSION: $5, Children $3

1769
Roswell Historical Society, Inc.
617 Atlanta St, 30077 [PO Box 1636, 30077]; (p) (770) 992-1665; www.accessatlanta.com/community/groups/roswellhistory; (c) Fulton

Private non-profit/ 1971/ Board of Directors/ staff: 2(p)/ members: 400/publication: *Roswell: A Pictorial History, Historic Roswell Cookbook, and others*

HISTORICAL SOCIETY: Preserves history through numerous programs.

PROGRAMS: Annual Meeting; Exhibits; Festivals; Guided Tours; Publication; Research Library/Archives

COLLECTIONS: [Mid 1800s-present] Deeds, ledgers, bank records, maps, photos, drawings, family history records, artifacts, textiles, vintage clothing, newspapers church, census, and cemetery records, books, decorative arts.

HOURS: Yr Office: T/Th 10-2; Research Library: M/Th 1-4:30

SAINT MARYS

1770
Cumberland Island Museum
Cumberland Island, 31558 [PO Box 796, 31558]; (p) (912) 269-3044; www.accessatlanta.com/community/groups/cumberland; (c) Camden

Private non-profit/ 1985/ staff: 2(v)/ members: 120

LIBRARY AND/OR ARCHIVES; RESEARCH CENTER: Holds research collection of natural and cultural history materials.

PROGRAMS: Lectures; Publication; Research Library/Archives

COLLECTIONS: [1900-present] Mostly vertebrates; large sea turtle collection; archaeological material from coast; artifacts of local inhabitation of island.

HOURS: Yr Daily 10-3 by appt

1771
Guale Historical Society
[PO Box 398, 31558-0398]; (p) (912) 882-4587; (c) Camden

Private non-profit/ 1978/ members: 130

HISTORICAL SOCIETY: Group interested in local history; publishes bimonthly newsletter.

1772
Plum Orchard Mansion
Cumberland Island (N end), 31558 [Cumberland Island National Seashore, PO Box 806, 31558]; (p) (912) 880-4335, (912) 258-3205; (f) (910) 882-6284

1898/ National Park Service

HOUSE MUSEUM: Built by Mrs. Lucy Carnegie, wife of Thomas Morrison Carnegie, for her newly married son, George.

COLLECTIONS: [1924-1973] Furnishings; household implements; art work.; Photographic history of the island.

HOURS: Yr

1773
Saint Marys Submarine Museum, Inc.
102 Saint Marys St West, 31558; submus@eagnet.com; (c) Camden

Private non-profit/ 1995/ Board of Directors/ staff: 1(f); 1(p); 2(v)/ members: 390

MARITIME MUSEUM: Displays submarine history, artifacts, photos, and models. Self-guided tour includes videos, photo library, computer displays.

PROGRAMS: Annual Meeting; Film/Video

COLLECTIONS: [1800-present] Approximately 4,000 artifacts on display; modern submarines; periscope; written historical information on every US submarine.

HOURS: Yr T-Sa 10-4, Su 1-5

ADMISSION: $3, Children $1; Under 6/Over 99 free

SAINT SIMONS ISLAND

1774
Arthur J. Moore Methodist Museum
Arthur J Moore Dr, 31522 [PO Box 20407, 31522]; (p) (912) 638-9801; methmuse@juno.com; (c) Glynn

Private non-profit/ 1964/ Board of Managers, South Georgia Conference of the United Methodist Church/ staff: 1(f); 2(p); 4(v)

HISTORY MUSEUM: Collections focus upon the arrival of John and Charles Wesley to the Island in 1736 and continue to the present. Museum is the official repository for the records of the Southern Georgia Conference of the United Methodist Church.

PROGRAMS: Community Outreach; Exhibits; Interpretation; Research Library/Archives

COLLECTIONS: [1736-present] Library and archives of the Southern Georgia Conference of the United Methodist Church. Includes hymnal collection, John Wesley and Bishop A.J. Moore collections.

HOURS: Yr T-Sa 9-4

1775
Coastal Georgia Historical Society
101 12th St, 31522 [PO Box 21136, 31522]; (p) (912) 638-4666; (f) (912) 638-6609; ssilight@darientel.net; www.saintsimonslighthouse.org; (c) Glynn

Private non-profit/ 1965/ staff: 4(f); 6(p); 90(v)/ members: 1100

HISTORICAL SOCIETY: Administers and maintains the St. Simons Island Lighthouse Museum and a 1936 USCG station. Collects, restores, and houses artifacts reflective of the history of coastal GA. Provides community and educational programming on heritage of the area.

PROGRAMS: Annual Meeting; Community Outreach; Concerts; Elder's Programs; Exhibits; Facility Rental; Family Programs; Film/Video; Garden Tours; Guided Tours; Interpretation; Lectures; Living History; Publication; Research Library/Archives; School-Based Curriculum

COLLECTIONS: [1810-present] 12,000 items including decorative arts, archaeology, historic postcards and photographs, slides, and a manuscript collection; all relating to local area especially during plantation period.

HOURS: Yr M-S 10-5, Su 1:30-5

ADMISSION: $4, Children $1; Under 6 Free

1776
Fort Frederica National Monument
6500 Frederica Rd, 31522 [Rt 9 Box 286-C, 31522]; (p) (912) 638-3639; (f) (912) 638-3639; FOFR_Administration@nos.gov; www.nps.gov/fofr; (c) Glynn

Federal/ 1945/ National Park Service/ staff: 11(f); 4(p); 12(v)/ members: 1

HISTORIC SITE: Preserves ruins of a British colonial fort built to protect Georgia from the Spanish.

PROGRAMS: Exhibits; Festivals; Film/Video; Guided Tours; Interpretation; Lectures; Theatre

COLLECTIONS: [1736-1760] Approximately 3,000 artifacts from the colonial period.

HOURS: Yr Daily 8-5

ADMISSION: $4/vehicle

1777
Lighthouse Keeper's Cottage
101 12th, 31522 [PO Box 21136, 31522-0636]; (p) (912) 638-4666; (f) (912) 638-6609; ssilighthouse@thebest.net; www.glynncounty.com/sts:monslight/index.html

1872/ staff: 3(f); 8(p); 71(v)

HOUSE MUSEUM: Lighthouse has been active since 1872.

COLLECTIONS: [Victorian] Artifacts relating to keeper's cottage; Victorian furnishings.; Relating to local maritime and plantation history.

HOURS: Yr

SANDERSVILLE

1778
Brown House, The
260 N Harris St, 31082 [PO Box 6088, 31082]; (p) (912) 552-2963

1852

HOUSE MUSEUM: Home of patriot William Griner Brown. The house was used as headquarters by General Sherman on his march to the sea in November, 1864.

COLLECTIONS: [Mid-to-late 19th c]

1779
Washington County Historical Society
268 N Harris St/129 Jones St, 31082 [PO Box 6088, 31082]; (p) (478) 552-1965, (478) 552-6965; www.rootsweb.com/~gawashin/washington/index.html; (c) Washington

Joint/ 1976/ County; Private non-profit/ Board of Directors/ staff: 35(v)/ members: 100/publication: Cotton to Kaolin; A History of Deepstep, Georgia; History of Deepstep Methodist Church and others

GENEALOGICAL SOCIETY; HISTORIC PRESERVATION AGENCY; HISTORIC SITE; HISTORICAL SOCIETY; HISTORY MUSEUM; HOUSE MUSEUM; RESEARCH CENTER: Supports and funds Brown House Museum. Exhibits historical artifacts and county archives. Supports and funds Genealogical Research Center with archival materials. Supports restored log jail, Georgia's oldest, located in Warthen.

PROGRAMS: Annual Meeting; Community Outreach; Elder's Programs; Exhibits; Facility Rental; Family Programs; Festivals; Garden

Tours; Guided Tours; Interpretation; Lectures; Living History; Publication; Reenactments; Research Library/Archives; School-Based Curriculu

COLLECTIONS: [1784-present] Historical artifacts including Civil War artifacts; genealogical resources, print and microfilm, photos.

HOURS: Yr T, Th 2-5

ADMISSION: No charge

SANDY SPRINGS

1780
Sandy Springs Historic Community Foundation, Inc.
135 Hildebrand Dr, 30358 [PO Box 720213, 30358]; (p) (404) 851-9111, (404) 851-9101; (f) (404) 851-9807; ssfoundation@mindspring.com; www.sandysprings.org/ssc; (c) Fulton

1985/ staff: 3(f); 2(p); 55(v)/ members: 650/publication: Sandy Springs Past Tense

PROGRAMS: Annual Meeting; Concerts; Family Programs; Garden Tours; Guided Tours; Lectures; Publication; Research Library/Archives

COLLECTIONS: [1870-1910] Museum artifacts, books, manuscripts, oral history interview transcriptions, photographs; natural springs, meadow, bog, forest; kitchen, garden.

HOURS: Yr T-F 10-4, Sa 9-1

ADMISSION: $3, Student $2, Children $1, Seniors $2

1781
Williams-Payne House
6075 Sandy Springs Circle, 30328 [PO Box 720213, 30358]; (p) (404) 851-9111, (404) 851-1327; (f) (404) 851-9807

1869/ County; Sandy Springs Foundation/ staff: 3(f); 2(p); 200(v)

COLLECTIONS: [1870-1900] Many kitchen implements and tools, and crockery

HOURS: Yr

SAVANNAH

1782
Andrew Low House
329 Abercorn St, 31401; (p) (912) 233-6854; Andrewlow@aol.com; (c) Chatham

Private non-profit/ 1847/ Natl Society of Colonial Dames of America in GA

HOUSE MUSEUM: This 1847 house was at one time the home of Juilette Magill Gordon Low, founder of the Girl Scouts, and is headquarters for the National Society of the Colonial Dames of America in the State of Georgia.

HOURS: Yr M-W, F-Sa 10:30-3:30, Su 12-3:30

ADMISSION: $7, Student $4.50; Under 5 free

1783
Coastal Heritage Society
303 Martin Luther King Jr Blvd, 31401; (p) (912) 651-6833; (f) (912) 651-6971; chsgeorgia.org; (c) Chatham

Private non-profit/ 1976/ Board of Trustees/ staff: 30(f); 45(p); 50(v)/ members: 300

HISTORIC SITE; HISTORICAL SOCIETY; HISTORY MUSEUM; LIBRARY AND/OR

ARCHIVES; LIVING HISTORY/OUTDOOR MUSEUM: Operates three historic sites with active programs.

PROGRAMS: Annual Meeting; Community Outreach; Concerts; Exhibits; Facility Rental; Family Programs; Festivals; Film/Video; Guided Tours; Interpretation; Lectures; Living History; Reenactments; Research Library/Archives; Theatre

COLLECTIONS: [19th c-early 20th c] Women's clothing, Georgia Railroad items, machinery and tools, military artifacts.

HOURS: Yr

ADMISSION: $3.50

1784
Congregation Mickve Israel
20 E Gordon St, 31401; (p) (912) 233-1547; (f) (912) 233-3086; mickveisr@aol.com; mickveisrael.org; (c) Chatham

Private non-profit/ 1733/ Rabbi Arnold Mark Belzer/ staff: 2(f); 7(p); 75(v)/ members: 300/publication: *The Contact*

HISTORIC SITE: Third oldest Jewish congregation in America, founded 1733 when GA was founded.

PROGRAMS: Annual Meeting; Community Outreach; Concerts; Elder's Programs; Exhibits; Facility Rental; Family Programs; Festivals; Film/Video; Guided Tours; Interpretation; Lectures; Living History; Publication; Research Library/Archives

COLLECTIONS: [18th-21st c] Various artifacts including a collection of Presidential letters and the oldest Torah in America.

HOURS: Yr M-F 10-12,2-4

ADMISSION: Donations requested

1785
Davenport House Museum
324 E State St, 31401; (p) (912) 236-8097

1820/ Private non-profit/ staff: 1(f); 6(p); 30(v)

COLLECTIONS: [1820-1840] House is furnished as it would have been in 1820-1840, the period of the Davenport family.

HOURS: Yr

1786
First African Baptist Church
23 Montgomery St, 31401; (p) (912) 233-6597; (f) (912) 234-7950; firstafrican@msn.com; www.oldestblackchurch.org; (c) Chatham

1773/ staff: 8(f); 1(p); 5(v)/ members: 500

HISTORIC SITE: Oldest black continuing congregation in North America.

PROGRAMS: Community Outreach; Exhibits; Facility Rental; Guided Tours

HOURS: Yr Daily 9-4

ADMISSION: No charge

1787
Flannery O'Connor Home Foundation
207 E Charlton St, 31401; (p) (912) 233-6014; www.armstrong.edu; (c) Chatham

Private non-profit/ 1989/ Board of Directors/ staff: 30(v)

HOUSE MUSEUM: Preserves the childhood home of writer Flannery O'Connor; Literary center and museum of O'Connor memorabilia.

PROGRAMS: Exhibits; Facility Rental; Guided Tours; Lectures

COLLECTIONS: [1924-1969]

HOURS: Yr

1788
Fort Pulaski National Monument
Hwy 80 E, 31410 [PO Box 30757, 31410]; (p) (912) 786-5787; (f) (912) 786-6023; fopu_ranger_activities@nps.gov; www.nps.gov/fopu; (c) Chatham

Federal/ 1924/ Natl Park Service, Dept of the Interior/ staff: 14(f); 5(p); 10(v)

HISTORIC PRESERVATION AGENCY; HISTORIC SITE; HISTORY MUSEUM; LIBRARY AND/OR ARCHIVES; LIVING HISTORY/OUTDOOR MUSEUM: Site set aside to commemorate and preserve a significant historic and natural resource.

PROGRAMS: Community Outreach; Concerts; Exhibits; Family Programs; Film/Video; Guided Tours; Interpretation; Lectures; Living History; Publication; Reenactments; Research Library/Archives; School-Based Curriculum

COLLECTIONS: [Civil War era] Principally "surface" collections and finds from the Fort area and most during the restoration in the 1930s. Also includes several purchases and gifts of inventories, letters, and diaries.

HOURS: Yr Daily 8:30-5:30, Mem Day-Labor Day 8:30-7

ADMISSION: $2; Under 16 free

1789
Georgia Historical Society
501 Whitaker St, 31401; (p) (912) 651-2125; (f) (912) 651-2831; ghs@georgiahistory.com; www.georgiahistory.com; (c) Chatham

Private non-profit/ 1839/ staff: 11(f); 4(p)/ members: 5000/publication: *Footnotes, Georgia Historical Quarterly*

HISTORICAL SOCIETY; HISTORY MUSEUM: Maintains library and archives; offers outreach programs.

PROGRAMS: Annual Meeting; Community Outreach; Exhibits; Family Programs; Guided Tours; Lectures; Publication; Research Library/Archives; School-Based Curriculum

COLLECTIONS: [1733-present] Archives and manuscripts, photos, maps, blueprints, rare books, newspapers, pamphlets, broadsides, portraits, and other artifacts.

HOURS: Yr T-Sa 10-5

1790
Green-Meldrim House
Bull St & Madison Sq, 31401 [1 W Macon St, 31401]; (p) (912) 233-3845; (f) (912) 232-5559; kaygunkel@email.msn.com; (c) Chatham

Private non-profit/ 1853/ Episcopal Church Women/ staff: 1(f); 100(v)

HOUSE MUSEUM: Historic house.

PROGRAMS: Facility Rental; Guided Tours

HOURS: Yr T,Th,F 10-4, Sa 10-1

ADMISSION: $5, Children $3

1791
Historic Savannah Foundation
321 E York St, 31402 [PO Box 7133, 31402]; (p) (912) 233-7787; (f) (912) 233-7706; (c) Chatham

Private non-profit/ 1955/ staff: 5(f); 1(p); 5(v)/ members: 1000/publication: *Historic Savannah*

HISTORICAL SOCIETY; HOUSE MUSEUM: Preserves and restores historic sites; protects Savannah's historic city plan; educates the public.

PROGRAMS: Annual Meeting; Community Outreach; Exhibits; Facility Rental; Festivals; Garden Tours; Guided Tours; Lectures; Publication

HOURS: Yr M-Sa 10-4, Su 1-4

ADMISSION: $5, Student $3, Children $3

1792
Isaiah Davenport House Museum
324 E State St, 31401; (p) (912) 236-8097; (f) (912) 233-7938; davenport@g-net.net; (c) Chatham

Private non-profit/ 1963/ staff: 1(f); 6(p); 35(v)

HOUSE MUSEUM: A Preserved example of Federal architecture from 1820.

PROGRAMS: Facility Rental; Garden Tours; Guided Tours

COLLECTIONS: [1820-1827] Period furnishings and decorative arts related to the period following Isaiah Davenport's death.

HOURS: Yr M-Sa 10-4, Su 1-4

ADMISSION: $6, Children $3

1793
Juliette Gordon Low Birthplace
10 E Oglethorpe Ave, 31401; (p) (912) 233-4501; (f) (912) 233-4659; (c) Chatham

Private non-profit/ 1956/ Girl Scouts of the USA/ staff: 11(f); 55(p); 75(v)

HOUSE MUSEUM: Serves as a memorial to the founder of the Girl Scouts of the USA; provides educational opportunities to Girl Scouts and students and interprets 19th c life for the public.

PROGRAMS: Community Outreach; Exhibits; Guided Tours; Interpretation; Research Library/Archives; School-Based Curriculum

COLLECTIONS: [1860-1927] Gordon and Low families' decorative arts and furnishings; art work by Juliette Low; Gordon and Low family archives; early Girl Scout Memorabilia.

HOURS: Yr M, T, Th-Sa 10-4, Su 12:30-4:30

ADMISSION: $6, Children $5

1794
King-Tisdell Cottage Foundation, Inc.
502 E Harris St, 31401; (p) (912) 234-8000; (f) (912) 234-8001; www.kingtisdell.org; (c) Chatham

Private non-profit/ 1985/ staff: 4(p)

HISTORY MUSEUM: Researches, collects, preserves, interprets, and presents African American historical and cultural artifacts.

PROGRAMS: Community Outreach; Exhibits; Facility Rental; Lectures

COLLECTIONS: [1800-present] African American historical and artistic artifacts; woodcarvings of Ulysses Davis (over 230 pieces).

HOURS: Yr

1795
Massie Heritage Interpretation Center
207 E Gordon St, 31401; (p) (912) 201-5070; (f) (912) 201-5227; (c) Chatham

County/ 1975/ Savannah-Chatham County Public School System/ staff: 3(f); 30(v)

HISTORIC SITE; LIBRARY AND/OR ARCHIVES: Interprets heritage educational themes for students and visitors; provides exhibits and other programs.

PROGRAMS: Concerts; Elder's Programs; Exhibits; Facility Rental; Family Programs; Festivals; Garden Tours; Guided Tours; Interpretation; Lectures; Living History; Research Library/Archives; School-Based Curriculum; Theatre

COLLECTIONS: [Late 19th c] School house from 1856; architectural artifacts school furnishings photos of Savannah Architecture and model of the city plan.

HOURS: Yr

1796
Mighty Eighth Air Force Heritage Museum, The
175 Bourne Ave, 31402 [PO Box 1992, 31402]; (p) (912) 748-8888; (f) (912) 748-0209; mighty8dev@aol.com; www.mighty8thmuseum.com; (c) Chatham

Private non-profit/ 1996/ Board of Trustees/ staff: 24(f); 3(p); 65(v)/ members: 6400

AVIATION MUSEUM: Displays and interprets artifacts related to the daily activities, sacrifices, and accomplishments of the "Mighty" Eighth Air Force team.

PROGRAMS: Concerts; Exhibits; Facility Rental; Family Programs; Festivals; Film/Video; Garden Tours; Guided Tours; Interpretation; Lectures; Living History; Research Library/Archives; School-Based Curriculum

COLLECTIONS: 4,000 artifacts, 350 art pieces, 6,000 books, 6,800 photos, and 8,000 personal and military archival documents.

HOURS: Yr Daily 9-6

ADMISSION: $7.50

1797
Old Fort Jackson
1 Fort Jackson Rd, 31404; (p) (912) 232-3945; (f) (912) 236-5126; ofj@g-net.net; www.chsgeorgia.org; (c) Chatham

Private non-profit/ 1977/ Coastal Heritage Society/ staff: 2(f); 5(p); 40(v)/ members: 400

HISTORIC SITE; LIVING HISTORY/OUTDOOR MUSEUM: Interprets Revolutionary War, War of 1812, and Civil War history of the site through various programs.

PROGRAMS: Elder's Programs; Exhibits; Facility Rental; Festivals; Interpretation; Living History; Reenactments; School-Based Curriculum

COLLECTIONS: [1861-1865] 19th century cannons, small arms, construction tools, and recovered artifacts and ship items.

HOURS: Yr Daily 9-5

ADMISSION: $2.50, Student $2, Seniors $2

1798
Ralph Mark Gilbert Civil Rights Museum
460 Martin Luther King, Jr Blvd, 31401; (p) (912) 231-8900; (f) (912) 234-2577; (c) Chatham

1996/ Chatham Co. Board of Commissioners/ staff: 2(f); 3(p); 50(v)/ members: 400

HISTORY MUSEUM: Preserves the history of and contributions of Savannah's African American community and others who have struggled for equality and justice during the Civil Rights Movement and educates the public about these individuals and struggles.

PROGRAMS: Exhibits; Facility Rental; Family Programs; Guided Tours; Interpretation; Lectures; Living History; School-Based Curriculum

COLLECTIONS: [1865-present] Three floors of photographic and interactive exhibits; church viewing area, fiber optic map of 87 significant Civil Rights sites and events; "sit-in," segregation, and judiciary exhibits.

HOURS: Yr M-Sa 9-5

ADMISSION: $4, Student $2, Seniors $3

1799
Richardson-Owens-Thomas House, The
124 Abercorn St, 31401; (p) (912) 233-9743; (f) (912) 233-0102; www.Telfair.org; (c) Chatham

Private non-profit/ 1951/ Telfair Museum of Art, Board of Trustees/ staff: 6(f); 16(p); 6(v)

HOUSE MUSEUM: A historic example of English Regency architecture in America.

PROGRAMS: Elder's Programs; Exhibits; Guided Tours; Research Library/Archives

COLLECTIONS: [1790-1951] British and American decorative arts and architecture, including Savannah-made textiles and silver

HOURS: Yr Su 2-5, M 12-5, T-Sa 10-5

ADMISSION: $8, Student $4, Children $2

1800
Roundhouse Railroad Museum, The
601 W Harris St, 31401; (p) (912) 651-6823; (f) (912) 651-3691; PT_HRS@g-net.net; www.chsgeorgia.org; (c) Chatham

1989/ Coastal Heritage Society Board of Trustees/ staff: 4(f); 4(p); 6(v)/ members: 450

HISTORY MUSEUM; RAILROAD MUSEUM: Coastal Heritage Society, non-profit organization.

PROGRAMS: Annual Meeting; Concerts; Exhibits; Facility Rental; Family Programs; Festivals; Guided Tours; Interpretation; Lectures; Reenactments; Research Library/Archives; Theatre

COLLECTIONS: [1850-1960] Repair shops of the mid 19th c; Central of Georgia Railway; machinery collection; turntable; ornament garden; restored 125 ft smokestack.

HOURS: Yr Daily

ADMISSION: $3.50

1801
Savannah Area Genealogical Association
[PO Box 15385, 31416]; (p) (912) 354-2078; (f) (912) 354-2078; SavSAGA@aol.com; (c) Chatham

Private non-profit/ 1983/ Board of Directors/ staff: 11(v)/ members: 138

GENEALOGICAL SOCIETY: Eeducational and research organization; assists genealogical research.

1802
Savannah Jewish Archives
501 Whitaker St, 31401; (p) (912) 651-2125; (f) (912) 651-2831; (c) Chatham

Private non-profit/ 1994/ Savannah Jewish Federation/ staff: 1(p); 6(v)

LIBRARY AND/OR ARCHIVES: Preserves, maintains, and makes available records of the Jewish community of the area.

PROGRAMS: Research Library/Archives

COLLECTIONS: [Late 1800s-mid1900s] Personal papers, oral histories, scrapbooks, synagogue and organization records, periodicals, books, manuscripts, and family histories.

HOURS: Yr T-Sa 10-5

1803
Ships of the Sea Maritime Museum
41 ML King Blvd, 31401; (p) (912) 232-1511; (f) (912) 234-7363; shipssea@bellsouth.net; www.shipsofthesea.org; (c) Chatham

Private non-profit/ 1966/ staff: 2(f); 8(p)/publication: *Flotsam and Jetsam, William Scarbrough's House History and Restoration*

HISTORIC SITE; HISTORY MUSEUM: Preserves and exhibits artifacts related to maritime and the history of Savannah as a port; creates educational programs and publications; maintain a historic house and garden.

PROGRAMS: Exhibits; Facility Rental; Family Programs; Film/Video; Garden Tours; Guided Tours; Lectures; Publication

COLLECTIONS: [19th c] Ship models, paintings, maritime antiques including navigational instruments; and video presentations.

HOURS: Yr T-Su

1804
Society for the Preservation of Laurel Grove, Inc.
802 W Anderson, 31412 [PO Box 10315, 31412]; (p) (912) 231-8166, (912) 238-4251; (f) (912) 231-8166; (c) Chatham

1992/ Board of Directors/ staff: 3(f); 4(p); 60(v)/publication: *Footstones*

HISTORIC PRESERVATION AGENCY: Preserves Laurel Grove Cemetery and offers programs related to it.

PROGRAMS: Annual Meeting; Concerts; Guided Tours; Living History; Publication; Reenactments

COLLECTIONS: [Mid 19th c] Coffins and funeral artifacts.

HOURS: Yr Daily 8-5

ADMISSION: $20 Living History Presentation

1805
Telfair Museum of Art
121 Barnard St, 31412 [PO Box 10081, 31412]; (p) (912) 232-1177; (f) (912) 232-6954; (c) Chatham

Private non-profit/ 1886/ staff: 28(f); 22(p)/ members: 1569

ART MUSEUM; HISTORIC SITE; HOUSE MUSEUM: Art museum housed in two historic homes built in 1818 by William Jay.

PROGRAMS: Concerts; Exhibits; Facility Rental; Family Programs; Festivals; Film/Video; Guided Tours; Lectures

COLLECTIONS: [19th-20th c] Paintings, drawings, decorative arts, sculpture.

HOURS: Yr Su 1-5, M 12-5, T-Sa 10-5

ADMISSION: Varies w/exhibit

SMYRNA

1806
Smyrna Historical and Genealogical Society
2861 Atlanta Rd, 30082 [825 Austin Dr, 30082]; (p) (770) 431-2858; Smyrnamuse@aol.com; (c) Cobb

Private non-profit/ 1985/ Board of Directors/ staff: 45(v)/ members: 250/publication: *Lives and Times*

HISTORICAL SOCIETY; HISTORY MUSEUM; RESEARCH CENTER: A membership organization which collects, preserves, and distributes local historical information, and operates the Smyrna Museum of History.

PROGRAMS: Community Outreach; Exhibits; Guided Tours; Lectures; Publication; Research Library/Archives

COLLECTIONS: [1850-present] Photographs, books, artifacts, archival materials, Civil War memorabilia.

HOURS: Yr M-Sa 10-4

ADMISSION: No charge/Donations

SOCIAL CIRCLE

1807
Historic Preservation Society of Social Circle
403 W Hwy, 30025 [PO Box 832, 30025]; (c) Walton

Private non-profit/ 1845/ members: 72

HISTORICAL SOCIETY

PROGRAMS: Annual Meeting; Community Outreach; Concerts; Exhibits; Facility Rental; Festivals; Guided Tours; School-Based Curriculum

HOURS: By appt

ADMISSION: No charge

SPARTA

1808
Sparta-Hancock County Historical Society, Inc.
353 E Broad St, 31087; (p) (706) 444-6411; (c) Hancock

Private non-profit/ 1994/ Sparta-Hancock County Historical Society, Inc/ staff: 4(v)/ members: 35

HISTORICAL SOCIETY: Restores old jail to house a museum; researches genealogy.

PROGRAMS: Community Outreach; Exhibits; Guided Tours; Interpretation; Publication

SPRINGFIELD

1809
Historic Effingham Society, Inc.
Pinet Early St, 31326 [PO Box 999, 31326]; (p) (912) 826-4705; (f) (912) 826-4706; Betndale@aol.com; (c) Effingham

Private non-profit/ 1986/ staff: 2(p); 4(v)/ members: 160/publication: *Echoes and Reflections*

HISTORICAL SOCIETY: Operates a museum with exhibits and programs.

PROGRAMS: Exhibits; Garden Tours; Lectures; Publication; Research Library/Archives

COLLECTIONS: [Prehistory-1900] Museum in old jail exhibits Native American artifacts, Revolutionary artifacts, and Confederate artifacts; one room is restored cabin set up with period kitchen furnishings.

HOURS: Yr Su 2-5

ADMISSION: No

ST. SIMONS ISLAND

1810
Moore Methodist Museum and Library
100 Arthur J Moore Dr, 31522 [PO Box 20407, 31522]; (p) (912) 638-4050; (f) (912) 634-0642; methmuse@darientel.net; www.epworthbythesea.org; (c) Glynn

Private non-profit/ 1968/ South GA Conference of the United Methodist Church/ staff: 1(f); 3(p); 4(v)/publication: *Historical Highlights*

HISTORICAL SOCIETY; HISTORY MUSEUM; LIBRARY AND/OR ARCHIVES

PROGRAMS: Exhibits; Film/Video; Lectures; Publication; Research Library/Archives

HOURS: Yr T-Sa 9-4

ADMISSION: Donations accepted

STATESBORO

1811
Georgia Southern University Museum
Rosenwald Bldg, Southern Dr, 30460 [PO Box 8061, 30460]; (p) (912) 681-5444; (f) (912) 681-0729; dharvey@gasou.edu; www2.gasou.edu/museum; (c) Bulloch

Private non-profit/ 1980/ Georgia Southern University/ staff: 5(f); 15(p); 25(v)/ members: 80

ART MUSEUM; HISTORY MUSEUM; NATURAL HISTORY MUSEUM: Interprets the natural and cultural history of the coastal plains.

PROGRAMS: Community Outreach; Elder's Programs; Exhibits; Family Programs; Festivals; Guided Tours; Lectures

COLLECTIONS: Mosasaur Fossil and other paleontological exhibits; Abercrombie camera collection; Wiss cutlery collection; Native American artifact collection.

HOURS: Yr M-F 9-5, Sa-Su 2-5

ADMISSION: No charge

STONE MOUNTAIN

1812
Antebellum Plantation
Stone Mountain Park, Hwy 78 E, 30086 [PO Box 778, 30086]; (p) (770) 498-5758, (770) 498-5600; (f) (770) 417-5084

State; Stone Mountain Park/ staff: 4(f); 12(p)

COLLECTIONS: [1860] Household furnishings, including several significant Georgia pieces (appearing in Henry Green's Furniture of the Georgia Piedmont Before 1830)

HOURS: Yr

SUMMERVILLE

1813
Chattooga County Historical Society
119 E Washington, 30747 [PO Box 626, 30747]; (p) (770) 973-2050; alusws@langarte.gsu.edu; (c) Chattooga

Private non-profit/ 1987/ members: 320/publication: *The CCHS Quarterly*

GENEALOGICAL SOCIETY: Preserves local historical and genealogical records and historic site; owns landmark Summerville Depot; manages pioneer Couey House Museum.

PROGRAMS: Annual Meeting; Community Outreach; Exhibits; Family Programs; Publication

COLLECTIONS: [1838-1900]

HOURS: Special occasions only

SWAINSBORO

1814
Emanuel County Historic Preservation Society
[PO Box 353, 30401]; (p) (912) 237-7317; (c) Emanuel

Private non-profit/ 1976/ Board of Directors/ staff: 1(v)/ members: 250

HISTORICAL SOCIETY; HISTORY MUSEUM: Maintains a museum, quarterly meetings on historical topics, and active with historical preservation issues.

PROGRAMS: Annual Meeting; Exhibits

COLLECTIONS: [Late 19th c-early 20th c] Farm and Home Museum contains agricultural equipment, timber products and industry tools, and domestic artifacts.

HOURS: By appt.

ADMISSIONS: Donations

TALLAPOOSA

1815
West Georgia Museum of Tallapoosa
185 Mann St, 30176 [PO Box 725, 30176]; (p) (770) 574-3125; (c) Haralson

City, non-profit/ 1991/ Board of Trustees/ staff: 1(f)/ members: 102

HISTORY MUSEUM: Collects, preserves, and displays local historical items.

PROGRAMS: Exhibits; Guided Tours; Research Library/Archives

COLLECTIONS: [Late 1800s-early 1900s] Artifacts of daily life; Civil War and Native American artifacts; 130 volumes of county records; and dinosaur models.

HOURS: Yr T-F 9-4, Sa 9-5

ADMISSION: $2,

TALLULAH FALLS

1816
Tallulah Gorge State Park
US Hwy 441 N, 30573 [PO Box 248, 30573]; (p) (706) 754-7970; (f) (706) 754-7974; tallulah@alltel.net; (c) Rabun

State/ 1993/ GA Dept of Natural Resources/ staff: 15(f); 5(p); 5(v)

STATE PARK

PROGRAMS: Exhibits; Festivals; Film/Video; Guided Tours; Interpretation

HOURS: Yr Daily

THOMASTON

1817
Pettigrew-White-Stamps House
Andrews Dr, 30286; (p) (706) 647-9686; (f) (706) 647-1703

1818
Thomaston-Upson Archives
301 S Center St, 30286 [PO Box 1137, 30286]; (p) (706) 646-2437; (f) (706) 646-3524; tuarch@inetnow.net; www.inetnow.net/~tuarch; (c) Upson

Joint/ 1996/ staff: 1(f); 2(p); 15(v)

LIBRARY AND/OR ARCHIVES: Archives for city-county-school records and repository for DAR-UDC-Upson Historical Society and family collections.

PROGRAMS: Community Outreach; Exhibits; Research Library/Archives

COLLECTIONS: [1824-present] Archives, family genealogies, county law library, civic organizations government records.

HOURS: Yr M-F 9-5, 1st Sa 9-1

1819
Upson Historical Society
Barron Ave, 30286 [PO Box 363, 30286]; (p) (706) 647-7952; (c) Upson

Private non-profit/ 1967/ Exec Board/ members: 220

HISTORICAL SOCIETY; HOUSE MUSEUM: Collects, preserves, and makes public local history.

PROGRAMS: Annual Meeting; Community Outreach; Interpretation; Living History; Research Library/Archives

COLLECTIONS: [1825-1900] Historic home, family histories, antiques.

HOURS: By appt

THOMASVILLE

1820
Heritage Foundation, Inc.
327A E Jackson St, 31799 [PO Box 2966, 31799]; (p) (912) 225-1514; (f) (912) 225-2148; (c) Thomas

1989/ Board of Directors/ staff: 2(p); 5(v)/ members: 100/publication: *Celebrate Ourselves*

HISTORY MUSEUM: Provides a setting for developing appreciation for the African American Humanities through art, poetry, drama, and history.

PROGRAMS: Annual Meeting; Community Outreach; Concerts; Exhibits; Family Programs; Publication

COLLECTIONS: First publication books and manuals; photos of historic African Americans.

HOURS: Yr M-Th 3-6

ADMISSION: No charge

1821
Lapham-Patterson House State Historic Site
626 N Dawson St, 31792; (p) (912) 225-4004; (f) (912) 227-2419; lphouse@rose.net; www.gastateparks.org; (c) Thomas

State/ 1974/ staff: 2(f); 1(p); 15(v)/ members: 53

HOUSE MUSEUM: Unique 1885 Queen Anne cottage with unusual architecture and features.

PROGRAMS: Annual Meeting; Community Outreach; Concerts; Elder's Programs; Family Programs; Guided Tours; Interpretation; Lectures; Theatre

COLLECTIONS: [1885-1905] Artifacts of life in a vacation cottage.

HOURS: Yr T, Sa-Su 9-5

ADMISSION: $3, Children $1.50

1822
Pebble Hill Plantation
1251 US Hwy 319 S, 31799 [PO Box 830, 31799]; (p) (912) 226-2344; (f) (912) 226-1780; php@rose.net; www.pebblehill.com; (c) Thomas

Private non-profit/ 1983/ Pebble Hill Foundation/ staff: 40(f); 4(p); 15(v)

HOUSE MUSEUM: Example of early 20th c shooting plantation.

PROGRAMS: Exhibits; Facility Rental; Film/Video; Guided Tours; Interpretation

COLLECTIONS: [Early 20th c] Three thousand acre estate including main house, stable complex, kennels, dog hospital, nurse's station, log cabin school; British and American sporting art, Audubon prints, antique furnishings, china, silver, glassware, Native American artifacts.

HOURS: Oct-Aug T-Sa 10-4, Su 1-4

ADMISSION: $10, Children $5

1823
Thomas College Library
1501 Millpond Rd, 31792; (p) (912) 226-1621; (f) (912) 226-1679; dnickers@thomascollege.com; (c) Thomas

Private non-profit/ 1950/ Thomas College/ staff: 4(f); 4(p); 6(v)

LIBRARY AND/OR ARCHIVES: Archives houses history and records of the college.

PROGRAMS: Research Library/Archives

COLLECTIONS: [1950-present]

HOURS: Yr M-Th 8-9, F 8-5, Sa 10-2

1824
Thomas County Historical Society
725 Dawson St, 31799 [PO Box 1922, 31799]; (p) (912) 226-7664; (f) (912) 226-7466; (c) Thomas

Private non-profit/ 1952/ staff: 2(f); 2(p); 100(v)/ members: 521

HISTORIC PRESERVATION AGENCY; HISTORICAL SOCIETY; HISTORY MUSEUM: Collects, preserves, and interprets county history.

PROGRAMS: Annual Meeting; Elder's Programs; Exhibits; Facility Rental; Family Programs; Film/Video; Guided Tours; Interpretation; Lectures; Living History; Publication; Research Library/Archives

COLLECTIONS: [1820-1940] County historical artifacts including exhibits on historic plantations, women's fashion, antique automobiles, 1860 log house, 1877 Victorian cottage, 1893 bowling alley.

HOURS: Yr M-Sa 10-12, 2-5

ADMISSION: $5, Children $1

1825
Thomasville Cultural Center, Inc.
600 E Washington St, 31799 [PO Box 2177, 31799]; (p) (912) 226-0588; (f) (912) 226-0599; tccstaff@rose.net; tccarts.org; (c) Thomas

Private non-profit/ 1982/ staff: 8(f); 21(p); 132(v)/ members: 810/publication: *Center Spotlight*

HISTORY MUSEUM: Regional arts center located in a former school.

PROGRAMS: Annual Meeting; Community Outreach; Concerts; Elder's Programs; Exhibits; Facility Rental; Family Programs; Festivals; Film/Video; Guided Tours; Interpretation; Lectures; Publication; Theatre

COLLECTIONS: [1900-present] Fine art collection focused on American and European paintings; 19th and 20th century decorative arts.

HOURS: Yr M-F 9-5, Sa-Su 1-5

ADMISSION: No charge

1826
Thomasville Genealogical, History, and Fine Arts Library, Inc.
135 N Broad St, 31799 [PO Box 1597, 31799]; (p) (929) 229-9640; (f) (929) 226-3199; glibrary@rose.net; www.rose.net/~glibrary; (c) Thomas

Private non-profit/ 1988/ Board of Directors/ staff: 2(f); 2(p); 9(v)/ members: 400/publication: *Origins*

LIBRARY AND/OR ARCHIVES: Large collection of genealogical research materials from the Southeastern United States and elsewhere.

PROGRAMS: Community Outreach; Family Programs; Lectures; Publication; Research Library/Archives; School-Based Curriculum

COLLECTIONS: [1700-present] Census records on microfilm; family, state, and county histories; US Revolutionary War pension applications on microfilm; marriage, death, and immigration records, and general reference works.

HOURS: Yr M-F 9-5, Sa 9-4

ADMISSION: No charge

1827
Thomasville Landmarks, Inc.

312 N Broad St, 31799 [PO Box 1285, 31799]; (p) (912) 226-6016; (f) (912) 226-6672; tli@rose.net; (c) Thomas

Private non-profit/ 1966/ Board of Directors/ staff: 2(f)/ members: 700/publication: *Oak Leaves, Newsletter*

HISTORY MUSEUM: Preserves heritage and architecture of the area.

PROGRAMS: Annual Meeting; Community Outreach; Guided Tours; Lectures; Publication; School-Based Curriculum

COLLECTIONS: [1830s-1850s]

HOURS: Yr F 2-4

ADMISSION: $2, Student $1

VALDOSTA

1828
Lowndes County Historical Society

305 W Central Ave, 31603 [PO Box 434, 31603]; (p) (229) 247-4780; (f) (229) 247-2840; lownhist@surfsouth.com; www.surf-south.com/~lownhist; (c) Lowndes

Private non-profit/ 1967/ staff: 1(f); 3(p); 10(v)/ members: 400/publication: *Yesterday and Today*

HISTORICAL SOCIETY; HISTORY MUSEUM; RESEARCH CENTER: Preserves and collects local history; maintain a museum for preservation and display of pictures, documents, and artifacts.

PROGRAMS: Annual Meeting; Exhibits; Interpretation; Lectures; Publication; Research Library/Archives

COLLECTIONS: [Prehistory-present] Letters, documents, club records, yearbooks, maps, photos, naval stores, farm implements, uniforms, clothing, Native American artifacts, genealogical and local research resources.

HOURS: Yr M-F 10-5, Sa 10-2

ADMISSION: No charge

1829
Valdosta State University Archives

VSU 1500 N Patterson St, 31698; (p) (912) 333-7150; (f) (912) 259-5059; dsdavis@valdosta.edu; books.valdosta.edu/arch/archives.html; (c) Lowndes

State/ 1981/ Valdosta State University/ staff: 2(f); 2(p)

LIBRARY AND/OR ARCHIVES: Collects, preserves, and makes available records, artifacts, letters, memoirs, reports, and other materials related to the activities, administration, and history of Valdosta State University, the history of South Georgia, and local historical artifacts.

PROGRAMS: Community Outreach; Exhibits; Guided Tours; Lectures; Research Library/Archives; School-Based Curriculum

COLLECTIONS: [1900-present] Papers of Presidents, faculty, students, and alumni of the University; early local land deeds state and local newspapers, artifacts of the University, archaeological finds, several thousand pictures.

HOURS: Yr M-F 8-12, 1-5

VIDALIA

1830
Altama Museum of Art and History

611 Jackson St, 30475 [PO Box 33, 30475]; (p) (912) 537-1911; (c) Toombs

Private non-profit/ staff: 1(p)

ART MUSEUM; HISTORY MUSEUM; HOUSE MUSEUM: Located at the neoclassic-style Brazell House (1911) and is on the National Register of Historic Places.

PROGRAMS: Community Outreach; Concerts; Exhibits; Festivals; Guided Tours

COLLECTIONS: [19th c] Norma Damon Libby Collection of Staffordshire porcelain. Artwork by John James Audubon, John Gould, William Morris, Jocob Studer, Elizabeth Graham, Curtis Ridgeway, Van Houtteano and other 20th century painters; wooden sculptures and furniture.

HOURS: Yr M-T, Th-F 10-4

1831
Toombs County Historical Society

[PO Box 2825, 30474]; (p) (912) 537-4430; bwarthen@cybersouth.com; (c) Toombs

Private non-profit/ members: 30

HISTORICAL SOCIETY: Holds monthly meetings, publishes records of local grave sites.

PROGRAMS: Lectures

COLLECTIONS: Photographs for an exhibit in a local art museum.

WARM SPRINGS

1832
Franklin Delano Roosevelt's Little White House Historic Site

GA Hwy 85 Alt & US Alt 27, 31830 [401 Little White House Rd, 31830]; (p) (706) 655-5870; (f) (706) 655-5872; www.gastateparks.org; (c) Meriwether

State/ 1947/ Department of Natural Resources/ staff: 21(f); 5(v)

HISTORIC SITE: Manages, protects, and preserves historic properties and resources.

PROGRAMS: Exhibits; Festivals; Film/Video; Guided Tours; Interpretation; Living History

COLLECTIONS: [1930-1945] FDR's home with original furnishings; personal belongings and gifts to him from home and abroad.

HOURS: Yr Daily 9-4:45

ADMISSION: $5, Children $2

WARNER ROBINS

1833
Museum of Aviation

Hwy 247 & Russel Pkwy, 31089 [PO Box 2469, 31089]; (p) (912) 926-6870; (f) (912) 926-5566; www.museum.robins/af/mil; (c) Houston

Federal/ 1984/ Robins AFB, GA/ staff: 43(f); 16(p); 100(v)/ members: 200

HISTORY MUSEUM; LIBRARY AND/OR ARCHIVES: Preserves and exhibits artifacts and history of the Air Force; operates educational programs.

PROGRAMS: Community Outreach; Concerts; Exhibits; Facility Rental; Family Programs; Film/Video; Guided Tours; Publication; Research Library/Archives; School-Based Curriculum; Theatre

COLLECTIONS: [1896-present] Aviation and USAF historical artifacts; WWII exhibits; pilot exhibits; Desert Storm exhibits.

HOURS: Yr Daily 9-5

ADMISSION: Free

WASHINGTON

1834
Robert Toombs House State Historic Site

216 E Robert Toombs Ave, 30673 [PO Box 605, 30673]; (p) (706) 678-2226; (f) (706) 678-7515; toombs@g-net.net; home.g-net/~toombs; (c) Wilkes

State/ 1973/ Georgia Dept of Natural Resources/ staff: 2(f); 25(v)

HISTORIC SITE; HOUSE MUSEUM

PROGRAMS: Exhibits; Festivals; Guided Tours; Interpretation; School-Based Curriculum

COLLECTIONS: [1837-1885] Period furnishings and personal articles.

HOURS: Yr T-Sa 9-5, Su 2-5

ADMISSION: $2.50, Children $1.50

1835
Washington Historical Museum

308 E Robert Toombs Ave, 30673; (p) (706) 678-2105; (c) Wilkes

City/ 1960/ City of Washington/ staff: 1(f); 1(p); 25(v)

HISTORICAL SOCIETY; HISTORY MUSEUM: Headquarters for local historical association.

PROGRAMS: Annual Meeting; Exhibits; Interpretation

COLLECTIONS: [1836-1900] Antique furniture; Native American artifacts; Confederate memorabilia; Revolutionary War weapons; busts of famous Georgians.

HOURS: Yr T-Sa 10-5, Su 2-5

ADMISSION: $2, Children $1

WAYCROSS

1836
Okefenokee Heritage Center

1460 N Augusta Ave, 31501; (p) (912) 285-4260; (f) (912) 283-2858; (c) Ware

Private non-profit/ 1975/ Okefenokee Heritage Center, Inc/ staff: 2(f); 2(p); 35(v)/ members: 150

CULTURAL CENTER; HISTORY MUSEUM: Located in Hilliard House (1843).

PROGRAMS: Community Outreach; Concerts; Exhibits; Facility Rental; Family Programs; Festivals; Guided Tours; Lectures

COLLECTIONS: [Prehistory-present] Artifacts representing Native American life, early Ware County, black heritage, and railroads; art collections which vary.

HOURS: Yr M-Sa 10-5, Su 1-5

ADMISSION: $2, Children $1

1837
Southern Forest World, Inc.
1440 N Augusta Ave, 331503; (p) (912) 285-4056; (f) (912) 283-2858; (c) Ware

Private non-profit/ 1981/ staff: 1(f); 2(p); 2(v)/ members: 75

NATURAL HISTORY MUSEUM: A small forestry museum with an emphasis on local forestry.

PROGRAMS: Community Outreach; Exhibits; Facility Rental; Guided Tours; School-Based Curriculum

COLLECTIONS: [1600-present] Artifacts from historical tree use.

HOURS: Yr M-Sa 10-4:30, Su 1-4:30

ADMISSION: $2, Children $2

WINDER

1838
Fort Yargo State Park
210 S Broad St, 30680 [PO Box 764, 30680]; (p) (770) 867-3489; (f) (770) 867-7517; ft_yargo@innerx.net; (c) Barrow

State/ 1954/ Georgia Dept of Natural Resources/ staff: 10(f); 5(v)

HISTORIC SITE: Last remaining blockhouse erected in 1972 by the Humphreys brothers; park with camping and boating.

PROGRAMS: Concerts; Exhibits; Facility Rental; Family Programs; Festivals; Film/Video; Guided Tours; Interpretation; Lectures; Living History; Reenactments

COLLECTIONS: [1792-present] Historic structures and park.

HOURS: Yr Daily 7-10pm

ADMISSION: $2 Parking

WINTERVILLE

1839
Carter-Coile Museum
125 N Church St, 30683 [PO Box 306, 30683]; (p) (706) 742-8600; (f) (706) 742-5476; wintervi@negia.net; (c) Clarke

Joint/ 1874/ City of Winterville/ staff: 4(v)

HISTORY MUSEUM; HOUSE MUSEUM: Former office of Dr. Warren D. Carter and later Dr. Frank W. Coile.

PROGRAMS: Festivals; Guided Tours

COLLECTIONS: Medical instrument and historical artifacts.

HOURS: By appt and for festivals

ADMISSION: No charge

WOODBINE

1840
Bryan-Lang Historical Library/ Gnale Historical Society
411 Camden Ave, 31569 [PO Box 725, 31569]; (p) (912) 576-5841; (c) Camden

County/ 1984/ Camden County/ staff: 1(f); 3(p); 5(v)

PROGRAMS: Community Outreach; Exhibits; Lectures; Research Library/Archives

COLLECTIONS: [Late 18th-early 20th c] County records, books dealing with the Civil War period, early American history, family histories and genealogy.

HOURS: Yr M-F 8-5

HAWAII

CAPTAIN COOK

1841
Amy B.H. Greenwell Ethnobotanical Garden
[PO Box 1053, 96726]; (p) (808) 323-3318; (f) (808) 323-2394; pvandyke@bishopmuseum.org; www.bishop.hawaii.org/bishop/greenwell; (c) Hawaii

Private non-profit/ 1974/ Bishop Museum/ staff: 2(f); 18(v)

GARDEN: The Garden supports Hawaiian cultural traditions of land use and plants and conserves the plant resources of traditional Hawaiian cultural activities.

PROGRAMS: Exhibits; Facility Rental; Garden Tours; Guided Tours; Interpretation

COLLECTIONS: [Hawaii before 1778] Extensive collection of rare native plants and Polynesian crop cultivars.

HOURS: Yr M-F 8:30-5

ADMISSION: $4

EWA

1842
Hawaiian Railway Society
91-1001 Renton Rd, 96706 [PO Box 60369, 96706]; (p) (808) 681-5461; (f) (808) 681-4860; hirailway@aol.com; www.members.aol.com/hawaiianrr; (c) Oahu

Private non-profit/ 1972/ staff: 6(p); 10(v)/ members: 200

HISTORIC PRESERVATION AGENCY: Restores historic rail equipment and preserves railroad history.

PROGRAMS: Annual Meeting; Exhibits; Living History

COLLECTIONS: Portable track, an 1890s Baldwin steam locomotive, a 12 ton coal burner locomotive, and Parlor Car 64.

HOURS: Yr 9-2

ADMISSION: Charge for train only

FORT SHAFTER

1843
U.S. Army Museum of Hawaii
Corner of Kalia Rd & Saratoga Rd, 96858 [APVG-GAR-LM, Stop 319, CRD, DCA USAG-HI, 96858]; (p) (808) 438-2821; (f) (808) 438-2819; fdcura@shafter.army.mil; (c) Honolulu

Federal/ 1976/ US Army Garrison, Hawaii/ staff: 3(f); 1(p); 12(v)

HISTORIC SITE; HISTORY MUSEUM: Collects, preserves, exhibits, and interprets the history of the US Army in the Pacific area, the military history of HI, and the contributions made by HI and its citizens to the nation's defense.

PROGRAMS: Community Outreach; Elder's Programs; Exhibits; Film/Video; Guided Tours; Interpretation; Research Library/Archives; School-Based Curriculum

COLLECTIONS: [1795-present] Military equipment, uniforms, weapons, and ephemera.

HOURS: Yr T-Su

HANA

1844
Hana Cultural Center
4974 Uakea Rd, 96713 [PO Box 27, 96713]; (p) (808) 248-8622; (f) (808) 248-8622; (c) Maui

Private non-profit/ 1971/ staff: 4(f); 3(p); 3(v)/ members: 1955/publication: Hana Cultural Center Newsletter

HISTORIC PRESERVATION AGENCY; HISTORIC SITE; LIVING HISTORY/OUTDOOR MUSEUM: Preserves historical and cultural items, sites, and information concerning the district of Hana, Maui, and Hawaii.

PROGRAMS: Annual Meeting; Exhibits; Family Programs; Film/Video; Garden Tours; Guided Tours; Living History; Publication; Research Library/Archives

COLLECTIONS: Hawaiian quilts, stone, artifacts, shells, photos, books, and historic papers.

HOURS: Yr Daily 10-4

ADMISSION: Donations accepted

HANALEI

1845
Ho'opulapula Haraguchi Rice Mill
4708 Ohiki Rd, 96714 [PO Box 427, 96714]; (p) (808) 826-6202; (f) (808) 826-6369; hvtaro@gte.net; (c) Kauai

Private non-profit/ 1983

HISTORIC SITE; LIVING HISTORY/OUTDOOR MUSEUM: Preserves and interprets the Haraguchi Rice Mill and the agrarian history of Hanalei Valley.

PROGRAMS: Community Outreach; Elder's Programs; Exhibits; Guided Tours; Interpretation; Living History

COLLECTIONS: [1924-present] Rice milling machinery, oral histories, agricultural artifacts, archival photos, newsletters, newspaper articles, and archival records.

HAUULA

1846
Kahana Valley State Park
52-222 Kamehameha Hwy, 96717; (p) (808) 237-7766; (f) (808) 237-7765; (c) Honolulu

State/ 1978/ HI State Dept of Land and Natural Resources/ staff: 1(f); 130(v)

HISTORIC SITE; LIVING HISTORY/OUTDOOR MUSEUM: Preserves, protects, perpetuates, and revitalizes the ahupua'a of Kahana through the protection, maintenance, preservation, and teaching stewardship of its environment, Hawaiian culture, and resources.

PROGRAMS: Elder's Programs; Interpretation; Living History; School-Based Curriculum

COLLECTIONS: [Pre Western contact-present]

HOURS: Yr Daily

HILO

1847
Lyman House Memorial Museum
276 Haili St, 96720; (p) (808) 935-5021; (f) (808) 969-7685; lymanwks@interpac.net; www.lymanmuseum.org; (c) Hawaii

Private non-profit/ 1931/ staff: 13(f); 10(p); 24(v)/ members: 292/publication: *Sarah Lyman's Journal; and others*

HISTORIC SITE; HISTORY MUSEUM; HOUSE MUSEUM: Interprets and disseminates Hawaiian history through the preservation of artifacts and records, exhibits, and public programs.

PROGRAMS: Annual Meeting; Community Outreach; Concerts; Elder's Programs; Exhibits; Facility Rental; Garden Tours; Guided Tours; Interpretation; Lectures; Publication; Research Library/Archives; School-Based Curriculum

COLLECTIONS: [Prehistory-present] 1839 Mission House; minerals and seashells; range of items which reflect HI's multi-ethnic history.

HOURS: Yr M-Sa 9-4:30

ADMISSION: $7, Student $2.50, Seniors $5

1848
Pacific Tsunami Museum
130 Kamehameha Ave, 96721 [PO Box 806, 96721]; (p) (808) 935-0926; (f) (808) 935-0842; tsunami@aloha.net; www.tsunami.org; (c) Hawaii

Private non-profit/ 1994/ staff: 22(v)/ members: 190/publication: *Tsunamis in Hawaii*

LIVING HISTORY/OUTDOOR MUSEUM: Disseminates public education about tsunamis; fosters research and cultural exchange; serves as a memorial to those who lost their lives to tsunamis.

PROGRAMS: Community Outreach; Exhibits; Film/Video; Guided Tours; Lectures; Publication

COLLECTIONS: [1800-present] Pictures, videos, and oral historical accounts of tsunamis in HI.

HOURS: Yr M-Sa

1849
Wailoa Center
900 Piopio St, 96720 [PO Box 936, 96720]; (p) (808) 933-0416; (f) (808) 933-0417

State/ 1978/ staff: 1(f); 1(p); 28(v)

ART MUSEUM: Promotes the arts and crafts of Hawaii's people.

PROGRAMS: Community Outreach; Elder's Programs; Exhibits; Family Programs; Film/Video; Lectures; Living History; Research Library/Archives

COLLECTIONS: [18th-19th c] Historical Hawaiian data and artwork.

HOURS: Yr

HONAUNAU

1850
Pu'uhonua o Honaunau National Historic Park
Honaunau Bay off HWY 160, 96726 [PO Box 129, 96726]; (p) (808) 328-2326; (f) (808) 328-9485; www.nps.gov/puho; (c) Hawaii

Federal/ 1961/ National Park Service/ staff: 15(f); 11(p); 2(v)

HISTORIC SITE: Operates and manages significant Hawaiian cultural site, includes a place of refuge, royal grounds, temple sites, fishponds, holua slides, and house sites.

PROGRAMS: Exhibits; Festivals; Guided Tours; Interpretation; Lectures; Research Library/Archives; School-Based Curriculum

COLLECTIONS: [Pre 1819] Hawaiian artifacts and carvings.

HOURS: Yr Daily

ADMISSION: $2

HONOLULU

1851
Bernice Pauahi Bishop Museum
1525 Bernice St, 96817; (p) (808) 847-3511; (f) (808) 841-8968; ask@bishopmuseum.org; www.bishopmuseum.org; (c) Honolulu

Private non-profit/ 1889/ staff: 200(f); 30(p); 550(v)/ members: 10000/publication: *Ka'Elele*

HISTORY MUSEUM: The Bishop Museum stimulates awareness and appreciation of the natural and cultural world with emphasis on Hawaii and the Pacific.

PROGRAMS: Community Outreach; Concerts; Exhibits; Facility Rental; Festivals; Garden Tours; Guided Tours; Interpretation; Lectures; Publication; Research Library/Archives; School-Based Curriculum

COLLECTIONS: [1778-present] All periods of Hawaiian/Pacific natural and cultural history: 1.2 million cultural objects, 13.5 million insects, 6 million shells, 500,000 plant specimens, 700,000 animal specimens, 1 million photographs, manuscripts, audio, video, and 110,000 books.

HOURS: Yr Daily 9-5

ADMISSION: $14.95, Children $11.95, Seniors $11.95; Under 6 free

1852
Center for Oral History, Social Science Research
2424 Maile Way, SSB 724, 96822; (p) (808) 956-6259; (f) (808) 956-9794; wnishimo@hawaii.edu; www2.soc.hawaii.edu/css/oral_hist; (c) Honolulu

State/ Univ of HI/ staff: 3(f); 3(p)

RESEARCH CENTER: Collect, preserve, and make available historic materials related to Hawaii.

PROGRAMS: Lectures; Publication; Research Library/Archives

COLLECTIONS: [1900-present] Oral histories.

HOURS: Yr M-F 8-4:30

1853
Contemporary Museum, The
2411 Makiki Heights Dr, 96822; (p) (808) 526-1322; (f) (808) 536-5973; glagoria@tcmhi.org; www.tcmhi.org; (c) Honolulu

Private non-profit/ 1988/ Board of Trustees/ staff: 24(f); 18(p); 450(v)/ members: 2400/publication: *The Contemporary Museum News*

HISTORY MUSEUM; HOUSE MUSEUM: Strives to develop a public appreciation and understanding of contemporary art through exhibition and educational programs; collects and preserves art; maintains and presents the historic Spalding House and Gardens.

PROGRAMS: Community Outreach; Exhibits; Family Programs; Festivals; Garden Tours; Guided Tours; Lectures; Publication; Research Library/Archives

COLLECTIONS: [1940-present]

HOURS: Yr T-Sa 10-4, Su 12-4

ADMISSION: $5, Student $3, Seniors $3

1854
Daughters of Hawaii
Hulihe'e Palace, 75-5718 Ali'i Dr, 96817 [2913 Pali Hwy, 96817]; (p) (808) 329-1877; (f) (808) 329-1321; doh@pixi.com; www.daughtersofhawaii.org; (c) Honolulu

Private non-profit/ 1903/ Board of Directors/ staff: 1(f); 10(p); 40(v)/ members: 1300/publication: *Hawaiian Furniture and Hawaii's Cabinetmakers, and others*

HISTORIC SITE; HISTORICAL SOCIETY; HOUSE MUSEUM: Preserves two historic site museums and one non-building site; perpetuates and preserves the language, culture, and spirit of old Hawai'i.

PROGRAMS: Annual Meeting; Community Outreach; Exhibits; Facility Rental; Festivals; Garden Tours; Guided Tours; Lectures; Publication

COLLECTIONS: [1848] Furnishings, belongings, artifacts, and memorabilia of the royal families of Hawai'i.

HOURS: Yr M-Su 9-4

ADMISSION: $5, Children $1, Seniors $4; $4 Residents

1855
Friends of 'Lolani Palace, The
364 S King St, 96804 [PO Box 2259, 96804]; (p) (808) 522-0822; (f) (808) 532-1051; (c) Honolulu

Private non-profit/ 1966/ Board of Directors/ staff: 22(f); 1(p); 200(v)/ members: 800

HISTORIC SITE; HOUSE MUSEUM: Spearheaded the restoration of 'Lolani Palace and manages the national historic site as a historic house museum.

PROGRAMS: Annual Meeting; Concerts; Exhibits; Film/Video; Guided Tours; Interpretation

COLLECTIONS: [1882-1893] Original 'Lolani Palace furnishings and artifacts from the Royal collection.

HOURS: Yr T-Sa 9-2:15

ADMISSION: $15, Children $5

1856
Friends of Honolulu Botanical Gardens
180 N Vineyard Blvd, 96817; (p) (808) 537-1708; (f) (808) 537-6274; friends.honolulubotgdns@gte.net; (c) Honolulu

Private non-profit/ 1961/ staff: 1(p); 100(v)/ members: 600

GARDEN: An educational and conservation corporation organized to support the programs and goals of the five sites comprising Honolulu Gardens.

PROGRAMS: Annual Meeting; Community Outreach; Exhibits; Garden Tours; Guided Tours; Lectures

COLLECTIONS: World wide botanical species from rainforest to tropical desert: trees, palms, orchids, aroids, and native Hawaiian species; rare and endangered species are a collection priority.

HOURS: Yr Daily

ADMISSION: No charge

1857
Hawaii Heritage Center
1168 Smith St (Chinatown), 96837 [PO Box 37520, 96837]; (p) (808) 521-2749; (f) (808) 988-7253; (c) Honolulu

Private non-profit/ 1980/ Board of Directors/ staff: 50(v)/ members: 350/publication: *Humanities Viewers Guides on the Chinese and Puerto Ricans of Hawaii*

HISTORIC PRESERVATION AGENCY: Interprets and preserves the history and culture of Hawaii's diverse ethnocultural groups through exhibits, public forums, publications, surveys, performances and other activities for educational purposes.

PROGRAMS: Annual Meeting; Community Outreach; Exhibits; Guided Tours; Interpretation; Lectures; Publication

COLLECTIONS: [1820-present] Original English language newspapers from 1820-1940s, photos, slides, videotapes, artifacts.

HOURS: Yr F

ADMISSIONS: Donations requested

1858
Hawaii Maritime Center
Pier 7, Honolulu Harbor, 96813; (p) (808) 523-6151; (f) (808) 536-1519; bmoore@bishopmuseum.org; www.bishopmuseum.org; (c) Honolulu

Private non-profit/ 1988/ staff: 8(f); 8(p)

HISTORY MUSEUM: Perpetuates and shares the maritime history of HI.

PROGRAMS: Exhibits; Facility Rental; Guided Tours

COLLECTIONS: Maritime artifacts, four masted fully rigged sailing ship, and a voyaging canoe.

HOURS: Yr Daily 8:30-5

ADMISSION: $7.50, Children $4.50

1859
Hawaii Museums Association
[PO Box 4125, 96812-4125]; (p) (808) 254-4292; (f) (808) 254-4153; dpope@lava.net; www.openstudio.hawaii.edu/hma; (c) Honolulu

Private non-profit/ 1968/ staff: 1(p); 15(v)/ members: 400/publication: *Economic Impact of Hawaii Museums, Directory of Hawaii Museums*

ALLIANCE OF HISTORICAL AGENCIES: State museum association that provides training, networking, research, publications, and advocacy.

PROGRAMS: Annual Meeting; Lectures; Publication

1860
Hawaii State Archives
'Iolani Palace Grounds, 96813; (p) (808) 586-0329; (f) (808) 586-0330; (c) Honolulu

State/ 1905/ Dept. of Accounting and General Services/ staff: 12(f); 2(v)

LIBRARY AND/OR ARCHIVES: Collects, preserves, and makes available records related to the Hawaiian Kingdom, the Republic of Hawaii, and territorial and state governments.

PROGRAMS: Research Library/Archives

COLLECTIONS: [1840-present] Record of Executive branch agencies, Legislative records, Governor's records, and Judiciary records; private papers, manuscripts, and photos.

HOURS: Yr M-F 9-4

1861
Hawaiian Historical Society
560 Kawaiahao St, 96813-5023; (p) (808) 537-6271; (f) (808) 537-6271; bedunn@lava.net; www.hawaiianhistory.org; (c) Honolulu

Private non-profit/ 1892/ Board of Trustees/ staff: 1(f); 1(p); 4(v)/ members: 1200/publication: *The Hawaiian Journal of History*

HISTORICAL SOCIETY: Collect, preserves, and makes accessible the documentary history of HI and the Pacific.

PROGRAMS: Lectures; Publication; Research Library/Archives

COLLECTIONS: [1783-1940] Books, serial newspapers, manuscripts, photographs, Hawaiian language books and newspaper, and accounts of voyages to Hawaii and the Pacific.

HOURS: Yr

1862
Historic Hawai'i Foundation
680 Iwilei Rd #690, 96806 [PO Box 1658, 96806]; (p) (808) 523-2900; (f) (808) 523-0800; hhfd@lava.net; www.historichawaii.org; (c) Honolulu

Private non-profit/ 1974/ staff: 3(f); 200(v)/ members: 2000/publication: *Historic Hawaii*

HISTORICAL SOCIETY: Encourages the preservation of historic buildings, objects, and sites relating to state history; promotes an awareness of and respect for all that is historically significant and architecturally distinctive about HI.

PROGRAMS: Annual

1863
History and Humanities Program of the State Foundation on Culture and the Arts
44 Merchant St, 96813; (p) (808) 586-0300; (f) (808) 586-0308; sfca@sfca.state.hi.us; www.state.hi.us/sfca

State/ 1965/ State Foundation on C & A Board of Commissioners/ staff: 23(f); 2(p)/publication: *Guides to Historical Resources, and others*

HISTORY MUSEUM: Promotes, perpetuates, preserves, and encourages culture, the arts, history, and the humanities in HI; coordinates,

administers, and appraises history programs for and in the state.

PROGRAMS: Community Outreach; Exhibits; Festivals; Publication

COLLECTIONS: [20th c] 5,000 works of art largely produced by HI artists.

HOURS: Offices: Yr M-F 7:45-4:30

1864
Honolulu Botanical Gardens
50 N Vineyard Blvd, 96817; (p) (808) 522-7060; (f) (808) 522-7050; heidibg@juno.com; www.co.honolulu.hi.us/parks/hbg/; (c) Honolulu

City; Private non-profit/ 1850/ C and C Honolulu/ staff: 40(f); 9(p); 150(v)/ members: 400/publication: *The Frond*

GARDEN: Maintains five botanical garden systems in five different microclimates.

PROGRAMS: Annual Meeting; Community Outreach; Concerts; Elder's Programs; Exhibits; Facility Rental; Family Programs; Festivals; Garden Tours; Guided Tours; Interpretation; Lectures; Living History; Publication

COLLECTIONS: [1960s-present] Tropical plant collection: old historic trees, orchids, and native Hawaiian plants.

HOURS: Yr Daily

ADMISSION: Foster Garden:$5, Others Free

1865
Honolulu Police Department Law Enforcement Museum
801 S Beretania St, 906813; (p) (808) 529-3511; (f) (808) 529-3028; hpd@honolulupd.org; www.honolulupd.org; (c) Oahu

City/ 1984/ staff: 1(f)

HISTORY MUSEUM: Depicts the evolution of law enforcement in HI and the evolution of the Honolulu Police Department from the pre-Cook era to the present.

PROGRAMS: Exhibits; Guided Tours; Interpretation; Lectures; School-Based Curriculum

COLLECTIONS: [1750-present] Antique weapons, uniforms, and books along with narcotic and gambling displays; model display of police vehicles dating to 1900; historic pictures and documents.

HOURS: Yr

1866
Japanese Cultural Center of Hawaii
2454 S Beretania St, 96826; (p) (808) 945-7633; (f) (808) 944-1123; jcch@lava.net; (c) Honolulu

Private non-profit/ 1987/ Board of Directors/ staff: 8(f); 1(p); 350(v)/ members: 2053/publication: *The Legacy of the Japanese in Hawaii: Cuisine*

HISTORIC PRESERVATION AGENCY: Center for public access to information, resources, and activities relative to the learning, appreciation, and perpetuation of the legacy of Japanese in Hawaii.

PROGRAMS: Annual Meeting; Community Outreach; Concerts; Elder's Programs; Exhibits; Facility Rental; Family Programs; Festivals; Guided Tours; Interpretation; Lectures; Living History; Publication; Research Library/Archives

COLLECTIONS: [1868-present] Artifacts of

Japanese in Hawaii, newspapers, photos, books, and oral histories.

HOURS: Yr T-Sa 10-4

ADMISSION: $3, Student $2, Children

1867
Judiciary History Center
417 S King St, Rm 102, 96813; (p) (808) 369-4999; (f) (808) 539-4996; jhc@aloha.net; www.jhchawaii.org; (c) Honolulu

State/ 1989/ staff: 3(f); 2(p); 14(v)/publication: *Kaulike, and others*

HISTORIC SITE; HISTORY MUSEUM: Enhances public understanding of HI's unique legal history through educational activities, exhibits, and research.

PROGRAMS: Community Outreach; Exhibits; Film/Video; Publication; Reenactments; School-Based Curriculum

COLLECTIONS: Authentic furnishings, a replicated territorial courtroom, photos, documents, and artwork.

HOURS: Yr M-F 10-4

1868
Mission Houses Museum
553 S King St, 96813; (p) (808) 351-0481; (f) (808) 545-2280; mhm@lava.net; www.lava.net/~mhm/main.htm; (c) Honolulu

Private non-profit/ Hawaiian Mission Children's Society/ staff: 10(f); 13(p); 12(v)/ members: 900/publication: *Grapes of Canaan, Ka Pa'i Palapala*

HISTORIC SITE; HISTORICAL SOCIETY; HISTORY MUSEUM; LIVING HISTORY/OUTDOOR MUSEUM; RESEARCH CENTER: Interprets the cultural interaction of Native Hawaiians, missionaries, and other immigrants in 19th c Hawaii.

PROGRAMS: Exhibits; Facility Rental; Family Programs; Festivals; Guided Tours; Interpretation; Lectures; Living History; Publication; Research Library/Archives; School-Based Curriculum

COLLECTIONS: [1820-1900] Missionary artifacts, Hawaiian artifacts, textiles, Hawaiian quilts, letters, journals, Hawaiian language books, photos, daguerreotypes, and engravings.

HOURS: Yr T-Sa 9-4

ADMISSION: $8, Student $4, Children $3, Seniors $6; $7 Residents/Military

1869
Pacific Aerospace Museum
HIA 300 Rodgers BL #7, 96819-1897; (p) (808) 839-0777; (f) (808) 836-3267; (c) Honolulu

Private non-profit/ 1991/ staff: 1(f); 10(p); 125(v)

AVIATION MUSEUM; HISTORY MUSEUM: Presents the history of aviation in the Pacific from ancient Polynesian voyaging canoes to modern space flight.

PROGRAMS: Exhibits

COLLECTIONS: [Prehistory-WWII]

HOURS: Yr Daily 9-6

ADMISSION: $3, Student $2.50, Children $1

1870
Queen's Historical Room, The
1301 Punchbowl St, 96813; (p) (808) 538-9011; Marshall@hml.org; www.queens.org/qmc/about/history/misshist.html; (c) Honolulu

Private non-profit/ 1965/ staff: 1(f); 2(v)

HISTORY MUSEUM: Presents the history of medicine in Hawaii and the history of The Queen's Hospital, founded in 1860.

PROGRAMS: Exhibits; Research Library/Archives

COLLECTIONS: [1850s-present] Photos, original documents, record, letters, and clippings.

HOURS: Yr M-F 8:30-3:30

ADMISSION: No charge

1871
USS Arizona Memorial
1 Arizona Memorial Pl, 96818; (p) (808) 422-2771; (f) (808) 483-8608; (c) Honolulu

Federal/ 1980/ National Park Service/ staff: 21(f); 10(p); 20(v)

HISTORIC SITE: Collects, preserves, interprets, and commemorates the Pearl Harbor attack and the loss of the USS Arizona.

PROGRAMS: Exhibits; Film/Video; Guided Tours; Interpretation; Lectures; Research Library/Archives; School-Based Curriculum; Theatre

COLLECTIONS: [Early Pacific War 1941-1942] 25,000 photographs, 2,000 museum artifacts, 300 oral histories, and 400 books.

HOURS: Yr Daily 7:45-5

1872
USS Bowfin Submarine Museum and Park
11 Arizona Memorial Dr, 96818; (p) (808) 423-1341; (f) (808) 422-4201; bowfin@aloha.net; www.aloha.net/bowfin; (c) Honolulu

Private non-profit/ 1978/ Pacific Fleet Submarine Memorail Association/ staff: 55(f); 1(p)/publication: *On Eternal Patrol*

HISTORIC SITE; HISTORY MUSEUM: Preserves the history and unique heritage of the US submarine force.

PROGRAMS: Community Outreach; Elder's Programs; Exhibits; Film/Video; Guided Tours; Publication; Research Library/Archives; School-Based Curriculum; Theatre

COLLECTIONS: [WWII Submarine] Documents that relate to America's involvement and development of submarine warfare; WWII war patrol reports and files on submarines since 1900.

HOURS: Yr Daily

KAILUA

1873
Hawaiian Music Hall of Fame and Museum
Bishop Museum, 96734 [PO Box 1619, 96734]; (p) (808) 235-4742; (f) (808) 235-4742; hsqa@lava.net; www.hawaiimusicmuseum.org; (c) Honolulu

Private non-profit/ 1994/ staff: 11(v)/ members: 110/publication: *Ho'oha'i*

HISTORY MUSEUM: Preserves, protects, and promotes 165 years of traditional Hawaiian music and its significant contribution to Hawai'i's cultural history.

PROGRAMS: Concerts; Exhibits; Lectures; Publication; Research Library/Archives; School-Based Curriculum

COLLECTIONS: [1850-1970] Exhibits depicting Hawai'i's Royal music patrons, historical composers, musicians, and vocalists.

HOURS: Yr Daily 9:30-4:30

KAILUA KONA

1874
Hulihe'e Palace
75-5718 Ali'i Drive, 96740; (p) (808) 329-1877, (808) 329-9555; (f) (808) 329-1321

1838/ staff: 3(f); 4(p); 22(v)

COLLECTIONS: [1885] Hawaiian royalty - tapa, portraits, featherwork, quilts, furniture.; Hawaiian royalty clothing, jewelry etc.

HOURS: Yr

1875
Maritime Museum of the Pacific, The
Ali'i Dr at the Historic Kona Inn Shopping Village, 96745 [PO Box 4774, 96745]; (p) (808) 322-4779; MarMusPac@aol.com; www.members.aol.com/MarMusPac/index

1998/ Hawaii Maritme School/ staff: 5(v)/ members: 5

MARITIME MUSEUM: Specializes in the social and cultural maritime history of Hawaii and the Pacific rim.

PROGRAMS: Exhibits

COLLECTIONS: [1700s-present]

ADMISSION: Donations

KALAUPAPA

1876
Kalaupapa National Historical Park
Kalaupapa Settlement, 96742 [PO Box 2222, 96742]; (p) (808) 567-6802; (f) (808) 567-6729; KALA_Interpretation@nps.gov; www.nps.gov/kala/; (c) Kalawao

Federal/ 1980/ National Parks Service/ staff: 17(f); 2(v)

HISTORIC SITE: Preserves and interprets the historic Hansen's disease (leprosy) isolation settlements of Kalawao and Kalaupapa; protects the privacy and lifestyle of the patients that desire to remain in the settlements.

PROGRAMS: Exhibits; Guided Tours

COLLECTIONS: [1866-present] 40,000 items, primarily personal property of former patients and equipment from the medical facilities, plus archaeological material.

HOURS: Yr M-Sa, Scenic Overlook: Daily

KAMUELA

1877
Historic Parker Ranch Homes
66-1304 Mamalahoa Hwy, 96743 [PO Box 458, 96743]; (p) (808) 885-5433, (808) 885-7311; (f) (808) 885-5602

1862/ staff: 3(f); 1(p)

COLLECTIONS: [1809-present] French impressionists & neo-impressionists and Tang, Ming, Peking glass chinese pieces.

HOURS: Yr

KAPOLEI

1878
Hawaii State Historic Preservation Office
601 Kamokila Blvd #555, 96707; (p) (808) 692-8015; (f) (808) 692-8020; www.hawaii.gov/dlnr/hpdhpgreeting.htm; (c) Honolulu

State/ staff: 24(f)

HISTORIC PRESERVATION AGENCY

KEALAKEKUA

1879
Kona Historical Society
81-6551 Mamalahoa Hwy, 96725 [PO Box 398, Captain Cook, 96725]; (p) (808) 323-3222; (f) (808) 323-2398; khs@ilhawaii.net; www.konahistorical.org; (c) Hawaii

1976/ staff: 8(f); 16(p); 10(v)/ members: 800/publication: *Guide to Old Kona*

HISTORIC SITE; HISTORICAL SOCIETY; HISTORY MUSEUM: Collects, preserves, and disseminates information on Kona's history during the post-contact period; operates 2 National Register sites; maintains research archives.

PROGRAMS: Annual Meeting; Community Outreach; Concerts; Elder's Programs; Exhibits; Family Programs; Film/Video; Garden Tours; Guided Tours; Interpretation; Lectures; Living History; Publication; Research Library/Archives; School-Based Curriculum

COLLECTIONS: [1850-1950] Artifacts, photos, archival materials primarily concerned with agricultural activities, ranching, coffee farming, and commercial activities in Kona.

HOURS: Yr 9-3

ADMISSION: Donations requested

KEKAHA

1880
KoKe'e Natural History Museum-Huio Laka
15 Mile Marker, Koke'e Rd, 96752 [PO Box 100, 96752]; (p) (808) 335-9975; (f) (808) 335-6131; kokee@aloha.net; www.aloha.net/~kokee/; (c) Kauai

Private non-profit/ 1952/ Huio Laka/ staff: 2(f); 5(p); 275(v)/ members: 445

HISTORIC SITE; HISTORY MUSEUM; LIVING HISTORY/OUTDOOR MUSEUM; RESEARCH CENTER: Promotes, stimulates, and encourages scientific and educational interest in the natural history of Kauai.

PROGRAMS: Annual Meeting; Community Outreach; Elder's Programs; Exhibits; Family Programs; Festivals; Guided Tours; Interpretation; Lectures; Reenactments; Research Library/Archives; School-Based Curriculum

COLLECTIONS: Small collection of Hawaiian stone artifacts, sea shells, and historic regional photos and papers.

HOURS: Yr Daily 9-4

ADMISSION: No charge

LAHAINA

1881
Lahaina Restoration Foundation
120 Dickenson St, 96761; (p) (808) 661-3262; (f) (808) 661-9309; lrf@maui.net; www.lahainarestoration.org/; (c) Maui

Private non-profit/ 1962/ staff: 3(f); 9(p); 240(v)

ALLIANCE OF HISTORICAL AGENCIES; HISTORIC SITE; HISTORY MUSEUM: Maintains the town of Lahaina, the first capital of the Hawaiian Islands, and restores it to Monarchy period. Properties include the Baldwin Home

PROGRAMS: Elder's Programs; Exhibits; Facility Rental; Guided Tours; Lectures; Research Library/Archives

COLLECTIONS: [1820-1950] Documented and pictorial history of the town, island, and the town, island, and the state.

HOURS: $3, Family $5, Seniors $2

LAUPAHOEHOE

1882
Ho'oikaika
35-2065 Old Mamalahoa Hwy, 96720 [PO Box 189, 96720]; (p) (808) 962-2200; (f) (808) 962-2202; (c) Hawaii

State/ 1996/ Laupahoehoe High and Elementary School/ staff: 5(p)/publication: *April Fools:The 1946 Tradegy of Laupahoehoe*

HISTORICAL SOCIETY: A student organization whose goal is to preserve and perpetuate the culture and history of the community.

PROGRAMS: Publication

COLLECTIONS: [1946] Oral histories documenting the effects of a tsunami which struck the community of Laupahoehoe on April 1, 1946.

1883
Laupahoehoe Train Museum
36-2377 Mamalahoa Hwy, 96764 [PO Box 358, 96764]; (p) (808) 962-6300; (f) (808) 962-6957; ltmhawaii@aol.com; (c) North Hilo

Private non-profit/ 1997/ Officers and Board of Directors/ staff: 10(v)/ members: 100

HISTORIC SITE; HISTORY MUSEUM; HOUSE MUSEUM: Preserves, promotes, and protects the historic, cultural, educational, social, civic, and economic interests of the N. Hilo and Hamakua districts while highlighting the history of railroads on the island of Hawaii.

PROGRAMS: Annual Meeting; Community Outreach; Elder's Programs; Exhibits; Festivals; Garden Tours; Guided Tours; Interpretation

COLLECTIONS: [1800s-1940s] Photos, memorabilia, and stories of railroads on the island; restored track and two pieces of rail stock.

HOURS: Yr M-F 9-4:30, Sa-Su 10-2

ADMISSION: $3, Student $2, Seniors $2; Under 5 free

LIHU'E

1884
Kaua'i Historical Society
4396 Rice St, 96766 [PO Box 1778, 96766]; (p) (808) 245-3373; (f) (808) 245-8693; khs@hawaiian.net; www.kauaihistoricalsociety.org; (c) Kaua'I

Private non-profit/ 1914/ Board of Directors/ staff: 2(f); 1(p); 50(v)/ members: 610

HISTORIC PRESERVATION AGENCY; HISTORIC SITE; HISTORICAL SOCIETY: Collects, preserves, and disseminates the oral, written, and pictorial history of Kauai; provides educational programs.

PROGRAMS: Annual Meeting; Elder's Programs; Film/Video; Guided Tours; Lectures; Living History; Publication; Research Library/Archives

COLLECTIONS: [1700-present] Historical archive on Kauai: photos, manuscripts, maps, and an audio visual collection.

HOURS: Yr M-F 8-4

ADMISSION: Donations accepted

1885
Kaua'i Museum Association
4428 Rice St, 96766 [PO Box 248, 96766]; (p) (808) 245-6931; (f) (808) 245-6864; info@hawaii.net; www.kauaimuseum.org; (c) Kaua'I

Private non-profit/ 1960/ Board of Trustees/ staff: 8(f); 4(p); 75(v)/ members: 1000/publication: *Kaua'i Museum Quilt Collection*

ART MUSEUM; HISTORIC SITE; HISTORY MUSEUM: Promotes an appreciation and respect for the indigenous and immigrant people of Kaua'i and Ni'ihau and their cultural heritages.

PROGRAMS: Annual Meeting; Elder's Programs; Exhibits; Family Programs; Festivals; Film/Video; Guided Tours; Interpretation; Lectures; Publication; Research Library/Archives; School-Based Curriculum

COLLECTIONS: Research archives containing oral histories, newspaper titles, manuscripts, books, 100 maps, and 5,000 photographs; 75 portraits and paintings and 3,000 artifacts.

HOURS: Yr M-F 9-4, Sa 10-4

ADMISSION: $5, Student $3, Children $1, Seniors $4

PAPAIKOU

1886
Hawaii Tropical Botanical Garden
27-717 Old Mamalahoa Hwy, 96781 [PO Box 80, 96781]; (p) (808) 964-5233; (f) (808) 964-1338; htbg@i_lhawaii.net; www.htbg.com

Private non-profit/ 1984/ Board of Directors/ staff: 15(f); 2(p)/ members: 3275/publication: *Garden News*

GARDEN; HISTORIC SITE; HISTORY MUSEUM; RESEARCH CENTER: Collects, preserves, and studies tropical rainforest plants; protects the existing rainforest ecology of Onomea Valley; promotes environmental awareness through education.

PROGRAMS: Annual Meeting; Exhibits; Garden Tours; Guided Tours; Interpretation; Living History; Publication; Research Library/Archives; School-Based Curriculum

COLLECTIONS: Focuses on the plant families: orchidaceae, zingiberaceae, heliconaiceae, maramtaceae, palmae, and araceae.

HOURS: Yr Daily 9-4

ADMISSION: $15, Children $5

PUUNENE

1887
Alexander and Baldwin Sugar Museum
3957 Hansen Rd, 96784 [PO Box 125, 96784]; (p) (808) 871-8058; (f) (808) 871-7663; sugar mus @maui.net; www.sugarmuseum.com; (c) Maui

Private non-profit/ 1980/ staff: 1(f); 6(p); 25(v)

HISTORY MUSEUM: Historical and cultural museum, adjacent to an operating sugar factory, that preserves and presents the history and heritage of the sugar industry and the multi-ethnic plantation life the industry engendered.

PROGRAMS: Community Outreach; Exhibits; School-Based Curriculum

COLLECTIONS: [1920s-1940s] Artifacts, photographs, and documents pertaining to the sugar industry and plantation life on Maui circa 1865-1965

HOURS: Yr M-Sa 9:30-4:30

ADMISSION: $5, Children $2

SCHOFIELD BARRACKS

1888
Tropic Lighting Museum
Bldg 361 Waianae Ave, 96858 [APVG-GAR-LM, DCA, USAG-HI, Fort Shafter, 96858-5000]; (p) (808) 655-0438; (f) (808) 655-8301; troplight1@juno.com; Heelin@schofield.army.mil; (c) Honolulu

Federal/ 1958/ Center of Military History, Dept of the Army/ staff: 2(f); 4(v)/publication: *25th I.D. History*

HISTORY MUSEUM: Collects, preserves, interprets, and displays the history and material culture of Schofield Barracks and the 25th infantry division.

PROGRAMS: Exhibits; Guided Tours; Publication; Research Library/Archives

COLLECTIONS: [1909-present] Artifact, memorabilia, and documents related to Schofield Barracks or the 25th infantry division.

HOURS: Yr T-Sa 10-4

ADMISSION: No charge

WAILUKU

1889
Bailey House Museum
2374-A Main St, 96793 [2374-A Main St, 96793]; (p) (808) 244-3326; (f) (808) 244-3920; www.mauigateway.com/~imctrigg/

1833/ staff: 3(f); 2(p)

COLLECTIONS: [17th c] 1,000 Hawn artifacts; 400 Missionary era artifacts; 19th century

paintings by Edward Bailey. Map's, manuscripts, documents, photos.

HOURS: Yr

1890
Maui Historical Society
2375 A Main St, 96793; (p) (808) 244-3326; (f) (808) 244-3920; www.mauimuseum.org

Private non-profit/ 1951/ staff: 3(f); 3(p); 100(v)/ members: 600/publication: *Maui Remembers, and others*

GARDEN; HISTORIC SITE; HISTORICAL SOCIETY; HISTORY MUSEUM: Collects and preserves the history and heritage of Maui; operates the Baily House Museum, an archival resource center, and historic gardens; conducts educational outreach lectures.

PROGRAMS: Annual Meeting; Community Outreach; Concerts; Elder's Programs; Exhibits; Garden Tours; Guided Tours; Interpretation; Lectures; Living History; Publication; Research Library/Archives; School-Based Curriculum

COLLECTIONS: [Precontact-1900] A mission home built in 1833 on the royal compound of Kahekili; Hawaiian artifacts, missionary era artifacts, 19th c oil paintings by Edward Baily, and other history materials.

HOURS: Yr M-Sa 10-4

ADMISSION: $4, Children $1, Seniors $3.50

1891
Maui Okinawa Kenjin Kai
688 Nukuwai Pl, 96793 [PO Box 1884, 96793]; (p) (808) 242-1560; (f) (808) 242-5952; (c) Maui

Private non-profit/ 1947/ Board of Directors/ staff: 1(p); 75(v)/ members: 395

HISTORY MUSEUM; HOUSE MUSEUM: Promotes, perpetuates, and encourages the appreciation of the Okinawan Heritage culture and arts; operates a museum.

PROGRAMS: Concerts; Elder's Programs; Exhibits; Facility Rental; Family Programs; Guided Tours; Lectures; Research Library/Archives

COLLECTIONS: [1920-present] Okinawan art, textiles, pottery, lacquerware, calligraphy, and dolls; display of first generation immigrants and artifacts.

HOURS: Yr

WAIPAHU

1892
Hawaii Okinawa Center
94-587 Ukee St, 96797-4214; (p) (808) 676-5400; (f) (808) 676-7811; (c) Honolulu

Private non-profit/ 1987/ Hawaii United Okinawa Assn/ staff: 3(f); 2(p); 80(v)

HISTORY MUSEUM: Honors the first Okinawan immigrants to HI and offers a place to perpetuate the Okinawan culture; home of the Hawaii United Okinawa Association.

PROGRAMS: Community Outreach; Exhibits; Facility Rental; Guided Tours; Research Library/Archives

COLLECTIONS: Artifacts and reference materials on the ethnic culture and immigrant history of Okinawans in HI.

HOURS: Yr M-F 8:30-5, Sa 9-3; or by appt

ADMISSION: Donations accepted

1893
Hawaii's Plantation Village
94-695 Waipahu St, 96797; (p) (808) 677-0110; (f) (808) 676-6727; alaike.lcc.hawaii.edu/openstudio/HPV/

Joint/ staff: 5(f); 4(p); 50(v)/ members: 1000/publication: *Friends Newsletter*

HISTORY MUSEUM; HOUSE MUSEUM: Preserves plantation history and maintains replicated plantation buildings: Puerto Rican House, Japanese Duplex, Filipino House, Okinawan House, and Korean House.

PROGRAMS: Annual Meeting; Community Outreach; Concerts; Elder's Programs; Exhibits; Facility Rental; Family Programs; Festivals; Garden Tours; Guided Tours; Interpretation; Lectures; Living History; Publication; Reenactments; Research Library/Archives; School-Based

COLLECTIONS: [Late 1900s-mid 1950s] Domestic artifacts, reconstructed and replicated structures that represent the material culture and ethnic diversity of early plantation history.

HOURS: Yr M-F 9-3, Sa 10-3

ADMISSION: $5, Children $3, Seniors $4

IDAHO

ALBION

1894
Albion Historical Museum
263 Whitman, 83311 [PO Box 83, 83311]; (p) (208) 673-6213; (c) Cassia

Private non-profit/ 1997/ ASN/SICE Alumni Association/ staff: 1(p); 1(v)/ members: 500

HISTORIC SITE; HISTORY MUSEUM; RESEARCH CENTER: Displays memorabilia and preserves the history of the state-abandoned college and of Albion's history as a stage stop and county seat.

PROGRAMS: Guided Tours

COLLECTIONS: [1893-1951] Photographs, memorabilia and written history of Albion State Normal and the Town of Albion.

HOURS: May-Sept Sa 10-5 or by appt

ADMISSION: Donations accepted

ALMO

1895
City of Rocks Historical Association
3010 Elba Almo Road, 83312 [PO Box 169, 83312]; (p) (208) 824-5519; (f) (208) 824-5563; cit@idpr.state.id.us; www.nps.gov/ciro/; (c) Cassia

Federal; State/ 1991/ City of Rocks National Reserve/ staff: 5(f); 9(p)/ members: 11

HISTORICAL SOCIETY: Promotes City of Rocks National Reserve through educational and interpretive services.

PROGRAMS: Annual Meeting; Community Outreach; Exhibits; Festivals; Guided Tours; Interpretation; Publication

HOURS: Yr May-Oct Daily 8-4:30, Nov-Apr M-F 8-4:30

AMERICAN FALLS

1896
Massacre Rocks State Park
3592 Park Ln, 83211; (p) (208) 548-2672; (f) (208) 226-2303; mas@idprstate.id.us; (c) Power

State/ Dept of Parks and Recreation/ staff: 3(f); 6(p)

HISTORIC SITE: Preserves local and natural history.

PROGRAMS: Festivals; Interpretation

COLLECTIONS: [1840-1869] Oregon Trail artifacts.

HOURS: Yr Oct-May M-F 8-8; June-Sept Daily 8-8

ADMISSION: $2

ARCO

1897
Craters of the Moon National Monument
Hwy 93 18 mi W of Arco, 83213 [PO Box 29, 83213]; (p) (208) 527-3257; (f) (208) 527-3073; www.nps.gov; (c) Butte

Federal/ 1924/ National Park Service/ staff: 12(f); 3(p); 10(v)/publication: *Unearthly Landscape, Around the Loop*

LIVING HISTORY/OUTDOOR MUSEUM: Preserves and interprets natural and cultural history through exhibits, guided walks and educational programs.

PROGRAMS: Exhibits; Family Programs; Film/Video; Guided Tours; Interpretation; Lectures; Living History; Publication

COLLECTIONS: Volcanic geology and associated natural and cultural history.

HOURS: Yr Daily

ATHOL

1898
Farragut State Park
13400 E Ranger Rd, 83801; (p) (208) 683-2425; (f) (208) 683-7416; far@idpr.st.id.us; www.idahoparks.org; (c) Kootenai

State/ 1965/ Dept of Parks and Recreation/ staff: 7(f); 11(p); 8(v)

HISTORIC PRESERVATION AGENCY: Natural, cultural, and historical interpretation.

PROGRAMS: Exhibits; Interpretation

HOURS: Visitor Center Yr Daily

ATLANTA

1899
Atlanta Historical Society
[PO Box 53, 83601]; (c) Elmore

Private non-profit/ 1989/ staff: 2(v)/ members: 25

GARDEN; HISTORIC SITE; HISTORICAL SOCIETY; HISTORY MUSEUM; HOUSE MUSEUM; LIVING HISTORY/OUTDOOR MUSEUM; RESEARCH CENTER: Preserves historic district, history of gold mining industries and pioneer cemetery.

PROGRAMS: Community Outreach; Concerts; Exhibits; Facility Rental; Festivals; Garden Tours; Guided Tours; Interpretation; Lectures; Publication; Reenactments; Research Library/Archives; School-Based Curriculum

COLLECTIONS: [1863-1910] Manuscripts, photos, 1910 jail building, 1880 log cabin, mining, and archives.

BELLEVUE

1900
Bellevue Historical Society, Inc.
209 N Main St, 83313 [PO Box 449, 83313]; (p) (208) 788-3628; (f) (208) 788-2092; (c) Blaine

1994/ staff: 25(v)

HISTORIC PRESERVATION AGENCY; HISTORIC SITE; HISTORICAL SOCIETY; HISTORY MUSEUM

PROGRAMS: Annual Meeting; Community Outreach; Exhibits; Lectures; Research Library/Archives

COLLECTIONS: [1883-1960] Original documents from the City of Bellevue government (day receipts, deeds, state communications), and photographs of mining activity in the

BLACKFOOT

1901
Bingham County Historical Museum
190 N Shilling, 83221 [581 N Ash, 83221]; (p) (208) 785-8065; (c) Bingham

County, non-profit/ 1974/ staff: 4(f); 2(p); 15(v)

HISTORIC SITE; HISTORY MUSEUM

PROGRAMS: Community Outreach; Exhibits; Facility Rental; Guided Tours; Interpretation

COLLECTIONS: [1880-1950] Native American artifacts, period furniture, photographs of Blackfoot, early 20th century clothing, and 1930 to 1969 newspapers.

HOURS: Apr-Oct W-F 1-4:30

ADMISSION: Donations accepted

1902
Idaho Potato Expo
130 NW Main, 83221 [PO Box 366, 83221]; (p) (208) 785-2517; potatoexpo@ida.net; (c) Bingham

Private non-profit/ 1990/ staff: 2(f); 4(p); 6(v)

HISTORY MUSEUM: Promotes the history of the potato-growing industry.

PROGRAMS: Exhibits; Guided Tours

COLLECTIONS: Housed in 1913 Oregon Short Line Railroad Depot; artifacts: Dan Quayle autographed potato, world's largest potato chip, exhibits and potato history video.

HOURS: May-Sept Daily 10-5

ADMISSION: $3, Family $8, Children $1, Seniors $3

BOISE

1903
Basque Museum and Cultural Center, Inc.
611 Grove St, 83702; (p) (208) 343-2671; (f) (208) 336-4801; (c) Ada

Private non-profit/ 1985/ Board President/ staff: 1(f); 1(p); 30(v)/ members: 600

HISTORY MUSEUM; HOUSE MUSEUM; RESEARCH CENTER: Interprets the history of the Basques in Idaho and their old world origins.

PROGRAMS: Annual Meeting; Community Outreach; Exhibits; Facility Rental; Guided Tours; Interpretation; Lectures; Research Library/Archives

COLLECTIONS: [1890s-present] Archives include oral histories, photographs, music archives, and extensive libraries regarding the Basques in the Western United States and their homeland.

HOURS: Yr T-F 10-4, Sa 11-3

ADMISSION: Donations accepted

1904
Friends of the Historical Museum
610 N Julia Davis Dr, 83702; (p) (208) 334-2120; (f) (208) 334-4059; (c) Ada

Private non-profit/ 1978/ Board of Directors/ staff: 4(p); 100(v)/ members: 200

HISTORICAL SOCIETY: Preserves Idaho's heritage through maintenance and support of Idaho Historical Museum.

PROGRAMS: Annual Meeting; Concerts; Exhibits; Facility Rental; Guided Tours; Lectures; Living History; Reenactments

COLLECTIONS: [1800] Fur trading, gold rush and pioneer settlement artifacts.

HOURS: Yr M-Sa 9-5,

1905
Idaho Association of Museums
610 N Julia Davis Dr, 83702; (p) (208) 334-2120; (c) Ada

Private non-profit/publication: *IAM Newsletter*

PROFESSIONAL ORGANIZATION

PROGRAMS: Annual Meeting; Community Outreach; Publication

1906
Idaho Black History Museum, Inc.
508 Julia Davis Dr, 83702; (p) (208) 433-0017; (f) (208) 433-0048; www.ibhm.org; (c) Ada

Private non-profit/ 1995/ Board of Directors/ staff: 1(f); 22(v)/ members: 750

HISTORIC SITE; HISTORY MUSEUM: Housed in historic Saint Paul Baptist Church building, Museum is dedicated to preserving the role Blacks in history and culture of Idaho.

PROGRAMS: Community Outreach; Concerts; Exhibits; Film/Video; Guided Tours; Publication

HOURS: Yr Tu-Sa 10-5, Su 1-5

ADMISSION: $2, Student $1, Seniors $1

1907
Idaho Botanical Gardens, Inc.
2355 N Penitentiary Dr, 83701 [PO Box 2140, 83701]; (p) (208) 343-8649; (f) (208) 343-3601; idbotgrd@micron.net; www.idahobotanicalgarden.org; (c) Ada

Private non-profit/ 1984/ Board of Directors/ staff: 3(f); 7(p); 130(v)/ members: 1155

GARDEN; HISTORIC SITE: Dedicated to the

advancement and appreciation of gardening, horticulture, and conservation, through plant collections and education programs.

PROGRAMS: Community Outreach; Concerts; Elder's Programs; Exhibits; Facility Rental; Family Programs; Festivals; Garden Tours; Guided Tours; Lectures; Publication; Research Library/Archives; School-Based Curriculum

COLLECTIONS: Gardens: herb, heirloom rose, alpine, English, Iris, meditation, water, cactus, peony, children's, Idaho native plant, butter fly/hummingbird and outlaw field.

HOURS: Apr-Sept M-Th 9-5, F 9-8, Sa-Su 10-6; Oct-Apr M-F 9-5, Sa-Su 12-4

ADMISSION: $3, Student $2, Seniors $2

1908
Idaho Historic Preservation Council, Inc.
[PO Box 1495, 83701-1495]; (p) (208) 424-5111; (f) (208) 242-6921; info@preservation idaho.org; www.preservationidaho.org; (c) Ada

Private non-profit/ 1972/ Board of Trustees and staff/ staff: 1(f); 15(v)/ members: 250

HISTORIC PRESERVATION AGENCY: Preserves the state's historic and cultural resources.

PROGRAMS: Annual Meeting; Guided Tours; Lectures; Publication; School-Based

1909
Idaho Military Historical Society/ Idaho Military History Museum
4040 W Guard, 83705 [4748 Lindberg, Bldg 924, Gowen Field, 83705]; (p) (208) 422-6128; (f) (208) 422-4837; gayle.alvarez@ idbois.ang.af.mil; www.inghro.state.id.us/ museum; (c) Ada

Private non-profit/ 1993/ Board of Directors/ staff: 1(f); 4(p); 30(v)/ members: 140/publication: *Pass in Review*

HISTORY MUSEUM: Preserves, displays and interprets military history and artifacts that have a geographical, cultural or historical tie to the people and state of Idaho.

PROGRAMS: Annual Meeting; Community Outreach; Exhibits; Guided Tours; Publication; Research Library/Archives

COLLECTIONS: [WWI-present] Model aircraft, pictorial history, uniforms, weapons and field equipment.

HOURS: Yr M-W 8-4, F-Su 12-4 and by special appt

ADMISSION: $2; Donations accepted

1910
Idaho Museum of Mining and Geology
2455 Old Penitentiary, 83712; (p) (208) 386-9876; idahomuseum@hotmail.com; (c) Ada

Private non-profit/ 1989/ staff: 20(v)/ members: 100

HISTORY MUSEUM: Promotes local history through educational programs and community outreach.

PROGRAMS: Annual Meeting; Community Outreach; Exhibits; Family Programs; Guided Tours; Interpretation; Lectures

COLLECTIONS: [1900-present] Historical photos, artifacts from early Idaho mining, gem and mineral specimens.

HOURS: April-Oct W-Su

1911
Idaho State Historical Museum
610 N Julia Davis Dr, 83702; (p) (208) 334-2120; (f) (208) 334-4059; jochoa@ishs.state.id.us; www2.state.id.us/ishs/index.html/; (c) Ada

State/ 1907/ Idaho State Historical Society/ staff: 9(f); 5(p); 300(v)

HISTORY MUSEUM: Preserves and interprets Idaho's cultural heritage through educational programs.

PROGRAMS: Community Outreach; Concerts; Exhibits; Facility Rental; Family Programs; Festivals; Guided Tours; Interpretation; Lectures; Living History; Publication; Reenactments; Research Library/Archives; School-Based Curriculum; Theatre

COLLECTIONS: Mining equipment, Chinese immigrant and apothecary items, armament, ethnographic, cameras, transportation.

HOURS: Yr M-Sa 9-5, Su 1-5

1912
Idaho State Historical Society
1109 Main St Ste 250, 83702-5642; (p) (208) 334-2682; (f) (208) 334-2774; sguerber@ishs.state.id.us; www2.state.id.us/ishs/index.html; (c) Ada

State/ 1881/ Board of Trustees/ staff: 37(f); 22(p); 328(v)/ members: 870/publication: *Idaho Yesterdays; Mountain Light; Timeline*

HISTORICAL SOCIETY: Identifies, preserves, and interprets Idaho's cultural heritage.

PROGRAMS: Community Outreach; Exhibits; Family Programs; Festivals; Guided Tours; Interpretation; Lectures; Living History; Publication; Reenactments; Research Library/ Archives

COLLECTIONS: [1863] Manuscripts, artifacts, photos, oral history, political history, genealogy, and ephemera.

1913
Old Idaho Penitentiary State Historic Site
2445 Old Penitentiary Rd, 83712; (p) (208) 334-2844; (f) (208) 334-3225; sthomas@ishs.state.id.us; www.state.is.us/ishs/index.html; (c) Ada

State/ 1974/ staff: 4(f); 5(p); 20(v)

HISTORIC SITE: Preserves and interprets this historic site and Idaho's cultural heritage.

PROGRAMS: Exhibits; Facility Rental; Film/Video; Guided Tours; Interpretation; School-Based Curriculum

COLLECTIONS: [1870-1973] Historic prison buildings including Territorial prison, Maximum Security, solitary confinement, death row and the gallows, prison artifacts, tattoo exhibit, transportation exhibit including historical motorized and non-motorized vehicles. J.C. weapons collection.

HOURS: June -Aug 10-5; Sept-May

BURLEY

1914
Cassia County Historical Society
East Main & Hiland, 83318 [PO Box 331, 83318]; (p) (208) 678-7172; (c) Cassia

County/ 1972/ staff: 2(f); 1(p)/ members: 153

HISTORICAL SOCIETY; HISTORY MUSEUM: Preserves local history.

PROGRAMS: Annual Meeting; Guided Tours; Living History; School-Based Curriculum

HOURS: Tu-Sa 10-5 and by appt

ADMISSION: Donation requested

CALDWELL

1915
Caldwell Kiwanis Events/Museum
2215 Washington Ave, 83605

LIVING HISTORY/OUTDOOR MUSEUM: Displays donated farm machinery.

PROGRAMS: Exhibits; Guided Tours

COLLECTIONS: Farm equipment.

HOURS: June 15-Sept 15 Su 1:30-4

ADMISSION: Donations accepted

CAMBRIDGE

1916
Cambridge Museum
15 N Superior, 83610 [PO Box 35, 83610]; (p) (208) 257-3485; shansen@cyberhighway.net; (c) Washington

City/ 1984/ staff: 7(v)

HISTORY MUSEUM: Maintains and displays elements of area history; small research area, active genealogical society.

PROGRAMS: Exhibits; Guided Tours; Interpretation; Lectures; Living History; Research Library/Archives

COLLECTIONS: [1868-1995] Artifacts, memorabilia and ephemera related to local history.

HOURS: W-Sa 10-4, Su 1-4

ADMISSION: Donations accepted

CATALDO

1917
Old Mission State Park
Exit 39, I-90, 83810 [Box 30, 83810]; (p) (208) 682-3814; (f) (208) 682-4032; old@idpr.state.id.us

State/ 1975/ Dept of Parks and Recreation/ staff: 2(f); 3(p)

HISTORIC SITE: Preserves and interprets Idaho's cultural and historical heritage, including Old Sacred Heart Mission.

PROGRAMS: Exhibits; Facility Rental; Festivals; Film/Video; Guided Tours; Interpretation; Lectures; Living History; Publication; School-Based Curriculum

COLLECTIONS: Coeur d'Alene Native American artifacts, Jesuit Missionary objects.

CHALLIS

1918
Land of the Yankee Fork Historical Association

12 mi up Yankee Fork, 83227 [PO Box 1086, 83227]; (p) (208) 838-2201; (c) Custer

1966/ staff: 3(f); 4(v)

HISTORIC PRESERVATION AGENCY; HISTORIC SITE: Preserves Custer's mining heritage through restoration and conservation efforts.

PROGRAMS: Annual Meeting; Exhibits; Film/Video; Guided Tours; Interpretation; Living History

COLLECTIONS: [1880] Mining artifacts, household items and period clothing.

HOURS: May-Sept Daily 10-6

1919
North Custer Historical Society

1203 S Main, 83226 [PO Box 776, 83226]; (p) (208) 879-2846; (c) Custer

Private non-profit/ 1978/ North Custer Historical Society/ staff: 10(v)

HISTORIC PRESERVATION AGENCY; HISTORICAL SOCIETY; HISTORY MUSEUM: Collects, preserves and maintains cultural and natural history of Custer County area and upper Salmon River.

PROGRAMS: Annual Meeting; Community Outreach; Exhibits; Interpretation

COLLECTIONS: Ranching, mining, logging artifacts, pioneer life, books, magazines, maps and documents.

HOURS: June-Oct F-Sa 11-5

ADMISSION: Donations accepted

COEUR D'ALENE

1920
Museum of North Idaho

115 NW Blvd, 83816 [PO Box 812, 83816-0812]; (p) (208) 664-3448; museumni@nidlink.com; (c) Kootenai

Private non-profit/ 1968/ Board of Trustees/ staff: 1(f); 30(v)/ members: 500

HISTORICAL SOCIETY; HISTORY MUSEUM: Preserves the history of Coeur d'Alene Region

PROGRAMS: Annual Meeting; Community Outreach; Exhibits; Facility Rental; Interpretation; Publication; Research Library/Archives

COLLECTIONS: [1890-1960] Artifacts related to agriculture, forest service, domestic life, textiles, railroads, photos and archive material.

HOURS: April-Oct Tu-Sa 11-5

COTTONWOOD

1921
Historical Museum at St. Gertrude's, The

Keuterville Rd, 83522 [HC 3 Box 121, 83522]; (p) (208) 962-7123; (f) (208) 962-8647; museum@camasnet.com; www.rc.net/boise/st_gertrude/history.html; (c) Idaho

1931/ Idaho Corporation of Benedictine Sisters/ staff: 3(f); 10(v)/ members: 35/publication: *Pioneer Days in Idaho County; Idaho Chinese Lore; and others*

HISTORY MUSEUM: Preserves and interprets natural and cultural history of Idaho.

PROGRAMS: Exhibits; Festivals; Interpretation; Lectures; Publication; Research Library/Archives; School-Based Curriculum

COLLECTIONS: [1870-1940] North Central Idaho settlement, mining, farming, ranching, medicine, weaponry, and monastery history.

HOURS: Yr T-Sa 9:30-4:30; May-Sept Su

COUNCIL

1922
Council Valley Museum

100 S Galena St, 83612 [PO Box 252, 83612]; dalefisk@juno.com; www.cyberhighway.net/~jcpeart; (c) Adams

City/ 1972/ staff: 5(v)

HISTORY MUSEUM: Preserves and interprets local history.

PROGRAMS: Exhibits; Guided Tours; Interpretation; Research Library/Archives

COLLECTIONS: [1876-1930] Artifacts, photos.

HOURS: June-Aug Tu-Sa 10-4, Su 1-4

CRAIGMONT

1923
Ilo-Vollmer Historical Society

109 E Main, 83523 [PO Box 61, 83523]; (p) (208) 924-5474; skuther@camasnet.com; www.rootsweb.com/~idlewis/; (c) Lewis

Private non-profit/ 1977/ staff: 20(v)

GENEALOGICAL SOCIETY; HISTORICAL SOCIETY: Preserves local history and genealogy.

PROGRAMS: Annual Meeting; Publication

COLLECTIONS: [1895-present] Birth, death and marriage records; area history books, military and census records, photos, oral histories, archives.

HOURS: Yr W 1:30-4:30

DUBOIS

1924
Heritage Hall

Reynolds St, 83423 [PO Box 53, 83423]; (p) (208) 374-5359; (c) Clark

City; County; State/ 1974/ City of Dubois/ staff: 6(p); 6(v)

HISTORIC SITE; HISTORY MUSEUM: Preserves Clark County archives and memorabilia in historic gothic revival Mission church.

PROGRAMS: Exhibits

COLLECTIONS: [1800] Period furnishing, tools, books and photos.

HOURS: June-Aug F 3-5 and by appt

FORT HALL

1925
Shoshone-Bannock Tribal Museum

Exit 80 I-15 Simplot Rd, 83203 [PO Box 793, 83203]; (p) (208) 237-9791; (c) Bannock

Tribal/ 1993/ Shoshone-Bannock Tribes/ staff: 1(f); 2(p); 1(v)

TRIBAL MUSEUM: Preserves and interprets tribal history and culture.

PROGRAMS: Exhibits; Festivals; Guided Tours; Interpretation

COLLECTIONS: [Prehistory-present] Baskets and tools, ceremonial clothing, dance regalia, horse ornamentation; Benedicte Wrensted photos of tribal members; beaded articles, buckskin crafts.

HOURS: Yr May-Aug

HAILEY

1926
Blaine County Historical Museum

220 N Main St, 83333 [PO Box 124, 83333]; (p) (208) 788-1801; (c) Blaine

Joint/ 1963/ Museum Board; City/ staff: 2(p); 10(v)

ART MUSEUM; GENEALOGICAL SOCIETY; HISTORIC PRESERVATION AGENCY; HISTORICAL SOCIETY

PROGRAMS: Annual Meeting; Exhibits; Guided Tours; Lectures; Living History

COLLECTIONS: All facets of the 115 year development of the City of Hailey with sections devoted to mining, the sheep industry and skiing. Holds an extensive political button collection.

HOURS: May-Sept W-M 10-5 or by appt

ADMISSION: Donations requested

HAYDEN LAKE

1927
Kootenai County Genealogical Society

8385 N Government Way, 83835; (p) (208) 772-5612; (f) (208) 772-5778; lachey@televar.com; www.ior.com/~jmakovec; (c) Kootenai

1979/ staff: 8(v)/ members: 28

GENEALOGICAL SOCIETY: Preserves local history through maintenance of area archives.

PROGRAMS: Research Library/Archives

COLLECTIONS: [1880-1990] Kootenai County civil records, marriage records, Cemeteries, census, criminal index, city directories, school census, newspapers, 16th century English parish records.

HOURS: Yr Su

IDAHO FALLS

1928
Bonneville Museum

200 N Eastern Ave, 83403 [PO Box 1784, 83403]; (p) (208) 522-1400; (f) (208) 522-3211; www.idahofallsmuseum.org; (c) Bonneville

Private non-profit/ 1975/ Bonneville County Historical Society/ staff: 3(p); 75(v)/ members: 308/publication: *City of Destiny*

HISTORY MUSEUM: Collects, preserves, cares for, studies, displays, and interprets the history of Bonneville County and its environs and makes that history available to the general public, local residents, public schools, researchers, historians, and specialists.

PROGRAMS: Annual Meeting; Community Outreach; Exhibits; Facility Rental; Guided Tours; Interpretation; Lectures; Publication; Research Library/Archives

COLLECTIONS: [1880s-present]

HOURS: Yr M-F

ISLAND PARK

1929
Herriman State Park of Idaho
HC66 Box 500, 83429; (p) (208) 558-7368; (f) (208) 558-7045; (c) Fremont

State/ Dept Parks and Recreation/ staff: 4(f); 7(p); 2(v)

HISTORIC SITE; LIVING HISTORY/OUT-DOOR MUSEUM: Preserves natural history.

PROGRAMS: Community Outreach; Exhibits; Facility Rental; Family Programs; Festivals; Guided Tours; Interpretation; Lectures; Living History; Research Library/Archives; School-Based Curriculum

COLLECTIONS: [1902-1977] Period furnishings, ranching and farming tools, personal effects of Union Pacific Railroad barons - Harriman, Guggenheim, and Jones Family.

HOURS: Yr Sunrise-Sunset

ADMISSION: $3

1930
Island Park Historical Society
4377 County Circle, 83429 [PO Box 224, 83429]; (p) (208) 558-7219, (208) 558-0991; cloudeg@fretel.com; (c) Fremont

Private non-profit/ 1992/ staff: 1(v)/ members: 62

HISTORICAL SOCIETY: Educates members about local history; preserves and protects historical information.

PROGRAMS: Annual Meeting; Exhibits; Guided Tours; Interpretation; Lectures; Publication; Research Library/Archives

COLLECTIONS: [1868-present] Artifacts, photos, audio and video cassettes, newspapers, written materials, books and magazines.

HOURS: Yr by appt

JEROME

1931
Jerome County Historical Society, Inc.
220 N Lincoln, 83338 [PO Box 50, 83338]; (p) (208) 324-5641; (c) Jerome

1981/ Board of Directors/ members: 105/publication: *JCHS Monthly Newsletter*

HISTORY MUSEUM: Preserves history of Southern Idaho.

PROGRAMS: Exhibits; Family Programs; Festivals; Interpretation; Living History; Research Library/Archives

COLLECTIONS: [20th c] Agricultural equipment, pioneer memorabilia.

HOURS: Yr T-Sa 1-5

ADMISSION: No charge

JULIAETTA

1932
Castle Museum
191 State St, 83535 [PO Box 454, 83535]; (p) (208) 276-3081; (c) Latah

Private non-profit/ 1970/ staff: 2(f)

HISTORIC SITE; HOUSE MUSEUM

PROGRAMS: Guided Tours

COLLECTIONS: [1890-present]

HOURS: Apr-Sept Su-Sa 10-4

ADMISSION: Donations accepted

KAMIAH

1933
Lewis County Historical Society
Main St, 83536 [PO Box 373, 83536]; (c) Lewis

County, non-profit/ 1977/ Board of Directors/ staff: 10(v)/ members: 38

HISTORIC PRESERVATION AGENCY; HISTORIC SITE; HISTORICAL SOCIETY: Preserves local history.

PROGRAMS: Elder's Programs; Exhibits; Family Programs; Film/Video; Lectures; Publication

COLLECTIONS: [19th c]

HOURS: June-Sept

KETCHUM

1934
Community Library Associaton-Regional History Dept
415 N Spruce Ave, 83340 [PO Box 2168, 83340]; (p) (208) 726-3493; wendyw@ketchum.lib.id.us; (c) Blaine

Private non-profit/ 1982/ Board of Directors/ staff: 2(f); 4(v)

HISTORY MUSEUM: Research center and depository for the preservation and storage of two dimensional historical materials relating to the Blaine County region.

PROGRAMS: Lectures; Research Library/Archives

COLLECTIONS: [1880-present] Books, journals, videos, ephemera, manuscripts, oral histories, audio tapes, newspapers, maps, scrapbooks, legal records, photographs, and periodicals.

HOURS: M-Sa

1935
Ketchum/Sun Valley Heritage and Ski Museum
First & Washington, 83340 [PO Box 2746, 83340]; (p) (208) 726-8118; (c) Blaine

Private non-profit/ 1995/ staff: 2(p); 12(v)/ members: 400

HISTORICAL SOCIETY; HISTORY MUSEUM: Preserves local history.

PROGRAMS: Annual Meeting; Community Outreach; Elder's Programs; Exhibits; Festivals; Guided Tours

COLLECTIONS: [1880] Ski equipment, clothing, ephemera; items related to fur trade, Native Americans, mining, WWI and II, Ernest Hemingway.

HOURS: June-Oct, Nov-Apr

LAVA HOT SPRINGS

1936
South Bannock County Historical Center Museum
110 E Main St, 83246 [PO Box 387, 83246]; (p) (208) 776-5254; (c) Bannock

1980/ Board of Directors/ staff: 3(p); 3(v)/ members: 90

HISTORICAL SOCIETY: Preserves and interprets local history.

PROGRAMS: Annual Meeting; Exhibits; Lectures; Publication; Research Library/Archives

COLLECTIONS: [1880-present] Hospital and pharmaceutical equipment, memorabilia.

HOURS: Yr Daily 12-5

ADMISSION: Donations accepted

LEWISTON

1937
Hells Gate State Park
3620 Snake River Ave, 83501; (p) (208) 799-5015; (f) (208) 799-5187; hellsgate@lewiston.com; (c) Nez Perce

State/ 1978/ Dept of Parks and Recreation/ staff: 6(f); 15(p); 10(v)

HISTORIC SITE

PROGRAMS: Exhibits; Family Programs; Guided Tours; Interpretation; Lectures; Living History

HOURS: Yr

ADMISSION: $2/vehicle

1938
Lewis-Clark Center for Arts and History
415 Main St, 83501; (p) (208) 799-2243; (f) (208) 799-2850; (c) Nez Perce

Private non-profit/ 1991/ staff: 2(f); 4(p); 258(v)/ members: 87

ART MUSEUM; HISTORY MUSEUM: Promotes local history and art.

PROGRAMS: Community Outreach; Concerts; Exhibits; Facility Rental; Festivals

HOURS: Yr M-F 11-4

ADMISSION: $1

1939
Nez Perce County Historical Society, Inc.
306 Third St, 83501; (p) (208) 743-2535; (c) Nez Perce

1960/ Board of Directors/ staff: 1(p); 6(v)/ members: 400/publication: *The Golden Age*

HISTORICAL SOCIETY: Collects and preserves history of Nez Perce County.

PROGRAMS: Annual Meeting; Community Outreach; Exhibits; Publication

COLLECTIONS: [1800-present] Native American and pioneer artifacts, exhibits, photos, archives, oral history Nez Perce County History.

HOURS: Mar-Dec Tu-Sa 10-4

ADMISSION: Donations accepted

MACKAY

1940
South Custer Historical Society
310 Capitol St, 83251 [PO Box 572, 83251]; (p) (208) 588-3148; (c) Custer

Private non-profit/ 1982/ staff: 20(v)/ members: 100

HISTORICAL SOCIETY: Preserves history and heritage of Lost River Valley; operates museum.

PROGRAMS: Publication

COLLECTIONS: [1900s] Mining and ranching tools, clothing, household items, railroad memorabilia, photos, early newspaper printing press.

HOURS: May-Sept Sa-Su 1-5

MALAD

1941
Oneida County Museum
86 W 400 N, 83253; (c) Oneida

County, non-profit/ staff: 1(p)

HISTORY MUSEUM

PROGRAMS: Exhibits

COLLECTIONS: [1864] Pioneer memorabilia, sewing machine, organs, clothing.

MCCALL

1942
Central Idaho Cultural Center
1001 State St, 83638 [PO Box 1761, 83638]; (p) (208) 634-4497; (f) (208) 634-7752; (c) Valley

Private non-profit/ 1992/ staff: 1(f); 1(p)/ members: 26

HISTORY MUSEUM; HOUSE MUSEUM; RESEARCH CENTER: Preserves local history through educational programs, exhibits and maintenance of regional historic archives.

PROGRAMS: Exhibits; Facility Rental; Guided Tours; Interpretation; Lectures; Research Library/Archives

COLLECTIONS: [Prehistory-present] Native American artifacts, maps, mining, logging, fire equipment, photos.

HOURS: Yr Sept-May M-F, June-Aug Su-Sa 10-5

MONTPELIER

1943
Bear Lake County Rails and Trails Museum
320 N 4th St, 83254 [Old Mill Rd, 83254]; (p) (208) 847-1069; www.oregontrailcenter.org; (c) Bear Lake

County; Private non-profit/ Bear Lake County Historical Society/ staff: 8(v)

HISTORIC PRESERVATION AGENCY; HISTORIC SITE; HISTORICAL SOCIETY; HISTORY MUSEUM

COLLECTIONS: Photographs of pioneer residents, artifacts, railroad exhibit, dairy exhibit and artifacts transported across the Oregon Trail.

HOURS: May-Sept

ADMISSION: Donations accepted

MOSCOW

1944
Appaloosa Museum and Heritage Center
2720 W Pullman Rd, 83843; (p) (208) 882-5578 x279; (f) (208) 882-8150; www.appaloosa.org; (c) Latah

Private non-profit/ 1975/ Board of Directors/ staff: 1(f); 1(p); 10(v)

HISTORY MUSEUM: Collects, preserves, studies and exhibits objects and information that illustrate the history of the Appaloosa horse.

PROGRAMS: Exhibits; Guided Tours; Lectures

COLLECTIONS: [1800-present] Native American artifacts, saddles and western artwork and photographs.

HOURS: Yr T-F 10-5, Sa 10-4

ADMISSION:

1945
Idaho Forest Fire Museum
310 N Main St, 83843; (p) (208) 882-4767; (f) (208) 882-0373; www.woodlandgifts.com; (c) Latah

Private non-profit/ 1996/ staff: 2(f); 4(p)

HISTORY MUSEUM: Preserves history of fire prevention through interpretive displays.

PROGRAMS: Exhibits; Interpretation

COLLECTIONS: [1910-present] Smokey Bear, fire prevention materials and equipment, archives.

HOURS: Yr M-F 9-4

1946
Latah County Historical Society
327 E Second, 83843; (p) (208) 882-1004; (f) (208) 882-0759; (c) Latah

Private non-profit/ 1968/ staff: 3(p); 40(v)/ members: 500

HISTORICAL SOCIETY; HISTORY MUSEUM; HOUSE MUSEUM; RESEARCH CENTER: Preserves local history through maintenance of historic house museum and educational exhibits.

PROGRAMS: Annual Meeting; Community Outreach; Exhibits; Family Programs; Garden Tours; Guided Tours; Interpretation; Lectures; Living History; Research Library/Archives; School-Based Curriculum

COLLECTIONS: [19th c-present] Archive, photos, Native American artifacts

HOURS: Yr Tu-Sa

1947
McConnell Mansion
110 S Adams St, 83843 [327 E Second, 83843]; (p) (208) 882-1004, (208) 882-0759

County/ 1886/ Latah County Historical Society/ staff: 3(p); 25(v)

HOUSE MUSEUM: The first owner of this early large home, the only Eastlake-style house in the area, was elected governor of ID.

COLLECTIONS: Furnishings, china glass.; Relate to the county history, residents genealogical

HOURS: Yr

1948
University of Idaho Library, Special Collections and Archives
Rayburn St, 83844-2351; (p) (208) 885-7951; (f) (208) 885-6817; speccoll@drseuss.lib. uidaho.edu; www.lib.uidaho.edu/special-collections/; (c) Latah

State/ University of Idaho/ staff: 4(f); 2(p)

HISTORY MUSEUM; LIBRARY AND/OR ARCHIVES: History of Idaho and the West.

PROGRAMS: Research Library/Archives

COLLECTIONS: [19th c-present] Materials related to Idaho, including books, correspondence, diaries, ledgers, financial records and photos.

HOURS: Yr M-F 8-5, summer

MULLAN

1949
Mullan Historical Society
229 Earle St, 83846 [PO Box 677, 83846-0677]; (p) (208) 744-1461; (c) Shoshone

Private non-profit/ 1985/ staff: 22(v)/ members: 20

HISTORIC PRESERVATION AGENCY; HISTORICAL SOCIETY; HISTORY MUSEUM: Preserves local history.

PROGRAMS: Annual Meeting; Exhibits; School-Based Curriculum

COLLECTIONS: [1880-present] Artifacts, memorabilia, period furnishing, mining, pioneer.

HOURS: June-Sept M-F

ADMISSION: Donations accepted

MURRAY

1950
Sprag Pole Museum, Inc.
General Delivery Box 425, 83874; (p) (208) 682-3901; (c) Shoshone

Private non-profit/ 1964/ State of ID/ staff: 8(v)

HISTORY MUSEUM: Gold and silver mining and logging history and areas history.

PROGRAMS: Community Outreach; Exhibits; Guided Tours

COLLECTIONS: [19th c-present] Over 100 separate collections; cameras, typewriters, rocks, bottles, guns, phonographs, medical equipment, toys, period furnishing, gems, minerals, mining equipment, logging, coins.

HOURS: Yr Su-Sa 8-8

ADMISSION: Donations accepted

NEZPERCE

1951
Nezperce Historical Society
412 Pine, 83543 [PO Box 14, 83543]; (p) (208) 937-2409; (c) Lewis

Private non-profit/ staff: 5(v)/ members: 5

HISTORIC PRESERVATION AGENCY

PROGRAMS: Exhibits; Guided Tours; Interpretation; Lectures; Publication

COLLECTIONS: [20th c]

HOURS: Summer by appt; July 2nd Sa

OAKLEY

1952
Oakley Valley Historical Association
140 W Main, 83346 [PO Box 239, 83346]; (c) Cassia

Private non-profit/ 1999/ staff: 6(v)/ members: 40

HISTORIC PRESERVATION AGENCY; HISTORICAL SOCIETY; HISTORY MUSEUM: Preserves history of Oakley Valley.

PROGRAMS: Annual Meeting; Exhibits; Guided Tours

COLLECTIONS: [1880-present]

HOURS: May-Sept M-Sa 10-5 or by appt

PARMA

1953
Parma Historical Society
Hwy 20/26 & Parma Rd, 83660 [PO Box 942, 83660]; (p) (208) 722-7608; atk@cyberhigh way.net; (c) Canyon

Private non-profit/ 1950/ staff: 12(v)/ members: 105

HISTORIC SITE; HISTORICAL SOCIETY; HISTORY MUSEUM: Preserves the history of Old Fort Boise and Oregon Trail.

PROGRAMS: Exhibits; Film/Video; Guided Tours; Interpretation

COLLECTIONS: Machinery, tools, clothing, transportation, furs, photos, Native American artifacts, blacksmith, books and artifacts related to Fort or Oregon Trail.

HOURS: June-Aug F-Su 1-4

ADMISSION: $1

POCATELLO

1954
Bannock County Historical Society
3000 Alvord Loop, 83204 [PO Box 253, 83204-0253]; (p) (208) 233-0434; (c) Bannock

Joint/ 1959/ staff: 1(f); 1(p); 3(v)/ members: 135/publication: *Annual newsletter*

HISTORICAL SOCIETY; HISTORY MUSEUM: Collects, preserves, exhibits, and interprets artifacts related to Bannock County history.

PROGRAMS: Annual Meeting; Exhibits; Guided Tours; Lectures; Research Library/Archives

COLLECTIONS: [1880s-1920s] Native American and railroad photographs, farm tools, stagecoach, 1916 La France pumper, belly dump/gravel wagon, printing press, two linotypes, clothing and toys.

HOURS: Sept-May T-Sa 10-2; June-Aug 10-6

ADMISSION: $2.50, Student $1.50, Children $0.50, Seniors $1.75

1955
Fort Hall Replica
911 N 7th, 83205 [PO Box 4169, 83205]; (p) (208) 234-6238; (f) (208) 234-6578; Adamnina@ci.pocatello.id.us; www.poky.inter speed.net/forthall/; (c) Bannock

City/ 1962/ staff: 3(p)

HISTORY MUSEUM: Preserves history of Old Fort and Oregon Trail through educational exhibits.

PROGRAMS: Exhibits; Guided Tours; Living History

COLLECTIONS: Replica of Old Fort Hall, blacksmith shop, Native American and frontiersman, fur trade.

HOURS: Daily 10-2; Summer Daily 10-6

1956
Idaho Museum of Natural History
5th & Dillon, 83209 [PO Box 8096, Idaho State Univ, 83209]; (p) (208) 236-3168; (f) (208) 236-5893; lancjean@isu.edu; (c) Bannock

State/ 1954/ staff: 9(f); 12(p)

HISTORY MUSEUM

PROGRAMS: Community Outreach; Concerts; Exhibits; Guided Tours; Publication

HOURS: M-Sa 10-4

ADMISSION: Donations

POST FALLS

1957
Post Falls Historical Society, Inc.
5th Ave & Frederick St, 83877 [PO Box 57, 83877-0057]; (c) Kootenai

Private non-profit/ 1988/ staff: 12(v)/ members: 200/publication: *Postfalls Historical Society News*

HISTORICAL SOCIETY: Preserves local history.

PROGRAMS: Annual Meeting; Exhibits; Festivals; Publication

COLLECTIONS: [1800] Oral history videos, photos, artifacts.

HOURS: Apr-Sept M-W 10-2

PRIEST LAKE

1958
Priest Lake Museum and Visitor Center
W Lakeshore Rd, 83856 [PO Box 44, Coolin, 83821-0044]; (p) (208) 443-2676; (c) Bonner

Federal; Private non-profit/ 1990/ Board of Directors/ staff: 50(v)/ members: 150/publication: *Museum Revue*

GARDEN; HISTORIC PRESERVATION AGENCY; HISTORIC SITE; LIVING HISTORY/OUTDOOR MUSEUM: Collects materials illuminating the cultural and natural history of the Priest Lake Region.

PROGRAMS: Annual Meeting; Exhibits; Family Programs; Guided Tours; Interpretation; Living History; Publication; Research Library/Archives

COLLECTIONS: [1930-1940] Exhibits related to logging, forestry, business, mining and Native Americans.

HOURS: May-Sept Tu-Su 10-4 and by appt

ADMISSION: Donations accepted

REXBURG

1959
Hess Heritage Museum
3409 E 1200 N, 83440 [275 S 2nd East, 83440]; (p) (208) 356-5674, (208) 356-5674; (c) Fremont

Private non-profit/ 1982/ staff: 40(v)/publication: *Journey in Time*

HISTORIC SITE; HISTORY MUSEUM; HOUSE MUSEUM; LIVING HISTORY/OUTDOOR MUSEUM: Preserves pioneer heritage.

PROGRAMS: Community Outreach; Exhibits; Facility Rental; Family Programs; Festivals; Film/Video; Guided Tours; Publication

COLLECTIONS: [1750-1920] 18th and 19th century furnishing, books, wagons, buggies, clothes, horse-drawn farm equipment, steam engines, tractors, snow travel, automobiles, school desks, and airplanes.

HOURS: Apr-Oct M, W-Sa by appt

ADMISSION: $3, Children $1

1960
Upper Snake River Valley Historical Society
51 N Center, 83440 [PO Box 244, 83440]; (p) (208) 356-9101; dhc@srv.net; (c) Madison

Private non-profit/ 1964/ staff: 15(v)/ members: 307/publication: *Snake River Echoes*

HISTORICAL SOCIETY; HISTORY MUSEUM: Preserves the history of Eastern Idaho, and the museum specializes in the collapse of the Teton Dam and its aftermath.

PROGRAMS: Annual Meeting; Exhibits; Film/Video; Guided Tours; Publication

COLLECTIONS: [1976] Collections include Teton flood exhibit and local history of Rexburg and upper Snake River valley.

HOURS: May-Sept M-Sa 10-5, Oct-Apr M-Sa 11-4

ADMISSION: $2,

RUPERT

1961
Minidoka County Historical Society
100 E Baseline, 83350 [PO Box 21, 83350]; (p) (208) 436-0336; (c) Minidoka

Private non-profit/ 1970/ Board of Directors/ staff: 1(f); 1(p); 20(v)/ members: 70

HISTORICAL SOCIETY: Operates Minidoka County Historical Society.

PROGRAMS: Annual Meeting; Exhibits; Guided Tours; Interpretation

COLLECTIONS: [1900] Russell steam engine, fire carts, household items, farm equipment; school, homestead, and jail memorabilia.

HOURS: Yr Daily 1-5

SAINT MARIES

1962
Hughes House Historical Society
538 Main St, 83861; (p) (208) 245-1501

1990/ staff: 25(v)/ members: 20

HISTORICAL SOCIETY; HOUSE MUSEUM

PROGRAMS: Community Outreach; Exhibits; Festivals; Interpretation

HOURS: W-Su 12-4

SALMON

1963
Lemhi County Historical Society Inc.
210 Main, 83467; (p) (208) 756-3342; (c) Lemhi
County/ 1960/ staff: 4(p)/ members: 23/publication: *Madame Charbonneau*

PROGRAMS: Publication

COLLECTIONS: Artifacts related to Native Americans, mining, medicine, railroad, and pioneer life.

ADMISSION: $1

SPALDING

1964
Nez Perce National Historic Park
3 mi N of Lapwai, Hwy 95, 83540 [Route One, Box 100, 83540]; (p) (208) 843-2261; (f) (208) 843-2001; nepesuperintendent@nps.gov

Federal/ 1965/ National Park Service/ staff: 30(f); 8(p); 10(v)

HISTORIC PRESERVATION AGENCY; HISTORIC SITE; HISTORY MUSEUM; RESEARCH CENTER: Preserves and interprets history of Nez Perce, including Missionary era, Westward expansion, mining, timber, transportation, Reservation era, Lewis and Clark Expedition. Sites include 1877 War battlefield, Nez Perce origins and archaeological sites.

PROGRAMS: Community Outreach; Elder's Programs; Exhibits; Family Programs; Film/Video; Guided Tours; Interpretation; Lectures; Research Library/Archives; School-Based Curriculum; Theatre

COLLECTIONS: [Prehistory-present] Plateau cultural material, photos, Watson's General Store artifacts and Spalding-Allen artifacts of Nez Perce Tribal collection.

HOURS: Yr Daily 8-5

STANLEY

1965
Sawtooth Interpretive and Historical Association
Hwy 75, 83278 [PO Box 75, 83278]; (p) (208) 774-3517; (f) (208) 774-3380; (c) Custer

Private non-profit/ 1972/ Board Directors/ staff: 1(f); 2(p); 11(v)/ members: 20

HISTORY MUSEUM: Promotes local history through education and interpretive exhibits.

PROGRAMS: Annual Meeting; Exhibits; Film/Video; Interpretation

COLLECTIONS: Gems

HOURS: May-Sept

SUN VALLEY

1966
Sun Valley Center for the Arts
191 Fifth St East, 83353 [PO Box 656, 83353]; (p) (208) 726-9491; (f) (208) 726-2344; svcenter@micron.net; www.sunvalleyid.com/svcenter; (c) Blaine

Private non-profit/ 1970/ staff: 9(f); 2(p); 400(v)/ members: 700

ART MUSEUM: Promotes art and art history through cultural and educational programs.

PROGRAMS: Annual Meeting; Community Outreach; Concerts; Exhibits; Family Programs; Festivals; Film/Video; Guided Tours; Interpretation; Lectures; Research Library/Archives; School-Based Curriculum; Theatre

COLLECTIONS: [13th c-present] 13th c illuminated manuscripts.

HOURS: Yr 9-5, Sa 11-5

TERRETON

1967
Mud Lake Historical Society
1055 E 1500 N, 83450 [PO Box 88, 83450]; (p) (208) 663-4376; (f) (208) 663-4376; potter@dedi.net; (c) Jefferson

Joint/ 1990/ staff: 5(v)

HISTORIC PRESERVATION AGENCY; HISTORICAL SOCIETY; HISTORY MUSEUM

PROGRAMS: Annual Meeting; Publication

COLLECTIONS: [1900] Pioneer artifacts.

HOURS: 1st and 3rd Th 1-4 and by appt

TWIN FALLS

1968
Twin Falls County Historical Society
Hwy 30, 3.5 mi W of city, 83301 [214 Meadows Lane, 83301]; (c) Twin Falls

County, non-profit/ 1957/ County Commissioners/ staff: 11(v)/ members: 25

HISTORICAL SOCIETY; HISTORY MUSEUM: Collects and promotes local history through museum preservation efforts.

PROGRAMS: Exhibits; Guided Tours

COLLECTIONS: [1850-1950] Bisbee photo archives, antique clothing, furnishings, tools, glassware, dolls and machinery.

HOURS: May-Sept Tu-Sa 1-5

WALLACE

1969
Northern Pacific Depot Museum
216 6th St, 83873 [PO Box 469, 83873]; (p) (208) 752-0111; (c) Soshone

Private non-profit/ 1983/ Northern Pacific Depot Foundation/ staff: 1(f); 3(p); 140(v)

HISTORY MUSEUM: Preserves history of Northern Pacific Railroad and its role in Shoshone County economic development.

PROGRAMS: Exhibits; Festivals

COLLECTIONS: [1886] Railroad artifacts, pictorial history.

ADMISSION: $2, Children $1, Seniors $1.50

1970
Sierra Silver Mine Tour
420 5th St, 83873 [PO Box 712, 83873]; (p) (208) 752-5151; (c) Shoshone

Joint/ 1981/ staff: 8(f); 2(p)

LIVING HISTORY/OUTDOOR MUSEUM: Preserves mining history through guided walking tours of local mines.

PROGRAMS: Exhibits; Guided Tours; Living History

COLLECTIONS: [1950-present] Mining equipment.

HOURS: May, June, Sept Daily 9-4; July-Aug Daily 9-6

1971
Wallace District Mining Museum
509 Bank St, 83873 [PO Box 469, 83873]; (p) (208) 556-1592; (c) Shoshone

Private non-profit/ 1956/ staff: 1(f); 3(p)

HISTORY MUSEUM; RESEARCH CENTER: Promotes the history of mining, pioneer life and mineral processing.

PROGRAMS: Exhibits; Family Programs; Film/Video; Guided Tours; Lectures; Research Library/Archives

COLLECTIONS: [1880-present] Mining artifacts, models, period furnishings, photos, paintings, quilts, interpretive signage, archives, newspapers, reference books, mineral specimens.

HOURS: Yr

ADMISSION: $2, Family $5, Children $0.50, Seniors $1.50

WINCHESTER

1972
Winchester Museum
McBeth Ave, 83555; (c) Lewis
City

HISTORY MUSEUM

COLLECTIONS: Pharmacy, lumbering, toys, agriculture, photos.

ILLINOIS

ADDISON

1973
Addison Historical Society
One Friendship Plaza, 60101-2786; (p) (630) 628-1433; (c) DuPage

City/ 1976/ staff: 1(p); 6(v)/publication: *Salt Creek Tattler*

HISTORY MUSEUM: Collects, preserves, and exhibits items pertaining to Addison history.

PROGRAMS: Exhibits; Guided Tours; Publication

COLLECTIONS: [Late 18th-early 19th c] Memorabilia pertaining to all periods of Addison's history.

HOURS: Sept-May Sa 10-2; June-Aug W 12-3

ALBION

1974
Edwards County Historical Society
212 W Main St, 62806; (p) (618) 445-2631; (f) (618) 445-3969; melrose@wworld.com; (c) Edwards

Private non-profit/ 1939/ staff: 6(v)/ members: 255/publication: *Edwards County Historical Society Newsletter*

GENEALOGICAL SOCIETY: Preserves history and genealogy of Edwards County, maintains the birthplace of former Illinois Governor Louis L. Emmerson, the 1859 Edwards County Jail, and a genealogical library.

PROGRAMS: Annual Meeting; Publication; Research Library/Archives

COLLECTIONS: [1818-present]

HOURS: Yr Th 6-9:30 and by appt

ALEDO

1975
Mercer County Historical Society
1402 SE 2nd Ave, 61231; (p) (309) 582-2280, (309) 584-4820; (c) Mercer

Private non-profit/ 1959/ staff: 2(p)/ members: 350

GENEALOGICAL SOCIETY; HISTORICAL SOCIETY; HISTORY MUSEUM: Preserves Mercer County history.

PROGRAMS: Annual Meeting; Community Outreach; Concerts; Exhibits; Facility Rental; Guided Tours; Lectures; Living History; Publication; Reenactments; Research Library/ Archives; School-Based Curriculum

COLLECTIONS: [1835-present] Period household items, agricultural, business, school books and records, local and county government records, and genealogy books and records.

HOURS: Apr-Oct W, Sa-Su 1-5

ADMISSION: No charge/Donations

ALTON

1976
Alton Area Historical Society
829 E 4th St, 62002 [PO Box 971, 62002]; (p) (618) 463-1795; mcgill@iw.edwpub.com; museum@altonweb.com; (c) Madison

Private non-profit/ 1948/ Board of Directors/ staff: 1(p); 35(v)/ members: 70/publication: *The Gentleman Giant, The Great Winged Monster of the Piasa Valley*

HISTORICAL SOCIETY

PROGRAMS: Annual Meeting; Lectures; Living History; Publication; Research Library/ Archives

COLLECTIONS: [1763-present] Books, manuscripts, letters, clippings, pamphlets, magazines, photographs, city directories and diaries.

HOURS: Yr Th-Sa 1-4

ADMISSION: Donations accepted

1977
Alton Area Landmarks Association
524 Belle St, 62002 [PO Box 232, 62002]; (p) (618) 463-5761; terryasharp@yahoo.com; (c) Madison

Private non-profit/ 1970/ members: 200

HISTORIC PRESERVATION AGENCY: Encourages the preservation and restoration of historic buildings and landmarks.

PROGRAMS: Community Outreach; Guided Tours; Lectures

COLLECTIONS: [19th-20th c] Includes historic Hart House.

1978
Elijah Lovejoy Memorial
[PO Box 214, 62002]; (p) (618) 466-5177; jer1008@yahoo.com

1947/ members: 171

HISTORICAL SOCIETY: Promotes the history of Elijah Lovejoy.

PROGRAMS: Annual Meeting; Exhibits; Interpretation; Lectures; School-Based Curriculum

COLLECTIONS: [WWII]

ANDOVER

1979
Andover Historical Society
418 Locust St, 61233 [PO Box 197, 61233]; (p) (309) 521-8378; (c) Henry

Private non-profit/ 1967

HISTORIC PRESERVATION AGENCY; HISTORIC SITE; HISTORICAL SOCIETY; HOUSE MUSEUM; RESEARCH CENTER

PROGRAMS: Annual Meeting; Community Outreach; Exhibits; Facility Rental; Family Programs; Festivals; Garden Tours; Guided Tours; Interpretation; Lectures; Living History; Monthly Meeting; Publication; Research Library Archives; School-Based Curriculum; Theatre

HOURS: June-Aug Su 1-4 or by appt

ADMISSION: Donations accepted

ANTIOCH

1980
Lakes Region Historical Society
817 Main St, 60002 [PO Box 240, 60002]; (p) (847) 395-7337; www.lake-online.com/lrhm; (c) Lake

Private non-profit/ 1973/ staff: 10(p); 15(v)/ members: 208

ALLIANCE OF HISTORICAL AGENCIES; HISTORIC PRESERVATION AGENCY; HISTORICAL SOCIETY; HISTORY MUSEUM: Preserves home, farm and business life of early Antioch and the Chain O'Lakes Region.

PROGRAMS: Community Outreach; Exhibits; Festivals; Guided Tours; Lectures; Publication; Research Library/Archives

COLLECTIONS: [1892-present] Schools, local organizations, farm, business, pioneer life.

HOURS: Mar-Dec Sa 11-3, and by appt

ADMISSION:

ARLINGTON HEIGHTS

1981
Arlington Heights Historical Society and Museum
110 W Fremont St, 60004; (p) (847) 255-1225; (f) (847) 255-1570; admuseum@ahpd.org; www.ahmuseum.org; (c) Cook

Joint/ 1957/ Village; Park District; AHHS/ staff: 1(f); 5(p); 150(v)/ members: 588/publication: *Chronicle of a Prairie Town; Pratorial History of Arlington Heights 1836-1936*

HISTORIC SITE; HISTORY MUSEUM: Searches out, collects, and preserves significant materials relating to the community. Includes Frederick W. Muller and Nathaniel M. Banta houses.

PROGRAMS: Annual Meeting; Concerts; Exhibits; Facility Rental; Festivals; Guided Tours; Interpretation; Lectures; Living History; Publication; Reenactments; Research Library/

Archives; School-Based Curriculum

COLLECTIONS: [1836-present] Photographs, maps, textiles, clothing, decorative arts, fine arts, tools, archival material, toys, oral histories and other information relating to local history.

HOURS: Yr Office: M-F 9-5; Gallery: Th-Su 1:30-4:30; Library: Th 1-4, F 9-12

ADMISSION: $2, Children $1; Donations accepted

AURORA

1982
Aurora Preservation Commission
44 E Downer Pl, 60507; (p) (630) 844-3648; (f) (630) 906-7430; (c) Kane

City/ 1979/ staff: 1(f); 1(p); 11(v)/publication: *Aurora, An Architectural Portrait*

HISTORIC PRESERVATION AGENCY: Designates, preserves, and promotes properties that reflect the city's historical, cultural, artistic or ethnic heritage or are representative of an architectural or engineering style.

PROGRAMS: Community Outreach; Publication; Research Library/Archives

HOURS: Yr M-F 8-5

1983
Aurora Regional Fire Museum
53 N Broadway, 60507 [PO Box 1782, 60507-1782]; (p) (630) 892-1572; (f) (630) 897-4147; (c) Kane

Private non-profit/ 1987/ Aurora Fire Station Preservation Corporation/ staff: 1(f)/ members: 38/publication: *Centennial Book*

HISTORY MUSEUM: Renovated 1894 Central Fire Station for its use as the charitable and educational Aurora Regional Fire Museum.

PROGRAMS: Exhibits; Facility Rental; Guided Tours; Publication; Research Library/Archives

COLLECTIONS: [1856-present] Artifacts, vehicles and photographs.

HOURS: Yr T-Sa 10-4

ADMISSION: $3.50, Children $1.50, Seniors $2.50

1984
Blackberry Farm's Pioneer Village
Galena Blvd & Barnes Rd, 60506 [100 S Barnes Rd, 60506]; (p) (630) 264-7405; (f) (630) 892-1661; www.foxvalleyparkdistrict.com; (c) Kane

1969/ Fox Valley Park District/ staff: 4(f); 80(p); 20(v)/ members: 1

LIVING HISTORY/OUTDOOR MUSEUM: Sixty acre park includes six living history sites, museums, barn area.

PROGRAMS: Community Outreach; Concerts; Exhibits; Facility Rental; Festivals; Garden Tours; Guided Tours; Interpretation; Lectures; Living History; Research Library/ Archives; School-Based Curriculum; Theatre

COLLECTIONS: [1840-1920] Agricultural implements, carriages, sleighs, household items, furniture and clothing.

HOURS: Apr-Sept Daily 10-4:30; Sept-Oct Fri-Sun 10-4:30

1985
Fox Valley Genealogical Society
5 E Galena Blvd, 60506; (p) (630) 896-1133;
(f) (630) 906-4127; thorn10@earthlink.net; (c)
Kane

Private non-profit/ 1957/ members: 450

1986
William Tanner House
305 Cedar St, 60506 [317 Cedar St, 60506];
(p) (630) 897-9029, (630) 905-0650; (f) (630)
905-0657

Joint/ 1856/ City; Aurora Historical Society/
staff: 1(f); 8(v)

COLLECTIONS: [1875-1900] High style Victorian furniture.

HOURS: Seasonal

AVON

1987
Avon Historical Society
AVCOM Park, 61415 [PO Box 483, 61415];
(p) (309) 465-7551; (c) Fulton

Private non-profit/ 1987/ members: 175

GENEALOGICAL SOCIETY; HISTORIC
PRESERVATION AGENCY; HISTORICAL SOCIETY: Operates a restored village depot as a
museum and a library in downtown Avon.

PROGRAMS: Annual Meeting; Community
Outreach; Exhibits; Festivals; Living History

COLLECTIONS: [1800-early 1900s] Railroad
tools, photographs, farming equipment, death
and marriage records, and local history.

HOURS: Aug F-Sa 4:30-6:30; Oct 1st two
weekends 8:30-5:30

ADMISSION: Donations accepted

BARRINGTON

1988
Barrington Area Historical Society, Inc.
212 W Main St, 60010; (p) (847) 381-1730; (f)
(847) 381-1766; (c) Lake

Private non-profit/ 1968/ staff: 1(f); 1(p); 600(v)

HISTORICAL SOCIETY; HISTORY MUSEUM;
RESEARCH CENTER: Keeps community history alive through preservation and education.

PROGRAMS: Annual Meeting; Community
Outreach; Exhibits; Guided Tours; Lectures;
Research Library/Archives; School-Based
Curriculum

BARTLETT

1989
Bartlett Historical Society
228 S Main St, 60103; (p) (630) 837-0800; (c)
Cook, DuPage, Kane

Private non-profit/ 1973/ staff: 1(p); 3(v)/ members: 25

HISTORY MUSEUM: Preserves the history of
Bartlett and the surrounding area.

PROGRAMS: Exhibits; Lectures

COLLECTIONS: [1873-present]

HOURS: Yr M-F 9-4:30, Sa 9-12

BEARDSTOWN

1990
Beardstown Museum, Inc.
101 W Third St, 62618; (p) (217) 323-3110;
(f) (217) 323-4029; (c) Cass

City/ 1829/ City of Beardstown/ staff: 25(v)

HISTORIC PRESERVATION AGENCY; HISTORIC SITE; HISTORICAL SOCIETY; HISTORY MUSEUM; PRESIDENTIAL SITE: Preserves the history of the town's courthouse
and its association with Abraham Lincoln, who
held court there.

PROGRAMS: Annual Meeting; Community
Outreach; Exhibits; Guided Tours; Interpretation; Reenactments

COLLECTIONS: [1890-1920] Arrowheads and
other Native American artifacts, paintings,
photographs, newspaper clippings, dishes,
guns, knives, swords, steamboat and aircraft
replicas, room settings, clothing, quilts, military
and railroad paraphernalia and the courtroom
where Lincoln practiced law.

HOURS: Yr Daily 8-5

ADMISSION: No charge

BELLEVILLE

1991
Belleville Public Library
121 E Washington St, 62220; (p) (618) 234-
0441, (618) 223-0441; (f) (618) 233-4947;
baa@lcls.org; (c) Saint Clair

City/ 1836/ staff: 14(f); 12(p); 5(v)

LIBRARY AND/OR ARCHIVES: One of the
oldest libraries in Illinois.

PROGRAMS: Community Outreach; Exhibits;
Facility Rental; Family Programs; Guided
Tours; Publication; Research Library/Archives

COLLECTIONS: [17th c-present] Serves the
interest of all ages through special collections
and archives that emphasize local and family
history; interlibrary loans through membership
in the Lewis and Clark Library System.

HOURS: Yr M-Th 9-8, F-Sa

1992
Saint Clair County Historical Society
602 Fulton St, 62220 [701 E Washington St,
62220]; (p) (618) 234-0600; (c) St Clair

Private non-profit/ 1905/ Board of Officers and
Directors/ staff: 1(f); 1(p); 50(v)/ members: 372

HOUSE MUSEUM; RESEARCH CENTER

PROGRAMS: Annual Meeting; Exhibits; Facility Rental; Family Programs; Research Library/Archives

COLLECTIONS: [1800s] 1830 furniture,
linens, dishes, and artifacts; St. Clair County
History books.

HOURS: 701 E Washington: M-F 10-2, 2nd Su
of Month 2-4; 602 Fulton: By appt

1993
St. Clair County Geneological Society
Belleville Public Library, 121 E Washington St,
62220 [PO Box 431, 62222-0431]; (p) (618)
295-2069, (618) 277-0848; www.compu-type.
net/rengen/stclair/stchome.htm; (c) St. Clair

Private non-profit/ 1977/ staff: 14(v)/ members:

500/publication: *The St Clair County Geneological Society Quarterly*

GENEALOGICAL SOCIETY: Preserves and
perpetuates ancestral records for educational
and historical purposes, encourages the study
of family history and teaches methods of research and publishes literature relating to the
purposes of the society.

PROGRAMS: Community Outreach; Lectures;
Publication; Research Library/Archives

COLLECTIONS: [1790-present] Microfilm and
photocopies of original church

BELLEVUE

1994
Margie Pfund Memorial Postmark Museum and Research Library
Historic Lyme Village Complex, St Rte 113 E,
44811 [1606 W Gilbert Ave, Peoria, IL,
61604]; (p) (309) 682-6774; (f) (309) 688-
4153; nextdayhill@prodigy.net; www.postmarks.org/museum/; (c) Sandusky

Private non-profit/ 1956/ Post Mark Collector's
Club/ staff: 1(f); 35(v)/ members: 800/publication: *The Postmark Bulletin*

HISTORIC PRESERVATION AGENCY; RESEARCH CENTER: Preserves postal history,
specifically postmark history.

PROGRAMS: Annual Meeting; Exhibits; Guided Tours; Publication; Research Library/
Archives

COLLECTIONS: [1800-present] Postal markings, archives, artifacts, and memorabilia related to postmark and postal history.

HOURS: May-Sept T-Su 12-4 and by

BELLFLOWER

1995
Bellflower Genealogical and Historical Society
Latcha St, 61724 [PO Box 140, 61724-0140];
(p) (309) 722-3458; (c) McLean

Private non-profit/ 1976/ staff: 5(v)/ members:
30

HISTORICAL SOCIETY: Collects Bellflower
items, newspaper articles, and cemetery
records.

PROGRAMS: Guided Tours

COLLECTIONS: [1871-present] High school
memorabilia, obituaries and scrapbooks.

HOURS: Yr by appt

ADMISSION: Donations accepted

BEMENT

1996
Bryant Cottage State Historic Site
146 E Wilson St, 61813 [PO Box 41, 61813];
(p) (217) 678-8184; (c) Piatt

State/ 1953/ Illinois Historic Preservation
Agency/ staff: 2(f)

HISTORIC PRESERVATION AGENCY; HISTORIC SITE; HOUSE MUSEUM: Built in 1856
as the home of businessman, Francis E.
Bryant, original structure of the mid-19th c.

PROGRAMS: Community Outreach; Festivals;
Interpretation; Reenactments

COLLECTIONS: [1818-1889] Original and period furnishings provide a glimpse of small town life in the mid-19th century.

HOURS: Mar-Oct Daily 9-5; Nov-Feb Daily 9-4

ADMISSION: $2, Children $1

BENSENVILLE

1997
Bensenville Historical Society
200 S Church Rd, 60106; (p) (630) 766-4642; (f) (630) 766-0788; jill@bensenville.lib.il.us; www.bensenville.lib.il.us/history; (c) DuPage

Private non-profit/ 1975/ staff: 12(v)/ members: 30

HISTORICAL SOCIETY; LIVING HISTORY/ OUTDOOR MUSEUM: Preserves and encourages an interest in the history of the community.

PROGRAMS: Community Outreach; Exhibits; Festivals; Guided Tours; Interpretation; Living History; Reenactments; Research Library/ Archives; School-Based Curriculum

COLLECTIONS: [1844-present] Photographs, oral histories and miscellaneous artifacts.

HOURS: Museum: Yr by appt; Library: Yr

BENTON

1998
Benton Public Library District
502 S Main St, 62812; (p) (618) 438-7511; (f) (618) 435-2150; www.sirin.lib.il.us; (c) Franklin

1916/ Board of Directors/ staff: 2(f); 5(p)

COLLECTIONS: [19th-20th c] Pamphlet file of local and county historical reference items, microfilm of the Benton Newspaper, local and state history books, and high school yearbooks.

HOURS: Yr M-Th 10-8, F-Sa 10-5:30, Su 1-5

BERWYN

1999
Berwyn Historical Society
1241 S Oak Park Ave, 60402 [PO Box 479, 60402]; (p) (708) 484-0020; (c) Cook

Private non-profit/ 1979/ Board of Directors/ staff: 50(v)/ members: 270/publication: *Stories of an Earlier Berwyn; Past-Times*

HISTORIC PRESERVATION AGENCY; HISTORICAL SOCIETY: Collects, preserves, and disseminates historical information relating to Berwyn and its residents.

PROGRAMS: Annual Meeting; Community Outreach; Exhibits; Guided Tours; Lectures; Publication

COLLECTIONS: [19th-20th c] Artifacts relating to the development of Berwyn and its people, museum artifacts, photographs and newspapers.

HOURS: Evenings/Weekends by appt

ADMISSION: Donations accepted

BISHOP HILL

2000
Bishop Hill Heritage Association
103 N Bishop Hill St, 61419 [PO Box 92, 61419]; (p) (309) 927-3899; (f) (309) 927-3010; bhha@winco.net; (c) Henry

Private non-profit/ 1962/ Board of Directors/ staff: 2(f); 4(p); 51(v)/ members: 230/publication: *Nobler Things to View; Bishop Hill Heritage Newsletter*

HISTORIC PRESERVATION AGENCY; HISTORIC SITE; HISTORY MUSEUM; LIVING HISTORY/OUTDOOR MUSEUM: Collects, preserves, and interprets the history of the Bishop Hill colonists and the town they built.

PROGRAMS: Annual Meeting; Community Outreach; Concerts; Exhibits; Facility Rental; Festivals; Guided Tours; Interpretation; Living History; Publication; Research Library/ Archives

COLLECTIONS: [1846-1920] Five colonial buildings, artifacts ,and archival pieces owned, produced or used by the original Bishop Hill colonists.

HOURS: Apr-Oct M-Sa 10-5, Su 12-5; Nov-Dec M-Sa 10-4, Su 10-4

ADMISSION: Donations accepted

2001
Bishop Hill State Historic Site
[PO Box 104, 61419]; (p) (309) 927-3345; (f) (309) 927-3345; (c) Henry

State/ 1946/ Illinois Historic Preservation Agency/ staff: 6(f); 4(p); 50(v)

HISTORIC SITE: Preserves, collects and interprets the remnants of the Bishop Hill Colony made up of three restored colonial structures and a contemporary museum.

PROGRAMS: Community Outreach; Concerts; Exhibits; Festivals; Interpretation

COLLECTIONS: [1846-1861] Material culture of the Bishop Hill Colony such as furniture, tools, ceramics, textiles, kitchen utensils, farm implements and archival items. Also includes Bishop Hill commemorative items and folk art works from Olaf Krans.

HOURS: Nov-Feb Daily 9-4; Mar-Oct Daily 9-5

ADMISSION: Donations

BLANDINSVILLE

2002
Blandin House Museum
215 S Chestnut St, 61420 [320 W Adams, 61420-9601]; (p) (309) 652-3673; (c) McDonough

Joint/ 1970/ Private non-profit; State/ staff: 12(v)/ members: 20

HOUSE MUSEUM: Collects and preserves memorabilia and artifacts of the community and provides a meeting place to share memories of the past.

PROGRAMS: Annual Meeting; Exhibits; Facility Rental; Guided Tours

COLLECTIONS: [20th c] Furniture, hand-crafted items, clothing, toys, hats, a history of the Blandin family, souvenirs of local celebrations, and photographs.

HOURS: Yr by appt; July 9-11: 2-9

ADMISSION: Donations accepted

BLOOMINGTON

2003
David Davis Mansion State Historic Site
1000 E Monroe Dr, 61701; (p) (309) 828-1084; (f) (309) 828-3493; www.state.il.us/hpa/davidd.htm; (c) McLean

1961/ State of Illinois/ staff: 4(f); 3(p); 120(v)

HISTORIC SITE; HOUSE MUSEUM: Preserves, researches and interprets Victorian social, political and cultural history.

PROGRAMS: Annual Meeting; Community Outreach; Exhibits; Facility Rental; Family Programs; Festivals; Garden Tours; Guided Tours; Interpretation; Lectures; School-Based Curriculum; Theatre

COLLECTIONS: [1872-1889] Architecture, ceramics, glass, furniture, historic objects, library and archival materials, musical instruments, paintings, photographic materials, textiles and costumes, watercolors, drawings and prints.

HOURS: Yr Th-M

2004
Illinois Great Rivers Conference Historical Society
1211 N Park St, 61702 [PO Box 515, 61702-0515]; (p) (309) 828-5092; (f) (309) 829-4820; www.gbgm-umc.org/igrac; (c) McLean

Private non-profit/ 1887/ The United Methodist Church/ staff: 4(p); 2(v)/ members: 300/publication: *Historical Messenger*

HISTORICAL SOCIETY; RESEARCH CENTER: Preserves records and resources of the Illinois Great Rivers Conference and predecessor domination of the United Methodist Church.

PROGRAMS: Annual Meeting; Community Outreach; Publication; Research Library/ Archives

COLLECTIONS: [1824-present] Local church histories, records, papers, Peter Cartwright memorabilia, predecessor denominations.

ADMISSION: No charge

2005
McLean County Museum of History
200 N Main St, 61701; (p) (309) 827-0428; (f) (309) 827-0100; mch@darkstar.rsa.lib.il.us; www.mchistory.org; (c) McLean

Private non-profit/ 1892/ McLean County Historical Society/ staff: 7(f); 5(p); 230(v)/ members: 1400/publication: *On The Square; and others*

HISTORIC SITE; HISTORICAL SOCIETY; HISTORY MUSEUM: Discovers and saves evidence of local history.

PROGRAMS: Annual Meeting; Community Outreach; Concerts; Exhibits; Facility Rental; Family Programs; Festivals; Guided Tours; Interpretation; Lectures; Publication; Research Library/Archives; School-Based Curriculum; Theatre

COLLECTIONS: [Prehistoric-present] Textiles, furniture, Native American artifacts; household, personal, military and farming items; library and archives of personal, business and organizational records; newspapers, periodicals, and photographs.

HOURS: Yr M-Th Sa 10-5, T 10-9; Sept-May Su 1-5

ADMISSION: $2, Children $1; Group rates

BOURBONNAIS

2006
Kankakee Valley Genealogical Society
250 W John Casey Dr, 60914 [PO Box 442, 60914]; (p) (815) 932-7567; (f) (815) 933-2516; marcias@keynet.net; www.rootsweb.com/~ilkankak; (c) Kankakee

Private non-profit/ 1968/ Board of Directors/Officers/ staff: 20(v)/ members: 150

GENEALOGICAL SOCIETY: Collects and preserves family, public and church records and promotes genealogical research.

PROGRAMS: Family Programs; Research Library/Archives

COLLECTIONS: [1800-present] Kankakee County historical, vital, church, census, cemetery and military records, publications from 40 genealogy societies.

HOURS: Yr M-Th 9-9; F, Sa 9-5

ADMISSION: No

BRIDGEPORT

2007
Lawrence County Genealogy Society
Route 1 Box 44, 62417; (p) (618) 945-7181; (c) Lawrence

1975/ staff: 4(v)/ members: 45

GENEALOGICAL SOCIETY; HISTORICAL SOCIETY: Promotes local history and provides genealogical research assistance.

HOURS: By appt

BRIMFIELD

2008
Jubilee College State Historic Site
11817 Jubilee College Rd, 61517; (p) (309) 243-9489; (c) Peoria

State/ 1985/ staff: 3(f); 4(p); 85(v)

HISTORIC PRESERVATION AGENCY; HISTORIC SITE: Promotes local history through preservation of Jubilee College as historic site.

PROGRAMS: Elder's Programs; Exhibits; Festivals; Guided Tours; Interpretation

COLLECTIONS: [1800s] Artifacts related to college, boarding school, seminary, prep school.

HOURS: Yr M-Su 9-5

ADMISSION: $2, Children $1

BUFFALO GROVE

2009
Raupp Memorial Museum
901 Dunham Lane, 60089 [530 Bernard Dr, 60089]; (p) (847) 459-2318; (f) (847) 459-3148; (c) Lake

1969/ Buffalo Grove Park District/ staff: 1(f); 1(p); 20(v)

HISTORY MUSEUM: Collects, preserves and interprets local history.

PROGRAMS: Exhibits; Family Programs; Fes-

tivals; Interpretation; Research Library/ Archives; School-Based Curriculum

COLLECTIONS: [1840-present] 3,000 artifacts, 500 photos, 300 documents and letters, 100 newspapers

HOURS: Yr M-W 2-5, Su 1-4

ADMISSION: No charge

BUSHNELL

2010
Bushnell Historical Society
300 Miller St, 61422 [c/o Donna Tracey, President, 22825 N 1900 Rd, 61422]; (p) (309) 772-3782; (c) McDonough

staff: 6(p); 40(v)

HISTORICAL SOCIETY; HISTORY MUSEUM

PROGRAMS: Annual Meeting; Exhibits; Festivals; Lectures

BYRON

2011
Byron Museum District
110 N Union St, 61010 [PO Box 186, 61010]; (p) (815) 234-5031; (f) (815) 234-7114; luciusread@mwci.net; (c) Ogle

Private non-profit/ 1991/ staff: 3(p); 20(v)/ members: 8

HISTORY MUSEUM: 1837 brick home that formed a portion of the Underground Railroad, owned by Lucius Read.

PROGRAMS: Exhibits; Facility Rental; Family Programs; Festivals; Guided Tours; Lectures; Publication; Reenactments; Research Library/Archives; School-Based Curriculum

COLLECTIONS: [1850-present] Artifacts include model of Byron, Civil War, WWI and WWII, 1900 school books and photos, agricultural equipment dating from early 1800s to early 1900s, including hand potato and corn planters.

HOURS: Yr Tu-F 9-3

CAHOKIA

2012
Cahokia Courthouse State Historic Site
107 Elm St, 62206; (p) (618) 332-1782; (f) (618) 332-1737; (c) St. Clair

State/ 1940/ Historic Preservation Agency/ staff: 3(f); 2(p); 65(v)

HISTORIC PRESERVATION AGENCY; HISTORIC SITE: Preserves and interprets Illinois' first French colonial settlement. Courthouse Museum examines Cahokia's influential role in the history of European and American domination of the Mississippi Valley.

PROGRAMS: Concerts; Exhibits; Festivals; Guided Tours; Interpretation; Living History; Reenactments

COLLECTIONS: [1740-1814] Focuses on cultural materials of the French and Native American Cahokians throughout the 18th-19th centuries. Uses artifacts, reproductions, graphics and texts displayed against Formica panels.

HOURS: Yr T-Sa 9-5

2013
Jarrot Mansion State Historic Site
124 E First St, 62206 [107 Elm St, 62206]; (p) (618) 332-1782; (f) (618) 332-1737; (c) St Clair

State/ 1807/ staff: 65(v)

HISTORIC PRESERVATION AGENCY; HISTORIC SITE: Preserves the 1810 Jarrot Mansion, oldest masonry building in Illinois.

PROGRAMS: Community Outreach; Concerts; Exhibits; Family Programs; Festivals; Guided Tours; Interpretation; Living History; Publication; Reenactments

COLLECTIONS: [1800-1818] Archaeological shards, period furnishing housed in historic

CAIRO

2014
Magnolia Manor
2700 Washington Ave, 62914 [PO Box 286, 62914]; (p) (618) 734-0201

1869/ staff: 1(f); 100(v)

COLLECTIONS: [1870s to 1900] Period furnishings and many original pieces.; Many 1st edition books.

HOURS: Yr; M- Sa 9-5, S; M- Sa 9-5, Su 1-5

CALUMET CITY

2015
Calumet City Historical Society
760 Wentworth Ave, 60409 [PO Box 1917, 60409]; (c) Cook

Private non-profit/ 1975/ Board of Directors/ staff: 10(v)/ members: 100

HISTORICAL SOCIETY; HISTORY MUSEUM: Operates a museum and archive and conducts meetings and programs monthly, in addition to a heritage day each September in an 1800's cabin with food, music and costumes.

PROGRAMS: Exhibits; Festivals; Guided Tours; Reenactments

COLLECTIONS: [Civil War-20th c] 20th century artifacts, clothes, municipal documents, maps, photos, US post office vestibule in oak and bronze, historic log cabin offsite.

HOURS: Yr Th 1-4, and by appt

CANTON

2016
Fulton County Historical and General Society
Parlin Public Library, E Chestnut, 61520 [PO Box 583, 61520]; (p) (309) 647-8817; wtjstracy@aol.com; (c) Fulton

Joint/ 1967/ County; Private non-profit/ staff: 20(v)/ members: 240

HISTORICAL SOCIETY: Provides assistance with genealogy and history research in Fulton.

PROGRAMS: Annual Meeting; Exhibits; Lectures; Publication; Research Library/Archives

COLLECTIONS: [1823-present] History and genealogy of Fulton County, along with global genealogy and military

CARBONDALE

2017
University Museum, Southern Illinois University
Faner Hall - C Wing, 62901 [Southern Illinois University, 62901-4508]; (p) (618) 453-5388; (f) (618) 453-7409; museum@siu.edu; www.museum.siu.edu; (c) Jackson

State/ 1869/ Southern Illinois Univ/ staff: 5(f); 21(p); 60(v)/ members: 75

ART MUSEUM; HISTORY MUSEUM: Preserves and promotes local and cultural history.

PROGRAMS: Community Outreach; Concerts; Exhibits; Facility Rental; Family Programs; Film/Video; Garden Tours; Guided Tours; Interpretation; Publication; Research Library/Archives; School-Based Curriculum

COLLECTIONS: [13th c-present] European and American paintings, drawings, prints, sculpture, metals, ceramics, musical instruments, opera costumes, period clothing, Oceania; geological and archaeological artifacts.

HOURS: Tu-Sa 9-3, Su 1:30-4:30

ADMISSION: No charge

CARMI

2018
Robinson-Stewart House Museum
110 S Main Cross St, 62821 [PO Box 121, 62821]

1814/ staff: 4(v)

COLLECTIONS: [1814-1900]

2019
White County Historical Society
218 E Main St, 62821 [PO Box 121, 62821]; (c) White

Private non-profit/ 1957/ staff: 20(v)/ members: 220/publication: *White County Historian*

HISTORIC SITE; HISTORICAL SOCIETY; HISTORY MUSEUM: Collects historical and genealogical material; maintains four museums and a genealogical library.

PROGRAMS: Annual Meeting; Community Outreach; Exhibits; Guided Tours; Publication; Research Library/Archives

COLLECTIONS: [1850-1950] Period furnishings, tools, genealogical material.

HOURS: Library: W 11-5; Museum: Oct 2nd Sa

CARTERVILLE

2020
Genealogy Society of Southern Illinois
c/o John Logan College, 700 Logan College Road, 62918; (p) (618) 985-3775, (618) 985-6213; dfozzard@midwest.net; www.jal.cc.il.us/gssi.html; (c) Williamson

Private non-profit/ 1973/ staff: 20(v)/ members: 1000/publication: *Saga of Southern Illinois; GSSI Newsletter*

GENEALOGICAL SOCIETY: Promotes and preserves genealogical research.

PROGRAMS: Annual Meeting; Publication

COLLECTIONS: Census, courthouse and cemetery records.

CARTHAGE

2021
Hancock County Historical Society
308 Walnut St, 62321 [PO Box 68, 62321-0068]; (p) (217) 357-0043; hancockhistory@yahoo.com; (c) Hancock

County, non-profit/ 1968/ staff: 15(v)/ members: 309/publication: *Hancock County Historical Society*

HISTORIC PRESERVATION AGENCY; HISTORIC SITE; HISTORICAL SOCIETY; HISTORY MUSEUM; LIBRARY AND/OR ARCHIVES: Preserves history of Hancock County.

PROGRAMS: Annual Meeting; Exhibits; Family Programs; Guided Tours; Lectures; Publication; Research Library/Archives

COLLECTIONS: [1835-present] Historical and vital records, newspapers, items related to genealogical and historical research.

HOURS: Yr M-F 9-3

ADMISSION: No charge

2022
Kibbe Hancock Heritage Museum
308 Walnut St, 62321 [306 Walnut St, 62321]; (c) Hancock

Private non-profit/ 1964/ Board of Directors/ staff: 1(p); 14(v)

ART MUSEUM; HISTORY MUSEUM: Preserves local history.

PROGRAMS: Community Outreach; Exhibits; Guided Tours

COLLECTIONS: [1938-1964] Biological and geological specimens from Alice Kibbe Chair of Biologic Studies-Carthage College, and local artifacts and county history.

HOURS: Yr 1-4

CATLIN

2023
Catlin Museum
210 N Paris, 61817; (p) (217) 427-5766

CHAMPAIGN

2024
Champaign County Historical Museum
102 E University Ave, 61820-4111; (p) (217) 356-1010; (f) (217) 356-1478; director@champaignmuseum.org; (c) Champaign

Private non-profit/ 1974/ Board of Trustees/ staff: 24(v)

HISTORY MUSEUM: Preserves local history.

PROGRAMS: Annual Meeting; Exhibits; Interpretation; Lectures; School-Based Curriculum

COLLECTIONS: [1875-present] Clothing, household articles, furniture, appliances, office equipment related to historic figures and institutions of Champaign County.

HOURS: Yr W-Su

2025
Illinois Heritage Association
602 1/2 E Green St, 61820; (p) (217) 359-5600; (f) (217) 344-6171; plmxiha@prairienet.org; www.illinoisheritage.prairienet.org; (c) Champaign

1981/ Board of Governors/ staff: 1(f); 1(p); 10(v)/ members: 300/publication: *Illinois Heritage Association Newsletter*

Promotes local and cultural history through research assistance, workshops, and classes.

COLLECTIONS: Extensive vertical file materials and books on museum and historic site administration, collection management and care, historic preservation, and local history.

HOURS: By appt

2026
Preservation and Conservation Association of Champaign
44 E Washington, 61825 [PO Box 2575 Station A, 61825]; (p) (217) 359-7222; (c) Champaign

Private non-profit/ 1981/ staff: 1(p); 35(v)/ members: 250

HISTORIC PRESERVATION AGENCY: Preserves history of Champaign County.

PROGRAMS: Annual Meeting; Community Outreach; Family Programs; Festivals; Guided Tours; Lectures

HOURS: Yr Sa 9:30-11

2027
Sousa Archives for Band Research
236 Harding Band Bldg, 1103 S 6th St, 61801; (p) (217) 244-9309; (f) (217) 333-2868; p-danner@uiuc.edu; www.library.uiuc.edu/sousa; (c) Champaign

1994/ University Library, U of Illinois at Urbana-Champaign/ staff: 1(f); 2(v)

LIBRARY AND/OR ARCHIVES: Maintains archives and music collections.

PROGRAMS: Community Outreach; Elder's Programs; Exhibits; Film/Video; Guided Tours; Lectures; Research Library/Archives; School-Based Curriculum

COLLECTIONS: Archival manuscript and published music collection of John Philip Sousa, Robert Clarke, Albert Austin Harding, Mark Hindsley, Harry Begian, and Richard Kent.

HOURS: Yr M-F 8:30-12, 1-5

ADMISSION: Donations accepted

CHAPIN

2028
Chapin Community Historical Society
Superior, 62628; (c) Morgan

Private non-profit/ 1977/ members: 26

HISTORICAL SOCIETY: Preserves local history.

PROGRAMS: Exhibits

COLLECTIONS: [1860-1960] Civil War, WWI, WWII, clothing, pictures, village ledgers and general stores.

HOURS: By appt only

ADMISSION:

CHARLESTON

2029
Coles County Genealogical Society
712 6th St, 61920 [PO Box 592, 61920]; (p) (217) 345-4913

Private non-profit/ 1975/ Board of Directors/ staff: 1(f); 1(v)/ members: 215/publication: *Among the Coles*

GENEALOGICAL SOCIETY; HISTORIC PRESERVATION AGENCY; RESEARCH CENTER: Collects and promotes genealogy and local history.

PROGRAMS: Annual Meeting; Publication; Research Library/Archives

COLLECTIONS: Genealogical and historical material, family files, census, cemetery and obituaries.

HOURS: Yr M-Th 10-8, F-S 10-6

2030
Coles County Historical Society
800 Hayes, 61920; (p) (217) 345-6755; (c) Coles

Private non-profit/ 1960

HISTORICAL SOCIETY; HISTORY MUSEUM

PROGRAMS: Exhibits; Publication;

CHENOA

2031
Chenoa Historical Society, Inc.
306 Green St, 61726 [PO Box 64, 61726]; (p) (815) 945-7356; (c) McLean

Private non-profit/ 1991/ staff: 10(v)/ members: 90

HISTORICAL SOCIETY: Researches, collects and preserves items related to the history of Chenoa to maintain a library and museum for historical materials. Conducts quarterly public programs and publishes a newsletter.

PROGRAMS: Exhibits; Lectures; Publication; Research Library/Archives

COLLECTIONS: [1854-present] Family histories, document, publications, local newspapers, pictures, scrapbooks, artifacts, school anvils and trophies.

HOURS: Yr by appt

ADMISSION: No

2032
Matthew T. Scott House
227 N 1st St, 61726; (p) (815) 945-4555

1855/ staff: 1(f)

HOUSE MUSEUM: Home of Matthew T. Scott, the founder of Chenoa. His sister-in-law married Adlai Stevenson I, later vice president of the US, in this house.

COLLECTIONS: Furnishings.

HOURS: Apr-Dec

CHESTER

2033
Randolph County Archives and Museum
Randolph County Courthouse, 62233 [1 Taylor St, 62233]; (p) (618) 826-5000; (f) (618) 826-2667; (c) Randolph

County, non-profit/ 1795/ Randolph County/ staff: 1(p); 15(v)

HISTORY MUSEUM; RESEARCH CENTER: Preserves and interprets first settlements and capital of Illinois.

PROGRAMS: Exhibits; Guided Tours; Interpretation; Research Library/Archives

COLLECTIONS: [Prehistory-1900] Photos, Native American artifacts, Kaskaskia manuscripts 1700-1800, documents, county artifacts.

HOURS: Yr M-F 8-4 and by appt

2034
Randolph County Genealogical Society
3rd Floor, 600 State St, 62233 [600 State St Rm 306, 62233]; (p) (618) 826-3807

Private non-profit/ 1990/ staff: 3(v)/ members: 170

GENEALOGICAL SOCIETY: Provides research and genealogical materials.

PROGRAMS: Guided Tours; Lectures; Publication; Research Library/Archives

COLLECTIONS: [Late 1800s-early 1900s] Birth, death and marriage records.

HOURS: Yr M, Tu 9-2

ADMISSION: No charge

2035
Randolph County Historical Society
104 Hillcrest Dr, 62233; (p) (618) 826-2667; (c) Randolph

Private non-profit/ 1953/ Board of Directors/ staff: 50(v)/ members: 110/publication: *Old Kaskia Days*

HISTORIC SITE; HISTORICAL SOCIETY; HOUSE MUSEUM: Collects, preserves, and interprets local history.

PROGRAMS: Annual Meeting; Exhibits; Family Programs; Festivals; Guided Tours; Interpretation; Publication

COLLECTIONS: [1690-1950] Furnished historic schoolhouse, Mississippi Transitional home, Shiloh College.

HOURS: By appt

ADMISSION: Donations requested

CHICAGO

2036
Adler Planetarium and Astronomy Museum
1300 S Lake Shore Dr, 60605; (p) (312) 322-0594; (f) (312) 341-9935; www.adlerplanetari um.org; (c) Cook

Private non-profit/ 1930/ staff: 100(f); 75(p); 100(v)/ members: 4500

HISTORY MUSEUM; RESEARCH CENTER

PROGRAMS: Annual Meeting; Community Outreach; Exhibits; Facility Rental; Interpretation; Lectures; Publication; Research Library/ Archives

COLLECTIONS: [1500-1900] Scientific instruments, books, documents relating to astronomy.

HOURS: Yr Daily 9-6

ADMISSION: $4; T free

2037
Archives of the Evangelical Lutheran Church in America
321 Bonnie Ln, 60631 [8765 W. Higgins Rd, 60631]; (p) (847) 960-9410; (f) (847) 960-9502; archives@elca.org; www.elca.org; (c) Cook

Private non-profit/ 1987/ Evangelical Lutheran Church in America/ staff: 8(f); 2(v)/publication: *ELCA Network News*

LIBRARY AND/OR ARCHIVES: Maintains an archives dating from Church's founding to the present.

PROGRAMS: Exhibits; Publication; Research Library/Archives

COLLECTIONS: [19th-20th c] Official archives of the Church and its predecessors. Includes records in all formats as well as the personal papers of church leaders and the official archives of several Lutherarn organizations.

HOURS: Yr M-F 8:30-5

2038
Canal Corridor Association
25 E Washington, Ste 1650, 60602; (p) (312) 427-3688; (f) (312) 377-2169; cca@canalcor. org; www.canalcor.org; (c) Cook

Private non-profit/ 1982/ Board of Directors/ staff: 6(f); 2(p)/publication: *Annual Report, Newsletters*

HERITAGE AREA: Promotes economic revitalization of the Illinois and Michigan Canal National Heritage Corridor through the preservation, conservation and enhancement of cultural and natural resources.

PROGRAMS: Community Outreach; Guided Tours; Interpretation; Lectures; Publication; School-Based Curriculum

COLLECTIONS: [1830-present]

HOURS: Yr M-F 9-5

2039
Chicago Architecture Foundation
224 S Michigan Ave, 60604; (p) (312) 922-3432; (f) (312) 922-2607; www.architecture.org; (c) Cook

1966/ Chicago Architecture Foundation/ staff: 24(f); 8(p); 450(v)/ members: 5000/publication: *A Walk Through Graceland Cemetery*

HISTORY MUSEUM

PROGRAMS: Community Outreach; Exhibits; Facility Rental; Family Programs; Guided Tours; Lectures; Publication

HOURS: Yr Daily

ADMISSION: $5

2040
Chicago Cultural Center
78 E Washington St, 60602; (p) (312) 744-6630; (f) (312) 744-2089; culture@ci.chi.il.us; www.ci.chi.il.us/Tour/CulturalCenter; (c) Cook

City/ 1991/ City of Chicago/ staff: 156(f); 125(v)/ members: 1000

COLLECTIONS: Housed in the first central Chicago Public Library, with largest Tiffany stained glass dome and permanent art collection.

HOURS: Yr M-W 10-6, Th 10-9, F 10-7, Sa 10-5, Su

2041
Chicago Genealogical Society
Box 1160, 60690; (p) (773) 725-1306; cphist@mc.net; (c) Cook

Private non-profit/ 1970/ staff: 12(v)/ members: 975/publication: *Chicago Genealogist*

GENEALOGICAL SOCIETY: Preserving and being a conduit for Chicago family history information and research.

PROGRAMS: Annual Meeting; Lectures; Publication

HOURS: 1st Sa Sept-June

2042
Chicago Heights Historic Preservation Advisory Committee
25 W 15th St, 60411; (p) (708) 754-0323; (f) (708) 754-0325; (c) Cook

1996/ staff: 11(v)

HISTORIC PRESERVATION AGENCY: Preserves local landmarks and historic structures.

PROGRAMS: Guided Tours

2043
Chicago Historical Society
1601 N Clark St, 60614-6099; (p) (312) 642-4600; (f) (312) 266-2077; brown@chicagohistory.org; www.chicagohistory.org; (c) Cook

Private non-profit/ 1856/ Chicago Historical Society/ staff: 109(f); 11(p); 87(v)/ members: 6000

HISTORICAL SOCIETY; HISTORY MUSEUM; RESEARCH CENTER: Research center specializing in evolving history of Chicago and Illinois.

PROGRAMS: Annual Meeting; Concerts; Elder's Programs; Exhibits; Family Programs; Guided Tours; Interpretation; Publication; Reenactments; Research Library/Archives; School-Based Curriculum

COLLECTIONS: [1600-present] 20 million objects, images and documents related to history of Chicago, Illinois and the US.

HOURS: Yr 9:30-4:30

ADMISSION: $5, Student $1,Seniors $3

2044
Chicago Jewish Historical Society
618 S Michigan Ave, 60605; (p) (312) 663-5634; (c) Cook

Private non-profit/ 1977/ Board of Directors/ members: 500

HISTORICAL SOCIETY: Preserves, collects, and shares the history of the Chicago Jewish community.

PROGRAMS: Annual Meeting; Exhibits; Guided Tours; Publication; Research Library/Archives

COLLECTIONS: [19th-20th c] Collections are held at the Chicago Jewish

2045
Chicago Lawn Historical Society
6120 S Kedzie Ave, 60629; (p) (312) 747-0639; (c) Cook

1938

HISTORIC PRESERVATION AGENCY; HISTORICAL SOCIETY

PROGRAMS: Annual Meeting; Community Outreach; Exhibits; Film/Video; Guided Tours; Research Library/Archives

COLLECTIONS: [1880-present] Artifacts, books and photos related to pioneer life, businesses and cultural groups.

HOURS: Yr 9-5

2046
Chicago Public Library Special Collections and Preservation Division
400 S State St, 60605; (p) (312) 747-4875; (f) (312) 747-4890; www.chipublib.org; (c) Cook

City/ 1873/ staff: 12(f); 1(p); 1(v)

LIBRARY AND/OR ARCHIVES: Collects, maintains, and preserves rare books, manuscripts, research and archival collections, art and artifact collections of Chicago Public Library

PROGRAMS: Community Outreach; Concerts; Exhibits; Facility Rental; Film/Video; Lectures; Research Library/Archives; Theatre

COLLECTIONS: [1820-present] 32,000 book volumes, manuscripts, photos, newspapers, ephemera, artifacts, artwork related to subject collections, WWII posters, weapons, uniforms, musical instruments relating to Civil War, theater archives and libraries public art collection.

HOURS: Yr Daily M 9-7, T, Th 11-7, W, F, S 9-5, Su 1-5

2047
Clarke House Museum
1821 S Indiana Ave, 60616 [1800 S Prairie Ave, 60616]; (p) (312) 745-0040; (f) (312) 745-0077

Joint/ 1982/ City of Chicago/ staff: 2(f); 35(v)/publication: *Candlesticks to Cupolas*

GARDEN; HISTORY MUSEUM; HOUSE MUSEUM: Interprets middle-class family life; highlights Greek Revival-style architecture and Chicago's history.

PROGRAMS: Community Outreach; Concerts; Exhibits; Garden Tours; Guided Tours; Interpretation; Lectures; Living History; Publication; Reenactments; School-Based Curriculum

COLLECTIONS: [1830-1860] Period furnishings, Native American trade silver, pre-1860 Chicago wallpapers, quilts, coverlets, food preparation tools, children's toys, architectural remnants, hunting accoutrements, maps and books on Chicago in the 1830s.

HOURS: Yr W-Su 12-4

ADMISSION: $8, Student $7

2048
Croatian Ethnic Institute
4851 S Drexel Blvd, 60615; (p) (773) 373-4670; (f) (773) 373-4746; croetljubo@aol.com; www.croatian-institute.org; (c) Cook

Private non-profit/ 1975/ Board of Directors/ staff: 1(f); 1(p); 40(v)/publication: *Croatian Almanac*

HISTORY MUSEUM: Maintains a central collection relating to 2.5 Million people of Croatian descent in the US and Canada, which includes archives, library, museum, and research center.

PROGRAMS: Community Outreach; Exhibits; Film/Video; Interpretation; Lectures; Living History; Publication; Research Library/Archives; School-Based Curriculum

COLLECTIONS: [1485-present] Old and rare books, Croatian periodicals and newspapers published in the US, books written and published by Croatian-Americans, folklore, artifacts, philately, records, and documents.

2049
DuSable Museum of African American History
740 E 56th Pl, 60637; (p) (773) 947-0600; (f) (773) 947-0677; www.dusablemuseum.org

Private non-profit/ 1961/ Board of Trustees/ staff: 40(f); 15(p); 30(v)/ members: 4289

HISTORY MUSEUM

PROGRAMS: Annual Meeting; Community Outreach; Concerts; Elder's Programs; Exhibits; Facility Rental; Family Programs; Festivals; Film/Video; Guided Tours; Lectures; School-Based Curriculum; Theatre

HOURS: Yr M-Sa 10-5, Su 12-5

ADMISSION: $3, Student $2, Children $1, Seniors $1

2050
Field Museum, The
1400 S Lake Shore Dr, 60605-2496; (p) (312) 922-9410; www.fmnh.org; (c) Cook

Private non-profit/ 1893/ Board of Trustees/ staff: 550(f); 200(p); 700(v)/ members: 22000

NATURAL HISTORY MUSEUM: Promotes natural history through exhibits and educational programs.

PROGRAMS: Community Outreach; Concerts; Exhibits; Facility Rental; Family Programs; Festivals; Film/Video; Guided Tours; Interpretation; Lectures; Research Library/Archives; School-Based Curriculum; Theatre

COLLECTIONS: 21 million biological and geological specimens and cultural objects, related books, periodicals, photos, illustrations, computer data, archive and instructional materials.

HOURS: Yr Daily 9-5

ADMISSION: $7, Student $4, Seniors $4

2051
Filipino American Historical Society of Chicago
3952 N Ashland Ave, 60615 [5472 S Dorchester Ave, 60615]; (p) (773) 947-8696; (f) (773) 955-3635; ealamar@aol.com; (c) Cook

Private non-profit/ 1986/ staff: 2(f); 5(v)/ members: 100

ART MUSEUM; HISTORIC PRESERVATION AGENCY; HISTORICAL SOCIETY; HISTORY MUSEUM; LIVING HISTORY/OUTDOOR MUSEUM; RESEARCH CENTER: Preserves Filipino American immigrant history in Chicago and surrounding area.

PROGRAMS: Annual Meeting; Community Outreach; Concerts; Exhibits; Family Programs; Festivals; Film/Video; Guided Tours; Lectures; Living History; Publication; Reenactments; Research Library/Archives; Theatre

COLLECTIONS: [1920-present] Photos, newspapers, memorabilia, artifacts, and archives of Filipino American immigrant community in Chicago.

HOURS: Yr Sa-Su 2-5 and by appt

ADMISSION: $3, Student $2, Seniors $2; Under 12 free

2052
Frank Lloyd Wright Building Conservancy
4657-B N Ravenswood Ave, 60640-4509; (p) (773) 784-7334; (f) (773) 784-7862; preservation@savewright.org; www.savewright.org/flw; (c) Cook

Private non-profit/ 1989/ staff: 2(f)/ members: 1200

HISTORIC PRESERVATION AGENCY: Facilitates the preservation of Wright-designed structures through education, advocacy, technical assistance and public outreach.

PROGRAMS: Annual Meeting; Publication

2053
Frederick C. Robie House
5757 S Woodlawn Ave, 60637 [951 Chicago Ave, Oak Park, 60302]; (p) (708) 848-1976

Joint/ 1909/ Univ of Chicago; Frank Lloyd Wright Home and Studio Foundation/ staff: 3(f); 4(p)

COLLECTIONS: [1909-1924] The Foundation's research center is located at the Frank Lloyd Wright Home and Studio.

HOURS: Yr

2054
Garfield Park Conservatory
300 N Central Park, 60624; (p) (312) 746-5100; (f) (773) 638-1777; (c) Cook

City; Joint/ 1908/ Chicago Park District/ staff: 30(f)

GARDEN: Historic glass conservatory preserving rare and endangered tropical plants, Unusual annuals, hardy perennials.

PROGRAMS: Exhibits; Facility Rental; Garden Tours; Lectures

COLLECTIONS: Endangered tropical plants, economic botany, annuals, perennials.

HOURS: Yr Daily 9-5

ADMISSION: No charge

2055
Glessner House Museum
1800 S Prairie Ave, 60616; (p) (312) 326-1480; (f) (312) 326-1397; www.glessnerhouse.org

Private non-profit/ 1994/ Board of Directors/ staff: 8(f); 130(v)/ members: 300/publication: *Prairie Avenue News; In Our House*

ART MUSEUM; HISTORIC SITE; HISTORY MUSEUM; HOUSE MUSEUM: Promotes diverse audiences in exploring urban life and design through preservation and interpretation of the historic home of John and Frances Glessner on Chicago's Prairie Avenue.

PROGRAMS: Exhibits; Family Programs; Guided Tours; Interpretation; Lectures; Publication; Research Library/Archives

COLLECTIONS: [19th c] English arts and crafts furnishing, fine art, fabrics, books, and household items.

HOURS: Yr W-Su 12-4

ADMISSION: $7, Student $6, Senior $6

2056
Hellenic Museum and Cultural Center
168 N Michigan Ave, 4th Flr, 60601; (p) (312) 726-1234; (f) (312) 726-8539; (c) Cook

Private non-profit/ 1992/ staff: 2(f); 2(p); 30(v)/ members: 800

HISTORY MUSEUM: Preserves history of Greek immigrant experience in the U.S., and promotes Greek heritage and culture.

PROGRAMS: Community Outreach; Exhibits; Facility Rental; Lectures

COLLECTIONS: [Early 1900s] Preserves the items related to Greek immigration into the U.S., hand embroidered cloth.

HOURS: Yr T-F 10-4

ADMISSION:

2057
Historic Pullman Foundation
11111 S Forrestville Ave, 60628-4649; (p) (773) 785-3828; (f) (773) 785-8182; PullmanHPF@aol.com; (c) Cook

Private non-profit/ 1973/ Board of Directors/ staff: 2(f); 40(v)/ members: 700/publication: *Historic Pullman; Update*

HISTORIC SITE; HISTORICAL SOCIETY; HISTORY MUSEUM: Collects, preserves, and interprets the Pullman Historic Landmark District. Operates HPF Visitor Center.

PROGRAMS: Annual Meeting; Community Outreach; Exhibits; Facility Rental; Family Programs; Guided Tours; Publication; Research Library/Archives; School-Based Curriculum

COLLECTIONS: [1880-present] Photographs, maps, books and museum artifacts all relating to the Pullman Company, the town of Pullman or George M. Pullman.

HOURS: Visitor Center M-F 12-2, Sa 11-2, Su 12-3

ADMISSION: Donations requested

2058
Illinois Labor History Museum
28 E Jackson #1012, 60604; (p) (312) 663-4107; ilhs@mcs.com; (c) Cook

1969/ staff: 2(v)/ members: 425

HISTORICAL SOCIETY; HISTORY MUSEUM: Promotes local history through book and video publications.

PROGRAMS: Annual Meeting; Guided Tours; Research Library/Archives

COLLECTIONS: Photos, artifacts, videos and labor history.

HOURS: Yr 9:30-3:30

ADMISSION: No charge

2059
International Museum of Surgical Science
1524 N Lakeshore Dr, 60610; (p) (312) 642-6502; (f) (312) 642-9516; info@imss.org; www.imss.org; (c) Cook

1953/ Internal College of Surgeons/ staff: 3(f); 5(v)/ members: 200

HOUSE MUSEUM: Preserves history of surgical science.

PROGRAMS: Community Outreach; Exhibits; Facility Rental; Lectures; School-Based Curriculum

COLLECTIONS: [1850] Surgically specialized instruments from medieval ages to 1950; surgical and medical items from around the globe.

HOURS: Yr Tu-Sa 10-4

ADMISSION: $5,

2060
International Polka Association
4608 S Archer Ave, 60632; (p) (773) 254-7771; (f) (773) 254-8111; (c) Cook

Private non-profit/ 1968/ Executive Board/ members: 1000

HISTORY MUSEUM: Honors outstanding polka personalities who have made significant contributions to the advancement and promotion of Polka music.

PROGRAMS: Research Library/Archives

COLLECTIONS: Recordings, sheet music, musical instruments, and artifacts.

HOURS: Yr T 7:30 and by appt

ADMISSION: No charge

2061
Irving Park Historical Society
[PO Box 34749, 60634-4749]; (p) (773) 763-4303; (c) Cook

Private non-profit/ 1984/ staff: 9(v)/ members: 160

HISTORICAL SOCIETY: Collects and interprets history of Irving Park Community.

PROGRAMS: Guided Tours; Lectures; Publication; Research Library/Archives

COLLECTIONS: [1869-1930] Artifacts, manuscripts and ephemera related to development of Irving.

2062
Jane Addams Hull-House Museum
800 S Halstead St, 60607; (p) (312) 413-5353; (f) (312) 413-2092; jahh@uic.edu; www.uic.edu/jaddams/hull; (c) Cook

State/ 1967/ Univ of Illinois/ staff: 3(f); 6(p)

HISTORIC SITE; HOUSE MUSEUM: Commemorates social reformer Jane Addams, Hull-House settlement house workers and the near West side neighborhood of Chicago.

PROGRAMS: Exhibits; Guided Tours

COLLECTIONS: [1889-1935] Artifacts that relate to the history of the Hull-House settlement house and the neighborhood.

HOURS: Yr M-F 10-4

2063
Landmarks Preservation Council of Illinois
53 W Jackson Ste 752, 60604; (p) (312) 922-1742; (f) (312) 922-8112; www.lpci.org; (c) Cook

Private for-profit/ staff: 6(f); 2(p)/ members: 1600/publication: *The Cornerstone*

HISTORIC PRESERVATION AGENCY: Preseres historic and prehistoric cultural resources in Illinois, through its education and advocacy programs.

PROGRAMS: Annual Meeting; Community Outreach; Guided Tours; Lectures; Publication

COLLECTIONS: Photos of Chicago historic architecture.

ADMISSION: No charge

2064
Museum of Broadcast Communications
Michigan Ave at Washington, Chicago Cultural Ctr, 60602 [78 E Washington, 60602-4801]; (p) (312) 629-6000; (f) (312) 629-6009; www.mbcnet.org; (c) Cook

Private non-profit/ 1987/ staff: 7(f); 8(p); 8(v)/ members: 800

RESEARCH CENTER: Promotes broadcast communications through interactive exhibits, featuring a working radio and television studio.

PROGRAMS: Exhibits; Facility Rental; Family Programs; Film/Video; Guided Tours; Lectures; Research Library/Archives

COLLECTIONS: 85,000 hours of archival footage, 20,000 radio shows, 30,000 television programs, 10,000 news broadcasts and

2065
Museum of Science and Industry
57th St and Lake Shore Dr, 60637; (p) (773) 684-9844; (f) (773) 684-0026; www.msichicago.org; (c) Cook

Private non-profit/ 1929/ staff: 325(f); 470(p); 300(v)/ members: 20000

HISTORY MUSEUM: Collects artifacts that best reflect the developments of science, technolgy, and industry.

PROGRAMS: Annual Meeting; Community Outreach; Elder's Programs; Exhibits; Facility Rental; Family Programs; Film/Video; Lectures; Living History; Publication; Research Library/Archives; School-Based Curriculum; Theatre

COLLECTIONS: [19th c]

HOURS: Yr Summer: Daily 9:30-5:30; Sept-May M-F 9-4, Sa-Su and holiday 9-5:30

ADMISSION: $7, Children $3.50, Seniors $6

2066
National Vietnam Veterans Art Museum
1801 S Indiana, 60616; (p) (312) 326-0270; (f) (312) 326-9767; nvvamart@cs.com; (c) Cook

Private non-profit/ 1996/ Board of Directors/ staff: 7(f); 1(p); 4(v)/ members: 164/publication: *Vietnam: Reflexes and Reflections*

ART MUSEUM; HISTORY MUSEUM: Collects, preserves, and exhibits Vietnam War artifacts and art.

PROGRAMS: Community Outreach; Concerts; Exhibits; Facility Rental; Film/Video; Lectures; Publication

COLLECTIONS: [1960-1975] Weapon artifacts and art collection; paintings, sculptures, drawings, colleges, poetry, photographs, Vietnam War related artifacts.

HOURS: Yr T-F

2067
Newberry Library, The
60 W Walton St, 60610; (p) (312) 943-9090; (f) (312) 255-3513; reference@newberry.org; www.newberry.org; (c) Cook

Private non-profit/ 1887/ Board of Trustees/ staff: 85(f); 31(p); 400(v)/ members: 2500

PROGRAMS: Annual Meeting; Community Outreach; Concerts; Exhibits; Facility Rental; Lectures; Research Library/Archives

COLLECTIONS: Artifacts and exhibits related to history of Western Europe from Middle Ages to mid-20th century, and the Americas from first contact between Europeans and Native Americans.

HOURS: Yr M, F-Sa 9-5, T-W, Th 10-6

2068
Norwood Park Historical Society
5624 N Newark Ave, 60631; (p) (773) 631-4633; (c) Cook

Private non-profit/ 1973/ staff: 1(p)/ members: 325/publication: *The Journal*

HISTORIC PRESERVATION AGENCY; HISTORIC SITE; HISTORICAL SOCIETY; HISTORY MUSEUM; HOUSE MUSEUM: Noble Seymour Crippen House on site of the first white settler to the area.

PROGRAMS: Annual Meeting; Community Outreach; Exhibits; Facility Rental; Garden Tours; Lectures; Publication; Research Library/Archives

COLLECTIONS: [1870-1950] Documents and artifacts related to Village of Norwood Park and northwest Chicago from 1870.

HOURS: Yr Sa 12-4

2069
Oriental Institute Museum, The
1155 E 58th St, 60637; (p) (773) 702-9514; (f) (773) 702-9853; oi-museum@uchicago.edu; (c) Cook

1896/ Univ of Chicago/ staff: 13(f); 21(p); 90(v)/ members: 1935

HISTORY MUSEUM: Preserves and exhibits collection of artifacts from ancient Egypt, Mesopotamia, Syria, Palestine, Persia, and Anatolia, and educates about the civilizations of the ancient Near East.

PROGRAMS: Community Outreach; Exhibits; Family Programs; Film/Video; Guided Tours; Lectures; School-Based Curriculum

COLLECTIONS: [Prehistory-early present era] 108,000 registered objects: 26,000 Egyptian, 16,000 Mesopotamian, 21,000 Iranian, 19,000 Syro-Palestinian, 2,700 Anatolian and 14,000 Nubian; 165,000 photos, 250 cubic feet of documents and other archival material.

HOURS: Yr T, Th-Sa 10-4, W 10-8:30, Su 12-4

ADMISSION: No charge

2070
Polish Genealogical Society of America
984 N Milwaukee Ave, 60622; pgsamerica@aol.com; www.pgsa.org; (c) Cook

Private non-profit/ 1978/ staff: 40(v)/ members: 2000

GENEALOGICAL SOCIETY; HISTORICAL SOCIETY: Provides assistance with Polish-American genealogical and historical research.

PROGRAMS: Annual Meeting; Exhibits; Lectures; Publication; Research Library/Archives

COLLECTIONS: [16th c-present] Genealogical records.

HOURS: Yr 11-3

ADMISSION: No charge

2071
Polish Museum of America
984 N Milwaukee Ave, 60622-4101; (p) (773) 384-3352; (f) (773) 384-3799; pma@prcua.org; www.prcua.org/pma; (c) Cook

Private non-profit/ 1935/ Board of Directors/ staff: 6(f); 3(p); 18(v)/ members: 800/publication: *The PMA Newsletter*

HISTORY MUSEUM: The Museum preserves, presents, and promotes the history and culture of Poles in America and the Polish American community by means of exhibits and archival material.

PROGRAMS: Community Outreach; Concerts; Exhibits; Family Programs; Guided Tours; Lectures; Publication; Research Library/Archives

COLLECTIONS: [19th-20th c] Includes memorabilia associated with Maestro Paderewski, a significant portion of the Polish pavilion from the 1939 New York World's Fair and materials reflecting on the Polish community in Chicago.

HOURS: Yr M-Su 11-4

ADMISSION: Donations requested

2072
Ridge Historical Society
10621 S Seeley Ave, 60643; (p) (773) 881-1675; (c) Cook

1972/ Board of Directors/ staff: 1(f); 30(v)/ members: 250/publication: *RHS Newsletter*

HISTORICAL SOCIETY; HISTORY MUSEUM; RESEARCH CENTER: Collects, preserves and interprets local and architectural history of Beverly Hills-Morgan Park neighborhood of Southside Chicago.

PROGRAMS: Community Outreach; Exhibits; Family Programs; Interpretation; Lectures; Living History; Publication; Reenactments; Research Library/Archives

COLLECTIONS: [1837-present] Rock Island RR Suburban Line, pioneer history, period costumes,

2073
Society of American Archivists
527 S Wells St, 60607; (p) (312) 922-0140; (f) (312) 347-1452; info@archivists.org; www.archivists.org; (c) Cook

Private non-profit/ 1936/ staff: 8(f); 2(p)/ members: 3500

PROFESSIONAL ORGANIZATION: Provides leadership to ensure the identification, preservation, and use of records of historical value.

PROGRAMS: Annual Meeting; Publication

2074
Spertus Museum/Spertus Institute of Jewish Studies
618 S Michigan Ave, 60605; (p) (312) 322-1747; (f) (312) 922-3934; musm@spertus.edu; (c) Cook

Private non-profit/ 1924/ Spertus Institute/ staff: 10(f); 10(p); 40(v)/ members: 2000

ART MUSEUM; HISTORY MUSEUM: Preserves Jewish legacy through educational programs and exhibits on Jewish culture, religion and history.

PROGRAMS: Community Outreach; Elder's Programs; Exhibits; Family Programs; Festivals; Film/Video; Guided Tours; Interpretation; Lectures; Research Library/Archives; School-Based Curriculum

COLLECTIONS: 10,000 Judaica objects and artifacts, works of art reflecting 5,000 years of Jewish history and culture.

HOURS: Yr Su-W 10-5, Th 10-8, F 10-3

ADMISSION: $5,

2075
Swedish American Historical Society
5125 N Spaulding Ave, 60625-4816; (p) (773) 583-5722; (c) Cook

Private non-profit/ 1949/ staff: 1(p)/ members: 1000

COLLECTIONS: Artifacts related to Swedish American presence in Chicago.

HOURS: By appt only

2076
Swedish American Museum Association of Chicago
5211 N Clark, 60640; (p) (773) 728-8111; (f) (773) 728-8111; museum@samac.org; www.samac.org; (c) Cook

1976/ staff: 3(f); 3(p); 56(v)/ members: 1300/publication: SAMAC News

HISTORY MUSEUM: Promotes Swedish language, culture, and history of Swedish immigration to US.

PROGRAMS: Annual Meeting; Community Outreach; Concerts; Elder's Programs; Exhibits; Facility Rental; Family Programs; Festivals; Film/Video; Guided Tours; Interpretation; Lectures; Publication; Reenactments; Research Library/Archives; School-Based Curriculum; Theat

COLLECTIONS: [19th c] Personal effects of early Swedish immigrants.

HOURS: Yr T-F 10-3, Sa-Su 10-4

ADMISSION: $4, Children $2; Members free

2077
Ukrainian National Museum
721 N Oakley Blvd, 60612; (p) (312) 421-8020; (f) (773) 693-7479; hankewych@msn.com; www.ukrntlmuseum.org; (c) Cook

Private non-profit/ 1952/ staff: 4(v)/ members: 312

HISTORY MUSEUM

PROGRAMS: Community Outreach; Exhibits; Research Library/Archives

COLLECTIONS: [1900-present] Traditional folk arts, artwork, musical instruments, Pyskany, woodcarving, ceramics, regional costumes and embroidery.

HOURS: Yr Th-Su 11-4

ADMISSION: Donations accepted

CHILLICOTHE

2078
Chillicothe Historical Society
3rd & Cedar St, 61523 [PO Box 181, 61523]; (p) (309) 274-4268; (c) Peoria

Private non-profit/ 1971/ staff: 6(p); 12(v)/ members: 133

GENEALOGICAL SOCIETY; HISTORIC PRE-SERVATION AGENCY; HISTORICAL SOCIETY: Preserves and promotes local history.

PROGRAMS: Exhibits; Family Programs; Festivals; Guided Tours

COLLECTIONS: [1900-1930] Vintage clothing display, schoolroom, kitchen, military uniforms, artifacts, Native American artifacts, cameras, railroad display photos, postcards.

HOURS: W 9-12; 1st Su 1-4

CLINTON

2079
C.H. Moore Homestead
219 E Woodlawn, 61727; (p) (217) 935-6066

1867/ staff: 1(f); 1(p); 20(v)

COLLECTIONS: [1880s-1900] Library furniture and decor; WWI and II items; Columbian pottery; Indian relics.

HOURS: Seasonal

COBDEN

2080
Union County Historical and Genealogy Society and Cobden Museum
206 Front St, 62920 [104 Clemens, 62920]; (p) (618) 893-2067; (c) Union

Private non-profit/ 1961/ staff: 1(v)/ members: 75

GENEALOGICAL SOCIETY; HISTORICAL SOCIETY; HISTORY MUSEUM: Promotes and preserves local history and genealogy.

PROGRAMS: Exhibits; Research Library/Archives

COLLECTIONS: Native American artifacts, Anna Kirkpatrick pottery, pioneer and period artifacts.

HOURS: April-Nov Sa-Su 12:30-4:30

ADMISSION: No charge

COLLINSVILLE

2081
Cahokia Mounds Museum Society
30 Ramey St, 62234; (p) (618) 344-7316; (f) (618) 346-5162; www.cahokiamounds.com; (c) Madison

Private non-profit/ 1976/ staff: 2(f); 4(p)/ members: 400/publication: Cahokia-City of the Sun

HISTORICAL SOCIETY: Promotes the educational and scientific aspects of Cahokia Mounds. Supports activities that preserve, develop, or interpret Cahokia Mounds.

2082
Cahokia Mounds State Historic Site
30 Ramey St, 62234; (p) (618) 346-5160; (f) (618) 346-5162; cahokiamounds@ezl.com; www.cahokiamounds.com; (c) Saint Clair-Madison

State/ 1925/ Historic Preservation Agency/ staff: 13(f); 165(v)

HISTORIC SITE: Interpretive center/museum on the site of the largest prehistoric Indian settlement in America.

PROGRAMS: Community Outreach; Exhibits;

Facility Rental; Festivals; Guided Tours; Interpretation; Lectures; Research Library/Archives; School-Based Curriculum

COLLECTIONS: [AD 800-1400] Artifacts primarily from Cahokia and other Mississippian culture materials.

HOURS: Center: Daily 9-5;

2083
Collinsville Historical Museum
Collinsville Memorial Library, 62234 [408 W Main St, 62234-3018]; (p) (618) 344-1112; (f) (618) 345-6410; cve_ill@vax.lcls.lib.il.us; www.gatenet.lcls.lib.il.us/cve/cmpl.html; (c) Madison

City/ 1976/ Friends of the Museum Executive Board/ staff: 7(v)

HISTORICAL SOCIETY; HISTORY MUSEUM: Preserves city history through museum programs.

PROGRAMS: Exhibits; Film/Video; Guided Tours; Lectures

COLLECTIONS: [1810-present] Artifacts, writings and

COLUMBUS

2084
Bartholomew County Historical Society
524 Third St, 47201; (p) (812) 372-3541; (f) (812) 372-3113; bchs@hsonline.net; (c) Bartholomew

Private non-profit/ 1921/ staff: 1(f); 2(p); 3(v)/ members: 495/publication: Quarterly Connection

HISTORICAL SOCIETY; HISTORY MUSEUM: Provides educational experiences for all ages through exhibits, programs, demonstrations and research.

PROGRAMS: Annual Meeting; Community Outreach; Exhibits; Facility Rental; Festivals; Garden Tours; Guided Tours; Publication; Research Library/Archives; School-Based Curriculum

COLLECTIONS: [Early 19th c-present] Artifacts that represent the heritage of Bartholomew County.

HOURS: Yr T-F 9-4

ADMISSION: Donations accepted

CREVECOEUR

2085
Fort Crevecoeur Inc.
301 Lawnridge, 61610 [508 Scenic Park Dr, 61610]; (p) (309) 694-3193; (c) Tazewell

Private non-profit/ 1974/ Fort Crevecoeur Board of Dir/ staff: 15(f); 200(v)

HISTORY MUSEUM: Preserves fort history.

PROGRAMS: Exhibits; Festivals; Guided Tours; Interpretation; Living History; Reenactments

COLLECTIONS: [1680-1785] Native American, French, colonial artifacts and pictures.

HOURS: April-Dec T-Su 8-4

CRYSTAL LAKE

2086
Crystal Lake Historical Society, Inc.
[PO Box 1151, 60014]; (c) McHenry

Private non-profit/ 2000/ members: 90

HISTORICAL SOCIETY: Preserves, protects, and promotes the history of Crystal Lake.

PROGRAMS: Annual Meeting; Community Outreach; Exhibits; Guided Tours

COLLECTIONS: [19th-20th c] Photographs, newspapers, and artifacts pertaining to local history.

2087
McHenry County Illinois Genealogical Society
Box 184, 60014; (p) (815) 653-9459; cphist@mc.net; www.mcigs.org; (c) McHenry

Private non-profit/ 1981/ staff: 70(v)/ members: 330

GENEALOGICAL SOCIETY: Preserves history of McHenry County and Illinois family data.

PROGRAMS: Lectures; Research Library/ Archives

COLLECTIONS: [1830-present] Illinois county histories, census indexes, print census, McHenry County collection.

ADMISSION: No charge

DANVERS

2088
Danvers Historical Society
102 S W St, 61732; (p) (307) 963-4249; (c) McLean

Private non-profit/ 1977/ staff: 1(p); 30(v)/ members: 30

GARDEN; HISTORIC SITE; HISTORICAL SOCIETY: Preserves local history.

PROGRAMS: Annual Meeting; Community Outreach; Concerts; Elder's Programs; Exhibits; Facility Rental; Family Programs; Festivals; Garden Tours; Guided Tours; Interpretation; Lectures; School-Based Curriculum

DANVILLE

2089
Danville Junction Chapter, NRHS
E Benton St, 61834 [PO Box 1013, 61834-1013]; (p) (217) 748-6615; rickschro@aol.com; www.prairienet.org/djc-nrhs/; (c) Vermilion

Private non-profit/ 1969/ staff: 10(v)/ members: 80/publication: *Danville Flyer*

HISTORICAL SOCIETY; HISTORY MUSEUM: Preserves history of Chicago and Eastern Illinois Railroad and railroads of Western IN.

PROGRAMS: Guided Tours; Interpretation; Publication

COLLECTIONS: [1849-1980] Records of the Chicago and Eastern Illinois Railroad from 1849–1969.

HOURS: May-Sept Sa-Su 12-4

ADMISSION: No charge

2090
Danville Public Library-Archives
319 N Vermillion St, 61832; (p) (217) 477-5228; (f) (217) 477-5230; rallen@LTnet.his.org; www.danville.lib.il.us/arch.html; (c) Vermilion

City/ 1883/ Board of Trustees/ staff: 2(f); 3(p); 1(v)

LIBRARY AND/OR ARCHIVES: Serves as local genealogical depository.

PROGRAMS: Research Library/Archives

COLLECTIONS: [1826-present] Genealogy of East Central Illinois and West Central Indiana, with material for states migrating into Illinois.

HOURS: Yr M-Th 9-8, F-Sa 9-5:30

2091
Illiana Genealogical and Historical Society
215 W N St, 61834 [PO Box 207, 61834-0207]; (p) (217) 431-8733; ighs@danville.net; www.danvillevirtual.com; (c) Vermilion

1964/ Executive Board of Illiana Genealogical and Historical Society/ staff: 40(v)/ members: 750/publication: *Illiana Genealogist*

GENEALOGICAL SOCIETY; HISTORICAL SOCIETY; RESEARCH CENTER: Researches, gathers, and compiles materials related to Eastern Illinois and Western Indiana.

PROGRAMS: Annual Meeting; Publication; Research Library/Archives

COLLECTIONS: Periodicals and maps related to Vermillion County, CDs and books.

ADMISSION: $2

2092
Lamon House
1031 N Logan Ave, 61832 [116 N Gilbert St, 61832]; (p) (217) 442-2922

1840/ staff: 16(v)

COLLECTIONS: [Late 1800s]

HOURS: Seasonal

2093
Vermilion County Conservation District
22296-A Henning Rd, 61834; (p) (217) 442-1691; (f) (217) 442-1695; vccd@soltec.net; www.vccd.org; (c) Vermilion

County/ 1966/ Board of Trustees/ staff: 20(f); 20(p); 80(v)/publication: *Conservationist*

GARDEN; LIVING HISTORY/OUTDOOR MUSEUM: Promotes local and natural history, conservation education, and historical interpretation.

PROGRAMS: Community Outreach; Elder's Programs; Exhibits; Facility Rental; Family Programs; Festivals; Garden Tours; Guided Tours; Interpretation; Lectures; Living History; Publication; Reenactments; School-Based Curriculum

COLLECTIONS: Period, pioneer, and reproduction homes and sites located in Bunker Hill historic area.

HOURS: May-Sept Daily 6am-11pm; Jan-Mar Daily 7-4:30; Apr, Oct-Dec Daily 7am-10pm

2094
Vermilion County Museum Society
116 N Gilbert St, 61832; (p) (217) 442-2922, (217) 442-2001; (c) Vermilion

Private non-profit/ 1964/ staff: 1(f); 4(p); 42(v)/ members: 758/publication: *The Heritage*

HISTORIC SITE; HISTORICAL SOCIETY; HOUSE MUSEUM: Preserves history related to Vermilion County.

PROGRAMS: Annual Meeting; Community Outreach; Facility Rental; Garden Tours; Guided Tours; Publication; Research Library/ Archives; School-Based Curriculum

COLLECTIONS: [1800-1900] Lincoln site built by pioneer doctor William Fithian, with period clothing, furnishing, books, photos, fine arts and artifacts related to Vermilion county.

HOURS: Yr T-Sa 10-5, Su 1-5

ADMISSION: $2

DARIEN

2095
Darien Historical Society
7422 Cass Ave, 60561; (p) (630) 964-7033; (c) DuPage

Private non-profit/ 1974/ staff: 11(v)/ members: 160

HISTORICAL SOCIETY: Preserves local history through educational programs and activities.

PROGRAMS: Annual Meeting; Facility Rental; Film/Video; Lectures

COLLECTIONS: [20th c] 1859 schoolhouse, textbooks, albums, agricultural tools and local government

DECATUR

2096
Decatur Genealogical Society Inc.
356 N Main St, 62525 [PO Box 1548, 62525-1548]; (p) (217) 429-0135; (c) Macon

Private non-profit/ 1964/ staff: 15(v)/ members: 600

GENEALOGICAL SOCIETY: Collects, preserves, and publishes genealogical records.

PROGRAMS: Annual Meeting

COLLECTIONS: Repository for Macon County records.

HOURS: Yr M 10-6, W Sa 10-4, Su 1-4

ADMISSION: Donation requested

2097
Governor Richard Oglesby Mansion
421 W William, 62522; (p) (217) 429-9422; (c) Macon

Private non-profit/ 1976/ Oglesby Mansion Board of Directors/ staff: 1(p); 50(v)/ members: 300/publication: *Oglesby Mansion News*

HISTORIC SITE: Preserves and restores home of Richard Oglesby, former governor, US Senator and Civil War Major General.

PROGRAMS: Guided Tours; Publication

COLLECTIONS: [1875-present]

HOURS: March-Dec last Su and by appt

ADMISSION: $2

2098
Homestead Prairie Farm/Trobaugh-Good House c/o Macon County Conservation District's Rock Springs Center
3939 Nearing Lane, 62521-9258; (p) (217) 423-7708; (f) (217) 423-2837; mccd@fgi.net; www.fgi.net/~mccd; (c) Macon

County/ 1980/ Conservation District Board of Trustees/ staff: 1(f); 2(p); 30(v)

HISTORIC SITE; HISTORY MUSEUM: Preserves local history through maintenance of historic farm and homestead.

PROGRAMS: Community Outreach; Family Programs; Guided Tours; Interpretation; Living History; School-Based Curriculum

COLLECTIONS: [1850-1860] Living history farm illustrating the transition from folk life to popular culture with advent of railroad.

HOURS: June-Oct Sa-Su 1-4 or by appt

ADMISSION: No charge

2099
James Millikin Homestead
125 N Pine St, 62526; (p) (217) 422-9003, (217) 428-3807

2100
Macon County Historical Society and Museum Complex
5580 N Fork Rd, 62521; (p) (217) 422-4919; (f) (212) 422-4773; mchs@fgi.net; www.fgi.net/~mchs; (c) Macon

County/ Macon County/ staff: 2(f); 3(p); 508(v)/ members: 508

COLLECTIONS: [1830-present]

HOURS: Yr T-Su 1-4

ADMISSION: $2, Children $1

DEERFIELD

2101
Deerfield Area Historical Society
Deerfield Road & Kipling Place, 60015 [PO Box 520, 60015]; (p) (847) 948-0680; (c) Lake

Private non-profit/ 1968/ Board of Directors/ members: 400/publication: *Newsletter*

HISTORICAL SOCIETY; HISTORY MUSEUM; HOUSE MUSEUM: Preserves significant historical sites, buildings, and area artifacts.

PROGRAMS: Annual Meeting; Concerts; Elder's Programs; Exhibits; Family Programs; Festivals; Guided Tours; Lectures; Publication; Research Library/Archives; School-Based Curriculum

COLLECTIONS: [1830s-present] Photos, clothing, household furnishings, pioneer, schools, museum artifacts, books, newspapers and maps.

HOURS: June-Sept Su 2-4

DEKALB

2102
Ellwood House Museum
509 N First St, 60115; (p) (815) 756-4609; (f) (815) 756-4645; (c) Dekalb

Private non-profit/ 1966/ Ellwood House Association, Inc./ staff: 2(f); 2(p)/ members: 600/publication: *Ellwood House Herald*

HISTORY MUSEUM; HOUSE MUSEUM: Collects, preserves, and exhibits materials related to the career of Isaac Ellwood and the barbed wire industry; operates a historic house museum illustrating the lifestyle of a wealthy midwestern family in the late 19th and early 20th c.

PROGRAMS: Annual Meeting; Community Outreach; Concerts; Corporate History; Elder's Programs; Exhibits; Facility Rental; Festivals; Garden Tours; Guided Tours; Interpretation; Lectures; Publication; School-Based Curriculum

COLLECTIONS: [1870s-1920s] Five historic structures, barbed wire history, furnishings, decorative and fine arts, photographs, archival materials related to the Ellwood family, carriages, sleighs, historical staffordshire, costumes and textiles.

HOURS: Visitor Center: Mar-mid-Dec, 12-4:30

ADMISSION: $5, Children $1

DELAVAN

2103
Delavan Community Historical Society
320 Locust, 61734 [306 Locust, 61734]; (c) Tazewell

Private non-profit/ 1967/ staff: 13(v)/ members: 275

HISTORIC PRESERVATION AGENCY; HISTORICAL SOCIETY: Preserves local history.

PROGRAMS: Annual Meeting; Community Outreach; Exhibits; Guided Tours; Interpretation; Research Library/Archives

COLLECTIONS: [1837-present] Genealogical records and local artifacts.

HOURS: By appt

ADMISSION: No charge

2104
Wings and Things Museum, Inc.
1840 Brownwood Rd, 61734; (c) Tazewell

Private non-profit/ 1968/ staff: 1(f)

AVIATION MUSEUM: Static, flying, and full-size aircraft artifacts.

PROGRAMS: Exhibits; Guided Tours; Interpretation

COLLECTIONS: [1900-present] Airline artifacts, models, static and flying

DES PLAINES

2105
Des Plaines Historical Society
789 Pearson St, 60016-4506; (p) (847) 391-5399; (f) (847) 297-1710; (c) Cook

Private non-profit/ 1967/ staff: 3(f); 3(p); 50(v)/ members: 350/publication: *Cobweb*

HISTORICAL SOCIETY; HISTORY MUSEUM; HOUSE MUSEUM; RESEARCH CENTER: Collects, preserves and interprets city history and surrounding townships through exhibits, programs and educational services.

PROGRAMS: Annual Meeting; Community Outreach; Exhibits; Family Programs; Festivals; Guided Tours; Interpretation; Lectures; Publication; Research Library/Archives; School-Based Curriculum

COLLECTIONS: [19th c-present] Oral histories, manuscripts, microfilm, newspapers, clippings, files, genealogical information and 8,000 photographs.

HOURS: Feb-Dec M-F 9-4, Su 1-4

ADMISSION: Donations accepted

DIXON

2106
John Deere Historic Site
8393 S Main St Grand Detour, 61021-9406; (p) (815) 652-4551; (f) (815) 652-3835

1836/ staff: 7(f)

COLLECTIONS: [1836-1847]

HOURS: Seasonal

2107
Lee County Historical Society
113 Madison Ave, 61021 [PO Box 58, 61021]; (p) (815) 284-1134; lchs1@cin.net; www.leecountyhistory.com; (c) Lee

Private non-profit/ 1902/ staff: 4(v)/ members: 137

HISTORICAL SOCIETY; RESEARCH CENTER: Operates a research center and maintains a 106 year old log cabin.

PROGRAMS: Annual Meeting; Exhibits; Guided Tours; Research Library/Archives

COLLECTIONS: [1830-present] Papers, photos, microfilm and computer databases.

HOURS: Yr T, Th, Sa 9-3

ADMISSION: No charge

2108
Loveland Community House Museum
513 W Second St, 61021; (p) (815) 284-2741; (c) Lee

County/ 1946/ staff: 1(p); 1(v)

HISTORY MUSEUM; HOUSE MUSEUM; RESEARCH CENTER

PROGRAMS: Exhibits

COLLECTIONS: Pictures and personal items of town's founder, John Dixon and pioneer home furnishings, early farm tools, Native American artifacts, war items and clothing.

HOURS: Yr W, Th, F 9-12, 1st Sa 9-3

ADMISSION: No charge

2109
Ronald Reagan Boyhood Home
816 S Hennepin Ave, 61021; (p) (815) 288-3404; (f) (815) 288-6757

DOWNER'S GROVE

2110
Downer's Grove Museum, The
831 Maple Ave, 60515; (p) (630) 963-1309; (f) (630) 963-0496; mharmon@xnet.com; (c) DuPage

City/ 1969/ Park District/ staff: 1(f); 4(p); 35(v)

HISTORY MUSEUM: Collects, preserves, and interprets artifacts related to Downer Grove heritage.

PROGRAMS: Community Outreach; Exhibits; Family Programs; Festivals; Guided Tours; Interpretation; Lectures; Reenactments; Research Library/Archives

COLLECTIONS: [1832-present] 15,000 items, including archival materials, photos, maps, museum artifacts, period clothing, instruments, quilts, coverlets, tools, and china.

HOURS: Office/Research Yr M-F

DUNLAP

2111
Peoria Regional Museum Society
736 Wonderview Dr, 61525; (p) (309) 243-5616; (c) Peoria

1957/ staff: 20(v)/ members: 50

HISTORICAL SOCIETY: Collects and preserves historic and industrial artifacts.

PROGRAMS: Annual Meeting; Exhibits

COLLECTIONS: [19th-20th c] Steam train components, fire-fighting apparatus and other artifacts.

HOURS: May-Oct W-Su 12-5

ADMISSION: $4, Children $1.50

EAST CARONDELET

2112
Martin/Boismenue House
2110 1st St, 62240 [121 Lake Forest Dr, Belleville, 62220]; (p) (618) 397-3990; (f) (618) 397-7216

1790/ Historic Preservation Agency/ staff: 6(v)

COLLECTIONS: [1790-1830]

HOURS: By appt

EDWARDSVILLE

2113
Louisa H. Bowen University Archives, Southern Illinois University
Lovejoy Library, Southern Illinois Univ, 62026 [Box 1063, Southern Illinois Univ, 62026-1063]; (p) (618) 650-2665; (f) (618) 650-2717; skerber@siue.edu; www.library.siue.edu/; (c) Madison

State/ 1980/ Chancellor, Southern Illinois Univ/ staff: 2(f)

LIBRARY AND/OR ARCHIVES: Preserves academic and administrative records of Southern Illinois University.

PROGRAMS: Research Library/Archives

COLLECTIONS: [1965-present] Records of Southern Illinois University and local history source materials related to Madison and Saint Clair counties in Illinois.

HOURS: Yr

2114
Madison County Historical Society
715 N Main, 62025; (p) (618) 656-7562; www.plantnet.com/~museum; (c) Madison

Private non-profit/ 1924/ staff: 11(f); 24(p); 25(v)/ members: 125

HISTORIC SITE; HISTORICAL SOCIETY; HISTORY MUSEUM; HOUSE MUSEUM; RESEARCH CENTER: Collects, preserves, and interprets Madison County and Illinois history.

PROGRAMS: Annual Meeting; Community Outreach; Exhibits; Facility Rental; Family Programs; Festivals; Guided Tours; Interpretation; Lectures; Publication; Research Library/

Archives; School-Based Curriculum

COLLECTIONS: [1700s-present] Period furnishings, antiques, costumes, quilts, Native American artifacts, tools, medical items, household goods, research archives, pictures, maps, manuscripts, and documents.

HOURS: Yr Su 1-4, W-F 9-4

ADMISSION: No charge/Donations

2115
Weir House-Madison County Historical Association, The
715 N Main St, 62025; (p) (618) 656-7562

1836/ staff: 1(f); 34(v)

COLLECTIONS: [1800s] Furniture, antiques, Indian artifacts, historic costumes and textiles. Pictures, maps, documents, books, manuscripts, newspapers.

HOURS: Yr Su 1-4; W-F 9-4

EFFINGHAM

2116
Effingham County Genealogical and Historical Society
100 E Market, 62401 [PO Box 1166, 62401]; (p) (217) 857-1525; mnburf@yahoo.com; (c) Effingham

1966/ staff: 12(v)/ members: 225

GENEALOGICAL SOCIETY: Preserves, collects and interprets local history and genealogy.

PROGRAMS: Annual Meeting; Lectures; Research Library/Archives

COLLECTIONS: [1831-present] Photos, books and textiles.

HOURS: Yr M-Sa 10-9

ADMISSION: No charge

ELBURN

2117
Elburn and Countryside Historical Society
525 N Main, Box 115, 60119; (p) (630) 365-6655; (c) Kane

Private non-profit/ 1986/ staff: 10(v)/ members: 10

HISTORICAL SOCIETY: Preserves local history.

PROGRAMS: Exhibits; Research Library/Archives

COLLECTIONS: [1930-1960] Photos, newspaper clippings, old school records and memorabilia.

HOURS: Yr by appt

ADMISSION: No charge

ELDORADO

2118
Eldorado Museum
Locust Drive, 62930 [1818 Organ St, 62930]; (p) (618) 273-7109; (c) Saline

Private non-profit/ Project BOUNCE/ staff: 4(v)

HISTORICAL SOCIETY: Preserves Eldorado and Countryside history.

PROGRAMS: Annual Meeting; Exhibits; Family Programs; Festivals; Lectures; School-Based Curriculum

COLLECTIONS: WWII, period costumes, artifacts related to church, business and social activities of Eldorado and surrounding areas.

HOURS: Yr F-Sa 1-4

ELGIN

2119
Elgin Genealogical Society
[PO Box 1418, 60121]; www.elginarea.org/egs/; (c) Kane

Private non-profit/ 1972/ members: 200

GENEALOGICAL SOCIETY: Promotes family history research by providing information, education and sharing opportunities.

PROGRAMS: Publication

COLLECTIONS: [19th-20th c]

2120
Elgin Public Museum
225 Grand Blvd, 60120; (p) (847) 741-6655; (f) (847) 931-6787; epm@mc.net; (c) Cook

City, non-profit/ 1907/ Board of Directors/ staff: 2(f); 4(p); 6(v)/ members: 135/publication: *EPM News*

HISTORY MUSEUM: Promotes natural history and anthropology through exhibits and educational programs.

PROGRAMS: Community Outreach; Exhibits; Family Programs; Interpretation; Lectures; Publication; School-Based Curriculum

COLLECTIONS: Natural history, anthropology, dinosaur exhibit, Native American hall, geology, endangered species, mounds and discovery room.

HOURS: Oct-April Sa-Su 12-4, May-Sept Su

2121
Fire Barn No. 5 Museum
533 St Charles St, 60120

Private non-profit/ 1991/ staff: 14(v)/ members: 120

HISTORIC PRESERVATION AGENCY; HISTORIC SITE; HISTORY MUSEUM: Restored 1904 fire barn housing historic firefighting equipment and history of Elgin.

PROGRAMS: Annual Meeting; Exhibits; Festivals; Guided Tours

COLLECTIONS: [1860-present] Fire department records, artifacts related to fire-fighting.

HOURS: Yr Sa 9-3, Su 12-4 and by appt

ADMISSION: $2, Student $1

ELK GROVE VILLAGE

2122
Farmhouse Museum
399 Biester Field Rd, 60007; (p) (847) 439-3994, (847) 228-2869; (f) (847) 228-3520

1857/ Park District; Elk Grove Historical Society/ staff: 1(f); 3(p); 5(v)

COLLECTIONS: [Late 19th c] Carriages and sleigh from 1800s, original pieces of furniture, ie., secretary desk, night tables, handcrafted by the original owner.

HOURS: Yr Su 1-4, T-F 9-12

ELLIS GROVE

2123
Pierre Menard Home State Historic Site
Rural setting, S of Ellis Grove, 62241 [4230 Kaskaskia Rd, 62241]; (p) (618) 859-3741; (c) Randolph

State/ 1927/ Illinois Historic Preservation Agency/ staff: 5(f); 1(p); 12(v)

HISTORIC PRESERVATION AGENCY; HOUSE MUSEUM: Preserves 1802 French colonial mansion.

PROGRAMS: Exhibits; Garden Tours; Guided Tours; Interpretation; Living History

COLLECTIONS: [1802-1840] Period furnishings and personal items of Pierre Menard, Illinois' first lieutenant governor.

HOURS: Yr Daily 9-4

ADMISSION: No charge

ELMHURST

2124
Elmhurst Historical Museum
120 E Park Ave, 60126; (p) (630) 833-1457; (f) (630) 833-1326; (c) DuPage

City/ 1957/ staff: 4(f); 4(p); 40(v)

HISTORY MUSEUM: Preserves local history.

PROGRAMS: Community Outreach; Concerts; Exhibits; Family Programs; Guided Tours; Interpretation; Lectures; Research Library/Archives; School-Based Curriculum

COLLECTIONS: [1850-present] Documents related to human experience in and around Elmhurst; manuscript and photo collection.

HOURS: Yr T-Su 1-5 and by appt

ADMISSION: No charge

2125
Theatre Historical Society of America
152 N York Rd, Ste 200, 60126-2806; (p) (630) 782-1800; (f) (630) 782-1802; execdir@historictheatres.org; www.historictheaters.org; (c) Cook

1969/ staff: 1(f); 25(v)/ members: 1100/publication: *Marquee; and others*

HISTORICAL SOCIETY; HISTORY MUSEUM; LIBRARY AND/OR ARCHIVES; RESEARCH CENTER: Documents and celebrates historic theaters of all types in the US. Operates the American Theatre Architecture Archives and the American Movie Palace Museum.

PROGRAMS: Community Outreach; Exhibits; Facility Rental; Guided Tours; Lectures; Publication; Research Library/Archives

COLLECTIONS: [1920-1950] Files on 9,000 theatres, including clippings, playbills and programs, books and magazines, uniforms, corporate and business records, blueprints, 1,500 vintage postcards, 11,000 photo images, 27,000 slides, Loews, Balaban and Katz collection, Michael Miller Collection with NYC inventory.

HOURS: Yr Archives: M- F 9-4 by appt; Museum M-F 9-4

ADMISSION: Donations accepted; research fees

ELSAH

2126
Historic Elsah Foundation
41 Mill St, 62028 [PO Box 117, 62028]; (p) (618) 374-1059; (c) Jersey

Private non-profit/ 1972/ Board of Trustees/ staff: 1(p); 10(v)/ members: 135/publication: *Elsah History*

HISTORICAL SOCIETY: Preserves historic buildings, promotes local history through publications, research and educational programmes.

PROGRAMS: Concerts; Facility Rental; Garden Tours; Lectures; Publication; Research Library/Archives

COLLECTIONS: [19th-20th c] Items related to founding and history of Elsah Village.

HOURS: April-Oct Sa-Su 1-4

2127
Village of Elsah Museum
26 LaSalle St, 62028 [PO Box 28, 62028]; (p) (618) 374-1568; www.elsah.org; (c) Jersey

Joint/ 1971

HOUSE MUSEUM: Collects and preserves local history through exhibits and educational programs.

PROGRAMS: Exhibits

COLLECTIONS: [19th c-present] 1,200 photos, period furnishing, farm tools, textiles, household items, school artifacts, pamphlets and memorabilia.

HOURS: Sa-Su

ADMISSION: No charge

EVANSTON

2128
Evanston Historical Society
225 Greenwood St, 60201; (p) (847) 475-3410; (f) (847) 475-3599; evanstonhs@nwu.edu

Private non-profit/ 1898/ Board of Trustees/ staff: 2(f); 4(p); 50(v)/ members: 990/publication: *Timelines*

HISTORIC SITE; HISTORICAL SOCIETY; HOUSE MUSEUM; RESEARCH CENTER: Collects, preserves, exhibits and interprets history of the city and township of Evanston.

PROGRAMS: Community Outreach; Exhibits; Facility Rental; Guided Tours; Lectures; Publication; Research Library/Archives

COLLECTIONS: [1830-present] Artifacts and archives related to history of Evanston.

HOURS: Yr Th-Su 1-5

ADMISSION: $5,

2129
Mitchell Museum of the American Indian
Kendall College, 2600 Central Park, 60201; (p) (847) 475-1030; (f) (847) 475-0911; mitchellmuseum@mindspring.com; (c) Cook

1977/ Kendall College/ staff: 2(f); 45(v)/ members: 300/publication: *Rituals*

HISTORY MUSEUM: Collects, preserves, and interprets material culture of Native Americans.

PROGRAMS: Community Outreach; Exhibits; Family Programs; Guided Tours; Lectures; Research Library/Archives; School-Based Curriculum

COLLECTIONS: [Prehistory-present] Native American material culture from Paleo-Indian period; 6,000 objects including pottery, lithics, beadwork, jewelry, textiles and art.

HOURS: Yr T, W, F, Sa 10-5, Th 10-8, Su 12-4

ADMISSION: Donations requested

FAIRBURY

2130
Fairbury Echoes Museum
105 E Walnut, 61739 [510 S Third, 61739]; (p) (815) 692-2191; (c) Livingston

Private non-profit/ 1979/ staff: 3(p)

HISTORY MUSEUM: Promotes local history.

PROGRAMS: Exhibits

COLLECTIONS: [1880-1980] Items relating to local individuals, businesses and organizations.

HOURS: Apr-Dec W, F 9-5

FAIRFIELD

2131
Wayne County Historical Society
300 SE 2nd, 62837; (p) (618) 842-4516; (c) Wayne

County; Private non-profit/ 1953/ staff: 10(v)/ members: 25

GENEALOGICAL SOCIETY; HISTORICAL SOCIETY; HISTORY MUSEUM; HOUSE MUSEUM: Preserves local history through educational programs and outreach.

PROGRAMS: Annual Meeting; Community Outreach; Concerts; Exhibits; Family Programs; Festivals; Film/Video; Guided Tours; Interpretation; Lectures; Living History; Publication; Research Library/Archives; School-Based Curriculum

COLLECTIONS: [1800-1930] Clothing, carpentry tools, Civil War, Spanish-American, WWI exhibits, Sexton factory, religion and education, exhibits, spinning wheel, local and county items, local history papers.

HOURS: Yr 1st and 3rd Sa10:30-4:30

FAIRMOUNT

2132
Fairmount Jamaica Historical Society, Inc.
116 S Main, 61481; (p) (217) 288-9278; (c) Ver

1987/ staff: 6(v)

GENEALOGICAL SOCIETY; HISTORICAL SOCIETY: Collects genealogy of area

PROGRAMS: Exhibits

COLLECTIONS: Photos, family history, school, census and church records, oral history, maps, newspapers.

HOURS: 1st Sa Sept-July 9-11

FOREST PARK

2133
Historical Society of Forest Park
Forest Park Library, 60130 [519 Jackson Blvd, 60130]; (c) Cook

Private non-profit/ 1976/ staff: 4(p); 60(v)/publication: *Chronicles*

HISTORICAL SOCIETY; HISTORY MUSEUM: Collects, displays and preserves local history.

PROGRAMS: Annual Meeting; Guided Tours; Lectures; Publication

COLLECTIONS: Memorabilia

HOURS: Yr W

FRANKLIN PARK

2134
Village of Franklin Park
9748 Franklin, 60194 [9500 Belmont, 60194]; (p) (847) 671-8235; (f) (846) 671-7806; (c) Cook

City/ staff: 20(v)

HISTORIC SITE

PROGRAMS: Festivals; Lectures

COLLECTIONS: [1880-1900] Building preservation.

ADMISSION: No charge

FREEPORT

2135
Silvercreek Museum
2954 S Walnut, 61032; (p) (815) 235-2198; (c) Stephenson

1989/ Stephenson County Antique Engine Club/ members: 500

HISTORY MUSEUM; LIVING HISTORY/OUTDOOR MUSEUM: Promotes local history.

PROGRAMS: Exhibits; Guided Tours

HOURS: May-Oct Sa-Su 11-5

ADMISSION: Donations requested

2136
Stephenson County Genealogical Society
[PO Box 514, 61032]; (c) Stephenson

1967/ staff: 10(v)/ members: 150/publication: *Stephenson County Swoghen*

PROGRAMS: Lectures; Publication; Research Library/Archives

HOURS: By appt

ADMISSION: No charge

2137
Stephenson County Historical Society
1440 S Carroll Ave, 61032; (p) (815) 232-8419; (f) (815) 297-0313; (c) Stephenson

Private non-profit/ 1944/ Stephenson County Historical Society/ staff: 1(f); 30(v)/ members: 230

HISTORICAL SOCIETY; HISTORY MUSEUM; HOUSE MUSEUM: Preserves and interprets local and regional history.

PROGRAMS: Annual Meeting; Exhibits; Family Programs; Guided Tours; Interpretation; Living History; Publication; School-Based Curriculum

COLLECTIONS: [Victorian] Period home, furnishings, clothing, items related to Taylor Family, pioneer artifacts, local industry, log cabin and one-room schoolhouse.

HOURS: May-Oct W-Su 12-4; Nov-Apr F-Su 12-4

ADMISSION: $2, Children $1

GALENA

2138
Belvedere Mansion, The
1008 Park Ave, 61036; (p) (815) 777-0747; (f) (815) 777-8118

1857/ staff: 1(f); 6(p)

COLLECTIONS: [1857] Original Tiffany, Belter, Seaves china; Boulle, 2 1700 wing chairs, European paintings. Furniture once owned by people such as Roosevelts, President Coolidge, Gen Rawlins (Civil War General from Galena) or from other historic places.

HOURS: June-Oct Sa 11-5, Su-F 11-4

2139
Elihu Benjamin Washburne House State Historic Site, The
908 Third St, 61036 [PO Box 333, 61036]; (p) (815) 777-9406, (815) 777-3310; (f) (815) 777-3310

State/ 1843/ Historic Preservation Agency

COLLECTIONS: [1845-46] Period artifacts. 3 pier mirrors original to the house.

HOURS: Yr Daily 9-4:45

2140
Galena/Jo Daviess County Historical Society and Museum
211 S Bench St, 61036; (p) (815) 777-9129; (f) (815) 777-9131; ghmuseum@galenalink. net; www.galenahistorymuseum.org; (c) Jo Daviess

Private non-profit/ 1938/ Board of Directors/ staff: 2(f); 3(p); 100(v)/ members: 560/publication: *The Miners' Journal*

HISTORICAL SOCIETY; HISTORY MUSEUM: Collects, preserves, and interprets the history of Galena, Jo Daviess County and the Upper Mississippi Lead District.

PROGRAMS: Annual Meeting; Exhibits; Guided Tours; Lectures; Living History; Publication; Research Library/Archives

COLLECTIONS: [1826-1950] Clothing, textiles, dolls, toys, geology, agriculture, lead mining, steamboating, Ulysses S. Grant, Civil War, regional industry products and crafts, along with decorative and utilitarian arts.

HOURS: Yr Daily 9-4:30

ADMISSION: $4, Student $3; Under 10 free

2141
Historic Galena Foundation
220 Diagonal St, 61036; (p) (815) 777-1250; (c) JoDavies

Private non-profit/ 1978/ staff: 10(p); 8(v)

HISTORIC SITE: Belvedere Mansion is Italian-Victorian home of J. Russell Jones, former Ambassador to Belgium. Dowling House and Trading Post preserves pioneer heritage.

PROGRAMS: Guided Tours; Interpretation

COLLECTIONS: Belvedere House: period furnishings, Tiffany chandelier. Dowling House and Trading Post: Refurbished trading post with 1826 period furnishing and trading goods, pottery.

2142
Ulysses S. Grant Home State Historic Site, The
500 Bouthillier St, 61036 [PO Box 333, 61036]; (p) (815) 777-0248, (815) 777-3310; (f) (815) 777-3310

1859/ IL Historic Preservation Agency/ staff: 7(f); 9(p); 2(v)

COLLECTIONS: Original furniture; personal items of US and Julia: jewelry, dresser objects, satchel, saddle, shoes, Bible.; Collection of Leslies Illustrated Newspaper, Puck, Harper's Weekly magazine.

HOURS: Yr Daily 9-4:45

GALESBURG

2143
Browning Mansion
325 N Kellogg St, 61401; (p) (309) 344-2839; www.galesburg.org/chamber/tourism/attract.htm

2144
Carl Sandburg State Historic Site
313 E Third St, 61401; (p) (309) 342-2361

State/ 1860/ Historic Preservation Agency/ staff: 2(f); 1(p)

HISTORIC SITE: The birthplace of author Carl Sandburg also represents a typical immigrant working class house of the period.

COLLECTIONS: [1878] Some furnishings in home belonged to Sandburg's family; Edward Steichen photo of Sandburg, original N.C. Wyeth drawing of Lincoln.

HOURS: Yr Daily 9-5

2145
Knox County Genealogical Society
[PO Box 13, 61402-0013]; (c) Knox

Private non-profit/ 1972/ members: 200/publication: *Knox County Genealogical Society Quarterly*

GENEALOGICAL SOCIETY: Promotes local history and genealogy.

PROGRAMS: Publication

COLLECTIONS: Housed at the Galesburg Public Library, collection includes books, microfilm, microfiche, CD-ROMs and family files.

HOURS: Sept-May M-Th

GALVA

2146
Galva Historical Society
906 W Division, 61434 [PO Box 24, 61434]; (p) (309) 932-8992; snelson2@inw.net; www.galva.com; (c) Hendry

Private non-profit/ 1988/ staff: 1(p)/ members: 480

HISTORICAL SOCIETY: Preserves local history.

PROGRAMS: Exhibits; Film/Video; Guided Tours; Lectures; Publication; Research Library/Archives

COLLECTIONS: [1864-present]

HOURS: Yr M-T, Th-F 11-4; May-Sept Su 1:30-4

GENEVA

2147
Fabyan Villa Museum
1511 S Batavia Ave, 60134; (p) (630) 232-4811; (f) (630) 377-6424; (c) Kane

County/ 1940/ staff: 4(p)

HISTORIC SITE; HOUSE MUSEUM: Redesigned by Frank Lloyd Wright, collects, preserves and interprets the home and collection of George and Nelle Fabyan.

PROGRAMS: Exhibits; Facility Rental; Family Programs; Garden Tours; Guided Tours; School-Based Curriculum

COLLECTIONS: [1907-1925] Frank Lloyd Wright architecture, code breaking equipment, Asian artifacts, natural history specimens, period furnishing, photos, Japanese garden, Dutch windmill.

HOURS: Yr May-Oct W-Sa 1-4:30; Nov-Apr by appt

2148
Friends of Fabyan
1511 & 1931 S Batavia Ave, 60134 [PO Box 801, 60134]; (p) (630) 232-2378; (f) (630) 879-1341; (c) Kane

Private non-profit/ 1979/ Board of Directors/ staff: 60(v)/ members: 265/publication: *Fabyan Images*

HISTORICAL SOCIETY: Preserves Riverbank estate (Forest Preserve) of Col. George and Nelle Fabyan through education and restoration programs.

PROGRAMS: Annual Meeting; Exhibits; Family Programs; Garden Tours; Guided Tours; Interpretation; Lectures; Publication; Research Library/Archives

COLLECTIONS: [1905-1939] Furnishings, photos, and natural history specimens.

HOURS: May-Oct W, Sa-Su 1-4:30

ADMISSION: No charge/Donations

2149
Geneva Historical Society
400 Wheeler Drive, 60134 [PO Box 345, 60134]; (p) (630) 232-4951; (f) (630) 232-6069; (c) Kane

Private non-profit/ 1943/ Board of Directors/ staff: 3(f); 2(p); 57(v)/ members: 660

HISTORIC PRESERVATION AGENCY; HISTORICAL SOCIETY; HISTORY MUSEUM; HOUSE MUSEUM: Collects, researches, interprets and exhibits collections and research materials.

PROGRAMS: Annual Meeting; Community Outreach; Exhibits; Family Programs; Guided Tours; Interpretation; Lectures; Living History; Reenactments; Research Library/Archives; School-Based Curriculum

COLLECTIONS: [1840-present] Artifacts.

HOURS: Apr-Dec W-Su 1-4

GENOA

2150
Kishwaukee Valley Heritage Society
700 W Parke Ave, 60135 [PO Box 59, 60135-0059]; (p) (815) 784-5498; (f) (815) 784-5559; (c) DeKalb

Private non-profit/ 1977/ staff: 10(v)/ members: 85

HISTORICAL SOCIETY; HISTORY MUSEUM: Promotes local history through maintenance of public museum.

PROGRAMS: Annual Meeting; Exhibits; Guided Tours; Living History

COLLECTIONS: [1900] Local merchants, factories, early families and historical photos.

HOURS: May-Dec Su 2-4 and by appt

ADMISSION: Donations accepted

GLEN ELLYN

2151
Glen Ellyn Historical Society-Stacy's Tavern
551 Geneva Rd, 60138 [PO Box 283, 60138]; (p) (630) 858-8696; (f) (630) 858-8696; historical@glen-ellyn.com; www.glen-ellyn.com/historical; (c) DuPage

Private non-profit/ 1968/ staff: 1(f); 25(v)/ members: 300/publication: *Messenger, A Village Remembered*

HISTORIC SITE; HISTORICAL SOCIETY: Researchs, studies, and communicates the history of Glen Ellyn and its environs. Stacy's Tavern is a restored wayside stagecoach inn built in 1846.

PROGRAMS: Annual Meeting; Community Outreach; Exhibits; Festivals; Guided Tours; Publication; Research Library/Archives

COLLECTIONS: [1846-1850] Period pieces to 1840s.

HOURS: Mar-Nov T, W, Su, 1:30-4:30

ADMISSION: Donations accepted

GLENVIEW

2152
Glenview Area Historical Society
1121 Waukegan Rd, 60025; (p) (847) 724-2235; (c) Cook

Private non-profit/ 1965/ staff: 1(p)/ members: 200

ALLIANCE OF HISTORICAL AGENCIES; HISTORICAL SOCIETY; HOUSE MUSEUM: Promotes history of Glenview through Farm Home Museum and Research Library.

PROGRAMS: Annual Meeting; Exhibits; Lectures; Research Library/Archives

COLLECTIONS: [1850-present] Historical furniture, toys, clothing, autographs, newspapers, obituaries, books, schools, government and township records.

HOURS: Museum: Yr Su 1-4; Library: T, Th 1-4

2153
Grove Heritage Association
1421 Milwaukee Ave, 60025 [PO Box 484, 60025-0484]; (p) (847) 299-6026; (f) (847) 299-0571; (c) Cook

City/ 1973/ Glenview Park District/ staff: 9(f); 53(p); 112(v)/ members: 300/publication: *The Rustlings*

HISTORIC SITE; HOUSE MUSEUM: Preserves the Grove as specimen prairie grove and historical Kennicott home site.

PROGRAMS: Annual Meeting; Community Outreach; Exhibits; Facility Rental; Family Programs; Festivals; Guided Tours; Interpretation; Lectures; Living History;

2154
Hartung's License Plate and Auto Museum
3623 W Lake Ave, 60025; (p) (847) 724-4354; (c) Cook

Private for-profit/ 1971/ Cook County/ staff: 1(f)

HISTORY MUSEUM: Preserves the history of automobile license plates of each state.

COLLECTIONS: [1899-present] Antique autos, trucks, tractors, motorcycles, bicycles, toys and license plates from US and Canada.

HOURS: Apr-Nov Sa-Su 10-4

ADMISSION: Donations accepted

2155
Kennicott House
1421 Milwaukee Ave, 60025; (p) (847) 229-6096; (f) (847) 229-0571

1856/ staff: 9(f); 25(p)

COLLECTIONS: [1856-1866] Furniture; Roberts Natural History collection; Kennicott family letters and journals dating to the early 1830s.

HOURS: June 13-Oct 11 Sa-Su 10-3; June 15-Aug 14 M-F 10-3

GOLCONDA

2156
Pope County Historical Society
Main & Columbus, 62938 [PO Box 837, 62938]; (p) (618) 683-3050; (c) Pope

Private non-profit/ 1966/ staff: 20(v)/ members: 200

GENEALOGICAL SOCIETY; HISTORIC PRESERVATION AGENCY; HISTORICAL SOCIETY; HISTORY MUSEUM: Preserves and researches oral and written history.

PROGRAMS: Annual Meeting; Community Outreach; Exhibits; Guided Tours; Interpretation; Lectures; Reenactments; Research Library/Archives

COLLECTIONS: [19th-20th c] Photos, printed materials, clothing, furniture, tools, toys, country store exhibit, farm wagons and quilts.

HOURS: Sa 9-12, Su

GOLDEN

2157
Golden Historical Society, Inc.
902 Prairie Mills Rd, 62339 [PO Box 148, 62339]; (p) (217) 696-2722; (f) (217) 696-2504; www.windmill.org; (c) Adams

Private non-profit/ 1986/ Board of Trustees/ staff: 27(v)/ members: 93/publication: *When the Wind Blows*

HISTORICAL SOCIETY: Preserves and restores Smock Windmill to original grinding condition; operates railroad museum.

PROGRAMS: Annual Meeting; Exhibits; Facility Rental; Guided Tours; Publication

COLLECTIONS: [1869-1930] Period clothing, farm implements and household items.

HOURS: June-Sept Su 1-4

ADMISSION: $3

GRAYSLAKE

2158
Grayslake Municipal Historical Museum

164 Hawley, 60030 [PO Box 185, 60030]; (p) (847) 223-7663; www.grayslakehistory.org; (c) Lake

Private non-profit/ 1976/ Grayslake Historical Association/ staff: 10(v)/ members: 235

HISTORICAL SOCIETY; HISTORY MUSEUM: Collects and preserves artifacts of the community and its citizens.

PROGRAMS: Community Outreach; Exhibits; Festivals; Guided Tours; Lectures; Reenactments; Research Library/Archives

COLLECTIONS: [1895-present] Farm equipment, clothing, military uniforms, schoolroom, country store, outdoor theatre, business souvenirs, fire truck, horse-drawn hearse, household items, barber chair.

HOURS: Yr Th 9-2, T during summer 1:30-3:30, 2nd Su 1:30-3:30

ADMISSION: Donations accepted

GREENVILLE

2159
Bond County Genealogical Society

Greenville Public Library, 414 E Main, 62246 [PO Box 172, 62246]; (p) (618) 664-3054; (f) (618) 664-3054; foulon@gvc.net; www.GreenvilleIllinois.com; (c) Bond

Private non-profit/ 1982/ staff: 3(f); 8(p)/ members: 272

GENEALOGICAL SOCIETY; RESEARCH CENTER: Preserves the history of the people, places and times of Bond County.

PROGRAMS: Guided Tours; Research Library/Archives; School-Based Curriculum

COLLECTIONS: [1814-present] Revolutionary War records, county and family histories, and newspapers on microfilm.

HOURS: Yr M-Th 12-8, F-Sa 9-6

2160
Bond County Historical Society

318 W Winter St, 62246 [PO Box 376, 62246]; (c) Bond

Private non-profit/ 1955/ staff: 4(v)/ members: 65

HISTORICAL SOCIETY; HISTORY MUSEUM: Preserves county history and the Hoiles-Davis Museum.

PROGRAMS: Annual Meeting; Concerts; Exhibits; Lectures; Reenactments

COLLECTIONS: [19th c] Local historical items.

HOURS: Spring-Fall 1st Su 1-4

ADMISSION: Donations accepted

HAMPTON

2161
Hampton Historical Society

601 1st Ave, 61256 [PO Box 68, 61256]; (p) (309) 255-0362; hamptonwells.email.msn.com; www.hometown.aol.jamnjane.com; (c) Rock Island

Private non-profit/ 1974/ Hampton Historical Society/ staff: 20(v)/ members: 150

HISTORIC SITE; HISTORICAL SOCIETY; HISTORY MUSEUM: Promotes local history through operation of Black's Store Museum.

PROGRAMS: Annual Meeting; Exhibits; Festivals; Guided Tours; Interpretation; Lectures

COLLECTIONS: [19th c] Tools and artifacts related to clamming industry, pottery and

HANOVER PARK

2162
Village of Hanover Park Historic Commission

2121 W Lake St, 60103; (p) (630) 372-4200; (f) (630) 372-4215; (c) Cook/Dupage

City, non-profit/ 1987/ Village of Hanover Park/ staff: 1(p); 4(v)

HISTORIC PRESERVATION AGENCY: Preserves history of Ontarioville and village buildings and sites.

PROGRAMS: Community Outreach; Film/Video

COLLECTIONS: [1880-present] Photos, books and pamphlets.

HARDIN

2163
Calhoun County Historical Society

Farm Bureau Bldg, County Rd, 62047 [PO Box 46, 62047]; (p) (618) 576-2660; (c) Calhoun

Private non-profit/ 1975/ Board of Directors/ staff: 1(p); 3(v)/ members: 120

GENEALOGICAL SOCIETY; HISTORICAL SOCIETY; HISTORY MUSEUM: Promotes and preserves the history of the people of Calhoun County.

PROGRAMS: Annual Meeting; Exhibits; Publication; Research Library/Archives

COLLECTIONS: [1825-present] Genealogical resources and miscellaneous artifacts from the area.

HOURS: Yr W 8-3

ADMISSION:

HARRISBURG

2164
Saline County Genealogical Society

[PO Box 4, 62946-0004]; (c) Saline

1985/ staff: 8(v)/ members: 300/publication: The Shawnee

GENEALOGICAL SOCIETY; RESEARCH CENTER: Preserves and maintains local history and records.

PROGRAMS: Annual Meeting; Publication;

Research Library/Archives

HOURS: Yr 3rd M 8-12

ADMISSION: No charge

HARVARD

2165
Greater Harvard Area

308 N Hart, 60033 [PO Box 505, 60033]; (p) (815) 943-6141; (c) McHenry

Private for-profit/ 1977/ staff: 12(v)/ members: 120

HISTORICAL SOCIETY: Preserves local history.

PROGRAMS: Annual Meeting; Community Outreach; Exhibits; Guided Tours

COLLECTIONS: [1865-present] Memorabilia and artifacts related to founding of Harvard.

HOURS: May-Oct W 9:30-12, Su 1:30-4

HENNEPIN

2166
Pulsifer House

Rte 26 & Power Rd, 61327 [PO Box 74, 61327]; (p) (815) 925-7560

1844/ City; Putnam County Historical Society/ staff: 1(p); 2(v)

COLLECTIONS: [1840s] Artifacts of life on prairie in 1840s; pioneer quilts and coverlets, Native American artifacts, empire furniture. ; Day books and ledgers of EF & S. Pulsifer Hardware, Groceries, & Dry Goods, complete 1840-1850; Duck Hunting Club history and record books (Hennepin was Duck Hunting capital of Illinois)

HOURS: Yr

2167
Putnam County Historical Society

Rt 71 & Power Plant Rd, 61327 [PO Box 74, 61327]; (p) (815) 925-7560; (c) Putnam

County/ 1963/ Board of Directors/ staff: 1(p); 35(v)/ members: 671/publication: Mount Palatine Newsletter

HISTORICAL SOCIETY; HISTORY MUSEUM: Collects, preserves, and interprets local history; promotes historical house.

PROGRAMS: Annual Meeting; Community Outreach; Exhibits; Family Programs; Festivals; Guided Tours; Interpretation; Lectures; Living History; Publication; Research Library/Archives; School-Based Curriculum

COLLECTIONS: [1817-present] 1844 house and furnishings, artifacts, newspapers, miscellaneous household equipment, textiles, toys, dolls, clothing, and genealogical resources.

HOURS: Yr T, W, F

HIGHLAND

2168
Highland Historical Society

RR3 Old Trenton Road, 62249 [PO Box 51, 62249]; (p) (618) 654-7957; (c) Madison

Private non-profit/ 1970/ members: 183

HISTORIC PRESERVATION AGENCY; HISTORIC SITE; HISTORICAL SOCIETY; HISTORY MUSEUM; LIVING HISTORY/OUTDOOR

MUSEUM; RESEARCH CENTER: Preserves local history through two museums and cemetery chapel.

PROGRAMS: Guided Tours

COLLECTIONS: [1870-1950] Period furnishings, Highland and Pet Milk memorabilia.

HOURS: By appt

ADMISSION: $2.50

HIGHLAND PARK

2169
Highland Park Historical Society
326 Central Ave, 60035 [PO Box 56, 60035]; (p) (847) 432-7090; (f) (847) 432-7307; hphis toricalsociety@worldnet.att.net; www.high-landpark.org/histsoc/; (c) Lake

Private non-profit/ 1967/ Board of Directors/ staff: 7(p); 500(v)/publication: *The Lamplighter*

HISTORIC SITE; HISTORICAL SOCIETY; HOUSE MUSEUM: Collects and preserves local history.

PROGRAMS: Annual Meeting; Community Outreach; Exhibits; Family Programs; Film/Video; Guided Tours; Lectures; Publication; Research Library/Archives; School-Based Curriculum

COLLECTIONS: [1850-present] Local maps, pictures, blueprints, clothing, toys, postcards, manuscripts; automotive, gardening and woodworking tools.

HOURS: Feb-Dec T-F 10-3,

2170
Phillip H. Sheridan Reserve Center
Sheridan Reserve Center, Bldg 475, 60037 [3155 Blackhawk Dr Ste 475, 60037-1289]; (p) (847) 266-3045, (847) 266-3047; (f) (847) 266-3049; (c) Lake

1888/ staff: 3(f)

HISTORIC SITE; HISTORY MUSEUM: Preserves military history.

PROGRAMS: Exhibits

COLLECTIONS: [20th c] Uniforms, military equipment of WWI and WWII.

HOURS: Yr M-F 7:30-4

ADMISSION: No charge

HILLSBORO

2171
Solomon Harkey House
Corner Broadway & Water Sts, 62049 [904 S Main St, 62049]; (p) (217) 532-3329, (217) 532-2958

1834/ staff: 6(v)

COLLECTIONS: [1830-1900] Household furnishings of 1830-1900; woodworking tools; Archival items have been donated to Hillsboro Public Library.

HOURS: Seasonal

HINSDALE

2172
Hinsdale Historical Society
15 S Clay St, 60522 [PO Box 336, 60522]; (p) (630) 789-2600; (f) (630) 325-4357; (c) DuPage

Private non-profit/ 1973/ Board of Trustees/ staff: 30(v)/ members: 400

HISTORICAL SOCIETY; HOUSE MUSEUM: Collects, preserves and promotes history of Hinsdale.

PROGRAMS: Community Outreach; Exhibits; Guided Tours; Research Library/Archives

COLLECTIONS: [1875-1895] Artifacts related to Hinsdale.

HOURS: Yr W 12-2 and by appt

ADMISSION: Donations accepted

HOMEWOOD

2173
Homewood Historical Society
2035 W 183rd St, 60430 [PO Box 1144, 60430]; (p) (708) 799-1896; (c) Cook

Private non-profit/ 1980/ Board of Directors/ staff: 40(v)/ members: 320

HISTORIC SITE; HISTORICAL SOCIETY; HISTORY MUSEUM; HOUSE MUSEUM: Preserves local history, operates 1891 workingman's cottage built of Homewood stamped brick, landmark preservation and resource center.

PROGRAMS: Annual Meeting; Community Outreach; Exhibits; Family Programs; Guided Tours; Lectures; Publication; Reenactments; Research Library/Archives; School-Based Curriculum

COLLECTIONS: [1890-present] Local history items.

HOURS: Yr T, Sa 1-3

ADMISSION: $1, Children $.50

2174
South Suburban Heritage Association
2035 W 183rd St, 60430 [PO Box 917, 60430]; (p) (708) 798-9535; (c) Cook

Private non-profit/ 1987/ Board of Directors/ staff: 10(v)/ members: 25/publication: *Portals in Time*

ALLIANCE OF HISTORICAL AGENCIES; HISTORICAL SOCIETY; RESEARCH CENTER: Promotes and preserves local history through annual conferences and workshops.

PROGRAMS: Community Outreach; Guided Tours; Lectures; Publication; Research Library/Archives; School-Based Curriculum

COLLECTIONS: [Mid-1800s-present]

HOURS: Various workshops and conferences throughout year

ADMISSION: No charge

ITASCA

2175
Itasca Historical Commission
100 N Walnut St, 60143 [Itasca Village Hall, 60143]; (p) (630) 773-0835; (c) DuPage

City/ 1985/ Itasca Village Board of Trustee/ staff: 1(p); 7(v)/publication: *Color Me Itasca; Blast to the Past*

HISTORIC PRESERVATION AGENCY: Promotes local and architectural history. Approves all fa‡ade changes within the Historic District, approves matching grants to historic facade work within the Historic District.

PROGRAMS: Publication; School-Based Curriculum

2176
Itasca Historical Depot Museum
101 Catalpa St, 60143; (p) (630) 773-3363; (c) DuPage

Joint/ 1976/ Itasca Park District/ staff: 1(p); 15(v)/ members: 100

HISTORY MUSEUM: Collects and preserves Itasca history.

PROGRAMS: Exhibits; Guided Tours; Interpretation; School-Based Curriculum

COLLECTIONS: [1890-1950] Photos, documents, clothing, furnishings and railroad memorabilia.

HOURS: Yr 2nd and 4th Su, 1-4

ADMISSION: Donations accepted

JACKSONVILLE

2177
Jacksonville Heritage Cultural Center
125 S Webster, 62650 [200 W Douglas, 62650]; (p) (217) 243-7488; (c) Morgan

City/ 1988/ staff: 1(p); 16(v)/ members: 250

HISTORY MUSEUM: Operates the Jacksonville Heritage Museum and sponsors events about local history.

PROGRAMS: Exhibits; Family Programs; Guided Tours

COLLECTIONS: [19th-20th c] Materials from Jacksonville community businesses, professions, communications, transportation, and personages.

HOURS: Yr W 1-4, and by appt

ADMISSION: Donations requested

2178
Morgan County Historical Society
[PO Box 1330, 62651]; (c) Morgan

County; Private non-profit/ 1904/ members: 100

HISTORIC PRESERVATION AGENCY; HISTORICAL SOCIETY; HISTORY MUSEUM; HOUSE MUSEUM; RESEARCH CENTER: Preserves local history through preservation programs.

PROGRAMS: Annual Meeting; Community Outreach; Exhibits; Family Programs; Guided Tours; Lectures; Publication; Research Library/Archives

COLLECTIONS: Illinois and local history.

2179
Prairieland Heritage Museum Institute
1004 W Michigan Ave, 62650 [PO Box 754, 62650]; (p) (217) 243-7262

Private non-profit/ 1969/ staff: 100(v)/ members: 200

HISTORIC PRESERVATION AGENCY: Preserves and promotes local history.

PROGRAMS: Exhibits; Facility Rental; Festivals; Guided Tours

COLLECTIONS: Antique farm equipment and pioneer life.

HOURS: Last wknd Sept and by appt

ADMISSION: $4

2180
Reverend James Caldwell Chapter NSDAR
4 Duncan Place, 62650-1842; (p) (217) 479-0234; (c) Morgan

1896/ Executive Board/ staff: 25(v)/ members: 131

HISTORIC PRESERVATION AGENCY; HISTORIC SITE; HISTORICAL SOCIETY; HISTORY MUSEUM; HOUSE MUSEUM; LIVING HISTORY/OUTDOOR MUSEUM: Owns and operates the Governor Duncan Home; promotes patriotism and historical preservation.

PROGRAMS: Community Outreach; Family Programs; Garden Tours; Guided Tours; Interpretation; Lectures; Living History

COLLECTIONS: [1830-1900] Period furnishings, clothing and memorabilia.

HOURS: June-Aug W, Sa 1-4 and by appt

ADMISSION: $2, Children $1

JERSEYVILLE

2181
Jersey County Historical Society
108 N Lafayette St, 62052 [PO Box 12, 62052]; (p) (618) 498-3511, (618) 498-3514; (f) (618) 498-4122; jersey1@gtec.com; www.jersey1.org; (c) Jersey

Private non-profit/ 1889/ Jersey County Historical Society/ staff: 12(v)/ members: 320/publication: *Prairie Schooner*

GENEALOGICAL SOCIETY; HISTORIC SITE; HISTORICAL SOCIETY; HISTORY MUSEUM; HOUSE MUSEUM: Promotes local history.

PROGRAMS: Annual Meeting; Exhibits; Facility Rental; Family Programs; Festivals; Film/Video; Garden Tours; Guided Tours; Lectures; Publication; School-Based Curriculum

COLLECTIONS: [1860-1950] Vintage clothing, war memorabilia, school memorabilia, tools and Victorian furniture.

HOURS: Yr Th-Su 1-4

ADMISSION: Donations

JOLIET

2182
Cathedral Area Preservation Association
[PO Box 3662, 60434]; (p) (815) 726-4163; capa2@usa.net; (c) Will

Private non-profit/ 1981/ staff: 20(v)/ members: 300/publication: *The Landmark*

HISTORIC PRESERVATION AGENCY: Preserves, maintains and promotes the Cathedral Area.

PROGRAMS: Annual Meeting; Exhibits; Festivals; Garden Tours; Guided Tours; Lectures; Publication

2183
Joliet Area Historical Society
17 E Van Buren St, 60434 [PO Box 477, 60434]; (p) (815) 722-7003; (c) Will

Private non-profit/ 1981/ staff: 8(v)/ members: 400

HISTORICAL SOCIETY: Preserves local history.

PROGRAMS: Annual Meeting; Community Outreach; Exhibits; Film/Video; Interpretation; Lectures

COLLECTIONS: [1800-present] 20,000 photos, historic artifacts, memorabilia, 1,500 tools and 20,000 nail collection.

HOURS: Yr T-F 12-3

ADMISSION: No charge

KAMPSVILLE

2184
Center for American Archaeology
Hwy 100, 62053 [PO Box 366, 62053]; (p) (618) 653-4316; (f) (618) 653-4232; caa@caa-archeology.org; www.coa-archaeology.org; (c) Calhoun

Private non-profit/ 1953/ Board of Directors/ staff: 25(f); 25(p)/ members: 750

ARCHAEOLOGICAL SITE/MUSEUM: Promotes archeology through research and educational programs.

PROGRAMS: Annual Meeting; Community Outreach; Exhibits; Family Programs; Guided Tours; Interpretation; Lectures; Publication; School-Based Curriculum

COLLECTIONS: 11 million archaeological and ecofactual specimens, one-half million supporting documents, photos, maps; comparative collections for archaeological botany, zoology and human osteology.

HOURS: Apr-Nov M-Sa 10-5, Su 12-5

KANKAKEE

2185
Riverview Historic District
Riverview Subd, 60901 [PO Box 571, 60901]; (p) (815) 933-4553; speechl@aol.com; (c) Kankakee

Private non-profit/ Riverview Historic Area/ staff: 13(v)

KEITHSBURG

2186
Sharon Reason-Keithsburg Museum
302 S 14th St, 61442 [PO Box 79, 61442]; (p) (309) 374-2659; (f) (309) 374-2346; shareail@mcics.com; (c) Mercer

1985/ City of Keithsburg/ staff: 1(v)

GENEALOGICAL SOCIETY; HISTORY MUSEUM: Promotes local history and art.

PROGRAMS: Exhibits; Guided Tours; Reenactments; Research Library/Archives

HOURS: Mar-Nov M-F 8-12, Su 1-5

ADMISSION: Donations accepted

KENILWORTH

2187
Kenilworth Historical Society
415 Kenilworth Ave, 60043 [PO Box 181, 60043-1134]; (p) (847) 251-2565; (c) Cook

Private non-profit/ 1922/ Board of Directors/ staff: 3(p); 42(v)/ members: 450/publication: *Joseph Sears and His Kenilworth*

HISTORICAL SOCIETY: Collects, preserves, and records history of Kenilworth.

PROGRAMS: Exhibits; Family Programs; Publication

COLLECTIONS: [1889-present] Photos, artifacts, archives, children's museu, and non-circulating library.

HOURS: Yr M 9-4:30, Th 9-12

ADMISSION: No

KEWANEE

2188
Henry County Genealogical Society
Kewanee Public Library, 61443 [PO Box 346, 61443]; srmorris@inw.net; www.rootsweb.com/~ilhenry/index; (c) Henry

Private non-profit/ 1983/ staff: 10(v)/ members: 235

GENEALOGICAL SOCIETY; RESEARCH CENTER: Promotes genealogical research in Henry County.

PROGRAMS: Lectures; Research Library/ Archives

COLLECTIONS: [1800-present] Books, marriage, death, cemetery and naturalization records, microfilm.

HOURS: Yr

2189
Kewanee Historical Society
211 N Chestnut St, 61443; (c) Henry

Private non-profit/ 1976/ staff: 8(v)/ members: 702

HISTORICAL SOCIETY: Preserves local history.

PROGRAMS: Family Programs

COLLECTIONS: Artifacts related to history of Kewanee, local churches, factories, businesses, agricultural history, cornhusking and 300 scrapbooks of family histories. Home of the National Cornhuskers Hall of Fame, display of over 1,800 miniature pigs, iron lung, streetcars, and prairie chickens.

HOURS: May-Oct Su

2190
Woodland Place at Francis Park
4 mi E of Kewanee on US Rt 34, 61443 [200 W 3rd St, 61443]; (p) (309) 852-0511, (309) 852-2611; (f) (309) 856-6001

1890/ City/ staff: 1(f); 2(p)

COLLECTIONS: [1890-1925] Furniture made by Francis; several oil paintings and graphite etchings. Encyclopedia of Physical Culture, other random text books from 1870s.

HOURS: Seasonal

KNOXVILLE

2191
Knox County Historical Sites, Inc.
Public Square, 61448; (p) (309) 289-2814; tbould@netins.net; www.web.winco.net/~tbould; (c) Knox

Private non-profit/ 1953/ staff: 25(v)/ members: 100

HISTORIC PRESERVATION AGENCY: Restores and preserves buildings and grounds in Knox County.

PROGRAMS: Annual Meeting; Exhibits; Facility Rental; Guided Tours

COLLECTIONS: [1800] Museum artifacts, books, photos, manuscripts, maps and newspapers.

HOURS: June-Mid Oct Su 2-4

ADMISSION: Donations accepted

LACON

2192
Marshall County Historical Society
314 5th St, 61540; (p) (309) 246-2349; (f) (309) 246-2349; mchs@lacon.net; (c) Marshall

County; Private non-profit/ 1956/ staff: 15(v)

GENEALOGICAL SOCIETY; HISTORICAL SOCIETY; HISTORY MUSEUM; RESEARCH CENTER

PROGRAMS: Annual Meeting; Community Outreach; Concerts; Exhibits; Family Programs; Guided Tours; Lectures; Publication; Research Library/Archives

COLLECTIONS: [19th-20th c]

HOURS: Yr M,W 9-12

ADMISSION: Donations accepted

LAFOX

2193
Garfield Farm Museum
3N016 Garfield Road, 60147 [PO Box 403, 60147-0403]; (p) (630) 584-8485; (f) (630) 584-8522; garfarm@elnet.com; www.elnet.com/~garfarm; (c) Kane

Private non-profit/ 1977/ Garfield Heritage Society and Campton Historic Agricultural Lands, Inc./ staff: 2(f); 2(p); 300(v)/ members: 1000

LIVING HISTORY/OUTDOOR MUSEUM: Illinois' only intact 1840s farmstead, restored as living history farm.

PROGRAMS: Festivals; Guided Tours; Interpretation; Lectures; Living History

COLLECTIONS: [1840] Rare livestock breeds, artifacts related to Garfield and Mitchell family.

HOURS: Yr June-Sept W, Su 1-4 and by

LAKE FOREST

2194
Lake County Historical Society Collection
Sheridan Rd at College Rd, 60045 [555 N Sheridan Rd, 60045]; (p) (847) 735-5064; (f) (874) 735-6296; amiller@lfc.edu; www.lib.lfc.edu/special/; (c) Lake

Private non-profit/ 1857/ staff: 1(f); 3(p); 2(v)

HISTORICAL SOCIETY; LIBRARY AND/OR ARCHIVES: Promotes local and Illinois history through archives and special collection holdings.

PROGRAMS: Community Outreach; Exhibits; Garden Tours; Guided Tours; Lectures; Research Library/Archives

COLLECTIONS: [1850-present] Rare books, manuscripts, photos, prints and maps.

HOURS: Yr M-F 1-5 and by appt

ADMISSION: No charge

2195
Lake Forest Lake Bluff Historical Society
361 E Westminster, 60045 [PO Box 82, 60045]; (p) (847) 234-5253; (f) (847) 234-5236; (c) Lake

Private non-profit/ 1972/ Board of Directors/ staff: 1(p); 60(v)/ members: 769

HISTORICAL SOCIETY; HISTORY MUSEUM; LIBRARY AND/OR ARCHIVES: Promotes local history through museum, library, and archives.

PROGRAMS: Exhibits

COLLECTIONS: Library, archives, artifacts, memorabilia, clothing, furnishings, archaeological fragments related to Lake Forest and Lake Bluff.

HOURS: Yr T-Th

LANSING

2196
Lansing Historical Society
2750 Indiana Ave, 60438 [PO Box 1776, 60438]; (p) (708) 474-6160; (c) Cook

Private non-profit/ 1976/ staff: 12(v)/ members: 60

HISTORICAL SOCIETY; HISTORY MUSEUM: Records and preserves Lansing history.

PROGRAMS: Annual Meeting; Exhibits; Guided Tours

HOURS: Yr M 6-8, W 2-5, Sa 10-12

ADMISSION: Donations accepted

LEBANON

2197
Lebanon Historical Society
c/o Lebanon Advertiser, 62254 [309 W Louis St, 62254]; (p) (618) 537-4498; (c) St. Clair

Private non-profit/ 1964/ members: 75

HISTORIC SITE; HISTORICAL SOCIETY; HISTORY MUSEUM; HOUSE MUSEUM: Preserves small hotel visited by Charles Dickens in 1842.

PROGRAMS: Exhibits; Film/Video; Garden Tours; Guided Tours; Lectures; Living History; Publication; Research Library/Archives

COLLECTIONS: [1800] Dickensian memorabilia.

HOURS: Apr-Dec Th-Sa 11-3

ADMISSION: No charge

LEMONT

2198
Camp Saqawau: Environmental Education Center Forest Preserve District of Cook County
12545 W 111th St, 60439; (p) (630) 257-2045; (f) (630) 257-8026; (c) Cook

County/ 1961/ Forest Preserve District/ staff: 4(f); 3(p); 6(v)

PROGRAMS: Festivals; Guided Tours;

2199
Lemont Area Historical Society
306 Lemont St, 60439 [PO Box 126, 60439]; (p) (630) 257-2972; www.township.com/ lemont/historical; (c) Cook

Private non-profit/ 1970/ Lemont Area Historical Society/ staff: 2(f)/ members: 235/publication: *Cornerstone Newsletter*

HISTORIC SITE; HISTORICAL SOCIETY; HISTORY MUSEUM: Preserves Lemont history through historic site museum.

PROGRAMS: Exhibits; Facility Rental; Guided Tours; Interpretation; Publication

COLLECTIONS: [1800-1940] Displays include livery stable, general store, doctor's office, school, military uniforms, WWI, WWII, archival photos, cemetery, local books, census records and newspapers 1800s-present on microfilm.

HOURS: May-Nov T, Th, Sa-Su; Dec-Apr Th, Sa-Su

ADMISSION: Donations requested

LENA

2200
Lena Area Historical Society
Grove St & Lake Rd, 61048 [PO Box 620, 61048]; (p) (815) 369-5598; (c) Stephenson

1982/ staff: 35(v)/ members: 100

HISTORICAL SOCIETY; HISTORY MUSEUM: Preserves local history.

PROGRAMS: Exhibits; School-Based Curriculum

COLLECTIONS: [1840-1950] Artifacts representing early families, homes, businesses, local genealogy, early photos, 1840s log schoolhouse, barn with antique vehicles and farm tools, restored summer kitchen, caboose, blacksmith shop.

HOURS: May-Sept Sa-Su 1-4

ADMISSION: Donations accepted

LERNA

2201
Lincoln Log Cabin State Historic Site
400 S Lincoln Hwy Rd, 62440 [PO Box 100, 62440]; (p) (217) 345-1845; (f) (217) 345-6472; tomandsarah@lincolnlogcabin.org; www.state.il.us/HPA/Sites/lincolnlog01.htm; (c) Coles

State/ 1936/ IL Historic Preservation Agency/ staff: 8(f); 1(p); 220(v)/ members: 220

HISTORIC SITE; LIVING HISTORY/OUTDOOR MUSEUM: Preserves the home of Thomas and Sarah Lincoln, parents of Abraham Lincoln.

PROGRAMS: Community Outreach; Exhibits; Interpretation; Living History; School-Based Curriculum

COLLECTIONS: [1840] Period household items, agriculture, textiles, and books.

HOURS: Site Yr 8:30-Dusk; Apr-Oct 9-5; Nov-Mar 9-4

ADMISSION: No charge

LEROY

2202
Rike House Museum Guild, Inc., The
406 N Chestnut, 61752 [PO Box 232, 61752]; (p) (309) 962-3311, (309) 962-9028; (c) McLean

1983/ Rike House Guild, Inc.

PROGRAMS: Community Outreach; Exhibits; Guided Tours

COLLECTIONS: Various period artifacts, including ten-piece commode set and period furnishings.

HOURS: By appt

LEWISTOWN

2203
Dickson Mounds Museum
10956 N Dickson Mounds Rd, 61542; (p) (309) 547-3721; (f) (309) 547-3189; info-dmm@museum.stole.il.us; www.museum.state.il/us/ismsites/dickson; (c) Fulton

State/ 1927/ State of Illinois/ staff: 15(f); 1(p); 20(v)/ members: 58/publication: *Fieldnotes*

HISTORIC SITE; HISTORY MUSEUM: Collects, preserves, and interprets the history of Native Americans in the Midwest through on-site rural archaeological museum.

PROGRAMS: Community Outreach; Concerts; Elder's Programs; Exhibits; Facility Rental; Family Programs; Festivals; Film/Video; Guided Tours; Interpretation; Lectures; Living History; Publication; Reenactments; School-Based Curriculum

COLLECTIONS: Native American artifacts from Illinois dating from 10,000 BC including lithics, ceramics, tools and ornaments of shell, stone, bone and copper.

HOURS: Yr Daily 8:30-5

ADMISSION: No charge

LIBERTYVILLE

2204
Lake County Genealogical Society
[PO Box 721, 60048-0721]; (p) (847) 336-7151; mwynn10775@aol.com; (c) Lake

Private non-profit/ 1978/ members: 205

GENEALOGICAL SOCIETY

PROGRAMS: Annual Meeting; Exhibits; Family Programs; Publication; Research Library/Archives

HOURS: Yr T-W

2205
Libertyville-Mundelein Historical Society
413 N Milwaukee Ave, 60048; (p) (847) 362-2330; (f) (847) 362-0006; (c) Lake

Private non-profit/ 1955/ Board of Directors/ staff: 50(v)/ members: 180

HISTORICAL SOCIETY; HOUSE MUSEUM; RESEARCH CENTER: Collects and preserves historical material and information related to Libertyville, Mundelein and surrounding areas; maintains the Ansel B. Cook Victorian home.

PROGRAMS: Guided Tours; Lectures; Publication; Research Library/Archives

COLLECTIONS: [1836-present] Victorian furnishings, 1860 Wide Awake banner, toys, tools, clothing, photos, manuscripts, personal items related to Libertyville and Mundelein.

HOURS: June-Aug Su 2-4; Dec 1st and 2nd weekend 1-5

ADMISSION: $2, Student $1, Seniors $1

2206
Marytown
1600 W Park Ave, 60048; (p) (847) 367-7800; mail@marytown.org; www.marytown.org; (c) Lake

Private non-profit/ 1950/ staff: 10(f); 10(p); 5(v)/publication: *Immaculate Magazine*

HISTORIC SITE: Promotes history of the life of Maximilian Kolbe, an Auschwitz death camp prisoner.

PROGRAMS: Community Outreach; Exhibits; Family Programs; Festivals; Guided Tours; Lectures; Publication

COLLECTIONS: [1930-present] Mosaics, stained glass, decorative arts, paintings.

LINCOLN

2207
Abraham Lincoln Tourism Bureau of Logan County
303 S Kickapoo, 62656; (p) (217) 732-8687; (f) (217) 732-6293; toursm@abelink.com; (c) Logan

County/ 1986/ staff: 1(f); 1(p)

Promotes Logan County through tourism.

PROGRAMS: Annual Meeting; Exhibits

HOURS: Yr

2208
Lincoln College Museum
300 Keokuk, 62656; (p) (217) 732-3155; (c) Logan

Private non-profit/ 1865/ staff: 3(p)

HISTORY MUSEUM: Preserves history of Abraham Lincoln's presidency.

PROGRAMS: Exhibits; Publication

COLLECTIONS: Artifacts and books related to Lincoln and Civil War.

HOURS: Feb-Dec M-F 10-4, Sa-Su 1-4

ADMISSION: No charge

2209
Logan County Genealogical and Historical Society
Pulaski, 62656 [11 Arcade Ct, 62656]; (c) Logan

Private non-profit/ 1978/ staff: 8(v)/publication: *Logan Roots and Branches*

GENEALOGICAL SOCIETY; HISTORICAL SOCIETY: Promotes local history.

PROGRAMS: Annual Meeting; Family Programs; Publication

COLLECTIONS: Books, newspapers, obituaries, family histories and family ancestry charts, DAR books, Revolutionary War, Civil War, WW I, WW II, military records, cemetery records, census, and heirship records.

HOURS: Yr W 1-4, Sa 10-12

ADMISSION: Donations accepted

2210
Logan County Regional Planning Commission
529 S McLean St, 62656; (p) (217) 732-8835; (f) (217) 732-7138; (c) Logan

County/ 1967/ staff: 1(f)/ members: 8

HISTORIC PRESERVATION AGENCY: Works with county and local communities on land use, planning zoning issues, administration, preservation issues and Illinois State Data Center affiliate organization.

PROGRAMS: Research Library/Archives

COLLECTIONS: [1970-present] Land use, zoning library, enterprise zone map and incentives, US Bureau of census documents.

HOURS: Yr M-F

2211
Mt. Pulaski Courthouse State Historic Site
113 S Washington, 62656 [PO Box 355, 62656-0355]; (p) (217) 732-8930; (c) Logan

State/ 1936/ Historic Preservation Agency/ staff: 1(f); 35(v)

HISTORIC SITE: Preserves original 1848 courthouse building.

PROGRAMS: Festivals; Guided Tours; Interpretation

COLLECTIONS: [1848-1855] Period office and courtroom furnishings.

HOURS: Mar-Oct T-Su 12-5;

2212
Postville Courthouse State Historic Site
914 Fifth St, 62656 [PO Box 355, 62656-0355]; (p) (217) 732-8930; (c) Logan

1953/ Historic Preservation Agency/ staff: 1(f)

HISTORIC SITE: Preserves history of first Logan County Courthouse.

PROGRAMS: Festivals; Guided Tours; Interpretation

COLLECTIONS: [1840-1848] Period office furnishings.

HOURS: Mar-Oct F-Sa 12-5; Nov-Feb F-Sa

LISLE

2213
Jurica Nature Museum
5700 College Rd, 60532; (p) (630) 829-6545; (f) (630) 829-6551; tsuchy@ben.edu; www.alt.ben.edu/resources/j_museum/index.htm; (c) DuPage

Private non-profit/ 1970/ staff: 2(p); 12(v)

HISTORY MUSEUM: Collects, preserves and interprets natural history.

PROGRAMS: Community Outreach; Exhibits; Family Programs; Guided Tours; School-Based Curriculum

COLLECTIONS: [1900-1970] Native American, African, Northern Illinois and specimen dioramas.

HOURS: Sept-Nov, Jan-Apr M-F 1-5, Su 2-4

ADMISSION: No charge

2214
Lisle Station Park
918-920 Burlington Ave, 60532 [1825 Short St, 60532]; (p) (630) 968-2747; (f) (630) 964-7448; (c) DuPage

1978/ Lisle Park District/ staff: 1(f); 5(p); 75(v)

HISTORY MUSEUM; HOUSE MUSEUM: Promotes mid to late 19th century Northern Illinois life focused on 1830s tavern and inn, 1850s farmhouse, 1870s train depot and 1880s wooden caboose.

PROGRAMS: Community Outreach; Concerts; Exhibits; Facility Rental; Family Programs; Festivals; Garden Tours; Guided Tours; Interpretation; Lectures; Living History; Reenactments; Research Library/Archives; School-Based Curriculum

COLLECTIONS: [1830-1900] Mid to late 19th c artifacts.

HOURS: April-Dec Su, T, Th 1-4; June-Aug Su, T-Th 1-4

2215
Netsley-Yender Farmhouse Museum
920 Burlington, 60532 [c/o Lisle Park District, 1825 Short St, 60532]; (p) (630) 968-2747, (630) 968-0499; (f) (630) 964-7448

1850/ Park District/ staff: 1(f); 5(p)

COLLECTIONS: [1850s-1860s] Netzley family bible including family records.

HOURS: Apr-Dec

LOCKPORT

2216
Gaylord Building Historic Site
200 W 8th St, 60441; (p) (815) 588-1100; (f) (815) 588-1101; www.nthp.org; (c) Will

Private for-profit/ 1997/ NTHP/ staff: 5(f); 2(p)

HISTORIC SITE: Preserves local history of Gaylord Building, partnership with the IL Dept of Natural Resources Visitor Center on exhibits and public programs.

PROGRAMS: Exhibits; Facility Rental; Guided Tours; Interpretation; Lectures

HOURS: Yr T-Sa

2217
Gladys Fox Museum
221 E 9th St, 60441 [1911 S Lawrence Ave, 60441]; (p) (815) 838-1183; (f) (815) 838-4974; (c) Will

Private non-profit/ 1840/ Lockport Township Park District/ staff: 1(f); 20(v)

HISTORY MUSEUM: Preserves local history.

PROGRAMS: Annual Meeting; Community Outreach; Concerts; Elder's Programs; Exhibits; Facility Rental; Family Programs; Festivals; Guided Tours; Lectures

COLLECTIONS: [1910-1940] Photos, artifacts related to canal town, boats.

HOURS: Yr Daily

2218
Illinois and Michigan Canal National Heritage Corridor Commission
15701 S Independence Blvd, 60441; (p) (815) 740-2047; (f) (815) 740-2026; ilmi_administration@nps.gov; www.nps.gov/ilmi; (c) Will

Federal/ 1984/ Federal Commission/ staff: 3(f); 1(p)

ALLIANCE OF HISTORICAL AGENCIES: Assists the State of IL and local agencies in preservation, improvement, and interpretation of cultural, natural, and recreational resources.

PROGRAMS: School-Based Curriculum

COLLECTIONS: [1818-present] Primary and secondary materials related to the Illinois and Michigan Canal, its structures and the corridor.

HOURS: M-F 8-4:30

ADMISSION: No charge

2219
Will County Historical Society
803 S State St, 60441; (p) (815) 838-5080; (c) Will

Private non-profit/ 1964/ staff: 1(f); 50(v)/ members: 800/publication: *WCHS Newsletters and quarterly publications.*

HISTORIC SITE; HISTORICAL SOCIETY; HISTORY MUSEUM; HOUSE MUSEUM; LIVING HISTORY/OUTDOOR MUSEUM: Operates a museum and pioneer settlement and oversees historic sites within the county.

PROGRAMS: Annual Meeting; Community Outreach; Exhibits; Festivals; Guided Tours; Interpretation; Publication

COLLECTIONS: [1830-1880s] Collection of items relative to planning, operation and demise of a single waterway in the nation. Also exhibits relating to Will County history, coal mining, limestone and barbed-wire.

HOURS: Yr M-Su 1-4

LOMBARD

2220
DuPage County Genealogical Society
[PO Box 133, 60148]; (p) (630) 548-9095; www.dcgs.org; (c) DuPage

Private non-profit/ 1974/ members: 400

GENEALOGICAL SOCIETY: Promotes genealogy and history through record preservation; publishes genealogical materials.

PROGRAMS: Annual Meeting; Publication

HOURS: By appt

2221
Lombard Historical Society
23 W Maple, 60148; (p) (630) 629-1885; (f) (630) 629-9927; www.tccafe.com/lhm.htm/; (c) DuPage

Private non-profit/ 1970/ Lombard Historical Society/ staff: 1(f); 1(p); 50(v)/ members: 350

HISTORICAL SOCIETY; HISTORY MUSEUM; HOUSE MUSEUM; RESEARCH CENTER

PROGRAMS: Annual Meeting; Exhibits; Festivals; Garden Tours; Guided Tours; Interpretation; Lectures; Publication; Research Library/Archives; Theatre

COLLECTIONS: [19th c] Preserves local history through exhibits, slide presentations, archives and library.

HOURS: Yr W, Sa-Su 1-4

ADMISSION: No charge

2222
National College of Chiropractic Heritage Museum
200 E Roosevelt, 60148; (p) (630) 889-6635; (f) (630) 889-6655; (c) DuPage

Private non-profit/ 1906/ staff: 1(p)

HISTORY MUSEUM

PROGRAMS: Community Outreach; Exhibits

COLLECTIONS: [1906-present] Artifacts related to Chiropractic

2223
Sheldon Peck Homestead Museum
355 E Parkside, 60148 [23 W Maple, 60148]; (p) (630) 629-1885; (f) (630) 629-9927; www.tccafecom/apeck6/peck0.html; (c) DuPage

1999/ Lombard Historical Society/ staff: 1(f); 1(p); 50(v)/ members: 300

ART MUSEUM; HISTORIC SITE; HISTORY MUSEUM; HOUSE MUSEUM: Preserves and promotes life of Sheldon Peck, 19th century folk painter.

PROGRAMS: Community Outreach; Exhibits; Family Programs; Festivals; Guided Tours; Interpretation; Lectures

COLLECTIONS: [1840-1860] Sheldon Peck paintings, memorabilia and period furnishings.

ADMISSION: No charge

LOUISVILLE

2224
Clay County Genealogical Society
S Church St, 62858 [PO Box 94, 62858]; (p) (618) 665-4544; (c) Clay

Private non-profit/ 1988/ staff: 10(v)/ members: 511

GENEALOGICAL SOCIETY: Serves as repository for genealogical records.

PROGRAMS: Research Library/Archives

COLLECTIONS: [1800-present] 400 family histories, marriage, census, death, probate birth, and cemetery records from 50 Illinois counties and 45 states.

HOURS: Yr Apr-Dec M 12-4, Sa 9-4; Dec-Apr 2nd M 12-4

LYONS

2225
Lyons Historical Commission
3910 Barrypoint Rd, 60534 [PO Box 392, 60534]; (p) (708) 447-5815; (c) Cook

City/ 1969/ staff: 11(v)

HISTORIC SITE; HISTORICAL SOCIETY; HISTORY MUSEUM: Promotes local history through museum.

PROGRAMS: Community Outreach; Exhibits; Festivals; Film/Video; School-Based Curriculum

COLLECTIONS: [1900-1950] Period furnishings, clothes, and pictures.

HOURS: Apr-Oct 2nd Su of month 1-4

ADMISSION: No charge

MACOMB

2226
Macomb Public Library District
235 S Lafayette St, 61455 [PO Box 220, 61455]; (p) (309) 833-2714; (f) (309) 833-2714; maco@darkstar.rsa.lib.il.us; www.macomb.lib.il.us; (c) McDonough

1903/ staff: 5(f); 6(p); 3(v)

GENEALOGICAL SOCIETY: Preserves local history.

PROGRAMS: Annual Meeting; Community Outreach; Exhibits; Family Programs; Guided

Tours; Research Library/Archives

COLLECTIONS: Carnegie built library housing local history collection and McDonough County Genealogical Society items.

HOURS: Yr

2227
Western Illinois University Archives and Special Collections
University Library, 61455 [1 University Circle, 61455]; (p) (309) 298-2717; msmcv@wiu.edu; www.wiu.edu/library/units/archives; (c) McDonough

State/ 1972/ Western Illinois University/ staff: 3(f); 4(p)

LIBRARY AND/OR ARCHIVES: Collects materials by and about Western Illinois University, historical and cultural materials relating to the western Illinois region.

PROGRAMS: Research Library/Archives

COLLECTIONS: [Mid-19th c-present] Books, manuscripts, photos, artifacts related to western Illinois region, yearbooks and newspapers.

HOURS: Yr M-F 8-4:30

MAHOMET

2228
Early American Museum
600 N Lombard, 61853 [PO Drawer 1040, 61853]; (p) (217) 586-2612; (f) (217) 586-3491; early@cu-online.com; www.advancenet.net/~early; (c) Champaign

County/ 1968/ Champaign County Forest Preserve District/ staff: 3(f); 4(p); 100(v)

HISTORY MUSEUM: Collects, preserves, and interprets the history of east central Illinois, specifically Champaign County.

PROGRAMS: Exhibits; Interpretation; Lectures; Research Library/Archives; School-Based Curriculum

COLLECTIONS: [Pre 1950] Agriculture, tools, domestic and rural life, textiles and textile production, clothing.

HOURS: June-Aug Daily 10-5; Apr-Oct Sa-Su

MANTENO

2229
Manteno Historical Society
192 W 3rd St, 60950; (p) (815) 468-8002; (f) (815) 468-8002; (c) Kankakee

Private non-profit/ 1987/ Board of Directors/ staff: 20(v)/ members: 203

HISTORICAL SOCIETY: Preserves local history through genealogical research.

PROGRAMS: Annual Meeting; Exhibits; Garden Tours; Guided Tours

COLLECTIONS: [1857-present] Local memorabilia.

HOURS: Saturdays by request

ADMISSION: No charge

MARION

2230
Williamson County Historical Society
105 S Van Buren, 62959; (p) (618) 997-5863; charla@midwest.net;

www.members.xoom.com/wmson_hs/wchs.htm; (c) Williamson

Private non-profit/ staff: 8(v)/ members: 200

GENEALOGICAL SOCIETY; HISTORICAL SOCIETY; HISTORY MUSEUM; RESEARCH CENTER: Preserves local history and assists with genealogical research.

PROGRAMS: Exhibits; Guided Tours; Publication; Research Library/Archives

COLLECTIONS: [1850-1950s] Exhibits of parlor, kitchen, weaving room, country store, emporium, jail cells, sheriff's office and Native American artifacts; research library.

HOURS: (Library) Feb-Nov Th 9-3; (Museum) Apr-Nov Th 9-3

ADMISSION: $2, Children $1

MARISSA

2231
Marissa Historical and Genealogical Society
610 S Main St, 62257 [PO Box 47, 62257-0047]; (p) (618) 295-2562; (c) St Clair

Private non-profit/ 1969/ members: 160/publication: *Branching Out From St. Clair County Illinois*

GENEALOGICAL SOCIETY

PROGRAMS: Annual Meeting; Community Outreach; Publication

COLLECTIONS: Census, church, death and marriage records; newspapers, genealogy.

HOURS: Wed by appt

ADMISSION: No charge

MARSHALL

2232
Clark County Genealogical Library
521 Locust, 62441 [PO Box 153, 62441]; (p) (217) 826-2864; (c) Clark

Private non-profit/ 1976/ staff: 3(f); 2(p)/publication: *The Newsletter*

GENEALOGICAL SOCIETY: Preserves family and local histories, maintains genealogical library.

PROGRAMS: Exhibits; Facility Rental; Lectures; Research Library/Archives

COLLECTIONS: [1820-present] Clark County Family Histories and Public Records, including birth, marriage, cemetery, census, copies from originals and indexed.

HOURS: Th, F, Sa 12:30-3 or by appt

MARTINSVILLE

2233
Lincoln School Museum
7400 E 1500 St, 62442 [PO Box 429, 62442]; (p) (217) 382-6666; (c) Clark

Private non-profit/ 1988/ Martinsville Chamber of Commerce/ staff: 1(p); 5(v)/ members: 15

HISTORIC SITE; HISTORY MUSEUM: Preserves local history through one-room school museum.

PROGRAMS: Community Outreach; Facility

Rental; Family Programs; Interpretation; School-Based Curriculum

COLLECTIONS: [1900-1920] Period school artifacts.

HOURS: June-Aug W-F, Su 2-4 and by appt

ADMISSION: $1.50, Children $0.50

MASCOUTAH

2234
Mascoutah Historical Society
504 N Jefferson St, 62258; (p) (618) 566-2567; (c) St. Clair

City, non-profit/ 1976/ staff: 20(v)/ members: 58

HISTORICAL SOCIETY: Preserves history of Mascoutah and Engelmann townships.

PROGRAMS: Community Outreach; Exhibits; Lectures

COLLECTIONS: [1860s] Family histories, advertising, school items, clothing, farm and hand tools.

ADMISSION: No charge

MATTESON

2235
Matteson Historical Museum
813 School Ave, 60443; (p) (708) 748-3033; (f) (708) 748-2326; lrmathis@lincolnnet.net; www.lincolnnet.net/users/lmattesn; (c) Cook

City, non-profit/ 1976/ Village of Matteson/ staff: 1(f); 2(v)

Preserves and promotes local history.

COLLECTIONS: [19th-20th c] Items related to Matteson; papers, government archives, objects, documents and photos.

HOURS: Yr M-F 9-4:30, Sa-Su varied

MATTOON

2236
Association for the Preservation of Historic Coles County
[PO Box 1999, 61938]; (p) (217) 345-5145; (c) Coles

Private non-profit/ 1977/ Active Membership/ members: 25

HISTORIC PRESERVATION AGENCY: Promotes public awareness and appreciation of historic and cultural resources. Encourages the use of historical buildings and sites for cultural, commercial, civic or tourists purposes.

PROGRAMS: Annual Meeting; Interpretation

HOURS: 1824-present

MCLEANSBORO

2237
Hamilton County Historical Society
c/o McCoy Library, W Side Sq, 62859; (p) (618) 643-2125; (c) Hamilton

Private non-profit/ 1965/ staff: 10(v)/ members: 30

HISTORIC SITE; HISTORICAL SOCIETY; HISTORY MUSEUM: Preserves local history through maintenance of museum.

PROGRAMS: Annual Meeting; Community

Outreach; Exhibits; Guided Tours; Lectures

COLLECTIONS: [1800-1900] Genealogy records, military uniforms and memorabilia depicting early life.

HOURS: Yr M,W,F 1-4

ADMISSION: $1

MENDOTA

2238
Mendota Museum and Historical Society
901 Washington St, 61342 [PO Box 433, 61342-0433]; (p) (815) 539-3373; (f) (815) 539-3922; info@mendotamuseums.org; www.mendotamuseums.org; (c) LaSalle

Private non-profit/ 1993/ Board of Directors/ staff: 1(f); 2(p); 115(v)/ members: 297

HISTORICAL SOCIETY; HISTORY MUSEUM: Promotes preservation of area history, archives for research and study.

PROGRAMS: Community Outreach; Elder's Programs; Exhibits; Family Programs; Festivals; Film/Video; Guided Tours; Lectures

COLLECTIONS: [1850-present] Wild Bill Hickok and Helen Hokinson exhibit, over 2,500 vintage photos, 1800s medical equipment, locally manufactured items, #4978 Steam Engine, Tender and Caboose, operating HOscale Railroad exhibit.

HOURS: Yr Hume Carnegie: Sa-Su 1-4; Union Depot Sept-May Sa-Su 12-5: June-Aug W-Su 12-5

ADMISSION: $2, Student $1; Members free

MEREDOSIA

2239
Meredosia Area Historical Society
321 Main St, 62665 [PO Box 304, 62665]; (p) (217) 584-1356; (f) (217) 584-1911; dld dosh@accessus.net; (c) Morgan

1986/ Board of Trustees/ staff: 2(f); 2(p); 5(v)/ members: 100

HISTORIC SITE; HISTORICAL SOCIETY: Preserves history of Illinois River.

PROGRAMS: Exhibits; Festivals; Guided Tours; Interpretation; Living History

COLLECTIONS: [1875-1950] Photos, artifacts and oral history.

HOURS: Yr W-F 1-5 or by appt

ADMISSION: Donations accepted

METAMORA

2240
Illinois Mennonite Heritage Center
Rte 116 W, 61548 [PO Box 1007, 61548]; (p) (309) 367-2551; (f) (309) 392-2518; gnafzig@juno.com; (c) Woodford

Private non-profit/ 1982/ Illinois Mennonite Historical and Genealogical Society/ staff: 70(v)/ members: 400

HISTORY MUSEUM: Provides educational opportunities and information regarding Mennonite history, beliefs and genealogy through library, archives, museum collections, programs and events.

PROGRAMS: Exhibits; Facility Rental; Guided Tours; Research Library/Archives

COLLECTIONS: [1830-1930] Church, household, personal and agricultural items; records of 1830s immigrants, restored grandfather house and large barn, native trees, prairie plants and grass on 6 acre

METROPOLIS

2241
Elijah P. Curtis Home and Museum
405 Market St, 62960

1870

COLLECTIONS: [1870-1900] History of Massac County.

HOURS: By appt

2242
Fort Massac State Park
1308 E 5th St, 62960; (p) (618) 524-4712; (f) (618) 524-9321; (c) Massac

State/ 1908/ Illinois Dept of Natural Resources/ staff: 9(f); 35(v)

HISTORIC SITE; HISTORY MUSEUM; LIVING HISTORY/OUTDOOR MUSEUM: Archaeological outline of the original French and American forts.

PROGRAMS: Exhibits; Film/Video; Guided Tours; Interpretation; Living History; Reenactments

HOURS: Yr Daily Winter 9-4:30, Summer 10-5:30

2243
Massac County Historical Society
405 Market St, 62960; (c) Massac

Private non-profit/ 1975/ members: 50

HISTORIC PRESERVATION AGENCY; HISTORIC SITE; HISTORICAL SOCIETY; HISTORY MUSEUM: Preserves local history and 1870 home.

PROGRAMS: Annual Meeting; Community Outreach; Exhibits; Garden Tours; Guided Tours; Publication

COLLECTIONS: [1870-1910] Period furnishings, clothing and photos.

HOURS: Yr

ADMISSION: No charge

MIDLOTHIAN

2244
Chicago and Eastern Illinois Railroad Historical Society
Watseka Union Station, 60445 [PO Box 606, 60445-0606]; (p) (708) 479-1059; www.justnet.com/cei; (c) Cook

Private non-profit/ 1982/ staff: 7(v)/ members: 325

HISTORICAL SOCIETY; HISTORY MUSEUM: Preserves history of Chicago and Eastern Illinois Railroad and its predecessor railroads.

PROGRAMS: Annual Meeting; Exhibits; Lectures; Publication; Research Library/Archives

COLLECTIONS: [1849-1957] Photos, records and artifacts.

HOURS: May-Oct 1st Sat 9-4

2245
Midlothian Historical Society
14801 Pulaski, 60445; (p) (708) 385-6375, (708) 389-0055; (c) Cook

1993/ Midlothian Village/ staff: 6(f)/ members: 10

HISTORIC PRESERVATION AGENCY; HISTORIC SITE; HISTORICAL SOCIETY: Collects and preserves local history.

PROGRAMS: Community Outreach; Elder's Programs; Exhibits; Film/Video

COLLECTIONS: Period clothing, artifacts, pictures, tapes, videos, paintings, books, newspaper articles related to Midlothian residents.

HOURS: Yr 1st and 3rd Sat 11-2

ADMISSION: Donations

MINOOKA

2246
Three Rivers Public Library Local History Collection
109 N Wabena Ave, 60447 [PO Box 370, 60447]; (p) (815) 467-1600; (f) (815) 467-1632; mhouchens@starbasel.htls.lib.il.us; (c) Grundy

1992/ staff: 1(p)

HISTORIC PRESERVATION AGENCY: Preserves local history.

PROGRAMS: Publication; Research Library/Archives

COLLECTIONS: [1830-present] County histories, maps, plat books and newspapers.

HOURS: Yr M-Sa by appt

ADMISSION: No charge

MOLINE

2247
Butterworth Center
1105 8th St, 61265; (p) (309) 765-7970; (f) (309) 765-9656; (c) Rock Island

Private non-profit/ 1955/ William Butterworth Memorial Trust/ staff: 10(f); 8(p)

GARDEN; HISTORIC SITE; HOUSE MUSEUM: Preserves and interprets the 1892 home of Katherine Deere Butterworth and William Butterworth.

PROGRAMS: Community Outreach; Concerts; Exhibits; Family Programs; Festivals; Garden Tours; Guided Tours; Lectures; Research Library/Archives; School-Based Curriculum

COLLECTIONS: [1892-1953] Processed manuscripts, photographs, artifacts, portraits, paintings, sheet music, orchestration plates and organ rolls.

HOURS: Yr M-Sa by appt

ADMISSION: Donations accepted

2248
Deere-Wiman House
817 11th Ave, 61265; (p) (309) 765-7971; (f) (309) 765-9656; (c) Rock Island

Private non-profit/ 1872/ William Butterworth Memorial Trust/ staff: 10(f); 8(p)

GARDEN; HISTORIC SITE; HOUSE MUSEUM

PROGRAMS: Community Outreach; Concerts; Exhibits; Garden Tours; Guided Tours; Lectures; Research Library/Archives; School-Based Curriculum

COLLECTIONS: [1870-1976] Artifacts related to Deere Family history, 12 linear feet processed manuscripts, 2,000 volumes, 3,500 photos, 4,000 artifacts, 100 portraits and paintings, 200 pieces of sheet music, orchestrion plates and organ rolls.

HOURS: Yr Daily by appt

ADMISSION: Donations

2249
John Deere Pavilion
1400 River Dr, 61265; (p) (309) 765-1000; (f) (309) 765-1003; jdpavilion@deere.com; www.deere.com; (c) Rock Island

Private for-profit/ 1997/ staff: 4(f); 24(p)

HISTORY MUSEUM: Promotes history of agricultural equipment.

PROGRAMS: Exhibits; Film/Video; Guided Tours

COLLECTIONS: [1800-present] Antique John Deere equipment, memorabilia, photos, multimedia and interactive displays.

HOURS: Yr M-F 9-6, Sa 9-5, Su 12:30-5

ADMISSION: No charge

2250
Rock Island County Historical Society
822 11th Ave, 61244-3421; (p) (309) 764-8590; (f) (309) 764-4748; richs@netexpress.net; www.netexpress.net/~richs/; (c) Rock Island

Private non-profit/ 1905/ Board of Directors/ staff: 1(f); 60(v)/ members: 400

HISTORICAL SOCIETY; HOUSE MUSEUM; RESEARCH CENTER: The Society initiates and encourages historical inquiry and collects, preserves, organizes and disseminates the materials of history, particularly relating to Rock Island, IL, but not necessarily limited to.

PROGRAMS: Annual Meeting; Community Outreach; Exhibits; Guided Tours; Research Library/Archives

COLLECTIONS: [19th-20th c] Collections include local history materials in various formats including books, archives, manuscripts, newspapers, journals, maps, atlases, microfilm, photographs, city directories, genealogical resources, audio/video history, ephemera and museum artifacts.

HOURS: Yr W-Sa 9-5

MONMOUTH

2251
Stewart House, The
1015 E Euclid, 61462; (p) (369) 734-5154

1865/ staff: 1(v)

COLLECTIONS: [1869] Minnie Stewart's button box, Louise Stevenson's album, a melodeon, and furniture of the 19th century.; Historic albums of pictures from 1869 until now. Newspaper articles depicting events held by the group.

HOURS: By appt

2252
Wyatt Earp Birthplace Historic House Museum
406 S 3rd St, 61462 [1020 E Detroit Ave, 61462-1453]; (p) (309) 734-6419; wyattearp birthp@webtv.net; www.misslink.net/misslink/earp.htm; (c) Warren

Private non-profit/ 1986/ Board of Trustees/ staff: 1(p); 30(v)/ members: 50/publication: *Wyatt Earp Birthplace Newsletter*

HISTORIC SITE; HOUSE MUSEUM; LIVING HISTORY/OUTDOOR MUSEUM; RESEARCH CENTER: The birthplace of Wyatt Earp, renowned Deputy U.S. Marshal of the Old West; promotes the study of the life and legend of Wyatt Earp.

PROGRAMS: Annual Meeting; Community Outreach; Exhibits; Facility Rental; Family Programs; Festivals; Guided Tours; Interpretation; Living History; Publication; Reenactments; Research

HOURS: May-Sept Su 1-4 and by appt

ADMISSION: $2, Children $1

MONTICELLO

2253
Monticello Railway Museum, Inc.
992 Iron Horse Place, 61856 [PO Box 401, 61856-0401]; (p) (800) 952-3396, (217) 762-9011; mrm@prairienet.org; www.prairienet.org/mrm; (c) Piatt

Private non-profit/ 1966/ staff: 75(v)/ members: 350

RAILROAD MUSEUM: Preserves railroad history through exhibits and railroad demonstration.

PROGRAMS: Exhibits; Festivals

COLLECTIONS: [1940s] Locomotives, freight, passenger equipment built between 1891 and 1977, tools, clothing, pictures, promotional items.

HOURS: May-Oct Sa-Su

2254
Piatt County Historical and Genealogical
Courthouse Annex, 61856 [PO Box 111, 61856]; (c) Piatt

Private non-profit/ 1979/ staff: 12(v)/ members: 178

GENEALOGICAL SOCIETY; HISTORICAL SOCIETY: Collects and preserves Piatt County history.

PROGRAMS: Annual Meeting; Publication; Research Library/Archives

COLLECTIONS: [1830-present] Piatt County cemeteries, census records 1840-1920, newspapers 1874-1968, Francis Brooks Collection of early Piatt County photos.

HOURS: Yr M, W 1-4

ADMISSION: No charge

2255
Piatt County Museum, Inc.
315 W Main St, 61856; (p) (217) 762-4341; (c) Piatt

Private non-profit/ 1965/ Board of Trustees/ staff: 14(v)/ members: 65

HISTORICAL SOCIETY; HISTORY MUSEUM: Offers a unique look at the heritage of a county that is rich in pioneer history. The museum includes Rayville, a model railroad museum.

PROGRAMS: Annual Meeting; Exhibits; Festivals; Guided Tours

COLLECTIONS: [Late 19th-early 20th c] The collections tell the story of the Native Americans and Pioneers who lives in a county rich in Civil War, agricultural and cultural history.

HOURS: May-Oct, Sa, Su or by appt

ADMISSION: $2, Children $1

MORRIS

2256
Goose Lake Prairie State Natural Area
5010 N Jugtown Rd, 60450; (p) (815) 942-2899; (f) (815) 942-2936; (c) Grundy

State/ 1969/ staff: 7(f); 4(p); 10(v)

LIVING HISTORY/OUTDOOR MUSEUM

PROGRAMS: Exhibits; Festivals; Guided Tours; Interpretation; Lectures; School-Based Curriculum

HOURS: Yr Park 6 am-sunset; Visitor Center Apr-Nov Daily 10-4; Dec-Mar M-F 10-4

MORRISON

2257
Morrison Historical Society
202 E Lincoln Way, 61270 [PO Box 1, 61270]; (p) (815) 772-3013; jott@sanasys.com; (c) Whiteside

Private non-profit/ staff: 25(v)/ members: 250/publication: *Historic Society Newsletter*

HISTORIC SITE; HISTORICAL SOCIETY; HISTORY MUSEUM: Preserves agricultural heritage and general history.

PROGRAMS: Annual Meeting; Community Outreach; Exhibits; Facility Rental; Guided Tours; Publication

COLLECTIONS: Agricultural tools and memorabilia.

HOURS: Apr-May, Sept-Nov Sa-Su 1-4; June-Aug T-Su 1-4

MORRISONVILLE

2258
Morrisonville Historical Society
604 Carlin, 62546 [PO Box 227, 62546]; (c) Christian

Private non-profit/ 1978/ staff: 8(v)/ members: 100

HISTORY MUSEUM: Preserves and promotes local history.

PROGRAMS: Annual Meeting; Festivals; Guided Tours

COLLECTIONS: [1872-present] Pictures, period clothing, Morrisonville Times microfiche.

HOURS: By appt only

MORTON GROVE

2259
Morton Grove Historical Museum

6240 W Dempster, 60053 [6834 W Dempster, 60053]; (p) (847) 965-0203; (f) (847) 965-7484; (c) Cook

Joint/ 1986/ staff: 3(p); 50(v)/ members: 200

HOUSE MUSEUM: Collects, preserves, and exhibits material related to history of Village of Morton Grove and local area communities; park district and historical society.

PROGRAMS: Exhibits; Film/Video; Guided Tours; Lectures; School-Based Curriculum

COLLECTIONS: [1880-1920] Contains agricultural, commercial, decorative and domestic items related to Morton Grove.

HOURS: Yr W 1-3, Su 2-4

ADMISSION: No charge

MOUNT CARMEL

2260
Burkett House Wabash County Museum

119 W 3rd St, 62863 [PO Box 512, 62863]; (p) (618) 262-8774; www.mtcarmel.com; (c) Wabash

1990/ Wabash County Museum District/ staff: 1(p); 25(v)

HISTORIC PRESERVATION AGENCY: Preserves the cultural heritage of the region and provides the opportunity to view an array of artifacts from the people of Wabash County.

PROGRAMS: Exhibits; Guided Tours; Lectures; Research Library/Archives

COLLECTIONS: [1860s-present] Antique books, furniture, photographs, ephemera, tools and gadgets donated by local people.

HOURS: Yr T,Th, Su 2-5 or by appt

ADMISSION: Donations accepted

MOUNT CARROLL

2261
Carroll County Historical Society

107 W Broadway, 61053 [PO Box 65, 61053-1124]; (p) (815) 244-3474; (c) Carroll

County; Joint; Private non-profit/ 1964/ staff: 3(p); 10(v)/ members: 100

HISTORIC PRESERVATION AGENCY; HISTORICAL SOCIETY; HISTORY MUSEUM; HOUSE MUSEUM; LIVING HISTORY/OUTDOOR MUSEUM: Collects and preserves Carroll County history.

PROGRAMS: Annual Meeting; Community Outreach; Exhibits; Facility Rental; Family Programs; Festivals; Film/Video; Guided Tours; Lectures; Living History; Publication; Research Library/Archives

COLLECTIONS: [1850-1940] Natural, civil, military, literary and ecclesiastical artifacts.

HOURS: Yr M-F 10-2, Sa 10-3, Su 12-3

ADMISSION: $2, Children $1

MOUNT PROSPECT

2262
Mount Prospect Historical Society

101 S Maple, 60056; (p) (847) 392-9006; (f) (847) 392-8995; mphist@aol.com; www.mphist.org; (c) Cook

Private non-profit/ 1976/ Board of Directors/ staff: 2(p); 50(v)/ members: 300

HOUSE MUSEUM: Promotes local history through maintenance of historic house museum.

PROGRAMS: Annual Meeting; Exhibits; Facility Rental; Film/Video; Garden Tours; Guided Tours; Lectures; Research Library/Archives; School-Based Curriculum

COLLECTIONS: [1900-1920] Photos, newspapers, furnishings, clothing, early village days.

HOURS: Yr Su, T, Th 1-3

ADMISSION: No charge

2263
Northwest Suburban Council of Genealogies

[PO Box AC, 60056]; www.mtprospect.org/nsgs; (c) Cook

Private non-profit/ 1977/ members: 100/publication: News from the Northwest

GENEALOGICAL SOCIETY: Promotes study of genealogy and history, and encourages the preservation of private and public records; provides genealogical research assistance.

PROGRAMS: Annual Meeting; Publication

COLLECTIONS: [1900-1926] Index of births, marriages and obituaries.

HOURS: Sept-May 3rd Th 7:30

ADMISSION: Members Free

MOUNT PULASKI

2264
Mt. Pulaski Township Historical Society

104 E Cooke St, 62548; (p) (217) 792-5758; (c) Logan

1994/ Executive Board/ staff: 26(v)/ members: 90

HISTORIC PRESERVATION AGENCY; HISTORIC SITE; HISTORICAL SOCIETY; HISTORY MUSEUM; RESEARCH CENTER

PROGRAMS: Exhibits; Festivals; Guided Tours; Interpretation; Reenactments; School-Based Curriculum

COLLECTIONS: [1836-1950] Artifacts and memorabilia related to schools, businesses and organizations of Mt Pulaski.

HOURS: Yr T-Sa 12-4

ADMISSION: No charge

MOUNT VERNON

2265
Mitchell Museum at Cedarhurst

Richview Rd, 62864 [PO Box 923, 62864]; (p) (618) 242-1236; (f) (618) 242-9530; mitchell@midwest.net; www.cedarhurst.org; (c) Jefferson

Private non-profit/ 1965/ John R. and Eleanor R. Michell Foundation/ staff: 12(f); 4(p);

25(v)/publication: Cedarhurst Quarterly

ART MUSEUM: Presents over 400 visual and performing arts programs for the public. Educational programs include interpretive and participatory activities.

PROGRAMS: Concerts; Exhibits; Family Programs; Festivals; Guided Tours; Interpretation; Lectures; Publication

COLLECTIONS: [Late 19th-early 20th c] The small, significant American painting collection includes works by Samuel Bellows, Mary Cassatt, Thomas Eakins, Childe Hassam, Robert Henri, George Luks, Maurice Prendergast, John Singer Sargent and Andrew Wyeth. Additional collections include contemporary art, sculpture and decorative arts.

HOURS: Yr Tu-Sa 10-5, Su, 1-5

MURPHYSBORO

2266
General John A. Logan Museum

1613 Edith St, 62966 [PO Box 563, 62966]; (p) (618) 684-3455; (c) Jackson

Private non-profit/ 1985/ Museum Board/ staff: 6(p); 10(v)

HISTORIC SITE; HISTORY MUSEUM: Collects, preserves, and interprets 19th century southern Illinois through exhibits of John Logan Family.

PROGRAMS: Community Outreach; Exhibits; Guided Tours; Interpretation; Living History; Reenactments

COLLECTIONS: [19th c] Campaign biographies, military items, maps, and political memorabilia.

HOURS: Yr June-Aug M, W-Sa 10-4, Su 1-4; Mar-May and Sept-Nov Sa 10-4, Su 1-4

ADMISSION: Donations requested

2267
Jackson County Historical Society

224 S 17th St, 62966 [1616 Edith St, 62966]; (p) (618) 684-6989; (c) Jackson

Private non-profit/ 1969/ staff: 20(v)/ members: 275/publication: The Ventilator

GENEALOGICAL SOCIETY; HISTORICAL SOCIETY; HISTORY MUSEUM; HOUSE MUSEUM; RESEARCH CENTER: Collects, preserves and displays history and culture of Jackson County and communities with library and archives.

PROGRAMS: Annual Meeting; Community Outreach; Exhibits; Facility Rental; Family Programs; Festivals; Guided Tours; Interpretation; Lectures; Living History; Publication; Research Library/Archives; School-Based Curriculum

COLLECTIONS: [1799-present] Newspapers on microfilm, books, family histories, obituaries, cemetery and courthouse records.

HOURS: Yr W-F 12-3, Th 6:30-9:30

ADMISSION: No charge

NAPERVILLE

2268
Naper Settlement

523 S Webster St, 60540; (p) (630) 420-6010; (f) (630) 305-4044; towncrier@naperville.il.us;

www.napersettlement.org; (c) DuPage

Private non-profit/ 1969/ Naperville Heritage Society/ staff: 19(f); 33(p)/ 1171(v)/ members: 1357/publication: *Heritage News Extra*

LIVING HISTORY/OUTDOOR MUSEUM: Naper Settlement is a 19th century village on 13 acres with 30 historic structures, including a Victorian mansion listed on the national Register of Historic Places, homes, businesses, a log house, fort, chapel, and one-room schoolhouse.

PROGRAMS: Annual Meeting; Exhibits; Facility Rental; Family Programs; Guided Tours; Interpretation; Lectures; Living History; Publication; Reenactments; Research Library/Archives; School-Based Curriculum

COLLECTIONS: [1831-1900] Artifacts related to 19th century Naperville life.

HOURS: Nov-Mar T-F 10-4; Apr-Oct T-Sa 10-4, Su 1-4; July-Aug Th 10-8

ADMISSION: $6.50, Student $4, Children $4, Seniors $5.50; Winter fees lower

NASHVILLE

2269
Washington County Historical Society
326 S Kaskaskia, 62263 [PO Box 9, 62263]; (c) Washington

County; Private non-profit/ 1965/ staff: 12(v)/ members: 75

GENEALOGICAL SOCIETY; HISTORIC PRESERVATION AGENCY; HISTORIC SITE; HISTORICAL SOCIETY; HISTORY MUSEUM; HOUSE MUSEUM; RESEARCH CENTER: Preserves local history.

PROGRAMS: Annual Meeting; Community Outreach; Elder's Programs; Exhibits; Facility Rental; Family Programs; Festivals; Garden Tours; Guided Tours; Interpretation; Lectures; Living History; Publication; Reenactments; Research Library/Archives; School-Based Curriculu

COLLECTIONS: Period clothing, furnishings, dolls, toys, documents.

HOURS: Yr by appt

NAUVOO

2270
Joseph Smith Historic Center
149 Water St, 62354 [PO Box 338, 62354]; (p) (217) 453-2246; (f) (217) 453-6414; jshisctr@nauvoo.net; www.joseph-smith.com; (c) Hancock

Private non-profit/ 1980/ RLDS World Church/ staff: 4(f); 1(p); 16(v)

HISTORIC SITE: Preserves and interprets history of Joseph Smith, founder of Reorganized Church of Jesus Christ of Latter Day Saints.

PROGRAMS: Community Outreach; Exhibits; Facility Rental; Film/Video; Guided Tours; Interpretation; Lectures; Living History; Theatre

COLLECTIONS: [1810-1846] Furnishings and personal belongings of Smith Family.

HOURS: Yr M-Sa 9-5, Su 1-5

2271
Nauvoo Historical Society
1380 Mulholland St, 62354 [PO Box 69, 62354]; (p) (217) 453-2767, (271) 453-6671; (c) Hancock

Private non-profit; State/ 1953/ Board of Directors/ staff: 15(v)/ members: 97

HISTORIC PRESERVATION AGENCY; HISTORIC SITE; HISTORICAL SOCIETY; HISTORY MUSEUM; HOUSE MUSEUM: Collects and preserves artifacts and buildings.

PROGRAMS: Annual Meeting; Exhibits; Guided Tours; Interpretation; Lectures; Research Library/Archives

COLLECTIONS: Period clothing, furnishings, farming, military materials, arrowhead collection.

HOURS: May15-Oct-15 Daily 1-5

ADMISSION: No charge

2272
Nauvoo Restoration Inc.
145 N Wells St, 62354 [PO Box 215, 62354]; (p) (217) 453-2233; (f) (217) 453-0282; nripa@nauvoo.net; (c) Hancock

Private non-profit/ 1962/ The Church of Jesus Christ of Latter-day Saints/ staff: 16(f); 11(p); 164(v)/publication: *Nauvoo Newsletter*

HISTORIC PRESERVATION AGENCY: Preserves historic Nauvoo.

PROGRAMS: Concerts; Exhibits; Family Programs; Film/Video; Guided Tours; Interpretation; Living History; Publication; Reenactments; Theatre

HOURS: Yr May-Aug Daily 9-6; Sept-Apr

2273
Wilford Woodruff House
SR 96 & Hotchkess St, 62354 [SR 96 & Hotchkess St, 62354]; (p) (217) 453-2716

HOUSE MUSEUM

NEW BOSTON

2274
New Boston Historical Society
302 Main St, 61272 [Box 284, 61272]; (p) (309) 587-8640; (f) (309) 587-8292; (c) Mercer

Private non-profit/ 1990/ staff: 1(f); 10(v)/ members: 50

GENEALOGICAL SOCIETY; HISTORY MUSEUM: Preserves history of New Boston and New Boston Township.

PROGRAMS: Annual Meeting; Community Outreach; Concerts; Exhibits; Facility Rental; Garden Tours; Guided Tours; Interpretation; Living History; Reenactments

COLLECTIONS: Indian arrowheads, furnishings, tools and genealogy.

HOURS: Apr-Oct Su 1-5

NEWARK

2275
Fern Dell Historic Association
502 Chicago Rd, 60541 [PO Box 254, 60541]; (c) Kendall

Private non-profit/ 1985/ Board of Directors/ staff: 40(v)/ members: 132/publication: *Fern Dell School District 80*

HISTORIC SITE; HISTORICAL SOCIETY: Preserves history of Newark.

PROGRAMS: Annual Meeting; Community Outreach; Exhibits; Family Programs; Guided Tours; Publication

COLLECTIONS: [1892-1952] School, desks, books, maps, bells, blacksmith shop, forge, bellows, anvils, Smithy tools, goat and horse treadmills, line shaft.

HOURS: Yr by appt

NILES

2276
Niles Historical Society Museum
8970 Milwaukee Ave, 60714; (p) (847) 390-0160; (c) Cook

1971/ staff: 20(p); 8(v)/ members: 300

GENEALOGICAL SOCIETY; HISTORICAL SOCIETY; HISTORY MUSEUM

PROGRAMS: Annual Meeting; Community Outreach; Family Programs; Film/Video; Research Library/Archives

HOURS: Yr W, F, 4th Su of month 10:30-3:30

ADMISSION: Donations accepted

NORTHBROOK

2277
Jewish Genealogical Society of Illinois
[PO Box 515, 60065-0515]; (p) (312) 666-0100; jrfraz@megsinet.net; www.jewishgen.org/jgsi; (c) Cook

Private non-profit/ 1981/ staff: 15(v)/ members: 200/publication: *Morasha*

GENEALOGICAL SOCIETY: Promotes Jewish family historical research.

PROGRAMS: Lectures; Publication; Research Library/Archives

COLLECTIONS: [19th-20th c] Non-circulating reference library with books, periodicals, microfilms, microfiche related to genealogy research techniques, Jewish communities.

HOURS: Yr

ADMISSION: No charge

2278
Northfield Inn
1776 Walters Ave, 60062 [PO Box 2021, 60065-2021]; (p) (847) 498-3404; nbhsoc@nsn.nslsilus.org; nsn.nslsilus.org/nbkhome/nbhsoc

1894/ staff: 40(v)

Second floor of the inn is a recreation of a late 19th-century home.

COLLECTIONS: [Victorian] Furnishings from local families.; Local and family history.

HOURS: Yr

NORWAY

2279
Norwegian Center Inc./Norsk Museum
, [1422 James Court, Ottawa, 61350]; (p) (815) 434-7478; (c) LaSalle

Joint/ 1980/ State; Private non-profit/ staff: 2(p); 10(v)

HISTORY MUSEUM: Preserves history related to Scandinavia.

PROGRAMS: Exhibits

COLLECTIONS: [1700-1800s] Antique dishes, old farm implements, Norwegian rosemaling, artifacts.

HOURS: June-Sept Sa-Su 1-5

ADMISSION: $1

O'FALLON

2280
O'Fallon Historical Society
101 W State St, 62269 [PO Box 344, 62269-0344]; (p) (618) 624-8409; (c) Saint Clair

County, non-profit; Private non-profit/ 1988/ Board of Directors/ staff: 15(v)/ members: 140/publication: *O'Fallon Historical Society Newsletter*

HISTORIC SITE; HISTORICAL SOCIETY; HISTORY MUSEUM: Promotes, collects and preserves local history.

PROGRAMS: Annual Meeting; Community Outreach; Exhibits; Guided Tours; Interpretation; Lectures; Publication; Research Library/Archives

COLLECTIONS: 15,000 photos, negatives, 4,000 journals, 100 scrapbooks, 1,000 books and pamphlets, 7,000 newspapers, 30 oral histories, 5,000 museum artifacts housed in 1903 historic bank building.

HOURS: Yr W, F-Sa 1-4 and by appt

ADMISSION: No charge

OAK BROOK

2281
Czechoslovak Heritage Museum
122 W 22nd St, 60523; (p) (630) 472-9909; (f) (630) 472-1100; czskmuseum@aol.com; www.csafraternallife.org/museum.htm; (c) DuPage

Private non-profit/ 1974/ CSA Fraternal Life/ staff: 2(f); 2(v)

HISTORIC PRESERVATION AGENCY: Preserves study of Czech, Moravian and Slovak history and culture.

PROGRAMS: Exhibits; Guided Tours; Research Library/Archives

COLLECTIONS: [19th c-present] Costumes, artwork, ceramics, dolls, puppets; research library with books, periodicals in English and Czech; genealogical materials, CSA records.

HOURS: Yr M-F, 2nd Sa 10-4

ADMISSION: No charge

2282
Fullersburg Historic Foundation
York Road & Spring Road, 60522 [PO Box 5131, 60522]

Private for-profit/ 1986/ staff: 20(v)

HISTORIC SITE

2283
Graue Mill and Museum
3720 York Road, 60522 [PO Box 4533, 60522]; (p) (630) 655-2090; (f) (630) 920-9721; administrator@grauemill.org; www.grauemill.org; (c) DuPage

Private non-profit/ 1852/ staff: 10(f); 60(v)/ members: 440

HISTORIC SITE; HISTORY MUSEUM; LIVING HISTORY/OUTDOOR MUSEUM: Preserves grist mill and underground railroad station.

PROGRAMS: Annual Meeting; Community Outreach; Concerts; Exhibits; Family Programs; Festivals; Film/Video; Guided Tours; Interpretation; Living History; Publication; Reenactments; School-Based Curriculum

COLLECTIONS: [19th c-present] Period history rooms reflect various modes of life; milling operation uses original equipment, pioneer crafts, artifacts related to Underground Railroad Station.

HOURS: Apr-Nov T-Su

2284
Oak Brook Historical Society
[PO Box 3821, 60522]; (p) (630) 833-8154; (f) (630) 833-8154; (c) DuPage

1975/ staff: 20(v)/ members: 140

HISTORICAL SOCIETY

PROGRAMS: Annual Meeting; Exhibits; Family Programs; Guided Tours; Interpretation; Lectures; Living History; Publication; Research Library/Archives

COLLECTIONS: [1950-present] Newspaper clippings, photos, farm tools, doll furniture, toys, business machines, musical instruments, books, journals, furniture, video and audio.

OAK FOREST

2285
Oak Forest Historical Society
15440 S Central Ave, 60452; (p) (708) 687-4050; (f) (708) 687-8817; (c) Cook

1970

HISTORICAL SOCIETY: Preserves records and memorabilia related to local history.

COLLECTIONS: Photos, newspaper articles, artifacts, letters and books.

OAK LAWN

2286
Oak Lawn Public Library-Local History Section
9427 S Raymond Ave, 60453; (p) (708) 422-4990; (f) (708) 422-5061; www.lib.oak-lawn.il.us; (c) Cook

City/ staff: 1(p)

LIBRARY AND/OR ARCHIVES: Sub-area of general public library which gathers and stores information concerning aspects of the village.

PROGRAMS: Concerts; Exhibits; Family Programs; Lectures; Research Library/Archives

COLLECTIONS: [1920-present] Small, non-circulating book collection dealing with Chicago metropolitan area newspaper clippings, local documents, maps, and an obituary index.

HOURS: Yr M-Th 9-9, F-Sa 9-5, Sept-May Su 1-5

OAK PARK

2287
Cheney Mansion, The
220 N Euclid, 60302; (p) (708) 383-2612; (f)

(708) 383-6485; (c) Cook

1985/ Park District of Oak Park/ staff: 1(f)

Historic 1913 mansion promoting cultural events.

HOURS: Yr by appt

2288
Ernest Hemingway Foundation of Oak Park, The
333 N Oak Park Ave, 60303 [PO Box 2222, 60303-2222]; (p) (708) 848-2222; (f) (708) 386-2952; efhop@theramp.net; www.hemingway.org/hemingway; (c) Cook

Private non-profit/ 1983/ staff: 2(f); 2(p); 1100(v)/ members: 400

HISTORY MUSEUM; HOUSE MUSEUM: Promotes the life and work of Ernest Hemingway, with an emphasis on his Oak Park birthplace.

PROGRAMS: Community Outreach; Concerts; Exhibits; Family Programs; Festivals; Guided Tours; Interpretation; Lectures; Research Library/Archives; School-Based Curriculum

COLLECTIONS: [1899-1920] Material culture interpreting the literature, life and experiences of Ernest Hemingway, especially his early Oak Park years.

HOURS: Yr 4-7

ADMISSION: $6, Seniors $4.50

2289
Frank Lloyd Wright Preservaton Trust
931 Chicago Ave, 60302; (p) (708) 848-1976; (f) (708) 848-1248; (c) Cook

Private non-profit/ 1974/ staff: 25(f); 14(p); 550(v)/ members: 2530

HISTORIC SITE; HOUSE MUSEUM: Manages two sites as historic house museums - Frank Lloyd Wright's home and studio and Robie House.

PROGRAMS: Annual Meeting; Community Outreach; Exhibits; Family Programs; Guided Tours; Interpretation; Lectures; Research Library/Archives; School-Based Curriculum

COLLECTIONS: [1889-1909] Frank Lloyd Wright designed furnishings; ceramics, paintings, dinnerware, books, serials, toys, textiles, reference library.

HOURS: Yr Daily

2290
Historical Society of Oak Park and River Forest
217 Home Ave, 60303 [PO Box 771, 60303-0771]; (c) Cook

Private non-profit/ 1968/ staff: 1(f); 2(p)/ 50(v)/ members: 700/publication: *Nature's Choicest Spot Hemingway*

HISTORICAL SOCIETY; HISTORY MUSEUM; HOUSE MUSEUM; RESEARCH CENTER: Operates a museum and research center and conducts educational outreach programs to preserve, interpret and disseminate information and artifacts on sister villages.

PROGRAMS: Annual Meeting; Community Outreach; Exhibits; Facility Rental; Family Programs; Festivals; Guided Tours; Lectures; Living History; Research Library/Archives; School-Based Curriculum

COLLECTIONS: [19th-20th c] Photos, newspapers, records of clubs and organizations, biographical information and area costumes. Artifacts related to suburban life in America from late 19th century until WWII.

HOURS: Mar-Nov Th-Su 11:30-3:30; Dec-Feb 11:30-1:30

ADMISSION: $5

2291
Oak Park Conservatory, The
615 Garfield St, 60304; (p) (708) 386-4700; (f) (708) 386-3221; (c) Cook

Private non-profit/ 1929/ staff: 3(f); 3(p); 21(v)/ members: 900

NATURAL HISTORY MUSEUM: Conservation that has tropical sub Tropical Desert and Mediterranean plant collection.

PROGRAMS: Annual Meeting; Community Outreach; Exhibits; Facility Rental; Family Programs; Festivals; Garden Tours; Guided Tours; Interpretation; Lectures; Publication; School-Based Curriculum

COLLECTIONS: Live plant material from different parts of the world.

HOURS: Yr M 2-4, T 10-4, Th-Su 10-4

ADMISSION: $1, Children $0.50

2292
Pleasant Home Foundation
217 Home Ave, 60302; (p) (708) 383-2654; (f) (708) 383-2768; phf@enteract.com; (c) Cook

Private non-profit/ 1990/ Pleasant Home Foundation/ staff: 2(f); 1(p); 75(v)/ members: 500/publication: *Pleasant Home News*

HISTORIC PRESERVATION AGENCY; HISTORIC SITE; HISTORY MUSEUM; HOUSE MUSEUM: Maintains, operates and restores the Maher Home, a historic site.

PROGRAMS: Annual Meeting; Community Outreach; Exhibits; Facility Rental; Family Programs; Guided Tours; Interpretation; Lectures; Publication

COLLECTIONS: [1897-1910] Original furnishings and fixtures designed by architect George Maher.

HOURS: Mar-Nov Th-Su 11:30, 12:30, 1:30, 2:30; Dec-Feb Th-Su 11:30, 12:30

ADMISSION: $5, Student $3

OAKLAND

2293
Landmarks Inc.
14 S Pike St, 61543; (p) (217) 346-2282; andyt@net66.com; www.oaklandil.com; (c) Coles

Private non-profit/ 1969/ staff: 25(v)

HISTORY MUSEUM: Promotes life of prominent attorney Dr. H. Rutherford.

PROGRAMS: Community Outreach; Concerts; Exhibits; Facility Rental; Garden Tours; Guided Tours; School-Based Curriculum

2294
Museum of Christian Heritage
Corner of Walnut & Washington, 61943 [109 E Main St, 61943]; (p) (217) 346-3274; (f) (217) 346-2005; (c) Coles

Private non-profit/ 1991/ Oakland Historical Foundation/ staff: 6(v)/ members: 85

HISTORY MUSEUM: Collects histories and memorabilia of churches.

PROGRAMS: Community Outreach; Concerts; Exhibits; Facility Rental; Family Programs; Guided Tours; Lectures; Living History; Research Library/Archives

COLLECTIONS: Bibles, quilts, song books, Tiffany stained glass windows.

HOURS: May-Dec Daily

OAKWOOD

2295
Illiana Civil War Historical Society
205 Green St, 61858 [PO Box 365, 61858]; (p) (217) 354-4519; (c) Vermilion

Private non-profit/ 1985/ staff: 8(v)/ members: 28

LIVING HISTORY/OUTDOOR MUSEUM: Promotes Civil War history with exhibits and school presentations.

PROGRAMS: Exhibits; Lectures; Living History; Reenactments

COLLECTIONS: [1859-1865] Arms, military regalia, books, pictures, period clothing.

HOURS: By appt

ADMISSION: No charge

OKAWVILLE

2296
Heritage House and Museum of Okawville
114 W Walnut St, 62271 [PO Box 305, 62271]; (p) (618) 243-5535; (c) Washington

Private non-profit/ 1982/ Heritage House and Museum of Okawville/ staff: 1(p); 35(v)/ members: 100

HOUSE MUSEUM: Preserves local history through maintenance of historic home and museum.

PROGRAMS: Exhibits; Festivals; Guided Tours; Interpretation

COLLECTIONS: [20th c] Original furnishings from 1890-1957, 1890 harness shop with unsold stock, 1903 commercial laundry, personal effects of Frank Schlosser Family.

HOURS: Yr M, W, F 1-4, Sa-Su 12-4

ADMISSION: $2

OLNEY

2297
Richland County Illinois Genealogical and Historical Society
Olney Central College, 62450 [PO Box 202, 62450]; (p) (618) 869-2425; jdoan40@hotmail.com; (c) Richland

1977/ staff: 20(v)/ members: 250/publication: *Footprints Past and Present*

GENEALOGICAL SOCIETY; HISTORICAL

SOCIETY: Preserves local genealogical records.

PROGRAMS: Exhibits; Guided Tours; Publication

COLLECTIONS: [1600-present] Southeast Illinois genealogical records.

HOURS: M-Th 7:30-8, F 8-4:30

ADMISSION: No charge

2298
Richland Heritage Museum Assoc
[PO Box 153, 62450]; elbos@wworld.com; (c) Richland

Private non-profit/ 1984/ Board of Directors/ staff: 12(v)/ members: 155

HISTORY MUSEUM: Promotes local, state, and Midwest history.

PROGRAMS: Community Outreach; Exhibits; Guided Tours; Interpretation

COLLECTIONS: [1850-present] Exhibits depicting local communities.

HOURS: Apr-Nov Su 1-4 and by appt

OREGON

2299
Ogle County Genealogy Society
[PO Box 251, 61061]; (c) Ogle

Private non-profit/ members: 125

GENEALOGICAL SOCIETY

2300
Ogle County Historical Society
111 N 6th St, 61061 [PO Box 183, 61061]; (p) (815) 732-6876; (c) Ogle

Private non-profit/ 1954/ Board/ staff: 6(v)/ members: 267/publication: *Gazette*

HISTORICAL SOCIETY; HISTORY MUSEUM: Promotes local history.

PROGRAMS: Annual Meeting; Exhibits; Guided Tours; Publication

COLLECTIONS: [1800-present] Period furnishing, dolls, tools, photos and archives.

HOURS: May-Oct Su 1-4

ADMISSION: No charge

OSWEGO

2301
Oswegoland Heritage Association
72 Polk St, 60543 [Box 23, 60543]; (p) (630) 554-2999; (f) (630) 554-7560; 71540.1756@compuserve.com; (c) Kendall

Private non-profit/ 1975/ staff: 9(v)/ members: 150/publication: *The Bell Tower*

HISTORIC SITE; HISTORICAL SOCIETY; HISTORY MUSEUM; RESEARCH CENTER: Collects, preserves and interprets materials related to the history and heritage of Oswego township.

PROGRAMS: Annual Meeting; Community Outreach; Exhibits; Garden Tours; Guided Tours; Interpretation; Lectures; Publication; Research Library/Archives; School-Based Curriculum

COLLECTIONS: [1835-present] 2,400 cataloged collection, artifacts and archival materials, 3,000 uncataloged photos, 1,000 3-D museum artifacts.

HOURS: Sept-June 1st and 3rd Su 2-5 and by appt

PALATINE

2302
Palatine Historical Society
224 E Palatine Rd, 60078 [PO Box 134, 60078]; (p) (847) 991-6460; (f) (847) 963-0605; Claysonmus@aol.com; (c) Cook

Private non-profit/ 1955/ Board of Directors/ staff: 1(f); 20(v)/ members: 300/publication: *Hillside Cemetery; Slice of Life; Palaver Newsletter*

HISTORIC SITE; HISTORICAL SOCIETY; HOUSE MUSEUM; RESEARCH CENTER: Collects and preserves materials related to Palatine and provides educational services; operates Clayson House Museum.

PROGRAMS: Annual Meeting; Community Outreach; Exhibits; Family Programs; Festivals; Guided Tours; Publication; Research Library/Archives; School-Based Curriculum

COLLECTIONS: [1870] 45 linear ft boxed indexed archival materials, 3,000 slides, 1,000 photos, early maps, 500 museum artifacts, 1870s furnishing and textiles.

HOURS: Yr T, Th 9-4, Su 1:30-4:30

ADMISSION: Donations accepted

PALESTINE

2303
Palestine Preservation Projects Society
Main & Grand Prairie St, 62451 [PO Box 87, 62451]; (p) (618) 586-9418; (c) Crawford

Private non-profit/ 1988/ Palestine Preservation Projects Society/ staff: 20(v)/ members: 75

ART MUSEUM; HISTORIC PRESERVATION AGENCY; HISTORIC SITE; HISTORICAL SOCIETY; HISTORY MUSEUM; HOUSE MUSEUM; RESEARCH CENTER: Preserves written and oral history of Palestine, Illinois; also serves as cultural center.

PROGRAMS: Annual Meeting; Community Outreach; Concerts; Elder's Programs; Exhibits; Facility Rental; Family Programs; Festivals; Film/Video; Guided Tours; Living History; Reenactments; Research Library/Archives; School-Based Curriculum; Theatre

COLLECTIONS: [1898-1960] Historic clothing, furniture and photographs.

HOURS: Yr Th 9-2

ADMISSION: Donations accepted

PALOS PARK

2304
Palos Historical Society
12332 Forest Glen Blvd, 60464; (p) (708) 361-3118; (c) Cook

Private non-profit/ 1957/ Board of Directors/ staff: 4(p); 6(v)/ members: 65/publication: *Palos Historical Society Newsletter*

HISTORICAL SOCIETY: Preserves and promotes local and pioneer history.

PROGRAMS: Annual Meeting; Community Outreach; Exhibits; Guided Tours; Lectures; Publication

COLLECTIONS: [1800s-present] Photos, newspapers, letters, magazine articles, local theater brochures,

PARIS

2305
Edgar County Historical Society
408 & 414 N Main St, 61944 [408 N Main St, 61944]; (p) (217) 463-5305, (217) 463-4209; (c) Edgar

1922/ Board of Directors/ staff: 1(p)/ members: 220/publication: *'Tense' Past, Present, Future*

GENEALOGICAL SOCIETY; HISTORICAL SOCIETY; HISTORY MUSEUM; LIVING HISTORY/OUTDOOR MUSEUM: Preserves local county history with pioneering, historic preservation and genealogy.

PROGRAMS: Annual Meeting; Exhibits; Family Programs; Festivals; Guided Tours; Publication; Reenactments; Research Library/Archives

COLLECTIONS: Housed in Victorian home and pioneer log cabin with genealogy library.

HOURS: Feb-Dec W-F 9-4

PARK FOREST

2306
Park Forest Historical Society
400 Lakewood Blvd, 60466; (p) (708) 748-3731; (f) (708) 748-8829; www.lincolnnet.net/users/lrpfhs; (c) Cook and Will

Private non-profit/ 1985/ staff: 1(p); 4(v)/ members: 200/publication: *Park Forest-The Early Years 1945-1955*

HISTORICAL SOCIETY: Promotes local history through educational programs.

PROGRAMS: Annual Meeting; Community Outreach; Exhibits; Guided Tours; Lectures; Publication; Research Library/Archives; School-Based Curriculum

COLLECTIONS: [1946-present] 72 oral history transcripts, 2,274 photos and negatives, videos, ephemera, memorabilia, scrapbooks.

HOURS: Yr M-Th 10-9, F 10-6, Sa 10-5; Su 2-5 (Sept-May only)

PARK RIDGE

2307
Park Ridge Historical Society
41 Prairie Avenue, 60068; (p) (847) 696-1973; (c) Cook

Private non-profit/ 1973/ Board of Trustees/ staff: 12(v)/ members: 67

HISTORIC SITE; HISTORICAL SOCIETY; HISTORY MUSEUM; HOUSE MUSEUM: Promotes local history.

PROGRAMS: Annual Meeting; Community Outreach; Exhibits; Family Programs; Guided Tours; Lectures; Living History; Reenactments; Research Library/Archives

COLLECTIONS: [1830-1993] Memorabilia belonging to Park Ridge residents.

HOURS: Mar-Dec Sa

PAXTON

2308
Ford County Historical Society
201 W State St, 60957 [PO Box 115, 60957]; www.rootsweb.com/~ilford; (c) Ford

Private non-profit/ 1968/ staff: 19(v)/ members: 253/publication: *The Ford County Historical Messenger*

GENEALOGICAL SOCIETY; HISTORIC PRESERVATION AGENCY; HOUSE MUSEUM: Provides genealogical and research information.

PROGRAMS: Annual Meeting; Exhibits; Family Programs; Festivals; Guided Tours; Lectures; Publication; Research Library/Archives

2309
Illinois Central Railroad Historical Society
250 N Market St, 60957 [PO Box 288, 60957]; (p) (217) 379-2261; (f) (217) 379-4078; www.icrrhistorical.org; (c) Ford

Private non-profit/ members: 1000

HISTORICAL SOCIETY

PROGRAMS: Annual Meeting; Festivals; Publication

COLLECTIONS: [1915-present] Photos, drawings, 1915 valuation records.

HOURS: Yr Sa 10-3

ADMISSION: No charge

PEKIN

2310
Everett McKinley Dirksen Congressional Leadership Research Center, The
301 S 4th St Ste A, 61554; (p) (309) 347-7113; (f) (309) 347-6432; evdirksen@pekin.net; www.pekin.net/dirksen; (c) Tazewell

Private non-profit/ 1963/ staff: 2(f); 1(p); 120(v)/ members: 120

LIBRARY AND/OR ARCHIVES; RESEARCH CENTER: Promotes Congress through archives, research and educational programs.

PROGRAMS: Community Outreach; Facility Rental; Garden Tours; Lectures; Publication; Research Library/Archives; School-Based Curriculum

COLLECTIONS: [Post WWII] Papers of Everett Dirksen, Harold Velde and Robert Michel.

HOURS: Yr M-F

2311
Tazewell County Genealogical and Historical Society
719 N 11th St, 61555 [PO Box 312, 61555-0312]; (p) (309) 477-3044; tcghs@ancestry.com; www.rootsweb.com/~iltcghs; (c) Tazewell

1978/ staff: 50(v)/ members: 450/publication: *TCGHS Monthly*

GENEALOGICAL SOCIETY; HISTORICAL

SOCIETY: Preserves local history.

PROGRAMS: Publication; Research Library/ Archives

COLLECTIONS: [1800] Books and microforms, county histories, government and military records.

ADMISSION: $2 Non members

PEORIA

2312
Central Illinois Landmarks Foundation
416 Hamilton Blvd, 61651 [PO Box 495, 61651]; (p) (309) 694-7121; (f) (309) 694-7146; l-kenyon@umtec.com; (c) Peoria

1972/ staff: 1(p)/ 30(v)/ members: 1000

PROGRAMS: Exhibits; Living History; Reenactments

2313
Illinois Historical Water Museum
100 Lorentz St, 61602 [123 SW Washington, 61602]; (p) (309) 671-3701; (f) (309) 671-4841; satherto@illinoisamerican.com; illinoisamerican.com/educate.html; (c) Peoria

1988

HISTORIC SITE; HISTORY MUSEUM: Documents advances and techniques in the drinking water treatment industry, housed in historic building.

PROGRAMS: Exhibits; Guided Tours; School-Based Curriculum

COLLECTIONS: [1880] Artifacts used to treat drinking water, including wooden water pipes, water meters, hydrants, laboratory equipment and photos.

HOURS: By appt

2314
Peoria County Genealogical Society
[PO Box 1489, 61655-1489]; www.usgennet.org/~ilpeoria/pcgs.html; (c) Peoria

Private non-profit/ 1973/ members: 300/publication: *Prairie Roots*

GENEALOGICAL SOCIETY: Preserves and promotes local history and genealogy.

PROGRAMS: Lectures; Publication; Research Library/Archives

COLLECTIONS: [1825-present] Peoria County records, cemetery inscription books, census books, 1850, 1860, 1870.

2315
Peoria Historical Society
942 NE Glen Oak Ave, 61603; (p) (309) 674-1921; (f) (309) 674-1882; (c) Peoria

1934/ Board of Trustees/ staff: 3(f); 60(v)/ members: 600/publication: *Timeline*

HISTORIC SITE; HISTORICAL SOCIETY; HOUSE MUSEUM; RESEARCH CENTER: Collects, preserves, and exhibits local history.

PROGRAMS: Annual Meeting; Community Outreach; Exhibits; Facility Rental; Family Programs; Festivals; Guided Tours; Interpretation; Lectures; Living History; Publication; Reenactments; Research Library/Archives

COLLECTIONS: Books, photos, paintings, textiles and artifacts.

HOURS: Yr Daily

2316
Pettingill-Morron House
1212 W Moss Ave, 61606; (p) (309) 674-4745, (309) 674-1921; (f) (309) 674-1882; www.peoria.org/members/listing.dog?main_cat=Attractions

PETERSBURG

2317
Edgar Lee Masters Memorial Museum
Corner of Seventh & Jackson Sts, 62675 [123 W Stephenson, 62675]; (p) (217) 632-2187

2318
Lincoln's New Salem State Historic Site
2 mi S of Petersburg on IL Rt 97, 62675 [RR1 Box 244A, 62675]; (p) (217) 632-4000; (f) (217) 632-4010; newsalem@fgi.net; www.lincolnnewsalem.com; (c) Menard

State/ 1919/ IL Historic Preservation Agency/ staff: 21(f); 40(p); 350(v)/ members: 200

HISTORIC PRESERVATION AGENCY; HISTORIC SITE; LIVING HISTORY/OUTDOOR MUSEUM: Manages a reconstructed village where Abraham Lincoln lives as a young adult from 1831-1837.

PROGRAMS: Community Outreach; Concerts; Exhibits; Facility Rental; Festivals; Film/Video; Interpretation; Lectures; Living History; Reenactments; School-Based Curriculum; Theatre

COLLECTIONS: [1830s] 23 buildings furnished with period artifacts.

HOURS: Yr M-Su 9-5

PINCKNEYVILLE

2319
Perry County Historical Society
108 W Jackson St, 62274; (p) (618) 357-2225; (c) Perry

Private non-profit/ 1983/ Perry County Historical Society/ staff: 10(v)/ members: 130/publication: *Perry County History*

ART MUSEUM; GENEALOGICAL SOCIETY; HISTORICAL SOCIETY; HISTORY MUSEUM; HOUSE MUSEUM: Preserves local history.

PROGRAMS: Annual Meeting; Community Outreach; Exhibits; Facility Rental; Family Programs; Guided Tours; Interpretation; Living History; Publication; Research Library/ Archives

COLLECTIONS: [Late 19th-early 20th c]

HOURS: Mar-Dec

ADMISSION: No charge

PIPER CITY

2320
Piper City Community Historical Society
39 W Main, 60959 [222 E Vine St, 60959]; (p) (815) 686-9234, (815) 686-2651; (c) Ford

Private non-profit/ 1988/ Piper City Community Historical Society/ members: 53/publication: *The Panhandle Piper*

GENEALOGICAL SOCIETY; HISTORIC

PRESERVATION AGENCY; HISTORICAL SOCIETY: Preserves local history.

PROGRAMS: Annual Meeting; Community Outreach; Concerts; Elder's Programs; Exhibits; Family Programs; Publication

COLLECTIONS: Housed in a former harness shop; equestrian accessories.

HOURS: June-Aug 1st Sa of month 9-11

ADMISSION: No charge

PLAINFIELD

2321
Plainfield Historical Society
217 E Main St, 60544; (p) (815) 436-4703; (c) Will

Private non-profit/ 1976/ staff: 10(v)/ members: 150

GENEALOGICAL SOCIETY; HISTORIC PRESERVATION AGENCY; HISTORICAL SOCIETY; HISTORY MUSEUM: Collects and preserves local artifacts.

PROGRAMS: Annual Meeting; Community Outreach; Concerts; Exhibits; Family Programs; Guided Tours; Interpretation; Lectures; Research Library/Archives; Theatre

COLLECTIONS: [1830-present] Household items, agricultural items, village history.

HOURS: Yr by appt

ADMISSION: No charge

PLANO

2322
Farnsworth House
14520 River Rd, 60545 [PO Box 194, 60545]; (p) (630) 552-8622; (f) (630) 552-8687; www.farnsworthhouse.com; (c) Kendall

Private for-profit/ 1951/ Bannockburn Corp/ staff: 1(f); 9(p)/publication: *The Farnsworth House*

HOUSE MUSEUM: Preserves Mies van der Rohe designed home and sculpture garden.

PROGRAMS: Garden Tours; Guided Tours; Lectures; Publication

COLLECTIONS: [1940-present] Sculptures by Andy Goldworthy, Sir Anthony Cavo, Barry Bertoia, Donald Judd, George Rickey and Wendy Taylor.

HOURS: Mar-Nov Th-T 10-4; Dec-Feb by appt

POLO

2323
Polo Historical Society
123 N Franklin, 61064; (p) (815) 946-4142; (c) Ogle

1900/ Board of Directors/ staff: 1(v)/ members: 95

HISTORIC SITE; HISTORICAL SOCIETY; HISTORY MUSEUM; HOUSE MUSEUM: Preserves, restores and promotes local history.

PROGRAMS: Annual Meeting; Exhibits; Guided Tours; School-Based

PONTIAC

2324
Catherine V. Yost Museum and Art Gallery
298 W Water St, 61764 [298 W Water St, 61764]; (p) (815) 844-7401, (815) 842-3457

1898/ City/ Livingston County Historical Society/ staff: 31(v)

COLLECTIONS: [Victorian Era-1898] Art work by Catherine Yost and the others; textile collection from the Yost family.; Letters dating back to the mid 1800's; records, reports and documents from the family's lives; original plans and specifications for the house.

HOURS: Seas + By appt; ; May-Dec Su 2-4; and by appt

2325
Jones House, The
314 E Madison St, 61764 [PO Box 680, 61764]; (p) (815) 842-3457

1858/ staff: 50(v)

COLLECTIONS: [Late 1800s] Victorian furnishings, arrowhead collection

HOURS: Seasonal; May-De; May-Dec Su 2-4; or by appt

2326
Livingston County Historical Society
115 W Howard St, 61764; (p) (815) 842-3457; (c) Livingston

Private non-profit/ 1924/ staff: 60(v)/ members: 142

HISTORICAL SOCIETY; HISTORY MUSEUM; HOUSE MUSEUM: Preserves Jones House.

PROGRAMS: Annual Meeting; Community Outreach; Concerts; Exhibits; Family Programs; Lectures; School-Based Curriculum

COLLECTIONS: [1800-1930] Clothing, books, letters, art, music and items by Zoath Freeman Yost Family.

HOURS: (Jones House) May-Dec Su 2-4; (Yost House) Yr M-F 9-4:30

ADMISSION: $2; Jones House Free

PRAIRIE DU ROCHER

2327
Henry-Lee-Brickey Creole House
220 Market St, [c/o EC Guebert, 209 Locust St, Red Bud, 62278]

staff: 1(v)

COLLECTIONS: [1860] Furniture; clothing; items from archaeological dig.

HOURS: By appt

PRINCETON

2328
Bureau County Historical Society
109 Park Ave W, 61356; (p) (815) 875-2184; (c) Bureau

Private non-profit/ 1911/ Board of Directors/ staff: 1(f); 7(p); 14(v)/ members: 500

COLLECTIONS: [19th-20th c] Local history, genealogy, pioneers, agriculture, military, photography, historic preservation, library and archives.

HOURS: Feb-Dec 23: W-Su 1-5

ADMISSION: Donations requested

2329
Owen Lovejoy Homestead
East Peru St, 61356 [Rt 3, 61356]; (p) (815) 879-9151

1838/ City/ staff: 3(p); 10(v)

COLLECTIONS: [1830-1890]

HOURS: Seasonal

PRINCEVILLE

2330
Historical Association of Princeville
130 N Walnut, 61559 [PO Box 206, 61559]; (c) Peoria

Private non-profit/ 1987/ Elected Officers/Trustees/ staff: 24(v)

HISTORICAL SOCIETY; HISTORY MUSEUM: Preserves local history.

PROGRAMS: Annual Meeting; Exhibits; Film/Video; Guided Tours

COLLECTIONS: [1800-present] Photos, scrapbooks and utensils.

HOURS: May-Oct Sa 9-11

QUINCY

2331
All Wars Museum at the Illinois Veterans Home
1707 N 12th St, 62301; (p) (217) 222-8641; (f) (217) 222-9621; (c) Adams

State/ staff: 12(v)

HISTORY MUSEUM: Located at a home for the Illinois veterans and their spouses.

PROGRAMS: Exhibits; Guided Tours; Living History

COLLECTIONS: [World War II] Military exhibits and artifacts of all United States wars with a heavy emphasis on uniforms.

HOURS: Yr M-Sa

2332
Friends of the Dr. Richard Eells House
415 Jersey St, 62306 [PO Box 628, 62306]; (p) (217) 222-1799; (c) Adams

Private non-profit/ 1990/ staff: 15(v)/ members: 100

HISTORIC SITE: Preserves legacy of Quincy abolitionist Richard Eells.

PROGRAMS: Annual Meeting; Guided Tours

COLLECTIONS: [1800-1850] Glass, china, metal, wood, wallpaper unearthed during excavation and interior restoration.

HOURS: Yr by appt

2333
Gardner Museum of Architecture and Design
332 Maine St, 62301; (p) (217) 224-6873; (f) (217) 224-3303; (c) Adams

Private non-profit/ 1974/ Board of Directors/ staff: 2(f); 1(p); 30(v)/ members: 339/publication: *Gardner Museum Newsletter*

HISTORY MUSEUM: Preserves architectural and design heritage of Quincy area through exhibits, programs, collections, archives and preservation activities.

PROGRAMS: Annual Meeting; Community Outreach; Concerts; Exhibits; Facility Rental; Family Programs; Garden Tours; Guided Tours; Interpretation; Lectures; Living History; Publication; Research Library/Archives

COLLECTIONS: [1819-present] Architectural photos, blueprints, archives, area atlases, insurance maps, tax records, city directories, and books.

HOURS: Mar-Dec T-Su 1-5

ADMISSION: $2, Student $.50, Seniors $1

2334
Historical Society of Quincy and Adams County
425 S 12th St, 62301; (p) (217) 222-1835; (c) Adams

Private non-profit/ 1896/ staff: 4(p); 60(v)/ members: 400

HISTORICAL SOCIETY; HOUSE MUSEUM: Located in Governor John Wood Mansion.

PROGRAMS: Annual Meeting; Community Outreach; Exhibits; Facility Rental; Family Programs; Interpretation; Lectures; Research Library/Archives; School-Based Curriculum

COLLECTIONS: [1835-1880] Objects related to history of Quincy and Adams County, 1100 volume library, 1000 piece doll collection, funishings for 1835 Governor John Wood Mansion.

HOURS: (Mansion) Sa-Su 1-4, M-F 10-2

ADMISSION: $2, Student $1

2335
Quincy Museum
1601 Main St, 62301; (p) (217) 224-7669; (f) (217) 224-9323; (c) Adams

Private non-profit/ 1962/ staff: 3(f); 2(p); 120(v)/ members: 520

HISTORIC SITE; HISTORY MUSEUM: Promotes local and natural history in restored 1890s Romanesque mansion.

PROGRAMS: Annual Meeting; Community Outreach; Concerts; Elder's Programs; Exhibits; Family Programs; Festivals; Film/Video; Garden Tours; Guided Tours; Interpretation; Lectures; Living History; Publication; Reenactments; School-Based Curriculum

COLLECTIONS: [Prehistory-1890] Victoriania, Mississippi River natural history.

HOURS: Yr T-Su 1-5

ADMISSION: $2, Children

2336
Villa Kathrine
532 Gardener Expy, 62306 [PO Box 732, 62306]; (p) (217) 224-3688

HOUSE MUSEUM

RANTOUL

2337
Octave Chanute Aerospace Museum
1011 Pacesetter Dr, 61866 [PO Box 949, 61866]; (p) (217) 893-1613; (f) (217) 892-5774; www.aeromuseum.org; (c) Champaign

Private non-profit/ 1993/ Octave Chanute Aerospace Museum Foundation/ staff: 3(f); 3(p); 120(v)/ members: 450/publication: *Chanute News*

HISTORY MUSEUM: Preserves the history of Chanute Air Force Base.

PROGRAMS: Annual Meeting; Concerts; Exhibits; Festivals; Guided Tours; Publication; Theatre

COLLECTIONS: [1917-present] Artifacts, books on Chanute, aerospace, military history, mansucripts, base newspapers and photos.

HOURS: Yr 10-5

ADMISSION: $5, Student $3, Seniors $4

RARITAN

2338
Henderson County Historical Society
407 N Front St, 61471 [310 E Main St, 61471]; (p) (309) 746-6103, (309) 627-2069; allaman@hcil.net; (c) Henderson

Private non-profit/ 1962/ staff: 7(v)/ members: 35

HISTORIC SITE; HISTORICAL SOCIETY; HISTORY MUSEUM; HOUSE MUSEUM: Collects and preserves history of Henderson County through Henderson County Museum in Raritan and Alexic Phelsp House in Oquawka.

PROGRAMS: Annual Meeting; Festivals; Guided Tours; Lectures; Living History; Theatre

COLLECTIONS: [1850-1950] Museum displays rural country life from 1900-1950; Phelps House has period furnishings to represent home of Oquawka

RIVER GROVE

2339
River Grove Historical Commission
8455 W Grand Ave, 60171 [2621 Thatcher Ave, 60171]; (p) (708) 453-8000; (f) (708) 453-0761; (c) Cook

1988/ Village of River Grove

HISTORIC SITE

PROGRAMS: Guided Tours

COLLECTIONS: [1874-1915]

HOURS: By appt

ADMISSION: No charge

RIVERDALE

2340
Riverdale Historical Society
208 W 144th St, 60827; (p) (708) 841-3311; (f) (708) 841-1805; rds@sls.lib.il.us; www.sls.lib.il.us/rds/; (c) Cook

County/ 1978/ Riverdale Public Library District/ staff: 3(v)

HISTORICAL SOCIETY

PROGRAMS: Exhibits

COLLECTIONS: Village minutes, newspaper articles, regalia.

ROBINSON

2341
Crawford County Historical Society
13673 E 1150th, 62454 [PO Box 554, 62454]; (p) (618) 544-3087; olecrawf@frsb.net; www.rootsweb.com/ilcchs/county.html; (c) Crawford

Private non-profit/ staff: 5(v)/ members: 187/publication: *Ole Crawford*

HISTORICAL SOCIETY; HISTORY MUSEUM: Promotes local history.

PROGRAMS: Annual Meeting; Community Outreach; Concerts; Exhibits; Facility Rental; Family Programs; Guided Tours; Lectures; Publication; School-Based Curriculum

COLLECTIONS: [1800] Pioneer, Native American, railroad, war, oil, medical, aviation, and agricultural artifacts.

HOURS: Yr Sa-Su 2-4 and by appt

ADMISSION: Donations

ROCHESTER

2342
Rochester Historical Preservation Society
201 S Walnut St, 62563 [PO Box 13, 62563]; (p) (217) 498-8101; (f) (217) 498-8489; (c) Sangamon

Private non-profit/ 1988/ staff: 2(p); 20(v)/ members: 82

HISTORICAL SOCIETY: Promotes and preserves historical sites, buildings and artifacts related to Rochester.

PROGRAMS: Annual Meeting; Family Programs; Lectures; Living History

COLLECTIONS: [1830-1860] Log home, stone house and reconstruction of historic village site with period garden.

HOURS: Yr

ADMISSION: No charge

ROCK ISLAND

2343
Black Hawk State Historic Site/Hauberg Indian Museum
Route 5, 61201 [1510 46th Ave, 61201]; (p) (309) 788-9536; (f) (309) 788-9865; hauberg-museum@juno.com; (c) Rock Island

State/ 1929/ Illinois Historic Preservation Agency/ staff: 4(f); 1(p); 50(v)

HISTORIC SITE; HISTORY MUSEUM; TRIBAL MUSEUM: Preserves ethnological material culture related to the Sauk and Mesquakie (Fox) Indians, as well as numerous other tribes.

PROGRAMS: Annual Meeting; Community Outreach; Exhibits; Facility Rental; Guided Tours; Interpretation; Lectures; School-Based Curriculum

COLLECTIONS: [1750-1831] Museum artifacts of various Native American groups, emphasizing Eastern Woodlands culture; lithic tools; and photographs of Civilian Conservation Corps work.

HOURS: Mar-Oct Daily 9-12/1-5; Nov-Feb Daily 9-12/1-4

ADMISSION: Donations requested

2344
Blackhawk Genealogical Society of Rock Island and Mercer Counties, Illinois
401 19th St, 61204 [PO Box 3912, 61204-3912]; (p) (309) 786-3058; (c) Rock Island

1972/ members: 170/publication: *Blackhawk Genealogical Society Quarterly*

PROGRAMS: Annual Meeting; Publication

COLLECTIONS: Book and microform collection of genealogical interest, especially on Rock Island and surrounding counties.

HOURS: Yr M-Th 9-9, F-Sa 9-5; Sept-May M-Th 9-9, F-Sa 9-5, Su 1-4

2345
Colonel Davenport Historical Foundation, The
N shore of Arsenal Island, 61204 [PO Box 4603, 61204-4603]; (p) (309) 786-7336; (c) Rock Island

Private non-profit/ 1977/ Board of Directors/ staff: 45(v)/ members: 235/publication: *Your Obedient Servant George Davenport*

HISTORIC SITE: Preserves Colonel Davenport House and site and interprets social history and material culture of early 19th century.

PROGRAMS: Annual Meeting; Community Outreach; Exhibits; Family Programs; Guided Tours; Interpretation; Lectures; Publication

COLLECTIONS: [Early 19th c] Historical research materials related to the Davenport House; photos, business records, furnishings and cultural materials retrieved from site.

HOURS: May-Oct Th-Su 12-4

ADMISSION: $3, Family $7, Student $2

2346
Rock Island Arsenal Museum
Bldg 60, Rock Island Arsenal, 61299 [Attn: SMRI-CFS-M, 1 Rock Island Arsenal, 61299]; (p) (309) 782-5021; (f) (309) 782-3598; leinickekeria@army.mil; www.ria.army.mil; (c) Rock Island

Federal/ 1905/ US Army/ staff: 2(f); 30(v)

HISTORY MUSEUM: Displays the history of Rock Island Arsenal, as well as the history of small arms development.

PROGRAMS: Community Outreach; Exhibits; Film/Video; Guided Tours; Lectures; Research Library/Archives; Theatre

COLLECTIONS: [1862-present] Products of the Arsenal and equipment used to produce those products, military, civilian, US and foreign small arms.

HOURS: Yr Sa-Su,10-4

2347
Rock Island Preservation Commission
1528 3rd Avenue, 61201-8678; (p) (309) 732-2900; (f) (309) 732-9305; doakja@ri.lincon.org; www.rigov.org; (c) Rock Island

1984/ City of Rock Island/ staff: 1(p); 12(v)

HISTORIC PRESERVATION AGENCY

PROGRAMS: Community Outreach; Guided Tours; Lectures; Publication

COLLECTIONS: [1860-1955]

HOURS: M-F 8-5

2348

Special Collections, Augustana College Library

3435 9 1/2 Ave, 61201 [639 38th St, 61201]; (p) (309) 794-7317;
specialcollections@agustana.edu; www.agustana.edu/library/special/index2.htm; (c) Rock Island

Private non-profit/ 1860/ Augustana College/ staff: 1(f); 1(v)

HISTORY MUSEUM; LIBRARY AND/OR ARCHIVES; RESEARCH CENTER: Houses the college archives and a large research collection of materials related to the upper Mississippi Valley.

PROGRAMS: Exhibits; Research Library/ Archives

COLLECTIONS: [1860-present] Contains a large local history manuscript collection, early 1900 glass plates and photographs, and a print collection of upper Mississippi valley and Native American material.

HOURS: Yr M-F 1-5

2349

Swenson Swedish Immigration Research Center

Denkmann Hall, 3520 7th Ave, 61201 [Augustana College, 639 38th St, 61201-2296]; (p) (309) 794-7204; (f) (309) 794-7443; sag@augustana.edu; www.augustana.edu/administration/swenson/; (c) Rock Island

Private non-profit/ 1981/ Augustana College/ staff: 1(f); 2(p); 2(v)/ members: 600/publication: *Swenson Center News; Swedish American Genealogist*

RESEARCH CENTER: National archives and genealogy research institute for the study of Swedish immigration to North America, serving as repository for records of organizations and institutions.

PROGRAMS: Lectures; Publication

COLLECTIONS: [1850-1930] Books and periodicals on the subject of immigration and Swedish immigration to North America, microfilms of Swedish-American church records, Swedish port indexes.

HOURS: Yr by appt

ADMISSION: $10 non-members

ROCKFORD

2350

Burpee Museum of Natural History

737 & 813 N Main St, 61103 [737 N Main St, 61103]; (p) (815) 965-3433; (f) (815) 965-2703; info@burpee.org; www.burpee.org; (c) Winnebago

Private non-profit/ 1942/ staff: 10(f); 11(p); 60(v)/ members: 650/publication: *Newsletter*

HISTORIC SITE; NATURAL HISTORY MUSEUM: Collects, preserves and interprets the natural and cultural heritage of the Rock River Valley, Illinois and Wisconsin with cultural emphasis on Native Americans.

PROGRAMS: Annual Meeting; Community Outreach; Exhibits; Facility Rental; Festivals; Guided Tours; Interpretation; Lectures; Publication; School-Based Curriculum

COLLECTIONS: Cultural, geological and paleontological objects; zoological and botanical

specimens; and library/archives.

HOURS: Yr T-Su 10-5

ADMISSION: $4, Children $3

2351

Ethnic Heritage Museum

1129 S Main St, 61101; (p) (815) 962-7402; (c) Winnebago

Private for-profit/ 1989/ Board of Directors/ staff: 22(p); 5(v)/ members: 225

ART MUSEUM; HISTORIC PRESERVATION AGENCY; HISTORY MUSEUM; HOUSE MUSEUM: Preserves history of Irish, Italian, Lithuanian, Polish and Hispanic immigrants in Rockford and the African American experience.

PROGRAMS: Annual Meeting; Community Outreach; Concerts; Exhibits; Facility Rental; Festivals; Guided Tours; Living History; Publication; School-Based Curriculum

COLLECTIONS: [1836-present] Displays related to ethnic groups in Rockford.

HOURS: Yr Su

2352

Graham-Ginestra House, Inc.

1115 S Main St, 61103 [1422 National Ave, 61103]; (p) (815) 964-8333; (c) Winnebago

1857/ Board of Directors/ staff: 25(v)/ members: 100

GARDEN; HISTORIC SITE; HOUSE MUSEUM; LIVING HISTORY/OUTDOOR MUSEUM: Preserves history of Greek Revival and Italianate limestone house and city of Rockford.

PROGRAMS: Community Outreach; Exhibits; Facility Rental; Festivals; Garden Tours; Guided Tours; Lectures; Living History

2353

Haight Village Restoration Society

404 S First St, 61104; (p) (815) 968-5352

Private non-profit/ staff: 4(p); 4(v)/ members: 60

HISTORIC SITE; HISTORICAL SOCIETY: Preserves 13-block historic district.

PROGRAMS: Guided Tours

COLLECTIONS: [1800]

2354

Kishwaukee Genealogists

[PO Box 5503, 61125]; (c) Winnebago

Private non-profit/ 1987/ members: 61

GENEALOGICAL SOCIETY: Collects genealogical records.

PROGRAMS: Lectures

COLLECTIONS: Cemeteries, census, obituaries, early marriages, funeral home and church records, society

2355

Midway Village and Museum Center

6799 Guilford Rd, 61107; (p) (815) 397-9112; (f) (815) 397-9156; MidwayVill@aol.com; (c) Winnebago

Private non-profit/ 1974/ Rockford Museum Association/ staff: 8(f); 16(p); 750(v)

HISTORY MUSEUM: Interprets history of Rockford through exhibits.

PROGRAMS: Community Outreach; Exhibits;

Facility Rental; Family Programs; Interpretation; Lectures; Living History; Reenactments; Research Library/Archives; School-Based Curriculum

COLLECTIONS: [1840-present] 80,000 objects representing industrial, social and domestic history of Rockford and Winnebago County, Illinois.

HOURS: Apr-Oct T-Su

2356

Rockford Historic Preservation Commission

425 E State St, 61104; (p) (815) 987-5600; (f) (815) 967-6933;
ginny.gregory@ci.rockford.il.us; www.ci.rockford.il.us; (c) Winnebago

1978/ City of Rockford/ staff: 2(p); 7(v)/publication: *Design Guidelines*

HISTORIC PRESERVATION AGENCY: Administers Rockford's historic preservation ordinance, including surveys of resources, designation of landmarks and districts, and mandatory design review.

PROGRAMS: Annual Meeting; Publication; Research Library/Archives

COLLECTIONS: Surveys of historic resources, 1979-1981, 1985, 1994, 1997-1999.

2357

Rockford Historical Society

6799 Guilford Rd, 61107; (p) (815) 226-4884; (c) Winnebago

1962/ members: 202/publication: *Nuggets of History*

HISTORICAL SOCIETY

PROGRAMS: Annual Meeting; Publication

2358

Swedish Historical Society of Rockford

404 S 3rd St, 61104; (p) (815) 963-5559; (c) Winnebago

Private non-profit/ 1938/ staff: 1(p); 40(v)/ members: 600

HISTORIC SITE; HISTORICAL SOCIETY; HOUSE MUSEUM: Preserves Swedish heritage through operation of Erlander Home Museum.

PROGRAMS: Annual Meeting; Exhibits; Family Programs; Festivals; Film/Video; Guided Tours; Research Library/Archives

COLLECTIONS: [1870-1920] Personal items belonging to early Swedish immigrants.

HOURS: Yr Su 2-4

ADMISSION: $3

2359

Tinker Swiss Cottage Museum

411 Kent St, 61102; (p) (815) 964-2424; (f) (815) 964-2466; www.tinkercottage.com; (c) Winnebago

Private non-profit/ 1943/ Board of Trustees/ staff: 3(f); 2(p); 75(v)/ members: 422

HOUSE MUSEUM: Preserves historic house of Robert Hall Tinker Family.

PROGRAMS: Guided Tours; School-Based Curriculum

COLLECTIONS: In-situ collection including

furniture, art, family journals.

HOURS: Yr T-Su Guided Tours 1, 2, 3

ADMISSION: $4, Student $1, Children $1, Seniors $3.50

2360
Winnebago and Boone Counties Genealogical Society
[PO Box 10166, 61131-0166]; (p) (815) 226-4884; (c) Winnebago

Private non-profit/ 1986/ members: 231

GENEALOGICAL SOCIETY

PROGRAMS: Annual Meeting; Publication

ROCKTON

2361
Stephen Mack Home and Whitman Trading Post
316 N Black Hawk Blvd, 61072; (p) (815) 624-7600

HOUSE MUSEUM

ROMEOVILLE

2362
Isle a la Cache Museum
501 E 135th St, 60446; (p) (815) 886-1467; (f) (815) 886-6803; (c) Will

County, non-profit/ 1990/ staff: 5(f); 5(v)

HOUSE MUSEUM: Preserves history of fur trade between 18th century explorers and Native Americans.

PROGRAMS: Exhibits; Family Programs; Festivals; Film/Video; Guided Tours; Interpretation; Reenactments

COLLECTIONS: [1750] Reproductions depicting fur trade, Native American tools, encampment re-creation, beaver lodge.

HOURS: Yr T-Sa 10-4, Su 12-4

ADMISSION: No charge

2363
Lewis University Canal and Regional History Collections
1 University Pl, 60446-2298; (p) (815) 838-0500; (f) (815) 838-9456; imcanal.lewisu.edu; (c) Will

Private non-profit/ 1984/ Lewis University/ staff: 1(f); 1(p)

HISTORY MUSEUM: Collects and preserves history of Northern Illinois, and the Illinois and Michigan Canal.

PROGRAMS: Community Outreach; Exhibits; Guided Tours; Lectures; Research Library/ Archives

COLLECTIONS: [1800-1950] Books, pamphlets, and manuscripts on US canals; canal artifacts and maps, photographs of canals and associated individuals and industries.

HOURS: Aug 26-Aug 9 M-Th 12-4

2364
Romeoville Area Historical Society
101 Normantown & Dalhart, 60446 [PO Box 7504 Romeo Road, 60446-0504]; (p) (630) 257-7954; (c) Will

1980/ staff: 4(v)/ members: 197

HISTORICAL SOCIETY: Preserves history of DuPage township.

PROGRAMS: Community Outreach; Elder's Programs; Guided Tours

COLLECTIONS: [1835-present] Farm tools, school artifacts and records, kitchen appliances, war artifacts, clothing, uniforms, photos.

HOURS: Jan-July, Sept-Oct, Dec 4th W

ADMISSION: No charge

ROSELLE

2365
Law Enforcement Memorial Association, Inc.
[PO Box 72883, 60172]; (p) (847) 795-1547; (f) (847) 795-2469; rvrbigred@aol.com; www.w8ca.com/lema; (c) Cook

1989/ staff: 1(p); 5(v)/ members: 300/publication: *LEMA News*

HISTORICAL SOCIETY; RESEARCH CENTER: Collects research from 1700s to present on law officer deaths with plans to build a memorial library.

PROGRAMS: Publication

COLLECTIONS: [1717-present] Research data and photos on slain officers and also on all those who have been executed or lynched for the crime. Collection also includes badges, books and uniforms

ROSEVILLE

2366
Warren County Historical Society
190 E Penn, 61473 [PO Box 325, 190 E Penn, 61473]; (p) (309) 426-2304; (c) Warren

County, non-profit; Private non-profit/ 1968/ staff: 6(p); 4(v)/ members: 30

HISTORICAL SOCIETY; HISTORY MUSEUM; RESEARCH CENTER: Promotes local history.

PROGRAMS: Annual Meeting; Community Outreach; Exhibits; Family Programs; Festivals; Guided Tours; Lectures; Living History; Publication; Research Library/Archives

COLLECTIONS: [1850-present] Four floors featuring, general store, country school, doctor's office, three-room home display, large agricultural equipment room, a Warren County room, a small tool room, library, and general exhibit hall.

HOURS: Yr by appt, Mem Day-Labor Day Su 1-5

ADMISSION: Donations

ROSICLARE

2367
American Fluorite Museum, The
Hwy 34, Main St, 62982 [PO Box 755, 62982]; (p) (618) 285-3513; (f) (618) 285-6232; (c) Hardin

Private non-profit/ 1989/ The Hardin County Fluorspar Museum Board/ staff: 13(v)

HISTORIC SITE; HISTORICAL SOCIETY; HISTORY MUSEUM: Located on a historic mine site. Preserves and presents the mineral fluorite and its colorful mining history.

PROGRAMS: Festivals; Guided Tours; Interpretation

COLLECTIONS: [Early 19th c-present] Collections of fluorite and associated minerals primarily from Southern Illinois, mining memorabilia, equipment, photographs, publications, mining stories and buildings.

HOURS: Mar-Dec F, Su 1-5, Sa 10-5

ROSSVILLE

2368
Rossville Historical and Genealogical Society
108 W Attica St, 60963 [PO Box 263, 60963]; (p) (217) 748-4080; roshisoc@soltec.net; rossville@rossville.com; (c) Vermilion

Private non-profit/ 1982/ Board of Directors/ staff: 15(v)/ members: 581

GENEALOGICAL SOCIETY; HISTORICAL SOCIETY; HISTORY MUSEUM: Preserves history of Ross/South Ross Townships.

PROGRAMS: Exhibits; Guided Tours; Publication; Research Library/Archives

COLLECTIONS: [1850-present] Military artifacts, jail, drugstore, doctor's office; death, marriage and birth files, antique tools, clothing, family hstories, microfilms, Rossville newspapers, Vermilion Co. and Warren Co. census.

HOURS: Yr T-Sa 12-4 and by appt

ADMISSION: Donations accepted

RUSHVILLE

2369
Schuyler County Historical and Genealogical Society
200 S Congress, 62681; (p) (217) 322-3283; (c) Schuyler

1967/ Board of Directors/ staff: 80(v)/ members: 400

HISTORICAL SOCIETY: Preserves local history and genealogy.

PROGRAMS: Annual Meeting; Festivals; Living History

SAINT CHARLES

2370
Pioneer Sholes School Society
LeRoy Oakes Forest Preserve, Dean St, 60174 [PO Box 1275, 60174]; (p) (217) 762-3366; (c) Kane

Private non-profit/ 1979/ staff: 1(p); 20(v)/ members: 125

HISTORIC SITE; HISTORY MUSEUM: Restored one-room school, circa 1872

PROGRAMS: Guided Tours; Interpretation; Living History; Research Library/Archives

COLLECTIONS: Historical documents, artifacts, textbooks.

HOURS: June-Oct Su 1-4 and by appt

ADMISSION: Donations accepted

SALEM

2371
Society for the Historical Preservation of the 22nd North Carolina Tropos, Inc.
221 W Broadway, 62881 [PO Box 254, 62881]; (p) (618) 548-4808; (c) Marion

1981/ staff: 4(p)/ members: 30

HISTORICAL SOCIETY: Preserves and promotes history of North Carolina confederate military units during Civil War through special collections and military reenactments.

PROGRAMS: Exhibits; Lectures; Living History; Reenactments

COLLECTIONS: [1861-1865] 2,000 pieces of arms and equipment related to the Civil War.

HOURS: Yr

2372
William Jennings Bryan Birthplace Museum
408 S Broadway, 62881 [101 S Broadway, 62881]; (p) (618) 548-7791; (c) Marion

City/ 1907/ staff: 1(p)

HOUSE MUSEUM: Promotes local figure and native son William J. Bryan's life through museum and education programs.

PROGRAMS: Guided Tours

COLLECTIONS: [1860-1925] Artifacts, articles, photos, memorabilia related to life of William Jennings Bryan.

HOURS: Yr F-W 1-5

SANDWICH

2373
Sandwich Historical Society
315 E Railroad, 60548 [PO Box 82, 60548]; (p) (815) 786-7936; (c) Dekalb

Private non-profit/ 1969/ staff: 10(v)/ members: 25

HISTORICAL SOCIETY; HOUSE MUSEUM: Maintains and promotes local Store Mill Museum.

PROGRAMS: Annual Meeting; Exhibits; Guided Tours

COLLECTIONS: [1800-present] Period furnishings, agriculture, artifacts.

HOURS: April-Sept Su 1-4

ADMISSION: Donations

SAVANNA

2374
Carroll County Genealogical Society
326 3rd St, 61074 [PO Box 354, 61074]; (c) Carroll

Private non-profit/ 1977/ Board of Officers/ staff: 10(v)/ members: 67

GENEALOGICAL SOCIETY; HISTORIC PRESERVATION AGENCY: Collects and promotes genealogy materials.

PROGRAMS: Lectures; Research Library/ Archives

COLLECTIONS: [1850-present] Cemetery readings.

HOURS: Yr M-T 1-5, W 10-5, F 1-5, Sa 9-1

SCHAUMBURG

2375
Chicago Athenaeum: Museum of Architecture and Design, The
190 S Roselle Road, 60193; (p) (847) 895-3950; (f) (847) 895-0951; www.chi-athenaeum.org; (c) Cook

Joint/ 1988/ staff: 10(f); 2(p); 5(v)

ART MUSEUM; HISTORY MUSEUM: Promotes art, architecture, and design through education.

PROGRAMS: Community Outreach; Exhibits; Facility Rental; Family Programs; Festivals; Film/Video; Guided Tours; Publication; Research Library/Archives

COLLECTIONS: [20th c] National and international industrial design, 20th century chairs, Japanese graphics and design, photo archive.

HOURS: Yr T-Sa 11-6, Sun 12-00-5

ADMISSION: $3, Student $2, Seniors $2

2376
St. Peter Lutheran Church
208 E Schaumburg Rd, 60194; (p) (847) 885-3350; (f) (847) 885-1106; (c) Cook

1847

HISTORIC PRESERVATION AGENCY: Promotes local history.

PROGRAMS: Exhibits; Guided Tours

COLLECTIONS: [1847-present] Pioneer artifacts, household furnishings, farm, church, cemetery.

HOURS: Yr

2377
Volkening Heritage Farm at Spring Valley
1111 E Schaumburg Rd, 60194; (p) (847) 985-2100; (f) (847) 985-9692; (c) Cook

1983/ Schaumburg Park District/ staff: 8(f); 25(p); 250(v)/publication: *Natural Enquirer*

LIVING HISTORY/OUTDOOR MUSEUM: Preserves and interprets agricultural heriatage of typical German-American from Shaumburg Township.

PROGRAMS: Exhibits; Family Programs; Festivals; Interpretation; Lectures; Living History; Publication

COLLECTIONS: [1870-1890] Illinois farm life, German agricultural community artifacts.

HOURS: May-Oct Th-M 10-4

ADMISSION: No charge

SCHILLER PARK

2378
Schiller Park Historical Commission
4200 Old River Road, 60176 [9526 W Irving Park Road, 60176]; (p) (847) 671-8513; (c) Cook

City, non-profit/ 19900/ Village of Schiller Park/ staff: 7(f); 8(v)

HISTORICAL SOCIETY: Promotes local history.

PROGRAMS: Community Outreach; Exhibits; Research Library/Archives; School-Based Curriculum

COLLECTIONS: Photos, maps, oral and writ-

ten history, Native American history, agriculture, manufacturing, government.

HOURS: Yr May-Sept M 9-12, 2nd Su of month 12-4 and by appt

ADMISSION: No charge

SESSER

2379
Goode-Barren Historical-Genealogical Society
201 E Callie, 62884 [PO Box 1024, 62884]; (p) (618) 625-2851; cb72750@midwest.net; (c) Franklin

Private non-profit/ staff: 8(v)/ members: 40/publication: *Goode-Barren Historical-Genealogical Society Newsletter*

GENEALOGICAL SOCIETY; HISTORICAL SOCIETY: Preserves history and genealogy of townships.

PROGRAMS: Publication; Research Library/ Archives

HOURS: Yr M 10-1, W 10-3

SHAWNEETOWN

2380
Shawneetown Bank Historic Site
280 Washington St, 62984; (p) (618) 269-3303; (c) Gallatin

1839/ staff: 1(f)

HISTORIC PRESERVATION AGENCY: Preserves oldest bank building in Illlinois.

PROGRAMS: Guided Tours

HOURS: Apr-Oct Daily 8-4 and by appt

ADMISSION: No charge

SHEFFIELD

2381
Sheffield Historical Society
Washington and Cook, 61361; (p) (815) 454-2758; (c) Bureau

Private non-profit/ 1968/ staff: 3(f)

GENEALOGICAL SOCIETY; HISTORIC SITE; HISTORICAL SOCIETY; HISTORY MUSEUM; RESEARCH CENTER: Promotes local history through collections housed in restored Danish church.

PROGRAMS: Annual Meeting; Community Outreach; Exhibits; Family Programs; Festivals; Guided Tours; Interpretation; Lectures; Living History; Publication; Research Library/Archives; School-Based Curriculum

COLLECTIONS: Military, period furnishings, glassware, art.

HOURS: Yr Daily 12-4 or by appt

SHELBYVILLE

2382
Shelby County Historical Society/Museum
151 S Washington, 62565 [PO Box 286, 62565]; (p) (217) 774-2260; (c) Shelby

Private non-profit/ 1968/ staff: 2(p); 10(v)/ members: 240

HISTORICAL SOCIETY: Collects and preserves local history and genealogical records.

PROGRAMS: Annual Meeting; Community Outreach; Exhibits; Facility Rental; Guided Tours; Interpretation; Lectures; Publication; Research Library/Archives

COLLECTIONS: [1827-present] Genealogical records.

HOURS: Yr M, F-Sa 10-4

SHIPMAN

2383
Southwestern Farm and Home Museum
203 Park St, 62685 [PO Box 132, 62685]; (p) (618) 729-4186, (618) 836-5840

1982/ staff: 2(v)

COLLECTIONS: [1850-1920] Bottles; shaving mugs; calendar plates; snuff bottles; tools; jugs; Indian arrow collection.

HOURS: Apr-Nov

SHIRLEY

2384
Funk Prairie Home and Funk Gem and Mineral Museum
RR1 Box 75A, 61772; (p) (309) 827-6792; (c) McLean

1971/ staff: 1(f); 3(p)

HOUSE MUSEUM: Promotes history through preservation of late Civil War era home.

PROGRAMS: Exhibits; Guided Tours; Interpretation; School-Based Curriculum

COLLECTIONS: [1865-1910] Period furnishings, artifacts, gems, minerals, fossils, Indian artifacts, buggies, sleighs.

HOURS: Mar-Dec T-Sa

SIDNEY

2385
Sidney Historical Society
Sidney Community Library, 61877 [PO Box 87, 61877]; (c) Champaign

1986

HISTORICAL SOCIETY: Promotes local history.

PROGRAMS: Exhibits

COLLECTIONS: [1900-1980] Local newspapers.

SKOKIE

2386
Holocaust Memorial of Illinois
4255 Main St, 60076-2063; (p) (847) 677-4640; (f) (847) 677-4684; holmemil@flash.net

Private non-profit/ 1981/ staff: 2(f); 1(p); 50(v)/ members: 1500

HISTORY MUSEUM: Preserves holocaust history through educational programs, community outreach programs, museum and library.

PROGRAMS: Annual Meeting; Community Outreach; Exhibits; Facility Rental; Family Programs; Film/Video; Guided Tours; Lectures; Living History; Publication; Research Library/Archives; School-Based Curriculum; Theatre

COLLECTIONS: [1933-1945] Photos, arti-facts, memorabilia, pre-war Jewish life, Nazi holocaust, art.

HOURS: Yr Su 12-4, M-Th 9-4:30, F 9-3

SOUTH ELGIN

2387
Fox River Trolley Association, Inc.
365 S LaFox St, 60177 [PO Box 315, 60177-0315]; (p) (847) 697-4676; infor@foxtrolley.org; www.foxtrolley.org; (c) Kane

Private non-profit/ 1962/ Board of Directors/ staff: 42(v)/ members: 204/publication: *Fox River Lines*

HISTORY MUSEUM: Preserves and interprets Chicago's electric transport era.

PROGRAMS: Community Outreach; Exhibits; Facility Rental; Family Programs; Festivals; Guided Tours; Interpretation; Publication

COLLECTIONS: [1890-1960] 25 historic railway

SOUTH HOLLAND

2388
South Holland Historical Society, The
16250 Wausua Ave, 60473 [PO Box 48, 60473]; (p) (708) 596-2722; (c) Cook

1969/ staff: 15(v)/ members: 105

HISTORY MUSEUM: Promotes South Holland history through museum exhibits.

PROGRAMS: Community Outreach; Exhibits; Festivals; Guided Tours; Publication; Research Library/Archives

COLLECTIONS: [1846-present] Artifacts, peri-od furnishings and clothing, farm equipment, photos, books, main street model.

HOURS: Yr Sa 1-4

ADMISSION: $1, Children $0.50

2389
South Suburban Genealogical and Historical Society
320 E 161st Place, 60473 [PO Box 96, 60473-0096]; (p) (708) 333-9474; ssghs@hotmail.com; www.rootsweb.com/~ssghs/ssghs.htm; (c) Cook

1968/ staff: 25(v)/ members: 350

GENEALOGICAL SOCIETY

PROGRAMS: Lectures; Research Library Archives

COLLECTIONS: General genealogy reference.

HOURS: Yr M 10-4, T 1-5, W 10-11:30 / 12:30-4, F 10-4; 1st, 2nd and 3rd Sat of month 11-4

SPRINGFIELD

2390
Abraham Lincoln Association
One Old State Capitol Plaza, 62701; (p) (217) 782-2118; (f) (217) 785-7937; www.alincolnassoc.com; (c) Sangamon

1908/ staff: 1(p); 35(v)/publication: *Journal of the Abraham Lincoln Association*

HISTORICAL SOCIETY: Produces and supports Lincoln studies, providing the general public with authoritative publications and lectures on Lincoln and his time.

PROGRAMS: Annual Meeting; Lectures; Publication

2391
Dana-Thomas House State Historic Site
301 E Lawrence Ave, 62703; (p) (217) 782-6776; (f) (217) 788-9450; (c) Sangamon

State/ 1981/ State of Illinois/Illinois Historic Preservation Agency/ staff: 6(f); 4(p); 125(v)/ members: 500

ART MUSEUM; HISTORIC PRESERVATION AGENCY; HISTORIC SITE; HOUSE MUSE-UM: Historic site designed by American architect Frank Lloyd Wright.

PROGRAMS: Annual Meeting; Exhibits; Facility Rental; Family Programs; Festivals; Guided Tours; Interpretation; Lectures; Research Library/Archives; School-Based Curriculum

COLLECTIONS: [20th c] Frank Lloyd Wright accessories with art glass, furniture and decorative

2392
Daughters of Union Veterans of the Civil War, 1861-1865
503 S Walnut, 62704-1932; (p) (217) 544-0616; duvcw@comp.net; (c) Sangamon

1885/ staff: 1(f)/ members: 4000/publication: *General Orders, Drumbeat*

HISTORICAL SOCIETY; HISTORY MUSEUM; RESEARCH CENTER: Promotes memories of Civil War ancestors through genealogical, ed-ucational, historical, patriotical, service and community projects.

PROGRAMS: Community Outreach; Exhibits; Film/Video; Guided Tours; Interpretation; Pub-lication; Research Library/Archives

COLLECTIONS: [Civil War] Videos, genealog-ical files, member records, library of Civil War histories, military and regimental records, war artifacts, historical records pertaining to Grand Army of the Republic.

HOURS: Yr M-F 9-4 and by appt

2393
Edwards Place Historic Home
700 N 4th St, 62702; (p) (217) 523-2631; www.online-springfield.com/sites/edplace.html

2394
Illinois Association of Museums
500 E Madison, 62701 [1 Old State Capitol, 62701]; (p) (217) 524-7080; (f) (217) 785-7937; mturner@hpa084r1.state.il.us; (c) Sangamon

Private non-profit/ 1994/ Illinois Association of Museums/ members: 320

ALLIANCE OF HISTORICAL AGENCIES: Statewide network of art, science and history musuems, historical and genealogical soci-eties, zoos, nature centers, arboreta and other cultural agencies to facilitate exchange of ideas among members who share goals relat-ed to preservation and interpretation of histo-ry, prehistory and natural history.

PROGRAMS: Research Library/Archives; School-Based Curriculum

2395
Illinois Historic Preservation Agency
500 E Madison, 62701 [1 Old State Capitol, 62701]; (p) (217) 524-7080; (f) (217) 785-7937; mturner@hap084r1.state.il.us; www.state.il.us/hpa/ihpa/home/default.htm; (c) Sangamon

State/ 1985/ State of Illinois/ staff: 218(f); 8(p)

HISTORIC PRESERVATION AGENCY

PROGRAMS: Publication; Research Library/ Archives

HOURS: Yr M-F 8:30-5

2396
Illinois National Guard and Militia Historical Society, Inc.
Camp Lincoln, 1301 N MacArthur Blvd, 62702-2399; (p) (217) 761-3975; (f) (217) 761-3709; whitlockm@il-arng.ngb.army.mil; www.ilng-history.org; (c) Sangamon

Private non-profit/ 1990/ staff: 3(p); 3(v)/ members: 380

HISTORICAL SOCIETY: Preserves, interprets, and presents information on history of the Illinois Militia.

PROGRAMS: Annual Meeting; Interpretation; Publication

COLLECTIONS: [1700-present] Flag restoration program.

2397
Illinois State Historical Society
210 1/2 S 6th St, 62701 [1 Old State Capitol Plaza, 62701-1507]; (p) (217) 782-2635; (f) (217) 524-8042; ishs@eosinc.com; www.prairienet.org/ishs; (c) Sangamon

Private non-profit/ 1899/ staff: 3(f); 2(p)/ members: 2700/publication: *Journal of the Illinois State Historical Society*

HISTORICAL SOCIETY: Collects, preserves and interprets history through publication and member/public service outreach programs.

PROGRAMS: Annual Meeting; Guided Tours; Interpretation; Lectures; Publication

HOURS: Yr M-F 9-5

ADMISSION: No charge

2398
Illinois State Military Museum
1301 N MacArthur Blvd, 62702-2399; (p) (217) 761-3910; (f) (217) 761-3709; mark.whitlock@il-arng.ngb.army.mil; mil-museum-il.il-arng.mb.army.mil/; (c) Sangamon

State/ 1878/ Illinois Dept of Military Affairs/ staff: 2(f); 4(p); 10(v)/publication: *Sharpshooter*

HISTORIC SITE; HISTORY MUSEUM: Preserves and interprets Illinois military heritage.

PROGRAMS: Community Outreach; Exhibits; Guided Tours; Interpretation; Publication; Research Library/Archives

COLLECTIONS: [Civil War, WWI] Weapons, vehicles, equipment, clothing, document, photos, Revolutionary War through present artifacts.

HOURS: Yr M-F

2399
Illinois State Museum
Spring and Edwards Sts, 62706-5000; (p) (217) 782-7387; (f) (217) 782-1254; (c) Sangamon

State/ 1877/ Dept of Natural Resources/ staff: 117(f); 32(p); 163(v)/ members: 664/publication: *The Living Museum*

ART MUSEUM; HISTORY MUSEUM; RESEARCH CENTER: Preserves, collects, and interprets natural history, art and anthropology.

PROGRAMS: Annual Meeting; Community Outreach; Exhibits; Facility Rental; Family Programs; Film/Video; Guided Tours; Lectures; Publication; Research Library/Archives

COLLECTIONS: [Prehistory-present] Anthropology, archaeology, botany, geology, zoology, entomology, herbarium, herpetology, natural history, paleontology, fine arts, decorative arts, and art history of Illinois.

HOURS: Yr M-Sa 8:30-5, Su 12-5

ADMISSION: No charge

2400
Lincoln Home National Historic Site
413 S 8th St, 62701-1905; (p) (217) 492-4241; (f) (217) 492-4673; lincolnhome@nps.gov; www.nps.gov/liho

Federal/ 1887/ Dept of the Interior/National Park Service/ staff: 30(f); 30(p); 30(v)

HISTORIC SITE; HOUSE MUSEUM; PRESIDENTIAL SITE: History of Abraham Lincoln and Family from 1844-1861 and mid 19th century American political and social history.

PROGRAMS: Exhibits; Family Programs; Film/Video; Guided Tours; Interpretation; Lectures; School-Based Curriculum

COLLECTIONS: [1860] Historic house furnishings, artifacts related to Lincoln Family, architecture, archaeology, and archives.

HOURS: Yr Daily

2401
Lincoln Library's Sangamon Valley Connection
326 S 7th St, 62701; (p) (217) 753-4900; (f) (217) 753-5329; (c) Sangamon

City, non-profit/ 1970/ staff: 3(f); 1(p); 8(v)

GENEALOGICAL SOCIETY; LIBRARY AND/OR ARCHIVES: Preserves local history.

PROGRAMS: Community Outreach; Exhibits; Research Library/Archives; School-Based Curriculum

COLLECTIONS: [1820-present] Genealogical information on Springfield, Sangamon County, special collection on poet Vachel Lindsay, obituaries.

HOURS: Yr Daily M-Th 9-9, F 9-6, Sa 9-5, Su

2402
Lincoln Tomb State Historic Site
Oak Ridge Cemetery, 62702 [1500 Monument Ave, 62702]; (p) (217) 782-2717; (c) Sangamon

State/ 1874/ State of Illinois/ staff: 5(f); 4(p); 15(v)

HISTORIC PRESERVATION AGENCY; HISTORIC SITE: Tomb of Abraham Lincoln, Mary, and their children.

PROGRAMS: Interpretation; Lectures; Living History

COLLECTIONS: [1860-1865] Items related to Lincoln's death and tomb history.

HOURS: Mar-Oct 9-5, Nov-Feb 9-4

ADMISSION: No charge

2403
National Woman's Relief Corps Auxiliary to the Grand Army of the Republic, Inc.
629 S Seventh St, 62703; (p) (217) 522-4373; (c) Sagamore

Private non-profit/ 1883/ National Convention/ staff: 1(f); 6(p)/ members: 2000

HISTORY MUSEUM: Promotes military history.

PROGRAMS: Exhibits; Research Library/ Archives

COLLECTIONS: [1861-present] Civil War memorabilia, convention badges, journals, photos, flags, ammunition, soldiers' personal effects, books.

HOURS: March-Dec T-Sa 10-4 and by appt

ADMISSION: No charge

2404
Old State Capitol Complex
1 Old State Capitol Plaza, 62701; (p) (217) 785-7960; (f) (217) 557-0282; (c) Sangamon

1970/ Illinois Historic Preservation Agency/ staff: 12(f); 10(p); 100(v)/ members: 180

HISTORIC SITE: Maintains and interprets three historic sites - Old State Capitol, The Lincoln/Herndon Law Offices, and the Vachel Lindsay Home for the Illinois Historic Preservation Agency.

PROGRAMS: Community Outreach; Exhibits; Facility Rental; Family Programs; Festivals; Guided Tours; Interpretation; Living History; Reenactments; Theatre

COLLECTIONS: [1800-1900] Memorabilia from the home of Poet Vachel Lindsay; Period artifacts illustrating state government and legal practices.

HOURS: Yr Daily

ADMISSION: Donations accepted

2405
Pearson Museum Dept of Medical Humanities
801 N Rutledge, 62794 [Southern Illinois, PO Box 19635, 62794-9635]; (p) (217) 785-2128; (f) (217) 782-9132; bmason@siumed.edu; (c) Sangamon

State/ 1974/ Board of Trustees of Southern Illinois University/ staff: 1(f); 3(p)

HISTORY MUSEUM: Provides research materials for medical students and faculty.

PROGRAMS: Community Outreach; Exhibits; Guided Tours; Lectures

COLLECTIONS: [18th-20th c] Artifacts, photos, papers and books reflecting health sciences history, primarily in Mississippi

2406
Sangamon County Genealogical Society
2856 S 11th St, 62705 [PO Box 1829, 62705-1829]; (p) (217) 529-0542; Dbutton2@aol.com; (c) Sangamon

Private non-profit/ 1968/ members: 350

GENEALOGICAL SOCIETY: Collects and preserves genealogical history.

PROGRAMS: Interpretation; Lectures; Publication; Research Library/Archives

COLLECTIONS: [1821-present] Housed within the Sangamon Valley Collection of Springfield's Lincoln Library.

2407
Sangamon County Historical Society
308 E Adams St, 62701; (p) (217) 522-2500; (c) Sangamon

Private non-profit/ 1961/publication: *Historico*

HISTORICAL SOCIETY: Preserves and supports the history of Sangamon County.

PROGRAMS: Annual Meeting; Lectures; Publication

2408
Vachel Lindsey Home State Historic Site
Fifth & Edwards Sts, 62701 [603 S Fifth St, 62701]; (p) (217) 785-7960

IL Historic Preservation Agency

HISTORIC SITE:; HOUSE MUSEUM; Birthplace and home of poet Vachel Lindsey.

COLLECTIONS: Furnishings; fixtures; books; artwork by Lindsey; Lindsey's writings.

ST. CHARLES

2409
Preservation Partners of the Fox Valley
8 Indiana St, 60174 [PO Box 903, 60174]; (p) (630) 377-6424; (c) Kane

1974/ Board of Directors/ staff: 2(f); 2(p); 100(v)/ members: 400

HISTORIC SITE; HOUSE MUSEUM: Preserves architectural and local history.

PROGRAMS: Community Outreach; Exhibits; Family Programs; Guided Tours; Interpretation; Lectures; Research Library/Archives; School-Based Curriculum

COLLECTIONS: [1840-1939] Restored furnished farmhouse, Oriental artifacts, arts & crafts furniture, code breaking devices, local history, 1850s furnishings, decorative arts.

2410
St. Charles Heritage Center
215 E Main St, 60174; (p) (630) 584-6967; (f) (630) 584-6077; info@stcmuseum.org; www.stcmuseum.org; (c) Kane

Private non-profit/ 1933/ staff: 3(f); 10(v)/ members: 240

HISTORIC SITE; HISTORY MUSEUM; RESEARCH CENTER: Collects, preserves, and presents St. Charles history; oversees the St. Charles History Museum and the 1839 Dunham-Hunt House at 304 Cedar Ave.

PROGRAMS: Annual Meeting; Exhibits; Research Library/Archives

COLLECTIONS: [1830-1920] Artifacts related to St. Charles.

HOURS: Yr T-F 10-4, Sa, Su 12-4

ADMISSION: Donations accepted

STAUNTON

2411
Macoupin County Genealogical Society
[PO Box 95, 62088]; www.rootsweb.com/~ilmacoup/macoupin.htm; (c) Macoupin

Private non-profit/ 1980/ staff: 20(v)/ members: 250/publication: *Macoupin County Searcher*

GENEALOGICAL SOCIETY: Collects and preserves county history.

PROGRAMS: Annual Meeting; Lectures; Publication; Research Library/Archives

COLLECTIONS: County census on microfilm, cemetery, biographical histories, newspaper on microfilm.

STERLING

2412
Dillon Home Museum
1005 E 3rd, 61081 [PO Box 958, 61081-0958]; (p) (815) 622-6202; (f) (815) 622-6210; parks@cin.net

Joint/ 1980/ Board of Commissioners/ staff: 2(f); 30(v)

HISTORIC SITE; HOUSE MUSEUM: Displays, interprets

PROGRAMS: Exhibits; Facility Rental; Guided Tours; Interpretation

COLLECTIONS: [18th c-present] Decorative arts, art, photos, labor and industrial history, architectural and railroading, manuscripts, and newspaper clippings.

HOURS: Yr T, Th, Sa 10-12/1-4, Su 1-5

ADMISSION: $2, Seniors $1

2413
Sterling Rock Falls Historical Society Museum
1005 E 3rd St, 61081 [PO Box 65, 61081]; (p) (815) 288-4088; (c) Whiteside

Private non-profit/ 1959/ Board of Directors/ staff: 1(f); 1(p); 25(v)/ members: 170

HISTORICAL SOCIETY; HISTORY MUSEUM: Preserves, interprets, and researches the history of Sterling-Rock Falls.

PROGRAMS: Annual Meeting; Exhibits; Family Programs; Guided Tours; Lectures; Research Library/Archives; School-Based Curriculum

COLLECTIONS: Manuscripts, maps, newspapers, volumes, paintings, museum artifacts, photos.

HOURS: Yr T,Th,Sa 10-12, Su 1-5

ADMISSION: Donations accepted

2414
Whiteside County Genealogists
[PO Box 145, 61081]; www.serve.com/bmosher/WSCGen/wscgen.htm; (c) Whiteside

Private non-profit/ 1976/ staff: 5(v)/ members: 101/publication: *Whiteside Genealogist Newsletter*

GENEALOGICAL SOCIETY: Preserves genealogical information and history of Whiteside County.

PROGRAMS: Monthly Meeting; Publication

STREAMWOOD

2415
Streamwood Park District/Streamwood Historical Society
700 W Irving Park Road, 60107; (p) (630) 213-9706; (f) (630) 372-1893; (c) Cook

Joint/ 1966/ Park District; Historical Society/ staff: 1(f); 4(p); 30(v)/ members: 25

GARDEN; HISTORICAL SOCIETY; HISTORY MUSEUM; RESEARCH CENTER

PROGRAMS: Annual Meeting; Community Outreach; Concerts; Elder's Programs; Exhibits; Facility Rental; Family Programs; Festivals; Film/Video; Garden Tours; Guided Tours; Interpretation; Lectures; Living History; Reenactments; Research Library/Archives; School-Based

COLLECTIONS: [1850-present]

HOURS: Mar-Dec F-Su 1-4 and by appt

ADMISSION: Donations accepted

STREATOR

2416
Streatorland Historical Society
306 S Vermillion St, 61364; (p) (815) 672-2443; (c) LaSalle

Private non-profit/ 1974/ staff: 2(p)/ members: 450/publication: *Unionville Dispatch*

GENEALOGICAL SOCIETY; HISTORICAL SOCIETY; HISTORY MUSEUM; RESEARCH CENTER

PROGRAMS: Annual Meeting; Exhibits; Family Programs; Festivals; Guided Tours; Publication; Research Library/Archives

COLLECTIONS: Artifacts, photos.

HOURS: Yr M-F 9:30-2:30, Su 1-4

ADMISSION: Donations accepted

SULLIVAN

2417
Moultrie County Historical and Genealogical Society
117 E Harrison, 61951 [PO Box 588, 61951]; (p) (217) 728-4085; (c) Moultrie

Private non-profit/ 1973

GENEALOGICAL SOCIETY; HISTORY MUSEUM: Preserves history of Moultrie County.

PROGRAMS: Annual Meeting; Exhibits; Publication; Research Library/Archives

COLLECTIONS: [1845-present] Historical and genealogical data and artifacts.

HOURS: Yr Sa, M

SYCAMORE

2418
DeKalb County Historical Genealogical Society
[PO Box 295, 60178]; (c) DeKalb

members: 150/publication: *Cornsilk*

GENEALOGICAL SOCIETY; HISTORICAL SOCIETY: Promotes local and genealogical history.

PROGRAMS: Annual Meeting; Lectures; Publication

TAMPICO

2419
Ronald Reagan Birthplace Museum
111 S Main St, 61283; (p) (815) 438-2130; (c) Whiteside

1981/ staff: 25(v)

HISTORIC SITE; HISTORY MUSEUM; PRESIDENTIAL SITE: Preserves Ronald Reagan's home and birthplace.

PROGRAMS: Exhibits; Festivals

COLLECTIONS: [Early 1900-present] Pictures, articles, memorabilia and books related to Ronald Reagan.

HOURS: Feb-Mar Sa 10-4, Su 1-4; Apr-Nov M-Sa 10-4, Su 1-4

ADMISSION: Donations accepted

2420
Tampico Area Historical Society
119 S Main St, 61283; (p) (815) 438-6175; (c) Whiteside

1991/ staff: 15(v)/ members: 28

HISTORICAL SOCIETY; PRESIDENTIAL SITE: Collects and preserves local history.

PROGRAMS: Film/Video; Guided Tours; School-Based Curriculum

COLLECTIONS: [1861-present] Pioneer artifacts, Ronald Reagan memorabilia.

HOURS: Apr-Nov Sa-Su 1-4

ADMISSION: Donations accepted

TAYLORVILLE

2421
Christian County Genealogical Society
Pence Bldg, Rts 29 & 48, 62568 [PO Box 28, 62568-0028]; (p) (217) 526-3701; isloman@chipsnet.com; www.homepage.macomb.com/~tkuntz/christianco.htm; (c) Christian

Private non-profit/ 1983/ Board of Elected Officers/ staff: 10(v)/ members: 125

GENEALOGICAL SOCIETY: Promotes, preserves and publishes materials of genealogical and historical nature, pertaining to early Christian County.

PROGRAMS: Community Outreach; Family Programs; Lectures; Research Library/ Archives

COLLECTIONS: [1839-present] Genealogical research books and microfilm of Christian County and adjacent counties of IL.

HOURS: Library: Apr-Nov W-Sa 11-4, Su 1-4; Dec-Mar Sa 11-4

ADMISSION: $2; Members Free

2422
Christian County Historical Society Museum
Pence Bldg, Rts 29 & 48, 62568 [PO Box 254, 62568]; (p) (217) 824-6922; (c) Christian

Private non-profit/ 1967/ staff: 1(p)/ 7(v)/ members: 250/publication: *Persimmons; Letters to Home 1861-1864*

GENEALOGICAL SOCIETY; HISTORIC PRESERVATION AGENCY; HISTORICAL SOCIETY; HISTORY MUSEUM: Preserves and presents the history of Christian County, IL.

PROGRAMS: Annual Meeting; Community Outreach; Exhibits; Guided Tours; Interpretation; Publication; Research Library/Archives; School-Based Curriculum

COLLECTIONS: [1820-present] Historic buildings.

HOURS: W-Su 10-4

ADMISSION: $2

TEUTOPOLIS

2423
Teutopolis Monastery Museum
110 S Garrott, 62467 [106 W Walter, 62467]; (p) (217) 857-3586; (c) Effingham

Private non-profit/ 1975

HISTORIC SITE; HISTORY MUSEUM: Promotes history of the Franciscan friars.

PROGRAMS: Annual Meeting; Exhibits; Guided Tours

COLLECTIONS: [19th-20th c] Artifacts, memorabilia and books of early Franciscans and early pioneer families since 1839.

HOURS: Apr-Nov 1st Su 12:30-4 and by appt

ADMISSION: $2, Children $1

THORNTON

2424
Village of Thornton Historical Site
114 N Hunter, 60476 [PO Box 34, 60476]; (p) (708) 877-6569; (c) Cook

Private non-profit/ 1974/ staff: 20(v)/ members: 40

HISTORICAL SOCIETY: Preserves history of Village of Thornton settlement.

PROGRAMS: Community Outreach

COLLECTIONS: [1875-1940] Artifacts and books.

HOURS: May-Sept Sa 1-4

ADMISSION: No charge

TILTON

2425
Tilton Historical Society
201 W 5th St, 61833; (p) (217) 442-9309; (c) Vermillon

Private non-profit/ 1988/ staff: 6(v)/ members: 105

GENEALOGICAL SOCIETY; HISTORICAL SOCIETY; HISTORY MUSEUM; HOUSE MUSEUM: Collects and preserves Tilton history.

COLLECTIONS: School house classrooms with memorabilia, clothing; railroad and mining artifacts.

HOURS: Yr Th 9-12

ADMISSION: No charge

TINLEY PARK

2426
Tinley Park Historical Society
6727 W 174th St, 60477 [PO Box 325, 60477]; (p) (708) 429-4210; lrtphist@lincolnnet.net

Private non-profit/ 1974/ staff: 10(v)

HISTORIC SITE; HISTORICAL SOCIETY; HISTORY MUSEUM

PROGRAMS: Exhibits; Lectures; Research Library/Archives

HOURS: W 10-2

TREMONT

2427
Tremont Museum and Historical Society
Madison & S Sampson St, 61568 [PO Box 738, 61568-0738]; (p) (309) 925-5262, (309) 925-5903; (c) Tazewell

Joint/ 1987/ City; Historical Society/ staff: 30(v)/ members: 175/publication: *Tales and Trails*

HISTORICAL SOCIETY; HISTORY MUSEUM: Preserves history of Tremont township and School District 702.

PROGRAMS: Annual Meeting; Community Outreach; Exhibits; Family Programs; Guided Tours; Interpretation; Lectures; Publication; Reenactments; School-Based Curriculum

COLLECTIONS: [1830s-present] Local artifacts, advertising, and photos.

HOURS: Yr 2nd Su 2-4

ADMISSION: $1

TUSCOLA

2428
Korean War Veterans National Museum and Library
700 S Main St, 61953; (p) (217) 253-5813; (f) (217) 253-3228; kwmuseum@netgg.com; www.theforgottenvictory.org; (c) Douglas

Private non-profit/ 1997/ staff: 1(f); 1(p); 6(v)/ members: 675

HISTORY MUSEUM: Preserves history of Korean War.

PROGRAMS: Annual Meeting; Community Outreach; Lectures; Publication; Research Library/Archives

COLLECTIONS: [1950-present] Korean

2429
Museum Association of Douglas County
700 S Main St, 61953; (p) (217) 253-2535; (f) (217) 253-3228; dcmuseum@net66.com; (c) Douglas

Private non-profit/ 1984/ staff: 1(f); 10(v)/ members: 1000/publication: *Cabin Chatter*

HISTORY MUSEUM; LIBRARY AND/OR ARCHIVES: Preserves and interprets local history.

PROGRAMS: Annual Meeting; Community Outreach; Concerts; Exhibits; Facility Rental; Family Programs; Guided Tours; Interpretation; Lectures; Publication; Research Library/Archives

COLLECTIONS: [1860-present] Manuscripts; artifacts from military, advertising, industry, medical; decorative arts; clothing and textiles.

HOURS: Yr M-F 9-4, Sa 1-4

UNION

2430
Illinois Railway Museum Inc.
7000 Olson Rd, 60180 [PO Box 427, 60180]; (p) (815) 923-4391; (f) (815) 923-2006; (c) McHenry

Private non-profit/ 1953/ staff: 2(f); 1(p); 150(v)/ members: 2400/publication: *Rail & Wire*

RAILROAD MUSEUM: Preserves and promotes railway history.

PROGRAMS: Exhibits; Living History; Publication

COLLECTIONS: [1900-1970] Over 350 pieces of railway transportation equipment, including electric powered streetcars, interurban cars, trolley buses, mainline railroad equipment, 25 steam locomotives, 35 diesels, 54 passenger coaches, 80 freight cars, Pullman Company drawings.

HOURS: May-Sept Daily 10-5; Oct Sa-Su 10-5

ADMISSION: Varies

2431
McHenry County Historical Society
6422 Main St, 60180 [PO Box 434, 60180]; (p) (815) 923-2267; (f) (815) 923-2271; info@mchsonline.org; www.mchsonline.org/; (c) McHenry

Private non-profit/ 1963/ staff: 2(f); 1(p); 250(v)/ members: 800/publication: *The Tracer*

HISTORICAL SOCIETY; HISTORY MUSEUM; LIBRARY AND/OR ARCHIVES: Identifies, preserves, presents, and promotes McHenry County history. Includes a museum with several preserved buildings and a local history research library.

PROGRAMS: Annual Meeting; Community Outreach; Exhibits; Family Programs; Festivals; Lectures; Publication; Research Library/Archives

COLLECTIONS: [1830-present] Documentary materials, artifacts of McHenry county life. An 1847 log cabin; an 1885 town hall; an 1895 one-room school house used for c.1900 school programs; and a 20th c modern tourist cabin.

HOURS: Society: Yr M-F 9-4:30; Museum: May-Oct Su, T-F 1-4; Library: Yr M-F by appt only

ADMISSION: $3, Student $2, Seniors $2; Members free

URBANA

2432
Champaign County Historical Archives
201 S Race St, 61801-3283; (p) (217) 367-4025; (f) (217) 367-4061; www.urbanafreelibrary.org; (c) Champaign

City/ 1874/ staff: 2(f); 4(p); 8(v)

PROGRAMS: Exhibits; Guided Tours; Research Library/Archives

COLLECTIONS: [1833-present] Genealogy and local history records for Champaign County, with an emphasis on east-central IL, and genealogy of the migration route from the east

2433
Spurlock Museum, The
600 S Gregory, 61801; (p) (217) 333-2360; (f) (217) 244-9419; darobbin@uiuc.edu; www.spurlock.uiuc.edu; (c) Champaign

State/ 1911/ Univ of IL/ staff: 13(f); 12(p); 70(v)/ members: 400

HISTORY MUSEUM; NATURAL HISTORY MUSEUM: Collects, preserves, and interprets natural history; history and culture.

PROGRAMS: Community Outreach; Concerts; Exhibits; Facility Rental; Family Programs; Guided Tours; Interpretation; Lectures; School-Based Curriculum

COLLECTIONS: 45,000 specimens and cultural artifacts spanning 500,000 years and six continents; natural history collections include substantial and significant research collections in herpetology, mammology, ornithology, malacology, and geology.

ADMISSION: No charge

URBANA-CHAMPAIGN

2434
Illinois Historical Survey-University of Illinois Library
1408 W Gregory Dr, 61801 [Library 346, 61801]; (p) (217) 333-1777; (c) Champaign

1910/ staff: 1(f); 2(p)

COLLECTIONS: [18th-20th c] Manuscripts

ADMISSION: No charge

UTICA

2435
LaSalle County Historical Society
Mill & Canal Sts, 61373 [PO Box 278, 61373]; (p) (815) 667-4861; (f) (815) 667-5121; (c) LaSalle

Private non-profit/ 1907/ staff: 1(f); 2(p); 25(v)/ members: 645

HISTORIC SITE; HISTORICAL SOCIETY; HISTORY MUSEUM: Preserves history of LaSalle County.

PROGRAMS: Annual Meeting; Community Outreach; Exhibits; Facility Rental; Family Programs; Festivals; Interpretation; Lectures; Publication; Research Library/Archives; School-Based Curriculum

COLLECTIONS: [1848-present]

HOURS: Mar-Dec W-Su 12-4

ADMISSION: Donations accepted

VANDALIA

2436
Vandalia State House Historic Site
315 W Gallatin, 62471; (p) (618) 283-1161; (c) Fayette

State/ IL Historic Preservation Agency/ staff: 3(f); 25(v)

HISTORIC PRESERVATION AGENCY: Preserves oldest Capitol building in Illinois.

PROGRAMS: Festivals; Guided Tours; Interpretation

COLLECTIONS: [1836-1839] Period artifacts.

HOURS: Mar-Oct Daily 8:30-5; Nov-Feb 8-4

ADMISSION: $2, Student $1

VERNON HILLS

2437
Cuneo Museum and Gardens
1350 N Milwaukee, 60061; (p) (847) 362-3042; (c) Lake

1991/ Cuneo Foundation/ staff: 12(f); 2(p); 2(v)

HOUSE MUSEUM: Collects, preserves, interprets and exhibits the collection of John Cuneo Family.

PROGRAMS: Concerts; Exhibits; Facility Rental; Festivals; Guided Tours; Lectures; Theatre

COLLECTIONS: [Renaissance] Renaissance Italian art, European furnishings, oriental rugs housed in Italianate villa.

HOURS: Feb-Dec T-Su 10-5

ADMISSION: $10, Student $5, Seniors $9

VIENNA

2438
Johnson County Genealogical and Historical Society/Powell House Museum and Research Center
404 Vine St, 62995; (p) (618) 658-4911, (217) 258-0459; (f) (217) 258-0426; members.nbci.com/jcghs/powellhouse.html

Joint/ 1850/ Paul Powell Charitable Trust; JCGHS

HISTORICAL SOCIETY; HOUSE MUSEUM; RESEARCH CENTER: Interprets life and political career of Paul Powell as well as the history and genealogy of Johnson County, IL.

PROGRAMS: Exhibits

COLLECTIONS: [20th c] Political memorabilia of Paul Powell; quilts.

HOURS: Yr W, F, Sa 1-4

VIRGINIA

2439
Cass County Historical and Genealogical Society
[PO Box 11, 62691]; (c) Cass

Private non-profit/ 1963/ staff: 5(v)/ members: 120/publication: *Cass County Historian*

GENEALOGICAL SOCIETY; HISTORICAL SOCIETY: Preserves history of Cass County through collection of tombstone, birth, and death records.

PROGRAMS: Annual Meeting; Publication

COLLECTIONS: [1847-present] Items related to local history, housed at Virginia Memorial Public Library.

ADMISSION: No charge

WARRENVILLE

2440
Warrenville Historical Society
35530 Second St, 60555 [PO Box 311, 60555]; (p) (630) 393-4215; (c) DuPage

Private non-profit/ 1983/ staff: 10(v)/ members: 85/publication: *Historic Update*

HISTORICAL SOCIETY: Collects, preserves, exhibits and interprets materials related to history of domestic, farm, political and business life of Warrenville.

PROGRAMS: Annual Meeting; Community Outreach; Concerts; Exhibits; Film/Video; Guided Tours; Lectures; Publication; Research Library/Archives; School-Based Curriculum

COLLECTIONS: [1840-present] Adam Albright paintings, 1,000 Native American artifacts, Greek Revival architecture, Chicago Aurora and Elgin railroad artifacts.

HOURS: June-Aug W, Su 1-4; Apr-May, Sept-Nov Su 1-4

WARSAW

2441
Warsaw Historical Society and Museum
401 Main St, 62379; (c) Hancock

Private non-profit/ 1980/ staff: 30(v)/ members: 50

HISTORIC SITE; HISTORICAL SOCIETY; HISTORY MUSEUM: Preserves area history.

PROGRAMS: Annual Meeting; Exhibits; Festivals; Guided Tours; Lectures; Research Library/Archives

COLLECTIONS: [1830-1910] Photos, abstracts, diaries, business related items, artifacts from Warsaw history; local school, individual and community photos, with emphasis on early settlers, family histories and Warsaw's famous people and buildings.

HOURS: May-Oct F-Sa 1-4

WASHINGTON

2442
Washington Historical Society
105 Zinger Place, 61571 [PO Box 54, 61571]; (p) (309) 444-4793; (f) (309) 444-4239; (c) Tazewell

1980/ staff: 30(v)/ members: 200/publication: *Washington Heritage Herald*

HISTORIC SITE; HISTORICAL SOCIETY; HISTORY MUSEUM; HOUSE MUSEUM: Preserves and interprets local history.

PROGRAMS: Annual Meeting; Community Outreach; Exhibits; Facility Rental; Festivals; Garden Tours; Guided Tours; Publication; Research Library/Archives

COLLECTIONS: Newspapers, books, photos, local Civil War journals and artifacts.

HOURS: Yr W-Th, Sa 10-1, F 10-4

WATERLOO

2443
Monroe County Historical Society
709 S Church St, 62298 [PO Box 48, 62298]; (p) (618) 939-5230; mocohis@htc.net; (c) Monroe

Private non-profit/ 1960/ staff: 10(v)/ members: 51

HISTORIC SITE; HISTORICAL SOCIETY; HISTORY MUSEUM; HOUSE MUSEUM: Preserves the history of Monroe County.

PROGRAMS: Annual Meeting; Community Outreach; Concerts; Exhibits; Facility Rental; Guided Tours; Lectures; Publication; Research Library/Archives; School-Based Curriculum; Theatre

COLLECTIONS: [1800s] Farmhouse, period furnishings, school and military rooms, battle shed, smokehouse, agricultural equipment, log corn crib.

HOURS: Apr-Oct Sa-Su 1-5, Dec

2444
Peterstown Heritage Society
275 N Main St, 62298; (p) (618) 939-4222; (c) Monroe

1972/ staff: 1(p); 1(v)/ members: 25

HISTORIC SITE; HOUSE MUSEUM

PROGRAMS: Community Outreach; Exhibits; Facility Rental; Family Programs; Guided Tours

COLLECTIONS: [1885-1910] Period furnishings, country store display, war memorabilia, 19th c farm tools, log cabins, restored ballroom.

HOURS: Yr Sa-Su 1-5

WATSEKA

2445
Iroquois County Genealogy Society
103 W Cherry, 60970-1524; (p) (815) 432-3730; (f) (815) 432-3732; iroqgene@techiater.com; (c) Iroquios

County, non-profit/ 1978/ staff: 1(p); 6(v)/publication: *Iroquios Stalker*

GENEALOGICAL SOCIETY: Public library with emphasis on local history and genealogy.

PROGRAMS: Annual Meeting; Lectures; Publication; Reenactments

COLLECTIONS: [1833-1900] Local pioneer history and biographies, census data, cemetery records, and obituaries.

HOURS: Yr M-F 10:30-4:30

2446
Watseka Union Depot
121 S Second St, 60970 [PO Box 118, 60970]; (f) (815) 432-4688; (c) Iroquois

Private non-profit/ 1989/ Board of Directors/ staff: 10(v)

HISTORIC SITE: Preserves Watseka Railroad Depot for public use.

PROGRAMS: Annual Meeting; Exhibits; Facility Rental; Festivals; Guided Tours

COLLECTIONS: Railroad memorabilia, historic train depot.

HOURS: Apr-Oct Sa 10-2

ADMISSION: Donations

WAUCONDA

2447
Lake County Discovery Museum
27277 Forest Preserve Dr, 60084; (p) (847) 968-3400; (f) (847) 526-0024; lcmuseum@co.lake.il.us; (c) Lake

County/ 1976/ staff: 13(f); 4(p)/ members: 1

HISTORY MUSEUM: Preserves local history.

PROGRAMS: Community Outreach; Exhibits; Facility Rental; Family Programs; Festivals; Guided Tours; Lectures; Living History; Reenactments

COLLECTIONS: Native American artifacts, postcard archives, regional history archives.

HOURS: Yr M-Sa 11-4:30, Su 1-4:30

ADMISSION: $5, Student $2.50

2448
Wauconda Township Historical Society
711 N Main St, 60084 [PO Box 256, 60084]; (p) (847) 526-9303; (c) Lake

Private non-profit/ 1973/ staff: 25(v)/ members: 170

HISTORIC SITE; HISTORY MUSEUM: Preserves local history.

PROGRAMS: Annual Meeting; Exhibits; Festivals; Guided Tours; Lectures; Reenactments; Research Library/Archives; School-Based Curriculum

COLLECTIONS: [1900] Housed in Greek Revival brick farmhouse; photos, locally made furniture, agriculture.

HOURS: May-Sept Su 1-4

WAUKEGAN

2449
Bowen Heritage Circle
1911 N Sheridan Rd, 60087; (p) (847) 360-4770; (f) (847) 662-0592; (c) Lake

City/ Waukegan Park District/ staff: 1(f); 1(p)

HISTORIC SITE; HISTORICAL SOCIETY; HOUSE MUSEUM

PROGRAMS: Community Outreach; Exhibits; Festivals; Guided Tours; Lectures; Living History; Reenactments; Research Library/Archives; School-Based Curriculum

HOURS: Yr W-F 10-2:30; Library: Yr M 3-8, T,F 10-2

2450
Waukegan Historical Society, Haines House Museum
1917 N Sheridan Rd, 60079 [PO Box 857, 60079]; (p) (847) 336-1859; (f) (847) 662-0592; (c) Lake

Joint/ 1968/ Waukegan Park District; WHS/ staff: 1(p); 20(v)/ members: 120/publication: *Historically Speaking*

HISTORIC SITE; HISTORICAL SOCIETY; HISTORY MUSEUM; HOUSE MUSEUM: Collects, preserves, interprets, and exhibits materials related to Waukegan area.

PROGRAMS: Annual Meeting; Exhibits; Guided Tours; Publication; Research Library/Archives; School-Based Curriculum

COLLECTIONS: [1870-1900]

HOURS: Yr M 3-8, T, F 10-2:30

WEST CHICAGO

2451
West Chicago City Museum
132 Main St, 60185; (p) (630) 231-3376; (f) (630) 293-3028; wegomuseum@aol.com; (c) DuPage

City/ 1975/ staff: 4(f); 30(v)

HISTORY MUSEUM: Collects, preserves, and interprets history of West Chicago.

PROGRAMS: Community Outreach; Exhibits; Family Programs; Guided Tours; Interpretation; Lectures; Research Library/Archives; School-Based Curriculum

COLLECTIONS: [1849-present] 3,000 train related photos, 200 maps, manuscript collection of Burlington, newspapers, genealogies, photos, church and school records.

HOURS: Jan-Apr T-F 10-3:30; May-Dec Sa 11-3

2452
West Chicago Historical Society
Kruse House Museum, 527 Main St, 60186 [PO Box 246, 60186-0246]; (p) (630) 231-0564; (c) DuPage

Private non-profit/ 1975/ staff: 15(v)/ members: 110/publication: *Olde News Now*

HISTORICAL SOCIETY; HOUSE MUSEUM: Preserves 1917 Kruse House Museum and history of West Chicago.

PROGRAMS: Annual Meeting; Exhibits; Garden Tours; Guided Tours; Interpretation; Publication

COLLECTIONS: [1920] Period furnishings and artifacts.

HOURS: May-Sept Sa 11-3

WEST DUNDEE

2453
Dundee Township Historical Society
426 Highland Ave, 60118; (p) (847) 426-6996; (c) Kane

Private non-profit/ 1964/publication: *Dundee Township*

HISTORICAL SOCIETY: Collects, preserves and interprets history of township for the education and enjoyment.

PROGRAMS: Annual Meeting; Community Outreach; Exhibits; Family Programs; Garden Tours; Guided Tours; Publication; Research Library/Archives

COLLECTIONS: [1825-present] Artifacts; clothing; household business and agricultural items; photographs; slides; clippings; materials related to township families, businesses, schools; genealogies;, census and cemetery records.

HOURS: Mar-Dec W-Su 2-4

ADMISSION: $1

WESTERN SPRINGS

2454
Western Springs Historical Society
[PO Box 134, 60558]; (p) (708) 246-9230; (c) Cook

Private non-profit/ 1966/ Board of Directors/ staff: 30(v)/ members: 360

HISTORIC SITE; HISTORICAL SOCIETY; HISTORY MUSEUM

PROGRAMS: Exhibits; Guided Tours

HOURS: Sa 11-1

WESTMONT

2455
Westmont Historical Society
117 S Linden Ave, 60559 [75 E Richmond St, 60559]; (p) (630) 960-3392; scorpio003@juno.com; (c) DuPage

Joint/ 1976/ Westmont Park District; WHS/ staff: 2(p); 24(v)

HISTORICAL SOCIETY: Collects the history of Westmont area.

PROGRAMS: Concerts; Exhibits; Family Programs; Guided Tours; Interpretation; Living History; Research Library/Archives

COLLECTIONS: [1920-1940]

HOURS: Yr 1-3

2456
William L. Gregg House Museum, The
117 S Linden Ave, 60559 [75 E Richmond St, 60559]; (p) (630) 960-3392, (630) 964-4174; (f) (630) 963-5259

1872/ staff: 3(p); 28(v)

Home of William L. Gregg, local brick manufacturer.

COLLECTIONS: Photographs of local dairy farm; oral histories on cassette; local newspapers; recollections of old timers by local teacher.

HOURS: Yr

WHEATON

2457
Billy Graham Center Archives
501 E College Ave, 60187; (p) (630) 752-5910; (f) (630) 752-5916; bgcarc@wheaton.edu; www.wheaton.edu/bgc/archives; (c) DuPage

Private non-profit/ 1975/ Wheaton College/ staff: 4(f); 3(p)

RESEARCH CENTER: Collects, preserves, and makes available documents on North American, Protestant, and nondenominational Christian evangelism efforts.

PROGRAMS: Exhibits; Publication; Research Library/Archives

COLLECTIONS: [20th c] Records of organizations, papers of individuals, oral history interviews, and records of congresses and conferences.

HOURS: Yr M-F 10-5, Sa 10-2

2458
Billy Graham Center Museum
500 E College Ave, 60187; (p) (630) 752-5909; (f) (630) 752-5916; bgcmus@wheaton.edu; www.wheaton.edu/bgc/museum; (c) DuPage

Private non-profit/ 1975/ Wheaton College/ staff: 3(f); 6(p); 4(v)/publication: *Center Line; The Gospel in America—Guide to the Collections*

ART MUSEUM; HISTORY MUSEUM; RESEARCH CENTER: Provides a visual overview of the history of Christian evangelism and its influence on society.

PROGRAMS: Community Outreach; Elder's Programs; Exhibits; Facility Rental; Film/Video; Guided Tours; Interpretation; Publication; Research Library/Archives

COLLECTIONS: [18th-20th c] Artifacts documenting the story of Evangelical Christianity in America through prints, rare books, posters, manuscripts, photographs, postcards, audio recordings, fine art, ephemera, and tracts.

HOURS: Yr M-Sa 9:30-5:30, Su 1-5

ADMISSION: Donations requested

2459
DuPage County Historical Museum
102 E Wesley St, 60187; (p) (630) 682-7343; (f) (630) 682-6549; museum@mcs.net; (c) DuPage

County/ 1965/ staff: 5(f); 1(p); 30(v)

Housed in an 1891 Richardsonian Romanesque building in downtown Wheaton, museum highlights county history.

COLLECTIONS: [1830-present] 19th and 20th century material culture and archives related to history of DuPage County; Colonial Coverlet Guild of America collection.

HOURS: Yr M, W, F-Sa 10-4, Su 1-4

ADMISSION: No charge

2460
First Division Museum and Colonel Robert McCormick Research Center
1 S 151 Winfield Rd, 60187; (p) (630) 260-8185; (f) (630) 260-9298; Fdmuseum@xnet.com; www.rrmtf.org/firstdivision; (c) DuPage

Private non-profit/ 1992/ staff: 13(f); 3(p); 30(v)

CORPORATE ARCHIVES/MUSEUM; HISTORY MUSEUM; LIBRARY AND/OR ARCHIVES; RESEARCH CENTER: Preserves the history of the First Infantry Division, the Chicago Tribune, and general Chicago area.

PROGRAMS: Community Outreach; Concerts; Exhibits; Facility Rental; Guided Tours; Interpretation; Lectures; Publication; Research Library/Archives; School-Based Curriculum

COLLECTIONS: [20th c] Artifacts-uniforms, flags and colors, insignia, medals and decorations, and art. Art collection-over one thousand World War I posters, original drawings, paintings, and sculptures. General military and unit histories, reference books on military related subjects, microform records including the official records of the 1st Division in W W II, oral histories from 1st Division veterans, and periodicals on military history, veterans' associations and the military service. Tribune Company Archives.

HOURS: Feb F-Su 10-4; Mar-Mem Day, Labor Day-Dec T-Su 10-4; Mem Day-Labor Day T-Su 10-5

2461
Wheaton Historic Preservation Council/Wheaton History Center
606 N Main St, 60189 [PO Box 373, 60189-0373]; (p) (630) 682-9472; (f) (630) 682-9913; (c) DuPage

Private non-profit/ 1980/ Board of Directors/ staff: 5(f); 4(p); 42(v)/ members: 370

HISTORY MUSEUM: Promotes local history.

PROGRAMS: Annual Meeting; Community Outreach; Exhibits; Facility Rental; Family Programs; Festivals; Guided Tours; Interpretation; Lectures; Research Library/Archives; School-Based Curriculum

COLLECTIONS: [1837-present] Artifacts, photos, images, publications, ledgers, advertisements, archival material related to business, government, education, church, social history of Wheaton.

HOURS: Yr M-W, Sa 10-4, Su 1-4

ADMISSION: $2, Family $5, Student $1

WHEELING

2462
Wheeling Historical Society
251 N Wolf Road, 60090 [PO Box 3, 60090]; (p) (847) 537-3119; archclr@aol.com; www.nsn.nslisilus.org/wgkhome; (c) Cook

City/ 1968/ Wheeling Park District/ staff: 20(v)/ members: 80

GENEALOGICAL SOCIETY; HISTORIC SITE; HISTORICAL SOCIETY; HISTORY MUSEUM: Preserves and interprets Wheeling history.

PROGRAMS: Annual Meeting; Community Outreach; Exhibits; Guided Tours; Lectures; Publication; Research Library/Archives

COLLECTIONS: [1894-1930] Photos and archives.

HOURS: Mar-Oct Su 2-4, Th 9-12

WILLOW SPRINGS

2463
Little Red Schoolhouse Nature Center
9800 Willow Springs Rd, 60480; (p) (708) 839-6897; (c) Cook

County/ 1955/ Forest Preserve District/ staff: 5(f); 2(p); 5(v)

HISTORIC SITE; HISTORY MUSEUM: Promotes natural and local history.

PROGRAMS: Community Outreach; Concerts; Exhibits; Family Programs; Festivals; Garden Tours; Interpretation; School-Based Curriculum

COLLECTIONS: Native wildlife specimens and interpretive center housed in period one-room schoolhouse.

HOURS: Sept-May Sa-Th 9-4:30, June-Aug Sa-Th 9-4

ADMISSION: No

WILMETTE

2464
Wilmette Historical Society and Museum
609 Ridge Rd, 60091; (p) (847) 853-7666; (f) (847) 853-7706; www.wilmette.com/museum.htm; (c) Cook

Joint/ 1951/ Village of Wilmette and Wilmette Historical Society/ staff: 1(f); 2(p); 35(v)/ members: 300/publication: *Wilmette: A History; Wilmette Heritage*

HISTORICAL SOCIETY; HISTORY MUSEUM: Collects, preserves, and interprets the history of Wilmette, Gross Point, and the North Shore.

PROGRAMS: Annual Meeting; Community

Outreach; Elder's Programs; Exhibits; Facility Rental; Family Programs; Guided Tours; Interpretation; Lectures; Publication; Research Library/Archives; School-Based Curriculum

COLLECTIONS: [1800-present] Artifacts, photos, newspapers, maps, documents, books, clothing and textiles related to Wilmette and environs, art and archives.

HOURS: Yr T, Th 10-4, Su, W 1-4

ADMISSION: No charge

WILMINGTON

2465
Wilmington Area Historical Society
104 N Water St, 60481 [PO Box 1, 60481]; (p) (815) 476-5109; (f) (630) 257-1718; vasko@aol.com; (c) Will

1965/ staff: 20(v)/ members: 67/publication: *Wilmington Eagle*

HISTORIC PRESERVATION AGENCY; HISTORIC SITE; HISTORICAL SOCIETY; HISTORY MUSEUM: Promotes local history through restoration programs.

PROGRAMS: Exhibits; Interpretation; Living History; Publication

COLLECTIONS: [1840-1960] Farm equipment, letters, photos.

WINFIELD

2466
Kline Creek Farm
IN600 County Farm Road, 60189 [PO Box 5000, Glen Ellyn, 60189]; (p) (630) 876-5900; (f) (630) 293-9421; www.dupageforest.com/EDUCATION/klinecreek.html; (c) DuPage

County, non-profit/ 1989/ Forest Preserve District/ staff: 5(f); 1(p); 75(v)/ members: 20

LIVING HISTORY/OUTDOOR MUSEUM: Promotes local history with 1890s working farm with full complement of livestock and crops, a restored farmhouse, barn, smokehouse and 12 other reconstructed farm buildings.

PROGRAMS: Community Outreach; Exhibits; Facility Rental; Family Programs; Festivals; Garden Tours; Guided Tours; Interpretation; Lectures; Living History; School-Based Curriculum

COLLECTIONS: [1885-1905] Agricultural implements, household furniture, and educational collection of games.

HOURS: Yr Th-M 9-5

ADMISSION: No charge

WINNETKA

2467
North Suburban Genealogical Society
768 Oak St, 60093; (p) (847) 446-7220; (c) Cook

Private non-profit/ 1975/ members: 220/publication: *Newsletter of the NSGS*

GENEALOGICAL SOCIETY: Promotes genealogical research and documentation.

PROGRAMS: Lectures; Publication

COLLECTIONS: 6,000 volumes, census records on microfilm/fiche.

2468
Winnetka Historical Society
[PO Box 365, 60093]; (p) (847) 501-6025; (f) (847) 501-3221; (c) Cook

Private non-profit/ 1932/ staff: 2(p); 30(v)/ members: 400/publication: *Winnetka Architecture: Where Past Is Present*

HISTORICAL SOCIETY: Collects, preserves, and presents artifacts representing Winnetka history.

PROGRAMS: Annual Meeting; Community Outreach; Exhibits; Family Programs; Guided Tours; Interpretation; Lectures; Publication

COLLECTIONS: [1835-present] Photos, documents, costumes, oral histories, videos, films, local house files, locally made and used tools, and machines.

HOURS: By appt only

WOOD DALE

2469
Wood Dale Historical Society and Yesterday's Farm Museum
850 N Wood Dale Rd, 60191 [PO Box 13, 60191]; (p) (630) 595-8777; (c) DuPage

Private non-profit/ 1972/ staff: 30(v)/ members: 94

HISTORICAL SOCIETY; HOUSE MUSEUM: Preserves local history through museum and educational programs.

PROGRAMS: Annual Meeting; Exhibits; Facility Rental; Family Programs; Festivals; Film/Video; Guided Tours; Interpretation

COLLECTIONS: [1840-1945] Period clothing, furnishings, toys, dolls, farm equipment, silo, smoke house, tractor, outhouse, photos, oral histories, newspapers, cameras, typewriters, sewing machines.

HOURS: Su

WOODSTOCK

2470
Chester Gould-Dick Tracy Museum
101 N Johnson St, 60098 [PO Box 44, 60098]; (p) (815) 338-8281; (c) McHenry

Private non-profit/ 1991/ Board of Directors/ staff: 1(f); 25(v)/ members: 200

ART MUSEUM: Displays, promotes and honors the work of Chester Gould, creator of the "Dick Tracy" comic strip.

PROGRAMS: Annual Meeting; Community Outreach; Exhibits; Family Programs; Festivals; Publication

COLLECTIONS: [1931-1977] Chester Gould's original drawing board and chair; original cartoon art, photographs, and memorabilia.

HOURS: Yr Th-Sa 11-5, Su 1-5

ADMISSION: Donations accepted

WYANET

2471
Wyanet Historical Society
Main St, 61379 [PO Box 169, 61379]

Joint/ 1977/ City; Private non-profit/ staff: 1(f); 6(v)/ members: 30

HISTORICAL SOCIETY: Preserves local history.

PROGRAMS: Annual Meeting; Community Outreach; Elder's Programs; Festivals; Film/Video; Reenactments; School-Based Curriculum

COLLECTIONS: [1865-present] Civil War clothing, newspapers, cemetery records, WWI and WWII

YORKVILLE

2472
Kendall County Historical Society
107 W Center St & Lyon Farm and Village, Rte 71, 60560 [PO Box 123, 60560]; (p) (630) 553-6700; (c) Kendall

Private non-profit/ 1970/ members: 230

GARDEN; GENEALOGICAL SOCIETY; HISTORIC PRESERVATION AGENCY; HISTORIC SITE; HISTORICAL SOCIETY; HISTORY MUSEUM; HOUSE MUSEUM; LIVING HISTORY/OUTDOOR MUSEUM; RESEARCH CENTER: Collects, preserves and displays historical and genealogical documents and artifacts related to the county at Chapel on the Green/Heritage Hall. Lyon Farm and Village is a working farm with original and restored buildings.

PROGRAMS: Annual Meeting; Concerts; Exhibits; Facility Rental; Family Programs; Festivals; Film/Video; Garden Tours; Guided Tours; Interpretation; Living History; Reenactments; Research Library/Archives

COLLECTIONS: [1850-present] Kendall County histories, indexed maps and atlases, census and vital records, photos; oral histories; genealogies in Chapel on the Green.

HOURS: Chapel on the Green: Mar-Jan W 9-12; Lyon Farm and Village: Mar-Dec for special events

ADMISSION: $4, Children $2; Chapel on the Green Free

ZION

2473
Zion Genealogical Society
2400 Gabriel Ave, 60099; (p) (847) 360-0360; (f) (847) 623-3501; ziongensoc@aol.com; www.nsn.org/wkkhome/zion; (c) Lake

Private non-profit/ 1979/ members: 60/publication: *Zion Death Register List, Zion Genealogical Society Surname Book*

GENEALOGICAL SOCIETY: Collects, preserves and disseminates genealogical and related historical and biographical data.

PROGRAMS: Lectures; Publication; Research Library/Archives

COLLECTIONS: 800 volumes PERSI, IGI-US (1992), IL Death Index 1916-1945, partial index to early IL marriages.

HOURS: Yr M-Th 9-9, F 9-6, Sa 9-5, Su 1-5

2474
Zion Historical Society
1300 Shiloh Blvd, 60099-2622; (p) (847) 746-2427; (c) Lake

Private non-profit/ 1967/ staff: 15(v)/ members: 120

HISTORICAL SOCIETY; HOUSE MUSEUM: Preserves Shiloh House, home of Zion founder John Dowie.

PROGRAMS: Annual Meeting; Concerts; Exhibits; Facility Rental; Guided Tours

COLLECTIONS: [1900-1907] Photos and archives.

HOURS: June-Aug Sa-Su 2-5

ADMISSION: $2, Children $1

INDIANA

ANDERSON

2475
Gruenewald Historic House
626 Main St, 46016; (p) (765) 648-6875; (c) Madison

Private non-profit/ 1974/ Board of Directors/ staff: 2(p)/ members: 400

HOUSE MUSEUM

PROGRAMS: Annual Meeting; Community Outreach; Guided Tours; Living History

COLLECTIONS: [1875-1900] Original furnishings in Victorian house.

HOURS: Apr-mid Dec T-F 10-3, Sa 9-3

ADMISSION: $4, Student $2; Group rates

2476
Gustav Jeenings Museum of Bible and Near East Studies
1123 University Blvd, 46012 [1100 E 5th St, 46012]; (p) (765) 649-9071; (f) (765) 641-3851; www.anderson.edu; (c) Madison

Private non-profit/ 1963/ Anderson University/ staff: 1(p); 1(v)/publication: *Illumination*

HISTORY MUSEUM: Small ancient history museum.

PROGRAMS: Exhibits; Guided Tours; Publication

COLLECTIONS: [4,000 BC-AD 400] Ancient Egyptian, Babylonian, Greek, Roman, and Palestinian pottery, coins, and statues, all arranged by social context.

HOURS: Yr

2477
Madison County Historical Society, Inc.
1931 Brown St, Ste 2, 46016; (p) (765) 683-0052; beth@apl.acsc.net; (c) Madison

Private non-profit/ 1926/ Board of Directors/ staff: 30(v)/ members: 302

HISTORICAL SOCIETY: Promotes, studies, and preserves historical facts and materials of the area.

PROGRAMS: Lectures

COLLECTIONS: [Prehistory-present] Documents and artifacts.

HOURS: Yr M-F 9-4

AUBURN

2478
Auburn Cord Duesenberg Museum
1600 S Wayne St, 46706-0271; (p) (219) 925-1444; (f) (219) 925-6266; www.acdmuseum.org; (c) DeKalb

Private non-profit/ 1974/ Auburn Automotive Heritage, Inc./ staff: 13(f); 9(p); 109(v)/ members: 1624/publication: *The Accelerator*

AUTOMOBILE MUSEUM; HISTORY MUSEUM: Housed in the 1930 art deco national headquarters of the former Auburn Automobile Company.

PROGRAMS: Annual Meeting; Community Outreach; Concerts; Exhibits; Facility Rental; Festivals; Guided Tours; Interpretation; Lectures; Publication; Research Library/Archives

COLLECTIONS: [1890s-1970s] Gasoline, steam and electric automobiles; archives of automotive literature, photographs, and small artifacts.

HOURS: Yr Daily 9-5

ADMISSION: $7, Student $4.50

2479
DeKalb County Historical Society
Box 686, 46706; (p) (219) 925-4560; (f) (219) 925-4563; smithlaw@fwi.com; (c) DeKalb

Private non-profit/ 1965/ members: 100

GENEALOGICAL SOCIETY; HISTORIC PRESERVATION AGENCY; HISTORICAL SOCIETY; HISTORY MUSEUM; RESEARCH CENTER: Preserves and interprets history of people, businesses, and industry of county.

PROGRAMS: Annual Meeting; Guided Tours; Lectures; Publication; Research Library/Archives

COLLECTIONS: [1830-present]

2480
National Automotive and Truck Museum of the United States, Inc.
1000 Gordon M Buehrig Pl, 46706 [PO Box 686, 46706]; (p) (219) 925-9100; (f) (219) 925-8695; natmus@ctlnet.com; www.natmus.com; (c) DeKalb

Private non-profit/ 1989/ staff: 3(f); 3(p); 100(v)/ members: 530/publication: *Pastlane*

AUTOMOBILE MUSEUM: Collects and interprets cars, trucks, toys, models, and related artifacts; located in restored original factory buildings.

PROGRAMS: Annual Meeting; Community Outreach; Facility Rental; Festivals; Interpretation; Lectures; Publication; Reenactments

COLLECTIONS: [1895-present] Cars, trucks, toys, and models; literature, advertising, and roadside history pertaining to impact of cars and trucks on American

AURORA

2481
Hillforest Historical Foundation, Inc.
213 Fifth St, 47001 [PO Box 127, 47001]; (p) (812) 926-0087; (f) (812) 926-1075; hillforest@ seidata.com; www.dearborncounty.org/history/hillfor.html; (c) Dearborn

Private non-profit/ 1956/ Board of Governors/ staff: 1(f); 3(p); 60(v)/ members: 500/publication: *Hillforest Happenings*

HISTORY MUSEUM: Restores, maintains, and interprets Hillforest, the 1855 home of Thomas and Sarah Gaff.

PROGRAMS: Annual Meeting; Community Outreach; Concerts; Exhibits; Facility Rental;

Family Programs; Festivals; Guided Tours; Interpretation; Lectures; Publication; School-Based Curriculum

COLLECTIONS: [1855-1891] Decorative arts; furniture, glass, silver, ceramics, textiles, clothing; archives; photos, books, documents, telegrams; and distillery and brewery artifacts.

HOURS: Apr-Dec T-Su 1-5; Mem Day-Labor Day M 1-5

ADMISSION: $4, Student $2

BATTLE GROUND

2482
Museums at Prophetstown, Inc., The
3549 Prophetstown Trail, 47920 [PO Box 331, 47920-0331]; (p) (765) 567-4700; (f) (765) 567-4736; nlclark@prophetstown.org; www.prophetstown.org; (c) Tippecanoe

Private non-profit/ 1995/ staff: 5(f); 1(p); 325(v)/ members: 2800

HISTORY MUSEUM; LIVING HISTORY/OUTDOOR MUSEUM; NATURAL HISTORY MUSEUM: 338 acre museum campus featuring the Kampen Eagle Wing Visitor and Education Center, the 88 acre 1920s Wabash Valley Living History Farm, 200 acre Prophetstown Prairie Environmental Center and the 1810 recreated Prophetstown Native American Living History Village.

PROGRAMS: Reenactments; Research Library/Archives; School-Based Curriculum; Theatre

COLLECTIONS: [1810-present] Represents 1920s agriculture, 1810 frontier life, and prairie specimens.

HOURS: Yr Daily

ADMISSION: $5, Children $3; Group rates

BERNE

2483
Swiss Heritage Society
1200 Swiss Way, 46711 [PO Box 88, 46711]; (p) (219) 589-8007; (c) Adams

Private non-profit/ 1985/ Board of Directors/ staff: 1(f); 2(p); 40(v)/publication: *Swiss Echoes*

HISTORIC PRESERVATION AGENCY; HISTORICAL SOCIETY; HISTORY MUSEUM: Outdoor historical museum; preserves and interprets culture and past of Swiss-Americans.

PROGRAMS: Annual Meeting; Community Outreach; Exhibits; Family Programs; Festivals; Garden Tours; Guided Tours; Interpretation; Publication

COLLECTIONS: [1860-1900] Twelve historic buildings including homestead, summer kitchen, smokehouse, cheese house, bank barn, cider press, old doctor's office, 1840 log cabin, Baumgartner Mennonite Church.

HOURS: May-Oct M-Sa 9-4

ADMISSION: $3.50,

BEVERLY SHORES

2484
Beverly Shores Historic South Shore Line Passenger Depot
525 Broadway, 46301 [PO Box 305, 46301]; (p) (219) 871-0832; (c) Porter

Private non-profit/ 1998/ staff: 12(v)

ART MUSEUM; HISTORIC SITE; HOUSE MUSEUM; RAILROAD MUSEUM

PROGRAMS: Exhibits

COLLECTIONS: [1927-1950]

HOURS: May-Oct Th-Su 1-4

BLOOMINGTON

2485
Monroe County Historical Society
202 E 6th St, 47408; (p) (812) 332-2517; (f) (812) 355-5593; mchm@kiva.net; www.kiva.net/~mchm/monroe.html; (c) Monroe

Private non-profit/ 1980/ staff: 3(f); 2(p); 40(v)/ members: 600/publication: *The Monroe County Historian*

HISTORICAL SOCIETY; HISTORY MUSEUM: Housed in 1918 Carnegie Library building; collects, preserves, interprets, and exhibits historical and cultural artifacts of the county and state.

PROGRAMS: Annual Meeting; Community Outreach; Concerts; Exhibits; Facility Rental; Guided Tours; Lectures; Publication; Research Library/Archives; School-Based Curriculum; Theatre

COLLECTIONS: [Early-mid 20th c]

HOURS: Yr T-Sa 10-4, Su 1-4

ADMISSION: No charge

2486
Monroe County Public Library, Indiana Room
303 E Kirkwood Ave, 47408; (p) (812) 349-3080; www.monroe.lib.in.us; (c) Monroe

County/ 1818/ Board of Trustees/ staff: 2(f); 4(p); 1(v)

LIBRARY AND/OR ARCHIVES: Special collection devoted to family history and genealogy, IN history, Monroe county history.

PROGRAMS: Family Programs; Lectures

COLLECTIONS: [1816-present] State and local history, genealogy with emphasis on IN and region, local newspaper on microfilm, maps, city directories, yearbooks, magazines, and newsletters, clippings.

HOURS: Yr M-Th 9-9, F 9-6, Sa 9-5, Su 1-5

2487
Oral History Research Center, Indiana University
Ashton-Aley 264, 47405; (p) (812) 855-2856; (f) (812) 855-4869; ohrc@indiana.edu; ww.indiana.edu/~ohrc; (c) Monroe

State/ 1968/ IN Univ/ staff: 1(f); 3(p); 2(v)

RESEARCH CENTER: Collects first-person historically relevant interviews.

PROGRAMS: Publication

COLLECTIONS: [1900-2000] Over 1600 oral history interviews covering local and national

2488
Prairie Aviation Museum
Central Illinois Airport, Frontage Rd Rt 9 E, 61702 [PO Box 856, 61702]; (p) (309) 663-7632; (f) (309) 663-8411; (c) McLean

Private non-profit/ 1983/ staff: 1(f); 150(v)/ members: 350

AVIATION MUSEUM

PROGRAMS: Annual Meeting; Community Outreach; Exhibits; Film/Video; Guided Tours; Interpretation; Lectures

COLLECTIONS: [1920-present] Restored DC-3.

HOURS: Yr Tu 5-8

2489
William Hammond Mathers Museum
416 N Indiana Ave, 47408 [601 E 8th St, 47408]; (p) (812) 855-6873; (f) (812) 855-0205; mathers@indiana.edu; www.indiana.edu/~mathers/; (c) Monroe

State/ 1963/ Indiana University/ staff: 9(f); 2(p); 20(v)/ members: 60

ANTHROPOLOGY MUSEUM: A museum of diverse cultures, anthropology, and folklore.

PROGRAMS: Elder's Programs; Exhibits; Facility Rental; Family Programs; Festivals; Guided Tours; Interpretation; Lectures

COLLECTIONS: [19th-20th c] 22,000 artifacts from around the world and local community; 10,000 historical photos.

HOURS: Yr T-F 9-4:30, Sa-Su 1-4:30

ADMISSION: No charge

2490
Wylie House Museum
317 E 2nd St, 47401; (p) (812) 855-6224; jburges@indiana.edu; www.indiana.edu/~lib wylie; (c) Monroe

State/ 1960/ Indiana Univ/ staff: 2(f); 1(p); 25(v)/ members: 150

HOUSE MUSEUM: Restored 1835 home of first IN Univ president, Andrew Wylie, and his family; grounds include large garden of early 19th c vegetables.

PROGRAMS: Concerts; Garden Tours; Guided Tours; Interpretation; Lectures; Living History

COLLECTIONS: [1840-1850] Many original furnishings and artifacts.

HOURS: Mar-Nov T-Sa

BLUFFTON

2491
Wells County Historical Society
420 W Market St, 46714 [PO Box 143, 46714]; (p) (219) 824-9956; www.parlorcity.com; (c) Wells

Private non-profit/ 1935/ Board of Directors/ staff: 10(v)/ members: 220

HISTORICAL SOCIETY; HISTORY MUSEUM: Collects and preserves cultural, economic, and political artifacts and documents related to county history.

PROGRAMS: Annual Meeting; Community Outreach; Exhibits; Festivals; Guided Tours; Research Library/Archives

COLLECTIONS: [1860-present] Papers, books, files, and records; 1902 Oldsmobile; furniture; medical equip; bank and postal artifacts.

HOURS: May-Dec W, Su 1-4

ADMISSION: No charge

BOONVILLE

2492
Warrick County Museum, Inc.
217 S First St, 47601 [PO Box 581, 47601]; (p) (812) 897-3100; (c) Warrick

County/ staff: 3(p); 7(v)/ members: 130

HISTORY MUSEUM: Preserves and exhibits local historical artifacts.

PROGRAMS: Annual Meeting; Community Outreach; Exhibits; Festivals; School-Based Curriculum

COLLECTIONS: [Victorian] Replica of school-room; Victorian living room; military collection; clothing; quilts; art room; other artifacts.

HOURS: Yr M-Th 11-2, Su 2-4

ADMISSION: No charge

BRAZIL

2493
Clay County Historical Society
100 E National Ave, 47834; (p) (812) 446-4036; (c) Clay

Private non-profit/ 1925/ Board of Directors/ staff: 1(p); 20(v)/ members: 80

HISTORIC PRESERVATION AGENCY; HISTORIC SITE; HISTORICAL SOCIETY; HISTORY MUSEUM; LIVING HISTORY/OUTDOOR MUSEUM: Displays local historical artifacts in the old Brazil post office building.

PROGRAMS: Annual Meeting; Community Outreach; Exhibits; Family Programs; Festivals; Guided Tours; Interpretation; Lectures; Living History; Publication; Research Library/Archives; School-Based Curriculum

COLLECTIONS: [20th c] Two early 1900s pianos built by Knight-Brinkerhoff Co. of Brazil; antique furniture; 1949 TV; ca. 1900 kitchen; late 1800s linen chest made from Clay County wood; exhibits on mines, clay factories, and railroads.

HOURS: Mar-Dec M-F 1-4

ADMISSION: No charge

BRISTOL

2494
Elkhart County Historical Society, Inc. and Museum
304 W Vistula, 46507 [PO Box 434, 46507]; (p) (219) 848-4322; (f) (219) 848-5703; echm@juno.com; (c) Elkhart

Joint/ 1896/ ECHS; County-Parks & Rec Dept/ staff: 4(f); 4(p); 40(v)/ members: 275

HISTORY MUSEUM: Collects and preserves local historical artifacts and documents.

PROGRAMS: Annual Meeting; Exhibits; Facility Rental; Guided Tours; Interpretation; Lectures; Publication; Research Library/Archives; School-Based Curriculum

COLLECTIONS: [1830s-1940s] Railroad, agricultural, and pioneer artifacts; home furnishings, clothing; research library and archives.

HOURS: Feb-Nov

CAMBRIDGE CITY

2495
Huddleston Farmhouse Inn Museum
838 National Rd (US 40), 47327 [PO Box 284, 47327]; (p) (765) 478-3172; (f) (765) 478-3410; huddleston@historiclandmarks.org; www.historiclandmarks.org; (c) Wayne

Private non-profit/ 1960/ Historic Landmarks Foundation of IN/ staff: 2(f); 7(v)

HISTORIC SITE; HOUSE MUSEUM: Restored 1841 "mover's House" with period interiors, also springhouse, smokehouse, and barn. Also, Eastern Regional headquarters of IN Historic Landmarks Foundation.

PROGRAMS: Annual Meeting; Community Outreach; Facility Rental; Family Programs; Festivals; Guided Tours; Reenactments; School-Based Curriculum

COLLECTIONS: [1840-1860] Primitive and Empire Style furnishings; glassware; hearth cooking utensils; weaving equipment; spinning wheels; Huddleston family archives.

HOURS: Feb-Dec T-Sa 10-4; May-Aug Su 1-4

ADMISSION: Donations accepted

CARMEL

2496
Carmel Clay Historical Society
211 First St SW, 46032; (p) (317) 846-7117; (c) Hamilton

Private non-profit/ 1975/ Board of Directors/ staff: 1(p); 25(v)/ members: 225/publication: CCHS Newsletter

HISTORICAL SOCIETY; HISTORY MUSEUM; RESEARCH CENTER: Local history organization housed in 1880s railroad depot; collects source materials and artifacts for exhibits; sponsors programs.

PROGRAMS: Community Outreach; Exhibits; Family Programs; Guided Tours; Interpretation; Publication

COLLECTIONS: [1800-early 1900s] Manuscripts, letters, and journals of early residents; photos, maps, and oral history interviews; turn of the century clothing; Monon railroad memorabilia.

HOURS: Yr F 9-12/1-5, Sa 10-2

ADMISSION: Donations accepted

CEDAR LAKE

2497
Cedar Lake Historical Association, Inc.
7405 Constitution Ave, 46303 [PO Box 421, 46303]; (c) Lake

Joint/ 1977/ City; Private non-profit/ staff: 30(v)/ members: 60

HISTORICAL SOCIETY: Collects, preserves, researches, exhibits, and interprets artifacts and specimens related to Cedar Lake history.

PROGRAMS: Exhibits; Facility Rental; Guided Tours; Interpretation

COLLECTIONS: [1830-1930] Donated/on-loan items from Cedar Lake documenting local history; mostly 1920s.

HOURS: May-Sep Th-Su 1-4; Oct, May and by appt

ADMISSION: $2; Children $.50

COLUMBIA CITY

2498
Whitley County Historical Museum
108 W Jefferson St, 46725; (p) (219) 244-6372; (f) (219) 244-6384; home.whitley.net.org/historical/; (c) Whitley

Joint/ 1899/ County; WCHS/ staff: 3(p)/ members: 500

HISTORIC PRESERVATION AGENCY; HISTORY MUSEUM; HOUSE MUSEUM; LIBRARY AND/OR ARCHIVES: Collects and preserves artifacts related to county history.

PROGRAMS: Annual Meeting; Exhibits; Facility Rental; Family Programs; Festivals; Guided Tours; Lectures; Publication; Research Library/Archives; School-Based Curriculum

COLLECTIONS: 30,000 museum artifacts including textiles, photos, and volumes.

HOURS: Feb-Dec M-W 9-2, and by appt

CONNERSVILLE

2499
Blommel Historic Automotive Data Collection
427 E County Rd, 47331; (c) Fayette

1928/ staff: 1(f)/publication: Indiana's Little Detroit

HISTORIC PRESERVATION AGENCY; RESEARCH CENTER: Presents over 70 years of automotive history.

PROGRAMS: Guided Tours; Publication

CORYDON

2500
Corydon Capitol State Historic Site
202 E Walnut St, 47112; (p) (812) 738-4890; corydoncapitol@disknet.com; www.state.in.us/ism/sites/corydon/; (c) Harrison

State/ 1930/ IN DNR Div of Museums & Historic Sites/ staff: 4(f); 4(p); 30(v)/ members: 30

HISTORIC SITE: Historic site including old capitol building and The Constitution Elm building.

PROGRAMS: Community Outreach; Concerts; Facility Rental; Festivals; Guided Tours; Interpretation; Living History; School-Based Curriculum

COLLECTIONS: [1800-1900] IN artifacts from statehood, pioneer era, and Victorian era; tree trunk under which the first constitution was written.

HOURS: Mid Mar-mid Dec T-Sa 9-5, Su 1-5

ADMISSION: No charge

2501
Posey House Museum, The
225 Oak St, 47112 [c/o L Keasling, 870 Yankee Way SW, 47112]; (p) (812) 738-6921, (812) 347-2260

1817/ staff: 3(v)

1817 Federal style house.

COLLECTIONS: [1820 to post Civil War] Furniture dating from 1810, chair and table used by the first State Governor; rare step-stove; Civil war items and a Hessian gun from the Revolutionary war; farming tools of wood; hair wreaths; portrait and death masks from 1861. Collection of old books, some dating from the 1790s; D.A.R. publications from the early 1900s.

HOURS: May-Oct T-Sa 10-4

CRAWFORDSVILLE

2502
Ben-Hur Museum/General Lew Wallace Study
Wallace Ave at Pike St, 47933 [501 W Pike St, 47933]; (p) (765) 362-5769; (f) (765) 364-5179; study@wico.net; www.Ben-Hur.com; (c) Montgomery

City/ 1941/ Park and Recreation Department/ staff: 3(p); 2(v)

HISTORIC SITE; HISTORY MUSEUM: Preserves, exhibits, and interprets materials relating to General Lew Wallace's contributions to 19th c American history and literature as a soldier, politician, diplomat, and author of *Ben-Hur*.

PROGRAMS: Exhibits; Facility Rental; Guided Tours; Interpretation; Lectures; Living History; Reenactments

COLLECTIONS: [1827-1905/1880-present] General Lew Wallace's personal memorabilia and interior furnishings of the study he designed himself; his grandsons' W W I collection; and materials relating to *Ben-Hur* as a book, play, and film.

HOURS: Apr-Oct T-Su 1-4:30; June-Aug W-Sa 10-4:30

ADMISSION: $2, Children $0.50

2503
Montgomery County Historical Society, Inc.
212 S Water St, 47933 [PO Box 127, 47933]; (c) Montgomery

Joint/ staff: 1(f); 12(v)/ members: 600

GENEALOGICAL SOCIETY; HISTORICAL SOCIETY; HOUSE MUSEUM: Located in Henry S. Lane Historic Home, restored Greek Revival home built in 1845.

PROGRAMS: Annual Meeting; Community Outreach; Concerts; Exhibits; Facility Rental; Family Programs; Festivals; Garden Tours; Guided Tours; Interpretation; Lectures; Living History; Publication; Reenactments; Research Library/Archives; School-Based Curriculum

COLLECTIONS: [1700-1920] Decorative arts; Henry S. Lane Historic Home; documents related to county

2504
Old Jail Museum
225 N Washington St, 47933 [PO Box 771,

47933]; (p) (317) 362-5222; (c) Montgomery County; Private non-profit/ 1975/ Montgomery County Cultural Foundation, Inc./ staff: 1(p); 35(v)/ members: 132

HISTORIC SITE; HISTORY MUSEUM: Site of the only working rotary cell block in the US; attached Sheriff's residence exhibits items of local interest.

PROGRAMS: Annual Meeting; Exhibits; Festivals; Guided Tours

COLLECTIONS: [1881-present] Jail artifacts and records, industrial artifacts, clothing and photos.

HOURS: Apr-May, Sept-Oct W-Su 1-4:30; June-Aug T, Su 1-4:30, W-Sa 10-4:30

ADMISSION: Group rates

DANA

2505
Ernie Pyle State Historic Site
107 Maple, 47847 [PO Box 338, 47847]; (p) (765) 665-3633; (f) (765) 665-9312; erniepyleshs@jobax.net; (c) Vermillion

State/ IN DNR Div of Museums & Historic Sites/ staff: 2(f); 2(p)

HISTORIC SITE: Ernie Pyle's birth home; visitor center.

PROGRAMS: Community Outreach; Exhibits; Festivals; Guided Tours; Interpretation; Research Library/Archives; School-Based Curriculum

COLLECTIONS: [1900-1945] Ernie Pyle's personal items from before WW II; other WW II artifacts.

HOURS: Mid Mar-mid Dec T-Sa 9-5, Su 1-5

ADMISSION: Donations accepted

DANVILLE

2506
Hendricks County Historical Society
170 S Washington, 46122; (p) (317) 745-9617; (c) Hendricks

Private non-profit/ 1965/ staff: 4(p); 6(v)/ members: 185/publication: *History Bulletin*

HISTORICAL SOCIETY: Collects, preserves, and interprets artifacts and information on Hendricks County.

PROGRAMS: Community Outreach; Exhibits; Publication

COLLECTIONS: [1824-1974] Manuscripts and photographs; artifacts located in 1866 sheriff's residence and jail.

HOURS: Mar-Dec T 9:30-3:30, Sa

2507
Indiana Room, Danville Public Library
101 S Indiana St, 46122; (p) (317) 745-2604; (f) (317) 745-0756; dplind@dpl.in.us; www.dpl.lib.in.us; (c) Hendricks

City/ Library Board of Trustees/Center Township/ staff: 11(f); 11(p)

LIBRARY AND/OR ARCHIVES: Preserves historical and genealogical materials related to the county and state.

PROGRAMS: Exhibits; Guided Tours; Lectures; Research Library/Archives; School-

Based Curriculum

COLLECTIONS: [1800-present] Local newspapers, photos, yearbooks; birth, cemetery, and marriage indexes; CD-ROM reference collection.

HOURS: Yr M-Th 9-8, F-Sa 9-5, Su 2-5

ADMISSION: No charge

DECATUR

2508
Adams County Historical Museum
420 W Monroe St, 46733 [PO Box 262, 46733-0262]; (p) (219) 724-3493; historian@decaturnet.com; (c) Adams

Private non-profit/ 1957/ Adams County Historical Society/ staff: 10(v)/ members: 350/publication: *Trumpeter*

HISTORICAL SOCIETY; HISTORY MUSEUM; HOUSE MUSEUM: Collects, preserves, cares for and exhibits relics relating to early history of Adams County.

PROGRAMS: Annual Meeting; Community Outreach; Exhibits; Festivals; Publication

COLLECTIONS: [1836-present] Furniture, decorations, photos, books, newspapers, courthouse records, scrapbooks, farm implements and variety of medical instruments.

HOURS: June-Sept, 1st wknd in Dec Su 1-4

ADMISSION: Donations accepted

DELPHI

2509
Carroll County Historical Society Museum
11 W Main, 46923 [PO Box 277, 46923]; (p) (765) 564-3152; (f) (765) 564-3624; cchs@dcwi.com; dcwi.com/~cchs; (c) Carroll

County/ 1967/ staff: 1(f); 2(p); 5(v)/ members: 200

HISTORICAL SOCIETY; HISTORY MUSEUM; LIBRARY AND/OR ARCHIVES

PROGRAMS: Annual Meeting; Community Outreach; Exhibits; Festivals; Guided Tours; Research Library/Archives

COLLECTIONS: [Early-mid 1800s] Covered wagon, sleigh, documents; Native American artifacts; Mexican War and Civil War artifacts; genealogical material.

HOURS: Yr M, T, Th, F 8-5, W 8-12, and by appt

ADMISSION: Donations accepted

2510
Carroll County Wabash and Erie Canal, Inc.
1030 N Washington St, 46923 [3198 N 700 W, 46923]; (p) (765) 564-6297; mccain@carlnet.org; www.carlnet.org/canal; (c) Carroll

Private non-profit/ 1971/ staff: 150(v)/ members: 675

HISTORIC SITE; HISTORY MUSEUM; HOUSE MUSEUM; LIVING HISTORY/OUTDOOR MUSEUM: Interprets development of early 1800s transportation in the Wabash River Valley. Archaeological sites highlight canal structures along 2.5 mile watered section.

PROGRAMS: Annual Meeting; Exhibits; Facility Rental; Family Programs; Festivals; Guided Tours; Interpretation; Lectures; Living History; Reenactments

COLLECTIONS: [1830-1875] Restored 1844 Reed Case House; artifacts of the canal era; 3 log cabins.

HOURS: Apr-Dec 1st Su 2-4; by appt

ADMISSION: Donations requested

DUGGER

2511
Dugger Coal Museum
Main St, 47848; (c) Sullivan

Private non-profit/ 1980/ Board of Directors/ staff: 3(f); 80(p); 5(v)/ members: 158

HISTORY MUSEUM: Displays and preserves coal mining history and artifacts.

HOURS: Sept 16-23, and by appt

ADMISSION: Donations accepted

DUNKIRK

2512
Glass Museum, The
309 S Franklin St, 47336 [c/o Dunkirk Public Library, 127 W Washington St, 47336]; (p) (765) 768-6872; (f) (765) 768-6872; dunkirkli brary@netscape.net; www.dunkirkpublicli brary.com; (c) Jay

City/ 1976/ Dunkirk Public Library/ staff: 3(p); 13(v)

HISTORY MUSEUM: Preserves local glass industry history and more, includes items from 115 factories around the world.

PROGRAMS: Exhibits; Guided Tours

COLLECTIONS: [1860-] 5000 items from 115 factories around the world including glass canes, chandeliers, and stain-glass windows.

HOURS: May 1-Oct 31 T-Sa 10-4

ADMISSION: $2

DYER

2513
Dyer Historical Society, Inc.
1 Town Square, 46311; (p) (219) 865-6108; (f) (219) 865-4233; council@dyeronline.com; (c) Lake

1975/ staff: 15(v)

HISTORICAL SOCIETY

PROGRAMS: Annual Meeting; Community Outreach; Exhibits; Family Programs; Film/Video; Guided Tours; Lectures; Publication; Research Library/Archives

COLLECTIONS: [1800s-1900s] School, government, fire, police, and hospital related artifacts; photos and video of various events.

HOURS: Yr W 8-12, Th 6pm-9pm, Sa 9-12

ADMISSION: Donations accepted

EAST CHICAGO

2514
East Chicago Room of The East Chicago Public Library, The
2501 E Columbus Dr, 46312; (p) (219) 397-2456; ecpl@ecpl.lib.in.us; www.ecpl.org; (c) Lake

City/ 1987/ Public Library Board of Trustees/ staff: 3(f); 2(p)

LIBRARY AND/OR ARCHIVES: Traces local history through historical documents, biographical information, photos, archival material, and artifacts.

PROGRAMS: Community Outreach; Publication; Research Library/Archives

COLLECTIONS: [1892-present] historical information, photos, archives, artifacts, and books related to East Chicago history.

HOURS: Yr M, W 9-8, T, Th, F 9-5, Sa 9-5:30

ELKHART

2515
National New York Central Railroad Museum
721 S Main St, 46515 [PO Box 1708, 46515]; (p) (219) 294-3001; (f) (219) 295-9434; artscul@michiana.org; nycrrmuseum.railfan.net; (c) Elkhart

City/ 1987/ Museum Board of Commissioners/ staff: 1(f); 2(p); 15(v)/ members: 350/publication: *New York Central News*

HISTORIC SITE; HISTORY MUSEUM; RESEARCH CENTER: Collects, preserves, and interprets the history and heritage of the New York Central Railroad.

PROGRAMS: Community Outreach; Exhibits; Facility Rental; Guided Tours; Interpretation; Lectures; Publication; Research Library /Archives; School-Based Curriculum

COLLECTIONS: [1833-present] Three locomotives (steam, diesel, and electric), 20 pieces of rolling stock, 10,000 photographs, 1,000 volumes, 12,000 documents and assorted paper ephemera, and 1,000 museum artifacts.

HOURS: Yr T-F 10-2, Sa 10-4, Su 12-4

ADMISSION: $2, Children $1, Seniors $1

2516
Ruthmere
302 E Beardsley Ave, 46514; (p) (219) 264-0330; (f) (219) 266-0474; kagray@ruthmere.com; www.ruthmere.com; (c) Elkhart

Private non-profit/ 1973/ The Beardsley Foundation/ staff: 4(f); 13(p); 10(v)

HOUSE MUSEUM: 1910 house museum; preserves site, building, archives, and collections.

PROGRAMS: Community Outreach; Concerts; Elder's Programs; Exhibits; Facility Rental; Family Programs; Guided Tours; Interpretation; Lectures; Publication; Research Library/Archives

COLLECTIONS: [1910-1944] Elaborate window treatments; silk and velvet wall coverings; fine arts including sculptures by Rodin; ceramics; family memorabilia; period clothes; presidential china.

HOURS: Apr-Jun Sept-Dec T-Sa; July-Aug T-Su

ADMISSION: $6, Student $3, Children $3, Seniors $5

EVANSVILLE

2517
Angel Mounds State Historic Site
8215 Pollack Ave, 47715; (p) (812) 853-3956; (f) (812) 479-5783; curator@angelmounds.org; www.state.in.us/ism/sites/angelmounds/; (c) Vanderburgh

State/ 1972/ IN DNR Div of Museums & Historic Sites/ staff: 5(f); 2(p)

HISTORIC SITE: Preserves, collects, and interprets cultural and natural history of the Mississippian period; acts as cultural resource center to interpret other cultures and history. Indoor exhibits and outdoor site with earth mounds and reconstructed houses.

PROGRAMS: Community Outreach; Exhibits; Family Programs; Festivals; Guided Tours; Interpretation; Lectures; Research Library/Archives; School-Based Curriculum

COLLECTIONS: [1100-1450] Eleven earth mounds, and artifacts uncovered onsite.

HOURS: Mid Mar-Mid Dec T-Sa 9-5, Su 1-5

2518
Historic Southern Indiana
8600 University Blvd, 47720; (p) (812) 465-7014; (f) (812) 465-7061; hsi@usi.edu; www.usi.edu/his; (c) Vanderburgh

State/ 1986/ Univ of Southern IN/ staff: 3(f); 50(v)/ members: 110

ALLIANCE OF HISTORICAL AGENCIES; HISTORIC PRESERVATION AGENCY: Preserves, protects, enhances, and promotes historical, cultural, and natural resources of Southern IN.

PROGRAMS: Annual Meeting; Community Outreach; Guided Tours; Interpretation; Lectures; Research Library/Archives; School-Based Curriculum

2519
Reitz Home Preservation Society, Inc., The
224 SE First St, 47706 [PO Box 1322, 47706]; (p) (812) 426-1871; (f) (812) 426-2179; reitz@evansville.net; reitzhome.evansville.net; (c) Vanderburgh

Private non-profit/ 1974/ Board of Trustees/ staff: 2(f); 4(p); 125(v)/ members: 430

HISTORY MUSEUM; HOUSE MUSEUM: Preserves and restores the Reitz Home as an historical, educational, and cultural museum for students and visitors.

PROGRAMS: Annual Meeting; Facility Rental; Interpretation; Lectures; Living History

COLLECTIONS: [1890-1920] Reitz family original furnishings including decorative ceilings, chandeliers, mantels, parquet floors, stained glass window panels; textiles, costumes, watercolors; photos.

HOURS: Mid Jan-Dec T-Sa 11-3:30, Su 1-3:30

ADMISSION: $5, Student $2.50, Children $1.50

2520
Southwestern Indiana Historical Society
435 S Spring St, 47714-1550; (p) (812) 477-6777; (c) Vanderburgh

1920/ members: 50

HISTORICAL SOCIETY: Hosts seven meet

ings per year with historical programs of local, national, and international focus; annual day trip to a an area of historical interest.

2521
Vanderburgh County Historical Society
[PO Box 2626, 47728]; (p) (812) 465-7014; (f) (812) 465-7061; dbigham@usi.edu; (c) Vanderburgh

Private non-profit/ 1981/ staff: 15(v)/ members: 120

HISTORICAL SOCIETY: Promotes study of local history through programs and publications.

PROGRAMS: Annual Meeting; Guided Tours; Lectures; School-Based Curriculum

2522
Willard Library
21 First Ave, 47710; (p) (812) 425-4309; (f) (812) 421-9742; willard@willard.lib.un.us; www.willard.lib.in.us; (c) Vanderburgh

Private non-profit/ 1885/ Board of Trustees/ staff: 10(f); 12(p); 50(v)/ members: 1

LIBRARY AND/OR ARCHIVES: Provides access to historical, recreational, educational, and cultural resources and services to community members.

PROGRAMS: Annual Meeting; Community Outreach; Exhibits; Family Programs; Garden Tours; Guided Tours; Lectures; Publication; Research Library/Archives

COLLECTIONS: [Victorian] Genealogy, local history, and slavery and abolition artifacts; steamboats; Abraham Lincoln manuscript and photo collection; artbook library.

HOURS: Yr M-T 9-8, W-F 9-5:30, Sa

FERDINAND

2523
Ferdinand Historical Society
[PO Box 194, 47532]; (p) (812) 367-1803; (c) Dubois

Private non-profit/ 1982/ staff: 35(v)/ members: 35

HISTORICAL SOCIETY: Preserves local history through photo, books, artifacts, collectibles, and architecture.

PROGRAMS: Annual Meeting; Community Outreach; Exhibit; Publication

FISHERS

2524
Conner Prairie
13400 Allisonville Rd, 46038; (p) (317) 776-6000; (f) (317) 776-6014; dfreas@conner-prairie.org; www.connerprairie.org; (c) Hamilton

Private non-profit/ 1964/ Earlham College/ staff: 82(f); 120(p); 365(v)/ members: 3/publication: Closer Look

LIVING HISTORY/OUTDOOR MUSEUM: Serves as a local, regional, and national center for research and education about the lives, times, attitudes, and values of early 19th-c settlers in the Old Northwest Territory, based upon the Indiana experience. Includes Museum Center, special facilities, and five historic areas on a 210 acre site along the White River

in central IN.

PROGRAMS: Community Outreach; Concerts; Elder's Programs; Exhibits; Facility Rental; Family Programs; Festivals; Film/Video; Garden Tours; Guided Tours; Interpretation; Lectures; Living History; Publication; Reenactments; Research Library/Archives; School-Based Curriculum; Theater

COLLECTIONS: [1790-1940] Artifacts relevant to Conner Prairie history, farm life in 1886 and 1936, and settlement of the Old Northwest Territory.

HOURS: Museum: Yr T-Sa 9:30-5, Su 11-5; Historic Areas: Mar 31-Nov 25 T-Sa 9:30-5, Su 11-5

ADMISSION: $10, Children $6, Seniors $9; Under 5 free

FORT WAYNE

2525
Allen County-Ft. Wayne Historical Society
302 E Berry St, 46802; (p) (219) 426-2882; (f) (219) 424-4419; (c) Allen

Private non-profit/ staff: 6(f); 2(p); 30(v)/ members: 700/publication: Old Fort News

HISTORICAL SOCIETY

PROGRAMS: Annual Meeting; Community Outreach; Exhibits; Facility Rental; Guided Tours; Interpretation; Lectures; Publication

COLLECTIONS: Artifacts pertaining to northeast Indiana, Fort Wayne, business history, Victorian lifestyles, Miami Indian culture, French and Indian Wars, and Germanic heritage and settlement.

HOURS: Feb-Dec T-F 9-5, Sa-Su 12-5

ADMISSION: $3, Student $2, Seniors $2; Under 5 free

2526
Canal Society of Indiana
5205 Wapiti Dr, 46804 [PO Box 40087, 46804]; (p) (219) 432-0279; indcanal@aol.com; www.indcanal.org; (c) Allen

Private non-profit/ 1982/ staff: 3(v)/ members: 350/publication: Canal Society of Indiana Newsletter

HISTORICAL SOCIETY: Interprets, preserves and restores canal structures and history.

PROGRAMS: Annual Meeting; Exhibits; Festivals; Guided Tours; Interpretation; Lectures; Publication

COLLECTIONS: [1832-1872] Books, maps, engineer's reports on canal history and structures.

2527
Fort Wayne Railroad Historical Society
15808 Edgerton Rd, 46855 [PO Box 11017, 46855]; (p) (219) 493-0765; www.steamloco765.org; (c) Allen

Private non-profit/ 1972/ staff: 25(v)/ members: 270

HISTORICAL SOCIETY: Preserves and operates historical railroad equipment and offers tours.

PROGRAMS: Exhibits

COLLECTIONS: [1900-1950] Two steam locomotives, two wooden cabooses, a wooden box car, a railroad wreck train, several other historic pieces.

HOURS: Mar-Nov Sa 9-4; call first

ADMISSION: Donations accepted

2528
Historical Genealogy Department, Allen County Public Library
900 Webster St, 46801 [PO Box 2270, 46801]; (p) (219) 421-1225; (f) (219) 422-9688; cwitcher@acpl.lib.in.us; www.acpl.lib.in.us/genealogy/; (c) Allen

County/ 1961/ Board of Trustees/ staff: 16(f); 15(p); 37(v)

LIBRARY AND/OR ARCHIVES; RESEARCH CENTER: Assists genealogical research.

PROGRAMS: Lectures; Publication; Research Library/Archives; School-Based Curriculum

COLLECTIONS: [1700-present] Printed volumes and microtext covering local and family history, photos.

HOURS: Yr M-Th 9-9, F, Sa 9-6; Su 1-6 (winter only)

ADMISSION: No charge

2529
Lincoln Museum, The
200 E Berry St, 46801 [PO Box 7838, 46801]; (p) (219) 455-3864; (f) (219) 455-6922; ekehoe@LNC.com; www.thelincolnmuseum.org; (c) Allen

Private non-profit/ 1928/ Lincoln National Foundation/ staff: 12(f); 9(p); 150(v)/ members: 505

HISTORY MUSEUM: Interprets and preserves the history of Abraham Lincoln through research, exhibits, and education.

PROGRAMS: Annual Meeting; Community Outreach; Concerts; Exhibits; Facility Rental; Family Programs; Film/Video; Guided Tours; Interpretation; Lectures; Living History; Publication; Reenactments; Research Library/Archives; School-Based Curriculum; Theatre

COLLECTIONS: [Mid 1800s] 300 signed Lincoln documents, 18,000 volume library; 7,000 prints, engravings, and newspapers; 5,000 photographs; 200,000 item vertical file; 350 sheet music titles; period artifacts, Lincoln family belongings, and manuscripts.

HOURS: Yr T-Sa 10-5, Su 1-5

ADMISSION: $2.99, Children $1.99, Seniors $1.99; Under 5 free

FOUNTAIN CITY

2530
Levi Coffin House Association, Inc.
113 US 27 N, 47341 [PO Box 77, 47341]; (p) (765) 847-2432; (f) (765) 847-2498; coffinhs@infocom.com; www.state.in.us/ism/sites/levicoffin/; (c) Wayne

State/ 1967/ IN DNR Div of Museums & Historic Sites/ staff: 24(v)/ members: 45

HOUSE MUSEUM: Preserves and maintains the Coffin House as a historic house museum and interprets its significance to the public.

PROGRAMS: Annual Meeting; Guided Tours; Interpretation

COLLECTIONS: [1826-1847] Furniture, textiles, cooking utensils typical of a Quaker family of the period in Indiana.

HOURS: June-Aug T-Sa 1-4, Sept-Oct Sa 1-4

ADMISSION: $2, Student $1

FOWLER

2531
Benton County Hsitorical Society

404 E 6th St, 47944 [PO Box 341, 47944-1536]; (p) (765) 884-8839; (c) Benton

County, non-profit/ 1967/ Elected officers/ staff: 1(p)/ members: 144/publication: *Reflections*

HISTORICAL SOCIETY; HISTORY MUSEUM: Offers genealogy research assistance, local programs and preserves donated artifacts in a small museum.

PROGRAMS: Exhibits; Facility Rental; Monthly Meeting; Publication

COLLECTIONS: [1830-1960] Books, newspapers, clothing, army uniforms, GAR items, photographs, Native American artifacts, local school certificates, programs, annuals, and metal and wood tools.

HOURS: Yr M-F

FRANKFORT

2532
Clinton County Historical Society, Inc.

Old Stoney Bldg, 301 E Clinton St, 46041; (p) (765) 659-2030, (765) 659-4079; (f) (765) 654-7773; CCHSM@geetel.net; geetel.net/~cchsm/; (c) Clinton

Private non-profit/ 1921/ staff: 1(f); 1(p); 25(v)/ members: 152/publication: *Historical Notes*

GENEALOGICAL SOCIETY; HISTORIC PRESERVATION AGENCY; HISTORIC SITE; HISTORICAL SOCIETY; HISTORY MUSEUM; HOUSE MUSEUM; LIBRARY AND/OR ARCHIVES: Operates museum and archives.

PROGRAMS: Annual Meeting; Community Outreach; Elder's Programs; Exhibits; Family Programs; Festivals; Guided Tours; Lectures; Publication; Research Library/Archives; School-Based Curriculum

COLLECTIONS: [1800-1900] Parlor, kitchen, bedroom, school room, dentist and doctor office, general store, telephones and switchboard, farming exhibit, and train room; archives and library.

HOURS: Yr T-Su

ADMISSION: Donations accepted

FRANKLIN

2533
Johnson County Museum of History

135 N Main St, 46131; (p) (317) 736-4655; (f) (317) 736-5451; map@netdirect.net; www.co.johnson.in.us/countyoffices/museum.html; (c) Johnson

Joint/ 1931/ staff: 3(f); 2(p); 15(v)/ members: 386/publication: *Nostalgia News*

GENEALOGICAL SOCIETY; HISTORICAL SOCIETY; HISTORY MUSEUM: Collects, preserves, and interprets the cultural material and history of the region.

PROGRAMS: Annual Meeting; Community Outreach; Exhibits; Facility Rental; Family Programs; Guided Tours; Living History; Publication

COLLECTIONS: [Prehistory-1940s] Tools, clothing, furniture, decorative arts, photos, textiles.

HOURS: Yr M-F 9-4, 2nd Sa 10-3

ADMISSION: No charge

GARY

2534
Gary Historical and Cultural Society, Inc.

Fourth & Rutledge, 46401 [Box M-603, 46401]; (p) (219) 882-6873; (c) Lake

Private non-profit/ 1976/ Board/ staff: 4(p); 10(v)/ members: 250

HISTORICAL SOCIETY: Housed in the first building constructed in Gary in 1906; promotes historical programs; publishes materials

PROGRAMS: Annual Meeting; Community Outreach; Concerts; Exhibits; Family Programs; Festivals; Guided Tours; Lectures; Living History; School-Based Curriculum; Theatre

COLLECTIONS: [1906-present]

HOURS: Yr by appt

GAS CITY

2535
Gas City Historical Society

210 W North A St, 46933 [PO Box 192, 46933]; (p) (765) 674-2906; (f) (765) 677-3082; (c) Grant

City/ 1986/ staff: 8(v)/ members: 86

HISTORIC SITE; HISTORICAL SOCIETY: Discovers, collects, and preserves materials related to local history.

PROGRAMS: Annual Meeting; Exhibits; Festivals; Guided Tours

COLLECTIONS: Yearbooks, paintings, pottery, newspapers, military uniforms, postcards, furniture, medical instruments, glassware, and other artifacts.

HOURS: Yr by appt

ADMISSION: Donations accepted

GENEVA

2536
Limberlost State Historic Site

200 E Sixth St, 46740 [PO Box 356, 46740]; (p) (219) 368-7428; (f) (219) 368-7007; limberlost@adamswells.com; www.state.in.us/ism/sites/limberlost/; (c) Adams

State/ 1948/ IN DNR Div of Museums & Historic Sites/ staff: 1(f); 4(p); 20(v)/ members: 100

HISTORIC SITE: Home of author, naturalist, and photographer Gene Stratton-Porter. Ongoing restoration of Limberlost Swamp.

PROGRAMS: Family Programs; Guided Tours; Interpretation

COLLECTIONS: [1895-1913] Stratton-Porter's original paintings, moth collection, bedroom furniture, photos, and other related artifacts.

HOURS: Mid Mar-mid

GENTRYVILLE

2537
Colonel William Jones State Historic Site

Boone St, 47537 [RR 1 Box 60 D, 47537]; (p) (812) 937-2802; (f) (812) 937-7038; coljones@psci.net; www.state.in.us/ism/sites/jones/

State/ 1835/ IN DNR Div of Museums & Historic Sites/ staff: 1(f); 3(p); 4(v)

HISTORIC SITE; HOUSE MUSEUM: Restored Federal style home of Colonel William Jones, merchant, farmer, politician and soldier.

COLLECTIONS: [1840] Very few primary Jones materials; some material from later resident (1890s-1930s) who was local historian.

HOURS: Mid Mar-mid Dec W-Sa 9-5, Su 1-5

ADMISSION: Donations accepted

GOSHEN

2538
Goshen Historical Society

124 S Main St, 46526 [PO Box 701, 46526]; (p) (219) 533-1053; rnofziger@aol.com; (c) Elkhart

Private non-profit/ 1981/ Advisory Board/ members: 220

HISTORIC SITE; HISTORICAL SOCIETY: Offers programs, publications, and soon a museum.

PROGRAMS: Annual Meeting; Family Programs; Guided Tours; Lectures; Publication

GREENCASTLE

2539
Archives and Special Collections of DePauw University and Indiana United Methodism

400 S College Ave, 46135 [PO Box 37, 46135]; (p) (765) 658-4406; (f) (765) 658-4423; archives@depauw.edu; www.depauw.edu/library/archives/archiveshome.htm; (c) Putnam

Private non-profit/ 1951/ Depauw Univ/ staff: 2(f); 3(p); 1(v)

LIBRARY AND/OR ARCHIVES: Joint archives of DePauw University and the United Methodist Church in Indiana; documents the history of the university and the church.

PROGRAMS: Exhibits; Research Library/Archives

COLLECTIONS: [1808-present] Records of local churches, church agencies, and university offices; manuscripts of ministers, university alumni, faculty and staff, including letters, diaries, scrapbooks, office records, and photographic media.

HOURS: Winter: MWThF 8-5, T 8am-9pm; Summer: M-F 8-4

ADMISSION: No charge

GREENFIELD

2540
Hancock County Historical Society
Apple St & Main St, 46140 [PO Box 375, 46140]; (c) Hancock

Private non-profit/ 1963/ Board of Directors/ staff: 2(p)/ members: 300/publication: *Images of Hancock County*

HISTORIC PRESERVATION AGENCY; HISTORIC SITE; HISTORICAL SOCIETY; HISTORY MUSEUM; LIBRARY AND/OR ARCHIVES: Operates two museums that house material related to county history.

PROGRAMS: Annual Meeting; Exhibits; Family Programs; Guided Tours; Lectures; Publication; Research Library/Archives

COLLECTIONS: [Late 19th c] Books, letters, photos, family heirlooms, artifacts.

HOURS: Apr-Nov Sa, Su 1-4

ADMISSION: $0.50

2541
James Whitcomb Riley Birthplace
250 W Main St, 46016; (p) (317) 462-8539, (317) 462-8527; www.greenfieldin.org/parks/rileyhouse.htm

City/ Parks & Recreation Dept

James Whitcomb Riley's (the "Hoosier Poet") boyhood home and museum

HOURS: Apr 3-Nov 13 T-Sa 10-4, Su 1-4

GREENSBURG

2542
Decatur County Historical Society
222 N Franklin St, 47240 [PO Box 163, 47240]; (p) (812) 663-2764; (f) (812) 663-4275; gchamber@hsonline.net; www.treecity.com; (c) Decatur

Private non-profit/ 1916/ Board of Directors/ staff: 35(v)/ members: 300

HISTORICAL SOCIETY; HISTORY MUSEUM; HOUSE MUSEUM: Operates 1834 brick two-story museum home that displays local history.

PROGRAMS: Annual Meeting; Community Outreach; Exhibits; Facility Rental; Guided Tours; Interpretation; Lectures; Publication; Research Library/Archives

COLLECTIONS: [1800s-present] Historic furniture, pictures, documents, textiles, and art pieces.

HOURS: May-Oct Sa 10-1, Su

HAMMOND

2543
Hammond Historical Society
564 State St, 46320; (p) (219) 852-2255; (c) Lake

Private non-profit/ 1960/ members: 300/publication: *Flashback*

PROGRAMS: Annual Meeting; Guided Tours; Lectures; Publication

HARTFORD CITY

2544
Blackford County Historical Society
321 S High St, 47348 [PO Box 264, 47348]; (p) (765) 348-4028; sacastello@hotmail.com; www.surfmydotcom/bchistoricalsociety.htm; (c) Blackford

Private non-profit/ staff: 5(v)/ members: 50/publication: *Newsletter*

HISTORICAL SOCIETY

PROGRAMS: Facility Rental; Publication; Research Library/Archives

COLLECTIONS: [1890] The Cecil Beeson Library contains local genealogical sources with books, maps, newspapers and photographs.

HOURS: Apr-Nov Su 1-4

HAYDEN

2545
Hayden Historical Museum Inc.
6715 W County Rd 20 S, 47245 [PO Box 58, 47245]; (p) (812) 346-8212; haydenmu@sei-data.com; (c) Jennings

Private non-profit/ 1990/ staff: 8(v)/ members: 318

HISTORY MUSEUM: Highlights history of local community; has research library for local genealogy, and research materials on local heritage.

PROGRAMS: Annual Meeting; Community Outreach; Concerts; Exhibits; Facility Rental; Family Programs; Festivals; Film/Video; Guided Tours; Interpretation; Lectures; Living History; Publication; Reenactments; Research Library/Archives; School-Based Curriculum

COLLECTIONS: [Prehistory-present] 19th c bedroom, 1939 kitchen, 1965 living room, mid 1950 school room; Edgar Whitcomb, former IN governor, exhibit; displays on military, churches, baseball, merchants, pioneers, and agriculture.

HOURS: Mid Aug-May M-Th 3:30-5, W 3:30-8, Su 1-4

ADMISSION: No charge

HIGHLAND

2546
Highland Historical Society
2450 Lincoln St, 46322 [2611 Highway Ave, 46322]; (c) Lake

Private non-profit/ 1977/ staff: 20(v)/ members: 50

HISTORICAL SOCIETY: Collects and preserves historical records and artifacts of Highland; maintains one-room museum; prints newsletter.

PROGRAMS: Annual Meeting; Community Outreach; Exhibits; Facility Rental; Family Programs; Festivals; Guided Tours; Interpretation; Lectures; Living History; Publication; Reenactments; Research Library/Archives

COLLECTIONS: [1880-present] Local pre-settlement artifacts; manuscripts, photos, and town artifacts.

HOURS: Yr Sa 9:30-11 and by appt

ADMISSION: $2.50

HOBART

2547
Hobart Historical Society, Inc.
706 E Fourth St, 46342 [PO Box 24, 46342]; (p) (219) 942-0970; (c) Lake

Private non-profit/ 1965/ staff: 12(p); 12(v)/ members: 300/publication: *Growing Up In Hobart; Hobart Memories*

HISTORICAL SOCIETY: Preserves local heritage.

PROGRAMS: Annual Meeting; Exhibits; Guided Tours; Interpretation; Lectures; Publication; Research Library/Archives; School-Based Curriculum

COLLECTIONS: [1845-present] Documents, images, and artifacts related to local history.

HOURS: Yr Sa

HUNTINGTON

2548
Dan Quayle Center and Museum, The
815 Warren St, 46750 [PO Box 856, 46750]; (p) (219) 356-6356; (f) (219) 356-1455; dqcm@huntington.in.us; www.np.huntington.in.us/quayle; (c) Huntington

Private non-profit/ 1993/ The Dan Quayle Commemorative Foundation, Inc./ staff: 2(f); 1(p); 10(v)/ members: 275

HISTORY MUSEUM: Educational institution with exhibits, collections, and educational programs concerning the vice presidents of the US, especially those from IN.

PROGRAMS: Annual Meeting; Community Outreach; Exhibits; Facility Rental; Family Programs; Film/Video; Guided Tours; Lectures; Research Library/Archives; School-Based Curriculum

COLLECTIONS: [1947-present] Artifacts including photos related to Dan Quayle, other vice presidents from IN, and the US vice presidency in general.

HOURS: Yr T-Sa 10-4, Su 1-4

ADMISSION: No charge

2549
Historic Forks of the Wabash
US 24 at SR9, 46750 [PO Box 261, 46750]; (p) (219) 356-1903; (f) (219) 356-6371; historicforks@juno.com; (c) Huntington

Private non-profit/ 1987/ staff: 1(f); 1(p); 130(v)/ members: 475

HISTORIC SITE; HOUSE MUSEUM: Interprets interaction between Miami Indians, settlers, and the US government before the 1846 Miami Removal.

PROGRAMS: Annual Meeting; Community Outreach; Exhibits; Facility Rental; Family Programs; Festivals; Guided Tours; Interpretation; Lectures; Publication; Reenactments; Research Library/Archives; School-Based Curriculum

COLLECTIONS: [1846] Home of last Miami chief before removal; home of a German immigrant family; remnants of Wabash and Erie canals; artifacts of Woodland Indian and Pioneer cultural history.

HOURS: May-Oct Th-Su 1-5

ADMISSION: $2, Children $1

2550
Huntington County Historical Society, Inc.

315 Court St, 46750 [315 Court St, 46750]; (p) (219) 356-7264; (f) (219) 356-7265; (c) Huntington

1925/ Board of Directors/ staff: 1(f); 1(p); 10(v)/ members: 80

PROGRAMS: Exhibits; Family Programs; Lectures

COLLECTIONS: [1850-present]

HOURS: Yr T-F 10-4, Sa 1-4

ADMISSION: Donations accepted

IDAVILLE

2551
Parrish Farm Museum

[PO Box 184, 47950]; (p) (219) 826-4163; (c) White

Private for-profit/ 1979/ staff: 2(f); 10(p)

LIVING HISTORY/OUTDOOR MUSEUM: Interprets IN history from 1834-1850.

PROGRAMS: Festivals; Guided Tours; Living History; School-Based Curriculum

COLLECTIONS: [1834-1850] Folk art; early transportation, decorative arts, blacksmithing, early woodworking, Native American artifacts.

HOURS: June-Aug Daily 11-5 and Sep by appt

ADMISSION: $4, Children $2

INDIANAPOLIS

2552
American Legion, The

700 N Pennsylvania St, 46206 [PO Box 1055, 46206]; (p) (317) 630-1200; (f) (317) 630-1223; tal@legion.org; www.legion.org; (c) Marion

Private non-profit/ 1919/ National Executive Committee/ staff: 240(f); 10(p)

CORPORATE ARCHIVES/MUSEUM: Corporate museum representing the interests of its members.

PROGRAMS: Guided Tours

COLLECTIONS: [20th c] Published material relating to 20th c American military activity; strong collection of unit histories and original war posters; archives of American Legion; museum display.

HOURS: Yr M-F 8-4

ADMISSION: No charge

2553
Association of Indiana Museums Inc.

7452 Nutmeg Ct, 46224 [PO Box 24428, 46224-0428]; (p) (317) 882-5649; (f) (317) 865-7662; wildcat@iquest.net; (c) Marion

Private non-profit/ 1972/ staff: 1(p); 30(v)/ members: 400/publication: *The AIM Bulletin; The Directory of Indiana Museums*

Supports museums, their staffs, volunteers and patrons through the promotion of statewide public awareness of museums, the encouragement of better communication among museums, and the availability of technical information.

2554
Department of Natural Resources, Division of Historic Preservation and Archaeology

402 W Washington St, Rm 274, 46204; (p) (317) 232-1646; (f) (317) 232-0693; dhpa@dnr.state.in.us; www.ai.org/dnr; (c) Marion

State/ IN General Assembly/ staff: 17(f); 1(p)

HISTORIC PRESERVATION AGENCY: Promotes conservation of IN's cultural resources through public education, financial incentives, and administration of state/federally

2555
Eiteljorg Museum of American Indians and Western Art

500 W Washington St, 46204; (p) (317) 636-9378; (f) (317) 264-1724; museum@eiteljorg.org; www.eiteljorg.org; (c) Marion

Private non-profit/ 1989/ staff: 46(f); 9(p); 800(v)/ members: 3000

ART MUSEUM; HISTORY MUSEUM: Presents Western art and Native American environment through exhibits, performances, and hands-on workshops with artists.

PROGRAMS: Exhibits; Facility Rental; Family Programs; Festivals; Film/Video; Guided Tours; Lectures; Reenactments; School-Based Curriculum

COLLECTIONS: [Mid 19th c-present] Native American ethnographic collection; American Western art both historic and contemporary.

HOURS: Yr 10-5

ADMISSION: $5, Student $2, Children $2, Seniors $4

2556
Freetown Village, Inc.

[PO Box 1041, 46206]; (p) (317) 631-1870; (f) (317) 631-0224; freetown@ameritech.net; freetown.org; (c) Marion

Private non-profit/ 1982/ Board of Directors/ staff: 3(f); 12(p); 7(v)/ members: 100

HISTORY MUSEUM; LIVING HISTORY/OUTDOOR MUSEUM: Interprets lives of African Americans in IN after the Civil War through living history performances; preserves artifacts and offers exhibits and programs.

PROGRAMS: Annual Meeting; Community Outreach; Concerts; Exhibits; Family Programs; Festivals; Film/Video; Interpretation; Living History; Reenactments; Theatre

COLLECTIONS: [1850-1900] Living history and exhibits,

HOURS: Yr T-Sa 9:30-1:30, Su 1-4

ADMISSION: Museum free

2557
Historic Landmarks Foundation of Indiana

340 W Michigan St, 46202; (p) (317) 639-4534; (f) (317) 639-6734; info@historiclandmarks.org; www.historiclandmarks.org; (c) Marion

Private non-profit/ 1960/ Board of Directors/ staff: 40(f); 9(p); 205(v)/ members: 6100/publication: *The Indiana Preservationist*

HISTORIC PRESERVATION AGENCY; HISTORIC SITE; HOUSE MUSEUM; LIBRARY AND/OR ARCHIVES: Statewide preservation group; restores and protects historic structures; offers education, advocacy, and financial support for preservation.

PROGRAMS: Annual Meeting; Community Outreach; Exhibits; Facility Rental; Guided Tours; Lectures; Publication; Research Library/Archives; School-Based Curriculum

HOURS: Yr M-F 8:30-5 (Hdqtrs)

2558
Hugh Thomas Miller Rare Book Room, Butler University Libraries

4600 Sunset Ave, 46208; (p) (317) 940-9265; (f) (317) 940-9711; edavis@butler.edu; www.butler.edu/library/rare/; (c) Marion

Private non-profit/ 1980/ Butler Univ/ staff: 1(f); 1(p)

LIBRARY AND/OR ARCHIVES: Houses archives and special collections; open for research.

PROGRAMS: Exhibits; Lectures; Research Library/Archives

COLLECTIONS: [19th-20th c] Butler University Archives; William F. Charters South Seas collection; Indiana Federation of Advertising Agencies collection.

HOURS: Yr M-F 9-5

ADMISSION: No charge

2559
Indiana Historical Bureau

140 N Senate Ave, Rm 408, 46204; (p) (317) 232-2535; (f) (317) 232-3728; ihb@statelib.lib.in.us; www.state.in.us/history; (c) Marion

State/ 1915/ IN Library and Historical Board/ staff: 10(f); 1(p); 100(v)/publication: *The Indiana Historian, Indiana History Bulletin*

Publishes, educates, collaborates, and makes citizens aware of their history. Activities cover all interpretive

2560
Indiana Historical Society

450 W Ohio St, 46202-3269; (p) (317) 232-1882; (f) (317) 233-3109; www.indianahistory.org; (c) Marion

Private non-profit/ 1830/ Board of Trustees/ staff: 66(f); 21(p); 70(v)/ members: 9000/publication: *Traces of Indiana and Midwestern History; The Hoosier Genealogist; Black History News and Notes*

HISTORICAL SOCIETY; LIBRARY AND/OR ARCHIVES: Collects and preserves records of IN past and interprets and shares knowledge through research, publications, exhibits, and other programs.

PROGRAMS: Annual Meeting; Community Outreach; Concerts; Elder's Programs; Exhibits; Facility Rental; Family Programs; Festivals; Film/Video; Guided Tours; Interpretation; Lectures; Publication; Research Library/Archives; School-Based Curriculum; Theatre

COLLECTIONS: [1763-present] William Henry Smith Memorial Library: research-oriented repository of over 60,000 books and pamphlets, 7,000 manuscripts and archives, 1.5 million photos, 1,000 maps, and other historical material.

HOURS: Yr WFSa 10-5, TTh 10-8, Su 12-5 (except library)

ADMISSION: No charge

2561

Indiana Religious History Association

c/o Mbrshp Secty, 3200 Cold Spring Rd, 46222; (p) (317) 293-4607; jdivita@marian.edu; (c) Marion

Private non-profit/ 1976/ Board of Directors/ members: 44

HISTORICAL SOCIETY: Supports IN religious history.

PROGRAMS: Annual Meeting; Community Outreach; Guided Tours; Lectures

2562

Indiana State Archives

140 N Senate Ave, 46204; (p) (317) 232-3660; (f) (317) 233-1085; arc@icprlan.state.in.us; www.ai.org/icpr/web-file/archives/homepage.html; (c) Marion

State/ 1816/ Oversight Cmte on Public Records/ staff: 10(f); 10(v)

LIBRARY AND/OR ARCHIVES: Receives and preserves the records of official and historical value of state and local government in IN. Makes these records available to official and private researchers.

PROGRAMS: Exhibits; Lectures; Research Library/Archives

COLLECTIONS: [1816-present] Records of state government offices and agencies and some local government offices' records.

HOURS: Yr M-F

2563

Indiana State Library

140 N Senate Ave, 46204; (p) (317) 232-3675; (f) (317) 232-3736; www.statelib.lib.in.us; (c) Marion

State/ 1825/ IN Library and Historical Board/ staff: 71(f); 4(p)

Provides library services to governments staff and the public; also collects IN materials, serves visually impaired persons, and supports state library services.

COLLECTIONS: [1816-present] Historical and genealogical materials such as books, audio tapes and artifacts; federal and state documents; newspapers and manuscripts.

HOURS: Yr M-F

2564

Indiana State Museum and Historic Sites

202 N Alabama St, 46204; (p) (317) 232-1637; (f) (317) 232-7090; inmuseum@ismhs.org; www.state.in.us/ims; (c) Marion

State/ 1869/ staff: 80(f); 150(p); 150(v)/ members: 1000

HISTORIC PRESERVATION AGENCY; HISTORY MUSEUM; STATE AGENCY: Collects, preserves, and interprets cultural and natural history of IN.

PROGRAMS: Community Outreach; Exhibits; Facility Rental; Family Programs; Festivals; Guided Tours; Lectures; Publication; School-Based Curriculum

COLLECTIONS: [Prehistory-present]

HOURS: Museum:Yr Daily 9-5

ADMISSION: No charge

2565

Indianapolis-Marion County Public Library

40 E St Clair St, 46206 [PO Box 211, 46206]; (p) (317) 269-1700; (f) (317) 269-1768; www.imcpl.lib.in.us; (c) Marion

City/ 1873/ Public Library Board/publication: *Reading in Indianapolis*

Houses collections and supports educational programs for county residents.

COLLECTIONS: Archival collections of local interest.

HOURS: Yr M-F 9-9, Sa 9-5, Su 1-5

ADMISSION: No charge

2566

Irvington Historical Society

5350 University Ave, 46219 [66 Johnson Ave, 46219]; (p) (317) 353-8874; diebold@tcon.net; www.historicirvington.com; (c) Marion

Private non-profit/ 1964/ Board of Directors/ staff: 25(v)/ members: 400/publication: *Greater Irvington*

ART MUSEUM; HISTORICAL SOCIETY; LIBRARY AND/OR ARCHIVES

PROGRAMS: Annual Meeting; Concerts; Guided Tours; Lectures; Publication

COLLECTIONS: [1840-1945] Personal papers, photos, postcards, news clippings, books, art.

2567

James Whitcomb Riley Museum Home

528 Lockerbie St, 46202; (p) (317) 631-5885; (c) Marion

Private non-profit/ 1922/ J WR Memorial Assn/ staff: 3(f); 3(p); 20(v)

HOUSE MUSEUM: Preserved home in which James Whitcomb Riley lived the last 23 years of his life.

PROGRAMS: Guided Tours

COLLECTIONS: [Late Victorian] Original furnishings, wall coverings, carpets, and personal artifacts.

HOURS: Late Jan-Dec T-Sa 10-3:30, Su 12-3:30

ADMISSION: $3, Student $0.50, Seniors $2

2568

Morris-Butler House

1204 N Park Ave, 46202; (p) (317) 636-5409; (f) (317) 636-2630; mbhouse@indy.net; www.historiclandmarks.org; (c) Marion

Private non-profit/ 1960/ Historic Landmarks Foundation of IN/ staff: 2(f); 4(p); 20(v)/ members: 1

HISTORIC SITE

PROGRAMS: Exhibits; Facility Rental; Family Programs; Festivals; Guided Tours; Interpretation; Lectures; School-Based Curriculum; Theatre

COLLECTIONS: [1840-1900] American and European decorative arts.

HOURS: Yr T-Sa 10-4, Su 1-4

ADMISSION: $5, Children $2, Seniors $4

2569

National Council on Public History

425 University Blvd, Cavanaugh Hall 327, 46202; (p) (317) 274-2716; (f) (317) 274-2347; ncph@iupui.edu; www.ncph.org; (c) Marion

Private non-profit/ 1980/ Board of Directors/ staff: 3(p)/ members: 1700/publication: *The Public Historian, Public History News*

HISTORIC PRESERVATION AGENCY: Stimulates interest in history by promoting the use of history at all levels of society, advising historians, and helping

2570

President Benjamin Harrison Foundation

1230 N Delaware St, 46202; (p) (317) 631-1888; (f) (317) 632-5488; harrison@surf-ici-com; www.surf-ici.com/harrison; (c) Marion

Private non-profit/ 1966/ staff: 8(f); 4(p); 60(v)/ members: 250/publication: *The Statesman*

HISTORIC SITE; HISTORY MUSEUM; HOUSE MUSEUM; LIBRARY AND/OR ARCHIVES; PRESIDENTIAL SITE: Maintains and preserves home and property of the 23rd Pres; offers numerous educational programs.

PROGRAMS: Community Outreach; Elder's Programs; Exhibits; Facility Rental; Family Programs; Festivals; Garden Tours; Guided Tours; Interpretation; Lectures; Publication; Research Library/Archives; School-Based Curriculum

COLLECTIONS: [1875-1901] 1875 brick Italianate home and surrounding grounds; Harrison papers; personal items; furnishings; and political memorabilia; 11,075 objects and library materials.

HOURS: Yr M-Sa 10-3:30, Su 12:30-3:30

ADMISSION: $5, Children $1, Seniors $4

2571

Wishard Nursing Museum

1001 W 10th St, 46202; (p) (317) 630-6233; (c) Marion

Private non-profit/ 1980/ Wishard Memorial Hospital Alumni Association/ staff: 10(v)

HISTORY MUSEUM: Houses artifacts related to nursing and medicine.

PROGRAMS: Exhibits; Guided Tours

COLLECTIONS: [1883-present] Historical objects, photographs, and archives.

HOURS: Yr W 9-2 and by appt

ADMISSION: Donations accepted

JASPER

2572

Dubois County Historical Society, Inc.

737 W 8th St, 47546; (p) (812) 482-3074; (c) Dubois

County/ 1927/ members: 90

HISTORICAL SOCIETY: Preserves local history.

PROGRAMS: Annual Meeting

2573

Dubois County Museum, Inc.

1103 Main St, 47547 [PO Box 1086, 47547]; (p) (812) 634-7733; (c) Dubois

Private non-profit/ 1998/ staff: 30(v)/ members: 294

HISTORY MUSEUM: Located in historic Gramelspacher-Gutzweiler building; traces region's history.

PROGRAMS: Annual Meeting; Exhibits; Family Programs; Guided Tours; Lectures; Reenactments

COLLECTIONS: [1800-1950] Log cabin reconstruction exhibit; death ritual exhibit; mercantile display; military items agricultural implements; photos.

HOURS: Yr F-Sa 10-2, Su

JEFFERSONVILLE

2574
Howard Steamboat Museum/Clark County Historical Society, Inc.
1101 E Market St, 47131 [PO Box 606, 47131]; (p) (812) 283-3728; (f) (812) 283-6049; (c) Clark

Private non-profit/ 1958/ Board of Directors/ staff: 1(f); 1(p); 6(v)/ members: 500/publication: *Scenes From Memory*

HISTORICAL SOCIETY; HISTORY MUSEUM: Offers tours and interpretation of Victorian home and steamboat history; artifacts associated with the Howards of Jeffersonville, builders of steamboats.

PROGRAMS: Annual Meeting; Exhibits; Facility Rental; Festivals; Garden Tours; Guided Tours; Interpretation; Lectures; Publication; Research Library/Archives

COLLECTIONS: [1834-1941] Original furnishings of 1894 Victorian mansion; wood carvings, steamboat models, tools, artifacts, books, photos, and documents.

HOURS: Yr T-Sa 10-4, Su 1-4

ADMISSION: $4, Student $2, Children $1, Seniors $3

KOKOMO

2575
Elwood Haynes Museum
1915 S Webster, 46902; (p) (765) 456-7500; (c) Howard

City/ 1967/ staff: 1(f); 1(p)

HISTORIC SITE; HISTORY MUSEUM; HOUSE MUSEUM: Former home of inventor Elwood Haynes.

PROGRAMS: Exhibits; Festivals; Film/Video; Guided Tours; Publication

COLLECTIONS: [1857-1925] Four Haynes cars from 1905-1924; period furniture, china, glass; industrial displays; photos, samples of metals; bombs; first canned tomato juice.

HOURS: Yr T-Sa 1-4, Su 1-5

ADMISSION: No charge

2576
Howard County Historical Society
1200 W Sycamore, 46901; (p) (765) 452-4314; (f) (765) 452-4581; director@howard-countymuseum.org; www.howardcountymuseum.org; (c) Howard

Joint/ 1972/ County; Private non-profit/ staff: 3(f); 6(p); 150(v)/ members: 600/publication: *Museum Highlights*

HISTORIC SITE; HISTORICAL SOCIETY;

HISTORY MUSEUM; HOUSE MUSEUM; LIBRARY AND/OR ARCHIVES; RESEARCH CENTER: Local history museum in historic house.

PROGRAMS: Annual Meeting; Community Outreach; Concerts; Exhibits; Facility Rental; Family Programs; Festivals; Guided Tours; Interpretation; Lectures; Living History; Publication; Reenactments; Research Library/Archives; School-Based Curriculum

COLLECTIONS: [Early 1800s-1950s] Local history collection.

HOURS: Feb-Dec T-Su 1-4

ADMISSION: $2

LAFAYETTE

2577
Tippecanoe County Historical Association
909 S St, 47901; (p) (765) 476-8411; (f) (765) 476-8414; kevin@tcha.mus.in.us; www.tcha.mus.in.us; (c) Tippecanoe

Private non-profit/ 1925/ Board of Governors/ staff: 6(f); 5(p); 50(v)/ members: 1136

GENEALOGICAL SOCIETY; HISTORIC SITE; HISTORICAL SOCIETY; HISTORY MUSEUM; HOUSE MUSEUM; LIBRARY AND/OR ARCHIVES; RESEARCH CENTER: Operates the Fowler House, the Battleground Museum, Fort Ouiatenon, and the McCollough Library.

PROGRAMS: Annual Meeting; Exhibits; Facility Rental; Family Programs; Festivals; Guided Tours; Interpretation; Lectures; Living History; Reenactments; Research Library/Archives; School-Based Curriculum

COLLECTIONS: [Early 1800s-present] Material related to development of the county and historic sites.

HOURS: Feb-Dec T-Su 1-5

ADMISSION: $3, Children $1.50; Mbrs free

LAWRENCEBURG

2578
Dearborn County Historical Society
508 W High St, 47025; (p) (812) 537-4075; (c) Dearborn

Private non-profit/ 1984/ Board of Directors/ staff: 1(p); 3(v)/ members: 175

GENEALOGICAL SOCIETY; HISTORICAL SOCIETY; HISTORY MUSEUM: Collects and preserves historical materials.

PROGRAMS: Annual Meeting; Exhibits; Family Programs; Publication; Research Library/Archives

COLLECTIONS: [Late19th-early 20th c] Books, pictures, textiles, china, and other artifacts of local historical significance.

HOURS: Yr T-W 9-4, Th 9-3, F

LEAVENWORTH

2579
Crawford County Historical and Genealogical Society, Inc.
[PO Box 133, 47137]; (c) Crawford

Private non-profit/ 1985/ members: 40

GENEALOGICAL SOCIETY; HISTORICAL SOCIETY: Collects and preserves artifacts and records relevant to local history and genealogy.

PROGRAMS: Publication

COLLECTIONS: Pictures, cemetery records, and local history books.

LEBANON

2580
Boone County Historical Society
404 W Main St, 46052 [PO Box 141, 46052-0141]; (p) (765) 483-9414; (c) Boone

Joint/ 1979/ County; Private non-profit/ staff: 5(v)/ members: 70

HISTORICAL SOCIETY

PROGRAMS: Annual Meeting; Community Outreach; Concerts; Exhibits; Facility Rental; Festivals; Guided Tours; Interpretation; Lectures; Publication; Reenactments; Research Library/Archives

COLLECTIONS: [Late 19th c-present] Cragun Home, a Victorian structure, and its contents.

LINCOLN CITY

2581
Lincoln Boyhood National Monument
[PO Box 1816, 47552]; (p) (812) 937-4541; (f) (812) 937-9929; LIBO_secretary@nps.gov; www.nps.gov/LIBO; (c) Spencer

Federal/ 1962/ National Park Service/ staff: 10(f); 10(p)

LIVING HISTORY/OUTDOOR MUSEUM; PRESIDENTIAL SITE: Preserves site where Abraham Lincoln spent 14 years of his youth, and the site of his mother's burial.

PROGRAMS: Community Outreach; Exhibits; Family Programs; Guided Tours; Interpretation; Living History; Research Library/Archives

COLLECTIONS: [Early 19th c] Historic artifacts of daily life; research material and official records.

HOURS: Yr Daily 8-5

ADMISSION: $2, Family $4

LOGANSPORT

2582
Cass County Historical Society Museum
1004 E Market, 46947; (p) (219) 753-3866; (f) (219) 753-3866; (c) Cass

Joint/ 1907/ County; CCHS/ staff: 1(p); 1(v)/ members: 280

HISTORIC SITE; HISTORICAL SOCIETY; HISTORY MUSEUM: Displays local historical artifacts.

PROGRAMS: Annual Meeting; Elder's Programs; Exhibits; Family Programs; Festivals; Guided Tours; Interpretation; Lectures; Publication; Research Library/Archives; School-Based Curriculum

COLLECTIONS: [1907-present] Native American artifacts; art; genealogy; log house and barn; photographic county history; other artifacts.

HOURS: Yr T-Sa 1-5

ADMISSION: No charge

MADISON

2583
Historic Madison, Inc.
500 W St, 47250; (p) (812) 265-2967; (f) (812) 273-3941; hmihmfi@seidata.com; (c) Jefferson

Private non-profit/ 1960/ staff: 4(f); 1(p); 100(v)/ members: 750/publication: *Early Architecture of Madison, Indiana; A Horse-and-Buggy Doctor in Southern Indiana*

HISTORIC PRESERVATION AGENCY; HISTORICAL SOCIETY; HOUSE MUSEUM: Preserves Madison's historic architecture; owns, operates, and maintains several historic house museums; and restores buildings.

PROGRAMS: Annual Meeting; Community Outreach; Concerts; Exhibits; Facility Rental; Guided Tours; Publication

COLLECTIONS: [1820-1900] Judge Jeremiah Sullivan House ca. 1818; Dr. W.D. Hutchings Office ca. 1903; Architect Francis Costigan House ca. 1850; St Michael the Archangel Church ca. 1835, Schroeder Saddletree Factory ca. 1878.

HOURS: Mid Apr-Oct M-S 10-4:30, Su 1-4; Costigan House: Sa-M 1-4:30

ADMISSION: $2

2584
Jefferson County Historical Society
615 W First St, 47250; (p) (812) 265-2335; jchs@seidata.com; www.seidata.com/~jchs; (c) Jefferson

Joint/ 1850/ County; Private non-profit/ staff: 1(f); 1(p); 100(v)/ members: 550

ART MUSEUM; GENEALOGICAL SOCIETY; HISTORIC SITE; HISTORICAL SOCIETY; HISTORY MUSEUM; HOUSE MUSEUM; RESEARCH CENTER: Maintains modern county museum and restored 1895 Madison Railroad Station.

PROGRAMS: Annual Meeting; Community Outreach; Elder's Programs; Exhibits; Facility Rental; Family Programs; Festivals; Guided Tours; Lectures; Living History; Publication; Research Library/Archives; School-Based Curriculum

COLLECTIONS: [Mid 1800s] 16,000 fossil items; Native American artifacts; local nuclear power plant artifacts.

HOURS: Last week April-Oct Daily M-Sa 10-4:30, Su 1-4; Nov-Apr M-F 10-4:30

ADMISSION: $3

2585
Lanier Mansion State Historic Site
511 W First St, 47250; (p) (812) 265-3526; (f) (812) 265-3501; lanier@seidata.com; www.state.in.us/ism/sites/lanier; (c) Jefferson

State/ 1926/ IN DNR Div of Museums & Historic Sites/ staff: 4(f); 7(p); 25(v)

HISTORIC SITE: 1844 Greek Revival home of J.F.D. Lanier, banker and financier; features restored interior and period gardens.

PROGRAMS: Community Outreach; Facility Rental; Festivals; Garden Tours; Guided Tours; Interpretation

COLLECTIONS: [1844-1860] Original family artifacts and other period artifacts.

HOURS: Yr T-Sa 9-5, Su 1-5; Winter hours vary

ADMISSION: Donations accepted

MARION

2586
Grant County Historical Society
[PO Box 1951, 46952]; (p) (765) 664-6520; sunray@comteck.com; (c) Grant

Joint/ 1905/ County; Private non-profit/ staff: 12(v)/ members: 80/publication: *Battle of the Mississinewa, The Northcutt Diary, Historic Landmarks of Grant County*

GENEALOGICAL SOCIETY; HISTORIC PRESERVATION AGENCY; HISTORIC SITE; HISTORICAL SOCIETY; HISTORY MUSEUM; HOUSE MUSEUM; RESEARCH CENTER: Offers historical community programs.

PROGRAMS: Annual Meeting; Community Outreach; Exhibits; Family Programs; Guided Tours; Interpretation; Lectures; Living History; Publication; Reenactments; Research Library/Archives

2587
Marion Public Library—Museum Services
600 S Washington St, 46953; (p) (765) 668-2900; (f) (765) 668-2911; mpl@comteck.com; www.marion.lib.in.us; (c) Grant

City/ 1884/ staff: 2(f); 1(p)

HISTORY MUSEUM; LIBRARY AND/OR ARCHIVES: Preserves local history through print resources, objects, and oral history.

PROGRAMS: Exhibits; Guided Tours; Research Library/Archives

COLLECTIONS: [1831-present] Local historical and genealogical collections; museum artifacts.

HOURS: Mem Day-Labor Day MWF 9-8; TTh 9-5:30, Sa 9-5; Labor Day-Mem Day M W F 9-9, TTh 9-5:30, Sa 9-5

ADMISSION: No charge

METAMORA

2588
Whitewater Canal State Historic Site
19083 Clayborn St, 47030 [PO Box 88, 47030]; (p) (765) 647-6512; (f) (765) 647-2734; wwcshs@cnz.com; www.state.in.us/ism/sites/whitewater/; (c) Franklin

State/ 1946/ IN DNR Div of Museums & Historic Sites/ staff: 5(f); 7(p)

HISTORIC SITE: Working gristmill built in 1900 and 14 mi restored canal with operating

1840s era canal boat.

PROGRAMS: Community Outreach; Concerts; Facility Rental; Festivals; Interpretation

COLLECTIONS: [1840s-1850s]

HOURS: Mill: Mid Mar-mid Dec T-Su 9-5; Boat: May 1-Oct 31 T-Su 12-4

ADMISSION: $1; No charge for Mill

MICHIGAN CITY

2589
Barker Mansion
631 Washington, 46360; (p) (219) 873-1520; (f) (219) 873-1520; (c) La Porte

City/ 1968/ staff: 2(f); 3(p); 60(v)/ members: 75

GARDEN; HISTORIC SITE; HOUSE MUSEUM: 1905 house museum with all original furnishings and art objects.

PROGRAMS: Exhibits; Facility Rental; Festivals; Garden Tours; Guided Tours; Interpretation

COLLECTIONS: [1890-1920] Clothing, textiles, accessories, sculptures, paintings, silver, and glassware.

HOURS: Yr Daily

ADMISSION: $4, Children $2; Under 3 free

2590
Michigan City Historical Society
Heisman Harbor Road, Washington Park, 46360 [PO Box 512, 46360]; (p) (219) 827-6133; (c) LaPorte

Private non-profit/ 1923/ staff: 1(p); 23(v)/ members: 284

HISTORICAL SOCIETY: Preserves 1858 Light Station used as a museum; records and interprets local history.

PROGRAMS: Annual Meeting; Exhibits; Guided Tours

COLLECTIONS: [1800s-present] Fresnel lenses; Native American artifacts; 1858 furniture; Great Lakes cargo shipping artifacts; local industry and church artifacts.

HOURS: Mar-Dec T-Su 1-4

ADMISSION: $2, Student $1, Children $0.50

MITCHELL

2591
Spring Mill State Park
Hwy 60 E, 47446 [PO Box 376, 47446]; (p) (812) 849-4129; (f) (812) 849-4004; spring@tima.com; (c) Lawrence

State/ 1926/ IN Dept of Natural Resources/ staff: 16(f); 40(p); 200(v)

HISTORIC SITE

PROGRAMS: Community Outreach; Concerts; Exhibits; Facility Rental; Family Programs; Festivals; Garden Tours; Guided Tours; Interpretation; Lectures; Living History; Reenactments

COLLECTIONS: [1832] Pioneer Village; 1832 furnishings including tools, artwork, textiles; 2,500 artifacts; NASA collection: Gemini Capsule, Space Suit, photos

HOURS: Yr Daily 9-5

ADMISSION: $2-$5/vehicle

MONTPELIER

2592
Montpelier Historical Society, Inc.
109 E Huntington St, 47359; (c) Blackford

Private non-profit/ 1969/ staff: 10(v)/ members: 100

PROGRAMS: Exhibits

COLLECTIONS: Local donated historical artifacts.

HOURS: Special events only

ADMISSION: No charge

MOORES HILL

2593
Carnegie Historic Landmarks Preservation Society, Inc.
14687 Main St, 47032 [PO Box 118, 47032]; (p) (812) 744-4015; chall@seidata.com; (c) Dearborn

1987/ staff: 2(p)/ members: 115

HISTORIC SITE: Maintains and preserves Carnegie Hall, built in 1907 as part of Moores Hill Male and Female Collegiate Institute.

PROGRAMS: Exhibits; Facility Rental; Guided Tours

COLLECTIONS: [1907-1978] Artifacts and records related to the hall's use in the college (1907-1917) and then as a public school (1918-1978), including yearbooks, photos, and more.

HOURS: Yr by appt

ADMISSION: No charge

MOUNT VERNON

2594
Posey County Historical Society
207 Main St, 47620 [PO Box 171, 47620]; (c) Posey

Private non-profit/ 1974/ staff: 20(v)/ members: 139

GENEALOGICAL SOCIETY; HISTORIC PRESERVATION AGENCY; HISTORICAL SOCIETY; LIBRARY AND/OR ARCHIVES: Preserves and makes available local history.

PROGRAMS: Annual Meeting; Lectures; Publication; Research Library/Archives

HOURS: Yr M-T 1-3

ADMISSION: No charge

MUNCIE

2595
Delaware County Historical Alliance
120 E Washington St, 47305; (p) (765) 282-1550; (f) (765) 282-1058; dcha@iquest.net; www.iquest.net/~dcha; (c) Delaware

Private non-profit/ 1952/ Board of Directors/ staff: 1(f); 1(p); 6(v)/ members: 271

RESEARCH CENTER: Operates the Moore-Youse Home Museum and Heritage Genealogy Research Library; publishes local genealogy and historical journal.

PROGRAMS: Annual Meeting; Community Outreach; Guided Tours; Publication; Research Library/Archives; School-Based Cur-

riculum

COLLECTIONS: [Victorian] Furnishings and artifacts from Civil War time-1930.

HOURS: Museum: Mar 1-Oct 1 by appt; Library: M-F

2596
Minnetrista Cultural Center and Oakhurst Gardens
1200 N Minnetrista Pkwy, 47303; (p) (765) 282-4848; (f) (765) 741-5110; (c) Delaware

Private non-profit/ 1988/ Minnetrista Cultural Foundation, Inc/ staff: 36(f); 14(p); 680(v)/ members: 1329

ART MUSEUM; GARDEN; HISTORY MUSEUM; LIBRARY AND/OR ARCHIVES

PROGRAMS: Concerts; Exhibits; Facility Rental; Festivals; Garden Tours; Guided Tours; Interpretation; Lectures; Research Library /Archives

COLLECTIONS: [1800-2000] Exhibits and archival materials in history, art, science, and industry.

HOURS: Yr M-Sa 10-5, Su 1-5

ADMISSION: $5, Family $15, Student $3, Children $3, Seniors $3

2597
National Model Aviation Museum
5151 E Memorial Dr, 47302; (p) (765) 289-4236; (f) (765) 289-4248; michaels@modelaircraft.org; www.modelaircraft.org; (c) Delware

Private non-profit/ 1936/ Academy of Model Aeronautics/ staff: 2(f); 1(p); 6(v)/ members: 150000/publication: *AMA-Model Aviation Museum-Cloud 9 Newsletter*

AVIATION MUSEUM: Collects, preserves, and exhibits the historic, scientific, technical, and artistic legacy of model aviation.

PROGRAMS: Exhibits; Guided Tours; Publication; Research Library/Archives

COLLECTIONS: [20th c] Model aircraft, trophies and contest material.

HOURS: Yr M-F 8-4, Sa-Su

NASHVILLE

2598
Brown County Historical Society
1934 N Hwy 135, 47448 [PO Box 668, 47448]; (p) (812) 988-6089; (c) Brown

Private non-profit/ 1957/ Board of Directors/ staff: 64(v)/ members: 197

GENEALOGICAL SOCIETY; HISTORIC PRESERVATION AGENCY; HISTORIC SITE; HISTORICAL SOCIETY; HISTORY MUSEUM; HOUSE MUSEUM; RESEARCH CENTER: Collects and preserves county history; maintains museum.

PROGRAMS: Annual Meeting; Community Outreach; Exhibits; Facility Rental; Festivals; Guided Tours; Lectures; Living History; Monthly Meeting; Publication; Research Library/ Archives; School-Based Curriculum

COLLECTIONS: [1830-1900] Log cabin, log jail, blacksmith shop, doctor's office, and loom room.

HOURS: May-Oct Sa-Su 1-5

ADMISSION: $1.50; Under 11 free

2599
T.C. Steel State Historic Site
4220 TC Steele Rd, 47448; (p) (812) 988-2785; (f) (812) 988-8457; tcsteele@bloomington.in.us; (c) Brown

State/ 1946/ IN DNR Div of Museums & Historic Sites/ staff: 3(f); 5(p); 10(v)/ members: 54/publication: *The Singing Winds*

ART MUSEUM; HISTORIC SITE: Preserves the home and studio of noted IN impressionist Theodore Clement Steele.

PROGRAMS: Annual Meeting; Community Outreach; Family Programs; Festivals; Garden Tours; Guided Tours; Interpretation; Lectures; Publication

COLLECTIONS: [1907-1926] Over 80 paintings in two large historic buildings; original furnishings.

HOURS: Mid Mar-mid Dec T-Sa

NEW ALBANY

2600
Carnegie Center for Art and History
201 E Spring St, 47150; (p) (812) 944-7336; (f) (812) 981-3554; (c) Floyd

Joint/ 1971/ Carnegie Center; NA/FC Public Library/ staff: 3(f); 2(p); 5(v)/ members: 485/publication: *Musings*

ART MUSEUM; HISTORY MUSEUM: Contemporary art gallery and local history museum.

PROGRAMS: Annual Meeting; Community Outreach; Exhibits; Facility Rental; Family Programs; Garden Tours; Lectures; Publication

COLLECTIONS: [Prehistory-present] 2,000 items of local historical importance; artwork by local artists.

HOURS: Yr T-Sa 10-5:30

ADMISSION: No charge

2601
Culbertson Mansion State Historic Site
914 E Main St, 47150; (p) (812) 944-9600; (f) (912) 949-6134; culbertson@disknet.com; www.state.in.us/ism/sites/culbertson/; (c) Floyd

State/ 1976/ IN DNR Div of Museums & Historic Sites/ staff: 2(f); 4(p); 40(v)/ members: 60

HISTORIC SITE: Community resource for those interested in Victorian architecture and local history.

PROGRAMS: Community Outreach; Exhibits; Facility Rental; Family Programs; Guided Tours; Living History; Research Library/ Archives

COLLECTIONS: [1870-1900] 20,000 sq. ft French Empire style mansion, built in 1869; furniture, fine arts, decorative arts; over 2,000 accessioned artifacts.

HOURS: Mid Mar-mid Dec T-Sa 9-5, Su 1-5

ADMISSION: No charge

2602
Floyd County Historical Society
[PO Box 455, 47150]; (c) Floyd

Private non-profit/ members: 50/publication: *History of Floyd County*

NEW CASTLE

2603
Henry County Historical Society Museum
606 S 14th St, 47362; (p) (765) 529-4028; hchisoc@kiva.net; www.kiva.net/~hchisoc/museum.htm; (c) Henry

County/ 1887/ Board of Trustees/ staff: 4(p); 20(v)/ members: 750/publication: *The Historicalog*

HISTORICAL SOCIETY; HISTORY MUSEUM: Preserves and interprets mid 19th c life in Henry County.

PROGRAMS: Annual Meeting; Exhibits; Facility Rental; Guided Tours; Publication; Research Library/Archives

COLLECTIONS: [Pre 1920s] Pictures, books, bibles, and artifacts on early history of the county. Furniture, sculptures, paintings, clothing, war memorabilia related to county residents.

HOURS: Yr M-Sa 1-4:30

ADMISSION: $2, Student $1; Under 12/Mbrs free

NEW HARMONY

2604
Historic New Harmony
506 1/2 Main St, 47631 [PO Box 579, 47631]; (p) (812) 682-4488; (f) (812) 682-4313; harmony@usi.edu; www.newharmony.org; (c) Posey

Joint/ 1974/ Univ of Southern IN; IN DNR/ staff: 4(f); 28(p); 3(v)/ members: 514

HISTORIC SITE; HOUSE MUSEUM: House museums and various collections.

PROGRAMS: Community Outreach; Exhibits; Facility Rental; Family Programs; Festivals; Film/Video; Garden Tours; Guided Tours; Interpretation; Living History; School-Based Curriculum

COLLECTIONS: [1800-1900] House museums of the Harmonist and Owen periods (1814-1834); geological and natural science collections of the earliest geological surveys; early theatre collection; manuscripts; 81 hand-colored lithographs.

HOURS: Mar-Dec; Winter Daily 9-4; Summer Daily 9-5

ADMISSION: $8, Children $3

2605
New Harmony State Historic Site
410 Main St, 47631 [PO Box 607, 47631]; (p) (812) 682-3271; (f) (812) 682-5526; newharmonyshs@dynasty.net; www.state.in.us/ism/sites/newharmony/; (c) Posey

State/ 1939/ IN DNR Div of Museums & Historic Sites/ staff: 3(f)/publication: *In Harmonie*

HISTORIC SITE: Site of two of America's earliest utopian communities: the Harmony Society and Owen-Maclure Community.

PROGRAMS: Community Outreach; Concerts; Elder's Programs; Exhibits; Facility Rental; Family Programs; Festivals; Guided Tours; Interpretation; Lectures; Publication

COLLECTIONS: [1814-1890] 19th c decorative arts; furniture; archival collections; books; printing equipment; theatrical costumes and memorabilia; maps; photographs.

HOURS: Mar-Dec Daily 9-4

ADMISSION: $3-$8

2606
New Harmony Workingmen's Institute
407 W Tavern St, 47631 [Box 368, 47631]; (p) (812) 682-4806; (f) (812) 682-4806; (c) Posey

1838/ Board of Trustees/ staff: 2(f); 3(p)/ members: 26

ART MUSEUM; HISTORIC SITE; HISTORY MUSEUM; LIBRARY AND/OR ARCHIVES: Oldest continuously operating public library in IN; houses museum and archive of New Harmony history.

PROGRAMS: Exhibits; Family Programs; Research Library/Archives

COLLECTIONS: [1814-1900] Manuscripts from Owen Community, rare books, artifacts from Harmonist and Owen communities, natural science collections from early WMI members, and art—Italian and local.

HOURS: Yr

NEW HAVEN

2607
Besancon Historical Society
5335 Lincoln Hwy East, 46774; (p) (219) 622-4067; (c) Allen

Private non-profit/ 1994/ staff: 5(f); 4(v)/ members: 72/publication: *Chronicle*

HISTORICAL SOCIETY: Preserves the histories and genealogies of the early French immigrants of Allen County.

PROGRAMS: Annual Meeting; Exhibits; Publication; Research Library/Archives

COLLECTIONS: Family genealogies of early French immigrants.

HOURS: Yr W 9:30-1

ADMISSION: Donations accepted

NEWBERRY

2608
Greene County Historical Society
3 E Main St, 47449 [RR1 Box 45, 47449]; (c) Greene

Private non-profit/ 1972/ staff: 6(v)/ members: 65

HISTORIC SITE; HISTORICAL SOCIETY; HISTORY MUSEUM; HOUSE MUSEUM

PROGRAMS: Annual Meeting; Community Outreach; Exhibits; Facility Rental; Family Programs; Garden Tours; Guided Tours; Lectures; Publication; Research Library/Archives

COLLECTIONS: Material for genealogical and historical research.

HOURS: Yr T, Th, F 10-3

ADMISSION: No charge

2609
Scotland Historical Society, Inc.
Corner of Main & Jackson St, 47449 [RR 1 Box 45, 47449]; (c) Greene

1971/ members: 100

HISTORICAL SOCIETY; HISTORY MUSEUM: Manages a museum of historical artifacts.

PROGRAMS: Exhibits; Festivals

COLLECTIONS: [1880s-1920s] Furniture, pictures, and literature.

HOURS: Sept, 3rd Sa 9-4

ADMISSION: No charge

NOBLESVILLE

2610
Hamilton County Historical Society
[PO Box 397, 46060]; (p) (317) 770-0775; (f) (317) 770-0775; historical society@noblesville.com; www.noblesville.com/history.htm; (c) Hamilton

Private non-profit/ 1962/ staff: 1(f); 20(v)/ members: 250

HISTORIC SITE; HISTORICAL SOCIETY; HISTORY MUSEUM: Preserves and interprets historical artifacts and structures of the county.

PROGRAMS: Annual Meeting; Community Outreach; Exhibits; Guided Tours; Lectures

COLLECTIONS: Textiles, paper goods, photos, furniture, and personal items.

HOURS: Yr Sa 10-2 and by appt

ADMISSION: Donations requested

NOTRE DAME

2611
Holy Cross History Association
Douglas Road, 46556 [101 Bertrand Hall, St Mary's, 46556-5000]; (p) (219) 284-5662; (f) (219) 284-5779; dreppen@CSCSisters.org; (c) St. Joseph

Private non-profit/ 1984/ Officers and Council/ staff: 9(v)/ members: 124/publication: *Holy Cross History*

HISTORICAL SOCIETY: Promotes historical study of those religious communities that trace their origin to the Rev. Basil Moreau of Le-Mans, France.

PROGRAMS: Annual Meeting; Publication

COLLECTIONS: [1821-present] Papers given at the annual Conference on the History of the Congregations of Holy Cross, 1982-present.

PERU

2612
Circus City Festival, Inc.
154 N Broadway, 46970; (p) (765) 472-3918; (f) (765) 472-2826; perucirc@perucircus.com; www.perucircus.com; (c) Miami

Private non-profit/ 1960/ staff: 1(f); 1(p); 500(v)/ members: 225

HISTORY MUSEUM: Preserves history of the circus in Indiana, especially the amateur circus of Peru.

PROGRAMS: Facility Rental; Festivals

COLLECTIONS: [Late 1800s-present] Artifacts and memorabilia.

HOURS: Yr M-F 9-4

ADMISSION: No charge

2613
Grissom Air Museum State Historic Site
6500 Hoosier Blvd, 46970; (p) (765) 688-

2654; (f) (765) 688-2956; gamuseum@iquest.net; www.state.in.us/ism/sites/grissom/; (c) Miami

Joint/ 1984/ State; Private non-profit/ staff: 2(f); 1(p); 20(v)/ members: 425

HISTORY MUSEUM: Preserves and presents aviation history.

PROGRAMS: Community Outreach; Exhibits; Facility Rental; Festivals; Film/Video; Guided Tours; Interpretation; Research Library/Archives; School-Based Curriculum

COLLECTIONS: [1940-present] Eighteen historic aircraft including B-17 Flying Fortress and B-58; equipment, uniforms, flight trainers, photos, models, survival gear, engines, art, and memorabilia.

HOURS: Feb-mid Dec T-Sa 10-4

ADMISSION: Donations accepted

2614
Miami County Museum and Historical Society
51 N Broadway, 46970; (p) (765) 473-9183; (f) (765) 472-3880; mchs@netusa1.net; www.netusa1.net~mchs; (c) Miami

Private non-profit/ 1916/ staff: 5(f); 1(p); 55(v)/ members: 250/publication: *Times Past*

HISTORICAL SOCIETY; HISTORY MUSEUM; LIBRARY AND/OR ARCHIVES: Collects, preserves, and publishes historical information of local importance; operates museums.

PROGRAMS: Annual Meeting; Community Outreach; Exhibits; Family Programs; Film/Video; Guided Tours; Lectures; Publication; Research Library/Archives; School-Based Curriculum

COLLECTIONS: [1800-1900] Artifacts related to prehistoric Miami County, the Miami Indians, pioneers of Miami County, circus history, Cole Porter, railroads, and business and industry.

HOURS: Yr T-Sa 9-5

ADMISSION: Donations accepted

PLAINFIELD

2615
Guilford Township Historical Collection of the Plainfield-Guilford Public Library
1120 Stafford Rd, 46168; (p) (317) 839-6602; (f) (317) 839-4044; scarter@plainfield.lib.in.us; history.plainfield.lib.in.us/; (c) Hendricks

City, non-profit/ 1967/ Library Board of Trustees/ staff: 1(f); 3(p); 4(v)

LIBRARY AND/OR ARCHIVES: Collects, preserves, and makes available for research, material on the township's, county's, and state's history.

PROGRAMS: Exhibits; Family Programs; Lectures

COLLECTIONS: [1824-present] Historical and genealogical material of area; local newspapers, 13,000 books, photos, clippings, pamphlets, and manuscripts; other archival materials.

HOURS: Yr M-Th 9-8, F, Sa 9-5

ADMISSION: No charge

2616
Guilford Township Historical Society
1120 Stafford Rd, 46168; (p) (317) 839-6602; (c) Hendricks

Private non-profit/ 1963/ Board of Directors/ staff: 4(v)/ members: 37

HISTORICAL SOCIETY: Preserves local historical resources; assists public library's local history section.

PROGRAMS: Annual Meeting; Quarterly Meeting

PLYMOUTH

2617
Marshall County Historical Society, Inc.
123 N Michigan St, 46563; (p) (219) 936-2306; (f) (219) 936-9306; mchist@kconline.com; (c) Marshall

Joint/ 1957/ County; Board of Trustees/ staff: 3(f); 45(v)/ members: 590/publication: *Marshall County Quarterly*

HISTORICAL SOCIETY; LIBRARY AND/OR ARCHIVES: Library of local information and exhibits on county history.

PROGRAMS: Annual Meeting; Community Outreach; Exhibits; Family Programs; Guided Tours; Publication; Research Library/Archives

COLLECTIONS: [1850-1980] Ten exhibit rooms representing historic Marshall County; 1880s parlor, kitchen, entertainment, medical, agricultural, and other artifacts. Microfilm of county newspapers, and photographs.

HOURS: Yr T-F 9-5, Sa 10-4

ADMISSION: Donations accepted

PORTLAND

2618
Headwaters Heritage, Inc.
109 S Commerce St, 47371 [138 E Main St, 47371]; (p) (219) 726-4809; (c) Jay

Private non-profit/ 1984/ Board of Directors/ members: 50

HISTORIC PRESERVATION AGENCY: Educates public on architecture and restoration.

PROGRAMS: Annual Meeting; Community Outreach; Exhibits; Guided Tours; Lectures; Research Library/Archives; School-Based Curriculum

COLLECTIONS: [1823-present] Photos, maps, blue prints; donated archival items related to historic sites; structures; informational brochures and resource books.

HOURS: Yr by appt

2619
Jay County Historical Society
903 E Main St, 47371 [PO Box 1282, 47371]; (p) (219) 726-6680; (c) Jay

1914/ Board of Directors/ staff: 1(p); 15(v)/ members: 170

HISTORICAL SOCIETY: Collects and displays local historical artifacts.

PROGRAMS: Annual Meeting; Community Outreach; Exhibits; Guided Tours; Interpretation

COLLECTIONS: [Early 1900s] Artifacts of early settlers; industrial and cultural exhibits.

HOURS: 2nd Su Mar-Oct, 3rd wknd Sept 1-5

ADMISSION: Donations accepted

PRINCETON

2620
Gibson County Historical Society, Inc.
[PO Box 516, 47670]; (p) (812) 385-4745; (c) Gibson

Private non-profit/ 1985/ staff: 10(v)/ members: 113/publication: *County Lines*

HISTORICAL SOCIETY: Preserves the history and culture of the area; transcribes and indexes cemetery records.

PROGRAMS: Annual Meeting; Guided Tours; Lectures; Publication

COLLECTIONS: [1813-present]

RENSSELAER

2621
Jasper County Historical Society
479 N Van Rensselaer, 47978; (c) Jasper

County; Private non-profit/ 1967/ members: 25

HISTORICAL SOCIETY; HISTORY MUSEUM: Operates history museum and historic sites.

PROGRAMS: Annual Meeting; Community Outreach; Exhibits; Family Programs; Festivals; Film/Video; Guided Tours; Interpretation; Lectures; Publication; Reenactments; Research Library/Archives; School-Based Curriculum; Theatre

COLLECTIONS: [1840-1920] Donated items; pictures, clothing, military artifacts; log cabin, school house, post office.

HOURS: By appt

ADMISSION: No charge

RICHMOND

2622
Gaar House Museum
2593 Pleasant View Rd, 47374; (p) (765) 966-7184, (765) 962-5295

1876/ staff: 3(f); 6(p); 3(v)

COLLECTIONS: [1870s-1880s] Original chandeliers, furniture, china, Family Bibles, photos, paintings of Agnes & Abram, period clothing, house plans, furniture bills of sale.

HOURS: Seasonal

2623
Wayne County Historical Society and Museum
1150 N 'A' St, 47374; (p) (765) 962-5756; (f) (765) 939-0909; micheleb@infocom.com; (c) Wayne

Private non-profit/ 1930/ staff: 2(f); 4(p); 50(v)/ members: 800

HISTORIC SITE; HISTORICAL SOCIETY; HISTORY MUSEUM; LIVING HISTORY/OUTDOOR MUSEUM; RESEARCH CENTER: Collects, preserves, and interprets local history.

PROGRAMS: Annual Meeting; Community Outreach; Exhibits; Facility Rental; Family Programs; Festivals; Guided Tours; Interpretation; Living History; Research Library/Archives; School-Based Curriculum

COLLECTIONS: [1830-1999] Pioneer life, Victorian, Egyptian mummies, horse drawn carriages, vintage school buses and cars, airplanes, Starr-Gennett Jazz Collection, decorative arts, quilts, coverlets, women's clothing.

HOURS: Tu-F 9-4, Sa-Su 1-4

RISING SUN

2624
Ohio County Historical Society
212 S Walnut St, 47040 [212 S Walnut St, 47040]; (p) (812) 438-4915; (f) (812) 438-4925; ohiocohist@seidata.com; (c) Ohio

Private non-profit/ 1966/ staff: 1(f); 5(p); 25(v)/ members: 97

HISTORICAL SOCIETY; HISTORY MUSEUM: Collects, preserves, and displays artifacts and memorabilia.

PROGRAMS: Community Outreach; Exhibits; Facility Rental; Guided Tours; Interpretation; Research Library/Archives; School-Based Curriculum

COLLECTIONS: [19th and 20th c] Over 5,000 artifacts including "Hoosier Boy;" vignettes of 19th c daily life.

HOURS: Yr M-T, Th-Sa 11-4, Su 1:30-4:30

ADMISSION: $2.50, Student $1, Seniors $2

ROCHESTER

2625
Fulton County Historical Society, Inc.
4 Mi N of Rochester on US 31, 46975 [37 E 375 N, 46975]; (p) (219) 223-4436; wwillard@rtcol.com; icss.net/~fchs; (c) Fulton

Private non-profit/ 1963/ Board of Directors/ staff: 2(f); 2(p); 14(v)/ members: 500/publication: *Fulton County Images, Folk Finder*

HISTORICAL SOCIETY: 35 acres with museum, Round Barn Museum, living history village; answers genealogical queries.

PROGRAMS: Annual Meeting; Community Outreach; Concerts; Exhibits; Facility Rental; Family Programs; Festivals; Film/Video; Lectures; Living History; Publication; Reenactments; Research Library/Archives; School-Based Curriculum; Theatre

COLLECTIONS: [1860-present] Manuscripts, maps, newspapers, books, genealogy reference books and materials, pictures, and 10,000 artifacts.

HOURS: Yr M-Sa 9-5

ADMISSION: No charge

ROCKVILLE

2626
Mansfield Roller Mill State Historic Site
6 mi S of US 36 off SR S9, 47872 [160 S Raccoon Pkwy, 47872]; (p) (765) 344-1412; (f) (765) 344-1772; www.state.in.us/ism/sites/mansfield/; (c) Parke

State/ 1880/ IN DNR Div of Museums & Historic Sites/ staff: 1(f); 2(p); 2(v)

HISTORIC SITE: Roller mill that exemplifies the transitional period in milling accompanying the change from stone to roller grinding.

PROGRAMS: Community Outreach; Family

Programs; Festivals; Guided Tours; Interpretation

COLLECTIONS: [1880s]

HOURS: Apr 1-Mem Day F-Su; Mem Day-Last Wknd in Oct Daily Su-F 9-4, Sa 9-5

ADMISSION: No charge/Donations

2627
Parke County Historical Society, Inc.
503 W Ohio, 47872 [PO Box 332, 47872]; (p) (765) 569-2223; wswern@ticz.com; (c) Parke

Private non-profit/ 1894

HISTORICAL SOCIETY; HISTORY MUSEUM: Society and museum concerned with history of the county and its people.

PROGRAMS: Annual Meeting

COLLECTIONS: [1821-present] Artifacts depicting pioneer life and the history of Parke county and its people.

HOURS: June-Oct W-Su 1-4

ADMISSION: $1; Members free

ROME CITY

2628
Gene Stratton-Porter State Historic Site
1205 Pleasant Point, 46784 [PO Box 639, 46784]; (p) (219) 854-3790; (f) (219) 854-9102; www.state.in.us/ism/sites/porter/

State/ 1913/ IN DNR Div of Museums & Historic Sites/ staff: 3(f); 6(p); 2(v)

Second home of author and nature photographer Gene Stratton-Porter.

COLLECTIONS: [1863-1924] Stratton-Porter's personal library, photographs, writings, furniture, pottery.

HOURS: Mid Mar-mid Dec T-Sa 9-5, Su 1-5

ADMISSION: Donations accepted

SALEM

2629
Washington County Historical Society
307 E Market St, 47167; (p) (812) 883-6495; (c) Washington

Private non-profit/ 1897/ staff: 2(f); 100(v)/ members: 1000

HISTORICAL SOCIETY; HISTORY MUSEUM; HOUSE MUSEUM: Operates the John Hay Center, including the John Hay Birthplace, and the Stevens Memorial Museum.

PROGRAMS: Annual Meeting; Exhibits; Festivals; Guided Tours; Reenactments; Research Library/Archives

COLLECTIONS: [1700-present] 1840 house with period furnishings; pioneer and other artifacts of local historical significance.

HOURS: Yr T-Sa 9-5

ADMISSION: $2

SHERIDAN

2630
Sheridan Historical and Genealogical Society
308 Main St, 46069; (p) (317) 758-5054; (c)

Hamilton

Private non-profit/ 1969/ staff: 4(v)

HOURS: Yr T, F 1-4

ADMISSION: No charge

SHIRLEY

2631
Jane Ross Reeves Octagon House Foundation
400 S Railroad St, 47384; (p) (765) 737-6518; (c) Hancock

Private non-profit/ 1994/ Board of Directors/ members: 30

GENEALOGICAL SOCIETY; HISTORIC PRESERVATION AGENCY; HISTORY MUSEUM; LIBRARY AND/OR ARCHIVES; LIVING HISTORY/OUTDOOR MUSEUM: Restores historic Octagon House.

PROGRAMS: Annual Meeting; Community Outreach; Elder's Programs; Exhibits; Facility Rental; Family Programs; Festivals; Living History

COLLECTIONS: [1879-present]

2632
Shirley Centennial and Historical Society
204 Railroad St, 47384 [2484 Grant City Rd, 47384]; (c) Hancock

Private non-profit/ 1990/ staff: 6(v)/ members: 60

HISTORICAL SOCIETY; HISTORY MUSEUM: Preserves local historical artifacts; maintains train depot as a museum; restores old Doctor's office.

PROGRAMS: Annual Meeting; Community Outreach; Exhibits; Festivals; Guided Tours; Living History; Reenactments

COLLECTIONS: [1890-to present] Railroad depot; musical instruments, furniture, switchboard, tools, books, and pictures; old jail.

HOURS: Apr-Oct Sa-Su 1-4

ADMISSION: Donations accepted

SOUTH BEND

2633
College Football Hall of Fame
111 S St Joseph St, 46601; (p) (219) 235-9999; (f) (219) 235-5720; collegefootball.org; (c) St. Joseph

Private non-profit/ 1995/ National Football Foundation/ staff: 10(f); 6(p); 60(v)/ members: 10000

HISTORY MUSEUM; LIBRARY AND/OR ARCHIVES

COLLECTIONS: [1869-present] Physical artifacts from the game of college football; films, photos, and books.

HOURS: Yr Daily June-Nov 10-7; Dec-May 10-5

ADMISSION: $9, Student $6, Children $4, Seniors $6

2634
Copshaholm, the Oliver Mansion
808 W Washington, 46601; (p) (219) 235-9664; (f) (219) 235-9059; nich@michiana.org;

www.centerforhistory.org; (c) St. Joseph

Private non-profit/ 1867/ Northern IN Historical Society/ staff: 14(f); 8(p); 120(v)/ members: 700

GARDEN; HOUSE MUSEUM: Former home of J.D. Olivor and family.

PROGRAMS: Community Outreach; Exhibits; Garden Tours; Guided Tours; Interpretation; School-Based Curriculum

COLLECTIONS: [1895-1972] House with original furnishings; paintings, prints, silver, ceramics, photos, and archival materials.

HOURS: Yr T-Sa 10-5, Su 12-5

ADMISSION: $8

2635
Dom Robotnika, The Worker's Home Museum
808 W Washington, 46601; (p) (219) 235-9664; (f) (219) 234-9059; nich@michiana.org; www.centerforhistory.org; (c) St. Joseph

Private non-profit/ 1867/ Northern IN Historical Society/ staff: 18(f); 7(p); 120(v)/ members: 700

HISTORY MUSEUM: Interprets the ethnic heritage of the St. Joseph River Valley and the lifestyle of a Polish-American working-class family of the 1930s.

PROGRAMS: Community Outreach; Exhibits; Guided Tours; Interpretation; Living History; School-Based Curriculum

COLLECTIONS: [1930-1940] Furniture, knick-knacks, periodicals, and ephemera from 1915-1939.

HOURS: Yr

2636
Northern Indiana Center for History
808 W Washington St, 46601; (p) (219) 235-9664; nich@michiana.org; business.michiana.org/nich; (c) St. Joseph

Private non-profit/ Northern IN Historical Society/ staff: 14(f); 8(p); 120(v)/ members: 700

HISTORICAL SOCIETY; HISTORY MUSEUM; HOUSE MUSEUM; LIBRARY AND/OR ARCHIVES: Houses exhibits on exploration, travel and local history; Kidsfirst Children's museum features interactive activities based on history.

PROGRAMS: Annual Meeting; Community Outreach; Concerts; Exhibits; Facility Rental; Family Programs; Film/Video; Guided Tours; Interpretation; Lectures; Research Library/ Archives; School-Based Curriculum

COLLECTIONS: [Prehistory-present] Pioneer and Native American artifacts; art pieces, decorative arts; military, industrial, costumes, toys, dolls, tools, games; repository for the All-American Girls Professional Baseball League; archives include fur trading journals, regional newspapers 1830-1960, court documents and records, genealogical records, diaries, letters, bound volumes, photos, sheet music.

HOURS: Yr T-Sa 10-5, Su 12-5

2637
Northern Indiana Historical Society
808 W Washington St, 46601; (p) (219) 235-9664; (f) (219) 235-9059; nich@michiana.org; www.centerforhistory.org; (c) St. Joseph

Private non-profit/ 1896/ staff: 18(f); 7(p); 120(v)/ members: 700

GARDEN; HISTORICAL SOCIETY; HISTORY MUSEUM; HOUSE MUSEUM; LIBRARY AND/OR ARCHIVES: Collects, preserves, interprets, exhibits, and teaches heritage of St. Joseph River Valley region.

PROGRAMS: Community Outreach; Concerts; Exhibits; Facility Rental; Family Programs; Festivals; Film/Video; Garden Tours; Guided Tours; Interpretation; Lectures; Living History; Research Library/Archives; School-Based Curriculum; Theatre

COLLECTIONS: [1825-present] Includes costumes, textiles, decorative arts, toys,

TELL CITY

2638
Tell City Historical Society
516 Main St, 47586 [PO Box 728, 47586]; (p) (812) 547-9695; (c) Perry

Private non-profit/ members: 60

HISTORICAL SOCIETY: Researches, records, and maintains history and objects from Tell City's past.

PROGRAMS: Annual Meeting; Film/Video; Guided Tours

COLLECTIONS: [1858-present] Photographs and objects dating from city's founding.

HOURS: By appt; during local festivals

ADMISSION: No charge

TERRE HAUTE

2639
Eugene V. Debs Foundation
451 N 8th St, 47808 [PO Box 843, 47808]; (p) (812) 237-3443; (f) (812) 237-8072; (c) Vigo

Private non-profit/ 1962/ staff: 2(p); 5(v)/ members: 600

HISTORY MUSEUM; HOUSE MUSEUM: Owns, maintains, and exhibits the home of Eugene Debs, interpreting his labor leadership and political activism.

PROGRAMS: Annual Meeting; Guided Tours; Interpretation; Publication

COLLECTIONS: [Late19th-early 20th c] House, personal furniture, photos, campaign memorabilia, and murals that chronicle Debs' life.

HOURS: Yr W-Su 1-4:30 and by appt

ADMISSION: No charge

2640
Native American Museum
5170 E Poplar St, 47803; (p) (812) 877-6007; (f) (812) 232-7313; (c) Vigo

City/ 1834/ Parks and Recreation Dept/ staff: 1(f); 4(p); 4(v)

GARDEN; HISTORY MUSEUM; LIBRARY AND/OR ARCHIVES: Presents Native American cultural artifacts; offers educational programs and events; collects, preserves, and interprets material culture of regional tribes.

PROGRAMS: Community Outreach; Elder's Programs; Exhibits; Facility Rental; Family Programs; Garden Tours; Guided Tours; Interpretation; Lectures; Living History; Research Library/Archives; School-Based Curriculum

COLLECTIONS: Over 500 lithic materials; research library; video collection; over 1,000 photos and slides; beaded textiles, pottery, postcard, native dolls, weapons, and other artifacts.

HOURS: Yr M-Sa 9-5, Su 12-5

ADMISSION: No charge

2641
Vigo County Public Library, Special Collections/Archives
Corner of 7th & Poplar, 47807 [One Library Square, 47807]; (p) (812) 232-1113; (f) (812) 232-3208; vax1.vigo.lib.in.us; (c) Vigo

County/ 1882/ staff: 3(f); 3(p)

LIBRARY AND/OR ARCHIVES: Collects and preserves local historical material.

PROGRAMS: Community Outreach; Exhibits; Family Programs; Research Library/Archives

COLLECTIONS: [1810-present] County histories, city directories, newspapers, census records, personal manuscripts, and community organizational records.

HOURS: Yr M-Th 9-9, F 9-6, Sa 9-5; and Labor Day-Mem Day Su 1-5

THORNTOWN

2642
Sugar Creek Historical Society
124 W Main St, 46071 [PO Box 23, 46071]; (p) (765) 436-2202; clwhite@in-motion.net; www.bccn.boone.in.us/tpl/schs/index.htm

Private non-profit/ 1972/ staff: 2(p); 4(v)/ members: 40

HISTORICAL SOCIETY; HISTORY MUSEUM; HOUSE MUSEUM: Collects, preserves, and shares history of local community; supports the Thorntown Heritage Museum.

PROGRAMS: Community Outreach; Exhibits; Family Programs; Festivals; Guided Tours; Interpretation; Publication

COLLECTIONS: [1800-present] Native American baskets from Great Lakes area, period clothing, Anson Mills military items, musical instruments, arrow heads and stones, photos.

HOURS: May-Sept Sa-Su 11-5 and by appt

ADMISSION: Donations accepted

VALPARAISO

2643
Historical Society of Porter County
153 S Franklin St, 46383; (p) (219) 465-3595; (c) Porter

Private non-profit/ 1912/ staff: 2(p)/ members: 100

HISTORICAL SOCIETY: Preserves county's historical artifacts; operates small museum in old jail/sheriff's house.

PROGRAMS: Annual Meeting; Community Outreach; Exhibits; Guided Tours; Lectures; Publication; Research Library/Archives

COLLECTIONS: [1800s-1900s] Agricultural

and domestic implements, possessions of a fur trader and a cowboy, war memorabilia, pictorial marquetry, mastodon bones.

HOURS: Yr W,F,Sa 1-4

ADMISSION: Donations accepted

VERNON

2644
Jennings County Historical Society; Our Heritage, Inc.

134 E Brown St, 47282 [PO Box 335, 47282]; (p) (812) 346-8989; (c) Jennings

Private non-profit/ 1961/ staff: 1(p); 20(v)/ members: 102/publication: *History of Jennings County*

HISTORICAL SOCIETY: Presents, preserves, and documents county history through a historical museum and programs.

PROGRAMS: Annual Meeting; Exhibits; Facility Rental; Family Programs; Festivals; Guided Tours; Living History; Publication; Reenactments

COLLECTIONS: [1770-1930] American artifacts; loom, spinning wheels, and quilts.

HOURS: Yr M-W 11-4, Th-F 9-4

ADMISSION: No charge

VINCENNES

2645
Indiana Military Museum, Inc.

2074 N Old Bruceville Rd, 47591 [PO Box 977, 47591]; (p) (812) 882-8668; (c) Knox

Private non-profit/ 1981/ staff: 12(v)/ members: 121

HISTORY MUSEUM: Military museum.

PROGRAMS: Exhibits; Guided Tours; Living History

COLLECTIONS: [1861-present] Artillery, vehicles, uniforms, equipment, insignia, and captured enemy items.

HOURS: Apr 1-Sep 30 Daily 12-4

ADMISSION: $2, Children $1

2646
Old French House

509 N 1st St, 47591; (p) (812) 882-7886, (800) 886-6443; (c) Knox

1806

HOUSE MUSEUM: One-and-a-half-story house made of hand-hewn logs set on end on a sandstone foundation and daubed with mud. One of the few remaining examples of this unique French form of frontier construction.

PROGRAMS: Guided Tours; Interpretation

HOURS: Mem Day-Labor Day T-Sa 9-12/1-5, Su 1-5; and by appt

2647
Vincennes Historical and Antiquarian Society

[PO Box 487, 47591]; (p) (812) 882-1873; (c) Knox

Private non-profit/ members: 82

Holds meetings; publishes historical materials.

COLLECTIONS: Collection of historical documents signed by US presidents including

George Washington and George Bush.

2648
William Henry Harrison Museum

3 W Scott St, 47591; (p) (812) 882-2096; (c) Knox

Private non-profit/ 1909/ Francis Vigo Chapter, DAR/ staff: 1(f); 5(p); 25(v)

HOUSE MUSEUM; PRESIDENTIAL SITE: Three-story mansion designed and built by Harrison; his home while governor of IN Territory until 1812.

PROGRAMS: Community Outreach; Exhibits; Guided Tours; Interpretation; School-Based Curriculum

COLLECTIONS: [1804-1812] Fifteen rooms, restored with authentic and original furnishings; campaign artifacts from 1840.

HOURS: Yr Jan-Feb Daily 11-4; Mar-Dec M-Sa 9-5, Su 11-5

ADMISSION: $5, Student $3, Children $2

WAKARUSA

2649
Wakarusa Historical Museums

403 S Wabash Ave, 46573 [Box 2, 46573]; (p) (219) 862-4407; (c) Elkhart

Private non-profit/ 1975/ Wakarusa Historical Society, Inc/ staff: 15(f); 25(v)/ members: 65

HISTORY MUSEUM; HOUSE MUSEUM: Several restored and preserved historical structures.

PROGRAMS: Annual Meeting; Exhibits; Festivals; Guided Tours; Publication; School-Based Curriculum

COLLECTIONS: [1860-1950s] Various buildings including veterinary office, school house, and train depot; donated artifacts; photos.

HOURS: June-Sep 4th Su 2-4, and by appt

ADMISSION: Donations accepted

WASHINGTON

2650
Daviess County Historical Society

RR #2, Donaldson Rd, 47501 [1303 S Meridian St, 47501]; (p) (812) 254-5122; bmcguire@dmrtc.net; (c) Daviess

County/ 1966/ staff: 1(p); 2(v)/ members: 115

HISTORICAL SOCIETY; HISTORY MUSEUM: Displays and interprets county history and artifacts.

WINCHESTER

2651
Randolph County Historical Society and Museum

416 S Meridian, 47394; (p) (765) 584-1334; (c) Randolph

Joint/ 1959/ County; Private non-profit/ members: 200

HISTORICAL SOCIETY; HOUSE MUSEUM; LIBRARY AND/OR ARCHIVES: 1858 house containing artifacts. Genealogical and historical research library.

PROGRAMS: Annual Meeting; Community Outreach; Exhibits; Guided Tours; Lectures;

Research Library/Archives; School-Based Curriculum

COLLECTIONS: [1818-present] Household items, clothes, furniture, art, and others.

HOURS: Yr M-F 10-4:30

ADMISSION: Donations accepted

WOLCOTT

2652
Anson Wolcott Historical Society

400 N Range St, 47995 [PO Box 417, 47995]; (p) (219) 279-2123; (f) (219) 279-2561; (c) White

Private non-profit/ 1975/ staff: 9(p); 9(v)/ members: 85

HISTORIC SITE; HISTORICAL SOCIETY: Restores and maintains Wolcott House, home of town founder Anson Wolcott.

PROGRAMS: Annual Meeting; Facility Rental; Family Programs; Festivals; Guided Tours

COLLECTIONS: [Late 1800s-early 1900s] National Register listed house.

HOURS: By appt

ADMISSION: Donations accepted

ZIONSVILLE

2653
P.H. Sullivan Museum; Zionsville Munce Art Center

225-205 W Hawthorne St, 46077 [PO Box 182, 46077]; (p) (317) 873-4900; (c) Boone

Private non-profit/ 1973/ Patrick Henry Sullivan Foundation/ staff: 3(f); 1(p)/ members: 125

ART MUSEUM; HISTORY MUSEUM: Museum offers family genealogies and research, collecting, preserving, and displaying IN artifacts.

PROGRAMS: Community Outreach; Elder's Programs; Exhibits; Facility Rental; Guided Tours; Lectures; Research Library/Archives

COLLECTIONS: [1830-1940] Military collections; toys and dolls, photos including 1939 photo essay collection; artifacts pertaining to disappearing farms in IN; local coverlets and quilts; glassware and china; pioneer items; hat collection; 1917 player piano in working condition; 1920 records player with records; 1900 music box; paintings.

HOURS: Museum: Mid Jan-mid Dec T-Sa 10-4; Art Ctr: Th-Sa 12-5

ADMISSION: No charge

IOWA

ACKLEY

2654
Ackley Heritage Center

Upper Level Municipal Bldg, 50601 [737 State and Main, 50601]; (p) (515) 847-2067; (f) (515) 847-3204; ackleych@cnsinternet.com

Private non-profit/ 1987/ staff: 21(p); 3(v)/ members: 350

HISTORICAL SOCIETY; HISTORY MUSEUM; HOUSE MUSEUM: Preserves and interprets local history.

PROGRAMS: Annual Meeting; Exhibits; Garden Tours; Guided Tours; Interpretation; Lectures; Living History; Research Library/Archives

COLLECTIONS: [1857-present] Negatives, contact prints of 19th c photographs within the photograph preservation program; research material for families of East Friesland descent, and artifacts of local historical interest.

HOURS: Yr M-F, Su 1-5

ALBERT CITY

2655
Albert City Historical Association
212 N 2nd St, 50510 [PO Box 431, 50510]; (p) (712) 843-5684; (c) Buena Vista

Private non-profit/ 1974/ Board of Directors/ staff: 1(p); 15(v)/ members: 65

HISTORIC SITE; HISTORICAL SOCIETY; HISTORY MUSEUM; HOUSE MUSEUM: Preserves the history of the Albert City area from 1870 to the present, including histories of families, churches, schools, and businesses.

PROGRAMS: Annual Meeting; Exhibits; Guided Tours

COLLECTIONS: [1900-1950] Household items, clothing, automobiles, fine china and glassware, Goebel Hummel figurines and plates, guns, music boxes, pioneer laundry equipment, farm shop, carpentry tools, and wooden corn planter.

HOURS: June-Aug Su 2-5

ADMISSION: $3, Student $0.50

ALLISON

2656
Butler County Hall of Fame
On the Allison Courthouse Lawn, 50602 [PO Box 14, 50602-0014]; (p) (319) 278-4321; jpoppen@nations.net; (c) Butler

Private non-profit/ 1957/ Butler County Historical Society/ staff: 32(v)

HISTORY MUSEUM: Recognizes present and past residents of Butler County who have achieved recognition at the county, state, national, and international level.

PROGRAMS: Annual Meeting; Community Outreach; Exhibits; Guided Tours

COLLECTIONS: [1856-present] Photographs and resumes of noted county residents, military displays, and works of various Butler County authors.

HOURS: May-Oct by appt

ADMISSION: $1

2657
Butler County Museum
2191/2 S Main on Butler Co Fairgrnds, 50602 [PO Box 14, 50602-0014]; (p) (319) 278-4321; jpoppen@natins.net; (c) Butler

Private non-profit/ 1957/ Butler County Historical Society/ staff: 21(v)/ members: 22

HISTORICAL SOCIETY; HISTORY MUSEUM: Collects and preserves artifacts relating to Butler County history.

PROGRAMS: Annual Meeting; Community

Outreach; Exhibits; Guided Tours

COLLECTIONS: [Late 1870s-1950] Artifacts related to business, the Butler County fair, medicine, domestic life, and farming.

HOURS: May-Oct 3-8, or by appt

ADMISSION: $1

2658
Little Yellow Schoolhouse
On the Allison Courthouse Lawn, 50602 [219 1/2 S Main, PO Box 14, 50602-0014]; (p) (319) 278-4321; jpoppen@natins.net; (c) Butler

Private non-profit/ 1957/ Butler County Historical Society/ staff: 21(v)/ members: 22

HISTORICAL SOCIETY; HISTORY MUSEUM: Collects and interprets items of past education in the county.

PROGRAMS: Annual Meeting; Community Outreach; Exhibits; Guided Tours

COLLECTIONS: [1880-1950] Slay desks, pot belly stove, organ, school books, maps, and items dealing with nature.

HOURS: May-Oct by appt

ADMISSION: $1

AMANA

2659
Amana Heritage Society
705 44th Ave, 52203 [PO Box 81, 52203]; (p) (319) 622-3567; (f) (319) 622-6481; amherit@juno.com; www.amanaheritage.org; (c) Iowa

Private non-profit/ 1968/ Board of Directors/ staff: 3(f); 25(p); 10(v)/ members: 650/publication: Newsletter

HISTORICAL SOCIETY; HISTORY MUSEUM: Collects, preserves, and interprets the cultural heritage of the Amana Colonies from their religious origins in 18th c Germany to the present.

PROGRAMS: Annual Meeting; Community Outreach; Exhibits; Facility Rental; Festivals; Guided Tours; Interpretation; Lectures; Publication; Research Library/Archives; School-Based Curriculum

COLLECTIONS: [1700-present] 12,000 museum artifacts, primarily from communal era 1855-1932; 10,000 manuscripts, books and maps that document history of the community 1700-present; 5,000 photographs 1880-present.

HOURS: Apr-Oct Daily 10-5 and by appt

ADMISSION: $5, Children $1

AMES

2660
Ames Heritage Association
417 Douglas, 50010 [PO Box 821, 50010]; (p) (515) 232-2148; (c) Story

Private non-profit/ 1981/ staff: 50(v)/ members: 200

HISTORICAL SOCIETY; HISTORY MUSEUM: Preserves and interpretes local history.

PROGRAMS: Annual Meeting; Exhibits; Guided Tours; Lectures

COLLECTIONS: Bauge Family Log House and Hoggatt School, a one-room schoolhouse; artifacts and archives relating to local history.

HOURS: W, F 12-4, Sa 10-5, Su 2-5

ADMISSION: Donations accepted

2661
Farm House Museum
Knoll Rd, Iowa State Univ, 50011 [University Museum, 290 Scheman Bldg, 50011]; (p) (515) 294-7426; (f) (515) 294-7070; www.museums.iastate.edu; (c) Story

State/ 1976/ IA State Univ/ staff: 2(f); 2(p); 15(v)/ members: 250/publication: Farm House: College Farm to University Museum

HISTORIC SITE

PROGRAMS: Community Outreach; Exhibits; Facility Rental; Family Programs; Festivals; Guided Tours; Interpretation; Lectures; Publication

COLLECTIONS: [1860-1910] Original household objects reflecting former home of presidents of the college and college faculty.

HOURS: Yr M-F 12-4, Su 1-4

2662
Story Center, The
417 Douglas, 50010 [PO Box 821, 50010]; (p) (515) 232-2148; (c) Story

Private non-profit/ 1999/ Ames Heritage Assn/ staff: 20(v)/ members: 150

HISTORY MUSEUM: Operates a local history museum focusing on the scientific, engineering, and technological events that have occurred in Ames and Story County.

COLLECTIONS: [20th c]

HOURS: M 5-8, W 11-2, Sa 10-5, Su 2-5

ADMISSION: Donations requested

ARNOLDS PARK

2663
Abbie Gardner Cabin
34 Monument Dr, 51331 [PO Box 74, 51331]; (p) (712) 332-7248, (712) 332-2643; www.state.ia.us/gov/dca/shsi; (c) Dickenson

State/ 1856/ State Historical Society of IA/ staff: 1(p)/ members: 1550/publication: Annals of Iowa

HISTORIC SITE: Known as one of the sites of the 1857 "Spirit Lake Massacre" and as one of IA's first tourist attractions, the site interprets the story of Abbie Gardner and the Dakota leader, Inkpadutah.

PROGRAMS: Guided Tours; Interpretation; Publication

COLLECTIONS: [19th c] Restored 1856 log house with furnishings and early tourist souvenirs.

HOURS: May-Sept M-F 12-4, Sa-Su 9-4

2664
Iowa Great Lakes Maritime Museum
243 W Broadway, 51331 [PO Box 726, 51331]; (p) (712) 332-5264; (f) (712) 332-5366; currator@ncn.net; www.okobojimuseum.org; (c) Dickenson

Private non-profit/ 1984/ staff: 1(f); 4(p); 25(v)/

members: 125

HISTORY MUSEUM; MARITIME MUSEUM: Collects, preserves, and displays the nautical heritage of Lake Okoboji, the IA Great Lakes, and the wooden boat builders of the midwestern US.

PROGRAMS: Annual Meeting; Exhibits; Guided Tours; Interpretation; Lectures; Research Library/Archives; Theatre

COLLECTIONS: [1880-present] 25 classic wooden boats, area and regional nautical artifacts, 250 lakes area historical photos, wooden boat magazine collection (1,200), and 2,000 archival photographs.

HOURS: Yr M-F 10-5; Summer + Sa-Su

ADMISSION: No charge

AUDUBON

2665
Audubon County Historical Society
Hwy 71, 50025 [1745 160th St, 50025]; (p) (712) 563-3984; (c) Audubon

County, non-profit/ 1965/ members: 150

HISTORIC SITE; HISTORICAL SOCIETY; HISTORY MUSEUM; LIVING HISTORY/OUTDOOR MUSEUM: Collects and preserves the history of Audubon County.

PROGRAMS: Annual Meeting; Community Outreach; Exhibits; Festivals; Guided Tours; Living History; Research Library/Archives

COLLECTIONS: [1880-1960] Household articles, agricultural implements, military uniforms and artifacts, rural school house and record books, and nail collection.

HOURS: May 1-Sept 1 Sa-Su

AURELIA

2666
Aurelia Heritage Society
228 Main St, 51005 [PO Box 33, 51005]; (c) Cherokee

1973/ Board of Directors/ staff: 12(v)/ members: 50

HISTORIC PRESERVATION AGENCY; HISTORICAL SOCIETY: Preserves the history and heritage of the town of Aurelia.

PROGRAMS: Annual Meeting; Community Outreach; Exhibits; Guided Tours

COLLECTIONS: [Late 19th c-present] Cutglass china, early 19th c clothing, school memorabilia, kitchen furnishings, and service uniforms.

HOURS: Yr Th 9-11 and by appt

ADMISSION: Donations accepted

AVOCA

2667
Newtown-Avoca Historical Society
504 N Elm, 51521 [PO Box 57, 51521]; (p) (712) 343-2693; (c) Pottawattamie

Private non-profit/ 1993/ members: 60

HISTORICAL SOCIETY; HISTORY MUSEUM: Collects and preserves local historic articles and genealogical records.

PROGRAMS: Facility Rental; Festivals; Guided Tours

COLLECTIONS: Early American artifacts, musical instruments, household items, needlework, and Bing-Grondahl plate collection; mastodon bones and taxidermied animals.

HOURS: Daily 1-4

ADMISSION: Donations accepted

BEDFORD

2668
Taylor County Historical Society
1001 Pollock, 50833; (p) (712) 523-2041; (c) Taylor

Joint/ 1976/ County; Private non-profit/ staff: 75(v)

GENEALOGICAL SOCIETY; HISTORICAL SOCIETY; LIVING HISTORY/OUTDOOR MUSEUM: Collects local history and artifacts.

PROGRAMS: Annual Meeting; Community Outreach; Exhibits; Festivals; Guided Tours; Living History; Publication; Reenactments; Research Library/Archives

COLLECTIONS: [1890-1940] Farm objects and genealogical material.

HOURS: Apr-Dec T-Su

BELLEVUE

2669
Young Historical Museum
406 N Riverview, 52031 [106 N Third St, 52031]; (p) (319) 872-5830, (800) 653-2211; (f) (319) 872-4094

City/ 1890/ staff: 5(p)

HOUSE MUSEUM: Home of Joe and Grace Young, prominent city residents.

COLLECTIONS: [Victorian] Parian ware, a large collection of depressionware glass, salt & peppers

HOURS: Mem Day-Oct 29 Sa-Su 1-5

BONAPARTE

2670
Bonaparte Historical Association
Second & Washington, 52620 [PO Box 158, 52620]; (p) (319) 592-3677; (c) Van Buren

Private non-profit/ 1971/ staff: 1(p); 10(v)/ members: 20

HISTORIC SITE; HISTORICAL SOCIETY: Saves and restores Aunty Green Hotel, which is used as a library and museum.

PROGRAMS: Community Outreach; Guided Tours

COLLECTIONS: [1870-1930] Donated historical items that relate to the history of Bonaparte.

HOURS: May-Nov T, Th, Sa 10-5

ADMISSION: Donations accepted

BOONE

2671
Boone County Historical Society
602 Story St, 50036; (p) (515) 432-1907; bchs@opencominc.com; (c) Boone

Joint/ 1966/ County; Private non-profit/ staff: 1(f); 1(p); 25(v)/ members: 750

HISTORICAL SOCIETY: Collects, preserves, and displays documents and other valuable material, encourages historical research, and sponsors publications and events related to Boone County heritage.

PROGRAMS: Annual Meeting; Community Outreach; Concerts; Exhibits; Facility Rental; Festivals; Guided Tours; Interpretation; Lectures; Publication; Reenactments; Research Library/Archives

COLLECTIONS: Natural history; military, mining, transportation, local, rural school, geological, and Native American history; genealogy; and photographs.

2672
Iowa Railroad Historical Society
225 10th St, 50036 [PO Box 603, 50036]; (p) (515) 432-4249; (f) (515) 432-4253; www.scenic-valleyrr.com; (c) Boone

Private non-profit/ 1983/ staff: 6(f); 2(p); 200(v)/ members: 700/publication: *Keeping Track*

HISTORICAL SOCIETY: Interprets the history of the railroads.

PROGRAMS: Annual Meeting; Facility Rental; Guided Tours; Lectures; Publication; Reenactments

HOURS: Yr 8:30-4:30

ADMISSION: Museum free

2673
Mamie Doud Eisenhower Birthplace
709 Carroll St, 50036 [PO Box 55, 50036]; (p) (515) 432-1896, (800) 266-6312; (f) (515) 432-2571; (c) Boone

Private non-profit/ 1970/ staff: 1(f); 2(p); 50(v)/ members: 300/publication: *Newsletter*

HISTORIC SITE; PRESIDENTIAL SITE: Maintains the birthplace of Mamie Doud Eisenhower, a museum, and a library.

PROGRAMS: Community Outreach; Exhibits; Facility Rental; Film/Video; Guided Tours; Lectures; Publication; Research Library/Archives; School-Based Curriculum

COLLECTIONS: [1865-1979] Restored house with original furnishings and personal effects; books, photos, letters, and memorabilia about the Eisenhower era.

HOURS: Apr-May T-Su 1-5, June-Oct 10-5; and by appt

ADMISSION: $3, Children $1

BRITT

2674
Hancock County Historical Society
266 2nd St SE, 50423 [679 2nd St NW, 50423]; (p) (515) 843-3282; (c) Hancock

Private non-profit/ 1969/ staff: 12(v)/ members: 299

HISTORIC PRESERVATION AGENCY; HISTORIC SITE; HISTORICAL SOCIETY; HISTORY MUSEUM; LIBRARY AND/OR ARCHIVES: Preserves relevant history of

Hancock County.

PROGRAMS: Annual Meeting; Exhibits; Family Programs; Guided Tours; Lectures; Publication; Research Library/Archives

COLLECTIONS: [1890-1960] County artifacts

HOURS: May-Sept Alternate Sa/Su 1-4

ADMISSION: $1, Children $0.50

BURLINGTON

2675
Des Moines County Genealogical Society
[PO Box 493, 52601-0493]; dmcgs@yahoo.com; www.geocities.com/heartland/valley/9825/; (c) Des Moines

Private non-profit/ 1972/ members: 190/publication: *Des Moines County Genealogical Society Quarterly*

GENEALOGICAL SOCIETY: Promotes the study of genealogy and maintains a collection of research materials at the Burlington public library.

PROGRAMS: Lectures; Publication; Research Library/Archives

COLLECTIONS: [1840-present] Collection focuses on SE Iowa and SE Des Moines County and encompasses books, microfilm, microfiche, and some CDs.

HOURS: Yr Winter M-Sa M-Th 9-9, F-Sa 9-5; Summer M-Th 9-8

2676
Des Moines County Historical Society
1616 Dill St, 52601-4008; (p) (319) 753-2449; (f) (319) 753-2449; (c) Des Moines

Private non-profit/ 1942/ Board of Directors/ staff: 2(p); 140(v)/ members: 368/publication: *DMCHS Newsletter*

HISTORIC SITE; HISTORICAL SOCIETY; HOUSE MUSEUM: Operates three museums dedicated to the preservation of county history: The Apple Trees, The Phelps House, and The Hawkeye Log Cabin.

PROGRAMS: Exhibits; Guided Tours; Lectures; Publication

COLLECTIONS: [Early 1800s-mid 1900s] Artifacts associated with Des Moines County and IA, a doll collection, and a costume collection.

HOURS: Office: Yr M-F 9-12; Apple Trees Museum: May-Oct W, Su 1:30-4:30

ADMISSION: $2, Children $1; Phelps House; Others Free

2677
Hawkeye Log Cabin Museum
2915 S Main St, 52601 [c/o Des Moines County Hist Soc, 1616 Dill St, 52601]; (p) (319) 753-2449, (319) 753-5981

Private non-profit/ Des Moines County Historical Society

HOUSE MUSEUM

HOURS: May-Oct W, Su 1:30-4:30

2678
Phelps House
521 Columbia St, 52601 [c/o Des Moines County Hist Soc, 1616 Dill St, 52601]; (p) (319) 753-2449, (319) 753-5880

Private non-profit/ 1851/ Des Moines County Historical Society/ staff: 2(p)

HOUSE MUSEUM

COLLECTIONS: [1830s -1970s] House, furniture and other household items from the Rorer, Garrett, & Phelps families.

HOURS: May-Oct Sa-Su 1:30-4:30

CARROLL

2679
Carroll County Historical Society
123 E 6th, 51401 [704 W 15th, 51401-1301]; (p) (712) 792-3933; (c) Carroll

Private non-profit/ 1967/ staff: 63(v)/ members: 85

HISTORIC PRESERVATION AGENCY; HISTORICAL SOCIETY; HISTORY MUSEUM; HOUSE MUSEUM; LIVING HISTORY/OUTDOOR MUSEUM: Gathers, preserves, displays, and presents the history of Carroll County.

PROGRAMS: Annual Meeting; Community Outreach; Exhibits; Facility Rental; Family Programs; Festivals; Film/Video; Guided Tours; Lectures; Living History; Publication; Research Library/Archives

COLLECTIONS: [1850s-present] Military articles from Civil War to Desert Storm; period fashions, household items, toys, farm machinery, and tools.

HOURS: Yr Daily 1-4

CEDAR FALLS

2680
Cedar Falls Historical Society
308 W 3rd, 50613 [303 Franklin St, 50613]; (p) (319) 266-5149; (f) (319) 268-1812; www.its-ps.uni.edu:205; (c) Black Hawk

Private non-profit/ 1962/ staff: 2(f); 1(p); 275(v)/ members: 700/publication: *Quarterly Newsletter*

HISTORICAL SOCIETY; HOUSE MUSEUM: Operates five museums: Victorian Home, Ice House Museum, Bennington Township Schoolhouse #5, The George Wyth House, and Viking Pump Museum; preserves local, county, and state history.

PROGRAMS: Community Outreach; Exhibits; Family Programs; Garden Tours; Guided Tours; Interpretation; Lectures; Publication; Research Library/Archives; School-Based Curriculum

COLLECTIONS: [1850-1950] Period furnishings, decorative arts, household items, ice harvesting equip, horse drawn transportation items, agricultural collection, historic photographs, regional archives, and the William J. Lenoir model train collection.

HOURS: Victorian Home: Yr W-Sa 10-4, Su 1-4; Wyth House: May-Dec 2-4; Other Museums: May-Oct W, Sa-Su 20-4:30

ADMISSION: No charge

2681
University of Northern Iowa Museums Collections
3219 Hudson Rd, 50614 [University of Northern Iowa, 50614-0199]; (p) (319) 273-2188; (f) (319) 273-6924; sue.grosboll@uni.edu;

www.uni.edu/museum; (c) Black Hawk

State/ 1892/ Univ of Northern IA/ staff: 3(f); 10(p); 65(v)/ members: 160

HISTORY MUSEUM: Collects, preserves, exhibits, and interprets artifacts related to the history of early education in IA in addition to international materials related to biology, anthropology, and geology.

PROGRAMS: Annual Meeting; Community Outreach; Concerts; Exhibits; Facility Rental; Family Programs; Festivals; Film/Video; Guided Tours; Interpretation; Lectures; School-Based Curriculum

COLLECTIONS: [1850-present] 15,000 historical artifacts (rural education, university history, military, exchange mediums, photographs, costumes, state history); 5,900 anthropological artifacts, 9,500 archaeological artifacts, 18,000 biological specimens, and 19,100 geological specimens.

HOURS: Yr M-F 9-4:30, Sa-Su 1-4 and by appt

ADMISSION: No charge

CEDAR RAPIDS

2682
African American Heritage Foundation of Iowa
1035 3rd Ave, SE, 52406 [PO Box 2756, 52406]; (p) (319) 298-9772; (f) (319) 399-1805; valjoe@aol.com; (c) Linn

Private non-profit/ 1993/ staff: 1(f); 4(p); 25(v)/ members: 225/publication: *African American Pride*

HISTORY MUSEUM; RESEARCH CENTER: Interprets the history of African American Iowans.

PROGRAMS: Exhibits; Facility Rental; Interpretation; Lectures; Publication; Research Library/Archives; School-Based Curriculum

COLLECTIONS: [1848-present]

HOURS: Yr M-F 8-5

2683
Brucemore, Inc.
2160 Linden Dr, SE, 52403; (p) (319) 362-7375; (f) (319) 362-9418; mail@brucemore.org; www.brucemore.org; (c) Linn

Private non-profit/ 1981/ National Trust For Historic Preservation/ staff: 12(f); 8(p); 140(v)/ members: 600/publication: *Brucemore Newsletter; The Story of Brucemore*

CULTURAL CENTER; GARDEN; HISTORIC SITE; HOUSE MUSEUM: An 1886 Queen Anne mansion on park-like estate.

PROGRAMS: Concerts; Exhibits; Facility Rental; Festivals; Garden Tours; Guided Tours; Interpretation; Lectures; Publication; Research Library/Archives; School-Based Curriculum; Theatre

COLLECTIONS: [Early 20th c] Artifacts-furniture, art, and other furnishings; archival material-photographs, home movies, diaries, correspondence, and other documents; historical structures; and landscape features.

HOURS: Feb-Dec T-Sa 10-3, Su 12-3

ADMISSION: $5, Student $2

2684
History Center
615 First Ave SE, 52401; (p) (319) 362-1501;
(f) (319) 362-6790; www.historycenter.org; (c)
Linn

Private non-profit/ 1969/ Linn County Historical Society/ staff: 6(f); 2(p); 85(v)/ members:
900

HISTORY MUSEUM: Collects, preserves, and
interprets local history.

PROGRAMS: Annual Meeting; Community
Outreach; Concerts; Elder's Programs; Ex-
hibits; Facility Rental; Family Programs; Guid-
ed Tours; Interpretation; Lectures; Publication;
Research Library/Archives; School-Based
Curriculum

COLLECTIONS: [Mid-19th c] 10,000 archival
documents, 500 textiles, local artifacts, business and agricultural history artifacts and
archives, photographic records, and city directories.

HOURS: Yr T-W, F-Sa 10-4, Th 10-8, Su 12-4

2685
Iowa Masonic Library and Museums
913 First Ave SE, 52406 [PO Box 279,
52406-0279]; (p) (319) 365-1438; (f) (319)
365-1439; Grand_Lodge_IA@msn.com;
www.freemasonry.org/gl.ia; (c) Linn

Private non-profit/ 1845/ Grand Lodge of Iowa,
AF and AM/ staff: 1(f); 10(v)

LIBRARY AND/OR ARCHIVES

PROGRAMS: Exhibits; Lectures; Research Li-
brary/Archives

COLLECTIONS: [19th-20th c] Items of local
and regional interest (Masonic and general),
articles related to Native American, military,
and pioneer history. Volumes on Freemasonry,
IA history, religion, and special collections on '
Waite, Abraham Lincoln, and Robert Burns.

HOURS: Yr M-F 8-12, 1-5

2686
**National Czech and Slovak Museum
and Library**
30 16th Ave SW, 52240; (p) (319) 362-8500;
(f) (319) 363-2209; clangel@ncsml.org;
www.ncsml.org

Private non-profit/ 1974/ staff: 10(f); 2(p);
150(v)/ members: 1000/publication: *Slovo
Magazine*

HISTORY MUSEUM: Preserves and interpretes the history and culture of Czechs and
Slovaks in the Old World and in the US.

PROGRAMS: Annual Meeting; Community
Outreach; Concerts; Exhibits; Facility Rental;
Family Programs; Film/Video; Guided Tours;
Lectures; Publication; Research Library/
Archives; School-Based Curriculum

COLLECTIONS: [18th c-present] Fine and folk
art, archives, maps, glass, and ceramics; immigrant items, military objects, and a large textile collection.

HOURS: Yr T-Sa 9:30-4, Su 12-4

2687
Ushers Ferry Historic Village
5925 Seminole Valley Tr NE, 52411; (p) (319)
286-5763; (f) (319) 286-5764; (c) Linn

City/ 1975/ staff: 3(f); 16(p); 55(v)

LIVING HISTORY/OUTDOOR MUSEUM: Recreation of a small Iowa town at the turn of the
19th and 20th centuries.

PROGRAMS: Community Outreach; Concerts; Exhibits; Facility Rental; Family Programs; Festivals; Garden Tours; Guided Tours;
Interpretation; Lectures; Living History; Reenactments; Research Library/Archives; School-
Based Curriculum; Theatre

COLLECTIONS: [1890-1910] Artifacts from
homes, businesses, schools, churches, social
functions, and Usher family artifacts; exhibits
of Tokheim pumps and measuring devices.

HOURS: Apr-Dec 1-4

ADMISSION: $3, Children $2

CHARITON

2688
Lucas County Historical Society
217 N 17th, 50049 [Rt 1 Box 10, 50049]; (p)
(515) 774-4467; (c) Lucas

County/ 1965/ staff: 16(v)/ members: 202

HISTORICAL SOCIETY: Operates a county
historical museum, a schoolhouse, barn machine shed, and log cabin.

PROGRAMS: Annual Meeting; Exhibits; Festivals; Guided Tours; Living History

HOURS: June-Sept Su, W 1:30-4:30

CHARLES CITY

2689
**Floyd County Historical Society
Museum**
500 Gilbert St, 50616; (p) (515) 228-1099; (f)
(515) 228-1157; (c) Floyd

Private non-profit/ 1953/ staff: 2(f); 1(p); 10(v)/
members: 400/publication: *Past Harvests,
Floyd County Heritage*

HISTORICAL SOCIETY; HISTORY MUSEUM:
Interprets county history including the history
of the Hart-Parr and Oliver Company, a former
tractor manufacturer.

PROGRAMS: Annual Meeting; Community
Outreach; Exhibits; Guided Tours; Publication;
Research Library/Archives

COLLECTIONS: [1850-present] Hart-Parr and
Oliver Company records, tractors, pharmaceutical items from the late 19th c, photos, and
sales literature.

HOURS: Yr M-F 9-4:30, May-Sept + Sa 1-4

ADMISSION: $2, Student $1, Children $0.25

CHEROKEE

2690
Sanford Museum and Planetarium
117 E Willow St, 51012; (p) (712) 225-3922;
sanford@cherokee.k12.ia.us; www.chero
kee.k12.ia.us/mainfolder/sanford/sanhome;
(c) Cherokee

Private non-profit/ 1951/ Tiel Sanford Memorial Trust Fund/ staff: 3(f); 4(p); 12(v)/ members:
175/publication: *NWIAS Newsletter*

HISTORY MUSEUM: Interprets the history of

NW Iowa's people and its skies through exhibits, classes, and public programs.

PROGRAMS: Community Outreach; Exhibits;
Family Programs; Guided Tours; Interpretation;
Lectures; Publication; School-Based Curricu-
lum

COLLECTIONS: [1850s-1920s] NW Iowa Archaeology, history, and paleontology.

HOURS: Yr M-F 9-5, Sa-Su 12-5

ADMISSION: No charge

CLARINDA

2691
Glenn Miller Birthplace
107 E Main, 51632 [PO Box 61, 51632]; (p)
(712) 542-2461

CLERMONT

2692
Clermont Historical Society
505 Larrabee, 52135 [PO Box 103, 52135];
(p) (319) 423-5561; (f) (319) 422-3854; (c)
Fayette

Private non-profit/ 1967/ staff: 12(v)/ members:
24

HISTORIC SITE; HISTORICAL SOCIETY:
Preserves historic sites, collections, memorabilia, and research material.

PROGRAMS: Annual Meeting; Concerts; Exhibits; Family Programs; Guided Tours; Interpretation; School-Based Curriculum

COLLECTIONS: Military, school, Native American, and medical artifacts.

HOURS: Feb, Apr-Oct Daily 8-5

2693
Montauk
26223 Harding Rd, 52135 [PO Box 272,
52135]; (p) (319) 423-7173; (f) (319) 423-
7378; nwest@max.state.ia.us; (c) Fayette

State/ State Historical Society of Iowa/ staff:
2(f); 6(p); 2(v)

HISTORIC SITE; HISTORICAL SOCIETY;
HOUSE MUSEUM: Maintains home of IA's
12th governor.

PROGRAMS: Interpretation

COLLECTIONS: [1874-1930s] Original furnishings and family's personal collection of
world art, music, and books.

HOURS: May-Oct Daily 12-4

ADMISSION: No charge

CLINTON

2694
Clinton County Historical Society
601 S 1st St, 52732 [PO Box 3135, 52732];
(p) (319) 242-1201, (319) 243-3464; (c)
Clinton

Private non-profit/ 1965/ staff: 19(v)/ members: 150

GENEALOGICAL SOCIETY; HISTORIC
PRESERVATION AGENCY: Preserves and
displays artifacts.

PROGRAMS: Annual Meeting; Community Outreach; Exhibits; Family Programs; Festivals; Guided Tours; Lectures; Living History

COLLECTIONS: [Prehistory-present] Arrow heads, farm machinery, 1900 and 1924 kitchens, genealogy, quilts, dresses, and a hand pump fire engine.

2695
Clinton Women's Club
420 Fifth Ave S, 52732; (p) (319) 242-8556, (319) 242-7895; (f) (319) 242-0267

1883/ staff: 1(p); 30(v)

Home of Congressman George M. Curtis.

COLLECTIONS: Original fireplaces; furniture, kitchen, tin ceiling in dining room; many stained glass windows.

HOURS: May-Aug

COGGON

2696
Coggon Community Historical Society
126 E Main St, 52218 [2014 Coggon Rd, 52218]; (p) (319) 435-2050; (c) Linn

Private non-profit/ 1981/ staff: 10(v)/ members: 30

HISTORIC PRESERVATION AGENCY; HISTORICAL SOCIETY; HISTORY MUSEUM: Restored an old hotel, displays local items, provides genealogical assistance.

PROGRAMS: Annual Meeting; Community Outreach; Exhibits; Guided Tours

COLLECTIONS: [1800s-1920s] Period furniture, calendars, clothing, school artifacts, microfilm, clippings, and other local items.

HOURS: By appt

ADMISSION: No charge/Donations

CORALVILLE

2697
Johnson County Historical Society
310 Fifth St, 52241 [PO Box 5081, 52241]; (p) (319) 351-5738; (f) (319) 351-5310; (c) Johnson

Private non-profit/ 1976/ staff: 2(f); 2(p); 125(v)/ members: 850

HISTORICAL SOCIETY; HOUSE MUSEUM: Collects, interprets, teaches, and publishes local history; operates the Heritage Museum, manages Plum Grove Historic Home, and interprets the county's first asylum.

PROGRAMS: Annual Meeting; Community Outreach; Exhibits; Family Programs; Garden Tours; Guided Tours; Interpretation; Lectures; Living History

HOURS: Yr W-Sa 1-5, Su 1-4

ADMISSION: No charge

CORNING

2698
Adams County Centurama Historical Society
1000 Benton, 50841 [1203 Davis Ave, 50841]; (p) (515) 322-3241; (c) Adams

County/ staff: 20(v)/ members: 150

HISTORICAL SOCIETY: Acquires and preserves items related to county history.

PROGRAMS: Annual Meeting; Guided Tours

COLLECTIONS: [1850-present] Military items, clothing, dishes, quilts, flags, pictures, books, advertising, and medical items.

HOURS: May-Sept Su 1-4

CORRECTIONVILLE

2699
Rural Woodbury County Historical Society
Main St, 51016; (p) (712) 372-4341; (c) Woodbury

Private non-profit/ staff: 11(f); 12(v)/ members: 60

HISTORIC SITE; HISTORICAL SOCIETY; HISTORY MUSEUM: Restores Copeland Park and the Old Merchant State Bank, and preserves local history.

PROGRAMS: Annual Meeting; Community Outreach; Exhibits; Facility Rental; Festivals

COLLECTIONS: Photographs, school records, WWII, and Norman E. Lee.

HOURS: May-Aug Sa 10-2, Su 2-4

ADMISSION: Donations

CORYDON

2700
Wayne County Historical Society/Prairie Trails Museum
Hwy 2 East, 50060 [PO Box 104, 50060]; (p) (515) 872-2211; (f) (515) 872-2664; (c) Wayne

Private non-profit/ 1942/ staff: 1(f); 1(p); 30(v)/ members: 800/publication: *The Prarie Trails Newsletter*

HISTORICAL SOCIETY; HISTORY MUSEUM: Collects, preserves, and exhibits items related to county history.

PROGRAMS: Annual Meeting; Community Outreach; Exhibits; Guided Tours; Interpretation; Publication; Research Library/Archives

COLLECTIONS: [1850-1950] Farm implements, tools, period clothing, quilts, and other items representative of rural life.

HOURS: June-Aug M-Sa 10-5, Su 1-5; Apr-May, Sept-Oct Daily 1-5

ADMISSION: $3, Student $1, Children $0.50

COUNCIL BLUFFS

2701
Historic General Dodge House
621 3rd St, 51503; (p) (712) 322-2406; (c) Pottawattamie

Joint/ 1963/ City; Private non-profit/ staff: 2(f); 12(p); 50(v)/ members: 376

HISTORIC SITE; HOUSE MUSEUM: Preserves, restores, maintains and manages, the historic house, grounds, and collection associated with Gen. Grenville M. Dodge, chief engineer Union Pacific RR and Civil War general.

PROGRAMS: Exhibits; Facility Rental; Garden Tours; Guided Tours; Interpretation

COLLECTIONS: [1869-1916] Personal furnishings, memorabilia, pressed glass collection, clothing, period furniture, and textiles.

HOURS: Feb-Dec T-Sa 10-5, Su 1-5

2702
Historical Society of Pottawattamie County
1512 S Main St, 05102 [PO Box 2, 5102-0002]; (p) (712) 323-5182, (712) 323-2509; (c) Pottawattamie

Private non-profit/ 1961/ staff: 8(p); 30(v)/ members: 250

HISTORIC SITE; HISTORICAL SOCIETY; HISTORY MUSEUM: Operates the former 1899 Rock Island Railroad Depot and the former Squirrel Cage style county jail.

PROGRAMS: Annual Meeting; Community Outreach; Exhibits; Facility Rental; Family Programs; Film/Video; Lectures; Research Library/Archives

COLLECTIONS: [1850s-present] Artifacts and memorabilia of local history; county jail and railroad items, 2 steam engines, lounge car, railway post office railcar, cabooses.

HOURS: Call for hours

ADMISSION: $3, Children $1.50

2703
Kanesville Tabernacle Visitor Center
222 E Broadway, 51503-4407; (p) (402) 453-9372; (f) (402) 453-1538; (c) Pottawattamie

Private non-profit/ 1996/ The Church of Jesus Chirst of Latter- Day Saints/ staff: 3(p); 16(v)

Helps visitors experience Mormon Pioneer spirit as they traveled from Nauvoo, Illinois, to the Salt Lake Valley with interactive displays, paintings, statues and artifacts.

PROGRAMS: Concerts; Elder's Programs; Exhibits; Family Programs; Film/Video; Guided Tours; Interpretation; Lectures; Reenactments; Research Library/Archives; Theatre

COLLECTIONS: [1840-1890] Mormon Battalion Rosters (5 Companies) volunteer unit attached to the Army of the West, Mexican War 1846. Mormon pioneers artifacts, hand crafts, covered wagon, hand carved ox yokes, paintings.

HOURS: Yr Apr-Sept Daily 9-7; Oct-Mar Daily 10-5

ADMISSION: No charge

2704
Western Historic Trails Center
3434 Richard Downing Ave, 51501; (p) (912) 366-4900; (f) (912) 366-5080; www.iowahistory.org/sites/western_trails/western_trails.html; (c) Pottawattamie

State/ 1997/ State Historical Society of Iowa/ staff: 4(f); 2(p); 25(v)

HISTORY MUSEUM: Interprets the experience of the Lewis and Clark, Oregon, Mormon, and California Trails through exhibits, films, maps, and sculpture.

PROGRAMS: Exhibits; Guided Tours; Interpretation; Lectures; Reenactments

COLLECTIONS: Interpretative panels and sculptures.

CRESCO

2705
Howard County Historical Society
324 4th Ave W, 52136 [722 Gillette Ave, 52136]; (p) (319) 547-3434, (800) 373-6293;

vlhaak@stbek.net; (c) Howard

Joint/ 1924/ County; Private non-profit/ staff: 70(v)/ members: 125

HISTORIC SITE; HISTORICAL SOCIETY; HISTORY MUSEUM; HOUSE MUSEUM; LIBRARY AND/OR ARCHIVES; RESEARCH CENTER: Preserves the history, lifestyle, and artifacts of county residents from the late 18th and early 19th c. Museum housed in 1880 Kellow House.

PROGRAMS: Annual Meeting; Community Outreach; Concerts; Exhibits; Facility Rental; Family Programs; Festivals; Guided Tours; Interpretation; Lectures; Living History; Publication; Reenactments; Research Library/ Archives; School-Based Curriculum

COLLECTIONS: [Late Victorian, early 19th c] Furnished Victorian house, farming, business, and domestic artifacts.

HOURS: June-Aug Sa-Su 1-5

ADMISSION: $1, Children $0.50

CRESTON

2706
Union County Historical Society
1101 N Vine, 50801; (p) (515) 782-8159; (c) Union

County, non-profit/ 1966/ staff: 3(p); 15(v)/ members: 25

GENEALOGICAL SOCIETY; HISTORICAL SOCIETY; HISTORY MUSEUM; RESEARCH CENTER: Preserves the history of Union County.

PROGRAMS: Annual Meeting; Community Outreach; Concerts; Exhibits; Facility Rental; Family Programs; Festivals; Guided Tours; Interpretation; Lectures; Living History; Publication; Research Library/Archives; School-Based Curriculum

COLLECTIONS: [Early 1800s-early 1900s]

HOURS: June-Aug Daily 1-5

ADMISSION: No charge

DAKOTA CITY

2707
Humboldt County Historical Museum
905 1st Ave N, 50548; (p) (515) 332-5280; (c) Humboldt

1879/ Humboldt County Historical Society
Museum located in 1879 house.

COLLECTIONS: [1800s] 1879 brick house, log cabin, barn, jail.

HOURS: May-Sept M-T, Th-Sa 10-4:30, Su 1:30-4:30

DAVENPORT

2708
Antoine Le Claire House Historical Interpretive Center
630 E 7 St, 52801 [226 W 4 St, 52801]; (p) (319) 326-7756; (c) Scott

City/ 1976/ members: 100

HISTORIC SITE; HISTORY MUSEUM; HOUSE MUSEUM

PROGRAMS: Community Outreach; Facility Rental; Guided Tours; Interpretation; Lectures;

Living History

COLLECTIONS: [1815-present] Slide programs: frontier opening, fur trade, steamboating, log rafting, railroading, Civil War, archaeology, historic preservation, and renovation techniques.

2709
Palmer Foundation for Chiropractic History
1000 Brady St, 52803; (p) (319) 884-5404; (f) (319) 884-5616; callender_a@palmer.edu; (c) Scott

Private non-profit/ 1990/ staff: 2(f)

HISTORIC SITE; HOUSE MUSEUM: Preserves chiropractic history.

PROGRAMS: Exhibits; Guided Tours; Lectures; Research Library/Archives

COLLECTIONS: Chiropractic artifacts, including the historic home of B.J. Palmer and his osteological collection.

2710
Putnam Museum of History and Natural Science
1717 W 12th St, 52804; (p) (319) 324-1933; (f) (319) 324-6638; museum@putnam.org; www.putnam.org; (c) Scott

Private non-profit/ 1867/ staff: 26(f); 5(p); 190(v)/ members: 1703/publication: *Putnam Museum MuseLetter; Watching the River, Walking the Land: A Natural History of eastern Iowa and western Illinois*

HISTORY MUSEUM: Collects and preserves the cultural and natural heritage of eastern IA and western IL.

PROGRAMS: Community Outreach; Concerts; Elder's Programs; Exhibits; Facility Rental; Family Programs; Festivals; Film/ Video; Guided Tours; Interpretation; Lectures; Publication; Research Library/Archives; School-Based Curriculum; Theatre

COLLECTIONS: [300 BC-present] 87,000 archival documents and photographs, 25,200 natural science specimens, 9,000 earth science specimens, 10,400 archaeology artifacts, 4,600 ethnology artifacts.

HOURS: Yr T-F 9-5, Sa 10-5, Su 12-5

ADMISSION: $4, Children $2, Seniors $3

2711
Scott County Historic Preservation Society
[PO Box 2331, 52809]; (p) (319) 324-0257; (c) Scott

Private non-profit/ 1968/ members: 125

HISTORIC PRESERVATION AGENCY

PROGRAMS: Annual Meeting; Community Outreach; Elder's Programs; Exhibits; Guided Tours; Lectures; School-Based Curriculum

2712
Scott County Historical Society
Utica Ridge Rd @Blackhawk Trail, 52805 [PO Box 565, 52805-0565]; (p) (319) 326-1229; (f) (319) 332-5986; (c) Scott

1969/ staff: 30(v)/ members: 72

HISTORICAL SOCIETY; HISTORY MUSEUM

PROGRAMS: Annual Meeting; Community Outreach; Elder's Programs; Exhibits; Facility

Rental; Family Programs; Guided Tours; Interpretation; Lectures; Research Library/ Archives; School-Based Curriculum

COLLECTIONS: Pictures, books, articles, letters, Summit Cemetery Information.

HOURS: Yr

2713
Scott County Iowa Genealogical Society
321 Main St, 52808 [PO Box 3132, 52808-3132]; (p) (319) 326-7832; (f) (319) 326-7809; gemayhew@revealed.net; www.ancestry.com/ societyhall; (c) Scott

Private non-profit/ 1973/ members: 212/publication: *Iowan*

GENEALOGICAL SOCIETY: Collects and preserves the records of ancestors, founders, and early settlers of the county; aids individuals in their genealogical pursuits.

PROGRAMS: Annual Meeting; Publication; Research Library/Archives

COLLECTIONS: [1880-present] Books, maps, microfilm, and microfiche concentrates on vital records, cemetery entries, and census record for Scott County.

DECORAH

2714
Porter House Museum
401 W Broadway St, 52101; (p) (563) 382-8465, (563) 382-1867; (c) Winneshiek

1867

Italian Tuscan Villa built of native brick in 1867.

HOURS: Mem Day-Labor Day Daily 1-5; Labor Day-Mem Day Sa-Su 1-5; or by appt

ADMISSION: Varies

2715
Vesterheim Norwegian-American Museum
523 W Water St, 52101 [PO Box 379, 52101-0379]; (p) (563) 382-9681; (f) (563) 382-8828; vesterheim@vesterheim.org; www.vesterheim.org; (c) Winneshiek

Private non-profit/ 1877/ Board of Trustees/ staff: 19(f); 41(p); 668(v)/ members: 7255/publication: *Vesterheim News*

HISTORY MUSEUM; HOUSE MUSEUM; RESEARCH CENTER: Collects, preserves, and exhibits materials documenting the life and culture of Norwegians in America. 16 properties included in main complex and 2 outside of town.

PROGRAMS: Annual Meeting; Community Outreach; Elder's Programs; Exhibits; Facility Rental; Family Programs; Festivals; Guided Tours; Lectures; Publication; Research Library/Archives

COLLECTIONS: [1860s-1920s] 21,000 museum artifacts, including fine, decorative, and folk arts, the tools and machinery of early agriculture, lumbering, and other immigrant industries; 11,000 volumes; and 17,000 photos and archival documents.

HOURS: Yr Daily May 1-Oct 31 9-5; Nov 1-Apr 30 10-4

ADMISSION: $5, Student $3; Group rates

DENISON

2716
Crawford County Historical Society
1428 1st Ave N, 51442 [2134 Rocky Run, 51442]; (p) (712) 263-2693; (c) Crawford

Private non-profit/ 1966/ staff: 15(v)/ members: 269

HISTORICAL SOCIETY; HISTORY MUSEUM: Preserves artifacts related to Crawford County.

PROGRAMS: Annual Meeting; Community Outreach; Concerts; Exhibits; Facility Rental; Family Programs; Guided Tours; Lectures; Publication; School-Based Curriculum

COLLECTIONS: [1830-1998] Period clothing; Civil War guns; tins, jars, crocks for items in a General Store; rocks, bones, tools, art work

HOURS: May-Aug W-Th, Su 1-4

ADMISSION: $2

DES MOINES

2717
Flynn Mansion at Living History Farms
2600 NW 111th St, 50322; (p) (515) 278-5286, (515) 278-2400; (f) (515) 278-9808; www.lhf.org

1870/ staff: 1(f); 2(p); 22(v)

HOUSE MUSEUM: Home of successful entrepreneur Martin Flynn and his family.

COLLECTIONS: [1875] Furniture ranging from Empire through Renaissanse Revival to early Eastlake; textile collection.

HOURS: May-Oct

2718
Hoyt Sherman Place
501 Woodland, 50309; (p) (515) 244-0507; (f) (515) 237-3582

1877/ staff: 5(f); 15(p); 200(v)

HOUSE MUSEUM:Home of prominent pioneer businessman Hoyt Sherman, brother of Civil War general William Tecumseh Sherman.

COLLECTIONS: [Late 1800s] Furniture; paintings; decorative arts; statuary; stained glass.

HOURS: Yr

2719
Iowa Genealogical Society
6000 Douglas Ave, Ste 145, 50322 [PO Box 7735, 50322-7735]; (p) (515) 276-0287; igs@iowagenealogy.org; www.iowagenealogy.org; (c) Polk

Private non-profit/ 1965/ staff: 3(p); 50(v)/ members: 2700/publication: *Hawkeye Heritage and IGS Newsletter*

GENEALOGICAL SOCIETY: Preserves, records, and promotes the study of family history; research library, affiliated with 90 county chapters.

PROGRAMS: Annual Meeting; Lectures; Publication; Research Library/Archives

COLLECTIONS: [1790-1920] Federal and State census records, immigration, IA vital records, cemetery records, county histories, military records, personal family histories, and German and Irish resources.

HOURS: Yr M, F-Sa 10-4, T-Th

2720
Polk County Historical Society
SW 1st & Elm St, 50312 [317 SW 42nd St, 50312]; (p) (515) 255-6657; (c) Polk

Private non-profit/ 1938/ Board of Directors/ staff: 7(v)/ members: 150/publication: *Newsletter*

HISTORIC SITE; HISTORICAL SOCIETY; HISTORY MUSEUM; HOUSE MUSEUM; TRIBAL MUSEUM: Collects information pertaining to the history of Polk County and Des Moines; offers public programs related to local history.

PROGRAMS: Annual Meeting; Community Outreach; Exhibits; Facility Rental; Family Programs; Festivals; Film/Video; Garden Tours; Guided Tours; Interpretation; Lectures; Publication; Research Library/Archives

COLLECTIONS: [Pioneer-present] Newsletters from 1962, books, photos, and artifacts.

HOURS: By Appt

2721
Salisbury House Foundation
4025 Tonawanda Dr, 50312; (p) (515) 274-1777; salhouse@dwx.com; www.salisburyhouse.org; (c) Polk

Private non-profit/ 1993/ staff: 4(f); 1(p); 30(v)

HOUSE MUSEUM: Restores, preserves, and safeguards the Salisbury House.

PROGRAMS: Concerts; Exhibits; Facility Rental; Family Programs; Festivals; Guided Tours; Lectures; Living History; Publication; School-Based Curriculum; Theatre

COLLECTIONS: [Prehistory-1940] A 42 room, Tudor style mansion featuring 16th c English oak, flintwork, and rafters; original art, historic furnishings, tapestries, and rare books.

HOURS: Yr M-F

ADMISSION: $5

2722
State Historical Society of Iowa, Iowa Historical Building
600 E Locust St, 50319; (p) (515) 281-6412; (f) (515) 282-0502; www.iowahistory.org; (c) Polk

State/ 1856/ staff: 46(f); 12(p); 150(v)/ members: 1550/publication: *Annals of Iowa; Iowa Heritage Illustrated; and others*

HISTORIC PRESERVATION AGENCY; HISTORICAL SOCIETY; HISTORY MUSEUM; LIBRARY AND/OR ARCHIVES: Main headquarters for the State Historical Society of Iowa including the state museum, state archives and records program, research library, community programs, and SHPO.

PROGRAMS: Annual Meeting; Community Outreach; Concerts; Exhibits; Facility Rental; Family Programs; Festivals; Guided Tours; Interpretation; Lectures; Publication; Research Library/Archives; School-Based Curriculum; Theatre

COLLECTIONS: [19th-20th c] 26,500 linear feet of state records and private manuscripts, 500,000 photos, 70,000 volumes in the library, and 25,000 reels of microfilm.

HOURS: Yr Museum: T-Sa 9-4:30, Su 12-4:30; Library T-Sa 9-4:30

ADMISSION: No charge

2723
Terrace Hill, Iowa's Governor's Residence and Museum
2300 Grand Ave, 50312; (p) (515) 281-3604; (f) (515) 281-7267; (c) Polk

State/ 1971/ Terrace Hill Commission/ staff: 5(f); 45(v)

HOUSE MUSEUM: Maintains the governor's mansion, completed in 1869.

PROGRAMS: Exhibits; Guided Tours

COLLECTIONS: [1869-1900] Second Empire architectural style mansion with period furnishings, J.H. Belter parlor furniture.

HOURS: Mar-Dec T-Sa 10-2

ADMISSION: $5, Children $2

DEWITT

2724
Central Community Historical Society
628 6th Ave, 52742 [2503 340th Ave, 52742]; (p) (319) 659-3686; (c) Clinton

Private non-profit/ 1977/ staff: 25(v)/ members: 120

GENEALOGICAL SOCIETY; HISTORICAL SOCIETY: Preserves county genealogy and artifacts.

PROGRAMS: Annual Meeting; Exhibits; Guided Tours

COLLECTIONS: [1850-present] Genealogy, farm machinery, fire trucks, camera equipment, and survey equipment; period furniture, clothes, photos, arrowheads, army items, and fancy work and type telephones; school house and kitchen displays.

HOURS: Su 1-4:30

ADMISSION: Donations accepted

DEXTER

2725
Dexter Historical Museum
318 Marshall St, 50070; (p) (515) 789-4550; (c) Dallas

City/ staff: 5(v)

HISTORY MUSEUM

COLLECTIONS: Blacksmith shop.

ADMISSION: Donations accepted

DOW CITY

2726
Dow House Historic Site
S Prince St, 51528 [PO Box, 51528]; (p) (712) 674-3734, (712) 263-2693; (c) Crawford

County/ 1969/ Conservation Board/ staff: 3(f); 3(p); 60(v)

HISTORIC SITE: Preserves the Dow House, late 19th c home of a prosperous farmer and civic leader.

PROGRAMS: Guided Tours; Living History; Publication; School-Based Curriculum

COLLECTIONS: [1865-1900] Period furnishings and household items.

HOURS: W-Su 1-5

ADMISSION: $1, Children $0.50

DUBUQUE

2727
Dubuque County Historical Society/Mississippi River Museum
400 E Third St, 52004 [PO Box 266, 52004-0266]; (p) (319) 557-9545; (f) (319) 583-1241; rivermuse@mwci.net; www.mississippiriver museum.com; (c) Dubuque

Private non-profit/ 1950/ staff: 1(f); 40(p); 100(v)/ members: 495

HISTORICAL SOCIETY; HISTORY MUSEUM: Explores, collects, preserves, and interprets history of Dubuque County, the MS river, and other rivers of the US. Operates Mississippi River Museum, National Rivers Hall of Fame, and Mathias Ham House Historic Site.

PROGRAMS: Annual Meeting; Community Outreach; Concerts; Exhibits; Facility Rental; Family Programs; Festivals; Film/Video; Guided Tours; Interpretation; Lectures; Living History; Publication; Research Library/Archives; School-Based Curriculum

COLLECTIONS: [1600-1999] Historic house furnishings, records and regional artifacts.

HOURS: Yr Daily 10-5:30

ADMISSION: $6, Children $3; Under 5 free

2728
Dubuque County-Key City Genealogical Society
1155 Locust St, 52004 [PO Box 13, 52004-013]; dckcgs@hotmail.com; www.rootsweb.com/~iadckgs/; (c) Dubuque

Private non-profit/ 1976/ staff: 11(v)/ members: 175

GENEALOGICAL SOCIETY; LIBRARY AND/OR ARCHIVES; RESEARCH CENTER: Collecst, preserves, and makes available genealogical materials.

PROGRAMS: Annual Meeting; Exhibits; Publication; Research Library/Archives

COLLECTIONS: Family histories; county, state, national genealogy materials.

HOURS: Yr Th 6-8,

2729
Mathias Ham House Historic Site
2241 Lincoln Ave, 52004 [PO Box 266, 52004-0266]; (p) (319) 557-9545; (f) (319) 583-1241; rivermus@mwci.net; (c) Dubuque

Private non-profit/ 1964/ staff: 1(f); 8(p); 100(v)/ members: 555

HISTORIC SITE; HOUSE MUSEUM: Collects, preserves, and interprets the history of the diverse people and culture of Dubuque County, the history of Mathias Ham, and his Victorian home.

PROGRAMS: Annual Meeting; Community Outreach; Concerts; Elder's Programs; Exhibits; Family Programs; Festivals; Film/Video; Guided Tours; Interpretation; Living History; Publication; School-Based Curriculum

COLLECTIONS: [1850-1900] Domestic, utili-

tarian, and decorative arts; clothing, toys, and quilts.

HOURS: May-Oct Daily 10-4:30

ADMISSION: $3.50, Children $1.50

DYERSVILLE

2730
Dyersville Area Historical Society
Dyer-Botsford Museum, 331 1st Ave E, 52040 [120 3rd St SW, 52040]; (p) (319) 875-2504; (c) Dubuque

Private non-profit/ 1984/ staff: 2(f); 1(p); 30(v)/ members: 451

HISTORIC SITE; HISTORICAL SOCIETY: Maintains a local genealogy library and the Dyer-Botsford house, the original home of the city's founder.

PROGRAMS: Annual Meeting; Exhibits; Guided Tours

COLLECTIONS: [Victorian] Hand carved circus and miniature castle replicas, over 1,000 dolls, period furnishings, local artifacts, and over 20,000 obituaries.

HOURS: Apr-Nov M-F 10-4, Sa-Su 1-4

ADMISSION: $3

DYSART

2731
Dysart Historical Society
612 Crisman, 52224 [PO Box 62, 52224]; (c) Tama

Joint/ 1997/ City; DHS/ staff: 35(v)/ members: 109

HISTORY MUSEUM: Housed in a late 19th c church building, exhibits artifacts representing local history.

PROGRAMS: Annual Meeting; Exhibits; Facility Rental; Family Programs

COLLECTIONS: [1875-present] Photos and small local artifacts.

HOURS: Jun-Sep Su 2-4

ADMISSION: No charge.

ELDON

2732
American Gothic House
Main St, 52554 [c/o State Historical Society of Iowa, 600 E Locust, Des Moines, 50319]; (p) (515) 281-6412; www.iowahistory.org/sites/gothic_house/gothic_house.html; (c) Wapello

State/ 1880/ SHSI

HISTORIC SITE: The site preserves the house used as the backdrop for Grant Wood's painting, "American Gothic." External viewing only at this time.

COLLECTIONS: [20th c]

ADMISSION: No charge

ELDORA

2733
Hardin County Historical Society
[PO Box 187, 50627]; (p) (515) 858-5173; (c) Hardin

County/ 1972/ staff: 10(v)/ members: 160/publication: *Hardin County Family History Book*

HISTORIC SITE; HISTORICAL SOCIETY; HOUSE MUSEUM: Preserves county history and maintains a historic house and carriage house.

PROGRAMS: Annual Meeting; Community Outreach; Exhibits; Facility Rental; Family Programs; Festivals; Guided Tours; Lectures; Publication; Research Library/Archives

COLLECTIONS: [1850-present]

HOURS: May-Sep 2nd Su 1-4

ADMISSION: Donations accepted

ELK HORN

2734
Bedstemor's (Grandmother's) House
2105 College, 51531 [c/o Danish Immigrant Museum, PO Box 470, 51531]; (p) (712) 764-6082, (712) 764-7001; (f) (712) 764-7002; DKMUS@netins.net

1908/ staff: 2(p); 12(v)

COLLECTIONS: [1910s-1920s] House; furniture, dishes, pots/pans, bedding; a few letters, family photos, community business photos.

HOURS: May-Oct 1 M-Sa 10-4, Su 1-4

2735
Danish Immigrant Museum, The
2212 Washington St, 51531 [Box 470, 51531]; (p) (712) 764-7001; (f) (712) 764-7002; dkmus@netins.net; www.dkmuseum.org; (c) Shelby

Private non-profit/ 1983/ staff: 6(f); 6(p); 125(v)/ members: 3012

CULTURAL CENTER; HISTORY MUSEUM: Disseminates the story of Danish Immigrants and the Danish-American experience; collects, preserves, and studies, interprets their material, culture, and traditions.

PROGRAMS: Annual Meeting; Concerts; Exhibits; Facility Rental; Festivals; Guided Tours; Interpretation; Publication; Research Library/Archives

COLLECTIONS: [Late 19th c-present] Documents, photos, paintings, agricultural tools and equip, costumes, textiles, porcelains, kitchen utensils, furniture, household accessories, religious and ceremonial items, dolls, toys, printing tools and equip; family, place, and church histories.

HOURS: June-Sept M-F 9-6, Sa 10-6, Su 12-6; Oct-May M-F 9-5, Sa 10-5, Su 12-5

ADMISSION: $3, Children $1.50

2736
Danish Mill Corporation
4038 Main, 51531 [PO Box 245, 51531]; (p) (712) 764-7472; (f) (712) 764-7475; windmill@netins.net; www.dnishwindmill.com; (c) Shelby

Private non-profit/ 1975/ Board of Directors/ staff: 3(f); 10(p); 7(v)/ members: 150/publication: *Velkommen*

HISTORY MUSEUM: Restoration of an 1848 60 ft authentic Danish windmill from Denmark and rebuilt in Elk Horn in 1976.

PROGRAMS: Annual Meeting; Community Outreach; Concerts; Festivals; Film/Video; Guided Tours; Interpretation; Lectures; Living History; Publication

COLLECTIONS: [1840s] Windmill restored to working condition, grinds grain by wind power.

HOURS: Yr Daily Fall/Winter: M-Sa 9-5, Su 12-5; Spring/Summer: M-Sa 8-7, Su 10-7

ADMISSION: $2, Children $1

ELLSTON

2737
Cornwall Restored Pioneer Home
Ringgold County Pioneer Ctr, County Rd P 64 & J 20, 50074 [Main St (Rd J 20), 50074]; (p) (515) 772-4419, (515) 464-2140; (c) Ringgold

1864/ Ringgold County Historical Society

HOUSE MUSEUM: Site includes the old brick telephone Mfg. building and Hazel Glen Country Schoolhouse.

PROGRAMS: Exhibits

COLLECTIONS: [Late 19th c-early 20th c] Local paintings, historical, archival & photographs on Cornwall family and early Ringgold County.

HOURS: June-Aug Sa-Su 1-5

ADMISSION: $1, Children

EMMETSBURG

2738
Palo Alto County Historical Association
1703 Main, 50536; (c) Palo Alto

Private non-profit/ 1969/ staff: 8(v)/ members: 70/publication: *History of Palo Alto County*

HISTORICAL SOCIETY; HISTORY MUSEUM; HOUSE MUSEUM: Preserves the history of Palo Alto County.

PROGRAMS: Exhibits; Guided Tours; Publication

COLLECTIONS: [1870s-present] Tools, clothing, doctors supplies, school memorabilia, butcher's set up, farm tools, office equip, and period furnishings.

HOURS: Mar-Oct by Appt

ESTHERVILLE

2739
Emmet County Historical Society
1720 3rd Ave, 51334 [PO Box 101, 51334]; (c) Emmet

Private non-profit/ 1964/ staff: 1(p); 60(v)/ members: 100

HISTORICAL SOCIETY; HISTORY MUSEUM: Operates a historical museum and research archives.

PROGRAMS: Annual Meeting; Exhibits; Guided Tours; Interpretation; Lectures; Living History; Research Library/Archives

COLLECTIONS: [1855-1980] Museum artifacts and photographs.

HOURS: June-Aug Daily 2-5

ADMISSION: Donations accepted

FARLEY

2740
Farley Area Historical Society
Farley Memorial Hall, 52046 [Box 174, 52046]; (p) (319) 744-3491; (f) (319) 744-3606; (c) Dubuque

Private non-profit/ 1996/ Board of Directors/ staff: 10(v)/ members: 90/publication: *History of Farley 1896-1996*

GENEALOGICAL SOCIETY; HISTORICAL SOCIETY; RESEARCH CENTER: Catalogues information and documents pertaining to city and pioneer history.

PROGRAMS: Annual Meeting; Community Outreach; Exhibits; Film/Video; Publication; Research Library/Archives

COLLECTIONS: [1852-present] Obituaries, biographies, photos, maps, old buildings, railroad history, and a bank collection.

HOURS: M-F by Appt

FOREST CITY

2741
Lunstrum Swedish Immigrant Log Cabin
36400 165th Ave, 50436; (p) (515) 581-4196

1870/ staff: 2(v)

COLLECTIONS: [1870-1900] Large immigrant dove-tailed chest immigrant tool chest, log house construction tools.; Family bible, church history book with family picture

HOURS: Seasonal

FORT DODGE

2742
Fort Dodge Historical Foundation
Bus Rt 20 & Museum Rd, 50501 [PO Box 1798, 50501]; (p) (515) 573-4231; (f) (515) 573-4231; thefort@frontiernet.com; www.fort.org; (c) Webster

Private non-profit/ 1962/ Board of Directors/ staff: 3(f); 15(p); 32(v)/ members: 173

HISTORY MUSEUM; LIVING HISTORY/OUTDOOR MUSEUM: Operates the Fort Museum and Frontier Village, composed of a replica 1862 militia fort and village of 12 original and replica buildings.

PROGRAMS: Exhibits; Facility Rental; Festivals; Guided Tours; Living History; Reenactments

COLLECTIONS: [1850-1950] Military, pioneer, and Native American exhibits relating to the history of Fort Dodge and NW Iowa.

HOURS: May-mid Oct Daily 9-6

ADMISSION: $4, Student $2

2743
Webster County Historical Society
Fort Dodge Public Library, 500 Central Ave, 50501 [Box 543, 50501]; rjnatte@dodgenet.com; www.dodgenet.com/~bqibbs/history; (c) Webster

Private non-profit/ 1971/ staff: 10(v)/ members: 100

GENEALOGICAL SOCIETY; HISTORICAL SOCIETY; HISTORY MUSEUM: Collects, preserves, and promotes interest in the history of North Central IA; maintains a library and archives of local history.

PROGRAMS: Annual Meeting; Community Outreach; Elder's Programs; Exhibits; Guided Tours; Lectures; Publication; Research Library/Archives

COLLECTIONS: [1850-present] Documentary, photographic, and manuscript collections of north central IA; 10,000 photos and negatives.

HOURS: Yr T-F 10-4

FORT MADISON

2744
Santa Fe Depot Museum and Historic Center
10th St & Hwy 61, 52627 [PO Box 285, 52627]; (p) (319) 372-7661; (f) (319) 372-1825; (c) Lee

Private non-profit/ 1968/ Board of Directors/ staff: 1(p); 25(v)/ members: 300

HISTORIC SITE; HISTORICAL SOCIETY; HISTORY MUSEUM: Maintains museum of railroad history, fire fighting, and fountain pens housed in a mission revival style building.

PROGRAMS: Annual Meeting; Community Outreach; Exhibits; Festivals; Guided Tours; Interpretation; Lectures; Living History; Publication; School-Based Curriculum

COLLECTIONS: [1840-present] Sheaffer fountain pen collection, Native American artifacts, 1876 Silsby fire engines, Santa Fe railroad exhibits, farm equipment, law enforcement memorabilia, and Civil War items.

GARDEN GROVE

2745
J.J. McClung House
Main and Vine, 50103; (p) (515) 443-2277; (f) (515) 443-3969

GARNAVILLO

2746
Garnavillo Historical Society
205 N Washington, 52049 [Box 371, 52049]; (p) (319) 964-2341; (f) (319) 964-2485; gsb@netins.net; (c) Clayton

Private non-profit/ 1965/ staff: 25(v)/ members: 25

HISTORIC PRESERVATION AGENCY; HISTORICAL SOCIETY; HISTORY MUSEUM

PROGRAMS: Annual Meeting; Community Outreach; Guided Tours

COLLECTIONS: [Pre-Civil War-WWII] Regional memorabilia and Judge Crosby papers.

HOURS: Sa-Su 1-4

GLENWOOD

2747
Mills County Historical Society
Glenwood Lake Park, 51534 [PO Box 255, 51534]; (p) (712) 527-5038; carriemerritt@hotmail.com; (c) Mills

Private non-profit/ 1959/ Board of Directors/ staff: 120(v)/ members: 50

HISTORIC PRESERVATION AGENCY; HISTORICAL SOCIETY; HISTORY MUSEUM: Preserves and interprets county history.

PROGRAMS: Annual Meeting; Community

Outreach; Exhibits; Film/Video; Guided Tours; Interpretation; Lectures; Living History

COLLECTIONS: [1840s-present] Native American artifacts, pioneer items, agricultural equip, military items, music related items, and clothing.

HOURS: June-Aug Sa-Su 1:30-4, and by appt

GRAFTON

2748
Grafton Heritage Depot
Main St, 50440 [3rd St, 50440]; (p) (515) 748-2337; (c) Worth

Private non-profit/ 1975

HISTORIC SITE: Restored turn of the century railroad depot.

PROGRAMS: Guided Tours

HOURS: June-Aug 1:30-5

ADMISSION: No charge

GREENFIELD

2749
Adair County Historical Society
Hwy 92 W, 50849 [PO Box 214, 50849]; (p) (515) 743-2232; (c) Adair

Joint/ 1959/ County; Private non-profit/ members: 93

ART MUSEUM; HISTORIC PRESERVATION AGENCY; HISTORICAL SOCIETY; HISTORY MUSEUM; HOUSE MUSEUM; LIVING HISTORY/OUTDOOR MUSEUM; RESEARCH CENTER: Preserves and interprets local history.

PROGRAMS: Annual Meeting; Community Outreach; Exhibits; Facility Rental; Festivals; Guided Tours; Interpretation; Lectures; Living History; Publication; Research Library/ Archives

COLLECTIONS: [19th-early 20th c] Memorabilia and artifacts related to education, machinery, church, depot, country school, and local history.

HOURS: May-Sept Daily 1-4:30

ADMISSION: $3, Children $1.50

2750
Henry A. Wallace Country Life Center
2773 290th St, 50849 [PO Box 363, 50849]; (p) (515) 337-5019; (f) (515) 337-5019; (c) Adair

Private non-profit/ 1993/ Board of Govenors/ staff: 1(f); 1(p); 15(v)/ members: 45

HISTORIC SITE; LIVING HISTORY/OUTDOOR MUSEUM: Maintains gardens, art exhibits, woodland, prairie, and cropland that interpret accomplishments of VP Henry A. Wallace.

PROGRAMS: Annual Meeting; Community Outreach; Exhibits; Festivals; Garden Tours; Guided Tours; Interpretation; Living History; Theatre

COLLECTIONS: [Early 20th c]

HOURS: Mar-Oct Daily 10-4

ADMISSION: Donations accepted

2751
Iowa Aviation Museum
2251 Airport Rd, 50849 [PO Box 31, 50849];

(p) (641) 343-7184; aviation@mddc.com; www.netins.net/showcase/jmass/iapa; (c) Adair

Private non-profit/ 1990/ Antique Preservation Assn of Greenfield/ staff: 1(f); 2(p)/ members: 200

HISTORY MUSEUM: Displays antique aircraft and related memorabilia; focus on IA's aviation history; home of the IA Aviation Hall of Fame.

PROGRAMS: Annual Meeting; Exhibits; Facility Rental; Festivals; Guided Tours; Publication; Research Library/Archives

COLLECTIONS: [Late 1920s-present] Rare aircraft: 7 early civil aircraft, four gliders, two military; related objects

GRINNELL

2752
Grinnell Historical Museum
1125 Broad St, 50112 [631 Park St #206, 50112]; (c) Poweshiek

Private non-profit/ 1965/ staff: 20(v)/ members: 200

HISTORIC PRESERVATION AGENCY; HISTORY MUSEUM; HOUSE MUSEUM: Repository for local historical items and research material.

PROGRAMS: Community Outreach; Exhibits; Guided Tours; Research Library/Archives

COLLECTIONS: [1850s-1970s] Locally manufactured items, clothes, dolls, photos, 30,000 obituaries, and an 1895 house.

HOURS: June-Aug T-Su 2-4

GRISWOLD

2753
Cass County Historical Society Museum
302 Cass St & 410 Main St, 51535 [Box 254, 51535]; (p) (712) 778-2700, (712) 778-4182; (c) Cass

1963/ staff: 12(v)/ members: 12

HISTORIC SITE; HISTORICAL SOCIETY; HISTORY MUSEUM: Collects, preserves, and interprets county history.

PROGRAMS: Annual Meeting; Elder's Programs; Exhibits; Family Programs; Festivals; Guided Tours; Interpretation; Lectures; Publication; Research Library/Archives; School-Based Curriculum

COLLECTIONS: [1850s-present] Native American, farming, advertising, military, education, Boy and Girl Scouts, and household artifacts.

HOURS: May-Nov Su 1:30-4:30

GRUNDY CENTER

2754
Grundy County Historical Society
c/o Sara Lee Yder, 705 10th St, 50638; (c) Grundy

Private non-profit/ 1974/ members: 14/publication: *Grundy County Remembers, Vol. 1&2*

2755
Ostfriesen Heritage Society
515 N Adam (Library), 50638 [905 E Ave, 50638]; (p) (319) 824-6321; (f) (515) 869-

5234; markstea@ostfriesenteashop; (c) Grundy

Private non-profit/ 1997/ staff: 10(v)/ members: 347/publication: *Neues Blatt*

GENEALOGICAL SOCIETY; HISTORIC PRESERVATION AGENCY; HISTORICAL SOCIETY; RESEARCH CENTER: Preserves North German heritage and the lowland German language.

PROGRAMS: Community Outreach; Elder's Programs; Exhibits; Facility Rental; Family Programs; Festivals; Film/Video; Lectures; Living History; Publication; Research Library/ Archives

HOURS: Yr T-Sa

ADMISSION: No charge

HAMPTON

2756
Franklin County Historical Society Museum
Hwy 3 W, 50441 [PO Box 114, 50441]; (p) (515) 456-5777; (c) Franklin

Private non-profit/ 1976/ staff: 20(v)

HISTORICAL SOCIETY

PROGRAMS: Annual Meeting; Community Outreach; Exhibits; Living History; Reenactments; Research Library/Archives

COLLECTIONS: [1800s-present] Period personal items of county residents.

HOURS: June-Sept 1-4

HARPERS FERRY

2757
Effigy Mounds National Monument
151 Hwy 76, 52146; (p) (319) 873-3491; (f) (319) 873-3743; www.nps.gov/efmo; (c) Allamakee/Clayton

Federal/ 1949/ National Park Service/ staff: 9(f); 9(p); 30(v)

HISTORIC PRESERVATION AGENCY: Preserves prehistoric burial and ceremonial mounds and the natural environment in which they exist.

PROGRAMS: Exhibits; Family Programs; Film/Video; Guided Tours; Interpretation; School-Based Curriculum

COLLECTIONS: [Prehistory-1500 AD] Artifacts and records associated with excavations of prehistoric Native American burial and ceremonial mounds in NE Iowa.

HOURS: Yr Daily 8-4:30

ADMISSION: $2;

HAVERHILL

2758
Matthew Edel Blacksmith Shop/Historical Society of Marshall County
, [Box 304, Marshalltown, 50158]; (p) (505) 752-6664; www.iowahistory.org/sites/edel_blacksmith/edel_blacksmith.html; (c) Marshall

State/ 1884/ State Historical Society of Iowa/ staff: 2(p)/ members: 1550

HISTORIC SITE: Preserves the blacksmith shop built by German immigrant, Mattew Edel, in 1884.

PROGRAMS: Guided Tours; Interpretation

COLLECTIONS: [19th-ealry 20th c] Shop contains line shaft, wagon shop, farriering area, and production forge; inventions patented and manufactured by Edel.

HOURS: June-Aug Daily 12-4

ADMISSION: No

HAWARDEN

2759
Big Sioux River Valley Historical Society
c/o Myrna C Ver Hoef, 1115 15th St, 51023; (p) (712) 552-2797; (c) Sioux

1979/ staff: 60(v)/ members: 115

HISTORICAL SOCIETY: Collects, preserves, and displays local history.

PROGRAMS: Annual Meeting; Community Outreach; Exhibits; Guided Tours

COLLECTIONS: [1860-present] Artifacts; more than 950 photographs, and Calliope Village, a fifteen building re-creation of the first settlement of Calliope and Hawarden.

HOURS: June-Sept Su or by appt

2760
Historical House and Photo Exhibit
803 Ave H, 51023 [c/o Glenn Gregg, 826 Central Ave, 51023]; (p) (712) 552-2233

IDA GROVE

2761
Moorehead House Museum
410 Moorehead St, 51445; (p) (712) 364-3816

INDEPENDENCE

2762
Buchanan County Genealogical Society
113 1/2 4th Ave, 50644 [PO Box 4, 50644-0004]; (p) (319) 334-9333; (c) Buchanan

County/ 1976/ staff: 11(v)/ members: 30

GENEALOGICAL SOCIETY

PROGRAMS: Research Library/Archives

COLLECTIONS: [1846-present] Probate, birth, marriage, death, and census records; poll tax; and newspapers from 1869 on microfilm.

HOURS: Yr M 10-2, Th 4-7

INDIANOLA

2763
Warren County Historical Society, The
1400 W 2nd Ave, 50125 [Box 256, 50125]; (p) (515) 961-8085

Private non-profit/ 1933/ staff: 75(v)/ members: 502/publication: *Monthly Newsletter*

HISTORICAL SOCIETY: Collects, preserves, and creates interest in the cultural, political, and economic heritage of Warren County; maintains county heritage, museums, and other property.

PROGRAMS: Annual Meeting; Community Outreach; Exhibits; Facility Rental; Family Programs; Festivals; Film/Video; Guided Tours; Lectures; Publication; Research Library/Archives; School-Based Curriculum

COLLECTIONS: [1964-present]:

IOWA CITY

2764
Old Capitol Museum
24 Old Capitol, Univ of Iowa, 52242-1000; (p) (319) 335-0548; (f) (319) 335-0558; ann-smothers@uiowa.edu; (c) Johnson

State/ 1840/ Univ of IA Board of Regents/ staff: 2(f); 10(p); 40(v)

HISTORIC SITE; HISTORY MUSEUM: Restored original state capitol serves as a living museum, representing territorial and state history.

PROGRAMS: Community Outreach; Concerts; Exhibits; Guided Tours; Interpretation; School-Based Curriculum

COLLECTIONS: [1840-1850s] 600 artifacts including period decor and furnishings.

HOURS: Yr M-Sa 10-3, Su 12-4; Fall Sa 9-12

ADMISSION: Donations accepted

2765
Plum Grove Historic Home
1030 Carroll St, 52240 [PO Box 5081, Coralville, 52241]; (p) (319) 351-5738; (f) (319) 351-5310; www.iowahistory.org/sites/plum_grove/plum_grove.html

State/ 1844/ State Historical Society of Iowa/ staff: 1(p); 10(v)

HISTORIC SITE: Home of Iowa's first Territorial Governor, Robert Lucas. Seven-room Greek Revival house furnished with pieces from the 1844-45 period. Seasonal archaeological research on the grounds.

PROGRAMS: Family Programs; Garden Tours; Guided Tours

COLLECTIONS: [1844-45] Furnishings and decorative arts for the period 1844-45.

HOURS: Mem Day-Oct 31 W-Su 1-5

ADMISSION: No charge

2766
State Historical Society of Iowa, Centennial Building
402 Iowa Ave, 52240; (p) (319) 335-3916; (f) (319) 335-3935; www.iowahistory.org; (c) Johnson

State/ 1856/ staff: 18(f)/ members: 1550/publication: *Annals of Iowa; Iowa Heritage Illustrated; and others*

HISTORICAL SOCIETY; STATE AGENCY: Houses a research library and special collections, provides technical support for both State Historical Society libraries, and houses the Society's publications program.

PROGRAMS: Annual Meeting; Publication; Research Library/Archives

COLLECTIONS: [19th and 20th c] 215,000 accessioned volumes, 25,000 reels of microfilm, 5,000 linear feet of manuscripts, 3,000 sheets of maps, and 1 million photographs.

HOURS: Yr T-Sa 9-4:30; June-Aug + M

2767
University of Iowa Hospitals and Clinics Medical Museum
200 Hawkins Dr, 52242; (p) (319) 356-7106; (f) (319) 384-8141; adrienne-drapkin@uiowa.edu; www.uihealthcare.com/depts/medmuseum/; (c) Johnson

State/ 1989/ staff: 1(f); 3(p); 1(v)

HISTORY MUSEUM: Promotes understanding and appreciation of medical history and health-related issues.

PROGRAMS: Community Outreach; Elder's Programs; Exhibits; Guided Tours; Interpretation; Lectures; Research Library/Archives; School-Based Curriculum

COLLECTIONS: 5,000 medically-related museum artifacts, 500 photos, and 300 books.

HOURS: Yr Daily M-F 8-5, Sa-Su 1-4

ADMISSION: No charge

IRETON

2768
Ireton Historical Society
301 Ash, 51027 [501 Ash Box 235, 51027]; (p) (712) 278-2203; (c) Sioux

staff: 12(v)/ members: 20

HISTORY MUSEUM: Maintains a history house, an old school, and the old City Hall; offers walking tours of the town.

PROGRAMS: Annual Meeting; Guided Tours; Living History; School-Based Curriculum

COLLECTIONS: Pioneer tools, books, and clothing.

HOURS: Apr-Dec by appt

JOHNSTON

2769
Iowa National Guard Gold Star Museum
7700 NW Beaver Dr, 50131; (p) (515) 252-4531; (f) (515) 252-4139; gordenj@ia-arng.ngb.army.mil; (c) Polk

Joint/ 1985/ Federal; State/ staff: 2(f); 30(v)

HISTORIC PRESERVATION AGENCY; HISTORY MUSEUM; RESEARCH CENTER: Collects, interprets, and presents the military history of Iowans from 1846 to the present and the history of Camp Dodge, IA.

PROGRAMS: Elder's Programs; Guided Tours; Interpretation; Lectures; Research Library/Archives

COLLECTIONS: [1846-present] Military uniforms, accoutrements, equipment, weapons, and major military arms and equipment (tanks, aircraft, etc); photos, records and journals, and a 4,000 volume military library.

HOURS: Yr Jan-Dec Library: M-Sa 9-4; Museum: T-Sa

KALONA

2770
Kalona Historical Society
411 9th, 52247 [Box 292, 52247-0292]; (p) (319) 656-3232; (c) Washington

Private non-profit/ 1969/ staff: 1(f); 27(p)/ members: 170

HISTORIC PRESERVATION AGENCY; HISTORICAL SOCIETY: Maintains artifacts in a 13 building historical village.

PROGRAMS: Annual Meeting; Exhibits; Facility Rental; Festivals; Guided Tours; Living History; Reenactments

COLLECTIONS: [Early 1900s]

HOURS: Apr-Oct M-Sa 9:30-4; Nov-Mar 11-3

ADMISSION: $6, Family $20, Children $2.50

2771
Mennonite Historical Society
411 9th, 52247 [PO Box 576, 52247]; (p) (319) 656-3732; (c) Washington

Private non-profit/ 1948/ staff: 5(p)/ members: 120/publication: *Reflections*

HISTORICAL SOCIETY; HISTORY MUSEUM: Maintains Mennonite and Amish archives and museum.

PROGRAMS: Family Programs; Guided Tours; Interpretation; Lectures; Publication; Research Library/Archives

COLLECTIONS: [1846-1940] Genealogical books, publications by Mennonite and Amish authors, historical charts and maps, tools, clothing, church items, dishes, and quilts.

HOURS: Apr-Nov M-Sa 10-4

ADMISSION: $4

KELLOGG

2772
Kellogg Historical Society
218 High St, 50135 [PO Box 295, 50135-0295]; (p) (515) 526-3430; www.rootsweb.com/ ~iajasper/museum.htm; (c) Jasper

Private non-profit/ 1980/ Board of Directors/ staff: 9(v)/ members: 540/publication: *Kellogg Enterprise*

HISTORICAL SOCIETY: Operates a seven building complex, housing local and area historical items; preserves and promotes town heritage.

PROGRAMS: Annual Meeting; Exhibits; Guided Tours; Publication

COLLECTIONS: Machinery, tools, farm related items, and factory items; 1,151 pitcher collection, washing machines, church and school items, cemetery and genealogy books, household items, and military uniforms.

HOURS: June-Aug M-F 9-4, Su 1:30-5

ADMISSION: Donations accepted

KEOKUK

2773
George M. Verity Riverboat Museum Commission
Keokuk Waterfront, 415 Blondeau, 52632 [PO Box 400, 52632]; (p) (319) 524-4765; (f) (319) 524-1365; iakeokum@interl.net; (c) Lee

City/ 1962/ staff: 30(v)

HISTORIC SITE; HISTORY MUSEUM: Museum focuses on Mississippi River transportation and steamship history, housed in a "retired" paddle wheel steamboat.

PROGRAMS: Annual Meeting; Exhibits; Guid

ed Tours; Interpretation

COLLECTIONS: [1850-1962] Steam boat artifacts, pictures and technology.

HOURS: Apr-May, Sept-Oct F-Su 9-5; June-Aug Daily 9-5

ADMISSION: $3, Children $2

2774
Lee County Genealogical Society of Iowa
210 N 5th St, 52632 [PO Box 303, 52632-0303]; (c) Lee

Private non-profit/ 1964/ members: 52/publication: *Gleanings*

GENEALOGICAL SOCIETY: Preserves and promotes genealogical and historical information; prepares records for public use.

PROGRAMS: Lectures; Publication; Research Library/Archives

COLLECTIONS: [1850-present] County histories, atlases, microfilm of newspapers, census records, marriage, and death records.

HOURS: Yr M-Th 9:30-7, F-Sa 9-5

2775
Miller House Museum
318 N 5th St, 52632 [PO Box 125, 52632]; (p) (319) 524-7283; www.keokukia.com/ Historical/KeoRegister/Miller.html

1859/ Lee County Historical Society/ staff: 25(v)

HOUSE MUSEUM: 1859 home of Supreme Court Justice Samuel L. Miller

COLLECTIONS: [1847-1913] Clothes, Civil War to WWI; Indian artifacts of Sac and Fox tribe; coverlets and quilts; items relating to building of the dam, powerhouse and lock; and medical colleges; portraits

HOURS: June-Aug F-Su 1-4; and by appt

KEOSAUQUA

2776
Pearson House
Intersection of Dodge & County, 52565 [PO Box 177, 52565]; (p) (319) 293-3311, (319) 293-3689

HOUSE MUSEUM: Brick and stone house built 1845-47. Upper floor was used at one time used for Methodist Church services, and it was a station on the Underground Railroad. Grounds also include log cabin, refurbished country school, and 100 year-old split rail fence.

HOURS: Su 1-4 and by appt

KNOXVILLE

2777
National Sprint Car Hall of Fame and Museum
One Sprint Capital Place, 50138 [PO Box 542, 50138]; (p) (641) 842-6176; (f) (641) 842-6177; sprintcarhof@sprintcarhof.com; www.sprintcarhof.com; (c) Marion

Private non-profit/ 1986/ staff: 3(f); 3(p); 20(v)/ members: 2000

HISTORY MUSEUM: Preserves the history of the sport of sprint car racing.

PROGRAMS: Annual Meeting; Exhibits; Facility Rental; Film/Video; Guided Tours; Publication; Research Library/Archives

COLLECTIONS: [20th c] "Big Cars," sprint cars, and sprint car memorabilia.

HOURS: Yr Daily 10-6

ADMISSION: $3, Student $2, Children $2, Seniors $2; Members free

LAKE VIEW

2778
Lake View Iowa Historical Society
114 Crescent Park Dr, 51450 [PO Box 483, 51450]; (p) (712) 657-8010; (c) Sac

Private non-profit/ 1994/ Board of Directors/ staff: 9(p)/ 80(v)/ members: 150

HISTORICAL SOCIETY: Preserves and displays the history of Lake View.

PROGRAMS: Annual Meeting; Exhibits; Film/Video; Guided Tours

COLLECTIONS: [Late 1880s-early 1900s] Mounted Birds, pictures, newspapers, furniture, military items, tools, class graduation pictures from 1889.

HOURS: June-Sept Sa-Su 2-5 and by appt

LAMONI

2779
Graceland University DuRose Rare Book Room
700 College Ave, 50140; (p) (515) 784-5301; (f) (515) 784-5497; library@graceland.edu; www2.graceland.edu; (c) Decatur

Private non-profit/ 1895/ Graceland Univ

LIBRARY AND/OR ARCHIVES: Preserves a collection of materials relating to the histories of Mormonism (RLDS and LDS), Lamoni, and Graceland University.

LEMANS

2780
Plymouth County Historical Museum
335 1st Ave SW, 51031; (p) (712) 546-7002; (c) Plymouth

1965/ staff: 3(p)/ members: 500/publication: *Museum Times*

HISTORIC SITE; HISTORY MUSEUM; RESEARCH CENTER: Preserves county history.

PROGRAMS: Annual Meeting; Exhibits; Facility Rental; Guided Tours; Publication; Research Library/Archives

COLLECTIONS: [1870-present] Musical instruments, Civil War era log cabin, 1940s cafe, military memorabilia.

HOURS: Yr T-Su 1-5

LEWIS

2781
Hitchcock House Advisory Committee
63788 567th Ln, 51544; (p) (712) 769-2323; (c) Cass

County/ 1988/ Conservation Board/ staff: 1(f); 25(v)/ members: 100

HISTORIC SITE: Maintains the historic 1856 Hitchcock House and its artifacts.

PROGRAMS: Annual Meeting; Festivals; Guided Tours; Interpretation

COLLECTIONS: [1850-1865] House, household furnishings, and farming equipment.

HOURS: May-Sept

LOGAN

2782
Harrison County Historical Society
119 W 4th St, 51546; (p) (712) 644-2941; (c) Harrison

Private non-profit/ 1968/ members: 183/publication: *Harrison County Historical Society*

HISTORIC PRESERVATION AGENCY; HISTORIC SITE; HISTORICAL SOCIETY; HISTORY MUSEUM; HOUSE MUSEUM: Preserves and promotes interest in county history.

PROGRAMS: Annual Meeting; Community Outreach; Exhibits; Guided Tours; Lectures; Publication

HOURS: Yr M-Sa 9-5, Su 12-5

ADMISSION: $2, Children $0.75

LOWDEN

2783
Lowden Historical Society
90 Main St, 52255; (p) (319) 941-5859; (c) Cedar

Private non-profit/ 1973/ Board of Directors/ staff: 18(v)/ members: 40

HISTORIC PRESERVATION AGENCY; HISTORICAL SOCIETY: Preserves town history, including business, trading, and pioneer history.

PROGRAMS: Annual Meeting; Community Outreach; Exhibits; Guided Tours; Publication; Research Library/Archives

COLLECTIONS: Tools, kitchen utensils, railroad and military items; early edition newspapers, scrapbooks, photo albums, Cedar County books.

HOURS: By Appt

ADMISSION: Donations accepted

LUCAS

2784
John L. Lewis Memorial Museum of Mining and Labor
102 Division St Box 3, 50151; (p) (515) 766-6831; (c) Lucas

Private non-profit/ 1986/ John L. Lewis Commission/ staff: 2(f); 4(p); 10(v)/ members: 133

HISTORY MUSEUM: Preserves, interprets, and exhibits the history of John L Lewis (1880-1969), mining, and labor.

PROGRAMS: Annual Meeting; Exhibits; Festivals; Film/Video; Guided Tours; Research Library/Archives; Theatre

COLLECTIONS: [1880-1960] Life size bronze statue, photos, and documents pertaining to Lewis, research material on coal mining and labor history, and early mining tools.

HOURS: Apr-Oct T-Sa 9-3 and by appt.

MADRID

2785
Madrid Historical Society and Museum
103 W 2nd St, 50156; (p) (515) 795-3249; (c) Boone

Private non-profit/ 1982/ Board of Directors/ staff: 12(v)/ members: 55

HISTORICAL SOCIETY; HISTORY MUSEUM: Preserves and exhibits mining artifacts and local history.

PROGRAMS: Exhibits; Guided Tours

COLLECTIONS: [Early 1800s-present] Mining artifacts and replicas and exhibits of underground and horizontal mines; doll and teddy bear collection, clothing, and local historical artifacts.

HOURS: May-Oct 3rd Su 2-5

ADMISSION: Donations accepted

MAQUOKETA

2786
Jackson County Historical Society
1212 Quarry, Fairgrounds, 52060 [PO Box 1245, 52060]; (p) (319) 652-5020; (f) (319) 652-5020; (c) Jackson

County/ 1964/ staff: 2(p); 60(v)/ members: 420

GENEALOGICAL SOCIETY; HISTORICAL SOCIETY; HISTORY MUSEUM; HOUSE MUSEUM; RESEARCH CENTER: Features local history, preserves and exhibits artifacts, and sponsors educational programs.

PROGRAMS: Annual Meeting; Community Outreach; Exhibits; Facility Rental; Family Programs; Festivals; Guided Tours; Interpretation; Lectures; Living History; Publication; Research Library/Archives; School-Based Curriculum

COLLECTIONS: [1840s-1940s] Log cabin, horsedrawn agricultural equipment, natural history, merchant artifacts, and photography archives.

HOURS: Yr T-F

MARBLE ROCK

2787
Marble Rock Historical Society
313 Bradford, 50653 [2790 Jersey Ave, 50653]; (p) (515) 397-2287; (c) Floyd

1972/ Board of Directors/ staff: 20(v)

HISTORICAL SOCIETY: Collects and displays historical items; maintains three museum buildings.

PROGRAMS: Annual Meeting; Community Outreach; Exhibits; Guided Tours

COLLECTIONS: [1850s-1930s] Furniture, home equipment, clothing, quilts, photos, business items, farming and railroad equipment, school memorabilia, scrapbooks, documents, and sports items.

HOURS: June-Aug Su

MARENGO

2788
Iowa County Historical Society
675 E S St, 52301 [PO Box 288, 52301]; (p) (319) 642-3054, (319) 642-7018

Private non-profit/ 1963/ Board of Directors/ members: 425/publication: *Newsletter*

HISTORICAL SOCIETY; HISTORY MUSEUM; LIVING HISTORY/OUTDOOR MUSEUM: Manages a museum complex that includes a log house, log cabin, railroad station, 1930s filling station, and a museum building and resource library.

PROGRAMS: Annual Meeting; Exhibits; Family Programs; Festivals; Film/Video; Guided Tours; Lectures; Publication; Research Library/Archives; School-Based Curriculum

COLLECTIONS: [1800-present] Items related to the development and lifestyle of IA.

HOURS: May-Sept Th-Sa 1-4; by appt

ADMISSION: Donations accepted

MARION

2789
Granger House Museum
970 10th St, 52302; (p) (319) 377-6672; grangerhou@aol.com

Private non-profit/ Marion Historical Museum Inc

HOUSE MUSEUM: The home of the Granger family for over a century, restored to its appearance in the late 1870s.

HOURS: May 1-Sept 13 Sa-T 1-4; Nov 20-Dec 19 Sa-Su 1-4

MARSHALLLTOWN

2790
Historical Society of Marshall County
202 E Church St, 50158 [PO Box 304, 50158]; (p) (515) 752-6664; hsmc@mtnia.com; www.marshallnet.com; (c) Marshall

Private non-profit/ 1908/ Board of Directors/ staff: 1(f); 25(v)/ members: 160/publication: *Then and Now*

HISTORICAL SOCIETY; HISTORY MUSEUM: Interprets county history.

PROGRAMS: Annual Meeting; Community Outreach; Exhibits; Guided Tours; Interpretation; Lectures; Publication

COLLECTIONS: [1850-present] Documents, photos, and artifacts related to county

MASON CITY

2791
George C. and Eleanor Stockman House, The
530 1st St NE, 50401 [431 First St SE, 50401]; (p) (515) 424-3494, (515) 424-3444; (c) Cerro Gordo

1908/ River City Society for Historic Preservation/ staff: 2(p); 1(v)

Frank Lloyd Wright Prairie School house.

COLLECTIONS: [1900-1910] West rooms: Arts & Crafts furniture. East rooms: furniture (reproductions) designed by Frank Lloyd Wright before 1908.

HOURS: Jun-Aug: M-Sa

2792
Kinney Pioneer Museum and Historical Society of North Iowa
91846 265th St, 50402 [PO Box 421, 50402-0421]; (p) (641) 423-1258; fran@netconx.net; (c) Cerro Gordo

Private non-profit/ 1965/ staff: 1(f); 1(p); 27(v)/ members: 175

HISTORICAL SOCIETY; HISTORY MUSEUM: Preserves North Iowa history.

PROGRAMS: Annual Meeting; Exhibits; Living History

HOURS: May-Sept W-F, Su 12-5, June-Aug also Sa 12-5

ADMISSION: $2.50

2793
River City Society for Historic Preservation
430 First St NE, 50401 [PO Box 565, 50401]; (p) (515) 423-1923; mccoy.robert@mcleodusa.net; www.radiopark.com/stockmanhouse; (c) Cerro Gordo

Private non-profit/ 1988/ staff: 1(p); 90(v)/ members: 85/publication: *Newsletter*

HISTORIC PRESERVATION AGENCY; HOUSE MUSEUM: Education about and preservation of significant historic buildings in Mason City; operation and maintenance of the Frank Lloyd Wright Stockman House.

PROGRAMS: Annual Meeting; Guided Tours; Interpretation; Publication

COLLECTIONS: [1900s] Period arts and crafts furniture, reproductions of furniture designed by Wright, embroidery, Japanese woodblock prints from Wright's collection.

HOURS: May-Oct

ADMISSION: $3, Children $1

MAYWELL

2794
Community Historical Society, The
Main St, 50161 [11272 W 124th St N, Collins, 50055]; (p) (515) 385-2376; (c) Story

Private non-profit/ 1964/ staff: 10(v)

HISTORICAL SOCIETY: Interprets history of central IA.

PROGRAMS: Annual Meeting; Guided Tours; School-Based Curriculum

COLLECTIONS: [1850s-present] 2 buildings, steel shed; artifacts used in homes and on farms; clothing; natural history; rocks; military.

HOURS: Yr Su 1-4 by appt

ADMISSION: Donations accepted

MISSOURI VALLEY

2795
Steamboat Berthand Museum, DeSoto National Wildlife Refuge
1434 316th Lane, 51555; (p) (712) 642-2772; (f) (712) 642-2877; r3Bertrand@mail.fws.gov; refugeses.fws.gov/NWRSFiles/CulturalResourc; (c) Harrison

Federal/ 1970/ U.S. Fish and Wildlife Service/ staff: 3(f); 10(p); 10(v)

HISTORIC SITE; HISTORY MUSEUM: Preservation and interpretation of excavated cargo from 1865 steamboat Bertrand found within borders of DeSoto National Wildlife Refuge. Natural and cultural history focus for public use, education, and wildlife preservation.

PROGRAMS: Exhibits; Film/Video; Guided Tours; Interpretation; Research Library/ Archives; School-Based Curriculum

COLLECTIONS: [1865] Cargo excavated from sunken 1865 Steamboat Bertrand including mining, farming, logging, and Western frontier settlement supplies. Foodstuffs, alcoholic beverages, clothing, and dioramas.

HOURS: Yr Daily 9-4:30

ADMISSION: $3/vehicle

MONONA

2796
Monona Historical Society
302 S Egbert St, 52159 [Box 434, 52159-0434]; (p) (319) 539-2640; (f) (319) 539-4271; marting@netins.net; (c) Clayton

Private non-profit/ 1971/ staff: 4(p); 3(v)/ members: 20

HISTORIC PRESERVATION AGENCY; HISTORICAL SOCIETY; HISTORY MUSEUM: Preservation of local history.

PROGRAMS: Annual Meeting; Community Outreach; Exhibits; Festivals; Guided Tours; Publication

COLLECTIONS: Handcarved chains and artifacts related to the region.

HOURS: May-Sept Su

MONTEZUMA

2797
Poweshiek County Historical and Genealogical Society
206 N Mill St, 50171 [PO Box 280, 50171]; (p) (515) 623-3322; fernor@pcpartner.net; (c) Poweshiek

County/ 1978/ staff: 10(v)/ members: 209/publication: *The Searcher*

GENEALOGICAL SOCIETY; HISTORICAL SOCIETY; HISTORY MUSEUM: Maintains historic house with added library.

PROGRAMS: Annual Meeting; Exhibits; Facility Rental; Publication; Research Library/ Archives

COLLECTIONS: County genealogical data.

HOURS: Yr M, Th, Sa 9-4

ADMISSION: No charge

MONTROSE

2798
Montrose Township Historical Society
3rd & Chestnut St, 52639 [PO Box 141, 52639]; (c) Lee

Private non-profit/ 1981/ staff: 25(v)/ members: 35

HISTORIC SITE; HISTORICAL SOCIETY: Owns St. Barnabas Wedding Chapel, built in

1869 from native limestone.

PROGRAMS: Annual Meeting; Community Outreach

HOURS: By appt.

MORAVIA

2799
Moravia Area Historical Society
W North St, 52571 [811 Pamela St, 52571]; (p) (515) 724-3777; (f) (515) 724-9009; wmburkla@lisco.net; (c) Appanoose

Private non-profit/ staff: 30(v)/ members: 65/publication: *Depot News*

HISTORIC PRESERVATION AGENCY; HISTORIC SITE; HISTORICAL SOCIETY; HISTORY MUSEUM: Owns and operates the Wabash Railroad Depot museum, an example of a rural combination depot.

PROGRAMS: Annual Meeting; Exhibits; Family Programs; Festivals; Guided Tours; Publication; Reenactments

COLLECTIONS: Railroad and local artifacts.

HOURS: May-Nov

MOULTON

2800
Moulton Historical Society
Main St (Hwy 202), 52572 [33864 497th St, 52572]; (p) (515) 642-3790; (c) Appanoose

Private non-profit/ 1976/ staff: 8(v)/ members: 35/publication: *Moulton History Book*

HISTORICAL SOCIETY; RAILROAD MUSEUM: Preserves local history and a railroad museum.

PROGRAMS: Annual Meeting; Community Outreach; Exhibits; Festivals; Guided Tours; Publication

COLLECTIONS: [1800s-present] Dental, dairy, post office, railway, and ice equipment.

HOURS: Yr Daily

ADMISSION: Donations accepted

MOUNT AYR

2801
Ringgold County Historical Society
603 N Hayes, 50854; (p) (515) 464-2140; (c) Ringgold

County/ 1939/ Board of Directors

HISTORICAL SOCIETY; HISTORY MUSEUM: Collects, preserves, and promotes county history at the Mount Ayr public library and the Pioneer Center Museum in Ellston.

PROGRAMS: Annual Meeting; Exhibits; Family Programs; Festivals; Guided Tours; Research Library/Archives

COLLECTIONS: Printed and microfilm materia, artifacts, and collection of early farm machinery.

HOURS: June-Aug Sa-Su

MOUNT PLEASANT

2802
Harlan-Lincoln Home
101 W Broad St, 52641 [601 N Main St, 52641]; (p) (800) 582-2383; (f) (319) 385-

6324; (c) Henry

Private non-profit/ 1959/ Iowa Weslyan College/ staff: 1(p)

HISTORIC SITE: Maintains the home of US Senator James Harlan and his daughter, who married Robert Todd Lincoln.

COLLECTIONS: [Mid-late 1800s] Items belonging to Mrs. Abraham Lincoln, the Harlan family, and the Robert Todd Lincoln family.

HOURS: Yr by Appt

ADMISSION: Donations accepted

2803
Midwest Old Settlers and Threshers Association
405 E Threshers Rd, 52641; (p) (319) 385-8937; (f) (319) 385-0563; info@oldthreshers.org; www.oldthreshers.org; (c) Henry

Private non-profit/ 1950/ Board of Directors/ staff: 9(f); 6(p); 700(v)

HISTORY MUSEUM; LIVING HISTORY/OUTDOOR MUSEUM; RESEARCH CENTER: Preserves the agricultural history of the Midwest.

PROGRAMS: Annual Meeting; Community Outreach; Exhibits; Facility Rental; Family Programs; Festivals; Guided Tours; Interpretation; Lectures; Living History; Publication; Reenactments; Research Library/Archives; School-Based Curriculum; Theatre

COLLECTIONS: [1860s-1950] Traction steam engines, stationary steam engines, antique unstyled tractors, historical farm implements, and other local artifacts.

HOURS: Yr M-F 8-4, Apr-Oct + Sa-Su 9-4:30

ADMISSION: $3

NEVADA

2804
Dyer Dowell Victorian House
922 Fifth St, 50201; (p) (515) 382-4876

NEW LONDON

2805
Dover Historical Society
213 W Main St, 52645; (p) (319) 367-2573, (877) 468-7700; (c) Henry

Private non-profit/ 1994/ staff: 29(v)/ members: 94

HISTORICAL SOCIETY; HISTORY MUSEUM; HOUSE MUSEUM: Collects and preserves local history.

PROGRAMS: Annual Meeting; Community Outreach; Concerts; Elder's Programs; Exhibits; Facility Rental; Family Programs; Garden Tours; Guided Tours; Interpretation; Lectures; Research Library/Archives

COLLECTIONS: [1900s-1960s] Artifacts, photos, books of early area history, and WWII scrapbooks of area service men and women.

HOURS: June-Dec F-Sa 1-4

NEW PROVIDENCE

2806
Honey Creek Church Preservation Group
31031 PP Ave, 50206 [30293 O Ave, 50206-

8008]; (p) (515) 497-5458; (c) Hardin

Joint/ 1979/ staff: 14(v)

HISTORIC PRESERVATION AGENCY; HISTORIC SITE; HISTORY MUSEUM: Preserves the historic Honey Creek Friends Church and local history.

PROGRAMS: Annual Meeting; Community Outreach; Concerts; Exhibits; Facility Rental; Family Programs; Interpretation; Research Library/Archives

COLLECTIONS: [1852-present] Local genealogy and early school's records.

HOURS: On request

NEWELL

2807
Newell Historical Society
2006 640 St, 50568 [Box 5, 50568]; (p) (712) 272-3691; (c) Buena Vista

1989/ Board of Directors/ staff: 25(v)/ members: 400

HISTORIC SITE; HISTORICAL SOCIETY; HISTORY MUSEUM; HOUSE MUSEUM: Preserves the history of Newell; maintains historic Allee Mansion.

PROGRAMS: Annual Meeting; Exhibits; Facility Rental; Family Programs; Garden Tours; Guided Tours; Interpretation; Lectures; Living History

COLLECTIONS: [Late 1800s, Victorian]

HOURS: June-Aug Su 1-4

ADMISSION: $3

NEWTON

2808
Jasper County Historical Society
1700 S 15th Ave W, 50208 [PO Box 834, 50208]; (p) (515) 792-9118; (c) Jasper

Private non-profit/ 1973/ staff: 1(f); 2(p); 80(v)/ members: 1450/publication: *Newsletter*

HISTORICAL SOCIETY; HISTORY MUSEUM: Owns, operates, and maintains a museum, an 1875 barn, and a 1920 Minneapolis Steam Engine.

PROGRAMS: Annual Meeting; Community Outreach; Exhibits; Family Programs; Festivals; Film/Video; Guided Tours; Interpretation; Lectures; Publication; Reenactments; Research Library/Archives; School-Based Curriculum; Theatre

COLLECTIONS: [1843-1950] Washing machine exhibit, agricultural display, a Victorian house, a 1930s house, and a 1910 store.

HOURS: Daily 1-5, or by appt

ADMISSION: $2

OAKLAND

2809
Oakland Historical Society/Nishna Heritage Museum
118-123 N Main, 51560 [38780 Hickory, 51560]; (p) (712) 482-6802; (c) Pottawattamie

1975/ staff: 6(v)

HISTORICAL SOCIETY; HISTORY MUSEUM;

RESEARCH CENTER: Preserves the history of SW Iowa.

PROGRAMS: Annual Meeting; Elder's Programs; Guided Tours; Lectures; Publication

COLLECTIONS: [Prehistory-present] Prehistoric animal bones, Native American artifacts, Victorian furniture, and rural IA artifacts.

HOURS: Yr

ADMISSION: Donations accepted

ODEBOLT

2810
Peterson Pioneer House
S Walnut, 51458; (p) (712) 668-2231

City/ 1886/ staff: 5(v)

HOUSE MUSEUM

COLLECTIONS: [Late 1880-90s] Clothing, books, toilet articles, and kitchen and dining utensils of the period.

HOURS: June-Aug

OELWEIN

2811
Oelwein Area Historical Society
900 2nd Ave SE, 50662 [PO Box 445, 50662]; (p) (319) 440-5322, (319) 283-4220; (c) Fayette

Private non-profit/ 1973/ Board/ staff: 20(v)/ members: 25

HISTORICAL SOCIETY: Collects and preserves historic items from Oelwein and the surrounding area.

PROGRAMS: Community Outreach; Exhibits; Guided Tours

COLLECTIONS: [1865-present]

HOURS: June-Sept Su 1-4

ADMISSION: No charge

OKOBOJI

2812
Higgins Museum, The
1507 Sanborn Ave, 51355 [PO Box 54, 51355]; (p) (712) 332-5859; (f) (712) 332-5859; hm1978@rconnect.com; www.higginsmuseum.com; (c) Dickinson

Private non-profit/ 1978/ Wm. R. Higgins Jr. Foundation, Inc./ staff: 1(f); 2(p); 5(v)

HISTORY MUSEUM; LIBRARY AND/OR ARCHIVES: Dedicated to the history of national banking and the preservation of national bank notes; houses numismatic research library.

PROGRAMS: Community Outreach; Exhibits; Publication; Research Library/Archives; School-Based Curriculum

COLLECTIONS: [1863-1935] Notes from national banks in IA and adjoining states and territories; 16,000 period post cards and 5,000+ volume numismatic research library.

HOURS: May-Oct T-Su 11-5:30

ADMISSION: No charge

ORANGE CITY

2813
Sioux County Historical Society
115 3rd St SW, 51041 [311 Florida Ave SW, 51041]; (p) (712) 737-8533; (c) Sioux

Private non-profit/ 1972/ Board of Directors/ staff: 20(v)

HISTORIC PRESERVATION AGENCY; HISTORICAL SOCIETY; HISTORY MUSEUM

PROGRAMS: Community Outreach; Exhibits; Festivals; Interpretation

COLLECTIONS: Native American artifacts, clocks, and bullets.

ADMISSION: $2, Children $1

OSAGE

2814
Mitchell County Historical Society
N 6th St & Mechanic, 50461 [PO Box 51, 50461]; (p) (515) 732-1269; (c) Mitchell

Private non-profit/ 1963/ Executive Board/ staff: 1(f)/ members: 150

GENEALOGICAL SOCIETY; HISTORICAL SOCIETY; HISTORY MUSEUM; RESEARCH CENTER: Maintains a local historical museum, a historic fort, and a collection of antique steam engines and farm equipment.

PROGRAMS: Annual Meeting; Community Outreach; Exhibits; Facility Rental; Festivals; Guided Tours; Living History; Publication; Reenactments; Research Library/Archives

COLLECTIONS: Quilts, medical equipment, clothing, genealogy information, early school records, and film equipment; antique farming implements, and steam engine.

HOURS: Museum: June-Aug Sa-Su 2-5

OSKALOOSA

2815
Mahaska County Historical Society
2294 Oxford Ave, 52577 [Box 578, 52577]; (p) (515) 672-2989; (c) Mahaska

Private non-profit/ 1945/ Board of Directors/ staff: 1(f); 2(p)/ members: 400

GENEALOGICAL SOCIETY; HISTORIC PRESERVATION AGENCY; HISTORY MUSEUM; RESEARCH CENTER: Preserves local historical artifacts and buildings.

PROGRAMS: Annual Meeting; Community Outreach; Exhibits; Festivals; Guided Tours; Living History; Research Library/Archives

COLLECTIONS: [1815-1940] Artifacts and machinery related to IA history.

HOURS: May-Oct T-Sa 10-4:30, Su 1-4

ADMISSION: $4, Student $1

OTTUMWA

2816
Airpower Museum, Inc.
22001 Bluegrass Rd, 52501-8569; (p) (515) 938-2773; (f) (515) 938-2773; aaaapmhq@ pcsia.com; www.aaa-apm.org/; (c) Wapello

Private non-profit/ 1965/ staff: 50(v)/publication: Airpower Museum Bulletin

HISTORY MUSEUM: Preserves aviation histo-

ry from 1903 through the Korean War.

PROGRAMS: Annual Meeting; Exhibits; Guided Tours; Living History; Publication; Research Library/Archives

COLLECTIONS: [1920-1940] 57 full-size antique and classic airplanes, 40 antique aircraft engines, models, clothing, photos, art, simulators, posters, instruments, and a library of several thousand books.

2817
Antique Airplane Association, Inc.
22001 Bluegrass Rd, 52501-8569; (p) (515) 938-2773; (f) (515) 938-2773; aaaapmhl@ pcsia.com; www.aaa-apm.org/; (c) Wapello

Private non-profit/ 1953/ staff: 4(f); 1(p); 15(v)/ members: 6500/publication: Antique Airplane News

HISTORICAL SOCIETY; RESEARCH CENTER: Finds, restores, and flies antique and classic airplanes. Twenty-two chapters in the United States promote regional fly-ins.

PROGRAMS: Annual Meeting; Living History; Publication

COLLECTIONS: [1903-1960] Aircraft and engine manuals, lithographs, aircraft photographs, blueprints, books, and periodicals.

HOURS: Yr M-F 9-5

2818
Wapello County Historical Society
210 W Main St, 52501; (p) (515) 682-8676; (c) Wapello

Joint/ 1959/ County; Private non-profit/ staff: 3(f); 50(v)/ members: 354/publication: Sweet Days of Old

HISTORICAL SOCIETY; HISTORY MUSEUM: Identifies, collects, and preserves Wapello County history. Operates a museum.

PROGRAMS: Annual Meeting; Community Outreach; Exhibits; Facility Rental; Family Programs; Guided Tours; Lectures; Publication; Research Library/Archives

COLLECTIONS: [1838-1950] Documents, printed materials, images and artifacts from county history.

HOURS: Yr 10-4

ADMISSION: $2, Children $0.50

PALMER

2819
Wiegert Prairie Farmstead
RR-East of Palmer, 50571 [58640 330th Ave, Gilmore City, 50541]; (p) (712) 359-7778, (712) 776-2350; (c) Pocahontas

1897/ Pocahontas Historical Society/ staff: 30(v)

LIVING HISTORY/OUTDOOR MUSEUM

PROGRAMS: Festivals; School-Based Curriculum

COLLECTIONS: [1900] Barn, garage/carriage house, tool shed, hog house, machine shed, church, schoolhouse.

HOURS: By appt

PARKERSBURG

2820
Parkersburg Historical Home
401 Fifth St, 50665; (p) (319) 346-1849, (319) 346-1511; (c) Butler

HOUSE MUSEUM: Victorian home built in 1895 featuring local history.

HOURS: June-Sept F-Su 1-4

PELLA

2821
Pella Historical Society
507 Franklin St, 50219 [PO Box 145, 50219]; (p) (641) 628-2409; (f) (641) 628-9192; pellatt@ kdsi.net; www.kdsi.net/~pellatt; (c) Marion

Private non-profit/ 1935/ staff: 2(f); 6(p); 100(v)/ members: 750

HISTORIC SITE; HISTORICAL SOCIETY; HOUSE MUSEUM: Maintains 3 historic properties designed to preserve and promote the area's Dutch heritage.

PROGRAMS: Annual Meeting; Concerts; Elder's Programs; Exhibits; Facility Rental; Family Programs; Festivals; Film/Video; Garden Tours; Guided Tours; Lectures; Publication; Research Library/Archives; School-Based Curriculum

COLLECTIONS: [1850s-1900s] Dutch furnishings, silver, costumes, jewelry, copper and brass, Delft, books, street organ, bakery, wooden shoes, miniature village, European antiques, blacksmith, woodworking, grist mill, founder's home, furnished country school, and pioneer artifacts.

HOURS: Yr M-F 9-5; Apr-Dec + Sa 9-5

ADMISSION: $5, Children $1

2822
Scholte House Museum
728 Washington St, 50219; (p) (515) 628-3684; (c) Marion

Private non-profit/ 1847/ Pella Historical Society/ staff: 1(f); 120(v)

GARDEN; HISTORIC SITE; HOUSE MUSEUM: Maintains the home of Pella's founder, Dominic Scholte; interprets the history of Dutch immigrants.

PROGRAMS: Concerts; Festivals; Film/Video; Guided Tours; School-Based Curriculum

COLLECTIONS: [1847-1987] Original furnishings, 2 bronze statues, books, pictures, and a tulip garden.

HOURS: Mar-Dec M-Sa 1-4; and by appt

ADMISSION: $4, Children $1

PERRY

2823
Forest Park Museum and Arboretum
1477 K Ave, 50220; (p) (515) 465-3577; (f) (515) 465-3579; info@dallas25.org

County/ 1966/ Conservation Dept/ staff: 2(f); 4(p); 10(v)/publication: Dallas County Conservation Department Newsletter

HISTORY MUSEUM; NATURAL HISTORY MUSEUM: Exhibits natural, cultural, and historical events and artifacts of central IA.

PROGRAMS: Concerts; Festivals; Garden Tours; Guided Tours; Publication

COLLECTIONS: Agricultural equipment, hand tools, photos, and historical newspapers.

HOURS: May-Oct M-Sa 9-4:30, Su 1-4:30

ADMISSION: No charge

PRIMGHAR

2824
O'Brien County Historical Society
Heritage Rd, 51245 [Box 385, 51245]; (c) O'Brien

Joint/ 1970/ County; Private non-profit/ staff: 9(v)/ members: 200

HISTORIC PRESERVATION AGENCY; HISTORICAL SOCIETY; HISTORY MUSEUM; HOUSE MUSEUM: Preserves NW Iowa history, particularly rural and military related.

PROGRAMS: Annual Meeting; Guided Tours

COLLECTIONS: [1890-present] County history books and articles pertaining to the agricultural lifestyle of NW Iowa.

HOURS: Su by appt

ADMISSION: Donations accepted

PRINCETON

2825
Buffalo Bill Cody Homestead
28050 230th Ave, 52768; (p) (319) 225-2981

1847/ staff: 2(f); 2(p); 2(v)

HOUSE MUSEUM: Boyhood home of Buffalo Bill Cody.

COLLECTIONS: [1847-1860] Arrowheads; pottery from surrounding area.

HOURS: Apr-Oct

QUASQUETON

2826
Cedar Rock
2611 Quasqueton Diagonal Blvd, 52326 [PO Box 25, 52326]; (p) (319) 934-3572; (f) (319) 934-3565

1950/ Dept of Natural Resources/ staff: 1(f); 5(p)

One of Frank Lloyd Wright's most complete designs, his involvement extending to the design of the furniture and the selection of carpets, draperies, and household accessories.

COLLECTIONS: [1948-52] Wright-designed furniture; Wright-chosen carpets, drapery, and accessories.

HOURS: May-Oct

RADCLIFFE

2827
Radcliffe Historical Society
310 Isabella, 50230 [603 Catherine St, 50230]; (p) (515) 899-7851; (c) Hardin

Private non-profit/ 1985/ staff: 7(v)/ members: 10

HISTORIC PRESERVATION AGENCY; HISTORICAL SOCIETY: Preserves items related to local history.

PROGRAMS: Annual Meeting; Exhibits; Guided Tours

COLLECTIONS: [Late 1880s-present] Tools, medical items, school and church memorabilia, pictures

RED OAK

2828
Montgomery County Historical Society
2700 N Fourth, 51566 [Box 634, 51566]; (p) (712) 623-2289; bmckena@ redoak.heartland.net; (c) Montgomery

Private non-profit/ 1956/ Board of Curators/ staff: 1(p); 15(v)/ members: 500/publication: *Montgomery County Historical Society*

HISTORICAL SOCIETY; HISTORY MUSEUM; LIVING HISTORY/OUTDOOR MUSEUM: Preserves local history and maintains a research library.

PROGRAMS: Annual Meeting; Community Outreach; Exhibits; Facility Rental; Family Programs; Interpretation; Lectures; Publication; Research Library/Archives; School-Based Curriculum

COLLECTIONS: [1856-present] Records and artifacts relating to county history, Thos. D. Murphy Company art calendars, and military and agricultural history.

HOURS: Mar-Dec T-Su 1-5; Dec-Mar 1-5

ADMISSION: Donations accepted

ROCK RAPIDS

2829
Lyon County Historical Society Museum Complex
110 N Story St, 51246 [Box 14, 51246]; (p) (712) 472-3101; (c) Lyon

Joint/ 1972/ County; Private non-profit/ members: 376/publication: *Newsletter*

HISTORIC PRESERVATION AGENCY; HISTORIC SITE; HISTORICAL SOCIETY; HISTORY MUSEUM: Preserves and displays local historic items.

PROGRAMS: Annual Meeting; Exhibits; Facility Rental; Festivals; Guided Tours; Interpretation; Living History; Publication; Reenactments; School-Based Curriculum

COLLECTIONS: Military exhibition from Civil War-present, Native American artifacts from Blood Run, medical display, and newspaper display; caboose, windmill, and school house.

HOURS: June-Aug Su 1-5, May & Sept by appt

ADMISSION: $1

SAC CITY

2830
Sac City Historical Museum
13th & Main, 50583 [3225 210th St, 50583]; (c) Sac

City/ 1987/ staff: 12(v)/ members: 250

HISTORY MUSEUM; HOUSE MUSEUM: Interprets city and farming history.

PROGRAMS: Annual Meeting; Exhibits; Festivals; Guided Tours; Reenactments

COLLECTIONS: [1850-present] Farm implements, tools, room settings, military items, and schoolhouse furnishings.

HOURS: May-Sept Sa-Su 1:30-4:30

SALEM

2831
Lewelling Quaker Shrine
401 S Main, 52649 [PO Box 28, 52649]; (p) (319) 258-2541, (319) 258-4341; (c) Henry

Private non-profit/ 1958/ staff: 5(v)/ members: 100

HISTORIC SITE; HISTORICAL SOCIETY; HOUSE MUSEUM: Maintains the Lewelling Quaker house, a stop on the underground railroad, emphasizing the anti-slavery period.

PROGRAMS: Annual Meeting; Guided Tours

COLLECTIONS: [Mid 1800s-1900s] Kitchen utensils, books, furniture, clothing, dishes, and period furnishings.

HOURS: May-Sept Su 1-4 and by appt

ADMISSION: $2

SHELDON

2832
Sheldon Historical Society
10th St & 4th Ave, 51201 [323 10th St, 51201]; (c) O'Brien

Joint/ City; Private non-profit/ staff: 7(v)/ members: 330

GENEALOGICAL SOCIETY; HISTORIC PRESERVATION AGENCY; HISTORICAL SOCIETY: Preserves and publicizes Sheldon history.

PROGRAMS: Annual Meeting; Community Outreach; Exhibits; Facility Rental; Guided Tours; Interpretation; Publication; Research Library/Archives

COLLECTIONS: [1872-present] Artifacts and documents related to local history.

HOURS: Yr M-Sa

SHENANDOAH

2833
Greater Shenandoah Historical Society
405 W Sheridan Ave, 51601 [PO Box 182, 51601-0182]; (p) (712) 246-1669; (c) Page

Private non-profit/ 1971/ Board of Directors/ staff: 1(f); 50(v)/ members: 418

HISTORICAL SOCIETY: Preserves and promotes local history.

PROGRAMS: Annual Meeting; Exhibits; Garden Tours; Guided Tours; Lectures; Publication

COLLECTIONS: [Mid 1850s-present] Artifacts related to the Mormon Manti Settlement, early radio KMA and KFNF, businesses, and local history.

HOURS: Yr W, F, Su 1:30-4:30

SIBLEY

2834
Osceola County Historical Society, McCallum Museum/Brunson Heritage Home
5th St & 8th Ave, 51249 [724 3rd Ave, 51249]; (p) (712) 754-4000, (712) 754-3882; verstoff@heartlandtel.com; (c) Osceola

Private non-profit/ staff: 1(p); 10(v)/ members: 60

HISTORICAL SOCIETY; HISTORY MUSEUM: Operates three county historical sites: the McCallum Museum and Brunson Home, the Tracy House, and the DeBoer Grocery Museum.

PROGRAMS: Exhibits; Lectures; Research Library/Archives

COLLECTIONS: [1890s-1930] 1908 Sears auto buggy, sleigh, tools and agricultural implements; Civil War muskets, ammunition pouches, and sabers; stoneware, china, stoves, office equipment, photos, and period furnishings; fire fighting equipment.

HOURS: Mem Day-Labor Day

SIGOURNEY

2835
Keokuk County Historical Society
East & Elm St, 52591 [Box 123, 52591]; (c) Keokuk

Joint/ 1962/ County; Private non-profit/ staff: 15(v)/ members: 108

GENEALOGICAL SOCIETY; HISTORIC PRESERVATION AGENCY; HISTORIC SITE; HISTORICAL SOCIETY; HISTORY MUSEUM: To preserve the history and artifacts related to Keokuk County.

PROGRAMS: Annual Meeting; Exhibits; Guided Tours

COLLECTIONS: [1843-present] Obituaries, marriage, school records, old maps, books.

HOURS: Apr-Nov W-Th 9-4

ADMISSION: No charge

SIOUX CENTER

2836
Sioux Center Heritage Board
335 1st Ave NW, 51250; (p) (712) 722-0761; (f) (712) 722-0760; (c) Sioux

City/ 1987/ staff: 1(p); 26(v)

HISTORIC PRESERVATION AGENCY; HISTORICAL SOCIETY; LIVING HISTORY/OUTDOOR MUSEUM: Maintains a Heritage Village and preserves items from Sioux Center's history.

PROGRAMS: Exhibits; Festivals; Guided Tours; Living History

COLLECTIONS: [Mid-late 1800s] Pioneer equip, horse drawn farm equip, period clothing, blacksmith shop, school, sawmill.

ADMISSION: $2

SIOUX CITY

2837
Sergeant Floyd River Museum
1000 Larson Park Rd, 51102; (p) (712) 279-0198; (f) (712) 279-6934; (c) Woodbury

City/ 1989/ Sioux City Public Museum/ staff: 1(f); 3(p); 20(v)

HISTORY MUSEUM: Operates as a combined Missouri River Transport Museum and the Interstate Highway information center, located aboard a dry-docked 1932 diesel riverboat; displays river history and art.

PROGRAMS: Community Outreach; Exhibits; Family Programs; Film/Video; Interpretation; Lectures; Living History; Reenactments; School-Based Curriculum

COLLECTIONS: Scale model keelboats, steamboats, towboats, barges, river construction, river construction equip, and small craft; original photos, engineering drawings, period maps, river art and prints

2838
Sioux City Public Museum
2901 Jackson St, 51104-3697; (p) (712) 279-6174; (f) (712) 252-5615; scpm@sioux-city.org; www.sioux-city.org/museum; (c) Woodbury

City/ 1886/ staff: 6(f); 8(p); 40(v)/ members: 425

HISTORY MUSEUM: Collects and interprets the history of the tri-state region through system of four sites.

PROGRAMS: Annual Meeting; Community Outreach; Exhibits; Family Programs; Guided Tours; Interpretation; Lectures; Publication; Reenactments; Research Library/Archives; School-Based Curriculum

COLLECTIONS: [Late 19th-early 20th c] Material culture, research materials, and ephemera related to the history and culture of Sioux City and its surrounding region.

HOURS: Yr T 9-8, W-Sa 9-5, Su 1-5

ADMISSION: No charge

SLOAN

2839
Sloan Historical Society
419 Evans St, 51055 [302 4th St, 51055]; (c) Woodbury

Private non-profit/ 1969/ staff: 6(v)/ members: 100

HISTORICAL SOCIETY; HISTORY MUSEUM: Operates a museum concentrated on Sloan and local school history.

PROGRAMS: Annual Meeting; Exhibits

COLLECTIONS: [Early 1900s-present]

HOURS: June-Aug Sa 9-12

ADMISSION: Donations accepted

SOUTH AMANA

2840
Henry Moore Museum Trust, Barn Museum
2 Blks N of Hwy 6 on 220 Trail, 52334 [413 P St Box 124, 52334]; (p) (319) 662-3058; (f) (319) 642-3620; minibarn@cc-cci.net; (c) IA

Private for-profit/ 1976/ staff: 2(f)

HISTORY MUSEUM: Presents the history of rural American agriculture and architecture, through miniature replicas.

PROGRAMS: Exhibits; Interpretation

COLLECTIONS: [1880-1930] 200 miniature replicas of rural agriculture and architecture.

HOURS: Apr-Oct Daily 9-5

SPENCER

2841
Parker Museum of Clay County
300 E 3rd St, 51301 [PO Box 91, 51301]; (p) (712) 262-3304; (f) (712) 262-5761; (c) Clay

Private non-profit/ 1960/ Board of Directors/ staff: 2(p)/ members: 411/publication: *History of Clay County*

HISTORICAL SOCIETY; HISTORY MUSEUM; HOUSE MUSEUM: Collects, preserves, and interprets the history of Clay County. Housed in a 1916 Arts and Crafts style home.

PROGRAMS: Annual Meeting; Community Outreach; Exhibits; Facility Rental; Family Programs; Festivals; Film/Video; Guided Tours; Interpretation; Lectures; Living History; Publication; Reenactments; Research Library/Archives; School-Based Curriculum

COLLECTIONS: [1860-1945] Antique furniture, 1918 La France fire truck, Victorian organs, textiles, clothing, and photos.

HOURS: Yr T-F 11:30-3:30, June-Sept also Su 2-4

ADMISSION: Donations accepted

SPILLVILLE

2842
Bily Clock Museum, The
[PO Box 258, 52168]; (p) (319) 562-3569; (f) (319) 534-4373; si10127@cedarnet.org; (c) Winneshiek

City/ 1948/ staff: 2(f); 5(p)

HISTORY MUSEUM

PROGRAMS: Annual Meeting; Concerts; Exhibits; Festivals; Guided Tours; Research Library/Archives

COLLECTIONS: [1913-1958] Hand-carved clocks with musical discs, Dvorak memorabilia, and Bily Brothers books.

HOURS: May-Nov: Daily 8:30-5

ADMISSION: $3.50, Children $1.25

STANTON

2843
Stanton Historical Society/Swedish Heritage and Cultural Center
410 Hilltop Box 231, 51573; (p) (712) 829-2840; (f) (712) 829-2393; (c) Montgomery

Private non-profit/ 1971/ staff: 1(f); 1(p); 15(v)/ members: 230

CULTURAL CENTER; HISTORY MUSEUM: Operates the Swedish Heritage and Cultural Center, which relates the history of Swedish immigration to the Halland settlement.

PROGRAMS: Annual Meeting; Community Outreach; Exhibits; Facility Rental; Festivals; Reenactments; Research Library/Archives

COLLECTIONS: [1870s-1940s] Artifacts of the Swedish immigrants to SW Iowa including trunks, clothing, tools, a loom, spinning wheels, and photos.

HOURS: Yr Dec 1-Apr 1 W-Su 1-4; Apr 1-Dec 1 T-Su 1-4

ADMISSION: $2

STORM LAKE

2844
Buena Vista County Historical Society
214 W 9th St, 50588 [214 W 5th St, 50588]; (p) (712) 732-4955; (c) Buena Vista

Private non-profit/ 1960/ staff: 1(p); 100(v)/ members: 375

HISTORICAL SOCIETY: Preserves, interprets, and enhances the history of Buena Vista County; supports active interest in state and local history.

PROGRAMS: Annual Meeting; Community Outreach; Exhibits; Festivals; Guided Tours; Lectures

COLLECTIONS: [1850s-present] Frank L. Van Voorhis Native American artifact collection. 1870s Norwegian log house; 1900 county schoolhouse.

HOURS: Yr M-F 12-4

ADMISSION: $2, Children $1

STRAWBERRY POINT

2845
Wilder Memorial Museum, Inc.
123 W Mission, 52076; (p) (319) 933-4461; (c) Clayton

Private non-profit/ 1960/ staff: 3(f); 2(p)/ members: 100

ART MUSEUM; HISTORICAL SOCIETY; HISTORY MUSEUM

PROGRAMS: Annual Meeting; Family Programs; Film/Video; Guided Tours

COLLECTIONS: [1750-present] Art glass, Victorian hanging lamps, Victorian furniture, European figures, paintings, doll collection, rock and shell collection, primitive farm tools, area history memorabilia.

HOURS: May-Sept Daily 10-5

ADMISSION: $2.50

SWEDESBURG

2846
Swedish Heritage Society
107 James Ave, 52652-0074; (p) (319) 254-2317; (c) Henry

Private non-profit/ 1986/ staff: 45(v)/ members: 421/publication: *Swedish Heritage Society Newsletter*

HISTORICAL SOCIETY; HISTORY MUSEUM; HOUSE MUSEUM: Preserves the values and traditions of Swedish immigrants; operates the Swedish Museum, which preserves and shares documents and information related to Swedesburg's early settlement and observes Swedish festivals.

PROGRAMS: Community Outreach; Exhibits; Festivals; Guided Tours; Lectures; Publication

HOURS: Yr M-T, Th-Sa 9-4

ADMISSION: Donations accepted

TABOR

2847
Tabor Historical Society
705 Park St, 51653 [PO Box 417, 51653]; (p) (712) 629-2675; (c) Fremont

Private non-profit/ 1969/ staff: 8(v)/ members: 50

HISTORIC SITE

PROGRAMS: Community Outreach; Elder's Programs; Exhibits; Guided Tours; Interpretation

COLLECTIONS: [Civil War] 1853 home, station on underground railroad, and period furnishings.

HOURS: By appt

ADMISSION: $1, Children $0.25

2848
Todd House, The
405 Park St, 51653 [PO Box 417, 51653]; (p) (712) 629-2675; (f) (712) 629-3535; www.community.heartland.net/tabor-library/ historical.htm; (c) Fremont

1853/ Tabor Historical Society/ staff: 4(v)

HOUSE MUSEUM: Home of abolitionist Reverend John Todd. The house served as a stop on the Underground Railroad.

COLLECTIONS: [Late 19th c] Furniture; diaries and letters.

HOURS: By appt

TOLEDO

2849
Tama County Historical Society
200 N Broadway St, 52342; (p) (515) 484-6767; (c) Tama

Joint/ 1942/ County; Private non-profit/ staff: 12(v)/ members: 150

GENEALOGICAL SOCIETY; HISTORICAL SOCIETY; HISTORY MUSEUM: Preserves artifacts and genealogical material of the county.

PROGRAMS: Annual Meeting; Exhibits

COLLECTIONS: [1853-present] Pioneer artifacts; genealogical material; 2,500 microfilm of passenger lists, censuses, and local newspapers.

HOURS: Yr T-Sa 1-4:30

TROY

2850
Troy Academy and Historical Society
Wheat Ave, 52537 [403 E Arkansas Ave, Bloomfield, 52537]; (p) (515) 664-1929; (c) Davis

1853/ staff: 4(v)/ members: 150

HISTORIC SITE; HISTORICAL SOCIETY; HISTORY MUSEUM: Restoring the academy.

PROGRAMS: Annual Meeting; Exhibits; Living History

COLLECTIONS: [1850-1925] Textbooks, agricultural implements, clothing, and other objects used in the academy.

HOURS: June-Oct

URBANDALE

2851
Living History Farms
2600 NW 111th St, 50322; (p) (515) 278-5286; (f) (515) 278-9808; www.lhf.org; (c) Polk

Private non-profit/ 1969/ staff: 26(f); 75(p); 600(v)/ members: 1000

LIVING HISTORY/OUTDOOR MUSEUM: Operates a 600 acre outdoor museum depicting the changes in Midwestern agriculture and rural life.

PROGRAMS: Community Outreach; Facility Rental; Family Programs; Festivals; Interpretation; Living History; School-Based Curriculum

COLLECTIONS: [1850-1950] 300 quilts and coverlets; farm implements, machinery, hand tools, livestock and seeds; domestic tools and household furnishings.

HOURS: May-Oct Daily 9-5

VINTON

2852
Benton County Historical Society
612 1st Ave,, 52349 [PO Box 112, 52349]; (p) (319) 472-4325; bchs@www.mebbs.com; www.rootsweb.com/~iabenton/bchs/:htm; (c) Benton

Private non-profit/ 1970/ Board of Directors/ staff: 25(v)/ members: 130

GENEALOGICAL SOCIETY; HISTORICAL SOCIETY; HISTORY MUSEUM; HOUSE MUSEUM; LIBRARY AND/OR ARCHIVES; RAILROAD MUSEUM: Preserves and educates about Benton County history through an archives and museum, a Victorian mansion, and a railroad museum.

PROGRAMS: Annual Meeting; Community Outreach; Exhibits; Facility Rental; Festivals; Guided Tours; Interpretation; Publication; Reenactments; Research Library/Archives

COLLECTIONS: [1860-present] Railroad and local history memorabilia and artifacts.

WADENA

2853
Johnson-Erickson Museum
Mill St, 52169 [Box 12, 140 S River St, 52169]; (p) (319) 774-3205; (c) Fayette

1971/ staff: 22(v)

HISTORY MUSEUM: Preserves articles related to local historical people and their accomplishments.

PROGRAMS: Annual Meeting; Community Outreach; Exhibits; Festivals; Guided Tours

COLLECTIONS: Doctors tools, horse related items, school items, historic literature, carpenter tools, and blacksmith tools.

ADMISSION: Donations accepted

WALKER

2854
Walker Historical Society
Rowley St, 52352 [PO Box 173, 52352]; (c) Linn

Private non-profit/ 1977/ Board of Directors/ staff: 10(v)/ members: 30

HISTORIC PRESERVATION AGENCY; HISTORIC SITE; HISTORICAL SOCIETY: Preserves railroad depot and the history of Walker.

PROGRAMS: Exhibits; Guided Tours; Living History

COLLECTIONS: [Late 1800s-1950] Railroad items and a Rock Island Caboose; living quarters with period furnishings.

HOURS: June-Sept 1st and 3rd Su 2-4

ADMISSION: No charge

WAPELLO

2855
Louisa County Historical Society
609 N US 61, 52653; (p) (319) 523-8381; (c)

Louisa

Private non-profit/ 1964/ staff: 20(p); 30(v)/ members: 330/publication: *Louisa's Story*

HISTORICAL SOCIETY; HISTORY MUSEUM; HOUSE MUSEUM

PROGRAMS: Annual Meeting; Community Outreach; Exhibits; Family Programs; Festivals; Film/Video; Lectures; Publication; Research Library/Archives

COLLECTIONS: [1880-present]

HOURS: Museum: Sa-Su 2-4

ADMISSION: Donations accepted

2856
Toolesboro Mounds National Historic Landmark
8 mi S of Wapello on Hwy 99, 52653 [Box 261, 52653]; (p) (319) 523-8381; www.iowahistory. org/sites/toolsboro/toolesboro_mounds.html; (c) Louisa

State/ State Historical Society of Iowa/ staff: 1(p)

LIVING HISTORY/OUTDOOR MUSEUM: Preserves the mounds at Toolesboro, remnants of Hopewellian culture in IA; maintains visitor center.

PROGRAMS: Exhibits; Guided Tours; Interpretation

COLLECTIONS: [2nd c BC]

HOURS: June-Aug Daily 12-4; Sept-Oct Sa-Su 12-4

ADMISSION: No charge

WASHINGTON

2857
Conger House Museum
309 E Washington, 52353 [2676 240th St, 52353]; (p) (319) 653-3125, (319) 653-6988

1847

COLLECTIONS: [Late 1800s] Washington County history, manufactured items, war memorabilia, medical items, Native American artifacts; Washington County photos & documents.

HOURS: June-Aug Su

2858
Washington County Historical Society, Inc.
903 E Washington, 52353 [2676 240th St, 52353]; (p) (319) 653-3125; (c) Washington

Joint/ 1960/ County; Private non-profit/ staff: 300(v)/ members: 300

GARDEN; HISTORIC SITE; HISTORICAL SOCIETY; HISTORY MUSEUM; HOUSE MUSEUM: Preserves county history through operation and maintenance of a house museum, a one room school house, and a country store.

PROGRAMS: Annual Meeting; Exhibits; Family Programs; Festivals; Garden Tours; Guided Tours; Lectures; Publication; Research Library/Archives

COLLECTIONS: [1847-1930] Period military, medical, archaeology, and manufactured articles; early 1900s general store merchandise and period school items.

HOURS: June-Aug + 1st 2 wks Dec Su 2-5

ADMISSION: $2, Children $1

WASHTA

2859
Grand Meadow Heritage Commission, Inc.
630th St & D Ave, 51061 [6211 E Ave, 51061]; (p) (713) 447-6429; htrt@pionet.net; (c) Cherokee

Private non-profit/ 1975/ staff: 3(p); 30(v)/ members: 25

HISTORY MUSEUM: Collects and displays historic memorabilia chiefly depicting the life and activities of early residents of the area.

PROGRAMS: Annual Meeting; Festivals; Guided Tours; Publication; Theatre

COLLECTIONS: [Prehistoric and Early 1900s] Former consolidated school, one-room school, log cabin, service station, and barn; artifacts of farm equipment and tools, household furnishings, toys, music, railroad artifacts, and Native American items.

HOURS: May-Sept Su 2-4

ADMISSION: Donations accepted

WATERLOO

2860
Grout Museum of History and Science
503 S St, 50701; (p) (319) 234-6357; (f) (319) 236-0500; grout@cedarnet.org; www.cedar net.org/grout; (c) Black Hawk

Private non-profit/ 1956/ H.W. Grout Trust/ staff: 8(f); 11(p); 350(v)/ members: 473/publication: *Collections Newsletter*

HISTORY MUSEUM: Collects, preserves, and interprets history and scientific principles, along with cultural and natural history of the region.

PROGRAMS: Community Outreach; Exhibits; Facility Rental; Family Programs; Guided Tours; Interpretation; Lectures; Living History; Publication; Research Library/Archives; School-Based Curriculum

COLLECTIONS: [1833-present] Primarily science related artifacts; items related to ethnology, pioneer, and natural history.

2861
Rensselaer Russell House Museum
520 W 3rd St, 50701 [503 S St, 50701]; (p) (319) 233-0262; (f) (319) 236-0500; grout@cedarnet.org; www.cedarnet.org/grout; (c) Black Hawk

Private non-profit/ 1965/ Grout Museum of History and Science/ staff: 1(f); 1(p); 40(v)/ members: 530

HOUSE MUSEUM: Preserves and interprets the history of Waterloo, Black Hawk County, IA, the Russell Family, and the Victorian Era.

PROGRAMS: Exhibits; Family Programs; Guided Tours; Reenactments; Theatre

COLLECTIONS: [Victorian Era] Italiante House Museum with Victorian furnishings, including original family pieces.

HOURS: Apr-May, Sept-Oct T-Su 1-4:30; June-Aug T-F 10-4:30, Sa-Su 1-4:30

ADMISSION: $3.50, Children $2.50

WAUKON

2862
Allamakee County Historical Society
107 Allamakee St, 52172 [PO Box 95, 52172]; (p) (319) 568-2954; bristol@rconnect.com; (c) Allamakee

Private non-profit/ 1965/ staff: 1(p); 20(v)/ members: 150

HISTORICAL SOCIETY

PROGRAMS: Annual Meeting; Exhibits; Facility Rental

COLLECTIONS: Courthouse records dating from 1860, Victorian clothing, parlor bedroom and kitchen, rural school artifacts, agricultural tools, and Norwegian-style log building, Native American, dolls.

HOURS: June-July, Aug-Sept W-Sa 10-4

ADMISSION: $2

WAVERLY

2863
Bremer County Historical Society
402 W Bremer Ave, 50677 [219 Main St, PO Box 218, Plainfield, 50666-0218]; (p) (319) 276-4674; (c) Bremer

Private non-profit/ 1958/ staff: 10(p); 10(v)/ members: 100

HISTORIC PRESERVATION AGENCY; HISTORIC SITE; HISTORICAL SOCIETY; HISTORY MUSEUM: Preserves and displays the history and artifacts of Waverly and Bremer County.

PROGRAMS: Annual Meeting; Exhibits; Guided Tours; School-Based Curriculum

COLLECTIONS: [1840-1960] Period artifacts and furniture displayed in theme rooms (central living room, bedroom, kitchen, and country store); former Field Museum curator C.J. Albrecht's animal collection.

HOURS: May-Oct M-Sa 1:30-4, Su 2-4

ADMISSION: $1

WEST BEND

2864
West Bend Historical Society
3rd St SE & 1st Ave SW, 50597 [4473 550 Ave, 50597]; (p) (515) 887-4356, (515) 887-3956; (c) Palo Alto

Joint/ City; Private non-profit/ staff: 5(p); 12(v)/ members: 75

HISTORIC SITE; HISTORICAL SOCIETY: Preserves and exhibits local historical artifacts, a replica of a sod house, an old post office and a restored country school.

PROGRAMS: Community Outreach; Exhibits; Guided Tours; Reenactments

COLLECTIONS: [1890-1940s] Period furnishings and clothing.

HOURS: June-Aug Sa-Su

WEST BRANCH

2865
Herbert Hoover Library
210 Parkside Dr, 52358 [PO Box 488, 52358-0488]; (p) (319) 643-5301; (f) (319) 643-5825;

hoover.library@nara.gov; hoover.nara.gov; (c) Cedar

Federal/ NARA

HOURS: Yr

2866
Herbert Hoover National Historic Site
110 Parkside Dr, 52358 [PO Box 607, 52358]; (p) (319) 643-2541; (f) (319) 643-5367; www.nps.gov/heho; (c) Cedar

Federal/ 1965/ National Park Service/ staff: 12(f); 25(p); 200(v)

HISTORIC SITE; PRESIDENTIAL SITE: Commemorates life of Herbert Hoover at site that includes cottage where Hoover was born, a blacksmith shop, the first West Branch schoolhouse, the Friends Meetinghouse; also on site is the Herbert Hoover Presidential Library-Museum, the gravesites of President and Mrs. Hoover, and a 76-acre tallgrass prairie.

PROGRAMS: Community Outreach; Exhibits; Family Programs; Festivals; Guided Tours; Interpretation

COLLECTIONS: [1874-1884] Historic buildings are furnished with period books, furnishings, blacksmithing, and woodworking tools.

HOURS: Yr Daily 9-5

ADMISSION: $2, Seniors $1

WEST DES MOINES

2867
Jordan House
2001 Fuller Rd, 50265; (p) (515) 225-1286

1850/ staff: 1(p)

HOUSE MUSEUM: 1850 Victorian mansion that was a stop on the Underground Railroad and home of town's first white settler, James C. Jordan and his family.

PROGRAMS: Exhibits; Guided Tours

COLLECTIONS: [Mid to late 1800s] Home furnishings 1850-1890s, underground railroad display.

HOURS: Seasonal

WEST UNION

2868
Fayette County Helpers Club and Historical Society
100 N Walnut, 52175; (p) (319) 422-5797; (c) Fayette

Private non-profit/ 1975/ staff: 8(v)

GENEALOGICAL SOCIETY; HISTORIC SITE; HISTORY MUSEUM: Operates a county museum and genealogy room, housed in a 1903 hospital building

PROGRAMS: Facility Rental; Guided Tours; Lectures

COLLECTIONS: Early agriculture and home-making exhibits; military uniforms and memorabilia, medical instruments, wheelchairs, and optical displays; political buttons, banners, and voting booths and machinery.

HOURS: May-Oct M-F 10-4, Nov-Apr M-F 10-3

ADMISSION: Donations accepted

WILTON

2869
Cedar County Historical Society
Courthouse, 52778 [2125 Old Muscatine Rd, 52778]; (p) (319) 732-2902; jkaufman@eiccd.cc.ia.us; (c) Cedar

Private non-profit/ 1958/ Board of Directors/ staff: 30(v)/ members: 500/publication: *Cedar County Historical Review*

HISTORICAL SOCIETY; HISTORY MUSEUM: Preserves county history of Cedar County; maintains museum.

PROGRAMS: Annual Meeting; Exhibits; Facility Rental; Family Programs; Festivals; Guided Tours; Interpretation; Living History; Publication; Reenactments; Research Library/ Archives

COLLECTIONS: [1836-1950] Pictures, legal documents, biographical data, newspapers, books, tools, machinery, uniforms, home furnishings, and archaeological materials from historic people, places, and events.

WINFIELD

2870
Winfield Historical Society
114 S Locust, 52659 [PO Box 184, 52659]; (c) Henry

Private non-profit/ 1997/ Board of Directors/ staff: 9(f); 20(v)/ members: 80

HISTORICAL SOCIETY; HISTORY MUSEUM: Maintains a museum to preserve local history and artifacts.

PROGRAMS: Annual Meeting; Exhibits

COLLECTIONS: Local history materials and artifacts.

HOURS: Yr M 10-2 and by appt

ADMISSION: No charge

WINTERSET

2871
Birthplace of John Wayne
224 S Second St, 50273 [216 S Second St, 50273]; (p) (515) 462-1044; www.john-waynebirthplace.org; (c) Madison

Private non-profit/ 1982/ John Wayne Birthplace Society, Ltd./ staff: 1(f); 13(p)

Museum with a campus that includes the house in which John Wayne was born and a park.

COLLECTIONS: Family photographs, movie stills, lobby cards, eyepatch John Wayne wore in "True Grit," hat he wore in "Rio Lobo," and a suitcase used in "Stagecoach."

HOURS: Yr Daily 10-4:30

ADMISSION: $2.50, Children $1

2872
Madison County Historical Society
815 S 2nd Ave, 50273 [PO Box 15, 50273]; (p) (515) 462-2134; (c) Madison

Private non-profit/ 1904/ staff: 1(f); 6(p); 187(v)/ members: 394/publication: *Scenic Madison County, IA; and others*

HISTORIC SITE; HISTORICAL SOCIETY; HISTORY MUSEUM; HOUSE MUSEUM; RE-

SEARCH CENTER: Acquires, preserves, and exhibits artifacts of the social, cultural, and natural history of the Madison County region.

PROGRAMS: Annual Meeting; Community Outreach; Exhibits; Facility Rental; Family Programs; Festivals; Guided Tours; Interpretation; Lectures; Publication; Research Library/ Archives; School-Based Curriculum

COLLECTIONS: [1860s-present] Rock, mineral, and fossil collection of Amel Priest; military uniforms, primitive toys, books, clothing, housewares, furniture, radios, and school memorabilia.

HOURS: May-Oct M-Sa 11-4, Su 1-5

ADMISSION: $5; Group rates

KANSAS

ABILENE

2873
Dickinson County Historical Society
412 S Campbell, 67410; (p) (785) 263-2632; (f) (785) 263-0380; dchs@ikansas.com; (c) Dickinson

Private non-profit/ 1928/ staff: 1(f); 6(p); 100(v)/ members: 617/publication: *The Gazette*

GENEALOGICAL SOCIETY; HISTORICAL SOCIETY; HISTORY MUSEUM: Collects and preserves artifacts, documents, and other items representing our country's history.

PROGRAMS: Annual Meeting; Community Outreach; Exhibits; Family Programs; Festivals; Film/Video; Guided Tours; Interpretation; Lectures; Living History; Publication; Research Library/Archives

COLLECTIONS: [1855-1900] Pioneer and early farming history; 1901 C.W. Parker Carousel.

HOURS: Yr Daily M-Sa 10:-4, Sun 1-5

ADMISSION: $2.50; Under 12 free

2874
Dwight D. Eisenhower Library & Museum, The
200 SE 4th St, 67410-2900; (p) (785) 263-4751; (f) (785) 263-4218; eisenhower.library@nara.gov; www.eisenhower.utexas.edu; (c) Dickinson

Federal/ NARA

Complex of library, museum, and burial place of Dwight & Mamie Eisenhower.

COLLECTIONS: [1890-1946] Presidential papers, audiovisual materials, and other items. House and related artifacts.

HOURS: Yr Daily Museum: 9-5, Summer 8-5:45; Library & Home: 9-4:45

2875
Museum of Independent Telephony
412 S Campbell, 67410; (p) (785) 262-2681; (f) (785) 263-0380; dchs@ikansas.com; (c) Dickinson

Private non-profit/ 1973/ staff: 1(f); 3(p); 60(v)

Tells the story of the independent telephone industry.

COLLECTIONS: [1870s-1970s] Artifacts in all areas of telephony; research library; 1,500 artifacts, 2,000 library volumes. Exhibits include a timeline of telephones from 1895-1976, films, and inter-activities.

HOURS: Yr Daily M-Sa 10-4, Su 1-4

ADMISSION: $2.50

2876
Seelye Mansion
1105 N Buckeye Ave, 67410-1942; (p) (785) 263-1084; (f) (785) 263-3741

2877
State of Kansas Sports Hall of Fame
213 N Broadway, 67410 [PO Box 35, 67410]; (p) (785) 263-7403; (f) (785) 263-0416; kshof@oz-onloine.net; www.kshof.org; (c) Dickinson

Private non-profit/ 1961/ staff: 3(f); 3(p); 6(v)/ members: 150/publication: *Kansas Sports Magazine*

HISTORY MUSEUM: Preserves the history of sports for the state of KS.

PROGRAMS: Exhibits; Guided Tours; Interpretation; Publication; Research Library/Archives

COLLECTIONS: Sports related exhibits and archives.

HOURS: Jan-Dec Daily M-Sa 9-4:30, Su

ALDEN

2878
AT & SF Railroad Museum
Main St, 67512 [PO Box 158, 67512]; (p) (316) 534-2425; (f) (316) 534-4021; prflrcraft@aol.com; (c) Rice

County/ 1970/ Coronado Quivire Museum

HISTORY MUSEUM

HOURS: By appt

ALMA

2879
Wabaunsee County Historical Society
227 Missouri, 66401 [PO Box 387, 66401]; (p) (785) 765-2200; (c) Wabaunsee

Private non-profit/ 1968/ staff: 1(f); 8(p)/ members: 228

ART MUSEUM; GENEALOGICAL SOCIETY; HISTORIC PRESERVATION AGENCY; HISTORIC SITE; HISTORICAL SOCIETY; HISTORY MUSEUM; HOUSE MUSEUM; RESEARCH CENTER; TRIBAL MUSEUM: Preserves the historic artifacts of the county.

PROGRAMS: Annual Meeting; Community Outreach; Exhibits; Facility Rental; Guided Tours; Publication; Research Library/Archives

COLLECTIONS: [early 1800s-present] Grouped artifacts including storefronts and household rooms.

HOURS: Mar 1-Nov 31 T-Sa 10-4, Su 1-4; Dec-Mar 1 T-F 10-4

ADMISSION: Donations accepted

ANTHONY

2880
Historical Museum of Anthony, Inc.
502 W Main, 67003 [PO Box 185, 67003]; (p)

(316) 842-3852; (c) Harper

Private non-profit/ 1975/ staff: 2(p)/ members: 97

HISTORICAL SOCIETY: Maintains museum housed in Old Santa Fe Railroad Depot built in 1928.

PROGRAMS: Annual Meeting; Exhibits; Guided Tours

COLLECTIONS: School materials, displays.

HOURS: Yr Th-Sa 9-12/1-5

ADMISSION: Donations

ARGONIA

2881
Salter House and Museum
220 W Garfield, 67004; (p) (620) 435-6990; (c) Sumner

1884/ Argonia and Western Sumner County Historical Society

Home of Susanna Madora Salter, first woman mayor in the USA, elected mayor of Argonia in 1887.

COLLECTIONS: [late 1800s] 1884 brick house, artifacts, antiques.

ARKANSAS CITY

2882
Cherokee Strip Land Rush Museum
S on Hwy 77, 67005 [PO Box 778, 67005]; (p) (316) 442-6750; (f) (316) 441-4426; museum@horizon.hit.net; www.arkcity.org/csm.html; (c) Cowley

City/ 1966/ staff: 1(f); 2(p); 6(v)/ members: 74

GENEALOGICAL SOCIETY; HISTORIC PRESERVATION AGENCY; HISTORY MUSEUM: Dedicated to the Cherokee Strip Land Rush of September 17, 1893.

PROGRAMS: Exhibits; Film/Video; Research Library/Archives; School-Based Curriculum

COLLECTIONS: [1890s-early 1900s] Artifacts of the period concerning the Cherokee Strip Land Rush, early Arkansas City, and North Central OK.

HOURS: Yr Apr-Aug T-Sa 10-5, Su 1-5; Sept-Mar T-Sa 10-4, Su 1-4

ADMISSION: $2.50, Children $1, Seniors $2.25

ASHLAND

2883
Clark County Historical Society
430 W 4th Hwy 160, 67831 [PO Box 862, 67831-0862]; (p) (316) 635-2227; rogers@ucom.net; (c) Clark

Private non-profit/ 1939/ staff: 2(p); 50(v)/ members: 478/publication: *Notes on Early Clark County, Kansas; Cattle Ranching South of Dodge City-The Early Years (1870-1920)*

GENEALOGICAL SOCIETY; HISTORIC PRESERVATION AGENCY; HISTORICAL SOCIETY; HISTORY MUSEUM; RESEARCH CENTER: Operates a museum and research library.

PROGRAMS: Annual Meeting; Community Outreach; Exhibits; Facility Rental; Family Programs; Festivals; Film/Video; Guided Tours; Lectures; Living History; Publication; Research Library/Archives; School-Based Curriculum

COLLECTIONS: [1880s] Dish, guns, military uniforms and artifacts, fossils, quilts, photographs, musical instruments, barb wire, farm implements, buggies, dolls, elephants, clocks, lamps, irons, clothing, machinery, tools, trophies, tapestries, office machinery, books, histories.

HOURS: Yr M-S 10-12/1-5, Su 1-5

ADMISSION: Donations accepted

ATCHISON

2884
Amelia Earhart Birthplace Museum
223 N Terrace, 66002; (p) (913) 367-4217; aemuseum@lvnworth.com; www.ameliaearhartmuseum.org; (c) Atchison

Private non-profit/ 1984/ Ninety-Nines International Organization of Women Pilots/ staff: 2(p); 50(v)

HISTORIC SITE; HISTORY MUSEUM; HOUSE MUSEUM: Birthplace of Amelia Earhart restored to the period of her childhood.

PROGRAMS: Community Outreach; Exhibits; Festivals; Guided Tours; Lectures; Research Library/Archives

COLLECTIONS: Original family and Amelia Earhart artifacts, including portraits. Most of the dwelling retains the original floors, woodwork, and siding.

HOURS: Yr Daily 9-4

ADMISSION: $2, Children $0.50

2885
Atchison County, Kansas Historical Society
200 10th St, 66002 [PO Box 201, 66002]; (p) (913) 367-6238; atchhistory@journy.com; (c) Atchison

Private non-profit/ 1966/ Board of Directors/ staff: 1(f); 12(v)/ members: 200/publication: *Newsletter*

HISTORICAL SOCIETY; HISTORY MUSEUM: Preserves, promotes, shares, and records the history and historical artifacts of Atchison County, KS.

PROGRAMS: Annual Meeting; Community Outreach; Exhibits; Guided Tours; Lectures; Publication

COLLECTIONS: [1854-present] Collection of Atchison-specific artifacts.

HOURS: Yr M-F 8-5, Sa 10-4, Su 12-4

ADMISSION: Donations accepted

2886
Evah C. Cray Historical Home Museum
805 N 5th St, 66002; (p) (913) 367-3046, (913) 367-1948; (c) Atchison

Private non-profit/ 1979/ Evah Cray Charitable Trust/ staff: 1(f); 7(p)

GARDEN; HOUSE MUSEUM: 25-room Victorian mansion with gardens.

PROGRAMS: Community Outreach; Elder's Programs; Exhibits; Facility Rental; Family Programs; Guided Tours; School-Based Curriculum

COLLECTIONS: [Victorian Era] Circa 1882 Victorian mansion; Amelia Earhart-Carriage House; Victorian furnishings, ornate fireplaces, drapes, artifacts, 3 stained glass windows, two towers, early toys/dolls, quilts, bedroom suites; World's Fair bedroom, 1906; Amelia Earhart large picture collection.

HOURS: Jan-Feb Sa 10-4; Su 1-4; Mar-Apr M-F 10-4, Sa-Su 1-4; May-Oct M-Sa 10-4, Su 1-4

AUGUSTA

2887
Augusta Historical Society, Inc.
303 & 305 State, 67010 [303 State, 67010]; (p) (316) 775-5655; (c) Butler

Private non-profit/ 1938/ Board of Directors/ staff: 1(f); 1(p); 35(v)/ members: 150

GENEALOGICAL SOCIETY; HISTORIC SITE; HISTORICAL SOCIETY; HISTORY MUSEUM: Collects, preserves, and exhibits artifacts of historical significance to Augusta, Butler County, and the State of KS.

PROGRAMS: Annual Meeting; Exhibits; Facility Rental; Research Library/Archives

COLLECTIONS: [1868-1940]

HOURS: Yr M-Sa 11-3, Su 1-4

BALDWIN CITY

2888
Baker University Archives
518 Eighth St, 66006 [PO Box 65, 66006]; (p) (785) 594-8380; (f) (788) 594-6721; day@harvey.bakeru.edu; www.bakeru.edu/library; (c) Douglas

Private non-profit/ 1858/ staff: 1(p)

LIBRARY AND/OR ARCHIVES: Teaching and research facility.

PROGRAMS: Research Library/Archives

COLLECTIONS: [1854-present] Records and documents relating to Baker University and the KS East Conference of the United Methodist Church.

HOURS: Yr T-F 1-4

2889
Old Castle Museum Complex
515 Fifth St, 66006 [PO Box 65, 66006]; (p) (785) 594-6809; (f) (785) 594-2522; day@ harvey.bakeru.edu; www.bakeru.edu; (c) Douglas

Joint/ 1958/ Baker Univ; Private non-profit/ staff: 1(f); 2(p); 2(v)

HISTORIC SITE; HISTORY MUSEUM: The museum collects, preserves, and interprets Baker University, Methodist, Santa Fe Trail, and local Kansas history for the education and entertainment of present and future generations.

PROGRAMS: Community Outreach; Elder's Programs; Exhibits; Family Programs; Festivals; Guided Tours; Living History; Publication; Research Library/Archives

COLLECTIONS: [19th c] Kansas history, 12 processed manuscripts, 20 maps, 300 volumes, 30 portraits and paintings, 20,000 museum artifacts, and 300 photographs.

BAXTER SPRINGS

2890
Baxter Springs Heritage Center and Museum
8th & E Ave, 66713 [PO Box 514, 66713]; (p) (316) 856-2385; (c) Cherokee

Joint/ 1958/ Baxter Springs Historical Society; Board/ staff: 1(f); 100(v)/ members: 90

HISTORIC PRESERVATION AGENCY; HISTORIC SITE; HISTORICAL SOCIETY; HISTORY MUSEUM

PROGRAMS: Exhibits; Guided Tours; Interpretation; Lectures; Research Library/Archives

COLLECTIONS: [1858-1945] Civil War, WW I & II, Victorian, Baxter Springs history, and school collections: photographs, maps, machinery, and specimens of local lead and zinc mining industry.

HOURS: Apr-Oct T-Su 10:30-4:30

BELLEVILLE

2891
Republic County Historical Society and Museum
2726 Hwy 36, 66935 [PO Box 218, 66935]; (p) (785) 527-5971; repcomuse@nckcn.com; (c) Republic

County/ 1962/ staff: 2(p); 6(v)/ members: 233

HISTORICAL SOCIETY; HISTORY MUSEUM: Collects, preserves, and exhibits artifacts that tell the story of Republic County.

PROGRAMS: Annual Meeting; Community Outreach; Exhibits; Guided Tours

COLLECTIONS: [1862-1960] Five structures: Log Cabin, Highland Baptist Church, Parkhill School, Caboose and Motor Car for railroad, Blacksmith shop.

HOURS: Yr M-F 1-5, Su 1:30-4:30

ADMISSION: Donations accepted

BELOIT

2892
Mitchell County Historical Society
402 W Eighth, 67401 [PO Box 472, 67401]; (p) (785) 738-5355; MCHS@nckcn.com; (c) Mitchell

1961/ Board of Directors/ staff: 1(f); 2(p); 3(v)/ members: 302

GENEALOGICAL SOCIETY; HISTORICAL SOCIETY; HISTORY MUSEUM; RESEARCH CENTER: Collects items relating to Mitchell County.

PROGRAMS: Annual Meeting; Community Outreach; Exhibits; Facility Rental; Festivals; Guided Tours; Living History; Publication; Reenactments; Research Library/Archives

COLLECTIONS: [1868-present] Artifacts, genealogies, obituaries, clippings, pioneer items, dishes, tools, clothes, military items, furniture

BONNER SPRINGS

2893
National Agricultural Center and Hall of Fame, The
630 Hall of Fame Dr, 66012; (p) (913) 721-1075; (f) (913) 721-1202;

www.aghalloffame.com; (c) Wyandotte

Private non-profit/ 1960/ staff: 3(f); 14(p); 164(v)/ members: 250/publication: *At the Ag Center*

HISTORY MUSEUM: Celebrates and communicates the heritage of the American farmer and leaders in agriculture.

PROGRAMS: Annual Meeting; Community Outreach; Exhibits; Facility Rental; Family Programs; Festivals; Film/Video; Garden Tours; Guided Tours; Interpretation; Lectures; Living History; Publication; Research Library/ Archives; School-Based Curriculum

COLLECTIONS: [1850-1980] Agricultural equipment and related material.

HOURS: Mid-Mar-Nov 30 M-Sa 9-5, Su 1-5

ADMISSION: $6.50, Children $3, Seniors $5; Under 5 free

BURLINGTON

2894
Coffey County Historical Society and Museum, The
1101 Neosho St, 66839; (p) (316) 364-2653; (f) (316) 364-8933; artifacts@kans.com; (c) Coffey

County, non-profit/ staff: 3(f); 100(v)/ members: 300

HISTORICAL SOCIETY; HISTORY MUSEUM

PROGRAMS: Annual Meeting; Community Outreach; Elder's Programs; Exhibits; Facility Rental; Family Programs; Festivals; Film/Video; Guided Tours; Interpretation; Lectures; Living History; Publication; Research Library/Archives; School-Based Curriculum

COLLECTIONS: [19th-20th c] 800 dolls, century old general store items, Victorian parlor, quilts, restored church and school, 1902 steel bridge, and playground area.

HOURS: Summer M-F 10-5, Sa, Su 1-4; Winter M-F 10-5

ADMISSION: No charge/Donations

CHANUTE

2895
Martin and Osa Johnson Safari Museum
111 N Lincoln Ave, 66720; (p) (316) 431-2730; (f) (316) 431-3848; www.safarimuseum.com; (c) Neosho

Private non-profit/ 1961/ staff: 4(f); 1(p); 15(v)/ members: 300/publication: *Wait-A-Bit News*

HISTORY MUSEUM: Preserves the achievements of early documentary film explorers Martin and Osa Johnson; encourages further research into their fields of study.

PROGRAMS: Community Outreach; Exhibits; Facility Rental; Family Programs; Film/Video; Guided Tours; Interpretation; Lectures; Publication; Research Library/Archives; School-Based Curriculum

COLLECTIONS: [First half of 20th c] Items directly related to work and lives of filmmakers, photographers, and authors Martin and Osa Johnson, related ethnographic collections from Africa, Borneo, and the South Pacific and natural history oriented library and art.

HOURS: Yr Daily M-Sa 10-5, Su 1-5

ADMISSION: $4, Student $3, Children $2, Seniors $3; Under 6 free

CHENEY

2896
Souders Historical Farm Museum
MacArthur Rd, 1/2 mi W of town, 67025 [PO Box 527, 67025]; (p) (316) 542-3573

HISTORY MUSEUM; HOUSE MUSEUM

COLLECTIONS: Pioneer chapel with furnishings from the first churches; washhouse with kitchen range and early day washing machines, and other household equipment. An original claim house, for preempting a 160-acre farm under the Homestead Act, restored and equipped with appropriate furnishings.

CLAY CENTER

2897
Clay County Museum
2121 7th St, 67432; (p) (785) 632-3786; (c) Clay

Private non-profit/ 1973/ staff: 3(p); 15(v)/ members: 346

HISTORY MUSEUM; RESEARCH CENTER: Collects, preserves, and displays artifacts connected with local history, and serves as a center for local and genealogical history.

PROGRAMS: Annual Meeting; Community Outreach; Exhibits; Festivals; Guided Tours; Living History; Publication; Reenactments; Research Library/Archives

COLLECTIONS: [1880-present] Artifacts and written history material connected with both the rural and urban history of the county and surrounding trade area.

HOURS: Yr T-Sa

CLIFTON

2898
Clifton Community Historical Society
Clifton and Railroad, 66937; (p) (785) 455-3555; (c) Washington/Clay

Private non-profit/ 1974/ staff: 40(v)/ members: 158/publication: Courier

HISTORIC PRESERVATION AGENCY: Holds meetings and assists in the cataloguing of donations.

PROGRAMS: Guided Tours; Publication

COLLECTIONS: Clothing, glassware, toys, military, school districts books, farming tools, church items, and memorabilia from the area.

HOURS: Su 2-4

ADMISSION: Donations accepted

COFFEYVILLE

2899
Brown Mansion
Eldridge & S Walnut, US 166, 67337 [PO Box 843, 67337]; (p) (316) 251-0431, (316) 251-2550; lbarndollar@terraworld.net;

www.terraworld.net/lbarndollar/Brown/brown.htm

Private non-profit/ 1904/ Coffeyville Historical Society

HOUSE MUSEUM: Preserves home of WP Brown.

COLLECTIONS: [1900-1930] Family furnishings and possessions.

HOURS: Mem Day-Labor Day Daily 9-5; Spring/Fall Daily 1-5

ADMISSION: $4, Student $2; Under 12 free w/adult; Group rates

2900
Coffeyville Historical Society/Dalton Defenders Museum
113 E 8th St, 67337 [PO Box 843, 67337]; (p) (316) 251-5944; (f) (316) 251-5448; lbarndollar@terraworld.net; www.terraworld.net/lbarndollar/; (c) Montgomery

Private non-profit/ 1953/ Board/ staff: 10(f); 12(p)

HISTORY MUSEUM; HOUSE MUSEUM: Collects and preserves items relating to area's history. Operates the Brown Mansion and the Dalton Defenders Museum.

PROGRAMS: Exhibits; Facility Rental; Festivals; Guided Tours

HOURS: Yr Daily Mem Day-Labor Day 9-7; Labor Day-Mem Day 9-5

ADMISSION: $3, Student $2; Under 12 free w/adult; Group rates

2901
Montgomery County Genealogical Society
310 W 10th, 67337 [PO Box 444, 67337]; (p) (316) 251-0716; (c) Montgomery

Private non-profit/ 1967/ members: 45/publication: Descender

GENEALOGICAL SOCIETY: Assists with genealogical searches and organizes genealogical material for public use.

PROGRAMS: Community Outreach; Publication; Research Library/Archives

COLLECTIONS: [1869-1925] Publications, books housed at the public library.

HOURS: M-Sa 9-5

ADMISSION: No charge

COLBY

2902
Thomas County Historical Society/ Prairie Museum of Art and History
1905 S Franklin, 67701 [PO Box 465, 67701]; (p) (785) 462-4590, (785) 462-4592; (f) (785) 462-4592; prairiem@colby.ixks.com; www.prairiemuseum.org; (c) Thomas

Private non-profit/ 1959/ staff: 3(f); 9(p); 15(v)/ members: 1100/publication: Prairie Winds Newsletter

ART MUSEUM; HISTORICAL SOCIETY; HISTORY MUSEUM; LIVING HISTORY/OUTDOOR MUSEUM: County supported historical society that maintains archives and records for Thomas County.

PROGRAMS: Annual Meeting; Community Outreach; Exhibits; Facility Rental; Family Programs; Festivals; Interpretation; Lectures; Publication; Research Library/Archives; School-

Based Curriculum

COLLECTIONS: [18th c-present] European and American glass, ceramics, dolls, silver, textiles, furniture, and toys.

HOURS: Yr Daily M-F 9-5, Sa-Su 1-5; June-Aug M-Sa open until 7; Closed M Nov 1-Mar 31

ADMISSION: $4, Children $1

COLUMBUS

2903
Cherokee County Kansas Genealogical/Historical Society
100 S Tennessee, 66725 [PO Box 33, 66725-0033]; (p) (316) 429-2992; (c) Cherokee

Private non-profit/ 1980/ staff: 1(p); 5(v)/ members: 188/publication: Relatively Seeking

GENEALOGICAL SOCIETY; HISTORICAL SOCIETY: Collects and records Cherokee County history.

PROGRAMS: Publication; Research Library/ Archives

COLLECTIONS: [1850-present] Books (1860s-present); microfilm of all available county newspapers.

HOURS: Yr M-Sa 1-5

ADMISSION: No charge

CONCORDIA

2904
Cloud County Historical Society
635 Broadway, 66901; (p) (785) 243-2286; (c) Cloud

County/ 1959/ staff: 3(f); 8(p); 3(v)/ members: 315/publication: Cloud Comments

HISTORICAL SOCIETY; HISTORY MUSEUM; RESEARCH CENTER: Collects, preserves, and displays historical records and items of Cloud County and KS.

PROGRAMS: Annual Meeting; Exhibits; Family Programs; Guided Tours; Publication; Research Library/Archives

COLLECTIONS: Memorabilia of agriculture, homemaking, railroads, medical, military and communications. Prisoner of War Camp rooms, dolls, library, photographs, gems, and minerals, microfilm of all county newspapers and card files on all births, deaths, and marriages in the county.

HOURS: Yr 1-5

COTTONWOOD FALLS

2905
Chase County Historical Society
301 Broadway, 66845; (p) (316) 273-8500; (c) Chase

County/ 1934/ staff: 1(f); 1(p)/ members: 450

HISTORICAL SOCIETY; HISTORY MUSEUM: Collects, compiles, and preserves the county's early pioneer history.

PROGRAMS: Annual Meeting; Exhibits

COLLECTIONS: [Late 1880s-early 1900s] Quilts, cameras, barbed wire, typewriters.

HOURS: Jan-Feb M-Sa; Mar-Dec Daily

COUNCIL GROVE

2906
Kaw Mission State Historic Site
500 N Mission, 66846; (p) (316) 767-5410; kawmission@cgtelco.net; www.kshs.org/places/kawmiss.htm; (c) Morris

State/ 1850/ KS State Historical Society/ staff: 1(f); 2(p); 15(v)/ members: 101

HISTORIC SITE: One of 15 state historic sites; built in 1850 as a mission school for children of the Kansa Tribe-the Native Americans for whom Kansas is named. The Santa Fe Trail passed nearby.

PROGRAMS: Annual Meeting; Community Outreach; Festivals; Guided Tours; Interpretation; Lectures

COLLECTIONS: [1851-1871] Artifacts from the Kansa tribe; old council grave, rendezvous point on the Santa Fe Trail.

HOURS: Yr T-Sa 10-5, Su 1-5

ADMISSION: Donations accepted

2907
Morris County Historical Society
303 W Main, 66846; (p) (316) 767-5716; (f) (316) 767-7312; bmcks@yahoo.com; (c) Morris

Private non-profit/ 1950/ staff: 11(v)/ members: 205

ALLIANCE OF HISTORICAL AGENCIES; GARDEN; HISTORIC SITE; HISTORICAL SOCIETY; HISTORY MUSEUM; HOUSE MUSEUM: Operates and maintains the Post Office Oak House Museum and the Seth Hays Home.

PROGRAMS: Annual Meeting; Community Outreach; Concerts; Exhibits; Facility Rental; Family Programs; Garden Tours; Guided Tours; Interpretation; Lectures; Research Library/Archives; School-Based Curriculum

COLLECTIONS: [1873-1984] Furnishings of the 18th and 19th c; china plates and other artifacts.

HOURS: Mem Day-Oct 31 Su 1:30-4:30

ADMISSION: Donations accepted

2908
Seth Hays Home
Wood & Hall Sts, 66846 [303 W Main, 66846]; (p) (316) 767-5413, (316) 767-5559; cgrove@mail.midusa.net

1867/ Morris County Historical Society

COLLECTIONS: [1870s] Located at Council Grove Public Library

HOURS: Mem Day-Oct 31 Su 1:30-4:30

DERBY

2909
Derby Historical Society
208 N Westview, 67037 [PO Box 544, 67037]; (p) (316) 788-7307; (f) (316) 788-6861; (c) Sedgwick

Private non-profit/ staff: 12(v)

HISTORICAL SOCIETY; HISTORY MUSEUM: Preserves the history of Derby; maintains a historical museum.

PROGRAMS: Annual Meeting; Exhibits; Facility Rental; Festivals; Guided Tours; Lectures; Living History

HOURS: Yr Daily by appt

ADMISSION: No charge

DIGHTON

2910
Lane County Historical Society
333 N Main, 67839 [PO Box 821, 67839]; (p) (316) 397-5652; (c) Lane

County/ 1976/ staff: 1(f); 1(p); 20(v)/ members: 180

HISTORICAL SOCIETY; HISTORY MUSEUM: Preserves and promotes the history of Lane County; collects and preserves items; operates machinery park and full-scale sod house.

PROGRAMS: Annual Meeting; Community Outreach; Exhibits; Guided Tours; Publication; Research Library/Archives; School-Based Curriculum

COLLECTIONS: [1890-1930] Photographs, tools and implements, clothing, oral histories, cemetery records, census records, marriage licenses, archeology, home furnishings, advertising items of early Lane County, country store, county newspapers on microfilm, Kansas books.

HOURS: Yr T-Sa 1-5, Su 2-5; May-Sept T-Sa 1-5

ADMISSION: No charge/Donations

DODGE CITY

2911
Boot Hill Museum, Inc.
Front St, 67801; (p) (316) 227-8188; (f) (316) 227-7673; frontst@pld.com; www.boothill.com; (c) Ford

Private non-profit/ 1947/ Board of Directors/ staff: 9(f); 250(p); 150(v)/ members: 190/publication: *Front Street Times*

HISTORY MUSEUM: Village museum located on the original site of Boot Hill Cemetery; interprets 19th c Dodge City.

PROGRAMS: Community Outreach; Exhibits; Facility Rental; Festivals; Guided Tours; Interpretation; Living History; Publication; Reenactments; Research Library/Archives; School-Based Curriculum

COLLECTIONS: [1870s] Common late 19th and early 20th c

2912
Dodge City Area Arts Council/Carnegie Center for the Arts
701 Second Ave, 67801 [PO Box 945, 67801]; (p) (316) 225-6388; carnegie@dodgecity.net; (c) Ford

Private non-profit/ 1973/ staff: 2(f); 1(p); 25(v)/ members: 260/publication: *Illuminations*

ART MUSEUM; HISTORIC SITE: Preserves and interprets the 1907 Carnegie Library building; promotes the arts.

PROGRAMS: Annual Meeting; Community Outreach; Concerts; Exhibits; Family Programs; Festivals; Guided Tours; Lectures; Publication

COLLECTIONS: 1907 library building; works of local, regional, and national contemporary artists.

HOURS: Feb-Dec T-F 12-5, Sa 11-3

2913
Ford County Historical Society
[PO Box 131, 67801]; (p) (316) 227-8808; (c) Ford

Private non-profit/ staff: 1(f); 6(p); 30(v)/ members: 253/publication: *FCHS Newsletter*

GENEALOGICAL SOCIETY; HISTORIC PRESERVATION AGENCY; HOUSE MUSEUM: Collects, preserves, and researches the pioneer period of old west settlement, and the frontier days of Dodge City, Fort Dodge, and Ford County.

PROGRAMS: Annual Meeting; Exhibits; Family Programs; Festivals; Guided Tours; Lectures; Publication; Research Library/Archives

COLLECTIONS: [1860-1900] Mueller-Schmidt House, 1879. Original furniture and artifacts of 1879 home and store; 3,000 photographs of old west; personal items of Dodge City founders.

HOURS: June-Aug

2914
Home of Stone and Ford County Museum
112 E Vine, 67801 [PO Box 131, 67801-0131]; (p) (316) 227-6791, (316) 227-8808; (c) Ford

Joint/ 1881/ Ford County; Ford County Historical Society, Inc./ staff: 1(f); 4(p); 2(v)

COLLECTIONS: [1880s]

HOURS: June-Aug

2915
Kansas Genealogical Society, Inc.
2601 Central, 67801 [PO Box 103, 67801-0103]; (c) Ford

Private non-profit/ staff: 30(v)/ members: 525/publication: *The Treesearcher*

GENEALOGICAL SOCIETY: Provides research library and educates on local genealogy.

PROGRAMS: Publication; Research Library/Archives

COLLECTIONS: [17th-20th c]

HOURS: Yr M-F 1-5

ADMISSION: No charge

2916
Kansas Heritage Center
1000 N 2nd Ave, 67801 [PO Box 1207, 67801-1207]; (p) (316) 227-1616; (f) (316) 227-1701; info@ksheritage.org; www.ksheritage.org; (c) Ford

Private non-profit/ 1965/ Dodge City USD 443/ staff: 3(f); 2(p)/publication: *399 Kansas Characters; Santa Fe Trail Adventures*

RESEARCH CENTER: Collectes, creates, and publishes resource materials for use by students, teachers and others interested in the history of KS, the Great Plains, and the Old West.

PROGRAMS: Community Outreach; Elder's Programs; Family Programs; Film/Video; Lectures; Research Library/Archives; School-Based Curriculum

COLLECTIONS: 7,500 volumes, 300 pieces of sheet music, 4,000 photographs, microfilm of Dodge City

DOUGLASS

2917
Douglass Historical Museum and Society
318 S Forest, 67039 [PO Box 95, 67039]; (c) Butler

1950/ staff: 1(f); 5(p); 15(v)/ members: 90

HISTORIC PRESERVATION AGENCY; HISTORICAL SOCIETY; HISTORY MUSEUM: Gathers, preserves, and displays the records, art, literature, memorabilia, pictures, and relics of the Douglass Pioneer.

PROGRAMS: Community Outreach; Elder's Programs; Guided Tours

COLLECTIONS: [1860-1940] Artifacts, newspaper microfilm 1884-1984, genealogy, town history, military, pioneer, pictures, Indian artifacts, school material, textiles, barbwire, medical, farming, bit and spurs, saddles, and church.

HOURS: Yr M-F

DOWNS

2918
Historical Society of Downs Carnegie Library
504 S Morgan, 67437 [416 S Morgan, 67437]; (p) (785) 454-3401; (c) Osborne

Private non-profit/ 1991/ members: 40/publication: *Downs Historical Society Newsletter*

HISTORICAL SOCIETY: Preservation of history of town and surrounding area.

PROGRAMS: Community Outreach; Elder's Programs; Exhibits; Family Programs; Film/Video; Guided Tours; Lectures; Publication; Research Library/Archives

COLLECTIONS: [1870-present] Books, photos, papers, and some artifacts.

EL DORADO

2919
Butler County Historical Society/Kansas Oil & Gas Museum
383 E Central, 67042 [PO Box 696, 67042]; (p) (316) 321-9333; bchs@powwwer.net; skyways.lib.ks.us/museums/kom/; (c) Butler

Private non-profit/ 1956/ Board of Trustees/ staff: 4(f); 4(p); 60(v)/ members: 362/publication: *The Kingdom of Butler*

HISTORICAL SOCIETY; HISTORY MUSEUM; LIBRARY AND/OR ARCHIVES; LIVING HISTORY/OUTDOOR MUSEUM: Collects, preserves, interprets, and exhibits the county's history. Operates museum as a center for the study and exhibition of Kansas oil history.

PROGRAMS: Annual Meeting; Exhibits; Guided Tours; Interpretation; Publication; Research Library/Archives

COLLECTIONS: [1860s-present] Objects and documents related to the history of the Kansas oil industry, oilfield equipment, original buildings; objects related to county development through ranching and farming. Structures: 1930s oil field lease house, 1858 Conner Log Cabin, 3 1930s oil field town businesses, 1930s cable tool rig, 1950s rotary rig.

HOURS: Yr M-Sa 9-5, Su 1-5

ADMISSION: $2, Student $1, Seniors $1.50; Under 6/Mbrs free

ELKHART

2920
Morton County Historical Society Museum
302 E Hwy 56, 67950 [PO Box 1248, 67950]; (p) (316) 697-2833; (f) (316) 697-4390; (c) Morton

County/ 1987/ staff: 3(f); 1(p); 28(v)/ members: 168

HISTORICAL SOCIETY; HISTORY MUSEUM: Interprets and exhibits local history.

PROGRAMS: Annual Meeting; Community Outreach; Exhibits; Facility Rental; Family Programs; Festivals; Film/Video; Guided Tours; Interpretation; Lectures; Living History; Publication; Reenactments; Research Library/Archives; School-Based Curriculum; Theatre

COLLECTIONS: [1541-present] Local county and Santa Fe Trail history; mounted animals including a life-size buffalo; dugout, teepee, covered wagon with horses, steam engines, antique tractors and cars, schoolhouse, barn, and caboose.

HOURS: June-Aug T-F 10-5, Sa-Su 2-4; Sept-May T-F 1-5, Sa-Su by appt

ADMISSION: Donations accepted

ELLINWOOD

2921
Ellinwood Community Historical Society
100 N Main, 67526 [Box 111, 67526]; (c) Barton

Private non-profit/ 1982/ staff: 15(v)/ members: 63

HISTORY MUSEUM: Small museum with underground tunnels used by early merchants who had stores in the underground.

PROGRAMS: Annual Meeting; Exhibits; Living History

COLLECTIONS: [1800-present]

HOURS: June-Sept Su 2-4

ADMISSION: No charge

ELLIS

2922
Bukovina Society of the Americas
718 Washington, 67637 [PO Box 81, 67637]; (p) (785) 726-3388; members.aol/Ljensen/bukovina.html; (c) Ellis

Private non-profit/ 1988/ staff: 1(f); 2(v)/ members: 250

HISTORICAL SOCIETY; HISTORY MUSEUM: Preserves Bukovina heritage.

PROGRAMS: Annual Meeting; Festivals; Publication

HOURS: Yr 1-4

ADMISSION: Donations accepted

2923
Walter P. Chrysler Boyhood Home and Museum
102 W 10th St, 67637; (p) (785) 726-3636

Private non-profit/ 1889/ staff: 4(p)

HOUSE MUSEUM: Boyhood home of Walter P. Chrysler, founder of the Chrysler Corporation.

COLLECTIONS: [Victorian] Walter P. Chrysler's duck hunting rifle, metal banks, jewelry. Books and photographs of Chrysler.

HOURS: May-Sept M-Sa 9:30-4:30, Su 12:30-4:30; Oct-Apr M-F 11-3, Su 12:30-4:30

ADMISSION: $3, Student $1, Seniors $2.50; Under 8 free w/adult

ELLSWORTH CITY

2924
Hodgden House Museum Complex
104 SW Main, 67439 [PO Box 144, 67439]; (p) (785) 472-3059

1878/ staff: 1(f); 2(p); 6(v)

HISTORIC SITE; HISTORY MUSEUM; HOUSE MUSEUM; LIVING HISTORY/OUTDOOR MUSEUM: Complex of restored house, stable, log cabin, and other buildings.

COLLECTIONS: [1870s-1900] 1878 Hodgden House, 1880s livery stable, 1912 one room school, 1880s church, small log cabin, modern building that houses, a general store and farm equipment, 1911 caboose, turn-of-the-century wooden windmill, 160 year old Dominion piano Household, commercial, and agricultural items from the late 1800s. Large collection of photographs, written material, 1880 census and genealogical material.

HOURS: May-Sept T-Sa 9-12/1-5, Su 1-5; Oct-Apr, T-F 1-5, Sa 9-1

EMPORIA

2925
Flint Hill Genealogical Society
[PO Box 555, 66801-0555]; lyoncoks@bigfoot.com; (c) Lyon

1973/ members: 60

GENEALOGICAL SOCIETY: Promotes genealogical and historical research; preserves and makes available historical and vital records.

PROGRAMS: Annual Meeting; Family Programs; Lectures

COLLECTIONS: Collections housed at the Emporia Public Library Genealogy section.

2926
Lyon County Historical Museum
118 E 6th Ave, 66801; (p) (316) 342-0933; lycomu@valu-line.net; www.emporia.com/lyoncountymuseum; (c) Lyon

1938/ staff: 1(f); 5(p); 20(v)/ members: 340

GENEALOGICAL SOCIETY; HISTORIC PRESERVATION AGENCY; HISTORIC SITE; HISTORICAL SOCIETY; HISTORY MUSEUM; HOUSE MUSEUM; LIVING HISTORY/OUTDOOR MUSEUM: Preserves, protects, and exhibits county history.

PROGRAMS: Annual Meeting; Community Outreach; Concerts; Elder's Programs; Exhibits; Family Programs; Guided Tours; Interpretation; Lectures; Living History; Reenactments; Research Library/Archives; School-Based Curriculum

COLLECTIONS: [1850-present] 150,000 artifacts, 100,000 pieces of archival material representing all phases of life in Lyon

EUREKA

2927
Greenwood County Historical Society
120 W 4th, 67045; (p) (315) 583-6682; (c) Greenwood

Private non-profit/ 1973/ staff: 1(p); 7(v)/ members: 540/publication: *Pioneer Spirit*

HISTORICAL SOCIETY; HISTORY MUSEUM; RESEARCH CENTER: Preserves history of people, events, and artifacts of the county.

PROGRAMS: Exhibits; Publication; Research Library/Archives

COLLECTIONS: Artifacts, newspapers, family histories, photographs of local people.

HOURS: Yr M-F 9-4

ADMISSION: No charge/Donations

FAIRWAY

2928
Friends of the Shawnee Indian Mission, Inc.
3403 W 53rd St, 66205; (p) (913) 262-0867; (c) Johnson

Private non-profit/ 1989/ members: 60/publication: *Friends Newsletter*

HISTORIC SITE: Supports the Shawnee Indian Mission through additional funding and volunteers at special events, educational programs, and outreach.

2929
Shawnee Indian Mission State Historic Site
3403 W 53rd St, 66205; (p) (913) 262-0867; shawneemission@KSHS.org; www.kshs.org/ places/shawnmis.htm; (c) Johnson

State/ KS State Historical Society/ staff: 3(f); 1(p); 6(v)

HISTORIC SITE; HISTORICAL SOCIETY: Preserves and interprets the history of the Shawnee Indian Mission.

PROGRAMS: Annual Meeting; Community Outreach; Concerts; Festivals; Guided Tours; Interpretation; Lectures; Living History; Reenactments; Research Library/Archives

COLLECTIONS: [1839-1870] Period furniture, looms, spinning wheels, dishes, farm and other tools from 1800s.

HOURS: Yr T-Sa 10-5, Su 1-5

FLORENCE

2930
Harvey House Museum/Florence Historical Society
Third & Marion St, 66851 [PO Box 147, 66851]; (p) (316) 878-4296; (c) Marion

staff: 1(p); 6(v)/ members: 200

HISTORIC SITE; HISTORICAL SOCIETY; HOUSE MUSEUM: Preserves the first Fred Harvey Hotel and Restaurant in Florence.

PROGRAMS: Exhibits; Facility Rental; Guided Tours

COLLECTIONS: [Late 1800s-early 1900s] Fred Harvey information and material displays; Harvey Girl memorabilia; period furniture.

HOURS: Yr T 12-2, W-Sa 12-5 by appt

ADMISSION: No charge/Donations

FORT LEAVENWORTH

2931
Combined Arms Research Library
250 Gibbon Ave, 66027-2314; (p) (913) 758-3101; (f) (913) 758-3014; www.cgsc.army.mil/carl/; (c) Leavenworth

Federal/ 1881/ US Army/ staff: 30(f); 4(p)

RESEARCH CENTER: Comprehensive military science reference and research center supporting the U.S. Army command and general staff college.

PROGRAMS: Research Library/Archives

COLLECTIONS: International affairs, military arts and sciences, military doctrine and history, security studies, tactics, warfare.

HOURS: Yr Daily

2932
Fort Leavenworth Historical Society
100 Reynolds Ave, 66027 [PO Box 3356, 66027]; (p) (913) 651-7440; (c) Fort Leavenworth

Joint/ 1950/ Federal; Private non-profit/ staff: 1(f); 4(p); 30(v)/ members: 40

HISTORICAL SOCIETY: Promotes local history.

PROGRAMS: Family Programs; Guided Tours; Lectures

HOURS: Yr Daily M-F 9-4, Sa 10-4, Su 12-4

ADMISSION: No charge

2933
Frontier Army Museum
Bldg 801 Reyolds Ave, 66027 [A12L-MU, 66027]; (p) (913) 684-3767; (f) (913) 684-3192; (c) Fort Leavenworth

Federal/ staff: 4(f); 2(p); 150(v)

HISTORIC SITE; HISTORY MUSEUM; LIVING HISTORY/OUTDOOR MUSEUM; RESEARCH CENTER

PROGRAMS: Exhibits; Festivals; Guided Tours; Interpretation; Lectures; Living History; Reenactments; Research Library/Archives; School-Based Curriculum; Theatre

COLLECTIONS: [1827-present]

HOURS: Yr Daily M-F 9-4, Sa 10-4, Su 12-4

ADMISSION: No charge

FORT RILEY

2934
Custer House
Bldg 24A, Sheridan St, 66442 [PO Box 2160, 66442]; (p) (785) 239-2737; (f) (785) 239-6243; vanmetet@riley-emhl.army.mil

Federal/ 1854/ staff: 2(f)

HOUSE MUSEUM

COLLECTIONS: [1880s] Typical furnishings for the time period. Photographs and archival materials pertaining to early establishment of Fort Riley.

HOURS: May-Sept

2935
First Territorial Capitol of Kansas
Hwy 18 Huebner Rd, 66442 [PO Box 2122, 66442]; (p) (785) 784-5535; (f) (785) 272-8681; (c) Riley

State/ 1855/ KS History Center/ staff: 3(p); 60(v)/ members: 200

HISTORIC SITE; HISTORICAL SOCIETY; HISTORY MUSEUM: Preserves and interprets the first territorial capitol of Kansas Territory; 1855 period.

PROGRAMS: Annual Meeting; Community Outreach; Exhibits; Facility Rental; Family Programs; Festivals; Guided Tours; Interpretation; Lectures; Living History; Reenactments; School-Based Curriculum

COLLECTIONS: [1855-present] 1855 stone two story building (restored). Collections include: Kaw Indians, military, Pawnee land company, early 1855 era politics, Civil War weapons, household items, military items, a scale model of the 1855 area, and early area photographs.

HOURS: Yr T-Sa 10-5, Su 1-5

ADMISSION: Donations requested

2936
U.S. Cavalry Museum
Bldg 205, 66442 [PO Box 2160, 66442]; (p) (785) 239-2737; (f) (785) 239-6243; vanmetet@riley.army.mil; (c) Riley

Federal/ 1957/ US Army/ staff: 6(f)/publication: *Bugle Call, Fort Riley Driving Tour; and others*

HISTORY MUSEUM: Preserves and interprets history of the US Cavalry from 1775-1950.

PROGRAMS: Exhibits; Lectures; Publication; Research Library/Archives

COLLECTIONS: [1775-1950] Artifacts pertaining to the history of the U.S. Cavalry including uniforms, flags, weapons, documents, photographs, and art.

HOURS: Yr Daily M-Sa 9-4:30, Su 12:30-4:30

ADMISSION: No charge

FORT SCOTT

2937
Fort Scott National Site
Old Fort Boulevard, 66701 [PO Box 918, 66701]; (p) (316) 223-0310, (316) 223-0188; (f) (316) 223-0188; fosc_interpretation@gov; www.nps.gov/fosc; (c) Bourbon

Federal/ 1978/ National Park Service/ staff: 10(f); 4(p)

HISTORIC SITE; RESEARCH CENTER: Site includes 20 historic structures with 33 furnished rooms, three museum areas, a visitor center, bookstore, and five acres of restored tall grass prairie.

PROGRAMS: Concerts; Exhibits; Family Programs; Film/Video; Guided Tours; Interpretation; Lectures; Living History; Research Library/Archives; School-Based Curriculum

COLLECTIONS: [1842-1873] Mixed collection of civilian and military objects covering daily life of a frontier military installation.

HOURS: Yr

2938

Lyons' Victorian Mansion
742 S National Ave, 66701; (p) (316) 223-3644; (f) (316) 223-3665; lyonshse@terraworld.net; www.lyonsmansion.com; (c) Bourson

Private non-profit/ 1992/ staff: 1(f)

GARDEN; HOUSE MUSEUM; LIVING HISTORY/OUTDOOR MUSEUM: Operates Fort Scott's landmark Victorian residence, circa 1876.

PROGRAMS: Facility Rental; Family Programs; Garden Tours; Guided Tours; Living History

COLLECTIONS: [1876-1890]

HOURS: Yr by appt

2939

Old Fort Genealogical Society of Southeastern Kansas, Inc.
502 S National Ave, 66701-1327; (p) (316) 223-3300; (c) Bourbon

Private non-profit/ 1974/ staff: 15(v)/ members: 200/publication: *Old Fort Log*

GENEALOGICAL SOCIETY: Collects, preserves, and makes available records of families and communities.

PROGRAMS: Annual Meeting; Family Programs; Publication; Research Library/Archives

COLLECTIONS: [1840-present] Bourbon County newspapers, local military records, land and court records, genealogical periodicals and instruction books.

HOURS: Yr M-Sa 1-4

ADMISSION: No charge

FREDONIA

2940

Wilson County Historical Museum
420 N 7th, 66736; (p) (316) 378-3965; (c) Wilson

Private non-profit/ 1962/ staff: 2(p)/ members: 134/publication: *Fredonia City Cemetery*

GENEALOGICAL SOCIETY; HISTORIC PRESERVATION AGENCY; HISTORIC SITE; HISTORICAL SOCIETY; HISTORY MUSEUM; HOUSE MUSEUM

PROGRAMS: Annual Meeting; Exhibits; Family Programs; Film/Video; Guided Tours; Lectures; Publication

COLLECTIONS: [Late 1800s-present] Former Wilson County sheriff's home and jail; exhibits in the rooms and cells.

HOURS: Yr M-F 12:30-4:30

ADMISSION: No charge/Donations

FULTON

2941

Fulton County Genealogical Society
312 Main St, 42041 [PO Box 1031, 42041]; (p) (270) 472-3439; (f) (270) 472-6241; fultonpl@aplex.net; (c) Fulton

Private non-profit/ 1972/ staff: 2(v)/ members: 124

GENEALOGICAL SOCIETY; HISTORICAL SOCIETY: A group dedicated to preserving and transcribing records pertaining to genealogy and family research.

PROGRAMS: Family Programs; Publication

COLLECTIONS: [1845-present] Genealogy books.

HOURS: T- W, F-Sa 9-12:30/1:30-5

ADMISSION: No charge

GALENA

2942

Galena Mining and Historical Museum
319 W 7th, 66739; (p) (316) 783-2192; (c) Cherokee

Private non-profit/ 1984/ staff: 3(v)/ members: 72

HISTORY MUSEUM: Preserves the history of the local lead and zinc mining community.

PROGRAMS: Exhibits; Guided Tours

COLLECTIONS: [1870-1970] Mining tools, lamps, hats, lunch buckets, mineral specimens, group pictures, painting, switch engine, caboose and smelting artifacts.

HOURS: Yr M-Sa 9-11/1-3:30

ADMISSION: No charge/Donations

GARDEN CITY

2943

Finney County Historical Society
403 S 4th St, 67846 [Box 796, 67846]; (p) (316) 272-3664; (f) (316) 272-3662; fico.historical@gcnet.com; (c) Finney

Joint/ 1948/ County; Private non-profit/ staff: 3(f); 6(p); 28(v)/ members: 400/publication: *The Sequoyan; Constant Frontier; and others*

HISTORIC PRESERVATION AGENCY; HISTORICAL SOCIETY; HISTORY MUSEUM: Preserves local history. On site: Pleasant Valley one-room schoolhouse and Mrs. Fulton's Herb Garden.

PROGRAMS: Annual Meeting; Community Outreach; Exhibits; Facility Rental; Festivals; Garden Tours; Guided Tours; Lectures; Living History; Publication; Research Library/Archives; School-Based Curriculum; Theatre

COLLECTIONS: [1879-present] Artifacts associated with the founding and development of Finney County, local and regional history reference materials including extensive collections of archival photographs, microfilmed newspapers, and county records.

HOURS: Yr Summer M-Sa 10-5, Su 1-5; Winter Daily 1-5

ADMISSION: No charge

GIRARD

2944

Museum of Crawford County, Inc.
300 S Summit, 66743 [378 S 80th, 66743]; (p) (316) 724-8592; (c) Crawford

County/ 1970/ staff: 20(v)/ members: 100

HISTORY MUSEUM

PROGRAMS: Exhibits; Festivals; Guided Tours

COLLECTIONS: Farm machinery, quilts, cloths

HOURS: May-Sept Su 2-4, or by appt.

GOESSEL

2945

Mennonite Heritage Museum
200 N Poplar St, 67053 [PO Box 231, 67053]; (p) (316) 367-8200; (c) Marion

Private non-profit/ 1974/ staff: 4(p); 20(v)/ members: 200

HISTORY MUSEUM: Collects, preserves, and interprets the history of the Alexanderwohl Mennonite congregation.

PROGRAMS: Annual Meeting; Community Outreach; Exhibits; Facility Rental; Festivals; Film/Video; Garden Tours; Guided Tours; Interpretation; Lectures; Living History; Publication; Research Library/Archives

COLLECTIONS: [1874-1920s] Material culture related to the Alexanderwohl congregation including photos, documents, furniture, agricultural equipment, and personal items; historic structures.

HOURS: Mar-Apr, Oct-Dec T-Su 1-4; May-Sept T-F 10-5, Sa-Su 1-5

ADMISSION: $3

GOODLAND

2946

High Plains Museum
1717 Cherry St, 67735; (p) (785) 899-4595; (c) Sherman

City/ 1959/ staff: 1(f); 3(p); 3(v)/ members: 100/publication: *Sodbuster*

HISTORY MUSEUM

PROGRAMS: Annual Meeting; Community Outreach; Exhibits; Guided Tours; Lectures; Publication; Research Library/Archives

COLLECTIONS: [Late 1800s-1950s] Local history artifacts including local history archival documents and newspapers.

HOURS: Yr Daily

ADMISSION: Donations accepted

GREELEY

2947

Anderson County Historical Society
6th & Maple St, 66033 [PO Box 217, 66033]; (p) (785) 448-5740, (785) 867-2966; (c) Anderson

County/ 1968/ staff: 10(v)/ members: 130/publication: *6 County Historical Newsletter*

HISTORICAL SOCIETY; HISTORY MUSEUM; RESEARCH CENTER

PROGRAMS: Annual Meeting; Exhibits; Guided Tours; Lectures; Publication; Research Library/Archives

COLLECTIONS: [1854-present] Military, school, home, medical, church, country store, and farm artifacts; also 1884 Harris House.

HOURS: May 1-Oct 1 T-Su 1-4

ADMISSION: Donations accepted

HANOVER

2948

Hollenberg Station State Historic Site
2889 23rd Rd, 669459634; (p) (785) 337-2635; www.kshs.org/places/hollenbg.htm; (c)

Washington

State/ KS State Historical Society/ staff: 1(f); 1(p); 15(v)

HISTORIC SITE: Maintains the Hollenberg Pony Express Station built in 1857-58 and still in its original location.

PROGRAMS: Family Programs; Festivals; Garden Tours; Interpretation; Living History

HAYS

2949
Ellis County Historical Society

100 W 7th St, 67601; (p) (785) 628-2624; historical@spidome.net; (c) Ellis

Private non-profit/ 1971/ staff: 1(f); 5(p); 10(v)/publication: *Homesteader, Gallery Guide*

HISTORIC SITE; HISTORICAL SOCIETY; HISTORY MUSEUM: Highlights regional history from the Wild West to the present.

PROGRAMS: Annual Meeting; Exhibits; Facility Rental; Interpretation; Publication; Research Library/Archives

COLLECTIONS: [1867-present] Primarily artifacts related to the history of Ellis County and W KS, including approximately 25,000 artifacts and 400 linear feet of archival material.

2950
Fort Hays State Historic Site

1472 US Hwy 183 Alt, 67601-9212; (p) (785) 625-6812; (f) (785) 625-4785; thefort@dailynews.net; www.kshs.org/places/forthays.htm; (c) Ellis

State/ 1967/ KS State Historical Society/ staff: 3(f); 1(p); 33(v)/ members: 100/publication: *The Post Returns*

HISTORIC SITE; HISTORY MUSEUM; HOUSE MUSEUM; LIVING HISTORY/OUTDOOR MUSEUM: Preserves and interprets the history of Fort Hays, a U.S. Army post active 1865-1889.

PROGRAMS: Annual Meeting; Community Outreach; Concerts; Exhibits; Family Programs; Festivals; Film/Video; Guided Tours; Interpretation; Lectures; Living History; Publication; Reenactments; Research Library/Archives; School-Based Curriculum

COLLECTIONS: [1865-1889] Small display of archeological material, military artifacts, period furnishings in historic structures, fort records available on microfilm, small research library.

HOURS: Yr Daily T-Sa 9-5, Su-M 1-5

ADMISSION: Donations requested

2951
Sternberg Museum of Natural History

3000 Sternberg Dr, 67601; (p) (785) 628-5664; (f) (785) 628-4578; jchoate@fhsu.edu; www.fhsu.edu/sternberg; (c) Ellis

State/ 1926/ staff: 13(f); 56(p); 300(v)/ members: 700

NATURAL HISTORY MUSEUM: Exhibits and interprets environmental history, natural history, and paleontology.

PROGRAMS: Community Outreach; Exhibits; Facility Rental; Family Programs; Guided Tours; Interpretation; Lectures

COLLECTIONS: [Prehistory-present] Fossil

collections; collections of plants, insects, fishes, amphibians, reptiles, birds, and mammals; small historical, archaeological, and ethnological collection.

HOURS: Yr Daily T-Sa 9-9, Su-M 1-9

ADMISSION: $4, Children $2, Seniors $2

HERINGTON

2952
Tri-County Historical Society and Museum, Inc.

800 S Broadway, 67449-3060; (p) (785) 258-2842; (c) Dickinson

Private non-profit/ 1975/ Board of Directors/ staff: 1(f); 14(v)/ members: 213

GENEALOGICAL SOCIETY; HISTORICAL SOCIETY; HISTORY MUSEUM

PROGRAMS: Annual Meeting; Exhibits; Guided Tours; Research Library/Archives

COLLECTIONS: [1859-present] Agricultural tools and machinery, Herington Family collection, Rock Island Railroad, baggage car annex and Cotton Belt Caboose, military uniforms, church histories through artifacts and microfilm.

HOURS: Yr May-Aug M-F 9-5; Sept-Apr M-F 10-4

ADMISSION: No charge

HIGHLAND

2953
Native American Heritage Museum

1737 Elgin Rd, 66035; (p) (785) 442-3304; nahm@kshs.org; www.kshs.org/places/highland.htm; (c) Doniphan

State/ 1938/ KS State Historical Society/ staff: 1(f); 4(p); 24(v)/ members: 50

HISTORIC SITE: Housed in former Presbyterian Mission house, museum highlights the culture of the many different tribes of the area, including the Sac and Fox and the Ioway nation.

PROGRAMS: Community Outreach; Exhibits; Facility Rental; Family Programs; Guided Tours; Interpretation; Lectures; School-Based Curriculum

COLLECTIONS: [1804-present] Beadwork and ribbon work from 1900; main focus is a collection of modern Native American artists; oral histories quotes, photos.

HOURS: Yr W-Sa 10-5, Su 1-5

ADMISSION: Donations

HILL CITY

2954
Graham County Historical Society

414 N W St, 67642; (c) Graham

1971/ staff: 10(v)/ members: 50

GENEALOGICAL SOCIETY; HISTORICAL SOCIETY

PROGRAMS: Exhibits; Film/Video; Monthly Meeting

COLLECTIONS: [1875-present] County newspaper-obituaries, family histories, photographs, school records, books, quilts, maps, WW I and II veteran records.

HOURS: Yr Sa and by appt

ADMISSION: No charge

HILLSBORO

2955
Hillsboro Historical Society and Museums

501 S Ash St, 67063; (p) (316) 947-3775; (c) Marion

1958/ staff: 1(f); 3(p); 20(v)/ members: 110

HISTORIC SITE; HISTORICAL SOCIETY; HISTORY MUSEUM; HOUSE MUSEUM; LIVING HISTORY/OUTDOOR MUSEUM: Collects, preserves, and interprets the cultural history of the community, focusing on immigrant settlement during the 1870s; includes Pioneer Adobe House and William Schaeffler House.

PROGRAMS: Annual Meeting; Community Outreach; Exhibits; Facility Rental; Festivals; Guided Tours; Interpretation; Lectures; Reenactments

COLLECTIONS: [1870s-1920] Pioneer handmade furniture, hand operated and horse drawn farm tools, machinery, immigrant trunks, pioneer portraits, photograph collection, textiles, carpenter tools, area maps, and atlases.

HOURS: Mar-Dec T-F 10-12/1:30-4, Sa-Su 2-4

ADMISSION: $2, Student $1

HOLTON

2956
Jackson County Historical Society

216 & 327 New York Ave, 66436 [216 New York Ave, 66436]; (p) (785) 364-2087, (785) 364-4991; alwilhelm@holton.net; (c) Jackson

Private non-profit/ 1979/ Board of Directors/ staff: 20(v)/ members: 150

GENEALOGICAL SOCIETY; HISTORICAL SOCIETY; HISTORY MUSEUM; HOUSE MUSEUM; RESEARCH CENTER: Discovers, collects, preserves, and maintains information, materials, and artifacts that illustrate the county history.

PROGRAMS: Annual Meeting; Community Outreach; Exhibits; Facility Rental; Family Programs; Festivals; Guided Tours; Interpretation; Lectures; Living History; Publication; Research Library/Archives; School-Based Curriculum

COLLECTIONS: [1855-1975] Pioneer artifacts associated with agriculture and housekeeping chores and business; genealogy surname files, and research folders.

HOURS: Museum: Apr-Dec F-Sa 10-4, Su 2-4; House: by appt only

HOXIE

2957
Sheridan County Historical Society

[PO Box 274, 67740]; (p) (785) 675-3501; schs@ruraltel.net; (c) Sheridan

Joint/ 1975/ County; Private non-profit-BOD/ staff: 1(f); 5(v)/ members: 200

HISTORICAL SOCIETY; HISTORY MUSEUM: Collects, preserves, and catalogues county historical materials; operates the Mickey Museum on local history.

PROGRAMS: Annual Meeting; Community Outreach; Exhibits; Guided Tours; Interpretation; Lectures; Publication; Research Library/Archives

COLLECTIONS: [1880-present] Birth, marriage, death, funeral, school, and census records; microfilm newspapers; family histories, cataloged photographs, and files containing historical information; naturalization applications; indexed manuscripts of first land owners of Sheridan County.

HUGOTON

2958
Stevens County Gas and Historical Museum, Inc.
905 S Adams, 67951 [PO Box 87, 67951]; (p) (316) 544-8751; (c) Stevens

County/ 1961/ staff: 1(f)/ members: 72/publication: *The Hugoton Gas Field*

HISTORICAL SOCIETY; HISTORY MUSEUM: Preserves and interprets the development of Stevens County, including agriculture, local history preservation, and history.

PROGRAMS: Annual Meeting; Exhibits; Guided Tours; Publication

COLLECTIONS: Local depot, grocery store, furnished county one-room schoolhouse, furnished century old house, 1885 original jail, 1905 church house, transportation and gas related artifacts.

HOURS: Yr Daily M-F 1-5, Sa-Su 2-4

ADMISSION: No charge/Donations

HUMBOLDT

2959
Humboldt Historical Museum and Society
2nd & Charles St, 66748 [416 N 2nd St, 66748]; (c) Allen

Private non-profit/ 1968/ members: 150/publication: *History of Humboldt, Kansas*

GENEALOGICAL SOCIETY; HISTORIC SITE; HISTORICAL SOCIETY; HISTORY MUSEUM; HOUSE MUSEUM; RESEARCH CENTER: Museum housed in 1867 structure.

PROGRAMS: Annual Meeting; Community Outreach; Exhibits; Family Programs; Guided Tours; Living History; Publication; Reenactments

COLLECTIONS: [Mid-1800s-present] Homestead, school house, machine shop, pole barn, exhibition hall; manuscripts, maps, newspapers, books, sheet music, paintings, museum artifacts and pictures, farm machinery, hearses, doctor's buggy, birthing bed of Walter Johnson.

HOURS: Mem Day-Oct 15 Daily 10-4 by appt

ADMISSION: No charge/Donations

HUTCHINSON

2960
Reno County Museum
100 S Walnut, 67504 [PO Box 664, 67504-0664]; (p) (316) 662-1184; (f) (316) 662-0236; renomus@mindspring.com; (c) Reno

Private non-profit/ 1961/ staff: 3(f); 4(p); 16(v)/

members: 582/publication: *Legacy: The Journal of the RCHS*

HISTORICAL SOCIETY; HISTORY MUSEUM

PROGRAMS: Annual Meeting; Community Outreach; Elder's Programs; Exhibits; Facility Rental; Family Programs; Festivals; Lectures; Living History; Publication; Research Library/Archives; School-Based Curriculum

COLLECTIONS: [1868-present] 32,000 items reflecting Reno County history including business, manufacturing, industries (especially salt), agriculture, early settlements, residential and personal items, and vehicles.

HOURS: Yr T-Sa 9-5, Su

INDEPENDENCE

2961
Independence Historical Museum
123 N 8, PO Box 294, 67301; (p) (316) 331-3515; (c) Montgomery

Private non-profit/ 1882/ staff: 1(p); 30(v)/ members: 150

HISTORY MUSEUM: Collects, preserves, and displays artifacts related to the history of Independence and Montgomery County.

PROGRAMS: Annual Meeting; Community Outreach; Concerts; Exhibits; Facility Rental; Family Programs; Guided Tours

COLLECTIONS: [1882] Former post office on National Register.

HOURS: Yr W-Sa 10-2, Su 1-5

ADMISSION: Donations requested

2962
Little House on the Prairie
13.5 mi SE of Independence on Hwy 75, 67301 [PO Box 386, 67301]; (p) (316) 882-3606; (f) (316) 331-1899; clamber@horizon.hit.net; (c) Montgomery

Private for-profit/ staff: 1(f)

HISTORIC SITE

PROGRAMS: Guided Tours; Publication

HOURS: May 15-Sept 1 M-Sa 10-5, Su 1-5

ADMISSION: Donations requested

INGALLS

2963
Santa Fe Trail Museum of Gray County, Inc.
206 W Main St, 67853 [PO Box 143, 67853]; (p) (316) 335-5220; (c) Gray

Private non-profit/ 1974/ staff: 2(p); 5(v)

HISTORICAL SOCIETY; HISTORY MUSEUM: Museum housed in 2 Santa Fe Railroad depots.

PROGRAMS: Annual Meeting; Exhibits; Guided Tours

COLLECTIONS: Old dishes, household items, furniture, farm, military, and railroad articles.

HOURS: May-Oct 9-11/1-4

IOLA

2964
Boyhood Home of Major General Frederick Funston, The
14 S Washington, 66749 [207 N Jefferson,

66749]; (p) (316) 365-3051, (316) 365-6728; (f) (316) 365-6833

1860/ Allen County Historical Society/ staff: 2(v)

HOUSE MUSEUM: Boyhood home of Major General Frederick Funston, an important botanist and US military figure.

COLLECTIONS: [Victorian] Furniture, collection of rare literature and other books, artifacts and photographs pertaining to the life and career of Frederick Funston; manuscripts, correspondence, and other documents pertaining to Frederick Funston, his family, and events he was associated with.

HOURS: May-Sept

JUNCTION CITY

2965
Geary County Historical Society Museum
530 N Adams, 66441; (p) (785) 238-1666; (f) (785) 238-3955; gchsm@jc.net; (c) Geary

1972/ staff: 3(f); 50(v)/ members: 540/publication: *Geary Glimmers*

GENEALOGICAL SOCIETY; HISTORICAL SOCIETY; HISTORY MUSEUM; RESEARCH CENTER: Preserves and interprets local and state history and artifacts.

PROGRAMS: Annual Meeting; Community Outreach; Concerts; Exhibits; Facility Rental; Guided Tours; Lectures; Living History; Publication; Reenactments; Research Library/Archives; School-Based Curriculum

HOURS: Yr T-Su 1-4

ADMISSION: Donations accepted

KANSAS CITY

2966
Grinter Place Museum
1420 S 78th St, 66111; (p) (913) 299-0373; grinter@kshs.org; www.kshs.org/places/grinter.htm; (c) Wyandotte

State/ KS State Historical Society

HISTORIC SITE; HOUSE MUSEUM: Red brick, modified Federal style home of Moses Grinter, early settler who traded with the Native Americans and operated a ferry on the Kansas River.

PROGRAMS: Exhibits; Festivals; Guided Tours; Interpretation; Living History

COLLECTIONS: [19th c] House; 1880s-90s furniture and d,cor; portraits; maps of the Frontier Military Road

KINGMAN

2967
Kingman County Historical Society, Inc.
400 N Main, 67068 [PO Box 281, 67068]; (p) (316) 532-5274; (c) Kingman

1969/ staff: 1(p); 10(v)/ members: 188

HISTORICAL SOCIETY; HISTORY MUSEUM; RESEARCH CENTER: Collects and preserves local and county history.

PROGRAMS: Annual Meeting; Community Outreach; Exhibits; Family Programs; Guided Tours; Publication; Research Library/Archives

COLLECTIONS: [Pre-Civil War-present] Sheet music, obituaries, fire trucks, history volumes, local and state histories, photographs of local and county business and portraits, cessna old plane parts and murals.

HOURS: Yr F 9-4:30, and by appt

KINSLEY

2968
Edwards County Historical Society
Hwy 56, 67547 [PO Box 64, 67547]; (p) (316) 659-2420; (c) Edwards

County/ 1953/ staff: 1(f)/ members: 80

HISTORICAL SOCIETY; HISTORY MUSEUM: Preserves local history; operates Sod House, replica of early pioneer home.

PROGRAMS: Annual Meeting; Concerts; Exhibits

COLLECTIONS: [1880-present] Artifacts relating to Edwards County, including clothing, furniture, newspapers, photographs.

HOURS: May 1-Sept Daily 10-5

ADMISSION: No charge

LACROSSE

2969
Kansas Barbed Wire Museum
120 W 1st St, 67548 [PO Box 578, 67548-0578]; (p) (785) 222-9900; (c) Rush

Private non-profit/ 1971/ staff: 3(p); 10(v)/ members: 80

HISTORY MUSEUM: Exhibits artifacts relevant to the settling of the Midwest, and effects of the development of barbed wire on the region.

PROGRAMS: Annual Meeting; Exhibits; Festivals; Guided Tours; Interpretation; Lectures; Research Library/Archives; Theatre

COLLECTIONS: [Late 19th c] Barbed wire, fencing items, barbed wire tools, fencing tools, reference materials, books, periodicals, newspaper articles.

HOURS: Daily

ADMISSION: Donations accepted

2970
Rush County Historical Society, Inc.
202 W 1st St, 67548 [PO Box 473, 67548-0473]; (p) (785) 222-2719; (c) Rush

Private non-profit/ 1960/ staff: 9(p); 7(v)/ members: 27

HISTORIC PRESERVATION AGENCY; HISTORICAL SOCIETY; HISTORY MUSEUM; HOUSE MUSEUM: Depicts the mining of post rock limestone and its uses, fossils and tools used; collects and preserves memorabilia of early Rush County.

PROGRAMS: Annual Meeting; Exhibits; Guided Tours

COLLECTIONS: Tools, artifacts, photos, new articles, clothing, and memorabilia from early settlers.

HOURS: May-Sept M-Sa 10-4:30, Su 1-4:30

LAKIN

2971
Kearny County Museum
101-111 S Buffalo, 67860 [PO Box 329,

67860]; (p) (316) 355-7448; (c) Kearny

County/ 1958/ Board of Directors/ staff: 3(p)/ members: 418

HISTORICAL SOCIETY; HISTORY MUSEUM: Presents Kearny County history.

PROGRAMS: Annual Meeting; Community Outreach; Concerts; Exhibits; Facility Rental; Family Programs; Festivals; Guided Tours; Interpretation; Lectures; Living History; Publication; School-Based Curriculum

COLLECTIONS: [1872-present] Artifacts from early pioneer families and their descendants.

HOURS: Yr T-F, Su 1-4

ADMISSION: Donations accepted

LANSING

2972
Lansing Historical Society, Inc.
115 E Kansas Ave, 66043 [115 E Kansas St, 66043-1667]; (p) (913) 727-3731; (c) Leavenworth

Private non-profit/ 1989/ staff: 12(p); 12(v)/ members: 250/publication: *Society Cookbook; Q and R Newsletter*

HISTORICAL SOCIETY; HISTORY MUSEUM: Relocated and restored historic railroad depot and manages museum.

PROGRAMS: Annual Meeting; Exhibits; Publication

COLLECTIONS: [1925-1965] Prison artifacts, photos and other artifacts depicting rural life, small town life and business, Santa Fe (local) artifacts, history.

HOURS: Yr Sa 10-4, Su 1-4 and by appt

ADMISSION: No charge

LARNED

2973
Fort Larned Historical Society, Inc.
2 mi W of Larned on Hwy 156, 67550 [Santa Fe Trail Center, Rte 3, 67550]; (p) (316) 285-2054; (f) (316) 285-7491; trailctr@larned.net; www.larned.net/trailctr/; (c) Pawnee

Private non-profit/ 1957/ Board of Directors/ staff: 3(f); 4(p); 89(v)/ members: 313/publication: *Trail Ruts II*

HISTORICAL SOCIETY; HISTORY MUSEUM: Owns and operates the Santa Fe Trail Center museum/research library, which preserves the history of the Santa Fe Trail, an early transportation route.

PROGRAMS: Annual Meeting; Community Outreach; Exhibits; Facility Rental; Film/Video; Guided Tours; Lectures; Living History; Publication; Research Library/Archives

COLLECTIONS: [Prehistory-1950] Artifacts, photographic materials, archival collections, and a research library pertaining to the geographical area of the Santa Fe Trail.

HOURS: Yr May-Sept Daily 9-5; Sept-May T-Su 9-5

ADMISSION: $3, Student $2, Children $1

2974
Fort Larned National Historic Site
6 mi W of Larned on Hwy 156, 67550 [Route 3, 67550]; (p) (316) 285-6911; (f) (316) 285-

3571; fols_superintendent@nps.gov; www.nps.gov/fols/; (c) Pawnee

Federal/ 1964/ National Park Service/ staff: 14(f); 12(p); 253(v)

HISTORIC SITE; HISTORY MUSEUM; HOUSE MUSEUM; LIVING HISTORY/OUTDOOR MUSEUM; RESEARCH CENTER: Site includes museum, historic buildings, barracks, post hospital, bakery, carpenter and blacksmith shops; new commissary with post school, blockhouse, old commissary and arsenal, Quartermaster building, officer's quarters.

PROGRAMS: Annual Meeting; Community Outreach; Exhibits; Family Programs; Guided Tours; Interpretation; Lectures; Living History; Publication; Reenactments; Research Library/Archives; Theatre

COLLECTIONS: [1859-1878] Military 1859-1878 including uniforms, weapons, accouterments, for furnishings, archeological collections.

HOURS: Yr Daily 8:30-5

ADMISSION: $2; Under 17 free

LAWRENCE

2975
Douglas County Historical Society/ Watkins Community Museum of History
1047 Massachusetts St, 66044-2923; (p) (785) 841-4109; wcmhist@sunflower.com; www.ci.lawrence.ks.us/museum/watkins.html; (c) Douglas

Private non-profit/ staff: 2(f); 4(p); 35(v)/ members: 712/publication: *Douglas County Historical Society Newsletter*

HISTORIC SITE; HISTORICAL SOCIETY: Collects, preserves, and studies f historical material relating to Lawrence, Douglas County, and the State of Kansas.

PROGRAMS: Annual Meeting; Community Outreach; Exhibits; Facility Rental; Family Programs; Guided Tours; Interpretation; Lectures; Publication; Research Library/Archives; School-Based Curriculum

COLLECTIONS: [1854-1945] 4,970 photographs and illustrations; 3,210 documents, 1,753 textiles items, 154 toys/dolls, 309 tools and agricultural equipment, 1879 children's playhouse, 1920 Milburn Electric automobile, 1900 Surrey; Mexican War cannon used in 1854-1865 conflicts.

HOURS: Yr T-Sa 10-4, Su 1:30-4

ADMISSION: Donations accepted

2976
Natural History Museum, Division of Entomology, Snow Collection
University of Kansas, 66045; (p) (785) 864-3065; (f) (785) 864-5620; ksem@kuhub.cc.ukans.edu; www.ron.nhm.ukans.edu/ksem/; (c) Douglas

State/ 1870/ staff: 2(p); 14(v)

NATURAL HISTORY MUSEUM; RESEARCH CENTER: Collects, preserves, and provides a research and teaching facility.

PROGRAMS: Exhibits; Lectures; Research Library/Archives

COLLECTIONS: [1870-present] 3.5 million in

sect collection includes bees, scorpionflies, leaf hoppers, plant hoppers, crane flies, and New World rove beetles.

2977
University of Kansas Museum of Anthropology
Univ of Kansas, 14th & Jayhawk Blvd, 66045 [Spooner Hall, 66045]; (p) (785) 864-4245; (f) (785) 864-5243; cadaniel@ukans.edu; www.ukans.edu/~kuma/; (c) Douglas

State/ 1980/ staff: 3(f); 7(p); 25(v)/ members: 250/publication: *Cultures*

ANTHROPOLOGY MUSEUM; RESEARCH CENTER: Researches, preserves, and interprets material culture from around the world.

PROGRAMS: Community Outreach; Elder's Programs; Exhibits; Family Programs; Festivals; Film/Video; Guided Tours; Interpretation; Lectures; Publication; School-Based Curriculum; Theatre

COLLECTIONS: [Pre history-present] Ethnographic collections: historic North America, Africa, Australia, and contemporary Latin America. Archaeological collections: prehistoric North America and pre Colombian Latin America.

HOURS: Yr Daily M-Sa 9-5, Su 1-5

ADMISSION: No charge

2978
University of Kansas Natural History Museum and Biodiversity Research Center, The
Dyche Hall, 66045-2454; (p) (785) 864-4450; (f) (785) 864-5335; kunhm@ukans.edu; www.nhm.ukans.edu; (c) Douglas

Joint; State/ 1866/ staff: 44(f); 14(p); 132(v)/ members: 800/publication: *Nature in Kansas Series*

NATURAL HISTORY MUSEUM; RESEARCH CENTER: Discovers, documents, and disseminates knowledge of biological diversity and natural environments, past and present.

PROGRAMS: Community Outreach; Elder's Programs; Exhibits; Facility Rental; Family Programs; Festivals; Lectures; Publication

COLLECTIONS: Six million specimens of plants and animals emphasizing the New World.

HOURS: Yr Daily M-F 8-5, Sa 10-5, Su 12-5

LEAVENWORTH

2979
Leavenworth County Historical Society/ The Edward Carroll Victorian Mansion
1128 Fifth Ave, 66048-3213; (p) (913) 682-7759; (f) (913) 682-2089; lvcohistsoc@lvnworth.com; leavenworth-net.com/lchs/; (c) Leavenworth

1954/ staff: 1(f); 2(p); 50(v)/ members: 300

HISTORICAL SOCIETY; HOUSE MUSEUM: Discovesr, preserves, and shares the heritage of the area; operates the Carroll Mansion (1857).

PROGRAMS: Facility Rental; Festivals; Garden Tours; Guided Tours; Lectures; School-Based Curriculum

COLLECTIONS: [Late 1880s-1890s] Victorian mansion and furniture, Victorian textiles, clothing and quilts. Files on Leavenworth County History, 30,000 19th c photo negatives; some

county archives, death, birth, marriage, and land records.

HOURS: Sept-Apr T-Sa 1-4:30; May-Aug T-Sa 10:30-4:30, Su 1-4:30

ADMISSION: $4, Children $2, Seniors $3; Under 5/Mbrs free

LECOMPTON

2980
Lecompton Historical Society
609 Woodson, 66050; (p) (785) 887-6148; (f) (785) 887-6148; www.lecomptonkansas.com; (c) Douglas

Private non-profit/ 1969/ staff: 1(p); 65(v)/ members: 553/publication: *Bald Eagle*

HISTORIC SITE; HISTORICAL SOCIETY; HISTORY MUSEUM: Promotes the Pre-Civil War history of Lecompton and the role it played in the nation's history; operates Territorial Capital Museum and Constitution Hall, a National Landmark.

PROGRAMS: Annual Meeting; Community Outreach; Exhibits; Facility Rental; Festivals; Guided Tours; Publication; Research Library/Archives

COLLECTIONS: [Mid 19th-early 20th c] Artifacts, memorabilia, and ephemera; turn-of-the-century Lane Univ artifacts and music rooms; household materials, furniture.

HOURS: Yr W-Sa 11-4, Su 1-5

ADMISSION: No charge/Donations

LENEXA

2981
Legler Barn Museum Complex
14907 W 87th St Pkwy, 66215; (p) (913) 894-4928; lhskc@kc.net; www.kc.net/~lhskc; (c) Johnson

Private non-profit/ 1983/ staff: 2(p); 15(v)/ members: 200

HISTORY MUSEUM: Museum housed in a relocated 1864 stone barn; exhibits in 1911-12 Lenexa Depot, Strang-Line Waiting Station, Caboose, and Prairie Schooner.

PROGRAMS: Community Outreach; Exhibits; Festivals; Lectures; Publication; Research Library/Archives

COLLECTIONS: [Late 19th-early 20th c] Material objects that contribute to the story of Lenexa's history.

HOURS: Yr Feb-Nov T-Sa 10-4, Su 1-4; Dec-Jan T-Sa 10-4

ADMISSION: No charge

LEOTI

2982
Wichita County Historical Society
201 N 4th St, 67861 [PO Box C, 67861]; (p) (316) 375-2316; (c) Wichita

Joint/ 1970/ County; Private non-profit/ staff: 1(p); 6(v)/ members: 98

GENEALOGICAL SOCIETY; HISTORIC PRESERVATION AGENCY; HISTORICAL SOCIETY; HISTORY MUSEUM

PROGRAMS: Annual Meeting; Exhibits; Lectures

COLLECTIONS: [Early America]
HOURS: Yr 4 days/wk 2-4

LIBERAL

2983
Dorothy's House and Coronado Museum
567 E Cedar St, 67901; (p) (316) 624-7624; (f) (316) 624-7656

2984
Mid America Air Museum
2000 W 2nd St, 67905 [PO Box 2199, 67905-2199]; (p) (316) 624-5263; (f) (316) 624-5454; (c) Seward

City/ 1984/ staff: 4(f); 1(p); 30(v)/ members: 260

HISTORY MUSEUM: Collects, exhibits, an terprets aircraft history.

PROGRAMS: Exhibits; Facility Rental; Family Programs; Guided Tours

COLLECTIONS: [20th c] 96 aircraft and hundreds of items of memorabilia.

HOURS: Yr Daily M-Sa 10-5, Su 1-5

ADMISSION: $5, Student $2, Seniors $4

LINCOLN

2985
Lincoln County Historical Society
214 W Lincoln Ave, 67455 [PO Box 85, 67455]; (p) (785) 524-4614; (c) Lincoln

County/ 1978/ Board of Directors/ staff: 12(v)/ members: 90

GARDEN; HISTORIC PRESERVATION AGENCY; HISTORIC SITE; HISTORICAL SOCIETY; HISTORY MUSEUM; HOUSE MUSEUM; LIVING HISTORY/OUTDOOR MUSEUM: Maintains: pioneer, native stone house with annex; one-room Topsy School; Victorian style Yohe House and garden; and collects, preserves, and interprets local history.

PROGRAMS: Annual Meeting; Community Outreach; Elder's Programs; Exhibits; Family Programs; Festivals; Garden Tours; Guided Tours; Interpretation; Lectures; Living History; Publication; Reenactments; Research Library/Archives; School-Based Curriculum

COLLECTIONS: Victorian House furnished in 1920s fashion with original furnishings, and one-room school; paintings, portraits, photographs, 1,000 artifacts, farm tools, fence-making equipment, uniforms and articles from 6 wars, articles of the 1881 Women's Relief Corps of the Grand Army of the Republic.

HOURS: Summer Su 1-5

ADMISSION: Donations accepted

2986
Yohe House
316 S 2nd, 67455 [Lincoln County Historical Society, PO Box 85, 67455]; (p) (785) 524-4934, (785) 524-4744

1885

HOUSE MUSEUM

LITTLE RIVER

2987
Young Historical Library
201 Main St, 67457 [PO Box 126, 67457-0126]; (p) (316) 897-6236; lilliew@midusa.net; (c) Rice

City/ 1977/ staff: 1(v)

LIBRARY AND/OR ARCHIVES; RESEARCH CENTER: Small historical library, provides research facility preserving records, newspapers, and photographs.

PROGRAMS: Community Outreach; Research Library/Archives

COLLECTIONS: [1886-present] Newspapers published in Little River, local cemetery records, old school records, photographs, family genealogy collection.

HOURS: Yr Th

LYNDON

2988
Osage County Historical Society
631 Topeka Ave, 66451 [PO Box 361, 66451]; (p) (785) 828-3477; research@kanza.net; www.osagechs.org; (c) Osage

County/ 1965/ Board of Directors/ staff: 1(f); 2(v)/ members: 225/publication: *The Hedgepost*

GENEALOGICAL SOCIETY; HISTORICAL SOCIETY; HISTORY MUSEUM; RESEARCH CENTER: Collects and displays artifacts, and compiles histories relating to the county.

PROGRAMS: Annual Meeting; Exhibits; Guided Tours; Publication; Research Library/ Archives

COLLECTIONS: [1861-1950] Agricultural implements, railroad and coal mining artifacts, Native American artifacts, actual paper files, docket books of district court 1861-1954, and pedigree files.

HOURS: Apr 1- Oct 31 W-Sa 12-5

ADMISSION: No charge

LYONS

2989
Rice County Historical Society
105 W Lyon, 67554; (p) (316) 257-3941; (c) Rice

Private non-profit/ 1927/ staff: 4(f); 3(p); 6(v)/ members: 236

HISTORIC SITE; HISTORICAL SOCIETY; HISTORY MUSEUM; HOUSE MUSEUM: Operates the Coronado Quivira Museum and archives.

PROGRAMS: Annual Meeting; Exhibits; Facility Rental; Family Programs; Festivals; Film/ Video; Guided Tours; Interpretation; Lectures; Publication; Research Library/Archives; School-Based Curriculum

COLLECTIONS: Prehistoric artifacts; memorabilia, artifacts, and objects related to: Quiviran Indians, Coronado's trek north, Santa Fe Trail, and rural America

MANHATTAN

2990
Marianna Kistler Beach Museum of Art
701 Beach Ln, 66506; (p) (785) 532-7718; (f) (785) 532-7498; klwalk@ksu.edu; www.ksu.edu/bma; (c) Riley

State/ 1996/ KS State Univ/ staff: 8(f); 30(p); 40(v)/ members: 300

ART MUSEUM: Acquires, preserves, documents, interprets, and exhibits significant works of art, particularly those that reflect the cultural traditions of Mid-America.

PROGRAMS: Annual Meeting; Community Outreach; Concerts; Exhibits; Facility Rental; Family Programs; Festivals; Guided Tours; Interpretation; Lectures; Publication; School-Based Curriculum

COLLECTIONS: [20th c] 2,500 20th century American paintings, prints, drawings, and photographs, with a regional focus, including works by Regionalist artists.

HOURS: Yr T-Sa 10-5, Th10-8:30, Su 1-5

2991
Riley County Historical Society and Museum
2309 Claflin Rd, 66502; (p) (785) 565-6490; (c) Riley

Joint/ 1914/ County; Private non-profit/ staff: 2(f); 5(p); 100(v)/ members: 850

HISTORICAL SOCIETY; HISTORY MUSEUM; HOUSE MUSEUM: Collects, preserves, and displays historical artifacts and records of Riley County and the West; encourages interest in local history.

PROGRAMS: Annual Meeting; Community Outreach; Exhibits; Facility Rental; Guided Tours; Living History; Research Library/ Archives

COLLECTIONS: [1855-present] Five Structures: Hartford house (1855 pre-fab construction), Pioneer Log Cabin Museum, Wolf House Museum (19th c limestone home), Rocky Ford School (one-room schoolhouse), Randolph Jail (19th c jail). 19th c pioneer household and farm equipment, furniture, toys, glass, china, clothing, school and medical equipment, dolls, quilts, photos, newspapers, tools, musical instruments; city, county, club, church, and school records.

HOURS: Yr T-F 8:30-5, Sa-Su 2-5

ADMISSION: No charge/Donations

2992
Wolf House Museum
630 Fremont St, 66502 [630 Fremont, 66502]; (p) (913) 776-7344, (913) 565-6490

Joint/ 1868/ County; RCHS/ staff: 3(p)

COLLECTIONS: [1868] 1860-1900 furnishings all on exhibit.

HOURS: Yr

MANKATO

2993
Jewell County Historical Society
210N Commercial, 66956 [RR 1 Box 101, 66956]; (c) Jewell

Private non-profit/ 1959/ staff: 1(p); 10(v)/ members: 180

HISTORICAL SOCIETY: Operates museum.

PROGRAMS: Annual Meeting; Community Outreach; Exhibits; Family Programs; Festivals; Research Library/Archives

COLLECTIONS: [1800-present] Artifacts, memorabilia, ephemera; general household, farm machinery, general store, pharmacy, post office, doctor and dental equipment, clothing, dolls, period rooms.

HOURS: Apr 15-Oct 15 Th-Sa 1-5

ADMISSION: No charge/Donations

MARQUETTE

2994
Marquette Historical Society
113 N Washington, 67464 [PO Box 401, 67464]; (p) (785) 546-2205; (f) (785) 546-2777; (c) McPherson

Private non-profit/ 1989/publication: *Pioneers on the Prairie*

HISTORICAL SOCIETY: Preserves community history.

PROGRAMS: Guided Tours

COLLECTIONS: Community history and pioneer memorabilia, one-room school preservation.

HOURS: Daily by appt

ADMISSION: No charge

MARYSVILLE

2995
Doll House Museum
912 Broadway, 66508; (p) (785) 562-4077; (f) (785) 562-2990; candc@midusa.net; (c) Marshall

Private non-profit/ 1997/ staff: 2(f); 1(p)/publication: *Doll Lovers Gazette*

HISTORY MUSEUM

PROGRAMS: Exhibits; Guided Tours; Interpretation; Lectures; Publication; School-Based Curriculum

COLLECTIONS: [1840-present] Dolls dressed in vintage clothing, antiques, and collectibles.

HOURS: Yr T-Sa 9-12/1-4

ADMISSION: $2, Children $1

2996
Koester House Museum
919 Broadway, 66508 [209 N 8th, 66508]; (p) (785) 562-2417, (785) 562-5331

City/ 1873/ staff: 1(f)

COLLECTIONS: [19th c Victorian] White bronze statuary, original items owned by the Koester family; children's clothes and toys, unique and "newest" kitchen gadgets.

HOURS: Yr

2997
Marshall County Historical Society
1207 Broadway, 66508; (p) (785) 562-5012; mchs@mvleadvocate.com; skyways.lib.ks.us/museums/mchc/index.html; (c) Marshall

1971/ Administrative Board/ staff: 1(p); 25(v)/ members: 310/publication: *Magpie*

GENEALOGICAL SOCIETY; HISTORICAL SOCIETY; HISTORY MUSEUM; RESEARCH CENTER: Collects, preserves, and displays historical records and items of Marshall County and KS; preserves the Historic Courthouse; maintains and makes available county genealogical records.

PROGRAMS: Annual Meeting; Community Outreach; Concerts; Exhibits; Family Programs; Guided Tours; Lectures; Publication; Quarterly Meeting; Research Library/Archives

COLLECTIONS: [1880-present] Manuscripts; court dockets; marriage, naturalization, and burial records; town and family histories, museum artifacts, photographs.

HOURS: Yr Labor Day-Mem Day M-F 1-4; Mem Day-Labor Day Daily 1-4

ADMISSION: $1; Donation requested

MCPHERSON

2998
McPherson County Historical Society, Inc.
540 E Hill, 67460; (p) (316) 241-2699; (c) Matherson

County/ 1962/ staff: 1(p); 10(v)/ members: 270

HISTORICAL SOCIETY

PROGRAMS: Annual Meeting; Community Outreach; Lectures; Research Library/ Archives

2999
McPherson Museum
1130 E Euclid, 67460; (p) (316) 245-2574; (f) (316) 245-2574; (c) McPherson

Joint/ 1968/ City; Private non-profit/ staff: 7(p)

HISTORY MUSEUM: Collects, preserves, and exhibits materials on local and regional history.

PROGRAMS: Annual Meeting; Community Outreach; Exhibits; Facility Rental; Festivals; Guided Tours; Living History; Research Library/Archives; School-Based Curriculum

COLLECTIONS: [1875-1925] Over 30,000 objects of local history, paleontology, Southwest Native American artifacts, Chinese and African arts.

HOURS: Yr 1-5

ADMISSION: No charge

MEADE

3000
Dalton Gang Hideout and Museum
502 S Pearlette St, 67864 [PO Box 515, 67864]; (p) (800) 354-2743, (620) 873-2731; (c) Meade

The Whipple house, hideout for the Dalton Gang; escape tunnel; barn museum; and Heritage House, a restored ca. 1900 Meade County home.

HOURS: Yr Daily M-Sa 9-6, Su 1-6; Labor Day-Mem Day 9-5/1-5

ADMISSION: $2

3001
Meade County Historical Museum
200 E Carthage, 67864 [PO Box 893, 67864]; (p) (620) 873-2359; (c) Meade

1974/ staff: 2(f); 10(v)

HISTORICAL SOCIETY; HISTORY MUSEUM

PROGRAMS: Annual Meeting; Exhibits

COLLECTIONS: [1885] Artifacts and memorabilia including artifacts from a local archeological dig; one room school house; a windmill; and early farm equipment.

HOURS: Yr Daily M-Sa 9-6, Su 1-6; Winter 9-5 Su1-5

ADMISSION: Donations accepted

MEDICINE LODGE

3002
Carry A. Nation Home and Museum
211 W Fowler Hwy 160, 67104 [Box 132, 67104]; (p) (316) 886-3553; (c) Barber

Joint/ 1950/ City; Private non-profit/ staff: 2(p); 6(v)

HOUSE MUSEUM

PROGRAMS: Family Programs; Guided Tours

COLLECTIONS: [1900s] Photographs, artifacts, and memorabilia of Carry A. Nation.

HOURS: Yr Daily 10:30-5

ADMISSION: $4, Children $2, Seniors $3.50

MOUNDRIDGE

3003
Swiss Mennonite Cultural and Historical Association
109 E Hirschler, 67107; (p) (316) 345-2844; (c) McPherson

Private non-profit/ 1973/ staff: 10(v)/ members: 160

HISTORICAL SOCIETY: Disseminates information on the cultural history of Mennonites of Swiss origin and maintains the memorial marker that tells their story.

PROGRAMS: Annual Meeting; Festivals

COLLECTIONS: Seven plaques on the memorial marker that tell the story of the Swiss Mennonite Memorial Center.

HOURS: Yr Daily Dawn-Dusk

ADMISSION: No charge

MULVANE

3004
Mulvane Historical Society
300 W Main, 67110 [PO Box 117, 67110]; (p) (316) 777-0506; (c) Sumner

Private non-profit/ 1972/ staff: 1(f); 15(v)/ members: 110

HISTORICAL SOCIETY; HISTORY MUSEUM: Located in a former Santa Fe Depot built in 1910; collects, preserves, and makes available the history of Mulvane.

PROGRAMS: Exhibits; Facility Rental; Festivals; Guided Tours

COLLECTIONS: [1879-present] Caboose, rail car, old city jail, railroad artifacts, farm and woodworking tools, doctor's instruments and mementos, WW II nurses exhibits, photographs, and artifacts.

HOURS: Yr T-Sa 10-4

ADMISSION: Donations accepted

3005
Sumner County Historical Society
[PO Box 213, 67110]; (c) Sumner

Private non-profit/ staff: 5(f)/ members: 125

HISTORICAL SOCIETY: Preserves and collects the history of Sumner County.

PROGRAMS: Lectures; Research Library/ Archives

HOURS: Jan-May, Aug-Nov 4th M 6:30-8:30

NEODESHA

3006
Norman #1 Oil Well Museum
First & Main, 66757 [105 S First St, 66757]; (p) (316) 325-5316; (f) (316) 325-5316; (c) Wilson

Joint/ 1962/ City; Private non-profit/ staff: 2(f); 3(v)/ members: 585

HISTORIC SITE; HISTORY MUSEUM: Site of the first commercial oil well west of the Mississippi River; preserves and exhibits artifacts.

PROGRAMS: Community Outreach; Guided Tours; Reenactments; School-Based Curriculum

COLLECTIONS: [1870-1935] WPA dolls depicting clothes from 1620-1900; pictures of oil wells, artifacts, and some tools; Army and Navy uniforms; 1901 wedding dress; a derrick depicting the original well drilled in1892.

3007
W.A. Rankin Memorial Library
502 Indian, 66757; (p) (316) 325-3275; rankin.library@ student.neodesha.ks.12.us; members.tripad.com/~neodesha_kansas/library ; (c) Wilson

City/ 1912/ staff: 3(f); 2(p); 2(v)

LIBRARY AND/OR ARCHIVES: Preserves local history materials and the holdings of the Heritage Genealogy Society disbanded in 1992.

PROGRAMS: Research Library/Archives

COLLECTIONS: [1870-present] Federal/state census records, local newspapers on microfilm, Wilson County history, local history, genealogy records, indexes and publications for many states where KS settlers originated, local obituaries and birth indexes, and Wilson County marriages.

HOURS: Yr M 9:30-8, T-F 9:30-5:30, Sa 9-12

NESS CITY

3008
Ness County Historical Society
123 S Pennsylvania Ave, 67560-1907; (p) (784) 798-3298; (c) Ness

State/ 1930/ staff: 4(p)/ members: 200

HISTORICAL SOCIETY; HISTORY MUSEUM: Displays artifacts connected to Ness County.

PROGRAMS: Annual Meeting; Exhibits; Guided Tours; Publication; Research Library/ Archives

COLLECTIONS: [1880-1960] Quilts, dishes, furniture, tools, books, pictures, clothing, military uniforms.

HOURS: Yr T-F 1-5

ADMISSION: No charge/Donations

NEWTON

3009
Harvey County Historical Society
203 Main, 67114 [PO Box 4, 67114]; (p) (316) 283-2221; (c) Harvey

Private non-profit/ 1960/ staff: 4(p); 40(v)/ members: 150

HISTORICAL SOCIETY; LIVING HISTORY/ OUTDOOR MUSEUM: Encourages and preserves local history.

PROGRAMS: Annual Meeting; Community Outreach; Exhibits; Lectures; Living History; Research Library/Archives

COLLECTIONS: [1870-present]

HOURS: Yr W-Su 1-4

ADMISSION: $2, Children $1

3010
Warkentin House Association
211 E First, 67114; (p) (316) 283-3113; www.infonewtonks.com/tourism/ warkentin.htm; (c) Harvey

Private non-profit/ 1969/ Board of Directors/ staff: 20(v)/ members: 35

HISTORIC SITE; HOUSE MUSEUM: Interprets history of house and its inhabitants.

PROGRAMS: Annual Meeting; Community Outreach; Concerts; Elder's Programs; Exhibits; Facility Rental; Family Programs; Guided Tours; Interpretation; Lectures; School-Based Curriculum

COLLECTIONS: [1887-1920] 1887 Victorian house, furniture of original owners; gazebo and carriage house.

HOURS: Jan-Mar by appt; Apr-May, Sept-Dec Sa-Su 1-4:30; June-Aug T-Su 1-4:30

ADMISSION: $3, Children $1.50; Under 5 free

NORTH NEWTON

3011
Mennonite Library and Archives
300 E 27th St, 67117-0531; (p) (316) 284-5304; (f) (316) 284-5286; mla@bethelks.edu; www.bethelks.edu/services/mla; (c) Harvey

Private non-profit/ 1936/ staff: 3(p); 5(v)/publication: *Mennonite Life*

LIBRARY AND/OR ARCHIVES: Collects, preserves, and makes available documentation on Mennonite history, theology, and culture; focus on Mennonites of the Plains states.

PROGRAMS: Exhibits; Publication; Research Library/Archives

COLLECTIONS: [1850-present] Materials, objects, and literature.

HOURS: Yr M-Th 10-12/1-5

ADMISSION: No charge

NORTON

3012
Adobe Home
Prairie Dog State Park, 4 mi W & 1 mi S of Norton, 67654 [PO Box 431, 67654]; (p) (785) 877-2953; (f) (785) 877-2479

State/ 1892/ KS Wildlife and Parks

COLLECTIONS: [1890s]

HOURS: By appt.

3013
Norton County Historical Society and Museum
105 E Lincoln, 67654 [PO Box 303, 67654]; (p) (785) 877-5107; www.nex-tech.com/ clients/nchistory/; (c) Norton

Joint/ County; Private non-profit/ staff: 7(p);

11(v)/ members: 70

HISTORICAL SOCIETY; HISTORY MUSEUM: Operates museum dedicated to preserving the pioneer history of Norton County and Northwest KS.

PROGRAMS: Annual Meeting; Exhibits; Guided Tours; Interpretation

COLLECTIONS: [1880-1930]

HOURS: Museum: W, Sa 2-4

ADMISSION: Donations

3014
Station 15 Stagecoach Stop
Wayside Park Hwy 36, 67654 [PO Box 132, 67654]; (p) (785) 877-2501; (f) (785) 877-3300; (c) Norton

City/ 1859

HISTORIC SITE: Window view museum.

COLLECTIONS: Material on Horace Greeley and Billy the Kid.

HOURS: Yr Daily

OAKLEY

3015
Fick Fossil and History Museum
700 W 3rd, 67748; (p) (785) 672-4839; (f) (785) 672-3497; cmullen@ruraltel.net; www.oakley-kansas.com/fick; (c) Logan

City/ 1975/ staff: 1(f); 2(p); 3(v)

HISTORY MUSEUM; NATURAL HISTORY MUSEUM: Collects, preserves, and interprets the artifacts and history of Northwest KS.

PROGRAMS: Exhibits; Guided Tours

COLLECTIONS: Fossils, rocks, minerals, fossil folkart, antique clothing, antique merchandise, local history items, photos, wood carvings, and over 11,000 cretaceous period shark teeth found in the area.

HOURS: Yr May-Sept M-Sa 9-5, Su 2-4; Oct-Apr M-Sa 9-5

ADMISSION: Donations accepted

OBERLIN

3016
Decatur County Museum, Inc.
258 S Penn, 67749; (p) (785) 475-2712; decaturmuseum@nwkansas.com; (c) Decatur

Private non-profit/ 1958/ staff: 2(f); 1(p); 4(v)/ members: 120

GENEALOGICAL SOCIETY; HISTORICAL SOCIETY; HISTORY MUSEUM: Site includes 13 buildings depicting the life and times of the pioneers, Native Americans, and peoples of the Plains

PROGRAMS: Annual Meeting; Exhibits; Festivals; Guided Tours; Research Library/Archives

COLLECTIONS: [1890-1940] Sod house, depot, country school, Dr. office, land office, grocery, and livery. Native American arrowheads; quilts; dolls; dishes; military memorabilia; farm tools; clothing; and items depicting Pioneer life.

HOURS: Apr-Nov T-Sa 10-12/1-5

ADMISSION: $3, Children $1.50

OKETO

3017
Oketo Community Historical Society Trust
102 E Center, 66518 [208 S E St, 66518]; (p) (785) 744-3460; (c) Marshall

Private non-profit/ 1971/ staff: 6(v)/ members: 24

HISTORIC PRESERVATION AGENCY; HISTORIC SITE; HISTORICAL SOCIETY; HISTORY MUSEUM: Maintains museum.

PROGRAMS: Community Outreach; Exhibits

COLLECTIONS: [1860s] Indian collections, rock quarry tools, period room displays, old telephones, bank equipment, Overland Trail artifacts, farm machinery and tools.

HOURS: By appt

ADMISSION: No charge

OLATHE

3018
Ensor Farmsite & Museum
18995 W 183rd St, 66062-9278; (p) (913) 592-4141

Home of Marshall H. and Loretta Ensor.

COLLECTIONS: [Early 20th c]

HOURS: June-Labor Day F-Sa 1-8, Su 1-5

ADMISSION: No charge

3019
Mahaffie Stagecoach Stop and Farm
1100 Kansas City Rd, 66061; (p) (913) 782-6972; (f) (913) 397-5114; mahaffie@unicom.net; (c) Johnson

Joint/ 1981/ City; Private non-profit/ staff: 6(f); 1(p); 50(v)/ members: 60

HISTORIC SITE: Site on the Santa Fe Trail; last remaining stage stop, limestone house, historic farm, wood peg barn

PROGRAMS: Concerts; Facility Rental; Family Programs; Festivals; Garden Tours; Guided Tours; Interpretation; Living History; Reenactments

COLLECTIONS: [1857-1880] House furnished for the time period, tools, and farm equipment, blacksmith tools, replica stagecoach, turn of the century doctor buggy, replica prairie schooner.

HOURS: Feb-Mar M-F 10-4; Apr-Dec M-Sa 10-4, Su 12-4

ADMISSION: $3, Children $1.75; Group rates

OSAWATOMIE

3020
Adair Cabin/John Brown Museum State Historic Site
10th & Main, 66064 [PO Box 37, 66064]; (p) (913) 755-4384; (f) (913) 755-4164; (c) Miami

Joint/ 1928/ State; City/ staff: 2(p); 3(v)/ members: 100

HISTORIC SITE; HISTORY MUSEUM: The log cabin of John Brown's half sister her husband; on the site of the Battle of Osawatomie.

PROGRAMS: Annual Meeting; Community Outreach; Exhibits; Festivals; Guided Tours; Interpretation; Lectures; Living History; Reenactments

COLLECTIONS: [1854-1898] 1850s log home and furnishings.

HOURS: Yr Su 1-5, T-Sa 11-5

ADMISSION: Donations accepted

3021
Osawatomie Museum Foundation
628 Main, 66064; (p) (913) 755-6781;
museum@paola-online.net; (c) Miami

Joint/ 1989/ County; Private non-profit/ staff: 1(f); 30(v)/ members: 77

HISTORIC PRESERVATION AGENCY; HOUSE MUSEUM: Preserves local history.

PROGRAMS: Annual Meeting; Community Outreach; Guided Tours

COLLECTIONS: [Pre Civil War-present] Artifacts, memorabilia, and ephemera relating to local history; state hospital, schools, pre-Civil War rural culture, and social history.

HOURS: Yr

OSBORNE

3022
Osborne County Genealogical and Historical Society
929 N Second St, 67473; (p) (587) 346-2418; (c) Osborne

Private non-profit/ 1976/ staff: 1(f); 1(p); 22(v)/ members: 92

GENEALOGICAL SOCIETY; HISTORICAL SOCIETY: Preserves genealogical records; collects, preserves, and interprets local history publications, pictures, and artifacts.

PROGRAMS: Annual Meeting; Community Outreach; Guided Tours; Interpretation; Research Library/Archives

COLLECTIONS: [1880s-1950s] Historical photographs, correspondence, county records, military uniforms, genealogical records, horse drawn farm machinery, turn of the century kitchen utensils, corporate stamps, rifles, restored school house, old books, adding machines, wind mill, and out house.

HOURS: Summer Su-Th 2-4

ADMISSION: No charge/Donations

OSKALOOSA

3023
Jefferson County Genealogical Society
Hwy 59, 66066 [PO Box 174, 66066-0174]; (p) (785) 863-2070; (c) Jefferson

Private non-profit/ 1979/ members: 150

GENEALOGICAL SOCIETY

PROGRAMS: Family Programs; Lectures

COLLECTIONS: [1850-present] Large microfilm collection of census records, county, newspapers, county records, obituaries, and cemetery records.

HOURS: Apr 1-Nov Sa 1-5, Su 1:30-5, M 7pm-8:30

ADMISSION: No charge

3024
Jefferson County Historical Society-Old Jefferson Town
Hwy 59, 66066 [PO Box 146, 66066]; (p) (785) 863-2070; www.digitalhistory.com/schools/oskaloosa.old _jeff_town.html; (c) Jefferson

County; Private non-profit/ 1966/ staff: 2(p); 128(v)/ members: 175/publication: *Newsletter and Yesteryears*

HISTORICAL SOCIETY; HISTORY MUSEUM: Creates interest in the history of Jefferson County and preserves, records, and displays representative buildings and artifacts from around the county.

PROGRAMS: Annual Meeting; Community Outreach; Exhibits; Facility Rental; Family Programs; Festivals; Guided Tours; Living History; Publication; Research Library/Archives

COLLECTIONS: [1880-1920] Historic buildings, including furnishings, museum collection, photographic collection from communities in Jefferson County; John Steuart Curry boyhood home museum, Nincehelster House, Country Church, one-room schoolhouse, general store, jail, blacksmith, statue, cemetery records, maps, books, photographs, local history materials, county newspapers.

HOURS: Research Center: Sa 1-5, Apr-Nov M 7-8:30pm, Su 1:30-5 by appt; Museum: May-Sept Sa 1-5, Su 1:30-5 by appt

ADMISSION: No charge/Donations

OSWEGO

3025
Oswego Historical Society, Inc.
410 Commerical, 67356; (p) (316) 795-4500; history@Oswego.net; (c) Labette

Private non-profit/ 1968/ staff: 2(p); 3(v)

ART MUSEUM; GENEALOGICAL SOCIETY; HISTORICAL SOCIETY; HISTORY MUSEUM: Collects and preserves local history materials, including a log cabin on the original site; operates historical museum and genealogy department.

PROGRAMS: Annual Meeting; Community Outreach; Exhibits; Guided Tours; Living History; Research Library/Archives; School-Based Curriculum

COLLECTIONS: [1840-present] Artifacts, photographs, records, and documents; burial and wedding records, complete genealogy department, including microfilm of all Oswego newspapers.

HOURS: June-Oct M-F 1-5

ADMISSION: No charge

OTTAWA

3026
Franklin County Historical Society, Inc.
S Main, 66067 [PO Box 145, 66067]; (p) (785) 242-1232; history@att.net; (c) Franklin

Private non-profit/ 1837/ staff: 1(f); 3(p); 40(v)/ members: 145/publication: *The Headlight*

HISTORICAL SOCIETY; HISTORY MUSEUM; HOUSE MUSEUM; RESEARCH CENTER: Preserves, collects, researches, and presents local history.

PROGRAMS: Annual Meeting; Community

Outreach; Exhibits; Family Programs; Festivals; Guided Tours; Interpretation; Lectures; Publication; School-Based Curriculum

COLLECTIONS: [1854-present] 10,000 cataloged photographs; 19th c Franklin County newspapers; 5,000 objects of daily life; artifacts of Ottaws Chatanques, Silkville Commune, John Brown's Pottawatomie Massacre, Ottawa Manufacturing Company.

HOURS: T-Sa 10-4, Su 1-4

ADMISSION: $2; Students/Children/Mbrs free

OVERBROOK

3027
Clinton Lake Historical Society, Inc.
Clinton Lake, 66524 [261 N 851 Diagonal Rd, 66524]; (p) (785) 748-0800; (c) Douglas

Private non-profit/ 1973/ staff: 1(f); 3(p); 3(v)/ members: 144

HISTORIC SITE; HISTORY MUSEUM: Collects, preserves, and interprets the histories of the 10 Clinton Lake Communities affected by construction on Clinton Lake by the Army Corps of Engineers.

PROGRAMS: Annual Meeting; Community Outreach; Exhibits; Facility Rental; Family Programs; Guided Tours; Interpretation; Reenactments

COLLECTIONS: [1854-1873] Photographs, documents, artifacts, genealogical material; exhibits include weather, education, religion, agriculture, transportation, Indian.

HOURS: May-Oct Sa 1-6, Su 1-5 or by appt

ADMISSION: No charge

PARSONS

3028
Parsons Historical Society
401 S 18th St, 67357; (c) Labette

Joint/ 1969/ City; County/ staff: 6(p); 14(v)/ members: 50

HISTORICAL SOCIETY; HISTORY MUSEUM: Collects, preserves, and displays historical memorabilia from Parsons and the surrounding area.

PROGRAMS: Annual Meeting; Exhibits; Guided Tours

COLLECTIONS: [1890-present] Books: city directories and school annuals; period rooms with furniture; farm machinery and tools; handwork and period clothing; photographs; video interviews with older residents.

PEABODY

3029
Peabody Historical Society
Cor of Walnut & Division Sts, 66866 [c/o Marilyn Jones, RR 2, 66866]; (p) (316) 983-2815; (c) Marion

1961/ staff: 1(p); 15(v)/ members: 75

GARDEN; HISTORIC PRESERVATION AGENCY; HISTORICAL SOCIETY; HOUSE MUSEUM: Saved the first free library in KS; promotes, portrays, and preserves local, state, and national history.

PROGRAMS: Community Outreach; Exhibits; Family Programs; Festivals; Garden Tours; Living History; Publication; Reenactments; Research Library/Archives

COLLECTIONS: [1880s-1960] Dolls, early day printing equipment. Five structures: Peabody Museum, Peabody Carnegie Library, 1881 Morgan House, ADA Outhouse, Peabody Printing Museum.

HOURS: June-Aug W-Su 1-4 and by appt; Carnegie Library: Yr M-Sa

PITTSBURG

3030
Crawford County Historical Museum
651 S Hwy 69, 66762; (p) (316) 231-1440; (c) Crawford

Private non-profit/ 1970/ Board of Directors/ staff: 20(v)/ members: 85

HISTORIC PRESERVATION AGENCY; HISTORICAL SOCIETY; HISTORY MUSEUM: Operates the museum.

PROGRAMS: Annual Meeting; Community Outreach; Exhibits; Festivals; Guided Tours

COLLECTIONS: [1865-1950] Artifacts and papers concerning history of coal mines in SE Kansas; country one room schoolhouse and Mom and Pop Grocery Store.

HOURS: Yr W-Su 1-5

ADMISSION: No charge/Donations

3031
Special Collection and Archives, Leonard H. Axe Library, Pittsburg State University
1605 S Joplin, 66762 [1701 S Broadway, 66762]; (p) (316) 235-4883; (f) (316) 235-4090; speccoll@mail.pittstate.edu; library.pittstate.edu/spcoll/; (c) Crawford

State/ 1903/ staff: 1(f); 1(p)

LIBRARY AND/OR ARCHIVES: Collects, preserves, and makes available the historical and cultural records of the Univ and SE Kansas.

PROGRAMS: Community Outreach; Exhibits; Lectures; Research Library/Archives

COLLECTIONS: [1850-present] Historical KS materials and the university archives; specialty is printed materials of SE Kansas culture and inhabitants, and the correspondence, libraries, business titles, and other memorabilia of significant SE Kansans.

HOURS: Yr M-F

PLEASANTON

3032
Linn County Historical Society and Museum
307 E Park, 66075 [PO Box 137, 66075]; (p) (913) 352-8739; (f) (913) 352-8739; (c) Linn

Private non-profit/ 1968/ staff: 1(f); 2(p)/ 4(v)/ members: 250/publication: LCHS Newsletter

GENEALOGICAL SOCIETY; HISTORICAL SOCIETY; HISTORY MUSEUM; RESEARCH CENTER: Maintains and operates the museum.

PROGRAMS: Annual Meeting; Exhibits; Family Programs; Film/Video; Guided Tours; Living History; Publication; Reenactments; Research Library/Archives

COLLECTIONS: [1860s-1920s] Indian and Civil War artifacts; period furniture and clothing; military uniforms 1898-1960s; general store items; genealogy library; census, land, cemetery, and marriage records; county and family histories.

HOURS: Yr T-Th 9-5, Sa-Su

3033
Trading Post Historical Society and Museum
15710 N 4th St, 66075; (p) (913) 352-6441; (c) Linn

1974/ Board of Directors/ staff: 1(f); 1(p); 2(v)/ members: 75/publication: Coal Mining in Linn County Then and Now

GENEALOGICAL SOCIETY; HISTORICAL SOCIETY; HISTORY MUSEUM; LIBRARY AND/OR ARCHIVES: Preserves and exhibits the history of the area—Indian, Bleeding Kansas, Civil War, and Territorial Kansas eras.

PROGRAMS: Annual Meeting; Community Outreach; Family Programs; Festivals; Interpretation; Living History; Publication; Reenactments; Research Library/Archives

COLLECTIONS: [17c-present] Collections: fur trade, early pioneer, John Brown, Civil War, Native Americans, 1870 cabin, 1886 one room schoolhouse, antique farm machinery, coal mining equipment, John Brown. Records: cemetery, school, census, tax, newspapers, store ledgers, township records, diaries, obituaries, birth, and marriage records.

HOURS: Mar 21-Nov 1 T-Sa 9-5, Su 1-5

ADMISSION: Donations requested

PRATT

3034
Pratt County Historical Society and Museum
208 S Ninnescah St, 67124; (p) (316) 673-7874; (c) Pratt

Private non-profit/ 1968/ staff: 30(v)/ members: 400

HISTORICAL SOCIETY; HISTORY MUSEUM: Maintains a county historical museum and an archives on county history, families, and businesses.

PROGRAMS: Exhibits; Guided Tours; Research Library/Archives

COLLECTIONS: [1870-present] Artifacts on local history including Native American and military artifacts; model rooms of the pioneer days; indoor Main Street and model shops; chapel .

HOURS: Yr Daily 2-4

ADMISSION: Donations accepted

REPUBLIC

3035
Pawnee Indian Village State Historical Site
Hwy 266, 66964 [RR 1 Box 475, 66964]; (p) (785) 361-2255; (f) (785) 361-2255; pawnee@cjetworks.com; www.kshs.com; (c) Republic

State/ 1968/ staff: 1(f); 3(p); 6(v)/ members: 65

HISTORIC SITE; HISTORICAL SOCIETY; HISTORY MUSEUM; LIVING HISTORY/OUTDOOR MUSEUM; RESEARCH CENTER; TRIBAL MUSEUM: Collects, preserves, and interprets the Pawnee Nation's past.

PROGRAMS: Annual Meeting; Community Outreach; Exhibits; Family Programs; Film/Video; Guided Tours; Interpretation; Lectures; Living History; Research Library/Archives; School-Based Curriculum

COLLECTIONS: [1800s-present] Books pertaining to Pawnee culture and Plains Indian culture; photos, maps, manuscripts, newspapers, and artifacts.

HOURS: Yr W-Sa 10-5, Su 1-5

ADMISSION: Donations requested

RUSSELL SPRINGS

3036
Butterfield Trail Association and Historical Society of Logan County
1 Museum Drive, 67755; (p) (913) 751-4242; (c) Logan

1965/ staff: 1(f)/ members: 120

COLLECTIONS: [1870s-present]

HOURS: May-Sept 4 T-Sa 9-12/1-5, Su 1-5

SABETHA

3037
Albany Historical Society, Inc.
415 Grant, 66534; (c) Nemaha

Private non-profit/ 1965/ staff: 70(v)/ members: 50

HISTORIC SITE; HISTORICAL SOCIETY; HISTORY MUSEUM; HOUSE MUSEUM; LIVING HISTORY/OUTDOOR MUSEUM: Features local history.

PROGRAMS: Annual Meeting; Exhibits; Facility Rental; Festivals; Living History

COLLECTIONS: [1900-1965] Agricultural equipment and automobiles.

HOURS: May-Sept Sa-Su 1-5 or by appt

ADMISSION: Donations accepted

SAINT FRANCIS

3038
Cheyenne County Historical Society
Hwy 36, 67756 [Box 611, 67756]; (p) (785) 332-2504; (c) Cheyenne

staff: 1(p); 65(v)

GENEALOGICAL SOCIETY; HISTORIC SITE; HISTORICAL SOCIETY; HISTORY MUSEUM: Preserves area history.

PROGRAMS: Annual Meeting; Exhibits; Guided Tours

COLLECTIONS: [1885-present]

HOURS: Yr M-F 1-4

ADMISSION: No charge/Donations

SAINT PAUL

3039
Osage Mission-Neosho County Historical Society, Inc.
203 Washington, 66771 [PO Box 113, 66771-0113]; (p) (316) 449-2320; (c) Neosho

Private non-profit/ 1984/ staff: 1(p); 23(v)/ members: 248/publication: *The Beacon*

HISTORICAL SOCIETY; HISTORY MUSEUM: Collects, preserves, interprets, and displays history of town and county.

PROGRAMS: Annual Meeting; Exhibits; Facility Rental; Publication

COLLECTIONS: [1847-present] Exhibits, artifacts, publications, and genealogy materials.

HOURS: Yr

SALINA

3040
Central Kansas Flywheel, Inc.
1100 W Diamond Dr, 67401; (p) (785) 825-8473; (c) Saline

Private non-profit/ 1977/ staff: 30(v)/ members: 125/publication: *Nuts and Bolts*

HISTORY MUSEUM: Preserves the history of the area's farming community.

PROGRAMS: Annual Meeting; Exhibits; Facility Rental; Living History; Publication

COLLECTIONS: [1900-present] Agricultural machinery; artifacts of family life, school, office, and home; farm equipment manuals; print shop; household appliances; law library; tools; radios; post office; barber shop.

HOURS: May-Sept T-Su 1-5

ADMISSION: $2

3041
Smoky Hill Museum
211 W Iron Ave, 67402 [PO Box 101, 67402-0101]; (p) (785) 826-7460; (f) (785) 826-7414; dee.harris@salina.org; (c) Saline

City/ 1983/ staff: 6(f); 4(p); 100(v)/ members: 250

HISTORY MUSEUM: Housed in 1937 federal building, includes library and archives.

PROGRAMS: Community Outreach; Concerts; Exhibits; Facility Rental; Family Programs; Film/Video; Guided Tours; Interpretation; Lectures; Living History; Theatre

COLLECTIONS: [1800s-1900s] More than 20,000 artifacts, archives with manuscripts, photos.

HOURS: Yr T-F 12-5, Sa 10-5, Su 1-5

ADMISSION: No charge/Donations

SCANDIA

3042
Scandia Museum
Main St, 66966 [PO Box 153, 66966]; (c) Republic

City/ 1947/ staff: 17(v)

HISTORY MUSEUM: Preserves and interprets the history of Scandia and the community.

PROGRAMS: Exhibits

COLLECTIONS: [1868-present] Scrapbooks and records, newspapers, photos, albums, 10,000 artifacts; carriages and buggies; drug store fountain; Indian artifacts; primitive tools.

HOURS: May-Sept 2-4 and by appt

SEDAN

3043
Emmett Kelly Historical Museum
202-204 E Main, 67361; (p) (620) 725-3470; (c) Chautauqua

City/ 1969/ staff: 1(f)/ 20(v)/ members: 5/publication: *Emmett Kelly Historical Museum*

HISTORIC SITE; HISTORY MUSEUM

PROGRAMS: Exhibits; Film/Video; Garden Tours; Publication

COLLECTIONS: [1860-present] Memorabilia of Emmett Kelly and D. W. "Sparky" Washburn; 1,500 decanters, antique print shop; Civil War, World War I and II memorabilia; Sedan school records; hats; doctors' instruments; Indian artifacts, and radios.

HOURS: May 1-Oct T-Sa 9-12/1-5

ADMISSION: Donations accepted

SENECA

3044
Nemaha County Historical Society
113 N 6th St, 66538; (p) (785) 336-6366; (c) Nemaha

Private non-profit/ 1976/ staff: 2(p); 16(v)

HISTORICAL SOCIETY

PROGRAMS: Concerts; Guided Tours; Publication; Research Library/Archives

HOURS: May-Aug M-F 10-3

ADMISSION: $1, Family $3, Children $0.50

SHAWNEE

3045
1950s All-Electric Model House
6305 Lackman Rd, 66217; (p) (913) 631-6709; (f) (913) 631-6359; jcmuseum@jocoks.com; www.digitalhistory.com; (c) Johnson

County/ 1994/ Museum Advisory Council

COLLECTIONS: [1950s]

HOURS: Yr T-Su 1-4:30

ADMISSION: $2, Children $1

3046
Johnson County Museum
6305 Lackman Rd, 66217; (p) (913) 631-6709; (f) (913) 631-6359; www.digitalhistory.com; (c) Johnson

County/ 1967/ staff: 8(f); 4(p); 50(v)/ members: 425/publication: *Album*

HISTORIC SITE; HISTORY MUSEUM: Preserves and interprets county history; operates museum of history, 1950s All-Electric Model House, Lanesfield School Historic Site, and a research facility.

PROGRAMS: Community Outreach; Exhibits; Family Programs; Guided Tours; Interpretation; Lectures; Living History; Publication; Research Library/Archives; School-Based Curriculum

COLLECTIONS: [1820-present] 25,000 county history artifacts with special focus on post-WWII suburbia; 6000 photos; 2500 manuscripts

HOURS: Yr T-Sa 10-4:30, Su 1-4:30

3047
Lanesfield School Historic Site
18745 S Dillie Road, 66217 [6305 Lackman Rd, 66217]; (p) (913) 893-6645; (f) (913) 631-6359; jcmuseum@jocoks.com; www.digitalhistory.com; (c) Johnson

County/ 1967

HOURS: Yr T-Su 1-5

ADMISSION: No charge

3048
Old Shawnee Town
11110 Johnson Dr, 66203; (p) (913) 248-2360; (f) (913) 248-2363; www.cityofshawnee.org; (c) Johnson

City/ 1966/ staff: 2(f); 2(p); 10(v)

HISTORY MUSEUM; LIVING HISTORY/OUTDOOR MUSEUM: Consists of 17 original and replica buildings from the 1800s and 1900s; interprets the history of Shawnee.

PROGRAMS: Community Outreach; Concerts; Exhibits; Facility Rental; Festivals; Interpretation; Living History

COLLECTIONS: [1843-1924] 7 historic buildings; archival collection, 7,000 artifacts relating to decorative arts, farming and agricultural implements, tools, machinery, folk art, fine art, textiles, objects used in commerce and objects relating to natural history.

HOURS: Feb 1-Mid-Dec T-Sa 12-5

ADMISSION: $1

STAFFORD

3049
Stafford County Historical Society
100 S Main, 67578 [PO Box 249, 67578]; (p) (316) 234-5664; (c) Stafford

County/ 1978/ staff: 1(f)/ members: 250/publication: *Reflections*

GENEALOGICAL SOCIETY; HISTORIC PRESERVATION AGENCY; HISTORICAL SOCIETY; HISTORY MUSEUM; LIVING HISTORY/OUTDOOR MUSEUM

PROGRAMS: Annual Meeting; Exhibits; Facility Rental; Family Programs; Guided Tours; Publication

COLLECTIONS: [1885]

HOURS: Yr T-Th 1:30-3:30, Sa 2-4

ADMISSION: Donations accepted

STOCKTON

3050
Rooks County Historical Society, Frank Walter Museum
921 S Cedar, 67669 [PO Box 43, 67669]; (p) (785) 425-7217; (c) Rooks

Private non-profit/ 1970/ staff: 1(f); 3(p); 3(v)

HISTORICAL SOCIETY; HISTORY MUSEUM: Preserves and interprets county history.

PROGRAMS: Annual Meeting; Community Outreach; Elder's Programs; Exhibits; Family Programs; Film/Video; Guided Tours

COLLECTIONS: [1860s-present] Rooks County artifacts

HOURS: Yr M-W 9-4

ADMISSION: Donations accepted

STUDLEY

3051
Cottonwood Ranch State Historic Site
US Hwy 24, 67740 [Rt 1 Box 57 M, 67740-9326];
(p) (785) 627-5866; www.kshs.org/places/
cottonwo.htm; (c) Sheridan

State/ 1985/ staff: 1(f); 2(p); 12(v)/publication:
Cottonwood Clippings

HISTORIC SITE; HOUSE MUSEUM: Sheep
Ranch constructed from 1885-1896 by Eng-
lishman John Fenton Pratt.

PROGRAMS: Annual Meeting; Community
Outreach; Family Programs; Festivals; Guided
Tours; Interpretation; Lectures; Reenactments

COLLECTIONS: [1885-1930s] Some original
furnishings; photograph collection; 19th c outbuildings.

HOURS: Yr W-Sa 10-5, Su 1-5

ADMISSION: Donations accepted

SUBLETTE

3052
Haskell County Historical Society
N Fairgrounds, 67877 [PO Box 101, 67877-
0101]; (p) (316) 675-8344; (c) Haskell

County/ 1983/ staff: 3(p); 9(v)/ members: 65

HISTORICAL SOCIETY; HISTORY MUSEUM;
HOUSE MUSEUM: Collects and interprets
pertaining to the settlement of Haskell County
and southwest KS.

PROGRAMS: Annual Meeting; Community
Outreach; Exhibits; Family Programs;
Film/Video; Guided Tours; Interpretation; Lec-
tures; Publication; School-Based Curriculum

COLLECTIONS: [1900-present] Household,
farming, and vocational artifacts; Strohwig-
Murphy Indian artifact collection; rocks and
minerals; early medical equipment; quilts;
books, periodicals and records of area history;
1929 fire engine; buggy.

HOURS: Yr T-Su 1-5

ADMISSION: No charge

SYRACUSE

3053
Hamilton County Museum
108 E Highway 50, 67878; (p) (620) 384-
7496; skyways.lib.ks.us/towns/Syracuse/
museum.html; (c) Hamilton

HISTORY MUSEUM

PROGRAMS: Exhibits

COLLECTIONS: Room arrangements: parlor,
bedroom, kitchen; bibles, books & maps; pictures & cameras; tools, buggies, and farm
equipment ; clothing &quilts; Indian artifacts;
cars & trucks; hospital equipment; military
memorabilia; appliances; business machines;
barber shop & general store; guns.

HOURS: Summer: M-F 1-5; Winter: M-W 10-4

TONGANOXIE

3054
**Tonganoxie Community Historical
Society**
201 Evans Rd, 66086 [PO Box 325, 66086];

(p) (913) 845-2102; (c) Leavenworth

Private non-profit/ 1981/ staff: 5(p); 10(v)/
members: 120

HISTORIC SITE; HISTORICAL SOCIETY:
Maintains a 10 acre historic site.

PROGRAMS: Annual Meeting; Exhibits; Facility Rental; Family Programs; Living History;
Publication; School-Based Curriculum

COLLECTIONS: [1900-1950] Dairy industry
artifacts; one room schoolhouse; living history
camp.

HOURS: May-Sept W-Su 8-1 and by appt

ADMISSION: No charge

TOPEKA

3055
**Cedar Crest, Residence of the
Governor of Kansas**
One SW Cedar Crest Rd, 66606; (p) (785)
296-3636; (f) (785) 272-9024;
tours@cedarcrest.state.ks.us; (c) Shawnee

State/ 1928/ staff: 3(f); 2(p); 20(v)

HISTORIC SITE: State's Governor's residence
since 1962, includes a 220 acre wildlife preserve and park.

PROGRAMS: Garden Tours; Guided Tours

COLLECTIONS: [1962-present] Furnishings
and art.

HOURS: Jan-Nov M 1-3:30

3056
Combat Air Museum
Forbes Field-Hangar #602, 66619 [PO Box
19142, 66619]; (p) (785) 862-3303; (f) (785)
862-3304; camtopeka@aol.com;
www.combatairmuseum.org; (c) Shawnee

Private non-profit/ 1976/ staff: 2(f); 40(v)/
members: 350

HISTORY MUSEUM: Preserves and interprets
aircraft and aviation related artifacts, includes
two historic hangars.

PROGRAMS: Annual Meeting; Concerts; Exhibits; Facility Rental; Guided Tours; Interpretation; Lectures

COLLECTIONS: [1916-present] 32 aircraft,
vehicles, professional model collection, five
missiles (rockets), 15 aircraft engines (turbine,
reciprocating), simulators, walk through WC-
121, Ch-53A.

HOURS: Yr Daily M-Sa 9-4:30, Su 10-4:30

ADMISSION: $5, Children $3, Seniors $4

3057
Historic Ritchie House
1116 SE Madison, 66605 [PO Box 2201,
66601]; (p) (785) 234-6097

1856/ staff: 1(p)

HOUSE MUSEUM: Part of an historic area
linking Free State Territorial politics with the
Brown vs. Board of Education State Historic
Site.

COLLECTIONS: [1856-1887] House.

3058
Historic Ward-Meade Park
124 NW Fillmore St, 66606; (p) (785) 368-
3888; (f) (785) 368-3890; wardmeade@tope-
ka.org; www.topeka.org; (c) Shawnee

City/ 1975/ staff: 4(f); 9(p); 100(v)

GARDEN; HISTORIC SITE; HOUSE MUSE-
UM; LIVING HISTORY/OUTDOOR MUSEUM:
Maintains six acre complex with Victorian
home listed on the National Register of Historic Places, replica log cabin, turn-of-the-century town, and botanical garden.

PROGRAMS: Exhibits; Facility Rental; Festivals; Guided Tours

COLLECTIONS: [Mid 1800s-mid 1900s]
Clothing, toys, furniture, artwork, physician's
and dentist's equipment.

HOURS: Park: Yr Daily 8-dusk; Mulvane

3059
Kansas Museum Association
6425 SW Sixth Ave, 66615-1099; (p) (785)
272-8681; (f) (785) 272-8682;
bkeckeisen@kshs.org; (c) Shawnee

Joint; Private non-profit/ 1969/ staff: 17(v)/
members: 250/publication: *The Exchange*

PROFESSIONAL ASSOCIATION: Creates,
fosters, and promotes interest in the advancement and appreciation of Kansas museums;
increases and disseminates knowledge of the
museum field; encourages cooperation among
Kansas

3060
Kansas State Historical Society
6425 SW 6th Ave, 66615-1099; (p) (785) 272-
8681; (f) (785) 272-8682;
reference@kshs.org; www.kshs.org; (c)
Shawnee

Joint/ Private non-profit; State/ staff: 142(f);
222(v)/ members: 3159/publication: *Kansas
History; Kansas Heritage; and others*

HISTORIC PRESERVATION AGENCY; HIS-
TORICAL SOCIETY; HISTORY MUSEUM;
RESEARCH CENTER: Identifies, collects,
preserves, interprets, and disseminates materials and information pertaining to KS history
in order to assist the public in understanding
and appreciating their KS heritage and how it
relates to their lives. Oversees State: museum,
archives, records management, archaeology,
historic reservation, research library, historic
sites, education, and programming.

PROGRAMS: Annual Meeting; Community
Outreach; Concerts; Exhibits; Facility Rental;
Family Programs; Festivals; Film/Video; Guid-
ed Tours; Interpretation; Lectures; Publication;
Research Library/Archives; School-Based
Curriculum

COLLECTIONS: [1850-present] 242,380 pamphlets, 169,757 volumes, 461,449 photographs, 28,924 maps, 6,963 cubic feet of manuscripts, 26,742 cubic feet of state records,
99,448 museum objects. National Registries:
Shawnee Indian Mission, Fort Hays, Constitution Hall Hollenberg Pony Express Station.

HOURS: Yr Museum: M-Sa 9-4:30, Su 12:30-
4:30; Research Center M-Sa 9-4:30

ADMISSION: Donations requested

3061
**Shawnee County Historical Society,
Inc.**
1116 SE Madison Ave, 66601 [PO Box 2201,
66601]; (p) (785) 234-6097; (c) Shawnee

Private non-profit/ 1949/ staff: 15(v)/ members:

275

HISTORICAL SOCIETY: A publications and museum agency devoted to local history.

PROGRAMS: Annual Meeting; Guided Tours; Lectures; Publication; School-Based Curriculum

COLLECTIONS: [1850-present] Annual publications devoted to topics and themes

3062
Topeka and Shawnee County Public Library/Alice C. Sabatini Gallery
1515 SW 10th, 66611-1374; (p) (785) 231-0527; (f) (785) 233-2055; lpeters@tscpl.lib.ks.us; www.tscpl.org; (c) Shawnee

Joint/ 1873/ City; County/ staff: 1(f); 1(p)

ART MUSEUM: Library contains local Topeka history and works by or about Topekans; gallery collects regional paintings, national prints, and contemporary American ceramics, glass paperweights, African arts, and some Chinese decorative arts, New Mexican art.

PROGRAMS: Exhibits

COLLECTIONS: [Post WW II-present] Art Nouveau glass and ceramics, American Contemporary ceramics, late 1800 - 1900 Chinese decorative arts, West African cultural objects, U.S. and European glass paperweights, regional paintings and prints.

HOURS: Yr M-F 9-9, Sa 9-6, Su 2-6 (May-Sept closed Su)

ADMISSION: No charge

TRIBUNE

3063
Greeley County Historical Society
214 E Harper, 67879 [Box 231, 67879-0231]; (p) (316) 376-4996; (c) Greeley

Joint/ 1975/ City; County/ staff: 4(p); 6(v)/ members: 72

HISTORIC PRESERVATION AGENCY; HISTORIC SITE; HISTORICAL SOCIETY; HISTORY MUSEUM; HOUSE MUSEUM: Promotes genealogy and local history.

PROGRAMS: Annual Meeting; Community Outreach; Exhibits; Family Programs; Film/Video; Guided Tours; Living History; Research Library/Archives

COLLECTIONS: [1886-present] Period rooms, artifacts, mammoth skull, marbles, lanterns, farm related, school and military room, old jail, library, photography.

HOURS: Yr M-F 9-4, Su

3064
Horace Greeley Museum
214 E Harper, 67879-0231; (p) (316) 376-4996; (c) Greeley

County/ 1976/ staff: 1(f); 6(p)/ members: 105

GENEALOGICAL SOCIETY; HISTORIC PRESERVATION AGENCY; HISTORIC SITE; HISTORICAL SOCIETY; HISTORY MUSEUM; RESEARCH CENTER

PROGRAMS: Annual Meeting; Community Outreach; Exhibits; Film/Video; Living History; Publication; Research Library/Archives

COLLECTIONS: Photos, clothing, memorabilia, tools, old jail, artifacts, mammoth skull, pe-

riod rooms housed in the old courthouse built in 1890.

HOURS: Summer M-F 10-4; Winter varies

ADMISSION: Donations accepted

TROY

3065
Doniphan County Historical Society
105 N Main St, 66087; (c) Donphian

Private non-profit/ staff: 6(v)/ members: 140

HISTORIC SITE: Restores old historical structures from the mid 1800s where Abraham Lincoln spoke in 1859.

PROGRAMS: Annual Meeting; Community Outreach; Exhibits; Film/Video; Lectures; Monthly Meeting; Reenactments

COLLECTIONS: [Late 1800s-early 1900s]

ULYSSES

3066
Grant County Museum
300 E Oklahoma, 67880 [PO Box 906, 67880]; (p) (316) 356-3009; (c) Grant

County/ 1978/ staff: 3(f); 2(p); 20(v)/ members: 125

HISTORIC SITE; HISTORICAL SOCIETY; HISTORY MUSEUM: Maintains museum.

PROGRAMS: Annual Meeting; Community Outreach; Exhibits; Facility Rental; Festivals; Guided Tours; Interpretation; Research Library/Archives; School-Based Curriculum

COLLECTIONS: [1885-1970s] Artifacts from the high Plains region of Southwest KS, Native American artifacts, oil and gas production items.

HOURS: Yr Daily M-F 10-5, Sa-Su 1-5

ADMISSION: No charge/Donations

VALLEY FALLS

3067
Valley Falls Historical Society
310 Broadway, 66088-1302; (p) (785) 945-3244; (c) Jefferson

Private non-profit/ 1967/ staff: 12(v)/ members: 190

ART MUSEUM; HISTORICAL SOCIETY; HISTORY MUSEUM; RESEARCH CENTER: The society dedicated to the preservation of artifacts of local interest in a museum setting.

PROGRAMS: Annual Meeting; Community Outreach; Exhibits; Guided Tours; Research Library/Archives

COLLECTIONS: Working linotype press, picture, tools, glassware, china, furniture, clothing, books, stamps, pump organ, toys, Boston fern, school artifacts, trophies, paintings, business advertisements, 100 year old bank furniture, miniature Breyer horse collection.

HOURS: Yr Sa 10:30-4

ADMISSION: No charge

WALLACE

3068
Fort Wallace Museum
US Hwy 40, 67761 [Box 53, 67761]; (p) (785) 891-3564, (785) 891-3780; (c) Wallace

County/ 1925/ Board/ staff: 3(p)/ members: 134

HISTORIC SITE; HISTORY MUSEUM; HOUSE MUSEUM: Promotes history education; maintains a county museum which seeks to preserve the history of the of Wallace County with emphasis on Fort Wallace and the role it played during Indian conflicts.

PROGRAMS: Annual Meeting; Festivals

COLLECTIONS: [Late 19th-20th c] Original condition items which were used by pioneers, cowboys, Native Americans and founding citizens of Wallace; early photographs of the Fort, railroad, family activity in Wallace, and of interpretive artwork.

HOURS: May-Oct Daily 9-5 and by appt

ADMISSION: Donations accepted

WAMEGO

3069
Columbian Theatre, Museum Art Center
531 Linclon Ave, 66547 [PO Box 72, 66547]; (p) (800) 899-1893, (785) 456-2029; (f) (785) 456-9498; etheatre@kansas.net; www.kansas.net.~ctheatre; (c) Pott

Private non-profit/ 1994/ staff: 5(f); 2(p); 250(v)/ members: 450

HISTORIC SITE: Maintains the historic Columbian Theater houses.

PROGRAMS: Annual Meeting; Concerts; Exhibits; Facility Rental; Guided Tours; Interpretation; Research Library/Archives; School-Based Curriculum

COLLECTIONS: [1893-1950] Decorative arts from the 1893 Chicago World's Fair, including 6 beautifully restored murals and ephemera, publications, and artifacts pertaining to the fair or to the Colombian Theatre.

HOURS: Yr Daily M-Su

ADMISSION: Donations requested

3070
Log Cabin-Wamego Historical Museum
4th St, 66547 [PO Box 84, 66547]; (p) (785) 456-2040

1840

COLLECTIONS: [1866-present] Storybook dolls; music room with victrola and piano; china closet; bookcase with books; secretary's desk; baby buggy; furnishings; clothing; Books; newspapers; photographs.

WASHINGTON

3071
Washington County Historical Society
208 Ballard, 66968 [PO Box 31, 66968]; (p) (785) 325-2198

Private non-profit/ 1982/ staff: 10(v)/ members: 400

GENEALOGICAL SOCIETY; HISTORIC PRESERVATION AGENCY; HISTORIC SITE; HISTORICAL SOCIETY; HISTORY MUSEUM; HOUSE MUSEUM; RESEARCH CENTER: Researches genealogy and collects and displays local history and artifacts.

PROGRAMS: Annual Meeting; Community Outreach; Elder's Programs; Exhibits; Facility Rental; Family Programs; Festivals; Garden Tours; Guided Tours; Interpretation; Lectures; Living History; Publication; Reenactments; Research Library/Archives; School-Based Curriculum

COLLECTIONS: [1860-1950] Newspapers, household artifacts, clothing, W W I and II memorabilia.

HOURS: June-Aug T- W, F 1-4, Th 10-12/1-4, Su 2-4; Sept-May Th 10-12/1-4, Su 2-4

ADMISSION: Donations accepted

WELLINGTON

3072
Chisholm Trail Museum
502 N Washington, 67152; (p) (316) 326-3820; (c) summer

Private non-profit/ 1963/ staff: 10(v)/ members: 100

HISTORY MUSEUM: Promotes a museum of local history.

COLLECTIONS: [1865-present] Music, military, railroad, automobile, pioneer, Chisholm Trail, kitchen, laundry, general store, tool, sports, barber shop, weaning, dentist, school, parlor, Santa Claus, grandmothers. More than 40 rooms and 20,000 artifacts and pictures, most collected locally, some dating back to the Civil War.

WHITE CLOUD

3073
Ma Hush Kah Historical Society
Main St, 66094 [2326 Buffalo Rd, 66094]; (p) (785) 595-3320; (c) Doniphan

Private non-profit/ 1964/ staff: 10(v)/ members: 33

HISTORIC PRESERVATION AGENCY; HISTORIC SITE; HISTORICAL SOCIETY; HISTORY MUSEUM; RESEARCH CENTER: Maintains museum.

PROGRAMS: Exhibits; Festivals; Guided Tours; Research Library/Archives; School-Based Curriculum

COLLECTIONS: [WW II-present] Clothing, furniture, books, pictures, newspapers, school records, early Post Office, barbershop, Native American, some W W I.

HOURS: Apr-Oct 10-4, by appt

ADMISSION: Donations

WHITEWATER

3074
Frederic Remington Area Historical Society
Rt 1, 67154 [PO Box 133, 67154]; (p) (316) 799-2123; (f) (316) 799-2943; (c) Butler

Private non-profit/ 1978/ staff: 1(p)/ members: 65

HISTORICAL SOCIETY: Promotes history by holding meetings, presenting programs related to local history, maintaining a library, and preserving local history and family genealogy; copies of local newspapers on 100 microfilm reels.

PROGRAMS: Annual Meeting; Family Programs; Lectures; Research Library/Archives

COLLECTIONS: 75 books, 100 manuscripts, 15 archive volumes, 600 slides, and 100 reels of microfilm.

HOURS: Sept-May M-F 9-4

ADMISSION: No charge

WICHITA

3075
Allen-Lambe House Foundation
255 N Roosevelt, 67208; (p) (316) 687-1027; (f) (316) 687-2991; www2.southwind.net/~allenlam

Private non-profit/ 1990/ staff: 20(v)/ members: 84

HOUSE MUSEUM: Maintains restoration and conservation of the last prairie house designed by Frank Lloyd Wright in 1915 for Henry and Elsie Allen.

PROGRAMS: Exhibits; Festivals; Guided Tours; Lectures; Publication

COLLECTIONS: [1918-1923] Frank Lloyd Wright books, archive, designs, study collection, furnishings and owners' art collection.

HOURS: By appt.

3076
Kansas African American Museum, The
601 N Water St, 67203; (p) (316) 262-7651; (f) (316) 265-6953; TKAAM@AOL.com; (c) Sedgwick

Private non-profit/ 1972/ staff: 4(f); 2(p); 25(v)/ members: 129

HISTORY MUSEUM: Dedicated to the identification, acquisition, research, collections, presentation, and preservation of historic documents, programs, and visual art forms that are reflective of African American life and culture.

PROGRAMS: Annual Meeting; Concerts; Elder's Programs; Exhibits; Facility Rental; Family Programs; Festivals; Film/Video; Interpretation; Lectures; Living History; Reenactments; Research Library/Archives

COLLECTIONS: [1920s-present] Collection of KS and Wichita African American history, and a contemporary African and a contemporary African American art collection.

HOURS: Yr T-F 10-5, Su 2-6, special tours by appt

ADMISSION: Donations accepted

3077
Kansas Aviation Museum
3350 George Washington Blvd, 67210; (p) (316) 683-9242; (f) (316) 683-0573; kam3350@juno.com; www.saranap.com/kam.html; (c) Sedgwick

Private non-profit/ 1990/ staff: 2(f); 150(v)/ members: 600

HISTORIC SITE; RESEARCH CENTER: Preserves the birth and living heritage of KS aviation, educates the world on the past, present, and future of flight and promotes the sprit of flight.

PROGRAMS: Annual Meeting; Community Outreach; Elder's Programs; Exhibits; Facility Rental; Family Programs; Festivals; Film/Video; Guided Tours; Interpretation; Lectures; Living History; Publication; Research Library/Archives; School-Based Curriculum

COLLECTIONS: [1903-present] 35, aircraft, 50,000 slides, 100,00 photos, 100,000 negatives, 3,000 volumes, prints, films, videos, engine collection from 1911-present, aviation related artifacts, hot air balloons, kites, model airplanes, several paintings, and 2 cars.

HOURS: Yr T-F 9-4, Sa 1-5

ADMISSION: $2, Children $1; Under 6 free

3078
Kansas West Conference Archives
9440 E Boston Ste 198, 67207-3600; (p) (316) 684-0266; (f) (316) 684-0044; debumc@south wind.net; www.gbgm-umc.org/kansas-west; (c) Sedgwick

Private non-profit/ 1979/ staff: 1(p); 1(v)

LIBRARY AND/OR ARCHIVES: Collects church information on all pastors and churches in the Methodist Church in our Conference and those with connection to other dominations which merged to be called The United Methodist Church.

COLLECTIONS: [1856-present] Conference journals for most of the years mentioned for the now U.M.C. records of closed Churches, pastors who served in the conference, church histories, conference records.

HOURS: Yr 8:30-4:30

ADMISSION: No charge

3079
Mid-America All Indian Center, Inc.
650 N Seneca, 67203; (p) (316) 262-5221; (f) (316) 262-4216; icm@southwind.net; ww2.southwind.net/~icm/museum/museum.html; (c) Sedgwick

Private non-profit/ 1976/ staff: 4(f); 150(v)/ members: 400

TRIBAL MUSEUM: Preserve and showcase the cultures of Native North Americans through exhibits and public programs.

PROGRAMS: Exhibits

COLLECTIONS: Works of Southern Plains painters, pottery, textiles, beadwork, and other arts from the Plains and other cultures.

HOURS: Yr Daily M-Sa 10-5, Su 1-5

ADMISSION: $2, Children $1; Under 6 free, group rates

3080
Old Cowtown Museum
1871 Sim Park Dr, 67203; (p) (316) 264-0671; (f) (316) 264-2937; cowtown@southwind.net; www.old-cowtown.org; (c) Sedgwick

Private non-profit/ 1950/ staff: 14(f); 20(p); 100(v)/ members: 850/publication: Cowtown Chronicle

HISTORY MUSEUM; HOUSE MUSEUM; LIVING HISTORY/OUTDOOR MUSEUM: A living history museum dedicated to interpreting and preserving early Wichita and Sedgwick County history.

PROGRAMS: Community Outreach; Exhibits; Facility Rental; Family Programs; Interpretation; Lectures; Publication; Reenactments; School-Based Curriculum

COLLECTIONS: [1865-1880] Decorative arts, agricultural implements, and buildings.

HOURS: Apr-Oct M-Sa 10-5, Su 12-5

ADMISSION: $7, Children $3.50, Seniors $6.50

3081
Wichita Public Library
223 S Main, 67202; (p) (316) 261-8500; (f) (316) 262-4540; webmaster@wichita.lib.ks.us; www.wichita.lib.ks.us; (c) Sedgwick

Joint/ 1876/ City/ staff: 89(f); 51(p); 300(v)/publication: *Excerpts*

LIBRARY AND/OR ARCHIVES: Maintains the Wichita Public Library is a public library system with eleven branches, that offers a genealogy section and local history archives.

PROGRAMS: Community Outreach; Exhibits; Facility Rental; Family Programs; Lectures; Publication; Research Library/Archives

COLLECTIONS: [1860-present] Special Collection with historical and genealogical materials books, maps, documents, manuscripts, photographs, newspaper, microfilm sources relating to Wichita, Sedgwick County, and Kansas.

3082
Wichita-Sedgwick County Historical Museum
204 S Main, 67202; (p) (316) 265-9314; (f) (316) 265-9319; (c) Sedgwick

Private non-profit/ 1939/ staff: 6(f); 4(p); 100(v)/ members: 700

HISTORY MUSEUM: Preserves and interprets the history of Wichita and Sedgwick County for the educational benefit of the community and its visitors.

PROGRAMS: Exhibits; Guided Tours; Lectures; Publication; Research Library/Archives

COLLECTIONS: [1865-present] 45,000 museum artifacts including textiles, costumes, furniture, and decorative arts, toys, and Plains Indian artifacts; archival holdings include manuscripts, maps, books, business records, and 15,000 photographs of Wichita and Sedgwick County.

HOURS: Yr T-F 11-4, Sa-Su 1-5

ADMISSION: $2

WILSON

3083
Wilson Czech Opera House Corporation, Foundation
415 27th St (Hwy 40), 67490 [PO Box 271, 67490]; (p) (785) 658-3505, (785) 658-3343; (c) Ellsworth

Private non-profit/ 1986/ staff: 1(f); 10(p); 10(v)/ members: 81/publication: *Kansas Pioneers*

GENEALOGICAL SOCIETY; HISTORIC SITE; HISTORICAL SOCIETY; HISTORY MUSEUM; HOUSE MUSEUM; LIVING HISTORY/OUTDOOR MUSEUM: Maintains Opera House, constructed 1904, Czech lodges.

PROGRAMS: Annual Meeting; Community Outreach; Concerts; Elder's Programs; Exhibits; Facility Rental; Family Programs; Festivals; Film/Video; Guided Tours; Interpretation; Living History; Publication; Research Library/Archives; Theatre

COLLECTIONS: [1873-present] Indian Artifacts, Czech memorabilia, genealogical, historical books, handmade quilts, lace, tools, handmade, wood carvings, glassware from Czechoslovakia, Bohemia costumes, Czech books, library, medicine, food, traditions, musical instruments, art.

HOURS: Yr M-F 10-12/1-4, Sa-Su by appt

ADMISSION: Donations requested

WINFIELD

3084
Cowley County Historical Society
1011 Mansfield, 67156; (p) (316) 221-4811; (c) Cowley

Private non-profit/ 1931/ staff: 1(p); 25(v)/ members: 200

GENEALOGICAL SOCIETY; HISTORIC SITE; HISTORICAL SOCIETY; HISTORY MUSEUM; RESEARCH CENTER: Preservation of Winfield and northern Cowley County history.

PROGRAMS: Annual Meeting; Community Outreach; Exhibits; Festivals; Guided Tours; Research Library/Archives

COLLECTIONS: [1870-1950] Genealogy, farm, garden, dolls, glassware, domestic items, clothing.

HOURS: Yr T 8:30-11:30, Sa-Su 2-5

ADMISSION: No charge/Donations

WIREFIELD

3085
Cowley County Genealogical Society
1518 E 12th St, 67156-3923; (p) (316) 221-4591; (c) Cowley

Private non-profit/ 1979/ staff: 2(p)/ members: 22

GENEALOGICAL SOCIETY: Maintain and preserve local history and a library with books on many states.

COLLECTIONS: [1880-present] Cemetery readings, monument and company funeral home records, old newspaper clippings, and obituaries.

HOURS: Yr T-Su 10-4

ADMISSION: $2.50

KENTUCKY

ALEXANDRIA

3086
Campbell County Historical Society
19 E Main St, 41001; (p) (606) 635-6407; (c) Campbell

Private non-profit/ 1990/ staff: 15(v)/ members: 275

GENEALOGICAL SOCIETY; HISTORICAL SOCIETY: Protects, promotes, and educates the public on the history and genealogy of Campbell County.

PROGRAMS: Annual Meeting; Exhibits; Publication; Research Library/Archives

COLLECTIONS: [20th c] Historical papers, books, maps, photographs, veterans' records, and genealogical data.

HOURS: Yr T 12-8, Sa 10-3

ADMISSION: No charge

3087
Campbell County Log Cabin Museum
234 W Clay Ridge Rd, 41001; (p) (606) 635-5913; (c) Campbell

Private non-profit/ 1985/ staff: 2(v)

HISTORIC SITE; LIVING HISTORY/OUTDOOR MUSEUM: Preserves Campbell's agricultural past and the tools used for agriculture; maintains log cabin and 1850s cemetery where Daniel Boone's sister, Mary Boone Bryon, is buried.

PROGRAMS: Exhibits; Guided Tours; School-Based Curriculum

COLLECTIONS: [1860-1940] Horse-drawn farm equipment, two reconstructed log cabins, tools, books, household items, covered bridge, homemade Native American teepee and covered wagon.

HOURS: Apr-Oct

ASHLAND

3088
Boyd County Public Library, Minnie Crawford Winder Room
1740 Central Ave, 41101; (p) (606) 329-0090; bcpl.genealogy@mail.state.ky.us; thebookplace.org; (c) Boyd

Joint/ staff: 2(p)

GENEALOGICAL SOCIETY; HISTORICAL SOCIETY; RESEARCH CENTER: Houses collections of both the Boyd County Historical Society and the Eastern KY Genealogical Society.

PROGRAMS: Exhibits; Family Programs; Lectures; Research Library/Archives

COLLECTIONS: Photographs; KY vital records; Armco photograph collection; maps; correspondence, census, land, marriage, military, records; Federal census records for KY, PA, VA, WV (selected years), newspapers, county court records.

HOURS: Yr June-Aug M-Th 10-8, F-Sa 10-5; Sept-May M-Th 9-9, F-Sa 9-5, Su 1-5

3089
Eastern Kentucky Genealogical Society, Inc.
[PO Box 1544, 41105]; (p) (606) 329-0518; (f) (606) 329-0578; (c) Boyd

1977/ staff: 1(f); 2(p)/ members: 1000/publication: *Treeshaker*

GENEALOGICAL SOCIETY: Collects and publishes records including vital statistics, marriages, wills, cemeteries, and brief genealogies; mainly of Lawrence, Boyd, Carter counties, KY.

PROGRAMS: Publication

3090
Kentucky Highlands Museum
1620 Winchester Ave, 41105 [PO Box 1494, 41105]; (p) (606) 329-8888; (f) (606) 324-3218; KYHIMUS@AOL.com; (c) Boyd

Private non-profit/ 1984/ staff: 2(f); 2(p); 110(v)/ members: 420

HISTORY MUSEUM: Provide interactive learning experience for people of all ages; displays regional history artifacts; presents educational and community programs.

PROGRAMS: Annual Meeting; Community Outreach; Concerts; Exhibits; Facility Rental;

Family Programs; Festivals; Film/Video; Guided Tours; Interpretation; Lectures; Living History; School-Based Curriculum

COLLECTIONS: Native American artifacts; Civil War and WW II memorabilia; clothing; communication equipment; textiles and weaving; transportation; country music; Boy Scout artifacts; fire engine and equipment; Children's Discovery Center.

HOURS: Yr T-F 9-4, Sa 10-4

ADMISSION: $2, Student $1, Children $1, Seniors $1

BARBOURSVILLE

3091
Doctor Thomas Walker Cabin
HC 83, Box 868, 40906; (p) (606) 546-4400

BARBOURVILLE

3092
Knox Historical Museum
Libetry St & Daniel Boone Dr, 40906 [PO Box 1446, 40906]; (c) Knox

Private non-profit/ 1987/ Board of Directors/ staff: 6(v)/ members: 240

HISTORICAL SOCIETY; HISTORY MUSEUM: Accumulates and preserves historical and archival materials related to county history.

PROGRAMS: Exhibits; Film/Video; Guided Tours; Lectures; Publication; Research Library/ Archives

COLLECTIONS: Mining and farm tools, medical displays, local organizations, oral histories, local newsreels, and home movies.

ADMISSION: No charge

BARDSTOWN

3093
My Old Kentucky Home State Park
501 E Stephen Foster Ave, 40004 [PO Box 323, 40004]; (p) (800) 323-7803; (f) (502) 349-0054; (c) Nelson

State/ 1923/ KY Dept of Parks/ staff: 28(f); 23(p); 7(v)

HOUSE MUSEUM; STATE PARK

PROGRAMS: Concerts; Exhibits; Festivals; Guided Tours

COLLECTIONS: [1850s] 75% original collection; watercolors, oils, manuscripts, personal artifacts, textiles, and silver.

HOURS: Yr Daily Sep-May 8-5; June-Aug 8:30-6:30

ADMISSION: $4.50, Children $2.50, Seniors $4; Group rates

3094
Wickland
107 E Stephen Foster Ave, 40004 [PO Box 867, 40004]; (p) (502) 348-5428; www.state.ky.us/tour/bluegras/bardstow.htm

BARLOW

3095
Barlow House Museum
[PO Box 400, Hwy 60, 42024]; (p) (270) 334-3010; (c) Ballard

Private non-profit/ 1990/ staff: 1(f)

HOUSE MUSEUM: Maintains Historic House built in 1903 and listed on the National Register.

PROGRAMS: Community Outreach; Facility Rental; Festivals; Guided Tours

COLLECTIONS: [1900-1920]

HOURS: Yr M-F 1-4, 2nd & 4th Su of month 1-4

ADMISSION: $3

BENHAM

3096
Kentucky Coal Mining Museum
221 Main St & Hwy 160, 40807 [PO Box A, 40807]; (p) (606) 848-1530; (f) (606) 848-1546; (c) Harlan

County/ 1994/ Harlan County Fiscal Court/ staff: 1(f); 2(p); 8(v)

HISTORIC SITE; HISTORICAL SOCIETY: Collects, preserves, and exhibits early coal mining industry artifacts.

PROGRAMS: Elder's Programs; Exhibits; Festivals; Film/Video; Guided Tours; Interpretation; Lectures; School-Based Curriculum

COLLECTIONS: [1900-1950] 5,000 items including photos, newspapers, mining records, and artifacts.

HOURS: Yr M-Sa 10-5, Su 1-4

ADMISSION: $4, Student $1.50, Seniors $3

BOWLING GREEN

3097
Kentucky Museum, The
1400 Block of Kentucky St, 42101 [1 Big Red Way, Western KY Univ, 42101]; (p) (270) 745-2592; (f) (270) 745-4878; www.wku.edu/Library/museum; (c) Warren

State/ 1939/ Western KY Univ/ staff: 13(f); 10(p); 10(v)/ members: 350

HISTORY MUSEUM: Preserves KY history and heritage.

PROGRAMS: Community Outreach; Concerts; Exhibits; Facility Rental; Family Programs; Festivals; Guided Tours; Lectures; Reenactments; Research Library/Archives; School-Based Curriculum

COLLECTIONS: [1700-present] Clothing and textiles, particularly quilts; furniture; glassware; toys and dolls; tools and equipment; Shaker artifacts; sheet music; and political artifacts.

HOURS: Yr T-Sa 9:30-4, Su 1-4

ADMISSION: $2, Family $5, Children $1

3098
Landmark Association
912 1/2 State St, 42102 [PO Box 1812, 42102]; (p) (270) 782-0037; (f) (270) 782-0037; jonathan.jeffrey@wku.edu; (c) Warren

Private non-profit/ 1976/ Board of Directors/ staff: 1(p); 25(v)/ members: 250/publication: *Landmark Report*

HISTORIC PRESERVATION AGENCY: Preserve the archaeological, architectural, and cultural heritage of Bowling Green and Warren County.

PROGRAMS: Annual Meeting; Community Outreach; Exhibits; Guided Tours; Interpreta-

tion; Lectures; Publication; Research Library/ Archives

COLLECTIONS: [1790-1940] Files related to historic homes in the area; files on area history.

HOURS: Yr M-F 8-5

ADMISSION: Charge for tours

3099
Riverview at Hobson Grove
1100 W Main Ave, 42102 [PO Box 10059, 42102]; (p) (502) 843-5565; www.ci-bowling-green.ky; (c) Warren

City/ 1872/ Hobson House Commission/ staff: 1(f); 5(p)/ members: 180

HISTORIC SITE; HOUSE MUSEUM: Preserves historic tourist attraction; educates people about post Civil War KY.

PROGRAMS: Annual Meeting; Community Outreach; Facility Rental; Guided Tours

COLLECTIONS: [1860-1890] Historic house furnishings and personal items.

HOURS: Feb-Dec T-Sa 10-4, Su 1-4

ADMISSION: $3.50, Family $6, Student $1.50; Group rates

BROOKSVILLE

3100
Bracken County Historical Society
Old City Jail, 41004 [PO Box 307, 41004]; (p) (606) 735-3337; (c) Bracken

Private non-profit/ 1993/ County/ staff: 12(v)/ members: 200

GENEALOGICAL SOCIETY; HISTORIC SITE; HISTORICAL SOCIETY; HISTORY MUSEUM; RESEARCH CENTER

PROGRAMS: Annual Meeting; Community Outreach; Exhibits; Festivals; Guided Tours; Lectures; Living History; Publication; Research Library/Archives

HOURS: Yr

BURLINGTON

3101
Dinsmore Homestead Foundation
5656 Burlington Pike, 41005 [PO Box 453, 41005]; (p) (859) 586-6117; (f) (859) 334-3690; info@dinsmorefarm.org; www.dinsmorefarm.org; (c) Boone

Private non-profit/ 1988/ Board of Directors/ staff: 2(f); 1(p); 60(v)/ members: 125

HISTORIC SITE; HISTORY MUSEUM; HOUSE MUSEUM; LIVING HISTORY/OUTDOOR MUSEUM: Maintains house museum with interpretive emphasis on early Ohio River, Boone Co., and Northern KY culture.

PROGRAMS: Exhibits; Facility Rental; Family Programs; Festivals; Guided Tours; Living History; School-Based Curriculum

COLLECTIONS: [1842-1960s] Original family furnishings and possessions including books, photos, family papers, clothing, linens, carriages, china, and other artifacts; housed in large 1842 Federal farmhouse and log cabin.

HOURS: Apr 1-Dec 15 W, Sa, Su 1-5

ADMISSION: $5, Children $2, Seniors $3

CADIZ

3102
Cadiz Log Cabin, Cadiz/Trigg County Tourist Commission
22 Main St, 42211 [PO Box 735, 42211]; (p) (502) 522-3892; (f) (502) 522-6343; cadizky@apex.net; www.gocadiz.com; (c) Trigg

Board of Directors/ staff: 2(f); 2(p)

Promotes tourism within the county.

COLLECTIONS: Iron stove and pump organ.

HOURS: Yr M-F 9-5

CAMPBELLSVILLE

3103
Atkinson-Griffin Log House
Green River Reservoir, 8 miles S on Hwy 55 S, 42718 [112 Kensington Way, 42718]; (p) (270) 465-4463; (f) (270) 465-8726

Federal; Private non-profit/ 1840/ US Army Corps of Engineers/ staff: 1(v)

HOUSE MUSEUM: 1840 log house that served as a Confederate hospital.

PROGRAMS: Guided Tours

COLLECTIONS: [1830-65]

HOURS: Winter varies, Summer 8-5

3104
Hiestand House Museum
Old Hodgenville Rd, 42718 [1095 Campbellsville Bypass, 42718]; (p) (502) 465-4343; (c) Taylor

1992/ staff: 1(p)

HOUSE MUSEUM: 1823 Federal-style former house of Jacob Hiestend, tanner, distiller; presents history and cultural programs.

PROGRAMS: Annual Meeting; Community Outreach; Exhibits; Facility Rental; Family Programs; Guided Tours; Interpretation; Lectures

COLLECTIONS: [1820-1860] Period furnishings, kitchen utensils, toys, photos of early settlers, drawing of Main St in the 1880s; medical equipment; Bicentennial Quilt with related history of 440 Taylor County families.

HOURS: June 15-Aug 15

CARROLLTON

3105
Butler-Turpin Historic House
Hwy 227, General Butler State Resort Park, 41008 [PO Box 325, 41008]; (p) (502) 732-4384; (f) (502) 732-4270; (c) Carroll

State/ 1933/ Commonwealth of KY; Dept of Parks/ staff: 1(f); 10(v)

HOUSE MUSEUM: Collects, preserves and interprets the Butler family's military history and preserves the family cemetery and grounds for future generations. House museum and local history center.

PROGRAMS: Exhibits; Festivals; Garden Tours; Guided Tours; Interpretation; Lectures; Living History; Research Library/Archives

COLLECTIONS: [1780-1880] American and European furniture, archaeological artifacts, manuscripts, documents, books, farming implements, dolls, toys, textiles, portraits and paintings.

HOURS: Feb-Dec T-Sa 10-4, Su 1-4

ADMISSION: $3, Children $1

CLINTON

3107
Hickman County Museum
221 E Clay, 42031 [PO Box 284, 42031]; (c) Hickman

1994/ Board of Directors/ staff: 1(p); 40(v)/ members: 75/publication: *Museum Musings*

HISTORY MUSEUM: Collects, preserves, and interprets county history.

PROGRAMS: Exhibits; Guided Tours; Publication

COLLECTIONS: [1821-present] 2,000 museum artifacts from schools, churches, business, local government, and homes.

HOURS: Yr W, Sa 1-4

COLUMBUS

3108
Columbus-Belmont State Park
350 Park Rd, 42032 [Box 8, 42032]; (p) (502) 677-2327; (f) (502) 677-4013; cindy.lynch@mail.state.ky.us; www.kystateparks.com/agency/parks/columbus.htm; (c) Hickman

1934/ staff: 5(f); 12(p); 1(v)

HISTORIC SITE; HISTORY MUSEUM; STATE PARK: Civil War memorial.

PROGRAMS: Exhibits; Interpretation; Reenactments

COLLECTIONS: [Civil War] Uniforms, guns, pictures, medical artifacts, books; Native American artifacts.

HOURS: Yr Daily 9-5

ADMISSION: $0.50

COVINGTON

3109
Behringer-Crawford Museum
1600 Montague Rd, 41012 [PO Box 67, 41012]; (p) (606) 491-4003; (f) (606) 491-4006; (c) Kenton

Private non-profit/ 1950/ staff: 2(f); 20(v)/ members: 400

HISTORIC SITE; HISTORY MUSEUM

PROGRAMS: Community Outreach; Concerts; Exhibits; Facility Rental; Festivals; Guided Tours; Interpretation; Lectures; Living History

COLLECTIONS: [Prehistoric/1850-1920] Archaeological and paleontological artifacts, documents, photographs, and historic artifacts of Northern KY heritage.

HOURS: Feb-Dec T-F 10-5, Sa-Su 1-5

ADMISSION: $3, Children $2, Seniors $2

3110
Kenton County Historical Society
[PO Box 641, 41012]; (p) (606) 431-2666; nkyheritage.kchs@juno.com; www.keton.lib.ky.us/~histsoc/; (c) Kenton

Private non-profit/ 1977/ Board of Directors/ staff: 8(v)/ members: 365/publication: *Northern KY Heritage*

HISTORICAL SOCIETY: Collects, preserves, and publishes the history of the County; publishes regional magazine for 15 participating counties in the region.

PROGRAMS: Annual Meeting; Guided Tours; Lectures; Publication

COLLECTIONS: [1700-1980] Historic photos deposited with Kenton County Public Library, as well as unpublished research papers. Monthly newsletter

3111
Kenton County Public Library
502 Scott Blvd, 41011; (p) (606) 491-7610; (f) (606) 655-7956; www.kenton.ky.us; (c) Kenton

County/ 1972/ staff: 70(f); 30(p); 30(v)

LIBRARY AND/OR ARCHIVES: Public library with large local history collection, photo collection, and newspaper index.

PROGRAMS: Research Library/Archives

COLLECTIONS: [19th and 20th c] Local history collection; photo collection; complete newspaper index for Northern KY 1831-1931 and 1984-present.

HOURS: Yr M-Th 10-9, F 10-6, Sa 10-5, Su 1-5

3112
Mimosa Mansion Museum
412 E 2nd St, 41011 [412 E 2nd, 41011]; (p) (606) 261-9000

1853/ staff: 2(v)

COLLECTIONS: [1850s; late 1800s-early 1900s] Laminated Rococo furniture 1850's, gasoliers of highest quality working, electric light bulbs, Christmas decorations; 4,000 piano rolls

3113
Northern Kentucky African American Heritage Task Force, Inc.
824 Greenup St, 41012 [PO Box 2329, 41012]; (p) (606) 431-5502; (f) (606) 431-5502; marhen@webtv.net; (c) Kenton

Private non-profit/ 1992/ Board of Directors/ staff: 10(v)/ members: 100

PROFESSIONAL ORGANIZATION: Discovers and preserves historical information; promotes the integration of KY African American history into mainstream American history.

PROGRAMS: Annual Meeting; Community Outreach; Concerts; Elder's Programs; Exhibits; Family Programs; Guided Tours; Lectures; Publication

COLLECTIONS: [1800-present] Acts with local and state archives as a repository and conduit.

HOURS: Yr Daily By appt

CUMBERLAND

3114
Appalachian Archive at Southeast Community College, The
700 College Rd, 40823; (p) (606) 589-2145; (f) (606) 589-2275; rhgipe01@popuky.edu; (c) Harlan

State/ staff: 2(f); 2(p); 20(v)

LIBRARY AND/OR ARCHIVES: Collects and presents artifacts documenting the culture and history of the Appalachian coal fields.

PROGRAMS: Concerts; Exhibits; Facility Rental; Festivals; Guided Tours; Lectures; Research Library/Archives; Theatre

COLLECTIONS: [19th-20th c] Oral histories, photographs, works of art, pocket knives

CYNTHIANA

3115
Cynthiana-Harrison County Museum
13 S Walnut St, 41031 [PO Box 411, 41031]; (p) (606) 234-7179; (c) Harrison

1994/ Cynthiana-Harrison Co. Trust, Inc/ staff: 25(v)/ members: 70

HISTORY MUSEUM: Preserves and shares county history and provides related programs.

PROGRAMS: Annual Meeting; Community Outreach; Exhibits; Festivals; Guided Tours; Interpretation; Reenactments; School-Based Curriculum

HOURS: Yr F-Sa

DANVILLE

3116
McDowell House and Apothecary Shop
125 S 2nd St, 40422; (p) (606) 236-2804; (f) (606) 236-2804; (c) Boyle

Private non-profit/ 1939/ McDowell House Cambus-Kenneth Foundation/ staff: 4(p); 7(v)/ members: 322

HISTORIC SITE; HOUSE MUSEUM: Medical history was made in this museum, where, on Christmas Day 1809, Dr. Ephraim McDowell removed a 22.5 pound tumor from Jane Crawford without anesthetic.

PROGRAMS: Community Outreach; Guided Tours; Interpretation

COLLECTIONS: [1795-1830] Period furnishings; KY artifacts; portraits by early KY artists, books, apothecary shop.

HOURS: Apr-Oct M-Sa 10-2/1-4, Su 2-4

ADMISSION: $5, Student $2

DAWSON SPRINGS

3117
Dawson Springs Museum and Art Center
127 S Main St, 42408 [PO Box 107, 42408]; (p) (270) 797-3891; (c) Hopkins

1986/ Board of Directors/ staff: 48(v)/ members: 120

HISTORY MUSEUM: Preserves local history and displays art exhibits.

PROGRAMS: Community Outreach; Exhibits; Guided Tours; Research Library/Archives

COLLECTIONS: [1874-present] Photos (1,200) and other artifacts covering local history; Japanese art collection.

HOURS: Feb-Dec M-F 1-5

ADMISSION: No charge

EDDYVILLE

3118
Rose Hill: Lyon County Museum
110 Water St, 42038 [PO Box 811, 42038]; (c) Lyon

Private non-profit/ 1982/ Lyon County Historical Society/ staff: 25(v)/ members: 135

HISTORY MUSEUM: Preserves all available artifacts and documents about early settlement, lifestyles, and family histories of Eddyville, and Kuttawa.

PROGRAMS: Annual Meeting; Exhibits; Guided Tours; Lectures

COLLECTIONS: [1799-1965] Portraits of Lyon Family and collages of pioneer families from Vt to KY; Irvin S. Cobb; replica of iron furnace; Wm Kelly story; Civil War battle flag; other Civil War items; farm tools; prison artifacts; pictures of Eddyville

EDMONTON

3119
Metcalfe County Historical Society
Metcalfe Co Public Library, 42129 [Box 910, 42129]; (p) (270) 428-3391; (c) Metcalfe

Private non-profit/ 1978/ staff: 5(v)/ members: 50/publication: *Quarterly Cemetery Record*

HISTORICAL SOCIETY: Mainly local history; collects oral history, preserves artifacts.

PROGRAMS: Publication; Research Library/Archives

COLLECTIONS: [1800-present]

ELIZABETHTOWN

3120
Brown-Pusey House
128 N Main St, 42701; (p) (270) 765-2515; (c) Hardin

Private non-profit/ 1923/ Board of Trustees/ staff: 1(f); 1(p); 3(v)

GENEALOGICAL SOCIETY; HISTORIC SITE; HOUSE MUSEUM; RESEARCH CENTER: Maintains museum built in 1825; fine example of rural Federal architecture. Known for many years as "The Hill House," a boarding house and inn run by Aunt Beck Hill. Used by General George Custer and his wife in the 1870s.

PROGRAMS: Facility Rental; Garden Tours; Guided Tours; Lectures; Living History; Research Library/Archives

COLLECTIONS: [1793-1923] Genealogical library contains a nearly complete set of Hardin County records; gardens.

HOURS: Yr M-Sa 10-4

ADMISSION: $3

3121
Children's Museum of Elizabethtown
University Dr, 42701 [447 Kings Way, 42701]; (p) (270) 765-9696; (f) (270) 765-5614; (c) Hardin

Private non-profit/ 1996/ Board of Directors/ staff: 2(f); 271(v)

HISTORY MUSEUM: Provides children, families, and adults with participatory and educational experiences.

PROGRAMS: Community Outreach; Exhibits; Facility Rental; Family Programs; Festivals; Interpretation; Living History; School-Based Curriculum

COLLECTIONS: [1800s-present] Authentic KY log cabin that offers hands-on interaction with butter churns, spinning wheels, dough trays, and other elements of historical life.

3122
Hardin County Historical Society
[PO Box 381, 42702]; (c) Hardin

County; Private non-profit/ 1931/ staff: 15(v)/ members: 175

HISTORIC SITE; HISTORICAL SOCIETY; HOUSE MUSEUM: Gathers, studies, preserves, and disseminates information about the county; publishes books, presents programs, and organizes exhibits.

PROGRAMS: Annual Meeting; Community Outreach; Exhibits; Facility Rental; Family Programs; Festivals; Guided Tours; Lectures; Publication; Research Library/Archives

COLLECTIONS: [1775-1950]

3123
Lincoln Heritage House
Freeman Lake Park, 704 Woodland Dr, 42701; (p) (800) 437-0092; www.state.ky.us/tour/bluegras/elizabet.htm

3124
Sara Bush Johnston Lincoln Memorial
Freeman Lake Park, 42701 [PO Box 291, 42701]; (p) (502) 737-8727

1992/ staff: 2(v)

COLLECTIONS: [early 1800s] Documents and photos of the Bush family history in Hardin City, KY, and a connection to the Lincoln story.

HOURS: Jun-Oct Sa-Su; Jun-Oct Sa-Sun

3125
Schmidt Museum of Coca-Cola Memorabilia, The
1201 N Dixie Hwy, 42702 [PO Box 647, 42702]; (p) (502) 737-4000; (f) (502) 737-6665; (c) Hardin

1977

CORPORATE ARCHIVES/MUSEUM: Displays Coca-Cola memorabilia; operated by third generation Coca-Cola bottlers Bill Schmidt and his wife.

PROGRAMS: Exhibits

COLLECTIONS: [1886-1975] Most complete collection of Coca-Cola memorabilia and items related to bottling/canning, packaging, advertising, vending, and delivery industries.

HOURS: Yr M-F 9-4

ADMISSION: $2, Student $0.50, Seniors $1.50

FALMOUTH

3126
Pendleton County Historical Society, Inc.
Pendleton Co Library, Main St, 41040 [PO Box 130, 41040]; (p) (606) 654-3225; www.usgenweb.org/ky; (c) Pendleton

Private non-profit/ 1993/ staff: 4(p)/ members: 230/publication: *County Atlas; Pioneer Families*

HISTORICAL SOCIETY: Preserves local history; restores cemeteries.

PROGRAMS: Annual Meeting; Exhibits; Family Programs; Festivals; Guided Tours; Lectures; Publication; Research Library/Archives

FORT CAMPBELL

3127
United States Army Don F. Pratt Museum
5702 Tennessee Ave, 42223-5335; (p) (270) 798-3215; (f) (270) 798-2605; boggsr@emh2.campbell.army.mil; www.campbell.army.mil/pratt/; (c) Montgomery

Federal/ 1956/ US Army Ctr of Military History/ staff: 4(f); 3(v)

HISTORY MUSEUM; LIBRARY AND/OR ARCHIVES; RESEARCH CENTER: Preserves and interprets the historical records and physical artifacts of the 101st Airborne Division (Air Assault) and the military units at Ft. Campbell, KY.

PROGRAMS: Exhibits; Film/Video; Lectures; Research Library/Archives

COLLECTIONS: [20th c] Military artifacts and art depicting key period equipment, uniforms, and captured equipment.

HOURS: Yr Daily 9:30-4:30

ADMISSION: Donations accepted

FORT KNOX

3128
Patton Museum of Cavalry and Armor
4554 Fayette Ave, 40121 [PO Box 208, 40121]; (p) (502) 624-3812; (f) (502) 624-2364; museum@ftknox-enh3.army.mil; 147.238.100.101/museum; (c) Hardin

Federal/ 1949/ US Federal Gov/ staff: 7(f)

HISTORY MUSEUM: Houses collection of war related artifacts.

PROGRAMS: Exhibits; Reenacts; Research Library/Archives

COLLECTIONS: Gen. George S. Patton artifacts; armored weapons, especially WW II tanks.

HOURS: Yr Daily 9-4:30

ADMISSION: No charge

FORT MITCHELL

3129
Vent Haven Museum
33 W Maple Ave, 41011; (p) (606) 341-0461; (f) (606) 341-0461; www.venthaven.com; (c) Kenton

Private non-profit/ 1968/ staff: 1(f)

HISTORY MUSEUM: Maintains collection of ventriloquist figures (over 600) and memorabilia.

PROGRAMS: Community Outreach; Guided Tours

COLLECTIONS: [1800-present]

HOURS: May-Sep M-F 9-7 by appt only

ADMISSION: $2, Children $1

FORT THOMAS

3130
Kentucky Covered Bridge Association
62 Miami Pkwy, 41075; (p) (859) 441-7000; (f) (859) 441-2112; lkpatton@fuse.net; (c) Campbell

Private non-profit/ 1963/ staff: 2(v)/ members: 350/publication: *Timbered Tunnel Talk*

HISTORIC PRESERVATION AGENCY; HISTORICAL SOCIETY; LIBRARY AND/OR ARCHIVES: Preservaton and historical collection of photos and information on KY covered bridges.

PROGRAMS: Exhibits; Lectures; Publication

COLLECTIONS: Photos of nonexistent and current KY covered bridges.

HOURS: By appt

FRANKFORT

3131
Governor's Mansion
Capitol Bldg on Capitol Ave, 40601 [Capital Avenue, 40601]; (p) (502) 564-3449; (f) (502) 564-6505

3132
Historical Confederation of Kentucky
300 W Broadway, 40601 [100 W Broadway, 40601]; (p) (502) 564-1792; (f) (502) 564-0475; Kathey.Jones@mail.state.ky.us; www.kyhistory.org/agencies/khs/outreach/historical_confederation.htm; (c) Franklin

Private non-profit/ 1978/ Governing Board/ staff: 2(f)/ members: 140/publication: *The Circuit Rider; Directory of Kentucky Historical Organizations*

ALLIANCE OF HISTORICAL AGENCIES: Provides technical assistance, information, and services to KY organizations via publications, meetings, workshops, awards, grants, and special projects.

PROGRAMS: Annual

3133
Kentucky Heritage Council
300 Washington St, 40601; (p) (502) 564-7005; (f) (502) 564-5820; dmorgan@mail.state.ky.us; www.state.ky.us/agencies/KHC/KHCHOME.htm; (c) Franklin

State/ 1966/ staff: 20(f)

HISTORIC PRESERVATION AGENCY: State preservation office

PROGRAMS: Annual Meeting; Community Outreach

HOURS: Yr M-F 8-4:30

3134
Kentucky Historical Society
100 W Broadway, 40601; (p) (502) 564-1792; (f) (502) 564-4701; kevin.graffagnino@mail.state.ky.us; www.kyhistory.org; (c) Franklin

State/ 1836/ Executive Committee/ staff: 85(f); 2(p); 120(v)/ members: 4622/publication: *The Register of the Kentucky Historical Society*

HISTORIC SITE; HISTORICAL SOCIETY; HISTORY MUSEUM; LIBRARY AND/OR ARCHIVES; RESEARCH CENTER

PROGRAMS: Annual Meeting; Community Outreach; Elder's Programs; Exhibits; Facility Rental; Family Programs; Festivals; Guided Tours; Interpretation; Lectures; Publication; Research Library/Archives; School-Based Curriculum; Theatre

COLLECTIONS: 80,000 books; 6,000 oral history interviews; 10,000 reels of microfilm; 100,000 photos; 65,000 artifacts.

HOURS: Yr Museum: T- W, F, Sa 10-5, Th 10-8, Su 1-5; Library; M-W, F-S 8-4, Th 8-8

ADMISSION: No charge

3135
Kentucky Military History Museum
Main & Capitol Ave, 40602 [PO Box 1792, 40602]; (p) (502) 564-3265; (f) (502) 564-4054; Bill.Bright@mail.state.ky.us; www.kyhistory.org (c) Franklin

1974/ staff: 3(f); 1(p); 2(v)

HISTORIC SITE; HISTORY MUSEUM: Emphasizes service of the KY Militia, State Guard, and other volunteer military organizations, from the Revolution to the Gulf War.

PROGRAMS: Community Outreach; Elder's Programs; Exhibits; Lectures; Living History; Reenactments; Research Library/Archives

COLLECTIONS: [Civil War] Firearms, edged weapons, artillery, uniforms, flags, photos, personal effects, and other equipment.

HOURS: Yr T-Sa 10-5, Su 1-5

ADMISSION: No charge

3136
Liberty Hall Historic Site
218 Wilkinson St, 40601; (p) (502) 227-2560; (f) (502) 227-3348; libhall@dcr.net; www.libertyhall.org; (c) Franklin

Private non-profit/ 1938/ Liberty Hall Incorporated/ staff: 2(f); 3(p); 35(v)

HISTORIC SITE: Interprets life and times of Senator John Brown and his family and collects, documents, preserves, conserves, researches, and exhibits aspects of KY life from 1796.

PROGRAMS: Community Outreach; Exhibits; Facility Rental; Family Programs; Garden Tours; Guided Tours; Interpretation; Lectures; Living History; Publication; Reenactments; Research Library/Archives; School-Based Curriculum

COLLECTIONS: [1796-1850] 2,000 family furnishings, housewares, and personal possessions; 10 linear ft of archival manuscripts; 200 photos; prints, drawings, and archaeological materials.

HOURS: Mid Mar-early Dec

ADMISSION: No charge

3137
Old Governor's Mansion
420 High St, 40601; (p) (502) 564-5500; (f) (502) 564-4099

1796/ Finance Administration Cabinet/ staff: 4(f); 2(p)

COLLECTIONS: Portraits of early Kentucky Governors, 1780 Tree clock, 1827 sideboard made in Kentucky, 18th century federal mirror, Empire desk and Butler's desk, Former Gov. collection of silver.

HOURS: Yr

3138
Vest-Lindsey House
401 Wapping St, 40601; (p) (502) 564-6980

1820/ Division of Historic Properties/ staff: 2(f)

COLLECTIONS: Several good KY pieces, a

couple of portraits by Kentuckian Joseph Bush.

HOURS: Yr M-F 9-4

FRANKLIN

3139
African American Heritage Center, Inc.
Jefferson St, 42135 [PO Box 323, 42135]; (p) (502) 586-4615; (f) (502) 586-5719; CESinc@apex.net; (c) Simpson

Private non-profit/ 1992/ staff: 5(v)

HOUSE MUSEUM

PROGRAMS: Community Outreach; Guided Tours; Research Library/Archives

COLLECTIONS: [Early 20th c]

HOURS: Yr T-Th 1-4

GEORGETOWN

3140
Georgetown and Scott County Museum
229 E Main St, 40324; (p) (502) 863-6201; (c) Scott

1992/ staff: 2(f); 2(p); 19(v)/ members: 104/publication: *A History of Scott Co, KY*

HISTORY MUSEUM: Preserves local history.

PROGRAMS: Annual Meeting; Exhibits; Facility Rental; Guided Tours; Living History; Publication

COLLECTIONS: [Prehistory-present]

HOURS: Yr M-F 9-4

ADMISSION: No charge

GLASGOW

3141
South Central Kentucky Cultural Center
207 W Main, 42142 [PO Box 1714, 42142]; (p) (502) 651-9792, (888) 256-6941; (f) (502) 651-9792; museum@glasgow-ky.com; (c) Barren

Private non-profit/ 1987/ staff: 1(f); 10(v)/ members: 200

HISTORY MUSEUM; LIBRARY AND/OR ARCHIVES: Interprets culture and history of the surrounding area formerly known as "The Barrens."

PROGRAMS: Annual Meeting; Community Outreach; Exhibits; Lectures; Research Library/Archives; School-Based Curriculum

COLLECTIONS: Artifacts, works of art, publications, and archival materials.

HOURS: Yr M-F 9-4

ADMISSION: No charge

3142
South Central Kentucky Historical and Genealogical Society, Inc.
[PO Box 157, 42142]; (p) (270) 651-3659; (c) Barren

Private non-profit/ 1973/ Board of Directors/ members: 350

GENEALOGICAL SOCIETY; HISTORICAL SOCIETY: Meets monthly; offers programs on county and state history; publishes books on local history.

COLLECTIONS: Research books and microfilm at Weldon Public Library; census records and KY history; local family histories.

GOLDEN POND

3143
Homeplace-1850, The
100 Van Morgan Dr, 42211; (p) (615) 232-6457; (f) (615) 232-3032; msandrews@tva.gov; www.lbl.org; (c) Stewart

1978/ staff: 7(f); 8(p); 10(v)

LIBRARY AND/OR ARCHIVES; LIVING HISTORY/OUTDOOR MUSEUM: Maintains living history farm; presents lifestyle of people living between Cumberland and Tennessee Rivers in mid 19th c.

PROGRAMS: Exhibits; Family Programs; Festivals; Film/Video; Garden Tours; Guided Tours; Interpretation; Lectures; Reenactments; Research Library/Archives; School-Based Curriculum; Theatre

COLLECTIONS: [1850-1890] Agricultural tools; woodworking tools; furnishings; clothing; buildings; animals; library.

HOURS: Apr-Oct M-Sa 9-5, Su 10-5; Mar and Nov W-Sa 9-5, Su 10-5

ADMISSION: $3.50, Children

GREENVILLE

3144
Duncan Cultural Center
122 S Cherry, 42345 [PO Box 287, 42345]; (p) (270) 338-3545, (270) 338-2605; (f) (270) 338-3007; (c) Muhlenberg

1989/ City of Greenville City Council/ staff: 1(f); 1(p); 10(v)/ members: 150

ART MUSEUM; HISTORIC PRESERVATION AGENCY; HISTORICAL SOCIETY; HISTORY MUSEUM: Preserves and exhibits local historical materials; offers school programs.

PROGRAMS: Community Outreach; Concerts; Exhibits; Facility Rental; Guided Tours; Publication; School-Based Curriculum

COLLECTIONS: Coal museum shows industry history; area museum with local artifacts.

HOURS: Yr T-F 1-4, Su 2-4

ADMISSION: No charge

GUTHRIE

3145
Committee for the Preservation of the Robert Penn Warren Birthplace in Todd County, Inc.
3rd & Cherry St, 42234 [PO Box 296, 42234]; (p) (502) 483-2683; (c) Todd

Private non-profit/ 1987/ Board of Directors/ staff: 1(p); 12(v)

HOUSE MUSEUM: Maintains museum that is the restored birthplace house of writer and poet Robert Penn Warren; exhibits his works and history; offers numerous programs.

PROGRAMS: Exhibits; Film/Video; Guided Tours; Lectures

HOURS: Yr T-Sa 11:30-3:30

ADMISSION: Donations accepted

HARRODSBURG

3146
Old Fort Harrod State Park
100 College St, 40330 [PO Box 156, 40330]; (p) (859) 734-3314; (f) (859) 734-0794; www.kystateparks.com; (c) Mercer

State/ 1925/ KY Dept of Parks/ staff: 3(f); 18(p)

HISTORIC SITE; HISTORY MUSEUM; LIVING HISTORY/OUTDOOR MUSEUM; STATE PARK: Oldest permanent town in KY; reconstructed fort with living history exhibits and furnished cabins; mansion museum with Union and Confederate rooms.

PROGRAMS: Concerts; Festivals; Guided Tours; Living History; Reenactments; School-Based Curriculum

COLLECTIONS: [18th and 19th c] Pioneer furnishings and tools; Native American artifacts; historical documents; paintings; photos; Civil War collections; gun collection; antique musical instruments.

HOURS: Yr Daily

3147
Shaker Village of Pleasant Hill
3501 Lexington Rd, 40330; (p) (859) 734-5411; (f) (859) 734-7278; lcurry@ shakervillageky.org; www.shakervillageky.org; (c) Mercer

Private non-profit/ 1961/ Board of Trustees/ staff: 120(f); 75(p); 25(v)/ members: 2400/publication: *Pleasant Hill and its Shakers; The Gift of Pleasant Hill*

HISTORIC SITE; HISTORY MUSEUM; LIVING HISTORY/OUTDOOR MUSEUM: Shaker village; offers tours, demonstrations, historic farming, events, and riverboat excursions; lodging and dining in historic buildings.

PROGRAMS: Concerts; Elder's Programs; Exhibits; Facility Rental; Film/Video; Guided Tours; Interpretation; Lectures; Living History; Publication; Reenactments; Research Library/Archives

COLLECTIONS: [19th c] 33 original on-site buildings on 2,800 acres of farmland; 5,500 artifacts including tools, textile equipment and textiles, furnishings, and agricultural implements; archives include 2,500 books, 1,000 microfiche, 260 microfilm.

HOURS: Yr Daily Apr-Oct 9:30-5:30; Nov-Mar 10-4:30

ADMISSION: $10, Student $5, Children $3.50; Winter rates reduced

HAWESVILLE

3148
Hancock County Museum
110 River St, 42348 [PO Box 605, 42348]; (c) Hancock

Private non-profit/ 1987/ staff: 40(v)/ members: 175

HISTORIC SITE; HISTORY MUSEUM: Maintains local history museum in a restored railroad depot.

PROGRAMS: Community Outreach; Concerts; Exhibits; Guided Tours

COLLECTIONS: [1827-present] Restored 1867 courthouse and related artifacts; tools, home artifacts; steamboats; photos, Indian artifacts, and more.

HOURS: Apr-Oct Su 2-4

ADMISSION: No charge

HAZARD

3149
Bobby Davis Museum and Park, Hazard, Perry County, Kentucky, Inc.
234 Walnut St, 41701; (p) (606) 439-4325; (f) (606) 436-3252; (c) Perry

Private non-profit/ 1983/ Board of Trustees/ staff: 2(f); 1(p); 5(v)

HISTORY MUSEUM: Collects and preserves artifacts, photographs, and documents of area ancestors through exhibits, information services, publications, and special projects.

PROGRAMS: Community Outreach; Exhibits; Facility Rental; Festivals; Interpretation; Research Library/Archives; School-Based Curriculum

COLLECTIONS: [1795-1950] Artifacts, newspapers, photographs, ledgers, oral history tapes, local directories, slides, and local history topic files.

HENDERSON

3150
Henderson County Historical and Genealogical Society, Inc.
132-B S Green St, 42419 [PO Box 303, 42419-0303]; (p) (270) 830-7514; hendersoncounty@hotmail.com; www.rootsweb.com/~kyhender/henderson/ henderson.html; (c) Henderson

Private non-profit/ 1966/ Board of Directors/ staff: 6(v)/ members: 312

GENEALOGICAL SOCIETY; HISTORICAL SOCIETY: Collects, preserves, distributes, and publishes historical materials; preserves historic sites.

PROGRAMS: Annual Meeting; Publication; Research Library/Archives

COLLECTIONS: Research library covering IL, KY, NC, SC, TN, VA.

HOURS: Th 2-5

3151
John James Audubon Museum
3100 Hwy 41 N, 42419 [PO Box 576, 42419]; (p) (502) 827-1893; (f) (502) 826-2286; jaudubon@ henderson.net; www.go-henderson.com/ audubon.htm; (c) Henderson

State/ 1938/ KY Dept of Parks/ staff: 6(f); 3(p); 8(v)/ members: 220/publication: *The Warbler*

HISTORY MUSEUM: Collects and displays art and artifacts of the life and work of John James Audubon and his family; houses nature center with bird and other wildlife displays; offers programs related to art and natural history.

PROGRAMS: Community Outreach; Exhibits; Facility Rental; Family Programs; Festivals; Guided Tours; Interpretation; Lectures; Publication; Research Library/Archives

COLLECTIONS: [1780-1860] Complete collection of Audubon's publications including the "Double Elephant Folio," and the imperial edition of his "Quadrupeds of North America;"

largest collection of original oils and personal memorabilia from the Audubon family.

HOURS: Yr Daily 10-5

ADMISSION: $4, Family $10, Children $2.50; Group rates

HIGHLAND HEIGHTS

3152
Museum of Anthropology
200 LA, University Drive, 41099 [Northern Kentucky University, 41099]; (p) (859) 572-5259; (f) (859) 572-6086; www.nku.edu/~anthro; (c) Campbell

Joint; State/ 1976/ Northern Kentucky University/ staff: 2(p); 1(v)

HISTORIC PRESERVATION AGENCY; HISTORY MUSEUM: Serves as an educational, research, and conservational unit with responsibilities in selected areas of anthropology and archaeology.

PROGRAMS: Community Outreach; Exhibits; Guided Tours; Interpretation; Lectures; Research Library/Archives

COLLECTIONS: Ohio valley archaeological collection; small ethnographic collections representing contemporary Native American; small ethnographic collections from West Africa, Mexico, and New Guinea.

HOURS: Aug-May M-F 8:30-4:30

ADMISSION: No charge

HODGENVILLE

3153
Lincoln Boyhood Home
US 31E, 42748 [PO Box 183, New Haven, 40051]; (p) (502) 549-3741

3154
Lincoln Museum, Inc., The
66 Lincoln Sq, 42748; (p) (270) 358-3163; (f) (270) 358-8978; (c) LaRue

Private non-profit/ 1988/ staff: 2(f); 1(p); 5(v)/ members: 150

HISTORY MUSEUM: Promotes legacy and history of Abraham Lincoln, KY native.

PROGRAMS: Annual Meeting; Community Outreach; Exhibits; Facility Rental; Family Programs; Festivals; Film/Video; Guided Tours; Interpretation; Lectures; Living History; Publication; Reenactments; Research Library/ Archives; School-Based Curriculum

COLLECTIONS: [1800-1865] Lincoln-related dioramas; film, art, and special exhibits.

HOURS: Yr M-Sa 8:30-4:30, Su 12:30-4:30

3155
Abraham Lincoln Birthplace National Historic Site
2995 Lincoln Farm Rd, 42748; (p) (270) 358-3137, (270) 358-3138; (f) (270) 358-3874; ABLI_Adminstration@nps.gov; www.nps.gov/abli/index.html

1916/ National Parks Service

HISTORIC SITE; HISTORY MUSEUM; NATIONAL PARK; PRESIDENTIAL SITE: Site where Abraham Lincoln the 16th US President was born in 1809.

PROGRAMS: Exhibits; Film/Video; Interpreta-

tion; Lectures

COLLECTIONS: [1800s] Early 19c KY cabin, artifacts, axes, scythes, hayforks, Lincoln family Bible, period tools, and utensils.

HOURS: May-Sept Daily 8-6:45; Sept-May Daily 8-4:45

ADMISSION: No charge

LATONIA

3156
Railway Exposition Company, Inc., The
315 W Southern, 41015 [PO Box 36165, 41015]; (p) (606) 655-5200

Private non-profit/ 1974/ staff: 25(v)/ members: 75

PROFESSIONAL ORGANIZATION

PROGRAMS: Annual Meeting; Exhibits; Facility Rental; Festivals; Guided Tours; School-Based Curriculum

COLLECTIONS: [1935-1950] Railroad artifacts.

HOURS: May-Oct Sa, Su 12-4

ADMISSION: $4, Children $2

LEBANON

3157
Marion County Historical Society
201 E Main St, 40033; (p) (270) 692-4698; mary.parrott@lycos.com; (c) Marion

Private non-profit/ 1991/ County/ staff: 8(v)/ members: 100/publication: *Marion County Historical Society Quarterly; Marion County History*

HISTORIC SITE; HISTORICAL SOCIETY; HISTORY MUSEUM: Members meet monthly, operate a museum, and collect historical information and artifacts.

PROGRAMS: Annual Meeting; Community Outreach; Exhibits; Festivals; Guided Tours; Lectures; Publication; Research Library/ Archives

COLLECTIONS: [1800-present] Hundreds of pictures; Native American artifacts; Longhorn rifle, bayonet and powderhorn; inaugural gown of Governor Knott's wife

LEXINGTON

3158
American Saddlebred Museum
4093 Iron Works Pkwy, 40511; (p) (859) 259-2746; (f) (859) 255-4909; ashm@mis.net; www.american-saddlebred.com; (c) Fayette

Private non-profit/ 1962/ Board of Trustees/ staff: 3(f); 8(p); 20(v)/ members: 800

HISTORY MUSEUM; LIBRARY AND/OR ARCHIVES: Presents the traditions and heritage of the American Saddlebred through collection, preservation, and display of artifacts, fine arts, photography, and literature.

PROGRAMS: Annual Meeting; Community Outreach; Exhibits; Film/Video; Research Library/Archives

COLLECTIONS: [20th c] Books, documents, drawings, film, horse shoes, magazines, paintings, photos, prints, saddles, bridles, sculptures and trophies.

HOURS: May-Sept Daily 9-6; Sept-May Daily 9-5

3159
Ashland, the Henry Clay Estate
120 Sycamore Rd, 40502; (f) (606) 268-7266; HClay1777@aol.com; www.henryclay.org; (c) Fayette

Private non-profit/ 1926/ Henry Clay Memorial Foundation/ staff: 2(f); 8(p); 80(v)/ members: 1100/publication: *The Historic Grounds of Ashland*

HOUSE MUSEUM: House museum that interprets the life and times of Henry Clay and his family.

PROGRAMS: Concerts; Elder's Programs; Exhibits; Facility Rental; Family Programs; Festivals; Film/Video; Garden Tours; Guided Tours; Lectures; Living History; Publication; Reenactments; School-Based Curriculum

COLLECTIONS: [19th c] Mostly original Clay family pieces including furniture, fine and decorative arts, costumes and textiles; historical, archival, photographic, and archaeological materials.

HOURS: Feb-Dec M-Sa 10-4:30, Su 1-4:30; Nov-Mar closed M

ADMISSION: $6, Student $3, Children $2; Group rates

3160
Blue Grass Trust for Historic Preservation
253 Market St, 40507; (p) (606) 253-0362; (f) (606) 259-9210; bgtrust@mis.net; (c) Fayette

Private non-profit/ 1955/ staff: 2(f); 2(p); 120(v)/ members: 600

HISTORIC PRESERVATION AGENCY: Advocate for historic preservation that strives to protect, revitalize, and promote historic places in the region.

PROGRAMS: Annual Meeting; Community Outreach; Exhibits; Facility Rental; Guided Tours; Lectures; School-Based Curriculum

3161
Bodley-Bullock House Museum
200 Market St, 40507-1030; (p) (606) 259-1266; www.kytravel.com/ktg07.html

3162
Headley-Whitney Museum
4435 Old Frankfort Pk, 40510; (p) (606) 255-6653; (f) (606) 255-8375; hwmuseum@mind spring.com; headley-whitney-org; (c) Fayette

Private non-profit/ 1968/ Board of Directors/ staff: 6(f); 3(p); 26(v)/ members: 380

HISTORY MUSEUM: Decorative arts museum, founded by jewelry designer George W. Headley.

PROGRAMS: Annual Meeting; Community Outreach; Concerts; Elder's Programs; Exhibits; Facility Rental; Family Programs; Guided Tours; Interpretation; Lectures; Publication; Research Library/Archives

COLLECTIONS: Headley jewelry; Asian ceramics and textiles; KY-made silver.

HOURS: Feb-Dec T-F

3163
Historic Preservation Office, Lexington Fayette Urban County Government
200 E Main St, 40507; (p) (606) 258-3265; (f) (606) 258-3394; (c) Fayette

1976/ staff: 5(f)

HISTORIC PRESERVATION AGENCY: Responsible for historic preservation including design review of historic districts, national register nominations, architectural survey and documentation, technical assistance, and enforcing ordinances.

PROGRAMS: Community Outreach; Guided Tours

HOURS: Yr M-F 8-5

3164
Hunt-Morgan House
201 N Mill St, 40507 [BGTHP, Inc, 253 Market St, 40507]; (p) (606) 233-3290, (606) 253 0362; (f) (606) 259-9210; www.state.ky.us/tour/bluegras/lexdown.htm; (c) Fayette

3165
Lexington Cemetery Company, Inc.
833 W Main St, 40508; (p) (606) 255-5522; (f) (606) 258-2774; (c) Fayette

Private non-profit/ 1848/ staff: 26(f); 7(p)

HISTORIC SITE: 60,000 burials, including vets from all wars, Henry Clay, and other persons of national, state, and local importance; flower garden.

PROGRAMS: Exhibits; Garden Tours; Guided Tours

HOURS: Yr Daily 8-5

3166
Lexington History Museum, Inc.
c/o 200 N Upper St, 40507

Private non-profit/ 1998

HISTORY MUSEUM

3167
Lexington Public Library
140 E Main St, 40507; (p) (606) 231-5520; (f) (606) 231-5545; www.lexpublib.org; (c) Fayette

County/ 1898/ staff: 87(f); 104(p)

Four branches and central library; Kentucky Room Reference Collection located within the Central Library includes Lexington and KY history materials.

COLLECTIONS: [19th and 20th c] Local and state history with some genealogy; extensive index to local newspapers; subject files; photos.

HOURS: Yr Daily M-Th 9-9; F, Sa 9-5; Su 1-5

ADMISSION: No charge

3168
Mary Todd Lincoln House
578 W Main St, 40507 [PO Box 132, 40588]; (p) (606) 233-9999; (c) Fayette

1803/ staff: 1(f); 6(p)

Maints former home of Mary Todd, future wife of Abraham Lincoln, was in her teens when her upper-class family moved into this Georgian-style home. In the parlor she participated in political discussions with such illustrious guests as Henry Clay. Built as a tavern in 1803, the home was renovated in the early 1830s by Mary's father, Robert Todd, and influential banker and legislator.

COLLECTIONS: [1832-1849] Several of Mary's personal possessions: china, books, clothing; Todd furniture

3169
Robert H. Williams Cultural Center
644 Georgetown St, 40508; (p) (606) 255-5066; (f) (606) 255-5066; (c) Fayette

Private non-profit/ 1892/ Board of Directors/ staff: 1(f); 5(p); 10(v)/ members: 25/publication: *Lexington's Colored Orphan; Industrial Home: Building for the Future*

CULTURAL CENTER; HISTORIC PRESERVATION AGENCY; HISTORIC SITE: Provides educational and cultural enrichment via classes, workshops, exhibits, and after school programs; other activities include an African marketplace, summer camp, and a Kwanzaa program.

PROGRAMS: Community Outreach; Elder's Programs; Facility Rental; Family Programs; Lectures

3170
Senator John Pope House
326 Grosvenor Ave, 40508 [BGTHP, Inc, 253 Market St, 40507]; (p) (606) 253-0362, (606) 253 0362; (f) (606) 259-9210; www.state.ky.us/tour/bluegras/lexdown.htm; (c) Fayette

3171
Special Collections and Archives, Transylvania University Library
300 N Broadway, 40508 [Transylvania Univ, 40508]; (p) (859) 233-8225; (f) (859) 233-8779; bjgooch@transy.edu; www.transy.edu/library; (c) Fayette

Private non-profit/ 1784/ Transylvania University/ staff: 1(f); 1(p)

LIBRARY AND/OR ARCHIVES: Collects and preserves KY historical materials, University records; medicine and science in the 19th c; natural history.

PROGRAMS: Research Library/Archives

COLLECTIONS: [Late 18th-Early 19th c] Early printed books and pamphlets; British and American history and literature; early 19th c medicine and science; natural history

3172
University of Kentucky Art Museum
Rose St and Euclid Ave, 40506; (p) (859) 257-5716; (f) (859) 323-1994

State/ 1976/ Univ of KY/ staff: 8(f); 5(p); 50(v)/ members: 585

ART MUSEUM: Offers programs, changing exhibits, lectures, symposia, educational tours; scholarly archives and publications on exhibition related subjects.

PROGRAMS: Community Outreach; Exhibits; Family Programs; Guided Tours; Interpretation; Lectures; Publication; Research Library/Archives; School-Based Curriculum

COLLECTIONS: 3,500 works: 19th and 20th c European and American; Italian Baroque paintings and prints; contemporary prints; photography; decorative arts; regional works; art from Asia, Africa, and the Americas.

HOURS: Yr T-Su 12-5, F 12-8

ADMISSION: No charge

3173
Waveland State Historic Site
225 Waveland Museum Ln, 40514; (p) (606)

272-3611; (f) (606) 245-4269; (c) Fayette

State/ 1963/ KY Dept of Parks/ staff: 3(f); 4(p); 80(v)

HOUSE MUSEUM: Collects, preserves, and interprets social, domestic, economic, and agricultural aspects of KY antebellum life.

PROGRAMS: Community Outreach; Elder's Programs; Family Programs; Guided Tours; Interpretation; Lectures; Living History; School-Based Curriculum

COLLECTIONS: [1850-1860] 10,000 artifacts: textiles, farming implements, and decorative arts.

HOURS: Mar-mid Dec M-Sa 10-5, Su 1-5

ADMISSION: $6, Student $3, Seniors $5

3174
William S. Webb Museum of Anthropology
211 Lafferty Hall, U of KY, 40506; (p) (859) 257-8208; (f) (859) 232-2686; museum@pop.uky.edu; www.uky.edu/AS/Anthropology/Museum/museum.htm; (c) Fayette

State/ 1931/ Dept of Anthropology, Univ of KY/ staff: 2(f); 1(p); 1(v)

ANTHROPOLOGY MUSEUM: Acquires and maintains anthropological collections; encourages anthropological research, and disseminates knowledge, especially of prehistoric KY.

PROGRAMS: Community Outreach; Exhibits; Guided Tours; Lectures

COLLECTIONS: [14,000 BP-1950 AD] Archaeological materials and human skeletal remains from sites in KY; materials from Nubia; some ethnographic materials.

HOURS: Yr M-F May 15-Aug 15 8-4; Aug 15-May 15 8-4:30

ADMISSION: No charge

LIBERTY

3175
Bicentennial Heritage Corporation of Casey County, Kentucky
238 Middleburg St, 42539 [148 Wolford St, 42539]; (p) (606) 787-9381; ccplstaff@kih.net; (c) Casey

County/ 1975/ Casey County Public Library/ staff: 5(p); 5(v)/ members: 55

HERITAGE AREA; LIBRARY AND/OR ARCHIVES: Discovers and preserves local heritage.

PROGRAMS: Exhibits; Lectures; Research Library/Archives

COLLECTIONS: Books, county records, and newspapers on microfilm, family files indexed and cross-indexed, census records, Kentucky Vital Records, Civil War publications and oral tapes.

HOURS: Yr M-W, F 10-6, Sa 9-3

LORETTO

3176
Maker's Mark Distillery, Inc.
Hwy 52 E, 40037 [3350 Burks Spring Rd, 40037]; (p) (502) 865-2099; (f) (502) 865-2199; donna_nally@adws.com;

www.makersmark.com; (c) Marion

Private for-profit/ 1805/ Taylor William Samuels, Jr./ staff: 60(f); 8(p)

HISTORY MUSEUM: 1805 gristmill purchased and converted into distillery still in business today.

PROGRAMS: Guided Tours

HOURS: Yr M-Sa 10:30-3:30, Su

LOUISVILLE

3177
Belle of Louisville
401 W River Rd, 40202; (p) (502) 574-2992; (f) (502) 574-3030; www.belleoflouisvill.org; (c) Jefferson

Joint; Private non-profit/ 1914/ staff: 40(f); 20(p)/publication: *Belle of Louisville: A Window to the Past, A Door to the Future*

Oldest and most authentic operating Mississippi River-style steamboat in the United States.

COLLECTIONS: [Early-mid 20th c] Boat itself is the primary exhibit. Also, photographs document its history and the history of steamboats.

3178
Brennan Historic House and Medical Office Museum
631 S Fifth St, 40202; (p) (502) 540-5145; (f) (502) 587-6481; (c) Jefferson

Private non-profit/ 1982/ staff: 1(f); 5(v)/ members: 15

HISTORIC SITE; HISTORY MUSEUM; HOUSE MUSEUM

PROGRAMS: Exhibits; Facility Rental; Garden Tours; Guided Tours

COLLECTIONS: [1800-1920] Items from the Brennan Family who resided in the home 1884-1971.

HOURS: Mar-Dec T-Sa 1-5

ADMISSION: $4, Seniors $3.50

3179
Col. Harland Sanders Museum at KFC
1441 Gardiner Lane, 40213; (p) (502) 874-8353; (c) Jefferson

Private non-profit/ 1980/ KFC Corporation/ staff: 2(p)

CORPORATE ARCHIVES/MUSEUM: Documents life of Col. Harland Sanders, founder of Kentucky Fried Chicken.

PROGRAMS: Film/Video

HOURS: Yr M-F 8-5

ADMISSION: No charge

3180
Conrad/Caldwell House Museum
1402 St. James Ct, 40208; (p) (502) 636-5023; (f) (502) 636-1264; caldwell@iglou.com; (c) Jefferson

1987/ St. James Court Historic Foundation, Inc/ staff: 1(f); 1(p); 25(v)/ members: 50

HOUSE MUSEUM: Stone Victorian Romanesque Revival house; offers tours focused on local history and lifestyle of Louisville entrepreneurs.

PROGRAMS: Elder's Programs; Exhibits; Fa-

cility Rental; Guided Tours; Lectures; Publication; School-Based Curriculum

COLLECTIONS: [1890-1910] Furniture, decorative and fine arts, books, linens, and household goods.

HOURS: Yr W-F, Sa 10-4, Su 12-4

ADMISSION: $4, Student $2, Seniors $3

3181
Farmington Historic Home
3033 Bardstown Rd, 40205; (p) (502) 452-9920; (f) (502) 456-1976; (c) Jefferson

1957/ Historic Homes Foundation/ staff: 3(f); 3(p); 40(v)/ members: 600

GARDEN; HOUSE MUSEUM: 1815-1816 house, based on design by Thomas Jefferson; presents the story of a unique early 19th c KY house, its people, and their farm culture, through preservation, exhibitions, and education.

PROGRAMS: Exhibits; Facility Rental; Festivals; Film/Video; Garden Tours; Guided Tours; Interpretation; Lectures; School-Based Curriculum

COLLECTIONS: [1810-1850] 750 decorative arts objects.

HOURS: Yr T-Sa 10-4:30, Su

3182
Filson Club, The
1310 S Third St, 40208; (p) (502) 635-5083; (f) (502) 635-5086; filson@filsonclub.org; www.filsonclub.org; (c) Jefferson

1884/ Board of Directors/ staff: 16(f); 4(p); 25(v)/ members: 5100

LIBRARY AND/OR ARCHIVES: Operates an independent historical society; collects, preserves, and interprets history of KY, the Ohio River Valley, and the Upper South for education and research.

PROGRAMS: Community Outreach; Exhibits; Family Programs; Guided Tours; Interpretation; Lectures; Publication; Research Library/Archives; School-Based Curriculum; Theatre

COLLECTIONS: [1700-present] 1.5 million processed manuscripts; 2,000 pieces of sheet music; 55,000 library volumes; 400 portraits and paintings; 50,000 photos and prints; 10,000 museum artifacts.

HOURS: Yr M-F 9-5, Sa 9-12

ADMISSION: Library charge/Museum free

3183
Jefferson Office of Public History
810 Barret Ave, 40204; (p) (502) 574-5761; (f) (502) 574-6886; dneary@co.jefferson.ky.us; (c) Jefferson

County/ 1979/ Jefferson Co. Fiscal Court/ staff: 7(f); 2(p)

HISTORIC PRESERVATION AGENCY

PROGRAMS: Community Outreach

HOURS: Yr M-F 8-5

ADMISSION: No charge

3184
Kentucky Derby Museum
704 Central Ave, 40201 [PO Box 3513, 40201]; (p) (502) 637-1111; (f) (502) 636-5855; info@derbymuseum.org;

www.derbymuseum.org; (c) Jefferson

Private non-profit/ 1962/ Churchill Downs, Inc/ staff: 37(f); 50(p); 62(v)/ members: 1000

CORPORATE ARCHIVES/MUSEUM; HISTORY MUSEUM: Located at Gate 1 of Churchill Downs, includes exhibition galleries, auditorium, restaurant, gift shop, and archives.

PROGRAMS: Exhibits; Facility Rental; Guided Tours; Lectures; Research Library/Archives; School-Based Curriculum

COLLECTIONS: [20th c] Thoroughbred racing and equine artifacts; memorabilia, photos, archives, art work, and trophies.

HOURS: Yr Daily 9-5

ADMISSION: $6, Children $2, Seniors $5

3185
Locust Grove Historic Home
561 Blankenbaker Lane, 40207; (p) (502) 897-0103; (f) (502) 897-9845; lghh@locust grove.org; www.locustgrove.org; (c) Jefferson

Private non-profit/ 1961/ Locust Grove Board of Regents, a division of Historic Homes Foundation, Inc/ staff: 3(f); 10(p); 150(v)/ members: 728

GARDEN; HISTORIC SITE; HISTORY MUSEUM; HOUSE MUSEUM: Teaches about the life of George Rogers Clark, Western expansion, and early KY pioneer life; offers guided tours, classes, lectures, and other public programs.

PROGRAMS: Community Outreach; Concerts; Exhibits; Facility Rental; Family Programs; Film/Video; Guided Tours; Interpretation; Lectures; Reenactments; School-Based Curriculum

COLLECTIONS: [1760-1849] Furniture, prints, paintings, and domestic objects; military and personal artifacts of George Rogers Clark.

HOURS: Yr M-Sa 10-4:30, Su 1:30-4:30

ADMISSION: $4, Children $2, Seniors $3

3186
Marie and Eugene Callahan Museum of the American Printing House for the Blind
1839 Frankfort Ave, 40206; (p) (502) 895-2405; (f) (502) 899-2363; ctobe@aph.org; www.aph.org; (c) Jefferson

1994/ American Printing House for the Blind, Inc/ staff: 2(f)

HISTORY MUSEUM: Features educational history of blind people, and the history of the Printing House; exhibits are accessible to all with disabilities, with audio phones, Braille labels, and touchable exhibits for blind people; tours include manufacturing plant.

PROGRAMS: Community Outreach; Elder's Programs; Exhibits; Family Programs; Guided Tours; Interpretation; Research Library/Archives

COLLECTIONS: [1850-present] Tactile books, maps, educational aides, mechanical writers, Braille production machinery, "Talking Books," and audio recorders and players.

HOURS: Yr M-F 8:30-4:30

ADMISSION: No charge

3187
National Society Sons of the American Revolution, The
1000 S Fourth St, 40203; (p) (502) 589-1776; (f) (502) 589-1671; nssar@sar.org; www.sar.org; (c) Jefferson

1889/ staff: 9(f); 4(p)/ members: 26000

LIBRARY AND/OR ARCHIVES: Maintains library.

PROGRAMS: Research Library/Archives

COLLECTIONS: [18th-19th c]

HOURS: Yr M-F 9:30-4:30

3188
Papa John's International, Inc. Corporate Museum
11492 Bluegrass Pkwy, 40269 [PO Box 99900, 40269]; (p) (502) 261-4003; (f) (502) 261-4324; lisa-baize@papajohns.com; www.papajohns.com; (c) Jefferson

Private non-profit/ 1985/ staff: 3(f)

CORPORATE ARCHIVES/MUSEUM: Corporate museum showing company's role in industry history.

PROGRAMS: Annual Meeting; Guided Tours

COLLECTIONS: [1980s-present]

HOURS: Yr M-F 8-5

ADMISSION: No charge

3189
Photographic Archives, University of Louisville
Photo Archives/Special Coll Dept/Ekstrom Lib/Univ , 40292 [Photo Archives/Special Coll Dept/Ekstrom Lib/Univ Louisville, 40292]; (p) (502) 852-6752; (f) (502) 852-8734; special. collections@louisville.edu; www.louisville.edu/library/ekstrom/special/pa_info.html

1968/ University of Louisville/ staff: 7(f); 1(p); 4(v)

LIBRARY AND/OR ARCHIVES: Collects significant documentary photograph collections, organizes them, and makes them available to researchers and casual browsers.

PROGRAMS: Exhibits; Lectures; Research Library/Archives; School-Based Curriculum

COLLECTIONS: [20th c] 1.2 million photographs in hundreds of discrete collections including significant national documentary projects, local history photos, and a museum collection of fine prints.

HOURS: Yr M-F

ADMISSION: No charge

3190
Riverside, the Farnsley-Moorman Landing
7410 Moorman Rd, 40272-4572; (p) (502) 935-6809; (f) (502) 935-6821; www.Riverside-Landing.org; (c) Jefferson

Joint/ 1993/ Jefferson County Fiscal Court/ staff: 4(f); 1(p); 75(v)/ members: 200/publication: Riverside: The Restoration of a Way

HISTORIC SITE; HISTORY MUSEUM: Interprets 19th c Ohio River farm life; 300 acre site with Farnsley-Moreman House, built in 1837.

PROGRAMS: Concerts; Elder's Programs; Exhibits; Facility Rental; Family Programs; Festivals; Garden Tours; Guided Tours; Interpretation; Lectures; Publication; School-Based Curriculum

COLLECTIONS: [1830s-1885] House with mid 19th c detached kitchen, period household furnishings, farm implements, textiles, and photos; 2,000 objects.

HOURS: Yr T-Sa 10-4:30, Su 1-4:30

ADMISSION: $4, Children $2, Seniors $3.50

3191
Thomas Edison House
729-31 E Washington St, 40202; (p) (502) 585-5247; (f) (502) 585-5247; (c) Jefferson

1973/ Historic Homes Foundation, Inc./ staff: 1(f); 1(p); 30(v)

HISTORIC SITE; HISTORY MUSEUM; HOUSE MUSEUM: Maintains 1850s shotgun duplex and interprets Edison's formative years as a telegrapher and later as a prolific inventor.

PROGRAMS: Community Outreach; Exhibits; Facility Rental; Family Programs; Film/Video; Garden Tours; Guided Tours; Interpretation; Lectures

COLLECTIONS: [1847-1931] Examples of many inventions including light bulbs, cylinder and disk phonographs, and the kinetoscope.

HOURS: Yr T-Sa 10-2

3192
Tompkins-Buchanan-Rankin Mansion
851 S Fourth St, 40203; (p) (502) 585-9911; (f) (502) 585-7156; (c) Jefferson

Private non-profit/ 1871/ Spalding University

HISTORIC SITE: Maintains house designed by Henry Whitestone; then became main building of Spalding University; additional rooms have been added to the original building; entire structure is now used as administrative building.

PROGRAMS: Guided Tours; Lectures

HOURS: Yr M-F 8-5

ADMISSION: No charge

3193
Whitehall State Historic Site
3110 Lexington Rd, 40206; (p) (502) 897-2944; (f) (502) 897-7737

State/ 1855/ staff: 1(f); 2(p)

COLLECTIONS: [1909]

HOURS: Yr

LOUSVILLE

3194
E.P. "Tom" Sawyer State Park
3000 Freys Hill Rd, 40241; (p) (502) 426-8950; (f) (502) 425-3114; www.state.ky.us; (c) Jefferson

1970/ Commonwealth of KY/ staff: 15(f); 30(p); 40(v)

HISTORIC SITE; STATE PARK: Recreational state park; offers activities; former site of old Central State Hospital and Hite family plantation.

PROGRAMS: Concerts; Facility Rental; Family Programs; Festivals; Interpretation; School-Based Curriculum

COLLECTIONS: [Late 1800s]

HOURS: Yr Daily 7am-10pm

ADMISSION: No charge

3195
Historic Homes Foundation
3110 Lexington Rd, 40206; (p) (502) 899-5079; (f) (502) 899-5016; JCSHHF@aol.com; historichomes.org; (c) Jefferson

1957/ staff: 12(f); 18(p); 85(v)/ members: 626

HISTORIC SITE: Operates Farmington, Locust Grove, Whitehall, and Thomas Edison House.

PROGRAMS: Annual Meeting; Community Outreach; Concerts; Exhibits; Facility Rental; Family Programs; Festivals; Garden Tours; Guided Tours; Interpretation; Lectures; Publication; School-Based Curriculum

COLLECTIONS: [1790-1840] Homes contain Southern furniture and decorative arts.

ADMISSION: $4

MADISONVILLE

3196
Historical Society of Hopkins County
107 Union St, 42431; (p) (502) 821-3986; (c) Hopkins

1974/ staff: 2(p); 1(v)/ members: 400/publication: *Annual Yearbook*

HISTORICAL SOCIETY: Preserves history in oral, written, and photographic forms.

PROGRAMS: Publication

COLLECTIONS: [1750-present] Artifacts, photos, and written history.

HOURS: Yr M-F 1-5

3197
Ruby Laffoon Log Cabin
107 Union, 42431; (p) (502) 281-3986; www.state.ky.us/tour/western/wmadison.htm

MAPLE MOUNT

3198
Mount Saint Joseph Ursuline Archives
8001 Cummings Rd, 42356-9999; (p) (502) 229-4103; (f) (502) 229-4127; emma@cpc.brescia.edu; (c) Daviess

Private non-profit/ 1874/ Ursuline Sisters/ staff: 2(p)

HISTORIC SITE; HOUSE MUSEUM; LIBRARY AND/OR ARCHIVES; RESEARCH CENTER: Houses documents, manuscripts, photos, tapes, artifacts, and holdings pertinent to community and education; qualified researchers welcome.

PROGRAMS: Concerts; Exhibits; Festivals; Guided Tours; Research Library/Archives

COLLECTIONS: [1874-present] 450 linear ft of arranged, boxed, shelved, and indexed documents; 2,500 volumes of old and rare books; 5 file cabinets of photos of buildings, property, individuals, missions; 1000 books on KY history and genealogy.

MARION

3199
Ben E. Clement Mineral Museum, The
205 N Walker St, 42064 [PO Box 391, 42064]; (p) (270) 965-4263; (f) (270) 965-3085; becmus@apex.com;www.clement mineral.museum.com; (c) Crittenden

Private non-profit/ 1997/ staff: 2(f); 3(p); 11(v)

HISTORY MUSEUM

PROGRAMS: Community Outreach; Exhibits; Guided Tours; School-Based Curriculum

COLLECTIONS: [1920-1980] 50,000 minerals.

HOURS: Yr T-Sa 9-3

ADMISSION: $3

3200
Crittenden County Genealogical Society, Inc.
222 W Carlisle St, 42064 [PO Box 61, 42064]; (c) Crittenden

1991/ Board of Directors/ staff: 2(v)/ members: 90/publication: *Census Crittenden Co, 1860 & 1870*

GENEALOGICAL SOCIETY: Collects genealogical materials for members and others with Crittenden County family.

PROGRAMS: Publication

COLLECTIONS: Genealogical research material and family histories.

HOURS: Apr-Oct T-Sa 10-4

ADMISSION: No charge

3201
Crittenden County Historical Society: Bob Wheeler Museum
222 W Carlisle St, 42064 [PO Box 23, 42064]; (c) Crittenden

1967/ staff: 1(f); 1(p); 80(v)/ members: 100

HISTORICAL SOCIETY; HISTORY MUSEUM

PROGRAMS: Annual Meeting; Community Outreach; Exhibits; Family Programs; Festivals; Guided Tours; Lectures; Living History

COLLECTIONS: Farm related tools; doll collection; attached log cabin.

HOURS: Apr-Oct 10-4

ADMISSION: No charge

MASON

3202
Grant County Historical Society, Inc.
William Arnold Dr, 41054 [PO Box 33, 41054-9998]; (p) (606) 428-1717, (606) 823-2051; cgi.rootsweb.com/~genbbs.cgi/USA/Ky/GCHS Obits; (c) Grant

Private non-profit/ 1976/ staff: 15(v)/ members: 320

HISTORICAL SOCIETY: Offers monthly programs about historical activities in the area; publishes and disseminates reference books of cemeteries, court records, and newspapers; marks historical sites; shows museum; writes family histories.

PROGRAMS: Annual Meeting; Guided Tours; Lectures; Publication

COLLECTIONS: [1820-1920] Society owns and shows artifact collections in William Arnold Log House.

MAYSVILLE

3203
Mason County Museum
215 Sutton St, 41056; (p) (606) 564-5865; (f) (606) 564-4372; masonmuseum@ maysvilleky.net; webpages.maysvilleky.net/masonmuseum; (c) Mason

Private non-profit/ 1878/ Maysville and Mason County Library, Historical and Scientific Association/ staff: 3(f); 6(p); 35(v)/ members: 400/publication: *Bicentennial Minutes; Towns of Mason County: Their Past In Pictures; Maysville, KY: From Past To Present In Pictures*

ART MUSEUM; HISTORIC SITE; HISTORICAL SOCIETY; HISTORY MUSEUM; LIBRARY AND/OR ARCHIVES: Preserves and displays historical artifacts and records of the area.

PROGRAMS: Annual Meeting; Community Outreach; Exhibits; Film/Video; Guided Tours; Publication; Reenactments; Research Library/Archives; School-Based Curriculum

COLLECTIONS: [1784-present] Museum with permanent and rotating exhibits, art gallery, and research library which are of particular historical interest to Maysville and Ohio Counties, and Kentucky in general.

HOURS: Feb-Mar T-Sa 10-4; Apr-Dec M-Sa 10-4; Jan Closed

ADMISSION: $2.50, Student $0.50; Library $3.50/$.50

MIDDLESBORO

3204
Bell County Historical Society and Museum
207 N 20th St, 40965 [PO Box 1344, 40965]; (p) (606) 242-0005; bellhist_society@hotmail.com; www.geocities.com/Heartland/Hills/1810; (c) Bell

Private non-profit/ 1998/ Board of Directors/ staff: 15(v)/ members: 150/publication: *Gateway*

GENEALOGICAL SOCIETY; HISTORICAL SOCIETY; HISTORY MUSEUM: Collects and displays Bell County history.

PROGRAMS: Exhibits; Publication

COLLECTIONS: [1850-present] Artifacts relating to Native American culture, coal mining, logging and manufacturing industries, 500 photos.

HOURS: Yr M, W, F 10-2

ADMISSION: Donations accepted

3205
Middlesborough-Bell County Public Library
126 S 20th St, 40965 [PO Drawer 1677, 40965]; (p) (606) 248-4812; (f) (606) 248-8766; mborolib@tcnet.net; (c) Bell

1912/ Board of Trustees/ staff: 4(f); 3(p); 2(v)

LIBRARY AND/OR ARCHIVES: Public library with local and area history collection.

COLLECTIONS: Books, microfilm, local newspapers, and area census reports.

HOURS: Yr M-Th 9-7, F 9-7, S 10-4

MORGANTOWN

3206
Hammers House
2055 Main St, 42261 [227 W Porter, 42261]; (p) (502) 526-2300, (502) 526-4325; (c) Butler

Private non-profit/ 1880/ staff: 1(f)

HISTORIC SITE: Maintains historic house.

PROGRAMS: Community Outreach; Exhibits; Family Programs; Guided Tours; Lectures; Living History

COLLECTIONS: 1880 house with antique furnishings, owned by Hammers family since 1932.

HOURS: Yr by appt

MOUNT VERNON

3207
Rockcastle County Historical Society, Inc.
85 Spring St, 40456 [PO Boc 930, 40456]; (c) Rockcastle

Private non-profit/ 1984/ staff: 1(p); 1(v)/ members: 215

HISTORICAL SOCIETY: Collects census records and genealogical materials for public use.

COLLECTIONS: Census of Rockcastle and surrounding counties; Family file records.

HOURS: Yr M-Th 10-3

ADMISSION: No charge

MUNFORDVILLE

3208
Hart County Historical Society
109 Main St, 42765 [PO Box 606, 42765]; (p) (270) 524-0101; (c) Hart

Private non-profit/ 1969/ Board of Directors/ staff: 1(p); 8(v)/ members: 565

GENEALOGICAL SOCIETY; HISTORIC SITE; HISTORICAL SOCIETY; HISTORY MUSEUM; RESEARCH CENTER

PROGRAMS: Community Outreach; Exhibits; Publication; Reenactments; Research Library/Archives

COLLECTIONS: [Civil War] Civil War artifacts and family research material.

HOURS: Yr M-Sa 10-4

ADMISSION: No charge

MURRAY

3209
Murray Ledger and Times
1001 Whitnell Ave, 42071; (p) (270) 753-1916; (f) (270) 753-1927; mlt@murrayledger.com; (c) Calloway

State/ 1869/ Wrather Museum, Murray State Univ/ staff: 2(f); 2(p); 12(v)

HISTORY MUSEUM

PROGRAMS: Annual Meeting; Facility Rental

COLLECTIONS: Artifacts of the Jackson Purchase of KY.

HOURS: Yr M-Sa 9-4

3210
National Scouting Museum of the Boy Scouts of America, Inc.
16th & Calloway St, 42071 [Murray State University, PO Box 9, 42071]; (p) (502) 762-3383; (f) (502) 762-3189; (c) Calloway

Private non-profit/ 1986/ staff: 5(f); 30(p); 20(v)/ members: 397

HISTORY MUSEUM: Collects, preserves, and interprets the history of scouting; supports scouting programs.

PROGRAMS: Exhibits; Facility Rental; Guided Tours; Research Library/Archives; School-Based Curriculum

COLLECTIONS: [1910-present] Numerous scouting-related objects. Largest collection of Norman Rockwell scouting paintings. Library includes original scouting literature and personal papers of the four founders of scouting.

ADMISSION: $5, Children $4, Seniors $3.50; $3.50 Scouts

3211
Wrather West Kentucky Museum
Murray State Univ, 42071 [PO Box 9, 42071]; (p) (502) 762-4771; (f) (502) 762-4485; kate.reeves@murraystate.edu; www.murraystate.edu/info/wrather/wrather.htm; (c) Calloway

1982/ University and Board of Representatives/ staff: 2(f)

HISTORIC SITE: First building on campus; opened in 1924 as Murray Normal School; dedicated as a museum in 1982.

PROGRAMS: Community Outreach; Exhibits; Guided Tours; Lectures

COLLECTIONS: [Mid 19th c-present] Artifacts pertaining to the West KY and Jackson Purchase Area.

HOURS: Yr M-F 8:30-4, Sa 10-1

NEW HAVEN

3212
Kentucky Railway Museum
136 S Main St, 40051 [PO Box 240, 40051]; (p) (502) 549-5470; (f) (502) 549-5472; kyrail@bardstown.com; www.rrhistorical.com/krm; (c) Nelson

Private non-profit/ 1957/ staff: 3(f); 2(p); 40(v)/ members: 375/publication: *The Station Lamp*

LIBRARY AND/OR ARCHIVES; RAILROAD MUSEUM: Operating and stationary aspects of KY railroad history, including operating steam and diesel powered engines.

PROGRAMS: Annual Meeting; Community Outreach; Exhibits; Facility Rental; Family Programs; Film/Video; Interpretation; Publication

COLLECTIONS: [1902-1950] Rail equipment, tools, documents, and artifacts from various railroads operating in KY, primarily since 1900.

HOURS: Yr M-Sa 9-5, Su 12-5

ADMISSION: $3

OWENSBORO

3213
International Bluegrass Music Museum
101 Daviess St, 42303 [207 E 2nd St, 42303]; (p) (270) 926-7891; (f) (270) 686-7863; (c) Daviess

Private non-profit/ 1991/ staff: 1(f); 2(p); 25(v)/ members: 400

HISTORY MUSEUM: Collects, preserves, and shares the heritage of bluegrass music.

PROGRAMS: Community Outreach; Concerts; Exhibits; Facility Rental; Family Programs; Guided Tours; Lectures; Research Library/Archives; School-Based Curriculum; Theatre

COLLECTIONS: [1930-present] Includes instruments, music, memorabilia, and clothing; archive houses bluegrass magazines, newspapers, and regional newsletters as well as LPs, 78 rpm records, cassettes, and CDs.

HOURS: Yr T-Sa 10-4, Su 1-4

ADMISSION: $2, Student $1, Seniors $1

3214
Kentucky Room, Daviess County Public Library
450 Griffith Ave, 42301; (p) (270) 684-0211; (f) (270) 684-0218; kentucky@dcpl.lib.ky.us; www.dcpl.lib.ky.us; (c) Daviess

Joint/ 1911/ Board of Directors; Daviess County Public Library Taxing District/ staff: 3(f); 1(p)

Collects and preserves collections of local and state historical and genealogical resources.

COLLECTIONS: [1792-present] Local and state history with genealogical materials related to KY and its residents.

HOURS: Yr M-Th 9-9, F 9-8, Sa 9-6, Su 1-5

3215
Owensboro Area Museum of Science and History
220 Daviess St, 42303; (p) (270) 687-2732; (f) (270) 687-2738; (c) Daviess

Private non-profit/ 1966/ Board of Directors/ staff: 4(f); 4(p); 20(v)/ members: 400

HISTORY MUSEUM; NATURAL HISTORY MUSEUM: Collects, preserves, and interprets artifacts of the material culture and natural history of Western KY with an emphasis on the Ohio River region; maintains a hands-on science learning center.

PROGRAMS: Community Outreach; Exhibits; Facility Rental; Family Programs; Festivals; Guided Tours; Interpretation; Lectures

COLLECTIONS: [1700-present] 25,000 artifacts including textiles, photos, documents, and household items from all periods of KY history, especially 1840-1920.

HOURS: Yr T-Sa 10-5; Su 1-4

3216
Owensboro Museum of Fine Art
901 Frederica St, 42301; (p) (270) 685-3181; (f) (270) 685-3181; (c) Daviess

Private non-profit/ 1977/ staff: 6(f); 7(p); 500(v)/ members: 1300

ART MUSEUM; HISTORIC SITE: Organizes exhibitions documenting American cultural traditions; features changing exhibitions of national and international scope; decorative arts wing housed in Civil War era mansion; Stained Glass Gallery and Atrium Sculpture Court.

PROGRAMS: Community Outreach; Exhibits; Family Programs; Festivals; Film/Video; Guided Tours; Lectures; School-Based Curriculum

COLLECTIONS: [19th-20th c] American and European fine and decorative arts; 20th c studio art glass and American folk art.

HOURS: Yr T-F 10-4, Sa-Su 1-4

ADMISSION: Donations requested

OWENTON

3217
Owen County Historical Society
206 N Main St, 40359 [PO Box 84, 40359]; (p) (502) 484-2321; (c) Owen

Private non-profit/ 1963/ staff: 30(v)/ members: 184/publication: *Gone But Not Forgotten; Sweet Owen; Pictorial History of Owen County*

GENEALOGICAL SOCIETY; HISTORIC PRESERVATION AGENCY; HISTORICAL SOCIETY; HISTORY MUSEUM: Offers publications, displays, and programs related to county history.

PROGRAMS: Annual Meeting; Community Outreach; Exhibits; Family Programs; Festivals; Living History

COLLECTIONS: [1800s-present] Artifacts of farming and rural family life including work, home, church, stores, and medical artifacts; public library maintains genealogical reference materials.

HOURS: Library: Yr M-Sa

OWINGSVILLE

3218
Owingsville Banking Company
49 W Main St, 40360 [PO Box 575, 40360]; (p) (606) 674-6317; Jimbnkr@aol.com; (c) Bath

Private for-profit/ 1893

HISTORIC SITE: Commercial bank operating in a house attributed to renowned architect Benjamin Latrobe.

HOURS: Yr M-F 8:30-3:30, Sa 8:30-12

PADUCAH

3219
Alben W. Barkley Museum
533 Madison St, 42001; (p) (502) 444-9356, (502) 443-8161

1852/ Private non-profit/ staff: 20(v)

COLLECTIONS: [1850-Present] Barkely collection, period furniture, Saunders artifacts; Pictorial record of prominent Paducahans, 1875-1950; Paducah Police Court records, 1870-1900; Furniture and records from old City Hall.

HOURS: Seasonal

3220
Allen Barkley Young Historians, Inc.
533 Madison St, 42001 [502 N 7th St, 42001]; (c) McCracken

Private non-profit/ 1965/ staff: 10(v)

GARDEN; GENEALOGICAL SOCIETY; HISTORIC SITE; HISTORICAL SOCIETY; HISTORY MUSEUM; HOUSE MUSEUM; RESEARCH CENTER

PROGRAMS: Community Outreach; Exhibits; Facility Rental; Garden Tours; Guided Tours; Interpretation; Research Library/Archives; School-Based Curriculum

COLLECTIONS: [Mid 19th c-present]

HOURS: Yr Sa-Su 1-4 and by appt

ADMISSION: $1, Student $0.50

3221
McCracken County Genealogical and Historical Society
[PO Box 7651, 42002]; (c) McCracken

1977/ members: 45

GENEALOGICAL SOCIETY; HISTORICAL SOCIETY

PROGRAMS: Lectures; Publication

3222
Museum of the American Quilter's Society
215 Jefferson St, 42002 [PO Box 1540, 42002]; (p) (270) 442-8856; (f) (270) 442-5448; maqmus@apex.net; quiltmuseum.com; (c) McCracken

1991/ Board of Directors/ staff: 7(f); 9(p); 175(v)

HISTORY MUSEUM: Celebrates quiltmaking of past and present; exhibits contemporary quilts; offers educational programs.

PROGRAMS: Community Outreach; Concerts; Elder's Programs; Exhibits; Facility Rental; Family Programs; Festivals; Guided Tours; Interpretation; Lectures; Living History; Publication; Research Library/Archives

COLLECTIONS: [1980-present] 187 quilts, including award winning masterpieces.

HOURS: Yr M-Sa 10-5; Apr-Oct Su 1-5

ADMISSION: $5, Student $3; Group rates

3223
Tilghman Heritage Foundation, Inc.
631 KY Ave, 42002 [PO Box 8221, 42002]; (p) (502) 442-1058; (f) (502) 442-1049; (c) McCracken

Private non-profit/ 1992/ staff: 10(v)/ members: 125

HERITAGE AREA; PROFESSIONAL ORGANIZATION: Interprets Paducah and the Jackson Purchase's antebellum history; restores the historic landmark, former home of Gen. Lloyd Tilghman.

PROGRAMS: Exhibits; Facility Rental; Festivals; Guided Tours; Interpretation; Lectures; Living History; Reenacts

COLLECTIONS: [1852-1865] Civil War artifacts.

ADMISSION: $3.50, Children $2, Seniors $3

3224
William Clark Market House Museum
121 S 2nd St, 42002 [PO Box 12, 42002]; (p) (270) 443-7759; (c) McCracken

Private non-profit/ 1968/ staff: 1(f); 1(p); 25(v)

HISTORIC SITE; HISTORY MUSEUM: 4,800 sq ft of exhibits featuring railroad, river, regional, historical, biographical, Civil War, and local business artifacts, and prominent citizens of the area.

PROGRAMS: Annual Meeting; Community Outreach; Exhibits; Festivals; Guided Tours; Interpretation; Living History; School-Based Curriculum

COLLECTIONS: [1827-present] Local historical items including Civil War, WW I and WW II, railroad, prominent people, Victoriana, 1880s

drugstore, William Clark items.

HOURS: Mar-Dec M-Sa 12-4; Jan-Feb Closed

ADMISSION: $1.50, Children $0.50

PARIS

3225
Hopewell Museum
800 Pleasant St, 40361; (p) (606) 986-7274; hopemuse@bellsouth.net; (c) Bourbon

1995/ Historic Paris-Bourbon Co., Inc/ staff: 1(f), 85(v)/ members: 151

HISTORY MUSEUM: Collects, preserves, and interprets the historic and artistic heritage of Paris and Bourbon County.

PROGRAMS: Annual Meeting; Exhibits; Facility Rental; Family Programs; Guided Tours; Interpretation; Lectures; Publication; School-Based Curriculum

COLLECTIONS: Artifacts, furniture, manuscripts, maps, portraits, and paintings, newspapers, rare volumes, photos, and period clothing.

HOURS: Feb-Dec W-Sa 12-5, Su 2-4

ADMISSION: $2

PERRYVILLE

3226
Perryville Battlefield Preservation Association
[PO Box 65, 40468]; (p) (606) 332-1862; (f) (606) 332-1865; www.paracomm.com/perryville/; (c) Boyce

Private non-profit/ 1991/ Board of Directors/ staff: 1(f)/ members: 400

BATTLEFIELD; HISTORIC PRESERVATION AGENCY; HISTORIC SITE: Preserves, interprets, and restores KY's largest Civil War battlefield.

PROGRAMS: Community Outreach; Exhibits; Festivals; Living History; Reenactments

COLLECTIONS: [Civil War] Goods from a general store that was owned by the same family for a century: farm implements, clothing, pharmaceutical wares, household goods, and glass-plate negatives.

HOURS: Apr-Oct

PIKEVILLE

3227
Augusta Dils York Mansion
209 Elm St, 41501 [PO Box 2913, 41502]; (p) (606) 432-3092

1912/ staff: 2(v)

COLLECTIONS: [Civil War] Furniture from the last century; Old books: Byron, Shelley, Keats, Milton, Shakespeare, old law books and other collections.

HOURS: By appt

3228
Pike County Society for Historical and Genealogical Research
Allara Library, Pikeville College, 41502 [PO Box 97, 41502]; (p) (606) 432-9371; (f) (606) 432-9372; cmaddox@pc.edu; (c) Pike

Private non-profit/ 1994/ staff: 4(v)/ members:

200/publication: *Pike County Historical Review*

GENEALOGICAL SOCIETY; HISTORICAL SOCIETY; LIBRARY AND/OR ARCHIVES: Collects, preserves, and makes available material on the local history of the community and the genealogy of its residents.

PROGRAMS: Community Outreach; Exhibits; Lectures; Publication; Research Library/Archives

COLLECTIONS: Family genealogies, serials, photos, books, and clippings.

HOURS: Yr M-F 12-4

POINTSVILLE

3229
Johnson County Historical and Genealogical Association
444 Main, 41240 [PO Box 788, 41240]; (p) (606) 789-4355; (f) (606) 789-6758; (c) Johnson

Private non-profit/ 1983/ members: 186/publication: *Highland Echo*

HISTORICAL SOCIETY

PROGRAMS: Publication

COLLECTIONS: Materials related to local, eastern KY, and Civil War.

PRESTONBURG

3230
Friends of the Samuel May House, Inc.
N Lake Dr, 41653 [PO Box 1460, 41653]; shatcher@kymtnnet.org; mayhouse.org; (c) Floyd

1993/ Board of Trustees/ staff: 1(v)/ members: 180

HISTORIC SITE; HOUSE MUSEUM: Restores house as a living history museum.

PROGRAMS: Annual Meeting; Exhibits; Interpretation; Living History

COLLECTIONS: [1817-1865]

HOURS: Yr by appt

ADMISSION: Donations requested

PRINCETON

3231
Adsmore Museum
304 N Jefferson St, 42445; (p) (270) 365-3114; (c) Caldwell

Private non-profit/ 1986/ Caldwell County Library District/ staff: 3(f); 8(p)

HOUSE MUSEUM; LIVING HISTORY/OUTDOOR MUSEUM: Interprets lifestyle of a prominent Western KY family from 1901-1914 through eight yearly thematic tours.

PROGRAMS: Community Outreach; Concerts; Exhibits; Guided Tours; Interpretation; Living History

COLLECTIONS: [1790s-1914] American furniture (1790s-1900s), textiles, clothing, decorative and personal accessories, family papers, portraits, photographs, and Smith, Kevil, Garrett, and Osborne family memorabilia.

HOURS: Yr T-Sa 11-4, Su 1:30-4

ADMISSION: $5, Student $1, Children $2, Se-

niors $4.50; Group rates

RICHMOND

3232
Fort Boonesborough State Park
4375 Boonesboro Rd, 40475; (p) (606) 527-3131; (f) (606) 527-3328; phil-gray@mail.state.ky.us; www.state.ky.us/agencies/parks/ftboones.htm; (c) Madison/Clark

1963/ KY Dept of Parks/ staff: 12(f); 16(p)

HISTORIC SITE; HISTORY MUSEUM; LIBRARY AND/OR ARCHIVES; LIVING HISTORY/OUTDOOR MUSEUM: Promotes living fort history with craft demonstrations; archive of river history; native botanical restorations; special events for schools and public; seminars and educational outreach; exhibit gallery.

PROGRAMS: Concerts; Exhibits; Facility Rental; Festivals; Interpretation; Living History; Reenactments; Research Library/Archives; School-Based Curriculum

COLLECTIONS: [1700-present] Objects and archives related to early Euro-American settlement of KY; local Native American artifacts; KY River history and navigation; indigenous plant species; history of Daniel Boone and the Transylvania Land Company.

HOURS: Yr Apr-Sept Daily 9-5; Oct-Mar W-Su 9-5

ADMISSION: $4.50, Children $3

3233
White Hall State Historic Site
500 White Hall Shrine Rd, 40475; (p) (606) 623-9178; (f) (606) 626-8489; (c) Madison

State/ 1968/ KY Dept of Parks/ staff: 5(f); 7(p)

HISTORIC SITE; HISTORY MUSEUM; HOUSE MUSEUM: Former home of Cassius M. Clay, ambassador to Russia during the Civil War.

PROGRAMS: Concerts; Facility Rental; Guided Tours; Interpretation

COLLECTIONS: [1860s-1903] Period furnishings and historic documents.

HOURS: Apr-Oct W-Su 9-5:30

ADMISSION: $4.50, Children $2.50

RUSSELLVILLE

3234
Bibb House, The
183 W 8th, 42276 [PO Box 116, 42276]; (p) (502) 726-2085

1817

COLLECTIONS: [1880] Belter sofa, Duncan Phyfe tables, KY Huntboard, Old Paris Porcelain; KY documents regarding slavery and emancipation

HOURS: Yr

3235
Logan County Genealogical Society, Inc.
Logan Co Archives, W 4th St, 42276 [PO Box 853, 42276]; (p) (270) 726-8179; (c) Logan

Private non-profit/ 1978/ Board of Trustees/ staff: 5(v)/ members: 30/publication: *Logan County, KY Marriages; Logan Co. Confeder-*

ate/Union Soldiers; Logan Co. Abstracts of Wills and Settlements

GENEALOGICAL SOCIETY: Organizes county records; publishes books; maintains archives; purchases books for public use; answers queries; helps researchers; teaches genealogical research classes; and sponsors programs.

PROGRAMS: Lectures; Publication; Research Library/Archives

COLLECTIONS: [1792-present] Archives: genealogical topics; 600 books in archives; 400 in Logan Co. Public Library.

HOURS: Yr M-F 8-3

ADMISSION: No

SCOTTSVILLE

3236
Allen County Historical and Genealogy Society
301 N 4th St, 42164 [PO Box 393, 42164]; (p) (502) 237-3759; (f) (502) 237-5304; (c) Allen

Private non-profit/ 1981/ staff: 25(v)/ members: 200

GENEALOGICAL SOCIETY; HISTORICAL SOCIETY: Provides a depository for county memorabilia and items of historical interest.

PROGRAMS: Community Outreach; Festivals; Guided Tours; Interpretation; Research Library/Archives

COLLECTIONS: [18th-20th c] Revolutionary War and Civil War pension papers, artifacts, photographs, maps, scrapbooks, newspapers, and genealogy books.

HOURS: Twice monthly and by appt

SLADE

3237
Gladdie Creek Cabin
Ctr of Red River Gorge Geologic Area, 40376 [USDA FS, 705 W College Ave, Stanton, 40380]; (p) (606) 663-2852; (f) (606) 663-9097; www.r8web.com/boone

SMITHLAND

3238
Livingston County Historical and Genealogical Society, Inc.
Livingston, 42081 [PO Box 138, 42081]; (p) (502) 928-4656; (c) Livingston

Private non-profit/ 1984/ staff: 1(p); 12(v)/ members: 125

GENEALOGICAL SOCIETY; HISTORY MUSEUM; HOUSE MUSEUM: Operate 1840 log cabin museum; large genealogical library; quarterly newsletter; sell local genealogy books.

PROGRAMS: Exhibits; Publication; Research Library/Archives

COLLECTIONS: [1850-1940] Photos, furniture, accessories for 1840s log cabin; extensive genealogy library with trained genealogist available to assist research.

HOURS: Yr M-F 1-4

ADMISSION: No charge

SOMERSET

3239
Jacques Timothe Boucher Sieur de Montbrun Heritage Society
140 W Bolton Dr, 42503

Private non-profit/ 1975/ staff: 1(v)/ members: 300

GENEALOGICAL SOCIETY; HISTORICAL SOCIETY: Promotes study of French Lick area of middle TN, awareness of Timothy Demonbreun's role in TN, and American history.

PROGRAMS: Annual Meeting; Exhibits; Film/Video; Guided Tours; Lectures; Publication; Research

SOUTH UNION

3240
South Union Shaker Village
850 Shaker Museum Rd, 42283 [PO Box 30, 42283]; (p) (800) 811-8379; (f) (270) 542-7558; shakmus@logantele.com; www.logantele.com/~shakmus/; (c) Logan

Private non-profit/ 1960/ Shakertown Revisited, Inc/ staff: 4(f); 5(p); 30(v)/ members: 300

HERITAGE AREA; HISTORIC SITE: Preserves and maintains site of the former Shaker society; protects its buildings, landscape, folklife, and material culture.

PROGRAMS: Community Outreach; Exhibits; Facility Rental; Festivals; Guided Tours; Interpretation; Lectures; Living History; Research Library/Archives

COLLECTIONS: [1850-1900] Variety of South Union and general Shaker material culture including manuscripts, photos, baskets, textiles, and the largest collection of Western Shaker furniture.

HOURS: Mar 1-Dec 1 M-Sa 9-4, Su 1-4
ADMISSION: $4, Children $1

SPRINGFIELD

3241
Lincoln Homestead State Park
5079 Lincoln Park Rd, 40069; (p) (606) 336-7461; (f) (606) 336-0659

1946/ State/ staff: 1(f)

Maintains two houses, a replica blacksmith shop, and the Mordecai Lincoln House.

COLLECTIONS: [1786-1806] Cabinet and beds said to be made by Thomas Lincoln; tools; household items.

HOURS: May-Sept

STANFORD

3242
William Whitley House State Historic Site
625 Wm Whitney Rd, 40484; (p) (606) 355-2881; (f) (606) 355-2778; (c) Lincoln

State/ 1948/ KY Dept of Parks/ staff: 3(f); 2(p); 5(v)

HISTORIC SITE; HOUSE MUSEUM: Former home of pioneers William and Esther Whitley; built between 1785-1792; first brick house West of the Allegheny Mountains; site of first circular race track in America.

PROGRAMS: Facility Rental; Guided Tours; Interpretation; School-Based Curriculum

COLLECTIONS: [1785-1820] Period artifacts; family artifacts including long rifle, powder horn, Indian strap, textiles, and hand-forged pieces.

HOURS: Mar 16-May 30, Sept-Dec 31 T-Su 9-5; June 1-Sept Daily 9-5
ADMISSION: $3.50, Children $2, Seniors $3

TOLLESBORO

3243
Himes General Store
State Route 10, 41189 [RR 1 Box 807, 41189]; (p) (606) 798-3301; (f) (606) 798-3301; (c) Lewis

1892/ staff: 2(f); 1(p)

HISTORIC SITE: Oldest continually operating general store in Northern KY.

PROGRAMS: Living History
HOURS: Yr M-F 7-7, Sa 8-7

TOMPKINSVILLE

3244
Old Mulkey Meetinghouse State Historic Site
1819 Old Mulkey Rd, 42167; (p) (207) 487-8481; (f) (270) 487-8121; cindy.thrasher@mail.state.ky.us; www.state.ky.us/agencies/parks/mulkey.htm; (c) Monroe

State/ 1931/ KY Dept of Parks/ staff: 2(f); 1(v)/ members: 1

HISTORIC SITE; STATE PARK: Log church erected in 1804 during a religious revival; pioneer graveyard with graves of Revolutionary War veterans, and Hannah Boone (sister of Daniel Boone); park facilities.

PROGRAMS: Concerts; Facility Rental; Family Programs

VERSAILLES

3245
Jack Jouett House
255 Craig's Creek Pike, 40383 [255 Craigs Creek, 40383]; (p) (606) 873-7902

1797/ Woodford County Fiscal Court

COLLECTIONS: [1797-1809] Artifacts, memorabila, and original painting of Matthew Jouett.
HOURS: Seasonal

3246
Kentucky Hemp Growers Cooperative Museum and Library
149 Lexington St, 40383; (p) (606) 873-8957; (f) (606) 873-8957; kyhempmuse@aol.com; (c) Woodford

Private non-profit/ 1994/ Board of Directors/ staff: 1(f); 2(p)

HISTORIC PRESERVATION AGENCY: Preserves history of industrial hemp growing; offers educational programs.

PROGRAMS: Community Outreach; Exhibits; Film/Video; Lectures; Research Library/Archives

COLLECTIONS: Several rare pieces of agricultural equipment used for hemp harvesting and processing; documents and publications on industrial hemp industry, processing, historic and modern uses, and future potential.

HOURS: Yr T-F 12-6, Sa 10-4
ADMISSION: No charge

3247
Woodford County Heritage Committee
255 Craigs Creek Rd, 40383; (p) (606) 873-7902; (c) Woodford

Private non-profit/ staff: 1(p); 15(v)

HERITAGE AREA; HOUSE MUSEUM: Helps to maintain the historic Jack Jovett House.

PROGRAMS: Concerts; Guided Tours; Living History

COLLECTIONS: Portraits by KY painters, including Matthew Jovett and Henry Clay's favorite portrait of himself.

HOURS: Apr-Oct 1 Sa, Su 1-5 and by appt
ADMISSION: Donations accepted

3248
Woodford County Historical Society
121 Rose Hill, 40383; (p) (606) 873-6786; woodford@qx.net; (c) Woodford

1966/ staff: 1(p); 10(v)/ members: 225

GENEALOGICAL SOCIETY; HISTORICAL SOCIETY: Maintains genealogical and historical library and a small museum.

PROGRAMS: Annual Meeting; Exhibits; Lectures; Research Library/Archives

COLLECTIONS: Native American artifacts and Victorian clothing from Woodford County.

HOURS: Yr
ADMISSION: No charge

VINE GROVE

3249
Ancestral Trails Historical Society, Inc.
127 W Main St, 40175 [PO Box 573, 40175-0573]; (p) (270) 351-4757; www.aths.com; (c) Hardin

Private non-profit/ 1976/ staff: 15(v)/ members: 715

GENEALOGICAL SOCIETY; HISTORICAL SOCIETY: Gathers, processes, and preserves genealogical and historical information several KY counties and Harrison County in.

PROGRAMS: Monthly Meeting; Publication

WASHINGTON

3250
Harriet Beecher Stowe Slavery to Freedom Museum
[PO Box 184, 41096]; (p) (606) 759-4860; (c) Mason

Private non-profit/ 1997/ Board of Directors/ staff: 8(v)/ members: 30

HISTORICAL SOCIETY

PROGRAMS: Exhibits; Festivals; Guided Tours; Interpretation

COLLECTIONS: [1800-1865] Displays of slave documents, various editions of Uncle Tom's Cabin, slave shackle, books written by and about Harriet Beecher Stowe, pictures of and her Family; quilt she used.

HOURS: Mar-Dec M-F Sa-Su 11-4:30

ADMISSION: $1

WHITLEY CITY

3251
McCreary County Historical and Genealogical Society, Inc.
Main St, 42653 [PO Box 400, 42653]; (p) (606) 354-2946; ktrammell@highland.net; (c) McCreary

1996/ Membership/ staff: 20(v)/ members: 80

GENEALOGICAL SOCIETY; HISTORICAL SOCIETY: Preserves history, culture, and folklore of county.

PROGRAMS: Community Outreach; Festivals; Lectures; Publication

COLLECTIONS: [1912-present] Traveling folklife exhibit.

HOURS: Apr-Dec T-Su 8-5

ADMISSION: No charge

WICKLIFFE

3252
Wickliffe Mounds Research Center
94 Green St, 42087 [PO Box 155, 42087]; (p) (270) 335-3681; wmounds@brtc.net; campus.murraystate.edu/org/wmrc.wmrc.htm; (c) Ballard

State/ 1932/ Murray State Univ/ staff: 4(f); 3(p); 6(v)/ members: 20

ARCHAEOLOGICAL SITE/MUSEUM: Studies, interprets, and preserves the Wickliffe Mounds site, a Native American village site occupied AD 1100-1350.

PROGRAMS: Community Outreach; Exhibits; Guided Tours; Interpretation

COLLECTIONS: [AD 1100-1350 (Mississippian)] Archaeological specimens recovered from excavations of the Wickliffe Mounds site.

HOURS: Mar-Nov Daily 9-4:30; Dec-Feb M-F

WILLIAMSTOWN

3253
Grant County News, The
151 N Main St, 41097 [PO Box 247, 41097]; (p) (606) 824-3343; (f) (606) 824-5888; grantnews@comtechusa.net; grantky.com; (c) Grant

1906/ Landmark Community Newspapers, Inc/ staff: 9(f); 3(p)/publication: *Footsteps of the Past*

HISTORIC SITE; LIBRARY AND/OR ARCHIVES: Originally named the Williamson Courier (1870-1906); name changed 1906; community news source for the county; houses old newspaper archives.

PROGRAMS: Community Outreach; Publication

COLLECTIONS: [1872-present] Newspaper archives.

HOURS: Yr M-F 8-5 and by appt

WINCHESTER

3254
Holly Rood Clark Mansion
28 Beckner St next to the library, 40391 [c/o Robert Coney, 8 Windridge Dr, 40391]; (p) (606) 744-6616

WOODBURY

3255
Green River Museum
Off Hwy 403, 42288 [PO Box 111, 42288]; (p) (502) 526-2391

LOUISIANA

ABBEVILLE

3256
Abbeville Cultural and Historical Alliance
108 S State St, 70511 [PO Box 698, 70511-0698]; (p) (318) 898-4114; (f) (318) 893-4119; vivacadi@bellsouth.net; (c) Vermilion

Private non-profit/ 1998/ staff: 2(p); 12(v)/ members: 4

ALLIANCE OF HISTORICAL AGENCIES; ART MUSEUM; HISTORICAL SOCIETY; RESEARCH CENTER: Provides an art gallery dedicated to exhibiting local artists, a photography exhibit of areas around the world where Acadians once lived, and history of the parish.

PROGRAMS: Community Outreach; Exhibits; Guided Tours; Lectures; Research Library/Archives; School-Based Curriculum; Theatre

HOURS: Yr T-Sa 11-4

ALEXANDRIA

3257
Alexandria Historical and Genealogical Library
503 Washington St, 71301; (p) (318) 487-8556; (c) Rapides

Private non-profit/ 1976/ Library and Museum Association/ staff: 1(f); 2(v)

LIBRARY AND/OR ARCHIVES

PROGRAMS: Research Library/Archives

COLLECTIONS: All periods LA history, portraits, archives of original colonies, research materials on all states east of the Mississippi River, foreign research, Spanish legatos, French superior court records, census, CDs.

HOURS: Yr T-Sa 10-4

ADMISSION: No charge

3258
Kent House
3601 Bayou Rapides Rd, 71303; (p) (318) 487-5998; (f) (318) 442-4154; www.kenthouse.org

3259
Louisiana History Museum
503 Washington, 71301; (p) (318) 487-8556; (c) Rapides

Private non-profit/ 1996/ Library and Museum Association/ staff: 1(f); 1(p)

HISTORY MUSEUM: Museum dedicated to LA history.

PROGRAMS: Exhibits; Guided Tours; Lectures

COLLECTIONS: Collections relating to Native Americans, Spanish, and French eras, plantation culture, and city history.

ADMISSION: No charge

ANGOLA

3260
Louisiana State Penitentiary Museum
Hwy 66, 70712 [Gen. Delivery, 70712]; (f) (225) 655-2319; (c) W. Feliciana

Private non-profit/ 1998/ staff: 1(f); 3(p)

Preserves the history of LA penal system.

COLLECTIONS: [1835-present] Original electric chair, prison made weapons, reproductions of striped uniforms worn by inmates, inmate record books dating to 1889, guard's weapons, and old guard uniforms.

HOURS: Yr

ARCADIA

3261
Civil War Naval Museum
153 Museum Rd, 71001; (p) (318) 263-8247; (f) (318) 263-3852; www.arcadialouisiana.org; (c) Bienville

Private non-profit/ 1995/ staff: 1(f); 1(p)/publication: *North/South Naval Images*

HISTORY MUSEUM

PROGRAMS: Exhibits; Interpretation; Lectures; Publication; Research Library/Archives

COLLECTIONS: [Civil War] Civil War warships and oral and written history.

HOURS: Yr Th-Sa 10-4, Su 1-4

AVERY ISLAND

3262
McIlhenny Company and Avery Island, Inc., Archives, The
General Delivery, Hwy 329, 70513; (p) (337) 365-8173; (f) (337) 369-6326; archives@TABASCO.com; www.TABASCO.com; (c) Iberia

Private for-profit/ 1993/ McIlhenney Company and Avery Island, Inc./ staff: 1(f)

CORPORATE ARCHIVES/MUSEUM: Houses documents and artifacts concerning the history of Tabasco Brand Pepper Sauce, the Avery and McIlhenny families, Avery Island.

PROGRAMS: Research Library/Archives

COLLECTIONS: [1800-present] 550 file drawers and over 225 archival boxes of family and business correspondence, photos, and artifacts.

HOURS: By appt

ADMISSION: No charge

BATON ROUGE

3263
Foundation for Historical Louisiana
Old Govenor's Mansion, 502 N Blvd, 70821 [PO Box 908, 70821-0908]; (p) (225) 387-2464; (f) (228) 343-3989; Fhistorica@aol.com; www.fhl.org; (c) East Baton Rouge

HISTORIC PRESERVATION AGENCY; HISTORIC SITE; HISTORICAL SOCIETY; HISTORY MUSEUM; HOUSE MUSEUM; RESEARCH CENTER: Preserves the cultural and architectural history of LA, located in the historic Old Governor's Mansion.

PROGRAMS: Exhibits; Facility Rental; Guided Tours; Lectures; Reenactments; Research Library/Archives

COLLECTIONS: [1930-1960] Period furnishings and antiques from the various governors that have resided in the Mansion; vintage clothing, silver, and china.

HOURS: Yr T, Su 1-4, Th 10-4

ADMISSION: $4, Student $3, Children $2, Seniors $3

3264
L.S.U. Textile and Costume Gallery and Historic Collection
Tower Dr, Louisiana State University, 70808 [School of Human Ecology, Louisiana State Univ, 70808]; (p) (225) 388-6992, (225) 388-2403; (f) (225) 388-2697; textile@unixl.sncc.lsu.edu; www.sun.huec.lsu.edu/htcc.html; (c) East Baton Rouge

State/ 1930/ Louisiana State University/ staff: 3(p)/ members: 118/publication: *Stitches in Time*

ART MUSEUM; HISTORY MUSEUM; RESEARCH CENTER: Devoted to the promotion of textiles and apparel through teaching, research, preservation, and exhibition.

PROGRAMS: Annual Meeting; Exhibits; Guided Tours; Interpretation; Lectures; Publication; Research Library/Archives; School-Based Curriculum

COLLECTIONS: [19th-20th c] Over 10,000 pieces ranging from prehistoric and ethnic textiles to contemporary fashion.

HOURS: Yr M-F 8-4:30

ADMISSION: No charge

3265
Le Comite des Archives de la Louisiane
[PO Box 44370, 70804]; (p) (225) 355-9906; jj.a.riffel@att.net; www.sec.state.la.us/archives/; (c) East Baton Rouge

Private non-profit/ 1978/ staff: 5(v)/ members: 559/publication: *Le Raconteur*

GENEALOGICAL SOCIETY; RESEARCH CENTER: Preserves historical records, promotes and facilitates the use of the Louisiana State archives for genealogical and historical research and publishes genealogical records.

PROGRAMS: Annual Meeting; Guided Tours; Lectures; Publication; Research

3266
Louisiana Association of Museums
[PO Box 4434, 70821-4434]; (p) (225) 383-6800; (f) (225) 383-6880; info@louisianamuseums.org; www.louisianamuseums.org/; (c) East Baton Rouge

1979/ staff: 1(f)/ members: 250/publication: *Louisiana Museum*

ALLIANCE OF HISTORICAL AGENCIES: Facilitates better communication among museums and related organizations; strengthens

state museums so that they may better serve their communities.

3267
Louisiana Office of State Parks
1051 N Third St, 70802 [PO Box 44426, 70804]; (p) (225) 342-8111; (f) (225) 342-8107; parks@crt.state.la.us; www.lastateparks.com; (c) E Baton Rouge

State/ 1934/ State of LA/ staff: 325(f)

BATTLEFIELD; GARDEN; HISTORIC PRESERVATION AGENCY; LIVING HISTORY/OUTDOOR MUSEUM: To serve the people of LA and their visitors by preserving, protecting, and portraying historic and scientific sites of statewide importance.

PROGRAMS: Exhibits; Family Programs; Garden Tours; Guided Tours; Interpretation; Lectures; Living History; Reenactments

COLLECTIONS: [Pre-Columbian-1960] Wide variety of reproduction clothing, artifacts, furniture, Native American artifacts, and related cultural goods.

HOURS: Yr Daily Rec Site: 7-9; Historic Site: 9-5

3268
Louisiana Preservation Alliance
263 Third St, 70821 [PO Box 1587, 70821]; (p) (225) 344-6001; (f) (225) 344-7176; lapreserve@mindspring.com; (c) East Baton Rouge

Private non-profit/ 1979/ staff: 1(f); 1(p); 25(v)/ members: 900/publication: *Preservation Progress*

HISTORIC PRESERVATION AGENCY: Statewide historic preservation organization dedicated to the protection and promotion of LA's historic and cultural treasures.

PROGRAMS: Annual Meeting; Community Outreach; Guided Tours; Lectures; Publication

3269
Louisiana's Old State Capital
100 N Blvd at River Rd, 70801; (p) (225) 342-0500, (800) 488-2968; (f) (225) 342-0316; osc@sec.state.la.us; www.sec.state.la.us; (c) East Baton Rouge

State/ 1850/ Louisiana Secretary of State/ staff: 30(f); 10(p); 25(v)/ members: 140

HISTORIC SITE; HISTORY MUSEUM: Exhibits, classroom activities, and special events.

PROGRAMS: Exhibits; Facility Rental; Film/Video; Guided Tours; Lectures; Living History; Research Library/Archives; School-Based Curriculum

COLLECTIONS: Located in the restored 1850 Statehouse, 1 million feet of vintage film transferred to video, 2,000 artifacts and 10,000 photographs, with emphasis on political history.

HOURS: Yr T-Sa 10-4, Su 12-4

ADMISSION: $4, Student $2, Seniors $3

3270
LSU Rural Life Museum, The
4560 Essen Ln, 70809 [PO Box 80498, 70898]; (p) (225) 765-2437; (f) (225) 765-2639; rurallife.lsu.edu

1840/ LA State Univ/ staff: 6(f); 5(p); 205(v)

COLLECTIONS: [1800-1890] 20,000 artifacts; Slavery-related items and documents.

HOURS: Yr

3271
Magnolia Mound Plantation
2161 Nicholson Dr, 70802; (p) (225) 343-4955; (f) (225) 343-6739; magmound@aol.com; www.magnoliamound.org; (c) East Baton Rouge

City; Joint; Private non-profit/ 1966/ Friends of Magnolia Mound, Inc/ staff: 2(f); 8(p); 80(v)/ members: 130/publication: *The Magnolia Leaf*

HISTORIC SITE; HOUSE MUSEUM: Preserves, collects, and interprets the historic house and site as a demonstration of early plantation life in South LA.

PROGRAMS: Exhibits; Facility Rental; Family Programs; Guided Tours; Interpretation; Lectures; Living History; Publication; School-Based Curriculum

COLLECTIONS: [1800-1830] Furniture, ceramics, glass, metals, textiles, fine arts, religious, kitchen, toys, tools, books and photos.

HOURS: Yr T-Sa 10-4, Su 1-4

ADMISSION: $5, Student $2, Seniors $4

3272
Old Governor's Mansion
502 N Blvd, 70802 [502 N Blvd, 70802]; (p) (225) 344-5272

HOUSE MUSEUM

3273
Special Collections, LSU Libraries, Louisiana State University
LA State Univ, 70803-3300; (p) (225) 578-6544; (f) (225) 578-9425; www.lib.lsu.edu/special; (c) E Baton Rouge

State/ 1935/ LA State Univ/ staff: 23(f); 5(p)

LIBRARY AND/OR ARCHIVES: Collects, preserves, and makes available to researcher.

PROGRAMS: Exhibits; Research Library/Archives

COLLECTIONS: [19th c] Primary source materials, manuscripts, documents, books, and 18th c British books and natural history.

HOURS: Yr M-F 9-5, Sa

BERNICE

3274
Bernice Historical Society, Inc.
4th St & Louisiana Ave, 71222 [PO Box 186, 71222]; (p) (318) 285-9071; (f) (318) 285-9737; (c) Union

Private non-profit/ 1992/ Board of Directors/ staff: 1(p); 5(v)/ members: 82

HISTORIC SITE; HISTORICAL SOCIETY; HISTORY MUSEUM: Operates the 1899 Bernice Depot Museum for the preservation of railroad and area history.

PROGRAMS: Annual Meeting; Exhibits; Facility Rental; Publication; Theatre

COLLECTIONS: [Early 20th c] Rock Island Railroad memorabilia, early area artifacts, World War II items, genealogy collection, and toys and children's items.

HOURS: Yr M-F 10-12/1-3

ADMISSION: Donations accepted

BOSSIER CITY

3275
Bossier Parish Historical Center
2206 Beckett St, 71111; (p) (318) 746-7717;
(f) (318) 746-7768;
shannaf@netra.bossier.lib.la.us; (c) Bossier

1997/ Bossier Parish Library Board/ staff: 3(f);
2(p)

HISTORICAL SOCIETY; RESEARCH CENTER: Acquires and preserves items and documents related to local history, and educates through exhibits and programs.

PROGRAMS: Community Outreach; Exhibits; Guided Tours; Lectures; Research Library/ Archives

COLLECTIONS: [1200-1500, 1830-1950] Microfilm copies of Bossier Parish newspapers, hard copies of the Bossier Banner 1859-1994, documents, photographs, scrapbooks, books, oral histories, maps, models of historic structures, and artifacts related to Bossier Parish and its citizens.

HOURS: Winter: M-Th 9-9, F 9-6, Sa 9-5, Su 2-5; Summer: M-Th 9-8, F 9-6, Sa 9-5, Su 2-5

CLOUTIERVILLE

3276
Kate Chopin House
Bayou Folk Museum, 243 Hwy 495, 71416
[243 Hwy 495, 71416]; (p) (318) 379-2233,
(318) 357-7907

1809/ staff: 2(f); 1(p); 12(v)

COLLECTIONS: [1809-1884] Guns and war-related items, Civil War to Vietnam; Items that belonged to Kate Chopin; antique medical equipment, early farming tools.; Scrap books of information from newspapers, letters, etc. Large collection of newspaper head-lines dating back to 1893.

HOURS: Yr

COLUMBIA

3277
North Louisiana Folk Life, Inc., DBA Martin Homeplace
203 Martin Place Rd, 71418 [PO Box 196,
71418]; (p) (318) 649-6722; (f) (318) 679-
2874; (c) Caldwell

Private non-profit/ 1998/ staff: 1(f); 25(v)/
members: 125

GARDEN; HISTORIC SITE; HISTORY MUSEUM; HOUSE MUSEUM

PROGRAMS: Annual Meeting; Community Outreach; Family Programs; Guided Tours; Interpretation; Living History; School-Based Curriculum

COLLECTIONS: [1880-1940] Antique farm implements and homemade tools (1878-1940), hand made clothing, kitchen and laundry items, period furniture, and local history memorabilia.

HOURS: Yr T-F 9:30-4:30

3278
Schepis Museum, The
107 Main St, 71418 [PO Box 743, 71418]; (p)
(318) 649-9931; (f) (318) 649-0509;
mainst@caldwell.org; (c) Caldwell

Private non-profit/ 1994/ The Schepis Foundation/ staff: 1(p)/ members: 157

PROGRAMS: Community Outreach; Concerts; Exhibits; Facility Rental; School-Based Curriculum; Theatre

COLLECTIONS: Art guild paintings and sculpture, historical weapons, letters, and landscape photos.

HOURS: Yr T-Sa 10-4

ADMISSION: No charge

COVINGTON

3279
H.J. Smith's Son
308 N Columbia St, 70434 [PO Box 308,
70434]; (p) (504) 892-0460; (f) (504) 893-
6905; (c) Saint Tammany

Private non-profit/ 1876/ staff: 2(p)

HISTORIC SITE; HISTORY MUSEUM: Operates a museum focused on the history of Covington and the surrounding area.

PROGRAMS: Guided Tours

COLLECTIONS: [1900] Located in an original store building (1876), cast iron casket, gas pump, wagon, bottles, tools, and local photos.

HOURS: Yr M-T, Th-F 8:30-5, W 8:30, Sa 8:30-1

ADMISSION: No charge

CROWLEY

3280
Crystal Rice Plantation
6428 Airport Rd, 70526 [PO Box1425, 70526];
(p) (318) 783-6417; (f) (318) 788-0123; crystal_rice@compuserve.com; (c) Acadia

Private for-profit/ 1890/ staff: 7(f); 10(p)

HISTORIC SITE; HOUSE MUSEUM; LIVING HISTORY/OUTDOOR MUSEUM: Maintains a working rice and crawfish plantation (1890), the plantation home (1848), and a car museum.

PROGRAMS: Exhibits; Guided Tours

COLLECTIONS: [Antebellum-1900s] Antebellum furniture, glass, and silver; 20 antique cars.

HOURS: Yr M-F 10-4

ADMISSION: $6, Student $.50, Seniors $5.50

DESTREHAN

3281
River Road Historical Society
13034 River Rd, 70047 [PO Box 5, 70047]; (p)
(504) 764-9315; (f) (504) 725-1929; information@destrehanplantation.org; www.destrehanplantation.org; (c) Saint Charles

Private non-profit/ 1971/ staff: 3(f); 35(p); 4(v)/
members: 300/publication: Communique

HISTORIC SITE; HISTORICAL SOCIETY; HOUSE MUSEUM: Preserves and interprets the Destrehan Plantation and other historical sites along River Road, LA.

PROGRAMS: Annual Meeting; Community Outreach; Concerts; Elder's Programs; Exhibits; Facility Rental; Festivals; Guided Tours; Interpretation; Publication; Reenactments

COLLECTIONS: [1840-1860] Period furnishings and decorative arts.

HOURS: Yr Daily 9-4

ADMISSION: $8, Student $4, Children $2

3282
Destrehan Plantation
13034 River Rd, 70047 [PO Box 5, Luling,
70070]; (p) (504) 764-9315, (504) 524-5522;
(f) (504) 725-1929

DONALDSONVILLE

3283
Historic Donaldsonville Museum
318 Mississippi St, 70346 [PO Box 1085,
70346]; (p) (225) 746-0004; (f) (225) 746-0004;
(c) Ascension

Private non-profit/ 1997/ Ascension Heritage Association/ staff: 1(f); 8(v)/ members: 110

HISTORY MUSEUM: The Museum serves to preserve and present the heritage of Donaldsonville and the area; to promote tourism; and to inform the public of the history, architecture, culture, and technology of the area.

PROGRAMS: Exhibits; Guided Tours

COLLECTIONS: [1900-present]

HOURS: Yr T,Th,Sa

DUBACH

3284
Absalom Autrey House Museum
LA 151 W, 71235; (c) Lincoln

Private non-profit/ Lincoln Parish Museum/
staff: 10(v)/ members: 20

HISTORIC SITE; HOUSE MUSEUM

PROGRAMS: Guided Tours; Lectures

COLLECTIONS: [1849]

HOURS: Mar-Oct Sa-Su 1-4

ADMISSION: Donations accepted

ERATH

3285
Acadian Heritage and Culture Foundation, Inc.
203 S Broadway, 70533; (p) (318) 937-5468; (f)
(318) 235-4382; perrin@plddo.com; (c) Vermilion

Private non-profit/ 1991/ staff: 1(f); 50(p);
250(v)/publication: Our Town

HISTORY MUSEUM

PROGRAMS: Exhibits; Lectures; Living History; Publication

HOURS: Yr M-F 1-5

ADMISSION: No charge

FERRIDAY

3286
Lewis Family Living Museum
LA Ave, 71334 [905 8th St, 71334]; (p) (318)
757-2563, (318) 757-4422; (f) (318) 757-0709;
(c) Concordia

Private non-profit/ 1991/ staff: 4(v)

HISTORIC SITE; HISTORY MUSEUM; HOUSE MUSEUM: Maintains history and artifacts of Jerry Lee Lewis, Mickey Gilly, and Jimmy Lee Swaggart.

PROGRAMS: Guided Tours

COLLECTIONS: [1950s-present] Gold records, photos, furniture, clothing, show posters, and personal items.

HOURS: Yr Daily 1-6 and by appt

ADMISSION: Donations accepted

FORT POLK

3287
Fort Polk Military Museum
917 S Carolina Ave, 71459 [PO Box 3916, 71459-0916]; (p) (318) 531-7905; (f) (318) 531-4202; binghamd@polk-emh2.army.mil; (c) Vernon

Federal/ 1975/ US Army/ staff: 1(f)

HISTORY MUSEUM: Preserves the history of Fort Polk and the units that served there from 1941 to the present.

PROGRAMS: Exhibits; Film/Video; Guided Tours; Interpretation; Lectures; Research Library/Archives; Theatre

COLLECTIONS: [WWII-present]

HOURS: Yr W-F 10-2, Sa-Su 9-4

ADMISSION: No charge

FRANKLIN

3288
Grevemberg House Museum
407 Sterling Rd, 70538 [PO Box 400, 70538]; (p) (337) 828-2092; (f) (337) 828-2028; (c) Saint Mary's

City; Joint; Private non-profit/ 1972/ Louisiana Lord Mark's Society, St. Mary's Chapter/ staff: 1(f); 1(p); 25(v)/ members: 275

HISTORIC SITE; HISTORICAL SOCIETY; HOUSE MUSEUM: Restores and maintains Grevemberg House.

PROGRAMS: Concerts; Exhibits; Facility Rental; Garden Tours; Guided Tours; Interpretation; Reenactments

COLLECTIONS: [1820-1870] Period furnishings, Civil War memorabilia, antique toys, kitchen implements, Grevemberg family papers, nursery rhyme floor cloth, and courthouse furniture.

HOURS: Yr Daily 10-4

ADMISSION: $4, Student $3, Children $2, Seniors $3

3289
Oaklawn Manor
3296 E Oaklawn Dr, 70538; (p) (318) 828-0434

1837/ Private/ staff: 1(f); 2(p)

COLLECTIONS: Audubon prints and Selby's wood carvings of birds and ducks.

HOURS: Yr Daily

FROGMORE

3290
Frogmore Plantation and Gins
11054 Hwy 84, 71334; (p) (318) 757-2453, (800) 647-6724; (f) (318) 757-6535; frogmore@bayou.com; www.louisianatravel.com/frogmore; (c) Concordia

Private for-profit/ 1998/ staff: 1(f); 2(p); 3(v)

Focuses on the historical evolution of plantation life and cotton from the 1700s to the present.

PROGRAMS: Exhibits; Facility Rental; Family Programs; Film/Video; Guided Tours; Living History

COLLECTIONS: [1790s-1890s] 16 antebellum structures including a steam gin and slave quarters; kitchen items, tools, furniture, and spinning and weaving items.

HOURS: Yr M-Sa Call

ADMISSION: $7, Student $4.50; Under 6 Free

GIBSLAND

3291
Mount Lebanon Historical Society, Stagecoach Trail Museum
12801 Hwy 154, 71028; (p) (318) 843-6455, (813) 843-6255; (c) Bienville

Private non-profit/ 1968/ Board of Directors/ staff: 15(v)/ members: 179

HISTORIC SITE; HISTORICAL SOCIETY; HISTORY MUSEUM: Preserves local history and heritage.

PROGRAMS: Annual Meeting; Exhibits; Festivals

COLLECTIONS: Antique farm tools, black smith shop, dolls, WW I uniforms and equipment, dresses, and printed local and parish history.

HOURS: Yr F-Su 2-5

ADMISSION: Donations accepted

GONZALES

3292
River Road African American Museum and Gallery
3138 Hwy 44, 70707 [PO Box 1357, 70707-1357]; (p) (225) 562-7703; (f) (225) 562-7704; aamuseum@eatel.net; www.africanamericanmuseum.org; (c) Ascension

Private non-profit/ 1994/ staff: 1(f); 2(p); 10(v)/ members: 275

ART MUSEUM; HISTORY MUSEUM: Collects, preserves, and interprets art, artifacts, and buildings related to the history of African Americans in rural LA, primary focus is on slavery and achievements of African Americans.

PROGRAMS: Community Outreach; Concerts; Exhibits; Family Programs; Festivals; Film/Video; Guided Tours; Interpretation; Lectures; Research Library/Archives

COLLECTIONS: [Colonial Louisiana-present] Military memorabilia, dolls, Black Mardi Gras memorabilia, and other cultural artifacts.

HOURS: Yr W-Sa 10-5, Su 1-5

ADMISSION: $3

GRAND COTEAU

3293
Academy of the Sacred Heart
1821 Academy Rd, 70541 [PO Box 310, 70541]; (p) (318) 662-5275; (f) (318) 662-3011; morgorn98@yahoo.com; (c) St. Landry

Private non-profit/ 1821/ Society of the Sacred Heart/ staff: 85(f)

GARDEN; HISTORIC SITE; HOUSE MUSEUM: The site offers a unique glimpse into the history of Southern LA through personalized tours, a museum, and formal gardens.

PROGRAMS: Concerts; Facility Rental; Festivals

HOURS: Yr M-F 10-3 by appt

ADMISSION: $5, Seniors $3

GRETNA

3294
Gretna Historical Society
200-209 Lafayette St, 70054 [PO Box 115, 70054]; (p) (504) 362-3854; (c) Jefferson

Private non-profit/ 1969/ staff: 1(p); 7(v)/ members: 240/publication: *Gretna Chronicles*

HISTORIC SITE; HISTORICAL SOCIETY; HISTORY MUSEUM; HOUSE MUSEUM: Preserves and maintains the heritage of the City of Gretna; preserves and promotes the craft of blacksmith reaffirmation of marriages and anniversaries over the anvil in the 200 year tradition of Gretna's namesake, Gretna Green, Scotland.

PROGRAMS: Community Outreach; Exhibits; Guided Tours; Interpretation; Lectures; Publication

COLLECTIONS: [1836-present] Three 1840s Creole Cottages, period furnishings, and an 1859 fire station with life saving equipment.

HOURS: Yr

HAMMOND

3295
Southeast Louisiana Historical Association
Ctr for SE Louisiana Studies, Sims Library, 70402 [SLU 10730, 70402]; (p) (504) 549-2151; (f) (504) 549-2306; rheleniak@selu.edu; www.selu.edu/Academic/Depts/RegionalStudies

Private non-profit/ Board/ staff: 4(p); 4(v)/ members: 80

HISTORICAL SOCIETY: Promotes the study of the history and the cultures of Louisiana's Florida Parishes, SW Mississippi, and the surrounding areas.

PROGRAMS: Annual Meeting; Community Outreach; Lectures

COLLECTIONS: [19th c]

HOURS: M-F 8-4:30

HOMER

3296
Herbert S. Ford Memorial Museum
519 S Main St, 71040 [PO Box 157, 71040]; (p) (318) 927-9190; (c) Claiborne

Private non-profit/ 1982/ Board of Directors/ staff: 1(p); 25(v)/ members: 325

HISTORY MUSEUM: Center for arts, culture, and history of the North Louisiana Hill Country.

PROGRAMS: Annual Meeting; Exhibits; Guided Tours

COLLECTIONS: [1890-1920] Dugout canoe,

1860 log cabin, and original items from the Claiborne Parish Courthouse.

HOURS: Yr M, W, F 9:30-12/1:30-4, Su 2-4

ADMISSION: $3, Family $5, Children $1

HOUMA

3297
Bayou Terrebonne Waterlife Museum
7910 Park Ave, 70360; (p) (504) 580-7200; (f) (504) 580-7205; mmbtwm@cajun.net; www.terrebonne.org; (c) Terrebonne

County/ 1999/ Terrebonne Parish Consolidated Government/ staff: 2(f); 5(v)/ members: 300

ART MUSEUM; HISTORIC SITE: The Museum interprets the economic, social, and natural history of Terrebonne Parish and Southeast Louisiana's bayous, wetlands, and nearby Gulf waters. Peserves and promotes the area's connection to the seafood industry and water transportation.

PROGRAMS: Community Outreach; Concerts; Exhibits; Facility Rental; Festivals; Guided Tours; Lectures; Reenactments; School-Based Curriculum

COLLECTIONS: [18th-20th c]

HOURS: Yr M-F 9-5, Sa 10-4

ADMISSION: $3, Children $2

3298
Terrebonne Genealogical Society
Box 295, Station 2, 70360; www.rootsweb.com /~laterreb/tqs.htm; (c) Terrebonne

Private non-profit/ 1981/ Board of Directors/ members: 400/publication: *Terrebonne Life Lines*

GENEALOGICAL SOCIETY

PROGRAMS: Lectures; Publication; Research Library/Archives

COLLECTIONS: [Colonial-present] Genealogy and History from South LA.

HOURS: Yr M-Th 9-8, F-Sa 9-5

ADMISSION: No charge

3299
Terrebonne Historical and Cultural Society
1208 Museum Dr, 70360 [PO Box 2095, 70361]; (p) (985) 851-0154; (f) (985) 868-1476; southdown@mobiletel.com; www.southdown.org; (c) Terrebonne

Private non-profit/ 1972/ staff: 2(f); 100(v)/ members: 500

HISTORICAL SOCIETY; HISTORY MUSEUM: Preservation, programs, and exhibits of the Terrebonne Museum of local history, culture, and art located in the historic 19th c Southdown Plantation House.

PROGRAMS: Annual Meeting; Community Outreach; Concerts; Exhibits; Facility Rental; Festivals; Guided Tours; Lectures; Publication

COLLECTIONS: [1850-present] Artifacts, photos, and furnishings relating to Cajun culture; sugarcane plantations; Mardi Gras; Native Peoples; area industries; local art and literature; Sen. Allen Elender; Doughty and Boehm porcelain.

HOURS: Yr T-Sa 10-4

ADMISSION: $5, Student $3, Children $2, Seniors $3

JENNINGS

3300
Louisiana Telephone Pioneers Museum
311 N Main, 70546; (p) (337) 821-5532; (f) (337) 821-5527; www.jeffdavis.org; (c) Jeff Davis

Private non-profit/ 1992/ staff: 3(f); 3(p)

HISTORY MUSEUM: Promotes the ideals of the earliest telephone worker. Children's museum with hands on learning.

PROGRAMS: Exhibits; Film/Video

COLLECTIONS: [Early 1900s-present] Equip, tools, and telephones.

HOURS: Yr M-Sa 9:30-5:30

ADMISSION: $3, Student $1

3301
Zigler Museum Foundation
411 Clara St, 70546; (p) (318) 824-0114; (f) (318) 824-0120; (c) Jefferson Davis

Private non-profit/ 1963/ Board of Trustees/ staff: 2(f); 1(p); 10(v)/ members: 175

ART MUSEUM: An art museum and cultural center with an emphasis on art education and culture.

PROGRAMS: Concerts; Exhibits; Family Programs; Festivals; Guided Tours; Lectures

COLLECTIONS: Five c of European and American art (including Rembrandt, Durer, Pissaro, de Vlaminck), wildlife dioramas, wildfowl carvings, and decorative arts.

HOURS: Yr T-Sa 9-5, Su 1-5

ADMISSION: $2, Children $1

JONESBORO

3302
Jackson Heritage Museum and Fine Arts Association
515 Cooper Ave, S, 71251; (p) (318) 259-3119; (c) Jackson

County; Private non-profit/ 1990/ staff: 22(v)

HISTORIC PRESERVATION AGENCY; HOUSE MUSEUM

PROGRAMS: Exhibits; Facility Rental

HOURS: Yr Th-Sa 10-4

KAPLAN

3303
Le Musee de la Ville de Kaplan
405 N Cushing Blvd, 70548-4123; (p) (318) 643-1528; kaplanmuseum@kaplantel.net; www.vrml.k12.la.us/vermilion/kaplan/kapmuse.html; (c) Vermilion

City/ 1994/ staff: 1(f); 1(p)/ members: 37

HISTORY MUSEUM: Preserves the Acadian history and culture of the City of Kaplan, LA.

PROGRAMS: Exhibits

COLLECTIONS: [1895-present] Period tools, pictures, genealogy, and paintings.

HOURS: Yr M-F 8-4, Sa 12-4

ADMISSION: Donations accepted

KENTWOOD

3304
Kentwood Historical and Cultural Arts Museum
204 Ave E 1, 70444 [PO Box 685, 70444]; (p) (504) 229-4656; (f) (504) 229-4406; (c) Tangipahoa

Private non-profit/ 1995/ Kentwood Museum Trustees/ staff: 1(f); 2(v)/ members: 120

ART MUSEUM; HISTORY MUSEUM: Collects and interprets Kentwood history.

PROGRAMS: Community Outreach; Exhibits; Film/Video; Interpretation; School-Based Curriculum

COLLECTIONS: 450 pictures, artifacts, POW history, and video of the Kentwood military history.

HOURS: Yr T-Sa 10-4

ADMISSION: $2

LAFAYETTE

3305
Acadian Village
200 Greenleaf Dr, 70506; (p) (337) 981-2364; (f) (337) 988-4554; (c) Lafayette

Private non-profit/ 1976/ Lafayette Association for Retarded Citizens/ staff: 5(f); 3(p); 100(v)

HOUSE MUSEUM; LIVING HISTORY/OUTDOOR MUSEUM: A history program of authentic houses with French-speaking tour guides. Funds raised benefit the Lafayette Association for Retarded Citizens.

PROGRAMS: Exhibits; Festivals; Guided Tours; Interpretation

COLLECTIONS: [19th-early 20th c] Houses, musical instruments, and artifacts used by the Acadian people living in Southwest Louisiana during the 19th and early 20th c.

HOURS: Yr Daily

3306
Alexander Mouton House
1122 Lafayette, 70501; (p) (318) 234-2208; (f) (318) 234-2208

HOUSE MUSEUM: Home of former governor.

3307
Cathedral of Saint John the Evangelist Museum
914 Saint John St, 70502 [PO Drawer V, 70502]; (p) (318) 232-1322; (f) (318) 232-1379; www.lafayettetravel.com; (c) Lafayette

Private non-profit/ 1992/ Cathedra Museum Board/ staff: 22(v)/publication: *Cathedral of St. John the Evangelist*

HISTORIC PRESERVATION AGENCY; HISTORIC SITE; HISTORY MUSEUM: Operates a museum which chronicles church and community history.

PROGRAMS: Community Outreach; Exhibits; Film/Video; Guided Tours; Interpretation; Publication; Research Library/Archives

COLLECTIONS: [1821-present] Historical documents, artifacts, and memorabilia of religious and founding leader of the French-Acadian settlement of Vermillionville (renamed Lafayette).

HOURS: Yr M-F 9-12/1-4

3308
Lafayette Genealogical Society
[PO Box 52041, 70505]; (c) Lafayette

Private non-profit/ 1985/ staff: 60(v)/ members: 60/publication: *Les Memoires de Lafayette*

GENEALOGICAL SOCIETY: Collects and encourages interest in genealogy, preserves and makes available genealogical material, and assists the researcher in compiling material on family history.

PROGRAMS: Publication

3309
Lafayette Natural History Museum and Planetarium
637 Girard Park Dr, 70503; (p) (337) 291-5544; (f) (337) 291-5464; www.inhm.org; (c) Lafayette

City; County; Joint/ 1969/ Lafayette Consolidated Government/ staff: 5(f); 8(p); 20(v)/ members: 400

HISTORY MUSEUM: Maintains exhibits of area culture and the natural world; operates a planetarium.

PROGRAMS: Annual Meeting; Community Outreach; Concerts; Exhibits; Family Programs; Festivals; Film/Video; Guided Tours; Lectures; Research Library/Archives; School-Based Curriculum

COLLECTIONS: Materials related to LA cultures, nature, astronomy, and aerospace.

HOURS: Yr M, W-F 9-5, T 9-9, Sa-Su 1-5

ADMISSION: No charge

3310
Louisiana Historical Association
302 E Saint Mary St, 70504 [PO Box 42808, 70504]; (p) (318) 482-6871; (f) (318) 482-6028; grc6539@usl.edu; (c) Lafayette

Private non-profit/ 1960/ Board of Directors/ staff: 2(f); 2(p)/ members: 960/publication: *Louisiana History*

HISTORICAL SOCIETY

PROGRAMS: Annual Meeting; Lectures; Publication

COLLECTIONS: [Civil War] Documents and artifacts.

3311
Southwestern Archives and Manuscripts Collections, University of Southwestern Louisiana
302 E Saint Mary Blvd, 70504 [PO Box 40155, 70504]; (p) (337) 482-6031, (337) 482-5702; (f) (337) 482-5841; bturner@louisiana.edu; www.louisiana.edu/Infotech/Library; (c) Lafayette

State/ 1964/ Univ of LA at Lafayette/ staff: 4(f); 10(p); 1(v)

LIBRARY AND/OR ARCHIVES: Maintains archival collections on Southern LA.

PROGRAMS: Exhibits; Lectures; Research Library/Archives

COLLECTIONS: [19th-20th c] Genealogy, personal family papers, university records, organization records, photos, and oral histories.

HOURS: Yr

3312
Vermilionville
1600 Surrey St, 70501; (p) (337) 233-4077; (f) (337) 233-1694; vville@BellSouth.net; www.vermilionville.org; (c) Lafayette Parish

Joint; Private non-profit/ 1989/ The Vermilionville Foundation/Lafayette Parish Bayou Vermilion District/ staff: 7(f); 40(p); 5(v)/ members: 850

LIVING HISTORY/OUTDOOR MUSEUM: Operates a Cajun/Creole living history museum situated on 23 acres; preserves and interprets elements of the folklife and cultures of the Attakapas between 1765-1890.

PROGRAMS: Exhibits; Facility Rental; Guided Tours; Lectures; Living History

COLLECTIONS: 16 historic buildings, 2 water cisterns, historic outhouse, Acadian homespun blankets and other household textiles, split oak baskets, hand forged ironwork, and cypress furnishings.

HOURS: Yr Jan-Dec M-Su 10-5

ADMISSION: $8, Children $5

LAKE CHARLES

3313
Imperial Calcasieu Museum, Inc.
204 W Sallier, 70601; (p) (318) 439-4797; (f) (318) 439-6040; (c) Calcasieu

Private non-profit/ 1963/ staff: 1(f); 5(p)/ members: 300

ART MUSEUM; HISTORY MUSEUM

PROGRAMS: Exhibits; Facility Rental; Family Programs; Festivals; Guided Tours; Reenactments; Research Library/Archives; School-Based Curriculum

COLLECTIONS: [1850-1900] Artifacts, furniture, dolls, paintings, and prints from the region.

HOURS: Yr T-Sa 10-5

ADMISSION: $2, Student $1

LAKE PROVIDENCE

3314
Louisiana State Cotton Museum
Rt 2, Box 17, 71254 [PO Box 541, 71254]; (p) (318) 559-2041; (f) (318) 559-2217; (c) East Carroll

State/ 1989/ Secretary of State/ staff: 2(f); 1(p); 15(v)

HISTORY MUSEUM: Preserves the history and heritage of cotton cultivation and its influence on life in LA.

PROGRAMS: Annual Meeting; Exhibits; School-Based Curriculum

HOURS: Yr Jan-Dec M-F 9-4

LEESVILLE

3315
Museum Association of West Louisiana
803 S Third, 71446; (p) (318) 239-0927; mwl@dtx.net; www.dtx.net/~mwl; (c) Vernon

Private non-profit/ 1919/ staff: 1(f); 25(v)/ members: 300

HISTORIC PRESERVATION AGENCY; HISTORIC SITE; HISTORY MUSEUM; RESEARCH CENTER

PROGRAMS: Annual Meeting; Community Outreach; Elder's Programs; Exhibits; Festivals; Guided Tours; Interpretation; Research Library/Archives

COLLECTIONS: [Late 1800s-present]

HOURS: Yr

ADMISSION: No charge

3316
Museum of West Louisiana
803 S 3rd St, 71446; (p) (318) 239-0927; (c) Vernon

Private non-profit/ 1987/ staff: 1(f); 6(p); 25(v)/ members: 310

GENEALOGICAL SOCIETY; HISTORIC PRESERVATION AGENCY; HOUSE MUSEUM: Preserves and displays artifacts of the history, culture, and folk art, and resources of Vernon Parish and the west central area of LA.

PROGRAMS: Annual Meeting; Exhibits; Festivals; Guided Tours

COLLECTIONS: [1870] Archaeological artifacts, logging implements, railroad memorabilia, quilts, clothing, cooking and household items, furniture, POW paintings, WWI I memorabilia, toys, dolls, and pictures.

HOURS: Yr

LONG LEAF

3317
Southern Forest Heritage Museum and Research Center, Inc.
77 Longleaf Rd, 71448 [PO Box 101, 71448-0101]; (p) (318) 748-8404; (c) Rapides

Private non-profit/ 1994/ staff: 2(f); 4(p); 7(v)/ members: 319/publication: *Edgings and Trimmings*

HISTORIC SITE: Interprets the history of the Southern Forest through a 1910 sawmill complex.

PROGRAMS: Annual Meeting; Exhibits; Facility Rental; Guided Tours; Publication

COLLECTIONS: [1910-1969] 34 buildings including 1910 sawmill and planer mill, belt-drive machine shop, original mill machinery, 3 steam-powered logging machines, 3 steam locomotives, and unprocessed collection of documents.

HOURS: Yr Daily 9-5

MADISONVILLE

3318
Lake Pontchartrain Basin Maritime Musem, Inc.
Mabel Dr, 70447 [PO Box 323, 70447]; (p) (504) 845-9200; (f) (504) 845-9201; www.lpbmm/selu.edu; (c) Saint Tammany

Private non-profit/ 1991/ Board of Directors/ staff: 300(v)/ members: 200

HISTORY MUSEUM; RESEARCH CENTER: Preserves and advocates the maritime heritage of the area.

PROGRAMS: Annual Meeting; Community Outreach; Concerts; Exhibits; Facility Rental;

Festivals; Film/Video; Guided Tours; Interpretation; Lectures; Living History; Research Library/Archives; School-Based Curriculum

MANSFIELD

3319
Mansfield State Historic Site
15149 Hwy 175, 71052; (p) (888) 677-6267; (f) (318) 871-4345; mansfield@crt.state.la.us; (c) DeSoto

State/ 1957/ State of LA, Dept Culture, Recreation and Tourism/ staff: 6(f); 3(p)

HISTORIC SITE; HISTORY MUSEUM: Interprets the Battle of Mansfield (Apr 8, 1864) and the Red River Campaign of 1864.

PROGRAMS: Exhibits; Family Programs; Interpretation; Lectures; Living History; Reenactments; Research Library/Archives; School-Based Curriculum

COLLECTIONS: [1861-1865] Artifacts, letters, equipment and displays on the Battle of Mansfield and the Red River Campaign.

HOURS: Yr Daily 9-5

ADMISSION: $2

MARTHAVILLE

3320
Rebel State Historic Site
1260 Hwy 1221, 71450 [PO Box 127, 71450]; (p) (318) 472-6255; (f) (318) 472-6255; rebel@crt.state.la.us; (c) Natchitoches

State/ 1970/ Dept of Culture, Recreation, and Tourism/ staff: 2(f); 3(p)

HISTORIC SITE; HISTORY MUSEUM: Operates a music museum.

PROGRAMS: Community Outreach; Concerts; Exhibits; Family Programs; Festivals; Film/Video; Guided Tours; Interpretation; Research Library/Archives; School-Based Curriculum; Theatre

COLLECTIONS: Music memorabilia and antique musical

MELROSE

3321
Melrose Plantation Home Complex
Hwy 199, 71452 [General Delivery, Hwy 119, 71452]; (p) (318) 379-0055; (f) (318) 379-0055

HOUSE MUSEUM

MONROE

3322
Aviation Historical Museum of Louisiana
, 71203 [701 Central Ave, 71203]; (p) (318) 361-9020; (c) Oauchita

City/ 1995/ Board of Directors/ staff: 5(p); 18(v)/ members: 148

HISTORY MUSEUM: Bring more awareness to the public about our history. Restored WW II Barracks.

COLLECTIONS: W W II memorabilia, historical aviation, W W II air communication, uniforms, utensils, documents, and newspaper articles.

HOURS: Sa 9-5, Su 1-5

ADMISSION: $3, Children $1, Seniors $2

3323
Biedenharn Museum and Gardens
2006 Riverside Dr, 71201; (p) (318) 387-5281; (f) (318) 387-8253; bmuseum@bayou.com; www.bmuseum.org; (c) Ouachita

Private non-profit/ 1971/ Emy-Lou Biedenharn Foundation/ staff: 8(f); 14(p)

GARDEN; HISTORIC SITE; HISTORY MUSEUM: Joseph Biedenharn Home, first person to bottle Coca-Cola, Elsong Garden, and the Bible Museum which holds material from Gutenberg through the late 20th c.

PROGRAMS: Community Outreach; Concerts; Exhibits; Facility Rental; Garden Tours; Guided Tours; Interpretation; Lectures; Publication; Research Library/Archives

COLLECTIONS: [1400-present] Early 20th c southern house. Bibles and archaeological items from the Holy Land. Coca-Cola materials.

HOURS: Yr M-Sa 10-5, Su 2-5

ADMISSION: No

3324
Masur Museum of Art
1400 S Grand St, 71202; (p) (318) 329-2237; (f) (318) 329-2847; (c) Ouachita

City/ 1963/ City of Monroe/ staff: 3(f); 2(p); 24(v)/ members: 400/publication: *Museum News*

ART MUSEUM; HISTORIC SITE: Listed on the National Register of Historic Places; supports and fosters visual arts in the cultural and educational life of Northeast LA.

PROGRAMS: Community Outreach; Exhibits; Facility Rental; Film/Video; Guided Tours; Lectures; Publication; Research Library/Archives

COLLECTIONS: Prints, paintings, sculpture, photography, and mixed media pieces by regionally and nationally recognized contemporary artists including Clyde Connell, Ida Kohlmeyer, Lynda Benglis, Glenna Goodacre, John Baeder, Raphael Soyer, and Julian Stanczak.

HOURS: Yr T-Th 9-5, F-Su 2-5

ADMISSION: No charge

3325
Ouachita African American Historical Society
503 Plum St, 71210 [PO Box 168, 71210]; (p) (318) 323-1167; (f) (318) 323-1167; (c) Ouachita

Private non-profit/ 1996/ Board of Directors/ staff: 1(f); 3(p); 3(v)/ members: 40/publication: *Tall Talk*

HISTORICAL SOCIETY; HISTORY MUSEUM: Dedicated to the research, identification, acquisition, presentation, and preservation of visual art forms, historical documents, and artifacts that relate to the life and culture of the African American community.

PROGRAMS: Annual Meeting; Community Outreach; Exhibits; Festivals; Guided Tours; Publication; Research Library/Archives; School-Based Curriculum

COLLECTIONS: [Late 1800s-present] Heritage artifacts, African art and artifacts, paintings, books, videos, and recordings.

HOURS: Yr T-Sa 9-5

MORGAN CITY

3326
Turn of the Century House/Mardi Gras Museum
715 Second St, 70381 [PO Box 1218, 70381]; (p) (504) 380-4651; (f) (504) 384-7519; (c) Saint Mary

City/ 1983/ City of Morgan City/ staff: 1(f); 3(p)

HISTORY MUSEUM; HOUSE MUSEUM: Collects local artifacts and preserves local culture though exhibits.

PROGRAMS: Exhibits; Guided Tours

COLLECTIONS: Local artifacts, home furnishings, and local Mardi Gras costumes and memorabilia.

HOURS: Yr T-Su 10-5

ADMISSION: $3, Student $2

3327
Young-Sanders Center for Study of the War Between the States
501 Federal Ave, 70381 [PO Box 430, 70381]; (p) (504) 380-4650; (f) (504) 380-4662; www.youngsanders.org; (c) Saint Mary

City/ 1996/ City of Morgan City/ staff: 1(f); 2(p)

HISTORY MUSEUM; RESEARCH CENTER: Collects, preserves, and maintains the historical records of the State of LA in regards to the War Between the States, and makes those records available to the public.

PROGRAMS: Exhibits; Guided Tours; Research Library/Archives

COLLECTIONS: [Civil War] Armaments, letters, books, photos, and maps.

HOURS: Yr M-F 9-5, Sa 9-12

ADMISSION: $1

NATCHEZ

3328
Magnolia Plantation Home
5487 SR 119, 71456; (p) (318) 379-2221; www.nps.gov/cari/MagnoliaPlantation.htm

HOUSE MUSEUM

NATCHITOCHES

3329
Association for the Preservation of Historic Natchitoches
310 Jefferson St, 71457 [PO Box 2248, 71457]; (p) (318) 379-0055; (f) (318) 357-8341; melrose@worldnetla.net; (c) Natchitoches

Private non-profit/ 1944/ staff: 3(f); 4(p); 300(v)/ members: 380/publication: *Calico Courier*

HISTORIC PRESERVATION AGENCY; HISTORIC SITE; HOUSE MUSEUM

PROGRAMS: Annual Meeting; Community Outreach; Festivals; Guided Tours; Interpretation; Publication; Research Library/Archives; School-Based Curriculum

COLLECTIONS: [Turn of the century] Buildings, artifacts, and books

HOURS: Yr Melrose: Daily 12-4, Kate Chopin Home Daily 10-5

ADMISSION: $6, Student $4, Children $3

3330
Beau Fort Plantation
4078 Hwy 494, 71457 [PO Box 2300, 71457]; (p) (318) 352-9580; (f) (318) 352-7280; beau fort@worldnet.la.net; (c) Natchitoches

Private for-profit/ 1790/ staff: 1(f); 2(p); 1(v)

HISTORIC SITE

PROGRAMS: Facility Rental; Guided Tours

COLLECTIONS: [1790-1860] Early LA Empire furniture and French, English, and family heirlooms.

HOURS: Yr Daily 1-4

ADMISSION: $5, Student $3, Children $2

3331
Immaculate Conception Church Museum
145 Church St, 71457; (p) (318) 352-3422; (c) Natchitoches

Private non-profit/ Immaculate Conception Church/ staff: 3(v)

HISTORIC SITE; HISTORY MUSEUM: Maintains church, bishop's house, rectory, seminary building, and historical church related collection.

PROGRAMS: Exhibits

COLLECTIONS: [1700s-1800s] Old church artifacts, documents, paintings, and photographs.

HOURS: By Appt

ADMISSION: Donations accepted

3332
Kate Chopin Home/Bayou Folk Museum
243 Hwy 495, 71457 [PO Box 2248, 71457]; (p) (318) 379-2233; (c) Natchitoches

Private non-profit/ 1965/ Association for the Preservation of Historic Natchitoches/ staff: 1(f)/publication: *Calico Courier*

HISTORIC PRESERVATION AGENCY; HISTORIC SITE; HISTORICAL SOCIETY; HOUSE MUSEUM: Operates Melrose Plantation and Kate Chopin/Bayou Folk Museum, both listed on the National Register.

PROGRAMS: Festivals; Guided Tours; Publication

COLLECTIONS: [19th c-present] Doctor's office, blacksmith shop, newspaper articles, books, photographs, farm tools, and equipment.

HOURS: Yr M-Sa 10-5, Su 1-5

3333
Natchitoches Historic Foundation
550 Second St, 71457 [Box 2351, 71457]; (p) (318) 352-0990; (c) Natchitoches

Private non-profit/ 1994/ staff: 150(v)/ members: 350

ALLIANCE OF HISTORICAL AGENCIES; HISTORIC PRESERVATION AGENCY; HISTORIC SITE; HOUSE MUSEUM: Focuses on public education of the history and preservation of Natchitoches Parish.

PROGRAMS: Annual Meeting; Community Outreach; Facility Rental; Garden Tours; Guided Tours; Lectures; School-Based Curriculum

HOURS: Yr

3334
Old Courthouse Museum, Louisiana State Museum Branch
600 Second St, 71457; (p) (318) 357-2270; (f) (318) 357-7040; carolyn@cp-tel.net; (c) Natchitoches

1995/ LA State Museum Board of Directors/ staff: 6(f)/ members: 75

HISTORY MUSEUM: Collects, preserves and interprets the history of North LA for educational and exhibition purposes.

PROGRAMS: Annual Meeting; Community Outreach; Exhibits; Facility Rental; Guided Tours; Interpretation; Lectures; Living History; Research Library/Archives; School-Based Curriculum

COLLECTIONS: [19th-20th c]

HOURS: Yr M-Sa 9-5

ADMISSION: $3, Student $2, Seniors $2

3335
Williamson Museum
Kyser Hall, NSU, 71297 [Nothwestern State Univ, 71297]; (p) (318) 357-4364; gregoryh@alpha.nsula.edu; (c) Natchitoches

Joint/ 1900/ State; Tribal/ staff: 1(f); 2(p)

TRIBAL MUSEUM: A teaching facility focused on southeastern Indian culture; official repository for the LA Division of Archeology and the Caddo Tribe of OK.

PROGRAMS: Community Outreach; Exhibits; Guided Tours; Lectures

COLLECTIONS: [Preshistory-present] Artifacts, tapes, and archival files.

HOURS: Sept-July M-F 9-4

NEW IBERIA

3336
Conrad Rice Mill
307 Ann St, 70562 [PO Box 10640, 70562]; (p) (318) 364-7242, (800) 551-3245; (f) (318) 365-5806; (c) Iberia

Private for-profit/ 1912/ staff: 23(f); 7(p)

HISTORIC SITE: Maintains the historic Conrad Rice Mill, uses the belt drive power transmission syste, presents Cajun history and culture.

PROGRAMS: Guided Tours

COLLECTIONS: [Turn-of-the century]

HOURS: Yr M-Sa 9-5

ADMISSION: $2.75, Children $1.25, Seniors $2.25

3337
Jefferson Island
5505 Rip Van Winkle Rd, 70560; (p) (318) 365-3332; (f) (318) 365-3354

3338
Shadows-on-the-Teche
317 E Main St, 70560; (p) (337) 369-6446; (f) (337) 365-5213; (c) Iberia

Private non-profit/ 1961/ National Trust for Historic Preservation/ staff: 9(f); 10(p); 94(v)/ members: 430

HISTORIC SITE: Preserves, researches, and interprets the historic structure, landscape, and collections of the 19th c Southern LA plantation.

PROGRAMS: Community Outreach; Exhibits; Family Programs; Garden Tours; Guided Tours; Interpretation; Lectures; Living History; Publication; Reenactments; Research Library/Archives; School-Based Curriculum

COLLECTIONS: [1830s-1958s] Artifacts from four generations of residents.

HOURS: Yr M-Su

NEW ORLEANS

3339
1850 House, Lower Pontalba Building
523 Saint Anne St, 70116 [PO Box 2448, 70176]; (p) (504) 568-6968, (800) 568-6968; (f) (504) 568-4995; www.crt.state.la.us/crt/museum/lsmnet3.htm

1849/ LA State Museum/ staff: 4(f)

COLLECTIONS: [1850-Antebellum Era] New Orleans-retailed furniture of the era.

HOURS: Yr

3340
American-Italian Renaissance Foundation
537 S Peters St, 70176 [PO Box 2392, 70176]; (p) (504) 522-7294; (f) (504) 522-1657; www.mindspring.com/~cammami; (c) Orleans

Private non-profit/ 1978/ staff: 2(p); 4(v)/publication: *Italian American Digest*

RESEARCH CENTER: Sponsors the LA Italian Sports Hall of Fame, the periodical, "Italian American Digest," and activities honoring individuals and organizations from the region.

PROGRAMS: Exhibits; Festivals; Interpretation; Publication; Research Library/Archives

COLLECTIONS: [Early-mid 20th century] The museum displays items reflecting the lives of early 20th century Italian immigrants of the Gulf Coast region. The library holds published works on Italian affairs, publications by Italian Americans, and experiences of Italian immigrants to the U.S.

HOURS: Yr W-Sa 10-2:30

ADMISSION: Donations accepted

3341
Amistad Research Center, The
6823 St Charles Ave, 70118 [Tulane University, Tilton Hall, 70118]; (p) (504) 865-5535; (f) (504) 865-5580; arc@mailhost.tcs.tulane.edu; www.tulane.edu/~amistad; (c) Orleans

Private non-profit/ 1966/ staff: 12(f)/ members: 250/publication: *Amistad Report*

ART MUSEUM; HISTORIC PRESERVATION AGENCY; HISTORY MUSEUM; RESEARCH CENTER

PROGRAMS: Community Outreach; Exhibits; Guided Tours; Lectures; Publication; Research Library/Archives

COLLECTIONS: [1839-1985] Collections relate to United States ethnic history, race relations, civil rights, and United Church of Christ history and mission to United States' minorities. Art collections include works from the Harlem Renaissance period, African art, and contemporary

3342
Beauregard-Keyes House
1113 Chartres St, 70116; (p) (504) 523-7257; (c) Orleans

Private non-profit/ 1948/ The Keyes Foundation/ staff: 2(f); 4(p); 10(v)/publication: *Beauregard-Keyes House*

HOUSE MUSEUM: A restored 1826 mansion located in the French Quarter that includes the collections of writer, Frances Parkinson Keyes and confederate general, P.G.T. Beauregard.

PROGRAMS: Exhibits; Facility Rental; Garden Tours; Guided Tours; Interpretation; Publication

COLLECTIONS: [1820-1900] Keyes collections: dolls, veilleuses, fans, maps, folk costumes, books, photographs; Beauregard collections: portraits, furnishings, and artifacts; and Swiss exhibit: paintings, manuscripts, and books.

HOURS: Yr M-Sa

3343
Blaine Kern's Mardi Gras World
233 Newton St, 70114; (p) (504) 368-7821; (f) (504) 368-4628; briankern@mardigrasworld.com; www.mardigrasworld.com; (c) Orleans

Private for-profit/ 1947/ staff: 11(f)

HISTORIC SITE; HISTORY MUSEUM

PROGRAMS: Facility Rental; Guided Tours; Theatre

HOURS: Yr Daily 9:30-4:30

ADMISSION: $11.50, Children $5.50, Seniors $8.50

3344
Eisenhower Center for American Studies, The
923 Magazine St, 70130; (p) (504) 539-9560; (f) (504) 539-9563; awedekin@uno.edu; www.uno.edu/~eice

State/ 1983/ University of New Orleans/ staff: 3(f); 3(p); 2(v)/ members: 2000/publication: *The Crusade*

PROFESSIONAL ORGANIZATION: A research institute dedicated to the study and preservation of American history and leadership.

PROGRAMS: Lectures; Publication; Research Library/Archives

COLLECTIONS: [W W II] Large collection of oral histories of D-Day and Battle of the Bulge veterans; memoirs, photos, documents, memorabilia, and over 150 hours of WW II color footage.

HOURS: Yr M-F

3345
Friends of the Cabildo, Inc.
701 Chartres St, 70116; (p) (504) 523-3939; (f) (504) 524-9130; cabildo@gnofn.org; www.gnofn.org/~fcabildo; (c) Orleans

Private non-profit/ 1956/ staff: 2(f); 3(p); 280(v)/ members: 1700/publication: *New Orleans Architecture Series Vols I-8*

HISTORIC PRESERVATION AGENCY: To provide support for the LA State Museum, its projects, and its property.

PROGRAMS: Community Outreach; Guided Tours; Lectures; Publication; Research Library/Archives

3346
Garden District Association
938 Lafayette St, Ste 428, 70150 [PO Box 50836, 70150-0836]; (p) (504) 525-7608; (f) (504) 523-3680; sla@acadiacom.net

Private non-profit/ 1939/ members: 400

HISTORIC PRESERVATION AGENCY: Preserves the architecture, character, and zoning integrity of the Garden District; coordinates community activities.

PROGRAMS: Annual Meeting; Community Outreach; Garden Tours; Publication

3347
Genealogical Research Society of New Orleans
[PO Box 51791, 70151]; (p) (504) 581-3153; www.rootsweb.com/~lagrsno/; (c) Orleans

Private non-profit/ 1960/ Board of Directors/ members: 375/publication: *New Orleans Genesis*

GENEALOGICAL SOCIETY: Dedicated to encouraging genealogical studies; fostering maintenance of family records, locating, preserving, cataloging, and publishing records, and assisting researchers in tracing family lineage.

PROGRAMS: Annual Meeting; Lectures; Publication

3348
Hermann-Grima and Gallier Historic Houses
820 Saint Louis St, 70116 [820 Saint Louis St, 70116]; (p) (504) 525-5661; (f) (504) 568-9735; hggh@gnofn.org; www.gnofn.org/~hggh; (c) Orleans

1831/ The Women's Exchange/ staff: 11(f); 6(p); 60(v)/ members: 661

Mission is to preserve, maintain, and complete the restoration of the houses and to interpret their place in New Orleans history.

COLLECTIONS: [1830-present] Kitchen implements of the period; some family things; period furniture 1830-1860.

HOURS: Yr M-F10-4

ADMISSION: One Museum $6.00; $10 Both Museums

3349
Historic District Landmarks Commission
830 Julia St, 70113; (p) (504) 565-7440; (f) (504) 565-6269; (c) Orleans

City/ 1976/ City of New Orleans/ staff: 8(f)

HISTORIC PRESERVATION AGENCY: The regulatory agency for local historic districts and local landmarks.

PROGRAMS: Lectures

HOURS: Yr M-F 9-5

3350
Historic New Orleans Collection, The
533 Royal St, 70130; (p) (504) 523-4662; hnocinfo@hnoc.org; www.hnoc.org

Private non-profit/ 1966/ Kemper and Leila Williams Foundation/ staff: 45(f); 15(p); 10(v)/publication: *Historic New Orleans Quarterly*

HISTORY MUSEUM; LIBRARY AND/OR ARCHIVES; RESEARCH CENTER: Collects, preserves, and makes available to researchers item related to LA history and culture; operates a museum and research center for state and local history.

PROGRAMS: Elder's Programs; Exhibits; Film/Video; Guided Tours; Interpretation; Lectures; Publication; Research Library/Archives

COLLECTIONS: [19th-20th c] Research Center: documents, maps, books, photos, prints, drawings, and paintings.

HOURS: Yr T-Sa 10-4:30

ADMISSION: No charge

3351
Jackson Barracks Military Museum
6400 Saint Clude Ave, 70146 [Bldg 201, Jackson Barracks, 70146]; (p) (504) 278-8242; (f) (504) 278-8614; jbmuseum@la-arng.ngb.army.mil; www.la.ngb.army.mil/jbmhm.htm; (c) Orleans

State/ 1974/ LA National Guard/ staff: 3(f); 12(v)/ members: 200

HISTORY MUSEUM: LA National Guard Museum displays military vehicles, aircraft, weapons, and memorabilia used by the armed forces.

PROGRAMS: Exhibits; Family Programs; Film/Video; Guided Tours; Research Library/Archives

COLLECTIONS: [American Revolution-Desert Storm] Tanks, military vehicles, aircraft, weapons, flags, uniforms, helicopters, a 1917 Cadillac touring car, and a cutaway section of a WW II barracks building.

HOURS: Yr M-F 7:30-4, Sa 9-3

ADMISSION: No charge

3352
Jean Lafitte National Historical Park and Preserve
365 Canal St, Ste 2400, 70130; (p) (504) 589-3882; (f) (504) 589-3851; jela_interpretation@nps.gov; www.nps.gov/jela; (c) Orleans

Federal/ 1978/ National Park Service/ staff: 68(f); 5(p); 110(v)/ members: 1

HISTORIC SITE; HISTORY MUSEUM: Preserves examples of natural and historical resources and interprets cultural diversity in the Mississippi Delta Region; four units located throughout southern LA.

PROGRAMS: Exhibits; Facility Rental; Film/Video; Guided Tours; Interpretation; Living History; Reenactments; School-Based Curriculum

COLLECTIONS: [War of 1812] 82,000 archaeology, 4,850 history, 26,000 archival, and 1,573 biology items/specimens, includes cemetery records, research, studies, historic and prehistoric archeology, War of 1812 material, and post 1800 artifacts.

HOURS: Yr Daily 9-5

3353
Longue Vue House and Gardens
7 Bamboo Rd, 70124-1065; (p) (504) 488-5488; (f) (504) 486-7015; www.longuevue.com; (c) Orleans

Private non-profit/ 1968/ Longue Vue Foundation/ staff: 21(f); 19(p); 250(v)/ members: 1277

GARDEN; HISTORIC SITE; HOUSE MUSEUM: Maintains and interprets estate and its collection in relation to the wealthy and philanthropic Stern family who lived there in the mid 20th c.

PROGRAMS: Annual Meeting; Community Outreach; Exhibits; Family Programs; Garden Tours; Guided Tours; Interpretation; Lectures; Research Library/Archives; School-Based Curriculum

COLLECTIONS: [17th-20th c] Creamware-Pearlware collection; large textile collection, including needlework, printed textiles (chintzes and toiles); costume collection; rugs and carpets (Russian, French, Eastern European, North American) hooked rugs.; Original and copied landscape and architectural drawings and models; family papers; family photographs; photographs of gardens, interiors and exteriors.

HOURS: Yr M-Sa 10-4:30, Su 1-5

ADMISSION: $7, Student $3, Children $3, Seniors $6

3354
Los Islenos Heritage and Cultural Museum and Village
1357 Bayou Rd, 70130 [206 Decatur St, 70130-1016]; (p) (504) 682-9862, (504) 524-1659; (f) (504) 523-2254; (c) Saint Bernard

Joint/ 1980/ Los Islenos Heritage; Cultural Society and Parish Gov., St Bernard Recreation Department/ private non-profit/ staff: 1(f); 30(v)/ members: 671

HISTORICAL SOCIETY; HISTORY MUSEUM; HOUSE MUSEUM; RESEARCH CENTER: Maintains a 22 acre site dedicated to the interpretation and preservation of the Spanish influence in LA, particularly that of the Canary Islanders, the Islenos, who settled in St. Bernard Parish beginning 1778.

PROGRAMS: Exhibits; Facility Rental; Festivals; Interpretation; Lectures; Living History; Publication; Research Library/Archives

COLLECTIONS: [1778-present] Canarian exhibits, gifts from the Canary Island Gov Islenos items, pictures, boats, hunting and carving exhibits.

HOURS: Yr W-Su 11-4

ADMISSION: No charge

3355
Louisiana Historical Society
5801 Saint Charles Ave, 70115; (p) (504) 866-3049; wdrl@home.com; www. ouisianahistoricalsociety.org; (c) Orleans

Private non-profit/ 1836/ staff: 2(v)/ members: 608

HISTORICAL SOCIETY: Sponsors lectures, tours, and symposia on LA history.

PROGRAMS: Annual Meeting; Guided Tours; Lectures

3356
Louisiana Landmarks Society
1440 Moss St, 70119; (p) (504) 482-0312; (f) (504) 482-0312; (c) Orleans

Private non-profit/ 1950/ staff: 3(p); 12(v)/

members: 958/publication: *Preservation*

HISTORIC PRESERVATION AGENCY: Promotes preservation of LA landmarks and supports the Pilot House Museum.

PROGRAMS: Annual Meeting; Exhibits; Facility Rental; Guided Tours; Interpretation; Lectures; Publication; Reenactments

COLLECTIONS: [1810-1830] Plantation House on Bayou St. John, furnished with LA and American antiques associated with the period of James Pilot, first elected mayor of New Orleans.

HOURS: Yr W-Sa

3357
Louisiana State Museum
751 Chartes St, 70176 [PO Box 2448, 70176-2448]; (p) (504) 568-6968, (800) 568-6968; (f) (504) 568-4995; lsm@crt.state.la.us; lsm.crt.state.la.us; (c) Orleans

State/ 1911/ staff: 105(f); 600(v)/ members: 1800

HISTORIC PRESERVATION AGENCY; HISTORIC SITE; HISTORY MUSEUM; HOUSE MUSEUM; RESEARCH CENTER: Preserves and presents LA's unique cultural heritage through landmark properties in New Orleans and across the state.

PROGRAMS: Community Outreach; Concerts; Exhibits; Facility Rental; Family Programs; Festivals; Film/Video; Guided Tours; Interpretation; Lectures; Research Library/Archives

COLLECTIONS: Decorative arts, jazz memorabilia, maps and documents, paintings, photography, furniture, folk art, science and technology, costumes and textiles, and Mardi Gras memorabilia.

HOURS: Yr T-Su 9-5

ADMISSION: $5, Student $4, Seniors $4; $4 Military

3358
Memorial Hall's Confederate Museum
929 Camp St, 70130; (p) (504) 523-4522; (f) (504) 523-8595; memhall@aol.com; www.confederatemuseum.com

Private non-profit/ 1891/ staff: 2(f); 3(p); 10(v)/ members: 250

HISTORY MUSEUM: Preserves Confederate history and memorabilia.

PROGRAMS: Community Outreach; Exhibits; Facility Rental; Interpretation; Reenactments

COLLECTIONS: [1861-1865] Memorabilia and effects of the common soldier as well as top southern generals; flags, weapons, and uniforms.

HOURS: Yr M-Sa 10-4

ADMISSION: $5, Children $2, Seniors $4

3359
National D-Day Museum, The
923 Magazine St, 70130; (p) (504) 527-6012; (f) (504) 527-6088; info@ddaymuseum.org; www.ddaymuseum.org; (c) Orleans

Private non-profit/ 1991/ staff: 30(f); 10(p); 150(v)/ members: 3000

LIBRARY AND/OR ARCHIVES: Promotes the memory, history, and education of D-Day.

PROGRAMS: Exhibits; Facility Rental; Film/Video; Guided Tours; Lectures; Theatre

COLLECTIONS: [WW II] Military and homefront, 10,000 artifacts, 1,000 manuscripts, maps, and photographs.

HOURS: Yr M-Su 9-5

ADMISSION: $7, Student $5, Seniors $6

3360
New Orleans Notarial Archives
Room B-4, Civil District Courts Bldg, 70112 [421 Loyola Ave, 70112]; (p) (504) 680-9604; (f) (504) 680-9607; skrnona@gnofn.org; (c) Orleans

1867/ LA State/ staff: 17(f); 3(p)

LIBRARY AND/OR ARCHIVES: Preserves and makes available private sector legal instruments and notarial acts in the New Orleans area from 1731 to the present

PROGRAMS: Lectures; Research Library/Archives

COLLECTIONS: [1731-present] Authentic notarial acts derived from Roman-based system of civil law including property transfers, wills, inventories, marriage, and building contracts; 40,000 water color architectural drawings and blueprints.

HOURS: Yr

3361
New Orleans Pharmacy Museum
514 Chartes St, 70130; (p) (504) 565-8027; (f) (504) 565-8028; (c) Orleans

Private non-profit/ 1950/ Municipal Govt. Friends of Historical Pharmacy/ staff: 3(f); 5(v)/ members: 240/publication: *Rx News*

HISTORIC SITE; HISTORY MUSEUM: Operates a pharmacy and medical museum housed in an 1823 building constructed for Louis Joseph Dulfilho, first licensed pharmacist in the US.

PROGRAMS: Exhibits; Facility Rental; Guided Tours; Lectures; Publication; Research Library/Archives; School-Based Curriculum

COLLECTIONS: [19th c] Exhibits emphasize history of pharmacy and health care; apothecary bottles and jars; drugs, herbs, medical devices, trade journals, Civil War surgical instruments; cosmetics; 1855 soda fountain; voodoo gris-gris potions.

HOURS: Yr T-Su 10-5

ADMISSION: $2, Student $1, Seniors $1

3362
Preservation Resource Center of New Orleans
604 Julia St, 70130; (p) (504) 581-7032; (f) (504) 522-9275; prc@prcno.org; www.prcno.org; (c) Orleans

Private non-profit/ 1974/ staff: 18(f); 2(p); 400(v)/ members: 3000/publication: *Preservation in Print*

HISTORIC PRESERVATION AGENCY: Promotes the preservation of New Orleans' historic architecture and neighborhoods by expanding the constituency that understands the economic, cultural, and aesthetic importance of historic preservation by involving citizens in preservation projects and services.

PROGRAMS: Annual Meeting; Community Outreach; Exhibits; Guided Tours; Publication; Research Library/Archives

COLLECTIONS: Documents on historic preservation, city planning, architecture, and historic home repairs.

3363
Vieux Carre Commission
334 Royal, 70130; (p) (504) 528-3950; (f) (504) 528-3945; marcc@new-orleans.la.us; www.vcc.new-orleans.la.us; (c) Orleans

City/ 1936/ City of New Orleans/ staff: 9(f); 2(v)

HISTORIC PRESERVATION AGENCY: Preserves the French Quarter and issues restoration permits.

PROGRAMS: Research Library/Archives

COLLECTIONS: Records of the Vieux Carre Commission by individual address, historic and contemporary photos, architectural drawings.

HOURS: Yr M-F 9-5

OIL CITY

3364
Caddo-Pine Island Oil Museum
200 S Land Ave, 71061 [PO Box 897, 71061]; (p) (318) 995-6895; (f) (318) 995-6848; laoilmuseum@earthlink.net; www.sec.state.la.us; (c) Caddo

State/ 1968/ Board of Directors/State Governing Board/ staff: 2(f); 2(p); 12(v)/ members: 325

HISTORICAL SOCIETY; HISTORY MUSEUM: The Caddo-Pine Island Oil Museum collects and preserves records of the Caddo Pine oil field and Caddo Lake for the education and enjoyment of the general public.

PROGRAMS: Annual Meeting; Community Outreach; Exhibits; Facility Rental; Festivals; Guided Tours; Research Library/Archives; School-Based Curriculum

COLLECTIONS: Early oil field equipment, tools, and photographs, and artifacts related to Caddo Indians and the railroad.

HOURS: Yr M-F 9-4

OPELOUSAS

3365
Opelousas Museum and Interpretive Center
315 N Main St, 70571 [PO Box 712, 70571-0712]; (p) (337) 948-2589; (f) (337) 948-2592; musdir@hotmail.com; www.opelousas.com; (c) Saint Landry

City/ 1992/ City of Opelousas/ staff: 1(f); 2(p); 2(v)/ members: 15/publication: Dust and Cobwebs

HISTORY MUSEUM: Collects, preserves, and interprets objects and artifacts about the history and culture of the area.

PROGRAMS: Community Outreach; Concerts; Elder's Programs; Exhibits; Family Programs; Festivals; Film/Video; Guided Tours; Interpretation; Lectures; Living History; Publication; Reenactments; Research Library/Archives; School-Based Curriculum; Theatre

COLLECTIONS: [Prehistoric-present] Print, artifacts, photos, and music archives.

HOURS: Yr

3366
Wannamuse Institute for Arts, Culture, and Ethnic Studies
[PO Box 7239, 70571]; (p) (318) 826-3934; (f) (318) 826-3934; wondara@asbank; (c) Saint Landry

Private non-profit/ 1989/ Wannamuse Institute/ staff: 1(f); 1(p); 9(v)

RESEARCH CENTER: A research and educational organization concerned with the documentation, presentation, and preservation of rural African American cultural traditions.

PROGRAMS: Community Outreach; Exhibits; Facility Rental; Family Programs; Festivals; Garden Tours; Interpretation; Lectures; Research Library/Archives

COLLECTIONS: Audio and video tapes, newspaper clippings, photographs, artifacts, and fieldnotes related to oral traditions, especially folk medicine.

HOURS: Feb-June, Sept-Nov by Appt 1-6

ADMISSION: Donations accepted

PINEVILLE

3367
Old Town Hall Museum
731 Main St, 71361 [PO Box 3820, 71361]; (p) (318) 449-5690; (f) (318) 442-8373; www.pineville.net; (c) Rapides

City/ staff: 1(p)

HISTORY MUSEUM: Operates a museum of LA municipal government.

PROGRAMS: Exhibits; Film/Video; Guided Tours

COLLECTIONS: [1931-1970] Fire truck (1950), call box fire alarm, early radar equipment, photos, and video.

HOURS: M-F 10-2

PORT ALLEN

3368
West Baton Rouge Historical Association/West Baton Rouge Museum
845 N Jefferson Ave, 70767; (p) (225) 336-2422; (f) (225) 336-2448; www.intersurf.com/locale/wbrm; (c) West Baton Rouge

County/ 1968/ staff: 4(f); 5(p); 75(v)/publication: Chronicles of West Baton Rouge

HISTORICAL SOCIETY: Collects, preserves, and interprets artifacts pertaining to the West Baton Rouge Parish area with particular emphasis on sugar plantation history, culture, and folklife.

PROGRAMS: Annual Meeting; Community Outreach; Elder's Programs; Exhibits; Facility Rental; Family Programs; Festivals; Guided Tours; Interpretation; Lectures; Living History; Publication; Reenactments; Research Library/Archives; School-Based Curriculum

COLLECTIONS: [19th c] Paintings, prints, photos, manuscripts, clothing, furniture, and objects relating to local industry, professions, domestic life, education, folklife, and related memorabilia.

HOURS: Yr T-Sa 10-4:30, Su 2-5

ADMISSION: No charge

RESERVE

3369
San Francisco Plantation House, The
LA Hwy 44 (River Rd), 70084 [PO Drawer AX, 70084]; (p) (504) 535-2341; (f) (504) 535-5450; information@sanfranciscoplantation.org; www.sanfranciscoplantation.org; (c) St. John the Baptist Parish

Private non-profit/ 1975/ staff: 4(f); 12(p)

HOUSE MUSEUM: Restored and maintains the historic 1856 plantation.

PROGRAMS: Community Outreach; Facility Rental; Guided Tours; Interpretation

COLLECTIONS: Five hand painted ceilings, faux marbling and wood graining throughout, and antique furnishings Belter and Mallard.

HOURS: Yr Daily 10-4:30

ADMISSION: $8, Student $4, Children $3

RUSTON

3370
Lincoln Parish Museum and Histoical Society
609 N Vienna St, 71270; (p) (318) 251-0018; (c) Lincoln

Private non-profit/ 1975/ Lincoln Parish Museum and Historical Society Board/ staff: 1(p)/ members: 200

HISTORIC PRESERVATION AGENCY; HISTORICAL SOCIETY; HISTORY MUSEUM; HOUSE MUSEUM: Preserves an 1890 house.

PROGRAMS: Annual Meeting; Exhibits; Facility Rental; Guided Tours

COLLECTIONS: [1890-1920] Miniature doll houses, early farm tools and implements, and Long family memorabilia.

HOURS: Yr T-F 10-4

ADMISSION: Donations accepted

SAINT FRANCISVILLE

3371
Audubon State Commemorative Area
Louisiana Hwy 965, 70775 [PO Box 546, 70775]; (p) (888) 677-2838; (f) (225) 784-0578; audubon@crt.state.la.us; www.crt.state.la.us/crt/parks/audubon.htm; (c) West Feliciana

State/ 1954/ LA Office of State Parks/ staff: 9(f); 20(v)

HISTORIC SITE

PROGRAMS: Exhibits; Facility Rental; Guided Tours; Interpretation; Living History; School-Based Curriculum

COLLECTIONS: [American Federal period] Over 3000 items ranging from furniture, decorative art pieces, photographs, books, manuscripts, farm implements, and textiles.

HOURS: Yr Daily 9-5

ADMISSION: $2

3372
Oakley Plantation House
Audubon State Commemorative Area, 70775 [PO Box 546, 70775]; (p) (225) 635-3739

HOUSE MUSEUM

3373
West Feliciana Historical Society
11757 Ferdinand St, 70775 [PO Box 338, 70775]; (p) (225) 635-6330; (c) West Feliciana

Private non-profit/ 1970/ staff: 1(f)/ members: 475

HISTORICAL SOCIETY: Operates a local history museum.

PROGRAMS: Community Outreach; Exhibits; Garden Tours

COLLECTIONS: Artifact pertaining to West Feliciana, cotton, and the railroad; photographs.

HOURS: Yr Daily 9-5

ADMISSION: Donations accepted

SAINT MARTINVILLE

3374
Maison Olivier
1200 N Main St, 70582; (p) (318) 394-3754, (318) 394-4784; (f) (318) 394-3754; longfellow@crt.state.la.us

1815/ Office of State Parks/ staff: 8(f); 20(v)

COLLECTIONS: [1830s-40s] Furnishings, agricultural tools (cane, cotton & Spanish moss industry), Acadian textiles

HOURS: Yr

3375
Acadian Memorial
121 S New Market St, 70582 [PO Box 379, Dept AM, 70582]; (p) (337) 394-2258; (f) (337) 394-2260; info@acadianmemorial.org; www.acadianmemorial.org; (c) St. Martin

Joint/ 1990/ staff: 2(f); 4(p); 20(v)/ members: 205/publication: Calling All Cajuns

GENEALOGICAL SOCIETY; HISTORIC SITE; RESEARCH CENTER: Monument to LA's Acadian legacy, honoring the victims of the Acadian exile of the 18th c.

PROGRAMS: Annual Meeting; Facility Rental; Guided Tours; Interpretation; Lectures; Living History; Publication; Research Library/ Archives; Theatre

COLLECTIONS: [1764-1813] Mural of Acadian refugees; Wall of Names listing the 3,000 exiles; an Eternal Flame; and a computerized archive on LA Acadians.

HOURS: Yr Daily

3376
Longfellow Evangeline State Historic Site
1200 N Main St, 70582; (p) (337) 394-3754, (888) 677-2900; (f) (337) 394-3754; (c) Saint Martin

State/ 1934/ Dept of Culture Recreation and Tourism; Office of State Parks/ staff: 7(f); 4(p); 20(v)

HISTORIC SITE; HISTORY MUSEUM; HOUSE MUSEUM; LIVING HISTORY/OUTDOOR MUSEUM: Interprets the history of the French-speaking cultures along the Bayou Teche by comparing life on a French Creole Plantation of the 1800s to life on a small Acadian Farmstead.

PROGRAMS: Community Outreach; Elder's Programs; Exhibits; Family Programs; Guided

Tours; Interpretation; Living History; School-Based Curriculum

COLLECTIONS: [1790-1840] Raised Creole plantation house with period furnishings, Acadian Cabin with LA colonial furnishings, farm tools, and Acadian textiles.

HOURS: Yr Daily 9-5

ADMISSION: $2

3377
Saint Martinville Main Street
201 Main St, 70582 [PO Box 646, 70582]; (p) (318) 394-2250; (f) (318) 394-2265; (c) Saint Martin

1992/ City of Martinville/ staff: 3(f); 4(p); 12(v)

HISTORIC PRESERVATION AGENCY; HISTORIC SITE; HISTORICAL SOCIETY; HISTORY MUSEUM: Restores and preserves the city of Saint Martinville.

PROGRAMS: Annual Meeting; Community Outreach; Exhibits; Facility Rental; Festivals; Lectures; Reenactments; Theatre

COLLECTIONS: [1840-1880s] Pictures, furniture, and clothing.

HOURS: Yr Daily 10-4

ADMISSION: Donations accepted

SAINT ROSE

3378
La Branche Plantation Dependency Home
11244 River Rd, 70087; (p) (504) 468-8843; (f) (504) 468-3379; www.labrancheplantation.com

1790/ Private/ staff: 1(f); 1(v)

HOURS: Yr

SHREVEPORT

3379
Catholic Diocese of Shreveport Archives
3500 Fairfield Ave, 71104; (p) (318) 868-4441; (f) (318) 868-4605; crivers@dioshpt.org; www.dioshpt.org; (c) Caddo

Private non-profit/ 1986/ Diocese of Shreveport/ staff: 1(f)

Gathers, arranges, safeguards, and makes available for research records of continuing value to the Catholic Church in northern LA.

PROGRAMS: Publication; Research Library /Archives

COLLECTIONS: [1856-1925] Items related to the history of the Catholic Church in northern LA, its bishops, clergy, churches, and schools; sacramental records.

HOURS: M-F 8:30-3:30 by Appt

3380
National Society of the Colonial Dames of Louisiana Shreveport Committee
525 Spring St, 71101; (p) (318) 424-0964; sshm@shrevenet.net; www.springstreetmuseum.com; (c) Caddo

Private non-profit/ 1977/ Shreveport Committee of the Colonial Dames/ staff: 1(f); 3(p); 5(v)/ members: 150

HISTORIC SITE; HISTORICAL SOCIETY;

HISTORY MUSEUM; HOUSE MUSEUM

PROGRAMS: Exhibits; Family Programs; Festivals; Guided Tours; Interpretation; Lectures; Living History; School-Based Curriculum

COLLECTIONS: [1800-1940] Vintage clothing, textiles, furniture, and china; local photos and papers.

HOURS: Yr T-Sa 10-3

ADMISSION: $3, Children $1

3381
Noel Memorial Library, Archives, and Special Collections
One University Place, LSU in Shreveport, 71115-2399; (p) (318) 797-5378; (f) (318) 797-5156; lconerly@pilot.lsus.edu; (c) Caddo

State/ 1975/ staff: 3(f); 2(p)/publication: Guide to Archives and Special Collections

LIBRARY AND/OR ARCHIVES; RESEARCH CENTER: Gather, acquire, preserve, and make available the papers, photographs, film, and records relating to NW LA history.

PROGRAMS: Community Outreach; Exhibits; Lectures; Publication; Research Library/ Archives

COLLECTIONS: [1830-present] Manuscripts, photographs, maps, oral histories, architectural drawings, film relating to LA history.

HOURS: Yr M-F 8-4:30

ADMISSION: No charge

3382
Pioneer Heritage Center
One University Place, 71115; (p) (318) 797-5332, (318) 797-5339; (f) (318) 797-5395; mplummer@pilot.lsus.edu; (c) Caddo

Private non-profit/ 1977/ LA State Univ in Shreveport/ staff: 2(f); 30(v)

HISTORIC SITE; HISTORY MUSEUM; HOUSE MUSEUM; LIVING HISTORY/OUTDOOR MUSEUM: A "history laboratory" devoted to local history and folklore.

PROGRAMS: Exhibits; Family Programs; Festivals; Guided Tours; Interpretation; Living History; Reenactments; School-Based Curriculum

COLLECTIONS: Pioneer tools and equipment, furniture, clothing rare books, photos, farm implements, quilts, and cooking utensils.

HOURS: By Appt

3383
Shreveport Fire Fighters Ark-La-Tex Antique and Classic Vehicle Museum
601 Spring, 71101; (p) (318) 222-0227; (f) (318) 222-5042; (c) Caddo

Private non-profit/ 1995/ Board of Directors/ staff: 1(f); 2(p); 25(v)/ members: 200

HISTORIC SITE: An educational and historical venue featuring vehicles, costumes, historical sets, and a library.

PROGRAMS: Annual Meeting; Community Outreach; Elder's Programs; Exhibits; Facility Rental; Family Programs; Festivals; Film/Video; Guided Tours; Lectures; School-Based Curriculum

COLLECTIONS: 500 books, 400 newspapers, 300 photos, and 2,000 artifacts of transportation: railroad, flight, motorcycles, trucks, cars, bicycles, and emergency vehicles.

HOURS: Yr T-Sa 9-5, Su 1-5

ADMISSION: $5, Student $4, Children $3, Seniors $4

3384
Spring Street Historical Museum
525 Spring St, 71101; (p) (318) 424-0964; (f) (318) 424-0964; sshm@shrevenet.net; www.springstreetmuseum.com; (c) Caddo

Private non-profit/ 1977/ Shreveport Committee of the National Society of Colonial Dames/ staff: 1(f); 2(p); 4(v)

GENEALOGICAL SOCIETY; HISTORIC SITE; HISTORY MUSEUM; HOUSE MUSEUM: Interprets local history.

PROGRAMS: Community Outreach; Exhibits; Guided Tours; Interpretation; Lectures; School-Based Curriculum

COLLECTIONS: [1830-1930] Books, clothing, decorative arts, correspondence, and photographs.

HOURS: Yr T-Sa 10-3

ADMISSION: $3, Children $1

3385
Stephens African American Museum
2810 Lindholm St, 71108-2610; (p) (318) 635-2147; (f) (318) 636-0504; gwenfrazier@juno.com; (c) Caddo

Private non-profit/ 1994/ staff: 2(f); 3(p); 7(v)/ members: 200

ART MUSEUM; HISTORY MUSEUM; RESEARCH CENTER: Operates a living history museum dedicated to the preservation of African-American history, artifacts, and documents.

PROGRAMS: Community Outreach; Exhibits; Facility Rental; Family Programs; Festivals; Guided Tours; Interpretation; Lectures; Research Library/Archives

COLLECTIONS: [18th c] Pre-Civil War Slave "Bill of Sale" dated 1857, pictures, documents, clothes, furniture, magazines, and newspapers.

HOURS: Yr T-Sa 12-4

ADMISSION: $2, Student $1

SLIDELL

3386
Guardians of Slidell History
2020 First St, 70459 [PO Box 2273, 70459-2273]; (p) (504) 646-4375, (504) 643-2269; (f) (504) 643-4493; wmcarroll@juno.com; (c) St. Tammany

Private non-profit/ 1996/ staff: 160(v)/ members: 99/publication: *The Courier*

HISTORIC PRESERVATION AGENCY; HISTORIC SITE; HISTORICAL SOCIETY; HISTORY MUSEUM: Preserves local history and encourages the public participation.

PROGRAMS: Community Outreach; Exhibits; Festivals; Film/Video; Publication

COLLECTIONS: [Early 1900s-1976] Collections related to city govt, industry, churches, schools, and family histories.

HOURS: Yr Th 2-4

ADMISSION: No charge

SORRENTO

3387
Cajun Village
6482 Hwy 22, 70778; (p) (800) 460-6815, (504) 675-8068; www.crt.state.la.us /crt/tourism/scenic/dolouis.htm

SPRINGHILL

3388
City of Springhill Historic District Commission
400 N Giles St, 71075; (p) (318) 539-5699; (f) (318) 539-2500; jwillis@cbt,net; www.springhilllouisiana.com; (c) Webster

1996/ City of Springhill/ staff: 1(f); 17(v)

HISTORIC PRESERVATION AGENCY; HISTORIC SITE: Restoration, preservation, and revitalization of historic Main Street, Springhill.

SULPHUR

3389
Brimstone Historical Society
800 Picard Rd, 70663; (p) (337) 527-7142; (f) (337) 527-0860; (c) Calcasieu

1975/ staff: 1(p)/ members: 90

HISTORICAL SOCIETY; HISTORY MUSEUM

PROGRAMS: Annual Meeting; Exhibits; Festivals

COLLECTIONS: [Early 20th c]

HOURS: Yr M-F 9:30-5, Sa 12-3

TANGIPAHOA

3390
Camp Moore Historical Association, Inc.
70640 Camp Moore Rd, 70465 [PO Box 25, 70465]; (p) (504) 229-2438; (c) Tangipahoa

Private non-profit/ 1965/ staff: 10(v)

HISTORIC SITE; HISTORICAL SOCIETY; HISTORY MUSEUM; LIVING HISTORY/OUTDOOR MUSEUM: Provide information about the history of the United States, Camp Moore, the Confederate States of America, and the Civil War.

PROGRAMS: Exhibits; Lectures; Living History; Reenactments

COLLECTIONS: [1861-1865] Artifacts, Civil War material, and regional history.

HOURS: Yr Th-Sa 9-4

ADMISSION: $2, Children $1

THIBODAUX

3391
Lafourche Heritage Society, Inc.
[PO Box 913, 70301-0913]; (c) Lafourche

Private non-profit/ 1976/ staff: 287(v)/ members: 287

HISTORIC PRESERVATION AGENCY; HISTORICAL SOCIETY: Preserves and promotes the history and cultural heritage of the Bayou Laforche Region through publications, historical markers, preservation awards, and genealogical research.

PROGRAMS: Annual Meeting

TROUT

3392
Lasalle Parish Library
Hwy 127, 71371 [Rt 1 Box 234, 71371]; (p) (318) 992-5675; (f) (318) 992-7374; www.lasalle.lib.la.us; (c) Lasalle Parish

Private non-profit/ Lasalle Parish Police Jury/ members: 3

ALLIANCE OF HISTORICAL AGENCIES; GENEALOGICAL SOCIETY: Maintains genealogy, micro-fishe, books, obituaries materials, and confederate histories.

PROGRAMS: Community Outreach; Exhibits; Family Programs; Film/Video; Lectures; Living History; Research Library/Archives; School-Based Curriculum

HOURS: Yr M-F

VACHERIE

3393
Laura Plantation
2247 Hwy 18, 70090; (p) (225) 265-7690; (f) (225) 265-7960; creolaura@aol.com; www.lauraplantation.com; (c) Saint James

Private for-profit/ 1805/ Laura Plantation Co., L.L.C./ staff: 11(f); 12(p)/publication: *Memories of My Old Plantation Home; and others*

HISTORIC SITE; HOUSE MUSEUM: Preserves and interprets LA's Creole culture, detailing the actual lives of Creole women, slaves, and children on this site over its 200 year period.

PROGRAMS: Elder's Programs; Exhibits; Facility Rental; Festivals; Garden Tours; Guided Tours; Interpretation; Publication

COLLECTIONS: [1780s-1890s] 5,000 pages of documents, mostly in French, relating to this site including 'Memoirs of Laura', photos, heirlooms, business and slave records.

HOURS: Yr Daily 9-5

ADMISSION: $8, Student $4

3394
Oak Alley Plantation
3645 Hwy 18, 70090; (p) (504) 265-2151, (800) 442-5539; (f) (504) 265-7035; oalley@oal.com; www.louisianatravel.com/oal_alley

1830

COLLECTIONS: [1830s]

HOURS: Yr

VIVIAN

3395
Vivian Railroad Station Museum
100 W Front St, 71082 [PO Box 31, 71082]; scollier@prodigy.net; www.pages.prodigy.net /scollier/hsnc; (c) Caddo

Private non-profit/ 1992/ Board of Directors/ staff: 5(f); 10(p); 15(v)/ members: 35/publication: *Historic Northern Caddo Parish; and others*

HISTORICAL SOCIETY; HISTORY MUSEUM: Collects, preserves, and interprets local history through exhibits.

PROGRAMS: Annual Meeting; Exhibits; Festivals; Guided Tours; Interpretation; Publication

COLLECTIONS: [1835-1945] Artifacts representative of pioneering and steamboating, agriculture, timber, and petroleum industries.

HOURS: Yr M-F 9-3

ADMISSION: No charge

WHITE CASTLE

3396
Nottoway Plantation
30970 Hwy 405, 70788 [PO Box 160, 70788]; (p) (504) 545-2730, (504) 545-2409; (f) (504) 545-8632; nottoway@worldnety.att.net

1859/ staff: 20(f); 70(p)

COLLECTIONS: [1860s]

HOURS: Yr Daily

ZACHARY

3397
Port Hudson State Historical Site
756 W Plains/PH Rd, 70791; (p) (225) 654-3775, (888) 677-3400; (f) (225) 654-1048; (c) East Feliciana

State/ LA Office of State Parks/ staff: 9(f); 15(v)

HISTORIC SITE; HISTORY MUSEUM; LIVING HISTORY/OUTDOOR MUSEUM; RESEARCH CENTER: Commemorates and preserves the site of the longest continuos siege in American military history and the last Confederate stronghold on the Mississippi River.

PROGRAMS: Community Outreach; Exhibits; Festivals; Film/Video; Guided Tours; Interpretation; Lectures; Living History; Reenactments; Research Library/Archives

COLLECTIONS: [1861-1865] Civil War artifacts, cannons, guns, canteens, uniforms, and other related items; Research Library: regimental histories, unit rosters, letters, diaries, and published books.

HOURS: Yr Daily 9-5

ADMISSION: $2

MAINE

ALLAGASH

3398
Allagash Historical Society
Rt 161 from Fort Kent to Allagash, 04774 [RFD 1, Box 237, 04774]; (p) (207) 398-3335; Pockwock.mail.sjv.net; (c) Aroostook

Private non-profit/ 1978/ staff: 12(v)/ members: 50

HISTORIC PRESERVATION AGENCY; HISTORICAL SOCIETY; HISTORY MUSEUM: Seeks to preserve the settlement history of Allagash.

PROGRAMS: Annual Meeting; Community Outreach; Exhibits; Guided Tours

COLLECTIONS: [1830-present] Genealogy, military, lumbering, farming, and kitchen artifacts.

HOURS: May-Sept 15 F-Su 12-4

ATHENS

3399
Athens Historical Society
Somerset Academy Bldg, 04912 [PO Box 4068, 04912]; (p) (207) 654-3923; (c) Somerset

Private non-profit/ 1985/ staff: 4(p) 1(v)/ members: 36

HISTORICAL SOCIETY; HISTORY MUSEUM: Encourage citizens to preserve history by establishing a small museum and publishing an annual report.

PROGRAMS: Annual Meeting; Exhibits; Research Library/Archives

COLLECTIONS: [1802-present] Early records, photographs, maps, correspondence, and family history.

HOURS: Yr by appt

AUBURN

3400
Androscoggin Historical Society
County Bldg, 2 Turner St, 04210-5978; (p) (207) 784-0586; www.rootsweb.com/~meandrhs; (c) Androscoggin

Private non-profit/ 1923/ staff: 1(p); 4(v)/ members: 130/publication: *Androscoggin History*

GENEALOGICAL SOCIETY; HISTORICAL SOCIETY; HISTORY MUSEUM: Preserves and disseminates the history of Androscoggin County.

PROGRAMS: Annual Meeting; Exhibits; Lectures; Publication; Research Library/Archives; School-Based Curriculum

COLLECTIONS: [Colonial era-present] Native American material from pre-history.

HOURS: Yr W-F 9-12/1-5

ADMISSION: No Charge

AUGUSTA

3401
Maine Historic Preservation Commission
55 Capitol St, 04333; (p) (207) 287-2132; (f) (207) 287-2335; (c) Kennebec

State/ 1971/ staff: 10(f)

Administers the National Historic Preservation Act to identify and protect significant architectural and archaeological resources. Conducts surveys statewide, and nominates all significant buildings, sites, and districts to the National Register of Historic Places. Also reviews all federally-funded and federally-licensed projects for their effect upon historic resources.

HOURS: Yr M-F 8-5

3402
Old Fort Western
16 Cony St, 04330; (p) (207) 626-2385; (f) (207) 626-2304; oldfort@oldfortwestern.org; www.oldfortwestern.org; (c) Kennebec

Joint/ 1922/ City/ staff: 2(f); 12(p); 30(v)/ members: 250

HISTORIC SITE; HOUSE MUSEUM; LIVING HISTORY/OUTDOOR MUSEUM: Preserves and interprets the military, store, and residential history of Fort Western, a National Historic Landmark, 1754 to 1810, through a variety of on-site and outreach programs and special events.

PROGRAMS: Annual Meeting; Community Outreach; Concerts; Elder's Programs; Exhibits; Family Programs; Film/Video; Guided Tours; Interpretation; Lectures; Living History; Publication; Reenactments; School-Based Curriculum

COLLECTIONS: [1754-1810] Military, store merchandise, and household objects.

HOURS: May-Oct Daily (July 4-Sept M-F 10-4)

ADMISSION: $4.75, Children $3.75; Under 6 free

BANGOR

3403
Bangor Historical Society
159 Union St, 04401; (p) (207) 942-5766; (f) (207) 941-0266; bangorhistorical@hotmail.com; www.bairnet.org; (c) Penobscot

Private non-profit/ 1864/ staff: 1(f); 3(p); 60(v)/ members: 400

HISTORICAL SOCIETY; HOUSE MUSEUM

PROGRAMS: Annual Meeting; Community Outreach; Exhibits; Facility Rental; Guided Tours; Lectures

COLLECTIONS: [19th c] Photographs, 19th c furnishings, and Civil War era artifacts.

HOURS: Apr-Dec T-F 12-4, Sa 12-4 (June-Sept)

ADMISSION: $5; Under 12 free

3404
Cole Land Transportation Museum
405 Perry Rd, 04401; (p) (207) 990-3600; (f) (297) 990-2653; mail @colemuseum.com; www.colemuseum.org; (c) Penobscot

Private non-profit/ 1990/ Gale Cole Family Foundation/ staff: 2(f); 7(p); 70(v)

HISTORY MUSEUM: Collects, preserves, and interprets local history.

PROGRAMS: Exhibits; Facility Rental; Guided Tours; School-Based Curriculum

COLLECTIONS: [Mid 1800s-present] 200 Maine land transportation vehicle, roller skates, locomotive, 2,000 photos, covered bridge, fire engines, farm tractors, recreation-toys, work sleds, sleighs, wagons, autos, road construction, trucks, saws, box car, caboose, RR Station, military, blacksmith shops.

HOURS: May 1-Nov 11 Daily 9-5

ADMISSION: $3, Seniors $2; Under 19 Free

3405
Iasaac Farrar Mansion
166 Union St, 04401; (p) (207) 942-5766

HOUSE MUSEUM

BAR HARBOR

3406
Robert Abbe Museum of Stone Age Antiquities

26 Mount Desert St, 04609 [PO Box 286, 04609]; (p) (207) 288-3519; (f) (207) 288-8979; abbe@midmaine.com; www.abbemuseum.org; (c) Hancock

Private non-profit/ 1928/ Board of Trustees/ staff: 5(f); 3(p); 12(v)/ members: 525

Collects, preserves, interprets, and conducts research on the history and culture of Native American cultures in Maine, from prehistory to the present.

PROGRAMS: Annual Meeting; Community Outreach; Exhibits; Family Programs; Festivals; Film/Video; Guided Tours; Interpretation; Lectures; Publication; Research Library /Archives; School-Based Curriculum

COLLECTIONS: [Paleo Indian-present] Prehistoric stone, bone, and ceramic tools representing 12,000 years of Native American occupations. Ethnographic and contemporary baskets, jewelry, tools, and artwork document historic Native arts and cultures.

HOURS: May-June, Sept-Oct Daily 10-4; July-Aug 9-5

ADMISSION: $2, Children $0.50

3407
William Otis Sawtelle Collections and Research Center

Rt 233, McFarland Hill, Park Headquarters, 04609 [c/o Acadia Nat'l Park, PO Box 177, 04609]; (p) (207) 288-5463; (f) (207) 288-5507; Brooke_Childrey@nps.gov; www.nps.gov/acad; (c) Hancock

Federal/ 1999/ staff: 1(f); 2(v)

HISTORIC SITE; HISTORY MUSEUM; RESEARCH CENTER: Collects, preserves and interprets the natural and cultural history of Acadia National Park and Saint Croix Island International Historic Site.

PROGRAMS: Exhibits; Interpretation; Lectures; Research Library/Archives

COLLECTIONS: [1596-1960] 865,000 archival documents and historic artifacts covering the colonization of New France, settlement of the Cranberry Isles of Maine, history of Maine, genealogy of the settlers.

HOURS: Yr T-F 8:30-3:30

BASS HARBOR

3408
Tremont Historical Society

[PO Box 7, 04653]; (p) (207) 244-3410; great-grandpa@acadia.net; (c) Hancock

Private non-profit/ 1982/ members: 250

HISTORIC PRESERVATION AGENCY; HISTORICAL SOCIETY: Collects items pertaining to the history of the town of Tremont including oral histories, pictures, and photo reproductions.

PROGRAMS: Annual Meeting; Exhibits; Festivals; Film/Video; Guided Tours; Publication; Research Library/Archives

COLLECTIONS: [1848-present] Artifacts that are relevant to the history of the town of Tremont.

HOURS: June-Sept Daily 10-5

ADMISSION: No charge

BATH

3409
Maine Maritime Museum

243 Washington St, 04530; (p) (207) 443-1316; (f) (207) 443-1665; maritime@bath-maine.com; wwww.bathmaine.com; (c) Sagadahoc

Private non-profit/ 1962/ staff: 20(f); 5(p); 285(v)/ members: 1804

HISTORIC SITE; HISTORY MUSEUM: Collects, preserves, and interprets artifacts and memorabilia relating to the maritime history of ME.

PROGRAMS: Annual Meeting; Community Outreach; Exhibits; Facility Rental; Family Programs; Guided Tours; Interpretation; Lectures; Publication; Research Library/Archives; School-Based Curriculum

COLLECTIONS: [1850-1950] 17,000 art, artifacts, books, photographs, and documents relating to ME maritime history.

HOURS: Yr Daily 9:30-5

ADMISSION: $9, Children $6, Seniors $8.25; Under 6

3410
Sagadahoc Preservation, Inc.

[PO Box 322, 04530]; (p) (207) 442-8455; join@sagadahocpreservation.org; www sagadahocpreservation.org; (c) Sagadahoc

Private non-profit/ 1972/ members: 225/publication: Bath Architecture

HISTORIC PRESERVATION AGENCY: To identify, preserve, and maintain buildings, and places in the county of Sagadahoc.

PROGRAMS: Annual Meeting; Guided Tours; Publication; School-Based Curriculum

COLLECTIONS: Architectural historical survey of buildings in the city of Bath, ME built before 1920.

HOURS: June 15-Sept T-Th

ADMISSION: $10

BETHEL

3411
Bethel Historical Society, The

14 Broad St, 04217 [PO Box 12, 04217-0012]; (p) (800) 824-2910; (f) (207) 824-0882; history@bdc.bethel.me.us; orion.bdc.bethel.me.us/~history; (c) Oxford

Private non-profit/ 1966/ staff: 1(f); 2(p); 100(v)/ members: 1200

HISTORICAL SOCIETY; HISTORY MUSEUM; HOUSE MUSEUM: Period house museum, home of Dr. Moses Mason.

PROGRAMS: Annual Meeting; Community Outreach; Concerts; Exhibits; Facility Rental; Festivals; Garden Tours; Guided Tours; Interpretation; Lectures; Publication; Reenactments; Research Library/Archives; School-Based Curriculum

COLLECTIONS: [1813-present] 30,000 items, including photographs, newspapers, documents, books, microfilm, microfiche, artifacts, and historic structures.

HOURS: Sept-June T-F 1-4; July-Aug T-Su 1-4

ADMISSION: $3, Family $5.70, Children $1.50

BIDDEFORD

3412
Biddeford Historical Society

270 Main St, 04005 [PO Box 200, 04005]; (p) (207) 284-4181; (c) York

Private non-profit/ 1968/ Board of Directors/ staff: 1(v)/ members: 132

HISTORICAL SOCIETY: Preserves the history of Biddeford, York County, and the State of ME. Legal secondary depository of the City of Biddeford records.

PROGRAMS: Annual Meeting; Concerts; Interpretation; Lectures; Research Library/ Archives; School-Based Curriculum

COLLECTIONS: [1628-present] Original Town Records of Biddeford, the first Parish Meeting house, letters, books, photographs, and scrapbooks.

HOURS: Yr Th 9:30-12 or by appt

BOOTHBAY

3413
Boothbay Railway Village

Rt 27, 04537 [PO Box 123, 04537]; (p) (207) 633-4727; www.railwayvillage.org; (c) Lincoln

Private non-profit/ 1964/ staff: 7(f); 8(p); 15(v)/ members: 380

LIVING HISTORY/OUTDOOR MUSEUM

PROGRAMS: Annual Meeting; Facility Rental; Festivals; Guided Tours

COLLECTIONS: [1850-1950]

HOURS: Yr Daily 9:30-5

ADMISSION: $7, Children $3

BOOTHBAY HARBOR

3414
Boothbay Region Historical Society

72 Oak St, 04538 [PO Box 272, 04538]; (p) (207) 633-0820; (c) Lincoln

Private non-profit/ 1967/ Board of Trustees/ staff: 20(v)/ members: 470

HISTORICAL SOCIETY; HISTORY MUSEUM; RESEARCH CENTER: Devoted to the history of Boothbay, Boothbay Harbor, and Southport. The Society collects, preserves, and interprets the region's past and augments its research capabilities with exhibits.

PROGRAMS: Annual Meeting; Exhibits; Lectures; Research Library/Archives

COLLECTIONS: [1730-present] 10,000 photographic images, 225 account books and diaries, 95 maps, 3,000 newspapers, 500 books, ephemera, 50 document collections, 5,000 artifacts, 25 paintings, and 40 feet of history and genealogy files.

HOURS: July-Aug W, F-Sa 10-4; Sept-June Sa 10-2

BRIDGTON

3415
Bridgton Historical Society
Gibbs Ave, 04009 [PO Box 44, 04009]; (p)
(207) 647-3699; bhs@megalink.net;
www.megalink.net/~bhs; (c) Cumberland

Private non-profit/ 1953/ staff: 1(f); 2(p); 15(v)/
members: 206

GENEALOGICAL SOCIETY; HISTORIC SITE;
HISTORICAL SOCIETY; HOUSE MUSEUM;
LIVING HISTORY/OUTDOOR MUSEUM; RE-
SEARCH CENTER: Collects, preserves, and
interprets material that documents the history
of the Bridgton community.

PROGRAMS: Annual Meeting; Exhibits; Facility Rental; Festivals; Guided Tours; Interpretation; Lectures; Living History; Research Li-
brary/Archives; School-Based Curriculum

COLLECTIONS: Manuscripts, newspapers,
scrapbooks, photographs, journals and day
books, personal letters, and museum artifacts.

HOURS: Yr T,Th 1-4 or by appt

ADMISSION: $1

BROOKSVILLE

3416
Brooksville Historical Society
Rt 176, 04617; (p) (207) 326-8681;
mcmillen@acadia.net

Private non-profit/ 1967/ members: 160

HISTORICAL SOCIETY; HISTORY MUSEUM:
Studies the history of Brooksville maintains a
museum of local artifacts, and seeks to educate the public.

PROGRAMS: Annual Meeting; Community
Outreach; Guided Tours

COLLECTIONS: [Colonial-W W II] Genealogy
records and local artifacts relating to farming,
seafaring, rural life, and early tourism.

HOURS: July-Aug W, Su 1-4

BROWNVILLE

3417
**Brownville/Brownville Junction
Historical Society**
Church St, 04414 [PO Box 750, 04414];
fandg@kynd.net; (c) Piscataquis

Private non-profit/ 1979/ Board of Directors/
staff: 8(v)/ members: 70

HISTORICAL SOCIETY; HISTORY MUSEUM:
Collect, preserve, and display artifacts, teach,
publish, and educate the public about
Brownville's unique place in local and Maine
history.

PROGRAMS: Annual Meeting; Community
Outreach; Exhibits; Festivals; Guided Tours; Interpretation; Lectures; Living History; Research Library/Archives; School-Based Curriculum

COLLECTIONS: [Late 18th-present] Detailed
documents from the late 18th c to the present:
government, pioneers, founders, historians,
churches, and the military.

HOURS: May-Oct T, Sa 10-3 by

BRUNSWICK

3418
**Peary-MacMillan Arctic Museum and
Arctic Studies Center, The**
Hubbard Hall, 04011 [Bowdoin College, 9500
College Station, 04011-8495]; (p) (207) 725-
3062, (207) 725-3416; (f) (207) 725-3499;
www.bowdoin.edu/dept/arctic; (c) Cumberland

Private non-profit/ 1967/ staff: 5(f); 2(p); 20(v)

Museum and academic programs focus on anthropology, archaeology, and environmental
investigations of the Arctic. Museum mounts
exhibits and sponsors lectures, workshops,
education outreach programs.

PROGRAMS: Community Outreach; Exhibits;
Guided Tours; Lectures

COLLECTIONS: Equipment, paintings, and
photographs relating to the history of arctic exploration, natural history specimens, and artifacts and drawings made by Inuit and Indians
of Arctic North America.

HOURS: Yr T-Sa 10-5, Su 2-5

ADMISSION: No charge

3419
Pejepscot Historical Society
159 Park Row, 04011; (p) (207) 729-6606; (f)
(207) 729-6012; pejepscot@curtislibrary.com;
www.curtislibrary.com/pejepscot.htm; (c)
Cumberland

Private non-profit/ 1888/ staff: 2(f); 2(p); 75(v)/
members: 1100

Dedicated to the local history of Brunswick,
Topsham, and Harpswell; maintains two historic houses.

PROGRAMS: Annual Meeting; Elder's Pro-
grams; Exhibits; Guided Tours; Interpretation;
Lectures; Research Library/Archives; School-
Based Curriculum

COLLECTIONS: [1850-1925] Manuscripts,
photographs, and artifacts of local history;
complete original furnishings and documentation of Skolfield-Whittier House; restored home
of Joshus Chamberlain, Civil War hero, ME
governor and college president.

HOURS: Pejepscot Museum: Yr T-F 9-5, Th 9-
8, Sa 9-4; Skolfield-Whittier House and Joshua
Chamberlain Museum June-Oct T-Sa 10-4

CALAIS

3420
Saint Croix Historical Society
245 Main St, 04619 [PO Box 242, 04619];
chasbl@nemaine.com; (c) Washington

Private non-profit/ 1954/ staff: 10(v)/ members:
115

HISTORIC SITE; HISTORICAL SOCIETY;
HOUSE MUSEUM: Preserve and disseminate
St. Croix Valley History; to preserve 1800 Doctor's cottage and museum for all public preserve 1906 lighthouse; preserve photo collection, including 300 glass plate negatives.

PROGRAMS: Exhibits; Festivals; Guided
Tours; Living History; Publication

COLLECTIONS: [1850-1860] Period home,
furnishings, restored Doctor's Cottage including medical office; listed on the National Register.

HOURS: July-Aug M, Th, F 1-4

ADMISSION: No charge

CAPE ELIZABETH

3421
**Cape Elizabeth Historical
Preservation Society**
6 Scott Dyer Rd, 04107; (p) (207) 799-1720;
cehps@thomas.lib.me.us; (c) Cumberland

Private non-profit/ 1977/ Board of Directors/
staff: 12(v)/ members: 67/publication: *Cape
Elizabeth: Past to Present*

HISTORICAL SOCIETY

PROGRAMS: Community Outreach; Exhibits;
Lectures; Publication; Research Library/
Archives

COLLECTIONS: [1718-present] Town reports
and records, local family memorabilia, and
photographs relating to town history and architecture.

HOURS: Yr Th 9-12 or by appt

CHARLOTTE

3422
Charlotte Historical Society
1092 Ayers Junction Rd, 04666 [RR# 1 Box
382, 04666]; (p) (207) 454-8238; (f) (207)
454-2114; CARTERA2@AOL.COM; (c)
Washington

Private non-profit/ 1983/ staff: 8(v)/ members:
92/publication: *LOON II*

GENEALOGICAL SOCIETY; HISTORICAL
SOCIETY; HISTORY MUSEUM; HOUSE MU-
SEUM: Promotes interested in the preserva-
tion of the history and culture of Charlotte and
nearby communities surrounding the St. Croix
River and the Passamaquddy and Cobscook
Bays of Washington County.

PROGRAMS: Annual Meeting; Exhibits; Family Programs; Lectures; Publication; Research
Library/Archives

COLLECTIONS: [1800-1920] Material related
to agriculture, lumbering, household items and
family history and genealogical collection of
local families of Washington County; 1827
farm house.

HOURS: July-Sept W 1-4 and by appt

ADMISSION: Donations accepted

CHERRYFIELD

3423
**Cherryfield-Narraguagus Historical
Society**
Main St, 04622 [PO Box 96, 04622]; (c)
Washington

Private non-profit/ 1974/ staff: 4(v)/ members:
250

GENEALOGICAL SOCIETY; HISTORICAL
SOCIETY; HISTORY MUSEUM: Collects information about the town and surrounding area
making it available through the museum and
research archives, schools, and local libraries.

PROGRAMS: Annual Meeting; Guided Tours;
Publication; Research Library/Archives;
School-Based Curriculum

COLLECTIONS: [1850-1920] Tools, household items, farm and sawmill equipment, photographs, genealogical collection of town history and family history from time of settlement CA 1760.

HOURS: July-Aug W-F 1-4 and by appt

ADMISSION: No charge

COLUMBIA FALLS

3424
Ruggles House Society
Main St, 04623 [RR 1 Box 120, 04623]; (p) (207) 483-4689; (c) Washington

Private non-profit/ 1932/ staff: 3(p)/ members: 40

HISTORIC SITE: Maintains mansion built by a wealthy merchant.

PROGRAMS: Guided Tours

COLLECTIONS: [1790-1890] Period furnishings and accessories used in this small mansion during the 1790 - 1890 period.

HOURS: June 1-Oct 15 M-Sa 9:30-4:30, Su 11-4:30

ADMISSION: Donations requested

DEER ISLE

3425
Deer Isle Historical Society
Rt 15 A, 04627 [PO Box 652, 04627]; (c) Hancock

Private non-profit/ 1959/ staff: 30(v)/ members: 200

HISTORICAL SOCIETY; LIBRARY AND/OR ARCHIVES: Preserves history and genealogy.

PROGRAMS: Annual Meeting; Exhibits; Guided Tours; Publication; Research Library/ Archives

COLLECTIONS: [1800-1920] 1830 House, furnished in period style, Salome Sellers House, Exhibit Hall, Archives Building, Old Sunset Post Office.

HOURS: July, Aug W-F 1-4, Oct-June M, Th for research

DEXTER

3426
Dexter Historical Society, Inc.
Water St, 04930 [PO Box 481, 04930]; (p) (207) 924-5721; (c) Penobscot

Private non-profit/ 1966/ Dexter Historical Society/ staff: 1(p); 10(v)/ members: 40/publication: *Dexter, Spirit of an Age; Our Neighborly Neighbors - Rural Dexter 1800-2000; and others*

HISTORICAL SOCIETY; HISTORY MUSEUM; HOUSE MUSEUM; LIBRARY AND/OR ARCHIVES; RESEARCH CENTER: Operates three museums; collects, preserves and displays items pertaining to Dexter history.

PROGRAMS: Annual Meeting; Community Outreach; Exhibits; Guided Tours; Interpretation; Lectures; Living History; Publication; Research Library/Archives

COLLECTIONS: [1801-present] Personal and business artifacts, photographs, manuscript records, diaries, genealogies.

HOURS: Mid May-mid Sept M-F10-4, Sa 1-4

ADMISSION: Donations accepted

DIXFIELD

3427
Dixfield Historical Society
63 Main St, 04224 [PO Box 182, 04224-0182]; (p) (207) 562-7595; (c) Oxford

Private non-profit/ 1975/ staff: 10(v)/ members: 190/publication: *The Dixfield Star*

HISTORICAL SOCIETY: Collects and preserves artifacts and data from Dixfield's past, preserves historical materials, and promotes through education.

PROGRAMS: Annual Meeting; Exhibits; Publication; Research Library/Archives

COLLECTIONS: [1800-present] Kitchen pantry items, vintage clothing, and other historical artifacts; 1,200 antique tools.

HOURS: June-Sept

ADMISSION: Donations accepted

DRESDEN

3428
Dresden Historical Society
Brick School House Museum Rt 128, 04342 [PO Box 201, 04342]; (p) (207) 737-2326; www.agate.net/~dresden; (c) Lincoln

Private non-profit/ 1969/ members: 65

HISTORICAL SOCIETY; HISTORY MUSEUM: Collect, record, and disseminate information on the history of Dresden; maintain a place relating to the history of the town for exhibition.

PROGRAMS: Community Outreach; Exhibits; Film/Video; Interpretation; Publication; Research Library/Archives

COLLECTIONS: [18th-20th c] Early education, ice industry, diorama, photos, architecture, archaeology, military history.

HOURS: Yr Sa-Su 1-4

ADMISSION: No charge

EAST MACHIAS

3429
Heath Historical Society
[PO Box 658, 04630]; (p) (207) 255-4713; (c) Washington

Private non-profit/ 1975/ Board of Directors/ staff: 6(v)/ members: 15

HISTORICAL SOCIETY: Collects items of historical interest and exhibit them at local events to promote appreciation of the history of East Machias.

PROGRAMS: Exhibits

COLLECTIONS: Photographs, town documents, newspaper clippings, artifacts, and tools.

EASTPORT

3430
Border Historical Society
Washington St, 04631 [PO Box 95, 04631]; (c) Washington

Private non-profit/ staff: 5(v)/ members: 235

HISTORICAL SOCIETY: Preserves local histories of communities on the United States/Canadian border.

PROGRAMS: Annual Meeting; Exhibits; Publication; Research Library/Archives

COLLECTIONS: [Early 19th c-W W I] Publications, artifacts, photographs, and items of clothing.

HOURS: May-Sept M-Sa 1-4

ADMISSION: Donations accepted

3431
Quoddy Maritime Museum
Water St, 04631 [PO 98, 04631]; (p) (207) 853-4297; charlton@nemaine.com; (c) Washington

Joint; Private non-profit/ 1995/ staff: 14(v)

HISTORIC PRESERVATION AGENCY; HISTORICAL SOCIETY; HISTORY MUSEUM: Preserves artifacts relating to Eastport's Maritime history, particularly the Quoddy Dam Model.

PROGRAMS: Annual Meeting; Community Outreach; Exhibits; Film/Video; Guided Tours; Interpretation; Lectures; Living History; Publication

COLLECTIONS: [1800-1940] Quoddy Dam Model (14' by 16') built by President Franklin Roosevelt in 1935; oral history videos, and stories from 1900-1940.

HOURS: June-Sept M-Sa 10-5

ADMISSION: Donations accepted

ELIOT

3432
Eliot Historical Society
[PO Box 3, 03903]; (p) (207) 439-9411; TRBuzz9@aol.com; (c) York

Private non-profit/ 1897/ staff: 35(v)/ members: 35

HISTORICAL SOCIETY: Preserves and promotes Eliot's history through publications, talks, meetings, and displays.

PROGRAMS: Annual Meeting; Community Outreach; Film/Video; Lectures; Publication

COLLECTIONS: [1810-present] Clothing, manuscripts, photographs, furniture, diaries, artifacts.

ELLSWORTH

3433
Colonel Black Mansion
81 W Main St, 04605; (p) (207) 667-8671

3434
Stanwood Wildlife Sanctuary
289 High St, 04605 [PO Box 485, 04605]; (p) (207) 667-8460; (c) Hancock

Private non-profit/ 1959/ staff: 1(f); 15(v)/ members: 300

HOUSE MUSEUM: Home of Cordelia Stanwood, pioneer photographer, writer, ornithologist; nature center with displays.

PROGRAMS: Annual Meeting; Community Outreach; Exhibits; Family Programs; Guided Tours; Lectures; School-Based Curriculum

COLLECTIONS: [1910-present] 1,000 glass plate negatives of birds and wildlife; manuscripts on bird lore; personal letter of C. Stanwood.

HOURS: Grounds: Yr; Museum and Native Center: June 15-Oct 15 Daily 10-4

ADMISSION: Donations

FARMINGTON

3435
Maine Genealogical Society
[PO Box 221, 04938]

Private non-profit/ members: 1000

GENEALOGICAL SOCIETY: Collects, exchanges, preserves, and publishes genealogical records related documents and information; promotes, encourages interest, and scholarship in genealogy and family history.

PROGRAMS: Annual Meeting; Publication

COLLECTIONS: [1620-present]

3436
Nordica Memorial Association
Holley Rd, 04938 [RR 3, Box 3062, 04938]; (p) (207) 778-2042

1800

COLLECTIONS: [1857-1914] Her china; many pictures of her; several gowns; stage jewelry; gifts to her from admirers during her singing career.

HOURS: Seasonal

FORT KENT

3437
Fort Kent Historical Society
Market St, 04743 [PO Box 181, 04743]; (p) (207) 834-5258; (c) Aroostook

Private non-profit/ 1925/ Fort Kent Historical Society/ staff: 10(v)/ members: 50

HISTORICAL SOCIETY: Housed in a railroad station; promotes local history.

PROGRAMS: Annual Meeting; Exhibits; School-Based Curriculum

COLLECTIONS: [Early 1900] Railroad artifacts, early household artifacts, pictures, lumberman's artifacts.

HOURS: July T-Th 1-4

ADMISSION: No charge

FRANKLIN

3438
Franklin Historical Society
Hog Bay Rd Rte 200, 04634 [PO Box 317, 04634]; (c) Hancock

Private non-profit/ 1965/ Board of Directors/ staff: 50(v)/ members: 100

HISTORICAL SOCIETY; HISTORY MUSEUM: Operates entirely by volunteers and maintains four buildings including a museum and memorial park.

PROGRAMS: Annual Meeting; Community Outreach; Concerts; Exhibits; Facility Rental; Guided Tours; Interpretation; Lectures; Research Library/Archives

COLLECTIONS: [Late 1800s and early 1900s]

1,000 artifacts reflecting the area's industries, education, agriculture, with emphasis on granite quarrying, ship-building, family life.

HOURS: July-Aug Th-Sa 2-4

ADMISSION: No charge

FREEPORT

3439
Freeport Historical Society
45 Main St, 04032; (p) (207) 865-3170; (f) (207) 865-9055; (c) Cumberland

Private non-profit/ 1969/ staff: 2(f); 3(p); 30(v)/ members: 450

HISTORIC SITE; HISTORICAL SOCIETY; HISTORY MUSEUM; LIBRARY AND/OR ARCHIVES: Owns and operates two historic properties.

PROGRAMS: Annual Meeting; Community Outreach; Concerts; Exhibits; Family Programs; Festivals; Film/Video; Garden Tours; Guided Tours; Interpretation; Lectures; Living History; Publication; Research Library/Archives; School-Based Curriculum

COLLECTIONS: [Mid 19th c-present] Archival materials, maps, photographs, and artifacts.

HOURS: Yr

FRIENDSHIP

3440
Friendship Museum, Inc.
Corner of Rt 220 & Martin Point Rd, 04547 [PO Box 321, 04547]; (c) Knox

Private non-profit/ 1965/ staff: 3(v)/ members: 90

HISTORY MUSEUM: Housed in an old brick schoolhouse; artifacts and memorabilia.

PROGRAMS: Exhibits

COLLECTIONS: [1900s] Fishing gear, lobstering, photographs, household goods.

HOURS: July-Aug M-F 1-4, Sa, Su 2-4

ADMISSION: No charge

GILFORD

3441
Monson Historical Society
Main St, 04443 [PO Box 173, 04443]; ebennett@telplus.net; (c) Piscataquis

City/ 1967/ staff: 5(v)/ members: 128

HISTORICAL SOCIETY: Organization for collecting and preserving local history.

PROGRAMS: Annual Meeting; Community Outreach; Exhibits; Facility Rental; Family Programs; Festivals; Film/Video; Lectures; Publication; Research Library/Archives; School-Based Curriculum

COLLECTIONS: [1800s-1900s] Early life of Monson, Scandinavian influence, slate mining, schools, narrow gauge railroad.

GORHAM

3442
Baxter Museum
71 South St, 04038; (p) (207) 839-3878

Joint/ 1797/ Town; Baxter Memorial Library

Boyhood home of James Phinney Baxter, mayor of Portland, and governor of ME.

COLLECTIONS: [Colonial-present] Furnishings, artifacts, papers of James Phinney Baxter.

HOURS: Jul-Aug

3443
Gorham Historical Society
28 School St, 04038; (p) (207) 839-4313; USER149971@aol.com; (c) Cumberland

Private non-profit/ 1968/ Executive Committee/ staff: 12(v)/ members: 120

HISTORIC PRESERVATION AGENCY; HISTORIC SITE; HISTORICAL SOCIETY; HISTORY MUSEUM; LIBRARY AND/OR ARCHIVES: Classifying ephemera and photos and building data bases of local history.

PROGRAMS: Annual Meeting; Community Outreach; Exhibits; Guided Tours; Lectures; Research Library/Archives

COLLECTIONS: [1733-present] Ephemera, photographs, and local records.

HOURS: Apr-Oct Th 10-1

ADMISSION: No charge

GREENVILLE

3444
Moosehead Historical Society
Pritham Ave, 04441 [PO Box 1116, 04441-1116]; (p) (207) 695-2909; (f) (207) 685-3163; eparker@moosehead.net; (c) Piscataquis

Private non-profit/ 1962/ Board of Directors/ staff: 1(f); 3(p); 10(v)/ members: 125

HISTORICAL SOCIETY: Collects, preserves, and interprets history of the entire North Woods region.

PROGRAMS: Annual Meeting; Community Outreach; Exhibits; Family Programs; Film/Video; Guided Tours; Interpretation; Lectures; Research Library/Archives

COLLECTIONS: [Civil War -1950s] Displays, artifacts of early settlers of Moosehead region, logging, and lumbering industry, history of North Woods.

HOURS: June-Sept 1-4

ADMISSION: $2, Children $1; Members Free

HANCOCK

3445
Historical Society of the Town of Hancock, The
Point Rd, 04640 [PO Box 74, 04640]; (p) (207) 422-3080; (c) Hancock

Private non-profit/ 1979/ Board of Directors/ staff: 10(v)/ members: 110

HOUSE MUSEUM: Collects materials relating to Hancock history.

PROGRAMS: Annual Meeting; Community Outreach; Exhibits; Family Programs; Lectures; Research Library/Archives

COLLECTIONS: [1850-present] 1,200 file folders of Hancock History, town maps, government records, letters, and artifact.

HOURS: May-Oct T 10-12 and by appt

HARMONY

3446
Harrison Historical Society
[PO Box 83, 04942]; (c) Somerset

Private non-profit/ 1994/ Board of Directors/ members: 154/publication: *Historical Review*

HISTORIC PRESERVATION AGENCY; HISTORICAL SOCIETY; HISTORY MUSEUM: Preserves the history of Harmony.

PROGRAMS: Annual Meeting; Community Outreach; Exhibits; Guided Tours; Publication

COLLECTIONS: Artifacts, photographs, farm tools, kitchen utensils, blacksmith shop.

HOURS: By appt

ADMISSION: No charge

HARRISON

3447
Harrison Historical Society
121 Haskell Hill Rd, 04040; (p) (207) 583-6225; (c) Cumberland

1963/ members: 100

HISTORICAL SOCIETY; HISTORY MUSEUM; LIBRARY AND/OR ARCHIVES: Collects and displays artifacts and records pertinent to Harrison's past.

PROGRAMS: Exhibits

COLLECTIONS: [1850-1950] Journals, diaries, school pictures, research papers, toys, tools, household items, farm equipment, military items.

HOURS: July-Aug W 1-3 and by appt

ADMISSION: No charge

HINCKLEY

3448
L.C. Bates Museum
Rt 201, 04944; (p) (207) 453-4894; (c) Somerset

Private non-profit/ 1911/ staff: 1(f); 1(p); 53(v)/ members: 25/publication: *Beaver Paw Press*

ART MUSEUM; HISTORY MUSEUM; LIVING HISTORY/OUTDOOR MUSEUM: Offers educational tours, presents Maine's history, and offers outreach programs.

PROGRAMS: Community Outreach; Elder's Programs; Exhibits; Family Programs; Festivals; Guided Tours; Interpretation; Lectures; Living History; Publication; Reenactments; Research Library/Archives; School-Based Curriculum

COLLECTIONS: [1900s] L.C. Bates collections including arboretum of ME species, American Art, ME history, objects of Good Will-Hinckley Homes showing the social history of childcare, archaeology,anthropology.

ISLESFORD

3449
Islesford Historical Society
Little Cranberry Island, 04646; (p) (207) 244-7893, (703) 352-0846; hldwelley@aol.com; www.cranberryisles.com; (c) Hancock

Private non-profit/ 1990/ Board of Trustees/ staff: 4(v)/ members: 200/publication: *A Histo-*

ry of Little Cranberry Island, Maine; Memories of a Maine Island: Turn-of-the-Century Tales and Photographs; and others

HISTORICAL SOCIETY: Devoted to collecting, preserving, and publishing the local history.

PROGRAMS: Annual Meeting; Exhibits; Publication

COLLECTIONS: [1762-present] Documents and artifacts relating to the history of Little Cranberry Island.

HOURS: Yr T-Th 9-12

ADMISSION: No charge

KENNEBUNK

3450
Brick Store Museum, The
117 Main St, 04043; (p) (207) 985-4802; (f) (207) 985-6887; info@bricksstoremuseum.org; (c) York

Private non-profit/ 1936/ staff: 4(f); 2(p); 50(v)/ members: 475/publication: *Sketch of an Old River*

HISTORY MUSEUM: Preserving the cultural heritage of the Kennebunks.

PROGRAMS: Annual Meeting; Exhibits; Lectures; Publication; Research Library/Archives

COLLECTIONS: [1750-present] 45,000 objects, including paintings, furniture, photographs, costumes, ephemera, tools, toys, ceramics, navigation instruments and tools, maritime related objects, and archival material.

HOURS: Mar-Dec T-Sa

3451
Taylor-Barry House
24 Summer St, 04043 [PO Box 177, 04043]; (p) (207) 985-4296, (207) 985-4802; (f) (207) 985-6887; brickstore@cybertours.com; www.cybertours.com/~brickstore/

1803/ Private non-profit

HOUSE MUSEUM: Depicts the lifestyles of Captain Charles Williams, a master mariner and merchant during Kennebunk's shipbuilding era; and the artist's studio of his niece, Edith Barry.

COLLECTIONS: Household furnishings of the 1800s; paintings; a mid-20th c artist's studio and her numerous paintings and sculpture.

HOURS: July-Aug

KENNEBUNKPORT

3452
Kennebunkport Historical Society, The
125 N St, 04046 [PO Box 1173, 04046]; (p) (207) 967-2751; (f) (207) 967-1205; kports@gwi.net; www.kporthistory.org; (c) York

Private non-profit/ 1852/ staff: 1(f); 2(p); 80(v)/ members: 405/publication: *The Log*

HISTORICAL SOCIETY: Preserve local history.

PROGRAMS: Annual Meeting; Exhibits; Guided Tours; Interpretation; Lectures; Publication; Research Library/Archives

COLLECTIONS: [1650-1999] Mott House original furnishings, clothing; Town House School research center, exhibit hall and offices; 270 linear feet of archives, 7,000 photographs, 4,000 artifacts, 50 maps, 450 volumes, 4 newspaper titles, 50 oral histories.

HOURS: Yr Summer T-F 10-4, Sa 10-1; Winter T-F 10-4

3453
New England Electric Railway Historical Society / Seashore Trolley Museum
195 Log Cabin Rd, 04046 [PO Box A, 04046]; (p) (207) 967-2800; (f) (207) 967-0867; carshop@gwi.net; www.trolleymuseum.com; (c) York

1939/ Board of Trustees/ staff: 4(f); 3(p); 150(v)/ members: 1200

HISTORICAL SOCIETY; HISTORY MUSEUM: Preserves the history of the mass transit industry by collecting, restoring, displaying, operating, and interpreting vehicles and artifacts.

PROGRAMS: Community Outreach; Exhibits; Guided Tours; Interpretation; Research Library/Archives

COLLECTIONS: [1896-1971] 250 vehicles, 3,000 small items, books drawings, photographs, and artifacts.

HOURS: May-Oct Daily 10-5

ADMISSION: $7, Student $4.50; Under 6 Free

KINGFIELD

3454
Kingfield Historical Society
High St, 04947 [PO Box 238, 04947]; (p) (207) 265-4032; (c) Franklin

Private non-profit/ 1964/ staff: 12(v)/ members: 85

HISTORICAL SOCIETY: Preserves and interprets local area history.

PROGRAMS: Annual Meeting; Exhibits; Guided Tours

COLLECTIONS: [19th-early 20th c] Eclectic collection of artifacts housed in a Victorian house that is on the National Register.

HOURS: June-Sept W 9-4

3455
Stanley Museum, Inc.
School St, 04947 [PO Box 77, 04947]; (p) (207) 265-2729; (f) (207) 265-4700; www.stanleymuseum.org; (c) Franklin

Private non-profit/ 1981/ staff: 3(f); 1(p); 30(v)/ members: 700/publication: *Stanley Museum Quarterly*

HISTORY MUSEUM: Collects and shares the traditions of Yankee Ingenuity and creativity.

PROGRAMS: Annual Meeting; Exhibits; Guided Tours; Interpretation; Lectures; Publication; Research Library/Archives

COLLECTIONS: [1850-1985] Airbrush portraits, photographic equipment, steam cars, and violins of Francis and Freelan Stanley. Artwork and black/white photography of Chansonetta Stanley Emmons. Stanley family archives. Both museums housed in buildings designed by Stanley twins.

HOURS: Yr ME: May 1-Oct 31; Nov 1-Apr 30 M-F Daily 1-4 and by appt; CO: Yr call for times

LEWISTON

3456
Edmund S. Muskie Archives and Special Collections Library
Bates College, 70 Campus Ave, 04240-6018; (p) (207) 786-6354; (f) (207) 786-6035; muskie@bates.edu; www.bates.edu/ muskie_archives; (c) Androscoggin

Private non-profit/ 1985/ President and Trustees of Bates College/ staff: 3(f); 3(p)

LIBRARY AND/OR ARCHIVES: Collects, preserves, and makes available papers, office files, campaign records, and memorabilia Edmund S. Muskie, James B. Longley, and other political collections. Houses the Muskie Oral History Project; maintains rare books and manuscripts, collects works published by small ME press; and administers Archives of Bates College.

PROGRAMS: Community Outreach; Guided Tours; Interpretation; Lectures; Living History; Research Library/Archives; School-Based Curriculum

COLLECTIONS: [1946-1996] The Muskie collection, national politics in the post WW II period, 2,800 linear feet of materials.

HOURS: Yr M-F 9-4

ADMISSION: No charge

LIVERMORE

3457
Norlands Living History Center, Washburn Mansion
290 Norlands Rd, 04253; (p) (207) 897-4366; (f) (207) 897-4963

1867/ staff: 4(f); 25(p); 56(v)

HISTORY MUSEUM; RESEARCH CENTER

COLLECTIONS: [1870s] Political memorabilia from Washburn's relationships, notably Lincoln and Grant; dry-point etchings of Cadwallader Washburn; oil portraits by Healy; Victorian furnishings; Papers and journals of Washburns; Town archives of Livermore.

LUBEC

3458
Franklin D. Roosevelt Cottage
RCIP, PO Box 129, 04652; (p) (506) 752-2922; (f) (506) 752-6000; info@fdr.net; www.fdr.net

Federal/ 1897/ staff: 14(f); 29(p)

HISTORY MUSEUM; HOUSE MUSEUM: Preserves summer home of US President Franklin D. Roosevelt.

COLLECTIONS: [1897-1950] House, furniture, books, papers and personal effects.

MACHIAS

3459
Burnham Tavern Museum
Main St, Just off Rt 1, 04654 [2 Free St, 04654]; (p) (207) 255-4432; valdine@juno.com; (c) Washington

Private non-profit/ 1910/ Hannah Weston Chapter, DAR/ staff: 1(p); 3(v)

HOUSE MUSEUM: The oldest building in Eastern Maine and has a Revolutionary War history. The Tavern is preserved as a memorial to the early settlers of the Machias Valley.

PROGRAMS: Exhibits; Guided Tours

COLLECTIONS: [1763-1850]

HOURS: Mid June-Sept M-F 9-5

ADMISSION: $2.50, Children $0.25

MACHIASPORT

3460
Gates House
, 04655 [Machiasport Historical Society, PO Box 301, 04655]; (p) (207) 255-8461, (207) 255-8557

1800/ Private non-profit

COLLECTIONS: Early ship information; history of the area.

MADAWASKA

3461
Madawaska Historical Society
US # 1, 04756 [PO Box 258, 04756]; (p) (207) 728-4518; (c) Aroostook

Private non-profit/ 1969/ staff: 1(p); 12(v)/ members: 512

HISTORIC SITE; HISTORICAL SOCIETY; HOUSE MUSEUM: Preservation of local culture and history predominately Acadian.

PROGRAMS: Annual Meeting; Exhibits; Lectures; Publication; Reenactments

COLLECTIONS: [1785-present] Artifacts, papers, and documents pertaining to Acadians who settled the St. John Valley of Northern ME.

HOURS: June-Sept M-F 10:30-3:30, Su 1:30-3:30

MERCER

3462
Mercer Historical Society
, [RR 2 Box 930, Norridgewolk, 04957]; (p) (207) 758-7256; (c) Somerset

City/ 1983/ staff: 8(p)/ members: 8

HISTORICAL SOCIETY: Documents town history and collects tools and records related to the town.

PROGRAMS: Annual Meeting; Guided Tours; School-Based Curriculum

COLLECTIONS: [1804-1940] Records and artifacts.

HOURS: June-Sept by appt

ADMISSION: No charge

MONHEGAN ISLAND

3463
Monhegan Historical and Cultural Museum Association, Inc.
1 Lighthouse Hill, 04852; (p) (207) 596-7003; (c) Lincoln

Private non-profit/ 1984/ staff: 50(v)/ members: 300

HISTORY MUSEUM: A museum housed in a historic lighthouse complex that preserves and displays objects and information related to the history of Monhegan Island.

PROGRAMS: Annual Meeting; Exhibits; Research Library/Archives

COLLECTIONS: [1850-present] Artifacts related to Monhegan Island's history that include works of art and exhibits of natural history, local history, the fishing industry, the lighthouse, and early island life.

HOURS: July-Aug Daily 11:30-3:30, Sept

MONMOUTH

3464
Monmouth Museum
Main St, 04259 [PO Box 352, 04259]; (p) (207) 933-2287; (c) Rennebec

Private non-profit/ 1975/ staff: 15(v)

HISTORY MUSEUM; HOUSE MUSEUM; LIBRARY AND/OR ARCHIVES

PROGRAMS: Exhibits; Festivals; Guided Tours; Research Library/Archives

COLLECTIONS: [19th c] Objects and documents relating to 19th c life in rural ME; Carriage House, Blossom House, Stencil Shop, Freight Shed, Country Store.

ADMISSION: $3

MONSON

3465
Monson Museum
Main St, 04464 [182 Steward Rd, 04464]; (p) (207) 997-3792; (c) Piscataquis

Private non-profit/ 1972

HISTORY MUSEUM: Collection of local artifacts and memorabilia.

PROGRAMS: Exhibits

COLLECTIONS: [Early 1800s-present] Mostly farming, lumbering, and slate mining.

HOURS: Varies

ADMISSION: Donations accepted

MOUNT DESERT

3466
Mount Desert Island Historical Society
2 Oakhill Rd, 04660 [PO Box 653, 04660]; (p) (207) 244-5043; (f) (207) 244-3991; jroths@ acadia.net; www.ellsworthme.org/ mdihsociety; (c) Hancock

Private non-profit/ 1931/ Board of Directors/ staff: 1(f); 1(p); 10(v)/ members: 493/publication: *Desert Island Historical Society*

HISTORICAL SOCIETY; HISTORY MUSEUM: Preserves the heritage, protects the scenic and historic Mount Desert Island.

PROGRAMS: Annual Meeting; Exhibits; Family Programs; Festivals; Guided Tours; Lectures; Publication; Research Library/Archives

COLLECTIONS: [Late 18th-early 20th c] 3,000 artifacts, 5,000 documents, 6,000 photos

NAPLES

3467
Naples Historical Society
On the Village Green, Rt 302, 04055 [Naples town office, Village Green, 04055]; (p) (207)

693-6979; (f) (207) 693-3667; nic@pinot.net; www.napleschamber.com; (c) Cumberland

Joint; Private non-profit/ 1974/ staff: 3(v)/ members: 15/publication: *Now I Will Tell You*

GENEALOGICAL SOCIETY; HISTORICAL SOCIETY; HISTORY MUSEUM: Collect artifacts and memorabilia related to the town of Naples; archives with a focus on the Cumberland and Oxford Canal, Native American artifacts and historic buildings.

PROGRAMS: Annual Meeting; Community Outreach; Exhibits; Festivals; Film/Video; Lectures; Publication; School-Based Curriculum

COLLECTIONS: [1850-present] Native American, pottery shards, arrow heads, tools. Town records, cemetery records, family histories, photos, and genealogy. Farm machinery, folk lore artifacts, steamboat, architectural, and way of life artifacts.

HOURS: June-Aug F 10-2

ADMISSION: Donations accepted

NEW GLOUCESTER

3468
New Gloucester Maine Historical Society
[PO Box 531, 04260]; (c) Cumberland

Private non-profit/ 1934/ staff: 16(v)/ members: 125/publication: *Footnotes*

HISTORICAL SOCIETY; LIBRARY AND/OR ARCHIVES: Collects materials and items that relate to the history of New Gloucester; maintains a library and archives.

PROGRAMS: Annual Meeting; Exhibits; Family Programs; Festivals; Lectures; Publication; Research Library/Archives; School-Based Curriculum

COLLECTIONS: [1700s-present] Town records, both official and individual family records; vehicles, artifacts.

ADMISSION: By appt

3469
United Society of Shakers
707 Shaker Rd, 04260; (p) (207) 926-4597; brooks1@shaker.lib.me.us; www.shakerlib.me.us; (c) Cumberland

Private non-profit/ 1931/ staff: 4(f); 1(p); 40(v)

HISTORIC SITE; HISTORY MUSEUM: Exists as an educational corporation to help the public learn about the Shaker way of life through our Shaker museum and Shaker library.

PROGRAMS: Concerts; Elder's Programs; Exhibits; Guided Tours; Lectures; Publication; Research Library/Archives; School-Based Curriculum

COLLECTIONS: [1790s-1950s] 100,000 items that tell the Shaker story from the late 1700s and includes information on the Shaker Villages.

HOURS: May-Oct M-Sa 10-4:30

ADMISSION: $6, Children $2

NEW HARBOR

3470
Fishermen's Museum
Keeper's House/ Pemaquid Point Lighthouse, 04554 [Bristol Rd, 04554]; (p) (207) 677-2494; (c) Lincoln

Private non-profit/ 1972/ staff: 3(p); 20(v)

HISTORY MUSEUM: Preserves relics and tools of the local fishing industry; charts, scrap books, boat models.

PROGRAMS: Exhibits

COLLECTIONS: [Early 20th c] Artifacts of the fishing industry; large chart of ME Coast, pictures of the lighthouse, Fresnel lens, compasses, old pictures.

HOURS: Mid May-mid Oct Daily M-Sa 10-5, Su 11-5

NEWFIELD

3471
Willowbrook at Newfield Restoration Village
59 Elm St, 04056 [PO Box 80, 04056]; (p) (207) 793-2784; (c) York

Private non-profit/ 1970/ staff: 1(f); 6(p)

HISTORIC SITE; HISTORY MUSEUM; HOUSE MUSEUM: 19th c museum in New England with 37 structures.

PROGRAMS: Guided Tours

COLLECTIONS: [19th c] 10,000 artifacts, Herschell carousel and 60 horse drawn carriages and sleighs. Two homesteads, tools, farm equipment, barber shop, bank, school house, boats, gas engines, bicycles, photo shop, crafts such as cobbler, ice harvesting, and weaving.

HOURS: May 15-Sept 30 Daily 10-5

ADMISSION: $7, Student $3.50; Under 6 free

NOBLEBORO

3472
Nobleboro Historical Society
198 Center St, 04555 [PO Box 122, 04555]; (p) (207) 563-5874; (c) Lincoln

City/ 1978/ staff: 3(p); 10(v)/ members: 200

HISTORICAL SOCIETY; HISTORY MUSEUM: Collects and exhibits artifacts and makes available genealogies, and history records for town of Nobleboro.

PROGRAMS: Annual Meeting; Exhibits; Festivals; Interpretation; Lectures; Publication; Research Library/Archives

COLLECTIONS: [1830-present] Business account books; criminal term reports; genealogies; old building histories; published articles on Nobleboro History and artifacts.

HOURS: July-Aug Sa 1:30-4:30 and by appt.

NORTH ANSON

3473
Embden Historical Society
Across Town Rd, 04958 [16 Philpot Ln, 04958]; (p) (207) 643-2434; (c) Somerset

Private non-profit/ 1983/ staff: 15(v)/ members: 54

HISTORICAL SOCIETY: Preserves local history and cares for 19 local cemeteries.

PROGRAMS: Annual Meeting; Community Outreach; Exhibits; Guided Tours; Living History; Reenactments; School-Based Curriculum

COLLECTIONS: [1895-present] 100 years of town reports, photographs, various research reports.

HOURS: Feb-Nov 3rd M or by appt

ADMISSION: No charge

NORTH HAVEN

3474
North Haven Historical Society
Main St, 04853 [RR # 1 Box 858, 04853-9719]; (p) (207) 867-2248; (c) Knox

Private non-profit/ 1975/ staff: 12(v)/ members: 335

GENEALOGICAL SOCIETY; HISTORICAL SOCIETY; HISTORY MUSEUM; RESEARCH CENTER: Promotes interest in the history of North Haven Island and collects, preserves, exhibits, educates, and cooperates with other area Historical Societies.

PROGRAMS: Annual Meeting; Community Outreach; Exhibits; Film/Video; Interpretation; Lectures; Reenactments; Research Library/Archives; School-Based Curriculum

COLLECTIONS: [1785-present] Early 1900 display of home, store, barn, tool shed, and local Industry; oral histories, books, genealogical records, family photographs, local artwork.

HOURS: Museum: July-Aug T 2-5; Archives: Sept-June Th 2-5; by appt only

ADMISSION: No charge

NORTHEAST HARBOR

3475
Great Harbor Martitine Museum
125 Main St, 04662 [PO Box 145, 04662]; (p) (207) 276-5262; (f) (207) 276-5262; (c) Hancock

Private non-profit/ 1982/ Board of Directors/ staff: 2(p); 4(v)

Provides and presents: materials and artifacts relating to regions maritime traditions.

PROGRAMS: Community Outreach; Concerts; Exhibits; Family Programs; Festivals; Film/Video; Interpretation; Lectures; School-Based Curriculum; Theatre

COLLECTIONS: [1850-present] Maritime photographs and artifacts.

HOURS: May-Oct M-Sa 9-5

ADMISSION: Donations requested

OCEAN PARK

3476
Ocean Park Historical Society
Porter Hall, 04063 [PO Box 7308, 04063]; (c) York

Private non-profit/ 1976/ staff: 12(v)/ members: 30

HISTORICAL SOCIETY; HISTORY MUSEUM: Program meetings and exhibits.

PROGRAMS: Exhibits; Guided Tours; Lectures

COLLECTIONS: Photos, costumes, programs, artifacts, post cards.

HOURS: July-Aug Su 11:30

ADMISSION: No charge

OLD TOWN

3477
Old Town Canoe Company
58 Middle St, 04468 [PO Box 548, 04468]; (p)
(207) 827-5513; (f) (207) 827-2779; feedback@
oldtowncanoe.com; www.oldtowncanoe.com;
(c) Penobscot

Private non-profit/ 1898/publication: *Legacy:
The First 100 Years*

CORPORATE ARCHIVES/MUSEUM: The
largest and oldest continuous manufacturer of
canoes and kayaks in the world; in operation
since 1898; shaped by water-built by hand.

PROGRAMS: Publication; Research Library/
Archives

COLLECTIONS: [Early 1900s-present] Vintage canoes, authentic birchbark canoe from
the local Penobscot Nation.

HOURS: Yr Jan-Feb M-F 9-5; Mar-Oct M-Sa
10-3; Nov-Dec M-Sa 9-5

3478
Old Town Museum
138 S Main St, 04468 [PO Box 375, 04468];
(p) (207) 827-7256; ozamaine@aol.com; (c)
Penobscot

City, non-profit/ 1976/ staff: 1(f); 40(v)

HISTORY MUSEUM; LIVING HISTORY/OUT-
DOOR MUSEUM

PROGRAMS: Annual Meeting; Concerts; Exhibits; Facility Rental; Lectures; Living History;
School-Based Curriculum

COLLECTIONS: [1800s-1900s] Focuses on
local history and its industrial base; lumbering
textile, shoe, and paper manufactories.

HOURS: Apr-Dec

ADMISSION: No charge

ORONO

3479
Hudson Museum, University of Maine
Univ of ME, 04469 [5746 Maine Center for the
Arts, 04469-5746]; (p) (207) 581-1901; (f) (207)
581-1950; hudsonmuseum@unit.maine.edu;
www.umaine.edu/hudsonmuseum; (c)
Penobscot

1986/ staff: 2(f); 27(p); 29(v)/ members:
74/publication: *The Totem: Hudson Museum
News for Schools*

HISTORY MUSEUM: Promote research, exploration, and understanding of the diversity of
human experience through acquiring, documenting, preserving, scientifically investigating, interpreting, and exhibiting material culture.

PROGRAMS: Community Outreach; Elder's
Programs; Exhibits; Family Programs; Festi-
vals; Guided Tours; Lectures; Publication;
School-Based Curriculum

COLLECTIONS: [Neolithic-present] 8,000
ethnographic and archaeological objects included pre-Columbian holding as well as Native American, South American, African,
Oceanic, and Asian collections.

HOURS: Yr T-F 9-4, Sa-Su 11-4

ADMISSION: Donations accepted

3480
Maine Folklife Center
S Stevens Hall, Univ of Maine, 04469; (p)
(207) 581-1891; (f) (207) 581-1823;
www.umaine.edu/folklife; (c) Penobscot

State/ staff: 2(f); 2(p)/ members: 186/publica-
tion: *Northeast Folklore*

RESEARCH CENTER: Conducts public arts
and history programming including publication. Northeast Archives of folklore and oral
history collects and preserves documentation
of cultural heritage and community history in
Maine, New England and the Canadian Maritime Provinces.

PROGRAMS: Community Outreach; Exhibits;
Festivals; Lectures; Publication; Research Li-
brary/Archives

COLLECTIONS: [1880-present] 3,500 tapes
of recorded interviews and traditional music
(2,500 w/transcripts); 8,000 photos; 3,600
songs; 1,500 library volumes; 270 periodicals;
250 linear feet of manuscript materials; 300
LPs; 250 videos.

HOURS: Yr M-F 9-4

ADMISSION: No charge

3481
Maine Forest and Logging Museum
Rt 178, 04473 [PO Box 456, 04473]; (p) (207)
581-2871; ummflmus@saturn.caps.maine.edu;
(c) Penobscot

Private non-profit/ 1962/ staff: 2(f); 220(v)/
members: 280/publication: *Maine's Forest History: A Reader's Guide; The Logging Scott,
History and Design*

HISTORIC SITE; HISTORY MUSEUM: Preserving and sharing ME's forest history.
Leonard's Mills is a reconstructed logging and
milling community, where Maine's pioneers
and lumbering heritage are featured.

PROGRAMS: Annual Meeting; Community
Outreach; Exhibits; Facility Rental; Family Pro-
grams; Festivals; Guided Tours; Interpretation;
Living History; Reenactments; School-Based
Curriculum

COLLECTIONS: [Late 1700s-Present] Logging
and farming tools and equipment, broad axes,
peaveys, saws, log scales, bateaus, chainsaws;
blacksmithing tools; wood-working tools; barn
loom; Lombard log hauler; and related photographs; period buildings: water-powered sawmill,
blacksmith's shop, log cabin, trappers line camp
hovel, and early settlers' house.

HOURS: Nov-Mar by appt

ADMISSION: Donations accepted

OWLS HEAD

3482
Owls Head Transportation Museum
Rt 73, 04854 [PO Box 277, 04854]; (p) (207)
594-4418; (f) (207) 594-4410; ohtm@
midcoast.com; www.ohtm.org; (c) Knox

Private non-profit/ 1974/ staff: 10(f); 1(p);
175(v)/ members: 2750

AVIATION MUSEUM; HISTORY MUSEUM:
Collects, preserves, and exhibits pioneer aircraft, ground vehicles, and engines significant
to the evolution of transportation, and heavier-
than-air flight.

PROGRAMS: Community Outreach; Concerts; Exhibits; Facility Rental; Family Programs; Film/Video; Guided Tours; Interpretation; Lectures; Living History; Publication;
Reenactments; Research Library/Archives;
School-Based Curriculum

COLLECTIONS: [1890-1920] Aeroplanes, automobiles, engines, carriages, bicycles

PATTEN

3483
Patten Lumbermans Museum
Rt 159 Shin Pond Rd, 04765 [PO Box 300,
04765]; (p) (207) 528-2398; (c) Penobscot

Private non-profit/ 1962/ Board of Trustees/
staff: 1(f); 2(p); 15(v)/ members: 12

HISTORY MUSEUM

PROGRAMS: Annual Meeting; Exhibits; Family Programs; Film/Video; Reenactments; Research Library/Archives

COLLECTIONS: [Early 1800s-1920s]

HOURS: May-June F-Su 10-4; July-Aug T-Su
10-4; Sept 1-Oct 9 F-Su 10-4

ADMISSION: $3.50, Children $1

PEAKS ISLAND

3484
Fifth Maine Regiment Center
45 Seashore Ave, 04108 [PO Box 41, 04108];
(p) (207) 766-3330; fifthmaine@juno.com;
http://fifthmaine.home.att.net/; (c) Cumberland

Private non-profit/ 1954/ Fifth Maine Regiment
Community Association/ staff: 45(v)/ members: 365/publication: *Fifth Maine News*

HISTORICAL SOCIETY; HISTORY MUSEUM:
Preserves and interprets ME's history and the
Fifth Maine Infantry's roles in the Civil War as
well as the history of Peaks Island.

PROGRAMS: Annual Meeting; Community
Outreach; Exhibits; Facility Rental; Film/Video;
Guided Tours; Interpretation; Lectures; Publi-
cation; Reenactments

COLLECTIONS: [1860-1950] Photographs,
documents, maps, and artifacts.

HOURS: July 1-Sept M-F 1-4, Sa-Su 1-4;
Sept-July 1 Sa-Su 11-4

PEMBROKE

3485
Pembroke Historical Society
Leighton Point Rd, 04666 [RR 1 Box 220,
04666]; (p) (207) 726-4734; (c) Washington

Private non-profit/ 1995/ staff: 10(v)/ members:
225/publication: *The Pemmaquon Call*

HISTORICAL SOCIETY: Preservation and
publication of History of Pembroke.

PROGRAMS: Annual Meeting; Publication;
Research Library/Archives

COLLECTIONS: [1784-1900] Historical documents, vital statistics.

PITTSTON

3486
Arnold Expedition Historical Society
Arnold Rd, 04345 [RR #4, Box 6895,

Gardiner, 04345]; (p) (207) 582-7080; (c) Kennebec

Private non-profit/ 1968/ staff: 5(v)/ members: 150

HISTORIC PRESERVATION AGENCY; HISTORIC SITE; HISTORICAL SOCIETY; HISTORY MUSEUM; HOUSE MUSEUM: Preservation, research, and educational society that maintains a library and museum of the Arnold expedition to Quebec in 1775.

PROGRAMS: Annual Meeting; Community Outreach; Exhibits; Guided Tours; Publication

COLLECTIONS: [1775] Military artifacts from 1775, clothing, flags, and boats from a 1975 reenactment.

HOURS: July-Aug Sa-Su 10-4 or by appt

ADMISSION: $3

PORTER

3487
Parsonsfield-Porter Historical Society
92 Main St, 04068 [PO Box 92, 04068]; (c) Oxford

Private non-profit/ 1946/ staff: 14(v)/ members: 150

HISTORICAL SOCIETY; HOUSE MUSEUM: Collects and preserve artifacts, photographs, documents, and publications of historical significance that relate directly to the history of region; preserve and make available for research genealogical records.

PROGRAMS: Exhibits; Guided Tours; Lectures; Publication; Research Library/Archives

COLLECTIONS: [1800-present] Artifacts, photographs, documents, publications, local history, and genealogical records.

HOURS: Meeting 1Sa Apr-Nov and by appt.

PORTLAND

3488
Greater Portland Landmarks, Inc.
165 State St, 04101; (p) (207) 774-5561; (f) (207) 774-2509; gladma1@maine.rr.com; www.portlandlandmarks.org; (c) Cumberland

Private non-profit/ 1964/ Board of Trustees/ staff: 2(f); 3(p); 100(v)/ members: 1000

HISTORIC PRESERVATION AGENCY; LIBRARY AND/OR ARCHIVES: Works to increase public's awareness of and appreciation for this area's remarkable built environment.

PROGRAMS: Annual Meeting; Community Outreach; Garden Tours; Guided Tours; Lectures; Publication; Research Library/Archives; School-Based Curriculum

COLLECTIONS: Books, preservation, Maine history.

HOURS: Yr M-F 9-5

ADMISSION: No charge

3489
Maine Historical Society
485 Congress St, 04101; (p) (207) 774-1822; (f) (207) 775-4301; www.mainehistory.org; (c) Cumberland

Private non-profit/ 1822/ staff: 9(f); 6(p); 25(v)/ members: 2200

HISTORICAL SOCIETY: Houses the state's historical and genealogical library with over 125,000 books and two million manuscripts, maintains a museum collection with 8,000 objects, conducts a wide range of programs and outreach services and publishes works of significant historical scholarship.

PROGRAMS: Annual Meeting; Community Outreach; Exhibits; Facility Rental; Guided Tours; Lectures; Publication; Research Library/Archives; School-Based Curriculum

COLLECTIONS: 60,000 books, two million manuscripts, 5,000 artifacts.

HOURS: Library: Yr T-Sa 10-4;

3490
Maine Humanities Council
371 Cumberland Ave, 04112 [PO Box 7202, 04112]; (p) (207) 773-5051; (f) (207) 773-2416; info@mainehumanities.org; www.mainehumanities.org; (c) Cumberland

Private non-profit/ 1975/ staff: 4(f); 4(p)

NATURAL HISTORY MUSEUM; PROFESSIONAL ORGANIZATION: Support community programs in culture heritage contemporary issues, reading, and literacy as well as enrichment programs for teachers.

PROGRAMS: Annual Meeting; Community Outreach; Elder's Programs; Exhibits; Family Programs; Festivals;

3491
Maine Narrow Gauge Railroad Company Museum
58 Fore St, 04101; (p) (207) 828-0814; (f) (207) 879-6132; mnerr@clinic.net; www.datamaine.com; (c) Cumberland

Private non-profit/ 1993/ members: 400

HISTORIC SITE; HISTORY MUSEUM; RAILROAD MUSEUM; RESEARCH CENTER: Museums collects, maintain, preserves, and exhibits historic railroad materials and artifacts.

PROGRAMS: Community Outreach; Exhibits; Facility Rental; Festivals; Guided Tours; Lectures; Publication; Research Library/Archives; School-Based Curriculum

COLLECTIONS: [Late 1870-present] Thirty plus pieces of rolling stock one and a half miles of track, books, pictures, ephemera, library, and two-foot gauge railroad line, four steam engines, marine engines.

HOURS: Yr Daily 10-4

3492
Maine Preservation
500 Congress St, 04104 [PO Box 1198, 04104]; (p) (207) 775-3652; (f) (207) 775-7737; maineprs@gwi.net; mainepreservation.com; (c) Cumberland

Private non-profit/ 1971/ staff: 1(f); 1(p); 20(v)/ members: 1000/publication: *Beautiful in All Its Details: The Architecture of Maine's Public Library Buildings; and others.*

HISTORIC PRESERVATION AGENCY: Dedicated to preserving and protecting the irreplaceable architectural heritage, historic places, and communities of ME.

PROGRAMS: Annual Meeting; Community

3493
McLellan House
High St, 04101 [Portland Museum of Art, 7 Congress Square, 04101]; (p) (207) 775-6148; (f) (207) 773-7324; www.portlandmuseum.org

1800

COLLECTIONS: [1780-1850] Decorative arts c. 1780-1850 by Portland artisans; portraits of members of McLellan and Clapp families; artifacts owned by Margaret Mussey Sweat; Extensive documents relating to McLellan family and Portland, c. 1800.

HOURS: By appt only

3494
Tate House Museum
1270 Westbrook St, 04104 [PO Box 8800, 04104]; (p) (207) 774-9781; (f) (207) 774-6177; tate@gwi.net; (c) Cumberland

Private non-profit/ 1931/ staff: 1(f); 3(p); 60(v)/ members: 200/publication: *Tate House Gazette*

HISTORIC SITE; HOUSE MUSEUM: Maintains the Tate House Museum.

PROGRAMS: Community Outreach; Exhibits; Facility Rental; Family Programs; Garden Tours; Guided Tours; Interpretation; Lectures; Publication; School-Based Curriculum

COLLECTIONS: [Mid-late 18th c] Home (built in 1755) of Maine Mast agent, Captain George Tate, period furnishings.

HOURS: May-Oct T-Sa 10-4, Su

3495
Victoria Mansion, Inc.
109 Danforth St, 04101; (p) (207) 772-4841; (f) (207) 772-6290; victoria@maine.rr.com; www.portlandarts.com/victoriamansion; (c) Cumberland

Private non-profit/ 1943/ staff: 3(f); 15(p); 62(v)/ members: 260

HISTORICAL SOCIETY; HOUSE MUSEUM: Preserves, restores, and maintains Victoria Mansion, a National Historic Landmark, documents and interprets the history and significance of the buildings, furnishings, and residents as important expressions of 19th c American culture.

PROGRAMS: Annual Meeting; Exhibits; Facility Rental; Family Programs; Guided Tours; Interpretation; Lectures; Research Library/Archives; School-Based Curriculum

COLLECTIONS: [1860-1900] Morse-Libby Mansion (1858-60) and carriage house, original interior decoration by Gustave Herter, 400 objects original to the Morses and Libbys, furniture, silver, ceramics, glass, lighting fixtures, artwork.

HOURS: May-Oct T-Sa 10-4, Su 1-5

ADMISSION: $5

3496
Wadsworth-Longfellow House
487 Congress St, 04101 [485 Congress St, 04101]; (p) (207) 879-0427, (207) 774-1822; (f) (207) 775-4301; mainehistory.com

1785/ staff: 12(f); 4(p); 30(v)

COLLECTIONS: [1880s] Home to three generations; family papers from three generations including bills for original furniture.

RANGELY

3497
Wilhelm Reich Museum, The
Dodge Pond Rd, 04970 [PO Box 687, 04970]; (p) (207) 864-3443; (f) (207) 864-5156; wreich@rangeley.org; www.rangeley.org/~wreich/; (c) Franklin

Private non-profit/ 1960/ staff: 2(f); 5(p); 12(v)/publication: *Organomic Functionalism*

HISTORY MUSEUM: A Historic site and nature preserve which interprets the life and work of physician/scientist Wilhelm Reich (1897-1957) and the environment in which he investigated the energy functions in nature.

PROGRAMS: Annual Meeting; Community Outreach; Exhibits; Facility Rental; Family Programs; Film/Video; Guided Tours; Interpretation; Lectures; Publication

COLLECTIONS: [1897-1957] Scientific equipment, and library, photographs, paintings, furnishings, and personal items.

RICHMOND

3498
C.H.T.J. Southard House Museum
75 Main St, 04357; (p) (207) 737-8202; (c) Sagadahoc

Private non-profit/ 1990/ staff: 5(v)

HOUSE MUSEUM: Preserves and shares local culture and enriches the local community; preserve building.

PROGRAMS: Exhibits; Guided Tours

COLLECTIONS: [Late 1800s-early 1900s] Victorian sea captain's home and carriage house, consists of turn-of-the-century tools, toys, and textiles, including ice harvesting exhibits.

HOURS: Yr Sa 1-5 or by appt

ADMISSION: $1

ROCKLAND

3499
Island Institute
386 Maine St, 04841-3350; (p) (207) 594-9209; (f) (207) 594-9314; inquires@islandinstitute.org; www.islandinstitute.org; (c) Knox

Private non-profit/ 1983/ staff: 30(f); 3(p); 5(v)/ members: 3500/publication: *Working Waterfront, Island Journal*

RESEARCH CENTER: Community and economic development, resource management and research.

PROGRAMS: Community Outreach; Publication

HOURS: M-F

3500
Olson House
384 Hathorn Point Rd, 04841 [PO Box 466, 04841]; (p) (207) 596-6457; (f) (207) 596-0509; janice@farnsworth.midcoast.com; www.farnsworthmuseum.org; (c) Knox

Private non-profit/ 1991/ staff: 1(f); 3(p); 15(v)/ members: 2000

HISTORIC SITE; HOUSE MUSEUM: 1800 home of the Hathorn and Olson families better known as the site the American artist Andrew Wyeth painted from 1938-1968. Best known

Wyeth work from that era 1948 tempera painting "Christina's World."

PROGRAMS: Exhibits; Festivals; Guided Tours; Interpretation; Lectures; School-Based Curriculum

COLLECTIONS: [20th c] Reproductions of Andrew Wyeth's artwork.

HOURS: May-Oct 15 Daily 11-4

ADMISSION: $9, Student $5, Seniors $8; Under 18 free

3501
Shore Village Museum
104 Limerock St, 04841; (p) (207) 594-0311; (f) (207) 594-9481; knb@ine.net; www.tier.net/users/buster.sltirevillage; (c) Knox

City/ 1976/ staff: 2(f); 8(v)

3502
William A. Farnsworth Homestead
21 Elm St, 04841 [PO Box 466, 04841]; (p) (207) 596-6457; (f) (207) 596-0509; janice@farnsworth.midcoast.com; www.farnsworthmuseum.org; (c) Knox

Private non-profit/ 1935/ staff: 1(f); 3(p); 15(v)/ members: 2000

HOUSE MUSEUM: 1850 home of the museum's founder, Lucy Farnsworth. Maintained in original state since 1871.

PROGRAMS: Exhibits; Family Programs; Guided Tours; Interpretation; Lectures; School-Based Curriculum

COLLECTIONS: [Late 19th c] Original 1871 house, original furnishings, wallpaper, carpeting, gas lights, and family papers and books.

HOURS: May-Oct Daily 10-5

ADMISSION: $9

3503
William A. Farnsworth Library & Art Museum
352 Main St, 04841 [PO Box 466, 04841]; (p) (207) 596-6457; (f) (207) 596-0509; farnswth@midcoast.com; www.farnsworthmuseum.org; (c) Knox

Private non-profit/ 1948/ staff: 25(f); 40(p); 200(v)/ members: 2000/publication: *Maine in America: American Art at the Farnsworth Art Museum*

ART MUSEUM; LIBRARY AND/OR ARCHIVES: Art museum with a focus of American art related to the state of Maine.

PROGRAMS: Community Outreach; Concerts; Elder's Programs; Exhibits; Facility Rental; Family Programs; Festivals; Film/Video; Guided Tours; Interpretation; Lectures; Publication; Research Library/Archives; School-Based Curriculum

COLLECTIONS: [18 c-present] 19th and 20th c American art related to the state of ME including the works of Andrew and James Wyeth.

HOURS: Yr Daily summer 9-5; winter T-Sa 10-5, Su 1-5

ADMISSION: $9, Student $5, Seniors $8; Under 18 free

RUMFORD

3504
Rumford Area Historical Society
Congress, 04276 [Municipal Building, 04276]; (p) (207) 364-4773; (c) Oxford

Private non-profit/ 1970/ staff: 6(v)/ members: 78

GENEALOGICAL SOCIETY; HISTORIC SITE; HISTORICAL SOCIETY; HISTORY MUSEUM; RESEARCH CENTER: An archival organization open to the public for research and consultation.

PROGRAMS: Exhibits; Film/Video; Lectures; Reenactments; Research Library/Archives

COLLECTIONS: [Early 1800-present] Donated items.

HOURS: Museum:June-Sept W-F 10-5; Archives: Yr Th 9-2

SACO

3505
York Institute Museum
371 Main St, 04072; (p) (207) 283-0684; (f) (207) 283-0754; (c) York

Private non-profit/ 1866/ staff: 2(f); 20(v)/ members: 300

ART MUSEUM; HISTORY MUSEUM: Preserve and interpret the history and culture of the Saco River Valley.

PROGRAMS: Annual Meeting; Community Outreach; Exhibits; Family Programs; Guided Tours; Lectures; Research Library/Archives

COLLECTIONS: [1750-1950] Fine and decorative arts which represent the artistic heritage of Southern ME.

HOURS: Yr T,W,F 12-4, Th 12-8, Su 12-4

ADMISSION: $4, Family $10, Student $1, Seniors $3

SAINT AGATHA

3506
Saint Agatha Historical Society
Main St, 04772 [PO Box 237, 04772]; www.stagatha.com; (c) Aroostook

Joint/ 1977/ Directors; Town/ staff: 8(p); 20(v)/ members: 40

HISTORIC SITE; HISTORICAL SOCIETY; HOUSE MUSEUM: Preservation of local history - French Canadian, Acadian, and region.

PROGRAMS: Annual Meeting; Exhibits; Guided Tours; Publication

COLLECTIONS: [1900-present] Artifacts and memorabilia from early farmers, teachers, schools, local families, local historical material; photograph collection, historical house.

HOURS: June-Sept T- Su 1-4

ADMISSION: No charge/Donations

SCARBOROUGH

3507
Scarborough Historical Society and Museum
649 A US Rt 1, 04070 [PO Box 156, 04070-0156]; (p) (207) 883-3539; (c) Cumberland

Private non-profit/ 1961/ staff: 25(v)/ members: 130

HISTORICAL SOCIETY; HISTORY MUSEUM: Collects and displays artifacts and records relating the culture, heritage, and people of Scarborough.

PROGRAMS: Community Outreach; Exhibits; Research Library/Archives

COLLECTIONS: [1600-1900] Local history items including history and genealogical records and books, photographs, farm tools, household items, costumes, and personal artifacts.

HOURS: Yr T 9-12

ADMISSION: Donations accepted

SEARSPORT

3508
Penobscot Marine Museum
5 Church St, 04974 [PO Box 498, 04974]; (p) (207) 548-2529; (f) (207) 548-2520; pmmuseum@acadia.net; www.acadia.net/pmmuseum

Private non-profit/ staff: 12(f); 20(p); 110(v)/ members: 950/publication: At the Bay Chronicle

MARITIME MUSEUM: Preserve and interpret the maritime history of Maine in general and Penobscot Bay in particular.

PROGRAMS: Community Outreach; Elder's Programs; Exhibits; Facility Rental; Family Programs; Guided Tours; Interpretation; Lectures; Publication; Research Library/Archives; School-Based Curriculum

COLLECTIONS: [1840-1918]

HOURS: May-Oct Daily 10-5

ADMISSION: $6

SEBAGO

3509
Jones Museum of Glass and Ceramics
35 Douglass Mountain, 04029; (p) (207) 787-3370; (f) (207) 787-2800; (c) Cumberland

Private non-profit/ 1978/ staff: 4(f); 2(p); 30(v)/ members: 500/publication: Horizons

HOUSE MUSEUM; LIBRARY AND/OR ARCHIVES: Museum devoted to glass and ceramics, all historical periods, worldwide; research library.

PROGRAMS: Community Outreach; Exhibits; Guided Tours; Interpretation; Lectures; Publication; Research Library/Archives

COLLECTIONS: 10,000 pieces of glass and ceramics, Roman period to present; research library with 6,000 volumes, plus 10,000 slides, VF drawers, 300 microfiche.

HOURS: May-Nov M-Sa 10-5, Su 1-5

ADMISSION: $5, Student $3, Seniors $3.75; Under 12/Members free

SEBEC

3510
Sebec Historical Society
N Rd, 04481 [PO Box 101, 04481]; (p) (207) 564-7259; (f) (207) 654-8338; (c) Piscataquis

Private non-profit/ 1968/ staff: 8(v)/ members: 120/publication: News and Views

HISTORICAL SOCIETY

PROGRAMS: Exhibits; Publication

COLLECTIONS: [Early 1800-1935] Local historical items from families with heavy application of genealogy of people having lived in Sebec since the beginning of town history.

HOURS: July-Aug Su 2-4 and by appt

ADMISSION: No charge

SEDGWICK

3511
Sedgwick-Brooklin Historical Society
Rt 172, 04676 [PO Box 171, 04676]; (c) Hancock

Private non-profit/ 1964/ staff: 1(p); 20(v)/ members: 180/publication: Life and Times in a Coastal Village

GENEALOGICAL SOCIETY; HISTORIC SITE; HISTORICAL SOCIETY; HOUSE MUSEUM: Conserve, collect, and document all aspects of local history.

PROGRAMS: Annual Meeting; Community Outreach; Exhibits; Family Programs; Lectures; Publication; School-Based Curriculum

COLLECTIONS: [19th-early 20th c] Textiles, commercial cooper's equipment, shoemaker's bench and tools, farm equipment, household goods, furniture, restored hearse, pictures, drawings, watercolors, photographs, archives.

HOURS: July-Aug Su 2-4

ADMISSION: No charge

SKOWHEGAN

3512
Margaret Chase Smith Library
54 Norridgewock Ave, 04976; (p) (207) 474-7133; (f) (207) 474-8878; mcsl@somtel.com; (c) Somerset

Private non-profit/ 1982/ staff: 7(f); 1(p); 1(v)/publication: Margaret Chase Smith Newsletter

HISTORY MUSEUM; RESEARCH CENTER: Archives, museum, educational facility, and public policy center, promoting research into 20th-c political history, advancement of civic ideals, and discussion of policy issues.

PROGRAMS: Annual Meeting; Community Outreach; Exhibits; Guided Tours; Lectures; Publication; Research Library/Archives

COLLECTIONS: [1900-1995] 300,000 documents, 500 scrapbooks, 2,400 books, 2,400 photographs, 450 audio and video tapes, and 1,300 artifacts relating to the Congressional career of Senator Smith.

3513
Showhegan History House
40 Elm St, 04976-1202 [PO Box832, 04976-1202]; (p) (207) 474-6632; skowhegan.maineusa.com/KB/HistoryH/index.htm; (c) Somerset

HISTORIC SITE; HISTORICAL SOCIETY; HISTORY MUSEUM; HOUSE MUSEUM: Operates local history museum.

PROGRAMS: Guided Tours

COLLECTIONS: [1800s] House from 1800s.

HOURS: June-Aug T-F 1-5

ADMISSION: Donations Accepted

3514
Skowhegan History House
40 Elm St, 04976 [PO Box 832, 04976]; (p) (207) 474-6632; skowhegan.maineusa.com/kb/historyh/index.ht; (c) Somerset

City/ 1937/ staff: 1(p)

HISTORIC SITE; HISTORICAL SOCIETY; HISTORY MUSEUM; HOUSE MUSEUM: We are a local history museum open to the public.

PROGRAMS: Guided Tours

COLLECTIONS: [1800s] The house is set-up in 1800s style.

HOURS: June-Aug T-F 1-5

ADMISSION: Donations accepted

SOUTH BERWICK

3515
Hamilton House, SPNEA
40 Vaughan's Ln, 03908; (p) (207) 384-2454; www.spnea.org

Private non-profit/ 1785/ Society for the Preservation of New England Antiquities

HISTORY MUSEUM; HOUSE MUSEUM: C. 1785 house, restored in 1898.

PROGRAMS: Concerts; Exhibits; Family Programs; Garden Tours; Guided Tours; Lectures; School-Based Curriculum

HOURS: June 1-Oct 15 W-Su 11-5

ADMISSION: $5; SPNEA Mbrs/Town residents free

3516
Old Berwick Historical Society/Counting House Museum
Main & Liberty St, 03908 [PO Box 296, 03908]; (c) York

Private non-profit/ 1965/ staff: 25(v)/ members: 250/publication: Deephaven

HISTORICAL SOCIETY; HISTORY MUSEUM: Maintains a citizen group based in the Counting House, an 1831 Textile Mill building now serving as a small country museum, history education center, and archives repository.

PROGRAMS: Annual Meeting; Community Outreach; Exhibits; Facility Rental; Family Programs; Guided Tours; Lectures; Publication; Research Library/Archives; School-Based Curriculum

COLLECTIONS: [1600-1900] 4,000 documents, books, and photos; 10,000 artifacts from 1650 Humphrey Chadbourn archeological site; nautical models; 19th c tools, implements, and textiles.

HOURS: June-Oct Sa-Su 1-4

ADMISSION: Donations accepted

3517
Sarah Orne Jewett House, SPNEA
5 Portland St, 03908; (p) (207) 384-2454; www.spnea.org

Private non-profit/ 1774/ Society for the Preservation of New England Antiquities

HISTORY MUSEUM; HOUSE MUSEUM: Stately Georgian residence that was home to writer Sarah Orne Jewett, owned by her family since 1819.

PROGRAMS: Exhibits; Family Programs; Garden Tours; Guided Tours; Lectures; School-Based Curriculum

COLLECTIONS: [1880-1909] The author's bedroom exactly as she furnished it; one late 18th and two mid-19th century wallpapers.

HOURS: June 1-Oct 15 W-Su 11-5

ADMISSION: $5; SPNEA Mbrs/Town residents free

SOUTH PARIS

3518
Paris Cape Historical Society
163 Park St, 04281 [19 Park St, 04281]; (p) (207) 743-2462; cfi@megalink.net; (c) Oxford

Private non-profit/ 1981/ staff: 10(v)/ members: 115/publication: *The Second Hundred Years; Pictorial History of Paris; and others*

GENEALOGICAL SOCIETY; HISTORIC PRESERVATION AGENCY; HISTORICAL SOCIETY; HISTORY MUSEUM: Collect and preserve items connected with the history of the Town of Paris; to assist genealogists and historians: to publish books.

PROGRAMS: Annual Meeting; Exhibits; Family Programs; Lectures; Publication

COLLECTIONS: [1800s-1900s] Genealogies, complete set of Union Civil War History, town histories, town reports, artifacts demonstrating life during the period, scrapbooks covering 1894-1994, area cemetery listings.

HOURS: May-Sept Th 1-4 and by appt

ADMISSION: No charge

SOUTH PORTLAND

3519
Portland Harbor Museum
SMTC Campus, Fort Road, 04106; (p) (207) 799-6337; (f) (207) 799-6337; PortHarbMuseum@Juno.com; www.PortlandHarborMuseum.org; (c) Cumberland

Private non-profit/ 1985/ staff: 1(f); 2(p); 30(v)/ members: 250

HISTORIC SITE; RESEARCH CENTER: Maritime museum which preserves and interprets the history of Portland Harbor, its islands, and surrounding communities.

PROGRAMS: Community Outreach; Exhibits; Guided Tours; Interpretation; Lectures; Research Library/Archives; School-Based Curriculum

COLLECTIONS: [19th-20th c] Artifacts, documents, and photographs pertaining to the maritime and local history of Portland Harbor, its islands and surrounding communities.

HOURS: Apr-Dec, July-Sept Daily 10-4:30; call for hours for other months

ADMISSION: $3, Children $1; Under 6/Mbrs free; group rates

3520
South Portland-Cape Elizabeth Historical Society
Braeburn Ave, 04106 [PO Box 2623, 04106]; (p) (207) 799-1977; (c) Cumberland

Private non-profit/ 1964/ staff: 10(v)/ members: 30

HISTORICAL SOCIETY; HISTORY MUSEUM: Collect, display, and maintain historical photographs and documents; Erect historical signs and markers. Maintain a museum.

PROGRAMS: Community Outreach; Exhibits; Research Library/Archives

COLLECTIONS: [1900-present] Scrapbooks, photographs, antiques, clothing, documents. Historical accounts of South Portland and Cape Elizabeth.

HOURS: May-Oct 1st & 3rd Sa 1-4

ADMISSION: No charge

STANDISH

3521
Marrett House, SPNEA
Rt 25, 04084; (p) (207) 642-3032; www.spnea.org

Private non-profit/ 1789/ Society for the Preservation of New England Antiquities

HISTORY MUSEUM; HOUSE MUSEUM: Maintains house museum.

PROGRAMS: Garden Tours; Guided Tours

HOURS: June 1-Oct 15 Sa-Su 11-5

ADMISSION: $4; SPNEA Mbrs/Town residents free

3522
Standish Historical Society
Oakhill Rd, 04084 [PO Box 28, 04084]; (p) (207) 642-3216; (c) Cumberland

Private non-profit/ 1974/ staff: 1(p)/ members: 72/publication: *Pearson Town Press Quarterly Newspaper*

GENEALOGICAL SOCIETY; HISTORIC SITE; HISTORICAL SOCIETY; HISTORY MUSEUM; RESEARCH CENTER: Works to preserve the history of the town of Standish; maintains a museum in a historic church with exhibits and is open for research.

PROGRAMS: Annual Meeting; Community Outreach; Exhibits; Facility Rental; Guided Tours; Publication; Research Library/Archives

COLLECTIONS: [1800-present] Artifacts from town of Standish. Genealogy, antique clothing, photographs, resources for general research, restored classroom, oral histories.

HOURS: June-Aug T, Th 10:30-1:30; Sept M, W 10:30-1:30

ADMISSION: Donations requested

STOCKHOLM

3523
Stockholm Historical Society
280 Main St, 04783; (p) (207) 896-5759; (f) (207) 896-3177; jhede@mfx.net; www.aroostook.me.us; (c) Aroostook

Private non-profit/ 1976/ staff: 1(p)/ 12(v)/ members: 140

GENEALOGICAL SOCIETY; HISTORIC PRESERVATION AGENCY; HISTORIC SITE; HISTORICAL SOCIETY; HOUSE MUSEUM; LIBRARY AND/OR ARCHIVES: Owns and operates the Stockholm Museum located in the original Anderson Brothers Store. National Register of Historic Places.

PROGRAMS: Annual Meeting; Community Outreach; Exhibits; Festivals; Publication; Reenactments; Research Library/Archives

COLLECTIONS: [1880-present] Historic artifacts: connected with the Stockholm area, brought by early settlers, connected with the mills, stores, railroad, farms, and homes.

HOURS: July-Aug W-Su 1:30-4:30

ADMISSION: No charge

STRATTON

3524
Dead River Area Historical Society
172 Main St, 04982 [PO Box 150, 04982]; jhapson@somtes.com; (c) Franklin

Private non-profit/ 1979/ members: 68

HISTORICAL SOCIETY; HISTORY MUSEUM: Maintains museum.

PROGRAMS: Annual Meeting; Exhibits

COLLECTIONS: [Early 20th c] Electric collection, artifacts, tools, household goods, business records, family history.

HOURS: May-Sept Sa-Su 11-3

ADMISSION: $1

THOMASTON

3525
Montpelier-General Henry Knox Museum
High St, 04861 [PO Box 326, 04861]; (p) (207) 354-8062; (f) (207) 354-3501; www.midcoast.com/generalknoxmuseum; (c) Knox

Private non-profit/ 1931/ Friends of Montpelier/ staff: 1(f); 150(v)/ members: 175

HISTORY MUSEUM; HOUSE MUSEUM: Replica home of Major General Henry Knox, contains family artifacts and collection of furniture from original 1795 mansion.

PROGRAMS: Community Outreach; Concerts; Exhibits; Facility Rental; Family Programs; Festivals; Guided Tours; Interpretation; Lectures; Living History; Reenactments; School-Based Curriculum; Theatre

COLLECTIONS: [1760-1850] Furnishings and personal belongings of the Knox family.

HOURS: June-Oct T-Sa 10-4

3526
Thomaston Historical Society
Knox St, 04861 [PO Box 384, 04861]; (p) (207) 354-8835; catsmeow@mint.net; www.net/thomastonhistoricalsociety; (c) Knox

Private non-profit/ 1972/ staff: 20(v)/ members: 275

HISTORIC SITE; HISTORICAL SOCIETY; HISTORY MUSEUM; RESEARCH CENTER: Volunteer organization that preserves the building and collection of artifacts pertaining to the history of Thomaston beginning early 17th century. Publish books, present lectures of historic interest and provide tours to area schools.

PROGRAMS: Annual Meeting; Community Outreach; Exhibits; Family Programs; Film/Video; Guided Tours; Lectures; Publication; Research Library/Archives

COLLECTIONS: [17th c-present] Letters, journals, documents, photographs, newspapers articles, diaries from 1623 to present. Artifacts from early Colonial maritime history through ship building era 1795 to 1910.

HOURS: June-Aug T-Th 2-4 or by appt

ADMISSION: No charge

THORNDIKE

3527
Bryant Stove and Music, Inc.
Rich Rd, Box 2048, 04986; (p) (207) 568-3665; (f) (207) 568-3666; (c) Waldo

Private for-profit/ 1957/ staff: 3(f)

HISTORY MUSEUM: Collects, restores, and displays antique stoves in a showroom and a museum.

PROGRAMS: Exhibits; Guided Tours

COLLECTIONS: [1830s-1930s] A rare collection of antique stoves (column, base burners, bedroom stoves, templates, and fireplaces), urns, tow stoves, salesmen samples, antique automobiles, nickelodeons, player pianos, band organs, and other mechanical devices.

UNION

3528
Union Historical Society
343 Common Rd, 04862 [PO Box 154, 04862]; (p) (207) 785-5444; (c) Knox

Private non-profit/ 1972/ staff: 25(v)/ members: 150/publication: Sibley's History of Union; Cone Spring; and others

HISTORICAL SOCIETY: Collect, preserve, and make available Union's historical documents, relics, and records; manages and preserves the society's property and buildings; promotes interest in history through programs, activities, and publications.

PROGRAMS: Annual Meeting; Community Outreach; Exhibits; Facility Rental; Family Programs; Festivals; Guided Tours; Lectures; Publication; Research Library/Archives

COLLECTIONS: [1840-1940] Pioneer artifacts; locally made Victorian furniture and pump organ; 1840s house, clothing and furnishings, genealogy records, deeds, diaries, books, postcards, business cards, scrapbooks relating to local families and businesses.

HOURS: Yr Sa 10-12, Mar-Dec 1st W 7:30-9 pm

ADMISSION: No charge

VAN BUREN

3529
L'Heritage Vivant-Living Heritage
Main St Rt 1A, 04785 [PO Box 165, 04785]; (p) (207) 868-5042, (207) 868-2691; (c) Aroostook

Private non-profit/ 1973/ staff: 2(p); 3(v)/ members: 20

HISTORIC SITE; HISTORICAL SOCIETY: Operates the Acadian Village: the village depicts the mode of living from 1790-early 1900; consist of 16 reconstructed buildings furnished with artifacts of the past.

PROGRAMS: Exhibits; Facility Rental; Guided Tours

COLLECTIONS: [1790-1900] Household furniture, agriculture machinery, telephones, shoe shop, school house fully furnished, chapel with historical pieces.

VINALHAVEN

3530
Vinalhaven Historical Society
High St, 04863 [PO Box 339, 04863]; (p) (207) 863-4410; vhhissoc@midcoast.com; www.midcoast.com/~vhhissoc; (c) Knox

Private non-profit/ 1963/ staff: 2(f); 1(p); 7(v)/ members: 800

GENEALOGICAL SOCIETY; HISTORICAL SOCIETY; HISTORY MUSEUM: Collects, identifies, preserves, exhibits, interprets, and makes available for education and research, information and artifacts relating to local history.

PROGRAMS: Annual Meeting; Community Outreach; Exhibits; Film/Video; Guided Tours; Interpretation; Lectures; Publication; Research Library/Archives; School-Based Curriculum

COLLECTIONS: [1789-1983] Vinalhaven Vital and Property Records, genealogical records, granite industry records and tools, John A. Low collection of glass plate negatives (1890-1920) of Vinalhaven photographer William H. Merrithew, photographs, Civil War portraits.

HOURS: June-Sept Daily 11-3 and by appt

ADMISSION: No charge/Donations

WELD

3531
Museum House
[PO Box 31, 04285]; (p) (207) 585-2179

WELLS

3532
Historical Society of Wells and Ogunquit, Inc.
938 Post Rd, 04090 [PO Box 801, 04090]; (p) (207) 646-4775; (f) (207) 646-0832; wohistory@cybertours; (c) York

Private non-profit/ 1954/ Board of Directors/ staff: 2(p); 35(v)/ members: 450

HISTORIC SITE; HISTORICAL SOCIETY; LIBRARY AND/OR ARCHIVES: Listed on the National Register and maintains the 1860 Historic Meetinghouse, Museum, and Esselyn Perkins Genealogy Library and archives, dedicated to the history of Wells and Ogunquit.

PROGRAMS: Publication; Research Library/Archives; School-Based Curriculum

COLLECTIONS: [1700s-present] Museum: quilts, costumes, art, decorative arts, military, postal history, and schools. Archives: Ledgers, scrapbooks, journals, post cards, photographs, and maps. Library: 3,000 volumes of early York county families, general genealogy,

ME town histories, and complete census microfilms 1800-1920.

HOURS: Yr Winter W,Th 10-4; Summer T,W,Th, 10-4, Sa 10-1

ADMISSION: Donations requested

3533
Wells Auto Museum
1181 Post Rd (Rte 1), 040900496 [PO Box 496, 040900496]; (p) (207) 646-9064; wellsauto@aol.com; (c) York

Federal; Joint; Private non-profit/ 1980/ staff: 4(f); 1(p); 2(v)/ members: 100/publication: The Path Finder

HISTORY MUSEUM: Collects, preserves, and displays of the automobile form the earliest one cylinders through the sixties and up to V-12 engines. Also history of early pioneers in automotive history.

PROGRAMS: Annual Meeting; Exhibits; Family Programs; Lectures; Publication; School-Based Curriculum

COLLECTIONS: [1894-1960s] 85 auto, nickelodeons for public to play, Victorian arcade games and important marquees displayed: Pierce Arrow, Knox, Winton, Stanley Steamer, Model "T," and Packard.

WESTBROOK

3534
Westbrook Historical Society
756 Main St, 04098 [PO Box 161, 04098]; (c) Cumberland

Private non-profit/ 1975/ staff: 20(v)/ members: 100

HISTORICAL SOCIETY: Promote interested in the history of Westbrook and to discover and collect material and objects which establish and illustrate the history of the area.

COLLECTIONS: [Late 1800s-present] Scrapbooks of news clippings, school yearbooks and pictures, genealogies, information on old houses in the area, and area artifacts.

HOURS: Yr Sa 9-12

WESTPORT

3535
Westport Community Association, The
Center Church, 04578 [42 W Shore Rd, 04578]; (p) (207) 882-7689; bhchef1@gwi.net; (c) Lincoln

Private non-profit/ 1955/ staff: 12(v)/ members: 200/publication: Early Families of Westport; Westport Cemeteries; and others

PROFESSIONAL ORGANIZATION: To save the center church.

PROGRAMS: Annual Meeting; Concerts; Facility Rental; Family Programs; Publication

HOURS: Su 8:45-10

WILTON

3536
Wilton Historical Society/Wilton Farm & Home Museum
3 Canal St, 04294 [PO Box 33, 04294]; (p) (207) 645-3637; (c) Franklin

Private non-profit/ 1963/ staff: 25(v)/ members: 70

HISTORIC SITE; HISTORICAL SOCIETY; HOUSE MUSEUM

PROGRAMS: Annual Meeting; Exhibits; Facility Rental; Family Programs; Guided Tours; Lectures

COLLECTIONS: [1795-present] Farm equipment, local photographs, genealogy, school memorabilia, period clothing, restored Bass Boarding House rooms, home life & tools, antique bottle collection, G.H. Bass Shoe Co. items, and Boy & Girl Scout memorabilia.

HOURS: July-Aug Sa 1-4

ADMISSION: Donations accepted

WINDHAM

3537
Windham Historical Society, Inc.
234 Windham Center Rd, 04062 [PO Box 2233, 04062]; (p) (207) 892-1433; (c) Cumberland

Private non-profit/ 1967/ staff: 6(v)/ members: 200/publication: *Windham Historical Society News*

HISTORIC SITE; HISTORICAL SOCIETY; HISTORY MUSEUM: Organizes monthly meetings and offers genealogical research, monthly newsletter, and guided museum tours.

PROGRAMS: Annual Meeting; Guided Tours; Publication

COLLECTIONS: [1734-present] Items from early Windham homes, photographs, documents, letters, town reports, and records, books, family history material, maps, clothing, and rural school items.

HOURS: Apr-Nov

WISCASSET

3538
Castle Tucker, SPNEA
Lee St at High St, 04578; (p) (603) 436-3205; www.spnea.org

Private non-profit/ 1807/ Society for the Preservation of New England Antiquities

HISTORY MUSEUM; HOUSE MUSEUM

PROGRAMS: Guided Tours; Lectures

COLLECTIONS: Furniture, paintings, decorative arts, and household objects, documents.

HOURS: June 1-Oct 15 W-Su 15

ADMISSION: $4; SPNEA Mbrs/Town residents free

3539
Lincoln County Historical Association
Lincoln City Museum & Old Jail 133 Federal St, 04578 [PO Box 61, 04578]; (p) (207) 882-6817; lcha@wiscasset.net; www.wiscasset.net/lcha; (c) Lincoln

Private non-profit/ staff: 1(f); 5(p); 20(v)/ members: 275

HISTORICAL SOCIETY: Collect, preserve, and share the history, decorative arts, and material culture of Lincoln County.

COLLECTIONS: Lincoln County Old Jail and Pownal Borough Court House Museum.

3540
Musical Wonder House
18 High St, 04578; (p) (207) 882-7163; (f) (207) 882-6373; musicbox@musicalwonderhouse.co; www.musicalwonderhouse.con/

1852/ Private/ staff: 3(f); 2(p)

COLLECTIONS: [1745-1927] Antique music boxes, player pianos, and phonographs.; Original catalogs of phonograph records, music boxes, player piano rolls.

HOURS: May-Oct

3541
Nickels-Sortwell House, SPNEA
12 Main St, 04578; (p) (207) 882-6218; www.spnea.org

Private non-profit/ 1807/ Society for the Preservation of New England Antiquities

HISTORY MUSEUM; HOUSE MUSEUM: Maintains the Nickels-Sortwell House that was built by Captain William Nickels, a ship owner and trader.

PROGRAMS: Guided Tours; Lectures

COLLECTIONS: Collection of furniture paintings, decorative arts household objects, and documents.

HOURS: June 1-Oct 15 W-Su 11-5

ADMISSION: $5

YARMOUTH

3542
Yarmouth Historical Society-Museum of Yarmouth History
215 Main St, 04096 [PO Box 107, 04096]; (p) (207) 846-6259; (c) Cumberland

Private non-profit/ 1960/ staff: 1(f); 4(p); 12(v)/ members: 550

HISTORICAL SOCIETY; HISTORY MUSEUM: A non-profit educational organization whose purpose is to promote interest in the history of Yarmouth.

PROGRAMS: Annual Meeting; Community Outreach; Exhibits; Interpretation; Lectures; Research Library/Archives

COLLECTIONS: [19th c] 18th,19th and 20th c books, manuscripts, photographs, and artifacts related to the history of Yarmouth.

HOURS: Yr Sept-June T-F 1-5, Sa 10-5; July-Aug M-F

YORK

3543
Old York Historical Society
207 York St, 03909 [PO Box 312, 03909]; (p) (207) 363-4974; (f) (207) 363-4021; oyhs@oldyork.org; www.oldyork.org; (c) York

Private non-profit/ 1984/ staff: 7(f); 5(p); 200(v)/ members: 600

GENEALOGICAL SOCIETY; HISTORIC SITE; HISTORICAL SOCIETY; HISTORY MUSEUM; HOUSE MUSEUM: Promotes and preserves the history of the York region for the education and enjoyment of the public.

PROGRAMS: Annual Meeting; Community Outreach; Concerts; Elder's Programs; Exhibits; Family Programs; Festivals; Guided Tours; Interpretation; Lectures; Publication; Reenactments; Research Library/Archives; School-Based Curriculum

COLLECTIONS: [Colonial-Colonial Revival] 22,000 museum artifacts, including decorative arts, and textiles.

HOURS: June-Oct T-Sa 10-5, Su 1-5

ADMISSION: $7, Family $15, Children $3, Seniors $6

YORK HARBOR

3544
Sayward-Wheeler House, SPNEA
9 Barrell Lane Ext, 03911; (p) (207) 384-2454; www.spnea.org

Private non-profit/ 1718/ Society for the Preservation of New England Antiquities

Maintans the home of Jonathan Sayward, a local merchant and civic leader, who remodeled and furnished the house in the 1760s. Refurbished in the early 20th c, it still contains original furnishings and family portraits.

COLLECTIONS: [18th-20th c]

HOURS: June 1-Oct 15 Sa-Su 11-5

ADMISSION: $5; SPNEA Mbrs/Town residents free

MARYLAND

ABERDEEN

3545
Aberdeen Room Archives and Museum
18 Howard St, 21001 [PO Box 698, 21001]; (p) (410) 273-6325; (c) Harford

City/ 1987/ staff: 12(v)

GENEALOGICAL SOCIETY; HISTORIC PRESERVATION AGENCY; HISTORICAL SOCIETY; HISTORY MUSEUM; RESEARCH CENTER: Collects and interprets the history of Aberdeen.

PROGRAMS: Community Outreach; Exhibits; Guided Tours; Interpretation; Lectures; Living History; Publication; Reenactments; Research Library/Archives; School-Based Curriculum

COLLECTIONS: [1987-1999] Artifacts, maps, and original plat.

HOURS: Yr T,Th 10-1, 1st Sa 12-3 and by appt

ADMISSION: No charge

3546
U.S. Army Ordinance Museum
Maryland & Aberdeen Ave, 21005 [Aberdeen Proving Ground, 21005]; (p) (410) 278-3602, (410) 278-2396; (f) (410) 278-7473; museum@ocs2.apg.army.mil; (c) Harford

Federal/ 1919/ staff: 6(f); 1(p); 1(v)/ members: 125

HISTORY MUSEUM: Collects, preserves, and accounts for historically significant property that relates to the history of the US Army Ordinance Corps and the evolution and development of American military ordinance material from the colonial period to the present.

PROGRAMS: Exhibits; Film/Video; Guided Tours; Publication; Research Library/Archives; Theatre

COLLECTIONS: [WW I and WW II] Ordinance equipment, foreign military equipment (captured and donated) small arms from the 16th c, ammunitions exhibit, archives, and tanks.

ACCOKEEK

3547
Accokeek Foundation
3400 Bryan Point Rd, 20607; (p) (301) 283-2113; (f) (301) 283-2049; accofound@accokeek.org; www.accokeek.org; (c) Prince George's

Private non-profit/ 1957/ Board of Trustees/ staff: 9(f); 17(p); 90(v)/publication: *At the Farm*

GARDEN; LIVING HISTORY/OUTDOOR MUSEUM: The Accokeek Foundation uses its two farm sites, the historic National Colonial Farm and the modern-day Ecosystem Farm, as outdoor classrooms. Programs blend ecology, history, and economics, educating people of all ages about responsible land stewardship.

PROGRAMS: Concerts; Facility Rental; Festivals; Garden Tours; Guided Tours; Interpretation; Lectures; Living History; Publication; School-Based Curriculum

COLLECTIONS: [Colonial-mid 18th c] Heirloom seed saving program, two restored period buildings, and small collection of period tools.

HOURS: Yr Daily dawn-dusk

ADMISSION: $2, Family $5, Children $0.50

ANNAPOLIS

3548
Charles Carroll House of Annapolis
107 Duke of Gloucester St, 21401-2504; (p) (410) 269-1737; (f) (410) 269-1746; PAM@carrollhouse.com; www.carrollhouse.com; (c) Anne Arundel

Private non-profit/ 1987/ Charles Carroll House of Annapolis, Inc/ staff: 3(f); 4(p); 115(v)/ members: 465/publication: *Charles Carroll Chronicle Quarterly*

GARDEN; HISTORIC SITE; HOUSE MUSEUM; RESEARCH CENTER: Fosters and engages understanding of American history through the political, religious, social, and cultural worlds of four generations of the Charles Carroll family (1706-1832).

PROGRAMS: Concerts; Elder's Programs; Exhibits; Facility Rental; Family Programs; Festivals; Garden Tours; Guided Tours; Interpretation; Lectures; Living History; Publication; Research Library/Archives; School-Based Curriculum

COLLECTIONS: [1706-1832] Architectural, archaeological, archival, manuscript, engraving and photo collections relating to the historical development of the Charles Carroll family; special collections focus on African American Carroll slave artifacts traced back to Sierra Leone.

HOURS: Mar-Dec F, Su 12-4, Sa 10-2, M-F by appt

ADMISSION: $5, Student $3, Seniors $4

3549
Chase/Lloyd House
22 Maryland Ave, 21401; (p) (410) 263-2723; (c) Anne Arundel

Private non-profit/ 1769/ staff: 3(f); 3(p)

GARDEN; HISTORIC SITE: Maintains historic Chase/Lloyd house and gardens.

COLLECTIONS: Cantilevered stairway, palladium window, Chinese export china, artwork, silver, and colonial furniture.

HOURS: Mar-Dec M-Sa 2-4

ADMISSION: $2

3550
Governor's Mansion
State Circle & School St, 21401 [100 State Circle, 21401]; (p) (410)

3551
Hammond-Harwood House Association, Inc.
19 Maryland Ave, 21401; (p) (410) 263-4683; (f) (410) 267-6891; hammondharwood@annapolis.net; (c) Anne Arundel

Private non-profit/ 1938/ staff: 2(f); 14(p); 4(v)/ members: 250

HOUSE MUSEUM: Maintains and interprets a 1774 five-part Georgian colonial residence, designed by William Buckland.

PROGRAMS: Annual Meeting; Community Outreach; Concerts; Elder's Programs; Exhibits; Facility Rental; Family Programs; Festivals; Film/Video; Interpretation; Lectures; Living History

COLLECTIONS: [Pre-Revolutionary War] 11 works by the Peale family: Charles Wilson Peale, Rembrandt Peale, and James Peale

3552
Historic Annapolis Foundation
18 Pinkeney St, 21401; (p) (410) 267-8149; (f) (410) 267-6189; parkera@annapolis.org; www.annapolis.org; (c) Anne Arundel

Private non-profit/ 1952/ staff: 21(f); 18(p); 300(v)/ members: 1200/publication: *HAF Journal; The Scrivener*

HISTORIC PRESERVATION AGENCY; HISTORIC SITE; HOUSE MUSEUM; RESEARCH CENTER: Preserves the history of MD's capital city through museum programs, restoration, public advocacy, research, archaeology, collections, protective easements, and conservation of historic sites.

PROGRAMS: Annual Meeting; Community Outreach; Exhibits; Facility Rental; Family Programs; Festivals; Garden Tours; Guided Tours; Interpretation; Lectures; Publication; Research Library/Archives; School-Based Curriculum

COLLECTIONS: [18th c] Living plant collection, archaeological collection, six historic buildings, an archival collection, and a cultural artifacts/decorative arts collection.

HOURS: Yr Daily

ADMISSION: $7

3553
James Brice House, The
42 E St, 21401; (p) (410) 280-1305, (301) 261-1841; (f) (301) 261-2855; lobrien@imiweb.org

1766/ staff: 4(f)

HOURS: Appt

3554
Maryland Association of History Museums, Inc.
[PO Box 1806, 21404-1806]; (p) (410) 349-9375; (f) (410) 349-9376

Private non-profit/ 1996/ Board of Trustees/ staff: 1(p); 25(v)/ members: 40/publication:
Museum Guide

An alliance of historical, cultural, and educational institutions created to speak to enhance the professionalism and effectiveness of all organizations that collect, hold, interpret, and and protect the cultural and material heritage within the State.

3555
Maryland State Archives
350 Rowe Blvd, 21401; (p) (410) 260-6400; (f) (410) 974-3895; archives@mdarchives.state.md.us; www.mdsa.net

State/ 1934/ staff: 60(f); 20(v)

LIBRARY AND/OR ARCHIVES: Repository for government records of permanent value, along with extensive holdings in private papers and photos.

PROGRAMS: Community Outreach; Exhibits; Lectures; Publication; Research Library/Archives; School-Based Curriculum

COLLECTIONS: [1634-present]

HOURS: Yr T-F 8-4:30, Sa 8:30-4:30

3556
U.S. Naval Academy Museum
118 Maryland Ave, 21402; (p) (410) 293-2108; (f) (410) 293-5220; jsharmom@nadr.navy.mil; www.nadn.navy.mil/museum/; (c) Anne Arundel

Federal/ 1845/ US Naval Academy/ staff: 8(f); 1(p)

HISTORY MUSEUM: Preserves and interprets the history and heritage of the US Navy and the Naval Academy.

PROGRAMS: Community Outreach; Exhibits; Interpretation

COLLECTIONS: [1600-present] Memorabilia of the Naval Academy graduates and their contributions; "dockyard" ship models and historic Naval prints.

HOURS: Yr M-Sa 9-5, Su 11-5

ADMISSION: No charge

3557
William Paca House and Garden
186 Prince George St, 21401; (p) (410) 263-5553; (f) (410) 626-1031; www@annapolis.org

1763/ staff: 4(f); 11(p); 80(v)

COLLECTIONS: [1760-1780] 18th c plant material, furniture and decorative arts of the 18th c; Research on the people and properties of 18th c. Annapolis, photographic collection of the 19th & 20th c.

HOURS: Yr

BALTIMORE

3558
Archives of the Peabody Institute of The Johns Hopkins University
1 E Mount Vernon Pl, 21202; (p) (410) 659-8257; (f) (410) 727-5101; schaaf@peabody.jhu.edu; www.peabody.jhu.edu/ archives

Private non-profit/ 1857/ The Peabody Institute of The Johns Hopkins Univ/ staff: 1(f); 2(p); 2(v)

LIBRARY AND/OR ARCHIVES: Serve as the region's performing arts archives, maintaining the records of the Baltimore Symphony Orchestra and the Baltimore Opera, as well as materials on African American musicians.

PROGRAMS: Concerts; Exhibits

COLLECTIONS: [1860-present] Personal papers, photographs, recorded sound, institutional archives of the Peabody Institute and the Baltimore Symphony Orchestra, records of the Lyric Opera House, sheet music, and records of the Peabody Art Museum.

3559
B&O Railroad Museum
901 W Pratt St, 21223-2699; (p) (410) 752-2490; (f) (410) 752-2499; info@borail.org; (c) Baltimore City

Private non-profit/ 1987/ staff: 22(f); 50(p); 153(v)/ members: 3021/publication: *B & O Railroad Museum Guidebook*

RAILROAD MUSEUM: Operates the B&O Railroad Museum and preserves and interprets the history of American railroading through the B&O.

PROGRAMS: Annual Meeting; Community Outreach; Exhibits; Facility Rental; Festivals; Guided Tours; Interpretation; Lectures; Living History; Publication; Reenactments; Research Library/Archives; School-Based Curriculum; Theatre

COLLECTIONS: [1840-1940] 200 pieces of 19th and 20th c rolling stock; 2,500 models, tools, and textiles; 30,000 still images; 2,000 volumes; engineering drawings; and 300,000 documents.

HOURS: Yr M-Su 10-5

ADMISSION: $8, Children $5, Seniors $7

3560
Babe Ruth Birthplace Museum
216 Emory St, 21230; (p) (410) 727-1539; (f) (410) 727-1652; www.baberuthmuseum.com

Private non-profit/ 1973/ Babe Ruth Birthplace Foundation, Inc./ staff: 11(f); 5(p); 120(v)/ members: 600/publication: *Baselines*

HISTORIC SITE; HISTORY MUSEUM: Preserves, maintains, and interprets the life and baseball career of George Herman "Babe" Ruth, the Baltimore Orioles, and local baseball through exhibits and educational programs.

PROGRAMS: Annual Meeting; Community Outreach; Exhibits; Facility Rental; Festivals; Guided Tours; Interpretation; Lectures; Living History; Publication; Research Library/ Archives; School-Based Curriculum; Theatre

COLLECTIONS: [1880s-present] 3800 artifacts and 1200 photographs on it major themes: Babe Ruth, the Baltimore Orioles, and local baseball.

HOURS: Yr Daily 9-5

ADMISSION: $6, Children $3

3561
Ballestone Manor
1935 Back River Neck Rd, Rocky Point Golf Course, 21221 [1935 Back River Neck Rd, 21221]; (p) (410) 887-0218, (410) 686-5821

1780

COLLECTIONS: [1780-1880] Middle class furnishings including Federal, Empire 1820-1840, Victorian 1840-1880, at times special exhibits of ceramics, clothing, lamps etc.; Art finds - small photos 1840-1945

HOURS: Seasonal

3562
Ballestone Preservation Society
1935 Back River Neck Rd, 21221 [19 Lindsey Ct, 21221]; (p) (410) 887-0218, (410) 686-5801; (c) Baltimore

County, non-profit/ 1976/ staff: 25(v)/ members: 115

HISTORIC PRESERVATION AGENCY; HISTORIC SITE; HOUSE MUSEUM; LIVING HISTORY/OUTDOOR MUSEUM: House built c 1780 on land granted to William Ball, maternal great-grandfather of George Washington.

PROGRAMS: Concerts; Festivals; Guided Tours; Living History; Reenactments

COLLECTIONS: [Federal, Empire, Victorian] Ballestone Manor features American decorative arts and furnishings in several period room settings.

HOURS: May-June and appt

3563
Baltimore Conservatory and Botanical Gardens
3100 Swan Dr, 21209 [4915 Greenspring Ave, 21209]; (p) (410) 396-0180; (f) (410) 367-8039; (c) Baltimore

City, non-profit/ 1888/ staff: 5(f); 1(p); 25(v)

GARDEN; HISTORIC SITE: Operates and maintains a historical house and botanical gardens.

PROGRAMS: Community Outreach; Concerts; Exhibits; Festivals; Garden Tours; Living History

COLLECTIONS: [Late 1800s-present] Orchid hybrids and species, begonias, palms and cycads, desert collections, and Mediterranean and tropical plants.

3564
Baltimore Maritime Museum
Piers 3 & 5, Baltimore Inner Harbor, 21231 [802 S Caroline St, 21231]; (p) (410) 396-3453; (f) (410) 396-3393; www.livingclassrooms.org

Private non-profit/ 1986/ Living Classrooms Foundation/ staff: 15(f); 15(p); 60(v)/ members: 1000

HISTORIC SITE; HISTORY MUSEUM; LIVING HISTORY/OUTDOOR MUSEUM; MARITIME MUSEUM: Preserves and interprets the USCGC Taney, the submarine USS Torsk, the lightship Chesapeake, and the Seven Foot Knoll Lighthouse.

PROGRAMS: Exhibits; Facility Rental; Interpretation

COLLECTIONS: [W W II] USCGC Taney, submarine USS Torsk, lightship Chesapeake, Seven Foot Knoll Lighthouse, and related maritime artifacts.

HOURS: Jan-Feb Sa-Su; Mar-Dec Daily 10:30-6

ADMISSION: $5.50, Children $3, Seniors $4.50; Under 6 free

3565
Baltimore Public Works Museum, The
751 Eastern Ave, 21202; (p) (410) 396-5565; (f) (410) 545-6781; bpwm@erols.com

Private non-profit/ 1982/ staff: 4(f); 2(p)/ members: 130

ALLIANCE OF HISTORICAL AGENCIES; HISTORIC SITE; RESEARCH CENTER: Committed to educating a diverse community, and dedicated to the collection, preservation, exhibition, and interpretation of artifacts representative of public works projects. Cultivates an understanding of public works history as it relates to current public projects.

PROGRAMS: Annual Meeting; Community Outreach; Exhibits; Guided Tours; School-Based Curriculum

COLLECTIONS: [18th-20th c] 4,000 photographic images: prints, glass plate negatives, and lantern slides dating from 1905; public works artifacts: 18th and 19th century wooden water pipes and drains, early valves, weights and measures, surveying equipment, and maintenance equipment.

HOURS: Yr T-Su 10-4

ADMISSION: $2.50, Student $2, Seniors $2

3566
Baltimore Streetcar Museum, Inc
1901 Falls Rd, 21211 [PO Box 4881, 21211]; (p) (410) 547-0264; (f) (410) 547-0264; www.baltimoremd.com/streetcar/; (c) Independent City

Private non-profit/ 1966/ Board of Trustees/ staff: 40(v)/ members: 700/publication: *The Live Wire*

HISTORY MUSEUM: Collects and preserves the city's transportation artifacts for the enjoyment of the public through demonstration operations.

PROGRAMS: Community Outreach; Concerts; Exhibits; Facility Rental; Guided Tours; Interpretation; Lectures; Living History; Publication; Reenactments; Research Library/ Archives; School-Based Curriculum

COLLECTIONS: [1859-present] Artifacts, including 16 vehicles, streetcars.

HOURS: Yr Su 12-5

3567
Banneker Historical Park and Museum
300 Della Ave, 21228; (p) (410) 887-1081; (f) (410) 203-2747; (c) Baltimore

County/ 1998/ Recreation and Parks/ staff: 1(f); 5(p); 40(v)/ members: 500

HISTORIC SITE; HISTORY MUSEUM: Dedicated to preserving the legacy of Benjamin Banneker, the nation's first African American man of science, early American history, and the natural environment.

PROGRAMS: Community Outreach; Exhibits; Guided Tours; Interpretation; Reenactments

COLLECTIONS: [Colonial-present] Archaeological collection, original 18th c journals and artifacts, and various historical and contemporary African American documents and artifacts.

HOURS: Yr T-Sa 10-4

ADMISSION: Donations accepted

3568
Carroll Mansion
NE Corner of Front & Lombard St, 21202 [800 E Lombard St, 21202]; (p) (410) 396-3523

Maintains a 1811 Federal Style mansion where Charles Carroll, signer of the Declaration of Independence, lived.

3569
Carroll's Hundred
1500 Washington Blvd, 21210 [PO Box 16261, 21210]; (p) (410) 323-5236; (f) (410) 323-5236; karel100@aol.com; www.carrolls100.org

Private non-profit/ 1990/ Carroll Park Fdn, Inc/ staff: 3(f); 1(p); 5(v)/ members: 84

GARDEN; HISTORIC SITE; LIVING HISTORY/OUTDOOR MUSEUM; RESEARCH CENTER: Operates a living history revolutionary-era iron plantations and archaeological site specializing in the interpretation of horticulture, iron production, and African-American and European servitude.

PROGRAMS: Annual Meeting; Community Outreach; Exhibits; Facility Rental; Family Programs; Festivals; Garden Tours; Guided Tours; Interpretation; Living History; Reenactments

COLLECTIONS: [18th-19th c] Archaeological artifacts Revolutionary War and Civil War period items.

HOURS: Yr 8:30-3:30

ADMISSION: Donations accepted

3570
Commission for Historical and Architectural Preservation
417 E Fayette St, Ste 1037, 21202; (p) (410) 396-4866; (f) (410) 396-5662; (c) Baltimore

City/ 1964/ staff: 7(f); 1(v)

HISTORIC PRESERVATION AGENCY; HOUSE MUSEUM

PROGRAMS: Exhibits; Family Programs; Guided Tours; Lectures; Reenactments; Research Library/Archives

HOURS: Yr M-F 8:30-4:30

3571
Constellation Foundation, Inc.
Pier I, 301 E Pratt St, 21202-3134; (p) (410) 539-1797; (f) (410) 539-6238; webcentral@constellation.org; www.constellation.org; (c) Baltimore

Private non-profit/ 1996/ staff: 15(f); 5(p); 150(v)/ members: 3000

HISTORIC SITE; HISTORY MUSEUM; LIVING HISTORY/OUTDOOR MUSEUM: Dedicated to the restoration and preservation of the historic Naval ship U.S.S. Constellation.

PROGRAMS: Concerts; Exhibits; Film/Video; Guided Tours; Interpretation; Lectures; Living History; Reenactments

COLLECTIONS: [1860-1865] U.S.S. Constellation is the last all sail warship built for the US Navy and the last Civil War era vessel afloat.

HOURS: Oct-Apr 10-4; May-June 10-6, July-Aug 10-8

ADMISSION: $5.50, Children $3.50

3572
Doctor Samuel D. Harris National Museum of Dentistry
31 S Greene St, 21201-1504; (p) (410) 206-0600; (f) (410) 706-8313; www.dentalmuseum.umaryland.edu; (c) Baltimore

State/ 1996/ University of Maryland/ staff: 10(f); 1(p); 18(v)/publication: *The Articulator*

HISTORY MUSEUM: Operates a dental history museum which fosters an awareness, understanding, and appreciation of dental history, dentistry, and oral health.

PROGRAMS: Exhibits; Family Programs; Guided Tours; Publication; Research Library/Archives; School-Based Curriculum

COLLECTIONS: [19th-20th c] Dental artifacts including art, literature, instruments, equip, photos, and related objects.

HOURS: Yr 10-4

ADMISSION: $4.50, Children $2.50, Seniors $2.50

3573
Edgar Allan Poe House and Museum
203 N Amity St, 21203; (p) (410) 396-4866, (410) 396-7932; (f) (410) 396-5662

City

HOURS: W-Sa 12-4

3574
Eubie Blake National Jazz Institute and Cultural Center, The
34 Market Pl, Ste 323, 21202; (p) (410) 625-3113; (f) (410) 385-2916; eubieblake@vols.com; www.eubieblake.org; (c) Baltimore

Private non-profit/ 1970/ staff: 3(f); 9(p)/ members: 50

PROFESSIONAL ORGANIZATION: Preserves Baltimore jazz history including Eubie Blake, Billie Holiday, Cab Calloway, Chick Webb; operates an art gallery featuring local and national exhibitions.

PROGRAMS: Community Outreach; Concerts; Exhibits; Facility Rental; Family Programs; Festivals; Film/Video; Guided Tours; Lectures; School-Based Curriculum; Theatre

COLLECTIONS: [Harlem Renaissance] Memorabilia of Eubie Blake, ragtime and Broadway composer and piano player.

HOURS: Yr M,Th,F 4-8, Sa-Su 12-5

3575
Evergreen House
4545 N Charles St, 21210; (p) (410) 516-0341; (f) (410) 516-0864; bnowell@jhunix.hcf.jhu.edu; www.jhu.edu/evergreen; (c) Baltimore

1952/ Johns Hopkins Univ/ staff: 7(f); 5(p); 53(v)/ members: 258/publication: *View from Evergreen*

HOUSE MUSEUM: Maintains an Italianate building, owned by two generations of the Garrett family.

PROGRAMS: Community Outreach; Concerts; Exhibits; Facility Rental; Family Programs; Garden Tours; Guided Tours; Interpretation; Lectures; Publication; Research Library/Archives

COLLECTIONS: [Late 19th-mid 20th c] Rare books, post-Impressionist paintings, Tiffany glass, and Japanese netsuke

HOURS: Yr M-F 10-4, Sa-Su 1-4

ADMISSION: $6, Student $3, Seniors $5

3576
Fellspoint Museum and Cultural Programs, Inc.
Captain's House 1631 Aliceanna St, 21231; (p) (410) 228-7886; (c) Baltimore

Private non-profit/ 1958/ Board of Directors/ staff: 5(v)

HISTORIC PRESERVATION AGENCY; HISTORIC SITE; HISTORY MUSEUM; HOUSE MUSEUM: Maintains 5 Historic District buildings (1700-1840) and a collection of Dashiell-Mavine family personal artifacts (1700-1965).

PROGRAMS: Exhibits; Guided Tours

COLLECTIONS: [1700-1965] Personal effects of the Danshiell-Mavine family, along with their buildings.

3577
Fort McHenry National Monument and Historic Shrine
End of E Fort Ave, 21260-5393; (p) (410) 962-4690; (f) (410) 962-2500; fomc_superintendent@nps.gov; www.nps.gov/fomc; (c) Baltimore

1925/ National Park Service/ staff: 23(f); 16(p); 50(v)

HISTORIC SITE; HISTORY MUSEUM: Preserves the history of the successful defense of the fort against a British attack in the War of 1812, inspiring Francis Scott Key to write "The Star Spangled Banner."

PROGRAMS: Exhibits; Family Programs; Film/Video; Interpretation; Living History; Reenactments; Research Library/Archives

COLLECTIONS: [War of 1812, Civil War, W W I & II] Historical, archaeological, and architectural materials on the 1814 Battle of Baltimore and the writing of "The Star Spangled Banner."

3578
H.L. Mencken House
1524 Hollins St, 21202; (p) (410) 396-3523

3579
Homewood House Museum
3400 N Charles St, 21218; (p) (410) 516-5589; (f) (410) 516-7859; homewood@jhunix.hcf.edu; www.jhu.edu/news_info/to_do/homewood; (c) Baltimore

1987/ The Johns Hopkins Univ/ staff: 3(f); 4(p); 41(v)/ members: 271

HISTORIC SITE; HOUSE MUSEUM: Maintains the Homewood House built in 1801 by Charles Carroll, Jr.

PROGRAMS: Community Outreach; Exhibits; Facility Rental; Family Programs; Guided Tours; Lectures; Research Library/Archives

COLLECTIONS: [Early 19th c] Period furnishings, American and English fine and decorative arts reflecting the lifestyle of the Carroll family; archaeological artifacts, and archival materials.

HOURS: Yr T-Sa 11-4, Su 12-4

ADMISSION: $6, Seniors $5

3580
Lacrosse Museum and National Hall of Fame, The
113 W University Pkwy, 21210-3300; (p) (410) 235-6882; (f) (410) 366-6735; www.lacrosse.org; (c) Baltimore

Private non-profit/ 1959/ US Lacrosse/ staff: 1(f); 4(v)/ members: 42000

HISTORY MUSEUM: Historical preservation and promotion of lacrosse through the exhibiting and honoring of those who have developed the sport from its Native American origins.

PROGRAMS: Exhibits; Facility Rental; Film/Video; Interpretation; Publication

COLLECTIONS: [1636-present] Historical artifacts, publications, equipment, awards, photos, articles, art and paraphernalia.

HOURS: Yr M-Sa

3581
League of Historic American Theatres
34 Market Pl, Ste 320, 21202; (p) (410) 659-9533; (f) (410) 837-9664; info@lhat.org; www.lhat.org; (c) Baltimore City

Private non-profit/ 1976/ Board of Directors/ staff: 3(f)/ members: 530

HISTORIC PRESERVATION AGENCY: Support and facilitate the rescue, restoration, and reuse of historic theatres.

PROGRAMS: Annual Meeting; Community Outreach; Guided Tours; Lectures

COLLECTIONS: [19-early 20th c]

HOURS: Yr M-F 9:30-5

ADMISSION: No charge

3582
Maryland Historical Society
201 W Monument St, 21201; (p) (410) 685-3750; (f) (410) 385-2105; www.mdhs.org; (c) Baltimore

Private non-profit/ 1844/ staff: 45(f); 19(p); 120(v)/ members: 4000/publication: MHS News

HISTORICAL SOCIETY; HISTORY MUSEUM: MD historical artifacts; offers permanent and changing exhibits, a library, a publishing division, and educational programs.

PROGRAMS: Community Outreach; Concerts; Elder's Programs; Exhibits; Facility Rental; Family Programs; Festivals; Film/Video; Guided Tours; Interpretation; Lectures; Living History; Publication; Research Library/Archives; School-Based Curriculum

COLLECTIONS: 7.5 million objects, manuscripts, maps, photos, newspapers, and rare books; silver ceramics, paintings, textiles, furniture, and architectural drawings.

HOURS: Yr T-F 10-5, Sa 9-5, Su 11-5

ADMISSION: $4, Family $6, Student $3, Seniors $3

3583
Mother Seton House Paca St, Inc.
600 N Paca St, 21201-1920; (p) (410) 523-3443; (c) Baltimore

Private non-profit/ 1962/ staff: 16(v)/ members: 233/publication: Mother Seton House

HISTORIC SITE: Maintains the house where St. Elizabeth Ann Seton (1st American-born saint) lived from 1808-1809.

PROGRAMS: Guided Tours; Publication

COLLECTIONS: [1808] Furnishings.

HOURS: Nov-Feb Sa-Su 1-3;

3584
Mount Clare Museum House
Carroll Park, 21230 [1500 Washington Blvd, 21230-1727]; (p) (410) 837-3262; (f) (410) 937-0251; mountclaremuseumhouse@erols.com; www.erols.com/mountclaremuseumhouse; (c) Baltimore

Private non-profit/ 1917/ National Society of the Colonial Dames of America/ staff: 7(p); 40(v)/ members: 400/publication: Mount Clare

HOUSE MUSEUM: Maintains a collection of 18th and 19th c furnishings and decorative arts in the 18th c structure.

PROGRAMS: Community Outreach; Exhibits; Facility Rental; Family Programs; Festivals; Guided Tours; Interpretation; Lectures; Publication; School-Based Curriculum

COLLECTIONS: [1760-1817] Original furnishings, decorative arts, silverware, glass, and china.

HOURS: Feb-Dec T-F 11-4, Sa-Su1-4

3585
Mount Vernon Museum of Incandescent Lighting
717 Washington Pl, 21201; (p) (410) 752-8576, (410) 323-3454; (c) Baltimore

Private non-profit/ 1963/ staff: 1(f); 2(p); 4(v)

HISTORIC PRESERVATION AGENCY; HISTORY MUSEUM: Demonstrates the development of the incandescent lamp since 1879.

PROGRAMS: Elder's Programs; Exhibits; Lectures

COLLECTIONS: [1879-present] 10,000 artifacts including Edison lamps from the 1880s, Diehl induction lamp, 1st generation tungsten lamps, turn of the century Christmas lights, and Mercury-vapor lamp from the Statue of Liberty.

HOURS: Yr 9-5

3586
National Historic Seaport of Baltimore
USCGC Taney, Pier IV Pratt St, 21231 [Living Classrooms Foundation 802 S Caroline St, 21231]; (p) (410) 396-3453; (f) (410) 396-3398; NationalHistoricSeaport@erols.com; www.Livingclassrooms.org; (c) Baltimore

Private non-profit/ 1998/ Living Classrooms Foundation/ staff: 8(f); 10(p); 30(v)

ALLIANCE OF HISTORICAL AGENCIES; HISTORIC PRESERVATION AGENCY; LIVING HISTORY/OUTDOOR MUSEUM: A consortium of historic attractions surrounding Baltimore's waterfront maintained for the purposes of exploring Baltimore's rich maritime history.

PROGRAMS: Exhibits; Facility Rental; Interpretation; School-Based Curriculum

COLLECTIONS: [1600s-post WW II]

HOURS: Mar-Dec Daily 10-6

3587
Project Liberty Ship, Baltimore, Inc.
Pier One, Clinton St, 21224 [PO Box 25846, 21224]; (p) (410) 661-1550, (410) 558-0646; (f) (410) 558-1737; john.w.brown@usa.net; www.liberty-ship.com; (c) Baltimore

Private non-profit/ 1988/ Board of Trustees/ staff: 250(v)/ members: 3000/publication: The Ugly Duckling; Liberty Log

HISTORIC SITE; HISTORY MUSEUM; LIVING HISTORY/OUTDOOR MUSEUM; RESEARCH CENTER: Dedicated to the preservation of the WW II Liberty Ship John W. Brown as a living, steaming museum ship and memorial in Baltimore.

PROGRAMS: Community Outreach; Facility Rental; Guided Tours; Interpretation; Living History; Publication; Reenactments; Research Library/Archives

COLLECTIONS: [1942-1945] Ship is an artifacts from WW II and is filled with displays of equipment, materials, books, and papers of the era.

HOURS: Yr W, Sa 9-3 or by appt

ADMISSION: Donations requested

3588
Society for the Preservation of Federal Hill and Fell's Point
812 S Ann St, 21217; (p) (410) 675-6750; (f) (410) 675-6769; (c) Baltimore

Private non-profit/ 1967/ Board of Directors/ staff: 2(f); 300(v)/ members: 500

HISTORIC PRESERVATION AGENCY; HISTORIC SITE; HISTORY MUSEUM; HOUSE MUSEUM: Preservation and operation of two historic houses, a maritime museum, an 18th c coffee house, an 18th c Inn, and a visitor's center.

PROGRAMS: Annual Meeting; Community Outreach; Exhibits; Facility Rental; Family Programs; Festivals; Garden Tours; Guided Tours; Interpretation; Lectures; Living History; Publication

COLLECTIONS: [1730-1900] Household furnishings of a workingman's family (1765-1781), merchant's shop and furnishings (1810)

3589
St. Joseph Society of the Sacred Heart Archives
1130 N Calvert St, 21202; (p) (410) 727-1193; (f) (410) 385-2331; archvssj@aol.com; www.josephites.org; (c) Baltimore

Private non-profit/ staff: 1(f); 11(p); 1(v)/ members: 1

LIBRARY AND/OR ARCHIVES

PROGRAMS: Research Library/Archives

COLLECTIONS: [17th c-present] Official correspondence, manuscripts, newspapers, magazine clippings, dissertations, and audio and video

3590
Star Spangled Banner Flag House/The 1812 Museum
844 E Pratt St, 21202; (p) (410) 834-7193; (f) (410) 837-1712; info@flaghouse.org;

www.flaghouse.org; (c) Baltimore

Private non-profit/ 1927/ staff: 2(f); 7(p); 15(v)/ members: 550

HISTORIC SITE; HOUSE MUSEUM: Maintains the 1793 home of Mary Pickersgill, who sewed the flag, and a museum with displays of military artifacts from the War of 1812.

PROGRAMS: Facility Rental; Family Programs; Guided Tours; Lectures; Living History; Research Library/Archives

COLLECTIONS: [18th-19th c] Personal items belonging to Pickersgill and her family; furniture, ceramics, textiles, artwork, military artifacts, archives, and documents.

HOURS: Yr T-Sa 10-4

ADMISSION: $4, Children $2, Seniors $3

3591
Steamship Historical Society Collection
Langsdale Library, Univ of Baltimore, 1420 Maryland Ave, 21201; (p) (410) 837-4334; ghaitsuka@ubmail.ubalt.edu.; www.ubalt.edu/archives/ship/ship.htm

Maintains the collection of the Steamship Historical Society, which is located in Providence, RI.

COLLECTIONS: Photographs, brochures, ship plans, books, periodicals, and

3592
United Methodist Historical Society of Baltimore-Washington Conf. Inc.
2200 St. Paul St, 21218-5897; (p) (410) 886-4458; (c) Baltimore

1855/ staff: 3(p); 6(v)/ members: 500/publication: *Third Century Methodism*

HISTORICAL SOCIETY: Collects, preserves, and displays items of Methodist history; offers permanent and special exhibits, archives/library, tours, and programs.

PROGRAMS: Annual Meeting; Exhibits; Guided Tours; Lectures; Publication; Research Library/Archives

COLLECTIONS: [1740-present] Books, manuscripts, documents, conference, local church records, clergy files, and artifacts associated with Wesley, Asbury.

BEL AIR

3593
Hays House Museum
324 Kenmore Ave, 21014 [PO Box 366, 21014]; (p) (410) 238-7691; HARCHIS@aol.com; www.netgsi.com/~hshc/; (c) Hartford

Private non-profit/ 1885/ Hisotrical Society of Hartford County/ staff: 200(v)/ members: 500

HISTORICAL SOCIETY; HOUSE MUSEUM: Preserves the Hayes House which illustrates the life of rural gentry during 1788-1814.

PROGRAMS: Concerts; Exhibits; Facility Rental; Festivals; Guided Tours; Interpretation; Lectures; Reenactments

COLLECTIONS: [1788-1814] Period furnishings.

HOURS: Apr-Dec Su 1-4; Jan-Mar by appt

ADMISSION: Donations accepted

3594
Historical Society of Harford County, Inc., The
143 N Main St, 21014 [PO Box 306, 21014-0366]; (p) (410) 838-7691; www.netgsi.com/~hshc; (c) Harford

Private non-profit/ 1879/ Board of Directors/ staff: 4(p); 30(v)/ members: 568/publication: *Harford Historical Bulletin and Newsletter*

HISTORICAL SOCIETY: Collects and preserves information on Harford County and encourages research.

PROGRAMS: Annual Meeting; Exhibits; Lectures; Publication; Research Library/Archives

COLLECTIONS: [1773-present] Books, pamphlets, clippings, photos, church histories, old school lists, family histories, maps, artifacts, Historical Site surveys, post cards, calendars, periodicals, telephone books, catalogues, yearbooks, and original documents.

HOURS: Yr

ADMISSION: Donations accepted

3595
Liriodendron
502 W Gordon St, 21014; (p) (410) 879-4424; info@liriodendron.org; www.liriodendron.org; (c) Harford

Joint/ 1980/ County; Private non-Profit/ staff: 1(f); 1(p); 60(v)/ members: 260

ART MUSEUM; GARDEN; HOUSE MUSEUM: Maintains the former summer home of Dr. Howard A. Kelly of Johns Hopkins as a social and cultural facility.

PROGRAMS: Annual Meeting; Community Outreach; Concerts; Exhibits; Facility Rental; Family Programs; Garden Tours; Guided Tours

COLLECTIONS: Native American artifacts, sculpture, and local artwork.

3596
Tudor Hall
17 Tudor Ln, 21015; (p) (410) 838-0466; http://www.carolinejasper.com/tdrhll.htm

1850/ staff: 20(v)

Maintains home of Shakespearean actors Junius Brutus Wilkes and his son Edwin Booth, father and brother of John Wilkes Booth.

COLLECTIONS: [Civil War] Prints, lithographs of Booth family. Original letters of Edwin Thomas Booth. Theatre memorabilia. First editions of Booth Family history, Civil War and Abe Lincoln. Tour guides tell the story of the home and family; None, Researchers, scholars, actors, etc. are generally interested in the birthplace and the rooms occupied by the family and the preservation of a historical site on the National Register since 1973.

BERLIN

3597
Berlin Heritage Foundation, Inc./Calvin B. Taylor House Museum
208 N Main St, 21811 [PO Box 351, 21811]; (p) (410) 641-1019; (c) Worcester

Private non-profit/ 1981/ Board of Directors/ staff: 1(p); 50(v)/ members: 250

HISTORY MUSEUM; HOUSE MUSEUM: Administers the Calvin B. Taylor House Museum,

a restored early 19th c house. This town museum collects, preserves, and interprets local history.

PROGRAMS: Concerts; Exhibits; Facility Rental; Guided Tours

COLLECTIONS: [19th-20th c] 1840s furnishings, local memorabilia.

HOURS: June-Oct 31 M, W, F, Sa 1-4

ADMISSION: Donations requested

BETHESDA

3598
DeWitt Stetten, Jr. Museum of Medical Research
NIH Bldg 31 Rm 2B09 MSC 2092, 20892-2092; (p) (301) 496-6610; (f) (301) 402-1434; vharden@helix.mh.gov; www.nih.gov/od/museum; (c) Montgomery

Federal/ 1986/ National Institute of Health, DHHS/ staff: 2(f); 2(p); 2(v)

HISTORY MUSEUM: Collects, preserves, and exhibits the material culture of biomedical research and serves as the history office of the National Institutes of Health.

PROGRAMS: Guided Tours; Lectures

COLLECTIONS: [20th c] Biomedical research instruments, technologies, and NIH memorabilia.

HOURS: Yr Daily

ADMISSION: No charge

BIG POOL

3599
Fort Frederick State Park
11100 Fort Frederick Rd, 21711; (p) (301) 842-2155; (f) (301) 842-0028; (c) Washington

State/ 1922/ Dept of Natural Resouces/ staff: 10(f); 11(p); 1000(v)

HISTORIC SITE; LIVING HISTORY/OUTDOOR MUSEUM: Maintains a colonial stone fort (1756) and offers related living history programs.

PROGRAMS: Exhibits; Facility Rental; Festivals; Film/Video; Guided Tours; Interpretation; Living History; Reenactments; School-Based Curriculum

COLLECTIONS: [1756-1764] Archaeological artifacts including pottery, buttons, buckles, glass, and beads.

HOURS: Yr Daily Daylight-Dark

ADMISSION: $2

BOONSBORO

3600
Boonsborough Museum of History
113 N Main St, 21713-1007; (p) (301) 432-6969; (f) (301) 416-2222; (c) Washington

Private non-profit/ 1975/ staff: 1(p); 3(v)

HISTORY MUSEUM

PROGRAMS: Exhibits; Guided Tours; Interpretation; Lectures

COLLECTIONS: [19th c] Historical artifacts spanning 5000 years; displays of china, glassware, weapons, and ancient artifacts; and reconstruction of a cabinetmaker's shop, and a

19th c general store.

HOURS: May-Sept Su 1-5 or by appt

BOWIE

3601
Belair Mansion
12207 Tulip Grove Dr, 20715; (p) (301) 809-3088, (301) 809-3089; (f) (301) 809-2308; bowiemuseum@juno.com; www.cityofbowie.org

City/ 1745/ staff: 2(f); 3(p); 30(v)

COLLECTIONS: [1745-1955] Four paintings by Phillipe Mercier (1689-1760) original to this house; paintings and decorative arts; documents belonging to Gov. Samuel Ogle.

HOURS: Yr

3602
City of Bowie Museums
12207 Tulip Grove Dr, 20715-2340; (p) (301) 809-3088; (f) (301) 809-2308; bowiemuseum@juno.com; www.cityofbowie.org/comserv/museums.htm; (c) Prince George's

City/ 1969/ staff: 2(f); 6(p); 40(v)/ members: 300

GENEALOGICAL SOCIETY; HISTORIC SITE; HISTORY MUSEUM: Maintains a collection of five historic sites operating under a municipal system collecting, preserving, and interpreting the history of Bowie.

PROGRAMS: Annual Meeting; Community Outreach; Concerts; Exhibits; Facility Rental; Family Programs; Festivals; Guided Tours; Interpretation; Lectures; Living History; Publication; Reenactments; Research Library/ Archives

COLLECTIONS: [1683-present] Paintings, furniture, railroad equip, radios, and communications artifacts; carriages, horse track, archaeological holdings, manuscripts, and 4,000 volume genealogy library.

HOURS: Yr Th-Su 1-4

ADMISSION: $3, Children $1

BROOKEVILLE

3603
Brookeville Academy
5 High St, 20833 [Box 67, 20833]; (p) (301) 570-4465; (f) (301) 570-4465; (c) Montgomery

City/ 1997/ Town of Brookeville/ staff: 10(v)

HISTORIC SITE: Restored and maintains one of the first private academies in MD.

PROGRAMS: Annual Meeting; Facility Rental; Interpretation; Lectures; Publication; Research Library/Archives

COLLECTIONS: [1794-present] Photos, land records, genealogical info, store logs, and records.

BRUNSWICK

3604
Brunswick Railroad Museum
40 W Potomac St, 21716; (p) (301) 834-7100; www.bhs.edu/brun/rrmus/rrmus.html; (c) Frederick

Private non-profit/ 1974/ Brunswick Potomac Foundation/ staff: 2(p); 33(v)/ members:

240/publication: *The Rail Letter*

HISTORY MUSEUM: Two exhibition floors offer interpretation of B&O Railroad history, featuring equipment, historic photographs, costume, Victoriana, and other collections.

PROGRAMS: Annual Meeting; Community Outreach; Exhibits; Facility Rental; Festivals; Guided Tours; Interpretation; Lectures; Publication; Research Library/Archives

COLLECTIONS: [1880-1960] Historic photographs, B&O Railroad equipment, memorabilia, archives, labor history, HO scale model railroad, communications and medical equipment, Victorian furnishings, costumes, antique toys, domestic goods, and C&O Canal history.

HOURS: Apr-May, Oct-Dec Sa 10-4, Su 1-4; June-Sept Sa 10-4, Su 1-4, Th-F 10-2

ADMISSION: $4, Children $2.50, Seniors $2.50

CAMBRIDGE

3605
Harriet Tubman Organization
424 Race St, 21613; (p) (410) 228-0401; (c) Dorchester

Private for-profit/ 1984/ staff: 2(p); 8(v)/publication: *Harriet Tubman Lives*

HISTORY MUSEUM; RESEARCH CENTER: Operates a museum and an information center.

PROGRAMS: Exhibits; Festivals; Guided Tours; Lectures; Monthly Meeting; Publication; Research Library/Archives

HOURS: Yr M-F 10-5:30, Sa by appt

3606
Meredith House
902 LaBrange Ave, 21613; (p) (410) 228-7953

3607
Richardson Maritime Museum
401 High St, 21613 [PO Box 1198, 21613]; (p) (410) 221-1871, (410) 228-3967; (c) Dorchester

Private non-profit/ 1992/ staff: 24(v)/ members: 100

HISTORIC PRESERVATION AGENCY: Dedicated to the preservation of the history of wooden boat building on the Chesapeake Bay.

PROGRAMS: Annual Meeting; Exhibits; Family Programs; Festivals; Guided Tours

COLLECTIONS: Models of bugeyes, pungys, skipjacks, log canoes, and a merchant brig; original hand tools and photos.

HOURS: Apr-Oct W, Sa-Su

3608
Spocott Windmill Foundation, Inc.
[PO Box 836, 21613]; (p) (410) 228-7090; (f) (410) 228-7091; (c) Dorchester

Private non-profit/ 1971/ staff: 25(v)/ members: 100

HISTORIC SITE: Operation of English Post Windmill and 3 historic buildings: Colonial Tenant House (1800), Victorian One Room School House (1870), and a County Store Museum (1935).

PROGRAMS: Annual Meeting; Exhibits; Guided Tours

COLLECTIONS:

CATONSVILLE

3609
Catonsville Historical Society, Inc., The
1824 Frederick Rd, 21228 [PO Box 9311, 21228-0311]; (p) (410) 744-3034; (c) Baltimore

Private non-profit/ 1973/ staff: 1(p); 40(v)/ members: 500/publication: *Catonsville Heritage, and others*

HISTORICAL SOCIETY: Functions as a repository for any material which may help to establish or illustrate the history of Catonsville; preserves historical material.

PROGRAMS: Annual Meeting; Community Outreach; Elder's Programs; Exhibits; Garden Tours; Guided Tours; Lectures; Publication

COLLECTIONS: [20th c] Catonsville memorabilia.

HOURS: By Appt

CENTREVILLE

3610
Queen Anne's Museum of Eastern Shore Life
Dulin Clark Rd, 21617 [PO Box 525, 21617]; (c) Queen Anne's

Joint/ 1993/ County; Private non-profit/ staff: 15(v)/ members: 150

HISTORY MUSEUM

PROGRAMS: Annual Meeting; Exhibits; Festivals; Film/Video; Guided Tours

COLLECTIONS: [Late 1600s-1800] Kitchen items, steam engine, tractors, threshers, corn planters, and items related to woodworking, dairy, and blacksmithing.

CHARLESTOWN

3611
107 House/Tory House
Market & Cecil Sts, 21914 [PO Box 52, 21914]; (p) (410) 287-8262

1810/ staff: 7(v)

COLLECTIONS: [1810 Federal Period] Arrowheads, antique desk & chairs, antique cradle, old glassware, the original silver town seal, original ship models.

HOURS: Seasonal

CHESAPEAKE BEACH

3612
Chesapeake Beach Railway Museum
4155 Mears Ave, 20732 [PO Box 738, 20732]; (p) (410) 257-3892; (c) Calvert

County/ 1978/ Commissioners of Calvert County/ staff: 1(f); 5(p); 35(v)/ members: 300/publication: *The Chesapeake Dispatcher*

HISTORIC SITE; HISTORY MUSEUM: Maintains local history museum; offers exhibits, educational programs, and special events.

PROGRAMS: Community Outreach; Concerts; Exhibits; Family Programs; Film/Video;

Guided Tours; Interpretation; Lectures; Publication; Research Library/Archives; School-Based Curriculum

COLLECTIONS: [1900-present] Artifacts, archives, photos, oral histories, library materials relating to the history of the railway and resort towns.

HOURS: May-Sept Daily 1-4; Apr and Oct Sa-Su 1-4

CHESTERTOWN

3613
Geddes-Piper House
101 Church Alley, 21620 [PO Box 665, 21620]; (p) (410) 778-3499; kentcounty.com/historicalsociety/index.htm

3614
Historical Society of Kent County
101 Church Alley, 21620 [PO Box 665, 21620]; (p) (410) 778-3499; (c) Kent

Private non-profit/ 1938/ staff: 1(p); 45(v)/ members: 652/publication: *Historic Houses of Kent County 1640-1860*

HOUSE MUSEUM: Preserves and disseminates knowledge relative to the social, political, civil, military, architectural, and biographical history of Kent County, founded in 1642.

PROGRAMS: Annual Meeting; Exhibits; Facility Rental; Guided Tours; Lectures; Publication; Research Library/Archives

COLLECTIONS: [18th c] Period furniture, textiles, maps, Chinese export porcelain, genealogy, local and state history.

CHEVY CHASE

3615
Chevy Chase Historical Society
Box 15145, 20825; (p) (301) 656-5135; (c) Montgomery

Private non-profit/ 1981/ members: 300

HISTORICAL SOCIETY: Preserves and collects the history of Chevy Chase, an early 19th c planned suburb.

PROGRAMS: Annual Meeting; Community Outreach; Exhibits; Guided Tours; Lectures; Research Library/Archives

COLLECTIONS: [1892-present] Photos, oral histories, books, ephemera, and standing files of materials relating to Chevy Chase.

HOURS: By appt

CLINTON

3616
His Lordship's Kindness
7607 Woodyard Rd, 20735; (p) (301) 856-0358; (f) (301) 856-0358; waltonfd@erols.com; www.somd.lib.md.us/lordship; (c) Prince George's

Private non-profit/ 1995/ Walton Foundation, Inc/ staff: 1(f); 1(p); 8(v)

HISTORIC SITE; HOUSE MUSEUM: Preserves the National Landmark built by Robert Darnall in 1787 on land received from Lord Baltimore in 1703; maintains outbuildings; preserves the site through research, public programs, exhibitions, and tours.

PROGRAMS: Exhibits; Facility Rental; Family Programs; Guided Tours; Lectures; Reenactments

COLLECTIONS: [1780s-1950s] Outbuildings, gardens, and furnishings.

HOURS: Mar-Dec F 12-5, 2nd/4th Sa by appt

ADMISSION: $5, Children $3, Seniors $4

3617
Surratt House Museum
9118 Brandywine Rd, 20735 [PO Box 427, 20735]; (p) (301) 868-1121; (f) (301) 868-8177; www.clark.net/pub/surratt/surratt.html; (c) Prince George's

County/ 1975/ MD National Capital Park and Planning Commission/ staff: 1(f); 3(p); 60(v)/ members: 1300/publication: *Monthly Surratt Courier*

HOUSE MUSEUM; RESEARCH CENTER: Maintains historic house museum (1852) which focuses on Civil War life in southern MD and the site's role in events surrounding the Lincoln assassination.

PROGRAMS: Annual Meeting; Community Outreach; Elder's Programs; Exhibits; Family Programs; Guided Tours; Interpretation; Lectures; Living History; Publication; Reenactments; Research Library/Archives; School-Based Curriculum

COLLECTIONS: [Civil War Era 1840-1865] Furnishings and decorative arts reflective of a middle-class plantation of Southern MD with special emphasis on archival and research materials related to the Lincoln assassination.

HOURS: Yr Th-F 11-3, Sa-Su 12-4

ADMISSION: $3, Children $1, Seniors $2

COCKEYSVILLE

3618
Baltimore County Historical Society, Inc.
9811 Van Buren Ln, 21030-5099; (p) (410) 666-1876; www.bcpl.lib.md.us/branchpgs/bchs/bchshome.html; (c) Baltimore

Private non-profit/ 1959/ staff: 20(v)/ members: 350/publication: *History Trails*

HISTORICAL SOCIETY; HOUSE MUSEUM: Collects, preserves, and interprets material from the county's past for the edification and enjoyment of present and future generations.

PROGRAMS: Annual Meeting; Exhibits; Festivals; Lectures; Living History; Publication; Research Library/Archives

COLLECTIONS: Research library, maps, photographs, periodicals, artifacts, and school; mercantile exhibit rooms, and farm museum.

HOURS: Yr Library: Sa 10-3, W 1-4; Farm Museum/Exhibit Rooms: Apr-July and and Sept-Dec 2nd Sa 10-3 or by appt

COLLEGE PARK

3619
College Park Aviation Museum
1985 Corporal Frank Scott Dr, 20740; (p) (301) 864-6029; (f) (301) 927-6472; cathy_allen@pgparks.com; www.parksrec.org; (c) Prince George's

County/ 1980/ Maryland-National Capital Park and Planning Commission/ staff: 6(f); 5(p); 102(v)/ members: 54/publication: *The Wright Flyer*

HISTORIC SITE; HISTORY MUSEUM: Interprets aviation history.

PROGRAMS: Community Outreach; Exhibits; Facility Rental; Family Programs; Festivals; Guided Tours; Interpretation; Lectures; Publication; Research Library/Archives; School-Based Curriculum

COLLECTIONS: [1900-present] Early aviation memorabilia related to the history of College Park Airport and early pre-WW I aviation history.

HOURS: Yr Daily 10-5

3620
National Archives and Records Administration
8601 Adelphi Rd, 20740-6001; (p) (301) 713-6800; (f) (301) 713-6915; inquire@arch2.nara.gov; www.nara.gov/.; (c) Prince George

Federal/ 1934/ staff: 2211(f); 325(p); 300(v)

RESEARCH CENTER: Ensures, for citizens and federal officials, ready access to essential evidence that documents the rights of American citizens, the actions of federal officials, and the national experience.

PROGRAMS: Exhibits; Film/Video; Guided Tours; Lectures; Research Library/Archives

COLLECTIONS: [Revolutionary War-present]

HOURS: Exhibit Hall: Yr Winter Daily 10-5:30, Summer Daily 10-9; Research rooms Yr M-W 8:45-5, T-Th-F 8:45-9, Sa 8:45-4:45

3621
Nixon Presidential Materials Staff
8601 Adelphi Rd, 20740-6001; (p) (301) 713-6950; (f) (301) 713-6916; nixon@arch2.nara.gov; www.nara.gov; (c) Prince George

COLTON'S POINT

3622
St. Clement's Island-Potomac River Museum
38370 Point Breeze Rd, 20626; (p) (301) 769-2222; (f) (301) 769-2225; pineypoint@erols; www.somd.lib.md.us/ STMA/government/R/museum.htm; (c) St. Mary's

County/ 1975/ staff: 2(f); 6(p); 62(v)/ members: 405

HISTORY MUSEUM: Founded to commemorate the landing of the MD colonists on St. Clement's Island in 1634; collects, preserves, exhibits, and interprets the history and culture of St. Mary's County.

PROGRAMS: Annual Meeting; Community Outreach; Concerts; Elder's Programs; Exhibits; Facility Rental; Family Programs; Guided Tours; Interpretation; Lectures; Research Library/Archives; School-Based Curriculum

COLLECTIONS: [Prehistory-present] 2,000 Native American artifacts, fine art, maritime tools and boats, historic documents, photos, and maps.

HOURS: Apr-Sept M-F 9-5, Sa-Su 12-5; Oct-Mar W-Su 12-4

ADMISSION: $2

COLUMBIA

3623
African Art Museum of Maryland
5430 Vantage Point Rd, 21044 [PO Box 1105, 21044]; (p) (410) 730-7105; (f) (410) 715-3047; Africanartmuseum@Erols.com; www.africanartmuseum.org; (c) Howard

Private non-profit/ 1980/ Board of Trustees/ staff: 2(f); 1(p); 25(v)/ members: 400/publication: *The Quartet and Museum Memos*

ART MUSEUM; HISTORIC SITE: Dedicated to collecting, exhibiting, and preserving the art of Africa through a wide range of experiences, including exhibits, lectures, and tours to Africa.

PROGRAMS: Community Outreach; Concerts; Exhibits; Festivals; Guided Tours; Interpretation; Lectures; Publication; Research Library/Archives; School-Based Curriculum

COLLECTIONS: Art from traditional societies: masks, textiles, jewelry, musical instruments, sculptured figures, and baskets.

HOURS: Yr T-F 10-4, Su 12-4

ADMISSION: $2, Children $1, Seniors $1; Members free

3624
Columbia Archives
10221 Wincopin Circle, 21045; (p) (410) 715-3103; (f) (410) 715-3043; jkellner@erols.com; www.columbiaassociation.com; (c) Howard

City/ Columbia Association/ staff: 1(f); 1(p); 10(v)

LIBRARY AND/OR ARCHIVES: Collects, preserves, and makes available the documentation of the planning and development of Columbia, MD.

PROGRAMS: Community Outreach; Exhibits; Guided Tours; Lectures; Research Library/Archives; School-Based Curriculum

COLLECTIONS: [Mid 20th c-present] Documents, manuscripts, newspapers, and other periodicals; photographs, maps, artifacts, memorabilia, audio and videotapes, scrapbooks

3625
Historic Oakland
5430 Vantage Point Rd, 21044; (p) (410) 730-4801; (f) (410) 730-1823; caoaklan@erols.com; www.historic-oakland.com; (c) Howard

Private non-profit/ 1811/ Columbia Association/ staff: 3(f); 12(p)

HISTORIC SITE: Maintains a late-federalist building which houses a community association, African art museum, and foundation.

PROGRAMS: Concerts; Exhibits; Facility Rental; Family Programs; Festivals; Guided Tours

HOURS: Yr Daily 7-midnight

CRISTFIELD

3626
Cristfield Heritage Foundaiton
#3 9th St, 21817 [PO Box 253, 21817]; (p) (410) 968-2501; (f) (410) 968-3639; (c) Somerset

Private non-profit/ 1977/ staff: 2(f); 2(p); 50(v)/ members: 200

PROFESSIONAL ORGANIZATION: Preserves history, heritage, and culture of the Lower Eastern Shore of MD for educational purposes.

PROGRAMS: Annual Meeting; Exhibits; Facility Rental; Festivals; Guided Tours; Interpretation; Lectures; Living History; Research Library/Archives

COLLECTIONS: [Prehistory-present] Native American artifacts, Chesapeake Bay harvesting tools, decoys, memorabilia of Gov. Tames, and photo archives of the Lower Shore of MD.

HOURS: Oct-May M-F 9-4:30; June-Sept also Sa-Su 10-3

ADMISSION: $2.50

CUMBERLAND

3627
Allegany County Historical Society
218 Washington St, 21502; (p) (301) 777-8678; (f) (301) 777-8678; (c) Allegany

Joint/ 1937/ Board of Directors; County, non-profit; Private non-profit/ staff: 1(f); 1(p); 50(v)/ members: 500

GENEALOGICAL SOCIETY; HISTORY MUSEUM; HOUSE MUSEUM; RESEARCH CENTER: Maintains Victorian house museum.

PROGRAMS: Annual Meeting; Community Outreach; Concerts; Exhibits; Facility Rental; Garden Tours; Guided Tours; Interpretation; Lectures; Living History; School-Based Curriculum

COLLECTIONS: [1860-1950] Home furnishings, clothing, toys, art, photos, local history, carriage house, industry, transportation, and quilts.

HOURS: May-Oct T-Su 11-4; Nov-Apr T-Sa 11-4

ADMISSION: $5, Student $3

3628
Preservation Society of Allegany County, Inc.
310 Decatur St, 21501 [PO Box 1648, 21501-1648]; (p) (301) 722-5610; (c) Allegany

Private non-profit/ 1968/ staff: 5(f); 6(p); 10(v)/ members: 130/publication: *Heritage Press; Heritage Review*

HISTORIC PRESERVATION AGENCY; HISTORY MUSEUM: Cultivates and encourages an interest in preserving county buildings, sties, and structures of historic and aesthetic significance.

PROGRAMS: Annual Meeting; Exhibits; Guided Tours; Interpretation; Publication

COLLECTIONS: [1800s-present] Early photos, household objects, clothing, loom, spinning wheel, and models/exhibits of industry,

3629
Thrasher Carriage Museum
19 Depot St, 21501 [c/o ACCVB, PO Box 1445, 21501-1445]; (p) (301) 689-3380; (f) (301) 689-3380; www.cumberland.com/tharsher; (c) Allegany

Joint/ 1994/ Allegany County Commissioners; Private non-profit/ staff: 1(f); 4(p); 20(v)/publication: *Horse Drawn Vehicles; and others*

HISTORY MUSEUM

PROGRAMS: Exhibits; Facility Rental; Guided Tours; Interpretation; Lectures; Living History; Publication

COLLECTIONS: [1850-1910] Horses drawn vehicles, dog cart, glass enclosed hearse, open sleighs, and vehicles owned by wealthy American citizens.

HOURS: May-Oct T-Su 11-3; Nov-Dec Sa-Su 11-3

ADMISSION: $2, Children $1, Seniors $1.75

3630
Western Maryland Chapter, National Railway Historical Society
15 Canal St, 21501 [PO Box 1331, 21501-1331]; (p) (301) 722-2101; bieryins@gcnet.net; www.mes.loyola.edu/faculty/phs/wmar-nrhs.htm; (c) Allegany

Private non-profit/ 1977/ Board of Directors/ staff: 12(v)/ members: 69/publication: *The Automatic Block*

HISTORICAL SOCIETY: Promotes the appreciation of rail transportation and its heritage through historic preservation and public education.

PROGRAMS: Annual Meeting; Festivals; Film/Video; Lectures; Publication; Research Library/Archives

COLLECTIONS: [1842-present] Historic railway artifacts, documents, and photos with emphasis on the railroads and rail transit lines of Western MD and adjacent PN and W VA.

HOURS: May-Dec T-Su 10-4

ADMISSION: Donations accepted

DUNDALK

3631
Dundalk-Patapsco Neck Historical Society
4 Center Pl, 21222 [PO Box 21781, 21222]; (p) (410) 284-2331; (c) Baltimore

Private non-profit/ 1970/ staff: 32(v)/ members: 350

HISTORIC SITE; HISTORICAL SOCIETY; HISTORY MUSEUM; RESEARCH CENTER: Preserves the history of Patapseo Neck area for educational purposes.

PROGRAMS: Annual Meeting; Community Outreach; Concerts; Exhibits; Family Programs; Festivals; Film/Video; Guided Tours; Interpretation; Lectures; Living History; Publication; Research Library/Archives; School-Based Curriculum

COLLECTIONS: [Late 1600s-present] Manuscripts, maps, newspapers, photos, artifacts, furniture, library, slide shows, oral histories, school yearbooks, and genealogy.

HOURS: Yr M-F 10-5, Sa 1-5, Su by appt.

EARLEVILLE

3632
Mount Harmon Plantation
600 Mt. Harmon Rd, 21919 [PO Box 65, 21919]; (p) (410) 275-8819

Private non-profit/ 1730/ Friends of Mt. Harmon/ staff: 7(v)

HISTORIC SITE; HISTORY MUSEUM;

HOUSE MUSEUM: A typical frontier tobacco plantation of the colonial era.

PROGRAMS: Guided Tours

COLLECTIONS: [18th c] 18th-century furnishings.

HOURS: Apr-Oct

EARVILLE

3633
Friends of Mt. Harmon
600 Mt Harmon Rd, 21919 [PO Box 65, 21919]; (p) (410) 275-8819; (f) (410) 275-9016; (c) Cecil

Private non-profit/ Friends of Mt Harmon/ staff: 1(f); 1(p); 12(v)

HOUSE MUSEUM: Offers guided tours of a restored tobacco plantation.

PROGRAMS: Guided Tours

COLLECTIONS: [18th c]

HOURS: May-Oct T, Th 10-3, Su 1-4

ADMISSION: $5

EASTON

3634
Historical Society of Talbot County
25 S Washington St, 21601; (p) (410) 822-0773; (f) (410) 822-7911; director@hsts.org; www.hstc.org; (c) Talbot

Private non-profit/ 1954/ Board of Directors/ staff: 1(f); 4(p); 120(v)/ members: 550

HISTORICAL SOCIETY; HOUSE MUSEUM: Promotes public interest, knowledge, understanding, and appreciation of the heritage of Talbot County through the collection, preservation, documentation, and interpretation of the material culture of the county.

PROGRAMS: Annual Meeting; Exhibits; Facility Rental; Festivals; Guided Tours

COLLECTIONS: [Late18th-mid 20th c] Over 75,000 photographs, 5,000 artifacts, documents, decorative and fine arts, textiles, and furnishings.

HOURS: Yr T-F 11-3, Sa 10-4

EDGEWATER

3635
Historic London Town and Gardens
839 Londontown Rd, 21037; (p) (410) 222-1919; (f) (410) 222-1918; londntwn@clark.net; www.historiclondontown.com; (c) Anne Arundel

Private non-profit/ 1973/ London Town Foundation, Inc/ staff: 4(f); 6(p); 130(v)/ members: 450

GARDEN; HISTORIC SITE; HOUSE MUSEUM; LIVING HISTORY/OUTDOOR MUSEUM: Maintains a historic and archaeological site featuring National Historic Landmark William Brown House and an 8 acre woodland garden.

PROGRAMS: Annual Meeting; Community Outreach; Concerts; Exhibits; Facility Rental; Family Programs; Garden Tours; Guided Tours; Interpretation; Lectures; Living History; Publication; School-Based Curriculum

COLLECTIONS: [1680-1780] 1765 tavern furnishings and archaeological artifacts.

HOURS: Yr Daily 9:30-4

ADMISSION: $6, Children $3, Seniors $4

ELLICOTT

3636
Coalition to Protect Maryland Burial Sites, Inc.
[PO Box 1533, 21041]; (p) (410) 465-3439; www.preservenet.cornell.edu/cpmbs/coalition.htm; (c) Howard

Private non-profit/ 1991/ Board of Directors/ staff: 11(v)/ members: 93/publication: *Coalition Courier*

HISTORIC PRESERVATION AGENCY: Promotes the welfare of burial sites through legislative effort and community outreach.

PROGRAMS: Annual Meeting; Lectures; Publication

COLLECTIONS: [Colonial]

ELLICOTT CITY

3637
Ellicott City B&O Railroad Station Museum, The
2711 Maryland Ave, 21043; (p) (410) 461-1945; (f) (410) 461-1944; dshack5@juno.com; www.ref.usc.edu/~gkoma; (c) Howard

Private non-profit/ 1973/ Historic Ellicott City, Inc/ staff: 2(f); 2(p); 150(v)

LIVING HISTORY/OUTDOOR MUSEUM: Operates a 19th c living history program centered on the B&O Railroad; offers seasonal programs highlighting the railroad and the Civil War.

PROGRAMS: Community Outreach; Exhibits; Family Programs; Film/Video; Guided Tours; Interpretation; Lectures; Living History; Research Library/Archives; School-Based Curriculum

COLLECTIONS: [1827-1868] Railroad artifacts and memorabilia focusing on the early years of the B&O Railroad.

HOURS: Yr

ADMISSION: $4, Student $3, Children

3638
Howard County Historical Society
8328 Court Ave, 21041 [PO Box 109, 21041]; (p) (410) 461-1050, (410) 750-0370; (f) (410) 750-0370; hchs@clark.net; (c) Howard

Joint/ 1957/ County; Private non-profit/ staff: 3(p); 75(v)/ members: 500/publication: *The Legacy*

HISTORIC SITE; HISTORICAL SOCIETY; HISTORY MUSEUM; HOUSE MUSEUM; LIBRARY AND/OR ARCHIVES; RESEARCH CENTER: Collects, preserves, and protects county history.

PROGRAMS: Annual Meeting; Community Outreach; Concerts; Exhibits; Facility Rental; Family Programs; Festivals; Guided Tours; Interpretation; Lectures; Living History; Publication; Reenactments; Research Library/Archives; School-Based Curriculum

COLLECTIONS: [1750-present] Artifacts, oral histories, genealogy, marriage licenses, maps, and books.

HOURS: Yr Museum: T,Sa 12-5; Library: T 12-8, Sa 12-5

ADMISSION: No charge

EMMITSBURG

3639
National Shrine of St. Elizabeth Ann Seton
333 S Seton Ave, 21727; (p) (301) 447-6606; (f) (301) 447-6061; office@setonshrine.org; www.setonshrine.org; (c) Frederick

Private non-profit/ staff: 8(f); 2(p); 9(v)/publication: *The Seton Way*

HISTORIC SITE: Objective is to further knowledge of and devotion to Saint Elizabeth Ann Setton, America's first native-born saint who was canonized on Sept 14, 1975.

PROGRAMS: Exhibits; Film/Video; Guided Tours; Publication

COLLECTIONS: [1774-1975] Artifacts cover the period from Seton's birth through canonization.

HOURS: Apr-Oct T-Su 10-4:30; Nov-Mar Daily 10-4:30

ESSEX

3640
Heritage Society of Essex and Middle River, Inc.
516 Eastern Blvd, 21221; (p) (410) 574-6934; (c) Baltimore

Private non-profit/ 1968/ Executive Officers/ staff: 25(v)/ members: 100

HISTORIC SITE; HISTORICAL SOCIETY; HISTORY MUSEUM: Collects, preserves, and investigates the history of Essex and Middle River.

PROGRAMS: Community Outreach; Exhibits; Facility Rental; Family Programs; Festivals; Guided Tours; Lectures; Research Library/Archives; School-Based Curriculum; Theatre

COLLECTIONS: [1600s-present] Manuscripts, maps, newspaper articles, photos, and over 1,000 related artifacts.

HOURS: Mar-Dec Su 1-4

ADMISSION: Donations

FORT MEADE

3641
Fort George G. Meade Museum
Bldg 4674, Griffin Ave, 20755 [ANME-OPM, Fort Meade, 20755-5094]; (p) (301) 677-6966, (301) 677-7054; (f) (601) 677-2953; museum@meade-emh2.army.mil; (c) Anne Arundel

Federal/ Dept of the Army/ staff: 3(f); 10(v)/publication: *An Illustrated History of Fort George G Meade*

HISTORY MUSEUM: Collects, preserves, and exhibits items relevant to the history of the fort's installation and surrounding community.

PROGRAMS: Community Outreach; Exhibits; Festivals; Guided Tours; Interpretation; Lectures; Living History; Publication; Reenactments; Research Library/Archives

COLLECTIONS: [1917-present] Uniforms, equip, and other items used by soldiers from WW I to the present.

HOURS: Yr W-Sa 11-4, Su 11-4

3642
National Cryptologic Museum
Intersection of MD Rts 32 & 295, 20755
[9800 Savage Rd, 20755-6000]; (p) (301)
688-5848, (301) 688-5849; (f) (301) 688-
5847; NCM1@ix.netcom.com;
www.nsa.gov:8080/; (c) Ann Arundel

Federal/ 1993/ staff: 3(f); 15(v)

HISTORY MUSEUM: Exhibits of books, machines, computers, and artifacts from the 16th c
to the modern era on the history of cryptology.

PROGRAMS: Exhibits; Film/Video; Guided
Tours; Lectures; Reenactments; Research Li-
brary/Archives

COLLECTIONS: [WW II and Cold War] Cipher
machines, books, computers, radios, memorabilia, interactive exhibits, and a research library.

HOURS: Yr M-F 9-3, Sa 10-2

FORT WASHINGTON

3643
Fort Washington Park
16551 Fort Washington Rd, 20772; (p) (301)
763-4600; (f) (301) 763-1389;
Fort_Washington@nps.gov; (c) Prince
George's

Federal/ 1946/ National Park Service/ staff:
6(f); 2(p); 20(v)

HISTORIC SITE: Maintains an early 19th c
seacoast fort built to protect the Nation's Capital from naval attack, along with 8 concrete
batteries from the early 1900s.

PROGRAMS: Community Outreach; Exhibits;
Film/Video; Guided Tours; Interpretation; Lectures; Living History

COLLECTIONS: [Early 19th c] Military artifacts.

HOURS: Yr Daily 8-Sunset

ADMISSION: $4/vehicle; $2/pedestrian

FREDERICK

3644
Barbara Fritchie House and Museum
1154 W Patrick St, 21701 [105 W 2nd St,
21701]; (p) (301) 698-4050, (301) 698-0630;
(f) (301) 698-4052; rkline@fred.net

Private non-profit/ 1800/ staff: 1(f)

COLLECTIONS: [Civil War] China, furniture,
portraits, walking canes, linens, quilts, kitchen
ware, letters, documents, marriage license applications, family Bibles, newspapers, flag with
34 stars.

HOURS: Seasonal

3645
Francis Scott Key Memorial Foundation, Inc.
121 S Bentz St, 21701 [145 Kline Blvd,
21701]; (p) (301) 663-3540; (c) Frederick

Private non-profit/ 1961/ staff: 5(v)

HISTORIC SITE; HISTORY MUSEUM;
HOUSE MUSEUM: Promotes Francis Scott
Key and his brother-in-law Roger Brooke
Taney; maintains the statue of FSK and the
1799 home of Taney.

PROGRAMS: Exhibits; Guided Tours

COLLECTIONS: [1800-1900] 1800 furnished
house, wine cellar, and slave quarters.

HOURS: By appt

ADMISSION: $2; Children free

3646
Historical Society of Frederick County, Inc.
24 E Church St, 21701; (p) (301) 663-1188;
(f) (301) 663-0526; director@fwp.net;
www.fwp.net/hsfc; (c) Frederick

Private non-profit/ 1888/ staff: 1(f); 6(p);
100(v)/ members: 750

HISTORICAL SOCIETY: Collects, preserves, and
interprets information and artifacts pertaining to
the history of Frederick County; operates a museum and library and conducts public programs.

PROGRAMS: Annual Meeting; Community
Outreach; Exhibits; Facility Rental; Guided
Tours; Interpretation; Lectures; Living History;
Publication; Research Library/Archives

COLLECTIONS: [18th and 19th c] Fine and
decorative arts, including a collection of tall
case clocks; books, documents, photos, maps,
and ephemera.

3647
Monocacy National Battlefield
4801 Urbana Pike, 21704; (p) (301) 662-3515;
(f) (301) 662-3420; cathy_beeler@nps.gov;
www.nps.gov/mono/mo_visit.htm; (c) Frederick

1934/ National Park Service/ staff: 5(f); 7(p)

BATTLEFIELD; HISTORIC SITE; HISTORY
MUSEUM: Commemorates the July 9, 1864
battle that saved Washington DC from invasion by Confederates.

PROGRAMS: Community Outreach; Exhibits;
Family Programs; Guided Tours; Interpretation;
Lectures; Living History; Research Library/
Archives; School-Based Curriculum

COLLECTIONS: [1861-1865] Military artifacts.

HOURS: Apr 1-Oct 31 Daily 8-4:30; Nov 1-Mar
31 W-Su 8-4:30

3648
National Museum of Civil War Medicine
48 E Patrick St, 21705 [PO Box 470, 21705];
(p) (301) 695-1964; (f) (301) 695-6823; muse-
um@civilwarmed.org; www.civilwarmed.org;
(c) Frederick

1990/ Board of Directors/ staff: 4(f); 5(p); 70(v)/
members: 600/publication: Surgeon's Call

HISTORIC SITE; HISTORY MUSEUM; RE-
SEARCH CENTER: Operates the center for
the study and interpretation of the medical history of the Civil War, including understanding
the impact of Civil War medicine on modern
medical practice.

PROGRAMS: Annual Meeting; Community Out-
reach; Exhibits; Facility Rental; Family Programs;
Guided Tours; Interpretation; Lectures; Living
History; Publication; Reenactments; Research
Library/Archives; School-Based Curriculum

COLLECTIONS: [1861-1865] 3,000 medical
artifacts including the only known surviving
surgeon's tent, examples of Dr E.R, Squibb's
travelling medical chests, uniforms, stretchers,

medical and dental instruments, swords,
books, and documents.

HOURS: Yr M-Sa 10-5, Su 11-5

3649
Rose Hill Manor Children's Museum
1611 N Market St, 21701; (p) (301) 694-
1684, (301) 694-1646; (f) (301) 694-2595

3650
Schifferstadt Architectural Museum
1110 Rosemont Ave, 21701; (p) (301) 663-3883;
(f) (301) 663-3885; www.wam.umd.edu/
~maryster/index.html; (c) Frederick

Private non-profit/ 1972/ Frederick County
Landmarks Foundation, Inc/ staff: 65(v)/ members: 250/publication: Landmarks Quarterly

GARDEN; HISTORIC SITE; HOUSE MUSE-
UM: Interprets the design, construction, and
use of the 1756 stone farmhouse, an example
of German colonial architecture.

PROGRAMS: Community Outreach; Exhibits;
Festivals; Garden Tours; Guided Tours; Publication; School-Based Curriculum

COLLECTIONS: [18th-19th c] Architectural
features include half timbered construction,
vaulted cellar, 5 plate jamb stove, original
hardware, wishbone design central chimney,
bake oven, stone sink, and a period kitchen
garden.

HOURS: Apr-Dec T-Sa 10-4, Su 12-4

ADMISSION: $2

3651
Maryland Room, C. Burr Artz Central Library, Frederick County Public Libraries
110 E Patrick St, 21701; (p) (301) 631-3764;
(f) (301) 631-3789;
mm0028@mail.pratt.lib.md.us; www.co.freder-
ick.me.us/fcpl/md-hist.html; (c) Frederick

County/ 1982/ Board of Trustees/ staff: 1(p);
6(v)

RESEARCH CENTER: Provides a research
collection documenting MD history (economic,
social, political, and religious), MD genealogy,
and the Civil War; emphasis on Frederick
County.

PROGRAMS: Lectures; Publication; Research
Library/Archives

COLLECTIONS: 3,000 titles on MD history,
culture, and genealogy; maps, photos, newspapers, manuscripts, oral histories, prints, and
ephemera; government documents and publications relating to

FRIENDSVILLE

3652
Friend Family Association Heritage Museum and Genealogical Library
261 Maple St, 21531 [PO Box 96, 21531]; (p)
(301) 745-4590; (c) Garrett

Private non-profit/ 1985/ Board of Trustees/
staff: 1(p); 10(v)/ members: 400/publication:
Friendship News

HISTORY MUSEUM; LIBRARY AND/OR
ARCHIVES: Preserves family records, artifacts, and photos for local families and houses
their history in a museum and library.

PROGRAMS: Community Outreach; Exhibits; Lectures; Publication; Research Library/Archives

COLLECTIONS: [1750-present] Native American artifacts, 1,000 genealogical and historical books, files, photos, artifacts depicting life in the Appalachians.

FROSTBURG

3653
Frostburg Museum Association, Inc., The
Hill & Oak St, 21532 [PO Box 92, 21532]; (p) (301) 689-1195; (c) Allegany

Private non-profit/ 1977/ staff: 12(v)/ members: 220

HISTORY MUSEUM: Preserves the historical record of the Frostburg area.

PROGRAMS: Annual Meeting; Exhibits; Guided Tours; Lectures

COLLECTIONS: [Mid 1800s-present] Information on National Road, history of Frostburg, mining industry, domestic and industrial items, and genealogical information.

HOURS: Apr-Sept 1-4

ADMISSION: No charge

GAITHERSBURG

3654
Gaithersburg Historical Association
9 S Summit Ave, 20884 [PO Box 211, 20884]; (p) (301) 258-6160; www.gaithersburghistorical.org; (c) Montgomery

Private non-profit/ 1983/ City/ staff: 1(p); 5(v)/ members: 60

HISTORIC SITE; HISTORICAL SOCIETY; HISTORY MUSEUM: Collects, interprets, and presents the history of Gaithersburg and its role as a small agriculturally based town and a B&O Railroad commuter stop.

PROGRAMS: Annual Meeting; Community Outreach; Exhibits; Garden Tours; Guided Tours; Research Library/Archives; School-Based Curriculum

COLLECTIONS: [1873-1930] Documents, photos, local funeral records 1913-1985, and B&O railroadiana.

HOURS: Yr Th-Sa 10-2

ADMISSION: No charge

GERMANTOWN

3655
Gemantown Historical Society, The
[PO Box 475, 20875]; (p) (301) 972-0795; soderber@clark.net; www.clark.net/pub/soderber/ghs; (c) Montgomery

Private non-profit/ 1990/ staff: 6(v)/ members: 32/publication: *A History of Germantown, Maryland, and others*

A local historical, education, and preservation organization.

PROGRAMS: Annual Meeting; Community Outreach; Exhibits; Film/Video; Lectures; Publication; Research Library/Archives

COLLECTIONS: [1830-present] Historic photos and local genealogies.

GLEN ECHO

3657
Clara Barton National Historic Site
5801 Oxford Rd, 20812; (p) (301) 492-6245; www.nps.gov/clba; (c) Montgomery

Federal/ 1974/ National Park Service/ staff: 3(f); 10(v)

HISTORIC SITE; HOUSE MUSEUM: Preserves Clara Barton's home (1897-1912) and interprets the early history of the American Red Cross.

PROGRAMS: Guided Tours; Interpretation; School-Based Curriculum

COLLECTIONS: [187-1912] Restored rooms contain a variety of period and original furnishings and artifacts which represent Barton's use of her home as the headquarters for the American Red Cross.

HOURS: Yr Daily 10-4

ADMISSION: No charge

GLENN DALE

3658
Dorsey Chapel
10704 Brookland Rd, 20769 [5626 Bell Station Rd, 20769]; (p) (301) 352-5544; (f) (301) 464-5654; www.parksrec.org; (c) Prince George's

County/ 1996/ staff: 1(f); 1(p); 4(v)

HISTORIC SITE: Dotsey Chapel is a publicly owned and operated African American historic site; religion and community life emphasized.

PROGRAMS: Exhibits; Facility Rental; Guided Tours; Lectures

COLLECTIONS: [1890-1950] Early photos of the site and of members, minute books, and oral histories; original fixtures and memorabilia on display.

HOURS: Yr by appt

ADMISSION: $1.50, Student $0.50, Seniors $1

3659
Marietta House Museum/Prince George's County Historical Society
5626 Bell Station Rd, 20769; (p) (301) 464-5291; (f) (301) 464-5654; (c) Prince George's

County/ 1989/ Maryland National Capital Park and Planning Commission/ staff: 1(f); 1(p); 20(v)/publication: *News and Notes*

HISTORIC SITE; HISTORICAL SOCIETY; HOUSE MUSEUM: Maintains a historic site of period federal houses and outbuildings; headquarters of the Prince George's County Historical Society.

PROGRAMS: Annual Meeting; Community Outreach; Family Programs; Guided Tours; Living History; Publication; Reenactments; School-Based Curriculum

COLLECTIONS: [1815-1900] Antique and reproduction furniture, china, documents, genealogy, and books.

HOURS: Museum: Jan-Dec F 11-3, Su 12-4; Hist Soc: Sa 12-4

ADMISSION: $3, Student $1, Seniors $2

GRANTSVILLE

3660
Spruce Forest Artisan Village, Inc.
177 Casselman Rd, 21536; (p) (301) 895-3332; (f) (301) 895-4665; tmorgan@spruce-forest.org; www.spruceforest.org; (c) Garrett

Private non-profit/ 1989/ staff: 1(f); 90(v)

HISTORIC PRESERVATION AGENCY; HISTORIC SITE; HISTORY MUSEUM; HOUSE MUSEUM: Creates an atmosphere, opportunity, and facilities for the public to experience the stories of the county' heritage, culture, and values.

PROGRAMS: Community Outreach; Concerts; Elder's Programs; Exhibits; Facility Rental; Family Programs; Festivals; Guided Tours; Interpretation

COLLECTIONS: [1800s] School memorabilia and artifacts: writing instruments, desks, books, clothing, and maps; Miller family furniture, history and archive materials

GREENBELT

3661
Greenbelt Museum
10 B Crescent Rd, 20770 [15 Crescent Rd, 20770]; (p) (301) 407-6582; (f) (301) 441-8248; www.otal.umd.edu/~rg/; (c) Prince George's

Joint/ 1987/ Friends of the Greenbelt Museum; Private non-profit; city/ staff: 1(p); 40(v)/ members: 200

HISTORIC SITE; HISTORY MUSEUM; HOUSE MUSEUM; LIVING HISTORY/OUTDOOR MUSEUM: Operates a historic 1930s house museum, preserves a collection of furnishings, textiles, and art.

PROGRAMS: Annual Meeting; Community Outreach; Exhibits; Film/Video; Guided Tours; Interpretation; Lectures; Publication; Research Library/Archives; School-Based Curriculum; Theatre

COLLECTIONS: [1930s-1940s] Art deco furnishings and decorative arts; clothing, textiles, and furniture.

HOURS: Yr

ADMISSION: $2

HAGERSTOWN

3662
Hagerstown Roundhouse Museum, Inc.
300 S Burhans Blvd, 21871 [PO Box 2858, 21871-2858]; (p) (301) 739-4665; (f) (301) 739-5598; (c) Washington

Private non-profit/ 1990/ staff: 270(v)/ members: 270

HISTORY MUSEUM: Dedicated to the preservation of railroad history.

PROGRAMS: Annual Meeting; Exhibits

COLLECTIONS: [1870s-present] Photos, artifacts, and model train displays; full size H and F trolley, diesel and steam locomotive, cabooses, and other rolling stock.

HOURS: Yr F-Su 1-5

ADMISSION: $3

3663
Jonathan Hager House and Museum
110 Key St, 21740; (p) (301) 739-8393; (c) Washington

City/ 1962/ staff: 1(f); 1(p); 1(v)

HOUSE MUSEUM: Educates the public about the life of Jonathan Hager; maintains and exhibits his unique house of German architecture and a collection of 18th c furnishings.

PROGRAMS: Community Outreach; Exhibits; Festivals; Guided Tours; Interpretation; Living History; Publication

COLLECTIONS: [18th c] Over 35,000 artifacts, chiefly ceramic, glass, and metal.

HOURS: Apr-Dec T-Sa

3664
Washington County Historical Society, Inc.
135 W Washington St, 21740 [PO Box 1281, 21741-1281]; (p) (301) 797-8782; histsoc@intrepid.net; www.rootsweb.com/~mdwchs; (c) Washington

Joint/ 1911/ Board of Directors; County; Private non-profit/ staff: 1(f); 4(p); 40(v)/ members: 425

GARDEN; HISTORIC SITE; HISTORICAL SOCIETY; HISTORY MUSEUM; HOUSE MUSEUM; LIBRARY AND/OR ARCHIVES: County historical society housed in Miller House Museum; collects, preserves, and exhibits.

PROGRAMS: Annual Meeting; Exhibits; Family Programs; Festivals; Garden Tours; Guided Tours; Lectures; Publication; Research Library/Archives

COLLECTIONS: [1825-1865] Federal period mansion; furnishings; papers and artifacts from Revolutionary War; clocks; antique dolls.

HOURS: Museum: Apr-Dec W-Sa 1-4; Library: T-Sa 9-4

ADMISSION: $3, Seniors $2; Under 16/Mbrs free

HANCOCK

3665
Hancock Historical Society Museum
126 W High St, 21750 [PO Box 164, 21750]; (p) (301) 678-6308; (c) Washington

Private non-profit/ 1987/ Hancock Historical Society/ staff: 15(v)

GENEALOGICAL SOCIETY; HISTORIC PRESERVATION AGENCY; HISTORICAL SOCIETY; HISTORY MUSEUM; HOUSE MUSEUM; LIVING HISTORY/OUTDOOR MUSEUM: Displays artifacts pertaining to Hancock and surrounding area; genealogical information.

PROGRAMS: Exhibits; Interpretation; Lectures; Research Library/Archives

COLLECTIONS: [Pre-Revolution-present] Photographs, businesses materials, railroad and canal items.

HOURS: Apr-Oct 2nd and 4th Su of the month only 2-4

ADMISSION: No charge

HAVRE DE GRACE

3666
Chesapeake Heritage Conservancy, Inc.
Foot of Congress Ave, 21078 [121 N Union St Ste C, 21078]; (p) (800) 406-0766; (f) (410) 592-3344; www.newmc.com/martha_lewis; (c) Harford

Private non-profit/ 1994/ Board of Directors/ staff: 2(f); 6(p); 20(v)/ members: 105

LIVING HISTORY/OUTDOOR MUSEUM: Develops and supervises programs that focus on historic preservation, maritime heritage, estuarine studies, and conservation of the Chesapeake Bay.

PROGRAMS: Annual Meeting; Community Outreach; Concerts; Elder's Programs; Exhibits; Facility Rental; Family Programs; Festivals; Interpretation; Lectures; Living History; School-Based Curriculum

HOURS: Apr-Oct Sa-Su 2-7:30; School Programs: Daily 9-1

ADMISSION: $10, Children $5

3667
Havre de Grace Decoy Museum
215 Giles St, 21078 [PO Box 878, 21078]; (p) (410) 939-3739; (f) (410) 939-3775; maryjom@earthlink.net; www.decoymuseum.com; (c) Hartford

Private non-profit/ 1981/ staff: 4(f); 3(p); 100(v)/ members: 1450/publication: *The Canvasback*

HISTORY MUSEUM: Collects decoys and related items to document and preserve the historical and cultural legacy of waterfowling; fosters awareness for conservation of waterfowl and their habitats.

PROGRAMS: Exhibits; Festivals; Guided Tours; Publication; Research Library/Archives; School-Based Curriculum

COLLECTIONS: [Late 1800s-present] Decoys and related waterfowling items spanning 100 yrs of decoy making history; exhibits include boats, guns, and calls.

HOURS: Yr Daily

3668
Rock Run House
801 Stafford Rd, 21078 [3318 Rocks Chrome Hill Rd, Jarrettsville, 21084]; (p) (410) 557-7994; (f) (410) 557-9720

1804/ State/ staff: 1(p)

COLLECTIONS: [18150] Archer Family furniture and Bible

HOURS: Seasonal

3669
Steppingstone Museum Association, Inc.
461 Quaker Bottom Rd, 21078; (p) (410) 939-2299, (888) 419-1762; (f) (410) 939-2321; (c) Harford

Private non-profit/ 1970/ staff: 1(f); 2(p); 75(v)/ members: 200

HISTORIC SITE; HISTORY MUSEUM; HOUSE MUSEUM: Preserves and demonstrates the rural arts and crafts of 1880-1920, the Foard Blacksmith Shop (1883), J. Edmund Bull Woodworking Shop, Spinning and Weaving Room, General Store, Veterinarian's Office, Carriage Barn, and the Canning House.

PROGRAMS: Annual Meeting; Community Outreach; Exhibits; Facility Rental; Family Programs; Festivals; Guided Tours; Living History; Publication; Reenactments; School-Based Curriculum

COLLECTIONS: [1880-1920] Period antiques, extensive hand tool collection relative to the trades of woodworking, blacksmithing, spinning and weaving, cooperage, dairy farming, veterinary medicine, farm and gardening, wheelwrighting, and the canning industry.

HOURS: May-Sept Sa-Su 1-5

ADMISSION: $2

3670
Susquehanna Museum of Havre de Grace
817 Conesteu St, 21078 [PO Box 253, 21078]; (p) (410) 939-5780; susqmuseum@erols.com; www.erols.com/susqmuseum/Index.html; (c) Harford

Private non-profit/ 1970/ staff: 2(p); 65(v)/ members: 200

HISTORIC SITE; HISTORY MUSEUM; HOUSE MUSEUM: Collects, preserves, and interprets the history of the Susquehanna and Tidewater Canal and the Havre de Grace area.

PROGRAMS: Annual Meeting; Community Outreach; Concerts; Elder's Programs; Exhibits; Facility Rental; Family Programs; Festivals; Film/Video; Guided Tours; Interpretation; Lectures; Living History; Reenactments; Research Library/Archives

COLLECTIONS: [1800s]

HOURS: May-Oct 1-5

ADMISSION: $2, Seniors $1

HOLLYWOOD

3671
Sotterley Plantation
44300 Sotterley Ln, 20636 [PO Box 67, 20636]; (p) (301) 373-2280, (800) 681-0850; (f) (301) 373-8474; sotterleyoffice@mail.ameritel.net; www.sotterley.com; (c) St Mary's

Private non-profit/ 1961/ Sotterley Foundation/ staff: 7(f); 1(p); 65(v)/ members: 200/publication: *News from the Customs House*

GARDEN; HISTORIC SITE; HOUSE MUSEUM: Preserves, researches, and interprets the Sotterley Plantation and its diverse cultures and environments, serving as a public resource.

PROGRAMS: Community Outreach; Concerts; Exhibits; Family Programs; Garden Tours; Guided Tours; Interpretation; Lectures; Publication; School-Based Curriculum

COLLECTIONS: [Early 18th-early 20th c] Manor house, slave cabin, outbuildings, and garden; furnishings and collections relating to periods of occupancy and plantation life.

HOURS: May-Oct T-Su 10-4

ADMISSION: $2 Grounds

HYATTSVILLE

3672
Office of Black Catholics, Archdiocese of Washington
5001 Eastern Ave, 20782; (p) (301) 853-4579; (f) (301) 853-7671; Wilson@adw.org; www.adw.org; (c) Prince George

Private non-profit/ 1974/ Archbishop of Washington/ staff: 2(f); 2(v)/publication: *Black Catholic History, A Select Bibliography of Works Located in Maryland and Washington, CD Archives and Libraries; and others*

HISTORIC PRESERVATION AGENCY; LIBRARY AND/OR ARCHIVES; RESEARCH CENTER: Listens to needs and concerns of Black Catholics, and responds or assists the Church in its response.

PROGRAMS: Community Outreach; Exhibits; Lectures; Publication; Research Library/ Archives

COLLECTIONS: [1634-present] Researched and archival materials/information on Black Catholics in Baltimore and Washington area.

HOURS: Call

LA PLATA

3673
Friendship House
c/o Charles County Community College, 20643 [PO Box 261, Port Tobacco, 20677]; (p) (301) 934-2251

1750/ C. C. Community College/ staff: 6(v)

COLLECTIONS: [1700s] Collection of cooking utensils from the 1700's & 1800's

HOURS: By appt.

3674
Southern Maryland Studies Center
8730 Mitchell Rd, 20646 [PO Box 910, 20646]; (p) (301) 942-2251; (f) (301) 934-7699; smsc@charles.cc.md.us; www.charles.cc.md.us; (c) Charles

1976/ Charles Community College Board of Trustees/ staff: 2(p); 5(v)

LIBRARY AND/OR ARCHIVES; RESEARCH CENTER: Provides a location for research on the history of Southern Maryland.

PROGRAMS: Research Library/Archives

COLLECTIONS: [19th-20th c] Print materials includes books, unpublished documents, newspapers, photos, slides, maps, and oral history tapes drawn from public and private sources.

HOURS: Yr Documents Rm: M-F 1-4; Reading Rm: Daily

LAUREL

3675
Laurel Museum, The
817 Main St, 20707; (p) (301) 725-7975; (f) (301) 725-7975; laurelmuseum@juno.com; www.laurelhistory.org; (c) Prince George's

City; Private non-profit/ 1996/ The Laurel Hisotrical Society, Inc/ members: 220

HISTORIC SITE; HISTORY MUSEUM: Interprets the history of Laurel through changing exhibits, educational efforts, and programs; museum is located in a renovated 1840's millworker's home.

PROGRAMS: Annual Meeting; Community Outreach; Exhibits; Family Programs; Garden Tours; Guided Tours; Interpretation; Lectures; Research Library/Archives; School-Based Curriculum

COLLECTIONS: [Lte 19th-early 20th c] Sadler photography collection of 1,300 glass plate negatives (1905-1917), additional photos of Laurel, mill tools, papers, diaries, artifacts from local business.

HOURS: Mar-Dec W 10-2, Su 1-4

ADMISSION: No charge

3676
Montpelier Mansion
9401 Montpelier Dr, 20708; (p) (301) 953-1376; (f) (301) 953-7572; www.parkdrec.org; (c) Prince George's

County/ 1961/ Maryland-National Capital Park and Planning Commission/ staff: 1(f); 7(p); 25(v)/ members: 292

HISTORIC SITE; HOUSE MUSEUM: Restored and maintains an 18th c Georgian mansion, built by Maj Thomas Snowden (1783), along with garden, grounds, and a summer house.

PROGRAMS: Community Outreach; Concerts; Exhibits; Facility Rental; Family Programs; Festivals; Guided Tours; Interpretation; Lectures; Reenactments

COLLECTIONS: [1830s] Antiques and reproduction furnishings.

HOURS: Yr Su 12-4

LEONARDTOWN

3677
St. Mary's County Historical Society, Inc.
41625 Courthouse Dr, 20650 [PO Box 212, 20650]; (p) (301) 475-2467; www.somd.lib.md.us/smchs; (c) St Mary's

Private non-profit/ 1951/ staff: 2(p); 25(v)/ members: 650

Preserves the history and heritage of MD; operates the Old Jail Museum and Tudor Hall Research Center.

PROGRAMS: Annual Meeting; Community Outreach; Exhibits; Guided Tours; Interpretation; Research Library/Archives

COLLECTIONS: [1634-present] Maps, documents, furniture, clothing, toys, and household items; genealogical materials including birth, death, tax, and census records.

HOURS: Old Jail Museum: Yr M-F 12-4; Research Center: Jan-Nov W-F 12-4, Sa 10-4

ADMISSION: Museum: Free, Research Center: $2.50/day

LINTHICUM

3678
Benson-Hammond House
[Poplar Lane and Aviation Blvd, 21090]; (p) (410) 768-9518

3679
Historical Electronics Museum
1745 W Nursery Rd, 21090 [PO Box 746 M/S 4015, Baltimore, 21203]; (p) (410) 765-3803; (f) (410) 765-0240; radarmus@erols.com; www.erols.com/radarmus; (c) Anne Arundel

Private non-profit/ 1980/ Board of Directors/ staff: 2(f); 1(p); 30(v)/ members: 167/publication: *Reflections*

HISTORY MUSEUM: Exhibits and interprets historically significant artifacts and documents related to electronics technology and the evolution and importance of electronics of the past century.

PROGRAMS: Community Outreach; Exhibits; Facility Rental; Guided Tours; Interpretation; Lectures; Publication; Research Library/ Archives

COLLECTIONS: [1900s] Emphasis on radar, communications, electro-optical systems, and components for both defense and commercial applications.

HOURS: Yr M-F 9-3, Sa 10-2

ADMISSION: No charge

LUTHERVILLE

3680
Fire Museum of Maryland
1301 York Rd, 21093; (p) (410) 321-7500; (f) (410) 769-8433; firemuseumofmaryland@erols.com; www.firemuseummd.org; (c) Baltimore

Private non-profit/ 1971/ staff: 2(f); 5(p); 29(v)/ members: 101

HISTORY MUSEUM; RESEARCH CENTER: Maintains and displays collection of fire fighting apparatuses and fire engines.

PROGRAMS: Community Outreach; Exhibits; Facility Rental; Family Programs; Guided Tours; Interpretation; Research Library/ Archives; School-Based Curriculum

COLLECTIONS: [1806-1957] Hand drawn, horse drawn, and self-propelled apparatuses and over 40 fire engines.

ADMISSION: $5, Children $3, Seniors $4

3681
Lutherville Historical Colored School #24 Museum
1426 School Ln, 21093; (p) (410) 825-6114; hlcteacher@yahoo.com; (c) Baltimore

Private non-profit/ 1908/ Chapman Foundation, Inc/ staff: 2(f); 3(p); 3(v)

GARDEN; HISTORIC SITE; HISTORY MUSEUM: Preservation of the original school house and original items.

PROGRAMS: Annual Meeting; Community Outreach; Exhibits; Facility Rental; Film/Video; Guided Tours; Lectures; Living History

COLLECTIONS: Oil lamps, textbooks, teacher rollbooks, report cards, photos, artifacts, desks, paintings, rare books, library, curriculum, gardens, chalkboard, and oral histories.

HOURS: Yr T-W 10-4

ADMISSION: $3, Children $2

MARBURY

3682
Smallwood State Park/Smallwood's Retreat
2750 Sweden Point Rd, 20658; (p) (301) 743-7613; (f) (301) 763-9605; www.dnr.state.md.us; (c) Charles

State/ 1958/ Dept of Natural Resources/ staff: 15(v)

HISTORIC SITE; HOUSE MUSEUM: Maintains reconstructed plantation house of William Smallwood, Revolutionary War officer and Governor of MD.

PROGRAMS: Exhibits; Guided Tours; Interpretation; Living History

COLLECTIONS: [Colonial-late 1700s] Original and period furnishings.

HOURS: Apr-Oct Su 1-5

ADMISSION: $2

NORTH EAST

3683
Upper Bay Museum
Walnut St at the River, 21901 [Box 275, 21901]; (p) (410) 287-2675; (c) Cecil

Private non-profit/ 1972/ Cecil-Harford Hunter's Assn. Inc./ staff: 15(v)/ members: 211

HISTORY MUSEUM

PROGRAMS: Annual Meeting; Guided Tours; Interpretation

COLLECTIONS: [Late 19th-early 20th c] Native American artifacts; hunting and fishing boats, guns, and nets.

HOURS: May-Oct Sa-Su 11-4

ADMISSION: Donations requested

OCEAN CITY

3684
Ocean City Life-Saving Station Museum
813 Boardwalk at the Inlet, 21843 [PO Box 603, 21843]; (p) (410) 289-4991; curator@ocmuseum.org; www.ocmuseum.org; (c) Worcester

City; Private non-profit/ 1977/ Ocean City Museum Society, Inc/ staff: 2(f); 4(p)/ members: 600/publication: *Shipwrecks and Rescues, and others*

HISTORY MUSEUM: Dedicated to preserving the history of the US Life-Saving Service on the Delmarva Peninsula and the history of Ocean City.

PROGRAMS: Exhibits; Family Programs; Guided Tours; Publication

COLLECTIONS: [Mid 1800s-1960s] US Life-Saving Service equipment, shipwreck artifacts, antique bathing suits, doll house replicas of old Ocean City hotels, aquariums with local marine life and sands from around the world.

HOURS: May, Oct Daily 11-4; June-Sept Daily 11-10; Nov-Apr Sa-Su 11-4

ADMISSION: $2, Children $1

ODENTON

3685
Epiphany Chapel and Church House
1417 Odenton Rd, 21113 [Box 11, 21113]; (p) (410) 674-8819; (f) (410) 269-6543; phebe@erols.com; www.mh105.infi.net/~wmcox; (c) Anne Arundel

Private non-profit/ 1917/ Epiphany Episcopal Church/ staff: 1(f)

HISTORIC SITE: Maintains a World War I chapel, built to support the soldiers deployed through Camp Meade enroute to France.

PROGRAMS: Exhibits

COLLECTIONS: [WW I]

HOURS: Yr Su

PASADENA

3686
Old Harford Town Maritime Center and Museum
10215 River Landing Rs, 21122 [146 Cornfield Rd, 21122]; (p) (410) 437-6975; (f) (410) 437-6975; cwsjr@erols.com; (c) Caroline

Private non-profit/ 1992/ staff: 1(f); 10(v)

HISTORY MUSEUM: A museum and educational center with focus on Chesapeake Bay Rivering and Trade.

PROGRAMS: Community Outreach; Exhibits; Festivals; Lectures

COLLECTIONS: Archival maritime records and Chesapeake Bay shipjack "F.C, Lewis, Jr" featured as a land based exhibit.

HOURS: Yr T-Th 10-2

PATUXENT RIVER

3687
Patuxent River Naval Air Museum
Rte 235 & Shangrila Dr, 20670 [PO Box 407, 20670]; (p) (301) 863-7418; (f) (301) 342-7947; paxmuseum@erols.com; www.nawcad.navy.mil; (c) St Mary's

County; Private non-profit; State/ 1978/ Naval Air Warfare Center Aircraft Division/ staff: 1(f); 3(p); 56(v)/ members: 1200/publication: *Quarterly Newsletter*

HISTORY MUSEUM; RESEARCH CENTER: The Navy's aviation technology museum preserves and interprets the research, development, testing, and evaluation of naval aircraft and their related systems.

PROGRAMS: Community Outreach; Exhibits; Film/Video; Guided Tours; Interpretation; Publication; Research Library/Archives; School-Based Curriculum

COLLECTIONS: [1943-present] 30,000 photographs, 1,700 films, 1,550 models, 1,000 aviation artifacts; 500 cubic feet of documents and memorabilia and an extensive research library.

HOURS: Yr T-Su 10-5

ADMISSION: No charge

POCOMOKE

3688
Costen House Museum and Rose Garden
204 Market St, 21851; (p) (410) 957-4364, (410) 957-0972

3689
Spirit of Newtown Committee, Inc./Costen House
206 Market St, 21851 [PO Box 430, 21851]; (p) (410) 957-1297; (f) (410) 957-0680; (c) Worcester

Private non-profit/ 1974/ staff: 25(v)/ members: 40/publication: *House Call*

GARDEN; HOUSE MUSEUM: Interprets the lifestyle of a small town doctor and his family (1870-1920) and preserves their Victorian Italiante house and gardens.

PROGRAMS: Annual Meeting; Community Outreach; Concerts; Elder's Programs; Exhibits; Facility Rental; Festivals; Garden Tours; Guided Tours; Publication; Research Library/Archives; School-Based Curriculum

COLLECTIONS: [1875-1920] Furniture, textiles, art objects, photographs, books, household utensils, doctors' instruments, newspapers and letters, toys, and games.

PORT DEPOSIT

3690
Port Deposit Heritage Corporation
98 N Main St, 21904 [PO Box 101, 21904]; (p) (410) 378-4480, (410) 378-3841; (c) Cecil

Private non-profit/ 1975/ Port Deposit Heritage Corp Officers and Board of Directors/ staff: 10(v)/ members: 200

GENEALOGICAL SOCIETY; HISTORIC PRESERVATION AGENCY; HISTORIC SITE; HISTORICAL SOCIETY; HISTORY MUSEUM; RESEARCH CENTER: Repository of history, archives, and records for Port Deposit, founded in 1729; preserves historic sites including former Naval Preparatory Academy at Tome School, Bainbridge.

PROGRAMS: Annual Meeting; Community Outreach; Concerts; Exhibits; Facility Rental; Festivals; Guided Tours; Lectures; Living History; Research Library/Archives; School-Based Curriculum

COLLECTIONS: [1800s-1900s] Civil War letters, uniforms, and swords; original documents, photos, and artifacts related to industry, business, granite, railroad, canal, and river arks; artifacts of Beaux-Arts Jacob Tome Schools, Bainbridge Naval Training Center; oral histories.

HOURS: May-Oct 2nd and 4th Su 1-4 or by appt

ADMISSION: No charge

PORT REPUBLIC

3691
One Room School of Calvert Retired Teacher's Association
Broomes Island Rd, 20676; (p) (410) 586-0482, (410) 586-0109; (c) Calvert

Private non-profit/ 1976/ Calvert Retired Teachers Assoc/ staff: 20(p); 20(v)/ members: 100

HISTORY MUSEUM; HOUSE MUSEUM: Restoration and preservation of a one room schoolhouse.

PROGRAMS: Interpretation

COLLECTIONS: [1865-1932] Fully furnished one room school of seven grades as it existed in 1932; desks, books, photos, and tapes.

HOURS: June-Aug Su 2-4

ADMISSION: No charge

PORT TOBACCO

3692
Society for the Restoration of Port Tobacco, Inc.
Chapel Point Rd, 20677 [PO Box 302, 20677]; (p) (301) 934-4313; (c) Charles

Private non-profit/ 1948/ Board of Directors/ staff: 4(p); 25(v)/ members: 125

HISTORIC SITE; HISTORY MUSEUM: Preserves the history of the original Charles County seat of government; maintains the Charles County Museum in the reconstructed court house.

PROGRAMS: Annual Meeting; Community Outreach; Elder's Programs; Exhibits; Facility Rental; Film/Video; Guided Tours; Interpretation; Reenactments

COLLECTIONS: [19th c] Civil War artifacts and items related to tobacco production.

HOURS: Apr-Aug

3693
Thomas Stone National Historic Site
Rosehill Rd, 20677; (p) (301) 934-6027; (f) (301) 934-8793; www.nps.gov/thst/; (c) Charles

PRINCE FREDERICK

3694
Calvert County Historical Society, Inc.
[PO Box 358, 20678]; (p) (410) 535-2452; www.somd.lib.md.us/CALV/cchs; (c) Calvert

Private non-profit/ 1953/ staff: 1(p); 3(v)/ members: 365/publication: *Calvert Historian and News and Notes*

GENEALOGICAL SOCIETY; HISTORIC SITE; HISTORICAL SOCIETY; RESEARCH CENTER

PROGRAMS: Annual Meeting; Community Outreach; Exhibits; Interpretation; Lectures; Publication; Research Library/Archives

COLLECTIONS: Library, family files, some objects which reflect Calvert life, paintings, and furnishings.

HOURS: Yr T-Th 10-3

ADMISSION: $3.50

PRINCESS ANNE

3695
Somerset County Historical Society
11736 Mansion St, 21853 [PO Box 181, 21853]; (p) (410) 651-4256; (c) Somerset

Private non-profit/ 1960/ staff: 50(v)/ members: 145

GENEALOGICAL SOCIETY; HISTORICAL SOCIETY; HOUSE MUSEUM: Dedicated to the research, preservation, and exhibition of Somerset County and MD history; operates a house museum in the mansion built by Littleton Dennis Teackle 1802-1819.

PROGRAMS: Annual Meeting; Exhibits; Facility Rental; Film/Video; Garden Tours; Guided Tours; Lectures; Publication; Research Library/Archives

COLLECTIONS: [Early 19th c] Furniture, paintings, and decorative items.

HOURS: Apr-Dec W,Sa-Su 1-3; Jan-Mar Su 1-3

3696
Teackle Mansion, Olde Princess Anne Days, Inc., The
11736 Mansion St, 21853 [PO Box 855, 21853]; (p) (410) 651-2238; (f) (410) 651-9288; Landmark@sea-east.com; (c) Somerset

Private non-profit/ 1956/ Board of Directors/ staff: 68(v)

Educates the public about early 19th c life and offers a collection of 19th c furniture and decorative arts.

PROGRAMS: Community Outreach; Facility Rental; Festivals; Guided Tours; Interpretation; Lectures; Living History; School-Based Curriculum

COLLECTIONS: [Early 19th c] Decorative arts, household objects, and local history artifacts; furniture, rugs, ceramics, costumes, metal objects, pictures, and books.

RIVERDALE

3697
Prince George's County Historical Society
5626 Bell Station Rd, 20738 [PO Box 14, 20738-0014]; (p) (301) 464-0590; (c) Prince George's

Private non-profit/ 1952/ Board of Directors/ staff: 20(v)/ members: 350/publication: *News and Notes*

HISTORICAL SOCIETY: Preserves and promotes county history through publications, a library, educational programs, and collections.

PROGRAMS: Annual Meeting; Community Outreach; Publication; Research Library/Archives; School-Based Curriculum

COLLECTIONS: [19th-20th c] Maps, books, newspapers, and photos; textiles, furniture, and personal items.

HOURS: Yr Sa 12-4 or by appt

RIVERDALE PARK

3698
Riverdale
4811 Riverdale Rd, 20737 [6005 48th Ave, 20737]; (p) (301) 864-0420; (f) (301) 927-3498; (c) Prince George's

County; Joint; State/ 1992/ Maryland-National Capital Park and Planning Commission/ staff: 1(f); 3(p); 40(v)/ members: 300/publication: *The Riversdale Letter*

HOUSE MUSEUM: Maintains historic house museum, interpreted through the letters of its mistress, Rosalie Stier Calvert.

PROGRAMS: Community Outreach; Exhibits; Facility Rental; Guided Tours; Lectures; Living History; Publication; Reenactments

COLLECTIONS: [1801-1838] Antique furniture and decorative arts, family items, and copies of Calvert's letters.

ROCK HALL

3699
Rock Hall Waterman's Museum
20880 Rock Hall Ave, 21661; (p) (410) 778-6697; (f) (410) 639-2971; havenhbr@friendly.net; www.havenharbour.com; (c) Kent

Private non-profit/ 1992/ Brawner Company

LIVING HISTORY/OUTDOOR MUSEUM

PROGRAMS: Exhibits; Guided Tours

COLLECTIONS: Photos, artifacts, writings, tools, and crafts used by watermen of the Chesapeake Bay over the last century.

HOURS: Yr Daily 10-4:30

ADMISSION: No charge

ROCKVILLE

3700
Montgomery County Historical Society, Inc., The
103 W Montgomery Ave, 20850 [111 W Montgomery Ave, 20850]; (p) (301) 762-1492; (f) (301) 340-2871; mchistory@mindspring.com; www.montgomeryhistory.org; (c) Montgomery

Private non-profit/ 1944/ staff: 3(f); 5(p); 125(v)/ members: 1100/publication: *Montgomery County Story*

HISTORICAL SOCIETY: Preserves and interprets county history through the operation of a library, two museums, and public programs.

PROGRAMS: Annual Meeting; Community Outreach; Exhibits; Family Programs; Festivals; Guided Tours; Interpretation; Lectures; Publication; Research Library/Archives; School-Based Curriculum

COLLECTIONS: [Late 18th-20th c] Books, maps, newspapers, manuscripts, decorative arts, archaeological artifacts, and medical items.

HOURS: Yr T-Su 12-4

ADMISSION: $3, Student $2, Seniors $2

3701
Peerless Rockville Historic Preservation, Ltd
29 Courthouse Sq #110, 20849 [PO Box 4262, 20849-4262]; (p) (301) 762-0096; (f) (301) 762-0961; peerless@millkern.com; www.millkern.com/peerless; (c) Montgomery

City; Joint; Private non-profit/ 1974/ Board of Directors/ staff: 1(f); 2(p); 500(v)/ members: 400/publication: *Historic and Architectural Guide to Rockville Pike, and others*

HISTORIC PRESERVATION AGENCY; HISTORIC SITE; HISTORY MUSEUM; RESEARCH CENTER: Safeguards Rockville's past by preserving buildings, spaces, objects, and information important to the city's heritage.

PROGRAMS: Community Outreach; Exhibits; Family Programs; Guided Tours; Interpretation; Lectures; Publication; Research Library/Archives

COLLECTIONS: [19th-20th c] Photographs, artifacts, business records, drugstore soda fountain, research files on historic properties, referral data on preservation specialists.

HOURS: Yr

SAINT LEONARD

3702
Jefferson Patterson Park and Museum
10515 Mackall Rd, 20685; (p) (410) 596-8500; (f) (410) 586-0080;

JPPM@dhcd.state.md.us;
www.ari.net/mkshpo/jppm.html; (c) Calvert

State/ 1983/ staff: 26(f); 18(p); 150(v)/ members: 160/publication: *Patterson Points*

HISTORIC PRESERVATION AGENCY; HISTORY MUSEUM; LIVING HISTORY/OUTDOOR MUSEUM; RESEARCH CENTER: Archaeological, historical, and agricultural museum and research institution that interprets the diverse cultures of MD and the Chesapeake Bay region on a 544 acre historic waterfront farm.

PROGRAMS: Annual Meeting; Community Outreach; Concerts; Exhibits; Facility Rental; Family Programs; Festivals; Garden Tours; Guided Tours; Interpretation; Lectures; Living History; Publication; Reenactments; Research Library/Archives; School-Based Curriculum

HOURS: Apr-Oct W-Su 8:30-5

ADMISSION: No charge

SAINT MARY'S CITY

3703
Historic St. Mary's City
Rosecroft Rd & Rt 5, 20686 [PO Box 39, 20686]; (p) (301) 862-0990; (f) (301) 862-0968; kbstanford@osprey.smcm.edu; www.smcm.edu/hsmcl; (c) St. Mary's

State/ 1966/ Historic St Mary's City Commission/ staff: 38(f); 38(p); 211(v)/ members: 710/publication: *A Briefe Relation*

HISTORIC SITE; HISTORY MUSEUM; LIVING HISTORY/OUTDOOR MUSEUM: Operates an archaeology and open-air living history museum on the site of MD's first capital (1634), National Historic Landmark.

PROGRAMS: Annual Meeting; Community Outreach; Concerts; Elder's Programs; Exhibits; Facility Rental; Family Programs; Festivals; Film/Video; Garden Tours; Guided Tours; Interpretation; Lectures; Living History; Publication; Reenactments; Research Library/Archives;

COLLECTIONS: [17th c] Archaeological materials

HOURS: Mar-Nov W-Su 10-5

ADMISSION: $7.50, Student $6, Children $3.50, Seniors $6

SAINT MICHAELS

3704
Chesapeake Bay Maritime Museum, Inc.
Mill St/ Navy Point, 21663 [PO Box 636, 21663]; (p) (410) 745-2916; (f) (410) 745-6088; comments@cbmm.org; www.cbmm.org; (c) Talbot

Private non-profit/ 1965/ Board of Directors/ staff: 36(f); 15(p); 285(v)/ members: 6026/publication: *The Weather Gauge*

HISTORY MUSEUM: Interprets the Chesapeake's cultural heritage in small boats, light houses, steamboating, waterfowling, the fisheries, and a working boat shop.

PROGRAMS: Community Outreach; Concerts; Exhibits; Facility Rental; Family Programs; Festivals; Guided Tours; Interpretation; Lectures; Publication; Research Library/Archives

COLLECTIONS: [19th-20th c] Photos, manuscripts, oral histories, ships plans, and 7,500 historic objects including boats, artworks, decoys, tools, models, navigational instruments, fisheries gear, vessel accessories from anchors to yawl boats, and historic structures.

HOURS: Yr Daily

ADMISSION: $7.50, Children $3, Seniors $6.50

SALISBURY

3705
Blackwell Library, Salisbury State University
1101 Camden Ave, 21801; (p) (410) 543-6131; (f) (410) 543-6203; jkfischer@ssu.edu; www.ssu.edu; (c) Wicomico

State/ 1925/ Salisbury State University/ staff: 22(f); 32(p)

LIBRARY AND/OR ARCHIVES: Provides library resources and services to a college campus and the larger community.

PROGRAMS: Research Library/Archives

COLLECTIONS: [State history] Special emphasis on the Eastern Shore and the Delmarva Peninsula (3,225 volumes) and on Civil War history (1,600 volumes).

HOURS: Yr

3706
Edward H. Nabb Research Center for Delmarva History and Culture at Salisbury State University
1101 Camden Ave, PP 190, 21801; (p) (410) 543-6312; (f) (410) 548-5559; redhac@ssu.edu; www.ssu.edu/community/RCDHAC.htm; (c) Wicomico

State/ 1988/ Salisbury State University/ staff: 2(f); 1(p); 5(v)/ members: 300/publication: *Shoreline*

RESEARCH CENTER: Operates a repository for documents and artifacts pertaining to the Delmarva Peninsula.

PROGRAMS: Exhibits; Lectures; Publication; Research Library/Archives

COLLECTIONS: [WWII] 2,000 maps, 12,000 volumes, 2,500 microfilm reels of public records (1632-1900), and 3,000 photos.

HOURS: Yr M 9:30-9, T-F 9:30-4:30

ADMISSION: $5

3707
Pemberton Hall and Park
Pemberton Dr, 21801; (p) (410) 860-2447

3708
Poplar Hill Mansion
117 Elizabeth St, 21801-4108; (p) (410) 749-1776

3709
Wicomico Historical Society, Inc.
Pemberton Dr, 21803 [PO Box 573, 21803]; (p) (410) 960-0447; (f) (410) 960-1441; history@shore.intercom.net; www.skipjack.net/le_shore/whs/; (c) Wicomico

Private non-profit/ 1932/ staff: 1(f); 1(p); 50(v)/ members: 200/publication: *Wicomico Recollections*

HISTORICAL SOCIETY; HISTORY MUSEUM; LIVING HISTORY/OUTDOOR MUSEUM: Interprets and preserves local history through rotating exhibits and educational programs at the Heritage Center Museum.

PROGRAMS: Community Outreach; Exhibits; Guided Tours; Interpretation; Lectures; Publication

COLLECTIONS: [18th-early 20th c] 5,000 artifacts including political memorabilia, tools, weaving apparel, books, bibles, portraits, military, household items, photographs.

SANDY SPRING

3710
Sandy Spring Museum
17901 Bentley Rd, 20860; (p) (301) 774-0022; (f) (301) 774-8149; ssmfp@worldnet.att.net; (c) Montgomery

Private non-profit/ 1980/ Board of Trustees/ staff: 4(p); 100(v)/ members: 700/publication: *Legacy*

HISTORY MUSEUM: Preserves the history and culture of the rural 19th c farming community through exhibits, lectures, children's activities, and special events.

PROGRAMS: Annual Meeting; Community Outreach; Concerts; Exhibits; Facility Rental; Family Programs; Festivals; Garden Tours; Guided Tours; Interpretation; Lectures; Publication; Research Library/Archives; School-Based Curriculum

COLLECTIONS: [19th c rural community] Documents, photos, textiles, farming equip and tools, furniture, fine art, and local family artifacts representing banking, women's rights, and general rural info.

HOURS: Yr M, W-Th 11-4, Sa-Su 12-4

ADMISSION: $2

SCOTLAND

3711
Point Lookout State Park
11175 Point Lookout Rd, 20687 [PO Box 48, 20687]; (p) (301) 872-5688; (f) (301) 872-5084; www.dnr.state.md.us; (c) St Mary's

State/ 1965/ State of Maryland/ staff: 12(f); 25(p); 30(v)

HISTORIC SITE: Maintains historic site of a Union Civil War Prisoner of War Camp and a small Civil War Museum.

PROGRAMS: Exhibits; Family Programs; Guided Tours; Interpretation; Reenactments

COLLECTIONS: [Civil War] Civil War artifacts and recreations associated with the POW camp.

HOURS: Park: Yr; Museum: Apr-May, Sept-Oct Sa-Su 10-6, June-Aug Daily 10-6

SHADY SIDE

3712
Captain Salem Avery House Museum
1418 E W Shady Side Rd, 20764 [PO Box 89, 20764]; (p) (410) 864-4486; Mdaly@aol.com

1860/ staff: 35(v)

COLLECTIONS: [1860-1890] Furnishings and clothing, tools, boat models, boats; Oral and video tapes, photographs, newspaper clippings

HOURS: Yr; Su 1-4; by a; Su 1-4; by

3713
Shady Side Rural Heritage Society
1418 EW Shady Side Rd, 20764 [PO Box 89, Sahdy Side, 20764]; (p) (410) 867-4486; MDaly4942@aol.com; (c) Anne Arundel

Private non-profit/ 1985/ Board of Directors/ staff: 35(v)/ members: 375/publication: *Miss Ethel Remembers, and others*

HISTORICAL SOCIETY; HOUSE MUSEUM: Operates the Capt. Salem Avery House Museum, a waterman's museum; preserves the history and traditions of the region.

PROGRAMS: Concerts; Exhibits; Festivals; Interpretation; Lectures; Publication

COLLECTIONS: [1860-1900] Restored waterman's home.

HOURS: Mar-Dec Su 1-4; May-Sept Sa 1-4

SHARPSBURG

3714
Antietam National Battlefield
[PO Box 158, 21782-0158]; (p) (301) 432-5124, (301) 432-7648; (f) (301) 432-4590; ANTI_Superintendent@nps.gov; www.nps.gov/anti/pphtml/contacts.html

1890/ National Park Service

BATTLEFIELD; HISTORIC SITE: This Civil War site marks the end of General Robert E. Lee's first invasion of the North in September 1862.

PROGRAMS: Interpretation; Lectures

COLLECTIONS: [Civil War Era] Napoleon cannon, model 1857, cemetery.

HOURS: Summer Daily 8:30-6: Winter Daily 8:30-5

3715
C&O Canal National Historical Park
[PO Box 4, 21782]; (p) (301) 739-4200; (f) (301) 739-5275; www.nps.gov/choh; (c) Numerous

Federal/ 1971/ National Park Service/ staff: 100(f)

HISTORIC SITE; LIVING HISTORY/OUT-DOOR MUSEUM: Preserves the remnants of the C&O Canal and the related historic structures in the 184.5 mile park.

PROGRAMS: Community Outreach; Exhibits; Family Programs; Festivals; Guided Tours; Interpretation; Lectures; Living History; Publication; School-Based Curriculum

COLLECTIONS: [Mid 19th]

SILVER SPRING

3716
George Meany Memorial Archives, The
10000 New Hampshire Ave, 20903; (p) (301) 431-5451; (f) (301) 431-0385; ldeloach@clark.net; www.georgemeany.org; (c) Montgomery

Private non-profit/ 1981/ The George Meany Center for Labor Studies/ staff: 9(f); 1(p)/publication: *Labor's Heritage*

LIBRARY AND/OR ARCHIVES: The official archives of the AFL-CIO, collects, researches, and interprets labor's heritage.

PROGRAMS: Exhibits; Facility Rental; Guided Tours; Lectures; Publication; Research Library/Archives; School-Based Curriculum

COLLECTIONS: [1881-present] Processed records (100 linear ft), audio-visual holdings (1,500 linear ft), artifacts (5,000), microfilm (1,000 reels), books (11,000), newspapers and journals (400 titles), and serials (323 titles).

HOURS: Yr M-F 9-4:30

3717
Montgomery County Historic Preservation Commission
8787 Georgia Ave, 20910; (p) (301) 563-3400; (f) (301) 563-3412; wright@mncppc.org; www.mncppc.org; (c) Montgomery

County/ 1979/ staff: 2(f); 6(p)

HISTORIC PRESERVATION AGENCY; HISTORIC SITE; HOUSE MUSEUM: Administers the Montgomery County Historic Preservation Ordinance and local rehabilitation tax credit program; organizes public use and events at historic sites.

PROGRAMS: Community Outreach; Exhibits; Facility Rental; Family Programs; Festivals; Film/Video; Interpretation; Lectures

COLLECTIONS: [1850-1915]

3718
National Capital Historical Museum of Transportation
1313 Bonifant Rd, 20905; (p) (301) 384-6088; (f) (301) 384-6352; nctm@dctrolley.org; www.dctrolley.org; (c) Montgomery

Private non-profit/ 1959/ staff: 1(p); 30(v)/ members: 150

HISTORY MUSEUM: Preserves and interprets electric street railway history for the National Capital area.

PROGRAMS: Exhibits; Facility Rental; Family Programs; Film/Video; Interpretation; School-Based Curriculum

COLLECTIONS: [1890s-1960s] 17 street cars, 10,000 postcards depicting street cars, 4,000 photos, artifacts.

HOURS: Yr Sa-Su 12-5

ADMISSION: $2.50, Children $2

3719
Sandy Spring Slavery Museum and African Art Gallery Inc.
18524 Brooke Rd, 20905 [c/o Winston Anderson, 1629 Hopefield Rd, 20905]; (p) (202) 806-6950; (f) (202) 806-6950; wanderson@howard.edu; (c) Montgomery

Private non-profit/ 1988/ staff: 1(f); 3(v)

HISTORY MUSEUM; LIVING HISTORY/OUT-DOOR MUSEUM: Interprets and disseminates information on the heritage of blacks from their origin in Africa through the transatlantic passage, the civil rights struggles, and their accomplishments and contributions in the US; educates all county residents on the advantages of cultural diversity.

PROGRAMS: Community Outreach; Elder's Programs; Exhibits; Film/Video; Reenactments; School-Based Curriculum

COLLECTIONS: [1800-present] Exhibits of the middle passage, living conditions of slaves, and an African American round house with over 400 objects of art from the African Diaspora.

HOURS: Yr Sa-Su 11-5

ADMISSION: No charge

SNOW HILL

3720
Furnace Town Historic Site
3816 Old Furnace Rd, 21863 [PO Box 207, 21863]; (p) (410) 632-2032; www.dol.net/~ebola/ftown.htm; (c) Worcester

Private non-profit/ 1982/ Furnace Town Foundation, Inc/ staff: 1(f); 15(p); 10(v)/ members: 400

HISTORIC SITE: Maintains exhibits on the wooded 12 acre site, providing an educational look at life in Furnace Town.

PROGRAMS: Concerts; Exhibits; Facility Rental; Family Programs; Festivals; Guided Tours; Interpretation; Living History

COLLECTIONS: [1820-1850] Items related to iron manufacturing and village life (broom making, weaving, blacksmithing, woodworking, gardening)

HOURS: Apr-Oct

3721
Julia A. Purnell Museum
208 W Market St, 21863; (p) (410) 632-0515; (c) Worchester

Private non-profit/ 1942/ Board of Directors/ staff: 1(f); 1(p); 20(v)/ members: 150

ART MUSEUM; HISTORIC SITE; HISTORY MUSEUM: A regional history museum housed in a Gothic Church maintains a collection of Worchester County artifacts spanning the past 400 years.

PROGRAMS: Community Outreach; Exhibits; Family Programs; Festivals; Guided Tours; Interpretation; Research Library/Archives

COLLECTIONS: [16th-20th c] Toys, tools, textiles, furniture, decorative arts, folk art pieces, and needle art work by Julia A Purnell.

HOURS: T-Sa

3722
Mt. Zion One Room School
Ironshire St, 21863 [230 S Washington St, 21863]; (p) (410) 632-1265; kfisher@shore.intercom.net; (c) Worcester

Worchester County Retired Teachers and Board of Education/ staff: 10(v)/ members: 100

HISTORY MUSEUM: Preserves and interprets a one room schoolhouse.

PROGRAMS: Exhibits; Guided Tours; Interpretation

COLLECTIONS: [1890s-1950s] Textbooks, lunch pails, desks, and other related items.

HOURS: July-Aug W-Su 1-4

ADMISSION: $1, Children $0.50

3723
Worcester County Historical Society
[PO Box 111, 21863]; (p) (410) 632-1265; kfisher@shore.intercom.net; (c) Worcester

Private non-profit/ 1968/ staff: 12(v)/ members: 125

HISTORICAL SOCIETY: Dedicated to preserving and helping interpret the local history found throughout Worcester County; funds raised are dedicated to the seven local museum sites.

PROGRAMS: Annual Meeting; Community Outreach; Research

SOLOMONS

3724
Calvert Marine Museum
14200 Solomons Island Rd, 20688 [PO Box 97, 20688]; (p) (410) 326-2042; (f) (410) 326-6691; information@calvertmarinemuseum.com; www.calvertmarinemuseum.com; (c) Calvert

County/ 1970/ Calvert County Board of Commissioners/ staff: 26(f); 27(p); 250(v)/ members: 2200/publication: *Bugeye Times*

HISTORY MUSEUM; NATURAL HISTORY MUSEUM: Dedicated to the presentation of regional paleontology, estuarine life, and maritime history of the Patuxent River and the Chesapeake Bay.

PROGRAMS: Community Outreach; Concerts; Exhibits; Facility Rental; Festivals; Guided Tours; Interpretation; Lectures; Living History; Publication; Research Library/Archives; School-Based Curriculum

COLLECTIONS: [19th-20th c] Regional paleontology, estuarine biology, and cultural history; maritime and local history

HOURS: Yr Daily 10-5

ADMISSION: $5, Children $2, Seniors $4

STEPHENSVILLE

3725
Cray House
Cockney's Lane, 21666 [POBox 321, 21666]; (p) (410) 643-5969

SUDLERSVILLE

3726
Sudlersville Train Station Museum
100 S Linden St, 21668 [PO Box 2, 21668]; (p) (410) 438-3501; (c) Queen Anne

Private non-profit/ 1991/ Sudlersville Community Betterment Club, Inc/ staff: 5(v)

HISTORIC SITE; HISTORY MUSEUM: Preserves Sudlersville history and promotes pride in the community.

PROGRAMS: Exhibits

COLLECTIONS: Last train station on the original site in QA Co, local artifacts, photos, and Jimmy Foxx memorabilia.

HOURS: May-Oct 3rd Sa

SUITLAND

3727
Airmen Memorial Museum
5211 Auth Rd, 20746; (p) (800) 638-0594; (f) (301) 899-8136; Staff@afsahq.org; www.afsahq.org; (c) Prince George's

Joint; Private non-profit/ 1986/ Board of Trustees/ staff: 3(f); 1(p)/ members: 130000/publication: *Airmen Heritage Series*

HISTORY MUSEUM: Collects, interprets, and exhibits the enlisted history of the U.S. Air Force and its predecessor organizations.

PROGRAMS: Community Outreach; Exhibits; Guided Tours; Publication; Research Library/Archives; School-Based Curriculum

COLLECTIONS: [1861-present] 4500 artifacts, 2000 volume library, 20,000 leaves archives, 6500 photographic images and slides, 7500 veterans surveys, and oral histories.

HOURS: Yr M-F 8-4:45

3728
National Museum of the American Indian Cultural Resources Center
4220 Silver Hill Rd, 20746; (p) (301) 238-6600

Federal/ 1989/ Smithsonian Institution

ART MUSEUM; HISTORY MUSEUM; LIVING HISTORY/OUTDOOR MUSEUM: Recognizes and affirms the historical and contemporary achievements and culture of the indigenous peoples of the Western Hemisphere.

PROGRAMS: Community Outreach; Exhibits; Festivals; Film/Video; Interpretation; Lectures; Research Library/Archives; School-Based Curriculum; Theatre

HOURS: Yr Daily

3729
Washington National Records Center
4205 Suitland Rd, 20746-8001; (p) (301) 457-7000; (f) (301) 457-7117; center@suitland.nara.gov; www.nara.gov; (c) Prince George

TAKOMA PARK

3730
Historic Takoma, Inc.
Tulip St, bet Maple & Cedar, 20913 [PO Box 5781, 20913]; (p) (301) 588-1605; heron25@aol.com; (c) Montgomery

Private non-profit/ 1978/ staff: 20(v)/ members: 300/publication: *Portrait of a Victorian Suburb*

HISTORIC PRESERVATION AGENCY; HISTORIC SITE

PROGRAMS: Annual Meeting; Community Outreach; Exhibits; Festivals; Film/Video; Interpretation; Lectures; Publication; Research Library/Archives

COLLECTIONS: [1880-1920] 1880s carriage in carriage house, farm implements; 1920s agricultural home and automotive items; archives.

HOURS: May-Aug Sa-Su 12-4

TOWSON

3731
Hampton National Historic Site
535 Hampton Lane, 21286; (p) (410) 823-1309; (f) (410) 823-8394

1783/ National Park Service/ staff: 6(f); 2(p); 282(v)

COLLECTIONS: [1790-1890] Furnishings belonging to the Ridgely family, including examples of Baltimore painted furniture.; microfilm of Ridgely papers, archive of Ridgely papers on ironworks, slaves, furnishings.

HOURS: Yr

UNION BRIDGE

3732
Hard Lodging
4625 Ladiesburg Rd, 21791 [c/o 210 E Main St, Westminster, 21157]; (p) (410) 857-3223, (410) 848-6494; hscc@carr.org; www.carr.org/hscc

1800

COLLECTIONS: [1950s] 18th - 20th century decorative arts; Historical photographs of Robert Wyndham Walden

HOURS: Yr

UPPER FAIRMOUNT

3733
Fairmount Academy Historical Association
[PO Box 133, 21867]; (p) (410) 651-0351; (c) Somerset

Private non-profit/ 1971/ staff: 13(f); 5(p); 30(v)/ members: 200

HISTORIC SITE; HISTORICAL SOCIETY; HISTORY MUSEUM; LIVING HISTORY/OUTDOOR MUSEUM

PROGRAMS: Festivals; Guided Tours; Living History

HOURS: Yr by appt

ADMISSION: Donations accepted

UPPER MARLBORO

3734
Billingsley House Museum
6900 Green Landing Rd, 20772; (p) (301) 627-0730; (f) (301) 627-7085; www.parks.com; (c) Prince George's

County/ 1990/ MD National Capital Park and Planning Commission/ staff: 3(p); 3(v)

HISTORIC SITE; HOUSE MUSEUM: Named for the first landowner, this 18th c Tidewater Colonial style plantation home, situated on 430 acres overlooking the confluence of the Patuxent River and the Western Branch, was built by James Weems.

PROGRAMS: Community Outreach; Facility Rental

HOURS: Yr M-F 9-4, Su 12-4

ADMISSION: $3, Student $2, Seniors $2

3735
Darnall's Chance
14800 Governor Oden Bowie Dr, 20773 [PO Box 32, 20773]; (p) (301) 952-8010; (f) (301) 952-1773; www.pgparks.com/; (c) Prince George's

County/ 1998/ Maryland National Capital Park and Planning Commission/ staff: 2(p); 20(v)

HISTORIC SITE; HOUSE MUSEUM: Maintains the probable birthplace of Daniel Carroll, signer of the US Constitution, and John Carroll, 1st Catholic Bishop in North America; preserves an 18th c underground burial vault.

PROGRAMS: Community Outreach; Concerts; Exhibits; Facility Rental; Family Programs; Festivals; Guided Tours; Interpretation; Lectures; Living History; Theatre

COLLECTIONS: [1696-1776] Original and re-produced William and Mary furnishings.

HOURS: Yr T-Th 10-4 by appt; F 10-4, Su 12-4

3736
Duval Tool Museum
Patuxent River Park, 20772 [16000 Croom Airport Rd, 20772-8395]; (p) (301) 627-6074; (f) (301) 952-9754; (c) Prince George's

Maryland-National Capital Park and Planning Commission/ staff: 1(f); 8(v)

HISTORY MUSEUM: Preserves and main-tains W. Henry Duvall's collection of 19th c tools and antique implements.

PROGRAMS: Guided Tours; Interpretation; Living History

COLLECTIONS: [1850-1930] Over 2,000 19th c tools and antique implements including peri-od carpenter tools, farm tools, and local den-tist's equip.

HOURS: Apr-Oct Su 1-4

ADMISSION: No charge

WALDORF

3737
Doctor Samuel A. Mudd Society, Inc.
Dr Samuel A Mudd Rd, [PO Box 1043, La Plata, 20646]; (p) (301) 934-8464; fluhartd@bellatlantic.net; (c) Charles

Private non-profit

HOUSE MUSEUM: Maintains the home of Dr Samuel A Mudd.

PROGRAMS: Annual Meeting; Exhibits; Inter-pretation; Living History

COLLECTIONS: [1830-1911] Personal items belonging to Dr. and Mrs. Mudd.

HOURS: Apr-Nov W 11-3, Sa-Su 12-4

ADMISSION: $3

WESTMINSTER

3738
Carroll County Farm Museum
500 S Center St, 21157; (p) (410) 876-2667; (c) Carroll

County/ 1965/ staff: 8(f); 5(p); 100(v)

HISTORIC SITE; HOUSE MUSEUM; LIVING HISTORY/OUTDOOR MUSEUM

PROGRAMS: Exhibits; Facility Rental; Festi-vals; Guided Tours; Interpretation; Living Histo-ry; Reenactments; Research Library/Archives

COLLECTIONS: [1880s-1910] Victorian heir-looms, period antiques, a springhouse, black-smith shop, accoutrements of a working 1800s farm.

HOURS: Apr-Dec T-Su 10-4

ADMISSION: $3,

3739
Historical Society of Carroll County
210 E Main St, 21157-5225; (p) (410) 848-6494; (f) (410) 848-3596; hscc@carr.org; www.carr.org/hscc; (c) Carroll

Private non-profit/ 1939/ Board of Directors/ staff: 2(f); 1(p); 100(v)/ members: 800/publica-tion: *Carroll County History Journal*

HISTORIC SITE; HISTORICAL SOCIETY: Collects and interprets objects significant to Carroll County history; presents educational programs and publishes local history titles.

PROGRAMS: Annual Meeting; Community Outreach; Exhibits; Facility Rental; Family Pro-grams; Guided Tours; Interpretation; Lectures; Publication; Research Library/Archives; School-Based Curriculum

COLLECTIONS: [18th-20th c] Decorative and fine arts, manuscripts, photos, costumes, and

3740
Kimmey House
210 E Main St, 21157; (p) (410) 848-6494

3741
Sherman-Fisher-Shellman House
206 E Main St, 21157 [c/o 210 E Main St, 21157]; (p) (410) 848-6494; hscc@carr.org; www.carr.org/hscc

1807/ staff: 2(p)

COLLECTIONS: [1807-1842] 18th - 19th cen-tury decorative arts

HOURS: Yr

3742
Union Mills Homestead, The
3311 Littlestown Pike, 21158; (p) (410) 858-2288; www.union.edu/PUBLIC/ECODEPT/kleind/unionmills/; (c) Carroll

Private non-profit/ 1964/ Union Mills Home-stead Foundation, Inc./ staff: 1(f); 2(p); 150(v)/ members: 350/publication: *Union Mills*

HISTORIC SITE; HOUSE MUSEUM: Home-stead begun in 1797 by brothers David and Andrew Shriver. Site of grist mill, saw mill and Shriver family home occupied until 1960s.

PROGRAMS: Annual Meeting; Exhibits; Festi-vals; Guided Tours; Publication

COLLECTIONS: [1797-1956]

HOURS: June-Aug T-F 10-4, Sa-Su 12-4; May and Sept Sa-Su

WYE MILLS

3743
Wye Grist Mill and Museum
Rt 662, 21679 [PO Box 277, 21679]; (p) (410) 829-6909; (c) Talbot/Queen Anne

Private non-profit/ 1996/ Friends of Wye Mill, Inc/ staff: 4(p); 15(v)/ members: 160

HISTORIC SITE; HISTORY MUSEUM: Ex-hibits the importance of wheat productions on MD's eastern shore from 1790-1820; main-tains a working 1810 grist mill.

PROGRAMS: Annual Meeting; Community Outreach; Exhibits; Facility Rental; Festivals; Guided Tours; Interpretation; Lectures; Living History; Reenactments; School-Based Cur-riculum

COLLECTIONS: [1810-1850] Working grist mill equipment (1810), steel roller mill, farm equip, historic flour bags, and model of village of Wye Mills.

HOURS: Apr-Nov M-F 10-1, Sa-Su 10-4

ADMISSION: $2

MASSACHUSETTS

ABINGTON

3744
Dyer Memorial Library
28 Centre Ave, 02351 [PO Box 2245, 02351]; (p) (781) 878-8480; (c) Plymouth

Private non-profit/ 1932/ Dyer Marietta W Cot/ staff: 1(f); 1(p); 2(v)

HISTORY MUSEUM; RESEARCH CENTER: Provides library for genealogical and military research (Revolutionary and Civil Wars) and meeting place for the Historical Society of Old Abington.

PROGRAMS: Exhibits; Guided Tours; Re-search Library/Archives; School-Based Cur-riculum

HOURS: Yr T-F 1-5, 2nd and 4th Sa 12-4; or by appt.

ADMISSION: No charge

ACTON

3745
Iron Work Farm in Acton, Inc.
5 High St, 01720 [PO Box 1111, 01720]; (p) (978) 263-2227; (f) (978) 263-2227; (c) Middlesex

Private non-profit/ 1964/ Board of Directors/ staff: 25(v)/ members: 150

HOUSE MUSEUM: Owns and operates 2 house museums, the 1707 Faulkner House and the 1732/1818 Jones Tavern, both in South Acton.

PROGRAMS: Annual Meeting; Community Outreach; Guided Tours; Interpretation

COLLECTIONS: [18th and early 19th c] Furni-ture and artifacts belonging to the Jones and Faulkner families and associated with the de-velopment of the town of Acton.

HOURS: Apr-Oct, 4th Su 3-5

ADMISSION: $1, Children $0.50

AMESBURY

3746
Bartlett Museum, Inc.
270 Main St, 01913 [PO Box 692, 01913]; (p) (978) 388-2271; (c) Essex

Private non-profit/ 1965/ Board of Directors/ staff: 1(p)/ members: 90

HISTORY MUSEUM; HOUSE MUSEUM; LIV-ING HISTORY/OUTDOOR MUSEUM; TRIBAL MUSEUM

PROGRAMS: Annual Meeting; Exhibits; Guid-ed Tours; Interpretation; Lectures; Publication; School-Based Curriculum

COLLECTIONS: [1750-present] Tools, equip-ment, bird specimens, carriages and railroad memorabilia.

HOURS: May-Sept 1-4

3747
John Greenleaf Whittier Home
86 Friend St, 01913; (p) (508) 338-1337; www.bostonnortheast.com/history.html

AMHERST

3748
Amherst History Museum at the Strong House
67 Amity St, 01002; (p) (413) 256-0678; (c) Hampshire

Private non-profit/ 1916/ Amherst Historical Society/ staff: 1(f); 1(p); 25(v)/ members: 340

HISTORIC SITE; HISTORY MUSEUM: Collects, preserves and displays objects that provide insight into the past.

PROGRAMS: Annual Meeting; Community Outreach; Exhibits; Facility Rental; Festivals; Garden Tours; Guided Tours; Interpretation; Lectures; Living History; Reenactments; School-Based Curriculum

COLLECTIONS: [1750-1900] Decorative and fine arts, textiles, period clothing, material culture artifacts, agricultural tools and other artifacts representing daily life.

HOURS: May-Oct W-Sa 12:30-3:30; Oct-May F-Sa 12:30-3:30

ADMISSION: $3

3749
Dickinson Homestead
280 Main St, 01002; (p) (413) 542-8161; csdickinson@amherst.edu; www.amherst.edu/~edhouse; (c) Hampshire

Private non-profit/ 1965/ Trustees of Amherst College/ staff: 1(f); 25(p); 1(v)

HISTORIC SITE; HOUSE MUSEUM: Birthplace and home of poet of Emily Dickinson. Dedicated to educating audiences about Dickinson's life, writings and relevance. Preserves and interprets the family homestead.

PROGRAMS: Community Outreach; Exhibits; Guided Tours; Interpretation

COLLECTIONS: [Mid 19th c] Objects related to the life and times of Emily Dickinson and her family.

HOURS: Mar-Dec days vary seasonally

3750
Martha Dickinson Bianchi Trust
The Evergreens, 214 Main St, 01004 [PO Box 603, 01004-0603]; (p) (413) 253-5272; (c) Hampshire

Private non-profit/ 1991/ Martha Dickinson Bianchi Trust/ staff: 3(p); 12(v)

HOUSE MUSEUM: Preserves and maintains the Evergreens, an Italianate residence closely associated with the life and work of poet Emily Dickinson.

PROGRAMS: Guided Tours; Interpretation; Lectures

COLLECTIONS: [1856-1943] Artworks and furnishings owned by the Dickinson family.

HOURS: By appt

3751
National Yiddish Book Center
Weinberg Building, 1021 W St, 01002; (p) (413) 256-4900; (f) (413) 256-4700; yiddish@bikher.org; www.yiddishbookcenter.org; (c) Hampshire

Private non-profit/ 1980/ Board of Directors/ staff: 22(f); 10(v)/ members: 27000/publication: *Pakn Treger*

CULTURAL CENTER; GARDEN; HISTORICAL SOCIETY; HISTORY MUSEUM: Has saved 1.5 million Yiddish books and redistributed them to libraries and readers worldwide.

PROGRAMS: Concerts; Exhibits; Facility Rental; Film/Video; Guided Tours; Lectures; Publication; Theatre

COLLECTIONS: [1860-1950] 1.5 million Yiddish novels, poetry, drama, essays, history, and other genres printed in Eastern Europe and America.

HOURS: Yr Su-F 10-3:30

ADMISSION: No charge

3752
Special Collections and Archives, W.E.B. Du Bois Library, University of Massachusetts
154 Hicks Way, 01003 [Univ of Massachusetts Amherst, 01003]; (p) (413) 545-2780; (f) (413) 577-1399; linda.seidman@library.umass.edu; www.library.umass.edu/spcoll/spec.html; (c) Hampshire

State/ 1973/ Trustees, University of Massachusetts/ staff: 4(f); 1(p)

LIBRARY AND/OR ARCHIVES: Collects archival records of the University Historical Manuscript Collection and publishes materials, especially concerning local history.

PROGRAMS: Community Outreach; Exhibits; Research Library/Archives

COLLECTIONS: [19th-20th c] Documentation of the political, social, economic and cultural life of the region, including social and labor history, African Americans and immigrant groups, especially Polish Americans and Southeast Asians.

HOURS: Yr M-F 10-3

ADMISSION: No charge

ANDOVER

3753
Andover Historical Society
97 Main St, 01810; (p) (978) 475-2236; (f) (978) 470-2741; andhists@ma.ultranet.com; www.ultranet.com/~andhists; (c) Essex

Private non-profit/ 1911/ Board of Directors/ staff: 3(f); 5(p); 150(v)/ members: 825/publication: *Andover, A Century of Change*

HISTORIC PRESERVATION AGENCY; HISTORIC SITE; HISTORICAL SOCIETY; HOUSE MUSEUM; RESEARCH CENTER: Maintains a research library and archives, local and regional history and genealogical resources. Offers tours of the house and barn museum, and displays temporary exhibits.

PROGRAMS: Annual Meeting; Community Outreach; Exhibits; Facility Rental; Family Programs; Festivals; Garden Tours; Guided Tours; Interpretation; Lectures; Living History; Monthly Meeting; Publication; Research Library/Archives; School-Based Curriculum; Theatre

COLLECTIONS: [1820-1840] American and imported furnishings, costumes, textiles, household agricultural and trade implements, genealogy and local history research materials. Also has a 1819 house and barn.

HOURS: Yr T-F 9-5, Sa 9-3

ADMISSION: $4, Student $2, Seniors $2; Mbrs free

3754
Andover's Historical Museum and Research Center
97 Main St, 01810; (p) (978) 475-2236, (978) 475-3488; (f) (978) 470-2741; Andhists@ma.ultranet.com; www.ultranet.com/~andhists/ 1819/ staff: 3(f)

COLLECTIONS: [1820-1860] Mostly 19th century costumes; tools for farm and industry; and household furnishings.; Journals, diaries, correspondence, Andover church records, AHS organizational records, genealogical material for Andover families beginning in 1646.

HOURS: Jan-Dec, T- Sa 9; Jan-Dec, T- Sa 9-5; July-Aug T-F 9-5; M

3755
Northeast Document Conservation Center
100 Brickstone Sq, 01810-1494; (p) (978) 470-1010; (f) (978) 475-6021; nedcc@nedcc.org; www.nedcc.org; (c) Essex

Private non-profit/ 1973/ staff: 35(f); 5(p)/publication: *Preservation of Library and Archive Collections: A Manual*

Nonprofit regional conservation center specializing in the treatment and preservation of paper-based materials. Provides bookbinding, microfilming, photographic duplication and field services.

PROGRAMS: Publication

HOURS: Yr M-F 8:30-4:30

ADMISSION: No charge

ARLINGTON

3756
Arlington Historical Society, The
7 Jason St, 02476; (p) (781) 648-4300; www.arlhs.org; (c) Middlesex

Private non-profit/ 1897/ staff: 2(p); 20(v)/ members: 250

HISTORICAL SOCIETY; HOUSE MUSEUM: Collects, preserves, and interprets the history of Arlington. Maintains the 1740s Jason Russell House, site of battle on the first day of the Revolutionary War.

PROGRAMS: Annual Meeting; Community Outreach; Exhibits; Guided Tours; Interpretation; Lectures; Living History; Reenactments; Research Library/Archives; School-Based Curriculum

COLLECTIONS: [18th c-present] Photographs, books, documents, textiles, furnishings, ephemera and maps.

HOURS: Jason Russell House: Mid Apr-Nov T-Sa 1-5; Smith Museum: Mar-Dec T-Sa 1-5

ADMISSION: $2, Children

3757
Old Schwamb Mill
17 Mill Ln, 02476; (p) (781) 643-0554; (f) (781) 648-8809; schwambmil@aol.com; www.oldschwambmill.org; (c) Middlesex

Private non-profit/ 1969/ The Schwamb Mill Preservation Trust/ staff: 1(f); 2(p); 30(v)/ members: 130

HISTORIC PRESERVATION AGENCY; HISTORIC SITE; HISTORY MUSEUM; LIVING HISTORY/OUTDOOR MUSEUM: Preserves the longest continuously operating mill site in the western hemisphere and educates the public to the concept of evolution of industrial technology in rural settings.

PROGRAMS: Community Outreach; Exhibits; Guided Tours; Interpretation; Living History; School-Based Curriculum

COLLECTIONS: [1650-present] Shaft and pulley belt-driven system of operating 19th c woodworking machinery, using water, steam, and electric power.

HOURS: Yr M-F 10-3

ADMISSION: Donations accepted

ASHLAND

3758
Ashland Historical Society
2 Myrtle St, 01721 [PO Box 145, 01721]; (p) (508) 881-8183; (c) Middlesex

City, non-profit; Private non-profit/ 1909/ staff: 8(v)/ members: 100

HISTORICAL SOCIETY; HISTORY MUSEUM; HOUSE MUSEUM

PROGRAMS: Annual Meeting; Exhibits; Guided Tours; Lectures; Publication; Research Library/Archives

COLLECTIONS: [1830-1900] Assorted items and papers concerning Ashland and neighboring towns.

HOURS: Yr W 7-9, Sa 9-12, 2nd Su 2-5

ASHLEY FALLS

3759
Colonel John Ashley House
Cooper Hill Rd, 01262 [PO Box 792, Stockbridge, 01262]; (p) (413) 298-3239, (413) 229-8600; (f) (413) 298-5239; Westregion@ttor.org

1735/ The Trustees of Reservations/ staff: 1(f); 5(p)

COLLECTIONS: [1750-1800] American Redware, kitchen tools, colonial furniture; Pre & post restoration photographs, ledgers from Ashley General Store, deeds.

HOURS: Yr;; Sa-Su, Mon holidays 1-5

BELCHERTOWN

3760
Belchertown Historical Association
20 Maple St, 01007 [PO Box 1211, 01007]; (p) (413) 323-6573; (c) Hampshire

Private non-profit/ 1903/ staff: 1(p); 20(v)/ members: 200

HISTORICAL SOCIETY; HISTORY MUSEUM: Interprets local and area history in a house setting utilizing 19th century furniture, ceramics, paintings, costumes and accessories.

PROGRAMS: Annual Meeting; Community Outreach; Exhibits; Guided Tours; Lectures; Research Library/Archives; School-Based Curriculum

COLLECTIONS: [1820-1860] Town and church records, family journals, photographs, historical Blue Stafforshire, fabrics, mourning jewelry, country furniture, carriages and sleighs made in Belchertown, as well as farm equipment and tools.

HOURS: Yr W, Sa 2-5

ADMISSION: $3

BEVERLY

3761
Beverly Historical Society and Museum
117 Cabot St, 01915; (p) (978) 922-1186; (f) (978) 922-7387; (c) Essex

Private non-profit/ 1891/ staff: 1(f); 3(p); 19(v)/ members: 1000/publication: *Chronicle*

GENEALOGICAL SOCIETY; HISTORIC SITE; HISTORICAL SOCIETY; HISTORY MUSEUM; HOUSE MUSEUM; LIVING HISTORY/OUTDOOR MUSEUM; RESEARCH CENTER: Preserves, interprets and shares Beverly's social and cultural history through three 17th and 18th century houses.

PROGRAMS: Exhibits; Guided Tours; Interpretation; Lectures; Living History; Publication; Reenactments; Research Library/Archives

COLLECTIONS: [17th-20th c] Furniture, decorative arts; nautical, military, transportation and social history artifacts.

HOURS: Yr T-F 10-4, Sa 12-4

3762
Reverend John Hale House, Beverly Historical Society and Museum
39 Hale St, 01915

1694/ staff: 1(f); 1(p)

COLLECTIONS: [1694; 1850-1900] 18th century beaufait or shell cupboard with original paint; Nathan Hale signet ring.; John Hale's book, A Modest Inquiry into the Nature of Witchcraft.

BILLERICA

3763
Billerica Historical Society
36 Concord Rd, 01821 [PO Box 381, 01821]; (p) (978) 667-7020; (c) Middlesex

Private non-profit/ 1894/ Board of Directors/ members: 250/publication: *Yankee Doodle Times*

HISTORICAL SOCIETY; HOUSE MUSEUM

PROGRAMS: Annual Meeting; Community Outreach; Exhibits; Guided Tours; Lectures; Publication; Research Library/Archives; School-Based Curriculum

COLLECTIONS: [18th-20th c]

HOURS: Apr-Sept Su 1-5 and Sa by appt

ADMISSION: Donations accepted

BOSTON

3764
Ancient and Honorable Artillery Company of Massachusetts
Armory, Faneuil Hall, 02109; (p) (617) 227-1638; (f) (617) 227-7221; (c) Suffolk

Military/ 1638/ staff: 2(f)/ members: 792

ART MUSEUM; HISTORIC SITE; HISTORY MUSEUM: A military organization, chartered 1638, that trains officers for the existing militia. Today the Company is the Ceremonial Guard for the Governor of the Commonwealth.

PROGRAMS: Exhibits; Guided Tours; Interpretation

COLLECTIONS: [1638-present] Weapons, uniforms, medals, military hats, buckles, china, silver, photographs, and a 4000 volume library of military history, military science, and church sermons.

HOURS: Yr M-F 9-4:30

3765
Boston Athenaeum, The
10 1/2 Beacon St, 02108; (p) (617) 227-0270; (f) (617) 227-5266; www.bostonathenaeum.org; (c) Suffolk

Private non-profit/ 1807/ Proprietors of the Boston Athenaeum/ staff: 37(f); 10(p); 70(v)/ members: 5000

ART MUSEUM; RESEARCH CENTER: An independent membership and research library incorporated in 1807 that occupies a National Historic Landmark building built in 1849.

PROGRAMS: Community Outreach; Concerts; Exhibits; Facility Rental; Guided Tours; Lectures; Research Library/Archives

COLLECTIONS: [19th-20th c] Archives, manuscripts, microfilm, newspapers, periodicals, prints and photographs.

HOURS: Labor Day-Mem Day M-F 9-5:30, Sa 9-4

3766
Boston Fire Museum
344 Congress St, 02210; (p) (617) 482-1344; (c) Suffolk

Private non-profit/ 1983/ staff: 6(v)/ members: 160

HISTORIC PRESERVATION AGENCY; HISTORIC SITE; HISTORY MUSEUM: Dedicated to preserving and memorializing the history of firefighting in the Boston area and educating the public about fire prevention and safety.

PROGRAMS: Community Outreach; Exhibits; Facility Rental; Guided Tours; Living History

COLLECTIONS: [1840s-1970s] Six pieces of fire fighting apparatus, hand-operated and self-propelled; fire tools, memorabilia, and photographs, including the Arthur Fiedler collection.

HOURS: Apr-Oct Sa 12-4 or by appt.

3767
Boston National Historical Park
Charlestown Navy Yard, 02129; (p) (617) 242-5644; (f) (617) 242-6006; BOST_email@nps.gov; www.nps.gov/bost; (c) Suffolk

Federal/ 1974/ National Park Service/ staff: 120(f); 51(v)

HISTORIC SITE; HISTORY MUSEUM: Includes Charlestown Navy Yard, Bunker Hill Monument, Dorchester Heights, Paul Revere House, Old North Church, Old State House, Old Meeting House, and Faneuil Hall.

PROGRAMS: Community Outreach; Concerts; Exhibits; Facility Rental; Guided Tours; Interpretation; Lectures; Living History; Publication; Reenactments; Research Library/Archives

COLLECTIONS: [1760-1974] Archives relate to USS Cassin Young and Charlestown Navy Yard; chain, rope and other products produced in the Yard; prints and memorabilia from Boston's Freedom Trail sites.

3768
Boston Public Library
700 Boylston St, 02116; (p) (617) 536-5400; www.bpl.org; (c) Suffolk

City/ 1848/ Board of Trustees/ staff: 500(f); 100(p); 50(v)

LIBRARY AND/OR ARCHIVES: Develops, maintains and preserves comprehensive collections of a research and archival nature.

PROGRAMS: Community Outreach; Concerts; Exhibits; Guided Tours; Lectures; Research Library/Archives

COLLECTIONS: [17th-20th c] Books, periodicals, maps, musical scores, manuscripts, prints, drawings, water colors, photographs, government documents and patents.

HOURS: Yr

3769
Boston Symphony Orchestra Archives
Symphony Hall, 02115; (p) (617) 638-9434; (f) (617) 638-9433; bcarr@bso.org; www.bso.org; (c) Suffolk

Private non-profit/ 1881/ Board of Trustees/ staff: 1(f); 1(p); 10(v)

LIBRARY AND/OR ARCHIVES: Collects, preserves, and makes available for scholarly use materials that document the Boston Symphony Orchestra, the Boston Pops, Symphony Hall, Boston Music Hall, Tanglewood Festival, Tanglewood Music Center, and the Tanglewood Estate.

PROGRAMS: Exhibits; Research Library/Archives

COLLECTIONS: [1881-present] Printed concert programs, press clippings and reviews, official records, administrative files, manuscript collections, recordings of live concerts, photographs, architectural records, and posters.

HOURS: Yr

3770
Bostonian Society, The
206 Washington St, 02109; (p) (617) 720-1713; library@bostonhistory.org; www.bostonhistory.org

Private non-profit/ 1881/ Board of Directors/ staff: 8(f); 13(p); 10(v)/ members: 1200

HISTORICAL SOCIETY; HISTORY MUSEUM: Committed to preserving and interpreting the city's history.

PROGRAMS: Annual Meeting; Community Outreach; Exhibits; Facility Rental; Guided Tours; Interpretation; Lectures; Reenactments; Research Library/Archives; School-Based Curriculum

COLLECTIONS: [Mid 18th-19th c] Revolutionary War and military artifacts; maritime objects, prints, drawings, paintings, domestic furnishings, books on Boston, photographs, maps and pieces of Boston ephemera.

HOURS: Yr Daily 9-5

3771
Congregational Christian Historical Society
14 Beacon St, 02108; (p) (617) 523-0470; (f) (617) 523-0491; hworthley@14beacon.org; (c) Suffolk

Private non-profit/ 1952/ Board of Directors/ staff: 2(p)/ members: 850

HISTORICAL SOCIETY: Teaches keeping accurate records by local churches, preservation of those records according to archival standards, and their use in scholarly research; and documents anniversary celebrations in Congregational Christian church life.

PROGRAMS: Annual Meeting; Interpretation; Research Library/Archives

COLLECTIONS: [1620-present] Holdings from the Congregational Library.

HOURS: Yr M-F

3772
Congregational Library
14 Beacon St, 02108; (p) (617) 523-0470; (f) (617) 523-0491; hworthley@14beacon.org; www.14beacon.org; (c) Suffolk

Private non-profit/ 1853/ Board of Directors/ staff: 5(f); 1(p)/ members: 165/publication: *Bulletin of the Congregational Library*

LIBRARY AND/OR ARCHIVES; RESEARCH CENTER: Lending (by mail) and research library of 230,000 books, journals and archives serves all who would access Congregational Christian, religious and family history, providing loans and reference services.

PROGRAMS: Annual Meeting; Interpretation; Publication; Research Library/Archives

COLLECTIONS: [1620-present] History and doctrine of the Congregational Christian churches; general religious studies and local church and organizational archives.

3773
Council of American Maritime Museums, USS Constitution Museum
[PO Box 1812, 02129]; (p) (617) 426-1812; (f) (617) 242-0496; (c) Suffolk

Private non-profit/ 1974

ALLIANCE OF HISTORICAL AGENCIES: Offers professional support to institutions that preserve and interpret America's maritime heritage, promoting fellowship and cooperation among member museums.

3774
First Church of Christ, Scientist, Church History Department, The
175 Huntington Ave, 02115; (p) (617) 450-3501; (f) (617) 450-3415; mbehist@csps.com; (c) Suffolk

Private non-profit/ staff: 24(f); 9(p); 3(v)

HISTORIC SITE; HOUSE MUSEUM; RESEARCH CENTER

PROGRAMS: Community Outreach; Exhibits; Guided Tours; Interpretation; Lectures; Research Library/Archives

COLLECTIONS: [1821-present] Mary Baker Eddy Historic Homes and papers; Archives of the First Church of Christ, Scientist

HOURS: Yr call for days and hours

ADMISSION: No charge

3775
Gibson House Museum
137 Beacon St, 02116; (p) (617) 267-6338

1859/ staff: 5(p); 2(v)

COLLECTIONS: [1860-1920] Daguerreotypes, European and American clocks, China trade porcelain; manuscripts, poems, letters of Charles Hammond Gibson

HOURS: Yr

3776
Isabella Stewart Gardner Museum
280 The Fenway, 02115 [2 Palace Rd, 02115]; (p) (617) 566-1401; (f) (617) 232-8039; www.boston.com/gardner; (c) Suffolk

Private non-profit/ 1903/ Board of Trustees/ staff: 72(f); 42(p)/ members: 4500

ART MUSEUM; GARDEN: Museum in a building styled after a 15th c Venetian palazzo, designed and built at the turn of the century by Isabella Stewart Gardner.

PROGRAMS: Community Outreach; Concerts; Exhibits; Facility Rental; Family Programs; Garden Tours; Guided Tours; Lectures; Research Library/Archives; School-Based Curriculum

COLLECTIONS: [Italian Renaissance] Gardner collection of 2,500 artworks including paintings, sculptures, drawings, prints, furniture, and textiles, along with glass and ceramic objects; letters, manuscripts, rare books and architectural elements.

HOURS: Yr T-Su 11-5

ADMISSION: $10, Student $5, Seniors $7; Under 18/Mbrs free

3777
John F. Kennedy Library and Museum
Columbia Point, 02125-3398; (p) (617) 929-4500; (f) (617) 929-4538; library@kennedy.nara.gov; www.nara.gov; (c) Suffolk

Federal

HISTORY MUSEUM; LIBRARY AND/OR ARCHIVES; PRESIDENTIAL SITE

PROGRAMS: Concerts; Elder's Programs; Exhibits; Facility Rental; Lectures; Research Library/Archives

3778
Massachusetts Archives and Commonwealth Museum
220 Morrissey Blvd, 02125; (p) (617) 727-2816; (f) (617) 288-8429; archives@sec.state.ma.us; www.state.ma.us/sec/arc; (c) Suffolk

State/ Secretary of the Commonwealth of Massachusetts/ staff: 15(f); 5(p); 45(v)

HISTORY MUSEUM; LIBRARY AND/OR ARCHIVES: The official repository of records of the Massachusetts state government.

PROGRAMS: Community Outreach; Exhibits; Facility Rental; Guided Tours; Lectures; Research Library/Archives; School-Based Curriculum

COLLECTIONS: [1629-present] State government records, beginning with the documents founding the Massachusetts Bay Company.

HOURS: Yr M-F 9-5, Sa 9-3

ADMISSION: No charge

3779
Massachusetts Historical Society
1154 Boylston St, 02215; (p) (617) 536-1608; (f) (617) 859-0074; www.masshist.org; (c) Middlesex

Private non-profit/ 1791/ staff: 26(f); 3(p); 5(v)/ members: 1000

HISTORICAL SOCIETY: Research library with publications and fellowship programs, sponsor of Adams Papers and co-sponsor of New England Quarterly.

PROGRAMS: Annual Meeting; Community Outreach; Exhibits; Facility Rental; Lectures; Research Library/Archives

COLLECTIONS: [18th c-present] 10 million manuscripts; 250,000 books; more than 100,000 photographs; and 400 paintings.

HOURS: Yr M-F 9-4:45, Sa 9-1

ADMISSION: No charge

3780
Massachusetts Society of Mayflower Descendants
100 Boylston St, #750, 02116-4610; (p) (617) 338-1991; (f) (617) 338-6085; msmd@tiac.net; www.massmayflowersociety.com; (c) Suffolk

Private non-profit/ 1896/ staff: 1(f); 1(p)/ members: 3100/publication: Mayflower Descendant

GENEALOGICAL SOCIETY: Statewide society for Mayflower descendants.

PROGRAMS: Annual Meeting; Publication; Research Library/Archives; School-Based Curriculum

COLLECTIONS: [1600s] Book collection focusing on New England, transcribed/copied records, and small manuscript collection.

HOURS: Yr T-Th 9-4

ADMISSION: No charge

3781
New England Historic Genealogical Society
99 Newbury St, 02116 [101 Newbury St, 02116-3007]; (p) (888) 286-3447, (617) 536-5740; (f) (617) 536-7307; membership@nehgs.org; www.NewEnglandAncestors.org; (c) Suffolk

Private non-profit/ 1845/ Board of Trustees/ staff: 55(f); 10(p)/ members: 18000/publication: New England Historical and Genealogical Register

GENEALOGICAL SOCIETY; HISTORICAL SOCIETY; RESEARCH CENTER: Works to help people understand their heritage through library research, educational programs, a lending library, informative publications, and a book sales department.

PROGRAMS: Annual Meeting; Facility Rental; Guided Tours; Lectures; Publication; Research Library/Archives; School-Based Curriculum

COLLECTIONS: [17th-20th c] State and local histories, manuscripts, census records and published genealogies from every U.S. region, Canada, England and Ireland.

HOURS: Yr T,F-Sa 9-5; W-Th 9-9

ADMISSION: $15/day non-members

3782
New England Museum Association
Boston NHP, Charlestown Navy Yard, 02129; (p) (617) 242-2283; (f) (617) 241-5797; www.nemanet.org; (c) Norfolk

Private non-profit/ 1919/ Board of Trustees/ staff: 4(f)/ members: 1670

PROFESSIONAL ASSOCIATION: Supports and furthers communication, ethical conduct and professional development among, by, and for New England's museums and their personnel and promotes museums in the region.

3783
Nichols House Museum, Inc.
55 Mount Vernon St, 02108; (p) (617) 227-6993; (f) (617) 723-8026; nhm@channelL.com; (c) Suffolk

Private non-profit/ 1961/ Board of Governors/ staff: 1(f); 2(p); 9(v)/ members: 250

HOUSE MUSEUM: Offers glimpse into 19th and early 20th c life on Boston's Beacon Hill.

PROGRAMS: Annual Meeting; Community Outreach; Guided Tours; Interpretation; Lectures

COLLECTIONS: [1885-1920] Family furnishings from 17th-early 20th c, paintings, prints, rugs, ceramic sculptures and needlework.

HOURS: Feb-Apr, Nov-Dec Th-Sa; May-Oct T-Sa; 12:15-4:15

ADMISSION: $5

3784
Northeast Museum Services Center
Charlestown Navy Yard, Building I/4, 02129; (p) (617) 242-5613; (f) (617) 242-1833; duncan_hay@nps.gov; www.nps.gov/neso/resources/cultural/museumsc.htm; (c) Suffolk

Federal/ 1995/ National Park Service/ staff: 18(f); 2(p)/publication: Annual Report

Provides professional support and service for museum programs throughout the Northeast Region of the National Park Service.

COLLECTIONS: [17th-20th c] Archives, manuscripts, large scale industrial machinery, fine art

3785
Paul Revere Memorial Association
19 North Square, 02113; (p) (617) 523-2388; (f) (671) 523-1776; staff@paulreverehouse.org; www.paulreverehouse.org; (c) Suffolk

Private non-profit/ 1907/ Board of Directors/ staff: 7(f); 20(p); 15(v)/ members: 200/publication: Revere House Gazette, Revere Dispatch

HISTORIC SITE; HISTORY MUSEUM; HOUSE MUSEUM: Preserves and interprets two of Boston's oldest homes by providing a range of educational experiences related to social history themes from the 17th-20th centuries.

PROGRAMS: Community Outreach; Concerts; Elder's Programs; Exhibits; Family Programs; Garden Tours; Guided Tours; Interpretation; Lectures; Living History; Publication

COLLECTIONS: [18th c] Artifacts, reproductions, research library, slides, photographs, and a Revere/Hitchborn genealogical reference collection.

HOURS: mid-Apr-Oct M-Su 9:30-5:15; Nov-mid-Apr M-Su 9:30-4:15

ADMISSION: $2.50, Student $2, Children $1, Seniors $2; Group rates

3786
Preservation Studies at Boston University
226 Bay State Rd, Rm 106, 02215; (p) (617) 353-2948; (f) (617) 353-2556; amnesp@bu.edu; www.bu.edu/psp; (c) Suffolk

Private non-profit/ 1970/ Boston University/ staff: 1(f); 3(p)

An interdisciplinary course-based program designed to provide students with the knowledge necessary for effective and judicious management of cultural resources. Graduates receive a Masters of Arts in Preservation Studies.

PROGRAMS: Lectures; School-Based Curriculum

HOURS: Yr M-F 9-5

3787
Society for the Preservation of New England Antiquities (SPNEA)
Harrison Gray Otis House, 141 Cambridge St, 02114; (p) (617) 227-3956, (617) 227-3957; (f) (617) 227-9204; www.spnea.org; (c) Suffolk

Private non-profit/ 1910/ staff: 67(f); 77(p); 280(v)/ members: 5000

HISTORIC PRESERVATION AGENCY; HOUSE MUSEUM; LIBRARY AND/OR ARCHIVES: Harrison Gray Otis House houses headquarters of SPNEA, SPNEA's library and archives, and the historic house. SPNEA operates a museum of cultural history; owns and operates 35 historic properties in five states and uses its collections to educate the public on New England history.

PROGRAMS: Community Outreach; Concerts; Exhibits; Facility Rental; Family Programs; Festivals; Garden Tours; Guided Tours; Lectures; Publication; School-Based Curriculum

COLLECTIONS: [17th c-present] House: Original period furnishings and wallcoverings; gothic revival furniture; paintings; decorative arts; household objects; documents. Library and Archives: SPNEA institutional archives; social history ephemera; multiple family papers and account books; more than 20,000 architectural drawings and specifications, American builders' guides, pattern books, and decorating manuals, and trade catalogues and other advertising ephemera that provide information about architectural ornament and building materials. The work of more than 450 architects working from c. 1800-1960s is represented.

HOURS: Yr House: W-Su 11-5; Library & Archives: W-F 9:30-4:45 by appt only

ADMISSION: $5, Children $2, Seniors $3.50

3788
USS Constitution Museum
Charlestown Navy Yard, 02129 [Box 1812, 02129]; (p) (617) 426-1812; (f) (617) 242-0496; info@ussconstitutionmuseum.org; www.ussconstitutionmuseum.org; (c) Suffolk

Private non-profit/ 1972/ staff: 18(f); 15(p); 30(v)/ members: 3500

HISTORY MUSEUM: Interpretive complement to USS Constitution, the oldest commissioned warship afloat in the world.

PROGRAMS: Annual Meeting; Community Outreach; Exhibits; Facility Rental; Family Programs; Film/Video; Guided Tours; Interpretation; Lectures; Living History; Research Library/Archives; School-Based Curriculum; Theatre

COLLECTIONS: [19th c] Photographs, prints, paintings, crew members' personal gear, flags, uniforms, ship models and souvenirs related to the ship's travels and restorations.

HOURS: Spring-Summer Daily 9-6; Fall-Winter Daily 10-5

ADMISSION: No charge

BOURNE

3789
Bourne Historical Society, Inc.
30 Keene St, 02532 [PO Box 3095, 02532-0795]; (p) (508) 759-8167; bournehs@capecod.net; (c) Barnstable

Private non-profit/ 1921/ Board of Trustees/ staff: 3(p); 100(v)/ members: 334/publication: *Post Scripts*

Collects, preserves, and interprets the history of the Town of Bourne; operates the 1627 reconstructed Aptucxet Trading Post Museum.

PROGRAMS: Annual Meeting; Community Outreach; Exhibits; Facility Rental; Festivals; Garden Tours; Guided Tours; Interpretation; Publication; Reenactments

COLLECTIONS: [Archaic-present] Manuscripts, maps, books, portraits, paintings, museum artifacts, photographs, post cards, and furniture.

HOURS: May1-Oct Su 2-4, T-F 10-4; July-Aug M-F 10-4, Su 2-5

BOYLSTON

3790
Boylston Historical Society, Inc.
7 Central St, 01505 [PO Box 459, 01505]; (p) (508) 869-2720; boyhisoc@ma.ultranet.com; www.ultranet.com/~boyhisoc/index.shtml; (c) Worcester

Private non-profit/ 1971/ staff: 7(v)/ members: 138/publication: *The Potpourri*

HISTORICAL SOCIETY; HISTORY MUSEUM: Publishes books on local history; collects, preserves, exhibits artifacts, archives, maintains research library, and offers educational programs.

PROGRAMS: Annual Meeting; Exhibits; Facility Rental; Lectures; Publication; Research Library/Archives

COLLECTIONS: [1720-present] Town and state history, real estate transactions, genealogy, maps, photographs, scrap books, correspondence, local history, neighboring community history, state history.

HOURS: Yr

3791
Worcester County Horticultural Society
11 French Dr, 01505 [PO Box 598, 01505-0598]; (p) (508) 869-6111; (f) (508) 869-0314; thbg@towerhillbg.org; www.towerhillbg.org; (c) Worcester

Private non-profit/ 1842/ Board of Trustees/ staff: 19(f); 20(p); 200(v)/ members: 4734/publication: *Grow With Us; Learn With Us*

GARDEN: Owns and operates Tower Hill Botanic Garden, 132 acres of formal gardens, meadows, woodland trails, and 1742 Farmhouse.

PROGRAMS: Annual Meeting; Community Outreach; Concerts; Elder's Programs; Exhibits; Facility Rental; Family Programs; Garden Tours; Guided Tours; Interpretation; Lectures; Publication; School-Based Curriculum

COLLECTIONS: Trees, shrubs, vines, herbaceous perennials and bulbs indigenous to Central Massachusetts; books, periodicals and catalogues.

HOURS: Yr T-Su 10-5

ADMISSION: $7, Children $3, Seniors $5

BRAINTREE

3792
Braintree Historical Society, Inc.
31 Tenney Rd, 02184; (p) (781) 848-1640; (f) (781) 380-0731; www.Braintree historical soc.org; (c) Norfolk

Private non-profit/ 1930/ staff: 1(f); 3(p); 27(v)/ members: 650

HISTORICAL SOCIETY: Collects, preserves, and interprets Old Braintree's history and culture for the education and enjoyment of present and future generations.

PROGRAMS: Annual Meeting; Community Outreach; Exhibits; Festivals; Guided Tours; Interpretation; Lectures; Living History; Publication; Research Library/Archives; School-Based Curriculum

COLLECTIONS: 50 portraits and paintings, 10,500 artifacts, 6,000 volumes, 1,050 maps, full run Braintree Newspaper, and 1,000 photographs.

HOURS: Yr Sa-W 10-4:30

BROOKLINE

3793
Antique Auto Museum of Massachusetts
15 Newton St, 02445; (p) (617) 522-6547; (f) (617) 524-0170; www.mot.org

Private non-profit/ 1952/ Museum of Transportation/ staff: 9(f); 12(p); 50(v)/ members: 799

Historic automobiles in the collection's original home on the grounds of Larz Anderson Park.

PROGRAMS: Annual Meeting; Community Outreach; Exhibits; Facility Rental; Family Programs; Guided Tours; Lectures; Research Library/Archives; School-Based Curriculum

COLLECTIONS: [1899-1942] Larz Anderson Motor Car Collection, pre-war automobiles, carriages, sleighs, motorcycles, bicycles; library and archives of Anderson artifacts.

HOURS: Yr

ADMISSION: $5, Children $3, Seniors $3; Under 6/Mbrs free

3794
John Fitzgerald Kennedy National Historic Site
83 Beals St, 02146; (p) (617) 566-7937; (f) (617) 730-9884; frla_kennedy_nhs@nps.gov; www.nps.gov/jof

1908/ National Park Service/ staff: 6(f)

COLLECTIONS: [1917] Early 20th century pieces original to family; photographs

HOURS: Seasonal

CAMBRIDGE

3795
Arthur and Elizabeth Schlesinger Library on the History of Women in America, The
3 James St, 02138 [Radcliffe College, 10 Garden St, 02138]; (p) (617) 495-8647; (f) (617) 496-8340; slref@Radcliffe.edu; www.Radcliffe.edu.Schles; (c) Middlesex

Private non-profit/ 1943/ Radcliffe College/ staff: 13(f); 7(p); 4(v)/ members: 15000/publication: *Newsletter*

RESEARCH CENTER: Books, manuscripts, periodicals, photographs, and oral histories document the social history of women in the U.S.

PROGRAMS: Community Outreach; Exhibits; Guided Tours; Lectures; Publication; Research Library/Archives

COLLECTIONS: [1850-present] Over 2000 manuscript collections, including the papers of Susan B. Anthony, Dorothy West, Julia Child, Amelia Earhart, and Betty Friedan; over 60,000 volumes of books on the social history of women in the U.S.; and over 400 periodicals.

HOURS: Yr M-F

3796
Cambridge Historical Commission
831 Massachusetts Ave, 02139; (p) (617) 349-3116; (f) (617) 349-6165; HistComm@ci.cambridge.ma.us; (c) Middlesex

1963/ City of Cambridge/ staff: 4(f); 3(p)

HISTORIC PRESERVATION AGENCY

PROGRAMS: Community Outreach; Exhibits; Interpretation; Lectures; Research Library/Archives

COLLECTIONS: [1860-present] An inventory with photos of 13,000 buildings compiled in 1964-1973; historic photos, surveys, maps, plans, and city documents; and information on individuals, groups, and companies.

HOURS: Yr M-F 8:30-5; Research hours T-F 9:30-11:30/2-4

3797
Cambridge Historical Society, The
159 Brattle St, 02138-3300; (p) (617) 547-4252; (f) (617) 661-1623; (c) Middlesex

Private non-profit/ 1905/ Board of Councillors/ staff: 2(p); 30(v)/ members: 450/publication: *Proceedings*

HISTORIC SITE; HISTORICAL SOCIETY; HISTORY MUSEUM; HOUSE MUSEUM: Presents educational programming related to the preservation and promotion of the history of Cambridge, and maintains the Hooper-Lee-

Nichols House and a research library.

PROGRAMS: Annual Meeting; Community Outreach; Concerts; Exhibits; Facility Rental; Garden Tours; Guided Tours; Interpretation; Lectures; Living History; Publication; Reenactments; Research Library/Archives

COLLECTIONS: [17th-20th c] Cambridge-related materials including books, manuscripts, photographs, ephemera, furniture, textiles, industrial products, and electronic media.

HOURS: Yr T-Th

ADMISSION: $5, Seniors $3

3798
Longfellow National Historic Site
105 Brattle St, 02138; (p) (617) 876-4491; (f) (617) 497-8718; www.nps.gov/long

Federal/ 1970/ National Park Service/ staff: 8(f); 4(v)/ members: 400/publication: *Longfellow House Bulletin*

HISTORIC SITE; HOUSE MUSEUM: Served as George Washington's headquarters from 1774-75 and was the home of poet Henry Wadsworth Longfellow from 1837-1882.

PROGRAMS: Community Outreach; Concerts; Exhibits; Festivals; Garden Tours; Guided Tours; Interpretation; Lectures; Publication; Research Library/Archives; School-Based Curriculum

COLLECTIONS: [1840s-1910s] Longfellow family papers and manuscripts, fine and decorative arts, Asian arts and a 10,000 volume historic library.

HOURS: Apr-Dec W-Su

3799
MIT Museum
265 Massachusetts Ave, 02139 [77 Massachusetts Ave, N52-2nd floor, 02139-4307]; (p) (617) 253-4444, (617) 253-5653; (f) (617) 253-8994; janep@mit.edu; web.mit.edu/museum/; (c) Middlesex

Private non-profit/ 1971/ Massachusetts Institute of Technology/ staff: 10(f); 5(p); 2(v)

HISTORY MUSEUM: Documents, interprets and communicates the activities and achievements of MIT and the worldwide impact of its innovation, particularly in science and technology.

PROGRAMS: Community Outreach; Exhibits; Facility Rental; Family Programs; Interpretation; Lectures

COLLECTIONS: [19th c-present] Scientific instruments and artifacts ; Architectural Collections; Hart Nautical Collections; and the Holography Collection.

HOURS: Yr T-F 10-5, Sa-Su

3800
Mount Auburn Cemetery
580 Mount Auburn St, 02138; (p) (617) 547-7105; (f) (617) 876-4405; friends@mtauburn.com; www.mtauburn.com; (c) Middlesex

Private non-profit/ 1831/ staff: 45(f); 5(p)/ members: 1000

GARDEN; HISTORIC SITE: First garden cemetery in the US.

PROGRAMS: Community Outreach; Elder's Programs; Garden Tours; Guided Tours; Inter-

pretation; Lectures; School-Based Curriculum

COLLECTIONS: [19th-20th c] 174 acres, including memorial art, architecture and horticulture collections; business papers, maps and ephemeral materials.

HOURS: Yr M-Su 8-5; M-Su 8-7 during daylight savings

ADMISSION: No charge

3801
Museum Loan Network
MIT, 265 Massachusetts Ave, N52-439, 02139-4307; (p) (617) 252-1888; (f) (617) 252-1899; loanet@mit.edu; www.loanet.mit.edu/web; (c) Middlesex

Private non-profit/ 1995/ staff: 3(f)

Awards grants to non-profit institutions in the US that are interested in borrowing or lending art works on a long-term basis.

COLLECTIONS: Online directory of objects available for long-term loan.

3802
Peabody Museum of Archaeology and Ethnology
Harvard University, 11 Divinity Ave, 02138; (p) (617) 496-1027; (f) (617) 495-7535; www.peabody.harvard.edu; (c) Middlesex

Private non-profit/ 1866/ President and Fellows of Harvard College/publication: *Corpus of Maya Hieroglyphic Inscriptions*

HISTORY MUSEUM: Preserves, interprets, exhibits, acquires, and makes accessible anthropological objects for teaching, research and public education.

PROGRAMS: Community Outreach; Exhibits; Facility Rental; Family Programs; Guided Tours; Lectures; Publication

COLLECTIONS: [Paleolithic-present] 450,000 catalogue records representing over 5 million objects including archaeological and ethnographic material from all regions of the world, over 1,200 linear feet of paper archives and 550,000 photographs.

HOURS: Yr M-Sa 9-5, Su 1-5

ADMISSION: $5, Children $3, Seniors $4; Sa 9-12 free

3803
Semitic Museum, Harvard University
6 Divinity Ave, 02138; (p) (617) 495-4363; (f) (617) 496-8904; davis4@fas.harvard.edu; www.fas.harvard.edu/~semitic; (c) Middlesex

Private non-profit/ 1889/ staff: 3(f); 6(p); 8(v)/ members: 153/publication: *Harvard Semitic Series; Harvard Semitic Monographs*

ARCHAEOLOGICAL SITE/MUSEUM: Conducts research, publications and exhibitions on the ancient Near East with Harvard University's Department of Near Eastern Languages and Civilizations.

PROGRAMS: Exhibits; Guided Tours; Lectures; Publication; Research Library/Archives

COLLECTIONS: [Bronze and Iron Ages] Over 40,000 ancient Near Eastern archaeological artifacts from Egypt, Syria-Palestine, Mesopotamia, Anatolia and Iran.

HOURS: Yr M-F

CENTERVILLE

3804
Centerville Historical Museum
513 Main St, 02632; (p) (508) 775-0331; (f) (508) 862-9211; chsm@capecod.net; (c) Barnstable

Private non-profit/ 1952/ Centerville Historical Society, Inc., Board of Trustees/ staff: 1(f)/ members: 203/publication: *The Chequaquet Log*

HISTORIC SITE; HISTORY MUSEUM; HOUSE MUSEUM: Collects, preserves, exhibits and interprets Centerville's past for the education and enjoyment of present and future generations.

PROGRAMS: Annual Meeting; Community Outreach; Concerts; Exhibits; Family Programs; Guided Tours; Interpretation; Lectures; Publication

COLLECTIONS: [18th-19th c] Tools, marine artifacts, decorative arts and textiles, including extensive costume and quilt collection; 1840 historic house with colonial kitchen; Crowell carved bird collection; Civil War collection; Dodge MacKnight paintings.

HOURS: Mid-June-mid-Sept W-Sa 1-5

ADMISSION: $3, Children $1, Seniors $2

CHATHAM

3805
Chatham Historical Society/Atwood House Musuem
347 Stage Harbor Rd, 02633 [PO Box 381, 02633]; (p) (508) 945-2493; (f) (508) 945-1205; chs@capecod.net; www.atwoodhouse.org; (c) Barnstable

Private non-profit/ 1924/ Executive Board/ staff: 1(p); 80(v)/ members: 990

HISTORIC PRESERVATION AGENCY; HISTORICAL SOCIETY; HISTORY MUSEUM; HOUSE MUSEUM: Preserves and records the history of Chatham and displays in its museum objects and artifacts; maintains the 1752 Atwood House.

PROGRAMS: Annual Meeting; Exhibits; Guided Tours; Interpretation; Lectures; Research Library/Archives; School-Based Curriculum

COLLECTIONS: [1750-present] Paintings of local scenes and persons, china, glassware, photographs, old letters, deeds, ships logs, account books.

HOURS: Mid-June-Sept T-F 1-4

ADMISSION: $3; Under 12 free

3806
Mayo House
540 Main St, 02633 [104 Crowell Rd, 02633]; (p) (508) 945-4084

1818/ staff: 1(p); 6(v)

HOUSE MUSEUM

COLLECTIONS: [19th c] Furnishings include original antiques and reproductions

HOURS: Seasonal

CHELMSFORD

3807
Chelmsford Historical Society
40 Byam Rd, 01824; (p) (978) 256-2311; (c) Middlesex

Private non-profit/ 1930/ staff: 10(v)/ members: 140

HISTORICAL SOCIETY; HISTORY MUSEUM; HOUSE MUSEUM: Stimulates interest in the history of Chelmsford; shows the manner of living during Chelmsford's development by collecting and preserving records of Chelmsford citizens and their accomplishments.

PROGRAMS: Annual Meeting; Elder's Programs; Exhibits; Family Programs; Film/Video; Garden Tours; Guided Tours; Living History; Research Library/Archives; School-Based Curriculum

HOURS: June-Sept, 2nd and 4th Su, 2-4

3808
Garrison House
105 Garrison Rd, 01824; (p) (978) 256-8832

HOUSE MUSEUM

CHESTNUT HILL

3809
Longyear Museum, Mary Baker Eddy Historic House
1125 Boylston St, 02467; (p) (800) 277-8943; (f) (617) 278-9003; letters@longyear.org; www.longyear.org; (c) Grafton; Merrimack

Private non-profit/ 1923/ Board of Trustees/ staff: 17(f); 5(p); 12(v)/ members: 4000/publication: *Longyear Historical Review*

HISTORIC SITE: Collects, preserves, and shares historical records of the life of Mary Baker Eddy and her students. Maintains 3 historic houses.

PROGRAMS: Concerts; Exhibits; Facility Rental; Film/Video; Guided Tours; Lectures; Publication; Research Library/Archives

COLLECTIONS: [1821-1892] Letters, books, periodicals, reminiscences, other documents, artifacts and artwork related to Mary Baker Eddy, her family and early Christian Scientists.

CHICOPEE

3810
Edward Bellamy Memorial Association
91-93 Church St, 01020; (p) (413) 594-6496; (c) Hampden

Private non-profit/ 1972/ Edward Bellamy Memorial Association, Inc./ staff: 1(p)/ members: 110

HISTORIC PRESERVATION AGENCY; HISTORIC SITE; HISTORICAL SOCIETY; HISTORY MUSEUM; HOUSE MUSEUM: Maintains the memory of Edward Bellamy, his life and his works; serves as a historical resource for the City of Chicopee.

PROGRAMS: Annual Meeting; Facility Rental; Film/Video; Guided Tours; Lectures; School-Based Curriculum

COLLECTIONS: [1880s] Over 5,000 items connected with the career of 19th c Utopian writer Edward Bellamy.

HOURS: Yr Daily 8-3:30, weekends by appt

ADMISSION: No charge

COHASSET

3811
Caleb Lothrop House
14 Summer St, 02025; (p) (718) 383-1434

Private non-profit/ 1821/ Cohasset Historical Society/ staff: 1(f)

COLLECTIONS: [19th c] Oil paintings, furniture; General archives plus archive of Cohasset theater history.

HOURS: Appt

3812
Captain John Wilson-David Nichols Historical House
2 Elm St, 02025 [14 Summer St, 02025]; (p) (781) 383-1434

Private non-profit/ 1810/ Cohasset Historical Society

COLLECTIONS: [Early 1800s] Home furnishings, kitchen ware, toys.

HOURS: Seasonal

3813
Cohasset Historical Society
14 Summer St, 02025; (p) (781) 383-1434; (c) Norfolk

Private non-profit/ 1928/ staff: 1(f); 50(v)/ members: 310

HISTORICAL SOCIETY: Preserves and presents the history of the Town of Cohasset. Maintains two seasonal (summer) museums, a headquarters house, archives and library.

PROGRAMS: Annual Meeting; Exhibits; Guided Tours; Lectures; Living History; Research Library/Archives; Theatre

COLLECTIONS: [19th-20th c] Houses, costumes, local artwork, maritime artifacts, general historical and documentary archives, all r

CONCORD

3814
Concord Museum
200 Lexington Rd, 01742 [PO Box 146, 01742]; (p) (978) 369-9763; (f) (978) 369-9660; cm1@concordmuseum.org; www.concordmuseum.org; (c) Middlesex

Private non-profit/ 1886/ Board of Governors/ staff: 9(f); 23(p); 250(v)/ members: 950

HISTORY MUSEUM: Collects, preserves and interprets objects made or used in the Concord area. Promotes understanding and appreciation of Concord's history and its relationship to the cultural history of the nation.

PROGRAMS: Exhibits; Facility Rental; Family Programs; Garden Tours; Guided Tours; Lectures; School-Based Curriculum

COLLECTIONS: [18th-19th c] Objects made or owned in Concord; includes Emerson's study, Thoreau's possessions, and a signal lantern associated with Paul Revere.

HOURS: Jan-Mar M-Sa 11-4, Su 1-4; Apr-Dec M-Sa 9-5, Su 12-5

ADMISSION: $7, Family $16, Children $3, Seniors $6

3815
Louisa May Alcott Memorial Association/Orchard House
399 Lexington Rd, 01742 [PO Box 343, 01742-0343]; (p) (978) 369-5617, (978) 369-4118; (f) (978) 369-1367; louisa@acunet.net; www.louisamayalcott.org; (c) Middlesex

Private non-profit/ 1911/ Louisa May Alcott Memorial Association/ staff: 5(f); 27(p); 64(v)/ members: 600

Preserves the Orchard House, the home of Louisa May Alcott and the setting for Little Women, as a museum and educational center.

PROGRAMS: Community Outreach; Exhibits; Facility Rental; Family Programs; Guided Tours; Interpretation; Lectures; Living History; Research Library/Archives; School-Based Curriculum

COLLECTIONS: [19th c] Objects owned by the Alcotts: furniture, artwork, textiles, ceramics/glassware, prints, photographs, documents and books.

HOURS: Apr-Oct M-Sa 10-4:30; Nov-Mar M-F 11-3, Sa 10-4:30, Su 1-4:30

ADMISSION: $5.50, Children $3

3816
Old Manse, The
269 Monument St, 01742 [PO Box 572, 01742-0572]; (p) (978) 369-3909; (f) (978) 287-6154; (c) Middlesex

Private non-profit/ 1939/ The Trustees of Reservations/ staff: 1(f); 18(p); 30(v)/ members: 20518/publication: *The Old Manse Muse*

GARDEN; HOUSE MUSEUM: Explores history through the eyes of its inhabitants, including Ralph Waldo Emerson and Nathaniel Hawthorne. House built in 1770 by Emerson's grandfathe with landscape and gardens.

PROGRAMS: Annual Meeting; Community Outreach; Elder's Programs; Family Programs; Garden Tours; Guided Tours; Interpretation; Lectures; Living History; Publication; Reenactments; School-Based Curriculum

COLLECTIONS: [1720-1920] Family furnishings, artifacts, books, paintings and etchings.

HOURS: Mid Apr-Oct M-Sa 10-5, Su and holidays 12-5

ADMISSION: $6, Student $5, Children $4, Seniors $5

3817
Ralph Waldo Emerson House
28 Cambridge Tpk, 01742; (p) (978) 369-2236; (c) Middlesex

Private non-profit/ 1829/ J.M. Forbes, RWE Memorial Association/ staff: 14(p)

HOUSE MUSEUM: Details the life and times of Ralph Waldo Emerson.

PROGRAMS: Guided Tours

COLLECTIONS: [19th c] Art and original memorabilia.

HOURS: Mid Apr-Oct Th-Sa 10-4:30, Su 2-4:30

3818
Wayside, The
455 Lexington Rd, 01742; (p) (508) 369-6975; www.visit-massachusetts.com/north/places/history.htm

CONTUIT

3819
Samuel B. Dottridge Homestead
1148 Main St, 02635 [PO Box 1484, Cotuit, 02635]; (p) (508) 428-0461, (508) 428-2199; jrg@care.com

1790/ staff: 45(v)

COLLECTIONS: [1850-1900] Scrimshaw, maritime, medical, oystering; Photographs, letters, postcards

HOURS: Seasonal

CONWAY

3820
Conway Historical Society
50 Main St, 01341; (c) Franklin

Private non-profit/ 1973/ Board of Trustees/ staff: 15(v)/ members: 50

HISTORIC PRESERVATION AGENCY; HISTORIC SITE; HISTORICAL SOCIETY; HISTORY MUSEUM; HOUSE MUSEUM: Collects and preserves historical materials and data relating to people, places, and events associated with Conway.

PROGRAMS: Annual Meeting; Community Outreach; Exhibits; Family Programs; Festivals; Guided Tours; Interpretation; Lectures; Living History; Research Library/Archives; School-Based Curriculum

COLLECTIONS: [19th-early 20th c] Agricultural and manufacturing items; household items, personal papers, diaries, letters, books, and photographs.

HOURS: July-Aug Su 1-4 and by appt

ADMISSION: No charge

CUMMINGTON

3821
Cummington Historical Commission
41 Main St, 01026 [PO Box 10, 01026]; (p) (413) 634-5527; (c) Hampshire

City/ Town of Cummington/ staff: 8(v)/publication: *Only One Cummington; Vital Records of Cummington*

HISTORICAL SOCIETY; HOUSE MUSEUM: Town historical commission and archives; runs Kingman Tavern Historical Museum.

PROGRAMS: Exhibits; Guided Tours; Publication; Research Library/Archives

COLLECTIONS: [1700s-present] Archives and artifacts.

HOURS: July-Aug Sa 2-5

ADMISSION: Donations accepted

3822
William Cullen Bryant Homestead
207 Bryant Rd, 01026-9639; (p) (413) 634-2244; (f) (413) 634-2244; bryanthomestead@ttor.org; www.thetrustees.org/TTOR/TT; (c) Hampshire

1927/ Trustees of Reservations/ staff: 4(p); 30(v)

HOUSE MUSEUM: Home of William Cullen Bryant—political figure, poet, traveler, editor of the New York Evening Post. A National Historic Landmark and a Massachusetts Archaeological/ Historic Landmark.

PROGRAMS: Exhibits; Facility Rental; Festivals; Guided Tours; Interpretation; Lectures

COLLECTIONS: [18th-19th c] Memorabilia from the Bryant and Snell families, many items from Bryant's New York estate, and pieces he collected on his travels to Europe and Asia.

HOURS: Landscape: Yr Daily; House: late June-early Sept F-Su 1-5, Mid Sept-mid Oct Sa-Su 1-5

ADMISSION: $5, Children $2.50, Seniors $4; Group rates; Landscape free

CUTTYHUNK ISLAND

3823
Cuttyhunk Historical Society
Lookout Rd, 02713; (p) (508) 626-6146, (617) 484-0613; ERTBELMONT@aol.com; (c) Dukes

Private non-profit/ 1978/ Board of Directors/ staff: 1(p); 30(v)/ members: 350

HISTORICAL SOCIETY; HISTORY MUSEUM: Exhibits related to Cuttyhunk history and the work of local artists.

PROGRAMS: Annual Meeting; Community Outreach; Exhibits; Lectures

COLLECTIONS: [1860-1950] Photographs and genealogical information on early island families, cemetery survey, material on former Coast Guard Station, and artifacts related to island life.

HOURS: July-Aug T, F-Sa 10:30-12:30/2-4, Th 10:30-12:30, Su 10-4

DANVERS

3824
Danvers Historical Society
9 Page St, 01923 [PO Box 381, 01923]; (p) (978) 777-1666; (f) (978) 777-5028; (c) Essex

Private non-profit/ 1889/ staff: 4(f); 4(p); 3(v)/ members: 670

GARDEN; HISTORIC SITE; HISTORICAL SOCIETY: Three historic sites, burial ground, museum office, community programs, special events, restored gardens and Derby Summer House (1794), a National Historic Landmark.

PROGRAMS: Annual Meeting; Community Outreach; Concerts; Elder's Programs; Exhibits; Facility Rental; Family Programs; Festivals; Garden Tours; Guided Tours; Interpretation; Lectures; School-Based Curriculum

COLLECTIONS: [19th-early 20th c] Clothing, textiles, ceramics, decorative arts and shoes.

HOURS: Yr M-F 9-2

ADMISSION: $5

3825
Glen Magna Farms
Ingersoll St, 01923 [Danvers Historical Society, PO Box 381, 01923]; (p) (978) 774-9165; (f) (978) 777-5681

3826
Rebecca Nurse Homestead
149 Pine St, 01923; (p) (978) 774-8799; www.rebeccanurse.org/; (c) Essex

Private non-profit/ 1974/ Danvers Alarm List Company, Inc./ staff: 3(p); 10(v)/ members: 500

HISTORIC SITE: A recreated 18th century militia company that maintains a 30 acre homestead including 3 major buildings and a graveyard owned by the Nurse family. In 1692 Rebecca Nurse was tried and executed for witchcraft.

PROGRAMS: Exhibits; Family Programs; Festivals; Guided Tours; Interpretation; Lectures; Living History; Reenactments; School-Based Curriculum

COLLECTIONS: [1678-1783] Domestic materials.

HOURS: June 15-Labor Day T-Su 1-4:30; Sept-Oct Sa-Su 1-4:30

DEDHAM

3827
Dedham Historical Society
612 High St, 02027 [PO Box 215, 02027-0215]; (p) (781) 326-1385; (f) (781) 326-5762; society@dedhamhistorical.org; www.dedhamhistorical.org; (c) Norfolk

Private non-profit/ 1859/ Board of Directors/ staff: 1(f); 2(p); 85(v)/ members: 979

ART MUSEUM; GENEALOGICAL SOCIETY; HISTORIC PRESERVATION AGENCY; HISTORICAL SOCIETY; HISTORY MUSEUM; RESEARCH CENTER: Focuses on artifacts, books and documents pertaining to Dedham, Old Dedham, Massachusetts and New England.

PROGRAMS: Annual Meeting; Community Outreach; Exhibits; Facility Rental; Guided Tours; Interpretation; Lectures; Research Library/Archives

COLLECTIONS: [16th-19th c] Dedham and Chelsea pottery, Katharine Pratt silver, paintings, antique furniture, photographs, pre-Columbian stone tools, local and Civil War artifacts, along with a historical and genealogical library.

HOURS: (Library) Yr T-F 9-4; (Museum) Yr T-F 12-4, Sa 1-4

ADMISSION: $2; Members free; Library $5

3828
Fairbanks House
511 E St, 02026-3060; (p) (781) 326-1170; (f) (781) 326-2147; curator@fairbankshouse.org; www.fairbankshouse.org; (c) Norfolk

Private non-profit/ 1903/ Fairbanks Family in America, Inc./ staff: 1(f); 16(v)/ members: 1250/publication: *The Courier*

HOUSE MUSEUM: Preserves, interprets and administers its ancestral home, the Fairbanks House, the oldest surviving timber frame house in North America.

PROGRAMS: Annual Meeting; Family Programs; Guided Tours; Living History; Publication; Research Library/Archives

COLLECTIONS: [18th-20th c] Fairbanks family related objects, furnishings, textiles, artwork, books, diaries, letters and photographs.

HOURS: May-Oct T-Sa 10-5, Su 1-5

ADMISSION: $5, Children $2

DEERFIELD

3829
Allen House, Historic Deerfield
104 Old Main St, 01342

1730

COLLECTIONS: [1945-1970] American furniture, paintings, needlework, ceramics, and other household objects.

3830
Ashley House, Historic Deerfield
129A Old Main St, 01342

1730

COLLECTIONS: [1733-1780] Furniture, ceramics glass, prints, and other household objects of 18th century Connecticut Valley

3831
Dwight House, Historic Deerfield
37A Old Main St, 01342

1725

COLLECTIONS: [1740-1790] Boston and Connecticut Valley furniture; early American paintings; English ceramics; Chinese export porcelain ; early American medical equipment.

3832
Frary House, Historic Deerfield
60A Old Main St, 01342

1740

COLLECTIONS: [1890-92] Furniture, furnishings, and paintings of the colonial period and of the Arts & Crafts movement.

3833
Hinsdale and Anna Williams House, Historic Deerfield
128 Old Main St, 01342

1749

COLLECTIONS: [1816-1838] Furniture, ceramics, household objects (including a rotary cookstove and a washing machine) of the early 19th century. Original c. 1817 wallpaper.

3834
Historic Deerfield, Inc.
The Street, 01342 [PO Box 321, 01342]; (p) (413) 774-5581; (f) (413) 775-7220; grace@historic-deerfield.org; www.historic-deerfield.org; (c) Franklin

Private non-profit/ 1952/ Trustees of Historic Deerfield/ staff: 55(f); 82(p); 250(v)/ members: 2000

ART MUSEUM; HISTORIC PRESERVATION AGENCY; HISTORIC SITE; HISTORY MUSEUM; HOUSE MUSEUM; RESEARCH CENTER: Historic Deerfield's 14 museum houses and the Flynt Collection of Early New England Life sit along a mile-long street in the village of Deerfield; interprets the artifactual, archeological and architectural history of early America.

PROGRAMS: Annual Meeting; Community Outreach; Concerts; Exhibits; Facility Rental; Family Programs; Guided Tours; Interpretation; Lectures; Research Library/Archives; School-Based Curriculum

COLLECTIONS: [1650-1850] More than 25,000 objects including New England furniture, English and Chinese ceramics, American and English textiles, and American silver and pewter.

HOURS: Yr M-Su 9:30-4:30
ADMISSION: $12, Children $5

3835
Pocumtuck Valley Memorial Association
10 Memorial St, 01342 [PO Box 428, 01342]; (p) (413) 774-7476; (f) (413) 774-5400; pvma@shaysnet.com; www.deerfield-ma.org; (c) Franklin

Private non-profit/ 1870/ Council of the Pocumtuck Valley Memorial Association/ staff: 7(f); 22(p); 65(v)/ members: 550

HISTORY MUSEUM: Collects, preserves and interprets the multicultural history of the Deerfield and Connecticut River Valleys by maintaining a museum, crafts center, research library and children's museum.

PROGRAMS: Annual Meeting; Community Outreach; Concerts; Elder's Programs; Exhibits; Festivals; Guided Tours; Lectures; Living History; Reenactments; Research Library/ Archives; School-Based Curriculum; Theatre

COLLECTIONS: [16th-20th c] Documents the entire history of the region. Includes Native American objects, furniture, paintings, photographs, textiles, musical instruments, military artifacts, dolls and toys.

HOURS: May-Oct Daily 9:30-4:30
ADMISSION: $6, Children $3; Under 6 free

3836
Reverend John Farwell Moors House, Historic Deerfield
103 Old Main St, 01342

1848

COLLECTIONS: [1848-1900] Late 19th century archaeological artifacts.

3837
Sheldon-Hawks House, Historic Deerfield
125 Old Main St, 01342

COLLECTIONS: [Late 18th c]

3838
Stebbins House, Historic Deerfield
88A Old Main St, 01342

1799

COLLECTIONS: [1790-1840] Furniture and ceramics of the Federal period; paintings by Erastus Salisbury Field.

3839
Wells-Thorne House, Historic Deerfield
52 Old Main St, 01342

1720

COLLECTIONS: [1720-1850] Furniture and furnishings, c. 1700-1850

3840
Wright House, Historic Deerfield
130 Old Main St, 01342

1824

COLLECTIONS: [1760-1830] The George Alfred Cluett Collection of Early American Furniture and Clocks, Chippendale and Federal from Boston, Newport, New York and Philadelphia, 130 pieces. Chinese export porcelain, 420 pieces.

DENNIS

3841
1736 Josiah Dennis Manse Museum
77 Nobscusset Rd, 02638 [PO Box 963, 02638]; (p) (508) 385-2232; (c) Barnstable

Joint/ 1967/ staff: 30(v)

HOUSE MUSEUM: The 1736 saltbox home of Reverend Josiah Dennis, the town's first minister.

PROGRAMS: Exhibits; Guided Tours; Living History

COLLECTIONS: [1639-1880s] Artifacts of early Dennis families, Nobscusset Indians, Dennis genealogy, maritime history, and a spinning/weaving exhibit.

HOURS: Mid-June-Sept T 10-12, Th 2-4
ADMISSION: Donations accepted

DORCHESTER

3842
Dorchester Historical Society
195 Boston St, 02125; (p) (617) 472-7543; (c) Suffolk

Private non-profit/ 1843/ staff: 3(p); 25(v)/ members: 250

HISTORICAL SOCIETY: Collects, preserves and interprets town history for a diverse urban community. Settled in 1630, Dorchester became a commercial farming district and then streetcar suburb annexed to Boston.

PROGRAMS: Annual Meeting; Community Outreach; Concerts; Exhibits; Guided Tours; Interpretation; Lectures; Research Library/ Archives

COLLECTIONS: [17th-19th c] Colonial, Federal and Victorian middle-class domestic furnishings and textiles from Dorchester displayed in period settings; archival collection includes Baker's Chocolate records. Houses include rare example of West Anglia house-framing.

HOURS: Yr, 2nd and 4th Sa , 2-4
ADMISSION: No charge

DRACUT

3843
Dracut Historical Society
1660 Lakeview Ave, 01826; (p) (978) 957-1701; bud@m1.sprynet.com; www.dracut-ma.com; (c) Middlesex

Private non-profit/ Board of Directors/ staff: 20(v)/ members: 197

HISTORICAL SOCIETY: Provides historical data and displays artifacts about the Town of Dracut—all housed in a 16-room museum.

PROGRAMS: Exhibits; Facility Rental; Guided Tours; Lectures

COLLECTIONS: [1701-present] Artifacts of Dracut and surrounding area pertaining to farming and textiles manufacturing.

DUXBURY

3844
Alden Kindred of America
105 Alden St, 02331 [PO Box 2754, 02331]; (p) (781) 934-9092; (f) (781) 792-3947; director@alden.org; www.alden.org; (c) Plymouth

Private non-profit/ 1906/ staff: 2(p); 20(v)/ members: 1500/publication: *Alden's Progress*

HOUSE MUSEUM: Family organization operating historic museum and conducting ancillary activities.

PROGRAMS: Annual Meeting; Community Outreach; Exhibits; Facility Rental; Festivals; Interpretation; Lectures; Publication; Reenactments; Research Library/Archives

COLLECTIONS: [Early colonial] Colonial furnishings and artifacts.

HOURS: May Daily 10-5

ADMISSION: $2.50, Children $1

3845
Captain Gershom Bradford House
931 Tremont St, 02332; (p) (781) 934-6106

3846
Duxbury Rural and Historical Society
685 Washington St, 02331 [PO Box 2865, 02331]; (p) (781) 934-6106; (f) (781) 934-5730; (c) Plymouth

Private non-profit/ 1883/ Executive Committee/ staff: 1(f); 3(p); 500(v)/ members: 662

HISTORICAL SOCIETY; HOUSE MUSEUM: Preserves the historical and natural resources of the Town of Duxbury and encourages awareness and appreciation of the town's heritage and rural character.

PROGRAMS: Annual Meeting; Community Outreach; Concerts; Exhibits; Family Programs; Guided Tours; Lectures; Research Library/Archives

COLLECTIONS: [Federal]

HOURS: June-Sept W- Su 1-4

ADMISSION: $5

3847
King Caesar House
King Caesar Rd, 02331 [PO Box 2865, 02331]; (p) (781) 934-6101, (781) 934-2378; www.visit-massachusetts.com/south/places/history.htm

EAST SANDWICH

3848
Benjamin Nye Homestead
85 Old County Rd, 02537 [PO Box 134, 02537]; (p) (508) 888-4213, (508) 888-2366

1685/ staff: 5(p); 8(v)

COLLECTIONS: Marine collection

HOURS: Seasonal

3849
Thorton W. Burgess Society
6 Discovery Hill Rd, 02537-1399; (p) (508) 888-6870; (f) (508) 888-1919; tburgess@capecod.net; www.thorntonburgess.org; (c) Barnstable

Private non-profit/ 1976/ Board of Trustees/ staff: 5(f); 20(p); 100(v)/ members: 1800

HISTORICAL SOCIETY: Offers exhibits and programs that "inspire reverence for wildlife and concern for the environment" based on the life and works of children's author Thornton Burgess.

PROGRAMS: Annual Meeting; Community Outreach; Exhibits; Family Programs; Festivals; Garden Tours; Interpretation; Living History; Research Library/Archives; School-Based Curriculum

COLLECTIONS: [18th-20th c] Books, manuscripts, artwork, memorabilia from life and books of author Thornton Burgess. Both living and non-living natural history collections that contain over 45,000 individual items.

HOURS: (Museum) Apr-Oct; (Nature Center) Yr M-Sa 10-4, Su 1-4, closed Su-M during winter

ADMISSION: Donations accepted

3850
Wing Fort House
69 Spring Hill Rd, 02537; (p) (508) 888-3591

EASTHAM

3851
Captain Edward Penniman House
Governor Prence Rd, [Cape Cod National Seashore, 99 Marconi, Wellfleet, 02667]; (p) (508) 255-3421; (f) (508) 240-3291

3852
Eastham Historical Society
Schoolhouse Rd, 02642 [PO Box 8, 02642]; (p) (508) 255-0788; (c) Barnstable

Private for-profit/ 1963/ Elected Officers and Board of Directors/ staff: 100(v)/ members: 320/publication: *History of Eastham; History of Town Burying Grounds*

HISTORICAL SOCIETY; HISTORY MUSEUM; HOUSE MUSEUM: Local history museums and historic buildings open to the public.

PROGRAMS: Annual Meeting; Exhibits; Interpretation; Lectures; Publication

COLLECTIONS: [17th-19th c] Furniture, clothing, tools, coins, Indian artifacts, buildings, genealogical collection and documents pertaining to Cape Cod families.

3853
Swift Daley House and Museum
Route 6, 02642 [PO Box 167, 02642]; (p) (508) 240-1247; (c) Barnstable

Private non-profit/ 1974/ Eastham Historical Society/ staff: 2(f); 10(v)/ members: 300

HISTORIC PRESERVATION AGENCY; HISTORIC SITE; HISTORICAL SOCIETY; HISTORY MUSEUM; HOUSE MUSEUM: Operates the 1741 Swift Daley House, a typical Cape Cod house, blacksmith shop, and a tool museum.

PROGRAMS: Annual Meeting; Exhibits; Guided Tours; Research Library/Archives

COLLECTIONS: [19th-20th c] Furniture, costumes, tools.

HOURS: July-Aug M-F 1-4

ADMISSION: Donations accepted

EDGARTOWN

3854
Doctor Daniel Fisher House
96 Main St, 02539 [Martha's Vineyard Preservation, PO Box 5277, 02539]; (p) (508) 627-4440; (f) (508) 627-8088; www.vineyard.net/org/mvpt

3855
Martha's Vineyard Historical Society
59 School St, 02539 [PO Box 1310, 02539]; (p) (508) 627-4441; (f) (508) 627-4436; mvhist@vineyard.net; www.marthasvineyard historg.org; (c) Dukes

Private non-profit/ 1922/ Board of Directors/ staff: 5(f); 5(p); 60(v)/ members: 1400/publication: *Dukes County Intelligencer; Vineyard Voices*

HISTORICAL SOCIETY; HISTORY MUSEUM; HOUSE MUSEUM; LIVING HISTORY/OUTDOOR MUSEUM; RESEARCH CENTER: Collects and preserves information and materials, maintains museums and libraries, disseminates historical information and stimulates interest in the island's heritage.

PROGRAMS: Annual Meeting; Community Outreach; Exhibits; Guided Tours; Interpretation; Lectures; Living History; Publication; Research Library/Archives; School-Based Curriculum

COLLECTIONS:[Prehistoric-present] Archives and artifacts, natural history and geology. Books, photos, maps, genealogy materials, maritime items, tools, costumes, textiles, furnishings, art, toys and musical instruments.

HOURS: Mid Oct-mid June W-F 1-4, Sa 10-4; Mid June-mid Oct T-Sa 10-5

ADMISSION: $6, Children $4; Under 6/Mbrs free

3856
Vincent House
Church St, 02539 [PO Box 5277, 02539]; (p) (508) 627-4440; (f) (508) 627-8088; www.vineyard.net/org/mvpt

ESSEX

3857
Cogswell's Grant, SPNEA
Spring St, 01929; (p) (978) 768-3632; www.spnea.org; (c) Essex

Private non-profit/ 1910/ Society for the Preservation of New England Antiquities

HISTORY MUSEUM; HOUSE MUSEUM

PROGRAMS: Guided Tours; Lectures

HOURS: June 1-Oct 15 W-Su 11-5

ADMISSION: $6; SPNEA Mbrs/Town residents free

3858
Essex Historical Society and Shipbuilding Museum
28 & 66 Main St, 01930 [66 Main St, 01930]; (p) (978) 768-7541; (f) (978) 768-2541; (c) Essex

Private non-profit/ 1976/ Board of Directors/ staff: 3(p); 10(v)/ members: 600

HISTORIC SITE; HISTORICAL SOCIETY; HISTORY MUSEUM: Gathers, records and preserves the history of the Town of Essex with attention to the shipbuilding industry and its role in the development of the American fishing schooner.

PROGRAMS: Annual Meeting; Exhibits; Facility Rental; Family Programs; Guided Tours; Interpretation; Lectures; Research Library/Archives; School-Based Curriculum

COLLECTIONS: [19th-20th c] Documents, photographs, objects and information relating to the general history of the Town of Essex as well as its shipbuilding industry and the vessels built there.

HOURS: May-Oct T-Su 10-5; Nov-Apr Sa-Su 10-5 or by appt

ADMISSION: $4, Children $2.50, Seniors $3

FAIRHAVEN

3859
Coggeshall Museum Memorial House
6 Cherry St, 02719 [6 Cherry St, 02719]; (p) (508) 993-4877

FALMOUTH

3860
Falmouth Historical Society
55-65 Palmer Ave, 02541 [PO Box 174, 02541]; (p) (508) 548-4857; (f) (508) 540-0968; FHSoc@juno.com; www.falmouth historicalsociety.org; (c) Barnstable

Private non-profit/ 1900/ Board of Directors/ staff: 1(f); 2(p); 50(v)/ members: 800

HISTORIC SITE; HISTORICAL SOCIETY; HISTORY MUSEUM; HOUSE MUSEUM: Operates a museum and archives of Falmouth history and sponsors other activities that promote knowledge and awareness of local history.

PROGRAMS: Community Outreach; Exhibits; Guided Tours; Lectures; Research Library/Archives; School-Based Curriculum

COLLECTIONS: [18th-19th c] Documents and objects relating to Falmouth history, its involvement in whaling, salt making, the Revolutionary War and War of 1812, along with furnishings typical of a 1790 house on Cape Cod.

HOURS: June-Sept T-Sa 10-4

ADMISSION: $4

FITCHBURG

3861
Fitchburg Historical Society
50 Grove St, 01420 [PO Box 953, 01420]; (p) (978) 345-1157; (f) (978) 345-2229; (c) Worcester

Private non-profit/ 1892/ Board of Trustees/Staff/ staff: 1(f); 1(p); 6(v)/ members: 450

HISTORICAL SOCIETY: Collects, preserves and exhibits materials illustrating the history of Fitchburg for the purpose of promoting interest and research on the city.

PROGRAMS: Annual Meeting; Exhibits; Film/Video; Guided Tours; Lectures; Research Library/Archives; School-Based Curriculum

COLLECTIONS: [19th-early 20th c] Papers, photographs, industrial archives and machines, decorative arts, ceramics and textiles.

HOURS: Yr M-Th

FOXBOROUGH

3862
Foxborough Historical Commission
20 South St, 02035 [40 S St, 02035]; (p) (508) 543-1248; (c) Norfolk

City/ 1967/ Board of Selectmen/ staff: 14(v)

HISTORY MUSEUM: Preserves historical assets and displays artifacts and documents pertaining to Foxborough's past at Memorial Hall.

PROGRAMS: Elder's Programs; Exhibits; Film/Video; Guided Tours; Lectures; Research Library/Archives; School-Based Curriculum

COLLECTIONS: [18th-20th c] Civil War Memorial/Town Museum with artifacts from the straw hat era and other industries, 1800s fire apparatus, school memorabilia, tools, oil lamps, post office and Indian artifacts displays.

HOURS: Yr W 7-9; 2nd

3863
Foxborough Historical Society, Inc.
Boyden Library, 02035 [PO Box 450, 02035]; (p) (508) 543-1248; godinpaul@aol.com

Private non-profit/ 1898/ Board of Directors/ staff: 9(v)/ members: 100

HISTORICAL SOCIETY: Assists the Historical Commission of the Town of Foxborough in the preservation, promotion and development of the historical assets of the town.

PROGRAMS: Annual Meeting; Community Outreach; Elder's Programs; Family Programs; Lectures

HOURS: Jan-May, Sept-Nov, every 4th T, 7:30-9

FRAMINGHAM

3864
Framingham Historical Society
16 Vernon St, 01703 [PO Box 2032, 01703-2032]; (p) (508) 872-3780; townonline.koz.com/visit/framhistsoc/; (c) Middlesex

Private non-profit/ 1888/ Board of Directors/ staff: 3(p); 138(v)/ members: 524

HISTORICAL SOCIETY: Fosters an understanding and appreciation of Framingham's cultural heritage through acquisition, preservation, interpretation, exhibition and publication of materials that reflect the town's prehistoric and historic development.

PROGRAMS: Annual Meeting; Community Outreach; Exhibits; Guided Tours; Interpretation; Lectures; Research Library/Archives; School-Based Curriculum

COLLECTIONS: [Prehistoric-present] Maps, photographs, clothing, textiles, decorative arts, Native American objects, ceramics, period furniture, domestic and agricultural tools, and Japanese art objects.

HOURS: Yr W-Th 10-4, Sa 10-1

ADMISSION: Donations requested

GEORGETOWN

3865
Georgetown Historical Society
East Main St, 01833 [PO Box 376, 01833]; (c) Essex

Private non-profit/ 1960/ Board of Officers and Directors/ staff: 40(v)/ members: 120

HISTORICAL SOCIETY; HOUSE MUSEUM: Preserves early local history.

PROGRAMS: Exhibits; Guided Tours; Lectures

COLLECTIONS: [17th-20th c] Artifacts related to the history of Georgetown and its shoe industry.

HOURS: July-Oct Su 2-5; May-Nov special tours by appt

ADMISSION: Donations accepted

GLOUCESTER

3866
Beauport, SPNEA
The Sleeper-McCann House, 75 Eastern Point Blvd, 01930; (p) (978) 283-0800; www.spnea.org; (c) Essex

Private non-profit/ 1907/ Society for the Preservation of New England Antiquities

HOUSE MUSEUM: Fantasy house of 40 rooms overlooking Gloucester Harbor. Created by Henry Davis Sleeper, an interior designer and collector of the 1920s and 1930s.

PROGRAMS: Guided Tours; Lectures

COLLECTIONS: [19th-20th c] Antiques and reused architectural elements.

HOURS: May 15-Sept 12 M-F 10-5; Sept 15-Oct 15 M-Su 10-5

ADMISSION: $10, Student $3, Children $3, Seniors $5.50; SPNEA Mbrs/Town residents free

3867
Cape Ann Historical Association
27 Pleasant St, 01930; (p) (978) 283-0455; (f) (978) 283-4141; www.cape-ann.com/histori-calmuseum; (c) Essex

1873/ Board of Managers/ staff: 4(f); 4(p); 30(v)/ members: 1700

ART MUSEUM; HISTORICAL SOCIETY; HISTORY MUSEUM; HOUSE MUSEUM; RESEARCH CENTER: Promotes Cape Ann history and art; collects and preserves information and artifacts; and encourages community involvement.

PROGRAMS: Annual Meeting; Community Outreach; Exhibits; Lectures; Research Library/Archives

COLLECTIONS: [18th-20th c] Fine arts, decorative arts, fisheries and maritime objects, granite quarrying objects, books, primary source materials, and photographs.

HOURS: Jan, Mar-Dec T-Sa 10-5

3868
Gloucester Adventure, Inc.
4 Harbor Loop, Fitz Hugh Lane House, 01931 [PO Box 1306, 01931]; (p) (978) 281-8079; (f) (978) 281-2393; www.schooner-adventure.org

Private non-profit/ 1988/ staff: 1(f); 3(p); 150(v)/ members: 500/publication: The Adventure Queen of the Windjammers

HISTORIC SITE; HISTORY MUSEUM; LIVING HISTORY/OUTDOOR MUSEUM: Preserves the historic fishing schooner Adventure, serves as a community educational resource and operates the vessel at sea as a symbol of maritime history.

PROGRAMS: Annual Meeting; Community Outreach; Concerts; Elder's Programs; Exhibits; Facility Rental; Family Programs; Guided Tours; Interpretation; Lectures; Living History; Publication; Research Library/Archives; School-Based Curriculum

COLLECTIONS: [Early 20th c] 122 foot knock-about fishing schooner, historic film footage of Gloucester fisherman at work, historic fishing and maritime artifacts, videotaped oral histories.

HOURS: Apr-Oct Sa-Su 10-2; M-F by appt

ADMISSION: Donations accepted

3869
Hammond Castle Museum
80 Hesperus Ave, 01930; (p) (978) 283-7673; (f) (978) 283-1643; (c) Essex

Private non-profit/ 1930/ Hammond Museum, Inc./ staff: 4(f); 1(p); 70(v)/publication: *Hammond Recipe Book and Biography*

ART MUSEUM; GARDEN; HISTORIC SITE; HOUSE MUSEUM: The home of famous American inventor John Hays Hammond, Jr. The medieval castle fortress contains his collections and his laboratories.

PROGRAMS: Community Outreach; Concerts; Exhibits; Family Programs; Festivals; Garden Tours; Guided Tours; Living History; Publication; Reenactments; School-Based Curriculum; Theatre

COLLECTIONS: [300 BC-20th c] Ancient Roman tombstones, medieval decorative arts, early American furniture.

HOURS: Yr Daily

ADMISSION: $6, Student $5

3870
Sargent House Museum
49 Middle St, 01930; (p) (978) 281-2432; (f) (978) 281-2432; (c) Essex

Private non-profit/ 1919/ staff: 4(p); 15(v)/ members: 150

HISTORIC SITE; HOUSE MUSEUM: Example of high-style Georgian architecture, the 1782 house was built for philosopher, writer and activist Judith Sargent Murray (1751-1820). Her husband, Rev. John Murray, was the founder of Universalism in America.

PROGRAMS: Annual Meeting; Community Outreach; Concerts; Exhibits; Guided Tours; Lectures; Research Library/Archives; School-Based Curriculum

COLLECTIONS: [1760-1820] Focuses on early New England fine and decorative arts, maritime artifacts. Works by artist John Singer Sargent (1856-1925), a descendant of Murray's.

HOURS: Mem Day-Columbus Day F-M

GREENFIELD

3871
Association for Gravestone Studies
278 Main St, Ste 207, 01301; (p) (413) 772-0836; (f) (413) 772-0836; admin@gravestonestudies.org; www.gravestonestudies.org; (c) Franklin

Private non-profit/ 1977/ Board of Trustees/ staff: 4(p); 20(v)/ members: 1200/publication: *AGS Quarterly; Markers: The AGS Annual Journal*

HISTORIC PRESERVATION AGENCY; LIVING HISTORY/OUTDOOR MUSEUM: Fosters appreciation of the cultural significance of gravestones and burial grounds through their study and preservation.

PROGRAMS: Annual Meeting; Exhibits; Guided Tours; Lectures; Publication; Research Library/Archives

COLLECTIONS: [17th-20th c] Local cemeteries and historical graveyards.

HOURS: Yr M-F 10-3

3872
Historical Society of Greenfield
43 Church St, 01302 [PO Box 415, 01302]; (p) (413) 774-3663; (c) Franklin

Private non-profit/ 1907/ staff: 12(v)/ members: 155

HISTORICAL SOCIETY: Promotes historical, educational, literary and patriotic activities; acquires, preserves and exhibits objects of historical value related to the history of Greenfield.

PROGRAMS: Annual Meeting; Exhibits; Lectures; Research Library/Archives

COLLECTIONS: [1790-present] Industrial artifacts from die factories, railroad artifacts, decorative arts, advertising ephemera and dinosaur footprints.

HOURS: Oct-early Nov Su 12-4

ADMISSION: No charge

3873
Museum of Our Industrial Heritage, Inc.
77 Petty Plain Rd, 01301; (p) (413) 773-8838; (c) Franklin

Private non-profit/ 1996/ Board of Directors/ staff: 1(f); 20(v)/ members: 50

HISTORY MUSEUM: Emphasizes tool making and metal cutting from Native Americans to present. Greenfield was the birthplace of American cutlery industry and metal threading industries, now a plastics manufacturing center.

PROGRAMS: Annual Meeting; Community Outreach; Elder's Programs; Exhibits; Interpretation; Lectures

COLLECTIONS: [Late 18th c-present] Eight room house diplays tools, machines, photographs, artifacts of local firms, documentary tapes and a display of area during World War II.

HOURS: Varies seasonally; usually Th, Su pm

ADMISSION: Donations

GROTON

3874
Governor Boutwell House
172 Main St, 01450 [PO Box 202, 01450]; (p) (978) 448-2046; (f) (978) 448-5589

1851/ staff: 5(v)

COLLECTIONS: [1655-present] Revolutionary War; Civil War; Published books only.

HOURS: Seasonal

3875
Groton Historical Society
172 Main St, 01450 [PO Box 202, 01450]; (p) (978) 448-2046; (f) (978) 448-5589; artbeal@juno.com; (c) Middlesex

Private non-profit/ 1894/ Board of Trustees/ staff: 3(v)/ members: 120/publication: *George S. Boutwell: Human Rights Advocate; Groton Houses; and others*

HISTORIC PRESERVATION AGENCY; HISTORIC SITE; HISTORICAL SOCIETY; HISTORY MUSEUM: Located at the Governor Boutwell House Museum.

PROGRAMS: Annual Meeting; Exhibits; Festivals; Guided Tours; Lectures; Publication

COLLECTIONS: [18th-19th c] Victorian house, furnishings, toys, Revolutionary and Civil War artifacts, and historical artifacts pertaining to Groton's history.

HOURS: June-Sept Su 2-4 and by appt

ADMISSION: No charge

HADLEY

3876
Porter-Phelps Huntington Foundation, Inc.
130 River Dr, 01035; (p) (413) 584-4699; (c) Hampshire

Private non-profit/ 1948/ Board of Directors/ staff: 5(p); 14(v)/ members: 470

GARDEN; HISTORIC SITE; HISTORY MUSEUM; HOUSE MUSEUM: Preserves and provides access to its collection as an educational and cultural resource.

PROGRAMS: Community Outreach; Concerts; Exhibits; Facility Rental; Family Programs; Festivals; Garden Tours; Guided Tours; Interpretation; Lectures; Reenactments; Research Library/Archives; School-Based Curriculum; Theatre

COLLECTIONS: [1700-1965] House, gardens and agricultural property; furniture, textiles, works of art, books, papers, photographs and related items.

HOURS: Mid May-mid Oct Sa-W 1-4:30

ADMISSION: $4, Children $1

HARVARD

3877
Fruitlands Museum
102 Prospect Hill Rd, 01451; (p) (978) 456-3924; (f) (978) 456-8910; msaalfield@fruitlands.org; www.fruitlands.org; (c) Worcester

Private non-profit/ 1914/ staff: 12(f); 45(p)/ members: 700

HISTORY MUSEUM: Four museums of American art and history: Shaker museum, Indian museum, Fruitlands Farmhouse and Picture Gallery set on 218 acres of diverse ecosystems. Focuses on the natural and human history of the landscape.

PROGRAMS: Community Outreach; Concerts; Elder's Programs; Exhibits; Facility Rental; Family Programs; Festivals; Guided Tours; Interpretation; Lectures; Living History; Research Library/Archives; School-Based Curriculum

COLLECTIONS: Shaker furniture, textiles, Hudson River School paintings, American primitive portraiture and Native American material culture.

HOURS: mid-May-Oct M-Su 10-5

ADMISSION: $6, Student $4, Children $3, Seniors $5

3878
Harvard Historical Society
215 Still River Rd, 01451 [PO Box 542, 01451]; (p) (978) 456-8285; (c) Worcester

Private non-profit/ 1897/ staff: 15(v)/ members: 200/publication: *The Harvard Album; Directions of a Town*

HISTORICAL SOCIETY: Three buildings on a 4.5 acre plot, a 1832 former Baptist church, 1850s farmers cottage, and old summer house.

PROGRAMS: Annual Meeting; Concerts; Exhibits; Facility Rental; Interpretation; Lectures; Publication; Research Library/Archives

COLLECTIONS: [19th-20th c] Furniture, costumes, textiles, books, documents, paintings, glass and metal ware, farm implements, local family histories, musical instruments, Shaker artifacts and other local artifacts and memorabilia.

HOURS: Yr 3rd Su 3-5; Special

HARWICH

3879
Harwich Historical Society
80 Parallel St, 02645; (p) (508) 432-8089; hhs@capecodhistory.org; www.capecodhistory.org/harwich; (c) Barnstable

Private non-profit/ 1955/ Harwich Historical Society/ staff: 2(p); 50(v)/ members: 400

HISTORICAL SOCIETY; HISTORY MUSEUM: Operates a museum at Brooks Academy that collects, preserves and interprets Harwich's past for the education and enjoyment of present and future generations.

PROGRAMS: Annual Meeting; Community Outreach; Exhibits; Family Programs; Festivals; Film/Video; Interpretation; Lectures; Research Library/Archives; School-Based Curriculum; Theatre

COLLECTIONS: [1694-present] Artifacts, photographs, textiles, manuscripts and historical archives, art, maps, genealogical and library resources.

HOURS: June-Sept W-Sa 1-4 and by appt; Oct-May by appt only

ADMISSION: Donations accepted

HAVERHILL

3880
John Greenleaf Whittier Homestead
SR 110, 01833 [150 Whitter Rd, 01830]; (p) (978) 373-3979

1698/ Board of Trustees/ staff: 3(v)

COLLECTIONS: [1700-1800] Original Family furniture

HOURS: Yr

HINGHAM

3881
Old Ordinary
21 Lincoln St, 02360; (p) (617)749-0013; www.key-biz.com/ssn/Hingham/ordinary.html

HOLDEN

3882
Holden Historical Society, Inc.
1157 Main St, 01520 [PO Box 421, 01520-0421]; (p) (508) 829-5576; (c) Worcester

1967/ staff: 20(v)/publication: *Pictorial History of Holden*

HISTORICAL SOCIETY: Sponsors public programs and trips; collects, preserves and exhibits memorabilia and artifacts; makes its collections available for genealogical and historical research.

PROGRAMS: Annual Meeting; Exhibits; Lectures; Publication; Research Library/Archives

COLLECTIONS: [1875-present] Artifacts, photographs, manuscripts, printed material, and ephemera relating to the history of Holden.

HOURS: Yr Sa 9-12

ADMISSION: No charge

HOLYOKE

3883
Wistariahurst Museum
238 Cabot St, 01040; (p) (413) 534-2216; (f) (413) 534-2344; www.holyoke.org/mainpage.htm; (c) Hampden

City/ Holyoke Historical Commission/ staff: 2(f); 30(v)

HOUSE MUSEUM: Encourages and promotes an understanding of the history of Holyoke, including the manufacturing and working class who lived there.

PROGRAMS: Concerts; Exhibits; Family Programs; Guided Tours; Interpretation; Research Library/Archives; School-Based Curriculum

COLLECTIONS: [Early 20th c] Furniture, decorative arts (1870-1930), textiles and archival materials.

HOURS: Yr W, Sa-Su

ADMISSION: $5, Student $3, Seniors $3; Under 12 free

HULL

3884
Hull Lifesaving Museum Inc., The Museum of Boston Harbor Heritage
117 Nantasket Ave, 02045 [PO Box 221, 02045]; (p) (781) 925-5433; (f) (781) 925-0992; hullmuse@channel1.com; www.bostonharborheritage.org; (c) Plymouth

Private non-profit/ 1978/ staff: 5(f); 15(p); 100(v)/ members: 650/publication: *Log, Messenger Line*

HISTORIC SITE; LIVING HISTORY/OUTDOOR MUSEUM; RESEARCH CENTER

PROGRAMS: Annual Meeting; Community Outreach; Concerts; Elder's Programs; Exhibits; Family Programs; Festivals; Film/Video; Guided Tours; Interpretation; Lectures; Publication; Research Library/Archives

COLLECTIONS: [early 1900s] Artifacts from the Massachusetts Humane Society, US Lifesaving Service, US Coast Guard and Lighthouse service, related photos, literature and a fleet of 17 traditional boats.

HOURS: Yr Sept-June F-Su 10-4, July-Aug W-Su 10-4

ADMISSION: $2, Seniors $1.50; Under 18 free

HYDE PARK

3885
City of Boston, Office of the City Clerk, Archives and Records Management Division
30 Millstone Rd, 02136-2324; (p) (617) 364-8679; (f) (617) 361-5729; archives@ci.boston.ma.us; www.ci.boston.ma.us/archivesandrecords; (c) Suffolk

City/ 1988/ City of Boston, Office of the City Clerk/ staff: 4(f)

LIBRARY AND/OR ARCHIVES: Preserves the history of Boston municipal government since 1630, provides day-to-day access to this heritage, and assists city departments with cost-effective records management practices.

PROGRAMS: Research Library/Archives

COLLECTIONS: [1822-present] Records of continuing value created by or for city departments. Includes records of annexed towns of Brighton, Charlestown, Dorchester, Hyde Park, Roxbury and West Roxbury.

IPSWICH

3886
Ipswich Historical Society
54 S Main St, 01938; (p) (978) 356-2811; (f) (978) 356-2817; ihs@gis.net; (c) Essex

Private non-profit/ 1890/ Ipswich Historical Society/ staff: 1(f); 1(p); 50(v)/ members: 600

HISTORICAL SOCIETY; HOUSE MUSEUM: Operates two museums and offers programs. Owns John Whipple House Museum (1655), a National Historic Landmark with early furnishings, John Herd Museum (1800), China Trade and Arthur W. Dow collections.

PROGRAMS: Annual Meeting; Community Outreach; Concerts; Exhibits; Family Programs; Festivals; Garden Tours; Guided Tours; Interpretation; Lectures; Research Library/ Archives; School-Based Curriculum

COLLECTIONS: [17th-19th c] Decorative arts and furnishings from Massachusetts Bay Colony, American handmade bobbin lace, maritime and religious library, Native American artifacts, dolls, toys, carriages, gardens, and artwork by Arthur Wesly Dow.

HOURS: Early May-mid Oct W-Sa 10-4, Su 1-4

ADMISSION: $7, Children $3

3887
John Whipple House, Ipswich Historical Society
1 S Village Green, 01938

1655

Includes a garden designed by Arthur Shurcliff and replanted by garden scholar Isadore Smith, known as Ann Leighton.

COLLECTIONS: [Colonial] American handmade bobbin-pillow lace; period furnishings and decorative arts.

KINGSTON

3888
Bradford House
Landing Rd, 02364; (p) (781) 585-6300

LANCASTER

3889
Lancaster Historical Commission
Town Hall, 01523 [PO Box 351, 01523]; (p) (978) 368-1162; (f) (978) 368-8486; (c) Worcester

City/ 1964/ Town of Lancaster/ staff: 2(p)/publication: *The Narrative of the Captivity and Restoration of Mrs. Mary Rowlandson*

HISTORICAL SOCIETY: Preserves, protects and develops Lancaster's historical and archaeological assets. Conducts research for places of historical and archaeological value. Coordinates with the Massachusetts State Historical Commission to preserve historic material.

PROGRAMS: Publication; Research Library /Archives

COLLECTIONS: [1860-1930] Photographs: The Alice Greene Chandler and James Macdonald Collections; The Lancaster Iconographic Collection; letters and early records of military service.

HOURS: Yr T 10-2

ADMISSION: No charge

LAWRENCE

3890
Immigrant City Archives
6 Essex St, 01840; (p) (978) 686-9230; (f) (978) 975-2154; archives@ma.ultranet.com; (c) Essex

Private non-profit/ 1978/ staff: 2(f); 1(p); 50(v)/ members: 400/publication: *Lawrence, MA*

HISTORIC SITE; HISTORICAL SOCIETY: Collects, preserves and interprets the history of the people of Lawrence.

PROGRAMS: Annual Meeting; Community Outreach; Exhibits; Guided Tours; Lectures; Publication; Research Library/Archives; School-Based Curriculum

COLLECTIONS: [1847-present] Books, manuscripts, photographs, taped oral histories, maps, city records and memorabilia relating to many ethnic groups.

3891
Lawrence Heritage State Park
1 Jackson St, 01840; (p) (978) 794-1655; (f) (978) 794-9241; (c) Essex

State/ 1986/ Massachusetts Dept of Environmental Management, Forests and Parks System/ staff: 5(f); 3(p); 2(v)

HISTORIC SITE; HISTORY MUSEUM; STATE PARK: Exhibits history of Lawrence, programs offered. Also includes two riverfront parks and canal walk.

PROGRAMS: Concerts; Exhibits; Facility Rental; Festivals; Film/Video; Guided Tours; Interpretation; School-Based Curriculum

COLLECTIONS: [1845-present] Artifacts from Lawrence's industrial and social history.

HOURS: Yr Daily 9-4

ADMISSION: No charge

LENOX

3892
Edith Wharton Restoration at the Mount
2 Plunkett St, 01240 [PO Box 974, 01240]; (p) (413) 637-1899, (888) 637-1902; (f) (413) 637-0619; admin@edithwharton.org; www.edithwharton.org; (c) Berkshire

Private non-profit/ 1980/ staff: 5(f); 7(p); 5(v)/publication: *The Mount: Home of Edith Wharton*

HISTORIC SITE; HOUSE MUSEUM: Preserves and restores Edith Wharton's home, The Mount, and has established it as a cultural and educational center dedicated to the study and promotion of Edith Wharton, and to what she described as "the complex art of civilized living."

PROGRAMS: Exhibits; Garden Tours; Guided Tours; Lectures; Publication; Theatre

COLLECTIONS: [Late 19th-early 20thc] Portraits, personal items, original plans, elevations and drawings of The Mount, first editions by Edith Wharton, letters and correspondence.

HOURS: May Sa-Su, Mem Day-Oct Daily 9-3

ADMISSION: $6, Children $4.50, Seniors $5.50; Under 12 free

3893
Lenox Historical Society
1803 Main St, Lenox Academy Bldg, 01240 [PO Box 1856, 01240]; (p) (413) 637-1634; (f) (413) 637-0222; chazma@ugernet.net; (c) Berkshire

Private non-profit/ 1980/ Board of Directors/ staff: 15(v)/ members: 150

HISTORIC PRESERVATION AGENCY; HISTORIC SITE; HISTORICAL SOCIETY; HISTORY MUSEUM; RESEARCH CENTER: Collects, records and preserves artifacts, paper documents and histories of the people of Lenox.

PROGRAMS: Annual Meeting; Community Outreach; Exhibits; Family Programs; Festivals; Guided Tours; Lectures; Living History; School-Based Curriculum

COLLECTIONS: [Late 18th c-present] Artifacts and paper documents.

HOURS: June-Aug daily 12-3

ADMISSION: No charge

LEXINGTON

3894
Hancock-Clarke House
36 Hancock St, 02173; (p) (617) 861-0928

1738/ staff: 14(p)

COLLECTIONS: [1775-mid 1800s] Mulliken clocks, Pitcairn pistols, William Diamond's drum, period furnishings.; Interior details in the construction of the house itself.

HOURS: Seasonal

3895
Lexington Historical Society
1332 Massachusetts Ave, 02420 [PO Box 514, 02420]; (p) (781) 862-1703, (781) 862-2465; (f) (781) 862-9338; lexhissc@tiac.net; (c) Middlesex

Private non-profit/ 1886/ staff: 58(p); 60(v)

HISTORIC SITE; HISTORICAL SOCIETY: Studies the history of Lexington and preserves knowledge, documents, photographs, artifacts and landmarks.

PROGRAMS: Annual Meeting; Exhibits; Facility Rental; Family Programs; Festivals; Garden Tours; Guided Tours; Interpretation; Lectures; Research Library/Archives; School-Based Curriculum

HOURS: Hancock-Clarke House and Munroe Tavern: Apr-Oct M-Sa 10-5, Su 1-5; (Buckman Tavern) Late Mar-Nov M-Sa 10-5, Su 1-5

ADMISSION: $5, Children $3

3896
Museum of Our National Heritage
33 Marrett Rd, 02420 [PO Box 519, 02420-0519]; (p) (781) 861-6559; (f) (781) 861-9846; info@monh.org; www.mnh.org; (c) Middlesex

Private non-profit/ 1971/ Supreme Council, Ancient and Accepted Scottish Rite, Northern Masonic Jurisdiction, USA/ staff: 21(f); 16(p); 73(v)/ members: 293/publication: *Frank Lloyd Wright and George Mann Niedecken: Prairie School Collaborators; George Washington: American Symbol*

HISTORY MUSEUM: Offers changing exhibitions on American history and culture; and programming throughout the year.

PROGRAMS: Concerts; Exhibits; Facility Rental; Family Programs; Festivals; Guided Tours; Lectures; Publication; Research Library/Archives; School-Based Curriculum

COLLECTIONS: [1700-present] Freemasonry; the Revolutionary War; and general Americana. Research fields include: history of Freemasonry, symbolism of Masonic and fraternal organizations, and patriotic iconography.

HOURS: Yr M-Sa 10-5, Su 12-5

ADMISSION: Donations accepted

LINCOLN

3897
Codman House, SPNEA
The Grange, Codman Rd, 01773; (p) (781) 259-8843; www.spnea.org; (c) Middlesex

Private non-profit/ 1740/ Society for the Preservation of New England Antiquities

HISTORIC PRESERVATION AGENCY; HOUSE MUSEUM: Home to the last generations of Boston's Codman family. Reflects the cosmopolitan taste of 18th-19th c Bostonians through its furnishings, art, and landscaped gardens.

PROGRAMS: Facility Rental; Festivals; Garden Tours; Guided Tours; School-Based Curriculum

COLLECTIONS: [1740-1960s] Art and objects from America and Europe, especially France.

HOURS: June 1-Oct 15 W-Su 11-5

ADMISSION: $4, Student $3.50, Seniors $3.50; SPNEA Mbrs/Town residents free

3898
DeCordova Museum and Sculpture Park
51 Sandy Pond Rd, 01773; (p) (781) 259-8355; (f) (781) 259-3650; www.decordova.org; (c) Middlesex

Private non-profit/ 1950/ DeCordova and Dana Museum and Sculpture Park/ staff: 40(f); 10(p); 60(v)/ members: 4500

ART MUSEUM: Dedicated to the exhibition, interpretation and collection of modern and contemporary American art, with a particular focus on the New England region; year-round outdoor sculpture park.

PROGRAMS: Annual Meeting; Community Outreach; Exhibits; Facility Rental; Family Programs; Festivals; Guided Tours; Interpretation; Lectures; School-Based Curriculum

COLLECTIONS: [1940-present] Paintings, graphics, sculpture, photography and mixed media works by New England artists.

HOURS: Yr T-Su 11-5

ADMISSION: $6, Student $4, Children $4, Seniors $4; Under 5/Mbrs/Town residents free

3899
Gropius House, SPNEA
68 Baker Bridge Rd, 01773; (p) (781) 259-8098; www.spnea.org; (c) Middlesex

Private non-profit/ 1938/ Society for the Preservation of New England Antiquities

HISTORIC SITE; HISTORY MUSEUM; HOUSE MUSEUM: Family home of Walter Gropius, founder of the German design school known as Bauhaus.

PROGRAMS: Family Programs; Garden Tours; Guided Tours; Interpretation; Lectures

COLLECTIONS: [1938-1969] Bauhaus furniture designed by Marcel Breuer and modern art.

HOURS: June 1-Oct 15 W-Su 11-5; Oct 16-May 31 Sa-Su 11-5

ADMISSION: $8, Student $2.50, Seniors $4.50; SPNEA Mbrs/Town residents free

LITTLETON

3900
Littleton Historical Society, Inc.
4 Rogers St, 01460 [PO Box 721, 01460]; (p) (978) 486-8202; (f) (978) 486-8202; (c) Middlesex

Private non-profit/ 1894/ staff: 15(v)/ members: 326

HISTORICAL SOCIETY; HISTORY MUSEUM: Collects and preserves manuscripts, printed books, pamphlets, historical facts and relics, biographical anecdotes, and stimulates research in local history.

PROGRAMS: Annual Meeting; Exhibits; Family Programs; Research Library/Archives

COLLECTIONS: [17th c-present] Artifacts, written material and genealogical library relating to Littleton's past.

HOURS: Yr W 1-4, second Su 2-4

ADMISSION: No charge

LONGMEADOW

3901
Richard Salter Storrs House, The
697 Longmeadow St, 01106; (p) (413) 567-3600

1786/ staff: 1(p)

COLLECTIONS: [18th, 19th & some 20th c] Many tools representing farming and carpen-

try, some elementary school books, etc. furniture, china, glass.; Genealogies, account books, no reproductions of any furniture or artifacts.

LOWELL

3902
American Textile History Museum
491 Dutton St, 01854; (p) (978) 441-0400; (c) Middlesex

Private non-profit/ 1960/ staff: 27(f); 20(p)/ members: 4/publication: The Overshot

HISTORY MUSEUM: Dedicated to the study, preservation, and exhibition of the story of textile manufacture in America and to the conservation of textile materials.

PROGRAMS: Annual Meeting; Community Outreach; Exhibits; Facility Rental; Festivals; Guided Tours; Interpretation; Lectures; Publication; Research Library/Archives; School-Based Curriculum

COLLECTIONS: [1770-1950] American textile materials, including over 200 industrial machines, 1,000 pre-industrial tools, 5,000,000 fabric samples and 40,000 photographs.

HOURS: Yr M-Sa 9-5

ADMISSION: $5

3903
New England Quilt Museum
18 Shattuck St, 01852; (p) (978) 452-4207; (f) (978) 452-5405; nequiltmuseum@erols.com; www.nequiltmuseum.org; (c) Middlesex

Private non-profit/ 1987/ Board of Directors/ staff: 2(f); 5(p); 80(v)/ members: 950/publication: The NEQM Quilts

ART MUSEUM: Preserves and interprets antique, traditional and contemporary quilt making in New England.

PROGRAMS: Annual Meeting; Community Outreach; Elder's Programs; Exhibits; Festivals; Guided Tours; Interpretation; Lectures; Publication; Research Library/Archives

COLLECTIONS: [1800-present] Antique, traditional and contemporary quilts and coverlets, and quilt related objects.

HOURS: Yr T-Sa 10-4; May-Dec Su 12-4

ADMISSION: $4, Student $3, Seniors $3

3904
Tsongas Industrial History Center
400 John St, 01852; (p) (978) 970-5080; (f) (978) 970-5085; peter_oconnell@uml.edu; www.uml.edu/tsongas; (c) Middlesex

State/ 1991/ University of Massachusetts, Lowell and Lowell National Historical Park/ staff: 11(f); 20(p); 2(v)/ members: 2

HISTORIC SITE: Interprets the causes and consequences of the American Industrial Revolution to 50,000 children and teachers annually.

PROGRAMS: Community Outreach; Concerts; Exhibits; Facility Rental; Family Programs; Festivals; Guided Tours; Interpretation; Lectures; Living History; School-Based Curriculum

COLLECTIONS: [1820-1920] Mill and canal plans, mill records, diaries, letters, broadsides and other manuscripts, and photographs about Lowell and other textile cities.

3905
Whistler House Museum of Art
243 Worthen St, 01852; (p) (978) 452-7641; (f) (978) 454-2421; tomedmonds@whistlerhouse.org; www.whistlerhouse.org; (c) Middlesex

Private non-profit/ 1878/ Lowell Art Association, Inc./ staff: 2(f); 4(p); 10(v)/ members: 450

ART MUSEUM; HOUSE MUSEUM: Displays the works of contemporary regional artists. Home of the Lowell Committee, which celebrates Jack Kerouac and promotes the author's birth city. Also the birthplace of James McNeill Whistler.

PROGRAMS: Exhibits; Facility Rental; Guided Tours; Lectures

COLLECTIONS: [19th-20th c] American art, with special emphasis on the artists of New England.

LYNN

3906
Lynn Museum
125 Green St, 01902; (p) (781) 592-2465; (f) (781) 592-0012; (c) Essex

Private non-profit/ 1897/ staff: 3(f); 5(p)/ members: 900

HISTORY MUSEUM: Operates a research library and museum with permanent and changing exhibits.

PROGRAMS: Annual Meeting; Elder's Programs; Exhibits; Family Programs; Guided Tours; Lectures; Research Library/Archives; School-Based Curriculum

COLLECTIONS: [17th-20th c] Artifacts, furniture, fine and decorative arts, manuscripts, published works and ephemera connected with all aspects of Lynn's history.

HOURS: Yr M-F 9-4, Sa 1-4

ADMISSION: $4

MANCHESTER

3907
Trask House
10 Union St, 01944; (p) (508) 526-7230

3908
Manchester Historical Society
10 Union St, 01944; (p) (978) 526-7230; (f) (978) 526-0060; manchesterhistorical@prodigy.net; www.manchesterhistorical.org; (c) Essex

Private non-profit/ 1886/ Executive Board/ staff: 1(f); 20(v)/ members: 461

HISTORICAL SOCIETY; HISTORY MUSEUM: Preserves Manchester's heritage.

PROGRAMS: Community Outreach; Exhibits; Family Programs; Guided Tours; Interpretation; Lectures; Research Library/Archives; School-Based Curriculum

COLLECTIONS: [1823-present] Locally-made furniture and artifacts; archives of local history with photos and genealogies.

HOURS: Yr M-F 10-12; July-Aug Sa 10-4, Su 12-4

MARBLEHEAD

3909
Jeremiah Lee Mansion
161 Washington St, 01945 [170 Washington St, 01945]; (p) (781) 631-1768; (c) Essex

Private non-profit/ 1909/ Marblehead Historical Society/ staff: 4(p); 75(v)/ members: 1200

GARDEN; HISTORIC SITE; HISTORY MUSEUM; HOUSE MUSEUM: Late colonial Georgian mansion with original rococo interior carving and newly restored exterior simulating stone. Rare original hand-painted English scenic wallpaper, furnishings, decorative arts and garden.

PROGRAMS: Annual Meeting; Community Outreach; Exhibits; Facility Rental; Family Programs; Garden Tours; Guided Tours; Interpretation; Lectures; School-Based Curriculum

COLLECTIONS: [17th-20th c] Folk art, textiles, ceramics, furniture, woodwork, portraits, maritime paintings, maritime and military artifacts, toys, women's and children's shoes.

HOURS: June-mid Oct T-Sa 10-4, Su 1-4

ADMISSION: $5, Student $4.50, Seniors $4.50; Under 13 free

3910
King Hooper Mansion
8 Hooper St, 01945; (p) (781) 631-2608; (f) (781) 639-7890

1728/ staff: 3(f)

Promotes the art of members.

COLLECTIONS: [1728-1790] Marblehead pottery collection; furniture.; General history.

HOURS: Yr

3911
Marblehead Historical Society and J.O.J. Frost Folk Art Gallery
170 Washington St, 01945; (p) (781) 631-1768; (f) (781) 631-0971; (c) Essex

Private non-profit/ 1898/ Marblehead Historical Society/ staff: 3(f); 2(p); 300(v)/ members: 1200

GENEALOGICAL SOCIETY; HISTORICAL SOCIETY; RESEARCH CENTER: Preserves and perpetuates local history through collections representing Marblehead's maritime and social history.

PROGRAMS: Annual Meeting; Community Outreach; Concerts; Exhibits; Facility Rental; Family Programs; Interpretation; Lectures; Research Library/Archives; School-Based Curriculum

COLLECTIONS: [18th-19th c] Documents, photographs, decorative arts, portraits and maritime paintings, folk art, children's objects, maritime, shoemaking and military artifacts, and 20th century folk art by JOJ Frost.

HOURS: (Galleries) Yr T-Sa 10-4, Su 1-4; (Office and research

MARSHFIELD

3912
Historic Winslow House Association
Webster at Careswell, 02050 [PO Box 531, 02050]; (p) (781) 837-5753; www.marshfield.net/history/winslow.shtml; (c) Plymouth

Private non-profit/ 1920/ Board of Governors/ staff: 125(v)/ members: 400

GENEALOGICAL SOCIETY; HISTORIC SITE; HOUSE MUSEUM: Maintains, collects, interprets and preserves the 1699 Isaac Winslow House (built by the grandson of a Mayflower descendant) a 13 room mansion restored to the Jacobean and Georgian periods. Site of Daniel Webster's law office, a National Historic Landmark.

PROGRAMS: Annual Meeting; Community Outreach; Concerts; Exhibits; Facility Rental; Family Programs; Festivals; Garden Tours; Guided Tours; Interpretation; Lectures; Living History; Reenactments; Research Library/Archives; School-Based Curriculum

COLLECTIONS: [1690-1710; 1750-1820] Early 17th and 18th century antique furnishings, furniture, paintings and artifacts of the Federal Period.

HOURS: Mid June-mid Oct W-Su 11-3 by appt

ADMISSION: $3, Children $0.50

MATTAPOISETT

3913
Mattapoisett Museum and Carriage House
5 Church St, 02739; (p) (508) 758-2844; (c) Plymouth

Private non-profit/ 1958/ Mattapoisett Historical Society, Inc./ staff: 1(p); 60(v)/ members: 400/publication: *Mattapoisett and Old Rochester*

HISTORICAL SOCIETY; HISTORY MUSEUM: Creates and fosters an interest in the history, settlement and development of Mattapoisett and surrounding areas; maintains a museum and promotes historical research.

PROGRAMS: Annual Meeting; Community Outreach; Exhibits; Guided Tours; Lectures; Publication; Research Library/Archives

COLLECTIONS: [1750-1950] Antique farming equipment, period furniture, papers, books, clothing, whaling and shipbuilding memorabilia.

HOURS: July-Aug T-Sa 1-4:30

ADMISSION: $2.50

MEDFORD

3914
Royal House Museum
15 George St, 02155; (p) (617) 396-9032

1732/ staff: 1(p); 25(v)

COLLECTIONS: [1775] New England furniture and decorative arts; fragment of 18th c. summer house restored in garden; history of Royal House Association; documents.

HOURS: Seasonal

MIDDLEBORO

3915
Massachusetts Archaeology Society, Inc. and Robbins Museum of Archaeology
17 Jackson St, 02346 [PO Box 700, 02346]; (p) (508) 947-9005; (c) Plymouth

Private non-profit/ 1939/ Board of Trustees/ staff: 1(p); 9(v)/ members: 2191/publication: *Bulletin of the Massachusetts Archaeology Society/The Round Robbins*

ARCHAEOLOGICAL SITE/MUSEUM: Preserves, studies and interprets Massachusetts' archaeological heritage.

PROGRAMS: Annual Meeting; Exhibits; Lectures; Publication; Research Library/Archives; School-Based Curriculum

COLLECTIONS: [Prehistory] Over 70,000 artifacts such as stone and bone tools, projectile points, horticultural tools, pipes, beads, stone and ceramic vessels, and ethnographic objects.

HOURS: Yr W 10-3, Th 1-4

ADMISSION: Donations requested

MILTON

3916
Captain Forbes House Museum
215 Adams St, 02186; (p) (617) 696-1815; (f) (617) 696-1815; www.key-biz.com/ssn/Milton/Forbes.html; (c) Norfolk

Private non-profit/ 1984/ staff: 1(f); 2(p); 90(v)/ members: 300/publication: *Forbes House Jottings*

HOUSE MUSEUM: Concentrates on 19th c America through the Forbes family's activities, interests, and tastes.

PROGRAMS: Community Outreach; Exhibits; Facility Rental; Festivals; Guided Tours; Interpretation; Lectures; Publication; Research Library/Archives; School-Based Curriculum

COLLECTIONS: [19th c] Forbes family furnishings and personal objects, including the Abraham Lincoln collection of Mary Bowditch Forbes.

HOURS: Yr Su,T-Th 1-4

ADMISSION: $3, Student $1.50, Seniors $1.50

3917
Milton Historical Society
Canton Ave, 02186 [239 Thacher St, 02186]; (p) (617) 333-9700; (c) Norfolk

Private non-profit/ 1904/ staff: 5(v)/ members: 250

HISTORIC SITE; HISTORICAL SOCIETY; HISTORY MUSEUM

PROGRAMS: Annual Meeting; Community Outreach; Elder's Programs; Exhibits; Facility Rental; Festivals; Guided Tours; Interpretation; Lectures; Research Library/Archives; School-Based Curriculum

COLLECTIONS: [18th c] Furniture, publications, and artifacts from the Revolutionary War Period

HOURS: Yr Sa 2-4

ADMISSION: No charge

MONTEREY

3918
Bidwell House, The
100 Art School Rd, 01245 [PO Box 537, 01245]; (p) (413) 528-6888; (f) (413) 528-6888; (c) Berkshire

Private non-profit/ 1990/ Board of Directors/ staff: 2(f); 3(v)/ members: 287

HISTORIC SITE; HOUSE MUSEUM; LIVING HISTORY/OUTDOOR MUSEUM: To interpret the natural and cultural history of the Berkshires, from 1750 to the present, through the presentation and preservation of the resources of the Bidwell House Museum: its land, architecture, and its collections.

PROGRAMS: Community Outreach; Concerts; Exhibits; Festivals; Garden Tours; Guided Tours; Interpretation; Lectures; Living History; Reenactments; Research Library/Archives; School-Based Curriculum; Theatre

COLLECTIONS: [1750-1850] Furniture, domestic and agricultural tools, lighting devices, textiles, including early samplers, nineteenth century whole cloth coverlets, hand-woven linens and needlework, 150 pieces of redware and slipware, 19th c delph ware.

HOURS: May-Oct 15 T-Su 11-4

ADMISSION: $5, Children $1, Seniors $4

NANTUCKET

3919
1800 House, Nantucket Historical Association
8 Mill St, 02554 [PO Box 1016, 02554]

1800

3920
Egan Institute of Maritime Studies
The Coffin School, 4 Winter St, 02554; (p) (508) 228-2505; (f) (508) 228-7069; eganinst@nantucket.net; www.marinehome center.com/eganinstitute; (c) Nantucket

Private non-profit/ 1996/ Board of Directors/ staff: 2(f); 4(p)

ART MUSEUM; HISTORIC SITE; HISTORY MUSEUM: Advances the scholarly study and appreciation of the history, literature, art and maritime traditions of Nantucket Island.

PROGRAMS: Concerts; Exhibits; Facility Rental; Family Programs; Film/Video; Guided Tours; Interpretation; Lectures; Research Library/Archives

COLLECTIONS: [19th-20th c] Paintings, sculpture, decorative arts, ship models, archive of documents and library relating to Nantucket's maritime history.

HOURS: Late May-mid Oct daily 1-5

3921
Greater Light, Nantucket Historical Association
8 Howard St, 02554 [PO Box 1016, 02554]

1790

COLLECTIONS: [Early 20th c]

3922
Hadwen House, Nantucket Historical Association
96 Main St, 02554 [PO Box 1016, 02554]

1845

COLLECTIONS: [Mid-19th c] High style Boston & Rhode Island furniture, local portraiture

3923
Jethro Coffin House-The Oldest House
16 Sunset Hill, 02554 [PO Box 1016, 02554]

1686

COLLECTIONS: [17th c] Late 17th, early 18th century vernacular furniture, 18th century loom

3924
Macy-Christian House, Nantucket Historical Association
12 Liberty St, 02554 [PO Box 1016, 02554]

1745

COLLECTIONS: [Late 18th c; 1930 colonial revival] Collection of 18th c. island made furniture, and eclectic colonial revival furniture and arts.

3925
Nantucket Historical Association
15 Broad St, 02554 [PO Box 1016, 02554]; (p) (508) 228-1894; (f) (508) 228-5618; infon-ha@capecod.net; (c) Nantucket

Private non-profit/ 1894/ Board of Trustees/ staff: 18(f); 30(p); 50(v)/ members: 2600/publication: Historic Nantucket

HISTORICAL SOCIETY: The principle repository of Nantucket history, with extensive archives, collections of historic properties, and art and artifacts that broadly illustrate the island's past.

PROGRAMS: Annual Meeting; Community Outreach; Concerts; Exhibits; Guided Tours; Lectures; Publication; Research Library/ Archives

COLLECTIONS: [18th-20th c] Most of the definitive aspects of Nantucket history are represented, including whaling, land and sea transportation, Quaker religion, fine and decorative arts, farming, commerce and architecture.

HOURS: Apr, Nov Sa-Su 11-3; May, Oct Daily 11-3; June-Sept Daily 10-5

ADMISSION: $10, Children $5;

3926
Nantucket Maria Mitchell Association
2 Vestal, 1 Vestal, Milk St & Washington St, 02554 [2 Vestal St, 02554]; (p) (508) 228-2896; jfinger@mmo.org; www.mmo.org; (c) Nantucket

Private non-profit/ 1902/ staff: 10(f); 22(p); 50(v)/ members: 2700/publication: Comet, Annual Report

GARDEN; HOUSE MUSEUM; RESEARCH CENTER: The association uses Nantucket's unique natural environment and builds upon the scientific achievements of Maria Mitchell, America's first woman astronomer.

PROGRAMS: Annual Meeting; Community Outreach; Exhibits; Family Programs; Guided Tours; Interpretation; Lectures; Publication; Research Library/Archives

COLLECTIONS: [19th-20th c] Historic house from 1830, science museum, aquarium, observatory and library.

HOURS: June-Sept T-Sa 10-4

ADMISSION: $3, Children $1

3927
Thomas Macy House, Nantucket Historical Association
99 Main St, 02554 [PO Box 1016, 02554]

1770

COLLECTIONS: [1950s] An eclectic collection of Continental and American furniture, Japanese prints.

NEW BEDFORD

3928
New Bedford Whaling Museum
18 Johnnycake Hill, 02740; (p) (508) 997-0046; (f) (508) 997-0018; whaling@ma.ultra net.com; www.whalingmuseum.org; (c) Bristol

Private non-profit/ 1903/ Old Dartmouth Historical Society/ staff: 18(f); 12(p); 130(v)/ members: 2500

HISTORY MUSEUM: Preserves and presents local history, art and culture.

PROGRAMS: Annual Meeting; Concerts; Exhibits; Facility Rental; Family Programs; Lectures; Research Library/Archives; School-Based Curriculum

COLLECTIONS: [1830-1900] Artifacts related to whaling, local art, history, ethnology, harpoons and other whaling tools, ship models, objects of scrimshaw, paintings, prints, photographs, lamps, navigational instruments and ships' logs.

HOURS: Yr M-Su 9-5

3929
Rotch-Jones-Duff House and Garden Museum, Inc.
396 County St, 02740-4934; (p) (508) 997-1401; (f) (508) 997-6846; (c) Bristol

Private non-profit/ 1985/ staff: 4(f); 3(p); 60(v)/ members: 620

GARDEN; HOUSE MUSEUM: This Greek Revival mansion (1834) chronicles the economic, social, religious and political evolution of New Bedford. Urban gardens include a formal rose parterre garden, a cutting garden and wildflower walk

PROGRAMS: Concerts; Exhibits; Facility Rental; Festivals; Guided Tours; Lectures

COLLECTIONS: [1834-1981] Decorative arts, furnishings and accessories, costumes, family diaries and correspondence.

NEWBURY

3930
Coffin House, SPNEA
14 High Rd, Route 1A, 01951; (p) (978) 462-2634; www.spnea.org; (c) Essex

Private non-profit/ 1654/ Society for the Preservation of New England Antiquities

HOUSE MUSEUM

PROGRAMS: Exhibits; Family Programs; Guided Tours; Lectures; School-Based Curriculum

COLLECTIONS: 18th-20th c household objects and 19th c. French wallpaper.

HOURS: June 1-Oct 15 Sa-Su 11-5

ADMISSION: $4; SPNEA Mbrs/Town residents free

3931
Spencer-Peirce-Little Farm, SPNEA
5 Little's Lane, 01951; (p) (978) 462-2634; www.spnea.org

Private non-profit/ 1690/ Society for the Preservation of New England Antiquities

COLLECTIONS: [18th-20th c] 18th-20th c objects owned by Little family

HOURS: June 1-Oct 15 W-Su 11-5

ADMISSION: $5; SPNEA Mbrs/Town residents free

NEWBURYPORT

3932
Customs House Maritime Museum/Lowell's Boat Shop
25 Water St, 01950; (p) (978) 462-8681, (978) 388-0162; (f) (978) 462-8740; nms@shore.net; (c) Essex

Private non-profit/ 1969/ Newburyport Maritime Society/ staff: 2(f); 3(p); 35(v)/ members: 250

Preserves Newburyport's 1835 granite custom house as a local maritime history museum. Preserves Amesbury's 1860s Lowell's Boat shop as a traditional working shop and dory museum.

PROGRAMS: Annual Meeting; Exhibits; Family Programs; Lectures; School-Based Curriculum

COLLECTIONS: [1790-1900] Half-hull models, ship models, paintings, charts, maps, navigation equipment, manuals, maritime logs, journals, manuscripts, uniforms, trade items, early photographs, wooden boats, patterns, tools.

HOURS: (Custom House Maritime Museum) Apr-Dec M-Sa 10-4, Su 1-4; (Lowell's Boat Shop) Sept-June W-Sa 10-3; July-Aug Daily 10-3

ADMISSION: $3, Children $2, Seniors $2

3933
Historical Society of Old Newbury/Cushing House Museum
98 High St, 01950; (p) (978) 462-2681; (f) (978) 462-0134; hson4@juno.com; (c) Essex

Private non-profit/ 1877/ staff: 1(f); 2(p); 12(v)/ members: 500/publication: *98 High Street*

GARDEN; HISTORICAL SOCIETY; HOUSE MUSEUM: Operates the Cushing House Museum as well as maintaining and interpreting the history of Newburyport and the Newburys for future generations.

PROGRAMS: Annual Meeting; Elder's Programs; Exhibits; Garden Tours; Guided Tours; Lectures; Publication; Research Library/Archives

COLLECTIONS: [1820-1850] Silver, needlework, antique fans, American and imported furniture, clocks, portraits, hatboxes and toys.

HOURS: May-Oct T-F 10-4, Sa 12-3

ADMISSION: $4

NEWTON

3934
Jackson Homestead, Newton's Museum and Historical Society
527 Washington St, 02458; (p) (617) 552-7238; (f) (617) 552-7228; mlatimer@ci.newton.ma.us; www.ci.newton.ma.us/jackson; (c) Middlesex

City; Private non-profit/ 1950/ Newton Historical Society/ staff: 1(f); 5(p); 50(v)/ members: 900

HISTORICAL SOCIETY; HISTORY MUSEUM: Explores Newton's heritage through exhibitions and programs, including its role as an early railroad suburb and the Homestead's role as a station on the Underground Railroad.

PROGRAMS: Community Outreach; Concerts; Elder's Programs; Exhibits; Family Programs; Lectures; Research Library/Archives; School-Based Curriculum

COLLECTIONS: [19th-20th c] Manuscripts, maps, photographs, prints, paintings, furniture, decorative arts, costumes, textiles, household equipment, tools, toys and games.

HOURS: Yr M-Th 12-5; Sept-May Su 2-5

ADMISSION: $2, Student $1, Seniors $1; No charge for members

NORTH ADAMS

3935
Freel Library, Massachusetts College of Liberal Arts
Ste 9250 Church St, 01247; (p) (413) 662-5325; (f) (413) 662-5286; (c) Berkshire

State/ 1894/ staff: 9(f); 7(p)

LIBRARY AND/OR ARCHIVES: Maintains college archives and collects materials related to history of North Adams and vicinity. Staff works with students on area history projects.

PROGRAMS: Exhibits; Research Library/Archives

COLLECTIONS: [20th c] College archives, history of the college, North Adams and Berkshire County, including documents, photographs, books, tapes and artifacts.

NORTH ANDOVER

3936
North Andover Historical Society
153 Academy Rd, 01845; (p) (978) 686-4035; (f) (978) 686-6616; (c) Essex

Private non-profit/ 1913/ staff: 1(f); 2(p); 30(v)/ members: 376

GARDEN; HISTORIC SITE; HISTORICAL SOCIETY; HISTORY MUSEUM; RESEARCH CENTER: Collects, preserves and interprets historical materials of local and regional significance. The society owns and operates five buildings on two sites, exhibits in two galleries and operates a research center.

PROGRAMS: Annual Meeting; Community Outreach; Exhibits; Family Programs; Festivals; Guided Tours; Interpretation; Lectures; Research Library/Archives; School-Based Curriculum

COLLECTIONS: [17th-20th c] Decorative arts, personal artifacts, clothing, archives, photographs, manuscripts and tools.

HOURS: Yr T-F 10-4 and by appt

ADMISSION: $3, Student $1, Seniors $2

3937
Parson Barnard House, North Andover Historical Society
179 Osgood St, 01845

1715

HOUSE MUSEUM: Sits on land originally owned by Simon and Anne Bradstreet. The house tour features an innovative interpretation of architectural elements devised by Yale professor, Abbot Lowell Cummings.

COLLECTIONS: [1715-1830] Furniture from 1670 to 1830; textiles; household accessories.

3938
Stevens-Coolidge Place
139 Andover St, 01845; (p) (978) 682-3580, (978) 356-4351; (f) (978) 356-2143; www.thetrustees.org/TTOR/TT; (c) Essex

1962/ Trustees of Reservations

GARDEN; HISTORIC SITE; HOUSE MUSEUM: Summer home of John Gardner Coolidge and his wife, Helen Stevens Coolidge. Farm house and gardens remodeled between 1914-1945 by colonial revival architect, Joseph Everett Chandler.

PROGRAMS: Community Outreach; Garden Tours; Guided Tours

COLLECTIONS: [19th-20th c] House contains collections from Europe, the Far East and America. There is a serpentine brick wall copied from Thomas Jefferson's (Coolidge's great great grandfather) wall at the University of Virginia. Period gardens and greenhouse.

HOURS: Gardens: Yr Daily; House: Mid May-early Oct Su 1-5, June-Aug W 2-4

ADMISSION: $4, Children $1; Group rates; Gardens free

NORTH GRAFTON

3939
Willard House and Clock Museum
11 Willard St, 01536-2011; (p) (508) 839-3500; (f) (508) 839-3599; willardhouse@erols.com; www.nawcc.org/museums/willard/willard.html

1718/ Board of Trustees/ staff: 2(f); 1(p); 5(v)

COLLECTIONS: [1750-1800] Willard clocks; two John Ritto Penniman portraits dated 1804.; documents relating to the Willard family and clocks; Simon Willard's original patent; original Jefferson drawing.

HOURS: Y; T-Sa 10-4; Su; T-Sa 10-4; Sun 1-5

NORTH OXFORD

3940
Clara Barton Birthplace Museum
68 Clara Barton Rd, 01537 [PO Box 356, 01537]; (p) (508) 987-5375, (508) 987-2056; (f) (508) 987-2002; cbdiabetes@aol.com

1818/ staff: 2(p); 1(v)

Birthplace of Clara Barton, founder of the American Red Cross.

COLLECTIONS: [1821-1888] Furnishings from Barton Family; quilt signed by Civil War officers as gift to Barton.; Letters.

NORTHAMPTON

3941
Historic Northampton
46 Bridge St, 01060-2428; (p) (413) 584-6011; (f) (413) 584-7956; mailbox@historic-northampton.org; www.historic-northampton.org; (c) Hampshire

Private non-profit/ 1905/ staff: 2(f); 3(p); 20(v)/ members: 350/publication: *The Weathervane*

HISTORICAL SOCIETY; HISTORY MUSEUM; HOUSE MUSEUM: Collects, preserves, and interprets the history of Northampton and the upper Connecticut River Valley. Properties include Damon House (1830), Parsons House(1730) , and Shepherd House (1796), Shepherd Barn with blacksmith shop, and visitor center.

PROGRAMS: Annual Meeting; Exhibits; Guided Tours; Lectures; Publication; Research Library/Archives

COLLECTIONS: [1600s-present]

HOURS: Mar-Dec T-F 10-4, Sa-Su 12-4; researchers by appt

ADMISSION: Call

NORTHBOROUGH

3942
Northborough Historical Society
50 Main St, 01532 [PO Box 661, 01532]; (p) (508) 393-6298; (c) Worcester

Private non-profit/ 1906/ staff: 3(p); 5(v)/ members: 123/publication: *The Hourglass*

HISTORICAL SOCIETY; HISTORY MUSEUM: Collects and preserves Northborough's history.

PROGRAMS: Annual Meeting; Exhibits; Facility Rental; Family Programs; Guided Tours; Lectures; Publication; Research Library/ Archives

COLLECTIONS: [1750-present] Manuscripts, deeds, maps, and genealogical artifacts; clothing, photos, toys, games, books, tools and household, military and industrial items.

HOURS: May-June, Sept-Oct Su 2-4

NORWELL

3943
Jacob's Farmhouse
Jacobs Lane, 02061; (p) (781) 659-1888

NORWOOD

3944
Norwood Historical Society
93 Day St, 02062; (p) (781) 762-9197; (f) (781) 551-0767; DonAck88@aol.com; (c) Norfolk

Private non-profit/ 1907/ Board of Governors/ staff: 20(v)/ members: 300

HISTORICAL SOCIETY; HOUSE MUSEUM: Collects, preserves and interprets the town's history, along with the archive of photographer Fred Holland Day.

PROGRAMS: Annual Meeting; Community Outreach; Exhibits; Guided Tours; Interpretation; Lectures; Research Library/Archives

COLLECTIONS: [1880s-present] Furniture, paintings, artifacts, photographs, manuscripts, correspondence, toys and dolls.

HOURS: May-Oct Su 1-4

ADMISSION: $3

OAK BLUFFS

3945
Cottage Museum
1 Trinity Park, 02557 [PO Box 1176, 02557]; (p) (508) 693-7784, (508) 693-0525; (f) (508) 693-8661

1868/ staff: 4(p); 20(v)

COLLECTIONS: [mid to late 19th c] Household appliances, clothing, lamps, dolls, bathing suits, pump organ, victrola, antique chairs, historic campground

ONSET

3946
Porter Thermometer Museum
49 Zarahemla Rd, 02558 [PO Box 944, 02558]; (p) (508) 295-5504; thermometerman@aol.com; (c) Plymouth

Private non-profit/ 1994/ Richard T. Porter, Owner/Curator/ staff: 1(f); 1(p)

HISTORY MUSEUM; HOUSE MUSEUM: Features 5,000 medical, antique, souvenir and advertising devices.

PROGRAMS: Community Outreach; Elder's Programs; Exhibits; Family Programs; Festivals; Guided Tours; Lectures; School-Based Curriculum

COLLECTIONS: [16th c-present] All kinds of thermometers—old, rare, fever, advertising, ornate, and ordinary, including Galilleo's first device from 1593.

HOURS: Yr Daily by appt.

ORLEANS

3947
Orleans Historical Society
Corner of River Rd & Main St, 02653 [PO Box 353, 02653]; (p) (508) 240-1329; orleanshs@gis.net

Private non-profit/ 1958/ staff: 1(p); 12(v)/ members: 450

HISTORICAL SOCIETY; HISTORY MUSEUM: Collects, preserves and exhibits objects and papers relating to people that have lived in the town of Orleans.

PROGRAMS: Annual Meeting; Community Outreach; Exhibits; Lectures; Research Library/Archives; School-Based Curriculum

COLLECTIONS: [18th-20th c] Photographs, paintings, toys, clothing, ceramics related to 19th-20th c Orleans, Native American artifacts, an archive of books, maps, deeds, ships' logs and manuscripts related to Orleans.

HOURS: Mar-June, Sept-Dec M-T 10-1; July-Aug T-Sa 10-1

ADMISSION: $2

OSTERVILLE

3948
Osterville Historical Society
155 W Bay Rd, 02655 [PO Box 3, 02655]; (p) (508) 428-5861; (f) (508) 428-2241; ohs@capecod.net; (c) Barnstable

1931/ Board of Directors/ staff: 1(p); 15(v)/ members: 200

HISTORIC SITE; HISTORICAL SOCIETY; HISTORY MUSEUM; HOUSE MUSEUM: Operates a wooden boat museum, an historic Cape Cod Farmhouse and an Art and Antiques Museum housed in the Parker House. It also preserves artifacts, documents and photographs on the history of Osterville and Cape Cod.

PROGRAMS: Annual Meeting; Community Outreach; Exhibits; Family Programs; Guided Tours; Lectures; Research Library/Archives

COLLECTIONS: [19th-20th c] Artifacts, documents and photographs from the 19th and 20th century wooden boat building industry of Osterville including coastal schooners and Crosby catboats.

HOURS: June-Oct Th-Su 1:30-4:30

ADMISSION: $3; Children/Mbrs free; group rates

PALMER

3949
Palmer Historical Commission
Main St, 01069; (c) Hampden

City/ staff: 7(v)

HISTORICAL SOCIETY

PROGRAMS: Annual Meeting

COLLECTIONS: [1716-present] Statistical records, genealogies, ephemera and artifacts from town of Palmer, books, postcards, prints, maps, etc.

ADMISSION: No charge

PETERSHAM

3950
Petersham Historical Society, Inc.
10 N Main St, 01366; (p) (978) 724-3380; (c) Worcester

Private non-profit/ 1912/ staff: 4(v)/ members: 45

HISTORICAL SOCIETY; HISTORY MUSEUM: Meetings, tours, oral histories, research and collections of members.

PROGRAMS: Annual Meeting; Exhibits; Family Programs; Research Library/Archives

COLLECTIONS: [18th c-present] Town Reports, church records, house pictures, newspaper clippings (1900-present), folk art, genealogy, Daniel Shays material, clothing.

HOURS: May-Oct Su 2-5 or by appt

ADMISSION: Donations accepted

PITTSFIELD

3951
Berkshire County Historical Society, The
780 Holmes Rd, 01201; (p) (413) 442-1793; (f) (413) 443-1449; melville@berkshire.net; www.berkshirehistory.org; (c) Berkshire

Private non-profit/ 1962/ staff: 2(f); 2(p); 50(v)/ members: 500/publication: *News and Notes; The Gam*

HISTORIC SITE; HISTORICAL SOCIETY; HOUSE MUSEUM: A county-wide historical society that maintains local history object collections, a library/archives, educational programs, and operates Arrowhead (a house museum once the home of Herman Melville).

PROGRAMS: Annual Meeting; Community Outreach; Concerts; Exhibits; Festivals; Garden Tours; Guided Tours; Interpretation; Lectures; Living History; Publication; Reenactments; Research Library/Archives; School-Based Curriculum; Theatre

COLLECTIONS: 4,500 local history objects, including fine and decorative arts, tools, and other objects; 3,000 costumes and textiles; 14,000 photographs; and 500 linear feet of manuscripts.

HOURS: May-Oct Daily 9:30-5 or by appt

ADMISSION: $5, Student $3, Children $1, Seniors $4.50

3952
Berkshire Museum, The
39 S St, 01201; (p) (413) 443-7171; (f) (413) 443-2135; www.berkshiremuseum.org; (c) Berkshire

Private non-profit/ 1903/ Trustees of the Berkshire Museum/ staff: 22(f); 5(p); 940(v)/ members: 2100

HISTORY MUSEUM: The Berkshire Museum presents exhibitions, programs, and events in art, natural science, and history.

PROGRAMS: Concerts; Exhibits; Facility Rental; Festivals; Guided Tours; Interpretation; Lectures; Theatre

COLLECTIONS: The history collection includes 6,000 archival items and 9,000 museum artifacts.

HOURS: Jan-June, Sept-Dec T-Sa 10-5, Su 1-5; July-Aug M-Sa 10-5, Su 1-5

ADMISSION: $6, Children $4, Seniors $5; Under 3/Mbrs free

3953
Hancock Shaker Village, Inc.
Rtes 20 & 41, 01202 [PO Box 927, 01202]; (p) (800) 817-1137, (413) 443-0188; (f) (413) 447-9357; info@hancockshakervillage.org; www.hancockshakervillage.org; (c) Berkshire

Private non-profit/ 1960/ staff: 15(f); 50(p); 75(v)/ members: 890

GARDEN; HISTORY MUSEUM; RESEARCH CENTER: 200-year-old Shaker Village with 20 historic buildings, heritage breeds farm, heirloom vegetable and herb gardens. Demonstrations of Shaker crafts, technology and farming techniques with hands-on activities for families.

PROGRAMS: Exhibits; Facility Rental; Family Programs; Festivals; Garden Tours; Guided Tours; Interpretation; Lectures; Living History; Research Library/Archives; School-Based Curriculum

COLLECTIONS: [1790-1930] Shaker artifacts, manuscripts, photographs and ephemera in a restored Shaker site.

HOURS: May-Nov Daily 9:30-5; Nov-May Daily 10-3

ADMISSION: $13.50, Children $5.50

3954
Local History Dept, Berkshire Athenaeum
1 Wendall Ave, 01201; (p) (413) 499-9486; pittslhg@cwmars.org; (c) Berkshire

Private non-profit/ 1872/ Trustees of the Berkshire Athenaeum/ staff: 1(f); 4(p); 3(v)

RESEARCH CENTER: Provides library service; collects, maintains, preserves and creates access to information and materials.

PROGRAMS: Research Library/Archives

COLLECTIONS: [17th c-present] Historical and genealogical research materials relating to Pittsfield, Berkshire County, the New England states and adjacent areas of New York state. Collections on Herman Melville and the Shakers.

HOURS: Sept-June M-Th 9-9, F 9-5, Sa 10-5; July-Aug M, W, F 9-5, T, Th 9-9, Sa 10-5

ADMISSION: No charge

PLYMOUTH

3955
Harlow Old Fort House
119 Sandwich St, 02361 [PO Box 3773, 02361]; (p) (508) 746-0012; (f) (508) 746-7908; pasm@ici.net; (c) Plymouth

Private non-profit/ 1919/ Plymouth Antiquarian Society/ staff: 1(f); 3(p); 60(v)/ members: 500

GARDEN; HISTORY MUSEUM; HOUSE MUSEUM: Family homestead from the Pilgrim era (1677). Demonstrations of activities of daily colonial life.

PROGRAMS: Exhibits; Family Programs; Festivals; Guided Tours; Interpretation; Reenactments

COLLECTIONS: [Late 17th c] Household goods and furnishings, particularly those involved in fiber arts and food preparation.

HOURS: July-Aug F 10-4

ADMISSION: $4

3956
Hedge House
126 Water St, 02361 [PO Box 3773, 02361]; (p) (508) 746-0012; (f) (508) 746-7908; pasm@ici.net; (c) Plymouth

Private non-profit/ 1919/ Plymouth Antiquarian Society/ staff: 1(f); 3(p); 60(v)/ members: 500

GARDEN; HISTORY MUSEUM; HOUSE MUSEUM: An 1809 Grand Federal era mansion. Covers Plymouth history from early republic to Civil War.

PROGRAMS: Exhibits; Festivals; Guided Tours; Interpretation; Research Library/Archives

COLLECTIONS: [19th c] Furnishings and goods such as china and dinnerware from England, portraits, textiles, furniture, toys, dolls, samplers and kitchenware. Costume collection for research.

HOURS: July-Aug F 10-4

ADMISSION: $4, Children $2

3957
Mayflower Society Museum
4 Winslow St, 02360; (p) (508) 746-2590; www.destinationplymouth.com/historic/index.html

3958
Ocean Spray Cranberry World
225 Water St, 02360; (p) (508) 747-2350; (f) (508) 747-0037; www.oceanspray.com; (c) Plymouth

Private for-profit/ 1977/ Ocean Spray Cranberries, Inc./ staff: 2(f); 25(p)

HISTORY MUSEUM: Focuses on the cranberry industry from the days of the Pilgrims to present day and exhibits on growing and cultivation, as well as a working bog.

PROGRAMS: Community Outreach; Exhibits; Festivals; Guided Tours; School-Based Curriculum

COLLECTIONS: [1620s-present] Cranberry harvesting equipment.

HOURS: May-Nov M-Su 9:30-5

ADMISSION: No charge

3959
Pilgrim John Howland Society, Inc.
33 Sandwich St, 02360; (p) (508) 746-9590; (f) (508) 866-5056; (c) Plymouth

Private non-profit/ 1897/ staff: 7(p)/ members: 1500/publication: The Howland Quarterly

GENEALOGICAL SOCIETY; HISTORIC SITE; HOUSE MUSEUM: A family organization for the descendants of "Mayflower" passengers John Howland and Elizabeth Tilley Howland. The Jabez Howland House is where John Howland died in 1672.

PROGRAMS: Exhibits; Guided Tours; Interpretation; Publication

COLLECTIONS: [1670-1750] Artifacts from a dig of John Howland's house which burned in 1675.

HOURS: May-Oct Daily 10-4:30

ADMISSION: $3.50

3960
Pilgrim Society
75 Court St, 02360; (p) (508) 746-1620; (f) (508) 747-4228; pegbaker@ici.net; www.pilgrimhall.org; (c) Plymouth

1820/ Pilgrim Society/ staff: 2(f); 11(p); 50(v)/ members: 800

HISTORICAL SOCIETY; HISTORY MUSEUM: Operates Pilgrim Hall Museum; collects, preserves and interprets artifacts and records of the Pilgrims and 17th century Plymouth Colony.

PROGRAMS: Annual Meeting; Community Outreach; Exhibits; Family Programs; Guided Tours; Interpretation; Lectures; Research Library/Archives

COLLECTIONS: [17th c] Pilgrim and 17th c Plymouth Colony artifacts.

HOURS: Feb-Dec Daily

3961
Plimoth Plantation
137 Warren Ave, 02362 [PO Box 1620, 02362]; (p) (508) 746-1622; (f) (508) 746-4978; www.plimoth.org; (c) Plymouth

Private non-profit/ 1947/ members: 3566

LIVING HISTORY/OUTDOOR MUSEUM: Promotes history and research of the Pilgrim and Wampanoag communities and provides learning opportunities and understanding of the relationship between historical events to modern America.

PROGRAMS: Community Outreach; Exhibits; Facility Rental; Family Programs; Garden Tours; Interpretation; Lectures; Living History; Reenactments; Research Library/Archives; School-Based Curriculum

COLLECTIONS: [17th c] European/Colonial ceramics, furniture, glass, metal and military objects, prints, paintings, reproduction buildings, rare breed livestock, European/Colonial and Native American clothing and archaeological materials.

HOURS: Apr-Nov Daily 9-5

ADMISSION: $19, Children $11

3962
Plymouth Antiquarian Society
6 Court St, 02361 [PO Box 3773, 02361]; (p)
(508) 746-0012; (f) (598) 746-7908;
pasm@ici.net; (c) Plymouth

Private non-profit/ 1919/ Board of Trustees/
staff: 1(f); 3(p); 60(v)/ members: 500

GARDEN; HISTORY MUSEUM; HOUSE MU-
SEUM: Collects, preserves and interprets
local history.

PROGRAMS: Annual Meeting; Exhibits; Family Programs; Festivals; Guided Tours; Interpretation; Research Library/Archives

COLLECTIONS: [18th-19th c] 3 historic
homes; textiles, costumes, furnishings and domestic artifacts, portraits, prints, manuscript,
archives and books.

HOURS: June-Oct Th-Sa 10-4

ADMISSION: $4

3963
Spooner House, Plymouth
Antiquarian Society
27 N St, 02361 [PO Box 3773, 02361]; (p)
(508) 746-0012; (f) (508) 746-7908;
pasm@ici.net; (c) Plymouth

Private non-profit/ 1919/ Board of Trustees/
staff: 1(f); 3(p); 60(v)/ members: 500

GARDEN; HISTORY MUSEUM; HOUSE MU-
SEUM: Colonial house with garden showing
how one American family adapted to changing
tastes and technologies.

PROGRAMS: Exhibits; Family Programs;
Guided Tours; Interpretation; Research Li-
brary/Archives

COLLECTIONS: [Mid 18th-early 20th c] Historic home (1749), household goods and furnishings, textiles, toys, maritime memorabilia,
dinnerware and kitchenware.

PROVINCETOWN

3964
Pilgrim Monument and Provincetown
Museum
High Pole Hill, 02657 [PO Box 1125, 02657];
(p) (508) 487-1310; (f) (508) 487-4702;
www.pilgrim-monument.org; (c) Barnstable

Private non-profit/ 1892/ Cape Cod Pilgrim
Memorial Association/ staff: 5(f); 4(p)/ mem-
bers: 75/publication: *Art In Narrow Streets;
Blanche Lazzell; and others*

HISTORIC SITE; HISTORY MUSEUM: A 252
foot tall tower built to commemorate Provincetown as the first landing place of the Mayflower
Pilgrims. The museum has exhibits, archives,
and programs relating to Provincetown and
Lower Cape Cod history.

PROGRAMS: Annual Meeting; Community
Outreach; Concerts; Elder's Programs; Exhibits; Facility Rental; Guided Tours; Interpretation; Lectures; Publication; Research Li-
brary/Archives; School-Based Curriculum

COLLECTIONS: [1800-1950] Shows the material culture of the Outer Cape Cod, American
art history, early American theater, whaling,
pre-Plymouth Pilgrim history, Revolutionary

War history and part of the collection of Arctic
explorer Admiral Donald MacMillan.

HOURS: May-June and Sept-Nov Daily 9-5;
July-Aug Daily 9-7

ADMISSION: $5, Children $3; Under 4 free

QUINCY

3965
Adams National Historical Park
135 Adams St, 02169-1749; (p) (617) 770-
1175, (617) 773-1177; (f) (617) 472-7562;
adam_visitor_center@nps.gov;
www.nps.gov/adam

National Park Service

Includes three houses, the Stone Library, and
the United First Parish Church. The church
contains the crypts where John and Abigail
Adams and John Quincy and Louisa Adams
are buried.

HOURS: Apr-Nov

3966
Quincy Historical Society
Adams Academy Building, 8 Adams St,
02169; (p) (617) 773-1144; (f) (617) 472-
4990; (c) Norfolk

Private non-profit/ 1893/ Board of Trustees
and Officers/ staff: 6(p); 50(v)/ members:
1000/publication: *Quincy History*

HISTORIC SITE; HISTORICAL SOCIETY;
HISTORY MUSEUM: Collects, preserves and
interprets the history of Quincy and neighboring communities.

PROGRAMS: Annual Meeting; Community
Outreach; Concerts; Elder's Programs; Ex-
hibits; Family Programs; Film/Video; Lectures;
Publication; Research Library/Archives;
School-Based Curriculum; Theatre

COLLECTIONS: [1600s-present] Documents
Quincy's political, industrial, military, social,
family and intellectual history.

HOURS: Yr M-F 9-4

ADMISSION: Donations accepted

3967
Quincy Homestead, The
1010 Hancock St, 02169; (p) (617) 472-5117;
www.key-biz.com/ssn/src/interest.html#quincy

3968
Quincy House, SPNEA
20 Muirhead St, 02170; (p) (617) 227-3956;
www.spnea.org; (c) Middlesex

Private non-profit/ 1770/ Society for the
Preservation of New England Antiquities

Built as a country estate by the Revolutionary
leader Colonel Josiah Quincy, Quincy House
was originally surrounded by fields and pas-
ture overlooking Quincy Bay.

HOURS: June 1-Oct 15 Sa-Su 11-5

ADMISSION: $3; SPNEA Mbrs/Town residents

ROCKPORT

3969
Paper House
52 Pigeon Hill St, 01966; (p) (978) 546-2629;
(c) Essex

Private non-profit/ 1924/ staff: 1(f)

HOUSE MUSEUM: A two room home constructed over 70 years ago of newspaper. The
family of builder Elis Stenman offers the home
for public viewing.

COLLECTIONS: Unique furnishings, along
with durable, readable and artfully made
newspaper constructions.

HOURS: Apr-Oct Daily 10-5

ADMISSION: Donations

3970
Sandy Bay Historical Society and
Museums, Inc.
40 King St, 01966 [PO Box 63, 01966]; (p)
(978) 546-9533; (c) Essex

Private non-profit/ 1926/ staff: 30(v)/ members:
325

ART MUSEUM; GENEALOGICAL SOCIETY;
HISTORICAL SOCIETY; HOUSE MUSEUM;
RESEARCH CENTER: Preservation of local
history and genealogical library.

PROGRAMS: Annual Meeting; Exhibits; Interpretation; Lectures; Research Library/Archives

COLLECTIONS: [1650-present] Local art
works, period rooms, Victorian parlor, Keeping
Room, Children's Room circa 1800, and genealogical research library.

HOURS: Mid June-mid Sept M-Sa 2-5; Research: Yr M 9-1

ADMISSION: $3

ROXBURY

3971
Shirley-Eustis House Association
33 Shirley St, 02119; (p) (617) 442-2275; (f)
(617) 442-2270; tamseng@aol.com;
www.shirleyeustishouse.org; (c) Suffolk

Private non-profit/ 1913/ Board of Governors/
staff: 1(f); 1(p); 25(v)/ members: 152

HOUSE MUSEUM: Preserves and maintains
the buildings and grounds in its care, including
a Royal Governor's mansion built in 1747. Educates the general public about the history of
Massachusetts and Boston.

PROGRAMS: Community Outreach; Concerts; Exhibits; Facility Rental; Family Programs; Guided Tours

COLLECTIONS: Georgian and Federal architecture (Governor's Mansion and Carriage
House) is featured along with their furnishings.

HOURS: June-Sept Th-Su 12-4; Oct-May by
appt

ADMISSION: $5, Children $3, Seniors $3

SAGAMORE

3972
Pairpoint Crystal, Inc.
851 Sandwich Rd, 02561 [PO Box 515,
02561]; (p) (508) 888-2344; (f) (508) 888-
3537; www.pairpoint.com; (c) Barnstable

Private for-profit/ 1837/ staff: 11(f); 4(p)

HISTORY MUSEUM: Uses tools and techniques from the 1800s doing reproductions of
early American glass. Also does contemporary
glass blowing and hand pressing.

PROGRAMS: Guided Tours; Living History

COLLECTIONS: [19th c] Molds, presses for glass making, reproduction of glass for many museums and collections from the 1800s.

HOURS: Yr

SALEM

3973
Crowninshield-Bentley House, Peabody Essex Museum
126 Essex St, 01970 [Peabody Essex Museum, E India Square, 01970]; (p) (508) 745-1876; (f) (508) 744-6776; rob_saarnio@pem.org; www.pem.org

1727/ staff: 1(f); 4(p); 3(v)

COLLECTIONS: [1793-1807]

HOURS: Yr

3974
Gardner Pingree House, Peabody Essex Museum
128 Essex St, 01970 [Peabody Essex Museum, E India Square, 01970]; (p) (508) 745-1876; (f) (508) 744-6776; rob_saarnio@pem.org; www.pem.org

1804/ staff: 1(f); 4(p); 3(v)

COLLECTIONS: [1805-1814]

HOURS: Yr

3975
House of the Seven Gables Historic Site
54 Turner St, 01970; (p) (978) 744-0991; (f) (978) 741-4350; dolson@7gables.org; www.7gables.org; (c) Essex

Private non-profit/ 1908/ House of the Seven Gables Settlement Association/ staff: 20(f); 40(p); 100(v)/ members: 1000

GARDEN; HISTORIC SITE; HOUSE MUSEUM: Dedicated to interpreting and preserving the history of Salem through its historic site and collection of artifacts.

PROGRAMS: Annual Meeting; Community Outreach; Exhibits; Facility Rental; Family Programs; Festivals; Garden Tours; Guided Tours; Interpretation; Lectures; Living History; School-Based Curriculum; Theatre

COLLECTIONS: [17th-19th c] Three 17th century houses and Nathaniel Hawthorne's birthplace. Also, furnishings and household items from the 1800s as well as items pertaining to the life and work of author Nathaniel Hawthorne.

HOURS: Yr Daily 10-5

ADMISSION: $8, Children $5

3976
John Ward House, Peabody Essex Museum
Rear 132 Essex St, 01970 [Peabody Essex Museum, E India Square, 01970]; (p) (508) 745-1876; (f) (508) 744-6776; rob_saarnio@pem.org; www.pem.org

1684/ staff: 1(f); 4(p); 3(v)

COLLECTIONS: [1684-1700]

HOURS: Yr

3977
Peabody Essex Museum
161 Essex St, 01970 [East India Sq, 01970];
(p) (978) 745-9500, (800) 745-4054; (f) (978) 744-6776; pem@pem.org; www.pem.org; (c) Essex

Private non-profit/ 1799/ Board of Trustees/ staff: 89(f); 71(p); 222(v)/ members: 4000/publication: *The American Neptune*

ART MUSEUM; GARDEN; HISTORIC SITE; HISTORY MUSEUM; HOUSE MUSEUM; RESEARCH CENTER: Seeks to increase knowledge and appreciation of outstanding works of artistic and cultural expression created by people around the world. Research, preservation, acquisition, exhibition, education, and publication programs support this mission.

PROGRAMS: Community Outreach; Concerts; Exhibits; Facility Rental; Family Programs; Film/Video; Garden Tours; Guided Tours; Lectures; Publication; Research Library/Archives

COLLECTIONS: [18th-19th c] 30 galleries exhibiting world famous collections of maritime art and history, Native American, Asian, African and Pacific Islander art, American decorative arts, and natural history. The historic houses include 3 national historic landmarks.

HOURS: Yr Mon-Sa 10-5, Su 12-5; Nov 1-Mem Day T-Su

ADMISSION: $8.50, Family $20, Student $7.50, Children $5, Seniors $7.50

3978
Ropes Mansion, Peabody Essex Museum
318 Essex St, 01970 [Peabody Essex Museum, E India Square, 01970]; (p) (508) 744-0718, (508) 745-1876; (f) (508) 744-6503; rob_saarnio@pem.org; www.pem.org

1720/ staff: 1(f); 4(p); 3(v)

Garden was designed by Salem botanist John Robinson in 1912 in the Colonial Revival style.

COLLECTIONS: [1769-1904]

HOURS: Seasonal

3979
Salem 1630: Pioneer Village
Forest River Park, 01970 [54 Turner St, 01970]; (p) (978) 745-0525, (978) 745-5391; (f) (978) 741-4350; H7G0lson@aol.com; www.7gables.org; (c) Essex

Joint/ 1930/ The House of the Seven Gables Settlement Association and the City of Salem/ staff: 1(f); 30(p); 10(v)

LIVING HISTORY/OUTDOOR MUSEUM: Tells the story of one of the first English colonies in New England through reproduction of artifacts and reconstructed buildings typical of the early 17th century.

PROGRAMS: Facility Rental; Family Programs; Festivals; Interpretation; Living History; Reenactments

COLLECTIONS: [17th c] Reproductions of houses and household items.

HOURS: Apr-Nov M-Sa 10-5, Su 12-5

ADMISSION: $5, Children $3

3980
Salem Maritime National Historic Site
174 Derby St, 01970; (p) (978) 740-1680; (f) (978) 740-1685; www.nps.gov/sama; (c) Essex

1937/ National Park Service/ staff: 19(f); 39(p); 40(v)

HISTORIC SITE: Located along Salem's waterfront, the site's buildings and wharves are a complete example of the maritime infrastructure that evolved to serve the extensive world trade network.

PROGRAMS: Concerts; Exhibits; Facility Rental; Festivals; Film/Video; Guided Tours; Interpretation; Lectures; Research Library/Archives

COLLECTIONS: [1770-1870] Furniture and furnishings, customs service tools and equipment, site administration archival material, and extensive archaeological collections.

HOURS: Yr Daily 9-5

ADMISSION: Tour fee

3981
Salem Witch Museum
Washington Sq, 01970; (p) (978) 744-1692; (f) (978) 745-4414; facts@salemwitch museum.com; www.salemwitchmuseum.com; (c) Essex

Private non-profit/ 1972/ staff: 5(f); 40(p)

HISTORY MUSEUM: Audio-visual history of the Salem Witch trials of 1692 and an exhibit concerning definitions of the word witch.

PROGRAMS: Community Outreach; Exhibits; Interpretation; Lectures; School-Based Curriculum

COLLECTIONS: [17th c] Dioramas of 17th century Salem as well as items from various periods connected with the word witch.

HOURS: Yr Daily 10-5; July-Aug 10-7

3982
Stephen Phillips Memorial Trust House
34 Chestnut St, 01970; (p) (978) 744-0440; (f) (978) 740-1086; phillipstrust@nii.net; www.salemweb.com/org/phillipshouse; (c) Essex

Private non-profit/ 1973/ Board of Trustees/ staff: 2(f); 5(p); 1(v)

HISTORIC SITE; HOUSE MUSEUM: Maintains and operates a federal period home.

PROGRAMS: Guided Tours; Interpretation; Lectures

COLLECTIONS: [1694-1955] Furniture, Chinese export porcelains, rare carpets, antique carriages, automobiles and other prized possessions from the sailing ship era.

SANDWICH

3983
Heritage Plantation of Sandwich
67 Grove St, 02563-2147; (p) (508) 888-3300; (f) (508) 888-9535; art@heritage plantation.org; www.heritageplantation.org; (c) Barnstable

Private non-profit/ 1969/ Board of Trustees/ staff: 21(f); 4(p); 225(v)/ members: 3500

ART MUSEUM; GARDEN; HISTORY MUSEUM: A diversified museum of Americana, features automobile, military, and art museums with a 1912 working carousel. These buildings are set among 76 acres of landscaped grounds.

PROGRAMS: Community Outreach; Concerts; Elder's Programs; Exhibits; Facility Rental; Family Programs; Garden Tours; Guided Tours; Interpretation; Lectures; School-Based Curriculum

COLLECTIONS: [1800-1950] Living plants, military miniatures, firearms, Native American items, automobiles, paintings, sculptures, Currier and Ives lithographs, a carousel and a windmill.

HOURS: May-Oct M-Su 10-5

ADMISSION: $9, Children $4.50

3984
Hoxie House
16 Water St, 02563 [145 Main St, 02563]; (p) (508) 888-0340, (508) 888-1173

1675/ City/ staff: 8(p)

COLLECTIONS: [17th c] 17th century furnishings, implements, etc. including loom.

HOURS: Seasonal

3985
Sandwich Glass Museum
129 Main St, 02563 [PO Box 103, 02563]; (p) (508) 888-0251; (f) (508) 888-4941; sgm@capecod.net; www.sandwichglass museum.org; (c) Barnstable

Private non-profit/ 1907/ Sandwich Historical Society, Inc., Board of Trustees/ staff: 6(f); 5(p); 70(v)/ members: 500/publication: *Acorn, Vol. 1-10*

HISTORICAL SOCIETY; HISTORY MUSEUM: Collects, preserves and exhibits material relating to the history of Sandwich, the oldest town incorporated on Cape Cod.

PROGRAMS: Annual Meeting; Community Outreach; Exhibits; Facility Rental; Family Programs; Guided Tours; Lectures; Publication; Research Library/Archives; School-Based Curriculum

COLLECTIONS: [19th c] 6,000 pieces of glass made in Sandwich factories, period paintings, furniture, decorative arts, photographs, manuscripts, and maps.

HOURS: Feb-March W-Su 9:30-4; Apr-Dec Daily 9:30-5

ADMISSION: $3.50, Children $1

3986
Thornton Burgess Museum/Deacon Eldred House
4 Water St, Rte 130, 02563 [PO Box 972, 02563]; (p) (508) 888-4668; (f) (508) 888-1919; tburgess@capecod.net; www.capecod.net/burgess

1756/ staff: 7(f); 20(p); 100(v)

COLLECTIONS: Collections deal with the life and works of Thornton W. Burgess.; Collections deal with the life and works of Thornton W. Burgess

HOURS: Seasonal

SCITUATE

3987
Cudsworth House
First Parish Rd, 02040 [Scituate Historical Society, First Parish Rd, 02040]; (p) (781) 545-1083; www.visit-massachusetts.com/south/places/history.htm

3988
Mann Farmhouse and Historical Museum
Stockbridge Rd & Greenfield Lane, 02066 [PO Box 276, 02066]; (p) (781) 545-1083

SHEFFIELD

3989
Sheffield Historical Society
159-161 Main St, 01257 [PO Box 747, 01257]; (p) (413) 229-2694; shs@sheffield-history.org; (c) Berkshire

Private non-profit/ 1972/ Board of Trustees/ staff: 1(f); 50(v)/ members: 198

GENEALOGICAL SOCIETY; HISTORIC SITE; HISTORICAL SOCIETY; HISTORY MUSEUM; RESEARCH CENTER: Collects, preserves and interprets records and artifacts of Sheffield and its surrounding communities.

PROGRAMS: Annual Meeting; Community Outreach; Exhibits; Family Programs; Festivals; Guided Tours; Interpretation; Lectures; Living History; Publication; Research Library/Archives; School-Based Curriculum

COLLECTIONS: [1770s-1870s] Photos, manuscripts, tax records, books, furniture, tools and textiles.

HOURS: Research Center: Yr M, F 1:30-4 or by appt; House: late May-Oct Th-Sa 11-4; Nov-Apr by appt

ADMISSION: $5, Children $1, Seniors $4

SHERBORN

3990
Sherborn Historical Society
19 Washington St, 01770 [PO Box 186, 01770-0186]; (p) (508) 653-0560; (f) (508) 651-7854; (c) Middlesex

Private non-profit/ 1911/ Board of Directors/ staff: 3(v)/ members: 100

HISTORICAL SOCIETY: Quarterly meetings and small museum room in Town Office Building.

PROGRAMS: Annual Meeting; Exhibits; Family Programs; Interpretation; Research Library/Archives; School-Based Curriculum

COLLECTIONS: [19th c] Artifacts relating to the Town of Sherborn, mostly genealogy information along with some personal and business papers.

HOURS: Sept-June M 10-2; July-Aug by appt

ADMISSION: No charge

SHREWSBURY

3991
General Artemus Ward Home
786 Main St, 01545; (p) (508) 842-8900; www.ci.shrewsbury.ma.us/musetop.htm

SOUTH DENNIS

3992
Jericho House and Barn Museum
Trotting Park Rd at Old Main St, 02660 [Dennis Town Office, PO Box 1419, 02660]

1801/ staff: 20(v)

COLLECTIONS: [19th c] Tool collection, drift wood, archives

HOURS: Appt

SOUTH NATICK

3993
Natick Historical Society
58 Eliot St, 01760; (p) (508) 647-4841; elliot@ma.ultranet.com; www.ultranet.com/~elliot/; (c) Middlesex

Private non-profit/ 1870/ Historical, Natural History and Library Society of Natick/ staff: 3(v)/ members: 250/publication: *The Arrow, Images of America-Natick*

HISTORICAL SOCIETY: Preserves the history and artifacts that contribute to an understanding of the local heritage.

PROGRAMS: Annual Meeting; Community Outreach; Exhibits; Guided Tours; Interpretation; Lectures; Publication; Research Library/Archives; School-Based Curriculum

COLLECTIONS: [17th c-present] John Eliot's Praying Indian Village, maps, manuscripts, museum artifacts, reference library, photographs and clipping files.

HOURS: Yr T 6-8:30, W 2-4:30; Sept 15-June 15 Sa 10-12:30

SOUTHBOROUGH

3994
Southborough Historical Society, Inc.
25 Common St, 01772 [PO Box 364, 01772]; shs01772@aol.com; www.ultranet.com/~sobohist; (c) Worcester

Private non-profit/ 1965/ Board of Directors/ members: 75

HISTORICAL SOCIETY; HISTORY MUSEUM; RESEARCH CENTER: Protects, preserves and promotes the history of Southborough.

PROGRAMS: Annual Meeting; Exhibits; Festivals; Lectures; Living History; Research Library/Archives

COLLECTIONS: [1700-present]

SPRINGFIELD

3995
Connecticut Valley Historical Museum
The Quadrangle, cor State & Chestnut Sts, 01103 [220 State St, 01103]; (p) (413) 263-6800; (f) (413) 263-6898; www.quadrangle.org; (c) Hampden

Private non-profit/ 1927/ Springfield Library and Museums Association/ staff: 6(f); 2(p); 20(v)/ members: 3326/publication: *Library and Museums Quarterly*

HISTORY MUSEUM: Changing exhibits highlight the history of the Greater Springfield area.

PROGRAMS: Annual Meeting; Community Outreach; Exhibits; Family Programs; Lectures; Publication; Research Library/Archives; School-Based Curriculum

COLLECTIONS: [18th-19th c] Paintings by Joseph Whiting Stock, James Ellsworth and other itinerant artists; decorative arts and objects made in Springfield. Genealogies, local history materials, newspapers, photographs and manuscripts.

HOURS: Yr W-F 12-5, Sa-Su 11-4

ADMISSION: $6, Student $3, Children $2, Seniors $3; Under 6 free

3996
Springfield Library and Museums Association
The Quadrangle, corner of State & Chestnut Sts, 01103 [220 State St, 01103]; (p) (413) 263-6800; (f) (413) 263-6814; www.quadrangle.org; (c) Hampden

Private non-profit/ 1857/ Springfield Library and Museums Association/ staff: 150(f); 120(p)/ members: 3200/publication: *Library and Museums Quarterly*

ART MUSEUM; HISTORY MUSEUM: Connecticut Valley Historical Museum with Genealogy and Local History Library; Springfield Museum of Fine Arts; George Walter Vincent Smith Art Museum, Springfield Science Museum, and Springfield Library System.

PROGRAMS: Annual Meeting; Community Outreach; Concerts; Elder's Programs; Exhibits; Family Programs; Guided Tours; Lectures; Publication; Research Library/Archives; School-Based Curriculum

COLLECTIONS: [1700s-present] Four distinctive museums featuring American and European paintings; Islamic rugs, Asian decorative arts; African Hall, a life-sized tyrannosaurus rex, aviation history; a genealogy library and regional history.

HOURS: Yr W-Su 12-4

ADMISSION: $4, Children $1; Under 6 free

3997
Western Massachusetts Genealogical Society
[PO Box 80206, Forest Park Sta, 01108]; www.rootsweb.com/~mawmgs; (c) Hampden

Private non-profit/ 1972/ members: 187/publication: *American Elm*

GENEALOGICAL SOCIETY: Help members in their genealogical researches.

PROGRAMS: Annual Meeting; Lectures; Publication; Research Library/Archives

COLLECTIONS: Library maintained at the Connecticut Valley Museum

STOCKBRIDGE

3998
Chesterwood
4 Williamsville Rd, 01262 [PO Box 827, 01262-0827]; (p) (413) 298-3579; (f) (413) 298-3973; chesterwood@nthp.org/

1901/ National Trust for Historic Preservation/ staff: 7(f); 30(p)

COLLECTIONS: [1925-1931] Art works by Daniel Chester French.; 150 linear feet, including papers, photographs, soler prints, blueprints and ephemera relating to the French family, Chesterwood and the sculptor's works.

3999
Merwin House, SPNEA
Tranquility, 14 Main St, 01262; (p) (413) 298-4703; www.spnea.org; (c) Berkshire

Private non-profit/ 1825/ Society for the Preservation of New England Antiquities

HISTORY MUSEUM; HOUSE MUSEUM: This handsome brick structure, which dates from the late Federal period, was purchased by William and Elizabeth Doane as a summer home in 1875.

PROGRAMS: Guided Tours; Lectures

COLLECTIONS: Silver, jewelry and souvenirs from Doane family travels.

HOURS: June 1-Oct 15 Sa-Su 11-5

ADMISSION: $5; SPNEA

4000
Mission House, The
19 Main St, 01262 [PO Box 792, 01262-0792]; (p) (413) 298-3239; (f) (413) 298-5239; westregion@ttor.org

1739/ The Trustees of Reservations/ staff: 8(f); 6(p)

COLLECTIONS: [Colonial] Courting mirrors, candle stands, kitchen utensils, colonial furniture, Native American objects.

4001
Naumkeag
5 Prospect Hill Rd, 01262 [PO Box 792, 01262-0792]; (p) (413) 298-3239; (f) (413) 298-5239; westregion@ttor.org; www.thetrustees.org/

Private for-profit/ 1885/ The Trustees of Reservations/ staff: 8(f); 10(p)

Gabled 26 room mansion designed by Stanford White. Gardens and landscape designed by Nathan Barrett and later, Fletcher Steele.

COLLECTIONS: [Gilded Age] Original furniture, Chinese export porcelain, rugs, clocks, tapestry.

HOURS: Mem Day-Columbus Day Daily 10-5

ADMISSION: $8, Children

4002
Norman Rockwell Museum at Stockbridge
Route 183, 01262 [PO Box 308, 01262-0308]; (p) (413) 298-4100; (f) (413) 298-4142; rmaster@nrm.org; www.nrm.org; (c) Berkshire

Private non-profit/ 1969/ Norman Rockwell Museum at Stockbridge, Inc./ staff: 36(f); 40(p); 30(v)/ members: 2200/publication: *The Definitive Catalogue*

ART MUSEUM; HISTORIC PRESERVATION AGENCY; HISTORIC SITE; HISTORY MUSEUM; HOUSE MUSEUM; RESEARCH CENTER: Original Rockwell art and archives; exhibits other important illustrators both past and present.

PROGRAMS: Community Outreach; Concerts; Elder's Programs; Exhibits; Facility Rental; Family Programs; Festivals; Guided Tours; Lectures; Living History; Publication; Reenactments; Research Library/Archives; School-Based Curriculum; Theatre

COLLECTIONS: [1894-1978] Paintings, drawings, sketches, a studio building, reference center and archive, original magazines and models, correspondence, costumes, props and illustration resources.

HOURS: Nov-Apr M-F 10-4, Sa-Su 10-5; May-Oct Daily 10-5

ADMISSION: $9; Under 19 free

4003
Stockbridge Library Association Historical Collection
46 Main St, 01262 [PO Box 119, 01262]; (p) (413) 298-5501; (f) (413) 298-5501; (c) Berkshire

Private non-profit/ 1937/ Board of Trustees/ staff: 3(f); 3(p); 10(v)

LIBRARY AND/OR ARCHIVES: Collects and preserves artifacts and papers that illustrate the town's past and the role it has played in national and international history.

PROGRAMS: Annual Meeting; Concerts; Exhibits; Facility Rental; Family Programs; Guided Tours; Lectures; Research Library/Archives; School-Based Curriculum

COLLECTIONS: [1740-present] Stockbridge and pertinent Berkshire County history from the 1730s to present. Includes original Native American deeds and materials, early church records, Field and Sedgwick Family papers and artifacts, maps, photographs, works by local authors, and books on genealogy, biography, theology and reference.

HOURS: Library: Yr M-F 9-5, Sa 9-4; Historical Room: Yr T-F 9-5, Sa 9-4

ADMISSION: No charge

4004
Trustees of Reservations
19 Main St, 01262 [PO Box 792, 01262]; (p) (413) 298-3239; (f) (413) 298-5239; westregion@ttor.org; www.thetrustees.org; (c) Berkshire

Private non-profit/ 1891/ staff: 100(f); 150(p); 200(v)/ members: 20000

GARDEN; HISTORIC PRESERVATION AGENCY; HISTORIC SITE; HOUSE MUSEUM: Preserves for public use and enjoyment places of scenic, historic and ecological value throughout the Commonwealth of Massachusetts.

PROGRAMS: Annual Meeting; Community Outreach; Concerts; Elder's Programs; Exhibits; Facility Rental; Family Programs; Festivals; Garden Tours; Guided Tours; Interpretation; Lectures; Research Library/Archives

COLLECTIONS: [1735-1966] European, Asian and American furniture and decorative objects are exhibited in their original locations in eleven historic houses.

HOURS: Late May-mid Oct Daily 10-5

ADMISSION: $8

STONEHAM

4005
Stoneham Historical Society, Inc.
36 William St, 02180-3845; (p) (781) 438-4185, (781) 438-4542; (c) Middlesex

Private non-profit/ 1922/ Executive Board/ staff: 17(v)/ members: 95/publication: *Stoneham History Coloring Book*

HISTORICAL SOCIETY; HISTORY MUSEUM; RESEARCH CENTER: Collects and preserves articles of local historic value.

PROGRAMS: Exhibits; Lectures; Publication; Research Library/Archives; School-Based Curriculum

COLLECTIONS: [1840-1910] Objects related to the shoe industry. Also, memorabilia from six local Olympians, many Spanish-American War items, and articles from early automobile manufacturers in town: Phelps (1902-05) and Shawmut (1905-08).

HOURS: Feb-May, Sept-Nov By Appt

ADMISSION: Donations accepted

STOW

4006
Stow Historical Society
380 Great Rd, 01775; (c) Middlesex

Private non-profit/ 1961/ staff: 5(v)/ members: 50/publication: *The History of Stow; Recollections of Stow*

HISTORICAL SOCIETY: Assists in collecting, preserving and cataloguing town records.

PROGRAMS: Exhibits; Lectures; Publication; Research Library/Archives

COLLECTIONS: [1669-present] Microfiche files with vital records, documents on the Gardner and Randall families.

HOURS: By Appt

ADMISSION: No charge

STURBRIDGE

4007
Old Sturbridge Village
1 Old Sturbridge Village Rd, 01566; (p) (508) 347-3362; (f) (508) 347-0377; langdon@osv.org; www.osv.org; (c) Worcester

1946/ Board of Trustees/ staff: 120(f); 217(p); 101(v)/ members: 7000/publication: *Old Sturbridge Visitor*

HISTORY MUSEUM; HOUSE MUSEUM; LIVING HISTORY/OUTDOOR MUSEUM: Recreates the life of a rural New England community of the early 19th c and is a center for research, preservation and education in early US history.

PROGRAMS: Community Outreach; Concerts; Elder's Programs; Exhibits; Facility Rental; Family Programs; Garden Tours; Guided Tours; Interpretation; Lectures; Living History; Publication; Research Library/Archives

COLLECTIONS: [1790-1840] Fine arts, furniture, ceramics, glass, textiles, clothing, tools, implements, clocks, and research library.

HOURS: Apr-Oct 9-5; Nov-Mar 10-4

ADMISSION: $16, Children $8, Seniors $15; Under 6 free

SUTTON

4008
Waters Farm Preservation, Inc.
53 Waters Rd, 01590 [4 Uxbridge Rd, 01590]; (p) (508) 865-0101; (f) (508) 865-0101

City; Private non-profit/ 1974/ Waters Farm Preservation, Inc./ staff: 350(v)/publication: *The Cultivator-Farm Brochure*

HISTORIC PRESERVATION AGENCY; HISTORIC SITE; HISTORY MUSEUM; HOUSE MUSEUM; LIVING HISTORY/OUTDOOR MUSEUM: Educational, living history farm with 6 miles of trails open to horseback riding and other non-motorized uses. 130 acres, 250 year old house with 2,000 feet of water frontage.

PROGRAMS: Annual Meeting; Community Outreach; Concerts; Elder's Programs; Exhibits; Facility Rental; Family Programs; Festivals; Film/Video; Guided Tours; Interpretation; Lectures; Living History; Publication; Reenactments; Research Library/Archives; School-Based Curriculum

COLLECTIONS: [1757-1984] House and contents (including diaries) from farm continuously occupied by one family for over 200 years.

HOURS: Yr By appt

ADMISSION: Group rates

SWAMPSCOTT

4009
John Humphrey House
99 Paradise Rd, 01907

1635

HOURS: Seasonal

TAUNTON

4010
Old Colony Historical Society
66 Church Green, 02780-3445; (p) (508) 822-1622; (c) Bristol

Private non-profit/ 1853/ staff: 3(f); 3(p); 19(v)/ members: 700

HISTORICAL SOCIETY: Contains extensive collections representing the development of the Old Colony region of Massachusetts. The society also runs an active membership program.

PROGRAMS: Annual Meeting; Community Outreach; Concerts; Exhibits; Guided Tours; Lectures; Research Library/Archives; School-Based Curriculum

COLLECTIONS: [1638-1945] Portraits, furniture, silver, military artifacts, fire fighting equipment, industrial and domestic artifacts and toys.

HOURS: Yr T-Sa 10-4; closed on Saturdays preceding M holidays

ADMISSION: $2, Children $1, Seniors $1; $5 Library research

TEWKSBURY

4011
Public Health Museum in New England
365 E St, 01876; (p) (978) 851-7321; (f) (617) 355-7283; cosgrove@al.tch.harvard.edu; www.clapham.tch.harvard.edu/museum; (c) Middlesex

Private non-profit/ 1990/ Public Health Museum Executive Board/ staff: 1(p); 4(v)/ members: 150

HISTORIC SITE; HISTORY MUSEUM; RESEARCH CENTER: Attempts to link the past with the present and promote the future of public health through preservation and education.

PROGRAMS: Annual Meeting; Exhibits; Facility Rental; Guided Tours; Interpretation; Research Library/Archives

COLLECTIONS: [1850-present] Documents, films, books, furniture, hospital equipment, and instruments as related to public health and public facilities.

HOURS: Yr T,Th 1-4

ADMISSION: No charge

TOPSFIELD

4012
Parson Capen House
#1 Howlett St, 01983 [PO Box 323, 01983]; (p) (978) 887-3998

1643/ staff: 25(v)

Listed on the National Register of Historic Places, an example of Elizabethan architecture in America.

COLLECTIONS: [Colonial period] Furnishings from early 1700's and American Revolution; church records from 1600's, town and family records.

HOURS: Seasonal

4013
Topsfield Historical Society
1 Howlett St, 01983 [PO Box 323, 01983]; (p) (978) 887-3998; topshist@tiac.net; wwwtiac.net/users/topshist; (c) Essex

Private non-profit/ 1894/ staff: 25(v)/ members: 400/publication: *Topsfield and the Witchcraft Hysteria; History of Topsfield*

HISTORIC SITE; HISTORICAL SOCIETY; HOUSE MUSEUM: Collects, preserves and studies material related to the history of the town and its natural history. Preserves the Captain Joseph Gould Barn and Parson Capen House.

PROGRAMS: Exhibits; Facility Rental; Festivals; Guided Tours; Publication

COLLECTIONS: [1683-1710] Period artifacts and furnishings.

HOURS: Mid June-mid Sept W, F, Su 1-4:30

ADMISSION: $3; Donations requested; Children free

TOWNSEND

4014
Townsend Historical Society
72 Main St, 01469 [PO Box 95, 01469]; (p) (978) 597-2106; (c) Middlesex

Private non-profit/ 1896/ staff: 1(p); 20(v)/ members: 105

HISTORICAL SOCIETY; HOUSE MUSEUM: Encourages interest in town history by: collecting and preserving artifacts, archives and oral history; promoting research; marketing historic sites; restoring historic properties for public access; and conducting curriculum-based programs for adults and school children.

PROGRAMS: Annual Meeting; Guided Tours; Lectures; School-Based Curriculum

COLLECTIONS: [19th c] Five buildings, including a gristmill and a cooperage; Rufus Porter murals in the Reed Homestead; "Country Women's Clothing" collection (1790-1970); and a collection of photographs, archives and artifacts depicting Townsend's history.

HOURS: Yr T-F 9-2, some weekends

ADMISSION: $2

WALPOLE

4015
Walpole Historical Society
Deacon Willard Lewis House, 33 W St, 02081 [PO Box 1724, 02081]; www.walpole.ma.us/historic.htm; (c) Norfolk

Private non-profit/ 1898/ Board of Directors/ staff: 20(v)/ members: 100

HISTORICAL SOCIETY; HOUSE MUSEUM: Collects, preserves and facilitates community access to objects related to Walpole's history. Located in a town-owned house built circa 1826 and listed on the National Register of Historic Places.

PROGRAMS: Annual Meeting; Community Outreach; Exhibits; Facility Rental; Guided Tours; Lectures; Research Library/Archives

COLLECTIONS: [1649-present] Documents, books, memoirs, photographs, newspapers, letters, wills, deeds, town reports and antiques.

HOURS: Yr W, Sa 2-4

ADMISSION: No charge

WALTHAM

4016
American Jewish Historical Society
2 Thornton Rd, 02453; (p) (781) 891-8110; (f) (781) 899-9208; ajhs@ajhs.org; www.ajhs.org; (c) Middlesex

Private non-profit/ 1892/ Board of Trustees/ staff: 10(f); 5(p); 5(v)/ members: 2000/publication: *American Jewish History*

HISTORICAL SOCIETY: Collects, preserves, and disseminates materials and information documenting the Jewish experience in the United States.

PROGRAMS: Annual Meeting; Community Outreach; Exhibits; Lectures; Publication; Research Library/Archives

COLLECTIONS: [1570-present] Artifacts, documents, books, newspapers, journals, photographs

4017
Bay State Historical League
185 Lyman St, 02452; (p) (781) 899-3920; (f) (781) 893-7832; masshistory@earthlink.net; www.masshistory.org

Private non-profit/ 1903/ staff: 2(p)/ members: 450/publication: *Going Public*

Promotes the preservation, interpretation, presentation and enjoyment of history.

4018
Charles River Museum of Industry
154 Moody St, 02453; (p) (781) 893-5410; (f) (781) 891-3456; charles_river@msn.com; www.crmi.org/~crmi; (c) Middlesex

Private non-profit/ 1980/ staff: 2(f); 5(p); 125(v)/ members: 150/publication: *Canoeing the Charles*

HISTORY MUSEUM: Tells the story of the industrial revolution with exhibits and public programs.

PROGRAMS: Annual Meeting; Community Outreach; Concerts; Exhibits; Facility Rental; Family Programs; Festivals; Guided Tours; Publication; Reenactments; Research Library/Archives; School-Based Curriculum

COLLECTIONS: [1814-present] Machines from 1890s, early automobiles, locomotive models, watch and watch-making equipment exhibit.

HOURS: Yr T-Su 10-5

ADMISSION: $4, Student $2

4019
Gore Place
52 Gore St, 02453; (p) (781) 894-2798; (f) (781) 894-5745; gpsinc@erols.com; www.goreplace.org; (c) Middlesex

Private non-profit/ 1935/ Gore Place Society/ staff: 3(f); 6(p); 75(v)/ members: 600/publication: *House Servants Directory*

GARDEN; HISTORIC SITE; HOUSE MUSEUM: Preserves and interprets the 21 room country estate of Governor Christopher Gore, his wife Rebecca, their servants and farm workers. Contains neoclassical architecture surrounded by 45-acre park and farm.

PROGRAMS: Annual Meeting; Community Outreach; Concerts; Elder's Programs; Exhibits; Facility Rental; Family Programs; Festivals; Film/Video; Guided Tours; Interpretation; Lectures; Publication; School-Based Curriculum

COLLECTIONS: [1800-1830] Furniture, silver, ceramics, textiles, wallpapers and paintings; also costumes, vehicles, small archives and research library, gardens and farm animals.

HOURS: Mid Apr-mid Nov T-Sa 11-5, Su 1-5; by appt during rest of the year

ADMISSION: $7, Student $6, Children $5, Seniors $6

4020
Lyman Estate, The, SPNEA
185 Lyman St, 02452; (p) (781) 891-1985; www.spnea.org; (c) Middlesex

Private non-profit/ 1793/ Society for the Preservation of New England Antiquities

GARDEN; HOUSE MUSEUM: Designed by noted Salem architect Samuel McIntire in 1793, the Lyman Estate, also known as The Vale, is a country estate laid out in the English manner.

PROGRAMS: Facility Rental

HOURS: Yr Greenhouses: M-Sa 9:30-4; Grounds: Daily 9-5

ADMISSION: Donations accepted

4021
New England Heritage Center at Bentley College
175 Forest St, 02452-4705; (p) (781) 891-3481; (f) (781) 891-2896; estevens@bentley.edu; www.bentley.edu/resource/nehc; (c) Middlesex

Private non-profit/ 1986/ Board of Advisors/ staff: 1(f); 2(p)/publication: *New England Historical Resources Catalog*

ALLIANCE OF HISTORICAL AGENCIES: Fosters understanding of New England's historical and cultural heritage, and helps to link the academic community to the interested public and professionals dedicated to education and historic preservation.

4022
Waltham Museum
196 Charles St, 02453 [17 Noonan St, 02453]; (p) (781) 893-8017; (c) Middlesex

Private non-profit/ 1971/ staff: 2(f); 5(p)/ members: 130

HISTORY MUSEUM; HOUSE MUSEUM: Located in the James Baker House.

PROGRAMS: Annual Meeting

COLLECTIONS: [1630-present] Items related to the history of Waltham; black iron stoves, ice boxes, blacksmith tools, general store items.

HOURS: Late Mar-late Dec Su 1-4:30 and by appt

ADMISSION: $1

WATERTOWN

4023
Armenian Library and Museum of America, Inc.
65 Main St, 02472-4400; (p) (617) 926-2562; (f) (617) 926-0175; almainc@aol.com; (c) Essex

Private non-profit/ 1971/ staff: 1(f); 3(p); 30(v)/ members: 750/publication: *ALMA Newsletter*

ART MUSEUM; HISTORY MUSEUM; RESEARCH CENTER: Collects, conserves, and documents Armenian artifacts; preserves and promotes through exhibits and programs; and serves as a resource center for Armenian studies.

PROGRAMS: Community Outreach; Concerts; Exhibits; Facility Rental; Lectures; Publication; Research Library/Archives

COLLECTIONS: [1500-present Armenia and Ottoman Empire] 10,000 books, 1,500 oral history tapes, 300 serials, 170 rugs, 1200 pieces of artwork, 1800 sound recordings, and 9,000 archival items.

HOURS: Yr Su, F 1-5, T 1-5 / 7-9

ADMISSION: Donations requested

4024
Historical Society of Watertown
26-28 Marshall St, 02472; (p) (617) 923-6067; (c) Middlesex

Private non-profit/ 1888/ Council/ staff: 17(v)/ members: 130/publication: *Great Little Watertown/Watertown Papers*

HISTORIC SITE; HISTORICAL SOCIETY; HOUSE MUSEUM: Promotes the history of Watertown, the first inland settlement in Massachusetts, and its people. Located at the Edmond Fowle House, built circa 1740 and listed on the National Register of Historic Places. Site of committee meetings of the Executive Council of the Provincial Congress in 1775 and 1776.

PROGRAMS: Community Outreach; Family Programs; Festivals; Guided Tours; Lectures; Publication

COLLECTIONS: [18th-19th c] Publications, letters, papers, portraits, photos

4025
Project SAVE Armenian Photograph Archives
65 Main St, 02471 [PO Box 236, 02471-0236]; (p) (617) 923-4542; (f) (617) 924-0434; archives@projectsave.org; (c) Middlesex

Private non-profit/ 1975/ Board of Directors/ staff: 2(f); 2(p); 10(v)

HISTORIC PRESERVATION AGENCY; RESEARCH CENTER: Collects, documents, preserves, and presents vintage and modern photographic records of Armenian Americans.

PROGRAMS: Community Outreach; Exhibits; Lectures; Research Library/Archives

COLLECTIONS: [1860-present] Photographs, oral history tapes, volumes on Armenian history and culture.

HOURS: Yr M-F 11-5 by appt

ADMISSION: No charge

WELLESLEY

4026
Davis Museum and Cultural Center
Wellesley College, 106 Central St, 02481-8203; (p) (781) 283-2051; (f) (781) 283-2064; www.wellesley.edu/davismuseum/davismenu.html; (c) Middlesex

Private non-profit/ 1886/ Wellesley College/ staff: 12(f); 10(p); 40(v)/ members: 2000

ART MUSEUM: Over 6,000 works of art; teaching museum of Wellesley College.

PROGRAMS: Concerts; Family Programs; Festivals; Film/Video; Guided Tours; Interpretation; Lectures

COLLECTIONS: Emphasis on African, Classical, American, photography and modern art.

HOURS: Yr T-Sa 11-5, Su 1-5

ADMISSION: No charge

4027
Wellesley Historical Society
229 Washington St, 02481 [PO Box 81142, 02481]; (p) (781) 235-6690; (f) (781) 235-6690; www.wellesleyhsoc.com; (c) Norfolk

Private non-profit/ 1925/ staff: 1(f); 30(v)/ members: 500

HISTORICAL SOCIETY: Collects, preserves and interprets the history of the Town of Wellesley.

PROGRAMS: Annual Meeting; Community Outreach; Concerts; Exhibits; Family Programs; Festivals; Interpretation; Lectures; Research Library/Archives

COLLECTIONS: Historical artifacts, plus the Denton butterfly and moth collection and Oldham lace collection; published and unpublished materials, photographs, maps and plans.

HOURS: Yr M, W 2-4:30, Th 4:30-7:30, Sa 1:30-3:30

ADMISSION: No charge

WENHAM

4028
Wenham Museum
132 Main St, 01984; (p) (978) 468-2377; (f) (978) 468-1763; info@wenhammuseum.com; (c) Essex

Private non-profit/ 1921/ Board of Trustees/ staff: 3(f); 14(p); 200(v)/ members: 1260/publication: *Wenham in Pictures and Prose*

HISTORICAL SOCIETY; HISTORY MUSEUM: Family-centered museum of colonial life, the skills and traditions of domesticity and childhood artifacts, including a large collection of dolls and toys.

PROGRAMS: Annual Meeting; Community Outreach; Exhibits; Facility Rental; Family Programs; Festivals; Guided Tours; Lectures; Publication; Research Library/Archives; School-Based Curriculum

COLLECTIONS: [17th-20th c] 30,000 artifacts including dolls, toys, model trains, costumes, textiles, 17th c house with period furnishings and over 4,000 glass plate negatives from the late 19th c.

HOURS: Yr T-Su 10-4

ADMISSION: $4, Children $2

WEST SPRINGFIELD

4029
Josiah Day House
70 Park St, 01089 [PO Box 826, 01090]

1754

COLLECTIONS: [1750-1900] 18th century furniture

HOURS: Seasonal

4030
Storrowton Village Museum
1305 Memorial Ave, 01089; (p) (413) 787-0136; (f) (413) 787-0166; dpicard@thebige.com; www.thebige.com/; (c) Hampden

Private non-profit/ 1927/ Eastern States Exposition/ staff: 3(f); 3(p); 150(v)/publication: *The Cracker Barrel*

HOUSE MUSEUM; LIVING HISTORY/OUTDOOR MUSEUM: Nine restored 18th-19th century structures arranged around a village green. Each building was moved from its original site to the museum.

PROGRAMS: Community Outreach; Concerts; Exhibits; Family Programs; Festivals; Guided Tours; Interpretation; Lectures; Living History; Publication; Research Library/Archives; School-Based Curriculum

COLLECTIONS: [1760-1850] Various artifacts reflecting all parts of life in New England.

HOURS: June-Oct M-Sa 11-3:30; Yr by appt

ADMISSION: $5, Children $3; Under 6 free

WESTMINSTER

4031
Westminster Historical Society
110 Main St, 01473 [PO Box 177, 01473]; (p) (978) 874-5569; (f) (978) 874-5569; (c) Worcester

Private non-profit/ 1921/ staff: 1(p)/ members: 157

HISTORICAL SOCIETY: Collects, preserves and interprets Westminster's past for the education and enjoyment of present and future generations. Provides research facilities, along with public and school programs.

PROGRAMS: Annual Meeting; Community Outreach; Exhibits; Facility Rental; Family Programs; Guided Tours; Lectures; Research Library/Archives; School-Based Curriculum

COLLECTIONS: [1800-present] Artifacts reflecting everyday life in rural and small town America, household, agricultural and school items, books, photographs, and maps.

HOURS: Yr by appt.

WESTON

4032
Golden Ball Tavern Museum
662 Boston Post Rd, 02493 [PO Box 223, 02493]; (p) (781) 894-1751; (f) (781) 862-9178; joanb5@aol.com

Private non-profit/ 1964/ Golden Ball Tavern Trust/ staff: 1(f); 100(v)/ members: 325/publication: *Grapevine*

HISTORY MUSEUM: Presents, illustrates, preserves and teaches the architectural, social and decorative changes over 200 years of the Jones family residence through education, collaborations and tours.

PROGRAMS: Annual Meeting; Community Outreach; Concerts; Exhibits; Festivals; Guided Tours; Interpretation; Lectures; Publication; Research Library/Archives; School-Based Curriculum

COLLECTIONS: [1768-1930] Jones family house, barn, grounds, artifacts and archives.

HOURS: Apr-Nov W and Su 9:30-12, 1:30-4;

4033
Weston Historical Society
358 Boston Post Rd, 02493 [PO Box 343, 02493]; (c) Middlesex

Private non-profit/ 1964/ staff: 3(v)/ members: 420

HISTORICAL SOCIETY; HISTORY MUSEUM; HOUSE MUSEUM

PROGRAMS: Annual Meeting; Community Outreach; Concerts; Exhibits; Family Programs; Guided Tours; Lectures; Research Library/Archives

COLLECTIONS: [19th-20th c] Memorabilia of Weston history, documents, photographs, artifacts, brochures, and books used for purposes of research into local history.

HOURS: Yr by appt; Sept-June W 10-12

ADMISSION: No charge

WEYMOUTH

4034
Abigail Adams Historical Society, Inc., The
180 Norton St, 02188 [PO Box 350, 02188]; (p) (781) 335-4205; (c) Norfolk

Private non-profit/ 1947/ Executive Board/ staff: 30(v)/ members: 175/publication: *Two Farms*

HISTORIC SITE; HISTORICAL SOCIETY; HOUSE MUSEUM: Maintains the restored birthplace of Abigail Adams; exhibits the house and grounds to the public and area students; and sponsors community events appropriate to the life of Abigail Adams.

PROGRAMS: Annual Meeting; Community Outreach; Festivals; Guided Tours; Interpretation; Publication; School-Based Curriculum

COLLECTIONS: [Mid-18th century] Furniture and articles of daily living, Smith/Adams artifacts, Weymouth items, records of house restoration, and "Abigail" literature.

HOURS: May 1-Oct 15 by appt; July-Sept T-Su 1-4

ADMISSION: $1, Children $0.25

4035
Weymouth Historical Society
Weymouth Museum, Broad St, 02190 [PO Box 56, 02190]; (c) Norfolk

Private non-profit/ 1879/ Executive Board/ members: 185

HISTORICAL SOCIETY: Maintains a museum and library, brings in speakers, conducts open houses and other activities.

PROGRAMS: Annual Meeting; Exhibits; Guided Tours; Interpretation; Lectures; Research Library/Archives

COLLECTIONS: [1622-present] Represents the daily life of Weymouth; genealogy.

HOURS: Yr By Appt

ADMISSION: No charge

WILBRAHAM

4036
Atheneum Society of Wilbraham

Corner Main St & Mountain Rd, 01095 [450 Main St, 01095]; (p) (413) 596-4097; (c) Hampden

Private non-profit/ 1963/ staff: 8(p); 6(v)/ members: 100/publication: *Peppercorn*

HISTORICAL SOCIETY

PROGRAMS: Annual Meeting; Exhibits; Lectures; Publication

COLLECTIONS: [1835] Books, furniture, papers, photographs, toys, and linens.

HOURS: May-Dec 1st Su 2-4

WILLIAMSTOWN

4037
Williams College Archives and Special Collections

Stetson Hall, 01267; (p) (413) 597-2568; (f) (413) 597-3931; archives@williams.edu; www.williams.edu/library/archives/main.html; (c) Berkshire

Private non-profit/ Williams College/ staff: 2(f)

LIBRARY AND/OR ARCHIVES: Collects, preserves and makes available the official records of Williams College, papers of College staff, students, faculty and alumni, and materials relating to the history of the Williamstown area.

PROGRAMS: Community Outreach; Exhibits; Research Library/Archives

COLLECTIONS: [1750-present] Official archives, personal papers, rare books, historic photographs and prints, artifacts, blueprints, oral history tapes, maps, phonograph recordings, sheet music, films and videotapes, scrapbooks and albums, ephemera, reference works.

HOURS: Yr M-F 10-12 and 1-4:30

ADMISSION: No charge

4038
Williamstown Art Conservation Center

225 S St, 01267; (p) (413) 458-5741; (f) (413) 458-2314; wacc@clark.williams.edu; (c) Berkshire

Private non-profit/ 1977/ staff: 22(f)/ members: 57

PROGRAMS: Guided Tours

ADMISSION: No charge

WOODS HOLE

4039
Woods Hole Historical Museum

579 Woods Hole Rd, 02543 [PO Box 185, 02543]; (p) (508) 548-7270; (f) (508) 540-1969; www.woodsholemuseum.org; (c) Barnstable

Private non-profit/ 1973/ Woods Hole Public Library/ staff: 2(p); 50(v)/ members: 475/publication: *Diary of Ruth Anna Hatch; Jane's Island; and others*

HISTORICAL SOCIETY; HISTORY MUSEUM: Preserves objects and materials of cultural, historical and artistic value to illustrate town history. Features a model of Woods Hole in 1895, changing exhibits, a small boat museum and Victorian workshop.

PROGRAMS: Annual Meeting; Exhibits; Garden Tours; Guided Tours; Lectures; Publication; Research Library/Archives

COLLECTIONS: [Mid 19th c-present] Photographs, particularly by Baldwin Coolidge; 200 oral histories; papers of families and businesses; ships' logs from whaling era and China trade, boat models and other maritime items; paintings.

HOURS: Archives: Yr T, Th 10-2; Exhibits: mid June-mid Oct T-Sa 10-4

ADMISSION: Donations accepted

WORCESTER

4040
American Antiquarian Society

185 Salisbury St, 01609; (p) (508) 755-5221; (f) (508) 753-3311; library@mwa.org; www.americanantiquarian.org

Private non-profit/ 1812/ staff: 36(f); 12(p); 6(v)/publication: *Proceedings of the American Antiquarian Society*

RESEARCH CENTER: Research library that documents the life of Americans from the Colonial era through the Civil War and Reconstruction. The Society sponsors research fellowships and supports active publication and education programs.

PROGRAMS: Annual Meeting; Community Outreach; Concerts; Festivals; Guided Tours; Lectures; Publication; Research Library/Archives; School-Based Curriculum

COLLECTIONS: [American history through 1876] Books, pamphlets, newspapers, periodicals, broadsides, manuscripts, music, maps, graphic arts, and printed ephemera.

HOURS: Yr M-F 9-5

4041
John Woodman Higgins Armory Museum

100 Barber Ave, 01606; (p) (508) 853-6015; (f) (508) 852-7697; higgins@higgins.org; www.higgins.org; (c) Worcester

Private non-profit/ 1931/ Board of Directors/ staff: 12(f); 30(p); 10(v)/ members: 400

HISTORY MUSEUM: Dedicated to the exhibition, interpretation, research and preservation of arms and armor in a broad cultural context.

PROGRAMS: Annual Meeting; Community Outreach; Concerts; Exhibits; Facility Rental; Family Programs; Festivals; Guided Tours; Lectures; Reenactments; Research Library/Archives; School-Based Curriculum

COLLECTIONS: [Prehistory-19th c] Arms and armor from around the world, including Roman, Medieval and Renaissance periods.

HOURS: Yr T-Sa 10-4, Su 12-4

ADMISSION: $6.75, Children

4042
New England Antiquities Research Association

Membership, 1199 Main St, 01603; www.neara.org

Private non-profit/ 1964/ staff: 18(v)/ members: 370/publication: *NEARA Journal; NEARA Transit*

HISTORIC PRESERVATION AGENCY; LIVING HISTORY/OUTDOOR MUSEUM; PROFESSIONAL ORGANIZATION; RESEARCH CENTER: Fosters interdisciplinary research on enigmatic stone structures or markings in their cultural context, and on evidence of world-wide cultural diffusion.

PROGRAMS: Annual Meeting; Guided Tours; Interpretation; Lectures; Publication; Research Library/Archives

COLLECTIONS: [1800-present] Exeter, NH Public Library: 800 books and 25 serials on archaeology anthropology, cultural and biological geography, archaeoastronomy and lithic sites.

HOURS: Bi-annual meetings and field trips

4043
Salisbury Mansion

40 Highland St, 01609 [30 Elm St, 01609]; (p) (508) 753-8278; (f) (508) 753-8278; worchistmu@aol.com

1771

Home of Stephen Salisbury I, showing 18th c rural imitation and adaptation of Boston high style.

COLLECTIONS: [1830s] Objects that can be matched to an 1851 partial inventory of the contents.

4044
Worcester Historical Museum

30 Elm St, 01609; (p) (508) 753-8278; (f) (508) 753-9070; worchistmu@aol.com; (c) Worcester

Private non-profit/ 1875/ staff: 8(f); 12(p); 25(v)/ members: 800

HISTORICAL SOCIETY; HISTORY MUSEUM; HOUSE MUSEUM: Museum and library of the city of Worcester.

PROGRAMS: Annual Meeting; Community Outreach; Concerts; Exhibits; Facility Rental; Family Programs; Guided Tours; Interpretation; Lectures; Research Library/Archives; School-Based Curriculum

COLLECTIONS: [Prehistory-present] Full survey of the material culture of the city.

HOURS: Yr T-Su 10-4

ADMISSION: $2; Students/Mbrs free

YARMOUTH

4045
Captain Bangs Hallet House

11 Strawberry Lane, 02675 [PO Box 11, 02675]; (p) (508) 362-3021

1843/ staff: 3(p); 20(v)

COLLECTIONS: [19th c] Maritime, children's; Photograph collection of Yarmouth homes, activities, people, Yarmouth historical documents, ship logs.

HOURS: Seasonal

YARMOUTHPORT

4046
Winslow Crocker House, SPNEA
250 Route 6A, Old King's Hwy, 02675; (p) (508) 362-4385; www.spnea.org

Private non-profit/ 1780/ Society for the Preservation of New England Antiquities

HOUSE MUSEUM: A colonial Cape Cod house with a 20th c flavor.

COLLECTIONS: Furniture, hooked rugs, ceramics, and pewter, Jacobean, William and Mary, Queen Anne, and Chippendale styles.

HOURS: June 1-Oct 15 Sa-Su 11-5

ADMISSION: $5; SPNEA Mbrs/Town

4047
Historical Society of Old Yarmouth
11 Strawberry Lane, 02675 [PO Box 11, Yarmouth Port, 02675]; (p) (508) 362-3021

Private non-profit/ 1953/ staff: 1(p); 40(v)/ members: 400/publication: *West Yarmouth: A Village Ignored; The Breed Family; and others*

HISTORICAL SOCIETY; HOUSE MUSEUM

PROGRAMS: Annual Meeting; Community Outreach; Exhibits; Facility Rental; Film/Video; Guided Tours; Interpretation; Lectures; Publication; Research Library/Archives; School-Based Curriculum

COLLECTIONS: [19th c] Photographs and manuscripts; maritime, domestic and decorative objects

HOURS: Su 1-4

ADMISSION: $3, Children $0.50

MICHIGAN

ACME

4048
Music House Museum, The
7377 US 31 N, 49610 [PO Box 297, 49610]; (p) (231) 938-9300; (f) (231) 938-3650; www.musichouse@coslink.net; www.musichouse.org; (c) Grand Traverse

Joint; Private non-profit/ 1983/ staff: 4(f); 4(p); 4(v)/ members: 60

Museum of restored antique automated musical instruments with related historical settings.

COLLECTIONS: [1850-1950] Thousands of musical and period decor items; music boxes, phonographs, keyboard, and stringed instruments, organs, radios, TV, recordings, printed music and reference materials.

HOURS: May-Oct Daily M-Sa 10-4, Su 12-4; call for winter schedule

ADMISSION: $7, Children $2.50

ADA

4049
Ada Historical Society
7144 Thornapple River Dr, 49301 [PO Box 741, 49301]; (p) (616) 676-9346; (c) Kent

Private non-profit/ 1976/ staff: 10(v)/ members: 97/publication: *A Snug Little Place*

HISTORICAL SOCIETY; HISTORY MUSEUM: Promotes understanding and appreciation of the historical and cultural heritage of Ada Township and surrounding area. Collects, preserves, interprets and exhibits historical and cultural artifacts and sites.

PROGRAMS: Annual Meeting; Community Outreach; Exhibits; Lectures; Living History; Publication

COLLECTIONS: [1821-present] Items associated with area history.

ADMISSION: Donations accepted

ADRIAN

4050
Lenawee County Historical Society, Inc.
110 E Church, 49221 [PO Box 511, 49221]; (p) (517) 265-6071; (c) Lenawee

Private non-profit/ 1923/ staff: 1(f); 24(v)/ members: 800/publication: *From the Tower*

HISTORIC SITE; HISTORICAL SOCIETY; HISTORY MUSEUM; HOUSE MUSEUM: Seeks through its collections and its lectures, articles, books, and exhibits to inform the public about the value and inherent interest of our common local history.

PROGRAMS: Annual Meeting; Exhibits; Facility Rental; Festivals; Guided Tours; Lectures; Publication

COLLECTIONS: [1820-present] Objects and documents related to the history of the people of Lenawee, including items related to politics, war, and government, the home, church, school, shop, and the factory.

HOURS: Yr T-Sa 1-5

ADMISSION: No charge

ALBION

4051
Gardner House Museum
509 S Superior St, 49224; (p) (517) 629-5100; (c) Calhoun

Private non-profit/ 1958/ Albion Historical Society/ staff: 1(p); 75(v)/ members: 650

Preserves and displays the heritage of Albion and vicinity.

PROGRAMS: Annual Meeting; Exhibits; Garden Tours; Guided Tours

COLLECTIONS: [Victorian]

HOURS: May-Sept Sa-Su 2-4

ADMISSION: Donations accepted

ALDEN

4052
Helena Township Historical Society
10670 Coy St, 49612 [PO Box 204, 49612]; (p) (616) 331-4274; (c) Antrim

Private non-profit/ 1986/ staff: 20(v)/ members: 90

HISTORIC SITE; HISTORICAL SOCIETY; HISTORY MUSEUM: The Society collects, preserves and displays artifacts from the area/assists local organization in presenting festival, concerts and displays in the "Alden Depot Park and Museum."

PROGRAMS: Annual Meeting; Concerts; Elder's Programs; Exhibits; Festivals; Garden Tours; Lectures

COLLECTIONS: [1840s-1980s] The 1000 article collection includes lumbering, railroad, farming and household artifacts, period clothing and textiles. There are 1,500 photographs of the period with accompanying photographic equipment.

HOURS: July-Aug Th 9-4 & 6-9,

ALLEGAN

4053
Allegan County Historical Society and Museum
113 Walnut St, 49010; (p) (616) 673-4853; (c) Allegan

Private non-profit/ 1952/ Board of Directors/ staff: 10(v)/ members: 202

HISTORICAL SOCIETY; HISTORY MUSEUM: Preserves and presents county history to the public through museum and village tours, programs and school-related activities.

PROGRAMS: Annual Meeting; Exhibits; Festivals; Guided Tours; Lectures; Research Library/Archives

COLLECTIONS: [19th-20th c] Fifteen period rooms in Old Jail and Sheriff's Living Quarters; historical village at Allegan County Fairgrounds consists of fifteen reconstructed buildings; and two Farmers Museum barns.

HOURS: June-Sept F 2-5 or by appt

ADMISSION: Donations accepted

ALPENA

4054
Jesse Besser Museum
491 Johnson St, 49707; (p) (517) 356-2202; (f) (517) 356-3133; jbmuseum@northland.lib.mi.us; www.oweb.com/upnoth/museum; (c) Alpena

Private non-profit/ 1966/ staff: 4(f); 5(p)

ART MUSEUM; HISTORY MUSEUM; LIVING HISTORY/OUTDOOR MUSEUM: Preserves, studies, teaches, and exhibits artistic, historical, scientific and technological collections to the public.

PROGRAMS: Community Outreach; Concerts; Exhibits; Facility Rental; Family Programs; Festivals; Guided Tours; Lectures; Living History; Research Library/Archives; School-Based Curriculum

COLLECTIONS: History collection includes Native Americans, logging, farming, household, and merchant artifacts.

HOURS: Yr

ADMISSION: $2, Children $1, Seniors $1; Disabled free

ANN ARBOR

4055
Gerald R. Ford Library
1000 Beal Ave, 48109-2214; (p) (734) 741-2218; (f) (734) 741-2341; ford.library@nara.gov; www.ford.utexas.edu/; (c) Wastenaw

Federal/ National Archives and Records

4056
Historical Society of Michigan
2117 Washtenaw Ave, 48104-4599; (p) (734) 769-1828; (f) (734) 769-4267; hsofmich@leslie.k12.mi.us; at146.atl.mus.edu/hsm.html; (c) Washtenaw

Private non-profit/ 1828/ staff: 2(f); 1(p); 5(v)/ members: 2500

HISTORICAL SOCIETY: Foster and understanding and appreciation of Michigan history through programs and publications, and enhancing public support for the preservation and protection of Michigan history.

PROGRAMS: Annual Meeting; Lectures; School-Based Curriculum

HOURS: Yr M-F 9-5

4057
Kempf House Center for Local History
312 S Division St, 48104; (p) (734) 994-4898; (c) Washtenaw

City/ 1970/ staff: 25(v)/ members: 160

HISTORIC PRESERVATION AGENCY; HISTORIC SITE; HISTORY MUSEUM; HOUSE MUSEUM: Interprets the history of Ann Arbor and family life in the Victorian Era.

PROGRAMS: Annual Meeting; Community Outreach; Exhibits; Facility Rental; Guided Tours; Interpretation; Lectures; Research Library/Archives; School-Based Curriculum

COLLECTIONS: [Victorian Era] Greek Revival house built in 1853 with furnishings.

HOURS: Sept-Dec and Feb-June Su 1-4, W 12-1

4058
Ticknor-Campbell House, The, at Cobblestone Farm and Museum
2781 Packard St, 48108 [2781 Packard Rd, 48108]; (p) (734) 994-2928, (734) 971-8789; (f) (734) 971-9415; (c) Washtenaw

1844/ City; Cobblestone Farm Association/ staff: 1(f); 6(p); 35(v)

COLLECTIONS: [1850s] Country Sheraton & Empire furniture, farm implements, blue and white china, clothing.; Late 19th early 20th century wallpaper used in house. Historic photos of farmstead and house interior, 1900-1930.

HOURS: Seasonal

4059
University of Michigan Exhibit Museum of Natural History
1109 Geddes Ave, 48109-1079; (p) (734) 764-0478; (f) (734) 647-2767; aharris@umich.edu; www.exhibits.lsa.umich.edu/; (c) Washtenaw

State/ 1956/ staff: 10(f); 1(p); 20(v)/ members: 600

HISTORY MUSEUM: Exhibits and educational programs in separate research and collecting museums.

PROGRAMS: Community Outreach; Exhibits; Facility Rental; Family Programs; Guided Tours; Lectures; School-Based Curriculum

COLLECTIONS: [Prehistory] Prehistoric life, Native Americans, Michigan wildlife, geology, biology, and astronomy; collections are housed in research museums.

HOURS: Yr Daily M-Sa 9-5

4060
Washtenaw County Historical Society
[PO Box 3336, 48106-3336]; (p) (734) 662-9092; (f) (734) 663-0039; PopoWalt@aol.com; www.hvcn.org/info/gswc/society/socwashtenaw. htm; (c) Washtenaw

Private non-profit/ 1857/ staff: 20(p); 15(v)/ members: 400/publication: *Impressions*

HISTORIC SITE; HISTORICAL SOCIETY; HISTORY MUSEUM: Sponsors programs and runs museum to display our collections relating to local history.

PROGRAMS: Annual Meeting; Community Outreach; Exhibits; Facility Rental; Guided Tours; Interpretation; Lectures; Publication; Research Library/Archives; School-Based Curriculum

COLLECTIONS: [1830-2000] Vintage clothing from pioneers, household goods, business memorabilia, toys, Univ of MI artifacts, Indian artifacts, photographs, and ephemera.

HOURS: Sept-May W, Sa-Su 12-4 and by appt

ADMISSION: Donations

ARNHEIM

4061
Hanka Homestead Museum
, [PO Box 10, Pelkie, 49958]; (p) (906) 344-2601

AU GRES

4062
Arenac County Historical Society
304 Michigan Ave, 48703 [PO Box 272, 48703]; (p) (517) 876-6399; (c) Arenac

County/ 1970/ members: 200

HISTORIC PRESERVATION AGENCY; HISTORICAL SOCIETY; HISTORY MUSEUM: Preserves history and educates with programs and displays.

PROGRAMS: Annual Meeting; Community Outreach; Exhibits; Guided Tours; Publication; Research Library/Archives

COLLECTIONS: [19th-mid 20th c] Native American artifacts, furniture, and newspapers.

HOURS: May-Sept Sa-Su 1-4; Program last Th May-Sept 7:30pm

ADMISSION: $1; Under 12 free

AUBURN HILLS

4063
Walter P. Chrysler Museum
One Chrysler Dr / CTMS 488-00-00, 48326-2766; (p) (248) 966-0431; (f) (248) 944-0460; BD28@daimle.chrysler.com; www.chrysler heritage.com; (c) Oakland

1986/ staff: 9(f); 5(p); 60(v)

CORPORATE ARCHIVES/MUSEUM; HISTORY MUSEUM: Devoted to the American heritage of Daimler Chrysler, including collateral and predecessor companies.

PROGRAMS: Exhibits; Facility Rental; Festivals; Interpretation; Lectures; Publication; Research Library/Archives; School-Based Curriculum

COLLECTIONS: [20th c] Automobiles, engines, graphics, ephemera related to Walter P. Chrysler and the company and products related to the American history of Daimler Chrysler

HOURS: Yr T-Sa 10-6, Su 12-6

ADMISSION: $6, Student $3, Seniors $3

BATTLE CREEK

4064
Kellogg's Cereal City, USA
171 W Michigan Ave, 49017; (p) (616) 962-6230; (f) (616) 962-3787; pboyer@ kccusa.org; www.kelloggscerealcityusa.org; (c) Calhoun

1994/ staff: 12(f); 80(p)

CORPORATE ARCHIVES/MUSEUM; HISTORY MUSEUM: Conveys the development, growth, and impact of the cereal industry.

PROGRAMS: Exhibits; Facility Rental; Family Programs; Festivals; Film/Video

COLLECTIONS: [Early 1900s-present] Cereal premiums, equipment from Battle Creek Sanitarium, original paintings used in early Kellogg Company advertising.

HOURS: Yr May-Sept Daily; Sept-Oct 31 and Mar-May T-Su; Nov-Feb Sa-Su

ADMISSION: $7.95

4065
Kimball House Historical Museum
196 Capital Ave NE, 49017-3925; (p) (616) 966-2496; (f) (616) 966-2495

BAY CITY

4066
Bay County Historical Society/ Historical Museum of Bay County
321 Washington Ave, 48708; (p) (517) 893-5733; (f) (517) 893-5741; www.bchsmuseum.org; (c) Bay

Private non-profit/ 1919/ Board of Directors/ staff: 5(f); 2(p); 200(v)/ members: 500/publication: *The Museum Record*

HISTORICAL SOCIETY: Preserves, collects, and interprets Bay County history through research library facilities, exhibits, publications, and programs.

PROGRAMS: Annual Meeting; Exhibits; Guided Tours; Interpretation; Lectures; Living History; Publication; Reenactments; School-Based Curriculum

COLLECTIONS: [1840-present] Archival materials and museum objects, Monitor Sugar Corporate Archives, Patrol Craft Sailor's Association Archives.

HOURS: Yr M-F 10-5, Sa-Su 12-4

4067
Trombley House
901 John F Kennedy Dr, 48708 [Historical Museum of Bay County, 321 Washington , 48708]; (p) (517) 892-9431, (517) 893-5733; www.saginawvalley.com/csdir/WWW1165.HTM

BEAVER ISLAND

4068
Beaver Island Historical Society
26275 Main St, 49782 [PO Box 263, 49782]; (p) (616) 448-2254; (f) (616) 448-2106; wcashman@beaverisland.net; www.beaver island.net/history; (c) Charlevoix

Joint/ 1957/ Private non-profit; Beaver Falls Historical Society; Carnegie Free Library/ staff: 1(f); 1(p); 44(v)/ members: 305/publication: *Journal of Beaver Island History, Vol. 1-4*

GENEALOGICAL SOCIETY; HISTORIC SITE; HISTORY MUSEUM; TRIBAL MUSEUM: Collects, restores, preserves, interprets, and displays artifacts and information relating to Beaver Island history.

PROGRAMS: Annual Meeting; Concerts; Exhibits; Festivals; Lectures; Publication

COLLECTIONS: [1850-present] Represents the Mormon era (1848-1856), Native Americans, Dr. Proctor and nautical displays.

BELLAIRE

4069
Bellaire Area Historical Society
202 N Bridge St, 49615 [PO Box 616, 49615]; (p) (616) 533-8631; (c) Antrim

1976/ staff: 20(v)/ members: 65

HISTORICAL SOCIETY; HISTORY MUSEUM: Collects, preserves and displays items relating to Bellaire and its surrounding rural area, including its people, businesses and industry.

COLLECTIONS: [1865-1965] Depression glass; tools relating to farming, automobile repair, lumbering and cutting ice; clothing, furs, books, scrapbooks and items from all wars.

HOURS: June-Aug M-F 11-3

BELLEVILLE

4070
Belleville Area Museum
405 Main St, 48111; (p) (734) 697-1944; (c) Wayne

Joint/ 1989/ staff: 1(f); 60(v)/ members: 187

HISTORICAL SOCIETY; HISTORY MUSEUM: Changing exhibits, local history, and genealogy archives available to researchers; quilt show and festival of holiday trees.

PROGRAMS: Annual Meeting; Exhibits; Guided Tours; Lectures; Research Library/Archives

COLLECTIONS: [1850-1950]

HOURS: Yr T-Sa 12-4

ADMISSION: $1, Family $3, Children $0.50

BENTON HARBOR

4071
Josephine Morton Memorial Home
501 Territorial, 49022; (p) (616) 925-7011; www.parrett.net/~morton/; (c) Berrien

Private non-profit/ 1960/ staff: 30(v)/ members: 400

HISTORY MUSEUM; HOUSE MUSEUM: Operates the 9-room Morton House; preserves local history and shares it with the community.

PROGRAMS: Exhibits; Facility Rental; Family Programs; Festivals; Interpretation; Lectures

COLLECTIONS: [1800-1940] Maritime records, costume collection, artifacts, photographs.

HOURS: Mid Apr-Oct Th 1-4, Su 2-4 or by appt

BENZONIA

4072
Benzie Area Historical Society
6941 River Rd, 49616 [PO Box 185, 49616-0185]; (p) (231) 882-5539; (c) Benzie

Private non-profit/ 1969/ Board of Directors/ staff: 1(f); 60(v)/ members: 737/publication: *Benzie Heritage*

HISTORIC SITE; HISTORICAL SOCIETY; HISTORY MUSEUM: Preserves and interprets local historical events, artifacts, and information through exhibits and archival files.

PROGRAMS: Annual Meeting; Community Outreach; Exhibits; Festivals; Guided Tours; Lectures; Publication; Research Library/ Archives

COLLECTIONS: [1850-1940] Photographs of early Benzie pioneers, artifacts related to logging, car ferry, early settlers, and farming.

HOURS: June-Aug M-Sa 10-4; May, Sept-Nov Th-Sa 10-4

ADMISSION: $3

BERRIEN SPRINGS

4073
Berrien County Historical Association
1839 Courthouse Museum, 313 N Cass St, 49103 [PO Box 261, 49103]; (p) (616) 471-1202; (f) (616) 471-7412; bcha@berrien history.org; www.berrienhistory.org; (c) Berrien

Private non-profit/ 1967/ Board of Trustees/ staff: 3(f); 3(p); 36(v)/ members: 426/publication: *Historical Sketches of Berrien County, Volumes 1-3; and others*

HISTORIC SITE; HISTORICAL SOCIETY; HISTORY MUSEUM: Preserves and interprets historic structures on the 1839 Courthouse Square in Berrien Springs and operates the historic site as a county museum and archives.

PROGRAMS: Annual Meeting; Community Outreach; Concerts; Exhibits; Facility Rental; Festivals; Guided Tours; Interpretation; Lectures; Living History; Publication; Reenactments; Research Library/Archives; School-Based Curriculum; Theatre

COLLECTIONS: [1830-1930] Photographs, letters, diaries, Clark Equipment Company archives, blacksmithing and woodworking tools, clothing, marriage and death records, probate court files, maps and newspapers.

HOURS: Feb-Dec T-F 9-4, Sa-Su 1-5

ADMISSION: $2.50, Children $1; Under 6 free

BIRMINGHAM

4074
Oakland County Genealogical Society
[PO Box 1094, 48012-1094]; (p) (248) 553-2151; ShirleyMSB@aol.com; www.rhpl.org/OCGS; (c) Oakland

Joint; Private non-profit/ 1977/ staff: 25(v)/ members: 425/publication: *Acorns to Oaks*

GENEALOGICAL SOCIETY: Provides informational speakers at monthly meetings.

PROGRAMS: Lectures; Publication; Research Library/Archives

COLLECTIONS: [1800s-present]

BLOOMFIELD

4075
Cranbrook House and Gardens Auxiliary
380 Lone Pine Rd, 48303 [PO Box 801, 48303-0801]; (p) (248) 645-3147; (f) (248) 645-3151; www.cranbrook.edu; (c) Oakland

Private non-profit/ 1971/ staff: 2(f); 550(v)/ members: 550

GARDEN; HISTORIC SITE; HOUSE MUSEUM: Supports maintenance of gardens and 1908 Arts & Crafts home of George Gough Booth and Ellen Scripps Booth designed by Albert Kahn.

PROGRAMS: Garden Tours; Guided Tours

HOURS: Garden: May-Aug Daily M-Sa 10-5, Su 11-5; House: June-Oct Th 11-1:15, Su 1:30-3

ADMISSION: $10

BRIDGEPORT

4076
Historical Society of Bridgeport, The
6190 Dixie Hwy, 48722 [PO Box 337, 48722]; (p) (517) 777-5230; (c) Saginaw

Private non-profit/ 1969/ staff: 1(p); 35(v)/ members: 100/publication: *Recollections*

HISTORICAL SOCIETY: To obtain and record information concerning historic and prehistoric sites and any artifacts in the township of Bridgeport.

PROGRAMS: Annual Meeting; Community Outreach; Concerts; Exhibits; Festivals; Publication; School-Based Curriculum

COLLECTIONS: [Early American] Early American artifacts of household, farm, hand tools, books, newspapers, photographs, clothing, schools, government, and Indian objects

BRIMLEY

4077
Bay Mills Community College Library and Heritage Center
12214 W Lakeshore, 49715; (p) (906) 248-3354; (f) (906) 248-3351; rpilon@bmcc.org; (c) Chippewa

Private non-profit/ staff: 1(f); 3(p)

HISTORY MUSEUM; TRIBAL MUSEUM: Owned by the Bay Mills Indian Community; operates as both an academic and public library and museum.

PROGRAMS: Community Outreach; Elder's Programs; Exhibits; Film/Video; Research Library/Archives; School-Based Curriculum

COLLECTIONS: [Late 19th c-early 20th c] James O. Keene Native American Heritage Collection consists of around 135 historical objects.

HOURS: Yr June-Aug M-F 8-5, Sept-May M-F

4078
Bay Mills/Brimley Historical Research Society
M221, Bay St at Depot, 49715 [PO Box 273, 49715]; (p) (906) 248-3665; (c) Chippewa

Private non-profit/ 1981/ Elected Board/ staff: 20(v)/ members: 85

HISTORIC SITE; HISTORICAL SOCIETY; HISTORY MUSEUM: Preserves history of the Bay Mills/Brimley area, operates a local history museum, "Wheels of History" and maintains the Point Iroquois Lighthouse Museum in partnership with the USDA Forest Service.

PROGRAMS: Concerts; Exhibits; Festivals; Guided Tours; Interpretation; Lectures

COLLECTIONS: [1870s-present] Photographs and artifacts of Brimley Area, Bay Mills townsite, Point Iroquois Lighthouse operation, lighthouse family life, area railroads, early telephones, logging and fishing.

HOURS: May15-June 15 Sa-Su 10-4; June 15-Sept W-Su 10-4; Sept-Oct 15 Sa-Su 10-4

ADMISSION: No charge

CADILLAC

4079
Wexford County Historical Society
127 Beech St, 49601 [PO Box 124, 49601]; (p) (231) 775-1717; community.mlive.com/cc/cadillacmusuem; (c) Wexford

Private non-profit/ 1965/ staff: 1(f)/ members: 211

HISTORICAL SOCIETY; HISTORY MUSEUM: Discover, collect, display material which helps to establish of illustrate the history of the area.

PROGRAMS: Annual Meeting; Exhibits; Guided Tours; Interpretation

COLLECTIONS: [1890-present] Dentist's and doctor's office, bank teller, logging, dining, living rooms, kitchen, Main St. general store, barber shop, watch maker shop, switch board, parlor, railroad, fire truck.

CANTON

4080
Canton Historical Society
Canton Center Rd at Heritage Dr, 48187 [PO Box 87362, 48187]; (p) (734) 397-0088; (c) Wayne

Private non-profit/ 1975/ staff: 20(v)/ members: 130

HISTORICAL SOCIETY; HISTORY MUSEUM: Preserves the history of Canton Township.

PROGRAMS: Annual Meeting

CAPAC

4081
Capac Community Historical Society
401 E Kempf Ct, 48014; (c) Saint Clair

Private non-profit/ 1977/ Board of Trustees/ staff: 20(v)/ members: 65

HISTORICAL SOCIETY; HISTORY MUSEUM: Preserves the physical artifacts and records of the past for use by future generations.

PROGRAMS: Annual Meeting; Exhibits

COLLECTIONS: [1910-1940] Kempf Model City portrays the county in the 1920s-1930s.

CASPIAN

4082
Iron County Historical and Museum Society
100 Museum Rd, 49915 [Box 272, 49915]; (p) (906) 265-2617; (c) Iron

Private non-profit/ 1962/ staff: 1(f); 3(p); 80(v)/ members: 180

HISTORY MUSEUM: Oversees 22 buildings and offers programs for the community.

PROGRAMS: Annual Meeting; Community Outreach; Concerts; Exhibits; Facility Rental; Family Programs; Guided Tours; Research Library/Archives; School-Based Curriculum

COLLECTIONS: [1880-present] Mining, logging, transportation, agricultural, school, Victorian, wild life art, business, medical, Native American, ethnic, community leaders, Native Sons, religious materials.

CASSOPOLIS

4083
Historic Newton House
20689 Marcellus Hwy, 49031 [c/o M. Federowski, 24010 Hospital St, 49031]; (p) (616) 782-2008, (616) 445-9016; (c) Cass

County/ staff: 20(v)

HOURS: Su 1-4

ADMISSION: Donations accepted

CEDARVILLE

4084
Les Cheneaux Historical Association
[PO Box 301, 49719]; (p) (906) 484-2821; lcha@northernway.net; lescheneaux@northernway.net; (c) Mackinac

Private non-profit/ 1968/ staff: 1(f); 7(p); 65(v)/ members: 200/publication: *Martin Reef-From Light to Lighthouse; Of Fifty Summers*

HISTORICAL SOCIETY; HISTORY MUSEUM: Encourages appreciation of social and historical heritage and the natural history of Les Cheneaux Islands and vicinity, preserves items of historical and educational significance and maintains and operates the Historical Museum and the Maritime Museum.

PROGRAMS: Annual Meeting; Community Outreach; Concerts; Elder's Programs; Exhibits; Family Programs; Festivals; Film/Video; Guided Tours; Interpretation; Lectures; Publication; Research Library/Archives

COLLECTIONS: [Mid 1800s-1950s] Historical Museum: items from Native American and Pioneer periods, through logging, fishing, hotel, and tourism industry including models of early water transportation. Maritime Museum: boats and boat models marine paraphernalia, photos, library, and boat building shop.

HOURS: Late May-mid Sept Daily M-Sa 10-5, Su 1-5; and by appt

ADMISSION: $2, Family $5; Children free

CHARLOTTE

4085
Courthouse Square Association, Inc.
100 W Lawrence Ave, 48813 [PO Box 411, 48813]; (p) (517) 543-6999; (f) (517) 543-6999; goforth@pilot.msu.edu; (c) Eaton

Joint; Private non-profit/ 1993/ staff: 2(f); 20(v)/ members: 100/publication: *The Courthouse Square Ledger*

HISTORIC SITE; HISTORY MUSEUM: National Register site includes the 1885 Eaton County Courthouse and 1873 Sheriff's Residence, exhibits and programs.

PROGRAMS: Community Outreach; Concerts; Exhibits; Facility Rental; Family Programs; Festivals; Film/Video; Guided Tours; Interpretation; Lectures; Publication; Research Library/Archives; School-Based Curriculum; Theatre

COLLECTIONS: [19th c] Textiles, agricultural equipment, radios/TVs, Civil War, archival photos and letters, country records, and documents, furniture.

HOURS: Yr M-F 9-4, Sa 10-2

ADMISSION: Donations requested

CHASSELL

4086
Chassell Historical Organization, Inc.
202 Nancock, 49916 [PO Box 331, 49916]; (p) (906) 523-1155; www.einerlei.com/chassell/chassell.html; (c) Houghton

Private non-profit/ 1992/ staff: 20(v)/ members: 100/publication: *The Heritage*

HISTORICAL SOCIETY: Oversees and maintains the Chassell Heritage Center which houses the Chassell Museum and the Friends of Fashion Vintage clothing collection.

PROGRAMS: Annual Meeting; Community Outreach; Exhibits; Festivals; Guided Tours; Interpretation; Living History; Publication; Reenactments

COLLECTIONS: [1860-present] Vintage clothing and accessories; items from farming, schoo,; businesses, WWI and WWII, native inhabitants.

HOURS: July-Aug T 1-4, Th 4-7; and special events

CHEBOYGAN

4087
Historical Society of Cheboygan County
427 Court St, 49721 [PO Box 5005, 49721]; (p) (231) 627-9597; rojan@freeway.net; (c) Cheboygan

Private non-profit/ 1969/ staff: 1(p); 40(v)/ members: 190

HISTORICAL SOCIETY: To collect, preserve, and cultivate the past to create an appreciation of the rich County-wide heritage.

PROGRAMS: Annual Meeting; Exhibits; Festivals; Garden Tours; Guided Tours; Publication; Research Library/Archives

COLLECTIONS: [1870-1945] Furnishings for a turn-of-the-century home, fishing, school, household items, farming, clothing, and textiles, tools, country store items.

HOURS: M, F 1-4, Sa 11-3

ADMISSION: $2; Children free

CHELSEA

4088
Heritage Room Museum of Chelsea Retirement Community
805 W Middle St, 48118; (p) (734) 475-8633; (f) (734) 475-4421; (c) Washtenaw

Private non-profit/ 1971/ staff: 15(v)

HISTORY MUSEUM: Teaches how the lifestyles and society's views of the elderly have evolved

PROGRAMS: Community Outreach; Exhibits; Guided Tours; Research Library/Archives; School-Based Curriculum

COLLECTIONS: [Early 1900s] Daily life in the Home during early 1900s.

HOURS: Yr by appt

ADMISSION: No charge

CHESANING

4089
Chesaning Area Historical Society
602 W Broad St, 48616 [PO Box 52, 48616]; (p) (517) 845-3155; (c) Saginaw

Joint/ 1982/ staff: 31(v)/ members: 139/publication: *Riverside Times*

HISTORICAL SOCIETY; HISTORY MUSEUM: Area history; publishes historical newspaper; holds meetings.

PROGRAMS: Annual Meeting; Community Outreach; Concerts; Exhibits; Festivals; Guided Tours; Publication

COLLECTIONS: Early Indian Reservation, logging, farming, settlers, meat packing, school district.

HOURS: Jan-Dec Sa, Su 12-4:30, special events or by appt

ADMISSION: Donations accepted

CLARKSTON

4090
Clarkston Community Historical Society
6495 Clarkston Rd, 48346; (p) (248) 922-0270; (f) (248) 625-2499; www.clarkstonhistorical.com/; (c) Oakland

Joint; Private non-profit/ 1972/ staff: 7(v)/ members: 250/publication: *Heritage; Our Children's Heritage; and others*

HISTORICAL SOCIETY; HISTORY MUSEUM: Dedicated to the preservation of local history. Operates the Clarkston Heritage Museum.

PROGRAMS: Annual Meeting; Concerts; Exhibits; Family Programs; Festivals; Guided Tours; Lectures; Publication; School-Based Curriculum

COLLECTIONS: [1832-present] Photographs, documents, and settler artifacts; Native American artifacts.

HOURS: M-Th 10-9, F 10-6, Sa 10-5, Su 1-5

ADMISSION: No charge

CLAWSON

4091
Clawson Historical Museum
41 Fisher Ct, 48017 [425 N Main, 48017]; (p) (248) 435-4467; (c) Oakland

City/ 1973/ staff: 1(p); 6(v)

HISTORY MUSEUM; HOUSE MUSEUM: To collect, preserve, and reflect Clawson history from the time the first pioneers settled in area.

PROGRAMS: Exhibits; Guided Tours; Lectures

COLLECTIONS: [1813-present] 3,000 photographs and slides, civic organization scrapbooks and memorabilia, archives of city and school, newsclippings and large 11 room house furnished in 1920s era.

HOURS: Yr

CLINTON

4092
Southern Michigan Railroad Society, Inc., The
320 S Division, 49236 [PO Box K, 49236]; (p) (517) 456-7677; (c) Lenawee

Private non-profit/ 1982/ staff: 35(v)/ members: 223/publication: *Railway Express*

RAILROAD MUSEUM: Static railroad museum offering rail rides on historical equipment.

PROGRAMS: Annual Meeting; Publication

COLLECTIONS: [1836-1999] General railroad memorabilia.

HOURS: June 1-Oct 31 T-F

COLDWATER

4093
Branch County Historical Society
27 S Jefferson St, 49030 [PO Box 107, 49030-0107]; (p) (517) 278-2871; (c) Branch

Private non-profit/ 1878/ staff: 2(p)/ members: 300

HISTORIC SITE; HISTORICAL SOCIETY; HOUSE MUSEUM

PROGRAMS: Exhibits; Facility Rental; Guided Tours; Publication

COLLECTIONS: [1850-1900] Furniture, clothing and household items.

HOURS: Yr W-Su 1-5

ADMISSION: $2

COLOMA

4094
North Berrien Historical Society Museum
300 Coloma Ave, 49038 [PO Box 207, 49038]; (p) (616) 468-3330; (c) Berrien

Private non-profit/ 1946/ staff: 20(v)/ members: 80

HISTORIC PRESERVATION AGENCY; HISTORICAL SOCIETY; HISTORY MUSEUM: Dedicated to the history of the region.

PROGRAMS: Annual Meeting; Community Outreach; Exhibits; Facility Rental; Family Programs; Film/Video; Guided Tours; Publication; School-Based Curriculum

COLLECTIONS: [Pre-historic-present] Local people, artifacts, videos.

HOURS: May - Dec W, Sa, Su 1-4 and by appt

ADMISSION: Donations accepted

COLON

4095
Community Historical Society
Blackstone Ave, 49040 [Box 136, 49040-0136]; (p) (616) 432-3804, (616) 432-2462; (c) St. Joseph

Private non-profit/ 1974/ members: 100

HISTORICAL SOCIETY; HISTORY MUSEUM: Preserves the artifacts of the community.

PROGRAMS: Exhibits; Film/Video; Guided Tours

COLLECTIONS: [16th c-present] Local history, doctor's office, 1860s bedroom, school room, local arts, quilts and kitchen materials.

HOURS: June-Aug T, Th 2-4:30 and by appt

ADMISSION: Donations accepted

CONCORD

4096
Historic Mann House, The
205 Hanover St, 49237 [205 Hanover, 49237]; (p) (517) 373-1979, (517) 783-6101

1884/ Michigan Historical Commission/ staff: 2(p); 1(v)

COLLECTIONS: [Late 1800s] Furniture, china collection, clothing, travel souvenirs.

HOURS: By appt.

COOPERSVILLE

4097
Coopersville Area Historical Society
363 Main St, 49404; (p) (616) 837-7240; budphoto@i2k.com; www.coopersville.com; (c) Ottawa

Private non-profit/ 1980

HISTORIC SITE; HISTORICAL SOCIETY; HISTORY MUSEUM: Preserve the area's past and make its museum an educational and enjoyable place for people from within and outside the community.

PROGRAMS: Exhibits; Lectures

COLLECTIONS: [Late 1800s-present] 5,000 artifacts, railroad and interurban train artifacts and cars, local drugstore, recreation, area history exhibits, local newspaper, and village council records.

HOURS: Yr T 2-8, Sa 10-4; Aug- Sept Su 1-4:30

COPPER HARBOR

4098
Fort Wilkins Historic Complex
Fort Wilkins State Park, US-41, 49918 [PO Box 71, 49918]; (p) (906) 289-4215; (f) (906) 289-4939; www.sos.state.mi.us/history/history.html; (c) Keweenaw

Joint; State/ 1923/ staff: 2(f); 25(p)

HISTORIC SITE; HISTORY MUSEUM; LIVING HISTORY/OUTDOOR MUSEUM: Preserves and interprets Fort Wilkins (1848-1919), 1844 copper mine sites, and the

Copper Harbor Light Station (1848-1919) through exhibits, a/v programs and costumed interpretation.

PROGRAMS: Exhibits; Family Programs; Interpretation; Lectures; Living History

COLLECTIONS: [1844-1920] Military, domestic, and decorative arts; 22 historic buildings.

HOURS: Mid May-mid Oct daily 12-dusk

DEARBORN

4099
Automotive Hall of Fame
21400 Oakwood Blvd, 48124; (p) (313) 240-4000; (f) (313) 240-8641; (c) Wayne

Private non-profit/ 1939/ staff: 10(f); 8(p); 50(v)/ members: 1/publication: *The Chronicle*

AUTOMOBILE MUSEUM: Offers exhibits and programs to educate and foster higher levels of personal achievement using inductees from the international motor vehicle industry as examples.

PROGRAMS: Community Outreach; Exhibits; Facility Rental; Guided Tours; Interpretation; Lectures; Publication; School-Based Curriculum

COLLECTIONS: [20th c] Interactive exhibits, automobiles and personal effects.

4100
Dearborn Historical Museum
915 Brady St / 21950 Michigan Ave, 48124 [915 Brady St, 48124-2322]; (p) (313) 565-3000; (f) (313) 565-4848; dearbornhistorical museum@yahoo.com; (c) Wayne

City/ 1950/ staff: 5(f); 10(p); 100(v)/publication: *The Dearborn Historian*

HISTORIC PRESERVATION AGENCY; HISTORIC SITE; HISTORY MUSEUM; HOUSE MUSEUM; RESEARCH CENTER: Dedicated to the collection, preservation, and disseminating of all aspects of the Dearborn area's heritage.

PROGRAMS: Exhibits; Festivals; Film/Video; Guided Tours; Interpretation; Lectures; Living History; Publication; Research Library/ Archives; School-Based Curriculum

COLLECTIONS: [1830s-present] Artifacts and archival materials.

HOURS: Yr Nov-Apr M-Sa 1-5; May-DecM-Sa 9-5

4101
Henry Ford Estate-Fair Lane, The
4901 Evergreen Rd, 48128-1491; (p) (313) 463-9170; (f) (313) 593-5243; dwerling@ ab-fl.umd.umich.edu; www.umd.umich.edu/ fairlane; (c) Wayne

State/ 1981/ staff: 18(f); 30(p); 200(v)

AUTOMOBILE MUSEUM; HOUSE MUSEUM: A National Historic Landmark interpreting the personal side of Henry and Clara Ford.

PROGRAMS: Concerts; Facility Rental; Family Programs; Festivals; Garden Tours; Guided Tours; Interpretation; Lectures; Living History; School-Based Curriculum

COLLECTIONS: [1920s] The home, gardens, powerhouse, and laboratory of Henry Ford.

HOURS: Yr Daily

ADMISSION: $8

4102
Henry Ford Museum and Greenfield Village
20900 Oakwood Blvd, 48121 [PO Box 1970, 48121-1970]; (p) (313) 271-1620, (313) 982-6100; (f) (313) 982-6247; info@hfmgv.org; www.hfmgv.org; (c) Wayne

Private non-profit/ 1929/ staff: 290(f); 650(p); 839(v)/ members: 26500

AUTOMOBILE MUSEUM; GARDEN; HISTORIC SITE; HISTORY MUSEUM; LIVING HISTORY/ OUTDOOR MUSEUM; RESEARCH CENTER: Stories of innovation and ingenuity based on authentic American traditions and artifacts; houses museum, collections, 75 historic structures including the Wright Brothers family home and cycle shop, Henry Ford's birthplace and Thomas Edison's Menlo Park, NJ, Lab complex.

PROGRAMS: Community Outreach; Concerts; Exhibits; Facility Rental; Family Programs; Festivals; Film/Video; Garden Tours; Interpretation; Living History; Reenactments; Research Library/Archives; School-Based Curriculum; Theatre

COLLECTIONS: [17th-19th c] 25 million paper artifacts, historical papers of the Ford Motor Company and Ford family; large car collection, domestic arts, transportation, agriculture and furniture and lighting collections.

HOURS: Museum- Yr 9-5, Village - Apr-Dec

ADMISSION: $12.50, Children $7.50, Seniors $11.50

DELTON

4103
Bernard Historical Society and Museum
7135 Delton Rd, 49046; (p) (616) 623-5451; (c) Barry

Private non-profit/ 1962/ staff: 1(p); 25(v)/ members: 100/publication: *Years Gone By*

HISTORICAL SOCIETY; HISTORY MUSEUM: Preserves and displays local historical objects and collects written material and photographs relating to the area and its residents.

PROGRAMS: Exhibits; Festivals; Guided Tours; Publication; Research Library/Archives

COLLECTIONS: [1800-1930] Objects used in early pioneer life, tools, clothing, home furnishings, photographs, clippings, books, Native American artifacts, minerals and early medical equipment.

HOURS: July-Aug Daily 1-5; June, Sept Su 1-5

ADMISSION: Donations accepted

DETROIT

4104
Archives of Labor and Urban Affairs
Walter P. Reuther Library, Wayne State University, 48202; (p) (313) 577-4024; (f) (313) 577-4300; m.o.smith@wayne.edu; www.reuther.wayne.edu; (c) Wayne

State/ 1960/ Wayne State University/ staff: 18(f); 10(p); 4(v)

LIBRARY AND/OR ARCHIVES: Historical records related to the North American labor movement and urban history of Southeastern Michigan.

PROGRAMS: Community Outreach; Exhibits; Guided Tours; Interpretation; Research Library/Archives

COLLECTIONS: [1930-present] Collections of nine major labor unions, including the United Automobile Workers, the United Farm Workers, the American Federation of Teachers, and the Industrial Workers of the World.

HOURS: Yr M-T 11-7, W-F 9-5

4105
Burton Historical Collection
N Wing, Detroit Public Library, Main Branch, 48202 [5201 Woodward Ave, 48202]; (p) (313) 833-1480; (c) Wayne

1914/ Detroit Library Commission/ staff: 10(f)

LIBRARY AND/OR ARCHIVES: Local and family history collection housed in the Detroit Public Library.

PROGRAMS: Community Outreach; Exhibits; Guided Tours; Lectures; Research Library/ Archives

COLLECTIONS: [18th-19th c] History of Detroit and the old Northwest Territory. Rare books.

HOURS: Yr T,Th-Sa 9:30-5:30, W 1-9

4106
Charles H. Wright Museum of African American History
315 E Warren Ave, 48201-1443; (p) (313) 494-5800; (f) (313) 494-5855; (c) Wayne

Private non-profit/ 1965/ staff: 55(f); 22(p); 140(v)/ members: 5660

HISTORY MUSEUM: Documents, preserves and educates the public on the history, life, and culture of African Americans.

PROGRAMS: Concerts; Exhibits; Facility Rental; Family Programs; Festivals; Film/ Video; Guided Tours; Lectures; Research Library/Archives; Theatre

COLLECTIONS: 10,000 archival materials; photos, manuscripts, and documents; 2,000 volume library; 15,000 museum artifacts; sculpture, household goods, paintings, and textiles.

HOURS: Jan- Dec T-Su 9:30-5

ADMISSION: $5, Children $3

4107
Commanding Officer's Residence- Historic Fort Wayne
Historic Fort Wayne National Historic Site, 48209 [6325 W Jefferson, 48209]; (p) (313) 297-8376; (f) (313) 297-8361; www.detroit historical.org

1880/ City and County

COLLECTIONS: [1883] Victorian furnishings reflecting upper-middle-class lifestyle of a military officer.; Modest archival collection and reference library maintained for staff use.

4108
Detroit Historical Museums
5401 Woodward Ave, 48202; (p) (313) 833-1805; (f) (313) 833-5342; www.detroithistorical.org; (c) Wayne

1928/ staff: 37(f); 425(v)

HISTORIC PRESERVATION AGENCY; HISTORIC SITE; HISTORY MUSEUM: Presents the history of our region.

PROGRAMS: Annual Meeting; Community Outreach; Concerts; Elder's Programs; Exhibits; Facility Rental; Family Programs; Festivals; Film/Video; Guided Tours; Interpretation; Lectures; Publication; School-Based Curriculum

COLLECTIONS: [1701-present] 100,000 objects representing many aspects of the city's past; collections: costume, vehicle, and Native American; Great Lakes marine models, art and archival materials, military.

HOURS: Yr T-F 9:30-5, Sa-Su 10-5

ADMISSION: $4.50

4109
Detroit Historical Society
5401 Woodward Ave, 48202; (p) (313) 833-7934; (f) (313) 833-5342; www.detroithistorical.org; (c) Wayne

Private non-profit/ 1921/ staff: 9(f); 2(p); 200(v)/ members: 2000

HISTORICAL SOCIETY: Provides fundraising, marketing and volunteer support for the Detroit Historical Museums and promotes area history.

PROGRAMS: Community Outreach; Festivals; Guided Tours

4110
Fisher Mansion, The
383 Lenox Ave, 48215 [383 Lenox Ave, 48215]; (p) (313) 331-6740; (f) (313) 822-3748; fmansion@flash.net

1927/ staff: 4(f); 6(p); 24(v)

COLLECTIONS: [1920s] East Indian art collection of Alfred Ford.

HOURS: Yr

4111
Pewabic Pottery
10125 E Jefferson, 48214; (p) (313) 822-0954; (f) (313) 822-6266; pewabic@pewabic.com; www.pewabic.com; (c) Wayne

Private non-profit/ 1990/ staff: 15(f); 9(p); 45(v)/ members: 680

ART MUSEUM; HISTORIC SITE; HISTORY MUSEUM: Pewabic-produced art museum of historic tiles, vessels and furniture; also offers community outreach, production studio, educational programming

PROGRAMS: Community Outreach; Exhibits; Guided Tours; Interpretation; Lectures

COLLECTIONS: Artifacts, tiles, vessels, pottery, business records, commission drawings, photos, correspondence, equipment.

HOURS: Yr 10-6

ADMISSION: No charge

4112
Walter P. Reuther Library of Labor and Urban Affairs
5401 Cass Wayne State University, 48202; (p) (313) 577-4024; (f) (313) 577-4300; M.O.Smith@wayne.edu; www.Routter.wayne.edu; (c) Wayne

State/ 1960/ staff: 15(f); 10(p); 2(v)

Largest collection of historical records relating to the American Labor Movement in the world; Urban Affairs in Southeast Michigan collection.

PROGRAMS: Community Outreach; Exhibits; Facility Rental; Lectures; Publication; Research Library/Archives

COLLECTIONS: [20th c]

HOURS: Yr M-T 11-6:45, W-F 9-5

DEXTER

4113
Dexter Area Historical Society and Museum
3442 Inverness, 48130; (p) (734) 426-2519; dexmueu@hvcn.org; www.hvcn.org/info/dextermuseum; (c) Washtenaw

Private non-profit/ 1971/ staff: 75(v)/ members: 85

HISTORICAL SOCIETY; HISTORY MUSEUM: Gathers, preserves, and makes available the archives and artifacts of local history.

PROGRAMS: Annual Meeting; Community Outreach; Exhibits; Facility Rental; Family Programs; Festivals; Film/Video; Guided Tours; Lectures; Research Library/Archives

COLLECTIONS: [Late 1820s-present] Vintage print shop, artifacts; home, military, paintings, archives: farm tools, model train, toys, clothing, personal items, photos, genealogy, cemetery records, local newspapers, maps, atlases, school records

DOUGLAS

4114
Saugatuck-Douglas Historical Society and Museum
Park St at Mt Baldhead Park, 49406 [Box 617, 49406]; (p) (616) 857-7900; (c) Allegan

Private non-profit/ 1994/ staff: 215(v)/ members: 504

HISTORY MUSEUM: Local history

COLLECTIONS: [1830-present] Local history, regional art, leisure cottage history.

ADMISSION: No charge

DOWAGIAC

4115
Heddon Museum
414 W St, 49047 [204 W Telegraph St, 49047-1241]; (p) (616) 782-4068, (616) 782-5698; (f) (616) 782-5159; (c) Cass

Private non-profit/ 1996/ staff: 2(f); 2(v)

HISTORIC SITE; RESEARCH CENTER: Preserves and presents the history of the James Heddons Sons Company and the individual Heddon family members.

PROGRAMS: Exhibits; Research Library/Archives

COLLECTIONS: [1902-1984] 1,000 fishing lures, 140 rods, 125 reels, phototype and experimental items, research documents, 100 original factory prototype, equipment and information about contributions made by the Heddons.

HOURS: Yr T 6:30-8:30pm, last Su 1:30-4 and by appt.

4116
Southwestern Michigan College Museum
58900 Cherry Grove Rd, 49047; (p) (616) 782-1374; (f) (616) 782-1460; www.smc.cc.ini.uc; (c) Cass

1982/ staff: 2(f); 3(p); 40(v)/ members: 120/publication: *Identification Dating of Round Oak Heating Stoves*

HISTORY MUSEUM: To collect, preserve, and exhibit the history of lower southwest Michigan and the science-technology of the area.

PROGRAMS: Community Outreach; Exhibits; Family Programs; Interpretation; Lectures; Publication; Research Library/Archives; School-Based Curriculum

COLLECTIONS: [1830-present] Collection focus on local business, families, agriculture; photographs, papers, and three dimensional objects, Round Oak Heating Stove Company.

HOURS: Yr T,Th, F, Sa 10-5, W 10-8

EAGLE HARBOR

4117
Keweenaw County Historical Society
HC-1, Box 265L, 49950; (p) (906) 289-4990; (c) Keweenaw

Private non-profit/ 1980/ staff: 38(v)/ members: 778

HISTORIC SITE; HISTORICAL SOCIETY; HISTORY MUSEUM

PROGRAMS: Annual Meeting; Community Outreach; Exhibits; Guided Tours

COLLECTIONS: [1870-present] Historic structures, artifacts, photographs, memorabilia.

HOURS: June-Oct Daily 10:30-5

ADMISSION: $3

EAST LANSING

4118
Michigan State University Archives and Historical Collections
101 Conrad Hall, 48824-1327; (p) (517) 355-2330; (f) (517) 353-9319; msuarhc@pilot.msu.edu; www.msu.edu/unit/msuarhc; (c) Ingham

State/ 1969/ staff: 5(f); 10(p)

LIBRARY AND/OR ARCHIVES: Collects, preserves, and makes accessible for research the historical records of the University and those associated, as well as historical document collections.

PROGRAMS: Community Outreach; Exhibits; Guided Tours; Lectures; Research Library/Archives; School-Based Curriculum

COLLECTIONS: Manuscripts, maps, photographs, audio, visual, serials, newspapers,

4119
Michigan State University Museum
West Circle Dr, 48824-1045; (p) (517) 355-2370; (f) (517) 432-2846; dewhurs1@pilot.mus.edu; museum.cl.msu.edu; (c) Ingham

State/ 1857/ staff: 40(f); 30(p); 375(v)/publication: *Associate*

HISTORY MUSEUM: As Michigan's land grant museum, the museum is committed to understanding, interpreting, and respecting material and cultural diversity.

PROGRAMS: Annual Meeting; Community Outreach; Concerts; Elder's Programs; Exhibits; Facility Rental; Family Programs; Festivals; Film/Video; Guided Tours; Interpretation; Lectures; Living History; Publication; Research Library/Archives; School-Based Curriculum

COLLECTIONS: 2.5 million objects and specimens with a focus on Michigan and the Great Lakes

EAST TAWAS

4120
Iosco County Historical Society Museum
405 W Bay St, 48730; (p) (517) 362-8911; (c) Iosco

Private non-profit/ 1968/ staff: 1(f); 1(p); 20(v)/ members: 170

HISTORIC PRESERVATION AGENCY; HISTORICAL SOCIETY; HOUSE MUSEUM: To preserve local county history; oversees small museum.

PROGRAMS: Annual Meeting; Community Outreach; Exhibits; Family Programs; Guided Tours; Research Library/Archives

HOURS: Apr-June Sa-Su 1-4; June-Sept Th-T 1-4; Sept-Dec Sa-Su 1-4

FAIRVIEW

4121
Steiner Museum
1980 Reber Rd, 48621; (p) (517) 848-7233; (c) Oscoda

County/ 1966/ staff: 8(v)/publication: *Wilderness; Friends of Steiner Museum; and others*

HISTORIC PRESERVATION AGENCY; HISTORIC SITE; HISTORY MUSEUM: Operates museum, involvest of local community.

PROGRAMS: Exhibits; Festivals; Publication

COLLECTIONS: [1890-1940] Artifacts related to lumbering activity and pioneer life in northern lower Michigan, including logmarks, photographs, and Earl Steiner's personal life.

HOURS: Mid May - Mid Oct Th-Su 1-5 and by appt

ADMISSION: Donations accepted

FARMINGTON

4122
Governor Warner Mansion
33805 Grand River, 48335 [23600 Liberty, 48335]; (p) (248) 473-7275; (f) (248) 473-7261; brichard@wwnet.net; www.ci.farmington.mi.us; (c) Oakland

City/ 1982/ staff: 35(v)

HOUSE MUSEUM: Dedicated to the collection of Farmington area history and Governor Fred Warner artifacts.

PROGRAMS: Community Outreach; Garden Tours; Guided Tours

COLLECTIONS: [1865-1925] Furniture, clothing, artifacts, memorabilia of Farmington area history.

HOURS: Mar-Dec W 1-5, 1st Su

ADMISSION: $2

FLINT

4123
Alfred P. Sloan Museum
1221 E Kearsley St, 48503; (p) (810) 237-3450; (f) (810) 237-3451; sloandirflintcultural.org; (c) Genesee

Private non-profit/ 1966/ Flint Cultural Center Corporation/ staff: 11(f); 19(p); 60(v)/ members: 700/publication: *Sloan News*

HISTORY MUSEUM: Collects, preserves, and interprets local and regional history and hosts traveling exhibits on Science and American history.

PROGRAMS: Annual Meeting; Community Outreach; Concerts; Exhibits; Facility Rental; Festivals; Interpretation; Lectures; Living History; Publication; Reenactments; Research Library/Archives; School-Based Curriculum

COLLECTIONS: [1830-present] Automobiles, carriages, household, and business artifacts, photographs and documents on the history of Flint and the surrounding region.

HOURS: Yr M-F 10-5, Sa-Su 12-5

ADMISSION: $5, Children $3

4124
Crossroads Village and Huckleberry Railroad
6140 Bray Rd, 48506 [5045 Stanley Rd, 48506]; (p) (810) 736-7100; (f) (810) 736-7220; gencopks@concentric.net; www.geneseecountyparks.org; (c) Genesee

County; Joint/ 1976/ staff: 30(f); 100(p); 125(v)

LIVING HISTORY/OUTDOOR MUSEUM: A living history village of the 1860s with 33 historic buildings, operated in conjunction with an authentic steam railroad, three working mills and five historic amusement rides.

PROGRAMS: Concerts; Facility Rental; Family Programs; Festivals; Interpretation; Living History; Publication; Reenactments; School-Based Curriculum; Theatre

COLLECTIONS: [1860-1880] Period-furnished historic buildings.

HOURS: May-Aug T-F 10-5, 11-5:30; Sept Sa, Su 11-5:30

4125
Whaley Historical House Association, Inc.
624 E Kearsley St, 48503-1909; (p) (810) 235-6841; (f) (810) 235-6186; (c) Genesee

Private non-profit/ 1975/ staff: 1(p); 40(v)/ members: 160

HOUSE MUSEUM: Preserve the Whaley name, the family values and traditions by restoring and maintaining the house and its role in the cultural history of Flint.

PROGRAMS: Annual Meeting; Community Outreach; Exhibits; Facility Rental; Guided Tours; Interpretation; Lectures; Living History; Research Library/Archives

COLLECTIONS: [1885-1905] Victorian furnishings

HOURS: Sept-July 1st/3rd Su 2-4 ; 2nd F 6-9; Office hours T-F 9-3

ADMISSION: $4

FLUSHING

4126
Flushing Area Historical Society
431 W Main, 48433 [PO Box 87, 48433]; (p) (810) 487-0814; (c) Genesee

Private non-profit/ 1973/ staff: 30(v)/ members: 600/publication: *Flushing Sesquicentennial History Books, Vol. I, II, and III*

GENEALOGICAL SOCIETY; HISTORIC SITE; HISTORICAL SOCIETY: Collects and preserves artifacts and genealogical materials from the local area, with emphasis on the railroad and local pioneers. Located in a restored 1888 railroad depot.

PROGRAMS: Annual Meeting; Community Outreach; Exhibits; Facility Rental; Festivals; Guided Tours; Publication

COLLECTIONS: [1835-present] Local history, railroad artifacts, local artifacts, visual and written history of pioneers of the area, local genealogy, veterinarian tools, vintage clothing, fire fighting equipment.

HOURS: Apr-Nov Su 1-4 and by appt

ADMISSION: Donations accepted

FRANKENMUTH

4127
Frankenmuth Historical Association
613 S Main St, 48415; (p) (517) 652-9701; (f) (517) 652-9390; (c) Saginaw

1963/ staff: 2(f); 8(p); 50(v)/ members: 375

HISTORY MUSEUM: Preserve and communicate the heritage of the Franconian communities in Saginaw Valley.

PROGRAMS: Annual Meeting; Exhibits; Facility Rental; Family Programs; Guided Tours; Research Library/Archives; Theatre

COLLECTIONS: Building furnishings, clothing and accessories, tools and equipment, communication tools, transportation, photos, books, art, recreation.

HOURS: Yr M-Sa 10:30-5, Su 12-5

ADMISSION: $1, Children $0.50

FREELAND

4128
Tittabawassoe Township Historical Society
[PO Box 294, 48623]; (p) (517) 695-9439; Pigletmom@aol.com; (c) Saginaw

1991/ staff: 15(v)/ members: 15

HISTORICAL SOCIETY: To preserve history and to collect and publish data on cemetery sites.

PROGRAMS: Community Outreach; Festivals; Film/Video; Living History; Publication; Research Library/Archives

GALESBURG

4129
Galesburg Historical Museum
199 E Mich Ave, 49053 [PO Box 398, 49053]; (p) (616) 665-7507; (c) Kalamazoo

City/ 1970/ staff: 14(v)

HISTORY MUSEUM

PROGRAMS: Exhibits

COLLECTIONS: [Early 1900-present]

HOURS: Yr W 4:30-9, Sa 10-2 or by appt

ADMISSION: No charge/Donations

GARDEN

4130

Fayette Historic State Park

13700 1325 Lane, 49835; (p) (906) 644-2603; (f) (906) 644-2666; www.sos.state.mi.us/history.html; (c) Delta

Joint; State/ 1959/ staff: 3(f)

HISTORIC SITE: Preserves and interprets 19th century industrial community and company town; eight historic buildings.

PROGRAMS: Exhibits; Guided Tours; Interpretation; School-Based Curriculum

COLLECTIONS: [1867-1891] 19th century industrial, domestic and decorative arts; 19 surviving structures: furnace complex, lime and charcoal kilns, machine shop, office, company store, hotel, town hall, superintendent's residence and homes of mid-level company employees.

GOODELLS

4131

St. Clair County Farm Museum

8310 County Park Dr, 48027-1400; (p) (810) 325-1737

GRAND BLANC

4132

Grand Blanc Heritage Association and Museum

203 E Grand Blanc Rd, 48439-1303; (p) (810) 694-7274; (c) Genesee

1972/ staff: 30(v)/ members: 275

GENEALOGICAL SOCIETY; HISTORIC PRESERVATION AGENCY; HISTORIC SITE; HISTORICAL SOCIETY; HISTORY MUSEUM; RESEARCH CENTER: Collects, preserves, documents and exhibits materials relating to local history.

PROGRAMS: Annual Meeting; Community Outreach; Concerts; Facility Rental; Family Programs; Film/Video; Guided Tours; Living History; Publication

COLLECTIONS: [1800-present] Furniture, toys, quilts, clothing, books, cameras, looms, genealogical information, books, newspapers, pictures, antiques, letters, diaries, ledgers and public records.

HOURS: Sept-Nov and Jan-June W 10-2

ADMISSION: No charge

GRAND HAVEN

4133

Tri-Cities Historical Museum

1 N Harvor Dr, 49417 [PO Box 234, 49417]; (p) (616) 842-0700; (f) (616) 842-3698; tcmuseum@grandhaven.com/museum; www.grandhaven.com/museum; (c) Ottawa

Private non-profit/ 1972/ staff: 4(f); 9(p); 30(v)/publication: *The Packet and Riverwinds*

HISTORIC SITE; HISTORICAL SOCIETY; HISTORY MUSEUM: Located in an 1870 Depot on the Grand River bank, it is a learning center, artifact depository, and preserver of local history.

PROGRAMS: Community Outreach; Exhibits; Film/Video; Guided Tours; Interpretation; Lectures; Living History; Publication

COLLECTIONS: [Victorian] Photographs, furniture, textiles, a vehicle, household goods, general store, artifacts.

HOURS: Yr Summer T-F 10-9:30, Sa-Su 12-9:30; Winter M-F

GRAND LEDGE

4134

Grand Ledge Area Historical Society Museum

118 W Lincoln St, 48837 [PO Box 203, 48837]; (p) (517) 627-3149; (f) (517) 627-5170; www.grandledgemi.com; (c) Eaton

Private non-profit/ 1976/ staff: 27(v)/ members: 126/publication: *Thru the Years; Greetings from Grand Ledge*

HISTORICAL SOCIETY; HISTORY MUSEUM: Presents programs on local history, maintains a museum and an archive, publishes books.

PROGRAMS: Annual Meeting; Exhibits; Festivals; Film/Video; Guided Tours; Lectures; Publication; Research Library/Archives; School-Based Curriculum

COLLECTIONS: [1880s-1920] photographs, newspapers, journals, scrapbooks, quilts, Grand Ledge-produced furniture, sewer tiles, bricks, clay fold art, period clothing, advertising memorabilia.

HOURS: Mar-Dec Au 2-4, T 9-12 and special events or by appt

ADMISSION: Donations accepted

GRAND RAPIDS

4135

Gerald R. Ford Museum

303 Pearl St NW, 49504-5353; (p) (616) 451-9263; (f) (616) 451-9570; ford.museum@nara.gov; www.ford.utexas.edu/; (c) Kent

Federal/ National Archives and Records Administration

HOURS: Daily 9-5

ADMISSION: $4, Seniors $3; Under 16 free

4136

Grand Rapids Historical Commission

c/o Public Library, 60 Library St NW, 49503; (p) (616) 988-5402; (f) (616) 988-5401; golson@grpl.org; (c) Kent

City/ 1961/ City of Grand Rapids/ staff: 1(f)/publication: *Grand Rapids Sampler; Grand Rapids: A City Renewed; Voices From The Rapids*

Responsible for collecting, preserving, and publishing community's history for all its citizens.

COLLECTIONS: [1800-present]

4137

Grand Rapids Historical Society

111 Library St NW, 49503; (p) (616) 988-5402; (f) (616) 988-5421; mi@grpl.org; www.grhistory.org; (c) Kent

Private non-profit/ 1894/ staff: 1(p)/ members: 401

HISTORIC PRESERVATION AGENCY; HISTORICAL SOCIETY; LIBRARY AND/OR ARCHIVES; RESEARCH CENTER: To collect and preserve our heritage, passing it on to new generations through books, lectures, and educational projects.

PROGRAMS: Annual Meeting; Community Outreach; Garden Tours; Interpretation; Research Library/Archives

4138

Grand Rapids Public Library, Local History Department

111 Library St NW, 49503; (p) (616) 988-5402; (f) (616) 988-5421; mi@grpl.org; www.grpl.org; (c) Kent

City/ 1871/ Library Board of Commissioners/ staff: 4(f); 3(p); 6(v)

Responsible for collecting, preserving, and providing public access to local and family history records.

COLLECTIONS: [1800-present] Books, maps, manuscripts, photographs, periodicals, scrapbooks, ephemera, documenting the history of Grand Rapids.

HOURS: Yr M-Th 9-9, F-Sa 9-5, Su 1-5

ADMISSION: No charge

4139

Meyer May House

450 Madison Ave SE, 49503; (p) (616) 246-4821

1908/ staff: 1(p)

COLLECTIONS: [1918] Original furnishings plus replicas designed by Wright and George Niedeckan; all period furnishings, 1911 mural.; Original blueprints, all furnishings designs, Niedecken archives, Milwaukee Art

4140

Public Museum of Grand Rapids

272 Pearl NW, 49504; (p) (616) 456-3977; (f) (616) 456-3873; staff@grmuseum.org; www.grmuseum.org; (c) Kent

City/ 1854/ staff: 35(f); 150(p); 700(v)/ members: 3031/publication: *Museum Magazine; Discoveries*

HISTORY MUSEUM: Collects, preserves, and presents the national, cultural and social history of its region.

PROGRAMS: Annual Meeting; Community Outreach; Concerts; Elder's Programs; Exhibits; Facility Rental; Family Programs; Film/Video; Guided Tours; Interpretation; Lectures; Publication; Reenactments; School-Based Curriculum

COLLECTIONS: [19th and 20th c] Archaeology, ethnology, archival materials, books, historic buildings, architectural fragments, communication, decorative/fine arts, transportation artifacts, household furnishing, personal artifacts and clothing, recreation, tools, natural science items.

HOURS: Yr Daily M-Sa 9-5, Su 12-5

ADMISSION: $5, Children $2, Seniors $4

4141
Voigt House Victorian Museum, The
115 College Ave SE, 49503 [115 College Ave SE, 49503]; (p) (616) 456-4600, (616) 456-4602; (f) (616) 456-4603; staff@grmuseum.org; www.grmuseum.org; (c) Kent

1972/ staff: 3(p); 117(v)/publication: *Voigt House*

HOUSE MUSEUM: Contains original possessions of the Voigt Family; develops programs, participates in preservation and long range planning.

COLLECTIONS: [1890-1930] 20,000 objects, furniture, decorative objects, household items, clothing and accessories, personal artifacts; Family archives, business archives.

HOURS: Yr T 11-3, 2nd and 4th Su 1-3

ADMISSION: $3, Children $2, Seniors $2

GRASS LAKE

4142
Coe House Museum
371 W Mich, 49240 [PO Box 53, 49240]; (p) (517) 522-5141, (517) 522-4384

1871/ staff: 20(v)

COLLECTIONS: [Victorian era] Ledgers, Civil War uniforms & trunk, old books, post cards, glass pitchers

HOURS: Seasonal

GRAYLING

4143
Hartwick Pines State Park Logging Museum
State Route M-93, 2 mi east of I-75, exit 259, 49738 [4216 Ranger Rd, 49738]; (p) (517) 348-2537; (f) (517) 344-6803; rpburg@freeway.net; www.sos.state.mi.us/history/museum/musehar.html; (c) Crawford

State/ 1927/ staff: 5(f); 20(p); 75(v)

HISTORIC SITE; HISTORY MUSEUM: Preserves and interprets the important history of logging and how it related to the development of Michigan and its citizens.

PROGRAMS: Community Outreach; Exhibits; Family Programs; Festivals; Guided Tours; Interpretation; Lectures; Living History; School-Based Curriculum

COLLECTIONS: [1840s-1910] Over 1,100 museum artifacts pertaining to the logging history of Michigan and Hartwick Pines State Park. Books and videos.

HOURS: June-Sept Daily 9-7; May & Sept-Nov T-Su 9-4

ADMISSION: $4 parking fee

GROSSE ILE

4144
Grosse Ile Historical Society
East River Rd & Grosse Ile Pkwy, 48138 [PO Box 131, 48138]; (p) (734) 676-0046; (c) Wayne

Private non-profit/ 1959/ staff: 8(p)/ members: 368

HISTORICAL SOCIETY; HISTORY MUSEUM; HOUSE MUSEUM: To preserve the history of Grosse Ile Island community founded in 1776.

PROGRAMS: Annual Meeting; Exhibits; Festivals; Film/Video; Guided Tours; Lectures; Research Library/Archives; School-Based Curriculum

COLLECTIONS: [1800-present]

HOURS: Sa, Su 1-4

ADMISSION: No charge

GROSSE POINTE FARMS

4145
Grosse Pointe Historical Society
381 Kercheval Ave, 49236; (p) (313) 884-7010; (c) Wayne

Private non-profit/ 1945/ staff: 1(p); 50(v)/ members: 600

HISTORIC PRESERVATION AGENCY; HISTORIC SITE; HISTORICAL SOCIETY; HISTORY MUSEUM; HOUSE MUSEUM; RESEARCH CENTER: Operates 1823 Provincial-Weir Farmhouse; provides lectures, tours, scholarships, and historic marker programs; supports a resource center for preservation of local historical documents, photos, and artifacts.

PROGRAMS: Annual Meeting; Community Outreach; Exhibits; Facility Rental; Family Programs; Festivals; Film/Video; Guided Tours; Interpretation; Lectures; Publication; Research Library/Archives; School-Based Curriculum

COLLECTIONS: [19th-20th c] Books, pamphlets, manuscripts, 6000 photographs, maps, archives, postcards, abstracts, periodicals, oral histories, clippings, and memorabilia.

HOURS: House: Sept- June 2nd Sa of month 1-4; Resource Center: Yr T-W 10-12:30 / 1:30-4

ADMISSION: No charge

GROSSE POINTE SHORES

4146
Edsel and Eleanor Ford House
1100 Lake Shore Rd, 48236; (p) (313) 884-4222; (f) (313) 884-5977; info@fordhouse; www.fordhouse.org; (c) Wayne

Private non-profit/ 1976/ staff: 35(f); 65(p)

GARDEN; HISTORIC SITE; HOUSE MUSEUM: A 60 room estate on 87 lakefront acres on grounds designed by landscape architect Jens Jensen.

PROGRAMS: Exhibits; Facility Rental; Family Programs; Garden Tours; Guided Tours; Interpretation; Lectures

COLLECTIONS: French and English period furniture, paintings, graphic arts and ceramics.

HOURS: Yr T-Sa 10-4, Su 12-4

ADMISSION: $6, Children $4, Seniors $5; Under 5 free

HANOVER

4147
Hanover-Horton Area Historical Society
105 Fairview St, 49241 [PO Box 256, 49241]; (p) (517) 563-8927; (c) Jackson

Private non-profit/ 1977/ staff: 2(p); 100(v)/ members: 220

HISTORICAL SOCIETY: Maintain the Conklin Antique Organ Museum and to collect and preserve local historical artifacts and information; housed in a designated state Historical Site building.

PROGRAMS: Annual Meeting; Community Outreach; Concerts; Exhibits; Family Programs; Festivals; Guided Tours; Interpretation; Lectures; Publication; Research Library/ Archives

COLLECTIONS: [1875-1958] 100 restored reed organs and melodeons; restored early 1900s classroom; local artifacts; photographs and documents;1900 and 1930 restored fine engines and equipment.

HOURS: Apr-Oct Su and special events 1-5

ADMISSION: $4, Family $10, Children $1, Seniors $2; Members free

HARBOR BEACH

4148
Frank Murphy Memorial Museum
146 S Huron, 48441 [766 State St, 48441]; (p) (517) 479-3363; (f) (517) 479-3343; (c) Huron

City/ 1994/ staff: 1(f); 1(p); 7(v)

HOUSE MUSEUM: Collects and preserves items related to the life and times of Justice Frank Murphy.

PROGRAMS: Community Outreach; Exhibits; Family Programs; Festivals; Guided Tours; Lectures; School-Based Curriculum

COLLECTIONS: [1890-1949] Personal items, documents and photographs relating to Michigan and United States government in 1930s and 1940s, collection of Philippines cultural items from Murphy's governorship in 1930.

HOURS: June-Sept Th-M 10-6:30

ADMISSION: $2

HASTINGS

4149
Historic Charlton Park Village, Museum and Recreation Area
2545 S Charlton Park Rd, 49058; (p) (616) 945-3775; (f) (616) 945-0390; (c) Barry

County/ 1936/ staff: 7(f); 3(p); 150(v)/publication: *The Villager*

HISTORIC SITE; HISTORY MUSEUM; HOUSE MUSEUM: Country Park with 17 historic structures and a museum.

PROGRAMS: Exhibits; Facility Rental; Festivals; Garden Tours; Interpretation; Reenactments; Research Library/Archives; School-Based Curriculum

COLLECTIONS: [Mid-late 19c-early 20c] Approx 50,000 objects used to depict life in a rural Michigan community at the turn of the century.

HOURS: Village: May-Sept Daily 8-5, Sept-May M-F 8-5; Rec Area: May-Sept Daily 8-8, Sept-May M-F 8-8

HICKORY CORNERS

4150
Gilmore-Classic Car Club of America Museum
6865 Hickory Rd, 49060; (p) (616) 671-5089; (f) (616) 671-5843; gcccam@gilmorecarmuseum.org; www.gilmorecarmuseum.org; (c) Barry

Private non-profit/ 1966/ staff: 5(f); 14(p); 3(v)/ members: 135

AUTOMOBILE MUSEUM

PROGRAMS: Exhibits; Facility Rental; Festivals; Guided Tours; Interpretation

COLLECTIONS: [1899-1985] Over 140 antique, classic and collector cars displayed in historic barns.

HOURS: 1st Sa in May-last Su in Oct, Daily 10-5

ADMISSION: $6, Children $3, Seniors $5

HOLLAND

4151
Cappon House Museum
228 W 9th St, 49423 [31 W 10th St, 49423]; (p) (616) 394-1362, (616) 392-6740; (f) (616) 394-4756

1873/ staff: 25(v)

COLLECTIONS: [1874-1900] Original furniture and interiors; early wallpaper, carpeting, draperies, Grand Rapids furniture; photographs, records, books.

HOURS: Summer W-Sa 1-4, winter 1st Sa of month 1-4, and by appt

4152
Holland Historical Trust
31 W 10th St, 49423-3101; (p) (616) 394-1362; (f) (616) 394-4756; museum@hope.edu; www.hollandmuseum.org; (c) Ottawa

Private non-profit/ 1937/ staff: 4(f); 25(p); 260(v)/ members: 900

HISTORY MUSEUM; HOUSE MUSEUM: Catalyst for the dynamic interaction of past and present that enriches the Holland area; maintains the Holland Museum, 1874 Cappon House, 1867 Settlers House, and the Joint Archives of Holland.

PROGRAMS: Annual Meeting; Community Outreach; Elder's Programs; Exhibits; Facility Rental; Family Programs; Guided Tours; Interpretation; Lectures; Publication; Research Library/Archives; School-Based Curriculum

COLLECTIONS: [1835-present] Fine Dutch material collection, local history, archive, 2 historic structures and an education collection.

HOMER

4153
Homer Historical Society
1 mi W of Homer on M-60, 49245 [505 Grandview, 49245]; (p) (517) 568-3116; (c) Calhoun

Private non-profit/ 1974/ staff: 30(v)/ members: 85

HISTORIC PRESERVATION AGENCY; HISTORIC SITE; HISTORICAL SOCIETY; HISTORY MUSEUM; HOUSE MUSEUM: To preserve and protect the history of Homer and its artifacts, to establish and operate a museum and to work with all ages of people to further historical appreciation.

PROGRAMS: Annual Meeting; Community Outreach; Concerts; Exhibits; Family Programs; Festivals; Guided Tours; Lectures; Living History; School-Based Curriculum

COLLECTIONS: [1890-1910] Local artifacts representing pioneer farm life.

HOURS: Yr by appt

ADMISSION: No charge

HOUGHTON

4154
Society for Industrial Archeology
Rm 208, Academic Office Bldg, MTU, 49931 [Dept of Social Sciences, MI Technological Univ, 49931]; (p) (906) 487-1889; (f) (906) 487-1889; sia@mtu.edu; www.ss.mtu.edu/IA/sia.html; (c) Houghton

Joint; Private non-profit/ 1971/ staff: 1(p); 20(v)/ members: 1600/publication: *IA: Journal of the Society for Industrial Archeology; SIA Newsletter*

PROFESSIONAL ORGANIZATION: International society devoted to the study, preservation, and interpretation of industrial heritage through a program of meetings, tours, and publications.

PROGRAMS: Annual Meeting; Guided Tours;

HOUGHTON LAKE

4155
Houghton Lake Area Historical Society
1701 W Houghton Lake Dr, 48629 [PO Box 14, 48629]; (p) (517) 366-9124, (517) 366-8784; (c) Roscommon

Joint; Private non-profit/ 1982/ staff: 3(p); 10(v)/ members: 144

HISTORICAL SOCIETY; HISTORY MUSEUM: To discover and collect material that may help establish or illustrate the history of the area.

PROGRAMS: Annual Meeting; Community Outreach; Exhibits; Facility Rental; Family Programs; Festivals; Guided Tours; Interpretation; Living History; Publication; School-Based Curriculum

COLLECTIONS: [Late 1800s-1900s] Logging materials, working blacksmith ship, antique clothing, period furnishings, old farm implements, old operating printing presses, articles, pictures, artifacts, objects.

IMLAY CITY

4156
Imlay City Historical Museum
77 Main St, 48444; (p) (810) 724-1111, (810) 724-9245; (c) Lapeer

Private non-profit/ 1978/ staff: 15(v)/ members: 120

HISTORICAL SOCIETY: Preservation of local historical items.

PROGRAMS: Exhibits; Festivals; Film/Video; School-Based Curriculum

COLLECTIONS: [1850-1940s] Local historic articles and photographic views of the city.

HOURS: Last Sa in Apr-Mid Sept Sa 1:30-4:30

IRON MOUNTAIN

4157
Iron Mountain/Iron Mine
US-2, 49801 [PO Box 177, 49801]; (p) (906) 563-8077; ironmine@uplogon.com; www.iron-mountainironmine.com; (c) Dickinson

Private non-profit/ 1956/ staff: 3(f); 5(p)

HISTORIC SITE; HISTORY MUSEUM: Guided underground tours by train of the Vulcan Iron Mine.

PROGRAMS: Guided Tours

COLLECTIONS: [1870-1945] Mining equipment.

HOURS: June 1 - Oct 15 Daily 9-5

ADMISSION: $7, Children $6; Under 6 free

4158
Menominee Range Historical Foundation
300 E Ludington St, 49801 [PO Box 237, 49801]; (p) (906) 774-4276, (906) 563-8029; (c) Dickinson

Private non-profit/ 1969/ staff: 2(f); 2(p); 45(v)/ members: 350

HISTORICAL SOCIETY; HISTORY MUSEUM: For the perpetuation and preservation of the history of the Menominee Iron Range.

PROGRAMS: Community Outreach; Exhibits; Family Programs; Film/Video; Guided Tours; Research Library/Archives; School-Based Curriculum

COLLECTIONS: [1880-1920] Large steam-driven pumping engine, underground mining equipment; Ford WW II glider display, pioneer materials, archival collections.

HOURS: Historical Museum: M-Sa 10-4; Pump: Mid Apr-Oct M-Sa 9-5, Sun 12-4

ADMISSION: $4, Student $2, Seniors $3.50; Under 10 free

IRONWOOD

4159
Ironwood Area Historical Society
105 Lowell St, 49938 [PO Box 553, 49938]; (p) (906) 932-0287; (c) Gogebic

Private non-profit/ 1971/ staff: 12(v)/ members: 100

HISTORIC SITE; HISTORICAL SOCIETY; HISTORY MUSEUM; RESEARCH CENTER: Located in a former railroad depot, preserves past local mining, railroad, and cultural history.

PROGRAMS: Exhibits; Facility Rental; Festivals

COLLECTIONS: [1885-present] Photos, artifacts, exhibits on local history.

HOURS: May-Sept Daily 12-4 and by appt

ADMISSION: Donations

JACKSON

4160
Elisharp Museum
3225 4th St, 49203; (p) (517) 787-2320; (f) (517) 787-2933

4161
Ella Sharp Museum
3225 Fourth St, 49203; (p) (517) 787-2320; (f) (517) 787-2933; (c) Jackson

Private for-profit/ 1965/ staff: 11(f); 22(p); 160(v)/ members: 1197

ART MUSEUM; HISTORIC SITE; HISTORY MUSEUM: Preserves and interprets the Merroman-Sharp Historic Site; the history of Jackson County and offers traveling exhibits and programming in the visual arts.

PROGRAMS: Community Outreach; Elder's Programs; Exhibits; Facility Rental; Family Programs; Guided Tours; Interpretation; Lectures; Publication; School-Based Curriculum

COLLECTIONS: [1829-present] Materials connected to the Merroman-Sharp families and to Jackson history; archives, photos, furnishings.

HOURS: Yr

ADMISSION: $4, Children $2

JONESVILLE

4162
Grosvenor House Museum Association
211 Maumee St, 49250 [PO Box 63, 49250]; (p) (517) 849-9506; (c) Hillsdale

Private non-profit/ 1977/ staff: 30(v)/ members: 200

HISTORIC PRESERVATION AGENCY; HISTORIC SITE; HISTORICAL SOCIETY; HOUSE MUSEUM: To preserve the historical identity and heritage of Michigan.

PROGRAMS: Annual Meeting; Community Outreach; Exhibits; Facility Rental; Family Programs; Research Library/Archives; School-Based Curriculum

COLLECTIONS: [Victorian era] Mid to late Victorian furnishings, apparel and appurtenances, Kiddie Brush Company toys, school room furnishings and accessories.

HOURS: June-Sept Sa-Su 2-5 or by appt

ADMISSION: $3, Family $7, Children $2, Seniors $2

KALAMAZOO

4163
Archives and Regional History Collections, Western Michigan University
East Hall, WMU, 49008; (p) (616) 387-8490; (f) (616) 387-8484; arch_collect@wmich.edu; www.wmich.edu/library/archive; (c) Kalamazoo

1956/ Western Michigan University/ staff: 5(f); 4(p)/publication: *Guide to Regional History Collections*

LIBRARY AND/OR ARCHIVES: Houses records of Western Michigan University and Southwestern Michigan including records from a twelve county region on deposit from the state archives.

PROGRAMS: Community Outreach; Exhibits; Lectures; Publication; Research Library/Archives

COLLECTIONS: [1827-present] Western Michigan University, regional holdings, local government records.

HOURS: Sept-June T-F 8-5, Sa 9-4; July-Aug M-F 10-4

4164
Kalamazoo Aviation History Museum
3101 E Milham, 49002; (p) (616) 382-6555; (f) (616) 382-1813; rnewman@airzoo.org; www.airzoo.org; (c) Kalamazoo

Private non-profit/ 1977/ staff: 15(f); 5(p); 170(v)/ members: 1136

HOUSE MUSEUM: Dedicated to preserving the history of aviation.

PROGRAMS: Community Outreach; Exhibits; Facility Rental; Family Programs; Festivals; Film/Video; Guided Tours; Lectures; Research Library/Archives; School-Based Curriculum

COLLECTIONS: [All periods of aviation history] Magazines, technical manuals, related publications, books, uniforms, photographs, artifacts, posters, and aviation videos.

HOURS: Yr Daily M-Sa 9-5, Su 12-5

ADMISSION: $10, Children $5, Seniors $8; Under 6 free

4165
Kalamazoo Valley Museum
230 N Rose St, 49003 [PO Box 4070, 49003-4070]; (p) (616) 372-7990; (f) (616) 373-7997; pnorris@kvcc.edu; www.kvcc.edu; (c) Kalamazoo

Joint/ 1881/ staff: 15(f); 9(p); 170(v)

HISTORY MUSEUM: A participatory museum of history science, and technology linking southwest Michigan to the world.

PROGRAMS: Exhibits; Family Programs; Festivals; Film/Video; Interpretation; Lectures; Publication; School-Based Curriculum

COLLECTIONS: [1820-present] 40,000 objects focused on local and regional history, with comparative examples; photographs, documents and artifacts.

HOURS: Yr Daily M-Sa 10-6, W 10-9, Su and Holidays

KALISPELL

4166
Northwest Montana Historical Society and Central School Museum
124 Second Ave East, 59903 [PO Box 2293, 59903]; (p) (406) 756-8381; (f) (406) 257-5719; nwmhs@digis.net; www.digisys.net/museum; (c) Flathead

Private non-profit/ 1996/ staff: 1(f); 1(p); 20(v)/ members: 500

HISTORICAL SOCIETY; HISTORY MUSEUM: Collect, preserve, and exhibit the history and culture of Northwest Montana.

PROGRAMS: Annual Meeting; Community Outreach; Exhibits; Facility Rental

COLLECTIONS: [1894-1950] Focuses on agriculture and social history artifacts and memorabilia.

HOURS: Yr Winter M-F 11-4; Summer M-F 10-4

ADMISSION: $2, Student $1, Children $1,

LAKE LINDEN

4167
Houghton County Historical Society
5500 M26, 49945 [PO Box 127, 49945]; (p) (906) 296-4121; (c) Houghton

Private non-profit/ 1961/ staff: 21(v)/ members: 307

HISTORIC PRESERVATION AGENCY; HISTORICAL SOCIETY; HISTORY MUSEUM; RESEARCH CENTER: Dedicated to preserving the mining history of the area.

PROGRAMS: Annual Meeting; Concerts; Exhibits; Facility Rental; Research Library/Archives

COLLECTIONS: [1840-1960] Newspapers from 1890 to 1945, photographs, artifacts, mining exhibits, railroad exhibits, school house and 1870s church.

HOURS: May-Oct Daily 10-4:30

ADMISSION: $5

LANSING

4168
Library of Michigan
717 W Allegan, 48909 [PO Box 30007, 48909]; (p) (517) 373-1300; (f) (517) 373-5700; www.libofmich.lib.mi.us; (c) Ingham

State/ 1828/ staff: 101(f)/publication: *Access, Abrams Collection Genealogy Highlights*

LIBRARY AND/OR ARCHIVES: State Library agency for Michigan; maintains Michigan Library, Historical Center, and State Law Library.

PROGRAMS: Community Outreach; Exhibits; Guided Tours; Publication

COLLECTIONS: Special collections focusing on Michigan, genealogy and Federal Documents resources.

HOURS: Jan-Dec Daily M-F 9-6, Sa 9-5, Su 1-5

ADMISSION: No charge

4169
Michigan Historical Center
717 W Allegan, 48918; (f) (517) 373-0851; (c) Ingham

State/ staff: 60(f); 10(p); 165(v)/publication: *Michigan History Magazine*

HISTORIC PRESERVATION AGENCY; HISTORY MUSEUM: Collects, preserves, and interprets the states past through its publications, Museum, Archives, Archaeology and Historic Preservation units.

PROGRAMS: Community Outreach; Exhibits; Facility Rental; Family Programs; Festivals; Guided Tours; Interpretation; Lectures; Publication; Research Library/Archives

COLLECTIONS: [19th-20th c] A general collection covering broad spectrum of Michigan history from time of European contact to present.

HOURS: Yr Museum: M-F 9-4:30, Sa 10-4, Su 1-5; Center Office hours M-F 8-5

4170
Michigan Museum of Surveying
220 S Museum Dr, 48933; (p) (517) 484-6605; (f) (517) 484-3711; (c) Ingham

Private non-profit/ 1973/ staff: 1(p)/ members: 168

HISTORY MUSEUM

PROGRAMS: Exhibits; Film/Video; Reenactments; Research Library/Archives

COLLECTIONS: [19th and 20th c]

HOURS: Yr M-F 8-12 / 1-5 and by appt

ADMISSION: Donations accepted

4171
Michigan Museums Association
717 W Allegan, 48901 [PO Box 10067, 48901]; (p) (517) 482-4055; (f) (517) 482-7997; (c) Ingham

Private non-profit/ 1954/ staff: 1(f); 30(v)/ members: 420/publication: *Museums and Cultural Sites in Michigan*

ALLIANCE OF HISTORICAL AGENCIES: Provides services that promote professional growth of Michigan museums and advocates on their behalf.

PROGRAMS: Annual Meeting;

4172
Michigan Women's Historical Center and Hall of Fame

213 W Main St, 48933-2315; (p) (517) 372-9772; (f) (517) 372-0170; mwhfame@leslie.k12.mi.us; leslie.k12.mi.us/mwhfame; (c) Ingham

Private non-profit/ 1973/ Michigan Women's Studies Assn./ staff: 2(f); 1(p)/ members: 215/publication: *Michigan Women: Firsts and Founders Vol I and II; Historic Women of Michigan*

ART MUSEUM; HISTORIC SITE; HISTORY MUSEUM: Dedicated to giving visibility to the accomplishments of Michigan women.

PROGRAMS: Annual Meeting; Community Outreach; Exhibits; Facility Rental; Family Programs; Festivals; Guided Tours; Lectures; Publication; Research Library/Archives

COLLECTIONS: [19th and 20th c] Photo collection of women inducted into the Michigan Women's Hall of Fame, antique clothing, suffrage artifacts and photos, artifacts of Honorees.

HOURS: Yr W-F 12-5, Sa 12-4, Su 2-4

ADMISSION: $2.50, Children $1, Seniors $2

LELAND

4173
Leelanau Historical Museum

203 E Cedar St, 49654 [PO Box 246, 49654]; (p) (231) 256-7475; (f) (231) 256-7650; info@leelanauhistory.org; www.leelanauhistory.org; (c) Leelanau

Private non-profit/ 1957/ staff: 2(f); 1(p); 125(v)/ members: 525/publication: *Leemuse*

HISTORICAL SOCIETY; HISTORY MUSEUM; RESEARCH CENTER: Interprets diverse cultures in the Leelanau Peninsula and its islands.

PROGRAMS: Annual Meeting; Community Outreach; Concerts; Exhibits; Family Programs; Interpretation; Lectures; Publication; Research Library/Archives; School-Based Curriculum

COLLECTIONS: [1850-1930] Photographs, manuscripts, ephemera, county records, books, and oral histories; Tools, textiles, folk, and fine art; traditional Odawa Art.

HOURS: Yr Summer M-Su 10-4; Winter F-S 10-4

ADMISSION: $1, Student $0.50; Under 5 free

LINCOLN PARK

4174
Lincoln Park Historical Society

1335 Sfield, 48146; (p) (313) 386-3137; (c) Wayne

Private non-profit/ 1974/ staff: 16(v)/ members: 300/publication: *Lincoln Park Historical Society News Letter*

HISTORIC PRESERVATION AGENCY; HISTORICAL SOCIETY; HOUSE MUSEUM

PROGRAMS: Exhibits; Festivals; Lectures; Publication

COLLECTIONS: Items relevant to the Lincoln Park community; pioneer and Indian items.

LOWELL

4175
Fallasburg Historical Society

13944 Covered Bridge Rd, 49331; (p) (616) 897-0849; fhspres@iserv.net; (c) Kent

Joint; Private non-profit/ 1965/ staff: 25(v)/ members: 140/publication: *Fallasburg Historical Society Newsletter*

HISTORIC SITE; HISTORICAL SOCIETY; HISTORY MUSEUM: Collect, preserve, interpret, and publish Fallasburg history; restore historic structures; enhance public support for Fallasburg Historic Village.

PROGRAMS: Annual Meeting; Exhibits; Facility Rental; Festivals; Guided Tours; Publication

COLLECTIONS: [Mid 19th c] Eight properties including houses, barns, and land; artifacts, photographs, print/manuscript materials, school furnishings.

HOURS: May-Oct Su 2-6

ADMISSION: $1, Children $0.25; Under 13 free

LUDINGTON

4176
Mason County Historical Society/ White Pine Village

1687 S Lakeshore Dr, 49431; (p) (231) 843-4808; (f) (231) 843-7089; whitepine@masoncounty.net; www./umanet.org/whitepine; (c) Mason

Private non-profit/ 1937/ staff: 2(f); 1(p); 400(v)/ members: 585/publication: *1987 Pictorial History*

GENEALOGICAL SOCIETY; HISTORICAL SOCIETY; HISTORY MUSEUM; HOUSE MUSEUM; LIVING HISTORY/OUTDOOR MUSEUM; RESEARCH CENTER: Depicts the history of Mason County with 21 buildings in White Pine Village.

PROGRAMS: Concerts; Exhibits; Facility Rental; Guided Tours; Interpretation; Living History; Publication; Reenactments; Research Library/Archives; School-Based Curriculum

COLLECTIONS: [1850-1950] Books, obituaries, directories, photographs, information files, scrapbooks, and document boxes; artifacts from lumbering days, agricultural start, business and education.

HOURS: Apr-Oct T-Sa 11-5

ADMISSION: $5

MACKINAC ISLAND

4177
Mackinac State Historic Parks-Mackinac Island

Mackinac State Historic Park, 49757 [PO Box 370, 49757-0370]; (p) (906) 847-3328; (f) (906) 847-3815; mackinacparks@state.mi.us; www.mackinac.com/historicparks; (c) Mackinac

State/ 1895/ Mackinac Island State Park Commission/ staff: 45(f); 120(p); 375(v)/ members: 1500

HISTORIC PRESERVATION AGENCY; HISTORIC SITE; HISTORY MUSEUM; LIVING HISTORY/OUTDOOR MUSEUM: Preserves and interprets the natural and cultural resources of Mackinac Island State Park, Fort Mackinac, the Historic Downtown, and related land and historic structures.

PROGRAMS: Annual Meeting; Community Outreach; Exhibits; Facility Rental; Family Programs; Festivals; Film/Video; Guided Tours; Interpretation; Lectures; Living History; Publication; Reenactments; School-Based Curriculum

COLLECTIONS: [Pre history-present] One million archaeological artifacts, and 30,000 historical artifacts representing human cultural activity at the Straits of Mackinac.

HOURS: Daily May 7-June 10, Sept 24-Oct 14 9:30-4; June 11-June 15, Aug 20-Sept 23 9:30-5; June 16-Aug 19 9:30-6:30

ADMISSION: Varies

4178
Stuart House City Museum

Market St, 49757 [PO Box 1194, 49757-1194]; (p) (906) 847-8181; (f) (906) 847-6430; (c) Mackinac

City; Joint/ 1930/ staff: 5(p); 4(v)

HISTORIC SITE; HISTORY MUSEUM: Collects, preserves, and interprets the history of the City of Mackinac Island.

PROGRAMS: Exhibits; Interpretation; Publication

COLLECTIONS: [1750-1950] Photographs, material culture objects, ledgers of the American Fur Company, furniture, archaeological artifacts.

HOURS: Mid May-Mid June 10-4; Mid June-Sept Daily 10-5:30, T, Th evenings 7-9; Oct Daily 1-4;

ADMISSION: $3.50, Family $10, Student $1.50, Seniors $2

MACKINAW CITY

4179
Great Lakes Lighthouse Museum

100 Dock Dr, 49701 [PO Box 712, 49701-0712]; (p) (231) 436-3333; (f) (231) 436-7870; (c) Cheboygan

Private non-profit/ 1998/ staff: 1(f); 2(v)/ members: 525/publication: *Beginning Guide to Saving a Lighthouse*

HISTORIC PRESERVATION AGENCY; HISTORIC SITE; HISTORY MUSEUM: To broaden the public's appreciation, understanding, and support of America's Lighthouse Heritage through fine arts, preservation, archeology, and restoration.

PROGRAMS: Annual Meeting; Concerts; Elder's Programs; Festivals; Guided Tours; Interpretation; Publication; Research Library/ Archives

COLLECTIONS: [1820-present]

4180
Mackinac State Historic Parks- Mackinaw City
Mackinac State Historic Park, 49701 [PO Box 873, 49701]; (p) (231) 436-4100; (f) (231) 436-4210; mackinacparks@state.mi.us; www.mackinac.com/historicparks

State/ 1895/ Mackinac Island State Park Commission

HISTORIC PRESERVATION AGENCY; HISTORIC SITE; HISTORY MUSEUM; LIVING HISTORY/OUTDOOR MUSEUM: Preserves and interprets the natural and cultural resources of Colonial Michilimackinac, Historic Mill Creek, Old Mackinac Point Light, and related land and historic structures.

PROGRAMS: Annual Meeting; Community Outreach; Exhibits; Facility Rental; Family Programs; Festivals; Film/Video; Guided Tours; Interpretation; Lectures; Living History; Publication; Reenactments; School-Based Curriculum

COLLECTIONS: [Prehistory-present] One million archaeological artifacts, and 30,000 historical artifacts representing human cultural activity at the Straits of Mackinac.

HOURS: Daily May 7-June 15, Aug 20-Oct 14 9-5; June 16-Aug 19 9-6;

ADMISSION: Varies

MANISTEE

4181
Manistee County Historical Museum
425 River St, 49660; (p) (616) 723-5531; (c) Manistee

Private non-profit/ 1954/ staff: 1(f); 1(p); 20(v)/ members: 500

HISTORIC PRESERVATION AGENCY; HISTORIC SITE; HISTORICAL SOCIETY; HISTORY MUSEUM; RESEARCH CENTER: Collects, preserves, and interprets Manistee County history, the Victorian Era, Lake Michigan maritime history.

PROGRAMS: Annual Meeting; Community Outreach; Exhibits; Interpretation; Lectures; Research Library/Archives

COLLECTIONS: [1850-1900] artifacts, newspapers, books, maps, serials, photographs; 2 historic buildings.

HOURS: Yr T-Sa 10-5

ADMISSION: $2

MARIE

4182
River of History Museum
209 E Portage Ave / Sault Ste, 49783 [PO Box 627, Sault Ste Marie, 49783]; (p) (906) 632-1999; (f) (906) 635-6678; (c) Chippewa

Private non-profit/ 1990/ staff: 1(f); 7(p); 10(v)/ members: 200

HISTORIC SITE; HISTORICAL SOCIETY; HISTORY MUSEUM; RESEARCH CENTER: 8,000 years of local history and cultures de-

picted in 8 exhibition galleries: glacial past, Native Americans, French Fur trade, British Siege, Michigan statehood, industrial boom, 20th century heritage.

PROGRAMS: Annual Meeting; Community Outreach; Exhibits; Family Programs; Guided Tours; Interpretation; School-Based Curriculum

COLLECTIONS: [Pre history-19th c]

HOURS: May 15 - Oct 15 Daily M-Sa 10-5, Su 12-5

ADMISSION: $2.50, Children $1.25, Seniors

MARQUETTE

4183
John Burt House
Little Island Pt #25, 49855; (p) (906) 226-2413

4184
Marquette County Historical Society, Inc.
213 N Front St, 49855; (p) (906) 226-3571; mqtcohis@uproc.lib.mi.us; (c) Marquette

Private non-profit/ 1918/ staff: 3(f); 2(p); 5(v)/ members: 825

HISTORICAL SOCIETY; HISTORY MUSEUM; LIBRARY AND/OR ARCHIVES: Collects, preserves, and interprets artifacts, archival materials, and items relevant to the history of Michigan's Upper Peninsula.

PROGRAMS: Annual Meeting; Community Outreach; Concerts; Exhibits; Guided Tours; Interpretation; Lectures; Publication; Research Library/Archives

COLLECTIONS: [Cooper Culture-present] Artifacts, maps, business records, rare books, manuscripts, and photographs.

HOURS: Yr M-F 10-5, 3rd Th 10-9

ADMISSION: $3, Children $3; Under 13 free

MARSHALL

4185
Marshall Historical Society
107 N Kalamazoo, 49068 [PO Box 68, 49068]; (p) (616) 781-8544; dircherie@aol.com; (c) Calhoun

Private non-profit/ 1961/ staff: 1(f); 5(p)/ members: 318

HISTORICAL SOCIETY: Strives to preserve and promote 19th century structures, Marshall and Michigan history.

PROGRAMS: Exhibits; Guided Tours

HOURS: May 1 - Sept 30 Daily 12-5; Oct Th-Su 12-5

ADMISSION: $3,

MARYSVILLE

4186
Marysville Historical Commission
887 Huron Blvd E, 48040 [1111 Delaware Ave, 48040]; (p) (810) 364-5198, (810) 364-6613; (f) (810) 364-3940; mville@advnet.net; vikings.marysville.k12.mius/city/; (c) St. Clair

City/ Joint/ 1977/ staff: 20(v)/ members: 40

HISTORY MUSEUM: Preserves, records, and promotes the history of the city of Marysville and its environs.

PROGRAMS: Annual Meeting; Exhibits; Film/Video; Guided Tours; Publication; Research Library/Archives

COLLECTIONS: [Late 19th c-early 20th c] 1924 Wills Ste. Claire automobile, 1947 Garwood boat, birchbark canoe, ship models, photographs, artifacts, school papers, yearbooks, city records.

HOURS: Apri-Oct Sa-Su 1:30-4 and by appt

ADMISSION: $1, Children $0.50, Seniors $0.50

MASON

4187
Mason Area Historical Society
200 E Oak, 48854 [PO Box 44, 48854]; (p) (517) 676-9837; mahsmuseum@aol.com; (c) Ingham

Private non-profit/ 1976/ staff: 60(v)/ members: 130

HISTORIC PRESERVATION AGENCY; HISTORICAL SOCIETY; HISTORY MUSEUM: Operates a museum and has preserved a county school.

PROGRAMS: Annual Meeting; Community Outreach; Elder's Programs; Exhibits; Family Programs; Festivals; Film/Video; Garden Tours; Guided Tours; Interpretation; Research Library/Archives; School-Based Curriculum; Theatre

COLLECTIONS: micro-film "Ingham County News," books, artifacts.

HOURS: Yr T, Th 12-4, Sa 10-4

ADMISSION: $1

MENOMINEE

4188
Menominee County Historical Society, Inc.
904 11th Ave, 69858 [PO Box 151, 69858-0151]; (p) (906) 863-9000; (c) Menominee

Private non-profit/ staff: 1(f); 50(v)/ members: 350

HISTORIC SITE; HISTORICAL SOCIETY; HISTORY MUSEUM; RESEARCH CENTER: Collect, preserve, and display historical artifacts and provide material for research.

PROGRAMS: Annual Meeting; Exhibits; Guided Tours; Research Library/Archives

COLLECTIONS: [Late 1800s-1900s]

HOURS: May-Sept M-Sa 10-4:30

ADMISSION: Donations

4189
West Shore Fishing Museum
N5156 Hwy M-35, 49858 [N6634 Harbor Lane, 49858]; (p) (906) 863-3347; bejj@cybrzn.com; (c) Menominee

Private non-profit/ 1997/ staff: 30(v)/ members: 80/publication: *West Shore Fishing Museum Newsletter*

HISTORIC PRESERVATION AGENCY; HISTORIC SITE; HISTORY MUSEUM; HOUSE MUSEUM: Expected opening in 2007.

PROGRAMS: Annual Meeting

COLLECTIONS: [1890-1940] Commercial fishing artifacts, house items, Bailey family papers.

MIDLAND

4190
Chippewa Nature Center, Inc.
400 S Badour Rd, 48640; (p) (517) 631-0830; (f) (517) 631-7070; cnc@journey.com; www.chippewanaturecenter.com; (c) Midland

Private non-profit/ 1966/ staff: 13(f); 22(p); 800(v)/ members: 1375

LIVING HISTORY/OUTDOOR MUSEUM: Facilitates the enjoyment and understanding of local natural, historical and archaeolo9gical resources, promotes environmental awareness and fosters responsible stewardship.

PROGRAMS: Annual Meeting; Community Outreach; Elder's Programs; Exhibits; Facility Rental; Family Programs; Festivals; Interpretation; Lectures; Publication; School-Based Curriculum

COLLECTIONS: [Prehistory-1880s] Historical collection of 2,000 artifacts; archaeology collection of 15,000 artifacts from the area's pre and post contact history.

HOURS: Yr Daily M-F 8-5, Sa 9-5, 1-5

ADMISSION: No charge

MILFORD

4191
Kensington Metro Park Farm Center
2240 W Buno Rd, 48380-4410; (p) (248) 685-1561; (f) (248) 684-5836; (c) Oakland

1976/ staff: 3(f); 5(p)

LIVING HISTORY/OUTDOOR MUSEUM: Educates and informs the public about their rural heritage.

PROGRAMS: Exhibits; Family Programs; Festivals; Guided Tours; Interpretation

COLLECTIONS: Horse-drawn farm implements.

HOURS: Yr Daily M-F 9-5, Sa-Su 9-6

4192
Milford Historical Society and Museum
124 E Commerce St, 48381; (p) (248) 685-7308; (c) Oakland

Private non-profit/ 1973/ staff: 20(v)/ members: 296/publication: *Ten Minutes Ahead of the Rest of the World*

ART MUSEUM; HISTORIC PRESERVATION AGENCY; HISTORY MUSEUM; HOUSE MUSEUM; RESEARCH CENTER: Local history, genealogy and conducts home tours.

PROGRAMS: Annual Meeting; Community Outreach; Exhibits; Family Programs; Festivals; Guided Tours; Lectures; Publication; Research Library/Archives

COLLECTIONS: [1800s] 1832 log cabin; mid-Victorian furnished home.

HOURS: Apr-Dec W-Sa 1-4

ADMISSION: No charge

MONROE

4193
Monroe County Historical Museum
126 S Monroe St, 48161; (p) (734) 240-7780; (f) (734) 240-7788; co.monroe.mi.us/Museum/; (c) Monroe

County/ 1939/ staff: 6(f); 5(p); 16(v)

HISTORY MUSEUM: Collects, preserves, and interprets artifacts and documents relating to the entire history of Monroe County.

PROGRAMS: Exhibits; Guided Tours; Lectures; Reenactments; Research Library/Archives

COLLECTIONS: [Prehistory-20th c] Local history artifacts, General G. A. Custer, woodland Indians, tools, clothing, musical instruments, medical and dental equipment, ceramics, Victorian, household goods, photos and period documents, manuscript collection military.

HOURS: Yr May 1-Sept 30 Daily 10-5; Oct 1-Apr 30 W-Su 10-5

4194
Navarre-Anderson Trading Post
3775 N Custer Rd, 48161 [c/o Monroe Museum, 126 S Monroe St, 48161]; (p) (734) 240-7780; (f) (734) 240-7788; (c) Monore

County/ 1972/ Monroe County Historical Commission/ staff: 1(p); 12(v)

HOUSE MUSEUM: Main building is a restored French-Canadian style, piece-sur-piece construction, trading post dating from 1789.Other buildings date from 1810 and 1860.

PROGRAMS: Exhibits; Guided Tours; Interpretation; Living History

COLLECTIONS: [1789-1910] Early 20th c store goods.

HOURS: June-Aug W-Su

4195
River Raisin Battlefield Visitor Center
1403 E Elm Ave, 48161 [c/o Monroe Museum, 126 S Monroe St, 48161]; (p) (734) 240-7780; (f) (734) 240-7788; (c) Monroe

County/ 1990/ Monroe County Historical Museum/ staff: 3(p); 3(v)

HISTORIC SITE; HISTORY MUSEUM: Preserves and interprets site of the Battles and Massacre of the River Raisin, 1813.

PROGRAMS: Exhibits; Interpretation; Lectures

COLLECTIONS: [War of 1812] Artifacts and exhibits, dioramas, fiber-optic map and battle narration, site markers and commemorative monuments; commemoration activities.

HOURS: Yr Summer Daily 10-5, Winter Sa-Su 10-5

ADMISSION: No charge

MONTROSE

4196
Montrose Historical Telephone Pioneer Museum
144 E Hickory St, 48457 [PO Box 577, 48457]; (p) (810) 639-6644; telemusm@gfn.org; www.gfn.org/telemusm/; (c) Genesee

Private non-profit/ 1980/ staff: 1(p); 40(v)/ members: 250/publication: *Memory Lane Gazette*

HISTORY MUSEUM: Operates the museum, collection of area history, telephone collections, and private collections.

PROGRAMS: Annual Meeting; Community Outreach; Exhibits; Family Programs; Guided Tours; Interpretation; Living History; Publication; Research Library/Archives

COLLECTIONS: [1882-present] Telephone-sand local history.

HOURS: Yr Jan 1-Mar 31 Su 1-5;

MOUNT CLEMENS

4197
Macomb County Historical Society/Crocker House Museum
15 Union St, 48043; (p) (810) 465-2488; www.macombonline.com/users/admin/update.cgi; (c) Macomb

Private non-profit/ 1964/ staff: 3(p); 30(v)/ members: 260

HISTORICAL SOCIETY; HOUSE MUSEUM: To preserve local history and the history of the County seat, Mt. Clemens, Victorian House Museum displays period rooms and changing exhibits related to the area.

PROGRAMS: Exhibits; Garden Tours; Guided Tours; Living History; Publication; Research Library/Archives

COLLECTIONS: [1860-1910] Victorian furniture, clothing, household items, canvas art; history of house, businesses, mineral baths.

HOURS: Mar-Dec T-Th 10-4 and 1st Su of month 1-4

ADMISSION: Donations

4198
Michigan Transit Museum
200 Grand, 48046 [PO Box 12, 48046]; (p) (810) 463-1863; www.alexxi.com/mtm; (c) Macomb

Private non-profit/ 1973/ staff: 30(v)/ members: 140/publication: *Michigan Transit Gizette*

HISTORIC SITE; HISTORICAL SOCIETY; HISTORY MUSEUM; LIVING HISTORY/OUTDOOR MUSEUM; RAILROAD MUSEUM: To collect, preserve, exhibit, and operate items and artifacts of railroads and mass transit; to establish a museum, library, archives; housed in the Mt. Clemens Depot (built in 1859).

PROGRAMS: Annual Meeting; Exhibits; Film/Video; Interpretation; Lectures; Living History; Publication; Research Library/Archives

COLLECTIONS: [1859-present] Trolleys, interurban, and railways; railway equipment at Air National Guard Base.

MOUNT PLEASANT

4199
Clark Historical Library
Central Michigan University, 48859; (p) (517) 774-2160; (f) (517) 774-1803; clarke@cmich.edu; www.lib.cmich.edu/clarke; (c) Isabella

State/ 1955/ staff: 6(f); 2(p)

LIBRARY AND/OR ARCHIVES: Research library open to the public.

PROGRAMS: Community Outreach; Exhibits; Lectures; Research Library/Archives

COLLECTIONS: [1600-present] Michigan history; books, manuscripts, photographs, maps, graphics, children's books from the 19c, Africana and Afro-Americana.

HOURS: Yr M-F

4200
Museum of Cultural and Natural History
103 Rowe Hall, Central Michigan Univ, 48859; (p) (517) 774-3829; (f) (517) 774-3256; Lynn.Fauver@cmich.edu; www.csv.cmich.edu/museum.html; (c) Isabella

Joint; State/ 1970/ staff: 3(f); 10(p); 8(v)

HISTORY MUSEUM: Provides academic and research support to the faculty, staff, and students; serves as repository and caretaker for historic, cultural, and scientific collections for the university.

PROGRAMS: Community Outreach; Exhibits; Interpretation

COLLECTIONS: [Late 1800s to present] Local and regional history, Michigan archaeology, regional natural science, and contemporary Native American art.

4201
Zubiwing Cultural Society
6870 E Broadway, 48640; (p) (517) 775-4750; (f) (517) 775-4770; (c) Isabella

1994/ staff: 25(p); 25(v)

HISTORIC PRESERVATION AGENCY; HISTORICAL SOCIETY; RESEARCH CENTER; TRIBAL MUSEUM: To enlighten and educate tribal and community members, and all other peoples of the world to the culture, heritage, history, and goals of the Saginaw Chippewa Indian Tribe.

PROGRAMS: Community Outreach; Elder's Programs; Exhibits; Lectures; Publication

COLLECTIONS: [1800s-1900s] All aspects of the history of the Saginaw Chippewa Indian Tribe.

HOURS: Yr by appt

MUSKEGON

4202
Hackley and Hume Historic Site
472 Webster Ave, 49440 [430 W Clay Ave, 49440]; (p) (616) 722-7578; (f) (616) 728-4119; (c) Muskegon

Private non-profit/ 1986/ staff: 1(f); 1(p); 87(v)

HISTORIC SITE; HOUSE MUSEUM: Historic house complex that interprets the lives of the Charles H. Hackley and Thomas Hume families; Queen Anne architecture; late Victorian decorative arts, and Muskegon's history.

PROGRAMS: Community Outreach; Concerts; Family Programs; Lectures; School-Based Curriculum

COLLECTIONS: [1890-1915] Furnishings, barn and carriage implements and tools, portraiture, and documentary materials.

HOURS: May -Sept W-Su 12-4

4203
Muskegon County Museum
430 W Clay Ave, 49440; (p) (616) 722-0278; (f) (616) 728-4119; (c) Muskegon

Private non-profit/ 1937/ staff: 16(f); 5(p); 250(v)/ members: 320/publication: Muser Quarterly Newsletters

HISTORY MUSEUM: Collects, preserves, and interprets the natural and cultural history of Muskegon County.

PROGRAMS: Annual Meeting; Community Outreach; Exhibits; Facility Rental; Family Programs; Guided Tours; Interpretation; Lectures; Publication; Research Library/Archives; School-Based Curriculum

COLLECTIONS: [19th and 20th c] Artifacts of the history of Muskegon County; Queen Anne architecture.

HOURS: Yr M-F 9:30-4:30, Sat and Sun 12:30-4:30

ADMISSION: No charge

4204
SS Milwaukee Clipper
[PO Box 1370, 49443]; (p) (231) 755-0990; (f) (231) 821-0396; ssmilwkclipper@webtv.net; milwaukeeclipper.org; (c) Muskegon

Private non-profit/ 1997/ staff: 125(v)

HOURS: Sa-Su hours vary

ADMISSION: $5, Student $2.50; Under 5 free

NEGAUNEE

4205
Michigan Iron Industry Museum
73 Forge Rd, 49866; (p) (906) 475-7857; (f) (906) 475-9221; www.sos.state.mi.us/ history/history.html; (c) Marquette

State/ 1987/ staff: 2(f); 1(p)

HISTORIC SITE; HISTORY MUSEUM: Collects, preserves, and interprets the heritage of Michigan's three iron ranges.

PROGRAMS: Community Outreach; Concerts; Exhibits; Family Programs; Festivals; Interpretation; Lectures; Publication

COLLECTIONS: [1845-present] Mining industry, technology, and cultural including the c. 1868 vertical boiler mine haulage locomotive "Yankee"

HOURS: May 1- Oct 31 Daily 9:30-4:30

ADMISSION: No charge

NILES

4206
Fort St. Joseph Museum
508 E Main, 49120 [PO Box 487, 49120]; (p) (616) 683-4702; (f) (616) 684-3930; www.ci.niles.mi.us.; (c) Berrien

City/ 1932/ staff: 1(f); 2(p); 12(v)

HISTORY MUSEUM: Interprets Niles area history; particularly in the French Colonial period.

PROGRAMS: Community Outreach; Exhibits; Family Programs; Interpretation; Lectures

COLLECTIONS: [1827-present] 12 pictographs drawn by Chief Sitting Bull; Fort St. Joseph artifacts, Sioux Indian artifacts, Victorian decorative arts, local history

NORTHPORT

4207
Grand Traverse Lighthouse Foundation
15500 N Lighthouse Point Rd, 49670 [PO Box 43, 49670]; (p) (231) 386-7195; (f) (231) 386-7195; gtlthse@gtii.com; www.grandtraverse lighthouse.com; (c) Leelanau

Private non-profit/ 1985/ staff: 1(f); 5(p); 20(v)/ members: 225

HISTORICAL SOCIETY: Collects, preserves and interprets the history of the Grand Traverse Lighthouse; enhances knowledge and understanding of the area's history.

PROGRAMS: Annual Meeting; Community Outreach; Concerts; Facility Rental; Guided Tours; Interpretation; Living History; Research Library/Archives

COLLECTIONS: [1920s-1940s] Grand Traverse Lighthouse and Great Lakes Lighthouse artifacts, photographs, paintings, ship models, journals, books, general house artifacts.

HOURS: May, Sept, Oct Daily 12-4; June, Aug Daily 10-7

ADMISSION: $2

NORTHVILLE

4208
Northville Historical Society/Mill Race Village
Griswold, 48167 [PO Box 71, 48167]; (p) (248) 348-1845; (f) (248) 348-0056; (c) Wayne

Private non-profit/ 1972/ staff: 2(p); 55(v)/ members: 215

HISTORIC PRESERVATION AGENCY; HISTORIC SITE; HISTORICAL SOCIETY: To discover, collect, preserve, advance, and disseminate knowledge of the history of the Northville region.

PROGRAMS: Annual Meeting; Exhibits; Facility Rental; Family Programs; Festivals; Garden Tours; Guided Tours; Publication; Reenactments; Research Library/Archives; School-Based Curriculum

COLLECTIONS: [Mid-late 1800s] Historical village consisting of 9 buildings preserving the architectural style common to the Northville area.

HOURS: June-Oct Su 1-4

OKEMOS

4209
Friends of Historic Meridian
5113 Marsh Rd, 48805 [PO Box 155, 48805-0155]; (p) (517) 347-7300; (c) Ingham

Private non-profit/ 1971/ staff: 1(p); 40(v)/ members: 120/publication: The Gatekeeper

HISTORIC SITE; HISTORY MUSEUM; HOUSE MUSEUM: Five historic structures: 1849 Inn, 1864 Tin House, 1850 Tall Gate House, 1877 Blacksmith Shop, 1883 School, and Barn.

PROGRAMS: Community Outreach; Concerts; Elder's Programs; Exhibits; Facility Rental; Family Programs; Festivals; Guided Tours; Interpretation; Living History; Publication; School-Based Curriculum

COLLECTIONS: [1840-1910] Furnishings, artifacts, pictures and archival materials, oral histories.

HOURS: Apr-Dec M-F 9-1, Sa 10-1, by appt

ADMISSION: $2

4210
Meridian Historical Village
5151 Marsh Rd, 48805 [PO Box 155, 48805-0155]; (p) (517) 347-7300; (f) (517) 347-7300; woolseyd@pilot.msu.edu; (c) Ingham

Private non-profit/ 1974/ staff: 1(p); 25(v)/ members: 136/publication: *The Gatekeeper*

HISTORICAL SOCIETY; LIVING HISTORY/ OUTDOOR MUSEUM: Six historic structures that inform and teach the public about early Michigan history by creating a context of pioneer life in Meridian Township.

PROGRAMS: Concerts; Exhibits; Facility Rental; Family Programs; Festivals; Guided Tours; Interpretation; Publication; Research Library/Archives; School-Based Curriculum

COLLECTIONS: [1850-1900] Items of local significance; rural/agricultural, education, transportation, trades, folk arts, family life.

HOURS: July-Oct 10-1; Nov-June Sa 2-5

4211
Nokomis Learning Center
5153 Marsh Rd, 48864; (p) (517) 349-5777; (f) (517) 349-8560; wood.cameron@acd.net; www.nolomis.org; (c) Ingham

Private non-profit/ 1989/ staff: 1(f); 3(p); 6(v)/ members: 100/publication: *Nokomis News*

LIVING HISTORY/OUTDOOR MUSEUM; RESEARCH CENTER; TRIBAL MUSEUM: Preserves and presents the history, arts, and culture of the Great Lakes and Native Americans.

PROGRAMS: Annual Meeting; Community Outreach; Exhibits; Facility Rental; Festivals; Guided Tours; Interpretation; Lectures; Living History; Publication; School-Based Curriculum

COLLECTIONS: [Pre history-present] Native American artifacts, crafts, and art.

HOURS: Yr T-F 10-5, Sa 12-5

ADMISSION: Donations accepted

ONTONAGON

4212
Ontonagon County Historical Society
422 River St, 49953 [PO Box 92, 49953]; (p) (906) 884-6165; ochsmuse@up.lib.net; www.ontonagon.com/mi/ochs.html; (c) Ontonagon

Private non-profit/ 1957/ staff: 1(f); 1(p); 10(v)/ members: 200

HISTORICAL SOCIETY; HISTORY MUSEUM: To preserve the heritage and artifacts of Ontonagon County; to compile history and genealogy.

PROGRAMS: Annual Meeting; Exhibits; Publication; Research Library/Archives

COLLECTIONS: [1880-1965] Period room displays representing home, office, school, mining, carpentry, farming, railroad; photo and reading display of local history.

HOURS: Yr Winter M-Sa 9-5; Summer M-Sa 9-5, Su 10-4

ADMISSION: $2

OWOSSO

4213
Curwood Castle
224 Curwood Castle Dr, 48867; (p) (517) 723-0597; (c) Shiawassee

1922/ staff: 2(p)

COLLECTIONS: Curwood papers and related memorabilia including movie posters.; Shiawassee County records.

HOURS: Yr

4214
Michigan State Trust for Railway Preservation, Inc.
[PO Box 665, 48867]; (p) (517) 725-9464; (f) (517) 723-1225; twelve25@shianet.org; (c) Shiawassee

Private non-profit/ 1982/ staff: 1(f); 30(v)/ members: 750

HISTORIC PRESERVATION AGENCY; HISTORIC SITE; HISTORY MUSEUM: To educate the public about steam-era railroad technology and its impact on the culture and economy of the Great Lakes region by safely operating, preserving, exhibiting, demonstrating, and interpreting historic railroad equipment and processes.

PROGRAMS: Exhibits; Interpretation; Lectures; School-Based Curriculum

COLLECTIONS: [19th and 20th c] 1941 PM 1225 Steam Locomotive, PM Caboose, full shop of machine tools , 2 Ann Arbor Box Cars, 1 PM Box Car.

4215
Movie Museum, The
318 E Oliver at Hickory, 48867 [408 N Water St, 48867-2254]; (p) (517) 725-7621; (c) Shiawassee

Private non-profit/ 1973/ Board of Directors/ staff: 1(f); 2(p); 37(v)/ members: 300

HISTORY MUSEUM: Collects, teaches, presents, and preserves movie, stage, radio, and TV artifacts and information.

PROGRAMS: Community Outreach; Concerts; Facility Rental; Family Programs; Film/Video; Lectures; Research Library/ Archives; Theatre

COLLECTIONS: [1700-present] Movie making gear, books, costumes, records, films, photographs, props, posters, oral histories, slides, sheet music, clippings.

HOURS: Yr Daily

PLYMOUTH

4216
Plymouth Historical Museum
155 S Main St, 48170; (p) (734) 455-8940; (f) (734) 455-7797; Bstew03@aol.com; www.plymouth.lib.mi.us/~history; (c) Wayne

Private non-profit/ 1948/ staff: 1(f); 4(p); 40(v)/ members: 600/publication: *Museum Memo Monthly*

HISTORY MUSEUM: Dedicated to preserving history of Plymouth and surrounding area, including Civil War history.

PROGRAMS: Annual Meeting; Community Outreach; Exhibits; Facility Rental; Family Programs; Festivals; Guided Tours; Interpretation;

Lectures; Living History; Publication; Reenactments; Research Library/Archives; School-Based Curriculum

COLLECTIONS: [1860-1945] Focusing on Victorian Era from Civil War; Petz Abraham Lincoln Collection, clothing and textile collection.

HOURS: Yr W-Su

PONTIAC

4217
Pine Grove Museum/Governor Wisner House
405 Oakland Ave, 48342; (p) (248) 338-6732; (f) (248) 338-6731; ocphs@wwnet.net; wwnet.net/~ocphs/index.html; (c) Oakland

Private non-profit/ 1845/ Oakland County Pioneer and Historical Society/ staff: 1(f); 25(v)/ members: 400/publication: *Oakland Gazette*

HISTORIC SITE; HISTORICAL SOCIETY; HISTORY MUSEUM: Pine Grove is a National and State Historic Site; includes Governor Wisner House, a 1865 one room schoolhouse, and research library.

PROGRAMS: Annual Meeting; Community Outreach; Exhibits; Guided Tours; Interpretation; Lectures; Publication; Research Library/Archives; School-Based Curriculum

COLLECTIONS: [Victorian/Civil War] Greek Revival Mansion built in 1845, containing Governor Wisner family's furnishings and personal items; Victorian era textiles, pioneer tools, archival and manuscript collections.

HOURS: Yr Library and Office T-Sa 9-4; Tours by appt

ADMISSION: $4, Children $2

PORT AUSTIN

4218
Huron City Museum
7930 Huron City Rd, 48467; (p) (989) 428-4123; (c) Huron

Private non-profit/ 1951/ William Lyon Phelps FDN/ staff: 2(p)

HISTORIC SITE; HISTORY MUSEUM; HOUSE MUSEUM; LIBRARY AND/OR ARCHIVES: A logging village, historic site, and museum consisting of 10 buildings.

PROGRAMS: Exhibits; Facility Rental; Family Programs; Festivals; Guided Tours; Interpretation

COLLECTIONS: [1875-1940] 1886 Victorian home and furnishings, barn, school, store, pioneer log cabin.

HOURS: July 1-Sept W,Th,M 10-5

4219
Port Austin Area Historical Society
335 Washington, 48467; (p) (517) 738-8623; (c) Huron

Private non-profit/ 1997/ staff: 32(v)/ members: 32/publication: *Pioneer History, Historical Calendar*

GENEALOGICAL SOCIETY; HISTORICAL SOCIETY: Preserve local history, educate our citizens about the area, and provide maps, markers, and other materials about pioneer settlement at "Tip of the Thumb" Peninsula.

PROGRAMS: Annual Meeting; Publication

PORT HURON

4220
Port Huron Museum
1115 Sixth St, 48060; (p) (810) 982-0891; (f) (810) 982-0053; phmuseum@tir.com; (c) Saint Clair

Private non-profit/ 1967/ staff: 5(f); 2(p); 70(v)/ members: 1300

ART MUSEUM; HISTORIC SITE; HISTORY MUSEUM; RESEARCH CENTER: Community Center for arts, culture, history of Saint Clair County; features the Huron Lightship Museum and the Thomas Edison Depot Museum.

PROGRAMS: Annual Meeting; Community Outreach; Concerts; Exhibits; Facility Rental; Family Programs; Festivals; Guided Tours; Lectures; Living History; Research Library/ Archives; School-Based Curriculum

COLLECTIONS: Local history, local archeology, regional art, Great Lakes marine history.

HOURS: Yr W-Su 1-4:30

ADMISSION: $2, Student $1; Under 6/Mbrs free

PORT SANILAC

4221
Loop-Harrison Historic House
228 S Ridge Rd, 48469 [c/o Sanilac County Historic Museum, PO Box 158, 48469]; (p) (810) 622-9946; (c) Sanilac

1872/ staff: 1(f); 3(p); 8(v)

COLLECTIONS: [1872-1900] Medical collection; marine; Civil War; World Wars I & II; Victorian clothing and house furnishings; quilts; natural science; Native Americans.; Family history; Civil War letters; cemetery readings; vital records, medical records

PORTAGE

4222
Celery Flats Historical Area
6335 Garden Lane, 49002 [7900 S Westnedge Ave, 49002]; (p) (616) 329-4410; (f) (616) 329-4506; (c) Kalamazoo

1989/ staff: 1(f); 5(p); 10(v)

GARDEN; HISTORIC SITE; HISTORY MUSEUM; HOUSE MUSEUM; LIVING HISTORY/ OUTDOOR MUSEUM: Dedicated to history of area farms, a restored barn theater, an open-air amphitheater, a grain elevator and a house.

PROGRAMS: Community Outreach; Concerts; Elder's Programs; Exhibits; Facility Rental; Family Programs; Festivals; Garden Tours; Guided Tours; Living History; School-Based Curriculum; Theatre

COLLECTIONS: [Mid 1800s] Artifacts, photographs of Dutch farmers.

HOURS: May 1- Sept 30 F 12-5, Sa 10-7, Su 12-5 and by appt

ADMISSION: $3, Children $2

PT. SANILAC

4223
Sanilac County Historical Society
228 S Ridge, 48469 [PO Box 158, 48469]; (p) (810) 359-5903; (c) Sanilac

Private non-profit/ 1961/ staff: 1(f); 3(p); 13(v)/ members: 246/publication: *Aanilac County History 1834-1934*

HISTORIC SITE; HISTORICAL SOCIETY; HISTORY MUSEUM; HOUSE MUSEUM

PROGRAMS: Annual Meeting; Community Outreach; Exhibits; Facility Rental; Festivals; Garden Tours; Guided Tours; Interpretation; Living History; Publication; Theatre

COLLECTIONS: [1870-1930] Historic home, 1875 period medical, dairy industry, carriages, blacksmith, fish industry, 1920 general store, log cabin, one room schoolhouse.

HOURS: May-Sept T-Su

RAY

4224
Wolcott Mill Historic Center/Huron-Clinton Metropolitan Authority
63841 Wolcott Rd, 48096; (p) (810) 749-5997; (f) (810) 749-2835; metroprk@mail.oeonline.com; www.metroparks.com; (c) Macomb

1979/ staff: 1(f); 5(p); 500(v)

HISTORIC SITE; HISTORY MUSEUM: Preserves, interprets, and operates a 150 year old grist mill.

PROGRAMS: Concerts; Exhibits; Family Programs; Festivals; Guided Tours; Interpretation; Lectures; Living History; Reenactments; Research Library/Archives; School-Based Curriculum

COLLECTIONS: [1840s-1960s] Artifacts, pictures, and other memorabilia indicating human life in southeastern Michigan with specifics directed toward mills.

HOURS: Yr Apr - Nov Daily 9-5; Dec-Mar W-Su 9-5

ADMISSION: $3/day

REED CITY

4225
Old Rugged Cross Historical Society/ Museum
4918 Park St, 49677 [PO Box 27, 49677]; (p) (231) 832-5431; (c) Osceola

Private non-profit/ 1968/ staff: 17(v)/ members: 93

GENEALOGICAL SOCIETY; HISTORIC PRESERVATION AGENCY; HISTORICAL SOCIETY; HISTORY MUSEUM; RESEARCH CENTER: Contains mementos and relics from the home of Rev. George Bennard author of the hymn "The Old Rugged Cross" and archives of the Reed County Area Genealogical Society.

PROGRAMS: Guided Tours; Interpretation; Research Library/Archives

COLLECTIONS: [1870-present] Early farm equipment, shop tools, models of early logging equipment, Indian artifacts, antiques, 1930s era fire truck, furniture, personal items, music.

HOURS: May-Oct Daily 1-4

ADMISSION: Donations accepted

ROCHESTER

4226
Meadow Brook Hall
Oakland University, 48309 [Oakland University, 48309-4401]; (p) (248) 370-3140; (f) (248) 370-4260; landers@oakland.edu; www.mbhconcours.org; (c) Oakland

State/ 1929/ Oakland University/ staff: 22(f); 16(p); 600(v)

HISTORIC SITE: Operates 1929 Tudor-revival house with original furnishings; cultural programs.

PROGRAMS: Exhibits; Facility Rental; Guided Tours; Lectures

COLLECTIONS: Architecture, craftsmanship, original furnishings, art, textiles, ceramics, art glass, furniture, costumes.

HOURS: Yr Daily Sept-June10:30-1:30; July-Aug Daily 10:30-12 / 1:30-3

ADMISSION: $8, Children $4

4227
Meadow Brook Hall
480 S Adams Rd, 48309 [Oakland University, Rochester Hills, 48309-4401]; (p) (248) 370-3140; (f) (248) 370-4260; ashby@oakland.edu

1926/ Oakland University/ staff: 17(f); 15(p); 250(v)

COLLECTIONS: [Late 1920s-1930s] Fine art, furniture, ceramics,Tiffany glass, silver, textiles, and archival materials; costumes by Paul Poiret; architectural drawings, family and architectural photographs

ROCHESTER HILLS

4228
Rochester Hills Historic Districts Commission
100 Rochester Hills Dr, 48307; (p) (248) 656-4661; (c) Oakland

City/ 1978/ staff: 1(p)

HISTORIC PRESERVATION AGENCY: Commission that reviews and advises work to be done on designated historic districts.

4229
Rochester Hills Museum at Van Hoosen Farm
1005 Van Hoosen Rd, 48306; (p) (248) 656-4663; (f) (248) 608-8198; rhmuseum@ ameritech.net; www.rochesterhills.org; (c) Oaklsand

City; Joint/ 1979/ staff: 2(f); 2(p); 35(v)/publication: *Van Hoosen, Bertha; Petticoat Surgeon, and others*

HISTORIC SITE; HISTORY MUSEUM; HOUSE MUSEUM: Dedicated to the preservation and interpretation of local and regional history and the achievements of the Van Hoosen families.

PROGRAMS: Community Outreach; Concerts; Exhibits; Facility Rental; Family Programs; Festivals; Garden Tours; Guided Tours; Interpretation; Lectures; Living History; Publication; Reenactments; Research Library/ Archives; School-Based Curriculum

COLLECTIONS: [1920s] Documents, artifacts

of the Taylor-Van Hoosen family and the greater Rochester Hills community.

HOURS: Yr W-Sa 1-4

ADMISSION: $3, Student $2, Seniors $2

ROCKLAND

4230
Old Victoria Restoration Site
Victoria Dam Rd, 49960 [PO Box 43, 49960]; (p) (906) 886-2617, (906) 884-4941; pthorgrn@up.net

1899/ City/ staff: 2(p)

COLLECTIONS: [1899-1921] Home furnishings and hand tools; records of Victorian Copper Mining Co., cancelled checks from 1911 to 1918, photographs.

ROGERS CITY

4231
Presque Isle County Historical Museum
176 W Michigan Ave, 49779 [PO Box 175, 49779]; (p) (517) 734-4121; (c) Presque Isle

Private non-profit/ 1975/ staff: 2(p)/ members: 350/publication: *Rogers City, Its First 100 Years; and others*

HISTORIC SITE; HISTORY MUSEUM: Dedicated to the preservation of Presque Isle County history and Rogers City, home to Bradley Fleet. National Register of Historic Sites.

PROGRAMS: Annual Meeting; Exhibits; Publication

COLLECTIONS: [1871-1930s] "Billy Whiskers" 1st Edition books, Maritime Room, and associated history; Native American collection, baskets, arrowheads, bow and arrow; history of Molitor murder 1872, Victorian clothing and hats, period furniture.

HOURS: June-July M-Sa 12-4; Aug-Oct M-F 12-4

ROMEO

4232
Romeo Historical Society
[PO Box 412, 48065]; (p) (810) 752-4111; www.libcoop.net/romrhs; (c) Macomb

Private non-profit/ 1961/ staff: 1(p)/ members: 30

HISTORICAL SOCIETY; LIBRARY AND/OR ARCHIVES: To preserve, promote, and document local history and archives.

PROGRAMS: Annual Meeting; Exhibits; Festivals; Guided Tours

COLLECTIONS: [1830-present] Blacksmith shop of early working tools, artifacts, archives.

HOURS: Apr-Dec 1st Sa of month 1-3

ADMISSION: Donations accepted

ROSE CITY

4233
Rose City Area Historical Society, Inc., The
Public Library, Main St, 48654 [c/o Ogemaw District Library, PO Box 427, W Main St,

48654]; (p) (989) 685-3300, (989) 684-4647; (c) Ogemaw

1985/ Board of Directors/ members: 36

GENEALOGICAL SOCIETY; HISTORICAL SOCIETY: To collect, catalogue, preserve and make available articles, as related to area, people, events.

PROGRAMS: Annual Meeting; Community Outreach; Exhibits; Festivals; Lectures; Research Library/Archives

COLLECTIONS: [1870-present] Early photographs of town, people, logging, schools, classes; census reports, newspapers, cemetery records, military files, periodicals, books, magazines, tapes.

HOURS: Yr M-F 10-5

ADMISSION: No charge

SAGINAW

4234
Historical Society of Saginaw Co., Inc./Castle Museum of Saginaw Co. History
500 Federal Ave, 48606 [PO Box 390, 48606-0390]; (p) (517) 752-2861; (f) (517) 752-1533; saghist@concentric.net; (c) Saginaw

Private non-profit/ 1964/ staff: 7(f); 3(p) 100(v)/ members: 450

HISTORIC SITE; HISTORICAL SOCIETY; HISTORY MUSEUM: Operates the Castle Museum of Saginaw Co. History in a French Castle; home of Saginaw Voyageurs with Montreal canoe, archaeological repository, county history, Smithsonian exhibits.

PROGRAMS: Annual Meeting; Exhibits; Reenactments; Research Library/Archives; School-Based Curriculum

COLLECTIONS: [Pre history-present] Objects manufactured by General Motors, archaeological repository of pre-historic and historical objects including federally owned artifacts.

HOURS: Yr Daily M-Sa 10-4:30, Su 1-4

ADMISSION: $1, Children $0.50

SAINT CLAIR

4235
Saint Clair Historical Museum
308 S Fourth St, 48079; (p) (810) 329-6888; (c) Saint Clair

City/ 1976/ staff: 30(v)

HISTORIC SITE; HISTORICAL SOCIETY; HISTORY MUSEUM: Maintains the museum; preserving, collecting, and exhibiting local materials.

PROGRAMS: Exhibits; Guided Tours

COLLECTIONS: [Early 1900s] Artifacts pertaining to the city of Saint Clair and nearby areas, highlights early ship building, and salt industry.

HOURS: May - Nov Sa-Su 1:30-4:30 and by appt

ADMISSION: Donations accepted

SAINT CLAIR SHORES

4236
Historical Society of Saint Clair Shores
22500 Eleven Mile Rd, 48081-1399; (p) (810) 771-9020; (f) (810) 771-8935; woodfor_a@libcoop.net; www.libcoop.net/stclairshores; (c) Macomb

City, non-profit/ 1982/ staff: 1(p); 60(v)/ members: 185/publication: *Muskrat Tales*

GENEALOGICAL SOCIETY; HISTORICAL SOCIETY; HISTORY MUSEUM; HOUSE MUSEUM: Develop programs to collect, preserve, and record the history of the city of St. Clair Shores.

PROGRAMS: Annual Meeting; Community Outreach; Exhibits; Guided Tours; Publication; Research Library/Archives

COLLECTIONS: [1890s] Household items, photographs, negatives; Selinsky-Green Farmhouse Museum.

HOURS: Yr W, Sa 1-4

ADMISSION: No charge

4237
Selinsky-Green Farmhouse
22500 Eleven Michigan, 48081; (p) (810) 771-9020; (c) Macomb

1981/ staff: 1(f); 20(v)/publication: *Muskrat Tales*

GARDEN; HISTORIC SITE: Restored farmhouse and gardens.

PROGRAMS: Annual Meeting; Community Outreach; Elder's Programs; Exhibits; Facility Rental; Family Programs; Garden Tours; Guided Tours; Interpretation; Lectures; Living History; Publication; Research Library/Archives

COLLECTIONS: [1860-1900] Victorian furniture representing rural life.

HOURS: Yr Winte: Sa 1-4; Summer: W 1-4

ADMISSION: Donations accepted

SAINT IGNACE

4238
Father Marquette National Memorial and Museum
Boulevard Dr, 49781 [Straits State Park, 720 Church St, 49781]; (p) (906) 643-8620; (f) (906) 643-9329; www.sos.state.mi.us/history/history.html; (c) Mackinac

Joint; State/ 1980/ staff: 3(p)

HISTORY MUSEUM: Interprets the 17th century French Jesuit missionary and explorer, Jacques Marquette and the meeting of French and Native American cultures in the North American wilderness.

PROGRAMS: Exhibits; Family Programs; Film/Video; Interpretation; Lectures; Publication

COLLECTIONS: [1660-1760] Artifacts of French colonial and Native American heritage; fur trade

4239
Marquette Mission Park and Museum of Ojibwa Culture
500-506 N State, 49781 [500 N State, 49781]; (p) (906) 643-9161; (f) (906) 643-9380; (c) Mackinac

City/ 1987/ staff: 7(p)/ 20(v)/ members: 50

HISTORIC SITE; HISTORY MUSEUM: Portray regional life over 300 years ago when Ojibwa, Huron, Odawa, and French lifestyles met; French Jesuit Mission, archaeological site, natural landmark.

PROGRAMS: Community Outreach; Concerts; Exhibits; Family Programs; Festivals; Guided Tours; Interpretation; Lectures; Living History; Publication

COLLECTIONS: [1600-1800] Archaeological, Native American, French fur trade/missionary.

HOURS: May-mid Oct Daily, hours vary

ADMISSION: $2, Family $5, Student $2, Children $1; Under 5 free

SAINT JOHNS

4240
Paine-Gillam-Scott Museum/Clinton County Historical Society
106 Maple St/W side of Courthouse Sq, 48879 [PO Box 174, 48879]; (p) (517) 224-2894, (517) 224-7402; (c) Clinton

Private non-profit/ 1978/ staff: 12(v)/ members: 125

GENEALOGICAL SOCIETY; HISTORIC SITE; HISTORICAL SOCIETY; HOUSE MUSEUM: Collects, preserves, and interprets Clinton Co. history; restoration: furniture, architecture, 1860s house, and Doctor's Office.

PROGRAMS: Exhibits; Family Programs; Festivals; Guided Tours; Interpretation; Research Library/Archives

COLLECTIONS: [1860-1920] Furnishings; clothing, guns and war related items, and local history materials.

HOURS: Apr-Dec W 2-7, Su 1-4

ADMISSION: Donations accepted

SALINE

4241
Rentschler Farm Museum
1265 E Michigan Ave, 48176 [PO Box 302, 48176]; (p) (734) 429-9621; (c) Washtenaw

Private non-profit/ 1987/ staff: 20(v)/ members: 100

HISTORIC SITE: Early 20th Century farm with Queen Anne style frame house and eleven typical outbuildings, including a barn with hand-adzed timbers.

PROGRAMS: Annual Meeting; Exhibits; Interpretation

COLLECTIONS: [1900-1950] House collection is 1900-1930, typical of southeast MI German farm house; agricultural tools and implements.

HOURS: Mid May-mid Oct

4242
Saline Area Historical Society
402 N Ann Arbor St, 48176 [PO Box 302, 48176]; (p) (734) 429-9621; (c) Washtenaw

Private non-profit/ 1987/ staff: 25(p)/ members: 65

HISTORICAL SOCIETY; HISTORY MUSEUM: Dedicated to bringing local history to the attention of the community through preservation and education; through use of a depot and farm museum with related artifacts.

PROGRAMS: Exhibits; Family Programs; Guided Tours; Interpretation

COLLECTIONS: [1824-present] Railroad and agricultural materials, oral histories, maps, and photographs.

HOURS: Depot Yr Sa 10-2; Farm May-Sept Sa10-2

ADMISSION: No charge

SAULT SAINTE MARIE

4243
Great Lakes Shipwreck Historical Society
111 Ashmun St, 49783; (p) (906) 635-1742; (f) (906) 635-0860; glshs@up.net; www.ship-wreckmuseum.com; (c) Chippewa

Private non-profit/ 1978/ staff: 5(f); 16(p); 13(v)/ members: 1070

HISTORIC SITE; HISTORICAL SOCIETY: Dedicated to preservation and interpretation of Great Lakes maritime history.

PROGRAMS: Community Outreach; Exhibits; Lectures

COLLECTIONS: [1849-1975] Artifacts from historic Great Lakes Shipwrecks including bell of the Edmund Fitzgerald; artifacts of U.S. Lighthouse Service, U.S. Life Saving Service, U.S. Coast Guard; history of underwater diving.

HOURS: Mid May-mid Oct Daily 10-6

ADMISSION: $7, Children $4; Under 13 free

SOUTH HAVEN

4244
Doctor Liberty Hyde Bailey Birthsite Museum
903 S Bailey Ave, 49090 [903 S Bailey Ave, 49090-9701]; (p) (616) 637-3251

1854/ staff: 2(p); 11(v)

COLLECTIONS: [1860s-1900s] Personal items, knife collection, arrowheads and other Indian tools, rock and mineral collection, political ribbons and buttons, carpenter and harness making tools, saltcellar collection.; books by Dr. Bailey, papers, South Haven High School annuals, histories of South Haven families.

HOURS: Seasonal

4245
Michigan Maritime Museum
260 Dyckman Ave, 49090; (p) (616) 637-8078; (f) (616) 637-1594; (c) Van Buren

Private non-profit/ 1975/ staff: 2(f); 10(p); 10(v)/ members: 700/publication: *The Ship's Lamp*

HISTORY MUSEUM; MARITIME MUSEUM; RESEARCH CENTER: Maritime research, preservation and education which serves the general public and academic communities.

PROGRAMS: Annual Meeting; Community Outreach; Exhibits; Facility Rental; Family Programs; Festivals; Film/Video; Guided Tours; Interpretation; Lectures; Living History; Publication; Research Library/Archives; School-Based Curriculum

COLLECTIONS: [19th-20 c] Artifacts, books, photographs and negatives, postcards, historic documents.

HOURS: Yr T-Sa 10-5, Su 12-5

ADMISSION: $2.50,

SOUTH LYON

4246
South Lyon Area Historical Society
300 Dorothy St, 48178 [PO Box 263, 48178]; (p) (248) 437-9929; (c) Oakland

Private non-profit/ 1976/ staff: 2(p); 30(v)/ members: 525/publication: *Witch's Chatter*

HISTORIC PRESERVATION AGENCY; HISTORICAL SOCIETY; HISTORY MUSEUM: Dedicated to preserving local historic buildings; collect, conserve, and maintain artifacts; operates museum.

PROGRAMS: Exhibits; Facility Rental; Festivals; Lectures; Publication; Research Library/Archives

COLLECTIONS: [1900-1950] Railroad artifacts, pictures, Civil War, WWI photos, and artifacts with local emphasis; local history collections; photos, household items, jewelry, clothing, family histories, local merchants' items.

HOURS: Apr-Dec Th-Su 1-5

ADMISSION: No

STOCKBRIDGE

4247
Waterloo Area Historical Society
9998 Waterloo-Munith Rd, 49285 [PO Box 37, 49285]; (p) (517) 596-2254; scs.k12_mi.us/~waterloo/index.html; (c) Jackson

Private non-profit; State/ 1963/ staff: 5(p); 100(v)/ members: 150

HISTORIC PRESERVATION AGENCY; HISTORIC SITE; HISTORICAL SOCIETY; HISTORY MUSEUM; HOUSE MUSEUM: Dedicated to interpreting pioneer farm life and schooling.

PROGRAMS: Annual Meeting; Community Outreach; Exhibits; Facility Rental; Family Programs; Festivals; Guided Tours; Interpretation; Lectures; Living History; Publication; Reenactments; Research Library/Archives; School-Based Curriculum

COLLECTIONS: [1850-1900] Farm buildings and house display: furnishings, clothing, utensils, tools, and other belongings from a Michigan farm family.

HOURS: June 1- Sept 1 W-Su 1-5

ADMISSION: $3, Children $1, Seniors $2.50

STURGIS

4248
Sturgis Historical Society
200 Main St, 49091 [PO Box 392, 49091]; (p)
(616) 651-3990; (c) St. Joseph

Private non-profit/ 1995/ staff: 20(v)/ members:
210

HISTORICAL SOCIETY; HISTORY MUSEUM:
Small restored G.R. and I. railroad depot, preserving local history.

PROGRAMS: Annual Meeting; Exhibits; Publication; Reenactments

COLLECTIONS: [1700-1940] Artifacts from
Sturgis history.

HOURS: By appt

TRAVERSE CITY

4249
Dennos Museum Center
1525 E Front St, 49686 [1701 E Front St,
49686]; (p) (231) 922-1055; (f) (231) 922-
1597; dmc@nmc.edu; dmc.nmc.edu; (c)
Grand Traverse

State/ 1991/ Northwestern Michigan College/
staff: 4(f); 5(p); 160(v)/ members: 1200

ART MUSEUM: Collection of art; and the
preservation of exhibitions and programs in
the visual arts, sciences, and performing arts.

PROGRAMS: Community Outreach; Concerts; Exhibits; Facility Rental; Family Programs; Guided Tours; Interpretation; Lectures;
School-Based Curriculum

COLLECTIONS: [1950-present] Artwork: Contemporary Inuit, Canadian Indian, 18th and
19th century Japanese prints, American and
European paintings, and graphic arts, and
sculptures.

HOURS: Yr Daily M-Sa 10-5, Su 1-5

ADMISSION: $2

4250
Grand Traverse Heritage Center
Waterfront Clinch Park, 49684 [322 Sixth St,
49684]; (p) (213) 995-0314; (f) (231) 946-
6750; www.traverse.net/traversecity/
services/museum.htm; (c) Grand Traverse

City; Joint; Private non-profit/ 2000/ Board of
Directors/ staff: 2(f); 1(p); 50(v)/ members:
582/publication: *Traces*

HISTORY MUSEUM: Educate about the cultural heritage of the pioneers and Native
Americans of the Great Traverse Region.

PROGRAMS: Community Outreach; Elder's
Programs; Exhibits; Family Programs; Festivals; Guided Tours; Interpretation; Lectures;
Living History; Publication; Reenactments; Research Library/Archives; School-Based Curriculum

COLLECTIONS: [2000 BC-1950 AD] Stone
tools and projectile points, beaded clothing,
replica of bark wigwam; furnishings and photos from state asylum; blacksmith, farm and
fire fighting equipment, household tools and
furnishings, maritime, military items and guns.

HOURS: May-Sept Daily

TRENTON

4251
Trenton Historical Museum
306 St Joseph, 48183 [2800 Third St, 48183];
(p) (734) 675-2130; (c) Wayne

City/ 1965/ staff: 22(v)

HOUSE MUSEUM

PROGRAMS: Exhibits; Interpretation

COLLECTIONS: [Victorian] Victorian furniture,
artifacts, Trenton History, Indian arrowheads.

HOURS: Feb-July and Sept-Dec Sa 1-4

ADMISSION: No charge

TROY

4252
Troy Museum and Historic Village
60 W Wattles Rd, 48098; (p) (248) 524-3570;
(f) (248) 524-3572; averilltm@ci.troy.mi.us; (c)
Oakland

1927/ staff: 2(f); 5(p); 175(v)

HOUSE MUSEUM: Local history museum and
village including log cabin, Caswell House
1832, Poppleton School 1877, County Store
1880, 1900 print shop, Wagon shop 1875,
Town Hall 1864, City Hall 1927.

PROGRAMS: Community Outreach; Con-
certs; Exhibits; Family Programs; Festivals;
Guided Tours; Interpretation; Lectures; Living
History; Research Library/Archives; School-
Based Curriculum

COLLECTIONS: Agricultural equipment, early
pioneer living collection, local archives and
manuscripts.

HOURS: Yr T-Sa 9-5:30, Su 1-5

ADMISSION: No charge

UNION CITY

4253
Society for Historic Preservation
210 Charlotte St, 49094; (c) Branch

Private non-profit/ 1986/ members: 80

GENEALOGICAL SOCIETY; HISTORIC
PRESERVATION AGENCY; HISTORIC SITE;
HISTORICAL SOCIETY; HISTORY MUSEUM;
HOUSE MUSEUM: Preserve local and region-
al history.

PROGRAMS: Exhibits; Living History; Research Library/Archives

COLLECTIONS: [1866-present] School bell
tower, old sports trophies, portraits of former
residents, antique furniture, newspaper clippings, pictures, two school cornerstones, army
uniform, J.P. Palmer oil paintings.

HOURS: By appt

ADMISSION: No charge

UNIVERSITY CENTER

4254
**Marshall M. Fredericks Sculpture
Museum**
Saginaw Valley State Univ, 48710; (p) (517)
790-5667; (f) (517) 791-7721;
panhorst@svsu.edu; www.svsu.edu; (c)
Saginaw

1988/ staff: 2(f); 10(p); 5(v)

ART MUSEUM: 200 works spanning the career of Fredericks (1908-1998).

PROGRAMS: Exhibits

COLLECTIONS: [20th c] Houses original plaster models for the Spirit of Detroit, the Cleveland Fountain, and scores of other sculptures
by Fredericks.

HOURS: Yr T-Su 1-5 and by appt

WALLED LAKE

4255
**Multi-Lakes Association for Civil War
Studies, Inc.**
[PO Box 487, 48390]; (p) (248) 624-9339;
tx$coe@speedlink.net;
www.speedlink.net/~tx4coe/

Private non-profit/ 1995/ staff: 4(v)/ members:
40/publication: *The March 4th*

LIVING HISTORY/OUTDOOR MUSEUM:
Comprised of four groups: 4th Texas Co. ECW
reenactors, 8th MI Cav. N-SSA, Citizens for Independence, and a historical research and
preservation group.

PROGRAMS: Festivals; Interpretation; Living
History; Reenactments

COLLECTIONS: [1861-1865]

WARREN

4256
Warren Historical Society
Warren Community Center, Rm 113, 5460
Arden Rd, 48090 [PO Box 1773, 48090-
1773]; (p) (810) 264-8410; (c) Macomb

Private non-profit/ 1979/ staff: 50(v)/ members:
70

HISTORICAL SOCIETY: Includes Bunert
School Museum, Union Cemetery, award historical date plaques.

PROGRAMS: Annual Meeting; Exhibits; Facility Rental; Family Programs; Festivals;
Film/Video; Garden Tours; Guided Tours; Lectures; Publication; School-Based Curriculum

COLLECTIONS: [Early-mid 1900s] Newspapers from 1940s-1960; form utensils; one
room school items; photography; early artifacts
and records.

HOURS: By appt

WAYNE

4257
Wayne Historical Museum
1 Towne Square, 48184; (p) (734) 722-0113;
(c) Wayne

City/ 1956/ staff: 1(p)/ members: 50

HISTORIC SITE; HISTORY MUSEUM: Collects historic materials; promotes local preservation, historical awareness, and appreciation for the local community.

PROGRAMS: Community Outreach; Exhibits; Guided Tours; Lectures; Research Library/Archives

COLLECTIONS: [1824-present] Municipal, business, and cemetery records; Civil War documents and information about early Nankin Township, Detroit, Eloise, and others; farming, business, industry, political, social, and educational artifacts and memorabilia; photographs, vital records; church history, library.

HOURS: Yr F-Sa 1-4 and by appt

ADMISSION: No charge

WYANDOTTE

4258
Wyandotte Museum
2610 Biddle, 48192; (p) (734) 324-7297; (f) (734) 324-7283; wymuseum@ili.net; www.angelfire.com/mi/wumuseum; (c) Wayne

City/ 1958/ staff: 1(f); 4(p); 20(v)/ members: 450

HISTORY MUSEUM

PROGRAMS: Annual Meeting; Concerts; Exhibits; Facility Rental; Festivals; Garden Tours; Guided Tours; Interpretation; Lectures; Living History; Publication; Reenactments; Research Library/Archives

COLLECTIONS: [1850-1950]

HOURS: Yr M-F 12-4

ADMISSION: $1

YPSILANTI

4259
Ypsilanti Historical Museum
220 N Huron, 48197; (p) (734) 482-4990; (c) Washtenaw

Private non-profit/ 1968/ staff: 1(p); 35(v)/ members: 220/publication: *Gleanings*

HISTORICAL SOCIETY; HISTORY MUSEUM; HOUSE MUSEUM

PROGRAMS: Annual Meeting; Guided Tours; Publication

COLLECTIONS: [Late 1800s] Furniture, dishes, books, obituaries, history of early settlers.

HOURS: Museum: Feb-Dec Th, Sa, Su 2-4; Archives: Feb-Dec M-F 9-12

ADMISSION: No charge

ZEELAND

4260
Herman Miller, Inc. Corporate Archives and Records Services
455 W Washington, 49464 [855 E Main Ave, 49464]; (p) (616) 654-5680; (f) (616) 654-3597; Bob_Viol@hermanmiller.com; (c) Ottawa

Private for-profit/ 1905/ staff: 7(f)

CORPORATE ARCHIVES/MUSEUM: Acquires, catalogs, preserves and references historical material and active records relating to Herman Miller's people, products and corporate culture.

PROGRAMS: Research Library/Archives

COLLECTIONS: [1905-present] Records relating to the furniture industry in west Michigan and Herman Miller, Inc.

HOURS: By appt only

4261
Zeeland Historical Society/Dekker Huis Museum
37 Main Ave, 49464 [PO Box 165, 49464-0165]; (p) (616) 772-4079; (c) Ottawa

Private non-profit/ 1974/ staff: 50(v)/ members: 350/publication: *Timeline*

HISTORICAL SOCIETY; HISTORY MUSEUM; HOUSE MUSEUM: Preserve knowledge about Zeeland and vicinity; collect and classify objects, letters, pictures, records, documents; publish books and brochures.

PROGRAMS: Exhibits; Guided Tours; Interpretation; Publication

COLLECTIONS: [1840-present] Furnishings, pioneer room and cabin, replicas of Zeeland State Bank, Huizenga Corner Grocery Store, one room schoolhouse, Dutch room Zeeland Church room, ladies hats room, military room, Post Office, and fire department room.

HOURS: Apr-Oct Th 10-4, Sa10-1 and by appt.

MINNESOTA

AFTON

4262
Afton Historic Preservation Commission
3033 St Croix Tr, 55001; (p) (651) 436-5090; (f) (651) 436-1453; (c) Washington

City/ 1991/ City of Afton

HISTORIC PRESERVATION AGENCY: Seeks to preserve the historic character of Historic Old Village and the surrounding area.

PROGRAMS: Community Outreach; Research

4263
Afton Historical Society Museum
3165 St Croix Tr S, 55001 [PO Box 178, 55001]; (p) (651) 436-3500; scriv@pressen ter.com; www.pressenter.com/~aftnhist/; (c) Washington

Private non-profit/ 1980/ Board of Directors/ staff: 20(v)/ members: 173/publication: *Afton Remembered*

HISTORICAL SOCIETY; HISTORY MUSEUM; RESEARCH CENTER: Dedicated to collecting, preserving, and displaying early memorabilia from lower St. Croix River Valley and Afton.

PROGRAMS: Annual Meeting; Community Outreach; Exhibits; Festivals; Guided Tours; Interpretation; Publication; Library/ Archives

COLLECTIONS: [1839-1940s] 1000 artifacts, 20,000 photographs, primarily agriculture related, Ernie Pyle memorabilia, maps of St. Croix River, lumbering and sawmill maps, and two working looms.

HOURS: Yr W 1-8; May-Oct Su 1-4

ADMISSION: Donations accepted

AITKIN

4264
Aitkin County Historical Society
20 Pacific St, 56431 [PO Box 215, 56431]; (p) (218) 927-3348; achs@mlecmn.net; (c) Aitkin

County; Private non-profit/ 1948/ staff: 1(p); 35(v)/ members: 160/publication: *Seasons in Time*

HISTORICAL SOCIETY; HISTORY MUSEUM; RESEARCH CENTER

PROGRAMS: Annual Meeting; Community Outreach; Exhibits; Festivals; Publication; Reenactments; Research Library/Archives; School-Based Curriculum

COLLECTIONS: [Early 19th c-present] Artifacts in logging and agriculture, family birth and death histories, newspapers, and photographs.

HOURS: Sept-May W,F-Sa 10-4:30; June-Aug T-W,F-Sa 10-4:30

ADMISSION: Donations accepted

ALBANY

4265
Albany Heritage Society, Inc.
City Clerk's Office, 301 Railroad Ave, 56307 [PO Box 374, 56307]; (p) (320) 845-4257; (c) Stearns

Private non-profit/ 1986/ staff: 4(v)/ members: 60/publication: *Albany: The Heart of Minnesota*

HISTORIC PRESERVATION AGENCY; HISTORICAL SOCIETY: Gathers and makes available to the public items that show the record of past events in Albany, Minnesota, and the rural area immediately around it.

PROGRAMS: Annual Meeting; Publication

COLLECTIONS: [To 1990] Newspaper reports, oral histories.

ALBERT LEA

4266
Freeborn County Historical Society
1031 Bridge Ave, 56007; (p) (507) 373-8003; (c) Freeborn

Private non-profit/ 1959/ staff: 1(f); 5(p); 50(v)/ members: 930

HISTORICAL SOCIETY

PROGRAMS: Annual Meeting; Community Outreach; Elder's Programs; Exhibits; Facility Rental; Family Programs; Festivals; Guided Tours; Interpretation; Publication; Research Library/Archives

COLLECTIONS: [1850-1950] Mammoth bones, Native American artifacts, farm implements, family and home times, clothing, community business items, genealogical and historical library, and several historic buildings.

HOURS: May-Sept (museum&village) Oct-Apr (museum only) T-F 10-5, Sa-Su 1-5

ADMISSION: $5, Student $1; Members free

ALEXANDRIA

4267
Douglas County Historical Society
1219 Nokomis St, 56308; (p) (320) 762-0382; (f) (320) 762-9062; historic@rea-alp.com; www.real-alp.com/historic/; (c) Douglas

Private non-profit/ 1976/ Board of Trustees/ staff: 3(f); 3(p); 60(v)/ members: 600/publication: *DCHS newsletter*

HISTORICAL SOCIETY: Discover, preserve, and disseminate the history of Douglas Co and its citizens.

PROGRAMS: Annual Meeting; Community Outreach; Elder's Programs; Exhibits; Facility Rental; Family Programs; Festivals; Film/Video; Guided Tours; Interpretation; Lectures; Living History; Publication; Research Library/Archives

COLLECTIONS: [1858-present] Photos, family histories, family research library, clothing, uniforms, books, and artifacts pertinent to the county.

HOURS: Yr M-F 8-5, wkends by appt

ADMISSION: $2, Donations accepted

4268
Runestone Museum
206 Broadway, 56308; (p) (320) 763-3160; (f) (320) 763-9705; bigole@rea-alp.com; www.atc.tec.mn.us/runestone/; (c) Douglas

Private non-profit/ 1958/ Board of Directors/ staff: 2(f); 3(p); 20(v)/ members: 150/publication: *The Runestone*

HISTORY MUSEUM; RESEARCH CENTER: Collects, preserves, interprets local history, and the history and research of the Kensington Runestone.

PROGRAMS: Annual Meeting; Exhibits; Facility Rental; Festivals; Film/Video; Interpretation; Lectures; Publication; Reenactments; Research Library/Archives; School-Based Curriculum

COLLECTIONS: Agriculture equipment, pioneer household, and tool collection; Kensington Runestone and its research archives.

HOURS: Yr Summer M-Sa 9-5, Su 11-4; Winter M-Sa 9-5

ADMISSION: $5, Students $3, Seniors $4, Under 7 free

ANOKA

4269
Anoka County Historical Society
1900 3rd Ave S, 55303; (p) (612) 421-0600; (f) (612) 421-0601; (c) Anoka

1934/ Board of Directors/ staff: 4(p); 150(v)/ members: 400

GENEALOGICAL SOCIETY; HISTORIC SITE; HISTORY MUSEUM; HOUSE MUSEUM; RESEARCH CENTER

PROGRAMS: Annual Meeting; Community Outreach; Exhibits; Festivals; Guided Tours; Lectures; Living History; Research Library/ Archives; School-Based Curriculum

COLLECTIONS: [Late 1800s-present] Textiles, clothing, and artifacts.

HOURS: Yr T-F 9-4

ADMISSION: $2.50, Children $1, Family $5

ARGYLE

4270
Argyle Historical Society, Inc., The
Corner of Pacific Ave & 4th St, 56713 [PO Box 244, 56713]; (c) Marshall

City/ 1986/ Board of Directors/ staff: 3(p); 26(v)/ members: 49

HISTORICAL SOCIETY; HISTORY MUSEUM

PROGRAMS: Annual Meeting; Exhibits

COLLECTIONS: [1879-present]

HOURS: June-Aug Su 1-4

ASKOV

4271
Pine County Historical Society
Dannesbergsgade, 55072 [1601 Hwy 23 N, Sandstone, 55072]; (p) (320) 245-2176; (c) Pine

Private non-profit/ 1948/ staff: 2(p); 5(v)/ members: 109

HISTORICAL SOCIETY: Artifacts and antiques on display at the Depot Museum and old reference books and artifacts on display at the History Center. Vintage Machinery at Fire Hall Museum.

PROGRAMS: Annual Meeting; Exhibits; Guided Tours; Research Library/Archives

COLLECTIONS: [1890-present] Dictionaries, Bibles, WW I and WW II uniforms, baseball uniforms, vintage clothing and hats, kitchen appliances, logging equipment, postal display, books.

HOURS: May 29–Sept 6

AUSTIN

4272
Hormel Foods Corporation
1 Hormel Place, 55912; (p) (507) 433-5100; (f) (507) 437-9803; www.hormel.com; (c) Moner

Private for-profit/ 1990/ staff: 2(f); 1(p)

CORPORATE ARCHIVES/MUSEUM; HISTORY MUSEUM: Depicts evolution of company and products since 1891.

PROGRAMS: Festivals

COLLECTIONS: [1890-1970] Artifacts and memorabilia, product, advertising, sales.

HOURS: Yr

ADMISSION: No charge

4273
Mower County Historical Society
1303 SW 6 Ave, 55912; (p) (507) 437-6082; (f) (507) 437-6082; mchs@smig.net; (c) Mower

County/ 1949/ staff: 3(p); 6(v)/ members: 180

ART MUSEUM; GENEALOGICAL SOCIETY; HISTORIC PRESERVATION AGENCY; HISTORIC SITE; HISTORICAL SOCIETY; HISTORY MUSEUM; HOUSE MUSEUM; LIVING HISTORY/OUTDOOR MUSEUM; RESEARCH CENTER; TRIBAL MUSEUM

PROGRAMS: Annual Meeting; Community Outreach; Exhibits; Family Programs; Festivals; Film/Video; Guided Tours; Interpretation; Lectures; Living History; Library/ Archives

HOURS: Yr M-F 11-4

ADMISSION: $2

BECKER

4274
Sherburne County Historical Society
13122 First St, 55308; (p) (612) 261-4433; (f) (612) 261-4437; www.rootsweb.com/~mnschs; (c) Sherburne

Private non-profit/ 1972/ staff: 3(f); 2(p); 90(v)/ members: 545

HISTORICAL SOCIETY; HISTORY MUSEUM: Collects, preserves, and interprets the history of Sherburne County.

PROGRAMS: Annual Meeting; Community Outreach; Exhibits; Interpretation; Lectures; Publication; Research Library/Archives; School-Based Curriculum

COLLECTIONS: [1856-present] Three dimensional objects, household, personal effects; archival collections includes photographs, maps, census records, oral histories, and newspapers.

HOURS: Yr M-F 8-5, 1st & 3rd Sa 10-2

ADMISSION: No charge

BELLE PLAINE

4275
Belle Plaine Historical Society
410 N Cedar, 56011 [PO Box 73, 56011]; (p) (612) 873-6109; (c) Scott

1975/ members: 81

HISTORIC SITE; HISTORICAL SOCIETY; HISTORY MUSEUM; HOUSE MUSEUM

PROGRAMS: Festivals; Guided Tours; Interpretation

HOURS: Su 1-4 or by appt

ADMISSION: $2, Student $0.50

BENSON

4276
Swift County Historical Society
W Hwy 12, 56215 [2135 Minnesota Ave #2, 56215]; (p) (320) 843-4467; (c) Swift

Private non-profit/ 1929/ Board of Directors/ staff: 2(p)/ members: 335/publication: *Echo & Swift Co History Book*

HISTORICAL SOCIETY; RESEARCH CENTER: Collects and interprets the history of Swift County.

PROGRAMS: Annual Meeting; Community Outreach; Exhibits; Film/Video; Lectures; Publication; Research Library/Archives; School-Based Curriculum

COLLECTIONS: [1880s-1920s] Artifacts pertaining to the early history of Swift Co; census records, personal histories and county newspapers.

HOURS: Yr T-F 10-4:30, Sa 10-3

ADMISSION: No charge/Donations

BERTHA

4277
Bertha Historical Society, Inc.
2nd Ave W & Main St, 56437 [PO Box 307, 56437]; (p) (218) 924-4095; (c) Todd

City; Private non-profit/ 1970/ Board of Directors/ staff: 5(p); 5(v)/ members: 40

HISTORIC PRESERVATION AGENCY; HISTORICAL SOCIETY: Collects artifacts, photographs, and local history.

PROGRAMS: Annual Meeting; Exhibits; Guided Tours

COLLECTIONS: [1901-present] Local newspaper, 1901-1998, antique tools, machines, catalogues of old hardware articles, dolls, church histories, 1910 pump organ, typewriters, and a barber pole.

HOURS: June-Sept F evenings 7-9, 2nd Su 1:30-4:30

ADMISSION: Donations accepted

BLOOMINGTON

4278
Bloomington Historical Society
10600 W 102nd St, 55431 [2215 W Old Shakopee Rd, 55431]; (p) (612) 948-8881; (f) (612) 948-8715; (c) Hennepin

City/ 1964/ Board of Directors/ staff: 1(f); 20(v)/ members: 125

HISTORICAL SOCIETY; HISTORY MUSEUM: Dedicated to preservation and interpretation of local and state history.

PROGRAMS: Annual Meeting; Exhibits; Facility Rental; Festivals; Guided Tours; Interpretation; Lectures; Living History; Publication;

Reenactments; Research Library/Archives; School-Based Curriculum; Theatre

COLLECTIONS: [Early pioneer] Early settlement period furnishings and agricultural equipment; Native American, military, schools, Dan Patch, horse, and railroad artifacts.

HOURS: Su 1:30-4 and by appt

BLUE EARTH

4279
Faribault County Historical Society
405 E 6th St, 56013; (p) (507) 526-5421; (c) Faribault

State/ 1948/ Minnesota State Historical Society/ staff: 2(p); 12(v)/ members: 250

HISTORICAL SOCIETY; HOUSE MUSEUM: Board handles the business, provides information to the public.

PROGRAMS: Annual Meeting; Community Outreach; Concerts; Exhibits; Guided Tours; Interpretation; School-Based Curriculum

COLLECTIONS: [1860-present] Local interest concerning rural society.

HOURS: Yr T-S 2-5 and by appt

ADMISSION: No charge

BOVEY

4280
Itasca Genealogy Club
City Hall, 55709 [PO Box 261, 55709]; (c) Itasca

Private non-profit/ 1979/ Executive Board/ members: 40/publication: *Itasca Genealogy Club newsletter*

GENEALOGICAL SOCIETY: Collect genealogical, biographical and historical material relative to Itasca Co and Minnesota families.

PROGRAMS: Lectures; Publication; Research Library/Archives

HOURS: Yr M-F same as Bovey Public Library

BRAINERD

4281
Crow Wing County Genealogical Society
LDS Family History Center, 101 W Buffalo Hills, 56401 [2103 Graydon Ave, 56401]; (p) (218) 829-9738; 1kirk@brainerd.net; (c) Crow Wing

1970/ members: 30/publication: *Heir Mail*

GENEALOGICAL SOCIETY

PROGRAMS: Publication

COLLECTIONS: Genealogical books and family histories.

4282
Crow Wing County Historical Society
320 Laurel St, 56401 [PO Box 722, 56401]; (p) (218) 829-3268; history@twwn.com; (c) Crow Wing

Private non-profit/ 1927/ Board of Directors/ staff: 2(f); 1(p); 30(v)/ members: 400

HISTORICAL SOCIETY; HISTORY MUSEUM; HOUSE MUSEUM: Operates a county historical museum in the old county jail and sheriff's residence. Maintains a research library, buildings, programs.

PROGRAMS: Annual Meeting; Community Outreach; Exhibits; Family Programs; Guided Tours; Interpretation; Lectures; Research Library/Archives; School-Based Curriculum

COLLECTIONS: [Late 19th-early 20th c] Includes tools (logging, railroad & mining), artifacts from early settlement life (household items, dishes, furniture & clothing). Archives and photos (including 1950s postcard collection), historical artwork and WPA artwork.

HOURS: Yr Sept-May M-F 1-5, Sa 10-2; June-Aug M-F 9-5, Sa 10-2

ADMISSION: $3; Students/children free

BRECKENRIDGE

4283
Wilkin County Historical Society
704 Nebraska Ave, 56520; (p) (218) 643-1303; (c) Wilkin

Private non-profit/ 1965/ Board of Directors/ staff: 2(p); 7(v)/ members: 254

HISTORICAL SOCIETY: Collect and preserve materials that help define or illustrate the history of Wilkin Co.

PROGRAMS: Annual Meeting; Exhibits; Guided Tours

COLLECTIONS: [Early 1900s] Old newspapers, obituaries, family histories, photos, biographies and other historical artifacts on display, bedroom, pioneer kitchen and laundry room, small chapel, old bank and hospital room.

HOURS: Apr-Nov Su,W,Th 1:30-4

ADMISSION: No charge

BRICELYN

4284
Bricelyn Area Historical Society
408 4th St, 56014 [309 N Main, PO Box 338, 56014]; (p) (507) 653-4367; eziemer@means.net; co.faribault.mn.us/Bricelyn; (c) Faribault

Private non-profit/ 1998/ staff: 8(v)/ members: 205

HISTORIC SITE; HISTORICAL SOCIETY; HISTORY MUSEUM: Collects, preserves, and disseminates the history of the Bricelyn area.

PROGRAMS: Concerts; Exhibits

COLLECTIONS: [1899-present] Histories, newspapers, photographs, maps, Native American and pioneer artifacts, and oral history interviews.

HOURS: May-Sept Su 1-4 or by appt

ADMISSION: Donations accepted

BROOKLYN CENTER

4285
Brooklyn Historical Society
5637 Brooklyn Blvd, 55429 [PO Box 29345, 55429]; (c) Hennepin

Private non-profit/ 1970/ Board of Directors/ staff: 25(v)/ members: 110/publication: *Quarterly Newsletter*

HISTORICAL SOCIETY; HISTORY MUSEUM: Preserves and disseminates area history.

PROGRAMS: Annual Meeting; Community

Outreach; Exhibits; Festivals; Garden Tours; Guided Tours; Lectures; Publication; Research Library/Archives; School-Based Curriculum

COLLECTIONS: [1850-present] Newspapers; periodicals; maps; books; public records; journals; oral histories; slides of community events; farming, business, education, and household artifacts.

BUFFALO

4286
Wright County Historical Society
2001 Hwy 25 N, 55313; (p) (763) 682-7323; (c) Wright

Private non-profit/ 1942/ Board of Directors/ staff: 2(f); 2(p); 80(v)/ members: 300

HISTORICAL SOCIETY; HISTORY MUSEUM; RESEARCH CENTER: Collects, preserves, exhibits, and interprets material related to the history of Wright County and its relationship to Minnesota and the U.S.

PROGRAMS: Annual Meeting; Community Outreach; Exhibits; Family Programs; Guided Tours; Interpretation; Lectures; Research Library/Archives; School-Based Curriculum

COLLECTIONS: [1855-present] History and genealogical library, photographs, manuscripts, microfilm collection of local newspapers, census, naturalization and probate records, museum artifacts include the "Nelsonian" (a 32 piece one man band).

HOURS: Yr Oct-May M-F 8-4:30; June-Sept T-F 8-4:30, Sa 8-4

ADMISSION: No charge

CALENDONIA

4287
Houston County Historical Society
104 History Lane, 55921-1725; (p) (507) 725-3884; (c) Houston

County, non-profit/ 1960/ staff: 100(v)/ members: 250/publication: *Newsletter*

GENEALOGICAL SOCIETY; HISTORIC PRESERVATION AGENCY; HISTORIC SITE; HISTORICAL SOCIETY; HISTORY MUSEUM; HOUSE MUSEUM; RESEARCH CENTER: Collect, preserve, interpret, and disseminate the history of Houston County.

PROGRAMS: Annual Meeting; Community Outreach; Elder's Programs; Exhibits; Facility Rental; Family Programs; Film/Video; Guided Tours; Interpretation; Publication; Research Library/Archives

COLLECTIONS: [1854-1950] Manuscripts, maps, newspapers, books, artifacts, photographs and farm equipment.

HOURS: Yr M-W 10-4 and June-Sept Sa-Su 1-4

CAMBRIDGE

4288
Isanti County Historical Society
1400 Hwy 293, 55008 [PO Box 525, 55008]; (p) (763) 689-4229; (f) (763) 689-4229; varrow2@ecenet.com; (c) Isanti

1965/ staff: 3(p)/ members: 280/publication: *Isanti Cuttings*

HISTORICAL SOCIETY: Preserves local his-

tory and educate the public.

PROGRAMS: Annual Meeting; Community Outreach; Concerts; Exhibits; Family Programs; Festivals; Film/Video; Guided Tours; Interpretation; Lectures; Publication; Research Library/Archives; School-Based Curriculum; Theatre

COLLECTIONS: [1857-1998] Photos, microfilm, newspapers, books, clothes, and genealogies.

HOURS: Yr M,T,Th 9:30-3:30 and by appt

ADMISSION: No charge

CASS LAKE

4289
Leech Lake Tribal College Library
Rte 3 Box 100, 56633; (p) (218) 335-2828; (f) (218) 335-7845; chester@lltc.org; (c) Leech Lake Reservation

1990/ staff: 2(f); 2(p); 3(v)

HISTORIC PRESERVATION AGENCY; HISTORY MUSEUM; LIVING HISTORY/OUTDOOR MUSEUM; RESEARCH CENTER; TRIBAL MUSEUM

PROGRAMS: Community Outreach; Guided Tours

COLLECTIONS: Books on Native American history, government, law.

HOURS: Sept-May M-F 8-8

ADMISSION: No charge

CENTER CITY

4290
Center City Historic Preservation Commission
[PO Box 245, 55012]; (p) (651) 257-5284; lhackl2001@aol.com; (c) Chisago

City/ 1991/ staff: 5(v)/publication: *The Human Imprint*

HISTORIC PRESERVATION AGENCY: To study and evaluate those buildings, land, areas, districts or other onjects which are to be considered for designation as heritage preservation sites and to recommend in writing such sites to the City Council.

PROGRAMS: Annual Meeting; Community Outreach; Exhibits; Guided Tours; Interpretation; Lectures; Publication; Research Library/Archives

COLLECTIONS: [1851-present] The Human Imprint establishes historic contexts for the built environment of the city along with a written inventory with photos and descriptions.

HOURS: Yr

ADMISSION: No charge

CEYLON

4291
Ceylon Area Historical Society
112 W Main St, 56121 [104 W Main St, 56121]; (c) Martin

1997

CHATFIELD

4292
Chatfield Brass Band Music Lending Library
81 Library Lane, 55923 [PO Box 578, 55923]; (p) (507) 867-3275; (c) Fillmore

Private non-profit/ 1980/ staff: 3(p); 1(v)/ members: 200

Lending collection of out-of-print music, mainly for band.

COLLECTIONS: [1800-1900s]

HOURS: Yr M-W 8-12 / 1-4

CHISHOLM

4293
Iron Range Research Center
Hwy 169 W, 55719 [PO Box 392, 55719]; (p) (218) 254-3325; (f) (218) 254-4938; debf@ ironworld.com; (c) St. Louis

State/ 1980/ Iron Range Resources and Rehabilitation Board/ staff: 4(f); 10(v)

RESEARCH CENTER: Identifies, collects, processes, catalogs, preserves, displays, and makes easily accessible the historically significant written, oral, and visual records of Minnesota's Iron Ranges.

PROGRAMS: Community Outreach; Research Library/Archives

COLLECTIONS: Library: reference books, periodicals, microfilm collections, CD-ROM genealogical programs, AV, oral histories. Archives: repository for historical records, photos, and artifacts.

HOURS: Yr M-F 9-4

ADMISSION: No charge

4294
Minnesota Museum of Mining
W Lake St, 55719 [PO Box 271, 55719]; (p) (218) 254-5543; (c) St. Louis

City, non-profit/ 1954/ staff: 3(p); 10(v)/ members: 30

HISTORY MUSEUM; LIVING HISTORY/OUTDOOR MUSEUM

PROGRAMS: Exhibits; Facility Rental; Guided Tours

COLLECTIONS: Mining equipment, powershovels, locomotives, drills, trucks, pump buckets, railroad cars and caboose.

HOURS: June-Aug Daily 9-5

ADMISSION: $3, Family $8

CLOQUET

4295
Carlton County Historical Society
406 Cloquet Ave, 55720; (p) (218) 879-1938; cchs@cpinternet.com; (c) Carlton

Private non-profit/ 1949/ staff: 1(f); 3(p); 75(v)/ members: 475

HISTORY MUSEUM: Collecting and preserving Carlton Co. history.

PROGRAMS: Annual Meeting; Community Outreach; Concerts; Elder's Programs; Exhibits; Family Programs; Festivals; Lectures; Living History; Publication; Research Library/ Archives

COLLECTIONS: [1870-present] Material related to Carlton County history; artifacts, photographs, archival materials, microfilms of newspapers, census naturalization records, newspapers, books.

HOURS: Yr M 9-8, T-F 9-4 or by appt

ADMISSION: No charge

COKATO

4296
Cokato Museum & Akerlund Photography Studio
175 W 4th St, 55321 [PO Box 686, 55321]; (p) (320) 286-2427; (f) (320) 286-5876; cokatomuseum@cmgate.com; www.cokato. mn.us/cmhs/; (c) Wright

City/ 1976/ staff: 2(f); 1(p); 10(v)/ members: 300/publication: *In the Midst Of* (qtrly newsletter)

HISTORIC SITE; HISTORY MUSEUM: Collects, preserves, and interprets the history of Cokato and the surrounding townships in southwestern Wright County.

PROGRAMS: Annual Meeting; Community Outreach; Exhibits; Lectures; Publication; Research Library/Archives

COLLECTIONS: [1880-1920; 1950-1970] Artifacts; photographs; archives. photo negatives from the Gust Akerlund Photography Studio.

HOURS: Yr Daily, M-F 9-4:30, Sa-Su 1-4

ADMISSION: donations accepted

COTTAGE GROVE

4297
South Washington Heritage Society
7515 80th St S, 55016; (p) (651) 459-1082; albyrobinson@worldnet.att.net; (c) Washington

Private non-profit/ 1979/ members: 40

HISTORICAL SOCIETY: Collecting, presenting, and preserving data about local families and history of this area.

PROGRAMS: Annual Meeting; Festivals; Guided Tours; Lectures; Living History

COTTONWOOD

4298
Cottonwood Area Historical Society
61 E Main St, 56229 [PO Box 106, 56229]; (p) (507) 423-6488; (f) (507) 423-5368; cotm ngi@means.net; (c) Lyon

Private non-profit/ 1988/ Board of Directors/ staff: 15(v)

HISTORIC SITE: Preservation of local history and care and upkeep of historic Norseth/Larsen house on National Register of Historic Places.

PROGRAMS: Annual Meeting; Exhibits; Festivals; Garden Tours; Guided Tours; Interpretation

COLLECTIONS: [1890s-1910s]

HOURS: May-Sept Su 1-5

ADMISSION: $2; Members free

CROOKSON

4299
Polk County Historical Society
Hwy #2 East, 56716 [PO Box 214, 56716]; (p) (218) 281-1038; (c) Polk

County; Private for-profit; Private non-profit/ 1935/ Board of Directors/ staff: 4(p); 100(v)/ members: 375

HISTORIC SITE; HISTORICAL SOCIETY; HISTORY MUSEUM; HOUSE MUSEUM; TRIBAL MUSEUM: Maintains museum, school house, log cabin, restored blacksmith shop and farm machinery.

PROGRAMS: Annual Meeting; Community Outreach; Exhibits; Facility Rental; Family Programs; Festivals; Film/Video; Garden Tours; Guided Tours; Interpretation; Lectures; Publication; Research Library/Archives

COLLECTIONS: [1930-1950] Newspapers, plat maps, museum artifacts, cemetery records, and death records.

HOURS: May-Sept Daily 12-4:30

ADMISSION: Free, donations welcome

CROSBY

4300
Cuyuna Heritage Preservation Society
101 First ST SW, 56441; (p) (218) 546-8005; cuyunaheritage.org; (c) Crow Wing

Private non-profit/ 1989/ staff: 16(v)/ members: 400/publication: *Cuyuna Country*

HISTORIC PRESERVATION AGENCY; HISTORICAL SOCIETY

PROGRAMS: Annual Meeting; Community Outreach; Exhibits; Publication; Research Library/Archives

COLLECTIONS: [1870-present] WPA oral histories; several books in print and in process.

HOURS: Yr 10-6

ADMISSION: No charge

4301
Cuyuna Range Historical Society
101 1st St NW, 56441 [PO Box 128, 56441]; (p) (218) 546-6178; (c) Crow Wing

Private non-profit/ 1968/ staff: 2(p); 2(v)/ members: 125

HISTORIC SITE; HISTORICAL SOCIETY; HISTORY MUSEUM: Preserve the history of the Cuyuna Iron Range and surrounding areas, its early schools and churches, business community, located in 1910 former 500-line depot.

PROGRAMS: Annual Meeting; Exhibits;Festivals.

CURRIE

4302
End-O-Line Railroad Park and Museum
440 N Mill St, 56123; (p) (507) 763-3708; louise@endoline.com; www.endoline.com; (c) Murray

County/ 1972/ Murray County/ staff: 1(f); 7(p); 6(v)

HISTORIC SITE; HISTORY MUSEUM: To preserve and tell the story of the railroads and expansion growth of the West.

PROGRAMS: Exhibits; Guided Tours

COLLECTIONS: [1880s-1950s] A working railroad yard including a manual turntable, original CN&W depot, rebuilt engine house, water tower, section foreman's house, rebuilt coal bunker used as a picnic shelter and one room school house.

HOURS: May-Sept Daily M-F 10-12/1-5; Sa-Su 1-5

ADMISSION: $3, Children $2, Family $6

DETROIT LAKES

4303
Becker County Historical Society and Museum
714 Summit Ave, 56502 [PO Box 622, 56502]; (p) (218) 847-2938; (f) (218) 847-5048; bolerud@tekstar.com; (c) Becker

County/ 1935/ Board of Directors/ staff: 1(f); 2(p); 7(v)/ members: 900/publication: *BCHS Bi-Monthly Newsletter*

HISTORIC PRESERVATION AGENCY; HISTORICAL SOCIETY; HISTORY MUSEUM; RESEARCH CENTER: Depicts the history of Becker Co.; archive contains the written and oral history of Co.

PROGRAMS: Annual Meeting; Community Outreach; Exhibits; Festivals; Guided Tours; Interpretation; Living History; Publication; Research Library/Archives; School-Based Curriculum

COLLECTIONS: [1880-1950]

HOURS: Yr M-F 8:30-5, Sa 12-4

DODGE CENTER

4304
Dodge County Genealogical Society
Dodge Center Library, Main St, 55927 [PO Box 683, 55927]; (c) Dodge

County/ 1988/ members: 12/publication: *Dodge County Genealogical Newsletter*

GENEALOGICAL SOCIETY: To help preserve the history of the county and help people do research on families.

PROGRAMS: Community Outreach; Publication

COLLECTIONS: Country schools, obituaries, cemetery walkings, farms and military.

HOURS: Yr M-T-Th-F-Sa 10-5

ADMISSION: No charge

DULUTH

4305
Duluth Heritage Preservation Commission
c/o Planning Comm, Rm 409, City Hall, 55802; (p) (218) 723-3328; (f) (218) 723-3400; (c) St. Louis

City/ 1990/ staff: 1(p)

HISTORIC PRESERVATION AGENCY: To review historic/heritage preservation matters and for public education and advocacy for preserving Duluth's historic structures.

PROGRAMS: Community Outreach; Guided Tours; Lectures; Publication

4306
Duluth Preservation Alliance
[PO Box 252, 55801]; www.duluthpreservation.org; (c) St. Louis

Private non-profit/ 1976/ staff: 10(v)/ members: 100

HISTORIC PRESERVATION AGENCY: Promotes an appreciation of Duluth's architectural heritage while encouraging and advising those who have undertaken a restoration project.

PROGRAMS: Annual Meeting; Community Outreach

4307
Glensheen Historic Estate
3300 London Rd, 55804; (p) (218) 724-8864; (f) (218) 724-3779; glen@d.umn.edu; www.d.umn.edu/glen/; (c) St. Louis

State/ 1979/ Univ of Minnesota/ staff: 11(f); 30(p); 150(v)/ members: 150/publication: *Glensheen Calling Card*

GARDEN; HISTORIC SITE; HOUSE MUSEUM; LIVING HISTORY/OUTDOOR MUSEUM: Research, interpretation and preservation of our community history; 1908 estate of Chester Congdon, includes formal gardens, extensive grounds, boat house, gardener's cottage, carriage house with carriages, 39 room Jacobean style manor.

PROGRAMS: Community Outreach; Concerts; Exhibits; Facility Rental; Festivals; Garden Tours; Guided Tours; Interpretation; Lectures; Living History; Publication; Research Library/Archives; School-Based Curriculum

COLLECTIONS: [Late 19th-early 20th C] Original furnishings, and extensive archives.

HOURS: Yr summer (May-Oct) Daily 9:30-4; winter (Nov-Apr) F-Su 11-2

ADMISSION: $8.75, Student $7, Children $4, Seniors $7; under 6 free

4308
Lake Superior Maritime Visitor Center
600 Lake Ave S, 55802; (p) (218) 720-5271; (f) (218) 720-5270; (c) St. Louis

Federal/ 1973/ US Army Corps of Engineers/ staff: 6(f); 4(p); 8(v)/ members: 600/publication: *Nor'Easter*

HISTORY MUSEUM: Focus on Lake Superior commercial shipping and the Army Corps of Engineers.

PROGRAMS: Community Outreach; Exhibits; Family Programs; Guided Tours; Interpretation; Lectures; Publication; Research Library/Archives; School-Based Curriculum

COLLECTIONS: [1870-present] Artifacts and memorabilia from Great Lakes ships and harbors, records and photographs of ships, shipwrecks and Army Corps of Engineers operations.

HOURS: Yr Sept-May Daily 10-4:30; June-Aug 10-9

ADMISSION: No charge

4309
Lake Superior Railroad Museum
506 W Michigan St, 55802; (p) (218) 733-7590; (f) (218) 733-7596; lsrm@cpinternet.com; www.duluth.com/lrsm/; (c) St. Louis

1975/ Board of Directors/ staff: 4(f); 1(p); 50(v)/ members: 250/publication: *The Junction*

RAILROAD MUSEUM: Preserves, interprets and presents to the public the history of railroading.

PROGRAMS: Annual Meeting; Community Outreach; Exhibits; Guided Tours; Interpretation; Publication; Research Library/Archives; School-Based Curriculum

COLLECTIONS: [Late 1800s-present] More than 50 pieces of railroad equipment, railway china, objects, bells, lanterns, library and archival material.

HOURS: Yr Daily, Winter M-Sa 10-5, Su 1-5; Summer Daily 9:30-6

ADMISSION: $8, Children $5

4310
Northeast Minnesota Historical Center
10 University Dr, 55812; (p) (218) 726-8526; pmaus@d.umn.edu; www.umn.edu/lib/collections; (c) St. Louis

Joint; Private non-profit/ 1976/ staff: 1(f); 3(v)

PROGRAMS: Research Library/Archives

COLLECTIONS: [1830-present] Local and regional history collections, manuscripts, photos, archival drawings, public records and family papers.

HOURS: Yr 8-12, 1:15-4:30

ADMISSION: No charge

4311
Twin Ports Genealogical Society
[PO Box 16895, 55816-0895]; (c) St. Louis

Private non-profit/ Elected Officers and Board/ members: 76

GENEALOGICAL SOCIETY: To support, preserve, and encourage others in their genealogical quests.

PROGRAMS: Community Outreach; Exhibits; Lectures; Living History; Research

EAGLE BEND

4312
Eagle Bend Historical Society/Museum
127 E Main St, 56446; (c) Todd

Private non-profit/ 1981/ Board of Directors, Pres, V-Pres, Sec, & Treas/ staff: 1(p); 4(v)/ members: 65

HISTORY MUSEUM: To preserve and display historical artifacts of the community.

PROGRAMS: Annual Meeting; Exhibits; Festivals; Guided Tours; Lectures

COLLECTIONS: [1982-present] Historical artifacts reflecting the community.

HOURS: Yr M 1-7, T,Th 9-1 / 2-6, Sa 9-12

ADMISSION: No charge

EAST GRAND FORKS

4313
Heritage Foundation of the East Grand Forks Area, Inc., The
219 20th St NE, 56721 [Box 295, 56721]; (p) (218) 773-0406; mdtucker@gfherald.infi.net; (c) Polk

Private non-profit/ 1975/ Private/ staff: 1(f); 200(v)/ members: 250/publication: *The Legacy*

HISTORICAL SOCIETY: To preserve the past for future generations; interpretsa griculture and pioneers in the Red River Valley of the North; 17 acres containing 21 structures.

PROGRAMS: Annual Meeting; Community Outreach; Exhibits; Facility Rental; Festivals; Guided Tours; Publication; School-Based Curriculum

EDINA

4314
Edina Historical Society and Museum
4711 W 70th St, 55435; (p) (612) 928-4577; (c) Hennepin

Private non-profit/ 1969/ Board of Directors/ staff: 21(v)/ members: 250/publication: *Edina Historical Society Newsletter*

HISTORIC SITE; HISTORICAL SOCIETY; HISTORY MUSEUM: Collection and preservation of Edina's past.

PROGRAMS: Annual Meeting; Community Outreach; Exhibits; Publication; Library/Archives

COLLECTIONS: [1849-present] Maps, newspapers, oral histories, biographies, photographs, artifacts, city directories, school yearbooks, history books and grange material.

HOURS: Sept-July Th-Sa 9-12

ADMISSION: No charge

ELBOW LAKE

4315
Grant County Historical Society
Hwy 79E & 1st Ave NE, 56531 [PO Box 1002, 56531]; (p) (218) 685-4864; hist@runestone.net; (c) Grant

County, non-profit; Private non-profit/ 1944/ Board of Directors/ staff: 1(p); 2(v)/ members: 125

GENEALOGICAL SOCIETY; HISTORIC PRESERVATION AGENCY; HISTORIC SITE; HISTORICAL SOCIETY; HISTORY MUSEUM; HOUSE MUSEUM; RESEARCH CENTER: To collect, preserve, and interpret materials pertinent to the history of Grant County. To provide historical and genealogical research.

PROGRAMS: Annual Meeting; Community Outreach; Exhibits; Family Programs; Guided Tours; Interpretation; Lectures; Living History; Publication; Reenactments; Research Library/Archives

COLLECTIONS: [1870s-present] Artifacts, photographs, newspapers covering 1883 to present, Grant County plat books, census and naturalization records, and local history books.

HOURS: Yr May-Sept M-Sa, Sept-May M-F 10-12, 1-4

ADMISSION: $2, Children $1

ELK RIVER

4316
Oliver H. Kelley Farm
15788 Kelley Farm Rd, 55330-6234; (p) (612) 441-6896; (f) (612)

4317
Otsego Heritage Preservation Commission
8899 Nashua Ave NE, 55330; (p) (612) 441-4414; (f) (612) 441-8823; (c) Wright

City/ 1995/publication: *Ostego in the Beginning Local History*

HISTORIC PRESERVATION AGENCY

PROGRAMS: Community Outreach; Exhibits; Festivals; Publication; Research Library/Archives

COLLECTIONS: [1860-present] City records, photographs, oral history tapes, library of local history resource books.

ELY

4318
Dorothy Molter Memorial Foundation
2002 E Sheridan St, 55731 [PO Box 391, 55731]; (p) (218) 365-4451; dmlter@norlhern net.com; (c) St Louis

Private non-profit/ 1992/ Bea Brophey, Pres/ staff: 6(p)/ members: 110

HISTORY MUSEUM: Tell people of Dorothy's life in the wilderness.

PROGRAMS: Annual Meeting; Elder's Programs; Exhibits; Film/Video; Guided Tours

COLLECTIONS: Log cabins and persona; property of Dorothy Molter's.

HOURS: May Sa-Su 10-6; June-Aug Daily 10-6; Sept Sa-Su 10-6

ADMISSION: $3, Children $1.50; Group

4319
Ely-Winton Historical Society
1900 E Camp St, 55731; (p) (218) 365-3226; (f) (218) 365-3142; ewhs@mail.vcc.mnscu.edu; (c) St. Louis

Private non-profit/ 1961/ staff: 3(p); 15(v)/ members: 185

HISTORICAL SOCIETY; HISTORY MUSEUM: Collect and preserve objects of material culture and historical research material.

PROGRAMS: Annual Meeting; Elder's Programs; Exhibits; Family Programs; Festivals; Film/Video; Interpretation; Lectures; Research Library/Archives

COLLECTIONS: Books, photos, artifacts, microfilm, videos, furniture and artwork.

HOURS: May-Sept Daily 10-4

ADMISSION: $2, Children $1

ELYSIAN

4320
Le Sueur County Historical Society
301 N E 2nd St, 56028 [PO Box 240, 56028]; (p) (507) 267-4620; museum@lchs.mus.mn.us; www.lchs.mus.mn.us/museum; (c) Le Sueur

Board of Directors/ staff: 1(f); 6(p)/ members: 246

HISTORICAL SOCIETY: Collecting early American history with special emphases on the late 1800s and early 1900s.

PROGRAMS: Annual Meeting; Family Programs; Interpretation

COLLECTIONS: [Early 1900s] Church room, 1900s general store, house, art area.

HOURS: May-Sept M-F 1-5; June-Aug W-Su 1-5

ADMISSION: Donations accepted

EVANSVILLE

4321
Evansville Historical Foundation
#337 Gran St, 56326; (p) (218) 948-2010; (c) Douglas

Private non-profit/ 1988/ staff: 1(f); 9(p)

GENEALOGICAL SOCIETY; HISTORIC PRESERVATION AGENCY; HISTORIC SITE; HISTORICAL SOCIETY; HISTORY MUSEUM; HOUSE MUSEUM; RESEARCH CENTER: Preserves and provides a visual experience into the ways of pioneer life.

PROGRAMS: Annual Meeting; Community Outreach; Exhibits; Festivals; Film/Video; Guided Tours

EXCELSIOR

4322
Excelsior Heritage Preservation Commission
339 3rd St, 55331-1877; (p) (612) 474-5233; (f) (612) 474-6300; (c) Hennepin

City/ 1997/ staff: 7(v)

HISTORIC PRESERVATION AGENCY: Performs activities necessary to maintain the city's status as a certified local government (CLG).

PROGRAMS: Community Outreach

4323
Lake Minnetonka Division, Minnesota Transportation Museum, Inc.
328 Lake St, 553331; (p) (952) 474-2115, (952) 474-4801; (f) (952) 474-2192; exdir@mt museum.org; www.mtmuseum.org; (c) Hennepin

Private non-profit/ 1990/ Board of Trustees/ staff: 2(f); 110(v)/ members: 900/publication: *Minnegazette and Division Newsletter*

HISTORY MUSEUM; LIVING HISTORY/OUTDOOR MUSEUM: Operate the steamboat Minnehaha, raised from the lake bottom and restored, and a historic streetcar.

PROGRAMS: Elder's Programs; Exhibits; Interpretation; Living History; Publication

COLLECTIONS: [19th-20th c] Nautical and streetcar related artifacts.

HOURS: May-Oct W-Th, Sa-Su, Holidays

4324
Steamboat Minnehaha and Excelsior Trolley
City Pier, Foot of Water St, 55331 [328 Lake St, 55331]; (p) (612) 474-4801, (800) 711-2591; www.mtmuseum.org

ADMISSION: $9, Children $5, Seniors $8; under 5 free

FAIRMONT

4325
Martin County Genealogical Society
208 E 2nd St #1048, 56031 [PO Box 169, 56031]; (p) (507) 238-1130; (c) Martin

County; Private non-profit/ 1982/ Board of Directors/ staff: 12(v)/ members: 72/publication: *Tree Climber*

GENEALOGICAL SOCIETY; RESEARCH CENTER: Collect, preserve and disseminate the knowledge about the history and families of Martin Co and surrounding territories. Also, to aid researchers in locating families and their history.

PROGRAMS: Annual Meeting; Lectures; Publication; Research Library/Archives

COLLECTIONS: Records: marriage, obituary, auction, people, birth, surname, files, family histories, cemetery books, atlases, foreign and U.S. research material.

HOURS: Yr M 1-4, Th 9:30-11:30a, Sa 9-11:30a

ADMISSION: $2

4326
Martin County Historical Society
304 E Blue Earth Ave, 56031; (p) (507) 235-5178; (c) Martin

County; Private non-profit/ 1929/ Pioneer Museum/ staff: 4(p)/ members: 952

HISTORICAL SOCIETY; HISTORY MUSEUM; RESEARCH CENTER

PROGRAMS: Annual Meeting; Community Outreach; Elder's Programs; Exhibits; Film/Video; Guided Tours; Research Library/ Archives

COLLECTIONS: [early 1800s-present] Antiques, 1874 newspapers, arrowheads, military, pioneer history, school room, doctor, dentist, pioneer home set-up, farming tools, carpentry tools, photos, maps, research info, scrapbooks and history of Martin County.

HOURS: May-Sept Daily 1-4:30

ADMISSION: No charge

FALCON HEIGHTS

4327
Gibbs Farm Museum
2097 Larpenteur Ave W, 55113 [2097 W Larpenteur Ave, 55113]; (p) (612) 646-8629, (612) 222-0701; (f) (612) 223-8539; admin6@rchs.com

1854/ staff: 1(f); 10(p)

COLLECTIONS: [1835-1920] Basic house furnishings 1830-1940's, personal artifacts 1830-1940's, farm equipment 1880-1910.; Gibbs family correspondence records 1880-1960, Gibbs farm records, receipts, ledgers 1880-1930.

HOURS: Seasonal

FARIBAULT

4328
Alexander Faribault House
12 First Ave NE, 55021 [1814 2nd Ave NW, 55021]; (p) (507) 334-7913; (c) Rice

Private non-profit/ 1926/ Rice Co. Historical

Society/ staff: 4(p); 100(v)/ members: 500

HISTORIC SITE; HOUSE MUSEUM: Maintains Alexander Faribault home, the first frame home built in area.

PROGRAMS: Annual Meeting; Guided Tours; Interpretation

COLLECTIONS: [1850-1910] Furniture and household artifacts from the early years of Faribault's history.

HOURS: May-Sept M-F 1-4 and by appt

ADMISSION: $1

4329
Faribault Woolen Mills Company
1500 2nd NW, 55021; (p) (507) 334-1644; (f) (507) 334-9431; store@means.net; www.faribowool.com; (c) Rice

Private non-profit/ 1865/ staff: 158(f); 20(p)/ members: 98

HISTORIC SITE: Fully vertical woolen mill manufacturing primarily woolen blankets and throws. Established in 1865 by Carl Klemer.

PROGRAMS: Festivals; Guided Tours

HOURS: Yr M-Sa 9-5:30, Su 12-5

ADMISSION: No charge

4330
Rice County Historical Society
1814 2nd Ave NW, 55021; (p) (507) 332-2121; (c) Rice

Private non-profit/ 1926/ Board of Directors/ staff: 1(f); 2(p); 100(v)/ members: 600/publication: *The Historian*

HISTORIC SITE; HISTORICAL SOCIETY; HISTORY MUSEUM; HOUSE MUSEUM: To preserve and share the history of Rice County and the state of Minnesota.

PROGRAMS: Annual Meeting; Exhibits; Facility Rental; Family Programs; Festivals; Film/Video; Guided Tours; Interpretation; Lectures; Publication; Research Library/Archives; School-Based Curriculum

COLLECTIONS: [1850-present] Items from Rice County History; emphasis on Native Americans, agricultural and industrial.

HOURS: Yr M-F 9-4; Summer M-F 9-4, Sa-Su 1-4

ADMISSION: $1, Children $0.50

FARMINGTON

4331
Dakota City Heritage Village
4008 220th St, 55024 [Box 73, 55024]; (p) (651) 460-8050; (f) (651) 463-6908; (c) Dakota

Private non-profit/ 1978/ Board of Directors/ staff: 4(f); 2(p); 400(v)/ members: 500

HISTORY MUSEUM; LIVING HISTORY/OUTDOOR MUSEUM: Preserves and interprets rural agricultural and small town history.

PROGRAMS: Exhibits; Family Programs; Festivals; Guided Tours; Interpretation; Living History; School-Based Curriculum

COLLECTIONS: [1880-1920] Buildings, agricultural artifacts, commercial and domestic artifacts. Library with pre 1920 collection.

HOURS: May-Oct M-Sa 10-4

ADMISSION: $4; No charge

4332
Heritage Preservation Commission
325 Oak St, 55024; (p) (651) 463-1802; (f) (651) 463-2591; kfinstuen@farmington.mn.us; www.ci.farmington.mn.us; (c) Dakota

City/ 1994/ staff: 2(p); 7(v)

HISTORIC PRESERVATION AGENCY: Preserve historic elements of city according to the city code.

HOURS: Yr M-F 8-4:30

FERGUS FALLS

4333
Otter Tail County Genealogical Society
1110 Lincoln Ave W, 56537; (p) (218) 736-6038; (c) Otter Tail

Private non-profit/ 1983/ staff: 12(v)/ members: 100

GENEALOGICAL SOCIETY: Educate and encourage genealogical research.

PROGRAMS: Exhibits; Facility Rental; Family Programs; Garden Tours; Guided Tours; Interpretation; Lectures; Publication; Research Library/Archives; School-Based Curriculum

COLLECTIONS: Complete Filby's passenger and immigration lists index; Wuer Hemberg Emigration index vol. 1-5, genealogical dictionary of New England vol. 1-4.

HOURS: Yr M-F 9-5.

ADMISSION: $2

FINLAND

4334
Finland Minnesota Historical Society
County Rd 6, 55603 [PO Box 583, 55603]; (p) (218) 353-7380; (c) Lake

Private non-profit/ 1986/ members: 50/publication: *How We Remember; History of Finland, MN*

HISTORICAL SOCIETY; HISTORY MUSEUM: Provide for membership and public enjoyment, restore our heritage values and to maintain as aesthetic experience.

PROGRAMS: Annual Meeting; Community Outreach; Concerts; Exhibits; Facility Rental; Family Programs; Festivals; Publication

COLLECTIONS: [early 1900s] A forestry building and old Finnish homestead furnished with period decorations and a collection of pictures, books and artifacts.

HOURS: June-Sept Th-Su 10-4

ADMISSION: Donations accepted

FOREST LAKE

4335
Gammelgarden Museum
20880 Olinda Tr, 55025 [9885 202 St, 55025]; (p) (651) 433-5053; (f) (651) 641-3419; (c) Washington

Private non-profit/ 1972/ Elim Lutheran Church/ staff: 3(p); 40(v)/ members: 300

HISTORIC SITE; LIVING HISTORY/OUTDOOR MUSEUM: Preserve, promote and present Swedish immigrant history, life and culture in Minnesota.

PROGRAMS: Annual Meeting; Community

Outreach; Concerts; Exhibits; Facility Rental; Family Programs; Festivals; Guided Tours; Interpretation; Living History

COLLECTIONS: [1850-1880s] Articles brought from Sweden and made by immigrants.

HOURS: May-Oct T-Su 1-4

ADMISSION: $3; elementary age free

FRIDLEY

4336
Fridley Historical Society

611 Mississippi St NE, 55432; (p) (612) 571-0120; (c) Anoka

Private non-profit/ 1985/ members: 110

HISTORICAL SOCIETY: Collects artifacts regarding Fridley.

PROGRAMS: Annual Meeting; Concerts; Exhibits; Family Programs; Guided Tours

COLLECTIONS: Memorabilia from Fridley homes, city hall and the schools. Information on the first families.

HOURS: Yr Sa 12-2 & by appt

ADMISSION: No charge

GIBBON

4337
Gibbon Restoration Society, Inc.

1013 1st Ave, 55335 [PO Box 383, 55335]; (p) (507) 834-6504; (f) (507) 834-9710; (c) Sibley

Private non-profit/ 1993/ staff: 10(v)

HISTORIC SITE; HISTORY MUSEUM: Restoration of Gibbon's 1895 City Hall, and the preservation of area history and artifacts.

PROGRAMS: Exhibits; Festivals; Guided Tours; Publication

COLLECTIONS: [1895-present] Articles related to the construction or use of Gibbon's 1895 City Hall and articles related to rural life.

ADMISSION: No charge

GILBERT

4338
Iron Range Historical Society

19 S Broadway, 55741 [PO Box 786, 55741]; (p) (218) 749-3150; (c) St. Louis

Private non-profit/ 1973/ Board of Directors/ staff: 9(v)/ members: 120/publication: *Range Reminiscing*

HISTORICAL SOCIETY; HISTORY MUSEUM; RESEARCH CENTER: Collect, preserve and disseminate Iron Range history of northern Minnesota.

PROGRAMS: Annual Meeting; Exhibits; Guided Tours; Publication; Research Library/ Archives

COLLECTIONS: [1880s-present] 10,000 photographs, newspapers, family histories, oral tapes, family historical items, manuscripts and documents.

HOURS: Yr Oct-Apr M 9-2; May-Sept M,T 9-2

ADMISSION: No charge

GLENWOOD

4339
Pope County Historical Society

809 S Lakeshore Dr, 56333; (p) (320) 634-3293; pcmuseum@runestone.net; (c) Pope

Private non-profit/ 1931/ staff: 4(p); 4(v)/ members: 350

GENEALOGICAL SOCIETY; HISTORIC PRESERVATION AGENCY; HISTORICAL SOCIETY; HISTORY MUSEUM: Collects, preserves, and disseminates information about the history of Pope County and Minnesota.

PROGRAMS: Annual Meeting; Community Outreach; Exhibits; Guided Tours; Interpretation; Lectures; Reenactments; Library/Archives

COLLECTIONS: [1850-1950] Native American crafts, pioneer life and development of Pope County; genealogy files.

HOURS: Yr T-Sa 10-5

ADMISSION: $3, Children $0.50

GOLDEN VALLEY

4340
Minnesota Genealogical Society

5768 Olson Memorial Hwy, 55422; (p) (612) 595-9347; mgsdec@mtn.org; www.mtn.org/mgs; (c) Hennepin

Private non-profit/ 1969/ members: 1810/publication: *Minnesota Genealogist, MGS Newsletter*

GENEALOGICAL SOCIETY: To promote and encourage an interest in genealogy and family history; to educate members in pursuit of genealogies and to collect genealogical, historical and biographical material on Minnesota families.

PROGRAMS: Annual Meeting; Publication; Research Library/Archives

COLLECTIONS: [1600s-present] Genealogical books, microfilm, microfiche, periodicals and CD-ROMs from the US; ethnic collections.

HOURS: Yr W-Th-Sa 9-3; T,Th 6:30p-9:30

ADMISSION: $5

4341
Museum of Questionable Medical Devices

201 Main St SE, 55416 [549 Turnpike Rd, 55416]; (p) (612) 379-4046; (f) (612) 540-9999; quack@mtn.org; www.mtn.org/quack; (c) Hennepin

Private non-profit/ 1986/ staff: 2(f); 3(p)

HISTORY MUSEUM: Educate the public, using hands-on demonstrations, about health fraud.

PROGRAMS: Community Outreach; Exhibits; Facility Rental; Lectures

COLLECTIONS: [1790-1999] Medical devices on permanent loan from FDA, AMA, other sources.

HOURS: Yr T,W,Th 5-9; F,Sa 12-9, Su 12-5

ADMISSION: No charge

GRAND MARAIS

4342
Grand Portage National Museum

211 Mile Creek Rd, 55604 [PO Box 668, 55604]; (p) (218) 387-2788, (218) 475-2202; (f) (218) 387-2790; grpo_admin_clerk@nps.gov; www.nps.gov/grpo; (c) Cook

Federal/ 1958/ Nat'l Park Service/ staff: 9(f); 15(p); 135(v)/publication: *Grand Portage Story; Moccasins and Red Sashes*

HISTORIC SITE; LIVING HISTORY/OUTDOOR MUSEUM: Preserves and interprets a reconstructed fur trade post of the 1790s.

PROGRAMS: Annual Meeting; Community Outreach; Elder's Programs; Exhibits; Family Programs; Festivals; Film/Video; Garden Tours; Guided Tours; Interpretation; Lectures; Living History; Publication; Reenactments; Research Library/Archives

COLLECTIONS: [1760-1900] Archaeological collections from French and British period fur trade sites; archaeological, historical, iconographic, and ethnographic collections from prehistoric and historic village of Grand Portage, reconstructed and furnished buildings.

HOURS: Buildings open May-Oct, grounds and portage Yr, Daily 9-5

ADMISSION: $2, Family $5; Under 17 free

GRAND RAPIDS

4343
Forest History Center

2609 County Rd 76, 55744; (p) (218) 327-4482; (f) (218) 327-4483; foresthistory@mnhs.org; (c) Itasca

Private non-profit/ 1978/ Minnesota Historical Society/ staff: 3(f); 30(p)

HISTORY MUSEUM: Interpretation of northern Minnesota forest and human history site.

PROGRAMS: Exhibits; Facility Rental; Family Programs; Festivals; Film/Video; Guided Tours; Interpretation; Living History; School-Based Curriculum

COLLECTIONS: [10,000 BC-present]

HOURS: June-Oct 15 M-Sa 10-5, Su 12-5

ADMISSION: $6, Children

4344
Itasca County Historical Society

10 NW 5th St, 55744 [PO Box 664, 55744]; (p) (218) 326-6431; ichs@paulbunyan.net; (c) Itasca

Private non-profit/ 1948/ Board of Directors/ staff: 2(f); 3(p); 25(v)/ members: 530

HISTORICAL SOCIETY; HISTORY MUSEUM; RESEARCH CENTER: Collect, preserve, interpret, and disseminate the history of Itasca Co.

PROGRAMS: Annual Meeting; Community Outreach; Exhibits; Guided Tours; Interpretation; Lectures; Research Library/Archives

COLLECTIONS: [Late 19th c-present] Objects and archival materials relating to logging, mining, recreation, clothing, home life, etc.

HOURS: Yr Winter M-Sa, Summer Daily, M-F 9:30-5, Sa 9:30-4, Su 11-4

ADMISSION: $4, Children $2, Seniors $3; Members free

HANLEY FALLS

4345
Minnesota's Machinery Museum

RR 2 Box 87, 56245; (p) (507) 768-3522; (f) (507) 768-3522; www.prairiewaters.com; (c) Yellow Medicine

County/ 1980/ staff: 1(f); 30(v)/ members: 160

HISTORICAL SOCIETY; HISTORY MUSEUM: Focus on Minnesota's agricultural heritage as well as developing Ag Today program.

PROGRAMS: Annual Meeting; Community Outreach; Concerts; Elder's Programs; Exhibits; Family Programs; Festivals; Film/Video; Guided Tours; Living History; Research Library/Archives; School-Based Curriculum

COLLECTIONS: [1900s] Restored tractors, gas engines, implements. Country art, railroading artifacts, vintage automobiles, quilts, farm home and general store.

HOURS: May-Sept M, W-Su 1-5

ADMISSIONS: Donations accepted

HAWLEY

4346
Western Minnesota Steam Threshers Reunion, Inc.
RR #3 Box 46, 56549; (p) (218) 937-5404; rollagee@means.net

Private non-profit/ 1954/ staff: 1520(v)/ members: 4900

HISTORY MUSEUM; LIVING HISTORY/OUTDOOR MUSEUM: Annual reenactment of the "Harvesting of Grain" as was done from 1890-1939, using steam engines and gas tractors of the era.

PROGRAMS: Festivals; Interpretation; Living History; Reenactments

COLLECTIONS: [1850-1950] 50 steam traction engines, 400 gas tractors, 10 stationary steam engines, 200 stationary gas & oil engines, 3 saw mills, threshing machines, and other grain harvesting equipment.

HOURS: Labor Day wkend F-M 6am-midnight

ADMISSION: $8 day

HENDERSON

4347
Sibley County Historical Society
700 N Main, 56044 [PO Box 407, 56044]; (p) (507) 248-3434; schs@prairie.lakes.com; history.sibley.mn.us; (c) Sibley

Private non-profit/ 1940/ Board of Directors/ staff: 20(v)/ members: 90/publication: *SCHS Newsletter*

HISTORIC SITE; HISTORICAL SOCIETY; HISTORY MUSEUM: 1885 brick house with museum, facility for genealogical research.

PROGRAMS: Annual Meeting; Exhibits; Guided Tours; Publication; Research Library/Archives

COLLECTIONS: [Late 1800s-early 1900s] Furnishings and materials, tools, artifacts, and memorabilia.

HOURS: May-last Su in Oct Su 2-5

ADMISSION: Donations accepted

HEWITT

4348
Hewitt Historical Society
Wisconsin, 56453 [RR1, Box 90A, 56453-9607]; (p) (218) 924-2303; (c) Todd

Private non-profit/ 1981/ staff: 3(f); 13(v)/ members: 15

HISTORICAL SOCIETY

COLLECTIONS: Historic artifacts of local history.

HOURS: June-Sept Sa-Su 2-5 and by appt

ADMISSION: No charge

HIBBING

4349
Greyhound Bus Origin Museum
1201 Greyhound Bld, 55746; (p) (218) 263-5814; (f) (218) 263-4379; (c) St. Louis

Private non-profit/ 1991/ staff: 24(v)

CORPORATE ARCHIVES/MUSEUM; RESEARCH CENTER: Interprets the history of Greyhound.

PROGRAMS: Exhibits; Film/Video; Guided Tours; Interpretation; Lectures; Research Library/Archives; School-Based Curriculum

COLLECTIONS: [1914-present] 14 historical buses; model buses, uniforms, bus parts, signs, safety items, other bus related material.

HOURS: May-Sept Daily 9-5

ADMISSION: $3, Children $1

4350
Hibbing Historical Society & Museum
400 23rd St and 5th Ave E, 55746; (p) (218) 263-8522; (c) St. Louis

Private non-profit/ Board of Directors/ staff: 1(p)/ members: 90

HISTORICAL SOCIETY; HISTORY MUSEUM: Collects, preserves, and disseminates Hibbing's history for the general public.

PROGRAMS: Annual Meeting; Exhibits; Film/Video; Guided Tours

COLLECTIONS: Displays of early mining, model and video of North Hibbing, Hibbing Almanac.

HOURS: Summer M-Sa 9-4; Winter M-Th 10-3

ADMISSION: $2, Children $1; under 6 free

HINKLEY

4351
Hinckley Fire Museum, Inc.
106 Old Hwy 61, 55037 [PO Box 40, 55037]; (p) (320) 384-7338; (f) (320) 384-7338; hinkleyfire.com; (c) Pine

Private non-profit/ 1970/ staff: 1(f); 3(p); 4(v)/ members: 200

HISTORY MUSEUM: Interprets "The Great Hinckley Fire" of 1894.

PROGRAMS: Annual Meeting; Community Outreach; Elder's Programs; Exhibits; Facility Rental; Family Programs; Festivals; Film/Video; Guided Tours; Interpretation; Lectures; Living History; Research Library/Archives; School-Based Curriculum; Theatre

COLLECTIONS: [Pre 1900-1890s] Artifacts from fire, clothing, logging equipment, agricultural equipment, artwork 2,000 museum artifacts, 1,500 photos.

HOURS: May-Oct Daily 10-5

ADMISSION: $3, Student $1.50, Children $0.50, Seniors $2;

HOPKINS

4352
Hopkins Historical Society
33 14th Ave N, 55343 [1018 14th St S, 55343]; (p) (612) 935-5848; (c) Hennepin

City; Private non-profit/ 1922/ staff: 17(v)/ members: 102

GENEALOGICAL SOCIETY; HISTORICAL SOCIETY; HISTORY MUSEUM

PROGRAMS: Annual Meeting; Community Outreach; Exhibits; Guided Tours; Publication; Research Library/Archives

COLLECTIONS: [1900-present]

HOURS: Yr Daily 10-4

KELLOGG

4353
Lark Toys & Carousel
RR2 Box 5, 55945 [PO Box 39, 55945]; (p) (507) 767-3387; (f) (507) 767-4565; lark@wabasha.net; www.larktoys.com; (c) Wabasha

Private non-profit/ 1983/ staff: 4(f); 26(p)

HISTORY MUSEUM: Antique toys arranged around a 20 piece hand-carved rideable carousel.

PROGRAMS: Film/Video

COLLECTIONS: [1890-1960] Antique toys, games, dolls.

HOURS: Yr Daily Summer M-F 9-5, Sa-Su 10-5; Winter: varies

ADMISSION: No charge, $1 carousel ride

KENYON

4354
Gunderson House
Kenyon Area Historical Society, 107 Gunderson Blvd, 55946 [Kenyon Area Historical Society, 107 Gunderson Bl, 55946-1014]; (p) (507) 789-5954; www.daddezio.com/society/hill/SH-MN-003.html

KIESTER

4355
Gopher-Hawkeye Power Association
1736 600th Ave, 56051 [PO Box 253, 56051]; (c) Faribault

1984/ Board of Directors/ staff: 45(v)/ members: 100

LIVING HISTORY/OUTDOOR MUSEUM: Preserving past rural agricultural machinery, tools, skills and lifestyles.

PROGRAMS: Annual Meeting; Community Outreach; Exhibits; Family Programs; Festivals; Living History

COLLECTIONS: [1900-1950] Farm buildings, tools and machinery, both horse drawn and gas powered;school and household items and clothing.

LAKE ELMO

4356
Oakdale Lake Elmo Historical Society
8280 15th St N, 55042; (p) (651) 738-2450; (c) Washington

Private non-profit/ 1994/ staff: 3(v)/ members: 30

HISTORICAL SOCIETY: Preserve and present the history of Oakdale Township.

PROGRAMS: Annual Meeting; Exhibits; Guided Tours

COLLECTIONS: [1850-1950] Photographs, news clippings, oral histories on videotape.

LAKEFIELD

4357
Jackson County Historical Society
307 N Hwy 86, 56150 [PO Box 238, 56150]; (p) (507) 662-5505; (c) Jackson

Joint/ 1946/ County/ staff: 3(p)/ 50(v)/ members: 218/publication: *JCHS Jottings Newsletter*

GENEALOGICAL SOCIETY; HISTORICAL SOCIETY; HISTORY MUSEUM; HOUSE MUSEUM; RESEARCH CENTER: Collects and preserves county history and serves as an information center.

PROGRAMS: Annual Meeting; Community Outreach; Exhibits; Facility Rental; Family Programs; Festivals; Guided Tours; Interpretation; Lectures; Living History; Publication; Research Library/Archives; School-Based Curriculum

COLLECTIONS: [1860s-1950s] Home arts, main street, religious, medical, transportation, Heron Lake, recreation, Native American influence and wildlife.

HOURS: Yr May-Aug M-F 10-12, 1-4, Sept-Apr T,Th 10-12, 1-4

ADMISSION: Donations accepted

LANESBORO

4358
Lanesboro Historical Preservation Association
105 Pkwy S, PO Box 345, 55949; (p) (507) 467-2177; (c) Fillmore

City/ 1976/ Board of Trustees/ staff: 2(p); 1(v)/ members: 300

HISTORIC PRESERVATION AGENCY; HISTORY MUSEUM

PROGRAMS: Annual Meeting; Exhibits

COLLECTIONS: [Early 1800s-early 1900s] Clothing, furniture, art collections and business memorabilia, photograph collections from Lanesboro and surrounding area.

HOURS: Apr-Dec Daily 10-5

ADMISSION: No charge, donations accepted

LESUEUR

4359
LeSueur Historians
709 N 2nd St, 56058 [208 N Main St, 56058]; (c) LeSueur

County/ 1975/ LeSueur County Historical Society/ staff: 2(p); 20(v)/ members: 30

HISTORICAL SOCIETY; HISTORY MUSEUM

PROGRAMS: Exhibits; Lectures; Publication; Research Library/Archives

COLLECTIONS: [1860-present] History of Green Giant Co, old time drugstore, veterinary medicine, agriculture in valley, 75 radios and

local artists.

HOURS: Yr Summer Daily 1-4:30, rest of year T-F 8-4:30

ADMISSION: No charge

4360
Mayo House Interpretive Society
WW Mayo House, 118 N Main St, 56058; (p) (507) 665-3250; tvoyages@prairie.lakes.com; home.lesueur.mn.us; (c) LeSueur

Private non-profit/ 1986/ Board of Directors/ staff: 6(p); 8(v)/ members: 40

HISTORIC SITE: Preserves, maintains and interprets, for public benefit the history associated with the W.W. Mayo House.

PROGRAMS: Exhibits; Family Programs; Festivals; Guided Tours; School-Based Curriculum

COLLECTIONS: [1854-1864] Period room settings from the collection of the Minnesota Historical Society. A Gothic secretary-bookcase, folding traveling chair, portraits of William and Louise Mayo.

HOURS: May, Sept, Oct Sa-Su 10:30-4:30; June, July, Aug T-Sa 10:30-4:30, Su 1-4:30

ADMISSION: $2, Student $1, Seniors $1.50

4361
W.W. Mayo House
118 N Main St, 56058; (p) (507) 665-3250

1859/ Mayo House Interpretive Society; Minnesota Historical Society/ staff: 2(p)

COLLECTIONS: [1859-1864] From collection of Minnesota Historical Society. A secretary-bookcase built of butternut in Gothic style built by Dr. WW Mayo; folding traveling chair 1820-30 period owned by Louise Mayo; portraits of William and Louise.

LINDSTROM

4362
Chisago County Historical Society
13100 3rd Ave N, 55045 [PO Box 146, 55045-0146]; (p) (651) 257-5310; stirling@tc.umn.edu; (c) Chisago

Private non-profit/ 1963/ staff: 25(v)/ members: 500/publication: *Heritage and CCHS Connection*

GENEALOGICAL SOCIETY; HISTORIC SITE; HISTORICAL SOCIETY; HISTORY MUSEUM: Collects, preserves and interprets information and artifacts about Chisago Country.

PROGRAMS: Annual Meeting; Community Outreach; Exhibits; Facility Rental; Family Programs; Film/Video; Interpretation; Lectures; Publication; Research Library/Archives

COLLECTIONS: [1850s-1950s]

HOURS: Yr M-W-F 9-4

ADMISSION: No charge

4363
Lindstrom Historical Society
[PO Box 12, 55045]; (c) Chisago

County/ 1994/ Chisago County Historical Society/ members: 94

HISTORICAL SOCIETY: Renovation and preservation of an "immigrant" house located in a county park.

PROGRAMS: Annual Meeting

COLLECTIONS: [1865-1895]

HOURS: May-Oct Su 1-4

ADMISSION: Donations accepted

LITCHFIELD

4364
Forest City Stockade
6 mi NE of Litchfield on Hwy 24, 55355 [66608 MN Hwy 24, 55355]; (p) (320) 693-6782; (c) Meeker

County/ 1976/ staff: 20(v)

HISTORIC SITE: To honor and memorialize Native Americans and the early pioneers of Meeker County.

PROGRAMS: Exhibits; Festivals; Living History

COLLECTIONS: [1850-1900] Household items, farm tools and horse machinery.

HOURS: By appt to groups

ADMISSION: $1

4365
Meeker County Historical Society
308 N Marshall, 55355; (p) (320) 693-8911; (c) Meeker

City; County/ 1956/ staff: 2(f); 1(p); 10(v)/ members: 450

HISTORICAL SOCIETY

PROGRAMS: Annual Meeting; Community Outreach; Exhibits; Family Programs; Garden Tours; Guided Tours; Interpretation; Lectures; Research Library/Archives; School-Based Curriculum

COLLECTIONS: [1885-1910] Civil War artifacts, domestic, personal items and trade tools, newspaper collection from 1870, family history files, platbooks, obituary index and oral history tapes.

HOURS: Yr T-Su 12-4 & by appt

ADMISSION: $2

LITTLE CANADA

4366
Little Canada Historical Society
515 E Little Canada Rd, 55117; (p) (651) 766-4044; littlecanadahicCTR@hotmail.com; (c) Ramsey

City; Private non-profit/ 1977/ staff: 10(v)/ members: 102/publication: *The Grist Mill*

HISTORICAL SOCIETY; HISTORY MUSEUM; RESEARCH CENTER

PROGRAMS: Exhibits; Publication; Research Library/Archives; School-Based Curriculum

COLLECTIONS: [1660s-present] Computer-based genealogy, largely French Canadian (published) plus other local nationalities.

HOURS: Yr T,Th 5-9

LITTLE FALLS

4367
Charles A. Lindbergh House
1200 Lindbergh Dr S, 56345; (p) (320) 632-3154; (f) (320) 632-0502

1906/ staff: 1(f); 9(p)

COLLECTIONS: [1906-1920] Furnishings and possessions belonging to the Lindbergh family, plus memorabilia related to the New Yorkto-Paris flight.; family papers and photographs.

HOURS: May 1-Labor Day M-Sa 10-5; Su 12-5; Labor Day-late Oct

4368
Dewey-Radke House
1200 W Broadway, 56345; (p) (320) 632-8902

4369
Little Falls Heritage Preservation Commission
c/o City Hall, 100 NE 7th Ave, 56345; (p) (320) 632-2341; (f) (320) 632-2344; rcarlson@cityof littlefalls.com; (c) Morrison

City/ 1992/ staff: 1(p); 8(v)/publication: *Concept Study, Design Guidelines, & Historic Site Survey*

HISTORIC PRESERVATION AGENCY: Responsibility of recommending to the city council the adoption of ordinance designing areas, places, building structures, works of art and other objects having special historical, cultural or architectural interest for the community as heritage preservation landmark or districts.

PROGRAMS: Publication; School-Based Curriculum

HOURS: M-F 8-5

4370
Morrison County Historical Society
2151 Lindbergh Dr S, 56345 [PO Box 239, 56345-0239]; (p) (320) 632-4007; (f) (320) 632-8409; (c) Morrison

Private non-profit/ 1936/ staff: 4(p); 50(v)/ members: 200/publication: *MCHS Newsletter*

HISTORICAL SOCIETY; HISTORY MUSEUM; RESEARCH CENTER: Preserving artifacts and historical information regarding Morrison County and to educate the public about that history.

PROGRAMS: Annual Meeting; Community Outreach; Exhibits; Family Programs; Guided Tours; Interpretation; Lectures; Publication; Research Library/Archives

COLLECTIONS: [1850-1920] Photographs, manuscripts, and primary source materials, newspapers and artifacts relating to Co. history.

HOURS: Yr T-Sa 10-5, summer T-Su

LONG PRAIRIE

4371
Todd County Historical Society
333 Central Ave, 56347; (p) (320) 732-4426; (c) Todd

County/ 1928/ Board of Trustees/ staff: 1(f); 1(p)/ members: 265

HISTORICAL SOCIETY; RESEARCH CENTER: Collect and preserve the history and artifacts of Todd Co.

PROGRAMS: Annual Meeting; Exhibits; Festivals; Guided Tours

COLLECTIONS: [1900s] Artifacts and history of Todd Co.

HOURS: Yr M-F 10-12, 1-4

LONSDALE

4372
Trondhjem Community Preservation Society
8501 Garfield Ave, 55046 [PO Box 259, 55046]; (p) (651) 453-0437; (c) Rice

Private non-profit/ 1988/ Board of Directors/ staff: 50(v)/ members: 400/publication: *"Letter from Trondhjem"*

HISTORIC PRESERVATION AGENCY; HISTORIC SITE; HOUSE MUSEUM: Maintain and restore Old Trondhjem church building, collect and preserve documents, pictures, stories and history of the early community.

PROGRAMS: Annual Meeting; Concerts; Family Programs; Festivals; Publication

COLLECTIONS: [1870-1970] WW I church banner, early 1900's batismal dress and other clothing, photographs of families, students, villages, servicemen, farm activities, church confirmands, and other artifacts.

HOURS: 3rd Su in May festival and by appt.

ADMISSION: Donations accepted.

LUCAN

4373
Lucan Area Historical Society
406 1st St, 56255; (p) (507) 747-2598; (c) Redwood

Private non-profit/ 1976/ staff: 50(v)/ members: 50

HISTORICAL SOCIETY; HISTORY MUSEUM: Preserve the history of our area for the future generations.

PROGRAMS: Annual Meeting; Exhibits; Living History

COLLECTIONS: [1976-present] Antiques, 1930s Lucan fire truck and a room devoted to John Zwach.

HOURS: June-Sept by appt

ADMISSION: No charge

LUVERNE

4374
Hinkly House Museum
217 N Freeman Ave, 56156 [PO Box 741, 56156]; (p) (507) 283-2115, (507) 283-9849

1892/ staff: 13(v)

COLLECTIONS: [1890-1910] China closets, book cases, marble top tables, desk, parquet floors, fireplaces, chairs, beveled mirrors and stairway; letters, documents, rare books medical and law books, newspapers for 1879-1880, ledgers.

HOURS: Yr

4375
Rock County Historical Society
123 N Freeman Ave, 56156 [PO Box 741, 56156]; (p) (507) 283-2115; (c) Rock

Private non-profit/ 1955/ Board of Directors/ staff: 25(v)/ members: 200

GENEALOGICAL SOCIETY; HISTORIC SITE; HISTORICAL SOCIETY; HISTORY MUSEUM; HOUSE MUSEUM; RESEARCH CENTER: Exhibits pioneer/agricultural artifacts, inter-

prets and educates about multi-generation history; Native Sioux Quartzite home preserved/restored with Victorian interior.

PROGRAMS: Annual Meeting; Community Outreach; Concerts; Elder's Programs; Exhibits; Facility Rental; Family Programs; Festivals; Guided Tours; Interpretation; Lectures; Publication; Reenactments; Research Library/ Archives; School-Based Curriculum; Theatre

COLLECTIONS: [1870-present] Pioneer implements, guns, military uniforms, dolls, obituary files, research books/notebooks, natural history specimens; 1885-1910 family furniture, books, glassware/dishes, clothing, children's toys, magazines, victrola and records.

HOURS: May-Sept T, Th, Sa 2-4

ADMISSION: $2, Children $2, Seniors $1

MABEL

4376
Hesper-Mabel Area Historical Society
Steam Engine Park, 55954 [PO Box 56, 55954]; (p) (507) 493-5350; www.geocities.com/yosemite/forest/6432; (c) Fillmore

Private non-profit/ 1991/ Board of Directors/ staff: 2(p); 8(v)/ members: 55

HISTORICAL SOCIETY; HISTORY MUSEUM: Preserves and educates about area agricultural and local history, maintains the Steam Engine Museum.

PROGRAMS: Annual Meeting; Exhibits; Guided Tours; Living History

COLLECTIONS: [1890-1950] Full scale and scale model steam engines, antique tractors, antique gas engines, threshing machines and other antique farm equipment. Antique fire truck and paraphernalia from local Grenadiers band.

HOURS: June-Aug Daily M-Sa 10-5, Su 1-5; May and Oct by appt

ADMISSION: $2, under 16 free, group rates

MADELIA

4377
Watonwan County Historical Society
423 Dill Ave SW, 56062 [PO Box 126, 56062]; (p) (507) 642-3247; (c) Watonwan

Private non-profit/ 1966/ staff: 1(f); 3(p); 25(v)/ members: 450

GENEALOGICAL SOCIETY; HISTORICAL SOCIETY; HISTORY MUSEUM; RESEARCH CENTER

PROGRAMS: Annual Meeting; Concerts; Exhibits; Guided Tours

COLLECTIONS: [1870-1915] Early pioneer life, horse-drawn equipment, early business displays, genealogical research materials.

HOURS: Apr-Oct M-Th 9-4; June-Sept M-Th 9-4, Sa-Su 1-4

ADMISSION: No charge

MANKATO

4378
Blue Earth County Historical Society
415 E Cherry, 56001; (p) (507) 345-5566; (c) Blue Earth

Private non-profit/ 1901/ Board of Directors/ staff: 3(f); 1(p); 100(v)/ members: 515

HISTORICAL SOCIETY: Seeks to collect, preserve, and promote the history of Blue Earth County.

PROGRAMS: Annual Meeting; Exhibits; Guided Tours; Lectures; Research Library/Archives

COLLECTIONS: 12,000 artifacts from Blue Earth

4379
Evangelical Lutheran Dept. of History and Archives
6 Browns Ct, 56001; (p) (507) 344-7354; (c) Blue Earth

Private non-profit/ 1972/ Evangelical Lutheran Synod/ staff: 2(p)

HISTORY MUSEUM; LIBRARY AND/OR ARCHIVES

PROGRAMS: Exhibits; Research Library/Archives

COLLECTIONS: [1852-present] Documents that pertain to the history of the Synod and its institution, leaders, pastors and church records. Also books of historical and theological interest, and artifacts.

HOURS: Yr M, W, F 9-12

ADMISSION: No charge

4380
R.D. Hubbard House
606 S Broad St, 56001 [Blue Earth County Hist Soc, 415 E Cherry St, 56001]; (p) (507) 345-5566

1871/ staff: 2(f); 1(p); 13(v)

COLLECTIONS: [1905] Furniture and light fixtures.; Papers, photos, maps.

HOURS: Yr: Hubbard House: April-Nov: Gallery, offices and archives

MANTORVILLE

4381
Dodge County Historical Society
615 N Main St, 55955-0433; (p) (507) 635-5508; (c) Dodge

Private non-profit/ Board of Trustees/ staff: 2(p)

HISTORIC SITE; HISTORICAL SOCIETY; HISTORY MUSEUM

PROGRAMS: Annual Meeting; Exhibits; Festivals; Guided Tours; Publication; Research Library/Archives; School-Based Curriculum

HOURS: Yr May-Oct 15 T-Sa 10-4; Oct 16-Apr Th-Sa 10-4

ADMISSION: $2, Seniors $1.50; under 12 free

MARINE ON SAINT

4382
Stone House Museum
5th & Oak St, 55047 [9070 4th St, 55047]; (p) (651) 433-2061; (c) Washington

City, non-profit; Private non-profit/ 1963/ staff: 1(v)/ members: 39/publication: *Marine on St. Croix - 150 Years of Village Life*

HISTORIC SITE; HISTORY MUSEUM

PROGRAMS: Community Outreach; Exhibits; Garden Tours; Guided Tours; Publication;

Reenactments; Research Library/Archives

COLLECTIONS: [1840-present] Artifacts from Swedish immigrants and early settlers.

HOURS: July-Sept Sa-Su 2-5

ADMISSION: Donations accepted

MARSHALL

4383
Lyon County Historical Society Museum
114 N 3rd St, 56258-1325; (p) (507) 537-6580; (f) (507) 537-6580; (c) Lyon

Private non-profit/ 1934/ staff: 2(p); 1(v)/ members: 250/publication: *Lyon Tale Prairie Town: Marshall, MN*

HISTORICAL SOCIETY; HISTORY MUSEUM: Educate students.

PROGRAMS: Annual Meeting; Community Outreach; Exhibits; Festivals; Film/Video; Guided Tours; Interpretation; Lectures; Publication; Research Library/Archives; School-Based Curriculum

COLLECTIONS: [1860s-present] Log cabin exhibit, a prairie diorama, working soda fountain and history of County.

HOURS: Feb-Dec Daily 10-5

ADMISSION: No charge

MELROSE

4384
Melrose Area Historical Society
518 E 2nd St S, 56352; (p) (320) 256-4996; (f) (320) 256-4996; melroseahs@aol.com; www.melrosemnhistory.com; (c) Stearns

Private non-profit/ 1987/ Board of Directors/ staff: 20(v)/ members: 250/publication: *The Father of Melrose*

HISTORY MUSEUM; RESEARCH CENTER: Preserves and interprets the history of the Melrose area, including Freeport, Meire Grove, Greenwald, St. Rosa, Spring Hill and New Munich.

PROGRAMS: Annual Meeting; Community Outreach; Exhibits; Family Programs; Festivals; Guided Tours; Interpretation; Publication; Research Library/Archives; School-Based Curriculum

COLLECTIONS: [Prehistory-present] Artifacts, photos, maps, video tapes, oral histories, newspaper files, books relating to the Melrose area school district.

HOURS: May-Oct W 9-3, Sa 10-3

MENDOTA

4385
Sibley House Historic Site
1347 Sibley Mem Hwy, 55150 [PO Box 50772, 55150]; (p) (651) 452-1596; sibleyhouse@mnhs.org; www.mhnhs.org; (c) Dakota

Private non-profit/ 1910/ Sibley House Association/ staff: 1(f); 15(p); 20(v)/ members: 300/publication: *A Piece of History*

HISTORIC SITE; HOUSE MUSEUM: Preserves and interprets the vestiges of MN's oldest Euro-American settlement, Mendota, a headquarters for the American Fur Company.

PROGRAMS: Annual Meeting; Exhibits; Family Programs; Guided Tours; Interpretation; Publication; Reenacts

COLLECTIONS: [Mid-19th c] Late Federal/ early Victorian furniture, decorative arts, textile, and costume artifacts,ethnographic materials, rare volumes, and paintings.

HOURS: May-Oct T-Sa 10-5; Su 12-5

ADMISSION: $4, Students $1.50, Seniors $3

MINNEAPOLIS

4386
American Swedish Institute, The
2600 Park Ave, 55407-1090; (p) (612) 871-4907; (f) (612) 871-8682; info@americanswedishinst.org; www.americanswedishinst.org; (c) Hennepin

Private non-profit/ 1929/ staff: 14(f); 14(p); 432(v)/ members: 5100/publication: *ASI Posten*

ART MUSEUM; HISTORIC SITE; HISTORY MUSEUM; HOUSE MUSEUM: Housed within the 1904 Turnblad mansion, emphasizes the emigrant era in its collections of Swedish-Americana and celebrates Swedish cultural traditions.

PROGRAMS: Annual Meeting; Community Outreach; Concerts; Exhibits; Festivals; Guided Tours; Lectures; Publication; Research Library/Archives

COLLECTIONS: [1850-present] Emigrant artifacts and Turnblad memorabilia; Swedish and Swedish-American fine and decorative arts including wood carvings, textiles, and glass; traditional crafts; and archival materials

HOURS: Yr Su 1-5, W 12-8, T,Th-Sa 12-4

ADMISSION: $4, Children $2, Seniors $3

4387
Hennepin History Museum
2303 3rd Ave S, 55404; (p) (612) 870-1329; (f) (612) 870-1320; hhmuseum@mtn.org; www.mtn.org/~hhmuseum; (c) Hennepin

Private non-profit/ 1938/ Historical Society of Hennepin County/ staff: 1(f); 4(p); 15(v)/ members: 350/publication: *Hennepin History*

HISTORICAL SOCIETY; HISTORY MUSEUM; HOUSE MUSEUM: Promotes an understanding of the relationship between Co.'s past and its contemporary communities through collection and preserving the county's history.

PROGRAMS: Annual Meeting; Community Outreach; Exhibits; Festivals; Guided Tours; Interpretation; Lectures; Publication; Research Library/Archives; School-Based Curriculum

COLLECTIONS: [1850-present] Objects, clothing, decorative arts, dolls and toys, quilts, appliances, books, manuscripts, maps, photographs, and various documents.

HOURS: Yr T 10-2, W-Sa 1-5

ADMISSION: $2, Student $1, Seniors $1

4388
Historic Minnehaha Depot
Minnehaha Park, 55417 [4926 Minnehaha Ave, 55417-0240]; (p) (612) 228-0263, (612) 291-7588; www.mtmuseum.org; (c) Hennepin
HOURS: May-Sept Su & holidays 12:30-4:30
ADMISSION: No charge

4389

Humphrey Forum, The

301 19th Ave S, 55455; (p) (612) 624-5893; (f) (612) 625-3513; ssandell@hhh.umn.edu; (c) Hennepin

State/ 1989/ University of Minnesota/ staff: 5(f); 3(p)/publication: *Nineteenth Avenue*

HISTORICAL SOCIETY: Offers museum programs and publications for schools and general public.

PROGRAMS: Community Outreach; Exhibits; Guided Tours; Interpretation; Lectures; Publication; School-Based Curriculum

COLLECTIONS: [20th C] 10,000 photographs, 5,000 objects and 3,000 books documenting the public life and politics of Hubert H. Humphrey.

HOURS: Yr 8-5 & by appt

ADMISSION: No charge

4390

Immigration History Research Center, University of Minnesota

8311 Anderson Library, 222 21st Ave S, 55455; (p) (612) 625-4800; (f) (612) 626-0018; ihrc@umn.edu; ww.umn.edu/ihrc; (c) Hennepin

State/ 1965/ Regents of U of M & College of Liberal Arts/ staff: 4(f); 5(p); 8(v)/publication: *IHRC News; Spectrum*

LIBRARY AND/OR ARCHIVES: Resource on American immigration and ethnic history, promoting study and appreciation of ethnic pluralism.

PROGRAMS: Annual Meeting; Community Outreach; Exhibits; Festivals; Guided Tours; Lectures; Publication; Research Library/ Archives; School-Based Curriculum

COLLECTIONS: [1880s-present] Records of immigrants and their descendants, their organizations and activities, books, newspapers and serials, manuscripts, archival material, photographs, oral histories, audiovisual materials.

HOURS: Yr M-F 8:30-4:30, Sa by appt

ADMISSION: No charge

4391

Minneapolis Heritage Preservation Commission

Rm 210 City Hall, 350 S 5th St, 55415; (p) (612) 673-2597; (f) (612) 673-2728; www.ci. minneapolis.us/citywork/planning/sections/; (c) Hennepin

City/ 1972/ Minneapolis Planning Dept

HISTORIC PRESERVATION AGENCY: Preserves and celebrates city heritage; serves as a citizen advisory body to the Minneapolis City Council.

PROGRAMS: Annual Meeting; Community Outreach; Guided Tours

COLLECTIONS: Sanborn maps, city directories, books and periodicals pertaining to Minneapolis history and architecture, historic preservation and files on several thousand buildings in Minneapolis.

HOURS: M-F by appt

ADMISSION: No charge

4392

Minneapolis Public Library, Special Collections Dept

300 Nicollet Mall, 55401-1992; (p) (612) 630-6350; (f) (612) 630-6210; www.mpls.mn.us; (c) Hennepin

City, non-profit/ 1885/ Board of Trustees/ staff: 3(f); 1(p); 21(v)/ members: 1/publication: *Scrolling Forward*

PROGRAMS: Community Outreach; Exhibits; Lectures; Publication; Research Library/ Archives

COLLECTIONS: [19th-20th c]

HOURS: Yr M-Th 9-5:30, F 9-6, Sa 10-5:30

ADMISSION: No charge

4393

Minnesota Annual Conference Archive

Rm 400, 122 W Franklin Ave, 55404; (p) (612) 870-0058; (f) (612) 870-1260; thelma. boeder@mnumc.org; (c) Hennepin

Private non-profit/ 1969/ United Methodist Church/ staff: 1(p)

LIBRARY AND/OR ARCHIVES: Repository for organizational archives and manuscript collections related to Minnesota United Methodism; assists local congregations in their archival programs.

PROGRAMS: Community Outreach; Interpretation; Research Library/Archives

COLLECTIONS: [1837-] Archives, manuscripts and published materials

HOURS: Yr M-F by appt

ADMISSION: No charge

4394

Minnesota Chapter, Society of Architectural Historians

International Market Sq 275 Market St Ste 54, 55405; (p) (612) 338-6763; (f) (612) 338-7981

Private non-profit/ 1973/ Board of Directors/ staff: 4(v)/ members: 125/publication: *With Respect to Architecture*

PROFESSIONAL ORGANIZATION: Broaden awareness and appreciation of our architectural heritage; to promote research and preservation and recording of important architecture.

PROGRAMS: Annual Meeting; Guided Tours; Lectures; Publication

4395

Original Baseball Hall of Fame

910 S 3rd St, 55415; (p) (612) 375-9707; (f) (612) 375-0428; raycrump@domeplus.com; www.domeplus.com; (c) Hennepin

Private non-profit/ 1987/ staff: 3(f); 3(p)/publication: *Beneath the Grandstands*

HISTORY MUSEUM: Baseball museum for Washington Senators and Minnesota Twins.

PROGRAMS: Film/Video; Guided Tours; Publication

COLLECTIONS: Autograph baseballs, photos, baseball furniture, uniforms and bats.

HOURS: Yr M-F 9-4, Sa 3-11

4396

Preservation Alliance of Minnesota

275 Market St, Ste 54, 55405; (p) (612) 341-8140; (f) (612) 338-7981; info@mnpreserva tion.org; www.mnpreservation.org; (c) Hennepin

Private non-profit/ 1981/ Board of Directors/ staff: 1(f); 1(p); 75(v)/ members: 1500/publication: *The Minnesota Preservationist; Preserve Minnesota*

HISTORIC PRESERVATION AGENCY: Historic preservation advocacy and education organization offering assistance to citizens and communities throughout MN.

PROGRAMS: Annual Meeting; Community Outreach; Guided Tours; Lectures

4397

United Methodist Historical Society of Minnesota

Rm 400, 122 W Franklin Ave, 55404; (p) (612) 870-0058; (f) (612) 870-1260; thelma. boeder@mnumc.org; (c) Hennepin

Private non-profit/ 1981/ members: 85/publication: *Heritage & Heritage, Too*

HISTORICAL SOCIETY: Promote interest in the heritage of Minnesota United Methodism through preservation of historical writing, archived material and memorabilia and dissemination of relevant information.

PROGRAMS: Annual Meeting; Publication

COLLECTIONS: [1837]

4398

Upper Midwest Conservation Association

Minneapolis Institute of Arts, 55404 [2400 3rd Ave S, 55404]; (p) (612) 870-3120; (f) (612) 870-3118; umca@aol.com; www.preserve art.org; (c) Hennepin

Private non-profit/ 1977/ staff: 9(f); 1(p)/ members: 140

Regional center for the preservation of art and artifacts. It provides conservation treatment, education and training for the staff of museums, historical societies, libraries, archives and other cultural institutions.

4399

Wells Fargo Bank Museum

Sixth and Marquette, 2nd Fl, 55479; (p) (612) 667-4210

HISTORY MUSEUM: History of Wells Fargo Bank.

PROGRAMS: Exhibits; Guided Tours

COLLECTIONS: [19th-20th c] Concord Stagecoach; Wells Fargo banking and express history; California gold rush exhibits; gold specimens and coins.

HOURS: M-F 9-5

MINNESOTA LAKE

4400

Kremer House Library and Museum

317 Main St, 56068 [PO Box 225, 56068]; (p) (507)

MINNETONKA

4401
Charles H. Burwell House
13209 E McGinty Rd, 55345 [c/o K Magrew, City of Minnetonka,14600 Minnetonka, 55345]; (p) (612) 939-8218; (f) (612) 939-8244

Joint/ 1883/ City; Minnetonka Historical Society; MN DOT

COLLECTIONS: [1892] Burwell furnishings and others of the period.

4402
Minnetonka Historical Society
13209 E McGinty Rd, 55305; (p) (612) 633-1611; mhs@minnetonka-history.org; www.minnetonka-history.org/; (c) Hennepin

Private non-profit/ 1970/ staff: 7(v)/ members: 100/publication: *Minnetonka Township*

HISTORICAL SOCIETY: Record and exhibit history of Minnetonka Township and present city.

PROGRAMS: Annual Meeting; Community Outreach; Exhibits; Festivals; Guided Tours; Interpretation; Lectures; Living History; Publication

COLLECTIONS: [1850-present]

MONTEVIDEO

4403
Chippewa County Historical Society
151 Pioneer Dr, 56265 [PO Box 303, 56265]; (p) (320) 269-7636; cchs.june@juno.com; (c) Chippewa

Private non-profit/ 1936/ staff: 1(f); 5(p); 50(v)/ members: 394/publication: *Chippewa County History Book*

GENEALOGICAL SOCIETY; HISTORIC SITE; HISTORICAL SOCIETY; HISTORY MUSEUM; HOUSE MUSEUM; RESEARCH CENTER: Promotes and pursues the discovery, collection, dissemination, and preservation of historical knowledge about Chippewa County.

PROGRAMS: Annual Meeting; Community Outreach; Concerts; Exhibits; Facility Rental; Family Programs; Festivals; Guided Tours; Interpretation; Lectures; Living History; Publication; Research Library/Archives; School-Based Curriculum

COLLECTIONS: [1870-1920] Three dimensional pieces, photographs, literature, automobiles, newspapers, portraits, and paintings, textiles, Native American artifacts, and leather.

HOURS: Historic Chippewa: May-Sept M-F 9-5, Sa-Su 1-5; Farm Museum: May-Sept Su 1-5; Historical Society Yr M-F 9-5

ADMISSION: $3, Student $1, Seniors $2; Under 5 free

MONTICELLO

4404
Little Mountain Settlement Museum
511 Territorial Rd, 55362 [Box 581, 55362]; (p) (612) 295-2950; (c) Wright

1979/ staff: 1(f)

HISTORY MUSEUM

PROGRAMS: Community Outreach; Elder's Programs; Exhibits; Family Programs; Festivals; Guided Tours; Interpretation; Living History; School-Based Curriculum

COLLECTIONS: [1855-1875] 13 historic log buildings furnished authentically. Norwegian, Swedish, German cabins, school, blacksmith/wheelwright shop, leatherworkers shop, woodworkers shop, weaver's cabin, barn, broom and rope shop, store and sauna.

HOURS: May-Dec Sa-Su 1-5, wkdays by appt

ADMISSION: $3.50, Students $3, Children $2.50

MOORHEAD

4405
Clay County Historical Society
202 1st Ave N, 56561 [PO Box 501, 56561-0501]; (p) (218) 299-5520; mpeihl1@juno.com; (c) Clay

Joint/ 1932/ County/ staff: 3(f); 1(p); 30(v)/ members: 525/publication: *CCHS Newsletter*

HISTORIC PRESERVATION AGENCY; HISTORIC SITE; HISTORICAL SOCIETY; HISTORY MUSEUM; LIVING HISTORY/OUTDOOR MUSEUM: The collection, preservation and dissemination of the history of Clay County.

PROGRAMS: Annual Meeting; Community Outreach; Exhibits; Family Programs; Festivals; Guided Tours; Interpretation; Lectures; Living History; Publication; Research Library/Archives; School-Based Curriculum

COLLECTIONS: [1860-present] Archival materials and artifacts relating to settlement, development, archaeology and social history.

HOURS: Yr Daily M-Sa 910-5, Su 12-5, Th 10-9

ADMISSION: No charge

4406
Comstock Historic House
506 8th St S, 56560-3504; (p) (218) 291-4211; (c) Clay

Private non-profit; State/ 1882/ Minnesota Historical Society/ members: 125

HISTORIC SITE: Interpret lives of members of the Comstock family and their influence on local, state and national governments.

PROGRAMS: Family Programs; Festivals; Interpretation; Lectures; Living History

COLLECTIONS: Furniture and furnishings of the Solomon Comstock family.

HOURS: May-Sept Sa-Su 1-4:15

ADMISSION: $3, Children $1.50, Seniors $2; Under 5 free

4407
Northwest Minnesota Historical Center
1104 7th Ave S, 56563; (p) (218) 236-2343; (f) (218) 299-5924; shoptaug@mhd1.moorhead.msus.edu; www.moorhead.msus.edu/archives; (c) Clay

State/ 1973/ Moorhead State University/ staff: 1(f); 3(p)

RESEARCH CENTER: Collects and preserves information concerning the history and culture of the Red River Valley of the North: settlement, agriculture, government, business and heritage.

PROGRAMS: Community Outreach; Exhibits; Research Library/Archives

COLLECTIONS: [1875-present] Correspon-

dence, diaries, newspapers, business records, photographs and other materials.

HOURS: Yr M-F 8-4

ADMISSION: No charge

4408
Red River Valley Center at Moorhead
202 First Ave N, 56561 [PO Box 157, 56561]; (p) (218) 233-5604; (f) (218) 233-6209; hrc@rrnet.com; www.atpfargo.com; (c) Clay

Private non-profit/ 1982/ staff: 3(f); 3(p); 100(v)/ members: 300/publication: *Heritage Press and the Historian*

HISTORY MUSEUM: Houses the Hjemkomst Viking Ship and a replica of the Norwegian Hopperstand Stave Church.

PROGRAMS: Annual Meeting; Community Outreach; Concerts; Exhibits; Facility Rental; Family Programs; Festivals; Film/Video; Guided Tours; Interpretation; Lectures; Publication; School-Based Curriculum; Theatre

COLLECTIONS: Artifacts from Viking Ship and Church.

HOURS: Yr Daily M-W, F, Sa 9-5, Th 9-9, Su 12-5

ADMISSION: $3.50, Student $3, Children $1.50, Seniors $3; Under 4 free

MOOSE LAKE

4409
Moose Lake Area Historical Society
900 Foltz, 55767 [PO Box 235, 55767]; (p) (218) 485-4234; (c) Carlton

Private non-profit/ 1969/ staff: 3(p); 65(v)/ members: 130/publication: *Moose Lake Area History, Vol I & II; The Other West Side Story; Fire Stories*

HISTORIC SITE; HISTORICAL SOCIETY; HISTORY MUSEUM: Tells the story of the Fires of 1918.

PROGRAMS: Community Outreach; Exhibits; Festivals; Guided Tours; Interpretation; Lectures; Living History; Publication; Reenactments; Research Library/Archives; Theatre

COLLECTIONS: [1918] Artifacts, photos of victims of the 1918 fires, railroad, logging, Nemadji pottery, documents.

HOURS: May-Aug T-Sa 10-4, Su 11-4

ADMISSION: $2, Donations accepted

MORA

4410
Kanabec County Historical Society & History Center
805 W Forest Ave, 55051 [PO Box 113, 55051]; (p) (320) 679-1665; (f) (320) 679-1673; kanabechistory@ncis.com; www.kanabechistory.com; (c) Kanabec

Private non-profit/ 1968/ Board of Directors/ staff: 2(f); 2(p); 80(v)/ members: 398

GENEALOGICAL SOCIETY; HISTORICAL SOCIETY; HISTORY MUSEUM; RESEARCH CENTER: Collect and preserve historical data, structures and objects from county.

PROGRAMS: Annual Meeting; Exhibits; Facility Rental; Family Programs; Festivals; Publication; Research Library/Archives

COLLECTIONS: [1880] Artifacts and manuscript.

HOURS: Yr Daily M-Sa 10-4:30, Su 12:30-4:30

ADMISSION: $3, Family $8, Children $1

MORRIS

4411
Stevens County Genealogical Society, Inc.
Morris Public Library, 56267 [102 E 6th St, 56267]; (c) Stevens

Private non-profit/ 1983/ Executive Board/ staff: 12(v)/ members: 75

GENEALOGICAL SOCIETY: Gather and disseminate information on genealogical research.

PROGRAMS: Lectures; Publication; Research Library/Archives

COLLECTIONS: Books, periodicals, microfilmed newspapers, and newsletters.

HOURS: Yr M-Sa (Public Library Hours)

MORTON

4412
Renville County Historical Society
441 N Park Dr, 56270; (p) (507) 697-6147; rchs@rconnect.com; (c) Renville

Private non-profit/ 1940/ Board of Directors/ staff: 2(f); 2(p); 19(v)/ members: 282/publication: *Joseph Renville*

HISTORICAL SOCIETY; HISTORY MUSEUM; RESEARCH CENTER: Collects and preserves history of Renville County.

PROGRAMS: Annual Meeting; Community Outreach; Elder's Programs; Exhibits; Facility Rental; Family Programs; Festivals; Guided Tours; Lectures; Publication; Research Library/Archives

COLLECTIONS: Agricultural machines, glassware, and military, county history; newspapers and family research files.

HOURS: May-Sept T-Sa 10-4, Su 1-5; Oct-Apr by appt

ADMISSION: $1

MOUND

4413
Westonka Historical Society
3740 Enchanted Ln, 55364; (p) (952) 472-1885; (c) Hennepin

Private non-profit/ 1972/ Board Members/ staff: 9(v)/ members: 60/publication: *Historical Backgrounds of Mound/ Minnetrista Memories; and others*

HISTORICAL SOCIETY: Collect and preserve pictures, artifacts and written and taped articles regarding the western Lake Minnetonka area.

PROGRAMS: Elder's Programs; Guided Tours; Interpretation; Lectures; Publication

COLLECTIONS: Cassettes and video tapes newspapers, artifacts of early pioneers, pictures and postcards.

ADMISSION: No charge

MOUNTAIN LAKE

4414
Heritage Village, Inc.
County Rd #1 & Hwy 6, 56159 [PO Box 152, 56159]; (p) (507) 427-2023; (c) Cottonwood

Private non-profit/ 1971/ staff: 30(v)/ members: 125

Preserves the Mennonite heritage.
COLLECTIONS: [Early 1900s]
HOURS: 15 May-15 Sept Daily 1-5
ADMISSION: $3, Children $2

NEW BRIGHTON

4415
New Brighton Area Historical Society
Long Lake Regional Park, 55112 [PO Box 120624, 55112]; (p) (651) 633-1499; (c) Ramsey

Private non-profit/ 1980/ staff: 25(v)/ members: 100/publication: *Depot News*

HISTORICAL SOCIETY; HISTORY MUSEUM; RAILROAD MUSEUM: Operates a depot museum and caboose, tells the history of our area and collects relevant artifacts.

PROGRAMS: Annual Meeting; Community Outreach; Exhibits; Family Programs; Festivals; Interpretation; Lectures; Publication; School-Based Curriculum

COLLECTIONS: Railroad memorabilia, glassware, clothing, hats, photos, train artifacts, time tables, tickets artwork, plus area artifacts.

HOURS: June-Sept Sa-Su 1-4

NEW ULM

4416
August Schell Brewing Company Museum of Brewing
Schell's Park, 56073 [PO Box 128, 56073]; (p) (507) 354-5528; (f) (507) 359-9119; schells@schellsbrewery.com; www.schellsbrewery.com; (c) Brown

Private for-profit/ 1860/ August Schell Brewing Company/ staff: 1(f); 10(p)

GARDEN; HISTORIC SITE

PROGRAMS: Concerts; Exhibits; Festivals; Guided Tours

COLLECTIONS: [1860-present] Artifacts and memorabilia from the brewing industry and information on the founding family.

HOURS: May-Sept Daily 12-5

ADMISSION: $2

4417
Brown County Historical Society
2 N Broadway, 56073; (p) (507) 233-2616; (f) (507) 354-1068; bchs@newulmtel.net; (c) Brown

Private non-profit/ 1930/ staff: 1(f); 5(p); 200(v)/ members: 700/publication: *News Notes*

GENEALOGICAL SOCIETY; HISTORIC PRESERVATION AGENCY; HISTORIC SITE; HISTORICAL SOCIETY; HISTORY MUSEUM; HOUSE MUSEUM; RESEARCH CENTER: A general historical society that deals with genealogy, Native American studies, early settlement, government, and businesses in Brown County.

PROGRAMS: Annual Meeting; Community Outreach; Exhibits; Facility Rental; Festivals; Guided Tours; Lectures; Living History; Monthly Meeting; Publication; Research Library/Archives; School-Based Curriculum

COLLECTIONS: [1850s-present] Pioneer family files, Dakota War, Wanda Gag, and business and governmental files on Brown County.

HOURS: May-Oct M-F 10-5, Sa-Su 1-5; Nov-Apr M-Sa 10-5

ADMISSION: $2; Children/Students free

4418
John Lind House
622 Center St, 56073; (p) (507) 354-8802

4419
Wanda Gag House Assn., Inc.
226 N Washington, 56073 [PO Box 432, 56073]; (p) (507) 359-2632; (c) Brown

Private non-profit/ 1988/ Brown County Historical Society/ staff: 6(v)/ members: 150

HOUSE MUSEUM: Honors her birthplace and her work as a writer and illustrator of children's books.

PROGRAMS: Lectures

COLLECTIONS: [1900-1950] Books, lithographs and art work by Wanda Gag and her sister and father.

HOURS: Yr Sa-Su 1-4

ADMISSION: Donations accepted

NEW YORK MILLS

4420
Minnesota Finnish-American Historical Society, Chapter 13 of New York Mills/ Finn Creek Museum
5 1/2 mi SE of New York Mills, 56567 [PO Box 134, 56567]; (p) (218) 385-2233; (c) Ottertail

Private non-profit/ 1975/ Board of Directors/ members: 100

HISTORIC SITE; HISTORICAL SOCIETY; HISTORY MUSEUM; LIVING HISTORY/OUTDOOR MUSEUM: Preserves and displays Finnish-American rural heritage.

PROGRAMS: Annual Meeting; Facility Rental; Family Programs; Festivals; Guided Tours

COLLECTIONS: [1900-1950s] Clothing, home furnishings, farm equipment,and general store artifacts

HOURS: May-Sept Daily 12-5, Sept-May by appt

ADMISSION: Donations accepted.

NISSWA

4421
Nisswa Caboose Society
Main & City Hall St, 56468 [2151 City Rd 29, 56468-9705]; (p) (218) 568-8789; (c) Crow Wing

Private non-profit/ 1993/ staff: 35(v)/ members: 27/publication: *Telegraph*

HISTORY MUSEUM; RAILROAD MUSEUM: Maintains a historic railroad depot.

PROGRAMS: Annual Meeting; Exhibits; Film/Video; Guided Tours; Publication

COLLECTIONS: [1885-1995] Photographs, video tapes, and artifacts.

HOURS: June-Sept Daily 1-4

ADMISSION: No charge

NORTHFIELD

4422
City of Northfield Historic Preservation Commission
801 Washington St, 55057; (p) (507) 645-3005; (f) (507) 645-3055; (c) Rice

City/ Local Municipal govrnment/City Council/ staff: 1(p)/ members: 9

HISTORIC PRESERVATION AGENCY: Regulatory commission reviews and approves all alterations to structures within the Historic District.

HOURS: Yr 3rd Th 4:30, open to public

4423
Northfield Historical Society
408 Division St, 55057; (p) (507) 645-9268; (f) (507) 663-6080; nhsmuseum@microassist.com; (c) Rice

Private non-profit/ 1975/ staff: 1(p); 80(v)/ members: 409

HISTORIC SITE: Restores and preserves Northfield area history.

PROGRAMS: Annual Meeting; Community Outreach; Exhibits; Family Programs; Festivals; Guided Tours; Interpretation; Lectures; Publication; Reenactments; Research Library/ Archives

COLLECTIONS: [1890-1960] James/Younger Gang items. Business premium collection, WWII surveys and uniform collection, items related to area history.

HOURS: Yr T-Sa 10-4, Su 1-4

ADMISSION: $3, Children $1.50

4424
Norwegian-American Historical Association
1510 St Olaf Ave, 55057-1097; (p) (507) 646-3221; (f) (507) 646-3734; naha@stolaf.edu; www.naha.stolaf.edu; (c) Rice

Private non-profit/ 1925/ staff: 4(f); 3(p); 2(v)/ members: 1950

HISTORICAL SOCIETY; RESEARCH CENTER: Locates, collects, preserves and interprets the Norwegian-American part of American culture through our archives and publications program.

PROGRAMS: Publication; Research Library/ Archives

COLLECTIONS: [Early 19th C-present] Letters, papers, books, periodicals, and newspapers related to Norwegian-American life.

HOURS: Yr M-F 8-12 1-4

ADMISSION: No charge

ORTONVILLE

4425
Big Stone County Historical Society
Inter of Hwys 12 & 75, 56278 [RR 2, Box 31, 56278]; (p) (320) 839-3359; (c) Big Stone

County/ 1971/ Big Stone County/ staff: 3(p); 30(v)/ members: 207/publication: *History of Big Stone County, 1881-1981*

HISTORICAL SOCIETY; RESEARCH CENTER: Illustrates the natural and physical development of Big Stone County and interpret the area's agricultural history, navigation history, and the granite industry.

PROGRAMS: Annual Meeting; Exhibits; Facility Rental; Guided Tours; Lectures; Publication; Research Library/Archives; School-Based Curriculum

COLLECTIONS: Ducks and geese, Native American artifacts, and fossils.

HOURS: Yr M-Sa 10-5, Su 1-4

OSAKIS

4426
Osakis Area Heritage Center
Todd County Hwy 46 E, 56360 [PO Box 327, 56360]; (p) (320) 859-3777; (f) (320) 859-4794; osakis@midwestinfo.net; www.lakeosakis.com; (c) Todd

Private non-profit/ 1990/ staff: 1(p)/ members: 100

HISTORIC PRESERVATION AGENCY; HISTORICAL SOCIETY; RESEARCH CENTER: Discovers, preserves, and shares the history of Osakis and surrounding area.

PROGRAMS: Annual Meeting; Community Outreach; Exhibits; Family Programs; Lectures; Publication; Reenactments; Research Library/Archives

COLLECTIONS: [Early 1900s] Photographs, historical items.

HOURS: Yr M-F 9-5

ADMISSION: Donations accepted

OWATONNA

4427
Steele County Historical Society
Steele County Fairgrounds, 55060 [1448 Austin Rd, 55060]; (p) (507) 451-1420; (c) Steele

Private non-profit/ 1959/ Board of Directors/ staff: 2(p); 50(v)/ members: 400

HISTORICAL SOCIETY; HISTORY MUSEUM; HOUSE MUSEUM: Operates the Village of Yesteryear, a collection of 15 buildings moved to the site, which give visitors a taste of the past.

PROGRAMS: Annual Meeting; Community Outreach; Concerts; Elder's Programs; Exhibits; Facility Rental; Family Programs; Festivals; Film/Video; Guided Tours; Interpretation; Lectures; Living History; Publication; Research Library/Archives

COLLECTIONS: [Late 19th C] Log cabins, depot, caboose, church, farm machinery, schoolhouse, fire hall, museum of professions, and the Dunnell House.

HOURS: May-Sept T-Su 1-5

ADMISSION: $5, Students, $2, 12 and under free

PARK RAPIDS

4428
Hubbard County Historical Society
3rd St & Court, 56470 [PO Box 327, 56470]; (p) (218) 732-5237; (c) Hubbard

Private non-profit/ 1934/ staff: 1(f); 1(p); 4(v)/ members: 75

HISTORICAL SOCIETY; HISTORY MUSEUM

PROGRAMS: Exhibits; Guided Tours; Research Library/Archives

COLLECTIONS: [19th-20th C] Nine rooms with artifacts from Hubbard County: cabin, schoolroom, logging room, office room, and clothing room.

HOURS: May-Oct T-Su 11-5

ADMISSION: $1

PERHAM

4429
History Museum of East Otter Trail County, The
230 1st Ave N, 56573; (p) (218) 346-7676; museum@eot.com; www.lakersurfer.com/museum/musebro.htm

Private non-profit/ 1998/ staff: 1(f); 1(p); 18(v)/ members: 126

HISTORY MUSEUM: Presents area history through interpretive exhibits, motion picture footage and photographic displays.

PROGRAMS: Annual Meeting; Community Outreach; Exhibits; Film/Video; Guided Tours; Lectures; Research Library/Archives

COLLECTIONS: [Late 19th c-present] Books, audio-visual materials, newspapers, photographs and museum artifacts pertaining to early medicine, pioneers, Native Americans, Earl industry, and tourism.

HOURS: Yr Daily M-Sa 10-5, Su 1-4

ADMISSION: No charge

PETERSON

4430
1877 Peterson Station Museum
228 Mill St, 55962 [RR #1, Box 87B, 55962]; (p) (507) 895-2551; (c) Fillmore

City/ 1974/ City of Peterson/ staff: 1(p)

HISTORY MUSEUM; RAILROAD MUSEUM

PROGRAMS: Exhibits; Library/ Archives

COLLECTIONS: [1853-present] Photographs, business advertising items, genealogy books, early settler artifacts, and railroad memorabilia.

HOURS: May-Sept Sa-Su 12-4 or by appt

PINE CITY

4431
North West Company Fur Post
County Hwy 7, 55063 [PO Box 51, 55063]; (p) (320) 629-6356; nwfurpost@mnhs.org; www.mnhs.org; (c) Pine

Private non-profit/ 1849/ Minnesota Historical Society/ staff: 1(f); 8(p); 4(v)

HISTORIC SITE; HISTORICAL SOCIETY; LIVING HISTORY/OUTDOOR MUSEUM: Interprets site.

PROGRAMS: Exhibits; Family Programs; Festivals; Interpretation; Lectures; Living History; Reenactments

HOURS: May-Sept T-Sa 10-5, Su 12-5

ADMISSION: No charge

PINE RIVER

4432

Driftwood Family Resort Museum and Golf (Norske Course), The

6020 Driftwood Ln, 56474; (p) (218) 568-4221; (f) (218) 568-4222; ponyride@uslink.net; www.driftwoodresort.com; (c) Crow Wing

1900/ staff: 25(f); 2(p)

HISTORY MUSEUM: Tells the story of the hospitality industry in Minnesota.

PROGRAMS: Exhibits; Guided Tours; Interpretation; Lectures

COLLECTIONS: [1950-1985] Items found on property.

HOURS: May-Sept 10-5 or by appt

ADMISSION: $3, Children $2, Seniors $2

PIPESTONE

4433

Pipestone County Historical Society

113 S Hiawatha Ave, 56164; (p) (507) 825-2563; (f) (507) 825-2563; pipctymu@rcon nect.com; www.pipestoneminnesota.com/museum; (c) Pipestone

Private non-profit/ 1880/ staff: 3(f); 2(p); 1(v)/ members: 400/publication: *Coteau Heritage*

HISTORIC SITE; HISTORICAL SOCIETY; HISTORY MUSEUM; RESEARCH CENTER: Fosters an awareness of our county's history and its connection with the history of Minnesota, the region, and the nation.

PROGRAMS: Annual Meeting; Community Outreach; Exhibits; Guided Tours; Interpretation; Lectures; Living History; Publication; Reenactments; Research Library/Archives; School-Based Curriculum

COLLECTIONS: [Late 19th c-20th c] 17,000 artifacts: Native American, military, clothing, communication equipment, local newspapers, land records, photographic images 6,000, glass negatives 3,000, domestic artifacts, books, and manuscripts.

HOURS: Yr Daily 10-5

ADMISSION: $2; Under 13 free

4434

Pipestone Indian Shrine Association

Pipestone Natl Monument, 36 Reservation Ave, 56164 [PO Box 727, 56164]; (p) (507) 825-5463; (f) (507) 825-2903; pipe_cooperat ing-association@nps.gov; (c) Pipestone

Joint/ 1955/ National Park Service/ staff: 3(f); 3(p)/ members: 634

HISTORY MUSEUM: To promote the art of pipemaking to aid in the interpretive activities of the Pipestore National Monument.

PROGRAMS: Annual Meeting

HOURS: Yr Daily Winter 8-5; May-Sept M-Th 8-6, F-Su 8-8

ADMISSION: $2

PRINCETON

4435

Mille Lacs County Historical Sociey and Depot Museum

101 S 10th Ave, 55371; (p) (612) 389-1296; (c) Mille Lacs

Private non-profit/ 1955/ staff: 1(p)/ members: 80

HISTORIC SITE; HISTORICAL SOCIETY; HISTORY MUSEUM; RESEARCH CENTER: Collects, preserves, and teaches the history of the county.

PROGRAMS: Exhibits; Facility Rental; Festivals; Research Library/Archives

COLLECTIONS: [Mid 1850s-present] Microfilm: federal and Minnesota censuses, Princeton newspapers; vital records; photographs, albums and scrapbooks artifacts of area history and daily life.

HOURS: Yr W-Sa 11-4

ADMISSION: No charge/Donations accepted

RED LAKE

4436

Red Lake Nation Tribal Archives and Library

Hwy 1 E Tribal Council Hdqters, 56671 [PO Box 297, 56671]; (p) (218) 679-3341; (f) (218) 679-3378; (c) Beltrami

Tribal/ 1989/ Red Lake Band of Chippewa Indians/ staff: 2(f); 2(p); 1(v)

ART MUSEUM; HISTORIC PRESERVATION AGENCY; HISTORY MUSEUM; RESEARCH CENTER; TRIBAL MUSEUM: Collects, preserves, and makes available the history of the Red Lake Band of Chippewa Indians.

PROGRAMS: Community Outreach; Exhibits; Interpretation; Lectures; Research Library/Archives; School-Based Curriculum

COLLECTIONS: Oral history tapes and transcripts, photographs, baskets, paintings, dance regalia, videos, rare book collection, periodicals, library: books by American Indian authors; law library

HOURS: Yr M-F 8-4 and by appt

ADMISSION: No charge

RED WING

4437

Goodhue County Historical Society

1166 Oak St, 55066; (p) (651) 388-6024; (f) (651) 388-3577; research@clear.lakes.com; www.goodhuecounty.mus.mn.us; (c) Goodhue

Private non-profit/ 1869/ staff: 5(f); 5(p); 200(v)/ members: 800/publication: *Goodhue County Historical Society News*

HISTORICAL SOCIETY; HISTORY MUSEUM; RESEARCH CENTER: To collect, protect, preserve, and interpret materials relating to the natural and cultural history of Goodhue County and its people.

PROGRAMS: Annual Meeting; Community Outreach; Exhibits; Family Programs; Festivals; Guided Tours; Interpretation; Lectures; Publication; Research Library/Archives; School-Based Curriculum

COLLECTIONS: [1840s-1950s] Material objects used by early settlers and their descendants. Major areas include military, immigration, agriculture, textiles, research, archaeology, rural schools and Red Wing pottery.

HOURS: Yr Daily T-F 10-5, Sa-Su 1-5

ADMISSION: $2; Under 16 free

4438

Red Wing Heritage Preservation Commission

315 W Fourth St, 55066 [PO Box 34, 55066]; (p) (651) 385-3617; brian.peterson@red-wing.ci.mn.us; (c) Goodhue

City/ 1979/ City of Red Wing/ staff: 1(p); 7(v)

HISTORIC PRESERVATION AGENCY: Responsible for preservation of the historic, architectural, and archaeological significant sites and districts within the city of Red Wing.

PROGRAMS: Annual Meeting; Community Outreach

COLLECTIONS: [1850-1950] Information related to historic sites and districts located within the city.

REDWOOD FALLS

4439

Redwood County Historical Society and Museum

33965 Laser Ave, 56283 [RR 2, Box 12, 56283]; (p) (507) 637-3329; (c) Redwood

County/ 1948/ staff: 1(f); 1(p)/ members: 75

HOURS: May 1-Sept 30 Th-Su 1-5

ADMISSION: $2, Student $0.50; Under 13 free

RENVILLE

4440

Renville County Genealogical Society

221 N Main St, 56284 [PO Box 331, 56284]; (p) (320) 329-3215; (f) (320) 329-3242; (c) Renville

Private non-profit/ 1985/ Board of Directors/ staff: 20(v)/ members: 150/publication: *The Geneline*

Focus is on family history and Renville County and area history.

COLLECTIONS: [1860-present] Microfilms of all county newspapers, cemetery headstones, local history books, church books, school records, veterans, war and family histories and genealogical aids.

HOURS: Yr M-F 12-5:30

ADMISSION: No charge

ROCHESTER

4441

Historic Mayowood Mansion

3720 Mayowood Rd SW, 55902 [1195 County Rd 22 SW, 55902]; (p) (507) 282-9447

1910/ staff: 1(f); 13(p); 8(v)

COLLECTIONS: [1965] 18th & 19th century furnishings, library; Early Mayo Clinic and family photos.

HOURS: Yr

4442
Olmsted County Historical Society
1195 W Circle Dr SW, 55902; (p) (507) 282-9447; (f) (507) 289-5481; ochs@olmstedhistory.com; www.olmstedhistory.com; (c) Olmsted

Private non-profit/ 1926/ Board of Directors/ staff: 8(f); 12(p); 150(v)/ members: 525/publication: *Olmsted Historian*

HISTORICAL SOCIETY: Operates the history center which includes gallery, archives and research library.

PROGRAMS: Annual Meeting; Community Outreach; Concerts; Exhibits; Facility Rental; Family Programs; Garden Tours; Guided Tours; Interpretation; Lectures; Living History; Publication; Reenactments; Research Library/Archives; School-Based Curriculum

COLLECTIONS: [1849-present] Farm implements, machinery, decorative arts, medical history, computer industry artifacts and historic buildings.

HOURS: Yr T-Sa 9-5

ADMISSION: $4

ROCKFORD

4443
Rockford Area Historical Society
8131 Bridge St, 55373 [PO Box 186, 55373]; (p) (612) 477-5383; (c) Wright

Private non-profit/ 1986/ Board of Trustees/ staff: 1(p); 15(v)/ members: 85

HOUSE MUSEUM: To show changes in rural lifestyle in the context of the three families who lived in the Ames-Florida-Stork House.

PROGRAMS: Annual Meeting; Community Outreach; Concerts; Exhibits; Guided Tours; Living History; School-Based Curriculum

COLLECTIONS: [1860-1960] Clothing, dishes, textiles, furniture, artwork, books, correspondence.

HOURS: May-Dec by appt

ADMISSION: $3

ROSEAU

4444
Pioneer Farm and Village
2 mi W of Roseau on Hwy 11, 56751 [c/o AJ Kramer, 312 7th Ave NE, 56751]; (p) (218) 463-2187, (218) 463-2690; www.rrv.net/roseau/history.htm

4445
Roseau County Historical Society
110 2nd Ave N E, 56751; (p) (218) 463-1918; (f) (218) 463-3795; roseau@wikel.com; www.angelfire.com/mn/rchistsocmuseum; (c) Roseau

Private non-profit/ 1927/ staff: 2(f); 2(p); 5(v)/ members: 290

HISTORICAL SOCIETY: Dedicated to the collection, preservation, and dissemination of Roseau County history from the ice age to the present.

PROGRAMS: Annual Meeting; Community Outreach; Exhibits; Family Programs; Festivals; Guided Tours; Interpretation; Lectures; Publication; Research Library/Archives

COLLECTIONS: [1895-1950] Native American, pioneer life, early industry and trades, period rooms, Polaris Industries and Marvin windows, clothing, musical instruments, agriculture, medical, fossils, mounted birds and animals, written histories, church, school, cemetery, business, and organizational records, photographs.

HOURS: Yr Nov-Apr T-Sa 9-4; May-Oct T-F 9-5, Sa 9-4

ADMISSION: $2, Children $1

ROSEVILLE

4446
Roseville Historical Society
1446 Buske Ave W, 55113-5804; (p) (651) 415-2100, (651) 639-0431; (c) Ramsey

City; Private non-profit/ 1977/ City of Roseville/ staff: 16(v)/ members: 88

GENEALOGICAL SOCIETY; HISTORIC PRESERVATION AGENCY; HISTORIC SITE; HISTORICAL SOCIETY; HISTORY MUSEUM; RESEARCH CENTER: Maintains Heritage Room with displays in City Hall.

PROGRAMS: Annual Meeting; Community Outreach; Elder's Programs; Exhibits; Facility Rental; Festivals; Film/Video; Lectures; Publication; Research Library/Archives

COLLECTIONS: [1930s] Paintings, book collection, costumes.

HOURS: Yr by appt

SACRED HEART

4447
Sacred Heart Area Historical Society
500 5th Ave, 56285 [309 1st Ave, 56285]; (p) (320) 765-2274, (320) 765-2729; Sonja@hci net.net; (c) Renville

Private non-profit/ 1996/ staff: 15(v)/ members: 206/publication: *SHAHS*

HISTORICAL SOCIETY; HISTORY MUSEUM: Collects, preserves, and interprets area history in the Sacred Heart Area

PROGRAMS: Annual Meeting; Community Outreach; Exhibits; Festivals; Interpretation; Publication; Research Library/Archives

COLLECTIONS: [1850-present] artifacts, library aids: photographs, newspapers, books, pamphlets, tapes.

HOURS: Jan-Dec T-Th 1:30-4 by appt

ADMISSION: Donations accepted

SAINT CLOUD

4448
Stearns History Museum
235 33rd Ave S, 56301-3752; (p) (320) 253-8424; (f) (320) 253-2172; info@stearns-museum.org; www.stearns-museum.org; (c) Stearns

Private non-profit/ 1936/ Board of Directors/ staff: 8(f); 4(p); 140(v)/ members: 865/publication: *Crossings*

HISTORICAL SOCIETY; HISTORY MUSEUM; RESEARCH CENTER: Nurtures a knowledge of and appreciation for the history of Stearns County and Minnesota. Discovers, collects and preserves material and records of human culture relating to the Co.

PROGRAMS: Annual Meeting; Community Outreach; Concerts; Exhibits; Facility Rental; Family Programs; Festivals; Film/Video; Guided Tours; Interpretation; Lectures; Publication; Research Library/Archives; School-Based Curriculum

COLLECTIONS: [1850-1999] Ethnographic items from Germans, Luxembourgers and Scandinavians that settled the area represented by local industries (dairy farms, granite industry, eye glasses).documents and business records, photographic images, oral histories, genealogies, architectural blueprints, map and microfilm newspapers.

HOURS: Yr Daily M-Sa 10-5, Su 12-5 public hrs, M-F 8:30-5 business hrs

ADMISSION: $4, Family $10, Children $2

SAINT JOSEPH

4449
St. Benedict's Monastic Heritage Museum, Sisters of the Order of St. Benedict
104 Chapel Ln, 56374; (p) (320) 363-7098; (c) Stearns

Private non-profit/ 2000/ Sisters of the Order of Saint Benedict/ staff: 2(f); 1(p)/ members: 9

HISTORY MUSEUM: Maintaining and preserving historical artifacts of our Benedictine religious community, to collect, document, preserve, and exhibit objects related to the history of the American Benedictine Women who came to Minnesota.

PROGRAMS: Community Outreach; Concerts; Elder's Programs; Exhibits; Family Programs; Festivals; Film/Video; Guided Tours; Lectures; Living History; Research Library/Archives; School-Based Curriculum; Theatre

COLLECTIONS: [1868] 4,000 artifacts pertaining to the history of the Sisters of the Order of Saint Benedict.

HOURS: Yr T-F 10-4, Sa-Su 1-3

ADMISSION: No charge

SAINT LOUIS PARK

4450
St. Louis Park Historical Society
37th & Brunswick Ave, 55416 [3700 Monterey Dr, 55416]; (p) (612) 924-2538; (f) (612) 925-5663; bwynn@ci.saint-louis-park.mn.us; (c) Hennepin

City/ 1971/ staff: 1(p); 7(v)/ members: 75

HISTORICAL SOCIETY: Collection, preservation and dissemination of St. Louis Park history.

PROGRAMS: Annual Meeting; Community Outreach; Festivals

COLLECTIONS: [1890s]

SAINT PAUL

4451
Alexander Ramsey House
265 S Exchange St, 55102; (p) (651) 296-8760; (f) (651) 296-0100; (c) Ramsey

Private non-profit/ 1964/ Minnesota Historical Society/ staff: 5(f); 20(p); 50(v)/ members: 17000

HISTORIC SITE: Restored 1872 home of a Minnesota governor.

PROGRAMS: Guided Tours; Interpretation; Lectures

COLLECTIONS: [1872-1895] Original furnishings, artifacts, manuscript collection.

HOURS: May-Dec T-Su 10-3

ADMISSION: $6, Children $4, Seniors $5

4452
Archdiocese of St. Paul/Minneapolis Archives
226 Summit Ave, 55102; (p) (651) 291-4429; (f) (651) 290-1629; archeom@archspm.org; (c) Ramsey

1988/ Archdiocese of St. Paul/Minneapolis/ staff: 1(f); 1(p); 1(v)

LIBRARY AND/OR ARCHIVES: A Roman Catholic Archdiocese that maintains collections on the history of Catholicism in the Upper Midwest.

PROGRAMS: Exhibits; Research Library/Archives

COLLECTIONS: [1850-present] Papers of bishops/archbishops, parish histories, photographs, artifacts, and audio and video tape.

HOURS: Yr T, W by appt

ADMISSION: $10/day

4453
Aviation Art Museum
[PO Box 16224, 55116]; (p) (651) 291-7925; www.pioneerplanet.infi.net/~docwrite; (c) Ramsey

Private for-profit/ 1971/ staff: 1(f)

ART MUSEUM; RESEARCH CENTER: Designs and produces aviation art prints to various aviation gift shops and galleries; assists in aviation history research.

PROGRAMS: Exhibits; Lectures; Research Library/Archives

COLLECTIONS: [1900s-present] Aviation art collection created by one artist.

ADMISSION: No change

4454
Como-Harriet Streetcar Line, Linden Hills Station
2330 W 42nd St, 55101 [193 Pennsylvania Ave E., 55101]; (p) (800) 711-2591, (651) 228-0263; www.mtmuseum.org; (c) Hennepin

Operate, maintain and restore streetcars.

COLLECTIONS: [1900s] Collection of running and restored streetcars.

HOURS: Yr May-Sept Daily M-F 6:30p-dusk, Sa-Su 12:30-dusk; Sept-May Sa-Su 12:30-dusk

4455
Dakota County Historical Society
130 3W Ave Worth S, 55075; (p) (651) 451-6260; (f) (651) 552-7265; dchs@mtn.org; (c) Dakota

Private non-profit/ 1939/ staff: 2(f); 1(p); 30(v)/ members: 554/publication: Over the Years, Dakota County History

GENEALOGICAL SOCIETY; HISTORICAL SOCIETY; HISTORY MUSEUM; RESEARCH CENTER: Repository for Dakota County related

primary source material.

PROGRAMS: Annual Meeting; Community Outreach; Concerts; Elder's Programs; Exhibits; Facility Rental; Family Programs; Film/Video; Guided Tours; Interpretation; Lectures; Publication; Research Library/Archives; School-Based Curriculum

COLLECTIONS: [Late 19th-20th c] Artifacts, photographs, naturalization, census, and church records, family genealogies, plat maps, newspapers on microfilm.

HOURS: Yr T, W 9-5, Th 9-8, F 9-5, Sa 9-3

ADMISSION: No charge

4456
Governor's Residence
1006 Summit Ave, 55105; (p) (651) 297-2161; (f) (651) 297-2229; (c) Ramsey

State/ 1965/ staff: 10(f)

HISTORIC SITE

PROGRAMS: Guided Tours

HOURS: Yr F 1-3

ADMISSION: No charge

4457
H.B. Fuller Company Corporate Archives
3220 Labore Rd, 55110; (p) (651) 236-5554; (f) (651) 482-8945; liz.johnson@hbfuller.com; (c) Ramsey

Private for-profit/ 1987/ staff: 2(f); 2(v)

CORPORATE ARCHIVES/MUSEUM

COLLECTIONS: [1887-present] Business records, annual reports, minutes, presidents papers, publications and speeches.

4458
Hamline University Archive
Bush Library, 55104 [1536 Hewitt Ave, 55104]; (p) (651) 523-2080; (f) (651) 523-2199; tboeder@gw.hamline.edu; (c) Ramsey

Private non-profit/ 1854/ staff: 1(p); 2(v)

LIBRARY AND/OR ARCHIVES: Archive of university records.

PROGRAMS: Research Library/Archives

COLLECTIONS: [1854-present] Records of the university, primarily those created after the school's move to St. Paul in 1880.

4459
Historic Fort Snelling
Fort Snelling History Center, 55111; (p) (612) 726-1171; (f) (612) 725-2429; brend.williams@mnhs.org; www.mnhs.org/places/sites/hfs; (c) Hennepin

Joint/ 1849/ State/ MN Historical Society/ staff: 6(f); 45(p); 37(v)

HISTORIC SITE; LIVING HISTORY/OUTDOOR MUSEUM: Re-creation of the buildings and people of the frontier military garrison and surrounding community in 1827.

PROGRAMS: Exhibits; Family Programs; Film/Video; Guided Tours; Interpretation; Lectures; Living History; Reenactments; School-Based Curriculum; Theatre

COLLECTIONS: [Early 1800s] 4 original structures; archaeology collections from extensive site excavations.

HOURS: May-Oct Daily M-Sa 10-5, Su 12-5

ADMISSION: $6, Children $4, Seniors $5

4460
Institute for Minnesota Archaeology
287 E 6th St, Ste 260, 55101; (p) (651) 848-0095; (f) (651) 848-0096; ima@imnarch.org; www.imnarch.org; (c) Hennepin

Private non-profit/ 1982/ Board of Directors/ staff: 2(f); 1(p); 25(v)/ members: 150/publication: Friends Newsletter

RESEARCH CENTER: Investigates the past through long-term interdisciplinary research programs, engages and educates the public through participation in archaeology, and promotes stewardship.

PROGRAMS: Annual Meeting; Community Outreach; Exhibits; Guided Tours; Interpretation; Lectures; Publication; Research Library/Archives; School-Based Curriculum

COLLECTIONS: Donated archaeological collections ranging from paleo to historic times.

HOURS: Yr M-F 9:30-5:30

4461
Jackson Street Roundhouse
193 E Pennsylvania Ave, 55101; (p) (651) 228-0263; www.mtmuseum.org; (c) Ramsey

19620/ Minnesota Transportation Museum/ staff: 3(f); 300(v)/ members: 1100

RAILROAD MUSEUM: Museum with working round house.

COLLECTIONS: Railroad equipment

ADMISSION: $3

4462
James J. Hill House
240 Summit Ave, 55102; (p) (651) 297-2555; (f) (651) 297-5655; hill.house@mnhs.org; www.mnhs.org; (c) Ramsey

Private non-profit/ 1978/ Minnesota Historical Society/ staff: 58(f); 13(p)

ART MUSEUM; HISTORIC SITE; HISTORICAL SOCIETY; HOUSE MUSEUM: Interprets four floors in the house, especially regarding servants, technology, the arts, and neighborhood history.

PROGRAMS: Community Outreach; Concerts; Elder's Programs; Exhibits; Facility Rental; Family Programs; Festivals; School-Based Curriculum; Theatre

COLLECTIONS: [1891-1921] Permanent furnishings and other artifacts.

HOURS: Yr W-Sa 10-3:30

ADMISSION: $6, Children $4, Seniors $5; Under 6 free

4463
James J. Hill Reference Library, Manuscripts Division
80 W 4th St, 55102; (p) (651) 265-5442; (f) (651) 222-4139; emccormack@jjhill.org; www.jjhill.org; (c) Ramsey

Private non-profit/ 1921/ Board of Directors/ staff: 2(f)/ members: 600

RESEARCH CENTER: Contains extensive resources for buiness research.

PROGRAMS: Exhibits; Facility Rental; Lectures; Research Library/Archives

COLLECTIONS: [1860-1950] Correspondence, financial records, pamphlets, maps and blueprints, diaries, artifacts, and over 7,000 photographs.

4464
Jewish Historical Society of the Upper Midwest
Hamline Univ, 1536 Hewitt Ave, 55104; (p) (651) 523-2407; history@jhsum.org; www.jhsum.org; (c) Ramsey

Private non-profit/ 1984/ Board of Trustees/ staff: 2(p)/ 4(v)/ members: 1000

HISTORICAL SOCIETY: Connects the region's Jewish past with the present and future.

PROGRAMS: Annual Meeting; Community Outreach; Exhibits; Family Programs; Lectures; Research Library/Archives; School-Based Curriculum

COLLECTIONS: [1890s-1960s] Manuscripts, photos, oral and video histories of Jewish communal organization and families in MN and the Dakotas.

HOURS: Yr M, W 9-5

4465
Minnesota Air & Space Museum
Box 75654, 55175; (p) (651) 291-7925; Steco1911@aol.com; www.pioneerplanet.infi.net/~docwrite; (c) Ramsey

Private non-profit/ 1981/ staff: 6(v)/ members: 25

AVIATION MUSEUM; RESEARCH CENTER: Researchs, acquires, restores, maintains, demonstrates, educate, and displays artifacts from all phases of aviation.

PROGRAMS: Elder's Programs; Exhibits; Family Programs; Film/Video; Lectures; Publication; Research Library/Archives

COLLECTIONS: [Early 1900-present] Navigation equipment, props, radios and instruments, military uniforms, aviation tableware, historical maps, medals, memorabilia of Charles Lindbergh and Amelia Earhart, Charles "Speed" Holman, photos.

ADMISSION: No charge

4466
Minnesota Air National Guard Historical Foundation, Inc.
670 General Miller Dr, 55111 [PO Box 11598, 55111]; (p) (612) 713-2523; (f) (612) 713-2525; www.mnangmuseum.org; (c) Hennepin

Private non-profit/ 1980/ Board of Directors/ staff: 1(f); 1(p); 105(v)/ members: 465/publication: The Historian

AVIATION MUSEUM; HISTORIC PRESERVATION AGENCY; HISTORIC SITE: Preservation and display of the history of the Minnesota Air Guard and maintenance and display of aircraft flown by the MN Air Guard.

PROGRAMS: Annual Meeting; Community Outreach; Exhibits; Facility Rental; Family Programs; Film/Video; Guided Tours; Interpretation; Lectures; Living History; Publication; Reenactments; Research Library/Archives

COLLECTIONS: [1920-present] Historic fighter alert barn, 20 aircraft including a 1920 Curtis Oriole and a 12 Blackbird.

HOURS: Yr Summer: Sa-Su 11-4; Winter

2nd/4th Sa-Su 11-4

ADMISSION: $2 donation

4467
Minnesota Archaeological Society
Fort Snelling History Center, 55111; (p) (612) 726-1171; (c) Ramsey

Private non-profit/ 1936/ Board of Directors/ staff: 20(v)/ members: 250/publication: Minnesota Archaeologist

HISTORICAL SOCIETY: Preserves and studies the archaeological resources of the upper Midwest.

PROGRAMS: Annual Meeting; Community Outreach; Family Programs; Guided Tours; Lectures; Publication

4468
Minnesota Historical Society
345 Kellogg Blvd W, 55102; (p) (651) 296-6126; (f) (651) 297-3343; webmaster@mnhs.org; www.mnhs.org

Private non-profit/ 1849/ Executive Council/ staff: 310(f); 295(p); 1400(v)/ members: 15000/ publication: Minnesota History; and others.

HISTORIC PRESERVATION AGENCY; HISTORIC SITE; HISTORICAL SOCIETY; HISTORY MUSEUM; HOUSE MUSEUM: Collects, preserves, and tells the story of Minnesota's past; administers libraries and collections and 24 historic sites.

PROGRAMS: Annual Meeting; Community Outreach; Concerts; Exhibits; Facility Rental; Family Programs; Festivals; Film/Video; Garden Tours; Guided Tours; Interpretation; Lectures; Living History; Publication; Reenactments; Research Library/Archives; School-Based Curriculum

COLLECTIONS: [9000BP-present] 227,000 historic objects, 957,00 archaeological specimens, 20,000 maps, 338,000 photographs, 6,000 art works, 66,000 reels of newspaper on microfilm, 35,000 cubic feet of manuscripts, 52,000 cubic feet of government records, 170,000 books, 68,000 periodicals, and 166,000 pamphlets.

HOURS: Yr W-Sa 10-5, T 10-8, Su 12-5; July-Sept Daily

ADMISSION: Varies

4469
Minnesota Historical Society Library
345 Kellogg Blvd W, 55102-1906; (p) (651) 296-2143; (f) (651) 297-7436; reference@mnhs.org; www.mnhs.org; (c) Ramsey

Private non-profit/ 1849/ MN Historical Society/ staff: 16(f); 20(p); 62(v)/ members: 16000

LIBRARY AND/OR ARCHIVES

PROGRAMS: Research Library/Archives

COLLECTIONS: [Prehistory-present] Materials and records related to MN history.

HOURS: Yr M-Sa

4470
Minnesota Transportation Museum
193 Pennsylvania Ave E, 55101; (p) (651) 228-0263, (800) 711-2591; www.mtmuseum.org; (c) Ramsey

Private non-profit/ 1962/ Board of Trustees/ staff: 2(f); 2(p); 250(v)/ members: 850/publica-

tion: Minnegazette

HISTORY MUSEUM: Preserves and communicates Minnesota's surface public transportation history.

PROGRAMS: Annual Meeting; Community Outreach; Exhibits; Facility Rental; Family Programs; Festivals; Guided Tours; Interpretation; Living History; Publication; Reenactments; Research Library/Archives

COLLECTIONS: [1890-1960] Buses, steamboats, streetcars, locomotives, and coaches.

4471
Minnesota Veterinary Historical Museum
1365 Gortner Ave, 55108; (p) (651) 486-0312; (c) Ramsey

Private non-profit/ 1987/ Board of Trustees/ staff: 4(p)/publication: 100 Years of Progress

HISTORIC PRESERVATION AGENCY; HISTORY MUSEUM: Records the progress of the Minnesota veterinary profession.

PROGRAMS: Exhibits; Guided Tours; Publication

COLLECTIONS: [1850-present] Instruments, drugs, photos, cages, books, and manuscripts.

HOURS: Yr W 12-3

ADMISSION: No charge

4472
Mounds-Midway School of Nursing Historical Society
1700 University Ave, 55104; (p) (651) 232-5951; (f) (651) 636-6035; (c) Ramsey

Private non-profit; State/ 1991/ staff: 12(v)/ members: 104/publication: School of Nursing Newsletter

HISTORICAL SOCIETY; HISTORY MUSEUM: Collects and preserves the historical knowledge of nursing.

PROGRAMS: Exhibits; Film/Video; Guided Tours; Publication

COLLECTIONS: [1807-1983] Documents, photos, equipment, surgical instruments, uniforms, annual class books, furniture, books, nurse uniform dolls, Florence Nightingale collection, educational material, military uniforms and journals, newsletters, wheelchairs, hospital bed, folding screens, and Bible and Communion set.

HOURS: W 1-3

4473
Ramsey County Historical Society
323 Landmark Center, 75 W 5 St, 55102; (p) (651) 222-0701; (f) (651) 223-8539; admin@rchs.com; www.rchs.com; (c) Ramsey

Private non-profit/ 1949/ Board of Directors/ staff: 6(f); 1(p); 36(v)/ members: 1200

HISTORIC SITE; HISTORICAL SOCIETY; HISTORY MUSEUM; HOUSE MUSEUM; LIVING HISTORY/OUTDOOR MUSEUM

PROGRAMS: Annual Meeting; Community Outreach; Exhibits; Facility Rental; Family Programs; Festivals; Guided Tours; Interpretation; Lectures; Living History; Publication; Research Library/Archives; School-Based Curriculum

COLLECTIONS: [1800-1940] 40,000 photographs, negatives, 25 processed manuscripts collections, 60,000 artifacts, 2,000 volumes.

HOURS: May-Oct M-F 9-5, Sa 10-4, Su 12-4

ADMISSION:$4, Children $2, Seniors $3.50

4474
St. Paul Police History Museum
100 E 11th St, 55101; (p) (651) 292-3505; (f) (651) 292-3542; policeinfo@ci.st.paul.mn.us; www.st.paul.gov/police; (c) Ramsey

City/ 1978/ staff: 1(v)

HISTORY MUSEUM: Collects and preserves St. Paul police historical items in museum housed in police headquarters.

PROGRAMS: Exhibits; Guided Tours; Lectures; Living History; Research Library/ Archives

COLLECTIONS: [1854-present] Photos, newspaper articles, historical artifacts, weapons, badges, patches, uniforms, 19th c equipment.

HOURS: Yr M-F 8-4

SAINT PETER

4475
E. St. Julien Cox House
E St. Julien St, 56082 [Nicollet County Hist Soc, 1851 N Minnesota Ave, 56082]; (p) (507) 931-4309, (507) 931-2160; (f) (507) 931-0172; NicolletCty@aol.com; emuseum.mnsu.edu/history/treatycenter/cox/

Private non-profit/ 1871/ Nicollet County Historical Society/ staff: 3(f); 4(p)

HOUSE MUSEUM: Gothic/Italianate house restored according to the original blueprints, furnished to reflect the late Victorian period.

PROGRAMS: Garden Tours; Guided Tours

COLLECTIONS: [1880s] Furniture; family objects; Wisconsin law books used by Judge Cox; and his impeachment trial records.

HOURS: May/Sept Sa-Su 1-4; June-Aug W-Su 1-4

ADMISSION: NCHS mbrs free

4476
Nicollet County Historical Society
1851 N Minnesota Ave, 56082; (p) (507) 931-2160; (f) (507) 931-0172; NicolletCty@aol.com; emuseum.mnsu.edu/history/treatycenter/; (c) Nicollet

Private non-profit/ 1928/ Board of Directors/ staff: 3(f); 3(p); 150(v)/ members: 400/publication: *The Crossing*

GARDEN; HISTORIC SITE; HISTORICAL SOCIETY; HISTORY MUSEUM; LIVING HISTORY/OUTDOOR MUSEUM; RESEARCH CENTER: Discovers, preserves and disseminats knowledge about Nicollet Co. and state history.

PROGRAMS: Annual Meeting; Exhibits; Facility Rental; Family Programs; Garden Tours; Guided Tours; Interpretation; Lectures; Living History; Publication; Research Library/ Archives; School-Based Curriculum

COLLECTIONS: 1,000 manuscripts, 5,000 photographs, 1,500 books, 10,000 museum artifacts.

HOURS: Yr Daily M-Sa 10-4, Su 1-4

ADMISSION: $3; under 12 free

4477
Traverse des Sioux Genealogical Society
c/o Nicollett Co Hist Soc & Museum, 1851 N Minnesota Ave, 56082; (p) (507) 931-2160; (c) Nicollett

1970

SANBORN

4478
Sod House on the Prairie
R R #2 Box 75, 56083; (p) (507) 723-5138; sodhouse@juno.com

1987/ staff: 1(p)

COLLECTIONS: [1880s] Two authentically built and furnished replicas of the sod house on the prairie era. Step inside, examine, hand's on. Stay overnight for the experience - it's a bed and breakfast.

HOURS: Seasonal

SANDSTONE

4479
Sandstone History and Art Center
402 Main, 55072 [Box 398, 55072]; (p) (320) 245-2504; (c) Pine

City; Private non-profit/ 1990/ staff: 2(p); 10(v)/ members: 45/publication: *Sandstone, The Quarry City and others*

ART MUSEUM; GENEALOGICAL SOCIETY; HISTORIC SITE; HISTORICAL SOCIETY; HISTORY MUSEUM: Two story museum in 1894 building built with sandstone from local quarry.

PROGRAMS: Annual Meeting; Community Outreach; Exhibits; Guided Tours; Interpretation; Lectures; Publication

COLLECTIONS: [1885-present] Census, Quarry union records, quarry artifacts, 1894 fire records, school records, photographs, business artifacts, organization records.

HOURS: May-Oct Th-Sa

ADMISSION: $1, Family $3, Children $0.50

SAUK CENTRE

4480
Sinclair Lewis Boyhood Home Museum
810 Sinclair Lewis Ave, 56378 [PO Box 222, 56378]; (p) (320) 352-5201; (f) (320) 352-5202; (c) Stearns

1884/ staff: 2(p)

COLLECTIONS: [Early 1900s] Wooden framed bed, hot water heating system, maple flooring, pictures of family, vacuumed radio, father's medical diploma, wooden golf clubs/bag.; China cupboard with china, desk chair and rolltop desk.

HOURS: Seasonal

4481
Sinclair Lewis Foundation
Interstate I-94 & US Hwy 71, 56378 [1220 S Main St, PO Box 222, 56378]; (p) (320) 352-5201; (f) (320) 352-5202; chamber@saukcentre.com; www.saukcentre.com; (c) Stearns

Private non-profit/ 1960/ Officers & Board of

Directors/ staff: 2(p); 2(v)/ members: 100

HISTORIC SITE; HISTORY MUSEUM; HOUSE MUSEUM: Owns and operates the Sinclair Lewis Boyhood Home and the Sinclair Lewis Museum.

PROGRAMS: Annual Meeting; Exhibits; Festivals; Film/Video; Guided Tours; Research Library/Archives

COLLECTIONS: [Early 1900s] Items that once belonged to the Lewis family; period clothing, pictures, wood/coal cookstove, desk, chair, medicine box, and other artifacts and memorabilia.

HOURS: May-Sept M-F 8:30-5, Sa-Su 9-5

ADMISSION: $3, Student $2, Children $1.50, Seniors $2.50; Under 5 free

SAUK RAPIDS

4482
Benton County Historical Society
218 1St N, 56379 [115 N 2nd Ave, 56379]; (p) (320) 253-9614; (f) (320) 251-0422; (c) Benton

Private non-profit/ 1963/ staff: 7(v)

ART MUSEUM; GENEALOGICAL SOCIETY; HISTORIC PRESERVATION AGENCY; HISTORIC SITE; HISTORICAL SOCIETY; HISTORY MUSEUM; HOUSE MUSEUM; RESEARCH CENTER

PROGRAMS: Annual Meeting; Community Outreach; Exhibits; Facility Rental; Festivals; Guided Tours; Interpretation; Publication; Reenactments; Research Library/Archives

COLLECTIONS: Military and farming items.

HOURS: Yr W 10-8, Sa 10-4

SAUM

4483
Saum Community Club
HC 79 Box S-41, 57750-9801; (p) (218) 647-8877; (c) Boltrami

Private non-profit/ 1962/ staff: 15(v)/ members: 30

HISTORICAL SOCIETY: Maintains school building.

PROGRAMS: Annual Meeting; Facility Rental; Festivals

HOURS: Yr

ADMISSION: No charge

SEBEKA

4484
Minnesota Finnish American Historical Society, Chapter 38
Riverside Dr, 56477 [RR 3 Box 312, 56477]; (c) Wadena

Private non-profit/ 1947/ staff: 44(v)/ members: 44

HISTORICAL SOCIETY; HISTORY MUSEUM: Collect artifacts and maintain a museum.

PROGRAMS: Annual Meeting; Exhibits; Family Programs; Festivals; Film/Video; Guided Tours

COLLECTIONS: [1880-1945] A pioneer school house, a sauna, and old barn. The artifacts are pre-WWII and used in area farms especially Finnish-American pioneer farm houses.

HOURS: May-Sept Daily 9-5

SHAKOPEE

4485
Scott County Historical Society
235 Fuller St S, 55379; (p) (952) 445-0378; (f) (952) 445-4154; histor@co.scott.mn.us; (c) Scott

Private non-profit/ 1967/ staff: 3(f); 20(v)/ members: 125

HISTORICAL SOCIETY; HISTORY MUSEUM

PROGRAMS: Elder's Programs; Exhibits; Facility Rental; Family Programs; Guided Tours; Lectures; Research Library/Archives; School-Based Curriculum

COLLECTIONS: Artifacts, memorabilia, and photographs relating to Scott County history and to Maurice Stans, former Secretary of Commerce.

HOURS: Yr T-W 9-4, Th 9-8, F 9-4, Sa 11-3

ADMISSION: No charge

SHEVLIN

4486
Clearwater County Historical Society
Hwy 2 W, 56676 [PO Box 241, Bagley, 56621]; (p) (218) 785-2000; (c) Clearwater

Private non-profit/ 1968/ staff: 1(f); 2(p); 2(v)/ members: 768/publication: *Clearwater History News*

HISTORICAL SOCIETY; HISTORY MUSEUM: Offers a pioneer museum experience, operating a main museum with exhibits plus 1890 cabin and two schools.

PROGRAMS: Annual Meeting; Community Outreach; Exhibits; Lectures; Publication; Research Library/Archives; School-Based Curriculum

COLLECTIONS: [1900-1949] Pioneer artifacts and photographs; logging and agricultural items.

HOURS: Feb-Dec T-Sa 10-4

ADMISSION: No charge

SILVER BAY

4487
Bay Area Historical Society
Outer Dr, 55614 [PO Box 33, 55614]; www.silverbay.com; (c) Lake

Private non-profit/ 1985/ staff: 2(p); 15(v)/ members: 200

HISTORICAL SOCIETY: The mission of the Bay Area Historical Society is to preserve and promote the history of the Bay Area.

PROGRAMS: Annual Meeting; Community Outreach; Exhibits; Lectures; Research Library/Archives

COLLECTIONS: [1950-present Silver Bay, 1856-present Beaver Bay] Focus on collecting written and recorded history of the area to make available for research on area mining, fishing, and logging.

HOURS: May-1st week in October: Daily

SLAYTON

4488
Murray County Historical Society and Museum
2480 29th St, 56172 [PO Box 61, 56172]; (p) (507) 836-6533; (f) (507) 443-5012; society@frontier.net; swmnmall.com; (c) Murray

Private non-profit/ 1934/ Board of Directors/ staff: 3(p); 45(v)/ members: 65

HISTORICAL SOCIETY; HISTORY MUSEUM; RESEARCH CENTER: Collect, preserve and interpret the history of Murray Co.

PROGRAMS: Annual Meeting; Community Outreach; Elder's Programs; Exhibits; Guided Tours; Research Library/Archives

COLLECTIONS: [Late 1800s-1940] artifacts representing Co. history since 1858; microfilm of census and naturalization records, county newspapers, county and state books, scrapbooks, and family files; also photos, maps and plat books.

HOURS: Yr Winter T-Th 1-5; Fall M-F 1-5; Summer M-Sa 10-5

SLEEPY EYE

4489
Depot Museum
100 Oak St & 1st Ave NW, 56085 [PO Box 544, 56085]; (p) (507) 794-5053; depot@prairie.lakes.com; (c) Brown

City; Joint; Private non-profit/ 1984/ Sleepy Eye Historical Society/ staff: 1(p); 4(v)/ members: 75/publication: *Journey*

GENEALOGICAL SOCIETY; HISTORIC SITE; HISTORICAL SOCIETY; HISTORY MUSEUM; HOUSE MUSEUM; RAILROAD MUSEUM: The discovery, preservation and dissemination of historical knowledge about the City of Sleepy Eye and the County of Brown

PROGRAMS: Annual Meeting; Community Outreach; Exhibits; Facility Rental; Festivals; Guided Tours; Interpretation; Lectures; Publication

COLLECTIONS: [1872-present] History pertaining to Sleepy Eye and its surrounding townships, including the depot and the drum and bugle corps.

HOURS: May-Dec15 T-Sa 2-5

SPRING VALLEY

4490
Spring Valley Community Historical Society
220 W Courtland St, 55975; (p) (507) 346-7659; www.ci.spring-valley.mn.us; (c) Fillmore

Private non-profit/ 1956/ Exective Board/ staff: 1(f); 6(p); 25(v)/ members: 104

HISTORIC PRESERVATION AGENCY; HISTORICAL SOCIETY; HOUSE MUSEUM: To house, preserve, and display items of local historic interest; Laura Ingalls Wilder family home.

PROGRAMS: Annual Meeting; Community Outreach; Exhibits; Festivals; Guided Tours

COLLECTIONS: [1870s-1940s] Stained glass windows, artifacts from local churches, Ingalls/Wilder picture history, Victorian furniture, clothing from late 1800s, toys.

HOURS: June-Aug Daily 10-4 and by appt

STARBUCK

4491
Starbuck Depot Society
Main St, 56381 [c/o SACC, PO Box 234, 56381]; (p) (320) 239-4220; (c) Pope

Private non-profit/ 1986/ staff: 20(v)

HISTORIC PRESERVATION AGENCY: Restore and maintain the historic Starbuck depot.

PROGRAMS: Exhibits; Festivals; Guided Tours

COLLECTIONS: Depot building, caboose, motor car, 1 block of track, telegraph, hand switch, and tools.

HOURS: May-Sept by appt

ADMISSION: No charge

STILLWATER

4492
Saint Croix Collection, Stillwater Public Library
223 N Fourth St, 55082; (p) (651) 439-1675; (f) (651) 439-0012; www.ci.stillwater.mn.us/library/index.htm; (c) Washington

City/ 1897/ Board of Trustees/ staff: 3(p); 4(v)

LIBRARY AND/OR ARCHIVES: Focuses on the history of Stillwater and the St. Croix River valley in MN and WI.

PROGRAMS: Research Library/Archives

COLLECTIONS: [1840-present] Books, maps, periodicals, manuscripts, microfilm, oral histories, scrapbooks, city directories, Sanborn maps, local newspapers, Washington Co census and naturalization records.

HOURS: Yr

4493
St. Croix Collection/Stillwater Public Library
223 N 4th St, 55082; (p) (651) 439-1675; (f) (651) 439-0012; (c) Washington

City/ Board of Trustees/ staff: 3(p); 4(v)

PROGRAMS: Research Library/Archives

COLLECTIONS: [1860s-present] Collection is general in nature: maps, local histories, vertical files, photographs, directories, local newspaper on microfilm, building permits, Washington Co census and naturalization records.

4494
Warden's Home Museum
602 N Main St, 55082 [PO Box 167, 55082-0167]; (p) (612) 439-5956

1853/ staff: 1(f); 2(p); 12(v)

COLLECTIONS: [1890s] Military collections include items from Civil War, S-A War, WWI, WWII and Persian Gulf; lumbering collections; school records; prison records; large photograph collection.

HOURS: Seasonal

4495
Washington County Historic Courthouse
3rd & Pine St, 55082 [101 W Pine St, 55082]; (p) (651) 430-6233; (f) (651) 430-6238; his toriccourthouse@co.washington.mn.us; (c) Washington

County/ 1982/ staff: 3(f); 1(p); 95(v)/publication: *Dream for Zion's Hill*

HISTORIC SITE

PROGRAMS: Community Outreach; Concerts; Exhibits; Facility Rental; Family Programs; Festivals; Guided Tours; Lectures; Living History; Publication

COLLECTIONS: [1840-1965] County tax records, jail records, Board of Commissioners records, welfare records, artifacts, documents, photos and furniture directly related to the county courthouse.

HOURS: Yr M-F 8-4

4496
Washington County Historical Society
602 N Main St, 55082 [PO Box 167, 55082-0167]; (p) (651) 439-5956; wchsmn@wchsmn.org; www.wchsmn.org; (c) Washington

Private non-profit/ 1934/ staff: 1(f); 2(p); 15(v)/ members: 650/publication: *Historical Whisperings*

GENEALOGICAL SOCIETY; HISTORIC PRESERVATION AGENCY; HISTORIC SITE; HISTORICAL SOCIETY; HISTORY MUSEUM; HOUSE MUSEUM; RESEARCH CENTER: Collects, preserves, interprets, and disseminates the history of Minnesota's oldest county.

PROGRAMS: Annual Meeting; Community Outreach; Elder's Programs; Exhibits; Facility Rental; Family Programs; Festivals; Garden Tours; Guided Tours; Interpretation; Lectures; Living History; Publication; Reenactments; Research Library/Archives; School-Based Curriculum

COLLECTIONS: [1880-1990] Over 2,000 area photographs, lumber company records, birth and death records, indexed scrapbooks, Gazette photograph collection, and military records.

HOURS: Museum: May-Oct Su, T, Th, Sa 2-5; Library: May-Oct T, F, Su 12-5, W 3-9

ADMISSION: $3, Children $1

TAYLORS FALLS

4497
Taylors Falls Historical Society, The
272 W Government St, 55084 [PO Box 333, 55084-0333]; (p) (651) 465-5535; (c) Chisago

Private non-profit/ 1978/ Board of Directors/ staff: 105(v)/ members: 281/publication: *Life and Times in Taylors Falls*

HISTORICAL SOCIETY: Manages historic sites: 1855 W.H.C. Folsom House Museum, 1852 Town House School. Discoversr, collects, preserves, and disseminates historical knowledge of Taylors Falls area.

PROGRAMS: Annual Meeting; Community Outreach; Exhibits; Festivals; Guided Tours; Interpretation; Lectures; Publication; Research

Library/Archives; School-Based Curriculum

COLLECTIONS: [19th c] Furniture, artifacts, photographs, paintings and publications of local interest, account books of Folsom's WI and MN stores; and steamboat traffic on the St. Croix River.

HOURS: May-Oct 15 Daily 1-4:30

ADMISSION: $3, Children $1

TERRACE

4498
Terrace Mill Foundation
27165 Old Pond Rd, 56334; (p) (320) 278-3728; cpye@infolink.mounis.mn.us; (c) Pope

Private non-profit/ 1978/ staff: 1(p); 35(v)/ members: 175

ART MUSEUM; HISTORIC SITE; HISTORY MUSEUM: Restores the original mill, houses a collection of related artifacts.

PROGRAMS: Annual Meeting; Concerts; Exhibits; Facility Rental; Family Programs; Festivals; Guided Tours; Interpretation

COLLECTIONS: [1900-1940] Artifacts from milling, commerce and pioneer farms.

HOURS: June-Sept W-Su 12-9

THIEF RIVER FALLS

4499
Peder Engelstad Pioneer Village
Oakland Park Rd, 56701 [PO Box 127, 56701]; (p) (218) 681-5767; (c) Pennington

Joint/ 1976/ City/ County/ staff: 1(f); 1(p); 25(v)/ members: 205/publication: *PCHS Newsletter*

HISTORIC SITE; HISTORICAL SOCIETY; HISTORY MUSEUM; HOUSE MUSEUM; LIVING HISTORY/OUTDOOR MUSEUM: Maintains several historic structures; preserves and educates on local history.

PROGRAMS: Annual Meeting; Exhibits; Facility Rental; Festivals; Publication

COLLECTIONS: [1870-present] Farm equipment, antique cars, photographs, printing machines, newspapers, period-style artifacts and furniture.

HOURS: June-Sept Daily 1-5

ADMISSION: $3

TOFTE

4500
Tofte Historical Society/North Shore Commercial Fishing Museum
Hwy 61 & County Rd 2, 55615 [PO Box 2312, 55615-2312]; (p) (218) 663-7804; (f) (218) 663-7980; mah@boreal.org; www.boreal.org/nhistory/; (c) Cook

Private non-profit/ 1993/ staff: 1(p); 6(v)/ members: 402/publication: *North Shore Commercial Fishing Journal*

HISTORICAL SOCIETY; HISTORY MUSEUM; MARITIME MUSEUM: Preserve the heritage of the first settlers on the North Shore of Lake Superior.

PROGRAMS: Annual Meeting; Family Programs; Publication

COLLECTIONS: [1890-1945] Artifacts of the

commercial fishing industry; pictures and oral histories from the fishing families.

HOURS: Yr Daily Summer: 9-7; Winter 9-5

ADMISSION: $3, Family $5

TRACY

4501
Wheels Across the Prairie Museum
W Hwy #14, 56175 [PO Box 1132, 56175]; (p) (507) 629-3661; (c) Lyon

Private non-profit/ 1985/ staff: 3(f); 26(v)/ members: 112/publication: *Waggin' Wheels*

HISTORY MUSEUM

PROGRAMS: Annual Meeting; Exhibits; Family Programs; Guided Tours; Publication

COLLECTIONS: [1880-1930] Railroad history, small town economic and social structures, 1863 log cabin, agriculture.

HOURS: May-Sept Daily 10-5

ADMISSION: $2

TWO HARBORS

4502
Lake County Historical Society
520 S Ave, 55616; (p) (218) 834-4898; (c) Lake

Private non-profit/ 1925/ staff: 12(f); 25(v)/ members: 300/publication: *Lake County*

HISTORIC SITE; HISTORICAL SOCIETY; HISTORY MUSEUM; RESEARCH CENTER: Interprets and preserves history of Lake Co; operates 4 museums: the lighthouse at Two Harbors, Depot Museum, Edna O. Tugboat Museum, and the 3M Museum

PROGRAMS: Annual Meeting; Community Outreach; Elder's Programs; Exhibits; Facility Rental; Family Programs; Festivals; Guided Tours; Interpretation; Lectures; Living History; Publication; Reenactments; Research Library/Archives; School-Based Curriculum

COLLECTIONS: [1880-1950] Iron ore, logging, fishing veterans, shipwrecks, photos.

HOURS: Apr-Oct Daily 9-5

4503
Split Rock Lighthouse Rd
3713 Split Rock, 55616; (p) (218) 226-6372; (f) (218) 226-6373; splitrock@mnhs.org; www.mnhs.org; (c) Lake

State/ 1976/ Minnesota Historical Society/ staff: 4(f); 20(p); 2(v)

HISTORIC SITE; HISTORICAL SOCIETY; HISTORY MUSEUM; HOUSE MUSEUM; LIVING HISTORY/OUTDOOR MUSEUM: Preserves and interprets the buildings, grounds, and story of the lighthouse.

PROGRAMS: Community Outreach; Exhibits; Film/Video; Guided Tours; Interpretation; Living History

COLLECTIONS: [1910-1969] Artifacts, photographs, and manuscripts related to the light station and its keepers.

HOURS: Visitor Center: May 15-Oct 15 Daily 9-6; Oct 16-May 14 F-Su 9-5

ADMISSION: $6, Student $3, Seniors $4; Free in winter

VERNDALE

4504
Verndale Historical Society
204 N Farwell, 56481 [112 N Farwell, 56481]; (p) (218) 445-5745; (c) Wadena

City/ 1975/ Board of Trustees/ staff: 50(v)/ members: 140/publication: *Newsletter & Annual*

GENEALOGICAL SOCIETY; HISTORIC PRESERVATION AGENCY; HISTORIC SITE; HISTORICAL SOCIETY; RESEARCH CENTER: Collects and provides family histories.

PROGRAMS: Annual Meeting; Exhibits; Festivals; Guided Tours; Publication; Research Library/Archives

COLLECTIONS: [1879-present] Artifacts: armed services, farming families, school, churches, organizations, businesses and miscellaneous.

HOURS: Father's Day, 1st Sa Sept, and by appt

ADMISSION: No charge

VIRGINIA

4505
Virginia Area Historical Society
800 9th St N, 55792 [PO Box 734, 55792]; (p) (736) 741-1136; (c) St. Louis

1978/ Board of Directors/ staff: 1(p); 35(v)/ members: 375/publication: *Heritage News*

HISTORICAL SOCIETY; HISTORY MUSEUM: Collects history of the area, preserves archival material and artifacts for the use of the community, and maintains a museum in Olcott Park.

PROGRAMS: Annual Meeting; Exhibits; Family Programs; Festivals; Interpretation; Lectures; Publication; Research Library/Archives; School-Based Curriculum

COLLECTIONS: [Late 19th-early 20th c]

HOURS: Yr Summer: T-Sa; Winter: Th-Sa 11-4

WACONIA

4506
Carver County Historical Society
555 W First St, 55387; (p) (952) 442-4234; (f) (952) 442-3025; historical@co.carver.mn.us; (c) Carver County

Private non-profit/ 1940/ staff: 1(f); 4(p); 15(v)/ members: 350

GENEALOGICAL SOCIETY; HISTORICAL SOCIETY; HISTORY MUSEUM: Collects, preserves, and interprets the history of Carver County.

PROGRAMS: Annual Meeting; Community Outreach; Elder's Programs; Exhibits; Family Programs; Guided Tours; Lectures; Publication; Research Library/Archives; School-Based Curriculum

COLLECTIONS: [1790-present] Books, diaries, photos, letters, family histories, pre-contact artifacts, Swedish and German immigrant items, textiles, military, industrial and agricultural implements, artifacts of everyday life.

HOURS: Yr M, W-F 10-4:30, T 10-8, Sa 10-3

WADENA

4507
Wadena County Historical Society & Museum
603 N Jefferson, 56482; (p) (218) 631-9079; wchs@wadena.net; (c) Wadena

State/ 1992/ staff: 2(p); 60(v)/ members: 300/publication: *WCHS Newsletter*

HISTORICAL SOCIETY; HISTORY MUSEUM: Main repository for all records of Wadena County.

PROGRAMS: Annual Meeting; Community Outreach; Concerts; Exhibits; Facility Rental; Family Programs; Festivals; Interpretation; Lectures; Publication; Research Library/Archives; School-Based Curriculum

COLLECTIONS: Artifacts of every day life in the county.

HOURS: Yr 9-3 or by appt

ADMISSION: Donations requested

WALKER

4508
Cass County Museum & Pioneer School
201 Minnesota Ave W, 56484 [PO Box 505, 56484]; (p) (218) 547-7251; (c) Cass

Private non-profit/ 1949/ Cass County Historical Society/ staff: 1(p); 10(v)/ members: 200

HISTORICAL SOCIETY; HISTORY MUSEUM; RESEARCH CENTER: Depicts early settlement of Cass Co.

PROGRAMS: Annual Meeting; Exhibits; Guided Tours; Research Library/Archives

COLLECTIONS: [Early 1900s] Logging, farming, fur trade, transportation (railroads), Pioneer kitchen, bedroom and parlor. Tools: blacksmith, newspapers, carpentry, millinery and dressmaking, coopers 1800s replica of boarding school. Post office and pioneer log school.

HOURS: May-Sept M-Sa 10-5

ADMISSION: $3, Family $6, Children $1

WALNUT GROVE

4509
Laura Ingalls Wilder Museum & Tourist Center, Inc.
330 8th St, 56180; (p) (507) 859-2358; www.walnutgrove.org; (c) Redwood

Private non-profit/ 1974/ staff: 8(p); 20(v)

HISTORY MUSEUM: Operates a combined historical museum and tourist information facility that promotes the development of Walnut Grove.

PROGRAMS: Community Outreach; Exhibits; Guided Tours; Interpretation; Lectures; Research Library/Archives

COLLECTIONS: [1870-1920] Laura Ingalls Wilder related items and local historical artifacts.

HOURS: Apr-Oct Daily

WARREN

4510
Marshall County Historical Society
Fairgrounds, E Johnson Ave, 56762 [PO Box 103, 56762]; (p) (218) 745-4803; (c) Marshall

Private non-profit/ 1930/ staff: 2(p); 9(v)

GENEALOGICAL SOCIETY; HISTORICAL SOCIETY; HISTORY MUSEUM; RESEARCH CENTER

PROGRAMS: Annual Meeting; Community Outreach; Concerts; Exhibits; Family Programs; Guided Tours; Lectures; Publication; Research Library/Archives

COLLECTIONS: [1880s-1940s] Farm machinery, antique furniture and household goods, vintage clothing and personal items, relics of the fur trade, and railroad artifacts.

HOURS: May-Sept W-F 9-5

ADMISSION: No charge

4511
Minnesota's Historic Great Northwest
c/o Ethel Thorlacius, PO Box 103, 56762; (p) (218) 745-4803

Joint/ 1998/ eight counties/ staff: 8(v)

Identification of historic sites, the sharing of web sites, newsletters, brochures, and other opportunities to support each regional historical group.

COLLECTIONS: [Mid 1800s-mid 1900s]

WARROAD

4512
Warroad Heritage Center
Main S, 56763 [Box 688, 56763]; (p) (218) 386-2500; (c) Roseau

City/ 1969/ staff: 3(v)

HISTORICAL SOCIETY: Maintains and exhibits materials on Warroad history.

PROGRAMS: Exhibits; Festivals; Interpretation; Research Library/Archives; School-Based Curriculum

COLLECTIONS: Family histories, subject files, photos, newspapers from 1898 (also microfilm) and census 1900-1920, with exhibits on commercial fishing, logging, Native Americans and pioneers.

HOURS: Yr Daily M-Sa 1-5, Su 1-4

WASECA

4513
Farmamerica
Corner of Ct Rds 2 & 17, 56093 [PO Box 111, 56093]; (p) (507) 835-2052; (f) (507) 835-2053; farmamer@mnic.net; www.farmamerica.org; (c) Waseca

Private non-profit/ 1978/ Board of Directors/ staff: 4(f); 7(p); 504(v)/ members: 2000

LIVING HISTORY/OUTDOOR MUSEUM

PROGRAMS: Festivals; Guided Tours; Interpretation

COLLECTIONS: [1850-present] Vintage vehicles, tractors, items used for farming.

HOURS: May-Sept W-Su 11-4

ADMISSION: $1, Children $3

4514
Waseca County Historical Society
315 2nd Ave NE, 56093 [PO Box 314, 56093]; (p) (507) 835-7700; director@historical.waseca.mn.us; www.historical.waseca.mn.us; (c) Waseca

Private non-profit/ 1938/ staff: 2(f); 3(p); 20(v)/ members: 325

GENEALOGICAL SOCIETY; HISTORICAL SOCIETY; RESEARCH CENTER

PROGRAMS: Annual Meeting; Community Outreach; Exhibits; Research Library/Archives

COLLECTIONS: [1890-1915] One room school, research center, church, agriculture hall, general small town, 30,000 textiles.

HOURS: Yr Daily 8-12/1-5

WATERTOWN

4515
Watertown Area Historical Society
309 Lewis Ave S, 55388 [PO Box 836, 55388]; (p) (612) 955-2586; WAHisSoc@aol.com; (c) Carver

City/ 1998/ staff: 15(v)/ members: 45

HISTORICAL SOCIETY: Preserves, documents, and presents history of the Watertown area.

PROGRAMS: Annual Meeting; Exhibits; Festivals

COLLECTIONS: [early 1900s] 100 community photos, 200 railroading photos of Luce Electric Line, newspapers from 1940, and genealogy materials.

HOURS: Last Sa/Su July 9-9

ADMISSION: No charge

WAVERLY

4516
Hubert H. Humphrey Museum
607 Maple, 55390 [PO Box 508, 55390]; (p) (612) 658-4505; (f) (612) 658-4836; hhhmusm @lkdllink.net; www.humphreymuseum.org; (c) Wright

Private non-profit/ 1996/ staff: 1(p); 12(v)/ members: 112

HISTORY MUSEUM: Focuses on Hubert H. Humphrey's life and the effects he had on the nation.

PROGRAMS: Annual Meeting; Exhibits; Facility Rental; Guided Tours; Interpretation; Publication

COLLECTIONS: [1948-1978] Humphrey's papers and objects, political memorabilia.

4517
Wright Air Museum
4859 US Hwy 12 SW, 55390; (p) (612) 658-4102; (f) (612) 658-4102; rborrell@aol.com; (c) Wright

Private non-profit/ 1995/ staff: 7(v)/ members: 15

AVIATION MUSEUM; HISTORY MUSEUM: Preserving the memories of aviators and their aircraft.

PROGRAMS: Annual Meeting; Community Outreach; Living History

COLLECTIONS: [1900-1970] Aviation artifacts, books, tapes, aircraft and recorded stories and memories.

HOURS: By appt only

ADMISSION: No charge

WESTBROOK

4518
Westbrook Heritage Museum
301 1st Ave, 56183 [Box 354, 56183]; (p) (507) 445-3181; (c) Cottonwood

Private non-profit/ 1980/ staff: 30(v)/ members: 60

HISTORY MUSEUM: Illustrates the farming community of Westbrook in 1900.

PROGRAMS: Annual Meeting; Exhibits; Guided Tours

COLLECTIONS: [1900s] Household items; period clothing, uniforms, exhibits from local businesses and school, items from depot, farm tools, weaving loom and furnished log house.

HOURS: June-Aug Sa-Su 2-4

ADMISSION: No charge

WHITE BEAR LAKE

4519
White Bear Lake Area Historical Society
Corner of Lake Ave & Moorhead, 55110 [PO Box 10543, 55110]; (p) (651) 426-0479; (c) Ramsey

Private non-profit/ 1975/ Board of Directors/ staff: 1(f); 40(v)/ members: 500/publication: *Lake Area Preserver*

HISTORIC SITE; HOUSE MUSEUM: Collects, displays, and interprets all facets of local life; operates two museums: Fillebrown House and railroad depot.

PROGRAMS: Annual Meeting; Community Outreach; Concerts; Exhibits; Facility Rental; Festivals; Guided Tours; Interpretation; Lectures; Publication; Research Library/Archives; School-Based Curriculum

COLLECTIONS: [1850-present] Stickley-style Fillebrown house; artifacts of Victorian life; NP railroad memorabilia.

HOURS: Fillebrown: June-Aug Su 1-4; Depot: May-mid June M-F 10-4 1st/3rd Su 1-4; Mid June-May M-F 10-4, Th 10-9, Su 1-4

ADMISSION: $3

WILLMAR

4520
Heritage Searchers of Kandiyohi County, The
[PO Box 175, 56201-0175]; (c) Kandiyohi

Private non-profit/ 1981/ members: 35

GENEALOGICAL SOCIETY: Promotes interest in family history and preservation of public records.

PROGRAMS: Research Library/Archives

COLLECTIONS: [1870-present] Family histories and county records.

HOURS: Yr M-F

ADMISSION: No charge

4521
Kandiyohi County Historical Society
610 NE Hwy 1, 56201; (p) (320) 235-1881; kandhist@wecnet.com; (c) Kandiyohi

Private non-profit/ 1897/ staff: 1(f); 4(p); 50(v)/ members: 500

HISTORIC SITE; HISTORICAL SOCIETY; HISTORY MUSEUM; RESEARCH CENTER: Administers multiple sites to discover, preserve, interpret, and share county history.

PROGRAMS: Annual Meeting; Exhibits; Interpretation; Publication; Research Library/ Archives

COLLECTIONS: [1850s-current] Archives and manuscripts, audio-visual, microfilm newspapers and records, photos, books, and two- and three- dimensional objects, relating to the history and culture of Kandiyohi County.

HOURS: Yr Summer: Daily M-F 9-5, Sa-Su 1-5; Winter: M-F 9-5

ADMISSION: No charge

WINDOM

4522
Cottonwood County Historical Society
812 4th Ave, 56101; (p) (507) 831-1134; (c) Cottonwood

Private non-profit/ 1901/ Board of Trustees/ staff: 3(p); 25(v)/ members: 270

HISTORICAL SOCIETY; RESEARCH CENTER: To collect, preserve, and disseminate the knowledge about the history of Cottonwood County and the state of Minnesota.

PROGRAMS: Annual Meeting; Exhibits; Facility Rental; Lectures; Research Library/Archives

COLLECTIONS: [1850-present] Artifacts pertaining to county history: 3,500 research documents, 1,000+ photographs, 8,600 photo negatives, 800 textiles, and 1,500 artifacts.

HOURS: Yr M-F 8-4

ADMISSION: No charge

WINNEBAGO

4523
Winnebago Area Museum
18 1st Ave NE, 56098 [Box 35, 56098]; (p) (507) 893-4660; (c) Fairbault

Joint/ 1977/ City; Private non-profit/Board/ staff: 1(p); 20(v)

GENEALOGICAL SOCIETY; HISTORICAL SOCIETY; HISTORY MUSEUM; RESEARCH CENTER: Interprets the pioneer/business history of the area.

PROGRAMS: Annual Meeting; Exhibits; Guided Tours; Interpretation; School-Based Curriculum

COLLECTIONS: [1856] Pioneer: archaic, woodland and Mississippian artifacts, displays: bedroom, kitchen and farm tools from 1860, area school, business, genealogy, military, displays and files.

HOURS: Yr M-T 9-12, W 8-5, Th-F 12-5

ADMISSION: No charge

WINONA

4524
Polish Cultural Institute
102 Liberty St, 55987; (p) (507) 454-3431; (f) (507) 452-5570; winpole@hbci.com; www.rhometown.com; (c) Winona

Private non-profit/ 1979/ staff: 1(f); 1(p); 10(v)/

members: 500

GENEALOGICAL SOCIETY; HISTORY MU-
SEUM: Sustains and enhances awareness of
the Kashubian and Silesian Poles; maintains a
museum.

PROGRAMS: Annual Meeting; Concerts; Exhibits; Family Programs; Festivals; Film/Video;
Guided Tours; Lectures; Living History; Publication; Research Library/Archives; School-
Based Curriculum

COLLECTIONS: [Late 19th-20th c] Kashubian
artifacts, family heirlooms, religious articles,
folk art, photographs, Polish Bibles and prayer
books; Polish language newspapers "Wiarus."

HOURS: May 1-Sept 31 M-F 10-3, Sa 10-12,
Su 1-3; Nov-Apr 30 by appt

ADMISSION: Donations accepted

4525
Winona County Historical Society, Inc.

160 Johnson St, 55987; (p) (507) 454-2723;
(f) (507) 454-0006; wchs@luminet.net;
www.winonahistory.org; (c) Winona

Private non-profit/ 1935/ staff: 1(f); 7(p);
250(v)/ members: 1400/publication: *The Argus*

HISTORIC SITE; HISTORICAL SOCIETY;
HISTORY MUSEUM; HOUSE MUSEUM; RE-
SEARCH CENTER: Operates 3 museums list-
ed on the National Registry: Willard B. Bunnell
House, Arches Museum of Pioneer Life, and
Armory Museum.

PROGRAMS: Annual Meeting; Community
Outreach; Concerts; Exhibits; Facility Rental;
Family Programs; Festivals; Guided Tours; In-
terpretation; Lectures; Publication; Research
Library/Archives; School-Based Curriculum

COLLECTIONS: [1840-present] Especially
strong in Native American, clothing, photographs, agriculture, Mississippi River and local
businesses.

HOURS: Yr Daily M-F 9-5, Sa-Su 12-4

ADMISSION: $3, Children $1.50

WOODBURY

4526
Woodbury Heritage Society

8301 Valley Creek Rd, 55125; (p) (651) 714-
3564; (c) Washington

Private non-profit/ 1983/ Board of Directors/
staff: 1(p)/ members: 115/publication: *Heritage Happenings*

GARDEN; GENEALOGICAL SOCIETY; HIS-
TORIC SITE; HISTORICAL SOCIETY; LIVING
HISTORY/OUTDOOR MUSEUM; RESEARCH
CENTER: Preserves, documents, and edu-
cates about Woodbury's history, and maintains
1870s historic house.

PROGRAMS: Annual Meeting; Community
Outreach; Exhibits; Family Programs; Garden
Tours; Publication

COLLECTIONS: [1844-present] Family histories, oral histories, photographs, newspaper
clippings, research books, artifacts, school
photographs and stories, maps, church and cemetery records and census and naturalization records.

HOURS: Yr 1-3, or by appt

ADMISSION: No charge

WORTHINGTON

4527
Nobles County Historical Society, Inc.

407 12th St, Ste #2, 56187; (p) (507) 376-
4431; (c) Nobles

Private non-profit/ 1933/ Board of Directors/
staff: 2(f); 1(p); 60(v)/ members: 487/publica-
tion: *Newsletter*

GENEALOGICAL SOCIETY; HISTORICAL
SOCIETY; HISTORY MUSEUM; LIVING HIS-
TORY/OUTDOOR MUSEUM: Promotes, preserves, develops and interprets the history of
the county and its people.

PROGRAMS: Annual Meeting; Community
Outreach; Elder's Programs; Exhibits; Facility
Rental; Family Programs; Festivals; Guided
Tours; Living History; Publication

COLLECTIONS: [1870-present] Artifacts, documents, literary works.

HOURS: Mem War Building Yr M-F 1-5; Pioneer Village May-Sept M-Sa 10-5, Su 1-5

ADMISSION: $3

MISSISSIPPI

BALDWYN

4528
Brice's Crossroads Visitor and Interpretive Center

607 Grisham St, 38824; (p) (601) 365-3909;
(f) (601) 365-3969; bricexrd@network-
one.com; (c) Lee

City/ 1998/ Brice's Crossroads Museum Com-
mission/ staff: 1(f); 20(v)

BATTLEFIELD; HISTORIC PRESERVATION
AGENCY; HISTORIC SITE: Preserves and interprets the Battle of Brice's Crossroads.

PROGRAMS: Exhibits; Guided Tours; Interpretation; Living History

COLLECTIONS: [Civil War] Artifacts and replicas from the Claude Gentry collection, videos,
outdoor flag display.

BATESVILLE

4529
Panola Historical Genealogical Association

Hwy 51 N, Public Library, 38606 [210 Kyle St,
38606]; (p) (601) 563-7287; (c) Panola

1972/ staff: 5(v)/ members: 105

GENEALOGICAL SOCIETY; HISTORICAL
SOCIETY: Collects and preserves the history
of Panola county and northern Mississippi.

COLLECTIONS: [1800-present] Records, family histories, censuses of Panola County and
northern Mississippi.

BELZONI

4530
Ethel Wright Mohamed/Mama's Dream World

307 Central St, 39038; (p) (662) 247-1433; (f)
(662) 247-1433; (c) Humphreys

Private for-profit/ 1976/ staff: 2(v)

HOUSE MUSEUM: Operates museum of work
by the artist Ethel Wright Mohamed.

PROGRAMS: Guided Tours

COLLECTIONS: Photographs, embroidery,
pictures.

HOURS: Yr M-Su by appt

ADMISSION: $2; No charge for children

BILOXI

4531
Beauvoir, The Jefferson Davis Home and Presidential Library

2244 Beach Blvd, 39531; (p) (228) 388-9074;
(f) (228) 388-1313; beauvoir@netdoor.com;
www.beauvoir.org; (c) Harrison

Private non-profit/ 1941/ Mississippi Division,
United Sons of Confederate Veterans/ staff:
12(f); 12(p); 21(v)/ members: 211

HISTORIC SITE; HISTORY MUSEUM;
HOUSE MUSEUM; PRESIDENTIAL SITE:
Preserves the retirement estate of Confederate President Jefferson Davis, including the restored home and outbuildings, Confederate
museum, Presidential library and historic
cemetery. Beauvoir is a National Historic
Landmark and a Mississippi Historical Landmark.

PROGRAMS: Exhibits; Facility Rental; Festi-
vals; Interpretation; Living History; Publication;
Reenactments; Research Library/Archives;
School-Based Curriculum

COLLECTIONS: [19th c] Historic furnishings,
decorative arts, textiles, military items,
archives, vehicles and excavated artifacts.

HOURS: Sept-Feb Daily 9-4; Mar-Aug Daily 9-5

ADMISSION: $7.50, Children $4.50, Seniors
$6.75

4532
Ohr-O'Keefe Museum of Art

136 George E Ohr St, 39530; (p) (228) 374-
5547; (f) (228) 436-3641; angel@georgeohr.
org; www.georgeohr.org; (c) Harrison

Private non-profit/ 1989/ staff: 11(f); 5(p); 6(v)/
members: 607/publication: *The Crack'd Pot*

ART MUSEUM: Preserves and displays collection of pottery created by Biloxi native
George E. Ohr, and a wide range of work from
contemporary art to baroque; maintains three
rotating art galleries for coastal, regional and
national exhibits.

PROGRAMS: Community Outreach; Con-
certs; Exhibits; Facility Rental; Festivals; Guided Tours; Lectures; Publication

COLLECTIONS: [Late 1800s-early 1900s] Fine
art pottery, ceramic wares, pewter jewelry.

HOURS: Yr M-Sa 9-5

ADMISSION: $3, Seniors $2; Students/Chil-
dren free

4533
Old Brick House Museum

622 Bayview, 39530 [PO Box 508, 39533]; (p)
(228) 435-6121, (228) 435-6308; (f) (228)
435-6246; museum@biloxi.ms.us

1850/ City/ staff: 1(f); 1(p)

COLLECTIONS: [1850-1900]

4534
Tullis-Toledano Manor
360 Beach Blvd, 39530 [PO Box 508, 39533];
(p) (228) 435-6293, (228) 435-6308; (f) (228)
435-6246; museum@biloxi.ms.us

1856/ City/ staff: 2(f)

COLLECTIONS: [1850s-1880s] Highlights of
collections is a four poster bed made by Dutre
Barson, free man of color, cabinet maker in
New Orleans, 1840s.

CAMP SHELBY

4535
Armed Forces Museum
Museum Bldg, Forrest Ave, 39407-5500; (p)
(601) 558-2757; (c) Forrest

Private non-profit/ 1988/ Adjunct General's Office; Federal and State/ staff: 1(p); 6(v)/ members: 554

HISTORY MUSEUM: Preserves the past in
and shares our rich military heritage.

PROGRAMS: Exhibits; Guided Tours

COLLECTIONS: [WW II]

HOURS: Yr M-F 9-4; May-Aug Sa-Su 1-4

CLARKSDALE

4536
Delta Blues Museum
[PO Box 280, 38614]; (p) (601) 627-6820; (f)
(601) 627-7263; dbm@clarksdale.com;
www.deltabluesmuseum.org; (c) Coahoma

City/ 1979/ staff: 3(f); 1(p)/ members: 362

HISTORY MUSEUM: Collects, preserves, and
makes accessible to the public information,
programs, and related services concerning the
history and significance of the blues.

PROGRAMS: Exhibits

COLLECTIONS: [20th c] Photographs, memorabilia, small research collection.

HOURS: Yr M-Sa 9-5

ADMISSION: No charge

CLEVELAND

4537
Delta State University Archives
Charles W Capps Jr Bldg, 5th Ave, 38733
[PO Box 3137, 38733]; (p) (601) 846-4780; (f)
(601) 846-4782; mjohnsto@merlin.deltast.
edu; wwwlib.deltast.edu/aboutlib/depart
ments/archivesinfo.html; (c) Bolivar

1968/ Delta State Univ/ staff: 2(f); 4(p); 1(v)/
members: 1

HISTORY MUSEUM; RESEARCH CENTER:
Collects, preserves, and provides access to
primary documentation of the history of the
MS Yazoo Delta and records of DSU's history,
programs, and activities.

PROGRAMS: Community Outreach; Exhibits;
Facility Rental; Lectures; Research Library/
Archives

COLLECTIONS: [1830-present] Historical
manuscripts and interviews, university
records, maps, photographs, and archeological artifacts.

HOURS: Yr M-Th 8-5, F 8-4

ADMISSION: No charge

CLINTON

4538
**Mississippi Baptist Historical
Commission**
Mississippi College Library, College St, 39058
[PO Box 4024, 39058]; (p) (601) 925-3434; (f)
(601) 925-3435; mbhc@mc.edu;
www.mc.edu; (c) Hinds

Private non-profit/ 1888/ MS Baptist Conven-
tion/ staff: 1(f); 2(p)/publication: *Highlights of
Mississippi Baptist History; A History of Mississippi Baptists; and others*

HISTORIC PRESERVATION AGENCY; RE-
SEARCH CENTER: Promotes Baptist heritage
by collecting and preserving materials, making
them available to researchers, maintaining historic sites, and recognizing historic churches.

PROGRAMS: Publication

COLLECTIONS: [1700s-present] History and
records of Baptist denomination in Mississippi.

HOURS: Yr M-F 8:30-12/1-4:30

ADMISSION: No charge

COLUMBIA

4539
Marion County Historical Society
1 Hugh White Pl, 39429; (p) (601) 736-1763;
(f) (601) 731-3999; columbia@aol.com;
www.waidsoft.com/methdirt.html; (c) Marion

Private non-profit/ 1967/ Marion County/ staff:
1(f); 2(p); 25(v)/publication: *History of Marion
County*

HISTORIC SITE; HISTORICAL SOCIETY;
HISTORY MUSEUM: Historic John Ford home
in Sandyhook and Confederate library.

PROGRAMS: Annual Meeting; Community
Outreach; Exhibits; Festivals; Guided Tours;
Lectures; Publication; Research Library/
Archives

COLLECTIONS: [1800-1850] Family memorabilia in oldest frontier-style home in Pearl River
Valley, restored Methodist Church, and Confederate library with 250 volumes.

HOURS: Mar-Nov Sa-Su 2-5; Dec-Feb by appt

ADMISSION: $4, Children $2

COLUMBUS

4540
**Blewett-Harrison-Lee Home and
Museum**
316 7th St N, 39701; (p) (601) 327-8888

1844/ staff: 31(v)

COLLECTIONS: [1844-1918] Many portraits;
Civil War artifacts; ladies dress & accessories;
Scrapbooks including SD Lee's; minute books
of Cols. Riflemen, 1837-1862.

HOURS: Yr

4541
**Columbus Lowndes Historical
Society**
316 N 7th St, 38705 [132 Ridge Rd, 38705];
(p) (662) 327-8888; libba@ebicom.net; (c)
Lowndes

Private non-profit/ staff: 1(p); 25(v)/ members:
100

HISTORIC PRESERVATION AGENCY; HIS-
TORICAL SOCIETY; HISTORY MUSEUM;
HOUSE MUSEUM

PROGRAMS: Annual Meeting; Facility Rental;
Guided Tours

COLLECTIONS: [Civil War] Period furniture,
large portraits of family members, family artifacts. Donated clothing, china, silver, swords,
guns, and historic documents.

HOURS: Mar-Dec F 10-4 or by appt

CORINTH

4542
Curlee House
705 Jackson St, 38834 [c/o Ann Thompson,
301 Childs St, 38834]; (p) (601) 287-9501,
(800) 647-6724

4543
Northeast Mississippi Museum
204 E 4th St, 38835 [PO Box 993, 38835]; (p)
(662) 287-3120; (f) (662) 287-3120;
nemma@tsixroads.com; (c) Alcorn

1981/ Northeast MS Museum Association/
staff: 2(f); 6(v)/ members: 102

Community education.

COLLECTIONS: [Civil War/Reconstruction]
Fossils, minerals, Native American, quilts,
clothing, household items, and art.

HOURS: Yr M-Sa 10-5, Su 11-5

ADMISSION: No charge

DEKALB

4544
**Kemper County Historical
Association**
Hopper Ave, 39328 [PO Box 545, 39328]; (c)
Kemper

Private non-profit/ 1983/ KCHA Board of Di-
rectors/ staff: 12(v)/ members: 125

HISTORY MUSEUM: Presents programs and
maintains museum.

PROGRAMS: Annual Meeting; Exhibits

COLLECTIONS: [19th-20th c] Local artifacts
and memorabilia from the late U.S. Senator
John C. Stennis.

HOURS: By appt only

ADMISSION: No charge

FAYETTE

4545
Historic Springfield Foundation, Inc.
Hwy 553, 8 miles W of Fayette, 39069 [Rt 1,
PO Box 201, 39069]; (p) (601) 786-3802;
sprinfld@mail.iamerica.net; (c) Jefferson

Private non-profit/ 1977/ Historic Springfield
Foundation/ staff: 3(f); 4(p)/ members: 30/pub-
lication: *Marriage of Andrew Jackson/Spring-
field*

HISTORIC PRESERVATION AGENCY; HIS-
TORIC SITE; HISTORY MUSEUM; HOUSE
MUSEUM; LIVING HISTORY/OUTDOOR MU-
SEUM; PRESIDENTIAL SITE; RESEARCH
CENTER: Restoration and preservation of his-

toric Springfield Plantation and grounds, location where President Andrew Jackson was married in 1791.

PROGRAMS: Exhibits; Garden Tours; Guided Tours; Interpretation; Lectures; Living History; Publication; Research Library/Archives

COLLECTIONS: Period furniture, library, farming, transportation, government, early settlement, art, artifacts.

HOURS: Yr M-Su 9:30-sunset

ADMISSION: $7, Children $4

FLORA

4546
Mississippi Petrified Forest
124 Forest Park Rd, 39071 [PO Box 37, 39071]; (p) (601) 879-8189; (f) (601) 879-8165; mspforest@aol.com; (c) Madison

Private for-profit/ 1966/ staff: 2(f); 4(p)

LIVING HISTORY/OUTDOOR MUSEUM; NATURAL HISTORY MUSEUM: Preserves giant petrified logs and studies their geological history.

PROGRAMS: Exhibits; Guided Tours; School-Based Curriculum

COLLECTIONS: [Prehistory] Nature trail among gigantic stone logs, petrified wood, mineral, and fossil museum.

HOURS: Yr Daily 9-5

ADMISSION: $5, Student $4, Seniors $4; Group rates

FRENCH CAMP

4547
Col. James Drane Home
Mile Marker 181 on the Natchez Trace Pkwy, 39745 [1 Fine Place, 39745]; (p) (601) 547-6482, (601) 547-6001; (f) (601) 547-6790

1846/ staff: 2(p)

COLLECTIONS: [Mid 1800s] Drane home.

HOURS: Yr

FRIARS POINT

4548
Friars Point Historical Preservation Society
2nd St, 38631 [PO Box 95, 38631]; (p) (601) 383-2471; flo@tecinfo.com; (c) Coahoma

Private non-profit/ 1997/ Friars Point Historical Preservation Society/ staff: 45(v)

HISTORIC PRESERVATION AGENCY: Collects artifacts and oral histories, preserves historic structures, and establishes historic districts.

PROGRAMS: Annual Meeting; Community Outreach; Family Programs; Guided Tours; Interpretation; Lectures; Living History; School-Based Curriculum

COLLECTIONS: [Pre-historic-1900s]

HOURS: Yr

4549
North Delta Museum
2nd St, 38631 [PO Box 22, 38631]; (p) (601) 383-2436

staff: 1(f)

GREENVILLE

4550
Wetherbee House
503 Washington Ave, 38701; (p) (601) 332-2246; (f) (601) 332-9290; gac1@fecinso.com

1873/ City/ staff: 1(f)

COLLECTIONS: [19th c] Period furniture original to the house.

HOURS: Yr

GREENWOOD

4551
Cottonlandia Museum
1608 Hwy 82 West, 38930; (p) (662) 453-0925; (f) (662) 455-7556; (c) Leflore

Private non-profit/ 1969/ Cottonlandia Educational and Recreational Foundation, Inc./ staff: 2(f); 3(p); 45(v)/ members: 250

ART MUSEUM; HISTORY MUSEUM: Collects, preserves, and exhibits MS artifacts and educates the public about Delta history.

PROGRAMS: Annual Meeting; Community Outreach; Concerts; Exhibits; Facility Rental; Guided Tours; Interpretation; Lectures; Research Library/Archives

COLLECTIONS: [Prehistory-present] Regional archeology, local historical antiquities, prehistoric pottery, beadwork, natural history, and military history.

HOURS: Yr M-F 9-5, Sa-Su 2-5

ADMISSION: $4, Student $1

4552
Florewood River Plantation
Ft Loring Rd, 38930 [PO Box 680, 38935]; (p) (601) 455-3821; (f) (601) 453-2459

1976/ State/ staff: 10(f); 5(p)

COLLECTIONS: [Mid 19th-early 20th c] Furnishings; mid-19th and early-20th-c steam engines; 19th-c tools.

HOURS: Mar-Dec

HAMILTON

4553
Cedarwycke Plantation
40310 Hwy 373, 39746; (p) (601) 343-8400, (601) 343-8402

1852/ Private

COLLECTIONS: [1852-present] Tool collection and owner history.

HOURS: Appt

HATTIESBURG

4554
Hattiesburg Area Historical Society and Museum
723 Main St, Hattiesburg Cultural Center, 39403 [PO Box 1573, 39403-1573]; (p) (601) 582-5460, (601) 583-1362; (c) Forrest

Private non-profit/ 1970/ Officers and Board of Directors/ staff: 45(v)/ members: 300/publication: *The History of Forrest County, Mississippi; Facts About Hattiesburg; and others*

HISTORICAL SOCIETY; HISTORY MUSEUM: Promotes local history.

PROGRAMS: Annual Meeting; Community Outreach; Concerts; Elder's Programs; Exhibits; Family Programs; Festivals; Film/Video; Garden Tours; Guided Tours; Lectures; Living History; Publication; Reenactments; Research Library/Archives; School-Based Curriculum

COLLECTIONS: Historical artifacts, newspapers, publications, photographs, and memorabilia related to local and area interest.

HOURS: Yr M-Th 2-5 by appt

ADMISSION: No charge

4555
Junior Historical Society of Mississippi
Lab 456, Univ of S Mississippi, 2609 W 4th Ave, 39406 [PO Box 5047, 39406-5047]; (p) (601) 266-4333; Mary.farrell@usm.edu; www-dept.usm.edu/~history/mhday.html; (c) Forrest

State/ 1964/ MS Historical Society/ staff: 1(f)/ members: 800

Sponsors MS History Day and encourages local junior historical societies to participate in historical research and preservation.

ADMISSION: $5

4556
South Mississippi Genealogical Society
[PO Box 15271, 39404]; www.members.xoom.com/smsgensoc; (c) Forrest

Private non-profit/ 1980/ Elected presidents/ members: 90

GENEALOGICAL SOCIETY: Preserves and promotes genealogical research and outreach to researchers.

PROGRAMS: Family Programs; Lectures; Publication

4557
Special Collections Department, USM Libraries, University of Southern Mississippi
McCain Library & Archives, USM, 39406 [PO Box 5148, 39406]; (p) (601) 266-4345; (f) (601) 266-6269; www.lib.usm.edu/archives; (c) Forrest

State/ 1976/ Univ of Southern MS, USM Libraries/ staff: 8(f)

LIBRARY AND/OR ARCHIVES; RESEARCH CENTER: Contains printed materials and original manuscripts concerning the history of the state plus children's literature.

PROGRAMS: Exhibits; Guided Tours; Research Library/Archives; School-Based Curriculum

COLLECTIONS: [Late 19th-20th c] Books, maps, manuscripts, photographs and newspaper clippings concerning the state of Mississippi, the Civil War, and other specialized collections, including children's literature.

4558
Turner House Museum
500 Bay St, 39401; (p) (601) 582-4249; (f) (601) 582-4249

HERNANDO

4559
Genealogical Society of DeSoto County
3260 Hwy 51 S, 38632 [PO Box 607, 38632-0607]; (p) (601) 429-6204; desgenms@aol.com; (c) DeSoto

Private non-profit/ 1982/ staff: 10(p); 10(v)/ members: 162/publication: *DeSoto Descendants*

ALLIANCE OF HISTORICAL AGENCIES; GENEALOGICAL SOCIETY; RESEARCH CENTER: Offers genealogical research and beginning genealogical workshops.

PROGRAMS: Annual Meeting; Community Outreach; Film/Video; Publication; Research Library/Archives

COLLECTIONS: [1800s-present] Early records of DeSoto County, census films on five counties, IGI Fiche, Family Tree CDs and GRS CDs.

HOURS: Yr M-F 9-12/1-3

ADMISSION: No charge

HOLLY SPRINGS

4560
Kate Freeman Clark Museum of Art
300 E College, 38635 [PO Box 580, 38635]; (p) (662) 252-4211; (f) (662) 252-1845; (c) Marshall

Private non-profit/ 1957/ Kate Freeman Clark Trust/ staff: 5(v)

ART MUSEUM: Promotes and preserves artwork created by Kate Freeman Clark.

PROGRAMS: Exhibits; Facility Rental; Guided Tours

COLLECTIONS: [1890-1925] 1200 paintings, watercolors, and drawings.

HOURS: By appt

4561
Marshall County Historical Museum
220 E College Ave, 38635 [PO Box 806, 38635]; (p) (662) 252-3669; (c) Marshall

Joint/ 1970/ Marshall County Historical Society;Town and County/ staff: 3(f); 2(p)/ members: 100

ALLIANCE OF HISTORICAL AGENCIES; GENEALOGICAL SOCIETY; HISTORIC PRESERVATION AGENCY; HISTORICAL SOCIETY; HISTORY MUSEUM: Maintains structure built in 1903 as a college dormitory, the building has 3 floors, 22 rooms and 40,000 artifacts.

PROGRAMS: Elder's Programs; Exhibits; Festivals; Guided Tours; Lectures; Living History

HOURS: Yr M-F 10-5, Sa 10-2

HOUSTON

4562
Chickasaw County Historical and Genealogical Society
105 W Madison, 38851 [PO Box 42, 38851]; (p) (662) 456-3381; jeclark@network_one.com; (c) Chickasaw

Society Board/ members: 150/publication: *Times Past*

GENEALOGICAL SOCIETY: Preservation of genealogical and historical information.

PROGRAMS: Annual Meeting; Lectures; Publication; Research Library/Archives

COLLECTIONS: [1860-present] Chickasaw Co land, cemetery and family records, county history books, census film.

HOURS: Yr T-Sa 10-6

ADMISSION: No charge

4563
Houlka Historical Society
1248 CR 515 N, 38851; (p) (662) 456-3071; (f) (662) 456-3072; (c) Chickasaw

1970

HISTORICAL SOCIETY: Preserves old high school building and local history. Holds "talking history" sessions.

PROGRAMS: Annual Meeting; Festivals; Living History

JACKSON

4564
Federation of Misssissippi Historical Societies
100 S State St, 39205 [PO Box 571, 39205-0571]; (p) (601) 359-6850; (f) (601) 359-6975; webmaster@mdah.state.ms.us; www.mdah.state.ms.us; (c) Hinds

Private non-profit/ 1995/ MS Historical Society/ staff: 3(p)/ members: 67

HISTORICAL SOCIETY: Unifies MS's local historical societies and fosters cooperation among them and the MS Dept of Archives and History.

4565
Jackson State University, Margaret Walker Alexander National Research Center
1400 Lynch St, 39217 [PO Box 17008, 39217]; (p) (601) 979-2055; (f) (601) 979-5929; (c) Hinds

State/ JSU Margaret Walker Alexander National Research Center/ staff: 3(f); 1(p); 1(v)/ members: 62

HISTORIC SITE; HISTORY MUSEUM; RESEARCH CENTER: Studies and demonstrates archival, cultural, and historic preservation projects relative to the 20th c African American.

PROGRAMS: Exhibits; Family Programs; Festivals; Guided Tours; Lectures; Research Library/Archives

COLLECTIONS: [20th c] Information on the 20th c African American experience.

HOURS: General Public: Yr Daily 9:30-4; Research: Yr Daily 10-1 by appt

ADMISSION: No charge

4566
Manship House Museum
420 E Fortification St, 39202; (p) (601) 961-4724; (f) (601) 354-6043; www.mdah.state.us; (c) Hinds

State/ 1982/ MS Dept of Archives and History/ staff: 2(f); 3(p); 1(v)/publication: *Manship House Museum Guidebook*

HOUSE MUSEUM: Preserves and interprets the 19th c Gothic Revival home of Charles Henry Manship, decorative painter and Civil War mayor of Jackson, through educational programs and by collecting and exhibiting related artifacts.

PROGRAMS: Concerts; Elder's Programs; Exhibits; Family Programs; Film/Video; Guided Tours; Interpretation; Lectures; Living History; Publication; School-Based Curriculum

COLLECTIONS: [19th c] Household furnishings, personal artifacts, decorative arts, Gothic Revival house

4567
Mississippi Agriculture and Forestry/National Agricultural Aviation Museum
1150 Lakeland Dr, 39216; (p) (601) 354-6113; (f) (601) 982-4292; www.mdac.state.ms.us; (c) Hinds

State/ 1981/ MS Agriculture and Forestry/National Agricultural Aviation Museum Foundation/ staff: 11(f); 6(p); 60(v)

HOUSE MUSEUM: Promotes knowledge and appreciation of MS and the Deep South's cultural, economic, and social history. Collects and preserves exhibits and interprets materials related to persons, eras, and events in the state's history.

PROGRAMS: Annual Meeting; Community Outreach; Concerts; Exhibits; Facility Rental; Family Programs; Festivals; Film/Video; Guided Tours; Interpretation; Research Library/Archives

COLLECTIONS: [18th-20th c] Tools, implements, and machines used in agriculture and forestry in the Deep South from early 1800s to 1950s. Equipment and buildings used in a typical small Mississippi town in the 1920s and 1930s.

HOURS: Yr M-Sa 9-5; June-Aug Su 1-5

ADMISSION: $4, Children $2, Seniors $3

4568
Mississippi Department of Archives and History
100 S State St, 39205 [PO Box 571, 39205-0571]; (p) (601) 359-6850; (f) (601) 359-6975; webmaster@mdah.state.ms.us; www.mdah.state.ms.us; (c) Hinds

State/ 1902/ State of MS/ staff: 128(f); 33(p); 110(v)/publication: *Journal of Mississippi History*

ALLIANCE OF HISTORICAL AGENCIES; HISTORIC PRESERVATION AGENCY; HISTORIC SITE; HISTORICAL SOCIETY; HISTORY MUSEUM; HOUSE MUSEUM: Responsible for the care and custody of the state's official archives and for collecting material relating to the history of MS.

PROGRAMS: Community Outreach; Concerts; Exhibits; Facility Rental; Family Programs; Festivals; Film/Video; Guided Tours; Interpretation; Lectures; Living History; Publication; Reenactments; Research Library/Archives

COLLECTIONS: [Prehistory-present] Artifacts and documents relating to all aspects of MS history and prehistory.

HOURS: Yr, varies

ADMISSION: No charge

4569
Mississippi Governor's Mansion
300 E Capitol St, 39201; (p) (601) 359-6421, (601) 359-3175; (f) (601) 359-6473; (c) Hinds

State/ 1842/ MS Dept of Archives and History/ staff: 1(f); 41(v)/publication: *An Illustrated Guide to the Mississippi Governor's Mansion*

HISTORIC SITE; HOUSE MUSEUM: A National Historic Landmark that serves as an historic house museum and as the official residence of the governor of the state.

PROGRAMS: Exhibits; Facility Rental; Guided Tours; Publication

COLLECTIONS: [19th c] Furniture and furnishings, primarily Empire style.

HOURS: Yr T-F 9:30-11

ADMISSION: No charge

4570
Mississippi Historical Society
100 S State St, 39205 [PO Box 571, 39205-0571]; (p) (601) 359-6850; (f) (601) 359-6975; webmaster@mdah.state.ms.us; www.mdah.state.ms.us; (c) Hinds

Private non-profit/ 1858/ members: 1282/publication: *Journal of Mississippi History*

HISTORICAL SOCIETY: An association of professional historians and laypersons interested in MS history; publishes a quarterly academic journal and holds an annual meeting.

PROGRAMS: Annual Meeting; Guided Tours; Lectures; Publication

ADMISSION: Student $5

4571
Mississippi Sports Hall of Fame and Museum
1152 Lakeland Dr, 39236 [PO Box 16021, 39236-6021]; (p) (601) 982-8264, (800) 280-3263; (f) (601) 982-4702; msfame@bellsouth. net; www.msfame.com; (c) Hinds

Private non-profit/ MS Sports Foundation, Inc./ staff: 5(f); 1(p); 50(v)/ members: 200/publication: *Legends*

HISTORY MUSEUM: Artifact displays, numerous participatory exhibits and a three-screen, multi-media presentation in its theatre.

PROGRAMS: Annual Meeting; Exhibits; Facility Rental; Living History; Publication; Theatre

COLLECTIONS: [1980-present] Turn of the century baseball equipment, display on equestrian sports, access to interviews, archival footage and achievement data on four touch screen kiosks.

HOURS: Yr M-Sa 10-4, Su 1:30-4:30

ADMISSION: $5, Students, Seniors $3.50

4572
Museum of the Southern Jewish Experience
4915 I-55 N, Ste 204-B, 39236 [PO Box 16528, 39236]; (p) (601) 362-6357; (f) (601) 366-6293; information@msje.org; www.msje.org; (c) Hinds

1989/ Institute of Southern Jewish Life/ staff: 6(f); 3(p); 10(v)/ members: 700/publication: *Cultural Corridors: Discovering Jewish Heritage Along the Mississippi River; Clara Lowenburg Moses, Memoir of a Southern Jewish Woman*

HISTORIC PRESERVATION AGENCY; HISTORY MUSEUM; RESEARCH CENTER: Interprets, documents and preserves traditions of Southern Jewish life through exhibits, programs, publications and community outreach.

PROGRAMS: Community Outreach; Elder's Programs; Exhibits; Facility Rental; Film/Video; Guided Tours; Interpretation; Lectures; Publication; Research Library/Archives

COLLECTIONS: [19th-20th c] Historic properties, ceremonial items, southern Jewish artifacts and memorabilia, photography, family and congregational papers, and furniture and architectural elements from southern synagogues.

HOURS: Yr Daily 10-5 by appt

ADMISSION: $5, Student $4, Seniors $4; Group rates

4573
Mynelle Gardens
4736 Clinton Blvd, 39209-2402; (p) (601) 960-1894; (f) (601) 922-5759; (c) Hinds

City/ 1923

GARDEN; HOUSE MUSEUM: Horticultural activities and development.

PROGRAMS: Annual Meeting; Concerts; Facility Rental; Family Programs; Festivals; Garden Tours; Research Library/Archives

COLLECTIONS: [1920s] 1920s style garden.

HOURS: Yr Mar-Oct 9-5:15; Nov-Feb 8-4:15

ADMISSION: $2, Children $0.50

4574
Oaks House Museum , The
823 N Jefferson St, 39202-4140; (p) (601) 353-9339

1850/ staff: 3(f)

Maintains one of the oldest house in Jackson, and the oldest residence in the city to be continuously occupied.

COLLECTIONS: Furnishings.

HOURS: Yr

4575
Old Capitol Museum of Mississippi History
100 S State St, 39205 [PO Box 571, 39205]; (p) (601) 359-6920, (601) 359-6925; (f) (601) 359-6921; www.mdah.state.ms.us; (c) Hinds

State/ 1961/ MS Dept of Archives and History/ staff: 11(f); 10(p); 100(v)

HISTORY MUSEUM: Collects, preserves, researches, and interprets artifacts related to MS history for public education. Housed in a 19th c Greek Revival building and National Historic Landmark that served as the State Capitol from 1839 to 1903.

PROGRAMS: Community Outreach; Exhibits; Facility Rental; Guided Tours; Interpretation; Lectures

COLLECTIONS: [18th-20th c] 10,000 museum artifacts.

HOURS: Yr M-F 8-5, Sa 9:30-4:30, Su 12:30-4:30

ADMISSION: No charge

4576
Scott-Ford Historic Site, Farish St Historic District
136 & 138 Cohea St, 39202 [440 N Mill St, 39202]; (p) (601) 949-4000; (f) (601) 949-9919; farish1@bellsouth.net; (c) Hinds

Private non-profit/ 1995/ Scott-Ford House, Inc.

HISTORIC SITE; HOUSE MUSEUM

PROGRAMS: Community Outreach; Exhibits; Family Programs; Film/Video; Garden Tours; Guided Tours; Interpretation; Living History; Publication; School-Based Curriculum

KOSCIUSKO

4577
Attala Historical Society
N Huntington St & E Washington St, 39090 [PO Box 127, 39090]; (p) (662) 289-5516; (c) Attala

Private non-profit/ 1972/ staff: 20(v)/ members: 200

Collects, preserves, and disseminates historical material and information. Maintains the Mary Ricks Thornton Cultural Center.

COLLECTIONS: Delta Gamma Founders room furnished in period antiques and accessories, a large oil portrait of three founders by Jason Bouldin, and Romanesque American Victorian stained glass windows.

HOURS: Yr M-Sa 11-3

LONG BEACH

4578
Long Beach Historical Society
[PO Box 244, 39560]; (p) (228) 863-2387; (c) Harrison

Private non-profit/ 1997/ Board of Directors/ staff: 30(v)/ members: 235

HISTORIC PRESERVATION AGENCY; HISTORICAL SOCIETY: Preserves and records local history.

PROGRAMS: Annual Meeting; Community Outreach; Exhibits; Festivals; Guided Tours; Lectures; Living History; School-Based Curriculum

COLLECTIONS: [1745-present] Copies of early maps and deeds, photographs, and school memorabilia.

LUKA

4579
Tishomingo County Historical and Genealogical Society
204 N Main St, 38852; (p) (601) 423-1971; (f) (601) 423-2543; cdnelson@networkone.com; www.geocities.com/Heartland/Acres/1038; (c) Tishomingo

1996/ State of MS/ staff: 1(p); 2(v)/ members: 250/publication: *Chronicles and Epitaphs*

GENEALOGICAL SOCIETY; HISTORICAL SOCIETY: Promotes interested in Tishomingo County history and family genealogy, encourages preservation of records, promotes educational programs, and publishes literature related to local histories and genealogies.

PROGRAMS: Annual Meeting; Festivals; Lectures; Publication; Research Library/Archives

COLLECTIONS: [1830s-1960s]

HOURS: Yr T-Th 9-12/1-4

ADMISSION: No charge

MACON

4580
Noxubee County Historical Society, Inc.
King St, 39341 [PO Box 392, 39341]; (p) (601) 726-5218; www.rootsweb.com/~msnox-ube/society.html; (c) Noxubee

Private non-profit/ 1967/ staff: 10(v)/ members: 250

HISTORICAL SOCIETY; HISTORY MUSEUM: Collects and preserves manuscripts, presents programs, and exhibitions.

PROGRAMS: Exhibits; Living History

COLLECTIONS: [1850-present] All types of items pertaining to local history.

HOURS: By appt only

ADMISSION: $2

MANTACHIE

4581
Itawamba Historical Society
Museum Dr, 38855 [PO Box 7, 38855]; (p) (662) 282-7664; (c) Itawamba

Private non-profit/ 1981/ staff: 1(p)/ members: 450/publication: Itawamba Settlers

GENEALOGICAL SOCIETY; HISTORICAL SOCIETY; HISTORY MUSEUM; HOUSE MU-SEUM: Preserves and provides access to local and regional records.

PROGRAMS: Annual Meeting; Community Outreach; Exhibits; Facility Rental; Guided Tours; Publication; Research Library/Archives

COLLECTIONS: [1837-present] Family and county history, cemetery records, censuses, newspaper on microfilm and microfiche, research books, and artifacts.

HOURS: Yr T-F 10-3

MERIDIAN

4582
Meridian Restorations Foundation, Inc.
905 Martin Luther King Dr, 39301; (p) (601) 483-8439; (c) Lauderdale

Private non-profit/ 1968/ staff: 4(f); 3(p); 150(v)/ members: 150

HOUSE MUSEUM: Restores, furnishes, and maintains two historically important landmarks from the 19th c Merrehope and Frank W. Wilson House.

PROGRAMS: Annual Meeting; Community Outreach; Concerts; Exhibits; Facility Rental; Family Programs; Guided Tours; Interpretation; School-Based Curriculum

COLLECTIONS: [Antebellum and Victorian South] Two restored homes containing furniture of the period, along with artifacts, books, dolls and toys, clothing, paintings, and mirrors.

HOURS: Yr M-Sa 9-4

ADMISSION: $8, Seniors $5; Group rates

MONTICELLO

4583
Longino House
136 Caswell St, 39654 [PO Box 100, 39654]; (p) (601) 587-7732

NATCHEZ

4584
Grand Village of the Natchez Indians
400 Jefferson Davis Blvd, 39120; (p) (601) 446-6502; (f) (601) 446-6503; gvni@bkbank.com; www.mdah.state.ms.us; (c) Adams

State/ 1976/ MS Dept of Archives and History/ staff: 7(f); 2(p); 25(v)/publication: The Natchez Indians

ARCHAEOLOGICAL SITE/MUSEUM; HIS-TORIC SITE: Maintains a National Historic Landmark and museum.

PROGRAMS: Concerts; Elder's Programs; Exhibits; Festivals; Film/Video; Guided Tours; Interpretation; Publication

COLLECTIONS: [c. AD 1200-1730] Items associated with the Natchez Indians or with groups with whom they were in contact.

HOURS: Yr M-Sa 9-5, Su 1:30-5

4585
Historic Natchez Foundation
108 S Commerce St, 39120 [PO Box 1761, 39120]; (p) (601) 442-2500; (f) (601) 442-2525; hnf@natchez.org; (c) Adams

Private non-profit/ 1974/ staff: 4(f); 6(p); 1(v)/ members: 600/publication: Progressive Preservation

HISTORIC PRESERVATION AGENCY; HIS-TORICAL SOCIETY; RESEARCH CENTER: Preserves, develops, collects, promotes, and interprets the unique character of Natchez for purposes related to education, enjoyment, ethnic harmony, economic development, and general quality of life.

PROGRAMS: Annual Meeting; Community Outreach; Exhibits; Festivals; Guided Tours; Interpretation; Lectures; Publication; Research Library/Archives

COLLECTIONS: [1800s-present] Adams County Circuit Court Records, Natchez history research and site files, slide and photo collections, and local history library.

HOURS: Yr M-F 9-5; Appt necessary for accessing research material

ADMISSION: No charge

4586
Melrose, Natchez National Historical Park
1 Melrose-Montebello Pkwy, 39120 [504 S Canal St, 39120]; (p) (601) 446-5790, (601) 442-7047; (f) (601) 442-9554

1841/ National Park Service/ staff: 15(f)

COLLECTIONS: [1840-1865] Mid-19th c furniture original to the house or to Natchez; library of site-specific photographs, journals, and correspondence dating to the early 19th c.

HOURS: Yr

4587
Natchez Garden Club
215 S Pearl St, 39120; (p) (601) 443-9065, (601) 442-6672; (f) (601) 443-9065; (c) Adams

Private non-profit/ 1927/ Executive Board/ staff: 10(f); 3(p); 300(v)/ members: 500

GARDEN; HISTORIC PRESERVATION AGENCY; HISTORIC SITE; HOUSE MUSE-UM: Preserved and restored two houses.

PROGRAMS: Elder's Programs; Exhibits; Facility Rental; Garden Tours; Guided Tours; Lectures

COLLECTIONS: [19th c] Furniture, kitchen items and utensils, dolls and costumes. The House on Ellicot Hill was built circa 1798 and is located near the site where the American flag was raised for the first time in the Lower Mississippi Valley. Built in 1858, Magnolia Hall is an outstanding example of Greek Revival architecture and is listed in the National Register of Historic Places.

HOURS: Yr Daily 9-5

ADMISSION: $6

4588
Natchez Historical Society
[PO Box 49, 39121]; (p) (601) 446-7720; (c) Adams

Private non-profit/ 1954/ Natchez Historical Society/ members: 160

HISTORIC PRESERVATION AGENCY; HIS-TORICAL SOCIETY: Collects and preserves historical and genealogical material on the Old Natchez District and its early inhabitants.

PROGRAMS: Annual Meeting; Community Outreach; Exhibits; Film/Video; Lectures; Living History

4589
Natchez National Historical Park
210 State St, 39120 [504 S Canal St, 39120]; (p) (601) 446-7047, (601) 446-5790; (f) (601) 442-8845

1841/ National Park Service/ staff: 15(f)

COLLECTIONS: [1841-1857] Original furnishings and archaeological artifacts recovered during restoration; William Johnson's diary, 1835-1857, and his family papers are housed at LSU. The diary has been published by LSU Press.

HOURS: Appt

4590
Rosalie
100 Orleans St, 39120; (p) (601) 445-4555, (601) 446-5676; (f) (601) 445-9137; www.Rosalie.net; (c) Adams

Private non-profit/ 1938/ MS State Society Daughters of the American Revolution/ staff: 1(f); 14(p)

GARDEN; HOUSE MUSEUM: 19th c mansion surrounded by formal gardens and the original detached kitchen.

PROGRAMS: Concerts; Festivals; Garden Tours; Guided Tours

COLLECTIONS: [1790-1858] Belter furniture and oil paintings of daughter of second owner.

HOURS: Yr Daily 9-4:30

ADMISSION: $6, Children $3; Under 7 free

NEW ALBANY

4591
Union County Historical Society and Heritage Museum
114 Cleveland St, 38652 [PO Box 657, 38652]; (p) (662) 538-0014; (f) (662) 538-6019; (c) Union

Private non-profit/ 1991/ Board of Directors/ staff: 1(f); 1(p); 25(v)/ members: 350/publication: *Cookbook: Worth Savoring*

HISTORICAL SOCIETY; HISTORY MUSEUM: Promotes an appreciation of the county's culture and heritage by collecting, preserving, exhibiting, and interpreting important aspects of its history for the public's enjoyment and educational experience.

PROGRAMS: Annual Meeting; Community Outreach; Exhibits; Festivals; Lectures; Publication

COLLECTIONS: [1700s-present] Artifacts, books, letters, paintings, and photographs.

HOURS: Yr M-F 10-5, Sa-Su by appt

ADMISSION: Donations accepted

OCEAN SPRINGS

4592
Fort Maurepas Society
Front Beach Blvd, 39564 [PO Box 1741, 39564]; (p) (228) 875-4369; (c) Jackson

Private non-profit/ 1992/ Fort Maurepas Society Officers/ staff: 10(v)/ members: 50

HISTORICAL SOCIETY; LIVING HISTORY/ OUTDOOR MUSEUM: Preserves the history of Fort Maurepas and presents living history reenactments.

PROGRAMS: Guided Tours; Interpretation; Lectures; Living History; Reenactments

HOURS: By appt

ADMISSION: No charge

4593
Ocean Springs Genealogical Society
[PO Box 1765, 39564]; (p) (228) 875-4920; www.rootsweb.com/~msosgs/; (c) Jackson

Private non-profit/ 1978/ members: 50

GENEALOGICAL SOCIETY: Promotes and assists family research, maintains genealogy collection at local library, provides help 3 times a week in research room.

PROGRAMS: Annual Meeting; Community Outreach; Family Programs; Lectures; Research Library/Archives

OXFORD

4594
Rowan Oak, Home of William Faulkner
Old Taylor Rd, [University of Mississippi, University, 38677]; (p) (601) 234-3284; (f) (601) 236-3293

1848/ Univ of MS/ staff: 1(f); 3(p)

COLLECTIONS: [1962] Personal possessions and furnishings of Faulkners are the only collections on exhibit; All archival materials are

being re-located at the University of Mississippi library in the future.

HOURS: Yr

4595
Skipwith Historical and Genealogical Society
401 Bramlett Blvd, Lafayette Co Library, 38655 [PO Box 1382, 38655]; (p) (601) 234-5751; jmurphey@dixie-net.com; www.rootsweb.com~mslafaye/index.html; (c) Lafayette

Private non-profit/ 1967/ Elected Board/ staff: 12(v)/ members: 150/publication: *Lafayette County Heritage News*

GENEALOGICAL SOCIETY; HISTORICAL SOCIETY; RESEARCH CENTER: Studies, collects, preserves, and disseminates historical, genealogical, and biographical information about the local area and its founders.

PROGRAMS: Lectures; Publication; Research Library/Archives

COLLECTIONS: [1830s-present] Civil War records, periodical subscriptions, sets of local genealogical society newsletters, microfilm of all censuses, and local newspapers.

HOURS: Yr M-Th 9:30-8, F-Sa 9:30-5:30

ADMISSION: No charge

PASCAGOULA

4596
La Pointe-Krebs House and the Old Spanish Fort Museum
4602 Fort Ave, 39567; (p) (228) 769-1505; (f) (228) 769-1432; lpkhouse@aol.com; (c) Jackson

Private non-profit/ 1948/ Board of Directors, Jackson County Historical Society/ staff: 2(f)/ members: 125

HISTORICAL SOCIETY; HOUSE MUSEUM: Preserves and protects the La Pointe-Krebs House and the Old Spanish Fort Museum.

PROGRAMS: Exhibits; Facility Rental; Festivals; Guided Tours

COLLECTIONS: [18th c French Colonial] Early coins, a replica of the Fort Maurepas corner stone, and an original Civil War muster roll.

HOURS: Yr M-Sa 9:30-4:30, Su 12-4:30

ADMISSION: $4, Children $2, Seniors $3

4597
Scranton Floating Museum
River Side Park, 39568 [PO Box 908, 39568-0908]; (p) (228) 938-6612; (f) (228) 938-6795; (c) Jackson

1985/ City of Pascagoula/ staff: 3(f); 1(p)/ members: 10

HISTORY MUSEUM: An authentic 70 foot commercial shrimp boat that has been converted into a museum and educates the public about the shrimping industry.

PROGRAMS: Community Outreach; Exhibits; Film/Video; Guided Tours; Interpretation; Research Library/Archives

COLLECTIONS: [1940s-1950s] Displays: shrimping history, marsh lands, sea shells and cultural and natural history of MS.

HOURS: Yr T-Sa 10-4, Su 1-4

ADMISSION: No charge

4598
Scranton Nature Center Museum
3928 Nathan Hale, 39568 [PO Box 908, 39568-0908]; (p) (228) 938-6612; (f) (228) 938-6795; (c) Jackson

City/ 1998/ staff: 3(f); 1(p)/ members: 10

HISTORY MUSEUM: Promotes and preserves the cultural and natural history of MS.

PROGRAMS: Exhibits; Film/Video; Guided Tours; Interpretation; Research Library/ Archives

COLLECTIONS: [Pre-historic-present] An environmental learning center with exhibits on plants, rocks, minerals, fossils, live snakes, and other animals.

HOURS: Yr T-Sa 10-4, Su 1-4

PASS CHRISTIAN

4599
Pass Christian Historical Society
203 E Scenic Dr, 39571 [PO Box 58, 39571]; (p) (228) 452-0063; (c) Harrison

Private non-profit/ 1966/ Board of Trustees/ staff: 20(v)/ members: 268/publication: *Brief History of Pass Christian*

HISTORIC PRESERVATION AGENCY; HISTORICAL SOCIETY; HISTORY MUSEUM: Collects and preserves historical records, documents, and artifacts.

PROGRAMS: Annual Meeting; Exhibits; Family Programs; Lectures; Publication; Research Library/Archives; School-Based Curriculum

COLLECTIONS: [1800s-present] Publications, tapes of oral history interviews, photographs, artifacts.

HOURS: Yr M-F 10-3

ADMISSION: No charge

PICAYUNE

4600
Crosby Arboretum, Mississippi State Univ
370 Ridge Rd, 39466 [PO Box 1639, 39466]; (p) (601) 799-2311; (f) (601) 799-2372; crosby-yar@datastar.net; msstate.edu/dept/crec/camain.html; (c) Pearl River

State/ 1980/ MS State Univ/ staff: 5(f); 1(p); 20(v)/ members: 450

GARDEN; NATURAL HISTORY MUSEUM: Preserves, protects, and displays plants native to the Pearl River basin.

PROGRAMS: Annual Meeting; Community Outreach; Facility Rental; Festivals; Garden Tours; Guided Tours; Interpretation; Lectures; Research Library/Archives

COLLECTIONS: Interpretive center has walking trails through restored and created aquatic, savanna and woodland plant communities, and historic architecture by E. Fay Jones.

HOURS: Yr W-Su 9-4:30

PORT GIBSON

4601
Grand Gulf Military Monument Commission
Grand Gulf Rd, 39150 [Rt 2, PO Box 389, 39150]; (p) (601) 437-5911; (f) (601) 437-2929; park@grandgulf.state.ms.us; www.grandgulfpark.state.ms.us; (c) Clairborne

State/ 1958/ State of MS Commissioners/ staff: 6(f); 1(p)

BATTLEFIELD; HISTORIC SITE; HISTORY MUSEUM; HOUSE MUSEUM; LIVING HISTORY/OUTDOOR MUSEUM: Civil War battlefield and museum contains both Civil War items and county history.

PROGRAMS: Facility Rental; Living History

COLLECTIONS: [Civil War] Civil War relics, Indian arrowheads, antique buggies and coaches, cemetery, and historic houses.

HOURS: Yr M-Su 8-9

ADMISSION: $1.50, Students $0.75

4602
Mississippi Cultural Crossroads
507 Market St, 39150; (p) (601) 437-8905; (f) (601) 437-4430; dcrosby@lorman.alcorn.edu; (c) Claiborne

Private non-profit/ 1978/ staff: 2(f); 3(p); 10(v)/publication: I Ain't Lying

CULTURAL CENTER: Promotes educational, cultural, and economic development by providing programs in the arts and humanities and creating opportunities for people to celebrate their heritages and learn respect for other cultures.

PROGRAMS: Community Outreach; Elder's Programs; Exhibits; Facility Rental; Family Programs; Publication; School-Based Curriculum; Theatre

HOURS: Yr M-F 9-4

ADMISSION: No charge

SANDY HOOK

4603
John Ford Home
[c/o Marion County Hist Soc, One Hugh White Place, Columbia, 39429]; (p) (601) 736-4328, (601) 736-1763; (f) (601) 731-3999; www.waidsoft.com/methodist.html

1800/ staff: 1(p)

COLLECTIONS: Arrow heads, farm implements; Early slave records, land grants.

HOURS: Seasonal

SARDIS

4604
Heflin House Museum
304 S Main St, 38666; (p) (601) 487-3451, (601) 487-1047; (f) (601) 487-3389; rosalee@panola.com; (c) Panola

Private non-profit/ 1973/ Heflin House Heritage Association/ staff: 50(v)/ members: 100

HISTORY MUSEUM; HOUSE MUSEUM: Promotes the history of Panola County from Indian times through 1900.

PROGRAMS: Annual Meeting; Community Outreach; Exhibits; Facility Rental; Family Programs

COLLECTIONS: [18th-19th c] Artifacts of Panola County displayed throughout the home.

HOURS: Yr every 3rd Su 2-4 or by appt

ADMISSION: Donations accepted

SENATOBIA

4605
Tate County Genealogical and Historical Society
107 Robinson St, 38668 [PO Box 974, 38668]; (p) (601) 562-0390; www.rootsweb.com/~mstate/gensoc.html; (c) Tate

Private non-profit/ 1983/ Elected Board/ staff: 20(v)/ members: 175/publication: Tate Trails

GENEALOGICAL SOCIETY; HISTORICAL SOCIETY: A genealogical research library and county archives.

PROGRAMS: Publication; Research Library/Archives

COLLECTIONS: State censuses on microfilm, regional county records on microfilm, printed records from most states in US, census indices, family histories and general research material.

HOURS: Yr Th-F 10-4:30

TUPELO

4606
Elvis Presley Birthplace
306 Elvis Presley Dr, 38802 [PO Box 1339, 38802]; (p) (601)

4607
Mount Locust
Milepost 155, Natchez Trace Pkwy, 38801 [2680 Natchez Trace Pkwy, 38801]; (p) (601) 680-4024, (601) 445-4211; (f) (601) 680-4033; sara_amy_leach@nps.gov; www.nps.gov/natr

1780/ National Park Service/ staff: 1(f); 2(p)

COLLECTIONS: [1780-1820] Furniture, original family pieces, artifacts, Ferguson family papers.

HOURS: Feb-Nov

4608
Natchez Trace Parkway
Milepost 266, NTP, 38804 [2680 Natchez Trace Pky, 38804]; (p) (662) 680-4022; (f) (662) 680-4034; natr_interpretation@nps.gov; www.nps.gov/natr/; (c) Lee

Federal/ 1938/ National Park Service/ staff: 139(f); 157(v)

HISTORIC SITE: Maintains 444 mile parkway, library, and archives containing material on park's history.

PROGRAMS: Exhibits; Festivals; Film/Video; Interpretation; Research Library/Archives

COLLECTIONS: [1780-1830; 1930s] Old Southwest settlement and 20th c parkway construction: manuscripts, government correspondence, newspaper items, maps, drawings, photographs, house furnishings; archeological collection located off-site.

HOURS: Yr Daily 8-5

ADMISSION: No charge

4609
Northeast Mississippi Historical and Geneological Society
219 N Madison, 38802 [PO Box 434, 38802-0434]; (c) Lee

Private non-profit/ 1976/ staff: 20(v)/ members: 450/publication: The Northeast Mississippi Historical and Genealogical Society Quarterly

GENEALOGICAL SOCIETY; HISTORICAL SOCIETY: Preserves the history of Northeast MS and the families in the region.

PROGRAMS: Annual Meeting; Family Programs; Publication

UNIVERSITY

4610
University Museum, University of Mississippi
5th St and University Ave, 38677; (p) (601) 232-7073; (f) (601) 232-7010; museums@ole miss.edu; www.olemiss.edu/depts/u_museum; (c) Lafayette

1939/ Univ of MS/ staff: 5(f); 7(p); 80(v)/ members: 345/publication: Memories of Mississippi

HOUSE MUSEUM: Preserves and promotes the history of the University, Oxford, and north MS, as well as objects related to the curriculum in art, classical archeology, anthropology, physics, astronomy and engineering.

PROGRAMS: Annual Meeting; Community Outreach; Exhibits; Family Programs; Guided Tours; Interpretation; Lectures; Publication; School-Based Curriculum

COLLECTIONS: [1880-1926] Furniture, textiles, and decorative arts that relate to Oxford and north MS history.

4611
University of Mississippi, Music Library and Blues Archives
340 Farley Hall, Room 340, 38677; (p) (601) 232-7753; (f) (601) 232-5161; www.olemiss.edu/depts/general_library/files/music/bluesarc.html; (c) Lafayette

State/ 1984/ Univ of MS/ staff: 3(f); 8(p)

LIBRARY AND/OR ARCHIVES: A research-level collection devoted to American blues music, including that of the MS Delta, with a basic collection of Western classical music.

PROGRAMS: Research Library/Archives

COLLECTIONS: [1890-present] 42,000 recordings in 78, 33 1/3, and 45 rpm formats and compact discs, 12,000 books, and 700 magazine titles.

HOURS: Yr M-F 9-5

ADMISSION: No charge

4612
Walton-Young Historic House
5th St & University Ave, 38677 [University of Mississippi Museums, 38677]; (p) (601) 232-7073; www.olemiss.edu/depts/u_museum

1800/ Univ of MS/ staff: 1(p)

COLLECTIONS: [1880-1900] Historical collection covers family history from early Virginia to post Civil War decorative artifacts including glass, ceramics, silver; letters of Stark Young, family diaries.

HOURS: By appt

VAUGHAN

4613
Casey Jones Railroad Museum State Park

10901 Vaughan Rd #1, 39179; (p) (662) 673-9864; (f) (662) 673-9864; holmesp@ayrix.net; (c) Yazoo

State/ 1980/ MiS Dept of Wildlife, Fisheries, and Parks/ staff: 1(f)

HISTORIC SITE; HISTORY MUSEUM: Examines the role of trains in MS history and folk hero Casey Jones.

PROGRAMS: Exhibits; Festivals

HOURS: Yr M-T,Th-F 8-5; W and Sa 8-12

ADMISSION: $1, Children $0.50

VICKSBURG

4614
Balfour House

1002 Crawford St, 39181 [PO Box 781, 39181]; (p) (601) 638-7113; (f) (601) 638-8484; shumble@vicksburg.com; www.balfourhouse.com; (c) Warren

Private for-profit/ staff: 2(f); 4(p)

HISTORIC SITE

PROGRAMS: Facility Rental; Guided Tours; Living History; Reenactments

COLLECTIONS: [Civil War] Federal, Empire, and Victorian home furnishings; artifacts from "Siege of Vicksburg" found in home during restoration; and an authentic jug mine named "Infernal Machine."

HOURS: Mar-Dec M-Sa 10-5, Su by appt

4615
Columns, The

2002 Cherry St, 39180; (p) (601) 634-4751; (f) (601) 638-6108

1899/ Private/ staff: 1(v)

COLLECTIONS: [Victorian, Turn-of-the-century] Blank/colored demitasse cup/saucer - 1st made in America; 1750s plantation secretary; 17 ft. banquet table; butter tray. Rosewood suite made for Napoleon when Mayor Girod offered his home to deposed Emperor.

HOURS: Seasonal

4616
Gray and Blue Naval Society

1102 Washington St, 39183; (p) (601) 638-6500; (f) (601) 638-8746; grayblue@vicksburg.com; www.grayandbluenavalmuseum.usre.net; (c) Warren

Private non-profit/ 1993/ staff: 1(p); 2(v)

HISTORICAL SOCIETY; HISTORY MUSEUM: Preserves the history of the navies of the Civil War and operates a museum.

PROGRAMS: Elder's Programs; Exhibits; Facility Rental; Guided Tours; Lectures; Research Library/Archives

COLLECTIONS: [Civil War] Ship models, dioramas, and paintings.

HOURS: Yr M-Sa 9-5

ADMISSION: $2.50, Children $1.50

4617
Martha Vick House

1300 Grove St, 39183; (p) (601) 638-7036; (c) Warren

Private for-profit/ 1984/ staff: 2(f); 1(p); 10(v)

HOUSE MUSEUM: Last remaining Vick home, built for the daughter of the founder of Vicksburg in 1830.

PROGRAMS: Facility Rental

COLLECTIONS: [19th c] Paintings by French postimpressionist Frederick August Ragot.

HOURS: Yr M-Sa 9-5, Su 2-5

ADMISSION: $5; Group rates

4618
McRaven Tour Home

1445 Harrison St, 39180; (p) (601) 636-1663; www.mcraven.com

4619
USS Cairo Museum, Vicksburg National Military Park

3201 Clay St, 39183; (p) (601) 636-2199; (f) (601) 638-7329; vick_cirs_3@nps.gov; www.nps.gov/vick/backup; (c) Warren

Federal/ 1980/ National Park Service, Dept of Interior/ staff: 3(f); 1(p)

HISTORY MUSEUM: Preserves and protects the cultural and natural resources.

PROGRAMS: Exhibits; Film/Video; Interpretation

COLLECTIONS: [Civil War] Items recovered from the sunken ironclad USS Cairo, which includes a sailor's personal possessions, cookware, and weaponry.

HOURS: Yr M-Su Nov-Mar 8:30-5, April-Oct 9:30-6

ADMISSION: $4/car; No charge for museum

4620
Vicksburg and Warren County Historical Society

1008 Cherry St, 39183; (p) (601) 636-0741; (c) Warren

Private non-profit/ 1946/ Vicksburg and Warren County Historical Society/ staff: 5(f); 1(p)/ members: 400

HISTORICAL SOCIETY; HISTORY MUSEUM

PROGRAMS: Annual Meeting; Concerts; Exhibits; Festivals; Lectures; Research Library/Archives

COLLECTIONS: [1850s-1900]

HOURS: Yr M-Sa 8:30-4:30, Su 1:30-4:30

ADMISSION: $3, Student $2

4621
Vicksburg Foundation for Historic Preservation

1107 Washington St, 39181 [PO Box 254, 39181]; (p) (601) 636-5010; (f) (601) 636-5010; bccmuseum@bellsouth.net; (c) Warren

Private non-profit/ 1958/ staff: 2(f); 3(p); 50(v)/ members: 380

HISTORIC PRESERVATION AGENCY; HISTORIC SITE; HISTORY MUSEUM: Identifies, preserves, protects, and interprets the historic environment of Vicksburg and Warren County.

PROGRAMS: Annual Meeting; Community Outreach; Exhibits; Interpretation; Lectures

COLLECTIONS: [1886-present] Artifacts associated with veterinary science, Coca-Cola memorabilia and artifacts associated with the Biedenharn family, who were the first bottlers of Coca-Cola.

HOURS: Yr M-Sa 9-5, Su 1:30-4:30

ADMISSION: $2.95, Children $1.95

4622
Vicksburg Genealogical Society

[PO Box 1161, 39181-1161]; (p) (601) 634-4581, (601) 638-0744; DARDEAUEA@aol.com; www.rootsweb.com/~msvgs/index.htm; (c) Warren

Private non-profit/ 1982/ staff: 150(v)/ members: 150/publication: Mississippi River Routes

GENEALOGICAL SOCIETY: Promotes interest in genealogy, provides assistance and instruction on genealogical matters, cooperates with other societies having similar interests, publishes genealogical material, and fosters the acquisition of genealogical materials for the Warren County-Vicksburg Public Library.

PROGRAMS: Lectures; Publication

4623
Vicksburg National Military Parks

3201 Clay Street, 39183; (p) (601) 636-0583; (f) (601) 636-9497; VICK_Interpretation@nps.gov; www.nps.gov/vick/pphtml/contacts.html

1899/ National Parks Service

BATTLEFIELD; HISTORIC SITE; NATIONAL PARK: Established to commemorate the site of one of the most decisive battles of the American Civil War, the campaign, siege, and defense of Vicksburg.

PROGRAMS: Exhibits; Film/Video; Interpretation

COLLECTIONS: [Civil War Era] 1,325 historic monuments and markers, 20 miles of reconstructed trenches and earthworks, a 16 mile tour road, antebellum home, 144 emplaced cannon, restored Union gunboat-USS Cairo, and the Vicksburg National Cemetery.

HOURS: Nov-Mar 8:30-5; Apr-Oct 9:30-6

ADMISSION: $4/per vehicle

WASHINGTON

4624
Historic Jefferson College

16 Old N St, 39190 [PO Box 700, 39190]; (p) (601) 442-2901; (f) (601) 442-2902; hjc@bkbank.com; mdah.state.ms.us; (c) Adams

State/ 1977/ MS Dept of Archives and History/ staff: 9(f); 2(p); 25(v)/ members: 525

HISTORIC SITE; HISTORY MUSEUM: Maintains a museum, 19th c buildings, sales shop, and nature trails.

PROGRAMS: Concerts; Elder's Programs; Exhibits; Festivals; Guided Tours; Interpretation; Lectures; Living History

COLLECTIONS: [1798-1964] Items associated with the history of the MS Territory and with the history of Jefferson College.

HOURS: Yr M-Sa 9-5, Su 1-5

ADMISSION: No charge

WEST POINT

4625
Waverley Plantation Mansion, Inc.
1 mile off Hwy 50 between Columbus & W Point, 39773 [Rt 2, PO Box 234, 39773]; (p) (601) 494-1399; (c) Clay

Private for-profit/ 1852/ staff: 5(f); 15(v)

HISTORIC SITE; HOUSE MUSEUM: The National Historic Landmark, a privately owned plantation mansion is open daily.

PROGRAMS: Garden Tours; Guided Tours

COLLECTIONS: [18th-19th c] Period furnishings, some original.

HOURS: Sept-Feb Daily 9-5; Mar-Aug Daily 9-6

ADMISSION: $7.50; Group rates

WOODVILLE

4626
Rosemont Plantation
Hwy 24 East, 39669 [PO Box 814, 39669]; (p) (601) 888-6809; (f) (601) 888-8606; pbeacroft@aol.com; (c) Wilkinson

Private non-profit/ staff: 2(f)

HISTORIC SITE; HOUSE MUSEUM; PRESIDENTIAL SITE; RESEARCH CENTER: Preserves family home of President Jefferson Davis.

PROGRAMS: Exhibits; Garden Tours; Guided Tours; Interpretation; Lectures; Research Library/Archives

COLLECTIONS: [1810-1895] Memorabilia of Davis family, books, furnishings, plus archives of Davis family history.

HOURS: Mar-mid Dec M-F 10-5

ADMISSION: $6, Children $3

4627
Woodville Civic Club, Inc.
[PO Box 1055, 39669]; (p) (601) 888-3998; (c) Wilkinson

Private non-profit/ 1971/ staff: 40(v)/ members: 400/publication: *Journal of Wilkinson County History*

ART MUSEUM; HISTORIC PRESERVATION AGENCY; HISTORIC SITE; HISTORICAL SOCIETY; HISTORY MUSEUM

PROGRAMS: Annual Meeting; Community Outreach; Concerts; Exhibits; Guided Tours; Interpretation; Lectures; Publication; Reenactments; Research Library/Archives

HOURS: Yr M-Sa 10-12/2-4

ADMISSION: No charge

MISSOURI

ALTENBURG

4628
Perry County Lutheran Historical Society of Alterburg, Missouri, Inc., The
Church St, 63732 [866 Hwy "C", 63732]; (p) (573) 824-5542; (c) Perry

Private non-profit/ 1910/ staff: 12(v)/ members: 30

HISTORICAL SOCIETY: Preservation of Lutheran Historical Site of Saxon Immigration to Perry County, Missouri, 1839.

PROGRAMS: Exhibits; Guided Tours; Lectures; Research Library/Archives; School-Based Curriculum

COLLECTIONS: [1839] Theological books, Bibles, sermon books, church periodicals, church furniture.

ALTON

4629
Oregon County Genealogical Society
#1 Court Square, 65791 [% Courthouse, 65791]; (p) (417) 778-6414; (f) (417) 778-6414; janicerichardson@hotmail.com; ortrackm.missouri.org/~workst3/index.html; (c) Oregon

County/ 1980/ staff: 4(p); 4(v)/ members: 170

GENEALOGICAL SOCIETY: 500 genealogy books; microfilm county census records 1950-1910 and 3 county newspapers dating 1898-1950; volunteer assistance.

PROGRAMS: Research Library/Archives

COLLECTIONS: County census, marriage, probate, cemetery burials records; newspapers on microfilm, family histories, county histories.

HOURS: Yr M-F 8-4:30

ADMISSION: No charge

APPLEWOOD

4630
Lee's Summit Historical Society
Museum-Old Depot, Lee's Summit, 64063 [625 N E, 64063]; (p) (816) 524-3367; (c) Jackson

Private non-profit/ 1980/ members: 35

HISTORICAL SOCIETY; HISTORY MUSEUM: Preserve the history of Lee's Summit, MO.

PROGRAMS: Annual Meeting

ARROW ROCK

4631
Arrow Rock State Historic Site
Fourth & Van Buren, 65320 [PO Box 1, 65320]; (p) (660) 837-3330; (f) (660) 837-3300; dsparro@mail.dnr.state.mo.us; (c) Saline

State/ 1923/ Dept of Natural Resources, Division of State Parks/ staff: 7(f); 5(p)

HISTORIC SITE; HISTORY MUSEUM; HOUSE MUSEUM: Preserves and interprets history of Missouri's Boone's Lick Region. Emphasis is placed upon Arrow Rock as a landmark and river town circa 1800-1900 and the region's African American and Native American history.

PROGRAMS: Community Outreach; Exhibits; Festivals; Film/Video; Guided Tours; Interpretation; Lectures; Living History; Reenactments; Research Library/Archives; School-Based Curriculum

COLLECTIONS: [1700-1900] Native American materials dating from prehistory to European contact, house furnishings, artwork, textiles, documents, manuscripts, agricultural implements, military equipment, medical equipment, pioneer industry, and river and overland transportation.

HOURS: Mar-Nov Daily 10-4; Dec-Feb Sa, Su 10-4

4632
Bingham House-Arrow Rock State Historic Site
First & High St, 65320; (p) (660) 837-3330; (f) (660) 837-3300; www.arrowrock.org

1837/ MO Dept of Natural Resources/ staff: 7(f); 2(p)

COLLECTIONS: [1830s] 3 Bingham portraits, several prints, personal artifacts of Bingham family; Limited letters, newspaper obituaries pertaining to Bingham family and descendants.

HOURS: Seasonal

4633
Friends of Arrow Rock, Inc.
305 Main St, 65320; (p) (660) 837-3231; (f) (660) 837-3230; www. Arrowrock.org; (c) Saline

Private non-profit/ 1959/ staff: 2(f); 4(p); 50(v)/ members: 700/publication: *Arrow Rock: Where Wheels Started West; and others*

HISTORIC PRESERVATION AGENCY; HISTORIC SITE; HISTORY MUSEUM; HOUSE MUSEUM: Preserves and maintains ten historic buildings of Arrow Rock; interprets the history of these buildings and town.

PROGRAMS: Annual Meeting; Exhibits; Facility Rental; Festivals; Guided Tours; Interpretation; Lectures; Publication; Research Library/Archives

COLLECTIONS: [1820-1900] The historic village and building are furnished with period artifacts.

HOURS: Spring and fall Sa 9-5, Su 12-5; June-Aug Daily M-Sa 9-5, Su 12-5

4634
Sappington Cemetery State Historic Site
Rt TT, 5 miles SW of Arrow Rock, 65320 [c/o Arrow Rock State Historic Site, 65320]; (p) (660) 837-3300; (f) (660) 837-3300; dsparros@mail.dnr.state.mo.us; (c) Saline

State/ 1972

Family cemetery for the Sappington, Jackson, Marmadukel, and Price families, prominent in early Missouri medicine and politics.

COLLECTIONS: [1832-1960] Cemetery: 110 family graves dating back to 1832; Stone wall capped by iron picket fence dating to 1859; Graves of two Missouri Governors, M.M. Marmaduke (1844) and Claiborne F. Jackson (1860-1861).

HOURS: Yr Daily daylight hours

ADMISSION: No charge

AUGUSTA

4635
Friends of Historic Augusta
High & Webster Sts, 63332 [176 Jackson St, 63332]; (p) (636) 228-4303; (f) (636) 482-8020; diadon@usmo.com; (c) Saint Charles

Private non-profit/ 1988/ Town of Augusta; Friends of Historic Augusta/ staff: 12(v)/ members: 12/publication: *German Missouri Cookbook; Historic Augusta: Its Buildings and People 1820-1900*

GENEALOGICAL SOCIETY; HISTORIC SITE; HISTORICAL SOCIETY; HISTORY MUSEUM; HOUSE MUSEUM: Owns and operates an original 1856 German brick Vernacular building and have it furnished in period antiques.

PROGRAMS: Annual Meeting; Community Outreach; Family Programs; Guided Tours; Interpretation; Living History; Publication; Research Library/Archives

COLLECTIONS: [1820-1900] Artifacts, ephemera, and memorabilia: book, family genealogy, wine industry and other commercial enterprises, photos, and special events.

ADMISSION: $1, Children $0.50

AVA

4636
Douglas County Historical and Genealogical Society, Inc.
401 E Washington Ave, 65608 [PO Box 986, 65608]; (p) (417) 683-5799; (c) Douglas

Private non-profit/ 1988/ staff: 12(v)/ members: 115

GENEALOGICAL SOCIETY; HISTORICAL SOCIETY; HISTORY MUSEUM; HOUSE MUSEUM; RESEARCH CENTER: Collects and preserves items of history; photographs, compiles books for genealogical research and publication.

PROGRAMS: Annual Meeting; Exhibits; Guided Tours; Publication; Research Library/Archives

HOURS: Yr Sa 10-3

ADMISSION: Donations accepted

BALLWIN

4637
Ballwin Historical Society
14811 Manchester Rd, 63011; (p) (314) 227-8580; (f) (314) 207-2320; ballwin@tetranet.net; www.ballwin.mo.us; (c) St. Louis

City/ 1991/ staff: 30(v)

HISTORICAL SOCIETY: Seeks to discover, collect, preserve, and disseminate material that illustrates the history of Ballwin.

PROGRAMS: Exhibits; Festivals; Guided Tours; Living History; Reenactments

COLLECTIONS: [1849-1900] Documents, photographs, furniture, tools, clothing, and memorabilia.

HOURS: By appt

4638
Missouri Pacific Historical Society
[PO Box 456, 63022]; HHAWK0621@aol.com.; www.geocities.com/~mopac

Private non-profit/ 1980/ staff: 15(v)/ members: 700/publication: *The Eagle*

HISTORICAL SOCIETY; LIBRARY AND/OR ARCHIVES: Obtains, preserves, and shares information and material relating to the Missouri Pacific Railroad and its subsidiaries.

Archives housed in caboose at Museum of Transport.

PROGRAMS: Annual Meeting; Publication; Research Library/Archives

COLLECTIONS: Missouri Pacific archival material at Museum of Transport, St. Louis.

HOURS: Yr 2nd Sa 9:30-12

ADMISSION: No charge

BARNARD

4639
Barnard Community Historical Society
Hwy M, 64423 [37292 Katydid Rd, 64423]; cmartyla@netins.net

Private non-profit/ staff: 12(v)/ members: 100/publication: *Barnard History*

HISTORY MUSEUM

PROGRAMS: Annual Meeting; Guided Tours; Publication

COLLECTIONS: [1880-present]

HOURS: Yr Daily

BELTON

4640
Smoky Hill Railway and Historical Society, Inc.
502 Walnut, 64012-2516; (p) (816) 331-0630; BGKCINFO@AOL.COM; www.orgsites.com/mo/beltonrailroad; (c) Cass

Joint/ 1964/ staff: 100(v)/ members: 100/publication: *The Flyer*

RAILROAD MUSEUM: Dedicated to the preservation and experience of an American railroad.

PROGRAMS: Annual Meeting; Exhibits; Facility Rental; Family Programs; Festivals; Living History; Publication; Reenactments; School-Based Curriculum

COLLECTIONS: [1920s-1950s]

HOURS: Apr-Oct Sa-Su 8-4

BENTON

4641
Scott County Historical and Genealogy Society
Benton Library, Hwy 61, 63736 [PO Box 151, 63736]; (p) (573) 335-0989; (f) (573) 335-5782; www.ldd.net/genealogy; (c) Scott

Private non-profit/ 1985/ staff: 8(v)/ members: 92

GENEALOGICAL SOCIETY; HISTORICAL SOCIETY; RESEARCH CENTER: Collects and preserves historical manuscripts, newspapers, other historical source materials concerning Scott County; communicate and publish information on the history of Scott county and Southeast Missouri.

PROGRAMS: Annual Meeting; Publication; Research Library/Archives

COLLECTIONS: [1800-present] Ancestor charts, books, genealogies, micro film for Scott, Bollinger, Cape Girardeau, and Mississippi counties.

HOURS: Yr M-Sa 1-6

BETHANY

4642
Edna Cuddy Memorial House and Gardens
1218 W Main, 64424 [1607 S 17th Terr, 64424]; (p) (660) 425-3167, (660) 425-6811; ehjh.netins.net

1882/ staff: 6(v)

COLLECTIONS: [Late 1800s early 1900s] Furniture of the period, several oil paintings, quilts, rugs, lamps, old (1857) rosewood square grand piano, organ.; Toys, dishes, clothing - wedding dresses.

HOURS: Appt

4643
Harrison County Genealogical Society
2307 Central, 64424; (p) (660) 425-8039; pejames@metins.net; www.rootsweb.com/~moharris/hcgen.html; (c) Harrison

Private non-profit/ 1978/ staff: 5(v)/ members: 200

GENEALOGICAL SOCIETY: Collect family records and preserve them for our county and surrounding area and staffs society library.

PROGRAMS: Research Library/Archives

COLLECTIONS: [1845-present] Census, marriage, cemetery, deaths, and obituaries, newspapers, microfilm, microfiche, family histories, county histories, correspondence files, pioneer family computer, atlases, maps, school and church histories.

HOURS: Yr T-Th 1-5; Sa 2-4

4644
Harrison County Historical Society
1218 Main St, 64424 [1106 Ranchwood Rd, 64424]; (p) (660) 425-6811; ehjh@netins.net; (c) Harrison

Private non-profit/ 1965/ staff: 20(v)/ members: 46

HISTORIC PRESERVATION AGENCY; HISTORIC SITE; HISTORICAL SOCIETY; HISTORY MUSEUM; HOUSE MUSEUM: Maintains the 1882 Cuddy House and museum.

PROGRAMS: Annual Meeting; Community Outreach; Exhibits; Guided Tours; Lectures; Publication

COLLECTIONS: [Late 1800s-early 1900s] Edna Cuddy Memorial House and Gardens is filled with Victorian era furnishings and is on the National Register.

HOURS: Apr-Oct Daily by appt

ADMISSION: $2; Group rates

BETHEL

4645
Historic Bethel German Colony
[PO Box 127, 63434]; (p) (660) 284-6200; wendyb@marktwain.net; (c) Shelby

Private non-profit/ 1972/ staff: 2(p); 50(v)/ members: 150

HISTORIC SITE: Interprets the history of the Bethel German Colony (1844-1879); supports festivals, educational workshops, and maintains several original colony homes.

PROGRAMS: Annual Meeting; Exhibits; Family Programs; Festivals; Guided Tours; Lectures; Reenactments

COLLECTIONS: [1844-present] Original colony artifacts and collections from the late 1800s to the present.

HOURS: Yr Daily 6-8

BLACKBURN

4646
Blackburn Historical Society
RR 1, Box 129, 65321; (p) (660) 538-4639; (c) Saline

City/ 1978/ staff: 3(v)/ members: 42

HISTORICAL SOCIETY: Collects, preserves, and make accessible local history.

PROGRAMS: Annual Meeting

BLUE SPRINGS

4647
Blue Springs Historical Society
15th & Main, 64015 [PO Box 762, 64015]; (p) (816) 224-8979; (c) Jackson

Private non-profit/ 1976/ staff: 11(v)/ members: 75/publication: *A Pictorial History of Blue Springs, Missouri*

HISTORIC PRESERVATION AGENCY; HISTORIC SITE; HISTORICAL SOCIETY; HISTORY MUSEUM; HOUSE MUSEUM: Preserves and maintains the history of Blue Springs and its surrounding area.

PROGRAMS: Annual Meeting; Exhibits; Facility Rental; Guided Tours; Publication; School-Based Curriculum

COLLECTIONS: [Early 1900s] 1906 home; rooms furnished in period.

HOURS: Yr W 1-4

ADMISSION: No charge/Donations

BOLIVAR

4648
Historical Society of Polk County
201 W Locust, 65613 [PO Box 423, 65613]; (p) (417) 326-6850; (c) Polk

Private non-profit/ 1971/ staff: 1(p); 10(v)/ members: 148

HISTORICAL SOCIETY; HISTORY MUSEUM: Sponsors the Polk County Museum.

PROGRAMS: Exhibits; Family Programs; Guided Tours

COLLECTIONS: [1835-present] Materials relating to region.

HOURS: Mid May-Mid Sept M-Sa 1-4

ADMISSION: $2, Children $1

BOONSBORO

4649
Boone's Lick State Historic Site
Hwy 187, [c/o Arrow Rock Historic Site, Arrow Rock, 65320]; (p) (660) 837-3330; (f) (660) 837-3300; dsparro@mail.dnr.state.mo.us; (c) Howard

State/ 1959/ MO Dept of Natural Resources, Div of State Parks/ staff: 1(p)

HISTORIC SITE: Preserves and interprets a unique salt-water environment and archaeological features associated with the early 19th salt-manufacturing business of Nathan and Daniel Morgan Boone.

PROGRAMS: Exhibits

COLLECTIONS: [1805-1833] Wooden tools and remnants of structures associated with the salt-making industry.

HOURS: Yr Daily sunrise to sunset

BOONVILLE

4650
Friends of Historic Boonville
614 E Morgan, 65233 [PO Box 1776, 65233]; (p) (660) 882-7977; (f) (660) 882-9194; friendart@mid-mo.net; www.mid-mo/friendsart; (c) Cooper

Private non-profit/ 1971/ staff: 1(f); 5(p)/ members: 712

GARDEN; GENEALOGICAL SOCIETY; HISTORIC PRESERVATION AGENCY; HISTORIC SITE; HISTORICAL SOCIETY; HOUSE MUSEUM: Local cultural organization providing arts programs through its historic theater, house museum, and memorial garden; research, genealogy.

PROGRAMS: Annual Meeting; Concerts; Exhibits; Facility Rental; Family Programs; Festivals; Garden Tours; Guided Tours; Living History; Publication; Reenactments; Research Library/Archives; School-Based Curriculum; Theatre

COLLECTIONS: [1820-present] Family records, maps, photographs, county and city records, artifacts relating to local history.

HOURS: Yr May-Sept Daily 9-5, Sept-May M-F 9-5

4651
Roslyn Heights
821 Main St, 65233-0297 [PO Box 297, 65233-0297]; (p) (816) 882-5320; www.c-magic.com/boonvill/roslyn.htm

BOWLING GREEN

4652
Champ Clark Honey Shuck Restoration, Inc.
205 Champ Clark Dr, 63334 [PO Box 162, 63334]; (p) (573) 324-3154; tmcune@netmont.com; (c) Pike

Private non-profit/ 1973/ staff: 35(v)/ members: 100

HISTORIC PRESERVATION AGENCY; HISTORIC SITE; HISTORICAL SOCIETY; HISTORY MUSEUM; HOUSE MUSEUM: Promotes preservation and tourism.

PROGRAMS: Annual Meeting; Community Outreach; Exhibits; Facility Rental; Festivals; Film/Video; Guided Tours; Interpretation

COLLECTIONS: [1880-1940] Memorabilia and artifacts.

HOURS: June-Aug T-Su 1-4:30 and by appt

ADMISSION: Donations accepted

BRANSON

4653
Old Matt's Cabin-Shepherd of the Hills Homestead
4 miles W of Branson on Hwy 76, 65616 [5586 W Hwy 76, 65616]; (p) (417) 334-4191, (800) 653-6288; (f) (417) 334-4617; oldmatt@aol.com; oldmatt.com

1884/ staff: 250(f)

COLLECTIONS: [1880s-1907] Working tools, furnishings; Collection of Harold Bell Wright's works.

HOURS: Seasonal

4654
Shepherd of the Hills Historical Society
5586 W Hwy 76, 65616 [111 E Main, 65616]; (p) (417) 334-4191; (f) (417) 334-4617; shelly@oldmatt.com; www.oldmatt.com; (c) Stone

Private non-profit/ 1960/ staff: 25(f); 270(p)/publication: *The Shepherd of the Hills Gazette*

HISTORIC SITE; HISTORICAL SOCIETY; HISTORY MUSEUM: Promotes the knowledge and learning of the history of the area, especially through the novel The Shepherd of the Hills and its characters, listed on the National Registry.

PROGRAMS: Exhibits; Family Programs; Festivals; Guided Tours; Interpretation; Living History; Publication; Reenactments; School-Based Curriculum; Theatre

COLLECTIONS: [Late 1800s] Old Matt's Cabin, contains artifacts.

HOURS: Apr-Oct M-Sa 9-5:30

BUFFALO

4655
Dallas County Historical Society, Inc.
S Hwy 65, 65722 [PO Box 594, 65722-0594]; (p) (417) 345-7297, (417) 345-8694; (c) Dallas

Joint/ 1966/ County; Private non-profit/ staff: 10(v)/ members: 150

HISTORIC PRESERVATION AGENCY; HISTORICAL SOCIETY; HISTORY MUSEUM; RESEARCH CENTER: Preserves the history and historical items related to Dallas County and promotes the study of our heritage.

PROGRAMS: Annual Meeting; Exhibits; Family Programs; Festivals; Film/Video; Guided Tours; Publication; Research Library/Archives; School-Based Curriculum

COLLECTIONS: [1890-present] Dallas county family histories; photographs, original county records, old school equipment, home furnishings.

HOURS: May-Oct Sa-Su 1-4

ADMISSION: Donations accepted

BURFORDVILLE

4656
Bollinger Mill State Historic Site
113 Bollinger Mill Rd, 63739; (p) (573) 243-4591; (f) (573) 243-5385; NRBOLLS@mail.dnr.state.mo.us; (c) Cape Girardeau

State/ 1967/ MO Dept of Natural Resources/ staff: 2(f); 1(p); 5(v)

HISTORIC SITE: Preserves and interprets 19th c water-powered gristmill and adjacent Howe-truss covered bridge.

PROGRAMS: Annual Meeting; Concerts; Exhibits; Guided Tours; Interpretation

COLLECTIONS: [1860-1930] Machines, tools, and equipment associated with grain milling and items associated specifically with the site's various owners, including George Frederick Bollinger, Soloman R. Burford, and the Cape County Milling Company.

HOURS: Yr M-Sa 10-4, Su 12-4

ADMISSION: $2, Children $1.25

BUTLER

4657
Bates County Museum of Pioneer History
Bates County Museum, 100 E Ft Scott, 64730 [100 E Fort Scott, 64730]; (p) (660) 679-4777; (c) Bates

Private non-profit/ 1961/ Bates County Historical Society/ staff: 1(f)/ members: 50

HISTORY MUSEUM: Preserves and collects artifacts of early Bates County history.

PROGRAMS: Exhibits; Festivals; Guided Tours; Lectures; Reenactments

COLLECTIONS: [Pre-Civil War-post World War II] Pre-Civil War pioneer quilts and property, Civil War artifacts, early Bates County photographs, political histories, farm equipment, manual printing press, log cabin, depot, three floors of Old Jail Museum.

4658
Bates County Old Settlers Association
706 Parkview, 64730; (p) (660) 679-4603; (c) Bates

County/ 1897/ staff: 3(v)

HISTORIC PRESERVATION AGENCY

PROGRAMS: Annual Meeting; Exhibits

CALIFORNIA

4659
Moniteau County Historical Society
201 N High, 65018; (p) (573) 796-3563; (c) Moniteau

Private non-profit/ 1966/ staff: 20(v)/ members: 135/publication: *Moniteau County Historical Society Newsletter*

HISTORICAL SOCIETY; HISTORY MUSEUM; RESEARCH CENTER: Operates genealogy library and museum.

PROGRAMS: Annual Meeting; Facility Rental; Guided Tours; Publication; Research Library/ Archives

HOURS: Library: Apr-Oct Th-Sa 1-5: Museum: by appt

ADMISSION: Donations accepted

CAMPBELL

4660
Campbell Area Genealogical and Historical Society
104 S Ash St, 63933 [PO Box 401, 63933-0401]; (p) (573) 246-2112

Private non-profit/ members: 100

GENEALOGICAL SOCIETY; HISTORICAL SOCIETY: Provides historical and genealogical records through the Campbell Branch Library of Dunklin County.

COLLECTIONS: [1880-present] History books, Campbell Citizen newspaper, cemetery records, family histories.

HOURS: M-Sa 1-5

ADMISSION: No charge

CANTON

4661
Cedar Falls Historic Village and Toy Museum
Old Hwy 61 One mile S of Canton, 63435 [Rt 2 Box 226 A, 63435]; (p) (573) 288-3995; (c) Lewis

Private non-profit/ 1986/ staff: 1(f); 2(v)

HISTORIC SITE; HISTORY MUSEUM: A recreated historical village from the 1830s with a country school, general store, blacksmith shop, feed store, dry goods store, cemetery, and living history demonstrations.

PROGRAMS: Exhibits; Living History

COLLECTIONS: [1800-1876] Toy collection with 20,000 items on display; restored old 1830s town and school with living history demonstrations.

HOURS: Yr M-F 9-5 and by appt

ADMISSION: $4, Children $3

4662
Lewis County Historical Society/Library-Museum
112 N 4th St, 63435; (p) (573) 288-5713; (f) (573) 288-3513; (c) Lewis

Private non-profit/ 1969/ staff: 5(v)/ members: 41

HISTORICAL SOCIETY; HISTORY MUSEUM

PROGRAMS: Annual Meeting; Exhibits; Research Library/Archives

COLLECTIONS: [1600-present] Wills, obituaries, atlases, probate index, families, family group sheets, maps.

HOURS: Yr 8-4

ADMISSION: No charge

CAPE GIRARDEAU

4663
Cape River Heritage Museum
538 Independence, 63701; (p) (573) 334-0405; (c) Cape Girardeau

Private non-profit/ 1976/ Board of Directors/ staff: 2(p); 25(v)/ members: 100

HISTORIC SITE; HISTORY MUSEUM: Promotes Missouri history, the Mississippi River, and Cape Girardeau history and exhibits collection.

PROGRAMS: Community Outreach; Exhibits; Guided Tours; Interpretation; Lectures

COLLECTIONS: Local and regional artifacts and memorabilia.

HOURS: Mar-Mid Dec W, F-Sa 11-4

ADMISSION: $1

4664
Historical Association of Greater Cape Girardeau
325 S Spanish St, 63703; (p) (573) 334-1177; (c) Cape Girardeau

Private non-profit/ 1960/ staff: 15(v)/ members: 170

HISTORIC SITE; HISTORICAL SOCIETY; HOUSE MUSEUM: Preserves historic house depicting late 1800 Victorian, middle class life and maintains museum.

PROGRAMS: Community Outreach; Guided Tours; Lectures

COLLECTIONS: [Victorian Era] Artifacts: clothing, home furnishings of middle class Victorian era, displayed in Victorian home.

HOURS: May-Sept Sa-Su 1-4

CARROLLTON

4665
Carroll County Historical Society
510 N Mason, 64633; (p) (660) 542-1511, (660) 542-2691; (c) Carroll

Joint/ 1956/ Non-profit-public; County

HISTORIC PRESERVATION AGENCY; HISTORICAL SOCIETY; HISTORY MUSEUM; HOUSE MUSEUM; LIVING HISTORY/OUTDOOR MUSEUM: Maintains museum and promotes local history.

PROGRAMS: Annual Meeting; Community Outreach; Exhibits; Facility Rental; Family Programs; Festivals; Film/Video; Guided Tours; Lectures; Living History; Publication; Research Library/Archives

COLLECTIONS: [Early 1900s-1950s] 43 rooms featuring period furniture, log cabin and farm machinery, family collections, antique tools, early 1900s high school graduation pictures.

HOURS: Sa-Su 1-5

ADMISSION: $2, Children $1

CARTHAGE

4666
Battle of Carthage
[1009 Truman, Lamar, 64759]; (p) (417) 682-2279; (f) (417) 682-6304; (c) Jasper

State/ 1990/ Dept of Natural Resources/ staff: 3(f); 4(p); 2(v)

HISTORIC SITE; LIVING HISTORY/OUTDOOR MUSEUM: Site was a campground for the Union troops the night before the battle of Carthage and a campsite for the Confederate troops after the battle.

PROGRAMS: Annual Meeting; Community Outreach; Guided Tours; Interpretation; Living History

COLLECTIONS: [1861]

HOURS: Yr Daily 6-9

4667
Carthage Historic Preservation, Inc.
1146 Grand Ave, 64836 [PO Box 375, 64836]; (p) (417) 358-1776; (c) Jasper

Private non-profit/ 1978/ staff: 1(p); 60(v)/ members: 80

HISTORIC PRESERVATION AGENCY; HOUSE MUSEUM: Organized to put 3 districts on National Register and alert citizens to Victorian heritage; main focus on historic Phelps House.

PROGRAMS: Community Outreach; Facility Rental

COLLECTIONS: Victorian

4668
Kendrick Place, The
130 E N Woods, 64836 [PO Box 406, 64836]; (p) (417) 358-0636

1849/ staff: 1(f); 1(p); 4(v)

COLLECTIONS: [1860-1866] Artifacts are authentic, not reproduction, and highlight status of the owners during the Civil War. Artifacts are not original to the house as the Civil War ravaged it.

HOURS: Mar-Dec M-F 9-5

CARUTHERSVILLE

4669
Pemiscot County Historical Society
Archives Rm, 3rd Fl, Presbyterian Church, 63830 [PO Box 604, 63830-0604]; (c) Pemiscot

Private non-profit/ 1970/ staff: 3(v)/ members: 100/publication: *Pemiscot County Missouri Quarterly*

GENEALOGICAL SOCIETY; HISTORICAL SOCIETY: Collects, receives, and preserves artifacts, documents, and materials relating to the history of Pemiscot County, and publish Pemiscot County Missouri Quarterly, and maintains Archives Room.

PROGRAMS: Publication

COLLECTIONS: [1840-present] Quarterly publications—indexed surname card file 1975-present, County newspapers 1910-1945, local histories, small collection of genealogy and history.

CATHAGE

4670
Powers Museum
1617 W Oak, 64836 [PO Box 593, 64836]; (p) (417) 358-2667; pmuseum@ecarthage.com; www.powersmuseum.com; (c) Jasper

City/ 1981/ staff: 1(f); 2(p); 5(v)

HISTORY MUSEUM: Rotating traveling exhibits based on Carthage history, Missouri heritage, decorative or textile arts, as well as archival holdings on music performance, women's history, and local industries and business.

PROGRAMS: Community Outreach; Concerts; Exhibits; Family Programs; Festivals; Lectures; Publication; Research Library/Archives; School-Based Curriculum

COLLECTIONS: [1865-1975] 15,000 artifacts, photographs, archival holdings, reference library; local history material.

HOURS: Mar-Apr, Nov-Dec T-Sa 11-4; May-Oct T-Sa 10-5, Su 1-5

CENTRALIA

4671
Centralia Historical Society, Inc.
319 E Sneed St, 65240; (p) (573) 682-5711; (c) Boone

Private non-profit/ 1974/ staff: 1(p); 60(v)

HOUSE MUSEUM: Preserves and exhibits artifacts related to history of Centralia and surrounding area; makes history available to children through various exhibits.

PROGRAMS: Exhibits; Guided Tours; Publication

COLLECTIONS: [Victorian-present] Furnishings, dishes, clothing ranging from late 1800s - present, early 1900s farm and woodworking tools, small Civil War collection and historical items from the A. B. Chance Company and area.

HOURS: May-Nov Su and W 2-4

ADMISSION: No charge

CHAFFEE

4672
Chaffee Historical Society, Inc.
112 N Main, 63740 [Box 185, 63740]; (p) (573) 887-6225; roper@showmenet.com; (c) Scott

Private non-profit/ 1996/ staff: 12(v)/ members: 120/publication: *Chaffee This and That; Cementery Record*

HISTORICAL SOCIETY; HISTORY MUSEUM: Preserves the history of Chaffe and surrounding area.

PROGRAMS: Community Outreach; Festivals; Publication

COLLECTIONS: [1905-present] Railroad items.

HOURS: Yr T and by appt

ADMISSION: No charge

CHARLESTON

4673
Mississippi County Historical Society
403 N Main, 63834 [PO Box 312, 63834]; (p) (573) 683-3837; (c) Mississippi

Private non-profit/ 1966/ staff: 3(p); 3(v)/ members: 273

HISTORICAL SOCIETY; HOUSE MUSEUM: Collects and displays local historical material and provides a site for gatherings.

PROGRAMS: Annual Meeting; Community Outreach; Facility Rental; Festivals

COLLECTIONS: [Late 1800s-present] Furniture, fixtures, d,cor, photographs, artifacts, documents, maps, tools, toys.

HOURS: By Appt

ADMISSION: $2

CHESTERFIELD

4674
Faust County Park/Faust Historical Village/Thornhill
15185 Olive Blvd, 63017; (p) (314) 532-7298; (f) (314) 532-0604; jim_foley@co.st-louis.mo.us; www.st-louiscountyparks.com; (c) St. Louis

County/ 1996/ staff: 11(f); 5(p); 50(v)

GARDEN; HISTORIC PRESERVATION AGENCY; HISTORY MUSEUM; LIVING HISTORY/OUTDOOR MUSEUM: Maintains restored 19th c homes in reconstructed village and interprets local settlement.

PROGRAMS: Community Outreach; Concerts; Exhibits; Family Programs; Festivals; Garden Tours; Guided Tours; Living History; School-Based Curriculum

COLLECTIONS: Reconstructed village, Queen Anne carriage house, German brick cottage, blacksmith shop, antebellum home, log cabin, and several period gardens.

CHILLICOTHE

4675
Livingston County Genealogy Society
450 Locust St, 64601; (p) (660) 646-0547; travler1@aol.com; www.greenhills.net/~fwoods; (c) Livingston

Private non-profit/ staff: 6(v)/ members: 73/publication: *Lifelines*

GENEALOGICAL SOCIETY: Dedicated to collecting and preserving local history.

PROGRAMS: Lectures; Publication; Research Library/Archives

COLLECTIONS: [1900-present] Books of surveys and audits of county history; family histories; cemetery and census records; mapping of cemeteries.

HOURS: Yr M-Sa 9-5

ADMISSION: No charge

CHILLILOTHE

4676
Grand River Historical Society and Museum
1401 Forrest Dr, 64601 [PO Box 154, 64601]; (p) (660) 646-1341; (c) Livingston

Private non-profit/ 1978/ staff: 35(v)/ members: 484

HISTORICAL SOCIETY; HISTORY MUSEUM: Preserves and collects artifacts from Grand River area and maintains local history for future generations.

PROGRAMS: Annual Meeting; Exhibits; Family Programs; Festivals; Film/Video; Guided Tours; Interpretation; Lectures; Publication

COLLECTIONS: [Late 1800-present]

HOURS: Apr-Oct T-Su 1-4

ADMISSION: No charge

CLAYTON

4677
Martin Franklin Hanley House
7600 Westmoreland, 63105 [2 Mark Twain Circle, 63105]; (p) (314) 746-0427; (f) (314) 746-0494

1855/ City/ staff: 1(p)

COLLECTIONS: [1850s]

HOURS: Yr

4678
St. Louis County Department of Parks and Rec.
41 S Central Ave, 63105; (p) (314) 889-3357; (f) (314) 889-3696; Esley_Hamilton@stlouisco.com; www.st-louiscountyparks.com; (c) St. Louis

County/ 1951/ staff: 1(f)

HISTORIC PRESERVATION AGENCY: Identifies and researches historic properties throughout the county and encourages their preservation through publications, lectures, tours, and exhibits. Supports statutory advisory commission.

PROGRAMS: Exhibits; Guided Tours; Lectures; Research Library/Archives

COLLECTIONS: [1790-present] Historic inventory forms and other documentation for more than 5,000 historic buildings in St. Louis County.

HOURS: M-F 8-5

CLINTON

4679
Henry County Historical Society
[PO Box 65, 64735]; (p) (660) 885-8814; (f) (660) 890-2228; hcmus@midamerica.net; (c) Henry

Private non-profit/ 1967/ staff: 1(f); 1(p); 11(v)/ members: 550

HISTORICAL SOCIETY; HISTORY MUSEUM: Preserves the history and heritage of Henry County; Operates the Henry County Museum and Cultural Arts Center in Clinton.

PROGRAMS: Annual Meeting; Community Outreach; Concerts; Exhibits; Facility Rental; Family Programs; Guided Tours; Interpretation; Living History; Research Library/Archives; Theatre

COLLECTIONS: [Late 19th-early 20th c] Artifacts relating to Henry county; Primary focus on late Victorian era. Recreated 1900s village, dog trot log house and 1886 Anheuser-Busch building.

HOURS: Apr-Oct M-Sa 10-4

ADMISSION: $3, Children $1, Seniors $2; Under 13 free

COLE CAMP

4680
Cole Camp Historical Society
104 E Main, 65325 [PO Box 151, 65325]; (p) (660) 668-3887; (c) Benton

Private non-profit/ 1973/ County/ staff: 1(p)/ members: 51

HISTORICAL SOCIETY; RESEARCH CENTER: Preserves the written history of Benton County.

PROGRAMS: Film/Video; Interpretation; Research Library/Archives

COLLECTIONS: [1880s-1990s] Area history books, cataloging of area cemeteries, microfilm of county newspapers spanning a 110-year period.

HOURS: Yr T-Sa

ADMISSION: No charge

COLUMBIA

4681
Boone County Historical Society
3801 Ponderosa Dr, 65201; (p) (573) 443-8936; (f) (573) 875-5268; bchs@socket.net; (c) Boone

County; Private non-profit/ 1963/ Board of Directors/ staff: 3(f); 100(v)/ members: 550/publication: County Lines; Boone County Chronicles

HISTORICAL SOCIETY: The Boone County Historical Society collects, preserves, and interprets artifacts related to the history of Boone County, Missouri.

PROGRAMS: Annual Meeting; Community Outreach; Concerts; Exhibits; Facility Rental; Festivals; Guided Tours; Interpretation; Lectures; Publication; Reenactments; Research Library/Archives

COLLECTIONS: [1812-present] 500,600 photographic negatives, 2,000 artifacts, 1,000 manuscripts, 3,000 books and genealogical records, and 1,500 works of art.

HOURS: Apr-Oct T-Su 1-5; Nov-Mar W, F-Su 1-4

ADMISSION: Donations requested

4682
Genealogical Society of Central Missouri
3801 Ponderosa, 65205 [PO Box 26, 65205]; (p) (573) 443-8936; www.synapse.com/bocomogenweb; (c) Boone

Private non-profit/ 1975/ members: 236

GENEALOGICAL SOCIETY; RESEARCH CENTER: Collects and preserves material relative to genealogy and history of the area; compiles and publishes selected materials; and shares information and materials for education of members and public.

PROGRAMS: Lectures; Publication; Research Library/Archives

COLLECTIONS: 1,400 genealogical reference books, surname files and group sheets; newsletters/quarterlies from all over the U.S.; Central Missouri microfilm records; International Genealogical Index, microfiche records, genealogical software library with CD ROM.

HOURS: Apr-Oct T-Su 1-5; Nov-Mar W, Sa, Su 1-4

ADMISSION: No charge

4683
Maplewood
Nifong & Ponderosa, 65203 [3801 Ponderosa Dr, 65201]; (p) (573) 443-8936; bchs@socket.net

1877/ staff: 2(f); 1(p); 67(v)

COLLECTIONS: [Late 19th c] Original furnishings, clothing, dishes, medical supplies of 19th c, family photos.

HOURS: Seasonal

4684
Missouri Alliance For Historic Preservation
McReynolds Hall Univ of MO Rm 35, 65203 [PO Box 1715, 65203]; (p) (573) 443-5946; www.preservemo.org; (c) Boone

Private non-profit/ 1976/ members: 150

HISTORIC PRESERVATION AGENCY: Promotes and coordinates preservation activities throughout

4685
Museum of Art & Archaeology, University of Missouri
1 Pickard Hall, 65211; (p) (573) 882-3591; (f) (573) 884-4039; www.research.missouri.edu/museum; (c) Boone

State/ 1957/ staff: 10(f); 11(p); 175(v)/ members: 600/publication: Fatherhood: Commitment in Black America; The Samuel H. Kress Study Collection at the Universitry of Missouri; MVSE Annual of the Museum of Art

ART MUSEUM; RESEARCH CENTER: Dedicated to serving the teaching and research programs of the student body, faculty, and community of mid-Missouri.

PROGRAMS: Annual Meeting; Exhibits; Facility Rental; Family Programs; Guided Tours; Interpretation; Publication; Research Library/Archives; School-Based Curriculum

COLLECTIONS: Art and archaeological material, prints and drawings (1,500), 14 works from the Kress Collection.

HOURS: Yr T,W, F 9-5, Th 6-9, Sa-Su 12-5

ADMISSION: No charge

4686
State Historical Society of Missouri
1020 Lowry St, 65201-7298; (p) (573) 882-7083; (f) (573) 884-4950; shsofmo@umsystem.edu; www.system.missouri.edu/shs; (c) Boone

State/ 1898/ staff: 23(f); 1(p)/ members: 5500/publication: Missouri Historical Review

ART MUSEUM; HISTORICAL SOCIETY; RESEARCH CENTER: Collects, preserves, makes accessible, and publishes materials relating to the history of Missouri and the Middle West.

PROGRAMS: Annual Meeting; Community Outreach; Exhibits; Publication; Research Library/Archives

COLLECTIONS: [19th-20th C] 452,000 volumes; 712 periodical subscriptions; 46,079 microfilm reels of Missouri newspapers; 6,726 microfilm reels of census; 2,775 maps; 100,000 photographs; 1,650 l.f. manuscript material; fine art and editorial cartoon collections; oral history.

HOURS: M-F 8-4:30; Sa 9-4:30

ADMISSION: No charge

COMMERCE

4687
Commerce Historical and Genealogy Society
203 Missouri St, 63742 [PO Box 93, 63742]; (p) (573) 264-2199; (f) (573) 264-3507; commercemo@clas.net; www.clas.net/~commercemo; (c) Scott

Private non-profit/ 1997/ staff: 4(p)/ members: 125/publication: Commerce News Letter

GENEALOGICAL SOCIETY; HISTORICAL SOCIETY; HISTORY MUSEUM; HOUSE MUSEUM; RESEARCH CENTER: Promote the history of Commerce in Missouri and the surrounding area.

PROGRAMS: Annual Meeting; Exhibits; Living History; Publication; Reenactments; Research Library/Archives

COLLECTIONS: Pottery pieces, family photos old newspapers, Mississippi River artifacts.

HOURS: Feb-Dec Sa-Su 1-5 and by appt

ADMISSION: Donations requested

CRESTWOOD

4688
Sappington House Foundation
1015 S Sappington Rd, 63126; (p) (314) 822-8171, (314) 822-9469; (c) St. Louis

Joint; Private non-profit/ 1969/ City; Foundation/ staff: 1(f); 125(v)/ members: 150

HISTORIC SITE; HOUSE MUSEUM: Supports the continuing development and maintenance of the Sappington House complex, creates and maintains interest in the site. Staff the Historic House, Library.

PROGRAMS: Annual Meeting; Concerts; Exhibits; Guided Tours; Research Library/Archives

COLLECTIONS: [Federal Period] Furnishings-Federal Period; Library-American History, State History-Local History and decorative arts.

HOURS: Feb-Dec T-Sa 11-3

CROCKER

4689
Genealogy Society of Pulaski County, MO
Old Courthouse, 65452 [PO Box 226, 65452]; (p) (573) 774-6883; (c) Pulaski

State/ 1947/ members: 54

GENEALOGICAL SOCIETY: Promotes genealogy research, to instill interest in genealogy, and to encourage accurate research.

PROGRAMS: Publication; Research Library/Archives

COLLECTIONS: Genealogical and historical information for Pulaski County.

HOURS: 2nd Su and by appt

DAVISVILLE

4690
Dillard Mill State Historical Site
142 Dillard Mill Rd, 65456; (p) (573) 244-3120; (f) (573) 244-5672; (c) Crawford

State/ staff: 3(f); 6(p)

HISTORIC PRESERVATION AGENCY; HISTORIC SITE

PROGRAMS: Community Outreach; Festivals; Guided Tours; Interpretation; Lectures

COLLECTIONS: [1890-1930] Restored 1890 roller mill with most of its original equipment.

HOURS: Yr Daily 8-5

ADMISSION: $2, Children $1.25

DE SOTO

4691
Jefferson County Historical Society
721 W Kelley St, 63020; (p) (314) 586-3858; azz002@connect.more.net; (c) Jefferson

Private non-profit/ 1969/ County/ staff: 12(v)/ members: 60/publication: Post Offices of Jefferson County; Index to the 1876 Atlas of Jefferson County; and others

ART MUSEUM; GENEALOGICAL SOCIETY; HISTORIC SITE; HISTORICAL SOCIETY; HISTORY MUSEUM; HOUSE MUSEUM; RESEARCH CENTER: Collects Jefferson County school, cemetery, and local history related materials.

PROGRAMS: Annual Meeting; Community Outreach; Elder's Programs; Exhibits; Facility Rental; Family Programs; Festivals; Guided Tours; Lectures; Living History; Publication; Research Library/Archives; School-Based Curriculum

COLLECTIONS: [1800-1930s] Cemetery records, maps, books, photographs, and local history materials.

HOURS: Yr M- W, F 9-5; Th, Sa 9-2

ADMISSION: No charge

DEFIANCE

4692
Historic Daniel Boone Home
1868 Highway F, 63341; (p) (636) 798-2005; (f) (636) 798-2914; (c) Saint Charles

Private non-profit/ 1963/ staff: 7(f); 8(p)

HISTORIC SITE; HOUSE MUSEUM; LIVING HISTORY/OUTDOOR MUSEUM: Maintains Daniel Boone Home and Boonesfield Village interpretation of American frontier life.

PROGRAMS: Concerts; Facility Rental; Family Programs; Film/Video; Guided Tours; Interpretation; Lectures; Living History; Reenactments; Theatre

COLLECTIONS: [1740-1840] Showcases personal furnishings and artifacts of Daniel Boone and his family, including the house where Daniel Boone died; various historic buildings from the 1830s.

HOURS: Spring/Fall 11-4; Summer 9-6

ADMISSION: $7, Children $4, Seniors $6

DESOTO

4693
Desoto Historical Society
[PO Box 513, 63020]; (p) (314) 586-9242; (c) Jefferson

Private non-profit/ 1991/ staff: 38(v)/ members: 38/publication: DeSoto Missouri: A Pictorial History

HISTORICAL SOCIETY; HISTORY MUSEUM: Promotes local education and preservation.

PROGRAMS: Exhibits; Festivals; Interpretation; Living History; Publication

COLLECTIONS: [1800-1990] Artifacts pertaining to the local history of DeSoto.

HOURS: Apr-Oct Sa 10-12

ADMISSION: No charge

DEXTER

4694
Heritage House
Cor of Cooper & Market, 63841 [17257 Betty Dr, 63841]; (p) (573) 624-7458

DIAMOND

4695
George Washington Carver Birthplace Association
5646 Carver Rd, 64840; (p) (417) 325-4151; (f) (417) 325-4231; gwca_superintendent@nps.gov; www.nps.gov/gwca; (c) Newton

Private non-profit/ 1953/ staff: 12(f); 3(p); 10(v)/ members: 105/publication: Trailblazer

HISTORIC SITE: Assists with the preservation and protection of the birthplace and childhood home of George Washington Carver, distinguished African-American scientist, educator, humanitarian, artist, and musician.

PROGRAMS: Community Outreach; Exhibits; Family Programs; Film/Video; Guided Tours; Interpretation; Lectures; Living History; Publication; Research Library/Archives; School-Based Curriculum

COLLECTIONS: [1860-1940] 2,166 objects and documents of an archeological, ethnological, historical, archival, biological, paleontological, and geological nature related to George Washington Carver.

HOURS: Yr Daily 9-5

ADMISSION: No charge

DONIPHAN

4696
Ripely County Historical Society
101 Washington St, 63435; (p) (573) 996-5298; (f) (573) 996-2212; ripleyco@scmo.net; www.pbmo.net/ripleyco; (c) Ripley

Private non-profit/ 1991/ staff: 96(v)/ members: 96/publication: Ripley County Heritage

ALLIANCE OF HISTORICAL AGENCIES; HISTORIC SITE; HISTORICAL SOCIETY; HISTORY MUSEUM; HOUSE MUSEUM; LIVING HISTORY/OUTDOOR MUSEUM

PROGRAMS: Community Outreach; Exhibits; Facility Rental; Guided Tours; Lectures; Living History; Publication; Reenactments; Research Library/Archives

COLLECTIONS: [20th c] Items pertaining to rural Ripley County and early Doniphan MO.

HOURS: Yr

ADMISSION: No charge

ELLINGTON

4697
Reynolds County Genealogy and Historical Society, Inc.
200 S Main St, 63638 [PO Box 281, 63638-0281]; (p) (573) 663-3233; (c) Reynolds

Private non-profit/ 1983/ staff: 7(v)/ members: 200/publication: Kinfolks Search

GENEALOGICAL SOCIETY; HISTORICAL SOCIETY; HISTORY MUSEUM; RESEARCH CENTER: Collects and houses material of genealogical and historical importance.

PROGRAMS: Annual Meeting; Exhibits; Publication; Research Library/Archives

COLLECTIONS: Library: censuses, marriage, and cemetery, obituaries records, family biographies, county history, community history, military records; Museum: clothing, uniforms,

Civil War artifacts, lumbering history, railroad history, and artifacts, school display, kitchen equipment and utensils, laundry items, quilts, glass display, 2,000 volumes.

HOURS: Museum: Mar-Dec Th, F, 2nd Sa 10-4; Library: Yr M-F 9-5

ADMISSION: No charge

ELLSINORE

4698
Ellsinore Pioneer Museum
11 Herren St, 63937 [PO Box 74, 63937]; (p) (573) 322-5297; pioneermuseum@hotmail.com; geocities.yahoo.com/chill/parliament/4910; (c) Carter

Joint/ 1984/ staff: 3(p); 20(v)/ members: 24

HISTORIC PRESERVATION AGENCY; HISTORY MUSEUM; LIVING HISTORY/OUTDOOR MUSEUM: Preserves community and family histories by keeping family heirlooms, demonstrating forgotten arts, and encouraging appreciation of pioneer heritage and values.

PROGRAMS: Community Outreach; Concerts; Exhibits; Family Programs; Festivals; Interpretation; Lectures; Living History; Research Library/Archives

COLLECTIONS: [1880-1985] Native American and pioneer tools, history of local schools, and Civilian Conservation Corps of 1930s, veterans exhibit, pioneer kitchen, looms, spinning wheels, herbs and medicines.

HOURS: June-Aug W-Sa 10-5

ADMISSION: Donations requested

FAIR GROVE

4699
Fair Grove Historical and Preservation Society
Main St & Hwy 125, 65648 [PO Box 93, 65648]; (p) (417) 759-7077; (f) (417) 759-6063; (c) Greene

Private non-profit/ 1979/ members: 45

HISTORIC SITE; HISTORICAL SOCIETY: Restored the historic 1884 Wommack Mill; restores and preserves turn of the century agriculture equipment.

PROGRAMS: Facility Rental; Festivals

COLLECTIONS: [19th c] Hand and horse drawn farm tools and equipment.

HOURS: By Appt

ADMISSION: Donations accepted

FAYETTE

4700
Franklin or Bust, Inc.
202 E Morrison St, 65298 [PO Box 32, 65298-0032]; (p) (660) 248-5223; (f) (660) 248-1200; newspaper@mcmsys.com; (c) Howard

Private non-profit/ 1986/ staff: 4(v)/ members: 57

HISTORIC PRESERVATION AGENCY: To mark, preserve, and publicize the starting point of the Santa Fe Trail, in Old Franklin, MO.

PROGRAMS: Annual Meeting; Guided Tours

FLORISSANT

4701
Florissant Valley Historical Society
1896 S New Florissant Rd, 63032 [PO Box 298, 63032]; (p) (314) 524-1100; (c) St. Louis

Private non-profit/ 1958/ staff: 10(v)/ members: 200/publication: *Florissant Valley Quarterly*

COLLECTIONS: [1890-presernt] Period furnishing in period, costume collection.

HOURS: Mar-Dec Su 1-4

ADMISSION: $2, Children $1

4702
Friends of Old South Ferdinand, Inc.
#1 Rue St. Francois, 63032 [PO Box 222, 63032]; (p) (314) 837-2110; (c) St. Louis

Private non-profit/ 1955/ staff: 12(v)/ members: 150

HISTORIC SITE: Raises funds and works to preserve, protect, and make available to the public this historic site and the information about the people who participated in this historic place.

PROGRAMS: Annual Meeting; Concerts; Exhibits; Facility Rental; Family Programs; Festivals; Guided Tours; Interpretation; Lectures; Living History; Reenactments; Research Library/Archives

COLLECTIONS: [1819-present] Records: Parish activity, church rituals, art work, furniture, garments, books.

HOURS: Apr-Dec Su

ADMISSION: No charge

4703
Historic Florissant, Inc.
1067 Dunn Rd, 63031; (p) (314) 921-7055; (c) St. Louis

Private non-profit/ 1969/ staff: 9(v)/publication: *Florissant Valley Quarterly*

HISTORIC SITE: Preserve threatened landmarks and maintain library of local history.

PROGRAMS: Guided Tours; Publication; Research Library/Archives

COLLECTIONS: Preserve and maintain 5 National Register Sites; Florissant Landmark 1850-1900; Library Florissant History 1767-present.

HOURS: By appt

ADMISSION: No charge

4704
Museum of Western Jesuit Missions, The
700 Howdershell Rd, 63031 [PO Box 1095, 63031]; (p) (314) 361-5122; (f) (314) 758-7164; Archives@jesuits-mis.org; (c) St. Louis

1971/ staff: 5(p); 10(v)/ members: 78/publication: *Museum Message*

HISTORY MUSEUM: The museum is housed in a 1840 Federal Style stone building; focuses on St. Regis Indian School, the westward movement, frontier religion, immigrants, and missionary efforts among Native Americans.

PROGRAMS: Annual Meeting; Community Outreach; Concerts; Exhibits; Guided Tours; Lectures; Living History; Publication; Reenactments

COLLECTIONS: [16th c-present] Tools of pioneer days, modern American Indian art, rugs, ceramics.

HOURS: Mar 15-Dec 15 Su 1-4 and by appt

ADMISSION: No charge/Donations

4705
Taille de Noyer
1896 S Florissant Rd, on McCluer HS Campus, 63031 [PO Box 298, 63031]; (p) (314) 524-1100

1790

COLLECTIONS: Furnishings and costumes; History library maintained by Historic Florissant in the Gittemeier House.

HOURS: Seasonal

FORSYTH

4706
White River Valley Historical Society
[PO Box 506, Point Lookout, 65726-0555]; (p) (417) 369-2314; Lmyphinn@aol.com; (c) Taney

Private non-profit/ 1961/ staff: 15(v)/ members: 200

HISTORIC PRESERVATION AGENCY; HISTORIC SITE; HISTORICAL SOCIETY: Promotes the preservation, discovery, and history of the upper White River Valley and awakens public interest through programs and publications; cooperate with other historical societies in collecting and preserving significant historical materials.

PROGRAMS: Annual Meeting; Community Outreach; Exhibits; Guided Tours; Lectures; Publication

FORT LEONARD WOOD

4707
U.S. Army Engineer Museum
Bldg # 1607, 65473 [Attn: ATZT-PTM-M, 65473]; (p) (573) 596-0780; (f) (573) 596-0169; combsk@wood.army.mil; (c) Pulaski

Federal/ 1976/ staff: 3(f); 1(p); 6(v)

HISTORY MUSEUM

PROGRAMS: Community Outreach; Exhibits; Film/Video; Guided Tours; Interpretation; Reenactments

COLLECTIONS: [1775-present]

HOURS: Yr M-F 8-4, Sa 10-4

ADMISSION: No charge

FREDERICKTOWN

4708
Historic Madison
122 N Main St, 63645; (p) (573) 783-2722; (c) Madison

Private non-profit/ 1965/ staff: 10(v)/ members: 160/publication: *Historical Madison County 1818-1987; and others*

HISTORIC SITE; HISTORICAL SOCIETY; HISTORY MUSEUM: Dedicated to preserving local history and collecting genealogical family information; maintains information facility open to the public.

PROGRAMS: Exhibits; Guided Tours; Publication

HOURS: T 1-4

ADMISSION: No charge

FULTON

4709
Kingdom of Callaway Historical Society

513 Court St, 65251 [PO Box 6073, 65251-6073]; (p) (573) 642-0570; history. fulton.missouri.org; (c) Callaway

Private non-profit/ 1960/ staff: 50(v)/ members: 175/publication: *The Callawegian*

HISTORICAL SOCIETY: Seeks to document the history of the cultural, ethnic, religious, and occupational diversity of Callaway County through preservation of local history and by education.

PROGRAMS: Annual Meeting; Community Outreach; Exhibits; Family Programs; Guided Tours; Publication; Research Library/Archives

COLLECTIONS: [1800s-present] Artifacts, photographs, and documents.

HOURS: Yr T-F 10-4

ADMISSION: Donations accepted

GAINESVILLE

4710
Ozark County Genealogical and Historical Society

[PO Box 4, 65655]; (c) Ozark

Private non-profit/ 1986/ members: 150/publication: *Old Mill Run*

GENEALOGICAL SOCIETY; HISTORICAL SOCIETY: Dedicated to preserving valuable genealogical, historical, and biographical records relating to the ancestry of its members and early settlers of Ozark County and its nearby counties in Missouri and Arkansas.

PROGRAMS: Annual Meeting; Publication; Research Library/Archives

COLLECTIONS: [1850-1920] Genealogical and historical material relating to Ozark County, MO, and nearby counties: census records, cemetery records, marriage records; family histories, oral history tapes, and archival photographs.

HOURS: Yr M-F 9-3:30

GALENA

4711
Stone County Historical/Genealogical Society

Corner of 5th & Elm, 65656 [PO Box 63, 65656]; (c) Stone

Private non-profit/ 1976/ members: 92/publication: *History of Stone Co., Vols. 1 & 2*

GENEALOGICAL SOCIETY; HISTORICAL SOCIETY: Collect, instruct, preserve, and publish the history of Stone Co. for the education and enjoyment of present and future generations.

PROGRAMS: Annual Meeting; Exhibits; Family Programs; Interpretation; Publication

COLLECTIONS: [1831-present] Periodicals.

HOURS: Yr

ADMISSION: No charge

GOLDMAN

4712
Sandy Creek Covered Bridge State Historic Site

End of Old Lemay Ferry Rd, [1050 Museum Dr, Imperial, 63052]; (p) (636) 464-2976; (f) (636) 464-2976; cschmidt@mail.state.mo.us; (c) Jefferson

State/ 1968/ staff: 4(f); 3(p)

HISTORIC SITE: Protect important natural and cultural resources.

PROGRAMS: Annual Meeting

COLLECTIONS: [19th-20th c] Prehistoric and historic archaeological materials found on the 218 acre property.

HOURS: Yr Daily 8-dark

ADMISSION: No charge

GRANBY

4713
Granby Historical Society

[PO Box 45, 64844]; (p) (417) 472-3171; (c) Newton

Private non-profit/ 1985/ staff: 5(v)/ members: 50/publication: *Granby-Oldest Mining Town In The Southwest*

HISTORICAL SOCIETY; HISTORY MUSEUM: Perpetuates the history of Granby as a lead and zinc mining town.

PROGRAMS: Annual Meeting; Exhibits; Facility Rental; Publication

COLLECTIONS: [Early 1900s] Exhibits, mining artifacts, pictures, memorabilia, documents, pictures, and books.

HOURS: Apr-Oct varies

ADMISSION: No charge

GRANDVIEW

4714
Grandview Historical Society

1205 Jones, 64030 [PO Box 512, 64030]; (c) Jackson

Private non-profit/ 1980/ staff: 15(v)/ members: 128/publication: *History of Grandview*

HISTORICAL SOCIETY; HISTORY MUSEUM: Collects and preserves town history and operates the depot museum.

PROGRAMS: Annual Meeting; Exhibits; Publication

COLLECTIONS: [1912-present] Photographs and oral history of town and people who lived here from 1912-present.

HOURS: Apr-Dec F 1-4, Sa 11-2

ADMISSION: $1

HAMILTON

4715
J.C. Penney Museum and Boyhood Home

312 N Davis, 64644; (p) (816) 583-2168; (f) (816) 583-4929; (c) Caldwell

City/ 1976

HISTORIC SITE: Owned and operated by the City of Hamilton with assistance from local civil organizations and groups; preserves the JC Penney heritage.

PROGRAMS: Exhibits; Facility Rental; Festivals; Film/Video; Guided Tours; Living History

COLLECTIONS: [1875-1971] Memorabilia telling JC Penney's story - personal and career - the Boyhood Home has been renovated to the 1875-1900 time frame.

HOURS: Yr M-F 9-12-1-4

ADMISSION: Donations accepted

HANNIBAL

4716
Becky Thatcher Book Shop

209-211 Hill St, 63401; (p) (573) 221-0822; (f) (573) 221-4091; fnorth@compuserve.com; (c) Marion

Private for-profit/ 1970/ staff: 2(f); 3(p)

HOUSE MUSEUM: Maintains the bedroom and parlor of the home of Laura Hawkins, the "Becky Thatcher" of The Adventures of Tom Sawyer, are available for public viewing.

PROGRAMS: Guided Tours; School-Based Curriculum

COLLECTIONS: [1850] Bedroom and parlor restored to the 1850s.

HOURS: Summer: Daily 8-6:30; Winter: Daily 10-4; Fall, Spring: Daily 9-5

4717
Mark Twain Home Foundation

208 Hill St, 63401; (p) (573) 221-9010; (f) (573) 221-7975; (c) Mariou

Private non-profit/ 1974/ staff: 4(f); 8(p); 70(v)/ members: 391/publication: *The Fence Painter*

HISTORY MUSEUM; RESEARCH CENTER: Maintains properties related to Mark Twain: 3 historic buildings and 3 museum buildings.

PROGRAMS: Annual Meeting; Community Outreach; Exhibits; Interpretation; Lectures; Publication

COLLECTIONS: [1835-1910] Primary and secondary artifacts relating to Mark Twain and early Hannibal history.

HOURS: Yr Summer Daily 8-6; Winter Daily 10-4

ADMISSION: $6, Children $2.50

4718
Rockcliffe Mansion

1000 Bird St, 63401; (p) (573) 221-4140

1900

HOURS: Yr

HARRISONVILLE

4719
Cass County Historical and Genealogical Societies, Inc.

400 E Mechanic, 64701 [PO Box 406, 64701-0400]; (p) (816) 887-2393; (c) Cass

Private non-profit/ 1966/ staff: 2(p); 15(v)/ members: 150

GENEALOGICAL SOCIETY; HISTORICAL

SOCIETY; HOUSE MUSEUM; RESEARCH CENTER: Maintains a 2-room log cabin with basement museum; archives of county records to open to researchers.

PROGRAMS: Annual Meeting; Exhibits; Festivals; Publication; Research Library/Archives

COLLECTIONS: [1800s-present] Cass County legal records, scrapbooks, club records, published histories, death record files. Log home; furnishings.

HOURS: Yr M-F 8:30-5

HARTVILLE

4720
Wright County Historical and Genealogical Society
101 E Rolla St, 65667 [PO Box 66, 65667]; (p) (417) 741-6265; wchs@ windo.missouri.org; www.rootsweb.com/ ~mowright/wright.htm; (c) Wright

Private non-profit/ 1967/ staff: 1(f)/ members: 85/publication: *Familiy Histories*

GENEALOGICAL SOCIETY; HISTORICAL SOCIETY; HISTORY MUSEUM: Dedicated to the preservation of history of Wright County; researching, collecting in dispensing of historical and genealogical information.

PROGRAMS: Community Outreach; Exhibits; Publication; Research Library/Archives

HOURS: Yr M-F 9-4:30, Sa 9-12

ADMISSION: No charge

HAZELWOOD

4721
Hazelwood Historic Preservation Commission
6800 Howdershell Rd, 63042; (p) (314) 731-3424; (f) (314) 731-1976; (c) St. Louis

City/ 1978/ staff: 2(p)/publication: *The City of Hazelwood: Past Forms the Future*

HISTORIC PRESERVATION AGENCY: Create awareness and appreciation for historical buildings; seeking help in restoring Knobbe House.

PROGRAMS: Exhibits; Publication

COLLECTIONS: [Mid 1800s-present] Little Red Schoolhouse with furnishings, books, photos.

HOURS: Varies

ADMISSION: No charge

HERMANN

4722
Daniel Boone and Frontier Families Research Association
1770 Little Bay Rd, 65041; (p) (314) 291-0737, (314) 943-6423; (c) Gasconade

Private non-profit/ 1996/ staff: 1(f)/ 4(v)/ members: 280/publication: *History and Genealogy Research Letter*

RESEARCH CENTER: Research to establish the factual history related to Daniel Boone and the frontier families associated with him; Pennsylvania, Virginia, North Carolina, Tennessee, Kentucky, and Missouri -- 1734-1920.

PROGRAMS: Exhibits; Guided Tours; Interpretation; Publication; Research Library/Archives

COLLECTIONS: [1750-1820] Boone Family and frontier family related items 500, Books 100, maps, and 2,000 folders of documents, 30 microfilm reels, 30 computer CD's of vital data.

HOURS: By appt

ADMISSION: Donations accepted

4723
Deutschheim State Historic Site
109 W 2nd St, 65041; (p) (573) 486-2200; (f) (573) 486-2249; deutschh@ktis.net; www.deutschheim; (c) Gasconade

State/ 1978/ staff: 3(f); 2(p); 13(v)/ members: 100/publication: *German American History; Der Maibaum Quarterly*

HISTORIC SITE; HISTORY MUSEUM; HOUSE MUSEUM; LIVING HISTORY/OUTDOOR MUSEUM: Preserves, protects, and interprets the heritage, material and culture, buildings, landscape of Missouri's 19th c German immigrants and their descendants.

PROGRAMS: Community Outreach; Exhibits; Festivals; Garden Tours; Guided Tours; Interpretation; Lectures; Publication; Research Library/Archives; School-Based Curriculum

COLLECTIONS: [1830-1910] German immigrant and German American artifacts, daily life, tools, household gear, farm equipment, gardens; Missouri research library.

HOURS: Yr Daily 9-4

ADMISSION: $2, Children $1.25

HERMITAGE

4724
Hickory County Historical Society
Museum St, 65668 [PO Box 248, 65668]; (p) (417) 745-6716; (c) Hickory

County/ 1958/ staff: 20(v)

HISTORICAL SOCIETY: Preserve local history; maintains genealogical room and Anti-Bellum house furnished with family heirlooms.

PROGRAMS: Annual Meeting; Festivals

HOURS: By request

ADMISSION: No charge

HIGGINSVILLE

4725
Harvey J. Higgins Historical Society
2113 Main, 64037 [c/o Loberta Runge, 1107 Main, 64037-1125]; (p) (660) 584-3232; (c) Lafayette

Private non-profit/ 1985/ staff: 3(v)/ members: 25/publication: *Jeffersonian*

HISTORICAL SOCIETY; LIVING HISTORY/OUTDOOR MUSEUM: Preserves regional and railroad history.

PROGRAMS: Guided Tours; Publication; Research Library/Archives

HOURS: May-Sept

ADMISSION: Donations accepted

4726
Confederate Memorial State Historic Site
W 1st St, 64037 [Rt 1 Box 221 A, 64037]; (p) (660) 584-2853; (f) (660) 584-5134; (c) Lafayette

State/ 1954/ staff: 3(f); 1(p); 1(v)/ members: 1

HISTORIC SITE: Preserves and interprets the history of the Confederate Veterans Home of Missouri.

PROGRAMS: Annual Meeting; Community Outreach; Concerts; Exhibits; Facility Rental; Guided Tours; Interpretation; Lectures; Research Library/Archives

COLLECTIONS: [1861-1950] Confederate artifacts; home, Civil War, and Reconstruction history in Missouri; historical photographs of people and buildings associated with the Confederate Home.

HOURS: Yr Daily

HIGH RIDGE

4727
Jefferson County Genealogical Society
3033 High Ridge Blvd, 63049; (p) (636) 677-8186; (f) (636) 677-8243; CindyH@ angelfire.com; www.rootsweb.com/ ~mojeffer/jcm.htm; (c) Jefferson

Private non-profit/ 1996/ members: 84

GENEALOGICAL SOCIETY

PROGRAMS: Family Programs; Lectures

HILLSBORO

4728
Jefferson County History Center
1000 Viking Dr, 63050; (p) (636) 789-3000; (f) (636) 789-3954; LPONZAR@gateway.jeffco.edu; www.jeffco.edu; (c) Jefferson

County/ 1980/ staff: 1(f); 1(p)

LIBRARY AND/OR ARCHIVES: County Archive established to help preserve and make accessible Jefferson County records.

COLLECTIONS: [1820-1970] County probate, tax records, and other miscellaneous county records.

HOURS: Yr M-F 8-4:30 and by appt.

HOPKINS

4729
Hopkins Historical Society
113 N Third St, 64461 [PO Box 292, 64461]; (p) (660) 778-3429; (c) Nodaway

Private non-profit/ 1998/ City/ staff: 30(v)/ members: 180/publication: *Hopkins Cemetery Books*

GENEALOGICAL SOCIETY; HISTORICAL SOCIETY; HISTORY MUSEUM: Operates museum; preserves and collects Hopkins' newspaper files since 1893, catalogues obituaries, photographs, print press equipment, cemetery records, and other local historical items and data.

PROGRAMS: Annual Meeting; Community Outreach; Exhibits; Guided Tours; Publication; Research Library/Archives

COLLECTIONS: Obituaries, local family and community history, artifacts, and relics from businesses.

HOURS: By appt

ADMISSION: No charge

HOUSTON

4730
Texas County Missouri Genealogical and Historical Society
Memorial Bldg, 300 S Grand Ave, 65483 [Box 12, 65483]; (p) (417) 967-3126; (c) Texas

Private non-profit/ 1980/ County/ members: 275

GENEALOGICAL SOCIETY; HISTORICAL SOCIETY: Preserves and perpetuates ancestral records for education and historical purposes; encourages the study of family history, teaches methods of research, promotes publications (genealogical) of the society, and safeguards genealogical and historical data.

PROGRAMS: Research Library/Archives

COLLECTIONS: Family histories, census indexes, cemetery records; Civil War, Revolutionary War, and other war indices; local historical collections; church and school records; some states histories; society publications.

HUNTSVILLE

4731
Huntsville Historical Society/Museum and Log Cabin
107 N Main, 65259 [401 N Main, 65259]; (p) (660) 277-4486; (c) Randolph

Joint/ 1973/ staff: 25(v)/ members: 80/publication: *Huntsville Historical Society Newsletter*

HISTORIC PRESERVATION AGENCY; HISTORIC SITE; HISTORICAL SOCIETY; HISTORY MUSEUM: Provide a storehouse for collecting, preserving, and disseminating historical information and to create interest in the past; provide a visual display of our community's past.

PROGRAMS: Exhibits; Family Programs; Lectures; Publication

COLLECTIONS: [19th-20th c] Huntsville and Randolph County involvement in the Civil War, military uniforms, household furnishings and items of personal apparel from local homes and families, school and business memorabilia, primitives, and coal mining in the area.

HOURS: Apr-Oct Sa-Su 2-5

ADMISSION: No charge

IMPERIAL

4732
Mastodon State Historic Site
1050 Museum Dr, 63052; (p) (636) 464-2976; (f) (636) 464-3768; cschmidt@mail.state.mo.us; www.state.mo.us\dnr\dsp\homedsp.htm; (c) Jefferson

State/ 1976/ staff: 4(f); 4(p); 4(v)

HISTORIC SITE; HISTORY MUSEUM; RESEARCH CENTER: Protects important natural and cultural resources while educating the public about their value and providing compatible recreation.

PROGRAMS: Annual Meeting; Community Outreach; Exhibits; Facility Rental; Festivals; Film/Video; Guided Tours; Research Library/Archives; School-Based Curriculum

COLLECTIONS: [Pleistocene] Paleontological and archaeological collections from sites on the 425 acre property, listed on the National

Register, Kimmswick Bone Bed, archaeological collection from other state historic sites.

HOURS: Yr Daily M-Sa 9-4:30 Su 12-4:30

ADMISSION: $2, Student $2; Under 15 free

INDEPENDENCE

4733
1859 Jail, Marshal's Home & Museum
217 N Main St, 64050 [217 N Main, 64050]; (p) (816) 252-1892; (f) (816) 252-7792; jchsjail@coop.crn.com; www.jchs.org/jail/museum.html

1859/ staff: 1(f); 2(p); 15(v)

COLLECTIONS: [1859-1882] Regulatory equipment - locks, handcuffs, shackles, weapons confiscated from prisoners; Archival collections are managed at our Archive & Research Library at another location.

4734
Bingham-Waggoner Historical Society
313 W Pacific Ave, 64051 [PO Box 1163, 64051]; (p) (816) 461-3491; (c) Jackson

Joint/ 1979/ Board of Directors; City of Independence

HISTORIC SITE

PROGRAMS: Annual Meeting; Exhibits; Festivals; Guided Tours

COLLECTIONS: [1890-1900]

ADMISSION: $3, Children $1, Seniors

4735
Civil War Round Table of Western Missouri
4947 S Peck Ave, 64055; (p) (816) 478-7648; (c) Jackson

Private non-profit/ 1992/ staff: 20(v)/ members: 72

HISTORICAL SOCIETY: Fosters knowledge of Civil War conflicts and the life and times of western Missouri in the 1850s and 1860s through monthly programs, periodic tours, and book collections.

PROGRAMS: Annual Meeting; Community Outreach; Exhibits; Family Programs; Guided Tours; Lectures; Living History; Reenactments; School-Based Curriculum

COLLECTIONS: [1850-1860] Maineschien Collection of books on Civil War history and westward expansion.

4736
Genealogy and Local History Branch, Mid-Continent Public Library
317 W 24 Hwy, 64050 [15616 E 24 Hwy, 64050]; (p) (816) 252-7228; (f) (816) 254-7114; ge_librarian@mcpl.lib.mo.us; www.mcpl.lib.mo.us/ge; (c) Jackson

County/ 1965/ staff: 5(f); 23(p)

Genealogy and local history library open to the public.

PROGRAMS: Research Library/Archives

COLLECTIONS: [1600-present] 50,000 reference book collection focusing on Missouri genealogy and history and eastern states; Federal population census schedules 1790-1920 for all states; genealogy circulating collection, 50,000 microfilm, 1,500 maps, 100,000 microfiche.

4737
Harry S. Truman Courtroom and Office
Main & Lexington, 64050 [22807 Woods Chapel Rd, Blue Springs, 64015]; (p) (816) 881-4467, (816) 795-8200; (f) (816) 795-7938; (c) Jackson

County/ 1973/ staff: 1(p)

HISTORIC SITE; PRESIDENTIAL SITE: Maintains site where Harry S. Truman began his career in public service here.

PROGRAMS: Film/Video; Guided Tours

COLLECTIONS: [1933]

HOURS: Mar 1-Nov 30 F-Sa 9-4:30

ADMISSION: $2, Children $1, Seniors $1

4738
Harry S. Truman Library
500 W US Hwy 24, 64050-1798; (p) (816) 833-1400; (f) (816) 833-4368; library@truman.nara.gov; www.trumanlibrary.org; (c) Jackson

Federal/ 1957/ staff: 30(f); 5(p); 80(v)

HISTORY MUSEUM; PRESIDENTIAL SITE; RESEARCH CENTER: Preserves and provides access to collections of historical materials; operates a museum with exhibits on the life and career of Harry S. Truman; offers public and educational programs.

PROGRAMS: Community Outreach; Exhibits; Film/Video; Guided Tours; Lectures; Publication; Research Library/Archives

COLLECTIONS: [1884-1972] Papers of Truman and 400 other people; 35,000 museum objects focused on the life and career of Truman; 125,000 photographs; films; sound recordings; oral history interview transcripts.

HOURS: Yr Museum: Daily 9-5; Archives M-F 8:45-4:45

ADMISSION: $5, Children $3, Seniors $4.50; Under 6 free

4739
Harry S. Truman National Historic Site
Truman Home, 219 N Delaware, 64050 [223 N Main St, 64050-2804]; (p) (816) 254-2770, (816) 254-9929; (f) (816) 254-4491; www.nps.gov/hstr; (c) Jackson

Federal/ 1983/ National Park Service/ staff: 20(f); 4(p); 3(v)

HISTORIC SITE; HOUSE MUSEUM; PRESIDENTIAL SITE: Preserves, interprets, and protects the history of former 33rd President of the U.S., Harry S. Truman, his family's farm home, his aunt and uncle's home, and 2 other relative's homes. Truman Farm Home is located in Grandview, MO.

PROGRAMS: Community Outreach; Exhibits; Film/Video; Guided Tours; Interpretation

COLLECTIONS: [1885-1982] Thousands of artifacts, memorabilia, and ephemera related to the 33rd President.

HOURS: Yr T-Su 8:30-3

ADMISSION: $2

4740
Jackson County Genealogical Society
420 S Main, 64055 [PO Box 2145, 64055]; (p) (816) 252-8128; (c) Jackson

Private non-profit/ 1979/ staff: 50(v)/ members: 250/publication: *Pioneer Trails; Pioneer Wagon*

GENEALOGICAL SOCIETY: Devoted to furthering genealogical research and promoting interest in family history.

PROGRAMS: Annual Meeting; Lectures; Publication; Research Library/Archives

COLLECTIONS: [19th-20th c] Books, periodicals, and a large collection of Jackson County records on microfilm; marriage, will, probate indexes, birth, death records.

HOURS: Yr T-Th 10-4, Sa 9-5

ADMISSION: No charge

4741
National Frontier Trails Center
318 W Pacific St, 64050; (p) (816) 325-7575; (f) (816) 325-7579; frontiertrailscenter.com; (c) Jackson

City/ 1990/ staff: 3(f); 6(p); 10(v)/ members: 80/publication: *The Trail Scout*

HISTORY MUSEUM: Focuses on the major western trails which began near Independence: Oregon, California, and Santa Fe. Interpretation includes period of the Lewis and Clark expedition to trans-continental railroad.

PROGRAMS: Annual Meeting; Community Outreach; Exhibits; Facility Rental; Family Programs; Festivals; Guided Tours; Interpretation; Lectures; Publication; Reenactments; Library/Archives; School-Based Curriculum; Theatre

COLLECTIONS: [1800-1880] Artifacts used by pioneers in crossing the American West; covered wagons, 3,000 volume research library on western themes.

HOURS: Yr Daily M-Sa 9-4:30, Su 12:30-4:30

ADMISSION: $3.50, Children $2, Seniors $3

4742
Oregon-California Trails Association
524 S Osage, 64051 [PO Box 1019, 64051]; (p) (816) 252-2276; (f) (816) 836-0989; octa@gov.net; http://www.octa-trails.org/; (c) Jackson

Private non-profit/ 1983/ staff: 1(f); 2(p); 3(v)/ members: 2500/publication: *Overland Journal; Finding the Right Place; and others*

HISTORIC PRESERVATION AGENCY: Identifies, preserves, interprets, and improves accessibility to historic trail sites, landmarks, artifacts, and objects associated with the overland western historic trails of the Trans-Mississippi region.

PROGRAMS: Annual Meeting; Publication; Research Library/Archives

COLLECTIONS: [1840-1890]

HOURS: Yr 9-3:30

4743
Pioneer Spring Cabin
Noland & Truman Rds, 64050 [111 E Maple, 64050]; (p) (816) 325-7111

4744
Reorganized Church of Jesus Christ of Later Day Saints Museum
River at Walnut, 64051 [PO Box 1059, 64051]; (p) (816) 833-1000; (f) (816) 521-3089; mscherer@rlds.org; www.rlds.org; (c) Jackson

Private non-profit/ 1860/ staff: 1(f); 20(v)

LIBRARY AND/OR ARCHIVES: Church Museum at the world church headquarters; maintains a full service library and archives.

PROGRAMS: Community Outreach; Exhibits; Film/Video; Guided Tours; Interpretation; Lectures; Research Library/Archives

COLLECTIONS: [Early 19th c-present] Artifacts collection related to church growth and expansion; artifacts in each period of American history from early 19 c.

4745
Vaile Mansion/DeWitt Museum
1500 N Liberty, 64050; (p) (816) 325-7430, (800) 748-7323

1881/ staff: 3(v)

COLLECTIONS: [1880s] Antique furniture, glass, china.

HOURS: Seasonal

IRON MOUNTAIN

4746
Iron Mountain Historical Society
325 Hwy W, Box 2, 63650; (p) (573) 734-1175; davmayo@il.net; (c) St. Francois

Private non-profit/ 1998/ staff: 12(v)/ members: 24

HISTORIC SITE; HISTORICAL SOCIETY; HISTORY MUSEUM

PROGRAMS: Exhibits

COLLECTIONS: Mining samples and memorabilia, local and personal artifacts, Native American and early settler's artifacts.

HOURS: Apr-Oct 2nd Su and by appt.

IRONTON

4747
Iron County Historical Society, Inc.
123 W Wayne St, 63650-1327; (p) (573) 546-3513; (c) Iron

Private non-profit/ 1974/ staff: 4(v)/ members: 162

HISTORICAL SOCIETY: Collects and preserves materials pertaining to Iron County.

PROGRAMS: Annual Meeting; Guided Tours; Interpretation; Publication

COLLECTIONS: Memorabilia and artifacts associated with local history, business, and residents.

HOURS: May-Oct Sa-Su 1-4

ADMISSION: No charge

JACKSON

4748
Cape Girardeau County Genealogical Society
204 S Union, 63755 [PO Box 389, 63755]; (p) (573) 335-1507; weddlema@biology.semo.edu; www.rosecity.net/genealog.html; (c) Cape Girardeau

Private non-profit/ 1970/ staff: 15(v)/ members: 200

GENEALOGICAL SOCIETY: Stimulates interest in collecting information on local families with regard to dates, incidents, stories, and family records of immediate and past genera-

tions.

PROGRAMS: Lectures; Publication; Research Library/Archives

COLLECTIONS: [1790-present] Library collection of state, regional, and county history and records, 2500 books and 200 rolls of microfilm.

HOURS: Yr

4749
Cape Girardeau County Historical Society
Jackson City Library, 101 Count, 63755 [PO Box 251, 63755]; (c) Cape Girardeau

Private non-profit/ 1930/ members: 60

Maintains a small archival collection.

4750
Oliver House Museum
224 E Adams, 63755 [PO Box 352, 63755]; (p) (573) 243-0533

1858/ staff: 12(v)

COLLECTIONS: [1850-1900] Eastlake walnut furnishings; early 1900's kitchen and artifacts; 1000 local area historical photographs.

HOURS: May-Dec 1st Su, Dec 2nd & 3rd Su 1-4:30

JAMESPORT

4751
Hook and Eye Amish Dutch House
1 blk E of the four-way stop, 64648 [509 N Elm St, 64648]; (p) (660) 684-6179

JEFFERSON CITY

4752
Cole County Historical Society
109 Madison St, 65101; (p) (573) 635-1850; (c) Cole

Private non-profit/ 1936/ staff: 2(p); 25(v)/ members: 350

HISTORICAL SOCIETY; HISTORY MUSEUM; HOUSE MUSEUM; RESEARCH CENTER: Presents, preserves, educates, collects, and displays; history of Cole County with a museum building and a library.

PROGRAMS: Annual Meeting; Community Outreach; Elder's Programs; Exhibits; Guided Tours; Interpretation; Lectures; Publication; Research Library/Archives

COLLECTIONS: [1826-present] 3 historic buildings, feature historic furniture, historic clothes and toys, historic volumes in library, local history, and genealogy collection; includes collection of ball gowns of governor's wives from 1900s-present.

HOURS: Yr T-Sa 12:30-3:30

ADMISSION: $2, Children $0.50, Students $1

4753
Jefferson Landing State Historic Site
100 Jefferson St, 65101 [Rm B2, Capitol Bldg, 65101]; (p) (573) 751-2854; (f) (573) 526-2927; (c) Cole

State/ 1974/ staff: 8(f); 18(p)

HISTORIC SITE; HISTORY MUSEUM: Preserves and interprets the history of Jefferson City and its connection to river and rail travel and provides changing exhibits.

PROGRAMS: Exhibits; Interpretation; School-Based Curriculum

COLLECTIONS: [1840-1875] Collections center around the history of Jefferson City.

HOURS: Yr Daily 10-4

4754
Mid-Missouri Genealogical Society
[PO Box 715, 65102]; (p) (573) 635-4449; (c) Cole

Private non-profit/ 1977/ staff: 10(v)/ members: 91

GENEALOGICAL SOCIETY

PROGRAMS: Annual Meeting; Community Outreach; Exhibits; Lectures; Living History; Research Library/Archives

HOURS: Yr

4755
Missouri Department of Natural Resources, Division of State Parks
1659 E Elm St, 65102 [PO Box 176, 65102]; (p) (800) 334-6946; (f) (573) 751-8656; mopa rks@mail.dnr.state.mo.us; www.mostatepar ks.com; (c) Cole

State/ 1917/ staff: 565(f); 709(p)

HISTORIC PRESERVATION AGENCY; HISTORIC SITE; HISTORY MUSEUM; HOUSE MUSEUM: Governing agency for 81 facilities, including 32 state historic sites and the Missouri State Museum; oversees State Historic Preservation Office.

PROGRAMS: Concerts; Exhibits; Family Programs; Festivals; Guided Tours; Interpretation; Living History; Reenactments

4756
Missouri Forest Heritage Center, Inc.
520 Ellis Blvd, Ste M, 65101; (p) (573) 634-6002; (f) (573) 634-4192; nallyb@sockets.net; www.snr.missouri.edu/MOForwarHeritage/index.html; (c) Shannon

Private non-profit/ 1989/ staff: 1(f); 1(p)/ members: 296

HISTORIC PRESERVATION AGENCY; LIVING HISTORY/OUTDOOR MUSEUM: Preserve the rich forest legacy of Missouri for future generations; exhibits, education, illustration, and interpretation of natural resources.

PROGRAMS: Exhibits; Interpretation; Living History

COLLECTIONS: [1840-present] Artifacts: working sawmill, crow's nest fire tower, 1840s steam powered reciprocating sawmill, an early two person chain saw, shingle mill, stave mill, historical documents.

4757
Missouri Mansion Preservation, Inc.
100 Madison St, 65102 [PO Box 1133, 65102]; (p) (573) 751-4141, (573) 751-4939; (f) (573) 751-9219; MMPI@missourimansion.org; www.missourimansion.org; (c) Cole

Private non-profit/ 1974/ staff: 3(f); 1(p); 200(v)/ members: 3500

GARDEN; HISTORIC SITE; HOUSE MUSEUM; RESEARCH CENTER: Assists the State of MO in the restoration, preservation, and historical interpretation of Missouri's 1871 Gover-

nor's Mansion.

PROGRAMS: Community Outreach; Family Programs; Guided Tours; Interpretation; Living History; Publication; Research Library/Archives; School-Based Curriculum

COLLECTIONS: Restored Governor's Mansion, in 1970s Renaissance Revival style; one of the best collections of gasoliners of the period in the county.

HOURS: Jan-July; Sept-Nov T, Th 10-12/1-3

ADMISSION: No charge

4758
Missouri State Archives
600 W Main St, 65102 [PO Box 778, 65102]; (p) (573) 751-3280; (f) (573) 526-7333; archref@mail.sos.state.mo.us; mosl.sos.state.mo.us/rec-man/arch.html; (c) Cole

State/ 1965/ staff: 16(f); 3(p); 26(v)

RESEARCH CENTER: The repository for state records of permanent historical value.

PROGRAMS: Annual Meeting; Community Outreach; Concerts; Exhibits; Family Programs; Lectures; Publication; Research Library/Archives; School-Based Curriculum

COLLECTIONS: [1760-present] Executive, legislative, and judicial records; records of state departments and agencies, land records, military records, state publications, manuscripts, photographs, and reference collections.

HOURS: Yr M- W, F 8-5, Th 8-9, Sa 8:30-3:30

4759
Missouri State Museum
First Fl, Capitol Bldg, 65101 [Rm B2, Capitol Bldg, 65101]; (p) (573) 751-2854; (f) (573) 526-2927; dspjeffl@dnr.mail.state.mo.us; (c) Cole

State/ 1919/ staff: 15(f); 12(p)/publication: Souvenir Guide to Missouri Capitol

HISTORIC SITE; HISTORY MUSEUM: Collects, preserves, and interprets the natural and cultural resources of the state of MO.

PROGRAMS: Exhibits; Festivals; Guided Tours; Interpretation; Publication

COLLECTIONS: [Prehistory-present] 100,000 items dealing with all aspects of state history.

4760
Veterinary Museum/Missouri Veterinary Medical Foundation
2500 County Club, 65074; (p) (573) 636-8737; (c) Cole

Private non-profit/ 1975/ staff: 1(p); 2(v)/ members: 70/publication: Veterinary Dispatch

HISTORY MUSEUM: Exhibits explain the development of veterinary medicine.

PROGRAMS: Exhibits; Interpretation; Publication; Research Library/Archives

COLLECTIONS: [1890-1930s] Veterinary related artifacts; medical instruments and equipment, textiles, medicines, paper artifacts, 5,000 objects, library of 1,500 books.

HOURS: W-F 12-4, Sa by appt

ADMISSION: No charge

JENNINGS

4761
Jennings Historical Society
8720 Jennings Station Rd, 63136; (p) (314) 381-6650; (f) (314) 381-7378; schmerb@swb.net; (c) St. Louis

Private non-profit/ 1980/ members: 65/publication: 50th Anniversary Cookbook

HISTORICAL SOCIETY: Collect, preserve, and maintain local history and provides information and conducts tours of Bellefountain Cemetery.

PROGRAMS: Exhibits; Family Programs; Guided Tours; Publication

COLLECTIONS: [1839-1999] Photographs, 3,000 slides, Jennings and Fairview, high school yearbooks, Jennings family, maps, business, current newspaper articles.

JOPLIN

4762
Joplin Historical and Mineral Museum, Inc.
Schifferdecker Park, 64802 [PO Box 555, 64802]; (p) (417) 623-1180, (417) 623-2341; (f) (417) 623-6393; jopmusm@ipa.net; (c) Jasper

Private non-profit/ 1995/ staff: 4(f); 50(v)/ members: 285/publication: Mineral Museum News; Historical and Mineral News

HISTORY MUSEUM

PROGRAMS: Annual Meeting; Community Outreach; Exhibits; Facility Rental; Family Programs; Film/Video; Guided Tours; Interpretation; Lectures; Living History; Publication

COLLECTIONS: Local mineral specimens, historical artifacts, photographs, and period clothing.

HOURS: Yr T-Sa 9-4, Su 1-4

ADMISSION: No charge

4763
Missouri Southern State College Archives and Special Collections
Spiva Library, 64850 [3950 E Newman Rd, 64850]; (p) (417) 625-9552; (f) (417) 625-9734; nodler-c@mail.mssc.edu; www.mssc.edu/pages/library/libhome.htm; (c) Jasper

State/ 1969/ staff: 1(f); 2(p)/publication: Southern Footnotes

LIBRARY AND/OR ARCHIVES: Collects historical materials.

PROGRAMS: Exhibits; Guided Tours; Publication; Research Library/Archives

COLLECTIONS: [1900s] Tri-State mining history, congressional papers, manuscripts, maps, local history.

HOURS: Yr M-F 8-5

ADMISSION: No charge

KAHOKA

4764
Clark County Historical Society
252 N Morgan, 63445 [PO Box 202, 63445]; (p) (660) 727-1072; (c) Clark

Private non-profit/ 1960/ members: 80

GENEALOGICAL SOCIETY; HISTORIC

PRESERVATION AGENCY; HISTORICAL SOCIETY; HISTORY MUSEUM; RESEARCH CENTER

PROGRAMS: Annual Meeting; Community Outreach; Exhibits; Facility Rental; Family Programs; Festivals; Film/Video; Guided Tours; Lectures; Living History; Publication; Research Library/Archives; School-Based Curriculum

COLLECTIONS: Records of artifacts, documents, clothing, genealogies, bibles.

HOURS: Yr

ADMISSION: Donations accepted

KANSAS CITY

4765
Alexander Majors Historical Foundation
8201 State Line Rd, 64114; (p) (816) 333-5556; (c) Jackson

1984/ staff: 36(v)/ members: 190

HISTORIC SITE; HISTORICAL SOCIETY; HISTORY MUSEUM

PROGRAMS: Exhibits; Facility Rental; Guided Tours; Interpretation

COLLECTIONS: [1850s-1870s] An 1856 house with 1840s to 1870s furnishings.

HOURS: Apr-Dec Sa-Su 1-4

ADMISSION: $3, Children $1

4766
Church of the Nazarene Archives
6401 The Paseo, 64131; (p) (816) 333-7000; singersol@nazarene.org; www.nazarene.org/hoo/archives.html; (c) Jackson

Private non-profit/ 1932/ staff: 1(f); 3(p)

LIBRARY AND/OR ARCHIVES: Official repository of historical materials related to the Church of the Nazarene an international body.

PROGRAMS: Exhibits; Research Library/Archives

COLLECTIONS: [1887-present] The papers of the Church's general offices, Church agencies, documents, social ministries, colleges, universities, and leaders.

HOURS: Yr M-F 8-4:30

ADMISSION: No charge

4767
Donald Kirk Piper, MD, Memorial Medical Museum/Saint Joseph Health Center
1000 Carondelet Dr, 64114; (p) (816) 943-2183; (f) (816) 943-2796; (c) Jackson

Private non-profit/ 1971/ staff: 1(f); 6(p)

HISTORY MUSEUM: Dedicated to preserving, interpreting, and promoting the history of medicine in Kansas City, especially that provided at Saint Joseph Health Center since its founding in 1874.

PROGRAMS: Exhibits; Research Library/Archives

COLLECTIONS: [1874-present] Medical instruments, equipment, uniforms, medical texts, and records reflecting the practice of medicine at Saint Joseph, Kansas City, and the U.S.

HOURS: Yr Daily

4768
Hallmark Visitors Center, The
2501 McGee, #132, 64141 [PO Box 419580, 64141-6580]; (p) (816) 274-5745; (f) (816) 274-3148; mcagel@hallmark.com; www.hallmark.com; (c) Jackson

Private non-profit/ 1985/ staff: 4(f); 14(p)

CORPORATE ARCHIVES/MUSEUM: Illustrated in over 14 major exhibits; history of Hallmark Cards, Inc.; Displays depict the history of Hallmark and how Hallmark products are made. Employees working on products demonstrate processes used in greeting card production.

PROGRAMS: Exhibits; Film/Video; Guided Tours

COLLECTIONS: [1910-present] Creative and original art by Hallmark artists; artifacts, memorabilia, historical, and archival collections, some dating back over a century; Hallmark collectibles and corporate inventory dating back to early 1900s.

4769
Heritage League of Greater Kansas City
5100 Rockhill Rd, 64110 [007 Cockefair Hall, UMKC, 64110-2499]; (p) (816) 235-1339; (f) (816) 235-5723; jsvadlenak@planetkc.com; (c) Jackson

Private non-profit/ 1980/ staff: 100(v)/ members: 100/publication: *Heritage Advocate*

Dedicated to the preservation of our cultural heritage; sponsors workshops to improve professional practices, public events, and social events to provide networking opportunities among those working in area agencies.

4770
Historic Kansas City Foundation
[PO Box 414413, 64141-4413]; (p) (816) 931-8448; (f) (816) 931-8558; (c) Jackson

Private non-profit/ 1974/ staff: 1(p); 100(v)/ members: 450

PROFESSIONAL ORGANIZATION: Dedicated to the preservation of historic buildings and neighborhoods in Greater Kansas City through advocacy and education programs.

PROGRAMS: Community Outreach; Guided Tours; Lectures; Research

4771
Historic Kansas City Foundation
201 Wyandotte St, 64105-1250; (p) (816) 471-3391; (f) (816) 471-3915

4772
Historical Society of New Santa Fe, The
908 W Santa Fe Trail & 103rd State Live Rd, 64145 [712 W 121st St, 64145]; (p) (816) 942-5033; kcsun4.kcstar.com/schools/NewSantaFe/; (c) Jackson

Private non-profit/ 1977/ staff: 10(v)/ members: 25

HISTORIC SITE; HISTORICAL SOCIETY: Concentrates on the sites of New Santa Fe, the Fity Rugh/Watts Bill and the Ruts, Swales, and California Trails.

PROGRAMS: Annual Meeting; Festivals; Lectures; Research Library/Archives

COLLECTIONS: [1800s-1900] A few artifacts from wagon trains.

4773
John Wornall House Museum
146 W 61st Terr, 64113; (p) (816) 444-1858; jwornall@crn.org; jchs@crn.org; (c) Jackson

Private non-profit/ 1972/ staff: 1(f); 4(p); 150(v)/ members: 200

GARDEN; HISTORIC SITE; HISTORY MUSEUM; HOUSE MUSEUM; LIVING HISTORY/OUTDOOR MUSEUM: Collects, researches, and interprets materials related to the daily lives of farm families who migrated from the Southern States, emphasizing the period of 1830-1865.

PROGRAMS: Community Outreach; Concerts; Exhibits; Facility Rental; Garden Tours; Guided Tours; Interpretation; Lectures; Living History; Reenactments; School-Based Curriculum

COLLECTIONS: [1830-1875] Period furnishings, household items, decorative arts.

HOURS: Feb-Dec T-Sa 10-4, Su 1-4

ADMISSION: $3, Student $2, Children $2, Seniors $2.50; Under 5 free; group rates

4774
Kansas City Area Archivists
5100 Rockhill Rd, 64110-2499; (p) (816) 235-1543; (f) (816) 235-5500; boutrosd@umkc.edu; www.umkc.edu/KCAA/; (c) Jackson

Private non-profit/ 1978/ staff: 13(v)/ members: 185/publication: *The Dusty Shelf*

Professional association of archivists working in Eastern Kansas and Western Missouri.

4775
Kansas City Museum
3218 Gladstone Blvd, 64123; (p) (816) 483-8300; (f) (816) 483-9912; www.kcmuseum.com; (c) Jackson

Private non-profit/ 1939/ staff: 65(f); 11(p)/ members: 2100

HISTORY MUSEUM

PROGRAMS: Exhibits; Facility Rental; Family Programs; Research Library/Archives

HOURS: Yr T-Sa 9:30-4:30, Su 12-4:30

ADMISSION: Donations requested

4776
Kansas City Public Library Special Collections Department
311 E 12th St, 64106; (p) (816) 701-3400; (f) (816) 701-3401; SWC_Katherine@KCLIBRARY.ORG; www.KCLIBRARY.ORG; (c) Jackson

1973/ staff: 5(f); 3(p)

GENEALOGICAL SOCIETY: Collects, preserves, and provides access to resource materials in genealogy and in the history of the Kansas City metropolitan region primarily and secondarily in areas of western MO and eastern KS.

COLLECTIONS: [1800-1960] Materials in all formats for Kansas City regional history, Western Americana, Civil War; African-American resources and extensive genealogy collection including 19th c country histories.

HOURS: Yr

4777

Liberty Memorial Museum of World War One

100 W 26 St, 64108-4616; (p) (816) 931-0749; staff@libertymemorialmuseum.org; www.libertymemorialmuseum.org; (c) Jackson

Joint/ 1920/ staff: 2(f); 100(v)

HISTORIC SITE; HISTORY MUSEUM; RESEARCH CENTER: Dedicated to the history of WW I.

PROGRAMS: Annual Meeting; Community Outreach; Exhibits; Interpretation; Lectures; Living History; Research Library/Archives

COLLECTIONS: [1914-present] Personal and official documents, ephemera, photographs, posters, sheetmusic, uniforms, equipment, weapons, artillery, homefront objects, helmets.

HOURS: Call for hours

4778

Line Creek Museum of Archaeology

5940 NW Waukomis, 64151; (p) (816) 741-7201, (816) 587-8822; (f) (816) 505-1784; (c) Platte

City/ 1973/ staff: 2(f); 1(p)

ARCHAEOLOGICAL SITE/MUSEUM: Preserves and interprets prehistoric cultures, archaeology, and related fields engaging visitors actively in day's challenges.

PROGRAMS: Community Outreach; Guided Tours; Interpretation; Lectures; School-Based Curriculum

COLLECTIONS: [Prehistory] Artifacts covering Paleo through Post Mississippian period with focus on Kansas City Hopewell culture.

HOURS: Yr Sa-Su 11-4

ADMISSION: $1, Children $0.50; Under 2 free

4779

Midwest Afro-American Genealogical Interest Coalition

3700 Blue Pkwy, 64130 [PO Box 300972, 64130]; (p) (816) 921-5293; (c) Jackson

Private non-profit/ 1991/ members: 60/publication: *Generations*

GENEALOGICAL SOCIETY: Promotes genealogy and family history through presentation of structured classes, exhibition of genealogies, guest lectures and tours of agencies which are considered sources of genealogical interest.

PROGRAMS: Community Outreach; Exhibits; Publication

4780

Native Sons of Kansas City

[PO Box 10046, 64113]; (p) (816) 926-9397; (f) (816) 822-2136; (c) Jackson

Private non-profit/ 1932/ staff: 1(p)/ members: 300/publication: *Journal Notes*

HISTORICAL SOCIETY: Preserves Kansas City history, maintains archives of historical interest to the development of Kansas City, promotes interest in the welfare of Kansas City.

PROGRAMS: Annual Meeting; Community Outreach; Publication; Research Library/ Archives

COLLECTIONS: Manuscripts and research materials.

4781

Shoal Creek Living History Museum

7000 N E Barry Rd, 64156; (p) (816) 792-2655; (f) (816) 792-3469; amcole@gateway.net; (c) Clay

Joint/ 1975/ staff: 2(f); 1(p); 92(v)/publication: *The Mouse in the Attic*

GARDEN; HISTORIC SITE; HISTORY MUSEUM; HOUSE MUSEUM; LIVING HISTORY/ OUTDOOR MUSEUM: Depicts daily life in Missouri during the period of 1801-1900; The museum is presently comprised of 23 relocated and reconstructed period building on an 80 acre park site; our purpose is to kindle the imagination to a world of possibilities.

PROGRAMS: Annual Meeting; Community Outreach; Concerts; Exhibits; Facility Rental; Family Programs; Festivals; Garden Tours; Guided Tours; Interpretation; Living History; Publication; Reenactments; School-Based Curriculum

COLLECTIONS: [1801-1899] 23 buildings, furnishings, clothing, books, artifacts, and memorabilia.

HOURS: Yr T-Sa 9-3

ADMISSION: $1

4782

Thomas Hart Benton Home & Studio State Historic Site

3616 Belleview, 64111; (p) (816) 931-5722; (c) Jackson

State/ 1977/ staff: 3(f); 2(p)

HISTORIC SITE; HOUSE MUSEUM: Dedicated to interpreting the life of the American artist, Thomas Hart Benton.

PROGRAMS: Guided Tours; Interpretation

COLLECTIONS: [1939-1975] Personal possessions and household furnishings from the period of the Benton family's occupancy.

HOURS: Yr Daily M-Sa 10-4, summer Su 12-5, winter Su 11-4

ADMISSION: $2, Children $1.25; Under 6

4783

Toy and Miniature Museum of Kansas City

5235 Oak St, 64112; (p) (816) 333-9328; (f) (816) 333-2055; www.umkc.edu/tmm; (c) Jackson

Private non-profit/ 1982/ staff: 5(f); 2(p); 75(v)/ members: 350

HISTORICAL SOCIETY: Toy and miniature museum collects, preserves, and displays toys and scale miniatures for the education and enjoyment of the general public.

PROGRAMS: Exhibits; Guided Tours; Research Library/Archives

COLLECTIONS: [Late 19th-early 20th c] Museum contains antique toys, dolls, dolls houses, trains, cast iron banks, and scale miniatures, Russian lacquer boxes.

HOURS: Yr W-Sa 10-4, Su 1-4

ADMISSION: $4,Children $2, Seniors $3.50

4784

Union Cemetery Historical Society

227 E 28th Terr, 64108; (p) (816) 472-4990; (c) Jackson

Private non-profit/ 1857/ staff: 10(v)/ members: 93/publication: *Tombstone Inscriptions*

HISTORICAL SOCIETY

PROGRAMS: Community Outreach; Guided Tours; Living History; Publication; School-Based Curriculum; Theatre

COLLECTIONS: [1857-present] Records and genealogical records of all persons buried in Union Cemetery since 1857.

HOURS: Yr Daily 9-3:30

ADMISSION: No charge

4785

University of Missouri-Kansas City Archives

302 Newcomb Hall, UMKC, 5100 Rockhill Rd, 64111-2499; (p) (816) 235-1543; (f) (816) 235-5500; UMKCArchives@umkc.edu; www.umkc.edu/University_Archives; (c) Jackson

1978/ staff: 1(f); 1(p)

LIBRARY AND/OR ARCHIVES

PROGRAMS: Community Outreach; Research Library/Archives

COLLECTIONS: [1930s-present]

HOURS: Yr M-F 8-5

ADMISSION: No charge

4786

Western Historical Manuscript Collection, Kansas City

302 Newcomb Hall, UMKC, 5100 Rockhill Rd, 64110-2499; (p) (816) 235-1543; (f) (816) 235-5500; WHMCKC@umkc.edu; www.UMKC.EDU/WHMCKC/; (c) Jackson

Private non-profit/ 1980/ State/ staff: 2(f); 1(p)

Collects and makes available manuscripts, documents related to the history, and culture of MO and the Midwest, promotes history and the care of the historical records, sponsors and otherwise supports educational and outreach projects including exhibits, publications, symposia, and workshops.

COLLECTIONS: [1850-present] 12,000 cubic feet of documents.

HOURS: Yr

4787

Westport Historical Society

4000 Baltimore, 64111; (p) (816) 561-1821; www.westporthistorical.org; (c) Jackson

Private non-profit/ 1964/ staff: 10(v)/ members: 350/publication: *The Battle of Westport*

HISTORIC SITE; HISTORICAL SOCIETY; HOUSE MUSEUM: Promotes public interest in the history of Westport through its house museum, web site, tours, speaker's bureau, publications historical signage, and quarterly programs. National Registry.

PROGRAMS: Annual Meeting; Community Outreach; Exhibits; Facility Rental; Garden Tours; Guided Tours; Lectures; Publication; Research Library/Archives

COLLECTIONS: [1850-1870] Domestic furnishings for four rooms of the 1855 portion of the Harris-Kearney House. The Westport Historical Society "Quarterlies."

HOURS: Yr M-F 10:30-3 and by appt weekends

ADMISSION: $2, Student $1, Children $0.50, Seniors $1

KEARNEY

4788
Clay County Parks, Recreation, Historic Sites
21216 Jesse James Rd, 64060; (p) (816) 628-6065; (f) (816) 628-6676; jamesfarm@claycogov.com; (c) Clay

County/ 1978/ staff: 2(f); 20(p); 12(v)

HISTORIC SITE; HISTORY MUSEUM; RE-SEARCH CENTER: Site includes: Jesse James birthplace and museum, Jesse James bank museum - site of the first peacetime day-light bank robbery, Claybrook house -antebel-lum home of Jesse's daughter.

PROGRAMS: Annual Meeting; Community Outreach; Facility Rental; Family Programs; Guided Tours; Interpretation; Lectures; Reen-actments; Research Library/Archives

COLLECTIONS: [Civil War Era] Collection of James family certificates and Civil War related artifacts.

HOURS: Yr Daily 9-4

KIMMSWICK

4789
Kimmswick Historical Society
6000 Third St, 63053 [Box 41, 63053]; (p) (314) 464-8687; (c) Jefferson

Private non-profit/ 1977/ staff: 45(v)/ members: 45

HISTORICAL SOCIETY; HISTORY MUSEUM; HOUSE MUSEUM: Collects and preserves pictures, artifacts, and maps for the education and enjoyment of people today and tomorrow.

PROGRAMS: Festivals; Guided Tours; Lec-tures; Reenactments

COLLECTIONS: [1880-1920s] Pictures, maps, Indian artifacts, complete tool and work bench of early watch repair.

HOURS: Yr Sa-Su 1-4

ADMISSION: No charge

KING CITY

4790
Tri-County Historical & Museum Society of King City, MO, Inc.
508 N Grand & Jct Hwy 169, 64463 [PO Box 547, 64463]; (p) (660) 535-4472, (800) 411-9013; (f) (660) 535-4391; (c) Gentry

Private non-profit/ 1975/ staff: 1(p); 20(v)

HISTORICAL SOCIETY

PROGRAMS: Community Outreach; Exhibits; Family Programs; Guided Tours; Living Histo-ry; Reenactments; Research Library/Archives

COLLECTIONS: [1850-present] House hold items, small town displays, farm implements, railroad depot and articles of railroad, school memorabilia, church items, military display of Spanish American War, Civil War and WW I & II, log cabin, barn, working blacksmith shop, & genealogy library.

HOURS: May-Sept Sa-Su 2-5 or by appt

ADMISSION: Donations accepted

KIRKSVILLE

4791
Adair County Historical Society
211 S Elson St, 63501-3466; (p) (660) 665-6502; www.kirksvillecity.com/museums.html; (c) Adair

County; Private non-profit/ 1976/ Officers and Board of Directors/ staff: 1(f); 1(p); 4(v)/ mem-bers: 237/publication: *The Adair Historian*

ART MUSEUM; HISTORIC PRESERVATION AGENCY; HISTORICAL SOCIETY; HISTORY MUSEUM; HOUSE MUSEUM; LIVING HISTO-RY/OUTDOOR MUSEUM; RESEARCH CEN-TER: Discovers, collects, displays, and preserves the county and area archives and artifacts.

PROGRAMS: Annual Meeting; Community Outreach; Exhibits; Facility Rental; Festivals; Guided Tours; Interpretation; Lectures; Living History; Publication; Research Library/ Archives

COLLECTIONS: Family histories, 500 books, original probate court records, aboriginal arti-facts, 1,000 photographs, art and paintings, 35 maps/atlases, vital records, newspapers on microfilm, 180 directories, 100 yearbooks, manuscripts, diaries, and 460 periodicals.

HOURS: Yr W-F 1-4 and by appt

ADMISSION: Donations accepted

KIRKWOOD

4792
Kirkwood Historical Society, The
302 W Argonne, 63122 [PO Box 220602, 63122]; (p) (314) 965-5151; (f) (314) 821-2601; (c) St. Louis

Private non-profit/ 1961/ members: 501/publi-cation: *History of Kirkwood; Kirkwood Histori-cal Review*

HISTORICAL SOCIETY: Society discovers, collects, studies, and preserves the history of Kirkwood and surrounding areas, and pro-vides for the preservation of Mudd's Grove, the society's museum, library, and headquarters.

PROGRAMS: Annual Meeting; Community Outreach; Concerts; Exhibits; Facility Rental; Family Programs; Festivals; Film/Video; Gar-den Tours; Guided Tours; Lectures; Living His-tory; Publication; Reenactments; Research Li-brary/Archives

COLLECTIONS: [1840-present] Manuscripts, maps, newspapers articles, volumes of history dating from 1840-present, and decorative arts, artifacts, photographs, music, portraits, and paintings.

HOURS: Feb-July, Sept-Dec Su 1-4

ADMISSION: $2; Children free

KOSHKONONG

4793
Historical Society of Oregon County
Rt 2, Box 3A, 65692; (p) (417) 867-3285; (c) Oregon

Private non-profit/ 1990/ staff: 2(v)/ members: 20

HISTORICAL SOCIETY: Dedicated to the pur-pose of collecting and preserving the history of Oregon County.

PROGRAMS: Research Library/Archives

COLLECTIONS: Newspapers, books, letters, pho-tographs, some family genealogies, and written documents relating to Oregon County families.

HOURS: By request

ADMISSION: No charge

LACLEDE

4794
General John J. Pershing Boyhood Home
1000 Pershing Dr, 64651 [PO Box 141, 64651]; (p) (660) 963-2525; (f) (660) 963-2520; (c) Linn

State/ 1952/ staff: 3(f); 3(p)

HISTORIC SITE; HISTORY MUSEUM; HOUSE MUSEUM: Owned and operated by the Missouri Dept. of Natural Resources, Divi-sion of State Parks.

PROGRAMS: Annual Meeting; Exhibits; Festi-vals; Film/Video; Guided Tours; Interpretation; Research Library/Archives

COLLECTIONS: [1850-1900] Boyhood home of Gen. Pershing; displays that relate to local history, Gen. Pershing's career, one room Prairie Mound School where Pershing taught.

HOURS: Yr Apr 15-Oct 15 Daily M-Sa 8-4, Su 12-6; Oct 16-Apr 14 Su 12-5

ADMISSION: $2, Children $1.25; Under 6 free

LAMAR

4795
Barton County Historical Society
1004 Gulf St, 64759 [PO Box 416, 64759]; (p) (417) 682-4141; (c) Barton

Private non-profit/ 1968/ Board of Trustees/ staff: 1(p); 10(v)/ members: 75

GENEALOGICAL SOCIETY; HISTORICAL SOCIETY; HISTORY MUSEUM: Seeks to bring people together interested in the history of Barton County; collects material that illus-trates the area's settlement and development; and maintains an archives.

PROGRAMS: Community Outreach; Exhibits; Lectures; Research Library/Archives

COLLECTIONS: [Pre-Civil War-present] Bar-ton County memorabilia, tools, small farm equipment, arrowheads, historic photographs, postcards, quilts, dishes, glassware, clothing, family histories, and microfilm of "Lama Demo-crat" dating from 1882-1973.

4796
Harry S. Truman Birthplace State Historic Park
1009 Truman, 64759; (p) (417) 682-2279; (f) (417) 682-6304; (c) Barton

State/ 1959/ Dept of Natural Resources/ staff: 3(f); 4(p); 2(v)

HISTORIC SITE; HOUSE MUSEUM; PRESI-DENTIAL SITE: Maintains the original birth-place of President Truman, furnished with arti-facts from the 1840s-1890s.

PROGRAMS: Annual Meeting; Community Outreach; Family Programs; Guided Tours; In-terpretation; Living History; Reenactments; School-Based Curriculum

COLLECTIONS: [1840-1890s] Birthplace of President Truman, with 1840-90s furnishings.

HOURS: Yr Daily M-Sa 10-4, Su 12-4

ADMISSION: No charge/Donations accepted

LANCASTER

4797
Schuyler County Historical Society
Corner of Washington & Lynn, 63548 [Box 215, 63548]; (c) Schuyler

Private non-profit/ staff: 1(p)

HISTORICAL SOCIETY; HOUSE MUSEUM

PROGRAMS: Annual Meeting; Community Outreach; Exhibits

COLLECTIONS: [1860-present] Photographs of Schuyler, County businesses and residents, old clothing, Rupert Hughes novels, cemetery records, newspaper files.

HOURS: June-Aug T-F 10-12/1-5

ADMISSION: Donations accepted

LAWSON

4798
Family Tree Climbers
[PO Box 422, 64062]; (c) Ray

Private non-profit/ 1965/ members: 12

GENEALOGICAL SOCIETY: Preservation of the community, its history, and families by cataloging cemeteries, saving old newspaper obituaries, and its families history as well as our members families.

COLLECTIONS: [1750-1900] Genealogy books, local history books, obituaries, New England genealogy books, individual family histories.

4799
Watkins Woolen Mill State Historic Site and Park
26600 Park Rd N, 64062; (p) (816) 580-3387; (f) (816) 580-3784; dspwatkn@mail.dnr.state.mo.us; (c) Clay

State/ 1964/ staff: 13(f); 8(p); 62(v)

HISTORIC SITE; LIVING HISTORY/OUTDOOR MUSEUM: Maintains 19 c technological and agricultural site with only remaining fully equipped 19 c woolen factory, owner's home, outbuildings, visitors center houses exhibits and site's extensive archives. National Landmark.

PROGRAMS: Exhibits; Film/Video; Guided Tours; Interpretation; Living History; Research Library/Archives

COLLECTIONS: [1825-1945] 19th c woolen textile manufacturing machinery, agricultural and household artifacts, and related documents and archival materials relating to textile production, agriculture and Watkins family including rare early American powered textile machines.

HOURS: Yr Summer M-Sa 10-5, Su 11-5; Winter Su 12-4

ADMISSION: $2, Children $1.25

LEE'S SUMMIT

4800
Historic Longview Farm
3361 SW Longview Rd, 64081; (p) (816) 761-6669; (f) (816) 765-8545; ngoodman@tfs.net;

(c) Jackson

Private non-profit/ 1985/ staff: 10(f)

Creating adaptive reuses for rehabilitation, preservation for 15 structures listed on the National Register.

HOURS: Yr 8-5

4801
Missouri Town 1855
8108 E Park Rd, 64015 [22807 Woods Chapel Rd, Blue Springs, 64015]; (p) (816) 524-8770; (f) (816) 795-7938; www.co.jackson.mo.us; (c) Jackson

County/ 1973/ staff: 5(f); 2(p); 200(v)/publication: *Missouri Town 1855: A Program In Architectural Preservation*

LIVING HISTORY/OUTDOOR MUSEUM: Promotes a Missouri Antebellum community in a living history format, includes 20 buildings (1820-1870s).

PROGRAMS: Community Outreach; Festivals; Interpretation; Living History; Publication

COLLECTIONS: [1850s]

HOURS: Apr 15-Nov 15 W-S 9-4:30; Nov 15-Apr 15 Sa-Su 9-4:30

ADMISSION: $3, Student $2, Seniors $2;

LEXINGTON

4802
1830s Log House Museum
Main at Broadway St, 64067 [PO Box 132, 64067]; (p) (660) 259-4960, (660) 259-4711

1830/ staff: 2(v)

COLLECTIONS: [1800s] Furnished with pioneer era antiques, reproductions.

HOURS: By appt

4803
Battle of Lexington State Historic Site
Ext Hwy 13 N, 64067 [PO Box 6, 64067]; (p) (660) 259-4654; (f) (660) 259-2378; blex@iland.net; www.digitalhistory.com/schools/BattleofLexingtonSt; (c) Lafayette

State/ 1959/ staff: 4(f); 6(p); 50(v)

BATTLEFIELD; HISTORIC SITE; HISTORY MUSEUM; HOUSE MUSEUM: Preserves a Civil War Battle site with original battlefield. Home used as a field hospital during the siege, and built by Oliver Anderson in 1853.

PROGRAMS: Community Outreach; Exhibits; Festivals; Guided Tours; Interpretation; Living History; Reenactments; Research Library/Archives; School-Based Curriculum

COLLECTIONS: [1840-1880] Victorian furniture and decorative arts, military material, Lexington, Lafayette county histories incorporating mostly archival items.

HOURS: Visitor Center Yr M-Sa 9-5, Su 11:30-5; Anderson House Mar-Oct M-Sa 9-5, Su 11:30-5

ADMISSION: $2, Children $1.25; Under 6 free; group rates

4804
Lexington Historical Association
112 S 13th St, 64067 [PO Box 121, 64067]; (p) (660) 259-6313; (c) Lafayette

Private non-profit/ 1924/ staff: 30(v)/ members: 150/publication: *Lexington Historical Association Newsletter*

HISTORICAL SOCIETY: Maintain two museums with archives and various activities; aids in preserving and interpreting the history and culture of the Lexington area.

PROGRAMS: Annual Meeting; Community Outreach; Exhibits; Facility Rental; Family Programs; Festivals; Guided Tours; Interpretation; Lectures; Publication; Research Library/Archives

COLLECTIONS: [Mid 1800s-mid 1900s] Materials on the entire history of the Lexington area; artifacts deal with pre-civil War traders and the Civil War Battle of Lexington.

HOURS: May, Sept, Oct Sa-Su 10-4:30; June-Aug Daily 1-4:30

ADMISSION: $1, Children $0.50

4805
Missouri River Outfitters
1421 S St, 64067; (p) (660) 259-2900; (c) Lafayette

Private non-profit/ 1991/ staff: 10(v)/ members: 50/publication: *Missouri River Outfitters Newsletter*

HISTORICAL SOCIETY: Local chapter of the Santa Fe Trail Association sponsors various activities to preserve and interpret the Santa Fe Trail in Missouri and Eastern Kansas.

PROGRAMS: Annual Meeting; Community Outreach; Family Programs; Guided Tours; Interpretation; Lectures; Living History; Publication; School-Based

LIBERTY

4806
Clay County Archives and Historical Library, Inc.
219 E Franklin, 64069 [PO Box 99, 64069]; (p) (816) 781-3611; ccarch@qni.com; www.qni.com/~ccarch/index.htm; (c) Clay

Private non-profit/ 1979/ staff: 15(p); 15(v)/ members: 225/publication: *Clay County Mosaic*

LIBRARY AND/OR ARCHIVES: Preserves original county records, offering a source for genealogical and historical research to area citizens and Clay County descendants nationwide.

PROGRAMS: Annual Meeting; Publication; Research Library/Archives

COLLECTIONS: [1822-present] Original county records, obits, cemeteries, County censuses 1830-1920, abstracts, land records, marriage index, circuit court civil records, school records, family genealogies and histories, newspaper microfilm

4807
Clay County Museum and Historical Society
14 N Main St, 64068; (p) (816) 792-1849; (c) Clay

Joint; Private non-profit/ 1973/ staff: 1(p); 25(v)/ members: 300

HISTORIC SITE; HISTORICAL SOCIETY; HISTORY MUSEUM: To operate an historical museum of local artifacts within a historic building and to promote the history of Clay County.

PROGRAMS: Annual Meeting; Exhibits; Facility Rental; Lectures; Publication

COLLECTIONS: [1820-1950] Artifacts reflecting the daily life of people from Clay Co9unty, Missouri from 1820-1950, pharmacy items cira 1870-1920, Indian arrowhead collection dating to 1000 B.C.

HOURS: Feb-Dec T-Sa 1-4

ADMISSION: $1

4808
Historic Liberty Jail
216 N Main St, 64068; (p) (816) 781-3188; (f) (816) 781-7311; (c) Clay

Private non-profit/ staff: 14(v)

HISTORIC SITE

PROGRAMS: Guided Tours

COLLECTIONS: [1833-1856] Old Liberty Jail restored with original stones.

HOURS: Yr Daily 9-9

4809
Partee Center for Baptist Historical Studies
500 College Hill, 64068; (p) (816) 781-7700; (f) (816) 415-5027; parteecenter@william.jewell.edu; jewell.edu/academia/currylibrary/partee/partee.htm; (c) Clay

Private non-profit/ 1885/ staff: 1(f); 1(p); 2(v)

RESEARCH CENTER: Assists in the preservation and study of Baptist History; provides services such as microfilming of Church documents, prepares historical sketches, leads seminars on writing and preserving history; preserves photographs and collects publications.

PROGRAMS: Annual Meeting; Publication; Research Library/Archives

COLLECTIONS: [1820s-present] Religious records, biographical files, books, photographs, newspapers, magazines, and journals relating to Baptist and religious

LINN

4810
Osage County Historical Society
402 Main St, 65051 [PO Box 402, 65051]; (p) (573) 897-2932; (c) Osage

County; Joint; Private non-profit/ 1985/ staff: 4(p); 50(v)/ members: 550

GENEALOGICAL SOCIETY; HISTORICAL SOCIETY; HISTORY MUSEUM; HOUSE MUSEUM; RESEARCH CENTER: Formed to preserve, collect, and make available to the public artifacts, and data related to the periods comprising county's history and to mark historic sites in the county including buildings.

PROGRAMS: Annual Meeting; Exhibits; Guided Tours; Publication; Research Library/ Archives

COLLECTIONS: [1841-present] Furniture, clothing, Indian artifacts, photos, books, tools, microfilmed and original documents schools and communities; organ and piano at both houses.

HOURS: Yr Linn research Library: May-Oct; Museum at Linn Su 2-4, W 9-12/1-4; Museum

at Chamois by appt

ADMISSION: Donations accepted

LINN CREEK

4811
Camden County Historical Society & Museum
Hwy 54 & V Rd, 65052 [PO Box 19, 65052-0019]; (p) (573) 346-7191; (c) Camden

Private non-profit/ 1964/ Camden County Historical Society/ staff: 35(v)/ members: 250/publication: Historical Journals

GENEALOGICAL SOCIETY; HISTORIC SITE; HISTORICAL SOCIETY; HISTORY MUSEUM; HOUSE MUSEUM: The Society preserves and makes available the history of Camden County.

PROGRAMS: Community Outreach; Concerts; Exhibits; Family Programs; Festivals; Guided Tours; Interpretation; Lectures; Living History; Monthly Meeting; Publication; Research Library/Archives; School-Based Curriculum; Theatre

COLLECTIONS: [1860-1939] Donations from local people with early Camden County history. Material on the flooding of old Linn Creek and the building of Bagnall Dam, Indian, family, community, services exhibits, working 100 year old loom and textiles, tools, bank room, and archives.

HOURS: Apr-Oct M-F 10-4

ADMISSION: Donations accepted

LONE JACK

4812
Civil War Battlefield Museum
301 S Bynum Rd, 64070-8508; (p) (816) 566-2272; (c) Jackson

City/ 1963

COLLECTIONS: [1861-1865] Electronic map, artifacts, rosters of militia in Lone Jack Battle, maps, portraits, photographs, souvenirs, four large dioramas of battle scenes.

HOURS: Apr-Oct Daily M-Sa 9-5, Su 1-5; Nov-Mar Sa-Su 1-5

ADMISSION: Donations accepted

MACON

4813
Macon County Missouri Historical Society
[PO Box 462, 63552]; (p) (660) 385-3354; (c) Macon

County/ 1957/ staff: 5(v)/ members: 35

GENEALOGICAL SOCIETY; HISTORIC SITE; HISTORICAL SOCIETY: Preservation of local history and genealogical research in cooperation with Macon Public Library.

PROGRAMS: Annual Meeting; Community Outreach; Exhibits; Guided Tours; Lectures; Research Library/Archives

COLLECTIONS: [1850-present] Memorial display case, Macon County MO Courthouse, genealogy family records, library reference books from other states, cemetery, and obituaries records.

HOURS: Library M, Sa 10-3; W, F 10-5; Th 12-5

MALDEN

4814
Malden Historical Museum
201 N Beckwith, 63863 [PO Box 142, 63863]; (p) (573) 276-5008; www.maldenmuseum.com; (c) Dunklin

Private non-profit/ 1955/ staff: 2(p); 20(v)/ members: 96

HISTORY MUSEUM: Preserve local history and artifacts.

PROGRAMS: Exhibits

COLLECTIONS: [1860-1960] Clothing, Indian artifacts, Egyptian artifacts, military exhibits, history of Little River Drainage District.

HOURS: Yr W-Sa

MANCHESTER

4815
Old Trails Historical Society
Henry Ave & Spring Meadow Dr, 63011 [PO Box 852, 63011-1152]; (p) (314) 227-6246; (c) St. Louis

Private non-profit/ 1967/ members: 97

HISTORICAL SOCIETY: Dedicated to collecting and preserving local history; cabins used for our meetings in warm weather used to illustrate and educate children's groups local history, culture, and living in the 1800s.

PROGRAMS: Annual Meeting; Community Outreach; Exhibits; Family Programs; Festivals; Guided Tours; Lectures; Living History

COLLECTIONS: [Mid 1800s] Mostly typical of items used in a modest home around 1835; bed, dressing, washstand, cupboards, chairs, desk, cider press, utensils.

HOURS: Apr-Dec by appt

ADMISSION: No charge

MANSFIELD

4816
Laura Ingalls Wilder/Rose Wilder Lane Home & Museum
3068 Hwy A, 65704; (p) (417) 924-3626; (f) (417) 924-8580; liwhome@windowmissouri.org; www.bestoftheozarks.com/wilderhome; (c) Wright

Private non-profit/ 1957/ staff: 3(f); 20(p); 2(v)/ members: 250

HISTORIC SITE; HISTORY MUSEUM; HOUSE MUSEUM: Collects, preserves, and interprets artifacts from the Ingalls and Wilder families for the education and enjoyment of present and future generations.

PROGRAMS: Annual Meeting; Community Outreach; Exhibits; Festivals; Interpretation

COLLECTIONS: [1865-1957] Possessions of the Ingalls and Wilder families including Pa's fiddle and the original handwritten manuscript of the Little House books, and the Wilder home with personal effects and furnishings intact.

HOURS: Mar-Oct M-Sa 9-5, Su 1-5

ADMISSION: $6, Student $4, Seniors $5; Under 6 free

MARBLE HILL

4817
Bollinger County Historical Society, Inc.
[PO Box 290, 63764]; (p) (573) 238-2750; bocomo@clas.net; (c) Bollinger

Private non-profit/ 1977/ Executive Board/ staff: 20(v)/ members: 126

GENEALOGICAL SOCIETY; HISTORICAL SOCIETY; HOUSE MUSEUM: Seeks to discover, promote, and preserve local history.

PROGRAMS: Festivals; Lectures; Living History; Publication; Reenactments

COLLECTIONS: [1870-1940] A two-story log house built by Henry Massey c 1868 furnished with household artifacts common to daily living in Bollinger County in the early 20th c.

HOURS: May-June, Sept-Oct Sa 10-4, Su 1-4

4818
Massey House
Mill St, 63764 [PO Box 402, 63764]; (p) (573) 238-4374, (573) 866-2480

1869/ staff: 9(v)

COLLECTIONS: [Early 1900s] Kitchen/domestic tools and equipment a collection of fragments from a ceramic industry long since gone.

HOURS: Seasonal

MARCELINE

4819
Genealogy Researchers of Linn County Missouri
Rt 1 Box 247, 64658-9634; (p) (660) 376-2170; (c) Linn

Private non-profit/ 1979/ members: 10

GENEALOGICAL SOCIETY: Preserve genealogical information and assists persons in finding information on their ancestors.

PROGRAMS: Annual Meeting

COLLECTIONS: Cemetery, census, family histories, country and town histories, funeral homes, obituaries, all in book form, some microfilm.

MARSHFIELD

4820
Webster County Historical Society
219 S Clay, 65706 [PO Box 13, 65706]; (p) (417) 468-3505; hj4@juno.com; www.rootsweb.com/~mowebste/wchs.html; (c) Webster

Private non-profit/ 1975/ staff: 100(v)/ members: 40/publication: *1999 Webster County History Book*

GENEALOGICAL SOCIETY; HISTORICAL SOCIETY; HISTORY MUSEUM: Collect and preserve information, maps, mementos, and materials pertaining to County history; maintains a museum, honors County pioneers, and promotes interest and pride in County history.

PROGRAMS: Annual Meeting; Community Outreach; Elder's Programs; Exhibits; Guided Tours; Lectures; Publication; Research Library/Archives

COLLECTIONS: [Pre 1855-present] Materials related to local history; Indian artifacts, old records, newspapers, maps, pictures, family collections, military, and memorabilia.

HOURS: May-Oct M-F 10-4, Su 1-4 and by appt

ADMISSION: Donations accepted

MARYSVILLE

4821
Nodaway County Historical Society/Nodaway County Heritage Collection
110 N Walnut, 64468 [PO Box 324, 64468]; (p) (660) 582-8176; (f) (660) 562-1290; tcarnea@mail.nwmissouri.ed; (c) Nodaway

Private non-profit/ 1944/ staff: 12(v)/ members: 135

HISTORIC SITE; HISTORICAL SOCIETY; HISTORY MUSEUM; HOUSE MUSEUM: Collects, preserves, and protects the history and artifacts of Nodaway County.

PROGRAMS: Annual Meeting; Community Outreach; Exhibits; Facility Rental; Festivals; Guided Tours; Interpretation; Lectures; Research Library/Archives

COLLECTIONS: [1850-present] Artifacts, clothing, dolls, hats, military uniforms, horse show, and racing materials relating to Nodaway County.

HOURS: Feb 14-Dec 10 T-F 1-4

ADMISSION: No charge

MARYVILLE

4822
Caleb Burns House
422 W 2nd, 64468 [PO Box 324, 64468]; (p) (660) 582-8176, (660) 582-4955; (f) (660) 562-1290

1849

COLLECTIONS: [1850-1890] Period clothing and china ware; Museum has collection of local history.

HOURS: Yr

MAYSVILLE

4823
DeKalb County Historical Society
116 W Main, 64469 [PO Box 467, 64469-0467]; (p) (816) 449-5451; dchs@ccp.com; www.rootsweb.com/modekalb/dchs.html; (c) DeKalb

Private non-profit/ 1969/ County/ staff: 44(v)/ members: 400

GENEALOGICAL SOCIETY; HISTORIC PRESERVATION AGENCY; HISTORICAL SOCIETY; HISTORY MUSEUM; RESEARCH CENTER: Studies, records, and preserves our heritage.

PROGRAMS: Annual Meeting; Guided Tours; Lectures; Publication; Research Library/Archives

COLLECTIONS: [1845-present] 3,000 pieces of artifacts; clothing, tools, toys, books, photographs, war uniforms, schools, and communication.

HOURS: Apr-Nov M-F 9-3

ADMISSION: No charge

MEMPHIS

4824
Scotland County Historical Society
311 S Main St, 63555 [PO Box 263, 63555]; (p) (660) 465-2275, (660) 465-2259; (c) Scotland

Private non-profit/ 1978/ County/ staff: 1(p); 10(v)/ members: 20/publication: *Downing House Newsletter*

HISTORICAL SOCIETY; HOUSE MUSEUM: Assembles and displays Scotland County Historical memorabilia and artifacts, and preserves history or stories of the county. Maintains Boyer House and Downing House museum.

PROGRAMS: Annual Meeting; Exhibits; Publication

COLLECTIONS: [1841-present] Civil War collection, artifacts, and Ella Ewing displays.

HOURS: Apr-Sept T-F 1-4

ADMISSION: $2; Children free

MEXICO

4825
Audrain County Genealogical Society
c/o Mexico-Audrain County Library, 305 W Jackson, 65265-2789; (c) Audrain

members: 50

HOURS: Yr M-Th 9-4, W 6-8, F-Sa 1-4

4826
Audrain County Historical Society
501 S Muldrow, 65265 [PO Box 398, 65265]; (p) (573) 581-3910; (c) Audrain

Private non-profit/ 1959/ staff: 5(p); 8(v)/ members: 475/publication: *Graceland Gazette*

GARDEN; HISTORIC SITE; HISTORICAL SOCIETY; HOUSE MUSEUM; RESEARCH CENTER: Dedicated to preserving the history of Audrain County.

PROGRAMS: Annual Meeting; Exhibits; Facility Rental; Garden Tours; Guided Tours; Publication; Research Library/Archives

COLLECTIONS: [1859-1920s] Currier and Ives prints, extensive doll collection, lusterware, Thomas Hart Benton prints, textiles, clothing, quilts, and an extensive collection of Tom Bass articles.

HOURS: Feb-Dec T-Sa 1-4, Su 2-5

ADMISSION: $2, Children $0.50

4827
Graceland Museum
501 S Muldrow, 65265 [PO Box 3, 65265]; (p) (573) 581-3910

1857/ staff: 2(f); 3(p); 10(v)

COLLECTIONS: [1857-1920s] Currier and Ives collection, fashions, Lusterware, Three-face glass collection, dolls from around the world, George Caleb Bingham prints; Audrain County history books, telephone books. Cemetery records, family histories, city directories.

HOURS: Feb-Dec T-Sa 1-4, Su 2-5

MILAN

4828
Sullivan County Genealogy Library
N Water St, 63556; (p) (660) 265-3476; (c) Sullivan

Private non-profit/ 1978/ staff: 10(p); 10(v)

GENEALOGICAL SOCIETY: Contains local genealogy material and volunteers assists with research.

PROGRAMS: Research Library/Archives

COLLECTIONS: [1850-present] Family genealogy, census, funeral home records, cemetery records, and community history.

ADMISSION: No charge

MOBERLY

4829
Randolph County Historical Society
223 N Clark, 65270; (p) (660) 263-5621; (c) Randolph

Private non-profit/ 1966/ staff: 10(v)/ members: 180/publication: *Old N Newsletter*

HISTORIC SITE; HISTORICAL SOCIETY; HOUSE MUSEUM: The preservation and presentation of history of Randolph County.

PROGRAMS: Annual Meeting; Exhibits; Family Programs; Festivals; Guided Tours; Interpretation; Publication

COLLECTIONS: [1900-present] Items donated are from documents, family histories, military, railroad, quilts, clothing, religious and various items pertaining to everyday life.

HOURS: Feb-Nov M 10-12, Th 1-3, Sa 9-12

ADMISSION: No charge

MONTGOMERY CITY

4830
Montgomery County Historical Society, Inc.
112 W Second St, 63361; (c) Montgomery

Private non-profit/ 1976/ members: 375/publication: *Pictorial History Montgomery County, Missouri*

GENEALOGICAL SOCIETY; HISTORICAL SOCIETY: Preservation of Montgomery County History, memorabilia, family genealogy.

PROGRAMS: Annual Meeting; Community Outreach; Concerts; Exhibits; Facility Rental; Family Programs; Festivals; Garden Tours; Guided Tours; Interpretation; Lectures; Living History; Publication; Reenactments; Research Library/Archives; School-Based Curriculum

COLLECTIONS: [1800-present] Cemetery records, obituaries, family records, will abstracts, index Montgomery Co. census: 1850, 60, 70, 76; photograph collection

HOURS: By appt

ADMISSION: No charge

MOSCOW MILLS

4831
Lincoln County Missouri Genealogy Society
146 W 2nd St, 63362-1215; EAGLEFORK@aol.com; (c) Lincoln

Private non-profit/ 1980/ staff: 6(f); 4(v)/ members: 65

GENEALOGICAL SOCIETY; RESEARCH CENTER: Sharing and collecting early family history of Lincoln; researching military and

Afro-American family history.

PROGRAMS: Community Outreach; Facility Rental; Family Programs; Publication; Research Library/Archives

COLLECTIONS: Local, church, school, and town histories, family histories, organization histories, and miscellaneous materials.

HOURS: Yr by appt

ADMISSION: No charge

4832
Mills Historic Shapley Ross House
125 W 2nd St, 63362; (p) (314) 366-9825; show-me-missouri.com/heritage7.htm

MOUND CITY

4833
Holt County Historical Society
115 Ada St, 64470 [PO Box 55, 64470]; (p) (660) 582-5361, (660) 442-5949; (c) Holt

Private non-profit/ 1972/ County/ members: 200

GENEALOGICAL SOCIETY; HISTORIC SITE; HISTORICAL SOCIETY; HISTORY MUSEUM; HOUSE MUSEUM; RESEARCH CENTER: Preserves local and state history and events along with the people who developed and homesteaded the area.

PROGRAMS: Annual Meeting; Exhibits; Facility Rental; Family Programs; Festivals; Guided Tours; Lectures; Living History; Publication; Reenactments; Research Library/Archives

COLLECTIONS: [1840-present] Preserves and furnishes the 1869 Brick home, 1900 frame home, and the 1906 county school in each time period; Archival storage for photos, histories, and documents in the 1896 church building.

HOURS: May-Sept special events and by appt

NELSON

4834
Prairie Park
Hwy TT, 3 1/3 mile W of Arrow Rock, 65347 [Rt 1, 65347]; (p) (660) 837-3213, (660) 837-3231; (c) Saline

Private non-profit/ 1849

GARDEN; HOUSE MUSEUM: House museum available for guided tours through the Friends of Arrow Rock.

PROGRAMS: Guided Tours; Interpretation; Publication

COLLECTIONS: [1840-1880] Period furnishings, oil paintings, prints, and decorative arts relating to the period, 1849. Some original furnishings.

HOURS: Yr by appt

ADMISSION: $10; Group rates

NEOSHO

4835
Genealogy Friends of the Library
Located in City-County Library, W Spring St, 64850 [PO Box 314, 64850]; (p) (417) 451-4231; (c) Newton

Private non-profit/ 1986/ staff: 2(p); 5(v)/ members: 139

GENEALOGICAL SOCIETY: Promote interest in the field of genealogy through educational programs; collects and disseminates genealogy knowledge and information.

COLLECTIONS: Books, microfilm, microfiche, genealogy CD's, newspapers on microfilm, and census records; co. records on microfilm.

HOURS: Yr M-Th 9-9, F, Sa 9-5

4836
Newton County Historical Society
121 N Washington, 64850 [PO Box 675, 64850]; (p) (417) 451-4940; (f) (417) 455-1109; crossno@ipa.net; (c) Newton

Private non-profit/ 1956/ staff: 2(p); 2(v)/ members: 107/publication: *Newton County Saga*

HISTORIC SITE; HISTORICAL SOCIETY; HISTORY MUSEUM: Promotes an understanding and appreciation of the history of the Ozarks region, its culture, and its people through exhibitions and special programs.

PROGRAMS: Exhibits; Facility Rental; Family Programs; Guided Tours; Lectures; Living History; Publication; Research Library/Archives; School-Based Curriculum

COLLECTIONS: [1800s-present] County record books, artifacts, clothing and textiles, prints, portraits, photographs, newspaper articles, genealogy records, historic school library, reference library.

HOURS: Yr W-Su 12:30-4:30

ADMISSION: Donations accepted

NEVADA

4837
Vernon County Historical Society
212 W Walnut, 64772 [231 Main St, 64772]; (p) (417) 667-9602; info@bushwhacker.org; www.bushwhacker.org; (c) Vernon

Private non-profit/ 1965/ County/ staff: 1(f); 45(v)/ members: 500/publication: *The Bushwhacker Musings*

HISTORIC SITE; HISTORICAL SOCIETY; HISTORY MUSEUM; RESEARCH CENTER: Presents history of Vernon Co. from the Native American period through the 20th c by means of the Old Jail Historic Site and Bushwhacker Historical Museum.

PROGRAMS: Annual Meeting; Community Outreach; Exhibits; Facility Rental; Family Programs; Film/Video; Guided Tours; Lectures; Publication; Research Library/Archives; School-Based Curriculum

COLLECTIONS: [1850s-1940s] All periods of Vernon Co. history, emphasizing Osage Indians, Civil War, military, agriculture, life styles of the late 1800s to mid 1900s, recreation of 1900s doctor's office and home.

HOURS: May-Oct M-Su 10-4

ADMISSION: $3, Student $2, Children $1

NEW FRANKLIN

4838
South Howard County Historical Society
101 E Broadway, 65274 [PO Box 201, 65274]; members.xoom.com/shchs; (c) Howard

Private non-profit/ 1989/ staff: 7(v)/ members: 63

HISTORIC PRESERVATION AGENCY; HISTORICAL SOCIETY: Provides available information on various aspects of the local area: cemeteries, obituaries, family histories, some census records, pictures, brochures, homes, historic sites, old scrapbooks.

PROGRAMS: Annual Meeting; Community Outreach; Facility Rental; Festivals

HOURS: May-Oct Sa-Su 1-4

ADMISSION: No charge

NEW LEBANON

4839
New Lebanon Preservation Society
Hwy A, [5236 Hwy A, Bunceton, 65237]; (p) (660) 366-4482; (c) Cooper

Private non-profit/ 1998/ staff: 40(p)/ members: 40

HISTORIC PRESERVATION AGENCY; HISTORIC SITE; HISTORY MUSEUM: Preserve the history and the buildings in the New Lebanon Historic District which includes the Cumberland Presbyterian Church, one-room school house, and general store museum.

PROGRAMS: Exhibits; Festivals; Guided Tours; Living History

COLLECTIONS: [1819-present]

HOURS: May-Oct by appt

ADMISSION: $3

NEW MADRID

4840
Hunter-Dawson State Historic Site
113 Dawson Rd, 63869 [PO Box 308, 63869]; (p) (573) 748-5340; (f) (573) 748-7228; huntdaw@sheltonbbs.com; (c) New Madrid

Joint/ 1966/ staff: 4(f); 4(p); 2(v)

HISTORIC SITE: Preserves the Hunter-Dawson home an antebellum house built in 1859; 90 percent of interior furnishings are original to the house; interprets Southern culture in the Missouri Bootheel.

PROGRAMS: Exhibits; Family Programs; Festivals; Guided Tours; Lectures; Publication

COLLECTIONS: [1860-1880] Collection of Mitchell-Rammelsburg furniture, family papers, and belongings.

HOURS: Yr M-Sa 10-4, Su 12-5

ADMISSION: $2

4841
New Madrid Historical Museum
#1 Main St, 63869; (p) (573) 748-5944; (c) New Madrid

Private non-profit/ 1975/ staff: 1(f); 2(p); 5(v)/ members: 125

HISTORY MUSEUM: Maintains museum that houses exhibits on the Civil War, Mississippian Indian Artifacts, and local history.

PROGRAMS: Annual Meeting; Exhibits; Film/Video; Guided Tours

COLLECTIONS: Civil War, Native American, and agricultural artifacts; furniture, clothing pictures, hand-made antique quilts.

HOURS: Yr Daily May-Sept 9-4, Summer 9-5

ADMISSION: $2, Children $1, Seniors $1.50

NEW MELLE

4842
Boone-Duden Historical Society
Mill St, 63365 [PO Box 82, 63365]; ndnis soc@morm.org; www.norn.org/pub/other-orgs/bdhissoc; (c) St. Charles

Private non-profit/ 1986/ Advisory Council and Board of Directors/ staff: 16(v)/ members: 176/publication: *Boone-Duden Historical Society Newsletter*

HISTORIC PRESERVATION AGENCY; HISTORIC SITE; HISTORICAL SOCIETY; HISTORY MUSEUM; HOUSE MUSEUM: Preserves and collects the history of Daniel Boone, Gottfried Duden, and their followers for future generations to study and enjoy.

PROGRAMS: Annual Meeting; Community Outreach; Exhibits; Guided Tours; Publication; Research Library/Archives

COLLECTIONS: Articles and books about Daniel Boone, Gottfried Duden, and their followers, early family genealogies, maps, newspaper articles, census and tax records, photographs, and church and school records.

HOURS: Yr Su 1:30-4:30

ADMISSION: Donations accepted

NOVINGER

4843
Coal Miners Museum
Snyder, 63559 [RR 3 Box 199B, 63559]; (p) (660) 488-6818; (c) Adair

Private non-profit/ 1960/ Novinger Planned Progress Inc./ staff: 2(p); 10(v)/ members: 10

HISTORY MUSEUM: Collects, preserves, and interprets the area's past.

PROGRAMS: Exhibits; Film/Video; Guided Tours; Publication

COLLECTIONS: Unique store front display cases; antique tools; reproduction of underground coal mine; small model coal mine; farm room and early farming tools; early American lathe (working model), audio and video tapes; library room; pictures, clippings; mining records; books; mannequins.

HOURS: May-Aug Su 2-4 and by appt

ADMISSION: $1, Children $0.50

4844
Novinger Log Homestead
Snyder Ave & Coal St, 63559 [RR 3 Box 31, 63559]; (p) (660) 627-2140, (660) 488-5280; gloyd@socket.net; (c) Adair

1848/ Novinger Renewal Inc/ staff: 50(v)/ members: 300

1850s log cabin, log barn, and log smoke house.

COLLECTIONS: [1850s] Historic log structures furnished with period items.

HOURS: Mem Day-Labor Day M, W, F 1-3, Sa-Su 1-4, and by appt

ADMISSION: Donations requested

OLD MINES

4845
Old Mines Area Historical Society
Hwy 21, 63630 [Rt #1 Box 1466, 63630]; (p) (573) 438-2368, (314) 394-8543; puroner@sprintmail.com; (c) Washington

Private non-profit/ 1979/ staff: 10(f); 10(p); 100(v)/ members: 500/publication: *Diggins*

GENEALOGICAL SOCIETY; HISTORIC SITE; HISTORICAL SOCIETY; LIVING HISTORY/ OUTDOOR MUSEUM: Preserves French history and artifacts of early French settlers of Washington County; plans to establish French Village.

PROGRAMS: Annual Meeting; Community Outreach; Concerts; Exhibits; Family Programs; Festivals; Lectures; Living History; Publication; Research Library/Archives

COLLECTIONS: [17th-18th c] Genealogical records, photographs, buildings.

OSCEOLA

4846
St. Clair County Historical Society
[PO Box 376, 64776]; (p) (417) 644-7597; (c) St. Clair

Private non-profit/ 1994/ members: 47

HISTORICAL SOCIETY: Dedicated to the study and preservations of our county history, past and present.

PROGRAMS: Annual Meeting; Elder's Programs; Lectures; Publication

COLLECTIONS: Two published books, Vol. I Families and Vol. 2 Cemeteries.

OVERLAND

4847
Historical Societies of St. Louis
2315 Woodson Rd, 63114; (p) (314) 427-4810; (c) St. Louis

Private non-profit/ 1993

ALLIANCE OF HISTORICAL AGENCIES: Organized to provide an area for historical societies to share resources, ideas, and information and to undertake joint projects.

4848
Overland Historical Society
9711 Lackland Rd, 63114; (p) (314) 426-7027; (c) St. Louis

Private non-profit/ 1976/ members: 140/publication: *Overland Trails and Trials*

HISTORY MUSEUM; HOUSE MUSEUM; LIVING HISTORY/OUTDOOR MUSEUM: Operates museum, rebuilt two-story log house 1858, and log barn.

PROGRAMS: Annual Meeting; Exhibits; Guided Tours; Publication

COLLECTIONS: [Mid 1800s] Furniture, clothing, toys, tools, dishes, wagon: prairie schooner type, actually used by family in area.

HOURS: By appt.

ADMISSION: $1, Children free

OZARK

4849
Christian County Museum and Historical Society
202 E Church St, 65721 [PO Box 442, 65721]; (c) Christian

Private non-profit/ 1976/ members: 160

HISTORICAL SOCIETY; HISTORY MUSEUM: Promotes the preservation of county history through maintenance of a museum and library, presentations, programs, and publications.

PROGRAMS: Exhibits; Publication; Research Library/Archives

COLLECTIONS: [1880-present] Tax and probate records (1880-mid 1900s) and artifacts related to local individuals and history.

HOURS: Apr-Oct 3rd wkend F-Su 1-4

ADMISSION: Donations accepted

PARK HILLS

4850
Missouri Mines Museum Society
[PO Box 492, 63601]; (p) (573) 431-6226; (c) St. Francois

Private non-profit/ 1985/ staff: 38(v)/ members: 38

HISTORICAL SOCIETY: Provide financial and volunteer assistance to the Missouri Mines State Historic Site.

PROGRAMS: Annual Meeting; Exhibits

4851
Missouri Mines State Historic Site
75 Hwy 32, 63601 [PO Box 492, 63601]; (p) (573) 431-6226; dspmines@mail.dnr.state. mo.us; (c) St. Francois

State/ 1980/ staff: 4(f); 3(p); 17(v)

HISTORIC SITE; HISTORY MUSEUM: Preserve, document, and interpret the mining, milling, industry, and culture of the region.

PROGRAMS: Annual Meeting; Community Outreach; Exhibits; Festivals; Film/Video; Guided Tours; Interpretation; Publication

COLLECTIONS: [Prehistory-present] 50 large mining machines; 550 mining tools and artifacts; 500 foundry patterns; 1,500 mining documents, maps, ephemera; 1,000 mine photographs; 400 books, papers, periodicals; 5,500 Missouri and worldwide mineral and rock specimens.

HOURS: Yr Daily M-Sa 10-4, Su 12-5

ADMISSION: $2, Students $1.25, Under 6 free, group rates

PARKVILLE

4852
Missouri River Frontier Museum
126 S Main St, 64152; (p) (816) 741-5858; (c) Platte

Joint/ 1998/ State; Federal/ staff: 6(v)

HISTORIC PRESERVATION AGENCY; HISTORIC SITE; HISTORY MUSEUM; RESEARCH CENTER: Collects and preserves local history from early man to the Civil War.

PROGRAMS: Annual Meeting; Exhibits; Festivals; Interpretation

COLLECTIONS: Early maps, Indian history, Indian Items, farm tools, railroad items, frontier development items, river travel, and pictures.

HOURS: Yr T-Sa 1-4

ADMISSION: No charge

4853
Park College Library, Fishburn Archives
8700 NW River Park Dr, 64152-3795; (p) (816) 741-2000; (f) (816) 741-4911; aschultis@mial.park.edu; www.park.edu; (c) Platte

Private non-profit/ 1875/ staff: 2(p)/ members: 180/publication: *The Dusty Shelf*

LIBRARY AND/OR ARCHIVES: Collects and pressurs material related to the history of Park College.

PROGRAMS: Annual Meeting; Exhibits; Publication; Research Library/Archives

COLLECTIONS: [1850-present] College catalogs, yearbooks, photographs, and other materials related to the history of Park College and Parkville.

HOURS: Yr M-Th 8-9:30 pm, F 8-4:30, Sa 10-4, Su 4-9:30

ADMISSION: No charge

PERRYVILLE

4854
Perry County Historical Society
11 S Spring, 63775 [PO Box 97, 63775]; (p) (573) 547-2927; (c) Perry

Private non-profit/ 1971/ staff: 12(v)/ members: 300/publication: *Heritage and Newsletter*

ART MUSEUM; GENEALOGICAL SOCIETY; HISTORICAL SOCIETY; HISTORY MUSEUM; HOUSE MUSEUM: Collects and preserves the Historical and Genealogical History of the County.

PROGRAMS: Annual Meeting; Community Outreach; Exhibits; Facility Rental; Family Programs; Guided Tours; Interpretation; Living History; Publication; Research Library/ Archives

COLLECTIONS: [1830-present] Furnished House c Mid-1800s, museum military room, kitchen room, school room, genealogical material library.

HOURS: Apr-Oct Lib 1st and 3rd Sa 10-2, Museum W, Sa, Su 1-3

ADMISSION: Donations accepted

PIEDMONT

4855
Wayne County Historical Society
Rt 1 Box 1117, 63957; (p) (573) 223-7130; (c) Wayne

Private non-profit/ 1985/ County/ staff: 9(p); 15(v)/ members: 300/publication: *Wayne County Historical Society Newsletter*

GENEALOGICAL SOCIETY; HISTORICAL SOCIETY; HISTORY MUSEUM; HOUSE MUSEUM: Preserves the history of Wayne County.

PROGRAMS: Annual Meeting; Community Outreach; Concerts; Exhibits; Family Programs; Festivals; Film/Video; Guided Tours; Interpretation; Lectures; Living History; Publication; Research Library/Archives; School-Based Curriculum

COLLECTIONS: [1800-1900] Books, tools, family histories, medical equipment, household, materials pertaining to the past way of life or making a living.

HOURS: Mar-Nov 2nd Sa

PILOT GROVE

4856
Cooper County Historical Society
111 Roe St, 65276 [7400 A Hwy, 65276]; (p) (660) 834-4140; (c) Coo[er

Private non-profit/ 1990/ staff: 40(v)/ members: 160/publication: *Discover Cooper County*

GENEALOGICAL SOCIETY; HISTORICAL SOCIETY; HISTORY MUSEUM: Discovers and collects materials which will help to establish the history of the county; preserves, collects, and makes accessible; preserves historic buildings, monuments, and markers.

PROGRAMS: Annual Meeting; Community Outreach; Exhibits; Festivals; Guided Tours; Publication; Reenactments; Research Library/ Archives; School-Based Curriculum

COLLECTIONS: [1810-present] Includes family histories, cemetery records, county histories 1876-1995, old books, Civil War Dairy, vantage clothing, antiques, artifacts, maps, paintings, and photos.

HOURS: Apr-Oct W, Sa, Su 1-5

ADMISSION: No charge

4857
Pleasant Green
7045 Hwy 135, 65276; (p) (660) 834-3945; (f) (660) 834-3947

1820

COLLECTIONS: [1860s] Period clothing, old telephone service; Copies of early family land grants from Territorial years 17,000 acres.

HOURS: Seasonal

PILOT KNOB

4858
Fort Davidson State Historic Site
Hwy V at Hwy 21, 63663 [PO Box 509, 63663]; (p) (573) 546-3454; (f) (573) 546-2713; FRNTDV@mail.dnr.state.mo.us; (c) Iron

State/ 1972/ staff: 3(f); 1(p); 6(v)

BATTLEFIELD; HISTORIC SITE; HISTORY MUSEUM; STATE PARK: A museum and remains of a fort of one of the most intense Battles West of the MS, often called the Thermopylae of the West.

PROGRAMS: Exhibits; Film/Video; Interpretation

COLLECTIONS: [Civil War, Trans-Mississippi] Civil War exhibits, artifacts, multimedia, film and diorama displays, mainly of Price's 1864 raid and the Battle of Pilot Knob.

HOURS: Yr Daily

ADMISSION: No charge

PLATTE CITY

4859
Ben Ferrell Platte County 1882 Home Museum
220 Ferrell St, 64079 [PO Box 103, 64079]; (p) (816) 858-5121

1882/ staff: 1(p); 6(v)

COLLECTIONS: [1840-1900] America Brown Lowmiller Collection 101 Articles, household and domestic, originally to Platte Co. 1840. Billie Brown Burand Collection - 1840's to 1860's hand made furniture; Library room with genealogical collection of Platte Co. MO. family histories, genealogies and research books. Platte County Archives Room.

HOURS: Seasonal

PLATTSBURG

4860
Clinton County Historical and Genealogy Society, Inc.
102 W Broadway, 64477 [515 W Clay Ave, 64477-1373]; (p) (816) 930-1909; hrus25@aol.com; www.aolmembers/clintonco/ inde.html; (c) Clinton

Private non-profit/ staff: 10(v)/ members: 100

GENEALOGICAL SOCIETY; HISTORICAL SOCIETY; HOUSE MUSEUM: Maintains genealogy office, collections, house museum.

COLLECTIONS: [1800s-1920] Entire home filled with period furniture from late 1800s-1920. Clothes, memorabilia from WW II, quilts, cooking utensils, library of old books.

HOURS: By appt.

ADMISSION: Donations accepted

PLEASANT HILL

4861
Pleasant Hill Historical Society, Inc.
125 Wyoming St, 64080 [PO Box 31, 64080]; (c) Cass

Private non-profit/ 1970/ members: 77

HISTORIC PRESERVATION AGENCY; HISTORIC SITE; HISTORICAL SOCIETY; HISTORY MUSEUM: Discovers, collects, and preserves historical material, establishes and illustrates the history of the Pleasant Hill area; maintains genealogical files.

PROGRAMS: Annual Meeting; Exhibits; Film/Video; Lectures; Research Library/ Archives

COLLECTIONS: [1850-present] Artifacts and memorabilia relating to Pleasant Hill history.

HOURS: Yr W-F 3:15-5

ADMISSION: No charge

POINT LOOKOUT

4862
Ralph Foster Museum
College of the Ozarks, 65726; (p) (417) 334-6411; (c) Taney

Private non-profit/ 1920/ staff: 4(f); 35(p)

HISTORY MUSEUM: Collects, preserves, interprets, and exhibits the material relating to the natural and cultural history of the Ozarks region and the academic, spiritual, vocational, cultural, and patriotic goals of the College of the Ozarks.

PROGRAMS: Living History; Research Library/Archives

COLLECTIONS: Ozarks area history, clocks, watches, natural history, dolls, weapons, furniture,

history of the college and the original vehicle from the Beverly Hillbillies television show.

HOURS: Feb-mid Dec M-Sa 9-4:30; Feb-Mar M-F 9-4:30

ADMISSION: $4.50, Seniors $3.50; Under 18 free

POPLAR BLUFF

4863
Moark Regional Railroad Museum
303 Moran St, 63901; (p) (573) 785-4935; (c) Butler

Private non-profit/ 1951/ staff: 8(v)/ members: 64

HISTORIC SITE; HISTORY MUSEUM; RAILROAD MUSEUM: Preserves railroad history, the industry, the city-owned Frisco Depot, a National Historic site and maintains the railroad museum.

PROGRAMS: Community Outreach; Exhibits; Guided Tours; Interpretation; Lectures

COLLECTIONS: [1865-1980] Railroad photographs, books, dining car display, pictorial logging history, track crew tools, agents' office supplies, tickets, passes, Morse Code, antiques phones, lanterns, train shop, library.

HOURS: Yr 1-4 and tours by appt

ADMISSION: No charge/Donations

4864
Genealogical Society of Butler County
Box 426, 63901; (c) Butler

Private non-profit/ members: 100

GENEALOGICAL SOCIETY: Promotes an interest in genealogy and preserves our area genealogical and historical records by publishing a semi annual booklets to help persons researching their families.

PROGRAMS: Annual Meeting; Community Outreach; Exhibits; Family Programs; Lectures; Publication; Research Library/Archives; School-Based Curriculum

ADMISSION: No charge

POTOSI

4865
Mine Au Breton Historical Society, Inc.
Rt 1 Box 3154, 63664; (p) (573) 438-4973; (c) Washington

Private non-profit/ 1981/ staff: 30(v)/ members: 35

HISTORIC SITE; HISTORICAL SOCIETY: Restores and preserves historical sites and data.

PROGRAMS: Annual Meeting; Community Outreach; Exhibits; Festivals; Film/Video; Guided Tours

COLLECTIONS: [1763-1800s] Mining tools, collections of minerals and ore.

HOURS: Daily

PRINCETON

4866
Mercer County Genealogical and Historical Society, Inc.
601 Grant St, 64673; (p) (660) 748-4755, (660) 748-4104; backwood@netins.net; www.roots web.com/~momercer/index.html; (c) Mercer

Joint/ 1958/ State; County; private non-profit/ staff: 6(v)/ members: 153/publication: *Pioneer Traces*

GENEALOGICAL SOCIETY; HISTORIC PRESERVATION AGENCY; HISTORICAL SOCIETY; HISTORY MUSEUM; RESEARCH CENTER: Committed to collecting and preserving the history of Mercer County through research and dissemination of information and collecting artifacts for public viewing.

PROGRAMS: Community Outreach; Guided Tours; Lectures; Publication; Research Library/Archives

COLLECTIONS: [1840-1999] Printed materials and microfilms for genealogical purposes and a history room at the library as well as a room at the courthouse in which historical artifacts are displayed.

HOURS: Yr M-W, F 9-5, Th 9-8, Su 9-12

ADMISSION: No charge

QULIN

4867
Oller-Reynolds House
10 S St, 63961; (p) (573) 328-4488; www.show-me-missouri.com/heritage11.htm

RAYTOWN

4868
Raytown Historical Society and Museum
9705E 63rd St, 64133 [PO Box 16652, 64133]; (p) (816) 353-5033; (c) Jackson

1966/ staff: 25(v)/ members: 250/publication: *Raytown Missouri USA 1849-1999*

HISTORICAL SOCIETY; HISTORY MUSEUM: Dedicated to preserving the history of Raytown.

PROGRAMS: Exhibits; Interpretation; Publication; Research Library/Archives; School-Based Curriculum

COLLECTIONS: [Early 1800-present] Late 1800s county store, blacksmith shop and tools, parlor, school room, collection of historical and family pictures of early Raytown.

HOURS: Yr W-Sa 10-4, Su 1-4

ADMISSION: No charge/Donations accepted

REPUBLIC

4869
General Sweeny's Museum
5228 S State Hwy ZZ, 65738; (p) (417) 883-2101; www.civilwarmuseum.com; (c) Greene

Private for-profit/ 1992/ staff: 3(f); 1(v)

HISTORY MUSEUM: Collects, preserves, and interprets the Civil War in the Trans-Mississippi, including Missouri, Arkansas, Kansas, and Oklahoma) for the enjoyment of present and future generations.

PROGRAMS: Guided Tours; Interpretation

COLLECTIONS: [1860s] 5,000 original and rare artifacts including uniforms, letters, weapons, diaries, photographs, newspapers, flags, medical instruments, saddles, paintings, engravings, Medals of Honor.

4870
Wilson's Creek National Battlefield
6424 West Farm Road 182, 65738-9514; (p) (417) 732.2662; (f) (417) 732-1167; wicrnb@ hotmail.com; www.nps.gov/wicr/index.htm

National Park Service

BATTLEFIELD; HISTORIC SITE; HOUSE MUSEUM; NATIONAL PARK: Maintains Ray House c 1850s and historic battlefield site August 10, 1861, the first major Civil War engagement west of the Mississippi River. Ray House served as a temporary field hospital for Confederate soldiers. General Nathaniel Lyon injured during this battle, and taken to the Ray House, became the first Union general to met his death.

PROGRAMS: Exhibits; Festivals; Interpretation; Living History

COLLECTIONS: [Civil War Era] Weaponry, artifacts, memorabilia.

HOURS: Park: Yr; Ray House: May-Sept Sa-Su

REVERE

4871
Thome-Benning Cannonball House
Rt 1, Box 26, 63465; (p) (660) 877-3871, (660) 877-3884

1841/ Dept of Natural Resources/ staff: 2(f); 6(v)

Home of abolitionists Arthur and James Thome.

COLLECTIONS: [1840-1860] American Indian and Civil War collections; Historic photos and old newspaper files on the Civil War battle at Athens and area buildings and residents.

HOURS: Yr

RICHMOND

4872
Ray County Genealogical Association
901 W Royal St, 64085; (p) (816) 776-2305; (c) Ray

Private non-profit/ 1988/ staff: 1(f)/ members: 216/publication: Reflections

GENEALOGICAL SOCIETY; HISTORIC SITE; HISTORICAL SOCIETY; HOUSE MUSEUM: Educational organization sharing information, conducting educational programs, and assisting persons in family research; collectes, records, indexes, preserves and stores genealogical and historical records.

PROGRAMS: Annual Meeting; Publication

COLLECTIONS: Marriage and cemetery records, history, books, family files, family histories, regional county historical and genealogical material; research aids, census, books, mortality listings, agriculture census.

HOURS: Yr W-Sa 12-4

ADMISSION: No charge

ROCHEPORT

4873
Friends of Rocheport Society
101 Moniteau ST, 65279 [PO Box 122, 65279]; (p) (573) 698-3210; (c) Boone

Private non-profit/ 1979/ staff: 25(v)/ members: 150/publication: Chronicles

GARDEN; HISTORICAL SOCIETY; HISTORY MUSEUM: Preserve the historical and social aspect of Rocheport along with buildings and archives.

PROGRAMS: Annual Meeting; Community Outreach; Exhibits; Publication; Research Library/Archives

COLLECTIONS: [1830-1950] Local artifacts and memorabilia.

HOURS: Apr-Nov Sa-Su 1-4

ADMISSION: $1

ROLLA

4874
Dillon Log Cabin
302 Third St, 65402-1535 [c/o Phelps County Historical Society, PO Box 1535, 65402-1535]; (p) (573) 364-5977; www.umr.edu/~whmcinfo/pchs/

4875
Old Courthouse Preservation Committee
305 Third St, 65402 [PO Box 1861, 65402-1861]; (p) (573) 364-5977; www.umr.edu/~whmcinfo/ocpc/; (c) Phelps

Private non-profit/ 1992/ members: 100

HISTORIC SITE: Owns and maintains the old Phelps County Courthouse (1860-1994), listed on the National Register of Historic Places.

PROGRAMS: Annual Meeting; Exhibits; Guided Tours; Interpretation; Living History; Publication; Reenactments

COLLECTIONS: [1860-1994]

HOURS: Yr M-F 8-5 and special events

ADMISSION: No charge/Donations

4876
Phelps County Genealogical Society
Rm 308, Phelps County Courthouse, 65402 [PO Box 571, 65402-0571]; pcgs@ rollanet.org; www.umr.edu/~whmcinfo/pcgs/; (c) Phelps

Private non-profit/ 1982/ members: 200

GENEALOGICAL SOCIETY: Maintains a library and archives room in the Phelps County Courthouse, and publishes a quarterly journal.

PROGRAMS: Lectures; Publication; Research Library/Archives

COLLECTIONS: Materials relating to history and genealogy of Phelps County; library and archival materials.

HOURS: Yr T 12:30-5

4877
Phelps County Historical Society
302 Third St, 65402 [PO Box 1535, 65402-1535]; (p) (573) 364-5977; www.umr.edu/~whmcinfo/pchs/; (c) Phelps

Joint; Private non-profit/ 1938/ members: 200

ART MUSEUM; GENEALOGICAL SOCIETY; HISTORICAL SOCIETY; HISTORY MUSEUM: Maintains the Dillon Log Cabin Museum and Old Phelps County Jail, meets twice each year, and publishes a semi-annual journal.

PROGRAMS: Annual Meeting; Community Outreach; Exhibits; Facility Rental; Family Programs; Festivals; Guided Tours; Lectures; Publication; Research Library/Archives

COLLECTIONS: [1830s-present] Historical artifacts related to the settlement and development of Phelps County.

HOURS: May-Oct Th, Su

ADMISSION: Donations accepted

4878
Western Historical Manuscript Collection, Rolla
Rm G-3 Curtis Laws Wilson Library,Univ of MO-Rolla, 65409 [G-3 UMR Library, 1870 Miner Circle, 65409-0060]; (p) (573) 341-4874; whmcinfo@umr.edu; www.umr.edu/~whmcinfo/; (c) Phelps

State/ 1980/ staff: 2(f); 5(p)

Collects, catalogs, preserves, and makes available to researchers historical manuscripts, mostly from southern Missouri.

PROGRAMS: Lectures; Publication; Research Library/Archives

COLLECTIONS: [1850-present] Historical manuscripts; correspondence, diaries, business, and organizational records, and other unpublished materials; collected mostly from southern Missouri.

HOURS: Yr

SAINT JOSEPH

4879
Glore Psychiatric Museum
3406 Frederick Ave, 64506; (p) (816) 387-2310; (f) (816) 387-2170; glore_museum@ mail.dmh.state.mo.us; (c) Buchanan

Joint; State/ 1968/ staff: 2(f); 3(p); 35(v)/publication: History of St. Joseph State Hospital: 125th Anniversary

HISTORIC SITE; HISTORY MUSEUM: Educates the public about mental health and its treatment.

PROGRAMS: Community Outreach; Exhibits; Film/Video; Guided Tours; Interpretation; Lectures; Publication; Research Library/Archives

COLLECTIONS: [1874-present] Replicas, artifacts, and documents.

HOURS: Yr Daily M-Sa 9-5, Su 1-5

ADMISSION: No charge/Donation

SAINT CHARLES

4880
First Missouri State Capitol State Historic Site
200-216 S Main St, 63301 [200 S Main St, 63301]; (p) (636) 940-3322; (f) (636) 940-3324; (c) St. Charles

State/ 1961/ staff: 5(f); 6(p); 24(v)

HISTORIC SITE; LIVING HISTORY/OUTDOOR MUSEUM: Restores, preserves, and interpretes the First Missouri State Capitol State Historic Site.

PROGRAMS: Annual Meeting; Concerts; Elder's Programs; Exhibits; Facility Rental; Festivals; Film/Video; Garden Tours; Guided Tours; Interpretation; Lectures; Living History; Reenactments; Research Library/Archives; School-Based Curriculum

COLLECTIONS: [1800-1820] Eight rooms in the First Capitol have been restored to their original state and are furnished with 1,447 artifacts from the 1821-1826 period.

HOURS: Yr M-Sa 9-4, Su 11-5

ADMISSION: $2, Family $10, Children $1.25; Under 5 free

4881
Lewis and Clark Center
701 Riverside Dr, 63301; (p) (636) 947-3199; (f) (636) 916-0240; (c) St. Charles

Private non-profit/ 1985/ staff: 3(p)

HISTORIC SITE: Interprets the Lewis and Clark Expedition through exhibits, literature, and educational programs with a special focus on the time the Corps of Discovery spent in St. Charles.

PROGRAMS: Elder's Programs; Exhibits; Interpretation; Lectures; School-Based Curriculum

COLLECTIONS: [1803-1809] Items similar to those of the Lewis and Clark Expedition; Dioramas of the Expedition, Plants and animals described in the journals, Indian artifacts, maps, boat model, journal information, time and importance of St. Charles.

HOURS: Yr Daily 10:30-4:30

4882
St. Charles City-County Library District, Kathryn Linnemann Branch Library
2323 Elm St, 63301; (p) (636) 723-0232; (f) (636) 947-0692; aking01@mail.win.org; www.win.org/library/services/lhgen/cinmenu.htm; (c) St. Charles

County; Joint/ 1933/ staff: 9(f); 13(p); 10(v)

PROGRAMS: Publication; Research Library/ Archives

COLLECTIONS: [1800-present]

HOURS: Yr Daily M-Th 9-9, F-Sa 9-6, Su 1-5

ADMISSION: No charge

4883
St. Charles County Genealogical Society
3rd & Jefferson, 63302 [PO Box 715, 63302-0715]; www.rootsweb.com/mosccgs/; (c) St. Charles

State/ 1974/ staff: 6(v)/ members: 88/publication: *Tangled Roots*

GENEALOGICAL SOCIETY: Educates and shares ideas and informational records; collects, preserves, and makes accessible research material to the public.

PROGRAMS: Community Outreach; Publication; Research Library/Archives

COLLECTIONS: [1800-present] Self-help books on researching, local, state, and individual family histories, information on Irish, German immigrants, maps, indexes, church records, records of marriage, deaths, cemeteries, census records, and newsletter exchange with historical and genealogical societies from other states.

HOURS: Yr T 9-2, last T of month 7p-8:30p

ADMISSION: No charge

4884
St. Charles County Historical Society
101 S Main St, 63301; (p) (636) 946-9828; (c) St. Charles

Private non-profit/ 1956/ staff: 3(p); 10(v)/ members: 700/publication: *Heritage*

Preserves county records, dating back to pre-statehood and making them accessible to researchers.

COLLECTIONS: [1800-1900] Primary documents including probate packets, circuit court packets, deeds, funeral home registers, indexes of county's early churches, censuses, death and marriage records.

HOURS: Yr M,W,F 10-3, 2nd and 4th Sa

ADMISSION: No charge

SAINT CLAIR

4885
Phoebe Apperson Hearst Historical Society
2808 Sycamore Lane, 63077; (p) (314) 629-2596; (c) Franklin

Private non-profit/ 1963/ staff: 10(f)/ members: 42

GENEALOGICAL SOCIETY; HISTORIC SITE; HISTORICAL SOCIETY; RESEARCH CENTER

PROGRAMS: Annual Meeting; Exhibits; Family Programs; Film/Video; Guided Tours; Lectures

COLLECTIONS: Collections relating to Phoebe Apperson Hearst and husband, George Hearst.

HOURS: Yr daylight-dark

ADMISSION: No charge

4886
St. Clair Historical Society
208 Hibbard St, 63077 [Box 137, 63077]; (p) (314) 629-3199; (c) Franklin

Private non-profit/ 1989/ staff: 20(p)/ members: 125

HISTORY MUSEUM: Collects, preserves, and interprets the past.

PROGRAMS: Annual Meeting; Exhibits; Film/Video; Guided Tours

COLLECTIONS: [1890s-1940s] Mining, general store, drug store, post office, bank, Indian artifacts, laundry, Victorian clothing, school, doctors offices, kitchen, and Victorian parlor.

HOURS: Yr Sa-Su 1-4

ADMISSION: No charge

SAINT GENEVIEVE

4887
Amoureux House
327 St. Mary's Rd, 63670 [Felix Valle House SHS, PO Box 89, 63670]; (p) (573) 883-7102; (f) (573) 883-9630; http://www.ste-genevieve.com/histsite.htm

1792/ Dept of Natural Resources/ staff: 1(p)

COLLECTIONS: [1790-1840] 1792 vertical log house built in the rare poteaux-enterre style.

4888
Bolduc House Museum
125 S Main St, 63670; (p) (573) 883-3105; http://www.ste-genevieve.com/histsite.htm

4889
Felix Valle House State Historic Site
198 Merchant St, 63670 [PO Box 89, 63670]; (p) (573) 883-7102; (f) (573) 883-9630; dspvalle@mail.dnr.state.mo.us; (c) Ste. Genevieve

State/ 1970/ staff: 3(f); 3(p)

HISTORIC SITE: A historic site devoted to the interpretation and preservation of the early French culture of Missouri by preserving historic structures from the colonial and early territorial period.

PROGRAMS: Annual Meeting; Exhibits; Festivals; Interpretation; Lectures

COLLECTIONS: [1790-1840] Period furnishings, documents, and archaeological collections.

HOURS: Yr

4890
Guibourd Valle House
N 4th & Merchant St, 63670 [PO Box 88, 63670]; (p) (573) 883-9622; (f) (573) 883-9622

1806/ staff: 4(p)

COLLECTIONS: [Federal-First Empire] Louis XV & XVI antique gilt furnishings and silver; 18th & 19th century French antique furnishings.

4891
St. Genevieve Museum
Merchant and Dubourg, 63670; (p) (573) 883-3461; (c) St. Genevieve

Private non-profit/ 1935/ staff: 2(p)/ members: 50

HISTORY MUSEUM: Maintains a museum of artifacts pertaining to the history of St. Genevieve, 1735.

COLLECTIONS: [1700s-early 1900s] Indian artifacts, gun collections, dishes, meat curing log, salt spring kettles, photographs, hair jewelry & wreaths, safe from a bank Jesse James robbed, quilts.

HOURS: Yr Apr-Oct daily 9-4; Nov-Mar M-Sa 12-4, Su 11-4

ADMISSION: $1.50,Students $0.50

SAINT JAMES

4892
James Foundation, The
320 S Bourbeuse, 65559; (p) (573) 265-7124; (f) (573) 265-8770; t;f@tigernet.missouri.org; (c) Phelps

Private non-profit/ 1941/ staff: 25(f); 15(p)

HISTORY MUSEUM; PROFESSIONAL ORGANIZATION: Manages two parks, two museums, library.

PROGRAMS: Community Outreach; Festivals; Guided Tours; Interpretation

COLLECTIONS: [1826-1876] Artifacts from Ironworks period.

HOURS: Yr Daily dawn-dusk

ADMISSION: $3/car

SAINT JOSEPH

4893
Jesse James Home
1202 Penn St, 64502 [Box 1022, 64502]; (p) (816) 232-8206; www.stjoseph.net/ponyexpress; (c) Buchanan

Private non-profit/ 1882/ staff: 2(f); 3(v)/ members: 398/publication: *Pony Express Mail*

HISTORIC SITE; HISTORICAL SOCIETY; HOUSE MUSEUM: Operates the house where outlaw Jesse James was shot and killed, on the grounds of the Patee House Museum.

PROGRAMS: Annual Meeting; Festivals; Interpretation; Publication; Reenactments

COLLECTIONS: [1882] This house is furnished as it would have looked when Jesse James lived there. Artifacts from the grave when Jesse was exhumed for DNA tests in 1995: coffin handles, a bullet from his right lung and the tiny tie-pin he was wearing in his death photo; casting of Jesse's skull showing where the bullet entered.

HOURS: Yr Daily M-F 10-4, Sa-Su 10-5

ADMISSION: $2, Student $1, Seniors $1.50

4894
Knea-Von Black Archive and Museum
1901 Messanie, 64507; (c) Buchanan

Private non-profit/ 1994/ staff: 2(f); 2(p); 2(v)

HISTORIC PRESERVATION AGENCY; HISTORY MUSEUM: Display, preserve, and narrate black history, locally and nationally.

PROGRAMS: Exhibits; Festivals

COLLECTIONS: [1860-1999]

HOURS: By appt only

ADMISSION: $1, Student $0.50

4895
National Military Heritage Society, Inc.
701 Messanie St, 64501-2219; (p) (816) 233-4321; (f) (816) 279-9667; (c) Buchanan

Private non-profit/ 1989/ staff: 1(f); 4(p); 30(v)/ members: 210

HISTORIC SITE; HISTORY MUSEUM; LIVING HISTORY/OUTDOOR MUSEUM: Collects, studies, preserves, disseminates U.S. military heritage for all branches of service from 1800 to modern day; to include home front in the National Military Heritage Museum.

PROGRAMS: Annual Meeting; Community Outreach; Exhibits; Facility Rental; Family Programs; Film/Video; Guided Tours; Interpretation; Lectures; Living History; Research Library/Archives; School-Based Curriculum

COLLECTIONS: [1914-present] Military uniforms and equipment; 7,779 museum artifacts.

HOURS: Yr M-F 9-5, Sa 9-1

ADMISSION: $2, Students $0.50

4896
Northwest Missouri Genealogical Society
412 Felix, 64502 [PO Box 382, 64502]; (p) (816) 233-0524; (c) Buchanan

Private non-profit/ 1979/ staff: 20(v)/ members: 725

GENEALOGICAL SOCIETY: Maintains the depository for the Buchanan County courthouse records, open to the public for research.

COLLECTIONS: Buchanan County courthouse records, wills, probates, marriages, circuit court 1839-present, city directories, census, state records, county records from NW Missouri.

HOURS: Yr

ADMISSION: $2

4897
Pony Express Historical Association, Inc.
1202 Penn St Box 1022, 64502; (p) (816) 232-8206; www.stjoseph.not/ponyexpress; (c) Buchanan

Private non-profit/ 1963/ staff: 5(f); 2(p); 35(v)/ members: 398/publication: *Pony Express Mail*

HISTORIC SITE; HISTORICAL SOCIETY; HISTORY MUSEUM; HOUSE MUSEUM: Operates Patee House Museum, the headquarters for the Pony Express. This 1858 former hotel is now a museum of communications and transportation and National Landmark.

PROGRAMS: Annual Meeting; Exhibits; Facility Rental; Festivals; Interpretation; Publication; Reenactments; Research Library/Archives

COLLECTIONS: [1860-1930] 1860 Hannibal and St. Joseph Railroad locomotive and mail car, depot; antique cars, trucks and fire trucks; historic streets of Old St. Joseph featuring an early town; western on Wood 44 painting original art collection; antique telephones and radios, antique furniture, dishes large model railroad.

HOURS: Apr-Oct Daily 10-5

ADMISSION: $3, Student $1.50, Seniors $2.50; Under 6 free

4898
Pony Express Museum
914 Penn St, 64503; (p) (816) 279-5059; (f) (816) 253-9370; (c) Buchanan

Private non-profit/ 1950/ staff: 4(f); 6(p); 30(v)/ members: 300/publication: *Pony Trails*

HISTORIC SITE; HISTORY MUSEUM: Maintains museum that is housed in the original Pony Express Stables. Hands-on, inter-active exhibits.

PROGRAMS: Exhibits; Facility Rental; Festivals; Guided Tours; Interpretation; Lectures; Publication

COLLECTIONS: [1860] Original Pony Express artifacts in existence

HOURS: Yr Daily M-Sa 9-5, Su 1-5

ADMISSION: $3, Children $1.50, Seniors $2.50

4899
Saint Joseph Historical Society
3rd & Poulin, 64502 [PO Box 246, 64502]; (p) (816) 232-5861; (c) Buchanan

Private non-profit/ 1949/ staff: 1(f); 2(p); 5(v)/ members: 350/publication: *Saint Joseph Historical Society Journal*

HISTORICAL SOCIETY; HISTORY MUSEUM; HOUSE MUSEUM: Collects and preserves the history of St. Joseph and the surrounding area. Operates and maintains Robidoux Row Museum, home of our city's founder.

PROGRAMS: Annual Meeting; Exhibits; Facility Rental; Festivals; Lectures; Publication

COLLECTIONS: [1840-1870] 1,500 books, 450 photographs, 12 maps, 4,000 artifacts.

HOURS: Yr May-Sept T-F 10-4, Sa-Su 1-4; Oct-Apr T-F 12-4, Sa 1-4

ADMISSION: $2, Student $0.50; Under 12 free

4900
St. Joseph Museum
1100 Charles, 64052 [PO Box 128, 64052-0128]; (p) (816) 232-8471; (f) (816) 232-8482; sjm@stjosephmuseum.org; www.stjoseph museum.org; (c) Buchanan

Private non-profit/ 1927/ staff: 10(f); 2(p); 48(v)/ members: 306/publication: *Happenings*

HISTORY MUSEUM; HOUSE MUSEUM: Preserves collections, maintains museum collections, serves the public by educating through exhibits and programs; promotes research and encourages appreciation and understanding of St. Joseph's heritage.

PROGRAMS: Annual Meeting; Community Outreach; Elder's Programs; Exhibits; Facility Rental; Family Programs; Festivals; Guided Tours; Interpretation; Lectures; Publication; Research Library/Archives; School-Based Curriculum

COLLECTIONS: [19th c-present] Artifacts and memorabilia relating to St. Joseph, region, national history archaeology, ethnology, geology, zoology, paleontology, art, decorative arts, crafts, clothing, textiles, agricultural tools, medical equipment, transportation, business, political and social history, archives, library, and audio-visual materials.

HOURS: Yr Daily M-Sa 9-5, Su 1-5

ADMISSION: $2, Children $1; Members free; Su free

SAINT LOUIS

4901
Affton Historical Society
7801 Genesta, 63123 [Box 28855 Affton Post Office, 63123]; (p) (314) 352-5654; (f) (314) 849-3859; Aswantner@aol.com; (c) St. Louis

Private for-profit/ 1972/ staff: 1(p); 65(v)/ members: 595/publication: *Oakleaf News*

GARDEN; HISTORIC SITE; HISTORICAL SOCIETY; HOUSE MUSEUM; LIVING HISTORY/OUTDOOR MUSEUM: Collects information from the community and gives it back through programs of research, tours, luncheons, and holiday programs.

PROGRAMS: Annual Meeting; Community Outreach; Concerts; Exhibits; Facility Rental; Festivals; Garden Tours; Guided Tours; Interpretation; Lectures; Living History; Publication; Reenactments; School-Based Curriculum

COLLECTIONS: [19th c] Early photographs, original artifacts from early community residents, written manuscripts, and a restored 1850s stone mansion, home to St. Louis private banker, Louis A. Benoist.

HOURS: Apr-Sept Daily or by appt

4902
Archives of the Evangelical Synod of North America
Eden Theological Seminary Campus, 63119 [475 E Lockwood, 63119]; (p) (314) 961-3627; vdetjen@eden.edu; (c) St. Louis

Private non-profit/ 1925/ Board of Directors, Eden Theological Seminary/ staff: 2(p)

LIBRARY AND/OR ARCHIVES: Preserve the records generated by the Deutscher Evangelischer Kirchenverein des Westens 1840-1866 and successor, Evangelical Synod of North

America 1866-1934, its member churches, pastors, and institutions.

PROGRAMS: Exhibits; Research Library/ Archives

COLLECTIONS: [1840-1934] Organizational records and papers, pastoral records, congregational records, and published literature of Evangelical Synod of North American.

HOURS: Yr M,W-Th 8-4:30 or by appt

4903
Association of Midwest Museums
5585 Pershing, Ste 170 Rear, 63112 [PO Box 11940, 63112-0040]; (p) (314) 454-3110; (f) (314) 454-3112; mmcdirect2@aol.com; (c) St. Louis

Private non-profit/ 1937/ staff: 1(f); 3(v)/ members: 700/publication: *News Brief Products/ Services Directory*

4904
Bissell House Museum
10225 Bellefontaine Rd, 63137; (p) (314) 868-0973; (f) (314) 868-8435

1818/ Parks Dept/ staff: 1(f); 1(p); 3(v)

COLLECTIONS: [1800-1850] Large collection of Empire furnishings, documents signed by 4 of the first 5 Presidents; literature on the life of Daniel Bissell.

4905
Black World History Wax Museum, The
2505 St. Louis Ave, 63106; (p) (314) 241-7057; (f) (314) 241-7058; blkwaxmusm@aol.com

1992/ staff: 2(f); 3(p); 10(v)/ members: 150/publication: *Sankofa*

HISTORY MUSEUM: Interprets Missouri's rich African American heritage using life-size wax figures, artifacts, books, documents, and other artistic expressions.

PROGRAMS: Community Outreach; Exhibits; Facility Rental; Guided Tours; Interpretation; Lectures; Publication; Reenactments

COLLECTIONS: [1600-1950s] Wax figures, artifacts, documents, books, a slave cabin slave ship replica.

HOURS: Feb-mid Dec W-Sa 10-5; Summer W-Sa 10-5, Su 2-5

ADMISSION: $4.50, Student $3.50, Children $2, Seniors $3

4906
Campbell House Museum
1508 Locust St, 63103-1816; (p) (314) 421-0325; (f) (314) 421-0113; campbellhousemuseum@worldnet.att.net; (c) St. Louis

Private non-profit/ 1942/ staff: 1(f); 2(p); 40(v)/ members: 300

HISTORIC SITE: Maintains the museum.

PROGRAMS: Community Outreach; Exhibits; Guided Tours; Lectures; Research Library/ Archives

COLLECTIONS: [19th c] Original furnishings and memorabilia of Colonel Robert Campbell who was an active participant in the opening of the Rocky Mountain fur trade (1820-1830) and later a prominent St. Louis entrepreneur and civic leader. Assembled by the Campbell family.

HOURS: Mar-Dec T-Sa 10-4, Su 12-4

ADMISSION: $4, Children $2

4907
Carondelet Historical Society
6303 Michigan Ave, 63111; (p) (314) 481-6303; (c) Independent City

Private non-profit/ 1967/ staff: 40(p); 40(v)/ members: 412

HISTORIC SITE; HISTORICAL SOCIETY: Plans programs for educational and historical study for youth and adults; protects, preserves, and restores artifacts and data significant to Canondelet culture. Preserves site of the first continuous public school Kindergarten in the US, founded by Susan Blow.

PROGRAMS: Annual Meeting; Exhibits; Guided Tours; Publication; Research Library/ Archives

COLLECTIONS: [Mid 1800s-present] Children's education toys, exhibits, slide-show, art and historical memorabilia, pictorial history of Carondelet homes, genealogical records.

HOURS: Yr T- W, F 9:30-12, Sa 10:30-2

ADMISSION: $2, Children $1

4908
Chatillon-DeMenil House Foundation
3352 DeMenil Place, 63118; (p) (314) 771-5828; (f) (314) 771-3475; demenil@stlouis.missouri.org; (c) St. Louis

Private non-profit/ 1965/ staff: 2(f); 2(p); 15(v)/ members: 400

HOUSE MUSEUM: Preserves and maintains the historic Greek Revival mansion built by Henri Chatillon and later bought and inhabited by Nicolas DeMenil and his family.

PROGRAMS: Annual Meeting; Community Outreach; Concerts; Exhibits; Facility Rental; Family Programs; Guided Tours; Interpretation; Lectures; Living History; Publication; Reenactments; School-Based Curriculum

COLLECTIONS: [1860-1880] Furnishings mostly from the Mid-Victorian period, with some original pieces including etched crystal and Haviland Lamoge China, decorative arts including paintings by George Caleb Bingham, chairs and settees by Henry Belter, and tapestries by Fragonard.

HOURS: Mar 1-Dec 31 T-Sa 10-4

ADMISSION: $4, Children $1

4909
Concordia Historical Institute
801 DeMun Ave, 63105; (p) (314) 505-7900; (f) (314) 505-7901; chi@chi.lcms.org; chi.lcms.org/; (c) St. Louis

Private non-profit/ 1927/ staff: 7(f); 9(p); 15(v)/ members: 1300/publication: *Concordia Historical Institute Quarterly; Historical Footnotes*

HISTORICAL SOCIETY; HISTORY MUSEUM: Maintains a reference library, museum, and manuscript collection on Lutheranism in North America.

PROGRAMS: Exhibits; Publication; Research Library/Archives

COLLECTIONS: [Colonial era-present] 60,000 volumes, 2.5 million manuscripts, 5,000 museum artifacts, films, filmstrips, audio and video tapes, photographs, coins, and medals, microfilm.

HOURS: Yr M-F 8:30-12/1-4:30

ADMISSION: No charge

4910
Creve Coeur-Chesterfield Historical Society
Lake School Park & Conway Park, 63146 [1672 Redbluff Ct, 63146-3915]; (p) (314) 878-3142; (f) (314) 878-3142; (c) St. Louis

Private non-profit/ 1968/ staff: 15(v)/ members: 45/publication: *Heritage of the Creve Coear Area*

HISTORICAL SOCIETY; HISTORY MUSEUM; HOUSE MUSEUM: Collects and preserves historical information, educational programs for youth and adults to help understand our historic heritage; establishes historical museums.

PROGRAMS: Annual Meeting; Film/Video; Guided Tours; Publication

COLLECTIONS: [1875-1925] One room school authentically furnished 1897-1925; log house furnished; pioneer log house and Victorian house.

HOURS: Apr-Oct by appt

ADMISSION: No charge

4911
Eugene Field House and St. Louis Toy Museum
634 S Broadway, 63102; (p) (314) 421-4689; (c) St. Louis

Private non-profit/ 1936/ staff: 1(f); 1(p); 30(v)/ members: 300/publication: *Field Notes*

HOUSE MUSEUM: Birthplace and childhood home of Eugene Field the "Children's Poet" and "Father of the Personal Newspaper Column," home of Roswell Field the lawyer for Dred Scott and his family when they sued for their freedom.

PROGRAMS: Exhibits; Guided Tours; Lectures; Publication; School-Based Curriculum

COLLECTIONS: [Victorian era] Furniture and decorative arts owned by Rowell and Eugene Field, books and papers of Eugene and Roswell Field, and toy museum from early 1800s through to the 1970s.

HOURS: Mar-Dec W-Sa 10-4, Su 12-4

4912
General Daniel Bissell House Museum
10225 Belle Foutaine Rd, 63137; (p) (314) 868-0973; (f) (314) 868-8435; jb1826@aol.com; www.st-louiscountyparks.com; (c) St. Louis

County/ 1960/ staff: 6(f); 2(p); 25(v)/ members: 25

ART MUSEUM; GARDEN; HISTORIC SITE; HOUSE MUSEUM; LIVING HISTORY/OUT-DOOR MUSEUM: Preserves and interprets the history of General Daniel Bissell and his family including their involvement in the American Revolution, War of 1812, St. Louis, and the Civil War, role of soldier-settler, and slavery in the Missouri Territory.

PROGRAMS: Community Outreach; Exhibits; Facility Rental; Family Programs; Festivals; Film/Video; Guided Tours; Interpretation; Lectures; Living History; Library/ Archives

COLLECTIONS: Decorative arts, military, Bissell family items.

HOURS: Feb-Dec Sa-Su 12-4:30

ADMISSION: $2, Children $1

4913
International Bowling Museum and Hall of Fame

111 Stadium Plaza Dr, 63102; (p) (314) 231-6340; (f) (314) 231-4054; bowling@anet-stl.com; www.bowlingmuseum.com; (c) St. Louis

Private non-profit/ 1984/ staff: 6(f); 20(p)

HISTORY MUSEUM: Collects, preserves, and researches the history of bowling; provides a hall of fame, makes information and collections available globally for education, promotion and entertainment.

PROGRAMS: Exhibits; Facility Rental; Interpretation; Publication; Research Library/Archives; School-Based Curriculum

COLLECTIONS: [Mid-19th c-present] Photographs, film, and videos, library, and archival materials; bowling games, equipment, apparel, and ephemera.

HOURS: Yr Daily M-Sa 9-5, Su 12-5

ADMISSION: $5, Children $3, Under 5 free

4914
Jefferson Barracks Historic Site

533 Grant Rd, 63125; (p) (314) 544-5714; (f) (314) 638-5009; jb1826@aol.com; www.co.st-louis.mo.us/parks/jb-museum.html; (c) Saint Louis

County/ 1950/ staff: 6(f); 2(p); 100(v)/ members: 50

GARDEN; HISTORIC PRESERVATION AGENCY; HISTORIC SITE; HOUSE MUSEUM; LIVING HISTORY/OUTDOOR MUSEUM: Provides information about the history of the men and women who served in the United States military at Jefferson Barracks from 1826 to 1946 and their families and community.

PROGRAMS: Annual Meeting; Community Outreach; Concerts; Elder's Programs; Exhibits; Facility Rental; Family Programs; Festivals; Film/Video; Guided Tours; Interpretation; Lectures; Living History; Reenactments; Research Library/Archives; School-Based Curriculum

COLLECTIONS: [US Military 1826-1946] Studies the interaction of the military of Jefferson Barracks in the context of St. Louis, the nation and the world by interpreting and preserving the site structures and collecting artifacts appropriate to site.

HOURS: Feb-Dec T-F 10-4:30, Sa-Su 12-4:30

ADMISSION: No charge

4915
Jefferson National Expansion Memorial

11 N Fourth St, 63102; (p) (314) 655-1600; (f) (314) 655-1639; jeff_superintendent@nps.gov; www.nps.gov/jeff; (c) St. Louis

Federal/ 1935/ staff: 118(f); 25(p); 225(v)

HISTORIC SITE; HISTORY MUSEUM: National Park Service unit includes Gateway Arch, Old Courthouse, and Museum of Westward Expansion; interprets westward expansion of the United States and St. Louis history.

PROGRAMS: Concerts; Exhibits; Facility Rental; Film/Video; Guided Tours; Interpretation; Research Library/Archives; School-Based Curriculum

COLLECTIONS: Artifacts and archival collec-

tions pertaining to westward expansion, St. Louis history, and the park's administrative history.

HOURS: Yr May-Sept Daily 8-10; Sept-May Daily 9-6

4916
Landmarks Association of St. Louis, Inc.

917 Locust St, 7th fl, 63101-1413; (p) (314) 421-6474; (f) (314) 421-4104; landmark@stlouis.missouri.org; stlouis.missouri.org/501c/landmarks

Private non-profit/ 1959/ staff: 4(f); 2(p); 20(v)/ members: 1200/publication: *St. Louis: Historical Churches & Synagogues*

HISTORIC PRESERVATION AGENCY: Preserve and enhance St. Louis' architectural legacy.

PROGRAMS: Annual Meeting; Community Outreach; Lectures; Publication

HOURS: Yr M-F 9-5

4917
Midwest Jesuit Archives

4511 W Pine, 63108; (p) (314) 361-7765; (f) (314) 758-7182; archives@jesuits-mis.org

Private non-profit/ staff: 4(f)

LIBRARY AND/OR ARCHIVES: Serves scholars, authors, genealogists, and other researchers.

PROGRAMS: Publication; Research Library/Archives

COLLECTIONS: [1823-present] Records on all closed Midwest Jesuit institutions; files, photographs, books, and periodicals related to deceased Jesuits of the Midwest; special collections.

HOURS: Yr M-F 9-4

ADMISSION: No charge

4918
Missouri Historical Society

Jefferson Memorial Bldg, Forest Pk & 225 S Skiner, 63112 [PO Box 11940, 63112-0040]; (p) (314) 746-4599; (f) (314) 746-3162; (c) St. Louis

Private non-profit/ 1866/ staff: 140(f); 20(p); 200(v)/ members: 6200/publication: *Gateway Heritage*

HISTORY MUSEUM: Provides a forum to facilitate an inclusive discussion of enduring issues in the community; historical perspective; exhibits, programs, theater, publications, lectures, conferences, tours, and community collaboration.

PROGRAMS: Community Outreach; Concerts; Exhibits; Facility Rental; Family Programs; Guided Tours; Interpretation; Lectures; Publication; Research Library/Archives; School-Based Curriculum; Theatre

COLLECTIONS: [19th -20th c] St. Louis and Missouri history: exploration of the West, artifacts, broadsides, and maps, costumes, manuscripts, photographs, paintings, sculpture, Charles A. Lindbergh collections, library and archives.

HOURS: Yr Daily W-M 9-5, T 9-7

ADMISSION: No charge

4919
Missouri Humanities Council

543 Hanley Industral Ct, 63144-1905; (p) (314) 621-7705; (f) (314) 621-5850; mail@mohumanities.com; www.mohumanities.org; (c) St. Louis

Private non-profit/ 1971/ staff: 6(f); 1(p); 2(v)/publication: *Humanities News*

PROFESSIONAL ORGANIZATION: Humanities council helping people of Missouri learn about our history, literature, and ideas that shaped our democracy.

PROGRAMS: Publication

4920
Museum of Transportation

3015 Barrett Station Rd, 63122; (p) (314) 965-7998; (f) (314) 965-0242; www.st-louiscountyparks.com; (c) St. Louis

County/ 1944/ staff: 10(f); 5(p); 250(v)/ members: 3000

HISTORY MUSEUM: Collects, protectes, and interprets North America's transportation heritage.

PROGRAMS: Community Outreach; Exhibits; Facility Rental; Festivals; Guided Tours; Lectures; Research Library/Archives; School-Based Curriculum

COLLECTIONS: [1870-1970] Transportation history, notably railroad and automobile history: 150 rail artifacts, 300 vehicles, extensive library and archives.

HOURS: Yr Daily

ADMISSION: $4, Children $1.50, Seniors $1.50, Under 5 free

4921
Saint Louis University Archives

3650 Lindell Blvd, 63108 [Pius Library 307, 3650 Lindell Blvd, 63108]; (p) (314) 977-3109; (f) (314) 977-3108; waide@slu.edu; (c) Independent

Private non-profit/ 1989/ staff: 4(f); 2(p)

LIBRARY AND/OR ARCHIVES: Acquires, organizes, and preserves University records and personal papers relating to University activities or the St. Louis area and houses University and faculty/alumni publications and rare books.

PROGRAMS: Exhibits; Research Library/Archives

COLLECTIONS: [1818-present] 155 linear feet of processed records/papers, 96 linear feet of University office open files, 126 linear feet of University publications, 132 linear feet of personality files, 48,000 photographs, 17,500 volumes (7,500 rare).

HOURS: Yr M-F

4922
Samuel Cupples House

221 N Grand Blvd, 63108; (p) (314) 977-3025, (314) 977-3022; (f) (314) 977-3581; ambrosp2@slu.edu; www.slu.edu/the_arts/cupples

1890/ St. Louis University/ staff: 5(f); 3(p); 5(v)

COLLECTIONS: [1880-1900] 16th and 17th c Northern Renaissance paintings and furnishings brought to St. Louis by Jesuit founders of St. Louis University. Elaborate interior design including Tiffany windows. 1000-object collection of antique American and European glass.

HOURS: Feb-Dec W-Su 11; Feb-Dec W-Su 11-4

4923
School of Nations Museum, The
13201 Clayton Rd, 63131; (p) (314) 434-2100; (f) (314) 275-3504; drh@prin.edu; (c) St. Louis

Private non-profit/ 1927/ The Principia/ staff: 2(p)

CULTURAL CENTER; HISTORY MUSEUM: Helps students of the Principia understand other cultures through their artifacts.

PROGRAMS: Exhibits; School-Based Curriculum

COLLECTIONS: [Ancient-present] Art and artifacts from all parts of the world.

HOURS: Sept-June M-F 8:30-4:30

ADMISSION: No charge

4924
Scott Joplin House State Historic Site
2658 Delmar Blvd, 63103; (p) (314) 340-5790; (f) (314) 340-5793; DSPJOPL@mail.dnr.state.mo.us; (c) St. Louis

State/ 1991/ staff: 4(f); 6(p); 3(v)

HISTORIC SITE: Maintains the Scott Joplin House that consists of 3 downstairs galleries, Scott Joplin turn-of- the-century apartment.

PROGRAMS: Community Outreach; Concerts; Exhibits; Facility Rental; Festivals; Guided Tours; Interpretation; Lectures

COLLECTIONS: [1900-present] Three interpretive galleries featuring the Ragtime Music Era, a variety of classic pianos.

HOURS: Yr Daily M-Sa 10-4, Su 12-5

ADMISSION: $2, Children $1.25; Group

4925
Soldiers' Memorial Military Museum
1315 Chestnut, 63103; (p) (314) 622-4550; (f) (314) 622-4237; (c) St. Louis

City/ 1938/ staff: 4(f); 2(v)

HISTORY MUSEUM; RESEARCH CENTER: Collects, preserves, interprets, and displays artifacts associated with the military history of the citizens of the city of St. Louis.

PROGRAMS: Community Outreach; Elder's Programs; Exhibits; Facility Rental; Guided Tours; Interpretation; Lectures; Research Library/Archives

COLLECTIONS: [WW I-WW II] Uniforms, edged weapons, firearms, medals, letters, books. Artifacts collected by veterans from various conflicts.

HOURS: Yr Daily 9-4:30

4926
St. Louis Browns Historical Society
9388 White Ave, 63144; (p) (314) 961-5874; (f) (314) 961-6882; (c) St. Louis

State/ 1984/ staff: 4(v)/ members: 521/publication: Pop Flies

HISTORICAL SOCIETY: Education and historic preservation of the St. Louis Browns American League baseball team's history.

PROGRAMS: Annual Meeting; Exhibits; Publication

COLLECTIONS: [1902-1953] Photographs and written material.

4927
St. Louis Genealogical Society
#4 Surren Dr, Ste 140, 63143 [PO Box 43010, 63143]; (p) (314) 647-8547; (f) (314) 647-8548; stlgsmail@primary.net; www.rootsweb.com/~mostlogs/STINDEX.HTM; (c) St. Louis

Private non-profit/ 1966/ staff: 15(v)/ members: 2500

GENEALOGICAL SOCIETY: Promotes family history research by providing education and research opportunities, offers community services in related fields and collects, preserves, and publishes genealogical and historic records.

PROGRAMS: Annual Meeting; Lectures; Publication; Research Library/Archives; School-Based Curriculum

COLLECTIONS: A 20,000 volume research library for genealogy and local history.

HOURS: T, Th, Sa 9-12

ADMISSION: No charge

4928
St. Louis Mercantile Library, University of Missouri, St. Louis
8001 Natural Bridge Rd, 63121; (p) (314) 516-7240; (f) (314) 516-7241; mercantile@umsl.edu; www.umsl.edu/services/library; (c) North

State/ 1846/ staff: 10(f); 2(p)/ members: 900/publication: Cultural Cornerstone, 1846-1998

LIBRARY AND/OR ARCHIVES

PROGRAMS: Exhibits; Interpretation; Lectures; Publication; Research Library/Archives; School-Based Curriculum

COLLECTIONS: [1800-present] Primary and secondary research collections of Western expansion and the history and growth of the St. Louis region. The John W. Barriger III National Railroad Library focuses on American railroad history and the Herman T. Pott National Inland and Waterways Library on US rivers and inland waterways.

HOURS: Yr M-Th 8a-10:30p, F 8-5, Sa 9-5, Su 1-9

ADMISSION: No charge

4929
Terminal Railroad Association of St. Louis/Historical and Technical Society, Inc.
[PO Box 1688, 63188-1688]; (p) (314) 535-3101; (c) St. Louis

Private non-profit/ 1986/ staff: 5(v)/ members: 250

HISTORICAL SOCIETY: Focuses on the Terminal Railroad Association of St. Louis, the original owner of the St. Louis Union Station, the Eads, Merchants and McCarthur Bridges at St. Louis and related bits of railroad history in Southwestern Illinois.

PROGRAMS: Annual Meeting; Publication

COLLECTIONS: [1889-present] Quarterly

4930
Tower Grove House
Missouri Botanical Garden, 2345 Tower Grove, 63110 [c/o Missouri Botanical Garden, PO Box 299, 63166]; (p) (314) 577-5150, (314) 577-5100; (f) (314) 577-9598; www.mobot.org

1851/ Board of Trustees/ staff: 1(f); 4(p); 50(v)

COLLECTIONS: [1870-1910] Furnishings of the period of the house, household and business records of Henry Shaw, and writings of botanists affiliated with the garden - Engelmann, Steyermark, Trelease.

HOURS: Feb-Dec Daily 9:45-4

SAINT MARY

4931
Church of the Immaculate Conception
6450 Klein Ln, 63673; (p) (618) 366-2633; (f) (618) 826-2667; (c) Randolph

Private non-profit/ 1675/ Trustees/ staff: 30(v)/ members: 50/publication: Church of the Immaculate Conception

HISTORIC SITE: Preserves and interprets local history and historic site.

PROGRAMS: Community Outreach; Festivals; Guided Tours; Interpretation; Publication

COLLECTIONS: [1675-present] Religious artifacts from early French settlement and Native American mission, 1741 bronze bell.

HOURS: Yr Sa 3-5, Su 1-5

ADMISSION: Donations accepted

SALISBURY

4932
Chariton County Historical Society
115 E Second St, 65281; (p) (660) 388-5941; (c) Chariton

Private non-profit/ 1956/ staff: 1(p); 10(v)/ members: 290/publication: CCHS

HISTORICAL SOCIETY; HISTORY MUSEUM: Collects, preserves, and displays information pertaining to Clariton county and contributes to the education of future generations.

PROGRAMS: Exhibits; Facility Rental; Family Programs; Guided Tours; Publication; Research Library/Archives

COLLECTIONS: [1800-present] Genealogy research material, military items, clothing, pioneer artifacts, household and farm implements, tools homemade items.

HOURS: Apr-Oct T-Th, Sa, Su 2-4 or by appt

ADMISSION: Donations accepted

SAVANNAH

4933
Andrew County Museum and Historical Society
202 E Duncan Dr, 64485 [PO Box 12, 64485-0012]; (p) (816) 324-4720; (f) (816) 324-5271; andcomus@ccp.com; (c) Andrew

Private non-profit/ 1972/ Board of Directors/ staff: 1(f); 2(p); 100(v)/ members: 516/publication: Diggin' History; Andrew County: A Community, Vols 1 and 2; and others

HISTORICAL SOCIETY; HISTORY MUSEUM: Collects, preserves, and interprets Andrew

County's rich historical past for present and future visitors and researchers to enjoy.

PROGRAMS: Annual Meeting; Community Outreach; Exhibits; Facility Rental; Festivals; Guided Tours; Interpretation; Lectures; Living History; Publication; Reenactments; Research Library/Archives; School-Based Curriculum

COLLECTIONS: 4,000 page archive, 25 scrapbooks, 2,000 photographs, 25 atlases, 25 maps, 175 newspaper volumes, 1,000 book library, 50 portraits and paintings, and 10,000 museum artifacts.

HOURS: Yr M-Sa 10-4, Su 1-4

ADMISSION: Donations accepted

SEDALIA

4934
Bothwell Lodge State Historic Site
19349 Bothwell Park Rd, 65301; (p) (660) 827-0510; (f) (660) 827-4125; blshs@iland.net; (c) Pettis

State/ 1974/ Dept of Natural Resources/ staff: 3(f); 5(p); 20(v)

HISTORIC SITE: Interprets turn-of-the-century (1890-1929) life in Missouri through the thirty-room home of banker, lawyer, and state representative, Mr. Bothwell.

PROGRAMS: Community Outreach; Facility Rental; Festivals; Guided Tours; Research Library/Archives; School-Based Curriculum

COLLECTIONS: [1890-1960] Books and furnishings belonging to Mr. Bothwell, Native American collection.

HOURS: Yr M-Sa 10-4, Su 12-5

ADMISSION: $2

4935
Katy Railroad Historical Society
113 E Fourth, 65301; (p) (660) 826-2932; (f) (660) 826-2223; cofc@ilano.net

Private non-profit/ staff: 20(v)

HISTORICAL SOCIETY: Brings together all with a common interest in the Katy Railroad.

PROGRAMS: Annual Meeting; Publication

4936
Sedalia Heritage Museum
600 E 3rd, 65301 [113 E 4th, 65301]; (p) (660) 826-2222; (f) (660) 826-2223; cofc@iland.net; tourism.sedalia.mo.us; (c) Pettis

Private non-profit/ 1994/ staff: 3(f); 1(p); 20(v)

HISTORIC SITE; HISTORICAL SOCIETY; HISTORY MUSEUM: Preserves the Katy depot historic site and presents local, regional, and state history and heritage; provides public service through education, coordination and partnership.

PROGRAMS: Annual Meeting; Community Outreach; Exhibits; Facility Rental; Family Programs; Festivals; Film/Video; Guided Tours; Interpretation; Lectures; School-Based Curriculum

HOURS: Yr

SENECA

4937
County School Restoration
Near middle school, 64865 [14175 Bethel Rd,

64865]; (p) (417) 776-8232; (c) Newton

1988/ staff: 5(v)

HISTORY MUSEUM: Restoration, maintenance, and furnishing of old one room school house for visitors, events, and meetings.

PROGRAMS: Community Outreach; Exhibits; Festivals; Film/Video; Guided Tours; Interpretation; Living History

COLLECTIONS: Furnished school house with authentic desks, chairs, boobs, piano, stage curtain, and school pictures.

HOURS: Special events and appt

4938
Seneca Historical Committee
14175 Bethel Rd, 64865; (p) (417) 776-8232; (c) Newton

1980/ members: 2

Compile and publish history of the region.

SIBLEY

4939
Fort Osage National Historic Landmark
105 Osage, 64088 [22807 Woods Chapel Rd, Blue Springs, 64015]; (p) (816) 650-5737; (f) (816) 650-5740; (c) Jackson

County/ 1948/ staff: 4(f); 1(p); 100(v)

HISTORIC SITE; LIVING HISTORY/OUTDOOR MUSEUM: Maintains reconstructed fort and provides living history interpretes to illustrate the daily life of the fort's military and civilian population in 1812.

PROGRAMS: Community Outreach; Exhibits; Festivals; Film/Video; Interpretation; Living History; Reenactments; School-Based Curriculum

COLLECTIONS: [1812]

HOURS: Apr 15-Nov 15 W-Su 9-4:30; Nov 15-April 15 Sa-Su 9-4:30

ADMISSION: $3, Students $2, Seniors $2, Under 5 free

SMITHVILLE

4940
Smithville Missouri Historical Society
400 E Church St, 64089 [303 W Main, 64089]; (p) (816) 532-0255; (f) (816) 532-8444; (c) Clay

Private non-profit/ 1966/ staff: 8(p); 8(v)/ members: 27

HISTORICAL SOCIETY: Preserve community history.

PROGRAMS: Concerts; Exhibits; Festivals

COLLECTIONS: Artifacts, documents, and memorabilia related to Smithville history.

HOURS: Sa 8-5

ADMISSION: No charge

SPRINGFIELD

4941
Flower Pentecostal Heritage Center
1445 Boonville Ave, 65802; (p) (417) 862-2781; (f) (417) 862-6203; archives@ag.org; (c) Greene

Joint; Private non-profit/ 1977/ staff: 4(f); 2(p)/ members: 2400/publication: Assembly of God Heritage

HISTORY MUSEUM; RESEARCH CENTER: Preserves and collects materials created by the General Council of the Assemblies of God as well as personal collections of prominent members of the denomination.

PROGRAMS: Exhibits; Guided Tours; Publication; Research Library/Archives

COLLECTIONS: [Late 19th c-20th c] Documents, minutes, correspondence, books, personal papers, diaries, films, photographs, posters, recordings, artifacts, oral history, exhibits.

HOURS: Yr M-F

4942
Greene County Historical Society
[PO Box 3466 GS, 65808]; (p) (417) 881-6147; gsociety@mail.orion.org; www.rootsweb.com/~gcmohs/; (c) Greene

Private non-profit/ 1954/ staff: 1(v)/ members: 110/publication: Greene County Historical Society Bulletin

HISTORICAL SOCIETY: Foster and maintain an interest in the history of Greene County through programs, publications, projects, and observances.

PROGRAMS: Annual Meeting; Community Outreach; Exhibits; Facility Rental; Family Programs; Garden Tours; Guided Tours;

4943
History Museum for Springfield-Green County, The
830 Boonville, 65802; (p) (417) 864-1976; (f) (417) 864-2019; information@history museumsgc.org; www.historymuseumsgc.org

Private non-profit/ 1975/ staff: 4(f); 1(p); 40(v)/ members: 465/publication: Crossroads at the Spring

HISTORY MUSEUM: Endeavors to document the history of Springfield and Greene County and their people through the collection, preservation, and exhibition of historical objects and their research and interpretation.

PROGRAMS: Community Outreach; Exhibits; Film/Video; Guided Tours; Interpretation; Lectures; Publication; Research Library/Archives; School-Based Curriculum

COLLECTIONS: [1815-present] 80,000 items: photographs, documents, artifacts, costumes, and textiles. Documents all periods of history for Springfield and Greene County.

HOURS: Yr T-Sa 10:30-4:30

ADMISSION: Donations requested

4944
Ozarks Genealogical Society, Inc.
534 W Catalpa, 65808 [PO Box 3945, 65808-3945]; (p) (417) 831-2773; osociety@ mail.orion.org; /www.rootsweb.com/~ozarksgs; (c) Greene

Private non-profit/ 1969/ members: 560/publication: Ozark'kin

GENEALOGICAL SOCIETY: Educates members and general public in art of genealogical research; acquires genealogical and historical material; collects, preserves, and publishes material relating to the Missouri Ozarks region.

PROGRAMS: Community Outreach; Exhibits;

Publication; Research Library/Archives

COLLECTIONS: Books, periodicals, microfilm, and special collections.

HOURS: Yr T 6-8:30, W 1-4, Sa 10-4

STOCKTON

4945
Cedar County Historical Society

[PO Box 111, 65785]; (c) Cedar

Private non-profit/ 1970/ members: 35/publication: *Cedar County Quarterly*

HISTORICAL SOCIETY; HISTORY MUSEUM: Operates the county museum; open for research and visitors.

PROGRAMS: Annual Meeting; Exhibits; Facility Rental; Family Programs; Festivals; Guided Tours; Interpretation; Living History; Publication; Reenactments; Research Library/Archives

COLLECTIONS: [Early 1900s] Tools, portraits, Civil War items, books, newspapers, household items.

HOURS: Open last Sa of month 10-4 and by appt

ADMISSION: No charge/Donations accepted

STOUTSVILLE

4946
Mark Twain Birthplace State Historic Site

37352 Shrine Rd, 65283; (p) (573) 565-3449; (f) (573) 565-3718; dsptwab@MAIL.DNR.STATE. MO.US; www.mobot.org/Atateparks/twain birth_s.html; (c) Monroe

State/ 1960/ staff: 4(f); 4(p)

HISTORIC SITE: One of eighty historic sites and parks operated by MO Dept. of Natural Resources.

PROGRAMS: Exhibits; Festivals; Film/Video; Interpretation; Research Library/Archives

COLLECTIONS: [1835-1910] Artifacts associated with Mark Twain, including his birth house, the original manuscript of "Adventures of Tom Sawyer"; furniture from Hartford Home; and research library.

HOURS: Yr Daily M-Sa 10-4, Su 12-6

ADMISSION: $2, Children $1.25, Under 6 free

SWEET SPRINGS

4947
Brown County Historical Association

Miller St, 65351 [714 S Locust, 65351]; (p) (660) 335-6643; (c) Saline

Private non-profit/ 1986/ staff: 4(v)/ members: 30

PROFESSIONAL ORGANIZATION: Preserves the history of the Sweet Springs-Houstonia-Emma-Punksburg area during the years 1836 to 2000.

PROGRAMS: Annual Meeting; Community Outreach; Exhibits; Festivals

COLLECTIONS: [1870-1920] Newspapers, material objects, and Gusher fountain.

TIPTON

4948
Maclay Home

208 Howard St, 65081 [PO Box 4, 65081]; (p) (816) 433-2101, (816) 433-2176; (f) (816) 433-5631

1858/ staff: 25(v)

COLLECTIONS: [Late 1800s] Furnishings are all original to the time the Maclays and their ancestorsthat lived here. Letters, books.

HOURS: Seasonal

TRENTON

4949
Grundy County Museum

1100 Mabel, 64683; (p) (660) 359-2411; (c) Grundy

Private non-profit/ 1976/ staff: 18(f)/ members: 2500

HISTORIC PRESERVATION AGENCY; HISTORICAL SOCIETY; HISTORY MUSEUM

PROGRAMS: Annual Meeting; Elder's Programs; Exhibits; Family Programs; Guided Tours; Lectures

COLLECTIONS: Material items: agriculture, Civil War, Spanish American War, WW I and II, railroad, country school, medical, telephone, toys, furniture, and clothing.

HOURS: May-Oct Sa-Su and holidays 1-4

ADMISSION: $1, Children free

TURNEY

4950
Turney Historical Society

207 Sherman, 64493 [PO Box 102, 64493]; (p) (816) 664-2271; (c) Clinton

Private non-profit; State/ 1989/ staff: 7(f); 7(v)/ members: 85

HISTORIC PRESERVATION AGENCY; HISTORICAL SOCIETY; HISTORY MUSEUM: Collects and restores the Burlington depot of Turney.

PROGRAMS: Annual Meeting

COLLECTIONS: [1903-1955] Items pertaining to the ongoing of the railroad and depot, Brakeman lantern, large tools, office typewriter, phones, signal lights, conductor's complete uniform, and photographs.

HOURS: Daily 9-6

ADMISSION: No charge

TUSCUMBIA

4951
Miller County Historical Society

Hwy 52, 65082 [PO Box 57, 65082]; (p) (573) 793-6998; (c) Miller

Private non-profit/ 1979/ staff: 30(v)/ members: 250

HISTORICAL SOCIETY

PROGRAMS: Annual Meeting; Exhibits; Family Programs; Guided Tours; Publication; Research Library/Archives

COLLECTIONS: [Late 19th-20th c] Schools, tools, home furnishings, county store, clothing,

musical items, looms, spinning wheels, old lamps, medical equipment, Indian artifacts.

HOURS: May-Sept M, W, F 10-4

ADMISSION: Donations accepted

UNIONVILLE

4952
Putnam County Historical Society, Inc.

201 S 16th St, 63565 [2111 Stewart St, 63565]; (p) (660) 947-2955; (c) Putnam

County; Private non-profit/ 1964/ staff: 16(v)/ members: 127/publication: *The History of the Rural Schools of Putnam County 1843-1965*

HISTORICAL SOCIETY: Preserve the history of Putnam county Missouri.

PROGRAMS: Annual Meeting; Festivals; Guided Tours; Publication

COLLECTIONS: Coal mining, early drug store, Indian Artifacts, horse drawn hearse, dolls, furniture, pictures, farming equipment, dishes, maps, music.

HOURS: May-Oct F-Sa 1-4:30

ADMISSION: No charge

UNITY VILLAGE

4953
Unity Archives, Unity School of Christianity

1901 N W Blue Pkwy, 64065-0001; (p) (816) 524-3550; (f) (816) 251-3555; archives@unityworldhq.org; unityworldhq.org; (c) Jackson

Private non-profit/ 1942/ staff: 1(f); 1(p); 5(v)

LIBRARY AND/OR ARCHIVES: Preserves and makes available the historical records of the Unity School of Christianity and papers of individuals associated with the worldwide religious movement called Unity.

PROGRAMS: Exhibits; Guided Tours; Research Library/Archives

COLLECTIONS: [1889-present] Includes published materials of Unity: books, periodicals, pamphlets, promotional mailings, theses, and dissertations, manuscript and biographical collections of Unity ministers and teachers, multimedia, artifacts, and photographs.

UNIVERSITY CITY

4954
Historical Society of University City, The

Housed in the University City Public Library, 63130 [6701 Delmar Blvd, 63130]; (p) (314) 721-2473, (314) 726-4522; juddlittle@aol.com; (c) St. Louis

Private non-profit/ 1978/ staff: 16(v)/ members: 225

HISTORICAL SOCIETY: Collects, preserves, and presents to the public material and information on the history of University City.

PROGRAMS: Annual Meeting; Guided Tours; Lectures; Publication

COLLECTIONS: [1900-present] Newspapers, magazines, photographs, and artifacts relating to University

VAN BUREN

4955
Hidden Log Cabin Museum
Corner John & Ash, 63965 [PO Box 135, 63965]; (p) (573) 323-4563; (c) Carter

Private non-profit/ 1991

HISTORY MUSEUM: 18 foot by 24 foot log structure restored to turn-of-the-century period.

PROGRAMS: Lectures

HOURS: Apr-Nov M-Sa 9-5, Su 1-5

ADMISSION: $2, Children $1

VIENNA

4956
Historical Society of Maries County
Box 289, 65582; (p) (573) 422-3301; (c) Maries

Private non-profit/ 1956/ staff: 55(v)/ members: 350/publication: *The Maries Countian*

GENEALOGICAL SOCIETY; HISTORIC PRESERVATION AGENCY; HISTORIC SITE; HISTORICAL SOCIETY; HISTORY MUSEUM; HOUSE MUSEUM; LIVING HISTORY/OUTDOOR MUSEUM; RESEARCH CENTER: Collects and preserves history genealogy related to Maries County and assumes recognition and preservation of various historical landmarks.

PROGRAMS: Annual Meeting; Community Outreach; Concerts; Exhibits; Festivals; Guided Tours; Publication; Research Library/ Archives

COLLECTIONS: [1855-present] Old county records, family charts and records, published genealogies, and research materials.

HOURS: June, Sept, Oct Su 1-4

ADMISSION: Donations accepted

WALKER

4957
Osage Village State Historic Park
, [1009 Truman, Lamar, 64759]; (p) (417) 682-2279; (f) (417) 682-6363; (c) Vernon

State/ 1984/ staff: 3(f); 4(p); 2(v)

HISTORIC SITE; LIVING HISTORY/OUTDOOR MUSEUM; STATE PARK

PROGRAMS: Annual Meeting; Community Outreach; Family Programs; Guided Tours; Interpretation; Living History; Reenactments; School-Based Curriculum

COLLECTIONS: [1777] Part of an original Osage Indian Village, acreage with archeology site.

HOURS: Yr Daily

ADMISSION: No charge

WARRENSBUG

4958
Central Missouri State University Archives/Museum
James C. Kirkpatrick Library, 64093; (p) (660) 543-4649; www.cmsu.edu; (c) Johnson

State/ 1968/ staff: 1(f); 1(p)/ members: 1

HISTORY MUSEUM: Preserves the history of the University and various historical and natural history collections donated to the University; serves as an academic resource and laboratory, and provides exhibits and presentations for the campus and community.

PROGRAMS: Community Outreach; Exhibits; Guided Tours; Research Library/Archives

COLLECTIONS: [Late 19th c-present] University history; Natural history; Haymaker Latin American Collection, Rohmiller Shell Collection, Asian and Native American items.

HOURS: Yr M-F 8-4

ADMISSION: No charge

WARRENSBURG

4959
Johnson County Historical Society, Inc.
302 N Main, 64093 [PO Box 825, 64093]; (p) (660) 747-6480; (c) Johnson

County/ 1920/ staff: 1(p); 8(v)/ members: 300/publication: *Bulletin*

HISTORICAL SOCIETY; HISTORY MUSEUM: Collects and preserves records and artifacts pertaining to the families of Johnson County; Maintains 1838 Georgian Courthouse and Elm Schoolhouse.

PROGRAMS: Annual Meeting; Community Outreach; Exhibits; Facility Rental; Guided Tours; Lectures; Publication; Research Library/Archives

COLLECTIONS: [1835-present] Original survey equipment, pioneer household and land equipment, including musical instruments, dental, fine glassware, original county records.

HOURS: Yr M-Sa 1-4 and by appt

4960
West Central Missouri Genealogical Society and Library, Inc.
115 N Holden St, 64093 [705 Broad St, 64093-2032]; (p) (660) 747-6264; yunguns@iland.net; (c) Johnson

Private non-profit/ 1968/ members: 250/publication: *Prairie Gleaner; Pioneers of Pettis and Adjoining Missouri Counties; and others*

GENEALOGICAL SOCIETY

PROGRAMS: Publication

COLLECTIONS: Reference Materials: books, family histories, genealogy society quarterlies, microfiche.

HOURS: Yr Sa 1-4

ADMISSION: No charge

WARRENTON

4961
Warren County Historical Society
Market & Walton St, 63383 [PO Box 12, 63383]; (p) (314) 456-3820; (c) Warren

County, non-profit; Private non-profit/ 1970/ members: 200

HISTORICAL SOCIETY; HISTORY MUSEUM; RESEARCH CENTER: Receive, preserve, catalog, and display historical items relating to Warren County.

PROGRAMS: Annual Meeting; Community Outreach; Exhibits; Family Programs; Festivals; Guided Tours; Lectures; Living History; Publication; Research Library/Archives

COLLECTIONS: [1833-present] Records and artifacts relating to Warren County and the people of Warren County.

HOURS: 3rd weekend of Apr-Oct Sa 10-4, Su 1-4.

WARSAW

4962
Benton County Historical Society
700 Benton St, 65355 [PO Box 1082, 65355]; (p) (660) 438-6707; smithl@iland.net; (c) Benton

Private non-profit/ staff: 1(f)/ members: 20

ART MUSEUM; GENEALOGICAL SOCIETY; HISTORIC PRESERVATION AGENCY; HISTORIC SITE; HISTORICAL SOCIETY; HISTORY MUSEUM; HOUSE MUSEUM; RESEARCH CENTER: The Society maintains the Benton County Museum in the Old 1886 Schoolhouse on the Hill.

PROGRAMS: Annual Meeting; Community Outreach; Exhibits; Facility Rental; Festivals; Guided Tours; Interpretation; Publication; Reenactments; Research Library/Archives

COLLECTIONS: [Mid-19th c-present] Artifacts from pioneer Benton County families, including a piano shipped by steamboat on the Missouri River, original jail cell, antique household items and tools, photographs, and Native American artifacts.

HOURS: May - Sept T-Su 1-5

ADMISSION: $1, Children $5

WEBSTER GROVES

4963
Hawken House
1155 S Rock Hill Rd, 63119; (p) (314) 968-3184

1857/ staff: 2(p); 30(v)

Home of Christopher Hawken, son of Jacob Hawken, the maker of the Hawken rifle.

COLLECTIONS: [Late 19th c] Textile collection; furnishings; bridal gown collection.; Local history; Hawken rifles.

HOURS: Mar-Dec

4964
Webster Groves Historical Society
1155 S Rock Hill Rd, 63119; (p) (314) 968-1857; (c) St. Louis

Private non-profit/ 1966/ staff: 2(p); 30(v)/ members: 200

HOUSE MUSEUM: Operates and maintains historic Hawken House and houses the Society's archives collection; hosts special exhibits, events, and meetings.

PROGRAMS: Annual Meeting; Exhibits; Guided Tours; Lectures; Research Library/Archives

COLLECTIONS: [Late 19th c] 1857 Federal style house is furnished in the Victorian mode and features special exhibits; archival material.

HOURS: Mar-Dec T, Th 10-1, Su 1-4

ADMISSION: $250, Children $1

WEST PLAINS

4965
Harlin House Museum
505 Worcester St, 65775 [PO Box 444, 65775]; (p) (417) 256-7801; www.missouri tourism.org/heritage.htm

4966
South Central Missouri Genealogical Society
9 Court Sq, 65775 [1043 W 5th St, 65775]; (p) (417) 256-3966; (c) Howell

Private non-profit/ 1974/ staff: 7(v)/ members: 200

GENEALOGICAL SOCIETY: Preserves information on local and other MO counties, and states, immigration, Civil War.

PROGRAMS: Publication; Research Library/ Archives

COLLECTIONS: [1895-present] 1895-present newspapers microfilm, bound & loose from West Plains, MO, 200 microfilm, newspapers, census, 300 hard and soft bound books, 1,500 periodicals and exchange newsletters.

HOURS: Yr T-Sa 9-12, except 1st Sa 9-3

ADMISSION: No charge

WESTON

4967
Price-Loyles House
718 Spring St, 64098; (p) (816) 640-2383, (816) 891-6535

1857/ staff: 3(v)

COLLECTIONS: [1820s-WW II] Col. James Price and Civil War artifacts, journals, letters, greeting cards, advertising toys, movie memorabilia, sewing, bed.

HOURS: Yr

4968
Walter Herbert Bonnell Museum
20755 Lamar Rd, 64098 [PO Box 235, 64098]; (p) (816) 386-5587, (816) 532-3466

1800

COLLECTIONS: Arrowhead collection; pencil drawings by Bonnell.

4969
Weston Historical Museum, Inc.
601 Main, 64098 [PO Box 266, 64098]; (p) (816) 386-2977; (c) Platte

Private non-profit/ 1960/ staff: 1(p); 200(v)/ members: 400

HISTORIC PRESERVATION AGENCY; HISTORICAL SOCIETY; HISTORY MUSEUM: Maintains museum.

PROGRAMS: Annual Meeting; Community Outreach; Exhibits; Festivals; Guided Tours; Research Library/Archives

COLLECTIONS: [1830-1920s] Household items, clothing, and pictorial history.

HOURS: Mar 15-Dec 15 T-Sa 1-4, Su 1:30-5

ADMISSION: No charge

WESTPHALIA

4970
Westphalia Historical Society
Main St, 65085 [PO Box 244, 65085]; (c) Osage

Private non-profit/ 1974/ staff: 15(p); 15(v)/ members: 155/publication: *Klein Volksblatt*

HISTORICAL SOCIETY: Preserve items from the area's past.

PROGRAMS: Annual Meeting; Community Outreach; Exhibits; Guided Tours; Publication; Research Library/Archives

COLLECTIONS: [1840-1900] Items from the National Historic Site-listed parish church, household, agricultural items, immigrant tronks, immigrant papers, pictures, and primitives.

HOURS: Mar-Oct Su 1-5

ADMISSION: $1, Children $0.25

WINSTON

4971
Winston Historical Society
Hwy 69, 64689 [PO Box 177, 64689]; (p) (660) 749-5626; (c) Daviess

Private non-profit/ 1986/ staff: 6(v)/ members: 70/publication: *The Semaphore*

HISTORICAL SOCIETY: Maintains former Rock Island Railroad Depot that has been converted into a museum.

PROGRAMS: Annual Meeting; Exhibits; Festivals; Guided Tours; Publication; Theatre

COLLECTIONS: [1871-1938] General artifacts in use during late 19th and early 20th c.

HOURS: Sa-Su 2-4

ADMISSION: Donations accepted

MONTANA

BAKER

4972
O'Fallon Historical Society
723 S Main, 59313 [PO Box 285, 59313]; (p) (406) 778-3265; (c) Fallon

County, non-profit; Private non-profit/ 1968/ O'Fallon Historical Society and Museum/ staff: 1(f); 3(v)/ members: 60/publication: *O'Fallon Flashbacks*

HISTORIC SITE; HISTORICAL SOCIETY; HISTORY MUSEUM: Collects, preserves, and interprets local history.

PROGRAMS: Annual Meeting; Community Outreach; Exhibits; Guided Tours; Interpretation; Lectures; Publication; Research Library/Archives

COLLECTIONS: [1800-1900] Homestead era artifacts.

HOURS: Yr T-F, Su 9-12/1-5

ADMISSION: No charge

BELT

4973
Belt Museum
Castner St, 59412 [PO Box 473, 59412]; (p) (406) 277-3574; (c) Cascade

City/ 1975/ staff: 14(v)

HISTORIC SITE; HISTORY MUSEUM

PROGRAMS: Community Outreach; Exhibits; Guided Tours; Research Library/Archives; School-Based Curriculum

COLLECTIONS: [Early 20th c] Mining artifacts, agricultural displays, vintage clothing, dolls, dishes, and school art projects.

ADMISSION: Donations accepted

BIG TIMBER

4974
Crazy Mountain Museum/Sweet Grass Museum Society
Exit 367 W Interchange I-90 Cemetery Rd, 59011 [PO Box 83, 59011]; (p) (406) 932-5126; (c) Sweet Grass

Private non-profit/ 1992/ staff: 2(p); 80(v)/ members: 300/publication: *The New Breeze*

HISTORIC PRESERVATION AGENCY; HISTORICAL SOCIETY; HISTORY MUSEUM: Collects, preserves, and exhibit history of Sweet Grass County.

PROGRAMS: Annual Meeting; Exhibits; Facility Rental; Festivals; Guided Tours; Interpretation; Lectures; Publication; Research Library/Archives

COLLECTIONS: Photos, newspapers, research, biography files, oral histories, local history, books, annuals, scrapbooks, maps, music, archival papers, documents, paintings, artifacts.

HOURS: May-Sept T-Su 1-4:30

ADMISSION: No charge

BILLINGS

4975
Moss Mansion Historic House Museum
914 Division St, 59101; (p) (406) 265-5100; (f) (406) 252-0091; www.blgs.com/moss

1901/ staff: 2(f); 3(p); 1(v)

COLLECTIONS: [1901-1925] 2,986 original items and 329 items not original, three story brown sandstone building and a small wood frame garage. 440 original furnishings, 448 paintings and photographs, 659 documents, 482 personal artifacts, original laces and linens, and vintage costumes.

HOURS: Yr

4976
Museum of Women's History
2824 Third Ave N, 59101 [2423 Pine St, 59101]; (p) (406) 248-2015; (c) Yellowstone

Private non-profit/ 1995/ members: 100

HISTORY MUSEUM: Collects oral, audio, and video histories.

PROGRAMS: Annual Meeting; Exhibits

COLLECTIONS: Videos, pictorials, audio tapes, biographies, historical records.

HOURS: Yr W 12-2

ADMISSION: No charge

4977
Oscar's Park
4002 Story Rd, 59102 [3100 Harrow Dr, 59102]; (p) (406) 245-4598; (f) (406) 245-1788; (c) Yellowstone

Private for-profit/ 1972

HISTORIC SITE; LIVING HISTORY/OUTDOOR MUSEUM

PROGRAMS: Concerts; Elder's Programs; Exhibits; Facility Rental; Family Programs; Festivals; Guided Tours

COLLECTIONS: [1890-1930]

4978
Peter Yegen Jr. Yellowstone County Museum
1500 Terminal Circle, 59103 [PO Box 959, 59103]; (p) (406) 256-6811; (c) Yellowstone

County, non-profit/ 1953/ staff: 1(f); 1(p); 20(v)/ members: 100

HISTORY MUSEUM: Collects, preserves, and promotes local history.

PROGRAMS: Annual Meeting; Community Outreach; Exhibits; Interpretation

COLLECTIONS: [1870-1970] Pioneer, Native American, and Yellowstone Valley artifacts.

HOURS: M-F 10:30-5, Sa 10:30-3

ADMISSION: No charge

4979
Western Heritage Center
2822 Montana, 59101; (p) (406) 256-6809; (f) (406) 256-6850; heritage@ywhc.org; www.ywhc.org; (c) Yellowstone

County, non-profit/ 1971/ staff: 5(f); 1(p); 4(v)/ members: 348

HISTORY MUSEUM: Interprets natural and cultural history of Yellowstone River through educational programs and exhibits.

PROGRAMS: Annual Meeting; Community Outreach; Exhibits; Facility Rental; Family Programs; Guided Tours; Interpretation; Lectures; Living History

COLLECTIONS: [Prehistory] Everyday objects reflecting the work and lifestyles of the inhabitants of the Yellowstone Valley Region, including Native American artifacts.

HOURS: Yr T-Sa 10-5

ADMISSION: Donations accepted

BOZEMAN

4980
Gallatin County Historical Society and Pioneer Museum
317 W Main St, 59715; (p) (406) 522-8122; (f) (406) 522-0367; gchs@pioneermuseum.org; www.pioneermuseum.org; (c) Gallatin

Private non-profit/ 1977/ staff: 1(f); 2(p); 50(v)/ members: 700

GENEALOGICAL SOCIETY; HISTORICAL SOCIETY; HISTORY MUSEUM; RESEARCH CENTER: Preserves and promotes pioneer heritage of Gallatin.

PROGRAMS: Annual Meeting; Community Outreach; Exhibits; Facility Rental; Family Programs; Guided Tours; Interpretation; Lectures; Publication; Research Library/Archives

COLLECTIONS: [1860-1950] Gallatin County artifacts.

HOURS: June-Sept M-F 10-4:30, Sa 1-4; Oct-May T-F 11-4, Sa 1-4

ADMISSION: No charge

4981
Montana Preservation Alliance
321 E Main St, Ste 212, 59771 [PO Box 1872, 59771-1872]; (p) (406) 585-9551; (f) (406) 585-0468; (c) Gallatin

Private non-profit/ 1987/ staff: 2(p)/ members: 155

HISTORIC PRESERVATION AGENCY: Encourages and promotes historic preservation in MT.

PROGRAMS: Annual Meeting

4982
Museum of the Rockies
600 W Kagy Blvd, 59717 [Montana State University, 59717-2730]; (p) (406) 994-2251; (f) (406) 994-2682; sfischer@montana.edu; www.montana.edu/wwwmor/; (c) Gallatin

State/ 1957/ MT State Univ/ staff: 35(f); 40(p); 200(v)/ members: 3465

HISTORY MUSEUM; LIVING HISTORY/OUTDOOR MUSEUM: Preserves and interprets the natural and cultural history of the Northern Rocky Mountain region.

PROGRAMS: Community Outreach; Exhibits; Facility Rental; Family Programs; Film/Video; Guided Tours; Interpretation; Lectures; Living History; Research Library/Archives; School-Based Curriculum

COLLECTIONS: 280,000 items in archaeology, historic photography, history, textiles, paleontology, geology, and ethnology/anthropology.

HOURS: May-Sept Daily 8-8; Oct-Apr M-Sa 9-5, 12:30-5 Su

ADMISSION: $6, Children $4

BROADUS

4983
Powder River Historical Museum
[PO Box 575, 59317]; (p) (406) 436-2977; (c) Powder River

Private non-profit/ 1980/ staff: 60(v)

GENEALOGICAL SOCIETY; HISTORICAL SOCIETY; HISTORY MUSEUM: Preserves local history through preservation and educational efforts.

PROGRAMS: Research Library/Archives

COLLECTIONS: [1900] 2,300 sea shells, 1,700 arrowheads, Native American artifacts, 2,230 minerals, guns, bit and spur collection.

HOURS: June-Sept M-Sa 9-5

ADMISSION: No charge

BROWNING

4984
Museum of the Plains Indian
Junction of HWY 2 & 89 W, 59417 [PO Box 410, 59417]; (p) (406) 338-2230; (f) (406) 338-7404; mpi@3rivers.net; (c) Glacier

1941/ US Dept of the Interior, Indian Arts and Crafts Board/ staff: 3(f); 1(p)

HISTORY MUSEUM: Promotes Native American history, art, and development of contemporary Native American arts and crafts.

PROGRAMS: Exhibits

COLLECTIONS: [19th c] Traditional costumes, art forms related to social and ceremonial aspects of tribal cultures of the Region.

HOURS: Oct-May M-F 10-4:30; June-Sept Daily 9-4:45

ADMISSION: $4, Children $1; Under 6 free; Group rates

BUTTE

4985
Butte Historical Society
[PO Box 3913, 59702]; (p) (406) 497-6226; www.coppercity.com; (c) Butte-Silverbow

Private non-profit/ 1978/ Board of Directors/ members: 60/publication: *Historical Butte; Mine Maps of Butte; and others.*

Promotes the history of Butte-Silverbow, MT through historical, educational, and governmental agencies and individuals.

4986
Butte-Silver Bow Public Archives
17 W Quartz St, 59701 [PO Box 81, 59701]; (p) (406) 723-8262; (c) Silver Bow

Joint/ 1981/ City; County/ staff: 2(f); 2(p); 4(v)

HISTORIC SITE; RESEARCH CENTER: Manages government records and processes documents about Butte history. Preserves and maintains the collections, making them accessible to educators, writers, and genealogists.

PROGRAMS: Community Outreach; Exhibits; Guided Tours; Interpretation; Lectures; Research Library/Archives; School-Based Curriculum

COLLECTIONS: [1864-present] Government and labor records for Montana's major unions. Over 1,000 collections pertaining to the history and industrial growth of Butte-Silver Bow.

HOURS: Yr M-F 9-5

4987
Copper King Mansion
219 W Granite, 59701; (p) (406) 782-7580

4988
World Museum of Mining and Hell Roarin' Gulch, The
W end of Park St, 59703 [PO Box 33, 59703]; (p) (406) 723-7211; (f) (406) 723-7211; www.miningmuseum.org; (c) Silver Bow

Private non-profit/ 1963/ Board of Directors/ staff: 2(f); 9(p); 20(v)/ members: 250

HISTORY MUSEUM: Preserves historical legacy of mining and the social, ethnic, and cultural history of Butte.

PROGRAMS: Annual Meeting; Community Outreach; Concerts; Elder's Programs; Exhibits; Facility Rental; Guided Tours; Interpretation; Research Library/Archives; School-Based Curriculum

COLLECTIONS: [1880-1920] Hell-Roarin' Gulch: reproductions of bank, funeral parlor, jail, post office, city hall, union hall, school, church, and Chinese laundry. World Museum of Mining: mining artifacts, Orphan Girl

CHARLO

4989

Ninepipes Museum of Early Montana
40962 US Hwy 93, 59824; (p) (406) 644-3435; (f) (406) 644-2928; (c) Lake

Private non-profit/ 1998/ staff: 2(f); 3(p); 7(v)/ members: 22

HISTORY MUSEUM: Preserves history of Flathead Reservation and early settlers.

PROGRAMS: Exhibits; Guided Tours; Lectures

COLLECTIONS: [1880-1940] 1,150 Native American and Western artifacts, 250 black and white photos, 75 portraits and paintings, 20 life-size mounts.

HOURS: June-Aug Daily 8-7, Sept-May Daily 10-6

ADMISSION: $4, Student $2.75, Children $1.75

CHESTER

4990

Liberty County Museum Association
210 2nd St East, 59522 [PO Box 410, 59522]; (p) (406) 759-5256, (406) 759-5274; (c) Liberty

County, non-profit/ 1968/ staff: 5(p); 3(v)

ALLIANCE OF HISTORICAL AGENCIES; HISTORIC PRESERVATION AGENCY; HISTORICAL SOCIETY; HISTORY MUSEUM: Preserves and displays local history.

PROGRAMS: Guided Tours

HOURS: June-Sept Daily 2-5/7-9

ADMISSION: Donations accepted

CHINOOK

4991

Blaine County Museum
501 Indiana, 59523 [PO Box 927, 59523]; (p) (406) 357-2590; (f) (406) 357-2199; (c) Blaine

County/ 1977/ staff: 1(f); 1(p); 6(v)

HISTORY MUSEUM: Emphasizes the Homestead Era, early West, paleontology and Native American culture.

PROGRAMS: Guided Tours; Interpretation

COLLECTIONS: [Late 19th-early 20th c] Fossils and artifacts relating to Native American culture, the Homestead and Cowboy eras, early churches, schools, doctors, dentists, the military, W W I and II, and Bear Paw Battlefield.

HOURS: June-Aug M-Sa 8-12/1-5, Su 12-5; May-Sept M-F 8-12/1-5; Oct-Apr M-F 1-5

CHOTEAU

4992

Old Trail Museum
823 N Main, 59422; (p) (406) 466-5332; otm@erivres.net; oldtrailmuseum.org; (c) Teton

Private non-profit/ 1968/ Board of Directors/ staff: 3(f); 10(v)/ members: 500

HISTORY MUSEUM: Preserves, researches, and interprets the physical and cultural heritage of the Rocky Mountain region.

PROGRAMS: Elder's Programs; Exhibits; Family Programs; Guided Tours; Lectures

COLLECTIONS: Native American artifacts, local history display.

HOURS: June-Aug Daily 9-6

ADMISSION: $2

CIRCLE

4993

McCone County Museum
801 1st Ave S, 59215 [PO Box 127, 59215]; (p) (406) 485-2414; (c) McCone

Private non-profit/ 1953/ McCone County Commissioners/ staff: 1(f); 4(v)/ members: 95

HISTORICAL SOCIETY; HISTORY MUSEUM: Preserves local history.

PROGRAMS: Exhibits; Research Library/ Archives

COLLECTIONS: [1870-present] Tools, pioneer artifacts.

HOURS: May-Sept M-F 8-5

ADMISSION: $2

COLSTRIP

4994

Schoolhouse History and Art Center
400 Woodrose, 59323 [PO Box 430, 59323]; (p) (406) 748-4822; (c) Rosebud

Private non-profit/ 1987/ Board of Directors/ staff: 1(f); 100(v)/ members: 85

ART MUSEUM; HISTORY MUSEUM

PROGRAMS: Annual Meeting; Concerts; Exhibits; Facility Rental; Family Programs

COLLECTIONS: [1920-1990] Coal mining, photos of Colstrip.

HOURS: Yr

ADMISSION: No charge

COLUMBUS

4995

Stillwater Historical Society
440 E 5th Ave N, 59019 [Box 1, 59019]; (p) (406) 322-4588; (c) Stillwater

County/ 1993/ staff: 60(v)/ members: 200

HISTORICAL SOCIETY: Operates the Museum of Beartooths.

PROGRAMS: Annual Meeting; Exhibits; Lectures; Living History; Research Library/ Archives

COLLECTIONS: Pioneer, homesteading, Albert Johnson furnishing, farm tools, military memorabilia, railroad caboose.

HOURS: June-Sept T-Su 1-5

ADMISSION: Donations accepted

CONRAD

4996

Pondera History Association
[PO Box 921, 59425]; (p) (406) 278-5434; (f) (406) 278-5097; (c) Pondera

Private non-profit/ 1976/ members: 20

HISTORICAL SOCIETY: Promotes historical preservation of North Central MT.

PROGRAMS: Annual Meeting; Concerts; Exhibits; Lectures

CROW AGENCY

4997

Little Bighorn Battlefield National Monument
Exit 510 on I-90 JCT Hwy 212, 59022 [PO Box 39, 59022]; (p) (406) 638-2621; (f) (406) 638-2623; ken_woody@nps.gov; www.nps.gov/libi; (c) Bighorn

Federal/ 1879/ Dept of Interior, NPS/ staff: 13(f); 15(p); 5(v)

BATTLEFIELD; HOUSE MUSEUM: Preserves history of Battle of the Little Bighorn, June 25-26, 1876

PROGRAMS: Exhibits; Family Programs; Film/Video; Guided Tours; Interpretation; Lectures; Living History

COLLECTIONS: [1876-present] George Armstrong Custer personal effects, weapons, Northern Plains Indian material cutlure, photos.

HOURS: Yr Daily 8-4:30

ADMISSION: $6/vehicle

CULBERTSON

4998

Culbertson Museum
Hwy #2 East, 59218 [PO Box 95 Highway # 2 East, 59218]; (p) (406) 787-6320; (c) Roosevelt

Private non-profit/ 1984/ Culbertson Museum, Board of Directors/ staff: 6(p); 30(v)/ members: 45

HISTORY MUSEUM: Preserves pioneer ranching, homestead and early railroad town.

PROGRAMS: Community Outreach; Exhibits; Family Programs; Guided Tours; Interpretation; Publication

COLLECTIONS: [1880-1940] Religious, school, general store, post office, medical, homestead rooms, military, toys, barber and beauty shop, railroad memorabilia.

HOURS: May, Sept Daily 9-6, June-Aug Daily 8-8

ADMISSION: No charge

4999

Northeastern Montana Threshers and Antique Association
1 mile SE, 59218 [PO Box 168, 59218]; (p) (406) 787-5265; (c) Roosevelt

Private non-profit/ 1963/ staff: 20(v)/ members: 87

HISTORIC PRESERVATION AGENCY; HISTORY MUSEUM; LIVING HISTORY/OUTDOOR MUSEUM: Preserves local history.

PROGRAMS: Annual Meeting; Exhibits; Reenactments

COLLECTIONS: [1900-1960] Tractors, engines, equipment, homesteaders, agriculture, pioneer.

HOURS: Varies

ADMISSION: $6

DARBY

5000
Darby Historical Center-Darby Ranger District
712 N Main, 59829 [PO Box 388, 59829]; (p) (406) 821-3913; (f) (406) 821-3675; (c) Ravalli

Federal/ USDA Forest Service/ staff: 13(v)

HISTORIC SITE; HISTORY MUSEUM

PROGRAMS: Exhibits; Interpretation

COLLECTIONS: [1930-1940] Early office equipment, tools.

HOURS: May-Nov M-Sa 9-5, Su 1-5

ADMISSION: No charge

DEER LODGE

5001
Grant-Kohrs Ranch National Historic Site
210 Missouri Ave, 59722 [PO Box 790, 59722]; (p) (406) 846-2070; (f) (406) 846-3962; darlene_koontz@nps.gov; www.nps.gov.grko; (c) Powell

Federal/ 1972/ U.S. National Park Service/ staff: 13(f); 15(p); 12(v)

HISTORIC SITE; LIVING HISTORY/OUTDOOR MUSEUM; NATIONAL PARK: Preserves and interprets the frontier cattle era. Active from 1860 to 1972, the 1,500 - acre site's structures, features, and landscapes are managed for educational and resource management values as a working cattle ranch.

PROGRAMS: Community Outreach; Exhibits; Festivals; Guided Tours; Interpretation; Living History; Publication; Library/ Archives

COLLECTIONS: [1860-1990] 26,000 site-original ranch objects and furnishings, and ranch archive dating 1860-1972.

HOURS: Yr Daily Sept 15-Apr 30 8-5:30, May 1-Sept 14 9:30-4

ADMISSION: No charge

5002
Yesterday's Play Things
1017 Main St, 59722 [1106 Main St, 59722]; (p) (406) 846-1480; (f) (406) 846-3156; (c) Powell

Private non-profit/ 1986/ Powell County Museum and Arts Foundation/ staff: 1(f); 1(p)

HISTORY MUSEUM: Collects and preserves antique dolls and toys.

PROGRAMS: Exhibits

COLLECTIONS: [1850-present] Dolls, toys, memorabilia.

HOURS: May 15-Sept 30 Daily 9:30-5

ADMISSION: $7.95

DILLON

5003
Bannack State Park
25 miles SW of Dillon, 59725 [4200 Bannack Rd, 59725]; (p) (406) 834-3413; (f) (406) 834-3548; bannack@montana.com; (c) Beaverhead

State/ 1954/ Montana Fish, Wildlife and Parks/ staff: 3(f); 4(p); 300(v)/ members: 180

HISTORIC SITE; STATE PARK: 1,000 acre site commemorating Montana's First Territorial Capital. Bannack, a town that developed after the 1862 gold rush, was the site of Montana's first jail, hotel, Masonic Lodge, electric gold dredge, quarts stamp mill, and commercial sawmill.

PROGRAMS: Festivals; Guided Tours; Interpretation; Lectures; Reenactments; School-Based Curriculum

COLLECTIONS: [1860-1930] Over fifty buildings, oral history interviews, archaeological artifacts, and historic photographs.

HOURS: Yr/Daily 8-5

ADMISSION: $4/vehicle

5004
Beaverhead County Museum
15 S Montana, 59726; (p) (406) 683-5027

County/ 1950/ Beaverhead County Commissioners/ staff: 1(f); 15(v)/ members: 285

GENEALOGICAL SOCIETY; HISTORIC PRESERVATION AGENCY; HISTORICAL SOCIETY; HISTORY MUSEUM: Preserves county history for future generations.

PROGRAMS: Annual Meeting; Community Outreach; Exhibits; Facility Rental; Guided Tours; Interpretation; Lectures; Research Library/Archives; School-Based Curriculum; Theatre

COLLECTIONS: [1860s-present] Dinosaur bones, Native American artifacts, county history and artifacts.

HOURS: May-Sept M-F 8-5, Sa 12-4; Oct-Apr M-F 1-5

ADMISSION: $2

EKALAKA

5005
Carter County Museum
100 Main St, 59324 [PO 547, 59324]; (p) (406) 775-6886; (c) Carter

1936/ Carter County Genealogical Society/ staff: 1(f); 1(p); 1(v)/ members: 35

HISTORY MUSEUM: Promotes natural and local history of Carter County.

PROGRAMS: Exhibits

COLLECTIONS: [Prehistory] Paleontology exhibit, Native American life, pioneer life

HOURS: Yr Sa-Su 1-5, T-F 9-5

ADMISSION: No charge

EUREKA

5006
Tobacco Valley Historical Society
S end of Dewey, 59917 [PO Box 1452, 59917]; (c) Lincoln

Private non-profit/ 1972/ Tobacco Valley Improvement Association/ staff: 25(v)/ members: 15

HISTORICAL SOCIETY: Collects, preserves, and displays the history of the Tobacco Valley.

PROGRAMS: Annual Meeting; Community Outreach; Exhibits; Facility Rental; Family Programs; Festivals; Guided Tours; Interpretation; Lectures; Research Library/Archives; School-Based Curriculum

COLLECTIONS: [1890-1945] Artifacts, maps, photos, journals, home furnishings, reference materials, housed in various historic buildings.

HOURS: June-Aug Daily 1-5

ADMISSION: No charge

5007
Tobacco Valley Improvement Association Historical Village
S End, Dewey Ave, 59917 [PO Box 325, 59917]; (c) Lincoln

Private non-profit/ 1972/ staff: 20(v)

HISTORY MUSEUM; HOUSE MUSEUM: Preserves local history and maintains historical records.

PROGRAMS: Annual Meeting; Community Outreach; Exhibits; Facility Rental; Family Programs; Festivals; Guided Tours; Interpretation; Research Library/Archives; School-Based Curriculum

COLLECTIONS: [1890-1950] Photos, oral histories, archives, period clothing, restoration of period village: store, school, train depot, home, church, blacksmith shop, lookout tower, log cabin.

HOURS: Daily 1-5

ADMISSION: No charge

FORT BENTON

5008
River and Plains Society/Museum of the Upper Missouri/Montana Agricultural Center and Museum
20th & Washington, 59442 [PO Box 262, 59442]; (p) (406) 622-5316; (c) Chouteau

Private non-profit/ 1998

HISTORICAL SOCIETY: Promotes local history through preservation and operation of historic buildings and two museums in Fort Benton.

PROGRAMS: Interpretation

GERALDINE

5009
Geraldine Historical Committee, The
1 Railroad Ave, 59446 [200 Brewster, 59446]; (p) (406) 737-4368; hamrice@ttc-cmc.net; (c) Chouteau

Private non-profit/ 1994/ members: 32

PROFESSIONAL ORGANIZATION: Preserves local history.

PROGRAMS: Annual Meeting; Facility Rental; Guided Tours

HOURS: By appt

ADMISSION: No charge

GLASGOW

5010
Valley County Pioneer Museum
Hwy 2 W, 59230 [PO Box 44, 59230]; (p) (406) 228-8692; (c) Valley

County, non-profit/ 1968/ staff: 2(p); 125(v)/ members: 75

GENEALOGICAL SOCIETY; HISTORICAL SOCIETY: Preserves local history.

PROGRAMS: Exhibits; Guided Tours

COLLECTIONS: [1890-1930] Native American artifacts, homesteading.

HOURS: M-Sa 9-7, Su 1-5

ADMISSION: No charge

GLENDIVE

5011
Frontier Gateway Museum and Foundation

Belle Prairie Frontage Rd, 59330 [PO Box 1181, 59330]; (p) (406) 377-8168; (c) Dawson

County, non-profit/ 1963/ Dawson County and F.G. Museum Association/ staff: 3(p); 1(v)/ members: 400

HISTORICAL SOCIETY; HISTORY MUSEUM; RESEARCH CENTER: Preserves local history.

PROGRAMS: Annual Meeting; Elder's Programs; Guided Tours; Interpretation; Lectures; Research Library/Archives

COLLECTIONS: Large farm machinery

HOURS: June-Aug M-Sa 9-1, Su 1-5; May, Sept Su-Sa 1-5

ADMISSION: No charge

5012
Makoshika State Park

1301 Snyder Ave, 59330 [PO Box 1242, 59330]; (p) (406) 365-6256; (f) (406) 365-8043; makoshikapark@mcn.net; (c) Dawson

State/ 1953/ Fish, Wildlife, and Parks/ staff: 2(f); 6(p); 20(v)

HISTORIC PRESERVATION AGENCY; HISTORY MUSEUM; STATE PARK: Preserves natural history.

PROGRAMS: School-Based Curriculum; Theatre

COLLECTIONS: [Prehistory] Native American artifacts; dinosaur exhibit, including Triceratop, Tyrannosaurus Rex, Hadrosaur specimens.

HOURS: Yr Daily 8-6

ADMISSION: $4/vehicle

GREAT FALLS

5013
C.M. Russell Museum

400 13th St N, 59401; (p) (406) 727-8787; (f) (406) 727-2402; edear@cmrussell.org; (c) Cascade

1951/publication: *Russell's West*

Collects, preserves, researches, and interprets the art and life of C.M. Russell and other artists that depict the culture, and life of the West.

PROGRAMS: Community Outreach; Concerts; Elder's Programs; Exhibits; Facility Rental; Family Programs; Guided Tours; Interpretation; Lectures; Publication; Research Library/Archives

COLLECTIONS: [19th-20th c] CM Russell paintings, drawings, sculptures, personal effects, photo archives, material culture, housed in CM Russell home and studio.

HOURS: Yr Daily 10-5

ADMISSION: $4, Students $2, Seniors $3

5014
Cascade County Historical Museum and Archives

High Plains Heritage Center, 59405 [422 2nd St S, 59405]; (p) (406) 452-3462; (f) (406) 761-3805; (c) Cascade

Private non-profit/ 1972/ Cascade County Historical Society/ staff: 3(f); 6(p); 100(v)/ members: 420

HISTORIC SITE; HISTORICAL SOCIETY; HISTORY MUSEUM; RESEARCH CENTER: Collects, preserves, and interprets Central MT history.

PROGRAMS: Annual Meeting; Community Outreach; Elder's Programs; Exhibits; Family Programs; Festivals; Film/Video; Guided Tours; Interpretation; Lectures; Living History

COLLECTIONS: [1870-1970] 70,000 material culture; artifacts; 15,000 photographic images.

HOURS: May-Sept M-F 10-5, Sa-Su 12-5

ADMISSION: No charge

5015
Cascade County Historical Society

In the Plains Heritage Center, 59405 [422 2nd St S, 59405]; (p) (406) 452-3462; (f) (406) 761-3805; (c) Cascade

Private non-profit/ 1972/ staff: 2(f); 5(p); 125(v)

HISTORICAL SOCIETY; HISTORY MUSEUM: Preserves historical and folk heritage of Central MT.

5016
Lewis and Clark National Historic Trail and Interpretive Center

4201 Giant Springs Road, 59403 [PO Box 1806, 59403]; (p) (406) 727-8733; (f) (406) 453-6157; (c) Cascade

Federal/ 1998/ USDA Forest Service/ staff: 8(f); 8(p); 120(v)

LIVING HISTORY/OUTDOOR MUSEUM; NATIONAL PARK: Chronicles the expedition's portage around the Great Falls and relations with Plains and Pacific Northwest Indians.

PROGRAMS: Community Outreach; Exhibits; Facility Rental; Family Programs; Festivals; Guided Tours; Interpretation; Lectures; Living History; Research Library/Archives; School-Based Curriculum; Theatre

COLLECTIONS: [1803-1806] Reproductions of items used by the Corps of Discovery or the Native peoples they encountered, animal mounts, temporary exhibit of artwork and artifacts.

HOURS: Oct-May T-Sa 9-5, Su 12-5; June-Sept Daily 9-6

ADMISSION: $5, Student $4, Children $2, Seniors $4

HAMILTON

5017
Bitter Root Valley Historical Society/Ravalli County Museum

205 Bedford, 59840; (p) (406) 363-3338; rcmuseum@cybernet1.com; www.cybernet1.com/rcmuseum/; (c) Ravalli

Private non-profit/ 1955/ staff: 1(f); 3(p); 50(v)/ members: 300/publication: *Bitter Root Trails*

HISTORIC SITE; HISTORICAL SOCIETY; HISTORY MUSEUM; LIBRARY AND/OR ARCHIVES: Collects, gathers, preserves, and interprets history and culture of the Bitter Root Valley and Lewis and Clark. Maintains Ravalli County Museum.

PROGRAMS: Annual Meeting; Community Outreach; Concerts; Exhibits; Facility Rental; Festivals; Interpretation; Lectures; Publication; Research Library/Archives; School-Based Curriculum

COLLECTIONS: [1880-1970] Native American exhibit, Richetts Room depicting pioneer scientists in search of spotted fever vaccine, hunter/trapper exhibit, period rooms, pioneer and Ernst Peterson photographs.

HOURS: Yr Th-M 10-4

5018
Daly Mansion Preservation Trust

251 Eastside Hwy, 59840 [PO Box 223, 59840]; (p) (406) 363-6004; (f) (406) 375-0048; daly@bitterroot.net; www.bitterroot.net/dmpt/daly.html; (c) Ravalli

Joint/ 1986/ State; Montana Historical Society/ staff: 1(f); 4(p); 60(v)/ members: 425

GARDEN; HISTORIC SITE; HOUSE MUSEUM: Promotes local history through preservation of Daly Mansion.

PROGRAMS: Annual Meeting; Concerts; Facility Rental; Family Programs; Guided Tours; Interpretation

COLLECTIONS: [1890-1941] Period furnishings, clothing.

HOURS: Apr 15-Oct 15 Daily 11-4

ADMISSION: $5, Children $3

HARDIN

5019
Big Horn County Historical Society and Museum

Rt 1, Box 1206 A, 59034; (p) (406) 665-1671; (f) (406) 665-3068; bhchistorical@juno.com; (c) Big Horn

Joint/ 1979/ County; Historical Society/ staff: 2(f); 2(p); 20(v)/ members: 959

HISTORIC PRESERVATION AGENCY; HISTORICAL SOCIETY; HISTORY MUSEUM; HOUSE MUSEUM; RESEARCH CENTER: Maintains historic buildings which interpret the area's past.

PROGRAMS: Annual Meeting; Community Outreach; Exhibits; Facility Rental; Guided Tours; Interpretation; Lectures

COLLECTIONS: [1900-1940s] Collection of photographs and buildings which represent Big Horn County. Each Building displays a collection of artifacts which interpret early settlement in Montana. These include: farmhouses, log cabins, service station, depot, general store, post office, church, doctor's office, schoolhouse, farm exhibits, barn, slaughterhouse and tipis.

HOURS: Main Building Yr; Peripheral buildings: May-Oct M-Su, 8-5

HARLOWTON

5020
Upper Musselshell Historical Society
11 S Central Ave, 59036 [PO Box 364, 59036-0364]; (p) (406) 632-5519; rcbrown@mcn.net; (c) Wheatland

County/ 1975/ Upper Musselshell Historical Society/ staff: 1(f); 1(p); 15(v)/ members: 150

HISTORIC PRESERVATION AGENCY; HISTORICAL SOCIETY; HISTORY MUSEUM; RESEARCH CENTER: Preserves, displays, and gathers history of Upper Musselshell area.

PROGRAMS: Annual Meeting; Exhibits; Film/Video; Lectures; Publication

COLLECTIONS: [1800-1900] Period clothing, weapons, tools, Milwaukee Railroad memorabilia, Native American arrowhead, military uniforms, paleontology exhibit.

HOURS: May-Sept M-F 10-5, Su 1-5

ADMISSION: Donations accepted

HAVRE

5021
H. Earl Clark Museum
306 3rd Ave, 59501 [315 4th St, 59501]; (p) (406) 265-4000; (f) (406) 265-4000; mcgregord@mail.msun.edu; theheritagecenter.com; (c) Hill

County, non-profit/ 1964/ Hill County/ staff: 1(f); 1(p); 15(v)/ members: 50

ART MUSEUM; HISTORIC SITE; HISTORY MUSEUM: Preserves local history in former post office listed on National Registry of Historic Places.

PROGRAMS: Annual Meeting; Community Outreach; Exhibits; Facility Rental; Guided Tours; Interpretation; Lectures; Research Library/Archives; School-Based Curriculum

COLLECTIONS: [1890-1930] Artifacts from bison kill site, paleontology, railroad, homesteaders, boot leggers.

HOURS: Yr June-Aug 10-6; Sept-May 12-5

ADMISSION: $3, Student $1.50

HELENA

5022
Kleffner Ranch
1 mile S of E Helena, [PO Box 427, East Helena, 59635]; (p) (406) 227-6645; (f) (406) 441-9191; dove@initco.net; www.helenamt.com/kleffner

1880/ Private/ staff: 1(p); 1(v)

Maintains historic house that was built of glacial rock by stone masons from Italy. The site is still a working cattle ranch.

COLLECTIONS: [1880s-1890s]

HOURS: May-Oct

5023
Little Red Schoolhouse, Inc.
1635 Sierra Rd E, 59602; (p) (406) 458-9249; (c) Lewis and Clark

Private non-profit/ 1888/ staff: 1(f); 1(v)/publication: LRSH, Inc.

HISTORIC SITE: Restores and preserves the 111 year old school.

PROGRAMS: Annual Meeting; Guided Tours; Lectures; Publication; School-Based Curriculum

COLLECTIONS: [1888] Teaching artifacts, equipment

HOURS: By appt

ADMISSION: No charge

5024
Montana Heritage Preservation and Development Comission
600 N Park, 59620 [PO Box 201204, 59620-1204]; (p) (406) 841-4014; (f) (406) 841-4004; karlees@state.mt.us; (c) Lewis & Clark

State/ 1997/ staff: 5(f); 10(p); 100(v)

HISTORIC PRESERVATION AGENCY; HISTORIC SITE; HISTORY MUSEUM; LIVING HISTORY/OUTDOOR MUSEUM: Preserves historic properties.

PROGRAMS: Concerts; Elder's Programs; Exhibits; Family Programs; Festivals; Guided Tours; Interpretation; Lectures; Living History; Publication; Reenactments; Research Library/Archives; School-Based Curriculum; Theatre

COLLECTIONS: [1863-1945] Over 200 buildings in historic Virginia City and Nevada City, with 300,000 artifacts, 1910 steam locomotive and 30 gauge railroad track.

5025
Montana Historical Society
225 N Roberts, 59620 [PO Box 201201, 59620-1201]; (p) (406) 444-2694; (f) (406) 444-2696; www.his.mt.gov; (c) Lewis & Clark

1865/publication: Montana, the Magazine of Western History

HISTORIC PRESERVATION AGENCY; HISTORICAL SOCIETY; HISTORY MUSEUM: Promotes understanding of MT history through collection, preservation and interpretation efforts, and by providing access to historical resources maintained by the Society.

PROGRAMS: Community Outreach; Exhibits; Family Programs; Garden Tours; Guided Tours; Interpretation; Lectures; Publication; Research Library/Archives

COLLECTIONS: 100,000 volumes, 7,000 maps, 14,000 microfilm, 3,500 oral history tapes, 3,000 ephemera, 350,000 photos, 5,000 artwork, 43,000 artifacts, 15,000 linear ft of govt records, manuscripts, and business records.

HOURS: Yr Sept-May M-F 8-5; June-Aug M-F 8-5, Sa-Su 9-5

ADMISSION: No charge

5026
Montana's Original Governor's Mansion
304 N Ewing, 59601 [PO Box 201201, 59620-1201]; (p) (406) 444-4710, (406) 442-3115; (f) (406) 444-2696; www.his.state.mt.us/ (for MHS, not just OGM)

1888/ Montana Historical Society/ staff: 6(p); 20(v)

COLLECTIONS: [1913-1920] Furniture, household furnishings and textiles; children's toys; ceramic tiles; carriages and other horse-drawn vehicles; oriental rugs.

HOURS: Apr-Dec; Mem Day; Mem Day-Labor Day T-Su 12-5; Labor Day-Dec 31 T-Sa 12-5

5027
Pioneer Cabin
200 S Park, 59601; (p) (406) 443-7641

HOBSON

5028
Utica Museum and Historical Society
Main St, 59452 [HC 81-Box 58, 59452]; (p) (406) 423-5209; (c) Judith Basin

Private non-profit/ 1965/ staff: 12(v)/ members: 17/publication: Utica I and II

HISTORIC PRESERVATION AGENCY; HISTORICAL SOCIETY; HISTORY MUSEUM: A locally owned and operated museum.

PROGRAMS: Annual Meeting; Exhibits; Publication

COLLECTIONS: [19th c-present] Agriculture and homesteading artifacts.

HOURS: May-Sept Sa, Su 10-5

HUNTLEY

5029
Huntley Project Museum of Irrigated Agriculture
Hwy 312 E, 59037 [PO Box 141, Ballantine, 59006-0141]; (p) (406) 967-2619; dhoefer@mcn.net; (c) Yellowstone

Private non-profit/ 1973/ staff: 1(f); 1(p); 20(v)/ members: 60

HISTORIC PRESERVATION AGENCY; HISTORY MUSEUM: Preserves history of homesteading and second irrigation project.

PROGRAMS: Annual Meeting; Community Outreach; Elder's Programs; Publication

COLLECTIONS: [1863-1930] 5,000 items, including homesteader clothing, agriculture equipment, wooden threshing machines, Ruth-dredger, homestead homes, zippo lighters.

HOURS: May-Sept M-Sa 9-4

ADMISSION: No charge

HYSHAM

5030
Treasure County 89ers Museum
Elliott Ave, 59038 [PO Box 324, 59038]; (p) (406) 342-5452; (c) Treasure

Private non-profit/ 1989/ staff: 50(v)/ members: 450/publication: Treasure County 89ers Newsletter

HISTORIC PRESERVATION AGENCY; HISTORY MUSEUM: Preserves history of the area with displays, exhibits, memorabilia.

PROGRAMS: Annual Meeting; Community Outreach; Exhibits; Guided Tours; Publication

COLLECTIONS: [1892] Treasure County artifacts.

HOURS: June-Sept M-Sa 1-5

ADMISSION: No charge

KALISPELL

5031
Conrad Mansion National Historic Site Museum
6 blocks E of Main on 4th St E, 59903 [PO Box 1041, 59903]; (p) (406) 755-2166; (c) Flathead

Private non-profit/ 1976/ Directors/ staff: 1(f); 20(p); 30(v)/publication: *Half Interest in a Silver Dollar*

HISTORIC SITE; HOUSE MUSEUM: Preserves local history and restored home of city founder C.E. Conrad.

PROGRAMS: Garden Tours; Guided Tours; Interpretation; Publication; School-Based Curriculum

COLLECTIONS: [1890-1920] Period clothing, toys, dolls, books, letters, photos, magazines.

HOURS: May 15-June 14 10-5:30; June 15-Sept 15 9-8; Sept 16-Oct 15 10-5:30

ADMISSION: $7, Children $1, Seniors $6

5032
Northwest Montana Historical Society, Central School Museum
124 2nd Ave E, 59903 [PO Box 2293, 59903]; (p) (406) 756-8381; (f) (406) 257-5719; nwmhs@digisys.net; (c) Flathead

Private non-profit/ 1987/ Northwest MT Historical Village and Museum/ staff: 1(f); 1(p); 70(v)/ members: 214/publication: *Looking Back: A Pictorial History of the Flathead Valley, Montana*

HISTORIC SITE; HISTORICAL SOCIETY; HISTORY MUSEUM: Promotes local history.

PROGRAMS: Community Outreach; Concerts; Exhibits; Facility Rental; Family Programs; Garden Tours; Lectures; Publication; School-Based Curriculum

COLLECTIONS: [1880-present] Artifacts, photos, tools, furnishings, costumes related to Northwest MT and Flathead Valley

HOURS: Yr Winter M-F 11-4; Summer M-F 10-4

ADMISSION: $2, Children $1, Students $1, Seniors $1

LAMBERT

5033
Lambert Historical Society
Main St, 59243 [PO Box 31, 59243]; (p) (406) 774-3439; (c) Richland

County, non-profit/ 1977/ staff: 1(p); 2(v)

HISTORICAL SOCIETY: Preserves history of small dry land farm in Eastern MT.

PROGRAMS: Annual Meeting; Community Outreach; Exhibits; Facility Rental; Research Library/Archives; School-Based Curriculum

COLLECTIONS: [1900] Native American, farming, ranching, military, school exhibits. Family histories, photos, newspapers.

HOURS: May-Oct T-Th 10-2 and by appt

ADMISSION: No charge

LEWISTOWN

5034
Central Montana Historical Association, Inc.
408 NE Main, 59457; (c) Fergus

Private non-profit/ 1953/ Central MT Historical Assoc, Inc/ staff: 30(v)/ members: 25/publication: *Guarding the Carrell Trail*

HISTORY MUSEUM: Preserves the history of Central MT.

PROGRAMS: Annual Meeting; Facility Rental; Guided Tours; Publication

COLLECTIONS: [1880-present] Pioneer history, military, family photos, Native American artifacts, period clothing, guns.

HOURS: Yr M-F 8-5, Sa-Su 10-4

ADMISSION: Donations accepted

LIBBY

5035
Heritage Museum
1367 Hwy 2 S, 59923 [PO Box 628, 59923]; (p) (406) 293-7521; (c) Lincoln

Private non-profit/ 1973/ staff: 45(v)

HISTORY MUSEUM: Preserves historical culture of Northwest MT in a 2-story, 12-sided log structure.

PROGRAMS: Research Library/Archives

COLLECTIONS: Art gallery, outdoor exhibits, history of local culture, mining, lumbering, forestry, natural history, Kootenai Indians.

HOURS: June-Aug M-Sa 10-5, Su 1-5

ADMISSION: Donations accepted

LIVINGSTON

5036
Livingston Depot Foundation
200 W Park St, 59047 [PO Box 1319, 59047]; (p) (406) 222-2300; (f) (406) 222-2401; (c) Park

Private non-profit/ 1985/ Board of Trustees/ staff: 3(f); 4(p); 40(v)/publication: *Depot Center News*

HISTORY MUSEUM: Restores and preserves historic Northern Pacific depot, and community cultural center.

PROGRAMS: Annual Meeting; Community Outreach; Concerts; Elder's Programs; Exhibits; Facility Rental; Family Programs; Festivals; Film/Video; Guided Tours; Interpretation; Lectures; Living History; Publication; Reenactments; School-Based Curriculum

COLLECTIONS: [1870-1970] Railroad memorabilia, equipment, photos, ephemera.

HOURS: May-Sept M-Sa 9-5, Su 1-5

ADMISSION: $3, Children $2; Under 6, Free

LOLO

5037
Timber Heritage Foundation, The
6800 Hwy 12, 59847 [PO Box 129, 59847]; (p) (406) 273-6743; (f) (406) 273-6378; holtranch@marsweb.com; (c) Missoula

Private non-profit/ 1991/ staff: 2(v)

COLLECTIONS: [1800-present] Cowboy, stockman exhibits, Lewis and Clark, Nez Perce Indians.

HOURS: June-Sept W-Su 12-6

ADMISSION: Donations accepted

MALTA

5038
Phillips County Museum
Hwy #2 East, 59538; (p) (406) 654-1037; (c) Phillips

Private non-profit/ 1978/ County Commissioners Museum Board/ staff: 10(v)/ members: 50

HISTORIC PRESERVATION AGENCY; HISTORY MUSEUM; LIBRARY AND/OR ARCHIVES: Preserves local history.

PROGRAMS: Community Outreach; Exhibits; Family Programs; Guided Tours; Interpretation; Lectures; Research Library/Archives

COLLECTIONS: [1930] Native American clothing, artifacts, outlaw history, homestead era, school, implements, memorabilia, medical, military, fossils, and dinosaurs.

HOURS: Yr May-Sept Daily 10-5 and by appt

ADMISSION: $3

MILES CITY

5039
Range Riders Museum
Rt 1, Box 2003, 59301; (p) (406) 232-6146; (c) Custer

Private non-profit/ 1939/ staff: 2(f); 1(p)/ members: 300

HISTORY MUSEUM

PROGRAMS: Elder's Programs; Exhibits; Facility Rental; Family Programs; Festivals; Guided Tours; Lectures

COLLECTIONS: [1800-1930] Western, pioneer life.

HOURS: Apr-Oct Daily

ADMISSION: $4, Student $1, Children $0.50, Seniors $3

5040
Southeastern Montana Research Library
1411 Leighton, 59301 [PO Box 711, 59301]; (p) (406) 232-6736; www.geocities.com/heartland/fields/6175; (c) Custer

Private non-profit/ 1992/ Miles City Genealogical Society/publication: *Cemetery Index, 1920 Census Index*

GENEALOGICAL SOCIETY; HISTORICAL SOCIETY; RESEARCH CENTER: Preserves history of Southeastern MT.

PROGRAMS: Publication; Research Library/Archives

COLLECTIONS: [1876-present] Genealogy, blueprints of historic buildings, obituaries.

HOURS: Yr M 9-12, W 10-12, Sa 10-2

ADMISSION: No charge

MISSOULA

5041
Garnet Preservation Association
3255 Fort Missoula Rd, 59804; (p) (406) 329-3884; (f) (406) 329-3721; (c) Missoula

Joint/ 1984/ Garnet Ghost Town Management Plan/ staff: 1(f); 3(p); 5(v)/ members: 250/publication: *Garnet, Montana's Last Gold Camp*

HISTORIC SITE

PROGRAMS: Annual Meeting; Exhibits; Facility Rental; Family Programs; Guided Tours; Interpretation; Publication; School-Based Curriculum

COLLECTIONS: [1890-1915] Mining artifacts, golden

HOURS: Yr Daily 8-5

ADMISSION: $2

5042
Historical Museum at Fort Missoula
Bldg 322 Fort Missoula, 59804; (p) (406) 728-3476; (f) (406) 543-6277; ftmslamuseum@ montana.com; www.montana.com/ ftmslamuseum; (c) Missoula

County, non-profit/ 1974/ Missoula County/ staff: 3(f); 1(p); 40(v)/ members: 345

HISTORIC SITE; HISTORY MUSEUM: Preserves and interprets history of Missoula, Fort Missoula, and the forest industry.

PROGRAMS: Annual Meeting; Community Outreach; Elder's Programs; Exhibits; Facility Rental; Festivals; Guided Tours; Interpretation; Lectures; Publication; Research Library/ Archives; Theatre

COLLECTIONS: 22,000 artifacts, 750 volume library, 13 historic structures on 32 acres.

HOURS: Yr June-Sept T-Sa 10-5; Oct-May T-Sa 12-5

ADMISSION: $3, Student $1, Seniors $2; Under 6 free

PABLO

5043
People's Center, The
53253 Hwy 93, 59860 [PO Box 278, 59860]; (p) (406) 675-0160; (f) (406) 675-0260; director@ peoplescenter.org; www.peoplescenter.org; (c) Lake

Tribal/ 1990/ Confederated Salish and Kootenai Tribes/ staff: 4(f); 4(p); 10(v)/ members: 200

TRIBAL MUSEUM: Collects, preserves, and promotes tribal history of Salish Kootenai and Pend d'oreille band.

PROGRAMS: Annual Meeting; Community Outreach; Elder's Programs; Exhibits; Facility Rental; Family Programs; Festivals; Film/Video; Guided Tours; Interpretation; Lectures; Living History; Library/ Archives

COLLECTIONS: [Prehistoric] 50,000 archaeological items, material culture, tribal artifacts.

HOURS: Sept-May M-F 9-5; June-Aug M-F 9-5, Sa-Su 10-4

PLENTYWOOD

5044
Sheridan County Museum
Hwy 16, 59254 [111 Wellliver Rd, 59254]; (c)

Sheridan

County, non-profit/ 1960/ staff: 1(p); 4(v)/ members: 84

ART MUSEUM; HISTORICAL SOCIETY; HISTORY MUSEUM: Preserves history of Sheridan County.

PROGRAMS: Annual Meeting; Exhibits; Guided Tours; Interpretation; Lectures

COLLECTIONS: [Prehistory] Native American artifacts, homestead, Montana artists.

ADMISSION: No charge

POLSON

5045
Miracle of America Museum, Inc.
58176 Hwy 93, 59860; (p) (406) 883-6804; museum@cyberport.net; www.cyberport.net/museum; (c) Lake

Private non-profit/ 1985/ Board of Directors/ staff: 2(f); 10(p); 12(v)/ members: 380

HISTORY MUSEUM: Preserves and displays Americana 'From the Walking Plow to Walking on the Moon' educational program.

PROGRAMS: Annual Meeting; Community Outreach; Concerts; Exhibits; Facility Rental; Family Programs; Festivals; Guided Tours; Interpretation; Lectures; Living History; Publication; Research Library/Archives

COLLECTIONS: [1850-1950] 100,000 objects depicting America's progress.

HOURS: June-Aug Daily 8-8, Sept-May M-Sa 8-5, Su 1:30-5

ADMISSION: $3, Children $1

5046
Polson Flathead Historical Museum
708 Main, 59860 [PO Box 206, 59860]; (p) (406) 883-3049; (f) (406) 883-1236; (c) Lake

Private non-profit/ 1946/ Flathead Historical Museum/ staff: 15(p)/ members: 150

HISTORIC PRESERVATION AGENCY; HISTORY MUSEUM; LIVING HISTORY/OUTDOOR MUSEUM; TRIBAL MUSEUM: Preserves and displays local historical projects.

PROGRAMS: Annual Meeting; Exhibits; Festivals; Living History

COLLECTIONS: [1946-1970] Native American artifacts, pioneer, cowboy, homesteading, logging, sawmills exhibit.

HOURS: May-Aug M-F 9-6, Su 12-6

ADMISSION: $2; Donations

POPLAR

5047
Fort Peck Assiniboine and Sioux
Cultural Center, 59255 [602 Court Ave, 59255]; (p) (406) 768-5155; (f) (406) 768-5478; cultres@nemontel.net; (c) Roosevelt

Private non-profit; Tribal/ 1978/ Cultural Resources Department/ staff: 5(f)

HISTORIC PRESERVATION AGENCY; TRIBAL MUSEUM: Preserves tribal history through museum and archives.

PROGRAMS: Annual Meeting; Community Outreach; Concerts; Elder's Programs; Exhibits; Festivals; Interpretation; Lectures; Research Library/Archives; School-Based Curriculum; Theatre

COLLECTIONS: Artifacts of Fort Peck and Assiniboine and Sioux tribes.

HOURS: Yr M-Sa 8-5:30

PRYOR

5048
Chief Plenty Coups Museum and State Park
3/4 miles W of Pryor, 59066 [PO Box 100, 59066]; (p) (406) 252-1289; (f) (406) 252-6668; (c) Big Horn

State/ 1965/ Montana Fish, Wildlife and Parks/ staff: 1(f); 6(p); 1(v)/ members: 100/publication: *Friends of Chief Plenty Coups Newsletter*

HISTORY MUSEUM; STATE PARK; TRIBAL MUSEUM: Preserves history of Chief Plenty Coups and burial site.

PROGRAMS: Exhibits; Guided Tours; Interpretation; Publication

COLLECTIONS: [1884-1932] Preservation Era; settlement of Crow Reservation; Native American artifacts, photos.

HOURS: May-Sept Daily 8-8; Museum 10-5

ADMISSION: $1; $4/car

RED LODGE

5049
Carbon County Historical Society
224 N Broadway Ave, 59068 [PO Box 881, 59068-0881]; (p) (406) 446-3667; (f) (406) 446-1920; (c) Carbon

County/ 1974

HISTORICAL SOCIETY; HISTORY MUSEUM; RESEARCH CENTER: Operates the Peaks to Plains Museum which houses and preserves historical artifacts and exhibits pertaining to Carbon County's history.

PROGRAMS: Annual Meeting; Exhibits; Facility Rental; Guided Tours; Lectures; Living History; Publication; Research Library/Archives

COLLECTIONS: [1800-present] Museum exhibits, photographs, newspapers, oral histories, local history files, county records, genealogical materials and mining maps.

HOURS: Yr

ADMISSION: $3, Children $2, Seniors $2; Members free

RICHEY

5050
Richey Historical Society
Main St, 59259 [PO Box 218, 59259]; (c) Dawson

County/ 1973/ staff: 1(f)/ members: 20

HISTORICAL SOCIETY; HISTORY MUSEUM: Preserves local history.

PROGRAMS: Exhibits

COLLECTIONS: [1910-1925] Homesteader artifacts.

HOURS: June-Sept M, W, F 2-5

ADMISSION: No charge

RONAN

5051
Garden of the Rockies Museum
400 Round Butte Rd, 59864 [128 Main St SW, 59864]; (p) (406) 676-5210; (c) Lake

City, non-profit/ 1972/ staff: 2(p); 6(v)/ members: 100

HISTORY MUSEUM; HOUSE MUSEUM; LIVING HISTORY/OUTDOOR MUSEUM; TRIBAL MUSEUM: Preserves local history.

PROGRAMS: Community Outreach; Exhibits; Guided Tours

COLLECTIONS: [1880-1950] Farm machinery, household items, Native American artifacts, logging/mining equipment, log construction house, church.

HOURS: May-Sept M-Sa 11-4

ADMISSION: No charge

ROUNDUP

5052
Musselshell Valley History Museum
524 1st W, 59072; (p) (406) 323-1403; (c) Musselshell

Private non-profit/ 1972/ Board of Directors/ staff: 1(p); 22(v)/ members: 165

HISTORIC PRESERVATION AGENCY: Promotes local history.

PROGRAMS: Annual Meeting; Exhibits; Facility Rental

COLLECTIONS: [1850-present] Pioneer school, 1890 home, coal mine, Native American artifacts, prehistoric fossils, 1920 hospital, military uniforms and equipment, 1884 log cabin, printing press.

HOURS: May-Sept Daily 1-5

ADMISSION: Donations accepted

SAINT IGNATIUS

5053
Flathead Indian Museum
32621 Hwy 93, 59865 [PO Box 460, 59865]; (p) (706) 745-2951; (f) (406) 745-2961; jeanine@allardauctions.com; (c) Lake

Private non-profit/ 1975/ staff: 2(f); 5(p)

HISTORY MUSEUM: Promotes tribal history.

PROGRAMS: Exhibits; Lectures

COLLECTIONS: [1880-1930] Native American clothing, costumes, photos, tools.

HOURS: Yr Daily 9-5:30

ADMISSION: No charge

5054
St. Ignatius Catholic Mission
Church St, 59865 [PO Box 667, 59865]; (p) (406) 745-2768; (c) Lake

Private non-profit/ 1854/ staff: 3(f); 3(p); 9(v)

HISTORIC SITE; HISTORY MUSEUM: Preserves history of mission church on Flathead Indian Reservation.

PROGRAMS: Exhibits; Guided Tours

COLLECTIONS: 58 historical and religious murals.

HOURS: Yr Daily 9-5

ADMISSION: No charge

SCOBEY

5055
Daniels County Museum Association
7 County Road, 59263 [Box 133, 59263]; (p) (406) 487-5965; (f) (406) 487-2849; charlymt@newmontel.net; (c) Daniels

Private non-profit/ 1965/ staff: 2(p); 60(v)

LIVING HISTORY/OUTDOOR MUSEUM: Preserves local history.

PROGRAMS: Annual Meeting; Community Outreach; Exhibits; Guided Tours; Living History; Theatre

COLLECTIONS: [1900] Local history artifacts

HOURS: May-Sept Daily 12:30-4:30

ADMISSION: $3, Children $1.50

SHELBY

5056
Marias Museum of History and Art
206 12th Ave N, 59474 [Box 895, 59474]; (p) (406) 434-2551; (c) Toole

Private non-profit/ 1960/ staff: 1(p); 12(v)/ members: 18

HISTORIC PRESERVATION AGENCY; HISTORY MUSEUM; HOUSE MUSEUM: Preserves historical objects.

PROGRAMS: Annual Meeting; Community Outreach; Exhibits; Film/Video

COLLECTIONS: [1880-present]

HOURS: May 15-Sept 15 1-5, 7-9; Sept 15-May 15 T 1-5

ADMISSION: No charge

SIDNEY

5057
Mondak Heritage Center
120 3rd Ave, 59270 [PO Box 50, 59270]; (p) (406) 482-3500; (c) Richland

Private non-profit/ 1967/ staff: 2(f); 2(p); 30(v)/ members: 475

ART MUSEUM; GENEALOGICAL SOCIETY; HISTORICAL SOCIETY; HISTORY MUSEUM

PROGRAMS: Annual Meeting; Community Outreach; Exhibits; Facility Rental; Family Programs; Festivals; Guided Tours

COLLECTIONS: [1900]

HOURS: Feb-Dec W-F 10-4; Sa-Su 1-4 (summer hours also)

ADMISSION: $2.50, Student $1, Children $1

STANFORD

5058
Judith Basin County Museum
20 3rd St S, 59479 [PO Box 38, 59479]; (p) (406) 566-2277, (406) 566-2974; (c) Judith Basin

County, non-profit/ 1970/ staff: 1(f)

HISTORY MUSEUM: Preserves local history.

COLLECTIONS: 50,000 buttons, 1,000 pairs of salt and pepper shakers, Native American artifacts, photos.

HOURS: June-Aug M-F 9-12/1-5

ADMISSION: Donations accepted

STEVENSVILLE

5059
Historic St. Marys Mission Inc.
W End 4th St, 59870 [PO Box 211, 59870]; (p) (406) 777-5734; (c) Ravalli

Private non-profit/ 1983/ staff: 3(f); 5(p); 9(v)

HISTORIC SITE; HISTORY MUSEUM: Restores, preserves, and maintains the 1866 site of St. Mary's Mission and related artifacts.

PROGRAMS: Community Outreach; Exhibits; Facility Rental; Guided Tours; Interpretation; Lectures; Research Library/Archives; School-Based Curriculum

COLLECTIONS: [1823-1939] Log chapel/residence, furnishings, log house, pharmacy and related equipment, Native American cabin, photos, paintings, tools, research library with 500 rare volumes, maps, photos.

HOURS: Su-Sa 10-5

ADMISSION: $3, Students $1

SUPERIOR

5060
Mineral County Museum and Historical Society
302 2nd Ave E, 59872 [PO Box 533, 59872]; (p) (406) 822-4626; (c) Mineral

County, non-profit/ 1975/ Mineral County/ staff: 2(v)/ members: 25/publication: *Mullan Chronicles*

HISTORICAL SOCIETY: Collects and preserves local history.

PROGRAMS: Annual Meeting; Publication; Research Library/Archives

COLLECTIONS: [1880] Photos, railroad memorabilia, Mullan Military Road.

ADMISSION: No charge

TERRY

5061
Prairie County Museum, Inc.
101 Logan Ave, 59349 [PO Box 368, 59349]; (p) (406) 635-4040; (c) Prairie

Private non-profit/ 1975/ Prairie County Museum, Inc./ staff: 15(v)

THOMPSON FALLS

5062
Sanders County Historical Society
Madison & Maiden Lane, 59873 [PO Box 755, 59873]; (c) Sanders

1980/ staff: 15(v)

HISTORICAL SOCIETY; HISTORY MUSEUM: Preserves and maintains Old County Jail Museum

PROGRAMS: Exhibits; Guided Tours

COLLECTIONS: [1865-present] Photos, jail memorabilia, artifacts.

HOURS: May-Sept Daily 12-4

ADMISSION: Donations accepted

THREE FORKS

5063
Three Forks Area Historical Society
202 S Main St, 59752 [PO Box 116, 59752];
(p) (406) 285-3644; (c) Gallatin

Private non-profit/ 1981/ staff: 40(v)/ members:
250

HISTORIC PRESERVATION AGENCY; HISTORICAL SOCIETY; HISTORY MUSEUM; LIVING HISTORY/OUTDOOR MUSEUM: Maintains the Three Forks Heritage Museum, located in the 1910 bank building.

PROGRAMS: Exhibits; Guided Tours

COLLECTIONS: [Late 19th-early 20th c] Thousands of artifacts from local families, including a barbed wire collection, railroad memorabilia, millitary momentos, an 1810-era anvil.

HOURS: June-Oct M-Sa 9-5, Su 1-5

ADMISSION: Donations accepted

ULM

5064
Ulm Pishkun State Park
342 Ulm-Vaughn Road, 59485 [PO Box 109, 59485]; (p) (406) 866-2217; (f) (406) 866-2218

State/ Montana Fish, Wildlife and Parks/ staff: 4(f)

HISTORIC SITE; STATE PARK; TRIBAL MUSEUM: Preserves history of Native and nonnative communities in the area.

PROGRAMS: Exhibits; Festivals; Interpretation; Lectures; School-Based Curriculum

COLLECTIONS: [Prehistory] Plains Indian artifacts including full-sized buffalo hide tipi, housed in interpretive center.

HOURS: May-Sept Daily 10-6

VIRGINIA CITY

5065
Montana Heritage Commission/ Virginia and Nevada City Project
[PO Box 338, 59755]; (p) (406) 843-5247; (c) Madison

State/ 1997/ staff: 2(f); 20(p); 30(v)

HISTORIC SITE; LIVING HISTORY/OUTDOOR MUSEUM: Preserves and restores Virginia City's gold mining history.

PROGRAMS: Elder's Programs; Exhibits; Facility Rental; Interpretation; Lectures; Living History; Theatre

COLLECTIONS: [1863-1915] Restored original buildings and related displays.

HOURS: May-Sept Daily 9-7

5066
Vigilance Club of Virginia City Thompson-Hickman Museum, The
220 E Wallace St, 59755 [PO Box 295, 59755-0295]; (p) (406) 843-5238; (f) (406) 843-5347; (c) Madison

Private non-profit/ staff: 1(f); 1(p); 3(v)/ members: 15

HERITAGE AREA; HISTORIC PRESERVATION AGENCY; HISTORY MUSEUM: Preserves, interprets, and displays history of Virginia City through educational programs.

PROGRAMS: Community Outreach; Exhibits; Facility Rental; Family Programs; Interpretation

COLLECTIONS: [1864-1899] Artifacts and buildings from Montana's Territorial Capital.

HOURS: May-Sept Daily 10-5

ADMISSION: Donations accepted

5067
Virginia City Madison County Historical Museum
Wallace St, 59755 [PO Box 215, 59755]; (p) (406) 843-5500; (c) Madison

Private non-profit/ 1957/ staff: 3(f); 10(v)

HISTORY MUSEUM: Preserves local mining history.

COLLECTIONS: [1800-1900] Mining artifacts.

HOURS: May-Sept Daily 10-5

ADMISSION: Donations

WHITEHALL

5068
Jefferson Valley Museum, Inc.
303 S Division, 59759 [PO Box 902, 59759]; (p) (406) 287-7813; (c) Jefferson

Private non-profit/ 1990/ staff: 7(v)/ members: 216

HISTORY MUSEUM: Collects and preserves local history.

PROGRAMS: Annual Meeting; Exhibits; Guided Tours; Interpretation; Lectures

COLLECTIONS: [1800-1900] Pioneer artifacts, schools, photos, genealogy, railroad memorabilia housed in former horse and dairy barn.

HOURS: May-Sept T-Su 12-4

ADMISSION: No charge

WIBAUX

5069
Pierre Wibaux Museum Complex
East Orgain, 59353 [PO Box 74, 59353]; (p) (406) 796-9969; (f) (406) 795-2381; (c) Wibaux

County, non-profit/ 1970/ staff: 1(f); 1(v)

HISTORIC SITE; HISTORY MUSEUM; HOUSE MUSEUM

PROGRAMS: Community Outreach; Exhibits; Guided Tours; Interpretation

COLLECTIONS: [1800-present] Pierre Wibaux artifacts.

HOURS: May-Sept Daily 9-5

ADMISSION: No charge

WOLF POINT

5070
Wolf Point Area Historical Society
220 2nd Ave S, 59201 [PO Box 977, 59201]; (p) (406) 653-1912; (c) Roosevelt

Private non-profit/ 1972/ Historical Society Board/ staff: 2(f)/ members: 75

ALLIANCE OF HISTORICAL AGENCIES; HISTORICAL SOCIETY; HISTORY MUSEUM: Preserves history of early settlers in MT.

PROGRAMS: Annual Meeting; Exhibits

COLLECTIONS: [1800-1900] Arrowheads, dolls, cowboy saddles, military uniforms, Native American clothing.

HOURS: June-Aug M-F 10-5

ADMISSION: No charge

NEBRASKA

AINSWORTH

5071
Brown County Historical Society
5th St & Old Hwy 7, 69210 [HC 65 Box 158, 69210]; (p) (402) 387-2061; (c) Brown

Private non-profit/ 1976/ Board of Directors and Officers/ staff: 10(v)/ members: 27/publication: *Tales of Brown County, Nebraska*

GENEALOGICAL SOCIETY; HISTORIC PRESERVATION AGENCY; HISTORIC SITE; HISTORICAL SOCIETY; HISTORY MUSEUM; HOUSE MUSEUM; RESEARCH CENTER: Preserves the history of the county through artifacts, local history books, and programs.

PROGRAMS: Annual Meeting; Community Outreach; Exhibits; Facility Rental; Festivals; Guided Tours; Lectures; Living History; Monthly Meeting; Publication; Research Library/ Archives; School-Based Curriculum

COLLECTIONS: [1882-present] Pioneer tools, kitchenware, clothing, furniture, genealogy files, family files, small farm artifacts, and a local history file.

HOURS: By appt

ADMISSION: No charge/Donations accepted

5072
Coleman House Museum
Old Hwy 7 & 5th St, 69210 [RR 1, Box 189, 69210]; (p) (402) 387-0820

1918

COLLECTIONS: Clothing, library books, furniture; Working on a family history library.

5073
Sellors/Barton Museum
Hwy 20 & Main, 69210 [319 N Walnut, 69210]; (p) (402) 387-2494; (f) (402) 387-1234; www.nebpawer.com/ainswor; (c) Brown

City/ 1992/ City of Ainsworth/ staff: 1(f)

HISTORY MUSEUM

PROGRAMS: Film/Video; Guided Tours

COLLECTIONS: [1883-present] Artifacts, pictures, tools, clothing, furniture, illustrating life of the early settlers.

HOURS: May-Oct Daily

ADMISSION: Donations accepted

ALBION

5074
Boone County Historical Society
11th & Fairview St, 68620 [1025 W Fairview St, 68620]; (c) Boone

County; Private non-profit/ 1968/ Board of Trustees/ staff: 10(v)/ members: 111/publication: *Museum News*

HISTORICAL SOCIETY

PROGRAMS: Annual Meeting; Community

Outreach; Concerts; Exhibits; Facility Rental; Festivals; Guided Tours; Interpretation; Lectures; Publication; Reenactments; Library/Archives

COLLECTIONS: [Late 19th-20th c] Military uniforms and artifacts, vintage clothing, farm equipment, newspapers, vintage rooms, medical artifacts, community/county history, pioneer artifacts, and photographs.

HOURS: June-Aug Sa-Su 1-5

ADMISSION: Donations accepted

ALDA

5075
Merrick Auto Museum
Apollo Ave, Door #8, 68810 [PO Box 188, 68810]; (p) (308) 384-1780; (f) (887) 308-2277; info@antiqueauto.org; www.antiqueauto.org; (c) Hall

Private non-profit/ 1992/ Board of Directors/ staff: 3(f); 2(p)

AUTOMOBILE MUSEUM; RESEARCH CENTER: Collects, preserves, restores, and interprets antique automobiles, related automobiles, and literature.

PROGRAMS: Exhibits; Guided Tours; Interpretation; Research Library/Archives

COLLECTIONS: 65 restored antique autos; extensive auto library; operator's manuals; sales literature; early serials; auto repair manuals; photographs; model car collection; stock certificates; and automobilia.

HOURS: Jun-Aug Sa-Su by appt

ADMISSION: Donations accepted

ALLIANCE

5076
Knight Museum
908 Yellowstone, 69301 [Drawer D, 69301]; (p) (308) 762-2384; museum@panhandle.net; (c) Box Butte

City/ 1963/ City of Alliance/ staff: 1(f); 1(p); 18(v)/ members: 40

HISTORY MUSEUM; RESEARCH CENTER: Displays, houses and catalogs historic memorabilia about Alliance and Box Butte County. Research library for local information.

PROGRAMS: Exhibits; Family Programs; Festivals; Guided Tours; Lectures; Living History; Research Library/Archives

COLLECTIONS: [1880-1960] Pioneer, railroad, Native American, and agricultural displays.

HOURS: Yr May-Sept Daily 10-6; Sept-Apr T-Sa 12-5

ADMISSION: No charge

ARAPAHOE

5077
Furnas and Gosper Counties Museum
401 Nebraska Ave, 68922 [Box 202, 68922]; (c) Furnas

Private non-profit/ 1966/ Furnas and Gosper Counties Historical Society/ staff: 4(v)/ members: 24

HISTORICAL SOCIETY; HISTORY MUSEUM:
Collects, preserves, and displays artifacts from prehistory to present.

PROGRAMS: Annual Meeting; Exhibits; Festivals; Research Library/Archives

COLLECTIONS: [1860s-1970s] Archeological and paleontological collection from area including Native American pottery and stone tools, area newspapers from turn-of-the-century, tools, machinery, and furnishings.

HOURS: May-Sept Sa-Su 12-4 or by appt

ADMISSION: Donations accepted

ASHLAND

5078
Strategic Air Command Museum
I-80 Exit 426, 68003 [28210 W Park Hwy, 68003]; (p) (402) 944-3100; (f) (402) 944-3160; Wschmidt@SACmuseum.org; www.sacmuseum.org; (c) Cass

1972/ Board of Directors/ staff: 20(f); 20(p); 100(v)/ members: 2000/publication: Alert

AVIATION MUSEUM; HISTORY MUSEUM: Preserves and exhibits the history of the Strategic Air Command with aircraft and exhibits.

PROGRAMS: Community Outreach; Exhibits; Facility Rental; Guided Tours; Publication

COLLECTIONS: [Post WW II and Cold War era] Aerospace artifacts, aircraft and missals pertaining to the Strategic Air Command and its mission during the Cold War. Personal artifacts, a large documentary archival collection and an extensive photograph and video collection.

HOURS: Yr Daily 9-5

ADMISSION: $6, Children $3, Seniors $5, Under 5 free

ATKINSON

5079
Sturdevant-McKee Foundation Inc.
308 S Main St, 68713 [PO Box 225, 68713]; (p) (402) 925-2726; (f) (402) 925-2726; stumckee@inetnebr; (c) Holt

Private non-profit/ 1994/ staff: 1(p); 20(v)

HOUSE MUSEUM: Period home, built in 1887, consisting of 9 rooms, a horse barn, coal shed and another house for exhibits.

PROGRAMS: Exhibits; Facility Rental; Guided Tours

COLLECTIONS: [1890-1940] Household furnishings, dishes, letters, books scrapbooks, toys, decorations, clothing, family history, linens, photographs, sheet music, medical equipment, furniture, and artifacts.

HOURS: Yr M-F 10-12/1-4; Sa-Su 1-4

ADMISSION: Donations accepted

AURORA

5080
Hamilton County Historical Society, Plainsman Museum
210 16th St, 68818; (p) (402) 694-6531; smolak@hamilton.net; www.plainsmanmuseum.org; (c) Hamilton

County; Private non-profit/ 1935/ Board of Directors/ staff: 1(f); 1(p); 35(v)/ members:
350/publication: Plainsman Newsletter

ART MUSEUM; GENEALOGICAL SOCIETY; HISTORIC PRESERVATION AGENCY; HISTORICAL SOCIETY; HISTORY MUSEUM: Collects, preserves, and illustrates the history of Hamilton County, Nebraska, through education, exhibits, research, and maintenance of relevant archives and collections.

PROGRAMS: Annual Meeting; Community Outreach; Concerts; Exhibits; Family Programs; Festivals; Guided Tours; Interpretation; Lectures; Publication; Reenactments; Library/Archives; School-Based Curriculum

COLLECTIONS: [1840-1950] Doll collection, fashions, glassware, furniture, horse-drawn equipment, automobiles, railroad collection, Civil War, WW I & II collections, cane and iron toy collections, musical instruments, tractors.

HOURS: Yr Apr 1-Oct 31 M-Sa 9-5, Su 1-5 Nov 1- Mar 31 Daily 1-5

ADMISSION: $4600, Student $2, Seniors $4

BANCROFT

5081
John G. Neihardt Center
306 Elm St, 68004 [PO Box 344, 68004]; (p) (402) 648-3388, (888) 777-4667; (f) (402) 648-3388; neihardt@gpcom.com; www.neihardt.com; (c) Cuming

Joint/ 1965/ State of NE Hist Soc; John G. Neihardt Foundation/ staff: 2(f); 2(p)/ members: 385/publication: Neihardt Foundation News

GARDEN; HISTORIC SITE; RESEARCH CENTER: Dedicated to history and literature of the Plains, focusing on the works of John Neihardt.

PROGRAMS: Annual Meeting; Exhibits; Facility Rental; Family Programs; Festivals; Garden Tours; Guided Tours; Interpretation; Lectures; Publication; Research Library/Archives

COLLECTIONS: [1881-1973] Personal and period artifacts, video and audio tapes, works by and about John Neihardt and Native Americans of NE and SD.

HOURS: Yr Mar-Dec M-Sa 9-5, Su 1:30-5; Jan-Feb M-F 9-5

ADMISSION: Donations requested

BAYARD

5082
Bayard's Chimney Rock Museum
S end of Main St, 69334 [PO Box 313, 69334]; (c) Morrill

Private non-profit/ 1997/ Board Members/ members: 220

HISTORIC SITE; HISTORY MUSEUM: Seeks to gather and collect materials pertaining to the early days of the Bayard area.

PROGRAMS: Annual Meeting; Exhibits

COLLECTIONS: [1880-1960] Agriculture and business artifacts and collections reflective of area history and development.

HOURS: May-Sept M-9-12, Sa-Su 1-4

ADMISSION: Donations accepted

5083
Chimney Rock National Historic Site
5 miles S on Hwy 92 on Chimney Rock Rd, 69334 [PO Box F, 69334]; (p) (308) 586-2581; chimrock@scottsbluff.net; www.nps.gov/chro/

HISTORIC SITE; NATIONAL PARK: Preserves most famous site on Oregon Trail.

PROGRAMS: Exhibits; Film/Video

HOURS: Yr Apr 1-Sept 30 M-Su 9- 6; Oct 1- Mar 31 M-Su 9-5

ADMISSION: $1; Children w/adults free

BEATRICE

5084
Gage County Historical Society
101 N 2nd St, 68310 [PO Box 793, 68310]; (p) (402) 228-1679; www4.infoanalytic.com/H beatrice.HTML#Gage; (c) Gage

Private non-profit/ 1971/ staff: 2(f); 1(p); 100(v)/ members: 300/publication: *Quarterly Express*

HISTORIC SITE; HISTORICAL SOCIETY; HISTORY MUSEUM; LIVING HISTORY/OUTDOOR MUSEUM; RESEARCH CENTER: Collects and preserves significant artifacts on the history of Gage county people, industry, agriculture, medicine, and railroads.

PROGRAMS: Annual Meeting; Community Outreach; Concerts; Exhibits; Facility Rental; Family Programs; Festivals; Interpretation; Living History; Publication; Research Library/ Archives

COLLECTIONS: [1854-1960] 11,000 objects, including: 4,400 photographic images, 3,400 archival, 1,200 textiles, 400 communication equipment, 860 agricultural, 860 science and technology, 250 recreational, 220 Native America, and 90 transportation objects.

HOURS: Yr Summer: T-Sa 9-12/1-5, Su 1:30-5; Winter: T-F 9-12, 1-5, Su 1:30-5

ADMISSION: Donations accepted

5085
Homestead National Monument of America
4 miles W of Beatrice NE on Hwy 4, 68310 [Rt 3 Box 47, 68310]; (p) (402) 223-3514; (f) (402) 228-4231; www.nps.gov/home; (c) Gage

Federal/ 1936/ National Park Service/ staff: 8(f); 3(p); 30(v)/publication: *Homestead, Homestead Trail Guide*

HISTORIC SITE: Commemorates the (Homestead Act) free land idea site.

PROGRAMS: Community Outreach; Concerts; Exhibits; Family Programs; Festivals; Film/Video; Guided Tours; Interpretation; Living History; Publication; Reenacts; Research Library/Archives; School-Based Curriculum; Theatre

COLLECTIONS: [1862-1936] Items relating to the America homesteading era.

HOURS: Yr Daily M-F 8:30-5, Sa-Su 9-5

ADMISSION: No charge

5086
Palmer-Epard Cabin
4 miles W of Beatrice, NE on NE Hwy 4, 68310 [Rt #3, PO Box 46, 68310]; (p) (402) 223-3415; (f) (402) 228-4231; home_superintendent@nps.gov; www.nps.gov/

1867/ National Park Service

COLLECTIONS: [1862-1936] Photographs, documents, artifacts, diaries from homesteading era.

HOURS: Yr

BELLEVUE

5087
Sarpy County Historical Society
2402 Clay St, 68005-3932; (p) (402) 292-1880; (c) Sarpy

County/ 1934/ staff: 1(f); 45(v)/ members: 350

HISTORIC SITE; HISTORICAL SOCIETY; HISTORY MUSEUM: Operates the museum, old log cabin, the 1869 depot, and the Moses Merrill Mission site. Archives offer marriage records, obituaries, and court records.

PROGRAMS: Annual Meeting; Community Outreach; Exhibits; Facility Rental; Family Programs; Interpretation; Lectures; Publication; Research Library/Archives

COLLECTIONS: [1820s-1920s] Indian artifacts, fur trading artifacts, Pioneer and farming artifacts. 5 furnished period rooms.

HOURS: Yr T-Su 9-4

ADMISSION: $2, Children $1, Seniors $1

BOYS TOWN

5088
Boys Town Hall of History and Father Flanagan House
14057 Flanagan Blvd, 68010; (p) (402) 498-1186; (f) (402) 498-1159; lynccht@boystown.org; www.boystown.org; (c) Douglas

Private non-profit/ 1986/ Father Flanagan's Boys' Home/ staff: 2(f); 25(p); 25(v)/publication: *Boys Town Journal*

HISTORIC SITE; HISTORY MUSEUM; HOUSE MUSEUM: Preserves and interprets the local history.

PROGRAMS: Community Outreach; Exhibits; Garden Tours; Guided Tours; Publication; Research Library/Archives

COLLECTIONS: [Early 20th c] Collection of 500,000 photographs, a document collection of three million items, an artifact, film, and tape library in the Hall of History archives.

HOURS: May-Aug Daily 9-5; Sept-Apr 10-4:30

BREWSTER

5089
Blaine County History
HC 63, Box 33, 68821; (p) (308) 547-2474; (c) Blaine

Private for-profit/ 1988/ staff: 1(p)

GENEALOGICAL SOCIETY; HISTORICAL SOCIETY

COLLECTIONS: [1888-1954]

BROKEN BOW

5090
Custer County Historical Society
445 S 9th St, 68822; (p) (308) 872-5148; custer.county.history@navix.net; www.roots web.com/~necuster; (c) Custer

Private non-profit/ 1968/ staff: 1(p); 50(v)/ members: 165/publication: *Custer Connections (cookbook)*

GENEALOGICAL SOCIETY; HISTORIC SITE; HISTORICAL SOCIETY; HISTORY MUSEUM; HOUSE MUSEUM: Collects and preserves information, genealogies, and SD Butcher photographs relating to county.

PROGRAMS: Concerts; Exhibits; Film/Video; Guided Tours; Interpretation; Lectures; Publication; Research Library/Archives

COLLECTIONS: [1887- present] Local newspapers, rural school records, books on local history, genealogical files.

HOURS: Yr May-Sep M-Sa 10-5; Oct-Apr M-F 1-5

ADMISSION: No charge

BROWNVILLE

5091
Brownville Historical Society
Main St, 68321 [PO Box 1, 68321]; (p) (402) 825-6001; (c) Nemaha

Private for-profit/ 1949/ City/ staff: 15(f)/ members: 300

HISTORIC SITE; HISTORICAL SOCIETY; HISTORY MUSEUM; HOUSE MUSEUM

PROGRAMS: Annual Meeting; Community Outreach; Exhibits; Festivals; Guided Tours; Reenacts

COLLECTIONS: [19th-20th c] Furniture, clothing, buggies, and dental equipment.

HOURS: Apr-Sept Sa-Su 10-5 or by appt

ADMISSION: $1

5092
Captain Bailey Museum, The
5th & Main Sts, 68321 [Main St, 68321]; (p) (402) 825-6001

1877/ staff: 4(f); 5(v)

COLLECTIONS: Completely furnished house as lived in 1870; one children's room, one room with Gov. Furnas (1874) articles.

HOURS: Seasonal

BURWELL

5093
Fort Hartsuff State Historical Park
4 miles NW of Elyn, 68823 [Rt 1 Box 37, 68823]; (p) (308) 346-4715; (c) Valley

State/ 1874/ NE Government Parks Division/ staff: 2(f); 4(p); 4(v)

HISTORIC SITE; HISTORY MUSEUM; LIVING HISTORY/OUTDOOR MUSEUM; STATE PARK: 1870's period federal military post, original lime/ concrete buildings.

PROGRAMS: Exhibits; Interpretation; Living History

COLLECTIONS: [1874-1881] Well preserved lime/concrete buildings, period furnishings, firearms of the 1870s.

HOURS: Yr Daily

ADMISSION: $2/vehicle

CALLAWAY

5094
Seven Valleys Historical Society
Kimball & Grand Ave, 68825 [Rt 1 Box 45, 68825]; (p) (308) 836-2728; (c) Custer

Joint/ 1968/ City; County/ staff: 12(v)

HISTORICAL SOCIETY: Preserving local history and artifacts for future generations.

PROGRAMS: Annual Meeting; Guided Tours

COLLECTIONS: [1880- present] Local newspapers, publications; artifacts from local clubs and agencies; cemetery information; obituaries; family genealogies.

HOURS: Yr by appt

ADMISSION: Donations accepted

CHADRON

5095
Dawes County Historical Society, Inc.
341 Country Club Rd, 69337 [PO Box 1319, 69337]; (p) (308) 432-4999; (c) Dawes

Private non-profit/ 1935/ Dawes County Historical Society Board/ staff: 59(v)/ members: 280

HISTORICAL SOCIETY; HISTORY MUSEUM: Encourages research and inquiry into records, letters, articles, artifacts, places, and incidents of historical importance to Dawes county.

PROGRAMS: Annual Meeting; Exhibits; Facility Rental; Family Programs; Film/Video; Guided Tours; Interpretation; Lectures; Publication; Reenactments; Research Library/Archives

COLLECTIONS: [1885-present] Local and family histories, photos, artifacts, buildings, newspapers; county civil, criminal records; marriages, delayed birth records, caboose, genealogy research materials, cemetery records, obituaries, diaries, farm machinery.

HOURS: Jun-Sept M-Sa 10-4, Su 1-5

ADMISSION: Donations accepted

5096
Museum of the Fur Trade
6321 Hwy 20, 69337; (p) (308) 432-3843; (f) (308) 432-5963; museum@furtrade.org; www.furtrade.org; (c) Dawes

Private non-profit/ 1949/ staff: 1(f); 35(v)/ members: 3000/publication: *Museum of the Fur Trade Quarterly*

HISTORIC SITE; HISTORY MUSEUM: Presents, interprets, and exhibits history of the North American fur trade.

PROGRAMS: Exhibits; Facility Rental; Interpretation; Publication

COLLECTIONS: [1400-1900] All related to North American fur trade, large collection of NW guns, beadwork, blankets, trade silver, trade goods, traps, furs.

HOURS: May-Sept Daily 8-5

ADMISSION: $2.50

CHAPPELL

5097
Chappell Museum Association, The
701 5th St, 69129 [PO Box 324, 69129]; (p) (308) 874-3441; (c) Deuel

City/ 1981/ Sudman-Neumann Heritage House/ staff: 40(v)/ members: 91

HOUSE MUSEUM: Preserves historic house and furnishings for educational, historical and cultural purposes.

PROGRAMS: Annual Meeting; Community Outreach; Exhibits; Family Programs; Guided Tours

COLLECTIONS: [Early 20th c] Antique furniture, paintings and dishes; over 100 dolls - some Madame Alexander; 20 Aaron Pyle lithographs; historical picture display rack; ladies and men's vintage clothing; military uniforms of various wars.

HOURS: Yr Su 2-5

ADMISSION: $1

CHARDRON

5098
Mari Sandoz Heritage Society
1000 Main St, 69337; (p) (308) 432-6276; (f) (308) 432-6464; dgreen@csc.edu; (c) Dawes

Private non-profit/ 1971/ Mari Sandoz Heritage Society/ staff: 6(v)/ members: 158/publication: *Sandoz Society Newsletter*

HISTORY MUSEUM; RESEARCH CENTER: Educates about the objectives of the late Mari Sandoz, western writer.

PROGRAMS: Annual Meeting; Community Outreach; Exhibits; Lectures; Publication; Library/Archives; School-Based Curriculum

COLLECTIONS: [Late 19th-20th c] Artifacts, archives, library resources related to the work of Mari Sandoz and to the history and culture of the Northern Plains.

HOURS: Yr by appt

ADMISSION: No charge

CLARKSON

5099
Clarkson Historical Society Museum
221 Pine St, 68629 [319 E 4th St, 68629]; (p) (402) 892-3293; (c) Colfax

Private non-profit/ 1967/ staff: 10(v)/ members: 150

HISTORICAL SOCIETY: Preserves the history of Clarkson ancestors.

PROGRAMS: Annual Meeting; Community Outreach; Exhibits; Festivals; Guided Tours

COLLECTIONS: Czech clothing and articles pertaining to the pioneers who settled the town, antiques

HOURS: By appt only, last wknd June

ADMISSION: Donations accepted

CLAY CENTER

5100
Clay County Historical Society
316 W Gelnvil, 68933 [PO Box 201, 68933]; (p) (402) 762-3563; (c) Clay

County, non-profit; Private non-profit/ 1972/ Clay County Historical Society/ staff: 1(p); 140(v)/ members: 325/publication: *Historical News*

HISTORIC PRESERVATION AGENCY; HISTORIC SITE; HISTORICAL SOCIETY; HISTO-

RY MUSEUM; LIVING HISTORY/OUTDOOR MUSEUM: Preserves local history.

PROGRAMS: Annual Meeting; Community Outreach; Exhibits; Family Programs; Festivals; Guided Tours; Interpretation; Lectures; Living History; Publication; Research Library/Archives; School-Based Curriculum

COLLECTIONS: [1867-present] Early radio station, flour mill, woodworking shop, parlor, kitchen, one- room school, incubator factory, agricultural equipment, railroad caboose, moravian catholic church with furnishings.

HOURS: Yr Sa-Su 1-5, or by appt

ADMISSION: Donations accepted

COOMSTOCK

5101
Dowse Sod House
HCR 68 Box 72, 68828; (p) (308) 628-4231, (308) 527-3462; (c) Custer

Private non-profit/ 1900

HISTORIC SITE; HOUSE MUSEUM: Preserves historic sod house.

PROGRAMS: Concerts; Guided Tours; Living History

COLLECTIONS: [1900-present] Sod house.

HOURS: Yr Daily

ADMISSION: No charge, Donations accepted

COZAD

5102
Cozad Historical Society—The 100th Meridian Museum
206 E 8th St, 69130 [PO Box 325, 69130]; (p) (308) 784-1100; (c) Dawson

Private non-profit/ 1993/ Cozad Historical Society/ members: 310/publication: *100th Meridian News*

HISTORICAL SOCIETY: Preserves history and artifacts of local area.

PROGRAMS: Annual Meeting; Community Outreach; Concerts; Exhibits; Family Programs; Festivals; Guided Tours; Interpretation; Lectures; Living History; Publication; Research Library/Archives; School-Based Curriculum

COLLECTIONS: [1870s-present] Yellowstone touring coach for the Chamber of Commerce; 1927 Chevrolet truck, local displays.

HOURS: May-Sept M-F 10-5, Sa 1-5, Su by appt

ADMISSION: Donations requested

5103
Robert Henri Museum and Historical Walkway
218 E 8th St, 69130 [Box 355, 69130]; (p) (308) 784-4145; (c) Dawson

Private non-profit/ 1986/ Volunteer Board/ staff: 1(f); 12(v)/ members: 200

ART MUSEUM; HISTORIC SITE; HISTORICAL SOCIETY; HISTORY MUSEUM: Hotel and home of Robert Henri during that last quarter of the 1800s. Furnished in period furniture, with some of Henri's paintings (not originals) and early sketches.

PROGRAMS: Community Outreach; Exhibits;

Film/Video; Garden Tours; Guided Tours; Living History

COLLECTIONS: [1800s] Hotel, pony express station, church, one room school.

HOURS: May-Oct M-F 10-5, Sat 10-5 and by appt; Oct-May Su-F

ADMISSION: $2

CRAWFORD

5104
Fort Robinson Museum
3200 Hwy 20, Ft Robinson St Pk, 3 mi W of Crawford, 69339 [PO Box 304, 69339-3112]; (p) (308) 665-2919; (f) (308) 665-2917; fort rob@bbc.net; (c) Dawes

State/ 1956/ Nebraska Historical Society/ staff: 5(f); 5(p)

HISTORIC SITE; RESEARCH CENTER: Preserves and interprets the historic resources associated with Fort Robinson for public benefit, adds to those resources through research.

PROGRAMS: Exhibits; Guided Tours; Interpretation; Research Library/Archives

COLLECTIONS: [1873-1948] Artifacts connected with the history of Red Cloud Agency (1873-1877) and Fort Robinson (1874-1948).

HOURS: Oct 1-May 1 M-F 8-5; May 1- Oct 1 M-Su 8-5

ADMISSION: $2; Child w/adult free, group rates

DAKOTA CITY

5105
Dakota County Historical Society
[PO Box 971, 68731]; (p) (402) 698-2288; (c) Dakota

County/ 1963/ Executive Committee/ staff: 3(p); 17(v)/ members: 150/publication: History of Dakota County, Nebraska

HISTORICAL SOCIETY: Preserves Victorian era farm life with implements, schooling and church artifacts.

PROGRAMS: Exhibits; Facility Rental; Interpretation; Publication

COLLECTIONS: [1860-1900] Collection includes machinery, dental equipment, pioneer utensils, county newspapers, country school still in use.

HOURS: June-Aug Su 2-4 or by appt

ADMISSION: $1

DENTON

5106
Denton Community Historical Society
[PO Box 405, 68339]; (p) (402) 797-3245; cs20231@navix.net; www.geocities.com/heartland/prairie/1890/#home; (c) Lancaster

Private non-profit/ 1996/ staff: 12(v)/ members: 67/publication: Trails and Trails Newsletter

HISTORIC PRESERVATION AGENCY; HISTORIC SITE; HISTORICAL SOCIETY: Preserves history of Denton and surrounding areas of the community with photos and artifacts.

PROGRAMS: Annual Meeting; Community Outreach; Exhibits; Festivals; Film/Video;

Guided Tours; Publication

COLLECTIONS: [1871-present] Gun, furniture, pictures, oral history.

DEWITT

5107
Dewitt Historical Society
303 E Fillmore, 68341 [RRI Box 226, 68341]; (p) (402) 683-5815; jp52914@navix.net; (c) Saline

Private non-profit/ 1991/ staff: 6(v)/ members: 25

HISTORICAL SOCIETY: Collects and preserves the history and artifacts of DeWitt community.

PROGRAMS: Annual Meeting; Exhibits

COLLECTIONS: [1900-present] Personal lifetime collection of DeWitt history of Gerald Badman, over 100 years of DeWitt newspapers for genealogy research.

HOURS: Yr Su 2-4, and special occasions

ADMISSION: No charge

DORCHESTER

5108
Saline County Historical Society
Hwy 33, 68343 [1127 E 2nd St, Friend, 68359]; (p) (402) 947-2911; (f) (402) 947-2911; (c) Saline

County/ 1956/ staff: 2(p); 15(v)/ members: 35

GENEALOGICAL SOCIETY; HISTORICAL SOCIETY; HISTORY MUSEUM; HOUSE MUSEUM: Preserves items pertaining to history of Saline county.

PROGRAMS: Annual Meeting; Community Outreach; Exhibits; Research Library/Archives

COLLECTIONS: [1865-present]

HOURS: Mar-Dec Su 2-5 and by appt

ADMISSION: Donations accepted

ELGIN

5109
Elgin Historical Society
202 Bowen, 68636 [Box 30, 68636]; (c) Antelope

Private non-profit/ 1991/ Board of Directors/ members: 40

HISTORIC PRESERVATION AGENCY; HISTORICAL SOCIETY; HISTORY MUSEUM; LIVING HISTORY/OUTDOOR MUSEUM: Young organization focusing on fund-raising.

PROGRAMS: Annual Meeting; Festivals; Lectures

COLLECTIONS: [19th-20th c] Artifacts.

ELM CREEK

5110
Chevyland Auto Museum
7245 Buffalo Creek Rd, 68836; (p) (308) 856-4208; (c) Buffalo

Private for-profit/ 1975

HISTORY MUSEUM: Museum of classic automobiles.

PROGRAMS: Automobile Museum; Living History

COLLECTIONS: [1915-1970] 100 Classic Chevys, 50 motorcycles

HOURS: May-Sept Daily 8-5

ADMISSION: $4, Children $2, Under 10 free

ELMWOOD

5111
Bess Streeter Aldrich House and Museum
204 East F St, 68349 [PO Box 167, 68349]; (p) (402) 994-3855; marciab@hotmail.com; www.lincolnne.com/nonprofit/bsaf; (c) Cass

Private non-profit/ 1972/ Bess Streeter Aldrich Foundation/ staff: 1(p); 5(v)/ members: 260

HOUSE MUSEUM: Preserves and promotes the writings and memorabilia of Bess Streeter Aldrich, a nationally recognized author.

PROGRAMS: Annual Meeting; Facility Rental; Festivals; Garden Tours; Guided Tours; Interpretation; School-Based Curriculum

COLLECTIONS: [1920-1946] Manuscripts, family memorabilia, original furniture, literary displays, paintings, sculpture, photographs, and book covers.

HOURS: Yr W, Th, Sa-Su 2-5

ADMISSION: $3, Family $10

FAIRBURY

5112
Fairbury City Museum
1128 Elm St, 68352; (p) (402) 729-3707; (c) Jefferson

City/ 1952/ staff: 1(f); 7(v)

HISTORIC PRESERVATION AGENCY; HISTORICAL SOCIETY; HISTORY MUSEUM: Museum of the history of Jefferson County.

PROGRAMS: Exhibits; Guided Tours

COLLECTIONS: Railroad, schools, furniture, dishes, clothing, farm related, photo, military, and materials.

HOURS: Yr Th, Sa- Su 1-4 and by appt

ADMISSION: No charge

5113
Rock Creek Station State Historical Park
57425 710 Rd, 68352; (p) (402) 729-5777; www.ngpc.state.ne.us/parks/rcstat.html; (c) Jefferson

State/ 1980/ NE Game and Parks Comission/ staff: 3(f); 8(p)

HISTORIC SITE; HISTORY MUSEUM; STATE PARK: Historic interpretation of the California-Oregon Trail, Pony Express, and road ranching. Preserves area where deep trail ruts are visible. The park is noted as the starting point of the Wild Bill Hickok- David McCanles fracas.

PROGRAMS: Exhibits; Guided Tours; Interpretation; Living History; Theatre

COLLECTIONS: [1850-1865] Period artifacts pertaining to the California-Oregon Trail, Pony Express and road ranching, materials on the Hickok/ McCanles fracas.

HOURS: Apr Sa-Su 1-5; May-Sept Daily 9-5; Sept-Oct Sa-Su 1-5

ADMISSION: $2.50/vehicle

FAIRMONT

5114
Fillmore County Historical Society Museum
600 Fairmont Ave, 68354 [PO Box 373, 68354]; (p) (402) 268-3607; 1p71746@navix.net; (c) Fillmore

County/ 1987/ Fillmore County Historical Society/ staff: 12(p); 1(v)/ members: 112

HISTORICAL SOCIETY: Preserves local history.

PROGRAMS: Annual Meeting; Community Outreach; Exhibits; Guided Tours; Interpretation

COLLECTIONS: [1865-present] Photographs, medical artifacts, household utensils, farm implements and tools, clothing histories, war memorabilia especially WW II.

HOURS: Apr-Nov W and by appt, Nov-Mar by appt

ADMISSION: Donations accepted

FORT CALHOUN

5115
Fort Atkinson State Historical Park
7th & Madison, 68023 [PO Box 230, 68023]; (p) (402) 468-5611; (f) (402) 468-5066; ftat kin@ngpc.state.ne.us; www.ngpc.stat.ne.us; (c) Washington

State/ NE Game and Parks/ staff: 2(f); 4(p); 35(v)

HISTORIC SITE; HISTORY MUSEUM; LIVING HISTORY/OUTDOOR MUSEUM: In the process of reconstructing Fort Atkinson. Visitor center, museum and exhibits in the fort.

PROGRAMS: Film/Video; Guided Tours; Interpretation; Lectures; Living History

COLLECTIONS: [1820-1830] Artifacts from the archeological excavations including military items, tools, and personal items.

HOURS: May and Oct Daily 9-5

ADMISSION: $2/vehicle w/NE Park Sticker

5116
Washington County Historical Association
104 N 14th St, Box 25, 68023; (p) (402) 468-5740; info@huntel.net; www.newashcohist.org; (c) Washington

Private non-profit/ 1938/ staff: 4(p)/ members: 162/publication: *Newsletter*

HISTORIC SITE; HISTORICAL SOCIETY; HISTORY MUSEUM; HOUSE MUSEUM: Preserves history of Washington county, including Fort Atkinson, 1819-1827 and early pioneers who began occupying the area as early as the 1840s.

PROGRAMS: Annual Meeting; Exhibits; Guided Tours; Interpretation; Lectures; Publication; Research Library/Archives

COLLECTIONS: [1785-present]

HOURS: Mar-Dec W and F all day, Sa-Su 1:30-4:30

ADMISSION: Donations accepted

FREMONT

5117
Dodge County Historical Society/ Louis E. May Museum
1643 Nye Ave, 68025 [PO Box 766, 68025]; (p) (402) 721-4515; (f) (402) 721-8354; (c) Dodge

County/ 1955/ Dodge County/ staff: 3(p); 125(v)/ members: 400

GARDEN; HISTORIC SITE; HISTORICAL SOCIETY; HOUSE MUSEUM: Collects and preserves artifacts, documents, and local historic sites.

PROGRAMS: Annual Meeting; Concerts; Exhibits; Garden Tours; Guided Tours

COLLECTIONS: [1820-1920] Period furniture from 1820-1920, library, research materials, two gardens.

HOURS: Apr-Dec W-Su 1:30-4:30

ADMISSION: $2.50, Children $0.50; Under 6 free

5118
Louis E. May Museum
1643 N Nye Ave, 68025 [PO Box 776, 68026]; (p) (402) 721-4515; (f) (402) 721-8254; dchs-may@teknetwork.com; connect fremont.org

1874/ staff: 1(f); 3(p)

COLLECTIONS: [Late 1800s-early 1900s] Parlor set of John C. Fremont; furniture, photographics, city directories, and cemetery records.

HOURS: Apr-Dec W-Su 1:30-4:30

GERING

5119
Farm and Ranch Museum
2930 M St, 69341-0398; (p) (308) 436-1989; farm@bbc.net; museums2go.com/farm; (c) Scotts Bluff

Private non-profit/ 1986/ Farm and Ranch Museum/ staff: 30(v)/ members: 100

HISTORY MUSEUM: Volunteer organization to preserve history of western NE agriculture.

PROGRAMS: Annual Meeting; Community Outreach; Exhibits; Festivals; Guided Tours; Interpretation; Lectures; Living History

COLLECTIONS: [1880-1950] Describe, interpret, and preserve agriculture of the area.

HOURS: Jun-Oct M-Sa 10-5, Su 1-5

ADMISSION: No charge

5120
North Platte Valley Historical Association, Inc.
11th & J Sts, 69341 [Box 435, 69341]; (p) (308) 436-5411; (c) Scotts Bluff

1961/ Board of Directors/ staff: 1(f); 1(p); 50(v)/ members: 414/publication: *Museum Musings*

HISTORICAL SOCIETY; HISTORY MUSEUM: Collects, preserves, and interprets the history of the North Platte Valley in Western NE.

PROGRAMS: Annual Meeting; Community Outreach; Exhibits; Guided Tours; Interpretation; Lectures; Living History; Publication; Reenactments; Research Library/Archives

COLLECTIONS: [Pre-history- 1950s] Indian

artifacts, tools, furnishings, clothing of early settlers, horse drawn equipment, military, early quilts, and photographs.

HOURS: May-Sept Daily M-Sa 8:30-5, Su 1-5

ADMISSION: $3, Children $0.50

5121
Scotts Bluff National Monument
Hwy 92 W, 69341 [PO Box 27, 69341]; (p) (308) 436-4340; (f) (308) 436-7611; (c) Scotts Bluff

Federal/ 1919/ staff: 11(f); 10(p); 1(v)

HISTORY MUSEUM; NATIONAL PARK: Preserves and provides access to remnants of the Oregon Trail and the natural landscape within the monument's boundaries.

PROGRAMS: Exhibits; Film/Video; Guided Tours; Interpretation; Lectures; Living History; Research Library/Archives

COLLECTIONS: [1840s-1890] Oregon Trail relics, art, fossils, natural history specimens, archeological matter, and archival items, and William Henry Jackson collection of paintings, photos, and drawings.

HOURS: Yr Daily Sept-May 8-5 Jun-Aug 8-7

ADMISSION: $5/vehicle

GORDON

5122
Tri State Old Time Cowboys Museum
4th & Oak St, 69343 [PO Box 202, 69343-0202]; (c) Sheridon

Private non-profit/ 1967/ Royal McGaughey/ staff: 4(f)/ members: 300

HISTORIC PRESERVATION AGENCY; HISTORY MUSEUM; LIVING HISTORY/OUTDOOR MUSEUM: Old time rancher cowboy historical museum.

PROGRAMS: Annual Meeting; Community Outreach; Exhibits; Family Programs; Festivals; Film/Video; Publication

COLLECTIONS: Items donated by old timers and their families: saddles, spurs, chuck wagon, bridles, brands, old photos.

HOURS: June-Sept Daily 1-5 or by appt

ADMISSION: No charge

GOTHENBURG

5123
Gothenberg Historical Society
522 9th St, 69138 [PO Box 153, 69138]; (c) Dawson

Private non-profit/ 1982/ Board of Trustees/ staff: 4(v)/ members: 45

HISTORICAL SOCIETY; HISTORY MUSEUM: Preserve and display historical items and serve as a local history research center.

PROGRAMS: Annual Meeting; Exhibits; Research Library/Archives

COLLECTIONS: [1882-present] Local history including items of the local German and Swedish populations.

HOURS: June-Aug

ADMISSION: No charge

5124
Pony Express Station
15th & Lake Ave, 69138 [1617 Ave A, 69138];
(p) (308) 537-2680; (c) Dawson

City/ 1954/ staff: 3(f); 3(p)/publication: *Pony Express Times*

HISTORIC SITE; HISTORY MUSEUM: Preserves Pony Express station as museum.

PROGRAMS: Exhibits; Guided Tours; Publication

COLLECTIONS: [1860] Replica of Pony Express mailbag, maps of the trails (Pony Express, Oregon, Mormon), Indian artifacts, memorabilia of the era.

HOURS: May, Sept Daily 9-6; Jun-Aug 8-8

ADMISSION: No charge

5125
Sod House Museum
I-80 & Hwy 47, 69138 [1617 Ave A, 69138];
(p) (308) 537-2680; (c) Dawson

Private for-profit/ 1988/ Private/ staff: 3(f); 3(p)

HISTORIC SITE; HISTORY MUSEUM; HOUSE MUSEUM: Dedicated to preserving sod house history. A farmstead setting features a barn housing photographs and memorabilia, a sod house.

PROGRAMS: Exhibits; Family Programs; Festivals; Guided Tours

COLLECTIONS: [1870-1900] Indian artifacts; photos of sod houses; old wooden windmills; barbed-wire, sculptures of a buffalo, horse, and Indian; and a giant sod-breaking plow.

HOURS: May and Sept Daily 9-6; Jun-Aug 8-8

ADMISSION: No charge

GRAND ISLAND

5126
Stuhr Museum of the Prairie Pioneer
3133 W Hwy 34, 68802 [PO Box 1505, 68802];
(p) (308) 385-5316; (f) (308) 385-5028; www.
stuhrmuseum.org; (c) Hall

County; Private non-profit/ 1961/ Board of Trustees/ staff: 20(f); 85(p); 200(v)/ members: 2200

HISTORY MUSEUM: Preserves and portrays the story of the pioneer town builders who create the first communities in NE.

PROGRAMS: Community Outreach; Concerts; Elder's Programs; Exhibits; Facility Rental; Family Programs; Guided Tours; Interpretation; Lectures; Living History; Publication; Reenactments; Research Library/Archives; School-Based Curriculum

COLLECTIONS: [1840s-1920s] 125,000 late 19th and early 20th c. artifacts, including 61 original buildings; 10 railcars; 60,000 manuscripts and photographs; and 500 periodicals.

HOURS: Yr May-Sept Daily 9-5; Oct-Apr Daily M-Sa 9-5, Su 1-5

ADMISSION: $7.25, Children $4, Seniors $6.50, Under 7 free (less in winter)

GRANT

5127
Perkins County Historical Society
Central Ave & 6th St, 69104 [PO Box 192, 69104]; (c) Perkins

County; Private non-profit/ 1950/ Perkins County Historical Society/ staff: 1(p); 10(v)

HISTORIC PRESERVATION AGENCY; HISTORIC SITE; HISTORICAL SOCIETY; HISTORY MUSEUM; HOUSE MUSEUM: Volunteer organization that oversees the property, keeps it in repair and opens it to the public in the summer and for special tours if requested.

PROGRAMS: Annual Meeting; Community Outreach; Exhibits; Family Programs; Film/Video; Guided Tours

COLLECTIONS: [1890- present] Historical furnished house, country school complete with desks and supplies, a museum building with newspaper collection of the county and numerous exhibits of memorabilia of the early history of Perkins County.

HOURS: Jun-Aug Su 2-4:30 and by appt

ADMISSION: No charge

GREELEY

5128
Greeley County Historical Society
Court House, 68842 [Box 6, 68842]; (c) Greeley

Joint/ County; City/ staff: 4(v)

HISTORIC PRESERVATION AGENCY; HISTORIC SITE; HISTORICAL SOCIETY; HISTORY MUSEUM; HOUSE MUSEUM: Displays things of historical value and files historical information.

PROGRAMS: Annual Meeting; Community Outreach; Exhibits; Family Programs; Film/Video; Guided Tours; Living History; Research Library/Archives

COLLECTIONS: Books, military, tools, clothing, sports equipment, kitchen articles, photography equipment, and pictures, crafts, business equipment.

HOURS: Yr M-F 9-4:30

ADMISSION: No charge

HARRISBURG

5129
Banner County Historical Society
200 N Pennsylvania, 69345; (p) (308) 436-4514; (c) Banner

1968/ staff: 20(v)/ members: 75

HISTORICAL SOCIETY: Preserve the history of Banner County and the surrounding area through the collection and display of artifacts and family and oral histories.

PROGRAMS: Annual Meeting; Exhibits; Festivals; Guided Tours; Research Library/Archives

COLLECTIONS: [Late 19th-early 20th c] Artifacts pertinent to illustrating the settlement and the way of life of the area's prairie pioneers.

HOURS: May-Sept Su 1:30-5

HARRISON

5130
Agate Fossil Beds National Monument
301 River Rd, 69346; (p) (308) 668-2211; (f) (308) 668-2318; agfo_ranger_activities@nps.gov; www.nps.gov/agfo/; (c) Sioux

Federal/ 1965/ National Park Service/ staff: 7(f); 5(p); 2(v)

HISTORIC SITE; HOUSE MUSEUM; RESEARCH CENTER: Preserves a 3000 acre preserve along the upper Niobrara River and maintains a museum that features the history of paleontological excavations of Early Miocene mammals, a cameo Lakota Indian collection, and family archives of "Captain" James Cook's Agate Springs Ranch.

PROGRAMS: Exhibits; Guided Tours; Interpretation; Research Library/Archives

COLLECTIONS: [1870-1940] Remnants of the homespun Cook Museum of Natural History: fossils, archaeological artifacts, 500 High Plains Indian artifacts, family archives and photographs of the Agate Springs Ranch, and the Harold Cook Paleontological Library.

HOURS: Yr May-Sept Daily 8-6; Sept-May Daily 8-5

ADMISSION: $2

HASTINGS

5131
Adams County Historical Society
1400 N Burlington Ave, 68902 [PO Box 102, 68902]; (p) (402) 463-5838; achs@tcgcs.com; www.tcgcs.com/~achs/index.html; (c) Adams

Private non-profit/ 1965/ staff: 1(f); 20(v)/ members: 920/publication: *Historical News*

HISTORICAL SOCIETY; HISTORY MUSEUM: Maintains a research archive.

PROGRAMS: Annual Meeting; Community Outreach; Exhibits; Festivals; Guided Tours; Lectures; Monthly Meeting; Publication; Research Library/Archives; School-Based Curriculum

COLLECTIONS: [1870-present] Historical and genealogical collections that focus upon south central NE.

HOURS: Yr T-Sa 9:30-4

5132
Hastings Museum of Culture and Natural History
1330 N Burlington Ave, 68902 [PO Box 1286, 68902-1286]; (p) (402) 461-2399; (f) (402) 461-2379; museum@tcgcs.com; www.hastingsnet.com/museum/; (c) Adams

Joint/ 1926/ Board of Trustees: City/ staff: 17(f); 12(p); 75(v)/ members: 4211/publication: *Museum Highlights*

CULTURAL CENTER; HISTORY MUSEUM; NATURAL HISTORY MUSEUM: Collects, preserves, and interprets specimens and artifacts primarily from the Great Plains.

PROGRAMS: Exhibits; Facility Rental; Family Programs; Film/Video; Interpretation; Lectures; Publication; Research Library/Archives

COLLECTIONS: Zoological specimens, samples of geology, mineralogy, paleontology, archeological artifacts, stone artifacts, photographic artifacts, furniture and wood artifacts, firearms, and textiles.

HOURS: Yr Daily

5133
Nebraska Softball Association
220 N Hastings Ave, 68901-5144; (p) (402) 721-0347; (f) (402) 721-2765; (c) Dodge

Private non-profit/ 1991/ staff: 2(f)

HISTORY MUSEUM: Hall of fame museum for the history of softball.

PROGRAMS: Exhibits

HOURS: Yr M-F 8-5

ADMISSION: No charge

HOLDREGE

5134
Phelps County Historical Society
N Hwy 183, 68949 [PO Box 164, 68949]; (p) (308) 995-5015; (c) Phelps

Private non-profit/ 1966/ staff: 3(p); 94(v)/ members: 346/publication: *Stereoscope*

ART MUSEUM; GENEALOGICAL SOCIETY; HISTORICAL SOCIETY; HISTORY MUSEUM

PROGRAMS: Annual Meeting; Community Outreach; Exhibits; Facility Rental; Family Programs; Festivals; Guided Tours; Lectures; Publication; Research Library/Archives

COLLECTIONS: [1850s- present]

HOURS: Yr Daily M-Sa 10-5, Su 1-5

ADMISSION: Donations accepted

HOMER

5135
O'Connor House
1 mile E of Homer, NE on Blyburg Rd, 68030 [PO Box 971, Dakota City, 68731]; (p) (402) 698-2161, (402) 698-2288

1865/ staff: 4(v)

COLLECTIONS: [Late 1800s] Original handmade furniture, fireplace from Italy.

HOURS: Seasonal

HYANNIS

5136
Grant County Historical Society and Museum
Grant and Harrison, 69350; (p) (308) 458-2488; (c) Grant

County/ 1959/ Grant County Historical Society/ staff: 1(f); 1(p); 1(v)

HISTORICAL SOCIETY; HISTORY MUSEUM

PROGRAMS: Annual Meeting; Community Outreach; Exhibits; Family Programs; Guided Tours; Living History

HOURS: Yr M and by appt

ADMISSION: Donations accepted

KEARNEY

5137
Buffalo County Historical Society
710 W 11th St, 68848 [PO Box 523, 68848]; (p) (308) 234-3041; bchs@kearney.net; bchs.kearney.net; (c) Buffalo

Private non-profit/ 1960/ staff: 8(p); 25(v)/ members: 277/publication: *Buffalo Tales*

HISTORICAL SOCIETY: Preserves the history of Buffalo County and educates the public

through public meetings, publications, tours, archives, and the operations of Trails and Rails Museum.

PROGRAMS: Annual Meeting; Exhibits; Guided Tours; Publication; Research Library/Archives

COLLECTIONS: [1870-1900] Archival documents, artifacts, and historic buildings relating to the history of Buffalo County, Nebraska.

HOURS: May-Sept Su 1-5, M 10-5, T-Sa 10-8

ADMISSION: Donations accepted

5138
Fort Kearney State Historical Park
1020 V Rd, 68847; (p) (308) 865-5305; ftkrny @ngpsun.ngpc.state.ne.us; www.ngpc.state. us; (c) Kearney

State/ 1929/ Nebraska Game and Parks Commission/ staff: 2(f); 6(p); 2(v)

HISTORIC SITE; HISTORY MUSEUM; LIVING HISTORY/OUTDOOR MUSEUM; STATE PARK: Preseves the history of Fort Kearney as Americans traveled west.

PROGRAMS: Exhibits; Festivals; Film/Video; Guided Tours; Interpretation; Lectures; Living History; Reenactments; Research Library/Archives; School-Based Curriculum

COLLECTIONS: [1840s-1870s] Displays, buildings, and artifacts found at a major military fort from the mid 1800s.

HOURS: Mar, May-Sept Daily 9-5

ADMISSION: $2/vehicle w/NE Park Sticker

5139
George W. Frank House
UNK W Campus, W Hwy 30, 68845 [2010 W 24th St, 68845]; (p) (308) 865-8284; lundv@ platte.unk.edu; www.unk.edu/related_org/fra nk_house/home.html; (c) Buffalo

State/ 1889/ University Chacellor/ staff: 1(f); 3(p); 65(v)

HOUSE MUSEUM: Historic museum, owned and operated by the University of NE at Kearney.

PROGRAMS: Facility Rental; Guided Tours; Interpretation; School-Based Curriculum

COLLECTIONS: [Victorian] Victorian period furnishings, playable 1876 Steinway Square grand piano and collection of vintage clothing, jewelry, linens and laces, Satsuma buttons.

HOURS: June-Aug T-Su 1-5

ADMISSION: $3, Children $1, Student $2

LEIGH

5140
Leigh's House of Yester Year
Beech St, 68643 [PO Box 341, 68643]; (p) (402) 487-2283; (c) Colfax

City, non-profit; Private non-profit/ 1972/ Board of Directors

HISTORIC SITE; HOUSE MUSEUM: Maintains house that was general store, official post office, GAR meeting place, and home built in 1876.

PROGRAMS: Annual Meeting; Festivals; Guided Tours

COLLECTIONS: [1870s-1920] Rooms with period furnishings: toy room, sewing room, mil-

itary room, library, original kitchen, living, dining, and bedrooms.

HOURS: May-Sept by appt

ADMISSION: Donations accepted

LEXINGTON

5141
Dawson County Historical Society
805 N Taft, 68850 [Box 369, 68850]; (p) (308) 324-5340; dawcomus@navix.net; (c) Dawson

Private non-profit/ 1963/ Dawson County Historical Society/ staff: 1(f); 3(p); 100(v)/ members: 362/publication: *Captive of Cheyenne, Ladder of Rivers, Plum Creek to Lexington*

GENEALOGICAL SOCIETY; HISTORICAL SOCIETY; HISTORY MUSEUM; LIVING HISTORY/OUTDOOR MUSEUM; RESEARCH CENTER: Collect, preserves, interprets, and displays the history of Dawson County.

PROGRAMS: Annual Meeting; Community Outreach; Elder's Programs; Exhibits; Facility Rental; Family Programs; Guided Tours; Interpretation; Lectures; Living History; Publication; Library/Archives; School-Based Curriculum

COLLECTIONS: [1860s-present] Fossils of Colombian Mammoth, and other pioneer to modern artifacts.

HOURS: Yr Daily M-Sa 9-5, Su 1:30-5

ADMISSION: Donations accepted

5142
Heartland Museum of Military Vehicles, The
600 Heartland Rd, 68850 [PO Box 699, 68850]; (p) (308) 324-6329; www.capc.com/heartl; (c) Dawson

Private non-profit/ Board of Directors/ staff: 4(v)/ members: 242

HISTORY MUSEUM

PROGRAMS: Exhibits; Guided Tours; Interpretation; Research Library/Archives

COLLECTIONS: [1917- Present] 50 preserved/ restored military vehicles,

HOURS: Yr M-F 10-5, Su 1-5

ADMISSION: Donations accepted

LINCOLN

5143
American Historical Society of Germans from Russia
631 D St, 68502-1199; (p) (402) 474-3363; (f) (402) 474-7229; ahsgr@aol.com; www.ahsgr .org; (c) Lancaster

Private non-profit/ 1968/ Board of Directors/ staff: 6(f); 1(p); 170(v)/ members: 5000/publication: *Clues*

GENEALOGICAL SOCIETY; HISTORICAL SOCIETY; HISTORY MUSEUM; HOUSE MUSEUM; LIVING HISTORY/OUTDOOR MUSEUM; RESEARCH CENTER: Committed to preserving the history and culture of this ethnic group by collecting objects, books, and records. Research, translation, and library services are available.

PROGRAMS: Annual Meeting; Exhibits; Guided Tours; Publication; Research Library/Archives

COLLECTIONS: [Late 19th-early 20th c] Extensive research collections include maps, genealogy database, obituary collection, and various records obtained from Russian and Ukrainian archives. The library holds large collection of books pertaining to the history and culture of German Russians in the USA.

HOURS: Sept-Feb: M-F 9-4; Mar-Aug M-F 9-4, Sa 9-1

5144
National Museum of Roller Skating
4730 South St, Ste 2, 68506; (p) (402) 483-7551; (f) (402) 483-1465; postmaster@roller skatingmuseum.com; www.rollerskatingmuseum.com; (c) Lancaster

Private non-profit/ 1980/ staff: 1(f); 1(p); 2(v)/ members: 400/publication: *Historical Roller Skating Overview*

HISTORY MUSEUM; RESEARCH CENTER: Committed to enriching people's lives by increasing their understanding and enjoyment of roller skating history.

PROGRAMS: Community Outreach; Exhibits; Family Programs; Film/Video; Guided Tours; Interpretation; Lectures; Publication; Research Library/Archives

COLLECTIONS: [1819-present] Roller skates dating back to 1819; patents; trophies; photographs and film collections; costumes; library materials; memorabilia dealing with roller sports and the roller industry.

HOURS: Yr M-F 9-5

ADMISSION: Donations accepted

5145
Nebraska Game and Parks Commission
2200 N 33rd St, 68503 [PO Box 30370, 68503]; (p) (402) 471-0641; (f) (402) 471-5528; jfuller@hgpc.state.ne.us; www.ngpc.state.ne.us; (c) Lancaster

State/ 1921/ staff: 16(f); 85(p)

HISTORIC SITE; HOUSE MUSEUM; LIVING HISTORY/OUTDOOR MUSEUM; STATE PARK: State park agency administrating and interpreting 11 state historical parks.

PROGRAMS: Exhibits; Film/Video; Guided Tours; Interpretation; Living History; Reenactments

COLLECTIONS: Buildings, grounds, furnishings.

HOURS: Varies

5146
Nebraska Humanities Council
215 Centennial Mall S, Ste 225, 68508; (p) (402) 474-2131; (f) (402) 474-4852; nehumanities@juno.com; www.lincolnne.com/non profit/nhc; (c) Lancaster

Private non-profit/ 1973/ Volunteer Board/ staff: 8(f); 1(p); 2(v)/ members: 500/publication: *Nebraska Humanities*

PROFESSIONAL ORGANIZATION: Grant making organization. State affiliate of the National Endowment for the Humanities. Goals are to connect state civically and culturally, to promote the exchange of culture and ideas between east and west, rural and urban, scholar and public, citizen and government. Works with organizations to bring programs to community that explore history and culture.

PROGRAMS: Annual Meeting; Community Outreach; Concerts; Elder's Programs; Exhibits; Family Programs; Festivals; Film/Video; Garden Tours; Guided Tours; Interpretation; Lectures; Living History; Publication; Reenactments

COLLECTIONS: Exhibits, humanities resources.

HOURS: Yr M-F 8-5

ADMISSION: No charge

5147
Nebraska State Capitol D.A.S. Building Division
1445 K St, 68508 [521 S 14th St, 68508-2707]; (p) (402) 471-6691; (f) (402) 471-6952; www.capitol.org; (c) Lancaster

State/ 1934/ D.A.S. Building Division State of Nebraska (Capitol Commission)/ staff: 33(f); 10(p)/publication: *Harmony of the Arts, Book and Brochures*

ART MUSEUM; HISTORIC SITE: State agency charged with the on-going preservation, restoration, enhancement, and promotion of the Nebraska state capitol and its environs.

PROGRAMS: Guided Tours; Interpretation; Lectures; Publication; Research Library/Archives; School-Based Curriculum

COLLECTIONS: [1920-1935] Over 200,000 unique items including drawings, specifications, correspondence, images, and artifacts.

HOURS: Yr M-F 8-5, Sa 10-5, Su 1-5; Collections: by appt only

5148
Nebraska State Historical Society
1500 R St, 68501 [PO Box 82554, 68501-2554]; (p) (402) 471-3270; (f) (402) 471-3100; nshs@nebraskahistory.org; www.nebraska history.org; (c) Lancaster

Private non-profit; State/ 1878/ Board of Trustees/ staff: 100(f); 20(p); 250(v)/ members: 3400/publication: *Nebraska History*

HISTORIC PRESERVATION AGENCY; HISTORIC SITE; HISTORICAL SOCIETY; HISTORY MUSEUM; RESEARCH CENTER: Umbrella Organization for nine historic sites around NE. Houses Museum and Archives on site.

PROGRAMS: Annual Meeting; Community Outreach; Exhibits; Facility Rental; Family Programs; Film/Video; Guided Tours; Interpretation; Lectures; Publication; Research Library/Archives; School-Based Curriculum

COLLECTIONS: [Prehistory-present]

HOURS: Yr Museum Daily M- F 9-4:30, Sa 9-5, Su 1:30-5; Library/ Archives Daily T-F 9:30-4:30, Sa 8-5

ADMISSION: No charge

5149
Nebraska United Methodist Historical Center
5000 St. Paul Ave, 68504 [PO Box 4553, 68504-0553]; (p) (402) 465-2175; mvetter@inebraska.com; (c) Lancaster

Private non-profit/ NE United Methodist Annual Conference/ Comission on Archives and History/ staff: 1(p)

HISTORY MUSEUM

PROGRAMS: Annual Meeting; Exhibits; Guided Tours; Research Library/Archives

COLLECTIONS: [Late 1800s-present]

HOURS: Yr T 1-5 by appt; W-Th 8-5

ADMISSION: No charge

5150
Preservation Association of Lincoln
c/o Rogers House 2145 B St, 68502; (c) Lancaster

Private non-profit/ 1992/ Board of Directors/ staff: 124(v)/ members: 275

HISTORIC PRESERVATION AGENCY: Promotes an awareness and respect for the historically and architecturally significant resources of Lincoln and Lancaster County.

PROGRAMS: Annual Meeting; Community Outreach; Festivals; Guided Tours; Lectures; Publication

5151
State Arsenal Museum, Nebraska National Guard Historical Society, Inc.
17th & Court St, 68508 [1300 Military Rd, 68508-1090]; (p) (402) 471-7124; (f) (402) 471-7202; (c) Lancaster

Private non-profit/ 1980/ Military Dept of NE; State/ staff: 4(p); 6(v)/ members: 125

HISTORIC SITE; HISTORICAL SOCIETY; HISTORY MUSEUM: Established to collect, preserve, and display military artifacts pertinent primarily to the Army and Air National Guard of NE.

PROGRAMS: Exhibits; Guided Tours; Interpretation; Living History

COLLECTIONS: [1854-present] Military artifacts from the various war periods as related to the NE National Guard, WW II related items and a chronology of the service of the NE National Guard 134th Infantry Regiment, 200 military model aircraft from many nations.

HOURS: NE State Fair 8-4, and by appt

ADMISSION: Donations accepted

5152
Steinauer Historical Society
c/o Lawrence D Obrist 5309 Antler Ct, 68516-2407; (p) (402) 423-7170; Lrn-Lsw.obrist@all tel.net; (c) Pawnee

Private non-profit/ 1975/ staff: 5(v)/publication: *Steinauer Family History and Genealogy*

HISTORICAL SOCIETY: Discovers, collects, and preserves materials illustrating the history of the area with main focus on pioneer period, records, archives, and historic town buildings, monuments, and markers.

PROGRAMS: Family Programs; Film/Video; Publication

COLLECTIONS: [1856-present] Steinauer Family History, photographs, and family souvenirs scattered among family members.

5153
Thomas P. Kennard House
1627 H, 68501 [PO Box 82554, 68501]; (p) (402) 471-4764; (f) (402) 471-4764

1869/ staff: 1(f); 2(p); 2(v)

COLLECTIONS: [1870s] 1870's Victorian furnishings, some of the furnishings belonged to early NE governors.

HOURS: Yr

5154
University of Nebraska State Museum
14th St & Memorial Oval, 68588 [307 Morrill Hall, 68588-0338]; (p) (402) 472-3779; (f) (402) 472-8899; www-museum.unl.edu; (c) Lancaster

State/ 1871/ Univ of NE/ staff: 42(f); 24(p); 121(v)/ members: 750

NATURAL HISTORY MUSEUM: Repository for specimens documenting natural history of NE and the Great Plains. Specimens available for research, teaching, interpretation and exhibits.

PROGRAMS: Interpretation; Lectures; Publication; Research Library/Archives; School-Based Curriculum

COLLECTIONS: Specimens mostly devoted to natural history, Native American, from archaic to immediate post- contact; African; Pacific; excellent fossil mammals of Nebraska; affiliated Lester Larson Tractor Museum.

HOURS: Yr Daily M-Sa 9:30-4:30, Su 1:30-4:30

ADMISSION: No charge

LONG PINE

5155
Long Pine Heritage Society
199 W 3rd St, 69217 [PO Box 182, 69217]; (p) (402) 273-4141; wardene@sscg.net; (c) Brown

Private non-profit/ 1985/ staff: 6(v)/ members: 50

GENEALOGICAL SOCIETY; HISTORIC PRESERVATION AGENCY; HISTORIC SITE; HISTORY MUSEUM: Preserves the history of the area with artifacts, photos, and written history.

PROGRAMS: Annual Meeting; Guided Tours; Research Library/Archives

COLLECTIONS: [1882-present] Items of history, photos.

HOURS: Sa 1-4

ADMISSION: Donations accepted

LOUP CITY

5156
Sherman County Historical Society
433 S 7th St, 68853; (p) (308) 745-1484; (c) Sherman

Private non-profit/ 1979/ Board of Directors; City; County/ staff: 16(v)/ members: 139

GENEALOGICAL SOCIETY; HISTORIC PRESERVATION AGENCY; HISTORIC SITE; HISTORICAL SOCIETY; HISTORY MUSEUM; HOUSE MUSEUM; LIVING HISTORY/OUTDOOR MUSEUM: Promotes historic site situated along creek where the Army lost all horses and mules in 1873 due to winter blizzard while in pursuit of Indians.

PROGRAMS: Annual Meeting; Community Outreach; Elder's Programs; Exhibits; Family Programs; Festivals; Film/Video; Guided Tours; Lectures; Living History; Publication; Research Library/Archives; School-Based

Curriculum

COLLECTIONS: Family histories, school records, newspapers and clippings, pictures, and artifacts.

HOURS: Mem Day-Labor Day Su 2-5; and by appt

ADMISSION: Donations accepted

MADISON

5157
Madison County Historical Society Museum
210 Ward St, 68748 [PO Box 708, 68748]; (p) (402) 454-2827; (f) (402) 454-2498; (c) Madison

Private non-profit/ 1965/ staff: 42(v)/ members: 176

HISTORIC PRESERVATION AGENCY; HISTORICAL SOCIETY

PROGRAMS: Annual Meeting; Community Outreach; Exhibits; Family Programs; Festivals; Film/Video; Guided Tours; Interpretation; Lectures; Living History; Reenactments; Research Library/Archives; School-Based Curriculum

COLLECTIONS: [1880-present] Communications, pioneer history, textiles, military, home life through the ages, local and county histories.

HOURS: Yr M-F 2-5 and by appt

ADMISSION: No charge

MASON CITY

5158
Muddy Creek Historical Society
[PO Box 62, 68855-0062]; (c) Custer

Private non-profit/ 1983/ members: 20

HISTORICAL SOCIETY: A group of 15-20 people interested in studying the history of the area and recording it for future generations.

MCCOOK

5159
High Plains Historical Society
421 Norris Ave, 69001; (p) (308) 345-3661; (c) Red Willow

Private non-profit/ 1965/ staff: 3(p); 35(v)/ members: 125

HISTORICAL SOCIETY; HISTORY MUSEUM: Promotes and exhibits local history and preserve a 1907 Carnegie Library listed on the National Register.

PROGRAMS: Annual Meeting

COLLECTIONS: [1870s-present] Photographs; artifacts from pioneer settlement days; Native American arrowheads; archeological specimens; turn-of-the-century toys, clothing, and furniture. Artifacts from Spanish American War, Civil War, WW I, WW II. Paintings by German prisoners of war, 1900-era pharmacy.

HOURS: Yr T-Sa 1-5, Su 2-4

ADMISSION: Donations accepted

5160
McCook County Airbase Historical Society
10 miles NW of McCook on Hwy 83, 69001 [PO Box B-29, 69001-1082]; (p) (308) 345-6097; cas515@yahoo.com; (c) Red Willow

Private non-profit/ 1987/ staff: 20(v)/ members: 300

HISTORIC PRESERVATION AGENCY; HISTORIC SITE; HISTORICAL SOCIETY; HISTORY MUSEUM; LIVING HISTORY/OUTDOOR MUSEUM: Preserves the property as well as resort buildings to wartime condition. Provides location for WW II memorabilia, documents, aircraft, and vehicles. Site listed on the National Historical Register.

PROGRAMS: Annual Meeting; Festivals; Guided Tours; Living History; Publication

COLLECTIONS: [1941-1945] WW II hanger at the airfield, Veterans Memorial Garden with sidewalk replica of runways and bronze plaques of bomb groups stationed at McCook. A barracks building complete with beds and blankets, stoves, clothing, and foot lockers. 1/4 scale model b-27 with 20 foot wing span. Norden Bomb site vault listed on National Historical Registry.

HOURS: June-Sept Sa-Su 1-4 and by appt

ADMISSION: No charge

5161
Senator George Norris State Historic Site
706 Norris Ave, 69001-3142; (p) (308) 345-8484; (f) (308) 345-8484; norris@wil-net.com; www.nebraskahistory.org; (c) Red Willow

State/ 1967/ NE State Historical Society/ staff: 1(f)/ members: 2547

HISTORIC SITE; HOUSE MUSEUM; STATE PARK: Preserves and interprets the home and furnishings of a nationally significant NE politician.

PROGRAMS: Community Outreach; Elder's Programs; Exhibits; Film/Video; Garden Tours; Guided Tours; Interpretation

COLLECTIONS: [1890-1944] Original furnishings and artifacts of Sen. Norris, oriental rug collection, spinning wheels, and a 1937 Buick.

HOURS: Yr W-Sa 10-12/1-5, T and Su 1:30-5

ADMISSION: $1, Children $0.25

MCCOOL JUNCTION

5162
Iron Horse Station G518
O St, 68401 [Box 126, 68401]; (c) York

Private non-profit/ 1991/ Board of Trustees

HISTORY MUSEUM: Preserve the depot and McCool History.

MERRIMAN

5163
Arthur Bowring Sandhills Ranch
N off US 20 on HWY 61, 69218 [PO Box 38, 69218]; (p) (308) 684-3428, (308) 684-3383; (f) (308) 684-3470; (c) Cherry

State/ 1894/ NE Game and Parks/ staff: 1(f); 7(p); 1(v)

LIVING HISTORY/OUTDOOR MUSEUM: Preserves Bowring Ranch as a working.

PROGRAMS: Community Outreach; Concerts; Exhibits; Guided Tours; Interpretation; Living History; Theatre

COLLECTIONS: [1894-present] Fine antique china, crystal, and silver; Ranch, homestead, geology, wildlife.

HOURS: May-Sept Daily 8-5

ADMISSION: $2/vehicle

MINDEN

5164
Harold Warp Pioneer Village
138 E Hwy 6, 68959 [PO Box 68, 68959-0068]; (p) (308) 832-1181, (800) 445-4447; (f) (308) 832-1181; www.pioneervillage.org; (c) Kearney

Private non-profit/ 1953/ staff: 21(f); 12(p)

HISTORY MUSEUM; HOUSE MUSEUM: Preserves and restores historic pioneer village.

COLLECTIONS: [1830-present] 50,000 items, 350 antique autos, airplanes china, old merry-go-round, crafts, Pony Express relay station and barn. The Pioneer Village complex comprises 28 buildings arranged in groups and also in the chronological order of their development.

HOURS: Yr Daily 8am-sundown

ADMISSION: $7, Children $3.50

5165
Kearney County Historical Society
6th & Nebraska, 68909 [1776 32nd, 68909]; (p) (308) 832-2676; (c) Kearney

County/ 1926/ staff: 1(p); 18(v)/ members: 210

HISTORIC PRESERVATION AGENCY; HISTORIC SITE; HISTORICAL SOCIETY; HISTORY MUSEUM: Maintains museum.

PROGRAMS: Annual Meeting; Exhibits; School-Based Curriculum

COLLECTIONS: [1860-present] Artifacts, photos, 6,000 articles, railroad depot, early business building.

HOURS: Yr Su 2-5

ADMISSION: No charge

MOCKSVILLE

5166
Davie County Historical and Genealogical Society
371 N Main St, 27028; (p) (336) 751-2023; (c) Davie

Private non-profit/ 1968/ staff: 4(v)/ members: 90

GENEALOGICAL SOCIETY; HISTORICAL SOCIETY: Collects genealogical and historical information, researches and publishes genealogical works. Housed within Davie County Public Library.

PROGRAMS: Annual Meeting; Family Programs; Lectures

COLLECTIONS: [1836-present] Artifacts, documents, books, microfilm, family histories, maps.

HOURS: Yr M-Th 9-8:30, F 9-5:30, Sa 9-4, Su 2-5

ADMISSION: No charge

MULLEN

5167
Hooker County Historical Society
NW 1st St, 69152 [PO Box 107, 69152]; (p) (308) 546-2530; (f) (308) 546-2432; pbridge@neb-sandhills.net; www.neb-sandhills.net/mullen; (c) Hooker

Private non-profit/ 1968/ Board of Directors/ staff: 20(v)/ members: 40

GENEALOGICAL SOCIETY; HISTORIC PRESERVATION AGENCY; HISTORIC SITE; HISTORICAL SOCIETY; HISTORY MUSEUM; HOUSE MUSEUM: Development stage of preserving and restoring historical hotel. Currently houses museum collection and genealogical records with 25 rooms for displays.

PROGRAMS: Community Outreach; Exhibits; Festivals; Theatre

COLLECTIONS: [Late 1800s-present] Boy and Girl Scout, Beauty and Barber Shop, laundry and Kitchen Utensils, appliances, linens, school room with slates, books, teaching aids, maps, millinery and vintage clothing, military uniforms, pictures, period tables, chairs, cupboards, dishes, benches, organ and musical instruments, music.

HOURS: By appt

ADMISSION: No charge

MURDOCK

5168
Mudock Historical Society
3rd & Nebraska, 68407 [9014 310th St, 68407]; (p) (402) 867-2545; du25655@navix.net; (c) Cass

Private non-profit/ 1993/ staff: 2(v)/ members: 50

HISTORICAL SOCIETY; HISTORY MUSEUM: Preserves the history of the Murdock area.

PROGRAMS: Annual Meeting; Exhibits; Facility Rental; Film/Video; Guided Tours

COLLECTIONS: [1890-present] Recreated stores, churches in museum building.

HOURS: Yr Sa 9-1, Su 1:30-5

ADMISSION: Donations accepted

NEBRASKA CITY

5169
Arbor Lodge State Historical Park
2300 W Second Ave, 68410 [PO Box 15, 68410]; (p) (402) 873-7222; (c) Otoe

State/ 1923/ NE Game and Parks Commission/ staff: 2(f); 17(p)

HISTORIC SITE; HOUSE MUSEUM; STATE PARK: Maintains the Arbor Day Lodge mansion and surrounding arboretum.

PROGRAMS: Exhibits; Living History; Reenactments

COLLECTIONS: [1855-1923] 2,000 artifacts, including furniture, glass, china, art, clothing, and textiles.

HOURS: Apr-Dec Daily

ADMISSION: $3, Children $1; Under 6 free

5170
Nebraska City Historical Society
711 3rd Corso, 68410 [Box 175, 68410]; (p) (402) 873-9360; (c) Otoe

Private non-profit/ 1937/ Board of Directors/ staff: 10(v)/ members: 56

HISTORIC SITE; HISTORICAL SOCIETY; HISTORY MUSEUM; HOUSE MUSEUM: Gathers and preserves historical information about Nebraska City. Identifies buildings, monuments, markers, sites and papers of historical value and encourages their preservation. Promotes research and provides a forum for discussing topics of historical interest.

PROGRAMS: Exhibits; Facility Rental; Guided Tours; Interpretation; Lectures; Research Library/Archives

COLLECTIONS: [1850s-present] Period portrayals, photographs, artifacts, Nelson House, a 1850's Greek revival style.

HOURS: By appt

ADMISSION: $2

5171
Wildwood Historic Center, The
Steinhort Park Rd, 68410; (p) (402) 873-6340; (c) Otae

City/ 1869/ staff: 1(f); 4(p)

HOUSE MUSEUM: Restored house from the Victorian era.

COLLECTIONS: [Victorian] Victorian furnishings, art by Midwestern artists.

HOURS: Apr-Oct T-Sa 11-5, Su 1-5

ADMISSION: $2, Children $0.50

NELIGH

5172
Antelope County Historical Society
609 L, 68756 [305 K, 68756]; (p) (402) 887-4999; (c) Antelope

County/ 1965/ staff: 1(p); 8(v)

HISTORIC PRESERVATION AGENCY; HISTORIC SITE; HISTORICAL SOCIETY; HISTORY MUSEUM

PROGRAMS: Annual Meeting; Community Outreach; Exhibits; Guided Tours; Publication; Research Library/Archives

COLLECTIONS: [1900] Local items: clothing and textiles, Native American artifacts, and genealogy sources.

HOURS: June-Aug, portions of May and Sept W-F, Su 1:30-4:30 and by appt

ADMISSION: $1

5173
Neligh Mill State Historic Site
N St at Wylie Dr, 68756 [PO Box 271, 68756]; (p) (402) 887-4303; www.nebraskahistory.org/sites/mill/; (c) Antelope

State/ 1873

HISTORIC SITE; HISTORICAL SOCIETY; STATE PARK: Preserves the history of the Neligh Mill, grist mill, and provide information about other water-powered mills once located throughout NE and the Midwest.

PROGRAMS: Exhibits; Film/Video; Guided Tours; Interpretation; Publication

COLLECTIONS: [1880s] Grist mill, restored mill office, original equipment, reconstructed flume and penstock, and the remains of the mill dam.

HOURS: May-Sept 30 M-Sa 8-3, Su 1:30-5; Oct 1-May M-F 8-5

ADMISSION: $2

NIOBRARA

5174
Niobrara Historical Society
Park Ave, 68760 [89054-519 Ave, 68760-6013]; (p) (402) 857-3794; (c) Knox

Private non-profit/ 1976/ Niobrara Historical Society/ staff: 20(v)/ members: 20

HISTORICAL SOCIETY: A small group of volunteers who are interested in preserving the history of the community.

PROGRAMS: Annual Meeting; Guided Tours

COLLECTIONS: Microfilms of newspapers printed in Niobrara. Photos from all stages of Niobrara's history: rural school's establishment, agricultural era, country store, country home, military area.

HOURS: May-Sept Sa 10-3, W 10-12 or by appt

ADMISSION: Donations accepted

NORFOLK

5175
Elkhorn Valley Museum and Research Center
515 Queen City Blvd, 68701; (p) (402) 371-3886; (f) (402) 371-3886; (c) Madison

Private non-profit/ 1958/ Elkhorn Valley Historical Society/ staff: 1(f); 2(p); 60(v)/ members: 348

HISTORY MUSEUM; RESEARCH CENTER: Preserves local history

PROGRAMS: Annual Meeting; Community Outreach; Exhibits; Facility Rental; Festivals; Guided Tours; Interpretation; Lectures; Publication; Research Library/Archives

COLLECTIONS: [1800-present] Medical, agricultural, and personal artifacts, including 1927 painted backdrop, 1918 tractor, photographs, newspapers, documents, and books.

HOURS: Yr T-Sa 10-4, Su 1-4

ADMISSION: No charge, donations accepted

NORTH BRIDGTON

5176
Spratt-Mead Museum
Waterford Rd, 04057 [c/o Bridgton Academy, PO Box 292, 04057]; (p) (207) 647-3322; (f) (207) 647-8513; stanc@mail.bacad.bridgton.me.us; www.bacad.bridgton.me.us/; (c) Cumberland

Private non-profit/ staff: 2(v)

HISTORY MUSEUM: Maintains a cabinet collection 1850, owns and oversees the museum.

PROGRAMS: Exhibits

COLLECTIONS: [1890-1930] 19th and 20th c cultural history artifacts and natural history specimens.

HOURS: May-Sept Sa 2-4

ADMISSION: No charge

NORTH PLATTE

5177
Buffalo Bill Ranch State Historical Park
Scouts Rest Ranch Rd, 69101 [RR 1, Box 229, 69101]; (p) (308) 535-8035; (f) (308) 535-8068; bbranch@ns.nque.com; www.ngpc.state.ne.us/cody.html; (c) Lincoln

State/ 1965/ NE Game and Parks Commission/ staff: 2(f); 14(p)

HISTORIC SITE; HOUSE MUSEUM; STATE PARK: Preserves William F. "Buffalo Bill" Cody's 1886 house, horse barn, and memorabilia, exhibits recreate the fascinating story of America's famous showman-scout.

PROGRAMS: Exhibits; Facility Rental; Guided Tours; Interpretation; Lectures

COLLECTIONS: [1868-1917] 1886 ranch house, 1887 horse barn, carriages, saddles, Buffalo Bill and Cody family memorabilia, photographs, and "The Life and Times of Buffalo Bill" video.

HOURS: May-Sept Daily 10-8; Apr-May, Sept-Oct M-F 9-12/1-5

ADMISSION: $2/vehicle

5178
Lincoln County Historical Society Museum and Village
2403 N Buffalo Bill, 69101; (p) (308) 534-5640; (f) (308) 534-5640; (c) Lincoln

Private non-profit/ 1972/ Board of Directors/ staff: 1(f); 250(v)/ members: 363

HISTORICAL SOCIETY; HISTORY MUSEUM: Preseves an 1860s village.

PROGRAMS: Annual Meeting; Community Outreach; Exhibits; Facility Rental; Festivals; Guided Tours; Living History; Publication

COLLECTIONS: [1860s-present] 1860s village with 4 log cabins; early houses; artifacts; research library; WW II canteen and photos; old machinery; medical and music artifacts.

HOURS: May-Sept Daily 9-8

ADMISSION: Donations accepted

O'NEIL

5179
Holt County Historical Society
401 E Douglas, 68763; (p) (402) 336-2344; (c) Holt

Private non-profit/ 1970/ Holt County Historical Society Board/ staff: 1(f); 10(v)/ members: 100/publication: *Holt County Historical Newsletter*

GENEALOGICAL SOCIETY; HISTORIC SITE; HISTORICAL SOCIETY; HISTORY MUSEUM; HOUSE MUSEUM; RESEARCH CENTER: Promotes the history of early pioneers.

PROGRAMS: Annual Meeting; Exhibits; Facility Rental; Family Programs; Festivals; Guided Tours; Lectures; Living History; Publication; Reenactments; Research Library/Archives

COLLECTIONS: [1880-1925] Photographic collections and 4,000 family histories.

HOURS: Feb-Dec M-Th 10-4

ADMISSION: Donations accepted

OGALLALA

5180
Front Street
519 E 1st St, 69153; (p) (308) 284-6000; (f) (308) 284-0865; frontstreet@lakemac.net; (c) Keith

1963

Restaurant, saloon, old west history museum, gift shop.

5181
Keith County Historical Society
1004 N Spruce, 69153 [619 Highland Dr, 69153]; (p) (308) 284-2832; (c) Keith

Private non-profit/ 1963/ Board of Directors/ staff: 1(f); 100(v)/ members: 50

HISTORIC PRESERVATION AGENCY; HISTORICAL SOCIETY; HOUSE MUSEUM: Preservation, protection and promotion of historical buildings and sites, gathering of historical data, encouraging research, and providing educational opportunities.

PROGRAMS: Annual Meeting; Exhibits; Facility Rental; Family Programs; Guided Tours

HOURS: May-Sept T-Sa 9-12/1-4; Su 1-4

ADMISSION: $2, Children $1

5182
Mansion on the Hill
W 10th and Spruce Sts, 69153; (p) (308) 284-4327

OMAHA

5183
City of Omaha Planning Department
1819 Farnam Rm 1100, 68183; (p) (402) 444-5770; (f) (402) 444-6140; (c) Douglas

City/ staff: 100(f); 3(p)

HISTORIC PRESERVATION AGENCY; PRESIDENTIAL SITE; RESEARCH CENTER: Networks and coordinates with other historical agencies.

PROGRAMS: Exhibits; Research Library/Archives

COLLECTIONS: [1890-1949] Files for national and local historic properties and photo surveys.

HOURS: Yr M-F 8-5

5184
Durham Western Heritage Museum
801 S 10th St, 68108; (p) (402) 444-5071; (f) (402) 444-5397; (c) Douglas

Private non-profit/ 1975/ staff: 25(f); 7(p); 150(v)/ members: 2389

HISTORIC SITE; HISTORY MUSEUM: Interprets railroad history of Omaha.

PROGRAMS: Concerts; Exhibits; Facility Rental; Family Programs; Festivals; Film/Video; Guided Tours; Lectures; Living History; Research Library/Archives; Theatre

COLLECTIONS: [1850-1960] Artifacts, archives, photographs, Union Pacific Railroad Historical Collection, Byron Reed Collection of rare coins, documents, and manuscripts

HOURS: Yr T-Sa 10-5, Su 1- 5

ADMISSION: $5, Children $3.50, Seniors $4

5185
Florence Historical
8502 N 30th, 68112 [PO Box 12331, 68112]; (p) (402) 453-4280; (c) Dougal

Private non-profit/ 1962/ Florence Historical/ staff: 18(v)/ members: 102

HISTORIC SITE; HISTORICAL SOCIETY; HISTORY MUSEUM: Oldest bank in NE, 1854-1888 railroad depot, two museums of pioneer life.

PROGRAMS: Annual Meeting; Exhibits; Festivals; Lectures

COLLECTIONS: [1860-1930s] Restored 1853 bank museum with managers living quarters upstairs, restored 1888 railroad depot, 3 pieces rolling stock telegraph office.

HOURS: May-Sept 1-5

ADMISSION: No charge

5186
Freedom Park, Inc.
2497 Freedom Park Rd, 68110; (p) (402) 345-1959; (f) (402) 345-3418; 420phish@home.com; www.freedomparknavy.org; (c) Douglas

Private non-profit/ 1971/ staff: 2(f); 3(p); 25(v)/ members: 150

HISTORY MUSEUM: Collects and houses military artifacts, especially from the Navy during WW II.

PROGRAMS: Community Outreach; Exhibits; Facility Rental; Family Programs; Interpretation; School-Based Curriculum

COLLECTIONS: [WW II] Houses the USS Hazard, a WW II mine sweeper; the LSM 45, a landing craft; USS Marlin, a training submarine; and various other military artifacts.

HOURS: Apr-Oct Daily 10-5

ADMISSION: $4, Children $2.50, Seniors $3

5187
Gerald R. Ford Conservation Center
1326 S 32nd St, 68105-2044; (p) (402) 595-1180

HISTORICAL SOCIETY; PRESIDENTIAL SITE: Preserve local history and the life history of Gerald Ford.

HOURS: M-F 10-5, Sa-Su 1-5

ADMISSION: $1; Children/Members free

5188
Historical Society of Douglas County
30th & Fort St, 68111 [5730 N 30th St, 68111-1657]; (p) (402) 455-9990; (f) (402) 453-9448; hsdc-lac@radiks.net; www.radiks.net/hsdc-lac; (c) Douglas

Private non-profit/ 1956/ Board of Directors/ staff: 4(f); 6(p); 30(v)/ members: 900/publication: *The Banner*

GARDEN; HISTORIC SITE; HISTORICAL SOCIETY; HOUSE MUSEUM; PRESIDENTIAL SITE; RESEARCH CENTER: Collects, preserves, and makes available materials relevant to the history of Douglas County thorough the General Crook House Museum and the Library and Archives Center.

PROGRAMS: Annual Meeting; Community Outreach; Exhibits; Facility Rental; Family Programs; Garden Tours; Guided Tours; Lectures; Living History; Publication; Research Library/Archives

COLLECTIONS: [1850s-present] 6 million newspaper clippings; government, corporate, organization and family records; 20,000 photographs; video and audio collection; map, plat book and atlases; city directories; 107 newspaper titles; local authors and local history works.

HOURS: Yr Crook House M-F 10-4, Su 1-4; Library/Archives T-Sa 10-4

ADMISSION: $3.50, Children $1.50; Members free

5189
Joslyn Castle
3902 Davenport St, 68131; (p) (402) 595-2199, (402) 595-3209; www.cityatlas.com/static/joslyncastle.htm

5190
Landmarks Inc.
The Joslyn Castle Carriage House, 68131 [3838 Davenport St, 68131]; (p) (402) 595-2553; (f) (402) 595-2556; (c) Douglas

Private non-profit/ 1965/ staff: 1(p)/ members: 250/publication: *Landmark's Link*

HISTORIC PRESERVATION AGENCY: Serves as an advocate for the preservation of Omaha's historic environment.

PROGRAMS: Annual Meeting; Guided Tours; Lectures; Publication; Research Library/Archives

HOURS: Yr M-F mornings

5191
Mormon Trail Center at Historic Winter Quarters
3215 State St, 68112; (p) (402) 453-9372; (f) (402) 453-1538; (c) Douglas

Private non-profit/ 1997/ The Church of Jesus Christ of Later-Day Saints/ staff: 3(f); 15(v)

HISTORY MUSEUM; LIBRARY AND/OR ARCHIVES: Promotes Mormon Pioneer history and trail experience from Nauvoo, IL to Salt Lake Valley, UT with interactive displays, paintings, statues, and artifacts.

PROGRAMS: Concerts; Elder's Programs; Exhibits; Family Programs; Festivals; Guided Tours; Interpretation; Lectures; Reenactments; Research Library/Archives; Theatre

COLLECTIONS: [1840-1890] Possessions that belonged to Mormon pioneers or authentic reproductions, covered wagon with stuffed oxen, furnished cabin, handcart, ship model, 1847 printing press, odometer.

HOURS: Yr Daily 9-9

ADMISSION: No charge

5192
Nebraska Jewish Historical Society
333 S 132nd St, 68154-2198; (p) (402) 334-6441; (f) (402) 334-1330; njhs@radiks.net; (c) Douglas

Private non-profit/ 1982/ NE Jewish Historical Society, Inc./ staff: 1(f); 1(p); 8(v)/ members: 708/publication: *Memories of the Jewish Midwest*

HISTORICAL SOCIETY; HISTORY MUSEUM: Collects, preserves, publishes, and displays materials which depict the landmarks, families, businesses, and social history of the Jewish communities of NE.

PROGRAMS: Annual Meeting; Community Outreach; Exhibits; Guided Tours; Publication

COLLECTIONS: [1856-present] Photograph, documents, objects primarily related to organizations and businesses.

HOURS: Yr M-F 9-5 and by appt

ADMISSION: No charge

5193
Servants of Mary
7400 Military Ave, 68134; (p) (402) 571-2547; (f) (402) 573-6055; mawatson@marian.creighton.edu; osms.org/america/; (c) Douglas

Private non-profit/ 1986/ staff: 1(f); 3(p)/ members: 1

LIBRARY AND/OR ARCHIVES: Houses the independent collections of the American Province. It has been created to care for existing collections, to collect additional materials, and to serve the reference and educational needs of the province.

PROGRAMS: Exhibits; Garden Tours; Guided Tours; Research Library/Archives

COLLECTIONS: [1871-present]

HOURS: M-F 9-3

ADMISSION: No charge

PAPILLION

5194
Papillion Area Historical Socierty
242 N Jefferson St, 68046; (p) (402) 339-6984; (c) Sarpy

Private non-profit/ 1979/ Papillion Area Historical Society, Inc./ staff: 49(v)/ members: 49/publication: *Sautter House Five*

HISTORIC PRESERVATION AGENCY; HISTORIC SITE; HISTORICAL SOCIETY; HISTORY MUSEUM; HOUSE MUSEUM: Preserves local history.

PROGRAMS: Annual Meeting; Exhibits; Family Programs; Festivals; Guided Tours; Interpretation; Lectures; Publication; Research Library/Archives; Theatre

COLLECTIONS: [1890-1916] Victorian housewares and furniture, 1860 John Sautter house listed on the National Registery, early school paraphernalia, and archival records dating from 1890 in the Portal school, a one- room school house.

HOURS: Yr by appt

PAWNEE CITY

5195
Pawnee City Historical Society
East edge of Pawnee City on Hwy 8 & 50, 68420 [Box 33, 68420]; (c) Pawnee

Private non-profit/ 1968/ staff: 90(v)/ members: 55

HISTORICAL SOCIETY; LIVING HISTORY/OUTDOOR MUSEUM: Preserves the items of Pawnee County for the enjoyment of future generations.

PROGRAMS: Annual Meeting; Exhibits; Facility Rental; Festivals; Guided Tours; Living History

COLLECTIONS: 16 buildings hold pioneer artifacts. 3 buildings hold farm machinery, a blacksmith shop, log cabin, first governor of Nebraska's home, dentist office, doctor's office.

HOURS: Winter T-Th 9-4, Summer T-F 9-2, Sa-Su 1-4

ADMISSION: $2; Under 12 free

PERU

5196
Peru Historical Society

5th St & California, 68421 [PO Box 243, 68421]; (p) (402) 812-7745; bp15624@naxix.net; www.cl.peru.ne.us; (c) Nemaha

Private non-profit/ 1986/ staff: 47(v)/ members: 155

HISTORY MUSEUM; HOUSE MUSEUM: Preserves history for the city of Peru and Peru State College.

PROGRAMS: Annual Meeting; Exhibits; Facility Rental; Family Programs; Festivals; Guided Tours; Interpretation; Lectures; Publication; Research Library/Archives

COLLECTIONS: [1890s] Indian artifacts, Peru State College annuals, obituaries, family histories, period clothing, military uniforms, Missouri river floods, high school memorabilia.

HOURS: May-Sept Su 2-4, or by appt

PIERCE

5197
Pierce Historical Society Museum Complex

N Mill St, 68767 [PO Box 122, 68767]; (p) (402) 329-4576; www.ptcnet.net/museum.htm; (c) Pierce

Private non-profit/ 1976/ staff: 80(v)/ members: 213

HISTORICAL SOCIETY; HISTORY MUSEUM: Preserves memorabilia and promotes local history.

PROGRAMS: Annual Meeting; Exhibits; Guided Tours

COLLECTIONS: [1860s-mid 1900s] 2,500 items pertaining to rural and urban living in early days.

HOURS: May-Sept Su 1:30-4:30

ADMISSION: Donations accepted

PLAINVIEW

5198
Plainview Historical Society

304 S Main St, 68769 [PO Box 495, 68769-0495]; (p) (402) 582-4713; dickh@plvwtelco.net; (c) Pierce

Private non-profit/ 1978/ Plainview Historical Society/ staff: 14(v)/ members: 14

HISTORICAL SOCIETY; HISTORY MUSEUM: Preserves artifacts from the Plainview area.

PROGRAMS: Exhibits; Guided Tours; Publication

COLLECTIONS: [1880-1950] Photos, clothing, depot agents, apartment, medical and dental equipment.

HOURS: May-Sept Su 2-4

ADMISSION: No charge

PLATTSMOUTH

5199
Cass County Historical Society Museum

646 Main St, 68048; (p) (402) 296-4770; (c) Cass

Private non-profit/ 1936/ Cass County Historical Society/ staff: 1(f); 1(p); 50(v)/ members: 345

HISTORIC SITE; HISTORICAL SOCIETY; HISTORY MUSEUM: Collects, preserves, and interprets the history of county.

PROGRAMS: Annual Meeting; Elder's Programs; Exhibits; Family Programs; Festivals; Guided Tours; Interpretation; Lectures; Publication; Research Library/Archives; School-Based Curriculum

COLLECTIONS: [1854-1930]

HOURS: Yr Apr-Oct T-Su 12-4; Nov-Mar T-Sa 12-4

ADMISSION: No charge

POTTER

5200
Potter Museum

3666 Rd 83, 69156 [Box 155, 69156]; (c) Cheyenne

Private non-profit/ 1983/ Village of Potter/ staff: 12(v)/ members: 25

HISTORIC SITE; HISTORY MUSEUM; LIVING HISTORY/OUTDOOR MUSEUM: Collects, preserves, and interprets the commonwealth's history.

PROGRAMS: Exhibits; Festivals; Guided Tours; Publication

COLLECTIONS: Artifacts and memorabilia related to farming, ranching, and railroad.

HOURS: June-Sept W and Sa 1-3 or by appt

ADMISSION: Donations accepted

RED CLOUD

5201
Willa Cather State Historical Site

326 N Webster St, 68970-2810; (p) (402) 746-2653; (c) Webster

1955/ Board of Governors/ staff: 4(f); 5(p)/ members: 1000

Preserves history of Pulitzer Prize winner author in her home town, Willa Cather Pioneer Memorial and Educational Foundation.

HOURS: M-Sa 8-5 (Seasonal)

ADMISSION: $5, Children $2; No charge

ROYAL

5202
Ashfall Fossil Beds State Historical Park

[PO Box 66, 68773]; (p) (402) 893-2000; (f) (402) 893-2044; museum.unl.edu; (c) Antelope

Joint/ 1991/ Univ of NE-Lincoln; NE Game & Parks Commission/ staff: 2(f); 5(p); 15(v)/ members: 200

NATURAL HISTORY MUSEUM; STATE PARK: Fossil site with summer excavations. Complete skeletons of rhinos and three-toed horses are left in-situ for public viewing in the rhino barn.

PROGRAMS: Interpretation; Living History; School-Based Curriculum

COLLECTIONS: [Miocene-Ice Age] Vertebrate fossils of Northeast and Northcentral NE.

HOURS: May-Oct

ADMISSION: $3, Student $2

RUSHVILLE

5203
Sheridan County Historical Society

2nd & Nelson Ave, 69360 [PO Box 274, 69360]; (p) (308) 327-2917; (f) (308) 327-2166; rwbuchan@gpcom.net; (c) Sheridan

Private non-profit/ 1933/ Scoiety Board; County/ staff: 1(p); 6(v)/ members: 100

HISTORICAL SOCIETY; HISTORY MUSEUM: Researches and preserves the history and prehistory of the area.

PROGRAMS: Annual Meeting; Community Outreach; Exhibits; Guided Tours; Interpretation; Lectures; Publication; Research Library/Archives

COLLECTIONS: [1800-present] Area pioneer and Native American artifacts.

HOURS: May-Sept M-F 1-4

ADMISSION: No charge

SIDNEY

5204
Post Commander's Home

1113 6th Ave, 69162 [PO Box 596, 69162]; (p) (308) 254-2150

1871/ staff: 2(p)

COLLECTIONS: [1867-1894] Ice skates used by family, toys, clothing used, cooking utincels used, feather mattresses.

HOURS: Seasonal

SPRINGVIEW

5205
Keya Paha County Historical Society

Courthouse Sq, 68778 [HC 80 Box 49, 68778-9729]; (p) (402) 497-2526; (c) Keya Paha

1968/ Board of Directors/ members: 25

HISTORICAL SOCIETY; HISTORY MUSEUM; HOUSE MUSEUM: Collects and preserves artifacts and memorabilia related to people that homesteaded in the county or live in Keya Paha County.

PROGRAMS: Annual Meeting; Community Outreach; Exhibits; Guided Tours; Research Library/Archives

COLLECTIONS: [1885-present] Clothing, toys, dishes, rural school, military display, Boy and Girl Scout display, doll display, tools, printing presses, and newspapers.

HOURS: May-Sept 1-4 and by appt

ADMISSION: Donations accepted

ST. PAUL

5206
Howard County Historical Society
902-915 6th St, 68873 [PO Box 304, 68873]; (p) (308) 754-4454; (f) (308) 754-5223; marion@cornhusker.net; www.cornhusker.net/~mine/hchs.htm; (c) Howard

County; Private non-profit/ 1901/ Board of Directors/ staff: 50(v)/ members: 250/publication: *Entering Howard County; Historically Speaking*

HISTORIC SITE; HISTORICAL SOCIETY; HISTORY MUSEUM; HOUSE MUSEUM; LIBRARY AND/OR ARCHIVES; RESEARCH CENTER: Preserves local history, collects and preserves social, ethnic, military, service and farming artifacts related to its settlement.

PROGRAMS: Annual Meeting; Community Outreach; Concerts; Exhibits; Facility Rental; Family Programs; Festivals; Guided Tours; Interpretation; Lectures; Living History; Publication; Reenactments; Research Library/Archives; School-Based Curriculum

COLLECTIONS: [1870-1930] Historical village (pioneer church, school, store, blacksmith shop, post office, and home).

HOURS: May-Sep Su 1-4 and by appt

ADMISSION: Donations accepted

STAPLETON

5207
Logan County Historical Association
245 Main St, 69163 [PO Box 7, 69163]; (p) (308) 636-2461; (c) Logan

Private non-profit/ 1980/ staff: 1(v)

GENEALOGICAL SOCIETY; HISTORIC PRESERVATION AGENCY: Collection of items donated to preserve the heritage of Logan County.

STRANG

5208
Strang Museum
Main St, 68444 [PO Box 62, 68444]; (c) Fillmore

Private non-profit/ 1986/ Strang CIP and Fillmore County Historical Society/ staff: 2(v)

HISTORY MUSEUM: Collects, preserves, and displays local history.

PROGRAMS: Exhibits

COLLECTIONS: [1885-present] Pictures, clothing reading material, trinkets, historical documents, artifacts, and other items relevant to life in the community since its beginning.

HOURS: By appt

ADMISSION: No charge

TARNOV

5209
St. Michael's Historical Society
309 3rd St, Ste 1, 68642; tarnov@hotmail.com; www.megavision.net/stmichaels; (c) Platte

Private non-profit/ 1993/ staff: 6(v)/ members: 75

HISTORICAL SOCIETY: Preserves National Register of Historic Places. Operates on membership and memorial.

PROGRAMS: Annual Meeting; Festivals; Guided Tours

HOURS: May-Sept 1st Su 1-5, and by appt

ADMISSION: $1

TAYLOR

5210
Loup County Historical Society
401 Murry St, 68879 [PO Box 102, 68879]; (p) (308) 942-3403; kevbrown@esu10.org; (c) Loup

Private non-profit/ 1940/ staff: 5(v)/ members: 145

GENEALOGICAL SOCIETY; HISTORICAL SOCIETY; HISTORY MUSEUM: Preserve local history.

PROGRAMS: Annual Meeting; Community Outreach; Concerts; Exhibits; Family Programs; Festivals; Guided Tours; Interpretation; Lectures; Research Library/Archives; School-Based Curriculum

COLLECTIONS: [1870s-1910s] Artifacts and memorabilia with special emphasis on those who came during the Homestead and Kinkaid Acts.

HOURS: Jun-Sep Su 1-5 and by appt

ADMISSION: No charge

TEKAMAH

5211
Burt County Museum/E.C. Houston House
319 N 13th St, 68061 [PO Box 125, 68061]; (p) (402) 374-1505; (c) Burt

Private non-profit/ 1967/ City/ staff: 4(p); 8(v)/ members: 706

GENEALOGICAL SOCIETY; HISTORIC SITE; HISTORY MUSEUM; HOUSE MUSEUM: Collects, preserves, and develops an appreciation of the history of Burt County.

PROGRAMS: Annual Meeting; Exhibits; Facility Rental; Garden Tours; Guided Tours; Publication; Research Library/Archives

COLLECTIONS: [1904-1940s] Agricultural artifacts, clothing, military artifacts, quilt collection, newspapers, and 2,000 photographs.

HOURS: Yr T,Th,Sa 1-5

ADMISSION: Donations accepted

THEDFORD

5212
Thomas County Historical Society
609 Court St, 69166 [PO Box 131, 69166]; (c) Thomas

Private non-profit/ 1989/ Board of Directors/ staff: 6(v)/ members: 44

HISTORIC PRESERVATION AGENCY; HISTORICAL SOCIETY; HISTORY MUSEUM: Dedicated to preserving historical collections of the area.

PROGRAMS: Annual Meeting; Elder's Programs; Exhibits; Facility Rental; Family Programs; Film/Video; Guided Tours; Interpretation; Lectures; Living History; Publication; Research Library/Archives

COLLECTIONS: [1900s] Quilts, military uniforms, army artifacts, local history books, history book on Thomas County, local artifacts.

HOURS: May-Sept 30 M-F 10-12/2-4:30 or by appt

ADMISSION: Donations accepted

TRENTON

5213
Hitchcock County Historical Society
311 E 1st St, 69044 [PO Box 511, 69044-0511]; (c) Hitchcock

County/ 1928/ Hitchcock County Musuem Board/ staff: 5(v)/ members: 100

HISTORICAL SOCIETY; HISTORY MUSEUM: Preserves history for future generations.

PROGRAMS: Annual Meeting; Exhibits

COLLECTIONS: [Late 19th c-present] Early American Indian artifacts, household items, old school house, general store, dishes, toys, old cars, farming implements.

HOURS: May-Sept Su 2- 5

ADMISSION: No charge

VALENTINE

5214
Centennial Hall Corp
3rd & Maycomb, 69201 [810 E 9th St, 69201]; (p) (402) 376-2418; (c) Cherry

Private non-profit/ 1983/ members: 150

HISTORIC SITE; HISTORY MUSEUM: Operates heritage museum housed in high school building built in 1897.

PROGRAMS: Exhibits; Festivals; Guided Tours

COLLECTIONS: Bell collection, china, clocks, antiques.

HOURS: May-Sept Th-Sa 1-5

ADMISSION: $2, Children $1

5215
Cherry County Historical Society
Main St & US 20, 69201 [PO Box 284, 69201]; (p) (402) 376-2015

VALLEY

5216
Valley Community Historical Society
218 W Alexander St, 68064 [PO Box 685, 68064]; (p) (402) 359-2678; (c) Douglas

Private non-profit/ 1966/ Directors/ members: 90/publication: *Annual Report*

HISTORIC SITE; HISTORICAL SOCIETY; HISTORY MUSEUM: Maintains Valley's 1873 school house, 1896 Baptist church, until 1918 when it became a Catholic church.

PROGRAMS: Annual Meeting; Community Outreach; Exhibits; Family Programs; Interpretation; Publication

COLLECTIONS: [1864-1925] Artifacts of Hairy Mammoth, Africa, Indians and settlers. War memorabilia from Civil to Vietnam, Early Platt books, farm and railroad tools, musical instruments. Many historical pictures, documents, and books.

HOURS: May-Sept Su 2-4 and by appt

ADMISSION: Donations accepted

WAHOO

5217
Hanson House
12th & Linden, 68066 [611 N Walnut Apt 11, 68066]; (p) (402) 443-3936

5218
Saunders County Historical Society
Hwy 77 & 3rd St, 68066 [240 N Walnut, 68066]; (p) (402) 443-3090; www.co.saunders.ne.us; (c) Saunders

Private non-profit/ 1963/ Board of Directors/ staff: 1(f); 2(p); 50(v)/ members: 450

HISTORICAL SOCIETY; HISTORY MUSEUM; RESEARCH CENTER: Interprets the history of Saunders County through exhibits in the main museum, six historic structures, and an agricultural building.

PROGRAMS: Annual Meeting; Exhibits; Facility Rental; Family Programs; Festivals; Film/Video; Guided Tours; Publication; Research Library/Archives

COLLECTIONS: [1860s-present] Artifacts from the county, archives, photos, genealogical items, and Native American artifacts.

HOURS: Apr-Oct T-Sa 10-4, Su 1:30-4:30; Nov- Mar T-Fr 10-4

ADMISSION: No charge

WELLFLEET

5219
Dancing Leaf Earth Lodge
6100 E Opal Springs Rd, 69170; (p) (308) 963-4233; (c) Lincoln

Private for-profit/ 1989/ Les and Jan Hosick/ staff: 2(f); 1(v)

LIVING HISTORY/OUTDOOR MUSEUM: Replicates pre-historic Native America life. Reconstructed earthen lodge, museum of Native American artifacts, nature trails.

PROGRAMS: Elder's Programs; Exhibits; Facility Rental; Family Programs; Guided Tours; Interpretation; Lectures; Living History; School-Based Curriculum

COLLECTIONS: [Prehistory-present] Paleontology and archeology findings of the Medicine Creek area in the Southwest NE Prairie.

HOURS: Yr by appt

ADMISSION: $7, Student $5

WILBER

5220
Dvoracek Memorial Library
419 W Third St, 68465 [PO Box 803, 68465-0803]; (p) (402) 821-2832; dvoraceklib@isp channel.com; www.ianr.unl.edu/ianr/saline/library.htm; (c) Saline

City/ 1968/ Board of Trustees/ staff: 1(f); 2(p); 3(v)

LIBRARY AND/OR ARCHIVES: Public library.

PROGRAMS: Exhibits; Facility Rental; Family Programs; Guided Tours; Research Library/ Archives

COLLECTIONS: Fiction and non-fiction, genealogy for county, music, Czech-Slovak books and music.

HOURS: Yr M-T, Th-F 9-5:30, W 9-8, Sa 11-4

ADMISSION: No charge

5221
Wilber Czech Museum
102 W 3rd St, 68465 [PO Box 253, 68465]; (p) (402) 821-2183; (c) Saline

Private non-profit/ 1965

HISTORY MUSEUM: Displays and exhibits items of Czech heritage.

PROGRAMS: Community Outreach; Exhibits; Guided Tours

COLLECTIONS: Displays of an old butcher shop, mercantile store, barber shop, dental office, and beauty shop.

HOURS: Yr Daily 1-4

ADMISSION: Donations accepted

WINNEBAGO

5222
Ho-Chunk Historical Society
Rt 1 Box 21 E, 68071; (p) (402) 878-2976; dsmith@lptc.cc.ne.us; www.lptc.cc.ne.us/; (c) Thurston

Tribal/ 1994/ staff: 4(v)/ members: 14

HISTORICAL SOCIETY; LIBRARY AND/OR ARCHIVES: Preserves the history and culture of the Winnebago tribe of NE.

PROGRAMS: Research Library/Archives

COLLECTIONS: 300 oil paintings of tribal leaders of the past. A collection of traditional Winnebago dolls.

HOURS: Yr M-F 6pm-10pm, Sa-Su 12-10

ADMISSION: Donations accepted

WINNETOON

5223
Winnetoon Board Walk Back in Time
W Main St, 68789 [PO Box 94 Main St, 68789]; (p) (402) 847-3368; (c) Knox

Private non-profit/ 1999/ Winnetoon Community Foundation/ staff: 1(f); 1(p); 5(v)

HISTORICAL SOCIETY; LIVING HISTORY/ OUTDOOR MUSEUM: Collects and Preserves local history.

PROGRAMS: Guided Tours; Research Library/ Archives

COLLECTIONS: [1888-1914] Drugstore, Jones Merchandise, post office, blacksmith shop, and other business building fronts line the boardwalk.

HOURS: Yr Daily M-F 9-3

ADMISSION: Donations accepted

YORK

5224
D.A.R. Anna Palmer Museum
211 E 7th St, 68467; (p) (402) 363-2630; (c) York

City/ 1967/ staff: 1(f); 1(p)

HISTORY MUSEUM: Artifacts and memorabilia related to York city and county.

PROGRAMS: Exhibits

COLLECTIONS: [1800s-present] Pioneer collections, Civil War artifacts, local artifacts and memorabilia.

5225
DAR Anna Palmer Museum
211 E 7th St, 68467; (p) (402) 363-2630; (c) York

City/ 1967/ staff: 1(f); 1(p); 1(v)

HISTORY MUSEUM: Items from or about the history of the city of York and the county of York.

PROGRAMS: Exhibits

COLLECTIONS: [1800s-present] Pioneer collections, civil war items, day to day living items used in area.

HOURS: Yr M-F 8-4

ADMISSION: No charge

NEVADA

BATTLE MOUNTAIN

5226
Lander County Historical Society
[PO Box 663, 89820]; (p) (775) 635-8581; (c) Lander

Private non-profit/ 1979/ staff: 5(v)/ members: 30

HISTORICAL SOCIETY: Raising money to open museum, have small exhibit in local store.

PROGRAMS: Exhibits

COLLECTIONS: [1840s-present] Mining equipment, personal artifacts, and photographs.

HOURS: Yr T-Sa 10-4

ADMISSION: No charge

BOULDER CITY

5227
Boulder City/Hoover Dam Museum
1305 Arizona St, Boulder Dam Hotel, 89006 [PO Box 60516, 89006]; (p) (702) 294-1988; (f) (702) 294-4380; (c) Clark

Private non-profit/ 1980/ Boulder City Museum and Historical Association/ staff: 1(f); 3(p); 5(v)/ members: 400/publication: *Boulder City/Hoover Dam Museum Newsletter*

HISTORIC SITE; HISTORICAL SOCIETY; HISTORY MUSEUM: Collects, preserves, and makes available for study records and artifacts detailing the personal, human side of Hoover Dam construction, life during the Great Depression, and the development of Boulder City, NV.

PROGRAMS: Annual Meeting; Exhibits; Publication; Research Library/Archives

COLLECTIONS: [Hoover Dam 1920s-1950s, Boulder City 1930s-present] Manuscript collections; photographs and artwork; posters and broadsides; maps; serials and monographs; legal documents; biography files; subject files; scrapbooks; oral history tapes; videotapes and film; and three-dimensional artifacts.

HOURS: Yr M-Sa 10-5, Su 12-5

ADMISSION: Donations accepted

CARSON CITY

5228

Bowers Mansion Regional Park

4005 US 395 N, 89704; (p) (775) 849-1825; (f) (775) 849-9568; (c) Washoe

County/ 1946/ Parks Dept/ staff: 3(f); 6(p)

HISTORIC SITE; HOUSE MUSEUM: Preserves and interprets the Comstock area's rich history of mining, lumbering, Native American culture, and colorful western pioneer life.

PROGRAMS: Exhibits; Facility Rental; Festivals; Guided Tours; Interpretation; Living History; School-Based Curriculum

COLLECTIONS: [1860-1880] A restored historical mansion containing period furniture, photographs, artifacts, dolls, books, pianos, and a harp.

HOURS: Mansion: May-Oct Daily 11-4:30; Park: Yr Daily

5229

Historic Preservation Office

100 N Stewart St, 89701; (p) (775) 687-1311; (f) (775) 687-3442; (c) Carson City

State/ 1977/ staff: 8(f)/ members: 1

HISTORIC PRESERVATION AGENCY: State Historic

5230

Mormon Station State Historic Park

2295 Main St, 89701 [1060 Mallory Way, 89701]; (p) (775) 782-2590; (f) (775) 687-8972; (c) Douglas

State/ 1851/ staff: 1(f); 2(p); 15(v)

HISTORIC SITE; STATE PARK: Museum and Stockade provide exhibits which tell the history of Mormon Station and the nearby area.

PROGRAMS: Community Outreach; Concerts; Elder's Programs; Exhibits; Facility Rental; Family Programs; Guided Tours; Interpretation; Lectures; Living History; Reenactments; School-Based Curriculum

COLLECTIONS: [1850-1910] Log cabin, stockade, and exhibits; materials and artifacts displayed in exhibits relating to period and area.

HOURS: Mid May-mid Oct Daily 9-5

ADMISSION: Donations accepted

5231

Nevada State Railroad Museum

2180 S Carson St, 89701-5552; (p) (775) 687-6953; (f) (775) 687-8294; (c) Carson City

State/ 1980/ staff: 13(f); 100(v)/ members: 800/publication: Sagebrush Headlight

HISTORY MUSEUM: Preserving and interpreting the railroad heritage of Nevada.

PROGRAMS: Annual Meeting; Community Outreach; Elder's Programs; Exhibits; Facility Rental; Festivals; Interpretation; Lectures; Publication; Research Library/Archives; School-Based Curriculum

COLLECTIONS: [1869-1950] Railroad related materials and artifacts.

HOURS: Yr W-Su 8:30-4:30

ADMISSION: $2

5232

Stewart Indian School Museum

5366 Snyder Ave, 89701; (p) (775) 882-6929; (f) (775) 882-6929; (c) Carson City

Private non-profit/ 1981/ staff: 4(v)

HISTORIC SITE; HISTORY MUSEUM; LIVING HISTORY/OUTDOOR MUSEUM: Maintains Stewart Indian boarding school which ran from 1890 to 1980.

PROGRAMS: Exhibits; Festivals; Guided Tours; Living History

COLLECTIONS: [1887-1980] School and local ancestral artifacts, Native American art, 46 buildings, museum in Superintendent's old house.

HOURS: Yr Daily 9-5

ADMISSION: No charge

EAST ELY

5233

East Ely Railroad Depot Museum

1100 Ave A, 89315 [PO Box 151100, 89315]; (p) (775) 289-1663; (f) (775) 289-1664; esm @idsely.com; (c) White Pine

State/ 1992/ staff: 2(f); 1(p); 60(v)

HISTORIC SITE; HISTORY MUSEUM; LIVING HISTORY/OUTDOOR MUSEUM; RESEARCH CENTER: Utilizes its collection to preserve, study, and interpret the rich heritage and industrial development of eastern NE. This is accomplished through exhibits, tours, and educational programming. Historic steam and diesel train excursions.

PROGRAMS: Community Outreach; Concerts; Exhibits; Facility Rental; Festivals; Guided Tours; Interpretation; Lectures; Living History; School-Based Curriculum

COLLECTIONS: [Early 20th C] Documents from the NE Northern Railroad, Nevada's last operation Shortline, complete payroll documents, financial reports, maps, and company correspondence.

HOURS: Yr M-F 8-4, some weekends

ADMISSION: Donations requested

5234

White Pine Historical Railroad Foundation

1100 Ave A, 89315 [PO Box 150040, 89315]; (p) (775) 289-2085; (f) (775) 289-6284; page s.prodigy.com/nevada_northern/; (c) White Pine

City, non-profit/ 1983/ staff: 4(f); 3(p); 100(v)

HISTORY MUSEUM; LIVING HISTORY/OUTDOOR MUSEUM: Operates historical railroad museum offering regularly scheduled steam and diesel excursions with all aspects of a rail yard and supporting facilities intact.

PROGRAMS: Exhibits; Facility Rental; Family Programs; Festivals; Guided Tours; Interpretation; Reenactments

COLLECTIONS: [1887-1952] Authentic locomotives, rolling stock, buildings, track, and support equipment showcasing the early days of mining in the old west.

HOURS: May-Oct Daily 8-5

ELKO

5235

Northeastern Nevada Museum

1515 Idaho St, 89801; (p) (775) 738-3418; (f) (775) 778-9318; (c) Elko

Private non-profit/ 1968/ staff: 5(f); 5(p); 6(v)/ members: 1300

ART MUSEUM; GENEALOGICAL SOCIETY; HISTORIC PRESERVATION AGENCY; HISTORICAL SOCIETY; HISTORY MUSEUM; RESEARCH CENTER: Interpretive displays, extensive gun collection, historical displays, natural history, mining exhibits, area wildlife displays, art gallery, gift shop, research library, archives, photo library, newspaper, research files.

PROGRAMS: Community Outreach; Concerts; Elder's Programs; Exhibits; Facility Rental; Family Programs; Festivals; Film/Video; Guided Tours; Publication; Research Library/Archives; School-Based Curriculum; Theatre

COLLECTIONS: Historical, Indian (Shoshone and Paiute), natural history, local interest, manuscripts, photographs, American mastodon, guns and other materials and artifacts.

HOURS: Yr M-Sa 9-5, Su 1-5

ADMISSION: Donations accepted

5236

Western Folklife Center

501 Railroad St, 89801; (p) (775) 738-7508; (f) (775) 738-2900; wfc@westernfolklife.org; www.westernfolklife.org; (c) Elko

Private non-profit/ 1980/ staff: 12(f); 1(p); 300(v)/ members: 980

PROFESSIONAL ORGANIZATION: Dedicated to presenting, preserving, perpetuating the folk research, documentation, and public performances, exhibits, and educational programs.

PROGRAMS: Community Outreach; Concerts; Exhibits; Facility Rental; Family Programs; Festivals

COLLECTIONS: [1980-present] Audio, video, and photographic collection drawn from original folklife fieldwork in the western states as well as documentation of Center events. Handcrafted contemporary cowboy gear.

HOURS: Yr T-Sa 10-5:30

ADMISSION: No charge

ELY

5237

Ely Field Office, Bureau of Land Management

702 N Industrial Way, 89301 [HC 33 Box 33500, 89301-9408]; (p) (775) 289-1800; (f) (775) 289-1910; (c) White Pine

Federal/ 1946/ staff: 75(f); 25(p); 10(v)

HISTORIC PRESERVATION AGENCY; LIVING HISTORY/OUTDOOR MUSEUM; RESEARCH CENTER: The headquarters for administration of nearly 12 million acres of public land resources.

PROGRAMS: Community Outreach; Exhibits; Family Programs; Guided Tours; Interpretation; Lectures; Research Library/Archives

COLLECTIONS: [Prehistory-present] 10,000 prehistoric and historic sites are protected and inventory records maintained including about 130 miles of the Pony Express National Historical Trail and several historical mine sites.

HOURS: Yr Daily

ADMISSION: No charge

EUREKA

5238
Eureka County Sentinel Museum
10 N Monroe St, 89316 [PO Box 284, 89316]; (p) (775) 237-5010; (f) (775) 237-6040; wcu chine@eurekanv.org; (c) Eureka

County/ 1983/ staff: 1(f); 1(p)/ members: 1

HISTORY MUSEUM: Part of the Eureka Co. government.

PROGRAMS: Exhibits; Guided Tours; Interpretation

COLLECTIONS: [Prehistoric-1800s] Displays and interprets the lead and silver mining history of the area as well as the newspaper history of the community.

HOURS: Yr T-Sa 9-5

ADMISSION: Donations accepted

FALLON

5239
Churchill County Museum & Archives
1050 S Maine St, 89406; (p) (775) 423-3677; (f) (775) 423-3662; ccmuseum@phonewave.net; ccmuseum.org; (c) Churchill

County/ 1967/ staff: 1(f); 9(p); 15(v)/ members: 525/publication: In Focus

HISTORY MUSEUM; LIBRARY AND/OR ARCHIVES: Collects, preserves and interprets Churchill County history.

PROGRAMS: Annual Meeting; Community Outreach; Concerts; Elder's Programs; Exhibits; Family Programs; Festivals; Guided Tours; Interpretation; Lectures; Living History; Publication; Reenactments; Research Library/ Archives; School-Based Curriculum

COLLECTIONS: [Prehistoric and 19th-20th c] 17,000 artifacts, 30,000 photographs, and 1,000 pieces of archival material, books.

HOURS: Yr Daily Jan-Mar M-Sa 10-4, Su 12-4; Apr-Dec M-Sa 10-5, Su 12-5

ADMISSION: Donations accepted

GARDNERVILLE

5240
Carson Valley Historical Society
1477 Hwy 395 N, 89410; (p) (775) 782-2555; cecileb_99@yahoo.com

Private non-profit/ 1969/ staff: 3(f); 60(v)/ members: 256

HISTORICAL SOCIETY; HISTORY MUSEUM; RESEARCH CENTER: Owns and operates two museums, one of which has a reference library, and maintains an extensive collection of NE pioneer documents and photographs.

PROGRAMS: Annual Meeting; Community Outreach; Concerts; Exhibits; Facility Rental; Festivals; Interpretation; Lectures; Living His-

tory; Publication; Reenactments; Research Library/Archives

COLLECTIONS: [1916-present] Farm and ranch implements, newspapers equipment, documents, books, photographs, extensive collection of taxidermy mounts, furniture, records of the first permanent settlement in NE.

HOURS: Yr Carson Valley Museum: T-Sa T-Sa 10-4; Genoa Courthouse Museum: May-Oct 10-4:30

ADMISSION: $2, Student $1; Donations requested

HENDERSON

5241
Clark County Museum
1830 S Boulder Hwy, 89015; (p) (702) 455-7955; (f) (702) 455-7948; www.co.clark.nv.us; (c) Clark

County/ 1979/ staff: 5(f); 17(p); 5(v)/ members: 167/publication: Clark County Aviation History

HISTORY MUSEUM; HOUSE MUSEUM; LIVING HISTORY/OUTDOOR MUSEUM: Maintains exhibit center and a collection of restored historic homes in a museum park setting. An annual series of traveling exhibits and programs combine with permanent exhibits.

PROGRAMS: Community Outreach; Concerts; Exhibits; Family Programs; Festivals; Film/Video; Interpretation; Lectures; Living History; Publication; Research Library/ Archives; School-Based Curriculum

COLLECTIONS: [1900-present] Southern NE cultural inventory with focus on Native American mining, aviation, gaming and entertainment, transportation and technology and county history.

HOURS: Yr Daily 9-4:30

ADMISSION: $1.50, Children $1, Seniors $1

5242
MacDonald Center For Ancient History
1700 Horizon Ridge #200, 89012-1833; (p) (702) 458-0001; (f) (702) 458-5570; macmu seum@aol.com; (c) Clark

Private non-profit/ 1996/ staff: 1(f)

HISTORY MUSEUM: New Museum which is in the process of fundraising and building.

PROGRAMS: Community Outreach; Lectures

LAS VEGAS

5243
Guinness World Records Museum
2780 Las Vegas Blvd S, 89109; (p) (702) 792-3766; (f) (702) 792-0530; lasvegas.com/ lv/guiness/; (c) Clark

Private for-profit/ 1990/ staff: 2(f); 3(p)

Brings The Guiness Book of World Records to life with life-sized replicas, record breaking videos, and unusual collections.

HOURS: Yr Daily 9-6

ADMISSION: $4.95, Student $3.95, Children $2.95, Seniors $3.95

5244
Howard W. Cannon Aviation Museum/Office and Collections Clark County Museum
McCarran International Airport, [1830 S Boulder Hwy, Henderson, 89015]; (p) (702) 455-7968; (f) (702) 455-7948; ccparks@co. clark.nv.us; http://www.co.clark.nv.us/parks/ Aviation_Museum.htm; (c) Clark

County/ 1992/ staff: 2(f); 2(p); 3(v)/publication: Desert Airways

AVIATION MUSEUM: Collects, preserves, and interprets the aviation history of Southern NE with an emphasis on commercial and general aviation.

PROGRAMS: Exhibits; Film/Video; Publication; Research Library/Archives

COLLECTIONS: [1920-present] Artifacts including uniforms, insignia, military, airline equipment, memorabilia and souvenirs; archival materials including books, articles, timetables, ephemera, maps and charts, photographs.

HOURS: Yr Daily 24 hours per day

ADMISSION: No charge

5245
Liberace Foundation and Museum, The
1775 E Tropicana Ave, 89119; (p) (702) 798-5595; (f) (702) 798-7386; sharris@liberace. org; www.liberace.org; (c) Clark

Private non-profit/ 1976/ staff: 8(f); 8(p); 20(v)/ members: 200

ART MUSEUM; HISTORY MUSEUM; RESEARCH CENTER: Grants scholarships to students pursuing careers in the Arts. Preserves and exhibits Liberace's collections and educates the public about Liberace scholars, the Arts, and Las Vegas history.

PROGRAMS: Community Outreach; Concerts; Elder's Programs; Exhibits; Facility Rental; Family Programs; Film/Video; Guided Tours; Interpretation; Lectures; Publication; Research Library/Archives; School-Based Curriculum

COLLECTIONS: [19th-20th c] Liberace's stage costumes and furs, jewelry, custom autos, pianos, and home furnishings. Archival collection of sound and video recordings, personal and professional photos, and periodicals.

HOURS: Yr M-Sa 10-5, Su 1-5

ADMISSION: $8, Student $5, Seniors $5; Under 13/Mbrs free

5246
Marjorie Barrick Museum of Natural History
4505 Maryland Pkwy, 89154-4012; (p) (702) 895-3381; (f) (702) 895-3094; hrcweb.1v-hrc. nevada.edu/mbm/index.html; (c) Clark

State/ 1967/ staff: 8(f); 3(p)

NATURAL HISTORY MUSEUM; RESEARCH CENTER: Maintains the museum's research center includes, cultural resource management, the State Archive, Southern Ne, and collections in herpetology, entomology, ornithology, anthropology, and archaeology.

PROGRAMS: Exhibits; Facility Rental; Garden Tours; Lectures

COLLECTIONS: Ornithology collection 7,500

specimens; Entomology collection; herpetology collection; anthropology dance masks, Native American artifacts, Mayan artifacts.

HOURS: Yr M-F 8-4:45, Sa 10-2

ADMISSION: No charge

5247
Nevada State Museum and Historical Society
700 Twin Lakes Dr, 89107-2104; (p) (702) 486-5205; (f) (702) 486-5172; (c) Clark

State/ 1982/ staff: 14(f); 1(p); 20(v)/ members: 225

HISTORY MUSEUM: Collects, preserves, and exhibits the history and natural history of Nevada, focusing on southern NV.

PROGRAMS: Community Outreach; Exhibits; Facility Rental; Guided Tours; Research Library/Archives; School-Based Curriculum

COLLECTIONS: [20th c] 10,000 photographs, 100 manuscripts, 200 historic maps, newspaper indexes, and 10,000 museum artifacts relating to NV history; mammals, lepidoptera of the region.

HOURS: Yr Daily 9-5

ADMISSION: $2, Under 18/Members free

5248
Nevada Test Site Historical Foundation
2330 Paseo del Prado, Ste C104, 89036 [PO Box 30182, 89036-0182]; (p) (702) 257-7900; (f) (702) 257-7999; mfg@ntsdev.com; www. lvrj.com/communitylink/ntshistorical; (c) Clark

Private non-profit/ 1998/ staff: 1(p); 40(v)/ members: 200

HISTORY MUSEUM: Promotes and supports a nuclear testing research center and exhibits for scientific, historical, educational, and charitable purposes.

PROGRAMS: Annual Meeting; Community Outreach; Exhibits; Film/Video; Guided Tours; Publication; Research Library/Archives

COLLECTIONS: [1950-present] Public historical and archival records, films, photographs, testing, and archaeological artifacts associated with the NV Test Site.

HOURS: Yr W-F

ADMISSION: No charge

5249
Old Las Vegas Mormon Fort State Historic Park
500 E Washington, 89158 [State Mail Rm, 89158]; (p) (702) 486-3511; (f) (702) 486-3734; cmack8@aol.com; www.state.nv.us/ stparks; (c) Clark

State/ 1991/ staff: 2(f); 2(p); 180(v)

HISTORIC SITE; STATE PARK: Collects, preserves, and interprets Southern Nevada's history.

PROGRAMS: Community Outreach; Exhibits; Festivals; Interpretation; Living History; Publication; Reenactments

COLLECTIONS: [1855-1930] Period building, furnishings and photographs of early Las Vegas. The site contains a remnant of the original European American Fort built in Las Vegas in 1855 making it the oldest building in the State of Nevada.

HOURS: Yr Daily 8:30-4

ADMISSION: $3/vehicle

NIXON

5250
Pyramid Lake Paiute Cultural Center
Hwy 446, 89424 [PO Box 256, 89424]; (p) (775) 574-1088; (f) (775) 574-1090; (c) Washoe

Private non-profit; Tribal/ 1976/ staff: 3(f); 10(v)

TRIBAL MUSEUM: Preserves the history contributions of the first inhabitants of the Great Basin and provides educational opportunities.

PROGRAMS: Exhibits; Film/Video; Interpretation; Lectures

COLLECTIONS: [Mid 1800-present] Artifacts collected in the Pyramid Lake area and adjacent area's of the Great Basin. Stone objects, basketry, beadwork, and fiber technology; photographic collection of Native Americans of the Great Basin.

HOURS: Yr Winter M-F 10-4:30; Summer Daily 10-4:30

ADMISSION: No charge

OVERTON

5251
Lost City Museum
721 S Moapa Valley Blvd, 89040 [PO Box 807, 89040]; (p) (702) 397-2193; (f) (702) 397-8987; kolson@comnett.net; www.com nett.net/kolson/; (c) Clark

State/ 1935/ staff: 6(f); 2(p); 14(v)/ members: 60

HISTORY MUSEUM: Preserves and interprets the prehistory and history of the Moapa Valley in Southern NV and educates the public through exhibits, public programs, and publications.

PROGRAMS: Community Outreach; Exhibits; Festivals; Guided Tours; Interpretation; Lectures; Research Library/Archives

COLLECTIONS: [1-1150 A.D.] 20,000 archaeological and ethnological artifacts, 2,000 geologic specimens, 200 photographs, 200 volumes, maps and 100 manuscripts.

HOURS: Yr Daily 8:30-4:30

ADMISSION: $2; Children free

RENO

5252
Lake Mansion, The
4598 S Virginia St, 89502; (p) (775) 829-1868; (f) (775) 826-6107; vsanevada@juno.com; www.nv.vsarts.org; (c) Washoe

Private non-profit/ 1972/ VAS Arts of Nevada/ staff: 2(f); 1(p); 100(v)

HOUSE MUSEUM: Restoring the home of the founder of Reno, Myron Lake.

PROGRAMS: Community Outreach; Exhibits; Facility Rental; Family Programs; Festivals

COLLECTIONS: [1880-1900] Period furnishings from 1880s-1900.

HOURS: By appt

ADMISSION: No charge/Donations accepted

5253
Liberty Belle Slot Machine Collection
4250 S Virginia St, 89502; (p) (775) 825-1776; (f) (775) 826-7411; libbelbks@aol.com; www. libertybellereno.com; (c) Washoe

Private non-profit/ 1958/ staff: 3(f)

HISTORIC SITE: Antique slots on public display including the original 3-reel slot and draw poker machine, both invented by the proprietor's grandfather; other old-west memorabilia.

PROGRAMS: Exhibits

COLLECTIONS: [1890-1950] Antique slot machines, saloon memorabilia, early advertising, horse drawn vehicle collection plus miscellaneous turn-of-the-century memorabilia.

HOURS: Yr Daily 11am-11pm

ADMISSION: No charge

5254
National Automobile Museum
10 Lake St S, 89501-1558; (p) (775) 333-9300; (f) (775) 333-9309; www.automuseum.org; (c) Washoe

Private non-profit/ 1989/ staff: 12(f); 7(p); 90(v)/ members: 700

The National Automobile Museum (The Harrah Collection) collects and preserves automobiles and tells the story of the automobile's impact on American Society.

COLLECTIONS: [1890-1999] 227 vehicles 1892-present; automotive library and archives, books, periodicals, photographs, sales literature, shop and owner's manuals; early automotive advertising signs, vintage clothing 1890-1910; auto-related artifacts.

HOURS: Yr Daily

ADMISSION: $7.50, Children $2.50, Seniors $6.50

5255
Nevada Historical Society
1650 N Virginia St, 89503; (p) (775) 688-1191; (f) (775) 688-2917; (c) Washoe

State/ 1904/ staff: 10(f); 1(p); 75(v)/ members: 900

HISTORICAL SOCIETY; HISTORY MUSEUM; LIBRARY AND/OR ARCHIVES; RESEARCH CENTER: Maintains research collections regarding the history of Nevada and the West.

PROGRAMS: Community Outreach; Concerts; Exhibits; Facility Rental; Family Programs; Festivals; Film/Video; Guided Tours; Interpretation; Lectures; Living History; Publication; Research Library/Archives; School-Based Curriculum

COLLECTIONS: [1850-present] History of Nevada and the Great Basin, library, photos, newspapers, maps, ephemera, exhibits.

HOURS: Museum: Yr M-Sa 10-5; Library: T-Sa 12-4

ADMISSION: $2; Under 18 free

5256
Wilbur D. May Museum
1502 Washington St, 89503; (p) (775) 785-5961; (f) (775) 785-4707; (c) Washoe

County/ 1985/ staff: 2(f); 4(p); 20(v)

HISTORY MUSEUM; NATURAL HISTORY MUSEUM: Preserves the artifacts that Wilbur

May spent a lifetime collecting and presents a view of his lifestyle and many talents to the people and visitors of his community.

PROGRAMS: Community Outreach; Exhibits; Facility Rental; Family Programs; Guided Tours; School-Based Curriculum

COLLECTIONS: [300 BC-present] Antiques and collectibles from Wilbur's 40 trips around the world. Dioramas and the trophy room provide a glimpse of his big game hunting years.

HOURS: Yr vary call for times

ADMISSION: $2.50, Children $1.50, Seniors $1.50

SEARCHLIGHT

5257
Searchlight Historic Museum and Guild
200 Michael Wendell Way, 89046 [PO Box 36, 89046]; (p) (702) 297-1201; (c) Clark

Private non-profit/ 1989/ staff: 1(p)/ members: 100

HISTORY MUSEUM: Gathers and preserves artifacts, photo collections, and finds items needed for the museum exhibits.

COLLECTIONS: Self-guided 500 foot inside history museum which features, early history, famous personalities, mining, railroad, and area. Outdoor mining displays.

HOURS: Yr M-F 9-5, Sa 9-1

ADMISSION: Donations accepted

SILVER SPRINGS

5258
Fort Churchill State Historic Site
10000 Hwy 95 A, 89429; (p) (775) 577-2345; (f) (775) 577-3941; (c) Lyon

State/ 1957/ staff: 2(f); 3(p)/publication: *Fort Churchill-1860 Outpost*

HISTORIC SITE; STATE PARK: Maintains 4,461 acre park with small Visitor Center, historic abode ruins.

PROGRAMS: Exhibits; Guided Tours; Interpretation; Living History; Publication; Reenactments

COLLECTIONS: [1860-1900] Two 1860s period canons, caissons and limbers, 1860 military artifacts, 1900s period blacksmith equipment, multiple historic photographs, manuscripts, newspaper articles. Museum artifacts stored in historic archives.

HOURS: Yr Daily 8-4

ADMISSION: $3/vehicle

SPARKS

5259
Sparks Heritage Museum
820 Victorian Ave, 89431; (p) (775) 355-1144; (c) Washoe

Private non-profit/ 1984/ staff: 1(p); 25(v)/ members: 498

HISTORIC PRESERVATION AGENCY; HISTORICAL SOCIETY; HISTORY MUSEUM; RESEARCH CENTER: Dedicated to the preservation of local history and artifacts and the education of local groups.

PROGRAMS: Annual Meeting; Community Outreach; Exhibits; Facility Rental; Film/Video; Guided Tours; Research Library/Archives

COLLECTIONS: [1850s-1940] Photos, books, documents, artifacts, dioramas, exhibits concerning local history.

HOURS: Yr T-F 11-4, Sa-Su 1-4

ADMISSION: Donations accepted

TONOPAH

5260
Central Nevada Historical Society/Museum
1900 Logan Field Rd, 89049 [PO Box 326, 89049]; (p) (775) 482-9676; (f) (775) 482-5423; (c) Nye

Private non-profit/ 1978/ staff: 1(f); 2(p); 8(v)/ members: 550/publication: *Central Nevada's Glorious Past*

HISTORICAL SOCIETY; HISTORY MUSEUM; RESEARCH CENTER: Preserve and display the history of Nye and Esmeralda counties with associated research library.

PROGRAMS: Annual Meeting; Community Outreach; Exhibits; Film/Video; Guided Tours; Interpretation; Lectures; Publication; Research Library/Archives

COLLECTIONS: [1850s-present] Prehistoric to modern mankind related to Nye/Esmeralda counties, research library 1,000 books, oral histories, films, videos, 30,000 photos, 500 maps, manuscripts, and albums.

HOURS: Yr Apr-Sept Daily 9-5; Oct-Mar M-Sa 11-5

ADMISSION: No charge

VIRGINIA CITY

5261
Mackay Mansion
129 S D St, 89440 [Box 971, 89440]; (p) (775) 847-0173; www.mackaymansoncom; (c) Storey

Private non-profit/ 1859/ staff: 2(f); 2(p)

GARDEN; HISTORIC SITE; HISTORY MUSEUM; HOUSE MUSEUM: Dedicated to preserving the foundation of the great Hearst fortune and the largest silver strike in world history, found by John Mackay.

PROGRAMS: Annual Meeting; Concerts; Facility Rental; Garden Tours; Guided Tours; Lectures

COLLECTIONS: [1870-1880] Original Mackay furnishings, Renaissance Revival, Victorian dolls, mining artifacts, and dishes dating from 1860-1880.

HOURS: Yr Daily 10-6

ADMISSION: $3; Under 5 free

5262
Way It Was Museum, The
113 N C St, 89440 [PO Box 158, 89440]; (p) (775) 847-0766; (f) (775) 847-9613; (c) Storey

Private non-profit/ 1958/ staff: 1(f); 1(p)

LIVING HISTORY/OUTDOOR MUSEUM: Walk through museum of historical Virginia City mining equipment, ores, various day to day living artifacts, fashions, fashions, from the "Bonanza" days on the Comstock.

PROGRAMS: Exhibits; Film/Video

COLLECTIONS: [1860-1890] Displays of period mining equipment, scale model operations, antique glassware, Victorian fashion, tools.

HOURS: Yr Daily 10-5

ADMISSION: $3, Under 11 free

WINNEMUCCA

5263
Humboldt Museum
Jungo Road & Maple Ave, 89446 [PO Box 819, 89446]; (p) (775) 623-2912; (f) (775) 623-5640; (c) Humboldt

Private non-profit/ 1978/ staff: 1(f); 1(p); 5(v)/ members: 450

HISTORICAL SOCIETY; HISTORY MUSEUM; RESEARCH CENTER: Maintains the parent organization of the Humboldt Museum whose goal is to serve this north central area as a permanent repository for historical data.

PROGRAMS: Exhibits; Facility Rental; Guided Tours; Publication; Research Library/Archives

COLLECTIONS: [1888-1930] Newspaper volumes, 1903 to 1955; 1,000 pieces of old sheet music; 2,000 museum artifacts including early antique automobiles; 1867 Epler survey map of Humboldt Valley; 4,000 old negatives; 1,500 early photographs.

HOURS: Yr M-Sa 10-12/1-4

ADMISSION: No charge/Donations accepted

NEW HAMPSHIRE

ALSTEAD VILLAGE

5264
Alstead Historical Society
Main St, 03602 [Rt 1, Box 168A, 03602]; (c) Cheshire

Joint/ 1978/ City; County; State/ staff: 4(v)/ members: 30/publication: *Alstead Through the Years*

HISTORIC SITE; HISTORICAL SOCIETY; HISTORY MUSEUM: Collects items pertaining to Alstead history.

PROGRAMS: Annual Meeting; Community Outreach; Exhibits; Research Library/Archives

COLLECTIONS: [1780-20th c] Photographs of local industry paper mills, mines, cobbler shops and blacksmiths, one-room schools, early township newspapers, and a military exhibition focusing upon the Civil War onward.

HOURS: May 30-Oct 30 Su

ALTON

5265
Alton Historical Society, Inc.
Gilman Library, Main St, 03809 [PO Box 536, 03809-0536]; (p) (603) 569-2629; (c) Belknap

Private non-profit/ 1950/ staff: 10(v)/ members: 35

HISTORICAL SOCIETY; HISTORY MUSEUM

PROGRAMS: Annual Meeting; Exhibits; Lectures; Research Library/Archives; School-Based Curriculum

COLLECTIONS: [1800s-present] Artifacts relating to Alton's rural and business activities and a library that houses local histories, photographs, and scrapbooks.

HOURS: June-Sept by appt

AMHERST

5266
Historical Society of Amherst
17 Middle St, 03031 [PO Box 717, 03031]; (c) Hillsborough

Private non-profit/ 1957/ members: 200/publication: *Amherst, New Hampshire 1881/1982: A Sleeping Town Awakens*

GENEALOGICAL SOCIETY; HISTORICAL SOCIETY; HISTORY MUSEUM; LIBRARY AND/OR ARCHIVES: Promotes and records the history of Amherst, and preserves artifacts and records of interest to the Society.

PROGRAMS: Annual Meeting; Community Outreach; Guided Tours; Interpretation; Lectures; Research Library/Archives

COLLECTIONS: [1760-present] Photographs, documents, publications, and artifacts directly associated with the history of Amherst.

HOURS: July-Aug Su 1:30-4:30

ADMISSION: No charge

ANDOVER

5267
Andover Historical Society
105 Depot St, 03216 [PO Box 167, 03216]; (c) Merrimac

Private non-profit/ 1982/ Governing Board/ staff: 50(v)/ members: 225/publication: *Newsletter of A.H.S.*

HISTORIC PRESERVATION AGENCY; HISTORIC SITE; HISTORICAL SOCIETY; HOUSE MUSEUM; RESEARCH CENTER: Collects, preserves, and interprets materials, information, buildings, monuments, and other objects of historical significance to the New England area, particularly the Town of Andover.

PROGRAMS: Annual Meeting; Community Outreach; Exhibits; Facility Rental; Family Programs; Festivals; Garden Tours; Guided Tours; Interpretation; Lectures; Living History; Monthly Meeting; Publication; Research Library/Archives; School-Based Curriculum; Theatre

COLLECTIONS: [All periods of New England history] Victorian railroad station, turn-of-the-century village store, railroad objects, farming implements, historical costumes, and photographs.

HOURS: June-Oct Sa 10-3, Su 1-3

ASHLAND

5268
Ashland Historical Society
14 Pleasant St, 03217 [PO Box 175, 03217]; (p) (603) 968-7716; (f) (603) 968-7716; (c) Grafton

Joint/ 1968/ City; private non-profit/ staff: 40(v)/ members: 80

HISTORICAL SOCIETY; HISTORY MUSEUM; HOUSE MUSEUM: Operates Whipple House

Museum, Pauline E. Glidden Toy Museum, and Ashland Railroad Station Museum.

PROGRAMS: Annual Meeting; Exhibits; Guided Tours; Lectures; Publication; Research Library/Archives

COLLECTIONS: [19th-20th c] Whipple House: local historic artifacts, antique furnishings; Pauline E. Glidden Toy Museum: antique American toys; Ashland Railroad Station: railroad artifacts and memorabilia.

HOURS: Whipple House Museum: July-Aug W, Sa 1-4; Glidden Museum W-Sa 1-4; RR Station 1-4

ADMISSION: Varies

ATKINSON

5269
Association of Historical Societies of New Hampshire
14 Ironwood Ln, 03811-2706; (p) (603) 362-6152; ilsleymf@de-inc.com

1950/ staff: 11(v)/ members: 264/publication: *The Associate*

HISTORICAL SOCIETY; HISTORY MUSEUM; LIVING HISTORY/OUTDOOR MUSEUM; RESEARCH CENTER: Organizes an association of local historical societies.

PROGRAMS: Annual Meeting; Exhibits; Festivals; Guided Tours; Interpretation; Lectures; Publication; Reenactments; Research Library/Archives

5270
Atkinson Historical Society
3 Academy Ave, 03811 [PO Box 863, 03811]; (c) Rockingham

Private non-profit/ 1954/ staff: 7(v)/ members: 35/publication: *Atkinson Then and Now*

The Atkinson Historical Society is dedicated to the preservation of the history of Atkinson, NH.

COLLECTIONS: [1800-present] Artifacts representative of Atkinson history and genealogy collections of early families.

HOURS: Yr W 2-4

AUBURN

5271
Auburn Historical Association
[PO Box 555, 03032]; (c) Rockingham

Private non-profit/ 1977/ Board of Trustees/ staff: 10(v)/ members: 30

HISTORICAL SOCIETY

PROGRAMS: Annual Meeting; Lectures

BARRINGTON

5272
Barrington New Hampshire Historical Society
Rt 9, 03825 [PO Box 462, 03825]; (p) (603) 664-2740; (c) Strafford

Private non-profit/ 1972/ members: 75

HISTORICAL SOCIETY

PROGRAMS: Monthly Meeting

BEDFORD

5273
Bedford Historical Society
24 N Amherst Rd, 03110; (p) (603) 471-6336; (c) Hillsborough

Private non-profit/ 1967/ members: 180/publication: *The History of Bedford, 1737-1971*

HISTORICAL SOCIETY: Seeks to preserve the local history and to foster interest through programs, its museum, and publications.

PROGRAMS: Annual Meeting; Exhibits; Lectures; Publication

COLLECTIONS: [1750-1900] Collections of artifacts pertaining to Bedford's past as a farming community and displays on Matthew Patten, John Goffe Rand, and the Dunlap Furniture Makers.

HOURS: Apr-Oct Su 2-4

BELMONT

5274
Belmont Historical Society
c/o Wallace Rhodes, President, 433 Hurricane Rd, 03220; (p) (603) 267-6272; wally1@worldbath.net; (c) Belknap

Private non-profit/ 1969/ staff: 5(v)/ members: 30

HISTORICAL SOCIETY: A community historical society engaged in encouraging preservation of local historic sites and artifacts and in researching local history.

PROGRAMS: Annual Meeting; Exhibits

COLLECTIONS: Photographs, artifacts, and memorabilia relating to local history.

BERLIN

5275
Berlin and Coos County Historical Society
119 High St, 03570 [PO Box 52, 03570]; (p) (603) 752-4590; (c) Coos

Private non-profit/ 1990/ staff: 10(v)/ members: 200

GENEALOGICAL SOCIETY; HISTORIC PRESERVATION AGENCY; HISTORICAL SOCIETY; HISTORY MUSEUM; RESEARCH CENTER: Operates the Moffett House as a local history museum.

PROGRAMS: Exhibits; Facility Rental; Guided Tours; Interpretation; Research Library/Archives

COLLECTIONS: [1880-present] Franco-American genealogy volumes, school yearbooks and periodicals, china and glass, photographs a slides, antiques, medical equipment, military items, postcards, and logging artifacts.

HOURS: Yr T-Sa 12-4

ADMISSION: Donations accepted

BOSCAWEN

5276
Boscowen Historical Society, Inc.
228 King St, 03303 [PO Box 3067, 03303]; (c) Merrimack

Private non-profit/ 1961/ staff: 15(v)/ members: 120

GENEALOGICAL SOCIETY; HISTORICAL SOCIETY

PROGRAMS: Annual Meeting; Community Outreach; Exhibits; Festivals

COLLECTIONS: [1850-1950]

HOURS: July-Aug Su 2-4

BRIDGEWATER

5277
Bridgewater Historical Society
773 River Rd, 03264; (p) (603) 968-7000; (c) Grafton

Private non-profit/ 1990/ staff: 5(f); 2(p); 8(v)/ members: 35/publication: *Bridgewater Advocate; Bicentennial History of Bridgewater*

HISTORIC SITE; HISTORICAL SOCIETY; HISTORY MUSEUM: Serves as repository for historical documents, antiques, artifacts, and genealogies.

PROGRAMS: Annual Meeting; Community Outreach; Exhibits; Guided Tours; Lectures; Living History; Monthly Meeting; Publication; Research Library/Archives

COLLECTIONS: [1700- present] Family genealogies, family histories, school records, census figures and voting lists, military records, publications, Bridgewater Gazetteers.

HOURS: Yr W evenings and by appt

BRISTOL

5278
Bristol Historical Society
Summer, 03222 [PO Box 400, 03222]; (c) Grafton

Private non-profit/ 1965/ staff: 7(v)/ members: 30

HISTORIC PRESERVATION AGENCY; HISTORIC SITE; HISTORICAL SOCIETY; HISTORY MUSEUM: Preserve the history of Bristol and provides a repository for artifacts, documents, photographs, and portraits.

PROGRAMS: Annual Meeting; Exhibits; Garden Tours; Lectures; Living History; Monthly Meeting; Publication; Research Library/Archives

COLLECTIONS: [1700-present] Dishes, clothing, farming implements, books, documents, Civil War and Revolutionary War memorabilia, photographs, and portraits.

ADMISSION: Donations accepted

BROOKLINE

5279
Brookline Historical Society
Meeting House Hill Rd, 03033 [Main St, 03033]; (p) (603) 673-3828; (c) Hillsborough

1982/ staff: 15(v)

HISTORICAL SOCIETY; HOUSE MUSEUM: Preserves and promotes the history of Brookline, New Hampshire and its people.

PROGRAMS: Annual Meeting; Exhibits

COLLECTIONS: [1800-1930]

CANAAN

5280
Canaan Historical Society
Canaan St, 03741 [PO Box 402, 03741]; (c) Grafton

1961/ staff: 8(v)/ members: 17/publication: *Canaan History*

HISTORICAL SOCIETY; HISTORY MUSEUM

PROGRAMS: Publication

COLLECTIONS: [1800-present] Over 300 museum artifacts, about 75 old photos of Canaan, a post card collection, and several historical articles on Canaan history.

HOURS: July-Sept Sa 1-4

ADMISSION: No charge

CANDIA

5281
Candia Historical Society
29 High St, 03034 [PO Box 300, 03034]; (c) Rockingham

Private non-profit/ 1975/ Board of Directors/ members: 24

HISTORIC PRESERVATION AGENCY; HISTORIC SITE; HISTORICAL SOCIETY: Collects and preserves information and memorabilia related to the town's history.

PROGRAMS: Annual Meeting; Exhibits; Facility Rental; Interpretation; Lectures; Living History; Research Library/Archives

COLLECTIONS: [1700s-present] Town memorabilia and artifacts, books, newspaper articles, pictures, photographs, historical reference materials, period furniture.

HOURS: Yr 4th T and by appointment

ADMISSION: No charge

5282
Fitts Museum
High St, 03034 [c/o Purington 146 High St, 03034]; (p) (603) 483-2320; (c) Rockingham

City/ 1901/ staff: 5(v)

GARDEN; HISTORY MUSEUM; HOUSE MUSEUM; RESEARCH CENTER: Collects and preserves local history, provides educational and cultural resource for schools and the public, and offers assistance to researchers.

PROGRAMS: Exhibits; Family Programs; Festivals; Guided Tours; Research Library/Archives; School-Based Curriculum

COLLECTIONS: Furniture and domestic equipment of early homes; coopering, shoemaking and farming tools; spinning and weaving equipment, paintings, and photographs, old documents, and manuscripts, Civil War items.

HOURS: July-Aug Sa 1-4 and by appt

ADMISSION: No charge

CANTERBURY

5283
Canterbury Shaker Village, Inc.
288 Shaker Rd, 03224; (p) (603) 783-9511; (f) (603) 783-9152; shakers@totalnetnh.net; www.shakers.org; (c) Merrimack

Private non-profit/ 1969/ staff: 16(f); 95(p); 150(v)/ members: 1400/publication: *Shaker*

Life, Art, and Architecture

GARDEN; HISTORIC SITE; HISTORY MUSEUM; LIVING HISTORY/OUTDOOR MUSEUM; RESEARCH CENTER: Maintains a National Historic Landmark with twenty-five original Shaker buildings on 694 acres of gardens, nature trails, and ponds.

PROGRAMS: Community Outreach; Concerts; Exhibits; Facility Rental; Festivals; Garden Tours; Guided Tours; Interpretation; Lectures; Living History; Publication; Research Library/Archives

COLLECTIONS: [1792-1992] 18,000 Shaker artifacts and 100,000 plus archival collections, representing Shaker design and ideology from late 18th through 20th c.

HOURS: May-Oct Daily 10-5; Nov-Apr Sa-Su 10-5

ADMISSION: $10, Children $5; Group rates

CENTER CONWAY

5284
Chatham Historical Society
Rt 113 B, 03813 [HCR 68 Box 242, 03813]; (p) (603) 694-2099; (c) Carroll

Private non-profit/ 1989/ staff: 3(v)/ members: 87

HISTORIC PRESERVATION AGENCY; HISTORICAL SOCIETY; HISTORY MUSEUM; HOUSE MUSEUM: Preserves the history of the town and surrounding area and collectes genealogical information on area families.

PROGRAMS: Annual Meeting; Exhibits; Guided Tours; Interpretation; Lectures; Research Library/Archives; School-Based Curriculum

COLLECTIONS: [1800-present] 550 photos, over 50 family histories, Chatham VRs from 1790 to present, Catham and regional cemetery records, town histories, published genealogical books, national and state papers.

HOURS: Yr W 1-4:30 and by appt

ADMISSION: No charge

CENTER HARBOR

5285
Center Harbor Historical Society
Plymouth St, 03226 [PO Box 98, 03226]; (p) (603) 258-7891; (c) Belknap

Private non-profit/ 1971/ staff: 45(v)/ members: 120

HISTORIC SITE; HISTORICAL SOCIETY; HISTORY MUSEUM; PRESIDENTIAL SITE

PROGRAMS: Annual Meeting; Community Outreach; Exhibits; Guided Tours; Lectures

COLLECTIONS: [1850-present] Kitchen utensils, bottle collection, farm tools, toys, clothes, fancy work, pictures, books.

HOURS: Apr-Nov by appt

ADMISSION: No charge

CENTER SANDWICH

5286
Sandwich Historical Society
4 Maple St, 03227 [PO Box 106, 03227]; (p) (603) 284-6269; (f) (603) 284-6269; (c) Carroll

Private non-profit/ 1917/ staff: 6(p); 32(v)/ members: 700

HISTORICAL SOCIETY; HOUSE MUSEUM: Maintains historic home and preserves and protects the history of Sandwich; library available for research related to town.

PROGRAMS: Annual Meeting; Exhibits; Guided Tours

COLLECTIONS: [Late 1800s-1900s] Household items, furniture, paintings, agricultural items, and some transportation items.

HOURS: Mid June-Sept T-Sa 11-5

ADMISSION: No charge

CHARLESTOWN

5287
Old Fort No. 4 Associates
267 Springfield Rd, Rt 11, 03603 [PO Box 1336, 03603]; (p) (603) 826-5700; (f) (603) 826-3368; fortat4@cyberportal.net; www.fort at4.com; (c) Sullivan

Private non-profit/ 1948/ staff: 3(f); 5(p); 75(v)/ members: 300

HISTORY MUSEUM; LIVING HISTORY/OUTDOOR MUSEUM: Dedicated to preserving the heritage of mid 18th c life in the Connecticut River Valley through demonstrations by interpreters in period dress.

PROGRAMS: Community Outreach; Guided Tours; Interpretation; Lectures; Living History; Publication; Reenactments; School-Based Curriculum

COLLECTIONS: [Mid-late 18th c] The fort is made up of 17 reconstructed and original buildings having original or reproduced furniture.

HOURS: Late May-late Oct Daily 10-4

ADMISSION: $8, Children $4.50, Seniors $7, Under 6 free

CHESTERFIELD

5288
Chesterfield Historical Society, Inc.
Rt 63, 03443 [PO 204, 03443]; (p) (603) 363-8018; (c) Cheshire

Private non-profit/ 1974/ staff: 30(v)/ members: 120/publication: *Journey's End to Hardscrabble: The Cemeteries and Burying-grounds of Chesterfield New Hampshire*

HISTORICAL SOCIETY: We work to stimulate an interest in and the documentation of the history of Chesterfield; offer programs, tours, and community outreach, and genealogy research; offer collections, archives and library.

PROGRAMS: Annual Meeting; Community Outreach; Exhibits; Guided Tours; Lectures; Publication; Research Library/Archives

COLLECTIONS: [1761-present] Early town records, tax books, day books, genealogy and vital histories files, and over 3,000 photographs.

HOURS: By appt

ADMISSION: No charge

CHICHESTER

5289
Chichester Historical Society
51 Main St, 03234 [54 Main St, 03234]; (p) (603) 798-5943; (c) Merrimack

Joint/ 1970/ City; Private-non profit/ staff: 15(v)/ members: 18

HISTORICAL SOCIETY; HISTORY MUSEUM

PROGRAMS: Annual Meeting; Community Outreach; Exhibits; Lectures; Research Library/Archives

COLLECTIONS: [1727-present] Artifacts related to local town histories, old photographs, and post cards relating to town.

HOURS: Yr 1st and 3rd T 6:30-8

ADMISSION: No charge

CLAREMONT

5290
Claremont, New Hampshire Historical Society, Inc., The
26 Mulberry St, 03743; (p) (603) 543-1400; (c) Sullivan

Private non-profit/ 1963/ staff: 25(v)/ members: 150

HISTORICAL SOCIETY: Preserves published historical information; collects, acquires, and preserves documents and artifacts significant to Claremont.

PROGRAMS: Annual Meeting; Community Outreach; Exhibits; Guided Tours; Lectures

COLLECTIONS: Books and documents, china, glass, and metalware, furniture, military articles, pictures, art work, textiles, tools, natural history collection, and Claremont-made items.

HOURS: Mid June-mid Sept Su 2-5

ADMISSION: $1

COLEBROOK

5291
Colebrook Area Historical Society
10 Bridge St, 03576 [PO Box 32, 03576]; (c) Coos

Private non-profit/ 1991/ members: 120

HISTORICAL SOCIETY; HISTORY MUSEUM: Collects and preserves items relating to Colebrook area's history, conducts monthly public programs and records interviews for an ongoing oral history.

PROGRAMS: Exhibits; Guided Tours; Lectures

HOURS: July-Aug Sa 10-2

CONCORD

5292
Department of Resources and Economic Development
172 Pembroke Rd, 03302 [PO Box 1856, 03302-1856]; (p) (603) 271-3556; (f) (603) 271-2629; nhparks@dred.state.nh.us; www.nhparks.state.nh.us

State/ 1935

HISTORIC SITE: Manages several historic sites and areas, historic homes, coastal fortifications.

PROGRAMS: Guided Tours; Interpretation; Living History

HOURS: Mid June-Sept

5293
New Hampshire Division of Records Management and Archives
71 S Fruit St, 03301-2410; (p) (603) 271-2236; (f) (603) 271-2272; fmevers@sos.state.nh.us; www.state.nh.us/state/archives.htm; (c) Merrimack

State/ 1959/ staff: 5(f); 3(p); 2(v)

LIBRARY AND/OR ARCHIVES: Manages records created by several hundred state agencies, preserves state records, and makes non-confidential records accessible for public research.

PROGRAMS: Research Library/Archives

COLLECTIONS: [1630-Present] Documents created by or for the State of New Hampshire.

HOURS: Yr M-F 8-4:30

ADMISSION: No charge

5294
New Hampshire Historical Society
30 Park, 03301; (p) (603) 225-3381, (603) 226-3189; (f) (603) 224-0463; library@nhhis tory.org; www.Nhhistory.org; (c) Merrimack

Private non-profit/ 1823/ staff: 26(p); 100(v)/ members: 4500/publication: *Historical New Hampshire*

HISTORICAL SOCIETY; HISTORY MUSEUM: Educates a diverse public about the significance of NH's past and its relationship to our lives today. Collects, preserves, and interprets materials pertaining to NH history.

PROGRAMS: Annual Meeting; Community Outreach; Concerts; Exhibits; Facility Rental; Family Programs; Guided Tours; Interpretation; Lectures; Publication; Research Library/Archives; School-Based Curriculum

COLLECTIONS: [1623-present] New Hampshire fine and decorative arts, military equipment, domestic artifacts, tools, industrials, vehicles representing 400 years of European occupation, as well as Native American tools and domestic artifacts representing 9,000 years of occupation.

HOURS: Yr Library: T-Sa 9:30-5; Museum: T-Sa 9:30-5 (Th evenings to 8:30), Su 12-5

ADMISSION: $5, Children $2.50, Seniors $4; Members free; group rates

5295
Pierce Brigade, Inc., The
14 Penacook St, 03301 [PO 425, 03302-0425]; (p) (603) 225-4555; (c) Merrimack

Private non-profit/ staff: 10(p); 10(v)/ members: 100

HOUSE MUSEUM; PRESIDENTIAL SITE: Maintains the Pierce Mance, home of President Franklin Pierce.

PROGRAMS: Annual Meeting; Facility Rental; Guided Tours

COLLECTIONS: [1860-1870] Period furniture in the home of U.S. President Franklin Pierce. Some material from the Pierce family.

HOURS: M-F 10-5

ADMISSION: $3, Children $1, Students $1

CONWAY

5296
Conway Historical Society
100 Main St, 03818 [PO Box 1949, 03818]; (p) (603) 447-5551; (f) (603) 447-5551; conhist@yahoo.com; members.tripof.com/~ConwayHistorical/index.; (c) Carroll

Private non-profit/ 1935/ staff: 1(f); 50(v)/ members: 375

HISTORIC PRESERVATION AGENCY; HISTORIC SITE; HISTORICAL SOCIETY; HISTORY MUSEUM; HOUSE MUSEUM: The society serves as a repository for facts and artifacts important to the Conways. Eastman-Lord House museum (1818).

PROGRAMS: Annual Meeting; Community Outreach; Exhibits; Family Programs; Festivals; Guided Tours; Interpretation; Lectures; Living History; Research Library/Archives; School-Based Curriculum

COLLECTIONS: [1818-1945] Seventeen rooms of period furniture and artifacts relating to the rich and varied history of the Conways.

HOURS: May- Sept T 6-8, W 2-4, Th 6-8, Oct by appt

ADMISSION: $3, Family $6

5297
Henney History Room-Conway Public Library
15 E Main St, 03818 [Box 2100, 03818]; (p) (603) 447-5552; (f) (603) 447-6921; henneyhr@hotmail.com; www.ncia.net/library/conway; (c) Carroll

Private non-profit/ 1975/ staff: 1(f); 2(p)/publication: *The Conways*

LIBRARY AND/OR ARCHIVES: Repository for Carroll County, NH and Oxford County, ME records.

PROGRAMS: Exhibits; Family Programs; Film/Video; Lectures; Publication; Research Library/Archives

COLLECTIONS: [1765-present] Special collections dealing with the history of Carroll County, NH and Oxford county, ME.

HOURS: Yr M,T 10-5, W 5:30-8:30

ADMISSION: No charge

CORNISH

5298
Cornish Historical Society
Rt 120 & Penniman Rd, 03745 [RR 2, Box 416, 03745-9727]; (p) (603) 675-6003; (c) Sullivan

Private non-profit/ 1976/ staff: 4(v)/ members: 75

HISTORICAL SOCIETY: Collect, maintain, and preserve items related to the history of the town of Cornish and the Cornish Art Colony.

PROGRAMS: Annual Meeting; Community Outreach; Exhibits; Garden Tours; Guided Tours; Interpretation; Lectures

COLLECTIONS: [18th-20th c] Artifacts, books, paintings, memorabilia, and handcrafts related to the town's history.

ADMISSION: No charge

5299
Saint-Gaudens National Historic Site
Saint-Gardens Rd of NH Rt 12 A, 03745 [RR # 3 Box 73, 03745]; (p) (603) 675-2175; (f) (603) 675-2701; Saga@valley.net; www.nps.Gov/saga; (c) Sullivan

Joint/ 1964/ Federal/ staff: 15(f); 10(p); 2(v)

GARDEN; HISTORIC SITE: Maintains the home, gardens, and studios of Augustus Saint-Gaudens, 1848-1907; protects and preserves the historically significant properties associated with the life and cultural achievements of the artist.

PROGRAMS: Community Outreach; Exhibits; Garden Tours; Guided Tours; Interpretation; Living History; Publication; School-Based Curriculum

COLLECTIONS: [1870-1907] 300 of the artist's works with many original pieces including bas relief and sculpture in the round, life-size and heroic-size sculptures including the Adams Memorial, the Shaw Memorial and Farragot Monument. The house contains the original furnishing of the Saint-Gauden's family, collection of art, culture, and lifestyles representative of the Gilded Age.

HOURS: Mid May-Oct 31 Daily 9-4:30

ADMISSION: $4

CROYDON

5300
Croydon Historical Society
879 NH Rt 10, 03773; (p) (603) 863-9183; (f) (603) 863-5353; (c) Sullivan

Private non-profit/ 1999/ staff: 20(v)/ members: 20

HISTORICAL SOCIETY: Collects, preserves, and interprets local town history: its people, buildings, life changes, written materials, photos, and audio records.

PROGRAMS: Annual Meeting

COLLECTIONS: [1750-present] Books, photographs, diaries, artifacts.

DANVILLE

5301
Hawke Historical Society
[PO Box 402, 03819]; (c) Rockingham

Private non-profit/ 1969/ members: 30/publication: *Reminiscences*

GENEALOGICAL SOCIETY; HISTORIC SITE; HISTORICAL SOCIETY; RESEARCH CENTER: Artifacts, photographs, papers, historical documents, and books.

PROGRAMS: Annual Meeting; Publication

COLLECTIONS: [1700-present] Town documents, photographs, genealogical material books, journals, and manuscripts.

DEERFIELD

5302
Deerfield Historical Society
The Town Hall, 03037 [141 Middle Rd, 03037]; (c) Rockingham

Private non-profit/ 1973/ members: 45

ALLIANCE OF HISTORICAL AGENCIES; HISTORICAL SOCIETY: Preserves the history and artifacts of Deerfield.

PROGRAMS: Annual Meeting; Community Outreach; Exhibits; Festivals; Film/Video; Guided Tours; Lectures; Research Library/ Archives

COLLECTIONS: [1975] Pictures, paintings, books, guns, old letters.

DERRY

5303
Charles Bartlett House, The
12 N Main St, 03038; (p) (603) 437-8969, (603) 432-6479

1834

Maintains the home of Charles Bartlett, first owner and publisher of the Derry News.

COLLECTIONS: [1897-1925] The original bedroom set from the Pinkerton's; several Bartlett pieces; local memorabilia; Large genealogical library; photo, birdseye view, and postcard collections; original copper plates by Charles Bartlett.

5304
Derry Historical Society and Museum
W Broadway, Fire Station at the Depot, 03038 [65 Birch St, 03038]; (p) (603) 432-3188; (c) Rockingham

City; Joint/ staff: 4(v)/ members: 37

HISTORICAL SOCIETY; HISTORY MUSEUM: Purpose of the DHS is to discover, secure, educate, and preserve whatever may relate to the natural, civil, literary, and religious history of the Town of Derry.

PROGRAMS: Community Outreach; Exhibits; Festivals; Guided Tours; Interpretation; Publication

COLLECTIONS: [1800-present]

HOURS: Yr Su 2-4 and by appt

5305
Robert Frost Farm
Rt 28, 03038 [PO Box 1075, 03038]; (p) (603) 432-3091

1885/ State/ staff: 1(f); 1(p); 1(v)

Home of poet Robert Frost from 1900 to 1911.

COLLECTIONS: [Early 1900s]

HOURS: Yr

DOVER

5306
Woodman Institute
182 Central Ave, 03821; (p) (603) 742-1038; www.seacoastnh.com/woodman/

HISTORY MUSEUM; HOUSE MUSEUM; NATURAL HISTORY MUSEUM: Museum complex features three historic buildings: The Woodman House (1818), the Damm Garrison House (1675) and the Hale House (1813).

COLLECTIONS: [17th-19th c] Woodman Institute: Rocks & minerals Indian artifacts, mammals & marine life, birds & butterflies, shells, snakes & turtles, dolls, military museum, maps & documents. Damm Garrison House: Furniture, colonial items, kitchen, child room, spinning wheels, cooking fireplace, Dover history display. Hale House: Hale family items. political ephemera, samples of Cocheco textiles, old toys and antique dolls, furniture, fire and maritime exhibits, Ben Franklin & Josiah Bartlett items, domestic and political exhibits.

HOURS: Apr-Nov W-Su 12:30-4:30; Dec-Jan Sa-Su 12:30-4:30

ADMISSION: $3, Student $1, Seniors $2; Under 14 free

DUBLIN

5307
Dublin Historical Society
Main St, 03444 [PO Box 415, 03444]; (p) (603) 563-8545; (c) Cheshire

Private non-profit/ 1920/ staff: 1(p); 1(v)/ members: 175

HISTORICAL SOCIETY: Preserves records and artifacts relating to Dublin and makes them available to the public.

PROGRAMS: Annual Meeting; Exhibits; Guided Tours; Lectures; Publication; Research Library/Archives

COLLECTIONS: [1760-present] Town records, family papers, miscellaneous artifacts, books by Dublin authors.

HOURS: Archives: Yr M-F 9-12; Schoolhouse Museum: varies

ADMISSION: No charge

DURHAM

5308
Durham Historical Association
Old Town Hall, 03824 [PO Box 305, 03824]; (p) (603) 868-5436; (c) Strafford

Private non-profit/ 1850/ staff: 15(v)/ members: 188

HISTORICAL SOCIETY; HISTORY MUSEUM; RESEARCH CENTER: Maintains a museum and produces a newsletter.

PROGRAMS: Annual Meeting; Community Outreach; Exhibits; Film/Video; Guided Tours; Lectures; Living History; Publication; Reenactments; Research Library/Archives; School-Based Curriculum

COLLECTIONS: [1600s-present] Documents, genealogy resources, photographs; artifacts.

HOURS: Yr T-Th and by appt

ADMISSION: No charge

5309
Milne Special Collections and Archives, University of New Hampshire Library
18 Library Way, 03820; (p) (603) 862-2714; (f) (603) 862-1919; special.collections@unh.edu; www.izaak.unh.edu; (c) Strafford

State/ 1974/ staff: 6(f); 6(p); 2(v)

HISTORY MUSEUM: Maintains special collections and archives department; university museum organized to collect, preserve, and interpret materials related to the history and culture of the State of NH and the University.

PROGRAMS: Community Outreach; Exhibits; Research Library/Archives

COLLECTIONS: [17th c-present] Books, manuscripts, archives, and museum artifacts, primarily related to the history and culture of NH

and the University of NH.

HOURS: Yr M-F 9-5, Sa during school year

ADMISSION: No charge

EAST DERRY

5310
First Parish Congregational Church
47 E Derry Rd, 03041 [Box 114, 03041]; (p) (603) 434-0628; www.fpc-ucc.org; (c) Rockingham

Private non-profit/ 1719/ staff: 2(f); 1(p)/ members: 400

HISTORIC SITE; HOUSE MUSEUM: Preserves the church, built in 1719 by Scots from Ireland, that has been in continuous use; strives to serve and educate the community. Listed on National Register.

PROGRAMS: Annual Meeting; Community Outreach; Exhibits; Guided Tours; Lectures; Research Library/Archives; School-Based Curriculum

COLLECTIONS: [1720-present] Museum items in meetinghouse area, paper record collection, photographs, 1700s founders graves in cemetery. Howard Steeple clock, 2,000 pound bell.

HOURS: By appt

ADMISSION: No charge

ENFIELD

5311
Enfield Historical Society
[PO Box 612, 03748]; (p) (603) 632-7740; (c) Grafton

Private non-profit/ 1976/ staff: 30(v)/ members: 75

HISTORICAL SOCIETY: Dedicated to the collecting and preservation of the town's history.

PROGRAMS: Annual Meeting; Exhibits; Lectures; Research Library/Archives

COLLECTIONS: [19th-20th c] Local history artifacts and memorabilia.

HOURS: Mid June-Sept Lockehaven Schoolhouse Su 2-4; Enfield Historical Society Sa 2-4

ADMISSION: No charge

5312
Enfield Shaker Museum
Rt 4 A, 03748 [24 Caleb Dyer Lane, 03748]; (p) (603) 632-4346; (f) (603) 632-4346; chosen.vale@valley.net; www.shakermuseum.org; (c) Grafton

1986/ staff: 3(f); 8(p); 60(v)/ members: 631

GARDEN; HISTORIC SITE; HISTORY MUSEUM; LIVING HISTORY/OUTDOOR MUSEUM: The museum preserves and protects the legacy of the Enfield Shaker community. We relate the unique Shaker experience and the Shaker's contribution to American society through a variety of tours, workshops, and educational forums.

PROGRAMS: Annual Meeting; Concerts; Exhibits; Facility Rental; Family Programs; Festivals; Interpretation; Lectures

COLLECTIONS: [1793-present] A wide variety of Shaker artifacts that illustrate the Shaker's home, work, and spiritual life.

HOURS: May -Oct M-Sa 10-5, Su 12-5; Winter weekends

EPSOM

5313
Daniel Webster Birthplace Living History Project
N Rd, 03234 [c/o Sharon Burnstou, 78 Center Hill Rd, 03234]; (p) (603) 736-8938; (c) Belknap

Joint/ 1997/ staff: 12(v)

HISTORIC SITE; HOUSE MUSEUM: Organizes and interprets the life of the average New Hampshire family of the 1780s, using living history as our medium and the Webster family as our example.

PROGRAMS: Community Outreach; Exhibits; Interpretation; Living History; School-Based Curriculum

COLLECTIONS: [1780s] Replica furnishings appropriate to our site, for hands-on interpretation; also exhibit- period artifacts and Daniel Webster memorabilia.

HOURS: June-Sept Sa-Su 12-5

ADMISSION: $2.50; NH residents, Seniors, and under 18 free

EXETER

5314
American Independence Museum
One Governors Ln, 03033; (p) (603) 772-2622; (f) (603) 772-0861; aim@independencemuseum.org; www.indenpendencemuseum.org; (c) Rockingham

Private non-profit/ 1991/ staff: 1(f); 10(p); 45(v)/ members: 350

HOUSE MUSEUM

PROGRAMS: Exhibits; Festivals; Guided Tours; Interpretation; Lectures; Living History; Reenactments; Research Library/Archives; School-Based Curriculum

COLLECTIONS: [18th c-present] Colonial furnishings, military uniforms and weapons, library and archives, portraits, and rare documents.

HOURS: May-Oct W-Su 12-5 or by appt

ADMISSION: $5, Students $3, Seniors $3

5315
Exeter Historical Society
47 Front St, 03833 [PO Box 924, 03833-0924]; (p) (603) 778-2335; (c) Rockingham

Private non-profit/ 1928/ staff: 2(p); 26(v)/ members: 326/publication: *Exeter, NH 1888-1988*

HISTORIC PRESERVATION AGENCY; HISTORIC SITE; HISTORICAL SOCIETY; HISTORY MUSEUM; RESEARCH CENTER: Promotes local history.

PROGRAMS: Annual Meeting; Community Outreach; Exhibits; Lectures; Publication; Research Library/Archives

COLLECTIONS: Artifacts: documents, genealogical papers, photographs 4,000, books, aqueduct sections, newspaper from 1831-present.

HOURS: Yr Sa,T,Th 2-4:30

ADMISSION: No charge

5316
Exeter Public Library
Founders Park, 03833; (p) (603) 772-3101; (f)
(603) 772-7548; dewey@nh.ultranet.com;
www.nh.ultranet.com/~dewey/; (c) Rockingham

City; Private non-profit/ 1853/ staff: 7(f); 5(p);
43(v)

LIBRARY AND/OR ARCHIVES: Provides information and materials for local and regional
residents.

PROGRAMS: Annual Meeting; Lectures; Research Library/Archives

COLLECTIONS: History of state, county, town,
and families in NH; Revolutionary and Civil
War regiment lists, and cemetery lisst for
Rockingham City.

HOURS: Yr M-Th 10-8, F-Sa 10-5

ADMISSION: No charge

5317
Gilman Garrison, SPNEA
12 Water St, 03833; (p) (603) 436-3205;
www.spnea.org

Private non-profit/ 1690/ Society for the
Preservation of New England Antiquities

HISTORY MUSEUM; HOUSE MUSEUM: Preserves a fortified house, strategically sited to
protect the valuable sawmills and waterpower
sites owned by John Gilman. Restored in the
1950s by local preservationist William Dudley
to reveal its early architecture and to commemorate the lives of its varied occupants
over the centuries.

PROGRAMS: Guided Tours

HOURS: June 1-Oct 15 Sa-Su 11-5

ADMISSION: $4; SPNEA Members/Town resi-
dents free

5318
Moses-Kent House Museum, The
One Pine St, 03833; (p) (603) 772-2044

Private non-profit

GARDEN; HISTORIC SITE; HOUSE MUSEUM

PROGRAMS: Garden Tours; Guided Tours

COLLECTIONS: [Early 1900s] Grounds attributed to Frederick Law Olmsted.

HOURS: Summer: varies

ADMISSION: $5; Grounds free

FARMINGTON

5319
Farmington Historical Society
Goodwin Library, 03835 [9 S Main St, 03835];
(p) (603) 755-2944; (c) Strafford

Private non-profit/ 1949/ members: 65/publica-
tion: *Images of America - Farmington*

HISTORICAL SOCIETY; HISTORY MUSEUM:
Promotes history by means of lectures and
discussion on historically related subjects;
maintains a museum in the town library.

PROGRAMS: Annual Meeting; Exhibits; Lectures; Publication

COLLECTIONS: [19th c] Photographs, paintings, scrapbooks, and museum artifacts related to local and state history.

ADMISSION: No charge

FITZWILLIAM

5320
Fitzwilliam Historical Society
On the Historic Fitzwilliam Common, 03447
[PO Box 87, 03447]; (p) (603) 585-7742; (c)
Cheshire

Private non-profit/ 1961/ staff: 10(v)/ members:
125

HISTORIC SITE; HISTORICAL SOCIETY;
HISTORY MUSEUM; HOUSE MUSEUM: Preserves the Amos J. Blake House Museum and
its furnishings.

PROGRAMS: Annual Meeting; Exhibits; Festivals; Guided Tours

COLLECTIONS: [Early 19th c] Valuable period
furnishings, 1837.

HOURS: May-Oct Sa 1-4

ADMISSION: No charge

FRANCONIA

5321
Franconia Heritage Museum
553 Main St, 03580 [PO Box 169, 03580]; (p)
(603) 823-5000; FHMuseum@ConnRiver.net;
www.magnetic-north.com/FHM/findex; (c)
Grafton

Private non-profit/ 1983/ staff: 20(p); 40(v)/
members: 150

HISTORICAL SOCIETY; HISTORY MUSEUM;
HOUSE MUSEUM; RESEARCH CENTER:
Operates a local history museum in a 1880
house, shed and barn, and an Iron Furnace Interpretive Center for the only blast furnace still
standing in NH.

PROGRAMS: Annual Meeting; Exhibits;
Film/Video; Guided Tours; Interpretation; Publication; Research Library/Archives

COLLECTIONS: [1800-1940] Documents, diaries, personal, household, business, industry,
farm tools, equipment, toys, books, clothing,
photos, maps, school records, linens: possessions of four generations of a family; early iron
industry books, tools, and products, genealogy, and records.

HOURS: Museum: June-Oct Th, Sa 1-4 and by
appt; Iron Furnace Interpretive Center: Yr

ADMISSION: No charge

5322
New England Ski Museum
Pkwy Exit 2, 03580 [PO Box 267, 03580-
0267]; (p) (603) 823-7177; (f) (603) 823-9505;
staff@skimuseum.org; www.skimuseum.org;
(c) Grafton

Private non-profit/ 1977/ staff: 2(f); 2(p)/ members: 1051

HISTORY MUSEUM: Collects, preserves, and
exhibits elements from the broad spectrum of
ski history for the purpose of research, education, and entertainment.

PROGRAMS: Exhibits; Facility Rental; Film/
Video

COLLECTIONS: [1900s] Ski equipment, clothing, literature, books, photographs, and artwork.

HOURS: May-Oct Daily 12-5; Dec 1-Mar 31 F-
T 12-5

FREEDOM

5323
Freedom Historical Society
Old Portland Rd, 03836 [PO Box 481, 03836];
(p) (603) 367-4626; (c) Carroll

Private non-profit/ 1965/ staff: 20(p)/ members: 200/publication: *Reminiscences of
French Wars, Quick Silver Times*

HISTORICAL SOCIETY; HOUSE MUSEUM:
Preserve the history of Freedom, fosters
awareness, and appreciation of our town's history through records, and collections in the Allard House and in the attached Barn Museum.

PROGRAMS: Annual Meeting; Community
Outreach; Exhibits; Family Programs; Guided
Tours; Interpretation; Publication; Research Li-
brary/Archives; School-Based Curriculum

COLLECTIONS: [Pre 1930] The Allard House
(1877) is furnished as it might have been between 1877 and the mid 1900s. Collections of
farm implements, wagons, tools, documents,
books, town maps, town records books and
over 4,000 artifacts.

HOURS: July, Aug Sa 10-12, Su 12-2 and by
appt

ADMISSION: No charge

FREMONT

5324
Fremont Historical Society
Main St, 03044 [225 S Rd, 03044]; (p) (603)
895-4032; (c) Rockingham

Private non-profit/ 1966/ staff: 1(p); 4(v)/ members: 64

HISTORICAL SOCIETY: Collects, preserves
and records the history of Fremont and provides programs that educate and promote the
importance of preserving local history and un-
dertaking preservation projects.

PROGRAMS: Concerts; Exhibits; Family Programs; Festivals; Guided Tours; Lectures;
Reenactments; Research Library/Archives

COLLECTIONS: [1740-present] Town and
family histories, furniture, old documents, military memorabilia, photographs, various memorabilia relating to the community.

HOURS: June-Sept Sa 10-3

ADMISSION: No charge

GILMANTON

5325
Gilmanton Historical Society
Gilmanton Academy Bldg, Gilmanton Corners,
03237 [PO Box 236, 03237]; (p) (603) 364-
7405; rparms@worldpath.net; (c) Belnap

Private non-profit/ 1967/ staff: 11(v)/ members:
100

HISTORICAL SOCIETY; HISTORY MUSEUM:
Promotes community interest in the history of
Gilmanton and surrounding area. Maintains a
museum, collects, catalogues and displays artifacts and documents.

PROGRAMS: Annual Meeting; Exhibits; Lectures

COLLECTIONS: [1790s-1910] 700 items: documents, photos, books, and other publications;

tools used in the 1790s-1900 time period.

HOURS: Yr by appt

ADMISSION: No charge

GILSUM

5326
Gilsum Historical Society
Church St, 03448 [115 Alstead Hill, 03448];
(p) (603) 352-6208; (c) Cheshire

Private non-profit/ members: 10

HISTORICAL SOCIETY; HISTORY MUSEUM: Collecting and recording information on artifacts of Gilsum.

PROGRAMS: Annual Meeting; Exhibits; Festivals; Film/Video; Guided Tours

COLLECTIONS: Historical artifacts and literature pertaining to Gilsum.

HOURS: Special occasions

GORHAM

5327
Gorham Historical Society
25 Railroad St, 03581; (c) Coos

Private non-profit/ 1974/ staff: 12(v)/ members: 113

HISTORIC PRESERVATION AGENCY; HISTORIC SITE; HISTORICAL SOCIETY; HISTORY MUSEUM; LIBRARY AND/OR ARCHIVES: Expand knowledge of the community's heritage with special emphasis on three principal focuses in Gorham's history: railroads, tourism, logging through museum exhibits, events, and lectures.

PROGRAMS: Annual Meeting; Community Outreach; Exhibits; Guided Tours; Lectures; Research Library/Archives

COLLECTIONS: [1830-present] Railroad memorabilia, collection of period post cards, photographs, historical registers, newspapers, and artifacts such as a model fishing schooner and Dolly Copp's spinning wheel.

HOURS: Late May-Nov Daily 1-5 and by appt

ADMISSION: No charge/Donations accepted

GRANTHAM

5328
Grantham Historical Society, Inc.
[PO Box 540, 03753]; (c) Sullivan

City; Private non-profit/ members: 34

HISTORICAL SOCIETY

PROGRAMS: Annual Meeting; Exhibits

GREENFIELD

5329
Greenfield New Hampshire Historical Society, The
Stephenson Menorical Library, 03047 [PO Box 213, 03047]; (p) (603) 547-3596; (c) Hillsborough

Private non-profit/ 1973/ staff: 8(v)/ members: 102

HISTORICAL SOCIETY: Promotes and supports the preservation of the heritage of Greenfield.

PROGRAMS: Annual Meeting; Exhibits; Lectures

COLLECTIONS: [1791-1950] Documents relating to the town of Greenfield.

HOURS: Yr 12-5

HAMPTON

5330
Hampton Historical Society/Tuck Museum
40 Park Ave, 03843 [PO Box 1601, 03843-1601]; (p) (603) 929-0781; www.nh.ultranet.com/~hhs/hhshome.htm; (c) Rockingham

Private non-profit/ 1924/ staff: 30(v)/ members: 400/publication: *Gatherings From The Green*

HISTORICAL SOCIETY; HISTORY MUSEUM: Collects, preserves, and interprets artifacts, documents, pictures, archival materials, and other items identified of specific interest to Hampton or region encompassed during settlement.

PROGRAMS: Annual Meeting; Community Outreach; Exhibits; Family Programs; Garden Tours; Guided Tours; Lectures; Living History; Publication; Research Library/Archives; School-Based Curriculum

COLLECTIONS: Photographs, manuscripts, Tuck Museum: relating to life in Hampton Founding through early 1900s; Farm Museum; Fire Museum; 1850s Schoolhouse.

HOURS: Mid June-Mid Sept W, F, Su 1-4

ADMISSION: No charge

HANCOCK

5331
Hancock Depot Association, Inc.
Depot Rd, 03449 [PO Box 152, 03449]; (f) (603) 535-9487; (c) Hillsborough

Private non-profit/ 1976/ staff: 12(v)/ members: 140

HISTORIC SITE: Maintains an old railroad station; organizes cultural and community events.

PROGRAMS: Annual Meeting; Community Outreach; Exhibits; Facility Rental; Family Programs

5332
Hancock Historical Society
7 Main St, 03449 [PO Box 138, 03449]; (p) (603) 525-9379; hhs@mcttelecom.com; (c) Hillsborough

Private non-profit/ 1903/ staff: 6(v)/ members: 140/publication: *Hancock Historical Society Newsletter*

HISTORICAL SOCIETY; HOUSE MUSEUM: The society collects and preserves archives and artifacts relating to the history of Hancock and its people. It fosters interest and education of history through programs and exhibits.

PROGRAMS: Annual Meeting; Community Outreach; Exhibits; Guided Tours; Lectures; Publication; Research Library/Archives

COLLECTIONS: [1780-1940] Furniture, paintings, decorative arts, household, farming and military artifacts, textiles, photographs, manuscripts, representing Hancock and its people exhibited in the society's building (1809 two-story brick Federal structure).

HOURS: June-Sept W-Sa 2-4; Office: Jan 2-Dec 15 W 9-11

ADMISSION: Donations accepted

HANOVER

5333
Hanover Historical Society
32 N Main St, 03755 [PO Box 142, 03755]; (p) (603) 643-3371; (c) Grafton

Private non-profit/ 1961/ staff: 30(v)/ members: 220

HISTORIC SITE; HISTORICAL SOCIETY; HISTORY MUSEUM: Society collects local historical and biographical materials maintains a small museum, documents, and catalogues town records; restores, repairs, conserves grave stones in nine burial grounds.

PROGRAMS: Annual Meeting; Exhibits; Guided Tours; Interpretation; Lectures; School-Based Curriculum

COLLECTIONS: [1780-1880] Furnishings of early farm house as well as those associated with Daniel Webster and Dartmouth College, and a few from Shaker community nearby.

HOURS: May 30-Oct 12 W, Sa, Su 2:30-4:30

ADMISSION: No charge

5334
Rauner Special Collections Library
6065 Webster Hall, Dartmouth College, 03755; (p) (603) 646-2037, (603) 646-0538; (f) (603) 646-0447; Rauner.Special.Collections.Reference@Dartmouth.EDU; www.dartmouth.edu/~speccoll/; (c) Grafton

Private non-profit/ 1769/ staff: 13(f); 1(p); 5(v)/publication: *Dartmouth College Library Bulletin; Friends of the Library Newsletter*

LIBRARY AND/OR ARCHIVES: Special Collections collects, preserves, and makes available resources which support the curriculum and research needs of Dartmouth College and the community.

PROGRAMS: Publication; Research Library/Archives

COLLECTIONS: [1600-present] Popular history; Dartmouth College history; presses; modern British and American literature; New Hampshire social, natural and political history; and Hanover history. New Hampshire's Cornish Colony and White Mountains are emphasized. Papers of Mayfield Parish, Sherman Adams, Richard Eberhart, Robert Frost, and the Stefensson collection of Polar Exploration. 16,500 l.f. boxed collections; 15,000 volumes; 300 sound recordings; 600,000 photographic images; 500 objects.

HOURS: Yr M-F 8-4:30

ADMISSION: No charge

HAVERHILL

5335
Haverhill Historic Society
Court St, 03765 [PO Box 52, 03765]; (c) Grafton

Private non-profit/ 1965/ staff: 4(v)/ members: 80

HISTORY MUSEUM; LIBRARY AND/OR ARCHIVES: Maintains museum and archives in local library; active in historic preservation;

owns mid-19th c schoolhouse currently under restoration as adjunct museum.

PROGRAMS: Annual Meeting; Exhibits; Guided Tours; Lectures; Research Library/Archives

COLLECTIONS: [1790-1900] Collection related principally to 19th c buildings, persons, events including local railroad and industrial history; research files on local buildings.

HOURS: June-Sept irregular schedule and by appt

ADMISSION: No charge

HENNIKER

5336
Henniker Historical Society
5 A Maple St, 03242 [PO Box 674, 03242]; (p) (603) 428-6267; (c) Merrimack

Private non-profit/ 1971/ staff: 30(v)/ members: 380/publication: *Henniker Historian*

HISTORICAL SOCIETY: Obtains, compiles, and maintains records and objects related to the town of Henniker; makes such information available to the public and supports education about the history of Henniker.

PROGRAMS: Annual Meeting; Exhibits; Guided Tours; Lectures; Publication; Research Library/Archives

COLLECTIONS: [1768-present] Museum artifacts, manuscripts, maps, unpublished genealogies, newspapers, cemetery records, obituary files, paintings, portraits, photographs, musical instruments, war artifacts.

HOURS: Yr Th-Sa 10-2

ADMISSION: No charge

HILL

5337
Hill Historical Society
265 Murray Hill Rd, 03243 [PO Box 193, 03243]; (c) Merrimack

Private non-profit/ 1982/ staff: 12(v)/ members: 160

HISTORICAL SOCIETY: Dedicated to the preservation of local historical records and photographs, promoting understanding of local historical events, and encouraging preservation of historic sites, buildings, and monuments.

PROGRAMS: Annual Meeting; Family Programs; Interpretation; Lectures; Publication; Research Library/Archives

COLLECTIONS: [1750-1950] Includes several hundred vintage photographs, retired town records, complete set of town annual reports, obituaries, news clippings, audiotapes and transcripts of oral histories, video tapes of significant town events.

HOURS: 2nd Sa June-Sept 10-2 or by appt

ADMISSION: No charge

HILLSBOROUGH

5338
Pierce Homestead
Rts 9 & 31, 03244 [PO Box 896, 03244]; (p) (603) 478-3165, (603) 478-3913; www.conk net.com/~hillsboro/pierce

Federal/ 1804/ State; Hillsborough Historical Society/ staff: 2(p); 35(v)

Maintains home of President Frankin Pierce from 1804-1834. Other residents of the home included John McNiel, hero of the Battle of Lundy's Lane in the War of 1812; Benjamin Pierce Cheney, a founder of the American Express Company and the Santa Fe and Great Northern Railroads; and Albert Baker, brother of Mary Baker Eddy.

COLLECTIONS: [1824-1834] Family portaits; furniture belonging to Pierce; painting of the formal surrender in Mexico City by Gualdi.

HOURS: May-Oct

HOLDERNESS

5339
Holderness Historical Society
Curry Place, 03245 [PO Box 319, 03245]; (c) Grafton

Private non-profit/ 1961/ staff: 15(v)/ members: 150

HISTORICAL SOCIETY: Promotes meetings, entertainment, book sales, concerts, tours.

PROGRAMS: Annual Meeting; Community Outreach; Concerts; Exhibits; Facility Rental; Festivals; Guided Tours; Lectures; Living History; Research Library/Archives

COLLECTIONS: [1700s-present] Old tools, pictures, memory quilts, organ, books by local authors, artifacts dating back to the 1700s, books on history of Holderness, clothes in trunk dating back to 1800s, replica of stage coach, dressmaker's form.

HOURS: July-Aug Sa 9-12 and by appt

ADMISSION: No charge

HOLLIS

5340
Hollis Historical Society
20 Main St, 03049 [PO Box 754, 03049-0754]; (p) (603) 465-3935; hollis-historical.org; www. hollis-historical.org; (c) Hillsborough

Private non-profit/ 1958/ staff: 30(v)/ members: 190

HISTORICAL SOCIETY; HOUSE MUSEUM

PROGRAMS: Annual Meeting; Community Outreach; Exhibits; Family Programs; Research Library/Archives

COLLECTIONS: Artifacts, memorabilia, and historical data significant to the town, local history publications, and genealogy assistance.

HOURS: Wheeler House Yr W 1-4; Engine House Apr-Oct 1st and 3rd Su 1-4

HOPKINTON

5341
New Hampshire Antiquarian Society
300 Main St, 03229; (p) (603) 746-3825; c_yod@conlcnet.com; (c) Merrimack

Private non-profit/ 1859/ staff: 2(p); 50(v)/ members: 455

HISTORICAL SOCIETY: Interprets, preserves, and celebrates the history of Hopkinton, New Hampshire.

PROGRAMS: Annual Meeting; Community Outreach; Concerts; Exhibits; Facility Rental; Family Programs; Festivals; Guided Tours; Interpretation; Lectures; Publication; Research Library/Archives

COLLECTIONS: [1700-1900] Portraits, paintings, clothing, costumes and accessories, fire fighting equipment, furniture, Indian artifacts, lamps, military equipment, needlework, photographs, textiles, tools, toys, weavings and equipment, historical publications, genealogy, publications, relative to NH.

HOURS: Yr Th-F 10-5, Sa 10-2

ADMISSION: No charge

HUDSON

5342
Hudson Historical Society
Alvirne Hills House 211 Derry Rd, Rt 102, 03051 [PO Box 475, 03051]; (p) (603) 882-7474; (c) Hillsborough

Private non-profit/ 1966/ staff: 1(p); 30(v)/ members: 105

HISTORIC PRESERVATION AGENCY; HISTORIC SITE; HISTORICAL SOCIETY; HISTORY MUSEUM: Dedicated to preserving the history of Hudson and its culture since its incorporation and maintains a museum of Hudson's history at historic Alvirne Hills House.

PROGRAMS: Annual Meeting; Community Outreach; Exhibits; Facility Rental; Festivals; Guided Tours; Research Library/Archives; School-Based Curriculum

COLLECTIONS: [Late 1800s-1900] Photographs, news clippings, books, furniture, household goods, large collection of vintage clothing.

HOURS: By appt

ADMISSION: $2

JACKSON

5343
Jackson Historical Society
Hwy 16, 03846 [PO Box 209, 03846]; (p) (603) 383-4060; (c) Carroll

Private non-profit/ 1977/ staff: 6(v)/ members: 130/publication: *The Jackson Villager*

HISTORIC PRESERVATION AGENCY; HISTORICAL SOCIETY: Collects and preserves documents pertaining to the history of Jackson and maintains the means to disseminate this historic information.

PROGRAMS: Annual Meeting; Community Outreach; Guided Tours; Interpretation; Lectures; Publication

COLLECTIONS: 1,500 originals and or copies of deeds, letters, articles.

HOURS: Yr by appt

JEFFERSON

5344
Jefferson Historical Society
Rt 2, 03583 [PO Box 143, 03583]; (p) (603) 586-7021; (c) Coos

Private non-profit/ 1977/ staff: 15(v)/ members: 80

HISTORICAL SOCIETY; HISTORY MUSEUM

PROGRAMS: Lectures; School-Based Curriculum

COLLECTIONS: [1850-present] Local memorabilia.

HOURS: June-Oct T, Th, Sa 11-2

ADMISSION: No charge

KEENE

5345
Historical Society of Cheshire County
246 Main St, 03431 [PO Box 803, 03431]; (p) (603) 352-1895; (f) (603) 352-9226; hscc@cheshire.net; (c) Cheshire

Private non-profit/ 1927/ staff: 1(f); 3(p); 80(v)/ members: 919

HISTORICAL SOCIETY; HISTORY MUSEUM; HOUSE MUSEUM; RESEARCH CENTER: Collects, preserves, and communicates the history of Cheshire County, offers genealogy and local history research collection, period house, exhibits, publications, lectures.

PROGRAMS: Annual Meeting; Community Outreach; Elder's Programs; Exhibits; Facility Rental; Guided Tours; Interpretation; Lectures; Publication; Reenactments; Research Library/Archives; School-Based Curriculum

COLLECTIONS: [1770-1890] 300,000 item genealogy and local history research collection; NH glass, pottery, local art, toys, and silver; 1760-1820 furniture and accessories.

HOURS: Yr M-T, Th-F 9-4, W 9-9, Sa 9-12

ADMISSION: No charge

5346
Horatio Colony House Museum
199 Main St, 03431 [PO Box 722, 03431]; (p) (603) 352-0460

1806/ staff: 1(f); 2(p)

COLLECTIONS: [1900-1976] Silver, china, figurenes, art work, European, Oriental, fine furnishings; Letters, diaries, manuscripts.

HOURS: Yr

5347
Westmoreland Historical Society
River Rd, 03431 [21 Page St, 03431]; (p) (603) 357-2282; (c) Cheshire

Private non-profit/ 1944/ members: 35

Serves as a historical society for the town and preserves the 1789 Corner Schoolhouse; protects and preserves historical artifacts and memorabilia.

COLLECTIONS: [1789-present] Artifacts and memorabilia related to local history.

LACONIA

5348
Belknap Mill Society
25 Beacon St East, 03246 [The Mill Plaza, 03246]; (p) (603) 524-8813; (f) (603) 528-1228; belknap@worldpath.net; (c) Belknap

Private non-profit/ 1970/ Board of Trustees/ staff: 2(f); 4(p); 118(v)/ members: 700/publication: Belknap Mill News

CULTURAL CENTER; HISTORICAL SOCIETY; HISTORY MUSEUM: Maintains Belknap

Mill, located in a former knitting mill as a cultural center with a permanent exhibit on industrial knitting, and a 1918 hydroelectric plant and offers changing exhibit on art and history.

PROGRAMS: Annual Meeting; Community Outreach; Concerts; Exhibits; Facility Rental; Festivals; Guided Tours; Interpretation; Lectures; Living History; Publication; Reenactments; Research Library/Archives; School-Based Curriculum; Theatre

COLLECTIONS: [1928-present] Items relating to industrial knitting.

HOURS: Yr M-F 9-5

5349
New Hampshire Antique and Classic Boat Museum
11B at Weirs Beach, 03246 [216 Union Ave, 03246]; (p) (603) 524-8989; museum@worldpath.net; www.nhacbm.org; (c) Belknap

Private non-profit/ 1994/ staff: 1(f); 50(v)/ members: 188/publication: Boat House News

HISTORY MUSEUM: Dedicated to preserving and interpreting the history of antique boats and how the boating community effected the lifestyles and economy of NH.

PROGRAMS: Annual Meeting; Community Outreach; Exhibits; Facility Rental; Festivals; Lectures; Publication

COLLECTIONS: [1910-1960] Boats and other maritime artifacts.

HOURS: May-Oct Daily M-Sa 10-5, Su 10-4

ADMISSION: $4, Children $2, Seniors $2

LANCASTER

5350
Wilder-Holton House
226 Main St, 03584 [PO Box 473, 03584]; (p) (603) 788-3004, (603) 271-3556

1780

COLLECTIONS: [1763-date] Furniture manufactured locally by E. C. Garland & Son, late 1800's. Civil War memorabilia, particularly 5th NH Vols. & Col. E. E. Cross, sword, saddle; books and albums. Children's clothes, toys, furniture; Bound volumes of Lancaster's weekly newspaper, 1901 to 1986. Pictures and newspaper clippings in re. visit of President Harding to John W. Weeks' summer home. Scrapbooks compiled by lawyer Fred W. Baker, a Lancaster native.

HOURS: By appt

LEBANON

5351
Lebanon Historical Society
E Park St, 03266 [PO Box 18, 03266]; (p) (603) 448-3118; (c) Gragfton

Private non-profit/ 1958/ staff: 1(p); 15(v)/ members: 80

HISTORIC SITE; HISTORICAL SOCIETY; HISTORY MUSEUM; HOUSE MUSEUM: Collects and preserves the town's history.

PROGRAMS: Exhibits; Film/Video; Garden Tours; Guided Tours; Lectures; Living History; Publication; Research Library/Archives

COLLECTIONS: [1800s-1900] Photographs,

military uniforms, items from local industry.

ADMISSION: No charge

LEE

5352
Lee Historical Society
7 Mast Rd, 03824; (c) Strafford

Private non-profit/ 1971/ staff: 10(v)

HISTORICAL SOCIETY: Operates a small museum.

COLLECTIONS: [1800s-1900s] Housed in the former South Lee Railroad Freight Depot. Railroad, agriculture, household items, ice harvesting tools, genealogy, and town records.

HOURS: By appt

ADMISSION: No charge

LEMPSTER

5353
Lempster Historical Society
Lempster St, 03605 [124 Lempster St, 03605]; (c) Sullivan

Private non-profit/ members: 20

HISTORICAL SOCIETY; HISTORY MUSEUM

PROGRAMS: Annual Meeting; Exhibits

COLLECTIONS: Historical articles and papers pertaining to the town of Lempster.

HOURS: By appt

ADMISSION: No charge

LINCOLN

5354
Upper Pemi Valley Historical Society
Church St, 03251; (p) (603) 745-8149; (c) Grafton

Private non-profit/ 1983/ staff: 40(v)/ members: 150

HISTORICAL SOCIETY: Collects and preserves all artifacts pertaining to the area of the Pemi Valley.

PROGRAMS: Annual Meeting; Exhibits

COLLECTIONS: [Late 1800-present] Collection of logging, logging camps and tools, and paper making equipment.

HOURS: June-Oct W, F, Su 2-4

ADMISSION: No charge

5355
Upper Pemigewasset Historical Society
Church St, 03251 [PO Box 963, 03251]; (p) (603) 745-8491, (603) 745-3325; (c) Grafton

Private non-profit/ 1985/ staff: 25(v)/ members: 155/publication: Upstream

HISTORICAL SOCIETY; HISTORY MUSEUM: Preserve the history of the region in an interesting manner from pioneering mountain folks, era of large hotels, the paper mill, ski resorts, and tourism.

PROGRAMS: Annual Meeting; Exhibits; Lectures; Publication; Reenactments

LITTLETON

5356
Littleton Area Historical Society
One Cottage St, 03561; (p) (603) 444-6435; (c) Grafton

Private non-profit/ 1970/ staff: 1(p); 24(v)/ members: 200

HISTORIC SITE; HISTORICAL SOCIETY; HISTORY MUSEUM; RESEARCH CENTER: Collects, preserves, and displays artifacts and information from Littleton's past for the education and enjoyment of present and future generations.

PROGRAMS: Annual Meeting; Community Outreach; Exhibits; Guided Tours; Interpretation; Research Library/Archives; School-Based Curriculum

COLLECTIONS: 1,500 photographs, 3,000 references, china, period clothing and accessories, antique toys and dolls, memorabilia from every period of Littleton's history.

HOURS: July-Oct W, Sa 1:30-4:30 and by appt

ADMISSION: No charge

LYME

5357
Lyme Historians, The
Academy Bldg, 03768 [c/o William Murphy 40 Preston Rd, 03768]; (p) (603) 795-2287; (c) Grafton

Private non-profit/ 1961/ members: 80

GENEALOGICAL SOCIETY; HISTORIC PRESERVATION AGENCY; HISTORICAL SOCIETY; HISTORY MUSEUM: Dedicated to the preservation of materials relevant to Lyme and the upper valley and to the education of people about their heritage.

PROGRAMS: Annual Meeting; Community Outreach; Exhibits; Festivals; Guided Tours; Lectures

COLLECTIONS: [1770-1990] Printed materials and artifacts.

MADBURY

5358
Madbury Historical Society
13 Town Hall Rd, 03820; (p) (603) 742-5131; (c) Strafford

Private non-profit/ 1978/ members: 50

HISTORIC PRESERVATION AGENCY; HISTORICAL SOCIETY: Encourages an interest in the history of Madbury including the collection, display, and of articles of historic interest.

PROGRAMS: Exhibits; Guided Tours; Lectures

COLLECTIONS: [1700-present] Processed manuscripts, maps, newspaper clippings, photographs, costumes, and living history tapes.

MADISON

5359
Madison Historical Society
Madison Corner/East Madison Rd, 03849 [PO Box 505, 03849]; (p) (603) 367-4535, (603) 367-4687; (c) Carroll

Private non-profit/ 1959/ staff: 6(v)/ members: 70

HISTORICAL SOCIETY; HISTORY MUSEUM; HOUSE MUSEUM: Maintains the museum and provides programs both local and regional.

PROGRAMS: Annual Meeting; Community Outreach; Exhibits; Guided Tours; Lectures; Research Library/Archives; School-Based Curriculum

COLLECTIONS: [1852-present] Merchant wagon, sleigh, and exhibits of a general store, school room, living room, belongings of E.E. Cummings.

HOURS: May-Sept T 2-4, Su 2-4 by appt

ADMISSION: No charge

MANCHESTER

5360
American-Canadian Genealogical Society
4 Elm St, 03108 [PO Box 6478, 03108-6478]; (p) (603) 622-1554; www.acgs.org; (c) Hillsboro

Private non-profit/ 1973/ Board of Directors/ staff: 20(v)/ members: 2800/publication: American-Canadian Genealogist

GENEALOGICAL SOCIETY: Collects information on births, marriages, and deaths in Canada and the United States. The focus is primarily French, but includes other groups, such as the Irish, Scottish, and Native Americans.

PROGRAMS: Annual Meeting; Publication; Research Library/Archives

COLLECTIONS: [1600-present] Church and civil records, United States and Canada, including the Arcadian and maritime provinces; a 2,000 volume library; and 5,000 microfilm and microfiche records.

HOURS: Yr W-F 9-9, Sa 9-4

ADMISSION: $5, Members free

5361
Diocesan Museum
140 Laurel St, 03103; (p) (603) 624-1729; (c) Hillsborough

Private non-profit/ 1990/ staff: 1(f); 1(p); 7(v)

HISTORIC SITE; HISTORY MUSEUM: Collects, preserves, interprets, and displays objects relevant to the history of Catholic life in NH, for the purposes of research and education housed in a 19th c convent chapel.

PROGRAMS: Elder's Programs; Exhibits; Interpretation; Lectures; Living History; Publication; Research Library/Archives; School-Based Curriculum

COLLECTIONS: [Late 17th c-present] Religious art, liturgical objects, and ephemera, photographs, bibles, manuscripts.

HOURS: Yr T-F 10-4 and by appt

ADMISSION: No charge

5362
Franco-American Center
52 Concord St, 03101-1806; (p) (603) 669-4045; (f) (603) 625-1322; iciFranAm@aol.com; www.aca-assurance.com; (c) Hillsborough

Private non-profit/ 1990/ staff: 4(p)/ members: 300/publication: Les Informations

ART MUSEUM; HISTORICAL SOCIETY; RESEARCH CENTER: Preserves and promotes the history, culture, and artistic expression of the French in North America.

PROGRAMS: Annual Meeting; Community Outreach; Concerts; Exhibits; Facility Rental; Family Programs; Festivals; Film/Video; Guided Tours; Interpretation; Lectures; Publication; Library/Archives; School-Based Curriculum

COLLECTIONS: [18th-20th c] Art, statuary, and literary collection. 30,000 volumes and manuscripts of an historic, folkloric and literary nature. Works of Canadian sculptor Alfred Laliberte, a student of France's Rodin.

HOURS: Yr M-F 9-4:30

ADMISSION: No charge

5363
Lawrence L. Lee Scouting Museum
Bodwell Rd, 03105 [PO Box 1121, 03105]; (p) (603) 669-8919; (f) (603) 641-6464; administrator@scoutingmuseum.org; www.scoutingmuseum.org; (c) Hillsborough

Private non-profit/ 1969/ staff: 2(p); 28(v)

Preserves Scouting's heritage for the youth of tomorrow.

COLLECTIONS: [1900-date] Local, national, and international Boy Scout uniforms and insignia, periodicals, books, and pamphlets, and stamps; Baden-Powell Boer War collectibles, and many unique Scouting-related items.

HOURS: July-Aug Daily 10-4; Sa the rest of the year and by appt

ADMISSION: No charge

5364
Manchester City Library, New Hampshire Room
NH Room, 03104-6199; (p) (603) 624-6550; (c) Hillsborough

City/ staff: 1(f)

GENEALOGICAL SOCIETY; HISTORICAL SOCIETY; LIBRARY AND/OR ARCHIVES: Reference collection of local history and genealogy pertaining to NH and the city of Manchester.

PROGRAMS: Research Library/Archives

ADMISSION: No charge

5365
Manchester Historic Association
129 Amherst St, 03101; (p) (603) 622-7531; (f) (603) 622-0822; history@mha.mv.com; www.manchester-historic.org; (c) Hillsborough

Private non-profit/ 1896/ staff: 7(f); 6(p); 60(v)/ members: 671/publication: Calendar of Events

HISTORY MUSEUM: Collects, preserves, and interprets, artifacts, photographs and documents relating to the history of Manchester; provides exhibits, programs, library services, and interprets materials.

PROGRAMS: Community Outreach; Concerts; Exhibits; Facility Rental; Family Programs; Film/Video; Guided Tours; Lectures; Publication; Research Library/Archives

COLLECTIONS: [10,000 BC-present] Corporate documents and artifacts, 1836-1936, and other area textile mills; Native American archaeological collection from area; 18th-20th c decorative arts and manufactured goods from area. Historic photographs and glass plate negatives.

HOURS: Yr T-Sa 9-4, Sa 10-4
ADMISSION: $4, Student $3, Seniors $3

MARLBOROUGH

5366
Marlborough Historical Society, Inc.
[PO Box202, 03455]; (p) (603) 876-3980;
dbutler@cheshire.net; (c) Cheshire

Private non-profit/ 1964/ staff: 15(v)/ members:
90

HISTORICAL SOCIETY; LIBRARY AND/OR
ARCHIVES: Works on preservation and education of town history from all ages, and stives to
be a vital link to our heritage as a dedicated non-
profit chartered corporation in the state of NH.

PROGRAMS: Annual Meeting; Community
Outreach; Exhibits; Guided Tours; Interpretation; Lectures; Living History; Publication; Research Library/Archives

COLLECTIONS: [1850-2000] Photos, books,
clothing, household articles, and other artifacts pertaining to the town's history.

MASON

5367
Mason Historical Society
16 Darling Hill Rd, 03048; (p) (603) 878-
2070; (c) Hillsborough

City/ 1968/ staff: 2(p); 15(v)

HISTORICAL SOCIETY: Collects, preserves,
and makes accessible local history and genealogical materials.

PROGRAMS: Annual Meeting; Community
Outreach; Exhibits; Festivals

COLLECTIONS: Mason county records.

HOURS: Yr W 1-3:30 and by appt

ADMISSION: No charge

MELVIN VILLAGE

5368
Tuftonboro Historical Society, Inc.
Governor Wentworth Hwy, 03850 [PO Box
372, 03850]; (c) Carroll

Private non-profit/ 1958/ staff: 100(v)/ members:
160

HISTORICAL SOCIETY; HISTORY MUSEUM
PROGRAMS: Annual Meeting; Exhibits

COLLECTIONS: [1795-present] Local town
history collections: steam boat builder, local
artists, farm pieces, post offices, Abenaki Indian artifacts, museum located in original one-
room schoolhouse.

HOURS: July-Aug M-Sa 2-4

ADMISSION: No charge

MEREDITH

5369
Meredith Historical Society
45 Main St, 03253 [PO Box 920, 03253]; (p)
(603) 279-1190; (c) Belknap

Private non-profit/ 1950/ staff: 1(p); 10(v)/
members: 160

HISTORICAL SOCIETY; HISTORY MUSEUM:
Presents monthly programs, maintains two

local museums, small library, genealogy, and
Meredith history
PROGRAMS: Annual Meeting; Exhibits; Fami-
ly Programs
COLLECTIONS: [Mid 1800s-1900s] Materials
relating to Meredith.
HOURS: Late May-mid Oct W-Sa 11-4; farm
museum W-Sa 12-4
ADMISSION: Donations accepted

MILTON

5370
New Hampshire Farm Museum
Rt 125 Plummus Ridge, 03851 [PO Box 644,
03851]; (p) (603) 652-7840; (f) (603) 652-7840;
www.farmmuseum.org; (c) Strafford

Private non-profit/ 1969/ staff: 2(f); 2(p); 253(v)/
members: 926

HISTORIC SITE; HOUSE MUSEUM; LIVING
HISTORY/OUTDOOR MUSEUM; RESEARCH
CENTER: Collects, preserves, and interprets
the agricultural history of the state of New
Hampshire, for the education and enjoyment of
the public through live demonstrations.

PROGRAMS: Annual Meeting; Community
Outreach; Exhibits; Facility Rental; Family Pro-
grams; Guided Tours; Interpretation; Living
History; Research Library/Archives; School-
Based Curriculum

COLLECTIONS: [1880-1930] Agricultural artifacts and household items.

HOURS: June-Oct W-Su 10-4

ADMISSION: $4, Children $1.50

MILTON MILLS

5371
Township of Milton Historical Society
Main St, 03852 [PO Box 28, 03852]; (c)
Strafford

Private non-profit/ 1976/ staff: 30(v)/ members:
25

HISTORICAL SOCIETY: Provides monthly
meetings, speakers, and members covering
historical events, town history, town buildings,
early families, cataloging of material, and re-
sponding to the publics' requests.

PROGRAMS: Annual Meeting; Community
Outreach; Exhibits; Lectures

COLLECTIONS: [1800s-1900s] Town records:
marriage, death, birth, deeds, town meeting
minutes; photographs of original buildings,
events, town residents; record books of organizations and businesses.

ADMISSION: No charge

MONT VERNON

5372
**Beaver Brook Farm and
Transportation Museum**
78 Brook Rd, 03057; (p) (603) 673-9001; (c)
Hillsborro

Private for-profit/ 1985/ Edward and Beth
Gilbert/ staff: 8(v)

HISTORY MUSEUM; LIVING HISTORY/OUT-
DOOR MUSEUM; RAILROAD MUSEUM: Pro-

vides displays and living history depicting history between the 17th c and the 1920s.

PROGRAMS: Annual Meeting; Exhibits; Festivals; Guided Tours; Living History

COLLECTIONS: [18th-19th c] Carriages,
sleighs, clothing, tools, railroads, toys, New
England heritage farm implements, NH recreation, and all major factors of New England
life.

HOURS: Dec Sa-Su 12-7

5373
Mont Vernon Historical Society
Main St, 03057 [PO Box 15, 03057]; (p) (603)
673-2886; (c) Hillsborough

Private non-profit/ 1975/ staff: 3(p); 10(v)/
members: 50

HISTORICAL SOCIETY; HISTORY MUSEUM:
Promotes interest in history, preserves,
records, acquires, publishs, and promotes
local and regional history.

PROGRAMS: Annual Meeting; Community
Outreach; Exhibits; Festivals; Guided Tours;
Lectures; Publication; Research Library/
Archives; School-Based Curriculum

COLLECTIONS: [1800-present] Rural, farming, early education, summer hotels, clocks,
and local genealogical materials.

HOURS: May-Sept Last full Sa and Su of
month

ADMISSION: No charge

MOULTONBOROUGH

5374
**Moultonborough Historical Society,
Inc.**
Rt 25, 03254 [PO Box 659, 03254]; (c) Carroll

Private non-profit/ 1958/ members: 215/publi-
cation: *Moultonboro Cemetery Records*

HISTORICAL SOCIETY: Promotes local history programs; exhibits; restored one-room
schoolhouse and former inn building.

PROGRAMS: Annual Meeting; Community
Outreach; Exhibits; Guided Tours; Lectures;
Publication

COLLECTIONS: [19th c] Household artifacts,
horse-drawn agricultural implements.

HOURS: July-Aug W 2-4

ADMISSION: No charge

NASHUA

5375
Abbot-Spalding House
1 Nashville St, 03060 [5 Abbott St, 03060];
(p) (603) 883-0015; (f) (603) 889-8515

1802/ staff: 1(f)

COLLECTIONS: [The Federal Era] Federal
furniture and historic house.

HOURS: Seasonal

5376
Nashua Historical Society, The
5 Abbott St, 03064; (p) (603) 883-0015; (c)
Hillsborough

Private non-profit/ 1872/ staff: 1(f); 1(p); 60(v)/
members: 219

HISTORICAL SOCIETY: Collects and preserves historical artifacts, properties, records, and documents with an emphasis on those used, produced, or relating to Nashua and surrounding area.

PROGRAMS: Annual Meeting; Community Outreach; Exhibits; Family Programs; Guided Tours; Interpretation; Research Library/Archives

COLLECTIONS: Eclectic collection focused on the history of Nashua in general.

HOURS: Mar-Nov T-Th 10-4, Sa 1-4

ADMISSION: No charge

NEW IPSWICH

5377
Barrett House, SPNEA
Forest Hall, Main St, 03071; (p) (603) 878-2517; www.spnea.org

Private non-profit/ 1800/ Society for the Preservation of New England Antiquities

HISTORY MUSEUM; HOUSE MUSEUM

PROGRAMS: Garden Tours; Guided Tours; Lectures

HOURS: June 1-Oct 15 Sa-Su 11-5

ADMISSION: $5; SPNEA Members/Town residents free

NEW LONDON

5378
New London Historical Society
Little Sunapee Rd, 03257 [PO Box 965, 03257]; (p) (603) 526-6564; (c) Merrimack

Private non-profit/ 1954/ staff: 100(v)/ members: 300

HISTORICAL SOCIETY; LIVING HISTORY/ OUTDOOR MUSEUM: Promotes local history; collects and preserves artifacts and information of historical significance; provides education about evolution of daily life.

PROGRAMS: Annual Meeting; Community Outreach; Facility Rental; Family Programs; Festivals; Guided Tours; Interpretation; Lectures; Living History; School-Based Curriculum

COLLECTIONS: [1830-1890] Twelve buildings: collection of horse-drawn vehicles; blacksmith shop; violin shop, furniture, clothing, and other artifacts from 19th c.

HOURS: June-Aug 10-5 and by appt

NEW MARKET

5379
New Market Historical Society
Stone School Museum Granite St, 03857 [PO Box 534, 03857]; (p) (603) 659-7420; (c) Rockingham

Private non-profit/ 1966/ staff: 10(v)/ members: 200

HISTORICAL SOCIETY; HISTORY MUSEUM: Maintains 1841 Stone School Museum and collects artifacts and material related to local history.

PROGRAMS: Annual Meeting; Community Outreach; Exhibits; Festivals; Interpretation; Lectures; School-Based Curriculum

COLLECTIONS: [17th-19th c] Local artifacts, old farm and blacksmith tools, materials relating to Granite textile mills 1823, shoe shops, and local industries.

HOURS: June-Aug Th 2-4 and by appt

ADMISSION: Donations accepted

NEWBURY

5380
Friends of John Hay National Wildlife Refuge
Rt 103 A, 03255 [PO Box 276, 03255]; (p) (603) 763-4789; (f) (603) 763-2452; fells@tds.net; www.thefells.org; (c) Merrimack

Private non-profit/ 1996/ staff: 1(f); 6(p); 150(v)/ members: 500

GARDEN; HISTORIC SITE: Preserves the buildings, gardens, and grounds of the Hay family property known as the Fells, and education in history, horticulture, and the environment as relates to this site.

PROGRAMS: Exhibits; Family Programs; Festivals; Garden Tours; Guided Tours; Interpretation

COLLECTIONS: [1880-present] Extensive living plant collections, Hay family photographs, books, and small collection of furnishings.

HOURS: Yr grounds and gardens Daily dawn-dusk; Historic house: late May-mid Oct Sa-Su, M and holidays 10-5

ADMISSION: $4

5381
Newbury Historical Society
Village Rd, 03255 [PO Box 176, 03255]; (p) (603) 938-2892; w_weiler@conknet.com; (c) Merrimack

Private non-profit/ 1986/ staff: 3(v)/ members: 60

Organizes, preserves, and protects the documentary heritage of the town and promotes the study of town history and genealogy.

COLLECTIONS: [1795-present] Town records from 1795 to 1989 published school reports, miscellaneous photos, and papers related to local history.

HOURS: May-Nov By appt

ADMISSION: No charge

NEWPORT

5382
Goshen, New Hampshire Historical Society, Inc.
Lear Hill Farm, 03773 [161 Lear Hill, Goshen, 03773]; (p) (603) 863-1718; (f) (603) 863-8758; learhillfarm@sugar-river.net; (c) Sullivan

Joint/ 1969/ State; Private non-profit/ members: 16

ALLIANCE OF HISTORICAL AGENCIES; HISTORICAL SOCIETY: Promotes interested in the history of Goshen and provides for the collection and preservation of material to help establish and illustrate local history.

PROGRAMS: Annual Meeting; Exhibits; Festivals; Guided Tours; Lectures; Publication; Research Library/Archives

COLLECTIONS: [1769-present] Written and photographic, many glass negatives from itinerant photographers, documents, memorabil-

ia, genealogical, and cemetery records.

HOURS: By appt

ADMISSION: No charge

5383
Sargent Museum, The
30 Central St, 03773 [PO Box 4212, 03302-4212]; (p) (603) 863-1944; (f) (603) 229-4966; info@mail.sargentmuseum.org; www.sargentmuseum.org; (c) Sullivan

Private non-profit/ 1994/ staff: 4(p); 3(v)/ members: 250

ARCHAEOLOGICAL SITE/MUSEUM; HISTORY MUSEUM: Preserves and interprets NH and Northern New England; past for the education and enjoyment of the public; performs research into our past and promotes public involvement in research and history to build community ties and commitment.

PROGRAMS: Annual Meeting; Community Outreach; Exhibits; Family Programs; Film/Video; Guided Tours; Lectures; Publication; Research Library/Archives

COLLECTIONS: Collections, library, and research materials of Howard R. Sargent. Includes 1,000,000 artifacts, 5,000 volumes, 10,000 manuscripts, 10,000 museum artifacts and 7,000 photographs covering Indian and European settlers history.

HOURS: Jan-Nov M, W, F 9-5

ADMISSION: No charge

NEWPSWICH

5384
Newipswich Historical Society
23 Main St, 03071 [PO Box 422, Newipswich, 03071]; (p) (603) 878-1132; (c) Hillsborogh

Private non-profit/ 1913/ staff: 12(v)/ members: 100

HISTORICAL SOCIETY; HISTORY MUSEUM: Collects, preserves, and interprets New Inpswich's history from 1750 to the present.

PROGRAMS: Annual Meeting; Exhibits; Lectures; Research Library/Archives

COLLECTIONS: [18th-19th c] 600 cataloged artifacts, 1,500 cataloged photographs, unprocessed manuscripts, and book collections related to the history of New Ipswich.

HOURS: June-Oct Su 1-5

ADMISSION: No charge

NEWTON

5385
Newton, New Hampshire Historical Society
S Main St, 03858 [34 Gale Village Rd, 03858]; (p) (603) 382-8649; (c) Rockingham

Private non-profit/ 1973/ staff: 20(v)/ members: 70

HISTORICAL SOCIETY: Discovers, collects and disseminates materials to establish or illustrate the history of our town.

PROGRAMS: Annual Meeting; Exhibits; Family Programs; Lectures

HOURS: By appt

ADMISSION: No charge

NORTH HAMPTON

5386
North Hampton Historical Society
[PO Box 17, 03862-0017]; (p) (603) 964-8829;
(c) Rockingham

Private non-profit/ 1971/ Executive Board/
members: 30

HISTORICAL SOCIETY: Collects, preserves
documents, artifacts, sites, buildings related to
North Hampton.

PROGRAMS: Family Programs; Lectures;
Monthly Meeting

COLLECTIONS: [1850-1950] Historical Documents, old photographs, old books, maps, old
memorabilia.

NORTH SUTTON

5387
**Muster Field Farm/Harvey
Homestead, Inc.**
Harvey Rd, 03260 [PO Box 118, 03260]; (p)
(603) 927-4276; (c) Merrimack

Private non-profit/ 1991/ staff: 1(f); 1(p); 30(v)/
members: 340

GARDEN; HISTORIC PRESERVATION
AGENCY; HISTORIC SITE; HISTORICAL SOCIETY; HISTORY MUSEUM; LIVING HISTORY/OUTDOOR MUSEUM: Preserves and promotes the traditions of NH farming; collects,
protects, and preserves artifacts pertaining to
the Harvey family, and promotes the early history of Sutton.

PROGRAMS: Annual Meeting; Community
Outreach; Concerts; Elder's Programs; Exhibits; Facility Rental; Family Programs; Festivals; Garden Tours; Guided Tours; Interpretation; Lectures; Living History; Publication;
Reenactments; Research Library/Archives

COLLECTIONS: [1783-1941] Our farm museum includes 18 farm buildings, blacksmith
shops, schoolhouse, church house, 1787 Harvey Homestead, vegetable and flower gardens
and a small orchard.

HOURS: Yr

ADMISSION: $3

NORTHWOOD

5388
Northwood Historical Society
School St, 03261 [PO Box 114, 03261-0114];
(p) (603) 942-8506; (f) (603) 942-5617; www.
rootsweb.com; (c) Rockingham

Private non-profit/ staff: 20(v)/ members:
65/publication: *Everlastings: Cemetery Index*

HISTORICAL SOCIETY: Brings together people interested in history to collect and preserve
related items and arouse interest and share information about our history.

PROGRAMS: Annual Meeting; Community
Outreach; Exhibits; Family Programs; Lectures; Publication

COLLECTIONS: [19th-20th] Items, documents, records, artifacts, materials related to
agriculture, shoemaking, tourism, local history.

HOURS: July-Aug 1st and 3rd Sa 1-3

ADMISSION: No charge

OSSIPEE

5389
Ossipee Historical Society
Rt 16 B, 03864 [PO Box 245, 03864]; (c)
Carroll

Private non-profit/ 1923/ staff: 5(p); 3(v)/ members: 284/publication: *Ossipee Journal of History*

HISTORICAL SOCIETY: The society preserves artifacts, documents, and records pertaining to Ossipee history and promotes the
study and acquisition of knowledge about Ossipee history to the public.

PROGRAMS: Annual Meeting; Exhibits; Lectures; Publication

COLLECTIONS: [16th c-present] Artifacts,
documents, photographs, and data, genealogical materials associated with the town of Ossippee, and New Hampshire.

HOURS: June 15th - Sept 15

ADMISSION: No charge

PENACOOK

5390
New Hampshire Archives Group
5 Penwood Dr # 3, 03303; (p) (603) 526-3687;
(f) (603) 526-3777; lhanson@colby-sawyer.edu

Private non-profit/ members: 100

ALLIANCE OF HISTORICAL AGENCIES: Is
dedicated to educating archives administrators
and practitioners in many types of institutional
settings.

PROGRAMS: Annual Meeting; Lectures

PENNSVILLE

5391
Church Landing Farmhouse Museum
86 Church Landing Rd, 08070; (p) (609) 678-
4453, (609) 678-5994

1860/ staff: 3(v)

COLLECTIONS: [1860] Collection of Indian artifacts (arrowheads, tools, etc.), collection of
articles from former amusement park
RIVERVIEW BEACH PARK.

HOURS: Mar-Jan

PETERBOROUGH

5392
Peterborough Historical Society
17 Grove St, 03458 [PO Box 58, 03458]; (p)
(603) 924-3235; (c) Hillsborough

Private non-profit/ 1902/ staff: 1(f); 2(p); 30(v)/
members: 400/publication: *Our Changing Town*

HISTORICAL SOCIETY; HISTORY MUSEUM:
Collects and preserves history of Peterborough.

PROGRAMS: Annual Meeting; Community
Outreach; Exhibits; Facility Rental; Guided
Tours; Interpretation; Lectures; Living History;
Publication; Research Library/Archives

COLLECTIONS: [19th-early 20th c] 10,000 artifacts and manuscripts related to Peterbough;
furniture, textiles.

HOURS: Yr M-F 10-4

ADMISSION: No charge

PITTSBURG

5393
Pittsburg Historical Society
Main St, 03592 [PO Box 2, 03592]; (c) Coos

Private non-profit/ 1982/ members: 400

HISTORIC PRESERVATION AGENCY; HISTORIC SITE; HISTORICAL SOCIETY; HISTORY MUSEUM: Located in Old Town Hall
across from town offices.

PROGRAMS: Exhibits; Guided Tours; Lectures

HOURS: July-Aug Sa 1-3 or by appt

ADMISSION: No charge

PITTSFIELD

5394
Pittsfield Historical Society
13 Elm St, 03263; (p) (603) 435-7575; (f)
(603) 435-5079; (c) Merrimack

Private non-profit/ 1971/ staff: 100(v)/ members:
100

HISTORICAL SOCIETY

PROGRAMS: Annual Meeting; Exhibits; Family Programs; Film/Video; Guided Tours; Lectures; Research Library/Archives

COLLECTIONS: [1768-present] Historical artifacts of Pittsfield, historic trail with 35 sites,
Hall of Fame pictures.

HOURS: By appt

ADMISSION: No charge

PLAINFIELD

5395
Plainfield Historical Society
Rt 12 A, 03781 [PO Box 107, 03781]; (p)
(603) 675-6866; (c) Sullivan

Private non-profit/ 1978/ staff: 35(v)/ members:
75

GENEALOGICAL SOCIETY; HISTORIC
PRESERVATION AGENCY; HISTORICAL SOCIETY; HISTORY MUSEUM: Promotes interest
in the history of Plainfield; collects and preserves artifacts related to the town; encourages
the preservation of historic structures; and disseminates information on the history of the
town.

PROGRAMS: Annual Meeting; Community
Outreach; Concerts; Exhibits; Family Programs; Guided Tours; Interpretation; Lectures;
Research Library/Archives; Theatre

COLLECTIONS: [1761-present] Anything pertaining to Plainfield, books, scrapbooks,
newsclippings, photos, locally-made items,
art, family records, business records, journals,
and items related to the Cornish Art Colony.

HOURS: Yr by appt

ADMISSION: No charge

PLAISTOW

5396
Plaistow Historical Society, Inc.
127 Main St, 03865 [PO Box 434, 03865]; (p)
(603) 382-1675; (c) Rockingham

City/ 1974/ members: 55

HISTORICAL SOCIETY: The society invokes

an interest in town history and future in its citizens; collects and preserves local history.

PROGRAMS: Exhibits; Festivals; Lectures

COLLECTIONS: Town memorabilia and articles of past history; collection of spear heads, extensive material on war remembrances, photos, articles, and collections of town folk family histories.

HOURS: Society meets 3rd T of every month

ADMISSION: No charge

PORTSMOUTH

5397
African American Resource Center
[PO Box 5094, 03801-5094]; (p) (603) 431-2768; pbhtrail@aol.com

5398
Albacore Park
600 Market St, 03801; (p) (603) 436-3680; (f) (603) 436-3680

Private non-profit/ 1984/ Portsmouth Submarine Memorial Association/ staff: 2(f); 2(p); 3(v)/ members: 750

MARITIME MUSEUM

PROGRAMS: Exhibits; Interpretation

COLLECTIONS: [1900-present] Submarine artifacts, memorabilia, and photographs.

HOURS: Yr Daily M-F May-Sept 9:30-5:30; Oct-Apr 9:30-4

ADMISSION: $5, Children $2, Seniors $3.50

5399
Governor John Langdon House, SPNEA
143 Pleasant St, 03801; (p) (603) 436-3205; www.spnea.org

Private non-profit/ 1784/ Society for the Preservation of New England Antiquities

HOUSE MUSEUM: House built by John Langdon, merchant, shipbuilder, signer of the Constitution, and 3 term governor of NH. At the end of the 19th c, Langdon descendants purchased the house and restored it to its 18th c look, adding on a substantial wing designed by McKim, Mead, and White to house modern conveniences.

PROGRAMS: Concerts; Garden Tours; Guided Tours; Lectures

HOURS: June 1-Oct 15 W-Su 11-5

ADMISSION: $6; SPNEA Members/Town residents free

5400
Jackson House, SPNEA
76 Northwest St, 03801; (p) (603) 436-3205; www.spnea.org

Private non-profit/ 1664/ Society for the Preservation of New England Antiquities

HISTORY MUSEUM; HOUSE MUSEUM: The oldest surviving wood frame house in NH and ME was built by Richard Jackson, a woodworker, farmer, and mariner, on his family's 25-acre plot.

PROGRAMS: Family Programs; Guided Tours

HOURS: June 1-Oct 15 Sa-Su 11-5

ADMISSION: $6; SPNEA Members/Town residents free

5401
John Paul Jones House Museum
43 Middle St, 03802 [PO Box 728, 03802-0728]; (p) (603) 436-8420; jpjhouse@seacoastnh.com; www.SeacoastNH.com/jpj; (c) Rockingham

Private non-profit/ 1919/ staff: 10(p)/ members: 300

GARDEN; HOUSE MUSEUM

PROGRAMS: Annual Meeting; Guided Tours; Lectures; Living History

COLLECTIONS: [18th-20th c] John Paul Jones, the father of the American Navy. Fine china, furniture, clothing, documents, naval artifacts.

HOURS: Yr Daily M-Sa 10-4, Su 12-4

ADMISSION: $5, Children $2.50

5402
Moffatt-Ladd House and Garden
154 Market St, 03801; (p) (603) 436-8221, (603) 430-7968; (f) (603) 431-9063; moffatt-ladd@juno.com; (c) Rockingham

Private non-profit/ 1913/ staff: 1(f); 10(p); 60(v)/ members: 203

GARDEN; HOUSE MUSEUM

PROGRAMS: Exhibits; Facility Rental; Garden Tours; Guided Tours; Research Library/ Archives

COLLECTIONS: [1760-1840] One of America's finest Georgian mansions and formal gardens; extensive collection of family manuscripts and furnishings.

HOURS: June 15 - Oct 15 Daily M-Sa 11-5, Su 1-5

ADMISSION: $5; Group rates

5403
Portsmouth Athenaeum
6-8 Market Sq, 03802 [PO Box 848, 03802]; (p) (603) 431-2538; (f) (603) 431-7180; athenaeum@juno.com; (c) Rockingham

Joint; Private non-profit/ 1817/ staff: 6(p); 50(v)/ members: 365/publication: *The Portsmouth Athenaeum Newsletter*

RESEARCH CENTER: Membership library; maintains publicly accessible local history research library and archives; exhibits art and artifacts and offers lectures on themes of local and regional significance.

PROGRAMS: Concerts; Exhibits; Lectures; Publication; Research Library/Archives

COLLECTIONS: [18th-20th c] Local and regional business, institutional, family papers, photographs, ephemera, genealogical and city architecture resources, portraits of people and ships, ship models, publications on military, maritime, art architecture, and decorative arts of region.

HOURS: Yr T,Th 1-4, Sa 10-4

5404
Portsmouth Public Library
8 Islington St, 03801-4261; (p) (603) 427-1540; (f) (603) 433-0981; www.cityofportsmouth.com/library/library.htm; (c) Rockingham

City/ 1896/ staff: 15(f); 5(p); 2(v)

The library serves the local population and houses a local history and genealogy collection.

COLLECTIONS: Over 109,000 books, 400 periodical subscriptions, audio and video cassettes, and local history and genealogy collection specializing in Portsmouth history, and is fully automated.

HOURS: Yr M-Th 9-9, F 9-5:30, Sa 9-5

ADMISSION: No charge

5405
Rundlet-May House, SPNEA
364 Middle St, 03801; (p) (603) 436-3205; www.spnea.org

Private non-profit/ 1807/ Society for the Preservation of New England Antiquities

HISTORY MUSEUM; HOUSE MUSEUM: Mansion built by merchant James Rundlet including the latest technologies of the time. Includes a formal garden and outbuildings.

PROGRAMS: Garden Tours; Guided Tours

COLLECTIONS: [19th c]

HOURS: June 1-Oct 15 Sa-Su 11-5

ADMISSION: $6; SPNEA Members/Town residents free

5406
Warner House Association
150 Daniel St, 03802 [PO Box 895, 03802]; (p) (603) 436-5909; (c) Rockingham

Private non-profit/ 1931/ staff: 9(p)/ members: 200

HOUSE MUSEUM: The association owns, preserves and protects the Macphecdres, Warner House, and English Georgian style brick mansion built in 1716 which was owned and occupied by generations of one family from 1716-1930.

PROGRAMS: Annual Meeting; Exhibits; Facility Rental; Guided Tours; Lectures

COLLECTIONS: [18th c] 18th and 19th century furnishings, memorabilia, textiles, and early 18th century wall mural.

HOURS: June-Oct T-Sa 10-4, Su 1-4

ADMISSION: $5, Children $2.50

5407
Wentworth-Coolidge Mansion
375 Little Harbor Rd, 03801; (p) (603) 436-6607

1720/ staff: 1(p); 10(v)

COLLECTIONS: [18th c] Original 1750 English flocked wallpaper in 2 rooms, mansion is a fine example of 18th century architecture with many period details.

HOURS: Seasonal

RICHMOND

5408
Richmond Archives
19th Winchester Rd, 03470 [c/o N Thibodeau, 480 Fitzwilliam Rd, 03470]; (p) (603) 239-4598; rflanders@juno.com; (c) Cheshire

City; Joint/ 1976/ staff: 3(p); 3(v)

LIBRARY AND/OR ARCHIVES: Repository for documents pertaining to local history, some memorabilia, photographs.

PROGRAMS: Research Library/Archives

COLLECTIONS: [Late 1700s-1900s] The archives is in the process of being organized into collections on various subjects in the town. Computerized lists of collections are being made, all based on local history and genealogy.

HOURS: Yr T-F 9-12 and by appt

ADMISSION: No charge

5409
Richmond Historical Society
480 Fitzwilliam Rd, 03470; rflanders@monad. net; (c) Cheshire

Joint; State/ 1974/ members: 40/publication: *History of the Town of Richmond*

HISTORICAL SOCIETY: Preserve, the history of Richmond.

PROGRAMS: Guided Tours; Publication

RINDGE

5410
Rindge Historical Society
47 School St, 03461; (c) Cheshire

Private non-profit/ staff: 2(p); 15(v)/ members: 168

HISTORICAL SOCIETY: The society collects and preserves articles relating to Rindge, record events of historic interest, foster general interest in history of Rindge.

PROGRAMS: Annual Meeting; Community Outreach; Exhibits; Guided Tours

COLLECTIONS: [Colonial-Victorian] Early household, furniture, clothing, quilts, children's carriages.

HOURS: Special events and by appt

ROCHESTER

5411
Rochester New Hampshire Historical Society
58 Hanson St, 03866 [PO Box 65, 03866-0065]; (p) (603) 330-3099; Storia@s-way. com; www.geocities.com/powerofz7; (c) Strafford

Private non-profit/ 1950/ staff: 12(v)/ members: 149

HISTORICAL SOCIETY; HISTORY MUSEUM: To promote interest in the collection, preservation, and study of historical and regional materials in and of the city of Rochester, New Hampshire, and to serve as a clearing house for the exchange of information among its members.

PROGRAMS: Research Library/Archives

COLLECTIONS: [1750-present] Annual town and city reports form 1888 - present; incomplete set of city directories; Rochester Courier Newspaper from late 1800s -present; photographs, genealogical, Civil War, Rochester Fair, and cemeteries materials, and artifacts of early Rochester.

HOURS: Yr T-Th 1-4; Every 3rd Sa of Month 11-3

ADMISSION: No charge

5412
Rochester Public Library
65 S Main St, 03867; (p) (603) 332-1428; (f) (603) 335-7582; (c) Strafford

City/ 1905/ staff: 9(f); 13(p); 5(v)

Public library

HOURS: Yr 11-5

ADMISSION: No charge

RUMNEY

5413
Groton Historical Society
District 4 Schoolhouse, 03266 [PO Box 50, 03266]; (p) (603) 786-2335; (c) Grafton

Private non-profit/ 1988/ members: 25

HISTORIC PRESERVATION AGENCY; HISTORIC SITE; HISTORICAL SOCIETY; HISTORY MUSEUM: Preserves Groton history and restores the schoolhouse for museum.

PROGRAMS: Annual Meeting; Exhibits; Festivals; Guided Tours; Lectures; Publication

COLLECTIONS: [1800-1950] Mining artifacts, photographs of structures, church bell, schoolhouse.

RYE

5414
Rye Historical Society
Off Olde Parrish Rd, 03870 [PO Box 583, 03870]

Private non-profit/ 1976/ staff: 20(v)/ members: 42

HISTORIC SITE; HISTORICAL SOCIETY: Newly organized.

PROGRAMS: Community Outreach; Exhibits; Facility Rental; Family Programs; Guided Tours; Interpretation; Lectures; Research

5415
Seacoast Science Center
Odiorne Point State Park, 03870 [570 Ocean Blvd, 03870-2104]; (p) (603) 436-8043; (f) (603) 433-2235; seacentr@nh.ultranet.com; www.seacentr.org; (c) Rockingham

Joint; Private non-profit/ 1992/ staff: 9(f); 43(p); 127(v)/ members: 1300

HISTORIC SITE; LIVING HISTORY/OUTDOOR MUSEUM: Interprets environmental and natural history of the seacoast through programs and exhibits for families, students, and groups in a natural and historic setting.

PROGRAMS: Community Outreach; Concerts; Elder's Programs; Exhibits; Facility Rental; Family Programs; Garden Tours; Guided Tours; Interpretation; Lectures; Publication; Library/Archives; School-Based Curriculum

COLLECTIONS: [1623-present]

HOURS: Yr Daily 10-5

ADMISSION: $1; Under 6 free

SANBORNTON

5416
Sanbornton Historical Society
520 Stage Rd, 03269 [PO Box 2, 03269]; (p) (603) 286-7227; (c) Belknap

Private non-profit/ 1952/ staff: 8(p)/ members: 185/publication: *Tavern Talk*

HISTORICAL SOCIETY: Collects, preserves, and interprets Sanbornton and New Hampshire history for the education and enjoyment

of present and future generations.

PROGRAMS: Annual Meeting; Exhibits; Guided Tours; Lectures; Publication

COLLECTIONS: [Late 1700s-1900s] Clothing, agricultural tools, photos, paintings and portraits, furniture.

HOURS: Summer by appt

SANDOWN

5417
Old Meeting House Historical Association
Fremont Rd, 03873 [PO Box 377, 03873]; (p) (603) 887-3453; kbassett@gsinet.net; (c) Rockingham

City; Private non-profit/ 1774/ members: 80

HISTORIC SITE: Historic Old Meeting House preserved as originally built in 1774.

PROGRAMS: Annual Meeting; Community Outreach; Facility Rental; Lectures

HOURS: By appt only

ADMISSION: No charge

5418
Sandown Historical Society and Museum
Depot Rd, 03873 [PO Box 300, 03873]; (c) Rockingham

Private non-profit/ 1978/ staff: 5(v)/ members: 18

HISTORICAL SOCIETY: Founded with purpose of restoring the station of B & M Railroad.

PROGRAMS: Exhibits; Festivals

COLLECTIONS: Depot, two flanger cars, railroad artifacts displayed and Sandown artifacts, memorabilia, tools, implements used by shoemakers, blacksmiths, farmers, and housewives.

HOURS: May-Oct Sa-Su 1-5

ADMISSION: No charge

SEABROOK

5419
Historical Society of Seabrook
Washington St, 03874 [PO Box 414, 03874]; (p) (603) 474-5066; ens@seacoast.com; (c) Rockingham

Private non-profit/ 1964/ staff: 10(v)/ members: 100

HISTORICAL SOCIETY: Preserves the artifacts, documents, and photographs of the organizations and people of the town of Seabrook.

PROGRAMS: Annual Meeting; Exhibits; Lectures

COLLECTIONS: [19th-20th c] Collection emphasizes photograph, written material, salt hay farming, oil painting, decoys, farming, fishing, and shoe industry, history of Quakers.

SOUTH EFFINGHAM

5420
Effingham Historic District Commission
Town House, 03882 [PO Box 12, 03882]; (p) (603) 539-7770, (603) 539-4803

Private non-profit/ 1987/ staff: 7(v)

HISTORIC PRESERVATION AGENCY: A land use zoning commission within town historic districts of the town of Lords Hill and Central Effingham.

PROGRAMS: Annual Meeting; Guided Tours

COLLECTIONS: [1772-present] Our collections are two separate villages: one a normal school plus 15-20 other buildings; Italinate town hall plus 8 other buildings.

SPRINGFIELD

5421
Springfield Historical Society
Four Corner Rd, 03284 [Box 6, 03284]; User500491@aol.com; (c) Sullivan

City/ 1984/ members: 100

HISTORICAL SOCIETY: The society brings together people interested in the town's history. It also preserves material of historical interest and disseminates historical information to anyone interested.

PROGRAMS: Annual Meeting; Community Outreach; Exhibits; Lectures

COLLECTIONS: [1780s-present] Picture collection-people, houses in town, growing genealogy, and cemetery information, farming implements, household items, small amount of furniture.

HOURS: June-Sept Sa 2-4

ADMISSION: No charge

STRATHAM

5422
Stratham Historical Society, Inc.
Portsmouth Ave, 03885 [PO Box 39, 03885]; (p) (603) 778-1347; (c) Rockingham

Private non-profit/ 1970/ staff: 10(p); 40(v)/ members: 90

HISTORIC PRESERVATION AGENCY; HISTORIC SITE; HISTORICAL SOCIETY; HISTORY MUSEUM; RESEARCH CENTER: Preserves, interprets, collects, and displays those items related to our goals; rotation and maintenance of artifacts through a small museum.

PROGRAMS: Annual Meeting; Community Outreach; Exhibits; Lectures; Research Library/Archives

COLLECTIONS: [19th and 20th c] Collection of 1,200 local photographs and extensive genealogies, 40 volumes of NH state papers, museum artifacts, manuscripts, documents.

HOURS: Yr T 9-11:30, Th, 2-4, 1st Su 2-4

ADMISSION: No charge

SUGAR HILL

5423
Sugar Hill Historical Museum
Rt 117, 03585; (p) (603) 823-5336; (f) (603) 823-8431; robt.harwood@mail.connriver.net; www.franconianotch.org; (c) Grafton

Private non-profit/ 1976/ staff: 4(p); 50(v)/ members: 116

GENEALOGICAL SOCIETY; HISTORY MUSEUM: The museum was established as a Bicentennial project to document and exhibit the

history and life of the Sugar Hill area and is maintained largely by local volunteers.

PROGRAMS: Community Outreach; Concerts; Exhibits; Family Programs; Guided Tours; Interpretation; Lectures; Research Library/Archives; School-Based Curriculum

COLLECTIONS: [Late 18th c-present] Crafts, clothing, and old photos, art displays, exhibits, hands-on demonstrations.

HOURS: Mid June - early Oct F, Sa, Su 1-4

ADMISSION: Donations accepted

TAMWORTH

5424
Remick Country Doctor Museum and Farm
58 Cleveland Hill Rd, 03886 [PO Box 250, 03886]; (p) (603) 323-7591, (800) 686-6117; (f) (603) 323-8382; www.remickmuseum.org; (c) Carroll

Private non-profit/ 1996/ staff: 7(f); 1(p); 50(v)

HISTORY MUSEUM; HOUSE MUSEUM; LIVING HISTORY/OUTDOOR MUSEUM: Provides an in-depth look into two hundred years of medical and agricultural history. The emphasis is on a fun hands-on, up close and personal, interactive experience with history.

PROGRAMS: Community Outreach; Concerts; Elder's Programs; Exhibits; Family Programs; Guided Tours; Interpretation; Lectures; Living History; Reenactments; School-Based Curriculum

COLLECTIONS: [1700-present] Two historic homes and working farms with animals; house furnishings, decorative arts, agricultural tools, and equipment, costumes, large family archives, letters, and photos.

HOURS: Yr July-Oct M-SA 10-4; Nov-June M-F 10-4

ADMISSION: No charge

5425
Tamworth Historical Socity
26 Greg's Way, 03886 [PO Box 13, 03886]; (p) (603) 323-8214; (c) Carroll

Private non-profit/ 1952/ staff: 20(v)/ members: 200

HISTORICAL SOCIETY

PROGRAMS: Annual Meeting; Exhibits; Guided Tours; Lectures

COLLECTIONS: [Late 1790-early 1900s] Artifacts and archives relating to Tamworth history.

HOURS: Apr-octTh 5-7pm, Sa 10-2 and by appt

ADMISSION: No charge

TEMPLE

5426
Historical Society of Temple, New Hampshire, Inc.
Rt 45 at Mansfield Library, 03084 [PO Box 114, 03084]; (p) (603) 878-3100; (c) Hillsborough

Private non-profit/ 1941/ members: 65/publication: *History of Temple, New Hampshire*

HISTORIC SITE; HISTORICAL SOCIETY: To stimulate interest and discover, secure, and preserve information and objects relating to all

facets of Temple's history and to exhibit artifacts, disseminate knowledge and provide genealogical information on families of Temple.

PROGRAMS: Annual Meeting; Exhibits; Festivals; Guided Tours; Publication; Research Library/Archives

COLLECTIONS: [1770-present] Artifacts Donated by Temple residents; from Revolutionary drum, glass, china, toys, clothing, glasswork from archeological dig, photos, and records.

HOURS: Yr M, T, W, F, Sa 1:30-5

ADMISSION: No charge

UNITY

5427
Unity Historical Society, Inc.
Unity Town Hall, 2nd NH Turnpike, 03773 [c/o Roberta Callum, HC 66, Box 140, 03773-8601]; (p) (603) 863-3468; (f) (603) 863-3468; romer@cyberportal.net; (c) Sullivan

Private non-profit/ 1983/ staff: 5(v)/ members: 15/publication: *Highlights in History of Unity; Early Families of Unity, New Hampshire*

HISTORICAL SOCIETY; HISTORY MUSEUM: Devoted to studying the history of this rural township. We hold monthly meetings and maintain a small collection of artifacts and historical records.

PROGRAMS: Community Outreach; Lectures; Publication; Research Library/Archives

COLLECTIONS: [1760-date] Bailey silver, other artifacts, chattel mortgages, school records, Methodist records, Micro-films, and photocopies; Sullivan County census returns, town records, Quaker records.

HOURS: By appt

ADMISSION: No charge

WAKEFIELD

5428
Museum of Childhood of Wakefield
Just off Rt 16 in Historic District, 03872 [Wakefield Corner, 03872]; (p) (603) 522-8073; (c) Carroll

Private non-profit/ 1989/ staff: 2(f); 1(p); 2(v)

HISTORY MUSEUM; HOUSE MUSEUM

PROGRAMS: Community Outreach; Elder's Programs; Exhibits; Family Programs; Festivals; Guided Tours; Interpretation; School-Based Curriculum

COLLECTIONS: [18th-19th c] 11 room, 3,500 dolls, trains, sleds 1890 one room school, 45 furnished doll houses, teddy bear room, 1890 child's room, junior prom, blacksmith shop, 1890 kitchen, teddy bear picnic.

HOURS: June-Sept W-Sa 11-4, M 11-4, Su 1-4

ADMISSION: $3, Children $1.25

WARNER

5429
Mount Kearsarge Indian Museum, Education and Cultrural Center
Kearsarge Mountain Rd, 03278 [PO Box 142, 03278-0142]; (p) (603) 456-3244; (f) (603) 456-3092; mkim@conknet.com; www.indian-museum.org; (c) Merrimack

Private non-profit/ 1990/ staff: 1(f); 11(p); 20(v)/ members: 425

HISTORY MUSEUM: Depicts the culture and heritage of American Indians; Eastern Woodlands, Southwest, and Plains Indian cultures featured in guided tours; Medicine woods offers self-guided walking tour of 2 acres of plants used as food, dyes, and medicines.

PROGRAMS: Community Outreach; Elder's Programs; Exhibits; Facility Rental; Family Programs; Festivals; Film/Video; Garden Tours; Guided Tours; Interpretation; Lectures; Publication; School-Based Curriculum

COLLECTIONS: [Post contact-present] Extensive collection of artifacts from Eastern Woodlands, Southwest, and Plains Indians. Lithic and ceramic prehistoric artifacts quillwork, basketry, pottery, clothing, beadwork, weaponry, horse regalia, textiles.

HOURS: May-Dec Daily M-Sa 10-5, Su 12-5

ADMISSION: $6, Children $5, Seniors $6; Group rates

WARREN

5430
Warren Historical Society
[PO Box 114, 03279]; (c) Grafton

Private non-profit/ 1985/ staff: 15(v)/ members: 200

HISTORICAL SOCIETY: Collects and preserves town history, population documents, pictures, and industries.

PROGRAMS: Annual Meeting; Exhibits; Facility Rental; Family Programs; Festivals; Film/Video; Garden Tours; Guided Tours; Lectures; Publication; School-Based Curriculum

COLLECTIONS: [1763-present] Collections: pictures, artifacts, journals, documents relating to town of Warren.

HOURS: M-Sa 1-4 and Su by request

ADMISSION: No charge

WEARE

5431
Weare Historical Society
N Stark Hwy, 03281 [PO Box 33, 03281]; (c) Hillsborough

Private non-profit/ 1971/ staff: 20(v)/ members: 94/publication: *Weare, New Hampshire A Visual History*

HISTORIC PRESERVATION AGENCY; HISTORIC SITE; HISTORICAL SOCIETY; HISTORY MUSEUM

PROGRAMS: Annual Meeting; Community Outreach; Exhibits; Guided Tours; Lectures; Publication

COLLECTIONS: [1750-present] Old ledgers, deeds, newspapers, pictures, photographs, small video library of local programs, period clothing, quilts, household equipment, furniture, shoe making, blacksmith, and farm tools, Boy Scout memorabilia, and models.

HOURS: By appt

ADMISSION: No charge

WEST SWANZEY

5432
Swanzey Historical Museum
Rt 10, 03469 [PO Box 416, 03469]; (c) Cheshire City/ 1987/ staff: 65(v)/ members: 100

HISTORICAL SOCIETY; HISTORY MUSEUM: Collects and displays local history artifacts.

PROGRAMS: Annual Meeting; Exhibits; Guided Tours

COLLECTIONS: [1733-present] Steam fire pumper, stage coach, 1930 Model A Ford, Denman Thompson artifacts, uniforms, furniture, pictures.

HOURS: May-Mid Oct Daily M-F 1-5, Sa-Su 10;00-5 and by appt

ADMISSION: No charge

WILMOT

5433
Wilmot Historical Society, Inc.
[PO Box 72, 03287]; (p) (603) 323-8214; (c) Merrimack

Private non-profit/ 1978/ staff: 3(v)/ members: 70

Promotes public education, appreciation, and greater awareness of regional history, establishes and maintains storage and public display of historical memorabilia and artifacts.

COLLECTIONS: Small collection of Wilmot's historical periods: newspapers, photographs, maps, deeds, and other ephemera, artifacts.

HOURS: June-Mid-Oct Sa 1st and last 10-12, W 2nd and 3rd 4-6

ADMISSION: No charge

WOLFEBORO

5434
E. Stanley Wright Museum Foundation, Inc.
77 Center St, 03894 [PO Box 1212, 03894]; (p) (603) 569-1212; (f) (603) 569-6326; wrmuseum@aol.com; wrightmuseum.org; (c) Carroll

1982/ staff: 5(f); 1(p); 40(v)/ members: 325

HISTORY MUSEUM: Dedicated to preserving the history of the years 1939-1945, homefront America during World War II.

PROGRAMS: Exhibits; Facility Rental; Family Programs; Festivals; Film/Video; Guided Tours; Lectures; Reenactments; Research Library/Archives; School-Based Curriculum

COLLECTIONS: [1939-1945] Over 23 military vehicles, over 150 uniforms and period clothing, extensive collection of photographs, maps, and homefront related ration cards, civil defense, daily life memorabilia, propaganda, toys, sports, home appliances.

HOURS: Mar-Nov M-Sa 10-4, Su 12-4; closed Dec-Feb

ADMISSION: $5, Children $2.50, Seniors $4

5435
Libby Museum
N Main, Rt 109 N, 03894 [PO Box 629, 03894]; (p) (603) 569-1035; (f) (603) 569-2246; (c) Carroll

City; Private non-profit/ 1912/ staff: 3(p); 7(v)/ members: 350

NATURAL HISTORY MUSEUM: Preserves a type of private museum called a Wunder Kammele which still exists today.

PROGRAMS: School-Based Curriculum

COLLECTIONS: [Prehistory-present] Natural History and ethnology; focusing on New England's flora, fauna; stone tools and projectile points, minerals and fossils.

HOURS: May-Sept 10-4

ADMISSION: $2, Children $1

5436
Wolfeboro Historical Society/Clark House
337 S Main St, 03894 [PO Box 1066, 03894]; (p) (603) 569-4997; (c) Carroll

Private non-profit/ 1925/ staff: 1(p); 30(v)/ members: 145/publication: *The Wellsweep*

HISTORIC SITE; HISTORICAL SOCIETY; HISTORY MUSEUM; HOUSE MUSEUM: Promotes interest in the history of Wolfeboro; administers the Clark House Museum Complex.

PROGRAMS: Annual Meeting; Exhibits; Guided Tours; Lectures; Publication; Research Library/Archives

COLLECTIONS: [1775-1850] Manages the 1778 farmhouse (Clark House); 1805 Pleasant Valley (one-room) schoolhouse; and Engine Company Firehouse Museum.

HOURS: July 5 - Oct M-F 10-4, Sa 10-2

ADMISSION: $4, Student $2; Under 12 free

NEW JERSEY

ALLAIRE

5437
Historic Allaire Village
Rte 524, 07727 [PO Box 220, 07727]; (p) (732) 919-3500; (f) (732) 938-3302; allairevillage@ bytheshore.com; www.allairevillage.org; (c) Monmouth

Private non-profit/ 1957/ Allaire Village, Inc./ staff: 3(f); 10(p); 150(v)/ members: 150

LIVING HISTORY/OUTDOOR MUSEUM: A restored industrial community composed of thirteen original buildings and a visitor center.

PROGRAMS: Community Outreach; Concerts; Exhibits; Festivals; Film/Video; Guided Tours; Interpretation; Lectures; Living History; Reenactments; Research Library/Archives; School-Based Curriculum; Theatre

COLLECTIONS: [1822-1858] Vintage clothing, decorative arts, original family documents, photos, record books and antique items produced by the local industries.

ATLANTIC HIGHLANDS

5438
Atlantic Highlands Historical Society
27 Prospect Ave, 07716 [PO Box 108, 07716]; (p) (732) 291-1861; (c) Monmouth

Private non-profit/ 1973/ Executive Board/ members: 270/publication: *Portland Poynts*

HOUSE MUSEUM: Promotes interest in the history of Atlantic Highlands and the region. Preserves and presents the Strauss Mansion, an 1893 Queen Anne cottage from the Golden Age of Monmoth County coastal resorts.

PROGRAMS: Exhibits; Festivals; Guided Tours; Lectures; Publication; Research Library/Archives

COLLECTIONS: [19th c] Victorian furniture, decorations, clothing, tools, stained glass, parquet,1,200 slides, photographs, maps, and Lenape artifacts and displays.

5439
Historical Society of Highlands
403 Navesink Ave, 07716; (p) (732) 291-9229; (c) Monmouth

County; State/ 1990/ staff: 5(v)/ members: 170

HISTORICAL SOCIETY

PROGRAMS: Guided Tours; Lectures

COLLECTIONS: Postcards, books, photos, and small artifacts that represent local history.

BARNEGAT

5440
Edwards House
E Bay Ave, 08008-1112; (p) (609) 698-8365; www.oceancountygov.com/discover/oc_sites.htm

HOUSE MUSEUM

5441
Lippincott-Falkenburgh House
E Bay Ave, 08005 [PO Box 381, 08005]; (p) (609) 698-6996

HOUSE MUSEUM

BARNEGAT LIGHT

5442
Barnegat Light Historical Society
W 5th St & Central Ave, 08006 [PO Box 386, 08006]; (p) (609) 494-8578; (c) Ocean

City/ staff: 10(v)/ members: 77

HISTORICAL SOCIETY

PROGRAMS: Exhibits

COLLECTIONS: School memorabilia, local artifacts, maritime items, first class 1857 French Fresnel Lens used at the lighthouse until 1929, decoys and photographs.

HOURS: June & Sept Sa-Su 2-5; July-Aug Daily 2-5

BASKING RIDGE

5443
Somerset County Park Commission Environmental Education Center
190 Lord Stirling Rd, 07920; (p) (908) 766-2489; (f) (908) 766-2687; cschrein@parks.co. someret.nj.us; www.park.co.somerset.nj.us; (c) Somerset

County/ 1956/ Somerset County Park Commission/ staff: 15(f)/publication: *Parks, Programs and People*

HISTORIC SITE; LIVING HISTORY/OUTDOOR MUSEUM: Located on the site of Lord Stirling's (William Alexander's) 1762 manor house and estate. An annual living history 1770s Festival is held on the site the first Sunday of October.

PROGRAMS: Exhibits; Family Programs; Festivals; Guided Tours; Interpretation; Lectures; Living History; Publication; Research Library/Archives

COLLECTIONS: [18th c-present] Archaeology artifacts, photocopy and printed material file of Stirling historical data.

HOURS: Yr Daily 9-5

ADMISSION: No charge

BEACH HAVEN

5444
Long Beach Island Historical Association
Beach & Engleside Ave, 08008 [PO Box 1222, 08008]; (p) (609) 492-0700; Lbi-museum@juno.com; www.neabcomm.com/lbi/index/htm; (c) Ocean

Private non-profit/ 1975/ members: 1256

HISTORICAL SOCIETY: Collects, preserves and interprets the history of Long Beach Island.

PROGRAMS: Annual Meeting; Exhibits; Guided Tours; Lectures

COLLECTIONS: [19th c] Kitchen, living room, bridal gowns, surf board exhibit, and school room.

HOURS: Late June-mid Sept Sa-M 2-4/7-9, T-F10-4/7-9

BELLE MEAD

5445
Van Harlingen Historical Society of Montgomery, Inc.
Gulick House, 506 Route 601, 08502 [PO Box 23, 08502]; (p) (908) 359-3498; (c) Somerset

Private non-profit/ 1966/ members: 215

HISTORIC SITE; HISTORICAL SOCIETY; HOUSE MUSEUM: Preserves and interprets the heritage of the Montgomery Township area, including historical sites and buildings.

PROGRAMS: Annual Meeting; Exhibits; Festivals; Lectures

COLLECTIONS: [19th c] Structures includes the Farm Museum, Dirck Gulick Historic House and Bedensville Schoolhouse.

BERGENFIELD

5446
Bergenfield Museum
84 Hickory Ave, 07621 [PO Box 95, 07621]; (p) (201) 384-8656; (c) Bergen

Private non-profit/ 1976/ staff: 12(p); 5(v)/ members: 325/publication: *Bergenfield's Hall of Fame; The Tree of Life: Selections from Bergen County Folk Art; and others*

HISTORY MUSEUM: Preserves local artifacts, provides lectures in schools and features exhibits, including a Bergenfield "Hall of Fame."

PROGRAMS: Annual Meeting; Community Outreach; Exhibits; Family Programs; Festivals; Film/Video; Garden Tours; Guided Tours; Lectures; Publication

COLLECTIONS: [19th-20th c] Textiles, toys, furniture, documents, photographs, books, tools, kitchen items, pottery and quilts.

HOURS: Yr M, Th, Sa 1-4

ADMISSION: $2, Children $1

BLOOMFIELD

5447
Bloomfield Historical Society, The
90 Broad St, 07003; (p) (973) 566-6220

Private non-profit/ 1966/ staff: 2(v)/ members: 132

PROGRAMS: Annual Meeting; Exhibits; Lectures

HOURS: Yr W 2-4:30

5448
Oakside Bloomfield Cultural Center
240 Belleville Ave, 07003; (p) (973) 429-0960; (f) (973) 429-0697; (c) Essex

Private non-profit/ 1980/ Oakside Board of Trustees/ staff: 1(f); 2(p)

GARDEN; HISTORIC SITE; HOUSE MUSEUM: Offers public events for the community. Facility available for private parties.

PROGRAMS: Exhibits; Facility Rental; Garden Tours; Theatre

HOURS: Yr M-F 9-3

ADMISSION: No charge

BRANCHBURG

5449
Branchburg Historical Society
671 Old York Rd, 08876 [65 Harlan School Rd, 08876]; (p) (908) 722-2124; (c) Somerset

Private non-profit/ 1990/ staff: 3(v)/ members: 30

HISTORICAL SOCIETY; HOUSE MUSEUM: Collects and preserves the history of Branchburg Township.

PROGRAMS: Annual Meeting; Research Library/Archives; School-Based Curriculum

COLLECTIONS: [Late 17th c-present] Books and manuscripts related to the history and genealogy of Branchburg and Somerset County.

HOURS: Yr by appt

BRICK

5450
Brick Township Historical Society
Havens Homestead Museum, 521 Herbertsville Rd, 08723 [PO Box 160, 08723]; (p) (732) 785-2500; jeffab@litenet.net; (c) Ocean

Private non-profit/ 1976/ staff: 60(v)/ members: 90/publication: *Changing Scenes*

HISTORICAL SOCIETY: Operates the Havens Homestead Museum, a restored farmhouse and inn dating to 1827.

PROGRAMS: Exhibits; Guided Tours; Lectures; Publication

COLLECTIONS: [1850s] 19th century rope beds, kitchen accessories, toys and clothes.

HOURS: Apr-Oct Sa 10-12, Su 12-2

ADMISSION: Donations accepted

BRIDGETON

5451
Bridgeton Antiquarian League
1 Mayor Aitken Dr, 08302 [353 Roadstown Greenwich Rd, 08302]; (p) (609) 451-4500; (c) Cumberland

Private non-profit/ 1968/ staff: 1(f); 1(p); 10(v)/ members: 50

HISTORIC PRESERVATION AGENCY; HISTORIC SITE; HISTORICAL SOCIETY: Preserves and displays cultural and industrial artifacts from the Bridgeton area.

PROGRAMS: Community Outreach; Exhibits; Guided Tours; Research Library/Archives

COLLECTIONS: [1815-present] Encompasses the cultural and industrial heritage of the Bridgeton

BRIDGEWATER

5452
Somerset County Historical Society
Van Veghten Lane, 08807; (c) Somerset

Private non-profit/ 1882/ staff: 14(f)/ members: 70

GENEALOGICAL SOCIETY; HISTORICAL SOCIETY; HOUSE MUSEUM: Provides information about the history of the county and its families. Headquarters located in the Van Veghten House, built circa 1740, and features a

research library. Offers year round programs.

PROGRAMS: Annual Meeting; Exhibits; Facility Rental; Film/Video; Garden Tours; Guided Tours; Lectures; Publication; Research Library/Archives

COLLECTIONS: [17th c-present]

HOURS: Apr-Dec T, Sa

ADMISSION: No charge

BRIELLE

5453
Union Landing Historical Society
[PO Box 473, 08730]; (p) (732) 528-5867; (c) Monmouth

Private non-profit/ 1973/ staff: 35(v)/ members: 35/publication: *Union Landing Revisited: A History of Brielle*

HISTORICAL SOCIETY: Studies the history of Brielle and surrounding area, involves as many residents as possible and disseminates that knowledge to the general populace. Has restored abandoned private burial ground with 21 graves belonging to the Osborn family.

PROGRAMS: Annual Meeting; Exhibits; Family Programs; Festivals; Guided Tours; Interpretation; Lectures; Publication

COLLECTIONS: [Late 1600s-present] Pictures, photos, deeds, mortgages, newspaper articles and letters.

HOURS: By request

ADMISSION: No charge

BURLINGTON

5454
Burlington County Historical Society
457 High St, 08016; (p) (609) 386-4773; (f) (609) 386-4828; historyctr@juno.com; (c) Burlington

Private non-profit/ 1915/ staff: 2(f); 3(p); 50(v)/ members: 900

HISTORIC SITE; HISTORICAL SOCIETY; HISTORY MUSEUM; HOUSE MUSEUM: Collects, preserves, and interprets the history of the area through the preservation of four historic sites, educational programs and projects, and the exhibition of the area's outstanding folk arts.

PROGRAMS: Annual Meeting; Community Outreach; Exhibits; Guided Tours; Interpretation; Lectures; Publication; Research Library/Archives; School-Based Curriculum

COLLECTIONS: [18th-19th c] Decorative arts, period furnishings, case clocks, Delaware River decoys, needlework samplers, pieced and appliqued quilts and library/archival materials pertaining to South Jersey.

HOURS: Yr Su 2-4, M-Th 1-4, 1st F night 6-9

ADMISSION: $5

CALDWELL

5455
Grover Cleveland Birthplace Memorial Association
207 Bloomfield Ave, 07006 [PO Box 183, 07006-0183]; (p) (973) 226-0001; (f) (973) 226-1810; (c) Essex

State/ 1913/ State of New Jersey, Dept of Environmental Protection, Parks and Forestry Division/ staff: 1(f); 1(p); 32(v)/ members: 110

HISTORIC SITE; HISTORICAL SOCIETY; HISTORY MUSEUM; HOUSE MUSEUM; PRESIDENTIAL SITE: Promotes and preserves the Grover Cleveland Birthplace for public education and enjoyment.

PROGRAMS: Community Outreach; Exhibits; Festivals; Guided Tours; Interpretation; Research Library/Archives; School-Based Curriculum

COLLECTIONS: [1832-1908] Largest personal and family collection in public hands regarding Glover Cleveland—the only US President born in New Jersey.

HOURS: Yr W-Su By Appt; closed Wednesdays following M holidays

ADMISSION: No charge

CALIFON

5456
Califon Historical Society, The
25 Academy St, 07830 [PO Box 424, 07830]; (p) (908) 832-0878; (c) Hunterdon

1970/ staff: 25(v)/ members: 75

HISTORICAL SOCIETY: Displays artifacts, maps, deeds, photographs and memorabilia which detail life in Califon over the past 150 years.

PROGRAMS: Exhibits; Lectures

COLLECTIONS: [1880-present] 1875 Railroad station, artifacts, maps, deeds, photographs and

CAMDEN

5457
Walt Whitman House
328 Mickle Blvd, 08103-1126; (p) (856) 964-5383; WhitmanHse@aol.com; (c) Camden

State/ 1923/ New Jersey Division of Parks and Forestry/ staff: 1(f); 1(p); 15(v)

HISTORIC SITE; HOUSE MUSEUM: Home of poet Walt Whitman from 1884 until his death in 1892. Guided tours available for general audiences and lesson plans are available for teachers.

PROGRAMS: Community Outreach; Guided Tours; Interpretation; Research Library/Archives

COLLECTIONS: [19th c] Original furnishings, personal belongings of Whitman, photographs, letters, memorabilia related to Whitman and his life in Camden, first editions of "Leaves of Grass."

HOURS: Yr W-Sa 10-12/1-4, Su 1-4

ADMISSION: No charge

CAPE MAY

5458
Emlen Physick Estate
1048 Washington St, 08204; (p) (609) 884-5404; (f) (609) 884-2006; mac4arts@jerseycape.com; www.beachcomber.com

1879/ staff: 30(f); 100(p)

COLLECTIONS: [1890s] There are about a dozen pieces of significant architect-designed furniture, including bedsteads, chests, a roll-top-desk, collection is mostly a mix of period pieces; furniture, textiles, about 400 period books, accessories.; There are about 10 period photographs of the exterior of the Physick Estate. Some Physick papers (wills, inventory -1935)

5459
Greater Cape May Historical Society
653 1/2 Washington St, 08204 [PO Box 495, 08204]; (p) (609) 884-9100; (c) Cape May

Private non-profit/ 1974/ staff: 60(v)/ members: 193

HISTORIC SITE; HISTORICAL SOCIETY; HISTORY MUSEUM; HOUSE MUSEUM: Collects, documents, preserves, interprets and shares local history; Perpetuates the heritage of early Cape Island as steward of the Colonial House.

PROGRAMS: Annual Meeting; Exhibits; Guided Tours; Interpretation; Lectures; Research Library/Archives

COLLECTIONS: [1760s-present] Archives: photographs, Frank Leach diaries, periodicals. Museum: Tools and household furnishings that illustrate early Cape Island life.

HOURS: Mid June-mid Sept Daily 10-2, closed Tuesdays; 10 days in Oct

ADMISSION: Donations requested; Mbrs/Children free

5460
Historic Cold Spring Village
720 Route 9, 08204; (p) (609) 898-2300; (f) (609) 884-5926; roblemaire@hcsv.org; www.hcsv.org; (c) Cape May

Private non-profit/ 1973/ Historic Cold Spring Village Foundation Advisory Board/ staff: 6(f); 40(p); 30(v)/ members: 600

LIVING HISTORY/OUTDOOR MUSEUM: As an educational institution, the Village uses living history to present the rich cultural past of Cape May County to summer visitors and school children.

PROGRAMS: Concerts; Exhibits; Facility Rental; Family Programs; Festivals; Guided Tours; Interpretation; Lectures; Living History; Reenactments; School-Based Curriculum

COLLECTIONS: [Early-Mid 19th c] Agricultural, craft and domestic tools.

HOURS: Late May Sa-Su 10-4:30; Late June-early Sept

5461
Mid-Atlantic Center for the Arts
1048 Washington St, 08204 [PO Box 340, 08204]; (p) (609) 884-5404; (f) (609) 884-5064; mac4arts@capemaymac.org; www.capemaymac.org; (c) Cape May

Private non-profit/ 1970/ Board of Trustees/ staff: 35(f); 115(p); 400(v)/ members: 4400

HISTORIC SITE; HOUSE MUSEUM: Collects, preserves, and interprets Victorian decorative arts, history and architecture at the Emlen Physick Estate and Cape May lighthouse. Offers architectural tours of Cape May.

PROGRAMS: Annual Meeting; Community Outreach; Concerts; Exhibits; Facility Rental; Family Programs; Festivals; Garden Tours; Guided Tours; Interpretation; Lectures; Living History; Research Library/Archives; School-Based Curriculum; Theatre

COLLECTIONS: [Late 19th c] Serves to furnish the Emlen Physick Estate as a Victorian house museum and consists of period and Physick family-owned furniture, decorative arts and textiles.

HOURS: Jan-mid Feb Sa-Su; mid Feb-Dec Daily

ADMISSION: $8, Children $4

CAPE MAY COURT HOUSE

5462
Cape May County Historical and Genealogical Society
504 Rt 9 N, 08210; (p) (609) 465-3535; (f) (609) 465-4274; cmcmuseum@aol.com

Private non-profit/ 1927/ Board of Trustees/ staff: 2(f); 3(p); 30(v)/ members: 500

GENEALOGICAL SOCIETY; HISTORIC SITE; HISTORICAL SOCIETY; HISTORY MUSEUM; HOUSE MUSEUM: Historical museum and genealogical library that seeks to preserve and educate the community on county history.

PROGRAMS: Annual Meeting; Community Outreach; Exhibits; Lectures; Reenactments; Research Library/Archives

COLLECTIONS: [18th-19th c] Objects and documents donated by county residents such as furnishings, china, glass, tools, textiles, carriages, decorative objects, costumes, Native American artifacts and military objects.

HOURS: Apr-Nov T-Sa 9-4; Dec-Mar Sa 9-4

ADMISSION: $2.50, Children $0.50

5463
John Holmes House
504 Rte 9, 08210; (p) (609) 465-3535

HOUSE MUSEUM

CEDAR GROVE

5464
Cedar Grove Historical Society
903 Pompton Ave, 07009 [PO Box 461, 07009]; (p) (973) 239-5414; (c) Essex

Private non-profit/ 1969/ staff: 20(v)/ members: 148

GARDEN; HISTORIC SITE; HISTORICAL SOCIETY; HOUSE MUSEUM: Operates a 14-acre site that includes a farm with house museum, barns and a cemetery. Preserves and interprets agricultural history of the area.

PROGRAMS: Annual Meeting; Community Outreach; Concerts; Exhibits; Film/Video; Guided Tours; Lectures

COLLECTIONS: [Early 20th c] Agricultural tools, equipment, letters, photographs and furniture.

HOURS: Yr W 9:30-1:30; By Appt

ADMISSION: No charge

CHATHAM

5465
Chatham Historical Society
[PO Box 682, 07928]; (c) Morris

Private non-profit/ 1923/ staff: 30(p)/ members: 290

HISTORIC PRESERVATION AGENCY; HISTORICAL SOCIETY; HISTORY MUSEUM; HOUSE MUSEUM

PROGRAMS: Annual Meeting; Exhibits; Guided Tours; Interpretation; Lectures; Research Library/Archives; School-Based Curriculum

COLLECTIONS: All records relating to Chatham's history.

5466
Historical Society of Chatham Township
24 Southern Blvd, 07928 [PO Box 262, 07928]; (c) Morris

Private non-profit/ 1975/ staff: 15(v)/ members: 110

HISTORIC SITE; HISTORICAL SOCIETY: Promotes knowledge and preservation of township history. The Red Brick Schoolhouse, built in 1860, houses a small local history museum.

PROGRAMS: Exhibits; Lectures

COLLECTIONS: [19th-20th c] Historical photographs, documents, household items, personal artifacts and tools from Chatham township.

HOURS: Yr M 9-12 and by appt; Sept-May 2nd or 3rd Su of the month 2-4; June-Aug 1st Su

ADMISSION: No charge

CHERRY HILL

5467
Barclay Farmstead
209 Barclay Ln, 08034 [209 Barclay Lane, 08034]; (p) (609) 795-6225; (f) (609) 795-9722

1816/ City/ staff: 15(p); 25(v)

COLLECTIONS: [1815-1825]

HOURS: Yr; T-Fri 9-4; c; T-Fri 9-4; call for Su hours

CHESTER

5468
Chester Historical Society, Inc.
[PO Box 376, 07930]; (p) (908) 879-0806; www.historicchesternj.com; (c) Morris

Private non-profit/ 1970/ staff: 30(v)/ members: 110/publication: *Historic Highlights of Chester; Chester's Iron Heyday; and others*

HISTORICAL SOCIETY: Preserves local historical landmarks, buildings and artifacts and builds oral histories.

PROGRAMS: Annual Meeting; Exhibits; Film/Video; Guided Tours; Publication

COLLECTIONS: [19th c] Primarily items reflecting the area's mining heydays

CLARK

5469
Clark Historical Society
430 Westfield Ave, Municipal Building, Room #30, 07066-2227; (p) (732) 388-3600; (c) Union

1970/ staff: 25(v)/ members: 85

ALLIANCE OF HISTORICAL AGENCIES; GARDEN; HISTORIC SITE; HISTORICAL SOCIETY; HISTORY MUSEUM; HOUSE MUSEUM; RESEARCH CENTER: Collects, preserves and interprets the history of Clark and maintains a 1690 house museum.

PROGRAMS: Exhibits; Film/Video; Garden Tours; Guided Tours; Interpretation; Living History; Reenactments; Research Library/ Archives; School-Based Curriculum

COLLECTIONS: [17th-18th c] Native American artifacts, transportation and domestic articles, historic house built in 1690 and Dr. William Robinson's will.

HOURS: Apr-Dec 1st Su 1-4; Special Tours

ADMISSION: No charge

CLIFTON

5470
Hamilton-Van Wagoner House Museum
971 Valley Rd, 07013; (p) (973) -744-5701

1740/ staff: 1(f); 6(v)

HOUSE MUSEUM

COLLECTIONS: [Late 1700s-early 1800s] Local period furniture, antique clothing

CLINTON

5471
Hunterdon Historical Museum
56 Main St, 08809 [PO Box 5005, 08809]; (p) (908) 735-4101; (f) (908) 735-0914; redmill@ptd.net; www.clintonnj.org; (c) Hunterdon

Private non-profit/ 1963/ Board of Trustees/ staff: 3(f); 2(p); 25(v)/ members: 300/publication: *The Mulligans: A Legacy in Stone*

HISTORIC SITE; HISTORY MUSEUM; LIVING HISTORY/OUTDOOR MUSEUM: Dedicated to preserving the rural, agricultural and commercial heritage of Hunterdon County through its historic buildings and artifacts.

PROGRAMS: Annual Meeting; Community Outreach; Concerts; Exhibits; Facility Rental; Family Programs; Festivals; Guided Tours; Interpretation; Lectures; Living History; Publication; Reenactments; Research Library/ Archives; School-Based Curriculum; Theatre

COLLECTIONS: [19th c] Over 40,000 artifacts that chronicle over 180 years of Hunterdon County history.

HOURS: Apr-Nov T-Sa 10-4, Su 12-5

ADMISSION: $4, Children $1, Seniors $3

COLLINGSWOOD

5472
Collingswood-Newton Colony Historical Society
771 Haddon Ave, 08108-3714; (p) (856) 858-0649; (c) Camden

Private non-profit/ 1971/ staff: 3(v)/ members: 65

HISTORICAL SOCIETY: Preserves and restores local historic sites and disseminates information about the life and times of the local area.

PROGRAMS: Annual Meeting; Community Outreach; Exhibits; Family Programs; Lectures; Publication

COLLECTIONS: [18th c-present] Books, photographs and manuscripts held in the New Jersey Room of the Collingswood Library for public use. Contains the World War II record of every student that attended Collingswood High School.

HOURS: Sept-May M-F 9:30-8:30, Sa 9:30-3:30; June-Aug M-F 9:30-1

ADMISSION: No charge

5473
Camden County Historical Society
Park Boulevard & Euclid Ave, 08108 [PO Box 378, 08108-0378]; (p) (856) 964-3333; (f) (856) 964-0378; cchsnj@voicenet.com; www.cchsnj.org; (c) Camden

Private non-profit/ Board of Trustees/ staff: 2(f); 6(p)

GENEALOGICAL SOCIETY; HISTORIC SITE; HISTORICAL SOCIETY; HISTORY MUSEUM; HOUSE MUSEUM: Collects, preserves, and disseminates Camden County and regional history, maintains a historical house, museum, and research library, and offers public and educational programs.

PROGRAMS: Annual Meeting; Community Outreach; Concerts; Exhibits; Family Programs; Festivals; Guided Tours; Interpretation; Lectures; Living History; Publication; Research Library/Archives; School-Based Curriculum; Theatre

COLUMBUS

5474
Mansfield Township Historical Society
3121 Route 206, 08022-2043; (p) (609) 298-4174; (c) Burlington

1973/ staff: 1(v)/ members: 57

HISTORICAL SOCIETY

PROGRAMS: Annual Meeting; Exhibits

COLLECTIONS: [1840-present] School and newspaper items, clothes, books and pictures.

HOURS: Yr by appt

ADMISSION: No charge

CRANBURY

5475
Cranbury Historical and Preservation Society
4 Park Place East, 08512 [PO Box 77, 08512]; (p) (609) 655-2611; (c) Middlesex

Private non-profit/ 1967/ Board of Trustees/ staff: 30(v)/ members: 500

HISTORIC SITE; HISTORICAL SOCIETY; HOUSE MUSEUM; RESEARCH CENTER: Private, non-profit and staffed by volunteers.

PROGRAMS: Annual Meeting; Community Outreach; Concerts; Exhibits; Garden Tours; Guided Tours; Lectures; Research Library/Archives; School-Based Curriculum

COLLECTIONS: [19th c] Victorian and colonial furnishings, herb garden, tools, maps, newspapers, oral and written histories, genealogical information, local, county and state history, costumes, quilts, china, glass, dolls and toys.

HOURS: (Museum) Yr Su 1-4 and by appt;

CRANFORD

5476
Crane-Phillips House
124 N Union Ave, 07016 [38 Springfield Ave, 07016]; (p) (908) 276-0082

1840/ staff: 1(p); 15(v)

HOUSE MUSEUM

COLLECTIONS: [1860-1880] Outstanding collection of vintage clothes.; Information as it relates to the founding of Crawford NJ, its founding families and its importance in the Revolutionary , Civil War and Union County.

HOURS: Seasonal

5477
Cranford Historical Society
Crane-Phillips House Museum, 124 N Union Ave, 07016 [Hanson House Annex, 38 Springfield Ave, 07016]; (p) (908) 276-0082; (c) Union

Private non-profit/ 1927/ Board of Trustees/ staff: 1(p); 50(v)/ members: 400/publication: *Mill Wheel*

HISTORICAL SOCIETY: Collects and preserves information and artifacts relevant to the Township of Cranford, its buildings and its residents. Offers tours, school programs, community speakers and other crafts and activities related to the Victorian era.

PROGRAMS: Annual Meeting; Exhibits; Festivals; Interpretation; Living History; Publication

COLLECTIONS: [19th c] Photographs, maps, archives, oral history tapes, costumes, furniture, arms and armaments, kitchen and farm tools, Native American artifacts and a Victorian young girl's bedroom.

HOURS: (Museum) Sept-June Su 2-4 and by appt; (Office) Sept-June M-F 9-12

ADMISSION: Donations accepted

EAST MILLSTONE

5478
Franklin Inn
2371 Amwell Rd, [Meadows Found, 1289 Easton Ave, Somerset, 08873]; (p) (732) 873-5244; www.themeadowsfoundation.pair.com

EASTAMPTON

5479
Burlington County Division of Cultural and Heritage Affairs
Smithville Rd, 08060 [PO Box 6000, 08060]; (p) (609) 265-5068; (f) (609) 265-5782; (c) Burlington

County/ staff: 4(f)/publication: *The County Bell*

HISTORIC SITE; HOUSE MUSEUM: Responsible for developing programs to promote public interest in local history, the arts and in the cultural values, goals, and traditions of the community. Runs Smithville Mansion house museum

PROGRAMS: Concerts; Exhibits; Facility Rental; Festivals; Guided Tours; Interpretation; Publication

COLLECTIONS: [1865-1890]

HOURS: May-Oct, last 3 weeks in Dec W-Su 1-3

EGG HARBOR CITY

5480
Egg Harbor City Historical Society
55 London Ave, 08215; (p) (609) 965-9073; (c) Atlantic

Private non-profit/ 1993/ Board of Trustees/ staff: 18(v)/ members: 150

HISTORIC SITE; HISTORICAL SOCIETY; HISTORY MUSEUM: Supports and fosters historical activities within the city of Egg Harbor City and its surrounding environs. Also maintains the historic site.

PROGRAMS: Annual Meeting; Community Outreach; Exhibits

COLLECTIONS: [1860-present] City records, community organization records, photos and local historical artifacts.

HOURS: Yr W 1-5, 2nd and 4th Sa 1-4

ADMISSION: No charge

ELIZABETH

5481
Belcher-Ogden Mansion
1046 E Jersey St, 07210 [PO Box 1, 07201]; (p) (908) 351-2500, (908) 289-8479; (f) (908) 351-2500

1680/ staff: 1(f); 6(v)

HOUSE MUSEUM

COLLECTIONS: [Belcher/Ogden periods] Display cases featuring articles found in attic and original cellars, along with articles found when restoration of Keeping room was done.

5482
Boxwood Hall State Historic Site
1073 E Jersey St, 07201-2503; (p) (973) -648-4540

1760/ NJ State Park Service/ staff: 1(f); 1(p)

HISTORIC SITE

COLLECTIONS: [1760-1820] High end American furniture, Dayton artifacts; Terrible

HOURS: Yr

5483
Union County Division of Cultural and Heritage Affairs
633 Pearl St, 07202; (p) (908) 558-2550; (f) (908) 352-3513; www.unioncountynj.org (c) Union

County/ County of Union/ staff: 4(f); 6(p)/publication: Union County Yesterday; Vantage Points

Promotes public interest and participation in local arts and history, fostering the opportunity for all to benefit from the county's multicultural arts and history.

COLLECTIONS: Books, newspaper clippings, deeds, maps, historic sites inventory and photographs on local history.

ENGLEWOOD

5484
Englewood Historical Society
500 Liberty Rd, 07631 [PO Box 8136, 07631]; (p) (201) 568-0678; (c) Bergen

Private non-profit/ 1977/ Board of Directors/ staff: 12(v)/ members: 105/publication: This Was Early Englewood; Liberty Square

HISTORICAL SOCIETY

PROGRAMS: Annual Meeting; Community Outreach; Exhibits; Guided Tours; Interpretation; Lectures; Publication

ENGLISHTOWN

5485
Battleground Historical Society
2 Water St, 07726 [PO Box 61, Tennent, 07763]; (p) (732) 462-0437; (c) Monmouth

Private non-profit/ 1969/ staff: 15(v)/ members: 83/publication: Matchaponix Journal

HISTORIC SITE

PROGRAMS: Festivals; Guided Tours; Lectures; Publication

COLLECTIONS: [18th c]

FAIR LAWN

5486
Garretson Forge and Farm Restoration
4-02 River Rd, 07410; (p) (201) 797-1775

1720/ staff: 15(v)

Continuously farmed for 200 years, the produce now grown on the farm is given to local emergency food pantries.

COLLECTIONS: [1770S-1870S] 1660 canal boat tool chest brought to the colonies; Dutch kas dating from the 1700s; furnishings; tools.; Maps and private papers of the Garretson family and the area.

HOURS: Apr-Oct

FARMINGDALE

5487
Farmingdale Historical Society
13 Asbury Ave, 07727 [2 Goodenough Rd, 07727]; (p) (732) 938-2008; (c) Monmouth

Private non-profit/ 1974/ members: 40

HISTORICAL SOCIETY: Collects data pertinent to small, semi-rural town.

PROGRAMS: Exhibits; Lectures

COLLECTIONS: [Late 19th-early 20th c] Photographs, clothing and books.

HOURS: Special Events Only

ADMISSION: No charge

FLEMINGTON

5488
Hunterdon County Historical Society
114 Main St, 08822; (p) (908) 782-1091; (c) Hunterdon

Private non-profit/ 1885/ Board of Trustees/ staff: 2(p)/ 20(v)/ members: 550

HISTORICAL SOCIETY; HOUSE MUSEUM: Dedicated to the collection, preservation and dissemination of material relating to county history and genealogy. Located in Doric House (1845).

PROGRAMS: Annual Meeting; Exhibits; Guided Tours; Research Library/Archives

COLLECTIONS: [18th-20th c] Manuscripts, artifacts, and publications, including newspapers, that represent over 200 years of local history.

HOURS: Yr Th 1-3, 7-9; Or By Appt

FORKED RIVER

5489
Lacey Historical Society
Old Schoolhouse Museum, Route 9, 08731 [PO Box 412, 08731]; (p) (609) 971-0467; (c) Ocean

Private non-profit/ 1962/ staff: 40(v)/ members: 160

HISTORICAL SOCIETY; HISTORY MUSEUM: Preserves regional artifacts, landmarks and folklore. Fosters public awareness of and appreciative concern for the unique history of Lacey Township.

PROGRAMS: Annual Meeting; Exhibits; Family Programs; Festivals; Film/Video; Guided Tours

COLLECTIONS: [18th-early 20th c] Clothing, personal artifacts, furnishings, photographs, paintings, tools and equipment.

HOURS: Yr by appt; June-Sept M, W, F 1-3, Sa 10-12

ADMISSION: Donations

FREEHOLD

5490
Monmouth County Historical Association
70 Court St, 07728; (p) (732) 462-1466; (f) (732) 462-8346; www.monmouth.com/; (c) Monmouth

Private non-profit/ 1898/ Board of Directors/ staff: 5(f); 6(p); 30(v)/ members: 825

HISTORICAL SOCIETY; HISTORY MUSEUM; HOUSE MUSEUM

PROGRAMS: Annual Meeting; Community Outreach; Exhibits; Facility Rental; Guided Tours; Lectures; Research Library/Archives; School-Based Curriculum

COLLECTIONS: [1665-present]

HOURS: (Museum) Yr T-Sa 10-4, Su 1-4; (Library) Yr W-Sa

GIBBSTOWN

5491
C.A. Nothnagle Log House
406 Swedesboro Rd, 08027-1706; (p) (609) 423-0911, (609) 423-4232; (f) (609) 423-2989

1700

COLLECTIONS: [17th c] Corner fireplace, construction, furniture.

GLEN RIDGE

5492
Glen Ridge Historical Society
[PO Box 164, 07028]; (p) (973) 743-0729; (f) (973) 743-0729; (c) Essex

Private non-profit/ 1976/ staff: 17(v)/ members: 400/publication: *Glen Ridge Centennial Book*

HISTORICAL SOCIETY: Celebrates, promotes and advances the history of the borough of Glen Ridge and the surrounding area. Seeks to educate the community and encourage an appreciation of history in general.

PROGRAMS: Annual Meeting; Community Outreach; Exhibits; Family Programs; Lectures; Publication; Research Library/Archives

COLLECTIONS: [1895-present] Artifacts and reference materials pertaining to Glen Ridge history.

GREENWICH

5493
Cumberland County Historical Society
960 Ye Greate St, 08323 [PO Box 16, 08323]; (p) (856) 455-4055; lummis2@juno.com; (c) Cumberland

Private non-profit/ 1908/ Board of Trustees/ staff: 3(p)/ 50(v)/ members: 1000

HISTORIC SITE; HISTORICAL SOCIETY; HISTORY MUSEUM; HOUSE MUSEUM; LIVING HISTORY/OUTDOOR MUSEUM; RESEARCH CENTER; TRIBAL MUSEUM

PROGRAMS: Annual Meeting; Community Outreach; Concerts; Exhibits; Facility Rental; Family Programs; Festivals; Guided Tours; Interpretation; Lectures; Living History; Publication; Reenactments; Research Library/Archives

COLLECTIONS: [17th c-present] Genealogical material, rare books, deeds, maps and decorative arts.

HOURS: Apr-Dec T-Su 1-4

ADMISSION: Donations accepted

HACKENSACK

5494
Bergen County Division of Cultural and Historic Affairs
One Bergen County Plaza, 4th Fl, 07601-7076; (p) (201) 336-7276; (f) (201) 336-7262; (c) Bergen

County/ 1979/ County of Bergen, Dept of Parks/ staff: 3(f); 2(p); 1(v)/publication: *Open Door to History; BC Tercentennial Monographs; and others*

RESEARCH CENTER: Serves as Bergen County's official art and heritage agency. Addresses the needs of the residents, cultural groups, artists, historians, preservationists, students, seniors, and people with disabilities.

PROGRAMS: Community Outreach; Exhibits; Festivals; Lectures; Publication; Research Library/Archives

COLLECTIONS: [19th-20th c] Archives include county government related documents; the Frederick W. Bogert Collection of Bergen County History; and Historic Sites Survey, Survey of Stone Houses, and Cemetery Inventory of Bergen County.

HOURS: Yr M-F 9-4:30

HACKETTSTOWN

5495
Hackettstown Historical Society
106 Church St, 07840; (p) (908) 852-8797; (c) Warren

City/ 1975/ Board of Trustees/ staff: 15(p)/ members: 73

HISTORICAL SOCIETY

PROGRAMS: Exhibits; Guided Tours; Publication; Research Library/Archives

COLLECTIONS: [1765-present] Books, vertical files of genealogy, archaeological artifacts, documents, newspaper clippings, maps, scrapbooks, loose-leaf notebooks on major historical people and events of the Hackettstown area's history.

HOURS: Yr W, F, Su 2-4; By

HADDONFIELD

5496
Historical Society of Haddonfield
Greenfield Hall, 343 King's Hwy East, 08033; (p) (609) 429-7375; (c) Camden

Private non-profit/ 1914/ staff: 1(p); 13(v)/ members: 400

HISTORICAL SOCIETY; HOUSE MUSEUM: Preserves the area's rich history and acquires articles of historic value for future generations.

PROGRAMS: Exhibits; Facility Rental; Festivals; Guided Tours; Lectures; Research Library/Archives

COLLECTIONS: [18th-19th c] Antique furniture, clocks, needlework, dolls, tools, ceramics, glassware and period clothing from the colonial/Victorian era.

HOURS: (Museum) Yr W-F 1-4 and by appt

5497
Indian King Tavern Museum
233 Kings Hwy East, 08033; (p) (856) 429-6792; www.levins.com/tavern.html; (c) Camden

State/ 1908/ New Jersey Division of Parks and Forestry/ staff: 1(f); 1(p); 23(v)

HISTORIC SITE; HOUSE MUSEUM: Site of where the 1777 Patriot-rebel Legislature of New Jersey formed its Council of Safety, adopted the State's Great Seal and technically formed a State. Furnished as a Revolutionary War tavern house.

PROGRAMS: Exhibits; Guided Tours; Interpretation; Living History

COLLECTIONS: [1770s] Furnishings, period antiques, artifacts and reproductions.

HOURS: Yr W-Sa 10-12/1-4, Su 1-4

ADMISSION: No

HALEDON

5498
Botto House American Labor Museum, Inc.
83 Norwood St, 07508; (p) (973) 595-7953; (f) (973) 595-7291; community.nj.com/cc/labormuseum; (c) Passaic

Private non-profit/ 1982/ staff: 2(f); 1(p)/ members: 1043/publication: *The Fragile Bridge*

HISTORY MUSEUM: Celebrates the history and contemporary issues of immigrants and working people through cultural and educational programs, community outreach, exhibits, and special events.

PROGRAMS: Annual Meeting; Community Outreach; Concerts; Exhibits; Facility Rental; Festivals; Garden Tours; Guided Tours; Interpretation; Lectures; Living History; Publication; Reenactments; Research Library/Archives; School-Based Curriculum; Theatre

COLLECTIONS: [Early 20th c] Labor union memorabilia like buttons, posters, photos, newspapers, due and contract books, and convention literature. Artifacts from working class immigrant's home such as chamber pots, irons, shoe and hat forms, pots and pans, mason jars, linens and photos.

HOURS: Yr W-Sa 1-4 or by appt

ADMISSION: Donations requested

HAMILTON

5499
Historical Society of Hamilton Township
2200 Kuren Rd, 08620 [PO Box 1776, 08620]; (p) (609) 585-1686; (c) Mercer

Private non-profit/ 1946/ Board of Trustees/ staff: 30(v)/ members: 100

HISTORIC SITE; HISTORICAL SOCIETY; HOUSE MUSEUM: Salt Box/Victorian farm house open to the public for tours every weekend.

PROGRAMS: Guided Tours; School-Based Curriculum

COLLECTIONS: [1740-1830] Original and reproduction furniture and artifacts from the colonial/Victorian era.

HOURS: Yr Sa-Su 12-5

ADMISSION: Donations requested

5500
Isaac Watson House
151 Westcott Ave, 08610; (p) (609) 888-2062; (c) Mercer

County; Private non-profit/ 1965/ Founders Committee, NJDAR/Mercer County/ staff: 20(v)

HOUSE MUSEUM: The 1708 Isaac Watson House is one of the earliest remaining examples of the fieldstone houses built by Quakers in New Jersey. It houses decorative arts from the 16th-19th centuries.

PROGRAMS: Guided Tours

COLLECTIONS: [18th c]

HOURS: Mar-June, Sept-Nov Sa 10-2

ADMISSION: No charge

5501
John Abbott II House
2200 Kuser Rd, 08690 [PO Box 1776, Yardville, 08620]; (p) (609) 585-1686

1730/ staff: 14(v)

COLLECTIONS: [1730]

HOURS: Yr

HAMMONTON

5502
Batsto Village
Wharton State Forest, 08037 [4110 Nesco Rd, 08037-3814]; (p) (609) 561-0024; (f) (609) 567-8116; (c) Burlington

State/ 1954/ State of New Jersey/ staff: 3(f); 5(p); 6(v)

HISTORIC SITE: Site of a former bog iron and glassmaking industrial center. Currently, it reflects the agricultural and commercial enterprises that existed in the late 19th century.

PROGRAMS: Community Outreach; Exhibits; Interpretation; Living History

COLLECTIONS: [1766-1867] Reflects the life of Batsto in the 18th-19th centuries, including household items, farm instruments, and items relating to bog iron and lumber industries.

HAMPTON

5503
Township of Lebanon Museum
1 mi off Rte 31 on left, White Schoolhouse, 08827 [57 Musconetcong River Rd, 08827]; (p) (908) 537-6464; (c) Hunterdon

1981/ Lebanon Township Historians/ staff: 2(p); 3(v)

HISTORICAL SOCIETY: A restored schoolhouse that continues to educate by reenacting a typical school day in 1870. Hosts art and quilt shows and rug exhibits, teaches craft classes for both adults and children, has changing exhibits, genealogy materials and more.

PROGRAMS: Exhibits; Living History; School-Based Curriculum

COLLECTIONS: [19th c] Local and private collections of individuals who are willing to share

5504
Union Township Historical Society
140 Perryville Rd, 08827; (p) (908) 730-9268; (c) Hunterdon

Private non-profit/ Board of Trustees/ staff: 30(v)/ members: 50/publication: *Reflections*

HISTORIC SITE; HISTORICAL SOCIETY: Preserves the historical foundation of the community.

PROGRAMS: Annual Meeting; Community Outreach; Elder's Programs; Exhibits; Family Programs; Film/Video; Guided Tours; Interpretation; Lectures; Publication; Research Library/Archives; School-Based Curriculum

HANCOCK'S BRIDGE

5505
Hancock House
3 Front St, 08038 [c/o Fort Mott State Park, 454 Fort Mott Rd, Pennsville, 08070]; (p) (609) 935-3218, (609) 339-9702; (f) (609) 935-7818

1734/ Park System/ staff: 10(v)

HOUSE MUSEUM: The home of Judge William Hancock, this was the site of a mas-

sacre by British troops on March 21, 1778.

COLLECTIONS: [Late 1700s] In development.

HOURS: Yr

HIGHLAND LAKES

5506
Vernon Township Historical Society
Vernon Township Municipal Bldg, Church St, 07422 [Barrett House Museum, 173 Barrett Rd, 07422]; (p) (973) 764-4055, (973) 764-8554; (c) Sussex

Private non-profit/ 1970/ staff: 12(v)/ members: 80

HISTORICAL SOCIETY: Small, community-based historical society that relies on volunteer curators and educators.

PROGRAMS: Annual Meeting; Community Outreach; Exhibits; Guided Tours; Lectures; School-Based Curriculum

COLLECTIONS: [17th c-present] Artifacts, papers and memorabilia from several families including the Barretts, Swanyes, Browns, DeKays and Rutherfords.

HOURS: (Barrett House Museum) Yr T, Th 10-2; (Office) Yr Sa-Su 1-4

ADMISSION: Donations requested

HIGHLAND PARK

5507
Highland Park Historical Society
[PO Box 4255, 08904]; (p) (732) 220-6618; ricekolva@monmouth.com; www.monmouth.com/~ricekolva; (c) Middlesex

Private non-profit/ 1995/ staff: 4(v)/ members: 64/publication: *Highland Park, New Jersey*

HISTORIC SITE; HISTORICAL SOCIETY; HOUSE MUSEUM: Sponsors exhibits of historical interest and advocates for historic preservation.

PROGRAMS: Annual Meeting; Community Outreach; Exhibits; Family Programs; Film/Video; Guided Tours; Lectures; Publication; Research Library/Archives; School-Based Curriculum

COLLECTIONS: [20th c] Memorabilia, photographs, vertical files items

HIGHLANDS

5508
Twin Light Historical Society
Lighthouse Rd, 07732; (p) (732) 872-1814; (f) (732) 872-0314; Society@twin-lights.org; www.twin-lights.org; (c) Monmouth

Private non-profit; State/ 1958/ State of New Jersey, Division of Parks and Forestry/ staff: 1(p); 30(v)/ members: 200/publication: *The Lighthouse Log*

HISTORIC SITE: Preserves and interprets the Twin Lights Historic Site. Provides funding for interpretive projects, volunteer staffing, and supports the State Park Service in managing the facility.

PROGRAMS: Exhibits; Guided Tours; Interpretation; Lectures; Publication

COLLECTIONS: [1820-1949] Objects, prints and research material relating to the Navesink

Lighthouse (Twin Lights Historic Site), local maritime history and the US Life-Saving Service.

HIGHTSTOWN

5509
Hightstown-East Windsor Historical Society
164 N Main St, 08520; (p) (609) 371-9580; (f) (609) 448-1031; (c) Mercer

Private non-profit/ 1971/ staff: 35(v)/ members: 260/publication: *Guide to Special Collections of the Hightstown-East Windsor Historical Society Library*

GENEALOGICAL SOCIETY; HISTORIC PRESERVATION AGENCY; HISTORICAL SOCIETY; HISTORY MUSEUM; HOUSE MUSEUM; RESEARCH CENTER: Built in the 1860s, the Ely House Museum contains furniture, paintings, maps, letters, photographs, currency printed in Hightstown Freight Station, newly renovated storing displays, farm and railroad equipment, trains, and fashion exhibits.

PROGRAMS: Annual Meeting; Festivals; Guided Tours; Lectures; Publication; Research Library/Archives; School-Based Curriculum

COLLECTIONS: [19th-20th c] Historical pictures of Hightstown, Woodrow Wilson and Clara Barton stories, transportation-railroad items, genealogies, history of local business, industry and schools, John Bull and aviation photos, newspapers and military history.

HOURS: Yr T twice a month 7-9

ADMISSION: No charge

HILLSIDE

5510
Hillside Historical Society, Inc.
111 Conant St, 07205; (p) (908) 353-8828, (908) 352-9270; (c) Union

Private non-profit/ 1973/ staff: 20(v)/ members: 250/publication: *The Cure*

HISTORIC SITE; HISTORICAL SOCIETY: Seeks to preserve history of Hillside; Owns and operates 1735 Woodruff House/Eaton Store with farm exhibits, barn, sports display and archival center.

PROGRAMS: Community Outreach; Exhibits; Guided Tours; Interpretation; Living History; Publication

COLLECTIONS: [19th-early 20th c] Furniture, textiles, china, glassware, kitchenware, farm equipment and artifacts, old store objects, photos, archival records.

HO-HO-KUS

5511
Hermitage, The
335 N Franklin Turnpike, 07423; (p) (201) 445-8311; (f) (201) 445-0437; info@thehermitage.org; www.thehermitage.org; (c) Bergen

Private non-profit; State/ 1972/ Board of Trustees/Friends of the Hermitage, Inc./State of New Jersey/ staff: 4(f); 6(p); 250(v)/ members: 600/publication: *The Hermitage News*

HISTORIC SITE; HOUSE MUSEUM: Maintains and interprets the 1847 Gothic Revival house on five acres. The site has a rich, early history that includes visits by many Revolutionary dignitaries. A National Historic Landmark.

PROGRAMS: Annual Meeting; Community Outreach; Elder's Programs; Exhibits; Facility Rental; Family Programs; Festivals; Film/Video; Garden Tours; Guided Tours; Interpretation; Lectures; Publication; Reenactments; Research Library/Archives; School-Based Curriculum; T

COLLECTIONS: [1740s-1900s] Victorian furniture and furnishings, clothing, period toys and games. Maps, photographs, books, personal and business correspondences.

HOURS: Yr W-Su 1-4

ADMISSION: $4, Children $2; Under 12 free

HOLMDEL

5512
Holmes-Hendrickson House
62 Longstreet Rd, 07733; (p) (908) 462-1466; www.exit109.com/~redbank/museums.html

HOUSE MUSEUM

5513
Longstreet Farm House
Holmdel Park, LongSt Rd, 07733 [805 Newman Springs Rd, Limecroft, 07738]; (p) (732) 946-3758; (f) (732) 946-0750

1775/ staff: 1(p); 8(v)

COLLECTIONS: [1890] House collection approximately 1/3 family pieces.; Local (Monmouth County) photographs and newspaper accounts limited personal correspondance and family items.

HOURS: Seasonal

5514
New Jersey Vietnam Veterans' Memorial and Vietnam Era Educational Center
1 Memorial Ln, Garden State Pkwy Exit 116, 07733 [PO Box 648, 07733]; (p) (732) 335-0033; (f) (732) 335-1107; kjones@njvvmf.org; www.njvvmf.org; (c) Monmouth

Private non-profit/ 1987/ New Jersey Vietnam Veterans' Memorial Foundation/ staff: 4(f); 60(v)

HISTORY MUSEUM; RESEARCH CENTER: Dedicated to telling the full story of the Vietnam War, as seen from the frontlines as well as from the home front. This is accomplished through photos, letters, text and personal stories.

PROGRAMS: Community Outreach; Exhibits; Facility Rental; Film/Video; Guided Tours; Interpretation; Lectures; Living History; Research Library/Archives; School-Based Curriculum

COLLECTIONS: [1959-1975] Photographs, historic timelines, films, interactive displays, personal letters, books, periodicals, CD-ROMS, educational and instructional material, and assorted memorabilia that reflect on personal, political, military, social and cultural perspectives.

HOURS: Yr T-Sa 10-4

ADMISSION: $4, Student $2, Seniors $2; Under 10/Veterans/Active military Free

HOWELL

5515
Howell Historical Society
427 Lakewood-Farmingdale Rd, 07731-8723; (p) (732) 938-2212, (732) 938-2231; Howellhist@aol.com; www.howellnj.com/historical; (c) Monmouth

Private non-profit/ 1971/ Board of Trustees/ staff: 16(v)/ members: 106/publication: *The History of Howell; Sketchbook of Howell Historical Museums*

HISTORICAL SOCIETY; HOUSE MUSEUM; RESEARCH CENTER: Preserves the history and culture of Howell Township.

PROGRAMS: Exhibits; Guided Tours; Interpretation; Publication; Research Library/Archives; School-Based Curriculum

COLLECTIONS: [19th c] Genealogies of local families, biographies, historical papers and maps.

HOURS: Museum: Yr Sa 9:30-12:30; Schoolhouse: Yr Last Su of the month 1-4

ADMISSION: Donations accepted

ISLAND HEIGHTS

5516
Island Heights Cultural and Heritage Association, Inc.
105 Simpson Ave, 08732 [PO Box 398, 08732]; (p) (732) 929-8499; (f) (732) 929-0695; (c) Ocean

Private non-profit/ 1990/ members: 120

HISTORICAL SOCIETY; HISTORY MUSEUM: Preserves the historic camp-meeting borough of Island Heights.

PROGRAMS: Annual Meeting; Exhibits; Guided Tours; Living History

JAMESBURG

5517
Jamesburg Historical Association
203 Buckelew Ave, 08831-1642; (p) (732) 521-2040; (c) Middlesex

Private non-profit/ 1977/ Marcia Kirkpatrick/ members: 140/publication: *House of Many Windows*

HISTORIC SITE; HISTORICAL SOCIETY; HISTORY MUSEUM; HOUSE MUSEUM

PROGRAMS: Exhibits; Festivals; Guided Tours; Publication

COLLECTIONS: [1685-1900] Model railroad and village, trophies and pictures.

HOURS: Yr by appt

ADMISSION: Donations accepted; School tours free

JERSEY CITY

5518
Hudson County Office of Cultural and Heritage Affairs
583 Newark Ave, 07306; (p) (201) 459-2070; (f) (201) 792-0729; (c) Hudson

County/ 1976/ staff: 2(f)

PROFESSIONAL ORGANIZATION: Provides funding and technical assistance to develop and promote local heritage.

PROGRAMS: Annual Meeting; Community Outreach; Exhibits; Guided Tours; Lectures; Research Library/Archives

COLLECTIONS: Maps, books, and artifacts.

HOURS: Yr M-F 9-5

ADMISSION: No charge

5519
Jersey City Museum
350 Montgomery St, 07302; (p) (201) 413-0303; (f) (201) 413-9922; info@jerseycity museum.org; www.jerseycitymuseum.org; (c) Hudson

Private non-profit/ 1901/ Board of Trustees/ staff: 12(f); 10(v)

ART MUSEUM; HISTORY MUSEUM: Preserves and interprets art and material culture from the region.

PROGRAMS: Community Outreach; Concerts; Exhibits; Family Programs; Guided Tours; Lectures; School-Based Curriculum

COLLECTIONS: [19th-20th c] Paintings and prints, Jersey City and New Jersey related artifacts.

HOURS: Yr T, Th-Sa 10:30-5, W 10:30-8; June-Sept Closed Sa

ADMISSION: Donations accepted

KEARNY

5520
Town of Kearny Museum
318 Kearny Ave, 07032; (p) (201) 977-6911; (c) Hudson

City/ 1978/ Town of Kearny/ staff: 26(v)

HISTORY MUSEUM

PROGRAMS: Exhibits; Guided Tours

HOURS: Yr W 2-4/6:30-8:30, Th 2-4, Sa 10-12

ADMISSION: No charge

KEYPORT

5521
Keyport Historical Society
Lower Broad St, 07735 [PO Box 312, 07735]; (p) (732) 739-6390; (c) Monmouth

Joint/ 1972/ City; Private non-profit/ staff: 25(p)/ members: 110

HISTORICAL SOCIETY; HISTORY MUSEUM: Maintains Steamboat Dock Museum.

PROGRAMS: Elder's Programs; Exhibits; Festivals; Guided Tours; Interpretation

COLLECTIONS: [1830-1940] Documents, photos and artifacts that delineate the birth and growth of a town.

HOURS: Mar-Dec Su 1-4, M 10-1

ADMISSION: No charge

LAMBERTVILLE

5522
Henry Phillips Farmhouse at Howell Living Historical Farm
Valley Rd, off Rt 29, 2 mi S of, [101 Hunter Rd, Titusville, 08560]; (p) (609) 737-3299; (f) (609) 737-6524; thefarm@bellatlantic.net; livinghistory.com/howellfarm

1790/ Parks Commission/ staff: 6(f); 2(p); 10(v)

COLLECTIONS: [1890-1910] Farm and barn equipment, photos of rural Pleasant Valley, 1890-1930; oral histories relating to horse-drawn

5523
Jamison Holcome Farmstead Museum
1605 Daniel Bray Hwy, 08530-2402 [PO Box 588, 08530-2402]; (p) (908) 995-2237

5524
Lambertville Historical Society
60 Bridge St, 08530 [PO Box 2, 08530]; (p) (609) 397-0770; (c) Hunterdon

State/ 1970/ staff: 1(p); 15(v)/ members: 220

HISTORIC SITE; HISTORICAL SOCIETY

PROGRAMS: Annual Meeting; Community Outreach; Exhibits; Guided Tours; Lectures

COLLECTIONS: [1812-1900] Period artifacts, documents, clothing, quilts.

HOURS: Yr 2 weekends/mo 1-5

ADMISSION: No charge

LANDING

5525
Lake Hopatcong Historical Museum
Hopatcong State Park, Lakeside Blvd, 07850 [PO Box 668, 07850-0668]; (p) (973) 398-2616; (f) (973) 361-8987; Lhhistory@world-net.att.net; www.hopatcong.org/museum; (c) Morris/Sussex

Private non-profit/ 1955/ Lake Hopatcong Historical Society/ staff: 20(v)/ members: 652

HISTORY MUSEUM: Exhibits and interprets artifacts and documents relating to the civil, political, social and general history of NJ's largest lake.

PROGRAMS: Exhibits; Film/Video; Lectures

COLLECTIONS: [1880-1940] Lenape tribe artifacts, Morris Canal, Lake artifacts.

HOURS: Mar-June, Sept-Nov Su 12-4

ADMISSION: No charge

LAWNSIDE

5526
Lawnside Historical Society, Inc.
[PO Box 608, 08045-0608]; (p) (856) 547-8489; (f) (856) 520-5804; lawn@juno.com; community.nj.com/cc/lawnsidehistory; (c) Camden

Private non-profit/ 1990/ staff: 6(v)/ members: 54

HISTORICAL SOCIETY; HOUSE MUSEUM: Preserves the Peter Mott House.

PROGRAMS: Community Outreach; Guided Tours

COLLECTIONS: [19th-20th c]

HOURS: Yr by appt

ADMISSION: $2, Children $1

LAWRENCEVILLE

5527
Lawrence Historical Society
4275 Province Line Rd, Fort Mercer Canal House, 08648 [PO Box 2065, 08648]; (p) (609) 895-1788, (609) 895-1728; www.thelhs.org; (c) Mercer

Private non-profit/ 1975/ staff: 15(v)/ members: 195

HISTORICAL SOCIETY: Preserves and promotes the historical records of Lawrence township; assists societies in restoring historic structures.

PROGRAMS: Annual Meeting; Community Outreach; Exhibits; Facility Rental; Family Programs; Festivals; Film/Video; Garden Tours; Guided Tours; Interpretation; Lectures; Living History; Reenactments; Research Library/Archives; School-Based Curriculum

COLLECTIONS: [1750-1840] Records, photos and archaeological artifacts.

HOURS: Yr 1st Sa 10-12, tours by appt

ADMISSION: No charge

5528
Medical History Society of New Jersey
2 Princess, Ste 101, 08648; (p) (609) 896-1901; (f) (609) 896-2317; (c) Mercer

Private non-profit/ 1980/ Exec Committee/ staff: 1(p)/ members: 100

HISTORICAL SOCIETY: Promotes medical history.

PROGRAMS: Annual Meeting; Lectures

HOURS: Yr M-F 8:30-4:30

LINWOOD

5529
Linwood Historical Society
16 Poplar Ave, 08221; (p) (609) 927-8293; www.linwoodnj.org; (c) Atlantic

Private non-profit/ 1981/ Board of Directors/ staff: 6(v)/ members: 325

HISTORIC PRESERVATION AGENCY; HISTORICAL SOCIETY; HISTORY MUSEUM: Preserves historic sites.

PROGRAMS: Annual Meeting; Exhibits; Family Programs; Lectures

COLLECTIONS: [19th-20th c] Photos, scrapbooks, ship models, furniture, clothing, architectural artifacts, historic documents, tools and household goods.

HOURS: Yr T 10-1 and by appt

ADMISSION: No charge

LONG VALLEY

5530
Washington Township Historical Society
6 Fairview Ave, 07853 [PO Box 189, 07853]; (p) (908) 876-9696; (c) Morris

Private non-profit/ members: 85

HISTORIC PRESERVATION AGENCY; HISTORICAL SOCIETY: Preserves landmarks in Washington Township area.

PROGRAMS: Annual Meeting; Community Outreach; Exhibits; Guided Tours; Lectures; Research Library/Archives

COLLECTIONS: [19th c] Genealogy records for Morris, Sussex, Warren and Hunterdon Counties. Early school room exhibit; prehistoric artifacts; church, farming and 19th c business documents.

HOURS: Yr Su 2-4 and by appt

ADMISSION: No charge

LYNDHURST

5531
Lyndhurst Historical Society
Riverside Ave, corner of Fern Ave, 07071 [PO Box 135, 07071]; (p) (201) 939-5425; (c) Bergen

Private non-profit/ 1984/ staff: 1(v)/ members: 98

HISTORIC SITE; HISTORICAL SOCIETY; HISTORY MUSEUM: Promotes local history and preservation; manages 1893 restored one-room schoolhouse leased from the Township of Lyndhurst.

PROGRAMS: Exhibits; Festivals; Guided Tours

COLLECTIONS: [1910-present] Photos, maps, local memorabilia, school items and books.

HOURS: Yr Su 2-4; Groups by appt.

MADISON

5532
General Commission on Archives and History of the United Methodist Church
36 Madison Ave, Methodist Archives, 07940 [PO Box 127, 07940]; (p) (973) 408-3189; (f) (973) 408-3909; gcah@gcah.org; www.gcah.org; (c) Morris

Private non-profit/ 1968/ staff: 5(f); 2(p); 2(v)

HISTORY MUSEUM; RESEARCH CENTER: Gathers, preserves and disseminates materials on the history of the United Methodist Church.

PROGRAMS: Exhibits; Guided Tours; Research Library/Archives

COLLECTIONS: [1784-present] Resource papers.

HOURS: Yr M-F

5533
Madison Historical Society
39 Keep St, 07940 [PO Box 148, 07940]; (p) (973) 377-0722; (c) Morris

Private non-profit/ 1922/ staff: 6(v)/ members: 150

HISTORICAL SOCIETY; HISTORY MUSEUM; HOUSE MUSEUM: Assembles, records and preserves Madison history.

PROGRAMS: Annual Meeting; Community Outreach; Exhibits; Guided Tours; Lectures; Research Library/Archives; School-Based Curriculum

COLLECTIONS: Photos, manuscripts and ledgers.

ADMISSION: No charge

5534
Madison Public Library
39 Keep St, 07940; (p) (973) 377-0722; (f) (973) 377-3142; www.rosenet.org/library; (c) Morris

City/ 1900/ Board of Trustees/ staff: 16(f); 22(p); 3(v)

LIBRARY AND/OR ARCHIVES

PROGRAMS: Exhibits; Research Library/ Archives

COLLECTIONS: [19th-20th c] Golden Hind Press, Arthur Rushmore's Washington Press and personal library; photos, correspondence and fugitive items; index to the Madison Eagle, local artifacts.

HOURS: Yr M-T, Th 9-9, W, F 9-6, Sa 9-5, Su 2-5

5535
Museum of Early Trades and Crafts
Main St at Green Village Rd, 07940; (p) (973) 377-2982; (f) (973) 377-7358; metc@msn.com; www.rosenet.org/metc; (c) Morris

Private non-profit/ 1969/ Board of Trustees/ staff: 3(f); 6(p); 25(v)/ members: 1042

HISTORIC SITE; HISTORY MUSEUM: Preserves and interprets NJ history.

PROGRAMS: Annual Meeting; Community Outreach; Elder's Programs; Exhibits; Facility Rental; Family Programs; Festivals; Guided Tours; Interpretation; Lectures; Living History; Reenactments; Research Library/Archives; School-Based Curriculum

COLLECTIONS: [18th-19th c] Tools and products: blacksmithing, shoe making, textile production, cabinet making, joinery, and wheel wrighting.

HOURS: Yr T-Sa 10-4, Su

MANALAPAN

5536
Monmouth County Archives
125 Symmes Dr, 07726; (p) (732) 308-3772; (f) (732) 409-4888; gsaretzk@shore.co.monmouth.nj.us; www.visitmonmouth.com/archives; (c) Monmouth

County/ 1994/ Monmouth County Clerk/ staff: 13(f)

LIBRARY AND/OR ARCHIVES: Preserves Monmouth County records.

PROGRAMS: Annual Meeting; Community Outreach; Exhibits; Guided Tours; Lectures; Publication; Research Library/Archives

COLLECTIONS: [1665-present] County government records and reference library.

HOURS: Yr M-W 9-4

ADMISSION: No charge

MARGATE

5537
Save Lucy Committee, Inc.
9200 Atlantic Ave, 08402 [PO Box 3336, 08402-0336]; (p) (609) 823-6473; (f) (609) 823-1895; ed@lucytheelephant.org; www.lucytheelephant.org; (c) Atlantic

Private non-profit/ 1970/ staff: 1(f); 45(v)

HISTORIC SITE: Restores, preserves and operates Lucy the Elephant, a National Historic Landmark built in 1881.

PROGRAMS: Annual Meeting; Concerts; Exhibits; Festivals; Guided Tours; Interpretation

COLLECTIONS: [1881-present] Building artifacts.

HOURS: Apr-Oct Daily 10-8

ADMISSION: $4,

MATAWAN

5538
Burrowes Mansion Museum
94 Main St, 07747 [Matawan Historical Society, PO Box 41, 07747]; (p) (732) 566-5605; www.matawan.com/ma05003.htm

HOUSE MUSEUM

5539
Madison Township Historical Society
4216 Route 516, 07747; (p) (732) 566-2108; (f) (732) 566-6943; (c) Middlesex

Private non-profit/ 1964/ Executive Board/ staff: 3(p)/ members: 122

GENEALOGICAL SOCIETY; HISTORIC SITE; HISTORICAL SOCIETY; HISTORY MUSEUM; RESEARCH CENTER

PROGRAMS: Guided Tours

COLLECTIONS: [18th-20th c] Genealogy papers, maps, photos, research files and books on NJ, Native American artifacts, fossils, household items, tools, sheet music and pottery.

HOURS: Yr W 9:30-12, 1st Su of month 1-4

ADMISSION: No charge

MAY'S LANDING

5540
Township of Hamilton Historical Society
49 Mill St, 08330 [PO Box 482, 08330]; (p) (609) 909-0272; (c) Atlantic

Private non-profit/ 1994/ staff: 4(v)/ members: 119

GENEALOGICAL SOCIETY; HISTORIC SITE; HISTORICAL SOCIETY; HISTORY MUSEUM: Preserves Township history.

PROGRAMS: Annual Meeting; Community Outreach; Exhibits; Family Programs; Interpretation; Lectures; Research Library/Archives

COLLECTIONS: [18th c-present] Maps, newspapers, museum artifacts, portraits, paintings, photos and carvings.

HOURS: Yr Th 6:30-9, Sa 10-4

ADMISSION: No charge

MAYWOOD

5541
Maywood Historical Committee
459 Maywood Ave, 07607; (p) (201) 843-1130; (c) Bergen

City/ 1986/ staff: 7(v)/publication: *Walking Tours*

HISTORICAL SOCIETY: Preserves town memorabilia and history.

PROGRAMS: Exhibits; Guided Tours; Publication

COLLECTIONS: [1894-present] Pictures, postcards, newspapers and glass hand-colored slides.

MENDHAM

5542
Ralston Historical Association
Rte 24 at Roxiticus Rd, 07945 [313 Mendham Rd West, 07945]; (p) (973) 543-4347; (c) Morris

Private non-profit/ 1941/ staff: 15(v)/ members: 200

HISTORICAL SOCIETY; HISTORY MUSEUM: Acquires, maintains, preserves, and exhibits objects and buildings of historic interest.

PROGRAMS: Annual Meeting; Exhibits; Interpretation; Lectures

COLLECTIONS: [18th c] Locally made tools, land transfer papers.

HOURS: June-Oct Su 2-5

ADMISSION: No charge

MERCHANTVILLE

5543
Merchantville Historical Society
Merchantville Community Ctr, 08109 [1 W Maple Ave, 08109]; (p) (609) 665-1819; (c) Camden

Borough/ 1974/ staff: 5(v)/ members: 120/publication: *The Annals of Merchantville*

HISTORIC PRESERVATION AGENCY; HISTORICAL SOCIETY: Identifies and preserves historic buildings.

PROGRAMS: Annual Meeting; Exhibits; Garden Tours; Guided Tours; Publication

COLLECTIONS: [1860s-present] Photos, clothing, books, real estate pamphlets, newspaper articles and other ephemera.

HOURS: Sept-June by appt

ADMISSION: No charge

MIDDLETOWN

5544
Murray Farmhouse at Poricy Park
345 Oak Hill Road, 07748 [PO Box 36, 07748]; (p) (732) 842-5966; (f) (732) 842-6833; poricypark@monmouth.com; www.monmouth.com/~poricypark/; (c) Monmouth

Private non-profit/ 1970/ Poricy Park Citizens Committee/ staff: 2(f); 12(p); 100(v)/ members: 900

HISTORIC SITE: Preserves integrity and authenticity of historic structures and surrounding land.

PROGRAMS: Family Programs; School-Based Curriculum

COLLECTIONS: [1770-1780] Period artifacts.

HOURS: Yr M-F 9-4, Su

MONTAGUE

5545
Montague Association for Restoration of Community History (MARCH)
320 River Rd, 07827; (p) (973) 293-3106; (c) Sussex

Private non-profit/ 1979/ staff: 35(v)/ members: 265/publication: *Notes, News and Nostalgia*

HISTORICAL SOCIETY: Preserves two historic homes.

PROGRAMS: Annual Meeting; Garden Tours; Guided Tours; Lectures; Living History; Publication; Research Library/Archives

COLLECTIONS: Quilts, vintage clothing, Native American artifacts, model covered bridge, photos, slides, oral history tapes and transcripts, American wars memorabilia, books, local paintings and colonial herb garden.

HOURS: Yr W 9:30-12; July-Aug Su 1-4

MONTCLAIR

5546
Montclair Historical Society
108-110 Orange Rd, 07042 [108 Orange Rd, 07042]; (p) (973) 744-1796; (f) (973) 783-9419; mtchistorical@viconet.com; (c) Essex

Private non-profit/ 1965/ Board of Trustees/ staff: 1(f); 3(p); 100(v)/ members: 600/publication: *Cranetown Crier; Thirteen Colonies Cookbook;*

HISTORIC SITE; HISTORICAL SOCIETY; HOUSE MUSEUM: Collects, preserves and interprets Montclair's history.

PROGRAMS: Annual Meeting; Exhibits; Family Programs; Festivals; Garden Tours; Guided Tours; Interpretation; Lectures; Living History; Publication; Research Library/Archives; School-Based Curriculum; Theatre

COLLECTIONS: [1796-1996] Local history of Montclair and surrounding area. Furniture and decorative arts of Federal, American Empire and Victorian periods.

HOURS: Sept-mid June Su 2-5, T-Th 9:30-12 by appt; (Library) T 10-12, W 2-4, Su 2-5

ADMISSION: $3, Children $1

MOORESTOWN

5547
Historical Society of Moorestown
12 High St, 08057 [PO Box 477, 08057]; (p) (856) 235-0353; historical@moorestown.com; (c) Burlington

Private non-profit/ 1970/ Board of Trustees/ staff: 100(v)/ members: 250

HISTORIC SITE; HISTORICAL SOCIETY; HOUSE MUSEUM

PROGRAMS: Annual Meeting; Exhibits; Guided Tours; Reenactments; Research Library/ Archives

COLLECTIONS: [1860-1950] Local history, Quaker and family information, manuscripts, maps and photos of Moorestown, newspaper clippings and scrapbooks.

HOURS: Sept-July T 1-3, W 10-12

ADMISSION: Donations requested

MORRIS PLAINS

5548
Craftsman Farms Foundation
2352 Route 10 W # 5, 07950; (p) (973) 540-1165; (f) (973) 540-1167; (c) Morris

Private non-profit/ 1989/ staff: 3(f); 2(p); 75(v)/ members: 700/publication: *Craftsman Farms: A Pictorial History*

HISTORIC SITE; HOUSE MUSEUM: Preserves and interprets Craftsman Farms, Gustav Stickley's home.

PROGRAMS: Community Outreach; Exhibits; Family Programs; Festivals; Garden Tours; Guided Tours; Interpretation; Lectures; Publication; Research Library/Archives; School-Based Curriculum

COLLECTIONS: [Early 20th c] Buildings, furniture, textiles and decorative objects.

HOURS: Apr-mid Nov W-F 12-3, Sa-Su 11-4; Three weekends in Dec

ADMISSION: $6, Student $5, Children $3, Seniors $5

MORRISTOWN

5549
Acorn Hall
68 Morris Ave, 07960-4212; (p) (973) -267-3462; (f) (973) -267-8773

1853/ staff: 2(f); 2(p)

COLLECTIONS: [1835-1902] Furniture, decorative arts, textiles, fine arts, costumes, accessories; artifacts: NJ governors, and US presidents.

HOURS: Yr; M, Th 10-4; Su 1-4

5550
Canal Society of New Jersey
Waterloo Village, 07063 [PO Box 737, 07063-0737]; (p) (908) 722-9556; (f) (908) 722-9556; bobandlindabarth@worldnet.att.net; canalsocietynj.org; (c) Sussex

Private non-profit/ 1969/ Board of Directors/ staff: 20(v)/ members: 1300

HISTORICAL SOCIETY; HISTORY MUSEUM: Studies the history of NJ towpath canals; preserves and restores canal remains and artifacts.

PROGRAMS: Annual Meeting; Exhibits; Festivals; Guided Tours; Interpretation; Lectures; Living History; Research Library/Archives

COLLECTIONS: [1830-1930] Artifacts and photos of the Morris, Delaware and Raritan

5551
Fosterfields Living Historical Farm
73 Kahdena Rd, 07960; (p) (973) 326-7645; (f) (973) 631-5023; www.parks.morris.nj.us; (c) Morris

County/ 1979/ Park Commission/ staff: 12(f); 15(p); 100(v)/ members: 670

HISTORIC SITE; HOUSE MUSEUM; LIVING HISTORY/OUTDOOR MUSEUM: Presents educational programs, tours and living history experiences interpreting the site's cultural and agricultural history.

PROGRAMS: Annual Meeting; Exhibits; Facility Rental; Family Programs; Guided Tours; Interpretation; Lectures; Living History; Reenact-

ments; School-Based Curriculum

COLLECTIONS: [1880-1940] Decorative arts, farming and agricultural implements in restored Victorian era mansion, cottage, farmhouse, barns and carriage house. Papers, periodicals, ephemera and photographs related to Foster family history and general agriculture topics.

HOURS: Apr-Oct W-Sa 10-5, Su 12-5

ADMISSION: $4, Children $2, Seniors $3; Under 6 free

5552
Local History and Genealogy Department, Joint Free Public Library of Morristown and Morris Township
1 Miller Rd, 07960; (p) (973) 538-3473; (f) (973) 267-4064; jochem@main.morris.org; www.jfpl.org; (c) Morris

1792/ Board of Trustees/ staff: 2(f); 6(p); 20(v)/publication: *In Lights and Shadows: Morristown in Three Centuries; Morris Township, NJ: A Glimpse into the Past; and others*

LIBRARY AND/OR ARCHIVES: Documents Morristown, Morris Township, Morris County and New Jersey history and genealogy with primary and secondary sources. Also has history and genealogy materials for New York, New England and the mid-Atlantic states.

PROGRAMS: Community Outreach; Exhibits; Guided Tours; Lectures; Publication; Research Library/Archives

COLLECTIONS: [1740-present] Printed books, books on microfiche, periodicals, New Jersey censuses, newspapers, maps, atlases, photographs, postcards, manuscripts, family papers, landscape drawings, vertical files, video and oral history tapes.

HOURS: Yr M-Th 9-9, F 9-6, Sa 9:30-5, Su 1-5; July-Aug Sa 10-2

ADMISSION: No charge

5553
MacCulloch Hall Historical Museum and Gardens
45 MacCulloch Ave, 07960; (p) (973) 538-2404; (f) (973) 538-9428; macchall@aol.com; www.machall.org; (c) Morris

Private non-profit/ 1950/ staff: 3(f); 2(p); 40(v)/ members: 300

ART MUSEUM; HOUSE MUSEUM: Preserves historic home.

PROGRAMS: Annual Meeting; Community Outreach; Concerts; Exhibits; Facility Rental; Garden Tours; Guided Tours; Lectures; Research Library/Archives; School-Based Curriculum; Theatre

COLLECTIONS: [18th-20th c] Decorative arts, MacCulloch-Miller archives, Morris Canal archives. Whig political archives and Thomas Nast collection.

HOURS: Yr W-Th, Su 1-4

ADMISSION: $3, Student $2, Seniors $2; Kids 12 and under free

5554
Morris County Heritage Commission
300 Mendham Rd, 07963 [PO Box 900, 07963-0900]; (p) (973) 829-8117; (f) (973) 631-5137; Heritage@co.morris.nj.us; www.co.morris.nj.us/heritage; (c) Morris

County/ 1970/ Board of Chosen Freeholders/ staff: 2(f); 9(v)/publication: *The County Circular*

LIBRARY AND/OR ARCHIVES: Promotes and preserves the history of Morris County.

PROGRAMS: Community Outreach; Exhibits; Lectures; Publication

COLLECTIONS: [1741-1973] County historical archives; county and court records.

HOURS: Yr M-F

5555
Morris County Historical Society
68 Morris Ave, Acorn Hall, 07960-4212; (p) (973) 267-3465; (f) (973) 267-8773; (c) Morris

Private non-profit/ 1945/ staff: 2(f); 5(p); 100(v)/ members: 485

ALLIANCE OF HISTORICAL AGENCIES; GARDEN; HISTORIC SITE; HISTORICAL SOCIETY; HISTORY MUSEUM; HOUSE MUSEUM: Discovers, preserves and makes known the history of Morris County and its people.

PROGRAMS: Annual Meeting; Community Outreach; Concerts; Exhibits; Facility Rental; Family Programs; Garden Tours; Guided Tours; Interpretation; Lectures; Research Library/Archives; School-Based Curriculum

COLLECTIONS: [19th c] European and American portraits and landscape paintings, Victorian furniture, ephemera, decorative arts, textiles, costumes, photos, restored period gardens.

HOURS: Yr M, Th 10-4, Su 1-4

ADMISSION: $5, Student $2, Children $1, Seniors $4

5556
Morristown Chapter DAR/Schuyler-Hamilton House
5 Olyphant Pl, 07960; (p) (973) 267-4039; prs1@flash.net; (c) Morris

Private non-profit/ 1895/ staff: 25(v)/ members: 71

HISTORIC SITE; HOUSE MUSEUM: Serves as DAR museum and headquarters.

PROGRAMS: Guided Tours

COLLECTIONS: [1750-1850] Period furnishing.

HOURS: Yr Su 1:30-4

ADMISSION: $4, Children $0.50, Seniors $3.50

5557
New Jersey Postal History Society
[PO Box 1945, 07962-1945]; njpostalhistory@aol.com; (c) Morris

Private non-profit/ 1972/ staff: 2(v)/ members: 125

HISTORICAL SOCIETY: Preserves and interprets postal and communications history in NJ.

PROGRAMS: Annual Meeting; Exhibits

5558
Roebling Chapter, Society for Industrial Archaeology
19 Budd St, 07960; (p) (973) 455-0491; (f) (973) 538-1828; www.ss.mtu.edu/IA/SIA.html; (c) Morris

Private non-profit/ 1980/ staff: 5(v)/ members: 430

PROFESSIONAL ORGANIZATION: Shares knowledge, explores structures and remains of industrial heritage in the greater NY area; serves as resource for historians, museums, and communities.

PROGRAMS: Lectures

5559
Vail Mansion
Historic Speedwell, 333 Speedwell Ave, 07960 [333 Speedwell Ave, 07960]; (p) (973) 540-0211; (f) (973) 540-0476; www.speedwell.org

1800/ staff: 1(p)

HOUSE MUSEUM

COLLECTIONS: [1800-1864] Diary of Stephen Vail.

HOURS: Vary

MOUNT HOLLY

5560
Friends of the Mansion at Smithville
Smithville Rd, 08060 [49 Rancocas Rd, 08060]; (p) (609) 261-3780; (f) (609) 265-5782; www.co.burlington.nj.us; (c) Burlington

County/ 1975/ Burlington County Freeholders/ staff: 1(p); 40(v)

HISTORIC SITE; HISTORY MUSEUM; HOUSE MUSEUM; LIVING HISTORY/OUTDOOR MUSEUM: Restores and adapts the Smithville Mansion Complex for use as a county cultural and heritage center. The 25-room mansion and annex were built in 1840. Residence of Hezekiah Bradley Smith from 1865 to 1887.

PROGRAMS: Annual Meeting; Community Outreach; Concerts; Exhibits; Facility Rental; Family Programs; Festivals; Garden Tours; Guided Tours; Interpretation; Lectures; Living History; Theatre

COLLECTIONS: [1865-1887] Antique furniture.

5561
John Woolman Memorial
99 Branch St, 08060; (p) (609) 267-3226

5562
Mt. Holly Historical Society
Park Drive, 08060 [PO Box 4081, 08060]; (p) (609) 267-8844; (c) Burlington

1965/ Mount Holly Township/ staff: 25(v)/ members: 88

HISTORICAL SOCIETY

PROGRAMS: Community Outreach; Exhibits; Guided Tours

COLLECTIONS: [18th c-present] Artifacts, newspapers, journals, period clothing, furniture, pictures, early deeds, ledgers and books.

HOURS: Apr-Oct F 11-1, Sa 10-5, Su

MOUNTAINVILLE

5563
Tewksbury Historical Society, Inc.
60 Water St, [PO Box 457, Oldwick, 08858]; (p) (908) 832-6734; (f) (908) 832-6734; scvd123@csnet.net; www.tewksburynj.com/history.shtml; (c) Hunterdon

Private non-profit/ 1989/ Executive Board/ staff: 25(v)/ members: 180

HISTORICAL SOCIETY: Gathers, preserves and disseminates the history of Tewksbury Township.

PROGRAMS: Annual Meeting; Community Outreach; Exhibits; Garden Tours; Guided Tours; Lectures; Research Library/Archives

COLLECTIONS: Photos, postcards, letters, maps and books.

HOURS: Yr Su 1-3

ADMISSION: No charge

MULLICA HILL

5564
Harrison Township Historical Society
Old Town Hall, S Main St & Woodstown Rd, 08062 [PO Box 4, 08062]; (p) (609) 478-4949; (c) Gloucester

Private non-profit/ 1971/ staff: 25(v)/ members: 200/publication: *Milestones*

HISTORICAL SOCIETY: Collects, preserves and interprets materials reflecting the social, civic and folk culture of Harrison Township and vicinity.

PROGRAMS: Annual Meeting; Exhibits; Publication; Research Library/Archives; School-Based Curriculum

COLLECTIONS: [1840-present] Agricultural artifacts, textiles, furniture, folk arts/crafts, manuscripts and photos.

HOURS: Apr-June, Oct-Dec Sa-Su

NEPTUNE

5565
Neptune Township Historical Society
25 Neptune Blvd, 07754; (p) (732) 775-8241; (f) (732) 774-1132; www.monmouth.edu/irs/library/melon/neptune/neptune.htm; (c) Monmouth

1971/ Township of Neptune/ staff: 1(f); 1(v)/publication: *Early Dutch Settlers by George Beekman; Neptune and Shark River Hills*

HISTORY MUSEUM: Preserves history of Neptune, Ocean Grove and Shark River Hills communities.

PROGRAMS: Community Outreach; Exhibits; Guided Tours; Lectures; Publication; Research Library/Archives; School-Based Curriculum

COLLECTIONS: [1880-1930] Artifacts: Lenape and Sand Hill Indians; early farming, carpentry, dairying, shoemaking, printing and pharmacy trades; costumes, survival gear of Arctic explorers; photos; local business ledgers.

NEW BRUNSWICK

5566
Buccleuch Mansion
George St/Eon Ave, Buccleuch Park, 08901 [114 Mine St, High Bridge, 08829]; (p) (732) 745-5094, (732) 638-6129; skene@noles.cc.bellcore.com

1739/ City/ staff: 2(v)

COLLECTIONS: [Revolutionary-early 1900s] Belter, Edgerton, Parsell furniture; costumes and accessories, DuFors scenic wallpaper, Micah Williams Folk art paintings.

HOURS: Varies

5567
Cornelius Low House/Middlesex County Museum
1225 River Rd, 08901 [703 Jersey Ave, 08901-3605]; (p) (732) 745-4177; (f) (732) 745-4507; info@cultureheritage.org; www.cultureheritage.org; (c) Middlesex

County/ 1979/ Cultural and Heritage Commission/ staff: 3(f); 3(p); 3(v)

HISTORIC SITE; HISTORY MUSEUM; HOUSE MUSEUM

PROGRAMS: Community Outreach; Exhibits; Family Programs; Guided Tours; Interpretation; Lectures

COLLECTIONS: [18th-20th c] Interpretive exhibits: medicine, immigration legends and oral traditions, Black professional baseball leagues, inventions and architecture.

HOURS: Yr T-F 8:30-4:15, Su 1-4

5568
East Jersey Olde Towne Village
1050 River Rd, 08901 [703 Jersey Ave, 08902]; (p) (732) 745-3030; (f) (732) 463-1086; www.cultureheritage.org/village.html; (c) Middlesex

County/ 1979/ Cultural and Heritage Commission/ staff: 3(f); 3(p); 25(v)

GARDEN; HISTORY MUSEUM; LIVING HISTORY/OUTDOOR MUSEUM: Interprets life in the Raritan Valley during the 18th-19th centuries.

PROGRAMS: Community Outreach; Concerts; Exhibits; Family Programs; Festivals; Guided Tours; Interpretation; Lectures; Research Library/Archives; School-Based Curriculum

COLLECTIONS: [18th-19th c] Original, replica and reconstructed buildings; architecture; farm and merchant communities of central NJ.

HOURS: Yr T-F 8:30-4:15, Su 1-4

ADMISSION: No charge

5569
Henry Guest House
60 Livingston Ave, 08901; (p) (732) 745-5175

1760

HOUSE MUSEUM

COLLECTIONS: [18th c]

HOURS: Yr

5570
Jewish Historical Society of Central Jersey
228 Livingston Ave, 08901; (p) (732) 249-4894; (f) (732) 249-4894; jhscj@cs.com; www.jewishgen.org/jhscj; (c) Middlesex

Private non-profit/ 1977/ Board of Directors/ staff: 1(p); 10(v)/ members: 470

GENEALOGICAL SOCIETY; HISTORIC PRESERVATION AGENCY; HISTORICAL SOCIETY; RESEARCH CENTER: Promotes American Jewish history in Central NJ.

PROGRAMS: Annual Meeting; Community Outreach; Concerts; Elder's Programs; Exhibits; Family Programs; Guided Tours; Lectures; Research Library/Archives; School-Based Curriculum

COLLECTIONS: [18th c-present] Institutional records, Jewish newspapers, books, manuscripts, photos, genealogies and memorabilia.

HOURS: Yr M-Th 10-2, F 9-12

ADMISSION: No charge

5571
Rutgers University Libraries, Special Collections and University Archives
169 College Ave, 08901-1163; (p) (732) 932-7006; (f) (732) 932-7012; rbecker@rci.rutgers.edu; www.libraries.rutgers.edu/rulib/spcol/spcol.htm; (c) Middlesex

State/ 1946/ Rutgers Univ/ staff: 13(f); 6(p); 1(v)

LIBRARY AND/OR ARCHIVES

PROGRAMS: Exhibits; Lectures; Research Library/Archives

COLLECTIONS: [17th c-present] NJ history, culture and genealogy; rare books, maps, pictorial materials, manuscripts and Rutgers Univ archives.

HOURS: Yr M-F 9-5; School Session Sa 1-5

ADMISSION: No charge

NEW PROVIDENCE

5572
New Providence Historical Society
Memorial Library, 07974 [Elkwood Ave, 07974]; (p) (908) 464-0163; (c) Union

Private non-profit/ 1968/ staff: 18(v)/ members: 126/publication: Turkey Tracks

HISTORICAL SOCIETY; HISTORY MUSEUM; HOUSE MUSEUM: Preserves the history of the Borough of New Providence.

PROGRAMS: Annual Meeting; Community Outreach; Exhibits; Guided Tours; Lectures; Publication; Research Library/Archives; School-Based Curriculum

COLLECTIONS: [Early 18th c-present] Photos, transcribed oral interviews, ledgers, maps and genealogy information on the town's founding families.

HOURS: (Museum) Yr 1st, 3rd Su 2-4; (Mason Room) Yr T 10-12, Th 10-12/2-5

ADMISSION: No charge

NEW VERNON

5573
Harding Township Historical Society
Village Rd, 07976 [PO Box 1777, 07976]; (p) (973) 292-3661, (973) 292-0161; (c) Morris

Private non-profit/ 1976/ staff: 3(p); 16(v)/ members: 550

HISTORICAL SOCIETY: Preserves the history of Harding Township; collects, maintains and interprets cultural material.

PROGRAMS: Annual Meeting; Lectures; Research Library/Archives

COLLECTIONS: [19th c] Artifacts: farming, newspapers.

HOURS: Vary

ADMISSION: No charge

NEWARK

5574
Ballantine House, The
PO Box 540, 07101 [49 Washington St, 07101]; (p) (973) 596-6550; (f) (973) 642-0459; (c) Essex

Private non-profit/ 1909/ Newark Museum Assoc/ staff: 95(f); 50(p); 50(v)/ members: 5000

HISTORIC SITE: Provides educational services, exhibits, historic preservation, junior history, living history and publications.

PROGRAMS: Exhibits; Guided Tours; Interpretation

COLLECTIONS: [19th c] Exhibits, artifacts and memorabilia.

HOURS: Yr W, Sa-Su 12-5, Th 12-8

5575
New Jersey Historical Society
52 Park Pl, 07102; (p) (973) 596-8500; (f) (973) 596-6957; (c) Essex

Private non-profit/ 1845/ Board of Trustees/ staff: 20(f); 9(p); 102(v)/ members: 2000/publication: New Jersey History

HISTORICAL SOCIETY: Promotes exploration of American culture.

PROGRAMS: Annual Meeting; Community Outreach; Concerts; Elder's Programs; Exhibits; Facility Rental; Family Programs; Festivals; Film/Video; Guided Tours; Interpretation; Lectures; Publication; Research Library/Archives; School-Based Curriculum

COLLECTIONS: [Prehistory-present] Folk art, furniture, fine and decorative arts, costumes, tools, photos, maps, manuscripts, plans and renderings by architects and industrial designers.

HOURS: Museum: Yr T-Sa

5576
Newark Museum Association
43-49 Washington St, 07101 [PO Box 540, 07101]; (p) (973) 596-6661; (f) (973) 596-6666; (c) Essex

City; Private non-profit; State/ 1909/ City of Newark/State of New Jersey/ staff: 100(f); 50(p); 100(v)/ members: 5000/publication: Exhibitions and Events

ART MUSEUM; HISTORIC SITE; HOUSE MUSEUM: Maintains Ballantine House, an 1885 beer brewer's townhouse, and art museum.

PROGRAMS: Annual Meeting; Community Outreach; Concerts; Elder's Programs; Exhibits; Facility Rental; Family Programs; Festivals; Film/Video; Guided Tours; Interpretation; Lectures; Publication; Research Library/Archives; School-Based Curriculum

COLLECTIONS: [18th c-present] American, Asian, African, Native American, pre-Columbian and Pacific Islander art; antiquities, numismatics, and household goods from Europe and America.

HOURS: Yr W-Su 12-5

ADMISSION: No charge

5577
Newark Preservation and Landmarks Committee
[PO Box 1066, 07101]; (p) (973) 622-4910, (973) 674-8194; (c) Essex

Private non-profit/ 1973/ staff: 1(p); 15(v)/ members: 225/publication: *Yesterday's News*

HISTORIC PRESERVATION AGENCY

PROGRAMS: Annual Meeting; Exhibits; Guided Tours; Publication

COLLECTIONS: [19th c-present] Documents, articles, correspondence and photos of historic buildings and sites in Newark.

HOURS: Not open to public

NORTH BRUNSWICK

5578
New Jersey Museum of Agriculture
103 College Farm Rd, 08902 [PO Box 7788, 08902]; (p) (732) 249-2077; (f) (732) 247-1035; Carl@agriculturemuseum.org; www.agriculturemuseum.org; (c) Middlesex

Private non-profit/ 1989/ Board of Trustees/ staff: 6(f); 7(p); 30(v)/ members: 650/publication: *Harvest Times*

HISTORIC PRESERVATION AGENCY; HISTORY MUSEUM; RESEARCH CENTER; TRIBAL MUSEUM

PROGRAMS: Annual Meeting; Community Outreach; Elder's Programs; Exhibits; Facility Rental; Family Programs; Festivals; Film/Video; Garden Tours; Guided Tours; Interpretation; Lectures; Publication; Reenactments; Research Library/Archives; School-Based Curriculum;

COLLECTIONS: [18th-20th c] Farming, barn and field working tools; machinery, equipment, vehicles and related crafts; photos.

HOURS: Yr T-Sa 10-5, Su 12-5

ADMISSION: $4, Children $2, Seniors $3; Members/Under 4 free

NORTH CALDWELL

5579
North Caldwell Historical Society
Borough Hall, 160 Gould Ave, 07006 [73 Evergreen Dr, 07006-4621]; (p) (973) 226-6786; (f) (973) 228-5596; (c) Essex

Private non-profit/ 1989/ members: 67/publication: *A Brief History of The Township of North Caldwell*

HISTORICAL SOCIETY

PROGRAMS: Annual Meeting; Community Outreach; Exhibits; Guided Tours; Lectures; Publication; School-Based Curriculum

COLLECTIONS: [1898-present] Records, newspapers clippings, postcards, certificates, pamphlets, tax bills and photos.

NORTHFIELD

5580
Northfield Cultural Committee and Museum
Burton Ave, Birch Grove Park, 08225 [1600 Shore Rd, 08225]; (p) (609) 645-1887, (609) 383-1505; (f) (609) 646-6175; (c) Atlantic

Joint/ 1972/ Private non-profit; Northfield Historical Society/ staff: 15(v)/ members: 101

HISTORICAL SOCIETY; HISTORY MUSEUM; HOUSE MUSEUM: Supports museum and Castro Project.

PROGRAMS: Concerts; Exhibits; Reenactments

COLLECTIONS: [1905-present] Memorabilia, local stories, news clippings and genealogy material.

HOURS: Yr Su-M, W 1-3

ADMISSION: No charge

NUTLEY

5581
Historic Restoration Trust, The
3 Kingsland St, 07110; (p) (973) 661-3410; (c) Essex

Private non-profit/ 1973/ The Trust (Township of Nutley)/ staff: 8(v)/ members: 1

HISTORIC SITE: Restores and preserves 1700s homestead, Kingsland Manor

PROGRAMS: Concerts; Facility Rental; Garden Tours; Guided Tours

COLLECTIONS: [1700s] Kingsland family artifacts.

HOURS: Meetings 2nd T

ADMISSION: Donations requested

5582
Nutley Historical Society and Museum
65 Church St, 07110; (p) (973) 667-1528; (c) Essex

Joint/ 1947/ Private non-profit;State/ staff: 14(v)/ members: 300/publication: *Nutley Yesterday and Today*

HISTORICAL SOCIETY

PROGRAMS: Annual Meeting; Community Outreach; Exhibits; Facility Rental; Festivals; Film/Video; Guided Tours; Interpretation; Living History; Publication; Research Library/Archives; School-Based Curriculum

HOURS: Sept-June T 7-9, Su 2-4

ADMISSION: Donations accepted

OAKHURST

5583
Township of Ocean Historical Museum
163 Monmouth Rd, 07755; (p) (732) 531-2136; (c) Monmouth

Private non-profit/ 1984/ staff: 12(v)/ members: 130/publication: *Images of America: Township of Ocean; Township of Ocean: Landmarks and Lore; and others*

HISTORIC SITE; HISTORICAL SOCIETY; HISTORY MUSEUM: Researches and preserves the history of Ocean Township.

PROGRAMS: Annual Meeting; Community Outreach; Exhibits; Family Programs; Festivals; Guided Tours; Interpretation; Lectures; Research Library/Archives; School-Based Curriculum

COLLECTIONS: [1850-1950] Photos, household and farm items, documents, books,

school memorabilia and family information.

HOURS: Yr T 1-4

ADMISSION: No charge

OCEAN CITY

5584
Friends of the Ocean City Historical Museum, Inc.
1735 Simpson Ave, 08226; (p) (609) 399-1801, (609) 525-9311; (f) (609) 349-0544; museumochm@aol.com; (c) Cape May

Private non-profit/ 1964/ staff: 2(f); 5(p); 125(v)/ members: 400

HISTORY MUSEUM: Collects, preserves and exhibits material relative to the history of Ocean City.

PROGRAMS: Annual Meeting; Community Outreach; Elder's Programs; Exhibits; Family Programs; Festivals; Film/Video; Guided Tours; Lectures; Reenactments; Research Library/Archives; School-Based Curriculum

COLLECTIONS: Hand written logs from original founders, photos, artifacts, furniture, glassware and clothing.

HOURS: May-Oct M-F 10-4, Sa 1-4; July-Aug Th 4-7; Nov-Apr M-Sa 1-4

ADMISSION: No charge

OCEAN GROVE

5585
Centennial Cottage
Corner of Central & McClintock Sts, 07756 [PO Box 446, 07756]; (p) (732) 774-1859; (f) (732) 775-5689; www.ogcma.com

1874/ staff: 36(v)

HOUSE MUSEUM

COLLECTIONS: [1869-1910] Clothing, toys, furniture and paintings, photos.

HOURS: June-Sept M-Sa 11-3

5586
Historical Society of Ocean Grove
50 Pitman Ave, 07756 [PO Box 446, 07756]; (p) (732) 774-1869; (c) Monmouth

Private non-profit/ 1970/ staff: 15(v)/ members: 600

HISTORICAL SOCIETY; HOUSE MUSEUM: Preserves the history of Ocean Grove.

PROGRAMS: Community Outreach; Concerts; Exhibits; Festivals; Guided Tours; Lectures; Research Library/Archives

COLLECTIONS: [19th c] History of Ocean Grove, Monmouth County, New Jersey , Victoriana, and camp meetings.

HOURS: June-Aug

OGDENSBURG

5587
Sterling Hill Mining Museum
30 Plant St, 07439; (p) (973) 209-7212; (f) (973) 209-8505; shm@tapnet.net; www.sterlinghill.org; (c) Sussex

Private non-profit/ 1989/ staff: 4(f); 11(p); 10(v)/ members: 325

HISTORY MUSEUM: Preserves and promotes mining history.

PROGRAMS: Exhibits; Guided Tours; School-Based Curriculum; Theatre

COLLECTIONS: [1890-present] Tools, lamps and mining equipment.

HOURS: Apr-Nov Daily 10-5; Mar, Dec Sa-Su 10-5

ADMISSION: $9, Student $8, Children $6

OXFORD

5588
Shippen Manor Museum/Warren County Cultural and Heritage Commission
8 Belvidere Ave, 07863; (p) (908) 453-4381; (f) (908) 453-4981; wcchc@nac.net; www.wcchc.org; (c) Warren

County/ 1979/ staff: 2(f); 1(p); 12(v)/ members: 9/publication: *The Furnace*

HISTORY MUSEUM: Operates Shippen Manor, the county museum, and Oxford Furnace, a colonial iron furnace.

PROGRAMS: Concerts; Exhibits; Festivals; Guided Tours; Lectures; Living History; Publication; Research Library/Archives

COLLECTIONS: [18th c-present] Artifacts: early iron industry and mining, Native American, early farm implements and photographs.

HOURS: Yr 1st and 2nd Su

PARK RIDGE

5589
Pascack Historical Society
19 Ridge Ave, 07656 [PO Box 285, 07656]; (p) (201) 573-0307; pashissoc@earthlink.net; (c) Bergen

Private non-profit/ 1942/ staff: 30(v)/ members: 300/publication: *Pascack Valley Tales*

HISTORIC SITE; HISTORICAL SOCIETY; HISTORY MUSEUM: Collects and preserves the history of the Pascack Valley.

PROGRAMS: Annual Meeting; Community Outreach; Exhibits; Guided Tours; Publication; Research Library/Archives

COLLECTIONS: [1860-1930] Area artifacts.

HOURS: Yr Su 2-4:30 and by

PATERSON

5590
Greater Falls Preservation and Development Corporation
Market & Square St, 07501 [2 Market St, 07501]; (p) (973) 279-1270; (f) (973) 279-6713; (c) Passaic

Private non-profit/ 1971/ staff: 3(f)/ members: 200

HISTORIC PRESERVATION AGENCY: Preserves and restores historic districts.

PROGRAMS: Annual Meeting

COLLECTIONS: [19th c] Architecture.

5591
Lambert Castle Museum
3 Valley Rd, 07503; (p) (201) 881-2761; www.dclink.com/castles/LAMBERT.HTM

5592
Passaic County Historical Society
317 Pennsylvania Ave, 07503; (p) (973) 881-2761; (f) (973) 357-1070; (c) Passaic

Private non-profit/ 1926/ staff: 1(f); 60(p)/ members: 1/publication: *Castle Genie, Historic County*

HISTORICAL SOCIETY; HISTORY MUSEUM; HOUSE MUSEUM; RESEARCH CENTER: Preserves and promotes the study and understanding of Passaic County's past; collects and preserves materials of local significance for the public.

PROGRAMS: Annual Meeting; Community Outreach; Concerts; Elder's Programs; Exhibits; Facility Rental; Family Programs; Festivals; Guided Tours; Lectures; Publication; Research Library/Archives; School-Based Curriculum

COLLECTIONS: [18th c] Fine and decorative arts, archaeological artifacts and textiles, photos.

PENNINGTON

5593
Hopewell Valley Historical Society
Hopewell Library, 245 Pennington-Titusville Rd, 08534 [PO Box 371, 08534-0371]; (p) (609) 466-1279; hvhist@aol.com; (c) Mercer

Private non-profit/ 1975/ Board of Trustees/ staff: 20(v)/ members: 125

HISTORICAL SOCIETY: Collects artifacts and records to make them available for educational purposes; encourages historic preservation.

PROGRAMS: Annual Meeting; Lectures; Research Library/Archives

COLLECTIONS: [18th-20th c] Personal and business documents, newspapers, photos pertaining to Hopewell Township and boroughs of Hopewell and Pennington.

PENNSAUKEN

5594
Griffith Morgan Committee, Inc.
243 Griffith Morgan Ln, 08110 [PO Box 522, 08110]; (p) (609) 486-9561, (609) 665-1948; (f) (609) 665-0082; (c) Camden

Joint/ 1972/ City; Private non-profit/ staff: 10(v)/ members: 150

HISTORIC SITE; HOUSE MUSEUM: Preserves Morgan family and Native American history.

PROGRAMS: Exhibits; Reenactments; Research Library/Archives; School-Based Curriculum

COLLECTIONS: [1693-1853] Period furniture, local artifacts, drawings, maps, articles of the Morgan family.

HOURS: 4 times/year and by appt; Sa-Su

5595
Pennsauken Historical Society
9201 Burrough Dover Ln, 08110 [PO Box 56, 08110]; (p) (856) 662-3002; (c) Camden

Private non-profit/ 1964/ Board of Directors/ staff: 12(p); 12(v)/ members: 200

HISTORIC SITE; HOUSE MUSEUM: Maintains and cares for the Burrough Dover House.

PROGRAMS: Festivals; Guided Tours

COLLECTIONS: [18th-19th c] Colonial and Victorian furniture, dishes and indentures.

HOURS: Apr, June, Aug, Dec One Sa 1-4

ADMISSION: No charge

PERTH AMBOY

5596
Kearny Cottage Historical Association
63 Catalpa Ave, 08861; (p) (732) 826-1826; (c) Middlesex

Private non-profit/ 1920/ staff: 4(v)/ members: 40

HISTORIC SITE; HOUSE MUSEUM: Preserves, maintains, and restores the Kearny Cottage homestead.

PROGRAMS: Annual Meeting; Garden Tours; Guided Tours; Lectures

COLLECTIONS: [18th-19th c] Letters, rare books, Kearny family possessions, Commodore Kearny's sea chest and naval artifacts; Perth Amboy artifacts.

HOURS: Yr by appt

ADMISSION: Donations accepted

5597
Proprietary House Association
149 Kearny Ave, 08861; (p) (732) 826-5527; (f) (732) 826-8889; (c) Middlesex

State/ 1967/ staff: 1(p); 24(v)/ members: 356/publication: *The Proprietary House in Amboy*

HISTORIC SITE; HISTORY MUSEUM; HOUSE MUSEUM: Restores and interprets the Royal Governor's mansion.

PROGRAMS: Annual Meeting; Community Outreach; Concerts; Exhibits; Facility Rental; Family Programs; Festivals; Guided Tours; Interpretation; Lectures; Living History; Publication; Reenactments; School-Based Curriculum; Theatre

COLLECTIONS: [1763-1846] Furniture, dishes, glassware, pictures and books.

HOURS: Yr W

PISCATAWAY

5598
Ivy Hall, Cornelius Low House
1225 River Rd, 08854 [Cultural & Heritage Comm, 703 Jersey Ave, New Brunswick, 08901]; (p) (908) 745-4177, (732) 745-4489; (f) (732) 745-4507;

HOUSE MUSEUM

5599
Metlar/Bodine House, The
Raritan Landing, 1281 River Rd, 08854 [Raritan Landing,1281 River Rd, 08854-5820]; (p) (732) 463-8363

1728/ staff: 2(p)

HOUSE MUSEUM

COLLECTIONS: [1750-present] Furniture, clocks, bells; local deeds, letters, ledger's, physician's office, general store.

HOURS: Yr

5600
Piscataway Historical and Heritage Society
1001 Maple, 08854; (p) (732) 752-5252; (c) Middlesex

Private non-profit/ 1976/ members: 45

HISTORICAL SOCIETY

PROGRAMS: Annual Meeting; Community Outreach; Family Programs; Guided Tours; Lectures

COLLECTIONS: [1666-present]

PLAINFIELD

5601
Historical Society of Plainfield
602 W Front St, 07060-1004; (p) (908) 755-5831; (f) (908) 755-0132; www.members.tripod.com/~drakehouse; (c) Union

Joint/ 1921/ City; Private non-profit/ staff: 1(p); 50(v)/ members: 300/publication: *The Communique*

HISTORICAL SOCIETY; HOUSE MUSEUM: Promotes interest in history; maintains and develops the Drake House Museum.

PROGRAMS: Exhibits; Guided Tours; Publication

COLLECTIONS: [18th-19th c] Furnishings, documents, quilts, clothing.

HOURS: Yr Su 2-4 Th-F by appt

ADMISSION: Donations accepted

5602
Plainfield Public Library
8th St at Park Ave, 07060; (p) (908) 757-1111; (f) (908) 754-0063; ekastel@lmxac.org; www.infolink.org/plainfieldpl/index.htm; (c) Union

City/ 1881/ staff: 18(f); 15(p); 10(v)

LIBRARY AND/OR ARCHIVES: Promotes historical research.

PROGRAMS: Community Outreach; Concerts; Exhibits; Facility Rental; Family Programs; Lectures; Research Library/Archives

COLLECTIONS: [1860s-present] Plainfield and regional history, Jerseyana, blueprints, historic photographs, postcards, genealogy, maps, newspapers, art.

HOURS: Yr M-Th 10-9, F, Sa 10-5 Su 1:30-5; During Summer: Sa 10-1

PLAINSBORO

5603
Plainsboro Historical Society
641 Plainsboro Rd, 08536; (p) (609) 799-9040; www.plainsboro.com; (c) Middlesex

City/ 1975/ Plainsboro Township/ members: 80

HISTORIC SITE; HISTORICAL SOCIETY; HISTORY MUSEUM

PROGRAMS: Annual Meeting; Exhibits; Guided Tours; Interpretation

COLLECTIONS: [1700 BC-present] Artifacts.

ADMISSION: No charge

POINT PLEASANT

5604
Bay Head Historical Society
1643 Bay Ave, 08742 [PO Box 127, Bay Head, 08742]; (p) (732) 295-2072; (f) (732) 295-4412; (c) Ocean

Joint/ 1992/ City; Private non-profit/ staff: 2(p); 25(v)/ members: 425

GARDEN; HISTORIC SITE; HISTORICAL SOCIETY; HOUSE MUSEUM: Preserves city history.

PROGRAMS: Annual Meeting; Community Outreach; Exhibits; Facility Rental; Festivals; Garden Tours; Lectures

COLLECTIONS: [1850-present] Maps, photos, small boats, books, business records, decoys and artifacts from three NJ coastal towns.

POINT PLEASANT BEACH

5605
Point Pleasant Historical Society
Borough Hall, 416 New Jersey Ave, 08742 [PO Box 1273, 08742]; (p) (732) 892-3091; www.membersbellatlantic.net/~ppthist/; (c) Ocean

Private non-profit/ 1976/ staff: 5(v)/ members: 60

HISTORICAL SOCIETY; HISTORY MUSEUM: Collects, preserves and interprets history of Jersey Shore communities.

PROGRAMS: Exhibits; Film/Video; Lectures; Research Library/Archives

COLLECTIONS: [1900-present] Local documents and maps, records, merchandise, shopkeepers; World War II scrapbooks.

HOURS: Yr 2nd Th 1-4, and by appt

ADMISSION: Donations accepted

PORT MONMOUTH

5606
Spy House Museum
119 Port Monmouth Rd, 07758; (p) (908) 787-1807

HOUSE MUSEUM

PRINCETON

5607
Drumthwacket
354 Stockton St, 08540; (p) (609) 683-0057, (609) 924-3044; (f) (609) 497-1680

1835/ staff: 6(f); 2(p)

COLLECTIONS: [18th c]

HOURS: Vary

5608
Historic Morven
55 Stockton St, 08540; (p) (609) 683-4495; (f) (609) 497-6390; www.historicmorven.org; (c) Mercer

Private non-profit/ 1987/ State/ staff: 1(f); 2(p); 10(v)

HISTORIC SITE: Preserves site that served as Governor's mansion, 1954-1981.

PROGRAMS: Exhibits; Facility Rental; Garden Tours; Guided Tours; Lectures; Research Library/Archives

COLLECTIONS: [1750-1950] Portraits, furnishings and archival items related to site, and history of NJ.

ADMISSION: No charge

5609
Historical Society of Princeton
158 Nassau St, 08542; (p) (609) 921-6748; (f) (609) 921-6939; www.princetonhistory.org; (c) Mercer

Private non-profit/ 1938/ staff: 5(f); 5(p); 60(v)/ members: 1100/publication: *Princeton History*

HISTORIC SITE; HISTORY MUSEUM: Collects and preserves materials pertaining to the town and its environs.

PROGRAMS: Annual Meeting; Community Outreach; Exhibits; Family Programs; Film/Video; Guided Tours; Interpretation; Lectures; Publication; Research Library/Archives; School-Based Curriculum

COLLECTIONS: [17th-20th c] Artifacts, manuscripts, photos, decorative art objects, art works and articles of clothing.

HOURS: Jan-Feb Sa-Su 12-4; Mar-Dec T-Su 12-4

ADMISSION: Donations accepted

5610
Princeton Battlefield State Park
500 Mercer Rd, 08540-4810; (p) (609) 921-0074; (f) (609) 921-0074; PBSP@aol.com; (c) Mercer

State/ 1946/ staff: 1(f); 1(p)

HOUSE MUSEUM: Preserves and interprets the site of the January 3, 1777 Revolutionary War Battle.

PROGRAMS: Community Outreach; Exhibits; Guided Tours; Interpretation; Lectures; Living History; Reenactments; School-Based Curriculum

COLLECTIONS: [18th c] Household furnishings, firearms, weapons and equipment, archaeological artifacts, paintings.

HOURS: (Clarke House) Yr W-Sa 10-12/1-4, Su 1-4; (Park) Yr Daily sunrise-sunset

ADMISSION: No charge

5611
Rockingham Association
108 CR 518, 08540; (p) (609) 921-8835; (f) (609) 921-8835; peggi@superlink.net; www.rockingham.net; (c) Somerset

Joint/ 1964/ Board of Trustees/NJ Dept of Environmental Protection, Parks and Forestry Division/ staff: 1(f); 1(p); 50(v)/ members: 300/publication: *The Sundial*

HISTORIC SITE; HISTORICAL SOCIETY; HISTORY MUSEUM; HOUSE MUSEUM; LIVING HISTORY/OUTDOOR MUSEUM; PRESIDENTIAL SITE: Promotes, preserves and interprets Rockingham and the site of General George Washington's 1783 stay.

PROGRAMS: Community Outreach; Exhibits; Garden Tours; Guided Tours; Interpretation; Living History; Publication; School-Based Curriculum

COLLECTIONS: [Late 18th-early 19th c] Period furniture, ceramics, linens, textiles, art and decorative arts.

HOURS: Yr W-Sa 10-12/1-4, Su 1-4

ADMISSION: Donations accepted

RAMSEY

5612
Ramsey Historical Association
538 Island Rd, Old Stone House Museum, 07446 [PO Box 76, 07446]; (p) (201) 825-1126; (c) Bergen

Private non-profit/ 1956/ staff: 18(v)/ members: 203

HISTORIC SITE; HISTORICAL SOCIETY; HOUSE MUSEUM: Manages, preserves and operates the Old Stone House Museum and Junior Museum.

PROGRAMS: Annual Meeting; Community Outreach; Exhibits; Family Programs; Guided Tours; Lectures; Research Library/Archives; School-Based Curriculum

COLLECTIONS: [1865-1940] Dutch Colonial farmhouse/tavern with period furnishing.

HOURS: Apr-June, Sept-Oct, Dec Selected Su 2-4

ADMISSION: Donations accepted

RIDGEWOOD

5613
Ridgewood Historical Society, Inc.
650 E Glen Ave, 07450; (p) (201) 447-3242; (c) Bergen

Private non-profit/ 1949/ staff: 20(v)/ members: 110

HISTORIC SITE; HISTORICAL SOCIETY; HISTORY MUSEUM: Preserves the objects, artifacts and documents significant to Bergen County's history and culture.

PROGRAMS: Annual Meeting; Exhibits; Family Programs; Guided Tours; Research Library/Archives; School-Based Curriculum

COLLECTIONS: [19th c] One room schoolhouse, Victorian parlor and kitchen, and historical artifacts from Dutch, Revolutionary and Civil War eras.

HOURS: May-Oct Su 2:30-4:30 and by appt

ADMISSION: No charge

RINGWOOD

5614
Forges and Manor of Ringwood, The
1304 Sloatsburg Rd, 07456; (p) (973) 962-2240; (f) (973) 962-2247; (c) Passaic

State/ 1939/ Division of Parks and Forestry/ staff: 2(f); 1(p); 2(v)

HISTORIC SITE: Interprets Cooper-Hewitt Family history.

PROGRAMS: Community Outreach; Concerts; Exhibits; Garden Tours; Guided Tours; Interpretation; Reenactments; Research Library/Archives; School-Based Curriculum

COLLECTIONS: [1740-1936] Documents, furnishings, costumes, firearms and sculptures.

HOURS: Yr W-Su 10-4

ADMISSION: $3

RIVER EDGE

5615
Campbell-Christie House
1201 Main St, 07661 [Bergen County Historical Society, PO Box 55, 07661]; (p) (201) 343-9492, (201) 646-2780; www.carroll.com/bchs/cchousehistory.html

HOUSE MUSEUM

5616
Demarest House
1207 Main St, 07661; (p) (201) 487-1739; www.carroll.com/bchs/cchousehistory.html

HOUSE MUSEUM

5617
Steuben House
1209 Main St, 07661; (p) (201) 487-1739; www.carroll.com/bchs/cchousehistory.html

HOUSE MUSEUM

RIVERTON

5618
Historical Society of Riverton
16 Carriage House Ln, 08077; (p) (609) 786-8660; (f) (609) 786-8660; www.riverton.k12.nj.us; (c) Burlington

Borough/ 1972/ staff: 12(v)/ members: 140

HISTORICAL SOCIETY: Promotes history and architecture of Riverton.

PROGRAMS: Annual Meeting; Film/Video; Guided Tours; Lectures

COLLECTIONS: [1851-1941] Clothing, books, photos, family history, local news articles.

ROSELLE

5619
Abraham Clark Memorial House
Chestnut St and W 9th Ave, 07203-1926; (p) (908) 486-1783; www.Roselle-Park.nj.us/

HOUSE MUSEUM

5620
Roselle Historical Society
116 E Fourth Ave, 07203; (p) (908) 245-9010; (c) Union

Private non-profit/ 1972/ staff: 10(v)/ members: 15

HISTORICAL SOCIETY: Collects and publicizes the history of Roselle.

PROGRAMS: Family Programs; Film/Video; Lectures

COLLECTIONS: [1664-present] Photographs, maps, personal histories, town records, artifacts and newspaper accounts.

ROSELLE PARK

5621
Roselle Park Historical Society
9 W Grant Ave, 07204; (p) (908) 245-1776; RPMuseum@aol.com; www.rosellepark.org/history/museum.htm; (c) Union

City/ 1972/ staff: 12(p); 12(v)/ members: 30/publication: The Family Album

HISTORICAL SOCIETY; HISTORY MUSEUM: Collects, preserves and exhibits memorabilia, documents, and photos relating to Roselle Park history.

PROGRAMS: Exhibits; Film/Video; Lectures; Publication; Research Library/Archives

COLLECTIONS: [17th-20th c] Revolutionary, Civil War and other US military memorabilia. Artifacts on Thomas Edison, early radio station WDY, architecture, photographs and the railroads.

HOURS: Yr M 7-9, W 10-2 and by appt

ADMISSION: No charge

RUTHERFORD

5622
Meadowlands Museum
91 Crane Ave, 07070 [PO Box 3, 07070]; (p) (201) 935-1175; (f) (201) 935-9791; (c) Bergen

Private non-profit/ 1960/ staff: 1(p); 12(v)/ members: 323

HISTORY MUSEUM: Collects, preserves and exhibits history and culture of NJ Meadowlands communities.

PROGRAMS: Annual Meeting; Exhibits; Family Programs; Guided Tours; Lectures

COLLECTIONS: [1850-1930s] Clothing, textiles, house wares, photographs, maps, manuscripts, posters, dolls, toys, local area rocks and minerals.

HOURS: Su 2-4, M,W, Sa 1-4

ADMISSION: Donations accepted

SALEM

5623
Salem County Historical Society
79-83 Market St, 08079; (p) (609) 935-5004; (f) (609) 935-0728; www.salemcounty.com/historicalsociety/index.html; (c) Salem

Private non-profit/ 1884/ Board of Officers and Trustees/ staff: 1(f); 1(p); 50(v)/ members: 800

HISTORIC SITE; HISTORICAL SOCIETY; HISTORY MUSEUM: Documents, preserves, interprets and perpetuates Salem County's heritage.

PROGRAMS: Annual Meeting; Community Outreach; Exhibits; Garden Tours; Guided Tours; Lectures; Research Library/Archives; School-Based Curriculum

COLLECTIONS: [17th-20th c] Regional furniture, fine folk and decorative arts, South Jersey glass, costumes, textiles, toys and dolls.

HOURS: Yr T-F, 2nd Sa of the month 12-4

ADMISSION: $3

SCOTCH PLAINS

5624
Historical Society of Scotch Plains and Fanwood
1840 E Front St, 07076 [PO Box 261, 07076]; (p) (908) 232-1199, (908) 322-6700; (f) (908) 232-2212; www.scotchplainsnj.com; (c) Union

Private non-profit/ 1972/ Board of Trustees/ staff: 22(v)/ members: 100/publication: Under the Blue Hills; Images of America: Scotch Plains and Fanwood

GARDEN; HISTORIC SITE; HISTORICAL SOCIETY; HOUSE MUSEUM: Preserves local history and depicts colonial/Victorian life in Scotch Plains and Fanwood.

PROGRAMS: Annual Meeting; Community Outreach; Exhibits; Family Programs; Film/Video; Garden Tours; Guided Tours; Interpretation; Lectures; Living History; Publication; Research Library/Archives

COLLECTIONS: [18th-19th c] Garments and artifacts depicting life in colonial and Victorian times.

HOURS: March-Dec 1st Su of the month 2-4

ADMISSION: No charge

5625
Osborn Cannonball House Museum
1840 Front St, 07076 [PO Box 261, 07076]; (p) (908) 232-1199; (f) (908) 232-2212; bousquet@westfieldnj.com; www.westfieldnj.com/bousquet

1740/ staff: 10(v)

HOUSE MUSEUM

COLLECTIONS: [Colonial] Garments; Early American, Revolution artifacts.

HOURS: Yr

SEWELL

5626
James and Ann Whitall House/Fort Mercer/Red Bank Battlefield
100 Hessian Ave, 08080 [6 Blackwood/Barnsboro Rd, 08080]; (p) (609) 853-5120; (f) (609) 468-4497; www.co.gloucester.nj.us/whitall.htm; (c) Gloucester

County/ 1979/ Parks and Recreation/ staff: 1(f), 45(v)/publication: *Whitall Family Daybook*

GARDEN; HISTORIC SITE; HOUSE MUSEUM; LIVING HISTORY/OUTDOOR MUSEUM

PROGRAMS: Community Outreach; Facility Rental; Family Programs; Festivals; Garden Tours; Guided Tours; Interpretation; Lectures; Living History; Reenactments; School-Based Curriculum

COLLECTIONS: [18th c] Quaker family life, Red Bank battle and field hospital.

HOURS: Yr W-F 9-12/1-4; Apr-Oct Sa-Su

ADMISSION: No charge

SHORT HILLS

5627
Millburn-Short Hills Historical Society
Westbound Short Hills train station building, 07078 [PO Box 234, 07078]; (p) (973) 564-9519; (f) (973) 564-9519; LKRanieri@home.com; www.community.nj.com/cc/millburn-shhistsoc; (c) Essex

Private non-profit/ 1975/ Board of Directors/ staff: 1(v)/ members: 500

HISTORICAL SOCIETY; HISTORY MUSEUM: Collects, preserves and houses local historical artifacts.

PROGRAMS: Annual Meeting; Community Outreach; Exhibits; Lectures; Research Library/Archives

COLLECTIONS: [1870-present] Early newspapers, photos, family histories, maps, oral histories, books and local architectural history.

HOURS: Yr T 5:30-7:30, W 3:30-5:30, 1st Su of the month 2-4

SHREWSBURY

5628
Shrewsbury Historical Society
419 Sycamore Ave, 07702 [PO Box 333, 07702]; (p) (732) 530-7974; (c) Monmouth

Private non-profit/ 1973/ staff: 2(f); 8(v)/ members: 96

HISTORICAL SOCIETY; HISTORY MUSEUM; RESEARCH CENTER: Preserves local history.

PROGRAMS: Annual Meeting; Exhibits; Garden Tours; Research Library/Archives

COLLECTIONS: [18th c] Books, legal documents, maps and periodicals focusing on local, county and state history.

HOURS: Yr T, Th, Sa 10-2

ADMISSION: Donations accepted

SOMERS POINT

5629
Atlantic County Historical Society, The
907 Shore Rd, 08244 [PO Box 301, 08244]; (p) (609) 927-5218; (c) Atlantic

Private non-profit/ 1913/ Board of Directors/ staff: 40(v)/ members: 500/publication: *The Atlantic County Historical Society Yearbook*

HISTORICAL SOCIETY: Promotes history and genealogy in Atlantic County and southern NJ.

PROGRAMS: Annual Meeting; Festivals; Guided Tours; Lectures; Publication; Research Library/Archives

COLLECTIONS: [1695-present] Land documents, vital records, genealogical data, photographs, lantern slides, glass plate negatives, Native American artifacts and Victoriana.

HOURS: Yr

5630
Risley Homestead
8 Virginia Ave, 08224 [PO Box 301, 08224]; (p) (609) 641-8976, (609) 927-5218; (c) Atlantic

Private non-profit/ 1989/ Atlantic County Historical Society, Executive Board/ staff: 1(f); 10(v)

HOUSE MUSEUM: Collects and preserves historical materials of Atlantic County and Southern NJ.

PROGRAMS: Annual Meeting; Festivals; Guided Tours; Interpretation; Lectures; Living History

COLLECTIONS: [Late 1800-1940]

HOURS: Apr-Nov Sa 10-4, Su 1-5

ADMISSION: No charge

5631
Somers Mansion
Shore Rd at Traffic Circle, 08244; (p) (609) 927-2212

HOUSE MUSEUM

SOMERSET

5632
Blackwells Mills Canal House
Canal Rd & Blackwells Mills Rd, 08873 [Meadows Found, 1289 Easton Ave, 08873];

(p) (732) 873-2958; www.themeadows foundation. pair.com

5633
Hageman Farm
209 S Middlebush Rd, 08873 [Meadows Found, 1289 Easton Ave, 08873]; (p) (732) 873-8718; www.themeadowsfoundation.pair.com

5634
Van Lieuw-Suydam House
S Middlebush Rd, 08873 [Meadows Found, 1289 Easton Ave, 08873]; (p) (908) 873-3417; www.themeadowsfoundation.pair.com

5635
Van Wickle House
1289 Eon Ave, 08873 [1289 Easton Ave, 08873]; (p) (732) 828-7418, (732) 249-6770; www.themeadowsfoundation.pair.com

1722/ Public non-profit

5636
Wycoff-Earretson House
S Middlebush Rd, 08873 [Meadows Found, 1289 Easton Ave, 08873]; (p) (732) 873-1792; www.themeadowsfoundation.pair.com

SOMERVILLE

5637
Dutch Parsonage
65 Washington Pl, 08876; (p) (908) 725-1015

5638
Friends of the Wallace House and Old Dutch Parsonage
38 Washington Pl, 08876 [PO Box 225, 08876]; (p) (908) 725-1015; (f) (908) 725-1015; (c) Somerset

State/ 1982/ staff: 1(f); 1(p)/ members: 65/publication: *Washington Place Dispatch*

HISTORICAL SOCIETY: Preserves and interprets cultural and material heritage of Wallace House and old Dutch Parsonage.

PROGRAMS: Annual Meeting; Community Outreach; Concerts; Facility Rental; Family Programs; Film/Video; Guided Tours; Lectures; Living History; Publication; Reenactments; School-Based Curriculum

COLLECTIONS: [1720-1780] American decorative arts, home furnishings and reproduction items.

HOURS: Yr W-Su 10-12 and 1-4

5639
Wallace House
38 Washington Pl, 08876; (p) (908) 725-1015

SOUTH ORANGE

5640
New Jersey Catholic Historical Records Commission
Fahy Hall, Seton Hall Univ, 07079 [History Dept, Seton Hall Univ, 07079]; (p) (973) 275-2773; (f) (973) 761-7798; mahonejo@shu.edu; (c) Essex

Private non-profit/ 1976/ staff: 1(p)

HISTORICAL SOCIETY: Collects, preserves and disseminates knowledge about Catholicism in NJ.

PROGRAMS: Exhibits; Lectures

5641
Seton Hall University Department of Archives
405 S Orange Ave, 07079; (p) (973) 761-9476, (973) 275-2378; (f) (973) 761-9551; (c) Essex

Private non-profit/ 1856/ Dean Arthur Hafner/ staff: 4(f); 6(p); 4(v)

GENEALOGICAL SOCIETY; HOUSE MUSEUM: Collects all the archives of Seton Hall Univ and the Archdiocese of Newark.

PROGRAMS: Exhibits; Film/Video; Lectures

HOURS: Yr M-F 9:30-4

ADMISSION: No charge

5642
Seton Hall University Museum
Fahy Hall, S Orange Ave, 07079; (p) (973) 761-9543; (f) (973) 761-9596; Krafther@lanmail.shu.edu; (c) Essex

Private non-profit/ 1960/ staff: 1(p); 2(v)/publication: *The Lenape-Delaware Indian Heritage; The Dutch, the Indians and the Quest for Copper*

HISTORY MUSEUM; RESEARCH CENTER: Promotes history of Lanape or Delaware Indians and prehistory of NJ and neighboring states.

PROGRAMS: Community Outreach; Exhibits; Guided Tours; Lectures; Publication

COLLECTIONS: [10,000 BC-1700 AD] Stone tools and weapons, ethnographic objects, prints and books relating to Native Americans.

SOUTH PLAINFIELD

5643
South Plainfield Historical Society
S Plainfield High School, 07080 [PO Box 11, 07080]; (p) (908) 756-9654; Kintut@erols.com; (c) Middlesex

City/ 1976/ Council/ members: 120

HISTORICAL SOCIETY: Collects town history.

PROGRAMS: Community Outreach; Exhibits; Lectures; Living History

COLLECTIONS: [19th c] Central Railroad of NJ Rail Car #1169.

SPRING LAKE

5644
Spring Lake Historical Society
Warren Ave & 5th, 07762 [PO Box 703, 07762]; (p) (732) 449-0772; www.springlake.org/home.html; (c) Monmouth

City/ 1977/ staff: 1(f); 1(p); 15(v)/ members: 274/publication: *Spring Lake: An Early History*

HISTORICAL SOCIETY; HISTORY MUSEUM; RESEARCH CENTER: Preserves history of Spring Lake.

PROGRAMS: Annual Meeting; Concerts; Exhibits; Family Programs; Film/Video; Guided Tours; Publication; Research Library/Archives

COLLECTIONS: [1800s-1970s] Furniture, clothes, pictures, Native American artifacts, and newspapers.

HOURS: Yr Th 10-12, Su 1:30-3:30 and by appt

ADMISSION: No charge

STANHOPE

5645
Waterloo Foundation For The Arts, Inc.
525 Waterloo Rd, 07874; (p) (973) 347-0900; (f) (973) 347-3573; info@waterloo.org; www.waterloovillage.org; (c) Sussex

Private non-profit/ 1964/ Waterloo Foundation For The Arts/ staff: 20(f); 50(p); 15(v)/ members: 250

LIVING HISTORY/OUTDOOR MUSEUM: Manages Waterloo, a 19th century canal village, a recreated Lenni Lenape Indian village, and 1825 farm site.

PROGRAMS: Community Outreach; Concerts; Elder's Programs; Facility Rental; Family Programs; Festivals; Guided Tours; Interpretation; Lectures; Living History; School-Based Curriculum

COLLECTIONS: [1625-1880s] Historic homes, waterpowered mills, store, canal structures, farm buildings, furnishings, tools and Lenni Lenape Indian artifacts.

HOURS: Apr-May M-F 10-4; June-Oct W-F 10-4, Sa-Su 11-5; Nov W-F 10-4

ADMISSION: $9, Children $7, Seniors $8

SUMMIT

5646
Carter House
92 Butler Pkwy, 07901 [PO Box 464, 07902-0464]; (p) (908) 277-1747

1741/ staff: 18(v)

HOUSE MUSEUM

COLLECTIONS: [1740-present] WWII Congressional Medal of Honor; costumes; maps; books; newspapers; postcards; genealogical records; scrapbooks; yearbooks; tax maps; biographical files.

5647
Reeves-Reed Arboretum, Inc.
165 Hobart Ave, 07901-2908; (p) (908) 273-8787; (f) (908) 273-6869; reeves-reedarboretum@juno.com; www.reeves-reedarboretum.org; (c) Union

Joint/ 1974/ City; Private non-profit/ staff: 150(v)/ members: 969

GARDEN; HISTORIC SITE; LIVING HISTORY/OUTDOOR MUSEUM

PROGRAMS: Concerts; Exhibits; Facility Rental; Family Programs; Festivals; Garden Tours; Guided Tours; Interpretation; Lectures; Research Library/Archives; School-Based Curriculum

HOURS: Yr Daily Dawn-Dusk

ADMISSION: Grounds free

5648
Summit Historical Society Carter House Museum
90 Butler Pkwy, 07902 [PO Box 464, 07902]; (p) (908) 277-1747; pemip@aol.com; (c) Union

Private non-profit/ 1949/ staff: 20(v)/ members: 400/publication: *Wish You Were Here: Summit, NJ*

GENEALOGICAL SOCIETY; HISTORIC SITE; HISTORICAL SOCIETY; HISTORY MUSEUM; HOUSE MUSEUM; RESEARCH CENTER: Promotes and preserves local history and makes materials available to the public through displays and archives in a 1740s house.

PROGRAMS: Annual Meeting; Community Outreach; Exhibits; Family Programs; Film/Video; Guided Tours; Interpretation; Lectures; Publication; Research Library/Archives; School-Based Curriculum

COLLECTIONS: [1740s-present] Genealogy records, maps, biography archives, photographs, postcards, city directories, period clothing, memorabilia, historic house survey, school yearbooks, newspapers.

HOURS: Yr T 9:30-12, W 1:30-4, one Su/mo, and by appt

ADMISSION: No charge

TENNENT

5649
Friends of Monmouth Battlefield, Inc.
Monmouth Battlefield State Park, 07763 [PO Box 122, 07763]; (p) (732) 951-9142; (f) (732) 951-9142; MonmouthB@aol.com; (c) Monmouth

Private non-profit/ 1990/ staff: 25(v)/ members: 155/publication: *Men of Color at the Battle of Monmouth; The Battle of Monmouth*

HISTORIC PRESERVATION AGENCY; HOUSE MUSEUM; LIVING HISTORY/OUTDOOR MUSEUM: Protects and promotes historical development of Monmouth Battlefield State Park/National Landmark.

PROGRAMS: Annual Meeting; Exhibits; Family Programs; Guided Tours; Interpretation; Lectures; Living History; Publication; Reenactments

COLLECTIONS: [Late 18th c] Artifacts, maps, weapons and household furnishings from the American Revolution.

HOURS: Fall-Winter Daily 9-4:30; Spring-Summer Daily 9-8:30

ADMISSION: No charge

TETERBORO

5650
Aviation Hall of Fame and Museum of New Jersey
400 Fred Wehran Dr, 07608; (p) (201) 288-6344; (f) (201) 288-5666; (c) Bergen

Private non-profit/ 1972/ Board of Trustees/ staff: 3(f); 4(p); 63(v)/ members: 1223

HISTORY MUSEUM; LIVING HISTORY/OUTDOOR MUSEUM; RESEARCH CENTER

PROGRAMS: Annual Meeting; Exhibits; Facility Rental; Guided Tours; Lectures; Research Library/Archives

COLLECTIONS: Balloons, jet and rocket engines, satellite development, astronauts uniforms, military equipment, fine art, models and a M.A.S.H unit.

HOURS: Yr T-Su 10-4

ADMISSION: $5, Children $3, Seniors $3

TITUSVILLE

5651
Howell Living History Farm
Valley Rd, off Rt 29, 2 mi S of Lambertville, 08560 [101 Hunter Rd, 08560]; (p) (609) 737-3299; (f) (609) 737-6524; thefarm@ bellatlantic.net; www.howellfarm.org; (c) Mercer

County/ Park Commission/ staff: 7(f); 8(p); 100(v)/ members: 200

LIVING HISTORY/OUTDOOR MUSEUM: Preserves early farming lifestyle.

PROGRAMS: Annual Meeting; Community Outreach; Exhibits; Facility Rental; Family Programs; Festivals; Interpretation; Living History

COLLECTIONS: [1900-1910] Farming implements, household articles, period clothing and oral histories.

HOURS: Late Jan-early Dec T-Sa 10-4, Su 12-4

ADMISSION: No

5652
Washington Crossing State Park-Johnson Ferry House
355 Washington Crossing/Permington Rd, 08560 [355 Washington Crossing-Pennington Rd, 08560]; (p) (609) 737-2515

1740/ Division of Parks and Forests/ staff: 1(f); 1(p); 2(v)

COLLECTIONS: [1750s] Delaware Valley Region artifacts.

HOURS: Yr

TOMS RIVER

5653
Ocean County Historical Society
26 Hadley Ave, 08754 [PO Box 2191, 08754-2191]; (p) (732) 341-1880; (f) (732) 341-4372; www.oceancountyhistory.org; (c) Ocean

Private non-profit/ 1950/ Board of Trustees/ staff: 4(f); 2(p); 60(v)/ members: 625/publication: *Along the Toms River; Chickaree in the Wall: One Room Schools in Ocean County*

HISTORICAL SOCIETY; HISTORY MUSEUM; RESEARCH CENTER: Maintains a museum and library/research center.

PROGRAMS: Annual Meeting; Community Outreach; Exhibits; Festivals; Guided Tours; Publication; Reenactments; Research Library/Archives; School-Based Curriculum

COLLECTIONS: [Late 19th-early 20th c] Native American items, early industrial artifacts, historic clothing, textiles, aviation materials, furniture, paintings, memorabilia, archives, photographs and postcards.

HOURS: (Research Center) T-Th 1-4, Sa 10-1; (Guided Tours) T, Th 1-3, Sa 10-4

ADMISSION: $2

5654
Ocean County Library
Bishop Building, 101 Washington St, 08753; (p) (732) 349-6200; (f) (732) 349-0478; ljbrown@oceancounty.lib.nj.us; www.ocean county.lib.nj.us; (c) Ocean

County/ 1924/ Library Commission/ staff: 4(f); 2(p)

LIBRARY AND/OR ARCHIVES: Historical and genealogical materials about Ocean County and New Jersey.

PROGRAMS: Exhibits; Family Programs; Lectures

COLLECTIONS: [17th c-present] Books, atlases, newspaper microfilms, CD-ROMs and Internet access.

HOURS: Yr M, W 1-9, T, Th-Sa 1-5

ADMISSION: No charge

TRENTON

5655
Contemporary Victorian Townhouse Museum
176 W State St, 08608; (p) (609) 392-9727; (c) Mercer

Private non-profit/ 1897/ The Contemporary, Inc./ staff: 1(f); 130(v)/ members: 140

HISTORIC PRESERVATION AGENCY; HISTORIC SITE; HISTORY MUSEUM; HOUSE MUSEUM; RESEARCH CENTER

PROGRAMS: Facility Rental; Guided Tours; Interpretation; Lectures; Research Library/Archives; School-Based Curriculum

COLLECTIONS: [19th c] Victorian Era furniture, clothing, woman's club records, fine and decorative arts.

HOURS: Yr 3rd Su 2-4 and by appt

ADMISSION: No charge

5656
Italianate Villa
Cadvalader Park, Parkside Ave, 08608 [319 E State St, 08608]; (p) (609) 989-3632; (f) (609) 989-3624

5657
New Jersey Historical Commission
225 W State St, 08625 [PO Box 305, 08625-0305]; (p) (609) 292-6062; (f) (609) 633-8168; marc.mappen@state.sos.nj.us; (c) Mercer

State/ 1967/ staff: 7(f)

HISTORICAL SOCIETY

PROGRAMS: Annual Meeting; Lectures

HOURS: Yr M-F 8:30-4:30

ADMISSION: No charge

5658
New Jersey State Museum
205 W State St, 08625 [PO Box 530, 08625]; (p) (609) 292-6464; (f) (609) 599-4098; www.state.nj.us/state/museum/musidx.html; (c) Mercer

State/ 1890/ staff: 35(f); 11(p); 120(v)/ members: 650

ART MUSEUM; HISTORY MUSEUM: Collects, exhibits and interprets in cultural history, archaeology, ethnology, fine arts and natural history.

PROGRAMS: Annual Meeting; Concerts; Exhibits; Facility Rental; Family Programs; Guided Tours; Interpretation; Lectures; Research Library/Archives; School-Based Curriculum; Theatre

COLLECTIONS: [17th c-present] Decorative arts objects made or used in New Jersey such as ceramics, glass, metalware and furniture.

Fine art collection of paintings, sculptures, prints, drawings and photographs. Items from natural history, paleontological and geological sciences describing New Jersey's environment. Data and artifacts relating to prehistoric New Jersey and other areas of North America.

HOURS: Yr T-Sa 9-4:45, Su 12-5

ADMISSION: No charge

5659
Old Barracks Museum
Barrack St, 08608; (p) (609) 396-1776; (f) (609) 777-4000; barracks@voicenet.com; www.barracks.org; (c) Mercer

Joint/ 1902/ Old Barracks Assoc/State/ staff: 16(f); 10(p)/ members: 579

HISTORIC SITE; HISTORY MUSEUM; LIVING HISTORY/OUTDOOR MUSEUM: Promotes and preserves colonial and revolutionary era NJ.

PROGRAMS: Annual Meeting; Community Outreach; Elder's Programs; Exhibits; Facility Rental; Family Programs; Interpretation; Lectures; Living History; Reenactments; School-Based Curriculum

COLLECTIONS: [18th-19th c]

HOURS: Yr Daily 10-5

ADMISSION: $6, Student $3, Seniors $3

5660
Preservation New Jersey, Inc.
30 S Warren St, 08608; (p) (609) 392-6409; (f) (609) 392-6418; info@preservationnj.org; www.preservationnj.org; (c) Mercer

Private non-profit/ 1978/ Board of Directors/ staff: 2(f); 1(p)/ members: 1000/publication: *Preservation Services Directory; Preserving New Jersey: A Handbook for Historic Preservation*

HISTORIC PRESERVATION AGENCY: Promotes and protects the state's historic resources, communities and landscapes.

PROGRAMS: Annual Meeting; Community Outreach; Guided Tours; Lectures; Publication; Research Library/Archives

COLLECTIONS: [Late 20th c] Newsletters, local sites, ordinances.

HOURS: Yr M-F 9-5

ADMISSION: No charge

5661
William Trent House Museum
15 Market St, 08611; (p) (609) 989-3027; (f) (609) 278-7890; (c) Mercer

City/ 1936/ staff: 3(f); 3(p); 10(v)/ members: 200

HISTORIC SITE; HOUSE MUSEUM

PROGRAMS: Annual Meeting; Community Outreach; Facility Rental; Family Programs; Festivals; Guided Tours; Interpretation; Lectures; Research Library/Archives; School-Based Curriculum

COLLECTIONS: [1680-1730] Colonial furniture, decorative arts, domestic objects, tools.

HOURS: Yr Daily 12:30-4 and by appt

ADMISSION: $2.50, Student $2, Children $1,

UNION

5662
Liberty Hall Museum
1003 Morris Ave, 07083; (p) (908) 527-0400; (f) (908) 352-8915; liberty-hall@juno.com; www.libertyhallnj.org; (c) Union

Private non-profit/ 1997/ Liberty Hall Foundation/ staff: 3(f); 8(p); 5(v)/ members: 75

GARDEN; HISTORIC SITE; HOUSE MUSEUM

PROGRAMS: Facility Rental; Family Programs; Festivals; Garden Tours; Guided Tours; Interpretation; Living History; Reenactments

COLLECTIONS: [1770-1990] Personal items, decorative arts, furnishings, household goods, family photos, papers and memorabilia.

HOURS: Apr-Dec W-Su 10-4

ADMISSION: $5, Children $3, Seniors $4; Under 6 free

5663
Union Township Historical Society
909 Caldwell Ave, 07083; (p) (908) 964-9047; (c) Union

Private non-profit/ 1957/ staff: 5(p); 10(v)/ members: 65/publication: *General William Maxwell; The New Jersey Brigade*

HISTORIC SITE; HISTORICAL SOCIETY: Maintains the Rev James and Hannah Caldwell Parsonage.

PROGRAMS: Annual Meeting; Community Outreach; Elder's Programs; Exhibits; Family Programs; Film/Video; Guided Tours; Interpretation; Lectures; Publication; Research Library/Archives; School-Based Curriculum

COLLECTIONS: [18th c] Photos, clothing, furniture, maps, military weapons, gravestone rubbings, pictures of Hannah and James Caldwell.

HOURS: Sept-Nov, Feb, Apr, June Su 1-4:30 and by appt

WALL

5664
Old Wall Historical Society
1701 New Bedford Rd, Allgor Barkalow Museum, 07719 [PO Box 1203, 07719]; (p) (732) 974-1430; (f) (732) 449-7888; (c) Monmouth

Private non-profit/ 1972/ staff: 12(v)/ members: 100

HISTORICAL SOCIETY; HOUSE MUSEUM

PROGRAMS: Annual Meeting; Community Outreach; Exhibits; Guided Tours

COLLECTIONS: [1830-1840] Period furniture; one-room schoolhouse.

HOURS: Yr Su 1-4, and by appt

ADMISSION: Donations accepted

WALPACK

5665
Walpack Historical Society
3 Main St, Walpack Ctr, 07881 [PO Box 3, 07881]; (p) (973) 948-6671; (c) Sussex

Private non-profit/ 1984/ staff: 12(v)/ members: 215/publication: *Over The Mountain: A Place Called Home*

GENEALOGICAL SOCIETY; HISTORIC PRESERVATION AGENCY; HISTORIC SITE; HISTORICAL SOCIETY; HOUSE MUSEUM: Preserves history and heritage of NJ Old Mine Road area and French and Indian War forts of upper DE River.

PROGRAMS: Annual Meeting; Community Outreach; Exhibits; Guided Tours; Interpretation; Lectures; Publication; Reenactments

COLLECTIONS: [1627-present] Letters, ledgers, tax records, oral histories, photos and memorabilia.

HOURS: May-Oct by appt; (Meetings) May-Oct Su 1-5

ADMISSION: No charge

WARREN

5666
AT&T Archives
5 Reinman Rd, 07059; (p) (908) 226-2386; (f) (908) 756-2105; (c) Union

Private for-profit/ 1921/ AT&T Corp/ staff: 14(f)

CORPORATE ARCHIVES/MUSEUM: Collects corporate history.

COLLECTIONS: [1876-present] Documents, photos, film, videos and artifacts of AT&T, Western Electric Co. and Bell Telephone Laboratories.

HOURS: Not open to the public

WAYNE

5667
Dey Mansion/Washington's Headquarters Museum
199 Totowa Rd, 07470; (p) (973) 696-1776; (f) (973) 696-1365; (c) Passaic

County/ 1934/ Parks and Recreation Dept and Board of Chosen Freeholders/ staff: 5(p); 3(v)/publication: *Dey Mansion Dispatch*

HISTORIC SITE; HISTORY MUSEUM; HOUSE MUSEUM; LIVING HISTORY/OUTDOOR MUSEUM; PRESIDENTIAL SITE

PROGRAMS: Exhibits; Facility Rental; Family Programs; Guided Tours; Lectures; Living History; Publication; Reenactments; Research Library/Archives; School-Based Curriculum

COLLECTIONS: [1740-1800] American/European furniture, textiles, paintings.

HOURS: Yr W-F 1-4, Sa-Su 10-12 and 1-4

ADMISSION: $1; Under 10 free

5668
Van Riper-Hopper House
533 Berdan Ave, 07470; (p) (973) 694-7192; www.waynetownship.com/history

HOUSE MUSEUM

WEST CALDWELL

5669
Historical Society of West Caldwell
289 Westville Ave, 07007 [PO Box 1701, 07007-1701]; (p) (973) 226-8976; (c) Essex

Private non-profit/ 1977/ staff: 12(v)/ members: 90

HISTORICAL SOCIETY; HOUSE MUSEUM: Restores Crane House; preserves local history and structures.

PROGRAMS: Annual Meeting; Community Outreach; Exhibits; Guided Tours; Interpretation; Lectures; Reenactments; Research Library/Archives

COLLECTIONS: [18th-20th c] Crane family furniture, records and memorabilia; paper records of West Essex communities; Norwood family records, local newspapers, clothing, costumes, textiles and accessories.

HOURS: Oct-June 2nd Th of month

WEST LONG BRANCH

5670
West Long Branch Historical Society
[PO Box 151, 07764]; (p) (732) 222-7375; (c) Monmouth

Private non-profit/ 1976/ members: 36/publication: *History of West Long Branch; Norwood Park: An Exclusive Summer Cottage Colony*

HISTORICAL SOCIETY

PROGRAMS: Annual Meeting; Exhibits; Lectures; Publication

WEST ORANGE

5671
Edison National Historic Site
Glenmont-Llewellyn Park, 07052 [Main St and Lakeside Ave, 07052]; (p) (973) 736-0550; www.nps.gov/edis

WESTFIELD

5672
Miller-Cory House Museum
614 Mountain Ave, 07091 [PO Box 455, 07091-0455]; (p) (908) 232-1776; (f) (908) 232-1740; mc@westfieldnj.com; www.westfieldnj.com; (c) Union

Private non-profit/ 1972/ Westfield Historical Society/ staff: 1(p); 60(v)/ members: 87/publication: *Groaning Board Cookbook*

HOUSE MUSEUM; LIVING HISTORY/OUTDOOR MUSEUM: Depicts colonial life.

PROGRAMS: Community Outreach; Concerts; Festivals; Guided Tours; Interpretation; Living History; Publication; School-Based Curriculum

COLLECTIONS: [1740-1820] Furnishing of colonial farm house, cooking utensils, farm tools and implements.

HOURS: Mid Sept-mid June Su 2-5, M-F by appt; Jan-Feb Su 2-4

ADMISSION: $2, Student $0.50; Under 6 free

5673
Westfield Historical Society
425 E Broad St, 07091 [PO Box 613, 07091-0613]; (p) (908) 789-4047; www.westfieldnj.com/history; (c) Union

Private non-profit/ 1969/ Board of Trustees/ staff: 50(v)/ members: 600

HISTORICAL SOCIETY: Collects and preserves local historical items.

PROGRAMS: Annual Meeting; Exhibits; Guided Tours; Lectures; Living History; Research Library/Archives

COLLECTIONS: [18th c-present] Newspapers, maps, photos, postcards, documents, artifacts, posters, flags, historic uniforms and attire, tools and audio-visual material.

HOURS: Yr M-W 8-12

ADMISSION: No charge

WESTHAMPTON TOWNSHIP

5674
Peachfield Plantation
180 Burrs Rd, 08060-9618; (p) (609) 267-6996

WHIPPANY

5675
Jewish Historical Society of Metrowest
901 Route 10 East, 07981-1156; (p) (973) 884-4800; (f) (973) 428-8237; jsettanni@ujfmetrowest.org; www.jhsmw.org; (c) Morris

Private non-profit/ 1990/ staff: 2(f); 2(p); 12(v)/ members: 400

HISTORICAL SOCIETY; RESEARCH CENTER: Documents and preserves local history.

PROGRAMS: Annual Meeting; Community Outreach; Elder's Programs; Exhibits; Guided Tours; Lectures; Research Library/Archives

COLLECTIONS: [1751-present] Maps, memorabilia, institutional records, private manuscripts, photographs, audiovisual material, ephemera, oral histories, videotapes and microfilm covering community agencies, families and individuals.

HOURS: Yr M-F 9-5

ADMISSION: No charge

5676
Morris County Library, New Jersey Collection
30 E Hanover Ave, 07981; (p) (973) 285-6974; (f) (973) 285-6965; heagney@main.morris.org; www.gti.metlmocolib1.html; (c) Morris

County/ 1920/ staff: 1(f); 1(p)

LIBRARY AND/OR ARCHIVES

PROGRAMS: Research Library/Archives

COLLECTIONS: [1639-present] State documents; reference materials: books, periodicals, maps, atlases, vertical file material, manuscripts, monographs and microfilm.

HOURS: Yr M-F 9-9, Sa 9-5, Su 12-5; July-Aug Closed Su

ADMISSION: No charge

5677
Township of Hanover Landmark Commission
1000 Rte 10, 07927 [PO Box 250, 07927]; (p) (973) 428-2500; (f) (973) 428-4374; (c) Morris

1979/ Township of Hanover/ staff: 9(v)

HISTORIC PRESERVATION AGENCY: Preserves local landmarks.

PROGRAMS: Community Outreach; Festivals

COLLECTIONS: [1710] Books and artifacts.

HOURS: Yr Every 3rd Thursday 7:30; Closed July-Aug

WHITE HOUSE STATION

5678
Readington Township Museums
Route 523; Potterstown Rd; Dreahook Rd, 08889 [509 County Rd #523, 08889]; (p) (908) 534-4051, (908) 236-2327; (f) (908) 534-5909; toad@blast.net; (c) Hunterdon

City/ 1989/ Readington Township/ staff: 1(p); 25(v)

HISTORIC SITE; HOUSE MUSEUM; LIVING HISTORY/OUTDOOR MUSEUM: Maintains two house museums, a stone one-room schoolhouse and historic garden.

PROGRAMS: Exhibits; Family Programs; Guided Tours; Interpretation; Living History; School-Based Curriculum

COLLECTIONS: [1740-1830] 19th c style school benches and seats, stove, teacher's desk and antique books.

HOURS: May-Nov by appt

ADMISSION: No charge

WILDWOOD

5679
Wildwood Historical Society, Inc./George F. Boyer Historical Museum
3907 Pacific Ave, Holly Beach Mall, 08260; (p) (609) 523-0277; www.the-wildwoods.com; (c) Cape May

1963/ Wildwood Historical Society, Inc./ staff: 1(f); 1(p); 8(v)/ members: 400

HISTORICAL SOCIETY: Gathers, preserves and presents the history of Wildwoods.

PROGRAMS: Annual Meeting; Exhibits; Festivals; Film/Video; Guided Tours; Research Library/Archives

COLLECTIONS: [1880-present] Photos, artifacts and memorabilia.

HOURS: Oct-Apr Th-Su 10:30-2:30; May-Sept M-F 9:30-2:30, Sa-Su 10:30-2:30

ADMISSION: Donations accepted

WOODBURY

5680
Gloucester County Historical Society
17 Hunter St & 58 N Broad St, 08096 [17 Hunter St, 08096-4605]; (p) (856) 845-4771, (856) 848-8531; (f) (856) 845-0131; gchs@net-gate.com; www.rootsweb.com/~njglouce/gchs; (c) Gloucester

Private non-profit/ 1903/ Board of Trustees/ staff: 2(f); 2(p); 26(v)/ members: 1785

GENEALOGICAL SOCIETY; HISTORIC SITE; HISTORY MUSEUM; HOUSE MUSEUM: Collects, exhibits and interprets 18th-19th c life in Gloucester County and south Jersey area.

PROGRAMS: Annual Meeting; Community Outreach; Exhibits; Guided Tours; Publication; Research Library/Archives

COLLECTIONS: [17th c-present] Furnishings, ceramics, clothing, military arms and accouterments, decorative arts, Native American artifacts, farm tools, household items, glass, toys, quilts, samplers and uniforms; books, periodicals, microfilm, microfiche, maps, atlases,

photographs, county records, oral history tapes and vertical files.

HOURS: (Library) Yr M-F 1-4 T, F 6-9:30, 1st Su of month 2-5; (Museum) Yr M, W, F 1-4, 1st Sa of month 10-5

ADMISSION: $2; Library free

WOODSTOWN

5681
Pilesgrove Woodstown Historical Society
42 N Main St, 08098 [209 N Main St, 08098]; (p) (609) 769-4588, (609) 769-1147; (c) Salem

Private non-profit/ 1976/ staff: 25(v)/ members: 205

HISTORIC SITE; HISTORICAL SOCIETY; HISTORY MUSEUM; HOUSE MUSEUM: Preserves community history.

PROGRAMS: Annual Meeting; Community Outreach; Exhibits; Festivals; Guided Tours; Reenactments

COLLECTIONS: [19th-early 20th c]

HOURS: Yr Sa 1-3

ADMISSION: No charge

NEW MEXICO

ABIQUIU

5682
Florence Hawley Ellis Museum of Anthropology
US Hwy 84 12 Mi N of Abiquiu, 87510 [HC 77, Box 11, 87510]; (p) (505) 685-4333; (f) (505) 685-4519; www.newmexico ghostranch.org; (c) Rio Arriba

Private non-profit/ 1980/ Ghost Ranch Conf Center, Presbyterian Church/ staff: 2(f); 1(p); 2(v)

HISTORY MUSEUM: Promotes prehistoric and historic use of the Chame River Valley and the descendants of Tewa Puebloans and Spanish inhabitants.

PROGRAMS: Community Outreach; Exhibits; Guided Tours; Interpretation; Lectures; School-Based Curriculum

COLLECTIONS: [1100-1400] Ethnographic material from modern Tewa Pueblos, Spanish, Navajo, Apache, and Ute; prehistoric artifacts from Tewa sites and Gallina culture.

HOURS: Jan-Nov T-Sa 9-12 and 1-5

ADMISSION: $2, Children $1, Seniors $1

5683
Georgia O'Keeffe Foundation, The
#13 County Rd 165, 87510 [PO Box 40, 87510]; (p) (505) 685-4539; (f) (505) 685-4428; (c) Rio Arriba

Private non-profit/ 1989/ staff: 12(f); 7(p)

HISTORICAL SOCIETY: Perpetuates the artistic legacy of Georgia O'Keeffe.

PROGRAMS: Guided Tours

HOURS: Apr-Nov T/Th/F by appt.

5684
Ruth Hall Museum of Paleontology
US Hwy 84, 12 mi N of Abiquiu, 87510 [HC 77 Box 11, 87510]; (p) (505) 685-4330; (f) (505) 685-4519; (c) Rio Arriba

1988/ Ghost Ranch Conference Center, Presbyterian Church/ staff: 2(f); 1(p); 2(v)

NATURAL HISTORY MUSEUM: Promotes natural history.

PROGRAMS: Community Outreach; Elder's Programs; Exhibits; Guided Tours; Interpretation; Lectures

COLLECTIONS: [Triassic period] Artifacts: Coelophysis dinosaur fossils, other Triassic reptiles.

HOURS: Jan-Nov T-Sa 9-12,

ALAMOGORDO

5685
Space Center, The
Top of NM Hwy 2001, 88310 [PO Box 533, 88310]; (p) (505) 437-2840; (f) (505) 434-2245; space-cur@nmsua.nmsu.edu; www.zianet.com/space; (c) Otero

State/ 1973/ Office of Cultural Affairs/ staff: 30(f); 25(p); 2(v)/publication: *Spacelog*

HISTORY MUSEUM: Promotes space history.

PROGRAMS: Community Outreach; Exhibits; Family Programs; Festivals; Film/Video; Guided Tours; Interpretation; Lectures; Living History; Publication; Research Library/Archives; School-Based Curriculum; Theatre

COLLECTIONS: [1950-Present] Astronautics, astronomy, and space exploration artifacts.

HOURS: Yr Daily

5686
Toy Train Depot Inc.
1991 N White Sands Blvd, 88310; (p) (505) 437-2855; (c) Otero

Private non-profit/ 1987/ staff: 1(p); 14(v)

HISTORY MUSEUM: Promotes Alamogordo area railroad history.

PROGRAMS: Exhibits; Family Programs; Guided Tours; School-Based Curriculum

COLLECTIONS: [1898-present] Over 1,200 feet of model railroad track hundreds of model and toy trains.

HOURS: Yr W-Su 12-5

ADMISSION: $2.50, Children $1.50

5687
Tularosa Basin Historical Society
1301 N White Sands Blvd, 88310; (p) (505) 434-4438; tbhs@zianet.com; www.alamogordo.com/tbhs; (c) Otero

Private non-profit/ 1964/ Board of Directors/ staff: 22(v)/ members: 165/publication: *Pioneer*

HISTORICAL SOCIETY

PROGRAMS: Annual Meeting; Exhibits; Publication; Research Library/Archives

COLLECTIONS: [1898-present] Archives, tools and instruments, prehistoric artifacts.

HOURS: Yr M-F 10-4, Sa 10-3

ADMISSION: Donations accepted

5688
Tularosa Basin Historical Society Museum
1503 White Sands Blvd, 88310; (p) (505) 434-4438; TBHS@zianet.com; www.alamogordo.com/tbhs/; (c) Otero

Private non-profit/ 1964/ Tularosa Basin Historical Society/ staff: 1(p); 27(v)/ members: 150/publication: *Otero County Family History*

HISTORY MUSEUM; RESEARCH CENTER

PROGRAMS: Annual Meeting; Community Outreach; Exhibits; Family Programs; Festivals; Film/Video; Interpretation; Lectures; Publication; Research Library/Archives

COLLECTIONS: [1800-1912]

HOURS: Yr M-F 10-4, Sa 10-3

ADMISSION: No charge

ALBUQUERQUE

5689
Albuquerque Museum of Art and History
2000 Mountain Rd NW, 87104; (p) (505) 243-7255; (f) (505) 764-6546; jmoore@cabq.gov; www.cabq.gov/museum; (c) Bernalillo

City/ 1967/ Cultural and Recreational Svcs Dept/ staff: 27(f); 3(p); 200(v)/ members: 1200

ART MUSEUM; HISTORY MUSEUM: Promotes art, history, and culture in the Southwest.

PROGRAMS: Annual Meeting; Community Outreach; Concerts; Exhibits; Facility Rental; Festivals; Garden Tours; Guided Tours; Interpretation; Lectures; Living History; Publication

COLLECTIONS: [17th-20th c] Albuquerque and middle Rio Grande Valley artifacts: arms and armor, Hispanic crafts, Victoriana, decorative arts, maps, textiles and photos.

HOURS: Yr T-Su 9-5

ADMISSION: No charge

5690
Center for Anthropological Studies
1517 Figueroa, NE, 87191 [Box 14576, 87191]; (p) (505) 296-6336; cas@nm.net; (c) Bernalillo

Private non-profit/ 1975/ Board of Directors/ staff: 7(f); 5(p)/ members: 300

RESEARCH CENTER: Conducts research into Southwest prehistoric and historic past.

PROGRAMS: Guided Tours; Publication

COLLECTIONS: [Prehistoric] Prehistoric pueblo material culture, historic Indian artifacts.

5691
Center for Southwest Research
General Library, The University of New Mexico, 87131; (p) (505) 277-6451; cswrref@unm.edu; www/unm.edu/~cswrref; (c) Bernalillo

State/ 1889/ UNM Regents/ staff: 11(f); 1(p); 3(v)

COLLECTIONS: [Prehistory-present] Literary manuscripts, business records, correspondence, diaries, legal documents, oral histories, architectural plans, photos, recordings, other archival materials.

HOURS: Yr M, Th 9-5, T-W 9-7, Sa-Su 12-4

ADMISSION: No charge

5692
Ernie Pyle Branch Library
900 Girard SE, 87106; (p) (505) 256-2065; (f) (505) 256-2069; epstf@rgv.lib.nm.us; cabg.gov/rgvls; (c) Bernalillo

City/ 1949/ staff: 2(f); 2(p)

COLLECTIONS: [1940] Memorabilia, newspaper and archives.

HOURS: Yr T-W 10-8, Th-Sa 10-6

5693
Indian Pueblo Cultural Center
2401 12th St NW, 87104; (p) (505) 843-7270; (f) (505) 842-6959; www.indianpueblo.org; (c) Bernalillo

Private for-profit/ 1976/ staff: 75(f); 10(p); 80(v)/ members: 900/publication: *Horizons*

HISTORY MUSEUM; TRIBAL MUSEUM: Promotes Pueblo culture.

PROGRAMS: Annual Meeting; Community Outreach; Concerts; Elder's Programs; Exhibits; Facility Rental; Family Programs; Festivals; Film/Video; Guided Tours; Interpretation; Lectures; Living History; Publication; Research Library/Archives; School-Based Curriculum; The

COLLECTIONS: [Prehistory-present] Pre-Columbian lithics, arts and crafts, dance regalia, architecture.

HOURS: Yr Daily 9-5:30

ADMISSION: $4, Student $1, Seniors $3

5694
Menaul Historical Library of the Southwest
301 Menaul Blvd NE, 87107; (p) (505) 343-7480; (c) Bernalillo

Private non-profit/ 1974/ Menaul School Board of Trustees/ staff: 18(v)

LIBRARY AND/OR ARCHIVES: Collects, preserves and catalogs history of the Southwest Presbyterian influence.

PROGRAMS: Research Library/Archives

COLLECTIONS: [1866-present] Manuscripts, photos and audio-visual materials, periodicals, books, and artifacts.

HOURS: T-F 10-4

5695
National Atomic Museum
Bldg 20358 Wyoming SE, Kirtland AFB, 87185 [PO Box 5800, 87185]; (p) (505) 284-3243; (f) (505) 284-3244; info@atomic museum.com; www.atomic.com; (c) Bernalillo

Federal/ 1969/ Natl Atomic Museum Foundation/ staff: 14(f); 4(p); 120(v)/ members: 230

HISTORY MUSEUM; RESEARCH CENTER: Collects historical artifacts.

PROGRAMS: Annual Meeting; Community Outreach; Exhibits; Facility Rental; Family Programs; Festivals; Film/Video; Guided Tours; Lectures; Publication; Research Library/Archives; School-Based Curriculum; Theatre

COLLECTIONS: [1900-present] Nuclear military items, historic materials and archives, medical equipment, energy-related texts.

HOURS: Yr Daily 9-5

ADMISSION: $3, Children $2, Seniors $2

5696
Petroglyph National Monument
4735 Unser Blvd NW, 87120 [6001 Unser Blvd NW, 87120]; (p) (505) 899-0205; (f) (505) 899-0207; www.nps.gov/petr/; (c) Bernalillo

Federal/ 1990/ National Park Service/ staff: 23(f); 3(p); 30(v)

HISTORIC SITE

PROGRAMS: Community Outreach; Interpretation; Lectures

COLLECTIONS: [1350-1500] Petroglyphs on Albuquerque's West Mesa escarpment.

HOURS: Yr Daily 8-5

ADMISSION: $2

5697
Special Collections Library, Albuquerque/Bernalillo County Library System
423 Central Ave NE, 87102; (p) (505) 848-1376; (f) (505) 764-1573; specialcollections@cabq.gov; www.cabq.gov/rgvls/specol.html; (c) Bernalillo

City/ 1901/ staff: 3(f); 1(p); 30(v)

LIBRARY AND/OR ARCHIVES

PROGRAMS: Exhibits; Interpretation; Research Library/Archives; School-Based Curriculum

COLLECTIONS: [1700-present]

HOURS: Yr T-Sa

5698
Telephone Pioneer Museum of New Mexico
110 4th St NW, 87103 [PO Box 1892, 87103]; (p) (505) 842-2937; lxturne@eni.net; www.nmculture.org; (c) Bernalillo

Private non-profit/ 1961/ staff: 63(v)

HISTORY MUSEUM: Promotes telephone and audio history.

PROGRAMS: Exhibits; Guided Tours; Research Library/Archives

COLLECTIONS: [1876-1998] Switchboards, telephones, teletypes, photos.

HOURS: Yr M-F 10-2

ADMISSION: $1, Children $0.50

5699
Turquoise Museum, The
2107 Central NW, 87104; (p) (505) 247-8650; (f) (505) 247-8765; (c) Bernalillo

Private for-profit/ 1993/ Zach-Low, Inc./ staff: 3(f); 1(p)

HISTORY MUSEUM: Educates about turquoise, history, geology, mythology, jewelry, and Native American studies.

PROGRAMS: Exhibits; Lectures

COLLECTIONS: Mines, tunnel display, turquoise and related jewelry.

HOURS: Yr M-Sa

5700
University of New Mexico Art Museum
UNM Center for the Arts, Rm 1017, 87131; (p) (505) 277-4001; (f) (505) 277-7315; mcerto@unm.edu; (c) Bernalillo

State/ 1963/ Board of Regents/ staff: 11(f); 2(p); 3(v)/ members: 250

ART MUSEUM; HISTORY MUSEUM: Preserves and develops collections; presents exhibits and programs; conducts and publishes scholarly research.

PROGRAMS: Community Outreach; Elder's Programs; Exhibits; Facility Rental; Film/Video; Guided Tours; Lectures; Research Library/Archives; School-Based Curriculum

COLLECTIONS: [19th-20th c] Photography, Spanish Colonial art.

HOURS: Yr T-F 9-4, Su 1-4, T

ARTESIA

5701
Artesia Historical Museum and Art Center
505 W Richardson Ave, 88210; (p) (505) 748-2390; (f) (505) 746-3886; (c) Eddy

City/ 1971/ staff: 1(f); 1(p)

HISTORY MUSEUM; HOUSE MUSEUM

PROGRAMS: Community Outreach; Exhibits; Garden Tours; Lectures

COLLECTIONS: [1890s-1970]

HOURS: Yr T-F 9-12/1-5, Sa 1-5

AZTEC

5702
Aztec Museum Association
125 N Main Ave, 87410; (p) (505) 334-9829; (f) (505) 334-7648; azmus@juno.com; www.cyber.port.com/aztec; (c) San Juan

Private non-profit/ 1974/ Board of Directors/ staff: 3(p); 114(v)/ members: 429/publication: *Aztec Museum Newsletter*

HISTORY MUSEUM: Preserves area history.

PROGRAMS: Annual Meeting; Community Outreach; Exhibits; Festivals; Living History; Publication; Reenactments

COLLECTIONS: [1880-present]

HOURS: May-Sept M-Sa 9-5; Sept-May M-Sa 10-4

ADMISSION: Donations

BELEN

5703
Valencia County Historical Society/Harvey House Museum
104 N First St, 87002 [PO Box 166, 87002]; (p) (505) 861-0581; (c) Valencia

Private non-profit/ 1969/ Board of Directors/ staff: 10(v)/ members: 100

HISTORICAL SOCIETY

PROGRAMS: Annual Meeting; Exhibits; Garden Tours; Lectures

COLLECTIONS: [1880-present] Artifacts related to the Fred Harvey Organization, Santa Fe Railroad, and Valencia County.

HOURS: Yr T-Sa 12:30-3:30

ADMISSION: Donations requested

BERNLILLO

5704
Coronado State Monument
485 Kuaua Rd W 44, 87004 [PO Box 95, 87004]; (p) (505) 867-5351; (f) (505) 867-1733; www.nmculture.org; (c) Sandoval

State/ 1940/ Museums of New Mexico/ staff: 3(f); 1(p); 8(v)/publication: *El Palacio*

HISTORIC SITE: Preserves ancient Pueblo ruins of Kuaua; interprets history of the Tiwa people and the Coronados Expedition.

PROGRAMS: Community Outreach; Exhibits; Facility Rental; Film/Video; Guided Tours; Interpretation; Lectures; Publication

COLLECTIONS: [1300-1600] Spanish Colonial and Pueblo Artifacts, pre-Columbian Murals.

HOURS: Yr Daily 8:30-5

ADMISSION: $3; Under 17 free

BLOOMFIELD

5705
San Juan County Museum Association
6131 US Hwy 64, 87413 [PO Box 125, 87413]; (p) (505) 632-2013; (f) (505) 632-1707; www.more2it.com/salmon; (c) San Juan

Private non-profit/ 1964/ Board of Directors/ staff: 7(f); 3(p); 10(v)/ members: 125

HISTORICAL SOCIETY; LIBRARY AND/OR ARCHIVES: Manages and operates the County Anthropological Research Center and Library; sponsors outdoor exhibits.

PROGRAMS: Annual Meeting; Community Outreach; Elder's Programs; Exhibits; Facility Rental; Guided Tours; Interpretation; Lectures; Publication

COLLECTIONS: [11th c-13th c and 1896-1918] Salmon Ruins (11th c pueblo) and artifacts excavated from site; pioneer homestead collection.

HOURS: Yr M-F 8-5, Sa-Su 9-5

ADMISSION: $3, Children $1, Seniors $2

CAPITAN

5706
Smokey Bear Historical Park
118 Smokey Bear Blvd, 88316 [PO Box 591, 88316]; (p) (505) 354-2748; (f) (505) 354-6012; (c) Lincoln

State/ 1978/ staff: 3(f); 1(v)

HISTORIC SITE: Exhibit topics related to wildfire prevention, forest health, fire ecology, wildland/urban interface problems.

PROGRAMS: Exhibits; Film/Video; Garden Tours; Interpretation; School-Based Curriculum

COLLECTIONS: [1942-present] Smokey Bear and the Cooperative Forest Fire Prevention Program artifacts: historic posters, and memorabilia.

HOURS: Yr

CAPULIN

5707
Capulin Volcano National Monument
Hwy 325, 88414 [PO Box 40, 88414]; (p)
(505) 278-2201; (f) (505) 278-2211;
cavo_superintendent@ups.gov;
www.nps.gov/cavo; (c) Union

Federal/ 1916/ National Park Service/ staff:
9(f); 3(p); 2(v)

HISTORIC SITE: Preserves the classic volcanic features and the scientific and scenic values of Capulin Volcano National Monument.

PROGRAMS: Community Outreach; Exhibits;
Interpretation; Publication

COLLECTIONS: [Late Cenozoic Volcanism]
Natural history specimens, herbarium, photographs and oral histories.

HOURS: Sept-May Daily 8-4; May-Sept Daily
7:30-6:30

ADMISSION: $4/vehicle

CARLSBAD

5708
Carlsbad Caverns National Park
3225 National Parks Hwy, 88220; (p) (505) 785-2232; (f) (505) 785-2232; cave_curatorial@
nps.gov; www.nps.gov/cave; (c) Eddy

Federal/ National Park Service/ staff: 3(f); 2(p)

HISTORIC SITE; LIBRARY AND/OR
ARCHIVES

PROGRAMS: Community Outreach; Exhibits;
Guided Tours; Interpretation; Lectures; Research Library/Archives

COLLECTIONS: [1900-present] Archives, archaeology, natural history artifacts related to Carlsbad Caverns National Park.

HOURS: Yr Daily 8:30-5

ADMISSION: $6

5709
Carlsbad Museum and Art Center
418 W Fox, 88220; (p) (505) 887-0276; (c)
Eddy

City/ staff: 1(f)

HOURS: Yr M-Sa 10-5

CEDAR CREST

5710
**Museum of Archaeology and Material
Culture**
22 Calvary Rd, 87008 [PO Box 582, 87008];
(p) (505) 281-2005; (c) Bernalillo

Private non-profit/ 1995/ staff: 2(f); 2(v)

HISTORY MUSEUM; RESEARCH CENTER:
Offers exhibits on archaeological techniques,
theory, and analysis.

PROGRAMS: Elder's Programs; Exhibits;
Family Programs; Film/Video; Guided Tours;
Interpretation; Lectures; Theatre

COLLECTIONS: [Prehistory-1900] Archaeological materials, historical artifacts from 1520-1900.

HOURS: May-Oct Daily 12-8

ADMISSION: $2.50

CHURCH ROCK

5711
Red Rock Museum
Red Rock State Park, 87311 [PO Box 10,
87311]; (p) (505) 863-1337; (f) (505) 863-1297; rrsp@ci.gallu.nm.us; www.ci.gallup.
nm.us; (c) McKinley

City/ 1951/ staff: 2(f); 1(p); 6(v)

ART MUSEUM; RESEARCH CENTER: Interprets the history of the Gallup area, including the Anasazi people, the modern Pueblo, and the Navajo people.

PROGRAMS: Community Outreach; Exhibits;
Family Programs; Garden Tours; Guided
Tours; Interpretation; Lectures

COLLECTIONS: [Prehistory-present] Ethnographic and archaeological artifacts; fine arts and crafts of Native Americans including the prehistoric Anasazi, Navajo, Juni, and Hopi;
photos.

HOURS: June-Aug M-F 8-6, Sa-Su 10-6; Sep-May M-Sa 8-4:30, Su 10-6

ADMISSION: Donations accepted

CIMARRON

5712
Old Mill Museum
RT 1 Box 62, 87714; (c) Colfax

Private non-profit/ 1967/ Cimarron Historical
Society/ staff: 1(f); 1(p)

HISTORIC SITE; HISTORICAL SOCIETY:
Presents a historic mill and various artifacts.

PROGRAMS: Exhibits

COLLECTIONS: [1848-present] Ute and
Apache Indians artifacts; Aztec mill.

HOURS: May F-W 9-4:30, June 1-Oct 1 M-W,
F 9-4:30

ADMISSION: $2, Children $1, Seniors $1; $1
Boy Scouts

5713
Philmont Museum
Philmont Scout Ranch, 87714 [Rt 1 Box 38A,
87714]; (p) (505) 376-2281; (f) (505) 376-2602; philmuseum@juno.com; (c) Colfax

Private non-profit/ 1942/ Boy Scouts of America/ staff: 5(f); 20(p)

ART MUSEUM; HISTORY MUSEUM; HOUSE
MUSEUM; LIBRARY AND/OR ARCHIVES;
LIVING HISTORY/OUTDOOR MUSEUM: Operates three museums: The Philmont Museum and Seton Memorial Library, Villa Philmonte, and Kit Carson Museum.

PROGRAMS: Exhibits; Facility Rental; Family
Programs; Guided Tours; Interpretation; Lectures; Living History; Reenactments; Research
Library/Archives

COLLECTIONS: [19th-20th c] Art; Artifacts:
Natural history, Southwest.

HOURS: Yr June-Aug Daily 9-5; Sep-May M-F
9-5

ADMISSION: $4

CLAYTON

5714
Herzstein Memorial Museum
Walnut & Second, 88415 [PO Box 75,
88415]; (p) (505) 374-2977; (c) Union

Private non-profit/ 1985/ Union County Historical Society/ staff: 1(f); 1(p); 10(v)/ members:
50

HISTORY MUSEUM: Collects, preserves, and
interprets local history.

PROGRAMS: Annual Meeting; Exhibits; Guided Tours; Lectures; Research Library/Archives

COLLECTIONS: [Late 1800s-early1900s]
Early settlers, Santa Fe Trail, dinosaurs, art.

HOURS: Yr T-Su 1-5

ADMISSION: No charge

CLEVELAND

5715
Historic Mora Valley Foundation
Hwy 518, 87715 [PO Box 287, 87715]; (p)
(505) 387-2645; (f) (505) 387-2645; (c) Mora

Private non-profit/ 1987/ staff: 2(v)

HISTORIC SITE; HISTORY MUSEUM: Operates the Cleveland Roller Mill Museum.

PROGRAMS: Exhibits; Festivals; Guided
Tours; Interpretation; Lectures

COLLECTIONS: [1900-1950] Photos.

HOURS: June-Oct Daily 10-5

ADMISSION: $2

CLIFF

5716
Hunter Trapper Trader Museum
8405 Hwy 180 W, 88028 [PO Box 377,
88028]; (p) (505) 535-2768; (c) Grant

Private non-profit/ 1995/ Board of Directors/
staff: 5(v)

HISTORY MUSEUM; LIVING HISTORY/OUTDOOR MUSEUM

PROGRAMS: Annual Meeting; Exhibits; Facility Rental; Family Programs; Film/Video; Guided Tours; Interpretation; Lectures; Living History; Research Library/Archives; School-Based
Curriculum

COLLECTIONS: [1850-present] Replica of c.
1875 trading post, animal pelts, antique traps and equipment, reference library of hunting and trapping books, magazines and videos.

HOURS: Yr Daily 11-6, and by appt

ADMISSION: Donations

CLOVIS

5717
Clovis Depot Model Train Museum
221 W First St, 88101; (p) (505) 762-0066,
(888) 762-0064; philipw@3lefties.com;
www.clovisdepot.com; (c) Curry

Private for-profit/ 1995/ staff: 2(f); 1(p)

HISTORY MUSEUM: Restored railroad station, with exhibits displaying local and worldwide railroad history.

PROGRAMS: Exhibits; Guided Tours; Interpretation; Research Library/Archives

COLLECTIONS: [1900-present] Railroad memorabilia, photos.

HOURS: Mar-Aug and Oct-Jan W-Su 12-5

ADMISSION: Call for prices

5718
H. A. "Pappy" Thorton Homestead and Museum
Ned Houk Park, 88101 [Clovis Chamber of Commerce, 215 N Main St, 88101]; (p) (505) 763-3435

DEMING

5719
Deming Luna Mimbres Museum
301 S Silver Ave, 88030; (p) (505) 546-2382; DLM-MUSEUM@ZIANET.com; (c) Luna

1978/ Luna County Historical Society/ staff: 75(v)/ members: 180

HISTORY MUSEUM; LIBRARY AND/OR ARCHIVES

PROGRAMS: Annual Meeting; Exhibits; Facility Rental; Guided Tours; Lectures; Research Library/Archives; School-Based Curriculum

COLLECTIONS: [900-1900] Artifacts of Mimbres Indians, farming, ranching, railroad, military, medical, and mining.

HOURS: Yr Daily 9-4

ADMISSION: Donations requested

DULCE

5720
Jicarillo Arts and Crafts Museum
Jicarilla Blvd, 87528 [PO Box 507, 87528]; (p) (505) 759-3242; (c) Rio Arriba

Private non-profit/ 1964/ staff: 14(f)

TRIBAL MUSEUM: Promotes tribal hsitory and culture.

PROGRAMS: Exhibits

COLLECTIONS: [Prehistory-present] Old Jicarilla baskets, pottery, and paintings.

HOURS: Yr Daily 8-5

FARMINGTON

5721
Bolack Electromechanical Museum
3901 Bloomfield Hwy, 87401; (p) (505) 325-4275; (f) (505) 325-1434; (c) San Juan

Private non-profit/ 1990/ staff: 2(f); 1(p)

HISTORY MUSEUM

PROGRAMS: Exhibits; Guided Tours

COLLECTIONS: [1890-1960] Electric power generation, radio and television broadcasting, and mechanical printing.

HOURS: Yr M-Sa 8-3

5722
Farmington Museum
3041 E Main St, 87402; (p) (505) 599-1174; (f) (505) 326-7572; frmngtnmuseum@juno.com; (c) San Juan

City/ 1980/ staff: 7(f); 2(p); 50(v)/ members: 327

ART MUSEUM; HISTORY MUSEUM: Collects, preserves, researches and interprets historical and natural artifacts.

PROGRAMS: Community Outreach; Elder's Programs; Exhibits; Facility Rental; Family Programs; Garden Tours; Guided Tours; Interpretation; Lectures; Research Library/Archives; School-Based Curriculum

COLLECTIONS: [1880-present] Pioneer artifacts; trading posts, development of oil and gas industry, photo archives.

HOURS: Yr M-Sa 9-5, Su 12-5

FOLSOM

5723
Folsom Museum
101 Main St, 88419 [PO Box 385, 88419]; (p) (505) 278-2122, (505) 278-3616; (c) Union

City, non-profit/ 1967/ Folsom Museum Board/ staff: 2(p)/ members: 6/publication: *Folsom Then and Now, 1888-1988*

HISTORIC PRESERVATION AGENCY; HISTORY MUSEUM: Preserves local historical artifacts.

PROGRAMS: Annual Meeting; Community Outreach; Exhibits; Garden Tours; Guided Tours; Interpretation; Publication; Research Library/Archives; School-Based Curriculum

COLLECTIONS: [Late 1800s-present] Historical, legal, Folsom Man, and other Indian artifacts, music center, clothing tools, household items, farming, ranch, and medical equipment of the Pioneer and homestead eras.

HOURS: Mem Day-Labor Day Daily 10-5; May and Sept Sa-Su

FORT SUMNER

5724
Billy the Kid Museum
1601 E Sumner Ave, 88119 [Rt 1, Box 36, 88119]; (p) (505) 355-2380; btkmuseum@plateautel.net; www.billythekid.nv.switchboard.com; (c) De Baca

Private for-profit/ 1953/ staff: 4(f)

HISTORY MUSEUM: Promotes history of Billy the Kid, the Lucien Bonaparte Maxwells, and Old Fort Sumner.

COLLECTIONS: [1850-1950] Guns, automobiles and paintings featuring Billy the Kid and Fort Sumner

5725
Fort Sumner State Monument
3 mi S of Hwy 60/84 on Billy the Kid Rd, 88119 [PO Box 356, 88119]; (p) (505) 355-2573; (c) De Baca

State/ 1968/ staff: 3(f); 3(v)

HISTORIC SITE

PROGRAMS: Community Outreach; Exhibits; Facility Rental; Guided Tours; Interpretation; Living History

COLLECTIONS: [1862-1869]

HOURS: Yr Daily

ADMISSION: $1; Under 17 free

GALLUP

5726
Gallup Cultural Center
201 E Hwy 66, 87301; (p) (505) 863-4131; kent@cia-g.com; (c) McKinley

Private non-profit/ 1997/ Southwest Indian Foundation/ staff: 7(f); 3(p); 2(v)

ART MUSEUM; HISTORY MUSEUM: Preserves Native American history.

PROGRAMS: Community Outreach; Concerts; Elder's Programs; Exhibits; Facility Rental; Family Programs; Festivals; Film/Video; Guided Tours; Interpretation; Lectures; Living History

COLLECTIONS: [400 AD-present] Native American artifacts, Kachinas, paintings, photos, displays, Spanish artifacts, railroad displays, military displays.

HOURS: May 31-Sep 6 T-Sa 9-4; Sep 6-May 31 M-F 9-4

HILLSBORO

5727
Black Range Museum
Hwy NM 152, 88042 [PO Box 454, 88042]; (p) (505) 895-5233; Hillsman@ziavms.enmu.edu; (c) Sierra

Private non-profit/ 1961/ staff: 1(f); 3(v)

HISTORIC SITE; HISTORY MUSEUM: Maintains historic Ocean Grove Hotel site as museum.

PROGRAMS: Exhibits

COLLECTIONS: [1880s-1940s] Farming, mining, and Native American artifacts.

HOURS: Th-Sa 11-4, Su 1-5

ADMISSION: Donations requested

HOBBS

5728
Lea County Cowboy Hall of Fame & Western Heritage Center
5317 Lovington Hwy, 88240; (p) (505) 392-1275; (f) (505) 392-5875; lburnett@nmjc.cc.nm.us; www.nmjc.cc.nm.us; (c) Lea

Private non-profit/ 1978/ New Mexico Junior College/ staff: 2(f); 1(p)/ members: 500

ART MUSEUM; HISTORICAL SOCIETY; HISTORY MUSEUM: Promotes Hall of Fame established to honor county residents.

PROGRAMS: Annual Meeting; Exhibits; Festivals; School-Based Curriculum

COLLECTIONS: [1897-present] Artifacts and memorabilia of Lea County.

5729
Linam Ranch Museum
9801 W Hwy 62-180, 88240 [PO Box 743, 88240]; (p) (505) 393-4784; (c) Lea

Private non-profit/ 1962/ staff: 4(v)

HISTORY MUSEUM

PROGRAMS: Guided Tours

COLLECTIONS: [1900-present] Artifacts of frontiers people.

HOURS: Apr-Nov Daily by appt

LAS CRUCES

5730
Branigan Cultural Center
500 N Water St, 88001; (p) (505) 541-2155; (f) (505) 525-3645; bcci@zinnet.com; www.lascruces-culture.org; (c) Dona Ana

City/ 1981/ City of Las Cruces/ staff: 6(f); 2(p); 30(v)/ members: 450

ART MUSEUM; HISTORY MUSEUM: Collects and preserves the history of Las Cruces and Dona Ana County. Interprets its collections for the education of citizens and visitors.

PROGRAMS: Annual Meeting; Community Outreach; Concerts; Exhibits; Facility Rental; Lectures; School-Based Curriculum

COLLECTIONS: [1850-1960] Regional and local history with major emphasis on early founding families in Las Cruces and Dona Ana County. Objects represent the late Victorian period through World War II with costumes, accessories, household items,

5731
Las Cruces Museum of Natural History
700 S Telshor Blvd, 88011; (p) (505) 522-3120; (f) (505) 522-3744; mnh@zianet.com; www.nmsu.edu/museum; (c) Dona Ana

City, non-profit/ 1986/ staff: 3(f); 1(p); 8(v)/ members: 350

HISTORY MUSEUM: Offers natural history and science exhibits.

PROGRAMS: Exhibits; Family Programs; Guided Tours; Lectures

HOURS: Yr M-Th 12-5, F 12-9, Sa 10-6, Su 12-6

ADMISSION: No charge

5732
New Mexico Farm and Ranch Heritage Museum
4100 Dripping Springs Rd, 88011; (p) (505) 522-4100; (f) (505) 522-3085; (c) Dona Ana

State/ 1998/ Office of Cultural Affairs/ staff: 23(f); 6(p); 131(v)/ members: 200/publication: NM Farm and Ranch Heritage News

HISTORY MUSEUM; LIBRARY AND/OR ARCHIVES: Promotes agricultural history.

PROGRAMS: Community Outreach; Exhibits; Facility Rental; Family Programs; Festivals; Film/Video; Garden Tours; Guided Tours; Lectures; School-Based Curriculum; Theatre

COLLECTIONS: [Prehistory-present] Artifacts of farming, ranching, and rural life in NM.

HOURS: Yr T-Sa 9-5; Su

5733
University Museum, New Mexico State University, The
Kent Hall, Univ Ave & Solano, 88003 [Box 3564 NMSU, PO Box 30001, 88003]; (p) (505) 646-3739; (f) (505) 646-3739; museum@nmsu.edu; www.nmsu.edu/~museum/; (c) Dona Ana

State/ 1959/ NM State Univ/ staff: 4(f); 30(p)/ members: 70

HISTORY MUSEUM: Promotes prehistory, history, and cultures of the American southwest.

PROGRAMS: Community Outreach; Exhibits;

Facility Rental; Family Programs; Guided Tours; Lectures; Research Library/Archives; School-Based Curriculum

COLLECTIONS: [Prehistory-present] Anthropological, ethnographic, and historical artifacts of the Southwest and Northern Mexico.

HOURS: Yr M-F 12-4

ADMISSION: No charge

LAS VEGAS

5734
City of Las Vegas Museum and Rough Riders Memorial Collection
727 Grand Ave, 87701 [Box 160, 87701]; (p) (505) 454-1401; (f) (505) 425-7335; (c) San Miguel

City/ 1965/ staff: 1(f); 3(p); 10(v)/ members: 30

HISTORY MUSEUM; PRESIDENTIAL SITE: Collects, preserves, and interprets regional territorial history and the role of New Mexican members of the US Volunteer Cavalry in the Spanish-American war.

PROGRAMS: Community Outreach; Concerts; Elder's Programs; Exhibits; Family Programs; Festivals; Interpretation; Lectures; Reenactments; Research Library/Archives; School-Based Curriculum

COLLECTIONS: [1860-1960] Uniforms, medals, artifacts related to Spanish-American War, Theodore Roosevelt memorabilia, books, photos, newspapers, costumes, ranch gear, domestic artifacts.

5735
New Mexico Highlands University Anthropology Laboratory
NMHU Anthropology Laboratory, 87701; (p) (505) 454-3283; (f) (505) 454-3331; mcpherson_b@ nmhu.edu; www.nmculture.org; (c) San Miguel

State/ 1893/ staff: 3(f); 2(p)

LIBRARY AND/OR ARCHIVES; RESEARCH CENTER

PROGRAMS: Research Library/Archives; School-Based Curriculum

COLLECTIONS: [1000-1900] Tecolote Pueblo collection, Tinsley Site collection, human osteometry collections, Valmora Sanitorium radiograph collection, Fred Howarth library and collections.

HOURS: Yr

LINCOLN

5736
Lincoln State Monument
Hwy 380, 88338 [PO Box 36, 88338]; (p) (505) 653-4372; (f) (505) 653-4372; (c) Lincoln

State/ 1979/ Museum of NM/ staff: 4(f); 2(p)

HISTORIC SITE: Interprets and preserves historic structures including those related to Billy the Kid and the Lincoln County War.

PROGRAMS: Community Outreach; Concerts; Exhibits; Facility Rental; Family Programs; Festivals; Film/Video; Guided Tours; Interpretation; Lectures; Living History; Reenactments; School-Based Curriculum

COLLECTIONS: [1800s] Documents, photos,

letters, original merchandise from 1990 mercantile, firearms, spurs, ledgers, other exhibits.

HOURS: Yr

LOS ALAMOS

5737
Los Alamos Historical Society and Museum
1921 Juniper St, 87544 [PO Box 43, 87544]; (p) (505) 662-6272, (662) 449-4493; (f) (505) 662-6312; historicalsociety@losalamos.com; losalamos.com/historicalsociety; (c) Los Alamos

Private non-profit/ 1968/ Los Alamos Historical Society/ staff: 4(p); 50(v)/ members: 600

HISTORICAL SOCIETY: Preserves and interprets local history.

PROGRAMS: Annual Meeting; Community Outreach; Elder's Programs; Exhibits; Family Programs; Festivals; Film/Video; Guided Tours; Interpretation; Lectures; Publication; Research Library/Archives

COLLECTIONS: [1200-present] Archives, artifacts

MADRID

5738
Old Coal Museum
2846 State Highway 14, 87010; (p) (505) 438-3780; (f) (505) 438-4418; oldcoalmine museum@aol.com; www.turquoisetrail.org; (c) Santa Fe

Private for-profit/ 1962/ Cato Enterprises, LLC/ staff: 1(f); 1(p)

HISTORIC SITE; LIBRARY AND/OR ARCHIVES; LIVING HISTORY/OUTDOOR MUSEUM

PROGRAMS: Exhibits; Facility Rental; Guided Tours; Theatre

COLLECTIONS: [1900-1956] Mining, railroading, office, medical, and fire fighting equipment; company records, memos, mining blueprints; miscellaneous vehicles and equipment.

HOURS: Yr Daily 10-5

ADMISSION: $3, Children $1

MAGDALENA

5739
Village of Magdalena Box Car Museum
108 N Main St, 87825 [PO Box 145, 87825]; (p) (505) 854-2261; (f) (505) 854-2273

City/ 1983/ staff: 2(v)

HISTORY MUSEUM: Displays railroad and mining history in the Magdalena area.

PROGRAMS: Exhibits

COLLECTIONS: [1800-early 1900s] Photos, mining equipment, railroad artifacts.

HOURS: Yr M-F 8-5

MOGOLLON

5740
Mining and Town Museum
5 Bursom Rd, 88039 [HC 61 Box 310, 88039]; (p) (505) 539-2016; (c) Catron

Private non-profit/ 1996/ Mogollon Enterprises/ staff: 1(p)

HISTORIC SITE; HISTORY MUSEUM: Old mining/ghost town museum.

PROGRAMS: Exhibits

COLLECTIONS: [1870-present] Furniture, clothes, mining implements, written history.

HOURS: May-Sept Sa-Su 10-5

ADMISSION: Donations requested

5741
Native Museum
17 Bursom Rd, 88039 [HC 61 Box 310, 88039]; (c) Catron

Private non-profit/ 1997/ Mogollon Enterprises/ staff: 1(p)

HISTORY MUSEUM: Native American Museum.

PROGRAMS: Exhibits

COLLECTIONS: [Prehistory-present] Pots, baskets, tomahawks, beadwork, other Native American artifacts.

HOURS: May-Sept Sa-Su 10-5

ADMISSION: Donations accepted

MOUNTAINAIR

5742
Salinas Pueblo Missions National Monument
Ripley & Broadway, 87036 [PO Box 517, 87036]; (p) (505) 847-2585; (f) (505) 847-2441; Jim_Boll@nps.gov; nps.gov/sapu; (c) Torrance

Federal/ 1980/ National Park Service/ staff: 16(f); 4(p); 4(v)

HISTORIC SITE: Preserves and interprets 17th c Spanish Colonial Mission ruins and associated prehistoric Indian Pueblos.

PROGRAMS: Community Outreach; Exhibits; Guided Tours; Interpretation; School-Based Curriculum

COLLECTIONS: [1600-1680] Spanish Colonial buildings and Indian pueblos.

HOURS: Yr Daily

ORGAN

5743
Space Murals, Inc.
12450 Hwy 70 E, 88052 [PO Box 243, 88052]; (p) (505) 382-0977; (f) (505) 382-7623; klin@zianet.com; www.zianet.com/SpaceMurals; (c) Dona Ana

Private non-profit/ 1993/ staff: 1(f); 2(p); 2(v)

HISTORY MUSEUM: Collects and displays cosmological artifacts.

PROGRAMS: Exhibits; Film/Video; Guided Tours

COLLECTIONS: [1950-present] Artifacts that have flown in space, Astronaut Gallery, air and space pictures, models, children's exhibits, X-15 rocket engine, and a Mercury capsule.

HOURS: Yr M-Sa 9-6, Su

PECOS

5744
Pecos National Historical Park
2 mi S of Pecos on Hwy 63, 87552 [PO Box 418, 87552]; (p) (505) 757-6414; (f) (505) 757-8460; PECO_Visitor_center@nps.gov; www.nps.gov/peco; (c) San Miguel

Federal/ 1965/ National Park Service/ staff: 15(f); 14(p); 10(v)

HISTORIC SITE: Promotes local history.

PROGRAMS: Community Outreach; Elder's Programs; Exhibits; Film/Video; Guided Tours; Interpretation; Lectures; Living History; Research Library/Archives; School-Based Curriculum

COLLECTIONS: [Prehistory-Civil War] Pecos Pueblo (1350-1838), Spanish Mission (1617-1826), ceramics and other artifacts related to these sites; Civil War battlefield.

HOURS: Yr Mem Day-Labor Day Daily 8-6; rest of year 8-5

ADMISSION: $2, Family $2

PORTALES

5745
Blackwater Draw Museum and Archaeological Site
US Hwy 70, 7 mi NE of Portales, 88130 [Ste 9, Eastern New Mexico University, 88130]; (p) (505) 562-2202; (f) (505) 562-2305; Matthew.Hillsman@enmu.edu; www.enmu.edu; (c) Roosevelt

State/ 1969/ Eastern New Mexico Univ/ staff: 2(f); 3(p)/publication: *ENMU Contributions in Anthropology*

ARCHAEOLOGICAL SITE/MUSEUM; LIVING HISTORY/OUTDOOR MUSEUM; RESEARCH CENTER: Preserves archaeological site related to Clovis, Folsom and later Paleoindian and Archaic Indian cultures of the Southwest.

PROGRAMS: Community Outreach; Exhibits; Facility Rental; Garden Tours; Interpretation; Lectures; Living History; Publication; Research Library/Archives

COLLECTIONS: [Paleoindian-Archaic] Stone tools and related artifacts and paleontological materials.

HOURS: Yr Daily 10-5

ADMISSION: $2, Seniors $1

5746
Dalley Windmills
1506 S Kilgore, 88130; (p) (505) 356-6263; windy@yucca.com; (c) Roosevelt

Private non-profit/ 1980

HISTORIC PRESERVATION AGENCY: Preserves historic windmills.

PROGRAMS: Exhibits; Guided Tours

COLLECTIONS: [Late 1800s-early 1900s] Power windmill, a railroad eclipse, wood-prop mills.

5747
Roosevelt County Historical Museum
ENMU, 88130 [ENMU-P, Station 9, 88130]; (p) (505) 562-2592; (f) (505) 562-2578; Mark.Romero@enmu.edu; www.enmu.edu/exhibits/rooseveltco.htm; (c) Roosevelt

State/ 1940/ Eastern New Mexico Univ/ staff: 1(f); 3(p)

HISTORY MUSEUM

PROGRAMS: Exhibits

COLLECTIONS: [1800-present] Artifacts: agricultural, medical, musical, and dental equipment, clothing

RAMAH

5748
El Morro National Monument
16 mi E of town, 87321 [RT 2 Box 43, 87321]; (p) (505) 783-4226; (f) (505) 783-4366

Federal/ National Park Service/ staff: 10(f); 4(p); 2(v)

HISTORIC SITE

PROGRAMS: Exhibits; Festivals; Film/Video; Guided Tours; Interpretation; Lectures

COLLECTIONS: [Prehistory-present]

HOURS: Yr Daily 9-4

ADMISSION: $4

RATON

5749
Colfax County Society of Art, History, and Archaeology
216 S First St, 87740; (p) (505) 445-9979; (c) Colfax

Private non-profit/ 1938/ staff: 1(f); 20(v)/ members: 130

ART MUSEUM; HISTORICAL SOCIETY: Preserves and displays local mining and ranching history.

PROGRAMS: Community Outreach; Exhibits; Guided Tours

COLLECTIONS: [1880] Photos, art, coal mine, railroad, and ranching artifacts.

HOURS: Summer T-Sa 9-5,

RIO RANCHO

5750
J and R Vintage Auto Museum and Bookstore
3650 A Hwy 528, 87174 [PO Box 15229, 87174]; (p) (505) 867-2881; (f) (505) 892-5722; INFO@jrvintageautos.com; www.jrvintageautos.com; (c) Sandovac

Private for-profit/ 1996/ staff: 3(f)

HISTORY MUSEUM

PROGRAMS: Exhibits; Facility Rental

COLLECTIONS: [1902-1972] 70 cars and books; toys, cars, bookstore.

HOURS: Yr M-Sa 10-5, Su 1-5

ADMISSION: $4, Children $3

ROSWELL

5751
Historical Center for Southwest New Mexico, Inc.
200 N Lea Ave, 88201; (p) (505) 622-8333; (f) (505) 622-8333; (c) Chaves

Private non-profit/ 1976/ staff: 2(p); 40(v)/ members: 2500

HISTORIC PRESERVATION AGENCY; HISTORIC SITE; LIBRARY AND/OR ARCHIVES: Preserves and interprets the social, cultural, and economic history of Southeastern NM.

PROGRAMS: Annual Meeting; Community Outreach; Exhibits; Facility Rental; Guided Tours; Living History; Publication; Research Library/Archives

COLLECTIONS: [1865-1940] Archival materials, household items, furniture, vintage clothing, military items, office equipment, farm and ranch

5752
Roswell Museum and Art Center
100 W Eleventh St, 88201; (p) (505) 624-6744; (f) (505) 624-6765; rufe@roswellmuseum.org; roswellmuseum.org; (c) Chaves

City/ 1937/ staff: 12(f); 6(p); 150(v)/ members: 1144

ART MUSEUM; HISTORY MUSEUM; LIBRARY AND/OR ARCHIVES: Displays art and historical artifacts.

PROGRAMS: Community Outreach; Concerts; Elder's Programs; Exhibits; Facility Rental; Family Programs; Festivals; Film/Video; Guided Tours; Interpretation; Lectures; Publication; Research Library/Archives; School-Based Curriculum; Theatre

COLLECTIONS: [1850-present] Art, rocket exhibits, and historical exhibits related to Native American, Spanish, Mexican, European American, and African American cultures.

HOURS: Yr M-Sa 9-5, Su 1-5

RUIDOSO DOWNS

5753
Hubbard Museum of the American West, The
841 Hwy 70 W, 88346 [PO Box 40, 88346]; (p) (505) 378-4142; moth@zianet.com; www.zianet.com/museum; (c) Lincoln

Private non-profit/ 1989/ staff: 17(f); 23(p); 150(v)/ members: 1100/publication: *Hoofprints*

HISTORY MUSEUM: Operates broad programs relevant to history of the horse and the American West.

PROGRAMS: Community Outreach; Concerts; Elder's Programs; Exhibits; Facility Rental; Family Programs; Festivals; Guided Tours; Interpretation; Lectures; Living History; Publication; Reenactments; Research Library/Archives; School-Based Curriculum; Theatre

COLLECTIONS: [1850-1950] Wheeled vehicles, horse racing, cowboys, Native Americans, Hispanic Americans, Lincoln County War, Billy the Kid, historic structures.

HOURS: Yr Daily 10-5

ADMISSION: $6, Seniors $5; $5 Military

SAINT PETER

5754
Saint Peter Heritage Preservation Commission
227 S Front St, 56082; (p) (507) 931-4840; (f) (507) 931-4917; (c) Nicollet

City/ 1989/ staff: 2(f)

HISTORIC PRESERVATION AGENCY: Conducts and promotes historic preservation.

PROGRAMS: Community Outreach

SANTA FE

5755
El Rancho de las Golondrinas
334 Los Pinos Road, 87505; (p) (505) 471-2261; (f) (505) 471-5623; erdlgolond@aol.com; www.golondrinas.org; (c) Santa Fe

Private non-profit/ 1972/ Rancho de las Golondrinas Charitable Trust/ staff: 9(f); 10(p); 170(v)/ members: 665

HISTORIC SITE; LIVING HISTORY/OUTDOOR MUSEUM: Preserves and displays artifacts of Spanish Colonial NM.

PROGRAMS: Elder's Programs; Exhibits; Facility Rental; Family Programs; Guided Tours; Interpretation; Lectures; Living History; Publication; Reenactments

COLLECTIONS: [1700-1890] Furniture, textiles, tools, traditional religious art.

HOURS: June-Sept

5756
Historical Society of New Mexico
[PO Box 1912, 87504]; (p) (505) 476-7955; (c) Santa Fe

Private non-profit/ 1859/ members: 315/publication: *La Cronica de Nuevo Mexico*

HISTORICAL SOCIETY: Encourages appreciation of NM historical, architectural, and cultural heritage.

PROGRAMS: Annual Meeting; Lectures; Publication

COLLECTIONS: [1598-1912] Institutional records.

5757
New Mexico Historic Preservation Division
228 E Palace Ave, 87501; (p) (505) 827-6320; (f) (505) 827-6338; www.museums.state.nm.us/hpd/; (c) Santa Fe

State/ Office of Cultural Affairs/ staff: 27(f); 2(p)

STATE AGENCY: Protects, preserves, and interprets NM history.

PROGRAMS: Community Outreach; Lectures; Publication; Research Library/Archives

HOURS: Yr M-F 8-5

ADMISSION: No charge

5758
New Mexico State Monuments
113 Lincoln Ave, 87504 [PO Box 2807, 87504]; (p) (505) 476-5085; (f) (505) 476-5088; (c) Santa Fe

State/ 1909/ staff: 22(f); 2(p); 10(v)

ALLIANCE OF HISTORICAL AGENCIES; HISTORIC SITE: Preserves, protects, and interprets state's cultural resources.

PROGRAMS: Annual Meeting; Community Outreach; Concerts; Elder's Programs; Facility Rental; Family Programs; Festivals; Film/Video; Garden Tours; Guided Tours; Interpretation; Lectures; Living History; Publication; Reenactments; Research Library/Archives; School-Based Curriculum

COLLECTIONS: [900-1880]
HOURS: Yr Daily 8:30-5
ADMISSION: Price varies

5759
New Mexico State Records Center and Archives
1205 Camino Carlos Rey, 87505; (p) (505) 476-7902; (f) (505) 476-7901; www.state.nm.us/cpr; (c) Santa Fe

State/ 1959/ NM Commission of Public Records/ staff: 30(f); 5(v)/publication: *Quipu*

LIBRARY AND/OR ARCHIVES; RESEARCH CENTER: Houses permanent historical records of NM from the Spanish colonial government, Mexican government, Territorial, and statehood.

PROGRAMS: Community Outreach; Film/Video; Lectures; Publication; Research Library/Archives

COLLECTIONS: [1621-present] Administrative, military, judicial, financial, and legislative records of NM government.

HOURS: Yr M-F 8-5

5760
Palace of the Governors Museum
105 W Palace Ave, 87504 [PO Box 2087, 87504-2087]; (p) (505) 476-5094; (f) (505) 476-5104; (c) Santa Fe

State/ 1909/ staff: 15(f); 3(p); 160(v)

HISTORY MUSEUM; LIBRARY AND/OR ARCHIVES

PROGRAMS: Exhibits; Facility Rental; Festivals; Guided Tours; Interpretation; Lectures; Living History; Research Library/Archives

COLLECTIONS: [1540-present]

HOURS: Yr

5761
Wheelwright Museum of the American Indian
704 Camino Lejo, 87502 [PO Box 5153, 87502]; (p) (505) 982-4636; (f) (505) 989-7386; www.collectorsguide.com; (c) Santa Fe

Private non-profit/ 1937/ Board of Directors/ staff: 15(f); 2(p); 200(v)/ members: 1100/publication: *The Messenger*

HISTORY MUSEUM: Houses library and research materials.

PROGRAMS: Annual Meeting; Exhibits; Guided Tours; Lectures; Publication; Research Library/Archives

COLLECTIONS: [Prehistory-present] Native American artistic and cultural artifacts from Navajo and NM tribes.

HOURS: Yr M-Sa 10-5, Su 1-5

SANTA TERESA

5762
War Eagles Air Museum
8012 Airport Rd, 88008; (p) (505) 589-2000; (f) (505) 589-0814; www.wareaglesairmuseum.com; (c) Dona Ana

Private non-profit/ 1989/ staff: 3(f); 40(v)

HISTORY MUSEUM: Collects, restores, and displays historic aircraft and other vehicles of the WWII and Korean Conflict eras.

PROGRAMS: Facility Rental; Guided Tours

COLLECTIONS: [Mid 20th C.-present] Military aircraft.

HOURS: Yr

SILVER CITY

5763
Billy the Kid Family Cabin
312 W Broadway, 88061; (p) (505) 538-5921

5764
Silver City Museum
312 W Broadway, 88061; (p) (505) 538-5921; (f) (505) 388-1096; scmuseum@zianet.com; (c) Grant

City/ 1967/ staff: 5(f); 6(p); 64(v)/ members: 275/publication: *Built to Last: An Architectural History of Silver City, New Mexico*

HISTORY MUSEUM: Collects, preserves, researches, and interprets history and objects relating to the peoples of Southwest NM.

PROGRAMS: Annual Meeting; Community Outreach; Exhibits; Facility Rental; Family Programs; Guided Tours; Lectures; Publication; Research Library/Archives; School-Based Curriculum

COLLECTIONS: [1800-present] 13,000 photos, 3,000 household and personal artifacts, business and industrial equipment, Mimbres pottery, Native American items.

HOURS: Yr T-F 9-4, Sa-Su

5765
Western New Mexico University Museum
10th St w/in campus, 88062 [PO Box 680, 88062]; (p) (505) 538-6386; (f) (505) 538-6178; www.wnmu.edu/univ/museum.htm; (c) Grant

1974/ Western New Mexico University/ staff: 2(f); 7(p); 14(v)/ members: 75

HISTORY MUSEUM: Presents prehistory and history of Southwest NM.

PROGRAMS: Community Outreach; Elder's Programs; Exhibits; Facility Rental; Family Programs; Festivals; Guided Tours; Interpretation; Lectures; Research Library/Archives; School-Based Curriculum

COLLECTIONS: [200-1350] Mimbres pottery and artifacts, Casas Grandes pottery and artifacts, mining history, history of Silver City, photos, andcampus collections.

SPRINGER

5766
Santa Fe Trail Museum
606 Maxwell Ave, 87747 [PO Box 488, 87747]; (p) (505) 483-5554; (f) (505) 483-2670; miketmgllc@yahoo.com; (c) Colfax

City/ 1967/ staff: 2(p); 3(v)

HISTORIC SITE; HISTORY MUSEUM: Promotes history and cultural heritage of the Santa Fe Trail.

PROGRAMS: Exhibits; Interpretation

COLLECTIONS: [Late 19th c-early 20th c] Early rural life and the Santa Fe Trail.

HOURS: Mem Day-Labor Day, M-Sa 9-4

TAOS

5767
Ernest L. Blumenschein Home
222 Ledoux St, 87571 [Kit Carson Historic Museums, PO Drawer CCC, 87571]; (p) (505) 758-0505; (f) (505) 758-0330

HOUSE MUSEUM

5768
Fechin Institute
227 Paseo del Pueblo Norte, 87571 [PO Box 832, 87571]; (p) (505) 758-1710; (c) Taos

Private non-profit/ 1981/ staff: 6(p); 11(v)

ART MUSEUM; HISTORIC SITE

PROGRAMS: Concerts; Exhibits; Lectures

HOURS: Yr W-Su 10-2

ADMISSION: $4

5769
Governor Bent Museum
117 Bent St, 87571 [PO Box 153, 87571]; (p) (505) 758-2376; (c) Taos

Private for-profit/ 1959/ Owner/ staff: 1(f)

HISTORIC SITE: Preserves former home of Charles Bent, First Civilian Governor of NM.

PROGRAMS: Guided Tours

COLLECTIONS: [19th and 20th c] Indian artifacts, Bent Family artifacts.

HOURS: Yr Daily 10-5

ADMISSION: $2, Children $1

5770
Hacienda Martinez
708 Hacienda Rd, 87571 [Kit Carson Historic Museums, PO Drawer CCC, 87571]; (p) (505) 758-0505; (f) (505) 758-0330

5771
Harwood Museum of the University of New Mexico
238 Ledoux St, 87571 [4080 NDCBU, 87571]; (p) (505) 758-9826; (f) (505) 758-1475; harwood@unm.edu; (c) Taos

State/ 1923/ Univ of NM/ staff: 7(f); 5(p); 12(v)/ members: 175/publication: *Alliance Newsletter*

ART MUSEUM; LIBRARY AND/ OR ARCHIVES: Promotes cultural heritage.

PROGRAMS: Annual Meeting; Community Outreach; Concerts; Exhibits; Facility Rental; Guided Tours; Interpretation; Lectures; Publication; Research Library/Archives

COLLECTIONS: [Late 18th c-present]

HOURS: Yr T-Sa 10-5, Su 12-5

ADMISSION: $5

5772
Kit Carson Historic Museums
222 Ledoux, 87571 [PO Drawer CCC, 87571]; (p) (505) 758-0330; nitkit@laplaza.org; www.laplaza.org/art/kitcarson; (c) Taos

Private non-profit/ 1952/ Board of Directors/ staff: 8(f); 15(p); 53(v)/ members: 184

HISTORIC SITE; LIBRARY AND/OR ARCHIVES: Collects, preserves, restores, and interprets artifacts and structures relevant to local history.

PROGRAMS: Annual Meeting; Community Outreach; Elder's Programs; Exhibits; Facility Rental; Family Programs; Festivals; Guided Tours; Interpretation; Lectures; Living History; Publication; Research Library/Archives; School-Based Curriculum

COLLECTIONS: [1804-1960] Furniture, personal belongings, and artwork related to the Spanish Colonial, Mexican, and American Territorial periods; photos and archives.

5773
La Hacienda de los Martinez
708 Hacienda Rd, 87571 [222 L'Doux St, 87571]; (p) (505) 758-0505; (f) (505) 758-0330; www.taosmuseums.org

1804

Restores home that served as trading post and ranching headquarters in the Spanish Colonial and Mexican Republic periods.

COLLECTIONS: [1820-1930] Late Spanish Colonial furniture; traditional crafts of northern NM.; 1,500-2,000 vertical files on individuals and events related to northern New Mexico; 14,000 historic images.

HOURS: Yr

5774
Millicent Rogers Museum
1504 Millicent Rogers Rd, 87571 [PO Box A, 87571]; (p) (505) 758-2462; (f) (505) 758-5751; mrm@newmex.com; www.millicentrogers.org; (c) Taos

Private non-profit/ 1956/ Board of Trustees/ staff: 7(f); 6(p); 10(v)/ members: 586

ART MUSEUM: Collects, preserves, and interprets the art and culture of Native American, Hispanic, and Anglo residents of the Taos area.

PROGRAMS: Community Outreach; Concerts; Exhibits; Family Programs; Festivals; Guided Tours; Lectures; School-Based Curriculum

COLLECTIONS: [Prehistory-present] Native and Pueblo jewelry, Navajo and Rio Grande textiles, Pueblo pottery, Maria Martinez family collection of ceramic art, Southwestern basketry, Rio Grande pueblo painting; Hispanic domestic, traditional, and devotional arts.

HOURS: Apr-Oct Daily 10-5, Nov-Mar T-Su 10-5

ADMISSION: $6, Family $12, Student $5, Children $1, Seniors $5; $4 NM Residents

5775
Taos County Historical Society, Inc.
121 C N Plaza, 87571 [PO Box 2447, 87571]; www.silverhawk.com/taos/tchs; (c) Taos

Private non-profit/ 1952/ Board of Directors/ staff: 12(v)/ members: 110/publication: *Ayer y Hoy en Taos*

HISTORICAL SOCIETY: Studies and preserves historical resources of Taos County and Northern NM.

PROGRAMS: Annual Meeting; Guided Tours; Lectures; Publication; Research Library/Archives

COLLECTIONS: [1950-present] Taos News, audio and video tapes of Taos personalities, society records.

TRUTH OR CONSEQUENCES

5776
Callahan's Auto Museum
410 Ceder St, 87901; (p) (505) 894-6900; (c)
Sierra

Private non-profit/ 1991/ staff: 8(v)

AUTOMOBILE MUSEUM: Preserves and displays automobiles.

PROGRAMS: Exhibits; Festivals; Guided
Tours; Interpretation

COLLECTIONS: [1900-1970] Restored automobiles, memorabilia, toys and auto related
items.

HOURS: Yr M-Sa 10-4:30

ADMISSION: $3

5777
**Sierra County Historical
Society/Geronimo Springs Museum**
211 Main, 87901; (p) (505) 894-6600; (f)
(505) 894-1968; (c) Sierra

Private non-profit/ 1972/ Sierra Co. Historical
Society/ staff: 3(p); 15(v)/ members: 250

HISTORICAL SOCIETY: Operates Geronimo
Springs Museum.

PROGRAMS: Annual Meeting; Community
Outreach; Exhibits; Facility Rental; Family Programs; Guided Tours; Lectures; Living History;
School-Based Curriculum

COLLECTIONS: [Prehistory-present] Mammoth
and mastodon skulls, prehistoric Mimbres pottery, modern pottery, arrowheads and tools, authentic log cabin, ranching, and military.

HOURS: Yr M-Sa 9-5

ADMISSION: $2

TUCUMCARI

5778
**Tucumcari Historical Research
Institute and Museum**
416 S Adams, 88401; (p) (505) 461-4201; (c)
Quay

City/ 1967/ staff: 3(f); 1(p)/ members: 128

HISTORY MUSEUM: Collects artifacts of local
area history.

PROGRAMS: Annual Meeting; Exhibits

COLLECTIONS: [Prehistory-present] Dinosaur bones, photos, artifacts such as saddles, arrowheads, furniture, machines.

HOURS: Yr Sep 2-June 2 T-Sa 9-5; June 2-
Sep 2 M-Sa 9-6

ADMISSION: $2.11, Children $0.53

TULAROSA

5779
Tularosa Village Historical Society
608 Central, 88352 [Box 662, 88352]; (p)
(505) 585-9597, (505) 585-2057; (c) Otero

1975/ Tularosa Village Historical Society/
members: 25

HISTORICAL SOCIETY: Operates a museum
which presents local artifacts.

COLLECTIONS: Pre-historic, Indian, Hispanic, Anglo.

HOURS: Yr M-F

WATROUS

5780
Fort Union National Monument
Exit 366 on I-25, 8 mi on NM161, 87753 [PO
Box 127, 87753]; (p) (505) 425-8025; (f) (505)
454-1155; founadminstration@nps.gov; (c)
Mora

Federal/ 1953/ Dept of the Interior/ staff: 13(f);
1(p); 2(v)

HISTORIC SITE; HISTORY MUSEUM: Displays artifacts of an army installation and the
Santa Fe Trail.

PROGRAMS: Community Outreach; Exhibits;
Film/Video; Guided Tours; Interpretation; Living History; School-Based Curriculum

COLLECTIONS: [1851-1891] Historical and
archaeological objects and associated field
records pertaining to the three Fort Unions,
and their significance in the development of
the Santa Fe Trail, the Civil War, and the settling of the West.

HOURS: Yr Daily Winter 8-5, Summer 8-6

ADMISSION: $2, Family $4

WINSTON

5781
Pioneer Store Museum
W Wall St, 87943 [HCR 30 Box 134, 87943];
(p) (505) 743-2736; edmund@zianet.com; (c)
Sierra

Private non-profit/ 1995/ staff: 2(p); 2(v)

HISTORIC SITE

PROGRAMS: Community Outreach; Elder's
Programs; Exhibits; Guided Tours; Interpretation; Lectures

COLLECTIONS: [1880-1923] Furnishings and
inventory of an operating 1880s dry goods
store in a silver-mining boom town, including
1890s women's clothing, photographs of local
residents, and town records from 1881-1923.

HOURS: Yr Daily 8-5, by appt.

ZUNI

5782
**A:shiwi A:wau Museum and Heritage
Center**
1222 Hwy 53, 87327 [PO Box 1009, 87327];
(p) (505) 782-4403; (f) (505) 782-4503; (c)
McKinley

Private non-profit/ 1989/ staff: 2(f); 3(p); 10(v)

CULTURAL CENTER; HISTORY MUSEUM:
Preserves cultural heritage of Zuni people.

PROGRAMS: Community Outreach; Exhibits;
Facility Rental; Festivals; Guided Tours; Interpretation; Lectures; Research Library/
Archives; School-Based Curriculum

COLLECTIONS: [Prehistoric-contemporary]
Materials related to the prehistory, history and
natural environment of the Zuni people and
culture.

HOURS: Yr M-Sa 9-5:30

ADMISSION: Donations requested

NEW YORK

ALBANY

5783
Albany Institute of History and Art
125 Washington Ave, 12210; (p) (518) 463-
4478; (f) (518) 462-1522;
www.albanyinstitute.org; (c) Albany

Private non-profit/ 1791/ staff: 33(f); 8(p);
300(v)/ members: 1600

ART MUSEUM; HISTORY MUSEUM: Collects, preserves, interprets, and promotes interest in the history, art, and culture of Albany
and the Upper Hudson Valley region.

PROGRAMS: Annual Meeting; Community
Outreach; Exhibits; Facility Rental; Festivals;
Guided Tours; Lectures; Research Library/
Archives; School-Based Curriculum

COLLECTIONS: [Late 17th c-present] Life and
culture of the Upper Hudson Valley region artifacts.

5784
**Destroyer Escort Historical
Foundation**
Hudson River, 12207 [11 Pruyn St, 12207];
(p) (518) 431-1943; (f) (581) 431-1943; (c)
Albany

Private non-profit/ 1993/ Destroyer Escort Historical Foundation/ staff: 2(f); 3(p); 60(v)/ members: 1300/publication: *Trim, But Deadly:
Newsletter of the DEHF; Slater Signals: Volunteer Newsletter*

HISTORIC SITE: Restores and maintains USS
Sater, WWII Destroyer Escort.

PROGRAMS: Elder's Programs; Family Programs; Guided Tours; Interpretation; Publication

COLLECTIONS: [WWII Naval History] 150
bound volumes; 2,300 WWII navigation charts;
600 naval architect/ engineering blueprints;
1,300 photographs; about 2 linear feet of
handwritten, printed and typewritten letters/
legal sized documents; and 3 16mm black and
white sound training films.

HOURS: Apr-Nov Th-Su 11-4

ADMISSION: $5, Children $2, Seniors $3

5785
Historic Cherry Hill
523 1/2 S Pearl St, 12202; (p) (518) 434-
4791; (f) (518) 434-4806; (c) Albany

Private non-profit/ 1964/ staff: 3(f); 6(p); 50(v)/
members: 250

HOUSE MUSEUM

PROGRAMS: Community Outreach; Exhibits;
Family Programs; Guided Tours; Interpretation;
Publication; Research Library/Archives;
School-Based Curriculum

COLLECTIONS: Van Rensselaer-Rankin family artifacts; 20,000 objects; 5,000 books;
3,000 photos; and 30,000 manuscripts.

HOURS: Feb-Dec Daily T-Sa 10-4, Su 1-4

ADMISSION: $3.50

5786
New York State Commission on the Restoration of the Capitol
Corning Tower, 40th Floor/ Empire State Plaza, 12242; (p) (518) 473-0341; (f) (518) 474-5635; (c) Albany

State/ 1979/ NYSC on the Restoration of the Capitol/ staff: 3(f); 13(v)

HISTORIC PRESERVATION AGENCY; HISTORIC SITE: Promotes restoration and rehabilitation of the NY State Capitol.

PROGRAMS: Exhibits; Guided Tours; Interpretation; Lectures; Publication

COLLECTIONS: [1879-1940]

HOURS: Yr Daily 9-6

ADMISSION: No charge

5787
New York State Museum
Madison Ave, 12230 [Rm 3140 CEC, 12230]; (p) (518) 474-5812; (f) (518) 486-3696; csiegfri@mail.nysed.gov; www.nysm.nysed.gov; (c) Albany

State/ 1836/ New York State/ staff: 118(f); 29(p); 214(v)/ members: 2300

HISTORY MUSEUM

PROGRAMS: Community Outreach; Exhibits; Facility Rental; Family Programs; Festivals; Interpretation; Lectures; Living History; Publication; School-Based Curriculum

COLLECTIONS: [Prehistory- present] 6 million objects in natural sciences and human history: paleontology, geology, zoology, botany, entomology, decorative arts, fine arts, industrial history.

HOURS: Yr

5788
Schulyer Mansion State Historic Site
32 Catherine St, 12202; (p) (518) 434-0834; (f) (518) 434-3821; (c) Albany

State/ 1917/ staff: 6(f); 4(p)

HISTORIC SITE; HOUSE MUSEUM: Preserves 18th c Georgian mansion of Revolutionary War Major-General Philip Schulyer and his family.

PROGRAMS: Community Outreach; Exhibits; Family Programs; Guided Tours; Interpretation; Reenactments; School-Based Curriculum

COLLECTIONS: [1733-1804] NY and New England furniture, English decorative arts of the Colonial and Federal periods. Chinese export porcelains; fine 18th c. furniture including Seymour sideboard; trapunto coverlets; English glassware.; New York Public Library Schuyler Papers on microfilm (40+ reels)

HOURS: Apr-Oct W-Sa 10-5 Su 1-5

ADMISSION: $3, Children $1, Seniors $2

5790
Shaker Heritage Society
Shaker Meeting House, Albany Shaker Rd, 12211; (p) (518) 456-7890; (f) (518) 452-7348; shakerwv@crisny.org; crisny.org/not-for-profit/shakerwv; (c) Albany

Private non-profit/ 1977/ Board of Directors/ staff: 2(f); 4(p); 150(v)/ members: 600

HISTORIC PRESERVATION AGENCY; HISTORIC SITE; HISTORICAL SOCIETY; HISTORY MUSEUM: Preserves Shaker culture and history.

PROGRAMS: Annual Meeting; Community Outreach; Concerts; Elder's Programs; Exhibits; Facility Rental; Family Programs; Festivals; Garden Tours; Guided Tours; Interpretation; Lectures; Publication

COLLECTIONS: [18th c-present] Books, papers, photographs and artifacts all relating to Shakers and Watervliet Shaker Community.

HOURS: Yr May, Nov, Dec T-Sa

5791
Ten Broeck Mansion
9 Ten Broeck Pl, 12210; (p) (518) 436-9826; (f) (518) 436-1489; www.tenbroeck.org; (c) Albany

Private non-profit/ 1948/ Albany County Historical Assoc/ staff: 1(f); 2(p); 4(v)/ members: 307/publication: *Mansion News*

HOUSE MUSEUM: Preserves and maintains Ten Broeck Mansion as an historic site.

PROGRAMS: Annual Meeting; Community Outreach; Concerts; Exhibits; Facility Rental; Guided Tours; Lectures; Living History; Publication; Reenactments

COLLECTIONS: [Federal/Empire] Paintings, furniture, and ceramics.

HOURS: May-Dec Th-Su 1-4

ADMISSION: $3, Children $1

ALEXANDRIA BAY

5792
Boldt Castle
New York-Canadian border, 1000 Island region, 13607 [PO Box 428, 13607]; (p) (315) 482-2501; (f) (315) 482-5925; info@boldtcastle.com; www.boldtcastle.com; (c) Jefferson

County/ 1900/ Thousand Islands Bridge Authority/ staff: 8(f); 35(p)

HISTORIC SITE; HISTORY MUSEUM: Preserves historic summer estate of George C. Boldt.

PROGRAMS: Exhibits; Facility Rental; Guided Tours; Interpretation

COLLECTIONS: [1890-1920] Furniture, china; artifacts related to life along the St. Lawrence River and 1000 Islands area.

HOURS: May-Sept M-Su 10-6:30

ADMISSION: $4.25, Children $2.50

5793
Casa Blanca
Cherry Island, 13607 [Box 27, 13607]; (p) (315) 482-2279; (f) (315) 482-4817; (c) Jefferson

Private for-profit/ 1895/ staff: 3(f)

HOUSE MUSEUM

COLLECTIONS: [1892-1929] Period furnishing; sites: ice house, pump house, boat house; boats, laundry house and cleaning equipment c. 1895.

HOURS: May-Sep by appt

ADMISSION: $15, Children $7.50

ALFRED

5794
Alfred Historical Society
[PO Box 1137, 14802]; (f) (607) 587-9780; (c) Allegany

Private non-profit/ 1968/ staff: 10(v)/ members: 75

Collects, protects, and interprets material pertaining to the history of Alfred.

COLLECTIONS: [1860-present] Photos, books, and ephemera.

AMENIA

5795
Wethersfield Estate and Gardens
Pugsley Hill, 12501 [PO Box 444, 12501]; (p) (914)

AMHERST

5796
Amherst Museum
3755 Tonawanda Creek Rd, 14228; (p) (716) 689-1440; (f) (716) 689-1409; (c) Erie

1972/ Town of Amherst/ staff: 17(f); 1(p); 250(v)/ members: 821

HISTORY MUSEUM; LIVING HISTORY/OUTDOOR MUSEUM: Collects, preserves, and interprets the history of Amherst and the surrounding communities of Western NY's Niagara frontier region.

PROGRAMS: Community Outreach; Concerts; Exhibits; Festivals; Guided Tours; Interpretation; Lectures; Living History; Reenactments; Research Library/Archives; School-Based Curriculum

COLLECTIONS: [1800-1960] Archives, textile collection, material culture, and twelve restored and furnished buildings.

HOURS: Yr T-F 9:30-4:30 and Apr-Oct 12:30-4:30, Sa-Su 12:30-4:30

ADMISSION: $4, Family

AMSTERDAM

5797
Guy Park Manor
355 W Main St, 12010 [PO Box 309, 12010]; (c) Montgomery

State/ 1773

HISTORIC SITE

COLLECTIONS: [Colonial era] Site: Colonial building and Erie Canal locks.

HOURS: Yr Daily 8:30- dusk

ANNANDALE-ON-HUDSON

5798
Montgomery Place Historic Estate
River Rd, 12504 [PO Box 32, 12504]; (p) (914) 758-5461; (f) (914) 758-0545; www.hudsonvalley.org; (c) Dutchess

Private non-profit/ 1988/ Historic Hudson Valley

GARDEN; HISTORIC PRESERVATION AGENCY; HISTORIC SITE; HOUSE MUSEUM; LIVING HISTORY/OUTDOOR MUSEUM: Significant and meticulously conserved county seat. 434 acre estate includes an elegant mansion, rolling lawns, gardens, and scenic views of the Hudson River and Catskill Mountains.

PROGRAMS: Facility Rental; Family Programs; Festivals; Garden Tours; Guided Tours; Interpretation; Lectures; Living History; School-Based Curriculum

COLLECTIONS: [18th-20th c.] Period furnishing; A.J. Davis architecture, A.J. Downing landscape.

HOURS: Apr-Oct W-M 10-5; Nov Sa-Su 10-5

ADMISSION: $6, Student $3, Seniors $5; Under 6 free, Grounds Pass $3

ARCADE

5799
Arcade Historical Society
331 W Main St, 14009 [PO Box 236, 14009]; (p) (716) 492-4466; (c) Wyoming

Private non-profit/ 1957/ staff: 1(p); 21(v)/ members: 125/publication: *Arcade Historical Society News*

HISTORICAL SOCIETY; HOUSE MUSEUM: Collects and preserves Arcade history.

PROGRAMS: Annual Meeting; Exhibits; Guided Tours; Publication

COLLECTIONS: [Late 1800s-present] Newspapers, clippings, photos.

ARMONK

5800
North Castle Historical Society, The
440 Bedford Rd, 10504; (p) (914) 273-4610; (c) Westchester

Private non-profit/ 1971/ staff: 50(v)/ members: 250/publication: *North Castle History*

HISTORICAL SOCIETY: Owns and maintains four structures: 1798 Quaker Meeting House; Colonial-era Smith's Tavern; Brundage Blacksmith Shop; one room East Middle Patent Schoolhouse.

PROGRAMS: Annual Meeting; Concerts; Exhibits; Facility Rental; Family Programs; Festivals; Film/Video; Interpretation; Publication; Research Library/Archives; School-Based Curriculum

COLLECTIONS: [1790s-present] Buildings, furnishings, costumes, photos.

ASTORIA

5801
American Museum of the Moving Image
35 Ave at 36 St, 11106 [36-01 35 Ave, 11106]; (p) (718) 784-4520; (f) (718) 784-4681; info@ammi.org; www.ammi.org; (c) Queens

Private non-profit/ 1977/ Board of Trustees/ staff: 41(f); 30(p); 30(v)/ members: 500

ART MUSEUM; HISTORIC SITE; HISTORY MUSEUM: Promotes history of film, television and digital media and their impact on society.

PROGRAMS: Exhibits; Facility Rental; Guided Tours; Interpretation; Lectures; School-Based Curriculum

COLLECTIONS: [20th c] 85,000 artifacts of material culture: cameras, props, costumes, and stage sets; film projectors and theater furnishings; merchandise tie-ins like lunch boxes and toys, fan magazines, and posters.

HOURS: Yr M 9-1(school groups only), T-F 12-5, Sa-Su

AUBURN

5802
Cayuga Museum
203 Genesee St, 13021; (p) (315) 253-8051; (f) (315) 253-9829; cayugamuseum@cayuganet.org; www.cayuganet.org/cayugamuseum; (c) Cayuga

Private non-profit/ 1936/ Board of Directors/ staff: 4(f); 2(p); 9(v)/ members: 237

HISTORIC SITE; HISTORY MUSEUM: Collects, preserves, and interprets the history of Cayuga County.

PROGRAMS: Community Outreach; Concerts; Elder's Programs; Exhibits; Family Programs; Festivals; Guided Tours; Lectures; Research Library/Archives

COLLECTIONS: 15,000 museum artifacts; 177 paintings; 2,000 photos; archives and manuscripts; decorative arts; case research lab collection.

HOURS: Feb-Dec T-Su 12-5

ADMISSION: No charge

5803
Harriet Tubman House
180 S St, 13021; (p) (315) 252-2081

5804
Seward House, The
33 S St, 13021; (p) (315) 252-1283; www.sewardhouse.org; (c) Cayuga

Private non-profit/ 1951/ staff: 3(f); 1(p); 12(v)/publication: *The Seward House*

HOUSE MUSEUM: Preserves historic home of politician W. H. Seward

PROGRAMS: Exhibits; Festivals; Garden Tours; Guided Tours; Interpretation; Publication; Research Library/Archives; School-Based Curriculum

COLLECTIONS: [19th c] Furnishing, paintings, furniture, libraries, toys, Alaskan Native American artifacts, Civil War material, photos, documents, costumes, political items.

HOURS: Feb 1-June 30 T-Sa 1-4; July 1-Oct 14 T-Sa 10-4, Su 1-4; Oct 15-Dec 31 T-Sa 1-4

ADMISSION: $4, Student $3, Seniors $3.50; Under 12 free

BALDWIN

5805
Baldwin Historical Society
1980 Grand Ave, 11510 [PO Box 762, 11510]; (p) (516) 223-6900; (c) Nassau

Private non-profit/ 1974/ staff: 6(v)/ members: 135

HISTORICAL SOCIETY; HISTORY MUSEUM: Preserves local history.

PROGRAMS: Exhibits; Lectures; School-Based Curriculum

COLLECTIONS: [1800-present] Photos, postcards, local artifacts, tools, and bicycles.

HOURS: Yr W Su 12-4

BALLSTON SPA

5806
National Bottle Museum
76 Milton Ave, 12020; (p) (518) 885-7589; (f) (518) 885-0317; nbm@crisny.org; (c) Saratoga

Private non-profit/ 1979/ Board of Trustees/ staff: 1(f); 1(p); 15(v)/ members: 500/publication: *The Bottle Muse*

HISTORY MUSEUM: Preserves and promotes bottling industry.

PROGRAMS: Annual Meeting; Exhibits; Festivals; Film/Video; Guided Tours; Interpretation; Lectures; Publication; Research

5807
Saratoga County Historical Society/Brookside
6 Charlton St, 12020; (p) (518) 885-4000; (f) (518) 885-7085; info@brooksidemuseum.org; www.brooksidemuseum.org; (c) Saratoga

Private non-profit/ 1972/ staff: 1(f); 3(p); 36(v)/ members: 349/publication: *Columns, The Grist Mill*

HISTORICAL SOCIETY: Collects, preserves and interprets Saratoga County history and culture.

PROGRAMS: Annual Meeting; Community Outreach; Concerts; Exhibits; Facility Rental; Family Programs; Publication

COLLECTIONS: [1800-1950] 11,000 objects, 5,000 photos, 1,000 volume library, items and documents made or used in Saratoga County.

HOURS: Yr T-Fr 10-4, Sa 12-4

ADMISSION: $2, Student $1.50, Children $1, Seniors $1.50

BATAVIA

5808
Genesee County History Department
3 W Main St, 14020; (p) (716) 344-2550; (c) Genesee

County/ 1941/ staff: 3(f); 1(p); 5(v)

HISTORICAL SOCIETY: Collects, preserves, researches, interprets, and promotes archival materials relating to the county.

PROGRAMS: Lectures; Research Library/Archives

COLLECTIONS: [1802-present] Genesee County Federal census, 1810-1880; cemetery records; bound newspapers, 1879-1974; atlases and maps, 1854-1900's; tax rolls, 1850-1993; church records; genealogy files; city and county directories; obituary records; Civil War records.

HOURS: Yr M-F 9-4:30

ADMISSION: No charge

5809
Holland Land Office Museum and Holland Purchase Historical Society
131 W Main St, 14020; (p) (716) 343-4727; (f) (716) 345-0023; hphs@eznet.net; (c) Genesee

Joint/ 1894/ County, non-profit; Private non-profit/ staff: 1(f); 3(p); 30(v)/ members: 250

HISTORICAL SOCIETY; HISTORY MUSEUM: Preserves, interpretes, and promotes an interest in the collective heritage of Genesee County.

PROGRAMS: Community Outreach; Exhibits; Facility Rental; Family Programs; Guided Tours; Lectures; Reenactments

COLLECTIONS: [1800-present]

BEACON

5810
Madam Brett Homestead
50 Van Nydeck Ave, 12508; (p) (845) 831-6533; (c) Dutchess

Private non-profit/ 1954/ Daughters of the American Revolution (Melzingah Chapter)/ staff: 25(v)/ members: 150

HOUSE MUSEUM: Preserves Dutch Colonial home.

PROGRAMS: Community Outreach; Exhibits; Garden Tours; Guided Tours; Interpretation; Lectures

COLLECTIONS: [1700s-1900s] Furnishings, personal effects.

HOURS: May-Dec 1st Su 1-4, July-Aug

ADMISSION: $4, Seniors $2

5811
Mount Gulian Historic Site
145 Sterling St, 12508; (p) (914) 831-8172; (f) (914) 831-8172; (c) Dutchess

Private non-profit/ 1966/ Mount Gulian Society/ staff: 2(f); 2(p); 25(v)/ members: 220/publication: *The History of A.I. Verplanck and His Male Descendents*

HISTORIC SITE: Collects, preserves, and interprets the history of the Verplanck family, the American Revolution, and the Society of the Cincinnati.

PROGRAMS: Annual Meeting; Community Outreach; Exhibits; Facility Rental; Family Programs; Garden Tours; Guided Tours; Interpretation; Living History; Publication; Reenactments; Research Library/Archives; School-Based Curriculum

COLLECTIONS: [18th-20th c] Historic house; Dutch Barn; 1,886 artifacts; 53 objects of fine art; 288 decorative arts; 202 Native American archeological objects; 1,301 archival objects; 20 botany objects; 22 military.

HOURS: Jan- Apr by appt; May-Oct W-Th and Su 1-5; Nov-Dec W and Su 1-5

ADMISSION: $3

BELLEROSE

5812
The Puerto Rican/Hispanic Genealogical Society Inc.
P.O. Box 260118, 11426-0118; (p) (516) 834-2511; prhgs@yahoo.com; www.rootsweb.com/~prhgs/

1996

GENEALOGICAL SOCIETY: Established to enable Puerto Ricans, Hispanics, and other interested persons develop and enhance their skills, knowledge and ability to conduct a competent genealogical search for their ancestors; sponsors conferences, seminars, training sessions and originates print and electronic publications, that are specifically designed to inform, train and otherwise educate people about genealogical investigation principals, methods and techniques.

BELLPORT

5813
Bellport-Brookhaven Historical Society
31 Bellport Ln, 11713; (p) (516) 286-0888; (c) Suffolk

Private non-profit/ 1960/ staff: 45(v)/ members: 245/publication: *The Barn Museum News*

HISTORIC PRESERVATION AGENCY; HISTORICAL SOCIETY; HISTORY MUSEUM

PROGRAMS: Annual Meeting; Concerts; Exhibits; Facility Rental; Festivals; Guided Tours; Interpretation; Lectures; Publication; Research Library/Archives

COLLECTIONS: [19th c] Furnished house; artifacts: decoys, period dolls, nineteenth century weaving and carpentry tools, stenciled tinware; blacksmith shop; Bellport ice scooter.

HOURS: May-Sept Th-Sa

BELMONT

5814
Allegany County Historical Society
11 Wells Ln, 14813; (p) (716) 208-7428; (c) Allegany

County, non-profit; Private non-profit/ 1895/ Allegany County/ staff: 1(f); 1(p)

GENEALOGICAL SOCIETY; HISTORY MUSEUM; HOUSE MUSEUM; RESEARCH CENTER

PROGRAMS: Annual Meeting; Community Outreach; Concerts; Exhibits; Facility Rental; Garden Tours; Guided Tours; Interpretation; Lectures; Living History; School-Based Curriculum

COLLECTIONS: [1806-present] Local products, cemetery records, and genealogy files.

HOURS: Fall-Spring M-F 9-5; Summer M-F 8:30-4

5815
Allegany County Museum
7 Court St, 14813; (p) (716) 268-9293; (f) (716) 268-9446; (c) Allegany

County/ 1972/ staff: 1(f)

HISTORY MUSEUM: Promotes local history; serves as county historian's office.

PROGRAMS: Exhibits; Interpretation; Lectures; Research Library/Archives

COLLECTIONS: [1806-present]

HOURS: Yr M-F 9-5

5816
American Manse/Whitney-Halsey House, The
Corner of Whitney Pl, 14813 [39 S St, 14813]; (p) (716) 268-5130; (c) Allegany

1964/ Ruth Czankus/publication: *Charles Smith Whitney I, Philanthropist*

HISTORIC SITE; HOUSE MUSEUM

PROGRAMS: Guided Tours; Publication; Research Library/Archives

COLLECTIONS: [1870]

HOURS: May-Nov by appt

ADMISSION: $4, Student $2, Children $1, Seniors

BINGHAMTON

5817
Broome County Historical Society
185 Court St, 13901; (p) (607) 778-3572; (c) Broome

Private non-profit/ 1919/ Board of Directors/ staff: 1(p); 12(v)/ members: 440/publication: *BCHS Newsletter*

HISTORICAL SOCIETY; RESEARCH CENTER

PROGRAMS: Annual Meeting; Exhibits; Publication; Research Library/Archives

COLLECTIONS: [1790-present]

HOURS: Yr M-F 10-4

5818
Phelps Mansion, The
191 Court St, 13901; (p) (607) 722-4872; phelps@tier.net; www.tier.net/phelps

1870

HOUSE MUSEUM: Preserves home of former mayor Sherman David Phelps.

COLLECTIONS: [Post-Civil War] Chandeliers; woodwork and marble fireplaces; mirrors; Hudson River School paintings.

HOURS: Jan-May, Sep-Dec

5819
Roberson Museum and Science Center
30 Front St, 13905; (p) (607) 772-0660; (f) (607) 771-8905; robmuseum@juno.com; www.roberson.org

1905/ staff: 25(f); 16(p); 13(v)

COLLECTIONS: [1890-1910] Furniture; 19th and 20th century clothing and textiles; quilts; 200 years of fans; pressed glass; silver; swords; dolls; farm tools.; 25,000 photos; city directories; immigration history archives; genealogical material.

BLUE MOUNTAIN LAKE

5820
Adirondack Museum, The
Route 28 N & 30, 12812 [PO Box 99, 12812]; (p) (518) 352-7311; (f) (518) 352-7653; www.adkmuseum.org; (c) Hamilton

Private non-profit/ 1957/ staff: 28(f); 5(p); 78(v)/ members: 4500/publication: *Guideline*

HISTORY MUSEUM: Explores and presents Adirondack region history.

PROGRAMS: Community Outreach; Concerts; Exhibits; Facility Rental; Festivals; Garden Tours; Guided Tours; Interpretation; Lectures; Living History; Publication; Research Library/Archives; School-Based Curriculum; Theatre

COLLECTIONS: [Mid 19th-mid 20th c] 500 art; furniture; vehicles; boats; tools; hunting; fishing, camping, and winter sports gear; 67,000 historical photos.

HOURS: May-Mid Oct: Daily 9:30-5:30

ADMISSION: $10, Seniors $9; Under 17 free

BOLTON LANDING

5821
Historical Society of the Town of Bolton
Main St, 12814 [PO Box 441, 12814]; (p) (518) 644-9960; (c) Warren

City/ 1972/ Trustees of Bolton Historical Museum/ staff: 1(f); 1(p); 30(v)/ members: 50

HISTORICAL SOCIETY

PROGRAMS: Exhibits; Film/Video; Lectures

COLLECTIONS: [1850-1950]

HOURS: May-Oct Daily M-Sa 11-4/ 7-9, Su 11-4

ADMISSION: Donations accepted

5822
Marcella Sembrich Memorial Association Inc.
4800 Lakeshore Dr, 12814 [PO 417, 12814]; (p) (518) 644-9839; (f) (518) 644-2191; sembrich@webTV.net; www.operamuseum.com; (c) Warren

Private non-profit/ 1937/ Board of Directors/ staff: 2(p); 25(v)/ members: 200

HISTORY MUSEUM: Mme. Marcella Sembrich, a Metropolitan Opera diva, spent her final 15 summers in Bolton Landing and taught Juilliard and Curtis students in her studio which since 1937 has been a memorial studio museum.

PROGRAMS: Annual Meeting; Concerts; Exhibits; Guided Tours; Lectures

COLLECTIONS: [1858-1935] Teaching studio, gowns, art work, mementos, signed photos of artists (Rachmaninoff, Bruckner, Verdi, and more), books, scores, and furniture.

HOURS: Jun 15-Sep 15 M-Su

BREWSTER

5823
Putnam County History Dept
68 Main St, 10509; (p) (845) 278-7209; (f) (845) 278-4865; putpast@bestweb.net; www.putnamcountyny.com/historian; (c) Putnam

County/ 1940/ staff: 3(p); 2(v)

HISTORY MUSEUM: Preserves and perpetuates the history of Putnam County.

PROGRAMS: Community Outreach; Exhibits; Festivals; Film/Video; Interpretation; Lectures; Research Library/Archives

COLLECTIONS: [1700-present] Native Americans, Civil War artifacts.

HOURS: Yr M-F 9-4; Research: T W F and by appt

ADMISSION: No charge

5824
Southeast Museum
67 Main St, 10509; (p) (914) 279-7500; (f) (914) 279-1992

Private non-profit/ 1965/ staff: 2(f); 2(p); 30(v)/ members: 300

HISTORY MUSEUM: Collects, preserves and interprets materials pertaining to Southeast including the Harlem railroad, Tilly Foster Iron Mine, Borden Milk Factory.

PROGRAMS: Annual Meeting; Concerts; Exhibits; Facility Rental; Family Programs; Guided Tours; Interpretation; Lectures; School-Based Curriculum

COLLECTIONS: [19th c] Americana, farm and household equipment, quilts, photos, textiles.

HOURS: Mar-Dec T, W, F-Sa

ADMISSION: Donations accepted

BRIDGE HAMPTON

5825
Bridge Hampton Historical Society, Inc.
2368 Main St, 11932 [PO Box 977, 11932]; (p) (516) 537-1088; (f) (516) 537-4225; (c) Suffolk

Private non-profit/ 1956/ Board of Trustees/ staff: 1(f); 1(p); 5(v)/ members: 300/publication: *The Bridge Hampton Times; The Bridge*

HISTORICAL SOCIETY: Preserves history of Bridge Hampton.

PROGRAMS: Annual Meeting; Community Outreach; Exhibits; Facility Rental; Guided Tours; Publication

COLLECTIONS: [1830s-1950] Period clothing and textiles, documents, letters, and deeds.

HOURS: Mar 1-May 31 M-F 11-4; June 1-Sept 15 Th-Sa 11-4; Sept 16-Dec 31 M-F 11-4 and by appt

ADMISSION: Donations accepted

BRONX

5826
Bartow-Pell Mansion Museum
895 Shore Rd, Pelham Bay Park, 10591; (p) (718) 885-1461; (f) (718) 885-9164

1840/ staff: 2(f); 3(p); 20(v)

COLLECTIONS: [1836-1860] 19th c American decorative arts.

HOURS: Yr; Sept-1st week Aug W Sa Su 12-4

5827
Bronx County Historical Society
3309 & 3313 Bainbridge Ave, 10467 [3309 Bainbridge Ave, 10467]; (p) (718) 881-8900; (f) (718) 881-4827; www.bronxhistoricalsociety.org; (c) Bronx

Private non-profit/ 1955/ staff: 7(f); 6(p); 20(v)/ members: 920

HISTORIC SITE; HISTORICAL SOCIETY; HISTORY MUSEUM; HOUSE MUSEUM; RESEARCH CENTER: Collects and preserves the material culture of the Bronx; operates two historic house museum, library, and Bronx County Archives.

PROGRAMS: Annual Meeting; Community Outreach; Concerts; Exhibits; Festivals; Guided Tours; Interpretation; Lectures; Publication; Research Library/Archives; School-Based Curriculum

COLLECTIONS: [1870-1930]

HOURS: Yr M-F 9-5, Sa 10-4, Su 1-5

5828
Edgar Allan Poe Cottage
E Kingsbridge Rd, Grand Concourse, 10467 [Bronx County Hist Soc, 3309 Bainbridge Ave, 10467]; (p) (718) 881-8900; www.fieldtrip.com/ny/88818900.htm

5829
Van Cortlandt House Museum
Van Cortlandt Park, Broadway at W 246th St, 10471; (p) (718) 543-3344; (f) (718) 543-3315; vancortlandthouse@juno.com; ilovethebronx.com; (c) Bronx

Private non-profit/ 1896/ The National Society of Colonial Dames in the State of NY/ staff: 2(f); 2(p); 15(v)/ members: 75

HISTORIC SITE; HOUSE MUSEUM: Promotes history of Van Cortlandt Family Plantation.

PROGRAMS: Concerts; Exhibits; Facility Rental; Family Programs; Festivals; Guided Tours; Lectures; Living History; Reenactments; School-Based Curriculum

COLLECTIONS: [Colonial and federal] 18th-19th decorative and fine arts.

HOURS: Yr T-F 10-3, Sa-Su

BROOKLYN

5830
Brooklyn Historical Society, The
128 Pierrepont St, 11201; (p) (718) 624-0890; (f) (718) 875-3869; bhs@panix.com; www.brooklynhistory.org; (c) Kings

Private non-profit/ 1863/ staff: 7(f); 7(p); 74(v)/ members: 900/publication: *Newsletter and curriculum guides*

GENEALOGICAL SOCIETY; HISTORIC SITE; HISTORICAL SOCIETY; HISTORY MUSEUM; RESEARCH CENTER: The Brooklyn Historical Society is a museum, library, and education center dedicated to collecting, preserving, and making available important materials representative of Brooklyn's diverse people and cultures, past and present.

PROGRAMS: Community Outreach; Exhibits; Facility Rental; Guided Tours; Interpretation; Lectures; Publication; Research Library/Archives; School-Based Curriculum

COLLECTIONS: [17th c-present] 200 oils on canvas; 3,000 works of art on paper; 100,000 photographs; 7,000 artifacts 100,000 volumes; 1700 linear feet archives; 3000 maps; 40,000 microforms; and extensive ephemera.

HOURS: Yr M, Th-Sa 12-5

ADMISSION: $2.50, Student $1, Seniors $1

5831
Brooklyn Museum of Art
200 Eastern Pkwy, 11238; (p) (718) 638-5000; (f) (718) 638-5931; bklynmus@echonyc.com; www.brooklynart.org; (c) Kings

Private non-profit/ 1823/ Board of Trustees Brooklyn Institute of Arts and Sciences/ staff: 300(f); 75(v)/ members: 12500

ART MUSEUM: Preserves world cultural heritage, art.

PROGRAMS: Community Outreach; Concerts; Exhibits; Facility Rental; Festivals; Guided Tours; Interpretation; Lectures; Research

Library/Archives; School-Based Curriculum

HOURS: Yr W-F 10-5, Sa-Su 11-5

ADMISSION: $4, Student $2, Seniors $1.50; Members/Under 12 free

5832
Brooklyn Public Library-Brooklyn Collection
Central Library, Grand Army Plaza, 11238; (p) (718) 230-2762; (f) (718) 857-2245; (c) Kings

City/ 1897/ Brooklyn Public Library/ staff: 4(f); 2(p); 2(v)

HISTORICAL SOCIETY: Collects Brooklyn's history and culture.

PROGRAMS: Exhibits; Lectures; Research Library/Archives

COLLECTIONS: [1900-present] Brooklyn Daily Eagle, 50,000 photos of Brooklyn, 4000 books, 500 maps, and 8000 clipping files.

HOURS: Yr T, Th 2-7:30, W 2-5:30, F 10-1, Sa 1-5:30

5833
Lefferts Homestead
In Prospect Park on Flatbush Ave, 11215 [Prospect Park Alliance, 95 Prospect Park W, 11215-3783]; (p) (718) 965-6505, (718) 965-8953; (f) (718) 965-8972; www.prospectpark.org

5834
New York Transit Museum
Boerum Place & Schermerhorn St, 11201 [130 Livingston St, 9th floor, Box E, 11201]; (p) (718) 243-8601; (f) (718) 522-5339; www.mta.nyc.ny.us; (c) Kings

Joint/ 1976/ Metropolitan Transportation Authority; Private non-profit/ staff: 16(f); 5(p); 18(v)/ members: 1000/publication: *Court St Shuttle*

HISTORIC SITE; HISTORY MUSEUM: Maintains transportation museum.

PROGRAMS: Community Outreach; Exhibits; Facility Rental; Festivals; Film/Video; Guided Tours; Lectures; Publication; Research Library/Archives; School-Based Curriculum

COLLECTIONS: [1800s-present] NY Metropolitan region public transportation systems; 1930 subway station, period subway and elevated cars, turnstiles, working signal tower.

5835
Pieter Cloesen Wyckoff House Museum
5816 Clarenden Rd, 11203 [PO Box 100-376, 11210]; (p) (718) 629-5400; (f) (718) 629-5400

1652/ City; Wyckoff Association/ staff: 2(f)

HOUSE MUSEUM

COLLECTIONS: Wyckoff Family artifacts.

HOURS: Apr 15-Dec 15 T-Th 1-4

5836
Roman Catholic Diocese of Brooklyn, Office of the Archivist
310 Prospect Park W, 11215; (p) (718) 965-7300; (f) (718) 965-7323; FXMLIB2@concentric.net; www.dioceseofbrooklyn.org; (c) Brooklyn

Private non-profit/ 1853/ staff: 3(f)

LIBRARY AND/OR ARCHIVES: Protects, preserves and makes available the records of the Roman Catholic Diocese of Brooklyn.

PROGRAMS: Exhibits; Research Library/Archives

COLLECTIONS: [1853-present] Parish files for Kings, Queens, Nassau and Suffolk counties, correspondence, photos and other material regarding bishops of Brooklyn, video and audio tapes.

HOURS: Yr M-F

BROWNVILLE

5837
Brown Mansion
216 Brown Blvd, 13615; (p) (315) 782-4508

HOUSE MUSEUM

BUFFALO

5838
Buffalo and Erie County Historical Society
25 Nottingham Ct, 14216; (p) (716) 873-9644; (f) (716) 873-8754; (c) Erie

Private non-profit/ 1862/ Board of Managers/ staff: 27(f); 2(p); 287(v)/ members: 1685

HISTORIC SITE; HISTORICAL SOCIETY; HISTORY MUSEUM: Explores the history of the Niagara Frontier.

PROGRAMS: Annual Meeting; Community Outreach; Exhibits; Facility Rental; Garden Tours; Guided Tours; Interpretation; Lectures; Research Library/Archives; School-Based Curriculum

COLLECTIONS: 80,000 artifacts, research library maintains 20,000 books, 200,000 photos, and 2000 manuscripts.

HOURS: Yr T-Sa 10-5, Su

5839
Buffalo and Erie County Naval and Military Park
One Naval Park Cove, 14202; (p) (716) 847-1773; (f) (716) 847-6405; npark@ci.buffalo.ny.us; www.buffalonavalpark.org; (c) Erie

Private non-profit/ 1979/ staff: 15(f); 20(p); 33(v)/ members: 325

HISTORIC PRESERVATION AGENCY; HISTORY MUSEUM; LIVING HISTORY/OUTDOOR MUSEUM: Preserves history of armed forces.

PROGRAMS: Annual Meeting; Community Outreach; Exhibits; Facility Rental; Guided Tours; Living History

COLLECTIONS: [World War II-present] Guided missile cruiser, a destroyer, a World War II submarine, jet aircraft, a helicopter.

HOURS: Apr-Oct Daily

5840
Buffalo Museum of Science
1020 Humboldt Pkwy, 14211; (p) (716) 896-5200; (f) (716) 897-6723; smith@sciencebuff.org; www.sciencebuff.org; (c) Erie

Private non-profit/ 1861/ Buffalo Society of Natural Sciences/ staff: 58(f); 14(p); 714(v)/ members: 6500

HISTORY MUSEUM: Promotes and preserves cultural and natural history of the Greater Niagara Region.

PROGRAMS: Annual Meeting; Community Outreach; Concerts; Exhibits; Facility Rental; Guided Tours; Interpretation; Lectures; Publication; Research Library/Archives; School-Based Curriculum

COLLECTIONS: 700,000 specimens and artifacts: ancient Middle Eastern civilizations to the indigenous peoples of North America, Africa, and Oceania.

HOURS: Yr T-Su 10-5

ADMISSION: $5.25, Student, Senior, Children $3.25

5841
Buffalo Transportation Museum, The
263 Michigan Ave, 14204 [24 Myrtle Ave, 14204]; (p) (716) 855-1931; (f) (716) 856-7135; msandoro@aol.com; (c) Erie

Private non-profit/ 1997/ staff: 5(v)

HISTORY MUSEUM: Promotes transportation history.

PROGRAMS: Exhibits

COLLECTIONS: [1880-1970] Automobiles, motorcycles, bicycles; some carriages and train, boat and aircraft items.

ADMISSION: $8

5842
Theodore Roosevelt Inaugural National Historic Site
641 Delaware Ave, 14202; (p) (716) 884-0095; (f) (716) 884-0330; www.nps.gov/thri; (c) Erie

Joint/ 1966/ National Park Service/ Theodore Roosevelt Inaugural Site Foundation/ staff: 7(f); 3(p); 400(v)/ members: 375/publication: *The Columns*

HISTORIC SITE; HOUSE MUSEUM: Preserves historic house museum.

PROGRAMS: Community Outreach; Exhibits; Facility Rental; Family Programs; Garden Tours; Guided Tours; Interpretation; Publication; Reenactments; Research Library/Archives; School-Based Curriculum

COLLECTIONS: [1895-1901] Ansley Wilcox House site; Artifacts: Roosevelt, inaugural.

HOURS: Yr M-F 9-5, Sa-Su 12-5

ADMISSION: $3, Children $1, Seniors $2

5843
University Archives of the State University of New York at Buffalo
420 Capen Hall, 14260; (p) (716) 645-2916; (f) (716) 645-3714; densmore@acsu.buffalo.edu; ublib.buffalo.edu/libraries/archives; (c) Erie

State/ 1966/ staff: 2(f)

LIBRARY AND/OR ARCHIVES: Collects, preserves and makes accessible the records of the State Univ of NY and Buffalo and western NY history.

PROGRAMS: Community Outreach; Exhibits; Lectures; Research Library/Archives

HOURS: Yr M-F 9-5

5844
Western New York Documentary Heritage Program
4455 Genesee St, 14225-0400 [PO Box 400, 14225-0400]; (p) (716) 633-0705; (f) (716) 633-1736; hbamford@wnylrc.org; www.wnylrc.org; (c) Erie

State/ 1989/ staff: 2(p)

PROFESSIONAL ORGANIZATION: Locates, preserves and promotes access to historical records; provides assistance and research services to local non-government organizations.

PROGRAMS: Community Outreach; Facility Rental; Publication

HOURS: Yr M-W 9-5

BURT

5845
Van Horn Mansion
2165 Lockport-Olcott Rd, 14028 [PO Box 155, 14028]; (p) (716) 778-7197

1823/ staff: 2(v)

HOUSE MUSEUM

COLLECTIONS: [1823-1900] Diaries

HOURS: Yr

CALEDONIA

5846
Big Springs Historical Society and Museum
3095 Main St, 14423 [PO Box 41, 14423]; (c) Livingston

Private non-profit/ 1936/ staff: 2(p); 15(v)/ members: 103

HISTORICAL SOCIETY: Promotes local history, heritage, and culture.

PROGRAMS: Annual Meeting; Community Outreach; Exhibits; Interpretation; Lectures

CAMDEN

5847
Carriage House Museum of the Queen Village Historical Society
2 N Park St, 13316 [PO Box 38, 13316]; (p) (315) 245-4652; (c) Oneida

Private non-profit/ 1975/ staff: 4(p); 2(v)/ members: 140/publication: *Architectural Heritage, Camden NY*

HOUSE MUSEUM: Collects and preserves Camden's history.

PROGRAMS: Annual Meeting; Community Outreach; Exhibits; Festivals; Guided Tours; Interpretation; Publication; Research Library/ Archives

COLLECTIONS: [1799-1999] Artifacts: local churches, schools, stores, industries, organizations, families, communication, transportation, census, cemetery and war records, clothing, needlework, quilts, furniture, agricultural implements, sports equipment, maps, newspapers; stamps.

CAMILLUS

5848
Wilcox Octagon House
5420 W Genesee St, 13031 [PO Box 314, 13031]; (p) (315) 488-7800, (315) 488-1234; (f) (315) 488-8983

1856/ Town; Octagon House Restoration Project, Inc./ staff: 10(v)

COLLECTIONS: [Pre-1900] Camillus Memorial Quilt; furnishing.

HOURS: By appt

CAMPBELL HALL

5849
Hill-Hold
Rte 416, 10916 [Rt 416, 10916]; (p) (914) 294-7661, (914) 291-2404; www.orangetourism.org/North_folder/North_History.html

5850
William Bull and Sarah Wells Stone House Association
183 County Rt 51, 10916-2924; (p) (914) 496-2855; (f) (914) 496-2855; bullstonehouse@fcc.net; (c) Orange

Private non-profit/ 1920/ Board of Directors/ staff: 3(p); 30(v)/publication: *History and Genealogy of the William Bull and Sarah Wells Family of Orange County, New York*

HISTORICAL SOCIETY: Preserves and manages the 1722 family homestead.

PROGRAMS: Annual Meeting; Community Outreach; Exhibits; Family Programs; Film/ Video; Guided Tours; Interpretation; Lectures; Living History; Publication; School-Based Curriculum

COLLECTIONS: [1712-present] Home furnishings, genealogical collection, local history books, maps, early tools and farm equipment. Sites: New World Dutch Barn (1718), Field Stone House (1722).

HOURS: Yr M-Sa by appt

ADMISSION: $1

CANAJOHARIE

5851
Mohawk Valley Heritage Corridor
66 Montgomery St, 13317; (p) (518) 673-1095; (f) (518) 673-1078; mvhc@telenet.net; (c) Montgomery

State/ 1997/ Mohawk Valley Heritage Corridor Commission/ staff: 4(f); 2(p); 20(v)

HISTORIC PRESERVATION AGENCY; HISTORIC SITE: Serves as regional heritage development and coordination umbrella for 8 county Mohawk River Valley; home of Iroquois Confederacy; Revolutionary War historic site; Erie Canal.

PROGRAMS: Community Outreach; Exhibits; Family Programs; Festivals; Interpretation; Lectures; Publication

COLLECTIONS: [Precontact- present] Natural, historic and cultural resources of Mohawk River Watershed area.

HOURS: Yr M-F 9-5

CANANDAIGUA

5852
Granger Homestead Association, Inc.
295 N Main St, 14424; (p) (716) 394-1472; (f) (716) 394-6958; www.ggw.org.freenet/s/granger/who.htm; (c) Ontario

Private non-profit/ 1946/ staff: 1(f); 4(p); 70(v)/ members: 503

HOUSE MUSEUM

PROGRAMS: Annual Meeting; Facility Rental; Festivals; Guided Tours

COLLECTIONS: [1816-1930] 1816 Federal style mansion with 9 period rooms.

HOURS: May-Oct M-Sa

5853
Ontario County Department of Records, Archives, and Information Management Service
County Rd #46, 14424 [3051 County Complex Dr, 14424]; (p) (716) 393-2910; (f) (716) 396-4390; MaryJo.Lanphear@ co.ontario.ny.us; www.raims.com/; (c) Ontario

County/ 1986/ Board of Supervisors/ staff: 7(f); 1(p); 4(v)

LIBRARY AND/OR ARCHIVES: Maintains inactive Ontario County government records.

PROGRAMS: Exhibits; Lectures; Publication; Research Library/Archives

COLLECTIONS: [1789-present] Deeds, will, mortgages, assessment, census, and court records.

HOURS: Yr M-F 9-4:30

ADMISSION: No charge

5854
Ontario County Historical Society
55 N Main St, 14424; (p) (716) 394-4975; (f) (716) 394-9351; ochs@eznet.net; www.ochs.org; (c) Ontario

Private non-profit/ 1902/ staff: 1(f); 4(p); 42(v)/ members: 752

HISTORICAL SOCIETY; HISTORY MUSEUM: Promotes history of Ontario County and early western NY.

PROGRAMS: Annual Meeting; Exhibits; Family Programs; Festivals; Guided Tours; Lectures; Publication; Research Library/Archives; School-Based Curriculum

COLLECTIONS: [1700-present] Ephemera, manuscripts, photos, books, 3D artifacts and textiles.

HOURS: Yr T, Th-Sa 10-4:30, W 10-9

ADMISSION: $2; Members free, Research room $5

5855
Sonnenberg Gardens
151 Charlotte St, 14424; (p) (716) 394-4922; www.sonnenberg.org; (c) Ontario

Private non-profit/ 1972/ staff: 15(f); 20(p); 495(v)/ members: 1000

GARDEN; HISTORIC SITE; HOUSE MUSEUM

PROGRAMS: Annual Meeting; Community Outreach; Exhibits; Facility Rental; Family Programs; Festivals; Garden Tours; Guided Tours; Interpretation

COLLECTIONS: [1870-1923] Gardens, mansion, buildings, statuary, furnishings. Structures: Lord & Burnham Conservatory Complex, Japanese Tea House.

HOURS: May-Oct M-Su 9:30-5:30

ADMISSION: $7.50, Children $3

CANTON

5856
St. Lawrence County Historical Association
3 E Main St, 13617 [PO Box 8, 13617]; (p) (315) 386-8133; (f) (315) 386-8134; slcha@northnet.org; www.slcha.org; (c) St. Lawrence

Private non-profit/ 1947/ Board of Trustees/ staff: 2(f); 2(p); 176(v)/ members: 950/publication: *Quarterly; St. Lawrence Chronicler*

HISTORICAL SOCIETY; HISTORY MUSEUM; HOUSE MUSEUM; RESEARCH CENTER: Collects, preserves, and interprets county history.

PROGRAMS: Annual Meeting; Community Outreach; Exhibits; Facility Rental; Family Programs; Guided Tours; Interpretation; Lectures; Living History; Publication; Reenactments; Research Library/Archives

COLLECTIONS: [1830-1870] Genealogy, maps, photos, 10,000 museum artifacts of local history, manuscripts.

HOURS: Yr T-Th, Sa 12-4, F 12-8

ADMISSION: Museum: free Archives $5, $2.50 students

CAZENOVIA

5857
Lorenzo State Historic Site
17 Rippleton Rd, 13035; (p) (315) 655-3200; (f) (315) 655-4303; Lincklaen@JUNO.com; (c) Madison

State/ 1968/ Office Parks, Rec and Hist Preservation/ staff: 8(f); 5(p); 40(v)/ members: 470

HISTORIC SITE

PROGRAMS: Community Outreach; Concerts; Exhibits; Facility Rental; Family Programs; Festivals; Film/Video; Garden Tours; Guided Tours; Interpretation; Lectures; Living History; Research Library/Archives; School-Based Curriculum

COLLECTIONS: [1808-1968] Personal effects, Federal and Empire furnishings, fine art, silver, china, decorative arts and ephemera.

HOURS: May-Sept W-Sa 10-5, Su

CENTERPORT

5858
Suffolk County Vanderbilt Museum
180 Little Neck Rd, 11721 [PO Box 0605, 11721]; (p) (516) 854-5580; (f) (516) 854-5591; vanderbilt@webscope.com/vanderbilt; www.webscope.com/vanderbilt; (c) Suffolk

County/ 1950/ staff: 18(f); 68(p); 8(v)/ members: 400/publication: *Eagle's Nest Newsletter*

HISTORIC SITE; HOUSE MUSEUM; LIVING HISTORY/OUTDOOR MUSEUM

PROGRAMS: Community Outreach; Concerts; Exhibits; Facility Rental; Family Programs; Guided Tours; Interpretation; Lectures; Living History; Publication; Reenactments; Research Library/Archives; School-Based Curriculum; Theatre

COLLECTIONS: [17th-20th c] Furnished home of William K Vanderbilt II; Artifacts: marine, ethnographic; decorative and fine arts, garden ornaments, 12,000 images and articles, photos, books.

HOURS: Yr Sep-Apr M-F 12-5, Sa-Su 12-5; May-Aug M-F 10-5, Sa 10-5, Su 12-5

ADMISSION: Grounds $5, Mansion Tour $3, Planetarium $3

CHAPPAQUA

5859
New Castle Historical Society
100 King St, 100514 [PO Box 55, 100514]; (p) (914) 941-0509; (f) (914) 941-0509; (c) Westchester

Private non-profit/ 1966/ New Castle Historical Society/ staff: 1(p); 87(v)/ members: 479

HISTORIC SITE; HISTORICAL SOCIETY; HISTORY MUSEUM: Discovers, preserves, and disseminates knowledge of the history of the town of New Castle.

PROGRAMS: Annual Meeting; Community Outreach; Exhibits; Family Programs; Festivals; Garden Tours; Guided Tours; Interpretation; Lectures; Living History; Publication; Research Library/Archives

COLLECTIONS: Horace Greeley collection; township and Quaker records and memorabilia; costumes; photos; maps; books; newspapers; artifacts; paintings and portraits.

HOURS: M-Th

CHARLTON

5860
Charlton Historical Society
2009 Maple Ave, 12019 [780 Charlton Rd, 12019]; (p) (518) 384-3441; (c) Saratoga

Private non-profit/ 1966/ Board of Directors/ staff: 40(v)/ members: 140/publication: *Charlton Historical Society News*

HISTORIC SITE; HISTORICAL SOCIETY; HISTORY MUSEUM: Gathers, preserves and displays materials relating to the early and current history of Charlton.

PROGRAMS: Annual Meeting; Community Outreach; Concerts; Exhibits; Facility Rental; Festivals; Garden Tours; Publication; Research Library/Archives

COLLECTIONS: [Late 18th-early 20th c] Artifacts; implements, clothing, home furnishings, maps, paintings, sketches, photos; 1800 era church furniture, stain glass windows architecture; period schoolhouse.

CHAZY

5861
Alice T. Miner Colonial Collection
9618 Main St, 12921 [PO Box 628, 12921]; (p) (518) 846-7336; (f) (518) 846-8771; minermuseum@westelcom.com; (c) Clinton

Private non-profit/ 1924/ Alice T. Miner Colonial Collection Board of Trustees/ staff: 1(f); 2(p); 10(v)

HOUSE MUSEUM: Preserves and interprets the Colonial Revival house museum.

PROGRAMS: Annual Meeting; Community Outreach; Concerts; Exhibits; Guided Tours; Interpretation; Lectures; Research Library/ Archives

COLLECTIONS: [18th-19th c] Furniture, decorative arts, books, historic documents, textiles, Native American items, military items, children's items, and weaving and spinning equipment.

HOURS: Feb-Dec T-Sa 10-4

ADMISSION: $3, Student $1, Seniors $2

CHERRY VALLEY

5862
Cherry Valley Historical Association
49 Main St, 13320 [PO Box 115, 13320]; (p) (607) 264-3303, (607) 264-3060; (c) Otsego

Private non-profit/ 1958/ Board of Regents/ staff: 2(p); 50(v)/ members: 100/publication: *Newsletter*

HISTORY MUSEUM: Preserves local history.

PROGRAMS: Annual Meeting; Exhibits; Publication

COLLECTIONS: [1778-present] Clothing, firefighting equipment, melodeons.

HOURS: May-Oct Daily 10-5

ADMISSION: $2, Seniors $1.50; Group rates

CLAYTON

5863
Thousand Islands Museum of Clayton
403 Riverside Dr, 13624 [PO Box 27, 13624]; (p) (315) 686-5794; (f) (315) 686-4867; timuseum@gisco.net; www.thousandislands.com; (c) Jefferson

Private non-profit/ 1964/ staff: 1(f); 3(p); 25(v)/ members: 150

HISTORY MUSEUM

PROGRAMS: Annual Meeting; Exhibits; Facility Rental; Guided Tours; Publication; Research Library/Archives; Theatre

COLLECTIONS: Intepretive rooms: school, country kitchen, railroad station, hotel, general store and Native American.

HOURS: May-Oct M-Su

COLD SPRING

5864
Putnam County Historical Society & Foundry School
63 Chestnut St, 10516; (p) (914) 265-4010; (f) (914) 265-2884; pchs@highlands.com; (c) Putnam

Private non-profit/ 1906/ Board of Trustees/ staff: 4(p)/ members: 450

GENEALOGICAL SOCIETY; HISTORIC SITE; HISTORICAL SOCIETY; HISTORY MUSEUM: Maintains and administers the Foundry School Museum archives, library and genealogical records.

5

PROGRAMS: Annual Meeting; Exhibits; Family Programs; Guided Tours; Lectures; Publication; Research Library/Archives

COLLECTIONS: [19th c] Historical and cultural materials relating to Philipstown area, the West Point Foundry and Putnam County.

HOURS: Mar-Dec Sa-Su, T-Th 2-5

ADMISSION: Donations accepted

CONSTABLEVILLE

5865
Constable Hall
John St and Summit Ave, 13325; (p) (315) 397-2323

COOPERSTOWN

5866
Farmers' Museum, The
Lake Rd, 13326 [PO Box 30, 13326]; (p) (607) 547-1450; (f) (607) 547-1404; nysha1@aol.com; www.farmersmuseum.org; (c) Otsego

Private non-profit/ 1943/ staff: 75(f); 88(p); 116(v)

HISTORY MUSEUM

PROGRAMS: Community Outreach; Concerts; Elder's Programs; Exhibits; Facility Rental; Family Programs; Festivals; Interpretation; Living History; School-Based Curriculum; Theatre

COLLECTIONS: [1800-1920] Agricultural tools and equipment, trades, crafts.

HOURS: Jun-Sep Daily 10-5; Oct-Nov T-Su 10-4; Apr-May T-Su 10-4

ADMISSION: $9, Children $4, Seniors $8

5867
Friends of Hyde Hall, Inc.
1 Mill Rd, 13326 [PO Box 721, 13326]; (p) (607) 548-5098; (f) (607) 547-8462; hydehall@juno.com; www.hydehall.org; (c) Otsego

Private non-profit/ 1964/ Hyde Hall, Inc/ staff: 2(f); 4(p); 10(v)/ members: 2000

HISTORIC SITE; HOUSE MUSEUM

PROGRAMS: Annual Meeting; Concerts; Exhibits; Facility Rental; Family Programs; Festivals; Guided Tours; Interpretation; Lectures; School-Based Curriculum

COLLECTIONS: [19th-early 20th c] George Clarke Family furnishings, documents.

HOURS: May-Oct Daily

5868
James Fenimore Cooper Society
8 Lake St, 13326-1016; (p) (607) 547-2118; jcooper@wpe.com; library.cmsu.edu/cooper/cooper.htm; (c) Otsego

Private non-profit/ 1989/ staff: 1(v)/ members: 125/publication: *Newsletter*

HISTORICAL SOCIETY: Promotes the study of the life and works of James Fenimore Cooper.

PROGRAMS: Publication

COLLECTIONS: [1789-1851]

5869
National Baseball Hall of Fame and Museum
25 Main St, 13326 [PO Box 590, 13326]; (p) (888) 425-5633; (f) (607) 547-2044; info@baseballhalloffame.org;www.baseballhalloffame.org; (c) Otsego

Private non-profit/ 1939/ staff: 73(f); 70(p); 5(v)/publication: *Memories and Dreams, Yearbook*

HISTORY MUSEUM; RESEARCH CENTER

PROGRAMS: Community Outreach; Concerts; Exhibits; Facility Rental; Family Programs; Festivals; Film/Video; Lectures; Research Library/Archives; School-Based Curriculum

COLLECTIONS: [1870-present] Baseball artifacts.

HOURS: Yr Oct-Apr 9-5 May-Sept 9-9

ADMISSION: $9.50, Children $4

5870
New York State Historical Association/Fenimore Art Museum
Lake Rd, 13326 [PO Box 800, 13326]; (p) (607) 547-1400; (f) (607) 547-1404; nysha1@aol.com; www.nysha.org; (c) Otsego

Private non-profit/ 1899/ staff: 65(f); 70(p); 79(v)/ members: 3510/publication: *Heritage and New York History*

ART MUSEUM; HISTORICAL SOCIETY: Preserves history of NY.

PROGRAMS: Annual Meeting; Community Outreach; Concerts; Elder's Programs; Exhibits; Facility Rental; Family Programs; Guided Tours; Interpretation; Lectures; Publication; Research Library/Archives; School-Based Curriculum; Theatre

COLLECTIONS: [1800-1900] American fine art, American folk art and Native American art; historic and contemporary photos; textiles; ceramics; glass; costumes; furniture; and James Fenimore Cooper memorabilia.

HOURS: Apr-May T-Su 10-4; June-Sept Daily 10-5; Oct-Dec T-Su 10-4

ADMISSION: $9, Children $4, Seniors $8

CORNING

5871
Corning Painted Post Historical Society
59 W Pulteney St, 14830; (p) (607) 937-5281; BenPatt@Juno.com; (c) Steuben

Private non-profit/ 1968/ Cornig Painted Post Historical Society/ staff: 1(f); 1(p); 75(v)/ members: 225/publication: *Camera on Corning*

HISTORIC SITE; HISTORICAL SOCIETY; HISTORY MUSEUM; HOUSE MUSEUM: Provides educational and preservation services to local area.

PROGRAMS: Annual Meeting; Elder's Programs; Exhibits; Facility Rental; Festivals; Guided Tours; Interpretation; Lectures; Living History; Publication; Reenactments; Research Library/Archives; School-Based Curriculum

COLLECTIONS: [Late 18th c-mid 19th c] Period building, furnishings; archival glass plates; pictures; vintage clothing.

HOURS: Mar-Dec M-F

5872
Rockwell Museum
corner of Cedar & Denison Pkwy (Rt 352), 14830 [111 Cedar St, 14830]; (p) (607) 937-5386; (f) (607) 974-4536; rmuseum@stny.1run.com; www.stny.1run.com/RockwellMuseum; (c) Steuben

1976/ Board of Trustees/ staff: 10(f); 6(p); 70(v)/ members: 600

ART MUSEUM: Collects, preserves, exhibits and interprets history of North American west, Carder Steuben glass and toys.

PROGRAMS: Community Outreach; Elder's Programs; Exhibits; Facility Rental; Family Programs; Guided Tours; Interpretation; Lectures; Publication; School-Based Curriculum

COLLECTIONS: [1820-1945] Paintings, sculptures, Native American art of Plains and Southwest, early Steuben glass, antique European and American toys.

HOURS: Yr M-Sa 9-5, Su 12-5

CORNWALL-ON-HUDSON

5873
Museum of the Hudson Highlands
The Boulevard, 12520 [PO Box 181, 12520]; (p) (914) 534-7781, (914) 534-5506; (f) (914) 534-4581; rzitomhh@frontiern.net; (c) Orange

Private non-profit/ 1959/ staff: 12(f); 12(p); 100(v)/ members: 1000/publication: *Museum Members Bulletin*

HISTORY MUSEUM: Museum of natural and cultural history of the Hudson Highlands.

PROGRAMS: Community Outreach; Concerts; Exhibits; Facility Rental; Family Programs; Festivals; Guided Tours; Interpretation; Lectures; Publication; School-Based Curriculum

COLLECTIONS: Farming artifacts.

HOURS: Yr M-Sa 10- 4

ADMISSION: $2

CORONA

5874
Louis Armstrong House
34-56 107th St, 11368 [Rosenthal Library, Room 332 Queens College, Flushing, 11367]; (p) (718) 997-3670; (f) (718) 997-3677; satchmo@qc.edu; www.satchmo.net

1910/ Queens College, CUNY/ staff: 3(f); 1(p)

HOUSE MUSEUM: Preserves home of jazz musician Louis Armstrong from 1943-1971.

COLLECTIONS: [Pre-1971] Furnishings; decorative items; musical instruments.; photographs; papers; scrapbooks; commercial and private recordings; memorabilia.

CORTLAND

5875
1890 House and Center for the Arts, The
37 Tompkins St, 13045-2555; (p) (607) 756-7551; (f) (607) 756-7551; (c) Cortland

Private non-profit/ 1974/ staff: 2(f); 12(p); 110(v)/ members: 700

HISTORIC SITE; HOUSE MUSEUM; RE-SEARCH CENTER

PROGRAMS: Annual Meeting; Community Outreach; Concerts; Exhibits; Facility Rental; Festivals; Garden Tours; Guided Tours; Interpretation; Lectures; Living History; Research Library/Archives

COLLECTIONS: [Victorian period] Original furnishings and period photos.

HOURS: Yr T-Su

5876
Cortland County Historical Society, Inc.
25 Homer Ave, 13045; (p) (607) 756-6071; (c) Cortland

Private non-profit/ 1925/ Cortland County Historical Society/ staff: 2(f); 1(p); 100(v)/ members: 750/publication: *News Notes, The Bulletin*

HISTORICAL SOCIETY; HOUSE MUSEUM; LIBRARY AND/OR ARCHIVES: Operates the Suggett House Museum.

PROGRAMS: Community Outreach; Exhibits; Facility Rental; Family Programs; Festivals; Film/Video; Guided Tours; Interpretation; Lectures; Publication; Research Library/Archives; School-Based Curriculum

COLLECTIONS: [19th-20th c.] Art, textiles, advertising, furniture, inventions, military, pottery, silver.

HOURS: Yr T-Sa Library: 1-5; Museum: 1-4

ADMISSION: $2; Members/students free

COXSACKIE

5877
Bronck Museum
Pieter Bronck Rd, 12051; (p) (518) 731-6490; (c) Greene

Private non-profit/ 1939/ Greene County Historical Society/ staff: 3(f); 1(p); 30(v)/ members: 800/publication: *Greene County Historical Journal*

HISTORIC SITE; HISTORICAL SOCIETY; HISTORY MUSEUM; HOUSE MUSEUM: Collects, preserves, and interprets the material culture and history of Greene County and the Catskill Mountains.

PROGRAMS: Exhibits; Guided Tours; Lectures; Publication; Research Library/Archives

COLLECTIONS: [1770-1870] Art, furniture, ceramics, glass, quilts, samplers, coverlets, household and agricultural equipment, sleighs and carriages, ice harvesting equipment, country store, and Catskill Mountain resort.

HOURS: May-Oct 15 T-Sa 10-4, Su

5878
Greene County Historical Society
90 CR 42, 12051; (p) (518) 731-1033, (518) 731-6490; (c) Greene

Private non-profit/ 1929/ Greene County Historical Society/ staff: 1(f); 1(p); 22(v)/ members: 824

HISTORIC SITE; HISTORICAL SOCIETY; HISTORY MUSEUM; HOUSE MUSEUM: Interprets county history.

PROGRAMS: Annual Meeting; Community

Outreach; Exhibits; Facility Rental; Family Programs; Garden Tours; Guided Tours; Lectures; Publication; Research Library/Archives

COLLECTIONS: [19th c.] Artifacts used by Greene County families; printed and manuscript holdings; decorative arts; photographs.

HOURS: Library: Yr T-W 10-4; Museum May-Oct M-F 10-4

ADMISSION: $4, Seniors $3.50; Members free; Library free to all

CROGHAN

5879
American Maple Museum
Main St, 13327 [PO Box 81, 13327]; (p) (315) 346-1107; (c) Lewis

Private non-profit/ 1977/ Board of Trustees/ staff: 1(p); 20(v)

HISTORY MUSEUM: Collects, preserves, displays, and interprets objects and artifacts related to the maple products industry.

PROGRAMS: Exhibits; Facility Rental; Guided Tours

COLLECTIONS: [1920-present] Tools, machinery, supplies, containers, and equipment.

ADMISSION: $2, Children $1

CROTON-ON-HUDSON

5880
Van Cortlandt Manor
525 S Riverside Ave, 10520 [525 S Riverside, 10520]; (p) (914) 271-8981; (f) (914) 271-9029; www.hudsonvalley.org

1750/ staff: 3(f); 25(p)

COLLECTIONS: [1790-1814] Furnishings, ceramics, pewter, letters, journals, account books.

HOURS: Vary

CROWN POINT

5881
Champlain Valley Heritage Network
Lake Champlain Visitor's Center "at the bridge", 12928 [Rt 1 Box 220, 12928]; (p) (528) 597-4646; (f) (518) 597-4648; lcvisit@capital.net; (c) Essex

Joint/ 1992/ staff: 1(p); 50(v)/publication: *Fields at Work; Champlain Valley Mapguide*

HISTORIC PRESERVATION AGENCY: Promotes natural, recreational, and cultural resources of Champlain Valley.

PROGRAMS: Community Outreach; Concerts; Exhibits; Interpretation; Lectures; Publication

COLLECTIONS: [Prehistory-present]

HOURS: Visitor

CUDDEBACKVILLE

5882
Neversink Valley Area Museum
D & H Canal Park, 12729 [PO Box 263, 12729]; (p) (914) 754-8876; moose2@frontiernet.net; (c) Orange

Private non-profit/ 1967/ staff: 1(f); 60(v)/ members: 400

HISTORIC SITE

PROGRAMS: Annual Meeting; Community Outreach; Exhibits; Family Programs; Film/Video; Guided Tours; Interpretation; Lectures; Living History; Research Library/Archives; School-Based Curriculum

COLLECTIONS: [19th c.] Working lock model; children's activity center; maps; videos; artifacts; photographs; and information on canal technology, history, boating and life on the canal.

HOURS: Mar-Dec Th-Su 12-4

ADMISSION: $2, Children

CUTCHOGUE

5883
Old House
Cutchogue Village Green, 11935 [PO Box 714, 11935]; (p) (516) 734-6977, (516) 734-7113

DEKALB JUNCTION

5884
Town of DeKalb Historical Association
696 E DeKalb Rd, 13630 [PO Box 111, 13630]; (p) (315) 347-1900; thompsbs@tds.net; (c) St. Lawrence

Private non-profit/ 1994/ staff: 15(v)/ members: 101/publication: *Williamstown Gazette*

HISTORICAL SOCIETY: Collects and preserves the history of DeKalb and the St. Lawrence Valley.

PROGRAMS: Annual Meeting; Exhibits; Festivals; Garden Tours; Publication; Research Library/Archives

COLLECTIONS: [1803-present] Books, Bibles, files, maps, photos.

HOURS: Yr T 9:30-11:30am, W 12-4

ADMISSION: Donations accepted

DELHI

5885
Delaware County Historical Association
3 mi N of Delhi, Rt 10, 13753 [RD 2 Box 201C, 13753]; (p) (607) 746-3849; (f) (607) 746-7326; DCHA@catskill.net; www.rootsweb.com/~nydelaha; (c) Delaware

Joint; Private non-profit/ 1945/ staff: 2(f); 3(p); 4(v)/publication: *Headwaters of History*

HISTORIC PRESERVATION AGENCY; HISTORIC SITE; HISTORICAL SOCIETY; HISTORY MUSEUM; HOUSE MUSEUM; RESEARCH CENTER: Preserves and exhibits the history and culture of Delaware County.

PROGRAMS: Annual Meeting; Community Outreach; Exhibits; Family Programs; Festivals; Guided Tours; Interpretation; Publication; Research Library/Archives; School-Based Curriculum

COLLECTIONS: [18th c-present] 4,500 artifacts; sites: Gideon Frisbee House and Barns, Husted Hollow School House.

HOURS: Historic Buildings: May-Oct T-Su 11-4:30; Library: Yr M-T 10-3; Exhibit Hall: Yr Nov-Apr M-F, May-Oct T-Su 10-3

ADMISSION: $3, Children $1.50

DRESDEN

5886
Robert Green Ingersoll Birthplace Museum
61 Main St, 14441 [PO Box 664, Amherst, 14226]; (p) (315) 536-1074; (f) (716) 636-1733; cfiflynn@aol.com; www.secularhumanism.org/ingersoll; (c) Yates

Private non-profit/ 1993/ Council for Secular Humanism/ staff: 2(p); 2(v)/ members: 300/publication: *Ingersoll Report*

HISTORY MUSEUM; HOUSE MUSEUM: Interprets Ingersoll's life; preserves regional history.

PROGRAMS: Exhibits; Guided Tours; Interpretation; Publication; Research Library/Archives

COLLECTIONS: [1833-1899] Publications, artifacts, images, ephemera, Yates County and village of Dresden.

HOURS: May-Oct Sa-Su

DRYDEN

5887
Dryden Township Historical Society
36 W Main St, 103053 [PO Box 69, 103053]; (p) (607) 844-9209; dths@juno.com; (c) Tompkins

Private non-profit/ 1981/ staff: 25(p); 25(v)/ members: 300/publication: *Barns of the Dryden Lake Area; From Richford's Rails to Freeville Stationmaster*

HISTORICAL SOCIETY

PROGRAMS: Annual Meeting; Exhibits; Family Programs; Guided Tours; Lectures; Publication

COLLECTIONS: [1783-present]

HOURS: Yr 10-2 or by appt

ADMISSION: Donations accepted

EAST AURORA

5888
Aurora Historical Society
5 S Grove, 14052 [PO Box 472, 14052]; (p) (716) 652-3280; (f) (716) 652-3507; (c) Erie

Joint/ 1951/ Private non-profit; state/ staff: 1(p); 30(v)/ members: 200/publication: *Aurora Courier*

HISTORICAL SOCIETY; HISTORY MUSEUM; HOUSE MUSEUM; PRESIDENTIAL SITE: Operates home of President Millard Fillmore and a museum dedicated to history of Elbert Hubbard of the Roycroft movement.

PROGRAMS: Annual Meeting; Community Outreach; Exhibits; Festivals; Garden Tours; Guided Tours; Interpretation; Lectures; Publication; Research Library/Archives

COLLECTIONS: [1825-1830, 1897-1938] Books.

HOURS: May-Sept W, Sa-Su 2-5

ADMISSION: $2

5889
Elbert Hubbard Roycroft Museum
363 Oakwood Ave, 14052; (p) (716) 652-4735; rin.buffalo.edu/c_erie/comm/cult/muse/roycroft.html

Aurora Historical Society, Inc.

COLLECTIONS: [1900s] House, furniture, sculpture, leather working tools and patterns, books, manuscripts, copper.

HOURS: June 1-Oct 15

5890
Millard Fillmore House
24 Shearer Ave, 14052

EAST DURHAM

5891
Irish American Heritage Museum
2267 Rt 145, 12324 [107 Washington Ave, Albany, 12210]; (p) (518) 432-6598; (f) (518) 449-2540; irishamermuseum@cs.com; irishamermuseum.org; (c) Greene

Private non-profit/ 1986/ Board of Trustees/ staff: 3(f); 1(p); 4(v)/ members: 500/publication: *Newsletter*

HISTORY MUSEUM: Presents and preserves Irish American history.

PROGRAMS: Community Outreach; Concerts; Elder's Programs; Exhibits; Family Programs; Guided Tours; Interpretation; Lectures; Publication; Research Library/Archives; School-Based Curriculum

COLLECTIONS: [19th c.-20th c.] Artifacts, documents, and archival materials.

HOURS: May-Oct W-Su 11-5

ADMISSION: $3.50, Family $9, Children $2, Seniors $2

EAST HAMPTON

5892
Home Sweet Home Museum
14 James Ln, 11937 [14 James Lane, 11937]; (p) (516) 324-0713

1680/ Village Government/ staff: 1(f); 1(p)

COLLECTIONS: [generally 1660-1852] Textiles, ceramics, pewter, furniture.

HOURS: Yr

5893
Osborn-Jackson House
101 Main St, 11937; (p) (516) 324-6850; (f) (516) 324-9885

5894
Pollack-Krasner House and Study Center
830 Fireplace Rd, 11937 [830 Fireplace Rd, 11937]; (p) (516) 324-4929; (f) (516) 324-8768; www.pkhouse.org

1879/ staff: 2(f); 1(p); 15(v)

Preserves home of Abstract Expressionist artists Jackson Pollock and Lee Krasner.

COLLECTIONS: [1945-1984] Furnishings and decorative objects, personal library, and records; photos.

HOURS: By appt

EAST MEADOW

5895
Museum Services Division
Department of Recreation and Parks
County of Nassau
Eisenhower Park, 11554; (p) (516) 572-0255; (f) (516) 572-0396; (c) Nassau

County/ 1970/ staff: 50(f); 47(p); 600(v)

HISTORIC SITE; HISTORY MUSEUM; LIVING HISTORY/OUTDOOR MUSEUM: Promotes natural and living history.

PROGRAMS: Exhibits; Facility Rental; Family Programs; Festivals; Film/Video; Guided Tours; Interpretation; Lectures; Living History; Reenactments; Research Library/Archives; School-Based Curriculum

COLLECTIONS: [18th-20th c.]

HOURS: Yr W-Su 10-5

ADMISSION: $6, Children $4

EAST MEREDITH

5896
Hanford Mills Museum
Corner of County Rt 10 & 12, 13757 [PO Box 99, 13757]; (p) (607) 278-5744; (f) (708) 278-6299; hanford1@hanfordmills.org; www.hanfordmills.org; (c) Otsego

Private non-profit/ 1973/ Board of Trustees/ staff: 7(f); 7(p); 25(v)/ members: 364/publication: *Made by Machine; The Hanford Photographs; East Meredith Memories, The Butter Business*

HISTORIC SITE; HOUSE MUSEUM; LIVING HISTORY/OUTDOOR MUSEUM: Promotes and preserves waterpowered sawmill, gristmill, woodworking shop and historic house.

PROGRAMS: Concerts; Elder's Programs; Exhibits; Facility Rental; Family Programs; Festivals; Film/Video; Guided Tours; Interpretation; Living History; Publication; Research Library/Archives; School-Based Curriculum

COLLECTIONS: [1890-1930] Original Hanford machinery, buildings, photos, and business records; related agricultural, industrial, and domestic artifacts.

HOURS: May-Oct Daily 10-5

ADMISSION: $6, Children $3, Seniors $5; Under 12 free

EAST ROCHESTER

5897
East Rochester Local History
901 Main St, 14445; (p) (716) 381-3023; (f) (716) 248-3354; erhistory@juno.com; (c) Monroe

City/ 1965/ staff: 3(p); 2(v)/ members: 1

HISTORY MUSEUM: Collects and preserves material, printed or verbal, on local history.

PROGRAMS: Exhibits; Living History; Research Library/Archives; School-Based Curriculum

COLLECTIONS: [1897-present] Old newspapers, schools yearbooks, tax assessors' roll books, files on organizations, industry, churches, schools, sports, vital statistics records, photographs.

HOURS: Yr T-F 9-12, Sa 10-1

ADMISSION: No charge

EASTCHESTER

5898

Eastchester Historical Society, The

388 California Rd, 10709 [Box 37, 10709]; (p) (914) 793-1900; (c) Westchester

Private non-profit/ 1959/ staff: 15(v)/ members: 340

HISTORICAL SOCIETY: Maintains restored 1835 marble school and Angelo H. Bianchi Reference Library.

PROGRAMS: Annual Meeting; Community Outreach; Guided Tours; Lectures; Research Library/Archives; School-Based Curriculum

COLLECTIONS: [Victorian-19th c.] Books of history and juvenile literature, toys, costumes, decorative arts.

HOURS: By appt

ADMISSION: $2

ELMIRA

5899

Chemung County Historical Society, Inc. (Chemung Valley History Museum)

415 E Water St, 14901; (p) (607) 734-1565; (f) (607) 734-1565; (c) Chemung

Private non-profit/ 1923/ Chemung County Historical Society/ staff: 4(f); 7(p); 50(v)/ members: 1250/publication: *Chemung Historical Journal*

HISTORICAL SOCIETY: Operates a museum, library and archivs.

PROGRAMS: Annual Meeting; Community Outreach; Elder's Programs; Exhibits; Facility Rental; Family Programs; Festivals; Interpretation; Lectures; Living History; Publication; Research Library/Archives; School-Based Curriculum

COLLECTIONS: [19th-20th c.] 17,000 museum artifacts; 20,000 photos; 30,000 manuscripts; 2,000 volumes; cemetery records; 2 historic structures.

HOURS: Yr M-F 9-5; Galleries:

ELMSFORD

5900

Lower Hudson Conference of Historical Agencies and Museums

2199 Saw Mill River Rd, 10523; (p) (914) 592-6726; (f) (914) 592-6946; lowerhudson@email.msn.com; www.lowerhudsonconference.org; (c) Westchester

Private non-profit/ 1978/ Board of Trustees/ staff: 2(p); 5(v)/ members: 360/publication: *History Keepers' Companion: Guide; Emergency Planning and Recovery Handbook*

ALLIANCE OF HISTORICAL AGENCIES: Povides professional training, networking and technical assistance support to museums and historic sites, libraries and historians in the Hudson Valley and metro NY-CT.

PROGRAMS: Annual Meeting; Community Outreach; Guided Tours; Publication

HOURS: Yr M-F 9:30-4:30

FABIUS

5901

Pioneer Museum

Highland Forest, 13063 [PO Box 31, 13063]; (p) (315) 683-5550; (f) (315) 683-5147

FISHKILL

5902

Fishkill Historical Society

509 Route 9, 12524 [PO Box 133, 12524-0133]; (p) (914) 896-9560; (f) (914) 896-4333; (c) Dutchess

Private non-profit/ 1962/ staff: 20(v)/ members: 489/publication: *Van Wyck Dispatch; Around Fishkil*

HISTORIC SITE; HISTORICAL SOCIETY; HISTORY MUSEUM; HOUSE MUSEUM: Collects, preserves and interprets the history of Fishkill; operates Van Wyck Homestead Museum.

PROGRAMS: Annual Meeting; Community Outreach; Concerts; Exhibits; Facility Rental; Family Programs; Festivals; Guided Tours; Interpretation; Lectures; Publication; Reenactments; Research Library/Archives; School-Based Curriculum

COLLECTIONS: [18th-19th c] Archaeological, local artifacts.

HOURS: Museum: May-Oct Sa-Su 1-5 and by appt.

FLORAL PARK

5903

Colonial Farmhouse Restoration Society of Bellerose, Inc. dba Queens County Farm Museum

73-50 Little Neck Pkwy, 11004; (p) (718) 347-3276; (f) (718) 347-3243; afischetti@queens-farm.org; www.queensfarm.org; (c) Queens

Private non-profit/ 1975/ Colonial Farmhouse Restoration Society of Bellerose/ staff: 5(f); 24(p); 68(v)/ members: 897/publication: *Broadside*

HOUSE MUSEUM; LIVING HISTORY/OUTDOOR MUSEUM

PROGRAMS: Annual Meeting; Community Outreach; Concerts; Exhibits; Facility Rental; Festivals; Guided Tours; Lectures; Living History; Publication; Reenactments

COLLECTIONS: [1697-1930s] Farm implements, vehicles, livestock.

HOURS: Yr M-F 9-5 Sa-Su 10-5

ADMISSION: No charge

FLUSHING

5904

Queens Historical Society

143-35 37th Ave, 11354; (p) (718) 939-0647; (f) (718) 539-9885; QHS@Juno.com; www.preserve.org/Queens; (c) Queens

Private non-profit/ 1968/ Board of Trustees/ staff: 1(f); 6(p); 50(v)/ members: 500

HISTORICAL SOCIETY: Researches and promotes historical heritage of Queens.

PROGRAMS: Annual Meeting; Community Outreach; Exhibits; Facility Rental; Family Programs; Festivals; Guided Tours; Lectures; Publication; Research Library/Archives; School-Based Curriculum

COLLECTIONS: [1800-present] Photos, textiles, maps, artifacts, manuscripts, memorabilia.

HOURS: Yr M-F 9:30-5 Sa-Su 2:30-4:30

ADMISSION: $3, Student $2,

5905

Queens Museum of Art

Flushing Meadows Park, 11368 [NYC Bldg, Flushing Meadows Corona Pk, 11368]; (p) (718) 592-9700; (f) (718) 592-5778; queensmuse.org; (c) Queens

Private non-profit/ 1972/ staff: 29(f); 11(p); 65(v)/ members: 500

ART MUSEUM; HISTORIC SITE: Preserves historic structure from 1939 and 1964 World's Fairs.

PROGRAMS: Community Outreach; Concerts; Exhibits; Family Programs; Film/Video; Guided Tours; Lectures; Theatre

COLLECTIONS: [20th c]

HOURS: Jan-Dec T-F 10-5, Sa-Su 12-5

ADMISSION: Donations requested

FONDA

5906

Montgomery County Department of History and Archives

Old Courthouse, Railroad St, 12068 [Old Courthouse, PO Box 1500, 12068-1500]; (p) (518) 853-8186; (f) (518) 853-8392; histarch@superior.net; www.amsterdam~ny/mcha; (c) Montgomery

County/ 1936/ staff: 2(f); 1(p); 2(v)/publication: *Catalog of Historical and Genealogical Materials; Steeple Chase: History of the Churches in the Town of Minden, Montgomery County, NY*

LIBRARY AND/OR ARCHIVES: Accumulates historical, archival, and genealogical information.

PROGRAMS: Exhibits; Guided Tours; Publication; Research Library/Archives

COLLECTIONS: [18th- early 20th c.] Historical, archival and genealogical records.

HOURS: Yr Sep-Jun M-F 8:30-4; Jul-Aug M, W-F 9-4, T

FORT EDWARD

5907

Fort Edward Historical Association, Inc.

22-29 Broadway, 12808 [PO Box 106, 12808-0106]; (p) (581) 747-9600; old-fort-house-museum@juno.com; (c) Washington

Private non-profit/ 1927/ Fort Edward Historical Assoc, Inc./ staff: 4(p); 93(v)/ members: 437

HISTORIC SITE; HISTORICAL SOCIETY; HISTORY MUSEUM; HOUSE MUSEUM; RESEARCH CENTER

PROGRAMS: Annual Meeting; Exhibits; Family Programs; Festivals; Guided Tours; Lectures; Publication; Research Library/Archives

COLLECTIONS: [1772-present] 200,000 artifacts: textiles, glass, furnishings, Fort Edward Pottery; 80,000 photos and 50,000 documents.

HOURS: June-Sept, Dec Daily 1-5 and by appt

ADMISSION: $2; Children free

FORT HUNTER

5908
Schoharie Crossing State Historic Site
129 Schoharie St, 12069 [PO Box 140, 12069-0140]; (p) (518) 829-7516; (f) (518) 829-7491; nysparks.state.ny.us; (c) Montgomery

Joint/ 1966/ staff: 3(f); 8(p); 6(v)

HISTORIC PRESERVATION AGENCY; HISTORIC SITE; LIVING HISTORY/OUTDOOR MUSEUM: Interprets and preserves over 10 structures of the Erie Canal, including culverts, locks and Schoharie Aqueduct.

PROGRAMS: Exhibits; Festivals; Guided Tours; Interpretation; Lectures; Publication; School-Based Curriculum

COLLECTIONS: [1817-1917] 40 archival and archaeological item; sites: 1840's Schoharie Aqueduct, Lock 28, Lock 29. 1822 East Guard Lock.

HOURS: Visitor Center: May-Oct W-Sa 10-5, Su 1-5 Grounds: Yr

ADMISSION: No charge

FORT PLAIN

5909
Fort Plain Museum
389 Canal St, 13339 [Box 324, 13339]; (p) (518) 993-2527; (c) Montgomery

State/ 1963/ Education Dept/ staff: 6(v)/ members: 150

HISTORIC SITE; HISTORY MUSEUM: Preserves 1848 house.

PROGRAMS: Community Outreach; Exhibits; Guided Tours

COLLECTIONS: [1600-present] Indian, revolutionary, costumes, agricultural, Erie Canal, local history.

HOURS: May-Sept W-F afternoons

ADMISSION: No charge

FRANKLINVILLE

5910
Ischua Valley Historical Society, Inc.
9 Pine St, 14737; (c) Cattaraugus

Private non-profit/ 1966/ staff: 50(v)/ members: 200

HISTORICAL SOCIETY; HISTORY MUSEUM: Preserves the history of Franklinville, NY and the Ischua Valley.

PROGRAMS: Annual Meeting; Community Outreach; Exhibits; Festivals; Lectures; Publication; Research Library/Archives; School-Based Curriculum

COLLECTIONS: [1814-present] Sites: Miner's Cabin and Howe-Prescott House.

HOURS: May-Sept Su 2-5 and by appt

ADMISSION: Donations accepted

FREDONIA

5911
Historical Museum of the D.R. Barker Library
20 E Main St, 14063 [7 Day St, 14063]; (p) (716) 672-2114; (f) (716) 679-3547; (c) Chautauqua

Private non-profit/ 1884/ Darwin R. Barker Library Assoc/ staff: 1(f); 1(p); 25(v)/ members: 177/publication: *A Diary Year: 1866; The Barker Library and Museum: A History*

GENEALOGICAL SOCIETY; HISTORIC SITE; HISTORY MUSEUM

PROGRAMS: Community Outreach; Concerts; Elder's Programs; Exhibits; Guided Tours; Lectures; Publication; Research Library/Archives

COLLECTIONS: Paintings; textiles; clothing; photos; military artifacts and uniforms; dolls and toys; agricultural/pioneer equipment; local education; decorative arts; businesses; musical instruments; rare and genealogical books

HOURS: Yr T 2:30-4:30,

FULTON

5912
Friends of History in Fulton, New York, Inc.
177 S First St, 13069 [PO Box 157, 13069]; (p) (315) 598-4616; www.fulton.com; (c) Oswego

Private non-profit/ 1979/ Fulton History Society/ staff: 1(f); 23(v)/ members: 285

HISTORICAL SOCIETY: Preserves John Wells Pratt house.

PROGRAMS: Annual Meeting; Community Outreach; Exhibits; Interpretation; Lectures; Research Library/Archives; School-Based Curriculum

COLLECTIONS: [1654-present] Clothing, photos, military.

HOURS: Yr M-F 9-4

ADMISSION: No charge

GARRISON

5913
Boscobel Restoration, Inc.
1601 Rt 9D, 10524; (p) (914) 265-3638; (f) (914) 265-4405; info@boscobel.org; www.boscobel.org; (c) Putnam

Private non-profit/ 1955/ staff: 10(f); 29(p); 15(v)/ members: 321/publication: *Federal Furniture and Decorative Arts at Boscobel*

ART MUSEUM; GARDEN; HOUSE MUSEUM: Collects, preserves, and interprets furniture and decorative arts of the federal period; explores the history of the 1808 mansion of States and Elizabeth Dyckman.

PROGRAMS: Concerts; Exhibits; Facility Rental; Garden Tours; Guided Tours; Lectures; Publication; School-Based Curriculum; Theatre

COLLECTIONS: Federal furniture, glass, ceramics, silver, paintings, prints, decorative arts;

HOURS: Apr-Oct W-M 9:30-5; Nov-Dec: W-M 9:30-4

GENESEO

5914
Livingston County Historical Society
30 Center St, 14454; (p) (716) 243-9147; www.livmalib.org; (c) Livingston

Private non-profit/ 1876/ Alberta S. Dunn, Pres/ staff: 1(f); 4(p); 10(v)/ members: 250

HISTORICAL SOCIETY; HISTORY MUSEUM; HOUSE MUSEUM: A five room cobblestone former schoolhouse now containing a museum of local history from Livingston County.

PROGRAMS: Annual Meeting; Community Outreach; Concerts; Exhibits; Family Programs; Lectures; School-Based Curriculum

COLLECTIONS: [1700s-present] Native American artifacts, domestic items, toys, furniture, clothing, musical instruments, Civil War and Shaker items.

GENEVA

5915
Geneva Historical Society
543 S Main St, 14456; (p) (315) 789-5151; (f) (315) 789-0314; genevhst@flare.net; (c) Ontario

Private non-profit/ staff: 7(f); 13(p); 100(v)/ members: 1000

HISTORIC PRESERVATION AGENCY; HISTORICAL SOCIETY; HISTORY MUSEUM; HOUSE MUSEUM: Maintains 4 historic properties which interpret life in Geneva from its earliest Native American settlers to the present.

PROGRAMS: Annual Meeting; Community Outreach; Exhibits; Family Programs; Guided Tours; Interpretation; Lectures; Living History; Reenactments; Research Library/Archives; School-Based Curriculum

COLLECTIONS: [1700s-present] Collections relate to the history of Geneva, New York and its environs. Items include archival materials, decorative arts, and products made in Geneva.

5916
Mike Weaver Drain Tile Museum, The
East Lake Road, off 96A, 14456 [Rose Hill Mansion, Box 464, 14456]; (p) (315) 789-3848; (c) Seneca

Private non-profit/ 1993/ Geneva Historical Society

HISTORY MUSEUM: Preserves 1821 house of John Johnston, father of tile drainage in US.

PROGRAMS: Guided Tours

COLLECTIONS: [100 BC- present] Tiling, historic house with furnishing, tools.

HOURS: May-Oct M-Sa 10-3

5917
Rose Hill Mansion
96A 1.25 mi S of 5 & 20, 14456 [Box 464, 14456]; (p) (315) 789-3848; (f) (315) 789-0314; (c) Seneca

Private non-profit/ 1966/ Geneva Historical Society/ staff: 2(f); 16(p); 10(v)/publication: *Rose Hill: A Greek Revival Mansion*

HISTORIC SITE; HOUSE MUSEUM

PROGRAMS: Guided Tours; Interpretation; Publication; Research Library/Archives

COLLECTIONS: [1825-1840] 1839 Greek Revival Restoration building, period furniture, drain tiling.

HOURS: May-Oct M-Sa 10-4, Su 1-5

ADMISSION: $3, Student $2, Seniors

GERMANTOWN

5918
Clermont State Historic Site
1 Clermont Ave, 12526; (p) (518) 537-4240; (f) (518) 537-6240; www.friendsofclermont.org; (c) Columbia

State/ 1968/ Office of Parks, Recreation, and Historic Preservation/ staff: 8(f); 16(p); 96(v)/ members: 550

GARDEN; HISTORIC SITE; HOUSE MUSEUM: Preserves historic house museum.

PROGRAMS: Annual Meeting; Community Outreach; Concerts; Exhibits; Facility Rental; Family Programs; Festivals; Garden Tours; Guided Tours; Interpretation; Lectures; Research Library/Archives; School-Based Curriculum

COLLECTIONS: [Colonial, Federal, 1930] Concentrations in American portraiture and French and American Furniture, decorative arts and books.

HOURS: Yr T-Su 8:30- Sunset

ADMISSION: $3, Children $1, Seniors $2

GLEN FALLS

5919
Chapman Historical Museum
348 Glen St, 12801; (p) (518) 793-2826; (f) (518) 793-2831; (c) Warren

Private non-profit/ 1967/ staff: 4(f); 1(p); 25(v)/ members: 360/publication: *Seneca Ray Stoddard Reproductions*

HISTORY MUSEUM: Preserves and shares the history of the southern Adirondacks.

PROGRAMS: Community Outreach; Exhibits; Family Programs; Guided Tours; Interpretation; Lectures; Publication; Research Library/ Archives; School-Based Curriculum

COLLECTIONS: [1860-1960] Seneca Ray Stoddard photos archive (7,000 manuscripts), Z.I. Delong house with period furnishings, costumes, artifacts.

HOURS: Yr M-F 10-5

ADMISSION: $2, Student $1, Seniors $1; Under 12 free

GLENVILLE

5920
Empire State Aerosciences Museum
250 Rudy Chase Dr, 12302; (p) (518) 377-2191; (f) (618) 388-1959; esam@crisny.org; www.cana.com/esam; (c) Schnectady

Private non-profit/ 1984/ Board of Trustees/ staff: 2(f); 7(p); 100(v)/ members: 950/publication: *AeroNotes*

HISTORY MUSEUM; RESEARCH CENTER: Collects and preserves historical aviation contributions of NY.

PROGRAMS: Community Outreach; Elder's Programs; Exhibits; Facility Rental; Family Pro-

grams; Guided Tours; Lectures; Publication; Research Library/Archives; School-Based Curriculum

COLLECTIONS: [1783-present] Represents the history and achievements of NY aviation.

HOURS: Yr T-Sa 10-4, Su 12-4

ADMISSION: $5, Student $2; Under 12 free w/adult

GLOVERSVILLE

5921
Fulton County Historical Society
237 Kingsboro Ave, 12078 [PO Box 711, 12078]; (p) (518) 725-2203; (c) Fulton

Private non-profit/ 1891/ Board of Directors/ staff: 2(p)/ members: 257

HISTORICAL SOCIETY: Preserves and displays Fulton County history.

PROGRAMS: Guided Tours; Lectures; Living History

COLLECTIONS: [1600-1900] Indian longhouse and artifacts; leather tanning display; glove making display; 19th c. room; weaving and spinning room; railroad display; country store; carpenter shop; school room; blacksmith shop; farm equipment.

HOURS: May-Nov M-F 9- 3, Sa 12-4

ADMISSION: Donations accepted

GOSHEN

5922
Harness Racing and Hall of Fame
240 Main St, 10924 [PO Box 590, 10924]; (p) (845) 294-6330; (f) (845) 294-3463; fame2@magiccarpet.com; www.harnessmuseum.com; (c) Orange

Private non-profit/ 1949/ staff: 8(f); 4(p)/ members: 600

HISTORY MUSEUM: Preserves the past, chronicles the present and promotes the future of Harness Racing.

PROGRAMS: Annual Meeting; Community Outreach; Concerts; Exhibits; Facility Rental; Family Programs; Film/Video; Guided Tours; Interpretation; Lectures; Research Library/ Archives; School-Based Curriculum

COLLECTIONS: [1850-present] Paper records, books, periodicals, photos, sound recordings, video tapes, motion picture film, microfilm/microfiche, computer media, objects, art, lithographs, textiles, metals, carriages.

HOURS: Yr Daily

ADMISSION: $7.50, Children $3.50, Seniors $6.50; Members free

GRANVILLE

5923
Slate Valley Museum
17 Water St, 12832; (p) (518) 642-1417; svm2@together.net; www.slatevalleymuseum.org; (c) Washington

Joint/ 1994/ Board of Directors; City/ staff: 3(p); 15(v)/ members: 250/publication: *Slate Valley Museum Newsletter*

HISTORY MUSEUM: Collects, interprets and exhibits materials relating to the history of slate quarrying.

PROGRAMS: Annual Meeting; Community Outreach; Concerts; Exhibits; Family Programs; Guided Tours; Interpretation; Lectures; Living History; Publication; Research Library/Archives; School-Based Curriculum

COLLECTIONS: [1850-present] Geological specimens, artifacts, small machines, resource archives, photographs, paintings, WPA mural.

HOURS: Yr T,Th-F 1-5 Sa 10-4

ADMISSION: $2.50, Student $1.50; Under 13 free; group rates

GRAVESEND

5924
Gravesend Historical Society, The
1937 W 6th St, 11223 [PO Box 1643, 11223]; (p) (718) 627-5617; (f) (718) 375-6831; (c) Kings

Private non-profit/ 1972/ State Education Dept/ staff: 1(f); 1(p); 3(v)/ members: 75/publication: *Historic Gravesend*

HISTORICAL SOCIETY: Preserves history of Gravesend.

PROGRAMS: Annual Meeting; Exhibits; Guided Tours; Lectures; Living History; Publication; Reenactments; School-Based Curriculum

COLLECTIONS: [20th c.] Books, textiles, and photographs.

GREENLAWN

5925
Greenlawn-Centerport Historical Association
31 Broadway, 11740 [Box 354, 11740]; (p) (631) 754-1180; (c) Suffolk

Private non-profit/ 1973/ NY Board of Regents/ staff: 1(f); 1(p); 50(v)/ members: 450

HISTORICAL SOCIETY: Researches, collects, preserves and records the history of area.

PROGRAMS: Annual Meeting; Concerts; Exhibits; Festivals; Film/Video; Guided Tours; Interpretation; Lectures; Research Library/ Archives; School-Based Curriculum

COLLECTIONS: [1800-1920] Over 2,000 photos; 6 portraits; 20 period maps local history library; house files; 1,000 museum artifacts; textile and clothing; scrapbooks.

HOURS: House and Barn May-Oct Su 1-4; Office Yr M-Sa 10-4

ADMISSION: No charge

GROTON

5926
Old Baptist Meeting House
168 Main St, 13073 [PO Box 44, 13073]; (p) (607) 898-5198

1819/ staff: 10(v)

Site of First Baptist formalized church body in central NY.

COLLECTIONS: [18th-19th c] Typewriters and adding machines.

HOURS: Yr

5927
Town of Groton Historical Association
168 Main St, 13073 [PO Box 142, 13073]; (p) (607) 898-5787; (c) Tompkins

County/ 1970/ Board of Directors/ staff: 20(v)/ members: 115

HISTORICAL SOCIETY; HISTORY MUSEUM

PROGRAMS: Annual Meeting; Community Outreach; Elder's Programs; Exhibits; Guided Tours; Lectures; Research Library/Archives

COLLECTIONS: [19th-20th c] Documents, letters, books, costumes, furniture, household utensils, photographs, paintings, Smith Corona Typewriter and adding machines manufactured in Groton, NY.

HOURS: Mar-Dec Sa 9-1

ADMISSION: Donations accepted

HAMMONDSPORT

5928
Glenn H. Curtiss Museum of Local History
8419 State Rt 54, 14840; (p) (607) 569-2160; (f) (607) 569-2040; (c) Steuben

Private non-profit/ 1961/ staff: 4(f); 4(p); 90(v)/ members: 978/publication: *Aerogramme; Glenn Curtiss, Architect of American Aviation; Tony's World*

HISTORY MUSEUM: Collects and exhibits early aviation.

PROGRAMS: Community Outreach; Elder's Programs; Exhibits; Facility Rental; Family Programs; Festivals; Film/Video; Guided Tours; Interpretation; Lectures; Publication; Research Library/Archives

COLLECTIONS: [1890-1930] 18 aircraft; 6 motorcycles; 2 autos; 1 travel trailer; 9,000 artifacts, art works; 40,000 photo images on early aviation.

HOURS: Yr Jan-Mar Th-Sa 10-4, Su 12-5; May-Oct M-Sa 9-5, Su 11-5; Nov-Apr M-Sa 10-4, Su 12-5

ADMISSION: $5, Student $2.50, Seniors $3.50; Under 7 free, group rates

HASTINGS-ON-HUDSON

5929
Hastings Historical Society
407 Broadway, 10706; (p) (914) 478-2249; (c) Westchester

Private non-profit/ 1971/ Board of Trustees/ staff: 15(v)/ members: 1200/publication: *Hastings Historian*

HISTORIC PRESERVATION AGENCY; HISTORICAL SOCIETY: Collects and preserves material that constitute Hastings' past.

PROGRAMS: Annual Meeting; Community Outreach; Exhibits; Family Programs; Festivals; Guided Tours; Lectures; Living History; Publication; Research Library/Archives

COLLECTIONS: [17th c-present] Village, county, and state references, Hastings authors, photos, slides, pamphlets, family papers, oral histories, maps, videos, artifacts, historical and biographical files, Society history, telephone directories, yearbooks.

HOURS: Yr M, Th 10-2 and by appt

ADMISSION: No charge

HEMPSTEAD

5930
Hofstra University & Nassau County Museum: Long Island Studies Institute
c/o Hofstra Univ W Campus 619 Fulton Ave, 11549; (p) (516) 463-6411; (f) (516) 463-6441; (c) Nassau

Joint/ 1985/ Nassau County Dept of Parks & Rec, Museum Div; Hofstra Univ Libraries/ staff: 4(f); 1(p); 3(v)

RESEARCH CENTER: Maintains research facility for the study of Long Island and NY history.

PROGRAMS: Lectures; Publication; Research Library/Archives

COLLECTIONS: [18th-19th c] Books, pamphlets, maps, photographs, manuscripts, deeds, estate inventories, directories, daybooks, and annual reports.

HOURS: Yr M-F 9-5 (May-Aug F 9-4)

HERKIMER

5931
Herkimer County Historical Society
400 N Main St, 13350; (p) (315) 866-6413; (c) Herkimer

Private non-profit/ 1896/ staff: 2(f); 1(p); 48(v)/ members: 560

HISTORICAL SOCIETY: Discovers, collects, preserves, exhibits and publishes the history, historical records and data of Herkimer County.

PROGRAMS: Annual Meeting; Exhibits; Guided Tours; Lectures; Research Library/Archives

COLLECTIONS: [1725-1925] 6,000 photos; 500 postcards; 2,000 slides; 500 bound volumes of newspapers (1820-1930); 4,100 manuscripts (1795-1930); military records (1861-1865); WWII posters; clothing; 35 Remington typewriters; Fairfield Seminary collection.

HOURS: Yr M-F 10-4

ADMISSION: Jail $1; Doll Houses $1.50; Combination $2

HICKSVILLE

5932
Hicksville Gregory Museum, Long Island Earth Center, The
Heitz Place and Bay Ave, 11801; (p) (516) 822-7505; (f) (516) 822-3227; members.aol.com/Hgmuseum; (c) Nassau

State/ 1963/ Board of Trustees/ staff: 1(f); 4(p); 21(v)/ members: 182/publication: *Cupola*

NATURAL HISTORY MUSEUM

PROGRAMS: Community Outreach; Exhibits; Facility Rental; Family Programs; Guided Tours; Lectures; Publication; School-Based Curriculum

COLLECTIONS: [1895-present] Photos, records and Hicksville artifacts; 15,000 specimens: rocks, minerals, shells, gems and fossils.

HOURS: Yr T-F 9:30-4:30, Sa-Su 1-5

ADMISSION: $3.50, Children $1.50,

HIGH FALLS

5933
Delaware and Hudson Canal Historical Society
Mohouk Rd, 12440 [PO Box 23, 12440]; (p) (914) 687-9311; (f) (914) 868-7895; 76440.1375@compuserve.com; www.mhrcc.org/kingston/kgndah.html; (c) Ulster

Private non-profit/ 1968/ Delaware and Hudson Canal Historical Society/ staff: 3(p); 12(v)/ members: 500/publication: *Delaware and Hudson Canal News, Local History Works*

HISTORIC SITE; HISTORICAL SOCIETY; LIBRARY AND/OR ARCHIVES: Interprets and preserves the history of the Delaware and Hudson Canal; maintains public access to nearby flight of locks.

PROGRAMS: Annual Meeting; Community Outreach; Elder's Programs; Exhibits; Facility Rental; Family Programs; Festivals; Guided Tours; Interpretation; Lectures; Publication; Research Library/Archives; School-Based Curriculum

COLLECTIONS: [1825-1898] Photos, objects, maps, ephemeral.

HILTON

5934
Antique Wireless Association Museum of Electronic Communication
2 S Ave, 14468 [187 Lighthouse Rd., 14468]; (p) (716) 392-3088; k2mp@eznet.net; www.antiquewireless.org; (c) Monroe

Private non-profit/ 1952/ Antique Wireless Assoc, Inc./ staff: 1(f); 20(v)/ members: 4000/publication: *Old Timer's Bulletin and Annual Review*

HISTORY MUSEUM; RESEARCH CENTER: Preserves history of electronic communication.

PROGRAMS: Annual Meeting; Community Outreach; Exhibits; Interpretation; Lectures; Publication; Reenactments; Research Library/Archives

COLLECTIONS: [1850-present] Telegraph keys and sounders, radio sets, crystal, vacuum tubes, television items, electrical items, spark transmitters, ham radio items, and large console

HOGANSBURG

5935
Akwesasne Cultural Center, Inc., aka Akwesasne Museum
321 State Rt 37, 13655-9705; (p) (518) 358-2461; (f) (518) 358-2649; akwmuse@ northnet.org; (c) Franklin

Private non-profit/ 1972/ Akwesasne Cultural Center, Inc. Board of Directors/ staff: 2(f); 1(p)

CULTURAL CENTER; HISTORY MUSEUM; TRIBAL MUSEUM: Dedicated to the preservation, promotion, and presentation of the continuing culture of the Akwesasne Mohawk people.

PROGRAMS: Exhibits; Guided Tours; Interpretation; Research Library/Archives

COLLECTIONS: Mohawk black ash basketry, early 20th c photographs, art and artifacts dating from pre-contact to the present.

HOURS: Yr M-Th 8:30-4:30, F 8-4, Sa 11-3

ADMISSION: $2, Children $1; Native American/Under 5 free

HOMER

5936
Homeville Museum
49 Clinton St, Rt 41, 13077-1024; (p) (607) 749-3105; (c) Cortland

Private non-profit/ 1976/ staff: 1(f); 1(v)

HISTORY MUSEUM: Military and model museum.

PROGRAMS: Exhibits; Guided Tours

COLLECTIONS: [1943-1968] Paratrooper's folding bicycle; army cargo truck; army cannon jeep; jeep trailer; main battle tank.

HOURS: May-Oct Th 7-9, 2nd and 4th Su of month 1-4

ADMISSION: Donations

HOWELLS

5937
Mt. Hope Historical Society Site/Eleazer Harding House
183 Old Mountain Rd, 10932 [PO Box 16, 10932]; (p) (914) 386-5945; (c) Orange

Private non-profit/ 1988/ Mt. Hope Historical Society/ staff: 5(v)/ members: 61

HISTORIC SITE; HISTORICAL SOCIETY; LIVING HISTORY/OUTDOOR MUSEUM: Dedicated to preserving and restoring old buildings in our area and showing how people lived in the area from 1790-1840.

PROGRAMS: Exhibits; Guided Tours; Interpretation; Living History

COLLECTIONS: [Early 19th c.] Furnishings and accessories demonstrating life of average subsistence farmer in this area from 1790-1840; journals, memorabilia.

HOURS: May-Oct, 4th Su 12-4

ADMISSION: Donations accepted

HOWES CAVE

5938
Iroquois Indian Museum
Caverns Rd, 12092 [PO Box 7, 12092]; (p) (518) 296-8949; (f) (518) 296-8955; INFO@ iroquoismuseum.org; www.iroquoismuseum.org; (c) Schoharie

Private non-profit/ 1980/ Board of Trustees/ staff: 3(f); 4(p); 50(v)/ members: 680/publication: Museum Notes

HISTORY MUSEUM

PROGRAMS: Community Outreach; Exhibits; Festivals; Guided Tours; Interpretation; Lectures; Publication; Research Library/Archives

COLLECTIONS: [20th c] Iroquois Native American contemporary arts, archaeological

collections from the Schoharie Valley region of NY state.

HOURS: Apr-Dec T-Su 10-5

ADMISSION: $7, Children $4

HUDSON

5939
Hendrick Hudson Chapter NSDAR/Robert Jenkins House
113 Warren St, 12534; (p) (518) 828-9764; (c) Columbia

Private non-profit/ 1896/ members: 90

HOUSE MUSEUM

PROGRAMS: Annual Meeting; Exhibits; Guided Tours; Research Library/Archives

COLLECTIONS: [1700s -present] Data related to whaling; Civil War and Revolutionary War; warbooks; bottles; and participants in such wars. Gun collection and uniforms, artifacts from past 200 years.

HOURS: July-Aug Su-M 1-3 and by appt

ADMISSION: Donations requested

5940
Olana State Historic Site
Rt 9G 1 mile S of the Rip van Winkle Bridge, 12534 [5720 Rt 9 G, 12534]; (p) (518) 828-0135; (f) (518) 828-6742; (c) Columbia

State/ 1967/ NY State Office of Parks, Recreation and Historic Preservation/ staff: 10(f); 21(p); 93(v)/ members: 800

ART MUSEUM; HISTORIC SITE; HISTORY MUSEUM; HOUSE MUSEUM; STATE PARK: Maintains home and garden of Frederic Edwin Church.

PROGRAMS: Annual Meeting; Community Outreach; Concerts; Family Programs; Film/Video; Garden Tours; Guided Tours; Interpretation; Lectures

COLLECTIONS: [19th c] Art works by Church and other Hudson River School artists, 400 drawings by Camille Pissarro and teacher Melbye, Middle Eastern carpets, metalwork, ceramics, Old Master paintings, Mexican colonial folk art, 4,500 photographs, household furnishings and artist's tools. Structures include Olana (1870), 11 outbuildings, carriage and animal barns, historic gardens, trails, drives, and a planned landscape.

HOURS: Apr-Oct W-Su 10-4

ADMISSION: $3, Student $1, Seniors $2

HUNTINGTON

5941
Arsenal, Home of Job Sammis, The
425 Park Ave, 11743 [c/o Huntington Town Historian, 228 Main St, 11743]; (p) (516) 351-3244

1740/ City/ staff: 11(v)

COLLECTIONS: [Colonial period-1776] Original furniture and loom.; Not stored at the Arsenal, but in town hall - original town documents of the town of Huntington before, during, and after the Revolutionary War.

HOURS: Jan 15-Dec 15 Su 1-4 and by appt

5942
Huntington Historical Society
209 Main St, 11743; (p) (516) 427-7045; (f) (516) 427-7056; hunthistory@juno.com; www.huntingtonli.org/hunthistorical; (c) Suffolk

Private non-profit/ 1903/ staff: 2(f); 5(p)/ members: 1050

GENEALOGICAL SOCIETY; HISTORIC SITE; HISTORICAL SOCIETY; HOUSE MUSEUM; RESEARCH CENTER: Dedicated to the preservation of Huntington's heritage through two house museums, research library, and collections.

PROGRAMS: Elder's Programs; Exhibits; Facility Rental; Family Programs; Festivals; Guided Tours; Lectures; Research Library/ Archives; School-Based Curriculum

COLLECTIONS: [1750-1890] Period rooms furnished in Colonial, Empire & Victorian styles, coverlets, quilts, textile preparation equipment, dolls, toys, kitchen equipment, pottery, extensive photograph collection, local genealog,y and history records.

HOURS: Yr T-Fr, Su 1-4

ADMISSION: $2.50, Family $5, Children $1

5943
Huntington Town Clerk's Archives
100 Main St, 11743-6991; (p) (516) 351-3035, (516) 351-3216; (f) (516) 351-3205; amattheou@town.huntington.ny.us; (c) Suffolk

1993/ staff: 1(f); 1(p)

LIBRARY AND/OR ARCHIVES: Collects, processes, preserves and makes available the town's historical records.

PROGRAMS: Community Outreach; Exhibits; Guided Tours; Research Library/Archives; School-Based Curriculum

COLLECTIONS: [18th-present] Minutes, vital statistics, land surveys, deeds, war records, licenses, correspondence, school,

5944
Joseph Lloyd Manor House
Lloyd Ln, 11743 [PO Box 148, Cold Spring Harbor, 11724]; (p) (516) 271-7760, (516) 692-4664; (f) (516) 692-5265; splia.com

1766/ staff: 4(p)

Home of Jupiter Hammon, a slave who became the first published African American poet.

COLLECTIONS: [18th c]

HOURS: Jun-Oct

HUNTINGTON STATION

5945
Walt Whitman Birthplace Association
246 Old Walt Whitman Rd, 11746-4148; (p) (631) 427-5240; (f) (631) 427-5247; www.nysparks.com; (c) Suffolk

Joint; State/ 1949/ NY State Office of Parks, Rec. and Hist. Preservation/ staff: 1(f); 12(p); 50(v)/ members: 500/publication: Starting from Paumanok

HISTORIC SITE; HISTORY MUSEUM; STATE PARK: Maintains the birthplace of Walt Whitman, fosters an appreciation of poetry and makes Whitman's life accessible to the public.

The Birthplace is a State of New York Historic Site with an 1819 farmhouse and an interpretive center.

PROGRAMS: Annual Meeting; Concerts; Exhibits; Facility Rental; Family Programs; Guided Tours; Interpretation; Lectures; Publication; Reenactments; Research Library/Archives; School-Based Curriculum

COLLECTIONS: [1819-1892] Newly restored farmhouse with authentic furnishings, library of 600 volumes, archives of Whitman and WWBA documents, photographs, a music collection, Whitman's desk and his voice on tape.

HOURS: Yr Summer: M, W-F 11-4, Sa-Su 12-5; Winter: W-F 1-4, Sa-Su 11-4

ADMISSION: $3, Student $2, Children $1, Seniors $2; Under 7 free

HURLEY

5946
Hurley Patentee Manor
464 Old Rt 209, 12443; (p) (914) 331-5414; (f) (914) 331-5414

1696

COLLECTIONS: [18th c] Indian arrowheads, stone knives, crushing stones, mortar and pestle, old letters, documents, books, papers, a few rare antiques, 18th c antiques in 9 rooms.

HOURS: Seasonal

HURLEYVILLE

5947
Sullivan County Historical Society
265 Main St, 12747 [PO Box 247, 12747]; (p) (914) 434-8044; schs@warwick.net; www.sullivancountyhistory.org; (c) Sullivan

Private non-profit/ 1896/ staff: 1(f); 12(v)/ members: 340/publication: The Observer

HISTORICAL SOCIETY: Organized to preserve and present the history of Sullivan County.

PROGRAMS: Annual Meeting; Community Outreach; Exhibits; Guided Tours; Interpretation; Lectures; Publication; Research Library/Archives; School-Based Curriculum

COLLECTIONS: [1800-1920] Collection consists of clothing, small artifacts and miscellaneous memorabilia. Extensive archived documents, obituary and personal history research materials.

HOURS: Yr W-Sa 10-4:30, Su 1-4:30

HYDE PARK

5948
Eleanor Roosevelt National Historic Site
Rt 9G, 12538 [519 Albany Post Rd, 12538]; (p) (845) 229-9115; (f) (845) 229-0739; ROVA_webmaster@nps.gov; www.nps.gov/elro/

1977

GARDEN; HISTORIC SITE; HOUSE MUSEUM; STATE PARK: Maintains the historic home and gardens owned by Eleanor Roosevelt called Val-Kill, the only National Historic site dedicated to a First Lady.

PROGRAMS: Exhibits; Guided Tours

COLLECTIONS: Furniture, documents, memorabilia.

HOURS: Yr May-Oct Daily 9-5; Nov-Apr Sa-Su 9-5

ADMISSION: $5

5949
Franklin D. Roosevelt Library & Digital Archives
4079 Albany Post Rd, 12538; (p) (845) 229-8114, (800) 337-8474; (f) (845) 229-0872; roosevelt.library@government.nara.gov; www.fdrlibrary.marist.edu/index.html; (c) Dutchess

Federal/ 1939/ National Archives and Records Administration/ staff: 18(f); 5(p); 14(v)

HISTORY MUSEUM; LIBRARY AND/OR ARCHIVES; RESEARCH CENTER: Archival repository for FDR's papers, public and private, those of his family and associates, a museum collection and exhibits, and an educational section.

PROGRAMS: Exhibits; Research Library/Archives

COLLECTIONS: [1910-1962] Personal papers, government records, heads of state gifts, gifts from private citizens, political campaign items, personal and family memorabilia, President Roosevelt's collection on U.S. Naval History.

HOURS: Yr Museum: Daily 9-5; Library Research Room: M-F 8:45-5

ADMISSION: $10

5950
Vanderbilt Mansion National Historic Site
Rt 9, 12538 [519 Albany Post Rd, 12538]; (p) (914) 229-7770; www.nps.gov/vama

1896/ National Park Service/ staff: 42(f)

COLLECTIONS: [1890-1938] Original furniture, including a tapestey collection, Paul Sormani cabinets, European fireplaces and furnishings, and an 1881 Steinway.

ITHACA

5951
DeWitt Historical Society of Tompkins County, The
401 E State St, 14850; (p) (607) 273-8284; (f) (607) 273-6107; dhs@lakenet.org; www.lakenet.org/dewitt; (c) Tompkins

Private non-profit/ 1935/ staff: 3(f); 3(p); 200(v)/ members: 600

HISTORICAL SOCIETY: Collects, preserves, and interprets the history of Tompkins County. Operates the Tompkins County Museum, site of exhibits, research and education programs, and the Eight Square Schoolhouse.

PROGRAMS: Annual Meeting; Community Outreach; Concerts; Elder's Programs; Exhibits; Family Programs; Festivals; Film/Video; Interpretation; Lectures; Living History; Publication; Research Library/Archives

COLLECTIONS: [Pre 19th- mid 20th c.] 100,000 images; 900 linear ft of archives; 4,000 books; 18,000 objects; maps. Historic structure-Eight Square Schoolhouse.

HOURS: Yr T-Sa 11-5

ADMISSION: Donations requested

5952
Paleontological Research Institution
1259 Trumansburg Rd, 14850; (p) (607) 273-6623; (f) (607) 273-6620; wda1@cornell.edu; www.engli6.cornell.edu/pri

Private non-profit/ 1932/ staff: 9(f); 1(p); 113(v)/ members: 900/publication: American Paleontologist; Bulletins of Paleontology; and others

HISTORY MUSEUM: Through its collections, exhibits, public outreach programs, and educational programs, the institution helps the public understand the history and diversity of life on Earth.

PROGRAMS: Annual Meeting; Community Outreach; Exhibits; Facility Rental; Family Programs; Interpretation; Lectures; Publication; Research Library/Archives; School-Based Curriculum

COLLECTIONS: 3 million fossils, shells, recent specimens, parts of the fossil and shell collections of Cornell University.

HOURS: Sept-May M-Sa 11-4; May-Sept, W-Sa 11-4

ADMISSION: Donations accepted

JAMAICA

5953
King Manor Museum
King Park, Jamaica Ave btwn 150 & 153 St, 11432 [90-04 161 Street, Ste 704, 11432]; (p) (718) 206-0545; (f) (718) 206-0541; (c) Queens

Private non-profit/ 1900/ King Manor Ass. Of L.I./ staff: 2(f); 4(p); 20(v)/ members: 175

HISTORIC SITE; HISTORY MUSEUM; HOUSE MUSEUM:

PROGRAMS: Community Outreach; Concerts; Exhibits; Family Programs; Festivals; Guided Tours; Interpretation; Lectures; School-Based Curriculum

COLLECTIONS: [18th-19th c] 1,400 objects, many related to Rufus King, his family and life in early Jamaica. Includes furniture; textiles and costumes; ceramics, china, and glass; children's clothing and toys; personal artifacts; armament; painting and prints; and memorabilia.

HOURS: Mar-Dec Sa-Su 12-4

ADMISSION: $2, Children $1

5954
Long Island Division Queens Borough Public Library
89-11 Merrick Blvd, 11432; (p) (718) 990-0770; (f) (718) 658-8342; www.queenslibrary.org/special/longisland.html

County/ staff: 4(f); 2(p); 2(v)

RESEARCH CENTER: Collects, preserves, and makes available material documenting the natural, social, economic, and political history of the four counties of Long Island-Kings, Queens, Nassau and Suffolk.

PROGRAMS: Research Library/Archives

COLLECTIONS: 800 linear ft of manuscripts, 31,000 books & volumes of serials, 75,000 photographs, 432 ft of vertical files, 168 newspaper titles, subscriptions to 49 journals, and 22 newspaper titles.

HOURS: Yr Jan-Dec M 10-9, T-Th 10-7, F 10-6, Sa 10-5:30, Su (Sept-May) 12-5

ADMISSION: No charge

JAMESTOWN

5955
Fenton History Center—Museum and Library

67 Washington St, 14701; (p) (716) 664-6256; (f) (716) 483-7524; (c) Chautauqua

Private non-profit/ 1964/ Board of Trustees/ staff: 1(f); 20(p); 40(v)/ members: 700

HISTORY MUSEUM; HOUSE MUSEUM: Local history center housed in 1863 mansion of NY Governor Reuben Fenton, offering period rooms, local history exhibits, education programs and reference and genealogy library, focusing on Jamestown, New York, and Southern Chautauqua County.

PROGRAMS: Annual Meeting; Community Outreach; Elder's Programs; Exhibits; Facility Rental; Family Programs; Festivals; Guided Tours; Interpretation; Lectures; Publication; Research Library/Archives; School-Based Curriculum

COLLECTIONS: [1850-present] Artifacts, textiles, photographs, and archival materials pertaining to the history of Jamestown, NY and Southern Chautauqua County.

HOURS: Yr Jan-Nov M-Sa 10-4; Dec M-Sa 10-4, Su 1-4

ADMISSION: $3.50, Student $2.50

JAMESVILLE

5956
Jamesville Community Museum

6492 E Seneca Tpk, 13078 [PO Box 76, 13078-0076]; (p) (315) 492-4890, (315) 469-1914; (c) Onondaga

Private non-profit/ 1978/ Board of Trustees/ staff: 1(p); 100(v)/ members: 390/publication: *Water, Wheels and Stone*

HISTORIC SITE; HISTORICAL SOCIETY; HISTORY MUSEUM: Maintains historic building as a center for community involvement and education about our heritage, with emphasis on the hamlet's geological, economic, and sociological development.

PROGRAMS: Annual Meeting; Community Outreach; Elder's Programs; Exhibits; Family Programs; Guided Tours; Interpretation; Lectures; Publication; Research Library/Archives; School-Based Curriculum; Theatre

COLLECTIONS: [Prehistoric-1790-present] New York State rocks and minerals; 15-foot diorama of the Solvay Process; artifacts, photographs, and documents related to quarrying, ice harvesting, farming, homemaking, and schools. Structures: Former St. Mark's Episcopal Church (1878) on State and National Registers of Historic Places.

HOURS: Yr Jan-Apr Su 2-4; May-Dec Sa-Su 1-4

ADMISSION: No charge

5957
John Burroughs Memorial State Historical Site

Route 30, 13078 [c/o NYS Parks Rec. Hist. Pres. 6105 E. Seneca Tpk, 13078-9516]; (p) (315) 492-1756; (f) (315) 492-3277; (c) Delaware

State/ 1966/ NY State Office of Parks, Rec. & Hist. Preservation

HISTORIC PRESERVATION AGENCY: John Burroughs, naturalist, author, philosopher, spent his boyhood in the Catskill Mountain area. His gravesite is located at Memorial Field at a large rock where Burroughs sat contemplating nature and drawing inspiration for his writings.

PROGRAMS: Interpretation

JOHNSTOWN

5958
Johnson Hall State Historic Site

Hall Ave, 12095; (p) (518) 762-8712; (f) (518) 762-2330; Wanda.burch@oprhp.state.ny.us; (c) Fulton

State/ 1763/ NYS Off. Of Parks, Rec. & Hist. Preservation/ staff: 3(f); 2(p)

HISTORIC SITE; HOUSE MUSEUM; STATE PARK: A Georgian house, 1763, originally owned by Sir William Johnson, landowner, military hero, entrepreneur and superintendent of Indian Affairs for the 6 Nations.

PROGRAMS: Community Outreach; Concerts; Family Programs; Festivals; Guided Tours; Interpretation; Lectures; Living History; Reenactments; Theatre

COLLECTIONS: [1763-1774] Period house set up with 1774 inventory. Structures include: 18th c stonehouse, 1763 Georgian house.

HOURS: May-Oct W-Sa 10-5, Su 1-5

ADMISSION: $3, Children $1, Seniors $2

5959
Johnstown Historical Society

17 N William St, 12095; (p) (518) 762-7076; (c) Fulton

Private non-profit/ staff: 10(v)/ members: 200

HISTORICAL SOCIETY; HISTORY MUSEUM: Preserves and researches city of Johnstown's history, resident, and historic homes.

PROGRAMS: Annual Meeting; Exhibits; Guided Tours; Interpretation; Lectures; Research Library/Archives

COLLECTIONS: [1860-1940] Artifacts, photographs, letters, newspapers.

HOURS: May-Sept W-Su 1-5 and by appt

ADMISSION: Donations accepted

KATONAH

5960
Caramoor Center for Music and Arts

149 Girdle Ridge Rd, 10536 [PO Box 816, 10536]; (p) (914) 232-5035; (f) (914) 223-5521; www.caramoor.com; (c) Westchester

Private non-profit/ 1946/ staff: 13(f); 7(p); 250(v)/ members: 1000/publication: *A Guide to the Collections of Caramoor*

ART MUSEUM; GARDEN; HOUSE MUSEUM: Offers a variety of programs, tours, education, architecture, and music, including the International Music Festival.

PROGRAMS: Community Outreach; Concerts; Exhibits; Facility Rental; Festivals; Garden Tours; Guided Tours; Lectures; Publication; School-Based Curriculum

COLLECTIONS: [Renaissance] Eastern, Medieval, Renaissance, and 18th c art and artifacts, paintings, textiles, and furniture; entire rooms from European villas; and jade collection.

HOURS: May-Oct W-Su 1-4; Nov-Apr M-F by appt

ADMISSION: $7; Under 17 free

5961
John Jay Homestead State Historic Site

400 Jay St, 10536 [PO Box 832, 10536]; (p) (914) 232-5651; (f) (914) 232-8085; (c) Westchester

State/ 1958/ NY State Office of Parks Recreation and Historic Preservation/ staff: 5(f); 2(p); 30(v)/ members: 400

HISTORIC SITE; HOUSE MUSEUM; STATE PARK: Preserves a five generation family estate with interpretations that reflect the Jay's lives from the era of Chief Justice John Jay through the 20th c and its last occupants. 64 acres of Northern Westchester farmland preserved with its buildings.

PROGRAMS: Annual Meeting; Community Outreach; Concerts; Exhibits; Facility Rental; Festivals; Garden Tours; Guided Tours; Interpretation; Lectures; School-Based Curriculum

COLLECTIONS: Fine arts, decorative arts, farm equipment, and other materials pertaining to the home and farm of the Jay family. Structures include five buildings; Main House; Barn; Carriage Barn; Coachman's House; Brick Cottage.

HOURS: Apr-Dec W-Su 10-4; Jan-Mar by appt

ADMISSION: $3, Children $1, Seniors $2

KINDERHOOK

5962
Columbia County Historical Society

5 Albany Ave, 12106 [PO Box 311, 12106]; (p) (518) 758-9265; (f) (518) 758-2499; (c) Columbia

Joint; Private non-profit/ 1916/ Board of Directors/ staff: 2(f); 3(p); 78(v)/ members: 670/publication: *The Columbian Repository*

HISTORIC SITE; HISTORICAL SOCIETY; HISTORY MUSEUM; HOUSE MUSEUM: The society encourages understanding, knowledge, and preservation of the county's history and culture through historical properties; a museum with changing exhibits, research archives, and library; collections, publications; and educational programming.

PROGRAMS: Annual Meeting; Exhibits; Festivals; Guided Tours; Interpretation; Lectures; Living History; Publication; Reenactments; Research Library/Archives; School-Based Curriculum

COLLECTIONS: [1730-present] Artifacts, manuscripts, photographs, books, and historical properties, exhibits, period rooms at three properties, Structures: Luykas Van Alen House (1737), James Vanderpoel House (1820), Ichabod Crane Schoolhouse (1850) and more.

HOURS: Yr Jan-Dec Museum: May-Nov M-F 10-4 Sa 1-4 Dec-Apr M, W, F, 10-4 Sa 1-4 Historic properties: May-Sept Th-Sa 11-5 Su 1-5

5963
Martin Van Buren National Historic Site
1013 Old Post Rd, 12106; (p) (518) 758-9689; (f) (518) 758-6986; mava@nps.gov; www.nps.gov/mava/home; (c) Columbia

Federal/ 1974/ staff: 12(f)/ members: 382

HISTORIC SITE; HOUSE MUSEUM; PRESIDENTIAL SITE: Preserves the Lindenwald home of 8th US President Martin Van Buren.

PROGRAMS: Concerts; Family Programs; Guided Tours; Interpretation; Lectures; School-Based Curriculum

COLLECTIONS: [1840-1860] Objects associated with Martin Van Buren, Lindenwald, the Van Buren family.

HOURS: LeRoy House: May-Oct M-F 1-4, Su 2-4, Nov-Apr by appt only; Jell-O Gallery: May-Oct M-Sa 10-4, Su 1-4, Nov-Apr M-F 10-4

ADMISSION: $2

KINGSTON

5964
Senate House State Historic Site
296 Fair St, 12401; (p) (914) 338-2786; (f) (914) 334-8173

1676/ NYS Office of Parks, Recreation and Historic Preservation, Bureau of Historic Sites/ staff: 6(f); 4(p)

HISTORIC SITE; STATE PARK: Preserves Senate House, 1777.

PROGRAMS: Exhibits

COLLECTIONS: [1777] Colonial furnishings in Senate House 18th & 19th c art, most by John Vanderlyn and 5,000 miscelaneous artifacts, largely decorative arts, Several thousand documents from the R. R. Hoeb collection and several other collections.

LAKE PLACID

5965
1932 and 1980 Lake Placid Winter Olympic Museum, The
Olympic Center, 12946; (p) (518) 523-4655; (f) (518) 523-9275; museum@orda.org; (c) Essex

Joint/ 1994/ staff: 3(f); 5(p)

HISTORY MUSEUM: Collects and preserves artifacts and archival materials associated with Lake Placid's winter sports and winter Olympic heritage, and interprets that heritage to the public.

PROGRAMS: Community Outreach; Exhibits; Facility Rental; Guided Tours; Interpretation; Lectures; Research Library/Archives; School-Based Curriculum

COLLECTIONS: [20th c] Winter sports/Olympic materials: 60 fine arts objects, 120 textiles, 80 numismatic objects, 10 pieces

of large equipment, 60 personal artifacts, 400 recreational artifacts, 10,000 slides and photographs, and 684 linear feet of archival holdings.

HOURS: W-Sa 10-5, Su 12-4

ADMISSION: $3, Children $1, Seniors $2

5966
John Brown Farm State Historic Site
2 John Brown Rd, 12946; (p) (518) 523-3900; (c) Essex

State/ 1870/ NY State Office of Parks, Rec & Hist. Preservation/ staff: 1(f); 2(p); 6(v)

HISTORIC SITE; HOUSE MUSEUM; STATE PARK: Preserves and interprets John Brown's final home, grave, raid on Harpers Ferry, arrest, and subsequent trial and execution.

PROGRAMS: Concerts; Exhibits; Interpretation; Reenactments

COLLECTIONS: [1850-1865] Artifacts relating to John Brown or members of immediate family, artifacts connected to Harpers Ferry raid, and period furnishings. Structures include: John Brown Farmhouse (1855), John Brown Barn (1854), Woodshed (1898), and others.

HOURS: May-Oct W-Sa 10-5, Su 1-5

LARCHMONT

5967
Larchmont Historical Society
740 W Boston Post Rd, 10538 [PO Box 742, 10538]; (p) (914) 381-2239; LHS@savvy.net; members.savvy.net/lhs; (c) Westchester

1980/ Board of Trustees/ staff: 1(p); 5(v)/ members: 500

HISTORICAL SOCIETY: Society collects, preserves, and interprets Larchmont's past.

PROGRAMS: Annual Meeting; Community Outreach; Exhibits; Family Programs; Lectures; Publication; Research Library/Archives

COLLECTIONS: [19th-20th c] 200 processed manuscripts, 150 maps, 250 volumes, 500 photographs, 30 linear feet of local information in 200 categories.

HOURS: Yr T-Th 9-2 and by appt

ADMISSION: No charge

LAWRENCE

5968
Friends of Rock Hall Museum
199 Broadway, 11559; (p) (516) 239-1157; (f) (516) 239-9436; (c) Nassau

City/ 1976/ Town of Hempsted Museum/ staff: 37(v)/ members: 400/publication: *Rock Hall and Narrative History*

HISTORIC SITE; HOUSE MUSEUM

PROGRAMS: Annual Meeting; Concerts; Exhibits; Family Programs; Festivals; Garden Tours; Guided Tours; Lectures; Publication; Reenactments; Research Library/Archives; School-Based Curriculum

COLLECTIONS: [18th-early 19th c.] Town furnishings, collection of Hepplewhite, Chippendale, and Federal furnishings.

HOURS: Yr W-Sa 10-4, Su 12-4

ADMISSION: No charge

LEROY

5969
LeRoy Historical Society
23 E Main St, 14482; (p) (716) 768-7433; (f) (716) 768-7579; (c) Genesee

Private non-profit/ 1940/ staff: 1(f); 1(p); 50(v)/ members: 350

HISTORICAL SOCIETY; HISTORY MUSEUM; HOUSE MUSEUM: Society maintains the history of LeRoy House and features the history of Jell-O which was invented in LeRoy.

PROGRAMS: Annual Meeting; Community Outreach; Exhibits; Family Programs; Guided Tours; Publication; Research Library/Archives; School-Based Curriculum

COLLECTIONS: [1800-present] Decorative arts of 19th c, Ingham University archives and art, Morganville pottery, western NY 19th c art and the history of Jell-O.

HOURS: Yr T-Fr 10-4, Su 2-4; Jell-O gallery May-Sept M-Su

ADMISSION: $3

LITTLE FALLS

5970
Herkimer Home State Historic Site
SR 167, Box 631, 13365; (p) (315) 823-0398; www.npac.syr.edu/projects/ltb/teacher_journeys/herk_title.html

5971
Little Falls Historical Society
319 S Ann St, 13365; (p) (315) 823-0643; (c) Herkimer

Private non-profit/ staff: 8(v)/ members: 60

HISTORICAL SOCIETY: Collects and preserves information about Little Falls and surrounding area.

PROGRAMS: Annual Meeting; Exhibits; Family Programs; Film/Video

COLLECTIONS: [18th c-present] Artifacts, clothing, maps, documents, pictures.

HOURS: May-Sept F-Su

LITTLE VALLEY

5972
Cattaraugus County Memorial Hospital and Historical Museum
Court St, 14755; (p) (716) 938-9111; (c) Cattaraugus

County/ 1914/ staff: 5(p); 1(v)

Maintains a local history museum and research library.

COLLECTIONS: [Early 1800s-WW II] Household artifacts, uniforms, and Iroquois Indian artifacts.

HOURS: Yr M-F 9-4:30

ADMISSION: No charge

LOCKPORT

5973
Niagara County Historical Society, Inc.
215 Niagara St, 14094-2605; (p) (716) 434-7433; (f) (716) 434-7433; (c) Niagara

Private non-profit/ 1947/ staff: 1(f); 2(p); 40(v)/ members: 800

HISTORICAL SOCIETY; HISTORY MUSEUM; HOUSE MUSEUM: Museum's collection deals with the Civil War, Iroquois Life, Erie Canal business and industry and owns a National Register Empire Period home built in 1823.

PROGRAMS: Annual Meeting; Community Outreach; Exhibits; Facility Rental; Family Programs; Festivals; Living History; Publication; Reenactments; Research Library/Archives; School-Based Curriculum

COLLECTIONS: [1805-1930] Artifacts relating to pioneer, military, medical, Iroquois, Erie Canal, paintings, business ledgers, textiles. 12 room Empire Period Home on National Register.

HOURS: Jan-Apr W-Sa 1-5; May-Dec Th-Su 1-5

ADMISSION: Donations accepted

LYONS

5974
Wayne County Historical Society
21 Butternut St, 14489; (p) (315) 946-4943; (f) (315) 946-0069; wchs4943@aol.com; members.aol.com/wchs4943; (c) Wayne

County; Private non-profit/ 1949/ staff: 2(p); 40(v)/ members: 756

GENEALOGICAL SOCIETY; HISTORICAL SOCIETY; HISTORY MUSEUM; HOUSE MUSEUM: Society collects, preserves, and displays artifacts with relevance to Wayne County history.

PROGRAMS: Annual Meeting; Community Outreach; Concerts; Exhibits; Family Programs; Festivals; Film/Video; Guided Tours; Interpretation; Lectures; Living History; Publication; Research Library/Archives; School-Based Curriculum

COLLECTIONS: [1812-present] Artifacts and items relating to industry and people of Wayne County

HOURS: Yr 15 T-F 10-4, Sa-Su or by appt

MALONE

5975
Almanzo and Laura Ingalls Wilder Association
177 Stacy Rd, 12953 [PO Box 283, 12953]; (p) (518) 483-1207; almanzo@northnet.org; www.almanzowilderfarm.com; (c) Franklin

Private non-profit/ 1987/ NY State Board of Regents/ staff: 18(v)/ members: 556

HISTORIC SITE; HISTORY MUSEUM; HOUSE MUSEUM: Maintains the Wilder farm restored to Laura Ingalls Wilder's description in "Farmer Boy" and offers tours of the house and barns.

PROGRAMS: Annual Meeting; Exhibits; Facility Rental; Guided Tours; Publication; Reenactments; School-Based Curriculum

COLLECTIONS: [1830-1875] Furniture, rugs, farm tools, buggies, and photographs.

HOURS: May-Sept T-Sa 11-4, Su 1-4

ADMISSION: $4, Children $2

5976
Franklin County Historical and Museum Society
51 Milwaulkee St, 12953 [PO Box 388, 12953]; (p) (518) 483-2750; (c) Franklin

Private non-profit/ 1903/ staff: 1(f); 35(v)/ members: 302/publication: *Franklin Historical Review*

HISTORICAL SOCIETY; HISTORY MUSEUM; HOUSE MUSEUM: Mission to encourage and facilitate research into the life and history of the area through the collection, preservation, and exhibition of materials relative to the history of Franklin County.

PROGRAMS: Annual Meeting; Exhibits; Guided Tours; Living History; Publication; Research Library/Archives

COLLECTIONS: [1750-1950] Period rooms, exhibition of artifacts related to area agriculture, industry, military, home life, research materials.

HOURS: June-Sept

MAMARONECK

5977
Mamaroneck Historical Society
136 Prospect St, 10543 [Box 766, 10543]; (p) (914) 777-2776; (c) Westchester

Private non-profit/ 1937/ Exec Board and Board of Trustees/ staff: 15(v)/ members: 500/publication: *Conversations*

HISTORICAL SOCIETY; HISTORY MUSEUM: Researches and preserves history of community through programs, exhibits, and local television show. Restores and operates an 1816 schoolhouse museum.

PROGRAMS: Annual Meeting; Community Outreach; Elder's Programs; Exhibits; Film/Video; Lectures; Publication

COLLECTIONS: [19th c-present] Local maps from 1868, county maps, local photographic archive, county history books, historical records, and biographies from 1896, small artifacts collection. Structures include Schoolhouse Museum (1816).

MARLBORO

5978
Gomez Mill House
11 Mill House Rd, 12542; (p) (845) 236-3126; (f) (845) 236-3365; gomezmillhouse@juno.com; www.gomez.org; (c) Orange

Private non-profit/ 1984/ staff: 2(f); 1(p); 19(v)/publication: *Gomez Mill House: Hudson Valley Treasure*

HISTORIC SITE; HOUSE MUSEUM: Built by a Sephardic Jew in 1714. Home of pioneers, patriots, arts and crafts.

PROGRAMS: Annual Meeting; Community Outreach; Elder's Programs; Exhibits; Family Programs; Festivals; Film/Video; Garden Tours; Guided Tours; Interpretation; Lectures; Living History; Publication; Reenactments; School-Based Curriculum

COLLECTIONS: [1705-present] Artifacts left on site by previous owners and gifts from the period. Certificate of Denization (1705), Stickley and Hunter pieces.

HOURS: Apr- Oct W-Su 10-4 and by appt

ADMISSION: $5, Children $1

5979
Marlboro Free Library
1251 Rt 9 W, 12542 [PO Box 780, 12542]; (p) (914) 236-7272; (f) (914) 236-7635; marlboro@sebridge.org; (c) Ulster

1911/ Marlboro Central School District/publication: *The Grapevine*

Public library that houses some collections focused on the town of Marlborough and the Hudson River Valley.

COLLECTIONS: Local history collection: town of Marlborough, Hudson River Valley, Frederic Goudy Collection.

HOURS: Yr M-Th 9:30-8:30, F 9:30-5, Sa 11-5, Su 1-5 (except July-Aug)

ADMISSION: No charge

MASTIC BEACH

5980
William Floyd Estate
245 Park Dr, 11951; (p) (516) 399-2030; www.sinc.sunysb.edu/ Class/est572/kammerman/

MAYFIELD

5981
Mayfield Historical Society
Riceville Rd, 12117 [PO Box 715, 12117]; (c) Fulton

Private non-profit/ 1981/ staff: 20(p)/ members: 200

HISTORIC PRESERVATION AGENCY; HISTORIC SITE; HISTORICAL SOCIETY; HISTORY MUSEUM; HOUSE MUSEUM

PROGRAMS: Annual Meeting; Automobile Museum; Concerts; Elder's Programs; Exhibits; Family Programs; Festivals; Garden Tours; Guided Tours; Living History; School-Based Curriculum

COLLECTIONS: [Late 1800s] Local artifacts, records and photos.

HOURS: May-Sept Sa-Su 12-4 and by

MIDDLEBURGH

5982
Best House-Dr. Christopher S. Best Medical Exhibit
34 Clauverwie Blvd, 12122 [PO Box 232, 12122]; (p) (518) 827-4239, (518) 827-7200; ahdoerge@midtel.net; www.cobleskill.edu/ schools/mcs/csbest

1885/ Middleburgh Library Association/ staff: 5(v)

COLLECTIONS: [1600s-Early 1900s] Household and medical artifacts, associated books, paperwork, bills, catalogs, photographs, diaries, books.

HOURS: Seasonal

5983
Doctor C.S. Best Home and Medical Exhibit
34 Clauverwie, 12122 [PO Box 232, 12122-0232]; (p) (518) 827-4239; ahdoerge@midtel.net; www. cobleskill.edu/schools/mcs/csbest; (c) Schoharie

Private non-profit/ 1991/ Middleburgh Library Association/ staff: 6(v)

HOUSE MUSEUM: Home and office of 2 generations of country doctors covering over 100 years from the mid 1800's.

PROGRAMS: Exhibits; Guided Tours

COLLECTIONS: [Mid 1800s-1980s] Original furnishings of home and office, paperwork, family letters, and genealogy, carriages, sleighs, photos of family and community, catalogs, diaries, automotive, newspaper, medical books, and

MIDDLETOWN

5984
Historical Society of Middletown and the Wallkill Precinct
25 E Ave, 10946 [PO Box 34, 10946]; (p) (914) 342-0941; enjine@aol.com; (c) Orange

Private non-profit/ 1923/ staff: 6(v)/ members: 160

HISTORICAL SOCIETY: Preserves local history.

PROGRAMS: Annual Meeting; Guided Tours; Research Library/Archives

COLLECTIONS: Historical artifacts, antique clothing, locally produced products.

HOURS: Yr W

MONROE

5985
Museum Village
Rt 17M, 10950 [1010 Museum Village Rd, 10950]; (p) (914) 782-8247; (f) (914) 781-6432; www.museumvillage.com; (c) Orange

Private non-profit/ 1950/ Board of Trustees/ staff: 3(f); 40(p); 250(v)/ members: 450

LIVING HISTORY/OUTDOOR MUSEUM: Museum Village is dedicated to the preservation, study, and interpretation of the historical and cultural heritage of the Hudson Valley and surrounding regions.

PROGRAMS: Community Outreach; Concerts; Exhibits; Facility Rental; Family Programs; Festivals; Guided Tours; Interpretation; Lectures; Living History; Reenactments; Research Library/Archives; School-Based Curriculum; Theatre

COLLECTIONS: [19th c] Farm hand- tools and machines; household furnishings; industrial machinery; fire- fighting equipment; local mercantile records; library; natural history specimens (including an almost complete mastodon); minerals; fossils; cultural artifacts.

HOURS: Apr-June W-F 10-2, Sa-Su 11-5; July-Aug 11-5, Sa-Su 11-5; Sept-Dec W-F 10-2, Sa-Su 11-5

ADMISSION: $8, Children $5, Seniors $6; Under 3 free

MORAVIA

5986
Millard Fillmore Cabin
Fillmore Glen State Park, 13118 [RD 3, Box 26, 13118]; (p) (315) 497-0130, (315) 497-9549; (f) (315) 497-0128

New York State Parks & Recreation

HOURS: Seasonal

MOUNT MORRIS

5987
Mount Morris Historical Society/ The Mills
14 Main St, Box 940, 14510; (p) (716) 658-3292; (c) Livingston

Private non-profit/ 1976/ staff: 1(p); 100(v)/ members: 300

HISTORIC SITE; HISTORICAL SOCIETY; HOUSE MUSEUM: Maintains restored historic house museum.

PROGRAMS: Annual Meeting; Exhibits; Guided Tours; Lectures; School-Based Curriculum

COLLECTIONS: [1820-1850] Empire furniture; period clothing; ceramics, including Pink Lustre and Spode; coverlets and quilts; newspapers; and archaeological shards.

HOURS: June-Sept F-Su 12-4, School programs Oct-Dec Daily 9:30- 1:30

ADMISSION: Donations requested

MUMFORD

5988
Genesee Country Village and Museum
1410 Flinthill Rd, 14511 [PO Box 310, 14511-0310]; (p) (716) 538-6822; (f) (716) 538-2887; gcvm@frontiernet.net; www.gcv.org; (c) Monroe

Private non-profit/ 1976/ staff: 27(f); 211(p); 495(v)/ members: 2100/publication: *Genesee Country Companion*

ART MUSEUM; GARDEN; HISTORIC SITE; LIVING HISTORY/OUTDOOR MUSEUM: Maintains a restored historic village, furnished buildings, the John L. Whale Gallery of Sporting Art, and the Genesee Country Nature Center.

PROGRAMS: Concerts; Exhibits; Facility Rental; Family Programs; Garden Tours; Guided Tours; Interpretation; Lectures; Living History; Publication; Reenactments; School-Based Curriculum

COLLECTIONS: [1790-1870] 57 restored buildings; over 20,000 artifacts reflecting the history of the Genesee River Valley. 400 Wildlife and hunting paintings and sculptures.

HOURS: May-Oct T-F 10-4, Sa-Su 10-5

ADMISSION: $11, Student $9.50, Children $6.50, Seniors $9.50

MUNNSVILLE

5989
Fryer Memorial Museum
Rt 46 & Willams Rd, 13409 [PO Box 177, 13409]; (p) (315) 495-5395, (315) 495-6148; (c) Madison

City/ 1976/ staff: 4(p); 1(v)

HISTORY MUSEUM: Housed in 1886 former Munnsville post office. Archives for local and genealogical research.

PROGRAMS: Exhibits; Lectures; Research Library/Archives

COLLECTIONS: [Mid 1800s-present] Local historical writings, photographs, obituaries, collection of local books, artifacts from local in-

dustries, Madison and surrounding counties cemetery records.

HOURS: Yr Daily by appt

ADMISSION: Donations accepted

NEW CITY

5990
Historical County of Rockland County, The
20 Zukor Rd, 10956; (p) (914) 634-9629; (f) (914) 634-8690; HSRockland@aol.com; (c) Rockland

Private non-profit/ 1965/ staff: 4(f); 4(p); 152(v)/ members: 1514

HOUSE MUSEUM: Operates a modern museum and the 1832 Jacob Blauvelt House; acquires, collects, preserves, and exhibits items related to Rockland County and the lower Hudson.

PROGRAMS: Annual Meeting; Community Outreach; Concerts; Exhibits; Facility Rental; Family Programs; Festivals; Guided Tours; Interpretation; Lectures; Publication; Research Library/Archives; School-Based Curriculum

COLLECTIONS: [19th-20th c.] Hudson Valley region furniture, textiles, painting, photographs, decorative arts, costumes, archeological artifacts, iron work tools, farm equipment, library/ archives contains family papers, genealogical data, unpublished manuscripts.

HOURS: Yr T-F 9:30-5, Sa-Su 1-5

ADMISSION: $4, Children $2; Members free

5991
Jacob Blauvelt House
20 Zukor Rd, 10956; (p) (914) 634-9629, (914) 634-9645; (f) (914) 634-8690

1832/ staff: 3(f); 2(p); 50(v)

COLLECTIONS: [1832-1860] 19th c Hudson Valley furniture; Rockland County specific pieces; 18th-19th c Hudson Valley; Rockland County, NY; Clarence Lexow papers; Drs. (Pierre and Viola) Sherwood map collection, Denoyelles papers, Claire Tholl papers.

HOURS: Yr T-Su 1-5

NEW PALTZ

5992
Huguenot Historical Society
18 Broadhead Ave, 12561; (p) (845) 255-1660; (f) (845) 255-0376; hhsoffice@hhs-newpaltz.org; www.hhs-newpaltz.org; (c) Ulster

Private non-profit/ 1894/ Board of Trustees/ staff: 13(f); 14(p); 25(v)/ members: 3500

HISTORIC PRESERVATION AGENCY; HISTORIC SITE; HISTORICAL SOCIETY; HISTORY MUSEUM: Promotes historic preservation, research, and education; acquires, preserves, and interprets the structures and collections associated with the Huguenot Community at New Paltz, NY.

PROGRAMS: Annual Meeting; Community Outreach; Concerts; Family Programs; Festivals; Guided Tours; Interpretation; Lectures; Living History; Research Library/Archives

COLLECTIONS: [1690-1950] 17th c National Landmark Historic District, National Register

Farmsite, 7,500 objects, and 290 cubic ft of French, Dutch, and English archival material spanning 17th-20th c.

HOURS: May 1-Oct 31 T-Su 10-4

ADMISSION: $6, Student $5, Children $3, Seniors $5; Varies

5993
Mohonk Mountain House
1000 Mountain Rest Rd, 12561; (p) (914) 255-1000; (f) (914) 256-2161; www.mohonk.com

NEW ROCHELLE

5994
Huguenot and New Rochelle Historic Association
20 Sicard Ave, 10804; (p) (914) 633-1776; (c) Westchester

Private non-profit/ 1886/ staff: 25(v)/ members: 200

HISTORICAL SOCIETY: Maintains and gives tours of the Thomas Paine cottage and a one room schoolhouse as well as hosting an annual Colonial Fair.

PROGRAMS: Annual Meeting; Community Outreach; Exhibits

COLLECTIONS: [18th c] Native American, Huguenot, and Colonial artifacts.

HOURS: May-Nov F-Su 2-5 and by appt

ADMISSION: Donations

5995
Thomas Paine National Historic Association
983 N Ave, 10804; (p) (914) 632-5376; (f) (914) 632-5376; brian.mccartin@nyu.edu; www.mediapro.net/cdadesign/paine; (c) Westchester

Private non-profit/ 1884/ Board of Trustees/ staff: 6(v)/ members: 125

HISTORICAL SOCIETY; HISTORY MUSEUM; RESEARCH CENTER: Promotes the history, ideas, and works of Thomas Paine; preserves and accumulates historic documents and artifacts of Paine for both civic education and scholarly research.

PROGRAMS: Annual Meeting; Exhibits; Facility Rental; Film/Video; Guided Tours; Lectures

COLLECTIONS: [18th c] First edition of Common Sense, Rights of Man, Age of Reason as well as biographies of Payne (Vail, Conway, VanderWyede, Fower) and artifacts-writing kit, writing trunk, hair, death masks, Romney painting.

HOURS: May-Oct F-Su 2-5

ADMISSION: Donations accepted

NEW YORK

5996
American Printing History Association
The New York Public Library, 5th Ave & 42nd St, 10163 [PO Box 4922, Grand Central Station, 10163]; (p) (212) 930-9220; scrook@nypl.org; wally2.rit.edu/cary/printinghistory.html

Private non-profit/ 1974/ staff: 1(p)/ members: 806/publication: *Printing History*

APHA encourages the study of printing history and its related arts and skills, including calligraphy, typefounding, papermaking, bookbinding, illustration, and publishing.

5997
Castle Clinton National Monument
Battery Park, Battery Place & State St, 10005 [26 Wall St, 10005]; (p) (212) 344-3262; (f) (212) 825-6874; www.nps.gov/cacl; (c) New York

Federal; Joint/ 1946/ National Park Service/ staff: 7(f)

HISTORIC SITE: Built as a fort before the War of 1812 to defend NY harbor, this site was renamed Castle Garden and became an entertainment center in 1824. America's first immigration station operated here 1854-1890. From 1896-1941 the NY Aquarium was housed in the structure until it was restored and reopened as a fort in 1975.

PROGRAMS: Concerts; Exhibits; Guided Tours; Publication;

5998
Chancellor Robert R. Livingston Masonic Library
71 W 23rd St, 10010-4171; (p) (212) 337-6620; (f) (212) 633-2639; livmalib@pipeline.com; www.rpi.edu/~nichot3/masonry/library/index.html; (c) New York

Private non-profit/ 1855/ staff: 2(f); 4(p); 15(v)

RESEARCH CENTER: Collects, preserves, interprets, and makes available for education and research materials related to the history, philosophy, culture, and organization of freemasonry with an emphasis upon NY State.

PROGRAMS: Community Outreach; Exhibits; Guided Tours; Interpretation; Lectures; Research Library/Archives

COLLECTIONS: [1781-present] Books, archives, periodicals, textiles, ceramics, photographs, and a wide range of other materials related to the history of freemasonry.

5999
Cooper-Hewitt National Design Museum
2 E 91st St, 10128; (p) (212) 849-8400; (f) (212) 849-8401; www.si.edu/ndm; (c) Manhattan

1976/ staff: 70(f); 30(p); 50(v)/ members: 4000

ART MUSEUM: Promotes library, archives, academic degree programs, fellowships, and internships.

PROGRAMS: Community Outreach; Concerts; Exhibits; Family Programs; Garden Tours; Guided Tours; Interpretation; Lectures; Publication; Research Library/Archives; School-Based Curriculum

COLLECTIONS: [Antiquity-present] Furnishings; drawings and prints; textiles; wallcoverings; 60,000 volumes dealing with ornament, architecture, decorative arts; archives of various design firms

HOURS: Yr T 10-9, W-Sa 10-5, Su 12-5

ADMISSION: $8, Children $5, Seniors $5

6000
Dyckman Farm House Museum, The
204th St & Broadway, 10034 [4881 Broadway, 10034]; (p) (212) 304-9422; (f) (212) 304-9422

1783/ City of New York Parks and Recreation/ staff: 3(f); 15(v)

COLLECTIONS: [1783-1850] Small collection of Revolution Era artifacts: bullets, cannonballs, barshot, Pike Points, 1 sword, 1 muscot uniform.

HOURS: Yr

6001
Equitable Life Assurance Society Archives
1290 Avenue of the Americas, 10104; (p) (212) 314-3133; (f) (212) 707-7783; jonathan.coss@equitable.com; www.equitable.com; (c) New York

Private for-profit/ 1969/ staff: 1(f)

LIBRARY AND/OR ARCHIVES: Collects, preserves, and maintains materials essential to documenting the history of the Equitable, its subsidiaries and affiliates, and makes this information accessible to employees of the company.

COLLECTIONS: Records of the Equitable, its subsidiaries, related insurance and financial services in domestic international operations. Company histories, executive files, reports, biographical and speech files.

6002
Federal Hall National Memorial
26 Wall St, 10005; (p) (212) 825-6888; (f) (212) 825-6874; www.nps.gov/feha; (c) New York

Federal; Joint/ 1939/ National Park Service/ staff: 9(f); 3(p)

HISTORIC SITE; HISTORY MUSEUM; NATIONAL PARK: Maintains this 1842 Greek Revival Customs House and Subtreasury Building now occupies the site of NYC's colonial City Hall and the first capitol of the United States. George Washington was inaugurated here on April 30, 1789.

PROGRAMS: Elder's Programs; Exhibits; Facility Rental; Guided Tours; Publication; School-Based Curriculum

COLLECTIONS: [1701-1952] Artifacts related to George Washington.

HOURS: Jan-Dec M-F 9-5; May-Aug M-Su 9-5

ADMISSION: No charge

6003
Frances Tavern Museum
Pearl St & Broad St, 2nd Fl, 10004 [54 Pearl St, 10004]; (p) (212) 425-1778; (f) (212) 509-3467; (c) New York

Private non-profit/ 1907/ staff: 6(f); 4(p); 10(v)/ members: 300

HISTORIC SITE; HISTORY MUSEUM: Promotes early American history and culture, maintains museum, housed in 18th c structure, interprets history of site and focuses on colonial and revolutionary NY.

PROGRAMS: Concerts; Exhibits; Facility Rental; Family Programs; Film/Video; Guided Tours; Lectures; School-Based Curriculum; Theatre

COLLECTIONS: [Colonial-Revolutionary] Artifacts relating to taverns, history paintings, images of George Washington, military artifacts (Revolutionary War), decorative arts.

HOURS: Yr Daily M-F 10-4:45, Sa-Su 12-4

6004
Frick Collection, The
1 E 70th St, 10021; (p) (212) 288-0700; (f) (212) 628-4417; info@frick.org; www.frick.org; (c) New York

Private non-profit/ 1920/ staff: 124(f); 41(p); 12(v)/ members: 1600

HOUSE MUSEUM: Housed in former NY residence of Henry Clay Frick, Pittsburgh coke and steel industrialist. Also Frick Art Reference Library.

PROGRAMS: Concerts; Exhibits; Lectures; Publication; Research Library/Archives

COLLECTIONS: [14th-19th c.] Well known paintings by European artists, sculpture, 18th c French furniture and porcelains, Limoges enamels.

HOURS: Yr T-Sa 10-6, Su 1-6

ADMISSION: $7, Students $5, Seniors $5

6005
General Grant National Monument
Riverside Dr & W 122 St, 10005 [26 Wall St, 10005]; (p) (212) 666-1640; (f) (212) 825-6874; www.nps.gov/gegr; (c) New York

Federal; Joint/ 1958/ National Park Service/ staff: 4(f); 2(p)

NATIONAL PARK; PRESIDENTIAL SITE: Grant's Tomb was completed in 1897 and reflects the popularity enjoyed by the Union commander who brought the Civil War to a close and served as the 18th President of the US.

PROGRAMS: Community Outreach; Concerts; Guided Tours; Lectures; Publication

COLLECTIONS: [19th c] Exhibits about the life and accomplishments of Ulysses S. Grant.

HOURS: Yr M-Su 9-5

ADMISSION: No charge

6006
Girl Scouts of the USA—National Historic Preservation Center
420 5th Ave, 10018-2798; (p) (212) 852-8676; (f) (212) 852-6517; mlevey@girlscouts.org; www.girlscouts.org; (c) New York

Private non-profit/ 1987/ Girl Scouts of the USA/ staff: 5(f)/publication: Annual Report; Highlights of Girl Scouting; Care and Handling Series

HISTORY MUSEUM; LIBRARY AND/OR ARCHIVES: Preserves and promotes an understanding of Girl Scout history, acts as a communication hub on the topic, serves as a role model for history collections of local affiliates.

PROGRAMS: Community Outreach; Exhibits; Guided Tours; Interpretation; Publication; Research Library/Archives

COLLECTIONS: [1912-present] 13,000 linear feet of records and archives, 10,000 photographs, 6,000 Girl Scout publication titles, 650

vintage uniforms, audiovisuals, various memorabilia and artifacts.

HOURS: Yr M-F 8:30-4:30

ADMISSION: No charge

6007
Glove Museum, The
304 5th Ave, 10001; (p) (212) 532-1956; (f) (212) 279-6863; glovemaster@webtv.com; www.wegloveyou.com; (c) New York

Private for-profit/ 1985/ staff: 1(f); 3(v)

HISTORY MUSEUM: Collects, preserves, and interprets all aspects of glove design, manufacture and glove history for the education and enjoyment of present and future generations.

PROGRAMS: Exhibits; Guided Tours; Lectures; Research Library/Archives

COLLECTIONS: [1850-present] 30,000 pairs of gloves; 2,000 glove stretchers; 1,500 glove button hooks; 500 glove boxes; 5,000 glove making artifacts; 10,000 glove-related paper ephemera.

HOURS: Yr M-Sa by appt

ADMISSION: No charge

6008
Gracie Mansion
E Ave at 88th St, 10128 [East Ave at 88th St, 10128]; (p) (212) 570-4751, (212) 570-0985

6009
Hamilton Grange National Memorial
Convent Ave & 141st St, 10005 [26 Wall St, 10005]; (p) (212) 283-5154; (f) (212) 825-6874; www.nps.gov/hagr; (c) New York

Federal/ 1962/ National Park Service/ staff: 3(p)

HOUSE MUSEUM; NATIONAL PARK: Home of Alexander Hamilton, Revolutionary leader, author of many of the "Federalist Papers," first US Secretary of the Treasury. Built in 1802

PROGRAMS: Exhibits; Guided Tours; Publication

COLLECTIONS: [Federalist Period] Exhibits depicting life and accomplishments of Alexander Hamilton.

6010
Historic House Trust of New York City
The Arsenal, Room 203, Central Park, 10021; (p) (212) 360-8282; (f) (212) 360-8201; www.nycparks.org; (c) New York

Private non-profit/ 1989/ City/ staff: 4(f)/ members: 1000/publication: Guide Books: Historic Houses in New York City Parks; Historic House News

HISTORIC PRESERVATION AGENCY; HOUSE MUSEUM: Enhances, promotes, and assists in the preservation and understanding of 19 historic house museums and their collections located on parkland New York City.

PROGRAMS: Concerts; Exhibits; Facility Rental; Family Programs; Festivals; Guided Tours; Interpretation; Lectures; Living History; Publication

COLLECTIONS: 19 historic houses with historical furnishings and personal artifacts.

6011
Huguenot Heritage
35 Sutton Pl, Ste 6-E, 10022-2464; (p) (212) 759-6222; (f) (212) 759-6222; (c) New York

Private non-profit/ 1984/ staff: 31(v)/publication: Huguenot Heritage

ART MUSEUM; HISTORIC PRESERVATION AGENCY; HISTORICAL SOCIETY; HISTORY MUSEUM; LIBRARY AND/OR ARCHIVES; RESEARCH CENTER: Research and publication of the cultural history of the Huguenots and their descendants from the 16th c to the present day.

PROGRAMS: Concerts; Exhibits; Film/Video; Guided Tours; Lectures; Publication; Research Library/Archives; Theatre

COLLECTIONS: [16th c-present] Manuscripts, maps, prints, paintings, books, art by or about Huguenots and their decendants.

ADMISSION: No charge

6012
International Center of Photography
1133 Ave of Americas, 10128 [1130 Fifth Ave, 10128]; (p) (212) 860-1777; (f) (212) 360-6490; info@icp.org; www.icp.org

Private non-profit/ 1974/ staff: 55(f); 24(p); 115(v)/ members: 6000

ART MUSEUM: Dedicated to the understanding and appreciation of photography, creates programs of the highest quality to advance knowledge of the medium, maintains both an uptown and a midtown facility.

PROGRAMS: Community Outreach; Elder's Programs; Exhibits; Facility Rental; Family Programs; Guided Tours; Lectures; Publication; Research Library/Archives; School-Based Curriculum

COLLECTIONS: [20th c] 45,000 images by over 1,000 photographers, primarily 20th c material in the documentary tradition. Robert Capa, Cornell Capa, Roman Vishniac, Weegee, and the Daniel Cowin Collection.

HOURS: Varies w/location

ADMISSION: Varies w/location

6013
John Burroughs Association, Inc., The
John Burroughs Dr, 10024 [15 West 77th St, 10024]; (p) (212) 769-5169; (f) (212) 769-5329; breslof@amnh.org; mimidi.amnh.org/burroughs/burroughs.html; (c) Manhattan

Private non-profit/ 1921/ staff: 21(v)/ members: 265/publication: Wake Robin

HOUSE MUSEUM

PROGRAMS: Annual Meeting; Community Outreach; Exhibits; Family Programs; Film/Video; Guided Tours; Lectures; Publication; School-Based Curriculum

COLLECTIONS: [Late 1880s -1921]

HOURS: Yr by appt

6014
Lower East Side Tenement Museum
97 Orchard St, 10002 [66 Allen St, 10002]; (p) (212) 431-0233; (f) (212) 431-0402; slong@tenement.org; www.wnet.org/tenement

Private non-profit/ 1988/ Board of Trustees/ staff: 26(f); 20(p); 25(v)/ members: 500/publication: Tenement Times and Tenement Story

HISTORIC SITE; HISTORY MUSEUM; HOUSE MUSEUM: Promotes tolerance and historical perspective through the presentation and interpretation on a variety of immigrants and migrant experiences on Manhattan's Lower East Side.

PROGRAMS: Community Outreach; Elder's Programs; Exhibits; Facility Rental; Family Programs; Film/Video; Guided Tours; Interpretation; Lectures; Living History; Publication; School-Based Curriculum; Theatre

COLLECTIONS: [1860-1940] Artifacts found at 97 Orchard St (landmarked tenement building) used by former residents, shopkeepers, and owners.

HOURS: Yr T-F 12-5, Sa-Su 11-5

ADMISSION: Varies w/program

6015
Merchant's House Museum
29 E Fourth St, 10003; (p) (212) 777-1089; (f) (212) 777-1104; NYC1832@aol.com; (c) New York

Joint/ 1936/ staff: 2(f); 2(p); 25(v)/ members: 1050

HISTORIC SITE; HOUSE MUSEUM: Maintains the Merchant's House Museum, a national and NYC landmark, is the city's only family home preserved intact, inside and out, from the 19th c.

PROGRAMS: Community Outreach; Concerts; Elder's Programs; Exhibits; Facility Rental; Family Programs; Festivals; Guided Tours; Interpretation; Lectures; School-Based Curriculum

COLLECTIONS: [19th c] 1832 rowhouse, which is among the finest examples of American architecture of the period, reflects in its original textiles, furniture, and decorative arts the lifestyle of the prosperous merchant family.

HOURS: Yr Su-Th 1-4

ADMISSION: $5, Student $3, Seniors $3; Members free

6016
Metropolitan Life Insurance Company
1 Madison Ave, 10010; (p) (212) 578-8818; (f) (212) 578-8071; Dmay@metlife.com; www.metlife.com

Private for-profit/ 1868/ staff: 1(f); 1(p)

CORPORATE ARCHIVES/MUSEUM: Documents history of MetLife corporation.

PROGRAMS: Guided Tours

COLLECTIONS: [1868-1980] Documents the enterprise and its business activities.

HOURS: By appt only

6017
Morris-Jumel Mansion, Inc.
160th St & Edgecombe Ave, 10032 [65 Jumel Terrace, 10032]; (p) (212) 923-8008; (f) (212) 923-8947; (c) New York

Private non-profit/ 1904/ Board of Directors/ staff: 3(f); 4(p); 25(v)/ members: 300

HISTORIC SITE; HOUSE MUSEUM: Built in 1765, the Georgian mansion highlights 200 years of NY history, including that of its British builder, Roger Morris, occupier George Washington, and later owners Eliza Jumel and Aaron Burr.

PROGRAMS: Community Outreach; Concerts; Exhibits; Facility Rental; Family Pro-

grams; Festivals; Guided Tours; Lectures; Publication; Research Library/Archives; School-Based Curriculum; Theatre

COLLECTIONS: [1765-1865] 20 present of collection original to the house, including New York Empire furniture, French Empire with Napoleonic provenance, Duncan Phyfe and Michael Allison pieces, and Chippendale style pieces. Numerous Colonial lithographs.

HOURS: Yr W-Su 10-4

ADMISSION: $3, Student $2, Seniors $2

6018
Mount Sinai Archives
100th St & Fifth Ave, 10029 [Box 1102, 1 Gustave L. Levy Pl, 10029-6574]; (p) (212) 241-7239; (f) (212) 831-2625; Barbara.Niss@mssm.edu; www.mssm.edu/library; (c) New York

Joint; Private non-profit/ 1986/ Mount Sinai School of Medicine/ staff: 2(p)

LIBRARY AND/OR ARCHIVES: Provides education and research in the biomedical sciences in an academic health care environment.

PROGRAMS: Exhibits; Publication; Research Library/Archives

COLLECTIONS: [20th c] Official repository of the Mt. Sinai Hospital (1852-), the Mt. Sinai School of Medicine (1963-), and the Mt. Sinai Hospital School of Nursing (1881-1971).

HOURS: Yr T, W, F 10-2 by appt only

ADMISSION: No charge

6019
Mount Vernon Hotel and Garden
421 E 61st St, 10021; (p) (212) 838-6878; (c) New York

1939/ Colonial Dames of America/ staff: 4(f); 15(v)/ members: 400

COLLECTIONS: [Early 19c] Decorative arts; Mount Vernon Hotel which operated in the building from 1826-1836.

HOURS: Yr T-Su 11-4 (In June & July open until 9, Closed M in Aug)

ADMISSION: $4, Student $3, Seniors $3; Under 12 free

6020
Museum of American Financial History
26 Broadway, 10004; (p) (212) 908-4519; (f) (212) 908-4601; bthompson@financialhistory.org; www.financialhistory.org; (c) New York

Private non-profit/ 1988/ Board of Trustees/ staff: 5(f); 4(p); 10(v)/publication: *Financial History Magazine*

HISTORY MUSEUM; LIBRARY AND/OR ARCHIVES: Independent public museum dedicated to business, finance, and the capital markets. Large museum archive of financial documents.

PROGRAMS: Exhibits; Facility Rental; Guided Tours; Lectures; Publication

COLLECTIONS: [Colonial-present] 10,000 items pertaining to business, investment, and the economy, including antique stocks and bonds, public and private financial documents—bearing famous signatures.

HOURS: Yr

6021
Museum of Jewish Heritage—A Living Memorial to the Holocaust
18 First Pl, 10004 [1 Battery Park Plaza, 10004-1484]; (p) (212) 968-1800; (f) (212) 968-1368; sslate@mjhnyc.org; www.mjhnyc.org; (c) New York

Private non-profit/ 1984/ staff: 62(f); 6(p); 205(v)

HISTORY MUSEUM

PROGRAMS: Community Outreach; Concerts; Elder's Programs; Exhibits; Facility Rental; Family Programs; Film/Video; Interpretation; Lectures; School-Based Curriculum

COLLECTIONS: [1880-present] Personal family and community related artifacts, documents, and photographs reflecting Jewish life worldwide 1880-1930, the Holocaust and post-war Jewish renewal.

HOURS: Yr Su-W 9-5, Th 9-8, F 9-4

ADMISSION: $7, Children $5, Seniors $5

6022
Museum of the American Piano, The
211 W 58th St, 10019; (p) (212) 246-4646; (f) (212) 333-7919; pmuseum@pianomuseum.com; www.pianomuseum.com; (c) New York

Joint/ 1984/ State; Private non-profit/ staff: 1(f); 1(p); 1(v)/ members: 895

HISTORY MUSEUM: Museum collects and restores early pianos of historical, technical and musical significance. Teaches traditional methods of working on and maintaining older and newer pianos including woodworking, wood finishing, tuning, repairing and restoring.

COLLECTIONS: [1895-present]

HOURS: Yr 10-5 by appt

6023
Museum of the City of New York
1220 5th Ave, 10029; (p) (212) 534-1672; (f) (212) 423-0758; rrmacdonald@mcny.org; www.mcny.org; (c) New York

Private non-profit/ 1923/ Museum of the City of New York/ staff: 56(f); 15(p); 40(v)/ members: 2000

HISTORY MUSEUM: Presents the history of New York City, and acquires and preserves original cultural materials buildings and sites that illustrate that history.

PROGRAMS: Community Outreach; Concerts; Elder's Programs; Exhibits; Facility Rental; Family Programs; Festivals; Film/Video; Guided Tours; Interpretation; Lectures; Publication; Research Library/Archives; School-Based Curriculum

COLLECTIONS: [1630-present] 1.5 million items including painting, photographs, prints, silver, furniture, costumes, textiles, toys, theater, marine built environment, politics.

HOURS: Yr W-Sa 10-5, Su 12-5

ADMISSION: No charge

6024
National Museum of the American Indian, Smithsonian Institution
George Gustav Heye Center, One Bowling Green, 10004; nmai.west@ic.si.edu; www.si.edu/nmai

Board of Trustees/ staff: 184(f); 4(p); 137(v)/ members: 52357

HISTORY MUSEUM: Dedicated to the preservation, study and exhibition of the life, languages, literature, history and arts of the Native Peoples of the Western Hemisphere.

COLLECTIONS: [Paleo-Indian-present] Native American ethnographic and archaeological objects from North, Central, and South America; Native American life prints and negatives; film, video, multi-media collection; archives.

HOURS: Yr F-W 10-5, Th 10-8

ADMISSION: No charge

6025
New York City Fire Museum
278 Spring St, 10013; (p) (212) 691-1303; (c) Manhattan

Private non-profit/ 1987/ staff: 2(f); 8(p); 12(v)/ members: 767/publication: *The Housewatch*

HISTORY MUSEUM: Maintains a museum in a restored firehouse, with a collection illustrating the history of fire-fighting.

PROGRAMS: Exhibits; Facility Rental; Family Programs; Guided Tours; Publication; Research Library/Archives

COLLECTIONS: [1970s-present] Historic hand drawn, horse drawn, and early motorized fire apparatus, tools and equipment. Fire related art and folk art, parade hats, belts, axes, speaking trumpets lamps, fire marks, models, and toys.

HOURS: Yr T-Su 10-4

ADMISSION: Donations accepted

6026
New York Genealogical and Biographical Society, The
122 E 58th St, 10022-1939; (p) (212) 755-8532; (f) (212) 754-4218; nygbs@nygbs.org; www.nygbs.org; (c) New York

Private non-profit/ 1869/ Board of Trustees/ staff: 9(f); 1(p); 5(v)/ members: 2700/publication: *New York Genealogical & Biographical Record*

GENEALOGICAL SOCIETY: Collects information on genealogy, biography, and local history, particularly as it relates to the people of New York State; maintains a research library and issues publications.

PROGRAMS: Annual Meeting; Facility Rental; Lectures; Publication; Research Library/Archives

COLLECTIONS: [17th-20th c] Genealogy and local history for all time periods and ethnic groups, manuscript collection with unpublished material on NY families.

HOURS: Yr T-Sa 9:30-5

ADMISSION: Research fee for nonmembers

6027
New York Historical Society, The
2 W 77th St, 10024; (p) (212) 873-3400; www.nyhistory.org; (c) New York

Private non-profit/ 1804/ Board of Directors/ staff: 50(f); 50(p); 100(v)/ members: 3000

HISTORICAL SOCIETY

PROGRAMS: Concerts; Exhibits; Facility Rental; Family Programs; Film/Video; Guided Tours; Interpretation; Lectures; Research Library/Archives; School-Based Curriculum

COLLECTIONS: [18th-20th c.]

HOURS: Museum: Yr T-Su 11-5; Library Mem Day-Labor Day T-F 11-5

ADMISSION: $5, Students, Seniors $3,

6028
New York Stock Exchange
20 Broas St, 10005 [11 Wall St, 10005]; (p) (212) 656-2252; (f) (212) 656-5629; swheeler@NYSE.com; www.nyse.com; (c) New York

Private non-profit/ 1979/ staff: 2(f)

CORPORATE ARCHIVES/MUSEUM: Corporate archives of the New York Stock Exchange, Inc.

PROGRAMS: Research Library/Archives

COLLECTIONS: [1817-present] Corporate records; minutes; correspondence; reports; legal and financial records; photographs; prints and motion pictures all pertaining to history of the stock market and Wall St.

HOURS: Yr M-F 9-5 by appt only

ADMISSION: No charge

6029
Saint-Gaudens Memorial
17 E 47th St, 10017; (p) (212) 750-3690; (f) (212) 750-3690; (c) New York

Private non-profit/ 1919/ staff: 1(p)/ members: 57

HISTORIC SITE: Supports the Saint-Gaudens National Historic Site in Cornish, NH with special programs, activities and funding that benefits the public, promotes Saint-Gaudens and American architecture.

COLLECTIONS: [1870-1910]

6030
South Street Seaport Museum
207 Front St, 10038; (p) (212) 748-8600; (f) (212) 748-8610; southseaport.org; (c) New York

Private non-profit/ 1967/ staff: 52(f); 300(v)/ members: 2700/publication: *Seaport Magazine*

HISTORY MUSEUM: Collects and interprets the maritime contributions to the commerce and culture of New York City, NY State, and the nation.

PROGRAMS: Community Outreach; Concerts; Elder's Programs; Exhibits; Facility Rental; Family Programs; Festivals; Film/Video; Guided Tours; Interpretation; Lectures; Living History; Publication; Research Library/Archives; School-Based Curriculum

COLLECTIONS: [18th-20th c] Historic ships, buildings, art, archaeological archives, and material culture reflecting the history of the port of NY.

6031
St. Paul's Church National Historic Site
897 S Columbus Ave, 10005 [26 Wall St, 10005]; (p) (914) 667-4116; (f) (914) 667-3024; www.nps.gov/sapa; (c) Westchester

Federal/ 1945/ National Park Service/ staff: 3(f); 2(p)

HISTORIC SITE: Maintains church that has been the center of an historic area in lower Westchester since 1665. The Battle of Pell's point took place in this area in 1776.

PROGRAMS: Guided Tours; Publication; Reenactments; School-Based Curriculum

COLLECTIONS: [17th-18th c] Exhibits of colonial life and events of the American Revolution.

HOURS: Yr M-F 9-5

ADMISSION: No charge

6032
Theodore Roosevelt Birthplace National Historic Site
28 E 20 St, 10005 [26 Wall St, 10005]; (p) (212) 260-1616; (f) (212) 825-6874; www.nps.gov/thrb; (c) New York

Federal; Joint/ 1962/ National Park Service/ staff: 4(f); 4(v)

HOUSE MUSEUM; NATIONAL PARK; PRESIDENTIAL SITE: Birthplace and childhood home of the 26th president of the US whose furnished rooms recreate the environment of Roosevelt's mid-19th c boyhood.

PROGRAMS: Concerts; Exhibits; Lectures; Publication; Research Library/Archives

COLLECTIONS: [1858-1916] Papers, photographs, artifacts, and memorabilia that illustrates the life and accomplishments of Theodore Roosevelt.

6033
Yeshiva University Museum
2520 Amsterdam Ave, 10033; (p) (212) 960-5390; (f) (212) 960-5406; herskowi@ymail.yu.edu; www.yu.edu/museu,; (c) New York

Private non-profit/ 1973/ staff: 5(f); 5(p); 36(v)/ members: 559

ART MUSEUM; HISTORY MUSEUM: Serves both Jewish and non-Jewish audiences with exhibitions, public programs, and publications focusing on Jewish themes.

PROGRAMS: Community Outreach; Concerts; Exhibits; Family Programs; Festivals; Film/Video; Guided Tours; Interpretation; Lectures; Research Library/Archives; School-Based Curriculum

COLLECTIONS: Diverse collection of artifacts representing Jewish cultural, intellectual, and artistic achievements, fine art, material culture objects.

HOURS: Jan-July, Sept-Dec Su 12-6, T-Th 10:30-5

NEWARK VALLEY

6034
Newark Valley Historical Society
Park St, 13811 [PO Box 222, 13811]; (p) (607) 642-9516; (f) (607) 642-9516; nvhistorical@juno.com; www.tier.net/nvhistory; (c) Tioga

Private non-profit/ 1975/ Board of Trustees/ staff: 2(f); 300(v)/ members: 550

HISTORIC SITE; HISTORICAL SOCIETY; HOUSE MUSEUM: Provides education programs via school, group and individual tours.

PROGRAMS: Community Outreach; Exhibits; Family Programs; Festivals; Guided Tours; Interpretation; Lectures; Living History; Reenactments; Research Library/Archives; School-Based Curriculum

COLLECTIONS: [1840s] Furniture, cook ware, art of 1800s. 1800s farmhouse with outbuildings. Railroad depot restored to 1910 with Lehigh valley memorabilia. Costumes and textiles. Woodworking and blacksmithing tools.

HOURS: Office: by appt only; RR Depot: July 5-Oct 6 Sa-Su 1:30-3; Farmstead July 5-Oct 6 Sa-Su 12-4

ADMISSION: $2, Student $1; Farmstead; Depot free

NEWBURGH

6035
Historical Society of Newburgh Bay
189 Montgomery St, 12550; (p) (845) 561-2585; (c) Orange

Private non-profit/ 1884/ Board of Trustees/ staff: 30(v)/ members: 100

HISTORICAL SOCIETY; HOUSE MUSEUM: Preserves and interprets the history of the Newburgh area through the collection and archives of the society and its headquarters, the David Crawford House and relevant programs.

PROGRAMS: Annual Meeting; Concerts; Exhibits; Facility Rental; Garden Tours; Guided Tours; Lectures; Publication; Research Library/Archives; School-Based Curriculum

COLLECTIONS: [Late 18th-mid 19th c.] Manuscripts; local maps; photographs; books of local interest, furniture, group of Hudson River school paintings, Hudson river boat models.

HOURS: June-Oct Su 1-4

ADMISSION: $2, Children $1

6036
Newburgh Free Library
124 Grand St, 12550; (p) (845) 561-1985; (f) (845) 561-2499; newburg1@sebridge.org; www.newburghlibrary.org; (c) Orange

City/ 1852/ Newburgh Enlarged City School District/ staff: 26(f); 62(p)

LIBRARY AND/OR ARCHIVES

PROGRAMS: Community Outreach; Concerts; Exhibits; Facility Rental; Family Programs; Festivals; Film/Video; Guided Tours; Lectures; Living History; Research Library/Archives; Theatre

COLLECTIONS: [Early history-present] Family histories, census and church records, maps, photos, periodicals and other materials.

HOURS: Yr Daily 8-8

ADMISSION: No charge

6037
Washington's Headquarters State Historic Site
Corner of Liberty & Washington streets, 12551 [PO Box 1783, 12551-1476]; (p) (845) 562-1195; (c) Orange

State/ 1850/ NY State/ staff: 5(f); 5(p)

HISTORIC SITE; HISTORY MUSEUM; HOUSE MUSEUM; PRESIDENTIAL SITE;

STATE PARK: Preserves the site of George Washington's army headquarters from Apr 1782-Aug 1783, his longest stay of the War of Independence. Birthplace of the Badge of Military Merit, forerunner of the Purple Heart.

PROGRAMS: Community Outreach; Concerts; Exhibits; Family Programs; Festivals; Guided Tours; Interpretation; Lectures; Research Library/Archives; School-Based Curriculum

COLLECTIONS: [1775-1814] Period furnishings, firearms, documents, and military artifacts of the War for Independence, Martha Washington's pocket watch, portraits of the Washington's by Asher B. Durand. Structures: Hasbrouck House (1750-1770), Tower of Victory monument (1887). Rooms furnished to the headquarters period. Museum has six galleries and is the first historic house museum in the US.

HOURS: Apr-Oct W-Sa 10-5, Su 1-5

ADMISSION: $3, Children $1, Seniors $2

NEWTONVILLE

6038
Friends of Pruyn House
207 Old Niskayuna Rd, 12128 [PO Box 212, 12128]; (p) (518) 783-1435; (f) (518) 783-1437; pruynhouse@wsg.net; www.colonie.org/pruyn; (c) Albany

Private non-profit/ 1985/ Board of Trustees/ staff: 2(f); 2(p); 6(v)/ members: 600

GARDEN; HISTORIC SITE: Restores and conserves the Pruyn House Complex as an educational, cultural, and social center.

PROGRAMS: Concerts; Facility Rental; Garden Tours; Guided Tours

COLLECTIONS: [Mid-1800s] House displays interior with original Greek revival details, furnished in 1800s period, antiques, papers, and records of the Pruyn family.

HOURS: Yr M-F 9-4:30 and by appt

NORTH BLENHEIM

6039
Lansing Manor House Museum
NY SR 30, 12131 [PO Box 898, 12131]; (p) (518) 827-6121; (f) (607) 588-9466

HOUSE MUSEUM

NORTH TARRYTOWN

6040
Philipsburg Manor
N Broadway, Rt 9, [Historic Hudson Valley, 150 White Plains Rd, Tarrytown, 10591]; (p) (914) 631-3992; (f) (914) 631-0089; 914-631-0089

HOUSE MUSEUM

NORTH TONWANDA

6041
Hirschell Carrousel Factory Museum
180 Thompson St, 14120 [PO Box 672, North Tonawanda, 14120]; (p) (716) 693-1885; (f) (716) 743-9018; (c) Niagara

Private non-profit/ 1979/ Carrousel Society at the Niagara Frontier/ staff: 2(f); 3(p); 50(v)/ members: 607

HISTORIC SITE: Dedicated to preserving amusement ride artifacts, carrousels, and historic Herschell factory buildings. Operates 1916 carrousel and 1948 kiddy carrousel.

PROGRAMS: Annual Meeting; Community Outreach; Concerts; Exhibits; Family Programs; Guided Tours; Interpretation; Lectures; Research Library/Archives; School-Based Curriculum

COLLECTIONS: [1880-1960] Carrousels, animals, amusement ride related to artifacts, Hershell Company records, blueprints, carving tools, carving classes, antique machinery, historic building.

HOURS: Apr-Dec W-Su 1-5

ADMISSION: $3, Children $1.50

NORTH WHITE PLAINS

6042
Washington's Headquarter Museum at the Miller House
140 Virginia Rd, 10603; (p) (914) 949-1236, (914) 941-0755; (f) (914) 242-6350; (c) Westchester

County/ 1917/ Westchester Co Parks/ staff: 1(f)

HOUSE MUSEUM; LIVING HISTORY/OUTDOOR MUSEUM: Historic house that preserves, collects, and interprets the county's colonial and Revolutionary War history.

PROGRAMS: Exhibits; Facility Rental; Family Programs; Guided Tours; Interpretation; Living History; Reenactments; School-Based Curriculum

COLLECTIONS: [18th c] Furniture including the table and chairs used by Washington during 1776 Battle of Whiteplains, artifacts found on the site.

NORTHPORT

6043
Northport Historical Society
215 Main St, 11768 [PO Box 545, 11768]; (p) (631) 757-9859; (f) (631) 757-9398; info@northporthistorical.org; www.northport historical.org; (c) Suffolk

Private non-profit/ 1962/ Board of Trustees/ staff: 5(p); 40(v)/ members: 385

HISTORICAL SOCIETY; HISTORY MUSEUM: Collects, preserves, and interprets Northport's past through exhibits and related programs.

PROGRAMS: Annual Meeting; Community Outreach; Exhibits; Festivals; Garden Tours; Guided Tours; Lectures; Research Library/Archives; School-Based Curriculum

COLLECTIONS: [1800-1900] Archival photographs, oral histories, slides, ship building tools, artifacts, textiles, and ephemera.

HOURS: Jan-Dec T-Su 1-4:30

ADMISSION: Donations requested

OGDENSBURG

6044
Frederic Remington Art Museum
303 Washington St, 13669; (p) (315) 393-2425; (f) (315) 393-4464; info@remindton-museum.org; www.remington-museum.org; (c) St. Lawrence

Private non-profit/ 1923/ Board of Trutees/ staff: 6(f); 2(p); 70(v)/ members: 851

ART MUSEUM; HISTORY MUSEUM: Dedicated to the life and works of Frederic Remington. Started by the artist's widow and sister-in-law, the museum continues to build its Remington collection and archives.

PROGRAMS: Community Outreach; Exhibits; Facility Rental; Family Programs; Interpretation; Lectures; School-Based Curriculum

COLLECTIONS: [1861-1909] Oil paintings, bronze sculpture, water colors, pen and ink illustrators. 1,000 photographs, artists tools, personal possessions, and sketchbooks.

HOURS: Yr May-Oct M-Sa 9-5; Nov-Apr Daily W-Sa 11-5, Su 1-5

ADMISSION: $4, Student $3, Seniors $3; Members/Under 5 free

OLD WESTBURY

6045
Old Westbury Gardens
71 Old Westbury Rd, 11568 [PO Box 430, 11568]; (p) (516) 333-0048; (f) (516) 333-6807

1906/ staff: 27(f); 35(p); 280(v)

COLLECTIONS: [1906-1950] Fine English furniture from the 1600s to the 1800s; 1,000 family photos and family correspondence.

HOURS: Seasonal

OLEAN

6046
Bartlett Historical House
302 Laurens St, 14760; (p) (716) 376-5642; www.oleanny.com/welcome2.htm

HOUSE MUSEUM

ONEIDA

6047
Madison County Historical Society/Cottage Lawn
435 Main St, 13421 [PO Box 415, 13421]; (p) (315) 363-4136; (c) Madison

Private non-profit/ 1900/ Board of Trustees/ staff: 2(f); 6(v)/ members: 500/publication: *Madison County Heritage*

HISTORIC SITE; HISTORICAL SOCIETY; HISTORY MUSEUM; HOUSE MUSEUM; RESEARCH CENTER: Collects, preserves, and promotes the history of Madison County and provides educational programs.

PROGRAMS: Annual Meeting; Community Outreach; Exhibits; Facility Rental; Family Programs; Festivals; Guided Tours; Interpretation; Lectures; Publication; Research Library/ Archives; School-Based Curriculum

COLLECTIONS: [19th c] Textiles, archival materials, library with genealogy and local history resources, memorabilia documenting 200 years of county's history.

HOURS: Yr M-F 9-4

ADMISSION: $2

6048
Oneida Community Mansion House
170 Kenwood Ave, 13421; (p) (315) 363-0745; (f) (315) 361-4580; ocmh@dreamscape.com;

www.oneidacommunity.org; (c) Madison

Private non-profit/ 1987/ Board of Trustees/ staff: 15(f); 15(p); 75(v)/ members: 300

GARDEN; HISTORIC SITE; HISTORY MUSEUM: Collects, preserves, and interprets the history of the 19th c utopian Oneida Community (1848-1880), the company that succeeded it, Oneida Community Ltd. (now Oneida Ltd.) and the 93,000 square foot, three-story brick Mansion House. A National Historical Landmark.

PROGRAMS: Annual Meeting; Community Outreach; Concerts; Exhibits; Facility Rental; Garden Tours; Guided Tours; Lectures

COLLECTIONS: [1848-1880] Photographs, books, artifacts, paintings.

6049
Shako:wi Cultural Center
5 Territory Rd, 13421-9304; (p) (315) 363-1424; (f) (315) 363-1843; www.oneida-nation.net; (c) Madison

Tribal/ 1993/ Oneida Indian Nation/ staff: 2(f); 2(p)

TRIBAL MUSEUM: Shares Oneida wisdom and skills through historical and contemporary exhibits, tours, craft and dance workshops, lectures, language, and literature classes.

PROGRAMS: Concerts; Elder's Programs; Exhibits; Film/Video; Interpretation; Lectures; Research Library/Archives

COLLECTIONS: [1000 AD-present] Oneida crafts & artwork of 19th and 20th c, archaeological collections from excavations, photo archives, small library, and manuscript archive.

ONEONTA

6050
Yager Museum
Hartwick College, 13820 [West St, 13820]; (p) (607) 431-4480; (f) (607) 431-4468; Abramsg@hartwick.edu

Private non-profit/ 1929/ Board of Trustees/ staff: 3(f); 3(p)

NATURAL HISTORY MUSEUM: Preserves natural history museum of Hartwick College with a focus in archaeology, ethnography, and fine arts with changing exhibitions.

PROGRAMS: Community Outreach; Exhibits; Guided Tours; Interpretation; Lectures

COLLECTIONS: [10,000 BC-present] Archaeological artifacts: 10,000 BC, Upper Susquehanna River Valley; Fine Arts: European Renaissance, Contemporary American, Folk Art.

HOURS: Yr T, Th-Sa 11-4:30, W 11-9, Su 1-4:30

ORCHARD PARK

6051
Town of Orchard Park Historical Museum & Society
4287 S Buffalos, 14127 [5800 Armor Rd, 14127]; (p) (716) 562-3285; (c) Erie

Private non-profit/ 1950/ staff: 25(v)/ members: 80

HISTORICAL SOCIETY; HISTORY MUSEUM; HOUSE MUSEUM: Collects and preserves items relating to local history in its 1870 house museum.

PROGRAMS: Exhibits; Guided Tours; Lectures

COLLECTIONS: Farm tools, dishes, costumes, books, and photographs.

HOURS: July-Aug Sa 1-4

ADMISSION: Donations accepted

ORIENT

6052
Oyster Ponds Historical Society
Village Lane, 11957 [PO Box 70, 11957]; (p) (516) 323-2480; (f) (516) 323-3719; (c) Suffolk

Private non-profit/ 1944/ Board of Trustees/ staff: 1(f); 1(p); 75(v)/ members: 600

HISTORICAL SOCIETY; HISTORY MUSEUM; HOUSE MUSEUM

PROGRAMS: Annual Meeting; Community Outreach; Concerts; Exhibits; Facility Rental; Family Programs; Festivals; Film/Video; Garden Tours; Guided Tours; Interpretation; Lectures; Reenactments; School-Based Curriculum

COLLECTIONS: [1850-1900]

HOURS: Yr June-Sept T-Su 10-5, Oct-May Th, Sa, Su 2-5

ADMISSION: $3, Children $0.50; Members free

ORISKANY

6053
Oriskany Battlefield State Historic Site
Rt 69 West, 13424; (p) (315) 768-7224; (f) (315) 337-3081; (c) Oneida

State/ NY State/ staff: 2(f); 3(p); 1(v)

BATTLEFIELD; HISTORIC SITE; LIVING HISTORY/OUTDOOR MUSEUM: Maintains historic site that provides battlefield tours and picnic facilities.

PROGRAMS: Concerts; Exhibits; Family Programs; Festivals; Guided Tours; Interpretation; Living History; Reenacts; School-Based Curriculum

COLLECTIONS: [1776]

HOURS: Mid May-mid Oct W-Sa 9-5, Su 1-5

OSSINING

6054
Ossining Historical Society Museum
196 Croton Ave, 10562; (p) (914) 941-0001; (f) (914) 941-0001; ohsm@worldnet.aaatt.net; home.att.net/˜ohsm; (c) Westchester

Private non-profit/ 1931/ Ossining Historical Society Museum/ staff: 1(f); 5(p); 15(v)/ members: 452

HISTORIC SITE; HISTORICAL SOCIETY; HISTORY MUSEUM; HOUSE MUSEUM: Educates the public in the history of Ossining by collecting, conserving, preserving, restoring, studying, and exhibiting items of historical importance.

PROGRAMS: Annual Meeting; Community Outreach; Exhibits; Research Library/ Archives; School-Based Curriculum

COLLECTIONS: [1880] Costumes; hat-boxes; flags; Civil War, Revolutionary War, WW I, and WW II memorabilia; minerals and rocks of the area; Birds native to Ossining; textiles and quilts; family bibles; slides and films of old Assigning; oral history tapes; Sing Sing Prison; photographs and daguerreotypes; maps; Genealogy files; Newspapers, dating 1818 to present.

HOURS: Yr M-Sa 1-4

ADMISSION: No charge/Donations

OSWEGO

6055
Fort Ontario State Historic Site
E 9th St, 13126 [1 E 4th St, 13126]; (p) (315) 343-4711; (f) (326) 343-1430; (c) Oswego

State/ 1949/ NY State Office of Parks, Recreation and Historic Preservation/ staff: 3(f); 9(p); 75(v)/ members: 150

HISTORIC SITE; HISTORY MUSEUM; LIVING HISTORY/OUTDOOR MUSEUM: Maintains military museum housed in 1839-1866 fortifications on site of 1755-1814 fortifications and battlefields situated at the outlet of Oswego River into Lake Ontario.

PROGRAMS: Community Outreach; Concerts; Exhibits; Family Programs; Festivals; Interpretation; Lectures; Living History; Reenactments

COLLECTIONS: [1867-1872] Military furnishings, firearms, equipment, uniforms, accoutrements, historic buildings, enlisted men's barracks, powder magazine, two officers quarters, two guardhouses and a series of casements.

HOURS: May-Oct W-Sa 10-5, Su 1-5 and by appt

ADMISSION: $3, Children $1; Group rates

6056
Oswego County Historical Society
135 E Third St, 13126; (p) (315) 343-1342; (c) Oswego

Private non-profit/ 1896/ Board of Trustees/ staff: 2(f); 3(p); 2(v)/ members: 350

HISTORIC SITE; HISTORICAL SOCIETY; HISTORY MUSEUM; HOUSE MUSEUM: Collects, preserves, and interprets materials relating to the history of Oswego County.

PROGRAMS: Annual Meeting; Community Outreach; Elder's Programs; Exhibits; Facility Rental; Family Programs; Guided Tours; Interpretation; Lectures; Research Library/ Archives; School-Based Curriculum

COLLECTIONS: [1800-present] 30,000 objects, documents, and photographs relating to Oswego County. The Richardson-Bates House contains 90% original 1880s furnishings.

HOURS: Yr T-F 10-5, Apr-Dec Sa-Su 1-5

6057
Richardson-Bates House Museum
135 E 3rd St, 13126 [135 E Third St, 13126]; (p) (315) 343-1342

1867/ staff: 2(f); 3(p); 3(v)

HOUSE MUSEUM

COLLECTIONS: [1800s] Drawing room designed and fabricated by Pottier & Stymus, NYC —furniture and architectural elements; Diaries, scrapbooks, correspondence of Richardson family, interior & exterior photos of

house c. 1867-1890, architectural drawings c. 1867-1887

HOURS: Yr

6058
Special Collections of Penfield Library, SUNY
7060 State Rt 104, Oswego State Univ of NY, 13126; (p) (315) 312-3537; (f) (315) 312-3194; archives@oswego.edu; www.oswego.edu/ library/archives/index.html; (c) Oswego

State/ 1973/ State Univ of NY (SUNY)/ staff: 3(p)

LIBRARY AND/OR ARCHIVES: Collects, arranges, and preserves the records of the SUNY College at Oswego and information pertaining to the campus and manuscripts of local, historical interest.

PROGRAMS: Research Library/Archives

COLLECTIONS: [19th c-present] 130 processed manuscripts, 470 linear feet of archives, 6,300 books, 320 oral history tapes, 150 maps and blueprints, several 1000 photographs and slides not indexed.

HOURS: Fall and Spring Terms: M, Th 1:30-4:30, appt

OWEGO

6059
Tioga County Historical Society
110 Front St, 13827; (p) (607) 687-2460; (f) (607) 687-7788; tiogamus@clarityconnect.com; www.tier.net/tiogahistory; (c) Tioga

Private non-profit/ 1914/ staff: 2(f); 4(p); 2(v)/ members: 450

HISTORICAL SOCIETY: Collects, preserves, and interprets the history of Tioga County from prehistoric times to the present.

PROGRAMS: Annual Meeting; Community Outreach; Concerts; Exhibits; Facility Rental; Family Programs; Guided Tours; Interpretation; Lectures; Research Library/Archives; School-Based Curriculum; Theatre

COLLECTIONS: [1791-present] Paintings of early county residents, Native American tools, objects manufactured by local industry, 1914 motorcycle, two locally made pianos, photographs, archives, a ledger from Matthew Brady's photographic studios.

HOURS: Yr T-Sa 10-4

ADMISSION: Donations accepted

OYSTER BAY

6060
Coe Hall at Planting Fields
Planting Fields Rd, 11771 [PO Box 58, 11771]; (p) (516) 922-0479; (f) (516) 922-9226; coehall@worldnet.att.net; (c) Nassau

Private non-profit/ 1974/ Planting Fields Foundation/ staff: 3(f); 4(p); 100(v)/ members: 200

GARDEN; HISTORIC SITE; HOUSE MUSEUM: Preserves 400 acre former estate with historic grounds and estate buildings. Greenhouses, nature walks, gardens.

PROGRAMS: Publication

6061
Friends of Raynham Hall
20 W Main St, 11771; (p) (516) 922-6808; (f) (516) 922-7640; (c) Nassau

Private non-profit/ 1954/ Friends of Raynham Hall/ staff: 1(f); 10(p); 20(v)/ members: 350

HISTORIC SITE; HOUSE MUSEUM: Historic home of the Townsend family of merchants who built the house around 1740. Used as headquarters by British troops during the Revolution.

PROGRAMS: Community Outreach; Exhibits; Family Programs; Guided Tours; Lectures

COLLECTIONS: [Mid 18th-later 19th c] Furnishings, decorative arts, and clothing from the 18th and 19th centuries. Exhibits on local history and important figures.

HOURS: Yr July-Aug T-Su 12-5; Sept-June T-Su 1-5

ADMISSION: $3, Student $2, Seniors $2

6062
Oyster Bay Historical Society
20 Summit St, 11771 [PO Box 297, 11771]; (p) (516) 922-5032; (f) (516) 922-6892; OBHistory@aol.com; members.aol.com/obhistory; (c) Nassau

Private non-profit/ 1960/ Board of Trustees/ staff: 1(f); 2(p); 40(v)/ members: 350/publication: *The Freeholder*

GARDEN; GENEALOGICAL SOCIETY; HISTORIC SITE; HISTORICAL SOCIETY; HISTORY MUSEUM; HOUSE MUSEUM; RESEARCH CENTER: Collects information and memorabilia relating to the town's history and disseminates information, headquartered in the Earle-Wightman House.

PROGRAMS: Annual Meeting; Community Outreach; Exhibits; Family Programs; Garden Tours; Guided Tours; Interpretation; Lectures; Living History; Publication; Reenactments; Research Library/Archives; School-Based Curriculum

COLLECTIONS: [1653-1950] 2,000 processed manuscripts, a library of 1,000 volumes, 2,500 photographs, 100 maps, and 2,000 artifacts.

HOURS: Yr T-F 10-2, Sa 9-1, Su 1-4

ADMISSION: Donations requested; Mbrs/ Under 12 free

6063
Sagamore Hill National Historic Site
20 Sagamore Hill Rd, 11771; SAHI_information@ NPS.GOV; www.nps.gov.sahi; (c) Nassau

Federal/ 1962/ National Park Service/ staff: 16(f); 16(p); 60(v)

HISTORIC SITE; HOUSE MUSEUM; NATIONAL PARK; PRESIDENTIAL SITE: Preserves the home of Theodore Roosevelt, 26th President of the US, furnished as it was during his lifetime that displays his many interests.

PROGRAMS: Concerts; Exhibits; Festivals; Film/Video; Guided Tours; Interpretation; Lectures; School-Based Curriculum

COLLECTIONS: [1884-1948]

HOURS: Yr Mar-Oct M-Su 9-4:45; Nov-Apr W-Su 9-4:45

PALMYRA

6064
Hill Cumorah Visitor's Center and Historic Sites
603 Rt, 21 S, 14522; (p) (315) 597-5851; (f) (315) 597-0165

1825/ The Church of Jesus Christ of Latter-Day Saints

Maintains the replica of the Peter Whitmer log home, the site of the organization of the Church of Jesus Christ of Latter-Day Saints; the Grandin Building is the site of the publication of the Book Of Mormon.

COLLECTIONS: [1818-1830]

HOURS: Yr

6065
Historic Palmyra, Inc.
132 Market St, 14522 [PO Box 96, 14522]; (p) (315) 597-6981; (c) Wayne

Private non-profit/ 1843/ Board of Directors/ staff: 1(f); 50(v)/ members: 300

HISTORICAL SOCIETY; HISTORY MUSEUM; HOUSE MUSEUM: Preserves and displays local historic items.

PROGRAMS: Exhibits; Festivals; Guided Tours; Lectures; Living History; Research Library/Archives

COLLECTIONS: [1790s-1970s] Homespun coverlets, original general store as seen in turn of the century with two story home upstairs, 10 rooms fully furnished with original items. Historic museum contains 23 rooms full of artifacts from all eras of Palmyra history.

PAWLING

6066
Historical Society of Quaker Hill and Pawling
126 E Main St, 12564 [PO Box 99, 12564]; (p) (845) 855-9316; www.pawhistory.com; (c) Dutchess

Private non-profit/ 1912/ Board of Directors/ staff: 30(v)/ members: 250

HISTORY MUSEUM; HOUSE MUSEUM: Memorabilia in 3 locations in Pawling: authentic Quaker meeting house, home of John Kane, one floor of exhibits at the Akin Free Library

PROGRAMS: Annual Meeting; Exhibits; Lectures

COLLECTIONS: [1750-present] Artifacts, Lowell Thomas memorabilia, pictorial history of Pawling.

HOURS: May-Oct Sa-Su 2-4

ADMISSION: No charge

PEEKSKILL

6067
National Maritime Historical Society
5 John Walsh Blvd, 10566 [PO Box 64, 10566]; (p) (914) 737-7878; nmhs@seahistory.org; www.seahistory.org; (c) Westchester

Private non-profit/ 1963/ Board of Trustees/ staff: 10(f); 3(p); 5(v)/ members: 16000/publication: Sea History Magazine; Sea History Gazette

HISTORICAL SOCIETY: Dedicated to preserving the skills, ships, and knowledge of seafaring heritage through the quarterly magazine, Sea History, and through education programs for children, teacher, and others.

PROGRAMS: Annual Meeting; Festivals; Lectures; Publication; Research Library/Archives

HOURS: Yr 9-5

PENFIELD

6068
Penfield Local History Room
1985 Baird Rd, 14526; (p) (716) 383-0557; kanaver@penfield.org; (c) Monroe

City/ 1985/ Town of Penfield/ staff: 2(v)

HISTORIC PRESERVATION AGENCY; HISTORY MUSEUM; RESEARCH CENTER: Collect and preserve written materials and objects that are related to early Penfield and provide a place where materials may be displayed, researched, and enjoyed. Have genealogical resources.

PROGRAMS: Community Outreach; Exhibits; Lectures; Research Library/Archives

COLLECTIONS: All permanent acquisitions relate to the history of Penfield, its people or events.

HOURS: Yr July-Aug M-T 1-5/7-9, Th 1-5; Sept-June M-T 1-5/7-9, Th 1-5, Su 2-5

PENN YAN

6069
Oliver House Museum
200 Main St, 14527; (p) (315) 536-7318; wcghs@linkny.com

PISECO

6070
Piseco Lake Historical Society
Old Piseco Rd, 12139; (c) Hamilton

Private non-profit/ 1986/ staff: 15(v)/ members: 85

HISTORICAL SOCIETY; HISTORY MUSEUM: Collects and preserves local history and is housed in two small historic buildings.

PROGRAMS: Annual Meeting; Community Outreach; Exhibits; Lectures; Research Library/Archives

COLLECTIONS: [1870-present] Photographs, books, artifacts relating to local and Adirondack history.

HOURS: July-Aug F-Su 1-4

PLAINVILLE

6071
Pioneer Experience at Plainville Farms, The
7830 Plainville Rd, 13137; (p) (315) 638-0226; (f) (315) 638-0659; plainvil@servtech.com; www.plainvillefarms.com; (c) Onondaga

Private non-profit/ 1998/ staff: 4(p)

HISTORY MUSEUM; HOUSE MUSEUM; LIVING HISTORY/OUTDOOR MUSEUM

PROGRAMS: Exhibits; Festivals

COLLECTIONS: [1650-1900] Reproduction primitive log cabin, 100s of household and agricultural artifacts used during the Northeast pioneer period of 1650-1900.

HOURS: May-Oct F-Sa 11-1

ADMISSION: $2.75

PLATTSBURGH

6072
Clinton County Historical Society
48 Court St, 12901; (p) (518) 561-0340; (f) (518) 561-0340; (c) Clinton County

County; Private non-profit/ 1946/ Regents, State University of New York/ staff: 1(f); 1(p); 6(v)/ members: 400/publication: Antiquarian, North Country Notes

GENEALOGICAL SOCIETY; HISTORIC PRESERVATION AGENCY; HISTORIC SITE; HISTORICAL SOCIETY; HISTORY MUSEUM; HOUSE MUSEUM; LIBRARY AND/OR ARCHIVES: Collects, preserves, and displays all artifacts, records of events, and citizens of the county. Maintains a six gallery museum; custodial caretakers of Bluff Pt. Lighthouse at Vancour Island; revolutionary period cannon; recently recovered anchor from the HMS Confiance, a British warship (1814).

PROGRAMS: Annual Meeting; Community Outreach; Elder's Programs; Exhibits; Family Programs; Festivals; Guided Tours; Lectures; Publication; Research Library/Archives; School-Based Curriculum

COLLECTIONS: [18th-early 19th c.] Maps dating from 1794; documents; artifacts from the earliest period of settlement; records of commerce; settlement and major events; establishment of the iron industry; prisons in the North Country; commercial establishments; and government in Clinton County.

HOURS: Feb-Dec T-Sa 12-4

ADMISSION: $2, Children $1

6073
Feinberg Library Special Collections, Plattsburgh State University
2 Draper Ave, 12901; (p) (518) 564-5206; (f) (518) 564-5209; millerwl@plattsburgh.edu; www.plattsburgh.edu/acadvp/libinfo/library/speccol; (c) Clinton

Joint; State/ 1965/ Univ of the State of NY/ staff: 5(p)

LIBRARY AND/OR ARCHIVES

PROGRAMS: Publication; Research Library/Archives

COLLECTIONS: [18th-20th c] Materials on NY state with particular emphasis on the Northern Counties of Clinton, Essex, Franklin, St. Lawrence, Hamilton, Herkimer, and Warren. Monographs, periodicals, pamphlets, ephemera, photographs, maps, manuscripts, indexing of periodicals. Special collections contains the college archives, the thesis collection

6074
Kent-Delord House Museum
17 Cumberland Ave, 12901; (p) (518) 561-1035; (f) (518) 561-1035; (c) Clinton

Private non-profit/ 1924/ Board of Trustees/ staff: 1(f); 3(p); 1(v)/ members: 390/publication: Kent-Delord Quarterly

HISTORIC SITE; HOUSE MUSEUM: Maintains the Kent-Delord House (1797), a documentary museum that preserves and exhibits the furnishings of the Delord family who occupied the house from 1810-1913.

PROGRAMS: Annual Meeting; Community Outreach; Concerts; Exhibits; Facility Rental; Family Programs; Festivals; Film/Video; Garden Tours; Guided Tours; Interpretation; Lectures; Living History; Publication; Reenactments; School-Based Curriculum

COLLECTIONS: [1810-1913] Portraits, furniture, china, silverware, decorative and personal objects of the Delord family from 19th c.

HOURS: Mar-Dec T-Sa 12-4

ADMISSION: $3, Student $2, Children $1, Seniors $2

PORT JEFFERSON

6075
Mather House Museum
115 Prospect St, 11777; (p) (516) 473-2665

PORT JERVIS

6076
Minisink Valley Historical Society
125-131 W Main St, 12771 [PO Box 659, 12771]; (p) (914) 856-2375; www.minisink.com; (c) Orange

Private non-profit/ 1889/ staff: 1(f); 1(p); 20(v)/ members: 350/publication: *The Mennisenck*

HISTORIC SITE; HISTORICAL SOCIETY; HOUSE MUSEUM: Dedicated to the preservation of the Minisink Valley's history.

PROGRAMS: Annual Meeting; Community Outreach; Exhibits; Family Programs; Guided Tours; Interpretation; Lectures; Publication

PORT WASHINGTON

6077
Port Washington Public Library
Main St, 11050 [One Library Drive, 11050]; (p) (516) 883-4400; (f) (516) 883-7927; library@pwpl.org; www.pwpl.org; (c) Nassau

1892/ Board of Trustees/ staff: 49(f); 42(p); 100(v)/publication: *It Looks Like Yesterday to Me: 200 years of African American roots in Port Washington; Particles of the Past: A Hist of the Port's Sandbanks*

LIBRARY AND/OR ARCHIVES: Operates a public library and community cultural center serving the Long Island and NY area with books, programs, exhibits and special collections.

PROGRAMS: Annual Meeting; Community Outreach; Concerts; Elder's Programs; Exhibits; Facility Rental; Family Programs; Festivals; Film/Video; Garden Tours; Guided Tours; Interpretation; Lectures; Publication; Research Library/Archives

COLLECTIONS: [19th-present] Items related to Port Washington & Long Island: 2,000 volumes of biography, genealogies, maps, books, manuscripts, photographs and 200 indexed and catalogued audio tapes and transcripts.

HOURS: Yr M-T, Th-F 9-9, W 11-9, Sa 9-5, Su 1-5

ADMISSION: No charge

POTSDAM

6078
Potsdam Public Museum
Civic Center, Park St, 13676 [Box 5168, 13676]; (p) (315) 265-6910; (c) St. Lawrence

Private non-profit/ 1940/ Village of Potsdam/ staff: 1(f); 4(p); 3(v)/publication: *Gallantry in the Field: Potsdam & The Civil War*

HISTORY MUSEUM: Museum collects, preserves, and interprets local history through archival research, exhibits, and programs.

PROGRAMS: Annual Meeting; Community Outreach; Exhibits; Family Programs; Interpretation; Lectures; Publication; Research Library/Archives; School-Based Curriculum

COLLECTIONS: [19th c-present] Decorative arts, objects of local history, Burnup Collection of English ceramics, furniture, costumes, textiles, art glass, tools, farm tools, Chinese art and costume.

HOURS: Yr T-Sa 2-5

ADMISSION: No charge

POUGHKEEPSIE

6079
Clinton House
549 Main St, 12602; (p) (914) 471-1630; (f) (914) 471-8777; www.pojonews.com/reweb/citypok.htm

6080
Dutchess County Historical Society
549 Main St, 01202 [PO Box 88, 1202-0088]; (p) (845) 471-1630; (f) (845) 471-8777; dchs@vh.net; (c) Dutchess

Private non-profit/ 1914/ Board of Trustees/ staff: 3(p); 5(v)/ members: 451/publication: *Annual Yearbook*

HISTORIC SITE; HISTORICAL SOCIETY; HOUSE MUSEUM; RESEARCH CENTER: Preserves and shares the history of Dutchess county, form its earliest peoples through chartering by the English Crown in 1683 as a county, to present.

PROGRAMS: Annual Meeting; Community Outreach; Exhibits; Guided Tours; Interpretation; Lectures; Publication; Research Library/Archives

COLLECTIONS: [19th c] 10,000 photographs, post cards, textiles, maps archival materials, and 3 dimensional objects.

HOURS: Yr T-F 10-3 by appt.

6081
Samuel F. B. Morse Historic Site
370 S Rd, 12601 [PO Box 1649, 12601]; (p) (914) 454-4500; (f) (914) 485-7122

Private non-profit/ 1979/ staff: 5(f); 30(p); 50(v)/ members: 200

GARDEN; HISTORIC SITE; HOUSE MUSEUM: Preserves and interprets the National Historic Landmark estate Locust Grove and collects and displays telegraph equipment and paintings by Samuel Morse.

PROGRAMS: Concerts; Elder's Programs; Exhibits; Facility Rental; Family Programs; Festivals; Garden Tours; Guided Tours; Interpretation; Lectures; Research Library/Archives;

School-Based Curriculum

COLLECTIONS: [1600-1975] American decorative arts 1700-1950, American & European paintings 1600-1950, telegraph equipment, 15,000 museum objects, 600 cubic feet of archival material.

HOURS: May-Oct M-Su 10-4; Nov, Dec, Apr by appt

ADMISSION: $5, Children $2, Seniors $4

POUND RIDGE

6082
Pound Ridge Historical Society
255 Westchester Ave, 10576 [PO Box 51, 10576]; (p) (914) 764-4333; (f) (914) 764-7642; (c) Westchester

Private non-profit/ 1970/ staff: 100(v)/ members: 230

HISTORIC SITE; HISTORICAL SOCIETY; HISTORY MUSEUM: Collects and preserves material related to history of the area.

PROGRAMS: Annual Meeting; Community Outreach; Exhibits; Guided Tours; Lectures; Publication; Research Library/Archives

COLLECTIONS: [20th c] Baskets, maps, documents, genealogy, tools, census, marriages, and more.

HOURS: Mar-Dec Sa-Su 2-4 and by appt

ADMISSION: Donations accepted

PRATTSBURGH

6083
Narcissa Prentiss House
7225 City Rt 75, 14873 [PO Box 384, 14873]; (p) (607) 522-4537

1805/ Private/ staff: 25(v)

COLLECTIONS: [First half of 19th c] Books and photos reflecting history of Prattsburgh and the surrounding area.

HOURS: June-Labor Day Sa-Su 1-4; by appt

6084
Prattsburgh Community Historical Society
Mill Pond Rd, 14873; (p) (607) 522-4537; (c) Steuben

Private non-profit/ 1987/ staff: 12(v)/ members: 45

HISTORIC SITE; HISTORICAL SOCIETY: Society preserves the birthplace of Narcissa Prentiss, the 1st white woman to cross the Rockies.

PROGRAMS: Annual Meeting; Community Outreach; Concerts; Exhibits; Guided Tours

COLLECTIONS: [1802-present] Pictures and artifacts of Prattsburg and of Narcissa Prentiss.

HOURS: Yr T 9-12, 1-3

ADMISSION: No charge

PRATTSVILLE

6085
Zadock Pratt Museum
Rt 23 Main St, 12468 [PO Box 333, 12468]; (p) (518) 299-3395

1828/ staff: 1(f); 2(v)

COLLECTIONS: [1840-1860] Photos and documents dealing with 19th c local and regional life; many papers, drawings, documents daybooks, dealing with Pratt's life and work.

RAQUETTE LAKE

6086
Sagamore Institute of the Adirondacks
Sagamore Rd, 13436 [PO Box 146, 13436-0146]; (p) (315) 354-5311; (f) (315) 354-5851; sagamore@telenet.net; www.sagamore.org; (c) Hamilton

Private non-profit/ 1897/ staff: 4(f); 10(p); 150(v)/ members: 400

HISTORIC SITE: Maintains National Historic site dating from 1897 dedicated to the preservation of Great Camp Sagamore that offers both residential programs and tours.

PROGRAMS: Concerts; Elder's Programs; Exhibits; Facility Rental; Family Programs; Guided Tours; Interpretation; Lectures; Living History

COLLECTIONS: [1897-present] 27 authentic wood and stone buildings, oral history tapes describing building and operation of Sagamore during Vanderbilt era.

HOURS: May-Oct M-Su

ADMISSION: $8, Children $3

REMSEN

6087
Steuben Memorial State Historic Site
Starr Hill Rd, 13438; (p) (315) 831-3737; (c) Oneida

State/ staff: 2(f); 1(p); 15(v)

HISTORIC SITE; HOUSE MUSEUM; LIVING HISTORY/OUTDOOR MUSEUM: Preserves the history of life in the 18th c.

PROGRAMS: Concerts; Family Programs; Festivals; Guided Tours; Interpretation; Living History; Reenactments; School-Based Curriculum

COLLECTIONS: [1777] Log home furnished with 18th c furniture.

HOURS: May-Oct W-Sa 9-5, Su 1-5

ADMISSION: No charge

RHINEBECK

6088
Rhinebeck Aerodrome Museum, Old Rhinebeck Aerodrome Airshows
44 Stone Church Rd, 12572 [PO Box 229, 12572]; (p) (914) 758-8610; (f) (914) 758-6481; www.oldrhinebeck.org; (c) Dutchess

State/ 1959/ staff: 4(f); 3(p); 40(v)/ members: 800/publication: Rotary Ramblings

AVIATION MUSEUM; HISTORY MUSEUM; LIVING HISTORY/OUTDOOR MUSEUM: Maintains the Old Rhinebeck Aerodrome presents antique aeroplanes from 1900-1940 through exhibits and vintage airshows.

PROGRAMS: Exhibits; Family Programs; Guided Tours; Living History; Publication

COLLECTIONS: [1900-1940] Collection of vin-

tage aircraft from Pioneer era (1900-1913), WW I (1914-1918), and Golden Age (1920-1940), automobiles, motorcycles, engines, and memorabilia.

HOURS: May-Oct M-Su 10-5

ADMISSION: $5, Children $2; Weekend airshows $12 adults, $5 ages 6-10

6089
Wilderstein Preservation Inc.
[PO Box 383, 12572]; (p) (914) 876-4818; (f) (914) 876-3336; wilderstein@wilderstein.org; wilderstein.org; (c) Dutchess

Private non-profit/ 1980/ Board of Directors/ staff: 1(f); 2(p); 100(v)/ members: 850/publication: News Line

HISTORIC SITE; HOUSE MUSEUM

PROGRAMS: Annual Meeting; Community Outreach; Exhibits; Facility Rental; Family Programs; Garden Tours; Guided Tours; Interpretation; Lectures; Publication; Research Library/Archives; School-Based Curriculum

COLLECTIONS: [1704-present] Family archives, textiles, books, art, costumes, furniture, personal objects, photographs, and furnishings dating from 1704-present. Structures include: 35 room Queen Anne-style

RICEVILLE

6090
Rice Homestead
328 Riceville Rd, [33 W Main St, Mayfield, 12117]; (p) (518) 661-5285

1790/ staff: 20(v)

COLLECTIONS: [1880s] Glove making articles, arrowhead collection from Mayfield area, photos, records, Revolutionary War materials,materials pertaining to the founders and men who built up our area.

RIVERHEAD

6091
Hallockville, Inc.
6038 Sound Ave, 11901; (p) (516) 298-5292; (f) (516) 298-0144; hallockville@ieaccess.net; hallockville.ieaccess.net; (c) Suffock

Private non-profit/ 1975/ staff: 2(f); 4(p); 75(v)/ members: 500

HISTORIC SITE; HOUSE MUSEUM; LIVING HISTORY/OUTDOOR MUSEUM: Dedicated to preserving and understanding Suffolk county's history, oral history, and cultural heritage relating to traditional occupations and to traditional community arts and lore.

PROGRAMS: Annual Meeting; Concerts; Exhibits; Facility Rental; Family Programs; Festivals; Guided Tours; Interpretation; Lectures; Living History; Reenactments; Research Library/Archives; School-Based Curriculum

COLLECTIONS: [1880-1910] Artifacts relating to Hallock family history and North Fork farming.

HOURS: Yr T-Sa 11-4 and by appt

ADMISSION: $4, Children $3, Seniors $3

6092
Suffolk County Historical Society
300 W Main St, 11901; (p) (631) 727-2881; (f) (631) 727-3467; histsoc@suffolk.lib.ny.us; (c) Suffolk

Private non-profit/ 1886/ Board of Directors/ staff: 4(f); 8(p); 25(v)/ members: 900/publication: Register

GENEALOGICAL SOCIETY; HISTORICAL SOCIETY; HISTORY MUSEUM: Collects, preserves, and interprets the history of Suffolk County and its people through its library, museum, and programs.

PROGRAMS: Annual Meeting; Community Outreach; Exhibits; Family Programs; Interpretation; Lectures; Publication; Research Library/Archives; School-Based Curriculum

COLLECTIONS: [19th-20th c] Native American artifacts, ceramics, textiles, agricultural implements, furniture, whaling, transportation, photographs, genealogical information, and manuscripts.

HOURS: Yr Museum: T-Sa 12:30-4:30; Library: W-Th, Sa 12:30-4:30

ADMISSION: Museum free, Library $2

ROCHESTER

6093
Baker-Cederberg Museum and Archives
Rochester General Hospital, 1425 Portland Ave, 14621; (p) (716) 336-3521; (f) (716) 339-5292; phil.maples@viahealth.org; www.via-health.org/archives; (c) Monroe

Private non-profit/ 1947/ staff: 1(f); 1(p); 12(v)/ members: 320/publication: Baker-Cederberg Notebook

HISTORICAL SOCIETY; HISTORY MUSEUM: Collects, preserves, exhibits, and disseminates information on the development of Rochester City and General Hospitals and their part in the greater Rochester community.

PROGRAMS: Annual Meeting; Community Outreach; Exhibits; Guided Tours; Lectures; Publication; Research Library/Archives

COLLECTIONS: [1847-present]

HOURS: Yr Daily

ADMISSION: No charge

6094
Campbell-Whittlesey House Museum, The
123 Fitzhugh St, 14608 [133 S Fitzhugh St, 14608]; (p) (716) 546-7029, (716) 546-7028; (f) (716) 546-4788

1835/ staff: 4(f); 4(p)

COLLECTIONS: [1835-1850] Outstanding collection of Empire furniture with stenciled decoration.

HOURS: Seasonal

6095
George Eastman House
900 East Ave, 14607; (p) (716) 271-3361; (f) (716) 271-3970; www.eastman.org; (c) Monroe

Private non-profit/ 1947/ George Eastman House/ staff: 62(f); 23(p); 300(v)/ members: 4200/publication: Image

GARDEN; HISTORIC SITE: Museum of photography and film and the landmark Colonial Revival mansion and gardens of Eastman Kodak Company.

PROGRAMS: Concerts; Exhibits; Facility Rental; Family Programs; Film/Video; Garden Tours; Guided Tours; Lectures; Publication; Research Library/Archives; School-Based Curriculum

COLLECTIONS: [Mid 19th c-present] 400,000 photographs; 15,000 technology artifacts; 43,000 books and periodicals about photography and motion pictures; 23,000 motion pictures, 5 million motion picture stills; George Eastman's restored house, gardens and related artifacts.

HOURS: Yr T-W and F-Sa 10-5, Th 10:30-8, Su 1-5

ADMISSION: $6.50, Student $5, Children $2.50, Seniors $5; Mbrs/Under 4 free

6096
Landmark Society of Western New York, The

Stone-Tolan House Museum, 2370 E Ave, 14608 [Campbell Whittlesey House Museum, 133 S Fitzhugh St, 14608]; (p) (716) 546-7029; (f) (716) 546-4788; lswny@yahoo.com; www.landmarksociety.org; (c) Monroe

Private non-profit/ 1937/ staff: 9(f); 11(p); 200(v)/ members: 3000/publication: *City of Frederick Douglass*

HISTORIC PRESERVATION AGENCY; HOUSE MUSEUM: Preserves and disseminates the community's architectural and historic heritage through two house museums and exhibits.

PROGRAMS: Annual Meeting; Community Outreach; Exhibits; Family Programs; Garden Tours; Guided Tours; Interpretation; Lectures; Living History; Publication; Research Library/Archives; School-Based Curriculum

COLLECTIONS: [1800-1850] Domestic furnishings and items related to 1805 Frontier tavern and farm and 1836 Greek Revival mansion, architectural artifacts, archives on historic structures in area. Structures: Campbell Whittlesey House Museum, Stone-Tolan House Museum, Hoyt-Potter House and more.

HOURS: Museums: Mar-Dec F-Su 12-4 or by appt; Library: Yr M-F by appt

ADMISSION: $3, Student $1

6097
Rochester Museum & Science Center

657 East Ave, 14607; (p) (716) 271-4320; (f) (716) 271-5935; Postmaster@rmsc.org; www.rmsc.org; (c) Monroe

Private non-profit/ 1912/ staff: 82(f); 70(p); 186(v)/ members: 8700

HISTORY MUSEUM; RESEARCH CENTER: Educates visitors and enables them to explore science and technology, the natural environment, and the region's cultural heritage.

PROGRAMS: Exhibits; Facility Rental; Family Programs; Guided Tours; Interpretation; Lectures; Living History; Publication; Research Library/Archives; School-Based Curriculum; Theatre

COLLECTIONS: [10,000 BC-present] 750,000 archaeological artifacts, 21,000 ethnographic artifacts, 164,000 historic objects costumes, textiles, domestic economy, home furnishings, communication devices, Rochester technology, 26,000 natural science specimens, 40,000 photographs, 60,000 documents and archives, 30,000 books.

HOURS: Yr M-Sa 9-5, Su 12-5

ADMISSION: $6, Children $3

6098
Stone-Tolan House

2370 E Ave, 14610 [133 S Fitzhugh St, 14608]; (p) (716) 442-4606, (716) 546-7029; (f) (716) 546-4788

1792/ staff: 4(f); 4(p)

COLLECTIONS: [1790-1820] Vernacular furnishings, tavern accessories, supplement with reproductions.

HOURS: Seasonal

6099
Strong Museum

One Manhattan Square, 14607; (p) (716) 263-2700; (f) (716) 263-2493; www.strongmuseum.org; (c) Monroe

Joint; Private non-profit/ 1968/ Board of Trustees/ staff: 73(f); 8(p); 55(v)/ members: 7100

HISTORY MUSEUM: Museum collects, explores, and interprets everyday life in the US to help people better understand themselves and each other, individually and collectively.

PROGRAMS: Community Outreach; Concerts; Exhibits; Facility Rental; Family Programs; Festivals; Interpretation; Publication; Research Library/Archives; School-Based Curriculum; Theatre

COLLECTIONS: [19th-20th c] 500,000 objects reflect everyday American life: toys, dolls, household furnishings, tablewares, clothing, prints, paintings, photographs, posters and 40,000 research library holdings.

HOURS: Yr M-Th, Sa 10-5, F 10-8, Su 12-5

ADMISSION: $6, Student $5, Children $4, Seniors $5

6100
Susan B. Anthony House, Inc.

17 Madison St, 14608; (p) (716) 235-6124; (f) (716) 235-6124; www.susanbanthonyhouse.org; (c) Monroe

Private non-profit/ 1946/ Board of Trustees/ staff: 4(f); 3(p); 80(v)/ members: 500/publication: *The Susan B. Anthony House Newsletter*

HISTORIC SITE; HOUSE MUSEUM: Preserves and maintains the national historic landmark home and collection of the famous leader in the woman's suffrage movement.

PROGRAMS: Community Outreach; Exhibits; Facility Rental; Festivals; Guided Tours; Publication; Research Library/Archives

COLLECTIONS: [19th-20th c] 2000 artifacts: furniture, textiles, photographs; 30 cubic feet of archives relating to Susan B. Anthony and others.

HOURS: Yr May-Aug T-Su 11-4; Sept-Apr 11-5

ADMISSION: $6, Children $2, Students $3, Seniors $4.50

6101
Woodside

485 E Ave, 14607 [485 East Ave, 14607]; (p) (716) 271-2705

1837/ staff: 1(f); 3(v)

Promotes local history.

COLLECTIONS: 600 portraits of Rochesterions important collection of handmade lace, photographic collection, business records, The Pioneer Register, extensive genealogical information, horticulture, 25 vols. on history of Rochester.

HOURS: Yr

ROME

6102
New York State Covered Bridge Society

6342 Martin Dr, 13440; (p) (315) 336-6341; rjwil@borg.com; www.nycoveredbridges.org; (c) Oneida

Private non-profit/ 1966/ NY State Covered Bridge Society/ members: 515/publication: *Empire State Courier*

HISTORICAL SOCIETY: Gathers information on covered bridges, documents their history, and puts out newsletters and a publication telling about covered bridges.

PROGRAMS: Annual Meeting; Guided Tours; Publication; Research Library/Archives

6103
Rome Historical Society

200 Church St, 13440; (p) (315) 336-5870; (f) (315) 336-5912; (c) Oneida

Private non-profit/ 1936/ Board of Directors/ staff: 1(f); 4(p); 15(v)/ members: 780/publication: *Annals and Recollections*

HISTORICAL SOCIETY; HISTORY MUSEUM: Society preserves the history of Rome and surrounding Oneida county through exhibits, archives,and programs.

PROGRAMS: Annual Meeting; Community Outreach; Concerts; Elder's Programs; Exhibits; Facility Rental; Guided Tours; Interpretation; Lectures; Publication

COLLECTIONS: [19th c-20th c] Textiles, photographs, archives, folk art, Rome Turney Radiator Records Collection 1905-1933.

HOURS: Yr Jan-Dec M-F 9-4, and by appt

ADMISSION: $5/day research library

ROOSEVELTOWN

6104
Mohawk Nation Council of Choices

Rt 37 Akwesasne Mohawk Territory, 13683 [PO Box 366, 13683]; (p) (518) 358-3381; (f) (518) 358-3488; mohawkna@slic.com

1142/ Haudenosaunce Confederacy/ staff: 45(f); 2(p); 300(v)/ members: 30000/publication: *Akwesasne Notes/ Indian Time*

TRIBAL MUSEUM: Historical and traditional government for the Mohawk Nation, as recognized by the 6 Nations (Iroquois) also known as the Houdenosauneer Confederacy.

PROGRAMS: Concerts; Elder's Programs; Exhibits; Family Programs; Festivals; Guided

Tours; Interpretation; Lectures; Living History; Publication; School-Based Curriculum

COLLECTIONS: [Pre-European contact-present] Oral history from creation story to philosophy; protocol and political structure of traditional people (Mohawk) with historic collections.

HOURS: Yr M-Sa 9-4

ADMISSION: No charge

ROSENDALE

6105
Snyder Estate
Rt 213, 12472 [PO Box 50, 12472-0150]; (p) (914) 658-9200; (f) (914) 658-9277

ROSLYN

6106
Bryant Library Local History Collection
2 Paper Mill Rd, 11576; (p) (516) 621-2240; (f) (516) 621-7211; www.nassaulibrary.org/bryant; (c) Nassau

1953/ The Bryant Library/ staff: 1(f); 1(p); 1(v)/publication: *Roslyn Then and Now*

LIBRARY AND/OR ARCHIVES: Housed in the oldest continuing public library in Nassau County, the Local History Collection actively collects and preserves the history and heritage of the Roslyn area of Long Island.

PROGRAMS: Exhibits; Publication; Research Library/Archives

COLLECTIONS: [1840-present] Visual and written materials documenting the history of Roslyn and the North Shore of Long Island.

6107
Roslyn Landmark Society
20 Main St, 11576 [PO Box 234, 11576]; (p) (516) 625-4363; (f) (516) 625-4363; (c) Nassau

Private non-profit/ 1961/ staff: 1(f); 45(v)/ members: 265

HISTORIC PRESERVATION AGENCY; HISTORIC SITE; HISTORICAL SOCIETY; HOUSE MUSEUM; LIVING HISTORY/OUTDOOR MUSEUM: Provides education about historic buildings, operates museum and monuments, and proviedes research in the Greater Roslyn area.

PROGRAMS: Annual Meeting; Community Outreach; Exhibits; Guided Tours; Interpretation; Lectures; Living History; Research Library/Archives; School-Based Curriculum

COLLECTIONS: [18th c-19th c] Photographs, maps, furnishings, decorative arts, primary source material: diaries, family archives, extensive research in Roslyn architectural heritage.

HOURS: Museum: June-Oct Sa-Su 1-4

ADMISSION: $1

6108
Van Nostrand-Starkins House
221 Main St, 11576 [PO Box 234, 11576]; (p) (516) 625-4060, (516) 487-1643; (f) (516) 625-4060

1680/ staff: 4(v)

COLLECTIONS: [1740] Dutch Kas (two) American ca 1740; Wm & Mary Low Boy ca. 1743; Wm & Mary Chairs; Country Queen Anne Chairs; vernacular furnishings, archaeological exhibit of site.

HOURS: Seasonal

RYE

6109
Rye Historical Society
One Purchase St, 10580; (p) (914) 967-7588; (c) Westchester

Private non-profit/ staff: 3(f); 2(p); 65(v)/ members: 1000

HISTORIC SITE; HISTORICAL SOCIETY: Society collects and preserves the history of Rye.

PROGRAMS: Community Outreach; Exhibits; Facility Rental; Family Programs; Guided Tours; Interpretation; Lectures; Research Library/Archives

COLLECTIONS: [18th c-19th c] 13,000 artifacts from 17th c to present, manuscripts and photographs.

HOURS: Yr T, Sa, Su 12:30-4:30 W- F

SACKETS HARBOR

6110
Sackets Harbor Battlefield State Historic Site
505 W Washington St, 13685 [PO Box 27, 13685]; (p) (315) 646-3634; (f) (315) 646-1203; (c) Jefferson

State/ 1933/ staff: 6(f); 16(p); 3(v)

BATTLEFIELD; HISTORIC SITE; LIVING HISTORY/OUTDOOR MUSEUM: Restored US Navy yard preserves and exhibits site of War of 1812 battlefield and other historic moments.

PROGRAMS: Community Outreach; Concerts; Exhibits; Guided Tours; Interpretation; Living History; Research Library/Archives; School-Based Curriculum

COLLECTIONS: [1812-1950] War of 1812 objects from the Brig Jefferson, armament accessories, military clothing, furnished 1850 commandants' house, 19th c household furniture.

HOURS: Grounds: Yr M-Su; Museum: May-Oct W-Sa 10-5, Su 1-5

SAG HARBOR

6111
Customs House
Garden & Main St, 11963 [PO Box 148, Cold Spring Harbor, 11724]; (p) (516) 725-0855, (516) 692-4664; (f) (516) 692-5265

staff: 4(p); 25(v)

Home to Sag Harbors' first US Customs Master, Henry Packer Dering.

COLLECTIONS: [1789-present] 18th and 19th c Long Island decorative arts; Dering family possessions.

HOURS: June-Oct

6112
Sag Harbor Whaling and Historical Museum
Main & Garden Sts, 11963 [PO Box 1327, 11963]; (p) (516) 725-0770; (f) (516) 725-0770; (c) Suffolk

Private non-profit/ 1945/ Board of Directors/ staff: 1(f); 4(p); 5(v)/ members: 100

HISTORIC SITE; HISTORY MUSEUM: Maintains museum housed in 1845 mansion built by shipping and whaling entrepreneur collects, preserves, and exhibits artifacts relating to the history of Long Island whaling in the 19th c and the history of Sag Harbor.

PROGRAMS: Annual Meeting; Community Outreach; Exhibits; Family Programs; Interpretation

COLLECTIONS: [1750-early 20th c] Scrimshaw, ship models, paintings, documents, toys, furniture, musical instruments, log books, tools, whaling implements, 1845 Greek Revival mansion.

HOURS: May-Sept M-Sa 10-5 Su 1-5

ADMISSION: $3, Children $1, Seniors $2; Group discounts

SAINT JOHNSVILLE

6113
Margaret Reaney Memorial Library
19 Kingsbury Ave, 13452; (p) (518) 568-7822; (f) (518) 568-7822; mrml@telenet.net; www2.telenet.net/community/mvla/stjo; (c) Montgomery

1909/ Board of Trustees/ staff: 2(f); 3(p); 2(v)

ART MUSEUM; GENEALOGICAL SOCIETY; HISTORICAL SOCIETY; HISTORY MUSEUM; RESEARCH CENTER: Provides materials, services, and programs in diverse formats to assist the community in obtaining information to meet their personal, educational, and professional needs and maintains a museum.

PROGRAMS: Community Outreach; Concerts; Elder's Programs; Exhibits; Family Programs; Guided Tours; Lectures; Research Library/Archives

COLLECTIONS: [Pre-Revolutionary-present] 76 original oil paintings, bronze sculpture, and exhibits about the Erie Canal, Civil War, and Palatine Germans; the library has an internationally recognized collection of genealogy and local history materials.

HOURS: Yr M, F 9:30-5/6:30-8:30, T-W 9:30-5, Th 1-5, Sa 9:30-12

ADMISSION: Donations accepted

SALAMANCA

6114
Seneca-Iroquois National Museum
794-814 Broad St, 14779; (p) (716) 945-1738, (716) 945-3895; (f) (716) 945-1760; seniroqm@localnet.com; (c) Cattaraugus

Private non-profit/ 1977/ Board of Trustees/ staff: 6(f)

TRIBAL MUSEUM: Museum collects and presents the prehistory, history, and contemporary culture of the Iroquois Nations through collection of relevant materials and contemporary Iroquois art.

PROGRAMS: Community Outreach; Exhibits; Family Programs; Guided Tours; Interpretation; Lectures; Living History

COLLECTIONS: [Early Woodland-present] Pre-historic artifacts, photographic record of

19th & 20th c cultural items, documentary materials, contemporary Iroquois art and audio-recorded history.

HOURS: Yr Sept-Dec, Feb-Apr M-F 10-5; May-Aug T-Su 10-5

SARANAC LAKE

6115
Robert Lewis Stevenson Memorial Cottage
11 Stevenson Ln, 12983; (p) (518) 891-1462, (518) 891-4480

1855/ staff: 2(v)

COLLECTIONS: [1887-1888] Large collection of Stevenson memorabilia, first editions, photographs, paintings, library.

HOURS: Seasonal

6116
Stevenson Society of America, Inc.
11 Stevenson Ln, 12983; (p) (518) 891-1462; (c) Essex

Private non-profit/ 1916/ staff: 3(v)/ members: 7

HISTORIC SITE; HISTORICAL SOCIETY; HOUSE MUSEUM: Society operates and maintains a house where author Robert Louis Stevenson spent winter of 1887-1888.

PROGRAMS: Elder's Programs; Guided Tours; Interpretation

COLLECTIONS: [1850-1894] Collection of Stevenson lore, personal memorabilia, photographs, paintings, original letters, first editions and original furniture.

HOURS: July-Sept T-Su 9:30-12/1-4:30, and Yr by appt

ADMISSION: $5; Under 12 free

SARATOGA SPRINGS

6117
National Museum of Racing and Hall of Fame
191 Union Ave, 12866; (p) (518) 584-0400; (f) (518) 584-4574; nmrhof96@race.saratoga; www.racingmuseum.org; (c) Saratoga

Private non-profit/ 1950/ staff: 15(f); 5(p); 25(v)/ members: 1900

ART MUSEUM; HISTORY MUSEUM: Maintains museum of history, art, and science, that interprets the history and conveys the excitement of Thoroughbred racing in America.

PROGRAMS: Exhibits; Facility Rental; Family Programs; Film/Video; Guided Tours; Lectures; Research Library/Archives; School-Based Curriculum

COLLECTIONS: [1664-present] Fine arts, artifacts, manuscripts, and books covering the subject of Thoroughbred racing.

HOURS: Yr Daily M-Sa 10-4:30, Su 9-5

ADMISSION: $5, Student $3, Seniors $3

6118
Ulysses S. Grant Cottage
Mt. McGregor Rd, 12866 [PO Box 990, 12866]; (p) (518) 587-8277; www.nysparks.state.ny.us; (c) Saratoga

1890/ NYS Office of Parks, Recreation, and Historic Preservation/ staff: 4(p); 15(v)/ members: 350

HISTORIC SITE; HOUSE MUSEUM; PRESIDENTIAL SITE: Maintains the site where Ulysses S. Grant went in the summer of 1885 to complete his memoirs and died of throat cancer on July 23rd.

PROGRAMS: Annual Meeting; Community Outreach; Concerts; Exhibits; Family Programs; Guided Tours

COLLECTIONS: [1885] House with original furnishings (1885) and personal items belonging to U.S. Grant.

HOURS: May-Sept W-Su 10-4; Sept-Oct Sa-Su 10-4

ADMISSION: $2.50, Children $1, Seniors $2

SAYVILLE

6119
Sayville Historical Society, The
Edwards St at Colton Ave, 11782 [PO Box 41, 11782]; (p) (516) 563-0186; (c) Suffolk

Private non-profit/ 1944/ Board of Directors/ staff: 1(p); 60(v)/ members: 124/publication: A History of Early Sayville

HISTORICAL SOCIETY: Preserves artifacts from the community and documents the history of the area.

PROGRAMS: Concerts; Exhibits; Family Programs; Guided Tours; Interpretation; Lectures; Publication; Reenactments; Research Library/Archives; School-Based Curriculum; Theatre

COLLECTIONS: [1830-present] Historic house, photographs, local business records.

HOURS: Oct-June 1st 3rd Su 2-4; or by appt.

SCARSDALE

6120
Cudner-Hyatt House
937 White Plains Post Rd, 10583 [PO Box 431, 10583-0431]; (p) (914) 723-1744; (f) (914) 723-2185

1734/ staff: 1(f); 6(p); 28(v)

COLLECTIONS: [1836-1886] Cast iron stove (1822-1823) restored but original; wood-burning - used for visiting school groups. Charles Eastlake suite in parlor, a working reed organ, a documented Friendship Quilt with squares signed and marked Scarsdale, dining room chairs; photographs, pamphlets, and memorabilia relating to Scarsdale and its history, both 19th and 20th c., books.

6121
Scarsdale Historical Society
937 Post Rd, 10583 [PO Box 431, 10583]; (p) (914) 723-1744; (f) (914) 723-2185; (c) Westchester

Private non-profit/ staff: 1(f); 8(p); 40(v)/ members: 850

HISTORICAL SOCIETY: Collects, preserves, and interprets local and surrounding history through lectures, exhibitions, and programs.

PROGRAMS: Annual Meeting; Community Outreach; Exhibits; Family Programs; Guided Tours; Interpretation; Lectures; Living History; Publication; Research Library/Archives; School-Based Curriculum

COLLECTIONS: [18th c-present] Cultural material related to middle-class 19th c farmhouse, objects, and archival material of 18th-20th c related to Scarsdale and environs.

HOURS: Yr W-F 1:30-4:30, Su 2-4:30

ADMISSION: $2.50, Children, Seniors $1.75

SCHENECTADY

6122
Special Collections, Schaffer Library, Union College
Union College, 12308; (p) (518) 388-6620; (f) (518) 388-6641; fladgere@union.edu; (c) Schenectady

Private non-profit/ 1974/ Union College; State/ staff: 2(f)

LIBRARY AND/OR ARCHIVES: Special Collections of Schaffer Library, Union College, houses the college archives and various special collections including the rare book collection.

PROGRAMS: Elder's Programs; Publication; Research Library/Archives

COLLECTIONS: [1795-present] Collections pertaining to Union College and various alumni and groups associated with the college.

HOURS: Yr M-F 9-12/1-4

ADMISSION: No charge

SCHOHARIE

6123
1743 Palatine House/Schoharie Colonial Heritage Association
Spring St, 12157 [PO Box 554, 12157]; (p) (518) 295-7505; (f) (518) 295-6001; scha@midtel.net; (c) Schoharie

Private non-profit/ 1963/ staff: 3(p); 40(v)/ members: 240/publication: The 1743 Palatine House

HISTORIC PRESERVATION AGENCY; HISTORIC SITE; HOUSE MUSEUM; LIVING HISTORY/OUTDOOR MUSEUM: Dedicated to preserving, acquiring, and making available to the public historic sites in and about Schoharie Village. 1743 Palatine House, the oldest existing building in Schoharie County and an old Lutheran parsonage, is a living museum.

PROGRAMS: Annual Meeting; Community Outreach; Concerts; Exhibits; Facility Rental; Festivals; Guided Tours; Living History; Publication

COLLECTIONS: [18th c]

HOURS: May-Oct Th-M 1-5

ADMISSION: $2.50; Group rates

6124
Schoharie Colonial Heritage Association
Palatine House Museum, Spring St, 12157 [PO Box 554, 12157]; (p) (518) 295-7505; (f) (518) 295-6001; scha@midtel.net; (c) Schoharie

Private non-profit/ 1963/ staff: 2(p); 50(v)/ members: 219/publication: Life in the Schoharie Valley: Diary 1759

HISTORIC SITE; HOUSE MUSEUM; LIVING HISTORY/OUTDOOR MUSEUM: Oldest existing house in Schoharie County on National Register of Historic Places.

PROGRAMS: Annual Meeting; Community Outreach; Concerts; Exhibits; Facility Rental; Guided Tours; Living History; Publication

COLLECTIONS: [18th c] 18th c household furnishings, loom, colonial garden, sleeping loft, jambless fireplaces.

HOURS: May-Oct Th-M 1-5

ADMISSION: $2.50; Family/Group rates

6125
Schoharie County Historical Society
N Main St, 12157 [RR 2 Box 30A, 12157]; (p) (518) 295-7192; (f) (518) 295-7187; (c) Schoharie

Joint/ 1889/ staff: 4(f); 5(p); 90(v)/ members: 700/publication: *Schoharie County Historical Review*

HISTORIC SITE; HISTORICAL SOCIETY; HISTORY MUSEUM: Preserves and promotes knowledge of the history and culture of Schoharie County.

PROGRAMS: Annual Meeting; Community Outreach; Concerts; Exhibits; Family Programs; Festivals; Guided Tours; Interpretation; Lectures; Living History; Publication; Reenactments; Research Library/Archives; School-Based Curriculum

COLLECTIONS: [18th-19th c] Materials relating to archaeology, technology, transportation, agriculture, military, textiles, decorative arts. Library holdings: genealogy, archival materials, and photographs. Structures: 18th c Palatine House, 18th c New World Dutch Barn.

HOURS: May-Oct T-Sa 10-5; Su 12-5; July-Aug M-Su

ADMISSION: $5, Children $1.50, Seniors $4.50

SCHUYLERVILLE

6126
General Philip Schuyler Home
Rt 4, 12871 [c/o Saratoga NHP 648 Rte 32, Stillwater, 12170]; (p) (518) 664-9821; (f) (518) 664-3349

1777/ National Park Service

COLLECTIONS: [1777-1804]

SEA CLIFF

6127
Sea Cliff Village Museum
95 Tenth Ave, 11579 [PO Box 72, 11579]; (p) (516) 671-0090; (f) (516) 671-2530; (c) Nassau

Joint/ 1979/ Board of Trustees/ staff: 1(p); 75(v)/ members: 415/publication: *Sea Cliff: 100 Years*

HISTORY MUSEUM: Collects, preserves, interprets, and displays material relating to the history of Sea Cliff.

PROGRAMS: Exhibits; Interpretation; Lectures; Publication; Research Library/Archives

COLLECTIONS: [1870-1940] Costume collection from Victorian era to 1940s, photograph and postcard collection, scale model of 1890's Sea Cliff home and more.

HOURS: Sept-July Sa-Su 2-5

ADMISSION: Donations

SELKIRK

6128
Town of Bethlehem Historical Association
1003 River Rd, 12158; (c) Albany

1965/ staff: 30(v)/ members: 180

HISTORIC SITE; HISTORICAL SOCIETY; HISTORY MUSEUM: Collects, preserves, and interprets documents pertaining to the history of the town of Bethlehem.

PROGRAMS: Annual Meeting; Community Outreach; Exhibits; Lectures; Living History

COLLECTIONS: [17th c-present] Books, paintings, prints, documents, and artifacts.

HOURS: Monthly meetings by appt

ADMISSION: No charge

SENECA FALLS

6129
Becker 1880 House Museum
55 Cayuga St, 13148; (p) (315) 568-8412; (f) (315) 568-8426; sfhs@nycc.edu

1855/ staff: 3(f); 40(v)

COLLECTIONS: [1880s] Local history, women's rights, Victoriana, period clothing, genealogy, extensive photographic archive focusing on local history.

HOURS: Yr M -F 9-5

6130
Seneca Falls Historical Society
55 Cayuga St, 13148; (p) (315) 568-8412; (f) (315) 568-8426; SFHS@flare.net; welcome.to/sfhs/; (c) Seneca

Private non-profit/ 1896/ Board of Directors/ staff: 3(f); 300(v)/ members: 1500

HISTORICAL SOCIETY; HOUSE MUSEUM: Preserves and interprets local history, housed in 23 room Victorian mansion.

PROGRAMS: Annual Meeting; Community Outreach; Concerts; Elder's Programs; Exhibits; Family Programs; Festivals; Film/Video; Garden Tours; Guided Tours; Interpretation; Lectures; Living History; Publication; Reenactments; Research Library/Archives; School-Based Curriculum

COLLECTIONS: [19th c] Victorian mansion, women rights history, local history, ethnic history, county history.

HOURS: Jan-Dec M-F 9-4; and July-Aug Sa-Su 1-4

6131
Women's Rights National Historic Park
32 Washington St, 13148 [136 Fall St, 13148]; (p) (315) 568-2991; (f) (315) 568-2141; davic_molone@nps.gov; www.nps.gov/wori

National Park Service

HISTORIC SITE; HOUSE MUSEUM; NATIONAL PARK: Preserves the site that commemorates the First Women's Rights Convention and the early leaders of the women's rights movement in the United States and consists of the remains of the Wesleyan Chapel where the Women's Rights Convention of 1848 took place, Declaration Park, Elizabeth Cady Stanton's house, Hunt House, and M'Clintock House.

COLLECTIONS: 1840's Greek Revival home of Elizabeth Cady Stanton, organizer and leader of the women's rights movement, the Wesleyan Chapel, site of the First Women's Rights Convention, Hunt House, home of Jane and Richard Hunt, the site where the idea for the First Women's Rights Convention was conceived, and the M'Clintock House, site where the Declaration of Sentiments was drafted.

HOURS: Yr

SETAUKET

6132
Sherwood-Jayne House
Old Post Rd, 11733 [PO Box 148, Cold Spring Harbor, 11724]; (p) (516) 751-6610, (516) 692-4664; (f) (516) 692-5265; splia.com

staff: 1(p); 10(v)

COLLECTIONS: 18th and 19th c decorative arts.

HOURS: June-Oct

6133
Thompson House
N Country Rd, 11733 [PO Box 148, Cold Spring Harbor, 11724]; (p) (516) 941-9716, (516) 692-4664; (f) (516) 692-5265; www.splia.com

1700/ staff: 1(p); 25(v)

Early Long Island furniture.

COLLECTIONS: [18th c] Early Long Island decorative arts.

HOURS: June-Oct

6134
Three Village Historical Society
93 N Country Rd, 11733-0076 [PO Box 76, East Setauket, 11733-0076]; (p) (516) 751-3730; (f) (516) 751-3936; tvhistsoc@aol.com; members.aol.com/tvhs1; (c) Suffolk

Private non-profit/ 1964/ Board of Trustees/ staff: 1(f); 4(p); 225(v)/ members: 1018/publication: *The Historian*

HISTORICAL SOCIETY: Collects and preserves artifacts, documents, and other materials of local significance as well as researching the history of the people who have lived in the Three Village area.

PROGRAMS: Annual Meeting; Community Outreach; Exhibits; Family Programs; Festivals; Guided Tours; Interpretation; Lectures; Publication; Research Library/Archives; School-Based Curriculum

COLLECTIONS: [17th c-present] Archives: local history 17th-20th c, seafaring; Artifacts: Native American, seafaring, Long Island's North Shore; 20th c collection of papers of Ward and Dorothy Melville.

HOURS: Yr M-F 9:30-5

ADMISSION: No charge

SHELTER ISLAND

6135
Havens House
16 S Ferry Rd, 11964 [PO Box 847, 11964]; (p) (516) 749-0025; (f) (516) 749-0025

1743/ Shelter Island Historical Society/ staff: 1(f); 22(v)

COLLECTIONS: [1743-1890] Artifacts related to local history, farming and fishing artifacts, children's room of artifacts, textiles, household items. Documents, newspapers, and photographs related to local history.

HOURS: Seasonal

6136
Shelter Island Historical Society
16 S Ferry Rd, 11964 [PO Box 847, 11964]; (p) (516) 749-0025; (f) (516) 749-1825; (c) Suffolk

Private non-profit/ 1922/ staff: 1(f); 28(v)/ members: 600

HISTORIC SITE; HISTORICAL SOCIETY; HISTORY MUSEUM; HOUSE MUSEUM: Collects, preserves, and disseminates knowledge of local history while operating an historic house, barn, and museum.

PROGRAMS: Annual Meeting; Concerts; Festivals; Garden Tours; Guided Tours; Lectures

COLLECTIONS: [1743-1926] Materials relating to history of Shelter Island.

HOURS: June-Sept F-Su 11-3

ADMISSION: $2

SLEEPY HOLLOW

6137
Kykuit, Rockefeller House and Gardens
Rt 9, [Historic Hudson Valley, 150 White Plains Rd, Tarrytown, 10591]; (p) (914) 631-8200; (f) (914) 631-0089

SMITHTOWN

6138
Smithtown Historical Society
5 N Country Rd, 11787-2142; (p) (516) 265-6768; (f) (516) 265-6768; (c) Suffolk

Private non-profit/ 1955/ staff: 1(f); 5(p); 26(v)/ members: 350/publication: Smithtown:1660-1929

HISTORIC PRESERVATION AGENCY; HISTORIC SITE; HISTORICAL SOCIETY; HOUSE MUSEUM: Maintains 10 historic buildings, collects, preserves and interprets archival material pertaining to Smithtown and provides educational programs to 13,000 children and adults.

PROGRAMS: Annual Meeting; Community Outreach; Exhibits; Facility Rental; Family Programs; Festivals; Guided Tours; Interpretation; Lectures; Publication; Reenactments; Research Library/Archives; School-Based Curriculum

COLLECTIONS: [1665-1900] 10 historic buildings, deeds, surveys from 1665, letters, ledgers, decorative arts, farm tools, furniture, household articles, costumes, textiles and books. Structures: 1700 Obadiah Smith House, 1740 Epenetus Smith Tavern, 1860 Judge J.L. Smith Homestead.

HOURS: Yr M-Sa 9-4

ADMISSION: Donations requested; group rates

SODUS POINT

6139
Sodus Bay Historical Society
7606 N Ontario St, 14555 [PO Box 94, 14555]; (p) (315) 483-4936; sodusbay@ix.netcom.com; www.peachey.com/soduslight; (c) Wayne

Private non-profit/ 1972/ staff: 1(f); 2(p); 100(v)/ members: 700

HISTORIC SITE; HISTORICAL SOCIETY: Collects, preserves, and exhibits historical records and artifacts related to the area; maintains the Sodus Point Lighthouse Museum.

PROGRAMS: Concerts; Elder's Programs; Exhibits; Festivals; Guided Tours; Interpretation; Living History; Research Library/Archives; School-Based Curriculum

COLLECTIONS: [1800-1940] Artifacts and historical records relating to maritime, cultural, and commercial activities in the area, maritime and local history library.

HOURS: May-Oct T-Su 10-5

SOUTHAMPTON

6140
Halsey Homestead, The
S Main St, 11969 [PO Box 303, 11969]; (p) (516) 283-3527, (516) 283-2494

1648/ staff: 1(f)

COLLECTIONS: [17th-18th c] 17th & 18th c furnishings selected by Henry DuPont in 1959, English furniture, local Dominy furniture, 4 stump work textiles.

HOURS: Seasonal

6141
Southampton County Historical Society
17 Meeting House Ln, 11969 [PO Box 303, 11969]; (p) (516) 283-2494; (f) (516) 283-2494; hismusdir@hamptons.com; (c) Suffolk

Private non-profit/ 1898/ staff: 1(f); 2(p); 80(v)/ members: 750

HISTORICAL SOCIETY: Collects, preserves and interprets materials relating to Southampton's history and culture and operates three museums and one historic site.

PROGRAMS: Exhibits; Family Programs; Festivals; Guided Tours; Interpretation; Lectures; Reenactments; Research Library/Archives; School-Based Curriculum

COLLECTIONS: [18th c-present] Artifacts related to Native Americans, whaling, carpentry, blacksmiths, agricultural tools, antique dolls and toys, and decorative arts.

HOURS: Yr Jan-May T-Sa 11-5; June-Dec T-Sa 11-5, Su 1-5

STAATSBURG

6142
Mills Mansion State Historic Site
Old Post Rd, 12580; (p) (914) 889-8851; (f) (914) 889-8321; (c) Dutchess

State/ 1938/ staff: 7(f); 7(p); 90(v)/ members: 300

HISTORIC SITE: Historic house museum, 1895.

PROGRAMS: Annual Meeting; Community Outreach; Concerts; Facility Rental; Family Programs; Guided Tours; Interpretation; Lectures; Research Library/Archives; School-Based Curriculum

COLLECTIONS: [1895-1920] Turn of the century furnishings including paintings, tapestries, decorative objects d'art, and furniture. Most in the styles of Louis XIV, XV, and XVI. All original to mansion.

HOURS: Mar-Nov W-Sa 10-5, Su 12-5

ADMISSION: $3, Children $1, Seniors $2

STATEN ISLAND

6143
Alice Austen House Museum
2 Hylan Blvd, 10305; (p) (718) 816-4506; (f) (718) 815-3959; (c) Richmond

Private non-profit/ 1969/ Friends of Alice Austen House, Inc./ staff: 2(f); 2(p); 8(v)/ members: 300/publication: Viewpoint

HOUSE MUSEUM: Commemorates one of the earliest female photographers, Alice Austen, and exhibits historic and contemporary photographers and photographic history.

PROGRAMS: Annual Meeting; Community Outreach; Concerts; Exhibits; Facility Rental; Festivals; Guided Tours; Lectures; Publication; School-Based Curriculum

COLLECTIONS: [Late Victorian] Period furnishings from the late Victorian period; Austen family artifacts; prints of Alice Austen's photographic works from 1880s through the early 1920s.

HOURS: Mar-Dec 31 Th-Su 12-5

6144
Conference House Association
7455 Hylan Blvd, 10307 [PO Box 171, 10307]; (p) (718) 984-6046; (c) Richmond

Private non-profit/ 1927/ Conference House Association/ staff: 1(f); 3(p); 30(v)/ members: 200/publication: Conference House Revisited

HISTORIC SITE; HOUSE MUSEUM: Historic house, site of 1776 Peace Conference attended by Benjamin Franklin, John Adams, Edward Rutledge. Colonial manor home of the Billop family.

PROGRAMS: Annual Meeting; Concerts; Exhibits; Festivals; Garden Tours; Guided Tours; Interpretation; Lectures; Living History; Publication; Reenactments; School-Based Curriculum

COLLECTIONS: [1776] Colonial furnishings.

HOURS: Mar-Dec F-Su 1-4

ADMISSION: $2, Children $1, Seniors $1

6145
Friends of Alice Austen House, Inc.
2 Hylan Blvd, 10305; (p) (718) 816-4506; (f) (718) 815-3959; (c) Richmond

Private non-profit/ 1979/ staff: 2(f); 4(p); 6(v)/ members: 250

HOUSE MUSEUM: Maintains historic house, interpretation to the 1890's, showcases photography of Alice Austen and other contemporary photographers.

PROGRAMS: Annual Meeting; Community Outreach; Concerts; Exhibits; Facility Rental; Family Programs; Festivals; Guided Tours; Lectures; Research Library/Archives; School-Based Curriculum

COLLECTIONS: [1840s-1900] Furniture, decorative arts, cameras, and other artifacts of Alice Austen and the Austen family. Also items that relate to the history of the Staten Island community.

HOURS: Mar-Dec Th-Su 12-5

6146
Garibaldi and Meucci Museum
420 Tompkins St, 10305; (p) (718) 442-1608; (f) (718) 442-8635

6147
Historic Richmond Town
441 Clarke Ave, 10306

6148
Staten Island Historical Society
441 Clarke Ave, 10306; (p) (718) 351-1611; (f) (718) 351-6057; (c) Richmond

Private non-profit/ 1856/ staff: 22(f); 15(p); 17(v)/ members: 700

HISTORIC SITE; HISTORICAL SOCIETY; HISTORY MUSEUM: Collects, preserves, and interprets the history and culture of Staten Island.

PROGRAMS: Annual Meeting; Concerts; Exhibits; Facility Rental; Family Programs; Festivals; Guided Tours; Interpretation; Lectures; Living History; Publication; Reenactments; Research Library/Archives; School-Based Curriculum

COLLECTIONS: [18th-19th c] 32 historic buildings, household items, furniture, textiles, clothing, tools, toys, vehicles, manuscripts, and archival materials.

HOURS: Yr W-Su 1-5

ADMISSION: $4, Children $2.50

STEPHENTOWN

6149
Stephentown Historical Society
4 Staples Rd, 12168 [PO Box 11, 12168]; (p) (518) 733-6070; (c) Rensselaer

Private non-profit/ 1973/ Board of Directors/ staff: 125(v)/publication: *Epitaphs in the only Stephentown on Earth; History of Stephentown; and others*

HISTORICAL SOCIETY; HISTORY MUSEUM: Preserves the history and artifacts of the town and maintains its 129 year old Heritage Center.

PROGRAMS: Annual Meeting; Exhibits; Lectures; Publication; Research Library/Archives

COLLECTIONS: [1790-present] Deeds, indentures (some from Stephen Van Rensselaer), war records, Rutland Railroad papers, church and school records, cemetery data, photographs, diaries, maps.

HOURS: Yr F 1-4

ADMISSION: No charge

STILLWATER

6150
Saratoga National Historical Park
648 Rt 32, 12170; (p) (518) 664-9821; (f) (518) 664-3349; sara_info@nps.gov; www.nps.gov/sara/; (c) Saratoga

Federal/ 1938/ staff: 16(f); 6(p); 20(v)

BATTLEFIELD; NATIONAL PARK: Preserves site of decisive battle that led to the surrender of British forces in American Revolutionary War.

PROGRAMS: Community Outreach; Exhibits; Family Programs; Festivals; Guided Tours; Interpretation; Lectures; Living History; Reenactments; Research Library/Archives; School-Based Curriculum

COLLECTIONS: [1776-1777] Decorative arts, military implements, library, and collection related to American Revolution, Burgoyne Campaign, and Battle of Saratoga.

HOURS: Yr M-Su 9-5

ADMISSION: $4

STONY BROOK

6151
Museums at Stony Brook, The
1208 Rt 25 A, 11790-1992; (p) (516) 751-0066; (f) (516) 751-0353; museum@mail.longisland.com; www.museumsatstonybrook.org; (c) Suffolk

Private non-profit/ 1939/ The Museums of Stonybrook/ staff: 25(f); 15(p); 250(v)/ members: 880

HISTORY MUSEUM: Preserves social and cultural history of America with focus on Long Island.

PROGRAMS: Community Outreach; Concerts; Exhibits; Facility Rental; Family Programs; Festivals; Garden Tours; Guided Tours; Interpretation; Lectures; Living History; Publication; Reenactments; Research Library/Archives; School-Based Curriculum

COLLECTIONS: [19th-20th c] American art, social history, horse-drawn transportation, research libraries, historic structures.

HOURS: Jan-June W-Sa 10-5, Su 12-5; July-Aug M-Sa 10-5, Su 12-5; Sept-Nov W-Sa 10-5, Su 12-5; Dec, July-Aug M-Sa 10-5, Su 12-5

ADMISSION: $4, Student $2, Seniors $3

STONY POINT

6152
Stony Point Battlefield State Historic Site
Park Rd, 10980 [Box 182, 10980]; (p) (914) 786-2521; (f) (914) 786-2521; spbattle@1hric.org; www2.1hric.org/spbattle/spbattle.htm; (c) Rockland

State/ 1902/ Palisades Interstate Park Commission/ staff: 2(f); 5(p); 4(v)

BATTLEFIELD; HISTORIC SITE: Battlefield is one of the few preserved Revolutionary War battlefields in NY state and is the location of the oldest lighthouse on the Hudson River.

PROGRAMS: Community Outreach; Exhibits; Film/Video; Guided Tours; Interpretation; Living History; School-Based Curriculum

COLLECTIONS: [18th-19th c] 600 artifacts relating to Battle of Stony Point & the 1826 lighthouse on the grounds on exhibit and in archives; 87 acres, buildings, and lighthouse are on the National Register.

SYRACUSE

6153
Milton J. Rubenstein Museum of Science and Technology
500 S Frankllin St, 13202; (p) (315) 425-9068; (f) (315) 425-9072; 76461.3464@compuserve.com; www.most.org; (c) Onondaga

Private non-profit/ 1979/ Board of Trustees/ staff: 31(f); 26(p); 280(v)/ members: 4300/publication: *Technologist*

HISTORY MUSEUM: Through exhibits, programs, shows, and lectures, the museum provides insight into the development of science and technology and an understanding of the underlying scientific principles.

PROGRAMS: Community Outreach; Exhibits; Facility Rental; Family Programs; Film/Video; Guided Tours; Interpretation; Lectures; Publication; School-Based Curriculum

COLLECTIONS: [1860-1920] Extensive significant collections in apothecary and the development of pharmaceutical sciences, primarily from the 1860's to the 1920's. Also artifacts about the history of communications.

HOURS: Yr Daily 11-5

ADMISSION: $4.75, Children $3.75, Seniors $3.75

6154
Erie Canal Museum
318 Erie Blvd E, 13202; (p) (315) 471-0593; (f) (315) 471-7220; www.syracuse.com/features/eriecanal; (c) Onondaga

Private non-profit/ 1962/ staff: 8(f); 8(p); 96(v)/ members: 400/publication: *Canal Packet*

HISTORIC SITE: Develops public appreciation of human history through Erie Canal related social science, art, and technology, by collecting, preserving, researching, exhibiting, and interpreting Erie Canal related artifacts and archival materials.

PROGRAMS: Elder's Programs; Exhibits; Facility Rental; Family Programs; Festivals; Guided Tours; Interpretation; Lectures; Publication; Research Library/Archives; School-Based Curriculum

COLLECTIONS: [Erie Canal era] Historic structure; 53,000 items in library and archival collections; 215 commemorative items; 145 pieces of boat equipment; 743 tools and canal related equipment; 520 items of clothing and personal items.

HOURS: Yr Daily 10-5

ADMISSION: Donations accepted

6155
Museum of Automobile History, The
321 N Clinton St, 13202; (p) (315) 478-2277; (f) (315) 432-8256; info@autolit.com; www.autolit.com; (c) Onondaga

Private for-profit/ 1995/ staff: 2(f)

AUTOMOBILE MUSEUM: Privately owned museum housing the collections of Walter

Miller. Displays a comprehensive history of the automobile in the United States and around the world.

PROGRAMS: Community Outreach; Exhibits; Facility Rental; Research Library/Archives; School-Based Curriculum

COLLECTIONS: [20th c.] 10,000 objects on display.

HOURS: Yr W-Su 10-5

ADMISSION: $4.75, Children $2.75, Seniors $3.75

6156
Onondaga Historical Association
321 Montgomery St, 13202; (p) (315) 428-1864; (f) (315) 471-2133; (c) Onondaga

Private non-profit/ 1863/ staff: 7(f); 4(p); 20(v)/ members: 1150

HISTORICAL SOCIETY; HISTORY MUSEUM; RESEARCH CENTER: Serves as the general history museum for the Greater Syracuse area and operates both museum galleries and a public research center.

PROGRAMS: Community Outreach; Concerts; Exhibits; Facility Rental; Family Programs; Film/Video; Guided Tours; Interpretation; Lectures; Publication; Research Library/Archives; School-Based Curriculum

COLLECTIONS: [19th-20th c] 50,000 museum artifacts including textiles, paintings, industrial and household items, over a million archival items including documents, photographs, maps, architectural drawings, books, manuscripts, and film.

HOURS: Yr W-Sa 11-4:30

ADMISSION: Museum free, research center $5 for non-members

6157
Parke S. Avery Historical House
650 James St, 13203; (p) (315) 475-0119

TARRYTOWN

6158
Historic Hudson Valley
150 White Plains Rd, 10591; (p) (914) 631-8200; (f) (914) 631-0089; mail@hudsonvalley.org; www.hudsonvalley.org; (c) Westchester

Private non-profit/ 1951/ staff: 68(f); 161(p); 200(v)/ members: 1200

GARDEN; HISTORIC SITE; LIVING HISTORY/OUTDOOR MUSEUM: Preserves the culture, landscape, and history of the Hudson River Valley and presents this heritage to the public through educational outreach, daily programming at historic properties and special events.

PROGRAMS: Exhibits; Facility Rental; Family Programs; Festivals; Garden Tours; Guided Tours; Interpretation; Lectures; Living History; Research Library/Archives

COLLECTIONS: [18th-20th c.] Six historic sites

HOURS: Apr-Dec W-M 10-4

ADMISSION: $8, Children $4

6159
Lyndhurst
635 S Broadway, 10591; (p) (914) 631-4481; (f) (914) 631-5634; www.Lyndhurst.org; (c) Westchester

Private non-profit/ 1964/ National Trust for Historic Preservation/ staff: 10(f); 30(p); 100(v)/ members: 1100/publication: Lyndhurst: A Guide to the House and Landscape

HISTORIC SITE; HOUSE MUSEUM: Lyndhurst is America's finest example of a Gothic Revival Villa. Located on the Hudson River, the house and its setting embody 19th c picturesque architecture and landscape design at its best.

PROGRAMS: Community Outreach; Concerts; Exhibits; Facility Rental; Family Programs; Festivals; Guided Tours; Interpretation; Lectures; Publication; Research Library/Archives; School-Based Curriculum

COLLECTIONS: [1838-1961] 15 historic buildings on 67 landscaped acres, 11,000 individual objects owned by three families who lived at Lyndhurst.

HOURS: Apr-Oct T-Su 10-5; Nov-Apr Sa-Su 10-4

ADMISSION: $10, Children $4, Seniors $9

6160
Sunnyside
W Sunnyside Ln, 10591 [150 White Plains Rd, 10591]; (p) (914) 591-8763; (f) (914) 591-4436; ww.hudsonvalley.org

1835/ staff: 3(f); 15(p); 10(v)

COLLECTIONS: [1835-1859] The house is furnished with an eclectic mix of objects and furniture from 1800-1859, some owned by Irving, some from the period.

TICONDEROGA

6161
Fort Ticonderoga
Fort Rd, 12883 [PO Box 390, 12883]; (p) (518) 585-2821; (f) (518) 585-2210; www.fort-ticonderoga.org; (c) Essex

Private non-profit/ 1909/ Board of Trustees/ staff: 18(f); 58(p); 1500(v)/ members: 1000/publication: Bulletin of the Fort Ticonderoga Museum; The Haversack; and others

GARDEN; HISTORIC SITE; HISTORY MUSEUM; LIVING HISTORY/OUTDOOR MUSEUM; RESEARCH CENTER: Preserves and interprets significant 18th c strategic chokepoint on Lake Champlain. The Pavilion (1826) and the King's Garden preserve and interpret 19th c development of heritage tourism and Fort Reconstruction.

PROGRAMS: Community Outreach; Concerts; Exhibits; Facility Rental; Garden Tours; Guided Tours; Interpretation; Lectures; Living History; Publication; Reenactments; Research Library/Archives

COLLECTIONS: [18th c.] 18th c military history at the Fort; 19th and 20th c decorative arts; USS Ticonderoga; library and manuscript collections; archaeological specimens recovered from the site; Carillon Battlefield; The King's Garden

HOURS: May-June Daily 9-5; July-Aug Daily 9-6; Sept-Oct Daily 9-5

TONAWANDA

6162
Historical Society of the Tonawandas
133 Main St, 14150-2129; (p) (716) 694-7406; (c) Erie

Private non-profit/ 1961/ Board of Trustees/ staff: 1(f); 40(v)/ members: 340

GENEALOGICAL SOCIETY; HISTORIC SITE; HISTORICAL SOCIETY; HISTORY MUSEUM; HOUSE MUSEUM; RESEARCH CENTER: Collects and preserves history of the Tonawanoas. Long homestead with artifacts from 1810-1840. History museum housed in 1870 New York Central railroad station with library.

PROGRAMS: Annual Meeting; Exhibits; Festivals; Guided Tours; Interpretation

COLLECTIONS: [1800-present] Maps, manuscripts, photographs, newspapers, genealogies, national census, models, marine, Erie canal, lumber, sheet music, museum artifacts, city directories, library.

HOURS: Yr W-F 10-4:30

TROY

6163
Hart-Cluett Mansion
59 Second St, 12180; (p) (518) 272-7232; (f) (518) 273-1264; rchs@crisny.org; www.crisny.org/not-fot-profit/rchs

1827/ staff: 5(f); 6(p); 362(v)

Preserves home of Richard and Betsey Hart, George and Amanda Cluett, and Albert and Caroline Cluett.

COLLECTIONS: [Mid 19th c] Fine and decorative arts; industrial and agricultural artifacts; vehicles; Manuscripts; photos; maps; published reference materials; family and business papers; organization archives.

HOURS: Feb-Dec

6164
Junior Museum, The
105 8th St, 12182; (p) (518) 235-2120; (f) (518) 235-6836; info@juniormuseum.org; www.juniormuseum.org; (c) Rensselaer

Private non-profit/ 1954/ Board of Trustees/ staff: 9(f); 17(p); 20(v)/ members: 150

HISTORY MUSEUM: Children's museum that provides educational experiences in science, history, and the arts for schools, families and youth groups.

PROGRAMS: Community Outreach; Concerts; Exhibits; Facility Rental; Family Programs; Festivals; Guided Tours; Interpretation; Living History; School-Based Curriculum; Theatre

COLLECTIONS: [1850-1950] Objects used in 19th c rural life, Victoriana, live animal collection.

HOURS: Yr Sa-Su 10-5

ADMISSION: $5, Children $5; Under 2 free

6165
Museum Association of New York, The
265 River St, 12180; (p) (518) 273-3400; (f) (518) 273-3416; info@manyonline.org; www.manyonline.org; (c) Rensselaer

Private non-profit/ 1962/ staff: 1(p)/ members:

260/publication: *Salary and Benefits Survey; Many Connections*

PROFESSIONAL ORGANIZATION: Statewide museum association. Membership based service and advocacy agency for museums and historical organizations in New York State and the and the individuals who work and volunteer for them.

6166
Rensselaer County Historical Society
59 Second St, 12180; (p) (518) 272-7232; (f) (518) 273-1264; info@rchsonline.org; www.rchsonline.org; (c) Rensselaer

Private non-profit/ 1927/ staff: 5(f); 6(p); 362(v)/ members: 535/publication: *Marble House in Second Street: Biography of a Town House and its Occupants 1825-2000*

HISTORICAL SOCIETY; HOUSE MUSEUM; RESEARCH CENTER: Society promotes interest in the history of the county through collection, research, and preservation.

PROGRAMS: Annual Meeting; Community Outreach; Exhibits; Family Programs; Festivals; Guided Tours; Interpretation; Lectures; Publication; Research Library/Archives; School-Based Curriculum

COLLECTIONS: [1714-present] Fine and decorative arts, textiles, clothing, agricultural and industrial objects, research material, photographs. Structures: General Joseph B. Carr Building, Hart-Cluett Mansion & Carriage House

HOURS: Feb-Dec Museum: T-Sa 10-4; Library: T-F 1-4 Sa 10-4

ADMISSION: $3; Children, Seniors $2

UTICA

6173
Matt Brewery
Corner of Court & Varick St, 13502 [811 Edward St, 13502]; (p) (315) 724-0246; (f) (315) 732-4296; www.saranac.com; (c) Oneida

Private for-profit/ 1888/ staff: 100(f); 25(p)

HISTORIC SITE: Brewery founded in 1888 that is currently run by 3rd and 4th generations of Matt family provides tours of nation's second oldest brewery.

PROGRAMS: Exhibits; Facility Rental; Festivals; Guided Tours

HOURS: Yr June-Aug M-Sa 10-4, Su 1-3; Sept-May M-Sa

ADMISSION: $3, Children $1

VAILS GATE

6167
National Temple Hill Association
1042 Rt 94, 12584 [PO Box 315, 12584]; (p) (845) 561-5073; www.flagguys.com; (c) Orange

Private non-profit/ 1933/ Trustees/ staff: 15(p); 15(v)/ members: 120/publication: *Last Cantonment: High Time for a Peace Author*

HISTORIC PRESERVATION AGENCY; HISTORIC SITE; HOUSE MUSEUM; LIVING HISTORY/OUTDOOR MUSEUM: Preserves portions of New Windsor cantonment, last

encampment of the American Revolution. Develops and interprets at Edmonston House and historic parklands.

PROGRAMS: Annual Meeting; Community Outreach; Exhibits; Interpretation; Lectures; Living History; Publication; Research Library/Archives

COLLECTIONS: [American Revolutionary War] Records of National Temple Hill Association 1933-present. Published materials pertaining to local history, military; Americana; maps.

HOURS: July-Sept Su 2-5

ADMISSION: Donations accepted

6168
Edmonston House, The
1042 Rt 94, 12584 [PO Box 315, 12584]; (p) (914) 561-5073

1755

COLLECTIONS: [1750s-1780s] Period furnishings, archaeiligical items indigenous to site; Local and Revolutionary War history, organization records 1933 to present.

HOURS: Seasonal

6169
Ellison House
289 Forge Hill Rd, 12584 [PO Box 207, 12584]; (p) (914) 561-5498

6170
Knox's Headquarters State Historic Site
Rt 94 & Forge Hill Rd, 12584 [PO Box 207, 12584]; (p) (914) 561-5498; (f) (914) 561-6577; (c) Orange

State/ 1922/ NYS Office of Parks, Rec & Hist Preservation/ staff: 4(f); 1(p); 10(v)

HISTORIC SITE; STATE PARK: Historic site of a 1754 Fieldstone house used as headquarters to Generals Henry Knox, Horatio Gates, and Nathanael Greene; ruins of a 1741 grist mill and native plant sanctuary.

PROGRAMS: Guided Tours; Lectures; Reenactments; School-Based Curriculum

COLLECTIONS: [1750-1780] English period and original furnishings, exhibits, 1754 house and remains of mill.

HOURS: Yr by appt; May-Aug 1-5

6171
New Windsor Cantonment State Historic Site
Temple Hill Rd (Rt 300), 12584 [PO Box 207, 12584]; (p) (914) 561-1765; (f) (914) 561-6577; nwc@orn.net; www.thepurpleheart.com; (c) Orange

Joint/ 1967/ Palisades Interstate Park Comm, NYSOPRHP/ staff: 6(f); 8(p); 200(v)

HISTORIC SITE; HISTORY MUSEUM; LIVING HISTORY/OUTDOOR MUSEUM: Revolutionary War period living history museum depicts the final winter encampment of the Continental Army (1782-3) with demonstrations of military drill, blacksmithing, women's roles, and military hospital.

PROGRAMS: Community Outreach; Concerts; Elder's Programs; Exhibits; Family Pro-

grams; Festivals; Film/Video; Guided Tours; Lectures; Living History; Publication; Reenactments; Research Library/Archives; School-Based Curriculum

COLLECTIONS: [1776-1782] Revolutionary War items: original 1782 Badge of Military Merit, the inspiration for the modern Purple Heart award, local manuscripts, late 18th c log building, 1891 monumental obelisk.

HOURS: Apr-Oct W-Sa 10-5, Su 1-5

ADMISSION: $3, Children $1, Seniors $2; Group rates

VALLEY STREAM

6172
Valley Stream Historical Society
143 Hendrickson Ave, 11580 [50 Payan Ave, 11580]; (p) (516) 872-0006; (f) (516) 872-2469; henrslla@l-2000.com; (c) Nassau

Private non-profit/ 1973/ staff: 25(v)/ members: 165/publication: *Panorama*

HISTORICAL SOCIETY; HOUSE MUSEUM: Collects and preserves local and regional history, geography, and culture and conduct tours of a restored Victorian house.

PROGRAMS: Annual Meeting; Exhibits; Family Programs; Guided Tours; Lectures; Publication

COLLECTIONS: [19th-20th c] Contents of restored Victorian house representing several generations of occupants, regional memorabilia, works of local artist and photographers.

HOURS: Yr Sa 1-4 or by appt

ADMISSION: No charge

WALDEN

6174
Jacob T. Walden House
N Montgomery St, 12586 [PO Box 48, 12586]; (p) (914) 778-5862

1700/ staff: 15(v)

COLLECTIONS: [Early 19th c] Pocketknives, personal items, museum quality furniture; bound local newspapers - early to mid 20th c - not yet catalogued.

HOURS: By appt

WAPPINGERS FALLS

6175
Wappingers Historical Society
Main St, 12590 [PO Box 174, 12590]; (p) (914) 462-7322; Guston@compuserve.com; (c) Dutchess

Private non-profit/ 1967/ staff: 20(v)/ members: 40

HISTORIC SITE; HISTORICAL SOCIETY; HISTORY MUSEUM; HOUSE MUSEUM: Collects and preserves history of the area and also has meetings with speakers that are open to the public.

PROGRAMS: Exhibits; Guided Tours; Lectures

COLLECTIONS: [17th c-present] Collection of 2,000 Native American artifacts, period dresses, uniforms, books.

HOURS: May, July-Aug Sa 1-5

ADMISSION: Donations accepted

WARWICK

6176
Shingle House, The
Historic Warwick Village, Forester Ave, 10990 [PO Box 353, 10990]

1764

COLLECTIONS: [18th-early 19th c] Kitchen equipment and utensils, for cooking fireplace and oven. Furnishings of railroad caboose, living arrangements for trainmen, early farming tools.

HOURS: Seasonal

WATER MILL

6177
Water Mill Museum
Old Mill Rd, 11976 [PO Box 63, 11976]; (p) (516) 726-4741; (c) Suffolk

Private non-profit/ 1969/ staff: 1(p); 35(v)/ members: 250/publication: *Water Mill Celebrating Community 1644-1994*

HISTORY MUSEUM: Collection preserves and exhibits the past uses of the water-powered mill, and the commercial, cultural, and social development of the Long Island community from 1644 to the present.

PROGRAMS: Annual Meeting; Exhibits; Family Programs; Guided Tours; Interpretation; Living History; Publication; Research Library/Archives

COLLECTIONS: [19th c] Items relating to the water-powered mill.

WATERFORD

6178
New York State Bureau of Historic Sites
Peebles Island State Park, 12188 [PO Box 219, 12188]; (p) (518) 237-8643; (f) (518) 235-4248; www.nysparks.com; (c) Saratoga

State/ 1974/ staff: 175(f); 200(p); 500(v)

GARDEN; HISTORIC PRESERVATION AGENCY; HISTORIC SITE; HOUSE MUSEUM; LIVING HISTORY/OUTDOOR MUSEUM; STATE PARK: As department in state government, administers over 185 state parks, and historic site facilities.

PROGRAMS: Community Outreach; Concerts; Exhibits; Facility Rental; Garden Tours; Guided Tours; Interpretation; Lectures; Living History; Reenactments

COLLECTIONS: [17th-early 20th c] Pre-Colombian through 19thc. Archaeological material and 17th through early 20th c. decorative and fine art, military collections reflective of state historic sites.

HOURS: Apr-Oct W-Sa 10-5, Su 1-5

ADMISSION: Varies

6179
Waterford Historical Museum & Cultural Center Inc.
2 Museum Ln, 12188 [PO Box 175, 12188]; (p) (518) 238-0809; (c) Saratoga

Private non-profit/ 1964/ Board of Trustees/ staff: 1(p); 11(v)/ members: 143/publication: *Museum News*

ART MUSEUM; HISTORY MUSEUM: Maintains museum, housed in Hugh White Homestead, collects, preserves, and interprets local history of Waterford, Cohoes, Halfmoon, and Lansingburgh.

PROGRAMS: Annual Meeting; Community Outreach; Concerts; Exhibits; Family Programs; Guided Tours; Lectures; Publication

COLLECTIONS: [19th c-present] Artifacts, maps, photos, postcards, manuscripts, volumes relating to Erie and Champlain Canal history and Dutch, English, Native American settlements.

HOURS: Apr-Nov Sa-Su 2-4 or by appt

WATERLOO

6180
Peter Whitmer, Sr. Farm
1451 Aunkst Rd, 13165; (p) (315) 539-2552

WATERTOWN

6181
Jefferson County Historical Society
228 Washington St, 13601; (p) (315) 782-3491; (f) (315) 782-2913; ns1.imcnet.net/jchs; (c) Jefferson

Private non-profit/ 1886/ staff: 5(f); 3(p); 60(v)/ members: 925

GARDEN; HISTORICAL SOCIETY; HISTORY MUSEUM: Promotes a county wide cultural, educational, and historical institution devoted to the preservation and interpretation of the history and heritage of Jefferson County.

PROGRAMS: Annual Meeting; Community Outreach; Exhibits; Facility Rental; Family Programs; Garden Tours; Guided Tours; Lectures; Publication; Research Library/Archives

COLLECTIONS: [1800-present] Tyler coverlets, quilts, 19th c water turbines, costumes, textiles, photographs, art, archives, farm tools, Civil War artifacts, vintage carriages and automobiles, Native American artifacts, decorative arts.

HOURS: Yr T-Fr 10-5, Sa 12-5

ADMISSION: Donations requested

WATERVLIET

6182
Watervliet Arsenal Museum
Watervliet Arsenal, 12189-4050; (p) (518) 266-5805; (c) Albany

Federal/ 1968/ Chief of Military History/ staff: 2(f); 2(p); 3(v)/publication: *Watervliet Arsenal*

HISTORY MUSEUM: Housed in the 1859 historic iron building, the museum interprets large caliber weapon design, development, and Watervliet Arsenal History.

PROGRAMS: Exhibits; Guided Tours; Publication; Research Library/Archives; School-Based Curriculum

COLLECTIONS: [1813-present] 3,000 artifacts, 10,000 photographs, technical manuals, reports, ordinance books, magazines, periodicals, letterbooks.

HOURS: Yr M-Th 10-3

WAYLAND

6183
Wayland Historical Society
100 S Main St, 14572 [PO Box 494, 14572-0494]; (p) (716) 728-3610; abennetg@frontiernet.net; (c) Steuben

Private non-profit/ 1992/ staff: 65(v)/ members: 430

HISTORY MUSEUM: Collects and preserves local history.

PROGRAMS: Annual Meeting; Community Outreach; Exhibits; Family Programs; Guided Tours; School-Based Curriculum

COLLECTIONS: Two old fire fighting pieces, Ladder wagon and hose cart, old farm wagon, horse drawn sower.

WELLSVILLE

6184
Mather Homestead Museum, Library and Memorial Park
343 N Main St, 14895 [PO Box 531, 14895]; (p) (716) 593-1636; (c) Allegheny

Private non-profit/ 1981/publication: *The Homestead Hoot*

ART MUSEUM; GARDEN; HISTORIC PRESERVATION AGENCY; HOUSE MUSEUM; LIVING HISTORY/OUTDOOR MUSEUM: Homestead from mid-1800s fosters the arts and preserves the local park.

PROGRAMS: Concerts; Exhibits; Family Programs; Guided Tours; Publication

COLLECTIONS: [1930s] Eclectic artifacts.

HOURS: Yr W, Sa 2-5 and by appt

WEST HENRIETTA

6185
New York Museum of Transportation
6393 E River Rd, 14586 [PO Box 136, 14586]; (p) (716) 533-1113; www.nymt.mus.ny.us; (c) Monroe

Private non-profit/ 1975/ Board of Trustees/ staff: 30(v)/ members: 180

HISTORY MUSEUM: Collects, preserves, displays, and interprets artifacts and provides information from the transportation history of upstate New York and surrounding area.

PROGRAMS: Community Outreach; Exhibits; Family Programs; Film/Video; Guided Tours; Interpretation; Living History; Research Library/Archives

COLLECTIONS: [1860-present] Horse drawn, trolley, interurban and railroad vehicles; artifacts; autos; trucks; bicycles; Archives and library for research, model railroad room, 2 miles of demonstration railroad with track, partially electrified for trolley operation.

HOURS: Yr Su 11-5 and by appt.

ADMISSION: $5, Student $3; Half price in winter

WEST POINT

6186
Constitution Island Association
United States Military Academy, 10996 [PO Box 41, 10996]; (p) (914) 446-8676; www.constitutionisland.org; (c) Orange

Private non-profit/ 1917/ Constitution Island

Association Board of Trustees/ staff: 3(p); 70(v)/ members: 240/publication: *Annual Report of the Constitution Island Association*

GARDEN; HISTORIC SITE; HISTORICAL SOCIETY; HOUSE MUSEUM: Operates Constitution Island, the site of ruins from the Revolutionary War fortifications, gardens, and the historic 19th c Warner House, a fully furnished farmhouse.

PROGRAMS: Annual Meeting; Community Outreach; Exhibits; Family Programs; Garden Tours; Guided Tours; Interpretation; Publication; Reenactments; Library/ Archives

COLLECTIONS: [1836-1915] Furniture, textiles, books, clothing, letters, manuscripts, paintings, kitchen equipment, personal belongings of the Warner family who lived at Constitution Island from 1835-1915.

HOURS: May-Sept W-Th 1-4

ADMISSION: $10, Children $9; Under 2 free

6187
Warner House
Constitution Island, 10996 [PO Box 41, 10996]; (p) (914) 446-8676

1777/ US Military Academy/ staff: 3(p); 65(v)

COLLECTIONS: Furniture, books; letters from graduates of West Point, letters from friends, account books, literary manuscripts.

HOURS: Seasonal

WEST SAYULLE

6188
Long Island Maritime Museum
86 W Ave, 11796 [PO Box 184, 11796]; (p) (516) 447-8679; (f) (516) 854-4974; (c) Suffolk

Private non-profit/ 1966/ staff: 2(f); 8(p); 156(v)/ members: 749/publication: *The Dolphin*

HISTORY MUSEUM; MARITIME MUSEUM: Museum preserves the history and heritage of Long Island's maritime history.

PROGRAMS: Annual Meeting; Community Outreach; Concerts; Elder's Programs; Exhibits; Facility Rental; Family Programs; Festivals; Film/Video; Guided Tours; Interpretation; Lectures; Publication; Research Library/ Archives; School-Based Curriculum

COLLECTIONS: [1880-1940] Region's largest and most comprehensive collection of small craft, vessels, art and artifacts.

HOURS: Yr M-Sa 10-3, Su 12-4

ADMISSION: $3; Children, Seniors $1.50

WEST SENECA

6189
West Seneca Historical Society Inc.
919 Mill Rd, 14224 [PO Box 2, 14224]; (p) (716) 674-4283; (c) Erie

Joint/ 1946/ staff: 1(p); 15(v)/ members: 390

HISTORY MUSEUM; HOUSE MUSEUM

PROGRAMS: Annual Meeting; Exhibits

COLLECTIONS: [BC-present] Native American artifacts, cut glass from factory, Victorian era furniture, pictures, books, musical instruments.

HOURS: Yr Sa-Su 10-4

WESTFIELD

6190
Chatauqua County Historical Society/ McClurg Museum
Village Park, 14787 [PO Box 7, 14787]; (p) (716) 326-2977; (c) Chautauqua

Private non-profit/ 1883/ staff: 1(f); 2(p); 25(v)/ members: 200

HISTORICAL SOCIETY; HISTORY MUSEUM: Fosters an interest in and knowledge of the history of Chautauqua County through the collection, preservation, and interpretation of objects and archival material of local historical significance.

PROGRAMS: Annual Meeting; Exhibits; Family Programs; Guided Tours; Lectures; Reenactments; Research Library/Archives

COLLECTIONS: [1800-1900] Archival materials, local genealogy, furnishings, fine art, and local artifacts from the collection of the CCHS.

HOURS: Winter M-F 10-4:30; Summer T-Sa 10-4:30

ADMISSION: $1.50, Students, Children $.50, Seniors $1

6191
McClurg Museum
Village Park, 14787 [PO Box 7, 14787]; (p) (716) 326-2977; obediah@netsync.net

1818/ staff: 1(f); 1(p); 2(v)

COLLECTIONS: [Late 19th c] Fine art and artifacts of mid 19th c and relating to the county's earliest settlement; Albion Tourge Papers - Law Schools, William B. Cushing - naval record.

HOURS: Yr

WHITE PLAINS

6192
Westchester County Genealogical Society
LDS Family Hist Library: Rt 134 801 Kitchawan Rd, 10603 [PO Box 518, 10603-0518]; (f) (914) 739-6481; pages.prodigy.com/ hfbk19a/wcgs.htm; (c) Westchester

Private non-profit/ 1982/ members: 400/publication: *Surname List, Westchester Connections*

GENEALOGICAL SOCIETY: Assists members and others in pursuit of genealogical research in addition to publishing material on Westchester County.

PROGRAMS: Lectures; Publication; Research Library/Archives

COLLECTIONS: [1600-present] Family produced family histories, genealogy books, local history.

HOURS: Yr T-Th 9-12/7-9

ADMISSION: $3

WILLSBORO

6193
1812 Homestead Educational Foundation
Reber Rd N, 12996 [PO Box 507, 12996]; (p) (518) 963-4071; (c) Essex

Private non-profit/ 1973/ Board of Directors/ staff: 2(f)/ members: 100

GARDEN; HISTORIC SITE; HISTORY MUSEUM; HOUSE MUSEUM; LIVING HISTORY/ OUTDOOR MUSEUM: Maintains a working farm and museum enjoyed by the public seasonally and school groups year round where hands-on experience teaches about 19th c life.

PROGRAMS: Community Outreach; Exhibits; Facility Rental; Festivals; Garden Tours; Guided Tours; Interpretation; Living History

COLLECTIONS: [1812-1850s]

HOURS: Late June-Early Oct Daily 12-4

ADMISSION: $2.50, Children $1

WYOMING

6194
Middlebury Historical Society
22 Academy St, 14591; (p) (716) 495-6692; (c) Wyoming

Private non-profit/ 1906/ New York State/ staff: 2(p); 20(v)/ members: 75

HISTORIC SITE; HISTORICAL SOCIETY; RESEARCH CENTER: Provides reference and research assistance, maintains historic collection of books, maps, letters, artifacts related to The town and its history. Museum housed in historic (1817) Middlebury Academy.

PROGRAMS: Annual Meeting; Exhibits; Guided Tours; Interpretation; Research Library/ Archives

COLLECTIONS: [Mid 1800s-WW II] Middlebury Academy (1817-1912) textbook collections; local historical documents; artifacts and early agricultural tools; local household furnishings; early fire-fighting apparatus; books, maps, letters, and photos related to town of Middlebury history.

HOURS: May-Oct Su 2-5, T 10-4

ADMISSION: Donations accepted

YERINGTON

6195
Lyon County Museum
215 S Main, 89447; (p) (775) 463-6576; (c) Lyon

Private non-profit/ 1978/ staff: 35(v)/ members: 130

HISTORIC PRESERVATION AGENCY; HISTORIC SITE; HISTORICAL SOCIETY; HISTORY MUSEUM: Maintains a museum featuring local historical displays including mining, agricultural, and recreational endeavors.

PROGRAMS: Annual Meeting; Exhibits; Guided Tours; Lectures

COLLECTIONS: Mining and agricultural materals, and a schoolhouse plus a natural history building.

HOURS: Yr Th-Su 1-4

ADMISSION: Donations accepted

YONKERS

6196
Glenview Mansion
511 Warburton Ave, 10701; (p) (914) 963-4550; (f) (914) 963-8558; hrm@hrm.org; www.hrm.org

1876/ staff: 28(f); 10(p); 120(v)

COLLECTIONS: [1876-1922] Late 19th c domestic decorative arts, paintings, Pabst side board, Eastlake inspired grand staircase; 19th c local and travel photography.

6197
Philipse Manor Hall State Historic Site
29 Dock St, 10702 [PO Box 496, 10702]; (p) (914) 965-4027; (f) (914) 965-6485; (c) Westchester

State/ 1972/ NY State Office Parks, Rec and Hist Preservation/ staff: 9(f); 3(p); 20(v)/ members: 100

HISTORIC SITE; STATE PARK: Preserves and interprets 300 years of Yonkers history through its architectural past.

PROGRAMS: Annual Meeting; Community Outreach; Concerts; Exhibits; Facility Rental; Family Programs; Festivals; Guided Tours; Interpretation; Lectures; Research Library/ Archives; School-Based Curriculum

COLLECTIONS: [1750-1868] Cochran collection of American portraiture of American heroes and statesman, High Georgian style, American Gothic architecture.

HOURS: Apr-Oct W-Sa 12-5, Su 1-4

ADMISSION: Donations accepted

YORKTOWN HEIGHTS

6198
Yorktown Museum
1974 Commerce St, 10598; (p) (914) 962-2970; (f) (914) 243-7058; www.yorktownmuseum.org; (c) Westchester

1966/ Town of Yorktown, NY/ staff: 2(p); 5(v)/ members: 150

HISTORY MUSEUM: Preserves and exhibits local history of Yorktown.

PROGRAMS: Community Outreach; Exhibits; Family Programs; Film/Video; Guided Tours; Interpretation; Research Library/Archives; School-Based Curriculum

COLLECTIONS: [17th c-present] Agricultural and household tools & equipment, costumes, manuscripts, textiles, archives, dollhouses, toys and dolls, ephemera, photographs, spinning & weaving equipment, 1,500 volume library.

HOURS: Yr T 12-4, Th 10-1

ADMISSION: Donations accepted

YOUNGSTOWN

6199
Old Fort Niagara Association
Fort Niagara State Park, 14174 [Box 169, 14174]; (p) (716) 745-7611; (f) (716) 745-9141; ofn@oldfortniagara.org; www.oldfort niagara.org

Private non-profit/ 1927/ Board of Directors/ staff: 10(f); 75(p); 2120(v)/ members: 900

HISTORIC SITE; HISTORY MUSEUM; LIVING HISTORY/OUTDOOR MUSEUM; RESEARCH CENTER: Preserves Fort Niagara Historic landmark and collects artifacts and documentary materials related to the history of

the site and the Niagara frontier.

PROGRAMS: Annual Meeting; Community Outreach; Concerts; Exhibits; Facility Rental; Family Programs; Festivals; Film/Video; Guided Tours; Interpretation; Lectures; Living History; Publication; Reenactments; Research Library/Archives; School-Based Curriculum

COLLECTIONS: [1726-1871] 18th c buildings, extensive fortifications constructed between 1726 and 1871, library, photographs, manuscripts, 100,000 artifacts recovered from the site. Structures include French Castle (1726), Powder Magazine (1757), 2 Redoubts (1770 & 1771), and a Bakehouse (1762).

HOURS: Yr Jan-Mar 9-5:30; April-May 9-5:30, Sa-Su 9-6:30; June 9-5:30, Sa-Su 9-7:30; July-Aug 9-7:30; Sept 9-5:30, Sa-Su 9-6:30

ADMISSION: $6.75, Children $4.50, Seniors $5.50

NORTH CAROLINA

ABERDEEN

6200
Malcolm Blue Historical Society
Bethesda Rd, 28315 [PO Box 603, 28315-0603]; (p) (910) 944-7558; (c) Moore

Private non-profit/ 1973/ staff: 1(p); 12(v)/ members: 300

HISTORIC PRESERVATION AGENCY; HISTORIC SITE; HISTORICAL SOCIETY; HISTORY MUSEUM; HOUSE MUSEUM: Interprets 19th c life in Moore County through preservation of artifacts significant to rural history, folk life programs that demonstrate cultural heritage, and farm presentations on typical activities of early Pine Barrens life.

PROGRAMS: Annual Meeting; Exhibits; Facility Rental; Festivals; Guided Tours; Lectures; Reenactments; School-Based Curriculum

COLLECTIONS: [1825-1900] Farm tools, medicines, logging industry artifacts, Civil War history, pottery, country store, basketry, Malcolm Blue family genealogy, and the Nationally Registered Malcolm Blue Homestead.

HOURS: Yr Th-Sa 1-4

ADMISSION: No charge

ALBEMARLE

6201
Snuggs House
112 N 3rd St, 28001

1850

HOUSE MUSEUM: Home of Buck Snuggs, a well-known and much respected county sheriff in the late 19th c. This is the 3rd oldest house in Albemarle and has a log cabin core.

COLLECTIONS: [Late 19th c] Victorian furniture and textiles, clothing, quilts, blankets.

6202
Stanly County Museum
245 E Main St, 28001; (p) (704) 986-3777; (f) (704) 986-3778; www.co.stanly.nc.us/Museum/index.htm; (c) Stanly

County/ 1973/ Stanly County Historic Preservation Commission/ staff: 2(f); 1(p); 40(v)/ members: 250/publication: *Museum News*

ALLIANCE OF HISTORICAL AGENCIES; HISTORIC PRESERVATION AGENCY; HISTORICAL SOCIETY; HISTORY MUSEUM; HOUSE MUSEUM; RESEARCH CENTER: Promotes Stanly County's heritage through a modern visitor center and two restored historic homes.

PROGRAMS: Community Outreach; Exhibits; Festivals; Guided Tours; Publication; Research Library/Archives

COLLECTIONS: [Prehistory-present] Artifacts from all periods of county history.

HOURS: Yr M-F 8:30-5; 1st Sa 10-2

ADMISSION: No charge

6203
Stanly County Historic Preservation Commission
245 E Main St, 28001; (p) (704) 986-3777; (f) (704) 986-3778; cdwyer@co.stanly.nc.us; www.co.stanly.nc.us/Departments/Museum/info.htm; (c) Stanly

County/ 1973/ Stanly County/ staff: 2(f); 1(p); 40(v)/ members: 300/publication: *Stanly County, North Carolina*

HISTORIC PRESERVATION AGENCY; HISTORIC SITE; HISTORICAL SOCIETY; HISTORY MUSEUM; HOUSE MUSEUM; RESEARCH CENTER: Researches, records, conserves, and interprets the history of Stanly County for the benefit of all North Carolinians.

PROGRAMS: Community Outreach; Exhibits; Family Programs; Film/Video; Guided Tours; Interpretation; Publication; Research Library/ Archives

COLLECTIONS: [1847-1940] Native American, industrial, military, and Southern history. Two historic houses, a research room and archived historical documents.

HOURS: Yr M-F 8:30-5, 1st Sa

ADMISSION: No charge

APEX

6204
Apex Historical Society
1101 Olive Chapel Rd, 27502 [PO Box 506, 27502]; (p) (919) 362-8980; (f) (919) 362-8980; (c) Wake

Private non-profit/ 1987/ Board of Directors/ staff: 20(v)/ members: 120/publication: *Dispatch*

GARDEN; GENEALOGICAL SOCIETY; HISTORIC PRESERVATION AGENCY; HISTORIC SITE; HISTORICAL SOCIETY; HISTORY MUSEUM; HOUSE MUSEUM

PROGRAMS: Annual Meeting; Community Outreach; Exhibits; Festivals; Garden Tours; Guided Tours; Interpretation; Lectures; Living History; Publication; Reenactments; Research Library/Archives; School-Based Curriculum

COLLECTIONS: [Late 1880s] Furniture, pianos, photographs, early home furnishings, horse-drawn farm equipment, and a 1870 farmhouse.

HOURS: Yr by appt

ASHEBORO

6205
Randolph County Genealogical Society
201 Worth St, Randolph County Public Library, 27204 [PO Box 4394, 27204]; (p) (336) 318-6815; (c) Randolph

Private non-profit/ 1977/ staff: 7(v)/ members: 502/publication: *The Genealogical Journal of Randolph County*

GENEALOGICAL SOCIETY: Assists patrons with research on Randolph County ancestors to learn more about them. Publishes a quarterly journal with source materials on Randolph County and its early inhabitants.

PROGRAMS: Guided Tours; Lectures; Publication; Research Library/Archives

COLLECTIONS: Family folders with miscellaneous materials, census records, some on microfilm, genealogy and heritage books, church histories, and cemetery records.

HOURS: Yr M,Th-Sa 9-5, T-W 9-9

ASHEVILLE

6206
Biltmore Estate
1 Biltmore Plaza, 28801 [1 N Pack Sq, 28801]; (p) (800) 543-2961; happenings@biltmore.com; www.biltmore.com; (c) Buncombe

Private for-profit/ 1895/ staff: 650(f); 275(p)

GARDEN; HISTORIC SITE; HOUSE MUSEUM: Privately-owned, national historic landmark. Includes George Vanderbilt's 250-room French Renaissance chateau (1895), along with 8,000 acres of forest, farmland, and pleasure gardens.

PROGRAMS: Concerts; Exhibits; Facility Rental; Festivals; Garden Tours; Guided Tours; Lectures; School-Based Curriculum

COLLECTIONS: [Late 19th-early 20th c] 250-room mansion faithfully preserved and filled with original furnishings, including works by artists Durer, Sargent, and Renoir. Biltmore House presents a detailed portrait of the great 19th c country estate.

HOURS: Jan-Mar Daily 9-5; Apr-Dec 8:30-5

ADMISSION: $29.95, Student $22.50; Under 9 free

6207
Biltmore Industries
111 Grovewood Rd, 28804; (p) (828) 253-7651; (f) (828) 254-2489; grovewood@grovewood.com; www.grovewood.com; (c) Buncombe

Private for-profit/ 1917/ staff: 8(f); 9(p)

HISTORIC SITE; HISTORY MUSEUM: Maintains Grovewood Gallery, Estes-Winn-Blomberg Automobile Museum, Biltmore Homespun Museum, and Grovewood Studios.

PROGRAMS: Exhibits

HOURS: Jan-Mar F-Sa 10-5; Apr-Dec M-Sa 10-5, Su 1-5

6208
Biltmore Village Historic Museum
7 Biltmore Plaza, 28803; (c) Buncombe

Private non-profit/ 1989/ staff: 2(p)/ members: 200

HISTORIC SITE: Houses information through photographs, maps, and drawings for the Biltmore Village Cottages, postcards, and vintage artifacts.

PROGRAMS: Guided Tours; Lectures

COLLECTIONS: [Late 19th c-present]

HOURS: Yr M-Sa 12-4

6209
Blue Ridge Parkway
1 W Pack Sq, Ste 400, 28801-3417; (p) (828) 271-4779; (f) (828) 271-4313; Jackie_Holt@nps.gov; www.nps.gov/parks.html; (c) Buncombe

Federal/ 1935/ Dept of Interior, National Park Service/ staff: 145(f); 10(p); 50(v)

HISTORIC PRESERVATION AGENCY: Links Shenandoah National Park in VA and the Great Smoky Mountains National Park in TN by way of a recreation-oriented motor road.

PROGRAMS: Exhibits; Guided Tours; Interpretation; Lectures; Living History; Research Library/Archives; School-Based Curriculum

COLLECTIONS: [1870-1930] Geology, Appalachian Mountain culture, furnishings, household items, archives and a herbarium collection.

6210
Old Buncombe County Genealogical Society, Inc.
Innsbruck Mall, Ste 22, 85 S Tunnel Rd, 28802 [PO Box 2122, 28802-2122]; (p) (828) 253-1894; obcgs@buncombe.main.nc.us; www.OBCGS.com; (c) Buncombe

Private non-profit/ 1979/ Board of Directors/ staff: 54(v)/ members: 560/publication: *A Lot of Bunkum*

GENEALOGICAL SOCIETY: Promotes interest in family history and genealogy through educational programs, workshops, and publications. Encourages and instructs members in the standards and techniques of genealogical research and compilation. Serves the community as a medium of exchange for genealogical information.

PROGRAMS: Annual Meeting; Exhibits; Lectures; Publication; Research Library/Archives; School-Based Curriculum

COLLECTIONS: [18th c-present] 9,000 volumes of computer cataloged resource material which includes land, tax and church records, cemetery inscriptions, published obituaries, and ancestors charts.

HOURS: Yr M 1-5/7-9, T-F 9-5, Sa 9-1

ADMISSION: $3; Mbrs free

6211
Preservation Society of Asheville and Buncombe County, Inc.
13 Biltmore Ave, 28802 [PO Box 2806, 28802]; (p) (828) 254-2343; (f) (828) 254-2343; (c) Buncombe

Private non-profit/ 1976/ staff: 1(f)/ members: 375

HISTORIC PRESERVATION AGENCY: Historic preservation through advocacy, education, technical assistance, and acquisition, protection, and resale of historical properties.

PROGRAMS: Annual Meeting; Guided Tours; Interpretation; Lectures

HOURS: Yr M-F 9-5

6212
Smith-McDowell House Museum
283 Victoria Rd, 28801; (p) (704) 253-9231; (f) (704) 253-9231; smith-mcdowell-house@worldnet.

1848/ staff: 1(f); 2(p); 30(v)

COLLECTIONS: [1840-1910] Furnishings, personal family-related items, Victoran from 1840-1910; family photographs, documents, newspaper articles.

6213
Southern Highland Handicraft Guild
275 Riceville Rd; Folk Art Center, Blue Ridge Pkwy, 28815 [PO Box 9545, 28815]; (p) (828) 298-7928; (f) (828) 298-7962; shcg@buncombe.main.nc.us; www.southernhighlandguild.org; (c) Buncombe

Private non-profit/ 1930/ Board of Trustees/ staff: 20(f); 30(p); 65(v)/ members: 700/publication: *Highland Highlights*

PROFESSIONAL ORGANIZATION: An educational organization that brings together the crafts and craftspeople of the Southern Highlands for the benefit of shared resources, education, conservation and marketing.

PROGRAMS: Community Outreach; Concerts; Exhibits; Family Programs; Festivals; Interpretation; Lectures; Publication

COLLECTIONS: [1920-present] Southern Appalachian region crafts and folk art with an extensive library and archive of the Appalachian Craft Revival.

HOURS: Jan-Mar Daily 9-5; Apr-Dec Daily 9-6

ADMISSION: No charge

6214
Thomas Wolfe Memorial State Historic Site
52 N Market St, 28801; (p) (828) 253-8304; (f) (828) 252-8121; WolfeMemorial@worldnet.att.net; wolfememorial.home.att.net; (c) Buncombe

State/ 1975/ NC Dept of Cultural Resources/ staff: 6(f); 5(p)

HISTORIC SITE: Maintains the boyhood home of the famous, American, 20th c writer. "Look Homeward, Angel," Wolfe's first and most famous novel was set in his mother's boarding house, now the Thomas Wolfe Memorial.

PROGRAMS: Exhibits; Festivals; Guided Tours; Interpretation; Living History

COLLECTIONS: [20th c] Original furnishings of Wolfe's boyhood home, his typewriters and contents of his New York apartment, and artifacts from the Woedfin Street home where he was born.

HOURS: Apr-Oct M-Sa 9-5, Su 1-4

6215
Western North Carolina Historical Association
Smith-McDowell House Museum, 28801 [283 Victoria Rd, 28801-4817]; (p) (828) 253-9231; (f) (828) 253-5518; smithmcdowellhouse@ msn.com; www.wnchistory.org; (c) Buncombe

Private non-profit/ 1952/ Board of Trustees/ staff: 2(f); 3(p); 20(v)/ members: 500/publication: *Around the House*

GARDEN; HISTORICAL SOCIETY; HOUSE MUSEUM: Promotes and preserves Western North Carolina's history. Its major project is the restoration and operation of Smith-McDowell House Museum, a 1840 structure that is Asheville's oldest house.

PROGRAMS: Annual Meeting; Community Outreach; Concerts; Elder's Programs; Exhibits; Facility Rental; Family Programs; Festivals; Garden Tours; Guided Tours; Interpretation; Lectures; Living History; Publication; Reenactments; Research Library/Archives; School-Based Curriculum

COLLECTIONS: [1840-1940] Furnishings, textiles, photographs, portraits, manuscripts, books, and decorative items used to interpret the Smith-McDowell House.

HOURS: Jan-Mar T-Sa 10-4; Apr-Dec T-Sa 10-4, Su 1-4

ADMISSION: $4.50, Student $3.50, Children $3.50, Seniors $3.50

6216
Western Office, North Carolina Division of Archives and History
1 Village Ln, Ste 3, 28803; (p) (828) 274-6789; (f) (828) 274-6995; rholland@ncsl.dcr.state.nc.us; (c) Buncombe

State/ 1978/ State of NC/ staff: 10(f)

PROFESSIONAL ORGANIZATION: Provides services to Western NC in the areas of archaeology, historic preservation, archives, and records management, historic sites education, museum, and historical society planning and development.

PROGRAMS: Exhibits; Lectures; Research Library/Archives

COLLECTIONS: National Register of Historic Places files, architectural and archaeological inventories, staff research collection.

HOURS: Yr M-F 7:30-5:30

ADMISSION: No charge

BAILEY

6217
Country Doctor Museum Foundation
6642 Peele Rd, 27807 [PO Box 34, 27807-0034]; (p) (252) 235-4165; (c) Nash

Private non-profit/ 1967/ staff: 5(p); 25(v)

HISTORY MUSEUM: Preserves and displays medical instruments and tools of pharmacy used by country doctors.

PROGRAMS: Annual Meeting; Exhibits; Garden Tours; Guided Tours; Interpretation

COLLECTIONS: [17th-20th c]

HOURS: Yr

ADMISSION: $3, Children $1, Seniors $2

BARNARDSVILLE

6218
Big Ivy Historical Society, Inc.
Dillingham Rd, Big Ivy Community, 28709 [PO Box 416, 28709]; (p) (828) 626-4143; westcrew@tds.net; (c) Buncombe

Joint; Private non-profit/ 1980/ Board of Trustees/ staff: 1(f), 55(v)/ members: 205/publication: *Dillinghams of Big Ivy; A Family Named Dillingham*

ALLIANCE OF HISTORICAL AGENCIES; HISTORIC PRESERVATION AGENCY; LIVING HISTORY/OUTDOOR MUSEUM: Preserves the history of the Big Ivy Community and promotes knowledge and appreciation for local history.

PROGRAMS: Annual Meeting; Community Outreach; Concerts; Exhibits; Facility Rental; Festivals; Garden Tours; Guided Tours; Interpretation; Lectures; Living History; Publication; Reenactments; School-Based Curriculum

COLLECTIONS: [Mid 19th c-present] Pre-Civil War, furnished dogtrot, detached kitchen and smoke house, spring house and 1898 schoolhouse known as the "Henry Stevens Carson Pre-Civil War Site."

HOURS: Apr-Oct Daily 10-5

ADMISSION: Donations accepted

BATH

6219
Historic Bath State Historic Site
207 Carteret St, 27808 [PO Box 148, 27808]; (p) (252) 923-3971; (f) (252) 923-0174; HistoricBath@tri-countynet.net; www.ah.dcr.state.nc.us/sections/hs/bath/bath. htm; (c) Beaufort

State/ 1962/ NC Dept of Cultural Resources/ staff: 5(f); 5(p)

HISTORIC SITE; HOUSE MUSEUM: Interprets 18th and 19th c life in NC's oldest town. Site includes Palmer-Marsh House, 1751 and Bonner House, 1830.

PROGRAMS: Exhibits; Family Programs; Film/Video; Guided Tours; Interpretation

COLLECTIONS: [18th-19th c] Upper class furnishings.

HOURS: Apr-Oct M-Sa 9-5, Su 1-5; Nov-Mar T-Sa 10-4, Su 1-4

ADMISSION: $2, Student $1, Under 6 free

BEAUFORT

6220
Beaufort Historic Preservation Commission
215 Pollock St, 28516 [PO Box 390, 28516]; (p) (252) 728-2141; (f) (252) 728-3982; (c) Carteret

Joint/ 1984/ Town of Beaufort/ staff: 2(f)

HISTORIC PRESERVATION AGENCY: Oversees and approves new growth or changes in the historic district; approves and issues certificates for plagued homes; and preserves historic structures and the maritime environment.

PROGRAMS: Community Outreach; Monthly Meeting

6221
Beaufort Historical Association
130 Turner St, 28516 [PO Box 1709, 28516]; (p) (252) 728-5225; (f) (252) 728-4966; bha@bmd.clis.com; www.blackbeardthepirate. com; (c) Carteret

Private non-profit/ 1960/ Board of Governors/ staff: 4(f); 8(p); 200(v)/ members: 1200

HISTORIC SITE; HISTORICAL SOCIETY; HISTORY MUSEUM; HOUSE MUSEUM

PROGRAMS: Annual Meeting; Exhibits; Facility Rental; Guided Tours; Interpretation; Lectures

COLLECTIONS: [1732-1859] Three restored homes with Victorian furnishings; 1859 apothecary/doctor's office; 1829 jail, 1796 courthouse and 1732 house used as art gallery.

HOURS: Apr-Oct M-Sa 9:30-5; Nov-Mar M-Sa 10-4

6222
North Carolina Maritime Museum
315 Front St, 28516; (p) (252) 728-7317; (f) (252) 728-2108; maritime@ncsl.dcr.state.nc.us; www.ah.dcr.state.nc.us/maritime; (c) Carteret

State/ 1975/ NC Dept of Cultural Resources/ staff: 18(f); 4(p); 100(v)/ members: 1300/publication: *Tributaries; The Waterline; and others*

HISTORY MUSEUM: Preserves and interprets all aspects of the rich maritime heritage of the state through educational exhibits, programs and field trips.

PROGRAMS: Annual Meeting; Community Outreach; Concerts; Elder's Programs; Exhibits; Facility Rental; Family Programs; Festivals; Film/Video; Guided Tours; Interpretation; Lectures; Living History; Publication; Research Library/Archives; School-Based Curriculum

COLLECTIONS: [1910-1960] Archives, rare books, photographs, textiles, decorative arts, small crafts, outboards, ship models, decoys, maritime tools, archaeological materials, fossils and natural history items.

HOURS: Yr M-F 9-5, Sa 10-5, Su 1-5

ADMISSION: No charge

BELHAVEN

6223
Belhaven Memorial Museum
210 E Main St, 27810 [PO Box 220, 27810]; www.beaufort-county/BelhavenMuseum.com; (c) Beaufort

Private non-profit/ 1965/ Board of Directors/ staff: 2(p); 5(v)/publication: *What's Cooking; The Wayfarer*

HISTORY MUSEUM: Folk heritage museum that collects, displays, and preserves artifacts of Beaufort County and Eastern NC.

PROGRAMS: Community Outreach; Exhibits; Festivals; Publication

COLLECTIONS: [19th-early 20th c] Artifacts reflecting people's connections with the farm and/or the sea such as tools, clothes, china, coins, furniture, and Civil War and other military items.

HOURS: Yr

BOONE

6224
Appalachian Consortium, Inc.
University Hall Dr, 28608 [PO Box 32017, Appalachian State University, 28608]; (p) (828) 262-2064; (f) (828) 262-6564; burlesonec@appstate.edu; www.uvawise.edu/appalcon; (c) Watauga

Private non-profit/ 1971/ Board of Directors/ staff: 2(f); 185(v)/ members: 20

ALLIANCE OF HISTORICAL AGENCIES: Preserves the heritage of Southern Appalachia. Publishes over 60 titles on the Appalachian region in fiction and non-fiction.

PROGRAMS: Annual Meeting; Exhibits

HOURS: Yr M-F 8-5

6225
Appalachian Cultural Museum, The
University Hall Dr, 28608 [University Hall, Appalachian State University, 28608]; (p) (828) 262-3117; (f) (828) 262-2920; watkinsca@appstate.edu; www.museum.appstate.edu; (c) Watauga

State/ 1984/ Appalachian State University/ staff: 3(f); 2(p); 25(v)

HISTORY MUSEUM: Interprets the history and culture of the mountains of Western NC from prehistory to the present.

PROGRAMS: Community Outreach; Concerts; Exhibits; Facility Rental; Festivals; Garden Tours; Guided Tours; Interpretation; Lectures; Living History; Research Library/ Archives; School-Based Curriculum

COLLECTIONS: [20th c] Artifacts relating to the Appalachian region and ranges from prehistoric Native American lithics to a section of the defunct mountain theme park, The Land of Oz, and two Winston cup race cars once owned by the legendary Junior Johnson.

HOURS: Yr T-Sa 10-5, Su 1-5

ADMISSION: $4, Children $2, Seniors $3.50; Under 10 free

6226
Genealogical Society of Watauga County
140 Queen St, 28607 [PO Box 126, 28607]; (p) (828) 264-7813; heatmjw@appstate.edu; (c) Watauga

State/ 1987/ staff: 1(f)/ members: 120/publication: *Watauga Ancestry*

GENEALOGICAL SOCIETY: Assists in local research for patrons of Watauga County Library and directs inquires to Sanna Gaffney.

PROGRAMS: Annual Meeting; Publication

6227
Hickory Ridge Homestead Living History Museum
591 Horn in the W Dr, 28607 [PO Box 295, 28607]; (p) (828) 264-2120; (f) (828) 268-0105; johnapeterson@hotmail.com; www.boonenc.org/saha; (c) Watauga

Private non-profit/ 1980/ Southern Appalachian Historical Association/ staff: 3(f); 5(p); 25(v)/ members: 40

HOUSE MUSEUM; LIVING HISTORY/OUTDOOR MUSEUM: Depicts everyday life in western NC during the late 18th c.

PROGRAMS: Community Outreach; Festivals; Guided Tours; Interpretation; Living History; Publication; Reenactments

COLLECTIONS: [1785-1805] Six cabins and a weaving house.

HOURS: May-mid June, mid Aug-late Oct Sa 9-4, Su 1-4; Mid June-mid Aug T-Su 1-8:30

ADMISSION: Donations requested

BOONVILLE

6228
Historic Richmond Hill Law School Commission
3801 River Rd, 27011 [PO Box 309, 27011]; (p) (336) 367-7251; (f) (336) 367-3637; yveddi@yadtel.net; (c) Yadkin

County/ 1970/ Yadkin County/ staff: 1(p); 15(v)

HISTORIC SITE

PROGRAMS: Guided Tours; Interpretation

COLLECTIONS: [1848-1878]

HOURS: Pearson Home: Apr-Oct Su; Nature Park: Yr Daily daytime, evening by appt

ADMISSION: Donations accepted

BREVARD

6229
Transylvania County Historical Society, Inc.
Silvermont Basement/Allison Deaver House, Hwy 280, 28712 [PO Box 2061, 28712]; (p) (828) 884-5137; (f) (828) 884-5137; (c) Transylvania

Private non-profit/ 1987/ Board of Directors/ staff: 80(v)/ members: 325

HISTORIC SITE; HISTORICAL SOCIETY; HOUSE MUSEUM: Fosters an appreciation of local cultural heritage. Preserves and revitalizes the livability of the community by encouraging preservation of the county's historic environment.

PROGRAMS: Annual Meeting; Community Outreach; Exhibits; Family Programs; Festivals; Garden Tours; Guided Tours; Interpretation; Lectures; Living History; Reenactments

COLLECTIONS: [1815-1865] Early farm implements and household furnishings.

HOURS: Apr-Oct F 1-4, Sa 10-4, Su 1-4 and by appt

BUIES CREEK

6230
North Carolina Association of Historians
D Rich Bldg, Campbell Univ, 27506 [PO Box 356, 27506]; (p) (910) 893-1485; (f) (910) 893-1424; martinj@mailcenter.campbell.edu; (c) Harnett

Private non-profit/ 1974/ staff: 6(v)/ members: 90/publication: *Journal of the North Carolina Association of Historians*

Promotes and stimulates an interest in history through research, teaching, and publication by historians.

BURGAW

6231
Pender County Historical Society
200 W Bridgers St, 28435 [PO Box 1380, 28435]; (p) (910) 259-8543; (c) Pender

Private non-profit/ 1962/ staff: 15(v)/ members: 90

HISTORICAL SOCIETY; HISTORY MUSEUM; RESEARCH CENTER

PROGRAMS: Exhibits; Facility Rental; Guided Tours; Research Library/Archives

COLLECTIONS: [1850-present] Artifacts, documents, photographs, and a genealogy collection open for research.

HOURS: Yr Th-Sa 1-4; Meetings: Feb, May, Sept, Nov 3rd Su in month 3-5

ADMISSION: No charge

BURLINGTON

6232
Alamance Battleground State Historic Site
5803 S NC Hwy 62, 27215; (p) (336) 227-4785; (f) (336) 227-4787; alamance@nesl.denstate.nc.us; (c) Alamance

State/ 1955/ N.C. Dept. of Cultural Resources/Division of Archives and History/ staff: 2(f); 3(p)/publication: *Alamance Battleground Brochure*

HISTORIC SITE; HISTORY MUSEUM; HOUSE MUSEUM; LIVING HISTORY/OUTDOOR MUSEUM: Preserves, interprets, and maintains historic resources pertaining to the Battle of Alamance (May 16, 1771) and life in the 18th c NC backcountry.

PROGRAMS: Community Outreach; Exhibits; Guided Tours; Interpretation; Lectures; Living History; Publication; Reenactments; Research Library/Archives; School-Based Curriculum

COLLECTIONS: [Mid-late 18th c] Military and domestic artifacts.

HOURS: Apr-Oct M-Sa 9-5, Su 1-5; Nov-Mar T-Sa 10-4, Su 1-4

ADMISSION: No charge

6233
Alamance County Genealogical Society
[PO Box 3052, 27215]; (c) Alamance

Board of Directors/ members: 170

GENEALOGICAL SOCIETY

PROGRAMS: Monthly Meeting; Publication

6234
Alamance County Historical Museum, Inc.
4777 S NC Hwy 62, 27215; (p) (336) 226-8254; (f) (336) 226-8254; (c) Alamance

Private non-profit/ 1976/ Board of Directors/ staff: 2(f); 1(p); 50(v)/ members: 600

GARDEN; HISTORIC SITE; HISTORY MUSEUM; HOUSE MUSEUM; LIVING HISTORY/OUTDOOR MUSEUM: Collects, preserves, displays, and interprets records, relics, and artifacts that contribute to an understanding and appreciation of the history of Alamance County and the NC Piedmont.

PROGRAMS: Annual Meeting; Community Outreach; Concerts; Exhibits; Facility Rental; Festivals; Garden Tours; Guided Tours; Interpretation; Lectures; Living History; Publication; Reenactments; Research Library/Archives; School-Based Curriculum

COLLECTIONS: [18th-19th c] Period furniture, porcelain, silver, textiles, paintings, photographs, and archival documents. Site includes 19th c plantation complex with house museum and period outbuildings.

HOURS: Yr T-F 9-5, Sa 10:30-5, Su 1-5

6235
Burlington Historic Preservation Commission
425 S Lexington Ave, 27216 [PO Box 1358, 27216-1358]; (p) (336) 222-5110; (f) (336) 513-5410; www.ci.burlington.nc.us; (c) Alamance

City/ 1978/ staff: 1(p); 9(v)

HISTORIC PRESERVATION AGENCY: Advises the city council regarding historic sites and preservation, reviews improvements to local historic properties, and provides technical assistance to owners of historic homes.

PROGRAMS: Guided Tours; Lectures; Monthly Meeting

COLLECTIONS: [1890-1930] Property surveys and photographs for most historic structures in Burlington.

HOURS: Yr M-F 8-5

CAMDEN

6236
County of Camden
117 N 343, 27921 [PO Box 190, 27921]; (p) (252) 338-1919; (f) (252) 333-1603; camdenco@interpath.com; (c) Camden

County/ 1777/ Board of Commissioners/ staff: 42(f); 5(p)

HISTORIC SITE: Maintains the historic 1847 Courthouse and grounds and the old jail (c.1910) that houses the election office and a restored jail upstairs plus a museum of Civil War memorabilia.

PROGRAMS: Exhibits; Guided Tours; Research Library/Archives

COLLECTIONS: [19th-20th c] Civil War and W W II memorabilia related to descendants in Camden County, a set of stocks and pillory.

HOURS: Yr M, W, F 9-1, and by appt

ADMISSION: No

CARTHAGE

6237
Bryant House/McLendon Cabin
6 miles from Pinehurst Traffic Cr, 28327 [SR 1210, Harris Crossroads, 28327]; (p) (910) 947-3995, (910) 692-7811; www.visitnc.com; (c) Moore

Maintains the Joel McLendon Cabin, c 1760, the James Bryant House c 1820.

COLLECTIONS: The Joel McLendon Cabin, c 1760, and the James Bryant House c 1820 both dwellings have been unaltered except for restoration.

HOURS: Su 2-5 and by appt

6238
McLendon Cabin
SR 1210, Harris Crossroads, 28327; (p) (910) 947-3995, (910) 692-2051; www.visitnc.com/

6239
Town of Cathage Historical Committee
203 W Barrett St, 28327 [PO Box 842, 28327]; (p) (910) 947-2331; (f) (910) 947-3079; toc@mail.ac.net; www.ac.net/~tocpw; (c) Moore

City/ staff: 10(v)

HISTORICAL SOCIETY; HISTORY MUSEUM: Collects, preserves, and interprets the community's past for the education, preservation, and enjoyment of present and future generations.

PROGRAMS: Community Outreach; Festivals; Guided Tours

COLLECTIONS: [18th-20th c] Photographs, Civil War, WW I and W W II costumes, buggies, newspaper clippings, coins, and museum artifacts.

HOURS: Yr

ADMISSION: No charge

CARY

6240
Page-Walker Arts and History Center
119 Ambassador Loop, 27512 [PO Box 8005, 27512]; (p) (919) 460-4963; (f) (919) 388-1141; smaultsb@ci.cary.nc.us; www.townofcary.org; (c) Wake

Private non-profit/ 1985/ Town of Cary/Friends of the Page-Walker Hotel, Inc./ staff: 2(f); 3(p); 35(v)/ members: 200/publication: *The Innkeeper*

ART MUSEUM; GARDEN; HISTORIC PRESERVATION AGENCY; HISTORIC SITE; HISTORY MUSEUM: Offers a full roster of classes and programs to fulfill its mission to provide arts, cultural, and historical programs.

PROGRAMS: Annual Meeting; Concerts; Exhibits; Facility Rental; Family Programs; Festivals; Film/Video; Garden Tours; Guided Tours; Interpretation; Lectures; Living History; Publication; Research Library/Archives; School-Based Curriculum; Theatre

COLLECTIONS: [19th c-present] Artifacts, displays, and documents highlighting the history of Cary and the region from the early 1800s through today.

HOURS: Yr M-W 10-9:30, Th 10-5, F 10-1

ADMISSION: No charge

CHAPEL HILL

6241
Chapel Hill Preservation Society
610 E Rosemary St, 27514; (p) (919) 942-7818; (f) (919) 942-7845; generalinfo@chps.org; www.chapelhillpreservation.com; (c) Orange

Private non-profit/ 1972/ staff: 1(f); 60(v)/ members: 400/publication: *Preservation Notes*

HISTORIC PRESERVATION AGENCY; HOUSE MUSEUM: Acts to protect, restore, and maintain historic structures including Betty Smith House and Horace Williams House.

PROGRAMS: Annual Meeting; Community Outreach; Concerts; Exhibits; Facility Rental; Family Programs; Guided Tours; Lectures; Publication

HOURS: Yr M-F 10-4, Su 1-4

ADMISSION: No charge

6242
North Carolina Collection, University of North Carolina at Chapel Hill
Wilson Library, CB 3930, 27514-8890; (p) (919) 962-1172; (f) (919) 962-4452; nccref@email.unc.edu; www.lib.unc.edu/ncc/; (c) Orange

State/ 1844/ Univ of NC at Chapel Hill/ staff: 13(f); 12(p); 3(v)/publication: *Annual Report of the North Caroliniana Society, Inc; The North Carolina Collection; and others*

LIBRARY AND/OR ARCHIVES: Collects library materials related to the Tar Heel State. It also holds publications by North Carolinians on non-state topics, plus distinguished Thomas Wolfe and Sir Walter Raleigh collections.

PROGRAMS: Exhibits; Guided Tours; Lectures; Publication; Research Library/Archives

COLLECTIONS: [16th c-present] 250,000 published items, 430,000 photographic images, 5,000 historical artifacts and a 10,000 piece numismatic collection.

HOURS: Yr M-F 8-5, Sa 9-1, Su 1-5

ADMISSION: No charge

6243
University of North Carolina at Chapel Hill, Manuscripts Department
Wilson Library, CB 3926, 27514-8890; (p) (919) 962-1345; (f) (919) 962-3594; mss@email.unc.edu; www.lib.unc.edu/mss/; (c) Orange

State/ 1930/ staff: 11(f); 20(p)

LIBRARY AND/OR ARCHIVES: Administers virtually all archival material held by the Academic Affairs Library of UNC at Chapel Hill. Contains one of the nation's foremost archival resources for the study of American folk music and popular culture.

PROGRAMS: Research Library/Archives

COLLECTIONS: [19th c-present] Southern Historical Collection with material on antebellum plantations, the Civil War and Reconstruction South. Includes manuscripts, photographs, audio recordings, film and video recordings.

CHARLOTTE

6244
Afro-American Cultural Center
401 N Myers St, 28202; (p) (704) 374-1565; (f) (704) 374-9273; www.aacc-charlotte.org; (c) Mecklenburg

Private non-profit/ 1976/ Board of Directors/ staff: 15(f); 1(p); 10(v)/ members: 400

CULTURAL CENTER: A cultural center that promotes and preserves African American art, history, and culture through visual arts, performing arts, and community and school-based educational programs.

PROGRAMS: Community Outreach; Concerts; Exhibits; Facility Rental; Festivals; Guided Tours; Interpretation; Lectures; School-Based Curriculum; Theatre

COLLECTIONS: Portraits, paintings, and three-dimensional installations from nationally as well as locally recognized artists.

HOURS: Yr T-Sa 10-6, Su 1-5

6245
Carolinas Historic Aviation Commission and Museum
4108 Airport Dr, 28208; (p) (704) 359-8442; (f) (704) 359-8442; chacboss@aol.com; (c) Mecklenburg

Private non-profit/ 1992/ Board of Directors

AVIATION MUSEUM: Preserves the aviation history of North and SC.

PROGRAMS: Annual Meeting; Family Programs; Film/Video; Guided Tours; Interpretation; Lectures; Research Library/Archives

COLLECTIONS: [1939-present] Aviation memorabilia, both military and commercial which includes aircraft and any pertinent material. Includes Piedmont Airlines DC-3 and two Vietnam OV-1's, all flyable. Other aircraft include Huey helicopters, A-4, T-28.

HOURS: Yr Daily 9-5

6246
Charlotte Historic District Commission
600 E Fourth St, 28203; (p) (704) 336-5994; (f) (704) 336-5964; pcjee@mail.charmeck.nc.us; (c) Mecklenburg

City/ 1976/ staff: 2(f); 1(p); 10(v)

HISTORIC PRESERVATION AGENCY

PROGRAMS: Community Outreach

6247
Charlotte Museum of History and Hezekina Alexander Homesite
3500 Shamrock Dr, 28215; (p) (704) 568-1774; (f) (704) 566-1817; cmhzhah@aol.com; (c) Mecklenburg

Private non-profit/ 1969/ Hezekiah Alexander Foundation/ staff: 12(f); 7(p); 54(v)

HISTORIC SITE; HISTORY MUSEUM: Educates visitors on the history and heritage of the region through exhibits, tours, events and public programs.

PROGRAMS: Exhibits; Facility Rental; Family Programs; Festivals; Garden Tours; Guided Tours; Interpretation; Lectures; Living History; Reenactments; Research Library/Archives; School-Based Curriculum

COLLECTIONS: [18th-20th c] Piedmont/Carolinas history archives, photos, documents, maps, furniture, quilts, coverlets, tools, toys, dolls, clothing, and educational hands-on materials. Fine collection of mid to late 18th c. southern furnishings and ceramics; 18th c maps and prints, (mid Atlantic - N.C./S.C.).

HOURS: Yr T-Sa 10-5, Su 1-5

ADMISSION: $6, Student $4, Children $2, Seniors $4

6248
Historic Rosedale Plantation
3427 N Tryon St, 28206; (p) (704) 335-0325; (f) (704) 335-0384; (c) Mecklenburg

Private non-profit/ 1987/ Board of Directors/ staff: 1(f); 1(p); 25(v)/ members: 200

GARDEN; HISTORIC SITE; HOUSE MUSEUM: Interprets backcountry NC plantation life. House is known for its faux-grained wainscoting and doors, original French wallpaper c 1815, hand carved woodwork and six treasure trees on property.

PROGRAMS: Exhibits; Family Programs; Garden Tours; Guided Tours; Interpretation; Lectures; Living History; School-Based Curriculum

COLLECTIONS: [1820s-1860s] House and gardens 19th c furnishings, family-related history, artifacts, and documents of the Davidsons, Caldwells, Frews, and slaves.

HOURS: Feb-Dec Th, Su 1-4

6249
Museum of the New South, Inc.
324 N College St, 28202; (p) (704) 333-1887; (f) (704) 333-1896; (c) Mecklenburg

Private non-profit/ 1991/ staff: 11(f); 3(p); 20(v)/ members: 500

HISTORY MUSEUM: Collects, exhibits, and interprets materials related to Southern history since the end of the Civil War, focusing on Carolina Piedmont, Charlotte, and surrounding area.

PROGRAMS: Community Outreach; Elder's Programs; Exhibits; Facility Rental; Family Programs; Festivals; Guided Tours; Interpretation; Lectures; School-Based Curriculum

COLLECTIONS: [1865-present] Artifacts and memoribilia related to Carolina Piedmont since the Civil War. Large collection of oral histories.

HOURS: Yr T-Sa 11-5

ADMISSION: $2; Students, Seniors, Educators $1

6250
Olde Mecklenburg Genealogical Society
[PO Box 32453, 28232-2453]; omgs002@ibm.net; (c) Mecklenburg

Joint/ 1981/ Board of Directors; County; Private non-profit/ staff: 13(v)/ members: 300/publication: Quarterly and Mecklenburg Messenger

GENEALOGICAL SOCIETY: Works to increase interest in and share knowledge of research aids through educational programs, workshops, and publications; encourages and acquaints members with sources of material and serves as a medium for the exchange of genealogical information.

PROGRAMS: Lectures; Publication

COLLECTIONS: Several books that have been authored by the Society and are available for purchase.

6251
Public Library of Charlotte and Mecklenburg County, Robinson-Spangler Carolina Room
310 N Tryon St, 28202; (p) (704) 336-2980; (f) (704) 336-6236; ncr@plcmc.lib.nc.us; www.plcmc.lib.nc.us/branch/main/NCR/; (c) Mecklenburg

County/ 1956/ Board of Trustees/ staff: 6(f); 1(p); 2(v)/publication: The Charlotte-Mecklenburg Story

LIBRARY AND/OR ARCHIVES: Collects, preserves, and presents resources in the areas of genealogy, local and state history, and current information.

PROGRAMS: Community Outreach; Exhibits; Lectures; Publication; Research Library/Archives

COLLECTIONS: [18th-20th c] Print volumes, microfilm reels, music recordings, periodicals, photographs, maps, state and local government

6252
Special Collections, Atkins Library, University of North Carolina at Charlotte
9201 University City Blvd, 28223; (p) (704) 684-2449; (f) (704) 687-2232; speccoll@email.uncc.edu; libweb.uncc.edu; (c) Mecklenburg

State/ 1946/ Board of Trustees/ staff: 5(f); 2(p)

LIBRARY AND/OR ARCHIVES; RESEARCH CENTER: A research collection of manuscripts, photographs, and architectural drawings that document the social, political, and architectural history of Mecklenburg and surrounding counties from the 18th c to the present.

PROGRAMS: Community Outreach; Exhibits; Lectures; Research Library/Archives

COLLECTIONS: 275 collections containing an estimated 1,000,000 manuscripts, 50,000 photos, and 7,500 architectural drawings.

HOURS: Yr M-F 9-5

CHEROKEE

6253
Great Smoky Mountains National Park Mountain Farm Museum
150 Hwy 441 N, 28719; (p) (828) 497-1900; (f) (828) 497-1910; (c) Swain

Federal/ 1953/ US National Park Service/ staff: 1(f); 10(v)

LIVING HISTORY/OUTDOOR MUSEUM: Comprised of nine historic log farm buildings moved from their original locations in Great Smokey Mountains National Park.

PROGRAMS: Exhibits; Festivals; Interpretation

HOURS: Yr Daily sunrise-sunset

ADMISSION: No charge

6254
Museum of the Cherokee Indian
Hwy 441 & Drama Rd, 28719 [PO Box 1599, 28719]; (p) (828) 497-3481; (f) (828) 497-4985; botaylor@cherokeemuseum.org; www.cherokeemuseum.org; (c) Swain

Private non-profit/ 1970/ staff: 12(f); 6(p); 10(v)/ members: 300/publication: Cherokee Studies

HISTORY MUSEUM; RESEARCH CENTER; TRIBAL MUSEUM

PROGRAMS: Annual Meeting; Community Outreach; Exhibits; Facility Rental; Interpretation; Lectures; Publication; Research Library/Archives

COLLECTIONS: [17th c-present] Archaeological and archival materials.

HOURS: June-Aug Daily 9-8; Sept-May Daily 9-5

ADMISSION: $8, Children $6

CHERRYVILLE

6255
C. Grier Beam Truck Museum
117 N Mountain St, 28021 [PO Box 238, 28021]; (p) (704) 435-3072; (f) (704) 445-9010; (c) Gaston

Private non-profit/ 1982/ staff: 4(p)

AUTOMOBILE MUSEUM; CORPORATE ARCHIVES/MUSEUM: Covers transportation/trucking in general and Carolina Freight Carriers Corporation in particular. Listed on the National Register of Historic Places.

PROGRAMS: Annual Meeting; Community Outreach; Exhibits; Festivals

COLLECTIONS: [1928-1995] Restored antique trucks and corporate history displays of the early trucking industry.

HOURS: Yr F 10-5, Sa 10-3

ADMISSION: $1; Children free

6256
Cherryville History Association
109 E Main St, 28021 [PO Box 856, 28021]; (p) (704) 435-8011; (c) Gaston

Private non-profit/ 1989/ staff: 8(v)/ members: 255

HISTORY MUSEUM: Oversees the restoration of historic buildings. The museum is located in a city hall built in 1910 that includes a fire and police department, courtroom, and jail.

PROGRAMS: Exhibits

COLLECTIONS: [1875-1935] Histories of local schools and industries, a 1921 La Franch fire truck, and photographs.

HOURS: Yr F 1-5, Sa 10-5, Su 2-5

ADMISSION: No charge

CLINTON

6257
Sampson County Historical Society
[PO Box 1084, 28328]; (p) (910) 594-0577; (c) Sampson

County/ 1979/ staff: 5(p); 5(v)/ members: 335/publication: *Huckleberry Historian*

GENEALOGICAL SOCIETY; HISTORICAL SOCIETY: Promotes interest in history and genealogy.

PROGRAMS: Lectures; Publication

HOURS: 2nd Sa Jan, Apr, July, Oct

ADMISSION: No charge

COINJOCK

6258
Albemarle Genealogical Society
142 Waterlily Rd, 27923; (p) (252) 453-2861; (c) Currituck

1981/ Current Officers/ members: 118

GENEALOGICAL SOCIETY: Organized to create and foster interest in genealogy through literary and educational means, and to gather and preserve genealogical and historical data and aid individuals in genealogical research by providing genealogical programs, discussions, lectures, and quarterly newsletters of genealogical information.

PROGRAMS: Lectures; Publication

COLLECTIONS: Journals, bulletins, and newsletters from other genealogical societies, books, family histories, microfilm.

HOURS: Library hours

COLUMBIA

6259
Tyrrell County Genealogical and Historical Society
[PO Box 686, 27925]; jimmyflemming@coastalnet.com; (c) Tyrrell

Private non-profit/ 1995/ members: 105

GENEALOGICAL SOCIETY; HISTORICAL SOCIETY: Meets monthly to promote history, genealogy, and research.

PROGRAMS: Family Programs; Lectures; Publication

HOURS: 4th Su

CONCORD

6260
Cabarrus Genealogy Society
57 Union St N, 28025 [PO Box 2981, 28025-0002]; (p) (704) 788-3167; cabgensoc@hotmail.com; www.rootsweb.com/~nccabarr/index.html; (c) Cabarrus

Private non-profit/ 1993/ staff: 10(v)/ members: 250/publication: *The Golden Nugget*

GENEALOGICAL SOCIETY: Publishes and disseminates information about Cabarrus County and its families.

PROGRAMS: Annual Meeting; Lectures; Publication

COLLECTIONS: [1792-present] Transcriptions of county records, family histories, and pedigree charts.

6261
Historic Cabarrus, Inc.
65 Union St S, 28026 [PO Box 966, 28026-0966]; (p) (704) 786-8515; (c) Cabarrus

Private non-profit/ 1973/ Board of Trustees/ staff: 1(p); 24(v)/ members: 239

HISTORIC PRESERVATION AGENCY; HISTORIC SITE; HISTORY MUSEUM: Promotes interest in county history and preserves its important historic sites and landmarks.

PROGRAMS: Annual Meeting; Community Outreach; Exhibits; Facility Rental; Research Library/Archives

COLLECTIONS: [18th c-present] Indian arrowheads and pottery through the present with an emphasis on household items and wartime memorabilia.

HOURS: Yr M, W 10-1, T, Th-F 9-12

COOLEEMEE

6262
Cooleemee Historical Association
14 Church St, 27014 [PO Box 667, 27014]; (p) (336) 284-6040; (f) (336) 284-2805; www.members.tripod.com/~cooleemee/; (c) Davie

Private non-profit/ 1989/ Board of Directors/ staff: 1(f); 2(p); 23(v)/ members: 1023

HISTORIC PRESERVATION AGENCY; HISTORICAL SOCIETY; HISTORY MUSEUM; RESEARCH CENTER: Operates Cooleemee's Textile Heritage Center and Mill Village Museum. Collected extensive archives. Created network of scholars and lay historians from over fifty southern mill towns.

PROGRAMS: Annual Meeting; Community Outreach; Elder's Programs; Exhibits; Facility Rental; Festivals; Interpretation; Living History; Research Library/Archives; School-Based Curriculum

COLLECTIONS: [1900-1950] Artifacts, photographs, documents, oral history interviews, and memorabilia relating to the history of Carolina mill village.

HOURS: Yr T-Th 9-2, Sa 11-2

ADMISSION: No charge

CRESWELL

6263
Somerset Place State Historic Site
2572 Lake Shore Rd, 27928; (p) (252) 797-4560; (f) (252) 797-4171; somerset@coastalnet.com; www.ah.dcr.state.nc.us/somerset/somerset.htm; (c) Washington

State/ 1959/ NC Dept of Cultural Resources, Division of Archives and History/ staff: 5(f); 6(p); 7(v)/ members: 25

HISTORIC SITE; HOUSE MUSEUM: A representative antebellum plantation offering an insightful view of life during the period before the Civil War.

PROGRAMS: Exhibits; Festivals; Guided Tours; Interpretation; School-Based Curriculum

COLLECTIONS: [1785-1865] Mansion, furniture.

HOURS: Apr-Oct M-Sa 9-5, Su 1-5; Nov-Mar M-Sa 10-4, Su 1-4

CULLOWHEE

6264
Jackson County Genealogical Society, Inc.
42 Asheville Hwy, 28723 [PO Box 2108, 28723]; www.main.nc.us/jcgs/; (c) Jackson

Private non-profit/ 1991/ staff: 10(v)/ members: 200/publication: *Journeys Through Jackson*

GENEALOGICAL SOCIETY: Collects and publishes genealogical data pertaining to Jackson County families.

PROGRAMS: Annual Meeting; Exhibits; Publication; Research Library/Archives

COLLECTIONS: [1851-present] Books, periodicals, family files relating to (but not limited to) Jackson County.

HOURS: Yr M-Th 5:30-8:30, Sa 9-1

ADMISSION: No charge

6265
Mountain Heritage Center
HF Robinson Bldg, Western Carolina Univ, 28723 [HF Robinson Building, Western Carolina Univ, 28723]; (p) (828) 227-7129; blethen@wcu.edu; www.wcu.edu/mhc; (c) Jackson

State/ 1975/ Western Carolina Univ/ staff: 3(f); 2(p)/ members: 190/publication: *Where the Ravens Roost*

HISTORY MUSEUM: Collects, interprets, and disseminates knowledge about the natural and cultural history of the Southern Appalachian region and its people.

PROGRAMS: Community Outreach; Concerts; Elder's Programs; Exhibits; Festivals; Lectures; Publication

COLLECTIONS: [19th-20th c] Regional artifacts from western NC with emphasis on agricultural implements, Native American materials, textile processing and communications equipment, land transportation, logging, woodworking, and food preparation tools.

HOURS: Nov-May M-F 8-5; June-Oct Su 2-5

ADMISSION: No charge

CURRIE

6266
Moores Creek National Battlefield
200 Patriots Hall Dr, 28435 [40 Patriots Hall Dr, 28435]; (p) (910) 283-5591; (f) (910) 283-5351; www.nps.gov/mocr; (c) Pender

Federal/ 1926/ staff: 6(f); 2(p); 3(v)

BATTLEFIELD; HISTORIC PRESERVATION AGENCY; HISTORIC SITE; LIVING HISTORY/OUTDOOR MUSEUM: Preserves the site of the first patriot victory in the American Revolution fought at Moores Creek bridge on February 27, 1776.

PROGRAMS: Exhibits; Facility Rental; Film/Video; Guided Tours; Interpretation; Lectures; Living History; Reenactments; School-Based Curriculum

COLLECTIONS: [18th c] Revolutionary War weapons and colonial artifacts.

HOURS: Yr Daily 9-5

ADMISSION: No charge

DOBSON

6267
Rockford Preservation Society, Inc.
1264 Rockford Rd, 27017; (p) (336) 374-3825; (f) (336) 374-3825; HHolyfield@surry.net; (c) Surry

Private non-profit/ 1974/ Board of Directors/ members: 50/publication: *The Story of Rockford*

HISTORIC PRESERVATION AGENCY: Preserves and maintains six buildings in the Historic District of the Village of Rockford; listed in the National Register of Historic Places. Maintained these buildings through grants, donations and fundraisers. Presents programs for the general public as well.

PROGRAMS: Annual Meeting; Concerts; Facility Rental; Family Programs; Guided Tours; Living History; Publication; Reenactments;

School-Based Curriculum

HOURS: Yr M-F by appt, Sa-Su 9-6

ADMISSION: Donations

6268
Surry County Genealogical Association
Surry Community College, 27017 [PO Box 997, 27017]; judyscard@aol.com; www.juliemorrison.com/surry/; (c) Surry

Private non-profit/ 1981/ members: 340/publication: *Quarterly Journal; The Heritage of Surry County, Volumes I and II*

GENEALOGICAL SOCIETY: Creates and fosters an interest in genealogy, preserves data, and assists individuals in genealogical research.

PROGRAMS: Lectures; Publication

COLLECTIONS: [1771-present] Family history and research books, family bible records, group sheets, pedigree charts, and maps.

HOURS: Yr M-F; Meetings: 2nd M at 7pm

DURHAM

6269
Bennett Place State Historic Site
4409 Bennett Memorial Rd, 27705; (p) (919) 383-4345; www.ah.dcr.state.nc.us/sections/hs/bennett/bennett.htm; (c) Durham

State/ 1962/ NC Dept of Cultural Resources/ staff: 3(f); 8(p); 6(v)

HISTORIC SITE: Location of the largest troop surrender of the Civil War. General Joseph E. Johnston surrendered his army to Major General William T. Sherman at the farm home of James Bennett.

PROGRAMS: Concerts; Exhibits; Guided Tours; Interpretation; Lectures; Living History; Publication; Reenactments; Research Library/Archives

COLLECTIONS: [Mid-19th c] Artifacts from antebellum era relating to domestic life, military, and a farm setting.

HOURS: Apr 1-Oct 31 M-Sa 9-5, Su 1-5; Nov 1-Mar 31 T-Sa 10-4, Su 1-4

6270
Duke Homestead State Historic Site and Tobacco Museum
2828 Duke Homestead Rd, 27705; (p) (919) 477-5498; (f) (919) 479-7092; duke@ncsl.dcr.state.nc.us; www.metalab.unc.edu/dukehome/index.html; (c) Durham

State/ 1974/ NC Dept of Cultural Resources/ staff: 5(f); 7(p); 75(v)

HISTORIC SITE; HISTORY MUSEUM; LIVING HISTORY/OUTDOOR MUSEUM: Maintains the 1852 home of Washington Duke and two of his early tobacco factories. The museum interprets tobacco history in North Carolina since 1600.

PROGRAMS: Annual Meeting; Community Outreach; Exhibits; Family Programs; Festivals; Film/Video; Garden Tours; Guided Tours; Interpretation; Lectures; Living History; Reenactments; Research Library/Archives; School-Based Curriculum

COLLECTIONS: [1850-1870] Tobacco products, memorabilia, advertisements, manufacturing equipment, and farm implements. Duke

family possessions, a tobacco history library, and a display of 1870 period rural home furnishings.

HOURS: Nov-Mar T-Sa 10-4, Su 1-4; Apr-Oct M-Sa 9-5, Su 1-5

ADMISSION: Donations accepted

6271
Duke University Rare Book, Manuscript and Special Collections Library
Science Dr, 27708 [PO Box 90185, 27708-0185]; (p) (919) 660-5820; (f) (919) 660-5934; specoll@mail.lib.duke.edu; www.scriptorium.lib.duke.edu; (c) Durham

Private non-profit/ 1931/ Duke Univ/ staff: 19(f); 5(p)

LIBRARY AND/OR ARCHIVES; RESEARCH CENTER: Preserves historical and cultural documentation and promotes its use by Duke University scholars, other academic users and the general public.

PROGRAMS: Exhibits; Lectures; Research Library/Archives

COLLECTIONS: Books, maps, newspapers, broadsides and pamphlets. Manuscripts ranging from ancient papyri to modern advertising. Focuses on Southern history and literature, African American and women's studies, advertising history, documentary photography and the history of economic thought.

HOURS: Fall-Spring M-Th 9-9, F 9-5, Sa 1-5; Summer M-F 9-5, Sa 1-5

ADMISSION: No charge

6272
Forest History Society
701 Vickers Ave, 27701; (p) (919) 682-9319; (f) (919) 682-2349; stevena@acpub.duke.edu; www.lib.duke.edu/forest/; (c) Durham

Private non-profit/ 1946/ staff: 7(f); 3(p)/ members: 1500/publication: *Forest History Today; Environmental History*

HISTORICAL SOCIETY; PROFESSIONAL ORGANIZATION; RESEARCH CENTER

PROGRAMS: Annual Meeting; Community Outreach; Exhibits; Film/Video; Interpretation; Lectures; Publication; Research Library/Archives; School-Based Curriculum

COLLECTIONS: [20th c] Forest, conservation and environmental history: volumes, serials, photographs, newspaper clippings, online bibliography and archival guide, US Forest Service History collection.

HOURS: Yr M-F 8-5

ADMISSION: No charge

6273
Historic Stagville
5825 Old Oxford Hwy, 27722 [PO Box 71217, 27722-1217]; (p) (919) 620-0120; (f) (919) 620-0422; stagvill@sprynet.com; www.ah.dcr.state.nc.us/sections/do/stagvill/default.htm; (c) Durham

State/ 1976/ NC Dept of Cultural Resources, Archives and History Division/ staff: 2(f); 2(p); 3(v)/ members: 100

HISTORIC SITE: A former plantation, the site includes original 18th and 19th c buildings that interpret antebellum plantation life, African

American history and preservation technology.

PROGRAMS: Guided Tours; Interpretation; Lectures; Living History; Reenactments

COLLECTIONS: [1787-1865] Seven locally and nationally significant buildings with period furnishings.

HOURS: Yr M-F 9-4

ADMISSION: No charge

6274
St. Joseph's Historic Foundation, Inc.
804 Old Fayetteville St, 27702 [PO Box 543, 27702]; (p) (919) 683-1709; (f) (919) 682-5869; hayti@hayti.org; www.hayti.org; (c) Durham

1975/ staff: 5(f); 4(p); 40(v)

ART MUSEUM; CULTURAL CENTER; HISTORIC SITE: Operates the Hayti Heritage Center, provides various cultural arts programs and classes relating to the African American experiences and its many contributions to world cultural. Activities include dance, visual arts, children's theater and special exhibits.

PROGRAMS: Community Outreach; Concerts; Elder's Programs; Exhibits; Facility Rental; Family Programs; Festivals; Film/Video; Guided Tours; Lectures

COLLECTIONS: [20th c]

HOURS: Yr M-F 10-7, Sa 10-4

ADMISSION: Donations accepted

6275
West Point on the Eno City Park
5101 N Roxboro Rd, 27704; (p) (919) 471-1623; bhighley@ci.durham.nc.us; (c) Durham

City/ 1973/ staff: 1(f); 4(p); 2(v)

HISTORIC SITE; LIVING HISTORY/OUTDOOR MUSEUM: A 388 acre natural and historic city park located along a two mile stretch of the scenic Eno River.

PROGRAMS: Concerts; Exhibits; Facility Rental; Family Programs; Festivals; Guided Tours; Interpretation; School-Based Curriculum

COLLECTIONS: [19th-20th c] Furnishings and artifacts.

HOURS: Yr Daily

EDENTON

6276
Cupola House Association, Inc.
408 S Broad St, 27932 [PO Box 311, 27932]; (p) (252) 482-2637; (c) Chowan

Private non-profit/ 1918/ staff: 25(v)/ members: 273/publication: *Deliverance of a Treasure: The Cupola House Association and Its Mission*

GARDEN; HISTORIC PRESERVATION AGENCY; HISTORIC SITE; HOUSE MUSEUM: Preserves the 1758 Cupola House. Restored in the mid-1960s as an historic house museum. A National Historic Landmark.

PROGRAMS: Annual Meeting; Family Programs; Publication; Research Library/Archives

COLLECTIONS: [1750-1775] Furnishings include English and Chowan River Basin pieces, primarily Queen Anne and Chippendale styles and portraits. Contains early regional documents.

ADMISSION: Prices vary

6277
Historic Edenton State Historic Site
108 N Broad St, 27932 [PO Box 474, 27932]; (p) (252) 482-2637; (f) (252) 482-3499; edentonshs@inteliport.com; www.ah.dcr.state.nc.us/sections/hs/iredell/iredell.htm; (c) Chowan

State/ 1951/ NC Dept of Cultural Resources/ staff: 7(f); 12(p); 37(v)

HISTORIC PRESERVATION AGENCY; HISTORIC SITE; HOUSE MUSEUM: Mantains the home of US Supreme Court Associate Justice James Iredell (1751-1799), Chowan County Courthouse National Historic Landmark (1767) and other historic properties in Edenton.

PROGRAMS: Community Outreach; Exhibits; Family Programs; Film/Video; Guided Tours; Interpretation

COLLECTIONS: [18th c] Household furnishings for historic house museum, includes Iredell family portraits and kitchen utensils.

HOURS: Apr-Oct M-Sa 9-5, Su 1-5; Nov-Mar T-Sa 10-4, Su 1-4

ADMISSION: Visitor Center free

ELIZABETH CITY

6278
Family Research Society of Northeastern North Carolina
410 E Main St, Ste 203, 27906 [PO Box 1425, 27906-1425]; (p) (252) 333-1640; (c) Pasquotank

Private non-profit/ 1991/ staff: 25(v)/ members: 314/publication: *Carolina Trees and Branches*

GENEALOGICAL SOCIETY; RESEARCH CENTER: Collects, researches, preserves, and exchanges genealogical and historical information on the counties of Camden, Chowan, Dare, Gates, Pasquotank, Currituck and Perquimans. Publishes over 30 genealogical and historical books. Answers queries and aids researchers all over the US with genealogical research on the seven local counties.

PROGRAMS: Annual Meeting; Interpretation; Lectures; Publication; Research Library/Archives

COLLECTIONS: [1600-present] Genealogies, maps and ancestor charts, printed materials and resource books with collections of funeral home, church and cemetery records.

HOURS: Yr T, Th, Sa 10-3

ADMISSION: Library is free

6279
Museum of the Albemarle
1116 US Hwy 17 S, 27909; (p) (252) 335-1453, (252) 335-2987; (f) (252) 335-0637; ncs1583@interpath.com; www.albemarle-nc.com/MOA; (c) Pasquotank

State/ 1967/ NC Dept of Cultural Resources/ staff: 6(f); 5(p); 21(v)/ members: 400

HISTORY MUSEUM: Through regional collections, historical interpretation and professional assistance, the museum encourages citizens and visitors to explore and understand the past, and to preserve regional history.

PROGRAMS: Exhibits; Family Programs; Festivals; Living History; Research Library/Archives

COLLECTIONS: [18th c-present] Regional history, Native American and agricultural artifacts, fire engines, lumbering, duck carvings, decoys, farming, fishing, US Coast Guard, tools and toys.

ELIZABETHTOWN

6280
Bladen County Historical Society, Inc.
[PO Box 848, 28337]; (c) Bladen

Private non-profit/ 1957/ Board of Directors/ staff: 3(v)/ members: 100/publication: *Back to Balden*

HISTORICAL SOCIETY: Collects and preserves relics, artifacts, memorabilia, and materials related to local history.

PROGRAMS: Publication; Quarterly Meeting

COLLECTIONS: [1734-present] Artifacts, original documents, photocopies of original documents, deed abstracts, Bible records, tax lists, brief family histories, church histories, cemetery records, and models.

HOURS: Yr by appt.

ADMISSION: Donations accepted

ELLERBE

6281
Rankin Museum of American Heritage
131 W Church St, 28338 [PO Box 499, 28338]; (p) (910) 652-6378; p_rankin@hotmail.com; www.rankinmuseum.com; (c) Richmond

Private non-profit/ 1985/ staff: 3(p); 2(v)/ members: 75

HISTORY MUSEUM

PROGRAMS: Exhibits; Festivals; Guided Tours; Lectures; School-Based Curriculum

COLLECTIONS: Exhibits on natural history, early Americana, archaeology and paleontology. A 500 gallon turpentine still, animal mounts, fossils, and Native American exhibits.

HOURS: Yr Daily

ADMISSION: $3, Student $1

FAIR BLUFF

6282
Greater Fair Bluff Historical Society
339 Railroad St, 28439 [PO Box 285, 28439]; (p) (910) 649-7707; (c) Columbus

Private non-profit/ 1990/ Executive Board/ staff: 10(v)/ members: 157

GENEALOGICAL SOCIETY; HISTORICAL SOCIETY; HISTORY MUSEUM; RESEARCH CENTER: Restored depot now used as museum that houses artifacts pertaining to the area.

PROGRAMS: Annual Meeting; Exhibits; Research Library/Archives

COLLECTIONS: [1700s-1940s] Artifacts and documents relating to area history and local family genealogies.

HOURS: Yr Su 2-4, T 10-4, and by appt

ADMISSION: No charge

FAIRFIELD

6283
**Hyde County Historical and
Genealogical Society**
20400 US 264, 27826 [7820 Liney Woods
Rd, 27826]; (p) (252) 925-9281; (f) (252) 925-
1092; romsandy@beachlink.com; (c) Hyde

1962/ staff: 10(v)/ members: 350/publication:
High Tides

GENEALOGICAL SOCIETY; HISTORIC
PRESERVATION AGENCY; HISTORICAL SO-
CIETY: Preserves county heritage through its
collection, community education, and journal
publication.

PROGRAMS: Annual Meeting; Publication;
Research Library/Archives

COLLECTIONS: [20th c] Volumes and microfilm.

HOURS: Yr M-Sa 10-5

ADMISSION: No charge

FAIRMONT

6284
Border Belt Historical Society, Inc., The
Thompson & Main St, 28340 [505 N Main St,
28340]; (p) (910) 628-9216; (c) Robeson

City, non-profit/ 1989/ Board of Directors/ staff:
1(p); 2(v)/ members: 78/publication: *Museum
Pieces*

HISTORICAL SOCIETY

PROGRAMS: Annual Meeting; Community
Outreach; Concerts; Exhibits; Festivals; Guided Tours; Interpretation; Publication

COLLECTIONS: [1899-present] History of tobacco farming, curing and sales; rural home
life; early education artifacts; local medical artifacts; and local history documents.

FARMVILLE

6285
**May Museum and Farmville Heritage
Center**
200 N Main St, 27828 [PO Box 86, 27828];
(p) (252) 753-5814; (f) (252) 753-3190;
ckendall@farmville-nc.com; (c) Pitt

City/ 1991/ staff: 2(f); 2(p); 10(v)

HISTORIC SITE; HISTORY MUSEUM;
HOUSE MUSEUM: Circa 1870 home built by
Farmville founding father James William May.

PROGRAMS: Community Outreach; Exhibits;
Facility Rental; Festivals; Guided Tours

COLLECTIONS: [18th-19th c] Home and commercial artifacts, photographs, quilt collection.

HOURS: Yr T-Sa 12-5

ADMISSION: Donations accepted

FAYETTEVILLE

6286
**Cumberland County Public Library
and Information Center, Local and
State History Room**
300 Maiden Ln, 28301; (p) (910) 483-3745;
(f) (910) 486-6661; www.cumberland.lib.nc.
us; (c) Cumberland

County/ staff: 3(f); 2(v)

LIBRARY AND/OR ARCHIVES: Develops and
maintains clipping files of local events, people,
historical and cultural activities.

PROGRAMS: Exhibits; Guided Tours; Lectures

COLLECTIONS: [18th c-present] NC historical, demographic, and statistical material,
state and local government documents, genealogical materials, local newspapers and
magazines.

HOURS: Yr M-Th 9-9, F-Sa 9-6, Su 2-6

ADMISSION: No charge

6287
**Fayetteville Independent Light
Infantry**
210 Burgess St, 28302 [PO Box 568, 28302];
(p) (910) 323-5936; (c) Cumberland

Private non-profit/ 1793/ NC Army National
Guard/ staff: 75(v)/ members: 75

HISTORY MUSEUM: Military command established in 1793, maintains a military museum
and color guard in its armory.

PROGRAMS: Guided Tours

COLLECTIONS: [1793-present] Military artifacts and records from the founding of the
company to the present day. Focus is on the
FILI, North Carolina, and US military history.

HOURS: Yr by appt

ADMISSION: No charge

6288
**Museum of the Cape Fear Historical
Complex**
801 Arsenal Ave, 28305 [PO Box 53693,
28305]; (p) (910) 486-1330; (f) (910) 486-
1585; mcfhc@infi.net; (c) Cumberland

State/ 1988/ NC Dept of Cultural Resources/
staff: 14(f); 4(p); 50(v)

HISTORIC SITE; HISTORY MUSEUM;
HOUSE MUSEUM: Chronicles the history of
southern NC. The 1897 Poe House depicts
family life (1903-1917) and Arsenal Park houses ruins of the federal and confederate arsenal, 1838-1865.

PROGRAMS: Community Outreach; Con-
certs; Exhibits; Family Programs; Festivals;
Guided Tours; Interpretation; Lectures; Living
History; School-Based Curriculum

COLLECTIONS: [18th-20th c] Artifacts on
southern NC history. Includes military materials relating to Fayetteville Arsenal (1838-
1865), Victorian household furnishings, tools
for marine stores, tobacco farming and textile
manufacturing.

HOURS: Yr T-Sa 10-5, Su 1-5

ADMISSION: No charge

6289
**Orange Street School Historical
Association**
600 Orange St, 28302 [PO Box 573, 28302];
(p) (910) 483-7038; (c) Cumberland

Joint/ 1987/ City of Fayetteville; Cumberland
County/ staff: 12(v)/ members: 18

HISTORIC SITE; HISTORY MUSEUM: Revitalizes the abandoned school building, which
was the first local school for blacks when it
was constructed in 1915. Following renova-
tions, it will be an African American Muse-
um/Civic Center.

PROGRAMS: Annual Meeting; Community
Outreach; Concerts; Elder's Programs; Exhibits; Family Programs; Guided Tours; Lectures

COLLECTIONS: [19th-20th c] Regional photographs and deeds. Artifacts discovered during
the renovation period dating back to the 19th c.

HOURS: Yr

ADMISSION: No charge

FLAT ROCK

6290
Carl Sandburg National Historic Site
1928 Little River Rd, 28731; (p) (828) 693-
4178; (f) (828) 693-4179; www.nps.gov.carl;
(c) Henderson

Federal/ 1968/ Dept of Interior, National Park
Service/ staff: 8(f); 3(p); 40(v)

HISTORIC SITE; HOUSE MUSEUM; LIVING
HISTORY/OUTDOOR MUSEUM: Home and
farm of author and poet, Carl Sandburg.

PROGRAMS: Exhibits; Guided Tours; Lectures; Living History

COLLECTIONS: [1930s-1960] Library, home
furnishings, and farm equipment of Carl Sandburg and his wife.

HOURS: Yr Daily 9-5

ADMISSION: $3; Under 17 free; Grounds free

FOREST CITY

6291
**Genealogical Society of Old Tryon
County**
102 W Main St, 28043 [PO Box 938, 28043-
0938]; (p) (828) 248-4010; (c) Rutherford

Private non-profit/ 1972/ staff: 14(v)/ members:
700

GENEALOGICAL SOCIETY; HISTORICAL
SOCIETY: Compiles, publishes, and preserves the historical and genealogical records
of the area.

PROGRAMS: Annual Meeting; Research Li-
brary/Archives

COLLECTIONS: [18th-19th c] Family histories,
books on the Revolutionary War, War of 1812
and the Civil War. Court proceedings, wills,
deeds, marriage bonds, birth and death certificates, cemetery and census records of many
counties and various states and personal family
files.

6292
Rutherford County Farm Museum
240 Depot St, 28043; (p) (828) 248-1248

FOUR OAKS

6293
**Bentonville Battlefield State Historic
Site**
5466 Harper House Rd, 27524; (p) (910)
594-0789, (910) 594-0222; (f) (910) 594-
0222; www.ah.dcr.state.nc.us/sections/hs/
bentonvi/bentonvi.htm

State/ 1855/ Dept of Cultural Resources/ staff:
4(f); 4(p)

BATTLEFIELD; HISTORIC SITE; HISTORY

MUSEUM: Site of the Battle of Bentonville. Includes visitor center, trails, monuments, outdoor exhibits, and the Harper House (ca. 1855), furnished as a Civil War field hospital. The site also includes a reconstructed kitchen and slave quarters.

PROGRAMS: Exhibits; Guided Tours; Living History

COLLECTIONS: [Civil War] Civil War medical equipment, mid 19th c NC furniture.

FRANKLIN

6294
Macon County Historical Society
36 W Main St, 28734; (p) (828) 524-9758; (c) Macon

Private non-profit/ 1946/ Board of Directors/ staff: 1(f); 10(v)/ members: 280/publication: *Heritage of Macon County I and II*

GENEALOGICAL SOCIETY; HISTORIC PRESERVATION AGENCY; HISTORIC SITE; HISTORICAL SOCIETY; HISTORY MUSEUM: Preserves Nikwasi Mound and continues historic site preservation. Aids in genealogy research and maintains a historical museum.

PROGRAMS: Annual Meeting; Community Outreach; Concerts; Festivals; Film/Video; Interpretation; Lectures; Living History; Publication; Research Library/Archives

COLLECTIONS: [Prehistory-20th c] Materials related to early Appalachian Mountain heritage.

HOURS: May-Oct Tu-Sa 10-5; Nov-Apr M-F 10-5

FREMONT

6295
Governor Charles B. Aycock Birthplace State Historic Site
264 Governor Aycock Rd, 27830 [PO Box 207, 27830]; (p) (919) 242-5581; (f) (919) 242-6668; aycock@ncsl.dcr.state.nc.us; www.ah.dcr.state.nc.us/hs/aycock/aycock.htm; (c) Wayne

State/ 1959/ NC Dept of Cultural Resources/ staff: 6(f); 5(p); 20(v)

HISTORIC SITE; HOUSE MUSEUM; LIVING HISTORY/OUTDOOR MUSEUM: Maintains the boyhood home (1893) of former Governor Aycock.

PROGRAMS: Community Outreach; Family Programs; Guided Tours; Living History

COLLECTIONS: [1850-1900] Period furnishings form a mid-19th c farmstead and an 1893 one-room schoolhouse, Aycock family pieces, and historic buildings.

HOURS: Apr-Oct M-Sa 9-5, Su 1-5; Nov-Mar T-Sa 10-4, Su 1-4

FRISCO

6296
Frisco Native American Museum and Natural History Center
53536 Hwy 12, 27936 [PO Box 399, 27936]; (p) (252) 995-4440; (f) (252) 995-4030; bfriend1@mindspring.com; www.nativeamericanmuseum.org; (c) Dare

Private non-profit/ 1986/ staff: 1(f); 1(p); 6(v)

HISTORY MUSEUM: Provides educational displays, interpretative exhibits, special seminars and workshops on Native American history and culture across the United States and Canada.

PROGRAMS: Community Outreach; Exhibits; Family Programs; Festivals; Film/Video; Guided Tours; Interpretation; Lectures; Living History; School-Based Curriculum

COLLECTIONS: [Prehistory-present]

HOURS: Yr T-Su 11-5

GASTONIA

6297
American Military Museum
115 W Second Ave, 28054 [307 Oakdale St, 28054]; (p) (704) 864-0267; (c) Gaston

Private non-profit/ 1930/ American Legion Post 23/ staff: 4(v)/ members: 150

HISTORY MUSEUM: Promotes military history and maintains military museum.

PROGRAMS: Exhibits; Guided Tours; Lectures

COLLECTIONS: [W W II] Uniforms, weapons, scale models, pictures, flags and war memorabilia, city histories, journals, books and letters.

HOURS: Yr Su 2-5 and by appt

GATES

6298
Gates County Historical Society
115 Court St, 27937 [PO Box 98, 27937]; (p) (252) 357-1733; (c) Gates

Private non-profit/ 1975/ staff: 15(v)/ members: 100/publication: *Forgotten Gates*

HISTORIC PRESERVATION AGENCY; HISTORIC SITE; HISTORICAL SOCIETY; HISTORY MUSEUM: Collects and preserves materials that illustrate county and state history. Disseminates historical and genealogical information through publications, visits, and tours.

PROGRAMS: Annual Meeting; Exhibits; Festivals; Publication

COLLECTIONS: [1940-1993] Memorabilia on Thad A. Eure, former Secretary of State of North Carolina and Gates County native. Bible and cemetery records.

GERMANTON

6299
Stokes County Historical Society
[PO Box 250, 27019]; (p) (336) 591-3044; stokeshistory@aol.com; www.actionsspeak.org/schs/; (c) Stokes

Private non-profit/ 1968/ Board of Directors/ staff: 9(v)/ members: 97/publication: *Heritage, Vol. I and II*

HISTORIC PRESERVATION AGENCY; HISTORICAL SOCIETY; HOUSE MUSEUM: Studies, collects, preserves, and educates about county and state history. Headquarters located at the Wilson Fulton House in Danbury, built in 1860 by local tanner and merchant, Mr. Wilson Fulton. Owns the 1774 Revolutionary Rock House, built by Colonel Jack Martin and located near Pinnacle.

PROGRAMS: Annual Meeting; Lectures; Publication

COLLECTIONS: [18th-20th c] Papers, books, records, relics, and historical artifacts.

HOURS: Rock House: Yr Daily; Library: M, W, F 9-5, T, Th 9-8, Sa 9-12

GOLDSBORO

6300
Goldsboro Historic District Commission
222 N Center St, 27533 [PO Drawer A, 27533]; (p) (919) 580-4334; (f) (919) 580-4315; schase@ci.goldsboro.nc.us; (c) Wayne

City/ 1986/ staff: 1(f)/ members: 12

HISTORIC PRESERVATION AGENCY: Reviews applications for Certificates of Appropriateness and assists the public with projects that would alter or improve property within the historic district.

6301
Wayne County Historical Association
116 N William St, 27533 [PO Box 665, 27533]; (p) (919) 734-1111, (919) 739-9989; (f) (919) 734-0877; (c) Wayne

Private non-profit/ 1953/ staff: 1(p); 10(v)/ members: 350/publication: *A History of Wayne County; Architectural Inventory of Goldsboro; and others*

ALLIANCE OF HISTORICAL AGENCIES; GENEALOGICAL SOCIETY; HISTORIC PRESERVATION AGENCY; HISTORIC SITE; HISTORICAL SOCIETY; HISTORY MUSEUM; LIVING HISTORY/OUTDOOR MUSEUM: Perpetuates and preserves the history and heritage of Wayne County.

PROGRAMS: Annual Meeting; Exhibits; Facility Rental; Festivals; Guided Tours; Lectures; Living History; Publication; Reenactments

COLLECTIONS: [18th-19th c] Eastern NC artifacts.

HOURS: Yr

ADMISSION: No charge

6302
Wayne County Museum
116 N William St, 27530; (p) (919) 734-5023; (f) (919) 705-1815; museum@esn.net; (c) Wayne

Private non-profit/ 1987/ Board Committee/ staff: 2(p)

HISTORY MUSEUM: Preserves and protects artifacts gathered by the citizens of Wayne County.

COLLECTIONS: [19th-20th c] Civil War artifacts including letter written by William T. Sherman to a local resident during the war.

HOURS: Yr T,Th 12-4, Sa 10-1

GREENSBORO

6303
Blandwood Mansion
447 W Washington St, 27415 [PO Box 13136, 27415]; (p) (336) 272-5003; (f) (336) 271-8049; tspitjard@blandwood.org; www.blandwood.org; (c) Guilford

Private non-profit/ 1966/ Preservation Greensboro, Inc/ staff: 1(f); 5(p); 80(v)/ members: 506

HOUSE MUSEUM: Former home of NC Governor John Motley Morehead (1841-1845).

Italianate architecture; listed as National Historic Landmark.

PROGRAMS: Annual Meeting; Community Outreach; Concerts; Facility Rental; Guided Tours; Interpretation; School-Based Curriculum

COLLECTIONS: [1844-1866] Period furnishings, artwork, and household items. Documented Morehead pieces used at Blandwood during the mid-19th c.

HOURS: Feb-Dec T-Sa 11-2, Su 2-5

ADMISSION: $5, Children $2, Seniors $4

6304
Greensboro Historical Museum
130 Summit Ave, 27401-3016; (p) (336) 373-2043, (336) 373-2610; (f) (336) 373-2204; linda.evans@ci.greensboro.nc.us; www.greensborohistory.org; (c) Guilford

Joint/ 1924/ City of Greensboro; Greensboro Historical Museum, Inc./ staff: 9(f); 17(p); 206(v)/ members: 922/publication: *Museum Journal*

HISTORY MUSEUM; HOUSE MUSEUM: Collects, preserves, exhibits, and interprets objects connected with the social, political, economic, and cultural history of the Greensboro region.

PROGRAMS: Annual Meeting; Community Outreach; Exhibits; Facility Rental; Guided Tours; Lectures; Publication; Research Library/ Archives; School-Based Curriculum; Theatre

COLLECTIONS: [17th c-present] Decorative arts, military artifacts, costumes, furniture, Dolly Madison and O. Henry collections. Documents, books, photographs, negatives and miscellaneous archival items.

HOURS: Yr T-Sa 10-5, Su 2-5

ADMISSION: Donations accepted

6305
Guilford County Historic Preservation Commission
201 S Eugene St, 27402 [PO Box 3427, 27402]; (p) (336) 373-3334, (336) 373-3728; (f) (336) 333-6988; jcurry@co.guilford.nc.us; www.co.guilford.nc.us; (c) Guilford

County/ 1980/ staff: 1(p)/ members: 11

HISTORIC PRESERVATION AGENCY: Oversees Landmark designations and considers Certificate of Appropriateness requests. Acts as a resource and advocate, and incorporates preservation into the planning process. Rural historic district established in 1995.

6306
Mattye Reed African Heritage Center, North Carolina Agricultural and Technical State University
Dudley & E Market Sts, 27411 [1601 E Market St, 27411]; (p) (336) 334-3209; (f) (336) 334-7837; (c) Guilford

State/ 1972/ NC University System/ staff: 2(f); 2(p); 3(v)

ART MUSEUM; HISTORY MUSEUM; RESEARCH CENTER

PROGRAMS: Exhibits; Family Programs; Festivals; Film/Video; Guided Tours; Lectures; Publication; School-Based Curriculum

COLLECTIONS: [20th c] African and African American art.

HOURS: Yr M-F by appt

GREENVILLE

6307
East Carolina Village of Yesteryear
Hwy 264 East, 27835 [PO Box 8027, 27835-8027]; (p) (252) 329-4200; simpson@mail.ecu.edu; (c) Pitt

Private non-profit/ 1990/ staff: 13(v)/ members: 100

HISTORY MUSEUM

PROGRAMS: Exhibits; Facility Rental; Guided Tours; School-Based Curriculum

COLLECTIONS: [1840-1940] Artifacts related to regional rural life. Nineteen donated or reconstructed buildings.

HOURS: Yr by appt

ADMISSION: $2, Children $1

6308
Greenville Historic Preservation Commission
306 S Greene St, 27835 [PO Box 7207, 27835]; (p) (252) 329-4486; (f) (252) 329-4483; (c) Pitt

City/ 1988/ staff: 1(f)/publication: *The Architectural Heritage of Greenville, North Carolina*

HISTORIC PRESERVATION AGENCY: Oversees twenty-one locally designated landmarks and the College View Historic District.

PROGRAMS: Community Outreach; Publication

COLLECTIONS: [20th c.]

6309
Pitt County Historical Society
[PO Box 1554, 27835-1554]; (c) Pitt

1927/ members: 172/publication: *The Historic Architecture of Pitt County*

HISTORICAL SOCIETY: Promotes the study, preservation and compilation of the history of Pitt County.

PROGRAMS: Annual Meeting; Lectures; Publication

6310
Special Collections Department, Joyner Library, East Carolina University
East Carolina Univ, 27858; (p) (252) 328-6671; (f) (252) 328-0268; demboj@mail.ecu.edu; www.lib.ecu.edu; (c) Pitt

State/ 1968/ East Carolina Univ/ staff: 3(f); 5(p)

LIBRARY AND/OR ARCHIVES: Collects, preserves, and makes accessible manuscripts, archives, and rare printed materials.

PROGRAMS: Exhibits

COLLECTIONS: [16th c-present] Manuscripts, maps, photographs, books, newspapers, serials, microforms, oral histories, and university records covering naval and maritime history, tobacco industry, NC, and missionary/religious history.

HOURS: Yr M-F 8-5, Sa 10-2

HALIFAX

6311
Halifax County Historical Association
[PO Box 12, 27839]; (p) (252) 583-7821; (f) (252) 583-7831; (c) Halifax

Private non-profit/ 1970/ Board of Directors/ members: 70

HISTORICAL SOCIETY: Discovers, collects, and preserves material related to county history and makes this knowledge available to the public.

PROGRAMS: Annual Meeting; Family Programs; Lectures

6312
Historic Halifax State Historic Site
25 Saintt David St, 27839 [PO Box 406, 27839]; (p) (252) 583-7191; (f) (252) 583-9421; histhalifax@coastalnet.com; www.visithalifax.com; (c) Halifax

State/ 1966/ NC Historic Sites/ staff: 5(f); 6(p); 6(v)

HISTORIC SITE: Interprets early history of Halifax and the adoption of the Halifax Resolves.

PROGRAMS: Exhibits; Festivals; Film/Video; Guided Tours; Interpretation; Living History; Reenactments; School-Based Curriculum

COLLECTIONS: [1760-1840] Furnishings in five restored buildings, archaeological artifacts, and a small museum.

HOURS: Apr-Oct M-Sa 9-5, Su 1-5; Nov-Mar T-Sa 10-4, Su 1-4

6313
Historical Halifax Restoration Association
25 Saint David St, 27839 [PO Box 406, 27839]; (p) (252) 583-7191; (f) (252) 583-9421; histhalifax@coastalnet.com; (c) Halifax

Private non-profit/ 1954/ staff: 6(v)/ members: 175

HISTORIC PRESERVATION AGENCY: Preserves historic buildings and sites and supports Historic Halifax State Historic Site.

PROGRAMS: Annual Meeting; Festivals

COLLECTIONS: [1760-1840] Household furnishings originating in southeast VA and northeast NC.

HAMILTON

6314
Fort Branch Battlefield Commission, Inc.
Fort Branch Rd, 27840 [PO Box 355, 27840]; (p) (252) 792-4902, (800) 776-8566; (f) (252) 792-8710; www.fortbranchcivilwarsite.com; (c) Martin

Private non-profit/ 1987/ staff: 100(v)/ members: 200

HISTORIC PRESERVATION AGENCY; HISTORIC SITE; HISTORY MUSEUM; LIVING HISTORY/OUTDOOR MUSEUM: Preserves and restores Fort Branch, a Confederate earthen fort on Rainbow Banks overlooking the Roanoke River.

PROGRAMS: Concerts; Exhibits; Facility Rental; Festivals; Guided Tours; Living History; Reenactments

COLLECTIONS: [18th-19c] Colonial, Civil War, and Native American artifacts. Primary to the collection are seven of the fort's original cannons which were raised from the Roanoke River in the 1970s.

HOURS: Apr-Nov Sa-Su 1:30-5:30, and by appt

ADMISSION: No charge

HAMLET

6315
National Railroad Museum and Hall of Fame, Inc.
2 Main St, 28345; (p) (910) 582-3317; (c) Richmond

Private non-profit/ 1976/ Board of Directors/ members: 100

HISTORY MUSEUM: Operated by the Old Seaboard Air Line Railway's depot, built in 1900, home to the NC Division of SAL a prime example of Victorian architecture.

PROGRAMS: Exhibits; Guided Tours

COLLECTIONS: [1930-present] Photographs, maps, model railroad layout, four pieces of rolling stock and a recreated telegraph office. SAL locomotive, 1114 SDP, and caboose SAL 5241 on display.

HOURS: Yr M-F by appt, Sa 10-5, Su 1-5

ADMISSION: Donations accepted

HARKERS ISLAND

6316
Core Sound Waterfowl Museum
1205 Island Rd, 28531 [PO Box 556, 28531]; (p) (252) 728-1500; (f) (252) 728-1742; amspacher@mail.clis.com; www.coresound.com; (c) Carteret

Private non-profit/ 1992/ State of NC/ staff: 2(f); 2(p); 100(v)/ members: 2000/publication: *Core Sounder; CSWM Yearbook*

ART MUSEUM; HISTORY MUSEUM; LIVING HISTORY/OUTDOOR MUSEUM: Preserves and perpetuates the cultural and natural history of North Carolina's coastal communities by documenting and celebrating the area's hunting and fishing traditions.

PROGRAMS: Annual Meeting; Community Outreach; Concerts; Elder's Programs; Exhibits; Family Programs; Festivals; Guided Tours; Interpretation; Lectures; Living History; Publication; Reenactments

COLLECTIONS: [19th c-present] Hunting artifacts such as decoys, boats, tools, and equipment; photographs, hunt club memorabilia, maps, and family histories.

HOURS: Yr M-Sa 10-5, Su 2-5

ADMISSION: Donations accepted

HAYESVILLE

6317
Clay County Historical and Arts Council
[PO Box 5, 28904]; (p) (828) 389-6814; (c) Clay

Private non-profit/ 1972/ staff: 1(p)/ members: 50

ART MUSEUM; HISTORIC SITE; HISTORY MUSEUM: Promotes arts in the schools and community and maintains museum.

PROGRAMS: Annual Meeting; Exhibits; Research Library/Archives

COLLECTIONS: [Early 20th c] Native American and early settler artifacts. Complete doc-

tors office with ledgers, instruments, and medicine bottles. Photographs of people and area.

HOURS: June-Aug T-Sa 10-4

HERTFORD

6318
Newbold-White House Historic Site
151 Newbold-White Rd, 27944 [PO Box 103, 27944]; (p) (252) 426-7567; (f) (252) 426-3538; nbwh@inteliport.com; www.albemarle-nc.com/newbold-white/; (c) Perquimans

Private non-profit/ 1973/ Perquimans County Restoration Association/ staff: 2(f); 1(p); 40(v)/ members: 215

HISTORIC SITE; HISTORICAL SOCIETY; HISTORY MUSEUM; HOUSE MUSEUM; LIVING HISTORY/OUTDOOR MUSEUM: Operates restored 1730 house, interpreted with period furnishings and archaeological artifacts.

PROGRAMS: Annual Meeting; Community Outreach; Exhibits; Family Programs; Festivals; Guided Tours; Interpretation; Lectures; Living History; School-Based Curriculum

COLLECTIONS: [17th-18th c] Period furnishings and archaeological artifacts.

HOURS: Mar-Nov T-Sa 10-4:30, Su 1-4:30; Dec Sa only

ADMISSION: $3, Student $1

HICKORY

6319
And That's The Way It Was
213 3rd St NE, 28601-5124; (p) (828) 324-0751; (f) (828) 466-0153; loribrom@twave.net; www.thewayitwas.com; (c) Catawba

Private for-profit/ 1995/ staff: 5(f); 1(v)

Dedicated to helping others see history through meticulously built historical miniature dioramas.

6320
Hickory Landmarks Society
542 2nd St, NE, 28603 [PO Box 2341, 28603]; (p) (828) 322-4731; (f) (828) 327-9096; HLS@abst.net; (c) Catawba

Private non-profit/ 1968/ staff: 1(f); 2(p); 60(v)/ members: 500/publication: *Tavern to Town*

HOUSE MUSEUM: Preserves the cultural and architecturally significant heritage sites of the Hickory area, including Maple Grove and the Propst House.

PROGRAMS: Annual Meeting; Community Outreach; Exhibits; Facility Rental; Family Programs; Festivals; Garden Tours; Guided Tours; Interpretation; Lectures; Living History; Publication; Research Library/Archives

COLLECTIONS: [1880-1910] Victoriana, including furniture and accoutrements. Archival records and library relating to historic properties and historical figures of Hickory.

HIDDENITE

6321
Hiddenite Center, Inc.
316 Church St, 28636 [PO Box 311, 28636]; (p) (828) 632-6966; (f) (828) 632-3783; HidNight@aol.com; www.Hiddenite.appstate.edu; (c) Alexander

Private non-profit/ 1981/ Board of Directors/ staff: 2(f); 9(p); 150(v)/ members: 350

ART MUSEUM; CULTURAL CENTER; HISTORIC SITE; HOUSE MUSEUM: Preserves and promotes the history, heritage, and culture of the area.

PROGRAMS: Annual Meeting; Community Outreach; Concerts; Exhibits; Facility Rental; Family Programs; Festivals; Guided Tours; Interpretation; Lectures; Living History; School-Based Curriculum; Theatre

COLLECTIONS: [1880-1925] Furniture, dolls, china, crystal, and art.

HOURS: Yr M-F 9-4:30, Sa-Su 2-4:30

ADMISSION: $2.50, Student $1.50, Seniors $1.50

6322
Lucas Mansion
Church St, 28636; (p) (704) 632-3783

HIGH POINT

6323
Angela Peterson Doll and Miniature Museum
101 W Green Dr, 27260; (p) (336) 885-3655; (f) (336) 884-4352; hpcvb@highpoint.org; www.highpoint.org; (c) Guilford

Private non-profit/ 1979/ Board of Directors/ staff: 2(p)

HISTORY MUSEUM: Educates, enlightens, and interprets the heritage of dolls and miniatures. Collects, preserves, and exhibits dolls, doll houses, and miniatures.

PROGRAMS: Community Outreach; Exhibits; Facility Rental; Guided Tours

COLLECTIONS: 1700 dolls from around the world. Includes a nativity scene with rare crˇche dolls, furnished replica of Mrs. Peterson's three story, 14-room home, Shirley Temple dolls, Bob Timberlake/Bette Ball dolls; wax, tin, bisque and paper dolls.

HOURS: Jan-Oct M-F 10-5, Sa 1-4:30, Su 1-4:30; Nov-Mar T-F 10-5, Sa 1-4:30, Su 1-4:30

ADMISSION: $3.50, Student $3, Children $1, Seniors $3; Under 3 free

6324
Furniture Discovery Center, Inc.
101 W Green Dr, 27260; (p) (336) 887-3876; (f) (336) 887-2159; (c) Guilford

Private non-profit/ 1992/ staff: 1(f); 3(p); 2(v)/publication: *Furniture Manufacturing in North Carolina: A Resource Guide*

CORPORATE ARCHIVES/MUSEUM; HISTORY MUSEUM: Devoted to furniture design and manufacturing. Utilizes static, hands-on and interactive displays.

PROGRAMS: Annual Meeting; Community Outreach; Exhibits; Facility Rental; Family Programs; Guided Tours; Interpretation; Lectures; Publication; School-Based Curriculum

COLLECTIONS: [1880-present]

HOURS: Yr M-Sa 10-5, Su 1-5

ADMISSION: $5, Children $2, Senior $4

6325
High Point Historical Society, Inc.
1859 E Lexington Ave, 27262; (p) (336) 885-1859; (f) (336) 883-3284; www.highpointmuseum.org; (c) Guilford

Private non-profit/ 1966/ Board of Trustees/ staff: 6(f); 9(p); 21(v)/ members: 1357/publication: *The Quill*

HISTORIC SITE; HISTORICAL SOCIETY; HISTORY MUSEUM; HOUSE MUSEUM: Operates the High Point Museum and Historical Park.

PROGRAMS: Annual Meeting; Community Outreach; Concerts; Elder's Programs; Exhibits; Facility Rental; Family Programs; Festivals; Guided Tours; Interpretation; Lectures; Living History; Publication; Reenactments; Research Library/Archives; School-Based Curriculum

COLLECTIONS: [1750s-present] Represents the social, religious (Quaker), military, industrial, and economic history of High Point and the Piedmont region of NC.

HOURS: Yr T-Sa 10-4:30, Su 1-4:30

ADMISSION: No charge

6326
High Point Museum and Historical Park
1859 E Lexington Ave, 27262; (p) (336) 885-1859; (f) (336) 883-3284; www.highpointmuseum.org; (c) Guilford

Private non-profit/ High Point Historical Society, Inc./ staff: 4(f); 4(p); 5(v)/ members: 510/publication: *The Quill*

HISTORIC SITE; HISTORICAL SOCIETY; HISTORY MUSEUM; HOUSE MUSEUM; LIVING HISTORY/OUTDOOR MUSEUM: Encourages a sense of heritage, place, and community through the history of Greater High Point for public enrichment.

PROGRAMS: Annual Meeting; Community Outreach; Elder's Programs; Exhibits; Family Programs; Guided Tours; Interpretation; Lectures; Publication; School-Based Curriculum

COLLECTIONS: [18th-20th c] Artifacts, photographs, and printed materials representing local and regional history including business, education, civic authority, and social life.

HOURS: Yr Sa 10-4, Su 1-4:30

ADMISSION: No charge

HILLSBOROUGH

6327
Alliance for Historic Hillsborough, The
150 E King St, 27278; (p) (919) 732-7741; (f) (919) 732-6322; alliance@historichillsborough.org; www.historichillsborough.org; (c) Orange

Private non-profit/ 1993/ Board of Directors/ staff: 2(f); 6(p); 2(v)/ members: 165/publication: *Annual Journal of the Hillsborough Historical Society*

ALLIANCE OF HISTORICAL AGENCIES; GARDEN; HISTORIC PRESERVATION AGENCY; HISTORIC SITE: Preserves Hillsborough's historic built and natural environments, develops interpretive programs, manages a public information program, and provides technical assistance to member organizations.

PROGRAMS: Annual Meeting; Community Outreach; Concerts; Exhibits; Family Pro-

grams; Festivals; Garden Tours; Guided Tours; Interpretation; Lectures; Living History; Publication; Reenactments; Research Library/Archives; School-Based Curriculum

COLLECTIONS: [Pre-colonial-present] Museum artifacts, manuscripts, printed material, photographs, portraits, and paintings.

HOURS: Yr M-Sa 10-4, Su 1-4

ADMISSION: No charge

6328
Ayr Mount
376 Saint Mary's Rd, 27278; (p) (919) (732) 6886

1815/ staff: 1(f); 1(p)

COLLECTIONS: [Early 19th c] Early American art and antiques; Historic maps and prints

HOURS: Seasonal

6329
Historic Hillsborough Commission
319 N Charton St, 27278 [150 E King St, 27278]; (p) (919) 732-7451; (c) Orange

Private non-profit/ 1965/ staff: 1(p); 32(v)

HISTORIC SITE; HOUSE MUSEUM; LIVING HISTORY/OUTDOOR MUSEUM: Interprets antebellum Hillsborough through exhibits, programs, lectures, guided and special group tours.

PROGRAMS: Community Outreach; Concerts; Exhibits; Facility Rental; Family Programs; Festivals; Garden Tours; Guided Tours; Interpretation; Lectures; Living History; Reenactments; School-Based Curriculum

COLLECTIONS: [1837-1860s]

HOURS: Yr Th-Sa 11-3, Su 1-4

ADMISSION: No charge

6330
Moorefields
2201 Moorfields Rd, 27278; (p) (919) (732) 4941; bjacobs@totalsports.net

1785/ staff: 1(f)

COLLECTIONS: [1785]

HOURS: By appt

HUNTERSVILLE

6331
Latta Plantation: A Living History Farm
5225 Sample Rd, 28078; (p) (704) 875-2312; (f) (704) 875-1724; www.lattaplantation.org; (c) Mecklenburg

Private non-profit/ 1972/ staff: 4(f); 3(p); 34(v)/ members: 150

HISTORIC SITE; LIVING HISTORY/OUTDOOR MUSEUM: 19th c living history farm demonstrating Piedmont history. Collects, preserves, and interprets early Catawba Valley history.

PROGRAMS: Annual Meeting; Exhibits; Facility Rental; Family Programs; Festivals; Interpretation; Lectures; Living History

COLLECTIONS: [1760-1840] 500 artifacts, 1,000 volumes.

HOURS: Yr Sept-May T-F 10-5, Sa-Su 12-5; June-Aug T-Su 10-5

ADMISSION: $4; Children $2; Students, Seniors $3

JACKSON

6332
Northampton County Museum
203 W Jefferson St, 27845 [PO Box 664, 27845]; (p) (252) 534-2911; (c) Northampton

Private non-profit/ 1986/ staff: 1(p)

HISTORY MUSEUM: Promotes local and regional history.

PROGRAMS: Community Outreach; Exhibits

COLLECTIONS: Native American projectile points, bottles, photographs of local interest, military weapons, and local maps.

HOURS: Yr W-F 11-1/2-5, Sa 9-2

ADMISSION: No charge

JACKSONVILLE

6333
Onslow County Genealogical Society
Onslow County Public Library, 58 Doris Ave East, 28541 [PO Box 1739, 28541-1739]; (c) Onslow

County/ 1989

GENEALOGICAL SOCIETY: Stimulates interest, support, and enjoyment of genealogical study. Provides research materials and promotes educational programs, publications, and workshops.

PROGRAMS: Research Library/Archives

HOURS: Sept-May 1st T

6334
Onslow County Historical Society
Helen's Kitchen, 2405-B Marine Blvd N, 28540 [PO Box 5203, 28540]; (p) (910) 347-5287, (910) 346-4696; (c) Onslow

County/ 1954/publication: *The Heritage of Onslow County*

HISTORICAL SOCIETY: Operates and maintains the Pelletier House, Jacksonville's oldest standing structure. Collects historical articles and papers for preservation. Participates in historical and genealogical research on subjects associated with Onslow County.

PROGRAMS: Publication

COLLECTIONS: Documents, court minutes, and cemetery records.

HOURS: Sept-May 3rd W

JAMESTOWN

6335
Historic Jamestown Society
603 W Main St, 27282 [PO Box 512, 27282]; (p) (336) 454-3819; (c) Guilford

Private non-profit/ staff: 1(p); 40(v)/ members: 260/publication: *Roads to Jamestown*

HISTORIC PRESERVATION AGENCY; HISTORIC SITE; HISTORICAL SOCIETY; HISTORY MUSEUM; HOUSE MUSEUM: Investigates, preserves, and makes available knowledge of the history of Jamestown and its environs and encourages preservation of its historic sites.

PROGRAMS: Annual Meeting; Community Outreach; Facility Rental; Guided Tours; Publication

COLLECTIONS: [1811-1900] Richard Mendenhall House, Madison Lindsay House,

19th c barn, and horse-drawn transportation including a slave wagon.

HOURS: Yr T-F 11-2, Sa 1-4, Su 2-4

ADMISSION: $2, Student $1

6336
Old Jamestown School Association, Inc.
200 Main St, 27282 [PO Box 1345, 27282]; (p) (336) 454-3312; (c) Guilford

Private non-profit/ 1986/ staff: 2(f); 30(v)/ members: 310

HISTORIC PRESERVATION AGENCY: Operates public library and historic school building.

PROGRAMS: Community Outreach; Concerts; Elder's Programs; Exhibits; Facility Rental; Festivals; Lectures; Research Library/ Archives

COLLECTIONS: 10,000 volumes of genealogical materials, videos, and educational archives of Jamestown.

HOURS: Yr

ADMISSION: No charge

KANNAPOLIS

6337
Cannon Village Textile Museum
200 W Ave, 28081; (p) (704) 938-3200; (f) (704) 932-4188

Private non-profit/ 1985/ Atlantic American Properties/ staff: 1(f); 5(p)

HISTORY MUSEUM: Maintains museum.

PROGRAMS: Community Outreach; Concerts

COLLECTIONS: Mummy wrappings, sheets, towels, and a wide variety of textiles. Holds the world's largest towel, an antique hand loom, and samples of textiles more than 1,200 years old.

HOURS: Yr M-Sa 9-5, Su 1-6

ADMISSION: No charge

KENANSVILLE

6338
Liberty Hall
SR 11/24/50, 28349 [PO Box 634, 28349]; (p) (910) 296-2175

KENLY

6339
Tobacco Farm Life Museum, Inc.
Hwy 301 N, 27542 [PO Box 88, 27542]; (p) (919) 284-3431; (f) (919) 284-9788; tobmuseum@ bbnp.com; www.tobmuseum.bbnp.com; (c) Johnston

Private non-profit/ 1983/ Board of Directors/ staff: 2(f); 6(p); 100(v)/ members: 300

HISTORY MUSEUM; HOUSE MUSEUM: Collects, preserves, and interprets the history and cultural heritage of an eastern NC farm family with emphasis on Depression Era farm life.

PROGRAMS: Community Outreach; Concerts; Exhibits; Facility Rental; Family Programs; Festivals; Guided Tours; Lectures; Research Library/Archives; School-Based Curriculum; Theatre

COLLECTIONS: [1880s-1950s] Agricultural

equipment, textiles, house wares, furniture, archival and library holdings, and various rural life artifacts.

KERNERSVILLE

6340
Korner's Folly
413 S Main St, 27284; (p) (336) 996-7922; (f) (336) 996-1199; www.kornersfolly.org; (c) Forsyth

Private non-profit/ 1995/ Korner's Folly Foundation, Inc./ staff: 1(f); 1(p); 65(v)/ members: 563

HOUSE MUSEUM: Maintains an eclectic Victorian house built c. 1880 by Jule Korner with original furnishings, decorations, and ceiling murals.

PROGRAMS: Festivals; Guided Tours; Theatre

COLLECTIONS: [1880-1910] Decorative arts including 15 fireplace surrounds and 9 mosaic tile floors by American Encaustic Tile Co. Murals by Jule Korner and Caesar Milch, furnishings by Jule Korner and paintings by Jean-Baptiste and Jule Korner.

HOURS: Yr Th 10-3, Sa 10-1, Su 1-5; by appt

ADMISSION: $6, Student $3

KILL DEVIL HILLS

6341
Wright Brothers National Memorial
Mile Post 8, US 158 By Pass, 27948 [PO Box 2539, 27948]; (p) (252) 441-7430; (f) (252) 441-7730; www.nps.gov/wrbr/wright.htm; (c) Dare

Federal/ 1927/ National Park Service/ staff: 4(f); 6(v)

HISTORIC SITE; HISTORY MUSEUM: Site of the world's first powered, controlled flights of an airplane, by Wilbur and Orville Wright on Dec 17, 1903.

PROGRAMS: Community Outreach; Exhibits; Family Programs; Guided Tours; Interpretation; Lectures

COLLECTIONS: [1900-1903] Archaeological and historical artifacts, archives, a monument, visitors center, quarters and hangar buildings.

HOURS: Yr Winter Daily 9-5; Summer Daily 9-6

KINSTON

6342
CSS Neuse State Historic Site and Governor Richard Caswell Memorial
2612 W Vernon Ave, 28502 [PO Box 3043, 28502]; (p) (252) 522-2091; (f) (252) 527-7036; cssneuse@ncsl.dcr.state.nc.us; www.ah.dcr.state.nc.us/sections/hs/neuse.htm; (c) Lenoir

State/ 1965/ staff: 4(f); 6(p)/publication: *A Question of Iron and Time*

HISTORY MUSEUM; LIVING HISTORY/OUTDOOR MUSEUM: Maintains the CSS Neuse Ironclad with interpretations of its history during the Civil War. Governor Richard Caswell Memorial.

PROGRAMS: Exhibits; Film/Video; Guided Tours; Living History; Publication; Reenactments

COLLECTIONS: [18th-19th c] Museum artifacts from CSS Neuse, USS Underwriter, Revolutionary War, and Governor Richard Caswell; Maps, pictures, slides and artifacts and material.

HOURS: Apr-Oct M-Sa 9-5, Su 1-5; Nov-Mar T-Sa 10-4, Su 1-4

ADMISSION: No charge

6343
Harmony Hall
109 E King St, 28501; (p) (252) 522-0421

1772/ staff: 1(p)

Home of Richard Caswell, first governor of NC after independence.

HOURS: By appt

KURE BEACH

6344
Fort Fisher State Historic Site
1610 Fort Fisher Blvd S, 28449 [PO Box 169, 28449]; (p) (910) 458-5538; (f) (910) 458-0477; fisher@ncsl.dcr.state.nc.us; www.ah.dcr.state.nc.us/hs/fisher/fisher.htm; (c) New Hanover

State/ 1965/ staff: 5(f); 5(p); 12(v)/publication: *The Telegraph*

BATTLEFIELD; HISTORIC SITE: Preserves, develops, interprets, operates, and maintains for public benefit the historic property (Civil War battlefield) and resources.

PROGRAMS: Community Outreach; Exhibits; Guided Tours; Interpretation; Living History; Publication; Reenactments; Research Library/ Archives; School-Based Curriculum

COLLECTIONS: [1861-1865] Civil War artifacts relating to site history, including blockade runner wrecks, projectiles, damaged artillery parts, photographs, maps, and lithographs.

HOURS: Apr-Oct M-Sa 9-5, Su 1-5; Nov-Mar T-Sa 10-4, Su 1-4

ADMISSION: Donations accepted

LAKE JUNALUSKA

6345
World Methodist Museum
575 Lakeshore Dr, 28745 [PO Box 518, 28745]; (p) (828) 456-9432; (f) (828) 456-9433; wmc6@juno.com; (c) Haywood

Private non-profit/ 1953/ World Methodist Council/ staff: 5(f); 15(v)/ members: 1/publication: *Saddlebag Notes; World Parish*

HISTORY MUSEUM: Maintains museum.

PROGRAMS: Exhibits; Film/Video; Guided Tours; Publication; Research Library/Archives

COLLECTIONS: [17th-18th c] Pottery, busts, oil paintings, original letters and manuscripts. Houses over 4,000 square feet of artifacts, original letters and manuscripts of John and Charles Wesley, Francis Asbury, George Whitefield and the Wesley family. Oil paintings by British artist Frank O. Salisbury. Bust by Enoch Wood and pottery by Josiah Wedgewood.

HOURS: Sept-May M-F 9-5; June-Aug M-Sa 9-5

LAKE WACCAMAW

6346
Lake Waccamaw Depot Museum, Inc.
201 Flemington Dr, 28450 [PO Box 386, 28450]; (p) (910) 646-1992; (c) Columbus

Private non-profit/ 1977/ Board of Directors/ staff: 1(f); 30(v)/ members: 299

HISTORY MUSEUM: Collects, preserves, and exhibits social and natural history.

PROGRAMS: Annual Meeting; Elder's Programs; Exhibits; Family Programs; Guided Tours; Lectures

COLLECTIONS: [Prehistory-20th c] Marine fossils recovered from freshwater lake bed, Native American and railroad artifacts, extensive photo collection from early 1900s and domestic items. Exhibits in 1904 Atlantic Coastline Railroad depot includes caboose and 300 year old Native American canoe.

HOURS: Yr T-F 1-5, Su 3-5 and by appt

ADMISSION: No charge

LAURINBURG

6347
Indian Museum of the Carolinas, Inc.
607 Turnpike Rd, 28352; (p) (910) 276-5880; (c) Scotland

Private non-profit/ 1972/ staff: 1(p); 12(v)

ARCHAEOLOGICAL SITE/MUSEUM: Educates the public about Native American heritage and culture and preserves archaeological heritage.

PROGRAMS: Community Outreach; Elder's Programs; Exhibits; Festivals; Guided Tours; Lectures; Research Library/Archives

COLLECTIONS: [Prehistory-present] Stone tools, other Southeast Native American artifacts and some ethnographic collections from tribes around the United States and Mexico.

HOURS: Yr

ADMISSION: Donations accepted

LENAIR

6348
Chapel of Rest Preservation Society
1964 Hwy 268, 28645 [PO Box 997, 28645]; (c) Caldwell

Private non-profit/ 1981/ Board of Directors/ staff: 10(v)/ members: 300

HISTORIC SITE: Preserves and maintains the Chapel.

PROGRAMS: Community Outreach; Concerts; Facility Rental; Lectures

HOURS: Yr Daily 8-8

ADMISSION: No charge

LENOIR

6349
Caldwell County Genealogical Society, The
Family History Room, Caldwell Public Library, 28645 [PO Box 2476, 28645-2476]; (p) (828) 758-1075; (c) Caldwell

County/ 1981/ Board of Directors/ staff: 2(f)/ members: 186/publication: *The Caldwell County Journal*

GENEALOGICAL SOCIETY: Brings together persons interested in family history research; fosters, stimulates, and promotes methods and practices in family research; acquires and preserves relevant materials.

PROGRAMS: Monthly Meeting; Publication

COLLECTIONS: [Mid 19th c-present] Family history collections, books, publications, microfilm, and microfiche.

HOURS: Yr M,W,F 8:30-5:30, T,Th 8:30-8:30, Sa 9-4

6350
Caldwell County Historical Society Heritage Museum
112 Vaiden St SW, 28645 [PO Box 2165, 28645]; (p) (828) 758-4004; (c) Caldwell

Joint/ 1950/ Board of Directors; Society; Private non-profit/ staff: 15(v)/ members: 125

HISTORICAL SOCIETY; HISTORY MUSEUM: Investigates, studies, and depicts the history of Caldwell County.

PROGRAMS: Annual Meeting; Exhibits; Guided Tours; Monthly Meeting

HOURS: Yr

LEXINGTON

6351
Davidson County Historical Museum
2 S Main St, 27292; (p) (336) 242-2035; choffmann@co.davidson.nc.us; (c) Davidson

County/ 1976/ staff: 2(f); 1(p); 8(v)

HISTORIC PRESERVATION AGENCY; HISTORIC SITE; HISTORY MUSEUM: Operates a historic site located in the 1858 Greek Revival Courthouse, interpretes courthouse history and architecture, and works on historic preservation initiatives in the community.

PROGRAMS: Community Outreach; Elder's Programs; Exhibits; Facility Rental; Family Programs; Guided Tours; Interpretation; Lectures; Research Library/Archives; School-Based Curriculum

COLLECTIONS: [1800-present] Manuscripts, images, and artifacts with concentrations in period costume, agricultural, economic areas, social, economic, and political history of Davidson County.

HOURS: Yr T-Sa 10-4, Su 2-4

ADMISSION: No charge

LILLINGTON

6352
Harnett County Historical Society
[PO Box 1865, 27546]; (p) (910) 893-3446; jpowell@nceye.net; (c) Harnett

Private non-profit/ 1954/ members: 250

HISTORICAL SOCIETY: Collects, preserves, interprets, and disseminates information on county history for the education and enjoyment of present and future generations.

PROGRAMS: Exhibits; Family Programs; Film/Video; Guided Tours; Lectures

COLLECTIONS: [1700-present]

LINCOLNTON

6353
Lincoln County Museum of History
403 E Main St, 28092; (p) (704) 748-9090; (f) (704) 732-9057; (c) Lincoln

Private non-profit/ 1991/ Lincoln County Historical Association/ staff: 1(f); 15(v)/ members: 350

HISTORIC SITE; HISTORICAL SOCIETY; HISTORY MUSEUM: Collects, preserves, studies, and exhibits artifacts and other historical materials relating to the history and heritage of Lincoln County.

PROGRAMS: Annual Meeting; Exhibits; Interpretation; Lectures; School-Based Curriculum

COLLECTIONS: [1790s-1990s] Manuscripts, photos, ephemera, and miscellaneous broadsides. Artifacts from Lincoln County, pottery from the Catawba Valley, looms, a spinning jenny, and coverlets from the local cottage industry.

HOURS: Yr T,Th 1-5, Su 2-5

ADMISSION: No charge

LUMBERTON

6354
Mill Prong Preservation, Inc.
Edinburg Rd, 28359 [PO Box 2878, 28359]; (c) Hoke

Private non-profit/ 1978/ Board of Directors/ staff: 15(v)/ members: 100

HISTORIC SITE: Preserves Scottish highlander heritage; listed on the National Register.

PROGRAMS: Annual Meeting; Exhibits; Facility Rental; Guided Tours; Interpretation

COLLECTIONS: [18th-19th c] Interior restored to original Federal period, decorations.

6355
Humphrey-Williams-Smith Plantation
5000 H C 211 W, 28358 [5000 H C 211 West, 28358-8701]; (p) (910) 739-6570

1846/ staff: 1(v)

COLLECTIONS: [Civil War-1900] Farm tools, blacksmith tools, barrel-builders, wheelright tools, tax documents, letters, and administrative records.

HOURS: By appt

6356
Robeson County Museum
101 S Elm St, 28359 [PO Box 988, 28359]; (p) (910) 739-3091; (c) Robeson

Private non-profit/ 1987/ Robeson County Public Library/ staff: 2(p); 20(v)/ members: 200

ART MUSEUM; HISTORIC SITE; HISTORICAL SOCIETY; HISTORY MUSEUM: Maintains historical and cultural artifacts with periodic new exhibits; administers Robeson County Public Library; sponsors seminars and community projects related to current exhibits.

PROGRAMS: Annual Meeting; Community Outreach; Exhibits; Festivals; Guided Tours; Interpretation; Lectures; Reenactments; School-Based Curriculum

COLLECTIONS: [Prehistory-present] Geological and archaeological artifacts.

HOURS: Yr T-F 1-5, Sa 11-2 and by appt

ADMISSION: No charge

MANTEO

6357
Outer Bank Group, Cape Hatteras National Seashore
1401 National Park Dr, 27954; (p) (252) 473-2111; (f) (252) 473-2595; www.nps.gov/caha; (c) Dare

Federal/ 1937/ US Dept of Interior, National Park Service/ staff: 110(f); 2(p); 80(v)

HISTORIC SITE; LIVING HISTORY/OUTDOOR MUSEUM; RESEARCH CENTER: Manages Cape Hatteras National Seashore, Fort Raleigh National Historic Site and Wright Brothers National Memorial collection and archives.

PROGRAMS: Community Outreach; Exhibits; Family Programs; Film/Video; Guided Tours; Interpretation; Living History; Research Library/Archives; School-Based Curriculum

COLLECTIONS: [19th-20th c] Local and natural history artifacts; library and archival materials.

HOURS: Yr Daily 9-5

6358
Outer Banks Conservationists, Inc.
Currituck Beach Lighthouse, PO Box 58, 27927; (p) (252) 453-8152; (f) (252) 453-8152; info@currituckbeachlight.com; www.currituckbeachlight.com; (c) Currituck

Private non-profit/ 1980/ staff: 2(f); 12(p)

HISTORIC SITE: Conserves the character of the Outer Banks, preserves, and operates the Currituck Beach Lighthouse in Corolla.

PROGRAMS: Community Outreach; Exhibits; Facility Rental; Family Programs; Interpretation

COLLECTIONS: [1875-1939] Lighthouse, two restored keepers houses, and outbuildings. Small keeper's house restored.

HOURS: Apr-Nov Daily 10-6

ADMISSION: $5, Children $5

6359
Roanoke Island Festival Park
1 Festival Park, 27954; (p) (252) 475-1500; (f) (252) 475-1507; RIFP.Information@ncmail.net; www.roanokeisland.com; (c) Dare

State/ 1983/ Dept of Cultural Resources and Roanoke Island Commission/ staff: 39(f); 41(p); 52(v)/ members: 554

HISTORIC SITE; HISTORY MUSEUM; LIVING HISTORY/OUTDOOR MUSEUM: Protects, preserves, develops, and interprets Roanoke Island's historical, cultural, and natural resources.

PROGRAMS: Annual Meeting; Community Outreach; Concerts; Elder's Programs; Exhibits; Facility Rental; Family Programs; Festivals; Film/Video; Guided Tours; Interpretation; Lectures; Living History; Reenactments; School-Based Curriculum; Theatre

COLLECTIONS: [1584-1900] Three wooden sailing vessels, including "Elizabeth II."

HOURS: Yr Winter Daily 10-5; Summer Daily 9-7

ADMISSION: $8, Student $6; Under 5 free; Group rates

MAYODAN

6360
Genealogical Society of Rockingham and Stokes Counties
[PO Box 152, 27027]; (p) (336) 548-6845; (c) Rockingham/Stokes

1993/ Board of Directors/ staff: 10(v)/ members: 300

GENEALOGICAL SOCIETY: Collects genealogy.

COLLECTIONS: Family histories collects deeds, tax, census, death, and birth records.

MILTON

6361
Thomas Day House/Union Tavern Restoration, Inc.
[PO Box 153, 27305]; (p) (336) 234-7215; (c) Caswell

Private non-profit/ 1989/ staff: 17(v)/ members: 94

HISTORIC SITE; HISTORY MUSEUM; HOUSE MUSEUM: Dedicated to the restoration of Union Tavern (c.1818), a National Historic Landmark.

PROGRAMS: Annual Meeting; Guided Tours

COLLECTIONS: [1818-1859] Residence, workshop, and furniture made by Thomas Day, a free black cabinetmaker c 1848-1859.

HOURS: Apr, July, Oct, Dec by appt

ADMISSION: No charge

MONROE

6362
Carolinas Genealogical Society
300 N Main St, The Old Union County Courthouse, 28111 [PO Box 397, 28111]; (p) (704) 289-6737; (c) Union

Private non-profit/ 1964/ staff: 10(v)/ members: 200/publication: Carolinas Genealogical Society Bulletin

GENEALOGICAL SOCIETY: Collects, preserves, disseminates, compiles, and publishes historical and genealogical information for educational and social purposes.

PROGRAMS: Exhibits; Guided Tours; Publication; Research Library/Archives

COLLECTIONS: [19th c-present] Family histories, census, cemetery, war, and marriage records. Surname files, scrapbooks, microfilm, microfiche, newspapers, church and school files, exchange bulletins, maps, and photographs.

HOURS: Yr M-W 10-3, Th 1-3

6363
Monroe-Union Historic Properties Commission
300 N Main St, The Old Union County Courthouse, 28111 [PO Box 282, 28111]; (p) (704) 289-6737; (c) Union

City; County/ 1981/ City of Monroe/Union County/ staff: 2(p); 8(v)

HISTORIC PRESERVATION AGENCY: Safeguards the heritage of the city and county by preserving any property that embodies important elements of its cultural, social, economic, political or architectural history. Promotes the use and conservation of these properties for the education, enjoyment and enrichment of local residents.

PROGRAMS: Exhibits; Guided Tours; Research Library/Archives

COLLECTIONS: [19th c-present] Architectural and historical inventory of Monroe and Union County published in a book, SWEET UNION. Photographs of properties dating back to the late 1880s; family histories.

HOURS: Yr M-W 10-3, Th 1-4

ADMISSION: No charge

MONTREAT

6364
Presbyterian Historical Society, Montreat Office
318 Georgia Terrace, 28757 [PO Box 849, 28757]; (p) (828) 669-7061; (f) (828) 669-5369; www.history.pcusa.org; (c) Buncombe

1927/ Presbyterian Church/ staff: 8(f); 1(p)/ members: 3300/publication: Journal of Presbyterian History; Presbyterian Heritage

HISTORICAL SOCIETY: Collects information related to Presbyterian history in the south and southern Presbyterian mission in other countries.

PROGRAMS: Publication; Research Library/Archives

COLLECTIONS: [1750-present] 10,000 cu ft manuscripts and archives; 60,000 volumes; 50,000 photos.

HOURS: Yr M-F 8:30-4:30

MOREHEAD CITY

6365
Carteret County Historical Society, Inc.
1008 Arendell St, 28557 [PO Box 481, 28557]; (p) (252) 247-7533; (f) (252) 247-7533; cchs@clis.com; www.rootsweb.com/~ncchs/; (c) Carteret

Private non-profit/ 1971/ Board of Directors/ staff: 1(f); 100(v)/ members: 1000/publication: The Researcher; Camp Glenn Dispatch

GENEALOGICAL SOCIETY; HISTORIC PRESERVATION AGENCY; HISTORICAL SOCIETY; HISTORY MUSEUM; RESEARCH CENTER: Promotes the preservation and study of the county's history, heritage, and genealogy through its library, museum, publications, and outreach programs.

PROGRAMS: Community Outreach; Exhibits; Facility Rental; Family Programs; Lectures; Publication; Research Library/Archives

COLLECTIONS: [18th c-present] Historical and genealogical research library covering eastern NC, VA, and New England. Museum exhibits interpret the history and culture of Carteret County and related areas.

HOURS: Yr T-Sa 1-4

ADMISSION: Donations accepted

MORGANTON

6366
Burke County Genealogical Society
[PO Box 661, 28680]; (c) Burke

Private non-profit/ 1982/ members: 300/publication: *Journal of Burke County Genealogical Society*

GENEALOGICAL SOCIETY: Publishes and sells transcriptions of old county records, cemetery and census books, and a quarterly journal.

6367
Burke County Public Library System
204 S King St, 28655; (p) (828) 437-5638; (f) (828) 433-1914; library@bcpls.org; www.bcpls.org; (c) Burke

Private non-profit/ 1923/ Board of Trustees/ staff: 12(f); 7(p); 3(v)

NC Room contains research material for Burke County and surrounding counties.

COLLECTIONS: [1777-present] Family histories, vertical files, microfilm, and books on NC, Burke County and other county histories.

6368
Historic Burke Foundation, Inc.
102 E Union St & 119 Saint Mary's Church Rd, 28680 [PO Box 915, 28680]; (p) (828) 437-4104; (c) Burke

Private non-profit/ 1982/ Board of Trustees/ staff: 1(f); 5(v)/ members: 458/publication: *Historic Burke: An Architectural Sites Inventory of Burke County; Under the Forest Floor, The Restoration of Quaker Meadows Cemetery*

HISTORIC PRESERVATION AGENCY; HISTORIC SITE; HISTORY MUSEUM; HOUSE MUSEUM: Promotes preservation and restoration of historic sites in Burke County. Operates the Heritage Museum in the Old Burke County Courthouse and 1812 Charles McDowell, Jr. House at Quaker Meadows Plantation.

PROGRAMS: Annual Meeting; Exhibits; Facility Rental; Film/Video; Guided Tours; Interpretation; Publication

COLLECTIONS: [19th c] Artifacts, memorabilia, and materials on different aspects of county history, Quaker Meadows, and Catawba Valley plantation life, 1812-1859.

HOURS: Heritage Museum: Yr T-F 10-4; Quaker Meadows: Apr-Oct Su 2-5 and by appt

ADMISSION: $3; No charge for Heritage Museum

MOUNT AIRY

6369
Edwards-Franklin House
11 mi W of Mount Airy on Haystack Rd, 27030 [c/o Cama C Merritt, 832 E Country Club Rd, 27030]; (p) (336) 786-8359; (f) (336) 786-1449

1799/ staff: 156(v)

COLLECTIONS: [Early 19th c] Original decorative painting on wainscoting, doors and mantels from 1823.

HOURS: Apr-Oct 2nd Sa-Su 1-5

6370
Gertrude Smith House
708 N Main St, 27030 [615 N Main St, 27030]; (p) (336) 786-6856, (800) 576-0231; (f) (336) 786-9193

1903/ staff: 1(f); 7(p); 6(v)

COLLECTIONS: [Victorian] Southern antiques, pottery and porcelain ware, artifacts, extensive library.

HOURS: Seasonal; Mar-May, Dec, Oct M, W, F, Sa 11-4

6371
Historic Preservation Commission
300 S Main St, 27030 [PO Box 70, 27030]; (p) (336) 786-3520; (f) (336) 719-7506; chegler@mountairy.org; (c) Surry

City/ 1992/ staff: 9(v)

HISTORIC PRESERVATION AGENCY: Protects Mount Airy's heritage by encouraging renovation of historic district and promotes preservation education.

PROGRAMS: Interpretation

6372
Mount Airy Museum of Regional History, Inc.
301 N Main St, 27030 [PO Box 6308, 27030]; (p) (336) 786-4478; (f) (336) 786-1666; (c) Surry

Private non-profit/ 1993/ staff: 3(f); 1(p); 65(v)/ members: 500/publication: *Historic Times*

HISTORY MUSEUM: Preserves the cultural and artistic heritage of the Hollows, a backcountry region of northwest NC and southwest VA.

PROGRAMS: Exhibits; Family Programs; Guided Tours; Publication; Research Library/ Archives

COLLECTIONS: [1700s-1950]

HOURS: Yr T-F 10-4, Sa 10-2

6373
Surry County Historical Society
832 E Country Club Rd, 27030; (p) (336) 786-8359; (f) (336) 786-1449; rmerritt@infoave.net; (c) Surry

Private non-profit/ 1972/ staff: 15(v)/ members: 380/publication: *Simple Treasures, Architectural Inventory of Surry County; Surry County Soldiers of the Civil War*

HISTORICAL SOCIETY: Collects, preserves, and interprets local history.

PROGRAMS: Annual Meeting; Exhibits; Festivals; Guided Tours; Interpretation; Lectures; Living History; Publication; Reenactments; Research Library/Archives

COLLECTIONS: [19th c] 1799 Edwards-Franklin House, antebellum Brower Mill Bridge, secondary sources, and a few manuscript.

HOURS: Apr-Oct 2nd Sa and Su 1-5

ADMISSION: No charge

MOUNT GILEAD

6374
Town Creek Indian Mound State Historic Site
509 Town Creek Mound Rd, 27306; (p) (910) 439-6802; (f) (910) 439-6441; tcim@ac.net; www.ah.dcr.state.nc.us/sections/town/town.htm; (c) Montgomery

State/ 1937/ North Carolina Department of Cultural Resources, Division of Archives and History/ staff: 5(f); 5(p)

HISTORIC SITE: Maintains, interprets and operates the site for the visiting public through reconstructions. Offers programs, exhibits and guided tours.

PROGRAMS: Community Outreach; Exhibits; Film/Video; Guided Tours; Interpretation; School-Based Curriculum

COLLECTIONS: [Prehistoric] Reconstructed 14th c Native American ceremonial center, based on archaeological data and early documents. Includes townhouse on an earthen mound, priest house, mortuary, game pole and stockade surrounding the ceremonial area. Exhibits interpret the lifestyle of Native Americans at Town Creek and include artifacts discovered during excavation of the site.

HOURS: Apr-Oct M-Sa 9-5, Su 1-5; Nov-Mar T-Sa 10-4, Su 1-4

ADMISSION: No charge

MURPHY

6375
Cherokee County Historical Museum
87 Peachtree St, 28906; (p) (828) 837-6792; (f) (828) 837-9684; (c) Cherokee

County/ 1977/ staff: 1(f)/publication: *The Heritage of Cherokee County*

HISTORIC PRESERVATION AGENCY; HISTORY MUSEUM: Collects, preserves, restores, studies, and exhibits artifacts, books, papers, photographs, and other materials significant to the history, culture, and heritage of Cherokee County.

PROGRAMS: Exhibits; Guided Tours; Publication

COLLECTIONS: [17th-19th c] Native American artifacts, antique farm implements, vintage household items, minerals, fairy crosses, dolls, old schoolhouse replica, Fort Butler exhibit, photographs, and publications about Cherokee County.

HOURS: Yr M-F 9-5

ADMISSION: No charge

NEW BERN

6376
Bellair Plantation and Restoration
1100 Washington Post Rd, 28560-9386; (p) (252) 637-3913; (f) (252) 637-3913

1700/ Private/ staff: 2(f); 1(v)

COLLECTIONS: [18th c]

HOURS: By appt

6377
New Bern Fireman's Museum
408 Hancock St, 28560 [PO Box 1129, 28560]; (p) (252) 636-4087; (f) (252) 636-1084; firechief-nb@admin.ci.new-bern.nc.us; (c) Craven

City/ 1955/ staff: 1(f); 2(p); 1(v)

HISTORIC PRESERVATION AGENCY; HISTORIC SITE; HISTORY MUSEUM: Interprets fire history and artifacts from the City of New Bern via a guided tour, which focuses on original fire equipment and the history of the New Bern Fire Department.

PROGRAMS: Exhibits; Guided Tours; Interpretation; Lectures

COLLECTIONS: [19th-20th c]

HOURS: Yr Summer Daily 10-4:30; Winter M-Sa 10-4:30, Su 1-5

ADMISSION: $2, Children $1

6378
New Bern Historic Preservation Commission
248 Craven St, 28563 [PO Box 1129, 28563-1129]; (p) (252) 636-4077; (f) (252) 636-2146; histprs-nb@admin.ci.new-bern.nc.us; (c) Craven

City/ 1981/ staff: 1(f); 9(v)

HISTORIC PRESERVATION AGENCY: Regulates exterior changes with locally designated historic districts.

PROGRAMS: Interpretation

6379
New Bern Historical Society Foundation, Inc.
510 Pollock St, 28563 [PO Box 119, 28563]; (p) (252) 638-8558; (f) (252) 638-5773; nbhistoricalsoc@coastalnet.com; (c) Craven

Private non-profit/ 1923/ Board of Directors/ staff: 2(f); 300(v)/ members: 750/publication: *Journal of the Historical Society; Ghost Stories of Old New Bern; and others*

HISTORIC SITE; HISTORICAL SOCIETY; HOUSE MUSEUM: Preserves New Bern's cultural and architectural heritage through education, publications and the collection, preservation, and exhibition of historical artifacts, and materials pertaining to local history.

PROGRAMS: Community Outreach; Exhibits; Facility Rental; Family Programs; Festivals; Guided Tours; Lectures; Publication; School-Based Curriculum

COLLECTIONS: [18th-19th c] Built in 1790, the Attmore-Oliver house was enlarged in 1834. Antique furnishings, Civil War memorabilia, and dolls.

HOURS: Apr-mid Dec T-Sa 1-4:30

ADMISSION: Donations accepted

6380
New Bern Preservation Foundation, Inc.
510 Pollock St, 28563 [PO Box 207, 28563]; (p) (252) 633-6448; (f) (252) 633-6448; (c) Craven

Private non-profit/ 1972/ Board of Directors/ staff: 1(f); 1(p)/ members: 425

HISTORIC PRESERVATION AGENCY: A revolving fund organization that offers programs, workshops and works with schools on educational programs. Has added two neighborhoods to the National Register.

PROGRAMS: Annual Meeting; Family Programs; Garden Tours; Guided Tours; Lectures; Research Library/Archives; School-Based Curriculum

6381
Tryon Palace Historic Sites and Gardens
610 Pollock St, 28563 [PO Box 1007, 28563]; (p) (252) 514-4900; (f) (252) 514-4876; tryon_palace@coastalnet.com; www.tryonpalace.org; (c) Craven

State/ 1945/ NC Dept of Cultural Resources, Division of Archives and History/ staff: 54(f);

100(p); 60(v)/ members: 600

GARDEN; HISTORIC SITE; HISTORY MUSEUM; HOUSE MUSEUM; LIVING HISTORY/OUTDOOR MUSEUM: Educates visitors about the contributions made by inhabitants of New Bern to state and national history and culture from initial European-Native American contact through the 19th c.

PROGRAMS: Concerts; Exhibits; Festivals; Film/Video; Garden Tours; Guided Tours; Interpretation; Lectures; Living History; Reenactments; Research Library/Archives; School-Based Curriculum

COLLECTIONS: [18th-19th c] Representative objects from England, America, and Asia including furniture, silver, porcelains, brass, glass, paintings, prints,and sculptures.

HOURS: Yr M-Sa 9-5, Su 1-5; Extended hours May-Sept

ADMISSION: $12, Children $6

NEWTON

6382
Catawba County Historical Association
30 N College, 28658 [PO Box 73, 28658]; (p) (828) 465-0383; (f) (828) 465-9813; ccha@w3link.com; (c) Catawba

Private non-profit/ 1949/ staff: 3(f); 7(p); 34(v)/ members: 1206/publication: *Past Times*

HISTORIC PRESERVATION AGENCY; HISTORIC SITE; HISTORICAL SOCIETY; HISTORY MUSEUM; HOUSE MUSEUM: Operates the Catawba County Museum of History and two historic sites, Historic Murray's Mill Complex and the 1894 Bunker Hill Covered Bridge. Provides publications, public programs and archives.

PROGRAMS: Annual Meeting; Community Outreach; Exhibits; Facility Rental; Family Programs; Festivals; Film/Video; Guided Tours; Interpretation; Lectures; Living History; Publication; Reenactments; Research Library/Archives; School-Based Curriculum

COLLECTIONS: [1747-present]

HOURS: Yr

ADMISSION: $4, Children $3, Seniors $3; Museum of History free

OCEAN ISLE BEACH

6383
Museum of Coastal Carolina
21 E Second, 28469; (p) (910) 579-1016; (f) (910) 579-1016; museum@nccoast.net; www.discoveryplace.org; (c) Brunswick

Private non-profit/ 1991/ Discovery Place, Inc./ staff: 1(f); 1(p); 70(v)/ members: 312

LIVING HISTORY/OUTDOOR MUSEUM; NATURAL HISTORY MUSEUM: Stimulates public interest in, and understanding of, the natural science, environmen, and cultural history of the coastal region of the Carolinas by providing educational facilities, activities, and exhibits.

PROGRAMS: Annual Meeting; Community Outreach; Exhibits; Facility Rental; Family Programs; Guided Tours; Interpretation; Lectures; Living History; School-Based Curriculum

COLLECTIONS: Native animals of the coastal region of the Carolinas including marine invertebrate and vertebrate specie as well as terrestrial species including Pre-Columbian and Post-European man.

HOURS: Yr M-Sa 9-5, Su 1-5

ADMISSION: $3.50, Children $1.50

OCRACOKE

6384
Ocracoke Preservation Society, Inc.
49 Water Plant Rd, 27960 [PO Box 491, 27960]; (p) (252) 928-7375; (f) (252) 928-4560; OPS@Beachlink.com; (c) Hyde

Private non-profit/ 1983/ staff: 2(f); 25(v)/ members: 375

GENEALOGICAL SOCIETY; HISTORIC PRESERVATION AGENCY; HISTORICAL SOCIETY; HISTORY MUSEUM; HOUSE MUSEUM: Preserves Ocracoke's rich historical, cultural, and environmental heritage.

PROGRAMS: Annual Meeting; Exhibits; Festivals; Film/Video; Lectures; Research Library/Archives

COLLECTIONS: [18th c-present] Artifacts and media related to the history of Ocracoke Village, Ocracoke Island, and maritime occupations.

HOURS: Apr-Nov Daily 10-4

ADMISSION: Donations accepted

OLD FORT

6385
Historic Carson House
Hwy 70 W, 28762 [Rt 1, Box 182, 28762]; (p) (828) 724-4948; (c) McDowell

Private non-profit/ 1964/ Board of Directors/ staff: 1(f); 3(v)

GENEALOGICAL SOCIETY; HISTORIC SITE; HISTORICAL SOCIETY; HISTORY MUSEUM; HOUSE MUSEUM: Genealogical records and memorabilia dating from pioneer days to early 1900 are maintained for study and research.

PROGRAMS: Community Outreach; Exhibits; Facility Rental; Festivals; Guided Tours; Interpretation; Reenactments; Research Library/Archives

COLLECTIONS: [19th c] Tools, utensils, clothing, needlework, and other homemade items.

HOURS: May-Oct T-Sa 10-5, Su 2-5

ADMISSION:$3, Children $1.50

6386
Mountain Gateway Museum
102 Water St, 28762 [PO Box 1286, 28762]; (p) (828) 668-9259; (f) (828) 668-0041; gateway@wnclink.com; (c) McDowell

State/ 1975/ North Carolina Museum of History/ staff: 3(f); 5(p)

HISTORY MUSEUM: Located on the banks of Mill Creek, the site includes a museum building and two log cabins.

PROGRAMS: Elder's Programs; Exhibits; Facility Rental; Family Programs; Festivals; Film/Video; Interpretation; Lectures; Living History

COLLECTIONS: [18th-19th c] Southern Appalachian rural household articles, farm tools, and personal items.

HOURS: Yr M-Sa 9-5, Su 2-5

ADMISSION: No charge

OXFORD

6387
Granville County Museum
110 Court St, 27565 [PO Box 1433, 27565]; (p) (919) 693-9706; (f) (919) 692-10309706; gcmuseum@gloryroad.net; (c) Granville

Private non-profit/ 1994/ Granville County Historical Society/ staff: 2(p); 72(v)/ members: 335/publication: *Heritage and Homesteads*

HISTORICAL SOCIETY; HISTORY MUSEUM: Preserves, raises awareness, and appreciation of Granville County's historical past.

PROGRAMS: Annual Meeting; Community Outreach; Exhibits; Facility Rental; Festivals; Film/Video; Guided Tours; Interpretation; Publication; School-Based Curriculum

COLLECTIONS: [1746-present] Papers, newspapers, photographs, and Civil War artifacts.

HOURS: Yr W-F 10-4, Sa 11-3

ADMISSION: No charge

PEMBROKE

6388
Museum of the Native American Resource Center
Old Main Bldg, 28372 [Univ of NC at Pembroke, 28372]; (p) (910) 521-6282; knick@nat.uncp.edu; www.uncp.edu/native-museum; (c) Robeson

State/ 1979/ Univ of NC at Pembroke/ staff: 2(f)

HISTORY MUSEUM; RESEARCH CENTER: Multi-faceted museum and research institute dedicated to the prehistory, history, culture, art and contemporary issues of Native Americans.

PROGRAMS: Exhibits; Festivals; Film/Video; Guided Tours; Lectures

COLLECTIONS: [Prehistory-present] Native American artifacts, arts, crafts, documents, recordings, and photographs.

HOURS: Yr M-F 8-5

ADMISSION: No charge

PINEVILLE

6389
James K. Polk Memorial State Historic Site
308 S Polk St, 28134 [PO Box 475, 28134]; (p) (704) 889-7145; (f) (704) 889-3057; polk-memorial@dasia.net; www.ah.state.nc.us/hs/polk/polk/htm; (c) Mecklenburg

State/ 1968/ NC Dept of Cultural Resources/ staff: 4(f); 6(p); 25(v)

HISTORIC SITE; HISTORY MUSEUM; HOUSE MUSEUM; PRESIDENTIAL SITE: Dedicated to interpreting significant events in James K. Polk's, (11th President of the United States) life and administration c 1795-1806. Site where James K. Polk was born.

PROGRAMS: Community Outreach; Exhibits; Family Programs; Film/Video; Interpretation;

Living History; Reenactments; School-Based Curriculum

COLLECTIONS: [1795-1806/1844-1849] Period pieces from early Mecklenburg County and NC, artifacts from the Polk presidency that includes a significant Mexican War collection.

HOURS: Apr-Oct M-Sa 9-5, Su 1-5; Nov-Mar T-Sa 10-4, Su 1-4

ADMISSION: No charge

PINNACLE

6390
Horne Creek Living Historical Farm
320 Hauser Rd, 27043; (p) (336) 325-2298; (f) (336) 325-3150; hornecreek@surry.net; www.ah.dcr.state.nc.us/sections/hs/horne/horne.htm; (c) Surry

State/ 1987/ NC Dept of Cultural Resources/ staff: 3(f); 4(p); 20(v)

GARDEN; HISTORIC SITE; LIVING HISTORY/OUTDOOR MUSEUM; RESEARCH CENTER: Outdoor museum and research center that studies, preserves, and interprets NC's agricultural and rural heritage, c 1900-1910.

PROGRAMS: Family Programs; Festivals; Garden Tours; Guided Tours; Interpretation; Lectures; Living History; Research Library/Archives; School-Based Curriculum

COLLECTIONS: [1900-1910] Agricultural equipment, tools, household furniture, kitchenware, photographs, and a series of oral history tapes.

HOURS: Apr-Oct T-Sa 9-5, Su 1-5; Nov-Mar T-Sa 10-4, Su 1-4

ADMISSION: No charge

PITTSBORO

6391
Chatham County Historical Association, Inc.
[PO Box 913, 27312]; (p) (919) 542-3603; (c) Chatham

Private non-profit/ 1966/ staff: 35(v)/ members: 275/publication: *Chatham Historical Journal*

HISTORICAL SOCIETY; HISTORY MUSEUM: Preserves and communicates local history through educational programs, newspaper clippings, guided tours, promotion of historic preservation, family history materials, and publications.

PROGRAMS: Annual Meeting; Exhibits; Guided Tours; Lectures; Publication

COLLECTIONS: Artifacts, primarily papers, related to Chatham County.

HOURS: Yr F 10-2

ADMISSION: No charge

PLYMOUTH

6392
Washington County Genealogical Society
Public Library, 27962 [PO Box 567, 27962]; (p) (252) 793-5236; (c) Washington

Private non-profit/ 1989/ Board of Directors/ members: 110

GENEALOGICAL SOCIETY: Maintains an or-

ganization of persons interested in the research of family histories associated with Washington and surrounding counties.

PROGRAMS: Publication

COLLECTIONS: [18th-19th c] Books, abstracts of wills, and colonial records.

HOURS: 3rd Su

RALEIGH

6393
Archives of the Episcopal Diocese of North Carolina
201 Saint Alban's Dr, 27619 [PO Box 17025, 27619]; (p) (919) 787-6313; (f) (919) 787-0156; tmalone@episdionc.org; www.episdionc.com; (c) Wake

Private non-profit/ 1817/ Episcopal Diocese of NC/ staff: 2(f)

LIBRARY AND/OR ARCHIVES: Repository for the official records of bishops conventions and parishes of the diocese. Library holds Episcopal Church-related journals, manuscripts, books, microfilm, and photographs.

PROGRAMS: Annual Meeting; Research Library/Archives

COLLECTIONS: [19th-20th c] Episcopal Church records, primarily from the Diocese of NC; papers of past bishops; microfilm of church newspapers (1861-1978); parish histories; records of closed churches; pamphlet and manuscripts.

HOURS: Yr M-F 9-5 by appt

6394
Capital Area Preservation, Inc.
128 E Hargett St, 27611 [PO Box 28072, 27611-8072]; (p) (919) 833-6404; (f) (919) 834-7314; CapPresInc@aol.com; (c) Wake

Private non-profit/ 1972/ staff: 3(f); 10(p); 50(v)/ members: 1000/publication: *Preservation Matters*

HISTORIC PRESERVATION AGENCY: Manages Mordecai Historic Park in cooperation with the City of Raleigh and operates a revolving fund that has helped save thirteen endangered properties.

PROGRAMS: Exhibits; Facility Rental; Garden Tours; Guided Tours; Interpretation; Lectures; Living History; Publication

COLLECTIONS: [Early 19th c] Park includes Mordecai Plantation House (1785) and several outbuildings, including the birthplace of President Andrew Johnson.

HOURS: Yr Su 1-3, M, W-Sa 10-3

6395
Federation of North Carolina Historical Societies
109 E Jones St, 27601; (p) (919) 733-7305; (f) (919) 733-8807; (c) Wake

Private non-profit/ 1976/ staff: 2(p); 12(v)

ALLIANCE OF HISTORICAL AGENCIES: Provides information and outreach for historical societies in NC. Operates a revolving fund for publishing local history and co-sponsors NC History Day.

PROGRAMS: Annual Meeting; Community Outreach; Lectures; School-Based Curriculum

6396
Haywood Hall Museum House and Gardens
211 New Bern Pl, 27601; (p) (919) 832-8357, (919) 832-4158; (c) Wake

Joint/ 1978/ Private non-profit; Haywood Hall Committee; Friends of Haywood Hall, Inc./ staff: 2(p); 16(v)/ members: 210

GARDEN; HISTORIC SITE; HISTORY MUSEUM; HOUSE MUSEUM: Maintains and enhances properties to educate the public about 200 years of Raleigh's history as well as Treasurer John Haywood's family.

PROGRAMS: Exhibits; Facility Rental; Film/ Video; Garden Tours; Guided Tours; Lectures; Research Library/ Archives; School-Based Curriculum

COLLECTIONS: [1800-1970] Family furniture, portraits, porcelains, glass, silver, children's clothing and toys.

HOURS: Mar-mid Dec Th 10:30-1:30

ADMISSION: Donations accepted

6397
Historic Oak View County Park
4028 Carya Dr, 27610; (p) (919) 250-1013; (f) (919) 250-1262; tburton@co.wake.nc.us; www.co.wake.nc.us/parksrec/; (c) Wake

County/ 1995/ Wake County Parks and Recreation/ staff: 2(f); 4(p); 50(v)

GARDEN; HISTORIC SITE; HISTORY MUSEUM; HOUSE MUSEUM; LIVING HISTORY/ OUTDOOR MUSEUM: Interprets and preserves the agricultural and rural farm heritage of NC through educational programs, special events, and exhibits and provides cultural enrichment and recreational activities.

PROGRAMS: Annual Meeting; Community Outreach; Concerts; Elder's Programs; Exhibits; Facility Rental; Family Programs; Festivals; Garden Tours; Guided Tours; Interpretation; Lectures; Living History; Reenactments; School-Based Curriculum

COLLECTIONS: [19th-20th c] Material culture specifically related to the site, such as items of agricultural and rural farm life that are consistent with the time period.

HOURS: Yr M-Sa 8:30-5, Su 1-5

ADMISSION: No charge

6398
Joel Lane Museum House
728 W Hargett St, 27603 [PO Box 10884, 27605]; (p) (919) 833-3431; ncneighbors.com

1760/ staff: 1(p); 4(v)

Home of Revolutionary War Colonel Joel Lane, and the site of the meeting at which the decision was made for state of NC to purchase Lane's land on which to build its capital.

COLLECTIONS: [1760-1800]

HOURS: Mar-Dec

6399
Mordecai Historic Park
1 Mimosa St, 27604; (p) (919) 834-4844; (f) (919) 834-7314; cappresinc@aol.com

1785/ staff: 1(f); 12(p); 10(v)

COLLECTIONS: [1785-1860] Artifacts, early Empire pieces, Mordecai family papers.

HOURS: Yr

6400
North Carolina Division of Archives and History
109 E Jones St, 27601; (p) (919) 733-7305; (f) (919) 733-8807; www.ah.dcr.state.nc.us; (c) Wake

State/ 1903/ staff: 400(f); 9(p); 250(v)/publication: *North Carolina Historical Review*

STATE AGENCY: Public historical agency with a full range of programs. Individual sections are Archives and Records, Historic Sites, Historical Publications, State Preservation Office, Maritime Museum, State Capitol/Visitor Services, and Tyron Palace.

PROGRAMS: Community Outreach; Exhibits; Family Programs; Garden Tours; Guided Tours; Interpretation; Lectures; Living History; Publication; Reenactments; Research Library/Archives; School-Based Curriculum

COLLECTIONS: [1584-present] Largest repository of the official records of the colony and state of NC and collections of prehistoric and historic artifacts.

6401
North Carolina Division of Parks and Recreation
512 N Salisbury St, Archdale Bldg, 7th Fl, 27611 [PO Box 27687, 27611-7687]; (p) (919) 733-4181, (919) 733-7275; (f) (919) 715-3085; tom_howard@mail.enr.state.nc.us; www.ils.unc.edu/parkproject/ncparks.html; (c) Wake

State/ 1915/ NC Dept of Environment and Natural Resources/ staff: 350(f)/ members: 1

STATE PARK: Manages 35 state parks and recreation areas including historic sites and monuments.

PROGRAMS: Community Outreach; Concerts; Exhibits; Facility Rental; Family Programs; Festivals; Film/Video; Interpretation; Lectures; Living History; School-Based Curriculum

6402
North Carolina Genealogical Society, Inc.
[PO Box 1492, 27602-1492]; ncgs@earthlink; www.ncgenealogy.org; (c) Wake

Private non-profit/ 1974/ staff: 3(p)/ members: 2000/publication: *North Carolina Genealogical Society Journal*

GENEALOGICAL SOCIETY: Promotes the collection, preservation, and utilization of manuscripts, documents, and other materials of genealogical and historical value.

PROGRAMS: Annual Meeting; Exhibits; Lectures; Publication

COLLECTIONS: Books and other materials.

6403
North Carolina Historic Sites
532 N Wilmington St, 27604; (p) (919) 733-7862; (f) (919) 733-9515; hs@ncsl.dcr.state.nc.us; www.ah.dcr.state.nc.us/sections/hs; (c) Wake

State/ 1955/ North Carolina Division of Archives and History/ staff: 140(f); 150(p); 4500(v)/publication: *Passport to North Carolina Historic Sites*

HISTORIC PRESERVATION AGENCY: Preserves and operates twenty-two historic properties spanning most of the state's geography and history.

PROGRAMS: Community Outreach; Exhibits; Family Programs; Festivals; Guided Tours; Interpretation; Lectures; Living History; Publication; Reenactments

COLLECTIONS: [Prehistoric-present] Material culture and archaeological artifacts representing the culture, people, and events significant to NC history.

HOURS: Apr-Oct M-Sa 9-5, Su 1-5; Nov-Mar T-Sa 10-4, Su 1-4

ADMISSION: No charge

6404
North Carolina Literary and Historical Association
109 E Jones St, 27601; (p) (919) 733-7305; (f) (919) 733-8807; (c) Wake

Private non-profit/ 1900/ staff: 2(p)/ members: 600/publication: *North Carolina Historical Review*

HISTORICAL SOCIETY: Fosters interest in the literature and history of NC. Encourages literary activity by conducting seven literary competitions annually and promotes local history.

PROGRAMS: Annual Meeting; Community Outreach; Lectures; Publication

6405
North Carolina Museum of History
5 E Edenton St, 27601; (p) (919) 715-0200; (f) (919) 733-8655; jcw@moh.dcr.state.nc.us.; www.nchistorydcr.state.nc.us/museums; (c) Wake

State/ 1902/ staff: 78(f); 24(p); 104(v)/ members: 7500/publication: *Cornerstone; Tarheel Junior Historian*

HISTORY MUSEUM: Promotes understanding of the history and material culture. Encourages individuals to explore and understand the past through collections and historical interpretation. Preserves state, regional, and local history.

PROGRAMS: Community Outreach; Concerts; Elder's Programs; Exhibits; Facility Rental; Family Programs; Festivals; Film/Video; Guided Tours; Interpretation; Lectures; Living History; Publication; Reenactments; Research Library/Archives; School-Based Curriculum; Theat

COLLECTIONS: [17th c-present] Artifacts relating to the history and culture of NC.

HOURS: Yr T-Sa 9-5, Su 12-5

ADMISSION: No charge

6406
North Carolina State Archives and Records Section
109 E Jones St, 27699 [4614 Mail Service Ctr, 27699-4614]; (p) (919) 733-3952; (f) (919) 733-1354; Archives@ncsl.dcr.state.nc.us; www.ah.dcr.state.nc.us; (c) Wake

State/ 1903/ NC Div of Archives and History/ staff: 74(f)

LIBRARY AND/OR ARCHIVES: The official repository for the state and its local entities.

PROGRAMS: Research Library/Archives

COLLECTIONS: [18th c-present] The official records of the state and its subdivisions. Manuscripts of various North Carolinians.

HOURS: Yr T-F 8-5:30, Sa 9-5

ADMISSION: No charge

6407
North Carolina State Capitol
1 E Edenton St, 27601 [4624 Mail Service Ctr, 27699-4624]; (p) (919) 733-4994; (f) (919) 715-4030; capitol@ncsl.dcr.state.nc.us; www.ah.dcr.state.nc.us/sections/capitol/; (c) Wake

State/ 1840/ NC Dept of Cultural Resources/ staff: 7(f); 9(p); 25(v)/ members: 150

HISTORIC SITE: Listed as National Historic Landmark, the state capitol is one of the best-preserved examples of a civic building in the Greek revival style.

PROGRAMS: Festivals; Guided Tours; Lectures; Living History; Reenactments

COLLECTIONS: [1840-1865] Legislative furnishings, 14 statues and monuments, and other period objects.

6408
North Carolina State Historic Preservation Office, Division of Archives and History
507 N Blount St, 27601 [109 E Jones St, 27601-2807]; (p) (919) 733-4763; (f) (919) 733-8653; hpo@ncst.dcr.state.nc.us; www.hpo.dcr.state.nc.us; (c) Wake

State/ 1974/ NC Dept of Cultural Resources/ staff: 43(f); 1(p); 100(v)/publication: Legacy at Work

ARCHAEOLOGICAL SITE/MUSEUM; HISTORIC PRESERVATION AGENCY; RESEARCH CENTER: Assists private citizens and institutions, local governments, and agencies of state and federal government in the identification, evaluation, protection, and enhancement of properties significant in NC history and archaeology.

PROGRAMS: Annual Meeting; Community Outreach; Exhibits; Interpretation; Lectures; Publication; Research Library/Archives; School-Based Curriculum

COLLECTIONS: [Prehistoric] Thousands of architectural survey and registration records and photographic materials. Curation and storage of most of the state's archaeological collections.

HOURS: Yr M-F 8-5

ADMISSION: No charge

6409
Olivia Raney Local History Library
4016 Carya Dr, 27610; (p) (919) 250-1196, (919) 212-0476; (f) (919) 212-0476; oliviaraney@co.wake.nc.us; www.co.wake.nc.us/library/locations/orl/; (c) Wake

County/ 1996/ Wake County Public Library System/ staff: 3(f)

RESEARCH CENTER: Collects and preserves materials that describe Wake County and its surrounding areas. Provides access for research on local and family history and serves as an archives for Wake County government materials.

PROGRAMS: Family Programs; Guided Tours; Lectures; Research Library/Archives

COLLECTIONS: [18th-20th c] Local history books, genealogical materials in print, and media such as microfilm, microfiche, audio tapes and CD-ROMs. Extensive Civil War titles and photographic collection of a local photographer.

HOURS: Yr M,Th 10-8, T-W 10-6, Sa 10-5

ADMISSION: No charge

6410
Preservation North Carolina
220 Fayetteville St Mall, Ste 300, 27611 [PO Box 27644, 27611-7644]; (p) (919) 832-3652; (f) (919) 832-1651; info@presnc.net; www.presnc.org; (c) Wake

Private non-profit/ 1939/ staff: 12(f); 14(p); 5(v)/ members: 5000/publication: North Carolina Preservation

HISTORIC PRESERVATION AGENCY: Protects and promotes buildings, sites, and landscapes important to the heritage of NC. Operates a revolving fund that purchases endangered historic properties throughout the state, provides educational opportunities, and an awards program.

PROGRAMS: Annual Meeting; Exhibits; Facility Rental

6411
Raleigh City Museum
Briggs Bldg, Ste 100, 220 Fayetteville St, 27601 [Briggs Building, Ste 100, 220 Fayetteville St Mall, 27601-1310]; (p) (919) 832-3775; (f) (919) 832-3085; JKulikowski@raleighcitymuseum.org; www.raleighcitymuseum.org; (c) Wake

Private non-profit/ 1992/ Board of Directors/ staff: 4(f); 1(p); 30(v)/ members: 350

HISTORY MUSEUM: Promotes understand of the City's present through knowledge of its past. Collects, preserves, and interprets materials pertaining to Raleigh's history and culture.

PROGRAMS: Annual Meeting; Community Outreach; Elder's Programs; Exhibits; Facility Rental; Family Programs; Guided Tours; Interpretation; Lectures; Research Library/Archives; School-Based Curriculum

COLLECTIONS: [20th c] Museum artifacts include decorative arts, portraits, paintings, statues, framed lithographs, maps, postcards, photographs, miscellaneous government and academic documents, and archival materials.

HOURS: Yr T-F 10-4, Sa-Su 1-4

ADMISSION: No charge

6412
Raleigh Historic Districts Commission, Inc.
222 W Hargett St, Room 400, 27602 [PO Box 829, Century Station, 27602]; (p) (919) 832-7238; (f) (919) 890-3690; rhdc@rhdc.org; www.rhdc.org; (c) Wake

Private non-profit/ 1961/ Board of Commissioners/ staff: 2(f)/publication: Culture Town: Life in Raleigh's African American Communities

HISTORIC PRESERVATION AGENCY: Serves as the city council's official historic preservation advisory body to identify, preserve, protect, and educate the public about Raleigh's historic resources.

PROGRAMS: Exhibits; Interpretation; Publication; Research Library/Archives

COLLECTIONS: [1961-present]

HOURS: M-F 8:30-5:15

6413
Society of North Carolina Archivists
[PO Box 20448, 27619]; www.rtpnet.org/snca; (c) Wake

Private non-profit/ 1984/ staff: 10(v)/ members: 125

Promotes cooperation and exchange of information among individuals and institutions interested in the preservation and use of the archival and manuscript resources.

6414
Wake County Historic Preservation Commission
337 S Salisbury St, 27602 [PO Box 550, 27602]; (p) (919) 856-6322; (f) (919) 856-6184; rpugh@co.wake.nc.us; www.co.wake.nc.us/planning/historic; (c) Wake

County/ 1993/ staff: 2(f); 12(v)/publication: The Historic Architecture of Wake County

HISTORIC PRESERVATION AGENCY: Identifies, preserves, and protects districts and landmarks promoting culture, history, architecture and prehistory.

PROGRAMS: Community Outreach; Guided Tours; Publication

6415
Wake County Historical Society
[PO Box 2, 27602]; (c) Wake

Private non-profit/ 1956/ Board of Directors/ staff: 15(v)/ members: 350

HISTORIC PRESERVATION AGENCY; HISTORICAL SOCIETY: Preserves historic properties in Wake County and promotes awareness of local history and heritage.

6416
Yates Mill Associates, Inc.
Penny Rd, 27605 [PO Box 10512, 27605-0512]; (p) (919) 515-5174; (c) Wake

Private non-profit/ 1989/ Board of Directors/ staff: 1(f); 1(p); 150(v)/ members: 150

HISTORIC SITE: Maintains restored an 18th c grist mill and developed an environmental - historical park.

PROGRAMS: Annual Meeting

COLLECTIONS: [1750-1950] An 18th c grist mill.

REIDSVILLE

6417
Chinqua-Penn Plantation Foundation, Inc.
2138 Wentworth St, 27320; (p) (336) 349-4576; (f) (336) 342-4863; www.chinquapenn.com; (c) Rockingham

Private non-profit/ 1992/ Board of Trustees/ staff: 17(f); 29(p); 60(v)/ members: 600

GARDEN; HOUSE MUSEUM: Maintains, promotes, and operates a 1920s mansion and 22-acre restored historic landscape and collection for the educational, scientific, cultural, and economic benefit of the people of NC.

PROGRAMS: Exhibits; Festivals; Film/Video; Garden Tours; Guided Tours; Interpretation; Lectures; School-Based Curriculum

COLLECTIONS: [16th-20th c] International art collection and furnishings in 1920s mansion with outdoor sculptures. Oriental Pagoda, 1928 greenhouse and horticulture garden.

HOURS: Mar-Dec

RICHLANDS

6418
Onslow County Museum
301 S Wilmington St, 28574 [PO Box 384, 28574]; (p) (910) 324-5008; (f) (910) 324-2897; ocmuseum@co.onslow.nc.us; (c) Onslow

County/ 1976/ Board of Commissioners/ staff: 5(f); 1(p); 200(v)/publication: *The Architectural History of Onslow County, North Carolina*

HISTORY MUSEUM; NATURAL HISTORY MUSEUM: Collects, preserves, exhibits, and interprets the cultural and natural history of Onslow County.

PROGRAMS: Community Outreach; Concerts; Exhibits; Family Programs; Festivals; Guided Tours; Interpretation; Lectures; Living History; Publication; Reenactments; Research Library/Archives; School-Based Curriculum

COLLECTIONS: [Prehistory-present] Artifacts, geologic specimens, agricultural equipment, naval stores, woodworking tools, textiles, and documentary artifacts.

HOURS: Yr T-F 10-4:30, Sa-Su 1-4

ADMISSION: No charge

ROCKY MOUNT

6419
Nash County Historical Association, Inc.
Stonewall Ln, 27804 [100 Salem Ct, 27804]; (p) (252) 443-4148; (f) (252) 937-4766; (c) Nash

Private non-profit/ 1970/ staff: 8(v)/ members: 75

HISTORIC SITE; HISTORICAL SOCIETY; HISTORY MUSEUM; HOUSE MUSEUM; LIVING HISTORY/OUTDOOR MUSEUM: Owns and operates Stonewall Manor, c.1830, a restored late Federal house.

PROGRAMS: Facility Rental; Guided Tours; Living History; Reenactments; School-Based Curriculum

COLLECTIONS: [19th c] Period bedcovers, furniture, and old farm hand tools.

HOURS: Yr 2nd Su 2-4:30

ADMISSION: $3, Seniors $2.50; Groups rates

ROXBORO

6420
Person County Museum of History
309 N Main St, 27573 [PO Box 1792, 27573]; (p) (336) 597-2884; www.esinc.net/personco-museum/; (c) Person

Private non-profit/ 1992/ Board of Directors/ staff: 2(p)/ 25(v)/ members: 100

HISTORY MUSEUM: Collects, preserves, and interprets the history of Person County for the education and enjoyment of present and future generations.

PROGRAMS: Annual Meeting; Community Outreach; Exhibits; Facility Rental; Guided Tours; Interpretation

COLLECTIONS: [19th c-present] Victorian furniture, linens, china, antique and collectable dolls, Enos Slaughter, WW I, WW II memorabilia.

HOURS: Yr T-Sa 10-2

RUTHERFORDTON

6421
Rutherford County Historical Society, Inc.
N Main at W Sixth St, 28139 [PO Box 1044, 28139]; (p) (828) 248-3512; (c) Rutherford

Private non-profit/ 1935/ Board of Directors/ members: 170

HISTORICAL SOCIETY: Promotes and preserves local history. Encourages education, identification, and marking of historical sites. Owns an 1849 Greek Revival restored church building.

PROGRAMS: Annual Meeting; Concerts; Facility Rental; Interpretation; Lectures

COLLECTIONS: [1800-1870] Artifacts relating to the gold industry in Rutherford County and history of the county.

HOURS: Yr 3rd T and by appt

ADMISSION: No charge

SALISBURY

6422
Doctor Josephus Wells Hall House Museum
226 S Jackson St, 28144 [PO Box 4221, 28145]; (p) (704) 636-0103, (704) 636-0106; (f) (704) 636-2522

1820

COLLECTIONS: [1850s] Original family antiques: china, silver, household furnishings.

HOURS: Yr

6423
Historic Salisbury Foundation
215 Depot St, 28145 [PO Box 4221, 28145-4221]; (p) (704) 636-0103; (f) (704) 636-2522; historicsal@historicsalisbury.org; www.historicsalisbury.org; (c) Rowan

Private non-profit/ 1972/ Board of Trustees/ staff: 2(f); 2(p); 400(v)/ members: 900

HISTORIC PRESERVATION AGENCY: Collects historically significant and endangered structures for resale for restoration. Operates events center in a restored railroad station, an 1820's house museum, and an 1890's roller mill museum.

PROGRAMS: Annual Meeting; Facility Rental; Family Programs; Guided Tours; Interpretation

COLLECTIONS: [1820-1900] 1820 Dr. Josephus Hall House, reproductions of the original wallpaper.

HOURS: Museum: Yr Sa-Su 1-4; Office: Yr M-F 9-4

ADMISSION: $3

6424
Old Stone House
114 S Jackson St, 28144 [202 N Main St, 28144]; (p) (704) 633-5946, (704) 279-3000; (f) (704) 633-9858; rowanmuseum@tarheel.net; www.tarheel.net/rowanmuseum

1766/ staff: 1(p)

HOUSE MUSEUM: Home of Michael Braun, one of Rowan County's early settlers.

COLLECTIONS: NC and PN furiture; pewter; books; cooking implements; agricultural tools; looms.

HOURS: Apr-Nov

6425
Rowan Museum, Inc.
202 N Main St, 28144; (p) (704) 633-5946; (f) (704) 633-9858; rowanmuseum@tarheel.net; (c) Rowan

Private non-profit/ 1953/ Board of Directors/ staff: 1(f); 6(p); 12(v)/ members: 500

GARDEN; HISTORIC SITE; HISTORICAL SOCIETY; HISTORY MUSEUM; HOUSE MUSEUM: Collects, preserves, displays, and educates the public on life and history of Rowan County citizens from early 1700s to present day.

PROGRAMS: Annual Meeting; Community Outreach; Exhibits; Facility Rental; Family Programs; Festivals; Guided Tours; Interpretation; Lectures; Living History; Reenactments; Research Library/Archives; School-Based Curriculum

COLLECTIONS: [18th c-present] Artifacts representing home, rural, and military life and period interpretations of life in the two historic houses.

HOURS: Yr Th-Su 1-4; Old Stone House: Apr-Nov

ADMISSION: $3, Children $1.50; Group rates

6426
Utzman-Chambers House
114 S Jackson St, 28144 [202 N Main St, 28144]; (p) (704) 633-5946; (f) (704) 633-9858; rowanmuseum@tarheel.net; www.tarheel.net/rowanmuseum

1815/ staff: 2(p)

COLLECTIONS: Salisbury Confederate prison flag; Revolutionary and Civil War artifacts; Daniel Boone chair; Hotel registers; Civil War-era materials.

HOURS: Yr

SANFORD

6427
House in the Horseshoe State Historic Site
324 Alston House Rd, 27330; (p) (910) 947-2051; (f) (910) 947-2051; horseshoe@ac.net; www.horseshoe@ncsl.dcr.state.nc.us; (c) Moore

State/ 1971/ State of NC/ staff: 3(f); 4(p); 200(v)

HOUSE MUSEUM: 1772 house museum with bullet holes from Whig-Tory skirmish. Home of NC Gov. Benjamin Williams.

PROGRAMS: Community Outreach; Guided Tours; Interpretation; Lectures; Living History; Reenactments; School-Based Curriculum

COLLECTIONS: [18th c] Furnishings from colonial period, NC, and Engand. Georgian house remodeled in early 1800s.

HOURS: Apr-Oct M-Sa 9-5, Su 1-5; Nov-Mar T-Sa 10-4, Su 1-4

6428
Lee County Genealogical Historical Society, Inc.
Local Library, 27331 [PO Box 3216, 27331-3216]; (c) Lee

Private non-profit/ 1986/ staff: 10(v)/ members: 112/publication: *The Times; Marriage Register of Lee County*

GENEALOGICAL SOCIETY; HISTORICAL SOCIETY: Encourages genealogical and historical research. Promotes collection and preservation of family records, manuscripts, and documents of historical value.

PROGRAMS: Family Programs; Lectures; Publication; Research Library/Archives

COLLECTIONS: [18th c-present] Books, papers, manuscripts, newspaper articles, family bible, and cemetery listings.

HOURS: Yr M-Sa 10-9, Su 1-6

SEAGROVE

6429
North Carolina Pottery Center
250 E Ave, 27341 [PO Box 531, 27341]; (p) (336) 873-8430; (f) (336) 873-8530; ncpc@atomic.net; www.ncpotterycenter.com; (c) Randolph

Private non-profit/ 1986/ staff: 1(f); 1(p)/ members: 400

ART MUSEUM; CULTURAL CENTER: A museum and educational center devoted to preserving the history and heritage of NC pottery and its ongoing tradition.

PROGRAMS: Annual Meeting; Exhibits; Facility Rental; Festivals; Lectures

COLLECTIONS: [18th c-present] NC pottery from the late 18th and 19th centuries, utilitarian wares of the early 20th c, contemporary art pottery, tools, related artifacts and documents.

HOURS: Yr T-Sa 10-4

ADMISSION: $3, Children $1; Mbrs free

SEDALIA

6430
Charlotte Hawkins Brown Historic Site
6136 Burlington Rd, 27342 [Drawer B, 27342]; (p) (336) 449-4846; (f) (336) 449-0176; palmermi@bellsouth.net; www.ah.dcr.state.nc.us/hs/chb/chb.htm; (c) Guilford

State/ 1987/ NC Historic Sites/ staff: 4(f); 8(p); 30(v)

HISTORIC SITE: Dedicated to the contributions of an African American and a woman. Lo-

cated on the former Alice Freeman Palmer Memorial Institute's campus.

PROGRAMS: Community Outreach; Concerts; Exhibits; Facility Rental; Family Programs; Festivals; Guided Tours; Interpretation; Lectures; School-Based Curriculum

COLLECTIONS: [1902-1971] Dr. Brown's personal residence, Canary Cottage, furniture, and other personal artifacts and memorabilia.

HOURS: Apr-Oct M-Sa 9-5, Su 1-5; T-Sa 10-4, Su 1-4

SHELBY

6431
Broad River Genealogical Society, Inc.
Cleveland County Fairgrounds, E Marion St, 28151 [PO Box 2261, 28151-2261]; (p) (704) 739-6874; jfs2246@hotmail.com; www.rootsweb.com/~ncclevel/brgs.htm; (c) Cleveland

Private non-profit/ 1980/ Executive and General Board of Directors/ staff: 15(v)/ members: 200/publication: *Eswau Huppeday*

GENEALOGICAL SOCIETY: Gathers and preserves area records. Disseminates genealogical and historical records and information through published books and a quarterly bulletin.

PROGRAMS: Annual Meeting; Festivals; Lectures; Monthly Meeting; Publication; Research Library/Archives

COLLECTIONS: Books published by members, Virginia Greene DePriest collection, exchange bulletins from other societies, copies of land grants for Cleveland, Lincoln, Rutherford, and Gaston Counties.

HOURS: Yr by appt

6432
Cleveland County Historical Museum
Court Sq, 28151 [PO Box 1333, 28151]; (p) (704) 482-8186; (f) (704) 482-8186; (c) Cleveland

Private non-profit/ 1976/ staff: 2(f)/ members: 1500

HISTORY MUSEUM: Preserves, promotes, and presents county history from 1806 to the present.

PROGRAMS: Exhibits; Guided Tours; Living History; Research Library/Archives

COLLECTIONS: [1806-present] Local histories.

HOURS: Yr T-F 9-4

SHERRILLS FORD

6433
North Carolina Society of Historians, Inc.
2263 Mollys Backbone Rd, 28673 [PO Box 93, 28673-0093]; (p) (828) 478-2469; (f) (828) 478-2469; ebsherrill@twave.net; (c) Catawba

Private non-profit/ 1941/ staff: 10(v)/publication: *From the Quill*

GENEALOGICAL SOCIETY; HISTORIC PRESERVATION AGENCY; HISTORICAL SOCIETY: Collects and preserves NC history, traditions, and folklore. Aids in the exchange of information between members and presents annual awards in history and genealogy.

PROGRAMS: Annual Meeting

SMITHFIELD

6434
Johnston County Genealogical and Historical Society
Johnston County Public Library, 27577 [PO Box 2373, 27577]; (c) Johnston

Private non-profit/ 1955/ staff: 1(p)/ members: 275/publication: *Johnston Journal*

GENEALOGICAL SOCIETY; HISTORICAL SOCIETY: Preserves and makes available local history and culture.

PROGRAMS: Publication; Research Library/Archives

COLLECTIONS: [1746-present] Books, papers, microfilm, maps, and vertical files on genealogy and local history.

6435
Johnston County Heritage Center
241 E Market St, 27577 [PO Box 2709, 27577]; (p) (919) 934-8146, (919) 934-2836; (f) (919) 934-7869; (c) Johnston

County/ 1997/ staff: 1(f); 5(p); 3(v)

HISTORY MUSEUM: Preserves the history and material culture of Johnston County for the educational benefit of its citizens and visitors. Promotes local through interpretive exhibits, programs, and publications.

PROGRAMS: Community Outreach; Concerts; Exhibits; Guided Tours; Lectures; Research Library/Archives; School-Based Curriculum

COLLECTIONS: [1746-present] Books, newspapers, microfilm of census, church, and courthouse records; maps, atlases, photographic images, and vertical files on genealogy, local history, and biographies.

SNOW CAMP

6436
Snow Camp Historical Drama Society, Inc.
1 Drama Rd, 27349 [PO Box 535, 27349]; (p) (336) 376-6948, (800) 726-5115; (f) (336) 376-1118; snowcampot@aol.com; (c) Alamance

Private non-profit/ 1972/ staff: 4(f); 75(p); 26(v)/ members: 148

HISTORIC SITE; HISTORICAL SOCIETY; HISTORY MUSEUM; HOUSE MUSEUM: Promotes the history of Piedmont and the African American community.

PROGRAMS: Festivals; Lectures; Living History; Theatre

COLLECTIONS: [1780-1820] 34 historical buildings, log kitchen, Quaker meeting houses, books, clothing, farm tools, household goods, working saw, and cider mills.

HOURS: Sept-May M-F 9-5; June-Aug Daily 9-8

SOUTH MILLS

6437
Dismal Swamp Canal Visitor Center
2356 Hwy 17 N, 27976; (p) (252) 771-8333; (f) (252) 771-2055; dscwelcome@coastal-guide.com; www.icw.net/dscwelcome; (c) Camden

County/ 1989/ Camden County/ staff: 2(f); 2(p); 12(v)

Greets travelers by both a major highway and historic waterway. Staff assists with highway conditions, directions, printed information, and reservations for lodging and ferries.

HOURS: May-Oct Daily 9-5

SOUTHERN PINES

6438
Moore County Historical Association, Inc.
Broad St & Morganton Rd, 28388 [PO Box 324, 28388]; (p) (910) 692-2051, (910) 947-3995; (c) Moore

Private non-profit/ 1946/ Board of Trustees/ staff: 1(p); 35(v)/ members: 335

HISTORIC PRESERVATION AGENCY; HISTORIC SITE; HISTORICAL SOCIETY; HOUSE MUSEUM: Preserves the heritage of Moore County and NC through its facilities and a variety of programs and services, including restored houses.

PROGRAMS: Annual Meeting; Community Outreach; Exhibits; Facility Rental; Festivals; Guided Tours; Interpretation; Living History; Reenactments

COLLECTIONS: [1758-1820] Historic houses furnished with period furniture.

HOURS: Mar-June, Sept-Dec T-Sa 1-4 and by appt

ADMISSION: No charge

6439
Weymouth Center/Boyd House
555 E Connecticut Ave, 28387 [PO Box 939, 28388]; (p) (910) 692-6261; (f) (910) 692-1815; weymouthcenter@pinehurst.net; www.weymouthcenter.org/

1925/ staff: 1(f); 1(p); 6(v)

NC Literary Hall of Fame is housed at the site. Writers-in-Residence program.

COLLECTIONS: [1921-1944] A few original furnishings.

HOURS: By appt

SOUTHPORT

6440
Southport Historical Society
Old Jail on Nash St, 28461 [PO Box 10014, 28461]; (p) (910) 457-6629; (c) Brunswick

Private non-profit/ 1976/ Board of Directors/ members: 337/publication: Architecture of Southport; Bald Head; and others

HISTORICAL SOCIETY: Meets six times a year and presents speakers to discuss local history, publishes books and maintains Old Jail for tours and as storage for files and books.

PROGRAMS: Annual Meeting; Guided Tours; Lectures; Publication

HOURS: Yr by appt

ADMISSION: No charge

SPENCER

6441
North Carolina Transportation Museum
411 S Salisbury Ave, 28159 [PO Box 165, 28159]; (p) (704) 636-2889, (877) 628-6386; (f) (704) 639-1881; www.nctrans.org; (c) Rowan

State/ 1977/ staff: 19(f); 13(p)/ members: 964/publication: Shop Talk

HISTORIC SITE; RESEARCH CENTER: Preserves and interprets inland transportation history from Native American canoes to current automobiles in three exhibit buildings.

PROGRAMS: Elder's Programs; Exhibits; Festivals; Guided Tours; Publication; Research Library/Archives

COLLECTIONS: [1860s-1970s] Artifacts and memorabilia; railroad equipment, automobiles, and airplanes.

HOURS: Apr-Oct Daily 9-5; Nov-Mar T-Su 10-4

SPRING HOPE

6442
Spring Hope Historical Museum
W Main St, 27882 [8839 Chantilly Rd, 27882]; (p) (252) 478-3239; (c) Nash

Private non-profit/ 1986/ staff: 15(v)/ members: 100

ART MUSEUM; GENEALOGICAL SOCIETY; HISTORIC PRESERVATION AGENCY; HISTORICAL SOCIETY; HISTORY MUSEUM: Preserves the history of the Town of Spring Hope for the enlightenment of future generations.

PROGRAMS: Annual Meeting; Community Outreach; Exhibits; Festivals; Guided Tours; Lectures

COLLECTIONS: [1900-1930]

HOURS: Sept-June Sa-Su 1-5

ADMISSION: No charge

STATESVILLE

6443
Allison Woods Foundation
Hwy 21, 28677 [437 Walnut St, 28677]; (p) (704) 872-1930; (f) (704) 872-1138; LauraWebb2@compuserve.com; (c) Iredell

Private non-profit/ 1991/ staff: 1(f); 3(p); 20(v)/ members: 95/publication: Allison Woods Foundation Newsletter

GARDEN; HISTORIC SITE

PROGRAMS: Community Outreach; Concerts; Facility Rental; Garden Tours; Guided Tours; Interpretation; Publication; School-Based Curriculum

COLLECTIONS: [Early 20th c]

HOURS: Yr by appt

ADMISSION: $1

6444
Fort Dobbs State Historic Site
438 Fort Dobbs Rd, 28625; (p) (704) 873-5866; (f) (704) 873-5866; fortdobbs@statesville.net; (c) Iredell

State/ 1973/ DCR, Historic Sites Section/ staff: 2(f); 2(p)

HISTORIC SITE: A French and Indian War fort built in 1756 to protect western settlements from Indian attack.

PROGRAMS: Exhibits; Guided Tours; Living History; Reenactments

COLLECTIONS: [1750s-1760s] Visitor center with three exhibit cases displaying artifacts found during archaeological excavations.

HOURS: Apr-Oct M-Sa 9-5, Su 1-5; Nov-Mar T-Sa 10-4, Su 1-4

6445
Genealogical Society of Iredell County
S Center St, 28687 [PO Box 946, 28687]; (p) (704) 878-5384; (c) Iredell

Private non-profit/ 1977/ staff: 4(v)/ members: 300/publication: Iredell County Tracks

GENEALOGICAL SOCIETY: Provides genealogical material for researchers at Iredell County Library and provides researchers with further assistance.

PROGRAMS: Publication; Research Library/Archives

COLLECTIONS: [1750s-present] Family, local history, and obituary files, maps, and limited publications.

HOURS: Yr T, F 10-2

SURF CITY

6446
Missiles and More Museum Missiles and More Museum
720 Channel Blvd, 28445 [PO Box 2645, 28445]; (p) (910) 328-8663, (910) 328-1950; (f) (910) 328-1950; evebrad@aol.com; (c) Pender

Private non-profit/ 1994/ Historical Society of Topsail Island/ staff: 40(v)/ members: 94

HISTORIC PRESERVATION AGENCY; HISTORICAL SOCIETY; HISTORY MUSEUM; RESEARCH CENTER: Preserves the history of three local communities and informs the public of a missile program conducted there in 1946-47 by the US government which was the beginning of the national space program.

PROGRAMS: Community Outreach; Exhibits; Festivals; Guided Tours; Research Library/Archives; School-Based Curriculum

COLLECTIONS: [Prehistoric-20th c] Native American, W W II, Blackbeard (pirate), Civil War blockade runner, military base in Holly Ridge (Camp Davis), and women in aviation.

HOURS: Apr-Oct Daily 2-4

ADMISSION: No charge

SWANSBORO

6447
Coastal Genealogical Society
Swansboro Town Hall, Bicentennial Room, 28584 [PO Box 1421, 28584]; (p) (910) 326-2660, (910) 326-3173

publication: The Tucker Littleton Notes, Vol. 1-3

GENEALOGICAL SOCIETY: Promotes family history for Onslow, Carteret, and Jones Counties.

PROGRAMS: Publication

HOURS: 4th M-Feb, May, Aug, and Nov

TARBORO

6448

Blount-Bridgers House/Hobson Pittman Memorial Gallery Foundation, Inc.

130 Bridgers St, 27886; (p) (252) 823-4159; (f) (252) 823-6190; eccac@coastalnet.com; (c) Edgecombe

Joint/ 1985/ Private non-profit; Board of Directors; Edgecombe County Cultural Arts Council, Inc./ staff: 2(f); 3(p); 20(v)/ members: 300/publication: *Around the House*

ART MUSEUM; GARDEN; HISTORIC SITE; HISTORY MUSEUM; HOUSE MUSEUM: Early 19th c plantation house with decorative arts, art by Edgecombe County native, Hobson Pittman.

PROGRAMS: Community Outreach; Concerts; Exhibits; Facility Rental; Festivals; Guided Tours; Interpretation; Lectures; Publication; Research Library/Archives

COLLECTIONS: [1760-1930] 20th c paintings by Hobson Pittman and related artists, furniture manufactured in Edgecombe County and Eastern NC (1750-1880), ceramics, tools, textiles, metals, and toys.

HOURS: Yr M-F 10-4, Sa-Su 2-4

ADMISSION: $2

6449

Edgecombe County Cultural Arts Council, Inc.

130 Bridgers St, 27886; (p) (252) 823-4159; (f) (252) 823-6190; eccac@coastalnet.com; (c) Edgecombe

Private non-profit/ 1985/ staff: 2(f); 3(p); 10(v)/ members: 350/publication: *Around The House*

ART MUSEUM; HOUSE MUSEUM: Operates an art/history museum in an historic house with library and archives focusing on county history and the career of local artist Hobson Pittman (1899-1972).

PROGRAMS: Annual Meeting; Community Outreach; Concerts; Exhibits; Facility Rental; Festivals; Guided Tours; Interpretation; Lectures; Publication; Research Library/Archives

COLLECTIONS: [18th-20th c] Art by Hobson Pittman, his associates, and students. Decorative arts, ceramics, textiles, furniture, tools, toys, photos, and documents related to Edgecombe County's social history.

HOURS: Yr M-F 10-4, Sa-Su 2-4; Dec-Feb Closed Sa

ADMISSION: $2

6450

Edgecombe County Historical Society

130 Bridgers St, 27886; (p) (252) 823-4159; (f) (252) 823-6190; eccac@coastalnet.com; www.coastalnet.com/~g3f3w5rm; (c) Edgecombe

Private non-profit/ 1962/ Edgecombe County Cultural Arts Council, Inc./publication: *Around The House*

HISTORIC SITE; HISTORY MUSEUM: Preserves and promotes Edgecombe County's cultural riches.

PROGRAMS: Community Outreach; Concerts; Exhibits; Facility Rental; Festivals; Guided Tours; Interpretation; Publication; Research Library/Archives

COLLECTIONS: [18th-20th c] Decorative arts, textiles, archives, tools, farming implements, and art by Hobson Pittman (1899-1972).

HOURS: Yr M-F 10-4, Sa-Su 2-4; Jan-Feb Closed Sa

ADMISSION: $2

TRYON

6451

Polk County Historical Association, Inc.

22 Depot St, 28782; (p) (828) 859-2287; (c) Polk

Private non-profit/ 1977/ Board of Directors/ staff: 32(v)/ members: 283/publication: *Polk County History*

HISTORICAL SOCIETY; HISTORY MUSEUM: Maintains museum.

PROGRAMS: Community Outreach; Exhibits; Family Programs; Festivals; Film/Video; Guided Tours; Interpretation; Lectures; Living History; Publication; Research Library/Archives; School-Based Curriculum

COLLECTIONS: [19th-20th c] Maps, tools, photos, clothing, military uniforms, dolls, books, manuscripts, deeds, land grants, scrapbooks, transcripts of meeting lectures, and living oral history tapes and videos, 500 artifacts.

HOURS: Sept-May T-Th 10-12 and by appt

ADMISSION: Donations

VALDESE

6452

Waldensian Presbyterian Church Museum

208 Rodoret St SE, 28690 [PO Box 216, 28690]; (p) (828) 874-2531; (f) (828) 874-0880; waldensian@hci.net; (c) Burke

Private non-profit/ 1955/ Historical Committee of the Session/ staff: 80(v)

HISTORIC PRESERVATION AGENCY; HISTORY MUSEUM: Preserves Waldensian artifacts, heritage and traditions brought by first settlers who came from Northwestern Italy in 1893. Maintains a repository of genealogical records.

PROGRAMS: Guided Tours

COLLECTIONS: [1893-1930] Books relating to Waldensian history and genealogy, photographs, household items, clothing, and tools.

HOURS: Apr-Oct Su 3-5; Mid June-mid Aug Su 5-8, and by appt

ADMISSION: Donations accepted

WADESBORO

6453

Anson County Historical Society, Inc

206 E Wade St, 28170; (p) (704) 694-6694; (f) (704) 694-3763; achs@vnet.net; (c) Anson

Private non-profit/ 1962/ staff: 1(p); 12(v)/ members: 340/publication: *Historical Society News*

HISTORICAL SOCIETY; HOUSE MUSEUM: Owns and operates Boggan-Hammond House and Alexander Little Wing museums.

PROGRAMS: Annual Meeting; Exhibits; Festivals; Guided Tours; Publication

COLLECTIONS: [1783-1839] Period furnishings and utensils.

HOURS: Yr M-F 9-11/12-2

WAKE FOREST

6454

Wake Forest College Birthplace Society, Inc.

414 N Main St, 27588 [PO Box 494, 27588]; (p) (919) 556-2911; (c) Wake

Private non-profit/ 1959/ Board of Directors/ staff: 30(v)/ members: 200

HISTORIC SITE; HISTORY MUSEUM: Keeper of town history.

PROGRAMS: Annual Meeting; Community Outreach; Concerts; Exhibits; Guided Tours; Interpretation

COLLECTIONS: [1834-1956] Photographs, books, college publications, furniture, documents, medical, law, and sports memorabilia representing town-school.

HOURS: Mar-Nov Su 3-5 and by appt

6455

Wake Forest Historic Preservation Commission

221 S Brooks St, 27587; (p) (919) 554-3911; (f) (919) 554-6607; (c) Wake

City/ 1979

HISTORIC PRESERVATION AGENCY: Early historic districts and property commissions in NC. Its purpose is to safeguard the heritage of the town by preserving districts and landmarks.

PROGRAMS: Community Outreach; Garden Tours

WASHINGTON

6456

Beaufort County Genealogical Society

[PO Box 1089, 27889-1089]; (p) (252) 946-4212; (c) Beaufort

1985/ members: 257/publication: *Pamteco Tracings*

GENEALOGICAL SOCIETY

PROGRAMS: Publication

WAXHAW

6457

Museum of the Waxhaws and Andrew Jackson Memorial

8215 Waxhaw Hwy, 28173 [PO Box 7, 28173]; (p) (704) 843-1832; (f) (704) 843-1767; mwaxhaw@perigee.net; www.perigee.net/~mwaxhaw; (c) Union

Private non-profit/ 1996/ Andrew Jackson Historical Foundation/ staff: 2(f); 1(p); 30(v)

HISTORY MUSEUM: Maintains regional history museum and memorial to the seventh President Andrew Jackson, a native of the Waxhaws region. Traces the area's history from 1500-1900.

PROGRAMS: Exhibits; Facility Rental; Film/Video; Guided Tours; Interpretation; Lectures; Living History; Reenactments

COLLECTIONS: [16th-19th c] Military, agricultural artifacts, and items related to Andrew Jackson.

HOURS: Yr W-Sa 10-5, Su 1-5

ADMISSION: $2, Children $1, Seniors $1; Under 7 free

WAYNESVILLE

6458
Haywood County Genealogical Society
38 S Main St, 28786 [PO Box 1331, 28786]; (p) (828) 452-4306; (f) (828) 452-1041; hcgs_nc@yahoo.com; www.rootsweb.com/~nchcgs; (c) Haywood

Private non-profit/ 1990/ staff: 25(v)/ members: 134/publication: *Balsam Roots; Census; and others*

GENEALOGICAL SOCIETY: Facilitates the study of genealogy, family, and local history. Encourages the preservation and availability of family and court records and promotes educational programs on these topics.

PROGRAMS: Family Programs; Guided Tours; Lectures; Publication; Research Library/Archives

COLLECTIONS: Genealogical books, family records, and research materials.

HOURS: Jan-Nov F 1-4 and by appt

WEAVERVILLE

6459
Zebulon B. Vance Birthplace State Historic Site
911 Reems Creek Rd, 28787; (p) (828) 645-6706; (f) (828) 645-6706

1795/ Dept of Cultural Resources, Archives and History, Historic Sites Section/ staff: 3(f); 7(p)

Birthplace of Zebulon B. Vance, North Carolina's Civil War Governor.

COLLECTIONS: [1830s] Early 19th c Southern Appalachian artitfacts.

HOURS: Yr

WENTWORTH

6460
Rockingham County Historical Society, Inc.
NC Hwy 65 (Main St), 27375 [PO Box 84, 27375-0084]; (p) (336) 342-5901; (c) Rockingham

Private non-profit/ 1954/ Board of Directors/ staff: 25(v)/ members: 400/publication: *Journal of Rockingham County History and Genealogy*

GENEALOGICAL SOCIETY; HISTORIC SITE; HISTORICAL SOCIETY; HOUSE MUSEUM: Preserves the heritage of Rockingham County

and encourages research and publications in the fields of local history and genealogy.

PROGRAMS: Community Outreach; Exhibits; Facility Rental; Festivals; Guided Tours; Interpretation; Lectures; Living History; Publication; Reenactments; Research Library/Archives

COLLECTIONS: [18th-19th c] 19th c inn, the Wright Tavern, and two Revolutionary War sites—High Rock Ford and Troublesome Creek Iron Works.

HOURS: Yr by appt

WILKESBORO

6461
Old Wilkes, Inc.
203 N Bridge St, 28697; (p) (336) 667-3712; (f) (336) 667-3712; oldwilkjb@aol.com; www.wilkesboro.com.OldWilkesInc; (c) Wilkes

Private non-profit/ 1968/ staff: 1(f); 30(v)/ members: 125

HISTORIC PRESERVATION AGENCY; HISTORY MUSEUM; HOUSE MUSEUM: Operates two museums, the old Wilkes Jail which housed the infamous "Tom Dooley" and the Robert Cleveland log house. Both are furnished in period furniture of the early and mid-19th c fashion.

PROGRAMS: Exhibits; Guided Tours; Interpretation; Lectures; Living History; Reenactments

COLLECTIONS: [1779-1915] Period furniture, authentic jail cell, roots herbs and bark. Piano, jewelry grinder, sterilizes, telephone and other first artifact to arrive in the county.

HOURS: Yr M-F 9-4

WILLARD

6462
Penderlea Homestead Museum
10034 Penderlea Hwy, 28478; (p) (910) 285-1934, (910) 283-5479; pjpatbob@intrstar.net; (c) Pender

State/ 1997/ staff: 1(p); 1(v)/ members: 2

HISTORIC SITE; HISTORY MUSEUM; RESEARCH CENTER: Promotes studies and fosters education concerning the history of the Penderlea community, which was a New Deal project of the Franklin D. Roosevelt administration.

PROGRAMS: Exhibits; Lectures; Research Library/Archives

COLLECTIONS: [20th c] Photocopies of documents acquired from the National Archives in Washington DC and Atlanta. Photographs from the Library of Congress and documents from the Franklin and Eleanor Roosevelt Library in Hyde Park, NY.

HOURS: Yr Sa-Su 1-5

ADMISSION: $3, Student $1, Seniors $2

WILLIAMSTON

6463
Asa Biggs House
100 E Church St, 27892 [PO Box 468, 27892]; (p) (252) 792-6605; (f) (252) 792-8710

1831/ staff: 1(f)

Maintains house, an excellent example of the side-hall plan that was characteristic of rural eastern NC during the early 19th c. The house serves as the main visitor center in Martin County.

COLLECTIONS: Heart-pine, locally-made early to mid-19th c; china used by the Biggs family; late 19th c quilt made in Martin County.

6464
Martin County Genealogical Society
Martin Community College Library Conference Room, 27892 [PO Box 121, 27892]; (p) (252) 792-5472; shepjr@coastalnet.com; (c) Martin

Private non-profit/ 1993/ County/ staff: 9(v)/ members: 45

GENEALOGICAL SOCIETY; RESEARCH CENTER: Maintains an association of persons interested in the research and preservation of family histories associated with Martin and surrounding counties.

PROGRAMS: Annual Meeting; Lectures; Publication; Research Library/Archives

COLLECTIONS: Titles that help members and the public to do research on eastern NC.

HOURS: 2nd T

ADMISSION: No Charge

6465
Martin County Historical Society
100 E Church St, 27892 [PO Box 468, 27892]; (p) (252) 792-6605; (f) (252) 792-8710; (c) Martin

Private non-profit/ 1957/ County/ staff: 20(v)/ members: 110

HISTORICAL SOCIETY; HISTORY MUSEUM; RESEARCH CENTER: Preserves and promotes county history and its historic sites. Maintains county's history room at local community college, oversees publications on county history, and organizes society's fundraisers.

PROGRAMS: Annual Meeting; Community Outreach; Elder's Programs; Exhibits; Film/Video; Guided Tours; Research Library/Archives

COLLECTIONS: [1831-present] 1931 Asa Biggs House, furnishings, and antiques.

HOURS: Yr M-F 8-5

ADMISSION: Donations accepted

WILMINGTON

6466
Battleship NORTH CAROLINA
Eagle Island, 28402 [PO Box 480, 28402-0480]; (p) (910) 251-5797; (f) (910) 251-5807; ncbb55@aol.com; www.battleshipnc.com; (c) New Hanover

State/ 1961/ USS North Carolina Battleship Commission/ staff: 26(f); 15(p); 19(v)/ members: 200/publication: *Battleship North Carolina*

HISTORIC SITE: Preserved W W II vessel, state W W II memorial, and a museum interpreting the history of ships named North Carolina.

PROGRAMS: Community Outreach; Concerts; Exhibits; Facility Rental; Interpretation; Lectures; Living History; Publication; Research

Library/Archives

COLLECTIONS: [1821-1947] Items associated with ships named NC, art, archives, artifacts, books, photographs, blueprints, uniforms, machinery, equipment, weapons, material printed aboard ship, memorabilia, souvenirs, and oral histories.

HOURS: May 16-Sept 15 Daily 8-8; Sept 16-May 15 Daily 8-5

ADMISSION: $8, Children $4, Seniors $7

6467
Bellamy Mansion Museum of History and Design Arts
503 Market St, 28402 [PO Box 1176, 28402]; (p) (910) 251-3700; (f) (910) 763-8154; bellamym@bellsouth.net; www.bellamymansion-museum.org; (c) New Hanover

Private non-profit/ 1994/ Preservation North Carolina/ staff: 2(f); 3(p); 75(v)/ members: 563

HISTORIC SITE; HISTORY MUSEUM; HOUSE MUSEUM: Manages Greek Revival mansion, slave quarters, and carriage house were completed in 1861.

PROGRAMS: Exhibits; Facility Rental; Garden Tours; Guided Tours; Interpretation; Lectures; Reenactments

COLLECTIONS: [19th c] 30,000 archaeological artifacts that are centered around the Bellamy family and the site itself.

HOURS: Yr W-Sa 10-5, Su 1-5

ADMISSION: $6, Children $3

6468
Burgwin-Wright Museum House and Gardens
224 Market St, 28401; (p) (910) 762-0570; (f) (910) 762-8650; (c) New Hanover

Private non-profit/ 1950/ National Society of the Colonial Dames of America, North Carolina Division/ staff: 2(f); 6(p); 10(v)/ members: 1525

GARDEN; HOUSE MUSEUM: Maintains Georgian-style townhouse built in 1770 for merchant, planter, and colonial official, John Burgwin. Restored and furnished with period pieces. Seven gardens planted with native Carolina species and 18th c plant types.

PROGRAMS: Garden Tours; Guided Tours

COLLECTIONS: [18th-early 19th c] Georgian-style architecture and furniture pieces from America, Europe, and Asia.

HOURS: Feb-Dec T-Sa 10-4

ADMISSION: $5, Student $2; Under 5 free

6469
Cape Fear Museum
814 Market St, 28401-4731; (p) (910) 341-4350; (f) (910) 341-4037; ssullivan@co.new-hanover.nc.us; www.co.new-hanover.nc.us/cfm/cfmmain.htm; (c) New Hanover

County/ 1898/ staff: 16(f); 3(p); 175(v)/ members: 530

HISTORY MUSEUM; RESEARCH CENTER: Collects, preserves, and interprets objects relating to the history, science and cultures of Lower Cape Fear, and makes those objects and their interpretation available to the public through educational exhibits and programs.

PROGRAMS: Annual Meeting; Community

Outreach; Concerts; Elder's Programs; Exhibits; Facility Rental; Family Programs; Festivals; Film/Video; Guided Tours; Interpretation; Lectures; Living History; Publication; Research Library/Archives; School-Based Curriculum; Theatre

COLLECTIONS: [Prehistory-20th c] Information and artifacts relating to the Civil War, Simmons Sea Skiff, Henry McMillan and Michael Jordan.

HOURS: Spring-Summer M-Sa 9-5, Su 2-5; Fall-Winter T-Sa 9-5, Su 2-5

ADMISSION: $4, Student $3, Children $1, Seniors $3

6470
Historic Wilmington Foundation, Inc.
702 Market St, 28402 [PO Box 1505, 28402]; (p) (910) 762-2511; (f) (910) 762-1551; www.historicwilmington.org; (c) New Hanover

Private non-profit/ 1966/ staff: 3(f); 2(p); 100(v)/ members: 1200

HISTORIC PRESERVATION AGENCY: Preserves and restores New Hanover County's historic buildings, sites, and resources.

PROGRAMS: Annual Meeting; Community Outreach; Exhibits; Family Programs; Garden Tours; Guided Tours; Lectures; Research Library/Archives

HOURS: Yr M-F 9-5

6471
Latimer House
Corner of S 3rd & Orange St, 28401 [126 S 3rd St, 28401]; (p) (910) 762-0492, (910) 763-5869; (f) (910) 763-5869; www.wilmington.org/latimer

1852/ staff: 1(f); 1(p)

COLLECTIONS: [Victorian] Period pieces, art works collected by the family, Latimer portraits, and family furnishings.

6472
Lower Cape Fear Historical Society
126 S 3rd St, 28401; (p) (910) 762-0492; (f) (910) 763-5869; latimer@wilmington.net; www.latimer.wilmington.org; (c) New Hanover

Private non-profit/ 1956/ Board of Directors/ staff: 1(f); 1(p); 47(v)/ members: 725/publication: Bulletin; For The Record

HISTORICAL SOCIETY; HOUSE MUSEUM; RESEARCH CENTER: Collects and preserves information and knowledge pertaining to the Lower Cape Fear area through its archives and house museum.

PROGRAMS: Annual Meeting; Concerts; Exhibits; Facility Rental; Garden Tours; Guided Tours; Lectures; Publication; Research Library/Archives

COLLECTIONS: [19th c] Two history libraries, genealogical files, original records, diaries, photographic/post card images, maps, and subject files related to NC with emphasis on the Cape Fear region.

HOURS: Yr M-F 10-3:30, Sa-Su 12-5

ADMISSION: $6, Student $2

6473
Old New Hanover Genealogical Society
New Hanover Public Library, 201 Chestnut St, 28402 [PO Box 2536, 28402]; onhgen@Wilmington.net; www.co.new-hanover.nc.us/lib/libmain.htm; (c) New Hanover

Private non-profit/ 1989/ members: 300/publication: The Clarendon Courier

GENEALOGICAL SOCIETY: Collects, preserves, and disseminates family histories from the southern region of NC.

PROGRAMS: Lectures; Publication

COLLECTIONS: [1715-present]

6474
Poplar Grove Plantation
10200 US Hwy 17 N, 28411; (p) (910) 686-9518; (f) (910) 686-4309; pgp@poplargrove.com; www.poplargrove.com; (c) Pender

Private non-profit/ 1980/ staff: 9(f); 7(p); 10(v)

HOUSE MUSEUM: Located on old peanut plantation in the South.

PROGRAMS: Community Outreach; Exhibits; Facility Rental; Family Programs; Festivals; Guided Tours; Interpretation; Lectures; Reenactments; School-Based Curriculum

COLLECTIONS: [19th c]

HOURS: Feb-mid Dec M-Sa 9-5, Su 12-5

ADMISSION: $7, Student $3, Seniors $6;

6475
Wilmington Railroad Museum Foundation, Inc.
501 Nutt St, 28401; (p) (910) 763-2634; (f) (910) 763-2634; www.wilmington.org/railroad/; (c) New Hanover

Private non-profit/ 1979/ Board of Directors/ staff: 1(f); 7(p); 59(v)/ members: 129/publication: Coast Line

HISTORIC SITE; HISTORY MUSEUM: Collects, preserves, and interprets the history of railroading, with particular emphasis on the eastern US. Displays artifacts and sponsors educational programs.

PROGRAMS: Annual Meeting; Community Outreach; Elder's Programs; Exhibits; Facility Rental; Family Programs; Guided Tours; Interpretation; Lectures; Publication; Research Library/Archives

COLLECTIONS: [1900-1960s] A building built in 1900, artifacts dealing with railroad history, two railroad working model layouts. A Baldwin steam engine, boxcar, caboose and machinery used in the maintenance and manufacture of railroad equipment.

HOURS: Apr-Oct M-Sa 10-5, Su 1-5; Nov-Mar call for hours

ADMISSION: $3, Children $1.50, Seniors $2; Under 5/Mbrs free

WILSON

6476
Wilson County Genealogical Society, Inc.
Wilson County Pub Lib Genealogy Rm, 27894 [PO Box 802, 27894-0802]; (p) (252) 243-1660; (f) (252) 243-0994; ancestor@wcgs.org; www.wcgs.org; (c) Wilson

Private non-profit/ 1991/ staff: 5(v)/ members: 200/publication: *Trees of Wilson; Wilson County Cemeteries; and others*

GENEALOGICAL SOCIETY: Undertakes programs of research, education, promotion, and preservation of the genealogical assets of Wilson County, including family histories, wills, legal documents, Bible records and photographs.

PROGRAMS: Annual Meeting; Family Programs; Festivals; Film/Video; Guided Tours; Interpretation; Lectures; Publication; Research Library/Archives

COLLECTIONS: [1607-present] Local and family histories, genealogical reference, resource items, and miscellaneous periodicals.

HOURS: Yr M-Th 9-9, F-Sa 9-6

ADMISSION: No charge

6477
Wilson Historic Properties Commission
112 N Goldsboro St, 27894 [PO Box 10, 27894-0010]; (p) (252) 399-2217; (f) (252) 399-2233; Lmonson@wilsonnc.org; www.wilsonnc.org; (c) Wilson

Joint/ 1976/ City; County/ staff: 1(f); 12(v)

HISTORIC PRESERVATION AGENCY: Architectural design review board for landmarks and historic districts in Wilson and Wilson County.

PROGRAMS: Exhibits; Film/Video; Guided Tours; Lectures

COLLECTIONS: Landmarks, National Registered Historic District nominations and technical materials related to the preservation of historic sites, properties, and landmarks.

HOURS: Yr M-F 8-5

WINDSOR

6478
Historic Hope Foundation, Inc.
312 Hope House Rd, 27983; (p) (252) 794-3140; (f) (252) 794-5583; hopeplantation@coastalnet.com; www.albemarlenc.com/hope/; (c) Bertie

Private non-profit/ 1966/ staff: 4(f); 11(p); 5(v)/ members: 750

GARDEN; HISTORIC SITE; HISTORY MUSEUM; HOUSE MUSEUM; LIVING HISTORY/ OUTDOOR MUSEUM; RESEARCH CENTER: Provides educational, cultural, and recreational benefits for the public by the preservation, maintenance, and administration of Hope Plantation, home of Governor David Stone (1770-1818).

PROGRAMS: Annual Meeting; Concerts; Exhibits; Facility Rental; Family Programs; Festivals; Film/Video; Garden Tours; Guided Tours; Interpretation; Lectures; Living History; Research Library/Archives; School-Based Curriculum; Theatre

COLLECTIONS: [17th-18th c] Academic and vernacular period architecture that displays collections of regional furniture.

HOURS: Yr M-Sa 10-5, Su 2-5

ADMISSION: $6.50, Student $2, Children $2, Seniors $6

WINNABOW

6479
Brunswick Town/Fort Anderson State Historic Site
Off Hwy 133 on Cape Fear River, 28479 [8884 Saint Philips Rd SE, 28479]; (p) (910) 371-6613; (f) (910) 383-3806; (c) Brunswick

State/ NC Dept of Cultural Resources/ staff: 5(f); 5(p)

HISTORIC SITE

PROGRAMS: Exhibits; Festivals; Guided Tours; Interpretation; Lectures; Reenactments

COLLECTIONS: [18th-19th c] Artifacts from the colonial period and Civil War.

HOURS: Spring-Summer M-F 9-5, Su 1-5; Fall-Winter T-Sa 10-4, Su 1-4

WINSTON-SALEM

6480
Dorothy Carpenter Medical Archives
E Fl, Gray Bldg, Hawthorne Rd, 27157 [Medical Center Blvd, 27157]; (p) (336) 716-3690; (f) (336) 716-2186; dyjohnso@wfubmc.edu; www.mero.lib.wfubmc.edu/archives/; (c) Forsyth

Private for-profit/ 1974/ Wake Forest University School of Medicine/ staff: 2(f)

LIBRARY AND/OR ARCHIVES: Collects historical materials associated with the Wake Forest University Baptist Medical Center.

PROGRAMS: Exhibits; Research Library/Archives

COLLECTIONS: [1942-present] Manuscript publications, oral histories, and museum objects associated with the history of medicine and the history of the Wake Forest University Baptist Medical Center.

HOURS: Yr M-F 9-4

ADMISSION: No charge

6481
Forsyth County Joint Historic Properties Commission
100 E First St, 27102 [PO Box 2511, 27102]; (p) (336) 727-2087; (f) (336) 748-3163; leannp@ci.winston-salem.nc.us; (c) Forsyth

Joint/ 1976/ City of Winston-Salem; Forsyth County/ staff: 1(f); 1(p)

HISTORIC PRESERVATION AGENCY: Protects and enriches Forsyth County's cultural, historical, and architectural heritage through identifying, designating, and preserving historic properties.

PROGRAMS: Community Outreach

6482
Historic Bethabara Park
2147 Bethabara Rd, 27106; (p) (336) 924-8191; (f) (336) 924-0535; www.co.forsyth.nc.us/Bethabara; (c) Forsyth

Joint/ 1970/ City of Winston-Salem/Forsyth County/ staff: 3(f); 25(p); 580(v)/publication: *Bethabara Diary*

GARDEN; HISTORIC PRESERVATION AGENCY; HISTORIC SITE; HISTORY MUSEUM; HOUSE MUSEUM; LIVING HISTORY/ OUTDOOR MUSEUM: Maintains site of the first Moravian settlement in NC listed as a National Historic Landmark. Preserves the 1788 Gemeinhaus, the 1782 Potter's House, the 1803 Brewer's House, archaeological ruins, reconstructed gardens, and a nature preserve.

PROGRAMS: Community Outreach; Concerts; Elder's Programs; Exhibits; Facility Rental; Family Programs; Festivals; Film/Video; Garden Tours; Guided Tours; Interpretation; Lectures; Living History; Publication; Reenactments; Research Library/Archives; School-Based Curriculum

COLLECTIONS: [1750-1850] Exhibits, archaeological ruins, and reconstructed gardens.

HOURS: Apr-Dec M-F 9:30-4:30, Sa-Su 1:30-4:30

ADMISSION: $1, Children $0.50

6483
Krause-Butner Potter's House
Historic Bethabara Park, 2147 Bethabara Rd, 27106; (p) (336) 924-8191

6484
Moravian Music Foundation, Inc.
457 S Church St, 27108 [PO Box L, Salem Station, 27108]; (p) (336) 725-0551; (f) (336) 725-4514; www.moravianmusic.org; (c) Forsyth

Private non-profit/ 1956/ staff: 3(f); 1(p)/ members: 1200/publication: *Moravian Music Foundation Newsletter*

HISTORIC PRESERVATION AGENCY: Archival and research facility for 18th and early 19th c music.

PROGRAMS: Annual Meeting; Community Outreach; Concerts; Festivals; Guided Tours; Lectures; Publication; Research Library/Archives

HOURS: Yr M-F 9-4:30 by appt

6485
Museum of Anthropology, Wake Forest University
Wingate Rd, 27109 [PO Box 7267, 27109]; (p) (336) 758-5282; (f) (336) 758-5116; moa@wfu.edu; www.wfu.edu/MOA; (c) Forsyth

Private non-profit/ 1963/ staff: 4(f); 2(p); 32(v)/ members: 200

ANTHROPOLOGY MUSEUM; HISTORY MUSEUM: Established by the faculty of the Anthropology Department to broaden the learning opportunities for their students.

PROGRAMS: Exhibits; Family Programs; Lectures; Research Library/Archives; School-Based Curriculum

COLLECTIONS: Objects from the Americas, Africa, Asia, and Oceania. Household and ceremonial items, textiles, hunting, and fishing gear.

HOURS: Yr T-Sa

6486
Museum of Early Southern Decorative Arts
924 S Main St, 27108 [PO Box 10310, 27108-0310]; (p) (336) 721-7360, (336) 721-7329; (f) (336) 721-7367; www.oldsalem.org; (c) Forsyth

Private non-profit/ 1965/ Old Salem, Inc./ staff: 25(f); 20(p); 10(v)/ members: 1200

HISTORY MUSEUM: Presents settings and galleries representing the decorative arts of seven southern states from the 17th-19th c.

PROGRAMS: Elder's Programs; Exhibits; Guided Tours; Lectures; Research Library/Archives

COLLECTIONS: [17th-19th c] Antiquities and architecture from diverse settings across the South.

HOURS: Yr M-Sa 9:30-4:30, Su 1:30-4:30

ADMISSION: $10

6487
North Carolina Baptist Historical Collection
Wake Forest Univ Campus, 27109 [PO Box 7777, 27109]; (p) (336) 758-5472, (336) 758-5089; (f) (336) 758-8831; woodarjr@wfu.edu; www.wfu.edu/Library/baptist; (c) Forsyth

Private non-profit/ 1880/ Board of Trustees/ staff: 3(f); 8(v)

RESEARCH CENTER: Collects, catalogs, indexes, preserves, and makes available to researchers records and information relating to NC Baptists, congregations, associations, missionaries, and denominational leaders, and organizations.

PROGRAMS: Annual Meeting; Community Outreach; Exhibits; Guided Tours; Lectures; Research Library/Archives

COLLECTIONS: [1729-present] Books, pamphlets, and printed items, microfilmed records of 1,045 NC Baptist churches; biographical files, vertical files for all NC churches including some African American, Primitive, Union, and Independent Baptist churches and collections of personal papers.

HOURS: Yr M-F 8:30-5

6488
Old Salem
600 S Main St, 27108 [PO Box F, Salem Station, 27108-0346]; (p) (336) 721-7300, (336) 721-7350; (f) (336) 721-7335; webmaster@oldsalem.org; www.oldsalem.org; (c) Forsyth

Private non-profit/ 1950/ Old Salem, Inc./ staff: 85(f); 80(p); 185(v)/ members: 1500

LIVING HISTORY/OUTDOOR MUSEUM: A living history town that interprets the Moravian settlement of Salem from 1766-1840.

PROGRAMS: Annual Meeting; Exhibits; Family Programs; Festivals; Film/Video; Guided Tours; Interpretation; Living History; Reenactments; Research Library/Archives; School-Based Curriculum

COLLECTIONS: [1769-1840] Crafts items, artifacts, and memorabilia relating to settlers in Old Salem during the late 18th and early 19th c.

HOURS: Yr M-Sa 9-5, Su 1-5:

6489
Reynolda House, Museum of American Art
2250 Reynolda Rd, 27116 [PO Box 11765, 27116]; (p) (336) 725-5325; (f) (336) 721-0991; reynolda@reynoldahouse.org; www.reynoldahouse.org; (c) Forsyth

1967/ Board of Directors/ staff: 16(f); 32(p); 275(v)/ members: 1

ART MUSEUM; GARDEN; HISTORIC SITE; HOUSE MUSEUM: Collects, preserves, and interprets American art and through educational programs, encourages participants to explore works of art in correlation with their counterparts in literature and music.

PROGRAMS: Community Outreach; Concerts; Elder's Programs; Exhibits; Family Programs; Festivals; Film/Video; Garden Tours; Guided Tours; Interpretation; Lectures; Living History; Research Library/Archives; Theatre

COLLECTIONS: [18th-20th c] American art history from 1755 to the present.

HOURS: Yr T 9:30-4:30, Su 1:30-4:30

ADMISSION: $6, Children $3, Seniors $5; Students free

6490
Wachovia Historical Society
924 S Main St, 27108 [PO Box 10310, 27108-0667]; (p) (336) 721-7373; (c) Forsyth

Private non-profit/ 1895/ staff: 1(p)/ members: 250

HISTORIC PRESERVATION AGENCY; HISTORICAL SOCIETY: Collects, preserves and disseminates information relating to the history and antiquities of the Moravian Church in the South.

PROGRAMS: Annual Meeting; Exhibits; Interpretation; Research Library/Archives

COLLECTIONS: [1750-1900] Photos, ceramics, written records of local and worldwide Moravian Church activities.

HOURS: Yr Daily 9:30-4:30

ADMISSION: Varies

YANCEYVILLE

6491
Caswell County Historical Association, Inc.
Old Jail, behind the Old Courthouse, 27379 [PO Box 278, 27379]; (p) (336) 694-6426; (c) Caswell

Private non-profit/ 1959/ Board of Directors/ staff: 3(p); 3(v)/ members: 200

ALLIANCE OF HISTORICAL AGENCIES; GENEALOGICAL SOCIETY; HISTORIC PRESERVATION AGENCY; HISTORIC SITE; HISTORICAL SOCIETY; HISTORY MUSEUM; HOUSE MUSEUM; LIVING HISTORY/OUTDOOR MUSEUM: Assisting in the restoration of 1862 courthouse.

HOURS: Yr by appt

NORTH DAKOTA

ABERCROMBIE

6492
Fort Abecrombie State Historic Site
816 Broadway St, 58001 [PO Box 148, 58001]; (p) (701) 553-8513; (f) (701) 825-6840; histsoc@state.nd.us; www.DiscoverND.com/hist; (c) Richland

1857/ staff: 2(f); 2(p)

HISTORIC SITE: Preserves military post of the Dakota Conflict of 1862.

PROGRAMS: Exhibits; Festivals; Interpretation; Publication

COLLECTIONS: [1862-1900] Military, frontier settlement.

HOURS: May-Sept W-Su 8-5

ADMISSION: $3, Student $0.75, Children $1.50

ALEXANDER

6493
Lewis and Clark Trail Museum
Hwy 85, 58831 [PO Box 22, 58831]; (p) (701) 828-3595; (c) McKenzie

1968/ staff: 1(f)

HISTORIC PRESERVATION AGENCY: Preserves local history.

PROGRAMS: Annual Meeting; Exhibits; Guided Tours

COLLECTIONS: [1900] Machinery, household items, Lewis and Clark artifacts.

HOURS: June-Aug M-Sa 9-5, Su 1-5

ADMISSION: $2, Student $1

BELCOURT

6494
Turtle Mountain Community
3 mi N of Belcourt, 58316 [PO Box 340, 58316]; (p) (701) 477-7812; (f) (701) 477-7870; eggerst@hotmail.com; www.turtle-mountain.cc.nd.us; (c) Rollette

Tribal/ 1972/ staff: 2(f)

PROGRAMS: Film/Video; Research Library/Archives

COLLECTIONS: [17th c-present] 1,200 books, Native American video/audio tapes, 14,000 artifacts.

HOURS: Yr

ADMISSION: No charge

BISMARCK

6495
Camp Hancock State Historic Site
101 W Main St, 58505 [ND Heritage Ctr, 612 E Boulevard Ave, 58505-0830]; (p) (701) 328-9664; (f) (701) 328-3710; histsoc@state.nd.us; www.DiscoverND.com/hist; (c) Burleigh

State/ State Historical Board/ staff: 1(f)

HISTORIC SITE: Preserves part of a military installation established as Camp Greeley in 1872.

PROGRAMS: Interpretation

COLLECTIONS: [1872-1950s] Railroad steam engine, oldest existing building in Bismarck, local 1880s-era church.

HOURS: Mid May-Sept W-Su 1-5

ADMISSION: Donations accepted

6496
Former Governor's Mansion State Historic Site
320 E Ave B, 58505 [612 E Boulevard Ave, 58505-0830]; (p) (701) 328-9529, (701) 382-2666; (f) (701) 328-3710; histsoc@state.nd.us; www.DiscoverND.com/hist; (c) Burleigh

State/ 1884/ State Historical Board/ staff: 2(f); 1(p); 20(v)/publication: *North Dakota's Fomer Governors' Mansion: Its History and Preservation*

HISTORIC SITE: Preserves historic site that served as residence for 21 governors of ND from 1893-1960.

PROGRAMS: Facility Rental; Festivals; Garden Tours; Interpretation; Publication

COLLECTIONS: [1893-1960] Period furnishings, photos and memorabilia.

HOURS: May

6497
Germans from Russia Heritage Society
1008 E Central Ave, 58501; (p) (701) 223-6167; (f) (701) 223-4421; grhs@btigate.com; grhs.com; (c) Burleigh

Private non-profit/ 1971/ staff: 1(f); 3(p); 250(v)/ members: 2235

GENEALOGICAL SOCIETY; HISTORICAL SOCIETY: Preserves Germanic-Russian heritage and history in North Dakota.

PROGRAMS: Annual Meeting

COLLECTIONS: [1800-present] Family histories, local histories, cemetery records, church history and records, obituaries, family records.

HOURS: Yr M-F 9:30-1

ADMISSION: No charge

6498
North Dakota Heritage Center, The
612 E Boulevard Ave, 58505-0830; (p) (701) 328-2666; (f) (701) 328-3710; histsoc@state.nd.us; www.DiscoverND.com/hist; (c) Burleigh

State/ 1981/ State Historical Board/ staff: 54(f); 22(p); 200(v)

HERITAGE AREA: Largest museum in the state. Features interpretive exhibits that explore the story of life on the Northern Plains. With the ND Geological Survey, houses the State Fossil Collection.

PROGRAMS: Annual Meeting; Community Outreach; Exhibits; Facility Rental; Family Programs; Interpretation; Lectures; Living History; Publication; Research Library/Archives

COLLECTIONS: [Prehistory-present] History, natural history and ethnology artifacts; archaeological items, books, periodicals, maps, photographs, historical manuscripts, archival records, newspapers, oral histories and films. Extensive genealogical resources.

HOURS: Yr M-F 8-5, Sa 9-5, Su 11-5; Library: Yr M-F 8-4:30

ADMISSION: No charge

6499
State Historical Society of North Dakota
ND Heritage Ctr, State Capitol, 58505 [612 E Boulevard Ave, 58505-0830]; (p) (701) 328-2666; (f) (701) 328-3710; histsoc@state.nd.us; www.DiscoverND.com/hist; (c) Burleigh

State/ 1895/ State Historical Board/ staff: 54(f); 22(p); 200(v)/ members: 1750

HISTORIC PRESERVATION AGENCY; HISTORIC SITE; HISTORICAL SOCIETY; HISTORY MUSEUM; HOUSE MUSEUM; LIVING HISTORY/OUTDOOR MUSEUM; RESEARCH CENTER: Manages 56 state historic sites and two state museums. Identifies, preserves, interprets and promotes the heritage of ND and its people.

PROGRAMS: Annual Meeting; Community Outreach; Concerts; Elder's Programs; Exhibits; Facility Rental; Festivals; Interpretation; Lectures; Living History; Publication; Research Library/Archives; School-Based Curriculum; Theatre

COLLECTIONS: [Prehistory-present] History, natural history and ethnology artifacts, archaeological items, books, periodicals, maps, photographs, historical manuscripts, archival records, newspapers, oral histories and film. Extensive genealogical resources.

BOTTINEAU

6500
Bottineau County Historical Society
N Main St, 58318 [c/o Velma Wondraek, 522 Sinclair, 58318]; (c) Bottineau

County/ 1935/ staff: 10(v)/ members: 12

HISTORICAL SOCIETY; HISTORY MUSEUM; RESEARCH CENTER

PROGRAMS: Annual Meeting; Community Outreach; Guided Tours; School-Based Curriculum

COLLECTIONS: [19th-20th c] Military, farm and Native American artifacts, newspapers, hardware, kitchen, dining room, parlor, bedroom, glassware, pottery, hospital, beauty and barber shops, ice cream parlor and 19th century fire engines.

HOURS: May-Oct Sa-Su 1:30-4:30

ADMISSION: Donations accepted

BOWDON

6501
Bowdon Museum and Library
232 40th Ave NE, 58418; (p) (701) 962-3736; (c) Wells

Private non-profit/ 1989/ staff: 1(p); 6(v)

HISTORY MUSEUM: Collects, preserves and displays local history.

PROGRAMS: Guided Tours

COLLECTIONS: [20th c]

HOURS: Late May-Aug W-Su 1-5

BOWMAN

6502
Bowman County Historical and Genealogical Society
12 First Ave NE, 58623 [PO Box 78, 58623-0078]; (p) (701) 523-3600; (f) (701) 523-3600; ptrm@ctctel.com; ptrm@ptrm.org; (c) Bowman

Private non-profit/ 1983/ Board of Directors/ staff: 1(p); 30(v)/ members: 227

GARDEN; GENEALOGICAL SOCIETY; HISTORIC PRESERVATION AGENCY; HISTORICAL SOCIETY; HISTORY MUSEUM; RESEARCH CENTER: Collects, preserves, interprets and displays local history; maintains museum, paleontology lab, and research facility.

PROGRAMS: Annual Meeting; Exhibits; Garden Tours; Guided Tours; Lectures; Research Library/Archives

COLLECTIONS: [Prehistoric-homesteading] Fossils, Native American artifacts, local and military history items, genealogy files and research papers in paleontology.

HOURS: Yr M-Sa 10-4; Winter M-Sa 9-6; Summer Su 1:30-5

ADMISSION: $2, Family $5

BUFFALO

6503
Buffalo Historical Society, Inc., Old Stone Church and Rectory Heritage Center
204-206 Wilcox Ave N, 58011-0014; (p) (701) 633-5259; (f) (701) 633-5115; bankers@ictc.com; (c) Cass

Private non-profit/ 1983/ Board of Directors/ staff: 25(v)/ members: 82/publication: *Historical Buffalo Express*

HISTORIC SITE; HISTORICAL SOCIETY; HISTORY MUSEUM; HOUSE MUSEUM; RESEARCH CENTER: Identifies, preserves, interprets and shares history of Western Cass County.

PROGRAMS: Annual Meeting; Community Outreach; Concerts; Exhibits; Festivals; Guided Tours; Interpretation; Lectures; Publication; Research Library/Archives; School-Based Curriculum

COLLECTIONS: [1879-present] Newspapers, photos, and artifacts of Buffalo.

HOURS: May-Sept Sa 10-3 or by appt

CAVALIER

6504
Northeastern North Dakota Heritage Assocation
5 mi W of Cavalier, 58220 [13571 Hwy 5, 58220]; (p) (701) 265-4561; (f) (701) 265-4443; isp@state.nd.us; www.state.nd.us/ndparks /parks /icelandic /home.htm; (c) Pembina

Joint/ 1989/ State; Private non-profit/ staff: 2(f); 12(p); 50(v)/ members: 200

GARDEN; GENEALOGICAL SOCIETY; HISTORIC PRESERVATION AGENCY; HOUSE MUSEUM: Preserves history of region and homesteaders.

PROGRAMS: Annual Meeting; Concerts; Elder's Programs; Exhibits; Facility Rental; Family Programs; Festivals; Film/Video; Guided Tours; Interpretation; Living History; Publication

COLLECTIONS: [1870-1920] Eight historic buildings with period furnishings, 1000 letters and books, photos.

HOURS: June-Aug Daily 8-9, Sept-May M-F 8-5, Su 1-5

CENTER

6505
Fort Clark State Historic Site
Fort Clark, 58530 [HC 2, Box 26, 58530]; (p) (701) 794-8832, (701) 623-4355; (f) (701) 328-3710; histsoc@state.nd.us; www.DiscoverND.com/hist; (c) Mercer

State/ staff: 1(f); 1(p)

HISTORIC SITE: Promotes history of site named for explorer William Clark of Lewis and Clark Expedition; served as a Mandan Indian earthlodge village and later as an Arikara village during the early to mid 19th c.

PROGRAMS: Interpretation; Publication

COLLECTIONS: [1822-1862] Archeological Mandan Indian village and Fort Clark Trading Post site.

HOURS: Mid May-Sept Th-M 8-5

ADMISSION: Donations accepted

DEVILS LAKE

6506
Devils Lake Historic Preservation Commission
522 7th St, 58301; (p) (701) 662-3334; (c) Ramsey

1991

HISTORIC PRESERVATION AGENCY: Preserves Devils Lake Historic buildings.

6507
Lake Region Heritage Center, Inc.
502 4th St, 58301 [PO Box 245, 58301-0245]; (p) (701) 662-3701; (f) (701) 662-2810; jschiele@stellarnet.com; www.lrhc.homestead.com; (c) Ramsey

Private non-profit/ 1974/ staff: 1(f); 5(p); 20(v)/ members: 200

HISTORICAL SOCIETY; HISTORY MUSEUM: Preserves and interprets local history in Old Post Office Museum; supports The Sheriff's Residence museum.

PROGRAMS: Annual Meeting; Community Outreach; Concerts; Elder's Programs; Exhibits; Facility Rental; Family Programs; Festivals; Guided Tours; Interpretation; Lectures; Living History; Research Library/Archives

COLLECTIONS: [1867-1910] Old Post Office Museum is Greco style, Vermont limestone 1910 structure. Pioneer clothing, furnishings, Native American artifacts, post office artifacts, 1906 automobile, fire fighting equipment, tools, farm implements.

HOURS: Yr Daily Sa-Su Noon-4; M-F 8:30-5, Mem Day-Labor Day 8:30-6

ADMISSION: Donations accepted

6508
Lake Region Pioneer Daughters
514 6th St, 58335; (p) (701) 766-4346; (c) Ramsey

1936/ staff: 2(p); 15(v)/ members: 142

HISTORY MUSEUM: Preserves history of North Dakota.

PROGRAMS: Exhibits; Interpretation

COLLECTIONS: [1880-present] Pioneer artifacts.

HOURS: May-Sept Daily 8-5

6509
Sheriff's Residence, The
416 6th St, 58301 [PO Box 245, 58301-0245]; (p) (701) 662-3701; (f) (701) 662-2810; jschiele@stellarnet.com; www.lrhc.homestead.com; (c) Ramsey

Private non-profit/ 1910/ Lake Region Heritage Center, Inc.

HISTORY MUSEUM; HOUSE MUSEUM: Former home of county sheriffs' families.

PROGRAMS: Exhibits

COLLECTIONS: [1800s-1950] Early 19th c furnishings, small farm implements, and store fixtures. Replica one-room school, all the furnishings from the Ceska 19th c dental office from Michigan City, ND.

HOURS: Mem Day-Labor Day Sa-Su Noon-4; and by appt

ADMISSION: Donations accepted

EDMORE

6510
Wheaton Manor
58330 [c/o Paul E Steffan, PO Box 121, 58330]; (p) (701) 644-2291, (701) 644-2777

EPPING

6511
Buffalo Trails Museum
Main St, 55843 [PO Box 22, 55843]; (p) (701) 859-4361; (c) Williams

Private non-profit/ 1966/ staff: 1(f); 2(p); 7(v)

ART MUSEUM; GENEALOGICAL SOCIETY; HISTORIC SITE; HISTORICAL SOCIETY; HISTORY MUSEUM; LIVING HISTORY/OUTDOOR MUSEUM; TRIBAL MUSEUM: Preserves local history.

PROGRAMS: Annual Meeting; Community Outreach; Concerts; Elder's Programs; Exhibits; Family Programs; Festivals; Film/Video; Guided Tours; Lectures; Living History; Library/Archives; School-Based Curriculum

COLLECTIONS: [1900-1960] Pioneer, homesteaders, implements, mercantile artifacts.

HOURS: T-Sa 10-6, Su 1-5

FARGO

6512
North Dakota Institute for Regional Studies
1305 19th Ave N, Rm 117, 58105 [PO Box 5599, 58105-5599]; (p) (701) 231-8914; (f) (701) 231-7138; archives@www.lib.ndsu.nodak.edu; www.lib.ndsu.nodak.edu/ndirs; (c) Cass

1950/ ND State Univ/ staff: 3(f); 4(v)

Promotes history of ND and environs.

PROGRAMS: Exhibits; Publication; Research Library/Archives

COLLECTIONS: [1865-present] 1,100 manuscript collection, 50,000 photographs, 5,000 publications on all aspects of ND history. German Russian collection.

HOURS: Yr M-F 8-4:30

6513
Plains Art Museum
704 First Ave N, 58108 [PO Box 2338, 58108-2338]; (p) (701) 232-3821; (f) (701) 293-1082; pam@rrnet.com; www.plainsart.org; (c) Cass

Private non-profit/ 1975/ Board of Directors/ staff: 26(f); 14(p); 65(v)/ members: 984

ART MUSEUM: Promotes art education and history programs in ND and MN.

PROGRAMS: Annual Meeting; Community Outreach; Concerts; Exhibits; Facility Rental; Family Programs; Guided Tours; Lectures; Publication; Research Library/Archives

COLLECTIONS: 2,500 objects, prints, photos, ethnographic artifacts of Ojibwe and Sioux.

HOURS: Yr T, Th 10-8, W, F-Sa 10-6, Su 12-6

ADMISSION: $3, Children $2, Students, Seniors $2.50

6514
Red River Valley Genealogical Society
112 N Univ Dr, 58106 [PO Box 9284, 58106]; (p) (701) 239-4129; rrvgs@rrnet.com; www.rrnet.com/~rrvgs; (c) Cass

Private non-profit/ 1969/ staff: 7(v)/ members: 2

GENEALOGICAL SOCIETY: Collects and preserves family history research.

PROGRAMS: Annual Meeting; Lectures; Publication; Research Library/Archives

COLLECTIONS: Cemetery records, funeral home records, family histories, research library, town histories.

HOURS: Yr T-Wed 1-4, Sa 10-4

ADMISSION: $1

FORT RANSOM

6515
Ransom County Historical Society
101 Mill Rd, 58033 [PO Box 5, 58033]; (p) (701) 845-0561; Sara_McManigle@ mail.vcsu.nodak.edu; www.members.tripod.com/rchsmuseum/; (c) Ransom

Private non-profit/ 1972/ Ransom County Historical Society/ staff: 1(p); 3(v)/ members: 42

HISTORIC SITE; HISTORICAL SOCIETY; HISTORY MUSEUM: Manages the Ransom County Historical Museum complex and the TJ Walker Historic Site.

PROGRAMS: Annual Meeting; Elder's Programs; Exhibits; Guided Tours; Interpretation; Publication; Research Library/Archives

COLLECTIONS: [19th c-present] Prehistoric, pioneer, Native American, farm implements, church organs.

HOURS: Yr May-Sept Daily 1-5

ADMISSION: Donations accepted

FORT TOTTEN

6516
Fort Totten State Historic Site
Fort Totten, 58335 [PO Box 224, 58335]; (p) (701) 766-4441; (f) (701) 766-1382; histsoc@state.nd.us; www.DiscoverND.com/hist; (c) Ramsey

State/ 1867/ State Historical Board/ staff: 2(f); 8(p); 15(v)/publication: *Fort Totten: Military Post and Indian School, 1867-1959*

HISTORIC SITE: Served as military fort from 1867-1890 and as an Indian Boarding School, then Community School, from 1891-1959. Example of frontier military post in the Trans-Mississippi West.

PROGRAMS: Community Outreach; Exhibits; Family Programs; Festivals; Interpretation; Publication

COLLECTIONS: [1867-1959] Military fort and later Indian Industrial School, Reservation Day School, 17 original buildings.

HOURS: Mid May-Sept Daily 8-5; Mid Sept-May Sa-Su 8-5

ADMISSION: $4, Children $1.50, Under 6 free

GARRETSON

6517
Garretson Area Historical Society and Garretson Heritage Museum
609 Main St, 57030 [PO Box 105, 57030]; (p) (605) 594-6094

1989/ members: 65

HISTORICAL SOCIETY: Preserves local history.

PROGRAMS: Annual Meeting; Exhibits; Festivals; Film/Video

COLLECTIONS: Pioneer, Devils Gulch Palisade Park memorabilia, toys, farming.

HOURS: May-Sept Th-Sa 9-5, Su 1-5

ADMISSION: Donations accepted

GARRISON

6518
Heritage Park Foundation
241 5th Ave NE, 58540-7352; (p) (701) 463-2519; (c) McLean

Private non-profit/ 1972/ Heritage Park Foundation/ staff: 12(v)

HISTORICAL SOCIETY; HISTORY MUSEUM; HOUSE MUSEUM: Preserves local history.

PROGRAMS: Annual Meeting; Community Outreach; Exhibits; Festivals; Guided Tours

COLLECTIONS: [1890-present] School, church, pioneer cabin, homestead houses and depot, history museum, period furnishing.

HOURS: May-Oct F 11-4 and by appt

ADMISSION: No charge

GLEN ULLIN

6519
Glen Ullin Museum and Association
207 S 10th St, 58631 [6315 46th St, 58631-9734]; (p) (701) 348-3295; (c) Morton

City, non-profit; Private non-profit/ 1984/ staff: 4(p); 10(v)/ members: 30

HISTORIC PRESERVATION AGENCY; HISTORY MUSEUM; HOUSE MUSEUM: Preserves local history.

PROGRAMS: Annual Meeting; Community Outreach; Exhibits; Festivals; Guided Tours

COLLECTIONS: [1883-present] 200 bibles, 1500 books, period furnishing, printing press, tractors, WWI army trucks.

HOURS: June-Sept Su 1-4

ADMISSION: Donations accepted

GRAFTON

6520
Walsh County Historical Society
600 Cooper Ave, 58237 [131 Prospect, 58237]; (p) (701) 352-0479; (c) Walsh

Private non-profit/ 1967/ members: 350/publication: *Walsh County Historical Society Newsletter*

HISTORIC PRESERVATION AGENCY; HISTORIC SITE; HISTORICAL SOCIETY; HISTORY MUSEUM; HOUSE MUSEUM; LIVING HISTORY/OUTDOOR MUSEUM: Maintains the history of Walsh County.

PROGRAMS: Annual Meeting; Exhibits; Festivals; Guided Tours; Lectures; Publication

COLLECTIONS: [1870] Artifacts of prairie settlement.

HOURS: Yr

ADMISSION: $3

GRAND FORKS

6521
Campbell House, The
2405 Belmont Rd, 58201; (p) (701) 776-2216

1878/ staff: 1(p); 3(v)

COLLECTIONS: [1878-1921] Period furnishing.

HOURS: Vary

6522
Elwyn B Robinson Department of Special Collections, University of North Dakota
University Ave & Centennial Dr, 58202 [Box 9000, Univ of ND, 58202-9000]; (p) (701) 777-4625; (f) (701) 777-3319; sandy_slater@mail.und.nodak.edu; www.und.nodak.edu/library/collections/spk.html; (c) Grand Forks

State/ 1951/ Univ. of North Dakota/ staff: 3(f); 1(p); 1(v)

Collects, preserves, and references published resources and historical records that document political, economic and cultural heritage of ND, Red River Valley, Grand Forks and the University of ND.

PROGRAMS: Community Outreach; Exhibits; Publication; Research Library/Archives

COLLECTIONS: [1860-present] 13,100 1 ft. manuscripts, 2900 1 ft. university archives, 53,000 photographs, 42,000 volumes, 8,000 theses and dissertations, 71 serials, 5,000 audio visuals, 1000 maps, 4400 reels of microfilm.

HOURS: Yr: Schoolyear M, T, Th 8-5, W 8-9pm, F 8-4:30; Other: M-F 8-4:30

ADMISSION: No charge

6523
Grand Forks Historic Preservation Commission
1405 1st Ave N, 58201; (p) (701) 772-8756; (f) (701) 746-2548; mgunderson@gfherald.com; (c) Grand Forks

1988/ staff: 1(f); 11(v)

HISTORIC PRESERVATION AGENCY: Preserves history of Grand Forks.

PROGRAMS: Exhibits

HATTON

6524
Hatton-Eielson Museum
405 Eielson St, 58240; (p) (701) 543-3726; (f) (701) 543-4013

HEBRON

6525
Hebron Historical and Art Society
c/o Lambert Kastrow, PO Box 394, 58638-0394; (p) (701) 878-4326; (f) (701) 878-4891; (c) Morton

Private for-profit/ 1975/ staff: 7(v)/ members: 35

ART MUSEUM; HISTORIC PRESERVATION AGENCY; HISTORICAL SOCIETY; HISTORY MUSEUM

PROGRAMS: Annual Meeting; Festivals; Film/Video; Research Library/Archives

COLLECTIONS: [1880-present] Pioneer settlers, immigrant population.

HOURS: By appt

ADMISSION: Donations accepted

HILLSBORO

6526
Traill County Historical Society
306 W Caledonia, 58045 [PO Box 173, 58045]; (p) (701) 436-5959; (c) Traill

Private non-profit/ 1965/ staff: 15(v)/ members: 100

HISTORICAL SOCIETY; HOUSE MUSEUM: Preserves heritage of Traill County pioneers.

PROGRAMS: Annual Meeting; Exhibits; Guided Tours

COLLECTIONS: [1870-1930] Period furnishing, Native American artifacts, farm tools, pioneer artifacts.

HOURS: May-Sept Sa-M 2-5

ADMISSION: $2

HOPE

6527
Steele County Historical Society
Steele Ave & 3rd St, 58046 [PO Box 144, 58046-0144]; (p) (701) 945-2394; (c) Steele

Private non-profit/ 1966/ Board of Directors/ staff: 3(p); 25(v)/ members: 75/publication: *Steele County of North Dakota, 1883-1983; Hope Through the Century*

HISTORICAL SOCIETY; HISTORY MUSEUM; HOUSE MUSEUM: Collects and preserves Steele County history; operates museum, cultural center and archives.

PROGRAMS: Annual Meeting; Community Outreach; Concerts; Elder's Programs; Exhibits; Facility Rental; Family Programs; Festivals; Film/Video; Guided Tours; Interpretation; Lectures; Living History; Publication; Research Library/Archives

COLLECTIONS: [1872-present] Newspapers, photos, manuscripts, family histories, atlases, portraits, art, textiles, furniture, farm machinery, tools, vehicles, toys, musical instruments, windmills, prairie life.

HOURS: Tu-F 9-12/1-5

ADMISSION: $2.50

JAMESTOWN

6528
National Buffalo Museum
500 17th St SE, 58402 [PO Box 1712, 58402-1712]; (p) (701) 252-8648; (f) (701) 253-5803; buffalo@daktel.com; (c) Stutsman

Private non-profit/ 1991/ North Dakota Buffalo Foundation/ staff: 2(f); 6(p); 25(v)/ members: 400/publication: *Buffalo Tales*

HISTORY MUSEUM: Promotes history of the American bison.

PROGRAMS: Exhibits; Facility Rental; Film/Video; Interpretation; Publication

COLLECTIONS: [1800s] 1,500 Native American objects and bison artifacts.

HOURS: May-Sept Daily 9-8, Oct-Apr 9-5

6529
Stutsman County Historical Society Museum
321 3rd Ave SE, 58401 [PO Box 1002, 58402-1002]; (p) (701) 252-6741

1907/ staff: 1(f); 18(v)

COLLECTIONS: [1800-1930] Interpretive rooms: country stores. homesteader's shanty, interior of sod house, Doll room, Library, Railroad room, sewing room, ballroom, parlor. Arrowheads, Indian hammers, pottery pieces, buffalo bones. Newspaper clippings, history books, photos, yearbooks, biographical annuals.

HOURS: Seasonal

KULM

6530
Whitestone Hill Battlefield State Historic Site
10 mi SE of Kulm, 58456 [7310 86th St SE, 58456]; (p) (701) 396-7731, (701) 825-6840; (f) (701) 328-3710; histsoc@state.nd.us; www.DiscoverND.com/hist; (c) Dickey

State/ 1863/ staff: 2(p)

HISTORIC SITE: Site of battle between Brigadier General Alfred Sully and Sioux warriors.

PROGRAMS: Exhibits; Interpretation; Publication

COLLECTIONS: [1860s] Artifacts, graves, and monuments commemorating the Battle of Whitestone Hill.

HOURS: Mid May-Sept Th-M 10-5

ADMISSION: Donations

LANGDON

6531
Cavalier County Historical Society
1213 12th Ave, 58245; (p) (701) 256-3650; (c) Cavalier

Private non-profit/ 1970/ CCHS Officers and Directors/ staff: 1(p)/ members: 300

HISTORIC SITE; HISTORICAL SOCIETY; HISTORY MUSEUM; HOUSE MUSEUM

PROGRAMS: Annual Meeting; Community Outreach; Concerts; Exhibits; Family Programs; Film/Video; Guided Tours; Living History; Research Library/Archives; School-Based Curriculum

COLLECTIONS: Pioneer family artifacts.

HOURS: June-Aug Su-M, W, F 2-5

ADMISSION: No charge

LIDGERWOOD

6532
Lidgerwood Community Museum
215 Park St SE, 58053 [PO Box 111, 58053-0111]; (p) (701) 538-4168; (c) Richland

City, non-profit/ 1985/ Board of Directors/ staff: 2(f); 9(v)

HISTORIC PRESERVATION AGENCY; HISTORIC SITE; HOUSE MUSEUM: Collects and preserves local history.

PROGRAMS: Annual Meeting; Exhibits; Festivals; Garden Tours; Guided Tours; School-Based Curriculum

COLLECTIONS: [1900-1945] Ida Prokop Lee feather pictures, paintings, Native American busts, military uniforms, WWI memorabilia, period clothing and furnishing.

HOURS: Yr Tu-F, 1st and 3rd Sa 1-5

ADMISSION: Donations accepted

MEDORA

6533
Billings County Historical Society
[PO Box 364, 58645]; (p) (701) 623-4389; (c) Billings

Private non-profit/ staff: 1(f); 1(p)/ members: 104

GENEALOGICAL SOCIETY; HISTORIC PRESERVATION AGENCY; HISTORICAL SOCIETY; HISTORY MUSEUM: Maintains historical museum.

PROGRAMS: Annual Meeting; Exhibits; Guided Tours; Interpretation

COLLECTIONS: [1880s-present] Military items from World War I through Desert Storm; ethnic and western items.

HOURS: May-Sept Daily 9-5

ADMISSION: $2, Student $75, Seniors $1.50; Under 12 free

6534
Chateau de Mores State Historic Site
W side of River overlooking Medora, 58645 [PO Box 106, 58645]; (p) (701) 623-4355; (f) (701) 623-4921; histsoc@state.nd.us; www.DiscoverND.com/hist; (c) Billings

Joint; State/ 1883/ staff: 2(f); 14(p); 10(v)

HOURS: May 16-Sept 15 Daily 8:30-6:30

ADMISSION: $5, Children $2.50, Students $1

6535
Theodore Roosevelt National Park
315 2nd Ave, 58695 [PO Box 7, 58695]; (p) (701) 623-4466; (f) (701) 623-4840; thro_interpretation@nps.gov; www.nps.gov/thro; (c) Billings

Federal/ 1947/ National Park Service Dept of the Interior/ staff: 4(f); 8(p); 15(v)

HISTORIC PRESERVATION AGENCY: Commemorates Theodore Roosevelt's contributions to national conservation efforts.

PROGRAMS: Community Outreach; Exhibits; Family Programs; Film/Video; Guided Tours; Interpretation; Lectures; Publication; Research Library/Archives; School-Based Curriculum

COLLECTIONS: [1880-present] Theodore Roosevelt memorabilia, CCC era, cattle ranching artifacts, Maltese Cross Cabin.

HOURS: Visitor's Center: Yr Daily July-Aug 8-8; Sept-June 8-:304; Park: 24 hours

MINNEWAUKAN

6536
Minnewaukan Historical Society
Hwy 281, 1st St, 58351 [PO Box 214, 58351-0214]; (p) (701) 473-5488; garvink@stellarnet.com; (c) Benson

Private non-profit/ 1983/ staff: 1(p)

HISTORICAL SOCIETY; HISTORY MUSEUM

PROGRAMS: Guided Tours

COLLECTIONS: [1870-1945]

HOURS: June-Aug Su 2-5 and by appt

ADMISSION: No charge

MINOT

6537
Minot Family History Center
2025 9th St NW, 58703; (p) (701) 838-4486; (c) Ward

Private non-profit/ 1985/ Church of Jesus Christ of Latter-Day Saints/ staff: 6(v)

GENEALOGICAL SOCIETY; RESEARCH CENTER: Preserves and researches family genealogy.

PROGRAMS: Research Library/Archives

COLLECTIONS: Microfilms/microfiche and written histories of various Scandinavian/ Northern European records.

HOURS: Yr W 6-9, Sa 10-1

ADMISSION: No charge

MINTO

6538
Walsh County Historical Museum
3rd St & Major Ave, 58261 [PO Box 312, 58261]; (p) (701) 248-3414; (c) Walsh

1971/ staff: 6(v)/ members: 500

HISTORIC SITE; HISTORICAL SOCIETY; HISTORY MUSEUM: Preserves history of Walsh County.

PROGRAMS: Exhibits; Festivals; Guided Tours

COLLECTIONS: [1750-present] Fur Trade artifacts, pioneer homes, agriculture, natural history, Native American.

HOURS: May-Sept Su 1-5 and by appt

MOHALL

6539
Renville County Historical Society, Inc.
1st St NE, 58761 [PO Box 261, 58761]; (p) (701) 756-6195; (c) Renville

County, non-profit/ 1976/ Renville County Historical Society/ staff: 1(p); 2(v)/ members: 35

PROGRAMS: Annual Meeting; Exhibits; Guided Tours

COLLECTIONS: [19th-20th c] Farm tools, household appliances, medical equipment, WWI and WWII memorabilia.

HOURS: June-Aug F-Su 2-5/7-9

ADMISSION: No charge

MOORETON

6540
Bagg Bonanza Historical Farm
8025 169th Ave SE, 58061 [PO Box 702, 58061]; (p) (701) 274-8989; (c) Richland

Private non-profit/ 1990/ staff: 20(v)/ members: 250

HISTORIC PRESERVATION AGENCY; HISTORIC SITE: Nation's remaining bonanza farm.

PROGRAMS: Annual Meeting; Community Outreach; Guided Tours; Interpretation; Living History; School-Based Curriculum

COLLECTIONS: [Late 1800s-1940s]

HOURS: May-Sept F-Su 12-6

ADMISSION: $3.50

NAPOLEON

6541
Logan County Historical Society
708 Lake Ave W, 58561 [800 Broadway St, 58561]; (p) (701) 754-2453; (c) Logan

Private non-profit/ 1975/ ND State Historical Society/ staff: 1(p); 10(v)/ members: 10

GENEALOGICAL SOCIETY; HISTORICAL SOCIETY; HISTORY MUSEUM: Preserves history of Logan County.

PROGRAMS: Annual Meeting; Exhibits; Publication

COLLECTIONS: Blacksmith, machinery, school, pioneer, agriculture, tools, church.

HOURS: May-Sept Su 1-4:30

ADMISSION: No charge

NEW TOWN

6542
Three Affiliated Tribes Museum, Inc.
[PO Box 147, 58763]; (p) (701) 627-4477; (f) (701) 627-3805; (c) McKenzie

Private non-profit/ 1964/ Board of Directors/ staff: 3(p); 3(v)

Preserves history and culture of Mandan, Hidatsa, and Arikara Natives.

PROGRAMS: Elder's Programs; Exhibits; Family Programs; Interpretation; School-Based Curriculum

COLLECTIONS: [1850-1950] Cultural artifacts of Mandan, Hidatsa, and Arikara tribes: clothing, implements, toys, photos.

HOURS: Apr-Nov Daily 10-6

ADMISSION: $3, Seniors $2

OAKES

6543
Dickey County Historical Society
Main Ave, 58474 [9225 104th Ave SE, 58474]; (p) (701) 783-4361; mkunrath@mail.oakes.k12.nd.us; (c) Dickey

County, non-profit/ 1974/ staff: 12(v)/ members: 101

HISTORICAL SOCIETY: Preserves local history.

PROGRAMS: Annual Meeting; Exhibits; Family Programs; Guided Tours; Interpretation; Research Library/Archives

COLLECTIONS: [1900]

HOURS: Apr-Sept Sa-Su 1-5

ADMISSION: $3, Seniors $2

PEMBINA

6544
Pembina State Museum
[PO Box 456/499, 58271]; (p) (701) 825-6840; (f) (701) 825-6383; mbailey@state.nd.us; www.DiscoverND.com/hist; (c) Pembina

State/ 1996/ State Historical Society of North Dakota/ staff: 1(f); 5(p); 4(v)

HISTORICAL SOCIETY; HISTORY MUSEUM: Interprets history of Red River Valley region.

PROGRAMS: Community Outreach; Concerts; Exhibits; Facility Rental; Guided Tours; Interpretation; Lectures; Reenactments

COLLECTIONS: [18th c-present] Natural history exhibit.

HOURS: June-Aug M-Sa 9-5, Su 1-5; Sept-May M-Sa 9-6, Su 1-6

ADMISSION: No charge

RUGBY

6545
Geographical Center Historical Society and Prairie Village Museum
US Hwy 2 & State Hwy 3, 58368 [102 Hwy 2 SE, 58368-2444]; (p) (701) 776-6414; (c) Pierce

1964/ staff: 3(f); 3(p); 10(v)/ members: 505

HISTORICAL SOCIETY; HISTORY MUSEUM; LIVING HISTORY/OUTDOOR MUSEUM: Preserves local history with restored village and museum.

PROGRAMS: Annual Meeting; Exhibits; Festivals; Guided Tours; School-Based Curriculum

COLLECTIONS: [1800-1900] Antique cars, machinery, period clothing, toys, dolls, guns, quilts, veterans artifacts.

HOURS: May-Sept M-Sa 8-7, Su 1-7

ADMISSION: $5, Children $1; Under 6 free

STANLEY

6546
Mountrail County Historical Society
Memorial Bldg, 58784 [PO Box 582, 58784]; gibbs@ndak.net; (c) Mountrail

Private non-profit/ 1974/ Board of Directors/ staff: 2(p)/ members: 12

GENEALOGICAL SOCIETY; HISTORICAL SOCIETY: Gathers, collects, and preserves Mountrail County history.

PROGRAMS: Annual Meeting; Exhibits; Publication; Research Library/Archives

COLLECTIONS: [1910-1990] Local county newspapers, cemetery records, phone directories.

HOURS: Yr M 2-4

ADMISSION: No charge

STRASBURG

6547
Ludwig and Christina Welk Homestead
3/4 mi N of Strasburg on US 83 then 2 mis W & 1/, 58573 [PO Box 52, 58573]; (p) (701) (336) 7519, (701) (336) 7777

staff: 7(p)

COLLECTIONS: [Late 1800s-1900s] Furniture, housewares; main house and summer kitchen are original sod houses.

HOURS: Vary

VALLEY CITY

6548
Barnes County Historical Society
315 Central Ave N, 58072 [PO Box 661, 58072-0661]; (p) (701) 845-0966; (f) (701) 845-0966; (c) Barnes

Private non-profit/ 1932/ Board of Directors/ staff: 1(f); 42(v)/ members: 502/publication: *Barnes County Quarterly*

ALLIANCE OF HISTORICAL AGENCIES; ART MUSEUM; GENEALOGICAL SOCIETY; HISTORIC PRESERVATION AGENCY; HISTORIC SITE; HISTORICAL SOCIETY; HISTORY MUSEUM; RESEARCH CENTER: Promotes all aspects of county history.

PROGRAMS: Annual Meeting; Community Outreach; Concerts; Exhibits; Festivals; Guided Tours; Interpretation; Lectures; Publication; Research Library/Archives; School-Based Curriculum; Theatre

COLLECTIONS: [19th-20th c] County and township records.

HOURS: Yr M-Sa 10-4

ADMISSION: Donations accepted

WALHALLA

6549
Gingras Trading Post State Historic Site
Off Hwy 32, near airport, NE of Walhalla, 58282 [10534 129 Ave NE, 58282]; (p) (701) 549-1775, (701) 825-6840; (f) (701) 358-3710; histsoc@state.md.us; www.DiscoverND.com/hist; (c) Cavalier

State/ 1840/ State Historical Board/ staff: 2(f); 1(p)

HISTORIC SITE: Preserves the home and trading post established by Metis trader Antoine Gingras.

PROGRAMS: Exhibits; Festivals; Interpretation; Publication

COLLECTIONS: [1840s] Fur trade building and home.

HOURS: Mid May-Sept Daily

WASHBURN

6550
North Dakota Lewis and Clark Bicentennial Foundation
2576 8th St SW, 58577 [PO Box 607, 58577]; (p) (701) 462-8535; (f) (701) 462-3316; info@ fortmandan.org; (c) Mclean

Private non-profit/ 1996/ staff: 5(f); 6(p); 20(v)/ members: 470/publication: *Lewis and Clark at Fort Mandan*

ART MUSEUM; LIVING HISTORY/OUTDOOR MUSEUM: Preserves history of Lewis and Clark Expedition and Fort Mandan period.

PROGRAMS: Annual Meeting; Exhibits; Festivals; Guided Tours; Interpretation; Living History; Publication

COLLECTIONS: [1800] Lewis and Clark Expedition rare books, prints by Swiss artist Karl Bodmer.

HOURS: June-Aug Daily 9-7; Sept-May Daily 9-5

ADMISSION: $5, Students $3

WEST FARGO

6551
Bonanzaville, USA
1351 W Main Ave, 58078 [PO Box 719, 58078]; (p) (701) 282-2822; (f) (701) 282-7606; info@bonanzaville.com; www.bonan zaville.com; (c) Cass

Private non-profit/ 1967/ Cass County Historical Society/ staff: 3(f); 7(p); 500(v)/ members: 500/publication: *Bonanzaville Times*

HISTORICAL SOCIETY; HISTORY MUSEUM: Historic village of forty-two buildings and over 400,000 artifacts, commemorating the bonanza farms that operated in the late 19th c.

PROGRAMS: Annual Meeting; Exhibits; Facility Rental; Festivals; Garden Tours; Guided Tours; Interpretation; Living History; Publication; School-Based Curriculum

COLLECTIONS: [1880-1940] Furnished and restored structures built in the late 18th and early 19th centuries, tractor, farm implements, automobiles, aircraft, and horse-drawn transports.

HOURS: May-Oct M-F 9-5; June-Sept Daily 9-5

ADMISSION: $6, Children $3; Under 6 free

WILLISTON

6552
Fort Buford State Historic Site
Hwys 58 & 1804, 58801 [15349 39th Lane NW, 58801]; (p) (701) 572-9034; (f) (701) 328-3710; histsoc@state.nd.us; www.Discov erND.com/hist; (c) Williams

Joint; State/ 1866/ State Historical Board/ staff: 1(f); 3(p)/publication: *Fort Buford and the Military Frontier of the Northern Plains*

HISTORIC SITE: Preserves history of frontier Plains military post.

PROGRAMS: Community Outreach; Exhibits; Interpretation

COLLECTIONS: [1866-1895] Military uniforms, guns, period furnishing.

HOURS: May-Sept Daily 9-6 and by appt

ADMISSION: $4, Student $1, Children $1.50

6553
Fort Union Trading Post National Historic Site
15550 Hwy 1804, 58801; (p) (701) 572-9083; (f) (701) 572-7321; www.nps.gov/fous; (c) Williams

Federal/ 1966/ National Park Service/ staff: 6(f); 6(p); 150(v)

HISTORIC SITE; LIVING HISTORY/OUT-DOOR MUSEUM: Preserves trading post of the American Fur Company on the upper Missouri and history of the Assiniboine, Crow, Cree, Ojibway and Blackfeet.

PROGRAMS: Exhibits; Film/Video; Guided Tours; Interpretation; Living History; Research Library/Archives; School-Based Curriculum

COLLECTIONS: [1828-1867] Archaeological and Native American artifacts.

HOURS: June-Aug Daily 8-8; Sept-May 9-5:30

ADMISSION: No charge

WIMBLEDON

6554
Wimbledon Community Museum
Center St, 58492 [1306 97th Ave SE, 58492]; (p) (701) 435-2239; (c) Barnes

1969/ Board of Directors/ staff: 15(v)

HISTORIC PRESERVATION AGENCY; HISTORY MUSEUM: Collects, preserves, and displays local materials.

PROGRAMS: Annual Meeting

COLLECTIONS: [1880-1950] Farm implements, railroad depot, medical, military, religious, business collections, railroad depot, one room school house.

HOURS: June-Aug by appt

ADMISSION: No charge/Donations

WOLFORD

6555
Dale and Martha Hawk Foundation and Museum
4 mi E & 3 mi N on SR 30, 58385 [Box 19B, 58385]; (p) (701) 583-2381, (701) 583-2152; www.hawkmuseum.com/; (c) Pierce

Private non-profit/ 1981/ Board of Directors/ staff: 3(f); 13(v)

HISTORY MUSEUM: Preserves local history.

PROGRAMS: Exhibits; Facility Rental; Guided Tours; Living History

COLLECTIONS: [1900] Steam engines, tractors, farm equipment, cars, household, schools, country store, church, dolls, clocks.

HOURS: Apr-Oct 8-7

ADMISSION: $4

NORTHERN MARIANA ISLANDS

SAIPAN

6556
CNMI Museum of History and Culture
Caller Box 10007, 96950; (p) (670) 664-2160; (f) (670) 664-2170; cnmimuseum@saipan. com; www.mariana-islands.gov.mp/history .htm

Joint/ 1996/ Commonwealth of the Northern Mariana Islands; Museum Board of Governors/ staff: 6(f); 3(v)

HISTORIC SITE; HISTORY MUSEUM: Maintains the museum and official repository of historical and cultural artifacts pertaining to the heritage of the Northern Marian Islands.

PROGRAMS: Annual Meeting; Community Outreach; Exhibits; Festivals; Interpretation; Lectures

COLLECTIONS: Indigenous Chamorro and Carolinian artifacts, gold, pottery from the 1638 shipwrecked Spanish galleon, Nuestra Senora de la Concepcion, original illustrations from the 1820s French explorer, Louis de Freycinet, and artifacts from the Spanish, German, Japanese and U.S administrations.

HOURS: Yr M-Sa 9-4:30, Su 1-4

ADMISSION: $3, Students $1, Under 12 and over 54 free

OHIO

AKRON

6557
Bath Township Historical Society
1249 Cleveland-Massilon Rd, 44333 [PO Box 1, Bath, 44210]; (c) Summit

Private non-profit/ 1968/ staff: 2(p)/ members: 275

Collects local history.

COLLECTIONS: [1818-present] Local photos, hand tools, family histories.

HOURS: Yr T 1-3

6558
Doctor Bob's Home
855 Ardmore Ave, 44302-1240; (p) (330) 864-1935; www.drbobs.com

6559
Hower House/The University of Akron
60 Fir Hill, 44325-2401; (p) (330) 972-6909; (f) (330) 384-2635; (c) Summit

State/ 1994/ Univ of Akron/ staff: 2(f); 2(p); 135(v)/ members: 400/publication: *Hower House News*

HISTORIC SITE; HOUSE MUSEUM: Second Empire Italianate house museum on the National Register, reflecting lifestyle of three generations of the Hower family.

PROGRAMS: Annual Meeting; Concerts; Exhibits; Facility Rental; Family Programs; Guided Tours; Publication

COLLECTIONS: [1871-1930] 28 furnished rooms; family memorabilia.

HOURS: Feb-Dec W-Sa 12-3:30, Su 1-4

ADMISSION: $5, Student $2, Seniors $4; Under 6

6560
Perkins Mansion
Copley Rd & S Portage Path, 44320 [550 Copley Rd, 44320]; (p) (330) 535-1120; (f) (330) 376-6868

6561
Stan Hywet Hall and Gardens
714 N Portage Path, 44303-1399; (p) (330) 836-5533; (f) (330) 836-2680; stanhywet.org; (c) Summit

Private non-profit/ 1956/ Board of Trustees/ staff: 58(f); 44(p); 800(v)/ members: 3500

GARDEN; HISTORIC SITE; HOUSE MUSEUM: Serves as cultural, educational, and horiticultural resource for northeast Ohio region, and former home of Goodyear co-founder F. A. Seiberling.

PROGRAMS: Community Outreach; Exhibits; Facility Rental; Family Programs; Garden Tours; Guided Tours; Interpretation; Lectures; Research Library/Archives; School-Based Curriculum; Theatre

COLLECTIONS: [1915-1930] Fine and decorative arts, manuscripts, personal belongings, historic buildings, garden rooms.

HOURS: Feb 1-Mar 31 T-Sa 10-4, Su 1-4; Apr 1-Dec 30 Daily 9-6

ADMISSION: $8, Children $4, Seniors $7

6562
Summit County Historical Society
550 Copley, 44320; (p) (330) 535-1120; (f) (330) 376-6868; www.neo.lrun.com/summit _county_histori cal_society; (c) Summit

Private non-profit/ 1925/ staff: 1(f); 5(p); 100(v)/ members: 490/publication: *Old Portage Trail Review (newsletter)*

HISTORIC SITE; HISTORICAL SOCIETY; HOUSE MUSEUM: Collects, preserves, interprets and educates about the history of Summit County.

PROGRAMS: Annual Meeting; Exhibits; Facility Rental; Family Programs; Festivals; Guided Tours; Lectures; Publication

COLLECTIONS: [1837-1890s] Early Americana; pottery; costumes; transportation; glass; manuscript collections; 1830 John Brown Home; 1837 Simon Perkins Mansion; 1839 Bronson Church; 1840 Old Stone School.

HOURS: Feb-Dec T-Su 1-4

ADMISSION: $5, Children $4, Seniors $4

ARCHBOLD

6563
Sauder Village
22611 St Rt 2, 43502 [PO Box 235, 43502]; (p) (419) 446-2541; (f) (419) 445-5251; vil lage@bright.net; saudervillage.com; (c) Fulton

1969/ Board of Trustees/ staff: 55(f); 300(p); 190(v)/ members: 850

HISTORY MUSEUM; LIVING HISTORY/OUTDOOR MUSEUM: Collects, preserves, and interprets the cultural, industrial, agricultural, and artistic heritage of the people of rural Northwest Ohio.

PROGRAMS: Community Outreach; Concerts; Elder's Programs; Exhibits; Facility Rental; Family Programs; Festivals; Interpretation; Living History

COLLECTIONS: [1830-1920] Tools, machinery, furnishings of Ohio rural life in the 19th c. Structures: Grime Home, Grime Barn, Elmira Depot.

HOURS: Apr-Oct M-Sa 10-5 Su 1-5

ADMISSION: $9.50,Students $4.75, Seniors $9

ASHLAND

6564
Ashland County Historical Society
414 Center St, 44805 [PO Box 484, 44805]; (p) (419) 289-3111; (c) Ashland

Private non-profit/ 1951/ Board of Directors/ staff: 2(p); 50(v)/ members: 565/publication: *The County Crier*

HISTORIC SITE; HISTORICAL SOCIETY; HISTORY MUSEUM; HOUSE MUSEUM: Maintains a museum of Ashland County artifacts.

PROGRAMS: Annual Meeting; Community Outreach; Exhibits; Facility Rental; Festivals; Guided Tours; Publication; Research Library/Archives; School-Based Curriculum

COLLECTIONS: [1890-1930] Victorian furniture, clothing, paper weights, cruets, goblets, paintings, artifacts from the Civil War through World War II, 13,000 insect specimens, Johnny Appleseed memorabilia, Ashland advertising and manufacturing

6565
Ashland University Archives
401 College, 44805; (p) (419) 289-5433; (f) (419) 289-5423; droepke@Ashland.edu; www.Ashland.edu; (c) Ashland

Private non-profit/ 1992/ Ashland Univ/ staff: 1(p)

LIBRARY AND/OR ARCHIVES: Collects documentation on Ashland Univ history and the papers of various conservative elected officials from OH dating from 1960-1980.

PROGRAMS: Community Outreach; Exhibits

COLLECTIONS: [1960-1980]

HOURS: Yr M-F

ASHVILLE

6566
Ashville Area Heritage Society
34 Long St, 43103; (p) (740) 983-9864; (c) Pickaway

City/ 1978/ staff: 1(f); 2(p); 6(v)/ members: 300/publication: *Ohio's Small-Town Museum*

GARDEN; HISTORIC SITE; HISTORICAL SOCIETY; HISTORY MUSEUM

PROGRAMS: Annual Meeting; Community

Outreach; Exhibits; Garden Tours; Guided Tours; Living History; Publication; Theatre

HOURS: Yr M-Sa 1-3

6567
Slate Run Living Historical Farm
9130 Marcy Rd, 43103; (p) (614) 833-1880; (c) Pickaway

1981/ staff: 4(f); 4(p); 60(v)

LIVING HISTORY/OUTDOOR MUSEUM: Depicts daily and seasonal activities of central Ohio family and farm in the 1880s.

PROGRAMS: Community Outreach; Family Programs; Interpretation; Living History; School-Based Curriculum

COLLECTIONS: [1880-1900] Late 19th c house and outbuilding furnishings of typical rural family life, agricultural tools and equipment, heirloom varieties of crops.

HOURS: Jun-Aug T-Th 9-4 F-Sa 9-6 Su 11-6; Jan-Mar W-Sa 9-4 Su 11-4; Apr-May Sep-Dec W-Sa 9-4 Su 11-4

ATHENS

6568
Archives and Special Collections, Ohio University Libraries
504 Alden Library, 45701 [Park Place, 45701-2978]; (p) (740) 593-2710; (f) (740) 593-0138; bain@ohio.edu; www.library.ohiou.edu/libin fo/depts/archives/; (c) Athens

State/ 1963/ Ohio University/ staff: 5(f); 1(p)

LIBRARY AND/OR ARCHIVES: Manages published and unpublished materials that document OH Univ, Southeastern OH.

PROGRAMS: Exhibits; Lectures; Research Library/Archives

COLLECTIONS: [1800-present] Ohio Univ archives, manuscript collections, rare book collections, and regional local government records.

HOURS: Yr M-F 8-5, Sa 12-4

6569
Athens County Historical Society and Museum
65 N Court St, 45701; (p) (740) 592-2280; achsm@frognet.net; www.frog.net/~achsm; (c) Athens

Private non-profit/ 1983/ ACHSM Board of Trustees/ staff: 1(f); 2(p); 12(v)/ members: 650/publication: *Bulletin*

GENEALOGICAL SOCIETY; HISTORICAL SOCIETY; HISTORY MUSEUM: Collects, preserves, and displays artifacts and archival materials about Athens County, OH.

PROGRAMS: Annual Meeting; Community Outreach; Exhibits; Facility Rental; Festivals; Guided Tours; Interpretation; Lectures; Publication; Research Library/Archives

COLLECTIONS: [Prehistory-present] Artifacts from prehistoric settlers; primitives; clothing; agriculture, business, military, religious, school, and transportation artifacts and papers; books; furniture; maps; photos; toys; and family papers.

HOURS: Yr M-F 1-4 and by appt

ATWATER

6570
Atwater Historical Society, The
[PO Box 38, 44201]; (p) (330) 947-2742; (c) Portage

Private non-profit/ 1995/ Federal-State/ staff: 10(v)/ members: 35

ALLIANCE OF HISTORICAL AGENCIES; HISTORIC PRESERVATION AGENCY; HISTORICAL SOCIETY; HISTORY MUSEUM: Preserves and displays history of growth and development of Western Reserve community.

PROGRAMS: Annual Meeting; Community Outreach; Exhibits; Festivals; Interpretation; Lectures; Living History; Research Library/ Archives

COLLECTIONS: [1800-1940] Photos, artifacts, and documents of CT Land Company settlement, depicting growth and development of town.

HOURS: Yr 1st and 3rd Su 1-4

AURORA

6571
Aurora Historical Society
115 E Pioneer Tr, 44202 [PO Box 241, 44202 -0241]; (c) Portage

Private non-profit; State/ 1968/ staff: 1(p); 175(v)/ members: 270/publication: *History of Aurora*

HISTORICAL SOCIETY; HISTORY MUSEUM; HOUSE MUSEUM; PRESIDENTIAL SITE: Interprets events and people of Aurora.

PROGRAMS: Annual Meeting; Community Outreach; Exhibits; Festivals; Garden Tours; Guided Tours; Interpretation; Lectures; Publication; Research Library/Archives

COLLECTIONS: [19th-20th c] Historic objects, records, and photos.

HOURS: Yr T,Th 1-4

AUSTINTOWN

6572
Austintown Historical Society
3979 S Raccoon Rd, 44515 [PO Box 4063, 44515]; (p) (330) 792-1129; (f) (330) 792-1129; (c) Mahoning

Private non-profit/ 1976/ Board of Directors/ staff: 100(v)/ members: 150

HISTORIC SITE; HISTORICAL SOCIETY; HISTORY MUSEUM; HOUSE MUSEUM

PROGRAMS: Annual Meeting; Community Outreach; Exhibits; Facility Rental; Festivals; Interpretation; Lectures; Living History

COLLECTIONS: [1814, 1830] Log cabin c 1814 with primitive furnishings; Strock Stone House c 1830 with furnishings.

HOURS: Yr 1st Su 1-4

ADMISSION: Donations accepted

AVON

6573
Avon Historical Society
2940 Stoney Ridge Rd, 44011; (p) (440) 934-6106; (c) Lorain

Private non-profit/ 1964/ staff: 15(v)/ members: 70

GENEALOGICAL SOCIETY; HISTORIC PRESERVATION AGENCY; HISTORICAL SOCIETY: Promotes local history.

PROGRAMS: Annual Meeting; Community Outreach; Exhibits; Festivals; Living History

AVON LAKE

6574
Peter Miller House Museum
33740 Lake Rd, 44012-1052; (p) (216) 933-6333; www.artcom.com/museums/oh.htm

BARNESVILLE

6575
Belmont County Historical Society
532 N Chestnut St, 43713 [PO Box 434, 43713]; (p) (740) 484-1350; (c) Belmont

Private non-profit/ 1966/ Board of Directors/ staff: 30(v)/ members: 150

HISTORIC PRESERVATION AGENCY; HISTORICAL SOCIETY; HOUSE MUSEUM: Collects and preserves objects, relics, documents, items, and materials that portray early local history.

PROGRAMS: Annual Meeting; Community Outreach; Concerts; Exhibits; Guided Tours; Interpretation; Lectures

COLLECTIONS: [1890s] Victorian furniture, glassware, china, lamps, textiles, clothing, dolls, toys, kitchen furnishings, silver, photos, and paintings.

HOURS: May 1-Nov 1 Th-Sa 1-4

ADMISSION: $4, Children $1; Group rates

BATAVIA

6576
Clermont County Historical Society
[PO Box 14, 45103]; (p) (513) 724-6222, (5130 753-5859; Rondhill@aol.com; (c) Clermont

Private non-profit/ 1958/ staff: 1(f); 25(v)/ members: 100/publication: *Clermont Historian*

HISTORICAL SOCIETY: Preserves, protects, and promotes historical heritage of Clermont County.

PROGRAMS: Community Outreach; Exhibits; Lectures; Publication; Research Library/ Archives

COLLECTIONS: 100 informational posters, rotating displays, books, photos, county records, buggy, farm equipment, needlework, 8 US flags, 2 man iron jail, articles, maps, uniforms.

BATH

6577
Hale Farm & Village
2686 Oak Hill Rd, 44210 [PO Box 296, 44210]; (p) (330) 666-3711; (f) (330) 666-9497; jguild@wvhs.org; www.wvhs.org; (c) Summit

Private non-profit/ 1958/ Western Reserve Historical Society/ staff: 30(f); 50(p); 50(v)/ members: 6000

LIVING HISTORY/OUTDOOR MUSEUM: Interprets life in Western Reserve Region of Ohio during the mid-19th c.

PROGRAMS: Community Outreach; Concerts; Facility Rental; Family Programs; Festivals; Interpretation; Lectures; Living History; Reenactments

COLLECTIONS: [1848] Material culture of the Western Reserve 1800-1850 including architecture, transportation, industry, agricultural tools, equipment, decorative arts and household accessories. Sites: Jonathan Hale Home, Robinson-Goldsmith House, Swetland Memorial Meeting House, and more.

HOURS: May-Oct T-Sa 10-5, Su 12-5

ADMISSION: $9, Seniors $7.50

BAY VILLAGE

6578
Bay Village Historical Society
27715 Lake Rd, 44140 [PO Box 40187, 44140]; (p) (440) 871-7338; (c) Cuyahoga

Private non-profit/ 1960/ staff: 20(v)/ members: 150/publication: *Bay Village: The Way of Life*

HISTORIC SITE; HISTORICAL SOCIETY; HOUSE MUSEUM: Preserves historical artifacts; promotes local history.

PROGRAMS: Annual Meeting; Exhibits; Festivals; Guided Tours; Lectures; Living History; Publication; Research Library/Archives; School-Based Curriculum

COLLECTIONS: [1818-1900] Vintage clothing, toys, boats, primitive furniture and utensils, tools, Victorian furniture, genealogy and local history library, furnished summer kitchen; 1810 replica log cabin with period furnishings.

HOURS: Mar-Dec Su 2-4

6579
Rose Hill Museum
27715 Lake Rd, 44140 [PO Box 40187, 44140]; (p) (614) 871-7338, (614) 871-0449; (f) (614) 696-8107 %E; wwwvictor/ana.com/ bvhs

1818/ Bay Village Historical Society

COLLECTIONS: [1818-1900] 1800's possessions of Cahoon and early residents; local history library; township documents; genealogy.

HOURS: Yr

BEAVERCREEK

6580
Beavercreek Historical Society
Wartinger Park, 3080 Kemp Rd, 45432 [1368 Research Park Dr, 45432-2818]; (p) (937) 427-5514; beavercreek.hcst.net/bckhissoc/; (c) Greene

Private non-profit/ 1987/ Board of Trustees/ staff: 65(v)/ members: 190/publication: *Log-by-Log; Beavercreek Chronicles*

HISTORIC PRESERVATION AGENCY; HISTORIC SITE; HISTORICAL SOCIETY; HOUSE MUSEUM; LIVING HISTORY/OUTDOOR MUSEUM: Preserves structures of historical significance.

PROGRAMS: Annual Meeting; Exhibits; Facility Rental; Festivals; Garden Tours; Guided Tours; Living History; Publication

COLLECTIONS: [1800-1850] Period house

furnishings and farm implements.

HOURS: Park: Yr; Historic structures: by appt

ADMISSION: $3.50; Park: No charge

BELLEFONTAINE

6581
Logan County Museum
521 E Columbus Ave, 43311 [PO Box 296, 43311]; (p) (937) 593-7557; (c) Logan

Private non-profit/ 1945/ Logan County Historical Society/ staff: 1(f); 1(p); 88(v)/ members: 700

HISTORICAL SOCIETY; HISTORY MUSEUM; HOUSE MUSEUM: 1906 Neo-classical mansion and attached museum with 13 exhibit rooms and temporary exhibits.

PROGRAMS: Annual Meeting; Exhibits; Facility Rental; Family Programs; Festivals; Guided Tours; Publication; Research Library/Archives; School-Based Curriculum

COLLECTIONS: [1850-present and prehistoric-1812] Native American artifacts, railroad memorabilia, locally manufactured items, clothes, farm equipment, military items.

HOURS: Yr May-Oct W, F-Su 1-4 ;Nov-Apr F-Sa 1-4

ADMISSION: Donations

BETHEL

6582
Bethel Historical Association, Inc.
562 S Charity, 45106; (p) (937) 379-1026; laceyann@ix.netcom.com; (c) Clermont

Private non-profit/ 1973/ staff: 6(p); 5(v)/ members: 25/publication: Bethel Historian

GENEALOGICAL SOCIETY; HISTORICAL SOCIETY; HISTORY MUSEUM; RESEARCH CENTER: Operates a museum, provides genealogy research, and publishes historical data.

PROGRAMS: Annual Meeting; Exhibits; Lectures; Living History; Publication; Research Library/Archives

COLLECTIONS: [Mid-20th c] Native American artifacts, memorabilia, photos, furniture, clothing, uniforms, books, rare documents, relics, newspapers, portraits, maps, and historical items.

HOURS: Yr by appt

BEVERLY

6583
Oliver Tucker Museum
[PO Box 122, 45715]

1835/ Lauer Muskingum Historical Society

COLLECTIONS: Revolutionary rifle, Civil War surgeons kit.; spinning wheel, loom, weaving rug.

HOURS: Seasonal

BOLIVAR

6584
Fort Laurens State Memorial
11067 Fort Laurens Rd NW, 44612 [PO Box 404, Zoar, 44697]; (p) (330) 874-2059; (f) (330) 874-2936; kmfzoar@compuserve.com; ohiohistory.org/places/ftlaurens; (c) Tuscarawas

Private non-profit; State/ 1917/ Ohio Historical Society/ staff: 1(f); 1(p)/publication: Fort Laurens 1778-1789

HISTORIC SITE: Maintains site of 1778 Revolutionary fort and resting place of 21 soldiers, with interpretive museum.

PROGRAMS: Exhibits; Film/Video; Publication; Reenactments

COLLECTIONS: [Late 18th c] Original and reproduction of military uniforms, artifacts, and weaponry and archaeological artifacts from fort excavation.

HOURS: Apr-May by appt only; Jun-Aug W-Sa 9:30-5, Su 12-5; Sep-Oct Sa-Su by appt

ADMISSION: $3, Children $1.25

BOWLING GREEN

6585
Association for Great Lakes Maritime History
[PO Box 7365, 43402]; (p) (715) 842-1762; (f) (715) 261-6333; rodonnel@uwc.edu; www.aglmh.org

Private non-profit/ 1984/ Board of Directors/ staff: 1(v)/ members: 200/publication: Association for Great Lakes Maritime History

ALLIANCE OF HISTORICAL AGENCIES: Organization of institutions, museums, societies, and individuals interested in preserving Great Lakes maritime history.

PROGRAMS: Annual Meeting; Community Outreach; Lectures; Publication

6586
Wood County Historical Center and Museum
13660 County Home Rd, 43402; (p) (419) 352-0967; (f) (419) 352-6220; wchisctr@wc net.org; wcnet.org/~wchisctr; (c) Wood

1955/ Local county Board of County Commissioners/ staff: 4(f); 125(v)/ members: 500

HISTORIC SITE; HISTORICAL SOCIETY; HISTORY MUSEUM: Collects, preserves, and interprets history and material record of Wood County, and Northwest OH.

PROGRAMS: Annual Meeting; Community Outreach; Exhibits; Facility Rental; Family Programs; Festivals; Garden Tours; Guided Tours; Interpretation; Living History

COLLECTIONS: [19th-20th c] Costumes, textiles, agricultural implements and tools, household furnishings, oil drilling, and pumping equipment, political memorabilia, Wood County infirmary, school memorabilia, Native American artifacts.

HOURS: Apr-Oct T-F 9:30-4:30, Sa-Su 1-4 ; Yr for research T-F 9:30-4:30

ADMISSION: Donations requested

BREWSTER

6587
Brewster Sugar Creek Township Historical Society
45 S Wabash, 44613; (p) (330) 767-0045; (c) Stark

Private non-profit/ 1976/ staff: 9(v)/ members: 140

HISTORIC SITE; HISTORICAL SOCIETY; HISTORY MUSEUM

PROGRAMS: Annual Meeting; Exhibits; Facility Rental; Guided Tours

COLLECTIONS: Railroad artifacts, photos; artifacts from Beach City, Wilmot, and Sugar Creek townships.

HOURS: Yr Sa-Su 8-3

ADMISSION: Donations

BROOKLYN

6588
Brooklyn Historical Society
4442 Ridge Rd, 44144-3353; (p) (216) 749-2804; (c) Cuyahoga

Private non-profit/ 1970/ staff: 50(v)/ members: 160

HISTORICAL SOCIETY; HISTORY MUSEUM: The Brooklyn Historical Society seeks to preserve and disseminate the history of the area.

PROGRAMS: Annual Meeting; Community Outreach; Exhibits; Festivals; Garden Tours; Guided Tours; Lectures; Publication; Research Library/Archives; School-Based Curriculum

HOURS: Apr-Mid Dec T 10-2, 1st and 3rd Su 2-5

BURTON

6589
Geauga County Historical Society
[PO Box 153, 44021-0153]; (p) (440) 834-4092; (f) (440) 834-4012; GCHS@jmzcom puter.com; (c) Geauga

Joint; Private non-profit/ 1938/ Board of Trustees/ staff: 2(f); 20(p); 125(v)/ members: 900

HISTORICAL SOCIETY; HISTORY MUSEUM; HOUSE MUSEUM; LIVING HISTORY/OUTDOOR MUSEUM: Restored Western Reserve village of 20 buildings from 1800-1900.

PROGRAMS: Annual Meeting; Community Outreach; Exhibits; Facility Rental; Family Programs; Festivals; Interpretation; Lectures; Living History; Publication; Reenactments; Research Library/Archives; School-Based Curriculum

COLLECTIONS: [1800-1900] Furniture and decorative arts from settlement era to 1900, transportation, agriculture, manuscripts, and primary source materials, 9,000 toy soldiers.

HOURS: May-Oct T-Su

ADMISSION: $5

CAMBRIDGE

6590
Cambridge Glass Museum, The
812 Jefferson Ave, 43725; (p) (740) 432-3045; (c) Guernsey

Private for-profit/ 1973/ staff: 1(f)

COLLECTIONS: [1901-1958] 5000 pieces of Cambridge glass made from 1901 to 1958; 200 pieces of Cambridge art pottery from 1901 to 1902.

HOURS: June-Oct M-Sa 1-4

ADMISSION: $2, Seniors $1

6591
Guernsey County Historical Society
218 N 9th St, 43725 [PO Box 741, 43725]; (p)
(740) 439-5884; (c) Guernsey

Private non-profit/ 1948/ Board of Trustees/
staff: 2(p)/ members: 243

HISTORICAL SOCIETY; HISTORY MUSEUM;
HOUSE MUSEUM: Collects, preserves, and
presents the cultural heritage of Guernsey
County.

PROGRAMS: Annual Meeting; Community
Outreach; Guided Tours; Interpretation; Lectures; Living History

COLLECTIONS: Victorian era furniture, clothing, glass, pottery, books, photos; County Hall
of Fame, John Glenn Room, military uniforms
and artifacts, farm tools.

HOURS: Mar-Dec T-F 1:30-4:00; by appt Jan-
Feb

ADMISSION: $1, Children $0.50

CAMP DENNISON

6592
**Christian Waldschmidt Homestead
and Camp Dennison Civil War
Museum**
7567 Glendale-Milford Rd, 45111 [PO Box
335, 45111]; (p) (513) 576-6327

1804/ Ohio Society Daughters of the American
Revolution/ staff: 22(v)

COLLECTIONS: [1804-1865] Flag collection,
lighting during 1800's collection, Herb garden,
Civil War Museum loaned items - guns, uniforms.; Buttons, gunballs, buckles, dishes,
quilts, etc.

HOURS: Vary

CANAL FULTON

6593
Canal Fulton Heritage Society
103 Tuscarawas St, 44614; (p) (330) 854-
3808; helena3@ohio-eriecanal.com; (c) Stark

Private non-profit/ staff: 10(v)/ members: 100

HISTORIC PRESERVATION AGENCY; HIS-
TORIC SITE; HISTORICAL SOCIETY; HISTO-
RY MUSEUM; HOUSE MUSEUM: Preserves
canal era history.

PROGRAMS: Annual Meeting; Exhibits; Guided Tours; Interpretation; Living History;
School-Based Curriculum

COLLECTIONS: [1848-present] Tools, models
of canal era, pictures of village, and canal boats.

HOURS: May-Oct Sa-Su 11:30-4:30; June-
Aug Daily 11:30-4:30

ADMISSION: No charge

CANFIELD

6594
Loghurst Farm Museum
3967 Boardman-Canfield Rd, 44406 [3967
Boardman-Canfield Rd, 44046]; (p) (330)
533-4330

1805/ Western Reserve Historical Society/
staff: 1(f); 3(p)

COLLECTIONS: [1870-1910] Furnishings;
photos; advertising and post cards, early 20th
century; photo album

HOURS: Yr

CANTON

6595
Pro Football Hall of Fame
2121 George Halas Dr NW, 44708; (p) (330)
456-8207; (f) (330) 456-8175; www.profoot
ballhof.com; (c) Stark

Private non-profit/ 1963/ staff: 21(f); 40(p)

HISTORY MUSEUM: Preserves origin, development, and growth of football as part of
American culture.

PROGRAMS: Exhibits; Festivals; Film/Video;
School-Based Curriculum

COLLECTIONS: [20th c] Professional football
artifacts.

HOURS: Yr Sep-May M-Su 9-5; Jun-Aug 9-8

ADMISSION: $12, Family $20, Children $6,
Seniors $8

6596
**Stark County Historical
Society/McKinley Museum**
800 McKinley Monument Dr NW, 44701 [PO
Box 20070, 44701]; (p) (330) 455-7043; (f)
(330) 455-1137; mmuseum@neo.rr.com; mc
kinleymuseum.org; (c) Stark

Private non-profit/ 1946/ staff: 6(f); 18(p);
160(v)/ members: 2350/publication: *William
McKinley and Our America*

HISTORICAL SOCIETY; HISTORY MUSEUM;
PRESIDENTIAL SITE: Collects, preserves, and
exhibits history and culture of Canton/Stark
county with educational interpretation and programs.

PROGRAMS: Annual Meeting; Community
Outreach; Concerts; Exhibits; Facility Rental;
Family Programs; Guided Tours; Publication;
Reenactments; Research Library/Archives;
School-Based Curriculum

COLLECTIONS: [1800-1920] McKinleyana,
Canton/Stark County history and genealogy,
Dueber Hampden watches, trains, post cards,
photos, furniture, ladies' gowns, hats, textiles
and Victoriana.

HOURS: Yr M-Sa 9-5, Su 12-5

ADMISSION: $6, Children $4, Seniors $5

CARLISLE

6597
Carlisle Area Historical Society
453 Park Dr, 45005 [PO Box 8261, 45005];
(p) (513) 746-7992; (c) Warren

Private non-profit/ 1983/ staff: 12(v)/ members:
90/publication: *Carlisle Area Historical Gazette*

HISTORICAL SOCIETY; HISTORY MUSEUM:
Preserves Carlisle area history.

PROGRAMS: Annual Meeting; Exhibits; Family Programs; Guided Tours; Lectures; Living
History; Publication

COLLECTIONS: Historical items of local interest on various topics.

HOURS: Apr-Dec Su 2-5

ADMISSION: Donations accepted

CARROLLTON

6598
**McCook House Civil War
Museum/Carroll County Historical
Society**
on the Square, 44615 [PO Box 174, 44615];
(p) (800) 600-7172, (330) 627-3345; stone-
jp@eohio.net; www.ohiohistory.org; (c) Carroll

Private non-profit/ 1971/ staff: 2(f); 2(p); 60(v)/
members: 800/publication: *CCHS Newsletter*

GARDEN; GENEALOGICAL SOCIETY; HIS-
TORIC PRESERVATION AGENCY; HIS-
TORIC SITE; HISTORICAL SOCIETY; HISTO-
RY MUSEUM; HOUSE MUSEUM: Preserves
history and heritage of county. Maintains Mc-
Cook House Civil War Museum.

PROGRAMS: Annual Meeting; Community
Outreach; Exhibits; Facility Rental; Family Programs; Festivals; Garden Tours; Guided Tours;
Publication; Reenactments; Research Li-
brary/Archives; School-Based Curriculum

CELINA

6599
Mercer County Historical Museum
130 E Market, 45822 [Box 512, 45822]; (p)
(419) 586-6065; histalig@bright.net; (c)
Mercer

Private non-profit/ 1959/ staff: 1(f); 1(p);
125(v)/ members: 250/publication: *Mercer
County Big Barns, Captain James Riley*

HISTORIC SITE; HISTORICAL SOCIETY;
HISTORY MUSEUM

PROGRAMS: Annual Meeting; Community
Outreach; Exhibits; Festivals; Film/Video; Interpretation; Lectures; Publication; Research Li-
brary/Archives

COLLECTIONS: [19th c] Period furniture, agricultural artifacts, pre-historic artifacts, Mercer
County archives.

HOURS: Yr W-F 8:30-4

ADMISSION: No charge

CENTERVILLE

6600
**Centerville-Washington Township
Historical Society, The**
89 W Franklin St, 45459; (p) (937) 433-0123;
(f) (937) 433-0310; www.mvcc.net/center
ville/histsoc; (c) Montgomery

Private non-profit/ 1966/ Board of Trustees/
staff: 1(f); 1(p); 100(v)/ members: 500

HISTORICAL SOCIETY; HISTORY MUSEUM:
Collects, preserves, and interprets history of
Centerville-Washington Township area; in-
cludes Walton House Museum.

PROGRAMS: Community Outreach; Exhibits;
Family Programs; Garden Tours; Guided
Tours; Interpretation; Lectures; Living History;
Research Library/Archives

COLLECTIONS: [prehistory-present] Photos,
furniture, china, glassware, clothing, textiles,
tools, books, oral history, interviews, family
and building files.

HOURS: Yr T-Sa 12-4

ADMISSION: No charge

CHARDON

6601
Geauga County Archives and Records Center

470 Center St Bldg 8, 44024; (p) (440) 285-2222; (f) (440) 285-8207; (c) Geauga County/ 1996/ staff: 2(f); 3(p); 2(v)

PRESIDENTIAL SITE: Preserves and provides access to noncurrent records of Geauga County government.

PROGRAMS: Research Library/Archives

COLLECTIONS: [1806-present] Over 3,000 ft of noncurrent records created by Geauga County government.

HOURS: Yr M-F 8-12 and by appt

ADMISSION: No charge

CHILLICOTHE

6602
Adena State Memorial: The Home of Thomas Worthington

848 Adena Rd, 45601 [PO Box 831, 45601-0831]; (p) (800) 772-1500; (f) (740) 775-2746; (c) Ross

Private non-profit/ 1953/ Ohio Historical Society/ staff: 2(f); 6(p)

GARDEN; HISTORIC SITE; HOUSE MUSEUM: Adena State Memorial is restored 1804 home/estate of Ohio's sixth governor.

PROGRAMS: Community Outreach; Garden Tours; Guided Tours; Interpretation; Reenactments

COLLECTIONS: [1790-1810] American antiques of the Federal period housed in restored 1807 mansion designed by Benjamin H. Latrobe.

HOURS: May-Sept W-Sa 9:30-5, Su and Holidays 12-5

ADMISSION: $5

6603
Ross County Historical Society

45 W 5th St, 45601; (p) (740) 772-1936; (f) (740) 773-1896; info@rosscountyhistorical.org; www.rosscountyhistorical.org; (c) Ross

Private non-profit/ 1896/ staff: 2(f); 4(p); 40(v)/ members: 500/publication: History-Mystery News, The Recorder

HISTORICAL SOCIETY; HISTORY MUSEUM; HOUSE MUSEUM; RESEARCH CENTER: Preserves and interprets the heritage of Chillicothe, Ross County, and OH.

PROGRAMS: Annual Meeting; Community Outreach; Exhibits; Family Programs; Guided Tours; Interpretation; Lectures; Publication; Research Library/Archives; School-Based Curriculum

COLLECTIONS: [prehistoric-present] Archives/Library: 13,000 volumes and 10,000 paper documents related to founding and history of Ohio; Museum: early to late 19th c art, furniture, decorative arts, military items, toys, vehicles, tools and textiles.

HOURS: Museum: Apr-Aug T-Su 1-5; Sep-Dec Sa-Su 1-5; Library: Yr Jan-Dec T W F Sa 1-5

ADMISSION: $4, Student $2, Seniors $2; Under 13 free

CINCINNATI

6604
Indian Hill Historical Society

8100 Given Rd, 45243; (p) (513) 891-1873; (f) (513) 891-1873; ihhist@one.net; indianhill.org; (c) Hamilton

Private non-profit/ 1973/ Board of Trustees/ staff: 3(p)/ members: 500/publication: From Camargo to Indian Hill, Treasured Landmarks of Indian Hill

HISTORIC SITE; HISTORICAL SOCIETY; HOUSE MUSEUM; RESEARCH CENTER: Preserves Indian Hill's history.

PROGRAMS: Annual Meeting; Community Outreach; Concerts; Exhibits; Facility Rental; Family Programs; Guided Tours; Lectures; Living History; Publication; Research Library/Archives; School-Based Curriculum

COLLECTIONS: [1795-present] Archives relating to local history and families.

HOURS: Yr Jan-Dec M-F by appt

ADMISSION: No charge

6605
Anderson Township Historical Society

6550 Clough Pk, 45230 [PO Box 30174, 45230-0174]; (p) (513) 231-2114; (c) Hamilton

Private non-profit/ 1968/ members: 200

GENEALOGICAL SOCIETY; HISTORIC SITE; HISTORICAL SOCIETY; LIVING HISTORY/OUTDOOR MUSEUM; RESEARCH CENTER

PROGRAMS: Exhibits; Festivals; Interpretation; Lectures; Research Library/Archives

COLLECTIONS: [1850-present] Cemetery records and various artifacts primarily from Anderson Township in Hamilton County, Ohio.

HOURS: May-Oct Every other Su 1-3

6606
Betts House Research Center

416 Clark St, Betts-Longworth Historic District, 45203; (p) (513) 651-0734; (f) (513) 651-2143; BettsHouse@Juno.com; (c) Hamilton

Private non-profit/ 1995/ The Colonial Dames of America, State of Ohio/ staff: 2(p); 24(v)/ members: 150/publication: The Betts House, Volumes I, II, III

HISTORIC SITE; HISTORY MUSEUM; HOUSE MUSEUM; RESEARCH CENTER: Promotes building arts;interpretive site of architectural renovation from two room farmhouse to Victorian dwelling.

PROGRAMS: Community Outreach; Publication

COLLECTIONS: [19th c] Architectural artifacts.

HOURS: Yr M-F 11-3, Sa-Su 11-2

ADMISSION: $2

6607
Cary Cottage

7000 Hamilton Ave, 45231; (p) (513) 522-3860; (f) (513) 728-3946; clovernook@clovernook.org; www.clovernook.org/carycottage.html; (c) Hamilton

Private non-profit/ 1832/ Board of Trustees/ staff: 10(v)

HISTORIC SITE; HOUSE MUSEUM: First home for blind women; site is listed on the National Register.

PROGRAMS: Community Outreach; Guided Tours

COLLECTIONS: [1830s] Cottage with period furnishing.

HOURS: Yr 1st Su 1-4, M-F 9-3 by appt

ADMISSION: Donations

6608
Cincinnati Fire Museum

315 W Court St, 45202; (p) (513) 621-5571; (f) (513) 621-5571; (c) Hamilton

Private non-profit/ 1978/ staff: 2(f); 4(p); 50(v)/ members: 500

HISTORIC SITE; HISTORY MUSEUM: Preserves over 200 years of firefighting history.

PROGRAMS: Annual Meeting; Elder's Programs; Exhibits; Facility Rental; Family Programs; Festivals; Film/Video; Guided Tours; Interpretation; Lectures; Research Library/Archives; School-Based Curriculum

COLLECTIONS: [1788-present] Interactive exhibits and artifacts.

HOURS: Yr T-F 10-4 Sa-Su 12-4

ADMISSION: $4.50, Children $2.50, Seniors $3

6609
Cincinnati Museum Center

1301 Western Ave, 45203; (p) (513) 287-7000, (800) 733-2077; (f) (513) 287-7029; www.cincymuseum.org; (c) Hamilton

Private non-profit/ 1990/ staff: 150(f); 150(p); 1000(v)/ members: 17000

HISTORIC SITE; HISTORICAL SOCIETY; HISTORY MUSEUM; LIVING HISTORY/OUTDOOR MUSEUM: Renovated art deco train station housing three interactive museums.

PROGRAMS: Community Outreach; Exhibits; Facility Rental; Family Programs; Festivals; Film/Video; Guided Tours; Interpretation; Lectures; Living History; Reenactments; Research Library/Archives; School-Based Curriculum; Theatre

COLLECTIONS: [19th c] Natural History; Ordovician Period; Ohio Valley ethnology; archaeology.

HOURS: Yr M-Sa 10-5 Su 11-6

ADMISSION: $6.50

6610
Cincinnati Nature Center-Gorman Heritage Farm

3035 Gorman Heritage Farm Ln, 45241; (p) (513) 563-6663; (f) (513) 563-6659; (c) Hamilton

Private non-profit/ 1996/ Board of Trustees/ staff: 6(f); 30(v)

GARDEN; HISTORIC SITE; LIVING HISTORY/OUTDOOR MUSEUM: Illustrates family life from 1835.

PROGRAMS: Community Outreach; Exhibits; Facility Rental; Family Programs; Festivals; Garden Tours; Guided Tours; Interpretation; School-Based Curriculum

COLLECTIONS: [1835-present] Farm machinery and household items.

HOURS: Yr Mar-Dec W-Sa 9-5, Su 1-5; Jan-Feb Sa-Su

ADMISSION: $5, Children $1

6611
College Hill Historical Society
[PO Box 24088, 45224]; 103107.3363@compuserve.com; (c) Hamilton

Private non-profit/ 1979/ staff: 5(v)/ members: 150/publication: *Heritage News*

HISTORICAL SOCIETY: Collects and preserves local history and genealogy.

PROGRAMS: Annual Meeting; Publication

COLLECTIONS: Underground Railroad artifacts.

6612
Delhi Historical Society
468 Anderson Ferry Rd, 45238 [PO Box 5103, 45205]; (p) (513) 451-9095, (513) 451-4313; (c) Hamilton

Private non-profit/ 1976/ Board of Directors/ staff: 50(v)/ members: 270

HISTORICAL SOCIETY: Collects information, artifacts about local history.

PROGRAMS: Annual Meeting; Community Outreach; Exhibits; Film/Video; Garden Tours; Guided Tours; Lectures; Research Library/ Archives

COLLECTIONS: [19th-20th c] Family history files, photos, social, educational, and agricultural information.

HOURS: Feb-Nov Su, T, Th 12-3

ADMISSION: Donations accepted

6613
Hebrew Union College Skirball Museum
3101 Clifton Ave, 45220; (p) (513) 221-1875; (f) (513) 221-1842; jlucas@huc.edu; www.huc.edu

Private non-profit/ 1913/ Board of Governors/Hebrew Union College/Burton Lehman/ staff: 2(f); 1(p); 30(v)/ members: 363

ART MUSEUM; HISTORIC SITE; HISTORY MUSEUM: Promotes and educates on Jewish identity.

PROGRAMS: Community Outreach; Exhibits; Facility Rental; Family Programs; Guided Tours; Lectures; Research Library/Archives; School-Based Curriculum

COLLECTIONS: [2000 BCE, 19th-present] Core exhibition: "An Eternal People: The Jewish Experience" focuses on contribution of Jewish people to the US; archaeological artifacts, Torah and Jewish celebrations and rituals, the Holocaust and diverse art and sculpture.

HOURS: Yr M-Th 11-4 Su 2-5

ADMISSION: No charge

6614
Historic Southwest Ohio
11450 Lebanon Pike Rt 42, 45262 [PO Box 62475, 45262]; (p) (513) 563-9484; (f) (513) 563-0914; (c) Hamilton

Private non-profit/ staff: 3(f); 7(p); 150(v)/ members: 450

ART MUSEUM; HISTORIC SITE; HISTORY MUSEUM; HOUSE MUSEUM; LIVING HISTORY/OUTDOOR MUSEUM: Collects, preserves and exhibits art, architecture, and artifacts of 19th c life; operates Heritage Village and Hauck House in the public trust.

PROGRAMS: Annual Meeting; Community Outreach; Concerts; Elder's Programs; Exhibits; Facility Rental; Family Programs; Festivals; Garden Tours; Guided Tours; Interpretation; Lectures; Living History; Publication; Reenactments; Research Library/Archives; School-Based

COLLECTIONS: [1804-1900] 10 historic structures, decorative and domestic arts and artifacts of 19th c life both rural and urban, resource library.

HOURS: Apr-Dec W-Su 12-4

ADMISSION: $5, Children $2, Seniors $3

6615
Jacob Rader Marcus Center of the American Jewish Archives
Hebrew Union College-Jewish Inst of Religion, 45220 [3101 Clifton Ave, 45220-2488]; (p) (513) 221-1875; (f) (513) 221-7812; aja@cn.huc.edu; huc.edu/aja

Private non-profit/ 1947/ staff: 9(f); 5(p)/publication: *The American Jewish Archives Journal*

LIBRARY AND/OR ARCHIVES: Preserves records of the American Jewish experience.

PROGRAMS: Lectures; Publication

COLLECTIONS: Collection in four areas: Western Hemisphere Judaism; Archives of the Reform Jewish Movement; Archives of Cincinnati/Midwestern Jewish history; Archive of Hebrew Union College-Jewish Institute of Religion.

HOURS: Yr M-F 9-5

ADMISSION: No charge

6616
John Hauck House Museum of Historic Southwest Ohio, Inc.
812 Dayton St, 45214; (p) (513) 721-3570, (513) 561-8842; (c) Hamilton

Private non-profit/ 1989/ Mrs. Cornelius W. Hauck/ staff: 2(p); 17(v)/ members: 450

GARDEN; HISTORIC SITE; HISTORY MUSEUM; HOUSE MUSEUM: Former home of brewer John Hauck.

PROGRAMS: Exhibits; Interpretation; Lectures; School-Based Curriculum

COLLECTIONS: [1880-1910] Period furniture, oil paintings, Cincinnati-made furniture, rookwood, clothing, decorative arts, iron garden fountain.

HOURS: Mar-Dec F and 4th Su 12-4, and by appt

ADMISSION: $3, Student $1, Children $1, Seniors $2

6617
Madeira Historical Society, The
5776 Kenwood Rd, 45243; (p) (513) 271-2129; indynovi@aol.com; (c) Hamilton

1972/ staff: 10(v)/ members: 98

HISTORICAL SOCIETY: Preserves city history.

PROGRAMS: Annual Meeting; Exhibits; Family Programs; Lectures

COLLECTIONS: [1820-present] Objects, writings and photos.

6618
Price Hill Historical Society
3640 Warsawave Ave, 45205 [PO Box 7020, 45205-7020]; (p) (513) 684-4104; www.price-hill.org; (c) Hamilton

Private non-profit/ 1990/ staff: 10(v)/ members: 350

HISTORICAL SOCIETY: Preserves history of Price Hill.

PROGRAMS: Community Outreach; Exhibits; Lectures; Living History; Publication

HOURS: Yr by appt

ADMISSION: No charge

6619
Public Library of Cincinnati and Hamilton County
800 Vine St, 45202-2071; (p) (513) 369-6900; (f) (513) 369-6993; comments@plch.lib.oh.us; plch.lib.oh.us; (c) Hamilton

1853/ Board of Trustees/ staff: 565(f); 331(p)

LIBRARY AND/OR ARCHIVES: Collects genealogy, local and regional history.

PROGRAMS: Community Outreach; Concerts; Exhibits; Family Programs; Guided Tours; Lectures

COLLECTIONS: [1800s-present] Maps, books, prints, slides, public documents, photographs, and ephemera related to genealogy and local/regional history.

HOURS: Yr Su 1-5, M-F 9-9, Sa 9-6

ADMISSION: No charge

6620
Sisters of Notre Dame-Ohio
701 E Columbia Ave, 45215-3999; (p) (513) 761-7636; (f) (513) 761-6159; louorth@aol.com; sndohio.org; (c) Hamilton

Private non-profit/ 1969/ staff: 1(f); 2(v)/ members: 1

HISTORY MUSEUM; LIBRARY AND/OR ARCHIVES: Collects, preserves, and interprets history and educational ministries of religious order.

PROGRAMS: Exhibits; Family Programs; Guided Tours; Research Library/Archives

COLLECTIONS: [late 1700s-present] Archives/Museum: 1,000 linear feet of processed manuscripts; 600 volumes (150 rare); 3000 museum artifacts; 1,500 photos; postcards; slides and video/audio cassettes.

HOURS: Yr Su-Sa and by appt

ADMISSION: No charge

6621
Taft Museum of Art
316 Pike St, 45202-4293; (p) (513) 241-0343; (f) (513) 241-7762; taftmuseum@taftmuseum.org; www.taftmuseum.org; (c) Hamilton

Private non-profit/ 1932/ Cincinnati Institute of Fine Arts/ staff: 21(f); 11(p); 132(v)/ members: 1632/publication: *Permanent Collections Catalogs*

ART MUSEUM; HISTORIC SITE: Art museum in Federal Villa.

PROGRAMS: Community Outreach; Concerts; Elder's Programs; Exhibits; Facility Rental; Family Programs; Festivals; Garden Tours; Guided Tours; Interpretation; Lectures; Publication; Research Library/Archives; School-Based Curriculum

COLLECTIONS: [600-1900] European paintings from 17th c Holland; English and 19th c Holland, England, Spain and America; European decorative artss; Chinese ceramics with a concentration in 18th c Qing dynasty; and 19th c American paintings, decorative arts, and architecture; American Federal furniture.

HOURS: Yr M-Sa 10-5, Su 1-5

ADMISSION: $4, Student $2, Seniors $2; Under 18 free

6622
William Howard Taft National Historic Site

2038 Auburn Ave, 45219-3025; (p) (513) 684-3262; (f) (513) 684-3627; wiho_superinten dent@nps.com; www.nps.gov/whio; (c) Hamilton

Federal/ 1969/ National Park Service/ staff: 9(f); 5(p); 20(v)/ members: 100

PRESIDENTIAL SITE: Interprets life and times of William Howard Taft, the 27th President and 10th Chief Justice of the United States.

PROGRAMS: Community Outreach; Exhibits; Family Programs; Guided Tours; Interpretation; School-Based Curriculum

COLLECTIONS: [19th-early 20th c] Artifacts associated with life and career of William Howard Taft.

HOURS: Yr M-Su 10-4

ADMISSION: No charge

CLEVELAND

6623
Archives, Diocese of Cleveland

1027 Superior Ave, 44114; (p) (216) 696-6525; (f) (216) 621-7332; krosel@ccd,cke-dioc.org; www.cle-dioc.org; (c) Cuyahoga

Private non-profit/ 1847/ Diocese of Cleveland/ staff: 2(f)

An institutional archives for a non-profit religious entity, the Roman Catholic Diocese of Cleveland, that documents the Catholic Church in northern Ohio, particularly the eight county area served by the Diocese. Open to researchers by prior appointment.

PROGRAMS: Community Outreach; Research Library/Archives

COLLECTIONS: [1847-present] The collection represents the correspondence, reports, microfilm copies of the diocesan newspapers (1874-present), photographs, and parish records that document the Diocese of Cleveland. Material pertains to parishes, religious organizations, Catholic charitable organizations, Catholic schools, and religious communities.

HOURS: Yr M-F 9-5 by appt

6624
Cleveland Grays

1234 Bolivar Rd, 44115; (p) (216) 621-5938; (f) (216) 621-5941; (c) Cuyahoga

Private non-profit/ 1837/ staff: 2(f); 3(v)/ members: 107/publication: Shako

RESEARCH CENTER: Maintains and improves Cleveland Grays Armory; maintains museum, library and archives of military history.

PROGRAMS: Concerts; Exhibits; Facility Rental; Guided Tours; Publication; Research Library/Archives

COLLECTIONS: [Revolutionary War-present] Military artifacts, photos and manuscripts.

HOURS: Yr M, W, F 1-3

ADMISSION: Donations accepted

6625
Cleveland Police Historical Society, Inc. and Museum

1300 Ontario St, 44113; (p) (216) 623-5055; (f) (216) 623-5145; museum@stratos.net; www.clevelandpolicemuseum.org; (c) Cuyahoga

Private non-profit/ 1983/ staff: 1(f); 2(p); 12(v)/ members: 1150/publication: CPHS Newsletter

HISTORICAL SOCIETY; HISTORY MUSEUM: Collects and preserves Cleveland's police history.

PROGRAMS: Community Outreach; Exhibits; Guided Tours; Living History; Publication

COLLECTIONS: [1866-1980] Archival materials: 5,000 photos and incomplete collections of annual reports, directories, manuals, police blotters, police orders, manuscripts, and scrapbooks; iniforms, equipment, furnishings and 3 vehicles.

HOURS: Yr M-F 10-4

ADMISSION: No charge

6626
Early Settlers Association of the Western Reserve, The

2030 W 19th St, 44113-3549; (p) (440) 779-1569; (f) (440) 779-1569; (c) Cuyahoga

Private non-profit/ 1879/ Board of Trustees/ staff: 20(v)/ members: 320/publication: The Pioneer and the Annals

HISTORICAL SOCIETY: Preserves history, culture and traditions of Western Reserve and Cleveland.

PROGRAMS: Annual Meeting; Community Outreach; Exhibits; Festivals; Guided Tours; Interpretation; Lectures; Living History; Publication

COLLECTIONS: [1879-present] Annals and published history, newsletter, the Hall of Fame mounted in Cleveland City Hall.

6627
Rock and Roll Hall of Fame and Museum

One Key Plaza, 44114; (p) (216) 515-1925; (f) (216) 515-1284; rockhall.com; (c) Cuyahoga

Private non-profit/ 1995/ staff: 105(f); 14(p)/ members: 15500/publication: Backbeat

HISTORY MUSEUM

PROGRAMS: Community Outreach; Con-

certs; Exhibits; Facility Rental; Family Programs; Film/Video; Guided Tours; Lectures; Living History; Publication

COLLECTIONS: [20th c] Rock and roll artifacts, films, and interactive exhibits.

HOURS: Yr M-Su 9-5

6628
Western Reserve Historical Society

10825 East Blvd, 44106; (p) (216) 721-5722; (f) (216) 721-0645; www.wrhs.org; (c) Cuyahoga

Joint; Private non-profit/ 1867/ staff: 95(f); 65(p); 400(v)/ members: 5500

GENEALOGICAL SOCIETY; HISTORICAL SOCIETY; HISTORY MUSEUM; HOUSE MUSEUM; LIVING HISTORY/OUTDOOR MUSEUM; PRESIDENTIAL SITE: Maintains seven historical properties in northeast OH: Crawford Auto-Aviation Museum, Library, History Museum, Hale Farm and Village, James A. Garfield National Historic Site, Shandy Hall, and Loghurst.

PROGRAMS: Community Outreach; Exhibits; Facility Rental; Family Programs; Festivals; Garden Tours; Guided Tours; Interpretation; Lectures; Living History; Publication; Reenactments; Research Library/Archives

COLLECTIONS: [1796-present]

HOURS: Yr

COLUMBUS

6629
Central Ohio Fire Museum & Learning Center

260 N Fourth St, 43215; (p) (614) 464-4099; (f) (614) 221-3132; cofmuseum@aol.com; (c) Franklin

Private non-profit/ 1982/ Board of Directors/ staff: 3(p)

HISTORIC SITE: Fire fighting history and fire prevention education Learning Center in restored 1908 fire station.

COLLECTIONS: [1850-present] Antique hand drawn, horse drawn and early motorized fire trucks; Fire fighting artifacts and memorabilia, Currier & Ives "Life of a Fireman" collection.

6630
Columbus Jewish Historical Society

1175 College Ave, 43209-2890; (p) (614) 238-6977; (f) (614) 237-2221; cjhs@tcjf.org; www.gcis.net/cjhs; (c) Franklin

1981/ Board of Trustees/ staff: 2(f); 2(p); 50(v)/ members: 535/publication: Reflections (newsletter)

HISTORICAL SOCIETY: Presents records of Jewish life; facilitates the collection, preservation, and publication of materials on the Jewish history of Columbus and central OH.

PROGRAMS: Annual Meeting; Community Outreach; Exhibits; Publication; Research Library/Archives

COLLECTIONS: Non-circulating collection of over 170 books and 150 oral history tapes, family portrait album, inventory of Jewish burials in 13 cemeteries, ceremonial art documentation, photos of early Jewish families and businesses, genealogy resources, and various

Jewish artifacts and clothing.

HOURS: Yr M-Th 8:45-5, F 8:45-4:30

ADMISSION: No charge

6631

Hilltop Historical Society

2300 W Broad St, 43204; (p) (614) 276-0060; (f) (614) 351-2580; (c) Franklin

Private non-profit/ 1986/ Board of Trustees/ members: 121/publication: *The Men and Women of Camp Chase*

HISTORIC PRESERVATION AGENCY; HISTORIC SITE; HISTORICAL SOCIETY: The society preserves the past of the Hilltop neighborhood of Columbus including Camp Chase Military Camp (1861-1865) and the National Road (Rt. 40).

PROGRAMS: Annual Meeting; Community Outreach; Exhibits; Guided Tours; Interpretation; Lectures; Publication; School-Based Curriculum

COLLECTIONS: [1861-1865] Civil War-related letters, books, National Road history, Jesse Owens history.

HOURS: Yr M-F 9-3

6632

Kelton House Museum and Garden

586 E Town St, 43215-4888; (p) (614) 464-2022; (f) (614) 464-3346; (c) Franklin

Private non-profit/ 1976/ Junior League of Columbus/ staff: 1(f); 1(p); 40(v)/ members: 200/publication: *The Keltonian*

HOUSE MUSEUM: Interprets urban life and decorative arts of 19th c Columbus.

PROGRAMS: Community Outreach; Exhibits; Facility Rental; Family Programs; Garden Tours; Guided Tours; Interpretation; Lectures; Living History; Publication; Reenactments; Research Library/Archives

COLLECTIONS: [19th c] Decorative arts, ceramics, glass, metals, furniture, painting, prints, rugs, tapestries, ivory, gems, books; Sophia and Fernando Cortez Family.

HOURS: Su 1-4, M-F 10-5 and by appt

ADMISSION: $3, Children $1.50, Seniors $2

6633

Ohio Association of Historical Societies and Museums

c/o Local Hist Office, OH Hist Soc 1982 Velma Ave, 43211-2497; (p) (614) 297-2340; (f) (614) 297-2318; bsuch@ohiohistory.org; www.ohiohistory.org; (c) Franklin

Private non-profit/ 1959/ staff: 3(f)/ members: 700/publication: *Local Historian*

HOURS: Yr M-F 7:30-5

6634

Ohio Historical Society

1982 Velma Ave, 43211-2497; (p) (614) 972-2330; (f) (614) 297-2318; jcole@ohiohistory.org; www.ohiohistory.org; (c) Franklin

Private non-profit/ 1885/ Board of Trustees/ staff: 360(f); 120(p); 1900(v)/ members: 11750

HISTORIC PRESERVATION AGENCY; HISTORIC SITE; HISTORICAL SOCIETY; HISTORY MUSEUM; HOUSE MUSEUM; LIVING HISTORY/OUTDOOR MUSEUM; PRESIDENTIAL SITE; RESEARCH CENTER: Collects,

preserves,and interprets OH history, cultural and natural environment.

PROGRAMS: Annual Meeting; Community Outreach; Concerts; Elder's Programs; Exhibits; Facility Rental; Family Programs; Festivals; Film/Video; Garden Tours; Guided Tours; Interpretation; Lectures; Living History; Publication; Reenactments; Research Library/Archives;School-Based Curriculum

COLLECTIONS: 1 million archaeological pieces, 93,000 natural history specimens, 300,000 historical artifacts, 131,000 books and pamphlets, 4,000 newspapers, 1 million audio-visual materials, and 28,000 cubic ft of state and local govt records.

HOURS: Yr M-Sa 9-5, Su 10-5

ADMISSION: $5, Children $1.25

6635

Ohio Museums Association

567 E Hudson St, 43211; (p) (614) 298-2030; (f) (614) 298-2068; oma@ohiohistory.org; (c) Franklin

Private non-profit/ 1976/ staff: 3(p); 30(v)/ members: 360/publication: *Ohio Museums Monthly; Ohio Museums Magazine*

Provides professional support services to OH museums.

6636

Palatines to America

611 E Weber Rd, 43211-1097; (p) (614) 267-4700; (f) (614) 267-4888; Pal-Am@juno.com; www.PalAm.org; (c) Franklin

Private non-profit/ 1975/ Board of Directors/ staff: 2(p); 100(v)/ members: 3500/publication: *Palatine Immigrant; Palatine Patter*

GENEALOGICAL SOCIETY: Promotes study of Germanic immigration to US.

PROGRAMS: Annual Meeting; Lectures; Publication; Research Library/Archives

COLLECTIONS: Ancestor charts; 5,000 monographs of genealogical guides and directories; religious and general biography; family histories; German language materials; European atlases; local histories and genealogical works for the US and Canada, German post code directories and phonebook; manuscripts, audiocassettes, microforms, and videotapes.

HOURS: W 12:30-4; 1st Sa 10-2, 3rd F 9-4 and by appt

ADMISSION: $5

6637

Thurber House, The

77 Jefferson Ave, 43215; (p) (614) 464-1032; (f) (614) 228-7445; TheCountry@thurberhouse.org; www.thurberhouse.org; (c) Franklin

Private non-profit/ 1980/ Board of Directors/ staff: 2(f); 8(p); 150(v)/publication: *The House Organ*

HOUSE MUSEUM: Restored boyhood home of James Thurber that serves as literary arts center.

PROGRAMS: Community Outreach; Exhibits; Facility Rental; Family Programs; Guided Tours; Lectures; Publication

COLLECTIONS: [early 1900s] Cartoons, letters, family photos, first edition books.

HOURS: Yr M-Su 12-4

ADMISSION: No charge

CONNEAUT

6638

Conneaut Chapter-National Railway Historical Society

Depot St, 44030 [PO Box 643, 44030]; (p) (440) 599-7878; (c) Ashtabula

Private non-profit/ 1964/ staff: 10(p); 5(v)/ members: 134/publication: *Semaphore*

HISTORIC SITE; HISTORICAL SOCIETY

PROGRAMS: Annual Meeting; Exhibits; Publication

COLLECTIONS: [1800-present] Railroad memorabilia.

HOURS: May-Sep M-Su 12-5

ADMISSION: Donations accepted

COSHOCTON

6639

Johnson-Humrickhouse Museum

300N Whitewoman St, 43812; (p) (740) 622-8710; (f) (740) 622-8710; (c) Coshocton

County, non-profit/ 1931/ Board of Trustees/ staff: 2(f); 3(p); 5(v)/ members: 276/publication: *The JHM*

HISTORY MUSEUM: Fosters respect, appreciation and understanding of other cultures.

PROGRAMS: Community Outreach; Exhibits; Facility Rental; Family Programs; Guided Tours; Interpretation; Lectures; Publication

COLLECTIONS: [19th and early 20th c] Native American artifacts, Asian fine and decorative arts and weaponry, 19th and early 20thc European and OH pioneer guns, and tools.

HOURS: Yr May-Oct M-Su 12-5; Nov-Apr T-Su 1-4:30

ADMISSION: $2, Children $1, Family $5

6640

Roscoe Village Foundation

600 N Whitewoman St, 43812 [381 Hill St, 43812]; (p) (740) 623-6548; (f) (740) 623-6545; rveducation@coshocton.com; www.roscoevillage.com; (c) Coshocton

Private non-profit/ 1969/ staff: 90(f); 107(p); 60(v)/ members: 750

HISTORIC SITE; LIVING HISTORY/OUTDOOR MUSEUM

PROGRAMS: Community Outreach; Concerts; Exhibits; Facility Rental; Festivals; Film/Video; Garden Tours; Guided Tours; Interpretation; Lectures; School-Based Curriculum; Theatre

COLLECTIONS: [1830-1913] Photos collection; Structures: Dr. Maro Johnson House, Craftsman House, Jacob Welsh-Toll House, Blacksmith Shop.

HOURS: Yr M-Su 10-5

CUYAHOGA FALLS

6641

Cuyahoga Falls Historical Society

[PO Box 108, 44222]; (p) (330) 923-2988; (c) Summit

1980/ staff: 14(v)/ members: 100/publication: *Monthly newsletter*

Collects and preserves local historical artifacts and memorabilia.

COLLECTIONS: [1800-present]

HOURS: Sep-Jun M 9-12:30

ADMISSION: Donations accepted

DAMASCUS

6642
Damascus Area Historical Society of Ohio, Inc.
US Rt 62, 44619 [PO Box 144, 44619]; (p) (330) 537-3939; (c) Columbiana

Private non-profit/ 1975/ members: 70/publication: *The Damascus Herald*

HISTORICAL SOCIETY: Preserves history and memories of Damascus area.

PROGRAMS: Exhibits; Facility Rental; Guided Tours; Publication

COLLECTIONS: [1850-present] Memorabilia from the Quaker heritage of the area and from rural farm life. Structures: The Pearce House Museum, The Quaker School & Meeting House.

HOURS: By appt

ADMISSION: No charge

DAYTON

6643
Carillon Historical Park, Inc.
1000 Carillon Blvd, 45409-2023; (p) (937) 293-2841; (f) (937) 293-5798; chpdayton@ main-net.com; www.carillon park.org; (c) Montgomery

Private non-profit/ 1950/ Board of Trustees/ staff: 10(f); 64(p); 40(v)/ members: 500/publication: *Carillon Courier*

HISTORY MUSEUM; LIVING HISTORY/OUT-DOOR MUSEUM: A sixty-five acre historical complex, is dedicated to preserving and interpreting this region's unique history.

PROGRAMS: Community Outreach; Concerts; Exhibits; Facility Rental; Festivals; Interpretation; Lectures; Publication; Reenactments

COLLECTIONS: [1790s-present] 3,300 accessioned artifacts, historic buildings, bridges, bicycles, automobiles, printing equipment, and original Wright brothers airplane; photos, and research files.

HOURS: Apr 1-Oct T-Sa 9:30-5, Su 12-5 and M & holidays 12-5

ADMISSION: $3, Student $2, Seniors $2.50

6644
Carriage Hill Metro Park Farm
7800 E Shull Rd, 45424; (p) (937) 879-0461; (f) (937) 879-8904; rmusselman@metroparks. org; (c) Montgomery

1968/ Five Rivers Metro Parks/ staff: 6(f); 6(p); 250(v)

HISTORIC SITE; LIVING HISTORY/OUT-DOOR MUSEUM: Interprets, and preserves farmstead and farm life.

PROGRAMS: Exhibits; Family Programs; Interpretation; Living History; School-Based Curriculum

COLLECTIONS: [1880s] Period and reproduction agricultural equipment, household furnishings, and utensils, historic animal breeds and heirloom seeds. Structures: Log barn, farm house, bank barn.

HOURS: Yr M-F 10-5, Sa-Su 1-5

ADMISSION: No charge

6645
Montgomery County Historical Society, The
224 N St. Clair St, 45402; (p) (937) 228-6271; (f) (937) 331-7160; mchsdayton@aol.com; (c) Montgomery

Private non-profit/ 1896/ Board of Trustees/ staff: 7(f); 5(p); 16(v)/ members: 500/publication: *Columns*

HISTORICAL SOCIETY: Collects and preserves the history of the Miami Valley and Dayton area museum and the Patterson Homestead.

PROGRAMS: Annual Meeting; Exhibits; Publication

COLLECTIONS: [1796-present] 3 million objects of local and regional history; corporate archives of the NCR Corporation; 1850 Montgomery County Court House, 1816-1850 Patterson Homestead.

HOURS: Yr Jan-Dec T-F 10-4:30 Sa 12-4

ADMISSION: No charge

6646
Patterson Homestead Museum, The
1815 Brown St, 45409-2414; (p) (937) 222-9724; (c) Montgomery

Joint/ 1953/ Montgomery County Historical Society/ staff: 1(f); 2(p); 12(v)

HOUSE MUSEUM: 1816-1850 Federal Style House that was the childhood home of the founders of National Cash Register Co, John H and Frank J. Patterson, furnished with antiques and family pieces ranging from Queen Anne to Empire.

PROGRAMS: Exhibits; Facility Rental; Family Programs; Interpretation; Living History; Reenactments

COLLECTIONS: [1760-1880] Approximately 700 objects: high style Sheraton and Hepplewhite items, Empire and hand crafted artifacts, Bird/Ship Lithographs and family memorabilia.

HOURS: May 15-Oct 31 W-Sa 1-4

ADMISSION: Donations requested

6647
Paul Laurence Dunbar State Memorial
219 N Paul Laurence Dunbar St, 45407 [PO Box 1872, 45401]; (p) (937) 224-7061, (937) 224-5626

1870/ State, Ohio Histor/ staff: 1(f); 2(p); 21(v)

HOUSE MUSEUM: Residence of African American author Paul Laurence Dunbar.

PROGRAMS: Exhibits

COLLECTIONS: [1900-1910] Dunbar's Native American collection, furniture, clothing, books, personal library.

HOURS: May-Oct

DEFIANCE

6648
Defiance Public Library
320 Fort St, 43512; (p) (419) 782-1456; (f) (419) 782-6235; ohioandp@plin.lib.oh.us; www.defiance.lib.oh.us; (c) Defiance

City/ 1904/ Trustees/ staff: 14(f); 31(p); 3(v)

LIBRARY AND/OR ARCHIVES: A public library with research center for history and genealogy; located next to Fort Defiance.

PROGRAMS: Community Outreach; Guided Tours; Research Library/Archives

COLLECTIONS: Historic maps, English and German newspapers, museum artifacts, photos, published local histories, microfilmed census.

HOURS: Yr Jun-Aug M-Th 9-8:30, F-Sa 9-6, Su 1-5; Sep-May Sa 9-12

DELAWARE

6649
Delaware County Historical Society, Inc.
157 E William St, 43015 [PO Box 317, 43015]; (p) (740) 369-3831; dchsdcgs@mido hio.net; www.midohio.net/dchsdcgs; (c) Delaware

Private non-profit/ 1948/ Board of Trustees/ staff: 50(v)

GENEALOGICAL SOCIETY; HISTORIC PRESERVATION AGENCY; HISTORICAL SOCIETY; HISTORY MUSEUM; HOUSE MUSEUM; RESEARCH CENTER: Collects, preserves, and shares items and information pertaining to county history; maintains Nash House museum.

PROGRAMS: Annual Meeting; Community Outreach; Exhibits; Facility Rental; Guided Tours; Lectures; Research Library/Archives

COLLECTIONS: Furnishings donated by people of Delaware County.

HOURS: Jan-Nov, May-Aug T-F 2-4:30; Nov-Feb S 2-4:30

DENNISON

6650
Dennison Railroad Depot Museum, The
400 Center St, 44621 [PO Box 11, 44621]; (p) (740) 922-0105; (f) (740) 922-0105; depot@tusco.net; web1.tusco.net/rail; (c) Tuscarawas

Private non-profit/ 1984/ Board of Trustees/ staff: 1(f); 2(p); 150(v)/ members: 700

HISTORY MUSEUM: Restored 1873 Pennsylvania Railroad Depot that houses museum.

PROGRAMS: Annual Meeting; Community Outreach; Exhibits; Family Programs; Festivals; Garden Tours; Interpretation; Lectures

COLLECTIONS: [1864-present] Artifacts pertaining to Dennison's railroad history and its role as a WWII servicemen's center.

HOURS: Yr Jan-Dec T-Su 10-5

ADMISSION: $3, Children $1.75

DOVER

6651
Dover Historical Society
325 E Iron Ave, 44622; (p) (330) 343-7040, (800) 815-2794; (f) (330) 343-6290; reeves@ tusco.net; web.tusco.net/tourism/reeves; (c) Tuscarawas

Private non-profit/ 1958/ staff: 1(f); 18(p); 25(v)/ members: 1000

HISTORICAL SOCIETY; HISTORY MUSEUM; HOUSE MUSEUM: Owns and operates a restored Victorian mansion and carriage house that serves as museum.

PROGRAMS: Annual Meeting; Community Outreach; Concerts; Elder's Programs; Exhibits; Facility Rental; Family Programs; Garden Tours; Guided Tours; Interpretation; Lectures; Research Library/Archives

COLLECTIONS: [1885-present] Furniture, china, glassware, clothing from 1885-1940, military uniforms, antique electric car and 1898 carriage. Structures: 17 room mansion, Carriage House.

HOURS: May-Oct T-Su 10-4

ADMISSION: $5, Student $2

6652
J.E. Reeves Victorian Home and Carriage House Museum
325 E Iron Ave, 44622; (p) (330) 343-7040; (f) (330) 343-6290; Reeves@tusco.net; web. tusco.net/reeves; (c) Tuscarawas

Private non-profit/ 1958/ Dover Historical Society/ staff: 2(f); 12(p); 35(v)/ members: 1017/publication: Dover Historical Society Newsletter

GARDEN; HISTORIC SITE; HISTORICAL SOCIETY; HISTORY MUSEUM; HOUSE MUSEUM: Restored 17 room mansion of industrialist Jeremiah Reeves.

PROGRAMS: Annual Meeting; Exhibits; Facility Rental; Festivals; Guided Tours; Lectures; Publication

COLLECTIONS: 17 room Victorian mansion and carriage house, Victorian furniture, original furnishings of J.E. Reeves family including personal items and clothing, fine China from England and Germany, a camera and radio collection, military display and carriages.

HOURS: May-Oct T-Su 10-4; Dec M-Su 12-8

ADMISSION: $5, Children $2

DOYLESTOWN

6653
Chippewa-Rogues' Hollow Historical Society
17500 Galehouse Rd, 44230 [PO Box 283, 44230]; (p) (330) 658-6771; (c) Wayne

Private non-profit/ 1958/ staff: 4(v)/ members: 30/publication: Rogues Hollow-History and Legends

HISTORICAL SOCIETY: Collects and preserves local history of the Doylestown and Chippewa Twp. Area.

PROGRAMS: Annual Meeting; Community Outreach; Exhibits, Interpretation; Publication

COLLECTIONS: [1827-present] Local memorabilia, coal mining tools and display, wool and weaving.

HOURS: May-Oct Su 1-4

EAST PALESTINE

6654
East Palestine Area Historical Society
555 Bacon Ave, 44413 [PO Box 176, 44413]; (p) (330) 426-9094; (c) Columbiana

Private non-profit/ 1974/ members: 51

HISTORICAL SOCIETY; HOUSE MUSEUM: Preserves local artifacts in historic log house.

PROGRAMS: Exhibits; Guided Tours

COLLECTIONS: Photos, books, post card albums, furniture, dishes, old clothing, miner's tools, 30 gallon apple butter kettles and paddles, Bibles.

HOURS: June-Aug, Dec Su 2-4

ADMISSION: No charge

EATON

6655
Preble County District Library
450 S Barron St, 45320-2402; (p) (937) 456-4970; (f) (937) 456-6092; pcroom@infinet. com; www.pcdl.lib.oh.us; (c) Preble

County; Joint/ 1959/ staff: 3(p); 1(v)/publication: Preble's

GENEALOGICAL SOCIETY; HISTORICAL SOCIETY

PROGRAMS: Publication; Research Library/ Archives

COLLECTIONS: [1808-present] Preble County records and archives. Records form Drake, Butler, Montgomery, and Warren Counties OH; and Franklin, Randolph, Union and Wayne Counties IN; various religious groups. 3,000 volumes.

HOURS: Yr M-F 9-8, Sa 9-5, Su 1-5

ADMISSION: No charge

6656
Preble County Historical Society
7693 Swartsel Rd, 45320; (p) (937) 787-4256; (f) (937) 787-9662; prcohs@infinet.com; (c) Preble

Private non-profit/ 1971/ Board of Trustees/ staff: 1(f); 1(p); 100(v)/ members: 500

HISTORICAL SOCIETY; HOUSE MUSEUM: Preserves and promotes knowledge of Preble County history ;provides for the collection, preservation and display of materials and objects with historical significance to county and state.

PROGRAMS: Annual Meeting; Community Outreach; Concerts; Exhibits; Facility Rental; Family Programs; Festivals; Interpretation; Lectures; Living History; Publication; Reenactments; Research Library/Archives

COLLECTIONS: Structures: 1860 Sayler-Swartsel House, 1813 Lewisburg Log House, 1830s Phillips Swartsel House.

HOURS: Yr M-F 9-4; May-Dec 1st Su 1-5

ADMISSION: No charge

ELYRIA

6657
Lorain County Historical Society
509 Washington Ave, 44035; (p) (440) 322-3341; (f) (440) 322-2817; (c) Lorain

Private non-profit/ 1889/ staff: 3(f); 1(p); 50(v)/ members: 275/publication: Hickory Leaves

HISTORICAL SOCIETY; HOUSE MUSEUM: Maintains Hickories Museum, an 1895 mansion; interprets late Victorian domestic life.

PROGRAMS: Annual Meeting; Community Outreach; Exhibits; Guided Tours; Interpretation; Lectures; Publication; Research Library/Archives; School-Based Curriculum

COLLECTIONS: [Late 1800s] Photos, costumes and textiles 1860-1950s, original artwork of Lorain County, artifacts 1800-1960 emphasizing late 19th and early 20th c furnishings, woodworking and textile tools/equipment, glassware, toys.

HOURS: T-F 10-5

ADMISSION: $3.50, Children $1

ENON

6658
Enon Community Historical Society
45 Indian Mound Dr, 45323 [PO Box 442, 45323]; (p) (937) 864-7080; echs@erinet. com; www.enonhistory.org; (c) Clark

Private non-profit/ 1974/ Board of Trustees/ staff: 15(v)/ members: 180

GENEALOGICAL SOCIETY; HISTORIC SITE; RESEARCH CENTER: Provides an archive of genealogy and history of the Enon area (Mad River Township); preserves and maintains Enon's Adena Indian Mound and 1830 house.

PROGRAMS: Annual Meeting; Exhibits; Festivals; Interpretation; Living History; Publication; Quarterly Meeting; Research Library/Archives

COLLECTIONS: [1830-1900] Native American (Adena) tools, Mad River Township genealogy, archives: books, articles, photos; photographic inventory of historic sites in and around Mad River Township, Clark Co; tapes, books, maps, and photos.

HOURS: Yr T 1-4, W 1-4/6-8, Sa 10-2

ADMISSION: No charge

FAIRPORT HARBOR

6659
Fairport Harbor Historical Society
129 Second St, 44077; (p) (440) 354-4825; (c) Lake

Private non-profit/ 1945/ staff: 50(v)/ members: 250

HISTORIC PRESERVATION AGENCY; HISTORIC SITE; HISTORICAL SOCIETY: Preserves history of Fairport Harbor; collects and displays artifacts relating to Great Lakes shipping.

PROGRAMS: Annual Meeting; Exhibits; Guided Tours; Research Library/Archives

COLLECTIONS: [early 1800s-present] Photos, books, maps, charts on Great Lakes shipping, artifacts from sailing vessels, pilot house, life car, original third order lens from Fairport Lighthouse.

HOURS: May-Sept W, Sa-Su

FAIRVIEW PARK

6660
Fairview Park Historical Society, The
[PO Box 26143, 44126-0143]; (c) Cuyahoga

Private non-profit/ 1960/ staff: 20(v)/ members: 122/publication: *Fairview Park's Historical Places, Fairview Park in Historical Review*

HISTORICAL SOCIETY: Maintains local history museum.

PROGRAMS: Annual Meeting; Exhibits; Lectures; Publication; Research Library/Archives

COLLECTIONS: Archives and artifacts of local history.

HOURS: Jan-Apr, Jun-Dec 2nd Su 2-4:30 and by appt

FINDLAY

6661
Hancock Historical Museum
422 W Sandusky, 45840; (p) (419) 423-4433; (c) Hancock

Private non-profit/ 1970/ staff: 2(f); 4(p); 50(v)/ members: 570/publication: *Herstory: Voices from the Past*

HISTORY MUSEUM; HOUSE MUSEUM: Promotes local history.

PROGRAMS: Annual Meeting; Community Outreach; Exhibits; Family Programs; Festivals; Interpretation; Lectures; Living History; Publication; Reenactments; Research Library/Archives; School-Based Curriculum

COLLECTIONS: [1880s-1920] Artifacts: mechanical, industrial, domestic, art, textiles, furniture; archives, toys, glass, pottery and military items. Structures: Hull House, Little Red Schoolhouse, Log House, and more.

HOURS: Yr T-F 1-4

ADMISSION: No charge

FORT LORAMIE

6662
Fort Loramie Historical Association
37 N Main St, 45845 [PO Box 276, 45845]; (p) (937) 295-3855; (c) Shelby

Private non-profit/ 1971/ staff: 1(p); 35(v)/ members: 43

HISTORICAL SOCIETY; HISTORY MUSEUM; HOUSE MUSEUM: Operates Wilderness Trail Museum, and 1853 boarding house/hotel.

PROGRAMS: Facility Rental; Festivals; Guided Tours; Lectures

COLLECTIONS: [1600s-1800s] Native American artifacts, doll room, millinery shop, period furniture, military room: Civil War, WWI, WWII; country store.

HOURS: Jun-Oct Su 1-4

ADMISSION: No charge

FOSTORIA

6663
Fostoria Historical Museum
123 W N St, 44830 [PO Box 142, 44830]; (p) (419) 435-4664; (c) Seneca

City; Private non-profit/ 1972/ staff: 6(p) 10(v)/ members: 180/publication: *monthly newsletter*

HISTORICAL SOCIETY; HISTORY MUSEUM

PROGRAMS: Annual Meeting; Film/Video; Lectures; Publication

COLLECTIONS: [1850-1960]

HOURS: Mar-Nov Sa 1:30-4:30

ADMISSION: No charge

FRANKLIN

6664
Franklin Area Historical Society
302 Park Ave, 45005; (p) (513) 746-8295; (c) Warren

Private non-profit/ 1965/ staff: 1(p)/ members: 140/publication: *FAHS Newsletter*

HISTORICAL SOCIETY: Preserves local history.

PROGRAMS: Community Outreach; Exhibits; Garden Tours; Guided Tours; Publication; Reenactments

COLLECTIONS: [1800-present] Clothing, tools, period furnishing.

HOURS: April-Dec Su 2-5

ADMISSION: $1, Children $0.25

FREMONT

6665
Rutherford B. Hayes Presidential Center
Spiegel Grove, 43420-2796; (p) (419) 332-2081; (f) (419) 332-4952; hayeslib@rbhayes.org; www.rbhayes.org; (c) Sandusky

Private non-profit/ 1916/ staff: 24(f); 24(p); 150(v)/ members: 650/publication: *The Statesman*

HISTORY MUSEUM; HOUSE MUSEUM; PRESIDENTIAL SITE: Maintains a research library and archives (emphasis 1860-1917) and is a museum that concentrates on the Hayes Presidency.

PROGRAMS: Concerts; Exhibits; Facility Rental; Guided Tours; Interpretation; Lectures; Publication; Reenactments; Research Library/Archives

COLLECTIONS: [1860-1917] The papers of Rutherford B. Hayes, his family and members of his administration; materials relating to history of northwest Ohio. Structures: Rutherford B. Hayes home, Rutherford B. Hayes Library and Museum.

HOURS: M-Sa 9-5 Su 12-5

ADMISSION: $5 Museum or Home; $8.50 both

GALION

6666
Galion Historical Society, Inc.
132 S Union St, 44833 [PO Box 125, 44833]; (p) (419) 468-9338; (c) Crawford

Private non-profit/ 1955/ staff: 25(v)/ members: 185

HISTORICAL SOCIETY; HISTORY MUSEUM: Maintains history museum; manages Victorian house museum.

PROGRAMS: Annual Meeting; Concerts; Exhibits; Guided Tours; Lectures; Publication

COLLECTIONS: [1817-1930s] Prehistoric artifacts of Arga, Pioneer exhibits, trains, medicine, dolls, glass, photographs, musical instruments, post office, organ and Victoriana.

HOURS: May-Nov Su 2-4

ADMISSION: $3, Student $1.50

GALLIPOLIS

6667
Gallia County Historical/Genealogical Society
430 Second Ave, 45631 [PO Box 295, 45631-0295]; (p) (740) 446-7200; (c) Gallia

Private non-profit/ 1974/ Board of Directors/ staff: 30(v)/ members: 500/publication: *Gallia County Glade (quarterly)*

GENEALOGICAL SOCIETY; HISTORICAL SOCIETY; RESEARCH CENTER: Preserves and publishes county history and genealogy.

PROGRAMS: Annual Meeting; Community Outreach; Exhibits; Facility Rental; Family Programs; Film/Video; Publication; Research Library/Archives; School-Based Curriculum

COLLECTIONS: [1803-present] Files and notebooks of local history, first families of Gallia County, revolutionary soldiers from Gallia, artifacts.

HOURS: Yr M-F 10-4 Sa 10-1

GENEVA

6668
Shandy Hall
6333 S Ridge Rd W, 44041; (p) (440) 466-3680; www.wrhs.org

1815/ Western Reserve Historical Society

HISTORY MUSEUM

COLLECTIONS: [1860s] Furnishings, texts, personal effects and documents of the Harper family.; personal letters, legal papers, reciepts, photos and sketches.

GEORGETOWN

6669
Brown County Historical Society
Corner of Cherry & Apple Sts, 45121 [PO Box 238, 45121]; (p) (937) 444-3521; (c) Brown

Private non-profit/ 1947/ staff: 2(v)/ members: 210/publication: *Bits of Heritage*

GENEALOGICAL SOCIETY; HISTORIC PRESERVATION AGENCY; HISTORIC SITE; HISTORICAL SOCIETY; HISTORY MUSEUM; HOUSE MUSEUM; RESEARCH CENTER: Maintains museum; collects, preserves, and displays items related to local history.

PROGRAMS: Annual Meeting; Community Outreach; Exhibits; Facility Rental; Festivals; Guided Tours; Lectures; Living History; Monthly Meeting; Publication; Research Library/Archives; School-Based Curriculum

COLLECTIONS: [Late 19th-20th c] Military artifacts, 1865-1910 county newspapers, Native American artifacts, and antiques.

HOURS: Yr Th 12-5

6671
Ulysses S. Grant Homestead
219 E Grant Ave, 45121 [7471 Doctor Faul Rd, 45121]; (p) (937) 378-3760, (800) 892-3586; (f) (937) 378-6430; www.ruthven.com; (c) Brown

1966/ staff: 4(v)

HISTORIC SITE; HOUSE MUSEUM; PRESIDENTIAL SITE: A collection of several buildings with historical significance to Ulysses S. Grant's boyhood years from 1823-1839.

PROGRAMS: Guided Tours; Interpretation; Research Library/Archives

COLLECTIONS: [1823-1840] U. S. Grant's gloves, Julia's headwear, family Bible and bed covering, cradle, chairs and sofa.; books on Grant and Civil War, newspapers, photos and prints. Furniture and family items as well as a library on the Civil War and U.S. President Grant.

HOURS: Yr M-Sa 9-1 2-5

ADMISSION: No charge

GERMANTOWN

6672
Historical Society of Germantown, The
47 W Center St, 45327 [PO Box 144, 45327]; (p) (937) 855-7951; (c) Montgomery

Private non-profit/ 1973/ Board of Trustees/ staff: 1(p); 15(v)/ members: 350/publication: *newsletter*

HISTORICAL SOCIETY: Collects, preserves, and interprets history of Germantown, the German Township.

PROGRAMS: Annual Meeting; Exhibits; Festivals; Film/Video; Guided Tours; Interpretation; Publication; Research Library/Archives

COLLECTIONS: [1804-present] 1,000 photos, 1,000 artifacts, newspaper articles relating to Germantown, German Township and areas surrounding.

HOURS: May-Dec Sa 10-12:30, Su 1-3

ADMISSION: No charge

GNADENHUTTEN

6673
Gnadenhutten Historical Society
352 S Cherry St, 44629 [PO Box 396, 44629]; (p) (740) 254-4143; (f) (740) 254-4986; gnadmuse@tusco.net; www.tusco.net/gnaden; (c) Tuscarawas

Joint/ 1843/ Board of Trustees/ staff: 2(f); 50(v)/ members: 15/publication: *A Brief History of Gnadenhutten*

HISTORIC SITE; HISTORICAL SOCIETY; HISTORY MUSEUM; LIVING HISTORY/OUTDOOR MUSEUM: Preserves histories of Gnadenhutten.

PROGRAMS: Annual Meeting; Community Outreach; Exhibits; Festivals; Film/Video; Guided Tours; Interpretation; Lectures; Living History; Publication; Reenactments; School-Based Curriculum

COLLECTIONS: [1700-1800s] Native American artifacts, old books and Bibles, household items, tools, maps, newspapers.

HOURS: Jun-Aug M-F, Sa 10-5, Su 12-5; Sep-Oct Sa 10-5, Su 12-5 and by appt

GOSHEN

6674
Goshen Township Historical Society
Box 671, 45122-0671; (c) Clermont

City/ 1988/ staff: 12(v)/ members: 50

HISTORIC SITE; HISTORICAL SOCIETY; HISTORY MUSEUM; HOUSE MUSEUM: Collects and preserves the local history of Goshen.

PROGRAMS: Community Outreach; Exhibits; Family Programs

HOURS: Yr F 9-5

ADMISSION: No charge

GRANVILLE

6675
Granville Historical Society
115 E Broadway, 43023 [PO Box 129, 43023]; (p) (740) 587-3951; (c) Licking

Private non-profit/ 1885/ staff: 50(v)/ members: 287/publication: *Granville Historical Times*

HISTORICAL SOCIETY: Preserves and collects artifacts and papers relating to history of Granville.

PROGRAMS: Annual Meeting; Community Outreach; Exhibits; Facility Rental; Family Programs; Guided Tours; Lectures; Publication; Research Library/Archives

COLLECTIONS: [19th c] Historic Granville furniture, memorabilia, documents relating to Granville.

HOURS: Apr-Oct Sa-Su 1-4

ADMISSION: Donations accepted

6676
Robbins Hunter Museum in the Avery-Downer House
221 E Broadway, 43023 [PO Box 183, 43023]; (p) (740) 587-0430; (c) Licking

Private non-profit/ 1981/ Licking County Historical Society/ staff: 1(f); 1(p); 25(v)

HOUSE MUSEUM: American Greek Revival Temple style house.

PROGRAMS: Community Outreach; Exhibits; Guided Tours; Interpretation; Lectures; Research Library/Archives

COLLECTIONS: [1830-1870] 18th and 19th c American and English furniture, paintings, rugs, lighting, ceramics, glass and decorative accessories, Clarence Hudson White photographs of the house and occupants 1902, platinum prints.

HOURS: May-Oct W-Su 1-4 also by appt

ADMISSION: $2, Group rates

GREENVILLE

6677
Darke County Historical Society
205 N Broadway, 45331-2222; (p) (937) 548-5250; (f) (937) 548-7645; (c) Darke

Private non-profit/ 1903/ staff: 2(f); 6(p)/ members: 234

GENEALOGICAL SOCIETY; HISTORY MUSEUM: Collects, preserves, and disseminates the history and heritage of Darke County; operates Garst Museum.

PROGRAMS: Annual Meeting; Exhibits; Guided Tours; Research Library/Archives

COLLECTIONS: [1790s-1900s] Artifacts: Annie Oakley and Lowell Thomas; Treaty of Greenville; military; early home and farm equipment.

HOURS: Feb-Dec T-Sa 11-5, Su 1-5

ADMISSION: $3, Children $1, Seniors $2

HAMDEN

6678
Vinton County Historical and Genealogical Society, Inc.
118 N Market St, 45634 [PO Box 312, 45634-0306]; (p) (740) 384-6305, (740) 384-2467; (c) Vinton

Private non-profit/ 1950/ Executive Committee/ staff: 1(v)/ members: 78/publication: *Vinton County Heritage*

GENEALOGICAL SOCIETY; HISTORICAL SOCIETY: Collects and preserves Vinton County artifacts and history.

PROGRAMS: Publication

COLLECTIONS: [1880-1960] Homer Pierce Genealogical Library, newspapers from 1872-1960.

HOURS: Yr M-F 12-4

ADMISSION: No charge

HAMILTON

6679
Butler County Historical Society Museum
327 N Second St, 45011; (p) (513) 896-9930; (f) (513) 896-9936; (c) Butler

Private non-profit/ 1949/ Board of Trustees/ staff: 1(f); 1(p); 12(v)/ members: 300/publication: *Butler County Historical Society Newsletter*

HISTORICAL SOCIETY; HISTORY MUSEUM; HOUSE MUSEUM: The Museum interprets the lifestyle of a prominent industrialist in Hamilton during the Gilded Age. Other exhibits expand upon the history of Butler County through significant people, events, and artifacts.

PROGRAMS: Annual Meeting; Community Outreach; Concerts; Exhibits; Guided Tours; Interpretation; Lectures; Publication; Research Library/Archives; School-Based Curriculum

COLLECTIONS: [19th c] 19th c household furnishings and decorative arts, dolls, toys, firearms, swords, and glassware.

HOURS: Yr T-Su 1-4

ADMISSION: $1

6680
Historic Hamilton, Inc.
319 N Third St, 45013; (p) (513) 863-1389;
(c) Butler

Private non-profit/ 1979/ members: 85

HISTORY MUSEUM; HOUSE MUSEUM: Preserves historic buildings and sites in Hamilton.

PROGRAMS: Annual Meeting; Guided Tours; Interpretation; Lectures

COLLECTIONS: [1860-1900] Restored Octagonal House partially used as offices, period furnishings, garden.

HOURS: Yr M-F 9-4:30

ADMISSION: No vharge

HARRISON

6681
Village Historical Society, The
10580 Marvin Rd, 45030 [6590 Kilby Rd, 45030]; (p) (513) 367-4984; gwoelfel@aol.com; (c) Hamilton

Private non-profit/ 1960/ staff: 20(v)/ members: 135

HISTORICAL SOCIETY: Restores historic sites.

PROGRAMS: Annual Meeting; Exhibits; Guided Tours; Lectures; School-Based Curriculum

COLLECTIONS: [1804-present]

HOURS: May-Oct 3rd Su 1:30-4

ADMISSION: No charge

HARVEYSBURG

6682
Harveysburg Community Historical Society
23 N St, 45032 [PO Box 105, 45032]; (p) (513) 897-6195; (c) Warren

Private non-profit/ 1977/ staff: 15(v)/ members: 30

HISTORICAL SOCIETY: Preserves community history with special focus on the first free Black School in Ohio and the west territory.

PROGRAMS: Exhibits

COLLECTIONS: [1800s-early 1900s] Books, ledgers, pictures, clothing, memorabilia,

HOURS: 3rd Su in May/3rd Su in Sept Su 2-4 and by appt

ADMISSION: Donations accepted

HILLIARD

6683
Northwest Franklin County Historical Society and Museum
Weaver Park, 4144 Main St, 43026 [PO Box 413, 43026-0413]; (p) (614) 777-4852; (c) Franklin

Private non-profit/ 1968/ Board Members/ members: 340/publication: *bi-monthly newsletter, Northwest Chronicle*

HISTORICAL SOCIETY: 18th c village with 6 relocated buildings and museum.

PROGRAMS: Annual Meeting; Exhibits; Facility Rental; Festivals; Guided Tours; Interpretation; Publication; School-Based Curriculum

COLLECTIONS: Military, dolls, home cooking equipment, farming, RR, agriculture.

HOURS: By appt

HILLSBORO

6684
Highland County Historical Society
151 E Main St, 45133; (p) (937) 393-3263; (c) Highland

Private non-profit/ 1965/ staff: 2(p); 35(v)/ members: 312

HISTORICAL SOCIETY; HOUSE MUSEUM: Collects and preserves heritage of Highland County.

PROGRAMS: Annual Meeting; Exhibits; Facility Rental; Family Programs; Guided Tours; Lectures; Research Library/Archives

COLLECTIONS: [19th c] Higland County artifacts and items relating to its history.

HOURS: Mar-Dec F 1-5, Su 1-4 and by appt

ADMISSION: Donations accepted

HOMEWORTH

6685
Western Columbiana County Historical Society
4355 Homeworth Rd, 44634 [24331 Georgetown Rd, 44634]; (p) (330) 525-7132; (c) Columbiana

County/ 1964/ staff: 6(v)/ members: 50/publication: *The Flinstones*

HISTORIC SITE; HISTORICAL SOCIETY; HISTORY MUSEUM: Collects and displays historical memorabilia.

PROGRAMS: Annual Meeting; Publication

COLLECTIONS: [late 1800s-1945] Historical memorabilia.

HOURS: Aug Su 1-4

ADMISSION: Donations accepted

HUDSON

6686
CHIPS
c/o Hudson Library, 22 Aurora St, 44236; (c) Summit/Portage

Private non-profit/ 1980/ staff: 1(v)

ALLIANCE OF HISTORICAL AGENCIES: Located in Summit and Portage counties.

6687
Hudson Library and Historical Society, The
22 Aurora St, 44236; (p) (330) 653-6658; (f) (330) 650-4693; www.hudsonlibrary.org; (c) Summit

Private non-profit/ 1910/ staff: 18(f); 25(p)

HISTORICAL SOCIETY; LIBRARY AND/OR ARCHIVES: Provides historical and genealogical research assistance.

PROGRAMS: Lectures; Research Library/ Archives

COLLECTIONS: [1799-present] Genealogical and historical materials relating to the community; manuscript collection on local resident John Brown.

HOURS: Yr Library: Su 12-5, M-Th 9-9, F-Sa 9-5; Archives: M W Th 9-9, T F Sa 9-5

ADMISSION: No charge

IRONTON

6688
Briggs Lawrence County Public Library
321 S 4th St, 45638; (p) (740) 532-1124; (f) (740) 532-4948; genblc@oplin.lib.oh.us; lawrencecountyohio.com; (c) Lawrence

County; Joint/ 1987/ staff: 2(f); 5(v)

LIBRARY AND/OR ARCHIVES

PROGRAMS: Publication

COLLECTIONS: [1817-present]

HOURS: Yr M-Th 9-8:30 F-Sa 9-5:30

ADMISSION: No charge

KALIDA

6689
Putnam County Historical Society
201 E Main, 45853 [PO Box 264, 45853-0264]; (p) (419) 532-3008; pchs@bright.net; nwoet.bgsu.edu/ode/putnamcounty.html; (c) Putnam

County/ 1873/ staff: 2(p); 40(v)/ members: 310/publication: *Putnam County Heritage*

HISTORICAL SOCIETY; HISTORY MUSEUM: The society collects and preserves artifacts and historical materials as well as disseminating knowledge concerning the history of Putnam County.

PROGRAMS: Annual Meeting; Community Outreach; Exhibits; Family Programs; Festivals; Guided Tours; Interpretation; Lectures; Living History; Publication; Research Library/Archives; School-Based Curriculum

COLLECTIONS: [1834-present] Collections reflect life in rural Ohio and the people of the county.

HOURS: Yr Jan-Dec W 9-12 Su 1-4

ADMISSION: No charge

KENT

6690
Kelso House, The
4158 State Rte 43, 44240 [PO Box 1231, 44240]; (p) (330) 673-1058

1833/ Brimfield Memorial House Association, Inc./ staff: 1(p); 1(v)

COLLECTIONS: [1875-1900] Hand tools, dolls, local diaries, deeds, organizational records, archives.

HOURS: Vary

6691
Kent Historical Society
152 Franklin Ave, 44240 [PO Box 663, 44240]; (p) (330) 678-2712; (f) (330) 678-2852; kenthist@aol.com; www.kenthist.org; (c) Portage

Private non-profit/ 1971/ Board of Trustees/ staff: 2(p); 1(v)/ members: 260/publication: *Kentennial*

HISTORICAL SOCIETY: Preserves local history.

PROGRAMS: Exhibits; Lectures; Publication; Research Library/Archives; School-Based Curriculum

KENTON

6692
Dougherty House
215 N Detroit St, 43326 [PO Box 521, 43326]; (p) (419) 673-0275; zeppo@kenton.com

1875/ County, Hardin Cou/ staff: 1(f); 3(p)

COLLECTIONS: [1850-1900]

HOURS: Vary

6693
Hardin County Historical Museums, Inc.
215 N Detroit St, 43326; (p) (419) 673-7147; (c) Hardin

Joint/ 1991/ staff: 1(f); 3(p); 75(v)

HISTORY MUSEUM: Collects, preserves, interprets, and promotes Hardin County's heritage.

PROGRAMS: Annual Meeting; Community Outreach; Exhibits; Family Programs; Festivals; Guided Tours; Interpretation; Lectures; Living History; Publication; Research Library/Archives; School-Based Curriculum

COLLECTIONS: [Mid-19th c-20th c] Artifacts: pioneer heirlooms, Kenton cast iron toys, agricultural implement; Native American, Victoriana, and Alaskan art; Fred Machetanz literature.

HOURS: Mar-Dec F-Su

KIRTLAND

6694
Kirtland Temple Historic Center
9020 Chillicothe Rd, 44094; (p) (440) 256-3318; temple@ncweb.com; www.kirtlandtemple.org; (c) Lake

Private non-profit/ 1830/ Reorganized Church of Jesus Christ of Latter Day Saints/ staff: 3(f); 8(p); 10(v)

HISTORIC SITE; HOUSE MUSEUM: Interprets Kirtland Temple.

PROGRAMS: Exhibits; Film/Video; Guided Tours; Interpretation; Lectures; Publication

COLLECTIONS: [1830-1838]

HOURS: Yr M-Sa 9-5, Su 1-5

ADMISSION: No charge

KIRTLAND HILLS

6695
Lake County Historical Society
8610 Mentor Rd, 44060; (p) (440) 255-8979; (f) (440) 255-8980; (c) Lake

Private non-profit/ 1936/ staff: 3(f); 1(p); 150(v)/ members: 1180

HISTORIC SITE; HISTORICAL SOCIETY; HISTORY MUSEUM; LIBRARY AND/OR ARCHIVES; RESEARCH CENTER: Operates a museum of local history, library, and archives.

PROGRAMS: Annual Meeting; Community Outreach; Elder's Programs; Exhibits; Facility Rental; Family Programs; Festivals; Guided

Tours; Interpretation; Lectures; Living History; Publication; Reenactments; Research Library/Archives; School-Based Curriculum

COLLECTIONS: [1800-present] 19th c agricultural life including tools, clothing, decorative arts in historic 1926 summer estate; Western Reserve History.

HOURS: Yr T-F 10-5; also Sa-Su 1-5 Apr-Dec

ADMISSION: Donations accepted

LAKEWOOD

6696
Lakewood Historical Society
14710 Lake Ave, 44107; (p) (216) 221-7343; (f) (216) 221-0320; lkwdhist@bge.net; lkwd-pl.org/histsoc; (c) Cuyahoga

Private non-profit/ 1952/ staff: 1(f); 6(p); 50(v)/ members: 500

GARDEN; HISTORIC SITE; HISTORICAL SOCIETY; HISTORY MUSEUM; HOUSE MUSEUM: Promotes study of regional cultural heritage especially as it pertains to Lakewood and Rockport Township.

PROGRAMS: Annual Meeting; Community Outreach; Exhibits; Facility Rental; Guided Tours; Lectures; Research Library/Archives; School-Based Curriculum

COLLECTIONS: Artifacts 1838-1870, textiles, photo files, archives, manuscripts.

HOURS: Feb-Nov W 1-4, Su 2-5

ADMISSION: No charge

LANCASTER

6697
Georgian Museum, The
105 E Wheeling St, 43130; (p) (740) 654-9923; (f) (740) 654-9890; (c) Fairfield

Private non-profit/ 1976/ staff: 1(f); 3(p); 150(v)/ members: 650/publication: *Fairfield Heritage Quarterly*

HOUSE MUSEUM: 1832 Federal Home with Regency features built for Samuel MacCracken.

PROGRAMS: Exhibits; Facility Rental; Family Programs; Guided Tours; Lectures; Publication; School-Based Curriculum

COLLECTIONS: [1830] Period furnishings, examples of Fairfield County and Ohio cabinetmaker's art.

HOURS: Apr-Dec T-Su 1-4

ADMISSION: $2.50, Student $1

6698
Sherman House, The
137 E Main St, 43130 [105 E Wheeling St, 43130]; (p) (740) 687-5891; (f) (740) 654-9890; (c) Fairfield

Private non-profit/ 1982/ staff: 1(f); 3(p); 100(v)/ members: 650/publication: *Fairfield Heritage Quarterly*

HOUSE MUSEUM: Birthplace of General William Tecumseh Sherman original 1811 restored dining room, Charles Sherman's 1816 Study and recreation of General Sherman's field tent.

PROGRAMS: Community Outreach; Exhibits; Facility Rental; Family Programs; Guided

Tours; Lectures; Publication; Reenactments; School-Based Curriculum

COLLECTIONS: [1800-1850] Daily tours, Heritage House tour, Civil War roundtable reception, materials on Civil War.

HOURS: Apr-Dec T-Su 1-4

ADMISSION: $2.50, Student $1

LEBANON

6699
Warren County Historical Society
105 S Broadway, 45036; (p) (513) 932-1817; (f) (513) 932-1817; wchs@compuserve.com; (c) Warren

County, non-profit; Private non-profit/ 1940/ Executive Board/ staff: 1(f); 4(p); 38(v)/ members: 562/publication: *Historica Log*

HISTORICAL SOCIETY; HISTORY MUSEUM; RESEARCH CENTER

PROGRAMS: Annual Meeting; Community Outreach; Exhibits; Family Programs; Festivals; Guided Tours; Lectures; Living History; Publication; Research Library/Archives

COLLECTIONS: [1796-present]

HOURS: Yr T-Su 9-4

ADMISSION: $3, Student $1

LIMA

6700
MacDonell House, The
632 W Market St, 45801 [632 W Market St, 45801]; (p) (419) 224-1113, (419) 222-9426 (ACHS); (f) (419) 222-0649; acmuseum@worc net.oh.us; www.worcnet.gen.oh.us~acmuseum

1893/ Allen County Historical Society/ staff: 1(f); 4(v)

COLLECTIONS: [1890s] Interpretive rooms of 19th c.

HOURS: Yr

LITCHFIELD

6701
Chatham Historical Society
6332 Avon Lake Rd, 44253 [5394 Richman Rd, 44253]; (p) (330) 667-2672; (c) Medina

Private non-profit/ 1994/ staff: 10(v)/ members: 40

HISTORIC PRESERVATION AGENCY; HISTORICAL SOCIETY; HISTORY MUSEUM; HOUSE MUSEUM: Collects, preserves and studies artifacts on township history.

PROGRAMS: Annual Meeting; Exhibits; Guided Tours; Interpretation; Lectures; Research Library/Archives; School-Based Curriculum

COLLECTIONS: [1818-present] Documents, photos, information on township history.

LONDON

6702
Madison County Historical Society Museum
260 E High St, 43140 [Box 124, 43140]; (p) (740) 852-2977; (f) (740) 852-2952; (c) Madison

Private non-profit/ 1960/ Board of Trustees/

staff: 10(v)/ members: 150

HISTORIC PRESERVATION AGENCY; HISTORICAL SOCIETY: Preserves artifacts of Madison County.

PROGRAMS: Annual Meeting; Community Outreach; Exhibits; Family Programs; Festivals; Film/Video; Guided Tours; Interpretation; Lectures; Living History; Reenactments; Research Library/Archives; School-Based Curriculum

COLLECTIONS: [mid 1800s] Nine permanent exhibits in the main building, four buildings on the grounds, train station, caboose, log cabin and two story log house.

HOURS: Mar-Dec W, 1st Sa-Su of every month 1-4:00

ADMISSION: No charge

LORAIN

6703
Black River Historical Society
309 Fifth St, 44052; (p) (440) 245-3563; (c) Lorain

Private non-profit/ 1981/ Board of Trustees/ staff: 30(v)/ members: 200

HISTORIC SITE; HISTORICAL SOCIETY; HISTORY MUSEUM; RESEARCH CENTER: Operates museum.

PROGRAMS: Annual Meeting; Community Outreach; Concerts; Exhibits; Facility Rental; Festivals; Guided Tours; Interpretation; Lectures; Living History; Publication; Research Library/Archives; School-Based Curriculum

COLLECTIONS: [Early 20th c] Artifacts relating to business, industry, and government; clothing; research files; photos of Lorain history.

HOURS: Yr Su, W 1-4, F

LOVELAND

6704
Chateau Laroche
12025 Shore Dr, 45140 [PO Box 135, 45140]; (p) (513) 683-4686

1929/ Knights of the Golden Trail/ staff: 16(v)

A one-fifth scale 16th century medieval castle built by Harry D. Andrews.

COLLECTIONS: Medieval weapons; items of builder's life.

HOURS: Yr

LUCAS

6705
Malabar Farm
4050 Bromfield Rd, 44843; (p) (419) 892-2784; (f) (419) 892-3988; malabar@richnet.net; malabarfarm.org; (c) Richland

State/ 1939/ staff: 9(f); 8(p); 150(v)

GARDEN; HISTORIC SITE; HOUSE MUSEUM; LIVING HISTORY/OUTDOOR MUSEUM: Promotes Louis Bromfield's farming philosophies through demonstration farm.

PROGRAMS: Annual Meeting; Community Outreach; Exhibits; Family Programs; Festivals; Garden Tours; Guided Tours; Interpretation; Living History; Reenactments; Research

Library/Archives; School-Based Curriculum

COLLECTIONS: [1930s-1960s] Belongings of Louis Bromfield, Pulitzer Prize winning author, farmer and conservationist; working farm with crops and livestock.

HOURS: Yr T-Su 10-5

ADMISSION: $3, Children $1

LUCASVILLE

6706
Lucasville Historical Society
North St, 45648 [PO Box 131, 45648]; (p) (740) 259-4777; (c) Scioto

Private non-profit/ 1984/ members: 40

HISTORIC PRESERVATION AGENCY; HISTORICAL SOCIETY: Collects and preserves local history.

PROGRAMS: Annual Meeting; Exhibits; Garden Tours

COLLECTIONS: Books toys, photos, school materials.

ADMISSION: No charge

MADISON

6707
Madison Historical Society
13 W Main St, 44057 [PO Box 91, 44057]; (p) (440) 428-6107; (c) Lake

Private non-profit/ 1978/ Board/ staff: 3(p)/ members: 120

HISTORICAL SOCIETY; HISTORY MUSEUM; HOUSE MUSEUM: Preserves local history.

PROGRAMS: Annual Meeting; Community Outreach; Exhibits; Guided Tours; Lectures; Research Library/Archives; School-Based Curriculum

COLLECTIONS: [1800s-1900] Agricultural implements, clothing from 1800s to 1960, pieces of Victorian furniture, Civil War items, artifacts and books.

HOURS: Apr-Dec W-Sa 11-4

ADMISSION: No charge

MALVERN

6708
Malvern Historical Society
[PO Box 80, 44644]; (p) (330) 863-0372; (c) Carroll

Private non-profit/ 1994/ members: 87/publication: *Malvern Historical Society Newsletter*

HISTORICAL SOCIETY: Promotes local history through newspaper and monthly meetings.

PROGRAMS: Family Programs; Publication

MANSFIELD

6709
Mansfield Fire Museum and Educational Center Inc.
1265 W Fourth St, 44906; (p) (419) 529-2573; (f) (419) 529-6460; (c) Richland

Private non-profit/ 1994/ staff: 3(v)

HISTORY MUSEUM: Preserves history of firefighting.

PROGRAMS: Exhibits; Festivals; Film/Video; Guided Tours

COLLECTIONS: [1850s-present] Firefighting equipment.

HOURS: Yr Jun-Sep Sa-W 1-4; Sep-Jun Sa-Su 1-4

ADMISSION: Donations accepted

MARIETTA

6710
Campus Martius Museum
601 Second St, 45750-2122; (p) (800) 860-0145; (f) (740) 373-3680; Cmmoriv@marietta.edu; www.ohiohistory.org/places/campus; (c) Washington

Private non-profit/ 1929/ Ohio Historical Society/ staff: 4(f); 2(p); 50(v)

HISTORIC SITE; HISTORY MUSEUM: Interpretive center for the history of settlement and migration in Ohio.

PROGRAMS: Annual Meeting; Community Outreach; Exhibits; Facility Rental; Interpretation; Lectures; Research Library/Archives; School-Based Curriculum

COLLECTIONS: [18th c-present] 18th c settlement of Marietta.

HOURS: Mar, Apr, Oct, Nov W-Sa 9:30-5, Su 12-5; May-Sept M-Sa 9:30-5, Su

6711
Castle, The
418 Fourth St, 45750; (p) (740) 373-4180; (f) (740) 373-4233; Castle@marietta.edu; www.marietta.edu/Castle; (c) Washington

Private non-profit/ 1994/ The Betsey Mills Corporation/ staff: 2(f); 5(p); 45(v)/ members: 199/publication: *The Calling Card*

HISTORIC SITE: Preserves and maintains the architectural and historical integrity of the Castle and its grounds.

PROGRAMS: Community Outreach; Concerts; Exhibits; Facility Rental; Family Programs; Garden Tours; Guided Tours; Interpretation; Lectures; Living History; Publication; School-Based Curriculum

COLLECTIONS: Gothic Revival period, community artifacts.

HOURS: Jun-Aug M-F 10-4, Sa-Su 1-4; Apr-May, Sept-Dec M,Th,F 10-4, Sa-Su 1-4

ADMISSION: $4, Student

6712
Local History and Genealogy Department of Washington County Public Library
418 Washington St, 45750-1902; (p) (740) 373-1057; ernie@wcplib.lib.oh.us; www.wcplib.lib.oh; (c) Washington

County/ Board of Trustees/Washington County Public Library/ staff: 2(f); 2(p); 4(v)

LIBRARY AND/OR ARCHIVES: Provides local and family history for Washington County and neighboring areas.

PROGRAMS: Community Outreach; Lectures; Research Library/Archives

COLLECTIONS: [1788-present] Family histories, books.

HOURS: Yr M-Th 9-8:30, F-Sa 9-5; Oct-May
Su 1-5

ADMISSION: No charge

MARION

6713
Marion County Historical Society, The
169 E Church St, 43302; (p) (740) 387-4255;
(f) (740) 387-0117; mchist@gte.net;
home1.gte.net/mchist; (c) Marion

Private non-profit/ 1969/ staff: 1(f); 2(p); 40(v)/
members: 360

HISTORICAL SOCIETY; LIBRARY AND/OR
ARCHIVES: Collects, preserves, and interprets history of Marion County; operates a museum and the Rinker/Hower Resource Center.

PROGRAMS: Annual Meeting; Community
Outreach; Exhibits; Facility Rental; Guided
Tours; Interpretation; Lectures; Publication;
Research Library/Archives; School-Based
Curriculum

COLLECTIONS: [1820-present] Artifacts: local
industries, Warren G. Harding.

HOURS: May-Oct W-Su 1-4 or by appt; Nov-
Apr Sa-Su 1-4 or by appt

ADMISSION: Donations accepted

6714
**President Warren G. Harding Home
and Museum**
380 Mount Vernon Ave, 43302 [380 Mt Vernon
Ave, 43302]; (p) (614) 387-9630, (800) 600-
6894; (f) (614) 387-9630; www.Ohiohistory.com

1891/ Ohio Historical Society

HISTORY MUSEUM; HOUSE MUSEUM

COLLECTIONS: [1890-1920] Harding Family
artifacts; political memorabilia.

HOURS: Mem Day to Labor Day: M-F 9:30am-
5pm

MARTINS FERRY

6715
Martins Ferry Area Historical Society
627 Hanover St, 43935 [PO Box 422, 43935];
(p) (304) 281-8329; (c) Belmont

Joint; Private non-profit/ 1966/ Board of
Trustees/ staff: 10(v)/ members: 150

HISTORIC SITE; HISTORICAL SOCIETY;
HISTORY MUSEUM: Collects, preserves, researches and interprets materials relating to
the history of the Martins Ferry area; involved
in preservation of Walnut Grove cemetery.

PROGRAMS: Annual Meeting; Community
Outreach; Family Programs; Guided Tours;
Publication; Research Library/Archives

COLLECTIONS: [1780s-present] Household
utensils, textiles, manufactured items, historical

MASON

6716
Mason Historical Society Inc.
207 W Church St, 45040 [PO Box 82, 45040];
(p) (513) 398-6750; (c) Warren

Private non-profit/ 1979/ staff: 25(v)/ members:
250/publication: *monthly newsletter*

GENEALOGICAL SOCIETY; HISTORIC SITE;
HISTORICAL SOCIETY; HISTORY MUSEUM;
HOUSE MUSEUM: Provides tours of Victorian
house.

PROGRAMS: Annual Meeting; Exhibits; Family Programs; Festivals; Guided Tours; Lectures; Publication; Research Library/Archives

COLLECTIONS: [1800-early 1900s] Artifacts.

HOURS: Yr Th-F 1-4 and by appt

MASSILLON

6717
Massillon Museum
121 Lincoln Way East, 44646; (p) (330) 833-
4061; (f) (330) 833-2925; (c) Stark

Private non-profit/ 1933/ staff: 5(f); 37(p)/
members: 525

ART MUSEUM; HISTORY MUSEUM

PROGRAMS: Community Outreach; Exhibits;
Facility Rental; Family Programs; Festivals;
Guided Tours

COLLECTIONS: [19th-20th c] 100,000 objects: folk art, historical costumes, glass, pottery, china, photos by Aaron Siskind and Nell
Dorr.

HOURS: Yr T-Sa 9:30-5 Su 2-5

ADMISSION: No charge

6718
Spring Hill Historic Home
1401 Spring Hill Lane, NE, 44646; (p) (330)
833-6749

1821/ Massillon Museum F/ staff: 3(p); 50(v)

COLLECTIONS: [1821] Mercury tube
baromter; glass, ceramics.

HOURS: Jun-Aug

MAUMEE

6719
**Lucas County/Maumee Valley
Historical Society**
1031 River Rd, 43537; (p) (419) 893-9602; (f)
(419) 893-3108; mvhs@accesstoledo.com;
www.maumee.org/wolcott/wolcott.htm; (c) Lucas

Private non-profit/ 1961/ staff: 2(f); 4(p); 50(v)/
members: 300

GARDEN; HISTORIC SITE; HISTORICAL SO-
CIETY; HISTORY MUSEUM; HOUSE MUSE-
UM

PROGRAMS: Annual Meeting; Community
Outreach; Exhibits; Festivals; Garden Tours;
Guided Tours; Interpretation; Lectures; Publi-
cation; Reenactments; Research Library/
Archives; School-Based Curriculum

COLLECTIONS: [19th c] Six historic buildings:
The Wolcott House; Log Home; Salt-box style
farmhouse ; Clover Leaf Railroad Depot and
Caboose and boxcar; Monclova Country
Church; paintings, prints, glass, furniture, cir-
cus memorabilia.

HOURS: Apr-Dec W-Su 1-4

ADMISSION: $3.50, Children $1.50

MCCONNELSVILLE

6720
Morgan County Historical Society
126 E Main St, 43756 [PO Box 524, 43756];
(p) (740) 962-4785; (c) Morgan

County; Private non-profit/ 1970/ staff: 12(v)/
members: 400/publication: *Elk Eye (quarterly)*

HISTORIC PRESERVATION AGENCY; HIS-
TORICAL SOCIETY; HISTORY MUSEUM;
HOUSE MUSEUM; RESEARCH CENTER:
Preserves artifacts and local history.

PROGRAMS: Annual Meeting; Community
Outreach; Exhibits; Family Programs; Guided
Tours; Lectures; Publication; Library/Archives

COLLECTIONS: [1830-1930] McConnelsville
founder's artifacts, literary works of local authors, Howard Chandler Christie art.

HOURS: Yr M-F 1-3, Su 10-12

ADMISSION: Donations accepted

MEDINA

6721
John Smart House
206 N Elmwood St, 44256 [PO Box 306,
44258]; (p) (330) 722-1341

1886/ Medina County Hist/ staff: 2(p); 10(v)

HOUSE MUSEUM: Preserves historic home.

COLLECTIONS: [1890s] Victorian furniture
and clothing; local family history.

HOURS: Mar-Dec

6722
Medina County Historical Society
206 N Elmwood St, 44258 [PO Box 306,
44258-0306]; (p) (330) 722-1341; (c) Medina

Private non-profit/ 1922/ Board of Trustees/
staff: 2(p); 15(v)/ members: 212

HISTORICAL SOCIETY; HISTORY MUSEUM:
Collects and preserves local artifacts.

PROGRAMS: Annual Meeting; Exhibits; Guided Tours; Lectures; Publication

COLLECTIONS: [Late 1800s] Local history artifacts, photos, newspapers, tax information,
Victorian furniture.

HOURS: Mar-Dec T, Th 9:30-5:30, 1st Su of
mo 1-4

MENTOR

6723
**James A. Garfield National Historic
Site**
8095 Mentor Ave, 44060; (p) (440) 255-8722;
(f) (440) 255-8545; (c) Lake

Joint/ 1936/ Western Reserve Historical Soci-
ety/ staff: 3(f); 15(p); 20(v)

HISTORIC SITE; PRESIDENTIAL SITE: Interprets life of 20th US president.

PROGRAMS: Community Outreach; Exhibits;
Facility Rental; Film/Video; Guided Tours; Interpretation; Lectures; School-Based Curriculum

COLLECTIONS: [1880-1885] James A.
Garfield artifacts.

HOURS: Yr M-Sa 10-5, Su 12-5

ADMISSION: $6, Children $4, Seniors $5;
Under 5

MIAMISBURG

6724
Miamisburg Historical Society, The
NW corner of Lock & Old Main streets, 45343
[PO Box 774, 45343-0774]; (c) Montgomery

Private non-profit/ 1967/ Board of Directors/
staff: 40(v)/ members: 200

HISTORICAL SOCIETY: Collects, preserves
and interprets historical artifacts pertaining to
Miamisburg and Miami Township; care and interpretation of Gebhart Tavern.

PROGRAMS: Annual Meeting; Community
Outreach; Exhibits; Family Programs; Guided
Tours; Interpretation; Lectures; Publication;
Research Library/Archives; School-Based
Curriculum

COLLECTIONS: Materials relating to all periods of Miamisburg and Miami Township history.

HOURS: May-Sep Su 2-5 or by appt

ADMISSION: No charge

MIDDLEFIELD

6725
Middlefield Historical Society
14979 S State Ave, 44062 [PO Box 1100,
44062-1100]; (p) (440) 632-0400; (c) Geauga

Private non-profit/ 1983/ Board of Trustees/
staff: 55(v)/ members: 180

HISTORICAL SOCIETY; HOUSE MUSEUM:
Collects, preserves, and disseminates Middlefield history and artifacts.

PROGRAMS: Annual Meeting; Exhibits; Facility Rental; Guided Tours; Research Library/
Archives

COLLECTIONS: [1900s] Furniture, clothing,
textiles, military uniforms, area photos.

HOURS: Railroad Depot T 7pm-9pm and by
appt

ADMISSION: Donations accepted

MILAN

6726
Edison Birthplace Association, Inc.
9 Edison Dr, 44846 [PO Box 451, 44846]; (p)
(419) 499-2135; (f) (419) 499-3241; edison
bp@accnorwalk.com; www.tomedison.org; (c)
Erie

Private non-profit/ 1950/ staff: 2(f); 15(p); 5(v)/
members: 88/publication: *Edison Inspiration to
Youth*

HISTORIC SITE; HOUSE MUSEUM: The association maintains and preserves the birthplace of Thomas Alva Edison, a National Historic Site.

PROGRAMS: Annual Meeting; Interpretation;
Lectures; Publication; School-Based Curriculum

COLLECTIONS: [1850-1880] Family furnishings, Edison memorabilia.

HOURS: Apr, May, Sept, Oct T-Su 1-5; Jun-
Aug T-Sa 10-5, Su

6727
Milan Historical Museum
10 Edison Dr, 44846 [10 Edison Dr, PO Box
308, 44846]; (p) (419) 499-2968; (f) (419)
499-9004; www.milanohio.com; (c) Erie

Private non-profit/ 1955/ Board of Trustees/
staff: 2(f); 16(p); 100(v)/ members: 95/publica-
tion: *The New Milan Ledger*

ART MUSEUM; GARDEN; HISTORIC SITE;
HISTORICAL SOCIETY; HISTORY MUSEUM;
HOUSE MUSEUM; RESEARCH CENTER:
Presents local history.

PROGRAMS: Concerts; Exhibits; Facility
Rental; Family Programs; Festivals; Guided
Tours; Interpretation; Lectures; Living History;
Publication; Reenactments; Research Li-
brary/Archives

COLLECTIONS: [19th c] Artifacts: glass, toys,
Civil War, local canal history, decorative arts,
costumes and accessories; interpretive sites:
General Store, Carriage Shed, Blacksmith
Shop, furnished period homes.

HOURS: Apr-May, Sep-Oct T-Sa 10-5, Su 1-5;
Jun-Aug T-Sa 10-5, Su 1-5; Nov-Dec, Feb-Mar
by appt

ADMISSION: Donations accepted

MINERVA

6728
Minerva Area Historical Society
128 N Market St, 44657 [PO Box 373, 44657-
0373]; (c) Stark

Private non-profit/ 1967/ Board of Trustees/
staff: 4(v)/ members: 200/publication: *Minerva
Historical Newsletter*

ART MUSEUM; GENEALOGICAL SOCIETY;
HISTORIC PRESERVATION AGENCY; HIS-
TORIC SITE; HISTORICAL SOCIETY; HISTO-
RY MUSEUM: Preserves and protects Miner-
va community and area history.

PROGRAMS: Annual Meeting; Community
Outreach; Elder's Programs; Exhibits; Facility
Rental; Family Programs; Film/Video; Guided
Tours; Interpretation; Lectures; Living History;
Publication; Research Library/Archives;
School-Based Curriculum

COLLECTIONS: [1800-1900] Oral and written
local history.

HOURS: Yr W 1-4, and by appt

ADMISSION: Donations accepted

MORELAND HILLS

6729
Moreland Hills Historical Society, The
4350 SOM Center Rd, 44022; (p) (440) 248-
1188, (440) 247-7282; (f) (440) 498-9588;
www.morelandhills.com; (c) Cuyahoga

Private non-profit/ 1980/ staff: 6(v)/ members:
50/publication: *Early Life of James A. Garfield*

HISTORICAL SOCIETY: Collects local history,
genealogy, memorabilia.

PROGRAMS: Annual Meeting; Community
Outreach; Festivals; Guided Tours; Interpretation; Living History; Publication; Research Li-
brary/Archives; School-Based Curriculum

COLLECTIONS: [1830-1850] James Abram
Garfield artifacts; photos, newspapers, cartoons, books, letters, memorabilia, commissioned statue, descriptive plaques.

HOURS: Yr M-F 9-4

ADMISSION: Donations accepted

MT. PLEASANT

6730
**Historical Society of Mount Pleasant,
Ohio Inc.**
Union St, 43939 [Box 35, 43939]; (p) (740)
769-2893; (c) Jefferson

Private non-profit/ 1948/ staff: 30(v)/ members:
200/publication: *The Town Crier*

GENEALOGICAL SOCIETY; HISTORIC
PRESERVATION AGENCY; HISTORIC SITE;
HISTORICAL SOCIETY; HOUSE MUSEUM;
RESEARCH CENTER: Collects, preserves,
and interprets Mt. Pleasant area history.

PROGRAMS: Annual Meeting; Community
Outreach; Exhibits; Facility Rental; Festivals;
Garden Tours; Guided Tours; Interpretation;
Lectures; Publication; Research Library/
Archives; School-Based Curriculum

COLLECTIONS: [1800-1900] Artifacts: Underground rail road, Quakers, textiles, photos,
books, letters, diaries, genealogy, documents,
quilts, furniture.

HOURS: Yr M-Sa 10-5, Su 1-5 by appt

ADMISSION: $7, Student $4; Under 5 free;
group rates

MUNROE FALLS

6731
Munroe Falls Historical Society
83 Munroe Falls Ave, 44262 [43 Munroe Falls
Ave, 44262]; Lown96@aol.com; www.munroe
falls.com; (c) Summit

Private non-profit/ 1976/ Executive Board/
staff: 5(v)/ members: 50/publication: *Olde Heritage*

HISTORICAL SOCIETY; HISTORY MUSEUM:
Collects, preserves, exhibits, and interprets
local history.

PROGRAMS: Annual Meeting; Exhibits; Interpretation; Lectures; Publication; Library/ Archives

COLLECTIONS: [Late 19th c-present] Memorabilia, 1809 river settlement.

HOURS: Feb-June, Sept-Dec 3rd Su of month
2-4 and by appt

ADMISSION: No charge

N. BLOOMFIELD

6732
**Association for Living History, Farm
and Agricultural Museums**
8774 Route 45 NW, 44450; (p) (440) 685-
4410; (f) (440) 685-4410; www.alhfam.org

Private non-profit/ 1970/ staff: 1(p); 2(v)/ members: 1000/publication: *ALHFAM Bulletin, ALH-
FAM Proceedings*

HISTORY MUSEUM: Organization for living
history, farm, and agricultural museums.

PROGRAMS: Annual Meeting; Publication;
Research Library/Archives

NAVARRE

6733
**Navarre-Bethlehem Township
Historical Society**
123 N High St, 44662 [PO Box 291, 44662];
(p) (330) 879-5938; (c) Stark

Private non-profit/ 1972/ staff: 25(v)/ members: 200

HISTORIC PRESERVATION AGENCY; HISTORIC SITE; HISTORICAL SOCIETY; HISTORY MUSEUM; HOUSE MUSEUM; RESEARCH CENTER

PROGRAMS: Annual Meeting; Exhibits; Festivals; Guided Tours; Interpretation; Lectures; Living History; Research Library/Archives; School-Based Curriculum

COLLECTIONS: [1850-present] Local artifacts.

HOURS: May-Nov 1st Su; Meeting: 2nd Su

ADMISSION: No charge

NEW BREMEN

6734
New Bremen Historic Association
122 N Main St, 45869 [PO Box 73, 45869-0073]; (c) Auglaize

Private non-profit/ 1973/ staff: 15(v)/ members: 750/publication: *The Towpath*

HISTORICAL SOCIETY; HISTORY MUSEUM; HOUSE MUSEUM: Collects and preserves history of German-settled area of New Bremen, Lock Two, and German Township.

PROGRAMS: Annual Meeting; Exhibits; Festivals; Publication; Research Library/Archives

COLLECTIONS: [1830s-1900s] New Bremen artifacts, Miami-Erie Canal memorabilia, ice-cutting equipment, clothing, photos, manufactured items, advertising items.

HOURS: Jun-Aug Su 2-4

ADMISSION: Donations

NEW LONDON

6735
New London Area Historical Society
42 E Main, 44851 [c/o VK Neel, 210 E Main St, 44851]; (p) (419) 929-3674; tito@accnorwalk.com; (c) Huron

Private non-profit/ 1985/ staff: 10(v)/ members: 95

HISTORICAL SOCIETY; HISTORY MUSEUM; RESEARCH CENTER: The society preserves and documents history of the community, buildings and families in New London Township and surrounding area.

PROGRAMS: Annual Meeting; Exhibits; Festivals; Guided Tours; Lectures; Research Library/Archives

COLLECTIONS: [1865-1945] 500 artifacts, 200 books, 1,000 photos, local newspapers, police records, genealogical papers.

HOURS: Yr 1st Su 1-4 or by appt.

NEW PHILADELPHIA

6736
Schoenbrunn Village State Memorial
1984 E High Ave, 44663 [PO Box 129, 44663-0129]; (p) (330) 339-3636; (f) (330) 339-4165; schoenbrunn@tusco.net; ohiohistory.org; (c) Tuscarawas

Joint; Private non-profit/ 1923/ Ohio Historical Society/ staff: 2(f); 6(p); 25(v)/publication: *Schoenbrunn: A Meeting of Cultures*

HISTORIC SITE; HISTORICAL SOCIETY; HISTORY MUSEUM; LIVING HISTORY/OUTDOOR MUSEUM: Preserves history of mission to Delaware Native Americans.

PROGRAMS: Exhibits; Family Programs; Guided Tours; Interpretation; Publication; Reenactments

COLLECTIONS: [Late 18th c] Reconstructed village with 17 log structures, field plantings; original cemetery.

HOURS: Apr-May by appt; Jun-Aug M-Sa 9:30-5, Su 12-5; Sep-Oct by appt, Sa 9:30-5, Su 12-5

ADMISSION: $5, Children $1.25

NEW WASHINGTON

6737
New Washington Historical Society, The
106 W Mansfield St, 44854 [Box 463, 44854]; (p) (419) 492-2829; (c) Crawford

Private non-profit/ 1985/ staff: 3(v)/ members: 20

HISTORICAL SOCIETY: Collects and preserves history of New Washington area.

PROGRAMS: Exhibits; Guided Tours; Lectures; School-Based Curriculum

COLLECTIONS: Local industry, agriculture artifacts.

NEWARK

6738
Heisey Collectors of America, Inc., National Heisey Glass Museum
169 W Church St, 43055; (p) (740) 345-2932; (f) (740) 345-9638; heisey@infinet.com; www.ahheisey.com; (c) Licking

Private non-profit/ 1971/ Heisey Collectors of America, Inc./ staff: 2(f); 4(p); 30(v)/ members: 3350/publication: *Heisey News*

HISTORY MUSEUM: History and preservation of Heisey Glassware and the A.H. Heisey Company.

PROGRAMS: Annual Meeting; Community Outreach; Exhibits; Guided Tours; Publication; Research Library/Archives

COLLECTIONS: [1896-1957] Glassware.

HOURS: Yr T-Sa 10-4, Su 1-4

ADMISSION: $2

6739
Institute of Industrial Technology
55 S First St, 43058 [PO Box 721, 43058-0721]; (p) (740) 349-9277; (f) (740) 345-7252; www.iitnewark.org; (c) Licking

Joint; Private non-profit/ 1996/ Board of Trustees/ staff: 1(f); 3(p); 50(v)/ members: 150

HISTORY MUSEUM: Collects and preserves industrial history of Licking County.

PROGRAMS: Community Outreach; Exhibits; Facility Rental; Guided Tours; Publication

COLLECTIONS: [1870-1950] 500 artifacts, 500 photos.

HOURS: Yr T-F 9-4, Sa-Su 12-4

ADMISSION: $4, Children $1, Seniors $3

6740
Sherwood-Davidson House
Veteran's Park, 6th St, 43058 [PO Box 785, 43058]; (p) (740) 345-4898, (740) 345-6525

6741
Webb House Museum, The
303 Granville St, 43055; (p) (740) 345-8540; webbhouse@nextek.net; (c) Licking

Private non-profit/ 1978/ Board of Trustees/ staff: 4(p); 3(v)

HOUSE MUSEUM: Depicts life in the 1920s.

PROGRAMS: Exhibits; Family Programs; Garden Tours; Guided Tours

COLLECTIONS: [early 20th c] Local artifacts, art.

HOURS: Apr-Dec Th-F, Su 1-4 or by appt

ADMISSION: No charge

NILES

6742
McKinley Memorial Library and Museum
40 N Main St, 44446; (p) (330) 652-1704; (f) (330) 652-5788; mckinley@oplin.liboh.us; www.mckinley.liboh.us; (c) Trumbull

Joint/ 1917/ staff: 17(f); 3(p)

HISTORY MUSEUM; PRESIDENTIAL SITE: Preserves and promotes history of William McKinley.

COLLECTIONS: [late 19th c] Political campaign buttons, McKinley artifacts.

HOURS: Yr Jun-Aug M-Th 9-8:30, F-Sa 9-5:30; Sep-May Su 1-5

6743
Niles Historical Society
503 Brown St, 44446 [PO Box 368, 44446]; (p) (330) 544-2143; (c) Trumbull

Private non-profit/ 1979/ staff: 20(v)/ members: 205

GARDEN; HISTORIC PRESERVATION AGENCY; HISTORIC SITE; HISTORICAL SOCIETY; HOUSE MUSEUM

PROGRAMS: Annual Meeting; Community Outreach; Exhibits; Family Programs; Festivals; Film/Video; Garden Tours; Lectures; Research Library/Archives

COLLECTIONS: [1774-present] Documents, books, clothing, artifacts, publications.

HOURS: Yr 1st Su 2-5 and by appt

ADMISSION: Donations

NORTH CANTON

6744
Hoover Historical Center
Inside Hoover Park, 44720 [1875 Easton St, 44720-3331]; (p) (330) 499-0287; (f) (330) 494-4725; (c) Stark

1978/ The Hoover Company/ staff: 2(f); 13(p); 110(v)

GARDEN; HISTORIC SITE; HISTORY MUSEUM; HOUSE MUSEUM: Preserves history of Hoover Company; located in the boyhood home of company founder, William H. Hoover.

PROGRAMS: Exhibits; Family Programs; Garden Tours; Guided Tours; Research Library/Archives

COLLECTIONS: [1850-present] Manual and electric vacuum cleaners.

HOURS: Yr T-Su 1-4

ADMISSION: No charge

NORTHFIELD

6745
Palmer House Museum, The
Olde 8 Rd, 44067 [PO Box 99, 44067]

1840/ Historical Society of Olde Northfield/ staff: 4(v)

COLLECTIONS: [1840s] Farm implements, books, pictures, household items, furniture.

HOURS: Yr

NORWICH

6746
National Road Zane Grey Museum
8850 E Pike, 43767; (p) (740) 872-3143; (f) (740) 872-3510; zanegrey@globalco.net; ohiohistory.org; (c) Muskingum

Private non-profit/ 1973/ Ohio Historical Society/ staff: 2(f); 3(p)

HISTORY MUSEUM: Site of the Ohio Historical Society and features three subject areas: the National Road, author Zane Grey, and Zanesville art pottery.

PROGRAMS: Exhibits; Family Programs; Festivals; Film/Video; Guided Tours; Interpretation; Lectures; School-Based Curriculum

COLLECTIONS: [1800-1940] National Road/US 40 era horsedrawn and motorized vehicles, Zane Grey related artifacts and Zanesville art pottery.

OBERLIN

6747
Oberlin Historical and Improvement Organization
Oberlin Heritage Center 73 1/2 S Professor St, 44074 [PO Box 0455, 44074]; (p) (440) 774-1700; (f) (440) 774-1502; history@oberlin.edu; www.oberlin.edu/EOG; (c) Lorain

Private non-profit/ 1903/ Board of Trustees/ staff: 2(f); 4(p); 200(v)/ members: 685/publication: The Gazette

HISTORIC PRESERVATION AGENCY; HISTORIC SITE; HISTORICAL SOCIETY; HISTORY MUSEUM; HOUSE MUSEUM: Preserves and shares Oberlin's heritage.

PROGRAMS: Annual Meeting; Community Outreach; Concerts; Exhibits; Family Programs; Festivals; Guided Tours; Interpretation; Lectures; Living History; Publication; Research Library/Archives; School-Based Curriculum

COLLECTIONS: [1833-1930] Period-furnished historic structures: Monroe House, Jewett House and Barn, School House.

HOURS: Yr T,Th, Sa 10:30-1:30

ADMISSION: $4

OREGON

6748
Oregon-Jerusalem Historical Society
1133 Grasser, 43616 [Box 167632, 43616-7632]; (p) (419) 666-9597; (f) (419) 691-7561; ojhs@juno.com; (c) Lucas

Private non-profit/ 1963/ Board of Trustees/ staff: 20(v)/ members: 125

HISTORICAL SOCIETY: Preserves local and rural history of the Oregon and Jerusalem area.

PROGRAMS: Community Outreach; Elder's Programs; Exhibits; Facility Rental; Festivals; Guided Tours; School-Based Curriculum

COLLECTIONS: [1863-present] Housed in an 1886 two-story brick schoolhouse listed on the National Register of Historic Places, displays of rural, educational and Civil War items.

HOURS: Yr Th, 1st Su

OXFORD

6749
Oxford Museum Association
3 locations, all just outside of Oxford, 45056 [PO Box 184, 45056]; (p) (513) 523-8005; cliohtd@aol.com; www.muohio.edu/oma; (c) Butler

Private non-profit/ 1959/ Board of Trustees/ staff: 90(v)/ members: 200/publication: Historical Perspective

GARDEN; HISTORIC PRESERVATION AGENCY; HISTORIC SITE; HISTORY MUSEUM; HOUSE MUSEUM: A museum association in three locations: Pioneer Farm Museum 1834; Black Covered Bridge 1876; DeWitt Log House 1804.

PROGRAMS: Annual Meeting; Community Outreach; Exhibits; Facility Rental; Family Programs; Festivals; Film/Video; Garden Tours; Guided Tours; Interpretation; Lectures; Publication

HOURS: Yr May-Aug M-F 12-4; or by appt yr round

ADMISSION: $1

6750
Smith Library of Regional History
15 S College Ave, 45056; (p) (513) 523-3035; (f) (513) 523-6661; elliotva@oplin.lib.oh.us; (c) Butler

1981/ Lane Public Library/ staff: 3(p); 4(v)/publication: Oxford and Miami University During World War II

LIBRARY AND/OR ARCHIVES: Collects, preserves, and disseminates information on the history of Oxford, Butler County, southwestern Ohio and nearby IN counties.

PROGRAMS: Community Outreach; Exhibits; Lectures; Publication; Research Library/ Archives

COLLECTIONS: [19th and early 20th c] Books, magazines, newspapers, wills, deeds, photos, archives, manuscripts, census, birth, death and marriage records.

HOURS: Yr M W F 10-12/1-5, Th 10-12/1-5/6-9, Sa 10-1

ADMISSION: No charge

6751
William Holmes McGuffey Museum
410 E Spring St, 45056; (p) (513) 529-2232; (f) (513) 529-6555; ellisocw@muohio.edu; www.muohio.edu/artmuseum; (c) Butler

State/ 1960/ Miami Univ/ staff: 2(f); 20(v)

HOUSE MUSEUM: National Historic Landmark, preserves history of William Holmes McGuffey and the McGuffey Eclectic Readers.

PROGRAMS: Guided Tours; Interpretation

COLLECTIONS: [1836-1900] Artifacts, library furniture.

ADMISSION: No charge

PARMA

6752
Parma Area Historical Association
6975 Ridge Rd, 44129 [PO Box 29002, 44129]; (p) (440) 884-8396; community.cleveland.com//cc/pahs; (c) Cuyahoga

City; Joint/ 1972/ City of Parma/ staff: 1(p); 12(v)/ members: 500

HISTORICAL SOCIETY; HOUSE MUSEUM; LIVING HISTORY/OUTDOOR MUSEUM: Operates Stearns Homestead, Parma's Historical Farm.

PROGRAMS: Annual Meeting; Exhibits; Facility Rental; Family Programs; Festivals; Guided Tours; Interpretation; Living History; Publication

COLLECTIONS: [1848 Stearns House, 1921-1973 Gibbs House] Donated household and farm items.

HOURS: Museum: May-Oct Sa-Su; Park: Yr Daily

ADMISSION: No charge

PAULDING

6753
John Paulding Historical Society, Inc.
600 Fairground Dr, 45879 [200 N Williams St, 45879]; (p) (419) 399-8218; (c) Paulding

Private non-profit/ 1978/ staff: 40(v)/ members: 400/publication: Atlas and newsletter

HISTORICAL SOCIETY; HISTORY MUSEUM: Depicts Paulding County agricultural community.

PROGRAMS: Annual Meeting; Community Outreach; Elder's Programs; Exhibits; Family Programs; Guided Tours; Lectures; Publication

COLLECTIONS: [1900-1945] Artifacts, including WWII.

HOURS: Yr Jan-Dec T10-4 and by appt

ADMISSION: No charge

PENINSULA

6754
Peninsula Library and Historical Society/Cuyayoga Valley Historical Museum
6105 Riverview Rd, 44264 [PO Box 236, 44264-0236]; (p) (330) 657-2665; (f) (330) 657-2311; Kim.Lyon@peninsula.Lib.oh.us; www.peninsula.Lib.oh.us/; (c) Summit

Joint/ 1943/ Board of Trustees/ staff: 6(f); 5(p); 20(v)/publication: Peninsula Library Newsletter; Architectural tour of Peninsula Village

HISTORICAL SOCIETY; HISTORY MUSEUM: Preserves communities of Peninsula, Boston Heights and Boston Township history.

PROGRAMS: Exhibits; Family Programs; Festivals; Lectures; Publication; Research Library/Archives

COLLECTIONS: Photos, maps, books, manuscripts, oral histories, clippings.

HOURS: Yr M-Th 9-8, F-Sa 9-5, Sun 12-5

ADMISSION: No charge

PERRY

6755
Perry Historical Society of Lake County

3885 Main St, 44081 [PO Box 216, 44081];
(p) (440) 259-2061; malonesd@aol.com; (c)
Lake

Private non-profit/ 1992/ Trustees/ staff: 40(v)/
members: 88/publication: *Perry Heritage
(newsletter)*

GENEALOGICAL SOCIETY; HISTORIC SITE;
HISTORICAL SOCIETY; HISTORY MUSEUM;
RESEARCH CENTER: Maintains museum
with a genealogy department.

PROGRAMS: Community Outreach; Exhibits;
Living History; Publication; Research Li-
brary/Archives; School-Based Curriculum

COLLECTIONS: [18th c-present] Artifacts,
photos, prints, audio-video, research material.

HOURS: Apr-Nov 2nd Sa 12-4 and by appt.

PICKERINGTON

6756
Motorcycle Hall of Fame Museum

13515 Yarmouth Dr, 43147; (p) (614) 856-
2222; (f) (614) 856-1921; info@motorcycle
museum.org; www.motorcyclemuseum; (c)
Fairfield

Private non-profit/ 1982/ American Motorcycle
Heritage Foundation/ staff: 4(f); 1(p); 15(v)

HISTORIC PRESERVATION AGENCY; HIS-
TORY MUSEUM: Preserves and presents the
history of motorcycling.

PROGRAMS: Exhibits; Facility Rental; Interpretation

COLLECTIONS: [20th c] Motorcycling industry
archives, photos, periodicals, memorabilia,
and machines.

HOURS: Daily

6757
Pickerington-Violet Township Historical Society

Corner Cols St & Lockville Rd, 43147 [PO
Box 80, 43147]; (c) Fairfield

Private non-profit/ 1987/ staff: 15(v)/ members:
104

HISTORIC PRESERVATION AGENCY; HIS-
TORIC SITE; HISTORICAL SOCIETY; HISTO-
RY MUSEUM

PROGRAMS: Annual Meeting; Exhibits;
Film/Video; Guided Tours; Lectures

COLLECTIONS: [1890-present] Local artifacts.

HOURS: Feb-Dec Sa 10-3

ADMISSION: No charge

PIQUA

6758
Piqua Historical Area State Memorial

9845 N Hardin Rd, 45356; (p) (937) 773-
2522; (f) (937) 773-4311; (c) Miami

Private non-profit/ 1972/ Ohio Historical Soci-
ety/ staff: 3(f); 9(p); 60(v)

HISTORIC SITE; LIVING HISTORY/OUT-
DOOR MUSEUM

PROGRAMS: Exhibits; Guided Tours; Interpretation; Lectures; Living History; Reenactments;
School-Based Curriculum

COLLECTIONS: [1808-1860] Agricultural,
Frontier Life, Native American, Canal. Structures: John Johnston Home, Johnston Springhouse, Cider House.

HOURS: May-Sept W-Sa 9:30-5, Su 12-5;
Sept-Oct Sa 9:30-5, Su 12-5

ADMISSION: $5, Children $1.25

6759
Flesh Public Library/Piqua Historical Museum Local History Department

509 N Main St, 45356 [124 W Greene St,
45356]; (p) (937) 773-6753; (f) (937) 773-
5981; crona@oplin.lib.oh.us; (c) Miami

City/ Piqua City Schools/ staff: 1(f); 2(p); 12(v)

HISTORY MUSEUM: Collects and interprets
local history.

PROGRAMS: Exhibits; Festivals; Guided
Tours; Interpretation; Research Library/
Archives; School-Based Curriculum

COLLECTIONS: [1840-present] Local industry, architecture, city development, and genealogical resources.

HOURS: Local Hist Dept Jan-Dec M-Th 9-8:30,
F-Sa 9-5:30; Museum: Apr-Oct T, Th-Sa 1-4

ADMISSION: No charge

PLYMOUTH

6760
Plymouth Heritage Center

7 E Main St, 44865; (p) (419) 687-5400;
SilverKing@willard-oh.com; (c) Richland

Private non-profit/ 1984/ staff: 1(f); 1(p); 6(v)/
members: 230/publication: *The Heritage Voice*

HISTORY MUSEUM: Collects and preserves
history relating to the village of Plymouth, and
Huron, Richland, and Crawford counties.

PROGRAMS: Annual Meeting; Exhibits; Facility Rental; Festivals; Guided Tours; Publication

COLLECTIONS: Fate, Root, Heath Co, Silver
King tractor.

HOURS: Apr-May, Sep-Dec W-F 8-5 ; Jun-Aug
M-Su 8-5

POLAND

6761
Poland Township Historical Society

Poland Center Rd, 44514 [2894 Algonquin
Dr, 44514]; (p) (330) 757-2613; (c) Mahoning

Private non-profit/ 1979/ staff: 50(v)/ members:
138

HISTORIC SITE; HISTORICAL SOCIETY:
Preserves local historic sites.

PROGRAMS: Annual Meeting; Community Outreach; Facility Rental; Guided Tours; Lectures

COLLECTIONS: Historical books, educational
materials and pictures.

HOURS: Yr

PORT WASHINGTON

6762
Port Washington-Salem Historical Society

109 E Main St PO Box 12, 43837; (p) (740)
498-8597; (c) Tuscarawas

1978/ staff: 8(v)/ members: 12/publication: *Old
Port Washington Road*

HISTORICAL SOCIETY; HISTORY MUSEUM:
Maintains Union Hall; promotes interest in
local history.

PROGRAMS: Exhibits; Family Programs; Publication

COLLECTIONS: [late 1800s-early 1900s]
Union Hall (National Register).

HOURS: Yr July-Oct last Su of month 2-4 or by
appt

ADMISSION: Donations accepted

PORTSMOUTH

6763
Scioto County Historical Society

1926 Waller, 45662 [Box 1810, 45662]; (p)
(740) 354-2369; (c) Scioto

Private non-profit/ 1947/ Board of Trustees/
staff: 32(v)/ members: 250

HOUSE MUSEUM: Maintains historic house.

PROGRAMS: Annual Meeting; Exhibits; Guided
Tours; Publication; School-Based Curriculum

COLLECTIONS: [1810-1946] Clothes, house
furnishings, and 500 dolls.

HOURS: May-Dec Sa-Su 2-4 and by appt.

PUT-IN-BAY

6764
Lake Erie Islands Historical Society

441 Catawba Ave, 43456 [PO Box 25,
43456]; (p) (419) 285-2804; (f) (419) 285-
3814; www.leihs.org; (c) Ottawa

Private non-profit/ 1985/ Board of Directors/
staff: 1(f); 3(p); 30(v)/ members: 385/publica-
tion: *newsletter*

HISTORICAL SOCIETY: Promotes local history.

PROGRAMS: Annual Meeting; Community
Outreach; Concerts; Facility Rental; Lectures;
Research Library/Archives; School-Based
Curriculum

COLLECTIONS: [1840-present] Great Lakes
Transportation, Battle of Lake Erie, Ford Tri-
motor, boating, historic plaques, oral history; 3
historic buildings.

HOURS: May-Oct M-Su 10-6

RAVENNA

6765
Portage County Historical Society

6549-51 N Chestnut St, 44266; (p) (330) 296-
3523; www/2clearlight.com/~pchs; (c) Portage
County; Private non-profit/ 1953/ staff: 23(v)/
members: 299

HISTORICAL SOCIETY; HISTORY MUSEUM;
HOUSE MUSEUM; LIVING HISTORY/OUT-
DOOR MUSEUM: Collects, preserves, and
displays Portage County history.

PROGRAMS: Annual Meeting; Community Outreach; Concerts; Exhibits; Facility Rental; Family Programs; Festivals; Film/Video; Garden Tours; Guided Tours; Interpretation; Lectures; Living History; Reenactments; Research Library/Archives; School-Based Curriculum

COLLECTIONS: Artifacts, letters, paintings.

HOURS: Yr Th-F Su 2-4

ADMISSION: Donations accepted

READING

6766
Reading Historical Society
22 W Benson St, 45215; (p) (513) 761-8535; (c) Hamilton

Private non-profit/ 1988/ staff: 12(v)/ members: 150/publication: *Bridging Time*

HISTORICAL SOCIETY; HISTORY MUSEUM; HOUSE MUSEUM: Collects, preserves, studies, exhibits and interprets records and artifacts related to Reading and surrounding areas.

PROGRAMS: Annual Meeting; Community Outreach; Exhibits; Lectures; Publication; Research Library/Archives

COLLECTIONS: [mid 1800s-present] Photographs, local history books, newspapers, military and band uniforms, early 1900s sheet music, paintings, drawings, local historic building sketches, political memorabilia.

RICHFIELD

6767
Richfield Historical Society
3907 Broadview Rd, 44286 [PO Box 215, 44286]; (p) (330) 659-6649; (c) Summit

Private non-profit/ 1950/ Board of Trustees/ staff: 20(v)/ members: 70

HISTORICAL SOCIETY; HISTORY MUSEUM: Collects, preserves and exhibits the community's past.

PROGRAMS: Annual Meeting; Community Outreach; Exhibits; Interpretation; Lectures; Publication; Research Library/Archives

COLLECTIONS: [1800s-present] Clothes, furniture, kitchen items, books, genealogy, tools, quilts, school items, postcards and photos.

RIPLEY

6768
Rankin House State Memorial
Rawkin Hill, 45167 [PO Box 176, 45167]; (p) (937) 392-1627

1828/ Ohio Historical Society/ staff: 1(p)

COLLECTIONS: [Abolitionist pre Civil War era] Rankin family items, furniture, abolitionists.

HOURS: Vary

6769
Ripley Museum
219 N 2nd St, 45167 [PO Box 176, 45167]; (p) (937) 392-4660

1837/ Ripley Heritage, Inc. / staff: 1(p)

COLLECTIONS: [1820-1930] 1883 Valley Gem Piano; Civil War era furniture; Toys (1800-1950); Clothing (1800-1950); 1891 Fire Engine hose carts; 1890 Funeral Wagon; WWI, WWII clothing/memorabilia; Turn-of-century kitchen; 1880-1980 newspapers; Civil War soldier's letters; Local cemetery records; Local History books; Local flood histories dating back to the 1800's.

HOURS: Seasonal

ROCKFORD

6770
Shanes Crossing Historical Society
[PO Box 92, 45882-0092]; (p) (419) 363-2998; www.bright.net/~noimvt; (c) Mercer

Private non-profit/ 1995/ members: 130/publication: *Shanes Crossing Chronicle*

HISTORICAL SOCIETY: Preserves and displays historical items.

PROGRAMS: Exhibits; Publication

COLLECTIONS: Pictures, tools, signs, articles.

SANDUSKY

6771
Eleutheros Cooke House and Garden
1415 Columbus Ave, 44870 [PO Box 1464, 44870]; (p) (419) 627-0640

1844/ Ohio Historical Society, owners/ staff: 2(p); 59(v)

COLLECTIONS: [1950s] Glassware, paintings, furniture; Sandusky books and slides.

HOURS: Yr

6772
Erie County Historical Society
[PO Box 944, 44871-0944]; (p) (419) 625-4341; (c) Erie

Private non-profit/ 1953/ members: 87

HISTORICAL SOCIETY; HOUSE MUSEUM: Sponsors local history exhibits; erects county historic markers.

PROGRAMS: Annual Meeting; Community Outreach; Concerts; Exhibits; Facility Rental; Family Programs; Festivals; Garden Tours; Guided Tours; Interpretation; Lectures; Living History; Publication; Reenactments; Research Library/Archives; School-Based Curriculum

6774
Merry Go Round Museum Inc.
301 Jackson, 44870 [PO Box 718, 44870]; (p) (419) 626-6111; (f) (419) 626-1297; merrygor@aol.com; www.carousel.net; (c) Erie

Private non-profit/ 1990/ staff: 3(f); 3(p); 100(v)/ members: 200/publication: *Stargazer*

HISTORY MUSEUM: Preserves, promotes and protects the history of the carousel; housed in former US Post Office.

PROGRAMS: Community Outreach; Exhibits; Facility Rental; Family Programs; Guided Tours; Interpretation; Publication; School-Based Curriculum

COLLECTIONS: [1880s-1940s] Carousel artifacts, photos, ephemera.

HOURS: Yr M-Sa 11-5 Su 12-5

ADMISSION: $4, Children $2, Seniors $3

6775
Old House Guild, The
1415 Columbus Ave, 44870 [1215 Columbus Ave/ PO Box 1464, 44870]; (p) (419) 627-0640; (c) Erie

Private non-profit/ 1978/ staff: 75(v)/ members: 350

PROFESSIONAL ORGANIZATION: Advises and educates on issues of historic preservation and Sandusky's architecture; operates Eleutheros Cooke House and Garden for the Ohio Historical Society.

PROGRAMS: Annual Meeting; Guided Tours; Lectures; Publication

COLLECTIONS: [18th c-1950s] Cranberry, ruby glass and porcelain figurines.

HOURS: Yr T-Sa 10-3 Su 12-3

6776
Sandusky Library Follett House Museum
404 Wayne St, 44870 [114 W Adams St, 44870]; (p) (419) 625-3834; (f) (419) 625-4574; comments@sandusky.lib.oh.us; www.sandusky.lib.oh.us; (c) Erie

1902/ staff: 2(f); 3(p); 6(v)/publication: *At Home in Early Sandusky, and more.*

LIBRARY AND/OR ARCHIVES: Preserves archives and local history.

PROGRAMS: Community Outreach; Exhibits; Guided Tours; Publication

COLLECTIONS: [1830-1940] Household objects, furniture, toys, artifacts of Sandusky, Erie County and Johnson's Island Civil War Confederate Officer's Prison.

HOURS: Jun-Aug 12-4; Apr-May, Sep-Dec Sa-Su 12-4

ADMISSION: Donations accepted

SAVANNAH

6777
Clear Creek Township Historical Society
6 Chambers St, 44874 [13 S Main, PO Box 75, 44874]; (p) (419) 962-4494; (c) Ashland

1993/ staff: 25(v)/ members: 150

HISTORICAL SOCIETY; HOUSE MUSEUM: Collects and preserves history of Clear Creek Township.

PROGRAMS: Exhibits

COLLECTIONS: [early 1800s-present] Pictures, school memorabilia, clothing, paper documents, military items, railroad and business memorabilia.

SEBRING

6778
Sebring Historical Society
126 N 15th St, 44672 [PO Box 127, 44672]; (c) Mahoning

1989/ Board of Directors/ members: 120

HISTORICAL SOCIETY: Preserves local history.

PROGRAMS: Annual Meeting; Community Outreach; Exhibits

COLLECTIONS: [1900-present] Pottery, movie posters, and theatre equipment.

HOURS: Yr by appt

SEVILLE

6779
Seville Historical Society
70 W Main St, 44273 [PO Box 312, 44273]; (c) Medina

1983/ Executive Board/ staff: 2(p); 8(v)/ members: 90

HISTORIC PRESERVATION AGENCY; HISTORIC SITE; HISTORICAL SOCIETY; HISTORY MUSEUM; HOUSE MUSEUM: Promotes local history.

PROGRAMS: Annual Meeting; Community Outreach; Elder's Programs; Exhibits; Family Programs; Festivals; Guided Tours; Publication; Research Library/Archives; School-Based Curriculum

COLLECTIONS: Items pertaining to local area. Structures: Museum/House, Summer Kitchen, Jail (National Register).

HOURS: Mar-Dec 1st Su 12-5

ADMISSION: Donations accepted

SHAKER HEIGHTS

6780
Shaker Historical Society and Museum
16740 S Park Boulevard, 44120; (p) (216) 921-1201; (f) (216) 921-2615; shakhist@ wviz.org; shakhist/shaker.htm; (c) Cuyahoga

Private non-profit/ 1947/ Executive Board/ staff: 1(f); 3(p); 150(v)/ members: 500/publication: *Hands on the Past, Celebrating the First 50 Years*

HISTORICAL SOCIETY; HISTORY MUSEUM; HOUSE MUSEUM: Promotes and preserves house museum on former Shaker lands.

PROGRAMS: Annual Meeting; Community Outreach; Elder's Programs; Exhibits; Facility Rental; Family Programs; Festivals; Guided Tours; Lectures; Living History; Publication; School-Based Curriculum

COLLECTIONS: [1860s-1930s] Shaker artifacts and furniture, architectural archives, Van Sweringen Brothers, North Union Shakers, the Manx settlers and the Warrens.

HOURS: Yr T-F, Su 2-5

ADMISSION: No charge; Group rates

SHARON CENTER

6781
Sharon Township Heritage Society
Sharon Center, 44274 [PO Box 154, 44274]; (p) (330) 336-3832; (c) Medina

Private non-profit/ 1968/ Board of Trustees/ members: 35

HISTORICAL SOCIETY: Promotes local history.

COLLECTIONS: Items related to Sharon Township.

SHARONVILLE

6782
Society of Historic Sharonville
Creek & Main Sts, 45241 [10900 Reading Rd, 45241]; (p) (513) 563-9756; www2.ci. sharonville/his_sh/historic.htm; (c) Hamilton

Joint; Private non-profit/ 1988/ staff: 1(p); 7(v)/ members: 90

HISTORICAL SOCIETY; HISTORY MUSEUM: Collects and preserves information and memorabilia pertaining to Sharonville; restores three pioneer cemeteries.

PROGRAMS: Community Outreach; Exhibits; Family Programs; Guided Tours; Interpretation; Publication; Research Library/Archives

COLLECTIONS: [1788-present] Family histories, railroad, artifacts, ephemera.

HOURS: Yr 1st Su 1-4

ADMISSION: No charge

SIDNEY

6783
Shelby County Historical Society
201 N Main Ave, 45365 [PO Box 376, 45365]; (p) (937) 498-1653; www.bright.net/~richnsus; (c) Shelby

County/ 1946/ staff: 1(p); 30(v)/ members: 500/publication: *Historical Highlights (newsletter)*

HISTORICAL SOCIETY; HISTORY MUSEUM; RESEARCH CENTER: Preserves historical resources in Shelby County.

PROGRAMS: Annual Meeting; Community Outreach; Exhibits; Family Programs; Festivals; Interpretation; Lectures; Living History; Publication; Research Library/Archives; School-Based Curriculum

COLLECTIONS: [1800-present] Artifacts of industry, business and family life.

HOURS: Yr

SMITHFIELD

6784
Smithfield Historical Society, Inc.
Box 32 1313 Main St, 43948; (p) (740) 733-7800; (c) Jefferson

Private non-profit/ 1974/ members: 75

HISTORIC SITE; HISTORICAL SOCIETY; HISTORY MUSEUM: Preserves and collects history of local area.

PROGRAMS: Annual Meeting; Community Outreach; Exhibits; Festivals; Reenactments

COLLECTIONS: [late 1800s] Hat made in Smithfield, Carbide lamp shades, village roll top desk, quilting frame, books and pictures.

HOURS: May, Sep, Nov, Dec T, Th-Su 10-9

ADMISSION: No charge

SOLON

6785
Solon Historical Society
33975 Bainbridge Rd, 44139; (p) (440) 248-6419; (c) Cuyahoga

1968/ staff: 12(v)/publication: *Pictorial History of Solon, Ohio*

HISTORIC PRESERVATION AGENCY; HISTORIC SITE; HISTORICAL SOCIETY: Preserves and disseminates knowledge about Solon and vicinity.

PROGRAMS: Annual Meeting; Community Outreach; Exhibits; Family Programs; Festivals; Guided Tours; Publication; School-Based Curriculum

COLLECTIONS: [1860-1950] Early Solon life and industry.

HOURS: Yr 2nd W

ST. MARYS

6786
Auglaize County Historical Society
223 S Main St, 45885; (p) (419) 394-7069; (c) Auglaize

County/ 1963/ Board of Trustees/ staff: 15(v)/ members: 150/publication: *County Atlas*

HISTORICAL SOCIETY: Operates two museums and historic site.

PROGRAMS: Annual Meeting; Exhibits; Guided Tours; Publication

COLLECTIONS: [1700s-present] Native American artifacts; Fort St. Mary's (1795), Ft. Amanda, Ft. Barbee (1812), and Civil War artifacts; Miami-Erie Canal, oil well, industry, and kitchen artifacts; photos.

HOURS: Yr 1st and 3rd Su 1-3

ADMISSION: $1

STEUBENVILLE

6787
Jefferson County Chapter, Ohio Genealogical Society
[PO Box 4712, 43952-8712]; fkrutill@weir.net; www.rootsweb.com/~ohjefogs

Private non-profit/ 19870/ staff: 5(v)/ members: 240/publication: *Jefferson County Lines Newsletter*

GENEALOGICAL SOCIETY: Preserves genealogical records.

PROGRAMS: Lectures; Publication; Research Library/Archives

COLLECTIONS: [1790s-present] Historical and genealogical records of Jefferson County.

HOURS: Yr T-F 10-3

ADMISSION: Donations accepted

STRONGSVILLE

6788
Strongsville Historical Society
13305 Pearl Rd, 44136; (p) (440) 572-0057; www.strongsville.ohio.com; (c) Cuyahoga

Private non-profit/ 1962/ staff: 25(v)/ members: 300

GENEALOGICAL SOCIETY; HISTORIC PRESERVATION AGENCY; HISTORICAL SOCIETY; HISTORY MUSEUM: Collects, preserves, records and interprets the local history.

PROGRAMS: Annual Meeting; Exhibits; Facility Rental; Family Programs; Festivals; Guided Tours; Research Library/Archives

COLLECTIONS: [1816-1940] 600 hats from 1850s-1970s, Pioneer farm tool collection, Doll collection, Chapman paintings, memorabilia, old quilts and antique clothing. Structures: Roe-Chapman House, Baldwin House.

HOURS: May-Oct W-Su 1-4

ADMISSION: $3, Children $1

STRUTHERS

6789
Struthers Historical Society and Museum
50 Terrace St, 44471; (p) (330) 750-1766; (c) Mahoning

1986/ staff: 20(v)/ members: 100

HISTORICAL SOCIETY; HOUSE MUSEUM: Preserves history of Struthers.

PROGRAMS: Exhibits; Guided Tours; Research Library/Archives

COLLECTIONS: [1928-present] Journal newspapers; artifacts from the Hopewell Furnace;furniture, clothing, books from Frankfort family; Paul Jenkins.

HOURS: Yr 1st Su 2-4 and by appt

ADMISSION: No charge

TALLMADGE

6790
Tallmadge Historical Society
Center Park, 44278 [PO Box 25, 44278-0025]; (p) (330) 630-9760; (c) Summit

Private non-profit/ 1858/ staff: 2(p); 50(v)/ members: 375/publication: *A History of Tallmadge, About Old Tallmadge*

GENEALOGICAL SOCIETY; HISTORIC PRESERVATION AGENCY; HISTORIC SITE; HISTORICAL SOCIETY; HISTORY MUSEUM: Provides schools and researchers with archives; maintains local history museum.

PROGRAMS: Annual Meeting; Exhibits; Facility Rental; Family Programs; Festivals; Film/Video; Guided Tours; Lectures; School-Based Curriculum

COLLECTIONS: [1807-1930] Tallmadge families archives, books. Structures: Olde Town Hall.

HOURS: Yr by appt

ADMISSION: No charge

TIFFIN

6791
Seneca County Museum
28 Clay St, 44883; (p) (419) 447-5955; (f) (419) 443-7940; (c) Seneca

County/ 1942/ staff: 1(f); 2(p); 15(v)

COLLECTIONS: [1850-1900] 16 rooms of historical items pertaining to Seneca County, Tiffin Glass Collection, fire equipment and tools.

HOURS: Yr Jan-May, Sep-Dec S-Su 2-5; Jun-Aug Th-Su 2-5

ADMISSION: No charge

TOLEDO

6792
Oliver House
27 Broadway St, 43602; (p) (419) 243-1302; (f) (410) 243-9256

6793
Toledo-Lucas County Public Library/ Local History and Genealogy Department
325 N Michigan St, 43624; (p) (419) 259-5233; (f) (419) 255-1334; www.library.toledo.oh.us; (c) Lucas

County/ 1940/ staff: 8(f); 4(p)

GENEALOGICAL SOCIETY; LIBRARY AND/ OR ARCHIVES

COLLECTIONS: Books, manuscripts, photographs, oral histories and maps.

HOURS: Yr Jan-Dec M-Th 9-9 F-Sa 9-5:30 Su 12:30-5:30

ADMISSION: No charge

6794
Ward M. Canaday Center, The University of Toledo
5th Fl, Carlson Library, The Univ of Toledo, 43606 [2801 W Bancroft, 43606]; (p) (419) 530-2170; (f) (419) 530-2726; barbara.floyd@utoledo.edu; (c) Lucas

State/ 1979/ Univ of Toledo/ staff: 1(f)

LIBRARY AND/OR ARCHIVES: Houses the rare book, manuscripts, and university archives collection.

PROGRAMS: Exhibits; Lectures; Research Library/Archives

COLLECTIONS: [1872-present] Records of Libbey-Owens-Ford, Inc; university history; rare book collection: women's history, African-American authors, southern authors, and Imagist poets.

HOURS: By appt

ADMISSION: No charge

6795
Western Lake Erie Historical Society
International Park, 43611 [PO Box 5311, 43611-0311]; (p) (419) 531-5280, (419) 936-3070; (f) (419) 936-3068; (c) Lucas

Private non-profit/ 1978/ Board of Trustees/ staff: 17(v)/ members: 84

HISTORIC PRESERVATION AGENCY; HISTORICAL SOCIETY; HISTORY MUSEUM; LIVING HISTORY/OUTDOOR MUSEUM: Collects, preserves, displays, and interprets the maritime past of the Great Lakes.

PROGRAMS: Elder's Programs; Exhibits; Facility Rental; Festivals; Guided Tours; Interpretation; Lectures

COLLECTIONS: [1840-1980] 617 ft retired lake freighter, photos, charts, brochures, books, magazines, marine artifacts.

HOURS: Yr Oct-May W-Su 10-5; Jun-Sep M-Su 10-5

ADMISSION: $5, Children $3

6796
Wildwood Manor House
5100 W Central Ave, 43615; (p) (419) 535-3056

TRENTON

6797
Trenton Historical Society
17 E State St, 45067; (p) (513) 988-9634, (513) 424-0740; (c) Butler

Private non-profit/ 1971/ members: 61

HISTORICAL SOCIETY; HISTORY MUSEUM: Operates historical museum in 1890 Victorian home.

PROGRAMS: Community Outreach; Festivals; Guided Tours

COLLECTIONS: [1890-present] Trenton development history.

HOURS: Apr-Aug 1st Sa 1-4; city festivals in Oct and Dec

ADMISSION: No charge

TROY

6798
Troy Historical Society
c/o Hayner Cultural Center 301 W Main, 45373; (p) (937) 339-0457; (c) Miami

Joint/ 1966/ Troy-Miami County Public Library/ staff: 1(f); 1(p); 40(v)/ members: 209

GENEALOGICAL SOCIETY; HISTORICAL SOCIETY; RESEARCH CENTER

COLLECTIONS: [1800-1920] Books, manuscripts, microfilms, local newspapers, court records, census records.

HOURS: Research Hours: Yr T-Sa 10-4; T-W 7pm-9pm, Su 1:30-4:30

6799
Waco Historical Society
105 S Market St, 45373 [PO Box 62, 45373]; (p) (937) 335-9226; (f) (937) 335-9647; general467@aol.com; www.wacoairmuseum.org; (c) Miami

Private non-profit/ Board of Trustees/ staff: 4(p); 76(v)/ members: 632/publication: *The WACO Word*

HISTORICAL SOCIETY: Preserves aviation heritage of the WACO aircraft company.

PROGRAMS: Annual Meeting; Exhibits; Family Programs; Festivals; Guided Tours; Living History; Publication; Research Library/ Archives; School-Based Curriculum

COLLECTIONS: [1900-1975] Flying aircraft, historical displays, photo archives, artifacts, written and audio-visual libraries, educational displays, aircraft restoration and training facilities.

HOURS: May-Nov Sa-Su 1-5

ADMISSION: No charge

UNIONTOWN

6800
Lake Township Historical Society
[PO Box 482, 44685]; (p) (330) 877-9220; (c) Stark

Private non-profit/ 1995/ staff: 20(v)/ members: 125

HISTORICAL SOCIETY

PROGRAMS: Annual Meeting; Community Outreach; Lectures; Living History

COLLECTIONS: Photos, news articles, and books.

URBANA

6801
Champaign County Historical Society
809 E Lawn Ave, 43078; (p) (937) 653-6721; (c) Champaign

County/ 1934/ Officers & Board of Trustees/ staff: 5(v)/ members: 200

HISTORICAL SOCIETY; HISTORY MUSEUM

PROGRAMS: Annual Meeting; Exhibits; Festivals; Guided Tours; School-Based Curriculum

COLLECTIONS: [19th-20th c] Artifacts and printed material.

HOURS: Yr T 10-4 or by appt

VAN WERT

6802
Van Wert County Historical Society
602 N Washington St, 45891 [PO Box 621, 45891-0621]; (p) (419) 238-5297; vwmuseum@bright.net; (c) Van Wert

1954/ Board of Trustees/ staff: 12(v)/ members: 200/publication: *Historical Happenings*

HISTORICAL SOCIETY; HISTORY MUSEUM; HOUSE MUSEUM: Collects and preserves local area artifacts.

PROGRAMS: Annual Meeting; Community Outreach; Exhibits; Family Programs; Festivals; Guided Tours; Lectures; Living History; Publication

COLLECTIONS: [1835-present] Area artifacts, interpretive Victorian home.

HOURS: Yr Su 2-4:30

VANDALIA

6803
Vandalia-Butler Historical Society
336 E Alkaline Springs Rd, 45377 [PO Box 243, 45377-0243]; (p) (937) 898-5300; (c) Montgomery

Private non-profit/ 1977/ members: 220

HISTORIC SITE; HISTORICAL SOCIETY; HISTORY MUSEUM; HOUSE MUSEUM

PROGRAMS: Concerts; Exhibits; Facility Rental; Guided Tours

COLLECTIONS: [Mid 1800s] Period-furnished two story log home, 1840s Federal Home, 1810 one room schoolhouse, Alkaline Springs; agricultural artifacts.

HOURS: Yr by appt

ADMISSION: No charge

VERMILION

6804
Brownhelm Historical Association
1355 Claus Rd, 44089 [PO Box 303, 44089]; (p) (440) 988-4550; (c) Lorain

1993/ Board of Trustees/Officers/ staff: 15(v)/ members: 90/publication: *The Brownhelm Bugle*

GENEALOGICAL SOCIETY; HISTORICAL SOCIETY

PROGRAMS: Exhibits; Festivals; Guided Tours; Living History; Publication; Reenactments; School-Based Curriculum

COLLECTIONS: [1840s-present] Photos, school memorabilia and artifacts.

HOURS: May-Dec by appt

ADMISSION: Donations accepted

6805
Great Lakes Historical Society, The
480 Main St, 44089 [PO Box 435, 44089]; (p) (440) 967-3467, (800) 893-1485; (f) (440)

967-1519; www.inlandseas.org; (c) Erie

Private non-profit/ 1944/ staff: 3(f); 7(p); 25(v)/ members: 3000/publication: *Inlandseas Quarterly Magazine*

HISTORICAL SOCIETY: Owns and operates Inlandseas Maritime Museum.

PROGRAMS: Annual Meeting; Community Outreach; Concerts; Exhibits; Facility Rental; Family Programs; Festivals; Film/Video; Guided Tours; Lectures; Living History; Publication

COLLECTIONS: [1800-present] Pictures, paintings, models, marine artifacts.

HOURS: Yr Jan-Dec M-Su 10-5

WADSWORTH

6806
Wadsworth Area Historical Society
555 Silvercreek Rd, 44281; (p) (330) 336-0062; (c) Medina

City/ 1991/ Board of Trustees/ staff: 120(v)/ members: 120/publication: *newsletter*

HISTORICAL SOCIETY: Preserves, studies and interprets Wadsworth area history.

PROGRAMS: Annual Meeting; Community Outreach; Exhibits; Family Programs; Festivals; Lectures; Living History; Publication

COLLECTIONS: [1814-present] Pictures, artifacts

WARREN

6807
Harriet Taylor Upton Association
380 Mahoning Ave, 44483; (p) (330) 395-1840; LanaE1776@aol.com; (c) Trumbull

Private non-profit/ 1989/ Board of Directors/ staff: 110(v)/ members: 201

GARDEN; HISTORIC SITE; HOUSE MUSEUM: Preserves the home of Suffragist Harriet Taylor Upton; collects, preserves and interprets materials related to suffrage movement.

PROGRAMS: Annual Meeting; Community Outreach; Exhibits; Facility Rental; Garden Tours; Guided Tours; Interpretation; Lectures; Research Library/Archives

COLLECTIONS: [1890-1920] Suffrage artifacts, books, furniture, costumes and textiles.

WASHINGTON

6808
Fayette County Historical Society Museum
517 Columbus Ave, 43160; (p) (740) 335-2953; (c) Fayette

Private non-profit/ 1948/ staff: 1(p); 30(v)/ members: 450

Preserves local history.

COLLECTIONS: [1890-1940] Native American artifacts, period clothing, regional furniture, area photos, glassware, tools, books. Structures: 1875 Morris Sharp Mansion and Carriage House.

HOURS: May-Oct Sa-Su 1-4

ADMISSION: Donations

WAVERLY

6809
Pike Heritage Museum
110 S Market St, 45690; (p) (740) 947-5281; (c) Pike

County/ 1972/ staff: 2(p); 20(v)/ members: 100

HISTORIC PRESERVATION AGENCY: Collects local historic artifacts.

PROGRAMS: Concerts; Family Programs; Festivals; Guided Tours; School-Based Curriculum

COLLECTIONS: Native American artifacts, early Pike County displays, pipe organ.

HOURS: Yr Sa-Su 1-4 and by appt

WAYNESVILLE

6810
Waynesville Historical Society
[PO Box 327, 45068]; (p) (513) 897-2960; (c) Warren

Private non-profit/ 1973/ Board of Trustees/ members: 43

Collects and preserves objects and materials relating to the history of the Waynesville area.

WELLINGTON

6811
Southern Lorain County Historical Society-Spirit of '76 Museum
201 N Main St, 44090 [PO Box 76, 44090]; (p) (440) 647-4367; (c) Lorain

Private non-profit/ 1970/ staff: 14(v)/ members: 225/publication: *The Spirit*

ART MUSEUM; HISTORICAL SOCIETY; HISTORY MUSEUM

PROGRAMS: Annual Meeting; Exhibits; Guided Tours; Publication; Research Library/ Archives

COLLECTIONS: [mid 19th-early 20th c]

HOURS: Apr-Oct Sa-Su 2:30-5

ADMISSION: No charge

WELLSVILLE

6812
Wellsville Historical Society
1003 Riverside Ave, 43968 [PO Box 13, 43968]; (p) (330) 532-1018; (c) Columbiana

Private non-profit/ 1966/ Board of Trustees/ staff: 20(v)/ members: 100

GENEALOGICAL SOCIETY; HISTORICAL SOCIETY; HISTORY MUSEUM; HOUSE MUSEUM: Collects and preserves Wellsville's heritage; sponsors the River Museum, Country Store, Fire House Museum and Caboose.

PROGRAMS: Exhibits; Festivals; Guided Tours; Living History; Research Library/ Archives

COLLECTIONS: [1800s-present] 11 interpretive rooms of city industries, businesses and local citizens.

HOURS: Jun-Sep Su 1-5:30

ADMISSION: Donations accepted

WEST LIBERTY

6813
Piatt Castles Company Inc., The
10051 Twp Rd 47, 43357 [PO Box 497, 43357]; (p) (937) 465-2821; (f) (937) 465-7774; macochee@logan.net; (c) Logan

Private for-profit/ 1912/ Board of Directors/ staff: 2(f); 16(p)

HOUSE MUSEUM: Started in 1864, Mac-A-Cheek Castle houses original collections of the Piatt family, and Mac-O-Chee Castle is known for its unique architecture.

PROGRAMS: Concerts; Exhibits; Facility Rental; Family Programs; Guided Tours; Lectures; Research Library/Archives; School-Based Curriculum; Theatre

COLLECTIONS: [1820s-1930s] Piatt family collections representing eight generations, Native American artifacts, Civil War artifacts, and a firearms collection.

HOURS: Apr-May M-Su 12-4; May-Aug M-Su 11-5; Sep-Oct 12-4

WESTERVILLE

6814
Amalthea Historical Society
975 S Sunbury Rd, 43081; (p) (614) 882-2347; (c) Franklin

Private non-profit/ 1977

HISTORICAL SOCIETY: Preserves, promotes, and interprets Amalthea (now Central College, Blendon Township, Central Cemetery, and Central College United Presbyterian Church) history.

PROGRAMS: Lectures; Living History; Research Library/Archives

COLLECTIONS: [1849-present] Local books, church programs, photos, and memorabilia.

6815
Westerville Historical Society
Hanby House 160 W Main St, 43081 [207 Patti Dr, 43081]; (p) (614) 891-6289, (800) 600-6843; mgale@ee.net; (c) Franklin

State/ 1941/ staff: 45(v)/ members: 300

GARDEN; HISTORIC SITE; HISTORICAL SOCIETY; HISTORY MUSEUM; HOUSE MUSEUM: Manages Hanby House, the home of Bishop William, co-founder of Otterbein College 1847, his son Ben Hanby and a site on the Underground Railroad.

PROGRAMS: Exhibits; Film/Video; Guided Tours; Interpretation; Publication; School-Based Curriculum

COLLECTIONS: [1863-1865] Collection of Hanby music, Judge Earl Hoover's collection, furnishing, musical instruments.

HOURS: May-Sep Sa-Su 1-4 and by appt

ADMISSION: $2, Children $0.75, Seniors $1.60

6816
Westerville Public Library, Local History Resource Center
126 S State St, 43081; (p) (614) 882-7277; (f) (614) 882-5369; weinharb@wpl.lib.oh.us; wpl.lib.oh.us/library/overview/loc_hist/2wv_loc .; (c) Franklin

1989/ staff: 1(f); 2(v)

RESEARCH CENTER: Collects, preserves, and shares local history information.

PROGRAMS: Community Outreach; Exhibits; Family Programs; Guided Tours; Lectures; Research Library/Archives; School-Based Curriculum

COLLECTIONS: [1800-present] Westerville history and genealogy yearbooks 1911-present, 2,000 indexed photos.

HOURS: Yr M-F 10-6

ADMISSION: No charge

WILBERFORCE

6817
National Afro-American Museum & Cultural Center
1350 Brush Row Rd, 45384 [PO Box 578, 45384-0578]; (p) (937) 376-4944; (f) (937) 376-2007; naamcc@erinet.com; www.ohiohistory.org; (c) Greene

Private non-profit/ 1980/ Ohio Historical Society/ staff: 17(f); 7(p); 125(v)/ members: 800

HISTORY MUSEUM

PROGRAMS: Community Outreach; Concerts; Exhibits; Facility Rental; Family Programs; Film/Video; Guided Tours; Lectures; Research Library/Archives; School-Based Curriculum

COLLECTIONS: Over 9,000 artifacts; manuscripts, Afro-American periodicals, collection of rare books, photos.

HOURS: Yr T-Sa 9-5, Su 1-5

WILMINGTON

6818
Clinton County Historical Society
149 E Locust St, 45177 [PO Box 529, 45177]; (p) (937) 382-4684; (f) (937) 382-5634; www.postcom.com/cc; (c) Clinton

County; Private non-profit/ 1948/ Board of Trustees/ staff: 1(f); 1(p); 20(v)/ members: 365/publication: *Rombach Recorder*

GENEALOGICAL SOCIETY; HISTORIC PRESERVATION AGENCY; HISTORIC SITE; HISTORICAL SOCIETY; HISTORY MUSEUM; HOUSE MUSEUM; LIBRARY AND/OR ARCHIVES: Collects, preserves, and disseminates Clinton County history and genealogy.

PROGRAMS: Annual Meeting; Community Outreach; Family Programs; Guided Tours; Publication

COLLECTIONS: [19th-20th c] Furnishings, housewares, clothing, and artifacts; Quaker clothing, artifacts; Eli Harvey sculpture, memorabilia of General James W. Denver.

HOURS: Mar-Dec W-F 1-4:00 or by appt

ADMISSION: No charge

WOOSTER

6819
Wayne County Historical Society and Museum
546 E Bowman St, 44691; (p) (330) 264-8856; (f) (330) 264-8856; www.wayne historical.org/; (c) Wayne

County; Private non-profit/ 1904/ Board of Trustees/ staff: 3(p); 55(v)/ members: 600

GENEALOGICAL SOCIETY; HISTORICAL SOCIETY; HISTORY MUSEUM; HOUSE MUSEUM

PROGRAMS: Annual Meeting; Community Outreach; Concerts; Exhibits; Family Programs; Festivals; Film/Video; Guided Tours; Interpretation; Lectures; Living History; Publication; Quarterly Meeting; Research Library/Archives; School-Based Curriculum

COLLECTIONS: [1815-1915] Agricultural implements, Native American artifacts, stuffed birds and animals, period furniture and china, military items, re-created General Store, furnished log cabin, horse drawn carriage, textiles and early fire engines.

HOURS: Feb-Dec W-Su 2-4:30

ADMISSION: $3

WORTHINGTON

6820
Worthington Historical Society
50 W New England Ave, 43085; (p) (614) 885-1247; (f) (614) 885-1040; worthhsoc@aol.com; (c) Franklin

Private non-profit/ 1955/ Executive Board/ staff: 2(p); 200(v)/ members: 600

HISTORICAL SOCIETY; HOUSE MUSEUM

PROGRAMS: Annual Meeting; Community Outreach; Concerts; Elder's Programs; Exhibits; Festivals; Garden Tours; Interpretation; Lectures; Publication; Research Library/Archives; School-Based Curriculum

COLLECTIONS: [1804-present] Early Federal-style house, furnishings 1810-1825, archival material relating to Worthington history, 19th c dolls. Structures: The Orange Johnson House Museum, The Old Rectory, The Jeffers Memorial Mound.

HOURS: Orange Johnson House: Su 2-5; Old Rectory: T-F 9-4 Sa 10-2

ADMISSION: $2, Children $1

WREN

6821
Wren Historical Society
Moser Memorial Park, 45832 [c/o Dudrey De Bolt, PO Box 387, Convay, 45832-0387]; (p) (419) 749-4093; (c) Van Wert

1975/ Trustees/ staff: 13(p)/ members: 25

HISTORICAL SOCIETY; HISTORY MUSEUM: Maintains local history museum.

PROGRAMS: Community Outreach; Exhibits

COLLECTIONS: Various household, school, farm artifacts in log cabin, 1 room school and summer kitchen.

HOURS: By appt.

WRIGHT-PATTERSON AFB

6822
United States Air Force Museum
1100 Spaatz St, 45433; (p) (937) 255-3286; (f) (937) 255-3910; www.wpafb.af.mil/museum

Federal/ 1923/ Dept of Defense/ staff: 94(f); 400(v)/ members: 15500/publication: *Friends Journal (quarterly)*

HISTORY MUSEUM: Collects and displays the USAF's material heritage.

PROGRAMS: Community Outreach; Concerts; Exhibits; Facility Rental; Family Programs; Festivals; Film/Video; Guided Tours; Lectures; Publication; Research Library/Archives; Theatre

COLLECTIONS: [1907-present] 62,000 USAF-related hardware artifacts from aircraft to button compasses; 1.5 million photos and archived documents. Structures: 8 major buildings.

HOURS: Yr M-Su 9-5

ADMISSION: No charge

XENIA

6823
Greene County Historical Society
74 W Church St, 45385; (p) (937) 372-4606; (f) (937) 372-5660; (c) Greene

Private non-profit/ 1929/ staff: 1(f); 1(p); 30(v)/ members: 450/publication: *Our Heritage*

HISTORIC SITE; HISTORICAL SOCIETY; HISTORY MUSEUM; HOUSE MUSEUM: Collects, preserves, and protects Greene County history for research and display.

PROGRAMS: Annual Meeting; Community Outreach; Exhibits; Facility Rental; Family Programs; Garden Tours; Guided Tours; Lectures; Publication; Research Library/Archives

COLLECTIONS: [1790-present] Railroad display diorama of Xenia, farm equipment, log house, Victorian House, military artifacts, research materials, photos, documents, medical, culinary, herb garden.

HOURS: Yr Jan-May, Sep-Dec T-F 9-12/1-3:30; Jun-Aug T-F 9-12/1-3:30, Sa-Su 1-4

ADMISSION: Donations

6824
James Galloway Log House, Greene County Historical Society Museum
74 W Church St , 45385 [74 W Church St, 45385]; (p) (937) 372-4606

1799/ Greene County Historical Society Museum/ staff: 1(f)

COLLECTIONS: [1797-1820] Furnishings; papers, documents.

HOURS: Yr

YOUNGSTOWN

6825
Business and Media Archvies of the Mahoning Valley
250 Federal Plaza E, 44555 [One University Plaza, 44555]; (p) (330) 744-7621; (f) (330) 743-7210; Business_Media_Archives@ msn.com; (c) Mahoning

Private non-profit/ 1995/ Board of Trustees/ staff: 1(f); 1(p)/ members: 1

LIBRARY AND/OR ARCHIVES: Collects, and preserves business and media records.

PROGRAMS: Research Library/Archives

COLLECTIONS: [1920-present] Business records, over 2 million feet of news film, 12 years of television news video tapes, audio recordings, television film, radio, video equipment, photos.

HOURS: Yr M-F 8:30-4:30

6826
Mahoning Valley Historical Society and The Arms Family Museum of Local History
648 Wick Ave, 44502-1289; (p) (330) 743-2589; (f) (330) 743-7210; mvhs@ mahoninghistory.org; (c) Mahoning

Private non-profit/ 1961/ Board of Trustees/ staff: 8(f); 15(p); 15(v)/ members: 700/publication: *Historic Happenings; Discover Greystone*

HISTORIC SITE; HISTORICAL SOCIETY; HISTORY MUSEUM; HOUSE MUSEUM: The society collects, preserves, and interprets the history of the Mahoning Valley while educating and raising awareness of the community's past through exhibits and other programs.

PROGRAMS: Annual Meeting; Community Outreach; Elder's Programs; Exhibits; Facility Rental; Family Programs; Guided Tours; Interpretation; Lectures; Publication

COLLECTIONS: [Prehistory-present] 109,330 artifacts in permanent collection, including historic house and contents, local hisotry collection from prehistory to present; archival collection; and business and media archives.

HOURS: Yr Jan-Dec Museum: M-F 1-4 Sa-Su 1:30-5 Library: T-F 9-4 Sa 1-5

ADMISSION: $3, Student $2, Seniors $2; Under 18 free

ZANESVILLE

6827
Pioneer and Historical Society of Muskingum County
115 Jefferson St, 43701-4905; (p) (740) 454-9500; (c) Muskingum

Private non-profit/ 1890/ Board of Trustees/ staff: 1(p); 10(v)/ members: 330/publication: *Muskingum Journal*

HISTORICAL SOCIETY; HISTORY MUSEUM; HOUSE MUSEUM: Perpetuates Muskingum County history.

PROGRAMS: Annual Meeting; Exhibits; Family Programs; Guided Tours; Lectures; Publication

COLLECTIONS: [1800-present] Interpretive rooms of military history, river life, and local pottery; Stone Academy Museum: revolving exhibits.

HOURS: Yr T-Sa 12-4

ADMISSION: $2

ZOAR

6828
Zoar Village State Memorial
State Rt 212, 44697 [PO Box 404, 44697]; (p) (330) 874-3011; (f) (330) 874-2936; kmfzoar@compuserve.com; ohiohistory.org/ places/zoar; (c) Tuscarawas

Private non-profit; State/ 1942/ Ohio Historical Society/ staff: 4(f); 14(p); 55(v)/publication: *Zoar: An Ohio Experiment in Communalism*

GARDEN; HISTORIC SITE; HOUSE MUSEUM; LIVING HISTORY/OUTDOOR MUSEUM: Restored site of 1817 German religious communal society.

PROGRAMS: Exhibits; Facility Rental; Festivals; Garden Tours; Guided Tours; Interpreta-

tion; Living History; Publication

COLLECTIONS: Furniture, textiles, pottery, artifacts.

HOURS: Apr-May, Sept-Oct Sa 9:30-5, Su 12-5; May-Sept W-Sa 9:30-5

ADMISSION: $5, Children $1.25

OKLAHOMA

ADA

6829
Pontotoc County Historical and Genealogical Society
221 W 16th, 74820; (c) Pontotoc

Private non-profit/ staff: 12(p); 12(v)/ members: 120

GENEALOGICAL SOCIETY; LIBRARY AND/OR ARCHIVES: Maintains library.

PROGRAMS: Research Library/Archives

COLLECTIONS: [20th c] History and genealogical literature for all states. Census for Oklahoma and others on microfilm.

HOURS: Yr M-W 12:30-4

ADMISSION: $2 non-members

AFTON

6830
National Rod and Custom Car Hall of Fame
Hwy 85A at 125, 74331 [Rt 3 Box 180, 74331]; (p) (918) 257-4234; (f) (918) 257-8224; ldmstar@galstar.com; (c) Delaware

Private non-profit/ 1995/ staff: 1(f); 1(p)

ART MUSEUM; AUTOMOBILE; HISTORY MUSEUM: Preserves heritage of the sport and profession of custom car and street rod building, the individuals and their machines.

PROGRAMS: Annual Meeting; Facility Rental; Film/Video; Theatre

COLLECTIONS: [Early 1950s-present] 40 customized automobiles, photos, magazine articles and biographies.

HOURS: Mar-Nov W-Sa 11-5

ADMISSION: $6, Children $3, Seniors $5

AHINE

6831
Sod House Museum
45 miles N of Cherokee Springs on Hwy 8, 73716 [Rt 3, 73716]; (p) (580) 463-2441; (c) Alfalfa

Private for-profit; State/ 1969/ Oklahoma Historical Society/ staff: 1(f); 5(p); 3(v)

HISTORIC SITE; HISTORY MUSEUM; HOUSE MUSEUM: Depicts early farm life in Oklahoma.

PROGRAMS: Exhibits; Family Programs; Festivals; Guided Tours

COLLECTIONS: [1893-1910] Farm, household and personal items in 1894 sod house.

HOURS: Yr T-F 9-5, Sa-Su 2-5

ADMISSION: Donations accepted

ALTUS

6832
Western Trail Historical Society and Museum of the Western Prairie
1100 Memorial Dr, 73522 [PO Box 574, 73522]; (p) (580) 482-1044; (f) (580) 482-0128; muswestpr@ok-history.mus.ok.us; www.ok-history.mus.ok.us/mus-sites/masnum18.htm; (c) Jackson

Private non-profit/ 1970/ Board of Directors/ staff: 12(f)/ members: 63/publication: *Trail News*

HISTORY MUSEUM: Depicts the history of Southwest Oklahoma.

PROGRAMS: Exhibits; School-Based Curriculum

COLLECTIONS: [Prehistory-present] 50,000 items: artifacts, documents and photos.

HOURS: Yr T-F 9-5, Sa-Su 2-5

ADMISSION: $1, Children $0.50; Donations

ALVA

6833
Cherokee Strip Museum Association
901 14th St, 73717-2542; (p) (580) 327-2030; (c) Woods

1976/ Board of Directors/ staff: 2(p); 60(v)

HISTORY MUSEUM: Preserves and presents local history.

PROGRAMS: Annual Meeting; Exhibits; Facility Rental; Festivals; Guided Tours

COLLECTIONS: [1890-1940] 40 interpretive rooms: dolls, country store, chapel, clothing, surgical, telephones, nursery, library, post office, furniture, DAR, Lincoln, military, POW.

HOURS: Sept-May Sa-Su 2-5; June-Aug T-Su 2-5

ADMISSION: Donations

ANADARKO

6834
Indian City USA, Inc.
25 mi on Hwy 8, 73005 [PO Box 695, 73005]; (p) (405) 247-5661, (800) 433-5661; (c) Caddo

Private for-profit/ 1954/ staff: 5(f); 12(p)

ART MUSEUM; HISTORIC SITE; HISTORY MUSEUM; LIVING HISTORY/OUTDOOR MUSEUM: Promotes Native American history and culture.

PROGRAMS: Exhibits; Facility Rental; Festivals; Film/Video; Guided Tours; Lectures; Living History; School-Based Curriculum; Theatre

COLLECTIONS: [1950-present] 7 Native American dwellings reconstruction; Native artifacts.

HOURS: Yr

6835
National Hall of Fame for Famous American Indians
Hwy 62 East, 73005 [PO Box 548, 73005-0548]; (p) (405) 247-5555; (f) (405) 247-5571; (c) Caddo

State/ 1952/ staff: 4(v)/ members: 300

LIVING HISTORY/OUTDOOR MUSEUM

PROGRAMS: Exhibits; Interpretation

COLLECTIONS: Sculptures of famous Native Americans by Allen Houser; Anna Hyatt Huntington animal sculptures.

HOURS: Yr M-Sa 9-5, Su 1-5

ADMISSION: No charge

APACHE

6836
Apache Historical Society and Museum
101 W Evans, 73006 [PO Box 101, 73006]; (p) (580) 588-3392; (f) (580) 588-3393; (c) Caddo

Private non-profit/ 1971/ Boad/ staff: 1(p); 3(v)/ members: 100

HISTORICAL SOCIETY; HISTORY MUSEUM: Collects and displays the history of the area and its citizens. Maintains the Bank Building listed on the National Register of Historic Places.

PROGRAMS: Annual Meeting; Exhibits; Guided Tours

COLLECTIONS: [1900-pesent] Tools, furniture, household items, pictures, Native American artifacts, documents and original bank fixtures.

ARDMORE

6837
Greater Southwest Historical Museum
35 Sunset Dr, 73401; (p) (580) 226-3857; history@ardmore.com; (c) Carter

Private non-profit/ 1965/ Board of Trustees/ staff: 5(f); 2(p); 25(v)/ members: 373

HISTORY MUSEUM: Collects, preserves and interprets south-central Oklahoma.

PROGRAMS: Annual Meeting; Community Outreach; Exhibits; Facility Rental; Guided Tours; Interpretation; School-Based Curriculum

COLLECTIONS: [19th c-present] Over 20,000 artifacts, photographs, maps, paintings, books and newspapers.

HOURS: Yr T-Sa 10-5, Su 1-5

ADMISSION: Donations accepted

ARNETT

6838
Ellis County Historical Society
RR 2, 73832; (p) (580) 885-7287; echslfox@pldi.net; (c) Ellis

Private non-profit/ 1973/ staff: 6(p); 2(v)/ members: 8/publication: *Ellis County Historical Society Cemetery Records*

HISTORIC SITE; HISTORICAL SOCIETY; HISTORY MUSEUM

PROGRAMS: Annual Meeting; Exhibits; Facility Rental; Interpretation; Publication; Research Library/Archives

COLLECTIONS: [20th c] Ellis County Heritage Vol. 1 and 2; Atlas of Ellis County, 1910 ; books, cemetery records of Dewey Bleaver and Roger Mills, Gnaudenfield Cemetery Higgins Cemetery (TX).

HOURS: Yr Daily 10-9

ADMISSION: No charge

6839
Log Cabin
211 E Barnes, 73832 [PO Box 337, 73832]; (p) (580) 885-7414

ATOKA

6840
Atoka County Historical Society
258 N Hwy 69, 74525 [PO Box 245, 74525]; (p) (580) 889-7192; (f) (580) 889-7192; (c) Atoka

County; Private non-profit/ 1969/ Board of Directors/ staff: 2(f); 1(p); 10(v)/ members: 50

HISTORIC PRESERVATION AGENCY; HISTORIC SITE; HISTORICAL SOCIETY; HISTORY MUSEUM: Operates Confederate Memorial Museum and Cemetery. Offers exhibits depicting local area history.

PROGRAMS: Exhibits; Guided Tours; Living History; Reenactments

COLLECTIONS: [1860-present] Civil War, military artifacts; vintage clothing; interpretive rooms.

HOURS: Yr M-Sa 9-4

BARNSDALL

6841
Bigheart Historical Museum
, 74002 [520 Main St, 74002]; (f) (918) 782-3192; (c) Osage

Private non-profit/ 1974/ staff: 15(v)/ members: 75

HISTORIC PRESERVATION AGENCY; HISTORICAL SOCIETY; HISTORY MUSEUM

PROGRAMS: Annual Meeting; Exhibits; Living History

COLLECTIONS: Artifacts: oil, cattle industry; Osage Indians and wax manufacturing.

HOURS: Apr-Oct T-F 1-5, Sa 9-1

BARTLESVILLE

6842
Bartlesville Area History Museum
401 S Johnstone, 74003; (p) (918) 338-4290; (f) (918) 338-4264; www.bartlesvillehistory.com; (c) Washington

City/ 1964/ City of Bartlesville/ staff: 1(f); 25(v)

HISTORY MUSEUM: Collects, preserves, and displays local history.

PROGRAMS: Community Outreach; Exhibits; Guided Tours; Interpretation; Lectures; Reenactments; School-Based Curriculum

COLLECTIONS: [Late 19th c-present] Early settlers, Native American tribal artifacts.

HOURS: Yr T-Sa

6843
Frank Phillips Home
1107 Cherokee, 74003-5027; (p) (918) 336-2491; (f) (918) 336-3529; fphillipshome@ok-hist.mus.ok.us; www.ok-history.mus.ok.us/; (c) Washington

State/ Oklahoma Historical Society/ staff: 2(f); 2(p); 20(v)/ members: 350

HISTORIC SITE; HOUSE MUSEUM

PROGRAMS: Annual Meeting; Community Outreach; Concerts; Elder's Programs; Family

Programs; Guided Tours; Interpretation; Lectures; Research Library/Archives

COLLECTIONS: [1930s] Neo-classical home (1909) with period furniture, decorative art.

6844
Woolaroc Lodge
Hwy 123, 74003 [Route 3, Box 2100, 74003]; (p) (918) 336-0307; (f) (918) 336-0084; Woolaroc1@aol.com; www.woolaroc.org; (c) Osage

Private non-profit/ 1926/ Frank Phillips Foundation. Inc./ staff: 7(f); 38(v)/ members: 295

HISTORIC SITE; HOUSE MUSEUM: Preserves country home of Frank Phillips of Phillips Petroleum Company.

PROGRAMS: Facility Rental; Guided Tours

COLLECTIONS: [1925-1950] Western art, period furnishings, taxidermy, Navajo rugs, personal effects.

HOURS: Yr T-Su 10-4:30, Summer: Daily

ADMISSION: Donations requested; under 12 free

6845
Woolaroc Museum
Hwy 123, 74003 [Route 3, Box 2100, 74003]; (p) (918) 336-0307; (f) (918) 336-0084; Woolaroc1@aol.com; www.woolaroc.org; (c) Osage

Private non-profit/ 1929/ Frank Phillips Foundation, Inc./ staff: 9(f); 4(p); 38(v)/ members: 295/publication: *Woolaroc, Woolaroc*

ANTHROPOLOGY MUSEUM; ART MUSEUM; HISTORY MUSEUM: Promotes Old West history.

PROGRAMS: Exhibits; Facility Rental; Guided Tours; Publication; Research Library/Archives

COLLECTIONS: [Pre-Columbian-mid 20th c] Cowboys, pioneers, Native American, archaeological and anthropological artifacts; Woolaroc airplane; Colt firearms.

HOURS: Yr T-Su 10-5; Open Daily during summer

ADMISSION: Donations requested; under 12 free

BEAVER

6846
Beaver County Historical Society
Fairgrounds, 73932 [PO Box 457, 73932]; (p) (580) 625-4439; (c) Beaver

Private non-profit/ 1982/ staff: 1(f); 1(p); 7(v)/ members: 52

GENEALOGICAL SOCIETY; HISTORIC PRESERVATION AGENCY

PROGRAMS: Annual Meeting; Community Outreach; Exhibits; Guided Tours

HOURS: Yr T-Sa 1-5

ADMISSION: Donations accepted

BINGER

6847
Caddo Cultural Center
Junction of Hwy 152 & 281, 73009 [PO Box 487, 73009]; (p) (405) 656-2901; (f) (405) 656-2892; nagpra@tanet.net; www.caddonation.com; (c) Caddo

Caddo Tribal Council/ staff: 2(f); 1(p); 5(v)

HISTORIC PRESERVATION AGENCY; HISTORY MUSEUM; RESEARCH CENTER; TRIBAL MUSEUM

PROGRAMS: Exhibits; Festivals; Lectures; Research Library/Archives

COLLECTIONS: [Prehistoric-historic] Archaeological, archival, historical artifacts, literature.

HOURS: Yr 8-4:30

BLACKWELL

6848
Top of Oklahoma Historical Museum
303 S Main, 74631; (p) (580) 363-0209; (f) (580) 363-0209; (c) Kay

City; Private non-profit/ 1972/ staff: 1(f); 75(v)/ members: 600

HISTORIC SITE; HISTORICAL SOCIETY; HISTORY MUSEUM

PROGRAMS: Annual Meeting; Community Outreach; Exhibits; Facility Rental; Film/Video; Guided Tours; Interpretation; School-Based Curriculum

COLLECTIONS: [1893-present] Farming, harvesting, pioneer family life, cameras, Blackwell Wine Company, meat markets, pianos and organs, church, post office, typewriters, dictating machines and Native American artifacts.

HOURS: Yr Daily 10-5

ADMISSION: No charge

BOISE CITY

6849
Cimarron Heritage Center, Inc.
1300 N Cimarron, 73933 [PO Box 214, 73933]; (p) (580) 544-3479; (f) (580) 544-3479; museum@ptsi.net; www.ptsi.net/user/museum; (c) Cimarron

Private non-profit/ 1994/ Board of Directors/ staff: 1(f); 2(p); 15(v)/ members: 300

HISTORICAL SOCIETY; HISTORY MUSEUM; LIVING HISTORY/OUTDOOR MUSEUM: Preserves and interprets the natural, historic and artistic heritage of Cimarron County.

PROGRAMS: Annual Meeting; Exhibits; Family Programs; Guided Tours; Lectures; Living History; Research Library/Archives

COLLECTIONS: [Prehistory-present] Bruce Goff designed house, Jack Hoxie, Santa Fe Trail, Dust Bowl, paleontology, Plains Indian artifacts, 1919 REO Truck, 1916 Dort hearse, 1941 Packard, antique farm equipment

BOLEY

6850
Boley Historical Museum
W Grant & Pecan, 74829 [PO Box 627, 74829]; (p) (918) 667-3711; hoh@brightok.net; (c) Okfuskee

City/ Boley Chamber of Commerce/ staff: 4(v)

HISTORIC SITE; HISTORY MUSEUM

PROGRAMS: Guided Tours

HOURS: Yr Sa 9-5

BROKEN ARROW

6851
Association of the Descendants of Nancy Ward, Beloved Woman of the Cherokee
[PO Box 2138, 74013]; dkhampton@home.com; www.nancyward.com

Private non-profit/ 1994/ staff: 1(v)/ members: 350

GENEALOGICAL SOCIETY: Promotes history and genealogy of Cherokee Nation and Nancy Ward.

PROGRAMS: Annual Meeting

HOURS: (Meetings) 4th Sa of March and Sa of Labor Day wknd

ADMISSION: No charge

6852
Broken Arrow Historical Society
1800 S Main St, 74013 [PO Box 371, 74013-0371]; (p) (918) 258-2616; (c) Tulsa

Private non-profit/ 1975/ Board of Directors/ staff: 1(f); 20(v)/ members: 250

HISTORICAL SOCIETY; HISTORY MUSEUM: Collects, preserves and interprets city history.

PROGRAMS: Annual Meeting; Community Outreach; Exhibits; Interpretation; Research Library/Archives

COLLECTIONS: [1900-1950] Home, farming and personal items, photos, newspapers.

HOURS: Yr

ADMISSION: Donations accepted

BROKEN BOW

6853
Gardner Mansion and Museum
6 mi E of Broken Bow, on US Hwy 70 N, 74728 [Route 1 Box 576, 74728]; (p) (580) 584-6588; (c) McCurtain

Private for-profit/ 1942/ staff: 1(f); 1(p)

HISTORIC SITE; HISTORY MUSEUM; HOUSE MUSEUM: Promotes Choctaw history in former Chief's home.

PROGRAMS: Community Outreach; Exhibits; Guided Tours

COLLECTIONS: [Prehistoric-modern times] Native American artifacts, fur trade items, fossils, architecture.

HOURS: Yr M-Sa 8-5, Su 2-5

ADMISSION: $3, Children $1

6854
Oklahoma Forest Heritage Center
Beavers Bend Resort Park, 74728 [PO Box 157, 74728]; (p) (580) 494-6497; (f) (580) 494-6689; fhc@beaversbend.com; www.beaversbend.com; (c) McCurtain

State/ 1977/ Oklahoma Department of Agriculture and Forestry/ staff: 2(f); 1(p)

HISTORY MUSEUM: Promotes conservation techniques, natural history.

PROGRAMS: Elder's Programs; Exhibits; Facility Rental; Festivals; Guided Tours; Research Library/Archives

COLLECTIONS: [Early 20th c-present] Lumber/timber industry photos and tools, Civilian

Conservation Corps memorabilia, wood sculptures, wood art gallery and dioramas.

HOURS: Yr Daily 8-8

BUFFALO

6855
Buffalo Museum
108 S Hoy, 73834 [PO Box 224, 73834]; (p) (405) 735-2008; www.shopoklahoma.com/museums.htm

CACHE

6856
Quanah Parker Star House
Eagle Park Ghost Town, Rte2, Box 9, 73527; (p) (405) 429-3238; www.shopoklahoma.com/museums.htm

CHANDLER

6857
Museum of Pioneer History
717-719 Manvel Ave, 74834; (p) (405) 258-2425; (f) (405) 258-2809; (c) Lincoln

Private non-profit/ 1954/ Lincoln County Historical Society/ staff: 1(f); 14(v)/ members: 400/publication: *Lincoln County, Oklahoma, History*

GENEALOGICAL SOCIETY; HISTORICAL SOCIETY; HISTORY MUSEUM; RESEARCH CENTER: Preserves history of Lincoln County.

PROGRAMS: Annual Meeting; Exhibits; Facility Rental; Film/Video; Guided Tours; Lectures; Publication; Research Library/Archives

COLLECTIONS: [1891-present] Artifacts: pioneer, militaryt, dental, medical, school, living quarters; two printing presses, photos, farm implements, tools, quilts, clothing, musical instruments, wagons, memorabilia of Deputy US Marshall Bill Tilghnam, and Route 66.

HOURS: Yr M-F 9:30-4

ADMISSION: Donations accepted

CHELSEA

6858
Hoque House
1001 S Olive, 74016; (p) (918) 789-3982; (c) Rogers

Private non-profit/ 1913

HOUSE MUSEUM: 1913 Sears-Roebuck precut Victorian home.

PROGRAMS: Family Programs; Guided Tours; Living History

COLLECTIONS: [Early 20th c]

HOURS: Yr Daily by appt

ADMISSION: No charge

CHEROKEE

6859
Alfalfa County Historical Society
117 W Main, 73728; (p) (580) 596-2960; alhistory@akslc.net; (c) Alfalfa

Private non-profit/ 1974/ Board of Directors/ staff: 2(p); 5(v)/ members: 100/publication: *Newsletter*

HISTORIC SITE; HISTORICAL SOCIETY; HISTORY MUSEUM: Preserves and interprets the prehistory and history.

PROGRAMS: Annual Meeting; Exhibits; Facility Rental; Guided Tours; Lectures; Living History; Publication; Research Library/Archives

COLLECTIONS: [1893-1949] Photos, manuscripts, books and research center.

HOURS: Yr T,Th-F 10-5 and by appt

CHEYENNE

6860
Black Kettle Museum
101 S LL Males, 73628 [PO Box 252, 73628]; (p) (580) 497-3929; (c) Roger Mills

State/ 1959/ Oklahoma Historical Society/ staff: 1(f); 1(p)

HISTORY MUSEUM: Interprets the Battle of the Washita, a military engagement between the Seventh U.S. Cavalry under Lt. Col. George Custer and the Cheyenne Indians under the leadership of Chief Black Kettle.

COLLECTIONS: [1868-early 1900s] Battle, local history artifacts.

HOURS: Yr T-Sa 9-5, Su 1-5; Summer additional hours

ADMISSION: Donations accepted

6861
Cheyenne City Park Museums
Cheyenne City Park, 73628 [PO Box 34, 73628]; (p) (580) 497-3318, (580) 497-2106; tdale55@aol.com; (c) Roger Mills

Private non-profit/ 1990/ Historic RMC Preservation Group/ staff: 2(f); 2(v)/ members: 70

HISTORIC PRESERVATION AGENCY: Restores historic buildings, including the Santa Fe Depot, Log Cabin, Veterans Display, Pioneer Museum, and One Room School.

PROGRAMS: Living History; School-Based Curriculum

COLLECTIONS: [Early 20th c] Schoolhouse, Santa Fe Depot, log cabin.

HOURS: Yr M-Sa 9-5, Su 1-5

ADMISSION: Donations accepted

6862
Washita Battlefield National Historic Site
426 Broadway, 73628 [PO Box 890, 73628]; (p) (580) 497-2742; (f) (580) 497-2712; www.nps.gov/waba; (c) Roger Mills

Federal/ 1996/ National Park Service/ staff: 4(f); 2(p); 9(v)

HISTORIC SITE: Preserves battle site of the Indian War.

PROGRAMS: Exhibits; Guided Tours; Interpretation

COLLECTIONS: [19th c] Cheyenne and Indian Wars.

HOURS: Yr Daily sunrise-sunset

ADMISSION: No charge

CHICKASHA

6863
Grady County Historical Society
415 Chickasha Ave, 73018 [PO Box 495, 73018]; (p) (405) 224-6480; (f) (405) 222-3730; angiecc@swbell.net; (c) Grady

Private non-profit/ 1985/ staff: 21(v)/ members: 100

HISTORICAL SOCIETY; HISTORY MUSEUM

PROGRAMS: Annual Meeting; Community Outreach; Exhibits; Guided Tours

COLLECTIONS: [1900-1960] County artifacts.

HOURS: Yr M-F 10-4

ADMISSION: Group rates

CHOCTAW

6864
Choctaw Historical Society and Caboose Museum
SE Corner NE 23rd St & Henney Rd, 73020 [PO Box 364, 73020]; (p) (405) 390-2771; (c) Oklahoma

City; Private non-profit; State/ 1976/ State of Oklahoma/ staff: 2(p); 2(v)

HISTORICAL SOCIETY; HISTORY MUSEUM; RESEARCH CENTER: Maintains and operates the Caboose Museum; local history research concerning Oklahoma County.

PROGRAMS: Exhibits; Guided Tours; Interpretation

COLLECTIONS: [1889-1920] Railway Caboose converted into museum with local history artifacts; pioneer, railroad photos.

HOURS: Mem Day-Labor Day Sa 10-4, Su 2-5; and by appt

ADMISSION: No charge

CLAREMORE

6865
Belvidere Mansion
121 N Chickasaw, 74017 [PO Box 774, 74018]; (p) (918) 342-1127; rchswr @ juno.com; www.rogersu.edu/claremore/historical

1907/ Rogers County Historical Society/ staff: 1(p); 10(v)

COLLECTIONS: [1800-1900] Vintage glassware and clothing (1920-30)

HOURS: Yr W-Sa, 10 - 3

6866
J.M. Davis Arms and Historical Museum
333 N Lynn Riggs Blvd, 74017 [PO Box 966, 74017]; (p) (918) 341-5707; (f) (918) 341-5771; www.state.ok.us/jmdavis/; (c) Rogers

State/ 1969/ State of Oklahoma/ staff: 5(f); 6(p)/publication: *Brochures and J.M. Davis Booklet*

HISTORIC PRESERVATION AGENCY; HISTORY MUSEUM

PROGRAMS: Exhibits; Festivals; Film/Video; Guided Tours; Lectures; Research Library/Archives; School-Based Curriculum

COLLECTIONS: [Prehistory-present] 20,000 guns and related items, 70 saddles, animal horns and trophy heads, musical instruments,

1,200 beer steins, swords, knives, Native American artifacts, John Rogers' statuary, over 600 World War I posters, firearms research library.

HOURS: Yr M-Sa 8:30-5, Su 1-5

ADMISSION: Donations accepted

6867
Will Rogers Memorial Museum
1720 Will Rogers Blvd, 74018 [PO Box 157, 74018]; (p) (918) 341-0719; (f) (918) 343-8119; wrinfo@willrogers.com; www.willrogers.com; (c) Rogers

State/ 1938/ Will Rogers Commission/State of Oklahoma/ staff: 13(f); 6(p)

HISTORY MUSEUM: Promotes life of humorist/philosopher Will Rogers.

PROGRAMS: Concerts; Exhibits; Family Programs; Festivals; Film/Video; Guided Tours; Interpretation; Living History; Research Library/Archives

COLLECTIONS: [1879-1935] Will Rogers artifacts.

HOURS: Yr Daily 8-5

ADMISSION: Donations accepted

CLINTON

6868
Cheyenne Cultural Center
2250 NE Route 66, 73601; (p) (580) 323-6224; (f) (580) 323-6225; (c) Custer

Private non-profit/ 1977/ Board of Trustees/ staff: 2(f); 2(p); 6(v)

CULTURAL CENTER: Focuses on the history, culture, and language of the Cheyenne tribe.

PROGRAMS: Community Outreach; Exhibits; Festivals; Guided Tours; Interpretation; Lectures

COLLECTIONS: [1830-1892] Primary material, photos, oral history recordings, Cheyenne Indian music, early reservation period and contemporary artifacts.

HOURS: Yr T-Sa 10-5:30; Su 1-5

6869
Oklahoma Route 66 Museum
2229 W Gary Blvd, 73601-5304; (p) (580) 323-7866; (f) (580) 323-2870; rt66mus@ok-history.mus.ok.us; www.Route66.org; (c) Custer

State/ 1995/ OK Historical Society/ staff: 2(f); 1(p); 14(v)

HISTORICAL SOCIETY; HISTORY MUSEUM: Explores the history of Route 66 and its cultural impact.

PROGRAMS: Community Outreach; Exhibits; Film/Video; Guided Tours; Interpretation; School-Based Curriculum

COLLECTIONS: [1920s-1970s] Automobile, popular culture, travel, Route 66 memorabilia.

HOURS: May-Aug M-Sa 9-7, Su 1-6; Sept-Apr M-Sa 9-5, Su 1-5; Dec-Jan T-Sa 9-5

ADMISSION: $3, Student $1, Seniors $2.50

COALGATE

6870
Coal County Historical and Mining Museum, Inc.
212 S Broadway, 74538; (p) (580) 927-2360; (c) Coal

Private non-profit/ 1975/ staff: 1(p); 9(v)/ members: 25

HISTORY MUSEUM: Preserves coal mining artifacts and historical records.

PROGRAMS: Community Outreach; Exhibits; Guided Tours; Lectures

COLLECTIONS: [1880-1930] Model mines, lunch boxes, drill bits, picks, lamps, shovels, mannequin, pictures, maps, antique toys, clothing, court, mining and census records.

HOURS: Yr

ADMISSION: No charge

CORDELL

6871
Washita County Historical Society
115 E First St, 73632 [PO Box 153, 73632]; (p) (580) 832-3681; wayneboothe@k.wash.net; (c) Washita

County/ Washita County/ staff: 8(v)/ members: 358

GENEALOGICAL SOCIETY; HISTORIC PRESERVATION AGENCY; HISTORICAL SOCIETY: Preserves local historical items.

PROGRAMS: Annual Meeting; Exhibits; Festivals; Guided Tours; Lectures

COLLECTIONS: [1892-1940s] Pioneer photos.

HOURS: Yr F 1-4 and by appt

ADMISSION: No charge

CUSHING

6872
Cimarron Valley Railroad Museum
S Kings Hwy & Eseco Rd, 74023 [PO Box 844, 74023]; (p) (918) 225-1657, (918) 225-3936; (c) Payne

Private non-profit/ 1970/ staff: 1(f); 4(v)

HISTORY MUSEUM; LIVING HISTORY/OUT-DOOR MUSEUM: Preserves regional and local railroad history.

PROGRAMS: Exhibits; Guided Tours; Interpretation; Lectures; Research Library/Archives

COLLECTIONS: [1900-1985] Santa Fe wooden depot, 1917 tank car, wooden Frisco caboose, 1897 DLCC box car, diesel switch locomotive, railroad library and artifacts.

HOURS: Yr by appt

ADMISSION: Donations accepted

DEWEY

6873
Tom Mix Museum
721 N Delaware, 74029 [PO Box 190, 74029]; (p) (918) 534-1555; (c) Washington

State/ 1968/ Oklahoma Historical Society/ staff: 2(p)/ members: 300

HISTORY MUSEUM: Preserves the personal property of Tom Mix, a leading actor, owner of Wild West Show and master horseman.

PROGRAMS: Elder's Programs; Exhibits; Family Programs; Festivals; Film/Video; Guided Tours; Living History; Theatre

COLLECTIONS: [1900-1940] Movie costumes and props, photos, guns.

HOURS: Feb Sa 10-4:30, Su 1-4:30; Mar-Dec T-Sa 10-4:30, Su 1-4:30

ADMISSION: Donations requested

DRUMRIGHT

6874
Drumright Historical Society
[PO Box 668, 74030]; (p) (918) 352-2204; (c) Creek

City/ 1964/ staff: 6(f)/ members: 300

HISTORICAL SOCIETY; HISTORY MUSEUM

PROGRAMS: Annual Meeting; Exhibits; Festivals; Guided Tours; Lectures; School-Based Curriculum

COLLECTIONS: [Early 20th c] Artifacts: Oilfield, yearbooks, dollhouse.

HOURS: Yr Su 1-5

ADMISSION: No charge

DUNCAN

6875
On The Chisholm Trail Association
1000 N 29th St, 73533; (p) (580) 252-6692; (f) (580) 252-6567; statue@texhoma.net; www.onthechisholmtrail.com; (c) Stephens

Private non-profit/ 1997/ staff: 2(f); 1(p); 2(v)

HISTORIC PRESERVATION AGENCY; HISTORIC SITE; HISTORY MUSEUM: Interprets Oklahoma's Chisholm Trail.

PROGRAMS: Exhibits; Family Programs; Festivals; Guided Tours; Interpretation; Lectures

COLLECTIONS: [1867-1885] Cattle drives, trail life, economic histories and artifacts.

HOURS: Yr M-Sa 10-5, Su 1-5

6876
Stephens County Historical Museum
N Hwy 81 & Beech, Fuqua Park, 73533 [PO Box 1294, 73533]; (p) (580) 255-2553, (580) 252-0717; (c) Stephens

1969/ staff: 1(f); 10(v)/ members: 400

HISTORIC SITE; HISTORICAL SOCIETY; HISTORY MUSEUM: Depicts OK pioneer life.

PROGRAMS: Annual Meeting; Community Outreach; Exhibits; Facility Rental; Festivals; Guided Tours; Living History; School-Based Curriculum

COLLECTIONS: [19th c] Archaeological samples, arrowheads, crafts, Native American lore, farming, pioneer drug store, blacksmith shop, legal, medical, rural school house.

HOURS: Yr T, Th-Sa 1-5

ADMISSION: No charge

DURANT

6877
Fort Washta Historic Site
HC 62 Box 213, 74701; (p) (580) 924-6502; (f) (580) 924-6502; (c) Bryan

State/ 1962/ Oklahoma Historical Society/ staff: 3(f); 1(p); 25(v)/ members: 25

HISTORIC SITE: Collects, preserves and interprets material relating to frontier military post.

PROGRAMS: Community Outreach; Exhibits; Festivals; Guided Tours; Interpretation; Living History; Reenactments

COLLECTIONS: [1842-1865] Restored buildings, military artifacts, documents.

HOURS: Yr M-Sa 9-5, Su 1-5

ADMISSION: No charge

EDMOND

6878
Edmond Historical Society
431 South Blvd, 73034; (p) (405) 340-0078; (f) (405) 340-2771; (c) Oklahoma

Private non-profit/ 1983/ Board of Directors/ staff: 3(f); 2(p); 65(v)/ members: 400

HISTORICAL SOCIETY; HISTORY MUSEUM: Collects, preserves and interprets the history of Edmond.

PROGRAMS: Annual Meeting; Community Outreach; Exhibits; Family Programs; Festivals; Guided Tours; Interpretation; Lectures; Living History; Research Library/Archives; School-Based Curriculum; Theatre

COLLECTIONS: [1889-1950] Edmond artifacts, photos.

HOURS: Yr T-F 10-4, Sa 1-4

ADMISSION: Donations accepted

ELK CITY

6879
National Route 66 Museum/Old Town Complex
2717 W Hwy 66, 73648 [PO Box 988, 73648]; (p) (580) 225-6266; (c) Beckham

City/ 1966/ staff: 4(f); 50(v)

HISTORY MUSEUM; LIVING HISTORY/OUTDOOR MUSEUM: Preserves history of people who lived, worked and traveled Route 66. Includes Pioneer Museum, Rodeo Hall Opera House, and Farm and Ranch Museum.

PROGRAMS: Annual Meeting; Exhibits; Facility Rental; Family Programs; Guided Tours; Living History

COLLECTIONS: [1910-1970] Artifacts: Pioneer living, local farming communities, lifestyle.

HOURS: Yr M-Sa 9-5, Su 2-5

ADMISSION: $5, Student $4, Seniors $4

ENID

6880
Garfield County Historical Society
506 S 4th St, 73701; (p) (580) 237-1907; (c) Garfield

Private non-profit/ 1955/ members: 10

HISTORICAL SOCIETY: Dedicated to the history of Garfield County; supports Museum of the Cherokee Strip.

PROGRAMS: Annual Meeting; Exhibits

COLLECTIONS: [1893-present]

6881
Midgley Museum
1001 Sequoyah Dr, 73703; (p) (580) 237-5918, (580) 233-6378; (c) Garfield

Private non-profit/ 1991/ Masonic Lodges/ staff: 1(f); 49(v)

HISTORIC SITE; LIVING HISTORY/OUTDOOR MUSEUM

PROGRAMS: Exhibits; Guided Tours

COLLECTIONS: [1895-1958] Natural history exhibits and artifacts.

HOURS: Spring-Summer M-F 10-5; Fall-Winter T-F 1-5

ADMISSION: No charge

6882
Oklahoma Historical Society's Museum of the Cherokee Strip
507 S 4th St, 73701; (p) (580) 237-1907; (f) (580) 242-2874; MCS1@onenet.net; (c) Garfield

State/ 1975/ Oklahoma Historical Society/ staff: 2(f); 30(v)/publication: *The Journal of the Cherokee Strip*

HISTORICAL SOCIETY; HISTORY MUSEUM: Interprets the pioneer settlement period of the Cherokee Strip portion of OK, cattle drive era.

PROGRAMS: Annual Meeting; Community Outreach; Exhibits; Facility Rental; Family Programs; Festivals; Film/Video; Guided Tours; Interpretation; Lectures; Living History; Publication; Reenactments; Research Library/Archives; School-Based Curriculum

COLLECTIONS: [1893-1930] Clothing, household goods, furniture and memorabilia.

HOURS: Yr T-F 9-5,

6883
Railroad Museum of Oklahoma
702 N Washington, 73701; (p) (580) 233-3051; (c) Garfield

Private non-profit/ 1988/ National Railway Historical Society/ staff: 8(v)/ members: 132/publication: *Making Tracks*

ART MUSEUM; HISTORICAL SOCIETY; HISTORY MUSEUM: Preserves and displays historical railroad artifacts.

PROGRAMS: Exhibits; Film/Video; Guided Tours; Publication; Research Library/Archives

COLLECTIONS: [1834-present] Engines, cars and cabooses; dining car china and silverware; maps of railroad lines, paintings, depot clocks, telegraph system, model trains, steam engine bells, lights, whistles and lanterns; reference books, photos and videotapes.

HOURS: Yr T-F 1-4, Sa 9-1, Su 2-5

ADMISSION: Donations requested

6884
Sons and Daughters of the Cherokee Strip Pioneers
506 S 4th St, 73702 [PO Box 465, 73702]; (p) (580) 237-1907; mcs1@onenet.net; (c) Garfield

Private non-profit/ 1932/ Board/ staff: 20(v)/ members: 600/publication: *Journal of the Cherokee Strip*

HISTORICAL SOCIETY; HISTORY MUSEUM; HOUSE MUSEUM: Preserves history of Cherokee Strip; supports Museum of the Cherokee Strip.

PROGRAMS: Annual Meeting; Exhibits; Facility Rental; Festivals; Guided Tours; Interpretation; Lectures; Living History; Publication; Reenactments; Research Library/Archives; School-Based Curriculum

COLLECTIONS: [1880-1950] Land Run of 1893.

HOURS: Yr T-F 9-5, Sa-Su 2-5

ADMISSION: Donations accepted

FORT GIBSON

6885
Fort Gibson Historic Site
907 N Garrison, 74434 [PO Box 457, 74434]; (p) (918) 478-4088; (f) (918) 478-4089; fortgibson@ok-history.mus.ok.us; www.geocities.com/TheTropics/Cove/4694; (c) Muskogee

State/ 1936/ Oklahoma Historical Society/ staff: 5(f); 2(p); 150(v)

HISTORIC SITE: Preserves and interprets area historic and archaeological resources.

PROGRAMS: Community Outreach; Exhibits; Facility Rental; Family Programs; Festivals; Guided Tours; Interpretation; Lectures; Living History; Reenactments; School-Based Curriculum

COLLECTIONS: [1824-1890] Military

HOURS: Yr M-F M-Sa 9-5, Su 1-5

ADMISSION: $3, Student $1, Seniors $2.50; Under 6 free

FORT SILL

6886
Fort Sill National Historic Landmark
437 Quanah Rd, 73503; (p) (580) 442-5123; (f) (580) 442-8120; spiveyt@doimexl.sil.army.mil; (c) Comanche

Federal/ 1934/ US Army/ staff: 7(f); 30(v)

HISTORIC SITE: Preserves the history of Fort Sill and field artillery.

PROGRAMS: Exhibits; Film/Video; Interpretation; Living History; Research Library/Archives

COLLECTIONS: [19th c-20th c] Indian Wars period fort; personal belongings of Geronimo, Quanah Parke, and other notable Native American leaders; cavalry, infantry and artillery items.

HOURS: Yr Daily 8:30-4:30

ADMISSION: No charge

FREDERICK

6887
Tillman County Historical Museum
201 N 9th St, 73542 [PO Box 833, 73542]; (p) (580) 335-5844, (580) 335-2989; www.frisco.org/msw/mswtil.htm; (c) Tillman

Private non-profit/ 1979/ Tillman County Historical and Educational Society/ staff: 1(f); 1(p)/ members: 250

HISTORIC PRESERVATION AGENCY; HISTORY MUSEUM: Preserves artifacts and information about Tillman County, housed in former Horse Creek School.

PROGRAMS: Annual Meeting; Community Outreach; Exhibits; Guided Tours; Living History; School-Based Curriculum

COLLECTIONS: [Early 20th c] Household items, farm machinery, poultry and cattle operation equipment, horse-drawn fire equipment and farming implements, wagons, tractor, toys, pictures, school, church.

HOURS: Yr M-Th 10-3, Sa-Su 2-4 and by

GATE

6888
GATEway to the Panhandle Museum Corporation
E Main, 73844 [PO Box 27, 73844]; (p) (580) 934-2004; (c) Beaver

City/ 1975/ staff: 3(f); 8(v)/ members: 40/publication: *Gate to the Panhandle*

HISTORICAL SOCIETY; HISTORY MUSEUM: Preserves local history.

PROGRAMS: Annual Meeting; Community Outreach; Exhibits; Facility Rental; Family Programs; Film/Video; Publication; Research Library/Archives; School-Based Curriculum

COLLECTIONS: [19th c] Civil War, farming, household items, ancient bones, Native American artifacts.

GEARY

6889
Canadian Rivers Historical Society
Main & Broadway, 73040 [Route 1, Box 78A, 73040]; (p) (405) 884-5456; (c) Blaine

City, non-profit/ 1968/ staff: 20(v)/ members: 20

ALLIANCE OF HISTORICAL AGENCIES; GENEALOGICAL SOCIETY; HISTORIC PRESERVATION AGENCY; HISTORICAL SOCIETY; HISTORY MUSEUM; RESEARCH CENTER; TRIBAL MUSEUM: Preserves history of Canadian Pacific.

PROGRAMS: Annual Meeting; Community Outreach; Exhibits; Guided Tours; Research Library/Archives

COLLECTIONS: [1881-1970] Photo archives, posters, advertising and promotional materials pertaining to CP railway, hotels, ships.

HOURS: Yr by appt

GOODWELL

6890
No Man's Land Historical Society, Inc.
207 W Sewell, 73939 [PO Box 278, 73939-0278]; (p) (580) 349-6697, (580) 349-2670; (f) (580) 349-2670; nmlhs@ptsi.net; (c) Texas

Private non-profit/ 1934/ Governing Council/ staff: 2(p); 6(v)/ members: 328/publication: *Recollections of No Man's Land: Memoirs of Fred Carter Tracy, Central High Plains History Series No. 1*

HISTORICAL SOCIETY; HISTORY MUSEUM: Supportsr No Man's Land Museum; collects and distributes history of OK Panhandle and borderlands.

PROGRAMS: Annual Meeting; Exhibits; Guided Tours; Interpretation; Lectures; Publication; Research Library/Archives

COLLECTIONS: [Prehistory-present] Artifacts.

HOURS: Yr T-Sa 9-12/1-5 and by appt

ADMISSION: No charge

GROVE

6891
Har-Ber Village Museum
4404 W 20th St, 74344; (p) (918) 786-3488, (918) 786-6446; (f) (918) 787-6213; harbervil@aol.com; www.harbervillage.com; (c) Delaware

Private non-profit/ 1968/ Board of Trustees/ staff: 9(f); 2(p); 20(v)

HISTORY MUSEUM: Collects, preserves and interprets local history.

PROGRAMS: Concerts; Exhibits; Family Programs; School-Based Curriculum

COLLECTIONS: [19th-20th c] China, household equipment, furnishings, dolls, glassware, brass in reconstructed log cabins.

HOURS: Mar 1-Nov 15 M-Sa 9-6, Su 11-6

GUTHRIE

6892
Oklahoma Sports Museum
315 W Oklahoma Ave, 73044 [PO Box 1342, 73044]; (p) (405) 260-1342; (f) (405) 260-1342; (c) Logan

Private non-profit/ 1993/ Oklahoma Sports Museum Association/ staff: 1(f); 4(p); 25(v)/ members: 200

ART MUSEUM; HISTORY MUSEUM: Recognizes Oklahoma athletes and coaches.

PROGRAMS: Community Outreach; Exhibits; Facility Rental; Lectures

COLLECTIONS: [1889-present] Photos, murals, sports art, bronze and clay sculptures, sports equipment and artifacts.

HOURS: Yr Su-M, W-Th 11-5, F-Sa 10-5 and by appt

ADMISSION: Donations accepted

6893
Oklahoma Territorial Museum/Carnegie Library
406 E Oklahoma, 73044; (p) (405) 282-1889; (c) Logan

State/ 1974/ Oklahoma Historical Society/ staff: 3(f); 1(p); 15(v)/ members: 45

HISTORIC SITE; HISTORY MUSEUM: Interprets the Land Run of 1889.

PROGRAMS: Community Outreach; Exhibits; Facility Rental; Family Programs; Interpretation; Lectures; Living History; Research Library/Archives

COLLECTIONS: [1866-1913] Land Run of 1889, transportation, textiles, tools, photos, documents and early records.

HOURS: Yr T-F 9-5, Sa 10-4, Su 1-4

ADMISSION: $2; Donations requested; children free

6894
State Capital Publishing Museum
301 W Harrison Ave, 73044; (p) (405) 282-4123; (c) Logan

State/ 1974/ Oklahoma Historical Society/ staff: 3(f); 1(p); 15(v)/ members: 45

HISTORIC SITE: Preserves history of print technology.

PROGRAMS: Community Outreach; Exhibits; Family Programs; Interpretation; Living History

COLLECTIONS: [1902-1974] Presses, bookbinding, print technology and historic records.

HOURS: Yr T-F 9-5, Sa 10-4, Su 1-4

ADMISSION: Donations requested

HARRAH

6895
Harrah Historical Society
East Main St, 73045 [PO Box 846, 73045]; (c) Oklahoma

Private non-profit/ 1976/ Harrah Historical Society/ staff: 1(p)/ members: 56

HISTORICAL SOCIETY; HISTORY MUSEUM: Preserves local history.

PROGRAMS: Annual Meeting; Community Outreach; Concerts; Exhibits; Interpretation; Lectures

COLLECTIONS: [Early 20th c] Local and railroad history, photos, documents, ephemera, subject files.

HOURS: Yr by appt

ADMISSION: No charge

HAWORTH

6896
Henry Harris Home
HC 60, Box 2070, 74740; (p) (405) 245-1129; www.shopoklahoma.com/museums.htm

HEAVENER

6897
Peter Conser House
4 mi S on US Hwy 59, 74937 [HC 64, Box 3725, 74937]; (p) (918) 653-2493

1894/ State/ staff: 1(f)

COLLECTIONS: [1894-1910]

HOURS: Yr

HOMINY

6898
Drummond House
305 N Price Ave, 74035-1007; (p) (918) 885-2374

1905/ Oklahoma Historical Society/ staff: 1(p)

COLLECTIONS: Period artifacts.

HOURS: Yr; Fri-Sat, 9-5, Sun, 1-5

IDABEL

6899
McCurtain County Historical Society
302 SE Adams, 74745; (p) (580) 584-6588, (580) 286-6314; (c) McCurtain

Private non-profit/ 1972/ staff: 1(p); 10(v)/ members: 150

HISTORIC PRESERVATION AGENCY; HISTORIC SITE; HISTORICAL SOCIETY: Preserves and promotes county history.

PROGRAMS: Annual Meeting; Community Outreach; Exhibits; Facility Rental; Guided Tours

COLLECTIONS: [Early 20th c] Victorian home furnishings, glassware and fans.

HOURS: Yr by appt

ADMISSION: No charge

6900
Museum of the Red River
812 E Lincoln Rd, 74745; (p) (580) 286-3616; (f) (580) 286-3616; www.museumoftheredriver.org; (c) McCurtain

Private non-profit/ 1975/ Herron Foundation/ staff: 3(f); 2(p)/publication: *Sherds*

CULTURAL CENTER; HISTORY MUSEUM: Preserves material culture of Native Americans.

PROGRAMS: Community Outreach; Elder's Programs; Exhibits; Facility Rental; Family Programs; Festivals; Film/Video; Guided Tours; Interpretation; Lectures; Publication; School-Based Curriculum

COLLECTIONS: [10,000 BC-present] Cultural art and artifacts.

HOURS: Yr T-F 10-5, Sa-Su 11-4

ADMISSION: No charge

INDIANOLA

6901
Choate House Museum
403 Walnut, 74442 [PO Box 239, Indianola, 74442]; (p) (918) 823-4421

1867/ Roy V. Bynum, - Ow

COLLECTIONS: [1853-1907] Indian Art

HOURS: By appt.

JAY

6902
Delaware County Historical Society
538 W Krause, 74346 [PO Box 855, 74346]; (p) (918) 253-4345; (c) Delaware

Joint/ 1981/ County; Private non-profit; Mariee Wallace Museum/ staff: 1(f); 6(v)/ members: 200/publication: *Heritage Of The Hills*

ART MUSEUM; GENEALOGICAL SOCIETY; HISTORICAL SOCIETY: Collects, preserves, and exhibits articles to illustrate local settlements, developments, activities, and progress.

PROGRAMS: Annual Meeting; Community Outreach; Exhibits; Festivals; Guided Tours; Lectures; Publication; Research Library/ Archives; School-Based Curriculum

COLLECTIONS: [Early 20th c] Early OK household artifacts, barber shop, Civil War mementos, buggies.

HOURS: Yr M-T, Th-F 9-5, W 1:30-5, Sa 9-1:30

ADMISSION: Donations

JENKS

6903
Doctor B.W. McLean Home and Office
123 E A St, 74037; (p) (918) 446-2745, (918) 299-8634; (c) Tulsa

Private non-profit/ 1986/ Family of Dr. McLean/ staff: 2(v)

HISTORIC SITE; HOUSE MUSEUM

PROGRAMS: Guided Tours

COLLECTIONS: [Early 20th c] Victorian home with original furnishings, documents, medical equipment, quilts, clothing and personal belongings.

HOURS: Yr Sa 3-4, or by appt

KAW CITY

6904
Kaw City Museum Association, Inc.
910 Washunga Dr, 74641 [PO Box 56, 74641]; (p) (580) 762-3046, (580) 269-2366; (c) Kay

City; Private non-profit/ 1974/ staff: 15(v)/ members: 110

GENEALOGICAL SOCIETY; HISTORIC SITE; HISTORY MUSEUM: Preserves history and artifacts of the Ox Bow Bend Area of the AR River.

PROGRAMS: Annual Meeting; Community Outreach; Elder's Programs; Exhibits; Facility Rental; Festivals; Film/Video; Guided Tours; Lectures; Research Library/Archives

COLLECTIONS: [Prehistory-20th c] Archaeological artifacts, Kanza Indian articles, Cherokee Strip and early OK items; photos, home interior, oral and written histories.

HOURS: Yr by appt; May-Sept Sa-Su 2-5

ADMISSION: No charge

KEOTA

6905
Overstreet-Kerr Historical Farm
10 mi S on Hwy 595, then W on Overstreet-Kerr Rd, 74941 [Rte 2, Box 693, 74941]; (p) (918) 966-3282, (918) 966-3396; (f) (918) 966-3282; (c) Le Flore

1890/ Kerr Center for Sustainable Agriculture/ staff: 2(f); 6(v)

COLLECTIONS: [1871-1914]

HOURS: Yr

KINGFISHER

6906
Chisholm Trail Museum/Governor Seay Mansion
605 Zellers Ave, 73750; (p) (405) 375-5176; (f) (405) 375-5176; reneem@ok-history.mus.ok.us; (c) Kingfisher

State/ 1967/ Oklahoma Historical Society/ staff: 2(f); 60(v)/ members: 200

HISTORIC SITE; HISTORY MUSEUM; HOUSE MUSEUM; LIVING HISTORY/OUTDOOR MUSEUM: Preserves artifacts pertaining to the cattle trail, pioneers and Native Americans.

PROGRAMS: Annual Meeting; Concerts; Exhibits; Family Programs; Guided Tours; Lectures; Living History; Reenactments; Research Library/Archives; School-Based Curriculum

COLLECTIONS: [19th c] Pioneer household items, farm implements, Native American artifacts, Victorian furniture, arrowheads, vintage clothing, horse-drawn hearse, chuck wagon, artifacts from land office, one-room schoolhouse, church, bank and two log cabins.

HOURS: Yr T-Sa 9-5, Su 1-5

LANGSTON

6907
Melvin B. Tolson Black Heritage Center
Langston University, Sandford Hall, 73050; (p) (405) 466-3346, (405) 466-3239; (f) (405) 466-3459; www.library2lunet.edu; (c) Logan

State/ 1976/ Board of Regents/ staff: 2(f); 1(p); 6(v)/ members: 35

LIBRARY AND/OR ARCHIVES: One of two libraries at Langston University.

PROGRAMS: Exhibits; Guided Tours; Lectures; Research Library/Archives; School-Based Curriculum

COLLECTIONS: [19th-20th c] Books, films, videos, periodicals, newspapers and microfilm concerning Africa and African Americans.

HOURS: Yr M, W, F 8-5, T,Th 8-10, Su 2-10; Summer M-F 8-5

ADMISSION: No charge

LAWTON

6908
Lawton Heritage Association, Inc.
1006 SW 5th St, 73502 [PO Box 311, 73502]; (p) (580) 357-1549; (f) (580) 252-6170; fish-pa@ascog.org; (c) Comanche

Private non-profit/ 1973/ Board of Directors/ staff: 50(v)/ members: 250

HISTORIC PRESERVATION AGENCY; HISTORIC SITE; HISTORICAL SOCIETY; HOUSE MUSEUM: Operates and owns Mattie Beal Home; promotes history and preservation in Comanche County and SW Oklahoma.

PROGRAMS: Annual Meeting; Community Outreach; Exhibits; Facility Rental; Family Programs; Festivals; Guided Tours; Interpretation; Living History

COLLECTIONS: [1907-1925] Artifacts in period mansion.

6909
Lawton Public Library
110 SW 4th St, 73501; (p) (580) 581-3450; (f) (580) 248-0243; reference@cityof.lawton.ok.us; www.cityof.lawton.ok.us/library/; (c) Comanche

City/ 1904/ staff: 14(f); 14(p)

LIBRARY AND/OR ARCHIVES: Preserves historical and genealogical materials.

PROGRAMS: Lectures; Research Library/ Archives

COLLECTIONS: 13,000 books.

HOURS: Yr M-Th 10-9, F 10-6, Sa 10-5, Su 1-5; June-Aug closed

6910
Museum of the Great Plains
601 NW Ferris, 73502 [PO Box 68, 73502];

(p) (580) 581-3460; (f) (580) 581-3458; mgp@sirinet.net; www.sirinet.net/~mgp; (c) Comanche

City/ 1961/ Museum of the Great Plains Trust Authority/ staff: 14(f); 20(v)/ members: 400/publication: *Great Plains Journal*

HISTORY MUSEUM; LIVING HISTORY/OUTDOOR MUSEUM; RESEARCH CENTER: Preserves the history of the Great Plains.

PROGRAMS: Annual Meeting; Community Outreach; Exhibits; Facility Rental; Guided Tours; Interpretation; Lectures; Living History; Publication; Reenactments; Research Library/Archives; School-Based Curriculum; Theatre

COLLECTIONS: [Prehistoric-present] Historical, archaeological, botanical, ethnological, geological and zoological materials and archives.

HOURS: Yr Daily 8-5

ADMISSION: $2, Children $1

6911
Southwestern Oklahoma Historical Society
[PO Box 3693, 73502]; (p) (580) 353-3632; (c) Comanche

Private non-profit/ 19634/ Board of Directors/ staff: 12(v)/ members: 375/publication: *Prairie Lore*

HISTORICAL SOCIETY: Preserves local history.

PROGRAMS: Annual Meeting; Family Programs; Publication

COLLECTIONS: [20th c] Publications.

LEEDEY

6912
Boswell Museum
Main St, 73654 [PO Box 128, 73654]; (p) (580) 488-3476; (c) Dewey

Private non-profit/ 1971/ Y.W.S. Club/ staff: 1(v)

HISTORY MUSEUM: Preserves the history of the community.

COLLECTIONS: Newspapers, artwork, photographs, saddles, buggies, dishes and furniture.

HOURS: May-Sept M-W 1-4

LINDSAY

6913
Murray-Lindsay Mansion
[PO Box 282, 73052]; (p) (405) 756-2121

1879/ Lindsay Community / staff: 1(f); 10(v)

COLLECTIONS: [1879-1900] Period furniture, farm machinery.

HOURS: Yr

MANGUM

6914
Old Greer County Museum
222 W Jefferson, 73554; (p) (580) 782-2851; (c) Greer

County; Private non-profit/ 1973/ Board of Directors/ staff: 2(v)/ members: 85

HISTORIC SITE; HISTORY MUSEUM; LIVING HISTORY/OUTDOOR MUSEUM: Preserves local history.

PROGRAMS: Annual Meeting; Festivals

COLLECTIONS: Interpretive rooms; family and school histories; Native American; local mineral and rock formations, and 256 monuments.

HOURS: Yr T-F 9-12/1-5

ADMISSION: $1, Children $0.50

MARIETTA

6915
Love County Historical Society, Inc.
101 SW Front St, 73430 [PO Box 134, 73430]; (p) (580) 276-5888; (c) Love

Private non-profit/ 1979/ staff: 4(v)/ members: 115

GENEALOGICAL SOCIETY; HISTORICAL SOCIETY; HISTORY MUSEUM: Maintains the Pioneer Museum.

PROGRAMS: Annual Meeting; Exhibits; Guided Tours; Research Library/Archives

COLLECTIONS: [19th-20th c] Pioneer living and farming, fossils, early household and clothing articles, photos, county, school and family histories.

HOURS: May-Oct Th-F 1-4 and by appt.

MEEKER

6916
Carl Hubbell Museum
Meeker City Hall, W Main St, 74855 [PO Box 186, 74855]; (p) (405) 279-3813; (c) Lincoln

Private non-profit/ 1983/ Carl Hubbell Museum Association/ staff: 2(v)

HISTORY MUSEUM: Promotes history of NY Giants' pitcher.

COLLECTIONS: [1920-1988] Autographed baseballs, trophies, photos, hall of fame memorabilia, and paintings.

HOURS: Yr M-F 8-5

MIAMI

6917
Dobson Museum
110 A SW, 74354; (p) (918) 542-5388; emoore@mmind.net; (c) Ottawa

Private for-profit/ 1960/ staff: 2(f); 49(p); 1(v)/ members: 92

ART MUSEUM; GARDEN; GENEALOGICAL SOCIETY; HISTORICAL SOCIETY; HISTORY MUSEUM; RESEARCH CENTER

PROGRAMS: Annual Meeting; Community Outreach; Exhibits; Facility Rental; Family Programs; Garden Tours; Interpretation; Living History; Research Library/Archives; School-Based Curriculum

COLLECTIONS: Native American bead works, art, clothes, pictures, manuscripts.

HOURS: Yr

ADMISSION: No charge

MUSKOGEE

6918
Ataloa Lodge Museum
Hwy 16 & 64, 74403 [2299 Old Bacone Rd, 74403]; (p) (918) 683-4581; (f) (918) 687-5913; (c) Muskogee

Private non-profit/ 1967/ Bacone College/ staff: 1(p); 5(v)/publication: *Baconian*

ART MUSEUM; HISTORY MUSEUM; HOUSE MUSEUM: Native American, natural history and foreign artifacts.

PROGRAMS: Community Outreach; Exhibits; Festivals; Guided Tours; Lectures; Theatre

COLLECTIONS: [1500-present] 20,000 artifacts from North, Central and South American Native peoples, fossil material from OK, Civil War and Trail of Tears period items, Native American art, photos.

HOURS: Yr M-F 10-4, Sa-Su by appt.

6919
Bacone College
2299 Old Bacone Rd, 74403; (p) (918) 683-4581; (f) (918) 687-5913; williamsu@mail.bacone.edu; www.bacone.edu; (c) Muskogee

Private non-profit/ 1880/ Board of Trustees/ staff: 2(f); 2(p); 5(v)

ART MUSEUM; HISTORY MUSEUM: Preserves history of Bacone College, formerly only institution of higher learning serving Native Americans.

PROGRAMS: Exhibits; Guided Tours; Research Library/Archives

COLLECTIONS: [1880-present] Native American art, artifacts, Baptist missionary diaries,

6920
Five Civilized Tribes Museum and Center for the Study of Indian Territory
Agency Hill, Honor Heights Dr, 74401; (p) (918) 683-1701; (f) (918) 683-3070; (c) Muskogee

Private non-profit/ 1966/ staff: 3(f); 3(p); 100(v)/ members: 950

ART MUSEUM; HISTORIC SITE; HISTORY MUSEUM: Promotes history of the Five Civilized Tribes and Indian Territory.

PROGRAMS: Exhibits; Guided Tours; Research Library/Archives

COLLECTIONS: [19th-20th c] Native American art, artifacts, and documents.

HOURS: Yr M-Sa 10-5, Su 1-5

ADMISSION: $2

6921
Muskogee County Genealogical Society
801 W Okmulgee, Muskogee Public Library, 74401-6840; (p) (918) 682-6657; muscogeso@yahoo.com; (c) Muskogee

Private non-profit/ 1983/ members: 85

GENEALOGICAL SOCIETY: Promotes preservation and research of family history in Muskogee County.

6922
Thomas-Foreman House
1419 W Okmulgee, 74401-6740; (p) (918) 682-6938

6923
Three Rivers Museum of Muskogee, Inc.
[PO Box 1813, 74402]; (p) (918) 686-6624; 3riversmuseum@muskogee.ok.us; www.3riversmuseum.muskogee.ok.us; (c) Muskogee

Private non-profit/ 1989/ members: 135/publication: *Three Rivers Historian*

HISTORY MUSEUM: Promotes regional history in former Midland Valley Railroad Depot.

PROGRAMS: Community Outreach; Exhibits; Facility Rental; Guided Tours; Interpretation; Lectures; Publication

COLLECTIONS: [19th c-present] Historical objects relating to the Three Rivers.

6924
War Memorial Park, USS Batfish
3500 Batfish Rd, 74402 [PO Box 253, 74402]; (p) (918) 682-6294; ussbatfish@yahoo.com; www.geocitites.com/ussbatfish; (c) Muskogee

Private non-profit/ 1972/ War Memorial Park Authority Trust/ staff: 1(f); 1(v)

HISTORY MUSEUM

PROGRAMS: Exhibits; Reenactments

COLLECTIONS: [1860-present] WWII artifacts.

HOURS: Mid March-mid Oct M, W-F 9-5, Su 12-5

ADMISSION: $4, Student $1.50, Seniors $3; Under 6 free; Group rates

NEWKIRK

6925
Newkirk Community Historical Society
101 S Maple, 74647 [500 W 8th, 74647]; (p) (580) 362-3330; (f) (580) 362-3724; (c) Kay

Private non-profit/ 1968/ staff: 14(v)/ members: 150/publication: *Jubilee; Newkirk Carved in Stone; Newkirk and Kay County Diamond*

HISTORICAL SOCIETY; HISTORY MUSEUM

PROGRAMS: Annual Meeting; Elder's Programs; Exhibits; Guided Tours; Lectures; Publication

COLLECTIONS: [1893-1947] Local Native American artifacts, agriculture related and early pioneer artifacts, mail buggy.

NORMAN

6926
Carl Albert Congressional Research and Studies Center
630 Parrington Oval, Rm 101, 73019-4031; (p) (405) 325-6372; (f) (405) 325-6419; www.ou.edu/special/albertctr/; (c) Cleveland

State/ 1979/ Univ of OK/ staff: 7(f); 7(p)/publication: *Extensions*

RESEARCH CENTER: Provides instruction and promotes scholarship related to the history, structure, processes, personnel and policies of the US Congress.

PROGRAMS: Community Outreach; Exhibits; Guided Tours; Lectures; Publication; Research Library/Archives

COLLECTIONS: [20th c]

6927
Cleveland County Historical Society Museum
508 N Peters, 73070 [PO Box 260, 73070]; (p) (405) 321-0156; (c) Cleveland

City; Private non-profit/ 1975/ staff: 1(f); 25(v)/ members: 175

HISTORICAL SOCIETY; HOUSE MUSEUM

PROGRAMS: Annual Meeting; Community Outreach; Exhibits; Facility Rental; Festivals; Guided Tours; Living History; School-Based Curriculum

COLLECTIONS: [1885-1910] Archive, library, lace, furniture and home built in 1899.

HOURS: Yr M-F 1-4 or by appt

ADMISSION: No charge

6928
Sam Noble Oklahoma Museum of Natural History
2401 Chautauqua Ave, 73072-7029; (p) (405) 325-4712; (f) (405) 325-7699; snomnh@ou.edu; www.snomnh.ou.edu; (c) Cleveland

State/ 1899/ Univ of OK/ staff: 87(f); 30(p); 400(v)/ members: 1000

HISTORIC PRESERVATION AGENCY; HISTORY MUSEUM; NATURAL HISTORY MUSEUM: Researches, collects and preserves the natural and cultural history of OK.

PROGRAMS: Community Outreach; Concerts; Exhibits; Facility Rental; Family Programs; Guided Tours; Interpretation; Lectures; School-Based Curriculum

COLLECTIONS: [Prehistory-present] Over 6 million natural history specimens and artifacts representing life, earth and social sciences; natural history, Native American art.

HOURS: Yr M-Sa 10-5, Su 1-5

NOWATA

6929
Glass Mansion
324 W Delaware, 74048 [PO Box 51, 74048]; (p) (918) 273-1191; www.shopoklahoma.com/museums.htm

6930
Nowata County Historical Society
121 S Pine St, 74048 [PO Box 87, 74048]; (p) (918) 273-1136; spjhp@fullnet.net; (c) Nowata

Private non-profit/ 1972/ Board of Trustees/Board of Directors/ staff: 100(v)/ members: 200

HISTORIC PRESERVATION AGENCY; HISTORIC SITE; HISTORICAL SOCIETY; LIVING HISTORY/OUTDOOR MUSEUM: Collects, preserves, maintains and displays the history of Nowata County.

PROGRAMS: Annual Meeting; Community Outreach; Facility Rental; Garden Tours; Guided Tours

COLLECTIONS: [1890-present] Period furniture, clothing, dolls, sewing and weaving, medical, business, law enforcement, education, oil production, music and military history.

HOURS: Yr T-Sa 1-4

ADMISSION: Donations accepted

OKEMAH

6931
Territory Town USA
I-40 (exit 217 N) on Hwy 48, 74859 [RR 2, Box 297-A, 74859]; (p) (918) 623-2599; (c) Okfuskee

1967/ staff: 1(f)

HISTORY MUSEUM: Replica of an entire old west ghost town.

COLLECTIONS: [Early 20th c] Guns, papers, Western relics, Civil War and Native American artifacts.

HOURS: Spring-Fall Daily 9-7; Winter Daily 9-5

ADMISSION: $2, Children $1

OKLAHOMA CITY

6932
45th Infantry Division Museum
2145 NE 36th St, 73111; (p) (405) 424-5313; (f) (405) 434-3748; museum45@aol.com; members.aol.com/museum45/index.html

State/ 1976/ State of OK/ staff: 2(f); 1(p); 63(v)

HISTORY MUSEUM: Preserves martial history of the State of OK.

PROGRAMS: Exhibits; Interpretation; Reenactments; Research Library/Archives; School-Based Curriculum

COLLECTIONS: [1939-1955] World War II and the Korean War, maps, military artifacts.

HOURS: Yr T-F 9-4:15, Sa 10-4:15, Su 1-4:15

6933
Harn Homestead and 1889ers Museum
313 NE 16th St, 73104; (p) (405) 235-4058; (f) (405) 235-4041; www.connections.oklahoman.net/harnhomestead; (c) Oklahoma

Joint; Private non-profit/ 1968/ Board of Directors/ staff: 2(f); 4(p); 2(v)

GARDEN; HISTORIC SITE; HISTORY MUSEUM; HOUSE MUSEUM; LIVING HISTORY/OUTDOOR MUSEUM: Collects, preserves and interprets territorial history of OK.

PROGRAMS: Elder's Programs; Exhibits; Facility Rental; Family Programs; Festivals; Guided Tours; Lectures; Living History; School-Based Curriculum

COLLECTIONS: [1889-1907] School textbooks, Victorian infant and children clothing, paintings of Alice Harn and Nellie and Lottie Shepherd.

HOURS: Aug 15-July 31 T-Sa 10-3

ADMISSION: $3, Children $1.50

6934
Henry Overholser Site
405 NW 15th St, 73103; (p) (405) 528-8485; (c) Oklahoma

State/ 1972/ Oklahoma Historical Society/ staff: 2(f); 6(v)

HISTORIC SITE; HISTORY MUSEUM; HOUSE MUSEUM

PROGRAMS: Annual Meeting; Exhibits; Facility Rental; Festivals; Guided Tours; Interpretation

COLLECTIONS: [1889-1970] Period furnishing, decorative arts in Victorian home.

HOURS: Yr T-Su

ADMISSION: $3, Seniors $2.50

6935
International Photography Hall of Fame and Museum
Kirkpatrick Ctr, 73111 [2100 NE 52nd St, 73111]; (p) (405) 424-4055; (f) (405) 424-4058; info@iphf.org; www.iphf.org; (c) Oklahoma

Private non-profit/ 1965/ Photographic Art and Science Museum/ staff: 2(f); 3(p); 1(v)/ members: 650

ART MUSEUM; HISTORY MUSEUM: Promotes public awareness and education of photographic imaging.

PROGRAMS: Community Outreach; Exhibits; Facility Rental; Family Programs; Guided Tours; Lectures; Research Library/Archives

COLLECTIONS: [1850s-present] Camera equipment, photographic prints.

HOURS: Yr Daily 9-5

ADMISSION: Mbrs free

6936
Kirkpatrick Science and Air Space Museum at Omniplex
2100 NE 52nd St, 73111; (p) (405) 602-6664, (800) 532-7652; (f) (405) 602-3768; omnipr@omniplex.org; www.omniplex.org; (c) Oklahoma

1958/ Board of Trustees/publication: *The Explorer*

ART MUSEUM; GARDEN; HISTORY MUSEUM: Promotes natural history.

PROGRAMS: Community Outreach; Exhibits; Facility Rental; Family Programs; Festivals; Film/Video; Garden Tours; Guided Tours; Publication; Research Library/Archives; School-Based Curriculum

COLLECTIONS: [Early 20th c-present] Natural history, Native American artifacts.

HOURS: Yr M-F 9-5, Sa 9-6, Su 11-6

ADMISSION: $7

6937
National Cowboy Hall of Fame and Western Heritage Center
1700 NE 63rd St, 73111; (p) (405) 478-2250; (f) (405) 478-4714; nchf@aol.com; www.cowboyhalloffame.org; (c) Oklahoma

Private non-profit/ 1956/ Board of Directors/ staff: 84(f); 16(p); 270(v)/ members: 5000/publication: *Persimmon Hill*

ART MUSEUM; HISTORY MUSEUM; RESEARCH CENTER: Collects, preserves and interprets the heritage of the American West.

PROGRAMS: Exhibits; Facility Rental; Family Programs; Publication; Research Library/ Archives

COLLECTIONS: [19th-20th c] Western and Native American fine art, material culture, firearms, ranch, cowboy rodeo, frontier military and popular culture artifacts.

HOURS: Spring-Summer Daily 8:30-6; Fall-Winter Daily 9-5

6938
Oklahoma Heritage Center/Judge R.A. Hefner Mansion
201 NW 14th St, 73103; (p) (405) 235-4458; (f) (405) 235-2714; oha@telepath.com; www.telepath.com/oha

1917/ Oklahoma Heritage / staff: 5(f); 4(p); 4(v)

Home of Judge Robert A. Hefner, OK State Supreme Court Justice.

COLLECTIONS: [1920s-1930s] Meissen china; bells; OK Hall of Fame archives.

HOURS: Yr

6939
Oklahoma Historical Society
2100 N Lincoln Blvd, 73105; (p) (405) 521-2491; (f) (405) 521-2492; www.ok-history.mus.ok.us; (c) Oklahoma

State/ 1893/ staff: 113(f); 700(v)/ members: 5809/publication: *The Chronicles of Oklahoma; Mistletoe Leaves*

HISTORIC PRESERVATION AGENCY; HISTORIC SITE; HISTORICAL SOCIETY; HISTORY MUSEUM; HOUSE MUSEUM; LIVING HISTORY/OUTDOOR MUSEUM; RESEARCH CENTER: Collects, preserves and interprets the history of OK.

PROGRAMS: Annual Meeting; Community Outreach; Elder's Programs; Exhibits; Facility Rental; Family Programs; Guided Tours; Interpretation; Lectures; Living History; Publication; Reenactments; Research Library/Archives; School-Based Curriculum

COLLECTIONS: [1880-1960] 100,00 photos, repository for National Archives for federal records of relocated tribes, 32 historic buildings; artifacts related to Native Americans, agriculture, military and women's clothing.

HOURS: Yr M-Sa 9-5

ADMISSION: No charge

6940
Oklahoma Museums Association
2100 NE 52nd St, 73111; (p) (405) 424-7757; (f) (405) 427-5068; oma@ionet.net; www.okmuseums.org; (c) Oklahoma

Private non-profit/ 1968/ staff: 2(f); 50(v)/ members: 380

Provides development training to employees and volunteers of OK museums and historical societies.

HOURS: Yr M-F 8-5

ADMISSION: No charge

6941
Red Earth, Inc.
2100 NE 52nd St, 73111; (p) (405) 427-5228; (f) (405) 427-8079; redearth@ilinkusa.net; www.redearth.org; (c) Oklahoma

Private non-profit/ 1979/ staff: 5(f); 4(p); 1200(v)/ members: 340

ART MUSEUM; HISTORY MUSEUM: Educates about Native American culture.

PROGRAMS: Community Outreach; Exhibits; Festivals; Film/Video; Lectures; Research Library/Archives; School-Based Curriculum

COLLECTIONS: [19th-20th c] Deupree cradleboard, Plains Indian culture, Northwest coast, Southwest and 20th century Native American art.

HOURS: Yr M-F 9-5, Sa 9-6, Su 11-6

ADMISSION: $7.60, Children $6.60

6942
Westerners International
National Cowboy Hall of Fame & Western Heritage, 73111 [1700 NE 63rd St, 73111]; (p) (800) 541-4650; wihomeranch@aol.com; www.westerners-intl.org; (c) Oklahoma

Private non-profit/ 1944/ staff: 1(p)/ members: 5000

RESEARCH CENTER: Promotes communication and cooperation between persons interested in all aspects of the American West.

PROGRAMS: Research Library/Archives

HOURS: Yr by appt

OKMULGEE

6943
Creek Council House Museum
106 W 6th, 74447; (p) (918) 756-2324; (f) (918) 756-3671; (c) Okmulgee

Private non-profit/ 1923/ Creek Indian Memorial Association/ staff: 3(f); 2(p)/ members: 100

HISTORIC SITE; HISTORY MUSEUM: Collects, preserves and interprets the cultures of Native American peoples; emphasis on Muscogee (Creek) Nation.

PROGRAMS: Exhibits; Festivals; Research Library/Archives

COLLECTIONS: [16th c-present] Muscogee (Creek) history: 15,000 photos, documents, art.

HOURS: Yr T-Sa 10-4

OOLAGAH

6944
Oolagah Historical Society
Cooweescoowee at Maple, 74053 [PO Box 609, 74053]; (p) (918) 443-2790; (f) (918) 443-2790; (c) Rogers

Private non-profit/ 1986/ Board of Directors/ staff: 2(p); 5(v)/ members: 100

HISTORICAL SOCIETY; HISTORY MUSEUM

PROGRAMS: Annual Meeting; Exhibits; Guided Tours

COLLECTIONS: [1890-present] Farm tools, local artifacts.

HOURS: Yr M-F 9-5, Sa 10-2

ADMISSION: Donations accepted

PARK HILL

6945
Murrell Home Site
Cor Murrell Rd & Keeler, 74451 [19479 E Murrell Home Road, 74451]; (p) (918) 456-2751; (f) (918) 456-2751; murrellhome@intellex.com; www.ok-history.mus.ok.us/mus-sites/masnum12.htm; (c) Cherokee

State/ 1948/ Oklahoma Historical Society/ staff: 2(f); 2(p); 4(v)

HISTORIC SITE; HISTORY MUSEUM: Collects, preserves and interprets the home and 19th century Cherokee Nation.

PROGRAMS: Interpretation; Living History; Reenactments

COLLECTIONS: [1830s-1907] Plantation home furnishings, textiles, artifacts and photographs.

HOURS: Yr Su 1-5; Apr-Labor Day W-Sa 10-5; Sept-Oct, Mar F-Sa 10-5; Nov-Feb Sa 10-5

ADMISSION: No charge

PAWHUSKA

6946
Osage County Historical Society Museum, Inc.
700 N Lynn Ave, 74056; (p) (918) 287-9924; (c) Osage

County; Private non-profit/ 1964/ staff: 1(f);
2(p); 5(v)/publication: *Osage County Profiles*

HISTORIC SITE; HISTORICAL SOCIETY;
HISTORY MUSEUM: Promotes local history.

PROGRAMS: Annual Meeting; Exhibits; Guided Tours; Publication

COLLECTIONS: [20th c] Native Americans, pioneers, western life, Scouting, oil artifacts.

HOURS: Yr M-Sa 9-5

ADMISSION: No charge

PAWNEE

6947
Pawnee Bill Ranch Site
1141 Pawnee Bill Rd, 74058 [PO Box 493,
74058]; (p) (918) 762-2513; (f) (918) 762-
2514; pawneebill@ok-history.mus.ok.us; (c)
Pawnee

State/ 1962/ Oklahoma Historical Society/
staff: 7(f); 3(p); 50(v)/ members: 113/publica-
tion: *Historic Site Highlight Series*

HISTORIC SITE; HISTORY MUSEUM

PROGRAMS: Annual Meeting; Community
Outreach; Exhibits; Facility Rental; Family Programs; Festivals; Film/Video; Guided Tours; Interpretation; Lectures; Living History; Publication; Reenactments; Research Library/
Archives

COLLECTIONS: [1900-1940] Furnishings,
Wild West Show memorabilia, Native American objects, photographs, documents, 7 historic structures.

HOURS: Yr Su-M 1-4; T-Sa 10-5

ADMISSION: Donations accepted

6948
Pawnee County Historical Society
and Museum
513 6th, 74058-9566; (p) (918) 762-4681; (f)
(918) 762-2549; djhpres@brightok.net; (c)
Pawnee

Private non-profit/ 1978/ staff: 2(p); 15(v)/
members: 114

HISTORIC PRESERVATION AGENCY; HIS-
TORICAL SOCIETY; HISTORY MUSEUM:
Preserves county history and genealogical
material.

PROGRAMS: Exhibits; Guided Tours; Research Library/Archives

COLLECTIONS: [20th c] Pioneer artifacts, military items and photos.

HOURS: Yr W-Sa 10-2

ADMISSION: No charge

PERRY

6949
Cherokee Strip Museum
2617 First Ave, 73077; (p) (580) 336-2405;
csmuseum@perryisp.net; (c) Noble

State/ 1967/ Oklahoma Historical Society/
staff: 2(f); 20(v)

HISTORY MUSEUM: Traces the history of the
Cherokee Outlet and its people.

PROGRAMS: Annual Meeting; Community
Outreach; Exhibits; Family Programs; Festivals; Interpretation; Lectures; Living History;

Research Library/Archives; School-Based
Curriculum

COLLECTIONS: [1893-1930] Artifacts, photos
and documents of Cherokee Outlet.

HOURS: Jan 15-Dec 31

PONCA CITY

6950
Marland Estate Mansion
901 Monument Rd, 74604; (p) (580) 767-0420;
(f) (580) 763-8054; adamsmk@ci.ponca-city.
ok.us; www.marlandmansion.com; (c) Kay

City/ 1976/ staff: 3(f); 3(p); 60(v)/ members:
300/publication: *Marland Estate Mansion and
E.W. Marland*

HISTORIC SITE; HOUSE MUSEUM: Interprets estate history.

PROGRAMS: Community Outreach; Exhibits;
Facility Rental; Festivals; Guided Tours; Interpretation; Publication

COLLECTIONS: [1928-1941] Furnishings,
personal items.

HOURS: Yr M-Sa 10-5, Su 1-5

ADMISSION: $5, Student $3, Seniors $4

6951
Marland's Grand Home
1000 E Grand, 74601; (p) (580) 767-0427; (f)
(580) 763-8068; adamsmk@poncacityok.com;
(c) Kay

City/ 1967/ staff: 1(f); 1(p); 20(v)/ members:
300

HISTORIC SITE; HISTORY MUSEUM;
HOUSE MUSEUM; RESEARCH CENTER:
Preserves and interprets the history of E.W.
Marland's first mansion.

PROGRAMS: Elder's Programs; Exhibits; Facility Rental; Guided Tours; Interpretation

COLLECTIONS: [1916-1928] Ponca City history and furnishings, memorabilia from ranch
and Wild West Shows, archaeological and Native American artifacts.

HOURS: Yr Tu-Sa 10-5

ADMISSION: $3, Student $1

6952
Pioneer Woman Museum
701 Monument Rd, 74604; (p) (580) 765-6108;
(f) (580) 762-2498; piown@ok-history.mus.ok.us;
www.ok-history.mus.ok.us; (c) Kay

State/ 1958/ Oklahoma Historical Society/
staff: 2(f); 15(v)

HISTORIC SITE; HISTORICAL SOCIETY;
HISTORY MUSEUM: Interprets and preserves
history of women pioneers.

PROGRAMS: Elder's Programs; Exhibits; Fa-
cility Rental; Family Programs; Film/Video;
Guided Tours; Interpretation; Lectures; Living
History; Research Library/Archives

COLLECTIONS: [1820s-present] Household
and personal artifacts, tools and equipment,
food processing and service related, agriculture, photos.

HOURS: Yr T-Sa 9-5, Su 1-5

ADMISSION: $3, Children $1, Seniors $2.50

POTEAU

6953
Robert S. Kerr Museum
Route 1, Box 1060, 74953; (p) (918) 647-
9579; (f) (918) 647-3952; (c) LeFlore

State/ 1968/ Carl Albert State College/Eastern
Oklahoma Historical Society/ staff: 1(f); 1(p);
15(v)/ members: 150

HISTORIC SITE; HISTORICAL SOCIETY;
HISTORY MUSEUM: Preserves Eastern Okla-
homa pioneer history and the contributions of
Senator Robert S. Kerr.

PROGRAMS: Annual Meeting; Elder's Programs; Exhibits; Guided Tours; Interpretation

COLLECTIONS: [1860-1960] Memorabilia of
Oklahoma Governor and US Senator Robert S.
Kerr, Spiro mound artifacts, pioneer tools, Viking
rune stones, clothing, quilts and jewelry.

HOURS: Yr T-Su 9-5

ADMISSION: Donations accepted

PRYOR

6954
Coo-Y-Yah Country Museum
S 8th & Hwy 69, 74361 [PO Box 969, 74361];
(p) (918) 825-2222; (c) Mayes

1982/ Mayes County Historical Society, Inc./
members: 250

HISTORICAL SOCIETY: Collects, preserves
and exhibits all materials and artifacts vital to
the history of Mayes County.

PROGRAMS: Annual Meeting; Exhibits; Guided Tours

COLLECTIONS: [20th c] Art and artifacts.

HOURS: Apr-Dec T-F 1-5

ADMISSION: No charge

PURCELL

6955
McClain County Oklahoma Historical
and Genealogical Society and Museum
203 W Washington, 73080; (p) (405) 527-
7883; (c) McClain

Private non-profit/ 1973/ staff: 1(p); 6(v)/ members: 95/publication: *McClain County History
and Heritage; Death and Marriage Records of
McClain County OK; and others*

GENEALOGICAL SOCIETY; HISTORICAL
SOCIETY; HISTORY MUSEUM: Researches,
preserves, and perpetuates the history of Mc-
Clain County.

PROGRAMS: Guided Tours; Publication; Research Library/Archives

COLLECTIONS: [1887-1950] 11 interpretive
rooms, photos and family histories.

HOURS: Yr M-F 12-4 by appt

SALLISAW

6956
Fourteen Flags Heritage Club
Cherokee Ave, 74955 [RR 1 Box 103 A,
74955]; (p) (918) 775-2608, (918) 774-0055;
(c) Sequoyah

Private non-profit/ 1986/ members: 55/publica-
tion: *Fourteen Flags Museum*

HISTORIC SITE; HISTORICAL SOCIETY; HISTORY MUSEUM; LIVING HISTORY/OUTDOOR MUSEUM: Exhibits artifacts of the 1800s through 1940s, including historic buildings and transportation modes.

PROGRAMS: Annual Meeting; Community Outreach; Exhibits; Family Programs; Festivals; Guided Tours; Interpretation; Living History; Publication

COLLECTIONS: [1800s-1940s] Tools, post office, transportation, gasoline pump, buggy, caboose and farming equipment.

HOURS: Yr Daily 9-5

ADMISSION: No charge

6957
Sequoyah's Cabin
Route 1, Box 141, 74955; (p) (918) 775-2413; (c) Sequoyah

State/ 1936/ Oklahoma Historical Society/ staff: 2(f); 3(v)

HISTORIC SITE: Promotes Sequoyah and Cherokee.

PROGRAMS: Elder's Programs; Family Programs; Guided Tours; Living History

COLLECTIONS: [19th c] Stone, metal tools; clothing, art and furniture.

HOURS: Yr T-F 9-5, Sa-Su 2-5

ADMISSION: Donations accepted

SAPULPA

6958
Sapulpa Historical Society, Inc.
100 E Lee St, 74067 [PO Box 287, 74067-0278]; (p) (918) 224-4871; saphistsoc@juno.com; (c) Creek

Private non-profit/ 1968/ Board of Trustees/ staff: 1(p); 45(v)/ members: 700/publication: *Sapulpa, OK 74066 Vol. I, II*

HISTORICAL SOCIETY; HISTORY MUSEUM: Maintains local history museum.

PROGRAMS: Exhibits; Guided Tours; Lectures; Publication; Research Library/Archives

COLLECTIONS: [1890s-present] Artifacts, industries, families, period exhibits, photos.

HOURS: Yr M-Th 10-3

SHATTUCK

6959
Shattuck Windmill Museum and Park, Inc.
Jct of State Hwy 15 & US Hwy 283, 73858 [PO Box 227, 73858]; (p) (580) 938-2881, (580) 938-5146; (c) Ellis

Private non-profit; State/ 1994/ Board of Trustees/ staff: 15(v)

LIVING HISTORY/OUTDOOR MUSEUM: Exhibits, interprets and demonstrates history of water and wind development of the High Plains and particularly Northwest OK.

PROGRAMS: Annual Meeting; Exhibits; Guided Tours; Interpretation

COLLECTIONS: [1854-1950] Wooden-wheeled and early steel windmills; 1900 homestead.

HOURS: Yr Daily

ADMISSION: Donations accepted

SHAWNEE

6960
Santa Fe Depot Museum
614 E Main, 74802 [PO Box 114, 74802]; (p) (405) 275-8412; SantaFeDepot@potawatomi.org; www.shawnee.com/museums.htm#OldSantaFeDepot; (c) Pottawatomie

Private non-profit/ 1982/ Historical Society of Pottawatomie County/ staff: 1(f); 1(p); 5(v)/ members: 150

HISTORIC SITE; HISTORICAL SOCIETY; HISTORY MUSEUM: Collects, interprets and preserves county artifacts.

PROGRAMS: Annual Meeting; Exhibits; Festivals; Guided Tours; Research Library/Archives

COLLECTIONS: [Late 19th-early 20th c] Native American tools, clothing, pioneer schoolhouse, dolls, toys, clothing, household items, Model-T Ford and medical equipment.

HOURS: Yr T-F 10-4, Sa-Su 2-4

ADMISSION: Donations accepted

SPENCER

6961
Spencer Museum
8622 NE 50th, 73084 [PO Box 394, 73084]; (p) (405) 771-4576, (405) 771-4494

1910/ Spencer Historical

COLLECTIONS: [1920s] Household furnishings.

HOURS: By appt

SPIRO

6962
Spiro Mounds Archaeological Center
Route 2, Box 339AA, 74959; (p) (918) 962-2062; spiromds@lpa.net; (c) LeFlore

Private non-profit; State/ 1978/ Oklahoma Historical Society/ staff: 2(f)/ members: 25

HISTORIC SITE: Preserves and interprets Native American sites in OK and US.

PROGRAMS: Annual Meeting; Exhibits; Family Programs; Festivals; Guided Tours; School-Based Curriculum

COLLECTIONS: [7th-15th c] Artifacts, reproductions, art.

HOURS: Yr W-Sa 9-5, Su 12-5

ADMISSION: Donations accepted

STILLWATER

6963
Oklahoma Museum of Higher Education
NE of University & Hester St, 74078 [Historic Old Central Oklahoma State University, 74078-0705]; (p) (405) 744-2828, (405) 744-2828; omhe@ok-history.mus.ok.us; (c) Payne

State/ 1981/ Oklahoma Historical Society/ staff: 1(f); 38(v)/ members: 75

HISTORIC SITE; HISTORY MUSEUM: Preserves history and advancement of higher education in OK.

PROGRAMS: Annual Meeting; Concerts; Elder's Programs; Exhibits; Facility Rental; Guided Tours; Lectures; Living History; Reenactments

COLLECTIONS: [1890-present] Photos of 1894 Old Central in 5 interpretive rooms.

HOURS: Yr T-F 9-5, Sa 10-4; Closed Mid-Dec-mid Jan

ADMISSION: $1, Children $0.50; Donations requested

6964
Sheerar Culture and Heritage Center
702 S Duncan, 74074; (p) (405) 377-0359; admin@sheerarmuseum.org; www.sheerarmuseum.org; (c) Payne

Private non-profit/ 1974/ Stillwater Museum Association Board of Trustees/ staff: 3(p); 20(v)/ members: 500/publication: *Stillwater Muse*

CULTURAL CENTER: Maintains a permanent exhibit of the history of Stillwater from 1889 to present. Presents an annual special exhibit based on a topic or event relevant to local history.

PROGRAMS: Community Outreach; Concerts; Exhibits; Facility Rental; Garden Tours; Guided Tours; Interpretation; Lectures; Publication; School-Based Curriculum

COLLECTIONS: [1889-present] Pioneer life objects, Stillwater and OSU memorabilia, furnishings, decorative arts, clothing, textiles, buttons, photos, documents, Native American dance costumes.

HOURS: Sept-July T-F 11-4, Sa-Su 1-4

ADMISSION: No charge

6965
Stillwater Airport Memorial Museum
2020-1 W Airport Rd, 74075; (p) (405) 372-7881; (f) (405) 372-8460; wgharr@hotmail.com; (c) Payne

Private non-profit/ 1994/ Stillwater Airport Memorial Museum Association/ staff: 10(v)/ members: 22

HISTORY MUSEUM

PROGRAMS: Exhibits; Guided Tours; Interpretation; Lectures

COLLECTIONS: [1917-present] Photos, posters, artifacts, clothing, instruments.

HOURS: Yr Su 1-5 and by appt.

6966
Washington Irving Trail Museum
[PO Box 1852, 74076]; (p) (405) 624-9130; Cchlouber@aol.com; www.cowboy.net/non-profit/irving/; (c) Payne

Private non-profit/ 1994/ Payne County and Central Oklahoma Museum Association/ staff: 1(f); 1(p); 8(v)

HISTORY MUSEUM: Promotes local and state history.

PROGRAMS: Annual Meeting; Exhibits; Guided Tours; Interpretation; Reenactments

COLLECTIONS: [19th-20th c] Southwest Native American, Settlement Era, cowboys, country western music.

HOURS: Yr W-Sa 10-5, Su 1-5

STROUD

6967
Sac and Fox National Public Library
5.5 mi S of Stroud on Hwy 99, 74079 [Route 2, Box 246, 74079]; (p) (918) 968-3526; (f)

(918) 968-4837; (c) Lincoln

Tribal/ 1988/ Sac and Fox Nation of OK/ staff: 2(f)

LIBRARY AND/OR ARCHIVES: Preserves Sac and Fox culture and history.

PROGRAMS: Community Outreach; Exhibits; Film/Video; Research Library/Archives

COLLECTIONS: [1860-present] Documents, photos and books focused on Native American life, history and traditions.

HOURS: Yr M-F 10-4:30

ADMISSION: No charge

SULPHUR

6968
Chickasaw National Recreation Area
Junction of Hwys 7 & 177, 73086 [PO Box 201, 73086]; (p) (580) 622-3161; (f) (580) 622-2296; www.nps.gov/chic; (c) Murray

Federal/ 1906/ National Park Service/ staff: 40(f); 30(p); 25(v)

HISTORIC SITE; LIVING HISTORY/OUTDOOR MUSEUM: Preserves and interprets the natural and cultural history of the area according to the mission of the National Park Service.

PROGRAMS: Community Outreach; Concerts; Exhibits; Facility Rental; Family Programs; Guided Tours; Interpretation; Lectures; Living History; Reenactments; School-Based Curriculum

COLLECTIONS: [Late 19th c-present] Platt National Park, Civilian Conservation Corps (CCC), and City of Sulphur; 500 maps and blueprints, 3,000 photos and 400 museum artifacts.

HOURS: Sept-May Daily 8-5; June-Aug Su-Th 8-7, F-Sa 8-9

ADMISSION: No charge

SWINK

6969
Apuckshunubbee District Chief's House
1/2 mi N of PO in Swink on Hwy 70 t, 74761 [PO Box 165, 74761]; (p) (405) 873-2301

1832/ staff: 2(v)

COLLECTIONS: [1830-1840]

HOURS: Yr

6970
Swink Historical Preservation Association
1800 Heritage Rd, 74761 [PO Box 165, 74761]; (p) (580) 873-2301; Swink1@oio.net; (c) Choctaw

Private non-profit/ 1994/ staff: 2(f); 5(p); 5(v)/ members: 92/publication: *The Gilded Age, Swink, Choctaw County, Oklahoma*

HISTORIC SITE; HOUSE MUSEUM; LIVING HISTORY/OUTDOOR MUSEUM: Owns and administers the district Choctaw Chief's house; rustic heritage trail at Swink.

PROGRAMS: Annual Meeting; Facility Rental; Guided Tours; Publication

COLLECTIONS: [1840-1920]

HOURS: Yr Daily 9-12/1-3

ADMISSION: Donations accepted

TAHLEQUAH

6971
Cherokee Heritage Center
21672 S Keeler, 74465 [PO Box 515, 74465]; (p) (918) 456-6007, (888) 999-6007; (f) (918) 456-6165; tourism@cherokeeheritage.org; www.cherokeeheritage.org; (c) Cherokee

Private non-profit/ 1963/ Cherokee National Historical Society/ staff: 55(f); 5(p); 20(v)/ members: 1100

ART MUSEUM; HISTORIC SITE; HISTORICAL SOCIETY; HISTORY MUSEUM; LIVING HISTORY/OUTDOOR MUSEUM; TRIBAL MUSEUM: Presents Cherokee history and culture through museum exhibits, living history village and the Trail of Tears.

PROGRAMS: Concerts; Exhibits; Facility Rental; Guided Tours; Interpretation; Lectures; Living History; Reenactments; Research Library/Archives; Theatre

COLLECTIONS: [Prehistory-present] Cherokee cultural items, art, manuscripts and archives; papers of Chief W.W. Keeler and General Counsel Estel Boyd Pierce.

HOURS: Feb-Dec M-Sa 10-5, Su 1-5

ADMISSION: $8.50, Children $4.25; Group rates

TALOGA

6972
Dewey County Jailhouse Museum and Annex
Riggs St, 73667 [PO Box 303, 73667]; (p) (580) 328-5485; (c) Dewey

County/ 1992/ Jailhouse Museum Board/ staff: 12(v)

HISTORIC SITE: Offers exhibits relating to outlaws and law enforcemen.

PROGRAMS: Annual Meeting; Community Outreach; Exhibits; Festivals

COLLECTIONS: [1890s-1930s]

HOURS: Yr by appt and special events

ADMISSION: No charge

TONKAWA

6973
A.D. Buck Museum of Science and History
N & Pine, 74653 [1220 E Grand, 74653]; (p) (580) 628-6477; (f) (580) 628-6209; rackerso@nocaxp.north-ok.edu; (c) Kay

State/ 1913/ Northern Oklahoma College/ staff: 1(f); 1(p)

HISTORY MUSEUM: Preserves and displays scientific and historic items.

PROGRAMS: Exhibits; Guided Tours; Lectures

COLLECTIONS: [1910-present] Birds, mammals, minerals and artifacts related to school history, pioneers, WWI, WWII.

HOURS: Mid Aug-Mid May M-Th 1-4

6974
McCarter Museum of Tonkawa History
220 E Grand Ave, 74653 [PO Box 27, 74653]; (p) (580) 628-2895; marilee@kskc.net; (c) Kay

Private non-profit/ 1972/ Tonkawa Historical Society/ staff: 26(v)/ members: 107

HISTORY MUSEUM: Collects, preserves and displays local history.

PROGRAMS: Exhibits; Guided Tours; Interpretation; Reenactments

COLLECTIONS: [1890-1950] Artifacts, memorabilia, pictures, unpublished manuscripts.

HOURS: Yr M-Sa 1-3 and by appt

ADMISSION: Donations accepted

TULSA

6975
Gilcrease Museum
1400 Gilcrease Museum Rd, 74127; (p) (918) 596-2700; (f) (918) 596-2770; www.gilcrease.org; (c) Tulsa

City; Private non-profit/ 1949/ staff: 55(f); 5(p); 300(v)/ members: 4500/publication: *Gilcrease Journal*

ART MUSEUM; HISTORY MUSEUM; RESEARCH CENTER: Promotes local history.

PROGRAMS: Annual Meeting; Community Outreach; Concerts; Exhibits; Facility Rental; Family Programs; Garden Tours; Guided Tours; Lectures; Publication; Research Library/Archives; School-Based Curriculum

COLLECTIONS: [pre-Colombian-present] American West, Native American, historical manuscripts, documents, maps, Mexican art, artifacts.

HOURS: Yr T-Sa 9-5, Su 11-5; Mem Day-Labor Day M 9-5

ADMISSION: $3

6976
International Linen Registry Foundation, Inc.
4107 S Yale Ave, Ste 247, 74150 [PO Box 50516, 74150-0516]; (p) (918) 622-5223; (c) Tulsa

1991/ Captola Thomas/ staff: 1(f); 23(v)/ members: 200

ART MUSEUM; HISTORIC PRESERVATION AGENCY: Preserves and restores needle art.

PROGRAMS: Community Outreach; Exhibits; Lectures

COLLECTIONS: [19th c-present] Fine linens, needlework, clothing.

HOURS: Yr M-Sa 10-9, Su 12-6

ADMISSION: No charge

6977
Tulsa Air and Space Center
7130 E Apache, 74115; (p) (918) 834-9900; (f) (918) 834-6723; (c) Tulsa

Private non-profit/ 1993/ staff: 2(f); 3(p); 100(v)/ members: 1000

HISTORY MUSEUM: Presents aerospace history of the Tulsa region.

PROGRAMS: Annual Meeting; Community Outreach; Exhibits; Facility Rental; Family Programs; Lectures; Living History; Research Library/Archives; School-Based Curriculum

COLLECTIONS: [1890-present] Vintage aircraft and power plants, photos, artifacts, and presentations on the space age and major aerospace events.

HOURS: Yr T-F 1-4, Sa 10-5, Su 1-5

ADMISSION: $4, Student $3, Children $2, Seniors $3; Under

6978
Tulsa Historical Society
1437 E 25th St, 74149 [PO Box 27303, 74149]; (p) (918) 712-9484; (f) (918) 712-1939; ths@intcon.net; (c) Tulsa

Private non-profit/ 1963/ staff: 2(f); 1(p)/ members: 600/publication: *Tulsa Past Times*

HISTORICAL SOCIETY; HISTORY MUSEUM; RESEARCH CENTER: Promotes local and state history.

PROGRAMS: Annual Meeting; Community Outreach; Exhibits; Facility Rental; Publication; School-Based Curriculum

COLLECTIONS: [Early 20th c] Decorative arts, oil field equipment, photos.

HOURS: Yr M-F 9-4

ADMISSION: No charge

TUSHKA HOMMA

6979
Choctaw Nation Museum
HC 64 Box 3270, 74574-9758; (p) (918) 569-4465; (f) (918) 569-4465

HISTORIC SITE; TRIBAL MUSEUM

PROGRAMS: Concerts; Exhibits; Facility Rental; Festivals; Guided Tours

COLLECTIONS: [19th c] Spoons made of bone, clay pots, arrowheads, Chief Pushmataha's bow, vintage clothing, old documents, Choctaw pottery, Trail of Tears, spinning wheel, iron pots.

HOURS: Yr M-F 8-4

VINITA

6980
Eastern Trails Museum
215 W Illinois, 74301 [PO Box 77, 74301]; (p) (918) 256-2115; (f) (918) 256-2309; staff@vinita.lib.ok.us; (c) Craig

City; Private non-profit/ 1950/ Oklahoma Historical Society/ staff: 1(f); 6(v)

ALLIANCE OF HISTORICAL AGENCIES; ART MUSEUM; GENEALOGICAL SOCIETY; HISTORIC PRESERVATION AGENCY; HISTORIC SITE; HISTORICAL SOCIETY; HISTORY MUSEUM; HOUSE MUSEUM; RESEARCH CENTER; TRIBAL MUSEUM

PROGRAMS: Exhibits; Guided Tours; Reenactments; Research Library/Archives; School-Based Curriculum

COLLECTIONS: [19th-mid 20th c] Pioneer, Native American artifacts, research history.

HOURS: Yr M-Sa

ADMISSION: No charge

WAURIKA

6981
Chisholm Trail Historical Museum Society
Hwys 70 & 81, 73573 [PO Box 262, 73573]; (p) (580) 228-2166; (f) (580) 228-3290; (c) Jefferson

State/ 1965/ OK Historical Society/ staff: 6(v)

HISTORY MUSEUM

PROGRAMS: Exhibits; Festivals; Film/Video; School-Based Curriculum; Theatre

COLLECTIONS: [1867-1930] Covered wagons, settlers' tools, Native American arrowheads and beadwork, drovers' equipment, antique clocks and barbwire.

HOURS: Yr

ADMISSION: No charge

WAYNOKA

6982
Waynoka Historical Society
200 S Cleveland, 73860 [PO Box 193, 73860]; (p) (580) 824-1886; (f) (580) 824-0921; sandieo@pldi.net; www.pldi.net/~harpo; (c) Woods

Private non-profit/ 1986/ staff: 27(v)/ members: 19/publication: *1906 Woods County Atlas; 1883 map of Cherokee Strip Ranches*

HISTORIC SITE; HISTORICAL SOCIETY; HISTORY MUSEUM: Operates an air/rail transportation museum in restored 1910 Harvey House. Preserves Waynoka's history.

PROGRAMS: Exhibits; Guided Tours; Interpretation; Publication; Research Library/Archives

COLLECTIONS: [1910-1960] Artifacts, photos, Transcontinental Air Transport, Harvey House, Ice Plant, rural and town schools. German prisoner of war paintings, John Holbird mural, Harvey memorabilia.

HOURS: Easter-Labor Day Sa-Su 2-4 and Yr by appt

ADMISSION: Donations requested

WEWOKA

6983
Seminole Nation Museum and Historical Society
526 S Wewoka Ave, 74884 [PO Box 1532, 74884]; (p) (405) 257-5580; semnationmus@onenet.net; (c) Seminole

Private non-profit/ 1974/ Board of Directors/ staff: 2(f); 1(p); 40(v)/ members: 150

ART MUSEUM; HISTORIC SITE; HISTORICAL SOCIETY; HISTORY MUSEUM; TRIBAL MUSEUM

PROGRAMS: Annual Meeting; Community Outreach; Festivals; Guided Tours

COLLECTIONS: [Mid 19th-mid 20th c] Native American, African American.

HOURS: Feb-Dec T-Su 1-5

ADMISSION: Donations accepted

WILBURTON

6984
Pate Enterprises
2307 E Main, 74578; (p) (918) 465-2216, (918) 465-3351

Private non-profit/ staff: 1(f)

HOUSE MUSEUM

PROGRAMS: Annual Meeting; Family Programs; Lectures

COLLECTIONS: [1890-1930] Restored Hailey Ola Coal Company (1901) and local mining artifacts.

HOURS: Yr Daily 9-12 and by appt

ADMISSION: No charge

WOODWARD

6985
Plains Indians and Pioneers Museum
2009 Williams Ave, 73801; (p) (580) 256-6136; (f) (580) 256-2577; plains@pldi.net; (c) Woodward

City; Private non-profit/ 1966/ Board of Directors/ staff: 4(f); 1(p); 20(v)/ members: 300

ART MUSEUM; HISTORY MUSEUM: Collects, preserves and interprets the history of the area for a 50 mile radius.

PROGRAMS: Annual Meeting; Community Outreach; Exhibits; Family Programs; Guided Tours; Interpretation; Lectures; Research Library/Archives

COLLECTIONS: [1900-1950] Photos, clothing, agricultural equipment, Temple Houston artifacts.

HOURS: Yr T-Sa 10-5, Su 1-4

ADMISSION: Donations accepted

WYNNEWOOD

6986
Wynnewood Historical Society
114 E Kerr, 73098; (p) (405) 665-5345; (f) (405) 665-4152; wwmainst@telepath.com; (c) Garvin

Private non-profit/ 1974/ staff: 40(v)/ members: 100/publication: *History of the City of Wynnewood*

HISTORICAL SOCIETY: Operates a museum housed in the Eskridge Hotel.

PROGRAMS: Annual Meeting; Community Outreach; Exhibits; Festivals; Guided Tours; Interpretation; Publication; Research Library/Archives; Theatre

COLLECTIONS: [Early 20th c] 24 interpretive rooms: city, county, state, lifestyle histories.

HOURS: Yr T-F 10-5:30, Sa 10-2

ADMISSION: $2, Children $1

YALE

6987
Jim Thorpe Home Site
706 E Boston, 74085; (p) (918) 387-2815

1916/ State, Oklahoma Historical Society/ staff: 2(f)

HOUSE MUSEUM: Home of Native American athlete Jim Thorpe.

COLLECTIONS: [1917-1923]

HOURS: Yr

OREGON

ALBANY

6988
Linn County Historical Society
1132 30th Pl SW, 97321-3419; (p) (541) 926-4680; (f) (541) 719-4707; harrison@cmieg.com; www.linnhistorical.com; (c) Linn

Private non-profit/ 1911/ Board of Directors/ staff: 12(p); 12(v)/ members: 110

HISTORICAL SOCIETY: Promotes conservation and preservation of local history.

PROGRAMS: Annual Meeting; Family Programs; Lectures; Publication; Research Library/Archives

COLLECTIONS: [1860-1960] Shedd family, town artifacts.

HOURS: May-Sept Sa 10-4

ASTORIA

6989
Captain George Flavel House
441 8th St, 97103 [1618 Exchange, 97103]; (p) (503) 325-2200; (f) (503) 338-6265; cchs@seasurf.net

1885/ Clatsop County Historical Society/ staff: 3(f); 1(p); 55(v)

COLLECTIONS: [Late Victorian 1880-1890] Eastlake style furniture; archives; 22,000 photos.

HOURS: Yr

6990
Clatsop County Historical Society
1618 Exchange St, 97103; (p) (503) 325-2203; (f) (503) 338-6265; cchs@seasurf.net; (c) Clatsop

Private non-profit/ 1948/ Board of Trustees/ staff: 4(f); 1(p); 65(v)/ members: 1001/publication: *Cumtux Quarterly Journal*

HISTORICAL SOCIETY; HISTORY MUSEUM; HOUSE MUSEUM: Collects, preserves, conserves and exhibits items pertaining to the history and culture of Clatsop County.

PROGRAMS: Annual Meeting; Exhibits; Facility Rental; Guided Tours; Interpretation; Lectures; Publication; Research Library/Archives

COLLECTIONS: Tools and period furnishing, industrial logging, fishing equipment, photo archives, firefighting equipment.

HOURS: May-Sept Daily 10-5; Oct-Apr Daily 11-4

ADMISSION: $5, Children $2.50, Seniors $4.50

6991
Columbia River Maritime Museum
1792 Marine Dr, 97103; (p) (503) 325-2323; (f) (503) 325-2331; columbia@seasurf.com; www.crmm.org; (c) Clatsop

Private non-profit/ 1962/ staff: 14(f); 6(p); 127(v)/ members: 1683/publication: *Quarterdeck*

HISTORY MUSEUM: Promotes history of Columbia River.

PROGRAMS: Annual Meeting; Community Outreach; Exhibits; Facility Rental; Family Programs; Guided Tours; Interpretation; Publica-

tion; Research Library/Archives; School-Based Curriculum

COLLECTIONS: [1700-present] Lightship, small craft, marine engines, naval weapons, nautical instruments, tools, miscellaneous marine artifacts, ship models, paintings, prints, photos, maps, books, manuscripts.

HOURS: Yr Daily 9:30-5

ADMISSION: $5

AURORA

6992
Aurora Colony Historical Society
15008 2nd St, 97002 [PO Box 202, 97002]; (p) (503) 678-5754; (f) (503) 678-5756; aurora_colony@juno.com; (c) Marion

Private non-profit/ 1963/ Board of Trustees/ staff: 1(f); 2(p); 100(v)/ members: 600

HISTORIC SITE; HISTORICAL SOCIETY; HISTORY MUSEUM; HOUSE MUSEUM; LIVING HISTORY/OUTDOOR MUSEUM

PROGRAMS: Annual Meeting; Community Outreach; Concerts; Exhibits; Festivals; Guided Tours; Interpretation; Lectures; Living History; Publication; Research Library/Archives

COLLECTIONS: [1856-1883] 21 buildings and 3,000 artifacts.

HOURS: Apr-Oct T-Sa 10-4, Su 12-4; Nov-Dec F-Sa 10-4, Su 12-4

ADMISSION: $3.50, Children $1.50, Seniors $3

BAKER CITY

6993
National Historic Oregon Trail Interpretive Center
Hwy 86 Flagstaff Hill, 97814 [PO Box 987, 97814]; (p) (541) 523-1845; (f) (541) 523-1834; Nhotic_Mail@or.blm.gov; www.or.blm.gov/NHOTIC; (c) Baker

Federal/ 1992/ USDI Bureau of Land Management (federal)/ staff: 12(f); 3(p); 150(v)

HISTORIC SITE: Interprets Oregon Trail history.

PROGRAMS: Exhibits; Festivals; Film/Video; Interpretation; Lectures; Living History; School-Based Curriculum

COLLECTIONS: [1830-1870] Wagons, pioneer lifeways, fur trade, mining, Bureau of Land Management history, artifacts and replicas.

HOURS: Apr-Oct 9-6; Nov-Mar 9-4

ADMISSION: $5, Student $3.50,

6994
Oregon Trail Regional Museum
2480 Grove St, 97814; (p) (541) 523-9308; (f) (541) 523-0244; (c) Baker

County/ 1982/ Baker County Museum Commission/ staff: 1(f); 1(p); 75(v)

HISTORIC SITE; HISTORY MUSEUM; RESEARCH CENTER: Preserves and interprets natural history.

PROGRAMS: Exhibits; Family Programs; Film/Video; Guided Tours; Interpretation; Lectures; Reenactments; Research Library/Archives

COLLECTIONS: [1800-1920] Archives, photos, artifacts, natural history related to Baker County.

HOURS: Apr-Oct Daily

BANDON

6995
Bandon Historical Society/Coquille River Museum
270 Fillmore & Hway 101, 97411 [PO Box 737, 97411]; (p) (541) 347-2164; (c) Coos

Private non-profit/ 1976/ staff: 1(f); 1(p); 50(v)/ members: 430

HISTORIC PRESERVATION AGENCY; HISTORICAL SOCIETY; HISTORY MUSEUM: Operates the Coquille River Museum; exhibits the history of Bandon and the Coquille River Area.

PROGRAMS: Elder's Programs; Film/Video; Guided Tours; Publication; Reenactments; School-Based Curriculum

COLLECTIONS: [1700-present] Native American artifacts, photos of local life, millitary artifacts, maritime collection, pioneer life depictions.

HOURS: Mem Day-end of Sep: M-Sa, 10-4, Su 12-3 Oct-Dec, Feb-Mem Day: M-Sa, 10-4

ADMISSION: $2; Under 12/Mbrs free

BEND

6996
Deschutes County Historical Society
129 NW Idaho St, 97708 [PO Box 5252, 97708]; (p) (541) 389-1813; (f) (541) 389-4356; (c) Deschutes

County/ staff: 2(f); 15(v)/publication: *Homesteaders*

HISTORICAL SOCIETY: Preserves and interprets the history of Deschutes County.

PROGRAMS: Annual Meeting; Exhibits; Facility Rental; Family Programs; Festivals; Film/Video; Guided Tours; Lectures; Living History; Publication

HOURS: Yr 10-4:30

ADMISSION: $2.50, Student $1

6997
Deschutes Historical Center
129 NW Idaho St, 97708 [PO Box 5252, 97708]; (p) (541) 389-1813; (c) Deschutes

Private non-profit/ 1975/ Deschutes County Historical Society/ staff: 3(f); 3(p); 40(v)/ members: 600

HISTORY MUSEUM: Preserves, protects, and exhibits regional artifacts.

PROGRAMS: Annual Meeting; Community Outreach; Exhibits; Family Programs; Film/Video; Interpretation; Lectures

COLLECTIONS: [1890-1950] High Desert and Cascade Mountain region artifacts.

HOURS: Yr T-Sa 10-4:30

ADMISSION: $2.50

6998
High Desert Museum
59800 S Highway 97, 97702; (p) (541) 382-4754; (f) (541) 382-5256; info@highdesert.org; www.highdesert.org; (c) Deschutes

Private non-profit/ 1974/ Board of Trustees/ staff: 60(f); 300(v)/ members: 5500

HISTORY MUSEUM; LIVING HISTORY/OUT-DOOR MUSEUM: Interprets natural and cultural history of High Desert of the Intermountain West.

PROGRAMS: Exhibits; Facility Rental; Family Programs; Festivals; Interpretation; Lectures; Living History; School-Based Curriculum

COLLECTIONS: [1800-present] Collects original objects, plant, and animal specimens.

HOURS: Yr Daily 9-5

ADMISSION: $7.75, Student $6.75, Children

BROOKINGS

6999
Blake House
15461 Museum Rd, 97415; (p) (541) 469-6651; www.ohwy.com/or/c/chetvhsm.htm

BROWNSVILLE

7000
Linn County Historical Museum
101 Park Ave, 97327 [PO Box 607, 97327]; (p) (541) 466-3390; (c) Linn

County, non-profit/ 1985/ staff: 3(p); 10(v)/ members: 100/publication: *Museum Tracks*

HISTORY MUSEUM: Collects, preserves, and interprets local history.

PROGRAMS: Annual Meeting; Community Outreach; Festivals; Film/Video; Guided Tours; Interpretation; Publication; Research Library/Archives; School-Based Curriculum; Theatre

COLLECTIONS: [1830-present] 7,500 items: artifacts, photos, portraits, books.

HOURS: Yr M-Sa 11-4, Su 1-5

ADMISSION: $2

7001
Moyer House
204 N Main, 97327 [PO Box 607, 97327]; (p) (503) 466-3070; (c) Linn

Private non-profit/ Linn County Parks and Recreation/ staff: 6(v)

HOUSE MUSEUM: Preserves historic house.

PROGRAMS: Elder's Programs; Festivals; Guided Tours; Reenactments; School-Based Curriculum

COLLECTIONS: [1800] Period furnishing; Seth Thomas clock.

HOURS: Yr Sa 11-4, Su 1-5 and by appt

ADMISSION: Donations

BUTTE FALLS

7002
Big Butte Historical Society
422 Pine St, 97522 [PO Box 379, 97522]; (p) (541) 865-3310; dhinc@cdsnet.net; (c) Jackson

County/ staff: 2(f); 2(p); 7(v)/ members: 125

HISTORICAL SOCIETY; HOUSE MUSEUM: Portrays town history.

PROGRAMS: Annual Meeting; Community Outreach; Exhibits; Garden Tours; Guided Tours; Living History

COLLECTIONS: [1920s-1960s] Ernest Smith photographs, Bill Edmondson carvings.

HOURS: Yr F, Su 1-4, Sa 10-4

ADMISSION: Donations accepted

CLATSKANIE

7003
Flippin House
620 Tichenor St, 97016 [PO Box 383, 97016]; (p) (503) 728-3608

1898/ Clatskanie Senior / staff: 4(f); 43(v)

COLLECTIONS: [Turn-of-c] Dishes, organ, piano.

HOURS: Yr; closed Jan;

COLUMBIA CITY

7004
Caples House Museum
1915 First St, 97018 [PO Box 263, 97018-0263]; (p) (503) 397-5390; (c) Columbia

Private non-profit/ 1969/ Oregon State Society DAR, Caples House Bldgs and Grounds Committee/ staff: 1(f); 5(v)/ members: 1600

HISTORIC SITE; HISTORY MUSEUM; HOUSE MUSEUM: Preserves the 1870 house and furnishings of the Oregon pioneer families, Caples and McBride.

PROGRAMS: Exhibits; Facility Rental; Garden Tours; Guided Tours

COLLECTIONS: [1848-1900] Early physician and dental instruments, antique lamps, kitchen and stove utensils, Eskimo and Native American artifacts, quilts, early pioneer furniture, old tools, washing and sewing machines, antique dolls and toys.

HOURS: Apr-Oct F-Su and Federal Holidays 1-5

ADMISSION: $2

7005
Charles Green Caples House Museum
1915 1st St, 97018; (p) (503) 397-5390

CONDON

7006
Gilliam County Historical Society
Hwy 19 at Burns Park, 97823 [PO Box 377, 97823]; (p) (541) 384-4233; (c) Gilliam

Private non-profit/ 1974/ Gilliam County Historical Society/ staff: 1(p); 40(v)/ members: 145

HISTORICAL SOCIETY; HISTORY MUSEUM: Preserves and displays history of Gilliam County.

PROGRAMS: Annual Meeting; Exhibits; Film/Video; Guided Tours; Research Library/Archives

COLLECTIONS: [18th-19th c] Agricultural, railroad, pioneer, community life, home life, machinery, historic buildings, photos, genealogy files.

HOURS: May-Oct W-Su 1-5

ADMISSION: Donations accepted

CORVALLIS

7007
Oregon State University Archives
15th & Jefferson, 97331 [94 Kerr Admin Bldg, 97331]; (p) (541) 737-0541; (f) (541) 737-0950; archives@orst.edu; osu.orst.edu/dept/archives; (c) Benton

State/ 1961/ staff: 4(f); 3(p); 1(v)

LIBRARY AND/OR ARCHIVES: Collects, interprets and preserves univ, local, and state history.

PROGRAMS: Exhibits; Publication; Research Library/Archives

COLLECTIONS: [1865-present] 260 manuscript collections, 210,000 photos, 3,000 films and videotapes, 500 publication titles, 400 oral history interviews, 2,500 general reference files.

HOURS: Yr M-F 8-5

ADMISSION: No charge

CRESWELL

7008
Creswell Area Historical Society
51 N 5th St, 97426 [PO Box 414, 97426]; (p) (541) 895-5161; (f) (541) 895-5161; (c) Lane

Private non-profit/ 1972/ Creswell Area Historical Society/ staff: 25(v)/ members: 25

HISTORICAL SOCIETY; HISTORY MUSEUM: Collects, preserves, exhibits, and interprets local area history.

PROGRAMS: Community Outreach; Concerts; Exhibits; Family Programs

COLLECTIONS: [1850-1940] Period artifacts.

HOURS: Yr Daily afternoons

ADMISSION: No charge

EAGLE CREEK

7009
Philip Foster Farm
29912 SE Hwy 211, 97022 [PO Box 1000, Estacada, 97023]; (p) (503) 637-6324, (503) 630-3885; (f) (503) 630-5044; www.endofthe-oregontrail.com

1883/ Jacknife-Zion-Hore/ staff: 2(p); 20(v)

Home of Philip and Mary Charlotte Foster; located at the end of the Barlow Road segment of the Oregon Trail.

COLLECTIONS: [1850s-1890]

HOURS: Jun-Sept

ECHO

7010
Chinese House Railroad Museum
100 S Bonanza, 97826 [PO Box 426, 97826]; (p) (541) 376-8411; (f) (541) 376-8218; www.ohwy.com/or/c/chinehrm.htm

HOUSE MUSEUM

7011
Echo Historical Museum
Bonanza & Main St, 97826 [PO Box 205, 97826]; (p) (541) 376-8150; (c) Umatilla

Private non-profit/ 1980/ staff: 8(v)/ members: 98

HISTORY MUSEUM: Preserves local history.

PROGRAMS: Exhibits
HOURS: May-Sept Sa-Su 1:30-4:30
ADMISSION: Donations accepted

EUGENE

7012
Associated Students for Historic Preservation (ASHP)
231 Pacific, Univ of Oregon, 97403 [Ste 4, EMU, Univ of Oregon, 97403]; (p) (541) 346-0726; ashp@darkwing.uoregon.edu; darkwing.uoregon.edu/~ashp/; (c) Lane

1988/ University of Oregon/ staff: 35(v)/publication: *ASHP Journal*

HISTORIC PRESERVATION AGENCY: Promotes historic preservation.

PROGRAMS: Community Outreach; Exhibits; Garden Tours; Guided Tours; Interpretation; Lectures; Publication; School-Based Curriculum

COLLECTIONS: Building pieces, photographs, prints

7013
Lane County Historical Museum
740 W 13th Ave, 97402; (p) (541) 682-4242; (f) (541) 682-7361; lchm@efn.org; www.home townonline.com/historical_museum; (c) Lane

Private non-profit/ 1951/ Friends of Lane County Historical Museum/ staff: 1(f); 5(p); 30(v)/ members: 100

HISTORY MUSEUM: Collects, preserves, documents and interprets Lane County history.

PROGRAMS: Annual Meeting; Exhibits; Guided Tours; Research Library/Archives; School-Based Curriculum

COLLECTIONS: [1850-1900] Settlement artifacts, archives.

HOURS: Yr W-F 10-4, Sa 12-4

ADMISSION: $2, Student $0.75, Seniors $1

7014
Shelton-McMurphey-Johnson House
W of 3rd & Pearl St, 97401 [303 Willamette St, 97401]; (p) (541) 484-0808; www.smjhouse.org; (c) Lane

Private non-profit/ 1990/ staff: 2(p); 45(v)

HOUSE MUSEUM: Preserves local history.

PROGRAMS: Community Outreach; Concerts; Exhibits; Facility Rental; Festivals; Guided Tours; Interpretation

COLLECTIONS: [1888-1930] Furnishing, photos, period artifacts.

HOURS: Yr T, Th, Su 1-4

ADMISSION: $3, Children $1

7015
University of Oregon Museum of Natural History
1680 E 15th Ave, 97403 [1224 University of Oregon, 97403-1224]; (p) (541) 346-3024; (f) (541) 346-5334; mnh@oregon.uoregon.edu; (c) Lane

State/ 1936/ staff: 3(f); 11(p); 100(v)/ members: 700

HISTORY MUSEUM

PROGRAMS: Annual Meeting; Community Outreach; Exhibits; Facility Rental; Family Pro-

grams; Guided Tours; Interpretation; Lectures; Research Library/Archives; School-Based Curriculum

COLLECTIONS: Archaeological specimens.

HOURS: Yr T-Su 12-5

ADMISSION: $2, Children $1.50

FOREST GROVE

7016
Harvey W. Scott Memorial Library Archives, Pacific University
2043 College Way, 97116; (p) (503) 359-2737; (f) (503) 359-2236; tothalek@pacificu.edu; www.pacificu.edu; (c) Washington

Private non-profit/ 1849/ staff: 1(p)

LIBRARY AND/OR ARCHIVES: Preserves history of Pacific University.

PROGRAMS: Research Library/Archives

COLLECTIONS: [1849-present]

HOURS: Yr M-F and by appt

FOSSIL

7017
Fossil Museum
Corner First & Main St, 97830 [PO Box 465, 97830]; (p) (541) 763-4481; (f) (541) 763-2620; (c) Wheeler

City, non-profit/ 1960/ Fossil/ staff: 1(p); 20(v)

HISTORY MUSEUM: Promotes local and natural history.

PROGRAMS: Annual Meeting; Exhibits; Facility Rental; Family Programs; Film/Video

COLLECTIONS: [1880] Newspapers, Native American artifacts, period clothing, farm tools.

HOURS: Yr

GRANTS PASS

7018
Josephine County Historical Society
512 SW 5th St, 97526; (p) (541) 479-7827; (f) (541) 472-8928; jchs@terragon.com; www.webtrail.com/jchs; (c) Josephine

Private non-profit/ 1960/ Board of Directors/ staff: 1(p); 20(v)/ members: 600/publication: *Local History*

HISTORICAL SOCIETY; HOUSE MUSEUM: Collects, preserves, and interprets county history.

PROGRAMS: Annual Meeting; Community Outreach; Exhibits; Facility Rental; Guided Tours; Interpretation; Lectures; Living History; Publication; Research Library/Archives

COLLECTIONS: [1890-1920] Manuscripts, maps, newspaper, books, serials, photos,

7019
Schmidt House
508 SW 5th St, 97526 [512 SW 5th St, 97526]; (p) (541) 479-7827; (f) (541) 472-8928; (c) Josephine

1901/ Josephine County H/ staff: 1(p); 1(v)

COLLECTIONS: [Early 1900] Toy and doll collections; handiwork (lace, tatting, needlepoint).; Papers, photos, documents, scrapbooks, correspondence.

GRESHAM

7020
Gresham Historical Society
410 N Main Ave, 97030; (p) (503) 661-0347; (c) Multnomah

Private non-profit/ 1976/ Gresham Historical Society/ staff: 1(f); 2(p); 75(v)/ members: 375/publication: *Gresham: Stories of our Past*

HISTORICAL SOCIETY; HISTORY MUSEUM: Preserves local history.

PROGRAMS: Annual Meeting; Elder's Programs; Exhibits; Facility Rental; Interpretation; Publication

COLLECTIONS: [1850-1950] 3,000 photos, local artifacts.

HOURS: Yr T, Th, Sa 10-4

HAINES

7021
Eastern Oregon Museum
3rd & School St, 97833; (c) Baker

Private non-profit/ 1959/ Eastern Oregon Museum, Inc./ staff: 25(v)/ members: 20

GENEALOGICAL SOCIETY; HISTORY MUSEUM: Preserves pioneer history of Northeastern Oregon.

PROGRAMS: Exhibits; Research Library/Archives

COLLECTIONS: [1800-1900] Mining, farming, railroad, school, household artifacts, toys, dolls, photos, histories, carriages, tools, school room, kitchen, parlor, barbershop, beauty shop, cowboy apparel.

HOURS: May-Sept Daily 9-5

ADMISSION: Donations

HEPPNER

7022
Morrow County Museum
440 N Main, 97836 [PO Box 1153, 97836]; (p) (541) 676-5524; mcmuseum@ptinet.net; www.ourworld.compuserve.com/homepages/mcmuseum; (c) Morrow

1960

HISTORY MUSEUM: Collects and interprets local history.

PROGRAMS: Community Outreach; Exhibits; Family Programs; Lectures; Living History; Publication; Research Library/Archives

COLLECTIONS: [1850-present] Pioneers, homesteaders, farmers, ranchers, Native American, natural history collections.

HOURS: Feb-Dec T-Su 1-5

ADMISSION: No charge

HILLSBORO

7023
Rice Northwest Museum of Rocks and Minerals
26385 NW Groveland Dr, 97124; (p) (503) 647-2418; (f) (503) 647-5207; info@ricenwmuseum.org; www.ricenwmuseum.org; (c) Washington

Private non-profit/ 1996/ staff: 2(f); 2(p); 20(v)

HISTORY MUSEUM: Preserves cultural and natural history.

PROGRAMS: Exhibits; Facility Rental; Family Programs; Lectures

COLLECTIONS: Geological, mineral and lapidary specimens, petrified wood.

HOURS: Yr W-Su 1-5

ADMISSION: $3, Student $2, Children $1; Under 6 free

HOOD RIVER

7024
Hood River County Historical Museum
Port Marina Park, 97031 [PO Box 781, 97031]; (p) (503) 386-6772; (c) Hood River

County, non-profit/ staff: 1(f); 66(v)

HISTORY MUSEUM: History of Hood River settlement.

PROGRAMS: Exhibits; Research Library/ Archives

COLLECTIONS: Native American artifacts, period clothing, Japanese, Finnish and Hispanic cultures, quilts.

HOURS: Apr-Aug Daily 10-4, Sept-Oct Daily 12-4

ADMISSION: Donations accepted

INDEPENDENCE

7025
Heritage Museum, The
112 S 3rd St, 97351 [PO Box 7, 97351]; (p) (503) 838-4989; herimusm@open.org; www. open.org/herimusm; (c) Polk

Joint/ 1976/ City; Board of Directors/ staff: 2(p); 16(v)/ members: 55

HISTORY MUSEUM; RESEARCH CENTER: Preserves and displays history and culture of the river town of Independence and neighboring communities.

PROGRAMS: Community Outreach; Concerts; Exhibits; Guided Tours; Lectures

COLLECTIONS: [1860-present] Covered wagon, blacksmith shop, medical/dental tools and equipment, high school yearbooks and class pictures, Native American artifacts, parlor area, war memorabilia, photos, oral history, tapes, cooper's tools, vintage clothing, newspapers.

HOURS: Yr W, Sa 1-5, Th, F 1-4

ADMISSION: Donations accepted

JACKSONVILLE

7026
Beekman House
Laurelwood & California Sts, 97530 [106 N Central Ave, Medford, 97520]; (p) (541) 773-6536; (f) (541) 776-7994; educate@sohs.org

County/ 1870/ staff: 3(f); 4(p); 30(v)

Former home of local banker Cornelius C. Beekman.

COLLECTIONS: [1911] Linens, books, paintings, furniture, paper, books.

HOURS: Jun-Aug

JOSEPH

7027
Wallowa County Museum
110 S Main St, 97846; (p) (541) 432-6095, (541) 432-4834; (c) Wallowa

County/ 1976/ Wallowa County Museum Board/ staff: 5(f); 15(v)/ members: 140

HISTORIC SITE; HOUSE MUSEUM: Preserves, protects, and displays pioneer, Nez Perce Indian and Wallowa County artifacts and documents.

COLLECTIONS: [1888-present] Nez Perce and Chief Joseph; clothes, cultural life of pioneers, and development of Wallowa County.

HOURS: May 28-3rd wknd Sept: M-Su 10-5

ADMISSION: Donations accepted

JUNCTION CITY

7028
Junction City Historical Society
655 Holly St, 97448; (p) (541) 988-6154; cgoodin253@aol.com; www.junctioncity.com/ history; (c) Lane

Private non-profit/ 1971/ staff: 12(v)/ members: 100

HISTORIC PRESERVATION AGENCY; HISTORICAL SOCIETY: Preserves and promotes history of Junction City.

PROGRAMS: Annual Meeting; Exhibits; Guided Tours

COLLECTIONS: Dr. Lee house: pioneer times to the 1960's; Mary Pitney House: restored 1874 home.

HOURS: Yr last Su 1-4, and by appt

KERBY

7029
Kerbyville Museum
24195 Redwood Hwy, 97531 [PO Box 3, 97531]; (p) (541) 592-5252, (541) 592-2631; www.kerbyvillemuseum.com

KIMBERLY

7030
John Day Fossil Beds National Monument
HC 92 Box 126, 97848; (p) (541) 987-2333; (f) (541) 987-2336; www.nps.gov/joda; (c) Grant

Federal/ 1975/ National Park Service/ staff: 12(f); 11(p)

RESEARCH CENTER: Preserves and interprets natural history.

PROGRAMS: Exhibits; Guided Tours; Interpretation

COLLECTIONS: [Prehistory] Plant and animal fossils.

HOURS: Mar-Nov Daily 9-5

ADMISSION: Donations accepted

KLAMATH FALLS

7031
Favell Museum of Western Art and Indian Artifacts
125 W Main, 97601 [PO Box 165, 97601]; (p) (541) 882-9996; (f) (541) 850-0125; favmuseum@intevnetcds.com; www.favellmuseum.com; (c) Klamath

Private for-profit/ 1972/ Gene Favell/ staff: 2(f); 1(p); 35(v)/publication: *Treasury of Our Western Heritage*

ART MUSEUM; HISTORY MUSEUM

PROGRAMS: Annual Meeting; Exhibits; Facility Rental; Publication

COLLECTIONS: [20th c] Contemporary Western art, wildlife art, Native American artifacts.

HOURS: Yr M-Sa 9:30-5:30

ADMISSION: $4, Children $2, Seniors $3

7032
Klamath County Museums
1451 Main St, 97601; (p) (541) 883-4208; (f) (541) 884-0219; (c) Klamath

County/ 1954/ staff: 2(f); 2(p); 40(v)

HISTORY MUSEUM: Interprets history of Klamath Basin.

PROGRAMS: Exhibits; Facility Rental; Festivals; Living History; Reenactments; Research Library/Archives

COLLECTIONS: Basketry, stone tools, Indian artifacts, documents, photos, period clothing.

HOURS: Yr T-Sa 9-5

ADMISSION: $2, Student $1, Seniors $1

LAFAYETTE

7033
Yamhill County Historical Museum
605 Market, 97127 [PO Box 784, 97127]; (p) (503) 864-2308; (f) (503) 434-8996; www.co.yamhill.or.us; www.onlinemac. com/users/dlin; (c) Yamhill

Private non-profit/ 1969/ Yamhill County Historical Society/ members: 200/publication: *The West Side*

HISTORIC PRESERVATION AGENCY; HISTORICAL SOCIETY; HISTORY MUSEUM; RESEARCH CENTER: Protects, preserves and shares history and heritage of Yamhill County.

PROGRAMS: Exhibits; Family Programs; Festivals; Film/Video; Guided Tours; Interpretation; Publication; Research Library/Archives; School-Based Curriculum

COLLECTIONS: Pioneer photos, documents.

HOURS: Sept-June Sa-Su 1-4 June-Sept F, Sa, Su 1-4

ADMISSION: Donations accepted

LAKEVIEW

7034
Schminch Memorial Museum
128 SE St, 97630; (p) (541) 947-3134; jenglenn@triax.com; (c) Lake

Private non-profit/ 1938/ staff: 1(f); 2(p)

HISTORY MUSEUM; HOUSE MUSEUM; RESEARCH CENTER: Promotes local history.

PROGRAMS: Exhibits; Research Library/Archives

COLLECTIONS: 7,000 items, quilts, dolls and toys, clothing, cooking utensils, American pressed glass goblets, tools.

HOURS: Feb-Nov T-Sa 10-4

ADMISSION: $2, Students $1

LINCOLN CITY

7035
North Lincoln County Historical Museum
4907 SW Hwy 101, 97367; (p) (541) 996-6614; (f) (541) 996-1244; curator@wcn.net; (c) Lincoln

County, non-profit; Private non-profit/ 1987/ Board of Directors/ staff: 1(f); 2(p); 30(v)/ members: 300

HISTORY MUSEUM: Preserves local history.

PROGRAMS: Annual Meeting; Community Outreach; Exhibits; Family Programs; Guided Tours; Interpretation; Lectures; Publication; Research Library/Archives

COLLECTIONS: [1900-present] Photos, documents, equipment, and memorabilia.

HOURS: Yr T-Sa

MADRAS

7036
Jefferson County Historical Society and Museum
34 SE D St, 97741; (p) (541) 475-3808; (f) (541) 475-4204; (c) Jefferson

County, non-profit/ 1958/ Board of Directors/ staff: 1(p); 15(v)/ members: 150

HISTORICAL SOCIETY: Preserves and collects Jefferson County history.

PROGRAMS: Annual Meeting; Community Outreach; Exhibits; Film/Video; Guided Tours; Publication; Research Library/Archives; School-Based Curriculum

COLLECTIONS: [1890-1950] Artifacts related to sheep ranching, railroad, businesses, schools, Oregon Trail.

HOURS: June-Sept T-F 1-5

ADMISSION: No charge

MEDFORD

7037
Southern Oregon Historical Society
106 N Central Ave, 97501-5926; (p) (541) 773-6536; (f) (541) 776-7994; director@sohs.org; www.sohs.org; (c) Jackson

Private non-profit/ 1946/ staff: 33(f); 6(p); 329(v)/ members: 1350

HISTORIC SITE; HISTORICAL SOCIETY; HISTORY MUSEUM; HOUSE MUSEUM; LIBRARY AND/OR ARCHIVES; LIVING HISTORY/OUTDOOR MUSEUM; RESEARCH CENTER: Collects, preserves, researches, and interprets local history.

PROGRAMS: Annual Meeting; Community Outreach; Elder's Programs; Exhibits; Facility Rental; Family Programs; Festivals;

Film/Video; Garden Tours; Guided Tours; Interpretation; Lectures; Living History; Publication; Research Library/Archives; School-Based Curriculum

COLLECTIONS: [1850-1970] 3,900 linear feet of manuscripts, 3/4 million photos, 27,000 books, maps, oral histories, periodicals, 81,000 objects including textiles, furniture, decorative arts, firearms, vehicles, baskets, manufacturing and technological equipment.

HOURS: Sept-May W-Sa 10-5, Su 12-5; June-Aug Daily 10-5

ADMISSION: $3, Children $2, Seniors $2; History Center free

MILL CITY

7038
Canyon Life Museum
143 Wall St, 97346 [PO Box 574, Gates, 97346]; (p) (503) 897-4088; nshs@wvi.com; www.wvi.com/~sherryp/santiam.htm; (c) Marion and Linn

Private non-profit/ 1988/ North Santiam Historical Society/ staff: 4(v)/ members: 300

HISTORICAL SOCIETY; HISTORY MUSEUM: Discovers, preserves, and shares the history of the North Santiam Canyon of Western Oregon .

PROGRAMS: Exhibits; Interpretation; Monthly Meeting; Publication; Research Library/Archives

COLLECTIONS: [1880-1955] Interpretive exhibits of early logging camps, source material from the North Fork mining district; photos, genealogical information.

HOURS: June-Sept

MILTON-FREEWATER

7039
Milton-Freewater Area Historical Society/Frazier Farmstead Museum
1403 Chestnut St, 97862; (p) (541) 938-4636; museum@bmi.net; (c) Umatilla

Private non-profit/ 1984/ Board of Directors/ staff: 1(f); 1(p); 30(v)/ members: 250

HISTORIC SITE; HISTORICAL SOCIETY; HISTORY MUSEUM; HOUSE MUSEUM: Collects, preserves, and interprets local history.

PROGRAMS: Annual Meeting; Exhibits; Facility Rental; Festivals; Guided Tours; Interpretation; Publication; Research Library/Archives

COLLECTIONS: [1860-1920] Restored 1892 home, Victoriana, period furnishing, decorative arts, artifacts, archives, pioneer memorabilia.

HOURS: Apr-Dec Th-Sa 11-4

ADMISSION: Donations

MILWAUKIE

7040
Milwaukie Historical Society and Museum Inc.
3737 SE Adams, 97222; (p) (503) 659-5780; (c) Clackamas

Private non-profit/ 1936/ staff: 10(v)/ members: 123

HISTORY MUSEUM: Collects, preserves and interprets local history.

PROGRAMS: Annual Meeting; Community Outreach; Elder's Programs; Exhibits; Facility Rental; Festivals; Guided Tours; Interpretation; Lectures; Research Library/Archives

COLLECTIONS: [1846-present]

HOURS: Yr Sa-Su 11-3

ADMISSION: Donations

MOLALLA

7041
Dibble House
616 S Molalla Ave, 97013 [Box 828, 97013]; (p) (503) 266-5571

1859/ Molalla Area Historical Society/ staff: 10(v)

COLLECTIONS: [1859-1900] Furnishings, quilts, tools, Oregon Flax; genealogy records.

HOURS: Yr

7042
Molalla Area Historical Society
623 S Molalla Ave, 97038 [PO Box 828, 97038]; (p) (503) 829-5521; (c) Clackamas

Private non-profit/ 1972/ staff: 20(v)/ members: 125

HISTORIC SITE; HISTORICAL SOCIETY; HISTORY MUSEUM; HOUSE MUSEUM

PROGRAMS: Exhibits; Family Programs; Festivals; Guided Tours; Interpretation; Living History; Research Library/Archives

COLLECTIONS: [1850-present] Period furnishing, toys, quilts, textiles, clothing.

HOURS: Yr F-Su 1-4

ADMISSION: Donations accepted

MONMOUTH

7043
Jensen Arctic Museum
590 W Church St, 97361 [Western Oregon Univ, 97361]; (c) Polk

State/ 1985/ Western Oregon Univ/ staff: 15(f); 3(p)/ members: 210

ART MUSEUM; TRIBAL MUSEUM: Collects, preserves and exhibits ecology and culture of the Arctic.

PROGRAMS: Annual Meeting; Community Outreach; Exhibits; Family Programs; Interpretation; Research Library/Archives

COLLECTIONS: 4,000 objects, 10,000 slides and photos, 1,000 volume research library.

HOURS: Yr W-Sa 10-4

ADMISSION: $2, Student $1, Children $1

7044
Polk County Historical Society
Polk County Fairgrounds, 97361 [PO Box 67, 97361]; (p) (503) 623-8548; (c) Polk

County; Private for-profit; Private non-profit/ 1959/ Polk County Historical Society/ staff: 19(v)/ members: 322/publication: *Poker; Historically Speaking*

HISTORIC SITE; HISTORICAL SOCIETY; HISTORY MUSEUM; HOUSE MUSEUM; TRIBAL MUSEUM: Collects, preserves, exhibits, interprets and publishes information related to history of Polk County.

PROGRAMS: Annual Meeting; Community Outreach; Exhibits; Facility Rental; Family Programs; Festivals; Film/Video; Garden Tours; Guided Tours; Interpretation; Lectures; Publication; Research Library/Archives

COLLECTIONS: [1843-1946] Agriculture, mining, logging, pioneers, Camp Adair.

HOURS: Yr S, M, W, Sa 1-4

MORO

7045
Sherman County Historical Society
200 Dewey St, 97039 [PO Box 173, 97039]; (p) (541) 565-3232; (f) (541) 565-3080; scmuseum@transport.com; (c) Sherman

Joint/ 1945/ Board of Trustees; Private non-profit/ staff: 95(p); 95(v)/ members: 830/publication: *Sherman County: For The Record; The Plow*

GENEALOGICAL SOCIETY; HISTORIC PRESERVATION AGENCY; HISTORIC SITE; HISTORICAL SOCIETY; HISTORY MUSEUM; HOUSE MUSEUM; LIVING HISTORY/OUTDOOR MUSEUM: Collects, preserves, interprets, and publishes materials related to Sherman County.

PROGRAMS: Annual Meeting; Community Outreach; Elder's Programs; Exhibits; Family Programs; Festivals; Film/Video; Guided Tours; Lectures; Living History; Publication; Research Library/Archives; School-Based Curriculum

COLLECTIONS: [1889-1950] Farm tools, photos, toys, period furnishing, Oregon Trail, pioneers, rural towns, military service.

HOURS: May-Oct Daily 10-5

ADMISSION: $3, Student $1

MYRTLE POINT

7046
Coos County Logging Museum
Corner 7th & Maple Sts, 97458 [PO Box 325, 97458]; (p) (541) 572-1014; (c) Coos

Private non-profit/ 1987/ Board of Directors/ staff: 30(v)

HISTORIC SITE; HISTORY MUSEUM: Collects logging equipment.

PROGRAMS: Annual Meeting; Exhibits

COLLECTIONS: [1900-1965] Logging pictures and equipment.

HOURS: End of May-Sept M-Sa 10-4, Su, 1-4

ADMISSION: Donations accepted

NEWBERG

7047
Hoover-Minthorn House Museum, The
115 S River St, 97132; (p) (503) 538-6629; (c) Yamhill

Private non-profit/ 1955/ National Society of Colonial Dames/ staff: 1(f); 1(p); 25(v)/ members: 180

HISTORIC SITE; HOUSE MUSEUM; LIVING HISTORY/OUTDOOR MUSEUM; PRESIDENTIAL SITE: Collects, preserves, exhibits and interprets materials, contents and buildings pertaining to Dr. Henry John Minthorn and to boyhood years of President Herbert Hoover.

PROGRAMS: Annual Meeting; Community Outreach; Exhibits; Festivals; Guided Tours; Lectures; Living History

COLLECTIONS: [1890-1900] Furnished Quaker home of 1885-90; Herbert Hoover's original bedroom set; Dr. Minthorn's medical and bible study books; Alfred Meakin Royal Ironstone, "Tea Leaf" china.

HOURS: Mar-Nov: W-Su 1-4 Feb, Dec Sa-Su 1-4

ADMISSION: $2, Student $1.50, Children $0.50, Seniors $1.50

NEWPORT

7048
Oregon Coast History Center
545 SW 9th St, 97365; (p) (541) 265-7509; (f) (541) 265-3992; coasthistory@newportnet.com; www.newportnet.com/coasthistory/home.htm; (c) Lincoln

Private non-profit/ 1948/ Lincoln County Historical Society/ staff: 3(f); 4(p); 45(v)/ members: 275

HISTORICAL SOCIETY; HISTORY MUSEUM: Preserves and interprets history of Lincoln County and central Oregon coast.

PROGRAMS: Annual Meeting; Community Outreach; Elder's Programs; Exhibits; Family Programs; Interpretation; Lectures; Publication; Research Library/Archives; School-Based Curriculum

COLLECTIONS: [1850-present] 45,000 artifacts related to logging, coastal settlement, Siletz Reservaion, railroad, maritime.

HOURS: June-Sept T-Su 10-5; Oct-May T-Su

NORTH BEND

7049
Coos County Historical Society Museum
1220 Sherman Ave, 97459; (p) (541) 756-6320; (f) (541) 756-6320; museum@harborside.com; (c) Coos

Private non-profit/ 1891/ staff: 1(f); 2(p); 2(v)/ members: 250

HISTORICAL SOCIETY; HISTORY MUSEUM: Preserves Coos County history.

PROGRAMS: Annual Meeting; Community Outreach; Elder's Programs; Exhibits; Interpretation; Publication; Research Library/Archives

COLLECTIONS: [1850-1950] Native American basketry, Pacific Rim memorabilia, photos/negatives of social history, textiles, toys/games, Merci Train heirlooms, maritime/waterways.

HOURS: June-Aug M-Sa 10-4; Sept-May T-Sa

7050
Coquille Indian Tribe
3050 Tremont St, 97459 [PO Box 783, 97420]; (p) (800) 622-5869; (f) (541) 756-0847; (c) Coos

Tribal/ CIT Tribal Council/publication: *Tribal Tidbits*

Preserves and promotes tribal history.

PROGRAMS: Annual Meeting; Community Outreach; Elder's Programs; Family Programs; Interpretation; Living History; Publication; Research Library/Archives

COLLECTIONS: [1850-present] Native American artifacts, language and oral history recordings.

HOURS: Yr M-F 8-5

NYSSA

7051
Nyssa Historical Society
117 Good Ave, 97913 [PO Box 2303, 97913]; (p) (541) 372-5069; (f) (541) 372-3193; (c) Malheur

Private non-profit/ 1993/ staff: 50(v)/ members: 150

HISTORICAL SOCIETY; HISTORY MUSEUM; HOUSE MUSEUM; LIVING HISTORY/OUTDOOR MUSEUM: Operates Nyssa Agricultural and Oregon Trail Museum, and promotes Nyssa Historical Walking Tour.

PROGRAMS: Annual Meeting; Community Outreach; Exhibits; Festivals; Guided Tours; Living History; Reenactments

COLLECTIONS: [1840] Agriculture, period furnishing, restored buildings.

HOURS: Apr-Oct F-Sa 10-5, Su 1-5

ADMISSION: $5 Walking Tour; Donations accepted

OAKLAND

7052
Oakland Museum Historical Society, Inc.
130 Locust St, 97462 [506 Green Valley Rd, 97462]; (p) (541) 459-3087; www.makewebs.com/oakland; (c) Douglas

Private non-profit/ 1969/ Board of Directors/ staff: 50(v)

HISTORICAL SOCIETY: Promotes local history.

PROGRAMS: Exhibits

COLLECTIONS: [1850-1950] Photos, musical instruments, toys, period clothing, furniture, tools, bottles.

HOURS: Yr Daily

ONTARIO

7053
Four Rivers Cultural Center and Museum
676 SW 5th Ave, 97914; (p) (541) 889-8191; (f) (541) 889-7628; free@micron.net; 4rcc.com; (c) Malheur

Private non-profit/ 1997/ staff: 7(f); 2(p); 70(v)/ members: 250

HISTORY MUSEUM: Promotes culture of Western Treasure Valley.

PROGRAMS: Community Outreach; Concerts; Exhibits; Facility Rental; Family Programs; Festivals; Guided Tours; Interpretation; Lectures; Living History; Research Library/Archives; School-Based Curriculum; Theatre

COLLECTIONS: [1850-present] 3,000 Native American artifacts, stone implements, basketry, pottery, flaked articles, beads, buckskin.

HOURS: Yr M-Sa 10-6, Su 12-6

OREGON CITY

7054
Clackamas County Historical Society
211 Tumwater, 97045; (p) (503) 655-5574; (f) (503) 655-0035; (c) Clackamas

Private non-profit/ 1952/ staff: 2(f); 1(p); 50(v)/ members: 450

HISTORICAL SOCIETY; HISTORY MUSEUM; HOUSE MUSEUM: Collects, preserves and interprets the culture and history of Clackamas County.

PROGRAMS: Annual Meeting; Community Outreach; Concerts; Exhibits; Facility Rental; Family Programs; Festivals; Guided Tours; Interpretation; Living History; Reenactments; School-Based Curriculum

COLLECTIONS: [1843-1950] Artifacts, photos, archival papers.

HOURS: Yr M-F 10-4, Sa-Su 1-5

ADMISSION: $4, Student $2, Seniors $3

7055
End of the Oregon Trail Interpretive Center
1726 Washington St, 97045; (p) (503) 557-9900; (f) (503) 557-8590; staff@endoftheoregontrail.org; (c) Clackamas

Private non-profit/ 1986/ Oregon Trail Foundation/ staff: 8(f); 17(p); 154(v)/ members: 200

LIVING HISTORY/OUTDOOR MUSEUM: Preserves history and culture of the End of the Oregon Trail.

PROGRAMS: Annual Meeting; Exhibits; Facility Rental; Family Programs; Interpretation; Living History; Publication; Reenactments; School-Based Curriculum

COLLECTIONS: [1843-1883] Donations, loans and reproduction of items related to Oregon Trail and early settlement in Pacific Northwest.

HOURS: Yr M-Sa 9-5, Su 10-5

ADMISSION: $5.50, Children $3, Seniors $4.50

7056
McLaughlin House National Historic Site/McLoughlin Memorial Association
713 Center, 97045; (p) (503) 656-5146; www.mcloughlinhouse.org; (c) Clackamas

Private non-profit/ 1909/ staff: 1(f); 2(p); 26(v)/ members: 100/publication: *Beaver Log Newsletter*

HISTORIC SITE; HISTORY MUSEUM; HOUSE MUSEUM: Preserves fur trade history and settlement.

PROGRAMS: Annual Meeting; Festivals; Guided Tours; Interpretation; Publication

COLLECTIONS: [1825-1870] Personal effects of John McLaughlin, period furnishing.

ADMISSION: $4, Student $2, Seniors $3

7057
Stevens Crawford Museum
603 Sixth St, 97045; (p) (503) 655-2866

1908/ Clackamas County H/ staff: 1(p); 16(v)

COLLECTIONS: [1908] Hats, clocks, Indian artifacts, clothing, Family letters, cards.

HOURS: Yr; Closed Jan

PARKDALE

7058
Jesse and Winifred Hutson Museum, The
4967 Baseline Dr, 97041 [PO Box 501, 97041]; (p) (541) 352-6808; (c) Hood River

Private non-profit/ 1992/ Board of Directors/ staff: 16(v)/ members: 157

HISTORY MUSEUM: Preserves and promotes Native American and local history.

PROGRAMS: Annual Meeting; Community Outreach; Exhibits

COLLECTIONS: [19th-20th c] Native American artifacts, agricultural, logging, local history, geological specimens.

HOURS: May-Sept T-F 11-4, Sa-Su 11-5:30; Oct-Nov W-F 11-4, Sa-Su

PENDLETON

7059
Tomastslikt Cultural Institute
72789 Hwy 331, 97801; (p) (541) 966-9748; (f) (541) 966-9927; www.umatilla.nsn.us/tamust.html; (c) Umatilla

Tribal/ 1998/ Confederated Tribes of the Umatilla Indian Reservation/ staff: 17(f); 4(p)

RESEARCH CENTER; TRIBAL MUSEUM: Promotes history of the Cayuse, Umatilla and Walla Walla tribes.

PROGRAMS: Exhibits; Facility Rental; Guided Tours; Interpretation; Lectures

COLLECTIONS: Tribal artifacts.

HOURS: Yr Daily 9-5

ADMISSION: $6, Children $4, Seniors $4

7060
Umatilla County Historical Society
108 SW Franzer Ave, 97801 [PO Box 253, 97801]; (p) (541) 276-0012; (f) (541) 276-7989; (c) Umatilla

Private non-profit/ 1974/ Umatilla County Historical Society/ staff: 2(f); 1(p); 400(v)/ members: 1000

HISTORICAL SOCIETY; HISTORY MUSEUM: Collects, preserves, and interprets history and prehistory of Umatilla County.

PROGRAMS: Annual Meeting; Exhibits; Family Programs; Lectures; Publication; Research Library/Archives

COLLECTIONS: [1860-present] Photos, museum artifacts.

HOURS: Yr T-Sa 10-4

ADMISSION: $2, Student $1; Under 5 free

PHILOMATH

7061
Benton County Historical Society
1101 Main St, 97370 [PO Box 35, 97370]; (p) (541) 929-6230; (f) (541) 929-6261; bchm@peak.org; (c) Benton

Private non-profit/ 1959/ Board of Directors/ staff: 6(f); 3(p); 50(v)/ members: 500

ART MUSEUM; GENEALOGICAL SOCIETY; HISTORIC PRESERVATION AGENCY; HISTORIC SITE; HISTORICAL SOCIETY; HISTORY MUSEUM; HOUSE MUSEUM; LIBRARY AND/OR ARCHIVES; RESEARCH CENTER: Collects, preserves, and uses cultural materials of Benton County history; maintains the Benton County History Center in Corvallis.

PROGRAMS: Annual Meeting; Community Outreach; Exhibits; Facility Rental; Festivals; Guided Tours; Interpretation; Publication; Reenactments; Research Library/Archives

COLLECTIONS: [19th-20th c] Manufactured objects, Native American materials, photos.

HOURS: Yr T-Sa 10-4:30

PORT ORFORD

7062
Cape Blanco Lighthouse/Friends of Cape Blanco
Cape Blanco State Park, near Port Orford, 97465 [c/o Friends of Cape Blanco, PO Box 285, 97465]; (p) (541) 756-0100; www.lighthousekeeper.com/blanco.html

Joint/ 1870/ US Coast Guard/Bureau of Land Mangement and others

HISTORIC SITE: Preserves history of 1870 Cape Blanco Lighthouse.

PROGRAMS: Guided Tours

COLLECTIONS: [1870-present] Photos, documents.

HOURS: Apr-Oct Th-M 10-3

ADMISSION: No charge

7063
Historic Hughes House, The
Cape Blanco Rd, [PO Box 285, Sixes, 97476-0285]; (p) (541) 332-0248

PORTLAND

7064
Bybee House and Agricultural Museum at Howell Territorial Park
13901 NW Howell Rd, 97205 [1200 SW Park Ave, 97205]; (p) (503) 222-1741; (f) (503) 221-2035; orhist@ohs.org; www.ohs.org; (c) Multnomah

Joint/ 1959/ Metro Regional Parks and Greenspaces/Oregon Historical Society/ staff: 3(p); 10(v)

HISTORIC SITE: Interprets rural lifestyle and history.

PROGRAMS: Exhibits; Facility Rental; Guided Tours; Interpretation

COLLECTIONS: [1858-1885] Social history, agricultural equipment.

HOURS: June-Aug Sa-Su

7065
Finnish-American Historical Society of the West
12602 SE 24th, 97228 [PO Box 5522, 97228-5522]; (p) (503) 654-0448; finamhsw@teleport.com; www.teleport.com/~finamhsw; (c) Clackamas

Private non-profit/ 1962/ Organization president/ staff: 10(f)/ members: 300/publication: *Pioneer Series*

HISTORICAL SOCIETY: Preserves Finnish heritage in the American West.

PROGRAMS: Publication

COLLECTIONS: [Start of immigration-1950s] Writings from individuals and groups are published in annual monographs.

HOURS: June-Labor Day: Sat, Su, holidays 11-5

7066
Northwest Archivists, Inc.
1206 SW Myrtle Dr, 97201; (p) (503) 306-5257; histdude@teleport.com; www.osu.orst.edu/dept/archives/misc/nwa

Private non-profit/ 1972/ members: 2000

Promotes archiving practices.

7067
Oregon Historical Society
1200 SW Park Ave, 97205-2483; (p) (503) 222-1741; (f) (503) 221-2035; orhist@ohs.org; www.ohs.org; (c) Multnomah

Private non-profit/ 1873/ staff: 55(f); 16(p); 300(v)/ members: 7500/publication: *Oregon Historical Quarterly*

HISTORIC SITE; HISTORICAL SOCIETY; HISTORY MUSEUM: Collects, preserves, interprets, and publishes materials related to the history of Oregon.

PROGRAMS: Annual Meeting; Community Outreach; Concerts; Exhibits; Facility Rental; Family Programs; Festivals; Guided Tours; Interpretation; Lectures; Publication; Reenactments; Research Library/Archives; School-Based Curriculum

COLLECTIONS: 100,000 museum artifacts, 2 million photos, 32,000 books, 3,000 rare books, 3,000 serieals, 30,000 maps, 12,000 linear feet of manuscripts, 6,000 oral history footage, 15,000 titles of moving images, 4,000 vertical files, government documents.

HOURS: Yr T-W, F-Sa 10-5, Th 10-8pm, Su 12-5

ADMISSION: $6, Student $3, Children $1.50

7068
Oregon Jewish Museum
310 NW Davis St, 97201; (p) (503) 226-3600; (f) (503) 226-1800; museum@ojm.org; (c) Multnomah

Private non-profit/ 1989/ staff: 3(p); 40(v)/ members: 400/publication: *The Jews of Oregon*

HISTORY MUSEUM; LIBRARY AND/OR ARCHIVES: Preserves history of Jews in Oregon.

PROGRAMS: Annual Meeting; Community Outreach; Exhibits; Facility Rental; Lectures; Publication; Research Library/Archives

COLLECTIONS: [1848-present] Synagogue histories, photos, papers, newspapers, artifacts.

HOURS: Yr T-F 11-2, Su 1-4

ADMISSION: No charge

7069
Oregon Maritime Center and Museum
113 SW Naito Pkwy, 97204; (p) (503) 224-7724; (f) (503) 224-7767; (c) Multnomah

Private non-profit/ 1980/ Board of Trustees/ staff: 1(p); 90(v)/ members: 500

HISTORIC PRESERVATION AGENCY; HISTORY MUSEUM: Preserves history of Columbia and Willamette Rivers.

PROGRAMS: Annual Meeting; Facility Rental; Guided Tours; Lectures; Research Library/ Archives

COLLECTIONS: [1850-present] Sail boats, nautical artifacts, maritime library, steam stern wheeler.

HOURS: Yr F-Su 11-4

ADMISSION: $3, Family $10, Children $2, Under 8 Free

7070
Oregon Sports Hall of Fame
321 SW Salmon, 97204; (p) (503) 227-7466; (c) Multnomah

Private non-profit/ 1980/ staff: 3(f); 4(p); 50(v)/ members: 1050/publication: *Scrapbook*

HISTORY MUSEUM: Interprets the history of sporting in the Northwest.

PROGRAMS: Annual Meeting; Community Outreach; Exhibits; Facility Rental; Family Programs; Guided Tours; Living History; Publication; School-Based Curriculum; Theatre

COLLECTIONS: Memorabilia, trophies, sports artifacts.

HOURS: Yr T-Su

7071
Pittock Mansion
3229 NW Pittock Dr, 97210; (p) (503) 823-3624; (f) (503) 823-3619; pkdanc@ci.portland.or.us; (c) Multnomah

Joint/ 1965/ Portland Parks and Recreation, Pittock Mansion Society/ staff: 3(f); 5(p); 205(v)/ members: 300/publication: *Newsletter: Pittock Papers*

HOUSE MUSEUM: Preserves and restores Pittock Estate.

PROGRAMS: Annual Meeting; Community Outreach; Exhibits; Facility Rental; Film/Video; Guided Tours; Interpretation; Lectures; Publication; School-Based Curriculum

COLLECTIONS: [17th-19th c] English, French, American furnishing, lusterware, Thomas Hill paintings.

HOURS: Feb-Dec Daily 12-4

ADMISSION: $5, Student $2.50, Seniors $4.50

7072
Portland Art Museum
1219 SW Park Ave, 97205; (p) (503) 226-2811; (f) (503) 226-4842; info@pam.org; www.pam.org; (c) Multnomah

Private non-profit/ 1892/ Board of Trustees/ staff: 93(f); 40(p); 1200(v)/ members: 18000

ART MUSEUM: Promotes art and cultural history of Pacific Northwest.

PROGRAMS: Community Outreach; Concerts; Elder's Programs; Exhibits; Facility Rental; Family Programs; Film/Video; Guided Tours; Interpretation; Lectures; Research Library/Archives; School-Based Curriculum

COLLECTIONS: European, African, Asian, Pre-Columbian, Native American art, photos, prints, drawings.

HOURS: Yr M-Sa 10-5, Su 12-5

ADMISSION: $7.50, Student $4, Children $4, Seniors $6

7073
Portland Police Historical Society and Police Museum
1111 SW Second Ave, 97208 [PO Box 4072, 97208]; (p) (503) 823-0019; (c) Multnomah

Private non-profit/ 1976/ Board of Directors/ staff: 2(f)

Preserves the history and paraphenalia of the Portland Police Department.

COLLECTIONS: [1851-present] Photos, uniforms, vehicles, guns and equipment.

HOURS: Yr M-Th 10-3

7074
Washington County Historical Society
17677 NW Springville Rd, 97229; (p) (503) 645-5353; (f) (503) 645-5650; wchs@teleport.com; (c) Washington

Private non-profit/ 1956/ Board of Directors/ staff: 3(f); 2(p); 35(v)/ members: 302/publication: *Express - This Far off Sunset Land*

GENEALOGICAL SOCIETY; HISTORIC PRESERVATION AGENCY; HISTORIC SITE; HISTORICAL SOCIETY; HISTORY MUSEUM; HOUSE MUSEUM; RESEARCH CENTER

PROGRAMS: Annual Meeting; Community Outreach; Elder's Programs; Exhibits; Facility Rental; Family Programs; Festivals; Garden Tours; Guided Tours; Interpretation; Lectures; Living History; Publication; Reenactments; Research Library/ Archives; School-Based Curriculum

COLLECTIONS: [Prehistory-present]

HOURS: Yr 10-4:30

ADMISSION: $2, Children $1

PRINEVILLE

7075
Crook County Historical Society
246 N Main St, 97754; (p) (541) 447-3715; (f) (541) 447-3715; bowmuse@netscape.net; (c) Crook

Private non-profit/ 1971/ staff: 1(f); 2(p); 10(v)/ members: 482

HISTORICAL SOCIETY; HISTORY MUSEUM

PROGRAMS: Annual Meeting; Community Outreach; Exhibits; Family Programs; Film/Video; Guided Tours; Lectures; Living History; Research Library/Archives

COLLECTIONS: [1800-present] Period clothing, firearms, household items, artifacts.

HOURS: Feb-Dec

ADMISSION: No charge

ROGUE RIVER

7076
Woodville Museum Inc.
Oak & First St, 97537 [PO Box 1288, 97537];
(p) (541) 582-3088; (c) Jackson

County/ 1986/ Southern Oregon Historical Society/ staff: 12(v)/ members: 144

HOUSE MUSEUM: Preserves historic home.

PROGRAMS: Annual Meeting; Community Outreach; Concerts; Exhibits; Festivals; Lectures

COLLECTIONS: Period furnishing, pioneer, mining artifacts.

HOURS: Sept-May T-Sa 12-4; June-Aug T-Su

ROSEBURG

7077
Douglas County Historical Society
544 SE Douglas, 97470 [733 W Ballf, 97470];
(c) Douglas

Private non-profit/ 1953/ Board of Directors/ staff: 1(p); 20(v)/ members: 325/publication: *The Umpqua Trapper*

HISTORICAL SOCIETY; HOUSE MUSEUM: Promotes local history.

PROGRAMS: Annual Meeting; Community Outreach; Concerts; Elder's Programs; Exhibits; Facility Rental; Family Programs; Festivals; Film/Video; Garden Tours; Guided Tours; Interpretation; Lectures; Living History; Publication; Reenactments; Research Library/ Archives;

COLLECTIONS: [1860-1890] Native American artifacts.

HOURS: Yr Sa-Su 1-4

ADMISSION: Donations

7078
Douglas County Museum of History and Natural History
123 Museum Dr, 97470; (p) (541) 957-7007; (f) (541) 957-7017; museum@co.douglas.or.us; www.co.douglas.or.us/museum/; (c) Douglas

County, non-profit/ 1969/ Douglas County/ staff: 4(f); 2(p); 30(v)/ members: 300/publication: *Friends*

HISTORY MUSEUM: Collects, preserves and interprets local history.

PROGRAMS: Exhibits; Facility Rental; Family Programs; Film/Video; Guided Tours; Interpretation; Publication; Research Library/Archives

COLLECTIONS: [Prehistory-present] 20,000 photos, Lavola Bakken Research library.

HOURS: Yr M-W, F 9-5, Th 9-8, Sa 10-5, Su

SALEM

7079
Brunk Pioneer Homestead
5705 Salem Dallas Hy NW, 97304 [PO Box 67, Monmouth, 97361]; (p) (503) 838-1807, (503) 838-6603

Private non-profit/ 1861/ Polk County Historical Society

COLLECTIONS: [1895-1920] 3 styles churns, flour bin, sugar barrel, pump organ, Indian artifacts, quilts, Oregon Trail items, local pottery, homemaker tools, toys, dolls, old deeds, maps, pioneer family histories, cemetery records, photos, scrapbooks.

HOURS: Appt

7080
Bush House Museum
600 Mission St SE, 97302; (p) (503) 363-4714; (c) Marion

Private non-profit/ 1953/ Salem Art Association/ staff: 1(f); 2(p); 60(v)/ members: 60

GARDEN; HISTORIC SITE; HOUSE MUSEUM: 1878 Victorian mansion with original furnishings, wallpaper, gas lights and seventy marble fireplaces.

PROGRAMS: Annual Meeting; Exhibits; Festivals; Guided Tours; Interpretation; Living History; Research Library/Archives

COLLECTIONS: [1870-1910]

HOURS: May-Sept T-Su 12-5; Oct-Apr T-Su 2-5

ADMISSION: $3, Student $2.50, Children $1.50

7081
Historic Deepwood Estate
1116 Mission St SE, 97302; (p) (503) 363-1725; deepwood@open.org; www.oregonlink.com/deepwood; (c) Marion

Private non-profit/ 1974/ Friends of Deepwood/ staff: 1(f); 4(p); 30(v)/ members: 125

GARDEN; HOUSE MUSEUM: Conserves, develops and interprets history of house, formal gardens and natural landscape.

PROGRAMS: Annual Meeting; Community Outreach; Concerts; Exhibits; Facility Rental; Family Programs; Garden Tours; Guided Tours; Interpretation; Lectures; School-Based Curriculum

COLLECTIONS: [1890-1930] Household furnishings, women's clothing, architectural fragments.

HOURS: May-Sept Su-F 12-5; Oct-Apr T-Sa 12-5

7082
Marion County Historical Society
260 12th St SE, 97301; (p) (503) 364-2128; (f) (503) 391-5356; mchs@open.org; www.open.org/mchs; (c) Marion

County; Private non-profit/ 1950/ Board of Directors/ staff: 1(f); 1(p); 30(v)/ members: 425/publication: *Historic Marion*

HISTORIC SITE; HISTORICAL SOCIETY; HISTORY MUSEUM: Preserves and interprets cultural and natural history.

PROGRAMS: Annual Meeting; Community Outreach; Exhibits; Festivals; Guided Tours; Lectures; Publication; Research Library/ Archives

COLLECTIONS: [1850-1950] 3,000 objects, 200,000 negatives, and photos, 1500 serials, 100 maps. President Herbert Hoover.

HOURS: Yr T-Sa 10-4:30

ADMISSION: $3, Children $1

7083
Mission Mill Museum/Mission Mill Museum Association
1313 Mill St SE, 97301; (p) (503) 585-7012; (f) (503) 588-9902; missionm@teleport.com; (c) Marion

Private non-profit/ 1962/ Executive Board/ staff: 9(f); 8(p); 200(v)/publication: *Milling Around*

HISTORIC SITE; HISTORICAL SOCIETY; HISTORY MUSEUM; LIVING HISTORY/OUTDOOR MUSEUM: Preserves history of 1896 brick woolen mill, Jason Lee Home, John D. Boon House, and Parsonage of the Methodist Mission.

PROGRAMS: Annual Meeting; Community Outreach; Exhibits; Family Programs; Festivals; Film/Video; Garden Tours; Guided Tours; Interpretation; Lectures; Living History; Publication; Research Library/Archives; School-Based Curriculum; Theatre

COLLECTIONS: [1840-present] Pioneer artifacts, woolen mill, archives, Methodist mission, settlers.

HOURS: Yr T-Sa 10-5

ADMISSION: $4, Student $2.25, Children $1.50, Seniors $4.50

7084
Oregon State Library
250 Winter St NE, 97301-3950; (p) (503) 378-4243; (f) (503) 588-7119; (c) Marion

State/ 1939/ staff: 45(f); 175(v)

GENEALOGICAL SOCIETY; HISTORIC PRESERVATION AGENCY; HISTORIC SITE; RESEARCH CENTER

COLLECTIONS: Federal and state documents, Oregoniana.

HOURS: Yr M-F 10-5

SCOTTS MILLS

7085
Scotts Mills Area Historical Society
210 Grandview Ave, 97375 [PO Box 226, 97375]; (p) (503) 873-6596; (c) Marion

Private non-profit/ 1979/ Board of Directors/ staff: 6(v)

GENEALOGICAL SOCIETY; HISTORICAL SOCIETY; HISTORY MUSEUM: Promotes historic preservation of materials and artifacts.

PROGRAMS: Annual Meeting; Exhibits; Guided Tours; Publication; School-Based Curriculum

HOURS: Mar-Oct, 2nd Su 1-5, or by appt

ADMISSION: Donations requested

SEASIDE

7086
Seaside Museum and Historical Society
570 Necanicum Dr, 97138 [PO Box 1024, 97138]; (p) (503) 738-7065; (f) (503) 738-0761; kirkham@westconnect.com; (c) Clatsop

Private non-profit/ 1973/ Board of Directors/ staff: 1(p); 44(v)/ members: 255/publication: *Making History Together*

HISTORICAL SOCIETY; HISTORY MUSEUM: Collects, preserves, and interprets Seaside history.

PROGRAMS: Annual Meeting; Concerts; Exhibits; Facility Rental; Festivals; Guided Tours; Interpretation; Publication; Research Library/Archives

COLLECTIONS: [Prehistory-1940] 2,000 glass negatives, Native American artifacts, Lewis and Clark, tourism, logging.

HOURS: Yr Summer Daily 11-4; Winter Daily 12-3

ADMISSION: $2, Student $1, Seniors $1.50

SILVERTON

7087
Silverton Country Historical Society
428 S Water St, 97381; (c) Marion

Private non-profit/ 1983/ Silverton County Historical Society/ staff: 20(v)/ members: 150

HISTORICAL SOCIETY; HISTORY MUSEUM

PROGRAMS: Annual Meeting; Community Outreach; Exhibits; Guided Tours; Interpretation

COLLECTIONS: [1840-present] Logging, farming, schools, pioneer exhibits; housed in 1908 house.

HOURS: Mar-Nov Th, Su 1-4

ADMISSION: $1, Children $0.50

SPRAY

7088
Spray Pioneer Museum
402 Willow St, 97874 [PO Box 83, 97874]; (p) (541) 468-2069; (f) (541) 468-2044; (c) Wheeler

City, non-profit/ 1992/ staff: 1(p); 32(v)

HISTORY MUSEUM: Collects, preserves and interprets local history.

COLLECTIONS: [1800-present] Pioneer memorabilia, photos, farm implements, household goods, obituaries.

HOURS: Yr Th-Su 9-3

ADMISSION: Donations

SPRINGFIELD

7089
Springfield Museum
590 Main St, 97477 [225 Fifth St, 97477]; (p) (541) 726-2300; (f) (541) 726-3689; kjensen@ci.springfield.or.us; (c) Lane

City, non-profit/ 1981/ staff: 1(f); 1(p); 61(v)/ members: 115

HISTORY MUSEUM: Promotes local history and culture.

PROGRAMS: Exhibits; Family Programs; Festivals; Garden Tours

COLLECTIONS: [1850-1920] Agricultural implements, photos.

HOURS: Yr T-F 10-5, Sa 12-5

ADMISSION: No charge

ST HELENS

7090
Columbia County Historical Society
Columbia County Courthouse Plaza, 97051 [PO Box 837, St. Helens, 97051]; (p) (503) 397-3868, (503) 397-9780; cchsb@columbia-center.org; (c) Columbia

Private non-profit/ 1920/ Board of Directors/ staff: 25(p); 25(v)/ members: 148/publication: *County History, Vol 1-24*

HISTORIC SITE; HISTORICAL SOCIETY; HISTORY MUSEUM; HOUSE MUSEUM: Collects and preserves Columbia County history.

PROGRAMS: Annual Meeting; Exhibits; Festivals; Guided Tours; Interpretation; Lectures; Living History; Publication; Reenactments; Research Library/Archives; School-Based Curriculum

COLLECTIONS: [1800-present] Local history artifacts.

HOURS: June-Aug Th-Sa 12-4, Su 1-4; Sept-May F-Sa 12-4, Su 1-4

ADMISSION: Donations

ST. PAUL

7091
Pioneer Mothers Memorial Cabin Museum
8035 Champoeg Rd NE, 97137-9709; (p) (503) 633-2237; darcabin@stpaultel.com; (c) Marion

Private non-profit/ 1931/ OR State Society, Daughters of the American Revolution/ staff: 2(f); 5(v)/ members: 1600/publication: *Men of Champoeg; Oregon Landmarks;*

HISTORY MUSEUM: Preserves pioneer history in OR.

PROGRAMS: Exhibits; Facility Rental; Family Programs; Garden Tours; Guided Tours; Interpretation; Living History; Publication

COLLECTIONS: [1775-1884] Historic furnishing, guns, quilts, dishware, wool carding, hand loom, shards, dishware, hand tools, wool spindle, covered wagon, pioneers artifacts.

HOURS: Mar-Oct F-Su 1-5

ADMISSION: $2, Children $1; Group rates

7092
Robert Newell House Museum
8089 Champoeg Rd NE, 97137-9709; (p) (503) 678-5537, (503) 678-5537; (c) Marion

Private non-profit/ 1859/ OR State Daughters of the American Revolution/ staff: 2(f); 5(v)/ members: 1600/publication: *Men of Champoeg; Oregon Landmarks*

HISTORIC SITE; HISTORY MUSEUM; HOUSE MUSEUM: Preserves and interprets OR history.

PROGRAMS: Exhibits; Facility Rental; Family Programs; Guided Tours; Interpretation; Publication

COLLECTIONS: [1850-1880] Native American clothing, baskets, stone artifacts; inaugural gowns of OR governors' wives. Period furnishing, quilts, schoolhouse, needlework, 1860s schoolhouse, 1850 Butte County jail, handcrafts, looms, coverlets, guns pioneer artifacts.

HOURS: Mar-Oct F-Su 1-5

ADMISSION: $2, Children $1, $3/Car

THE DALLES

7093
Columbia Gorge Discovery Center and Wasco County Historical Museum
500 Discover Dr, 97058; (p) (541) 296-8600; (f) (954) 298-8660; exdir@gorgediscovery.org; www.gorgediscovery.org; (c) Wasco

Private non-profit/ 1997/ Crate's Point Board of Directors/ staff: 12(f); 16(p); 150(v)/ members: 500

GARDEN; HISTORIC SITE; HISTORY MUSEUM; LIVING HISTORY/OUTDOOR MUSEUM: Interprets Native Americans, Lewis and Clark, and OR Trails history.

PROGRAMS: Annual Meeting; Community Outreach; Concerts; Elder's Programs; Exhibits; Facility Rental; Family Programs; Festivals; Film/Video; Garden Tours; Guided Tours; Interpretation; Lectures; Living History; Reenactments; Research Library/Archives; School-Based

COLLECTIONS: 1,000 manuscripts, 5,000 photos, 10,000 artifacts, archives, unpublished papers.

HOURS: Yr Daily except holidays, 10-6

ADMISSION: $6.50, Children $3, Seniors $5.50; Group rates

7094
Fort Dalles Museum
500 W 15th, 97058; (p) (541) 296-4547; (f) (541) 296-4547; (c) Wasco

City, non-profit/ 1905/ staff: 2(p); 6(v)

HISTORIC SITE; HISTORY MUSEUM: Preserves local history.

PROGRAMS: Facility Rental; Family Programs; Guided Tours; School-Based Curriculum

COLLECTIONS: [1850-1920] North American artifacts, pioneer tools, household articles, photos, textiles, horse-drawn and motor vehicles.

HOURS: Apr-Sept Daily 10-5; Oct-Mar Th-M 10-4

ADMISSION: $3

7095
Lewis Anderson Farmhouse and Granary
500 W 16th St, 97058-1602; (p) (541) 296-4542

7096
Wasco County Historical Society
300 W 13th, 97058; (p) (541) 296-1867; (c) Wasco

Private non-profit/ 1950/ staff: 30(v)/ members: 120/publication: *Wasco County Historical Society Quarterly; The Barlow Road*

HISTORICAL SOCIETY; HISTORY MUSEUM; HOUSE MUSEUM: Collects, preserves, and interprets history of Wasco County.

PROGRAMS: Annual Meeting; Community Outreach; Exhibits; Family Programs; Garden Tours; Guided Tours; Lectures; Publication

COLLECTIONS: [1900-1980] Household items, photos, documents, films, Rorick Family artifacts, The Dalles; housed in circa 1850 house.

HOURS: May-Sept F-Su 10-4

ADMISSION: No charge

TILLAMOOK

7097
Tillamook County Pioneer Museum
2106 2nd St, 97141; (p) (503) 842-4553; (f) (503) 842-4553; (c) Tillamook

Private non-profit/ 1935/ staff: 3(f); 2(p); 20(v)

HISTORY MUSEUM: Collects, preserves, displays, and interprets cultural and natural histories of Tillamook County.

PROGRAMS: Exhibits; Interpretation; Research Library/Archives

COLLECTIONS: [Prehistory] Natural history, archaeology, logging, pioneers, military, genealogical books and records, cheese industry, photos.

HOURS: Yr M-Sa 8-5, Su 12-5

ADMISSION: $2, Students $0.50, Seniors $1.50

TROUTDALE

7098
Troutdale Historical Society and Harlow House
104 SE Kibling Ave, 97060; (c) Multnomah

Private non-profit/ 1968/ Board of Directors/ staff: 1(f); 300(v)/ members: 700

HISTORICAL SOCIETY; HOUSE MUSEUM: Preserves and promotes local history.

PROGRAMS: Annual Meeting; Community Outreach; Exhibits; Facility Rental; Festivals; Guided Tours; Interpretation; Lectures

COLLECTIONS: [1900] Photos, oral history, smelt fishing, agriculture, railroad, housed in 1900 farm house.

HOURS: Oct-Apr Sa-Su 1-4

ADMISSION: $3

VALE

7099
Malhuer Historical Project-Stone House Museum
255 Main St, 97918 [PO Box 413, 97918]; (p) (541) 473-2070; (c) Malheur

County/ 1995/ staff: 30(v)/ members: 250

HISTORIC SITE; HISTORICAL SOCIETY; HISTORY MUSEUM; HOUSE MUSEUM; LIBRARY AND/OR ARCHIVES: Owns and operates the Museum; maintains a historical and genealogical library and surveys; protects local historical sites.

PROGRAMS: Festivals; Garden Tours; Guided Tours; Research Library/Archives

COLLECTIONS: [Paleolithic; 1850-1930] Artifacts, photos, documents, clothing, household goods of early OR and Malheur County.

HOURS: May-Oct T-Sa, 12-4:30

ADMISSION: Donations accepted

7100
Rinehart Stone House Museum
Main St, 97918 [PO Box 413, 97918]; (p) (541) 473-2070

1872/ Malheur Historical Project/ staff: 9(v)

COLLECTIONS: [1872-early 1900s] Period clothing, household furnishings, Indian artifacts, farm and carpenter tools; local historical documents, photos, books.

7101
Stone House Museum
255 Main St, 97918 [PO Box 413, 97918]; (p) (541) 473-2070; (c) Malheur

Joint/ 1995/ City; Private non-profit/ staff: 12(v)/ members: 250/publication: *Stone House Quarterly*

HISTORIC SITE; HISTORY MUSEUM: Preserves local history.

PROGRAMS: Community Outreach; Exhibits; Garden Tours; Guided Tours; Publication; Reenactments; Research Library/Archives

COLLECTIONS: [1830-1920] Native American artifacts, Oregon Trail, photos.

HOURS: March-Oct T-Sa 12-4

ADMISSION: No charge

WALDPORT

7102
Alsi Historical and Genealogical Society
320 NE Grant, 97394 [PO Box 822, 97394]; (p) (541) 563-7092; (c) Lincoln

Private non-profit/ 1981/ staff: 8(v)/ members: 47

GENEALOGICAL SOCIETY; HISTORY MUSEUM: Preserves and displays artifacts.

PROGRAMS: Community Outreach; Exhibits; Interpretation; Monthly Meeting; Research Library/Archives; School-Based Curriculum

COLLECTIONS: [1850-1950] Logging, clothing, school memorabilia, kitchenware, fishing gear and Native American artifacts.

HOURS: Yr Sa-Su 10-4

ADMISSION: Donations accepted

WARM SPRINGS

7103
Museum at Warm Springs, The
[PO Box C, 97761]; (p) (541) 553-3331; (f) (541) 553-3338; museum@madras.net; tmaws.org; (c) Jefferson

Private non-profit/ 1972/ Board of Directors/ staff: 11(f); 3(p); 500(v)/publication: *TWANAT Newsletter*

TRIBAL MUSEUM: Preserves and shares knowledge of cultural, traditional and artistic heritage of the Conf Tribes of Warm Springs.

PROGRAMS: Community Outreach; Concerts; Elder's Programs; Exhibits; Facility Rental; Family Programs; Guided Tours; Interpretation; Lectures; Living History; Publication; Research Library/Archives

COLLECTIONS: [1972-present] Native American artifacts.

HOURS: Yr Daily 10-5

ADMISSION: $6, Children $3, Seniors $5

WOODBURN

7104
French Prairie Historical Society and Settlemier House
355 N Settlemier Ave, 97071 [PO Box 405, 97071]; (p) (503) 982-1897; (c) Marion

Private non-profit/ 1970/ French Prairie Historical Society/ members: 150

HOUSE MUSEUM: Preserves and maintains Settlemier House.

PROGRAMS: Festivals; Guided Tours

COLLECTIONS: [1890-1940] Period furnishing, clothing, kitchen accessories.

HOURS: Mar-Dec 1st Su 1-4

ADMISSION: $3, Children $2

PENNSYLVANIA

AARONSBURG

7105
Penns Valley Area Historical Museum Association
116 W Plum St, 16820 [PO Box 80, 16820]; (p) (814) 349-8276; (c) Center

1968/ Aaronsburg Historical Museum Assoc/ staff: 1(v)/ members: 80

Collects, preserves, and interprets all aspects of eastern Center County history.

COLLECTIONS: Central PA agriculture..

HOURS: Yr W 7-9pm, Sa 1-4

ADDISON

7106
Old Petersburg-Addison Historical Society
Main St, 15411 [PO Box 82, 15411]; (p) (814) 395-3350; (c) Somerset

Private non-profit/ 1990/ staff: 3(v)/ members: 145/publication: *Youghiogheny River Towns-Somerfield*

HISTORICAL SOCIETY; HOUSE MUSEUM

PROGRAMS: Annual Meeting; Community Outreach; Festivals; Guided Tours; Publication

COLLECTIONS: [19th c] Artifacts, books, photos, paintings and genealogies.

HOURS: June-Aug Sa-Su 1-4

ADMISSION: No charge

ALBION

7107
Valley School Historical Society
1 Harthan Dr, 16401; (p) (814) 756-4116; (f) (814) 756-5331; (c) Erie

Joint/ 1997/ staff: 15(v)/ members: 10

LIVING HISTORY/OUTDOOR MUSEUM: Promotes local history.

PROGRAMS: Guided Tours; Living History; School-Based Curriculum

COLLECTIONS: School artifacts.

HOURS: Mar-Dec Su 2-4 and by appt

ALLENTOWN

7108
Frank Buchman House
117 N 11 St, 18012 [Old Courthouse, PO Box 1548, 18105]; (p) (610) 435-1074; (f) (610) 435-9812

1893/ Lehigh County Historical Society/ staff: 2(p)

COLLECTIONS: [1893-1963] Victorian furnishings; Dr. Buchman's personal library, books by and about Dr. Buchman and Moral Re-Armament.

HOURS: Yr

7109
Lehigh County Historical Society
Old Courthouse, Hamilton at 5th, 18105 [PO Box 1548, 18105-1548]; (p) (610) 435-4664; (f) (610) 435-9812; www.voicenet.com/~vpsoc/lchslibrary.html; (c) Lehigh

Private non-profit/ 1904/ staff: 7(f); 26(p); 40(v)/ members: 1240/publication: *Proceedings (journal)*

HISTORIC SITE; HISTORICAL SOCIETY; HISTORY MUSEUM; HOUSE MUSEUM: Preserves regional history; manages eight historic sites or houses, a central museum, and artifacts.

PROGRAMS: Annual Meeting; Community Outreach; Concerts; Elder's Programs; Exhibits; Family Programs; Festivals; Film/Video; Guided Tours; Interpretation; Lectures; Living History; Publication; Research Library/Archives; School-Based Curriculum

COLLECTIONS: [1740-present] Processed documents in Pennsylvania German materials, Lehigh County agricultural and industrial items, Allentown business records.

HOURS: (Museum) Yr M-F 9-5, Sa 10-4, Su 1-4; (Sites) May-Sept Sa 10-4, Su 1-4

7110
Lehigh Valley Jewish Archives/Holocaust Resource
702 N 22nd St, 18104; (p) (610) 821-5500; (f) (610) 821-8946; (c) Lehigh

Private non-profit/ 1981/ Jewish Federation of the Lehigh Valley/ staff: 2(p); 1(v)

LIBRARY AND/OR ARCHIVES: Collects and transcribes oral testimonies from Holocaust survivors; develops and maintains educational programs.

PROGRAMS: Community Outreach; Exhibits; Lectures; Research Library/Archives

COLLECTIONS: [20th c] Books, videos, photos, survivor testimonies, visual displays, memorabilia, paintings.

HOURS: Yr M-Th 1-4

ADMISSION: No charge

7111
Lenni Lenape Historical Society/Museum of Indian Culture
2825 Fish Hatchery Rd, 18103; (p) (610) 797-2121; (f) (610) 797-2801; lenape@epix.net; www.lenape.org; (c) Lehigh

Private non-profit/ 1981/ Board of Directors/ staff: 6(f); 8(p)/ members: 200

GARDEN; HISTORIC PRESERVATION AGENCY; HISTORIC SITE; HISTORICAL SOCIETY; HISTORY MUSEUM; LIVING HISTORY/OUTDOOR MUSEUM; TRIBAL MUSEUM: Preserves, promotes, and shares local Lenape (Delaware Indian) culture.

PROGRAMS: Annual Meeting; Community Outreach; Concerts; Elder's Programs; Exhibits; Facility Rental; Family Programs; Festivals; Film/Video; Garden Tours; Guided Tours; Interpretation; Lectures; Living History; Publication; Research Library/Archives; School-Based Curriculum

COLLECTIONS: [1600s-present] Stone and bone items, tools, crafts, toys, dolls, clothing, regalia, baskets, photos, portraits, and videos.

HOURS: General Public: Th-Su 12-3

ADMISSION: $3, Children $2, Seniors $2; Group rates

7112
Liberty Bell Shrine Museum
622 Hamilton Mall, 18101; (p) (610) 435-4232; (f) (610) 435-5667; www.geocities.com/Athens/Ithaca; (c) Lehigh

Private non-profit/ 1959/ staff: 6(p)/ members: 100

HISTORY MUSEUM: Maintains the museum that houses a replica of the Liberty Bell.

PROGRAMS: Annual Meeting; Exhibits; Guided Tours; Interpretation

COLLECTIONS: [18th c] Full-size replica of the Liberty Bell. Mural and audio tape.

HOURS: Feb-Apr, Nov-Dec Th-Sa 12-4; May-Oct M-Sa 12-4

ADMISSION: Donations accepted

7113
Trout Hall
4th & Walnut Sts, 18101 [Old Courthouse, PO Box 1548, 18105]; (p) (610) 435-4664, (610) 435-1074; (f) (610) 435-9812; www.voicenet.com/~vpsoc/lcslibrary.html

1770/ Lehigh County Historical Society

COLLECTIONS: [1770-1840] High-style furnishings of Colonial and Federal periods; Diary of James Allen, located in LCHS library (Old Courthouse, Allentown).

HOURS: Seasonal

ALLISON PARK

7114
Hampton Historical Commission
4743 S Pioneer Rd, 15101 [PO Box 174, 15101]; (p) (412) 486-0563; (c) Allegheny

1973/ Hampton Township/ staff: 15(v)/ members: 65

HISTORY MUSEUM; PROFESSIONAL ORGANIZATION: Preserves the history of the Depreciation Lands and the people that settled there.

PROGRAMS: Annual Meeting; Exhibits; Facility Rental; Family Programs; Festivals; Guided Tours; Publication

COLLECTIONS: [1776-present] Early household furnishings; farm, building and surveyor's tools; covered wagon, log house, maps, furnished replicas of one-room schoolhouse, and blacksmith shop.

HOURS: Apr-Dec Su 1-4 or by appt

ADMISSION: $1, Children $0.50

ALTOONA

7115
Blair County Historical Society
3419 Oak Ln, 16603 [PO Box 1083, 16603]; (p) (814) 942-3916; (f) (814) 942-7078; bchs@hotmail.com; (c) Blair

Private non-profit/ 1906/ Board of Trustees/ staff: 1(p); 25(v)/ members: 4041

HISTORICAL SOCIETY; HISTORY MUSEUM; HOUSE MUSEUM: Preserves, promotes, and interprets Blair County history.

PROGRAMS: Annual Meeting; Concerts; Exhibits; Facility Rental; Festivals; Guided Tours; Lectures; Reenactments

COLLECTIONS: [1850-1920] Blair County newspapers 1836 to the present, 2,500 photographs and prints, 3,000 volumes, extensive records of Alleghany Furnace and other Baker family businesses, Baker family archives, clothing, textiles, and furniture.

HOURS: Yr Library: T, F 9-12/1-4; Museum: Apr 15-May and Sept-Oct 31; May-Sept T-Su 1-4:30

ADMISSION: $4, Student $3.50, Children $2, Seniors $3.50; Members free

7116
Railroaders Memorial Museum, Inc.
1300 9th Ave & SR 4008, 16602 [1300 9th Ave, 16602]; (p) (814) 946-0834; (f) (814) 946-9457; admin@railroadcity.com; www.railroadcity.com; (c) Blair

Private non-profit/ 1972/ staff: 24(f); 4(p); 60(v)/ members: 1800

HISTORIC SITE; HISTORY MUSEUM: Museum complex dedicated to preservation and interpretation of the role of the PA Railroad in American history.

PROGRAMS: Annual Meeting; Community Outreach; Exhibits; Facility Rental; Family Programs; Festivals; Film/Video; Guided Tours; Interpretation; Lectures; Living History; Research Library/Archives; School-Based Curriculum; Theatre

COLLECTIONS: [1920-1940] PA Railroad, Altoona-built equipment and related objects and archives. Oral histories relating to railroad and community.

HOURS: Spring-Summer Daily 9-5; Fall-Winter T-Su 9-5

ADMISSION: Varies

ALTOONE

7117
Fort Roberdeau Association
SR 1013, 16601 [RR 3, Box 391, Altoona, 16601]; (p) (814) 946-0048; (c) Blair

County/ 1973/ staff: 2(f); 2(p)/ members: 115/publication: *Fort Roberdeau: The Garrison and Military Life*

HISTORIC SITE; LIVING HISTORY/OUTDOOR MUSEUM: Preserves the site of a 1778 frontier fort. Interprets the story of the lead miners, soldiers, and settlers who occupied the fort. Maintains a reconstructed stockade and cabins, barn, farmhouse and nature trails.

PROGRAMS: Annual Meeting; Community Outreach; Exhibits; Facility Rental; Family Programs; Guided Tours; Interpretation; Living History; Publication; Reenactments; School-Based Curriculum

COLLECTIONS: [1778-1781] The fort and the objects within it are reproductions.

HOURS: May-Oct T-Sa 11-5, Su-M 1-5

ADMISSION: $3, Children $1, Seniors $2.50; Group rates

AMBRIDGE

7118
Old Economy Village
14th and Church St, 15003; (p) (724) 266-4500; (f) (724) 266-7506; mlandis@phmc.state.pa.us; www.beavercounty.net/oldeconomy; (c) Beaver

State/ 1919/ PA Historical and Museum Commission/ staff: 10(f); 6(p); 273(v)/ members: 120

HISTORIC SITE: National Landmark Historic Site, interprets history of the communal Harmony Society, 1825-1905.

PROGRAMS: Annual Meeting; Community Outreach; Concerts; Exhibits; Facility Rental; Family Programs; Festivals; Garden Tours; Guided Tours; Interpretation; Lectures; Living History; Publication; Research Library/Archives; School-Based Curriculum

COLLECTIONS: [1825-1847] Early American decorative arts, crafts of the Harmony Society, European paintings, music c.1825, and early 19th c library.

HOURS: Mar-Dec T-Sa 9-5, Su 12-5

ADMISSION: $5, Family $13, Children $3, Seniors $4.50; Under 6 free

APOLLO

7119
Apollo Area Historical Society
317 N 2nd St, 15613 [PO Box 434, 15613]; (p) (724) 478-3037; (c) Armstrong

Private non-profit/ 1970/ Board of Directors/ staff: 15(v)/ members: 125/publication: *Our Heritage*

HISTORIC SITE; HISTORICAL SOCIETY; HISTORY MUSEUM; HOUSE MUSEUM: Owns and operates the Drake Log Cabin, c 1816, furnished to depict life on the western PA frontier including herb garden, spring house, and small waterfall.

PROGRAMS: Annual Meeting; Exhibits; Festivals; Guided Tours; Living History; Publication; Reenactments

HOURS: Open holidays and by appt

AVELLA

7120
Meadowcroft Museum of Rural Life
401 Meadowcroft Rd, 15312; (p) (724) 587-3412; (f) (724) 587-3414; mcroft@cobweb.net; www.meadowcroftmuseum.org; (c) Washington

Private non-profit/ 1969/ Board of Trustees/ staff: 4(f); 15(p); 30(v)

HISTORIC SITE; LIVING HISTORY/OUTDOOR MUSEUM: Manages the recreated 1890s village including log buildings, schoolhouse, and blacksmith shop. Exhibits on the Meadowcroft Rockshelter Archaeological Site, documenting the earliest evidence of man in North America.

PROGRAMS: Community Outreach; Exhibits; Family Programs; Festivals; Interpretation; Living History; School-Based Curriculum

COLLECTIONS: [19th-early 20th c] Historic buildings, horse-drawn vehicles, agricultural implements, tools of rural trade, blacksmith, carpenter, chairmaker, coal miner, harness maker. General store items, library, and photographs.

HOURS: May-Sept W-Sa 12-5, Su 1-5

ADMISSION: $6.50, Children $3.50, Seniors $5.50; Under 6 free

BEAVER

7121
Beaver Area Heritage Foundation
#1 River Rd, 15009 [PO Box 147, 15009]; (p) (724) 774-2459; (f) (724) 775-8648; (c) Beaver

Private non-profit/ 1967/ staff: 50(v)/ members: 417/publication: *Foundations*

HISTORIC PRESERVATION AGENCY; HISTORIC SITE; HISTORICAL SOCIETY; HISTORY MUSEUM: Promote awareness and appreciation of the rich history of the Beaver Area through research, documentation, education, and preservation activities.

PROGRAMS: Annual Meeting; Exhibits; Festivals; Lectures; Publication; Reenactments; Research Library/Archives

COLLECTIONS: [1700-1950]

HOURS: Mar-Dec W 10-4, Sa 1-4

ADMISSION: Donations

BEAVER FALLS

7122
Beaver Falls Historical Society Museum
1301 7th Ave, 15010 [c/o Carnegie Free Library, 1301 7th Ave, 15010]; (p) (724) 846-4340; (c) Beaver

Private non-profit/ 1948/ Beaver Falls Historical Society/Carnegie Free Library/ staff: 1(p)/ members: 30

HISTORIC SITE; HISTORICAL SOCIETY; HISTORY MUSEUM; RESEARCH CENTER: The Museum displays 125 years of Beaver Falls history.

PROGRAMS: Exhibits; Guided Tours; Lectures; Monthly Meeting; Research Library/Archives

COLLECTIONS: [1800-present] One hundred

twenty-five years of glassware, china, clothing, photographs, family histories, maps, and any other items relating to Beaver Falls history.

HOURS: Yr M,T,W, F 10-3

ADMISSION: Donations accepted

7123
Research Center for Beaver County
Carnegie Free Library, 15010 [1301 7th Ave, 15010]; (p) (724) 846-4340; (c) Beaver

Private non-profit/ 1971/ Board of Directors/ staff: 2(p); 2(v)

HISTORIC PRESERVATION AGENCY; RESEARCH CENTER: Provides a central place for referral, study, research, and preservation of historical and genealogical books and materials.

PROGRAMS: Research Library/Archives

COLLECTIONS: [18th-20th c] Books on local history, newspaper clippings, and pamphlets on local topics, surnames, firms, towns, churches, and schools.

HOURS: Yr M 3-8, T-Th 10-4, F-Sa 10-3

ADMISSION: No charge

BEDFORD

7124
Old Bedford Village
Business Rt 220, 15522 [220 Sawblade Rd, 15522]; (p) (814) 623-1156; (f) (814) 623-1158; village@bedford.net; www.bedford.net/village; (c) Bedford

Private non-profit/ 1976/ Board of Trustees/ staff: 8(f); 34(p); 88(v)

HISTORY MUSEUM: Preserves, interprets, and presents selected pre-20th c elements of Bedford County and central PA regional heritage for the educational benefit of existing and future generations.

PROGRAMS: Community Outreach; Concerts; Elder's Programs; Exhibits; Facility Rental; Guided Tours; Interpretation; Lectures; Living History; Reenactments; Research Library/Archives; School-Based Curriculum

COLLECTIONS: [18th-19th c] Residential and commercial life, including historical residential buildings, craft shops, household implements, furnishings, artisan tools, and fixtures.

HOURS: May 26-Sept 3 Th-T 9-5; Sept 6-Oct 28 Th-Sa 9-5, Su 10-4

ADMISSION: $8, Student $4; Under 6 free

7125
Pioneer Historical Society of Bedford County
242 E John St, 15522; (p) (814) 623-2011; (f) (814) 623-2011; (c) Bedford

Private non-profit/ 1936/ staff: 2(p); 15(v)/ members: 500

GENEALOGICAL SOCIETY; HISTORICAL SOCIETY; RESEARCH CENTER

PROGRAMS: Research Library/Archives

COLLECTIONS: Historical and genealogical material.

HOURS: Yr M-F 9-4, Sa 9-12

ADMISSION: No charge

BELLEFONTE

7126
Centre County Library and Historical Museum
203 N Allegheny St, 16823; (p) (814) 355-1516; (f) (814) 355-2700; paroom@centre-countylibrary.org; (c) Centre

County/ 1939/ staff: 1(f); 8(v)

HISTORY MUSEUM; HOUSE MUSEUM; RESEARCH CENTER: Pennsylvania Room and historical museum are part of the Centre County Library system and specialize in state genealogy and history.

PROGRAMS: Concerts; Exhibits; Guided Tours; Research Library/Archives

COLLECTIONS: [1700s-present] Spangler Records, 175 notebooks filled with genealogical information, 500 family histories, J. Marvin Lee collection, local newspapers, original county archives, census schedules.

HOURS: Yr M-F 9-5, Sa 9-12/1-5

ADMISSION: No charge

BETHLEHEM

7127
Burnside Plantation, Inc.
1461 Schoenersville Rd, 18018-1864 [459 Old York Rd, 18016-1305]; (p) (610) 868-5044; (f) (610) 868-5044; histbeth41@aol.com; www.historicbethlehem.org; (c) Lehigh

Private non-profit/ 1986/ Historic Bethlehem Partnership/ staff: 11(f); 6(p); 240(v)/ members: 1200/publication: *James Burnside Bulletin of Research*

GARDEN; HISTORIC SITE; HISTORY MUSEUM; HOUSE MUSEUM; LIVING HISTORY/ OUTDOOR MUSEUM: Preserves and promotes living history of colonial Moravian farm.

PROGRAMS: Facility Rental; Festivals; Garden Tours; Guided Tours; Interpretation; Lectures; Publication; School-Based Curriculum

COLLECTIONS: [1748-1848] Farm and domestic equipment, site maps, drawings, paintings, furniture, colonial toys and clothing.

HOURS: Yr Daily 8:30-5

7128
Goundie House
501 Main St, 18018 [PO Box 1305, 18016-1305]; (p) (610) 691-0603, (610) 882-0450; (f) (610) 882-0460; www.historicbethlehem.org

1810/ Historic Bethlehem/ staff: 7(f); 4(p); 5(v)

COLLECTIONS: [c 1820s] Furnishings.

HOURS: Summer

7129
Historic Bethlehem, Inc.
459 Old York Rd, 18016 [PO Box 1305, 18016-1305]; (p) (610) 882-0450; (f) (610) 882-0460; www.historicbethlehem.org; (c) Northampton

Private non-profit/ 1957/ staff: 10(f); 4(p); 20(v)/ members: 1000

HISTORIC SITE; HISTORY MUSEUM; HOUSE MUSEUM; LIVING HISTORY/OUT-DOOR MUSEUM; PROFESSIONAL ORGANIZATION: Interprets the trades, crafts, and industries of 18th c in the historic village of Moravian Bethlehem.

PROGRAMS: Elder's Programs; Family Programs; Garden Tours; Interpretation; Living History; Research Library/Archives; School-Based Curriculum

COLLECTIONS: [1748-1860] Documents trades, crafts, industries and technologies employed by the inhabitants of Bethlehem during the 18th and 19th c.

HOURS: Open Daily 8:30-5; Dec Sa-Su 12-4

7130
Kemerer Museum of Decorative Arts
427 N New St, 18016 [459 Old York Rd, 18016-1305]; (p) (610) 868-6888; (f) (610) 332-2458; histbeth41@aol.com; www.historic bethlehem.org; (c) Northampton

Private non-profit/ 1954/ Historic Bethlehem Partnership/ staff: 11(f); 6(p); 100(v)/ members: 1200

HISTORY MUSEUM: Gallery settings and changing exhibits to interpret 25 years of folk art, furnishings, paintings, textiles, glassware, and historical fine arts.

PROGRAMS: Exhibits; Facility Rental; Family Programs; Festivals; Garden Tours; Guided Tours; Interpretation; Lectures; Research Library/Archives; School-Based Curriculum

COLLECTIONS: Cast-iron toys, maps, print, and textiles. Colonial and Victorian era furniture, ceramics, Bohemian glass, landscape paintings, Oriental rugs, silve, and tall case clocks.

HOURS: Feb-Dec T-Su 12-4

ADMISSION: $5, Family $7, Student $3, Seniors $2; Under 6 free

7131
Moravian Museum of Bethlehem, Inc.
66 W Church St, 18018; (p) (610) 867-0173; (f) (610) 694-0960; histbeth41@aol.com; www.historicbethlehem.org; (c) Northampton

Private non-profit/ 1939/ Historic Bethlehem Partnership/ staff: 11(f); 6(p); 55(v)/ members: 1200

GARDEN; HISTORIC SITE; HOUSE MUSEUM: Encompasses three historic sites: the 1741 Gemeinhaus, 1752 Apothecary and Medicinal Herb Garden, and the 1758 Nain House.

PROGRAMS: Concerts; Elder's Programs; Exhibits; Facility Rental; Family Programs; Garden Tours; Guided Tours; Interpretation; Lectures

COLLECTIONS: [1730-1850] Artifacts related to the industry, home life, and religious practices of the area.

HOURS: Feb-Dec T-Su 12-4

ADMISSION: $5, Student $3; Under 6 free

7132
Sun Inn Preservation Association, Inc.
564 Main St, 18018 [556 Main St, 2nd fl, 18018-5891]; (p) (610) 866-1758, (610) 866-1772; (f) (610) 866-3360; (c) Northampton

Private non-profit/ 1982/ staff: 2(f); 1(p); 30(v)/ members: 600

ALLIANCE OF HISTORICAL AGENCIES; HISTORIC SITE; HISTORY MUSEUM: Visited by founding fathers and statesmen such as Washington, John Hancock, Marquis de Lafayette, Ethan Allan, John Adams, and now serves as a resource center.

PROGRAMS: Annual Meeting; Community Outreach; Concerts; Festivals; Guided Tours; Lectures; Living History; Publication

HOURS: Yr T-Sa 11:30-7:30

ADMISSION: $2, Family $5, Children $1

BIGLERVILLE

7133
Biglerville Historical and Preservation Society
154 W Hanover St, 17307 [PO Box 656, 17307]; (p) (717) 677-4556; (c) Adams

Private non-profit/ 1984/ PA Dept of State/ staff: 15(v)/ members: 316

HISTORIC PRESERVATION AGENCY; HISTORICAL SOCIETY: Fosters interest in the history of Biglerville and vicinity; conducts research; preserves records and objects; marks and preserves landmarks; celebrates patriotic anniversaries; and collects and displays Apple memorabilia.

PROGRAMS: Annual Meeting; Concerts; Exhibits; Facility Rental; Guided Tours; Interpretation; Research Library/Archives

COLLECTIONS: [Early 20th c] Agricultural tools and equipment; early apple processing machines, bee keeping, chemistry, country kitchen, Biglerville Country Store, and local colonial era land records.

HOURS: Sa 10-4, Su 12-4

ADMISSION: $2, Children $1

BIRDSBORO

7134
Daniel Boone Homestead
400 Daniel Boone Rd, 19508; (p) (610) 582-4900; (f) (610) 582-1744; jlewars@phmc.state.pa.us; (c) Berks

State/ 1938/ PA Historical and Museum Commission/ staff: 5(f); 5(p); 20(v)

HISTORIC SITE: Birthplace and home of Daniel Boone (1734-1750) located on 579 rural acres interpreting the diversity of 18th c life in Oley Valley through exhibits, tours, programs, and preservation of collections, architecture, and land patterns.

PROGRAMS: Elder's Programs; Exhibits; Facility Rental; Family Programs; Festivals; Guided Tours; Interpretation; Lectures; Living History; Reenactments; School-Based Curriculum

COLLECTIONS: [1730-1808] PA 18th c rural decorative arts, architecture, tools, textiles, furniture, and domestic items. 11-room stone farm house, operating water-powdered sawmill, 1750 PA German log house.

HOURS: Yr T-Sa 9-5, Su 12-5

ADMISSION: $4, Family $10, Children $2, Seniors $3.50

BLUE BELL

7135
Wissahickon Valley Historical Society
799 Skippack Pike, 19422 [PO Box 96, Ambler, 19002]; (p) (215) 646-6541; (c) Montgomery

Private non-profit/ 1975/ staff: 15(v)/ members: 150

HISTORIC PRESERVATION AGENCY; HISTORIC SITE; HISTORICAL SOCIETY; HISTORY MUSEUM: Local historical organization housed in 1895 Whitpain High School building that features library, museum, and meeting room.

PROGRAMS: Exhibits; Facility Rental; Festivals; Guided Tours; Interpretation; Lectures; Publication; Research Library/Archives

COLLECTIONS: [19th c] Photographs, documents, artifacts, material culture, newspapers, maps, and locally-made glassware.

HOURS: Yr by appt

ADMISSION: No charge

BOALSBURG

7136
Boalsburg Heritage Museum
[PO Box 346, 16827]; hah8@mail.psu.edu; (c) Centre

Private non-profit/ 1983/ staff: 12(v)/ members: 100

HISTORY MUSEUM; HOUSE MUSEUM

PROGRAMS: Annual Meeting; Community Outreach; Exhibits; Living History; School-Based Curriculum

COLLECTIONS: [1825-1983] Objects and furnishings of working class families.

HOURS: Yr T, Sa 2-4

7137
Columbus Chapel and Boal Mansion Museum
Business Rt 322, 16827 [PO Box 116, 16827]; (p) (814) 466-6210; (f) (814) 466-6210; boalmus@vicon.net; www.vicon.net/~boalmus; (c) Centre

Private non-profit/ 1952/ staff: 1(f); 5(p); 20(v)

HISTORIC SITE: Maintains a Columbus collection on the North American continent imported from Spain in 1909 to the Boal Mansion where the Boal family's original furnishings tell the story of America, 1789-present.

PROGRAMS: Concerts; Exhibits; Facility Rental; Festivals; Guided Tours; Interpretation; Lectures; Publication; Research Library/Archives

COLLECTIONS: [19th c] Photographs, documents, artifacts, material culture, newspapers, maps, and locally-made glassware.

HOURS: Yr by appt

ADMISSION: No charge

7138
PA Military Museum, The
East Boal Ave, 16827 [PO Box 160A, 16827]; (p) (814) 466-6263; (f) (814) 466-6618; wleech@phmc.state.pa.us; www.psu.edu/areospace/museum; (c) Centre

State/ 1969/ staff: 5(f); 3(p); 10(v)/ members: 95

HOUSE MUSEUM: Collects, preserves, and interprets PA's military history from 1747 to present. Shrine commemorates the sacrifices of those who served in the 28th Infantry Division, PA's National Guard.

PROGRAMS: Annual Meeting; Community Outreach; Concerts; Exhibits; Facility Rental; Festivals; Film/Video; Guided Tours; Interpretation; Lectures; Living History; Reenactments; Research Library/Archives; School-Based Curriculum

COLLECTIONS: [1747-present] Military uniforms, arms, equipment with a state provenance from all service branches. Special emphasis on 20th c artifacts and archival materials.

HOURS: Yr M-Sa 9-5; Th-Sa 10-4

ADMISSION: $3.50, Children $1.50, Seniors $3

BOSTON

7139
Elizabeth Township Historical Society
5811 Smithfield St, 15135; (p) (412) 754-2030; (f) (412) 754-2036; eths@sgi.net; www.15122.com/eths/info.htm; (c) Allegheny

Private non-profit/ 1976/ staff: 25(v)/ members: 210/publication: *Between Two Rivers*

HISTORICAL SOCIETY: Promotes local history and genology and maintains museum and reference library.

PROGRAMS: Annual Meeting; Community Outreach; Exhibits; Festivals; Guided Tours; Lectures; Publication; Research Library/Archives

COLLECTIONS: [1700s-1960s] Tools, household items, furniture, medical equipment, dolls, toys, glassware, guns, shoes, radios, lamps, books, pictures, and musical instruments.

HOURS: Yr T-Th 9-3, F 7-10

ADMISSION: Donations accepted

BOYERTOWN

7140
Boyertown Museum of Historic Vehicles
85 S Walnut Ave, 19512; (p) (610) 367-2090; (f) (610) 367-9712; museum@enter.net; www.boyertownmuseum.org; (c) Berks

Private non-profit/ 1965/ staff: 2(f); 2(p); 100(v)/ members: 400/publication: *Museum News*

HISTORY MUSEUM: Operates regional transportation museum interpreting Southeastern PA, horse and motor vehicles, their builders, and how changes influenced social, economic, and cultural life including exhibits, antique car show, library, television program, electric cars, trucks, and special events.

PROGRAMS: Annual Meeting; Community Outreach; Exhibits; Festivals; Interpretation; Lectures; Publication; Research Library/Archives; School-Based Curriculum

COLLECTIONS: [1800-1998] Vehicles built in Southeastern PA: horse-drawn carriages,

sleighs, and wagons, motorized automobiles, motorcycles, trucks by Charles Duryea and George Daniels, and electric vehicles.

HOURS: Yr T-Su 9:30-4

ADMISSION: $4, Student $2, Seniors $3.50

BRADDOCK

7141
Braddock's Field Historical Society
419 Library St, 15104; (p) (412) 351-5357; (f) (412) 351-6810; (c) Allegheny

Private non-profit/ 1979/ staff: 12(f); 8(p); 20(v)/ members: 300

ART MUSEUM; HISTORIC SITE; HISTORICAL SOCIETY; HISTORY MUSEUM: The Society restores and operates the first Carnegie Library in the United States and operates a museum and gallery that commemorates Braddock's defeat on July 9, 1755, in the French and Indian War.

PROGRAMS: Concerts; Exhibits; Facility Rental; Guided Tours; Interpretation; Lectures; Living History; Publication; Research Library/Archives; Theatre

COLLECTIONS: [French and Indian War and Andrew Carnegie] Over 250 artifacts and thirty prints or copies of all major artwork on the battle.

HOURS: Yr M-Th 9-7, F-Sa 9-4

ADMISSION: No charge

BRADFORD

7142
Zippo/Case Visitors Center
1932 Zippo Dr, 16701 [33 Barour St, 16701]; (p) (814) 368-2711; (f) (814) 368-2874; www.zippo.com; (c) McKean

Private non-profit/ 1993/ Zippo Manufacturing Company/ staff: 5(f); 5(p)

CORPORATE ARCHIVES/MUSEUM: Showcases Zippo lighters, case knives, interactive exhibits, Zippo repair clinic on display, and a retail store.

PROGRAMS: Community Outreach; Festivals; Guided Tours; Research Library/Archives

COLLECTIONS: [1920-present] Vintage Zippo lighters, Case Knives, and historical documents.

HOURS: Yr M-Sa 9-5; June-Dec Su 12-4

ADMISSION: No charge

BRIDGEVILLE

7143
Neville House
1375 Washington Pike, Kirwan Hts, 15017 [1080 Lafayette St, 15017]; (p) (412) 221-5797, (412) 221-0348

1780/ Neville House Associates/ staff: 20(v)

COLLECTIONS: [1780-1795] Late 18th c and early 19th c furniture and decorative arts.

HOURS: Seasonal

BRISTOL

7144
Margaret R. Grundy Memorial Museum, The
610 Radcliffe St, 19007; (p) (215) 788-9432; (c) Bucks

Private non-profit/ 1961/ The Grundy Foundation/ staff: 1(f); 4(p)

HISTORY MUSEUM: Maintains home and furnishings.

PROGRAMS: Guided Tours

COLLECTIONS: [19th c] Victorian home and furnishings.

HOURS: Yr M-F 1-4, Sa 1-3

ADMISSION: No charge

BROOKVILLE

7145
Jefferson County Historical and Genealogical Society
232 Jefferson St, 15825 [PO Box 51, 15825]; (p) (814) 849-0077; jchgs@penn.com; (c) Jefferson

1967/ Board of Directors/ staff: 1(p); 10(v)/ members: 350

GENEALOGICAL SOCIETY; HISTORICAL SOCIETY; HISTORY MUSEUM: Receives, collects, and preserves the historical and genealogical records of Jefferson County and maintains a library and museum.

PROGRAMS: Annual Meeting; Community Outreach; Elder's Programs; Exhibits; Festivals; Guided Tours; Interpretation; Lectures; Living History; Publication; Reenactments; Research Library/Archives; School-Based Curriculum

COLLECTIONS: [19th-20th c] Books, newspapers, documents, manuscripts, photographs, and artifacts that tell the stories of Jefferson County's people. Structures include Brady Craig House and Museum, Margaret Johnson Archives, Samuel Irvin Museum and Edelblute-Pearsall Building.

HOURS: Yr T-Su 2-5

ADMISSION: $15 non-member use fee

BROOMALL

7146
Delaware County Historical Society
85 N Malin Rd, 19008-1928; (p) (610) 359-1148; (f) (610) 359-4155; (c) Delaware

Joint/ 1895/ County; Board of Directors; Private non-profit/ staff: 1(f); 10(v)/ members: 400/publication: *The Bulletin*

ART MUSEUM; GENEALOGICAL SOCIETY; HISTORICAL SOCIETY: County historical society.

PROGRAMS: Annual Meeting; Community Outreach; Exhibits; Festivals; Guided Tours; Lectures; Publication; Research Library/ Archives; School-Based Curriculum

COLLECTIONS: [19th-20th c] Books, manuscripts, maps, photos, and microfilm.

HOURS: Yr T 1-8, W 9-4

ADMISSION: $3

7147
Marple Newtown Historical Society
1696 Thomas Massey House, 19008 [PO Box 755, 19008]; (p) (610) 353-4967, (610) 353-3644; mnhistsoc@juno.com; www.marple.net; (c) Delaware

Private non-profit/ 1965/ staff: 10(v)/ members: 75

HISTORICAL SOCIETY: Preserves local history and provides information about that history to the community.

PROGRAMS: Annual Meeting; Family Programs; Guided Tours; Interpretation; Lectures

COLLECTIONS: [17th-18th c] Genealogical, architectural, and social information about the community.

HOURS: Apr-Oct Su 2-4

ADMISSION: Donations

7148
Thomas Massey House
Lawrence & Springhouse Rds, 19008 [PO Box 18, 19008]; (p) (610) 353-3644; MNHISTSOC@juno.com; http://marple.net/township/massey.html

1696/ staff: 20(v)

Preseves historic house.

COLLECTIONS: [1696, 1730, 1840] Architecture details of the house, artifacts covering three c of the house, photographs, genealogy

HOURS: May-Oct Sun 2-4 or by appt

BROWNSVILLE

7149
Brownsville Historical Society
Front St, 15417 [PO Box 24, 15417]; (p) (724) 785-6882; www.nemacolincastle.org; (c) Fayette

County/ 1962/ staff: 2(p); 20(v)/ members: 160

HISTORIC SITE; HISTORICAL SOCIETY; HOUSE MUSEUM: Preserves Jacob Bowman's mansion and interprets two c of Americana through its architecture and furnishings.

PROGRAMS: Exhibits; Festivals; Guided Tours; Reenacts

COLLECTIONS: [1789-1850s] Household utensils, artifacts, furnishings, and Bowman records on display.

HOURS: June-Aug T-Su 11-5; Apr-May, Sept-Mid Oct Sa-Su 11-5

ADMISSION: $6, Children $3, Seniors $4

7150
Flatiron Building Heritage Center/BARC
69 Market St, 15417 [PO Box 97, 15417]; (p) (724) 785-9331; (f) (724) 785-8626; flatiron@lcsys.net; www.flatironcenter.com; (c) Fayette

Private non-profit/ 1989/ Board of Directors/ staff: 1(f); 5(p); 90(v)/ members: 183/publication: *Making of America*

HISTORICAL SOCIETY; HISTORY MUSEUM: Maintains museum featuring national road, river, railroad, coal, coke and a related art museum. BARC, established in 1989.

PROGRAMS: Annual Meeting; Community Outreach; Concerts; Festivals; Film/Video; Guided Tours; Interpretation; Lectures; Living History; Monthly Meeting; Research Library/Archives

COLLECTIONS: [19th-20th c] Local related artifacts, old and current photos, slides of old photos, art work, clothing, historic documents and information, advertisements, furniture, and machinery.

HOURS: Yr Summer M-Sa 11-8, Su 12-8; Winter 11/12-6

ADMISSION: No charge

BRYN ATHYN

7151
Glencairn Museum, Academy of the New Church
1001 Cathedral Rd, 19009 [Box 757, 19009]; (p) (215) 938-2600; (f) (215) 914-2986; www.glencairnmuseum.org; (c) Montgomery

Private non-profit/ 1874/ Academy of the New Church/ staff: 9(f); 3(p); 50(v)/ members: 250

HISTORY MUSEUM: Educates visitors about the history of religion.

PROGRAMS: Concerts; Exhibits; Family Programs; Festivals; Guided Tours; Lectures; School-Based Curriculum

COLLECTIONS: [Ancient/Medieval] Egyptian, classical, Near Eastern, Asian, and Native American items housed in a unique Romanesque-style former residence.

HOURS: Yr M-F 8:30-4:30 by appt only

ADMISSION: $5, Student $2, Seniors $4; Under 5 free

BRYN MAWR

7152
Bryn Mawr College Libraries
101 N Merion Ave, 19010; (p) (610) 526-5279; (f) (610) 526-7480; www.brvamawr.edu/Library/; (c) Montgomery

Private non-profit/ 1885/ Bryn Mawr College/ staff: 35(f); 4(p); 4(v)

LIBRARY AND/OR ARCHIVES: Preserves archival and library materials for Bryn Mawr College, Haverford College, Swarthmore College, University of Pennsylvania, and the local community.

PROGRAMS: Exhibits; Lectures; Research Library/Archives

COLLECTIONS: Archives of the college, manuscripts, rare books, prints and drawings, photographs, and fine art collection with a focus on history of women collections.

HOURS: Yr M-F

7153
Harriton Association
500 Harriton Rd, 19010 [PO Box 1364, 19010]; (p) (610) 525-0201; (f) (610) 525-0201; bcoopergil@aol.com; (c) Montgomery

Private non-profit/ 1962/ staff: 1(f); 2(p); 50(v)/ members: 535/publication: *Curator's Report*

HOUSE MUSEUM: Preserves, restores, and operates 1704 Harriton House, home of Charles Thomson, only secretary to the Continental Congress.

PROGRAMS: Annual Meeting; Facility Rental; Family Programs; Festivals; Guided Tours; Interpretation; Publication; Research Library/Archives

COLLECTIONS: [1780-1800] American decorative arts.

HOURS: Yr W-Sa 10-4 and by appt

BURGETTSTOWN

7154
Jefferson Township Historical Society
483 Eldersville Rd, 15021 [215 Eldersville Rd, 15021]; (c) Washington

Private non-profit/ 1990/ staff: 10(v)/ members: 83

HISTORICAL SOCIETY; HISTORY MUSEUM: Preserves and protects local artifacts to educate the public about the historical heritage of Jefferson Township.

PROGRAMS: Annual Meeting; Community Outreach; Exhibits; Festivals; Lectures

COLLECTIONS: Local artifacts, obituaries, historic newspapers, and publications.

HOURS: Summer-Fall F-Su 10-4

ADMISSION: No charge

BUTLER

7155
Butler County Historical Society
106 S Main St, 16003 [PO Box 414, 16003-0414]; (p) (724) 283-8116; (f) (724) 283-2505; bchissoc@isrv.com; www.butlercountyhistoricalsociety-pa.org; (c) Butler

Private non-profit/ 1960/ staff: 2(f); 2(p); 50(v)/ members: 400

HISTORICAL SOCIETY; HISTORY MUSEUM: Collects, preserves, and interprets county historical documents and artifacts through four museums.

PROGRAMS: Annual Meeting; Community Outreach; Exhibits; Facility Rental; Festivals; Guided Tours; Interpretation; Lectures; Living History; Research Library/Archives

COLLECTIONS: [1800-present] Cooper Cabin circa 1810, the Lowrie/Shaw House 1870-1890, Little Red Schoolhouse 1838-1874, and the Butler County Heritage Center.

HOURS: Yr

CALIFORNIA

7156
California Area Historical Society
429 Wood St, 15419 [PO Box 624, 15419]; (p) (724) 938-3250; (c) Washington

Private non-profit/ 1993/ staff: 10(v)/ members: 200/publication: *The California Crier*

GENEALOGICAL SOCIETY; HISTORIC SITE; HISTORICAL SOCIETY; RESEARCH CENTER: Seeks to bring together people interested in the history of the California area; to preserve and educate the public about the heritage of the land and the significance of its

settlers; and to aid persons in genealogical research.

PROGRAMS: Annual Meeting; Community Outreach; Exhibits; Guided Tours; Publication; Research Library/Archives

COLLECTIONS: [1849-present] 1,500 Photographs, 2,000 genealogy records, newspapers, Civil War records, and year books.

HOURS: Yr T-Th

CARLISLE

7157
Cumberland County Historical Society and Hamilton Library
21 N Pitt St, 17013 [PO Box 626, 17013-0626]; (p) (717) 249-7610, (717) 249-6931; (f) (717) 258-9332; info@historicalsociety.com; www.historicalsociety.com; (c) Cumberland

Private non-profit/ 1874/ staff: 4(f); 10(p); 300(v)/ members: 1600/publication: *Cumberland County History Journal*

HISTORIC SITE; HISTORICAL SOCIETY; HOUSE MUSEUM: Preserves and interprets county history. Maintains a library, museum, photo archives and the Two Mile House, located on Walnut Bottom Road, and is a site on the National Register of Historic Places.

PROGRAMS: Annual Meeting; Community Outreach; Exhibits; Facility Rental; Family Programs; Festivals; Guided Tours; Interpretation; Lectures; Living History; Publication; Reenactments; Research Library/Archives; School-Based Curriculum

COLLECTIONS: [1700s-present] Library contains primary and secondary materials related to county history; genealogical resources, microfilm, manuscripts, photographs, and Indian School materials.

HOURS: Yr M 7-9, T-F 10-4, Sa 10-1

ADMISSION: No charge; Library $4

7158
United States Army Military History Institute
22 Ashburn Dr, Carlisle Barracks, 17013-5008; (p) (717) 245-3611, (717) 245-3711; AWCC-DMH@awc.carlisle.army.mil; carlisle-www.army.mil/usamhi/; (c) Cumberland

Federal/ 1967/ United States Army/ staff: 35(f); 2(p); 47(v)

RESEARCH CENTER: Primary research facility for the historical study of the US Army. Central repository designated to collect, organize, preserve, and make available materials on American military history.

PROGRAMS: Exhibits; Garden Tours; Lectures; Research Library/Archives

COLLECTIONS: [18th-20th c] Books, photographs, manuscripts, maps, color slides, bound periodicals, periodical subscriptions and military publications, regulations, manuals, pamphlets.

HOURS: Yr M-T, Th 8-4:30, W 11:30-4:30

CARNEGIE

7159
Historical Society of Carnegie
1 W Main St, 15106 [Box 826, 15106]; (p) (412) 276-7447; (c) Allegheny

Joint/ 1990/ staff: 1(f); 10(p)/ members: 300

HISTORICAL SOCIETY: Preserves local history.

PROGRAMS: Annual Meeting; Community Outreach; Exhibits; Film/Video; Guided Tours; Lectures; Publication; Research Library/Archives

COLLECTIONS: [1861-1900s] Model of Carnegie's Main Street, local newspapers from 1872 on film with reader/printer available, school, church, club histories; Honus Wagner history and military wall. Housed in a 100 year old historic building.

HOURS: Yr M-F 10-5

ADMISSION: Donations accepted

CATASAUGUA

7160
George Taylor House
Lehigh & Poplar Sts, 18032 [Old Courthouse, PO Box 1548, Allentown, 18105]; (p) (610) 435-4664, (610) 435-1074; (f) (610) 435-9812; www.voicenet.com/~vpsoc/lchslibrary.html

1768/ Lehigh County Historical Society

COLLECTIONS: [1768-early 1800s] High-style Georgian & Federal furnishings. Archival material is housed at LCHS library.

HOURS: Seasonal

CHADDS FORD

7161
Barns-Brinton House
US Route 1, 19317 [PO Box 27, 19317]; (p) (610) 388-7376; (f) (610) 388-7480; cfhs@voicenet.com; www.voicenet.com/~cfhs; (c) Chester

Private non-profit/ 1968/ Chadds Ford Historical Society, Board of Directors/ staff: 3(p); 200(v)/ members: 700

Seeks to preserve the properties, records, and artifact, to interpret the history, and to educate the public concerning the lifeways of 18th c Chadds Ford.

COLLECTIONS: [18th c] Furniture, iron tools, kitchen equipment, textiles, photographs, and assorted archival materials.

HOURS: May-Sept Sa-Su 12-5

ADMISSION: $5, Children $2

7162
Brandywine Battlefield Park
US Route 1, 19317 [PO Box 202, 19317]; (p) (610) 459-3342; (f) (610) 459-9586; tcollins@phmc.state.pa.us; www.ushistory.org/brandywine; (c) Delaware

State/ 1949/ PA Historical and Museum Commission/Commonwealth of PA/ staff: 4(f); 7(p); 25(v)/ members: 200

HISTORIC SITE; HISTORY MUSEUM; HOUSE MUSEUM: Oversees a fifty acre commemorative park focusing on the Battle of Brandywine in the American Revolution with two historic houses and a visitor center.

PROGRAMS: Annual Meeting; Community Outreach; Exhibits; Guided Tours; Interpretation; Lectures; Living History; Reenactments

COLLECTIONS: [18th c] Restored 1745 Gideon Gilpin House, reconstructed Benjamin Ring House, 18th c military artifacts, muskets, bayonets, various military accessories, and period furnishings.

HOURS: Yr T-Sa 9-5, Su 12-5

ADMISSION: $3.50, Children $1.50, Seniors $2.50

7163
Brandywine Conservancy, Inc.
Routes 1 & 100, 19317 [PO Box 141, 19317]; (p) (610) 388-2700; (f) (610) 388-1197; inquiries@brandywine.org; www.brandywine museum.org; (c) Delaware

Private non-profit/ 1967/ staff: 61(f); 40(p); 250(v)/ members: 4000

ART MUSEUM; GARDEN; HISTORIC SITE: Housed in a restored 19th c grist mill, the museum showcases an extensive collection of Wyeth family art, illustrations, and other 19th and 20th c American art.

PROGRAMS: Exhibits; Facility Rental; Garden Tours; Guided Tours

COLLECTIONS: [19th-20th c] Collects and preserves American art with primary emphasis on the art history of the Brandywine Valley, the American landscape, and still life painting.

HOURS: Yr Daily 9:30-4:30

ADMISSION: $5, Student $2.50, Children $2.50, Seniors $2.50; Under 6 free

7164
Chadds Ford Historical Society
Rt 100 N, 1/4 mile N of US Rt 1, 19317 [PO Box 27, 19317]; (p) (610) 388-7376; (f) (610) 388-7480; cfhs@voicenet.com; www.voicenet.com/~cfhs/; (c) Delaware

Private non-profit/ 1968/ staff: 3(p); 200(v)/ members: 933

HISTORICAL SOCIETY; HOUSE MUSEUM; LIVING HISTORY/OUTDOOR MUSEUM: Preserves the properties, records, and artifacts; interprets local history and the 18th c Chadds Ford family history.

PROGRAMS: Exhibits; Family Programs; Festivals; Guided Tours; Interpretation; Lectures; Living History; Research Library/Archives; School-Based Curriculum

COLLECTIONS: [18th-19th c] House, furniture, iron tools, kitchen equipment, textiles, photographs, and assorted archival materials.

HOURS: Hdqtrs/The Barn: Yr M-F 9-2; House Museums: May-Sept Sa-Su 12-5

ADMISSION: $5, Children $2

7165
Christian C. Sanderson Museum, The
Rt 100 N, 19317 [PO Box 153, 19317]; (p) (610) 388-6545; (c) Delaware

Private non-profit/ 1967/ staff: 14(v)/ members: 250

HISTORY MUSEUM: Preserves the personal collection of Christian C. Sanderson.

PROGRAMS: Exhibits

COLLECTIONS: [1776-1945] Lifetime collection of Christian C. Sanderson 1890-1966: Andrew Wyeth portrait, Civil War items, sand from the digging of the Panama Canal, melted ice from the South Pole, and memorabilia.

HOURS: Mar-Dec Sa-Su 1-4:30

ADMISSION: Donations

CHAMBERSBURG

7166
Kittochtinny Historical Society, Inc.
175 E King St, 17201; (p) (717) 264-1667; (c) Franklin

Private non-profit/ 1898/ County/ staff: 31(v)/ members: 600

GARDEN; GENEALOGICAL SOCIETY; HISTORICAL SOCIETY; HISTORY MUSEUM; RESEARCH CENTER: Collects, preserves, and makes available to the public materials relating to the historical development of the Cumberland Valley, Franklin County, and its people.

PROGRAMS: Community Outreach; Exhibits; Garden Tours; Guided Tours; Lectures

COLLECTIONS: "The Old Jail" built in 1818 and survived the burning of Chambersburg during Civil War by the Confederates. This building of Georgian design is the third oldest in Chambersburg and was placed on the State and National Register of Historical Sites in 1978. Includes historical artifacts and library.

HOURS: Museum: Apr Th-Sa 9:30-4; Library: Nov-Apr T 5-8, W-Th 12-4; Sept-Nov T 5-8, Th-Sa 9:30-4; May-Aug T 5-8, W-Sa 9:30-4

CHESTER SPRINGS

7167
Historic Yellow Springs, Inc.
1685 Art School Rd, 19425 [PO Box 62, 19425]; (p) (610) 827-7414; (f) (610) 827-1336; (c) Chester

Private non-profit/ 1974/ staff: 3(f); 4(p); 75(v)/ members: 450

HISTORY MUSEUM: Preserves its buildings, conserves the open space, provides a resource center for education, interprets its pas,t and serves as a community learning center for present and future generations.

PROGRAMS: Annual Meeting; Community Outreach; Concerts; Elder's Programs; Exhibits; Facility Rental; Family Programs; Festivals; Garden Tours; Guided Tours; Interpretation; Lectures; Research Library/Archives; Theatre

COLLECTIONS: [1722-present] Paintings, drawings, plaster casts, documents, manuscripts, a small library, furniture, and photographs.

HOURS: Yr M-F 9-4 and by appt

ADMISSION: Grounds Free

CLARION

7168
Clarion County Historical Society
18 Grant St, 16214-1015; (p) (814) 226-4450; (f) (814) 226-7106; cchs@csonline.net; www.csonline.net/cchs; (c) Clarion

Private non-profit/ 1955/ staff: 1(f); 3(p); 4(v)/ members: 593

HISTORICAL SOCIETY; HOUSE MUSEUM: Owns and operates the Sutton-Ditz House, Museum, and Library. Collects, preserves and interprets the history of Clarion County, its industries, people, and events with special programming for the education of present and future generations.

PROGRAMS: Annual Meeting; Exhibits; Festivals; Guided Tours; Living History; Publication; Reenactments; Research Library/Archives

COLLECTIONS: [1840-present] Maps, newspapers, 2,000 volume library, periodicals, photographs, and museum artifacts.

HOURS: Yr

COATESVILLE

7169
Fallowfield Historical Society
Rt 82, 19320 [660 Buck Run Rd, 19320]; (p) (610) 383-1591; (c) Chester

1980/ members: 36

HISTORICAL SOCIETY: Preserves local history and maintains old historic Town Hall buildings built in 1847.

PROGRAMS: Annual Meeting; Exhibits; Festivals; Guided Tours

COLLECTIONS: Photos, books, deeds, maps, and newspapers.

HOURS: Jan-Mar, Apr-Oct

ADMISSION: Donations accepted

7170
Graystone Society, Inc.
76 S First Ave, 19320; (p) (610) 384-9282; (f) (610) 384-9022; (c) Chester

Private non-profit/ 1984/ staff: 1(f); 30(v)/ members: 125

HISTORICAL SOCIETY; HOUSE MUSEUM: Owns two houses as museums, Terracina and Graystone Mansion. Houses are in the Lukens Historic District, a National Historic Landmark and under restoration by the society.

PROGRAMS: Concerts; Exhibits; Festivals; Guided Tours; Lectures

COLLECTIONS: [1810-1930] Furniture, pictures, books relating to the houses, owners, iron, and steel industry.

HOURS: May-Dec Sa 1-4 and by appt

ADMISSION: $5

COCHRANTON

7171
Cochranton Heritage Society
[PO Box 58, 16314-0598]; (p) (814) 425-7700; (c) Crawford

Private non-profit/ 1980/ staff: 6(v)/ members: 100/publication: *Heritage Times*

HISTORICAL SOCIETY: Maintains historic railroad station with exhibits and artifacts.

PROGRAMS: Annual Meeting; Exhibits; Publication

COLLECTIONS: [1890-1950] Agricultural implements, school memorabilia, items from local businesses, and railroad office furniture.

HOURS: Varies

ADMISSION: No charge

COLLEGEVILLE

7172
Historical Society of Trappe
301 Main St, 19426 [PO Box 26708, 19426]; (p) (610) 489-7560; (c) Montgomery

Private non-profit/ 1964/ Board of Directors/ staff: 20(p); 2(v)/ members: 210/publication: *Trappe Chronicle*

HISTORIC SITE; HISTORICAL SOCIETY; HISTORY MUSEUM; HOUSE MUSEUM: Preserves history and buildings and educates about heritage of Perkiomen Valley.

PROGRAMS: Annual Meeting; Community Outreach; Exhibits; Family Programs; Interpretation; Lectures; Publication

COLLECTIONS: [18th-19th c] Farm, home, education, Muhlenberg Family, villages of Perkiomen Valley, and Native American artifacts.

HOURS: Yr by appt; June-Aug Su 12-5, 2nd T, last W evening

ADMISSION: Donations accepted

COLUMBIA

7173
Wrights Ferry Mansion
38 S 2nd St, 17512-1402 [PO Box 68, 17512-1402]; (p) (717) 684-4325; www.paheritage.com/lawright.html

CONCORDVILLE

7174
Concord Township Historical Society
659 Smith Bridge Rd/Concord Township, 19331 [PO Box 152, 19331]; (p) (610) 459-8911; (f) (610) 459-8917; crdtwp@twp.concord.pa.us; www.twp.concord.pa.us; (c) Delaware

Private non-profit/ 1967/ staff: 4(v)/ members: 120/publication: *Concord Township History, Vol. 1-2*

GENEALOGICAL SOCIETY; HISTORIC PRESERVATION AGENCY; HISTORIC SITE; HISTORICAL SOCIETY; HISTORY MUSEUM: Stimulates interest in the township, its heritage, and encourages active participation in the restoration and preservation of its landmarks.

PROGRAMS: Annual Meeting; Exhibits; Facility Rental; Guided Tours; Lectures; Publication

COLLECTIONS: [1683-present] Farm tools, genealogies of local families, copies of wills, deeds, tax records; photos of all old properties, atlases, maps, and scrapbooks.

HOURS: Yr by appt

CONNEAUT

7175
Conneaut Valley Area Historical Society
1625 Main St, 16406; (p) (814) 587-3782; bkovac@toolcity.net; www.toolcity.net/cvahs; (c) Crawford

Private non-profit/ 1989/ staff: 12(v)/ members: 168

GENEALOGICAL SOCIETY; HISTORIC PRESERVATION AGENCY; HISTORICAL SOCIETY; HISTORY MUSEUM: Preserves and protects materials relating to historic places and sites in the community. Encouraging historical research through the display of artifacts from the community and other activities.

PROGRAMS: Exhibits; Film/Video; Lectures; Reenactments; Research Library/Archives

COLLECTIONS: [Late 19th-early 20th c] School photos and records, military uniforms, local industrial artifacts and photos, county histories and index files for genealogical research.

HOURS: Yr Sa 12-2 or by appt

ADMISSION: No charge

CONNELLSVILLE

7176
Colonel William Crawford Log Cabin
275 S Pittsburgh St, 15425-3580; (p) (412) 628-5640

7177
Connellsville Area Historical Society
299 S Pittsburgh St, 15425; (p) (724) 628-5640; (f) (724) 628-5636; (c) Fayette

Private non-profit/ 1972/ staff: 2(v)/ members: 180

HISTORICAL SOCIETY

PROGRAMS: Annual Meeting; Research Library/Archives

COLLECTIONS: Photographs, family histories, cemetery listings, community artifacts, genealogy, local history books, and newspaper articles.

HOURS: Yr M-W

CONSHOHOCKEN

7178
Conshohocken Historical Society
120 E 5th Ave, 19428; (p) (610) 828-7869; (c) Montgomery

Private non-profit/ 1963/ Board of Directors/ staff: 8(p); 4(v)/ members: 200

HISTORICAL SOCIETY: Collects, preserves, and catalogs materials relating to town history.

PROGRAMS: Annual Meeting; Film/Video; Lectures; Research Library/Archives

COLLECTIONS: [1879-1963] Microfilm consisting of the Conshohocken Recorder; General history of churches, school, and industry.

HOURS: Yr Sa 10-12

ADMISSION: No charge

CORRY

7179
Corry Area Historical Society
945 Mead Ave, 16407 [PO Box 107, 16407]; (p) (814) 664-4749; (c) Erie

City/ 1967/ staff: 12(v)/ members: 110

HISTORICAL SOCIETY; HISTORY MUSEUM: Preserves local history, genealogy, and artifacts in all categories.

PROGRAMS: Annual Meeting; Exhibits; Guided Tours; Lectures; Research Library/Archives

COLLECTIONS: [Early 19th c-present] Climax Locomotive, items from Native Americans, commercial business, industrial and medical displays, bricks made in Corry, clothing.

HOURS: May-Oct Sa-Su 2-4 and by appt

ADMISSION: No charge

COUDERSPORT

7180
Potter County Historical Society
308 N Main St, 16915 [PO Box 605, 16915]; (p) (814) 274-8124; (c) Potter

Private non-profit/ 1919/ Potter County/ staff: 9(v)/ members: 340/publication: *Quarterly Bulletin*

GENEALOGICAL SOCIETY; HISTORICAL SOCIETY; HOUSE MUSEUM: Maintains a research library on genealogy and local history and museum. Collects, organizes, and preserves records and relics pertaining to Potter County.

PROGRAMS: Exhibits; Guided Tours; Interpretation; Lectures; Publication; Quarterly Meeting

COLLECTIONS: [1840-1940] Period rooms with Native American, Civil War, and local history artifacts.

HOURS: Yr M, F

DANVILLE

7181
Montgomery House Museum/Montour County Historical Society
1 Bloom St, 17821 [PO Box 8, 17821]; (p) (570) 271-0830; (c) Montour

County/ 1940/ staff: 15(v)/ members: 158

HISTORICAL SOCIETY; HOUSE MUSEUM: Preserves local history and is housed where William Montgomery settled in 1776.

PROGRAMS: Annual Meeting; Exhibits; Guided Tours; Lectures; School-Based Curriculum

COLLECTIONS: Montgomery belongings, Danville clocks, stoves and iron artifacts; musical instruments, photos, Civil War cannon, library, Native American artifacts and clothing.

HOURS: Yr by appt; June-Sept Su 2-4

ADMISSION: Donations accepted

DAWSON

7182
Linden Hall Mansion
Linden Hall Rd, 15428 [RD 1, 15428]; (p) (724) 429-7544; (f) (724) 529-0529; www.lindenhallpa.com

DAYTON

7183
Marshall House
N State St, 16222; (p) (814) 257-8260;
www.smicksburg-
dayton.com/Marshall_House.htm

DELTA

7184
Old Line Museum, Inc.
602 Main St, 17314 [PO Box 35, 17314]; (p)
(717) 456-5741; drrobinson@cyberia.com; (c)
York

Private non-profit/ 1974/ staff: 15(v)

HISTORY MUSEUM: Collects, preserves, and
interprets historic memorabilia of Delta and its
immediate area.

PROGRAMS: Annual Meeting; Exhibits; Family Programs; Festivals; Guided Tours

COLLECTIONS: [1850-present] Local newspapers, tax and school records, photographs
from schools, photos and other items relating
to local quarrying and industries; Maryland
and Pennsylvania Railroad items.

HOURS: May-Oct Su 1-5 and by appt

ADMISSION: Donations accepted

DILLSBURG

7185
**Northern York County Historical and
Preservation Society**
35 Greenbrier Ln, 17019 [PO Box 355,
17019]; (p) (717) 502-1440; (c) York

Private non-profit/ 1983/ Board of Directors/
staff: 100(v)/ members: 200

HISTORIC SITE; HISTORICAL SOCIETY;
HISTORY MUSEUM: Promotes the study, collection, and preservation of all aspects of the
historical, educational, and cultural heritage of
the Northern York County area.

PROGRAMS: Exhibits; Facility Rental; Festivals; Lectures; Publication; Reenactments

COLLECTIONS: State archives and colonial
records, central and eastern PA county histories, local newspapers, photographs, sheet
music, genealogical

DONORA

7186
**Tri-State Historical Steam Engine
Association, Inc.**
Rt 88, 15033 [448 7th St, 15033]; (p) (724)
379-4781; funz@westol.com; (c) Washington

Private non-profit/ 1956/ staff: 13(v)/ members:
207

HISTORICAL SOCIETY: Demonstrates how
land was farmed years ago.

PROGRAMS: Annual Meeting; Festivals;
Film/Video; Lectures

COLLECTIONS: [19th c] Twenty-eight running
antique farm traction engines, two stationary
engines, baker fan, gristmill, bailer thresher,
rock crusher, and shingle maker.

HOURS: Sept F-Su 9-sunset

DOWNINGTOWN

7187
Downingtown Historical Society
[PO Box 9, 19335]; (p) (610) 269-1167; (f)
(610) 269-1248; (c) Chester

Private non-profit/ 1978/ staff: 5(v)/ members:
150

HISTORICAL SOCIETY

PROGRAMS: Lectures; School-Based Curriculum

DOYLESTOWN

7188
Bucks County Historical Society
Pine St & Ashland St, 18901 [84 S Pine St,
18901]; (p) (215) 345-0210; (f) (215) 230-
0823; info@mercermuseum.org; www.mercer
museum.org; (c) Bucks

Private non-profit/ 1880

BCHS administers the Mercer and Fonthill Museums and the Spruancy Library.

HOURS: Yr M-Sa 10-5, Su 12-5; Mercer Museum T 5-9

ADMISSION: $6, Children $2.50, Seniors
$5.50; Mbrs/Under 6 free

7189
Fonthill Museum
E Court St & Rt 313, 18901 [84 S Pine St,
18901]; (p) (215) 348-9461; (f) (215) 348-
9462; www.libertynet.org\~bchs

1908/ Bucks County Historical Society/ staff:
1(f); 12(p)

COLLECTIONS: [1908-1912] Mercer's own
Moravian tiles, foreign tiles, Delft, Chinese,
Persia; Babylonian Clay Tablets, built in con-
crete furniture; 6,000 books.

HOURS: Yr

7190
James A. Michener Art Museum
138 S Pine St, 18901; (p) (215) 340-9800; (f)
(215) 340-9807; www.michenerartmuseum.org;
(c) Bucks

Private non-profit/ 1988/ staff: 12(f); 23(p);
80(v)/ members: 2300

ART MUSEUM: Collects, preserves, interprets, and exhibits the work of artists from the
Bucks County region. Educates the community about wider themes in art through changing
exhibitions and educational programs.

PROGRAMS: Community Outreach; Concerts; Elder's Programs; Exhibits; Facility
Rental; Family Programs; Festivals; Guided
Tours; Interpretation; Lectures; Research Li-
brary/Archives; School-Based Curriculum

COLLECTIONS: [19th-20th c] Works that represent the artistic tradition of Bucks County
and representative American sculpture.

HOURS: Yr T-F 10-4:30, Sa-Su 10-5

ADMISSION: $5, Student $1.50, Seniors
$4.50; Under 12 free

7191
Moravian Pottery and Tile Works
130 Swamp Rd, 18901; (p) (215) 345-6722;
(f) (215) 345-1361; www.buckscounty.org; (c)
Bucks

County/ 1969/ staff: 17(f); 3(p)

HISTORIC SITE: Manages working history
museum.

PROGRAMS: Community Outreach; Exhibits;
Facility Rental; Festivals; Guided Tours; Interpretation; Living History

COLLECTIONS: [1898-1956] Plaster molds,
architectural ceramic pieces, correspondences, notebooks, drawings, tools, machinery,
decorative tiles and mosaics made by hand in
the arts and crafts tradition, as begun in 1898
by Henry C. Mercer.

HOURS: Yr Daily 10-4:45

ADMISSION: $3, Children $1.50, Seniors
$2.50

EAST BERLIN

7192
**East Berlin Historical Preservation
Society**
332 W King St, 17316 [PO Box 73, 17316];
(p) (717) 259-0822; (c) Adams

Private non-profit/ 1975/ Board of Directors/
staff: 1(p)/ members: 170/publication: *The
Berlin Informer*

HISTORICAL SOCIETY: Preserves, restores
and teaches East Berlin history as well as
maintaining a museum, library and five historic
buildings.

PROGRAMS: Annual Meeting; Exhibits; Facility Rental; Family Programs; Festivals; Guided
Tours; Lectures; Publication; Library/Archives

COLLECTIONS: [19th-20th c] Artifacts pertaining to the society, Berlin history, genealogy
files, manuscripts, newspapers, photographs
of the local area and reference library.

HOURS: Yr W, Sa 10-4, Th 6-8:30

ADMISSION: No charge

EASTON

7193
Crayola Factory, The
30 Centre Sq, 18042; (p) (610) 515-8000; (f) (610)
559-6691; www.crayola.com; (c) Northampton

Joint/ 1996/ staff: 14(f); 25(p); 250(v)

CORPORATE ARCHIVES/MUSEUM: Combines displays of Binney and Smith's Corporate history, demonstrations of Crayola crayon
and marker manufacturing and interactive exhibits in the arts for family fun.

PROGRAMS: Community Outreach; Concerts; Exhibits; Facility Rental; Family Programs; School-Based Curriculum

COLLECTIONS: [1860-present] Binney &
Smith's corporate archives, artifacts, memorabilia, children's art.

HOURS: Sept 1-June 30 T-Sa 9:30-5, Su 12-5; July
1-Aug 31 M-Sa 9:30-5, Su 11-6

ADMISSION: $7

7194
**Hugh Moore Historical Park and
Museums, Inc./National Canal
Museum**
30 Centre Square, 18042-7743; (p) (610)
559-6613; (f) (610) 559-6690; ncm@canals.
org; www.canals.org; (c) Northampton

Private non-profit/ 1970/ staff: 11(f); 19(p); 56(v)/ members: 700

HISTORIC SITE; HISTORY MUSEUM; LIVING HISTORY/OUTDOOR MUSEUM: Preserves the artifacts, documents and structures of America's canal era. Educates people about the importance of historic canals and their contributions to the industrial revolution. Operates the National Canal Museum, library/ archives; offers canal boat rides for visitors to enjoy a valuable learning experience.

PROGRAMS: Community Outreach; Exhibits; Facility Rental; Family Programs; Festivals; Interpretation; Lectures; Living History; Publication; Research Library/Archives; School-Based Curriculum

COLLECTIONS: [1700s-present] Serves as national source of information on canals, inland waterways, anthracite coal mining and iron/steel production. Artifacts, videos, audio tapes, slides, photographs, negatives, engineering drawings, books, films and manuscripts. Permanent and changing exhibits, public programs, symposia, loan arrangements, research, and more.

HOURS: Museum: Yr T-Su; May-Aug Daily; Sept Sa-Su

ADMISSION: $8, Children $4, Seniors $7.50

7195
Northampton County Historical and Genealogical Society
101-107 S 4th St, 18042; (p) (610) 253-1222

Private non-profit/ staff: 1(f); 5(p); 30(v)/ members: 375

ART MUSEUM; GENEALOGICAL SOCIETY; HISTORIC PRESERVATION AGENCY; HISTORICAL SOCIETY; HISTORY MUSEUM; HOUSE MUSEUM: Collects, preserves, and interprets the intellectual and material culture of old Northampton County. Maintains two museums, a library and a history learning center.

PROGRAMS: Annual Meeting; Community Outreach; Exhibits; Guided Tours; Interpretation; Lectures; Publication; Research Library/Archives

COLLECTIONS: [1728-1900] Household accessories, decorative arts, industrial artifacts, fine arts, and costumes. Library has books, archives, photographs, family files and other materials.

HOURS: Yr M-F by appt

ADMISSION: $2; Under 14 free

EBENSBURG

7196
Cambria County Historical Society
615 N Center St, 15931; (p) (814) 472-6674; (c) Cambria

Private non-profit/ 1925/ Board of Directors/ staff: 1(f); 25(v)/ members: 415/publication: *Cambria County Heritage*

HISTORICAL SOCIETY; HISTORY MUSEUM: Seeks to preserve and promote the history of Cambria County through is museum collections, library, and archives.

PROGRAMS: Annual Meeting; Exhibits; Guided Tours; Publication; Research Library/Archives

COLLECTIONS: [1790-present] 3,000 bound volumes, large collection of newspapers, census reports, and a collection of maps, photographs, and artifacts.

HOURS: Yr T-F 10-4:30, Sa 9-1

ADMISSION: No charge

EDINBORO

7197
Edinboro Area Historical Society
Edinboro University of Pennsylvania, 16444 [EUP Library Archives, 16444]; (p) (814) 732-2415; (f) (814) 732-2883; (c) Erie

1998/ members: 150

Promotes interest in local history; identifies files and records, documents historical data and preserves artifacts unique to the Edinboro area for the sake of the community.

EGYPT

7198
Troxell-Steckel House & Farm Museum
4229 Reliance St, 18052 [PO Box 1548, Allentown, 18105]; (p) (610) 435-1074; (f) (610) 435-9812

1756/ Lehigh County Historical Society/ staff: 44(p); 2(v)

COLLECTIONS: [Mid-1700s-mid 1800s] Collections include domestic, agricultural, and craft implements of the late 18th, mid 19th c, furnishings typical of the PA Germans; All archival collections are at our central archive/library including genealogical materials, local buisiness records, photographs.

HOURS: Seasonal

ELIZABETHTOWN

7199
Elizabethtown Historical Society
57-59 S Poplar St, 17022 [PO Box 301, 17022]; (p) (717) 361-9382; (c) Lancaster

Private non-profit/ 1970/ Executive Board/ members: 185

HISTORICAL SOCIETY; HISTORY MUSEUM: Preserves and develops historical sites of Elizabethtown. Maintains a one-room schoolhouse museum.

PROGRAMS: Elder's Programs; Guided Tours; Lectures

COLLECTIONS: [19th c] Artifacts of Elizabethtown including schools, commerce, and housing.

HOURS: Yr by appt

ADMISSION: No charge

7200
Winters Heritage House Museum
41-43 E High St, 17022 [PO Box 14, 17022]; (p) (717) 367-4672; (f) (717) 367-9991; (c) Lancaster

Private non-profit/ 1988/ Elizabethtown Preservation Associates, Inc./ staff: 2(p); 100(v)/ members: 250

GARDEN; HISTORIC SITE; HISTORY MUSEUM: Preserves and promotes the historical and cultural experience of Elizabethtown and

surrounding communities through education, research, restoration, and cultural awareness.

PROGRAMS: Annual Meeting; Exhibits; Festivals; Guided Tours; Interpretation; Lectures; Living History; Research Library/Archives

COLLECTIONS: [1750-1850] Archaeological artifacts, oral history tapes. Genealogy library contains local family histories, cemetery records, Elizabethtown history, old deeds, atlases, and Lancaster County history.

HOURS: Mar-Dec Th 12-4, F 9-4, Sa 9-11:30

ADMISSION: Donations accepted

ELVERSON

7201
Hopewell Furnace National Historic Site
2 Mark Bird Ln, 19520; (p) (610) 582-8773; (f) (610) 582-2768; hofu_superintendent@nps.gov; www.nps.gov/hofu; (c) Berks/Chester

Federal; Joint/ 1938/ National Park Service/ staff: 15(f); 8(p); 191(v)

HISTORIC SITE; LIVING HISTORY/OUTDOOR MUSEUM: Preserves site as example of an early American iron plantation through living history, interpretive media, and an extensive museum collection.

PROGRAMS: Community Outreach; Elder's Programs; Exhibits; Festivals; Film/Video; Interpretation; Living History; Publication; Reenactments

COLLECTIONS: [1820-1850] Artifacts relevant to the industrial, agricultural and domestic lives of the community. Museum contains a variety of Ten Plate (a.k.a. Pennsylvania)

EMMAUS

7202
1803 House
55 S Keystone Ave, 18049; (p) (610) 965-0152

1803/ Board

COLLECTIONS: [1780-1840] Period coins and notes.

HOURS: By appt

7203
Shelter House Society
601 S 4th St, 18049 [PO Box 254, 18049]; (p) (610) 965-9258; (c) Lehigh

Private non-profit/ 1951/ members: 225/publication: *The Hearthstone*

HISTORIC SITE; HISTORICAL SOCIETY; HISTORY MUSEUM; HOUSE MUSEUM: Maintains and preserves log cabin built in 1734 and surrounding property.

PROGRAMS: Exhibits; Guided Tours; Living History; Publication; School-Based Curriculum

COLLECTIONS: [18th c] Furniture, books, and tools.

HOURS: Yr by appt

ADMISSION: Donations accepted

EPHRATA

7204
Ephrata Cloister

632 W Main St, 17522; (p) (717) 733-6600; (f) (717) 733-4364; (c) Lancaster

State/ 1941/ PA Historical and Museum Commission/ staff: 8(f); 6(p); 75(v)/ members: 450

HISTORIC SITE; HISTORY MUSEUM; HOUSE MUSEUM; LIVING HISTORY/OUTDOOR MUSEUM: Preserves and interprets the 18th c Germanic religious community which built the site.

PROGRAMS: Concerts; Exhibits; Facility Rental; Family Programs; Guided Tours; Interpretation; Lectures; Living History; Reenactments; Research Library/Archives; School-Based Curriculum

COLLECTIONS: [1732-present] Artifacts, furniture, baskets, and manuscripts. Structures include Saron Sister's House, Saal Meeting House, Conrad Beissel House.

HOURS: Jan-Feb T-Su 9-5; Mar-Dec Daily

7205
Historical Society of the Cocalico Valley, The

249 W Main St, 17522 [PO Box 193, 17522]; (p) (717) 733-1616; (c) Lancaster

Private non-profit/ 1957/ staff: 1(f); 20(v)/ members: 555/publication: *Journal of the Historical Society of the Cocalico Valley*

HISTORICAL SOCIETY; HOUSE MUSEUM: Collects, preserves, makes accessible, and interprets artifacts and research materials pertaining to the history and culture of the Cocalico Valley region of Lancaster County.

PROGRAMS: Exhibits; Garden Tours; Guided Tours; Lectures; Publication; Research Library/Archives

COLLECTIONS: [1720-present] Museum artifacts displayed in Victorian room settings after the period of society's headquarters (house erected in 1868). Books, research files, local newspapers, manuscripts, photographs, and microfilm.

HOURS: Yr M, W-Th 9:30-6, Sa 8:30-5

ADMISSION: $3

ERIE

7206
Erie County Historical Society

417 State St, 16501; (p) (814) 454-1813; (f) (814) 452-1744; echs@velocity.net; (c) Erie

Private non-profit/ 1903/ staff: 3(f); 5(p); 106(v)/ members: 650

HISTORICAL SOCIETY; HOUSE MUSEUM: Operates a local history library and archives, 1839 Cashier's House, and the Battles Museums of Rural Life.

PROGRAMS: Annual Meeting; Community Outreach; Concerts; Exhibits; Facility Rental; Family Programs; Festivals; Garden Tours; Guided Tours; Interpretation; Lectures; Living History; Publication; Reenactments; Research Library/Archives; School-Based Curriculum

COLLECTIONS: [1780-present] Books, vertical file materials, manuscripts, archives, county quarter session records, photographic images, maps, architectural plans, microfilm, and 3-D artifacts.

HOURS: Yr EHC: T-Sa 10-5; Battles Properties: May-Sept F-Sa 10-4, Su 12-4

7207
Erie Historical Museum and Planetarium

356 W 6th St, 16507; (p) (814) 871-5790; (f) (814) 879-0988; ehmp@erie.net; (c) Erie

Private non-profit/ 1899/ staff: 2(f); 5(p); 10(v)/ members: 800

HISTORY MUSEUM; HOUSE MUSEUM: Operates museum housed in 1891 Victorian mansion with planetarium in the original carriage house.

PROGRAMS: Community Outreach; Exhibits; Guided Tours; Interpretation; Lectures; Research Library/Archives

COLLECTIONS: Southwest Native American items, archives, dolls, WW II posters.

HOURS: T-F 10-5, Sa-Su 1-5

ADMISSION: $4, Children $2

7208
Erie Maritime Museum, Homeport US Brig Niagara

Bayview Commons, 150 E Front St, 16507 [150 E Front St, Ste 100, 16507]; (p) (814) 452-2744; (f) (814) 455-6760; sail@brigniagara.org; www.brigniagara.org; (c) Erie

Private non-profit; State/ 1948/ staff: 25(f); 6(p); 200(v)/ members: 1500

HISTORY MUSEUM; MARITIME MUSEUM: Homeport to US Brig Niagara, War of 1812 Museum, Great Lakes Fishing and Industry. Exhibits on USS Wolverine, the first iron warship.

PROGRAMS: Annual Meeting; Community Outreach; Concerts; Elder's Programs; Exhibits; Facility Rental; Family Programs; Film/Video; Garden Tours; Guided Tours; Interpretation; Lectures; Living History; Publication; Reenactments; Research Library/Archives; School-Base

COLLECTIONS: [1812-present]

HOURS: Yr M-Sa 9-5, Su 12-5

ADMISSION: $6, Children $4, Seniors $5

7209
Erie Society for Genealogical Research

419 State St, 16512 [PO Box 1403, 16512]; (p) (814) 454-1813; www.pa-roots.com/~erie/; (c) Erie

Private non-profit/ 1972/ staff: 20(v)/ members: 400/publication: *Keystone Kuzzins*

GENEALOGICAL SOCIETY: Locates, preserves, and shares genealogical information of Erie County individuals.

PROGRAMS: Publication; Research Library/Archives

7210
Firefighters Historical Museum, Inc.

428 Chestnut St, 16508 [3423 Hazel St, 16508-2632]; (p) (814) 456-5969, (814) 864-2156; (c) Erie

Private non-profit/ 1969/ staff: 12(v)/ members: 200

HISTORY MUSEUM: Preserves the history of firefighting with a collection of antique fire apparatus, equipment, tools, and uniforms from around the local area and the world.

PROGRAMS: Annual Meeting; Exhibits; Film/Video; Guided Tours

COLLECTIONS: [1800-present] Hose cart, uniforms, trumpets, fire buckets, nozzles, 1891 LaFrance 3rd class steamer, and 1858 Rumsey hand pulled fire pumper.

HOURS: May-Oct Sa 10-5, Su 1-5 and by appt

ADMISSION: $2.50, Children $1, Seniors $1.50, $1.50 firefighters

7211
Lawrence Park Historical Society

c/o Lawrence Park Township, 4230 Iroquois Ave, 16511; (p) (814) 899-7119; ferntree20@aol.com; (c) Erie

1979/ staff: 5(v)/ members: 65

HISTORICAL SOCIETY: Acquires and preserves the historical legacy of the Lawrence Park area. Familiarizes the community with its heritage, a company town built by the General Electric Company.

PROGRAMS: Community Outreach; Exhibits; Guided Tours; Interpretation; Lectures; Research Library/Archives

COLLECTIONS: [1910-present] History of company town, local school memorabilia, information on local organizations and personalities.

HOURS: Yr Sa 12-2 and by appt

7212
Museum of Erie GE History

2901 E Lake Rd, 16531; (p) (814) 875-2494; (c) Erie

Private non-profit/ 1995/ staff: 15(v)

CORPORATE ARCHIVES/MUSEUM: Exhibits the industrial products made during the 90 years since the plant was founded.

PROGRAMS: Garden Tours; Guided Tours; Interpretation; Research Library/Archives

COLLECTIONS: [1910-present] Photographs, artifacts, and publications displayed in a 2,000 square ft museum covering 90 years of plant existence.

HOURS: Yr Sa 10-2 and by appt

ADMISSION: No charge

FAIRVIEW

7213
Fairview Area Historical Society

4302 Avonia Rd, 16415 [PO Box 553, 16415]; (p) (814) 474-5855; (c) Erie

1976/ staff: 30(v)/ members: 100

GENEALOGICAL SOCIETY; HISTORICAL SOCIETY; HOUSE MUSEUM: Preserves local history through various means and disseminates local history.

PROGRAMS: Annual Meeting; Community Outreach; Exhibits; Facility Rental; Festivals; Guided Tours; Research Library/Archives; School-Based Curriculum

COLLECTIONS: [19th-early 20th c]

HOURS: Yr T-W 9-11:30 and by appt

ADMISSION: No charge

FALLSINGTON

7214
Historic Fallsington, Inc.
4 Yardley Ave, 19054; (p) (215) 295-6567; (f) (215) 295-6567; histfals@erols.com; (c) Bucks

Private non-profit/ 1953/ Board of Trustees/ staff: 1(f); 3(p); 70(v)/ members: 250

HISTORIC SITE; HISTORY MUSEUM: Preserves and makes available the 300 year old village of Fallsington.

PROGRAMS: Annual Meeting; Community Outreach; Exhibits; Facility Rental; Festivals; Guided Tours; Interpretation; Lectures; Reenactments

COLLECTIONS: [18th-19th c] Furnishings in three museum buildings. Supports the interpretation of early Quaker settlement and village life.

HOURS: May-Oct M-Sa 10-4, Su 1-4

ADMISSION: $3.50, Students $1, Seniors $2.50

FARMINGTON

7215
Fort Necessity National Battlefield
1 Washington Pkwy, 15437; (p) (724) 329-5512; (f) (724) 329-8682; fone_interpretation@nps.gov; www.nps.gov/fone; (c) Fayette

Federal/ 1931/ National Park Service/ staff: 35(f); 2(p); 10(v)

HISTORIC SITE: Commemorates the opening battle of the French and Indian War. Site of George Washington's first military campaign. Also tells the story of the National Road, America's first federally funded highway.

PROGRAMS: Community Outreach; Exhibits; Family Programs; Film/Video; Interpretation; Living History; School-Based Curriculum

COLLECTIONS: [Mid 18th-19th c] Archaeological artifacts such as post fragments, musket balls and accoutrements. Historic furnishings and domestic goods relating to operation of a stagecoach tavern on the National Road.

HOURS: Yr Daily 9-5

7216
Friendship Hill National Historic Site
RDI Box 149A, 15437 [c/o Fort Necessity NB, 1 Washington Pkwy, 15437]; (p) (724) 725-9190; (f) (724) 725-1999; www.nps.gov/frhi; (c) Fayette

Federal/ 1978/ Dept of the Interior, National Park Service/ staff: 6(f); 1(p); 4(v)

HISTORIC SITE: Historic western PA home of Albert Gallatin, Secretary of Treasury under presidents Jefferson and Madison.

PROGRAMS: Concerts; Exhibits; Family Programs; Festivals; Guided Tours; Interpretation; Lectures; Living History; School-Based Curriculum

COLLECTIONS: [1780-1830] Gallatin Papers on microfilm, period and Gallatin related artifacts.

HOURS: Yr Daily Park: sunrise-sunset; Gallatin House: 9-5

ADMISSION: No charge

FORT WASHINGTON

7217
Highlands Historical Society, The
7001 Sheaff Ln, 19034; (p) (215) 641-2687; (f) (215) 641-2556; (c) Montgomery

Private non-profit/ 1975/ staff: 2(f); 5(p); 59(v)/ members: 970

GARDEN; HOUSE MUSEUM: Restores, interprets, and preserves the Highlands Mansion and Garden, a 44-acre country estate, for the education and enjoyment of the public.

PROGRAMS: Concerts; Facility Rental; Family Programs; Garden Tours; Guided Tours; Interpretation; Lectures

COLLECTIONS: [1794-1970] 44-acre country estate featuring a 32 room Georgian Mansion with a two-acre formal garden, bank barn, springhouse, greenhouse, smokehouse, and Gothic Revival Gardner's Cottage.

HOURS: Yr M-F 10-4; Sa-Su by appt

ADMISSION: $4, Student $2, Seniors $3; Under 6 free

7218
Historical Society of Fort Washington
473 Bethlehem Pike, 19034; (p) (215) 646-6065; (c) Montgomery

Private non-profit/ 1936/ State/ staff: 30(v)/ members: 125/publication: The Bulletin

HISTORICAL SOCIETY; HISTORY MUSEUM; HOUSE MUSEUM: Housed in early 19th c Farmer Inn, with several furnished period rooms, library of local and state history and genealogy.

PROGRAMS: Annual Meeting; Community Outreach; Exhibits; Guided Tours; Lectures; Publication; Research Library/Archives

COLLECTIONS: [1700s-present] Period furniture and artifacts, books: local, state and national history, genealogy, biography, U.S. War histories.

HOURS: Mar-Dec W 12-2, 1st and 3rd Su

ADMISSION: Donations accepted

7219
Hope Lodge/Mather Mill
553 S Bethlehem Pike, 19034; (p) (215) 646-1595; (f) (215) 628-9471; smiller@pnmc.state.pa.us; ushistory.org/hope; (c) Montgomery

State/ 1958/ staff: 5(f); 2(p); 40(v)/ members: 114

HOUSE MUSEUM: Lodge is architecturally significant 18th c Georgian Manor house listed on the National Register. Noted for its quality preservation; a c 1820 grist mill on a 17th c foundation that is used for meetings.

PROGRAMS: Annual Meeting; Concerts; Exhibits; Facility Rental; Festivals; Guided Tours; Interpretation; Living History; Reenactments; School-Based Curriculum

COLLECTIONS: [Mid 18th-early 20th c] Decorative and fine arts.

HOURS: Yr T-Sa 9-5, Su 12-5

ADMISSION: $3.50, Children $1.50, Seniors $3; Under 6 free

FORTY FORT

7220
Denison Advocates
35 Denison St, 18704; (p) (717) 288-5531, (717) 288-5623; (c) Luzerne

Joint/ Denison Advocates;Commonwealth of PA/ staff: 22(v)/publication: Nathan Denison: Connecticut Settler in the Wyoming Valley

HISTORIC SITE; HISTORICAL SOCIETY: Educates the public about 1790 Denison House and the Denison's contributions to local, state, and national history.

PROGRAMS: Festivals; Film/Video; Guided Tours; Interpretation; Living History; Publication

COLLECTIONS: [1790-1840] Authentic period furnishings in each room.

HOURS: May-Aug Su 1-4

ADMISSION: $2, Children $0.50

FRANKLIN

7221
DeBence Antique Music World
1261 Liberty St, 16323; (p) (814) 432-8350; (f) (814) 437-7193; lynn@mail.usachoice.com; www.debencemusicworld.com; (c) Venango

Private non-profit/ 1993/ Oil Region Music Preservation Museum/ staff: 1(f); 50(v)/ members: 100

HISTORY MUSEUM: Collects and preserves automated musical instruments.

PROGRAMS: Guided Tours; Interpretation

COLLECTIONS: [1840-1920s] 100 mechanical musical instruments including calliopes, carousel band organs, music boxes, nickelodeons, phonographs, pump organs, player pianos, and orchestrations.

HOURS: Mar 15-Oct 31 T-Sa 11-4, Su 12:30-4; Nov 1-Dec 23 F-Sa 11-4, Su 12:30-4; Dec 24-Mar 15 by appt

ADMISSION: $8, Student $3, Children $3, Seniors $6

7222
Venango County Historical Society
301 S Park St, 16323 [PO Box 101, 16323]; (p) (814) 437-2275; (c) Venango

1959/ staff: 2(p); 95(v)/ members: 425

HOUSE MUSEUM: Located in house museum with genealogy, library, resource center, and publication sales room. Most publications are about local history, written, and published locally.

PROGRAMS: Annual Meeting; Exhibits; Lectures; Research Library/Archives

COLLECTIONS: [1825-1925] Household furnishings, china, tools, clothing, photographs, school memorabilia, ledgers, family histories, county records, business and industry artifacts.

HOURS: Jan-Apr Sa 10-2; May-Dec T-Th, Sa 10-2

FREEDOM

7223
Beaver County Historical Research and Landmarks Foundation
1235 Third Ave, 15042 [PO Box 1, 15042]; (p) (724) 775-1848; (f) (724) 775-1523; (c) Beaver

Private non-profit/ 1972/ staff: 1(p); 50(v)/ members: 275/publication: *Milestones*

HOURS: Yr M-F 10-2

ADMISSION: Donations accepted

GALLITZIN

7224
Allegeny Portage Railroad National Historic Site
Just off U.S. 22, 12 miles W of Altoona, 16641 [110 Federal Park Rd, PA, 16641]; (p) (814) 886-6150, (814) 886-6100; (f) (814) 884-0206; ALPO_Superintendent@nps.gov; www.nps.gov/alpo/index.htm

National Park Service

HISTORY MUSEUM; HOUSE MUSEUM; NATIONAL PARK; RAILROAD MUSEUM: The Allegheny Portage Railroad was the first railroad constructed over the Allegheny Mountains. This inclined plane railroad operated between 1834-1854 and was considered a technological wonder in its day and played a critical role in opening the interior of the United States to trade and settlement.

PROGRAMS: Community Outreach; Exhibits; Guided Tours; Interpretation

COLLECTIONS: Summit Level Visitor Center, the historic Lemon House, Engine House #6 Exhibit Shelter, the Skew Arch Bridge.

HOURS: Yr Daily

ADMISSION: $2

GERMANTOWN

7225
Grumblethorpe
5267 Germantown Ave, 19144; (p) (215) 843-4820, (215) 925-2251; (c) Philadelphia

1940/ Philadelphia Society for the Preservation of Landmarks

Maintains John Wister's, county residece built in 1744. Charles Jones Wister, a well-known astronomer, horticulturist and inventor made it his permanent residence in 1819.

COLLECTIONS: [1750-1900] Example of PA German architecture. Artifacts related to Wister family.

HOURS: Yr T, Th, Sa 1-4

ADMISSION: $3

GETTYSBURG

7226
Adams County Historical Society
Schmucker Hall, 111 Seminary Ridge, 17325 [PO Box 4325, 17325-4325]; (p) (717) 334-4723; (c) Adams

Private non-profit/ 1939/ staff: 1(f); 4(p); 14(v)/ members: 525

HISTORICAL SOCIETY; HISTORY MUSEUM: The officially recognized county historical society of Adams County, Pennsylvania.

PROGRAMS: Annual Meeting; Community Outreach; Exhibits; Festivals; Guided Tours; Lectures; Monthly Meeting; Publication; Research Library/Archives; School-Based Curriculum

COLLECTIONS: [1730-present] Primary and secondary sources for the study of many aspects of the history of Adams County from the time of settlement to the present.

HOURS: Yr W,Sa 9-5

7227
Eisenhower National Historic Site
200 Eisenhower Farm Ln, 17325 [97 Taneytown Rd, 17325]; (p) (717) 338-9114; (f) (717) 338-0821; eise_site_manager@nps.gov; www.nps.gov/eise; (c) Adams

Federal/ 1967/ National Park Service/ staff: 10(f); 4(p); 30(v)

HISTORIC SITE; PRESIDENTIAL SITE: Preserves and interprets the home and farm of General Dwight D. Eisenhower, 34th President of the United States.

PROGRAMS: Elder's Programs; Exhibits; Family Programs; Festivals; Guided Tours; Interpretation; Living History; Research Library/Archives; School-Based Curriculum

COLLECTIONS: Decorative arts, clothing, personal items, motorized vehicles, and farm equipment and tools owned by the Eisenhowers; memorabilia documenting Eisenhower's military and political careers; general WWII memorabilia; archaeology and archives.

HOURS: Apr-Oct Daily 9-4; Nov-Mar W-Su 9-4

ADMISSION: $5.25, Student $3.25, Children $2.25

7228
General Lee's Headquarters
401 Buford Ave, 17325; (p) (717) 334-3141; (f) (717) 334-1813

1700

COLLECTIONS: [1863] The finest collection of Civil War artifacts in the U. S. (privately owned).

HOURS: Seasonal

7229
Gettysburg National Military Park
97 Taneytown Road, 17325-2804; (p) (717) 334-1124; (f) (717) 334-1891; GETT_Superintendent@nps.gov; www.nps.gov/gett/pphtml/contacts.html

Federal/ 1895

BATTLEFIELD; HISTORIC SITE; HISTORY MUSEUM; NATIONAL PARK: Maintains site of the largest and bloodist Civil War battle. The Battle of Gettysburg began July 1, 1863 and closed two days later with "Pickett's Charge". Preserves site where President Abraham Lincoln delivered his Gettysburg Address.

PROGRAMS: Exhibits; Interpretation; Lectures

COLLECTIONS: [Civil War] Museum, cemetery, artifacts, memorabilia.

HOURS: Park Grounds: 6-10; Visitor Center: Daily 8-5

ADMISSION: No charge

7230
Historic Gettysburg-Adams County Inc.
12 Lincoln Square, 17325; (p) (717) 334-8188; (f) (717) 338-9491; www.gettysburg.com; (c) Adams

1974/ staff: 1(f); 1(p); 2(v)/ members: 400

HISTORIC PRESERVATION AGENCY: Preserves buildings and sites in Adams County.

PROGRAMS: Annual Meeting; Guided Tours; Lectures; Publication

HOURS: Yr Daily 9-5

7231
Jennie Wade House and Museum
548 Baltimore St, 17325 [777 Baltimore St, 17325]; (p) (717) 334-4100, (717) 334-6294; (f) (717) 334-9100

1800/ Heritage Inns, Inc/ staff: 5(p)

COLLECTIONS: [Civil War] Original furnishings.

HOURS: Mar-Nov

GIRARD

7232
Charlotte Elizabeth Battles Memorial Museum
306 Walnut St, 16417

1861

COLLECTIONS: [1952] 150 years of family artifacts and business papers.

7233
Yellow House
436 Walnut St, 16417

1857

COLLECTIONS: [1890] Battles family possessions.; Family and business papers covering three generations.

GLEN MILLS

7234
Millers House of the Newlin Grist Mill, The
219 S Cheyney Rd, 19342 [219 S Cheyney Rd, 19342]; (p) (610) 459-2359; (f) (610) 459-8709; nnf@erols.com

1704/ Nicholas Newlin Foundation/ staff: 3(f); 6(p); 12(v)

COLLECTIONS: [1704-1760] Domestic tools and furnishings appropriate to mid-18th c Artisan family. Emphasis on lighting and cooking; 100 years of Grist Mill Receipts.

HOURS: Yr

GLENMORE

7235
Springton Manor Farm
860 Springton Rd, 19343 [860 Springton Rd, 19343]; (p) (610) 942-3285; (f) (610) 942-3285; www.chesco.org/ccparks

GRANTHAM

7236
Brethren in Christ Historical Society
[PO Box 310, 17027]; (p) (717) 766-7767; (f) (717) 691-6042; msider@messiah.edu; (c) Cumberland

Private non-profit/ 1978/ Executive Committee/ staff: 1(f); 3(v)/ members: 560/publication: *Brethren in Christ History and Life*

PROGRAMS: Annual Meeting; Guided Tours; Lectures; Publication

COLLECTIONS: [19th-20th c] The Historical Society is affiliated with the Archives of Messiah College and the Brethren in Christ Church.

GREEN LANE

7237
Goschenhoppen Historians, Inc.
116-118 Gravel Pike, 18054 [PO Box 476, 18054-0476]; (p) (610) 234-8953, (610) 367-8286; (c) Montgomery

Private non-profit/ 1962/ Board of Directors/ staff: 1(p); 850(v)/ members: 300/publication: *Lest I Shall be Forgotten; Just a Quilt; and others*

HISTORICAL SOCIETY; HISTORY MUSEUM: Studies, collect, and interprets oral and material culture through annual folk festival and folklife museum.

PROGRAMS: Exhibits; Family Programs; Festivals; Interpretation; Lectures; Living History; Research Library/Archives; School-Based Curriculum

COLLECTIONS: [1730-1930] Local folk and material culture, audiotapes, and printed material, and a country store museum.

HOURS: Apr-Oct Su 1:30-4 and by appt

ADMISSION: Festival fees; under 12 free

GREENCASTLE

7238
Allison-Antrim Museum, Inc.
365 S Ridge Ave, 17225-1157; (p) (717) 597-9010; www.greencastlemuseum.org; (c) Franklin

Private non-profit/ 1995/ Board of Directors/ staff: 45(v)/ members: 170/publication: *Allison-Antrim Annals*

ART MUSEUM; HISTORY MUSEUM; HOUSE MUSEUM; RESEARCH CENTER: Allison-Antrim Museum exhibits, demonstrates, interprets, educates, and provides a research center for the study of local and regional history.

PROGRAMS: Annual Meeting; Community Outreach; Exhibits; Facility Rental; Guided Tours; Interpretation; Publication; Research Library/Archives

COLLECTIONS: Artifacts: local, regional, and state; books: history, research, and genealogy: 90 documents with PA governors' signatures; 15 paintings of internationally known early 12th c African American artist Walter Washington Smith.

HOURS: Yr 2nd Su 1-4 or by appt

ADMISSION: No Charge

GREENSBURG

7239
Westmoreland County Historical Society
951 Old Salem Rd, 15601; (p) (724) 836-1800; (f) (724) 836-1653; history@wchspa.com; www.wchspa.com; (c) Westmoreland

Private non-profit/ 1908/ staff: 3(f); 2(p); 25(v)/ members: 903/publication: *Westmoreland Chronicle*

GENEALOGICAL SOCIETY; HISTORIC SITE; HISTORICAL SOCIETY; HOUSE MUSEUM; RESEARCH CENTER: Operates the Hanna's Town historic site, first English courts west of the Allegheny Mountains; preserves genealogical and local history materials in research library.

PROGRAMS: Annual Meeting; Community Outreach; Exhibits; Facility Rental; Family Programs; Festivals; Guided Tours; Interpretation; Lectures; Living History; Publication; Reenactments; Research Library/Archives; School-Based Curriculum

COLLECTIONS: [1769-1782] Photographs, diaries, journals, maps, and papers; original General Order Book, Morning Book and Letter Book of the PA 11th Volunteers from the Civil War.

HOURS: Office/Library/Archives: Yr M-T, Th-F 9-5, W 9-8, Sa 10-1; Hanna's Town Historic Site Apr-Oct T-Sa 10-4, Su 1-4

ADMISSION: $2, Children $1; Hanna's Town; Library $2

HANOVER

7240
Hanover Area Historical Society
105 High St, 17331 [PO Box 305, 17331-2909]; (p) (717) 632-3207; (f) (717) 632-5199; carbrn@blagenet.net; www.hellohanover.com; (c) York

Private non-profit/ 1963/ staff: 1(f); 1(p); 50(v)/publication: *Hanover History*

GARDEN; HISTORIC SITE; HISTORICAL SOCIETY; HOUSE MUSEUM; RESEARCH CENTER: Collects, exhibits, and maintains area artifacts and conducts community programs.

PROGRAMS: Annual Meeting; Exhibits; Festivals; Garden Tours; Guided Tours; Lectures; Living History; Publication; Research Library/Archives; School-Based Curriculum

COLLECTIONS: [1800-present] Artifacts and papers pertaining to area.

HOURS: May-Oct T-F 9:30-2:30

ADMISSION: $1; Group rates

7241
NEAS House Museum
113 W Chestnut St, 17331 [PO Box 305, 17331]; (p) (717) 632-3207; (f) (717) 632-5199

1783/ Hanover Area Historical Society/ staff: 1(f); 1(p)

COLLECTIONS: [1800s] Early photos of area, deeds, indentures, coverlets; 75 reproduced Historical flags covering the Exploration, Colonial, Rev. War, Civil War, 1812, Expansion growth of our county to 50 states, and W W I & II.

HOURS: Seasonal

HARLEYSVILLE

7242
Heckler Plains Folklife Society
Morris & Landis Rd, 19438 [474 Main St, 19438]; (p) (215) 256-8087; (c) Montgomery

Private non-profit/ 1975/ staff: 25(v)/ members: 75

GARDEN; GENEALOGICAL SOCIETY; HISTORIC SITE; HISTORICAL SOCIETY; HISTORY MUSEUM; LIVING HISTORY/OUTDOOR MUSEUM: Maintains and restores Heckler Farmstead.

PROGRAMS: Exhibits; Festivals; Garden Tours; Guided Tours; Interpretation; Lectures; Living History; Reenactments; School-Based Curriculum

COLLECTIONS: [18th-19th c] Farming, household items, carpentry and blacksmithing tools.

HOURS: Yr by appt

7243
Mennonite Historians of Eastern Pennsylvania
565 Yoder Rd, 19438 [PO Box 82, 19438]; (p) (215) 256-3020; (f) (215) 256-3023; info@mhep.org; www.mhep.org; (c) Montgomery

Private non-profit/ 1974/ Board of Trustees/ staff: 1(f); 5(p); 60(v)/ members: 592/publication: *MHEP Quarterly*

HISTORICAL SOCIETY; HISTORY MUSEUM: Tells the story of the Mennonite faith and life in southeastern Pennsylvania. Also provides exhibits, library and archives on local history, church history and genealogy.

PROGRAMS: Exhibits; Festivals; Film/Video; Garden Tours; Guided Tours; Interpretation; Lectures; Publication; Research Library/Archives

COLLECTIONS: [1528-present] Information and artifacts on Mennonite life in southeastern Pennsylvania, including Bucks, Chester, Montgomery, Berks, Lehigh and Northampton Counties.

HOURS: Yr T-F 10-5, Sa 10-2

ADMISSION: Donations requested

HARMONY

7244
Historic Harmony Inc.
218 Mercer St, 16037 [PO Box 524, 16037-0524]; (p) (724) 452-7342, (888) 821-4822; (c) Butler

Private non-profit/ 1943/ Board of Directors/ staff: 1(p); 50(v)/ members: 375/publication: *Historic Harmony, Inc.*

HISTORY MUSEUM: Preserves and interprets town history from its founding in 1804 by German communal Harmony Society to later settlement by Mennonites and Victorian era.

PROGRAMS: Annual Meeting; Exhibits; Facility Rental; Family Programs; Festivals; Guided Tours; Lectures; Living History; Publication; Research Library/Archives

COLLECTIONS: Museum artifacts, 1,000 volumes.

HOURS: T-Su 1-4

ADMISSION: $3.50, Children $1.50

HARRISBURG

7245
Capitol Preservation Committee
3rd St, Capitol Complex, 17120 [Room 630, MC Bldg, 17120]; (p) (717) 783-6484; (f) (717) 772-0742; rkemper@legis.state.pa.us; cpc.leg.state.pa.us; (c) Daulphin

State/ 1982/ Capitol Preservation Committee and Dept. of General Services/ staff: 10(f)

HISTORIC PRESERVATION AGENCY; HISTORIC SITE: Coordinates and oversees programs to conserve, restore, preserve, and maintain the PA State Capitol and it historic contents for the future.

PROGRAMS: Exhibits; Guided Tours; Publication

COLLECTIONS: [1906] State Capitol Building, artwork, murals, sculpture.

7246
Dorothea Dix Museum/Harrisburg State Hospital
Cameron & Maclay St, 17105 [Harrisburg State Hospital, Pouch A, 17105]; (p) (717) 772-7561; (f) (717) 772-6015; jleopold@dpw.state.pa.us; www.paheritage.com/dadix.html; (c) Dauphin

State/ 1985/ staff: 1(f); 6(v)/publication: City on the Hill

HISTORY MUSEUM: Originally built in 1853 as a library for female patients, it was restored in 1985 and exhibits historic objects, documents, and photos that describe how the hospital served the mentally ill in PA for over a century.

PROGRAMS: Guided Tours; Publication; Research Library/Archives

COLLECTIONS: [1851-present] Historic photographs illustrating hospital life during the last century, original letters, records, old hospital furniture, medical equipment, art, documents describing innovative programs, clothing, and implements made at the hospital.

HOURS: Yr by appt

7247
Fire Museum of Greater Harrisburg
1820 N 4th St, 17102; (p) (717) 232-8915; (f) (717) 232-8916; (c) Dauphin

Private non-profit/ 1995/ members: 360/publication: Museum News

HISTORY MUSEUM: Restored 1899 Victorian-style fire station, apparatus, exhibits through video and sound displays and fire safety programs.

PROGRAMS: Annual Meeting; Exhibits; Facility Rental; Guided Tours; Lectures; Publication; School-Based Curriculum

COLLECTIONS: [1850-1960]

HOURS: Yr M-Sa 10-4

ADMISSION: $5

7248
Fort Hunter Mansion and Park
5300 N Front St, 17110; (p) (717) 599-5751; (f) (717) 599-5838; (c) Dauphin

County/ 1933/ staff: 2(f); 10(p); 20(v)/ members: 300

HISTORIC SITE; HOUSE MUSEUM: Explores PA history through buildings, interiors, photos, and archives housed in a 40-acre estate on the bank of the Susquehanna River.

PROGRAMS: Annual Meeting; Community Outreach; Concerts; Exhibits; Facility Rental; Family Programs; Garden Tours; Guided Tours; Interpretation; Lectures; Living History; Reenactments

COLLECTIONS: [1850-1910] Domestic items owned by Fort Hunter families: clothing, photographs, archives, books, furniture, and other decorative arts.

HOURS: May-Dec T-Sa 10-4:30, Su 12-4:30

ADMISSION: $4, Student $2, Seniors $3

7249
Historical Society of Dauphin County
219 S Front St, 17104-1619; (p) (717) 233-3462; (c) Dauphin

Private non-profit/ 1869/ staff: 5(p); 20(v)/ members: 400/publication: Oracle

HISTORICAL SOCIETY

PROGRAMS: Community Outreach; Exhibits; Facility Rental; Guided Tours; Publication; Research Library/Archives

COLLECTIONS: [Late 18th c-present] John Harris/Simon Cameron Mansion. Tall-case clocks, 1770 Philadelphia Chest-on-chest, fine arts, folk arts, quilts, coverlets, china, silver; Papers of Harrisburg founder; papers of Simon Cameron as Secretary of War and Minister to Russia; papers of John The Fighting Parson" elder of Revolutionary War fame; over a million photographic images available for reprint.

HOURS: Yr Library: M-F

7250
Pennsylvania Federation of Museums and Historical Organizations
400 N St, Commonwealth Keystone Bldg, 17120 [PO Box 1026, 17120-0053]; (p) (717) 787-3253; (f) (717) 772-4698; jean@pamusums.org; www.museumpa.org; (c) Dauphin

Private non-profit/ 1905/ staff: 2(f); 2(p)/ members: 500

Supports, sustains, invigorates, and expands the role that museums and historical organizations play in their communities and throughtout the commonwealth. It defines a shared vision for PA's community of museums and historical organizations

7251
Pennsylvania Historical and Museum Commission
300 N St, 17120-1024; (p) (717) 787-3362; (f) (717) 705-0482; www.phmc.state.pa.us; (c) Dauphin

State/ 1913/ staff: 333(f); 191(p); 2500(v)/publication: Pennsylvania Heritage

HISTORIC PRESERVATION AGENCY; HISTORIC SITE; HISTORY MUSEUM: Operates state museum and archives, 27 historic sites, and museums, state historic preservation program; records management program, and public history programs.

PROGRAMS: Community Outreach; Concerts; Exhibits; Facility Rental; Family Programs; Festivals; Film/Video; Garden Tours; Guided Tours; Interpretation; Lectures; Living History; Publication; Reenactments; Research

Library/Archives; School-Based Curriculum

COLLECTIONS: [18th-20th c] Government archives, manuscripts, photos and negatives, magazines, microfilm, archaeological artifacts, paleontology/geology specimens, natural science specimens, decorative art, and fine arts objects.

HOURS: M-Sa 9-5, Su 12-5

ADMISSION: State museum free; Sites and museum fees vary

7252
State Museum of Pennsylvania, The
300 N St, 17120-0024; (p) (717) 787-4980; (f) (717) 783-4558; museum@statemuseumpa .org; www.statemuseumpa.org; (c) Dauphin

State/ 1905/ Pennsylvania Historical and Museum Commission/ staff: 46(f); 33(p); 356(v)/ members: 385

HISTORY MUSEUM: Collects and preserves objects associated with state geology, paleontology, natural science, archaeology, history, and fine arts.

PROGRAMS: Annual Meeting; Community Outreach; Concerts; Exhibits; Facility Rental; Family Programs; Film/Video; Interpretation; Lectures; Publication; Research Library/ Archives; School-Based Curriculum; Theatre

COLLECTIONS: [320 million BC-present] Fine arts, Native American and historic archaeology; natural science; technology, geology, and paleontology.

HOURS: Yr T-Sa 9-5, Su 12-5

ADMISSION: No charge

7253
West Hanover Township Historical Society
7171 Allentown Blvd, 17112 [1033 Piketown Rd, 17112-9058]; (p) (717) 469-0730; donald7108@aol.com; (c) Dauphin

Private non-profit/ 19/ Board of Directors/ staff: 10(v)/ members: 35

HISTORICAL SOCIETY: Preserves local history.

PROGRAMS: Annual Meeting; Exhibits; Lectures

COLLECTIONS: [18th-20th c] Family histories, photographs, newspaper clippings, miscellaneous items and artifacts.

HOURS: Yr by appt

HARRISON CITY

7254
Bushy Run Battlefield
Rt 993, 15636 [PO Box 468, 15636-0468]; (p) (724) 527-5584; (f) (724) 527-5610; jgiblin@phmc.state.pa.us; (c) Westmoreland

State/ 1918/ PA Historical and Museum Commission/ staff: 2(f); 7(p); 60(v)/ members: 185

HISTORIC SITE: Preserves site of Pontiac's War and Pennsylvania's only recognized and interpreted Native American/European battlefield site.

PROGRAMS: Annual Meeting; Community Outreach; Exhibits; Facility Rental; Festivals; Guided Tours; Interpretation; Lectures; Living History; Reenactments; School-Based Curriculum

COLLECTIONS: [1758-1763] Military artifacts and artwork relating to the history of Fort Dusquesne, Fort Pitt, early Pittsburgh, and Native American culture.

HOURS: Yr W-Sa 10-4:30, Su 12-4:30

HATBORO

7255
Millbrook Society/Amy B. Yerkes Museum, The
32 N York Rd, 2nd fl, 19040 [PO Box 506, 19040-0506]; (p) (215) 675-0119; mill brook@voicenet.com; (c) Montgomery

Private non-profit/ 1984/ staff: 77(v)/ members: 170/publication: *The Grist*

HISTORICAL SOCIETY; HISTORY MUSEUM: Promotes and preserves local histor, maintains archaeological program and archive for research on topics of genealogy and history.

PROGRAMS: Annual Meeting; Exhibits; Publication; Research Library/Archives

COLLECTIONS: [18th-20th c] Artifacts, maritime archaeological materials, historic and genealogical archives and photographs.

HOURS: Yr T 7:30-9:30

ADMISSION: No charge

HAVERFORD

7256
Friends Historical Association
Haverford College Library, 370 Lancaster Ave, 19041; (p) (610) 896-1161; (f) (610) 896-1102; fha@haverford.edu; www.haverford.edu/library /fha/fha.html; (c) Delaware

Private non-profit/ 1873/ staff: 1(p); 21(v)/ members: 800/publication: *Quaker History*

Studies, preserves, and publishes material relating to the history of the Religious Society of Friends.

PROGRAMS: Annual Meeting; Lectures; Publication

7257
Haverford College Library, Special Collections
370 Lancaster Ave, 19041; (p) (610) 896-1161; (f) (610) 896-1102; elapsans@haver ford.edu; www.haverford.edu/library/sc/sc. html; (c) Delaware

Private non-profit/ 1833/ Board of Managers/ staff: 2(f); 1(p); 1(v)

LIBRARY AND/OR ARCHIVES: Collects and preserves history, biography, religious thought and fiction relating to Quakers and all special materials for college curriculum and archives.

PROGRAMS: Exhibits; Research Library/ Archives

COLLECTIONS: [1680-present] Books, manuscripts, and graphics relating to Society of Friends; other rare books, manuscripts, and graphics, and photographs.

HOURS: Yr M-F 9-12:30/1:30-4:30

HAVERTOWN

7258
Haverford Township Historical Society
Karakung Dr, 19083 [PO Box 825, 19083]; (p) (610) 446-7980; www.delcohistory.org/hths; (c) Delaware

Private non-profit/ 1939/ Board of Directors/ staff: 15(v)/ members: 175

HISTORIC SITE; HISTORICAL SOCIETY; HOUSE MUSEUM; LIVING HISTORY/OUTDOOR MUSEUM; RESEARCH CENTER: Preserves documents, property, and information relating to local history.

PROGRAMS: Annual Meeting; Exhibits; Festivals; Guided Tours; Interpretation; Lectures; Living History; School-Based Curriculum

COLLECTIONS: [1710-present] Welsh Society of Friends, books, Bibles, family documents, photographs, clothing, and newspaper articles.

HOURS: May-Oct 1st Sa-Su 1-4 and by appt

ADMISSION: $2, Student $1, Children $1

7259
Historic Grange Estate
Myrtle Ave and Warwick Rd, 19083; (p) (610) 446-4958; www.delcocvb.org/histor.htm

Township of Haverford

GARDEN; HOUSE MUSEUM: Maintains historic 18c home and gardens. Listed on National Register.

COLLECTIONS: [17c-present]

HERSHEY

7260
Derry Township Historical Society
50 N Linden Rd, 17033 [PO Box 316, 17033]; (p) (717) 520-0748; (f) (717) 520-0748; dths@hersheyhistory.com; (c) Dauphin

Private non-profit/ 1991/ Board of Directors/ staff: 50(v)/ members: 1364/publication: *Reflections*

HISTORICAL SOCIETY; HISTORY MUSEUM: Collects, preserves, and shares artifacts and papers relating to Derry Township, which includes the community of Hershey. Encourages the preservation of local history.

PROGRAMS: Annual Meeting; Exhibits; Festivals; Guided Tours; Lectures; Publication; Research Library/Archives

COLLECTIONS: [1875-present] Artifacts and papers of churches, schools, houses, organizations, people, events and growth of Derry Township; some historical buildings.

HOURS: Yr M 9-4:30, W 12-4:30, Sa 9-12

ADMISSION: No charge

7261
Hershey Community Archives
340 Pennsy Supply Rd, 17033 [PO Box 64, 17033]; (p) (717) 566-8116; (f) (717) 566-8004; pcassidy@hca.microserve.com; (c) Dauphin

Private non-profit/ 1985/ M.S. Hershey Foundation/ staff: 1(f); 2(p)

CORPORATE ARCHIVES/MUSEUM; LIBRARY AND/OR ARCHIVES: Promotes the study and understanding of Milton S. Hershey, his vision, legacy, and the community of Hershey. Collects and runs an active oral history program.

PROGRAMS: Community Outreach; Elder's Programs; Interpretation; Publication; Research Library/Archives

COLLECTIONS: [1903-present] Records of Hershey Foods Corporation and its subsidiaries, Hershey Entertainment and Resorts. Records that document Hershey, a planned model industrial town, including photographs and oral histories.

HOURS: Yr M-F 8-4:30

7262
Hershey Museum
170 W Hershey Park Dr, 17033; (p) (717) 534-3439; (f) (717) 534-8940; www.hershey-museum.microserve.net; (c) Dauphin

Private non-profit/ 1933/ M.S. Hershey Foundation/ staff: 10(f); 14(p); 365(v)/ members: 2560

CORPORATE ARCHIVES/MUSEUM; HISTORY MUSEUM: Interprets, collects, and preserves the history of Hershey, its founder Milton Hershey, and the chocolate company.

PROGRAMS: Community Outreach; Concerts; Elder's Programs; Exhibits; Facility Rental; Family Programs; Festivals; Guided Tours; Interpretation; Lectures; Living History; Publication; Research Library/Archives; School-Based Curriculum

COLLECTIONS: [19th-20th c] Hershey-related artifacts: vehicles, products, equipment, and decorative arts. Native American objects and PA-German regional artifacts.

HOURS: Yr Daily 10-5

ADMISSION: $5, Children $2.50, Seniors $4.50

HIGHSPIRE

7263
Highspire Historical Society
273 2nd St, 17034 [204 Frederick St, 17034]; (p) (717) 939-3518; (c) Dauphin

1977/ Executive Committee/publication: *Highspire Directory*

HISTORIC SITE; HISTORICAL SOCIETY; HISTORY MUSEUM: Collects, preserves, and interprets local history.

PROGRAMS: Annual Meeting; Community Outreach; Exhibits; Guided Tours; Interpretation; Publication

COLLECTIONS: [Mid 19th c-present] Historic sites (ex. 1832 brewery), furniture, printed material, pictures, maps, and artifacts.

HOURS: Yr by appt

HONESDALE

7264
Wayne County Historical Society
810 Main St, 18431 [PO Box 446, 18431]; (p) (570) 253-3240; (f) (570) 253-5204; wchs@ptd.net; (c) Wayne

Private non-profit/ 1917/ County/ staff: 1(f); 3(p); 50(v)/ members: 700

GENEALOGICAL SOCIETY; HISTORICAL SOCIETY; HISTORY MUSEUM: Collects and disseminates local history in museum and library.

PROGRAMS: Annual Meeting; Community Outreach; Concerts; Exhibits; Family Programs; Festivals; Film/Video; Guided Tours; Interpretation; Lectures; Living History; Publication; Research Library/Archives; School-Based Curriculum

COLLECTIONS: Artifacts, paintings and works on paper by local artists; working full-scale model of first locomotive to turn on track in the US.

HOURS: Jan, Feb Sa-Su 10-4; Mar-Dec T-Sa 10-4; Summer-Fall T-Sa 10-4, Su 12-4

ADMISSION: $3, Children $2; Under 12/Mbrs/students doing library research free

HORSHAM

7265
Graeme Park
859 County Line Rd, 19044; (p) (215) 343-0965; (f) (215) 343-2223; smile@pnmc.state.pa.us; (c) Montgomery

State/ 1957/ PA Historical and Museum Commission/ staff: 1(f); 2(p); 28(v)/ members: 54

HISTORIC SITE; HISTORY MUSEUM; HOUSE MUSEUM; LIVING HISTORY/OUTDOOR MUSEUM: Maintains architecturally significant 18th c house listed on the National Register. Noted for its untouched mid-18th c rooms; new research and interpretation of the African presence.

PROGRAMS: Annual Meeting; Exhibits; Facility Rental; Festivals; Guided Tours; Interpretation; Living History; School-Based Curriculum

COLLECTIONS: [Mid-late 18th c] Decorative arts, mostly furniture, and ceramics.

HOURS: Yr W-Sa 9:30-4:30, Su 12-4

ADMISSION: $3.50

HUNTINGDON

7266
Huntingdon County Historical Society
100-106 4th St, 16652 [PO Box 305, 16652]; (p) (814) 643-5449; (f) (814) 643-2711; hchs@vicon.net; www.huntingdon.net/hchs; (c) Huntingdon

Private non-profit/ 1937/ staff: 2(p); 8(v)/ members: 500

HISTORICAL SOCIETY: Promotes county history through programs, exhibits, publications, research facilities, house, church, and industrial museums.

PROGRAMS: Annual Meeting; Community Outreach; Exhibits; Facility Rental; Guided Tours; Interpretation; Lectures; Publication; Research Library/Archives

COLLECTIONS: [1750-present] Archives, photographs, fine arts, household furnishings, costumes, toys and children's books.

HUNTINGDON VALLEY

7267
Pennypack Ecological Trust
2955 Edge Hill Rd, 19006; (p) (215) 657-

0830; (f) (215) 657-1679; pennypack@compuserve.com; (c) Montgomery

Private non-profit/ 1970/ Board of Directors/ staff: 5(f); 2(p); 100(v)/ members: 2000/publication: Bulletin

PROFESSIONAL ORGANIZATION: Protects, restores, and preserves the natural landscape of the Pennypack Creek Valley.

PROGRAMS: Annual Meeting; Elder's Programs; Exhibits; Family Programs; Guided Tours; Interpretation; Publication; Research Library/Archives

COLLECTIONS: [Mid 19th c-present] Two stone arch bridges, three farmhouses, four mill and dam ruins, seven miles of hiking trails in a 640-acre natural area consisting of mature and second-growth forest, and meadowlands.

HOURS: Yr M-F 9-5, Sa 10-2, Su 1-3

INDIANA

7268
Historical and Genealogical Society of Indiana County, PA
200 S 6th St, 15701; (p) (724) 463-9600; (f) (724) 463-9899; clarkhs@microserve.net; www.rootsweb.com/~paicgs; (c) Indiana

Private non-profit/ 1938/ staff: 2(f); 30(v)/ members: 1300/publication: The Clark House News

GENEALOGICAL SOCIETY; HISTORICAL SOCIETY: Preserves artifacts, memorabilia, and information pertaining to county history and genealogy.

PROGRAMS: Annual Meeting; Exhibits; Publication; Reenactments

COLLECTIONS: [1850-present] Genealogical library contains documents, reference books, newspapers, family histories, cemetery records, period clothing, military artifacts, photographs, and local memorabilia.

HOURS: Yr M-F 9-4, Sa 10-3

7269
James M. Stewart Museum Foundation/ The Jimmy Stewart Museum, The
845 Philadelphia St, 15701 [PO Box 1, 15701]; (p) (724) 349-6112, (800) 835-4669; curator@jimmy.org; www.jimmy.org; (c) Indiana

Private non-profit/ 1993/ The James M. Stewart Museum Foundation/ staff: 2(f); 1(p); 25(v)/ members: 200/publication: The Stewart Sentinel

HISTORY MUSEUM: Preserves and interprets the life history and career of actor James Maitland Stewart.

PROGRAMS: Exhibits; Festivals; Film/Video; Lectures; Publication; Research Library/Archives; Theatre

COLLECTIONS: [1900-present] Scripts, costumes, uniforms, film stills, movie posters, photographs, awards, and artifacts relating to the history of the Stewart family, Indiana County, and Stewart's entertainment and military careers.

HOURS: Jan-Mar W-Su 10-5; Apr-Dec Daily 10-5

ADMISSION: $5, Student $4, Children $3, Seniors $4; Under 7 free

JAMISON

7270
Warwick Township Historical Society
1641 Old York Rd, 18929 [PO Box 107, 18929]; (p) (215) 918-1754; (f) (215) 491-5111; (c) Bucks

Private non-profit/ 1991/ members: 214/publication: Moland Gazette

HISTORICAL SOCIETY: Restores the Moldand House, Washington's Headquarters for 13 days in August 1777, while 11,000 troops camped nearby. It was at this site that Lafayette joined the American army.

PROGRAMS: Annual Meeting; Exhibits; Family Programs; Festivals; Guided Tours; Interpretation; Lectures; Living History; Publication; Reenactments; School-Based Curriculum

COLLECTIONS: [Late 18th c] Revolutionary War artifacts and ongoing archaeological site.

HOURS: Yr Sa 9-12

ADMISSION: $3, Student $1

JENKINTOWN

7271
Old York Road Historical Society
c/o Jenkintown Library, Vista and Old York Rd, 19046; (p) (215) 886-8590; (f) (215) 884-2243; (c) Montgomery

Private non-profit/ 1936/ Executive Council/ staff: 3(v)/ members: 250/publication: Old York Historical Society Bulletin

HISTORICAL SOCIETY: Collects, preserves, and makes available for research to the general public materials relating to the history of the communities along the Old York Road Corridor.

PROGRAMS: Annual Meeting; Guided Tours; Publication

COLLECTIONS: [1700s-present] Atlases, journals, individual research collections, community, and governmental records, Colonial and Civil War records, state archives, photographs, and genealogy materials.

HOURS: Yr M 7-9, T 11-2, W 10-3 and by appt.

JIM THORPE

7272
Harry Packer Mansion, The
Packer Hill, 18229 [PO Box 458, 18229]; (p) (717) 325-8566; mystery@murdermansion; www.murdermansion.com

1874/ staff: 3(f)

COLLECTIONS: [1874-1881]

HOURS: Yr

7273
Mauch Chunk Historical Society of Carbon County
14 W Broadway, 18229 [PO Box 273, 18229]; (p) (570) 325-4439; (c) Carbon

Private non-profit/ 1975/ staff: 1(f); 1(p); 450(v)

ART MUSEUM; HISTORICAL SOCIETY: Guardian of the historic heritage of this section of the Delaware and Lehigh National Heritage Corridor. Housed in the Marion House Exhibit Center, the first volunteer fire department in Carbon County.

PROGRAMS: Annual Meeting; Community Outreach; Concerts; Exhibits; Facility Rental; Festivals; Lectures; Research Library/Archives; Theatre

COLLECTIONS: [1840-present] Sears Collection of Old Mauch Chunk: coal mining, canals, and railroads.

HOURS: Yr Th-Su 12-5

ADMISSION: No charge, except concerts

JOHNSTOWN

7274
Johnstown Area Heritage Association
201 Sixth Ave, 15907 [PO Box 1889, 15907]; (p) (814) 539-1889; (f) (814) 535-1931; jaha@ctcnet.net; (c) Cambria

Private non-profit/ 1971/ staff: 11(f); 4(p); 18(v)/ members: 2200/publication: *JAHA Update*

HISTORY MUSEUM

PROGRAMS: Community Outreach; Exhibits; Facility Rental; Family Programs; Festivals; Film/Video; Guided Tours; Interpretation; Lectures; Research Library/Archives; School-Based Curriculum

COLLECTIONS: [19th-20th c] Local history artifacts and archive documenting the 1889 Johnstown Flood, regional steel and coal industries, ethnic groups.

HOURS: Yr Daily

KENNETT SQUARE

7275
Longwood Gardens
US Rt 1, 19348 [PO Box 501, 19348]; (p) (610) 388-1000; www.longwoodgardens.org; (c) Chester

Private non-profit/ 1906/ staff: 174(f); 177(p); 233(v)

GARDEN; HISTORIC SITE: Offers horticultural displays with 40 indoor/outdoor gardens; 11,000 types of plants; fountains, educational programs, annual horticultural, and performing arts events.

PROGRAMS: Community Outreach; Concerts; Exhibits; Facility Rental; Family Programs; Festivals; Garden Tours; Guided Tours; Interpretation; Lectures; School-Based Curriculum; Theatre

COLLECTIONS: [18th-20th c] 1,050 acres of gardens, woodlands, meadows, and a conservatory. Exhibits feature artifacts detailing the 300 year evolution of the property.

HOURS: Yr Daily

KULPSVILLE

7276
Welsh Valley Preservation Society
850 Weikel Rd, 10443 [PO Box 261, 19443]; (p) (215) 368-2480; (f) (215) 368-2480; wvps@morganloghouse.org; www.morganloghouse.org; (c) Montgomery

Private non-profit/ 1970/ staff: 2(f); 13(v)/ members: 51

HISTORIC SITE; HISTORY MUSEUM; HOUSE MUSEUM: Educates the public about the history of Towamencin Township, Montgomery County and its place in PA history as demonstrated by the architecture of the Morgan Log House, the lives of its past residents, and their material culture.

PROGRAMS: Community Outreach; Concerts; Exhibits; Family Programs; Festivals; Garden Tours; Guided Tours; Interpretation; Lectures; Living History; Publication; Reenactments; Research Library/Archives; School-Based Curriculum

COLLECTIONS: [17th-19th c] Domestic material culture, 700 books.

HOURS: Apr 1-Dec 30 F-Su 10-6 appt

ADMISSION: $3, Student $2, Seniors $2; Under 5 free

KUTZTOWN

7277
Pennsylvania Dutch Folk Culture Society
[PO Box 306, 19530]; (p) (610) 683-1589; (c) Berks

Private non-profit/ 1965/ staff: 1(f); 5(v)/ members: 380

GENEALOGICAL SOCIETY

PROGRAMS: Annual Meeting; Exhibits; Festivals; Research Library/Archives; School-Based Curriculum

COLLECTIONS: Artifacts and memorabilia related to German immigrants from the Pfaltz area in Germany and their subsequent lifestyles and folklore. Immigration, church and tax records; genealogy and Civil War history.

HOURS: Yr M, W, F

LANCASTER

7278
Amish Farm and House
2395 Rt 30 East, 17602; (p) (717) 394-6185; (f) (717) 394-4857; www.800padutch.com/ath.html

1805/ Privately owned/ staff: 5(f); 55(p); 1(v)

COLLECTIONS: [1730s-Present] Prehistoric, Archaic, and Woodland period Indian artifacts; conestoga wagon; early American farming equipment; blacksmith equipment.

HOURS: Yr

7279
Demuth Foundation
114 E King St, 17602; (p) (717) 299-9940; (f) (717) 299-9749; info@demuth.org; www.demuth.org; (c) Lancaster

Private non-profit/ 1981/ Board of Directors/ staff: 1(f); 4(p); 27(v)/ members: 371/publication: *Demuth Dialogue*

ART MUSEUM; GARDEN; HISTORIC SITE; HOUSE MUSEUM: Preserves and showcases the home, gardens, artworks, and family heritage of renowned early American modernist painter, Charles Demuth.

PROGRAMS: Annual Meeting; Community Outreach; Exhibits; Garden Tours; Guided Tours; Interpretation; Lectures; Publication; Research Library/Archives

COLLECTIONS: [1780-1935] House, gardens, family business, memorabilia, and over 25 original works of Charles Demuth.

HOURS: Feb-Dec T-Sa 10-4, Su 1-4

7280
Evangelical and Reformed Historical Society of the UCC
555 W James St, 17603; (p) (717) 290-8711; (f) (717) 393-4254; erhs@lts.org; www.lts.org/erhs/erhs.htm; (c) Lancaster

1863/ staff: 3(p); 1(v)/ members: 400

GENEALOGICAL SOCIETY; HISTORICAL SOCIETY: Acquires, maintains, and preserves the records of the Reformed and the Evangelical and Reformed Church. Makes available to visitors local church and genealogy records.

PROGRAMS: Annual Meeting; Lectures; Research Library/Archives

COLLECTIONS: [1700-1900s] Reformed Church records, Evangelical and Reformed Church records, their pastors, manuscripts, diaries, and genealogical collections.

HOURS: Yr M-Th 9-4

ADMISSION: $5/day gen rsrch

7281
Heritage Center of Lancaster County Inc.
Penn Square, 17603 [13 W King St, 17603]; (p) (717) 299-6440; (f) (717) 299-6916; heritage@paonline.com; www.lancasterheritage.com; (c) Lancaster

Private non-profit/ 1974/ staff: 4(f); 4(p); 41(v)/ members: 600

HERITAGE AREA: Uses the decorative and fine arts of Lancaster County to teach the history and diversity of the region.

PROGRAMS: Exhibits; Family Programs; Interpretation; Lectures

COLLECTIONS: [18th-20th c] Local history and arts such as furniture, silver, paintings, folk art, textiles, china, glass, industrial patterns, toys, and ornamental iron and metals.

HOURS: Apr-Dec T-Sa

7282
Historic Rock Ford Plantation
881 Rock Ford Rd, 17608 [PO Box 264, 17608-0264]; (p) (717) 392-7223; (f) (717) 392-7283; rockford@redrose.net; www.800padutch.com/rockford/html; (c) Lancaster

Private non-profit/ 1958/ staff: 2(f); 7(p); 75(v)/ members: 220

HOUSE MUSEUM: Maintains site to promote knowledge of General Edward Hand's life and times for the cultural and educational benefit of the public.

PROGRAMS: Annual Meeting; Community Outreach; Concerts; Exhibits; Facility Rental; Family Programs; Guided Tours; Interpretation; Reenactments

COLLECTIONS: [1794-1802] Regional period antiques conforming to Hand's estate inventory.

HOURS: Apr-Oct T-F 10-4, Su 12-4

ADMISSION: $4.50, Children $2.50, Seniors $3.50

7283
James Buchanan Foundation for the Preservation of Wheatland
1120 Marietta Ave, 17603; (p) (717) 392-8721; (f) (717) 295-8825; wheatland@wheatland.org; www.wheatland.org; (c) Lancaster

Private non-profit/ 1936/ staff: 4(f); 10(p); 80(v)/ members: 200

HISTORIC SITE; PRESIDENTIAL SITE: Preserves, restores, and maintains Wheatland, the home of President James Buchanan, provides education and interpretion about his life and times.

PROGRAMS: Annual Meeting; Community Outreach; Concerts; Exhibits; Facility Rental; Family Programs; Film/Video; Garden Tours; Guided Tours; Interpretation; Lectures; School-Based Curriculum

COLLECTIONS: [1848-1863] Artifacts associated with President James Buchanan and members of his family; period items furnish and interpret the mansion.

HOURS: Apr-Dec Daily 10-4

ADMISSION: $5.50, Student $3.50, Children $1.75, Seniors $4.50

7284
Lancaster County Historical Society
230 N President Ave, 17603; (p) (717) 392-4633; (f) (717) 293-2739; lchs@ptd.net; www.lanclio.org; (c) Lancaster

Private non-profit/ 1886/ staff: 3(f); 7(p); 106(v)/ members: 1850

GENEALOGICAL SOCIETY; HISTORICAL SOCIETY; RESEARCH CENTER: Tripartite focuses on library, archives, and artifacts.

PROGRAMS: Annual Meeting; Community Outreach; Exhibits; Family Programs; Interpretation; Lectures; Living History; Reenactments; Research Library/Archives; School-Based Curriculum

COLLECTIONS: [18th-20th c] Library: 12,000 volumes on local, regional, and family history. Archives contain extensive governmental and personal records dating from early 1700s, including 10,000 historic photos and artifacts reflecting 300 years of county history.

HOURS: Yr T, Th 9:30-9:30, W, F-Sa 9:30-4:30

ADMISSION: $5; Free to members

7285
Lancaster Mennonite Historical Society
2211 Millstream Rd, 17602-1499; (p) (717) 393-9745; (f) (717) 393-8751; (c) Lancaster

Private non-profit/ 1958/ staff: 7(f); 1(p); 100(v)/ members: 2800/publication: *Mirror; Pennsylvania Mennonite Heritage*

GENEALOGICAL SOCIETY; HISTORICAL SOCIETY; HISTORY MUSEUM; RESEARCH CENTER

PROGRAMS: Annual Meeting; Community Outreach; Concerts; Exhibits; Facility Rental; Family Programs; Festivals; Guided Tours; Lectures; Publication; Research Library/ Archives

COLLECTIONS: [1710-present] Focuses on historical background, religious thought and expression, culture, and family history of Mennonite and Amish related groups originating in PA and including their European background.

HOURS: Yr T-Sa

7286
Landis Valley Museum
2451 Kissel Hill Rd, 17601; (p) (717) 569-0401; (f) (717) 560-2147; stemiller@state.pa.us; www.landisvalleymuseum.org; (c) Lancaster

State/ 1953/ PA Historical and Museum Commission/ staff: 15(f); 55(p); 700(v)/ members: 500

HISTORY MUSEUM: Nationally significant living history museum that collects, conserves, exhibits, and interprets PA German material culture and heritage.

PROGRAMS: Community Outreach; Exhibits; Festivals; Film/Video; Garden Tours; Guided Tours; Interpretation; Lectures; Living History

COLLECTIONS: [1750-1940] Tools, equipment, ceramic, glass, textiles, iron objects, broadsides, toys, vehicles, books, plants, animals, diaries, trade catalogs, glass plate negatives, furniture, musical instruments, fine arts, and basketry.

HOURS: Mar-Dec M-Sa 9-5, Su 12-5

ADMISSION: $7, Children $5, Seniors $6.50

LANDISVILLE

7287
1852 Herr Family Homestead
1756 Nissley Rd, 17538 [PO Box 52, 17538]; (p) (717) 898-8822; (c) Lancaster

Private non-profit/ 1990/ Amos Herr House Foundation/ staff: 200(v)/ members: 410

GARDEN; HISTORIC PRESERVATION AGENCY; HOUSE MUSEUM: Portrays life on a 19th c non-Amish Lancaster County farm through its furnishings, interpretative tours, and activities.

PROGRAMS: Annual Meeting; Exhibits; Garden Tours; Interpretation; Lectures; Living History

COLLECTIONS: [1800-1910] Furnishings, archival library, vintage clothing, and accessories found in a farmhouse and barn that date 1800 to 1910.

HOURS: Apr-Oct Sa-Su 1-4 or by appt.

LANSDALE

7288
Lansdale Historical Society
137 Jenkins Ave, 19446 [PO Box 293, 19446]; (p) (215) 855-1872; (c) Montgomery

Private non-profit/ 1972/ Board of Directors/ staff: 8(v)/ members: 160

HISTORICAL SOCIETY: Collects, organizes, and preserves historical records and artifacts of the North Penn Area and makes them available to the public.

PROGRAMS: Annual Meeting; Guided Tours; Lectures

COLLECTIONS: [19th-20th c] Microfilm of The Reporter, local newspapers, northern PAa area genealogies, state archives, photographs, local histories, and yearbooks.

HOURS: Yr W 12-5

ADMISSION: $3; $3 research fee

LATROBE

7289
Latrobe Area Historical Society
1501 Ligonier St, 15650 [PO Box 266, 15650]; (p) (724) 539-8889; (c) Westmoreland

1974/ Board of Directors/ staff: 10(v)/ members: 200/publication: *The Latrobe Historical Gazette*

HISTORICAL SOCIETY: Collects, preserve, and catalogs artifacts and records and provides education for the community.

PROGRAMS: Community Outreach; Exhibits; Guided Tours; Interpretation; Lectures; Publication; Research Library/Archives; School-Based Curriculum

COLLECTIONS: [Late 18th-20th c] Archives and artifacts from industries, families, cemeteries, and schools include both photographs, oral histories, publications, records, and genealogies.

HOURS: Yr T 1-4, F 9-4

ADMISSION: Donations accepted

LAUGHLINTOWN

7290
Compass Inn Museum
Rt 30 East, 15655 [PO Box 167, 15655]; (p) (724) 238-4983; www.laurelhighlands.org/ compass; (c) Westmoreland

Private non-profit/ 1972/ Ligonier Valley Historical Society/ staff: 1(f); 1(p); 40(v)/ members: 350

HISTORY MUSEUM; HOUSE MUSEUM: Restored and furnished 1799 stagecoach stop that tells the story of transportation and life in the early 1800s.

PROGRAMS: Guided Tours; Living History

COLLECTIONS: [Early 1800s] Artifacts typically found in a tavern or a household such as cooking utensils, restored stagecoach and Conestoga wagon with a six-horse hitch, animal traps, farming, woodworking, and blacksmithing tools.

HOURS: May-Oct T-Sa 11-4, Su 12-4; Nov 2-5; mid Dec 2-8

ADMISSION: $5, Student $2

7291
Ligonier Valley Historical Society
Rt 30 East, 15655 [PO Box 167, 15655]; (p) (724) 238-6818; (c) Westmoreland

Private non-profit/ 1964/ staff: 1(f); 1(p); 100(v)/ members: 350

HISTORICAL SOCIETY: Discovers, collects, preserves, and interprets the history of Ligonier Valley.

PROGRAMS: Annual Meeting; Community Outreach; Lectures; Research Library/ Archives

COLLECTIONS: [1724-present] Small library of local history and some genealogy, documents, photographs, records relevant to Ligonier Valley.

HOURS: Yr T-Th 10-3

LEBANON

7292
Lebanon County Historical Society
924 Cumberland St, 17042; (p) (717) 272-1473; (f) (717) 272-7474; history@leba.net; www.leba.net/~history2; (c) Lebanon

Private non-profit/ 1898/ staff: 3(f); 1(p); 83(v)/ members: 1000

HISTORICAL SOCIETY; HOUSE MUSEUM: Collects, preserves, and exhibits historical and biographical data and artifacts pertaining to Lebanon County.

PROGRAMS: Annual Meeting; Exhibits; Guided Tours; Lectures; Publication; Research Library/Archives

COLLECTIONS: [18th-20th c] Artifacts related to the cultural history of Lebanon County; preserves historic tunnel.

HOURS: Yr Su 1-4:30, M 1-8, T-W, F 12:30-4:30, Th 10-4:30

LEECHBURG

7293
Leechburg Area Museum and Historical Society
118 First St, 15656 [PO Box 156, 15656]; (p) (724) 845-8914; www.apollotrust.com/~phillykid/mhs.html; (c) Armstrong

Private non-profit/ 1976/ staff: 25(v)/ members: 325/publication: *It's a Leechburg Thing (cookbook)*

HISTORICAL SOCIETY; HOUSE MUSEUM: Preserves the records and artifacts related to the Leechburg area and provides an understanding of local history.

PROGRAMS: Annual Meeting; Community Outreach; Exhibits; Garden Tours; Guided Tours; Publication; Research Library/Archives

COLLECTIONS: [19th-20th c] Local memorabilia, newspapers, military items, fashions, pictures, old school papers, and yearbooks.

HOURS: Feb-Dec W, Sa 12-3 and by appt

ADMISSION: No charge

LEWISBURG

7294
Packwood House Museum
8 Marker St, 17837 [15 N Water St, 17837]; (p) (570) 524-0323; (f) (570) 524-0548; packwood@jdweb.com; (c) Union

Private non-profit/ 1972/ Fetherston Foundation/ staff: 1(f); 4(p); 60(v)/ members: 400/publication: *Chanticleer*

GARDEN; HOUSE MUSEUM: Collects, preserves, interprets and exhibits a broad collection of 18th-20th century Americana, specializing in central Pennsylvania artifacts, for the educational benefit of all persons.

PROGRAMS: Exhibits; Facility Rental; Family Programs; Festivals; Guided Tours; Interpretation; Lectures

COLLECTIONS: [18th-20th c] Antique decorative arts from central PA region including furniture, quilts, textiles, glass, ceramics, metals, deeds, guns, and art.

HOURS: Yr T-Sa 10-4, Su 1-4

ADMISSION: $4, Student $1.75, Seniors $3.25

7295
Slifer House Museum
1 River Rd, 17837; (p) (570) 524-2245; sliferhs@postoffice.ptd.net; www.slifer.albrightcare.org; (c) Union

Private non-profit/ 1976/ staff: 1(f); 1(p); 40(v)/ members: 470

HISTORIC SITE; HOUSE MUSEUM: Designed by Philadelphia architect, Samuel Sloan, this Victorian mansion was the home of Eli Slifer, Secretary of PA during the Civil War.

PROGRAMS: Community Outreach; Concerts; Exhibits; Facility Rental; Family Programs; Festivals; Garden Tours; Guided Tours; Lectures; Publication; Reenactments; Research Library/Archives

COLLECTIONS: [1862-1915] Decorative arts of the Victorian period and memorabilia and artifacts related to the career of Eli Slifer and the house's subsequent history.

HOURS: Yr Jan-Apr 15 T-F 1-4; Apr 16-Dec T-Su 1-4 and by appt

ADMISSION: $4, Children $2, Seniors $3.50; Mbrs/Under 10 free; group rates

7296
Union County Historical Society
Union County Courthouse, 17837 [103 S 2nd St, 17837]; (p) (570) 524-8666; (f) (570) 524-8743; hstoricl@ptd.net; www.rootsweb.com/~paunion/society; (c) Union

Private non-profit/ 1963/ County/ staff: 2(p); 6(v)/ members: 350/publication: *Heritage*

GENEALOGICAL SOCIETY; HISTORICAL SOCIETY; HISTORY MUSEUM: Collects, interprets, and disseminates information on local history and assists researchers and those interested in preserving the past.

PROGRAMS: Annual Meeting; Community Outreach; Concerts; Exhibits; Facility Rental; Family Programs; Festivals; Guided Tours; Interpretation; Lectures; Living History; Publication; Research Library/Archives; School-Based Curriculum

COLLECTIONS: [1814-present] Local artifacts and memorabilia, photographs, slides, trade cards, account books and ledgers, quilts, clothing.

HOURS: Yr M-F 8:30-12/1-4:30

LEWISTOWN

7297
Mifflin County Historical Society
McCoy House, 1 N Market St, 17044 [1 W Market St, 17044]; (p) (717) 242-1022, (717) 248-4711; www.mccoyhouse.com; (c) Mifflin

Private non-profit/ 1921/ staff: 2(p); 32(v)/ members: 500

HISTORICAL SOCIETY; HOUSE MUSEUM: Preserves and records local history.

PROGRAMS: Annual Meeting; Exhibits; Guided Tours; Publication; Research Library/Archives

COLLECTIONS: [1860s-1930s] Thomas F. McCoy family's Victorian period rooms and memorabilia, Mifflin County Historical Society collection.

HOURS: Library: Yr T-W 10-4, 1st and 3rd Sa 10-3; Museum: May-Dec Su 1:30-4

ADMISSION: $5 Library/Museum free

LIGONIER

7298
Fort Ligonier Association
216 S Market St, 15658; (p) (724) 238-9701; (f) (724) 238-9732; FTLIG@westol.com; (c) Westmoreland

Private non-profit/ 1947/ Board of Directors/ staff: 6(f); 15(p); 20(v)/ members: 600

ART MUSEUM; HISTORIC SITE; HISTORICAL SOCIETY; HISTORY MUSEUM: Collects, preserves, researches, exhibits, and interprets the British-American fort and settlement, 1758-1766. Provides an opportunity to understand and appreciate a significant aspect of human experience in the 18th c through archaeology, art, and the reconstructed/restored historic site.

PROGRAMS: Annual Meeting; Community Outreach; Concerts; Elder's Programs; Exhibits; Family Programs; Film/Video; Garden Tours; Guided Tours; Interpretation; Living History; Publication; Reenactments

COLLECTIONS: [Mid-late 18th c] Archaeological objects recovered from local site. Fine arts such as original works by Reynolds, Ramsay, Copley, Peale, Penny, Morier and Houdon.

HOURS: May-Oct M-Sa 10-4:30, Su 12-4:30

ADMISSION: $5.50

LIMERICK

7299
Limerick Township Historical Society
545 W Ridge Pike, 19468; (p) (610) 495-5229; (c) Montgomery

Private non-profit/ 1984/ staff: 10(v)/ members: 175/publication: *A Journey Through Time: Limerick Township*

GENEALOGICAL SOCIETY; HISTORICAL SOCIETY; HISTORY MUSEUM; HOUSE MUSEUM: Preserves local history and genealogy.

PROGRAMS: Annual Meeting; Community Outreach; Exhibits; Family Programs; Festivals; Guided Tours; Publication; Research Library/Archives

COLLECTIONS: [19th-20th c] Items from local railroad, airport, organizations, schools, and other local artifacts

HOURS: Yr W 9-4 and by appt

LINESVILLE

7300
Linesville Historical Society, The
120 Erie St, 16424 [PO Box 785, 16424]; (p) (814) 683-4299; (c) Crawford

Private non-profit/ members: 100

HISTORICAL SOCIETY: Preserves local artifacts, photographs, and oral histories.

PROGRAMS: Annual Meeting; Exhibits; Lectures; Research Library/Archives

COLLECTIONS: [Late 19th c-present] Glass plate negatives and photographs, plus various artifacts covering a wide variety of subjects.

HOURS: May-Sept M-Sa 10-3

ADMISSION: Donations accepted

LITITZ

7301
Lititz Historical Foundation/Lititz Museum/Johannes Mueller House/Oheme Memorial Gardens
137-145 E Main St, 17543 [PO Box 65, 17543]; (p) (717) 627-4636; (c) Lancaster

Private non-profit/ 1965/ Board of Directors/ staff: 7(p)/ 50(v)/ members: 750/publication: *Historic Journal*

GARDEN; HISTORY MUSEUM; HOUSE MUSEUM: Interprets and preserves local history with emphasis on the Moravian Community from 1756-1856.

PROGRAMS: Annual Meeting; Community Outreach; Concerts; Exhibits; Facility Rental; Family Programs; Festivals; Garden Tours; Guided Tours; Lectures; Publication; Research Library/Archives; School-Based Curriculum

COLLECTIONS: [1750-1900] Mueller House depicts the 1800 Moravian home and gardens; Native American to 1888.

HOURS: May-Oct M-Sa 10-4

ADMISSION: $4, Student $2; $2 museum

7302
Lititz Moravian Archives and Museum
200 block of E Main St, 17543 [2 Church Square, 17543]; (p) (717) 626-8515; (c) Lancaster

Private non-profit/ 1952/ staff: 15(v)

HISTORIC SITE; HISTORY MUSEUM

PROGRAMS: Exhibits; Guided Tours; Research Library/Archives; School-Based Curriculum

COLLECTIONS: [1740-1900] Structures include church, museum, Corpse House, Brothers' House and Sisters' House.

HOURS: May-Sept Sa 10-4

ADMISSION: Donations accepted

7303
Wilbur Chocolate Candy Americana Museum and Store
48 N Bend St, 17543; (p) (717) 626-3249; (f) (717) 626-3455; www.800padutch.com/wilbur.html; (c) Lancaster

1972

HISTORIC SITE; HISTORY MUSEUM: Manages museum located in the Wilbur Chocolate Company founded in 1884 featuring the history of the candy industry.

PROGRAMS: Exhibits

COLLECTIONS: [20th c-present] Advertisements, packaging, equipment, antique chocolate pots, and a replica of an early 20th c candy kitchen.

HOURS: Yr M-Sa 10-5

ADMISSION: No charge

LOCK HAVEN

7304
Clinton County Historical Society
362 Water St, 17745; (c) Clinton

County; Private non-profit/ 1921/ Board of Directors/ staff: 4(p); 16(v)/ members: 178/publication: *News and Notes*

GENEALOGICAL SOCIETY; HISTORIC PRESERVATION AGENCY; HISTORIC SITE; HISTORICAL SOCIETY; HISTORY MUSEUM; HOUSE MUSEUM; LIBRARY AND/OR ARCHIVES

PROGRAMS: Annual Meeting; Community Outreach; Elder's Programs; Exhibits; Family

Programs; Festivals; Guided Tours; Lectures; Publication; Research Library/Archives; School-Based Curriculum

COLLECTIONS: [1800-1850] Artifacts pertaining to local historical significance; Heisey Museum located in Victorian home.

HOURS: Yr T-F 10-4

ADMISSION: $3, Student $5, Children $1; Donations requested, mbrs free

7305
Piper Aviation Museum Foundation
1 Piper Way, 17745; (p) (570) 748-8283; (f) (570) 893-8357; piper@cub.kcnet.org; www.kcnet.org/~piper; (c) Clinton

Private non-profit/ 1987/ Board of Directors/ staff: 2(f); 1(p); 31(v)/ members: 271

AVIATION MUSEUM; HISTORIC PRESERVATION AGENCY; HISTORY MUSEUM; RESEARCH CENTER

PROGRAMS: Community Outreach; Exhibits; Film/Video; Guided Tours; Publication; Research Library/Archives

COLLECTIONS: [1930s-1980s] Photographs, slides, films, videos, news clippings, company records,and letters. Airplane collection consists of unique airplanes, fuselages, and parts.

HOURS: Yr Daily 9:30-5

ADMISSION: $3, Children $1; Under 5 free

MANHEIM

7306
Manheim Historical Society
210 S Charlotte St, 17545; (p) (717) 665-3486; (f) (717) 295-1415; (c) Lancaster

Private non-profit/ 1964/ staff: 18(v)/ members: 630

HISTORIC PRESERVATION AGENCY; HISTORIC SITE; HISTORICAL SOCIETY; HISTORY MUSEUM; HOUSE MUSEUM; RESEARCH CENTER: Acquires, restores, preserves, and maintains historic buildings. Collects and preserves documents relating to business and people of the area.

PROGRAMS: Annual Meeting; Elder's Programs; Exhibits; Facility Rental; Guided Tours; Lectures; Research Library/Archives

COLLECTIONS: [1760-present] Documents, artifacts, photographs of Manheim and surrounding area; full set of Manheim newspaper 1841-1983.

HOURS: Yr F-Su

ADMISSION: No charge

MARIETTA

7307
Marietta Restoration Associates
418 Washington St, 17547 [PO Box 3, 17547]; (p) (717) 426-4736; (f) (717) 426-4440; (c) Lancaster

Private non-profit/ 1962/ Board of Trustees/ staff: 40(v)/ members: 250

HISTORIC PRESERVATION AGENCY; HISTORIC SITE; HISTORY MUSEUM; HOUSE MUSEUM: Promotes, encourages, and conducts the restoration, development, and preservation of the historical, cultural and aes-

thetic aspects of the Borough of Marietta. Restored The Old Town Hall c. 1847 and the Union Meeting House c. 1812. Maintains a local history museum in Town Hall.

PROGRAMS: Annual Meeting; Exhibits; Facility Rental; Guided Tours; Interpretation; Lectures

COLLECTIONS: Objects, furniture, goods, paintings, photographs, postcards, signs, and newspapers made in Marietta. Artifacts related to the PA Railroad and Canal, Susquehanna River, regional foundries, and the early lumber industry.

HOURS: Apr-Dec Sa 10-3, Su 1-3

ADMISSION: No charge

MCCONNELLSBURG

7308
Fulton County Historical Society, Inc.
Fulton House, 17233 [PO Box 115, 17233]; (c) Fulton

Private non-profit/ staff: 1(v)/ members: 600

HISTORICAL SOCIETY; HISTORY MUSEUM: Promotes knowledge of Fulton County history through programs, operation of a library, and a small museum.

PROGRAMS: Annual Meeting; Community Outreach; Concerts; Exhibits; Facility Rental; Family Programs; Festivals; Film/Video; Lectures; Living History; Publication; Reenactments; Research Library/Archives; School-Based Curriculum; Theatre

COLLECTIONS: [1850-present] Items of local historical relevance.

HOURS: Yr Th 1-4/7-9

ADMISSION: No charge

MCKEESPORT

7309
McKeesport Heritage Center
1832 Arboretum Dr, 15132; (p) (412) 678-1832; (c) Allegheny

Private non-profit/ 1985/ staff: 2(f); 1(p); 4(v)/ members: 600

GENEALOGICAL SOCIETY; HISTORIC PRESERVATION AGENCY; HISTORIC SITE; HISTORICAL SOCIETY; HISTORY MUSEUM; RESEARCH CENTER: Collects information and memorabilia from McKeesport area as well as giving shows, talks, and slide shows to many groups and schools.

PROGRAMS: Community Outreach; Exhibits; Facility Rental; Festivals; Film/Video; Guided Tours; Lectures

COLLECTIONS: [1790-present] Microfilmed local newspapers, census of Allegheny County, city directories and records, church and cemetery records, photographs, and corporate history of G.C. Murphy Company.

HOURS: Yr T-Th 9-5, Sa 9-3

ADMISSION: No charge

MEADVILLE

7310
**Crawford County Historical Society/
Baldwin-Reynolds House Museum**
639 Water St, 16335 [848 N Main St, 16335];
(p) (814) 724-6080; (f) (814) 333-8173;
brhouse@gremlan.org; visitcrawford.org; (c)
Crawford

Private non-profit/ 1874/ Board of Directors/
staff: 1(f); 8(p); 25(v)/ members: 480

HISTORICAL SOCIETY; HISTORY MUSEUM;
HOUSE MUSEUM

PROGRAMS: Annual Meeting; Community
Outreach; Concerts; Exhibits; Facility Rental;
Family Programs; Guided Tours; Lectures;
Publication; School-Based Curriculum

COLLECTIONS: [1843-1900] Paintings, furniture, and decorative arts; Greek Revival home
with 1860 kitchen and ice house; country doctor's office from 1938.

HOURS: May 31-Aug 31; Apr-Oct by appt

ADMISSION: $3, Student $1.50, Seniors $2;
Under 7 free

7311
John Brown Heritage Association
Village of New Richmond, 16335 [c/o Ed
Edinger, 291 Park Ave, 16335]; (p) (814) 724-
8625; (c) Crawford

Private non-profit/ 1974/ staff: 20(v)/ members:
100

HISTORIC PRESERVATION AGENCY; HISTORIC SITE; LIVING HISTORY/OUTDOOR
MUSEUM: Preserves and studies John
Brown, the abolitionist, and local hisory. Maintains site where the remains of his 1826 tannery are situated.

PROGRAMS: Annual Meeting; Exhibits; Festivals; Publication

COLLECTIONS: [1825-1900] Books and articles about John Brown and his times; commemorative decors of preservation efforts
since 1916.

HOURS: Yr Daily 24 hours

ADMISSION: No charge

MECHANICSBURG

7312
Mechanicsburg Museum Association
3 W Allen St, 17055; (p) (717) 697-6088; (f)
(717) 697-6285; (c) Cumberland

Private non-profit/ 1972/ Board of Directors/
staff: 1(p); 75(v)/ members: 504

HISTORIC SITE; HISTORY MUSEUM;
HOUSE MUSEUM; RESEARCH CENTER:
Cares for and maintains four historic buildings.
Conducts trips, programs, and demonstrations. Stores and maintains local artifacts.

PROGRAMS: Annual Meeting; Community
Outreach; Concerts; Exhibits; Family Programs; Festivals; Film/Video; Garden Tours;
Guided Tours; Interpretation; Lectures; Living
History; Publication; Reenactments; Research
Library/Archives; School-Based Curriculum

COLLECTIONS: [1800-present] Local memorabilia, newspapers, maps, books, pictures,
milk carts, signs, clothes, and Native American

artifacts. Structures include Frankerberger
Tavern, Stationmaster's House (on National
Registry) and Freight Station, which houses
the museum.

HOURS: Yr T-Sa 10-1

ADMISSION: No charge

MEDIA

7313
Colonial Pennsylvania Plantation
Ridley Creek State Park, 19064; (p) (610)
566-1725; (c) Delaware

Private non-profit/ 1973/ staff: 3(f); 20(p);
30(v)/ members: 150

GARDEN; LIVING HISTORY/OUTDOOR MUSEUM: Promotes understanding of 1760-1790
farm life in southwestern PA by providing a research-based experience for the public.

PROGRAMS: Community Outreach; Elder's
Programs; Guided Tours; Interpretation; Lectures; Living History; Reenactments

COLLECTIONS: [1760-1790] Household, agricultural artifacts, furnishings, antiques, and reproductions.

HOURS: Apr-Nov M-F 10-2, Sa-Su 10-5

ADMISSION: $4, Children $2, Seniors $2

MERCER

7314
Mercer County Historical Society
119 S Pitt St, 16137; (p) (724) 662-3490;
mchs@pathway.net; www.pathway.ent/mchs;
(c) Mercer

Private non-profit/ 1946/ Board of Directors/
staff: 1(f); 6(p); 8(v)/ members: 736/publication:
Mercer County Heritage

GENEALOGICAL SOCIETY; HISTORICAL
SOCIETY; HISTORY MUSEUM: Preserves
and presents county history through sites,
publications, and speakers.

PROGRAMS: Annual Meeting; Community
Outreach; Concerts; Exhibits; Facility Rental;
Guided Tours; Lectures; Living History; Publication; Reenactments; Research Library/
Archives; School-Based Curriculum

COLLECTIONS: [19th-20th c] Pioneer and
Underground Railroad artifacts, sports items,
doctor's equipment, and mortar supplies.

HOURS: Yr T-F 10-4:30, Sa 10-3

MIDDLEBURG

7315
Snyder County Historical Society
30 E Market St, 17842 [PO Box 276, 17842];
(p) (570) 837-6191; (f) (570) 837-4282; (c)
Snyder

Private non-profit/ 1898/ staff: 1(p)/ members:
1600

HISTORICAL SOCIETY; HISTORY MUSEUM:
Collects, preserves, and displays local history
artifacts and memorabilia and maintains library for historical and genealogical research.

PROGRAMS: Exhibits; Guided Tours; Lectures; Publication; Quarterly Meeting

COLLECTIONS: [19th-20th c] Local newspapers on microfilm, historical and genealogical

books, pictures, artifacts, carpentry tools, authentic 19th c gallows, and scale model of
early amusement park.

HOURS: Library: Yr Th-F 10-3:30; Museum:
May-Sept Su 1:30-5

ADMISSION: Lib fee/Donations for museum

MIDDLETOWN

7316
Middletown Area Historical Society
120 N Catherine St, 17057 [PO Box 248,
17057]; (p) (717) 944-3420; (c) Dauphin

Private non-profit/ 1972/ Board of Directors/
staff: 75(v)/ members: 250/publication: *Chronicles of Middletown*

HISTORIC PRESERVATION AGENCY; HISTORICAL SOCIETY; HISTORY MUSEUM;
HOUSE MUSEUM: Preserves local historical
information and artifacts and promotes local
history.

PROGRAMS: Community Outreach; Film/
Video; Lectures; Monthly Meeting; Publication;
School-Based Curriculum

COLLECTIONS: [Late 18th-20th c] Artifacts relating to the local community and adjacent area.

HOURS: Yr by appt and 4th M

MIFFLINBURG

7317
Mifflinburg Buggy Museum
523 Green St, 17844 [PO Box 86, 17844]; (p)
(570) 966-1355; (f) (570) 966-9231; buggymus@
csrlink.net; www./ycoming.org/buggy; (c) Union

Private non-profit/ 1978/ staff: 1(f); 1(p); 30(v)/
members: 200

HISTORIC SITE; HISTORY MUSEUM; HOUSE
MUSEUM: Housed in original buggy factory,
repository, and home. Representative of small
industry craft at the turn of the century.

PROGRAMS: Annual Meeting; Community
Outreach; Exhibits; Guided Tours; Interpretation; Lectures; School-Based Curriculum

COLLECTIONS: [1889-1920] Original parts,
tools and equipment used to manufacture
horse-drawn vehicles; period furnishings and
textiles.

HOURS: May-Oct Th-Su 1-5 and by appt

ADMISSION: No charge

MILFORD

7318
**Grey Towers National Historic
Landmark**
Old Owego Turnpike (off Rt 6), 18337 [PO
Box 188, 18337]; (p) (570) 296-9630; (f) (570)
296-9675; ccroston/na_gt@fs.fed.us;
www.pinchot.org/gt; (c) Pike

Federal/ 1963/ USDA Forest Service/ staff:
12(f); 8(p); 8(v)

HISTORIC SITE; HISTORY MUSEUM;
HOUSE MUSEUM: Continues and furthers the
conservation work of Gifford Pinchot, America's first Chief Forester, and two term Governor of PA.

PROGRAMS: Exhibits; Garden Tours; Guided
Tours; Interpretation; Lectures

COLLECTIONS: [19th c] Furnishings, family collectibles, memorabilia, books and other artifacts that belonged to Gifford Pinchot, and his family.

HOURS: Mem Day-Labor Day Daily 10-4; Labor-Veterans Day F-M 10-4

ADMISSION: Donations

7319
Pike County Historical Society
608 Broad St, 18337 [PO Box 915, 18337-0915]; (p) (570) 296-8126; (c) Pike

County/ 1930/ staff: 1(f); 1(p); 40(v)/ members: 230

HISTORICAL SOCIETY: Maintains and perpetuates the historical and cultural legacy of Pike County through preservation, leadership, and education.

PROGRAMS: Annual Meeting; Community Outreach; Exhibits; Guided Tours; Lectures; Publication; Research Library/Archives

COLLECTIONS: [19th-20th c] Lincoln Flag, Hiawatha Stagecoach, vintage clothing, genealogical materials, paintings, books, print resources, and photographs. Exhibits on Lincoln's assassination, the Civil War, and Pike County.

HOURS: Apr-Dec W, Sa-Su 1-4

ADMISSION: $3, Children $1

MILL RUN

7320
Fallingwater
Rt 381 S, 15464 [PO Box R, 15464]; (p) (724) 329-8501; (f) (724) 329-0881; fallingwater@paconserve.org; www.paconserve.org; (c) Fayette

Private non-profit/ 1963/ Board of Directors/ staff: 30(f); 47(p); 15(v)/ members: 12000/publication: Friends of Fallingwater

HISTORY MUSEUM: Designed by Frank Lloyd Wright in 1936 and completed three years later for the family of Pittsburgh department store owner Edgar J. Kaufmann. Presented to the WPC in 1963.

PROGRAMS: Community Outreach; Guided Tours; Publication

COLLECTIONS: [1936-1963] Frank Lloyd Wright designed house and furniture. Decorative arts include glass, ceramics, textiles; sculptures by Lipschitz, Arp and Voulkos; painting and graphic work by Picasso and Diego Rivera; 19th century Japanese print makers, J.J. Audubon.

HOURS: Mid Mar-Nov T-Su 10-4

ADMISSION: $8 weekdays; $12 weekends and holidays

MILLERSBURG

7321
Historical Society of Millersburg and Upper Paxton Township, The
330 Center St, 17061 [PO Box 171, 17061]; (p) (717) 692-4084; mbghist@epix.net; (c) Dauphin

Private non-profit/ 1980/ Board of Directors/ staff: 20(v)/ members: 385/publication: The Herald

HISTORICAL SOCIETY: Collects, preserves and displays local objects, photographs, and documents of historical value and makes them available for research.

PROGRAMS: Exhibits; Festivals; Publication; Research Library/Archives

COLLECTIONS: [1870s-present] Photographs, portraits, documents, deeds, maps, microfilmed newspapers and tax records, genealogy material, cemetery records, clothing, sheet music, art, and artifacts.

HOURS: May-Nov Sa-Su 10-3 and by appt

MONTOURSVILLE

7322
General John Burrows Historical Society of Montoursville
19 N Loyalsock Ave, 17754 [PO Box 385, 17754]; (p) (570) 368-7455; (f) (570) 368-1321; (c) Lycoming

Private non-profit/ 1987/ members: 140

Collects artifacts pertaining to local history and Andrew Burrows, Revolutionary War veteran and founder of Montoursville.

COLLECTIONS: [18th-20th c] Paintings of General John Burrows and wife Mary done by John Francis.

MONTROSE

7323
Susquehanna County Historical Society and Free Library Association
2 Monument Square, 18801; (p) (570) 278-1881; (f) (570) 278-9336; suspulib@epix.net; www.epix.net/~suspulib/hs.htm; (c) Susquehanna

1890/ Board of Directors/ staff: 2(f); 2(p); 10(v)/ members: 425

GENEALOGICAL SOCIETY; HISTORICAL SOCIETY; HISTORY MUSEUM: Collects and preserves Susquehanna County history in written, oral, and artifactual forms. Provides publications, museum exhibits, and programs.

PROGRAMS: Annual Meeting; Concerts; Exhibits; Festivals; Publication; Research Library/Archives

COLLECTIONS: [1790-present] Genealogy, local history museum, paintings, military items, textiles, maps, newspapers, and photographs.

HOURS: Yr May-Oct Apr M-F

MORGANTOWN

7324
Tri-County Heritage Society
8 Mill Rd, 19543 [PO Box 352, 19543]; (p) (610) 286-7477; tchslbry@voicenet.com; www.tchslibrary.com; (c) Berks

Private non-profit/ 1970/ staff: 2(f); 12(v)/ members: 400

GENEALOGICAL SOCIETY; HISTORIC PRESERVATION AGENCY; RESEARCH CENTER: Operates local history reference library, museum, and genealogy center housed in a restored an 18th c farm house. Maintains Old Welsh Cemetery located in Lancaster County, PA, as well as Nicholas Stoltzfus

House, Reading, Berks County, PA.

PROGRAMS: Annual Meeting; Community Outreach; Elder's Programs; Film/Video; Guided Tours; Lectures; Research Library/Archives; School-Based Curriculum

HOURS: By appt only M,T,F

ADMISSION: $5

MORRISVILLE

7325
Historic Morrisville Society
Hillcrest and Legion Ave, 19067; (c) Bucks

Private non-profit/ 1976/ staff: 25(v)/ members: 400

HISTORIC SITE; HISTORICAL SOCIETY; HISTORY MUSEUM; HOUSE MUSEUM: Preserves and maintains Summerseat Mansion and local history.

PROGRAMS: Annual Meeting; Community Outreach; Concerts; Elder's Programs; Exhibits; Facility Rental; Family Programs; Festivals; Guided Tours; Interpretation; Lectures; Living History; Reenactments; Research Library/Archives

COLLECTIONS: Antique and reproduction furniture, memorabilia, household items, pictures of past community activities, books.

HOURS: Yr 1st Sa

7326
Pennsbury Manor/Pennsbury Society, The
400 Pennsbury Memorial Rd, 19067; (p) (215) 946-0400; (f) (215) 295-2436; willpenn17@aol.com; www.pennsburymanor.org; (c) Bucks

Private non-profit/ 1939/ PA Historical and Museum Commission/ staff: 11(f); 10(p); 150(v)/ members: 150/publication: The Steward

HISTORICAL SOCIETY; HOUSE MUSEUM: Home of William Penn. Offers tours, lectures, and special programs.

PROGRAMS: Annual Meeting; Exhibits; Facility Rental; Family Programs; Festivals; Garden Tours; Guided Tours; Interpretation; Lectures; Living History; Publication; Research Library/Archives; School-Based Curriculum; Theatre

COLLECTIONS: [1680-1710] Reproductions and original artifacts that illustrate daily life during William Penn's stay at Pennsburg.

HOURS: Yr T-Sa 9-5, Su 12-5

ADMISSION: $5, Family $13, Children $3, Seniors $4.50

MOUNT JOY

7327
Donegal Society, The
Donegal Presbyterian Church, 17552 [1891 Donegal Springs Rd, 17552-8900]; (p) (717) 653-1943; (f) (717) 653-1352; donpreschurch@desupernet.net; (c) Lancaster

Private non-profit/ 1911/ staff: 4(v)/ members: 225

LIBRARY AND/OR ARCHIVES; RESEARCH CENTER: Perpetuates the memory of Donegal Church, built in 1721. Collects relics and artifacts of the church. Preserves and beautifies the grounds, buildings, and cemetery.

PROGRAMS: Annual Meeting; Exhibits; Festivals; Guided Tours; Interpretation; Research Library/Archives

COLLECTIONS: [1720-present] Church records and history, records of early Scots-Irish families, books, artifacts, and cemetery records. Structures include Stone Church building 1730; Session House 1811; Schoolhouse 1878

MUNCY

7328
Muncy Historical Society and Museum of History
40 N Main St, 17756 [PO Box 11, 17756]; (p) (570) 546-5917; (c) Lycoming

Private non-profit/ 1936/ members: 487

HISTORICAL SOCIETY; HOUSE MUSEUM: Collects, preserves, and interprets the history and heritage of Muncy and the surrounding area.

PROGRAMS: Annual Meeting; Exhibits; Facility Rental; Family Programs; Festivals; Guided Tours; Interpretation; Lectures; Publication; Reenactments; Research Library/Archives

COLLECTIONS: [Late 18th c-present] Area history, genealogy, and artifacts.

HOURS: May-Sept M, F 9-12 and by appt

ADMISSION: Donations accepted

MYERSTOWN

7329
Isaac Meier Homestead
Route 501 S, 17067 [PO Box 461, Myerstwon, 17067]; (p) (717) 866-2437

NAZARETH

7330
Jacobsburg Historical Society
402 Henry Rd, 18064 [PO Box 345, 18064]; (p) (610) 759-9029; schroedp@lafayette.edu; (c) Northampton

Private non-profit/ 1972/ staff: 100(v)/ members: 400/publication: Jacobsburg Record

HISTORIC SITE; HISTORICAL SOCIETY; HISTORY MUSEUM; HOUSE MUSEUM: Preserves and promotes the history of the Jacobsburg Historic District through programs and research focusing on the lives of the Henry gunmakers and early area inhabitants.

PROGRAMS: Annual Meeting; Exhibits; Family Programs; Festivals; Garden Tours; Guided Tours; Interpretation; Lectures; Publication; Reenactments; Research Library/Archives

COLLECTIONS: [19th c] Pennsylvania (primarily Henry) longrifles, firearms and accoutrements; original furnishings, decorative arts and art in 1832 John Joseph Henry House and Henry Homestead Museum.

HOURS: June-Dec 11-5

ADMISSION: $3

7331
Moravian Historical Society
214 E Center St, 18064; (p) (610) 759-5070; (f) (610) 759-2461; (c) Northampton

Private non-profit/ 1857/ Board of Managers/ staff: 2(f); 6(p); 50(v)/ members: 484/publication: The Moravian Historian; Transactions of the Moravian Historical Society

HISTORICAL SOCIETY; HISTORY MUSEUM: Collects, preserves, interprets, and publishes the history of the Moravian Church and its members.

PROGRAMS: Annual Meeting; Community Outreach; Concerts; Exhibits; Family Programs; Festivals; Guided Tours; Interpretation; Lectures; Publication; Research Library/Archives

COLLECTIONS: [17th-19th c] Concerns the history, art, music, lifestyle, and culture of the Moravian Church members who settled in America and of missions around the world. Structures include Whitefield House 1740, Gray Cottage 1740, Jordan House late 1800s, Kern House 1820, and Bell Cottage late 1800s.

HOURS: Yr Daily 1-4 and by appt

ADMISSION: $3, Children $1; Members/Under 5 free

NEW CASTLE

7332
Lawrence County Historical Society
408 N Jefferson St, 16103 [PO Box 1745, 16103]; (p) (724) 658-4022; (f) (724) 658-4022; history@lcix.net; www.ilovehistory.com; (c) Lawrence

Private non-profit/ 1938/ Board of Directors/ staff: 1(f); 3(p); 40(v)/ members: 400/publication: Bridges to the Past, Little Lawrence for Little People

HISTORICAL SOCIETY; HISTORY MUSEUM; HOUSE MUSEUM: Operates a history museum that features period rooms and interpretive displays. Sponsors an annual trivia competition in the schools, publishes, takes research requests, sponsors reading/discussion groups, holds monthly lecture series and operates an archiving program.

PROGRAMS: Annual Meeting; Community Outreach; Elder's Programs; Exhibits; Facility Rental; Guided Tours; Interpretation; Lectures; Publication; Research Library/Archives

COLLECTIONS: [1900-1960] Artifacts of local importance including Shenango China ware and documents.

HOURS: Yr M-Sa 9-5

ADMISSION: $2; Children free

NEW HOPE

7333
Friends of the Delaware Canal
145 S Main St, 18938; (p) (215) 862-2021; (f) (215) 862-2021; fodc@erols.com; www.fodc.org; (c) Bucks

Joint; Private non-profit/ 1982/ staff: 1(p); 20(v)/ members: 660

HOUSE MUSEUM: Preserves and restores the Delaware Canal. Maintains the Locktender's House, a c 1820 building, and presents lock history.

PROGRAMS: Annual Meeting; Community Outreach; Exhibits; Family Programs; Guided Tours; Lectures; Publication; School-Based Curriculum

COLLECTIONS: [1860-1875] Oral history tapes, photographs, newspaper clippings, books and booklets pertaining to Delaware Canal and other area canals.

HOURS: Jan-Apr, Nov-Dec M-F 11-4; May-Oct Sa-Su 1-4

ADMISSION: No charge

7334
New Hope Historical Society/Parry Mansion Museum
45 S Main St, 18938 [PO Box 41, 18938]; (p) (215) 862-5652; (c) Bucks

Private non-profit/ 1958/ staff: 1(p); 10(v)/ members: 300/publication: Walking Tour of New Hope

HISTORICAL SOCIETY; HOUSE MUSEUM: Historic local house restored and decorated in five periods from 1775-1900.

PROGRAMS: Annual Meeting; Garden Tours; Guided Tours; Publication

COLLECTIONS: [1775-1900] Furniture, paintings, clothing, and artifacts.

HOURS: Apr-Dec F-Su 1-5; and by appt

ADMISSION: $5, Student $4, Children $1, Seniors $4

NEWPORT

7335
Historical Society of Perry County
Little Buffalo State Park, 17074 [PO Box 81, 17074]; (c) Perry

Private non-profit/ 1880/ staff: 3(v)/ members: 164

HISTORICAL SOCIETY: Collects and preserves artifacts on local history and places them in the museum.

COLLECTIONS: [1700s-present] Kitchen gadgets, blacksmith tools, Native American artifacts, and pictures.

HOURS: June-Aug Su 2-4:30

ADMISSION: No charge

NEWTOWN

7336
Newtown Historic Association
Court Inn, Centre Ave & Court St, 18940 [PO Box 303, 18940]; (p) (215) 968-4004; www.twp.newtown.pa.us/historic/nha.; (c) Bucks

Private non-profit/ 1962/ members: 300

HISTORIC SITE; HOUSE MUSEUM: Preserves Newtown's colonial heritage.

PROGRAMS: Annual Meeting; Festivals; Guided Tours; Lectures; Research Library/Archives

COLLECTIONS: [1700-1900s] Colonial artifacts relating to local history.

HOURS: Yr T 9-3, Th 7-9 and by appt

ADMISSION: No charge

NEWTOWN SQUARE

7337
Newtown Square Historical Preservation Society
Saint Davids & Paper Mill Rd, 19073 [PO Box 3, 19073]; (p) (610) 975-0290; (c) Delaware

Private non-profit/ 1982/ staff: 30(v)/ members: 250

HISTORIC PRESERVATION AGENCY; HISTORIC SITE; HISTORICAL SOCIETY; HISTORY MUSEUM; HOUSE MUSEUM: Acquires and preserves all buildings, documents, artifacts, and memorabilia relevant to the history of Newtown Square. Sponsors museum.

PROGRAMS: Annual Meeting; Exhibits; Festivals; Lectures; School-Based Curriculum

NEWVILLE

7338
Newville Historical Society
69 S High St, 17241; (p) (717) 776-6210; jbrehm@epix.net; (c) Cumberland

Private non-profit/ 1965/ staff: 5(v)/ members: 125

HISTORICAL SOCIETY: Collects, preserves, and makes available to the public materials pertaining to the history of Newville and the surrounding townships and provides educational programs.

PROGRAMS: Exhibits; Guided Tours; Living History; Research Library/Archives

COLLECTIONS: [1730s-present] Artifacts and information relating to local area and the Civil War.

NORRISTOWN

7339
Historical Society of Montgomery County, The
1654 Dekalb St, 19401-5415; (p) (610) 272-0297; (f) (610) 272-2609; (c) Montgomery

Private non-profit/ 1881/ staff: 4(p); 5(v)/ members: 1176/publication: The Bulletin of the Historical Society of Montgomery County

HISTORICAL SOCIETY: Collects, preserves, interprets, and promotes the history of Montgomery County.

PROGRAMS: Annual Meeting; Exhibits; Facility Rental; Living History; Publication; Research Library/Archives

COLLECTIONS: [1784-present] Library contains manuscripts, photographs, and artifacts devoted to county history; deeds, tax records, and Norristown papers.

NORTH EAST

7340
Hornby School Restoration Society
10000 Colt Station Rd, 16428 [PO Box 270, 16428-0270]; (p) (814) 739-2720; (c) Erie

1973/ staff: 15(v)/ members: 125

HISTORIC SITE; HISTORICAL SOCIETY; HISTORY MUSEUM; LIVING HISTORY/OUTDOOR MUSEUM: On-going restoration and maintenance of wooden, one-room schoolhouse built in 1873. Receives and preserves

public education materials used over the last 128 years.

PROGRAMS: Annual Meeting; Community Outreach; Exhibits; Guided Tours; Living History; School-Based Curriculum

COLLECTIONS: [1873-1956] Textbooks, instructional materials, supplies used by students, furnishings, visual aids, desks, teacher souvenirs, memorabilia, school pictures, student personal items, community historic documents, papers and maps.

7341
Lake Shore Railway Historical Society
31 Wall St, 16428 [PO Box 521, 16428-0571]; (p) (814) 825-2724; (c) Erie

Private non-profit/ 1956/ staff: 1(p); 20(v)/ members: 225

HISTORIC SITE; HISTORICAL SOCIETY; HISTORY MUSEUM: Includes a railway library and archives in 1899 LS & MS masonry, passenger stations and 1869 frame combination station with railway locomotives, passenger, and freight cars displayed on grounds.

PROGRAMS: Annual Meeting; Community Outreach; Exhibits; Family Programs; Film/Video; Guided Tours; Interpretation; Lectures; Research Library/Archives

COLLECTIONS: [1850-present] General Electric locomotives and history; Heisley Locomotive Works locomotives and history; George M. Pullman cars and history; Lake Shore and Michigan Southern Railway cars, buildings and history; railroading in US in general.

HOURS: June-Aug W-Su 1-5; May, Sept-Oct Sa-Su 1-5

ADMISSION: Donations accepted

NORTH WALES

7342
Roth Living Farm Museum
502 DeKalb Pike, RD #2, 19454; (p) (215) 699-3994; (f) (215) 489-2290; webmaster@ devalcol.edu; www.devalcol.edu; (c) Montgomery

Private non-profit/ 1992/ Delaware Valley College/ staff: 1(f); 4(p); 20(v)

HISTORIC SITE; HOUSE MUSEUM; LIVING HISTORY/OUTDOOR MUSEUM: Depicts historical farm practices that provide a "hands-on" experience to visitors.

PROGRAMS: Community Outreach; Facility Rental; Family Programs; Festivals; Garden Tours; Guided Tours; Lectures; Living History; School-Based Curriculum

COLLECTIONS: [1850-1940] Household and farm equipment.

HOURS: Yr by appt

ADMISSION: $3

NORTHUMBERLAND

7343
Joseph Priestley House
472 Priestley Ave, 17857; (p) (570) 473-9474; (f) (570) 473-7901; mBashore@state.pa.us; (c) Northumberland

State/ 1959/ PA Historical and Museum Commission/ staff: 2(f); 1(p); 25(v)/ members: 150/publication: Joseph Priestley: A Comet in the System

HISTORIC SITE: American home of Joseph Priestley, preeminent English theologian and chemist, discoverer of oxygen, whose political thought influenced the authors of the Declaration of Independence and the Constitution.

PROGRAMS: Annual Meeting; Community Outreach; Exhibits; Family Programs; Film/Video; Guided Tours; Living History; Publication

COLLECTIONS: [1790-1810] Antique scientific equipment, decorative arts, and period furniture.

HOURS: Yr T-Sa 9-5, Su 12-5

PAOLI

7344
Historic Waynesborough
2049 Waynesborough Rd, 19301; (p) (610) 647-1779; (f) (610) 647-1015; (c) Chester

Joint/ 1980/ staff: 50(v)/ members: 50

HISTORIC SITE; HOUSE MUSEUM: Maintains the ancestral home of General Anthony Wayne and portrays the lives and times of seven generations of the Wayne family with emphasis on the general's life and military career.

PROGRAMS: Elder's Programs; Facility Rental; Guided Tours; Lectures; Research Library/Archives; School-Based Curriculum

COLLECTIONS: [1745-1902] Each room contains furnishings appropriate to the period portrayed, many from Wayne family members.

HOURS: Mar-Dec T, Th 10-4 Su 1-4

ADMISSION: $4, Family $10, Student $3, Seniors $3; Group rates

PENDED

7345
Hulmeville Historical Society, Inc.
Trenton Rd, 19047 [Box 7002, 19047]; (p) (215) 757-6886; (c) Bucks

City/ 1973/ members: 150/publication: Town Crier

HISTORICAL SOCIETY: Preserves and maintains historical buildings and collects artifacts from Hulmeville's past.

PROGRAMS: Elder's Programs; Exhibits; Family Programs; Publication; Research Library/Archives

COLLECTIONS: [18th-19th c] Variety of photographs, books, artifacts.

PENNSBURG

7346
Schwenkfelder Library and Heritage Center, The
105 Seminary St, 18073; (p) (215) 679-3103; (f) (215) 679-8175; info@schwenkfelder.com; www.schwenkfelder.com/; (c) Montgomery

Private non-profit/ staff: 3(f); 7(v)/publication: Fraktur Writings and Folk Art Drawings; Farming, Always Farming; and others

HISTORY MUSEUM; LIBRARY AND/OR ARCHIVES: Dedicated to the preservation of the history of the Schwenkfelders, a Protestant sect from Silesia that settled in southeastern PA in the early 18th c.

PROGRAMS: Community Outreach; Exhibits; Lectures; Publication; Research Library/ Archives

COLLECTIONS: [Late 18th c-present] Decorative arts, material culture, fine art, books, manuscripts, photographs, and ephemera, reflecting the Schwenkfelders and the Upper Perkiomen Valley region of PA.

HOURS: Yr T-W, F 9-4, Th 9-8, Sa 10-3, Su 1-4

ADMISSION: No charge

PERKASIE

7347
Pearl S. Buck House
520 Dublin Rd, 18944 [PO Box 181, 18944]; (p) (215) 249-0100; (f) (215) 249-9657; dbabcock@pearl-s-buck.org; www.pearl-s-buck.org; (c) Bucks

Private non-profit/ 1980/ staff: 30(f); 4(p); 200(v)/ members: 25

HISTORIC SITE; HOUSE MUSEUM: Preserves the legacy of Pearl S. Buck by educating visitors about her work as a humanitarian and author, spreading cultural awareness and understanding. National Historic Landmark.

PROGRAMS: Concerts; Exhibits; Facility Rental; Family Programs; Festivals; Guided Tours

COLLECTIONS: Artifacts collected by Pearl S. Buck throughout her life; Asian, European, and American art and furniture; prizes, awards and books; personal articles and photographs.

HOURS: Mar-Dec T-Sa 11, 1, 2, Su 1, 2

ADMISSION: $6, Family $15, Student $5, Seniors $5; Under 6 free/Group rates

7348
Perkasie Anniversary and Historical Society
513 W Walnut St, 18944; (c) Bucks

Private non-profit/ 1953/ staff: 30(v)/ members: 250

HISTORICAL SOCIETY: Preserves and protects items of interest to the history of Perkasie and maintains and operates the historic Menlo Park Carousel and the South Perkasie Covered Bridge.

PROGRAMS: Annual Meeting; Exhibits; Festivals; Guided Tours; Interpretation; Lectures

COLLECTIONS: [1850-1990] Books, photographs, newspapers, artifacts. Structures: Perkasie Historical Society Museum, Perkasie Menlo Park Carousel, South Perkasie Covered Bridge, and Stout Family Cemetery.

HOURS: Museum: May-Dec Sa-Su 1-4; Carousel: May-Dec Su 1-5 (Sa after Thanksgiving)

ADMISSION: $.35/carousel ride

PHILADELPHIA

7349
African American Museum in Philadelphia, The
701 Arch St, 19106; (p) (215) 574-0380; (f) (215) 574-3110; arosenberg@aampmuseum.org; www.aampmuseum.org; (c) Philadelphia

Private non-profit/ 1976/ staff: 25(f); 5(p); 80(v)/ members: 1000

ART MUSEUM; HISTORY MUSEUM; HOUSE MUSEUM; RESEARCH CENTER: Dedicated to collecting, preserving, and interpreting the material and intellectual culture of African Americans in Philadelphia, the Delaware Valley, the Commonwealth of PA, and the Americas.

PROGRAMS: Annual Meeting; Concerts; Exhibits; Facility Rental; Festivals; Guided Tours; Interpretation; Lectures; Research Library/Archives; School-Based Curriculum

COLLECTIONS: [20th c] 400,000 objects, images, and documents ranging from utilitarian and domestic objects to fine and folk art, memorabilia, furnishings, costumes, photographs and negatives, and books and periodicals.

HOURS: Yr T-Sa 10-5, Su 12-5

ADMISSION: $6, Student $4, Children $4, Seniors $4

7350
American Catholic Historical Society
263 S 4th St, 19105 [PO Box 84, 19105-0084]; (p) (215) 925-5752; www.amchs.org; (c) Philadelphia

Private non-profit/ 1884/ staff: 5(v)/ members: 635/publication: *Records of the American Catholic Historical Society*

GENEALOGICAL SOCIETY; HISTORIC SITE; HISTORICAL SOCIETY; HISTORY MUSEUM: Collects and preserves material relating to American history and the contribution of Catholics in the building of the Americas. It is the oldest existing Catholic historical organization in the United States.

PROGRAMS: Exhibits; Guided Tours; Lectures; Publication; Research

7351
American Flag House and Betsy Ross Memorial
239 Arch St, 19106; (p) (215) 861-2523; (f) (215) 686-1256; eileenvig@aol.com; (c) Philadelphia

Private non-profit/ 1898/ Historic Philadelphia, Inc./ staff: 7(p); 1(v)

HOUSE MUSEUM: Maintains the American Flag House and Betsy Ross Memorial, portrays the life and work of a typical working class person, and highlights the role of women in the Colonial period.

PROGRAMS: Facility Rental; Interpretation; Reenactments

COLLECTIONS: [1770s] Ceramics, furniture, and metalware items typical to a working class home of the Colonial period.

HOURS: Yr Summer Daily 10-5; Winter T-Su 10-5

7352
American Swedish Historical Museum
1900 Pattison Ave, 19145; (p) (215) 389-1776; (f) (215) 389-7701; ashm@libertynet.org; www.americanswedis.org; (c) Philadelphia

Private non-profit/ 1926/ Board of Governors/ staff: 7(f); 2(p); 150(v)/ members: 750

HISTORY MUSEUM: Thirteen galleries and a library focus on the history of Swedes in America from the establishment of the New Sweden Colony in 1638 to contemporary Swedish technology, architecture, and fine and decorative arts.

PROGRAMS: Annual Meeting; Community Outreach; Concerts; Exhibits; Facility Rental; Festivals; Guided Tours; Interpretation; Lectures; Reenactments; Research Library/Archives; School-Based Curriculum; Theatre

COLLECTIONS: [17th c-present] Models and correspondence of John Ericsson, Jenny Lind memorabilia, and examples of Swedish art.

HOURS: Yr T-F 10-4, Sa-Su 12-4

ADMISSION: $5, Student $4, Seniors $4

7353
Anthenaeum of Philadelphia, The
219 S Sixth St, 19106 [E Washington Sq, 19106-3794]; (p) (215) 925-2688; (f) (215) 925-3755; athena@philaathenaeum.org; www.philaathenaeum.org; (c) Philadelphia

Private non-profit/ 1814/ staff: 10(f); 2(p)/ members: 1375

HISTORIC SITE; HISTORY MUSEUM; LIBRARY AND/OR ARCHIVES; RESEARCH CENTER: Member-supported research library, specializing in American architecture, housed in a National Historic Landmark building near Independence Hall. The Athenaeum is operated as a historic site museum.

PROGRAMS: Annual Meeting; Concerts; Exhibits; Lectures; Publication; Research Library/Archives

COLLECTIONS: [1800-1930] 180,000 original architectural drawings, 50,000 photographs, and 100,000 rare books, several million manuscripts.

HOURS: Yr M-F 9-5

ADMISSION: No change

7354
Archives and Special Collections, MCP Hahnemann University
Conference Center, 3200 Henry Ave, 19129; (p) (215) 842-4700; (f) (215) 843-0349; archives.mcpho@drexel.edu; www.mcphu.edu; (c) Philadelphia

Private non-profit/ 1850/ MCP Hahnemann Univ/ staff: 2(f); 2(p)

LIBRARY AND/OR ARCHIVES; RESEARCH CENTER: The Archives and Special Collections is a research center for the history of the Woman's Medical College of PA MCP and Hahnemann Medical College, as well as the history of women in medicine and homeopathy.

PROGRAMS: Research Library/Archives

COLLECTIONS: [1848-present] 1,500 linear feet of manuscript material, historic book collection, 20,000 photographs, three-dimensional artifacts, and an 800 piece art collection.

7355
Awbury Arboretum Association
1 Awbury Rd, 19138-1505; (p) (215) 849-2855; (f) (215) 849-0213; www.awbury.org; (c) Philadelphia

Private non-profit/ 1916/ Board of Directors/ staff: 10(f); 8(p); 140(v)/ members: 500/publication: *The Arbor*

GARDEN; HISTORIC SITE; HOUSE MUSEUM: Preserves and manages an arboretum with a historical collection.

PROGRAMS: Community Outreach; Exhibits; Facility Rental; Garden Tours; Guided Tours; Interpretation; Publication; Research Library/

Archives; School-Based Curriculum

COLLECTIONS: [Late 18th c-present] Awbury collects, preserves, and makes available prints, books, manuscripts, artifacts, photographs, and audio tapes related to the history and development of Awbury, the Cope family, Quaker life, and garden development.

HOURS: Grounds: Yr Daily dawn-dusk; Cope House: Yr M-F 8-4

7356
Balch Institute for Ethnic Studies
18 S 7th St, 19106; (p) (215) 925-8090; (f) (215) 925-4392; balchlib@balchinstitute.org; www.balchinstitute.org

Private non-profit/ 1971/ staff: 14(f); 9(p); 52(v)/publication: *Perspective*

HISTORY MUSEUM: Maintains library, archives, museum, and education center and promotes greater intergroup understanding.

PROGRAMS: Community Outreach; Exhibits; Facility Rental; Lectures; Publication; Research Library/Archives

COLLECTIONS: [Early 20th c-present] Primary and secondary source materials and artifacts that document immigration, ethnic life, and multiculturalism in America: 60,000 volumes, 6,000 serial titles, 5,000 linear feet of archival material, 6,000 reels of microfilm, and 12,000 photographs.

7357
Belmont Mansion
2000 Belmont Mansion Dr, 19131; (p) (215) 878-8844; (f) (215) 878-9439; www.amerwomher.qpg.com; (c) Philadelphia

Private non-profit/ 1986/ American Women's Heritage Society, Inc. Board of Trustees/ staff: 4(f); 6(p); 225(v)/ members: 225/publication: *Belmont News*

HOUSE MUSEUM: Founded for the purpose of restoring and maintaining the 360-year-old Belmont Mansion, the most architecturally and historically significant house in Philadelphia's Fairmont Park.

PROGRAMS: Community Outreach; Concerts; Exhibits; Facility Rental; Guided Tours; Interpretation; Lectures; Publication

COLLECTIONS: [18th-early 19th c] Artifacts and documents associated with Belmont Mansion and the Peters family; recreations of homes of historically documented African American Philadelphians.

HOURS: Yr T-F 10-5, Sa-Su by appt

ADMISSION: $3, Children $1.50

7358
Carpenters' Company of the City and County, The
320 Chestnut St, 19106; (p) (215) 925-0167; (f) (215) 925-3880; (c) Philadelphia

Private non-profit/ 1724/ Managing Committee/ staff: 2(f); 4(p); 20(v)/ members: 141/publication: *Building Early America*

PROFESSIONAL ORGANIZATION: Consists of over 100 builders, engineers, and architects interested in preserving Carpenter's Hall, meeting place of the First Continental Congress.

PROGRAMS: Exhibits; Facility Rental; Guided Tours; Interpretation; Lectures; Publication

COLLECTIONS: [18th c-present] Windsor chairs, tools, Carpenters' Company and Continental Congress memorabilia dating from 1770 to present.

HOURS: Yr Jan-Dec T-Su 10-4

ADMISSION: No charge

7359
Cedar Grove
45 St & Parkside Ave, 19101 [PO Box 7647, 19101]; (p) (215) 763-8100

7360
Center for History of Foot Care and Footwear/Temple Univ School of Podiatric Medicine
8th and Race Sts, 19107; (p) (215) 625-5243; (f) (215) 629-1622; (c) Philadelphia

Private non-profit/ 1981/ Temple Univ/ staff: 1(p); 3(v)

HISTORY MUSEUM; RESEARCH CENTER: Serve as an important resource worldwide in history and literature of the foot, its care, treatment and coverings, as well as the chiropody/podiatry profession.

PROGRAMS: Exhibits; Guided Tours; Interpretation; Research Library/Archives

COLLECTIONS: [19th-early 20th c] 2,000 books, 500 pamphlets, 100 serial runs (many rare); 250 linear ft of archival material; 500 photographs; 350 medical artifacts; 800 item footwear collection.

7361
Chestnut Hill Historical Society
8708 Germantown Ave, 19118; (p) (215) 247-0417; (f) (215) 247-9329; chhist@aol.com; (c) Philadelphia

Private non-profit/ 1967/ staff: 2(f); 2(p)/ members: 400/publication: *Preserving Our Heritage*

HISTORIC PRESERVATION AGENCY; HISTORICAL SOCIETY: Preserves and nurtures the historical, physical, and cultural resources and character of Chestnut Hill.

PROGRAMS: Annual Meeting; Exhibits; Guided Tours; Lectures; Publication; Research Library/Archives

COLLECTIONS: [Late 18th c-1960] 15,000 photographs, maps, scrapbooks, local books, articles, and documents plus a few artifacts tracing the history of Chestnut Hill.

HOURS: Yr Gallery: M-F 9-5; Archives: T-F 9-5

ADMISSION: $4; Gallery free

7362
CIGNA Museum and Art Collection
TL07E, 1601 Chestnut St, 19192 [TLO7E, PO Box 7716, 19192-2078]; (p) (215) 761-4907; (f) (215) 761-5596; melissa.hough@cigna.com; (c) Philadelphia

Private non-profit/ 1925/ CIGNA Corporation/ staff: 4(f); 2(p)

CORPORATE ARCHIVES/MUSEUM; HISTORY MUSEUM: Operates with the Employee Services division of CIGNA Corporation.

PROGRAMS: Community Outreach; Exhibits; Guided Tours; Interpretation; Lectures; Publication; Research Library/Archives

COLLECTIONS: [1790-present] 10,000 art and historical artifacts: fire fighting and mar-

itime related objects including paintings, models, prints, equipment, apparatus, manuscripts.

HOURS: Yr M-F 9-5 and by appt

ADMISSION: No charge

7363
Civil War Library and Museum
1805 Pine St, 19103; (p) (215) 735-8196; (f) (215) 735-3812; cwlm@netreach.net; www.netreach.net/~cwlm; (c) Philadelphia

Private non-profit/ 1888/ Board of Governors/ staff: 2(f); 1(p); 30(v)/ members: 500

HISTORY MUSEUM; RESEARCH CENTER: Maintains a library and collection of artifacts to provide information on the Civil War to scholars and the general public.

PROGRAMS: Exhibits; Guided Tours; Interpretation; Lectures; Publication; Research Library/Archives

COLLECTIONS: [1861-1865] Weapons, flags, uniforms, paintings, photographs, and prints; 1,300 volumes, letters, and manuscripts.

HOURS: Yr T-Sa

7364
Cliveden of the National Trust
6401 Germantown Ave, 19144; (p) (215) 848-1777; (f) (215) 438-2892; cliveden@cliveden.org; www.cliveden.org; (c) Philadelphia

Private non-profit/ 1972/ Board of Trustees/ staff: 4(f); 25(p); 3(v)/publication: *The Surprise of Germantown*

HISTORIC SITE; HOUSE MUSEUM: Preserves site of the 1777 Revolutionary War Battle of Germantown. Documents the story of six generations of Philadelphia's Chew family through original furnishings.

PROGRAMS: Exhibits; Facility Rental; Festivals; Guided Tours; Interpretation; Publication; Reenactments

COLLECTIONS: [1763-1890] Artifacts: fine and decorative arts, archives, archaeological, architecture, and landscape documenting the Chew family's occupancy of the house: Cliveden, 1763-1970.

HOURS: Apr-Dec Th-Su 12-4

ADMISSION: $6, Student $4; Group rates

7365
Declaration House
7th & Market Sts, 19106 [Independence NHP, 313 Walnut St, 19106]; (p) (215) 597-8974; www.nps.gov/inde

1775/ Independence National Historical Park

Reconstruction of the house where Thomas Jefferson wrote the Declaration of Independence.

COLLECTIONS: [American Revolution and early Federal Era] 18th c furnishings; Materials dealing with Indepdendece National Historical Park and information related to the historic structures.

HOURS: Yr

7366
Deshler-Morris House
5442 Germantown Ave, 19106 [Independence NHP, 313 Walnut St, 19106]; (p) (215) 596-1748; (f) (215) 597-1416; www.nps.gov/inde/deshler-morris-house.html; (c) Philadelphia

Federal/ 1948/ National Park Service/publication: *Deshler-Morris House*

HISTORIC SITE; PRESIDENTIAL SITE: Maintains the house that was the temporary residence of President George Washington during the summers of 1793 and 1794, the oldest Presidential residence in the United States.

PROGRAMS: Guided Tours; Publication

COLLECTIONS: [1793-1794] Period pieces are used to recreate the interior of the home as it might have appeared when George Washington lived here with his family and when he conducted meetings at the residence.

HOURS: Apr-Dec T-Sa 1-4

ADMISSION: $2

7367
Ebenezer Maxwell Mansion, Inc.
200 W Tulpehocken St, 19144; (p) (215) 438-1861; (f) (215) 438-1861; (c) Philadelphia

1965/ Board of Trustees/ staff: 1(f); 1(p); 40(v)/ members: 115

HISTORIC SITE; HOUSE MUSEUM: Maintains restored Victorian house museum and gardens.

PROGRAMS: Garden Tours; Guided Tours; Lectures

COLLECTIONS: [1860-1890s] Rococo furniture and the Industrial Revolution's labor-saving devices in the kitchen, stencils from the Orient, Egypt and Rome; Renaissance Revival furniture.

HOURS: Apr-Dec F-Su 1-4

ADMISSION: $4, Student $2, Seniors $3

7368
Edgar Allan Poe National Historic Site
532 N 7th St, 19123; (p) (215) 597-8780; (f) (215) 597-1901; www.nps.gov/edal; (c) Philadelphia

Federal/ 1978/ National Park Service/ staff: 5(f); 2(p); 3(v)/publication: *Edgar Allan Poe Nationa Historic Site*

HISTORIC SITE: Preserves the temporary residence of Edgar Allan Poe. Three of his short stories, including The Tell-Tale Heart and The Black Cat were published when Poe lived at the residence.

PROGRAMS: Community Outreach; Exhibits; Film/Video; Guided Tours; Interpretation; Publication; Research Library/Archives

COLLECTIONS: 1843-1844 residence of Edgar Allan Poe.

HOURS: Jun-Oct M-Su 9-5; Nov-May W-Su 9-5

7369
Elfreth's Alley Association
126 Elfreth's Alley, 19106; (p) (215) 574-0560; (f) (215) 922-7869; (c) Philadelphia

Private non-profit/ 1934/ staff: 1(f); 1(p); 25(v)/ members: 50

HISTORIC SITE; HISTORY MUSEUM: Preservation, tourism, and education of working class 1702-1829 Philadelphia.

PROGRAMS: Annual Meeting; Community Outreach; Concerts; Exhibits; Facility Rental; Family Programs; Festivals; Guided Tours; Interpretation; Lectures; Living History

COLLECTIONS: [1702-1829] A living museum street with 2 museum houses open. Working class Mantua maker and Windsor Chair maker. Homes are interpreted and toured.

HOURS: Jan-Feb Sa 10-4 Su 12-4; Mar-Dec T-Sa 10-4 Su 12-4

ADMISSION: $2, Family $5

7370
Fireman's Hall Museum
147 N 2nd St, 19106; (p) (215) 923-1438; (f) (215) 923-0479; firemus@aol.com; (c) Philadelphia

Joint/ 1972/ Philadelphia Fire Dept Historical Corporation; City; Private non-profit/ staff: 2(f); 30(p)/publication: *Hike Out!*

HISTORIC PRESERVATION AGENCY; HISTORIC SITE; HISTORY MUSEUM; RESEARCH CENTER: Preserves county firefighting history, focuses on the human side of firefighting, and fire safety and preservation.

PROGRAMS: Community Outreach; Exhibits; Facility Rental; Family Programs; Guided Tours; Interpretation; Lectures; Living History; Publication; Research Library/Archives; School-Based Curriculum

COLLECTIONS: [1701-present] Photographs, newspaper articles, memorabilia, historic fire apparatus, 1920s stained glass window, firefighter's living quarters, inside of a fireboat, and a restored 1901 firehouse.

HOURS: Yr T-Sa 9-4:30

ADMISSION: Donations accepted

7371
Fort Mifflin on the Delaware
Fort Mifflin Rd, 19153; (p) (215) 492-1881; (f) (215) 429-1608; (c) Philadelphia

Private non-profit/ 1984/ staff: 5(f); 3(p); 200(v)/ members: 1/publication: *Fort Mifflin An Illustrated History*

HISTORIC SITE; LIVING HISTORY/OUTDOOR MUSEUM: Preserves, restores, and interprets Fort Mifflin, a National Historic Landmark; offers tours, education programs, and reenactments that tell the story of the 6 week battle that kept the British Navy out of Philadelphia in 1777.

PROGRAMS: Community Outreach; Concerts; Elder's Programs; Exhibits; Facility Rental; Family Programs; Festivals; Guided Tours; Interpretation; Lectures; Living History; Publication; Reenactments

COLLECTIONS: [Mid 1800s] 14 historic buildings, Revolutionary War artifacts.

HOURS: Apr-Nov W-Su 10-4 and by appt

ADMISSION: $5, Children $2, Seniors $4.50

7372
Friends of the Japanese House and Garden, The
Horticulture Center, W Fairmount Park, 19103 [PO Box 2224, 19103]; (p) (215) 763-8003; (f) (215) 763-7137; hopezoss@aol.com; www.libertynet.org/jhg; (c) Philadelphia

Private non-profit/ 1982/ staff: 2(f); 6(p); 75(v)/ members: 160

GARDEN; HOUSE MUSEUM: Maintains, preserves, and exhibits the house and garden and promotes intercultural understanding

through programming.

PROGRAMS: Annual Meeting; Community Outreach; Concerts; Facility Rental; Family Programs; Festivals; Garden Tours; Guided Tours; Interpretation; Lectures; Publication; School-Based Curriculum

COLLECTIONS: [17th c-present] Japanese dwelling is a representation of a 17th c house by Yoshimura Junzo and exhibited at MOMA. The traditional garden recalls the mountains, streams, and forests of Japan.

HOURS: May-Oct T-Su 10-4

ADMISSION: $2.50, Children $2, Seniors $2

7373
Genealogical Society of Pennsylvania, The
215 S Broad St, 7th Fl, 19107-5325; (p) (215) 545-0391; (f) (215) 545-0936; gsppa@aol.com; libertynet.org/gspa; (c) Philadelphia

Private non-profit/ 1892/ staff: 3(f); 2(p); 20(v)/ members: 1405/publication: *The Pennsylvania Genealogical Magazine; Penn In Hand Newsletter*

GENEALOGICAL SOCIETY: Makes available PA related genealogical information.

PROGRAMS: Annual Meeting; Community Outreach; Lectures; Publication; Research Library/Archives

COLLECTIONS: [17th and 18th c] Church registers, funeral, cemetery, Bible records, family papers, and correspondence, immigration, published genealogies, periodicals, military records, reference, some census, tax lists, public ledger indexes, obits, tombstone inscriptions, general reference.

HOURS: Yr M, T, W, Sa 10-4 by appt

ADMISSION: $5

7374
German Society of Philadelphia, The
611 Spring Garden St, 19123; (p) (215) 627-2332; (f) (215) 627-5297; GermanScty@aol.com; libertynet.org/gsp; (c) Philadelphia

Private non-profit/ 1764/ staff: 3(f); 2(p)/ members: 780

HISTORICAL SOCIETY: Promotes German-American history and German culture through extensive library, historic buildings, German language courses, concerts, and lectures.

PROGRAMS: Annual Meeting; Community Outreach; Facility Rental; Lectures; Research Library/Archives

COLLECTIONS: [1850-1950] German-Americana, 70,000 volumes (85% in German), 15 microfilms, 50 ft of unprocessed manuscripts, special collections; Oswald Seidensticker's German-Americana Collection, Carl Schultz Collection.

7375
Germantown Historical Society
5501 Germantown Ave, 19144; (p) (215) 844-1683; (f) (215) 844-2831; ghs@libertynet.org; www.libertynet.org/ghs; (c) Philadelphia

Private non-profit/ 1900/ Board of Directors/ staff: 2(f); 4(p); 96(v)/ members: 450/publication: *Now and Then; Germantown Crier*

HISTORY MUSEUM: Dedicated to preserving, protecting, and interpreting the significant national and local history of Germantown.

PROGRAMS: Annual Meeting; Community Outreach; Exhibits; Facility Rental; Guided Tours; Lectures; Publication; Research Library/Archives

COLLECTIONS: [1683-present] Objects, photographs, library and archive materials, costume, textiles including quilts, glass slides, negatives and lantern slides, paintings and works on paper, decorative arts all relating to Germantown and its history.

HOURS: T,Th 9-5, Su 1-5 and by appt; Visitor Center M-F 9-5, Su 1-5

ADMISSION: $4, Children $2

7376
Germantown Mennonite Historic Trust
6133 Germantown Ave, 19144; (p) (215) 843-0943; (f) (215) 843-6263; gmht@aol.com; (c) Philadelphia

Private non-profit/ 1952/ staff: 1(f); 1(p); 3(v)/ members: 480

HISTORIC SITE; HOUSE MUSEUM: Preserves and interprets the oldest Mennonite Meetinghouse in North America, built in 1770, but with a social history dating to the founding of Germantown in 1683 by the first German immigration to the New World.

PROGRAMS: Facility Rental; Interpretation

COLLECTIONS: [Colonial] German language religious books printed locally in the colonial period, table at which the Germantown Antislavery Protest of 1688 was signed.

HOURS: Mar-Dec by appt

ADMISSION: $3, Student $1.50

7377
Glen Foerd on the Delaware
5001 Grant Ave, 19114; (p) (215) 632-5330; (f) (215) 632-2312; glenfoerd@aol.com; (c) Philadelphia

Private non-profit/ 1983/ Glen Foerd Conservation Corp/ staff: 1(f); 120(v)/ members: 483

HISTORIC SITE; HOUSE MUSEUM: Preserves the last surviving riverfront estate in Philadelphia as a historic site and a center for providing historic and cultural experience to the public.

PROGRAMS: Community Outreach; Concerts; Facility Rental; Family Programs; Festivals; Guided Tours; Publication

COLLECTIONS: [1850-1934] Collection of the last resident-owner including: paintings, prints, textiles, antique furniture, and books.

7378
Grand Army of Republic Civil War Museum and Library
4278 Griscom St, 19124; (p) (215) 289-6484; GARMUSLIB@aol.com; suvcw.org/garmus.htm; (c) Philadelphia

Private non-profit/ 1926/ staff: 15(v)/ members: 230

HISTORIC SITE; HISTORY MUSEUM: Maintains museum in a historic house with a collection of Civil War and Grand Army of Republic artifacts deeded to them by Union Civil War veterans.

PROGRAMS: Annual Meeting; Exhibits; Family Programs; Lectures; Reenactments

COLLECTIONS: [1861-1865] Civil War artifacts from battles, prisons, and soldier's personal effects; 2,500 volume library; portraiture; photos, letters, armaments; records and memorabilia from Grand Army of Republic.

HOURS: Yr 1st Su of month 12-5, all Su in Jan and by appt

7379
Henry George Birthplace
413 S 10th St, 19147; (p) (215) 922-4278; (f) (215) 922-7089; georgist@bellatlantic.net; (c) Philadelphia

Private non-profit/ 1935/ Henry George School of Social Science/ staff: 1(f); 1(p); 10(v)

HISTORIC SITE

PROGRAMS: Lectures; School-Based Curriculum

COLLECTIONS: Books and memorabilia of Henry George, noted author of the economic classic, "Progress and Poverty," 1879. The bed in which he was born and the writing table on which "Progress and Poverty" was written.

HOURS: Yr by appt

7380
Historic Bartram's Garden
54th St & Lindbergh Blvd, 19143 [54th St and Lindbergh Boulevard, 19143]; (p) (215) 729-5281; (f) (215) 729-1047; bartram@libertynet.org

1731/ The John Bartram Association/ staff: 3(f); 7(p)

COLLECTIONS: [18th c] Historic collection, house, furnishings, and outbuildings; library collection of books, letters, documents writings, and photographs relating to the Bartrams.

HOURS: Yr

7381
Historic Philadelphia, Inc.
510 Walnut St, Ste 402, 19106; (p) (215) 629-5801; (f) (215) 629-5814; (c) Philadelphia

Private non-profit/ 1994/ staff: 5(f); 30(p)/publication: Historic Philadelphia Gazette

LIVING HISTORY/OUTDOOR MUSEUM: Provides programming on the City of Philadelphia's Historic District including the Town Crier Summer Theater-a troupe of 18th c re-enacters, fife and drum corps, 18th c singing quartet.

PROGRAMS: Concerts; Guided Tours; Interpretation; Living History; Publication

7382
Historic Rittenhouse Town Inc.
Lincoln Dr & Wissahickon Ave, 19144 [206 Lincoln Dr, 19144]; (p) (215) 438-5711; (f) (215) 849-6447; (c) Philadelphia

Private non-profit/ 1984/ staff: 2(f); 1(p); 25(v)/ members: 750

HISTORIC SITE; HISTORICAL SOCIETY; HISTORY MUSEUM; HOUSE MUSEUM: Preserves, restores, and interprets Rittenhouse-Town; a National Historic Landmark which is the site of America's first paper mill.

PROGRAMS: Annual Meeting; Community Outreach; Exhibits; Facility Rental; Family Programs; Festivals; Film/Video; Guided Tours; Interpretation; Lectures; Living History; Reenactments; School-Based Curriculum

COLLECTIONS: [1700-1900] Artifacts related to Rittenhouse Town as an early American industrial community and a German American colonial village which was dominated by papermaking.

HOURS: Yr Oct-Apr M-F 10-4; May-Sep M-Su 10-4

ADMISSION: Varies

7383
Historical Society of Pennsylvania, The
1300 Locust St, 19107; (p) (215) 732-6200; (f) (215) 732-2680; hsppr@hsp.org; www.hsp.org; (c) Philadelphia

Private non-profit/ 1824/ Board of Directors/ staff: 28(f); 9(p); 16(v)/ members: 2381/publication: Pennsylvania Magazine of History and Biography; Pennsylvania Legacies

Founded in 1824, HSP holds essential historical materials of national importance. It provides one of the nation's premier non-governmental repositories, housing more than 15 million books, graphics, and manuscript items.

COLLECTIONS: [17th-20th c] Library and archival holdings: emphasis on colonial, early national, and continuing regional, PA, and family history. Manuscript collection of 17th-19th c holdings that is internationally known.

HOURS: Library: Yr T, Th-F 9:30-4:45, W 1-8:45, Sa 10-4:45; Administrative Offices: M-F 9-5

ADMISSION: $6, Student $3

7384
Independence National Historical Park
313 Walnut St, 19106; (p) (215) 597-8787; (f) (215) 597-5556; www.nps.gov/indie; (c) Philadelphia

Federal/ 1948/ U.S. Dept. of the Interior, National Park Service/ staff: 154(f); 30(p); 60(v)

HISTORIC SITE; HOUSE MUSEUM: Oversees 70 historic structures including Independence Hall.

PROGRAMS: Exhibits; Family Programs; Film/Video; Guided Tours; Interpretation; Lectures; Publication; Research Library/Archives; School-Based Curriculum

COLLECTIONS: [18th c] Historic artifacts assembled in the mid 19th c for exhibition in Independence Hall. photograph collection featuring major figures of the Revolutionary and Federal eras painted from life. A sizeable collection of Revolutionary-era printed materials maps, pamphlets, books, decorative arts collections displayed in restored historic rooms which depict documented settings in which the political and social events of the late-18th c took place; liberty Bell.

HOURS: Yr Daily 9-5

ADMISSION: No charge, except select buildings

7385
Independence Seaport Museum
211 S Columbus Blvd, 19106; (p) (215) 925-5439; (f) (215) 925-6713; seaport.philly.com; (c) Philadelphia

Private non-profit/ 1961/ Board of Port Wardens/ staff: 35(f); 19(p); 25(v)/ members: 1200

MARITIME MUSEUM: Dedicated to exploring and making available art and artifacts of the Delaware River Valley and its maritime heritage.

PROGRAMS: Concerts; Elder's Programs; Exhibits; Facility Rental; Family Programs; Film/Video; Guided Tours; Interpretation; Lectures; Living History; Reenactments; Research Library/Archives; School-Based Curriculum

COLLECTIONS: [Late 19th-early 20th c] 1892 Cruiser Olympia the last remaining vessel of the Spanish-American War, diving equipment, ship models, and art.

HOURS: Yr M-Su

7386
International Congress of Distinguished Awards
705 Corinthian Ave, 19103 [PO Box 15782, 19103]; (p) (215) 765-1311; (f) (215) 765-2721; icda@icda.org; www.icda.org; (c) Philadelphia

Private non-profit/ 1994/ staff: 2(p)/ 5(v)/ members: 45/publication: *Awards Gazette*

PROFESSIONAL ORGANIZATION: A consortium of organizations presenting the world's most important prizes and awards in the arts and humanities, science and technology, literature and humanitarianism, the environment and peace.

PROGRAMS: Annual Meeting; Community Outreach; Festivals; Film/Video; Lectures; Publication

COLLECTIONS: [1901-present] Data and files on awards, honors, prizes, and their recipients from 1901 to the present; and sample awards.

7387
Lemon Hill Mansion
Fairmount Park, Lemon Hill & Sedgeley Dr, 19130 [149 Splitrail Lane, Blue Bell, 19422]; (p) (212) 232-4337, (215) 646-7084; (f) (215) 646-8472

1899/ City of Philadelphia Maintained Colonial/ staff: 1(p)

Conserves and preserves the site and educates the public about history especially Philadelphia during the period 1800-1836.

COLLECTIONS: [1800-1836] Furniture, painting, silver, glass, porcelain, decorative arts, and artifacts.

HOURS: Apr-Dec W-Su 10-5

ADMISSION: $2.50

7388
Library Company of Philadelphia, The
1314 Locust St, 19107; (p) (215) 546-3181; (f) (215) 546-5167; refdept@librarycompany.org; www.librarycompany.org; (c) Philadelphia

Private non-profit/ 1731/ Board of Directors/ staff: 19(f); 7(p); 4(v)/ members: 790

LIBRARY AND/OR ARCHIVES; RESEARCH CENTER: Provides research library for national and international constituency of scholars and exhibitions and program for the public free of charge.

PROGRAMS: Annual Meeting; Exhibits; Lectures; Publication; Research Library/Archives

COLLECTIONS: [17th-19th c] 500,000 rare books, prints, and photographs documenting every aspect of American history and culture and its European background.

7389
Masonic Library and Museum of Philadelphia, The
One N Broad St, 19107-2520; (p) (215) 988-1933; (f) (215) 988-1972; www.pagrandlodge.org; (c) Philadelphia

Private non-profit/ 1731/ staff: 9(f)/publication: *The Pennsylvania Freemason*

Guided tours and circulating library for PA Masons.

COLLECTIONS: Library: 70,000 volumes on all facets of Freemasonry, biography, history, religion, philosophy; Archives: manuscripts, broadsides, photographs, biographical files; Museum: 30,000 items including Washington's Lafayette Masonic apron, other regalia, glass, porcelain, textiles, silver, jewelry, and furniture.

7391
Morris Arboretum of the University of Pennsylvania
100 Northwestern Ave, 19118 [9414 Meadowbrook Ave, 19118]; (p) (215) 247-5777; (f) (212) 248-4439; www.openn.edu/morris; (c) Philadelphia

Private non-profit/ 1932/ members: 4400

GARDEN; HISTORIC SITE: A historic public garden and educational institution that promotes an understanding of the relationship between plants and people through programs that integrate science, art, and the humanities.

PROGRAMS: Community Outreach; Concerts; Exhibits; Facility Rental; Family Programs; Festivals; Garden Tours; Guided Tours; Interpretation; Lectures; School-Based Curriculum

COLLECTIONS: [1830-present] Over 14,018 labeled and scientifically documented trees and shrubs from around the world. Collections include medicinal plants, threatened populations, and urban suitable.

HOURS: Yr Nov-Mar M-Su 10-4; Apr-Oct 5 Sa-Su 10-5

ADMISSION: $6, Student $4, Seniors $5; Under 6 free

7392
Mount Pleasant Mansion
Mt Pleasant Dr, E Fairmount Park, 19131 [PO Box 7647, 19101]; (p) (215) 763-8100

7393
Mummers Museum
1100 S 2nd St, 19147; (p) (215) 336-3050; (f) (215) 389-5630; mummersmus@aol.com; www.mummers.com; (c) Philadelphia

Private non-profit/ 1975/ staff: 1(f); 5(p); 15(v)/ members: 480

HISTORY MUSEUM: Collects and preserves artifacts pertaining to the annual New Year's Day Parade (Mummers Parade) in Philadelphia.

PROGRAMS: Community Outreach; Concerts; Elder's Programs; Exhibits; Facility Rental; Guided Tours; Research Library/ Archives

COLLECTIONS: [1901-present] Photographs, videos, oral histories, and recordings.

HOURS: Yr M-Sa 9-5

ADMISSION: $2.50, Children $1.50, Seniors $1.50

7394
National Museum of American Jewish History
55 N 5th St, 19106; (p) (215) 923-3811; (f) (215) 923-0763; www.nmajh.org; (c) Philadelphia

Private non-profit/ 1976/ Board of Trustees/ staff: 18(f); 6(p); 90(v)/ members: 1000

HISTORY MUSEUM: Collects historical materials and presents educational programs that preserve, explore and celebrate the history of the Jews in America.

PROGRAMS: Community Outreach; Concerts; Elder's Programs; Exhibits; Facility Rental; Family Programs; Film/Video; Guided Tours; Interpretation; Lectures; Publication; Research Library/Archives; School-Based Curriculum; Theatre

COLLECTIONS: [1900-1950] 9,000 museum artifacts; 1,000 photographs; 40 linear ft of archival manuscripts.

HOURS: Yr M-Th 10-5, F 10-3, Su 12-5

7395
National Railway Historical Society
[PO Box 58547, 19102-8547]; (p) (215) 557-6606; (f) (215) 5576740; nrhs@compuserve.com; www.nrhs.com; (c) Philadelphia

Private non-profit/ 1936/ staff: 1(f); 150(v)/ members: 16800

HISTORICAL SOCIETY; LIBRARY AND/OR ARCHIVES: Preserves and promotes railroading nationwide.

PROGRAMS: Annual Meeting; Publication; Research Library/Archives

COLLECTIONS: [19th-20th c] NRHS chapter materials, railroad timetables, employee magazines, annual reports, postcards, railway-related periodicals, railway guides, ICC materials, accident reports, AAR publications, maps, stock and bond certificates, technical reports, ICC Blue Books 1888-1971.

HOURS: Yr W 9-3:30

7396
Old St. George's United Methodist Church and Museum
235 N 4th St, 19106; (p) (215) 925-7788; (c) Philadelphia

Private non-profit/ 1769/ Eastern PA Conference of the United Methodist Church/ staff: 3(f); 3(v)/ members: 67

HISTORIC SITE; HISTORICAL SOCIETY; HOUSE MUSEUM: Maintains the oldest Methodist Church in continuous use in the USA housing the conference archives, historical society, library and museum.

COLLECTIONS: [1769-present] Record books of over 100 closed United Methodist churches of the area, library volumes dating back 300 years, museum of artifacts including many old documents of Methodism.

HOURS: Yr

7397
Paley Design Center/Philadelphia College of Textiles & Science
4200 Henry Ave, 19144; (p) (215) 951-2860; (f) (215) 951-2662; www.philacol.edu/paley

1978/ staff: 2(f); 6(p); 2(v)

HISTORY MUSEUM: Devoted to the collection, care, and display of textiles.

PROGRAMS: Exhibits; Guided Tours; Lectures

COLLECTIONS: [1st c AD-present] Historic and contemporary textiles and a fine fabric archive consisting of over 300,000 original samples from many American and European textile mills.

HOURS: Yr T-F 10-4, Sa-Su

7398
Philadelphia Society for the Preservation of Landmarks

321 S 4th St, 19106; (p) (215) 925-2251; (f) (215) 925-7909; (c) Philadelphia

Private non-profit/ 1931/ Board of Trustees/ staff: 4(f); 11(p); 75(v)/ members: 315

HISTORIC SITE; HOUSE MUSEUM: Preserves and manages historic properties and collections and uses these cultural resources for education of present and future generations.

PROGRAMS: Annual Meeting; Concerts; Elder's Programs; Exhibits; Facility Rental; Family Programs; Garden Tours; Guided Tours; Interpretation; Lectures; Reenactments; Research Library/Archives; School-Based Curriculum

COLLECTIONS: [1740-1900] 4 historic houses: 320 period furniture piece, 50 painting, 550 books, 60 medical instruments, 10 military objects, 60 textiles, 60 documents, 5 musical instruments, 15 maps, 10 art works on paper. Structures: Grumble Thorpe, Powel House and Physick House. Physick House: home of Dr. Philip Syng Physick, "Father of American Surgery," Federal style townhouse, objects relating to Physick's contributions to American medicine and his occupancy of the house.

HOURS: Yr Th-Sa 12-4, Su 1-4

ADMISSION: $3

7399
Philadelphia Society of Numismatics

1812 Fairmount Ave, 19130; (p) (215) 769-6269; (c) Philadelphia

Private non-profit/ 1984/ Board of Directors/ staff: 12(v)/ members: 50/publication: *Panta Rei Ouden Menei*

HISTORIC PRESERVATION AGENCY; HOUSE MUSEUM: Collects ephemera and eclectic objects for the enjoyment and edification of the public.

PROGRAMS: Annual Meeting; Exhibits; Interpretation; Lectures; Publication; School-Based Curriculum

COLLECTIONS: Eclectic collection of various coins (ancient to present); Library: 2,000 volumes on medieval topics and architecture, 1st edition of Darwin's Origin of Species, Collected Works of E.M. Cioran and Horatio Jex; Brass Rubbings from England; dinosaur bones found in pre-historic Philadelphia; stuffed fur flamingo, farm implements from 16th c Trappist monastery in France.

HOURS: Feb-Apr Sa 9-4:30; Jun-Aug M, Th-Sa 9-4:30

ADMISSION: No charge

7400
Polish American Cultural Center Museum

308 Walnut St, 19106; (p) (215) 922-1700; (f) (215) 922-1518; mail@polishamericancenter.org; www.polishamericancenter.org; (c) Philadelphia

1981/ Board of Directors/ staff: 1(f); 2(p); 15(v)/ members: 1000/publication: *Polish American News*

HISTORY MUSEUM: Provides programs and exhibits featuring contributions of Poles and Polish Americans to the US, world history, and culture in such areas as scientific, artistic, musical, political, religious, and military achievement.

PROGRAMS: Annual Meeting; Community Outreach; Concerts; Elder's Programs; Exhibits; Family Programs; Festivals; Guided Tours; Interpretation; Lectures; Publication; School-Based Curriculum

COLLECTIONS: Museum features displays about Polish history and culture, paintings of "Great Men and Women of Poland" and a pictorial display of Poland at Arms, with WW II photographs from 1939-1944.

HOURS: Yr May-Dec M-Sa 10-4; Jan-Apr M-F 10-4

ADMISSION: No charge

7401
Powel House, The

244 S Third St, 19106; (p) (215) 627-0364; (f) (215) 627-1733; lswitzer@hotmail.com; (c) Philadelphia

1931/ The Philadelphia Society for the Preservation of Landmarks/ staff: 3(f); 5(p); 160(v)/ members: 450

GARDEN; HISTORIC SITE; HISTORICAL SOCIETY; HISTORY MUSEUM; HOUSE MUSEUM: Interprets the daily lives of Philadelphians at the time of the American Revolution.

PROGRAMS: Elder's Programs; Exhibits; Facility Rental; Guided Tours; Interpretation; Research Library/Archives

COLLECTIONS: [1769-1800]

HOURS: Yr Th-Sa 12-5, Su 1-5

ADMISSION: $3, Student $2, Seniors $2;

7402
Print Center, The

1614 Latimer St, 19103; (p) (215) 735-6090; (f) (215) 735-5511; print@libertynet.org; www.Printcenter.org; (c) Philadelphia

Private non-profit/ 1915/ Board of Governors/ staff: 4(f); 1(p); 10(v)/ members: 2000

HOUSE MUSEUM; LIBRARY AND/OR ARCHIVES: Provides exhibits as well as prints and photographs that are housed in a renovated carriage house.

PROGRAMS: Annual Meeting; Exhibits; Facility Rental; Family Programs; Festivals; Guided Tours; Lectures; Living History; Research Library/Archives

COLLECTIONS: 1,000 masterworks by historic and contemporary printmakers and photographers.

HOURS: Yr T-Sa 11-5:30

ADMISSION: No charge

7403
Rosenbach Museum and Library

2008-2010 DeLancey Place, 19103 [2010 DeLancey Place, 19103]; (p) (215) 732-1600; (f) (215) 545-7529; info@rosenbach.org; www.rosenbach.org; (c) Philadelphia

Private non-profit/ 1954/ staff: 14(f); 5(p); 36(v)/ members: 660

ART MUSEUM; HISTORIC SITE; HISTORY MUSEUM; HOUSE MUSEUM: Maintains the museum and library located in a historic house museum with rare books, manuscripts, and fine art, a regular schedule of exhibitions and programs, and a full-service library.

PROGRAMS: Community Outreach; Elder's Programs; Exhibits; Guided Tours; Interpretation; Lectures; Publication; Research Library/Archives

COLLECTIONS: [15th-20th c] Rare books, manuscripts, English and American furnishings, fine, and decorative arts. Collection strengths: Americana, British and American literature, works of art on paper related to book illustration.

HOURS: Sept-July T-Su 11-4; Research: M-F 9-5

ADMISSION: Varies

7404
Stenton

18th & Windrim streets, 19106 [4601 N 18th St, 19106-1026]; (p) (215) 329-7312; (f) (215) 329-7312; stenton@libertynet.org; (c) Philadelphia

Private non-profit/ 1899/ National Society of the Colonial Dames of America in the Commonwealth of Pennsylvania/ staff: 1(f); 1(p); 10(v)/ members: 110/publication: *Friends of Stenton*

HOUSE MUSEUM: Maintains Stenton 18th c plantation home of James Logan, William Penn's colonial agent an early Georgian brick house, kitchen wing and barn stand on a 3 acre wooded site.

PROGRAMS: Guided Tours; Interpretation; Publication

COLLECTIONS: [1730-1830] Stenton's handsome wood-paneled period rooms are furnished with a superb collection of furniture, decorative arts, and textiles. Many are fine Philadelphia-made pieces with Logan family provenance.

HOURS: Apr-Dec Th-Sa 1-4, T-W by appt; Jan-Mar by appt

ADMISSION: $5, Student $4; Under 6 free

7405
Thaddeus Kosciuszko National Memorial

301 Pine St, 19106 [Independence NHP, 313 Walnut St, 19106]; (p) (215) 597-9618; (f) (215) 597-1901; nps.gov/thko; www.nps.gov/thko; (c) Philadelphia

Federal/ 1976/ National Park Service/United States Department of the Interior/ staff: 5(f); 2(p)/publication: *Thaddeus Kosciuszko National Memorial*

HISTORIC SITE: Preserves the temporary residence of Thaddeus Kosciuszko, a Polish soldier who fought in the American Revolution and who led an unsuccessful insurrection for Polish independence.

PROGRAMS: Community Outreach; Exhibits; Film/Video; Interpretation; Publication

COLLECTIONS: [1797-1798] Kosciuszko's bed chamber has been recreated by utilizing reproduction wallpaper and period pieces.

7406
United States Mint at Philadelphia
5th & Arch Sts, 19106 [151 N Independence Mall E, 19106]; (p) (215) 408-0114; (f) (215) 408-2700; www.usmint.gov; (c) Philadelphia

Federal/ 1792/ Treasury Dept/ staff: 4(f)

HISTORY MUSEUM: Operates world's largest mint where one can see coins being produced and historical exhibits.

PROGRAMS: Exhibits; Publication

COLLECTIONS: [1792-present] Numismatic items from 1st Mint to present; coins, medals, coinage artifacts.

HOURS: Sep-Aug M-F 9-4:30; May-Jun M-Sa 9-4:30; July-Aug M-Su 9-4:30

7407
University of Pennsylvania Museum of Archaeology and Anthropology
33rd and Spruce Sts, 19104; (p) (215) 898-4000; (f) (215) 898-7961; pkosty@sas.upenn.edu; www.upenn.edu/museum; (c) Philadelphia

Private non-profit/ 1887/ staff: 101(f); 38(p); 250(v)/ members: 2900/publication: Expedition

ART MUSEUM; HISTORY MUSEUM: Dedicated to the study and understanding of human history and diversity. Conducts archaeological and anthropological expeditions around the world.

PROGRAMS: Community Outreach; Concerts; Exhibits; Facility Rental; Family Programs; Film/Video; Guided Tours; Interpretation; Lectures; Publication; Research Library/Archives; School-Based Curriculum; Theatre

COLLECTIONS: 1 million artifacts from around the world including materials from Ancient Egypt, Mesopotamia, Mesoamerica, Asia, and the Greco-Roman world and artifacts from native people of the Americas, Africa, and Polynesia.

HOURS: Yr T-Sa 10-4:30, Su 1-5; Summer, no Su

ADMISSION: $5, Student $2.50, Children $2.50, Seniors $2.50; Under 6 free

7408
Victorian Society in America, The
219 S Sixth St, 19106; (p) (215) 627-4252; (f) (215) 627-7221; info@victoriansociety.org; www.victoriansociety.org; (c) Philadelphia

Private non-profit/ 1966/ Board of Directors/ staff: 1(f); 2(v)/ members: 1600

HISTORICAL SOCIETY: Committed to historic preservation, protection, understanding, education, and enjoyment of our 19th c heritage.

PROGRAMS: Annual Meeting; Lectures

7409
Woodford Mansion
33rd & Dauphin St, E Fairmont Park, 19132 [33rd and Dauphin St, E Fairmont Park, 19132]; (p) (215) 229-6115

1756/ Naomi Wood Trust/ staff: 1(f); 1(p); 25(v)

COLLECTIONS: [1770-1800] American antiques: Chippendale, Federal and Queen Anne; some William & Mary; English delftware.

7410
Woodmere Art Museum
9201 Germantown Ave, 19118; (p) (215) 247-0476; (f) (215) 247-2387; (c) Philadelphia

Private non-profit/ 1940/ Board of Trustees/ staff: 9(f); 5(p); 66(v)/ members: 2270/publication: Exhibition Catalogues

ART MUSEUM; HISTORIC SITE: Focuses on the art and artists of the Philadelphia area, past and present, in a 19th c stone Victorian mansion.

PROGRAMS: Community Outreach; Concerts; Exhibits; Family Programs; Festivals; Guided Tours; Lectures; Publication; Research Library/Archives

COLLECTIONS: [18th-19th c] Fine arts featuring artist of the Delaware Valley; American and European decorative arts.

HOURS: Yr T-Sa 10-5, Su 1-5

ADMISSION: $3, Seniors $3; Donations requested

7411
Wyck
6026 Germantown Ave, 19144; (p) (215) 848-1690; (f) (215) 848-1690; wyck@libertynet.org

Joint/ 1700/ Wyck Charitable Trust; Core States Bank/ staff: 1(f); 5(p); 25(v)

COLLECTIONS: [1690-1973] 10,000 original furnishings, clothing, housewares; Strong ceramic, textile, furniture, natural history, Native American; 100,000 bills of sale, letters, diaries, estate papers; 2,000 volumes

PHOENIXVILLE

7412
Historical Society of the Phoenixville Area
Corner of Church & Main St, 19460 [PO Box 552, 19460]; (p) (610) 935-7646; (f) (610) 935-7646; www.voicenet.com/.com/~dstar; (c) Chester

Private non-profit/ 1977/ staff: 30(v)/ members: 350

HISTORICAL SOCIETY: Preserves information and artifacts relating to Phoenixville and adjacent townships.

PROGRAMS: Exhibits; Publication; Research Library/Archives

COLLECTIONS: [1700s-present] Local historical, genealogical information, and artifacts relating to Phoenixville and adjacent townships.

HOURS: Yr W, F 9-3

ADMISSION: No charge

7413
Pikeland Historical Society
Centennial Lutheran Church, Hares Hill Rd, 19460 [1289 W Evergreen, 19460]; (p) (610) 933-2867; (f) (610) 933-0900; (c) Chester

Private non-profit/ 1977/ Board of Directors/ staff: 8(v)/ members: 68

HISTORICAL SOCIETY: Collects and collates the history and pre-history of the Pikelands and protects and preserves the ancient Pikelands Friends Burial Ground at Kimberton.

PROGRAMS: Annual Meeting; Community Outreach; Exhibits; Family Programs; Festivals; Guided Tours; Interpretation; Lectures; Research Library/Archives

COLLECTIONS: [pre-historic-1900] Ephemera relating to pre-history and history of greater Kimberton, PA area including Native American and Quaker.

HOURS: Yr M-Su

PITTSBURGH

7414
Allegheny Cemetery Historical Association
4734 Butler St, 15201; (p) (412) 682-1624; (f) (412) 622-0655; tgpr@aol.com; allcem.com; (c) Allegheny

Private non-profit/ 1844/ Board of Directors/ staff: 3(p)/publication: Heritage

HISTORIC SITE

PROGRAMS: Exhibits; Festivals; Guided Tours; Living History; Publication

COLLECTIONS: [1844-present]

HOURS: Yr Daily 8-5

7415
Allegheny Foothills Historical Society
Pierson Run Rd, Boyce Park, 15239 [675 Old Frankstown Rd, 15239-2239]; (c) Allegheny

1979/ Board of Directors and Officers/ staff: 20(v)/ members: 90/publication: Where the Wild Plum Trees Grew

HISTORICAL SOCIETY: Preserves and interprets a part of the local history by maintaining the Carpenter Log House for the education and enjoyment of all generations in the greater Plum Borough area.

PROGRAMS: Community Outreach; Exhibits; Facility Rental; Festivals; Guided Tours; Living History; Publication; Reenactments

COLLECTIONS: [1870-1930s] Photographs, letters, and articles about the Plum Borough community and its people.

HOURS: May-Oct 1 Su 1-4

ADMISSION: Donations accepted

7416
Center for American Music
Stephen Foster Memorial, 4301 Forbes Ave, 15260 [Univ of Pittsburgh, 15260]; (p) (412) 624-4100; (f) (412) 624-7447; amerimus+@pitt.edu; www.library.pitt.edu/libraries/cam/cam.html; (c) Allegheny

State/ 1937/ Univ of Pittsburgh/ staff: 2(f)

LIBRARY AND/OR ARCHIVES: The center acquires, conserves, and makes accessible significant library holdings on music in American life between 1840 and 1940. It is the world's repository for information about Stephen Foster.

PROGRAMS: Community Outreach; Concerts; Exhibits; Family Programs; Guided Tours; Interpretation; Lectures; Publication; Research Library/Archives; School-Based Curriculum

COLLECTIONS: [1840s-1930s] Foster Hall Collection documents life and works of Stephen Collins Foster, 30,000 items in all formats including art works, recordings, printed media, photographs, instruments; other collections include Ethelbert Nevin, Charles H. Pace Gospel, Joe Negri, and Robert Schmertz collections.

HOURS: Yr M-F 9-4

ADMISSION: No charge, group rates

7417
Fort Pitt Museum
Point State Park, 15222 [101 Commonwealth Place, 15222]; (p) (412) 281-9284; (f) (412) 281-1417; jgiblin@PHMC.st.pa.us; (c) Allegheny

State/ 1964/ PA Historical and Museum Commission/ staff: 4(f); 2(p)

HISTORIC SITE: Depicts the French and Indian War era and "early" Pittsburgh, for the education and enjoyment of visitors through its collections, reenactments, and multimedia presentations.

PROGRAMS: Festivals; Guided Tours; Lectures; Living History; Reenactments

COLLECTIONS: [Mid 18th c-early 19th c]

HOURS: Yr W-Sa 10-4:30 Su 12-4:30

ADMISSION: $4, Family $10, Children $2, Seniors $3.50

7418
Frick Art and Historical Center, The
7227 Reynods St, 15208; (p) (412) 371-0600; (f) (412) 241-5393; info@frickart.org; www.frickart.org; (c) Allegheny

Private non-profit/ 1969/ Frick Art and Historical Center/ staff: 36(f); 84(p); 8(v)/ members: 2900/publication: *The Art and Life of a Pittsburgh Family*

GARDEN; HISTORY MUSEUM; HOUSE MUSEUM: The Frick's 5.5 acres of beautifully landscaped gardens and grounds include Clayton, the Victorian estate of industrialist Henry Clay Frick; The Frick Art Museum; Car and Carriage Museum; Greenhouse.

PROGRAMS: Community Outreach; Concerts; Exhibits; Facility Rental; Family Programs; Film/Video; Garden Tours; Guided Tours; Lectures; Publication

COLLECTIONS: [19th c] Museum: Italian Renaissance, French 18th c works, travelling exhibitions. Clayton: 19th c furniture, artwork, and decorative arts. Car and Carriage Museum: pre-1940 automobiles including a 1914 Rolls-Royce Silver Ghost.

HOURS: Yr T-Sa 10-5, Su 12-6

ADMISSION: $8, Student $6, Seniors $7; Art Museum and Car/Carriage Museum free

7419
Hartwood
215 Saxonburg Blvd, 15238; (p) (412) 767-9200; (f) (412) 767-0171; info.co.allegheny.pa.us/parks; (c) Allegheny

County/ 1929/ staff: 1(f); 5(p); 17(v)

HISTORIC SITE; HOUSE MUSEUM: Manages the Hartwood mansion houses a collection of English and American antiques.

PROGRAMS: Concerts; Facility Rental; Festivals; Guided Tours

COLLECTIONS: [15th-19th c] English and American antiques. Includes Bujar Carpet c. 1870, 1901 Steinway piano, and 17th c refectory table.

HOURS: Apr-Dec W-Sa 10-3, Su 12-4

7420
Historical Society of Western Pennsylvania
1212 Smallman St, 15222 [Sen. John Heinz Pittsburgh Reg Hist Ctr/, 15222]; (p) (412) 454-6000; (f) (412) 454-6031; hswp@usadr.net; www.eghistory.org; (c) Allegheny

Private non-profit/ 1884/ staff: 80(f); 31(p); 150(v)/ members: 5000/publication: *Western PA History*

HISTORICAL SOCIETY; HISTORY MUSEUM: Preserves and interprets regional history through a variety of programs.

PROGRAMS: Community Outreach; Concerts; Exhibits; Facility Rental; Family Programs; Festivals; Film/Video; Guided Tours; Interpretation; Lectures; Living History; Publication; Research Library/Archives; School-Based Curriculum

COLLECTIONS: [1750-present] Photographs, books, archives, costumes, tools, personal possessions, vehicles, household items related to western PA history; also archaeological collections related to Pittsburgh.

ADMISSION: $6, Children $4.50, Seniors $4.50

7421
Old St. Luke's Church, Burial Garden and Garden
Old Washington Pke, 15234 [c/o 217 Allenberry Dr, 15234]; (p) (412) 851-6541; (f) (412) 531-9820; www.oldsaintlukes.org; (c) Allegheny

Private non-profit/ 1765/ Episcopal Diocese of Pittsburgh/ staff: 30(v)/ members: 125/publication: *Rebellion and Revelation*

HISTORIC SITE

PROGRAMS: Family Programs; Festivals; Guided Tours; Lectures; Publication; School-Based Curriculum

COLLECTIONS: [1765-1800]

HOURS: Apr-Dec Su 1:30-4

7422
Pittsburgh History and Landmarks Foundation
450 One Station Sq, 15219; (p) (412) 471-5808; (f) (412) 471-1633; ron@phlf.org; www.phlg.org; (c) Allegheny

Private non-profit/ 1964/ staff: 20(f); 150(v)/ members: 3600

HISTORIC PRESERVATION AGENCY; HISTORICAL SOCIETY; RESEARCH CENTER: Dedicated to identifying and preserving the architectural landmarks, historic neighborhoods, and historic designed landscapes of Allegheny County and educating people about this regions architectural heritage and urban landscape design history.

PROGRAMS: Community Outreach; Elder's Programs; Exhibits; Family Programs; Festivals; Garden Tours; Guided Tours; Lectures; Publication; Research Library/Archives

COLLECTIONS: Books, manuscripts, periodicals, historic site survey data, photographs and other visual documentation, slides, maps, plat books, renderings and blueprints, and other materials pertaining to the activities of Landmarks, regional history, Allegheny County Historic Buildings Survey, African American History Survey, architecture, historic preservation, urban planning, engineering and technological development, interior design, and landscape design.

HOURS: Yr M-F 9-5

ADMISSION: No charge

PLYMOUTH MEETING

7423
Plymouth Meeting Historical Society
2130 Sierra Rd, 19462 [PO Box 167, 19462]; (p) (610) 828-8111; (f) (610) 828-0461; (c) Montgomery

Private non-profit/ 1932/ Board of Directors/ staff: 1(p); 1(v)/ members: 288

HISTORIC SITE; HISTORICAL SOCIETY: Headquartered in an old Quaker Farmstead, the society preserves local history through programs and exhibits as well as visiting community groups in order to share its knowledge.

PROGRAMS: Annual Meeting; Community Outreach; Exhibits; Guided Tours; Lectures; Research Library/Archives; School-Based Curriculum

COLLECTIONS: [1850s-present] Photographs, clothing (mostly Quaker), tools, books, photographs, furniture, written archives, videotapes, and artwork. Structures: Dickinson House, Albertson House, barn, smokehouse,and carriage shed.

HOURS: Yr T, F 10-4

ADMISSION: Donations accepted

PORTAGE

7424
Portage Area Historical Society
400 Lee St, 15946 [PO Box 45, 15946]; (p) (814) 736-9223; (c) Cambria

Private non-profit/ 1989/ Board of Directors/ staff: 14(v)/ members: 107/publication: *Portrait of a Town, Portage, Pennsylvania*

HISTORICAL SOCIETY; HISTORY MUSEUM: Collects and preserves artifacts and information that illustrate the region's rich heritage.

PROGRAMS: Annual Meeting; Community Outreach; Exhibits; Family Programs; Film/Video; Lectures; Publication; Research Library/Archives; School-Based Curriculum

COLLECTIONS: [1890-present] Mining, railroad artifacts, and other objects concerning "life along the Mainline."

POTTSTOWN

7425
Pottsgrove Manor
100 W King St, 19464; (p) (610) 326-4014; (f) (610) 326-9618; www.montcopa.org; (c) Montgomery

County/ 1952/ staff: 3(f); 1(p); 50(v)

HOUSE MUSEUM; LIVING HISTORY/OUTDOOR MUSEUM: Mantains Pottsgrove Manor, historic home of John Potts, colonial ironmaster and founder of Pottstown, PA. Provides educational programs that brings to life the world of the Potts family, their servants, and slaves.

PROGRAMS: Exhibits; Family Programs; Guided Tours; Interpretation; Lectures; Living History; Reenactments

COLLECTIONS: [1752-1783] Family period pieces and manuscripts.

HOURS: Yr T-Sa 10-4, Su 1-4

ADMISSION: No charge

7426
Pottstown Historical Society
871 N Hanover St, 19464 [Box 661, 19464]; (p) (610) 970-7355; (c) Montgomery

Private non-profit/ staff: 4(v)/ members: 310

HISTORICAL SOCIETY: Small library with a collection of local pictures, manuscripts, mostly related to the Potts family and their descendants. Local artifacts and library for genealogy research.

PROGRAMS: Lectures; Publication; Research Library/Archives

COLLECTIONS: [1700s-present] Manuscripts and ledgers relating to the local iron forges. Potts and Rutter Family history and genealogy, many other local genealogies, cemetery records, local newspapers on microfilm, historical maps and pictures of Pottstown.

POTTSVILLE

7427
Historical Society of Schuylkill County, The
14 N Third St, 17901; (p) (570) 628-3695; (f) (570) 628-2012; hward@voicenet.com; www.rootsweb.com/~flurion/hssc.html; (c) Schuylkill

Private non-profit/ 1903/ staff: 1(f); 1(v)/ members: 450

HISTORICAL SOCIETY: Collects information pertaining to the history of the Schuylkill County.

PROGRAMS: Annual Meeting; Lectures

COLLECTIONS: [19th c] Artifacts and memorabilia related to the history of Schuylkill County.

HOURS: Yr T-Su 10-12/1-4

ADMISSION: No charge

PROSPECT PARK

7428
Morton Homestead
100 Lincoln Ave, 19076; (p) (610) 583-7221, (610) 583-2349

QUAKERTOWN

7429
Quakertown Historical Society
26 N Main St, 18951 [PO Box 846, 18951]; (p) (215) 536-3298; (c) Bucks

Private non-profit/ 1965/ members: 182

HISTORIC SITE; HISTORICAL SOCIETY; HOUSE MUSEUM: Dedicated to the preservation of local history, maintaining historic buildings, and offering guided tours of the museum and local sites of interest.

PROGRAMS: Festivals; Guided Tours; Lectures

COLLECTIONS: Artifacts, furnishings, maps, newspapers, articles and photographs of local interest dating from early colonial to present day.

HOURS: By appt

QUARRYVILLE

7430
Solaneo Historical Society
2300 Robert Fulton Hwy, 17566 [PO Box 33, 17566]; (p) (717) 548-2679, (717) 548-2755; SLCHS@aol.com; members.aol.com/SLCHS/SLCHS.html; (c) Lancaster

Joint/ 1976/ State; Historical Society/ staff: 20(p); 8(v)/ members: 160

GENEALOGICAL SOCIETY; HISTORIC PRESERVATION AGENCY; HISTORIC SITE; HISTORICAL SOCIETY; HISTORY MUSEUM; RESEARCH CENTER: Maintains the Fulton birthplace, preserve local historic material, and are in the process of opening a museum of mining and agriculture of the area.

PROGRAMS: Community Outreach; Exhibits; Facility Rental; Garden Tours; Guided Tours; Lectures; Research Library/Archives; School-Based Curriculum

COLLECTIONS: [Early 1700s-present] Fulton House, period furniture, local history collection.

HOURS: Mem Day-Labor Day Sa 11-4, Su 1-5, or by appt

ADMISSION: $1

READING

7431
Historical Society of Berks County
940 Centre Ave, 19610; (p) (610) 375-4375; (f) (610) 375-4376; lorabec@epix.net; www.berksweb.com/histsoc; (c) Berks

Private non-profit/ 1869/ staff: 4(f); 9(p); 75(v)/ members: 2990

HISTORICAL SOCIETY; HISTORY MUSEUM: Dedicated to preserving, exhibiting, publishing, and disseminating the history of the county through programs, maintaining material artifacts, and printed material for research and education.

PROGRAMS: Annual Meeting; Community Outreach; Exhibits; Facility Rental; Family Programs; Guided Tours; Lectures; Publication; Research Library/Archives

COLLECTIONS: Art and artifacts related to all aspects of the county's history. Almshouse Paintings and articles unique to the county: the streetcar, Duryea Auto and 1802 organ.

HOURS: Yr M-F 9-4

ADMISSION: $2.50, Children $1, Seniors $2

7432
Reading Public Museum
500 Museum Rd, 19611; (p) (610) 371-5850; (f) (610) 371-5632; museum@ptd.net; www.readingpublicmuseum.org; (c) Berks

Private non-profit/ 1924/ staff: 15(f); 9(p); 467(v)/ members: 2100

HISTORY MUSEUM

PROGRAMS: Community Outreach; Concerts; Exhibits; Facility Rental; Family Pro-

grams; Festivals; Lectures; Research Library/Archives; Theatre

COLLECTIONS: Art, fine art collectionwith emphasis on American and foreign artists. Anthropology collection encompasses over 30,000 artifacts representing many cultures. Collection also includes PA German pieces. There are galleries devoted to Asian art and culture, to Judiac, Islamic and European Arms and Armor.

HOURS: Yr T, Th-Sa 11-5; W 11-8, Su 12-5

ADMISSION: $4

RED LION

7433
Red Lion Area Historical Society
Center Square, 17356 [PO Box 94, 17356]; (p) (717) 244-1912; (c) York

Private non-profit/ 1981/ members: 375

HISTORICAL SOCIETY; HISTORY MUSEUM: Collects, records, documents, preserves, extrapolates, and disseminates historical facts and information related to the Red Lion area. The exhibits feature a wide range of artifacts and memorabilia representative of the area's historical heritage.

PROGRAMS: Exhibits; Lectures; Publication

COLLECTIONS: [1880-present] Artifacts relating to hand rolling of cigars, artifacts and history of five major woodworking plants, 50th, 75th, and 100th Red Lion Anniversary items, scrap books, and school memorabilia.

HOURS: Yr W, F, Su 10-12

ADMISSION: Donations

RIDGWAY

7434
Elk County Historical Society
109 Center St, 15853 [PO Box 361, 15853]; (p) (814) 776-1032; (f) (814) 776-1032; (c) Elk

Private non-profit/ 1964/ staff: 2(p); 40(v)/ members: 567/publication: *History of Elk County*

HISTORICAL SOCIETY: Discovers, collects, and preserves materials pertaining to the history of Elk County and encourages the study and appreciation of this history.

PROGRAMS: Annual Meeting; Community Outreach; Exhibits; Family Programs; Festivals; Film/Video; Guided Tours; Publication; Research Library/Archives

COLLECTIONS: [1800-present] Elk County history, industry, ethnic/religious/cultural, genealogy, historic preservation, oral history, photos, and social history materials.

HOURS: Apr-Dec T-Th

ROBERTSDALE

7435
Broad Top Area Coal Miners Historical Society, Inc.
Main St, 16674 [PO Box 171, 16674]; (p) (814) 635-3807; (c) Huntingdon

Private non-profit/ 1990/ staff: 25(v)/ members: 205/publication: *Coal Miners Journal*

HISTORIC PRESERVATION AGENCY; HISTORIC SITE; HISTORICAL SOCIETY; HISTORY MUSEUM: Dedicated to the preservation and interpretation of the coal mining and railroading history of the Broad Top Coal Field.

PROGRAMS: Annual Meeting; Community Outreach; Exhibits; Facility Rental; Festivals; Guided Tours; Interpretation; Lectures; Publication; Research Library/Archives; Theatre

COLLECTIONS: [1800-present] Photographs, artifacts, records, audio/visual presentations, maps, and tools related to coal mining and railroads.

ROME

7436
P.P. Bliss Gospel Songwriters Museum
Main St, 18837 [RR 1 Box 293, 18837]; (p) (570) 247-7683; bview@epix.net; bradford-pa.com; (c) Bradford

1964/ P.P. Bliss Museum Board/ staff: 12(v)

HISTORY MUSEUM: Seeks to preserve a piece of local history in Bradford County.

PROGRAMS: Annual Meeting; Concerts; Exhibits; Guided Tours; Lectures

COLLECTIONS: [1838-1876] Museum contains music, books, pictures, letters and musical instruments associated with 19th c musicians, P.P. Bliss, James McGranahan, and D.B. Towner. Restored melodeon.

HOURS: May-Sept, W, Sa 1-4, other by appt

ADMISSION: No charge

RONKS

7437
Ressler Mill Foundation
2880 Stumptown Rd, 17572 [443 Newport Rd, 17572]; (p) (717) 656-7616; (f) (717) 656-6250; (c) Lancaster

Private non-profit/ 1967/ Board of Directors/ staff: 2(f); 20(p)

HISTORIC SITE; HOUSE MUSEUM; LIVING HISTORY/OUTDOOR MUSEUM: Administers a vigorous program of acquisition, restoration, and educational outreach. Researches and publishes material on the history of milling, milling technology, and the effects of the industry on the economy and culture of the region.

PROGRAMS: Exhibits; Guided Tours; Interpretation; Living History; School-Based Curriculum

COLLECTIONS: [1760-1977] Household and personal items of the Ressler family from the last 120 years. Machinery and equipment relating to the milling process. Mill still operates for visitors.

HOURS: May-Oct, M-Sa 9-4

ADMISSION: No charge

ROSEMONT

7438
Lower Marion Historical Society, The
1301 Montgomery Ave, 19010; (p) (610) 525-5831; lmhs@erols.com; (c) Montgomery

Private non-profit/ 1949/ staff: 15(p)/ members: 310/publication: *First 300: Amazing and*

Rich History of Lower Merion

The society promotes education, historical study and research of L.M. Township as well as collecting, preserving and publishing the history and historical records of the township.

PROGRAMS: Annual Meeting; Guided Tours; Lectures; Publication; Research Library/ Archives

COLLECTIONS: [1680s-1950s] Library, historic documents, railroad atlas, maps, local artifacts.

HOURS: Yr Th 12-4

SAINT MARYS

7439
St. Marys and Benzinger Historical Society
9 Erie Ave, 15857 [PO Box 584, 15857]; (p) (814) 834-6525; (c) Elk

Private non-profit/ 1965/ members: 384

HISTORICAL SOCIETY

PROGRAMS: Annual Meeting; Exhibits; Guided Tours; Publication; Research Library/ Archives

COLLECTIONS: [1800-present] Newspapers 1873-1970, early maps of St. Marys; 1,200 pictures of family and early industry on display, files, early history of the town.

HOURS: Yr T 10-4, Th 1-4, 6-8

ADMISSION: No charge

SAINT MICHAEL

7440
1889 South Fork Fishing and Hunting Club Historical Preservation Society
Main St, 15951 [PO Box 219, 15951]; (p) (814) 539-6752; (c) Cambria

Private non-profit/ 1986/ staff: 4(v)/ members: 552

HISTORIC SITE; HISTORICAL SOCIETY: Preserves the sites of the South Fork Fishing and Hunting Club, owners of a dam that collapsed causing the Johnstown Flood of 1889.

PROGRAMS: Festivals; Guided Tours

COLLECTIONS: [1880-1889] Original rocking chair, costumes, and photographs.

HOURS: May-Oct Daily 11-4

ADMISSION: Donations

SALTSBURG

7441
Rebecca B. Hadden Stone House Museum
105 Point St, 15681 [PO Box 12, 15681]; (p) (412) 639-9003, (724) 639-9038; (c) Indiana

Private non-profit/ 1964/ Saltsburg Area Historical Society/ members: 300

HISTORIC PRESERVATION AGENCY; HISTORIC SITE; HISTORICAL SOCIETY; HISTORY MUSEUM; LIVING HISTORY/OUTDOOR MUSEUM; RESEARCH CENTER: Maintains museum built in 1830 with Canal close.

PROGRAMS: Annual Meeting; Community Outreach; Elder's Programs; Family Programs; Festivals; Film/Video; Garden Tours; Guided

Tours; Lectures; Living History; Publication; Research Library/Archives; School-Based Curriculum

COLLECTIONS: [1800s] Artifacts and memorabilia of early history pertaining to Indians, Pioneers, Salt - including a salt replica of drilling; Canal listed on Historic Landmark; mining; manufacturing; schools; churches; floods; businesses; mills; factories.

HOURS: By appt

ADMISSION: No charge

SCHILLINGTON

7442
Governor Mifflin Historical Society
23 Pennsylvania Ave, 19607; (c) Berks

Private non-profit/ staff: 7(v)/ members: 425/publication: *Governor Mifflin Area History*

Publishes 3 magazines a year of local history, holds quarterly meetings, and has a banquet once a year.

SCHWENKSVILLE

7443
Pennypacker Mills
5 Haldeman Rd, 19473; (p) (610) 287-9349; (f) (610) 287-9567; (c) Montgomery

County/ 1981/ staff: 6(f); 2(p); 50(v)

HOUSE MUSEUM: Colonial Revival home redesigned for Samuel W. Pennypacker, containing original family antiques in a late Victorian gentleman's country estate. Landscape by Tho. Meehan, mansion by Arthur Brockie. Original structure 1720; Revolutionary War encampment site.

PROGRAMS: Exhibits; Family Programs; Festivals; Garden Tours; Guided Tours; Interpretation; Living History; Publication; Reenactments; Research Library/Archives

COLLECTIONS: [1700-1920 interpretation 1900-1916] Early PA decorative arts and manuscripts, family genealogy, government papers related to Samuel W. Pennypacker's term as governor (1903-1907), state capitol construction.

HOURS: Yr T-Sa 10-4, Su 1-4

ADMISSION: No charge

SCOTTDALE

7444
West Overton Museums and Village
Rt 819, 15683; (p) (724) 887-7910; (f) (724) 887-5010; womuseum@westol.com; (c) Westmoreland

Private non-profit/ 1928/ staff: 4(f); 4(p); 20(v)/ members: 500

GARDEN; HISTORIC SITE; HISTORICAL SOCIETY; HOUSE MUSEUM: A 19th c village of 19 original brick or stone houses dating from 1800 with yearly activities.

PROGRAMS: Reenactments; School-Based Curriculum; Theatre

COLLECTIONS: [1840-1890] Archives and artifacts belonging to Abraham Overholt and grandson H. C. Frick; household furnishings, mining, distilling, farming tools, and equipment.

HOURS: May-Oct T-Sa 10-4, Su 1-5

SCRANTON

7445
Lackawanna Historical Society
232 Monroe Ave, 18510; (p) (570) 344-3841; (f) (570) 344-3815; (c) Lackawanna

Private non-profit/ 1886/ Board of Trustees/ staff: 3(f); 15(v)/ members: 500/publication: *Society Journal*

HISTORICAL SOCIETY; HISTORY MUSEUM; HOUSE MUSEUM; RESEARCH CENTER: Promotes the preservation of the county's history through its collections, artifacts, books, historical programs, and by assisting in genealogical research.

PROGRAMS: Community Outreach; Exhibits; Family Programs; Guided Tours; Interpretation; Lectures; Publication; Research Library/ Archives

COLLECTIONS: [1790-present] Vertical and genealogical files: 5,000 photos; 4,000 books, atlases, 1,200 maps, limited microfilm of newspapers, manuscripts, letters, diaries, County prison records, some funeral records, oral histories, scrapbooks, musical scrapbooks.

HOURS: Yr T-F 10-5, Sa 12-3

ADMISSION: $5 library fee

7446
Pennsylvania Anthracite Heritage Museum
159 Cedar Ave, McDade Park, 18504 [RD 1, Bald Mountain Rd, 18504]; (p) (570) 963-4804, (570) 963-3208; (f) (570) 963-4194; (c) Lackawanna

State/ 1975/ PA Historical and Museum Commission/ staff: 5(f); 45(v)/ members: 350/publication: *The Miner's Lamp*

HISTORY MUSEUM: Promotes the story of the people who worked in the mines, mills and factories of northeastern PA's hard coal region.

PROGRAMS: Annual Meeting; Concerts; Exhibits; Facility Rental; Family Programs; Festivals; Film/Video; Guided Tours; Interpretation; Lectures; Publication; Research Library/ Archives; School-Based Curriculum

COLLECTIONS: [19th-20th c] Archives, library, and artifacts related to the hard coal industry and the people of northeastern PA as well as metals, silk, and transportation industries. Four massive stone blast furnaces of Lackawanna Iron and Coal Company built 1848-1857.

HOURS: Yr M-Sa 9-5, Su 12-5

ADMISSION: $3.50, Family $12, Children $2, Seniors $3

7447
Steamtown National Historic Site
Lackawanna & Cliff St, 18503 [150 S Washington Ave, 18503]; (p) (570) 340-5192; (f) (570) 340-5309; Stea_Superintendent@nps.gov; www.nps.gov/stea; (c) Lackawanna

Federal/ 1986/ National Park Service/ staff: 60(f); 20(p); 20(v)

HISTORIC SITE: Museum complex interpreting the impact and development of the steam locomotive.

PROGRAMS: Community Outreach; Exhibits; Film/Video; Guided Tours; Interpretation; Research Library/Archives; School-Based Curriculum

COLLECTIONS: [1900-1950] Objects and archives emphasizing regional railroads.

HOURS: Yr M-Su 9-5

ADMISSION: $7

SLIPPERY ROCK

7448
Old Stone House, The
Rt 8, 16057 [Dept of History, Slippery Rock University, 16057]; (p) (724) 738-2408

1822/ State/ staff: 1(f); 4(p)

Maintains old stone house where the Marquis de Lafayette visited the house.

COLLECTIONS: [1800s]

HOURS: May-Sept

SNOW SHOE

7449
Lions David House Trust, Inc.
206 N Fourth St, 16874 [PO Box 119, 16874-0019]; (p) (814) 387-4200; (f) (814) 387-6824; bilaine@juno.com; (c) Centre

Private non-profit/ 1989/ Board of Governors/ staff: 20(v)

HISTORIC PRESERVATION AGENCY; HISTORIC SITE; HISTORY MUSEUM: Manage the museum and its rich collection of local history.

PROGRAMS: Community Outreach; Exhibits; Guided Tours; Research Library/Archives

COLLECTIONS: [Early 19th-mid 20th c] Collection housed in a turn of the century coal miner's house, preserves Snow Shoe region history: photos, maps, related artifacts, and family genealogies.

HOURS: Yr M, W, Sa 1-5

SOMERSET

7450
Somerset Historical Center
10649 Somerset Pike, 15501; (p) (814) 445-6077; (f) (814) 443-6621; (c) Somerset

Joint/ 1970/ PA Historical and Museum Commission; State; County/ staff: 6(f); 5(p); 45(v)

HISTORICAL SOCIETY; HISTORY MUSEUM; LIVING HISTORY/OUTDOOR MUSEUM: Portrays southwestern PA rural life, from 18th c pioneer struggles through commercial agrarian enterprises of the mid 20th c. Preserves local history, customs and lifestyles through exhibits, collections, program, and genealogy library.

PROGRAMS: Annual Meeting; Exhibits; Facility Rental; Family Programs; Festivals; Guided Tours; Interpretation; Living History; Reenactments; Research Library/Archives; School-Based Curriculum

COLLECTIONS: [1750-present] Original tools, utensils, furnishings, clothing, books, machinery, restored buildings and structures, and artifacts related to daily life in Somerset County.

HOURS: Apr-Oct T-Su 9-5; Nov-Mar W-Su 9-5

ADMISSION: $3.50, Family $8.50, Children $1.50, Seniors $3

SPRINGDALE

7451
Rachel Carson Homestead
613 Marion Ave, 15144; (p) (724) 274-5459; (f) (724) 275-1259; homestead@rachelcarson.org; www.rachelcarson.org; (c) Allegheny

Private non-profit/ 1975/ Rachel Carson Homestead Association/ staff: 1(f); 2(p); 35(v)/ members: 150

HOUSE MUSEUM; LIVING HISTORY/OUTDOOR MUSEUM: Birthplace and childhood home of Ecologist and Silent Spring Author Rachel Carson. Guided Tours, education programs, publications, nature trail, bookstore, website.

PROGRAMS: Annual Meeting; Community Outreach; Exhibits; Family Programs; Festivals; Garden Tours; Guided Tours; Interpretation; Lectures; Publication; Research Library/Archives; School-Based Curriculum

COLLECTIONS: [1907-1964] Books, manuscripts, photographs, artifacts.

STATE COLLEGE

7452
Centre County Historical Society
1001 E College Ave, 16801; (p) (814) 234-4779; (f) (814) 234-1694; cchs@csrlink.net; centrecountyhistory.org; (c) Centre

Private non-profit/ 1904/ staff: 1(f); 30(v)/ members: 435/publication: *Centre County Heritage*

GARDEN; HISTORIC SITE; HISTORICAL SOCIETY; HISTORY MUSEUM; HOUSE MUSEUM: Collects, preserves, and makes available local historical materials. Operates the Centre Furnace Mansion as an historic house museum.

PROGRAMS: Annual Meeting; Community Outreach; Exhibits; Family Programs; Festivals; Guided Tours; Interpretation; Lectures; Publication; Research Library/Archives; School-Based Curriculum

7453
Centre Furnace Mansion
Corner of E College & Porter Rd, 16801 [1001 E College Ave, 16801]; (p) (814) 234-4779; (f) (814) 234-4779; spkelley@llpptn.pall.org

1820/ Centre County Historical Society/ staff: 1(f); 31(v)

COLLECTIONS: [1842-1891] Primarily Victorian furnishings from the family; Thompson family papers, collections of a few other Centre County figures, industrial history information, architectural and historic preservation collections, photos, surveys, National Register Nominations, library.

HOURS: Yr

STEWARTSTOWN

7454
Stewartstown Historical Society, Inc.
Mason-Dixon Library Bldg, 17363 [PO Box 82, 17363]; (p) (717) 993-6872; (c) York

Private non-profit/ 1984/ Board of Directors/ staff: 7(v)/ members: 109

HISTORICAL SOCIETY: Collects local documents and other items pertaining to the area.

PROGRAMS: Community Outreach; Festivals; Guided Tours; Interpretation; Lectures

COLLECTIONS: [1850-present] Local documents, artifacts, water powered grist mill, railroad, restored 1828 mill owned by County Parks Dept.

HOURS: Yr Daily by appt.

STRASBURG

7455
Railroad Museum of Pennsylvania

300 Gap Road, 17579 [PO Box 15, 17579]; (p) (717) 687-8628; (f) (717) 687-0876; ddunn@phmc.state.pa.us; www.rrhistorical.com/frm; (c) Lancaster

State/ 1974/ Commonwealth of PA/PA Historical and Museum Commission/ staff: 9(f); 3(p)/publication: *Milepost*

RAILROAD MUSEUM: Interprets the continuing history of PA's Railroad Industry through collecting, preserving, and documenting the significant contributions that PA railroading has made to the development of the nation.

PROGRAMS: Exhibits; Facility Rental; Family Programs; Guided Tours; Interpretation; Lectures; Living History; Publication; Research Library/Archives; School-Based Curriculum

COLLECTIONS: [1825-present] Steam, diesel electric, and electric locomotives; freight cars, passenger cars and non-revenue cars. Library and archival collections is augmented by railroadiana such as uniforms, china, tools, and equipment.

HOURS: Apr-Oct 7, Nov-Mar 6, M-Sa 9-5, Sun 12-5

ADMISSION: $6, Children $4, Seniors $5.50; Under 6 free

7456
Strasburg Heritage Society

122 S Decatur St, 17562 [PO Box 81, 17562]; (c) Lancaster

Private non-profit/ 1972/ staff: 100(v)/ members: 190

HISTORIC PRESERVATION AGENCY; HISTORY MUSEUM: Collects and preserves Strasburg area documents and artifacts, works to preserve Strasburg's historic area, and provides educational lectures on area history.

PROGRAMS: Annual Meeting; Community Outreach; Exhibits; Family Programs; Festivals; Garden Tours; Guided Tours; Interpretation; Lectures; Publication; Research Library/Archives

COLLECTIONS: [1710-present] Items made in Strasburg, local history, photographs, textiles, 100 years of Strasburg newspapers on microfilm.

7457
Train Collectors Association

300 Paradise Lane, 17579 [PO Box 248, 17579-0248]; (p) (717) 687-8623; (f) (717) 687-0742; toytrain@traincollectors.org; www.traincollectors.org; (c) Lancaster

Private non-profit/ 1954/ staff: 5(f); 7(p); 40(v)/ members: 32000/publication: *Train Collectors Quarterly*

RESEARCH CENTER: Preserve an important segment of history Tinplate Toy Trains through research, establishment of collecting standards, education, community outreach, fellowship, and to promote the growth and enjoyment of the hobby.

PROGRAMS: Exhibits; Publication; Research Library/Archives

COLLECTIONS: [1870-present] Toy trains and accessories.

HOURS: May-Oct Daily 10-5; Apr, Nov-Dec Sa-Su 10-5

ADMISSION: $3, Family $9, Children $1.50

STROMSBURG

7458
Friends of the Railroad Museum of Pennsylvania

[PO Box 125, 17579]; (p) (717) 687-8629; (f) (717) 687-0876; frm@redrose.net; www.rrhistorical.com/frm; (c) Lancaster

Private non-profit/ 1983/ staff: 5(f); 5(p); 150(v)/ members: 1260/publication: *Milepost*

RAILROAD MUSEUM: Provide staff, programs, and fund raising activities for the museum.

PROGRAMS: Annual Meeting; Family Programs; Guided Tours; Interpretation; Lectures; Living History; Publication; Research Library/Archives; School-Based Curriculum

COLLECTIONS: [1825-present]

HOURS: Yr Apr-Oct M-Sa 9-5, Su 12-5; Nov-Mar T-Sa 9-5, Su 12-5

ADMISSION: $6, Student $4

STRONGSTOWN

7459
Strongstown Homecoming and Historical Society

14895 Rt 422 Hwy E, 15957; (p) (814) 749-8228; (c) Indiana

Private non-profit/ members: 20

STROUDSBURG

7460
Monroe County Historical Association

900 Main St, 18360; (p) (570) 421-7703; (f) (570) 421-9199; mcha@ptdprolog.net; www.stroudsburg.com; (c) Monroe

Private non-profit/ 1921/ staff: 1(f); 2(p); 50(v)/publication: *Fanlight*

HISTORIC SITE; HISTORICAL SOCIETY; HISTORY MUSEUM; HOUSE MUSEUM: The association preserves and disseminates Monroe County history and educates a diverse audience through its variety of resources and programs.

PROGRAMS: Annual Meeting; Community Outreach; Exhibits; Facility Rental; Family Programs; Guided Tours; Lectures; Publication; Research Library/Archives

COLLECTIONS: Extensive local and family history files, cemetery, census, and newspapers. 1,500 researched Monroe County families.

HOURS: Yr T-F 10-4 Su

7461
Quiet Valley Living Historical Farm

1000 Turkey Hill Rd, 18360; (p) (570) 992-6161; qufarm@ptdprolog.net; www.pastconnect.com/quietValley; (c) Monroe

Private non-profit/ 1963/ staff: 3(f); 3(p); 500(v)/ members: 1000

HISTORIC SITE; LIVING HISTORY/OUTDOOR MUSEUM: Dedicated to preserving the Early American farming life.

PROGRAMS: Festivals; Guided Tours; Living History

COLLECTIONS: [19th c] Guided tours of original buildings, barn, smokehouse, drying house, outdoor bake oven, granddaddy house, springhouse, 1765 cellar kitchen, 1900 bedroom, parlor, and new kitchen with iron range.

HOURS: June-Sept T-Sa 10-5:30, Su 1-5:30

ADMISSION: $7

7462
Stroud Mansion

900 Main St, 18360; (p) (717) 421-7703; (f) (717) 421-9919; mcha.stroudsburg.com

1795/ Monroe County Historical Association/ staff: 1(f); 1(p); 10(v)

COLLECTIONS: [1795-1900] Native American points, tools, ceremonial artifacts, and weapons. Toys and dolls, weaving and tapestry, early PA German Fraktur; Monroe County census, cemetery, church records. 3,000 family files, books, and pamphlets.

SUNBURY

7463
Northumberland County Historical Society

1150 N Front St, 17801-1126; (p) (570) 286-4083; (c) Northumberland

Private non-profit/ 1925/ Board of Trustees/ staff: 1(p); 30(v)/ members: 480/publication: *Proceedings*

GENEALOGICAL SOCIETY; HISTORIC SITE; HISTORICAL SOCIETY; HISTORY MUSEUM; RESEARCH CENTER

PROGRAMS: Annual Meeting; Exhibits; Facility Rental; Family Programs; Festivals; Guided Tours; Lectures; Publication; Research Library/Archives; School-Based Curriculum

COLLECTIONS: [Pre-history-present] Documents, military, prehistoric

HOURS: Yr M,W,F 1-4

ADMISSION: Donations accepted

SWARTHMORE

7464
Swarthmore College Peace Collection

500 College Ave, 19081; (p) (610) 328-8557; (f) (610) 328-7329; www.swarthmore.edu/library/peace; (c) Delaware

Private non-profit/ 1930/ Swarthmore College/ staff: 2(f); 3(p); 2(v)

LIBRARY AND/OR ARCHIVES; RESEARCH CENTER: Collectes, preserve, and makes accessible to the general public materials on non-governmental efforts towards peace, worldwide.

PROGRAMS: Exhibits; Guided Tours; Lectures; Publication; Research Library/Archives

COLLECTIONS: [19th-20th c] Records of peace organizations and the personal papers of peace activists.

HOURS: Yr M-F 8:30-4:30, Sa 9-12

ADMISSION: No charge

TARENTUM

7465
Allegheny-Kiski Valley Historical Society

224 E Seventh Ave, 15084-1513; (p) (724) 224-7666; (f) (724) 224-7666; akvhs@salsgiver.com; AKValley.com/akvhs; (c) Allegheny

Private non-profit/ 1967/ Board of Directors/ staff: 1(p); 5(v)/ members: 200

HISTORIC PRESERVATION AGENCY; HISTORIC SITE; HISTORICAL SOCIETY; HISTORY MUSEUM: Preserves, interprets, and promotes the industrial and cultural heritage of Allegheny and Kiskiminetas Valleys in PA through educational programs, tours, publications, and museum operations.

PROGRAMS: Annual Meeting; Community Outreach; Exhibits; Festivals; Guided Tours; Interpretation; Lectures; School-Based Curriculum

COLLECTIONS: [1800-1900s] Military, aluminum, glass, agricultural, labor, working class, and ethnic histories.

HOURS: Yr M,W,F 8-3 and by appt

ADMISSION: $3, Children $2; Members free

THORNTON

7466
Thornbury Historical Society

Glen Mills Train Station, 19373 [c/o Joan Dehm, 7 Lake Rd, 19373]; (p) (610) 459-2307; (c) Delaware

Private non-profit/ 1976/ staff: 30(v)/ members: 300

HISTORIC SITE; HISTORICAL SOCIETY; HISTORY MUSEUM: Promotes the history of Thornbury Township through its collections and displays of local artifacts at the Glen Mills Train Station.

PROGRAMS: Annual Meeting; Community Outreach; Exhibits; Family Programs; Festivals; Lectures; Publication; Research Library/Archives

COLLECTIONS: [20th c] Books, artifacts, maps, memorabilia pertaining to the families, individuals.

HOURS: Spring and Fall: Sa-Su 12-4

TITUSVILLE

7467
Drake Well Museum

Drake Well Rd, 16354 [RR #3, Box 7, 16354-8902]; (p) (814) 827-2797; (f) (814) 827-4888; drakewell@sachoice.net; www.drakewell.org; (c) Venango

State/ 1934/ PA Historical and Museum Commission/ staff: 8(f); 6(p); 5(v)

HISTORIC SITE; HISTORY MUSEUM; LIVING HISTORY/OUTDOOR MUSEUM: Pre-

serves the birthplace of the petroleum industry with working oil machinery, outdoor and indoor exhibits which interpret the growth of PA's oil industry into a global enterprise. National Historic Landmark.

PROGRAMS: Community Outreach; Exhibits; Facility Rental; Guided Tours; School-Based Curriculum

COLLECTIONS: [1859] Items related to PA's oil industry including tools, lamps, models, fire fighting equipment, oil samples, machinery, photographs, glass plate negatives, and documents.

HOURS: Yr Nov-Apr T-Sa 9-5, Su 12-5; May-Oct M-Sa 9-5, Su 10-5

ADMISSION: $4, Family $10, Children $2, Seniors $3.50

TOWANDA

7468
Bradford County Historical Society and Museum

21 Main St, 18848; (p) (570) 265-2240; BCHS@Cyber-quest.com; (c) Bradford

Private non-profit/ 1870/ Board of Trustees/ staff: 1(f); 2(p); 10(v)/ members: 600/publication: The Settler

HISTORICAL SOCIETY; HISTORY MUSEUM; RESEARCH CENTER: Collects, preserves, and interprets the history and heritage of Bradford County for present and future generations.

PROGRAMS: Annual Meeting; Community Outreach; Exhibits; Guided Tours; Publication; Research Library/Archives

COLLECTIONS: [1813-1910] Early county records archives: assessment books, deed books, mortgage books, marriage ledgers, and wills. 300 family histories, 22 19th c newspapers, and 13,188 glass plate

7469
LaPorte House-French Azilum

TR 458, Asylum Twp, 18848 [RR 2, Box 266, 18848]; (p) (717) 265-3376

1836/ PA Historical & Museum Commission (PHMC) owns the site/ staff: 1(f); 5(p); 28(v)

COLLECTIONS: [1793-1871] 2,300 artifacts; furniture, china, glass, metal, tools, domestic implements, textiles, prints, and clothing, 4 musical instruments including a Sellers pianoforte c. 1790, 2 side chairs c. 1740, a cherry desk c. 1790, photographs, diaries, documents, deeds, bibles, and books.

HOURS: Seasonal

TYRONE

7470
Tyrone Area Historical Society

Washington Ave, 16686 [PO Box 1850, 16686]; (p) (814) 684-5141, (814) 632-5369; (f) (814) 632-5391; charma@nb.net; www.tyrone.k12.pa.us; (c) Blair

City, non-profit/ 1990/ Board of Directors/ staff: 10(v)/ members: 200

HISTORICAL SOCIETY; HISTORY MUSEUM: Promotes interest in and appreciation for the Tyrone Area's historic past.

PROGRAMS: Annual Meeting; Elder's Programs; Exhibits; Lectures; Research Library/Archives; School-Based Curriculum

COLLECTIONS: [19th-20th c] Photographs, postcards, railroad memorabilia, Fred Waring memorabilia, genealogies, and artifacts from the people who contributed to all aspects of the social history of Tyrone.

HOURS: Yr W 1-4

ADMISSION: No charge

UNIVERSITY PARK

7471
Matson Museum of Anthropology

2nd floor, Carpenter Bldg, Penn State, 16802 [409 Carpenter Building, Pennsylvania State Univ, 16802]; (p) (814) 865-3853; (f) (814) 863-1474; cmm8@psu.edu; www.anth.la.psu.edu/museum/mma.html; (c) Centre

Private non-profit/ 1966/ staff: 2(p); 30(v)

ANTHROPOLOGY MUSEUM: Educates a wide audience about the diversity of contemporary and ancient cultures, the history of human evolution, and scientific explanations for human cultural and biological variability.

PROGRAMS: Exhibits; Guided Tours

COLLECTIONS: [20th c] 28,000 items from around the world, particularly South America, Africa, and Afghanistan; prehistoric artifacts from the Americas, and hominid fossil casts.

HOURS: Sept-Apr M-F 9-4 June-July Sa 10-1

7472
Pasto Agricultural Museum

Russell E Larson Agricultural Research Center, 16802 [238 Agricultural Admin Bldg, Penn State Univer, 16802-2600]; (p) (814) 863-1383; (f) (814) 865-3103; pastoagmuseum@psu.edu; www.pasto.cas.psu.edu; (c) Centre

Joint/ 1978/ College of Agricultural Sciences; The PA State Univ/ staff: 1(p); 65(v)/publication: Pasto Agricultural Museum

HISTORY MUSEUM: Provides visitors with an historical account of early technological progress in agricultural production and home living, especially as it applies to rural areas of PA and the northeastern United States.

PROGRAMS: Community Outreach; Exhibits; Guided Tours; Publication

COLLECTIONS: 700 rare and unusual farm and household items dating back to the 1840s.

UPLAND

7473
Caleb Pusey House and Landingford Plantation

15 Race St, 19015 [PO Box 1183, 19015]; (p) (610) 876-5665; www.delcohistory.org/fcph; (c) Delaware

Private non-profit/ 1961/ The Friends of the Caleb Pusey House, Inc./ staff: 30(v)/ members: 400/publication: The Weathervane

HOUSE MUSEUM: Protects and preserves the home of the first English miller and business partner of William Penn and its artifacts for the education of present society.

PROGRAMS: Annual Meeting; Community

Outreach; Exhibits; Guided Tours; Interpretation; Lectures; Publication

COLLECTIONS: [17th-19th c] Historic house furnished with 17th c period pieces and implements of daily life.

HOURS: May-Oct Sa-Su 1-4

ADMISSION: Donations requested

VALENCIA

7474
Center for the History of American Needlework
6459 Old Rt 8, 16059 [PO Box 359, 16059]; (p) (724) 898-1423; charlotteann@hotmail.com; (c) Butler

Private non-profit/ 1974/ staff: 4(v)/ members: 250/publication: *Needlework Anthologies and Patterns*

HISTORICAL SOCIETY: Dedicated to the documentation and preservation of the work of the American Needleworker as it reflects the country's heritage.

PROGRAMS: Exhibits; Lectures; Living History; Publication

COLLECTIONS: [1600-present] 500 pieces of the textile and needle arts plus a library of nearly 2,000 books and 7,000 leaflets and patterns on needlework and related topics.

HOURS: By appt

VALLEY FORGE

7475
American Baptist Historical Society
588 N Gulph Rd, 19482 [PO Box 851, 19482-0851]; (p) (610) 768-2266; (f) (610) 768-2266; dbvanbro@abc-usa.org; www.abc-usa.org/abhs/; (c) Montgomery

Private non-profit/ 1853/ Board of Managers/ staff: 3(f); 2(p); 8(v)

HISTORICAL SOCIETY; RESEARCH CENTER: Repository for records of the American Baptist Churches, USA, formerly the Northern Baptist Convention.

PROGRAMS: Exhibits; Research Library/ Archives

COLLECTIONS: [1814-1970] Correspondence of home and foreign missionaries, records of the American Baptist Publication Society, personal papers of Baptist leaders, photographs, glass slides, and records of the Baptist World Alliance.

HOURS: Yr M-F 8:30-4:15 by appt for research

7476
Valley Forge Historical Society
Rt 23, 19481 [PO Box 122, 19481-0122]; (p) (610) 783-0535; (f) (610) 783-0957; vfhs@ix.netcom.com; www.valleyforgemuseum.org; (c) Montgomery

Private non-profit/ 1918/ Board of Directors/ staff: 3(f); 5(p); 15(v)/ members: 400

HISTORY MUSEUM: Collects, and interprets the history of the American Revolution, the Valley Forge encampment, and the histories of the men and women who lived during the Revolution.

PROGRAMS: Annual Meeting; Concerts; Elder's Programs; Exhibits; Family Programs;

Guided Tours; Interpretation; Lectures; Living History

COLLECTIONS: [1750-1799] Over 7,000 objects: art and artifacts; one of the largest George and Martha Washington collections in the world; decorative arts; original manuscripts, and archival materials.

HOURS: Jan-Mar W-Sa 10-4; Apr-Dec M-Sa 10-5, Su 1-5

ADMISSION: $2, Student $1.50, Seniors $1.50

7477
Valley Forge National Historic Park
[PO Box 953, 19482]; (p) (610) 783-1077; (c) Montgomery

Federal/ 1976/ National Park Service/ staff: 60(f); 35(v)

HISTORIC SITE: The historical park preserves and interprets the site of the 1777-1778 winter encampment of General George Washington's Continental Army.

PROGRAMS: Community Outreach; Film/ Video; Interpretation; Living History; School-Based Curriculum

COLLECTIONS: [1777-1778] Military items used during the Revolutionary War from muskets to personal items.

7478
Washington's Headquarters at Valley Forge (Isaac Potts House)
Valley Forge NHP, Rt 23 & N Gulph Rd, 19482 [PO Box 953, 19482]; (p) (610) 783-1000, (610) 783-1061; (f) (610) 783-1053

1768/ Valley Forge National Historical Park/ staff: 8(f); 10(v)

HISTORIC SITE; NATIONAL PARK: Preserves and protects historic site.

PROGRAMS: Exhibits

COLLECTIONS: [1777-1778] George C. Neumann collection of artifacts used in the American Revolution, some on display and used as study collection (at Visitor Center - study available through curator by appointment). John Reed collection of papers associated with George Washington and the encampment also available for study.

7479
Wharton Esherick Museum
Horseshoe Trail, [PO Box 595, Paoli, 19301-0595]; (p) (610) 644-5822; (f) (610) 644-2244

Private non-profit/ 1971/ staff: 2(f); 3(p); 28(v)/ members: 450/publication: *Museum Catalog*

ART MUSEUM; HISTORICAL SOCIETY: Promotes and preserves National Historic Landmark studio and home of Wharton Esherick (1887-1970), housing his paintings, woodcuts, sculpture, furniture, and furnishings.

PROGRAMS: Community Outreach; Elder's Programs; Exhibits; Guided Tours; Interpretation; Lectures; Publication

COLLECTIONS: [1920-1970] Wharton Esherick's studio, housing his collection of his works-paintings, woodcuts, sculpture, furniture, and furnishings.

HOURS: Mar-Dec M-F groups; Sa 10-5, Su 1-5

ADMISSION: $9

7480
World of Scouting, Inc., The
Behind Washington Memorial Chapel, 19482 [PO Box 2226, 19482-2226]; (p) (610) 783-5311; www.worldofscoutingmuseum.org; (c) Montgomery

Private non-profit/ 1994

Interpretative museum of the history of Boy and Girl Scouts. Not affiliated with the Boy or Girl Scout Organizations, but operated by dedicated volunteers from scouting.

COLLECTIONS: [1908-present] The exhibits include scarce uniforms predating WWI, badges, games, and photographs. The museum houses many one of a kind items including the prototype merit badge sash of the Boy Scouts, a bugle owned by the founder Dan Beard, and art work by Lord Baden Powell - the world wide founder.

HOURS: Feb-Dec Sa-Su 12-5

ADMISSION: $2, Children $1, Seniors $1

VANDERGRIFT

7481
Victorian Vandergrift Museum and Historical Society
128D Washington Ave, 15690 [PO Box 183, 15690]; (p) (724) 568-1990; vvmhs@kiski.net; (c) Westmoreland

Private non-profit/ 1990/ Board of Directors/ staff: 2(p); 10(v)/ members: 460

GENEALOGICAL SOCIETY; HISTORIC SITE; HISTORICAL SOCIETY; HISTORY MUSEUM: Preserves and promotes the history of Vandergrift and its founder, George G. McMurty.

PROGRAMS: Annual Meeting; Community Outreach; Exhibits; Family Programs; Festivals; Film/Video; Garden Tours; Guided Tours; Lectures; Publication; Research Library/ Archives

COLLECTIONS: [1895-present] Archival and material collection relating to the history of, and life in, Vandergrift and genealogy and reference library covering the area.

HOURS: Yr M,W 9-4:30, T 9-2, Th 10-2, F 9-3:30, Sa 10-3

ADMISSION: Donations accepted

WALLINGFORD

7482
Friends of Thomas Leiper House, Inc.
521 Avondale Rd, 19086; (p) (610) 566-6365; (c) Delaware

1977/ staff: 10(v)/ members: 125

HISTORIC SITE; HOUSE MUSEUM: Raises money, conducts tours, activities, and overseeing the restoration and maintenance of the 1785 country home of Philadelphia merchant Thomas Leiper.

PROGRAMS: Facility Rental; Guided Tours; Lectures

COLLECTIONS: [1800-1825] Country home with four outbuildings, main house furnished in early 19th c antiques, Leiper family portraits, silver and artifacts, and some furniture, and genealogy material.

HOURS: Apr-Dec Sa-Su 1-4

ADMISSION: $1, Children $0.50

WALNUTPORT

7483
Walnutport Canal Association, Inc., The
417 Lincoln Ave, 18088; (p) (610) 767-7887; (f) (610) 767-5156; (c) Northampton

Joint/ 1982/ Board of Trustees; Private non-profit/ staff: 75(v)/ members: 484

HOUSE MUSEUM; PROFESSIONAL ORGANIZATION: Maintains and preserves the Walnutport section of the Lehigh Canal and interprets the history of the Canal Era at the Locktender's House Museum.

PROGRAMS: Exhibits; Festivals; Guided Tours; Interpretation

COLLECTIONS: [1822-present Canal era] Canal related artifacts, documents, newspaper articles and photographs; 19th c house furnishings; 4 miles of watered canal with one guard lock, 4 lift locks (one restored) and one acquaduct.

HOURS: Canal: Yr; Locktender's House: May-Oct Su 1-4

WAMPUM

7484
Wampum Area Historical Society, Inc.
Main St Ext (Municipal Bld), 16157 [PO Box 763, 16157]; (p) (724) 535-4495; (c) Lawrence

Private non-profit/ 1989/ Board of Directors/ staff: 9(p); 47(v)/ members: 50/publication: *The Olde Times*

GARDEN; HISTORIC SITE; HISTORICAL SOCIETY; HISTORY MUSEUM: Dedicated to preserving and maintaining artifacts and memorabilia and promoting awareness of local history and genealogy.

PROGRAMS: Annual Meeting; Community Outreach; Concerts; Exhibits; Family Programs; Interpretation; Lectures; Living History; Publication; Research Library/Archives

COLLECTIONS: [1860-present] Historical writings, books of personal genealogy, artifacts, and memorabilia of our local history.

HOURS: Yr 2nd and 4th M

WARMINSTER

7485
Craven Hall Historical Society
599 Newtown Rd, 18974 [PO Box 2042, 18974]; (p) (215) 675-4698; (c) Bucks

Private non-profit/ 1978/ staff: 25(v)/ members: 100

HISTORIC SITE; HISTORICAL SOCIETY; HOUSE MUSEUM: Preserves, restores, and interprets the history of Craven Hall, a c 1726 building, and the c 1768 Craven/Vansant Burying Ground.

PROGRAMS: Annual Meeting; Community Outreach; Exhibits; Facility Rental; Family Programs; Festivals; Guided Tours; Interpretation; Lectures; Living History; Reenactments; School-Based Curriculum

COLLECTIONS: [1700-1850] Colonial and early federal era furnishings that assist in interpreting Craven Hall.

WARREN

7486
Warren County Historical Society
210 4th Ave, 16365 [PO Box 427, 16365]; (p) (814) 723-1795; (f) (814) 728-3479; warrenhistory@allegany.com; nathan.allegany.com/warrenhistory; (c) Warren

County, non-profit/ 1900/ staff: 2(f); 3(p); 81(v)/ members: 1000

HISTORICAL SOCIETY; HISTORY MUSEUM; RESEARCH CENTER: Promotes interest in Warren County history and preserves the county's heritage for the education and enjoyment of present and future generations.

PROGRAMS: Annual Meeting; Community Outreach; Exhibits; Family Programs; Festivals; Guided Tours; Lectures; Living History; Publication; Research Library/Archives

COLLECTIONS: [1795-present] General county history, library and archives, genealogy, and artifacts.

HOURS: Yr M-F 8:30-4:30, Sa 9-12

WASHINGTON

7487
David Bradford House Historical Association
175 S Main St, 15301 [PO Box 537, 15301]; (p) (724) 222-3604; mthart@pulsenet.com; www.bradfordhouse.org; (c) Washington

State/ 1960/ PA Historical and Museum Commission/ staff: 1(f); 10(v)/ members: 65/publication: *David Bradford's Escape*

HISTORIC SITE; HOUSE MUSEUM: Preserves and promotes history and education relating to the Whiskey Rebellion. Docents in period costumes give tours of the seven rooms in the David Bradford House.

PROGRAMS: Interpretation; Reenactments

COLLECTIONS: [Late 18th c] Furnishings are typical of those used in late 18th c PA; mahogany staircase.

HOURS: Apr-Dec W-Sa 11-4 Su by appt

ADMISSION: $4, Student $2, Seniors $3.50; Under 6 free

7488
LeMoyne House
49 E Maiden St, 15317; (p) (724) 225-6740; (f) (724) 225-8495; nmccomb@llpptn.pall.org; www.camconet.com/lemoyne

1812/ Washington County Historical Society/ staff: 4(f); 5(p)

COLLECTIONS: [1840-1870] Clothing, furniture belonging to the LeMoyne family; Letters and records dating back to the 18th c.

HOURS: Feb-Dec

7489
National Duncan Glass Society
525 Jefferson Ave, 15301 [PO Box 965, 15301]; (p) (724) 225-9950; museum@nb.net; www.duncanglass.com; (c) Washington

Private non-profit/ 1975/ Board of Directors/ staff: 20(v)/ members: 300

HISTORY MUSEUM: Displays Duncan and Duncan/Miller glassware.

PROGRAMS: Annual Meeting; Exhibits; Film/Video; Guided Tours; Research Library/Archives

COLLECTIONS: [1872-1955] Examples of glassware made by Geo. Duncan and related items also literature and catalogs.

HOURS: Apr-Oct Th-Su

7490
Pennsylvania Trolley Museum
1 Museum Rd, 15301-6133; (p) (724) 228-9256; (f) (724) 228-9675; ptm@pa-trolley.org; www.pa-trolley.org; (c) Washington

Private non-profit/ 1953/ staff: 1(f); 2(p); 125(v)/ members: 610

HISTORY MUSEUM: The museum preserves and interprets Pennsylvania's Trolley Era with a collection of 45 railway vehicles, photos, documents, and artifacts. Our visitors actually take 3 mile round trip rides aboard vintage trolley cars, guided walking tours of the museum's carbarn and restoration shop.

PROGRAMS: Concerts; Exhibits; Facility Rental; Family Programs; Festivals; Film/Video; Guided Tours; Interpretation; Lectures; Living History; Publication; Research Library/Archives; School-Based Curriculum

COLLECTIONS: [1885-present] Electric railway vehicles, railroad vehicles, photos, documents, movies, artifacts relating to the Trolley Era.

HOURS: Jun-Aug M-Su 11-5; Apr-May, Sep-Dec Sa-Su 11-5

ADMISSION: $6, Children $3.50, Seniors $5; Under 2 free

7491
Washington County Historical Society
49 E Maiden St, 15301; (p) (724) 225-6740; (f) (724) 225-8495; www.camconet.com/lemoyne; (c) Washington

County; Private non-profit/ 1900/ WCHS Board/ staff: 3(f); 2(p); 35(v)/ members: 350/publication: *Focus*

GENEALOGICAL SOCIETY; HISTORIC PRESERVATION AGENCY; HISTORIC SITE; HISTORICAL SOCIETY; HISTORY MUSEUM; HOUSE MUSEUM; RESEARCH CENTER: The society educates the public about the history and national significance of Washington County and administers historic sites for the enjoyment of present and future generations.

PROGRAMS: Annual Meeting; Community Outreach; Elder's Programs; Exhibits; Facility Rental; Family Programs; Festivals; Garden Tours; Guided Tours; Interpretation; Lectures; Living History; Publication; Reenactments; Research Library/Archives; School-Based Curriculum

COLLECTIONS: [19th c] Extensive 19th c textile collection (flags, dress, everyday attire, military); US Military artifacts, Underground Railroad-related documents; old photos; genealogical resources; 19th c medical collection; furniture; artifacts.

HOURS: Feb-Dec T-F 11-4 Sa-Su 12-4

ADMISSION: $4, Student $2

WASHINGTON CROSSING

7492
Washington Crossing Historic Park
1112 River Rd, 18977 [PO Box 103, 18977]; (p) (215) 493-4076; (f) (215) 493-4820; (c) Bucks

State/ 1917/ staff: 12(f); 4(p); 125(v)/ members: 125

HISTORIC SITE: Washington Crossing was founded in 1917 to perpetuate and preserve the site from which the Continental Army crossed the Delaware River. Included at the site is the early 19th c village of Taylorsville.

PROGRAMS: Exhibits; Family Programs; Garden Tours; Guided Tours; Interpretation; Lectures; Reenactments

COLLECTIONS: [18th c] House museums furnished with 18th-19th c artifacts made in Bucks County and the Philadelphia area.

HOURS: Yr T-Sa 9-5, Su 12-5

WATTSBURG

7493
Wattsburg Area Historical Society, Inc.
14430 Main St, 16442 [PO Box 240, 16442-0240]; (p) (814) 739-2952; tomjiggs@velocity.net; (c) Erie

Private non-profit/ 1983/ staff: 1(f); 20(v)/ members: 90

GENEALOGICAL SOCIETY; HISTORIC PRESERVATION AGENCY; HISTORICAL SOCIETY: Devoted to the preservation of the history and artifacts of Wattsburg Borough, Amity, Venango Townships, and nearby areas.

PROGRAMS: Annual Meeting; Elder's Programs; Family Programs; Festivals; Guided Tours

COLLECTIONS: [1823-1999]

HOURS: May-Oct Sa-Su 1-4

WAYNESBORO

7494
Renfrew Museum and Park
1010 E Main St, 17268; (p) (717) 762-4723; (f) (717) 762-4707; renfrewatinnernet.net; www.innernet.net/renfrew; (c) Franklin

City/ 1975/ Renfrew Committee Inc./ staff: 3(f); 20(v)/ members: 285

HISTORIC SITE: Collects high-style decorative arts from 1790-1830; 107 acre park with hiking trails, wetland area; 4-square and herb garden.

PROGRAMS: Exhibits; Family Programs; Festivals; Guided Tours; Interpretation; Lectures; Reenactments

COLLECTIONS: [1790-1830] Folk Art, painted boxes, tinware, to high style furniture-signed Colton sideboard, matching Baltimore card tables, 200 pieces of Bell Family pottery, examples of spatterware, pearlware, and canton.

HOURS: May-Dec F-Su 1-4

ADMISSION: $3, Children $1.75, Seniors $2.50

WAYNESBURG

7495
Greene Hill Farms
RR 201 DRT 21, 15370 [PO Box 127, 15370]; (p) (724) 627-3204; (f) (724) 627-3204; www.greenepa.net/~museum

1850/ Greene County Historical Society/ staff: 2(f); 2(p); 26(v)

COLLECTIONS: [Victorian] Monangehela Indian culture; Early ledgers of stores and business, school and tax records.

7496
Paul R. Stewart Museum
Waynesburg College, 15370; (p) (724) 852-3214; (f) (724) 627-6416; www.waynesburg.edu; (c) Greene

1930/ staff: 1(p)

HISTORY MUSEUM: Geology specimens, early American glass, local pottery industry, local newspapers, documents, and prehistoric to historic Native American artifact collection.

PROGRAMS: Community Outreach; Exhibits; Guided Tours; Lectures; Research Library/Archives

COLLECTIONS: [Prehistory-present]

HOURS: Yr M-F 9-12

WERNERSVILLE

7497
Heidelberg Heritage Society, Inc.
182 W Penn Ave, 19565 [Box 51, 19565]; (p) (610) 678-6202; (c) Berks

Private non-profit/ 1976/ Board of Directors and Staff/ staff: 40(v)/ members: 364/publication: The Heidelberger

GENEALOGICAL SOCIETY; HISTORIC PRESERVATION AGENCY; HISTORIC SITE; HISTORICAL SOCIETY; HISTORY MUSEUM: Preserves local museum housed in the second oldest house in the community, gathers local artifacts, and maintains a genealogical library promoting local history.

PROGRAMS: Annual Meeting; Community Outreach; Exhibits; Facility Rental; Guided Tours; Publication

COLLECTIONS: [1700-1900s] 2,000 artifacts: early Penna china, pre-revolutionary cannon balls, textiles, colonial dresses, uniforms, early agricultural tools, original parchment deed signed by Richard and Thomas Penn, photographs, Victorian furniture.

HOURS: By appt

ADMISSION: No charge

WEST CHESTER

7498
American Helicopter Museum and Education Center
1220 American Blvd, 19380; (p) (610) 436-9600; (f) (610) 436-8642; rotors@icdc.com; www.helicoptermuseum.org; (c) Chester

Private non-profit/ 1996/ staff: 5(f); 1(p); 325(v)/ members: 1000/publication: Vertika

AVIATION MUSEUM; HISTORIC PRESERVATION AGENCY; HISTORY MUSEUM; RESEARCH CENTER: Preserves the history of rotary wing aviation (helicopters) in the United States; highlights technological advances within the industry past, present, and future.

PROGRAMS: Community Outreach; Exhibits; Facility Rental; Guided Tours; Interpretation; Lectures; Living History; Publication; Research Library/Archives; School-Based Curriculum; Theatre

COLLECTIONS: [1928-present]

HOURS: Yr M-T by appt W-Sa 10-5, Su 12-5

ADMISSION: $5, Children $3.50, Seniors $4.50

7499
Chester County Archives and Records Services
601 Westtown Rd Ste 080, PO Box 2747, 19380-0990; (p) (610) 344-6760; (f) (610) 344-5616; (c) Chester

Private non-profit/ 1983/ County of Chester/ staff: 8(f); 1(p); 3(v)

LIBRARY AND/OR ARCHIVES: A repository of the county government records of the County of Chester from 1682-1933.

COLLECTIONS: [1682-1933] Historic county government records of Chester County including deeds, wills, tax records, criminal and civil court records, vital records, and administrative records.

HOURS: Yr

7500
Chester County Historical Society
225 N High St, 19380-2691; (p) (610) 692-4800; (f) (610) 692-4357; cchs@chesco.com; www.chesco.com/cchs; (c) Chester

Private non-profit/ 1893/ staff: 18(f); 3(p); 309(v)/ members: 2464/publication: History of Chester County, Pennsylvania; West Chester to 1865: That Elegant Notorious Place

HISTORICAL SOCIETY; HISTORY MUSEUM: Collects, preserves, and interprets the history of Chester County, the region and nation beyond. With six galleries, a lively hands-on exhibit, and extensive research library we tell the story of America's past through the lens of local history.

PROGRAMS: Community Outreach; Exhibits; Facility Rental; Family Programs; Festivals; Guided Tours; Lectures; Living History; Publication; Research Library/Archives; School-Based Curriculum

COLLECTIONS: 50,000 objects in the museum's collection that share a common history of use, manufacture, and ownership in Chester County. 70,000 photographic.

HOURS: Yr M-T, Th-Sa 9:30-4:30, W 9:30-8

ADMISSION: $5

WILKES-BARRE

7501
Wyoming Historical and Geological Society
49 S Franklin St, 18701; (p) (570) 823-6244; (f) (570) 823-9011; www.whgs.org; (c) Luzerne

Private non-profit/ 1858/ staff: 2(f); 4(p); 40(v)/ members: 628/publication: The Forecast

HISTORIC SITE; HISTORICAL SOCIETY; HISTORY MUSEUM; HOUSE MUSEUM; RESEARCH CENTER: Raise the consciousness of area residents concerning their heritage, thereby enabling them to better understand the area's uniqueness and its place in today's world.

PROGRAMS: Annual Meeting; Exhibits; Guided Tours; Interpretation; Lectures; Publication; Reenactments; Research Library/Archives

COLLECTIONS: [1750-1940] Luzerne County and Pennsylvania history; manuscripts, photographs, newspapers, maps, books, portraits, paintings, serials, museum artifacts.

HOURS: Yr T-F 12-4, Sa 10-4

ADMISSION: $5

WILLIAMSPORT

7502
Lycoming County Historical Society and Thomas T. Taber Museum
858 W Fourth St, 17701-5824; (p) (570) 326-3326; (f) (570) 326-3689; lchsmuse@csrlink.net; www.lycoming.org/lchsmuseum; (c) Lycoming

Private non-profit/ 1907/ staff: 3(f); 5(p)/ members: 989

HISTORICAL SOCIETY; HISTORY MUSEUM: Promotes education through museum, archives, and library. Its purpose is to discover, collect, preserve, and interpret the pre-historical, historical, and cultural heritage of north-central PA.

PROGRAMS: Annual Meeting; Community Outreach; Exhibits; Facility Rental; Family Programs; Guided Tours; Lectures; Publication; Research Library/Archives

COLLECTIONS: [1769-1900s] American Indian artifacts, costumes and textiles (1780-1970), tools of industry and technology, especially of the lumbering industry, fine and decorative arts, archival materials, 1,500 historical photographs.

HOURS: Yr T-F 9:30-4 Sa 11-4, Su 1-4

ADMISSION: $3.50, Children $1.50, Seniors $3

7503
Peter J. McGovern Little League Baseball Museum
Rt 15 S, 17701 [PO Box 3485, 17701]; (p) (570) 326-3607; (f) (570) 326-2267; Museum@littleleague.org; Littleleague.org/museum; (c) Lycoming

Private non-profit/ 1982/ Little League Baseball/ staff: 3(f); 7(p)

HISTORY MUSEUM: Preserves and protects the history of Little League Baseball and Softball.

PROGRAMS: Community Outreach; Exhibits; Family Programs; Film/Video; Guided Tours; Research Library/Archives; School-Based Curriculum; Theatre

COLLECTIONS: [1939-present] Artifacts and archival material relating to Little League Baseball and Softball; including Little League publications, photographs, rosters of players, international material, and video footage of games.

HOURS: Yr M-Sa 9-5, Su 12-5

WILLOW GROVE

7504
Delaware Valley Historical Aircraft Association
Naval Air Station, Rt 611, 19090 [Naval Air Station-JRB, 19090-5010]; (p) (215) 443-6039; (f) (215) 675-4005; www.dvhaa.org; (c) Montgomery

Private non-profit/ 1972/ Executive Board/ staff: 60(v)/ members: 400

AVIATION MUSEUM: The organization collects, restores, preserves, and displays aircraft and aviation artifacts of historical significance while offering citizens an opportunity to learn local, regional, and national, military, civilian, and aviation history.

PROGRAMS: Annual Meeting; Exhibits; Guided Tours

COLLECTIONS: [1940s-1970s] 16 restored 1940s-1970s navy fixed and rotary winged aircraft, a public access library, materials from the 1920s-present, 1,000 books, 1,500 magazines, films, videos, and photos.

WILLOW STREET

7505
1719 Hans Herr House
1849 Hans Herr Dr, 17584 [1849 Hans Herr Drive, 17584]; (p) (717) 464-4438; www.net conexinc.comhansherr

1719/ Lancaster Mennonite Historical Society/ staff: 1(f); 3(p); 35(v)

COLLECTIONS: [Mid 18th-19th c] 1,350 pieces, 800 artifacts related to agriculture and 100 of which are furnishings within the Herr House itself; land deeds, personal inventories, diaries. Most archival related matter is housed at parent organization, the Lancaster Mennonite Historical Society.

HOURS: Seasonal

WOMELSDORF

7506
Conrad Weiser Homestead
28 Weiser Rd, 19567-9718; (p) (610) 589-2934; (f) (610) 589-9458; (c) Berks

State/ 1928/ staff: 1(f); 1(p)/ members: 27

HOUSE MUSEUM: Preserves the home of the celebrated colonial diplomat who mediated the peace between PA and the powerful Iroquois Nation prior to 1760.

PROGRAMS: Community Outreach; Concerts; Facility Rental; Family Programs; Reenactments

COLLECTIONS: [1750-1780] PA Country furniture with a Germanic influence. Structures: Conrad Weiser House, Scheetz House.

HOURS: Yr W-Sa 9-5, Su 12-5; Grounds: Dawn-Dusk

ADMISSION: $2.50, Family $6, Children $1, Seniors $2

7507
Tulpehocken Settlement Historical Society
116 N Front St, 19567 [PO Box 53, 19567]; (p) (484) 589-2527; (c) Berks

Private non-profit/ 1970/ Board of Directors/ staff: 1(f); 6(v)/ members: 468/publication: *Die Shilgrut Fun Der Tulpehock*

HISTORICAL SOCIETY; HISTORY MUSEUM; RESEARCH CENTER: Preserve local and state history.

PROGRAMS: Annual Meeting; Exhibits; Guided Tours; Lectures; Publication

COLLECTIONS: [Mid 1800] Items manufactured in Womelsdorf and surrounding area; coverlets, pottery, tinware, original documents related to Womelsdorf's founding in 1762.

HOURS: Yr Daily except W, 1-4

WORCESTER

7508
Peter Wentz Farmstead
2100 Schultz Rd, 19490 [PO Box 240, 19490]; (p) (610) 584-5104; (f) (610) 584-6860; (c) Montgomery

County/ 1976/ staff: 5(f); 1(p); 75(v)/ members: 200

GARDEN; HISTORIC SITE; HOUSE MUSEUM; LIVING HISTORY/OUTDOOR MUSEUM

PROGRAMS: Annual Meeting; Community Outreach; Exhibits; Family Programs; Festivals; Guided Tours; Interpretation; Lectures; Living History; Reenactments; Research Library/Archives; School-Based Curriculum

COLLECTIONS: [1777 and earlier] Furniture and furnishings of 1777 and earlier, farm implements, redware, costumes.

HOURS: Yr T-Sa 10-4, Su 1-4

ADMISSION: Donations accepted

WRIGHTSVILLE

7509
Historic Wrightsville, Inc.
309 Locust St, 17368 [PO Box 125, 17368]; (p) (717) 252-1169; (c) York

Private non-profit/ 1976/ staff: 15(v)/ members: 375

HISTORICAL SOCIETY; HISTORY MUSEUM: Preserves the history of the Wrightsville area, and maintains historic architecture.

PROGRAMS: Annual Meeting; Community Outreach; Concerts; Exhibits; Festivals; Research Library/Archives

COLLECTIONS: [1727-present] Collection of Civil War books and local artifacts.

HOURS: Yr Su 1-4

ADMISSION: $2, Diorama; Museum: Donations accepted

WYOMING

7510
Swetland Homestead
885 Wyoming Ave, 18644 [49 S Franklin St, Wilkes-Barre, 18701]; (p) (717) 823-6244, (717) 693-2740; (f) (717) 823-9011

1797/ Wyoming Historical and Geological Society/ staff: 2(p); 6(v)

COLLECTIONS: [1762-1875] Period furnishings.

HOURS: May-Dec

WYOMISSING

7511
Berks County Heritage Center
Red Bridge Rd, Bern Township, 19610
[2201Tulpehocken Rd., 19610]; (p) (610) 374-
8839; (f) (610) 373-7049; www.fieldtrip.com/
pa/03748839.htm; (c) Berks

County/ 1981/ Berks County Parks and Recreation Department/ staff: 1(f); 5(p); 95(v)

HERITAGE AREA: Interprets early 20th c transportation and manufacturing at the Gruber Wagon Works and the importance and history of the Union and Schuylkill Canals.

PROGRAMS: Community Outreach; Concerts; Facility Rental; Festivals; Guided Tours; Interpretation; Lectures; Living History; Reenactments; School-Based Curriculum

COLLECTIONS: [1827-present] Gruber Wagon Works, 1882-1972: 19,000 wagon building artifacts and wagons; Hiester Canal Collection, 1827-1930; 1400 Schuylkill Navigation artifacts; and other artifacts of the period.

HOURS: May-Oct T-Sa 10-4, Su 12-5

ADMISSION: $5, Children $3, Seniors $4; Under 7 free

YARDLEY

7512
Pennsylvania Postal History Society
382 Tall Meadow Ln, 19067; (p) (215) 321-
3916; (c) Bucks

Private non-profit/ 1974/ staff: 5(v)/ members: 140/publication: *PA Postal Historian*

HISTORICAL SOCIETY: Preserves, collects, and promotes the postal history of PA, and encourages the preservation and acquisition of related materials.

PROGRAMS: Annual Meeting; Publication

YORK

7513
American Canal Society Inc., The
809 Rathon Rd, 17403-3349; www.black
sheep.org/canals/ACS/acs.html

Private non-profit/ 1972/publication: *American Canals*

Encourages the preservation, restoration, interpretation, and usage of the navigation canals of the US, past and present; cooperates with individual canal societies for action on threatened canals; and provides for the exchange of general canal information.

7514
Bonham House, The
152 E Market St, 17403 [250 E Market St, 17403]; (p) (717) 848-1587; (f) (717) 812-
1204; (c) York

Private non-profit/ 1967/ The Historical Society of York County Board of Directors/ staff: 1(f); 10(v)/ members: 2500

HOUSE MUSEUM

COLLECTIONS: [1840-1930] The collection consists of furniture and decorative arts collected by Elizabeth Bonham and her family from the 1840s to the 1940s, including paintings by Elizabeth's father, Horace Bonham.

7515
Historical Society of York County
157 W Market St, 17401; (p) (717) 845-2951,
(717) 848-1587

Historical Society/ staff: 1(f); 1(p); 16(v)

Prewserves historic sites including c. 1740 the Golden Plough Tavern.

HOURS: Mar-Dec

7516
Maryland and Pennsylvania Railroad Preservation Society
Village of Muddy Creek Forks, 17405 [PO Box 5122, 17405-5122]; (p) (717) 927-9565; www.jarrettsville.org/mapa; (c) York

Joint/ 1986/ Board of Directors; Private non-profit/ staff: 50(v)/ members: 200

HISTORIC PRESERVATION AGENCY; HISTORIC SITE; HISTORY MUSEUM; LIVING HISTORY/OUTDOOR MUSEUM: Preserves the history of the MD and PA Railroad and rural communities it serves as well as operating 5 miles of railroad and 10 buildings.

PROGRAMS: Annual Meeting; Exhibits; Festivals; Guided Tours; Interpretation; Living History; Publication

COLLECTIONS: [1890-1940] 6,000 catalogued photographs and documents; railroad tools and equipment, merchandise, fittings, implements, machinery from general store, post office, railroad station and mill; oral histories.

HOURS: Jun-Aug Su 1-5 and by appt

ADMISSION: Buildings free; train $3

7517
Police Heritage Museum, Inc.
54 W Market St, 17405 [PO Box 1941, 17405];
(p) (717) 845-2677; phm@yorkcity.org; phm.york
city.org; (c) York

Private non-profit/ 1995/ Board of Directors/ staff: 25(v)/ members: 50

HISTORY MUSEUM: Preserves police artifacts and the history of American law enforcement. Promotes a better understanding between law enforcement and the community.

PROGRAMS: Annual Meeting; Exhibits; Garden Tours; Guided Tours; Interpretation; Lectures

COLLECTIONS: [1750s-present] Uniforms, badges, and other "tools of the trade" used in peacekeeping, law enforcement, and criminal justice. Books, photographs, and other documents related to the history of law enforcement.

HOURS: Mid Apr-mid Oct Sa 9-4

ADMISSION: $2, Under 6 free

7518
York County Heritage Trust
250 E Market St, 17403; (p) (717) 848-1587;
(f) (717) 812-1204; (c) York

Private non-profit/ 1895/ Board of Directors/ staff: 14(f); 15(p); 117(v)/ members: 2500

HISTORIC SITE; HISTORICAL SOCIETY; HISTORY MUSEUM; HOUSE MUSEUM: Operates five historic house museums; Bonham House, c 1875; Gates House, c 1751; Plough Tavern, c 1741; Bobb Leg House, c 1812; and Workers' House, c 1910. Agricultural museum, industrial museum, research library and museum with permanent and changing exhibit galleries.

PROGRAMS: Community Outreach; Concerts; Elder's Programs; Exhibits; Facility Rental; Family Programs; Festivals; Guided Tours; Interpretation; Lectures; Research Library/Archives; School-Based Curriculum

COLLECTIONS: [1740-present] Clothing, decorative and fine arts, furniture, textiles, industrial and agricultural machines, folk art, historic local domestic, and cultural artifacts. Library of local and state history including published manuscripts, photographs, newspapers, genealogical, and business records.

ZELIENOPLE

7519
Zelienople Historical Society, Inc.
243 S Main St, 16063 [PO Box 45, 16063-
0045]; (p) (724) 452-9457; (c) Butler

Private non-profit/ 1975/ staff: 1(f); 1(p); 40(v)/ members: 460/publication: *List on request*

HISTORIC SITE; HISTORICAL SOCIETY; HISTORY MUSEUM; HOUSE MUSEUM: Operates two historic house museums: Passavant and Buhl Houses; preserves founding families' histories, area history, genealogy and history library/files, displays, research, outreach, tours, films, discussions.

PROGRAMS: Annual Meeting; Community Outreach; Exhibits; Family Programs; Festivals; Film/Video; Guided Tours; Interpretation; Lectures; Publication; Research Library/ Archives

COLLECTIONS: [1807-1920] Historic houses, antique family attire, furnishings, books, paintings, photographs, letters, legal documents, diaries; community memorabilia, signs, furniture, toys, documents, photos, family records, church records.

HOURS: Yr Office and Library: M-F 9-4

ADMISSION: $3.50, Student $2.50

PUERTO RICO

SAN JUAN

7520
Autoridad de los Puertos
Box 362829, 00936-2829

State/ staff: 1458(f); 232(p); 32(v)/ members: 1458

MARITIME MUSEUM: Preserves maritime history and artifacts.

PROGRAMS: Guided Tours

COLLECTIONS: Artifacts and memorabilia relating to ships and nautical history.

HOURS: Yr Su 9-4

7521
Conservation Trust of Puerto Rico, The
155 Tetuan St, 00902-0903 [PO Box 9020903, 00902-0903]; (p) (787) 722-5834; (f) (787) 722-5872; fideicomiso@fideicomiso.org; www.fideicomiso.org/

Private non-profit/ 1970/ Board of Trustees/ staff: 72(f)

LIVING HISTORY/OUTDOOR MUSEUM: Preserves and enhances Puerto Rico's national beauty and resources, primarily through land acquisition.

PROGRAMS: Exhibits; Guided Tours; Interpretation; Living History; Research Library/ Archives

COLLECTIONS: [19th-20th c] Restored 19th c coffee plantation, Hacienda Buena Vista and corn mill with historic buildings, machinery and artifacts; Original records, family documents, business papers, and old photographs.

HOURS: Yr W-Su 8:30-3:30

ADMISSION: $5

7522
El Morro Fortress
El Morro Fortress, 00901; (p) (787) 729-6960, (787) 729-6777; www.nps.gov/saju/morro.html

National Park Service

HISTORIC SITE; NATIONAL PARK: Maintains El Morro, six-level fortress with 18 ft wall 140 feet high built in the mid 1500s and extended in the mid 1700s, as the main defense for Puerto Rico. National Historic Site.

PROGRAMS: Exhibits

COLLECTIONS: [1540-present] Spanish fort, with dungeons, tunnels, barracks, outposts, cannons, sentry boxes, and ramps.

HOURS: Yr Daily 9-5

7523
Fort San Cristobal
Narzagaray St, 00901; (p) (787) 729-6960, (787) 729-6777; www.nps.gov/saju/sancristo bal.html

National Park Service

HISTORIC SITE; NATIONAL PARK: Maintains San Cristobal Fort, a partner to El Morro Fortress, construction began in 1634 ended in 1771, 150 ft tall on 27 acres, features 5 independent units, each connected by moat and tunnel, each fully self-sufficient should the others fall. National Historic Site.

PROGRAMS: Exhibits

COLLECTIONS: [1634-present] Spanish fort: battery, ramps, moats, chapel, tunnels, barracks.

HOURS: Yr Daily 9-6

7524
La Fortaleza, Governor's Residence
[PO Box 9020082, 00902-0082]; (p) (787) 721-7000

State

HISTORIC SITE: Maintains Governor's Residence built in 1540 as a fortress for Charles V. Has been the official Governor's Residence for 170 years.

PROGRAMS: Exhibits; Guided Tours

COLLECTIONS: [1540-present]

HOURS: Yr M-F 9-4

RHODE ISLAND

BARRINGTON

7525
Barrington Preservation Society
Pelk Library, 281 County Rd, 02806 [PO Box 178, 02806]; (p) (401) 246-0999; (c) Bristol

Private non-profit/ 1958/ staff: 1(f); 8(p); 25(v)/ members: 155

HISTORICAL SOCIETY; HISTORY MUSEUM; RESEARCH CENTER: Collects, preserves, and interprets town history through its museum, lectures, tours, school programs, historic plaque programs, and participation on town committees.

PROGRAMS: Annual Meeting; Community Outreach; Exhibits; Guided Tours; Lectures; Publication; Research Library/Archives; School-Based Curriculum

COLLECTIONS: [1617-present] Materials related to agriculture, genealogy, local history, architecture, toys and records of churches in Barrington.

HOURS: Yr T, Sa 10-2

BEECH ISLAND

7526
Redcliffe State Historic Site
181 Redcliffe Rd, 29841 [181 Redcliffe Road, RI, 29841]; (p) (803) 827-1473; (f) (803) 827-1473; redcliffe_plantation_sp@prt.st

State/ 1859/ staff: 3(f); 10(v)

Maintains the historic house.

COLLECTIONS: [1859-1975] The Hammond family's original furnishings including European art and finery and English and American furniture; the library is filled with much of the Hammond collection of books, papers, and photographs.

HOURS: Yr

BLOCK ISLAND

7527
Southeast Lighthouse Foundation
Mohegan Trail, 02807 [PO Box 949, 02807-0949]; (p) (401) 466-5009; selight@ids.net; (c) Washington

Private non-profit/ 1989/ Board of Directors/ staff: 1(f); 3(p)

HISTORIC PRESERVATION AGENCY; HISTORIC SITE; HOUSE MUSEUM: Restores and preserves Southeast Lighthouse.

PROGRAMS: Exhibits; Guided Tours; Interpretation

COLLECTIONS: [19th c]

HOURS: July-Aug Daily 10-4

ADMISSION: $5, Children $2.50, Seniors $2.50

BRISTOL

7528
Blithewold Mansion & Gardens
101 Ferry Rd, 02809 [PO Box 716, 02809-0716]; (p) (401) 253-2707; (f) (401) 253-0412

1908/ Heritage Trust of R I/ staff: 6(f); 12(p); 280(v)

Preserves gardens and mansion.

COLLECTIONS: [1895-1940] Silver collection, dolls, books, arboretum - unusual native and exotic trees; photographs, letters, diaries, home movies.

HOURS: Yr

7529
Coggeshall Farm Museum
Colt Drive, 02809 [PO Box 562, 02809]; (p) (401) 253-9062; coggmuseum@aol.com

Private non-profit/ 1973/ Board of Trustees/ staff: 1(f); 3(p)/ members: 425

HISTORY MUSEUM; LIVING HISTORY/OUTDOOR MUSEUM: Preserves and interprets RI coastal farming.

PROGRAMS: Annual Meeting; Exhibits; Festivals; Garden Tours; Guided Tours; Interpretation; Living History; Reenactments

COLLECTIONS: [1790] Agricultural, textile, and woodworking tools, period furnishings, artifacts.

HOURS: Yr Daily 10-6

ADMISSION: $1, Children $0.50, Seniors $0.50

7530
Friends of Linden Place
500 Hope St, 02809 [PO Box 328, 02809]; (p) (401) 253-0390; (f) (401) 254-0299; (c) Bristol

Private non-profit/ 1987/ Friends of Linden Place, Inc./ staff: 1(f); 2(p); 200(v)/ members: 500

GARDEN; HISTORY MUSEUM; HOUSE MUSEUM; PRESIDENTIAL SITE: Restores, operates, and promotes Linden Place, an 1810 federal period mansion, offering cultural and educational programs.

PROGRAMS: Annual Meeting; Community Outreach; Concerts; Exhibits; Facility Rental; Family Programs; Film/Video; Garden Tours; Guided Tours; Interpretation; Lectures; School-Based Curriculum

COLLECTIONS: [1800-1900] Period furnishing, portraits, china, paintings, sculpture, Ethel Barrymore collection of photos and ephemera.

HOURS: May-Oct Th-Sa 10-4, Su 12-4

ADMISSION: $5, Children $2.50

7531
Haffenreffer Museum of Anthropology
300 Tower St, 02809; (p) (401) 423-8388; (f) (401) 253-1198; kathleen_luke@brown.edu; www.brown.edu/facilities/haffenreffer; (c) Bristol

Private non-profit/ 1956/ Brown University/ staff: 9(f); 1(p); 30(v)/ members: 250/publication: *Contexts*

HISTORY MUSEUM: Preserves and interprets indigenous cultures.

PROGRAMS: Annual Meeting; Community Outreach; Exhibits; Family Programs; Festivals; Film/Video; Guided Tours; Interpretation; Lectures; Publication; Research Library/ Archives; School-Based Curriculum

COLLECTIONS: [Prehistory-present] Ethnographic artifacts including 6,700 from North

America, 6,700 from South and Central America, 2,500 from Africa, 2,200 from Eurasia, 1,700 from Southeast Asia, 600 from Oceania, 80,000 archaeological artifacts.

HOURS: Sept-May Sa-Su 11-5; June-Aug T-Su 11-5

ADMISSION: $2, Children $1, Seniors $1

7532
Historic Preservation Department, Roger Williams University
1 Old Ferry Rd, 02809 [Roger Williams Univ, 02809]; (p) (401) 254-3580; (f) (401) 254-3501; HP@alpha.rwu.edu; (c) Bristol

Private non-profit/ 1976/ Roger Williams Univ/ staff: 4(f); 3(p)

HISTORIC PRESERVATION AGENCY: Promotes conservation through educational programs and community lectures, workshops.

PROGRAMS: Facility Rental; Lectures; Research Library/Archives; School-Based Curriculum

COLLECTIONS: [1900] H.R. Hitchcock American Architecture books on microfilm, H.A.B.S. measured drawings, photos, data pages; Index of American Design.

HOURS: Yr

ADMISSION: No charge

CHEPACHET

7533
Glocester Heritage Society
1181 Main St, 02814 [PO Box 269, 02814]; (p) (401) 568-1866; (c) Providence

Private non-profit/ 1968/ Executive Board/ staff: 14(p); 4(v)/ members: 175

HISTORIC PRESERVATION AGENCY; HISTORIC SITE; HISTORICAL SOCIETY; HISTORY MUSEUM: Preserves local history.

PROGRAMS: Living History; Research Library/Archives

COLLECTIONS: [1860-1914] Town memorabilia, photos on glass negatives, Civil War Journal of Local Surgeon, artifacts from local mills, and school houses.

HOURS: Yr Sa 11-3

COVENTRY

7534
General Nathanael Greene Homestead
50 Taft St, 02816; (p) (401) 821-8630; www.brown.edu/Student_Services/Rhode_Island/points.html

Preserves historic homestead.

7535
Western Rhode Island Civic Historical Society/Paine House
7 Station St, 02816; (p) (401) 821-4095, (401) 395-5135; (c) Kent

Private non-profit/ 1954/ WRICHS/ staff: 1(v)/ members: 50/publication: *The Hinterlander*

HISTORICAL SOCIETY; HOUSE MUSEUM

PROGRAMS: Publication

HOURS: June-Sept Sa 1-4 and by appt

ADMISSION: $3, Student $1

CRANSTON

7536
Governor William Sprague Mansion
1351 Cranston St, 02920; (p) (401) 944-9226; www.geocities.com/heartland/4678

1790/ Cranston Historical Society/ staff: 5(v)

Home of William Sprague, Civil War governor of Rhode Island.

COLLECTIONS: [Late 1860s] Items belonging to Governor Sprague and his family; Photographs; maps; textbooks; city directories; Rhode Island books; scrapbooks of Cranston from 1900.

HOURS: By appt

7537
Joy Homestead
156 Scituate Ave, 02921; (p) (401) 463-6168

EAST GREENWICH

7538
New England Wireless and Steam Museum
1300 Frenchtown Rd, 02818; (p) (401) 885-0545; (f) (401) 884-0683; newsm@ids.net; www.users.ids.net/~nesm; (c) Kent

City, non-profit/ 1964/ staff: 60(v)

HISTORY MUSEUM

PROGRAMS: Community Outreach; Concerts; Exhibits; Facility Rental; Lectures

COLLECTIONS: [1860-1930]

HOURS: Yr by appt

ADMISSION: $6

7539
Varnum House Museum
1776 Revolution St, 02818; (p) (401) 884-1776; k8bcm@home.com; (c) Kent

Private non-profit/ 1907/ Varnum Continentals/ staff: 1(p); 6(v)/ members: 150

GARDEN; HOUSE MUSEUM: Preserves Federal mansion and colonial garden.

PROGRAMS: Annual Meeting; Garden Tours; Guided Tours; Lectures

COLLECTIONS: [1773-1781] Federal Period furnishing and colonial gardens.

HOURS: June-Aug Th-Sa 10-2; Sept Sa 10-2

ADMISSION: $2

EAST PROVIDENCE

7540
Carousel Park Commission
Carousel, Bullocks Pt Ave, 02914 [City Hall, 145 Taunton Ave, 02914-4505]; (p) (401) 435-7518; (f) (401) 435-7501; (c) Providence

Private non-profit/ 1895/ staff: 4(f); 25(p)

HISTORIC PRESERVATION AGENCY; HISTORIC SITE: Preserves, restores, and operates Crescent Park Carousel.

PROGRAMS: Community Outreach; Elder's Programs; Exhibits; Facility Rental; Festivals; Guided Tours; Lectures

COLLECTIONS: [1880-1895] 61 hand carved horses, camel, four chariots housed in onion-domed pavilion.

HOURS: Apr-Oct W-Su 12-8

ADMISSION: $0.75

7541
East Providence Historical Society
65 Hunts Mills Rd, 02916 [PO Box 4774, 02916]; (p) (401) 438-1750; (c) Providence

Private non-profit/ 1966/ staff: 15(v)/ members: 250/publication: *East Providence Historical Society Gazette*

GARDEN; HISTORIC SITE; HISTORICAL SOCIETY; HISTORY MUSEUM; HOUSE MUSEUM

PROGRAMS: Annual Meeting; Community Outreach; Exhibits; Facility Rental; Festivals; Guided Tours; Interpretation; Lectures; Living History; Publication; Research Library/Archives; School-Based Curriculum

COLLECTIONS: [1750-1866] Period furnishing, household artifacts, paintings, photos, papers, maps, books, tools, oral histories, tape recordings, advertising, textiles, decorative arts, mechanical machinery, genealogies.

HOURS: Mar-June and Sept-Dec T-Th 9-12, Su 1-3

FOSTER

7542
Foster Preservation Society
Howard Hill Rd, 02825 [Box 51, 02825]; (c) Providence

Private non-profit/ 1964/ staff: 6(v)/ members: 116

HISTORIC PRESERVATION AGENCY: Preserves natural and cultural history of Foster.

PROGRAMS: Annual Meeting; Community Outreach; Lectures; Publication

COLLECTIONS: [19th c-present] Photos, store ledgers, scrapbooks, artifacts, letters, documents, and family genealogy.

HOURS: Special events and by appt

ADMISSION: No charge

JAMESTOWN

7543
Jamestown Historical Society
92 Narragansett Ave, 02835 [PO Box 156, 02835]; (p) (401) 423-0784

Private non-profit/ 1912/ staff: 50(v)/ members: 300

HISTORICAL SOCIETY: Maintains 18th century windmill, Friends Meetinghouse, and town museum.

PROGRAMS: Annual Meeting; Exhibits; Guided Tours; Lectures; Research Library/Archives

COLLECTIONS: [1880-present] Artifacts related to Jamestown.

HOURS: (Museum) June-Aug W-Su 1-4; (Windmill) June-Aug Sa-Su 1-4

ADMISSION: Donations accepted

KINGSTON

7544
Pettaquamscutt Historical Society Inc.
2636 Kingstown Rd, 02881; (p) (401) 783-1328; (c) Washington

Private non-profit/ 1958/ Board of Directors/ staff: 2(p); 13(v)/ members: 250/publication: *The Reporter*

HISTORICAL SOCIETY: Collects, preserves, and exhibits Washington County artifacts.

PROGRAMS: Annual Meeting; Community Outreach; Exhibits; Guided Tours; Interpretation; Lectures; Publication; Research Library/Archives

COLLECTIONS: [1700-1945] Photos, library, genealogy files, historic clothing, household furnishing, toys, tools, arrowheads, Victorian furnishing, textiles, weaving, voting booth.

HOURS: T, Th, Sa 1-4

7545
University of Rhode Island Historic Textile and Costume Collection
55 Lower College Rd Ste 3, 02881; (p) (401) 874-4574; (f) (401) 874-2581; mordonez@ uri.edu; uri.edu/hss/tmd/gallery.htm

State/ 1951/ staff: 1(f); 2(p); 1(v)

HISTORY MUSEUM; RESEARCH CENTER

PROGRAMS: Community Outreach; Exhibits; Lectures; Research Library/Archives; School-Based Curriculum

COLLECTIONS: [18th c-present] Apparel, accessories, periodicals, textiles, ethnographic apparel.

HOURS: Yr M-F 8:30-4:30

ADMISSION: No charge

7546
University of Rhode Island Special Collections
15 Lippitt Rd, 02881; (p) (401) 874-2594; (f) (401) 874-4608; 5RW@URI.edu; www.URI.edu/library/special_collections; (c) South

State/ Univy of Rhode Island/ staff: 2(f)

LIBRARY AND/OR ARCHIVES: The library is a designated State Public Library and its materials are available to its citizens for research.

COLLECTIONS: [19th-20th c] Oral histories of Rhode Island life, records of the Episcopal Diocese of Rhode Island, papers, art of cartoonist Paul Loring, papers of Rhode Island politicians, Senator Pell and Senator Chafee, glass plates, and print collection of late 19th and 20th c college life.

HOURS: Yr M-F 8:30-4:30

LINCOLN

7547
Valentine Whitman House
Historic Great Rd, 02865 [Historic Great Road, 02865]; (p) (401) 333-1100 x 249

LITTLE COMPTON

7548
Little Compton Historical Society
548 W Main Rd, 02837 [PO Box 577, 02837]; (p) (401) 635-4035; (f) (401) 635-4906; hbridge@sprynet.com; www.rootsweb.com/ ~rinewpor/compton.html; (c) Newport

Private non-profit/ 1937/ Board of Directors/ staff: 25(v)/ members: 500

GARDEN; HISTORIC SITE; HISTORICAL SO-CIETY; HISTORY MUSEUM; HOUSE MUSEUM: Collects, preserves, and interprets town history.

PROGRAMS: Annual Meeting; Community Outreach; Exhibits; Guided Tours; Lectures; Publication; School-Based Curriculum

COLLECTIONS: [1680-1900] Ten period rooms of furnishing; sleighs, coaches; farm tools and equipment, photos, and paintings.

HOURS: June-Sept Th-M 2-5

ADMISSION: $5, Children $1

7549
Wilbor House
548 W Main Rd (SR 77), 02837 [PO Box 577, 02837]; (p) (401) 635-4035; 74561.3457@ compuserve.com

1690

COLLECTIONS: [1690-1860] Photographs of Little Compton.

HOURS: Seasonal

MIDDLETOWN

7550
Middletown Historical Society Inc.
Paradise & Prospect St, 02842 [PO Box 4196, 02842]; (p) (401) 849-1870; (c) Newport

Private non-profit/ 1976/ staff: 40(v)/ members: 400

HISTORICAL SOCIETY: Promotes history of Middletown. Owns and has restored 2 one room school houses, both on the National Register.

PROGRAMS: Annual Meeting; Elder's Programs; Exhibits; Lectures; School-Based Curriculum

COLLECTIONS: [1850-present] Historical documents, books, maps, newspapers, photos, letters, diaries, cemetery, history, tomb stones, dolls, uniforms, dresses, furnishing, tools housed in restored one room school-houses.

HOURS: July-Sept Su 2-4

ADMISSION: $2 Windmill

7551
Whitehall Museum House
311 Berkeley Ave, 02842; (p) (401) 846-3116; (c) Newport

Private non-profit/ 1900/ staff: 27(v)

HOUSE MUSEUM: Preserves home of philosopher Bishop George Berkeley.

PROGRAMS: Community Outreach; Guided Tours

COLLECTIONS: [1726-1731]

HOURS: July-Aug T-Su 10-5

ADMISSION: $3, Children $1

NARRAGANSETT

7552
South County Museum
100 Anne Hoxsie Lane, 02882 [Canochet Farm PO Box 709, 02882]; (p) (401) 783-5400; (f) (401) 783-0506; pricg@aol.com; www.southcountymuseum.org; (c) Washington

Private non-profit/ 1933/ staff: 3(p); 101(v)/ members: 700/publication: *Canonchet Gazette*

HISTORY MUSEUM: Interprets colonial history.

PROGRAMS: Annual Meeting; Community Outreach; Concerts; Elder's Programs; Exhibits; Family Programs; Festivals; Guided Tours; Interpretation; Lectures; Living History; Publication; Reenactments; School-Based Curriculum

COLLECTIONS: [1800-1940]

ADMISSION: $3.50, Children $1.75

NEWPORT

7553
Astors' Beechwood-Victorian Living History Museum
580 Bellevue Ave, 02840; (p) (401) 846-3772; (f) (401) 849-6998; astors@astors-beech wood.com; www.astors-beechwood.com; (c) Newport

Private for-profit/ 1982/ Historic Newport/ staff: 12(f); 9(p); 4(v)

HOUSE MUSEUM: Home of Caroline Astor, the creator of America's first social register and mother of Colonel John Astor, who died on the Titanic. A first person interpretive Victorian living history museum.

COLLECTIONS: [1891] Professional actors portray Mrs. Astor's family, friends, and domestics. One-third of the actual collection is original to the Astor family.

HOURS: Feb-Dec

ADMISSION: $8.75, Family $25

7554
Belcourt Castle
657 Bellevue Ave, 02840; (p) (401) 846-0669, (401) 849-1566; (f) (401) 846-5345; www.bel court.com

189194/ Royal Arts Foundation/ staff: 10(f); 3(v)

Home of Oliver H.P. Belmont, Alva Vanderbilt Belmont, and Harold Sterling Vanderbilt.

COLLECTIONS: [19th c] Comprehensive furniture collection.

HOURS: Feb-Dec

7555
Company of the Redwood Library and Athanaeum, The
50 Bellevue Ave, 02840; (p) (401) 847-0292; (f) (401) 841-5680; redwood@edgenet.net; www.redwood1747.org; (c) Newport

Private non-profit/ 1747/ Board of Directors/ staff: 10(f); 10(p); 50(v)/ members: 1350/publication: *Vetruvius Americana*

LIBRARY AND/OR ARCHIVES: Oldest surviving lending library in the US; operates museum, circulating, and research library.

PROGRAMS: Concerts; Exhibits; Family Programs; Guided Tours; Lectures; Publication; Research Library/Archives; Theatre

COLLECTIONS: [18th c] 162,000 volumes of general interest and special collections; fine and decorative arts.

HOURS: Yr Su 1-5, T-Th 9:30-8, M, F, Sa 9:30-5:30

ADMISSION: No charge

7556
Hammersmith Farm
Ocean Dr, 02840; (p) (401) 846-7346; (f) (401) 849-4973; www.hamersmithfarm.com; (c) Newport

Private for-profit/ 1977/ staff: 5(f); 25(p)

HOUSE MUSEUM: Preserves childhood home of Jackie Kennedy Onnasis and summer White House during JFK Administration.

PROGRAMS: Facility Rental; Guided Tours

HOURS: Apr-Nov Daily 10-5

ADMISSION: $8.50, Children $3.50

7557
International Tennis Hall of Fame
194 Bellevue Ave, 02840; (p) (401) 849-3990; (f) (401) 849-8780; www.tennisfame.org; (c) Newport

Private non-profit/ 1954/ staff: 20(f); 10(p); 12(v)/ members: 1500

HISTORY MUSEUM: Preserves history of the sport of tennis.

PROGRAMS: Concerts; Exhibits; Facility Rental; Film/Video; Guided Tours; Research Library/Archives

COLLECTIONS: [20th c] Tennis rackets, equipment, trophies, photos, prints, posters, paintings, tennis artifacts, costumes, archives, books, magazines.

HOURS: Yr Daily 9:30-5:30

ADMISSION: $8, Family $20, Children $4, Seniors $6

7558
Museum of Yachting, The
Fort Adams State Park, 02840 [PO Box 129, 02840]; (p) (401) 847-1018; (f) (401) 847-8320; museum@moy.org; www.moy.org; (c) Newport

Private non-profit/ 1980/ Board of Trustees/ staff: 3(f); 3(p); 90(v)/ members: 500/publication: *Spinnaker*

HISTORY MUSEUM; MARITIME MUSEUM: Preserves and presents history of yachting in Newport and Narragansett Bay through collections, programs, and archives.

PROGRAMS: Community Outreach; Concerts; Exhibits; Facility Rental; Family Programs; Festivals; Film/Video; Lectures; Publication; Research Library/Archives; Theatre

COLLECTIONS: [1800-present] Galleries depict the America's Cup history, mansions and yachts, small craft, singlehanded Hall of Fame and American Sailboat Hall of Fame. Reference library: 2,000 books, 35 monthly yachting magazine dating to 1908.

HOURS: May-Oct Su-Sa 10-5

ADMISSION: $4, Children $3, Seniors $3.50

7559
Naval War College Museum
686 Cushing Rd, 02841; (p) (401) 841-4052; (f) (401) 841-7689; Nicolosa@nwc.navy.mil; www.vistnewport.com/buspages/navy/; (c) Newport

Federal/ 1978/ US Navy/ staff: 3(f); 8(v)

HISTORIC SITE; HISTORY MUSEUM: Promotes history of naval warfare and naval heritage of Narragansett Bay.

PROGRAMS: Exhibits

COLLECTIONS: [19th-20th c] Artifacts, art, imprints, maps, memorabilia related to naval warfare.

HOURS: Oct-May M-F 10-4; June-Sept M-F 10-4, Sa-Su 12-4

ADMISSION: No charge

7560
Newport Historical Society
82 Touro St, 02840; (p) (401) 846-0813; (f) (401) 846-1853; (c) Newport

Private non-profit/ 1854/ staff: 10(f); 6(p); 55(v)/ members: 1500

HISTORICAL SOCIETY; HISTORY MUSEUM; HOUSE MUSEUM: Collects and preserves history of Newport County.

PROGRAMS: Annual Meeting; Community Outreach; Exhibits; Facility Rental; Guided Tours; Interpretation; Lectures; Publication; Research Library/Archives; Theatre

COLLECTIONS: [1630-present] 10,000 objects including paintings, Townsend-Goddard furnishings, clocks, textiles, 200,000 historic photos, genealogy archives, manuscripts, and maps.

HOURS: Tu-Sa 9:30-4:30

ADMISSION: No charge

7561
Nichols-Wanton-Hunter House
54 Washington St, 02840; (p) (401) 847-1000; www.rifog.com/recreation/travel/ri/newport/0005.shtml

7562
Preservation Society of Newport County
424 Bellevue Ave, 02840; (p) (401) 847-1000; (f) (401) 847-1361; info@newportmansions.org; (c) Newport

Private non-profit/ 1945/ Board of Trustees/ staff: 80(f); 330(p)/ members: 4200/publication: *Newport Gazette*

GARDEN; HISTORIC PRESERVATION AGENCY; HISTORIC SITE; HOUSE MUSEUM; RESEARCH CENTER: Preserves, restores, collects, and interprets 11 landmark buildings, fine and decorative arts, and historic landscapes of Newport County.

PROGRAMS: Annual Meeting; Concerts; Exhibits; Facility Rental; Family Programs; Festivals; Garden Tours; Guided Tours; Interpretation; Lectures; Living History; Research Library/Archives

COLLECTIONS: [1750-1900] 19th c topiary garden, 11 historic homes with period furnishing.

HOURS: Yr Daily

ADMISSION: Varies

7563
Samuel Whitehorne House
416 Thames St, 02840 [51 Touro St, 02840]; (p) (401) 847-2448

7564
Society of Friends of Touro Synagogue National Historic Site, Inc., The
85 Touro St, 02840; (p) (401) 847-0810; (f) (401) 847-8121; www.tourosynagogue.org; (c) Newport

Private non-profit/ 1948/ Board of Directors/ staff: 1(f); 11(p)/ members: 2600/publication: *Society Update*

HISTORIC SITE: Maintains and preserves Touro Synagogue, colonial Jewish cemetery, and Patriots Park; promotes religious freedom.

PROGRAMS: Annual Meeting; Concerts; Family Programs; Film/Video; Guided Tours; Interpretation; Lectures; Publication

COLLECTIONS: Religious artifacts and documents.

HOURS: Yr M-F, Su

ADMISSION: Group rates

PASCOAG

7565
Burrillville Historical and Preservation Society
16 Laurel Hill Ave, 02859 [PO Box 93, 02859]; (p) (401) 568-8534; (c) Providence

Private non-profit/ staff: 80(v)/ members: 80

HISTORICAL SOCIETY: Promotes historical education and preservation through newsletters, informational meetings, and research.

PROGRAMS: Annual Meeting; Community Outreach; Festivals

PAWTUCKET

7566
Daggett House
Later Memorial Park, 02861 [16 Second St, 02861]; (p) (401) 722-6931; (c) Providence

Private non-profit/ Pawtucket Chapter DAR/ staff: 12(v)/ members: 41

HISTORIC PRESERVATION AGENCY; HISTORIC SITE; HOUSE MUSEUM: Preserves and restores Daggett House.

PROGRAMS: Exhibits; Facility Rental; Guided Tours; Living History; Reenactments

COLLECTIONS: [17th-20th c] Revolutionary War and Civil War historical documents, period furnishings, and artifacts.

HOURS: May-Oct and by appt

ADMISSION: $2, Children $0.50

7567
Preservation Society of Pawtucket
67 Park Place, 02862 [PO Box 735, 02862]; (p) (401) 725-9581; (f) (401) 726-0973; psp@ici.net; www.preservepawtucket.com; (c) Providence

Private non-profit/ 1978/ Board of Directors/ staff: 1(f); 2(p); 20(v)/ members: 200

HISTORIC PRESERVATION AGENCY: Preserves historical, architectural, and cultural resources of Pawtucket.

PROGRAMS: Annual Meeting; Community Outreach; Concerts; Family Programs; Festivals; Guided Tours; Interpretation; Lectures; School-Based Curriculum

HOURS: Yr M-F 9-5

ADMISSION: No charge

7568
Slater Mill Historic Site
67 Roosevelt Ave, 02862 [PO Box 696, 02862]; (p) (401) 725-8631; (f) (401) 722-3040; samslater@aol.com; www.slatermill.org; (c) Providence

Private non-profit/ 1921/ Old Slater Mill Association/ staff: 3(f); 25(p); 10(v)/ members: 417

HISTORIC SITE; HOUSE MUSEUM: Museum complex dedicated to preserving site of first successful water powered cotton spinning mill, August 1793.

PROGRAMS: Annual Meeting; Concerts; Elder's Programs; Exhibits; Facility Rental; Family Programs; Interpretation; Lectures; Living History; Research Library/Archives; School-Based Curriculum

COLLECTIONS: [19th c] Textile machinery, textiles, fabric patterns, costumes, housed in historic Slater Mill, Wilkinson Mill, and Sylvanus Brown House.

HOURS: Yr M-Sa 10-5, Su 1-5

ADMISSION: $7, Children $5.50, Seniors $6

7569
Sylvanus Brown House
Roosevelt Ave, 02862 [c/o Slater Mill Historic Site, PO Box 696, 02862]; (p) (401) 725-8638, (401) 725-8639; (f) (401) 722-3040; SamSlater@aol.com; Slatermill.org

1758/ Old Slater Mill Association/ staff: 2(f); 21(p)

COLLECTIONS: [17th c-present] Machine tools, textile machines, textile processing equipment, textiles, photographic collections, some family and business records.

HOURS: M-Sa 10-5, Su 1-5; June 1-Nov 1; Nov 2-3rd wk

PEACE DALE

7570
Museum of Primitive Art and Culture
1053 Kingstown Rd, 02883 [PO Box A, 02883]; (p) (401) 783-5711; (c) Washington

Private non-profit/ 1892/ staff: 2(p); 8(v)/ members: 200/publication: *19th Century American Collector: A Rhode Island Perspective*

HISTORY MUSEUM: Collects, preserves, and interprets artifacts from native cultures through exhibits and outreach programs.

PROGRAMS: Community Outreach; Exhibits; Family Programs; Festivals; Film/Video; Garden Tours; Guided Tours; Interpretation; Lectures; Publication; School-Based Curriculum

COLLECTIONS: [Prehistory-present] Archaeological and ethnological artifacts from Africa, Native North America, Europe, Oceania, and South America.

HOURS: Sept-May T-Th 10-2

ADMISSION: Donations accepted

PORTSMOUTH

7571
Portsmouth Historical Society
870 E Main Rd, 02871 [PO Box 834, 02871]; (p) (401) 683-9178; (c) Newport

1938/ staff: 15(v)/ members: 175

HISTORIC SITE; HISTORICAL SOCIETY; HISTORY MUSEUM: Preserves and interprets history of Portsmouth.

PROGRAMS: Annual Meeting; Exhibits; Festivals; Film/Video; Guided Tours; Lectures; Publication; Research Library/Archives

COLLECTIONS: Housewares, toys, farm tools, and small library.

HOURS: May-Oct Su 2-4 and by appt

ADMISSION: No charge

7572
Prescott Farm
W Main Rd, 02871 [51 Touro St, Newport, 02840]; (p) (401) 847-6230

PROVIDENCE

7573
Betsey Williams Cottage
Roger Williams Park, 20905 [c/o Museum of Natural History, Roger Williams Pa, 20905]; (p) (401) 785-9457; (f) (401) 461-5146

1773/ Providence Parks Dept

COLLECTIONS: [1773-1873] House artifacts, archives include research and primary documents pertaining to the cottage and its former inhabitants, Williams family.

7574
Governor Stephen Hopkins House
15 Hopkins St, 02903; (p) (401) 421-0694

7575
John Brown House
52 Power St, 02906 [110 Benevolent St, 02906]; (p) (401) 331-8575; (f) (401) 351-0127; www.rihs.org

Private non-profit/ 1786/ RI Historical Society/ staff: 4(f); 1(p); 125(v)

COLLECTIONS: [1788-1941] Townsend and Goddard furniture of Newport, China, Trade porcelain, 18th and early 19th c paintings, including portraits of the members of the family, RI silver, reproduction wallpapers of John B. Wallpaper collection, R.I. furniture, textiles and family clothing remnants, pewter collection, 550 paintings not exhibited, Library materials, manuscripts, three dimensional objects.

HOURS: Jan-Feb F-Sa 10-5, Su 12-4; Mar-Dec T-Sa 10-5, Su 12-4

7576
John Nicholas Brown Center for the Study of American Civilization
357 Benefit St, 02912 [PO Box 1880, Brown University, 02912]; (p) (401) 272-0357; (f) (401) 272-1930; Joyce_Botelho@brown.edu; (c) Providence

Private non-profit/ 1985/ staff: 4(f); 3(p); 15(v)

HISTORIC SITE; RESEARCH CENTER: Promotes scholarship and education in American Studies.

PROGRAMS: Guided Tours; Lectures; Research Library/Archives

COLLECTIONS: [18th-20th c] Period furnishing, 700 linear feet of personal and business records.

HOURS: Yr F 1-4 and by appt

ADMISSION: $3, Students $2, Seniors $2

7577
Rhode Island Historical Society
110 Benevolent St, 02906; (p) (401) 333-8575; www.rihs.org; (c) Providence

Private non-profit/ 1822/ Board of Trustees/ staff: 21(f); 22(p); 150(v)/ members: 2000/publication: *Rhode Island History*

HISTORICAL SOCIETY; HISTORY MUSEUM; HOUSE MUSEUM; LIBRARY AND/OR ARCHIVES: Located in the Aldrich House, collects, preserves, and interprets RI history through operation of museum, research library, and John Brown House.

PROGRAMS: Annual Meeting; Community Outreach; Concerts; Exhibits; Facility Rental; Family Programs; Festivals; Guided Tours; Interpretation; Lectures; Publication; Research Library/Archives; School-Based Curriculum

COLLECTIONS: [17th-20th c] Film, photos, cartography, manuscripts, business records, decorative arts, textiles, costumes, China Trade material, silver and precious metals, jewelry, social history objects, models, and shipping equipment.

HOURS: Yr T-F 9-5

ADMISSION: $6

7578
Rhode Island Jewish Historical Association
130 Sessions St, 02906; (p) (401) 331-1360; (f) (401) 272-6729; rjhist@aol.com; www.dowtech.com/rijha/

1951/ staff: 3(p); 3(v)/ members: 600/publication: *Rhode Island Jewish Historical Notes*

HISTORICAL SOCIETY: Collects and preserves history of Jewish population of RI.

PROGRAMS: Annual Meeting; Exhibits; Publication; Research Library/Archives

COLLECTIONS: [1850-present] Artifacts related to Jewish presence in RI.

HOURS: Yr 9-2:30

ADMISSION: No charge

7579
Rhode Island State Archives
337 Westminster St, 02903; (p) (401) 222-2353; (f) (401) 222-3199; www.state.ri.us/archives

State/ 1647/ Dept of State

LIBRARY AND/OR ARCHIVES: Maintains the Rhode Island State Archives is the official custodian and trustee of all public records of permanent historical, legal material.

PROGRAMS: Exhibits; Lectures; Research Library/Archives

COLLECTIONS: [1638-present]

HOURS: Yr M-Sa 8:30-4:30

7580
Roger Williams National Monument
282 N Main St, 02903; (p) (401) 521-7266; (f) (401) 521-7239; rowl_interpretation@nps.gov; www.nps.gov/rowi; (c) Providence

1965/ National Park Service/ staff: 6(f); 2(p); 1(v)

HISTORIC SITE; NATIONAL PARK: Located at site of original settlement of Providence; collects and preserves history and contributions of Roger Williams.

PROGRAMS: Exhibits; Guided Tours; Interpretation; School-Based Curriculum

COLLECTIONS: [17th c]

HOURS: Yr Daily 9-4:30

ADMISSION: No charge

7581
Steamship Historical Society of America, Inc., The
300 Ray Dr, Ste 4, 02906; (p) (401) 274-0805; www.sshsa.org

Private non-profit/ 1975/ staff: 2(p); 2(v)/ members: 3500/publication: *Steamboat Bill*

HISTORICAL SOCIETY: Promotes history of steam navigation.

PROGRAMS: Annual Meeting; Publication; Research Library/Archives

COLLECTIONS: [1850-1990] See entry for Steamship Historical Society Collection under Baltimore, MD.

HOURS: Yr M-F 10-4

ADMISSION: No charge

SAUNDERSTOWN

7582
Casey Farm, SPNEA
2325 Boston Neck Rd, 02874; (p) (401) 295-1030, (614) 227-3956; (f) (401) 294-6957; www.spnea.org

1750/ Society for the Preservation of New England Antiquities

Maintains farm.

COLLECTIONS: [18thc-Present] Farm house and yard.

HOURS: June 1-Oct 15 T, Th, Sa 1-5

ADMISSION: $4

7583
Gilbert Stuart Museum
815 Gilbert Stuart Rd, 02874; (p) (401) 294-3001; (f) (401) 294-3869; (c) Washington

Private non-profit/ 1930/ staff: 2(f); 1(p); 14(v)/ members: 400

HOUSE MUSEUM: Promotes and interprets history art and literture of painter Gilbert Stuart through preservation of his work and his home.

PROGRAMS: Community Outreach; Exhibits; Family Programs; Festivals; Garden Tours; Guided Tours; Interpretation; School-Based Curriculum

COLLECTIONS: [18th-19th] Gilbert Stuart reproductions, artifacts, tools, period furnishing.

HOURS: Apr-Oct Th-M 11-4

ADMISSION: $5, Children $2

SMITHFIELD

7584
Historic Society of Smithfield
220 Stillwater Rd, 02917; (p) (401) 231-7363; (c) Providence

Private non-profit/ 1935/ staff: 25(v)/ members: 100

HISTORIC SITE; HISTORICAL SOCIETY;

HOUSE MUSEUM: Maintains and supports Smith-Appleby House Museum, historical cemeteries.

PROGRAMS: Facility Rental; Festivals; Guided Tours; Living History

COLLECTIONS: [18th-19th c] Period furnishing, artifacts, historical documents, and maps.

HOURS: May-Nov by appt

ADMISSION: $2, Children $1

7585
Smith-Appleby House
220 Stillwater Rd, 02917; (p) (401) 231-7363

1700/ The Historical Society of Smithfield, Inc.

COLLECTIONS: [1700s] Historic house.

HOURS: Appt

TIVERTON

7586
Chase-Cory House
3908 Main Rd, 02878; (p) (401) 624-2096

WARREN

7587
Massasoit Historical Association
59 Church St, 02885 [PO Box 203, 02885-0203]; (p) (401) 245-0392; (c) Bristol

Private non-profit/ 1907/ staff: 7(v)/ members: 100

HISTORICAL SOCIETY; HOUSE MUSEUM: Collects artifacts and preserves historic c. 1755 Maxwell House.

PROGRAMS: Annual Meeting; Community Outreach; Concerts; Festivals; Guided Tours; Interpretation; Lectures; Publication; Reenactments; Research Library/Archives; School-Based Curriculum

COLLECTIONS: [18th c] Artifacts related to Warren history, the Maxwell Family, and maritime history.

HOURS: Yr Sa 10-2

ADMISSION: No charge/donations accepted

WARWICK

7588
Warwick Historical Society
25 Roger Williams Circle, 02886; (p) (401) 467-7647, (401) 737-8160; (c) Kent

1938/ staff: 12(v)/ members: 130

GENEALOGICAL SOCIETY; HISTORICAL SOCIETY; HOUSE MUSEUM; RESEARCH CENTER: Promotes local history.

PROGRAMS: Community Outreach; Exhibits; Festivals; Guided Tours; Lectures; Research Library/Archives

COLLECTIONS: Native American artifacts, clothing, genealogy, photos, ephemera.

HOURS: Yr 9-1 and by appt

ADMISSION: Donations

WEST GREENWICH

7589
West Greenwich Historical Preservation Society
Louttit Library, Rt 102 Victory Hwy, 02817 [9 Sharpe St, 02817]; (p) (401) 397-4311; (c) Kent

1987/ staff: 6(v)/ members: 15

HISTORICAL SOCIETY: Preserves local history.

COLLECTIONS: [1800] Pictorial history of town and inhabitants.

HOURS: Yr 10-2

WESTERLY

7590
Babcock Smith House
124 Granite St, 02891; (p) (401) 596-5704, (401) 596-5704; lsmith9860@aol.com; (c) Washington

Private non-profit/ 1734/ staff: 1(p); 40(v)

ALLIANCE OF HISTORICAL AGENCIES; HISTORIC SITE; HOUSE MUSEUM

PROGRAMS: Annual Meeting; Community Outreach; Exhibits; School-Based Curriculum

COLLECTIONS: [18th-20th c] Babcock & Smith family genealogies, collections of Southern RI history books and papers, antique furniture, paintings, quilts, furniture, and toys.

HOURS: May-Sept Su 2-5; July-Sept W 2-5

ADMISSION: $3, Children $0.50

7591
Orlando R. Smith Trust (Babcock-Smith House)
124 Granite St, 02891; (p) (401) 596-5704; lsmith9860@aol.com; (c) Washington

1972/ Board of Trustees/ staff: 40(v)

HOUSE MUSEUM: Preserves home of Joshua Babcock, Westerly's first physician and postmaster and home of Orlando Smith, founder of Westerly granite industry.

PROGRAMS: Community Outreach; Elder's Programs; Exhibits; Guided Tours; Lectures; School-Based Curriculum

COLLECTIONS: [18th-19th c] Furnishing, paintings, quilts, colonial artifacts, family genealogy, local history books.

HOURS: May-June, Sept Su 2-5; July-Aug W, Su 2-5

ADMISSION: $3, Children $0.50

WICKFORD

7592
Smith's Castle
55 Richard Smith Dr, 02852; (p) (401) 294-3521; (c) Washington

Private non-profit/ 1949/ Cocumscussoc Association/ staff: 1(f); 60(v)/ members: 330

HISTORIC SITE; HOUSE MUSEUM: Preserves history of plantation house, 18th c garden and site of Roger Williams' 1637 trading post.

PROGRAMS: Facility Rental; Festivals; Guided Tours; Interpretation; Reenactments; School-Based Curriculum

COLLECTIONS: [1638-1813] Period furnishing, quilts, needlework, paintings, tools, kitchen utensils.

HOURS: May, Sept F-Su 12-4; June-Aug Th-M 12-4

ADMISSION: $3, Children $1

WYOMING

7593
Narragansett Indian Tribal Historic Preservation Office
[PO Box 700, 02898]; (p) (401) 364-3977; (f) (401) 539-4217; (c) Washington

Tribal/ 1985/ staff: 3(f); 2(p); 4(v)

HISTORIC PRESERVATION AGENCY; TRIBAL MUSEUM

PROGRAMS: Community Outreach; Exhibits; Garden Tours; Interpretation; Lectures; Living History

SOUTH CAROLINA

ABBEVILLE

7594
Abbeville County Historic Preservation Commission
400 N Main St, 29620 [PO Box 164, 29620]; (p) (864) 459-4297; (c) Abbeville

Joint/ 1964/ State; County/ staff: 10(v)

HISTORIC PRESERVATION AGENCY; HISTORIC SITE; HOUSE MUSEUM: Owns and operates the Burt Stark Mansion, site of the final meeting of the Confederate Cabinet on May 2, 1865.

PROGRAMS: Guided Tours

COLLECTIONS: [Victorian] Period furnishings.

HOURS: May-Aug T-Sa 1-5; Feb-May, Sept-Dec 1-5

ADMISSION: $4

7595
Burt-Stark Mansion
N Main & Greenville Sts, 29620 [Chamber of Commerce, 107 Court Square, 29620]; (p) (803) 459-4297, (864) 459-4600; (f) (864) 459-5462

AIKEN

7596
Aiken County Historical Museum
433 Newberry St SW, 29801; (p) (803) 642-2017; (f) (803) 642-2016; acmuseum@scescape.net; www.scescape.com; (c) Aiken

County/ 1970/ staff: 2(f); 1(p); 120(v)/ members: 425

HISTORY MUSEUM: Supports the history of Aiken County.

PROGRAMS: Annual Meeting; Concerts; Exhibits; Facility Rental; Festivals; Guided Tours; Lectures

COLLECTIONS: Two and three dimensional artifacts pertaining to county and regional history.

HOURS: Yr T-F 9:30-4:30, Sa-Su 2-5

7597
Aiken-Barnwell Genealogical Society
[PO Box 415, 29802-0415]; Lhutto@ifx.net; www.ifx.net/~lhutto/page2.html; (c) Aiken

Private non-profit/ 1984/ members: 225/publication: *News and Journal*

GENEALOGICAL SOCIETY: Seeks to further family history research.

PROGRAMS: Monthly Meeting; Publication

COLLECTIONS: Publications of news and journals since 1984 and eight cemetery books.

7598
Historic Aiken Foundation
433 Newberry St, Aiken County Historical Museum, 29802 [PO Box 959, 29802]; (p) (803) 648-0242; (c) Aiken

Private non-profit/ 1971/ staff: 1(p); 20(v)/ members: 150

HISTORICAL SOCIETY: Encourages the preservation and restoration of historic structures and sites.

PROGRAMS: Annual Meeting; Exhibits; Guided Tours; Lectures

ANDERSON

7599
Anderson Heritage, Inc.
[PO Box 58, 29622]; (p) (864) 375-1739; (c) Anderson

Private non-profit/ 1974/ staff: 20(v)/ members: 70

HISTORIC PRESERVATION AGENCY: Promotes the history and heritage of Anderson and restores its historic districts.

PROGRAMS: Annual Meeting; Community Outreach

BARNWELL

7600
Barnwell County Museum and Historical Board
Hagood & Marlboro Ave, 29812 [PO Box 3, 29812]; (p) (803) 259-1916; (c) Barnwell

County/ 1978/ staff: 1(f); 15(v)/ members: 80/publication: *Memoirs of Tarleton Brown*

ART MUSEUM; GENEALOGICAL SOCIETY; HISTORIC PRESERVATION AGENCY; HISTORICAL SOCIETY; HISTORY MUSEUM: Maintains exhibits and artifacts that relate to county history, sponsors cultural programs, provides art classes, and works closely with local schools.

PROGRAMS: Community Outreach; Concerts; Exhibits; Facility Rental; Guided Tours; Lectures; Publication; School-Based Curriculum

COLLECTIONS: [20th c] China, silver, documents, textiles, toys, pottery, and military items.

HOURS: Yr T-Th 3:30-5:30, Su 3-5:30

BEAUFORT

7601
Beaufort Historical Society
[PO Box 55, 29901]; (c) Beaufort

Private non-profit/ 1939/ staff: 6(v)/ members: 183

Sponsors speakers and assists the Beaufort County Library in supporting and gaining material for the library's local history room.

7602
Beaufort Museum
713 Craven St, 29901 [PO Drawer 1167, 29901]; (p) (843) 525-7077; (f) (843) 525-7013; bftmuseum@islc.net; www.beaufortcitysc.com; (c) Beaufort

City/ 1939/ City of Beaufort/ staff: 2(f)/ members: 400

HISTORY MUSEUM: Preserves and interprets the man-made history of the city of Beaufort, Beaufort County, and the South Carolina Lowcountry. Offers exhibits, programs, tours, lecture, and special events.

PROGRAMS: Annual Meeting; Community Outreach; Exhibits; Facility Rental; Family Programs; Interpretation; Lectures; Living History; Reenactments

COLLECTIONS: [18th-20th c] Arsenal and Carnegie Library, Native American artifacts, textiles, costumes, household, personal furnishings and accessories, Lowcountry artwork and photographs.

HOURS: Yr M-F 10-5

ADMISSION: $2, Student $0.50

7603
Historic Beaufort Foundation
801 Bay St, 29901 [PO Box 11, 29901]; (p) (843) 524-6334; (f) (843) 524-6240; (c) Beaufort

Private non-profit/ 1975/ Board of Trustees/ staff: 2(f); 3(p); 400(v)/ members: 666

GARDEN; HISTORIC PRESERVATION AGENCY; HISTORIC SITE: Preserves and protects historically significant buildings and places in Beaufort City and County, including John Mark Verdier House Museum.

PROGRAMS: Annual Meeting; Community Outreach; Exhibits; Facility Rental; Guided Tours; Interpretation

COLLECTIONS: [Early 19th c] Furnishings and artifacts: parlor, dining room, bed chamber, ballroom and retiring room.

HOURS: Yr M-F

BEECH ISLAND

7604
Beech Island Historical Society
144 Old Jackson Hwy, 29842 [PO Box 158, 29842]; (p) (803) 867-3600; (f) (803) 867-3600; psix@scescape.net; www.welcome.to/Beech-Island; (c) Aiken

Private non-profit/ 1985/ staff: 5(p)/ members: 300/publication: *Four Centuries and More*

HISTORICAL SOCIETY: Preserves and promotes the history of Beech Island.

PROGRAMS: Exhibits; Festivals; Guided Tours; Interpretation; Lectures; Living History; Monthly Meeting; Publication; Reenactments; Research Library/Archives

COLLECTIONS: [17th-19th c] Prehistoric Native American and colonial artifacts, photographs, letters, legal papers, and family histories.

HOURS: Yr T-W 11-2

BELTON

7605
Ruth Drake Museum
Main, 29627 [108 Carroll Lane, 29627]; (p)
(864) 338-7541; (c) Anderson

Private non-profit/ 1973/ Museum Board/ staff:
6(v)

HISTORIC SITE; HISTORY MUSEUM; RE-
SEARCH CENTER: Maintains museum located in a section of the historic Belton Depot
building.

PROGRAMS: Exhibits; Guided Tours

COLLECTIONS: [1850s-present] Artifacts pertaining to the area, including railroad displays,
farm implements, and textiles.

HOURS: Yr by appt

ADMISSION: No charge

7606
South Carolina Tennis Hall of Fame
Belton Depot, 101 Main St, 29627 [PO Box
843, 29627]; (p) (864) 338-7751; (f) (864) 338-
4034; RMAYN5224@aol.com; (c) Anderson

Private non-profit/ 1982/ SC Tennis Patrons
Foundation/ staff: 1(v)/ members: 100/publica-
tion: *Tennis Talk*

HISTORY MUSEUM: Honors individuals who
have contributed to SC tennis and preserves
artifacts from tennis history in the state. Provides a museum for the display and preservation of these tennis artifacts.

PROGRAMS: Annual Meeting; Community
Outreach; Guided Tours; Publication

COLLECTIONS: [1920-present] Old trophies,
racquets, pictures, publications and other tennis items of interest. Portraits of the inductees
done by Wayland Moore.

HOURS: Yr M,T,Th 11-1/2-8, W and Sa 9-1/2-
3:30, F 11-1

ADMISSION: No charge

BENNETTSVILLE

7607
Jennings-Brown House
121 S Marlboro St, 29512; (p) (803) 479-5624

1826/ Marlborough Historical Society/ staff:
1(f); 15(v)

COLLECTIONS: [1850] Pre-1850 furnishings,
belonging of family that lived in house, and
Marlborough County pieces.

HOURS: Yr

BISHOPVILLE

7608
South Carolina Cotton Museum, Inc.
121 W Cedar Lane, 29010; (p) (803) 484-4497; (f)
(803) 484-5203; sccottonmus@ftc-i.net; (c) Lee

1993/ Board of Trustees/ staff: 2(f); 2(p); 21(v)

HISTORY MUSEUM: Collects and preserves
artifacts and information concerning the history of cotton culture in SC and offers meeting
areas, classrooms for public use, and a public
park.

COLLECTIONS: [19th-20th c] Tools and
equipment used during the past two centuries
for growing and processing cotton. Cultural art

items directly related to cotton farming and
family life.

HOURS: Yr M-Sa 10-4, Su 1-4

ADMISSION: $5, Student $2, Seniors $3;
Under 6 free

BLACKSBURG

7609
Kings Mountain National Military Park
2625 Park Rd, 29702; (p) (864) 936-7921; (f) (864)
936-9897; www.nps.gov/kimo; (c) York/Cherokee

Federal/ 1931/ National Park Service/ staff:
11(f); 3(p); 74(v)

AVIATION MUSEUM; HISTORIC SITE: Commemorates an important Patriot victory during
the Revolutionary War. Contains nearly 4,000
acres and 1.5 mile trail with monuments and
wayside exhibits. Park has 20 buildings including four historic structures. Overmountain Victory National Historic Trail is a 310 mile path
once followed by frontier militiamen.

PROGRAMS: Community Outreach; Concerts; Exhibits; Film/Video; Guided Tours; Interpretation; Lectures; Living History; Research Library/Archives; School-Based
Curriculum

COLLECTIONS: [18th c] Miscellaneous
weapons, accoutrements, colonial cooking
and other houseware utensils. Reproductions
of like items and microfilm of Draper's manuscripts. Archives relating to Battle of Kings
Mountain and development of the military
park.

HOURS: Yr Daily 9-5

ADMISSION: No charge

7610
Kings Mountain State Park, Living History Farm
1277 Park Rd, 29702; (p) (803) 222-3209; (f)
(803) 222-6948; (c) York

State/ 1974/ SC Dept of Parks, Recreation and
Tourism/ staff: 1(f); 2(p); 11(v)

LIVING HISTORY/OUTDOOR MUSEUM:
Working farm that depicts farm life of mid 19th c.

PROGRAMS: Family Programs; Festivals;
Guided Tours; Living History; School-Based
Curriculum

COLLECTIONS: [1840-1850] Nine log buildings, including a furnished homeplace, wood-
wright shop, blacksmith, cotton gin, sorghum
mill, oven, and tool shed.

HOURS: Apr-mid Nov Daily 9-4:30

ADMISSION: $1.50

BLUFFTON

7611
Bluffton Historical Preservation Society
52 Boundary St, 29910 [PO Box 742, 29910];
(p) (843) 757-6293; (f) (843) 705-2938;
MayeBluff@aol.com; (c) Beaufort

Private non-profit/ 1981/ Board of Trustees/
staff: 1(f); 1(p); 15(v)/ members: 400

HISTORICAL SOCIETY; HISTORY MUSEUM:
Protects and preserves the history of Bluffton
and surrounding area for present and future

generations. Collects materials that document
and illustrate local history.

PROGRAMS: Annual Meeting; Exhibits; Facility Rental; Guided Tours; Lectures; Living History; Publication; Research Library/Archives

COLLECTIONS: [18th-20th c] Manuscripts,
photographs, newspapers, and maps.

HOURS: Yr W-Sa 10-3

ADMISSION: $2.50

BRANCHVILLE

7612
Branchville Railroad Shrine and Museum
7505 Freedom Rd, 29432; (p) (803) 274-
8820; (c) Orangeburg

City/ staff: 20(v)/ members: 85

HISTORIC SITE; RAILROAD MUSEUM

PROGRAMS: Festivals

COLLECTIONS: [19th c] Railroad artifacts.

BRATTONSVILLE

7613
Plantation House
Historic Brattonsville, [1444 Brattonsville
Road, McConnells, 29726]; (p) (803) 684-
2327; (f) (803) 684-0149

CAMDEN

7614
Bonds-Conway House
811 Fair St, 29020; (p) (803) 432-9841

7615
Camden Archives and Museum
1314 Broad St, 29020-3535; (p) (803) 425-
6050; (c) Kershaw

City/ 1975/ staff: 1(f); 3(p)

HISTORIC SITE; HISTORY MUSEUM; RE-
SEARCH CENTER: Preserves and makes
available items of historical interest related to
Camden and the surrounding area.

PROGRAMS: Exhibits; Guided Tours; Interpretation; Research Library/Archives; School-
Based Curriculum

COLLECTIONS: Publications, newspapers,
microfilm, manuscripts, photos, artifacts, and
microfiche.

HOURS: M-F 8-5; 1st & 3rd Su of month

7616
Historic Camden Revolutionary War Site
222 Broad St, 29020 [PO Box 710, 29020]; (p)
(803) 432-9841; (f) (803) 432-3815; hiscam
den@camden.net; www.Historic-camden.org;
(c) Kershaw

Private for-profit/ 1970/ Historic Camden
Found/ staff: 3(f); 3(p); 30(v)/ members: 560

HISTORIC SITE: Fosters public appreciation
and awareness of the historical, archaeological and military history of Camden from the
1730s to 1825, particularly its role as an inland
trade center and a British military base during
the American Revolution. Includes Kershaw-
Cornwallis house.

PROGRAMS: Community Outreach; Concerts; Exhibits; Facility Rental; Family Programs; Festivals; Film/Video; Guided Tours; Interpretation; Lectures; Living History; Reenactments; Research Library/Archives; School-Based Curriculum; Theatre

COLLECTIONS: [1730-1850] State and county archaeology and history artifacts, furniture, maps, portraits, paintings, books, and miscellaneous museum artifacts such as candlesticks, china, and assorted blacksmith tools.

HOURS: Yr T-Sa 10-5, Su 1-5

ADMISSION: Under 6/Self-guided

7617
Kershaw County Historical Society

811 Fair St, 29020 [PO Box 501, 29020]; (p) (803) 425-1123; kchistory@mindspring.com; www.go.to/~kchistory; (c) Kershaw

Private non-profit/ 1954/ Board of Directors/ staff: 2(p); 15(v)/ members: 480

HISTORICAL SOCIETY; HOUSE MUSEUM: Operates as a public benefit to seek, acquire, study, conserve, record, compile, and publish information concerning the history of Kershaw County.

PROGRAMS: Annual Meeting; Family Programs; Guided Tours; Interpretation; Publication

COLLECTIONS: [Mid 19th c] Furnished house restored by the society built c 1812 by an African-American believed to be the first to purchase his freedom in the United States.

HOURS: Yr Th 1-5 and by appt

ADMISSION: No charge

CATAWBA

7618
Landsford Canal State Park

2051 Park Dr, 29704; (p) (803) 789-5800; landsford_canal_sp@prt.state.sc.us; (c) Chester

State/ 1970/ SC Dept of Parks, Recreation and Tourism/ staff: 2(f); 1(p); 2(v)

HISTORIC SITE: Maintains the best preserved of SC's 19th c canals, includes stone lifting locks, culverts, bridges, mill ruins, tow path on the uppermost of four canals constructed on the Catawba-Wateree River system during the period 1820-1835.

PROGRAMS: Exhibits; Facility Rental; Guided Tours; Interpretation

COLLECTIONS: [1820-1850] SC's 19th c canals, includes stone lifting locks, culverts, bridges, mill ruins, and tow path.

HOURS: Yr Th-M 9-6; museum by appt

ADMISSION: $1.50

CAYCE

7619
Cayce Historical Museum

1800 12th St, 29171 [PO Box 2004, 29171]; (p) (803) 796-9020; (f) (803) 796-9072; (c) Lexington

Private non-profit/ 1991/ City of Cayce/Cayce Museum and Historical Commission/ staff: 3(p); 30(v)

HISTORIC SITE; HISTORY MUSEUM; HOUSE MUSEUM: Preserves and chronicles history of first European settlement in SC Midlands. Interprets agricultural, social, and cultural heritage of old Saxe-Gotha (1733), Granby, Cayce, and West Columbia. Exhibits emphasize periods of Colonial trade, agricultural development, and transportation.

PROGRAMS: Exhibits; Family Programs; Festivals; Guided Tours; Interpretation; Lectures; Living History; Reenactments; Research Library/Archives

COLLECTIONS: [18th c-present] Prehistoric Native American artifacts, agricultural, social, and cultural heritage of European settlers from 1733 to the present.

HOURS: Yr T-F 9-4, Sa-Su 2-5

ADMISSION: $2, Student $1, Children $0.50, Seniors $1; Su free

CHARLESTON

7620
Aiken-Rhett House

48 Elizabeth St, 29403; (p) (803) 723-1159; (f) (803) 805-6732; www.historiccharleston.org

1818/ Historic Charlesto

COLLECTIONS: Includes items obtained by Aiken family on trips to Europe, including crystal and bronze chandeliers, classical sculptue, and paintings.

HOURS: Yr

7621
Avery Research Center for African American History and Culture, College of Charleston

125 Bull St, 29424-0001; (p) (843) 953-7609, (843) 953-7608; (f) (843) 953-7607; FranksC@cofc.edu; www.cofc.edu/~averyrsc; (c) Charleston

State/ 1985/ Board of Trustees/ staff: 7(f); 2(p); 10(v)/publication: *The Avery Review*

RESEARCH CENTER: Collects, documents, exhibits, and interprets the African and African American experience in SC.

PROGRAMS: Community Outreach; Exhibits; Family Programs; Film/Video; Guided Tours; Interpretation; Lectures; Publication; Research Library/Archives; School-Based Curriculum

COLLECTIONS: [18th c-present] Processed manuscripts, African and African American artifacts, slides, photographs, portraits, paintings, documentarie, and serials.

HOURS: Yr M-Sa 12-5 by appt

ADMISSION: Donations accepted

7622
Calhoun Mansion

16 Meeting St, 29401; (p) (803) 722-8205

1876/ Privately owned/ staff: 1(f); 12(p)

COLLECTIONS: [Late 19th c] Some original furnishings; Senate records of John C. Calhoun

HOURS: Yr

7623
Charles Towne Landing State Historic Site

1500 Old Towne Rd, 29407; (p) (843) 852-4200; (f) (843) 852-4205; charles_towne_landing_sp@prt.state.sc.us; (c) Charleston

State/ 1970/ SC Dept of Parks, Recreation and Tourism/ staff: 29(f); 30(p); 100(v)/ members: 200

HISTORIC SITE; LIVING HISTORY/OUTDOOR MUSEUM: Preserve site of the first permanent English/African settlement in the Carolinas. A state historic site, a nature preserve, and an educational facility.

PROGRAMS: Community Outreach; Exhibits; Facility Rental; Family Programs; Film/Video; Guided Tours; Interpretation; Living History; School-Based Curriculum

COLLECTIONS: [1670-1735] Photographs, Native American artifacts, and archaeological findings.

HOURS: Yr Daily 8:30-5; July-Aug

7624
Charleston Library Society

164 King St, 29401; (p) (843) 723-9912; (c) Charleston

Private non-profit/ 1748/ Board of Trustees/ staff: 4(f); 3(p)/ members: 900

LIBRARY AND/OR ARCHIVES: Provides general circulating collection and research for all ages.

PROGRAMS: Annual Meeting; Exhibits; Lectures; Research Library/Archives

COLLECTIONS: [18th-19th]

HOURS: Yr M-F 9:30-5:30, Sa 9:30-2

ADMISSION: $3/day research fee

7625
Charleston Museum

360 Meeting St, 29403-6297; (p) (843) 722-2996; (f) (843) 722-1784; brumgard@bellsouth.net; www.charlestonmuseum.com; (c) Charleston

Private non-profit/ 1773/ staff: 35(f); 1(p); 100(v)/ members: 1800

HISTORY MUSEUM; HOUSE MUSEUM: Operates the main facility, two National Historic Landmark houses, Hewyard-Washington House and Joseph Manigault House, and a wildlife sanctuary with cultural features. Focuses on the cultural/natural history of the SC lowcountry.

PROGRAMS: Exhibits; Facility Rental; Family Programs; Interpretation; Lectures; Research Library/Archives; School-Based Curriculum

COLLECTIONS: [17th-19th c] Natural sciences, ornithology, cultural history, anthropology, historic archaeology, photographs, and documentary materials.

HOURS: Museum: Yr M-Sa 9-5, Su 1-5; Houses: Yr M-Sa 10-5, Su 1-5

ADMISSION: $8, Children $4; Multi-site rates

7626
Citadel Archives and Museum

171 Moultrie St, 29409; (p) (843) 953-6846; (f) (843) 953-6956; yatesj@citadel.edu; www.citadel.edu/archivesandmuseum; (c) Charleston

State/ 1960/ The Citadel, The Military College of South Carolina/ staff: 2(f); 3(p)

HISTORY MUSEUM; LIBRARY AND/OR ARCHIVES: Presents and preserves the history of The Military College of SC.

PROGRAMS: Exhibits; Guided Tours; Research Library/Archives

COLLECTIONS: [1842-present] Manuscripts, photographs, films, audio tape, and museum artifacts. The papers of General Mark W. Clark and archives collection.

HOURS: Museum: Su-F 2-5, Sa 12-5; Archives: M-F

7627
Drayton Hall, National Trust for Historic Preservation
3380 Ashley River Rd, 29414; (p) (843) 769-2600, (843) 769-2612; (f) (843) 766-0878; dhmail@draytonhall.org; www.draytonhall.org; (c) Charleston

Private non-profit/ 1977/ Board of Trustees/ staff: 12(f); 27(p); 40(v)/ members: 9000

HISTORIC SITE: Owned and operated by the National Trust for Historic Preservation. Preserves and interprets Drayton Hall, the only plantation house left on the Ashley River that survived both the Revolutionary and Civil Wars.

PROGRAMS: Community Outreach; Concerts; Facility Rental; Guided Tours; Interpretation; Lectures; School-Based Curriculum

COLLECTIONS: [18th-19th c] Built in 1738, Drayton Hall is an excellent example of Georgian Palladian architecture.

HOURS: Nov-Feb Daily 10-3; Mar-Oct Daily 10-4

ADMISSION: $8, Student $6, Children $4; Group rates

7628
Edmondston-Alston House
21 E Battery, 29401-2740; (p) (843) 722-7171; www.middletonplace.org; (c) Charleston

Private non-profit/ 1974/ Middleton Place Foundation/ staff: 2(f); 17(p); 38(v)

HOUSE MUSEUM: Operated through an educational trust, striving to sustain the highest levels of preservation and interpretation for the collections and programs for the House.

PROGRAMS: Elder's Programs; Exhibits; Facility Rental; Guided Tours; Interpretation; Lectures; Reenactments

COLLECTIONS: [1810-1850] Paintings, portraits, furniture, china, and silver.

HOURS: Yr Su-M 1:30-4:30, T-Sa 10-4:30

ADMISSION: $7

7629
Historic Charleston Foundation
40 E Bay St, 29402 [PO Box 1120, 29402]; (p) (843) 723-1623; (f) (843) 577-2067; www.historiccharleston.org; (c) Charleston

Private non-profit/ 1947/ Board of Trustees/ staff: 30(f); 50(p); 600(v)

HISTORIC PRESERVATION AGENCY; HOUSE MUSEUM: Preserves and protects the historical and architectural character of Charleston and its lowcountry environs through advocacy and participation in community planning, educational programs, heritage tours, neighborhood restoration, a covenant and easement program and revolving fund, a reproductions program, and the operation and interpretation of three museum properties.

PROGRAMS: Community Outreach; Exhibits; Garden Tours; Guided Tours; Interpretation; Lectures; Research Library/Archives

COLLECTIONS: [18th-19th c] Old Powder Magazine (c.1713) is the oldest public building in the Carolinas and interprets Charleston's formation as a walled city. The Nathaniel Russell House (c. 1808) is one of the nation's most significant neoclassical residences and is widely acclaimed for its architecture and important decorative arts collection. The Aiken - Rhett House (c. 1830) is interpreted as a unique example of a conserved antebellum urban plantation.

HOURS: Yr M-Sa 10-5, Su 2-5

ADMISSION: Varies

7630
John Rivers Communications Museum
College of Charleston, 58 George St, 29424; (p) (843) 953-5810; (c) Charleston

State/ 1989/ College of Charleston/ staff: 1(f); 2(p)

HISTORY MUSEUM: Focuses on the early history of communications which make possible today's information society.

PROGRAMS: Community Outreach; Exhibits; Film/Video; Guided Tours

COLLECTIONS: [1890s-1950s] Antique communications equipment that includes photographs, magic lanterns, motion picture projectors, radios, telegraphs, telephones, and televisions.

HOURS: Yr M-F 12-4

ADMISSION: No charge

7631
Karpeles Manuscript Library Museum
68 Spring St, 29403; (p) (803) 853-4651, (805) 969-3983; (f) (805) 969-0482; kmuseumsb@aol.com; www.karpeles.com; (c) Charleston

Private non-profit/ 1983/ Karpeles Manuscript Library/ staff: 4(f); 2(p)

HISTORIC PRESERVATION AGENCY; HISTORY MUSEUM: One of seven museums throughout the United States showing educational exhibits with free admission to everyone. Exhibits include original handwritten letters and documents of famous people throughout history.

PROGRAMS: Community Outreach; Concerts; Elder's Programs; Exhibits; Film/Video; Guided Tours; Lectures; Living History; Publication; Reenactments; Research Library/Archives; School-Based Curriculum; Theatre

COLLECTIONS: [Prehistory-present] One million manuscripts of important persons in the fields of science, music, technology, literature, art and history.

HOURS: Yr days vary 10-4

ADMISSION: No charge

7632
Macaulay Museum of Dental History/Waring Historical Library
175 Ashley Ave, PO Box 250181, 29425; (p) (843) 792-2288; (f) (843) 792-8619; brown jm@musc.edu; waring.library.musc.edu; (c) Charleston

State/ 1966/ Medical Univ of SC/ staff: 2(f); 1(p); 28(v)/ members: 272

HISTORY MUSEUM: Houses a large collection of dental artifacts and books.

PROGRAMS: Annual Meeting; Exhibits; Guided Tours; Lectures; Research Library/Archives

COLLECTIONS: [1670-2000] Artifacts chronicle progress in health sciences: dental chairs, an instrument designed by Paul Revere and early x-ray units. Library and archives provide resources in the history of health sciences.

HOURS: Yr M-F 8:30-5

ADMISSION: No charge

7633
Magnolia Plantation and Gardens
3550 Ashley River Rd, 29414; (p) (843) 571-1266; (f) (843) 571-5346; magnolia@internetx. net; www.magnoliaplantation.com; (c) Charleston

Private for-profit/ 1676/ staff: 75(f); 30(p)/ members: 600

ART MUSEUM; GARDEN; HISTORIC SITE; HOUSE MUSEUM; LIVING HISTORY/OUTDOOR MUSEUM: Features acres of garden with year round color, pre-Revolutionary War plantation house with museum-quality antiques, the Barbados Tropical Garden, nature train rides and horticulture maze.

PROGRAMS: Exhibits; Facility Rental; Garden Tours; Guided Tours

COLLECTIONS: [1676] Early American antiques, 900 varieties of camellias, 250 types of azaleas, year round bloom, rare botanical and ornithological prints and books.

HOURS: Mar-Oct Daily 8-5:30; Nov-Dec Daily 8-5, Dec-Feb Daily 8:30-4:30

ADMISSION: $10, Student $8, Children $5, Seniors $9; Under 6 free; Group rates

7634
Middleton Place
4300 Ashley River Rd, 29414; (p) (843) 556-6020; (f) (843) 766-4460; www.middletonplace.org; (c) Dorchester

Private non-profit/ 1974/ Middleton Place Found Bd of Trustees/ staff: 75(f); 35(p); 275(v)/ members: 1

GARDEN; HISTORIC SITE; HOUSE MUSEUM; LIVING HISTORY/OUTDOOR MUSEUM: Maintains oldest existing landscaped gardens in the United States. Birthplace of Arthur Middleton, signer of Declaration of Independence. Gardens, house and stable yards open to public.

PROGRAMS: Community Outreach; Concerts; Elder's Programs; Exhibits; Facility Rental; Family Programs; Garden Tours; Guided Tours; Interpretation; Lectures; Living History

COLLECTIONS: [18th-19th c] Middleton family collections: Benjamin West paintings, Thomas Elf breakfast table, English silver, china, Audubon prints, and first edition Mark Catesby.

HOURS: Yr Daily 9-5

ADMISSION: $8 house; $15 gardens

7635

Nathaniel Russell House

51 Meeting St, 29401; (p) (803) 724-8481; (f) (803) 805-6732; www.historiccharleston.org

1808/ Historic Charleston

COLLECTIONS: [Early 19th c] Period furnishings and works of art.

HOURS: Yr

7636

National Trust for Historic Preservation, Southern Office

456 King St, 29403; (p) (843) 722-8552; (f) (843) 722-8652; first_last@nthp.org; www.nationaltrust.com; (c) Charleston

Private non-profit/ 1949/ staff: 5(f); 2(p); 1(v)/ members: 275000/publication: *Preservation Magazine*

HISTORIC PRESERVATION AGENCY: Provides leadership, education, and advocacy to save America's diverse historic places and revitalize communities. This is done through six regional offices, 20 museum properties and the support of 275,000 members across the country.

PROGRAMS: Annual Meeting; Community Outreach; Lectures; Publication; Research

7637

Old Exchange Building

122 Eastbay St, 29401; (p) (843) 727-2165; (f) (843) 727-2163; oldexchange@infoave.net; www.oldexchange.com; (c) Charleston

State/ 1976/ Old Exchange Commission/ staff: 8(f); 8(p)

HISTORIC SITE; HISTORY MUSEUM: Preserves the Exchange and Customs House, 1771, holds an excavated portion of the fortification that surrounded Charles Towne dating to 1690. Museum interprets events from the founding of Charles Towne, the ratification of the US Constitution, Washington's Southern Tour as well as Colonial and postal history.

PROGRAMS: Exhibits; Facility Rental; Guided Tours; School-Based Curriculum

COLLECTIONS: [17th-18th c] Arms, textiles, furniture, china, and art.

HOURS: Yr Daily 9-5

ADMISSION: $6, Children $3.50

7638

Preservation Society of Charleston, The

147 King St, 29402 [PO Box 521, 29402]; (p) (843) 722-4630; (f) (843) 723-4381; preserve@preservationsociety.org; www.preservationsociety.org; (c) Charleston

Private non-profit/ 1920/ Board of Directors/ staff: 6(f); 1(p); 500(v)/ members: 2000/publication: *Preservation Progress*

HISTORIC PRESERVATION AGENCY: Advocates the preservation of Charleston's historic architectural resources through advocacy, education, and planning. The oldest community based historic preservation organization in the United States.

PROGRAMS: Annual Meeting; Community Outreach; Garden Tours; Lectures; Publication; Research Library/Archives; School-based Curriculum

7639

Robert Scott Small Library, Special Collections, College of Charleston

66 George St, 29424-0001; (p) (843) 953-8016; (f) (843) 953-8019; hollingsm@cofc.edu; www.cofc.edu/library/cofclib.html; (c) Charleston

State/ 1974/ State of SC/ staff: 4(f); 4(p); 6(v)

LIBRARY AND/OR ARCHIVES; RESEARCH CENTER: Preserves records and information of historical value pertaining to the College of Charleston, the State of South Carolina, the City of Charleston and the Lowcountry.

PROGRAMS: Elder's Programs; Exhibits; Research Library/Archives

COLLECTIONS: [19th-20th c] Illustrated ornithological books, papermaking and book arts, SC history, culture and architecture, College of Charleston and Spoleto festival archives, South Carolina Jewish Heritage collection.

HOURS: Yr M-F 9-1/2-4 and by appt

ADMISSION: No charge

7640

Save The Light, Inc.

Charleston Harbor, 29422 [PO Box 12490, 29422]; (p) (843) 795-8911; www.savethelight.org; (c) Charleston

Private non-profit/ 1998/ staff: 1(f); 1(p); 25(v)/ members: 400

HISTORIC PRESERVATION AGENCY; HISTORIC SITE: Saves and preserves the Morris Island Lighthouse for the people of SC.

COLLECTIONS: [1876-1962] Lighthouse is a 158 foot, 3,200 ton tower built in 1876 that now stands 1,600 feet offshore.

HOURS: Yr by appt

7641

Sea Island Historical Society

James Island, 29422 [PO Box 13405, 29422]; (p) (843) 406-1516; bostickd@bellsouth.net; (c) Charleston

Private non-profit/ 1998/ staff: 3(f); 50(v)

HISTORICAL SOCIETY: Dedicated to discovering, preserving, and celebrating the historical, cultural and natural resources of the SC Sea Islands.

PROGRAMS: Concerts; Elder's Programs; Exhibits; Family Programs; Film/Video; Guided Tours; Interpretation; Living History; Reenactments; Research Library/Archives; School-Based Curriculum

7642

South Carolina Historical Society

100 Meeting St, 29401-2299; (p) (843) 723-3225; (f) (843) 723-8584; david_percy@bell south.net; www.schistory.org; (c) Charleston

Private non-profit/ 1855/ staff: 14(f); 2(p); 10(v)/ members: 3800/publication: *The South Carolina Historical Magazine; The Carologue*

HISTORICAL SOCIETY; RESEARCH CENTER: Collects, preserves, and promotes the history of SC with an emphasis on non-official materials.

PROGRAMS: Annual Meeting; Community Outreach; Exhibits; Guided Tours; Lectures; Publication; Research Library/Archives

COLLECTIONS: [1610-present] Library of 35,000 volumes, 1 million manuscripts, 3,000 photographs, 1,000 works of art, plus maps, pamphlets, and architectural drawings focusing on SC.

HOURS: Yr T-F 9-4, Sa 9-2

ADMISSION: $6

7643

Studio Museum of Elizabeth O'Neill Verner

79 Church St, 29401 [38 Tradd St, 29401]; (p) (843) 722-4246; (f) (843) 722-1763; info@verner gallery.com; www.vernergallery.com; (c) Charleston

Private non-profit/ 1969/ staff: 2(f); 1(p)

ART MUSEUM: Museum of the works of Elizabeth O'Neill Verner in her last studio.

COLLECTIONS: [1920-1967] Works of Elizabeth O'Neill Verner.

HOURS: Yr M-Sa 10-5

ADMISSION: No charge

7644

Thomas Elfe House

54 Queen St, 29401; (p) (843) 722-9161; (c) Charleston

Private for-profit/ 1970/ staff: 2(f)

HISTORIC SITE; HISTORY MUSEUM; HOUSE MUSEUM: Preserves colonial Charleston cabinetmaker's house which dates c 1760.

PROGRAMS: Exhibits; Garden Tours; Guided Tours; Interpretation; Lectures; Living History

COLLECTIONS: [18th c] Pewter, furniture, cabinetry, books, lighting, pottery, glassware, needlework, and art.

HOURS: Yr M-Sa 10-12

ADMISSION: $5, Children $3

CHERAW

7645

Cheraw Lyceum

200 Market, Town Green, 29520 [221 Market St, 29520]; (p) (843) 537-8425; (f) (843) 537-5886; (c) Chesterfield

Private non-profit/ 1961/ Town of Cheraw/ staff: 1(p); 3(v)

HISTORIC SITE; HISTORY MUSEUM: Depicts Cheraw's 200 years of history through exhibits in an 1820s building.

PROGRAMS: Exhibits; Interpretation

COLLECTIONS: [Prehistory-present]

HOURS: Yr M-F 9-5 and by appt

ADMISSION: No charge

7646

Chesterfield County Historic Preservation Commission

Church St, 29520 [230 Third St, 29520]; (p) (843) 537-8425; (f) (843) 537-5886; (c) Chesterfield

County/ 1972/ staff: 8(v)/ members: 8

HISTORIC PRESERVATION AGENCY; HISTORIC SITE: Advises preservation efforts in the county. Operates and maintains Old St. David's Church, 1770, and used by four armies: British, American, Union and Confederate.

PROGRAMS: Facility Rental; Guided Tours; Interpretation; Publication; Reenactments

COLLECTIONS: [1770-1914]

HOURS: Yr M-F 9-5 and by appt

ADMISSION: No charge

7647
Historic Cheraw
230 Third St, 29520; (p) (843) 537-8425; (f) (843) 537-5886; (c) Chesterfield

Private non-profit/ members: 30

HISTORIC PRESERVATION AGENCY: Preserves and promotes Cheraw's history and architectural heritage.

PROGRAMS: Annual Meeting; Community Outreach; Guided Tours

COLLECTIONS: [18th c]

CHESNEE

7648
Cowpens National Battlefield
4001 Chesnee Hwy, 29323 [PO Box 308, 29323]; (p) (864) 461-2828; (f) (864) 461-7795; Pat_Ruff@cowpchiefranger; www.nps.gov/cowp; (c) Cherokee

Federal/ 1929/ National Park Service/ staff: 6(f); 3(p)

BATTLEFIELD; HISTORIC SITE; HISTORY MUSEUM: Protects and preserves the place where Daniel Morgan and his troops defeated Banastre Tarleton and the better-trained British army on January 17, 1781.

PROGRAMS: Exhibits; Interpretation; Living History

COLLECTIONS: [1781-1835] Reproduction grasshopper cannon and implements, weapons, and other artifacts from Revolutionary War.

HOURS: Yr Daily 9-5

ADMISSION: $1, Children $0.50

CLEMSON

7649
John C. Calhoun House-Fort Hill, The
Fort Hill St, 29634 [Trustee House, Clemson Univ, Box 345605H, 29634-5605]; (p) (864) 656-2475; (f) (864) 656-1026

COLUMBIA

7650
Chicora Foundation, Inc.
861 Arbutus Dr, 29202 [PO Box 8664, 29202-8664]; (p) (803) 787-6910; (f) (803) 787-6910; chicora@bellsouth.net; www.chicora.org; (c) Richland

1983/ staff: 3(f); 2(p)/publication: *Chicora Research Series; Chicora Research Contributions*

HISTORIC PRESERVATION AGENCY: Operates under a broad heritage preservation umbrella that includes programs in archaeological and historical research, public education, outreach, conservation, and preservation consulting for museums, libraries and archives.

PROGRAMS: Community Outreach; Interpretation; Publication; Research Library/Archives; School-Based Curriculum

COLLECTIONS: Research library of nearly 2,000 volumes, including regional archaeology, preservation, and general conservation. Archaeology collection includes pottery, lithics, ethnobotanical materials for SC, and coffin hardware and catalogs.

HOURS: Yr M-F 8:30-4:30

ADMISSION: No charge

7651
Hampton-Preston Mansion & Garden
1615 Blanding St, 29201; (p) (803) 252-1770, (803) 252-7742; (f) (803) 252-5001

1818/ Historic Columbia Foundation/ staff: 10(f); 11(p); 100(v)

COLLECTIONS: [1850s] Hampton and Preston family pieces, some original to house, others from their plantations throughout the Southeast.

HOURS: Yr

7652
Historic Columbia Foundation
1601 Richland St, 29201; (p) (803) 252-7742, (803) 252-1770; (f) (803) 929-7695; (c) Richland

Private non-profit/ 1961/ Board of Trustees/ staff: 11(f); 6(p); 225(v)/ members: 500

HISTORIC PRESERVATION AGENCY; HISTORIC SITE; HOUSE MUSEUM; PRESIDENTIAL SITE: Serves as advocate for community preservation and education by maintaining four historic house museums and displaying interpretive exhibitions. Tours of the city and county are offered; special programs and lectures are presented.

PROGRAMS: Annual Meeting; Community Outreach; Elder's Programs; Exhibits; Facility Rental; Family Programs; Festivals; Garden Tours; Guided Tours; Interpretation; Lectures; Living History; Research Library/Archives; School-Based Curriculum

COLLECTIONS: [19th c] Decorative arts, portraiture, textiles, furniture by several well-known cabinetmakers, and a variety of artifacts from the Hampton and Preston families.

HOURS: Yr T-Sa 10-4, Su 1-5

ADMISSION: $4

7653
Mann-Simons Cottage, Historic Columbia Foundation
1403 Richland St, 29201; (p) (803) 252-1770, (803) 252-7742; (f) (803) 252-5001

1850/ Historic Columbia Foundation/ staff: 10(f); 11(p); 100(v)

COLLECTIONS: [1850-1910] Original 1895 rosewood parlor suite, original dining chairs and pie safe, Charles Simm's tailoring irons, family portraits.

HOURS: Yr

7654
McKissick Museum
Corner of Bull & Pendleton Sts, 29208 [Univ of South Carolina, 29208]; (p) (803) 777-7251; (f) (893) 777-2829; robertson1@garnet.cla.sc.edu; www.cla.sc.edu/mcks/index.html; (c) Richland

State/ 1976/ Univ of SC/ staff: 11(f); 18(p); 39(v)/ members: 745

ART MUSEUM; HISTORY MUSEUM: Focuses on the history, art, folklife, and natural environment of the Southeastern United States.

PROGRAMS: Community Outreach; Exhibits; Family Programs; Festivals; Guided Tours; Interpretation; Lectures; Research Library/Archives; School-Based Curriculum

COLLECTIONS: Southern vernacular culture and traditions, folk arts, material culture, and natural history.

HOURS: Yr M-F 9-4, Sa-Su 1-5

ADMISSION: No charge

7655
Museum of Education, University of South Carolina
Green & Main St, 29208 [College of Education, Wardlaw Hall, USC, 29208]; (p) (803) 777-5741; (f) (803) 777-3090; musofed@sc.edu; www.ed.sc.edu/musofed/index.htm; (c) Richland

State/ 1970/ Univ of SC/ staff: 1(f); 1(p)

HISTORY MUSEUM; RESEARCH CENTER: Primarily an archival repository, the museum seeks to preserve, transmit, and expand the culture of educational life in SC and the US. Features exhibits, reference books, and special collections.

PROGRAMS: Exhibits; Lectures; Living History; Research Library/Archives

COLLECTIONS: [19th-20th c] 6,000 SC K-12 textbooks dating back to 1789, extinct school files, teachers' oral histories and biographies, photographs, papers of various prominent educators and the John B. Hawley Higher Education Collection with 20,000 postcards of colleges and universities.

HOURS: Call

ADMISSION: No charge

7656
South Carolina Archives and History Center
8301 Parklane Rd, 29223; (p) (803) 896-6100; (f) (803) 896-6167; hough@scdah.state.sc.us; www.state.sc.us/scdah; (c) Richland

State/ 1905/ staff: 90(f); 5(p); 2(v)/ members: 175/publication: *Currents*

HISTORIC PRESERVATION AGENCY; RESEARCH CENTER: Collects and provides public access to the public records of SC. Promotes state history through programs in education, records management, publications, and historic preservation.

PROGRAMS: Annual Meeting; Community Outreach; Exhibits; Facility Rental; Family Programs; Guided Tours; Lectures; Publication; Research Library/Archives; School-Based Curriculum

COLLECTIONS: [1671-present] 24,000 cubic feet of SC public records, with particular strength in the colonial period.

HOURS: Yr T-F 9-9, Sa 9-6, Su 1-6

ADMISSION: No charge

7657
South Carolina Confederate Relic Room and Museum
920 Sumter St, 29201; (p) (803) 898-8095; (f) (803) 898-8099; sschoon@crr.state.sc.us; www.crr.state.sc.us; (c) Richland

State/ 1896/ staff: 5(f); 2(p)

HISTORY MUSEUM: State operated museum with collection dating back to 1895. Initiated major $125,000 conservation program for flags and uniforms. Offers outreach education programs.

PROGRAMS: Community Outreach; Exhibits; Guided Tours; Interpretation; Lectures; Research Library/Archives

COLLECTIONS: [1860s] SC military history with strong emphasis on the Civil War era. Domestic items, textiles, quilts, dresses, sewing accoutrements, Confederate flags, military uniforms, and equipment.

HOURS: Yr M-F 8:30-5, 1st/3rd Saturdays 10-5

ADMISSION: No charge

7658
South Carolina Federation of Museums
301 Gervais St, 29202 [PO Box 100107, 29202-3107]; (p) (803) 898-4925; (f) (803) 898-4969; waiter@museum.state.sc.us; (c) Richland

Private non-profit/ members: 225/publication: *Good Muse!*

Represents and acts in the interest of museums in SC. Members strive to raise the standards of museum practice in the state. Sponsors an annual conference, variety of workshops and publishes quarterly newsletter.

7659
South Carolina Governor's Mansion
Cor of Richland & Lincoln Sts, 29201 [800 Richland St, 29201]; (p) (803) 737-1710; (f) (803) 737-3860; (c) Richland

State/ 1868/ staff: 5(f); 35(v)

GARDEN; HISTORIC SITE; HOUSE MUSEUM: Three historic homes and gardens are located within the Governor's Mansion complex. The Lace House is the official state guest house (built in 1850s). The Caldwell-Boylston houses offices and a gift shop.

PROGRAMS: Garden Tours; Living History

COLLECTIONS: [19th c] South Carolina art, furniture and state memorabilia.

7660
South Carolina Law Enforcement Officers Hall of Fame
5400 Broad River Rd, 29212-3540; (p) (803) 896-8199; (f) (803) 896-8067; (c) Richland

State/ 1979/ Advisory committee/ staff: 2(f)

HISTORY MUSEUM: Memorial to SC law enforcement officers who died in the line of duty and museum of historical and cultural aspects of state law enforcement.

PROGRAMS: Exhibits; Guided Tours

COLLECTIONS: [19th-20th c] Firearms and law enforcement related items.

HOURS: Yr M-F 8:30-5

ADMISSION: No charge

7661
South Carolina Military Museum
1 National Guard Rd, 29201-4766; (p) (803) 806-4440; (f) (803) 806-1071; scngmuseum@tag.scmd.state.sc.us; www.scguard.com; (c) Richland

Joint/ 1980/ SC Military Dept; Federal; State/ staff: 1(f); 10(v)

HISTORY MUSEUM: Historical holding of the SC National Guard and state militia.

PROGRAMS: Reenactments

7662
South Carolina State Museum
301 Gervais St, 29202 [PO Box 100107, 29202]; (p) (803) 898-4921; (f) (803) 898-4969; reception@museum.state.sc.us; www.museum.state.sc.us; (c) Richland

State/ 1973/ Museum Commission/ staff: 65(f); 65(p); 157(v)/ members: 6100

ART MUSEUM; HISTORY MUSEUM; NATURAL HISTORY MUSEUM: Collects, exhibits, and interprets the art, science, technology, and natural and cultural history of SC.

PROGRAMS: Annual Meeting; Community Outreach; Concerts; Exhibits; Facility Rental; Family Programs; Festivals; Film/Video; Guided Tours; Interpretation; Lectures; Living History; Publication; Reenactments; School-Based Curriculum

COLLECTIONS: [Prehistory-present] Textiles, furnishings, decorative arts, military, communications, transportation, social history, prints, paintings, photography, sculpture, space exploration, laser history, holography, fossils, minerals, and biological specimens.

HOURS: Yr M-Sa 10-5, Su 1-5

ADMISSION: $5, Student $4, Children $2, Seniors $4; $4 Military; Group rates

7663
University South Caroliniana Society
South Caroliniana Library, Univ of SC, 29208 [South Caroliniana Library, University of S Carolina, 29208]; (p) (803) 777-3131; (f) (803) 777-5747; (c) Richland

1937/ Executive Council/ staff: 17(f)/ members: 2100/publication: *Caroliniana Columns*

HISTORICAL SOCIETY; LIBRARY AND/OR ARCHIVES: Collects and makes available for scholarly research published, manuscript, and visual materials relating to the history, literature, and culture of SC from the 17th c to the present.

PROGRAMS: Annual Meeting; Community Outreach; Exhibits; Lectures; Publication; Research Library/Archives

COLLECTIONS: [17th c-present] 100,000 volumes, 11,000 linear feet of manuscripts, records, 16,000 microforms, 22,000 photographic images, and 2,500 maps.

HOURS: Yr

ADMISSION: No charge

7664
Woodrow Wilson Boyhood Home, Historic Columbia Foundation
1705 Hampton St, 29201; (p) (803) 252-1770, (803) 252-7742; (f) (803) 252-5001

1872/ Historic Columbia Foundation/ staff: 10(f); 11(p); 100(v)

COLLECTIONS: [1870-1874] Bed in which Woodrow Wilson was born, Janet Woodrow Wilson's Bible, a gift from her husband, the Rev. Joseph R. Wilson, some other family pieces, Woodrow Wilson's desk used when he was Governor of New Jersey; Wilson memorabilia, photographs.

HOURS: Yr

CONWAY

7665
Horry County Museum
428 Main St, 29526; (p) (843) 248-1542; (f) (843) 248-1854; hcmuseum@sccoast.net; www.horrycountymuseum.org; (c) Horry

County/ 1979/ Horry County Council/ staff: 4(f); 4(v)

HISTORY MUSEUM: Preserves, protects, and teaches the history, prehistory and natural history of Horry County and the coastal plain of SC.

PROGRAMS: Community Outreach; Exhibits; Festivals; Guided Tours; Interpretation; Lectures; Research Library/Archives; School-Based Curriculum

COLLECTIONS: [1880-1930] Photographs of rural SC around 1930, objects and artifacts associated with 19th c naval stores production, logging, and agriculture.

HOURS: Yr M-Sa 9-5

ADMISSION: No charge

DARLINGTON

7666
Darlington County Historical Commission
204 Hewitt St, 29532; (p) (843) 398-4710; (c) Darlington

County/ 1967/ staff: 2(f); 2(p); 2(v)

RESEARCH CENTER: Repository for local historical and genealogical archive material.

PROGRAMS: Research Library/Archives

COLLECTIONS: [1690-present] Archives for county government, schools, churches, business, plantation, and family genealogy.

HOURS: Yr M-F 9-5

ADMISSION: No charge

DILLON

7667
Dillon County Historical Society, Inc.
101 S Marion St, 29536 [PO Box 1806, 29536]; (p) (843) 752-9457; (c) Dillon

Private non-profit/ 1961/ staff: 30(v)/ members: 88

HISTORICAL SOCIETY; HISTORY MUSEUM: Preserves the culture and heritage of Dillon County and manages various community projects.

PROGRAMS: Exhibits; Guided Tours

COLLECTIONS: [18th c-present] Doctor's office, agricultural artifacts, military memorabilia, historical documents, history of Indigo, SC and J.W. Dillon House.

HOURS: Yr T,Th, Sa 10:30-12/1:30-4:30, Su 1:30-4:30

DURHAM

7668
Stagville Preservation Center
7 69th St, 27705 [PO Box 71217, 27705]; (p)
(919) 286-0055

EDGEFIELD

7669
Edgefield County Historical Society
320 Norris St, 29824 [PO Box 174, 29824];
(p) (803) 637-2233, (803) 637-5306; (f) (803)
637-6066; (c) Edgefield

Private non-profit/ 1939/ staff: 2(p); 25(v)/
members: 250/publication: *History of Johnston, South Carolina*

HISTORIC PRESERVATION AGENCY; HISTORIC SITE; HISTORICAL SOCIETY; HOUSE MUSEUM: Preserves and restores historical artifacts and collects genealogical information. Located in Magnolia-Dale house.

PROGRAMS: Annual Meeting; Concerts; Exhibits; Guided Tours; Interpretation; Lectures; Publication; Research Library/Archives; School-Based Curriculum

COLLECTIONS: [19th c-present] Archival materials and pottery.

HOURS: Yr by appt

ADMISSION: $3

7670
National Wild Turkey Federation
770 Augusta Rd, 29824-1510; (p) (803) 637-3106; (f) (803) 637-0034; (c) Edgefield

Private non-profit/ 1973/ staff: 125(f); 10(p); 200000(v)/ members: 200000/publication: *Turkey Call; The Caller; and others*

HISTORY MUSEUM; LIVING HISTORY/OUTDOOR MUSEUM; RESEARCH CENTER: Works with educational conservation organizations comprised of state and local affiliates working for the restoration and management of the American wild turkey and other valuable natural resources.

PROGRAMS: Annual Meeting; Community Outreach; Concerts; Exhibits; Family Programs; Film/Video; Guided Tours; Interpretation; Lectures; Publication; Research Library/Archives; School-Based Curriculum

COLLECTIONS: [Prehistory-present] 3-D dioramas depicting the five American wild turkey subspecies in their natural habitats, robotic old time storyteller, displays of historic turkey calls, and artifacts.

HOURS: Yr M-F 8:30-5

7671
Oakley Park Museum
300 Columbia Rd, 29824; (p) (803) 637-4027;
(c) Edgefield

Private non-profit/ 1946/ Edgefield Chapter, UDC/ staff: 1(p)/ 20(v)/ members: 30

HISTORIC SITE; HOUSE MUSEUM: Preserves house museum furnished in 1850-1880 period. Home of General Martin W. Gary, CSA and Governor John Gary Evans. Site of Mexican War muster and Reconstruction activities.

PROGRAMS: Exhibits; Family Programs; Interpretation; Lectures; Living History; Reenact-

ments

COLLECTIONS: [1850-1880] Furniture from Gary families including portraits, original photographs, artifacts, library from General Martin Gary, General N. G. Evans, and Governor John Gary Evans.

7672
Old Edgefield District Genealogical Society
104 Courthouse Square, 29824 [PO Box 546, 29824-0546]; (p) (803) 637-4010; Hardybryan1@AikenElectric.net; www.family-clan.net; (c) Edgefield

Joint/ 1985/ City; County; Private non-profit/ staff: 1(f); 12(v)/ members: 500/publication: *Quill*

GENEALOGICAL SOCIETY: Tompkins Library contains books, microfilm, and loose records on the families and history of the Old Edgefield District.

PROGRAMS: Annual Meeting; Community Outreach; Family Programs; Guided Tours; Lectures; Publication; Research Library/Archives

COLLECTIONS: [18th c-present] Family, state, and county histories, Civil War and Revolutionary War records, Old Edgefield County newspapers, loose family papers, wills, deeds, probate, coroner, census, church, and miscellaneous government records.

HOURS: Yr M-F 9-4

ADMISSION: First visit/Members free

EHRHARDT

7673
Rivers Bridge State Park
RR 1, Box 190a, 29081; (p) (803) 267-3675; rivers_bridge_sp@prt.state.sc.us; www.southcarolinaparks.com; (c) Bamberg

State/ 1945/ SC Dept of Parks, Recreation and Tourism/ staff: 3(f)

BATTLEFIELD; HISTORIC SITE: Preserves the site of the Battle of Rivers Bridge, February 2-3, 1865, the only major resistance encountered by General Sherman's army on its historic march through SC. The park includes confederate earthworks, memorial ground, cemetery, and visitor center.

PROGRAMS: Facility Rental; Guided Tours; Interpretation; Reenactments; School-Based Curriculum

COLLECTIONS: [1865-1940]

HOURS: Yr Daily 9-6

ADMISSION: No charge

EUTAWVILLE

7674
Eutaw Springs Battleground Museum
12656 Old #6 Hwy, Lake Marion Business Center, 29048 [PO Box 277, 29048]; (p) (803) 492-7111; (f) (803) 492-7111; (c) Orangeburg

Private non-profit/ 1988/ Tri-County Reg Chamber of Comm/ staff: 1(v)

BATTLEFIELD; HISTORIC SITE: Provides literature and information regarding the Battle of Eutaw Springs (Sept 8, 1781) and heritage trail and the two oldest working plantations in

the area: The Rocks and St. Julien.

PROGRAMS: Festivals; Interpretation

HOURS: Yr Daily

FLORENCE

7675
Florence Museum of Art, Science and History
558 Spruce St, 29501; (p) (843) 662-3351; flomus@bellsouth.net; (c) Florence

Private non-profit/ 1924/ Board of Trustees/ staff: 1(f); 3(p); 6(v)/ members: 250

ART MUSEUM; HISTORY MUSEUM: Preserves, collects, displays, and interprets the history and culture of the Pee Dee. Offers a look at the cultures of the past and around the world in a way that is educational and entertaining to visitors. Promotes the visual arts and culture with changing exhibits and competitions.

PROGRAMS: Annual Meeting; Community Outreach; Exhibits; Facility Rental; Family Programs; Guided Tours

COLLECTIONS: Local, historical, international, and ancient civilizations are all included at the Florence Museum. Special emphasis on Pee Dee area history, ancient civilizations, Asian artifacts, and Pueblo pottery.

HOURS: Yr T-Sa 10-5, Su 2-5

ADMISSION: Donations accepted

7676
War Between the States Museum
107 S Guerry St, 29501; (p) (843) 669-1266; nc@alltel.net; (c) Florence

Private non-profit/ 1988/ Sons of Confederate Veterans/ staff: 9(v)

HISTORY MUSEUM: Interprets the Civil War.

PROGRAMS: Exhibits; Family Programs; Festivals; Guided Tours; Interpretation; Living History; Reenactments; Research Library/Archives; School-Based Curriculum

COLLECTIONS: [1855-1870] Artifacts mainly from local area. Weapons used during the period, photographs of military and civilian participants. Documents and research materials available.

HOURS: Yr W, Sa 9-5

ADMISSION: $2, Children $1

FORT JACKSON

7677
U.S. Army Chaplain Museum
10100 Lee Rd, 29207-7090; (p) (803) 751-8827, (803) 751-8079; (f) (803) 751-8740; mcmanusm@usachcs-emh1.army.mil; (c) Richland

Federal/ 1957/ US Army Center of Military History/ staff: 1(f)

HISTORY MUSEUM: Collects, preserves, and maintains history of the US Army Chaplain Corps.

PROGRAMS: Research Library/Archives

COLLECTIONS: [19th c-present] Ecumenical clothing and equipment, military uniforms, equipage, and archives.

ADMISSION: No charge

GEORGETOWN

7678
Committee for African American History Observances
1623 Gilbert St, 29442 [PO Box 1507, 29442]; (p) (843) 546-1974; (f) (843) 546-1974; (c) Georgetown

Private non-profit/ 1978/ Board of Directors/ staff: 1(f); 5(p); 100(v)/ members: 100/publication: *Living Legends Calenders*

ART MUSEUM; HISTORIC SITE; HISTORY MUSEUM: Presents arts and cultural activities designed to promote appreciation for the contributions of African Americans to the larger society.

PROGRAMS: Concerts; Elder's Programs; Exhibits; Facility Rental; Family Programs; Festivals; Film/Video; Guided Tours; Lectures; Living History; Publication; Research Library/Archives

COLLECTIONS: [1860-present] The economical and political history of African Americans in Georgetown, South Carolina.

HOURS: Yr T-F 10-4

ADMISSION: No charge

7679
Georgetown County Historical Society
208 Cannon St, 29440; (p) (843) 527-2667; (c) Georgetown

Private non-profit/ 1955/ staff: 5(v)/ members: 250

HISTORICAL SOCIETY: The society collects, preserves, and disseminates the history of Georgetown County.

PROGRAMS: Guided Tours; Lectures

7680
Hopsewee Plantation
US #17 S, 29440 [494 Hopsewee Rd, 29440]; (p) (843) 546-7891; (c) Georgetown

Private for-profit/ 1970/ staff: 2(f); 2(p)

HISTORIC SITE; HOUSE MUSEUM: Preserves the birthplace of Thomas Lunch, Jr., a signer of the Declaration of Independence. The 1740 house, a National Historic Landmark, is furnished with 18th and 19th c furniture.

PROGRAMS: Guided Tours

COLLECTIONS: [1740-1900] Furniture.

HOURS: Mar-Oct T-F 10-4

ADMISSION: $6, Children $2

7681
Kaminski House Museum
1003 Front St, 29442 [PO Drawer 939, 29442]; (p) (843) 546-7706; (f) (843) 546-2126; (c) Georgetown

City/ 1972/ staff: 2(f); 6(p); 10(v)

HOUSE MUSEUM: Seeks to preserve history of SC's Lowcountry with primary interpretative emphases are furniture, decorative arts, architecture and social history as each pertains to the house and its collections.

PROGRAMS: Concerts; Exhibits; Facility Rental; Guided Tours; Interpretation; Lectures; Reenactments

COLLECTIONS: [18th-19th c] English and American furniture and artifacts from the Southeastern US with many pieces made in Charleston. Silver, porcelain, textiles, and paintings round out the collection.

HOURS: Yr M-Sa 9-5, Su 1-5

ADMISSION: $5, Children $2, Seniors $4; Under 6 free

GREENVILLE

7682
Greenville County Historical Society
211 E Washington St, 29603 [PO Box 10472, 29603]; (p) (864) 233-4103; (f) (864) 233-5541; info@greenvillehistory.org; www.greenvillehistory.org; (c) Greenville

Private non-profit/ 1962/ staff: 1(p)/ members: 400/publication: *Proceedings and Papers of the Greenville County Historical Society*

HISTORICAL SOCIETY: Collects and preserves the written and oral history of Greenville County.

PROGRAMS: Community Outreach; Exhibits; Publication; Research Library/Archives

COLLECTIONS: [19th-20th c] Photographs and limited research materials.

HOURS: Yr M 2-5, T-Th 1-5

7683
Greenville County Library
300 College St, 29601; (p) (864) 242-5000; (f) (864) 235-8375; sc_room@greenville.lib.sc.us; www.greenvillelibrary.org; (c) Greenville

County/ 1921/ staff: 4(f); 1(p)

LIBRARY AND/OR ARCHIVES: Collects historical and genealogical information focusing on SC, the southern states, and the migration routes leading south.

PROGRAMS: Community Outreach; Lectures; Research Library/Archives

COLLECTIONS: [18th c-present] Microfilm of census and local records, book and microfiche collection focusing on genealogy, local and family history, vertical file of local and biographical subjects.

HOURS: Yr M-F 9-9, Sa 9-6, Su 2-6

ADMISSION: No charge

GREENWOOD

7684
Greenwood County Historical Society
106 Main St, 29649 [PO Box 782, 29649]; (p) (864) 229-7093, (864) 229-3311; (f) (864) 229-9317; (c) Greenwood

Private non-profit/ 1970/ Executive Board/ members: 50

HISTORICAL SOCIETY; HISTORY MUSEUM; RESEARCH CENTER: Promotes local history and holds meetings four times a year with support of local museum.

PROGRAMS: Exhibits; Publication; Research Library/Archives

7685
Greenwood Museum, The
106 Main St, 29648 [PO Box 3131, 29648-3131]; (p) (864) 229-7093; (f) (864) 229-9317; pbwarner@greenwood.net; (c) Greenwood

Private non-profit/ 1969/ Board of Trustees/ staff: 1(f); 4(p); 70(v)/ members: 425

ART MUSEUM; HISTORY MUSEUM: A general museum with diverse collections in cultural and natural history, science, manufacturing, transportation, technology, and the arts, with particular emphasis on Greenwood County and the surrounding area. Also includes an international collection and The James West Durst exhibit gallery.

PROGRAMS: Annual Meeting; Community Outreach; Exhibits; Facility Rental; Family Programs; Festivals; Guided Tours; Interpretation; Lectures; School-Based Curriculum

COLLECTIONS: [1850s-1930s] Arrowheads, fossils, industrial robots, and Park Seed capsules, horse drawn vehicles, early period furniture, and Thomas Edison exhibit.

HOURS: Yr W-F 10-5, Sa-Su 2-5

ADMISSION: $2, Student $1, Seniors $1; Members free

HAMPTON

7686
Hampton County Museum
702 First St W, 29924 [104 Mulberry St, 29924]; (p) (803) 943-5484, (803) 943-3387; (c) Hampton

Private non-profit/ 1979/ Hampton County Historical Society/ staff: 3(p)

HISTORICAL SOCIETY; HISTORY MUSEUM: Maintains museum located at the old county jail across from the town hall.

PROGRAMS: Exhibits; Family Programs; Festivals; Interpretation; Research Library/Archives

COLLECTIONS: [1878-present] Variety of displays in old living quarters of jail and cell blocks: country store, natural history items, military artifacts, articles related to children, and extensive genealogical archives.

HOURS: Sept-July Th 10-12/4-7, Su 3-5

7687
Hampton Museum and Visitors Center
99 Elm St, 29924 [600 Harriet St, 29924]; (p) (803) 943-5318, (803) 943-2444; (c) Hampton

City/ 1989/ staff: 1(p); 20(v)/publication: *Self-Guided Walking Tour of Hampton*

HISTORY MUSEUM: Preserves and promotes the heritage of Hampton and its environs and encourages tourism in the area.

PROGRAMS: Community Outreach; Exhibits; Festivals; Lectures; Publication

COLLECTIONS: [1930s] Native American artifacts, communications, medical, watermelon festival, bank vault and safe, churches, art, children's room, military room, government, commercial and special exhibits.

HOURS: Yr Sa-Su 2-5

ADMISSION: No charge

HARTSVILLE

7688
Hartsville Museum
222 N Fifth St, 29551 [PO Box 431, 29551]; (p) (843) 383-3005; (f) (843) 383-2477; hvillemuseum@earthlink.net; (c) Darlington

City/ 1980/ staff: 2(f); 3(p); 15(v)/ members: 150

HISTORY MUSEUM: Maintains museum located in a 1930s post office building listed on the National Registry of Historic Places. Contains a gallery for changing exhibits of art and history.

PROGRAMS: Community Outreach; Exhibits; Guided Tours; School-Based Curriculum

COLLECTIONS: [1850-present] Photographs and artifacts documenting history of Hartsville and SC. The first local car, an 1899 locomobile steamer, a collection of silver plated hollowware featuring cotton boll and southern flower designs and highlights.

HOURS: Yr M-Sa 10-5

ADMISSION: No charge

7689
Jacob Kelley House Museum
2585 Kelleytown Rd, 29550 [104 Hewitt St, Darlington, 29532]; (p) (803) 398-4710

1820/ Darlington County Historical Commission/ staff: 25(v)

COLLECTIONS: [1820-1870] Joggling Board, pine and walnut rope bed with feather mattress and open headboard, rope bed with trundle and huntboard or slab, chests, tables, "sittin chairs"; Family portraits

HOURS: Seasonal

7690
John Hart Cottage
116 E Home Ave, 29550 [116 E Home Ave, 29550]; (p) (843) 332-6401

1845/ Hartsville Heritage/ staff: 12(v)

COLLECTIONS: [1850-1925] Furniture, photographs, and Bible from the Hart family.

HOURS: Mar-Dec 1st Su 3-5 PM

HEMINGWAY

7691
Three Rivers Historical Society
414 N Main St, 29554; (p) (843) 558-2355; (c) Williamsburg

Private non-profit/ 1977/publication: *Three Rivers Chronicle*

HISTORICAL SOCIETY: Acquires, preserves, and publishes local historical and genealogical records.

PROGRAMS: Annual Meeting; Community Outreach; Guided Tours; Interpretation; Publication

COLLECTIONS: [18th c-present] Historical and genealogical records, farmstead equipment, and cotton gin.

HOURS: May-Nov Sa 10-5, Su 1-5

ADMISSION: $2

HILTON HEAD ISLAND

7692
Coastal Discovery Museum on Hilton Head Island
100 Wilham Hilton Pkwy, 29925 [PO Box 23497, 29925-3497]; (p) (843) 689-6767; (f) (843) 689-6769; nhefter@coastaldiscovery.org; www.coastaldiscovery.org; (c) Beaufort

Private non-profit/ 1985/ staff: 4(f); 2(p); 100(v)/ members: 1200

HISTORY MUSEUM: Educates visitors and residents about the important heritage and natural history of Hilton Head through exhibits, interpretive programs, tours, and cruises.

PROGRAMS: Community Outreach; Exhibits; Family Programs; Film/Video; Garden Tours; Guided Tours; Interpretation; Lectures; School-Based Curriculum

COLLECTIONS: [18th-20th c] Archaeological materials from dig sites and artifacts.

HOURS: Yr Daily 9-5

ADMISSION: Varies

7693
Heritage Library, The
Courtyard Building, Ste 300, 29928; (p) (843) 686-6560; (f) (843) 341-6493; info@heritagelib.org; www.heritagelib.org; (c) Beaufort

Private non-profit/ 1997/ staff: 32(v)/ members: 234

GENEALOGICAL SOCIETY: Provides tools for the genealogist.

PROGRAMS: Concerts; Exhibits; Lectures; Research Library/Archives

COLLECTIONS: [19th c] 500 CD-ROMs and online genealogical subscription databases.

HOURS: Yr M,Th-Sa 9-2 and by appt

ADMISSION: No charge

7694
Hilton Head Island Historical Society
8 Moon Shell Rd, 29928-5444; (p) (843) 785-3967; (c) Beaufort

Private non-profit/ 1961/ staff: 10(p)/ members: 120/publication: *Robert Carse, Department of the South/Hilton Head Island in the Civil War; Robert Peeples, Tales of Antebellum Hilton Head Island Families*

HISTORIC SITE; HISTORICAL SOCIETY: Owns and maintains Fort Mitchell built in 1862 and Zion Chapel-of-Ease 1780s cemetery. Distributes Carse's "Hilton Head Island in the Civil War" and offers a quarterly lecture series.

PROGRAMS: Annual Meeting; Guided Tours; Lectures; Publication

HOURS: Yr Daily

HODGES

7695
Cokesbury College Historical and Recreational Commission
[PO Box 206, 29653]; (p) (864) 374-3237; (c) Greenwood

Joint/ 1854/ County; State/ staff: 1(p); 6(v)

PROFESSIONAL ORGANIZATION: Promotes historical preservation and interest in the county.

PROGRAMS: Annual Meeting; Community Outreach; Concerts; Exhibits; Facility Rental; Festivals; Garden Tours; Living History

COLLECTIONS: [19th c] Founders' pictures and old furniture.

HOURS: Yr Daily 10-5

ADMISSION: No charge

HUNTING ISLAND

7696
Hunting Island State Park
25555 Sea Island Pkwy, 29920; (p) (843) 838-2011; hunting_island_sp@prt.state.sc.us; (c) Beaufort

State/ 1938/ SC Dept of Parks, Recreation and Tourism/ staff: 17(f)

HISTORIC SITE; STATE PARK: Maintains historic resources including the c 1875 lighthouse and outbuildings, which are open to the public.

PROGRAMS: Family Programs; Guided Tours; Interpretation; School-Based Curriculum

COLLECTIONS: [1875-1933]

HOURS: Apr-Sept Daily 6-9; Oct-Mar Daily 6-6

ADMISSION: $2; Under 15

IVA

7697
Revitalize Iva Community Improvement Association (REVIVA)
Corner of Broad & Front St, 29655 [PO Box 402, 29655]; (p) (864) 348-6544; (f) (864) 348-6180; (c) Anderson

Private non-profit/ 1981/ staff: 100(v)/ members: 100

HISTORY MUSEUM: Maintains artifacts donated by local citizens and serves as a visitor information center.

PROGRAMS: Community Outreach; Exhibits; Festivals; Guided Tours; School-Based Curriculum

COLLECTIONS: [19th-20th c] Newspapers and photographs.

HOURS: Yr Sa 9-12 and by appt

ADMISSION: No charge

KINGSTREE

7698
Thorntree
101 E Main St, 29556 [Williamsburg Historical Society, PO Box 162, 29556]; (p) (843) 354-3306; www.carolina-now.com/hispeedee.htm#kingstreehistoricsites

7699
Williamsburgh Historical Society
[PO Box 162, 29556]; (p) (843) 354-6291; (f) (843) 354-7886; (c) Williamsburg

Private non-profit/ 1971/ staff: 2(v)/ members: 125

COLLECTIONS: [19th-present] Photographs and objects pertaining to the history of Williamsburg County.

HOURS: Yr by appt

ADMISSION: No charge

LAKE CITY

7700
Brown-Burrows House
SC 341, 29560; (p) (803) 558-2355

LANCASTER

7701
Andrew Jackson State Park
196 Andrew Jackson Park Rd, 29720; (p) (803) 285-3344; (f) (803) 285-3344; andrew_jackson_sp@prt.state.sc.us; www.state.sc.us; (c) Lancaster

State/ 1950/ SC Dept of Parks, Recreation and Tourism/ staff: 3(f); 2(p); 50(v)

HISTORY MUSEUM; PRESIDENTIAL SITE: Preserves the site of President Andrew Jackson's boyhood home. Museum contains exhibits that reflect life on a colonial backcountry farm in SC during the late 18th-early 19th c.

PROGRAMS: Facility Rental; Guided Tours; Interpretation; Living History; School-Based Curriculum

COLLECTIONS: [1767-1810] Period rooms and objects, including furnishings of a colonial backcountry farm and agricultural tools, that reflect the era of President Andrew Jackson's boyhood.

HOURS: Fall-Winter Daily 8-6; Spring-Summer Daily 9-9

LAURENS

7702
James Dunklin House, The
544 W Main St, 29360; (p) (864) 984-4735

MANNING

7703
Clarendon County Archives
211 N Brooks St, 29102; (p) (803) 435-0328; fscorbett@ftc-i.net; (c) Clarendon

County/ Board of Commissioners/ staff: 1(f); 1(v)/ members: 40

GENEALOGICAL SOCIETY; HISTORIC PRESERVATION AGENCY; HISTORICAL SOCIETY; RESEARCH CENTER

PROGRAMS: Annual Meeting; Community Outreach; Exhibits; Film/Video; Garden Tours; Guided Tours; Lectures; Reenactments; Research Library/Archives

HOURS: Yr T-F 9-4

ADMISSION: No charge

MARION

7704
Marion County Museum
101 Willcox Ave, 29571 [PO Box 220, 29571]; (p) (843) 423-8299; (c) Marion

County/ 1981/ Marion County Museum Commission/ staff: 1(f)/ members: 400

ART MUSEUM; HISTORIC SITE; HISTORY MUSEUM: Maintains museum located in an old schoolhouse (1886) and provides exhibits.

PROGRAMS: Community Outreach; Exhibits; Facility Rental; Family Programs; Guided Tours; Lectures; School-Based Curriculum

HOURS: Yr T-F 9-12/1-5

ADMISSION: No charge

MCCLELLANVILLE

7705
Hampton Plantation State Historic Site
1950 Rutledge Ave, 29458; (p) (843) 546-9361; hampton_plantation_sp@prt.state.sc.us; (c) Charleston

State/ 1973/ SC Dept of Parks, Recreation and Tourism/ staff: 4(f); 2(v)

HISTORIC SITE; HOUSE MUSEUM: Maintains a coastal rice plantation including the main house, gardens, kitchen building, and remains of rice fields.

PROGRAMS: Guided Tours; Interpretation; School-Based Curriculum

COLLECTIONS: [1750-1810] Predominantly original colonial architectural elements from the house.

HOURS: Yr Th-M 9-6

ADMISSION: Entrance free

7706
St. James-Santee Parish Historical Society
[PO Box 666, 29458]; (c) Charleston

Private non-profit/ 1989/ members: 100

HISTORICAL SOCIETY: Preserves the history and heritage of St. James-Santee Parish.

PROGRAMS: Annual Meeting; Community Outreach; Guided Tours

7707
Village Museum, The
401 Pinckney St, 29458 [PO Box 595, 29458]; (p) (843) 887-3030; (c) Charleston

Private non-profit/ 1999/ The Village Museum, Inc./ staff: 1(p); 4(v)/ members: 210

HISTORY MUSEUM: Presents the history and heritage of St. James-Santee Parish and the town of McClellanville, SC.

PROGRAMS: Community Outreach; Exhibits; Guided Tours; Interpretation; Lectures; Research Library/Archives

COLLECTIONS: [1696-1930] Illustrates the time of the Seewee Indians, rice and cotton plantation period, and founding of the parish and town.

HOURS: Yr Th-Sa 10-12/1-5

ADMISSION: $3, Children $2

MCCORMICK

7708
McCormick County Historical Commission
Cedar Hill Rd, 29835 [Rt 1, Box 2, 29835]; (p) (864) 465-2347; bkecedarhill@wctel.net; (c) McCormick

State/ 1975/ staff: 5(v)

HISTORIC PRESERVATION AGENCY: Records and preserves local history, sites, and buildings.

PROGRAMS: Guided Tours; Lectures; Reenactments

COLLECTIONS: [1760s-present]

HOURS: Special events and by appt

ADMISSION: No charge

MONCKS CORNER

7709
Berkeley Museum
950 Stony Landing Rd, 29461; (p) (843) 899-5101; (f) (843) 899-5101; reynoldsdd@aol.com; (c) Berkeley

Private non-profit/ 1989/ Board of Directors/ staff: 2(f); 2(p); 10(v)/ members: 120

HISTORY MUSEUM: Collects, preserves, researches, exhibits, and interprets Berkeley County's cultural and natural history. Strives to increase the appreciation and understanding of our common heritage.

PROGRAMS: Annual Meeting; Community Outreach; Exhibits; Facility Rental; Festivals; Lectures; Living History; Reenactments; Research Library/Archives; School-Based Curriculum

COLLECTIONS: [12,000 BC-present] Pleistocene mammal bones, mounted specimens, prehistoric and historic Native American materials, colonial, plantation era-modern medicine, blacksmithing, carpentry tools, modern appliances, electric, timber industry items, and art.

HOURS: Yr M-Sa 9-5, Su 1-5

ADMISSION: $2; Under 12 free

7710
Old Santee Canal State Historic Site
900 Stony Landing Rd, 29461; (p) (843) 899-5200; (f) (843) 899-5200; parkinfo@santeecooper.com; www.oldsanteecanalpark.org; (c) Berkeley

State/ 1989/ SC Public Service Auth/ staff: 6(f); 2(p)

HISTORIC SITE: Interprets the Santee Canal and the cultural and natural history that is related to the site.

PROGRAMS: Concerts; Elder's Programs; Exhibits; Facility Rental; Family Programs; Film/Video; Guided Tours; Interpretation; School-Based Curriculum

COLLECTIONS: [19th c] Artifacts that relate to the canal and the families that lived at Stony Landing Plantation.

HOURS: Yr Daily 9-5

ADMISSION: $3

MOUNT PLEASANT

7711
Charleston Chapter of National Railway Historical Society
456 King St, 29464 [133 Sampa Rd, 29464]; (p) (843) 973-7269; (c) Charleston

Private non-profit/ 1967/ staff: 6(p); 6(v)/ members: 20

HISTORIC PRESERVATION AGENCY; HISTORIC SITE; HISTORICAL SOCIETY; HISTORY MUSEUM: Preserves and displays local railroad artifacts for historical and educational use. Dedicated to education about railroads and their place in American history.

PROGRAMS: Annual Meeting; Exhibits; Research Library/Archives

COLLECTIONS: [1830-present] Models, photographs, documents, uniforms, books, timetables, and other memorabilia.

7712
Christ Church Parish Preservation Society

[PO Box 165, 29465]; (c) Charleston

Private non-profit/ 1972/ Officers/ staff: 4(v)/ members: 100/publication: *History of Mount Pleasant; Christ Church*

HISTORIC PRESERVATION AGENCY: A non-religious eleemosynary group that seeks to preserve the heritage of the local area, one of the ten parishes created in 1706, located east of Charleston, SC.

PROGRAMS: Annual Meeting; Lectures; Publication

7713
Patriots Point Naval and Maritime Museum

40 Patriots Point Rd, 29464-4377; (p) (843) 884-2727; (f) (843) 881-4232; patriotspt@infoave.net; www.state.sc.us/patpt; (c) Charleston

State/ 1973/ Patriots Point Development Authority/ staff: 110(f); 30(p); 120(v)

MARITIME MUSEUM: Features four historic ships: the carrier USS Yorktown, the destroyer USS Laffey, the submarine USS Clamagore and the Coast Guard cutter USCGC Ingham.

PROGRAMS: Community Outreach; Exhibits; Facility Rental; Film/Video; Guided Tours; Interpretation; Research Library/Archives; School-Based Curriculum

COLLECTIONS: [20th c] Photographs, documents, memorabilia, art and other artifacts illustrating the history of WW II, Korea and Vietnam as well as general 20th c naval and maritime history.

HOURS: Fall-Winter Daily 9-6:30; Spring-Summer Daily 9-7:30

ADMISSION: $10, Children $5, Seniors $9; Military $9; Group rates

MURRELLS INLET

7714
Huntington Beach State Park

16148 Ocean Hwy, 29576; (p) (843) 237-4440; huntington_beach_sp@prt.state.sc.us; (c) Georgetown

State/ 1960/ SC Dept of Parks, Recreation and Tourism/ staff: 10(f)

HOUSE MUSEUM; STATE PARK: Maintains historic Atalaya, the home of American sculptor Anna Hyatt Huntington, built circa 1930. National Historic Landmark.

PROGRAMS: Family Programs; Festivals; Guided Tours; Interpretation; School-Based Curriculum

COLLECTIONS: [1930s]

HOURS: Spring-Summer Daily 8-9; Fall-Winter Daily 9-6

ADMISSION: $4, Children $2

MYRTLE BEACH

7715
South Carolina Hall of Fame

21st Ave N & Oak St, 29578 [PO Box 1828, 29578]; (p) (843) 918-1225; (f) (843) 449-0887; (c) Horry

Private non-profit/ 1973/ staff: 2(v)

HISTORY MUSEUM: Honors South Carolinians, both living and deceased, who have made outstanding contributions to their state, the nation and the world. One deceased and one contemporary are inducted each year.

PROGRAMS: Annual Meeting; Exhibits

COLLECTIONS: [20th c] Portraits and video presentations of the inductees, interactive kiosk showing historical information.

HOURS: Yr M-Sa 8-5

ADMISSION: No charge

NEESES

7716
Neeses Farm Museum

6449 Savannah Hwy, 29107 [PO Box 70, 29107-0070]; (p) (803) 247-5811; (f) (803) 247-5811; (c) Orangeburg

Private non-profit/ 1976/ Town of Neeses/ staff: 2(v)

HISTORY MUSEUM: Maintains farm museum.

PROGRAMS: Guided Tours

COLLECTIONS: [19th c] Farm tools and equipment, household items such as wood burning cooking stove, churns, WW I & II artifacts, Native American pottery, and cultural display.

HOURS: Yr by appt

ADMISSION: No charge

NINETY SIX

7717
Ninety Six National Historic Site

1103 Hwy 248, 29666 [PO Box 496, 29666]; (p) (864) 543-4068; (f) (865) 543-2058; nisi_administration@nps.gov; www.nps.gov/nisi/; (c) Greenwood

Federal/ 1976/ National Park Service/ staff: 5(f); 20(v)

HISTORIC SITE; NATIONAL PARK: Dedicated to interpreting the era 1730-1860 in the SC backcountry.

PROGRAMS: Exhibits; Film/Video; Interpretation; Lectures; Living History; Reenactments

COLLECTIONS: [1730-1860] Original artifacts and reproductions that illustrate and interpret civilian and military life and activities of the SC backcountry.

HOURS: Yr Daily 8-5

ADMISSION: No charge

NORTH AUGUSTA

7718
North Augusta Historical Society

107 W Pine Grove Ave, 29841; (p) (803) 279-2951; (f) (803) 279-2951; (c) Aiken

Private non-profit/ 1969/ staff: 3(v)/ members: 25

HISTORICAL SOCIETY: Maintains and preserves local history.

PROGRAMS: Annual Meeting; Lectures; Living History

PARRIS ISLAND

7719
Parris Island Museum

Havana St, Bldg 111, 29905 [PO Box 19001, 29905-9001]; (p) (843) 525-2951; (f) (843) 525-3065; www.parrisisland.com; (c) Beaufort

Federal/ 1976/ US Marine Corps/ staff: 7(f); 3(p)

HISTORY MUSEUM: Promotes the history of the United States Marine Corps and the history of Parris Island from 5,000 years ago to the present.

PROGRAMS: Annual Meeting; Exhibits; Film/Video; Interpretation; Research Library/Archives

COLLECTIONS: [16th c-present] Papers and photographs relating to the early French and Spanish settlements on the island; Civil War and the wars of the 20th c.

HOURS: Yr Daily 10-4:30

ADMISSION: No charge

PENDLETON

7720
Ashtabula Plantation

Hwy 88, 29672 [PO Box 444, 29672]; (p) (864) 646-7249; (c) Anderson

Private non-profit/ 1960/ Pendleton Historic Foundation/ staff: 1(p); 15(v)/ members: 220/publication: *Pendleton Historic Foundation*

HOUSE MUSEUM: Promotes preservation, restoration, and exhibition of historic properties in the Pendleton area. Promotes knowledge of local history and the cultural heritage of the community.

PROGRAMS: Facility Rental; Garden Tours; Guided Tours; Interpretation; Publication; Research Library/Archives; School-Based Curriculum

COLLECTIONS: [1825-1865] Antique furnishings and decorative arts.

HOURS: Apr-Oct Su 2-6

ADMISSION: $5

7721
Pendleton District Historical, Recreational and Tourism Commission

125 E Queen St, 29670 [PO Box 565, 29670]; (p) (864) 646-3782; (f) (864) 646-2506; pendtour@innova.net; (c) Anderson

1966/ Pendleton District Commission/ staff: 3(f); 10(v)/ members: 75

HISTORIC PRESERVATION AGENCY; HISTORIC SITE: A tri-county commission that promotes and preserves regional history. Makes accessible local history archives and visitors center in an 1850 General Store. Promotes tourism, programs and local history projects. Agricultural museum at another site in town.

PROGRAMS: Community Outreach; Exhibits; Festivals; Guided Tours; Lectures; Research Library/Archives

COLLECTIONS: [1790-1960] Reference library and local history material concentrates on Anderson, Oconee, and Pickens counties in upstate SC. Includes family papers, records of textile mills, photographs, and oral history tapes.

HOURS: Yr M-F 9-4:30

ADMISSION: No charge

7722
Woodburn Plantation
130 History Lane, 29670 [PO Box 444, 29670]; (p) (864) 646-3782, (800) 862-1795; (f) (864) 646-7249; historicwoodburn@ bellsouth.net; (c) Anderson

Private non-profit/ 1828/ Pendleton Historic Foundation/ staff: 1(p); 3(v)/ members: 310

HISTORIC PRESERVATION AGENCY; HISTORIC SITE; HISTORICAL SOCIETY; HISTORY MUSEUM; HOUSE MUSEUM: Preserves and displays cultural items belonging to the three distinguished South Carolina families who resided at Woodburn Plantation from 1830-1910.

PROGRAMS: Annual Meeting; Facility Rental; Festivals; Garden Tours; Guided Tours; Living History; Reenactments

COLLECTIONS: [1830-1910] Victorian furnishings and personal items belonging to the three families.

HOURS: Apr-Oct Su 2-6, and by appt

PICKENS

7723
Hagood-Mauldin House
104 N Lewis St, 29671; (p) (864) 878-6799; www.clemson.edu/welcome/region/uphis.htm

7724
Pickens County Museum of Art and History/Hagood Mill
307 Johnson St, 29671; (p) (864) 898-5963; (f) (864) 898-5947; picmus@innova.net; www.co.pickens.sc.us/Cultural_events.asp#C ultural_Commission; (c) Pickens

1975/ Pickens County Cultural Commission/ staff: 2(f); 1(p); 20(v)/ members: 100/publication: *The Old Gaol Gazette*

ART MUSEUM; HISTORIC SITE; HISTORY MUSEUM; LIVING HISTORY/OUTDOOR MUSEUM: Collects, preserves, interprets, and teaches about the cultural, natural history of the county and region. Two facilities: 1902 Victorian Jail and 1845 restored Hagood Gristmill.

PROGRAMS: Community Outreach; Concerts; Exhibits; Festivals; Guided Tours; Interpretation; Lectures; Living History; Publication

COLLECTIONS: [19th-20th c] 8,000 artifacts, antiques, manuscripts, letters, photographs, and artworks representing regional history.

HOURS: Yr Museum: T 8:30-8:30, W-F 8:30-5, Sa 12-4; Mill: 3rd Sa and by appt

ADMISSION: Donations accepted

7725
Table Rock State Park
158 E Ellison Lane, 29671; (p) (864) 878-9813; table_rock_sp@prt.state.sc.us; (c) Pickens

State/ 1935/ SC Dept of Parks, Recreation and Tourism/ staff: 12(f)

STATE PARK: Constructed by the Civilian Conservation Corps during the 1930s. A lodge, cabins, picnic shelters and hiking trails all display the CCC's rustic architectural style.

PROGRAMS: Facility Rental; Family Programs; Guided Tours; Interpretation

COLLECTIONS: [1935-1940]

HOURS: Yr M-F

ADMISSION: $1.50; Under 15 free

RICHBURG

7726
Chester District Genealogical Society
203 N Main St, 29729 [PO Box 336, 29729]; (c) Chester

1978/ staff: 7(v)/ members: 750

GENEALOGICAL SOCIETY: Assists genealogical research for Chester, York, Lancaster, Union, and Fairfield Counties.

PROGRAMS: Annual Meeting; Lectures; Living History

COLLECTIONS: [18th c-present] Local families histories.

HOURS: Yr by appt

ADMISSION: No charge

RIDGELAND

7727
Jasper County Historical Society
Pauline Webel Museum, 123B E Wilson St, 29936 [PO Box 2111, 29936]; (p) (843) 726-3258; (f) (843) 987-9734; (c) Jasper

County/ 1976/ staff: 8(p); 25(v)/ members: 285/publication: *Pictorial History of Jasper County*

HISTORICAL SOCIETY; HISTORY MUSEUM: Provides historical information concentrating on the area's beginnings and its development.

PROGRAMS: Community Outreach; Exhibits; Family Programs; Festivals; Film/Video; Guided Tours; Interpretation; Lectures; Publication; Reenactments; Research Library/Archives; School-Based Curriculum; Theatre

COLLECTIONS: [1880-1950] Medical equipment, military artifacts, and photographs of early residents and landmarks.

HOURS: Yr M-F 9-5, or by appt Sa

ADMISSION: No charge

ROCK HILL

7728
Catawba Cultural Preservation Project
1536 Tom Steven Rd, 29730 [611 E Main St, 29730]; (p) (803) 328-2427; (f) (803) 328-5791; ccpp@cetlink.net; www.ccppcrafts.com; (c) York

Private non-profit/ 1989/ Tribal/ staff: 14(f); 3(p); 5(v)

HISTORIC PRESERVATION AGENCY; HISTORICAL SOCIETY; LIBRARY AND/OR ARCHIVES: Collects official records, private manuscripts, family photographs, and other records relating to the Catawba Nation, its people, and its land. Promotes research and study of Catawba history. Houses historical records from early 19th c to present.

PROGRAMS: Exhibits; Family Programs; Festivals; Film/Video; Guided Tours; Research Library/Archives

COLLECTIONS: [19th c-present] 100 cubic feet of historical records divided into three collections: Catawba Indian Nation tribal records, manuscripts and artifacts.

HOURS: Yr M-Sa 9-5

ADMISSION: No charge

7729
York County Culture and Heritage Commission
4621 Mount Gallant Rd, 29732; (p) (803) 329-2121; (f) (803) 329-5249; www.yorkcounty.org; (c) York

County; Private non-profit/ 1997/ York County/ staff: 38(f); 14(p); 280(v)/ members: 1300/publication: *Journal of the Carolina Piedmont*

ART MUSEUM; GENEALOGICAL SOCIETY; HISTORIC PRESERVATION AGENCY; HISTORIC SITE; HISTORICAL SOCIETY; HISTORY MUSEUM; HOUSE MUSEUM; LIVING HISTORY/OUTDOOR MUSEUM; NATURAL HISTORY MUSEUM; RESEARCH CENTER: Educates the public about the cultural, historical and natural heritage of the Carolina Piedmont. Governs the Museum of York County, Historic Brattonsville, and the Historical Center of York County.

PROGRAMS: Community Outreach; Exhibits; Facility Rental; Family Programs; Festivals; Film/Video; Guided Tours; Interpretation; Living History; Publication; Reenactments; Research Library/Archives; School-Based Curriculum

COLLECTIONS: [18th-20th c] Art, decorative arts, historical items, archives, natural history and anthropological specimens.

HOURS: Yr M-Sa 10-5, Su 1-5

ADMISSION: $6, Student $3, Seniors $3

ROEBUCK

7730
Price House
1200 Oak View Farms Rd, 29376 [1200 Otts' Shoals Rd, 29376]; (p) (864) 596-3501; (f) (864) 596-3501; (c) Spartanburg

Private non-profit/ 1961/ Spartanburg County Historical Association/ staff: 2(f); 13(p)/ members: 375

HISTORIC SITE; HOUSE MUSEUM: Preserves structure that served as stagecoach stop, general store, and post office. The house is unique to South Carolina upstate architecture of its time. Built around 1790 by Thomas and Ann Price.

PROGRAMS: Family Programs; Festivals; Guided Tours; Interpretation; Living History

COLLECTIONS: [1800-1840s]

HOURS: Yr Sa 11-5, Su 2-5

ADMISSION: $3.50, Student $1.50

7731
Walnut Grove Plantation
1200 Otts Shoals Rd, 29376; (p) (864) 576-6546; (f) (864) 576-4058; (c) Spartanburg

Private non-profit/ 1967/ Spartanburg County Historical Association/ staff: 1(f); 8(p); 2(v)

HISTORIC SITE: Preserves the plantation of Charles and Mary Moore.

PROGRAMS: Community Outreach; Concerts; Exhibits; Facility Rental; Family Programs; Festivals; Guided Tours; Interpretation; Living History; Reenactments; School-Based Curriculum

COLLECTIONS: [1765-1800] Personal items of Charles and Mary Moore, plantation house 1765, and includes manor house, academy, kitchen, doctors office, blacksmith shop, barn, wheat and smoke house, cemetery, and nature trail.

HOURS: Nov-Mar Sa 11-5, Su 2-5; Apr-Oct T-Sa 11-5, Su 2-5

ADMISSION: $4.50; Children $2

SAINT HELENA ISLAND

7732
Penn Center, Inc.
Martin Luther King, Jr, Dr, 29920 [PO Box 126, 29920]; (p) (843) 838-2432; (f) (843) 838-8545; Penncent@hargray.com; (c) Beaufort

Private non-profit/ 1862

ART MUSEUM; HISTORIC PRESERVATION AGENCY; HISTORIC SITE; RESEARCH CENTER

PROGRAMS: Community Outreach; Elder's Programs; Exhibits; Facility Rental; Festivals; Guided Tours; Lectures; Research Library/Archives; School-Based Curriculum

COLLECTIONS: [1862-present]

HOURS: Yr M-Sa 11-4

ADMISSION: $4, Student $2

SAINT MATTHEWS

7733
Calhoun County Museum and Cultural Center
303 Butler St, 29135; (p) (803) 874-3964; (f) (803) 874-4790; CALMUS@burg.NET; (c) Calhoun

County/ 1959/ Calhoun County Council/ staff: 2(f); 1(p); 15(v)/ members: 125/publication: Cemetery Book, Calhoun County

ART MUSEUM; HISTORY MUSEUM; LIVING HISTORY/OUTDOOR MUSEUM; RESEARCH CENTER: Provides multi-disciplinary arts programs and support services to stimulate community cultural economic growth.

PROGRAMS: Community Outreach; Exhibits; Festivals; Guided Tours; Publication; Research Library/Archives; School-Based Curriculum

COLLECTIONS: Art gallery, Native American artifacts, archives, silver, period rooms, costumes, farm room, and a general store.

HOURS: Yr M-F 9-5

SALLEY

7734
Old Salley School Museum
218 Pine St, 29137 [PO Box 441, 29137-0441]; (p) (803) 258-3230, (803) 258-3306; (c) Aiken

City/ 1990/ Old Salley School Museum Board/ staff: 10(v)

HISTORY MUSEUM: Collects and preserves community history.

PROGRAMS: Annual Meeting; Community Outreach; Exhibits; Facility Rental; Family Programs; Festivals; Guided Tours; Interpretation; Lectures

COLLECTIONS: [1750s-1950s] Furniture, clothing, papers, housewares, pictures, toys, church histories, books, quilts, first items in the community area and other oddities.

HOURS: Yr Daily by appt

ADMISSION: Donations requested

SPARTANBURG

7735
Archives, Sandor Teszler Library, Wofford College
429 N Church St, 29303-3663; (p) (864) 597-4309; (f) (864) 597-4329; stonerp@wofford.edu; www.wofford.edu; (c) Spartanburg

Private non-profit/ 1854/ Wofford College/ staff: 1(f)

LIBRARY AND/OR ARCHIVES: Maintains the records of Wofford College and the South Carolina Conference of the United Methodist Church.

PROGRAMS: Research Library/Archives

COLLECTIONS: [1800-present] Records, publications of Wofford College, its faculty and alumni, and of United Methodism in SC; indexes to obituaries in church newspaper; and records of Methodist ministers and churches.

HOURS: Yr M-F 9:30-12/1-3:30 by appt

7736
Spartanburg County Historical Association
[PO Box 887, 29304]; (p) (864) 596-3501; (f) (864) 596-3501; (c) Spartanburg

Private non-profit/ 1961/ staff: 3(f); 11(p); 5(v)/ members: 461/publication: The Drover's Post

HISTORIC SITE; HISTORY MUSEUM; HOUSE MUSEUM: Collects, preserves, and interprets the history of Spartanburg County through its four properties: Walnut Grove Plantation, Price House, Seay House, and the Regional Museum.

PROGRAMS: Annual Meeting; Community Outreach; Exhibits; Facility Rental; Family Programs; Festivals; Garden Tours; Guided Tours; Interpretation; Lectures; Living History; Publication; Reenactments; School-Based Curriculum

COLLECTIONS: [18th-21st c] Historic structures.

HOURS: Seay House: Yr by appt; Museum: Yr T-Sa 11-5

SUMMERTON

7737
Santee National Wildlife Refuge
2nd St Rd #803 & Hwys 301/15, exit #102 off I95, 29148 [Route 2, Box 370, 29148]; (p) (803) 478-2217; (f) (803) 478-2314; (c) Clarendon

Federal/ 1941/ US Fish and Wildlife Service/ staff: 5(f); 5(v)/ members: 4

HISTORIC SITE: Conserves, protects, and enhances fish and wildlife and their habitats. Historic site of Santee Indian Mound.

PROGRAMS: Exhibits

COLLECTIONS: [20th c] Numerous wildlife typical of local area. Living exhibits are fish typical of ones in Lake Marion. Indian Mound.

HOURS: Yr T-Sa 8-4

ADMISSION: No charge

SUMMERVILLE

7738
Old Dorchester State Historic Site
300 State Park Rd, 29485; (p) (843) 873-1740, (843) 873-7475; old_dorchester_sp@prt.state.sc.us; (c) Dorchester

State/ 1960/ SC Dept of Parks, Recreation and Tourism/ staff: 3(f); 1(p); 10(v)

HISTORIC SITE: Preserves the site of a Colonial village founded in 1697 by a group of New England Congregationalists. Historic resources include the remains of a c 1757 tabby fort, the ruins of St. George's Parish Church, and the outlines of the Colonial village.

PROGRAMS: Interpretation; School-Based Curriculum

COLLECTIONS: [1697-1795]

HOURS: Yr Daily 9-6

ADMISSION: $1.50; Under 16 free

7739
Summerville Preservation Society
201 W Carolina Ave, 29484 [PO Box 511, 29484]; (p) (843) 871-4276; (c) Dorchester

Private non-profit/ 1972/ staff: 221(v)/ members: 221

HISTORIC PRESERVATION AGENCY; HISTORIC SITE: Promotes interest in preservation of historic structures in the town, and houses a collection of material relating to local history.

PROGRAMS: Annual Meeting; Guided Tours; Lectures; Research Library/Archives

COLLECTIONS: [1850s-present] Articles and objects relating to the history of the Summerville area and nearby rice plantations.

HOURS: Yr special events

ADMISSION: No charge

7740
Summerville-Dorchester Museum
100 E Doty Ave, 29484 [PO Box 1873, 29484]; (p) (843) 875-9666; (c) Dorchester

Private non-profit/ 1991/ staff: 1(f); 1(p); 5(v)/ members: 203

HISTORY MUSEUM: Collects, preserves, and exhibits artifacts of the area and develops educational programs relating to the culture and history of Dorchester County.

PROGRAMS: Annual Meeting; Community Outreach; Exhibits; Family Programs; Guided Tours; Interpretation; Lectures; School-Based Curriculum

COLLECTIONS: [1765-1950s] Prehistoric fossils and early Native Americans artifacts; artifacts from early European settlement period, the Golden Era of the 1890s and the 1950s.

HOURS: Yr T-Sa 10-2

ADMISSION: $2, Children $1; Under 5 free

SUMTER

7741
Sumter County Museum
122 N Washington St, 29150 [PO Box 1456, 29150]; (p) (803) 775-0908; (f) (803) 436-5820; SCMuseum@aol.com; www.hometown. aol.com/scmuseum; (c) Sumter

Private non-profit/ 1989/ Board of Directors/ staff: 3(f); 6(p); 25(v)/ members: 325

GARDEN; HISTORIC SITE; HISTORY MUSEUM; LIVING HISTORY/OUTDOOR MUSEUM: Presents the history of the Old Sumter District (Sumter, Lee, and Clarendon counties) from c 1750 to the present.

PROGRAMS: Community Outreach; Exhibits; Facility Rental; Festivals; Guided Tours; Interpretation; Lectures; Living History; Research Library/Archives

COLLECTIONS: [1750-present] Buildings, machinery, textiles, objects d'art, images and documents that were made or owned by local residents.

HOURS: Yr T-Sa 10-5, Su 2-5

7742
Williams-Brice House
122 N Washington St, 29150 [PO Box 1456, 29150]; (p) (803) 775-0908

1916/ Sumter County Museum/ staff: 3(f); 5(p); 3(v)

COLLECTIONS: Textile collection from late 1700s to present.

HOURS: Yr

SUNSET

7743
Keowee Toxaway State Park, Cherokee Interpretive Museum
108 Residence Dr, 29685-9507; (p) (864) 868-2605; (f) (864) 868-2605; keowee_toxaway_sp@prt.state.sc.us; (c) Pickens

State/ 1974/ SC State Park Service/ staff: 3(f); 1(p)

HISTORY MUSEUM: Depicts the history and culture of the Cherokee Indians and the story of their relationship with European settlers of SC.

PROGRAMS: Exhibits; Interpretation; School-Based Curriculum

COLLECTIONS: [Prehistory-mid 19th c] Artifacts and collections depict the dress, tools, games, medicines, and dwelling structures of the Cherokee Indians.

HOURS: Sept-May Daily 11-12/4-5; June-Aug W-Su 10-5, M-T 11-12/4-5

ADMISSION: No charge

TAMASSEE

7744
Richards House
Oconee Station Rd, 29686 [Oconee Station/Richards House, 500 Oconee Station,

Walhalla, 29691]; (p) (864) 638-0079; www.upcountry-sc.org/attra-oco.htm

UNION

7745
Rose Hill Plantation State Historic Site
2677 Sardis Rd, 29379 [1205 Pendleton St, Columbia, 29201]; (p) (864) 427-5966; (f) (864) 427-5966; rose_hill_sp@prt.state.sc.us; www.southcarolinaparks.com; (c) Union

State/ 1960/ SC Dept of Parks, Recreation and Tourism/ staff: 2(f); 2(p); 5(v)

GARDEN; HISTORIC SITE; HOUSE MUSEUM; LIVING HISTORY/OUTDOOR MUSEUM: Preserves the house of William Henry Gist, SC's secession governor. Interpretation focuses on the Gist family, the house and grounds, African American slaves, and tenant farmers, and the natural history of the surrounding land and forest.

PROGRAMS: Exhibits; Family Programs; Garden Tours; Guided Tours; Interpretation; Living History; Reenactments; School-Based Curriculum

COLLECTIONS: [1830-1900] Period furnishings, clothing, and artifacts once belonging to Gov. William Henry Gist and his family.

HOURS: Yr Th-M 9-6 (Mansion 1-4)

ADMISSION: $2, Student $1, Children $1; SC seniors free

WAGENER

7746
Wagener Museum, The
Earle St, 29164 [PO Box 1004, 29164]; (p) (803) 564-5112, (803) 564-3412; (f) (803) 564-3412; (c) Aiken

City/ 1989/ staff: 6(v)

HISTORIC PRESERVATION AGENCY: Volunteers dedicated to the preservation of local history.

PROGRAMS: Guided Tours; Lectures

COLLECTIONS: [1887-present] Artifacts related to early and recent town development, includes Native American and farm implements, railroad relics, military uniforms, and period clothing.

HOURS: Yr by appt

ADMISSION: No charge

WALHALLA

7747
Oconee Station State Historic Site
500 Oconee Station Rd, 29691; (p) (864) 638-0079; oconee_station_sp@ prt.state.sc.us; (c) Oconee

State/ 1976/ SC Dept of Parks, Recreation and Tourism/ staff: 2(f)

HISTORIC SITE: Preserves the oldest structure in Oconee County was constructed c 1792 as part of a chain of fortified outposts established during a period of tension between white settlers and Native Americans. Also located in the park is the Richards House, c 1805. Both buildings are listed on the National Register of Historic Places.

PROGRAMS: Guided Tours; Interpretation; Living History

COLLECTIONS: [1792-1820]

HOURS: Mar-Dec Th-M 9-6

ADMISSION: No charge

WALTERBORO

7748
Colleton Museum
239 N Jefferies Blvd, 29488; (p) (843) 549-2303; (f) (843) 549-5775; museum@ lowcountry.com; (c) Colleton

County/ 1985/ staff: 2(p); 5(v)/ members: 140

HISTORIC SITE; HISTORY MUSEUM; NATURAL HISTORY MUSEUM: Maintains museum located in the "Old Jail" c 1855. Preserves and promotes the historical, natural and cultural heritage of Colleton County through the care and conservation of collections, research, exhibitions, tours, and educational programs.

PROGRAMS: Exhibits; Film/Video; Guided Tours; Interpretation; Lectures

COLLECTIONS: [Late 1800s-1940] Historic photographs, agricultural tools, and artifacts used in the home and on plantations.

HOURS: Yr T-F 10-1/2-5, Sa 12-4

ADMISSION: No charge

WINNSBORO

7749
Fairfield County Historical Museum
231 S Congress St, 29180 [PO Box 6, 29180]; (p) (803) 635-9811; (f) (803) 635-9811; (c) Fairfield

County/ 1976/ Fairfield County Council Historical Commission/County Historical Society/ staff: 1(f); 2(v)/ members: 200/publication: Fairfield County Sketchbook: Julian Bolick

GENEALOGICAL SOCIETY; HISTORY MUSEUM; HOUSE MUSEUM: Maintains three-story brick Federal style museum built as a home, housed a school for young women under Catherine Ladd during 1850-1860s. Listed on the National Historic Registry with a house museum on the first floor, genealogical library and exhibits on the second and exhibits on the third. A 1930s granite movie theater next door is now a cultural center.

PROGRAMS: Annual Meeting; Community Outreach; Concerts; Exhibits; Lectures; Publication; Reenactments; Research Library/ Archives

COLLECTIONS: [19th c] Prehistoric Native American artifacts and natural resource items. Professional tools: medical, dental, survey, quarrying, period clothing, agricultural, religious items, books, locally owned, and built antiques.

HOURS: Yr M,W, F 10:30-12:30/1:30-4:30, Sa 10:30-12:30 and by appt

ADMISSION: No charge

7750
South Carolina Railroad Museum, Inc.
110 Industrial Park Rd, 29180 [PO Box 645, 29180]; info@scrm.org; www.scrm.org; (c) Fairfield

Private non-profit/ 1972/ Board of Trustees/ staff: 30(v)/ members: 165

HISTORIC SITE; LIVING HISTORY/OUTDOOR MUSEUM: Owns a former quarry railroad built 1883-1900. Operates passenger excursion trains over a restored portion of the track. Works to preserve the history of railroading in SC.

PROGRAMS: Exhibits; Publication

COLLECTIONS: [20th c] Fifty pieces of vintage railroad equipment, including freight cars, passenger cars, cabooses, locomotives and a variety of small artifacts in exhibit gallery.

HOURS: May-Oct 1st/3rd Sa 9:30-4

ADMISSION: $5, Children $3

WOODRUFF

7751
Thomas Price House
1200 Oak View Farms Rd, 29388 [PO Box 887, Spartanburg, 29304]; (p) (864) 576-6546, (864) 476-2483; (f) (864) 576-4058

1795/ Spartanburg County Historical Association/ staff: 1(f); 3(p)

COLLECTIONS: [1790-1830] Furniture and kitchen implements; wonderful sideboard made in SC; Inventory of general store; store keeper journals 1810s.

HOURS: Yr

YORK

7752
York County Cultural and Heritage Commission Historical Center
212 E Jefferson St, 29745; (p) (803) 684-7262; (f) (803) 684-1866; hcyorksc@infoave.net; www.yorkcounty.org; (c) York

County/ 1989/ York County Cultural and Heritage Commission/ staff: 2(f); 2(p); 10(v)

RESEARCH CENTER: Makes available the County Historical Center' collection for research providing information on the Southern Piedmont.

PROGRAMS: Community Outreach; Exhibits; Lectures; Research Library/Archives

COLLECTIONS: [Prehistory-present] York County court records, family papers, church histories, photographs, and other collections related to the history of the Southern Piedmont.

HOURS: Yr M-F 10-4

ADMISSION: No charge

SOUTH DAKOTA

ABERDEEN

7753
Dacotah Prairie Museum
21 S Main, 57402 [PO Box 395, 57402-0395]; (p) (605) 626-7117; (f) (605) 626-4026; bcmuseum@midco.net; www.brown.sd.us/museum; (c) Brown

County/ 1969/ Brown County Commission/ staff: 4(f); 1(p); 60(v)/ members: 200/publica-

tion: *Dacotah Prairie Times*

HISTORY MUSEUM: Collects, preserves, and exhibits history of the Dakota Prairie.

PROGRAMS: Community Outreach; Exhibits; Family Programs; Guided Tours; Interpretation; Lectures; Publication; Research Library/Archives; School-Based Curriculum

COLLECTIONS: [1881-present] 3,000 photos, 5,000 pieces vintage clothing, small agricultural and household tools, archives, Hatterscheidt wildlife collection.

HOURS: Yr T-F 9-5, Sa-Su 1-4

ARMOUR

7754
Douglas County Historical Society and Museum
Courthouse Grounds, 57313 [PO Box 638, 57313]; (p) (605) 724-2115, (605) 724-2129; (c) Douglas

County, non-profit/ 1959/ staff: 1(p)

HISTORICAL SOCIETY; HISTORY MUSEUM; HOUSE MUSEUM: Maintains museum, historical house and country school.

PROGRAMS: Annual Meeting; Community Outreach; Exhibits; Guided Tours; Living History

COLLECTIONS: [1886-1940] Local newspaper on microfilm, memorabilia, artifacts.

HOURS: June-Sept F 1-5 and by appt

ADMISSION: No charge

BELLE FORUCHE

7755
Tri-State Memorial Museum
1222 9th Ave, 57717; (c) Butte

City, non-profit/ 1960/ City of Belle Fourche/ staff: 4(f)

HISTORIC PRESERVATION AGENCY; HISTORY MUSEUM: Preserves local history.

COLLECTIONS: Period clothing, furnishing, pianos, spinning wheels, Native American artifacts.

HOURS: May-Sept Su 2-8, M-Sa 8-8

ADMISSION: No charge

BELLE FOURCHE

7756
Tri-State Genealogical Society
Public Library 905 5th St, 57717; (p) (605) 892-4407; (c) Butte

members: 18/publication: *Wymondak Messenger*

GENEALOGICAL SOCIETY: Collects and preserves local genealogical material.

PROGRAMS: Publication

BLUNT

7757
Mentor Graham Museum
[PO Box 136, 57522]; (p) (605) 962-6445; www.state.sd.us/state/executive/tourism/musart.htm

BRITTON

7758
Marshall County Historical Society
[PO Box 249, 57430-0249]; (p) (605) 448-5179; (c) Marshall

County; Private non-profit/ 1977/ staff: 4(v)/ members: 65/publication: *Marshall County, SD*

GENEALOGICAL SOCIETY; HISTORICAL SOCIETY; HISTORY MUSEUM; RESEARCH CENTER: Preserves local history.

PROGRAMS: Annual Meeting; Community Outreach; Concerts; Exhibits; Family Programs; Guided Tours; Lectures; Publication; Research Library/Archives

COLLECTIONS: [1885-present] History books, microfilm, oral history tapes, family history, ghost town and modern settlement.

7759
Prayer Rock Museum, Inc.
Main St, 57430 [PO Box 201, 57430]; (p) (605) 448-5625; (c) Marshall

Private non-profit/ 1952/ staff: 2(p); 5(v)

HISTORY MUSEUM: Collects and preserves Native American history.

PROGRAMS: Elder's Programs; Exhibits; Guided Tours

COLLECTIONS: 4,500 year old prayer rock, Native artifacts, pioneer artifacts, log cabin.

HOURS: June-Aug M-Sa 11-4

ADMISSION: No charge

BROOKINGS

7760
Hodges Claim Shanty
925 11th St, 57007 [S Dakota State University Box 2207C, 57007]; (p) (605) 688-6226; (f) (605) 688-6303; agmuseum@mg.sdstate.edu; www.sdstate.edu/agmuseum

1882/ Agricultural Heritage Museum/ staff: 4(f); 1(p); 12(v)

COLLECTIONS: [1860-1950; 1880] Large home studies, photo archive.

HOURS: Yr M-Sa, 10; M-Sa, 10-5; Su, 1-5

7761
State Agricultural Heritage Museum
925 11th St, 57007 [SDSU Box 2207C, 57007]; (p) (605) 688-6226; agmuseum@mg.sdstate.edu; www.sdstate.edu/agmuseum; (c) Brookings

State/ 1967/ SD State Univ/ staff: 4(f); 1(p); 12(v)/ members: 240

HISTORY MUSEUM

PROGRAMS: Community Outreach; Exhibits; Facility Rental; Family Programs; Festivals; Film/Video; Guided Tours; Interpretation; Lectures; Living History; Research Library/Archives

COLLECTIONS: [1860-1950]

HOURS: Yr Daily

ADMISSION: No charge

CHAMBERLAIN

7762
Akta Lakota Museum and Cultural Center

N Main St, 57325 [Saint Joseph's Indian School, PO Box 89, 57325]; (p) (605) 734-3453; (f) (605) 734-3388; aktalakota@stjo.org; www.stjo.org; (c) Brule

Private non-profit/ 1991/ Congregation of the Priests of the Sacred Heart/ staff: 4(f); 5(p); 1(v)/publication: *Children of the Earth*

HISTORY MUSEUM: Educational outreach of St. Joseph's Indian School that serves the Lakota people of SD.

PROGRAMS: Community Outreach; Exhibits; Facility Rental; Guided Tours; Interpretation; Publication; Research Library/Archives; School-Based Curriculum

COLLECTIONS: Hundreds of authentic Lakota Sioux artifacts, including ceremonial regalia, tools, weaponry and pictographic robes. Contemporary Native American art, including paintings, pottery, doll,s and sculptures.

HOURS: Sept-May M-F 8-5; May-Sept M-Sa 8-6, Su 1-5

ADMISSION: Donations accepted

7763
Lyman-Brule Genealogical Society

110 E Lawler Ave, 57325 [PO Box 555, 57325]; (p) (605) 894-4242; (f) (605) 734-6474; barbara@easnet.net; www.geocities.com/heartland/ridge/8059/index.html; (c) Brule

Private non-profit/ 1986/ members: 40/publication: *Of Rails and Trails, a Centennial Journey 1889-1989*

GENEALOGICAL SOCIETY: Promotes and preserves genealogical data; provides research assistance.

PROGRAMS: Annual Meeting; Publication

COLLECTIONS: [1881-present] Obituaries, marriages, births, deaths, homestead, naturalization, military, cemetery, and baptism records.

HOURS: Yr M-Sa 10-6

ADMISSION: No charge

CLARK

7764
Clark County Historical Society

Hwy 212 & Dakota St, 57225 [201 N Commercial St, 57225-1525]; (p) (605) 532-5216; (c) Clark

Private non-profit/ 1975/ staff: 20(v)/ members: 85

GENEALOGICAL SOCIETY; HISTORIC PRESERVATION AGENCY; HISTORICAL SOCIETY; HISTORY MUSEUM; RESEARCH CENTER: Preserves local history.

PROGRAMS: Annual Meeting; Community Outreach; Exhibits; Facility Rental; Family Programs; Festivals; Film/Video; Guided Tours; Lectures; Living History; Publication; Research Library/Archives; School-Based Curriculum

COLLECTIONS: [1880-1940] Artifacts, period clothing, furniture, housed in eight restored

historic buildings.

HOURS: May-Oct F 2-5 and by appt

ADMISSION: No charge

CRAZY HORSE

7765
Crazy Horse Memorial

Avenue of the Chiefs, 57730-9506; (p) (605) 673-4681; (f) (605) 673-2185; memorial@crazyhorse.org; www.crazyhorse.org; (c) Custer

Private non-profit/ 1948/ Crazy Horse Memorial Foundation/ staff: 55(f)/publication: *Progress Report*

ART MUSEUM; HISTORIC SITE: Preserves Native American history through cultural and educational exhibits and projects.

PROGRAMS: Annual Meeting; Community Outreach; Concerts; Exhibits; Facility Rental; Family Programs; Film/Video; Guided Tours; Interpretation; Lectures; Living History; Publication; Research Library/Archives; School-Based Curriculum

COLLECTIONS: [Prehistory-present] Native American art and artifacts.

HOURS: Yr Daily 7-9

ADMISSION: $7.50; $17/vehicle

CUSTER

7766
Badger Clark Memorial

Custer State Park, 57730 [HC 83, Box 70, 57730]; (p) (605) 255-4515; (f) (605) 255-4460; craig.pugsley@state.sd.us; www.state.sd.us/sdparks/; (c) Custer

State/ 1957/ Board of Directors; State of SD/ members: 20

HISTORIC SITE: Promotes Badger Hole, home of SD's first poet laureate, is located within the environs of 73,000 acre Custer State Park.

PROGRAMS: Annual Meeting; Guided Tours; Interpretation; School-Based Curriculum

COLLECTIONS: [1927-1957] Charles Badger Clark collection including cabin, books and furnishings, which remain as he left them in 1957.

HOURS: May-Sept Daily 10-5

7767
Custer County Historical Society

411 Mt Rushmore Rd, 57730 [PO Box 826, 57730-0826]; (p) (605) 673-2443; (c) Custer

Private non-profit/ 1969/ staff: 4(p); 40(v)/ members: 124

GENEALOGICAL SOCIETY; HISTORIC SITE; HISTORICAL SOCIETY; HISTORY MUSEUM; HOUSE MUSEUM: Preserves history of Custer County and surrounding area of the Black Hills.

PROGRAMS: Concerts; Exhibits; Film/Video; Guided Tours; Interpretation; Lectures; Publication; Research Library/Archives

COLLECTIONS: [1870-1970] Rocks, minerals, pioneer, gold placer, and hard rock mining, forestry, 1900 rural school, photos, military uniforms, Lakota art and artifacts, antique ve-

hicles, hot type print shop, map, and blacksmith shop.

HOURS: May 26-Sept 3 M-Sa 9-9, Su 1-9; Sept 6-Sept 28 W-Sa 2-8 and by appt

7768
Doctor Flick Cabin

400 Block, Rushmore Rd, 57730 [PO Box 826, 57730]; (p) (605) 673-2443, (605) 673-4824; (f) (605) 673-2443

1875/ 1881 Courthouse Museum/ staff: 1(p); 40(v)

Home of Dr. D.W. Flick, early resident, physician, and city official.

COLLECTIONS: [1876] Furnishings.; Newspapers; family histories; books; photographs.

HOURS: June-Sept

DEADWOOD

7769
Adams House Museum

22 Van Buren St, 57732 [PO Box 252, 57732]; (p) (605) 578-1714; (f) (605) 578-3751; curator@adamsmuseumandhouse.org; www.adamsmuseumandhouse.org; (c) Lawrence

Joint/ 1998/ staff: 2(f); 5(p); 5(v)

COLLECTIONS: [Victorian-present]

HOURS: May-Sept M-Sa 9-6, Su 12-5; Oct-Apr M-Sa 10-4

ADMISSION: Donations accepted

7770
Adams Museum

54 Sherman St, 57732 [PO Box 252, 57732]; (p) (605) 578-1714, (605) 578-1928; (f) (605) 578-1714; director@adamsmuseumandhouse.org; www.adamsmuseumandhouse.org; (c) Lawrence

Private non-profit/ 1930/ staff: 6(f); 4(p); 10(v)

HOUSE MUSEUM: Educational organization dedicated to the acquisition, interpretation and preservation of Black Hills history, art, and natural history.

PROGRAMS: Community Outreach; Concerts; Exhibits; Guided Tours; Interpretation; Lectures; Research Library/Archives; School-Based Curriculum

COLLECTIONS: [Victorian-present] Relates to the mysteries, the tragedies, the bawdiness, and the dreams found in the history, art, and natural history of the Black Hills.

HOURS: May-Sept M-Sa 9-6, Su 12-5; Oct-Apr M-Sa 10-4

ADMISSION: Donations accepted

7771
Deadwood Historic Preservation Commission

108 Sherman St, 57732; (p) (605) 578-2082; (f) (605) 578-2084; hpc@deadwood.net; www.deadwood.net; (c) Lawrence

City, non-profit/ 1876

HISTORIC PRESERVATION AGENCY; HISTORIC SITE; HISTORICAL SOCIETY; HOUSE MUSEUM; RESEARCH CENTER: Promotes local history preservation.

PROGRAMS: Community Outreach; Concerts; Exhibits; Facility Rental; Family Programs; Festivals; Guided Tours; Interpretation; Lectures; Research Library/Archives

ADMISSION: No charge

7772
Galena Historical Society
HCR 73 Box 535, 57732; (c) Lawrence

Federal/ 1983

DELL RAPIDS

7773
Dell Rapid Society for Historic Preservation
407-409 4th St, 57022 [PO Box 143, 57022]; (p) (605) 428-4821; (c) Minnehaha

1994/ Board of Directors/ staff: 20(v)/ members: 197/publication: *Heritage Journal*

HISTORIC PRESERVATION AGENCY; HISTORICAL SOCIETY

PROGRAMS: Annual Meeting; Community Outreach; Exhibits; Facility Rental; Festivals; Guided Tours; Publication

COLLECTIONS: [1871-present] Period clothing, archaeological, and military artifacts.

HOURS: Apr-Feb Th-Su 10-4

ADMISSION: Donations accepted

DESMET

7774
Laura Ingalls Wilder Memorial Society
105 Olivet Ave, 57231 [PO Box 426, 57231]; (p) (605) 854-3383; (f) (605) 854-3064; liwms@iw.net; www.liwms.com; (c) Kingsbury

Private non-profit/ 1957/ Board of Directors/ staff: 2(f); 18(p)/ members: 850

PROFESSIONAL ORGANIZATION: Preserves and restores Ingalls-Wilder heritage.

PROGRAMS: Annual Meeting; Exhibits; Festivals

COLLECTIONS: [1800] 2,000 artifacts relating to the Ingalls family, two historic homes.

HOURS: Yr 9-4

ADMISSION: $5, Children $2

ELK POINT

7775
Union County Historical Society
124 Main St, 57025 [PO Box 552, 57025]; (c) Union

Joint/ 1987/ County; Private non-profit/ staff: 14(v)/ members: 230/publication: *Sands of Time*

GENEALOGICAL SOCIETY; HISTORICAL SOCIETY; HISTORY MUSEUM; RESEARCH CENTER

PROGRAMS: Annual Meeting; Community Outreach; Concerts; Exhibits; Facility Rental; Family Programs; Festivals; Guided Tours; Interpretation; Lectures; Living History; Publication; Research Library/Archives; School-Based Curriculum

COLLECTIONS: [1880-1940] Period furnishing, Native American artifacts, documents, libraries, family histories, maps, toys.

HOURS: Yr Sa-Su 1-4 and by appt

ADMISSION: No charge

ELKTON

7776
Elkton Community Museum
115 Elk St, 57026; (c) Brookings

City, non-profit/ 1986/ Elkton Museum Board/ staff: 1(p); 15(v)/ members: 45

HISTORY MUSEUM: Preserves local history.

PROGRAMS: Annual Meeting; Community Outreach; Exhibits

COLLECTIONS: [1880-1975] Clothing, guns, dishes, shoes, household, commercial, religious, educational agricultural.

HOURS: M-F 1-5 and by appt

ADMISSION: No charge

ELLSWORTH AIR FORCE BASE

7777
South Dakota Air and Space Museum
2890 Davis Ave, 57706 [28 BW/CVM, 57706]; (p) (605) 385-5188; (f) (605) 385-6295; (c) Pennington

Federal/ 1983/ United States Air Force/ staff: 3(f); 9(p); 10(v)

HISTORY MUSEUM: Portrays history of Ellsworth AFB and SD aviation through exhibits.

PROGRAMS: Exhibits; Guided Tours; Publication

COLLECTIONS: [1940-present] Ellsworth AFB artifacts, SD aviation history, 30 airfrafts.

HOURS: Yr Daily 8:30-4:30

ADMISSION: No charge

EUREKA

7778
Eureka Pioneer Museum
Hwy 10 W, 57437 [1210 N Lake Dr, 57437]; (p) (605) 284-2711; (c) McPherson

Private non-profit/ 1976/ Board of Directors/ staff: 2(f); 6(v)/ members: 500

GENEALOGICAL SOCIETY; HISTORICAL SOCIETY; HISTORY MUSEUM: Preserves pioneer culture.

PROGRAMS: Annual Meeting; Festivals; Guided Tours; School-Based Curriculum

COLLECTIONS: [1800-1900] Household, military, school, music, church, sod house, tools, agricultural machinery, general store.

HOURS: Apr-Oct W-F 9-5, Sa-Su 2-5

ADMISSION: No charge

FAULKTON

7779
Faulk County Historical Society, Inc.
900 8th Ave, 57438 [PO Box 584, 57438]; (p) (605) 598-4285; (c) Faulk

Private non-profit/ 1971/ Board of Directors/ staff: 1(p); 12(v)/ members: 82

HOUSE MUSEUM: Manages restored J.A. Pickler Mansion, Maloney school house, and Roberts Museum.

PROGRAMS: Annual Meeting; Community Outreach; Family Programs; Guided Tours; Lectures; Living History

COLLECTIONS: [1882-1935] Photographs, furniture, library, pottery, unique hat pins, small children's dishes, caloric cooker, coins, men's sports memorabilia and hard tack, dolls and restored dolls. J.A. Pickler Mansion who started the rural free mail delivery tested in Faulkton by a woman mail carrier.

HOURS: May-Sept Daily 1-5

ADMISSION: $5.25

FLANDREAU

7780
Moody County Genealogical Organization
501 First Ave W, 57028-1003; (p) (605) 997-2786; (c) Moody

Private non-profit/ 1993/ staff: 4(v)/ members: 10

GENEALOGICAL SOCIETY

PROGRAMS: Publication; Research Library/ Archives

COLLECTIONS: [1900] Atlas, census, newspaper microfilms.

7781
Moody County Historical Society
706 E Pipestone Ave, 57028 [PO Box 25, 57028]; (p) (605) 997-3191; (c) Moody

Private non-profit/ 1965/ staff: 1(p)/ members: 290/ publication: *Moody County Pioneer Newsletter*

Preserves local history.

COLLECTIONS: [1890-1940] Santee Sioux artifacts, church, depot, oral histories, newspaper microfilm, 'The Messenger' in Dakota language.

HOURS: Oct-Apr M-F 9-4; May-Sept Daily 9-4

ADMISSION: No charge

FORT MEADE

7782
Old Fort Meade Museum and Historic Research Association
Bldg 55, Sheridan Ave, 57741 [PO Box 164, 57741]; (p) (605) 347-9822; ftmeade@rapid-net.com; www.fortmeademuseum.org; (c) Meade

Private non-profit/ 1964/ staff: 4(p); 2(v)/ members: 100

HISTORIC SITE; HISTORY MUSEUM: Preserves cavalry history.

PROGRAMS: Annual Meeting; Community Outreach; Exhibits; Festivals; Interpretation; Lectures; Reenactments; Research Library/ Archives

COLLECTIONS: [1878-1944] Artifacts, photos, cemetery from Indian Wars era.

HOURS: May 15-31 Daily 9-5; June-Sept 15 8-6

ADMISSION: $3, Student $2

FORT PIERRE

7783
Wakpa Sica Historical Society
102 Oakwood, 57532 [PO Box 1, 57532]; (p) (605) 223-2518; (f) (605) 223-9522; (c) Stanley

Private non-profit/ 1989/ staff: 8(v)/ members: 20

HISTORICAL SOCIETY: Promotes local history.

PROGRAMS: Annual Meeting

GEDDES

7784
Charles Mix County Historical Restoration Society
3rd & Main St, 57342 [PO Box 97, 57342]; (p) (605) 337-2501; (f) (605) 337-3535; (c) Charles Mix

Private non-profit/ 1972/ staff: 6(p); 12(v)/ members: 20

HISTORIC PRESERVATION AGENCY; HISTORIC SITE; HISTORY MUSEUM: Preserves county history through restoration and conservation efforts.

PROGRAMS: Annual Meeting; Community Outreach; Festivals; Guided Tours

COLLECTIONS: [1840-1925] Period household, Papineau Trading Post, restored school house.

HOURS: May-Sept Daily 7-7

ADMISSIONS: Donations accepted

7785
Geddes Historical Restoration Society
3rd & Main St, 57342 [PO Box 92, 57342]; (p) (605) 337-2501; (f) (605) 337-3535; (c) Charles Mix

Private non-profit/ 1972/ staff: 15(v)/ members: 10

HISTORIC PRESERVATION AGENCY; HISTORIC SITE; HISTORICAL SOCIETY; HISTORY MUSEUM: Preserves local history.

PROGRAMS: Annual Meeting; Community Outreach; Exhibits; Festivals

COLLECTIONS: [1857-1900] Period furnishing and artifacts, restored trading post, and school house.

HOURS: May-Sept Daily 7-7

ADMISSION: Donations

GETTYSBURG

7786
Dakota Sunset Museum
205 W Commercial Ave, 57442; (p) (605) 765-9480; (c) Potter

Private non-profit/ 1984/ Board of Directors/ staff: 5(p); 12(v)/ members: 50

HISTORY MUSEUM: Collects and preserves Potter County's history.

PROGRAMS: Annual Meeting; Exhibits; Guided Tours; Reenactments; Research Library/ Archives

COLLECTIONS: [1880-1920]

HOURS: Summer Su-Sa 1-5; Winter T-Sa 1-5

ADMISSION: No charge/Donations

HIGHMORE

7787
Hyde County Historical and Genealogical Society
113 Iowa S, 57345 [PO Box 392, 57345-0392]; (p) (605) 852-3103; sgrable@

sullybuttes.net; www.usgenweb/sd/hyde/hyde.html; (c) Hyde

Private for-profit; Private non-profit/ 1973/ staff: 38(v)/ members: 44

GENEALOGICAL SOCIETY; HISTORIC PRESERVATION AGENCY; HISTORICAL SOCIETY: Preserves genealogical history.

PROGRAMS: Annual Meeting; Publication; Research Library/Archives

COLLECTIONS: Hyde County artifacts and memorabilia; donated items from local families.

HOURS: Tu and 4th Sa ; June 3rd weekend

ADMISSION: No charge

HOT SPRINGS

7788
Mammoth Site of Hot Springs, SD
1800 Hwy 18 Truck Rt, 57747 [PO Box 692, 57747-0692]; (p) (605) 745-6017; (f) (605) 745-3038; mammoth@mammothsite.com; www.mammothsite.com; (c) Fall River

Private non-profit/ 1975/ staff: 8(f); 2(p); 2(v)/ members: 360

NATURAL HISTORY MUSEUM

PROGRAMS: Exhibits; Guided Tours; Interpretation; Publication

COLLECTIONS: Fossils including three woolly mammoths.

HOURS: Yr Daily

ADMISSION: $5, Student $5, Children $3.25, Seniors $4.75

HURLEY

7789
Hurley Historical Society
Arthur Nelson Historical Museum, 57036; (p) (605) 238-5477; (c) Turner

Private non-profit/ 1975/ members: 18

HISTORICAL SOCIETY; HISTORY MUSEUM

PROGRAMS: Exhibits

COLLECTIONS: Household appliances, furnishing, farm implements, tools, photos, souvenirs, books, desk, children's toys, clothing.

HOURS: Yr Sa-Su 1-3:30 and by appt

ADMISSION: Donations

HURON

7790
Dakotaland Museum
SD State Fairgrounds, 57350 [PO Box 1254, 57350]; (c) Beadle

1960/ staff: 1(f); 4(p); 6(v)

HISTORIC PRESERVATION AGENCY; HISTORIC SITE; HISTORY MUSEUM: Preserves local history.

PROGRAMS: Exhibits; Research Library/ Archives

COLLECTIONS: [1881-present] Period clothing, furnishing, medical items, arrowheads, agriculture, music, photos, books, military, religious artifacts, quilts, toys.

HOURS: June-Sept Daily 9-11:30/1-4/6-8:30

ADMISSION: $1

7791
Heartland Historical Society, Inc.
[PO Box 1374, 57350]; (p) (605) 352-4623; (c) Beadle

Private non-profit/ 1985/ staff: 10(v)/ members: 50/publication: *Hearbeat*

HISTORICAL SOCIETY: Preserves history of east central South Dakota.

PROGRAMS: Annual Meeting; Festivals; Guided Tours; Lectures; Living History; Publication

COLLECTIONS: [Prehistory-1880] Native American artifacts, frontier rural life artifacts.

7792
James Valley Historical Society
[PO Box 607, 57350]; (p) (605) 352-8122; (c) Beadle

Preserves local history.

COLLECTIONS: School memorabilia.

HOURS: Sept T-M 8-7

7793
Pyle House Museum
376 Idaho SE, 57350; (p) (605) 352-2528; (c) Beadle

Private non-profit/ 1987/ Board of Directors/ staff: 1(f); 4(p); 6(v)

HOUSE MUSEUM: Preserves historic house and local history.

PROGRAMS: Exhibits; Guided Tours; Research Library/Archives; School-Based Curriculum

COLLECTIONS: [1893-94] Period furnishing, photos, personal items belonging to Pyle Family.

HOURS: Yr Daily 1-3:30

ADMISSION: $1.50

INTERIOR

7794
Badlands Natural History Association
Junction of Hwy 240 & 377, 57750 [PO Box 47, 57750]; (p) (605) 433-5489; (f) (605) 433-5484; (c) Jackson

Private non-profit/ 1959/ Board of Directors/ staff: 1(f); 6(p)/ members: 40

HISTORICAL SOCIETY; TRIBAL MUSEUM: Aids the interpretive, educational, and scientific programs of the National Park Service.

PROGRAMS: Annual Meeting; Guided Tours; Interpretation; Lectures; Living History

HOURS: Yr Daily 8-4:30

IPSWICH

7795
J.W. Parmley Historical Home Museum
317 4th St, 57451 [307 6th St PO Box 595, 57451]; (p) (605) 426-6949; (c) Edmunds

Private non-profit/ 1981/ staff: 9(f); 9(v)

HISTORIC SITE; HISTORY MUSEUM; HOUSE MUSEUM: Preserves history of Pioneer JW Parmley.

PROGRAMS: Exhibits; Guided Tours

COLLECTIONS: [1900s] Period furnishing,

personal items of Parmley Family, military uniforms, Native American artifacts.

HOURS: June-Aug Su, W, F 2-5

ADMISSION: Donations

KIMBALL

7796
Brule County Historical Society
213 Elm St, 57355 [PO Box 47, 57355]; (p) (605) 778-6490; (c) Brule

County, non-profit/ 1972/ Board of Directors/ staff: 1(f); 5(v)/ members: 35

HISTORY MUSEUM: Restores the 106 year-old church; installed and maintains museum.

PROGRAMS: Annual Meeting; Exhibits; Guided Tours; Research Library/Archives

COLLECTIONS: [19th c-present] Church related artifacts, reconstructed rural schoolroom.

HOURS: Yr by appt

LAKE CITY

7797
Fort Sisseton State Historic Park
11545 Northside Dr, 57247; (p) (605) 448-5701; (f) (605) 448-5572; roylakestp@ gfp.state.sd.us; (c) Marshall

State/ 1957/ staff: 3(f); 3(p); 40(v)/publication: Chilson's History of Fort Sisseton

HISTORIC SITE; HISTORY MUSEUM; LIVING HISTORY/OUTDOOR MUSEUM: Preserves history of Fort Sisseton.

PROGRAMS: Facility Rental; Family Programs; Festivals; Film/Video; Guided Tours; Interpretation; Living History; Publication; Reenactments; Research Library/Archives; Theatre

COLLECTIONS: [1864-1889]

HOURS: Apr-Oct Daily 10-6

ADMISSION: $3; $5/vehicle

LEAD

7798
Black Hills Mining Museum
323 W Main St, 57754 [PO Box 694, 57754]; (p) (605) 584-1605; www.mining-museum. blackhills.com; (c) Lawrence

Private non-profit/ 1986/ staff: 2(f); 8(p); 2(v)/ members: 250

HISTORY MUSEUM: Preserves and interprets the mining heritage of the Black Hills of South Dakota.

PROGRAMS: Annual Meeting; Exhibits; Guided Tours; Research Library/Archives

COLLECTIONS: [1876-present]

HOURS: May-Sept Daily 9-5; Oct-Apr M-F 9-5

ADMISSION: $4.25, Family $14, Student $3.25, Seniors $3.75; Under 7 free

7799
Homestake Gold Mine Visitor Center
160 W Main, 57754 [PO Box 887, 57754]; (p) (605) 584-3110; (f) (605) 584-2522; hvc@mato.com; www.homestaketour.com; (c) Lawrence

Joint; Private non-profit/ 1946/ Homestake Visitor Center/ staff: 1(f); 9(p)

HISTORY MUSEUM: Interprets history of gold and mining.

PROGRAMS: Guided Tours; Publication; School-Based Curriculum

HOURS: Yr Daily 8-5

ADMISSION: $4.25, Student $3.25, Senior $3.75

LEMMON

7800
Petrified Wood Park Museum
500 Main St, 57638; (p) (605) 374-5681; (f) (605) 374-5789; (c) Perkins

City, non-profit; Private non-profit/ 1930/ staff: 5(p); 5(v)

HISTORY MUSEUM; LIVING HISTORY/OUTDOOR MUSEUM: Collects, preserves and interprets local area history.

PROGRAMS: Exhibits; Film/Video; Interpretation

COLLECTIONS: Fossilized specimens.

HOURS: May-Sept Daily 8-7

ADMISSION: Donations accepted

MADISON

7801
Karl E. Mundt Historical and Educational Foundation
8th & Egan Ave, 57042 [PO Box 483, 57042]; (p) (605) 256-5211; (f) (605) 256-5208; Bonnie.Olson@dsu.edu; www.departments.dsu.edu/library/archive/ default.ht; (c) Lake

Private non-profit/ 1963/ Karl E. Mundt Historical and Educational Foundation/ staff: 1(f)/ members: 33

Preserves archives and memorabilia of former Senator Karl E Mundt.

COLLECTIONS: [1939-1972] 1.9 million documents catalogued and microfilmed, 15,000 pieces of memorabilia, 500 films, 100 tapes, 200 slides, 2500 photos, 100 scrapbooks.

HOURS: Yr M-F 8:30-4:30

ADMISSION: No charge

7802
Smith-Zimmermann Heritage Museum
Dakota State Univ Campus, 57042 [212 NE 8th St, 57042]; (p) (605) 256-5308; smith-zimmermann@dsu.edu; www. smith-zimmermann.dsu.edu; (c) Lake

Private non-profit/ 1961/ Lake County Historical Society/ staff: 1(p); 25(v)/ members: 250

HISTORICAL SOCIETY; LIBRARY AND/OR ARCHIVES: Operates the Smith-Zimmermann Heritage Museum; collects, preserves and interprets the history and historic artifacts of eastern SD.

PROGRAMS: Annual Meeting; Community Outreach; Concerts; Exhibits; Facility Rental; Guided Tours; Interpretation; Lectures; Living History; Publication; Reenactments; Research Library/Archives; School-Based Curriculum

COLLECTIONS: [1850-1950] Museum artifacts, historic county maps, archival books, and scrapbooks, local newspapers, and photographs and portraits.

HOURS: Yr T-F 9-4:30

ADMISSION: No charge

MARTIN

7803
Bennett County Genealogical Society
[PO Box 1054, 57551]; (p) (605) 685-6248; mriggs@gwtc.net; (c) Bennett

Private non-profit/ 1984

MARVIN

7804
American Indian Culture Research Center
46561 147th St, 57251 [Blue Cloud Abbey, PO Box 98, 57251-0098]; (p) (605) 398-9200; (f) (605) 398-9201; indian@bluecloud.org; www.bluecloud.org; (c) Grant

Private non-profit/ 1968/ staff: 3(f); 1(v)

HISTORICAL SOCIETY; HISTORY MUSEUM

PROGRAMS: Community Outreach; Facility Rental; Lectures

COLLECTIONS: [1880-present] Eastern Dakota, Native American clothing, tools and cultural artifacts. Library holds 300 books on Native American topics.

HOURS: Yr Daily

MEADOW

7805
Perkins County Historical Society
210 W Carr St, 57644 [13214 200th Ave, 57644]; (p) (605) 788-2279; (c) Perkins

Private non-profit/ 1975/ County/ staff: 10(v)/ members: 30

HISTORIC PRESERVATION AGENCY; HISTORIC SITE; HISTORICAL SOCIETY; HISTORY MUSEUM; HOUSE MUSEUM: Preserves local history.

PROGRAMS: Annual Meeting; Community Outreach; Exhibits; Family Programs; Film/Video; Guided Tours

COLLECTIONS: Period furnishing.

HOURS: June-Aug and by appt

ADMISSION: Donations accepted

MIDLAND

7806
Midland Pioneer Museum Association
Main St, 57552 [HCR61 Box 3, 57552]; (p) (605) 843-2150; (c) Haakon

Private non-profit/ 1973/ Board of Directors/ staff: 1(p)

HISTORIC PRESERVATION AGENCY; HISTORIC SITE; HISTORY MUSEUM

PROGRAMS: Annual Meeting; Exhibits

COLLECTIONS: [1900-present]

HOURS: June-Aug M-T, F 1:30-4

ADMISSION: No charge

MILBANK

7807
Grant County Historical Society
3rd St & 3rd Ave, 57252 [PO Box 201, 57252-0201]; (p) (605) 623-4538; (f) (605) 623-4215; alevisen@gdhscats.org; (c) Grant

County, non-profit; Private non-profit/ 1970/ Grant County Commissioners/ staff: 10(v)/ members: 300

GENEALOGICAL SOCIETY; HISTORIC PRESERVATION AGENCY; HISTORIC SITE; HISTORICAL SOCIETY; HISTORY MUSEUM; HOUSE MUSEUM; RESEARCH CENTER: Preserves and interprets early local history.

PROGRAMS: Annual Meeting; Community Outreach; Exhibits; Family Programs; Guided Tours; Interpretation; Lectures; Living History; Publication; Reenactments; Research Library/ Archives

COLLECTIONS: [1879-1920]

HOURS: May-Sept Su 2-5

ADMISSION: No charge

MILLER

7808
McWhorter House Museum and Depot
426 N Broadway, 57362-1438; (p) (605) 853-3281; www.state.sd.us/state/executive/tourism/ musart.htm

MINA

7809
North Central Genealogical Society
178 S Shore Dr, 57462; mkrueger@iw.net; (c) Edmunds

Private non-profit/ 1991/ members: 12

GENEALOGICAL SOCIETY: Collects and preserves family history.

COLLECTIONS: Family history, cemetery records.

MITCHELL

7810
Enchanted World Doll Museum
615 N Main, 57301; (p) (605) 996-9896; (f) (605) 996-0210; (c) Davison

1982/ staff: 1(f); 4(p)

HISTORY MUSEUM: Preserves history of dolls.

PROGRAMS: Exhibits; Facility Rental; Family Programs; Film/Video; Guided Tours; Lectures; Research Library/Archives; School-Based Curriculum

COLLECTIONS: [1800-1900] 4,700 vintage and modern dolls.

HOURS: Mar-Nov M-Sa 9-5, Su 1-5

ADMISSION: $3.50, Student $1.50, Seniors $2.50

7811
Louis Beckwith House
1311 S Duff St, 57301 [PO Box 1071, 57301]; (p) (605) 996-2122; (f) (605) 996-0323; fmb@mitchell.net

Private non-profit/ 1886/ Middle Border Museum of American Indian and Pioneer Life./ staff: 2(f); 1(p); 80(v)

Fully restored Italianate mansion.

COLLECTIONS: [Late 1800s-early 1900s] Late Victorian furnishings, Mrs. Beckwith's needlework; photos and other memorabilia of early settlers of the region; handwritten transcription of Jedediah Smith's diary.

HOURS: June-Aug, Mon-Sat, 8-6, Sun, 10-6; May and Sept, M-F, 9-5

7812
Middle Border Museum of American Indian and Pioneer Life
1311 S Duff St, 57301 [PO Box 1071, 57301]; (p) (605) 996-2122; (f) (605) 996-0323; fmb@mitchell.net; (c) Davison

Private non-profit/ 1939/ Board of Directors/ staff: 2(f); 2(p); 83(v)/ members: 406

HISTORY MUSEUM: Preserves heritage of Native American and immigrant settlers of the Upper River Valley Area.

PROGRAMS: Community Outreach; Exhibits; Facility Rental; Family Programs; Guided Tours; Lectures; Living History; Research Library/Archives; School-Based Curriculum

COLLECTIONS: [1600-1939] 3,500 volumes, 140 oral histories, journals, diaries, manuscripts, personal papers of Leland Case, Congressional papers of Francis Case, 2,000 photos and negatives, 100,000 Native American and settlement artifacts.

HOURS: June-Aug M-Sa 8-6, Su 10-6; May, Sept M-F 9-5, Sa-Su 1-5; Oct-Apr by appt

ADMISSION: $5, Children $3, Seniors $3

7813
Mitchell Area Historical Society
231 N Duff St, 57301 [PO Box 263, 57301]; dmmwn@santel.net; (c) Davison

Private non-profit/ 1988/ staff: 15(v)/ members: 26

HISTORICAL SOCIETY: Collects and preserves items related to exploration, settlement, development of Mitchell and surrounding area.

PROGRAMS: Annual Meeting; Research Library/Archives

COLLECTIONS: [1860-present] Memorabilia of settlement, Firesteel, Corn Palace, Mount Vernon and Ethan; cemeteries, newspapers, railroads.

7814
Mitchell Prehistoric Indian Village Museum and Archedome
Indian Village Rd, 57301 [PO Box 621, 57301]; (p) (605) 996-5473; www.mitchellindianvillage.org; (c) Davison

Private non-profit/ 1979/ staff: 2(f); 10(p); 12(v)/ members: 150

HISTORIC SITE; RESEARCH CENTER: Promotes Native American history through preservation of this national historic landmark and exhibits.

PROGRAMS: Annual Meeting; Exhibits; Family Programs; Festivals; Guided Tours; Lectures

COLLECTIONS: [Prehistory] Artifacts from local excavations.

HOURS: June-Aug Daily 8-6, M-F 9-4

ADMISSION: $4, Student $2, Seniors $3.50

MOBRIDGE

7815
Klein Museum
1820 W Grand Crossing, 57601; (p) (605) 845-7243; (c) Walworth

Private non-profit/ 1976/ Klein Foundation, Inc./ staff: 1(f); 3(p); 25(v)/ members: 250

HISTORY MUSEUM: Preserves local history.

PROGRAMS: Annual Meeting; Exhibits; Living History

COLLECTIONS: [1880-1960] Native American and Pioneer artifacts.

HOURS: Apr-Oct M-F 9-12/1-5, Sa-Su 1-5

ADMISSION: $1, Student $0.50

NEWELL

7816
Newell Museum
108 3rd St, 57760 [RR1, Box 110, 57760]; (c) Butte

City, non-profit/ 1985/ staff: 1(f); 4(v)

HISTORIC PRESERVATION AGENCY; HISTORY MUSEUM; RESEARCH CENTER: Preserves local history.

PROGRAMS: Exhibits; Family Programs; Guided Tours; Interpretation; Research Library/Archives

COLLECTIONS: [1900-1940] Family histories, agricultural items, 800 dolls, military memorabilia, natural history.

HOURS: May-Sept T-Sa 1-5 and by appt

ADMISSION: No charge

OELRICHS

7817
Oelrichs Historical Society
531 Walnut, 57763; (p) (605) 535-2421; (c) Fall River

Private non-profit/ 1982/ Oelrichs Historical Society/ members: 138/publication: *In the Shadow of the Butte, Oelrichs*

HISTORICAL SOCIETY: Collects and preserves history of Oelrichs and surrounding areas.

PROGRAMS: Publication

COLLECTIONS: [1885-1985]

OLDHAM

7818
Loriks Peterson Heritage House Museum
Williams St, 57051 [PO Box 243, 57051]

COLLECTIONS: Loriks Peterson artifacts.

HOURS: Mem to Labor Day on Su and by appt

PHILIP

7819
Prairie Homestead
HC 1 Box 51, 57567; (p) (605) 433-5400; klcrew@gwtc.net; www.prairiehomestead.com; (c) Jackson

Private non-profit/ 1962/ staff: 10(f)

HISTORIC SITE

PROGRAMS: Interpretation; Living History

HOURS: May-Sept Daily

ADMISSION: $4

7820
West River Museum Society
101 N Main St, 57567; (c) Haakon

Private non-profit/ 1964/ Museum Board/ staff: 3(v)

HISTORICAL SOCIETY

PROGRAMS: Annual Meeting

COLLECTIONS: Rural school, pioneer artifacts.

HOURS: By appt

ADMISSION: No charge

PIERRE

7821
Oahe Chapel Preservation Society
East End of Oahe Dam, 57501 [PO Box 7201, 57501]; (p) (605) 773-3458; (f) (605) 773-6041; www.state.sd.us/deca/cultural; (c) Hughes

Private non-profit; State/ 1984/ South Dakota State Historical Society/ staff: 1(f); 30(v)

HISTORIC PRESERVATION AGENCY; HISTORIC SITE; HISTORY MUSEUM; LIVING HISTORY/OUTDOOR MUSEUM: Preserves Oahe Chapel.

PROGRAMS: Annual Meeting; Family Programs

COLLECTIONS: Archives

HOURS: June-Aug 9-5

ADMISSION: No charge

7822
South Dakota National Guard Museum
301 E Dakota Ave, 57501-3225; (p) (605) 224-9991; (f) (605) 773-2475; sdngmuseum@aol.com; www.sodapop.dsu.edu; (c) Hughes

State/ 1982/ staff: 1(f); 1(p); 6(v)

HISTORIC PRESERVATION AGENCY; HISTORIC SITE; HISTORICAL SOCIETY; HISTORY MUSEUM; LIVING HISTORY/OUTDOOR MUSEUM; RESEARCH CENTER: Preserves South Dakota National Guard military history.

PROGRAMS: Annual Meeting

COLLECTIONS: 2,000 manuscripts, 4,500 pamphlets/magazines, maps, 1,200 portraits, 15,000 museum artifacts.

HOURS: Yr M, W, F 8-5

7823
South Dakota State Archives
900 Governors Dr, 57501-2217; (p) (605) 773-3804; (f) (605) 773-6041; archref@state.sd.us; www.sdhistory.org; (c) Hughes

State/ 1973/ South Dakota State Historical Society/ staff: 7(f); 13(v)

LIBRARY AND/OR ARCHIVES: Collects and preserves state and local history.

PROGRAMS: Community Outreach; Research

Library/Archives; School-Based Curriculum

COLLECTIONS: [19th-20th c] 10,000 cubic feet of government records, manuscripts, 12,000 microfilm rolls of newspapers, 100,000 photos, 15,000 volumes, maps, audio and video records.

HOURS: Yr M-F 1st Sa of month 9-4:30

ADMISSION: No charge

7824
South Dakota State Historical Society
900 Governors Dr, 57501; (p) (605) 773-3458; (f) (605) 773-6041; jeff.mammenga@sate.sd.us; www.state.sd.us/deca/cultural; (c) Hughes

State/ 1901/ Board of Trustees/ staff: 27(f); 5(p); 90(v)/ members: 2000/publication: *South Dakota History*

HISTORIC PRESERVATION AGENCY; HISTORY MUSEUM; HOUSE MUSEUM; RESEARCH CENTER: Promotes historical and cultural heritage of SD.

PROGRAMS: Annual Meeting; Community Outreach; Exhibits; Family Programs; Guided Tours; Living History; Publication; Research Library/Archives; School-Based Curriculum

COLLECTIONS: Native American artifacts, SD cultural, military, and political history.

HOURS: Yr M-F 9-4:30, Sa-Su 1-4:30

ADMISSION: $3

PINE RIDGE

7825
Heritage Center, The
Hwy 18 W, 57770 [Red Cloud Indian School, 57770]; (p) (605) 867-5491; (f) (605) 867-1291; rcheritage@basec.net; www.basec.net/rcheritage/; (c) Shannon

Private non-profit/ 1982/ The Heritage Center/ staff: 3(f); 1(p); 2(v)

HISTORY MUSEUM: Collects, preserves, exhibits and researches Native American art.

PROGRAMS: Community Outreach; Exhibits; Festivals; Guided Tours

COLLECTIONS: Native American, Lakota fine arts.

HOURS: Oct-May M-F 8-5; June-Sept Daily 8-5

ADMISSION: No charge

PLANKINTON

7826
Aurora County Historical Society
401 N Kimball, 57368 [PO Box 302, 57368]; (p) (605) 942-7452; (c) Aurora

County/ 1974/ staff: 5(f); 16(p); 10(v)/ members: 23

ART MUSEUM; GENEALOGICAL SOCIETY; HISTORIC PRESERVATION AGENCY; HISTORIC SITE; HISTORICAL SOCIETY; HOUSE MUSEUM

PROGRAMS: Annual Meeting; Community Outreach; Exhibits; Guided Tours; Lectures

COLLECTIONS: [1865-present] Restored farm home, photos, dishes, military uniforms, wedding dresses, and farm machinery.

HOURS: Apr-Oct Su 2-5 and by appt

ADMISSION: No charge/donations

PLATTE

7827
Heritage Club of Platte
Main St, 57369 [108 7th St, 57369]; (p) (605) 337-2459; (c) Charles Mix

Private non-profit/ 1981/ Heritage Club of Platte/ staff: 3(f)/ members: 7/publication: *Epic of the Great Exodus*

HISTORICAL SOCIETY: Preserves local history and genealogy records.

PROGRAMS: Publication

PRESHO

7828
Lyman County Historical Society
[PO Box 231, 57568-0231]; (p) (605) 895-9446; (c) Lyman

Private non-profit/ 1967/ Board of Directors/ staff: 2(p); 10(v)/ members: 150/publication: *Winds of Change*

HISTORICAL SOCIETY; HISTORY MUSEUM: Collects, interprets and preserves history of homestead settlement.

PROGRAMS: Annual Meeting; Exhibits; Research Library/Archives

COLLECTIONS: [1900] Maps, newspapers, photos, agriculture, ranching, Native American artifacts, arrowheads, pottery, dinosaurs, buildings, military, sailors, homestead.

HOURS: June-Sept Daily 3-8 and by appt

ADMISSION: Donations accepted

RAPID CITY

7829
Rapid City Historic Preservation Commission
300 Sixth St, 57701; (p) (605) 394-4120; (f) (605) 394-6636; (c) Pennington

City, non-profit/ staff: 2(p); 10(v)

HISTORIC PRESERVATION AGENCY: Promotes conservation through public education, National Register surveys and reviews.

PROGRAMS: Guided Tours; Lectures; Publication; Research Library/Archives

7830
Sioux Indian Museum
222 New York St, 57709 [PO Box 1504, 57709]; (p) (605) 394-2381; (f) (605) 348-6782; (c) Pennington

Federal/ 1939/ staff: 3(f)

HISTORY MUSEUM: Preserves history of the Sioux Nation.

PROGRAMS: Exhibits; Interpretation

HOURS: Summer: M-Su 9-5; Winter: M-Sa 10-5, Su 1-5

ADMISSION: $6, Student $4, Seniors $5; Under 11 free; group rates

REDFIELD

7831
Spink County Historical Society Museum
Courthouse Square, 57469; (c) Spink

staff: 1(p)/ members: 25

HISTORY MUSEUM

COLLECTIONS: [1880-WWII] Pioneer and Native American artifacts, natural history specimens.

HOURS: W-Su 1-5

ADMISSION: $1, Children $0.50

SAINT FRANCIS

7832
Buechel Memorial Lakota Museum
350 S Oak St, 57572 [PO Box 499, 57572]; (p) (605) 747-2745; (f) (605) 747-5057; (c) Todd

Private non-profit/ 1947/ Rosebud Educational Society/ staff: 1(f); 2(p); 1(v)

HISTORY MUSEUM: Collects, preserves and interprets artifacts, photographs, documents relating to Lakota culture and the history of Saint Francis Mission.

PROGRAMS: Exhibits; Guided Tours; Research Library/Archives

COLLECTIONS: [1900-1950] Photos, artifacts, manuscripts.

HOURS: May-Sept Daily 9-5

SCOTLAND

7833
Scotland Historic Preservation Committee
351 4th St, 57059; (p) (605) 583-4568; tlkluthe@gwtc.net; (c) Bon Homme

City, non-profit/ 1993/ staff: 2(v)

HISTORIC PRESERVATION AGENCY: Preserves local historic buildings.

COLLECTIONS: Preservation information.

HOURS: By appt

ADMISSION: None

7834
Scotland Historical Society
811 6th St, 57059 [PO Box 112, 57059-0112]; (p) (605) 583-2344; (c) Bon Homme

Private non-profit/ 1976/ members: 40

HISTORICAL SOCIETY: Promotes local history.

PROGRAMS: Annual Meeting; Exhibits

COLLECTIONS: [19th-20th c] Artifacts, genealogy.

HOURS: May-Sept Su 2-4

SIOUX FALLS

7835
Center for Western Studies
2001 S Summit Ave, 57197 [Box 727, Augustana College, 57197]; (p) (605) 274-4007; (f) (605) 274-4999; hthomps@inst.augie.edu; inst.augie.edu/CWS/; (c) Minnehaha

Private non-profit/ 1970/ Augustana College/

staff: 4(f); 2(p); 3(v)/ members: 800

ART MUSEUM; HISTORY MUSEUM: Promotes history of Northern Plains region.

PROGRAMS: Annual Meeting; Community Outreach; Exhibits; Interpretation; Lectures; Publication; Research Library/Archives

COLLECTIONS: [19th-20th c] 35,000 volumes on North Plains and American West, 4,500 linear feet of archives, original paintings, bronzes, Sioux clothing, Norwegian and Swedish rosemaled furniture. Lewis and Clark; Civil War.

HOURS: Yr M-F 8-12/1-5

ADMISSION: No charge

7836
Minnehaha County Historical Society
200 W 6th St, 57104; (p) (605) 334-7762; (f) (605) 373-0723; jbbsodak@aol.com; (c) Minnehaha

Private non-profit/ 1927/ staff: 35(v)/ members: 240

HISTORICAL SOCIETY: Studies and records the history of Minnehaha County through historical marker projects and restoration projects.

PROGRAMS: Annual Meeting; Community Outreach; Family Programs; Guided Tours

7837
Nordland Heritage Foundation of Augustana College, The
2001 S Summit, 57197; (p) (605) 336-4007; (f) (605) 336-4999; huseboe@inst.augie.edu; (c) Minnehaha

Private non-profit/ 1978/ staff: 1(v)/ members: 120/publication: The Nordlander

HOUSE MUSEUM: Maintains three historic buildings and Norwegian settlement in Dakota Territory.

PROGRAMS: Annual Meeting; Exhibits; Guided Tours; Lectures; Publication

COLLECTIONS: 1880s prairie home, an 1890s prairie church, 1909 one-room schoolhouse.

HOURS: June-Sept Su 2-4

ADMISSION: No charge

7838
North American Baptist Heritage Commission
1525 S Grange Ave, 57105-1526; (p) (605) 336-6588; (f) (605) 335-9090; NABarchives@nabs.edu; (c) Minnehaha

Private non-profit/ 1981/ staff: 2(p); 5(v)/ members: 80

HISTORICAL SOCIETY; HISTORY MUSEUM: Preserves research materials and depository for North American Baptist Conference.

PROGRAMS: Exhibits; Research Library/Archives

COLLECTIONS: [1860-present] Photos, archives, correspondence, slides, audio and video tapes.

HOURS: Yr M-F 1-4

ADMISSION: No charge

7839
Pettigrew Home & Museum
131 N Duluth Ave, 57104 [200 W 6th St,

57104]; (p) (605) 367-7097, (605) 367-7270; (f) (605) 331-0467

1889/ Siouxland Heritage Museum/ staff: 2(f); 6(p); 47(v)

COLLECTIONS: [1889-1926] Senator's and family's belongings; R. F. Pettigrew; manuscripts.

HOURS:Yr; T-F, 9-12 /1-5, Sa 9-5, Su 1-5

7840
Sioux Empire Medical Museum
1100 S Euclid Ave, 57117-5039; (p) (605) 333-6397; (c) Minnehaha

Private non-profit/ 1975/ staff: 40(v)

HISTORY MUSEUM: Promotes history of medicine in Sioux Falls area and state.

PROGRAMS: Exhibits

COLLECTIONS: Medical tools, medical books, surgery room, dental office, iron lung.

HOURS: Yr M-F 11-4

ADMISSION: No charge

7841
Sioux Falls Board of Preservation
224 W 9th St, 57104; (p) (605) 367-8863; (f) (605) 367-7801; www.sioux-falls.org; (c) Minnehaha

City, non-profit/ 1983/ staff: 1(p); 10(v)/ members: 10/publication: Historic Downtown Sioux Falls; When Trolley Rides Were a Nickel

HISTORIC PRESERVATION AGENCY: Preserves Sioux Falls' history.

PROGRAMS: Community Outreach; Exhibits; Film/Video; Interpretation; Publication

COLLECTIONS: [1857-1950] Photos, historic sites surveys, maps, National Register nominations.

7842
Sioux Valley Genealogical Society
200 W 6th St, 57104-6001; (p) (605) 528-6375; www.rootsweb.com/sdsvgs; (c) Minnehaha

Private non-profit/ 1972/ staff: 10(v)/ members: 10

GENEALOGICAL SOCIETY: Preserves genealogical records.

PROGRAMS: Annual Meeting; Community Outreach; Exhibits; Lectures; Research Library/Archives

COLLECTIONS: [1870-present] Books, microfilm, maps, card files, genealogical records in Minnehaha, Lincoln, Union, Clay and Turner Counties.

HOURS: Yr M-Sa 1-5

ADMISSION: No charge

7843
Siouxland Heritage Museums
200 W 6th St, 57104-6001; (p) (605) 367-4210; (f) (605) 367-6004; (c) Minnehaha

Joint/ 1974/ County of Minnehaha, City of Sioux Falls/ staff: 17(f); 7(p); 100(v)/ members: 270

HISTORY MUSEUM; HOUSE MUSEUM: Collects, preserves, and interprets the history of Minnehaha County and Sioux Falls.

PROGRAMS: Community Outreach; Concerts; Exhibits; Facility Rental; Family Programs; Festivals; Guided Tours; Lectures; Publication; Research Library/Archives; School-Based Curriculum

COLLECTIONS: [1850-present] 127,000 artifacts, general material culture related to history of southeastern SD, Minnehaha County, and city of Sioux Falls.

HOURS: Old Court House Museum: Yr M-Sa 9-5, Th 9-9, Su 12-5; Pethgrew Home Museum; Oct 1-Apr 30 12-5; May 1-Sept 30 M-Sa 9-5, Th 9-9, Su 12-5

ADMISSION: No charge

SISSETON

7844
Heritage Museum of Roberts County
SD Hwy 10 & Golf Course Rd, 57262 [PO Box 215, 57262]; (p) (605) 698-7672; (f) (605) 698-7906; jrsiston@tnics.com; (c) Roberts

Private non-profit/ 1989/ staff: 3(p)/ 5(v)/publication: *Journals of Joseph Nicollet; Dakota Encounter*

HISTORIC SITE; HISTORY MUSEUM: Preserves and interprets history of French cartographer Joseph Nicollet, Dakota Natives, Continental Divide, Red River Valley, Mississippi Valley Watershed, and Joseph Renville.

PROGRAMS: Annual Meeting; Exhibits; Facility Rental; Film/Video; Guided Tours; Interpretation; Publication

COLLECTIONS: [1930] Nicollet's report to US Senate, maps.

HOURS: May-Sept M-Sa 10-5, Su 1-5

ADMISSION: No charge

7845
Sisseton-Wahpeton Tribal Archives
Old Agency Box 689, 57262; (p) (605) 698-3966; (f) (605) 698-3132; aloma@mail.swcc.cc.sd.us; www.swcc.ca.sd.us/; (c) Roberts

Joint/ 1994/ staff: 1(f); 1(p)

HISTORIC PRESERVATION AGENCY

PROGRAMS: Community Outreach; Research Library/Archives

COLLECTIONS: [1970-present] Tribal records, cultural material.

HOURS: Yr 9-4

ADMISSION: No charge

SPEARFISH

7846
DC Booth Historic National Fish Hatchery
423 Hatchery Circle, 57783; (p) (605) 642-7730; (f) (605) 642-2336; r6ffa_dcb@fws.gov; www.fws.gov/r6dcbth/rcdcbooth.html; (c) Lawrence

Federal/ 1896/ staff: 5(f); 2(p); 75(v)/ members: 150

HISTORY MUSEUM: Collects fish cultural history, fish and wildlife service history; preserves 1899 hatchery building and 1905 superintendent's residence.

PROGRAMS: Annual Meeting; Community Outreach; Exhibits; Facility Rental; Family Programs; Festivals; Guided Tours; Interpretation; Lectures; Research Library/Archives; School-

Based Curriculum

COLLECTIONS: [1871-present] Fish cultural artifacts, documentary materials, Yellowstone boat, railroad fish car replica, underwater view windows, research materials.

HOURS: Grounds open Yr; Museum Mid May-mid Sept; research by appt

7847
High Plains Heritage Center Museum
825 Heritage Dr, 57783 [PO Box 524, 57783]; (p) (605) 642-9378; (f) (605) 644-0842; (c) Lawrence

Private non-profit/ 1977/ Board of Directors/ staff: 2(f); 1(p); 40(v)/ members: 40

ART MUSEUM; HISTORICAL SOCIETY; HISTORY MUSEUM; LIVING HISTORY/OUTDOOR MUSEUM: Preserves history of Old West pioneers and Native Americans of ND, SD, MT, WY, and NE.

PROGRAMS: Annual Meeting; Community Outreach; Concerts; Exhibits; Facility Rental; Family Programs; Festivals; Guided Tours; Lectures; Living History; Theatre

COLLECTIONS: [1850-1950] Western art, artifacts, family histories.

HOURS: Yr Daily 9-5 (summer hours 9-8)

ADMISSION: $4, Student $1, Seniors $3

7848
Leland D. Case Library for Western Historical Studies
Unit 9548 BHSU, 1200 Univ St, 57799; (p) (605) 642-6361; (f) (605) 642-6298; ckirby@mystic.bhsu.edu; www.bhsu.edu/resources/library/specialcollections; (c) Lawrence

State/ 1974/ Black Hills State Univ/ staff: 1(f)

LIBRARY AND/OR ARCHIVES: Collects, preserves and interprets Black Hills and Native American history.

PROGRAMS: Exhibits; Research Library/Archives

COLLECTIONS: Books, photos, maps, manuscript.

HOURS: Jan-July, Sept-Dec M-F 8-4:30

ADMISSION: No charge

STURGIS

7849
National Motorcycle Museum and Hall of Fame
1650 Lazelle St, 57785 [PO Box 602, 57785]; (p) (605) 347-4875; (f) (605) 347-4986; mcmuseum@sturgis.com; www.museumsturgis-rally.com; (c) Meade

Private non-profit/ 1989/ staff: 1(f); 2(p)/ members: 235

HISTORY MUSEUM: Preserves history of motorcycles and sport of cycling.

PROGRAMS: Exhibits

COLLECTIONS: [1900-present] Harley Davidson, Indian, European, Asian and racing/off road model motorcycles; memorabilia, photos, artwork, books.

HOURS: Yr Daily 9-5

ADMISSION: $5, Seniors $3

TABOR

7850
Czech Heritage Preservation Society
Main St, 57063 [PO Box 3, 57063]; (p) (650) 463-2476; (c) Bon Homme

Private non-profit/ 1974/ staff: 17(p)/ members: 240

HISTORIC PRESERVATION AGENCY: Preserves and promotes Czech heritage.

PROGRAMS: Annual Meeting; Guided Tours

TIMBER LAKE

7851
Timber Lake and Area Historical Society
[PO Box 181, 57656]; (p) (605) 865-3546; (f) (605) 865-3787; (c) Dewey

Private non-profit/ 1982/ Timber Lake and Area Historical Society/ staff: 1(f); 30(v)/ members: 250

HISTORICAL SOCIETY; HISTORY MUSEUM; RESEARCH CENTER; TRIBAL MUSEUM

PROGRAMS: Annual Meeting; Community Outreach; Exhibits; Guided Tours; Interpretation; Lectures; Living History; Publication; Research Library/Archives

COLLECTIONS: [1880-present] Native American, fossils, paintings.

HOURS: Yr M-F 9-5

ADMISSION: No charge

TYNDALL

7852
Bon Homme Heritage Association
101 W 14th, 57066 [PO Box 575, 57066]; (c) Bon Homme

County/ 1989/ Board of Directors/ members: 45

GENEALOGICAL SOCIETY; HISTORIC PRESERVATION AGENCY; HISTORY MUSEUM

PROGRAMS: Annual Meeting; Community Outreach; Exhibits; Guided Tours; Lectures; Living History; Research Library/Archives

COLLECTIONS: [1880-1948] Books, clothing, tools, maps, photos, cemetery and school records, dentist's office equipment, household furnishings, linotype printer, religious, genealogy and military items.

HOURS: June-Sept Sa-Su 1-4 or by appt

ADMISSION: Donations accepted

VERMILLION

7853
Austin Whittemore House
15 Austin Ave, 57069 [PO Box 332, 57069]; (p) (605) 624-8266, (605) 624-5539

1882/ staff: 3(v)

COLLECTIONS: [Late 1880s] Drug store tins; photos; toys; Victorian furniture; kerosene stove; wooden washing machine.

HOURS: App; Weekends anytime by calling

7854
Clay County Historical Society
15 Austin St, 57069-3055; (p) (605) 624-8266; (c) Clay

County, non-profit; Private non-profit/ 1965/ Board of Directors/ staff: 25(v)/ members: 200/publication: *CCHS Newsletter*

HISTORIC PRESERVATION AGENCY; HISTORIC SITE; HISTORICAL SOCIETY; HISTORY MUSEUM; LIVING HISTORY/OUTDOOR MUSEUM: Promotes local history, genealogy, family and oral history.

PROGRAMS: Annual Meeting; Community Outreach; Exhibits; Family Programs; Festivals; Guided Tours; Interpretation; Lectures; Living History; Publication; Research Library/Archives; School-Based Curriculum

COLLECTIONS: [1880-1920] Victorian furnishing, glassware, family and oral histories.

HOURS: May-Sept Daily 10-4 and by appt

ADMISSION: No charge

7855
W.H. Over Museum
1110 Ratingen St, 57069 [414 E Clark St, 57069]; (p) (605) 677-5228, (605) 677-5277; www.usd.edu/whover; (c) Clay

Private non-profit; State/ 1883/ staff: 2(f); 2(p)/ members: 410

HISTORY MUSEUM: Preserves local history.

PROGRAMS: Annual Meeting; Community Outreach; Elder's Programs; Exhibits; Facility Rental; Family Programs; Festivals; Garden Tours; Guided Tours; Lectures; Research Library/Archives

COLLECTIONS: [1860-1960] Native American, pioneer, Univ of SD, Vermillion artifacts; natural history specimens, photos.

HOURS: Yr M-F 9-5, Sa 10-4:30, Su 1-4:30

ADMISSION: Donations

VOLGA

7856
Brookings County Historical Society
Samara Ave, Volga City Park, 57071 [101 Lincoln Ln, 57071-9067]; (p) (605) 627-9149; (c) Brookings

County/ 1939/ Board of Directors/ staff: 40(v)/ members: 150

HISTORICAL SOCIETY; HISTORY MUSEUM

PROGRAMS: Annual Meeting; Exhibits; Guided Tours

COLLECTIONS: [1879-present] Books, documents, histories, photographs, clothing, military uniforms, household items, tools, farm equipment, furnished log cabin and country schoolhouse.

HOURS: June-Aug Daily 2-5

ADMISSION: Donations

WATERTOWN

7857
Codington County Historical Society
27 1st Ave SE, 57201; (p) (605) 886-7335; (f) (605) 882-4383; cchs@dailypost.com; www.cchsmuseum.org; (c) Codington

Private non-profit/ 1974/ staff: 2(f); 10(v)/ members: 300/publication: *Wagon Wheels*

HISTORICAL SOCIETY; HISTORY MUSEUM: Preserves and interprets history of Codington County.

PROGRAMS: Annual Meeting; Community Outreach; Exhibits; Guided Tours; Lectures; Publication

COLLECTIONS: [1890-1920] Victorian, military, pioneer, education, medicine.

HOURS: Yr 8-5

ADMISSION: No charge

7858
Mellette House
421 Fifth Ave, 57201 [816 S Broadway, 57201]; (p) (605) 886-5812, (605) 886-4730

1883/ Mellette Memorial / staff: 2(f)

COLLECTIONS: [Middle 1880s] Native American artifacts, political, family life; photos, letters, Watertown ephemera.

HOURS: Open 1st Su in May till Oct; Tues-Sun, 1-5

7859
Mellette Memorial Association
421 5th Ave NW, 57201 [824 Hidden Valley Dr, 57201]; (p) (605) 886-4730; (c) Codington

Private non-profit/ 1943/ staff: 3(p)

HISTORIC SITE; HOUSE MUSEUM: Preserves Mellette House, home of the first governor of SD.

PROGRAMS: Exhibits; Guided Tours; Interpretation; Reenactments

COLLECTIONS: [1883-1895] Period furnishing, clothing, pictures, artifacts, letters and papers of Mellette Family, Native American artifacts.

HOURS: May-Sept T-Su 1-5

WOOLSEY

7860
East River Genealogical Forum
17 5th SW, 57384 [20084 387th Ave, 57384-8433]; (p) (605) 883-4117; grudggr@santel.net; (c) Beadle

1970/ staff: 1(f)/publication: *People's History of Beadle County*

GENEALOGICAL SOCIETY; HISTORICAL SOCIETY: Preserves genealogical material.

PROGRAMS: Community Outreach; Exhibits; Family Programs; Interpretation; Living History; Publication; Research Library/Archives

COLLECTIONS: [1850-present] Oral and written histories, documents, records, photos.

HOURS: Yr

YANKTON

7861
Cramer-Kenyon Heritage House, Inc
509 Pine St, 57078 [PO Box 465, 57078]; (p) (605) 665-7470, (800) 888-1460; (c) Yankton

1888/ Board of Directors/ staff: 2(f); 16(v)

ART MUSEUM; GARDEN; HOUSE MUSEUM

PROGRAMS: Annual Meeting; Exhibits; Guided Tours; School-Based Curriculum

COLLECTIONS: [1863-1920] Period furnishing, artifacts, personal effects.

HOURS: May-Sept T-Sa 1-5

ADMISSION: $2

TENNESSEE

ADAMSVILLE

7862
Buford Pusser Home & Museum
342 Pusser St, 38310 [PO Box 301, 38310]; (p) (901) 632-4080, (901) 632-1401; (f) (901) 632-1779

1980/ City/ staff: 1(f); 3(p); 3(v)

COLLECTIONS: Photos, articles, stories, Pusser artifacts.

HOURS: Yr

ATHENS

7863
McMinn County Living Heritage Museum
522 W Madison Ave, 37303 [PO Box 889, 37303]; (p) (423) 745-0329; (f) (423) 745-0329; livher@usit.net; www.usit.com/livher; (c) McMinn

Private non-profit/ 1982/ Board of Trustees/ staff: 3(f); 3(p); 150(v)/ members: 825/publication: *Museum Pieces*

HISTORY MUSEUM: Presents local history of early settlers and Cherokee Indians.

PROGRAMS: Annual Meeting; Community Outreach; Exhibits; Family Programs; Festivals; Film/Video; Guided Tours; Interpretation; Lectures; Living History; Publication; Reenactments; Research Library/Archives; School-Based Curriculum

COLLECTIONS: [1800-1940] Clothing, tools, Cherokee artifacts, art, furniture, transportation, industry, business, toys, folk art and needlework.

BEERSHEBA SPRINGS

7864
Beersheba Springs Historical Society
[PO Box 148, 37305]; (p) (931) 692-3187; (f) (931) 692-3362; (c) Grundy

Private non-profit/ 1981/ Board of Directors/ staff: 20(v)/ members: 100/publication: *Beersheba Springs: A History*

HISTORICAL SOCIETY: Gathers and disseminates the history of Beersheba Springs.

PROGRAMS: Annual Meeting; Exhibits; Festivals; Garden Tours; Guided Tours; Lectures; Publication

COLLECTIONS: [1750-present] Letters, diaries, maps, newspapers, books, articles, arts, and artifacts.

BRENTWOOD

7865
Confederate Memorial Park at Winstead Hill
Columbia Hwy, 37024 [PO Box 3448, 37024]; (p) (615) 833-8977; (f) (615) 837-1109; (c) Williamson

Private non-profit/ 1968/ Sam Davis Camp, Sons of Confederate Veterans/ staff: 132(v)/ members: 132/publication: *The Hero's Herald*

HISTORIC SITE: Maintains the grounds and supervises the placement of monuments, plaques and historical markers at Winstead Hill.

PROGRAMS: Guided Tours; Interpretation; Lectures; Living History; Publication; Reenactments

COLLECTIONS: [1861-1865] 12 monuments, markers and plaques.

HOURS: Yr Daily

BROWNSVILLE

7866
Haywood County Museum
127 N Grand Ave, 38012 [115 Rooks Dr, 38012-2919]; (p) (901) 772-4883; (c) Haywood

Private non-profit/ 1991/ Haywood County Historical Society/ staff: 1(p); 10(v)/ members: 280

HISTORICAL SOCIETY; HISTORY MUSEUM: Preserves local history.

PROGRAMS: Annual Meeting; Exhibits

COLLECTIONS: Artifacts, documents, memorabilia; sports.

HOURS: Yr Su 1-5

BRUNSWICK

7867
Davies Manor Association, Inc.
9336 Davies Plantation Rd, 38014 [PO Box 56, 38014]; (p) (901) 386-0715; (f) (901) 388-4677; (c) Shelby

Private non-profit/ 1957/ Davies Manor Association, Inc./ staff: 2(f); 30(v)/ members: 200

HISTORIC SITE; HOUSE MUSEUM: Owns and operates Davies Manor house museum.

PROGRAMS: Community Outreach; Exhibits; Facility Rental; Family Programs; Guided Tours; Interpretation; Lectures; School-Based Curriculum

COLLECTIONS: [1830-1860] Pioneer furnishings.

HOURS: Apr-Dec T-Sa

BYRDSTOWN

7868
Cordell Hull Birthplace & Museum State Park
1300 Cordell Hull Memorial Dr, 38549; (p) (931) 864-3247; (f) (931) 864-6389; kerbaugh@ twlakes.net; (c) Pickett

Private non-profit; State/ 1969/ State of Tennessee, Conservation and Environment Division/ staff: 2(f); 4(v)/publication: The Back Porch

HISTORY MUSEUM; STATE PARK

PROGRAMS: Annual Meeting; Community Outreach; Exhibits; Facility Rental; Festivals; Guided Tours; Interpretation; Lectures; Publication; Research Library/Archives

COLLECTIONS: [1871-1955] Original log cabin birthplace; documents and artifacts.

HOURS: Yr M Sa 8-4, Su 12-4

ADMISSION: No charge/Donations

CASTALIAN SPRINGS

7869
Bledsoe's Lick Historical Association
210 Old Hwy 25, 37031; (p) (615) 452-5463; (f) (615) 452-6285; BLHA-Inc@excite.com; www.srlab.net/bledsoe; (c) Sumner

1972/ staff: 1(f); 2(p)/ members: 200

HISTORIC SITE; HISTORICAL SOCIETY; HOUSE MUSEUM: Preserves local history.

PROGRAMS: Annual Meeting; Community Outreach; Exhibits; Facility Rental; Festivals; Guided Tours

COLLECTIONS: Interpretive sites: Wynnewood State Historic Area, Bledsoe's Fort Historical Park, and the Nathaniel Parker cabin.

HOURS: Apr-Oct M-Sa 10-4, Su 1-5; Nov-Mar M-F 10-4

ADMISSION: $4, Seniors $3.50

7870
Historic Cragfont Inc.
200 Cragfont Rd, 37031; (p) (615) 452-7070; (c) Sumner

State/ 1962/ staff: 1(f); 12(v)/ members: 400

HISTORY MUSEUM

PROGRAMS: Annual Meeting; Concerts; Facility Rental; Film/Video; Guided Tours

COLLECTIONS: [Federal Period] 12 furnished rooms of Federal Period.

HOURS: Mid Apr-Oct T-Sa 10-4:30, Su 1-4:30

ADMISSION: $4, Children $0.50

CHATTANOOGA

7871
Chattanooga African American Museum
200 E Martin Luther King Blvd, 37403; (p) (423) 266-8658; (f) (423) 267-1076; (c) Hamilton

Private non-profit/ 1983/ staff: 4(f); 2(p); 10(v)/ members: 450

HISTORY MUSEUM

PROGRAMS: Community Outreach; Concerts; Exhibits; Facility Rental; Family Programs; Festivals; Guided Tours; Lectures; School-Based Curriculum; Theatre

COLLECTIONS: [1850-1950] Bessie Smith and African art; Chattanooga African-Americans; interpretive exhibits.

HOURS: Yr M, F 10-5, Sa 12-4

ADMISSION: $5

7872
Chattanooga-Hamilton County Bicentennial Library, Local History and Genealogy Department
1001 Broad St, 37402; (p) (423) 757-5317; library@lib.chattanooga.gov; www.lib. chattanooga.gov; (c) Hamilton

Joint/ 1888/ Board of Directors; City/County/ staff: 5(f); 1(v)

LIBRARY AND/OR ARCHIVES: Collects and preserves the history of the Chattanooga area.

PROGRAMS: Community Outreach; Exhibits; Research Library/Archives

COLLECTIONS: [19th-20th c] Books, newspaper clipping files, photos, oral histories and manuscripts; genealogical items: census records, books, TN county records on microfilm and index to local obituaries.

7873
National Knife Museum
7201 Shallowford Rd, 37424 [PO Box 21070, 37424-0070]; (p) (423) 892-5007; (f) (423) 899-9456; NKCA@aol.com; (c) Hamilton

Private non-profit/ 1972/ staff: 1(f); 1(p)/ members: 5000/publication: Knife World

Preserves the history of cutlery.

COLLECTIONS: [200 BC-present] 12,000 knives, swords and knife memorabilia.

HOURS: Yr T-F 10-3

ADMISSION: $2

7874
Tennessee Valley Railroad Museum, Inc.
4119 Cromwell Rd, 37421-2119; (p) (423) 894-8028; (f) (423) 894-8029; info@ tvrail.com; www.tvrail.com; (c) Hamilton

Private non-profit/ 1961/ staff: 12(f); 3(p); 24(v)/ members: 500/publication: Smoke and Cinders

RAILROAD MUSEUM: Preserves steam locomotives and passenger trains.

PROGRAMS: Annual Meeting; Exhibits; Facility Rental; Family Programs; Interpretation; Living History; Publication

COLLECTIONS: [1920-1950] Railway equipment.

HOURS: Apr-Oct, Daily; Nov Sa-Su

ADMISSION: $10.50, Children $5

CLARKSVILLE

7875
Clarksville-Montgomery County Museum
200 S Second St, 37041 [PO Box 383, 37041-0383]; (p) (931) 648-5780; (f) (931) 553-5179; museumcmc@aol.com; www.nashvillechamer.com/members/9539; (c) Montgomery

Private non-profit/ 1984/ Board of Trustees/ staff: 10(f); 7(p); 120(v)/ members: 900/publication: Ordeal By Fire; Edibles from the Archives

HISTORY MUSEUM: Collects, preserves and interprets historical, artistic and scientific material.

PROGRAMS: Community Outreach; Concerts; Elder's Programs; Exhibits; Facility Rental; Family Programs; Festivals; Guided Tours; Interpretation; Lectures; Living History; Publication; School-Based Curriculum; Theatre

COLLECTIONS: [19th-20th c] Archives, clothing, textiles, furniture, local businesses, military, agricultural and domestic items.

HOURS: Yr T-Sa 10-5, Su 1-5

ADMISSION: $3, Student $1, Seniors $2

CLEVELAND

7876
Museum Center at Five Points
200 Inman St, 37364 [PO Box 493, 37364-0493]; (p) (423) 339-5745; (f) (423) 476-7922; www.museumcenter.org; (c) Bradley

Private non-profit/ 1993/ staff: 5(f); 3(p)/ members: 1

HISTORY MUSEUM; LIVING HISTORY/OUTDOOR MUSEUM: Preserves and interprets the history and culture of the Oecor District of TN.

PROGRAMS: Community Outreach; Concerts; Elder's Programs; Exhibits; Facility Rental; Family Programs; Film/Video; Guided Tours; Lectures; Living History; School-Based Curriculum; Theatre

COLLECTIONS: [1700-1980] Regional artifacts, manufacturing, education, religion and culture.

HOURS: Yr

7877
Red Clay State Historical Park
1140 Red Clay Park Rd SW, 37311; (p) (423) 478-0339; (f) (423) 614-7251; (c) Bradley

State/ 1979/ TN Dept. of Environment & Conservation/ staff: 4(f); 3(p); 9(v)

HISTORIC SITE; HISTORY MUSEUM: Promotes history of Cherokee Nation and Trail of Tears.

PROGRAMS: Community Outreach; Elder's Programs; Family Programs; Festivals; Guided Tours; Interpretation; Lectures; Research Library/Archives; Theatre

COLLECTIONS: [19th c-present] Native American Studies; Cherokee history, culture, and genealogy; children's books, fiction, and biography; natural history.

HOURS: Yr Daily 8-4:30

COLLIERVILLE

7878
Biblical Resource Center and Museum
324 Poplar View Pkwy, 38017; (p) (901) 854-9578; (f) (901) 854-9883; donbassett@biblical-museum.org; www.Biblical-Museum.org; (c) Shelby

Private non-profit/ 1995/ Board of Directors/ staff: 2(f); 5(p); 4(v)/ members: 134/publication: *Journeys*

HISTORY MUSEUM: Promotes historical and cultural context of the Bible.

PROGRAMS: Exhibits; Interpretation; Lectures; Publication; Research Library/Archives

COLLECTIONS: Egyptian and Ancient Near Eastern archaeological artifacts and replicas.

COLUMBIA

7879
Athenaeum Rectory, The
808 Athenaeum St, 38402; (p) (931) 381-4822; (f) (931) 540-0745; www.athenaeum-rectory.com/; (c) Maury

Private non-profit/ 1837/ Assoc for the Preservation of TN Antiquities/ staff: 1(f); 25(v)

HISTORIC SITE: Preserves and promotes history of former 19th c girls school.

PROGRAMS: Annual Meeting; Community Outreach; Facility Rental; Festivals; Guided Tours; Reenactments

COLLECTIONS: [1835-1904] Furniture, paintings, flash glass windows, gasolier, Moorish architecture, and period musical instruments.

HOURS: T-Sa 10-4, Su 1-4 and by appt

ADMISSION: $5, Student $1, Seniors $4

7880
James K. Polk Memorial Association
301-305 W Seventh St, 38402 [PO Box 741, 38402]; (p) (931) 388-2354; (f) (931) 388-5971; jkpolk@usit.net; www.jameskpolk.com; (c) Maury

Private non-profit/ 1929/ James K. Polk Memorial Assoc/ staff: 2(f); 8(p); 68(v)/ members: 1253/publication: *A Special Home*

HISTORIC SITE; HOUSE MUSEUM; PRESIDENTIAL SITE: Operates and maintains the James K. Polk ancestral home.

PROGRAMS: Annual Meeting; Community Outreach; Elder's Programs; Exhibits; Family Programs; Film/Video; Guided Tours; Interpretation; Lectures; Publication; Reenactments

COLLECTIONS: [1795-1849] 1,500 artifacts and documents; original furnishings, White House china, and 1844 election memorabilia.

HOURS: Yr Apr-Oct M-Sa 9-5, Su 1-5; Nov-Mar M-Sa 9-4, Su 1-5

ADMISSION: $5, Student $2, Seniors $4

7881
Rattle & Snap Plantation
Hwy 243 between Columbia & Mt Pleasant, 38401 [1522 N Main, 38401]; (p) (931) 379-5861, (800) 258-3875; (f) (931) 379-0892; adevans@edge.net; www.rattleandsnap.com; (c) Maury

Private for-profit/ 1845/ staff: 10(f); 6(p)

HISTORIC SITE; HISTORY MUSEUM; HOUSE MUSEUM; LIVING HISTORY/OUTDOOR MUSEUM: Restored National Historic Landmark.

PROGRAMS: Exhibits; Facility Rental; Family Programs; Garden Tours; Guided Tours; Interpretation; Living History; School-Based Curriculum

COLLECTIONS: [1830-1865] Polk family period furnishings; archaeological artifacts.

HOURS: Yr M-Sa 10-5, Su 12-5

7882
Sons of Confederated Veterans
740 Mooresville Pk, 38402 [PO Box 59, 38402-0059]; (p) (931) 380-1844; (f) (931) 381-6712; scvihq@scv.org; www.scv.org; (c) Maury

Private non-profit/ 1896/ General Executive Council/ staff: 5(f); 1(p); 40(v)/ members: 27400/publication: *Confederate Veteran*

HISTORIC PRESERVATION AGENCY; HISTORIC SITE: Preserves history of the Confederate Army of Navy.

PROGRAMS: Guided Tours; Lectures; Publication

HOURS: Yr M-F 9-5

ADMISSION: $5

COOKVILLE

7883
Cookville Depot Museum
116 W Broad St, 38503 [PO Box 998, 38503]; (p) (931) 528-8570; (f) (931) 526-1167; (c) Putnam

City/ 1985/ staff: 3(p)/publication: *Time Table*

HISTORIC SITE; HISTORY MUSEUM

PROGRAMS: Exhibits; Interpretation; Publication; Research Library/Archives

COLLECTIONS: [1890-Present] Photos, artifacts, and memorabilia of local railroad life and history.

HOURS: Yr T-Sa 10-4

COVINGTON

7884
Tipton County Museum Veterans Memorial/Nature Center, The
751 Bert Johnston Ave, 38019 [PO Box 768, 38019]; (p) (901) 476-0242; (f) (901) 476-0261; tcmuseum@yahoo.com; (c) Tipton

City, non-profit/ 1998/ staff: 3(f); 2(v)/ members: 200

HISTORY MUSEUM: Preserves local, natural and veteran history.

PROGRAMS: Community Outreach; Elder's Programs; Exhibits; Facility Rental; Festivals; Garden Tours; Guided Tours; Lectures; School-Based Curriculum

COLLECTIONS: [1860s-present] 1,000 artifacts: nature, Civil War.

HOURS: Yr 9-5

DAYTON

7885
Scopes Trial Museum-Rhea County Courthouse, The
1475 Market St, 37321 [375 Church St, Ste 215, 37321]; (p) (423) 755-7801; (f) (423) 775-5553; (c) Rhea

County/ 1891/ staff: 1(p)

HISTORY MUSEUM: Promotes history of "Scopes Evolution Trial."

PROGRAMS: Festivals; Reenactments

COLLECTIONS: [1925] Courtroom artifacts: judge's bench, attorney's tables, dais rail, jury chairs, and spectator seats.

HOURS: Yr M-F 8-4:30

ELIZABETHTON

7886
Carter Mansion
E Broad St, 37643 [1651 W Elk Ave, 37643]; (p) (423) 543-6140; (c) Carter

7887
Sycamore Shoals State Historic Area
1651 W Elk Ave, 37643; (p) (423) 543-5808; (f) (423) 543-0078; (c) Carter

State/ 1976/ TN Dept. of Environmental & Conservation, Division of State Parks/ staff: 4(f); 2(p)

HISTORIC SITE

PROGRAMS: Community Outreach; Exhibits; Family Programs; Festivals; Film/Video; Guided Tours; Interpretation; Living History; Reenactments; School-Based Curriculum; Theatre

COLLECTIONS: [Revolutionary War era] Tools, spinning, weaving, dying and weapons.

HOURS: Yr Daily

ENGLEWOOD

7888
Englewood Textile Museum
17 S Niota Rd, 37329 [PO Box 253, 37329];
(p) (423) 887-5455; (f) (423) 887-7715; (c)
McMinn

Private non-profit/ 1994/ Community Action
Group of Englewood (CAGE)/ staff: 2(p);
15(v)/publication: *Then and Now: The Women
of Englewood's Textile Mills*

HOUSE MUSEUM: Promotes history of textile
industry.

PROGRAMS: Concerts; Exhibits; Festivals;
Guided Tours; Interpretation; Publication

COLLECTIONS: [1890-Present] Exhibits, artifacts, photographs, tape recordings all pertaining to Englewood's textile mills.

FARRAGUT

7889
Farragut Folklife Museum
11408 Municipal Center Dr, 37922; (p) (423)
699-7057; (f) (423) 675-2096; museum@far-
ragut.tn.us; www.farragut.tn.us; (c) Farragut

City; Joint/ 1987/ Town of Farragut/ staff: 6(p);
60(v)/ members: 114/publication: *Farragut
Folklife Museum Newsletter*

HISTORY MUSEUM: Collects, preserves and
interprets the history of Campbell's Station
and East TN.

PROGRAMS: Annual Meeting; Community
Outreach; Film/Video; Guided Tours; Interpre-
tation; Lectures; Publication; School-Based
Curriculum

COLLECTIONS: [1787-Present] Admiral Farragut artifacts; Civil War relics from the Battle
of Campbell's Station; photos;

FRANKLIN

7890
Carter House, The
1140 Columbia Ave, 37064; (p) (615) 791-
1861; www.carter-house.org

7891
Historic Carnton Plantation
1345 Carnton Lane, 37064; (p) (615) 794-
0903; (f) (615) 794-6563; carnton@mind-
spring.com; (c) Williamson

Private non-profit/ 1977/ Board of Directors,
Historic Carnton Plantation Association, Inc./
staff: 6(f); 1(p); 40(v)/ members: 500/publica-
tion: *Columns Quarterly Newsletter*

GARDEN; HISTORIC SITE; HOUSE MUSE-
UM: National Historic Landmark; interprets architectural, decorative and cultural arts of mid
19th century.

PROGRAMS: Concerts; Exhibits; Facility
Rental; Family Programs; Festivals; Garden
Tours; Guided Tours; Interpretation; Lectures;
Living History; Publication

COLLECTIONS: [1850s] 1826 home with period furnishings, portraits, etc. that served as
Civil War field hospital; slave quarters, spring
house, garden; Confederate cemetery with
1400 Confederate soldiers remains.

HOURS: Yr Daily

7892
Lotz House Museum
1111 Columbia Avenue, 37064; (p) (615)
791-6533; (f) (615) 791-5650;
lotzrebel@aol.com; www.lotzhouse.org; (c)
Williamson

Private non-profit/ 1995/ staff: 3(f); 2(p); 3(v)/
members: 115

GENEALOGICAL SOCIETY; HISTORIC SITE;
HISTORY MUSEUM: Promotes history of War
Between the States; maintains Confederate
and Yankee artifacts.

PROGRAMS: Annual Meeting; Exhibits; Guided Tours; Lectures; Research Library/Archives

HOURS: Yr Daily M-Sa 9-5, Su 12-5

ADMISSION: $5, Children $1.50, Seniors $4

GALLATIN

7893
Sumner County Museum
183 W Main St, 37066; (p) (615) 451-3738;
(c) Sumner

Private non-profit/ 1975/ Sumner County Museum Association/ staff: 4(p); 5(v)/ members: 152

HISTORY MUSEUM: Preserves and displays
regional and county artifacts.

PROGRAMS: Annual Meeting; Exhibits; Festivals; Guided Tours; School-Based Curriculum

COLLECTIONS: [Prehistoric-1950] Native American and pioneer artifacts; 24 exhibits: photography, farming, automobiles, schools, clothing, toys,
tools, the wars, trades and computers.

HOURS: Apr-Oct W-Sa 9-4:30, Su 1-4:30

ADMISSION: $2, Children $0.50

7894
Trousdale Place
183 W Main St, 37066; (p) (615) 452-1404,
(615) 452-5648; (c) Sumner

Private non-profit/ 1813/ Clark Chapter, United
Daughters of the Confederacy/ staff: 2(p); 2(v)/
members: 24

HISTORIC SITE: Historic home of former TN
Governor William Trousdale.

PROGRAMS: Community Outreach; Guided
Tours; Interpretation; Research Library/
Archives

COLLECTIONS: [1860-1865] Civil War; furniture of Trousdale family; family artifacts.

HOURS: Apr-Dec W-Sa 9-4, Su 1-5

ADMISSION: $3, Student $1, Children

GERMANTOWN

7895
PT Boats, Inc.
1384 Cordova Cove, Ste 2, 38183 [PO Box
38070, 38183-0070]; (p) (901) 755-8440;
ptboats@aol.com; www.ptboats.org; (c)
Shelby

Private non-profit/ 1946/ staff: 3(f); 1(p); 1(v)/
members: 16000

HISTORY MUSEUM: Promotes WWII and US
Navy Patrol Torpedo history.

PROGRAMS: Annual Meeting; Exhibits; Interpretation; Research Library/Archives

COLLECTIONS: [WWII] 8,000 uncatalogued
photos, film, blueprints, books, documents, diaries, action reports, maps, nautical charts.

HOURS: Yr M-F 8:30-4:30

ADMISSION: $9, Student $4.50, Children
$3.25, Seniors $6.75; Archives free

GOODLETTSVILLE

7896
Historic Mansker's Station Frontier
Caldwell Road/Moss-Wright Park, 37070 [705
Caldwell Dr, 37072]; (p) (615) 859-3678; (c)
Sumner

City/ 1987/ staff: 3(f); 2(p); 500(v)

HISTORIC SITE; HISTORY MUSEUM;
HOUSE MUSEUM; LIVING HISTORY/OUT-
DOOR MUSEUM: Promotes history of Cumberland Valley and Federal-style Bowen Plantation House.

PROGRAMS: Festivals; Garden Tours; Guided
Tours; Interpretation; Living History; Reenactments

COLLECTIONS: [18th c] Reproduction
firearms, furnishings, tools; Bowen Plantation
House furnished early TN and KY pieces and
reproductions.

HOURS: Mar-Dec T-Sa 9-4

ADMISSION: $5, Student $3

GRAND JUNCTION

7897
Ames Plantation
4275 Buford Ellington Rd, 38039 [PO Box
389, 38039]; (p) (901) 878-1067, (901) 878-
1068; (f) (901) 878-1068; amesplantation@
lunaweb.net; www.amesplantation.org; (c)
Fayette

Private non-profit/ 1847/ Trustees Hobart
Ames Foundation/ staff: 30(f); 4(v)

HISTORIC SITE; RESEARCH CENTER: Documents and preserves local history.

PROGRAMS: Guided Tours; Interpretation

COLLECTIONS: [19th c] Replica of 19th c
family farmstead with seven restored and furnished log structures, Ames Manor House, a
plantation home, and one-room school.

HOURS: Mar-Oct 4th Th 1-4, or by appt

ADMISSION: $2

GREENBRIER

7898
Greenbrier Historical Society
205 W College St, 37073 [PO Box 695,
37073]; (p) (615) 643-8461; (c) Robertson

Private non-profit/ 1997/ Board of Directors/
staff: 20(v)/ members: 500

HISTORICAL SOCIETY; HISTORY MUSEUM;
HOUSE MUSEUM: Interprets the history and culture of Greenbrier and southern Robertson County.

PROGRAMS: Exhibits; Guided Tours

COLLECTIONS: [1890-1945] Artifacts: Greenbrier, Granville Babb Sprouse family.

HOURS: Yr W-F 10-4, Sa 10-1

ADMISSION: No charge

GREENEVILLE

7899
Andrew Johnson National Historic Site and Homestead
209 S Main St, 37743 [PO Box 1088, 37744]; (p) (423) 638-3551, (423) 639-3711; (f) (423) 638-9194

Federal/ 1849/ National Park Service/ staff: 7(f); 2(p); 1(v)

HISTORIC SITE; HISTORY MUSEUM: Preserves history of Andrew Johnson.

COLLECTIONS: [1869-1875] Sites: Andrew Johnson's Tailor Shop and museum, the Andrew Johnson National Cemetery, Andrew Johnson Homestead, and 1830s-1851 house; Johnson Family artifacts.

HOURS: Yr

7900
Nathanael Greene City County Heritage Museum
101 W McKee St, 37743; (p) (423) 636-1558; (c) Greene

1982/ Museum Board of Directors/ staff: 1(f); 15(v)/ members: 175

HISTORIC PRESERVATION AGENCY; HISTORIC SITE; HISTORY MUSEUM: Collects, preserves, and presents natural history of Greene County and East Tennessee.

PROGRAMS: Exhibits; Family Programs; Guided Tours; Living History; School-Based Curriculum

COLLECTIONS: [Mid 1700s-Present] Galleries open: Early Agriculture 1780's to 1910; Military 1780- Present; Johnson Gallery; 1826-1880; Victorian Era, Special Exhibits; Great Forest 1700's; Sports Gallery late 1800's - present, Children's Gallery 1780's - 1890's; Main Street 1180-1900.

HOURS: Feb-Dec T-Sa 10-4

ADMISSION: Donations accepted

7901
President Andrew Johnson Museum
Box 5026 Tusculum College, 37743; (p) (426) 636-7348; agerhard@tusculum.edu

Private non-profit/ 1994/ staff: 2(f); 17(v)/ members: 68

HISTORY MUSEUM; PRESIDENTIAL SITE: Preserves history of Andrew Johnson.

PROGRAMS: Annual Meeting; Community Outreach; Elder's Programs; Interpretation

COLLECTIONS: [1808-1875] Johnson Family artifacts.

HOURS: Yr M-F 9-5

GREENSVILLE

7902
Doak House Museum/President Andrew Johnson Museum & Library
Tusculum College, 37743 [PO Box 5026, 37743]; (p) (423) 636-7348; (f) (423) 638-7166; gcollins@tusculum.edu; www.tusculum.edu; (c) Greene

Private non-profit/ 1994/ Tusculum College/Dept. of Museum Program and Studies/ staff: 3(f); 1(p); 20(v)

HOUSE MUSEUM; PRESIDENTIAL SITE: Doak House, the 1830 home of the college founder, and the President Andrew Johnson Museum and Library are maintained by the Dept of Museum Studies of Tusculum College.

PROGRAMS: Community Outreach; Exhibits; Family Programs; Garden Tours; Research Library/Archives; School-Based Curriculum

COLLECTIONS: [1794-1875] Artifacts: Tusculum College, Rev. Samuel Doak, President Andrew Johnson.

HOURS: Yr 9-5

ADMISSION: $2, Children $1; Museum: No charge

HARROGATE

7903
Abraham Lincoln Library and Museum
Cumberland Gap Pkwy, 37752 [PO Box 2006, 37752]; (p) (423) 869-6235; (f) (423) 869-6350; almuseum@inetlmu.lmunet.edu; www.lmunet.edu/museum/index.html; (c) Claiborne

1897/ staff: 5(f); 1(p); 7(v)/ members: 180/publication: *The Lincoln Herald*

HISTORY MUSEUM: Promotes the study of Lincolnia and the Civil War.

PROGRAMS: Community Outreach; Concerts; Exhibits; Facility Rental; Guided Tours; Interpretation; Lectures; Publication; Research Library/Archives

COLLECTIONS: [1809-present] 6000 books, 2500 pamphlets, 500 broadsides, 1000 sheets of music, 50 newspapers, 850 photographs, firearms, fine arts, uniforms, and edged weapons.

HOURS: Yr M-F 9-4, Sa 11-4, Su 1-4

ADMISSION: $3, Children

HENDERSONVILLE

7904
Friends of Rock Castle
139 Rock Castle Lane, 37075; (p) (615) 824-0502; (c) Sumner

State/ 1971/ staff: 2(p); 32(v)/ members: 88/publication: *The Surveyor*

HISTORIC SITE; HOUSE MUSEUM: Manages an 18 acre historic site.

PROGRAMS: Annual Meeting; Facility Rental; Family Programs; Festivals; Guided Tours; Publication; Reenactments; School-Based Curriculum

COLLECTIONS: [1790-1830] Artifacts, books belonging to Daniel Smith.

HOURS: Feb-Dec W-Sa 10-4, Su 1-4

ADMISSION: $3, Children $1.50, Seniors $2.50

HENNING

7905
Alex Haley House Museum, The
200 S Church St, 38041 [PO Box 500, 38041]; (p) (901) 738-2240; (f) (901) 738-2585

1918/ staff: 2(f); 2(p)

COLLECTIONS: [1920s] Furnishing, Alex Haley memorabilia, marble monument.

HOURS: T-Sa 10-5, Su 1-5

7906
Fort Pillow State Historic Park
3122 Park Road, 38041; (p) (901) 738-5581; (f) (901) 738-9117; (c) Lauderdale

State/ 1974/ staff: 8(f); 3(p)

HISTORIC SITE; HISTORY MUSEUM; LIVING HISTORY/OUTDOOR MUSEUM: Preserves history of Fort Pillow and the Civil War Battle of 1864.

PROGRAMS: Exhibits; Film/Video; Interpretation; Living History; Reenactments

COLLECTIONS: [1860s] Cannons, artifacts, literature, reproductions.

HERMITAGE

7907
Hermitage, The
4580 Rachel's Lane, 37076; (p) (615) 889-2941; (f) (615) 889-9289; info@thehermitage.com; www.thehermitage.com; (c) Davidson

Private non-profit; State/ 1889/ Ladies' Hermitage Association/ staff: 35(f); 40(p); 100(v)/ members: 1500

HOUSE MUSEUM: Preserves and collects Andrew Jackson history; maintains Jackson home.

PROGRAMS: Annual Meeting; Community Outreach; Elder's Programs; Exhibits; Facility Rental; Family Programs; Festivals; Film/Video; Garden Tours; Guided Tours; Interpretation; Lectures; Publication; Reenactments; Research Library/Archives; School-Based Curriculum; Theatre

COLLECTIONS: [1800-1860] Buildings, furnishings, personal possessions, archaeological material, photographs and books and manuscripts relating to Andrew Jackson.

HOURS: Jan-Dec Daily 9-5; Closed third week Jan

ADMISSION: $10, Children $5, Seniors $9

HOHENWALD

7908
Lewis County Historical Society
112 E Main St, 38462 [PO Box 703, 38462]; (p) (931) 796-4084; (c) Lewis

County, non-profit/ 1975/ members: 43/publication: *Lewis County Historical Quarterly*

HISTORIC PRESERVATION AGENCY; HISTORIC SITE; HISTORICAL SOCIETY: Preserves local history, records, and sites.

PROGRAMS: Elder's Programs; Exhibits; Family Programs; Film/Video; Lectures; Publication

HOURS: Yr 9-4:30

ADMISSION: $2, Student $0.50

7909
Lewis County Museum of Local and Natural History
108 E Main St, 38462; (p) (931) 796-1550; (c) Lewis

Private non-profit/ 1989/ Lewis County Historical Society/ staff: 1(p); 14(v)/ members: 40

HISTORICAL SOCIETY: Collects, preserves, and interprets local history.

PROGRAMS: Community Outreach; Exhibits; Festivals; Guided Tours

COLLECTIONS: [1809-present] Meriwether Lewis artifacts.

HOURS: Yr M-Sa 10-4, Su 1-4

ADMISSION: $2, Student $0.50

HUMBOLDT

7910
West Tennessee Regional Art Center
1200 Main St, 38343 [PO Box 951, 38343]; (p) (901) 784-1842, (901) 784-1787; (f) (901) 784-1787; WTRAC@aeneas.com; www.wtrac.tn.org; (c) Gibson

City/ 1994/ staff: 1(f); 1(v)

ART MUSEUM; HISTORY MUSEUM: Maintains West TN Historical Museum and Art Center in former city hall.

PROGRAMS: Exhibits; Lectures

COLLECTIONS: Paintings and sculptures: American Colonial and American Impressionist to African pieces and American Folk Art.

HOURS: Yr M-F 9-4

ADMISSION: $2

JACKSON

7911
Casey Jones Home and Railroad Museum
30 Casey Jones Ln, 38305; (p) (901) 668-1222; (f) (901) 668-6889; www.caseyjones village.com; (c) Madison

Joint/ 1956/ staff: 3(f); 4(p)

HISTORIC SITE; HOUSE MUSEUM: Maintains Casey Jones Family home.

PROGRAMS: Exhibits; School-Based Curriculum

COLLECTIONS: [Late 19th-early 20th c] Period furnishings, railroad, Casey Jones memorabilia.

HOURS: Yr Daily 8am-9pm

ADMISSION: $4, Children $3, Seniors $3.50

JEFFERSON CITY

7912
Glenmore Mansion
1280 N Chucky Pike, 37760 [PO Box 403, 37760]; (p) (423) 475-5014

JOHNSON CITY

7913
Carroll Reece Museum
Box 70660, 37614-0660; (p) (423) 439-4392; (f) (423) 439-4283; whiteb@etsu.edu; cass.etsu.edu/museum; (c) Washington

State/ 1965/ staff: 3(f); 11(p); 3(v)/ members: 175

ART MUSEUM; HISTORY MUSEUM: Promotes regional history.

PROGRAMS: Concerts; Exhibits; Guided Tours; Lectures

COLLECTIONS: [19th c] Regional settlement history and historical artifacts; household tools, farming implements, musical instruments, and furniture items; fine arts and craft items, paintings, prints, sculpture, ceramics and basketry.

HOURS: Yr M, T, W, F 9-4, Th 9-7, Sa-Su 1-4

ADMISSION: No charge

7914
Tipton-Haynes State Historic Site
2620 S Roan St, 37605 [PO Box 225, 37605]; (p) (423) 926-3631; pennym@tipton-haynes.org; www.tipton-haynes.org; (c) Washington

1944/ Tipton-Haynes Historical Association/ staff: 1(f); 7(v)/ members: 278

HISTORIC SITE: Collects, preserves, and interprets the history associated with Col. John Tipton and Landon Carter Haynes.

PROGRAMS: Annual Meeting; Facility Rental; Family Programs; Festivals; Guided Tours; Reenactments; Research Library/Archives

COLLECTIONS: [1780-1875] Furnishings, farm implements, a still and carriage.

HOURS: Yr Dec-Mar M-F 10-3; Apr-Nov M-Sa 10-4

ADMISSION: $3.50

JONESBOROROUGH

7915
Historical Jonesborough Foundation
117-1/2 W Main St, 37659; (p) (423) 753-9580; (c) Washington

Private non-profit/ 1992/ Board of Trustees/ staff: 2(f); 9(p)

HISTORIC PRESERVATION AGENCY: Provides preservation and restoration assistance.

PROGRAMS: Community Outreach; Exhibits; Lectures; Research Library/Archives

COLLECTIONS: 300 books and periodicals, photos, architectural salvage.

HOURS: Yr M-F 7:30-2

7916
Jonesborough-Washington County History Museum
117 Boone St, 37659; (p) (426) 753-1015; (f) (426) 753-1020; jbwchm@tricon.net; www.jonesborough.tricon.net/museum.html; (c) Washington

City/ 1982/ staff: 1(f); 1(p); 15(v)/ members: 30

HISTORY MUSEUM: Preserves and promotes local history.

PROGRAMS: Exhibits; Festivals; Guided Tours; Research Library/Archives; School-Based Curriculum

COLLECTIONS: [18th-20th c] Pioneer tools and utensils, textile-making, period interiors, blacksmithing, photography, early medicine, and early fire-fighting artifacts.

HOURS: Yr M-F 8-5, Sa-Su 10-5

ADMISSION: $2, Student $1, Seniors $1.50

7917
Washington County Historical Association
[PO Box 205, 37659]; (p) (423) 928-3829; www.uriel.com/history/washco.htm; (c) Washington

Private non-profit/ 1895/ members: 65/publication: *Washington County Historical Association Speeches 1987-88*

HISTORIC SITE; HISTORICAL SOCIETY; HISTORY MUSEUM; HOUSE MUSEUM: Studies, preserves, and disseminates history of Washington Co.

PROGRAMS: Annual Meeting; Exhibits; Guided Tours; Interpretation; Lectures; Publication; Research Library/Archives

COLLECTIONS: [1700-1900] Books, manuscripts, clipping, and photos.

KINGSPORT

7918
Exchange Place, Gaines-Preston Farm
4812 Orebank Road, 37664; (p) (426) 288-6071; (c) Sullivan

Private non-profit/ 1970/ Netherland Inn Association, Inc./ staff: 2(p); 125(v)/ members: 350

GARDEN; LIVING HISTORY/OUTDOOR MUSEUM: Interprets Preston family lifestyle through the restoration of their home and farm buildings.

PROGRAMS: Annual Meeting; Community Outreach; Family Programs; Festivals; Garden Tours; Guided Tours; Interpretation; Living History; School-Based Curriculum

COLLECTIONS: [1850] Representative furnishings and farm equipment of 1,200 acre farm in rural East TN.

HOURS: May-Oct Th, F 10-2, Sa-Su 1-4:30

KINGSTON

7919
Roane County Heritage Commission
119 Court St, 37763 [PO Box 738, 37763]; (p) (865) 376-9211; all@roanetnherigate.com; www.roanetnheritage.com; (c) Roane

Private non-profit/ 1974/ Board of Directors/ staff: 1(p); 8(v)/ members: 250

ART MUSEUM; HISTORIC PRESERVATION AGENCY; HISTORIC SITE; HISTORICAL SOCIETY; HISTORY MUSEUM; RESEARCH CENTER: Preserves and protects historic buildings, properties, sites, artifacts, documents, ephemera of Roane County.

PROGRAMS: Annual Meeting; Exhibits; Facility Rental; Festivals; Guided Tours; Publication; Research Library/Archives

COLLECTIONS: [Prehistory-1900] Civil War, prehistoric Roane County, court documents.

HOURS: Yr T-F 9-12/1-4

KNOXVILLE

7920
Armstrong-Lockett House/W.P. Toms Memorial Gardens
2728 Kingston Pk, 37919; (c) Knox

Private non-profit/ 1935/ staff: 4(f); 2(p)

HISTORIC SITE: Maintains house museum.

PROGRAMS: Exhibits; Festivals; Garden Tours

COLLECTIONS: [18th-early 19th c] American and English furniture, decorative arts, English silver.

7921
Beck Cultural Exchange Center
1927 Dandridge Ave, 37915; (p) (423) 524-8461; (f) (423) 524-8462; www.korrnet.org/beckcec; (c) Knox

Private non-profit/ 1975/ staff: 2(f); 1(p); 10(v)/ members: 800

HISTORY MUSEUM; RESEARCH CENTER: Researches, conserves, and displays the contributions of Knoxville area African-Americans.

PROGRAMS: Annual Meeting; Community Outreach; Exhibits; Guided Tours; Living History; Research Library/Archives

COLLECTIONS: [1864-1970] Photos, oral histories, biographical sketches, fine art, newspapers, and books by Knoxvillians.

HOURS: Yr T-Sa 10-6

7922
Blount Mansion Association
200 W Hill Ave, 37901 [PO Box 1703, 37901]; (p) (865) 525-2375, (888) 654-0016; (f) (865) 546-5315; info@blountmansion.org; www.blountmansion.org; (c) Knox

Private non-profit/ 1926/ Gov. William Blount Mansion Assoc/ staff: 3(f); 4(p); 45(v)/ members: 430/publication: *The Landmark*

CULTURAL CENTER: Promotes history of Blount Mansion and William Blount.

PROGRAMS: Annual Meeting; Elder's Programs; Exhibits; Facility Rental; Family Programs; Garden Tours; Guided Tours; Interpretation; Lectures; Publication; Reenactments; School-Based Curriculum

COLLECTIONS: [18th c] Historic structures, 18th c decorative arts, personal items; archaeological finds.

HOURS: Mar-Dec 15 M-Sa 9:30-5, Su 12:30-5; Dec 15-Feb M-F9:30-5

7923
Confederate Memorial Hall/ Bleak House
3148 Kingston Pike, 37919; (p) (423) 522-2371; www.korrnet.org/bhpa

7924
East Tennessee Development District (ETDD)
5616 Kingston Pike, 37939 [PO Box 19806, 37939]; (p) (865) 584-8553; (f) (865) 584-5159; EastTnDevD@aol.com; www.korrnet.org/etdd; (c) Knox

1966/ ETDD Board of Directors/ staff: 14(f)/ members: 72

PROFESSIONAL ORGANIZATION

PROGRAMS: Research Library/Archives

7925
East Tennessee Discovery Center
516 N Beaman St, 34914 [PO Box 6204, 34914]; (p) (423) 594-1494; edtc@usit.net; funnelweb.utcc.utk.edu/~loganj/etdc; (c) Knox

Joint; Private non-profit/ 1960/ Board of Trustees/ staff: 9(f); 3(p)/ members: 164

HISTORY MUSEUM: Promotes natural history.

PROGRAMS: Community Outreach; Exhibits; Facility Rental; Family Programs; Guided Tours; School-Based Curriculum

COLLECTIONS: Natural history exhibit.

HOURS: Yr M-F 9-5

ADMISSION: $3, Student $2, Children $1, Seniors $2

7926
East Tennessee Historical Society
314 W Clinch Ave, 37901 [PO Box 1629, 37901]; (p) (865) 215-8824; (f) (865) 215-

8819; eths@east-tennessee-history.org; www.east-tennessee-history.org; (c) Knox

Private non-profit/ 1834/ staff: 6(f); 4(p); 50(v)/ members: 1900

GENEALOGICAL SOCIETY; HISTORICAL SOCIETY; HISTORY MUSEUM: Preserves, interprets, and promotes East TN.

PROGRAMS: Annual Meeting; Community Outreach; Concerts; Facility Rental; Family Programs; Guided Tours; Interpretation; Lectures; Research Library/Archives; School-Based Curriculum

COLLECTIONS: [1750-Present] Paintings, textiles, furniture.

HOURS: Yr

7927
Frank H. McClung Museum
1327 Circle Park Drive, 37996-3200; (p) (865) 974-2144; (f) (865) 974-3827; jchapman@utk.edu; mcclungmuseum.utk.edu; (c) Knox

State/ 1963/ The University of Tennessee/ staff: 10(f); 2(p); 55(v)/ members: 525/publication: *Occasional Papers, Research Notes*

HISTORY MUSEUM: Collects and promotes local history.

PROGRAMS: Community Outreach; Exhibits; Family Programs; Lectures; Publication

COLLECTIONS: [Prehistory-present] Archaeological artifacts; Native American history; Civil War

7928
Hazen Historical Museum Foundation, Inc., The
1711 Dandridge Ave, 37915; (p) (423) 522-8661; (f) (423) 522-8661; mabry@korrnet.org; www.korrnet.org/mabry; (c) Knox

Private non-profit/ 1989/ Hazen Historical Museum Foundation, Inc. Bd./ staff: 1(f); 2(p); 25(v)/ members: 110

HISTORIC SITE; HISTORY MUSEUM; HOUSE MUSEUM; LIVING HISTORY/OUTDOOR MUSEUM: Preserves family life during the Victorian/Civil War Era; maintains Civil War cemetery.

PROGRAMS: Community Outreach; Exhibits; Facility Rental; Family Programs; Guided Tours; Interpretation; Lectures; Living History; Reenactments

COLLECTIONS: [1858-1920] Victorian home with period furnishing.

HOURS: Yr T-Sa

ADMISSION: $5, Student $2, Seniors $4.50; Under 5 free, group rates

7929
James White's Fort
205 E Hill Avenue, 37915; (p) (426) 525-6514; www.southdotnet/jameswhitesfort; (c) Knox

Private non-profit/ 1776/ JWF Assoc/ staff: 2(f); 7(p); 25(v)/ members: 519

HISTORIC SITE: Preserves and maintains history of James White.

PROGRAMS: Annual Meeting; Community Outreach; Facility Rental; Family Programs; Festivals; Garden Tours; Guided Tours; Interpretation; School-Based Curriculum

COLLECTIONS: [1780-1800] Period artifacts in home, guest house, blacksmith shop, loom

house, and smoke house.

HOURS: Mar-Dec 9:30-4:30

ADMISSION: $4, Children $2

7930
Knox County Old Gran Cemetery Educational, Historic and Memorial Association
543 N Broadway, 37901 [PO Box 806, 37901-0806]; (p) (423) 522-1424; oldgraynews@aol.com; www.Korrnet.org/oldgray; (c) Knox

Private non-profit/ 1850/ Board of Trustees/ staff: 2(p); 20(v)

HISTORICAL SOCIETY: Maintains 13 acres as an educational, historic and memorial park.

PROGRAMS: Garden Tours; Guided Tours; Research Library/Archives

COLLECTIONS: [1860-1940] Historical monuments and headstones; handwritten burial records; mature trees and plants.

HOURS: Yr Daily

7931
Marble Springs State Historic Farmstead
1220 W Gov John Sevier Hwy, 37920; (p) (423) 573-5508; (f) (423) 573-9768; (c) Knox

Joint; State/ 1946/ Governor John Sevier Memorial Assoc/ staff: 1(f); 2(p); 35(v)/ members: 225/publication: *News from Marble Springs*

LIVING HISTORY/OUTDOOR MUSEUM: Interprets pioneer history of East TN through 37 acre site with period buildings.

PROGRAMS: Annual Meeting; Community Outreach; Concerts; Exhibits; Facility Rental; Festivals; Guided Tours; Interpretation; Living History; Publication

COLLECTIONS: [18th-19th c] Gov John Sevier artifacts, intepretive rooms: kitchen, barn, loom house, tavern, retail shop.

HOURS: Yr T-Sa 10-5

ADMISSION: $5, Children $3, Seniors $4

7932
Ramsey House Plantation
2614 Thorngrove Pike, 37914; (p) (423) 456-0745; (f) (423) 456-0745

1797/ Assoc for the Preservation of TN Antiquities/ staff: 1(f); 3(p)

COLLECTIONS: [1797-1820] Period furnishing; original Annals of Tennessee by Dr. J.G.M. Ramsey.

HOURS: April 1-Dec 30, T-Sat, 10-4; Sun, 1-4

7933
TVA Historic Collections Program
400 W Summit Hill, 37902; (p) (423) 631-2190; (f) (423) 632-2195; MJdobrog@tva.gov; (c) Knox

Federal/ 1987/ Tennessee Valley Authority/ staff: 1(f); 2(p); 1(v)/ members: 1

HISTORIC PRESERVATION AGENCY: Preserves, documents, and illustrates the history and accomplishments of the Tennessee Valley Authority.

PROGRAMS: Community Outreach; Exhibits; Facility Rental; Family Programs; Film/Video; Guided Tours; Lectures; Research Library/Archives; School-Based Curriculum

COLLECTIONS: [1910-1960] Artifacts related to the history & accomplishments of the TVA, including electricity, power production, engineering, agricultural science, forestry, WWII, and river navigation.

HOURS: Yr Daily 8:30-4

LIMESTONE

7934
Davy Crockett Birthplace State Park
1245 Davy Crockett Park Rd, 37681; (p) (426) 257-2167; (f) (426) 257-2430; www.state.tn.us/environment/parks/davyshp/dcbp.htm; (c) Greene

State/ 1970/ staff: 6(f); 8(p)

HISTORIC SITE; HISTORY MUSEUM: Depicts life of frontier hero Davy Crockett.

PROGRAMS: Exhibits; Interpretation

COLLECTIONS: [1786-1836] Furnished log cabin replica of David Crockett birthplace.

HOURS: Yr Park: Sept-May M-F 8-dusk; May-Sept Daily dusk-9:30; Office & Museum Sept-May M-F 8-4:30, May-Sept M-F 8-4:30, Sa-Su 9-5

MANCHESTER

7935
Coffee Co/Manchester/Tullahoma Museum, Inc. Arrowheads/Aerospace Museum
24 Campground Rd, 37355; (p) (931) 723-1323; (c) Coffee

Private non-profit/ 1987/ Board of Directors/ staff: 2(f); 2(p); 30(v)/ members: 147

HISTORY MUSEUM; RESEARCH CENTER: Preserves and exhibits local history.

PROGRAMS: Annual Meeting; Community Outreach; Exhibits; Facility Rental; Family Programs; Festivals; Film/Video; Guided Tours; Interpretation; Lectures; School-Based Curriculum

COLLECTIONS: [1952] Artifacts: Native American war between the States, WWII, General Store, Barber Shop, Agriculture, Scouting, Sports, Decorative Arts, Toys, Lionel & other trains.

HOURS: Yr Daily 10:30-4:30

ADMISSION: $4, Student $2, Children $1

MARTIN

7936
Paul Meek Library & Special Collections Dept., University of Tennessee at Martin, The
c/o Richard Saunders, 38238; (p) (731) 587-7094; (f) (731) 587-7074; specoll@utm.edu; www.utm.edu/departments/acadpro/library/speccoll.h; (c) Weakley

State/ 1900/ Univ of Tennessee/ staff: 2(f); 2(p)

LIBRARY AND/OR ARCHIVES: Regional repository of state and regional history, genealogy, and institutional history.

PROGRAMS: Community Outreach; Exhibits; Guided Tours; Lectures; School-Based Curriculum

COLLECTIONS: [19th-20 c] Univ archives, manuscript collections, state and regional history, genealogy, and oral history.

MCKENZIE

7938
Gordon Browning Museum & Genealogical Library/Carroll Co. Historical Society
640 Main St N, 38201; (p) (901) 352-3510; (f) (901) 352-3456; gbm@excite.com; (c) Carroll

Private non-profit/ 1971/ Carroll Co. Historical Society/ staff: 1(f); 1(p); 10(v)/ members: 104/publication: Newsletter Lest We Forget

GENEALOGICAL SOCIETY; HISTORICAL SOCIETY; RESEARCH CENTER: Repository for historical artifacts of Carroll Co. and memorabilia of Gov. Gordon Browning.

PROGRAMS: Exhibits; Guided Tours; Publication; Research Library/Archives

COLLECTIONS: [1800-1999] Papers and memorabilia of Gov. Gordon Browning - Historical artifacts of Carroll Co. Pictures, furniture, farm implements - county loose records - micro-film genealogical research.

MEMPHIS

7939
C.H. Nash Museum/Chucalissa
1987 Indian Village Dr, 38109; (p) (901) 785-3160; (f) (901) 785-0519; lwweaver@memphis.edu; (c) Shelby

1957/ Univ of Memphis/ staff: 3(f); 5(p)

HISTORIC SITE; HISTORY MUSEUM; LIBRARY AND/OR ARCHIVES; RESEARCH CENTER: Promotes Native American history through reconstruction of 15th Native village, located on an ancient mound site.

PROGRAMS: Community Outreach; Concerts; Elder's Programs; Exhibits; Facility Rental; Family Programs; Festivals; Guided Tours; Interpretation; Research Library/Archives; School-Based Curriculum

COLLECTIONS: [900-1500 AD] Archaic, Woodland, and Mississippian eras artifacts, contemporary ethnographic artifacts from the Choctaw of Mississippi.

HOURS: T-Sa 1-5

ADMISSION: $5

7940
Coors Belle
5151 E Raines Rd, 38118; (p) (901) 375-2100; (f) (901) 375-2020; (c) Shelby

Joint/ 1972/ City;Private for profit/ staff: 2(f); 6(p)

Replica of an 1870s style steamboat grand salon.

COLLECTIONS: [1870s] Riverboat artifacts.

HOURS: Yr Th-Sa 12-5

7941
Dixon Gallery and Gardens, The
4339 Park Ave, 38117; (p) (901) 761-5250; (f) (901) 682-0943; adm1@dixon.org; www.dixon.org; (c) Shelby

Private non-profit/ 1976/ staff: 27(f); 5(p); 125(v)/ members: 4600/publication: DG&G Members Quarterly

ART MUSEUM: Promotes art history, horticulture.

PROGRAMS: Community Outreach; Concerts; Elder's Programs; Exhibits; Family Programs; Film/Video; Garden Tours; Guided

Tours; Interpretation; Lectures; Publication; Research Library/Archives; Theatre

COLLECTIONS: [18th-early 20th c] Paintings, drawings, prints and sculpture, pewter and 18th c German porcelain.

7942
Graceland, Elvis Presley Enterprises
3734 Elvis Presley Blvd, 38116; (p) (901) 332-3322; (f) (901) 344-3128; Graceland@Elvis-Presley.com; www.Elvis-Presley.com; (c) Shelby

Private for-profit/ 1982/ Elvis Presley Ent./ staff: 350(f); 100(p)

HISTORIC SITE; HOUSE MUSEUM: Preserves home of Elvis Presley, including his mansion, office, racquetball courts, gravesite, car museum, personal museum, trophy.

PROGRAMS: Annual Meeting; Concerts; Exhibits; Facility Rental; Festivals; Film/Video

COLLECTIONS: [1900-1970] Costumes, clothing, documents, photos, automobiles, musical instruments, awards, furnishings, memorabilia, recordings, film, Mansion, Heartbreak Hotel, car museum.

HOURS: Yr Daily 9-5

ADMISSION: $18

7943
Historic Elmwood Cemetery
824 S Dudley St, 38104; (p) (901) 774-3212; (f) (901) 774-0085; francat@bellsouth.net; www.elmwoodcemetery.org; (c) Shelby

Joint/ 1852/ Historic Elmwood Cemetery Board of Trustees;Private non-profit/ staff: 4(f); 2(p); 78(v)/publication: The Elmwood Journal

GARDEN; GENEALOGICAL SOCIETY; HISTORIC SITE; LIVING HISTORY/OUTDOOR MUSEUM; RESEARCH CENTER: Emphasizes historic, horticultural and educational aspects of cemetery.

PROGRAMS: Facility Rental; Family Programs; Lectures; Living History; Publication; Research Library/Archives; School-Based Curriculum

COLLECTIONS: [1852-present] Victorian memorial statuary.

HOURS: Yr Daily 8-4:30

7944
Hunt-Phelan Home, The
533 Beale St, 38103 [505 Beale St, 38103]; (p) (901) 525-8225; (f) (601) 525-5042; Hphelan@aol.com; www.Hunt-Phelan.com; (c) Shelby

Private non-profit/ 1992/ Williams B. Day, Jr./ staff: 3(f); 3(p); 1(v)

HOUSE MUSEUM: Promotes history of home used by Grant as Memphis headquarters.

PROGRAMS: Concerts; Exhibits; Facility Rental; Film/Video; Garden Tours; Guided Tours; School-Based Curriculum

COLLECTIONS: [1800-1900] Family artifacts: art, books, photographs, china, jewelry, silverware, war memorabilia, documents. Freedman's Bureau School house for freed slaves on property, slave documents.

HOURS: Yr

7945
Magevney House
198 Adams Ave, 38105 [652 Adams Ave,

38105]; (p) (901) 526-4464; (f) (901) 526-8666

1830/ Memphis Museum System/ staff: 1(f); 12(p)

COLLECTIONS: [1850s] Family history and artifacts.

HOURS: Mar-May, Sep-Dec, T-F, 10-2 Sat, 10-4; Jun-Aug, T-Sat

7946
Mallory-Neely House
652 Adams Ave, 38105; (p) (901) 523-1484; (f) (901) 526-8666

1852/ Memphis Museum System/ staff: 1(f); 12(p); 20(v)

COLLECTIONS: [1890s] Original architectural features of period home; artifacts; books.

HOURS: Mar-Dec, Sat, 10-4; Sun, 1-4

7947
Memphis Pink Palace Museum
3050 Central Ave, 38111; (p) (901) 320-6320; (f) (901) 320-6391; rbristr@memphis.magibox.net; www.memphismuseums.org; (c) Shelby

City/ 1930/ Memphis Park Comm/ staff: 62(f); 114(p); 238(v)/ members: 4200

HISTORY MUSEUM: Interprets the cultural and natural history of the mid South.

PROGRAMS: Community Outreach; Elder's Programs; Exhibits; Facility Rental; Family Programs; Festivals; Interpretation; Lectures

COLLECTIONS: [19th-20th c]

HOURS: Yr Daily 9-5

ADMISSION: $5.50, Children $4

7948
National Civil Rights Museum
450 Mulberry St, 38103; (p) (901) 521-9699; (f) (901) 521-9740; (c) Shelby

Private non-profit/ 1991/ staff: 17(f); 6(p); 45(v)/ members: 600/publication: *Precept and Example*

HISTORIC SITE; HISTORY MUSEUM: Preserves history of movements; Civil Rights Movements history.

PROGRAMS: Community Outreach; Concerts; Exhibits; Facility Rental; Family Programs; Film/Video; Guided Tours; Interpretation; Lectures; Living History; Publication; School-Based Curriculum; Theatre

COLLECTIONS: [1950-1960] Photos, court documents, organizational paper, oral testimonies, video footage, clothing items, transportation vehicles, books, serials, art work.

HOURS: Yr Jan-May, Sept-Dec W-M 9-5; June-Sept W-M 9-6

7949
National Ornamental Metal Museum
374 Metal Museum Dr, 38106; (p) (901) 774-6380; (f) (901) 774-6382; metal@wspice.com; Metal Museum.org; (c) Shelby

Private non-profit/ 1979/ staff: 8(f); 2(p); 20(v)/ members: 998/publication: *NOMM Newsletter*

ART MUSEUM; HISTORIC SITE; HISTORY MUSEUM; LIBRARY AND/OR ARCHIVES: Preserves and advances the art and craft of fine metal work.

PROGRAMS: Community Outreach; Exhibits; Facility Rental; Festivals; Guided Tours; Lectures

COLLECTIONS: [20th c] Architectural iron, jewelry, holoware, sculpture, paper, slides.

ADMISSION: $3, Student $2

7950
Woodruff Fontaine House/Memphis Chapter, APTA
680 Adams Ave, 38105; (p) (901) 526-1469; (f) (901) 526-4531; (c) Shelby

Private non-profit/ 1961/ APTA/ staff: 1(f); 6(p); 15(v)/ members: 120

HISTORIC PRESERVATION AGENCY: Preserves second Empire-style Victorian mansion.

PROGRAMS: Exhibits; Facility Rental; Festivals; Guided Tours; Interpretation

COLLECTIONS: [1870-1928] 19th and early 20th c furnishings, clothing, and accessories.

HOURS: Yr T-Sa 10-4, Su 1-4

ADMISSION: $5, Student $3, Seniors $4

MILLERSVILLE

7951
Museum of Beverage Containers & Advertising
1055 Ridgecrest Dr, 37072; (p) (615) 859-5236; (f) (615) 859-5238; mbca@gono.com; http://www.gono.com/vir-mus/museum.htm; (c) Sumner

Private for-profit/ 1986/ staff: 4(f); 2(p); 2(v)

HISTORY MUSEUM: Promotes history of soda production and advertising.

PROGRAMS: Exhibits

COLLECTIONS: [1950-1990] 36,000 beer and soda cans, bottles, and signs.

HOURS: Yr M-F 9-5

ADMISSION: $4

MORRISTOWN

7952
Crockett Tavern Museum
2002 Morningside Drive, 37814-5459; (p) (423) 587-9900; (c) Hamblen

Private non-profit/ 1852/ staff: 1(p); 1(v)/ members: 30/publication: *Trailblazer*

HISTORIC PRESERVATION AGENCY; HOUSE MUSEUM: Promotes early East TN history and the life of David Crockett.

PROGRAMS: Annual Meeting; Community Outreach; Exhibits; Facility Rental; Family Programs; Festivals; Guided Tours; Interpretation; Living History; Publication; Reenactments; School-Based Curriculum

COLLECTIONS: [1790-1820] Pioneer period artifacts furnishings, tools, spinning and weaving items in boyhood home of David Crockett.

HOURS: May-Oct T-Sa 9-5

ADMISSION: $4, Student $1, Children $1, Seniors $3.50

7953
Rose Center
442 W Second N St, 37816 [PO Box 1976, 37816]; (p) (423) 581-4330; (f) (423) 581-4307; rosecent@usit.net; www.rosecenter.org; (c) Hamblen

Private non-profit/ 1975/ staff: 2 (f); 2 (p);

CULTURAL CENTER: Presents arts and local history.

PROGRAMS: Community Outreach; Concerts; Exhibits; Facility Rental; Family Programs; Festivals; Guided Tours; Lectures; School-Based Curriculum; Theatre

COLLECTIONS: [1890-1940] Art, photos, and documents.

HOURS: Yr M-F 9-5

MURFREESBORO

7954
Cannonsburgh Village
312 S Front St, 37133 [PO Box 748, 37133-0748]; (p) (615) 890-0355; (f) (615) 849-2648; (c) Rutherford

City/ 1976/ Murfreesboro Parks and Rec Dept/ staff: 2(f); 2(p); 100(v)

HISTORIC SITE; HISTORICAL SOCIETY; HISTORY MUSEUM; HOUSE MUSEUM; LIVING HISTORY/OUTDOOR MUSEUM: Collects, preserves, and interprets local Middle TN artifacts.

PROGRAMS: Community Outreach; Concerts; Exhibits; Facility Rental; Festivals; Guided Tours; Interpretation; Living History; Reenactments; School-Based Curriculum

COLLECTIONS: [1860-mid 1900s] Village: Grist Mill, One-room Schoolhouse, Civil War Diorama, 1776-1876 Hayes Museum, 1920s Farm Implement Museum, Williamson Chapel, America Frontier Covered Wagon, 1800s General Store, stones River Garage, 1800s Blacksmith Shop.

HOURS: Late Apr-Dec 1 (Grounds open Yr) T-Sa 10-5, Su 1-5

ADMISSION: No charge

7955
Oaklands Historic House Museum
900 N Maney Ave, 37133 [PO Box 432, 37133]; (p) (615) 983-0022; (c) Rutherford

Private non-profit/ 1959/ Oaklands Association/ staff: 1(f); 1(p); 30(v)/ members: 400

HOUSE MUSEUM: Preserves, maintains, and interprets Oaklands antebellum plantation.

PROGRAMS: Annual Meeting; Exhibits; Facility Rental; Guided Tours; Interpretation; Lectures

COLLECTIONS: [1840-1865] Decorative arts; Rutherford County/Murfreesboro artifacts.

HOURS: Yr Tu-Sa 10-4, Su 1-4

ADMISSION: $4

7956
Stones River National Battlefield
3501 Old Nashville Hwy, 37129; (p) (615) 893-9501; (f) (615) 893-9508; STRI_Administration@nps.gov; www.nps.gov/stri; (c) Rutherford

Federal/ 1927/ National Park Service/ staff: 9(f); 7(p); 35(v)

LIVING HISTORY/OUTDOOR MUSEUM: Commemorates Civil War battle site.

PROGRAMS: Exhibits; Film/Video; Interpretation; Lectures; Living History; Research Library/Archives; School-Based Curriculum

COLLECTIONS: [1927-present] 18 liner feet regimental files, 2,500 volume research library, 10,000 museum artifacts, 25,000 archives.

NASHVILLE

7957
Association for Tennessee History, The
Acklen Station, Box 120735, 37212; (c) Davidson

1990/ staff: 1(p)/publication: *Tennessee History*

Promotes state history.

7958
Association for the Preservation of Tennessee Antiquities (APTA)
110 Leake Ave, 37205; (p) (615) 352-8247; (c) Davidson

Private non-profit/ 1952/ staff: 1(f); 30(v)/ members: 1980/publication: *APTA News*

ALLIANCE OF HISTORICAL AGENCIES; HISTORIC PRESERVATION AGENCY; HISTORY MUSEUM: Preserves local, regional, and state history.

PROGRAMS: Annual Meeting; Community Outreach; Concerts; Exhibits; Facility Rental; Festivals; Guided Tours; Interpretation; Lectures; Living History; Publication; Research Library/Archives

COLLECTIONS: [1780-1900]

HOURS: Yr Daily 9-5

7959
Belle Meade, Queen of Tennessee Plantations
5025 Harding Rd, 37205; (p) (615) 356-0501; (f) (615) 356-2336; bellemeade@home.com; www.bellemeadeplantation.com; (c) Davidson

Private non-profit/ 1952/ Assoc for the Preservation of TN Antiquities, Nashville Chapt./ staff: 17(f); 19(p); 262(v)/ members: 535

HISTORIC SITE; HOUSE MUSEUM: Preserves evolution of frontier cabin to a prosperous farm and nursery.

PROGRAMS: Annual Meeting; Community Outreach; Exhibits; Facility Rental; Festivals; Guided Tours; Interpretation; Lectures; School-Based Curriculum

COLLECTIONS: [1807-1906] Pioneer to Victorian history: 69 paintings, 389 photographs, 288 documents, 409 books, 687 furnishings, and 764 personal artifacts.

HOURS: Yr

7960
Belmont Mansion
1900 Belmont Blvd, 37212; (p) (615) 460-5459; (f) (615) 460-5688; brownm@mail.belmont.edu; www.citysearch.com/nas/belmontmansion; (c) Davidson

Private non-profit/ 1972/ Belmont Mansion Assoc/ staff: 2(f); 17(p); 35(v)/ members: 644/publication: *Belmont Mansion*

HOUSE MUSEUM: Restores 1850 Italian villa style summer home of Adelicia Acklen..

PROGRAMS: Community Outreach; Concerts; Exhibits; Facility Rental; Guided Tours; Interpretation; Lectures; Publication

COLLECTIONS: [1850-1860] Decorative arts.

HOURS: Sept-May T-Sa 10-4; June-Aug M-Sa 10-4, Su 2-5

ADMISSION: $6

7961

Cheekwood-Tennessee Botanical Garden & Museum of Art
1200 Forrest Park Drive, 37205; (p) (615) 356-8000; (f) (615) 353-2168; www.cheekwood.org; (c) Davidson

Private non-profit/ 1957/ Board of Trustees/ staff: 734(f); 50(p); 2500(v)/ members: 9500

ART MUSEUM; GARDEN; HOUSE MUSEUM: Preserves historic mansion.

PROGRAMS: Community Outreach; Concerts; Elder's Programs; Exhibits; Facility Rental; Family Programs; Film/Video; Garden Tours; Guided Tours; Interpretation; Lectures; Publication; Research Library/Archives; School-Based Curriculum

COLLECTIONS: [18th-20th c] American paintings, prints, drawings, photos, sculpture, Worcester porcelain; American & European silver; snuff bottles.

HOURS: Yr M-Sa 9-5, Su 11-5

ADMISSION: $10, Family $25, Student $5, Children $5, Seniors $8

7962
Country Music Foundation
4 Music Square E, 37203; (p) (615) 256-1639; (f) (615) 255-2245; (c) Davidson

1968/ staff: 35(f)/publication: *Journal of Country Music*

HISTORIC SITE; HISTORY MUSEUM; RESEARCH CENTER: Collects and preserves items, and artifacts related to country and folk music of the American South; conducts research on history and evolution of these musical forms.

PROGRAMS: Community Outreach; Exhibits; Facility Rental; Guided Tours; Publication; Research Library/Archives; School-Based Curriculum

COLLECTIONS: [1927-present] Artifacts, County Music Hall of Fame history.

HOURS: Yr Daily 9-5

ADMISSION: $10.75

7963
Disciples of Christ Historical Society
1101 19th Ave S, 37212; (p) (615) 327-1444; (f) (615) 327-1445; dishistsoc@aol.com; (c) Davidson

Private non-profit/ 1941/ Disciples of Christ Historical Society/ staff: 3(f); 5(p); 2(v)/publication: *Discipliana; We're History*

HISTORICAL SOCIETY: Collects, preserves, and disseminates information about the Campbell-Stone Movement (Christian Churches and Churches of Christ), Christian Church (Disciples of Christ and Churches of Christ).

PROGRAMS: Community Outreach; Exhibits; Guided Tours; Interpretation; Lectures; Publication; Research Library/Archives

COLLECTIONS: [1800-Present]

7964
Grassmere Historic Farm
3777 Nolensville Rd, 37211; (p) (615) 833-1534, (615) 832-8239; (f) (615) 333-0728; www.Nashvillezoo.org; (c) Davidson

Private non-profit/ 1997/ Nashville Zoo at Grassmere/ staff: 3(f); 2(p); 10(v)/ members: 5500

HISTORIC SITE; HOUSE MUSEUM; LIVING HISTORY/OUTDOOR MUSEUM: Preserves

historic house, farm, barn, family cemetery, and garden.

PROGRAMS: Exhibits; Facility Rental; Family Programs; Festivals; Garden Tours; Guided Tours; Interpretation; Living History

COLLECTIONS: [1850-1900] Furnishings, clothing and other textiles, books, glassware, silverware, photographic and written documents, artwork, and accessories.

HOURS: Yr Daily Zoo: Apr 1-Oct 31 9-6; Nov 1-Mar 31 9-4; Historic Barn: Apr 1-Oct 31 9-5; Nov 1-Mar 31 9-4

7965
Hartzler-Towner Multicultural Museum at Scarritt Bennett Center
1104 19th Ave S, 37212 [1008 19th Ave S, 37212]; (p) (615) 340-7481; (f) (615) 340-7463; museum.sbc@juno.com; www.umc.org/Scarritt/Museum.html; (c) Davidson

Private non-profit/ 1992/ Scarritt-Bennett Center Board of Trustees/ staff: 1(f); 2(p); 2(v)/ members: 25/publication: *Museum Newsletter*

ANTHROPOLOGY MUSEUM: Promotes cultural history.

PROGRAMS: Community Outreach; Exhibits; Family Programs; Festivals; Publication; School-Based Curriculum

COLLECTIONS: [1920-1970] 4,200 ethnographic artifacts, 700 dolls.

HOURS: Yr Daily M-F 8:30-8:30, Sa 9-6, Su 12-5

7966
Historic Nashville, Inc.
808 Lea Ave Ste 202, 37219 [PO Box 190516, 37219]; (p) (615) 244-7835; (f) (615) 244-7838; HNI@telalink.net; www.historicnashville.org; (c) Davidson

Private non-profit/ 1975/ staff: 1(f); 2(p); 50(v)/ members: 400/publication: *Historic Ink*

HISTORIC PRESERVATION AGENCY: Preserves Nashville architecture and development.

PROGRAMS: Annual Meeting; Exhibits; Family Programs; Guided Tours; Lectures; Publication

COLLECTIONS: Union Station, Nashville architecture.

HOURS: By appt

7967
Metropolitan Board of Parks and Recreation
3130 McGavock Pike, 37201 [Centennial Park Office, 37201]; (p) (615) 885-1112; (f) (615) 872-7528; (c) Davidson

City/ 1859/ staff: 3(f); 5(p); 110(v)

1859 Italianate Style mansion used as rental facility.

7968
Metropolitan Historical Commission of Nashville and Davidson County
209 10th Ave S, Ste 414, 37203; (p) (615) 862-7970; (f) (615) 862-7974; mhc@Nashville.Net; www.nashville.net/~mhc; (c) Davidson

City/ 1966/ staff: 7(f)/publication: *Nashville Architecture*

HISTORIC PRESERVATION AGENCY: Preserves historic buildings, documents architectural history.

PROGRAMS: Community Outreach; Interpretation

7969
Nashville City Cemetery Association
209 10th Ave S, Ste 414, 37203; (p) (615) 862-7970; (f) (615) 862-7974; ncca@Nashville.Net; www.nashville.net/~ncca; (c) Davidson

Private non-profit/ 1998/ Board of Directors/Members/ members: 65/publication: *NCCA Newsletter*

HISTORIC PRESERVATION AGENCY: Restores and preserves the history and architecture of Nashville's oldest remaining public cemetery.

PROGRAMS: Guided Tours; Interpretation; Living History; Publication

HOURS: Yr M-F 8-4:30

7970
Nashville Room Public Library of Nashville, The
2225 Polk Ave, 37203; (p) (615) 862-5783; (f) (615) 862-6884; nashvrm@wend.library. nashville.org; www.library.nashville.org; (c) Davidson

1904/ Board/ staff: 4(f)

LIBRARY AND/OR ARCHIVES: Collects, preserves, and restores Middle TN history.

PROGRAMS: Community Outreach; Exhibits; Lectures; Research Library/Archives

COLLECTIONS: 16,000 books, 1,000 slides, 3,000 photos, 500 oral histories, 500 postcards, maps, TN census, local posters and clippings.

HOURS: Yr M-F 9-8, Sa 9-5, Su 2-5

7971
Parthenon, The
Centennial Park, 37201 [Metro Postal Service, 37201]; (p) (615) 862-8431; (f) (615) 880-2265; info@parthenon.org; www.parthenon.org; (c) Davidson

Joint/ 1897/ Nashville/Davidson Co., Metropolitan Parks & Recreation/ staff: 11(f); 1(p); 23(v)/ members: 600/publication: *Cowan Catalogue; Tale of Two Parthenons*

ARCHAEOLOGICAL SITE/MUSEUM; HISTORY MUSEUM: Exhibits and collects visual art; educates the public concerning 5th c BC Greece and the TN Centennial.

PROGRAMS: Community Outreach; Concerts; Exhibits; Facility Rental; Guided Tours; Interpretation; Lectures; Publication; School-Based Curriculum

COLLECTIONS: [5th c BC -20th c] Statue of Athena and casts of the Elgin Marbles; art exhibits.

HOURS: Yr T-Sa 9-4:30, Su 12:30-4:30

ADMISSION: $2.50, Children $1.25, Seniors $1.25

7972
Scarritt-Bennett Center
1008 19th Ave S, 37212-2166; (p) (615) 340-7500; (f) (615) 340-7463; pr@scarrittbennett.org; www.scarrittbennett.org; (c) Davidson

Private non-profit/ 1988/ Board of Trustees/ staff: 30(f); 16(p); 250(v)

GARDEN; HISTORIC SITE; HISTORY MUSEUM

PROGRAMS: Concerts; Elder's Programs; Exhibits; Facility Rental; Family Programs; Festivals; Garden Tours; Guided Tours; Interpreta-

tion; Research Library/Archives; School-Based Curriculum

COLLECTIONS: Library: religion, women's issues, sociology.

HOURS: Yr M-F 8-8, Sa 9-5, Su 1-6

ADMISSION: No charge

7973
Society of Tennessee Archivists
c/o 403 Seventh Ave N, 37243-0312; (p) (615) 253-3471; (f) (615) 741-6471; drsowell@earthlink.net; www.arkay.net/tnarchivist; (c) Davidson

Private non-profit/ 1977/ staff: 5(v)/ members: 210/publication: *Tennessee Archivist*

PROFESSIONAL ORGANIZATION: Promotes the educational development and professionalism of archives in TN.

PROGRAMS: Annual Meeting; Community Outreach

7974
Southern Baptist Historical Library and Archives
901 Commerce St, #400, 37203-3630; (p) (615) 244-0344; (f) (615) 782-4821; bsumners@edge.net; www.sbhla.org; (c) Davidson

Private non-profit/ 1985/ Council of Seminary Presidents, Southern Baptist Convention/ staff: 4(f); 3(p); 1(v)

LIBRARY AND/OR ARCHIVES: Promotes Baptist life and history.

PROGRAMS: Exhibits; Research Library/Archives

COLLECTIONS: [1800-Present] Books, periodicals, microfilm, photos, audio-visuals, and archival material.

HOURS: Yr M-F 9-4

ADMISSION: No charge

7975
Tennessee Agricultural Museum
Ellington Agricultural Center, 37204; (p) (615) 837-5197; (f) (615) 837-5194; www.state.tn.us/agriculture/agmuseum.html; (c) Davidson

State/ 1979/ TN Dept of Agriculture/ staff: 1(f); 2(p); 3(v)/ members: 109

HISTORY MUSEUM

PROGRAMS: Annual Meeting; Exhibits; Festivals; Living History; School-Based Curriculum

COLLECTIONS: [1840-1900] 3,000 artifacts: household and kitchen items, blacksmithing, logging and woodworking tools, buggies, wagons, plows, pictorial exhibits, folk art sculptures; large farm and dairy equipment: butter press, wheat thresher, McCormick's reaper, steam engine, and pile driver.

7976
Tennessee Historical Commission
2941 Lebanon Rd, 37243-0442; (p) (615) 532-1550; (f) (615) 532-1549; (c) Davidson

State/ 1918/ staff: 15(f)/publication: *The Courier*

HISTORIC PRESERVATION AGENCY: Preserves state history, including historic sites, markers, publications; acts as state preservation agency under the National Historic Preservation Act.

PROGRAMS: Community Outreach; Publication

HOURS: Yr 8-4:30

7977
Tennessee Historical Society
War Memorial Building, 37243-0084; (p) (615) 741-8934; (f) (615) 741-8937; tnhissoc@isdn.net; (c) Davidson

Private non-profit/ 1849/ Tennessee Historical Society/ staff: 3(f); 1(p)/ members: 2000/publication: *Tennessee Historical Quarterly*

HISTORICAL SOCIETY: Collects, preserves, and interprets state history.

PROGRAMS: Annual Meeting; Community Outreach; Lectures; Publication

COLLECTIONS: Manuscripts, photos and print materials; museum artifacts.

HOURS: Yr M-F 8-4:30

7978
Tennessee State Library and Archives
403 Seventh Avenue N, 37243-0312; (p) (615) 741-2764; (f) (615) 741-6471; reference@mail.state.tn.us; www.state.tn.us/sos/statelib; (c) Davidson

State/ 1854/ staff: 98(f)

LIBRARY AND/OR ARCHIVES: Serves as official repository of State records; provides reference and research services through Public Services Section and Library for the Blind and Physically Handicapped; assists state regional libraries; provides educational, historical, and general information to the public.

PROGRAMS: Research Library/Archives

COLLECTIONS: [Prehistoric-Present] Books, journals, manuscripts, maps, photos, microfilm, audio/visual materials, and state agency records.

HOURS: Yr M-Sa 8-6

7979
Tennessee State Museum
5th Deaderick St, 37243 [505 Deaderick St, 37243-1120]; (p) (615) 741-2692; (f) (615) 741-7231; info@tnmuseum.org; (c) Davidson

State/ 1937/ staff: 40(f); 2(p); 25(v)/ members: 700/publication: *Exhibit Catalogs*

HISTORY MUSEUM: Promotes state history and culture.

PROGRAMS: Community Outreach; Exhibits; Facility Rental; Family Programs; Festivals; Guided Tours; Lectures; Publication; Research Library/Archives; School-Based Curriculum

COLLECTIONS: [1780-Present] 100,000 objects: silver, quilts, coverlets, furniture, and firearms, historic figures, military history, and events.

HOURS: Yr T-Sa 10-5, Su 1-5

7980
Travellers Rest Historic House Museum, Inc.
636 Farrell Pkwy, 37220; (p) (615) 452-8197; (f) (615) 832-8169; travrest@mindspring.com; travrest.home.mindspring.com; (c) Davidson

Private non-profit/ 1989/ staff: 4(f); 8(p); 1(v)/ members: 1500

HISTORIC SITE; HOUSE MUSEUM: Preserves, researches, and interprets historic house, collections, and grounds that represent life in Middle TN.

PROGRAMS: Concerts; Exhibits; Facility

Rental; Family Programs; Festivals; Guided Tours; Lectures; Reenactments; Research Library/Archives; School-Based Curriculum

COLLECTIONS: [1799-1833] 1,500 items: furniture, books and weaving equipment.

HOURS: Yr T-Sa 10-5

7981
Upper Room Chapel and Museum, The
1908 Grand Ave, 37212; (p) (615) 340-7207; (f) (615) 340-7293; kkimball@upperroom.org; www.upperroom.org; (c) Davidson

Private non-profit/ 1953/ The United Methodist Church/ staff: 3(f); 4(p)/publication: *The Upper Room Devotional Guide*

HISTORY MUSEUM

PROGRAMS: Exhibits; Guided Tours; Interpretation; Publication

COLLECTIONS: [1600-1900] Christian art and artifacts, manuscripts, English proclaims, nativity scenes, oriental rugs and furniture.

HOURS: Yr M-F 8-4:30

NORRIS

7982
Museum of Appalachia
Hwy 61, 37828 [PO Box 1189, 37828]; (p) (423) 494-7680, (426) 494-0514; (f) (423) 494-8957; (c) Anderson

Private for-profit/ 1969/ John Rice Irwin/ staff: 10(f); 18(p)

ART MUSEUM; HISTORIC SITE; HISTORY MUSEUM; HOUSE MUSEUM; LIVING HISTORY/OUTDOOR MUSEUM: Interprets 65 acre farm/village complex with 30 log cabins and buildings, the Appalachian Hall of Fame.

PROGRAMS: Concerts; Exhibits; Facility Rental; Festivals; Interpretation; Publication

COLLECTIONS: [1800-1900] Musical instruments, Indian relics, baskets, medical instruments, funeral items, folk art, quilts, pottery, agricultural artifacts.

PALL MALL

7983
Alvin C. York State Historic Site
2700 N York Hwy, 38577; (p) (931) 879-6456; (c) Fentress

State/ 1968/ State Park Division/ staff: 3(f); 1(p)

HISTORIC SITE

PROGRAMS: Lectures

COLLECTIONS: Portraits, photos.

HOURS: Yr M-Su 9-5

PARIS

7984
Paris-Henry County Heritage Center
614 N Poplar St, 38242 [PO Box 822, 38242-0822]; (p) (901) 642-1030; (f) (901) 642-1096; heritage@aeneas.net; (c) Henry

Private non-profit/ 1989/ Board of Trustees/ staff: 1(f); 1(p); 30(v)/ members: 350/publication: *Inkwell*

HISTORY MUSEUM: Preserves local history.

PROGRAMS: Annual Meeting; Exhibits; Facility Rental; Family Programs; Festivals; Film/Video; Guided Tours; Interpretation; Publication; Research Library/Archives; School-Based Curriculum

COLLECTIONS: [1826-1999] Artifacts, clothing, video, and photos.

HOURS: Yr M-F 9-5

PINEY FLATS

7985
Cobb-Massengill House
200 Hyder Hill Rd, 37686; (p) (423) 538-7396, (423) 538-9527; (f) (423) 538-5983; rmm@preferred.com

1770/ Rocky Mount Museum/ staff: 3(f); 13(p); 269(v)

COLLECTIONS: [1791] Early American coverlets.

PINSON

7986
Pinson Mounds State Park
460 Ozier Rd, 38366; (p) (901) 988-5614; (f) (901) 424-3909; Pinson@erc.jscc.cc.tn.us; erc.jscc.cc.tn.us/pinson; (c) Madison

State/ 1979/ TN Dept of Environment and Conservation, TN State Parks/ staff: 5(f); 3(p); 2(v)

HISTORIC SITE; HISTORY MUSEUM: Protects and preserves monumental mound complex built by prehistoric Native Americans during the Middle Woodland period and dates to 200 BC-500 AD.

PROGRAMS: Exhibits; Family Programs; Festivals; Film/Video; Guided Tours; Interpretation; Lectures; Research Library/Archives; Theatre

HOURS: Yr Mar-Nov M-Sa 8-4:30, Su 1-5; Dec-Feb M-F 8-4:30

PULASKI

7987
Giles County Historical Society
122 S 2nd St, 38478 [PO Box 693, 38478]; (p) (931) 363-2720; (c) Giles

Private non-profit/ 1974/ staff: 30(v)/ members: 600/publication: *Giles County Historical Society Bulletin*

GENEALOGICAL SOCIETY; HISTORIC PRESERVATION AGENCY; HISTORIC SITE; HISTORICAL SOCIETY; HISTORY MUSEUM; HOUSE MUSEUM; RESEARCH CENTER: Genealogical library and museum; striving to maintain the history of Giles County's past people and events.

PROGRAMS: Annual Meeting; Community Outreach; Exhibits; Guided Tours; Interpretation; Publication; Research Library/Archives

COLLECTIONS: [1809-1900] Civil War item, carry county history, church history, library of over 1800 books, over 680 rolls of micro-film and over 700 verti-fines of information.

7988
Sam Davis Memorial Museum
Sam Davis Ave, 38478 [PO Box 693, 122 S 2nd St, 38478]; (p) (931) 363-2720; (c) Giles

Joint/ 1963/ State; Private non-profit/ staff: 4(v)

HISTORIC SITE; HISTORY MUSEUM: Museum dedicated to the memory of Sam Davis, a Civil War soldier who was hung on this site.

PROGRAMS: Exhibits; Interpretation; Living History

COLLECTIONS: [1861-1863] Civil War items, including the iron shackles which bound Davis while he was a union prisoner in Pulaski; also items from the Davis family.

HOURS: 2nd Su 2-4

ROGERSVILLE

7989
Rogersville Heritage Association
415 S Depot St, 37857; (p) (426) 272-1961; (f) (426) 272-1961; (c) Hawkins

Private non-profit/ 1978/ Rogersville Heritage Association/ staff: 1(f)/ members: 350

HISTORIC PRESERVATION AGENCY; HISTORIC SITE; HISTORY MUSEUM: Preserves and restores artifacts related to local history.

PROGRAMS: Annual Meeting; Concerts; Exhibits; Facility Rental; Festivals

COLLECTIONS: [1800s] Newspapers; printing, railroad artifacts.

HOURS: Yr T-Th 10-4

ADMISSION: $1, Student $0.50

RUGBY

7990
Historic Rugby, Inc.
Hwy 52, 37733 [PO Box 8, 37733]; (p) (423) 628-2441; (f) (423) 628-2266; rigbytn@highland.net; www.historicrugby.org; (c) Morgan

Private non-profit/ 1966/ Historic Rugby/ staff: 25(f); 8(p); 30(v)/ members: 800/publication: *The Rugbeian*

HISTORIC SITE: Restores, preserves, and interprets the architectural, cultural, and natural resources of Rugby Colony National Register Historic District.

PROGRAMS: Annual Meeting; Community Outreach; Elder's Programs; Exhibits; Facility Rental; Family Programs; Festivals; Garden Tours; Guided Tours; Interpretation; Lectures; Living History; Publication; Research Library/Archives

COLLECTIONS: [1860-1900] Historic buildings, Victorian furnishings and decorative objects, 7,000 volume Victorian literature, archival manuscripts, historic photographs and colony records.

HOURS: Yr M-Sa 9:30-5, Su 11-5

ADMISSION: $4.50, Family $15, Student $2.25, Seniors $4

RUTHERFORD

7991
David Crockett Cabin-Museum
218 N Trenton St, 38369 [945 S Trenton St, 38369]; (p) (901) 665-7253; (f) (901) 665-6195

1955/ David Crockett Cabin Commission for the town of Rutherford.

Promotes David Crockett history.

COLLECTIONS: [1822-1856] Replica of period furnished home; artifacts: bearskin, beaver, bobcat, elk antlers, hornets nests, broad axes, froes, rifles, pistols kitchen utensils, tools, Indian rocks.

SAVANNAH

7992
Tennessee River Museum
507 Main St, 38372; (p) (901) 925-2364; (f) (901) 925-6987; teamhardin@centuryinter.net; www.tourhardincnty.org; (c) Hardin

Private non-profit/ 1992/ staff: 2(p); 3(v)

HISTORY MUSEUM: Preserves and presents natural, local, and military history.

PROGRAMS: Annual Meeting; Exhibits; Film/Video

COLLECTIONS: [Prehistory-present] Cretaceous fossils, archaeological artifacts, Shiloh Effigy Pipe, Civil War, steamboat.

HOURS: Yr Daily M-Sa 9-5, Su 1-5

ADMISSION: $2

SHELBYVILLE

7993
Tennessee Walking Horse National Celebration/Tennessee Walking Horse Museum
1110 Evans St, 37162 [PO Box 1010, 37162]; (p) (931) 684-5915; (f) (931) 684-5949; twhnc@twhnc.com; www.twhnc.com; (c) Bedford

Private non-profit/ 1939/ Celebration, Inc./ staff: 14(f)/publication: *Blue Ribbon Yearbook*

HISTORY MUSEUM: Interprets, presents, and exhibits history of TN Walking Horse Breed.

PROGRAMS: Community Outreach; Concerts; Exhibits; Facility Rental; Festivals; Guided Tours; Publication

COLLECTIONS: Walking Horse artifacts.

HOURS: Yr M-F 9-4:30

ADMISSION: $3, Children $2, Seniors $2

SHILOH

7994
Shiloh National Military Park
1055 Pittsburg Landing Road, 38376; (p) (901) 689-5275; (f) (901) 689-5450; shil_interpretation@NPS.gov; (c) Hardin

Federal/ 1894/ staff: 6(f); 6(p)

HISTORY MUSEUM: Promotes Civil War history.

PROGRAMS: Exhibits; Film/Video; Guided Tours; Interpretation; Living History

COLLECTIONS: [Mid-late 19th c] Union and Confederate artifacts.

HOURS: Yr M-Th 9-9, F-Sa 9-6, May-Sept Su 2-6

SMYRNA

7995
Sam Davis Memorial Association
1399 Sam Davis Rd, 37167; (p) (615) 459-2341, (888) 750-9524; (f) (615) 459-2341; (c) Rutherford

Private non-profit/ 1930/ Sam Davis Memorial Association/ staff: 2(f); 6(p); 140(v)/ members: 380

HISTORIC SITE: Promotes life of Sam Davis and 19th century farm family.

PROGRAMS: Annual Meeting; Community Outreach; Exhibits; Facility Rental; Festivals; Film/Video; Guided Tours; Interpretation; Reenactments

COLLECTIONS: [1840-1880] Confederate military items, textiles, furniture, and decorative arts.

HOURS: Yr May-Sept M-Sa 10-4, Su 1-4; June-Aug M-Sa 9-5, Su 1-5

ADMISSION: $5

SPARTA

7996
Rock House Shrine Sparta Rock House Chapter DAR
3663 Country Club Rd, 38583; (p) (931) 761-2885; (c) White

State/ 1930/ TN Historical Com/ staff: 2(p)/ members: 52/publication: *The Rock House Shrine*

HISTORIC PRESERVATION AGENCY

PROGRAMS: Facility Rental; Interpretation; Lectures; Living History; Publication; Research Library/Archives

COLLECTIONS: [1776-present] Period furnishing in home used as stage coach stop by Andrew Jackson.

HOURS: Mar-Dec W, F, Sa 10-2

ADMISSION: No charge

TAZEWELL

7997
Clairborne County Historical Society
[PO Box 32, 37879-0032]; (p) (426) 626-7261; (c) Clairborne

Private non-profit/ 1987/ members: 376/publication: *Reflections*

GENEALOGICAL SOCIETY: Collects and preserves county history.

PROGRAMS: Publication

COLLECTIONS: Collected histories, marriage records.

TRENTON

7998
City of Trenton
309 S College St, 38330; (p) (901) 855-2013; (f) (901) 855-1091; (c) Gibson

City/publication: *Rare Porcelain Veilleuses Collection*

Conduct tours of the Veilleuse Theieres collection and also of the house donated by the family.

COLLECTIONS: [1790-1890] 525 porcelain veilleuses theieres from Europe, Asia and North Africa

HOURS: Yr Daily 24 hrs

TULLAHOMA

7999
Mitchell Museum, Floyd & Margaret
404 S Jackson St, 37388 [PO Box 326,

37388]; (p) (931) 455-7239; (f) (931) 455-8340; sojack@midtnn.net; (c) Coffee

Private non-profit/ 1979/ South Jackson Civic Association/ staff: 1(f); 50(v)/ members: 236

HISTORY MUSEUM: Promotes local history.

PROGRAMS: Annual Meeting; Community Outreach; Concerts; Exhibits; Facility Rental; Family Programs; Festivals; Guided Tours; Theatre

COLLECTIONS: [1852-1952] Artifacts: Railroad, Civil War, World War II, Camp Forrest, and aerospace.

UNION CITY

8000
Obion Co. Museum, The
1400 Edwards, 38261; (p) (901) 885-6774; rebelc@eddn.com; (c) Obion

City/ 1963/ Board/ staff: 10(v)

HISTORY MUSEUM

PROGRAMS: Community Outreach; Exhibits; Guided Tours; Living History

COLLECTIONS: [1890-1940] Area photos, period clothing, tools, artifacts.

HOURS: Sa-Su 1-4

VONORE

8001
Fort Loudoun State Historic Area
338 Ft Loudoun Rd, 37885; (p) (423) 884-6217; (f) (423) 884-2287; (c) Monroe

State/ 1978/ Tennessee State Parks/ staff: 5(f); 4(p); 40(v)/ members: 120

HISTORIC SITE; HISTORY MUSEUM; LIVING HISTORY/OUTDOOR MUSEUM: Iinterprets life at the southwestern-most outpost of the British Empire and first English settlement west of Allegheny Mountains.

PROGRAMS: Concerts; Exhibits; Film/Video; Guided Tours; Interpretation; Lectures; Living History; Reenactments

COLLECTIONS: [18th c] Reconstruction of 18th c fortification, artifacts.

HOURS: Yr Daily 8-4:30

WINCHESTER

8002
Old Jail Museum
400 Dinah Shore Blvd, 37398; (p) (931) 967-0534; (c) Franklin

Joint/ 1973/ County; Nancy Hall/ staff: 1(f); 8(v)

HISTORIC SITE; HISTORY MUSEUM

PROGRAMS: Annual Meeting; Exhibits; Festivals; Guided Tours

COLLECTIONS: [18th-20th c] Interpretive rooms: pioneer room, Civil War, World War I, II.

HOURS: Mar-Nov 10-4

ADMISSION: $1, Children $0.50

TEXAS

ABILENE

8003
Grace Museum, The
102 Cypress St, 79601; (p) (915) 673-4587; (f) (915) 675-5993; moa@abilene.com; www.thegracemuseum.org; (c) Taylor

Private non-profit/ 1937/ staff: 10(f); 6(p); 80(v)/ members: 1000

ART MUSEUM; HISTORIC SITE; HISTORY MUSEUM: Collects, preserves and interprets local history.

PROGRAMS: Annual Meeting; Community Outreach; Concerts; Exhibits; Facility Rental; Family Programs; Festivals; Guided Tours; Interpretation; Lectures; Research Library/ Archives

COLLECTIONS: [1900-1950] 5,400 historical items, 400 photographs, oral histories and personal records. 6 period rooms display evolution of technology.

HOURS: Yr M-Sa 10-5

ADMISSION: $3, Children $1, Seniors $2

ALBANY

8004
Old Jail Art Center, The
201 S 2nd, 76430; (p) (915) 762-2269; (f) (915) 762-2260; ojac@camalott.com; www.albanytexas.com; (c) Shackelford

Private non-profit/ 1980/ staff: 4(f); 1(p); 50(v)/ members: 700

ART MUSEUM; LIBRARY AND/OR ARCHIVES: 20th century British and American art and history.

PROGRAMS: Community Outreach; Concerts; Exhibits; Facility Rental; Family Programs; Festivals; Film/Video; Lectures; Research Library/Archives

COLLECTIONS: [20th c] Pre-Columbian, Chinese tomb figures, paintings by Paul Klee, Modigliani, Picasso and Henry Moore.

HOURS: Yr T-Sa 10-5, Su 2-5

ADMISSION: No charge

ALPINE

8005
Museum of the Big Bend
Sul Ross State University, 79832 [PO Box C-210, 79832]; (p) (915) 837-8143; (f) (915) 837-8381; (c) Brewester

State/ 1926/ Sul Ross State University/ staff: 4(f); 5(p); 15(v)

HISTORY MUSEUM: Promotes Native American, Mexican and Anglo American history.

PROGRAMS: Community Outreach; Elder's Programs; Exhibits; Family Programs; Festivals; Film/Video; Guided Tours; Lectures; Research Library/Archives

COLLECTIONS: [6,000 BC-mid 20th c] Prehistoric Native American material; tools, textiles, firearms, decorative arts and household wares.

HOURS: Yr T-Sa 9-5, Su 1-5

ADMISSION: Donations accepted

ALVIN

8006
Alvin Museum Society
[PO Box 1902, 77512]; (p) (281) 585-2803; (c) Brazoria

Private non-profit/ 1976/ Alvin Museum Society Board of Trustees/ staff: 40(v)/ members: 275

HISTORICAL SOCIETY; HISTORY MUSEUM; HOUSE MUSEUM

PROGRAMS: Community Outreach; Exhibits; Interpretation; Lectures; School-Based Curriculum

COLLECTIONS: Alvin's history from settlement (circa 1870) to the present: artifacts; legal, commercial, and family documents; written and oral family histories; photographs; portraits and paintings; indexed censuses; and microfilmed newspapers, 1900-present.

AMARILLO

8007
American Quarter Horse Heritage Center and Museum
2601 I-40 East, 79104; (p) (806) 376-5181; (f) (806) 376-1005; museum@aqha.org; www.aqha.com; (c) Potter

Private non-profit/ 1988/ American Quarter Horse Foundation/ staff: 8(f); 5(p); 25(v)

HERITAGE AREA: Collects, preserves, and interprets the history and modern-day activities of the American Quarter Horse.

PROGRAMS: Exhibits; Facility Rental; Interpretation; Research Library/Archives

COLLECTIONS: [1940-present] 2000 historical items, including tack, race and show trophies, race memorabilia, sculptures and paintings; 20,000 archival items, including historical photos, manuscripts, corporate records and publications, periodicals, and film.

HOURS: Yr Su 12-5, M-Sa 9-5

ADMISSION: $4, Student $2.50, Seniors $3.50; Under 7 free

8008
Harrington House
1600 S Polk, 79102; (p) (806) 374-5490; (c) Potter

Private non-profit/ 1983/ Harrington House Foundation/ staff: 3(f); 1(p); 16(v)

HOUSE MUSEUM: Preserves home built by Amarillo pioneers and cattlemen Pat and John Landergin.

PROGRAMS: Exhibits; Guided Tours

COLLECTIONS: [1914-1980] French and English furnishings; decorative arts.

HOURS: Apr-mid Dec T-Th 10-12:30 by appt.

ANGLETON

8009
Brazoria County Historical Museum
100 E Cedar, 77515; (p) (479) 864-1208; (f) (479) 864-1217; bchm@bchm.org; bchm.org; (c) Brazoria

County, non-profit/ 1983/ staff: 8(f); 350(v)/ members: 400/publication: The Windowpane

HISTORIC SITE; HISTORICAL SOCIETY; HISTORY MUSEUM; RESEARCH CENTER: Collects, preserves, exhibits, and educates the public on the history of Brazoria County.

PROGRAMS: Annual Meeting; Community Outreach; Exhibits; Facility Rental; Festivals; Guided Tours; Interpretation; Lectures; Living History; Publication; Reenactments; Research Library/Archives

COLLECTIONS: [1820-present] 10,000 artifacts, letters, newspapers, maps, blueprints, and legal documents; 1,200 books; 200 tapes; 4,000 photos; and 800 vertical files housed in the research center.

HOURS: Yr M-F 9-5, Sa 9-3

ADMISSION: Donations accepted

ARLINGTON

8010
Legends of the Game Baseball Museum
1000 Ballpark Way, 76004 [PO Box 90111, 76004-3111]; (p) (817) 273-5600; (f) (817) 273-5093; www.texasrangers.com; (c) Dallas

Private for-profit/ 1994/ staff: 11(f); 15(p)

HISTORY MUSEUM

PROGRAMS: Community Outreach; Exhibits; Facility Rental; Family Programs; Guided Tours; Lectures; School-Based Curriculum; Theatre

COLLECTIONS: [1970-1990] National Baseball Hall of Fame exhibits; sporting artifacts.

HOURS: Apr-Oct M-Sa 9-6:30, Su 12-4; Nov-Mar T-Sa 9-4, Su 12-4

8011
University of Texas at Arlington, University Libraries, Special Collections Division
702 College St, 76019 [Box 19497, 76019-0497]; (p) (817) 272-3393; (f) (817) 272-3360; scref@library.uta.edu; www.uta.edu/library/SpecColl; (c) Tarrant

State/ 1974/ Univ of TX/ staff: 7(f); 3(p); 1(v)/publication: Compass Rose

LIBRARY AND/OR ARCHIVES: Preserves materials in all formats related to the history of TX, the Mexican American War, Mexico (1810-1920); cartographic history of TX and Gulf of Mexico.

PROGRAMS: Exhibits; Publication; Research Library/Archives

COLLECTIONS: [16th c-present] Books, archives/manuscripts, journals, maps, sheet music, graphics, photos, clippings, and oral histories.

HOURS: Yr M 9-7, T-Sa 9-5

ADMISSION: No charge

AUSTIN

8012
Austin Children's Museum
201 Colorado, 78704; (p) (512) 472-2499; (f) (512) 472-2495; www.austinkids.org; (c) Travis

Private non-profit/ 1983/ Board of Directors/ staff: 20(f); 51(p); 107(v)/ members: 1250

HISTORY MUSEUM: Provides innovative, participatory museum exhibits, programs, and resources.

PROGRAMS: Community Outreach; Concerts; Exhibits; Facility Rental; Festivals; Guided Tours;

8013
Center for American History, The University of Texas at Austin
2313 Red River, 78712 [Sid Richardson Hall 2101, Univ of Texas, 78712]; (p) (512) 495-4515; (f) (512) 495-4542; cahreA@ uts.cc.utexas.edu; www.cah.utexas.edu; (c) Travis

State/ Univ of Texas at Austin/ staff: 55(f); 7(v)

LIBRARY AND/OR ARCHIVES: Facilitates research; sponsors programs on the historical development of US.

PROGRAMS: Community Outreach; Exhibits; Facility Rental; Festivals; Guided Tours; Lectures; Publication; Research Library/Archives

COLLECTIONS: [19th-20th c] Archives, books, maps, newspapers, photos and sound recordings, the Southwest, the deep South and the Rocky Mountain West; Congress, the media, Civil Rights, traveling entertainment industry, Univ of TX and oral history program.

HOURS: (Research/Collections Div, UT Austin) Yr M-Sa 9-5

ADMISSION: No charge

8014
Elisabet Ney Museum
304 E 44th St, 78751; (p) (512) 458-2255; (f) (512) 453-0638; elisabetney@earthlink.net; (c) Travis

City/ 1911/ staff: 2(f); 2(p); 15(v)/ members: 110

ART MUSEUM; HISTORIC SITE; HISTORY MUSEUM: Preserves life and works of Elisabeth Ney.

PROGRAMS: Community Outreach; Exhibits; Family Programs; Guided Tours; Interpretation; Lectures; Research Library/Archives; School-Based Curriculum

COLLECTIONS: [1833-1907] Portraits, sculptures and personal memorabilia housed in Ney's former studio.

HOURS: Yr W-Sa 10-5, Su 12-5

ADMISSION: No charge

8015
Friends of the Governor's Mansion
[PO Box 2447, 78768]; (p) (512) 474-9960; (f) (512) 474-1164; admin@txfgm.org; www.txfgm.org; (c) Travis

Private non-profit/ 1979/ staff: 1(f); 175(v)/ members: 90

HOUSE MUSEUM: Provides curatorial services, educational programs and docents for the TX Governor's Mansion.

PROGRAMS: Guided Tours; School-Based Curriculum

COLLECTIONS: [19th c] American Federal and Empire decorative arts located in 1856 Greek Revival house that has been the residence of every TX governor since its completion.

HOURS: Yr M-F 10-12

ADMISSION: No charge

8016
Jourdan Bachman Pioneer Farm
11418 Sprinkle Cut Off Rd, 78754; (p) (512) 837-1215; (f) (512) 837-4503; jbfarmer@eden.com; www.pioneerfarm.org; (c) Travis

City/ 1977/ staff: 7(f); 4(p); 60(v)/ members: 100/publication: Guidebook; Sharecropper's Memoirs

LIVING HISTORY/OUTDOOR MUSEUM: Portrays the agrarian lifestyle of four different families typical to the area.

PROGRAMS: Annual Meeting; Community Outreach; Exhibits; Facility Rental; Family Programs; Festivals; Garden Tours; Guided Tours; Interpretation; Living History; School-Based Curriculum

COLLECTIONS: [1880s] Artifacts of commercial farmer, a small scale traditional farmer, an African American tenant farmer, and a German immigrant farmer. 10,000 items that depict life in rural central TX; furniture, textiles, farm equipment and tools.

HOURS: Yr M-Th 9:30-1, Su 1-5

ADMISSION: $4, Children $3

8017
Lyndon B. Johnson Library
2313 Red River St, 78705-5702; (p) (512) 916-5702; (f) (512) 916-5171; library@johnson.nara.gov; www.nara.gov; (c) Travis

8018
Neill-Cochran House
2310 San Gabriel St, 78705-5014; (p) (512) 478-2335

8019
O. Henry Museum
409 E 5th St, 78701; (p) (512) 472-1903; (f) (512) 472-7102; www.ci.austin.tx.us/parks/ohenry.htm; (c) Travis

City/ 1934/ staff: 1(f); 1(p); 10(v)/ members: 100

HISTORIC SITE; HOUSE MUSEUM: Collects, preserves, and interprets artifacts and archival materials.

PROGRAMS: Annual Meeting; Community Outreach; Exhibits; Family Programs; Festivals; Guided Tours; Interpretation; Lectures

COLLECTIONS: [1880s-1910] Articles and memorabilia.

HOURS: Yr W-Su 12-5

ADMISSION: No charge

8020
State Preservation Board
201 E 14th St, Ste 950, 78711 [PO Box 13286, 78711]; (p) (512) 463-5495; (f) (512) 475-3366; www.tspb.state.tx.us; (c) Travis

State/ 1983/ staff: 77(f)

HISTORIC SITE: Restores, preserves and maintains the capitol, the 1857 general land office building.

PROGRAMS: Exhibits; Guided Tours; Interpretation; Research Library/Archives; School-Based Curriculum

COLLECTIONS: [1888-1915] Original and period objects, artwork, furnishings and decorative arts.

HOURS: Yr M-F 8-5, Sa-Su 9-5

ADMISSION: No charge

8021
Texas Association of Museums
3939 Bee Caves Rd, Bldg A, Ste 1-B, 78746; (p) (512) 328-6812; (f) (512) 327-9775; tam@io.com; www.io.com/~tam; (c) Travis

Private non-profit/ 1975/ staff: 3(f)/ members: 830/publication: Museline; The Museum Forms Book

PROFESSIONAL ORGANIZATION: Fosters educational, cultural, and recreational opportunities; sponsors educational programs; encourages adherence to professional standards and practices.

PROGRAMS: Annual Meeting; Publication

8022
Texas Catholic Historical Society
1625 Rutherford Lane, Bldg D, 78754-5105; (p) (512) 339-9882; jd10@swt.edu; www.onr.com/user/cat/tchs.htm; (c) Travis

Private non-profit/ 1926/ staff: 7(v)/ members: 300/publication: Catholic Southwest: A Journal of History and Culture

HISTORICAL SOCIETY: Promotes and disseminates research regarding the state's Catholic heritage.

PROGRAMS: Annual Meeting;

8023
Texas Folklife Resources
1317 S Congress, 78704; (p) (512) 441-9255; (f) (512) 441-9222; tfr@10.com; www.main.org/tfr; (c) Travis

Private non-profit/ staff: 6(f); 1(p); 1(v)

CULTURAL CENTER: Perpetuates the traditional arts and culture of the Lone Star State.

PROGRAMS: Community Outreach; Concerts; Exhibits; Facility Rental; Family Programs; Festivals; Lectures; Research Library/Archives; School-Based Curriculum

COLLECTIONS: [19th-20th c] Photos, audio recordings of music, interviews of TX traditional artists.

8024
Texas Governor's Mansion
1010 Colorado, 78701; (p) (512) 463-5518; (f) (512) 463-1850; www.txfgm.org; (c) Travis

State/ 1856/ staff: 7(p); 100(v)/publication: Brochures

HISTORIC SITE; HOUSE MUSEUM

PROGRAMS: Garden Tours; Guided Tours; Publication

COLLECTIONS: [19th c] American Federal and American Empire furnishings.

HOURS: Yr M-F 10-12

ADMISSION: No charge

8025
Texas Historical Commission
1511 N Colorado, 78711 [PO Box 12276, 78711]; (p) (512) 463-6100; (f) (512) 475-4872; www.thc.state.tx.us; (c) Travis

State/ 1953/ staff: 100(f); 20(p)

Preserves the archaeological, historical, and cultural resources of TX.

HOURS: Yr M-F 8-5

8026
Texas Medical Association
401 W 15th St, 78701-1680; (p) (512) 370-1550, (800) 880-1300; (f) (512) 370-1634; tma_library@texmed.org; www.texmed.org; (c) Travis

Private non-profit/ 1853/ Board of Trustees/ staff: 175(f); 8(p)/ members: 37000

HISTORY MUSEUM: Promotes health care history in TX.

PROGRAMS: Exhibits; Research Library/ Archives

COLLECTIONS: [19th c] Bound volumes, clinical journals, video and audiotapes, slides, CD-ROMs, medical tools and equipment, rare books, papers, journals, historical prints and photos, medical postcards and postage stamps.

HOURS: Yr M-F 8:15-5:15, Sa 9-1

ADMISSION: Library access fee for non-members

8027
Texas Memorial Museum
2400 Trinity, 78705; (p) (512) 471-1604; (f) (512) 471-4794; tmmweb@uts.cc.utexas.edu; www.utexas.edu/depts/tmm; (c) Travis

State/ 1936/ The Univ of Texas/ staff: 25(f); 5(p); 12(v)/publication: Various

HISTORY MUSEUM; NATURAL HISTORY MUSEUM

PROGRAMS: Community Outreach; Exhibits; Guided Tours; Lectures; Publication; School-Based Curriculum

COLLECTIONS: [Prehistory-present] 4.5 million specimens and artifacts covering: geology, paleontology, zoology, botany, ecology, anthropology and history- emphasis on TX, the Southwest and Latin America.

HOURS: Yr M-F 9-5, Sa 10-5, Su 1-5

ADMISSION: No charge

8028
Texas Music Museum, Inc.
1009 E 11th St, 78761 [PO Box 16467, 78761]; (p) (512) 472-8891; cshorkey@mail.utexas.edu; members.tripod.com/~texasmusicmuseum/; (c) Travis

Private non-profit/ 1984

HISTORY MUSEUM: Collects, interprets, preserves and presents artifacts, achievements and memorabilia pertaining to the composition, performance, reproduction and promotion of the musical arts.

PROGRAMS: Concerts; Exhibits; Festivals; Guided Tours; Lectures

COLLECTIONS: [17th c-present] Musical instruments, recording, reproduction devices, music art, education, publishing and mechanical music devices.

HOURS: Yr M-F

8029
Texas State Historical Association
2306 Sid Richardson Hall, Univ of Texas, 78712; (p) (512) 471-1525; (f) (512) 471-1551; tsha@mail.utexas.edu; www.tsha.utexas.edu; (c) Travis

Private non-profit/ 1897/ staff: 16(f); 1(p); 1(v)/ members: 3000/publication: Southwestern His-torical Quarterly; The New Handbook of Texas

HISTORICAL SOCIETY: Fosters appreciation, understanding and teaching of the history of Texas.

PROGRAMS: Annual Meeting; Community Outreach; Publication

HOURS: Yr M-F 8-5

ADMISSION: No charge

BACLIFF

8030
Scow Schooner Project, The
4405 16th St, 77518 [PO Box 641, 77518]; (p) (281) 559-1092; (f) (281) 559-1092; (c) Galveston

Private non-profit/ 1997/ Galveston and Trinity Bay Marine Museum/ staff: 1(f); 5(p); 34(v)/ members: 112/publication: Schooner Times

HISTORY MUSEUM; LIVING HISTORY/OUTDOOR MUSEUM: Promotes maritime and shipbuilding history of Galveston and Trinity Bays.

PROGRAMS: Exhibits; Family Programs; Guided Tours; Interpretation; Lectures; Publication; Reenactments; School-Based Curriculum

COLLECTIONS: [Late 19th c] Demonstrations of traditional boat building-construction of Galveston Bay cargo schooner.

HOURS: Yr F-Sa 9-4, Su 1-4

ADMISSION: Donations accepted

BANDERA

8031
Frontier Times Museum
510 13th St, 78003 [PO Box 1918, 78003]; (p) (830) 796-3864; (c) Bandera

Private non-profit/ 1933/ staff: 3(p); 1(v)/ members: 65

ART MUSEUM; HISTORIC SITE; HISTORY MUSEUM: Exhibits artifacts and relics.

PROGRAMS: Guided Tours; Living History

COLLECTIONS: Coins, Native American artifacts, music boxes, old printing press, photos, iron works, saddles, educational materials, books, 15th c queen's throne chair .

HOURS: Yr M-F 10-4:30, Sa-Su 1-4:30

ADMISSION: $2, Children $0.25

BAY CITY

8032
Matagorda County Museum
2100 Avenue F, 77414; (p) (409) 245-7502; (f) (409) 245-1233; (c) Matagorda

Private non-profit/ 1963/ staff: 1(f); 3(p); 65(v)/ members: 195

HISTORIC SITE; HISTORY MUSEUM: Promotes local history.

PROGRAMS: Annual Meeting; Community Outreach; Exhibits; Facility Rental; Family Programs; Guided Tours; Interpretation; Research Library/Archives

COLLECTIONS: [1880s-present] Textiles, agricultural tools and personal effects.

HOURS: Yr W- Sa 1-5

ADMISSION: $2.50, Children $2.50, Seniors $2.50

BAYTOWN

8033
Bay Area Heritage Society/Baytown Historical Museum
220 W De fee St, 77520; (p) (281) 427-8768; (f) (281) 420-9029; (c) Harris

Private non-profit/ 1975/ staff: 3(f); 1(p); 35(v)/ members: 475/publication: Heritage Headlights

HISTORICAL SOCIETY: Preserves

PROGRAMS: Annual Meeting; Community Outreach; Exhibits; Guided Tours; Lectures; Publication; School-Based Curriculum

BEAUMONT

8034
Beaumont Heritage Society/John Jay French Museum
3025 French Rd, 77706; (p) (409) 898-0348; (f) (409) 898-8487; (c) Jefferson

Private non-profit/ 1967/ staff: 2(f); 3(p); 20(v)/ members: 400

HISTORIC SITE; HISTORICAL SOCIETY; HOUSE MUSEUM

PROGRAMS: Annual Meeting; Guided Tours; Interpretation; Lectures; School-Based Curriculum

COLLECTIONS: [1845-1865] Furnishings.

HOURS: Yr T-Sa 10-4

ADMISSION: $3

8035
McFaddin-Ward House
725 Third St, 77701; (p) (409) 832-1906; (f) (409) 832-3483; info@mcfaddin-ward.org; www.mcfaddin-ward.org; (c) Jefferson

Private non-profit/ 1983/ Board of Directors/ staff: 15(f); 8(p); 130(v)

HOUSE MUSEUM

PROGRAMS: Exhibits; Family Programs; Festivals; Garden Tours; Guided Tours; Lectures; Living History; Research Library/Archives; School-Based Curriculum; Theatre

COLLECTIONS: [1900-1950] 34,000 artifacts: decorative arts, furnishings, and objects.

HOURS: Yr T-Sa 10-4, Su1-4

8036
Texas Energy Museum
600 Main St, 77701; (p) (409) 833-5100; (f) (409) 833-4282; smithtem@msn.com; (c) Jefferson

Private non-profit/ 1987/ Texas Energy Museum, Inc./ staff: 3(f); 1(p); 25(v)

HISTORY MUSEUM: Interprets history, technology and science of petroleum industry from geological formation of oil to petrochemicals.

PROGRAMS: Community Outreach; Exhibits; Family Programs; Interpretation; Lectures; Research Library/Archives; School-Based Curriculum

COLLECTIONS: [20th c] 2,000 objects, photos and archives relating to TX oil, especially Spindletop, 1901.

HOURS: Yr T-Sa 9-5, Su 1-5

ADMISSION: $2, Children $1

BELTON

8037
Bell County Museum
201 N Main, 76513 [PO Box 1381, 76513]; (p) (254) 933-5243; (f) (254) 933-5756; museum@vvm.com; (c) Bell

County/ 1988/ Bell County/ staff: 2(f); 1(p); 40(v)/ members: 126

HISTORIC SITE; HISTORY MUSEUM: The Museum is devoted to the preservation and interpretation of the Bell County region with particular emphasis on the years 1850-1950.

PROGRAMS: Community Outreach; Exhibits; Guided Tours; Interpretation; Lectures; Research Library/Archives

COLLECTIONS: [1850-1950] The Museum maintains the Miriam A. Ferguson collection, the first female governor of Texas.

HOURS: Yr T-Sa 1-5

BIG SPRING

8038
Potton House
200 Gregg St, 79720; (p) (915) 267-8255

BONHAM

8039
Sam Rayburn House Museum
2 miles W of Bonham, Hwy 82, 75418 [Box 308, 75418]; (p) (903) 583-5558; (f) (903) 640-0800; srhmdir@texoma.net; www.thc.state.tx.us/sam2.html; (c) Fannin

State/ 1975/ Texas Historical Commission/ staff: 3(f); 2(p); 3(v)/ members: 150

HISTORIC SITE; HOUSE MUSEUM: Preserves 1916 farmstead and former home of Speaker of the House of Representative Sam Rayburn.

PROGRAMS: Annual Meeting; Community Outreach; Exhibits; Film/Video; Guided Tours; Lectures; School-Based Curriculum

COLLECTIONS: [Late 1800s-1970s] Family furnishings, photos, and political memorabilia relating to the career of Sam Rayburn.

BORGER

8040
Hutchinson County Museum
618 N Main, 79007; (p) (806) 273-0130; (f) (806) 273-0128; (c) Hutchinson

County/ 1977/ Board of Trustees/ staff: 3(f); 2(p); 18(v)/ members: 65/publication: *Hutchinson County History*

ART MUSEUM; HISTORIC SITE; HISTORICAL SOCIETY; HISTORY MUSEUM; LIVING HISTORY/OUTDOOR MUSEUM: Collects, preserves and interprets the heritage of Hutchinson County.

PROGRAMS: Annual Meeting; Community Outreach; Exhibits; Facility Rental; Family Programs; Guided Tours; Lectures; Publication; Reenactments; Research Library/Archives

COLLECTIONS: [1920-1930s] Two and three dimensional artifacts: oil boom and oil industry, Adobe Walls, Red River Wars, Native American tribes and pioneers.

HOURS: Yr M-F 9-5, Sa 11-4:30
ADMISSION: No charge

BROWNFIELD

8041
Terry County Heritage Museum
602 E Cardwell, 79316 [PO Box 1063, 79316]; (p) (806) 637-2467; tchm@juno.com; (c) Terry

County/ 1974/ Board of Directors/ staff: 1(p); 15(v)/ members: 185

HISTORIC SITE; HISTORY MUSEUM: Preserves history of the pioneers of Terry County.

PROGRAMS: Community Outreach; Exhibits; Guided Tours; Lectures; Research Library/ Archives; School-Based Curriculum

COLLECTIONS: [Prehistory-present] Prehistoric Native Americans to pioneer ranchers and farmers.

HOURS: Yr T-Sa 10-12/1-3 or by appt.

BROWNSVILLE

8042
Stillman House Museum
1305 E Washington St, 78520 [PO Box 846, 78522]; (p) (956) 542-3929, (956) 541-5560

City, non-profit/ 1850/ staff: 1(f); 1(p); 2(v)

The first battle of the Mexican war.

COLLECTIONS: [1820-1880] 1770 Grandfather clock; 1770 sofa; black and white Jasper chandelier; furnishings; Letter from Mexican President Porofino Diaz; early photos and histories of Brownsville.

HOURS: Aug-June

BRYAN

8043
Brazos Valley Museum of Natural History
3232 Briarcrest Dr, 77802; (p) (479) 776-2195; (f) (479) 774-0252; bvmnh@myriad.net; bvmuseum.myriad.net; (c) Brazos

Private non-profit/ 1961/ Board of Trustees/ staff: 4(f); 2(p); 20(v)/ members: 300/publication: *Newsletter*

HISTORY MUSEUM; LIVING HISTORY/OUTDOOR MUSEUM: Promotes local history.

PROGRAMS: Community Outreach; Exhibits; Facility Rental; Festivals; Guided Tours; Interpretation; Lectures; Publication; School-Based Curriculum

COLLECTIONS: [Prehistory-1940] 25,000 specimens: regional archaeology, history, geology, paleontology, zoology

BURNET

8044
Burnet County Heritage Society/Ft. Croghan Museum
705 Buchanan Dr, 78611 [PO Box 74, 78611]; (p) (512) 756-2462; (c) Burnet

Joint/ Burnet County and Heritage Society/ staff: 2(p); 10(v)/ members: 124

HISTORIC SITE; HISTORICAL SOCIETY; HISTORY MUSEUM; LIVING HISTORY/OUT-

---

DOOR MUSEUM: Preserves and demonstrates early living arts.

PROGRAMS: Festivals; Living History

COLLECTIONS: [1849-1999] Dwellings and furnishings of Burnet County, original fort building, costumes, early settlers, farming equipment, complete blacksmith shop, early schoolhouse.

HOURS: Apr-Aug Th, F, Sa 10-5
ADMISSION: Donations accepted

CANYON

8045
Panhandle-Plains Historical Museum
2401 Fourth Ave, 79016 [WTAMU Box 60967, 79016]; (p) (806) 651-2244; (f) (806) 651-2250; museum@WTAMU.edu; www.wtamu.edu/museum; (c) Randall

State/ 1933/ State of Texas/West Texas A&M Univ/ staff: 27(f); 13(p); 100(v)/ members: 750/publication: *Corral Dust, Panhandle-Plains Historical Review*

ART MUSEUM; HISTORIC SITE; HISTORICAL SOCIETY; HISTORY MUSEUM; RESEARCH CENTER: Promotes TX history.

PROGRAMS: Annual Meeting; Community Outreach; Exhibits; Family Programs; Guided Tours; Interpretation; Lectures; Living History; Publication; Reenactments; Research Library/Archives; School-Based Curriculum

COLLECTIONS: [1890-present] Comanche Chief Quanah Parker's eagle feather headdress, historic NM and TX art.

HOURS: Yr M-F 9-5, Sa 9-6, Su 1-6
ADMISSION: $4, Children $1, Seniors $3; Under 4 free; Group rates

CARROLLTON

8046
A.W. Perry Homestead Museum
1509 N Perry Rd, 75011 [PO Box 110535, 75011-0535]; (p) (972) 446-0442; (f) (972) 466-3175; (c) Dallas

City/ 1976/ City of Carrollton/ staff: 2(p); 10(v)

HISTORY MUSEUM; HOUSE MUSEUM: Preserves pioneer home life.

PROGRAMS: Concerts; Exhibits; Guided Tours

COLLECTIONS: [1890-1910] Artifacts: pioneer life,Perry family, development of Carrollton.

HOURS: Yr W-Sa 10-6

CENTER

8047
Shelby County Historical Society/Museum
230 Pecan St, 75935 [PO Box 1542, 75935]; (p) (409) 598-3613; jwarner@ktsnet.com; www.geocities.com/~rbarnett31; (c) Shelby

Private non-profit/ 1962/ staff: 2(p); 32(v)/ members: 516

ART MUSEUM; GENEALOGICAL SOCIETY; HISTORIC SITE; HISTORICAL SOCIETY; HISTORY MUSEUM; RESEARCH CENTER: Collects, preserves and interprets local history for the education and enjoyment of present and future generations.

PROGRAMS: Annual Meeting; Community Outreach; Exhibits; Facility Rental; Guided Tours; Interpretation; Lectures; Publication; Research Library/Archives

COLLECTIONS: [Prehistory-1960] Early Native American artifacts, 19th century furniture, clothing, genealogy research books, cemeteries, local artwork, early 20th century newspapers, photos.

HOURS: Yr M-F 12-4 and by appt

ADMISSION: Donations accepted

CLAUDE

8048
Armstrong County Museum, Inc.
120 N Trice, 79019 [PO Box 450, 79019]; (p) (806) 226-2187; (f) (603) 687-6852; armgem@amaonline.com; www.searchtexas.com/gen-theatre; (c) Armstrong

Private non-profit/ 1990/ Directors and Board/ staff: 2(p); 45(v)/ members: 425/publication: *Armstrong County Museum's Gem Theatre News*

HISTORY MUSEUM; RESEARCH CENTER: Collects and preserves history of Armstrong County, TX.

PROGRAMS: Annual Meeting; Community Outreach; Concerts; Exhibits; Facility Rental; Guided Tours; Interpretation; Lectures; Publication; School-Based Curriculum; Theatre

COLLECTIONS: [1874-present] 480 newspapers; 470 photos and paintings; 400 volumes, magazines, and maps; 326 personal artifacts; 360 tools and equipment; and 160 phonograph cylinders.

HOURS: Yr T-Sa 10-4, Su 1-5

ADMISSION: Donations accepted

CLEBURNE

8049
Layland Museum
201 N Caddo St, 76031; (p) (817) 645-0940; (f) (817) 641-4161; (c) Johnson

City/ 1963/ staff: 2(f); 25(v)

HISTORY MUSEUM; HOUSE MUSEUM; LIBRARY AND/OR ARCHIVES: Presents regional domestic life.

PROGRAMS: Community Outreach; Elder's Programs; Exhibits; Facility Rental; Family Programs; Festivals; Guided Tours; Interpretation; Lectures; Research Library/Archives; School-Based Curriculum; Theatre

COLLECTIONS: [Prehistory-1969] Domestic life artifacts, furnishings, and foodways, photos.

HOURS: Yr

CLIFTON

8050
Bosque Memorial Museum
301 S Ave Q, 76634 [PO Box 345, 76634]; (p) (254) 675-3845; (c) Bosque

1923/ Board of Trustees/ staff: 1(f); 25(v)/ members: 200

HISTORY MUSEUM; RESEARCH CENTER

PROGRAMS: Community Outreach; Exhibits; Facility Rental; Interpretation; Research Library/Archives; School-Based Curriculum

COLLECTIONS: [1915-1950] Norwegian immigrants' household items and furniture, guns, Native American artifacts, costumes, textiles, pioneer and Civil War artifacts, dolls and toys, Norwegian and TX history books.

HOURS: Yr T-Su 10-5

ADMISSION: $1, Children $0.50; Donations

COLORADO CITY

8051
Heart of West Texas Museum
340 E 3rd St, 79512; (p) (915) 728-8285; wtmuseum@bitstreet.com; (c) Mitchell

City/ 1959/ staff: 1(f); 1(p); 5(v)

HISTORY MUSEUM: Preserves history of Mitchell County and West TX.

PROGRAMS: Community Outreach; Exhibits; Guided Tours; Interpretation

COLUMBUS

8052
Alley Log Cabin, Magnolia Homes Tour
1224 Bowie St, 78934 [PO Box 817, 78934]; (p) (409) 732-5135; ccvb@intertex.net; intertex.net/users/ccvb

1836/ Magnolia Homes Tour, Inc./ staff: 8(v)

COLLECTIONS: [Texas colonial period] Furniture, quilts, arrowheads, furniture, photos.

HOURS: W -Su

8053
Dilue Rose Harris House Museum, Magnolia Homes Tour
602 Washington St, 78934 [PO Box 817, 78934]; (p) (409) 732-5135; ccvb@intertex.net; intertex.net/users/ccvb

1858/ Magnolia Homes Tour, Inc./ staff: 8(v)

COLLECTIONS: [1840s-1880] Furnishing.

HOURS: May 3rd wknd 9-5 and by appt

8054
Keith-Traylor House, Magnolia Homes Tour
808 Live Oak St, 78934 [PO Box 817, 78934]; (p) (409) 732-5135; ccvb@intertex.net; intertex.net/users/ccvb

1872/ Magnolia Homes Tour, Inc./ staff: 8(v)

COLLECTIONS: [1872-1900] Valentines, cosmetics, clothing, hats.

8055
Magnolia Homes Tour, Inc.
425 Spring St, 78934 [PO Box 817, 78934]; (p) (409) 732-5135; (f) (409) 732-5881; ccvb@intertex.net; www.colombustexas.org; (c) Colorado

Private non-profit/ 1962/ Board of Directors/ staff: 1(p); 3(v)/ members: 250

HISTORICAL SOCIETY: Owns four house museums, Santa Claus museum and 1886 opera house.

PROGRAMS: Annual Meeting; Facility Rental; Festivals; Guided Tours; Theatre

COLLECTIONS: [1836-1900] Furniture, household items, antique tools, clothing, photos, and opera house builder.

HOURS: Yr M-F 10-4 by appt

ADMISSION: $2

8056
Tate-Senftenberg-Brandon House, Magnolia Homes Tour
616 Walnut St, 78934 [PO Box 817, 78934]; (p) (409) 732-5135; ccvb@intertex.net; intertex.net/users/ccvb

1869/ Magnolia Homes Tour, Inc./ staff: 8(v)

COLLECTIONS: [1869-1900] Doll furniture and toys, early Murphy and hideaway beds, clothing.

HOURS: May 3rd weekend

COMMERCE

8057
Heritage House
2600 S Neal St, 75429 [PO Box 3425, 75429]; (p) (903) 886-5712; (f) (903) 886-5711

CONROE

8058
Heritage Museum of Montgomery County
1506 I-45 N, 77304 [PO Box 2262, 77304]; (p) (409) 539-6873; (f) (409) 539-6914; muse@lec.net; (c) Montgomery

Private non-profit/ 1984/ Board of Directors/ staff: 2(f); 40(v)/ members: 400

HISTORY MUSEUM: Collects, preserves, and exhibits artifacts significant to local history.

PROGRAMS: Exhibits; Facility Rental; Festivals; Film/Video; Guided Tours; Lectures; Research Library/Archives; School-Based Curriculum

COLLECTIONS: [1830-1990]

HOURS: Yr W-Sa 9-4

ADMISSION: $1

CORPUS CHRISTI

8059
Corpus Christi Museum of Science and History
1900 N Chaparral, 78401; (p) (361) 883-2862; (f) (361) 884-7392; (c) Nueces

City/ 1957/ staff: 18(f); 2(p); 100(v)/ members: 650

HISTORY MUSEUM

PROGRAMS: Elder's Programs; Exhibits; Facility Rental; Family Programs; Garden Tours; Guided Tours; Lectures

COLLECTIONS: [19th-20th c] Objects representing regional and natural history, shipwreck material, photos and archives.

HOURS: Yr T-Sa 10-5, Su 12-5

ADMISSION: $5, Children $3, Seniors $6; $6.50 Military

8060
Galvan House
1581 N Chaparral St, 78401; (p) (512) 883-9352; www.cctexas.org/cvb/attract.bak

8061
Sidbury House
1609 N Chaparral St, 78401-1107; (p) (512) 883-9352;
www.metrosurf.com/sights/hpark.htm

8062
USS Lexington Museum On The Bay
2914 N Shoreline Blvd, 78402; (p) (800) 523-9539, (512) 888-4873; (f) (361) 883-8361; www.usslexington.com; (c) Nueces

Private non-profit/ 1991/ USS Lexington Assoc/ staff: 60(f); 125(v)

HISTORIC SITE; HISTORY MUSEUM

PROGRAMS: Annual Meeting; Community Outreach; Concerts; Elder's Programs; Exhibits; Facility Rental; Family Programs; Festivals; Film/Video; Guided Tours; Interpretation; Lectures; Living History; Reenactments; Research Library/Archives; School-Based Curriculum; Theatre

COLLECTIONS: [20th c] US Navy artifacts, WWII.

HOURS: Yr Daily 9-5

ADMISSION: $9, Children $4, Seniors $7; $7 Military;

CROCKETT

8063
George W. and Hallis M. Crook Memorial, Inc.
707 E Houston, 75835 [PO Box 1251, 75835]; (p) (409) 544-5820; (c) Houston

Private non-profit/ 1974/ Board of Directors/ staff: 40(v)/ members: 200

HISTORIC SITE

PROGRAMS: Guided Tours

HOURS: Mar-Dec W, Sa-Su 2-4

ADMISSION: $2, Children $1

8064
Historical Projects of Houston County, Inc.
629 N 4th, 75835-4035; (p) (409) 544-3255; (f) (409) 544-8053; (c) Houston

Private non-profit/ 1975/ staff: 12(v)/ members: 12

HISTORIC PRESERVATION AGENCY: Educates, restores, and preserves local history.

PROGRAMS: Annual Meeting; Community Outreach; Elder's Programs; Exhibits; Family Programs; Festivals; Film/Video; Guided Tours; Interpretation; Lectures; Living History;

8065
Houston County Historical Commission
Courthouse, 1st Flr, 75835; (p) (409) 544-3255; (f) (409) 544-8053; (c) Houston

County; State/ 1961/ Texas Historical Commission/Houston County Commissioners Court/ staff: 15(v)/ members: 15

GENEALOGICAL SOCIETY; HISTORIC PRESERVATION AGENCY; HISTORICAL SO-CIETY; RESEARCH CENTER: Promotes local history; surveys historical buildings and sites; erects historical markers;

PROGRAMS: Annual Meeting; Community Outreach; Elder's Programs; Exhibits; Facility Rental; Family Programs; Festivals; Film/Video; Guided Tours; Interpretation; Lectures; Living History; Publication; Reenactments; Research Library/Archives

COLLECTIONS: [1840-1942] Genealogical records, photos, historical marker resumes.

HOURS: Yr

8066
Houston County Visitors Center/ Museum, Inc.
303 S First, 75835 [PO Box 449, 75835]; (p) (409) 544-9520; (c) Houston

Private non-profit/ 1993/ staff: 7(v)/ members: 21

HISTORY MUSEUM

PROGRAMS: Annual Meeting; Community Outreach; Exhibits; Family Programs; Festivals; Film/Video; Guided Tours; Interpretation; Lectures; Living History

COLLECTIONS: [1920-1970] Early settlers, railroad, veterans of WWI and WWII.

HOURS: Yr W 2-4; other days by appt

ADMISSION: Donations accepted

CROSBYTON

8067
Crosby County Pioneer Memorial
101 W Main St, 79322; (p) (806) 675-2331; (c) Crosby

City/ 1957/ staff: 4(f); 2(p); 17(v)

HISTORY MUSEUM

PROGRAMS: Community Outreach; Exhibits; Facility Rental; Family Programs; Festivals; Guided Tours; Interpretation; Publication; Reenactments; Research Library/Archives; School-Based Curriculum; Theatre

COLLECTIONS: [1876-1950] Cultural materials: prehistoric Plains Indians to 20th century pioneers.

HOURS: Yr T-Sa 9-12/1-5

ADMISSION: No charge

CUERO

8068
DeWitt County Historical Museum, The
312 E Broadway, Bates-Sheppard House, 77954 [PO Box 745, 77954]; (p) (512) 275-6322; (c) DeWitt

County/ 1973/ Commissioner's Court; Board of Directors/ staff: 2(f); 1(p); 5(v)/ members: 89

HOUSE MUSEUM: Depicts life during the late 19th and early 20th c.

PROGRAMS: Community Outreach; Exhibits; Facility Rental; Festivals; Garden Tours; Guided Tours; Interpretation; Living History; Reenactments; Research Library/Archives; School-Based Curriculum

COLLECTIONS: [Late 19th-early 20th c] Furnishings, clothing, literature, photos, tools, jewelry, letters, artifacts, and archival papers.

HOURS: Yr Th 9-4, F 9-5, Su 2-5; Apr Daily 9-5

DALHART

8069
XIT Museum
108 E 5th St, 79022 [PO Box 710, 79022]; (p) (806) 244-5390; xitmusm@xit.net; (c) Dallam

Private non-profit/ 1966/ Dallam-Hartley County Historical Society/ staff: 1(f); 3(p); 4(v)/ members: 95

HISTORICAL SOCIETY; HISTORY MUSEUM: Promotes and preserves bi-county history, ranching.

PROGRAMS: Annual Meeting; Community Outreach; Exhibits; Facility Rental; Film/Video; Guided Tours; Research Library/Archives

COLLECTIONS: [1880-present] 100,000 photohs, postcards, six buggies, an airplane, newspapers, books, archives.

HOURS: Yr T-Sa 9-5

ADMISSION: Donations accepted

DALLAS

8070
Age of Steam Railroad Museum, The
1105 Washington St, Fair Park, 75315 [PO Box 153259, 75315-3259]; (p) (214) 428-0101; (f) (214) 426-1937; info@dallasrailwaymuseum. com; www.dallasrailwaymuseum.com; (c) Dallas

Private non-profit/ 1963/ Southwest Railroad Historical Society/ staff: 3(f); 65(v)/ members: 320/publication: The Clearance Card

HISTORY MUSEUM: Restores and maintains railroad artifacts, entertains and educates visitors.

PROGRAMS: Annual Meeting; Community Outreach; Exhibits; Facility Rental; Family Programs; Interpretation; Lectures; Publication; Research Library/Archives; School-Based Curriculum

COLLECTIONS: [1890-1970] Railroad artifacts, lineside signals and structures, maintenance equipment, paper items.

HOURS: Yr

8071
American Museum of the Miniature Arts
2001 N Lamar St, 75202; (p) (214) 969-5502; (f) (214) 969-5997; (c) Dallas

Private non-profit/ 1982/ Board of Governors/ staff: 2(f); 53(v)/ members: 250/publication: Small Talk

HISTORY MUSEUM: Preserves history of miniature arts.

PROGRAMS: Annual Meeting; Community Outreach; Exhibits; Facility Rental; Guided Tours; Interpretation; Lectures; Living History; Publication; Research Library/Archives; School-Based Curriculum

HOURS: Yr T-Sa 10-4:30, Su 1-4:30

8072
Dallas Arboretum and Botanical Society
8617 Garland Rd, 75218-4332; (p) (214) 327-8263, (214) 327-4901; (f) (214) 327-6107; (c) Dallas

Joint/ 1977/ City; Private non-profit/ staff: 45(f); 20(p); 575(v)/ members: 12000

GARDEN; HISTORIC SITE; HOUSE MUSE-UM: Preserves period home of Nell and Everette DeGolyer.

PROGRAMS: Annual Meeting; Community Outreach; Concerts; Exhibits; Facility Rental; Family Programs; Festivals; Garden Tours; Guided Tours; Interpretation; Lectures; School-Based Curriculum

COLLECTIONS: [20th c] Period-furnished interpretive rooms.

HOURS: Yr Daily 10-6

ADMISSION: $6, Student $5, Children $3, Seniors $5

8073
Dallas Historical Society
3939 Grand Ave, 75315 [PO Box 150038, 75315-0038]; (p) (214) 421-4500; (f) (214) 421-7500; andy@dallashistory.org; www.dallashistory.org; (c) Dallas

Private non-profit/ 1922/ Board of Trustees/ staff: 7(f); 1(p); 50(v)/ members: 710/publication: *Dallas Rediscovered: A Photographic Chronicle of Urban Expansion, 1870-1925; When Dallas Became A City*

HISTORICAL SOCIETY: Collects, preserves, and exhibits historical material.

PROGRAMS: Annual Meeting; Exhibits; Facility Rental; Guided Tours; Interpretation; Lectures; Publication; Research Library/Archives; School-Based Curriculum

COLLECTIONS: [1840s-present] 2 million archival items, 15,000 books and 60,000 photos.

HOURS: Yr T-Sa 9-5, Su 12-5

8074
Dallas Memorial Center for Holocaust Studies
7900 Naven Rd, 75230; (p) (214) 750-4654; (f) (214) 750-4672; dmchs@mail.swbell.net; (c) Dallas

1984/ staff: 8(f); 4(p); 50(v)/ members: 900

HISTORY MUSEUM: Promotes holocaust history.

PROGRAMS: Annual Meeting; Community Outreach; Exhibits; Film/Video; Guided Tours; Lectures

COLLECTIONS: [1933-1945] Photos, artifacts, artworks, videotaped testimonies, documentaries, curriculum guides, books, periodicals, CD-ROMs, audio-visual materials.

HOURS: Yr M-F 9:30-4:30, Su 12-4

8075
Dallas Museum of Natural History
3535 Grand Ave, Fair Park, 75315 [PO Box 150349, 75315-0349]; (p) (214) 421-3466; (f) (214) 428-4356; abarker@dmnhnet.org; www.dallasdino.org; (c) Dallas

Private non-profit/ 1936/ Board of Trustees/ staff: 17(f); 33(p); 121(v)/ members: 1200/publication: *Bulletin of the Dallas Museum of Natural History*

LIBRARY AND/OR ARCHIVES; NATURAL HISTORY MUSEUM: Preserves and interprets natural history.

PROGRAMS: Annual Meeting; Community Outreach; Elder's Programs; Exhibits; Facility Rental; Family Programs; Festivals; Guided Tours; Interpretation; Lectures; Living History;

Publication; Research Library/Archives; School-Based Curriculum

COLLECTIONS: [Prehistory] 25 million specimens, 16,000 paleontology specimens, 20,000 archaeological specimens.

HOURS: Yr Daily 10-5

ADMISSION: No charge

8076
J.C. Penney Archives and Historical Museum
6501 Legacy Dr, 75301 [PO Box 10001, 75301-4118]; (p) (972) 431-5128; (f) (972) 431-5300; jpirt2@jcpenney.com; www.jcpenney.net/company/history/history.htm; (c) Collin

1993/ J.C. Penney Company, Inc/ staff: 1(f)

HISTORY MUSEUM: Preserves and documents the history of the J.C. Penney Company.

PROGRAMS: Community Outreach; Exhibits; Guided Tours; Research Library/Archives

COLLECTIONS: [20th c] Records, film, photos, audio library, J.C. Penney private brand merchandise and memorabilia, period clothing, accessories, artifact, and retail technology.

8077
Jerry Bywaters Special Collection
Hamon Arts Library, SMU, 75275-0356; (p) (214) 768-2303, (214) 768-1859; (f) (214) 768-1800; sratelif@mail.smu.edu; www.smu.edu/~hamon/spec.html; (c) Dallas

Private non-profit/ 1990/ Southern Methodist Univ/ staff: 2(f); 3(p)

LIBRARY AND/OR ARCHIVES: Acquires and preserves cultural history of American southwest.

PROGRAMS: Exhibits; Research Library/Archives

COLLECTIONS: [1900-1970] Clipping files, exhibition catalogues, correspondence, photos, scripts, slides, programs, art. 1,000 linear feet of papers belonging to TX artists Jerry Bywaters and Otis Dozier, sculptor Octavio Medellin, musician Paul van Katwijk and actress Greer Garson.

HOURS: Yr M-F 9-5; appt

8078
Sixth Floor Museum at Dealey Plaza
411 Elm St, Ste 120, 75202; (p) (214) 747-6660; (f) (214) 747-6662; jfk@jfk.org; www.jfk.org; (c) Dallas

Private non-profit/ 1989/ Dallas County Historical Foundation/ staff: 42(f); 1(p); 6(v)/ members: 50/publication: *Retrospect*

HISTORIC SITE; HISTORY MUSEUM; PRESIDENTIAL SITE; RESEARCH CENTER: Promotes legacy of President John F. Kennedy.

PROGRAMS: Exhibits; Facility Rental; Interpretation; Lectures; Publication

COLLECTIONS: [1960s] Newspapers, books, magazines, scrapbooks, documents, films and photos, videotapes, local and network audio tapes, three-dimensional artifacts, and oral histories.

HOURS: Yr Daily 9-6

ADMISSION: $10, Student $9, Seniors $9

8079
Southwest Museum of Science and Technology/The Science Place
1318 Second Ave, 75315 [PO Box 151469, 75315]; (p) (214) 428-5555; (f) (214) 428-2033; www.scienceplace.org; (c) Dallas

Private non-profit/ 1946/ Southwest Museums Foundation/ staff: 60(f); 45(p); 200(v)/ members: 7600/publication: *Pages*

HISTORY MUSEUM

PROGRAMS: Community Outreach; Exhibits; Facility Rental; Family Programs; Festivals; Lectures; Publication; School-Based Curriculum

HOURS: Yr Daily 9:30-5:30

ADMISSION: $6, Children $3, Seniors

DALLAS/FT. WORTH AIRPORT

8080
American Airlines C.R. Smith Museum
4601 Hwy 360 at FAA Rd, 75261 [PO Box 619617, 75261-9617]; (p) (817) 967-1560; (f) (817) 967-5737; Jay_Miller@AMRCORP.com; www.AA.com; (c) Tarrent

Private non-profit/ 1993/ American Airlines/ staff: 9(f); 3(p); 80(v)/ members: 13500

HISTORY MUSEUM: Collects, preserves, and interprets the history of American Airlines and the air transportation industry.

PROGRAMS: Exhibits; Facility Rental; Guided Tours; Lectures; Research Library/Archives

COLLECTIONS: [20th c] DC-3 Flagship Knoxville, aircraft engines, flight and ground crew uniforms, American Airlines memorabilia, 12,000 museum artifacts, 3000 photos, timetables, marketing research records, corporate publications, movie and video

DECATUR

8081
Wise County Historical Society, Inc.
1602 S Trinity, 76234 [PO Box 427, 76234]; (p) (940) 627-5586; (c) Wise

Private non-profit/ 1967/ staff: 2(p); 10(v)/ members: 340

HISTORIC SITE; HISTORICAL SOCIETY; RESEARCH CENTER

PROGRAMS: Exhibits; Facility Rental; Film/Video; Guided Tours; Research Library/Archives; Theatre

COLLECTIONS: [19th-20th c] County and family histories; cemetery, marriage and birth records; census, newspapes; Native American artifacts; pictures, and furniture.

HOURS: Yr M-F 9-4, Su1:30-5

DEL RIO

8082
Whitehead Memorial Museum
1308 S Main, 78840; (p) (830) 774-7568; director@whitehead-museum.com; www.whitehead-museum.com; (c) Val Verde

Joint/ 1962/ City; County/ staff: 4(f); 40(v)/ members: 40

HISTORIC SITE; HISTORY MUSEUM; LIVING HISTORY/OUTDOOR MUSEUM; RESEARCH CENTER: Preserves local history.

PROGRAMS: Community Outreach; Elder's Programs; Exhibits; Facility Rental; Family Programs; Festivals; Guided Tours; Interpretation; Lectures; Living History; Research Library/Archives

COLLECTIONS: Prehistoric artifacts, local Native American items, farming, transportation, log cabin, early settlers' articles, Jersey Lilly; grave of Judge Roy Bean and son.

HOURS: Yr T-Sa 9-4:30, Su 1-5

ADMISSION: $3, Student $2

DENISON

8083
Eisenhower Birthplace State Historical Park
208 E Day St, 75021; (p) (903) 465-8908; (f) (903) 465-8988; eisenhower@texoma.net; www.eisenhowerbirthplace.org; (c) Grayson

State/ 1945/ State of Texas/ staff: 1(f); 3(p); 10(v)/ members: 75/publication: *Commander's Post*

HISTORIC SITE; HOUSE MUSEUM; PRESIDENTIAL SITE; RESEARCH CENTER: Visitor center, gift shop, education center, library, pavilion for picnics and hiking trail. School and tour groups welcome. Education center and pavilion available to rent.

PROGRAMS: Annual Meeting; Community Outreach; Elder's Programs; Exhibits; Facility Rental; Family Programs; Film/Video; Guided Tours; Interpretation; Lectures; Living History; Publication; School-Based Curriculum

COLLECTIONS: [1890] House furnished with 1890 era pieces donated in 1940s by local residents, quilt made by Ike's mom, original Eisenhower painting, letters, photos and autographs.

HOURS: Yr M-Sa 10-4

ADMISSION: $2, Children $1

DENTON

8084
Denton County Courthouse-on-the-Square Museum
110 W Hickory, 76201; (p) (940) 565-5667; (f) (940) 565-5679; gcaraway@co.denton.tx.us; www.co.denton.tx.us/dept/hcm.htm; (c) Denton

County/ 1979/ Denton County Historical Commission/ staff: 4(f); 70(v)

HISTORIC SITE; HISTORY MUSEUM; RESEARCH CENTER: Provides and promotes programs that will, through educational outreach, bring about a better understanding and appreciation of Denton County history for all ages.

PROGRAMS: Community Outreach; Exhibits; Facility Rental; Family Programs; Guided Tours; Lectures; Research Library/Archives; School-Based Curriculum

COLLECTIONS: [Prehistory-mid 20th c] Native American pottery and artifacts, dolls, toys, weaponry, late 19th c home, Denton family materials, and Denton County pottery.

HOURS: Yr M-F 10-4:30 Sa 11-3

ADMISSION: No charge

8085
Denton County Historical Museum, Inc.
5800 I-35 N, Denton Factory Stores Mall Ste 30, 76202 [PO Box 2800, 76202]; (p) (940) 380-0877; (f) (940) 380-1699; (c) Denton

Private non-profit/ 1979/ staff: 1(f); 10(v)

HISTORY MUSEUM; RESEARCH CENTER: Provides educational opportunities and promotes local tourism.

PROGRAMS: Community Outreach; Concerts; Elder's Programs; Exhibits; Facility Rental; Family Programs; Festivals; Guided Tours; Interpretation; Lectures; Research Library/Archives; School-Based Curriculum

COLLECTIONS: [1846-1942] Photographs, Victorian furniture, dioramas, quilts, and library books.

HOURS: Yr M-F 10-6, Sa 10-4 and by appt

ADMISSION: No charge

DUBLIN

8086
Dr. Pepper Bottling of Texas
105 E Elm, 76446 [PO Box 307, 76446]; (p) (254) 445-3939; (f) (254) 445-4677; drpepper@drpep.com; www.drpep.com; (c) Erath

Private for-profit/ 1891/ staff: 13(f); 19(p)

HISTORIC SITE; HISTORY MUSEUM: Promotes history of Dr Pepper Bottling Co.

PROGRAMS: Exhibits; Facility Rental; Festivals; Guided Tours

COLLECTIONS: [19th c-present] Dr. Pepper memorabilia and advertisements.

HOURS: Yr M-F 9-5, Sa 10-5, Su 1-5

ADMISSION: $1.50, Children $0.50

DUMAS

8087
Moore County Historical Museum
810 S Dumas Ave #103, 79029; (p) (806) 935-3113; (f) (806) 935-3113; (c) Moore

Private non-profit/ 1976/ Board of Directors/ staff: 2(f); 30(v)/ members: 103

HISTORY MUSEUM: Preserves the history of Dumas and Moore County.

PROGRAMS: Annual Meeting; Community Outreach; Exhibits; Guided Tours; Research Library/Archives; School-Based Curriculum

COLLECTIONS: [20th c] Area wildlife, local artifacts.

HOURS: Spring-Summer M-Sa 10-5; Fall-Winter M-F 1-5

ADMISSION: Donations accepted

EDINBURG

8088
Hidalgo County Historical Museum
121 E McIntyre, 78539; (p) (956) 383-6911; (f) (956) 381-8518; hchm@hiline.net; www.riograndeborderlands.org/; (c) Hidalgo

Private non-profit/ 1967/ Board of Trustees/ staff: 12(f); 4(p); 35(v)/ members: 900

HISTORIC SITE; HISTORY MUSEUM; RESEARCH CENTER: Preserves and presents the history of South TX (south of the Nueces River to the Rio Grande) and Northeastern Mexico.

PROGRAMS: Community Outreach; Exhibits; Facility Rental; Family Programs; Festivals; Film/Video; Garden Tours; Guided Tours; Interpretation; Lectures; Publication; Research Library/Archives; School-Based Curriculum; Theatre

COLLECTIONS: [1000 AD-present] Native American through Spanish exploration and colonization, Mexican War, steamboat era, Civil War, early ranching and farming, border bandit wars.

HOURS: Yr T-F 9-5, Sa 10-5, Su 1-5

ADMISSION: $2

EL PASO

8089
El Paso Museum of History
12901 Gateway W, 79927; (p) (915) 858-1928; (f) (915) 858-4591; harrisra@ci.el-paso.tx.us; (c) El Paso

City/ 1974/ staff: 4(f)

HISTORY MUSEUM: Presents history of El Paso.

PROGRAMS: Exhibits; Guided Tours; Lectures

COLLECTIONS: [1881-present] Clothing, tools, bottles, military and transportation artifacts.

HOURS: Yr T-Sa 9-5, Su 1-5

ADMISSION: Donations accepted

8090
El Paso Public Library/Border Heritage Center
501 N Oregon, 79901; (p) (915) 543-5441; (f) (915) 543-5410; (c) El Paso

1885/ staff: 4(f); 1(p); 2(v)

GENEALOGICAL SOCIETY: Preserves the history of El Paso, early pioneers, architectural drawings, map files and archives.

PROGRAMS: Community Outreach; Exhibits;

8091
Magoffin Home State Historical Site
1120 Magoffin Ave, 79901; (p) (915) 533-5147; (f) (915) 544-4398; www.tpwd.state.tx.us; (c) El Paso

State/ 1976/ Texas Parks and Wildlife Dept/ staff: 2(f); 1(p); 10(v)

HOUSE MUSEUM: Preserves El Paso history.

PROGRAMS: Community Outreach; Concerts; Facility Rental; Guided Tours; Interpretation

COLLECTIONS: [1880-1910] Interpretive rooms.

HOURS: Yr Daily 9-4

ADMISSION: $2, Student $1; Under 6 free; Group rates available

8092
U.S. Border Patrol Museum and Memorial Library
4315 Transmountain Rd, 79914 [PO Box 4767, 79914]; (p) (915) 759-6060; (f) (915) 759-0992; www.NationalBPMuseum.org; (c) El Paso

Private non-profit/ 1985/ Board of Trustees and Directors/Board of Governors/ staff: 1(f); 2(p); 3(v)

HISTORY MUSEUM: Collects, preserves, and exhibits materials pertaining to the agency; provides information on the patrols' role in National Security.

PROGRAMS: Exhibits; Film/Video; Guided Tours; Research Library/Archives

COLLECTIONS: [1924-present] Photos, newspapers, boats, aircrafts.

HOURS: Yr T-Su 9-5

ADMISSION: No charge

EOLA

8093
Earnest and Dorthy Barrow Museum, The
4 mi E of Eola on US 765, 76937 [PO Box 688, 76937]; (c) Concho

Private non-profit/ 1976/ Board of Directors/ staff: 2(p)

HISTORY MUSEUM

PROGRAMS: Guided Tours

COLLECTIONS: [Early 20th c] Antiques, Hummels, Native American arrowheads, rocks, glass, cars, toys, barber shops, banks, dentist and doctor offices.

HOURS: Yr Th-Sa 10-5, Su 1-5

ADMISSION: Donations accepted

FAIRFIELD

8094
Freestone County Historical Museum
302 E Main St, 75840 [PO Box 524, 75840]; (p) (903) 389-3738; (c) Freestone

County/ 1967/ staff: 1(p); 1(v)/ members: 118

HISTORIC SITE; HISTORY MUSEUM; HOUSE MUSEUM: Promotes and preserves county history.

COLLECTIONS: [1840s-present] Sites: historic jail, 1930 country church, telephone museum, Pioneer artifacts, photos.

HOURS: Yr W, F 9:30-3:30, Sa 10-4, Su 1:30-4

ADMISSION: $2, Children $1; Donations accepted

8095
Moody-Bradley House
318 Moody St, 75840 [PO Box 857, 75840]; (p) (903) 389-7008, (908) 389-3164

1860/ The History Club

HOURS: By appt

FARMERS BRANCH

8096
Farmers Branch Historical Park
2540 Farmers Branch Ln, 75381 [PO Box 819010, 75381]; (p) (972) 406-0184; (f) (972) 247-3939; birdsald@ci.farmers-branch.tx.us; www.ci.farmers-branch.tx.us; (c) Dallas

City/ 1986/ staff: 5(f); 2(p); 60(v)/publication: *Once Upon A Time; Pictorial History of Farmers Branch, 1842-1996*

HISTORY MUSEUM: Establishes, collects, preserves, and interprets the history of TX.

PROGRAMS: Community Outreach; Concerts; Exhibits; Festivals; Guided Tours; Inter-

pretation; Lectures; Living History; Publication; Research Library/Archives

COLLECTIONS: [1840-1940] Peters Colony artifacts; books, photos, artifacts, and archival material.

HOURS: Spring-Summer M-Th 9:30-8, Sa-Su 12-8; Fall-Winter M-Th 9:30-6, Sa-Su 12-6

ADMISSION: No charge

FORT BLISS

8097
Fort Bliss Museum
Pershing & Pleasanton Rds, 79916 [Attn: ATSA-MM, 79916]; (p) (915) 568-6940; (f) (915) 568-6941; RogersJ@emh10.bliss.army.mil; (c) El Paso

Federal/ US Army/ staff: 3(f); 35(v)/publication: *Fort Bliss, 1857, Origins Of A Mexican-American Community*

HISTORY MUSEUM; LIVING HISTORY/OUTDOOR MUSEUM: Collects, preserves, and interprets the history of Fort Bliss.

PROGRAMS: Community Outreach; Exhibits; Family Programs; Guided Tours; Interpretation; Living History; Publication; Research Library/Archives; School-Based Curriculum

COLLECTIONS: [1848-present] Uniforms, personal equipment, weapons, vehicles, photos, and archival materials.

HOURS: Yr Daily 9-4:30

ADMISSION: No charge

8098
U.S. Army Air Defense Artillery Museum
Bldg 5000, Pleasanton Rd, 79916 [Attn: ATSA-MM, 79916-3802]; (p) (915) 568-5412; (f) (915) 586-6941; (c) El Paso

Federal/ 1974/ US Army, Department of Defense/ staff: 2(f); 2(v)

HISTORY MUSEUM: Maintains documents, reference materials, artifacts and unit histories.

PROGRAMS: Exhibits; Interpretation; Research Library/Archives

COLLECTIONS: [1917-present] Air Defense branch of the US Army artifacts.

HOURS: Yr Daily 9-4:30

ADMISSION: No charge

FORT DAVIS

8099
Fort Davis National Historic Site
Hwy 17-118, 79734 [PO Box 1456, 79734]; (p) (915) 426-3224; (f) (915) 426-3122; foda_superintendent@nps.gov; www.nps.gov/foda; (c) Jeff Davis

Federal/ 1961/ National Park Service/ staff: 16(f); 4(p); 20(v)

HISTORIC SITE: Preserves the foundations, ruins and structures of late 19th century military post in southwest.

PROGRAMS: Community Outreach; Exhibits; Festivals; Interpretation; Lectures; Living History; Publication; Reenactments; Research Library/Archives; School-Based Curriculum

COLLECTIONS: [1854-1891] Fort Davis artifacts.

HOURS: May-Sept Daily 8-6; Sept-May Daily 8-5

8100
Overland Trail Museum
2 blocks from Hwy 118, 79734 [PO Box 233, 79734]; (c) Jeff Davis

City; Private non-profit/ 1954/ Fort Davis Historical Society/ staff: 1(f); 2(v)/ members: 15/publication: *Jeff Davis County, Texas*

HISTORICAL SOCIETY; HISTORY MUSEUM: Preserves life, times, people, places and history of Jeff Davis County.

PROGRAMS: Annual Meeting; Community Outreach; Exhibits; Festivals; Guided Tours; Lectures; Living History; Publication

COLLECTIONS: [1880-present] County, early settlers artifacts.

HOURS: Mar-Nov T, F 1-5, Sa 10-5

ADMISSION: $2, Children $1

FORT MCKAVETT

8101
Fort McKavett State Historic Park
Farm Rd 864/1674, 76841 [PO Box 867, 76841]; (p) (915) 396-2358; (f) (915) 396-2818; mckavett@airmail.net; (c) Menard

State/ 1968/ Parks and Wildlife Dept/ staff: 3(f); 1(p); 1(v)

HISTORIC SITE; HISTORY MUSEUM: Interprets 19th c frontier fort.

PROGRAMS: Exhibits; Facility Rental; Family Programs; Festivals; Guided Tours; Interpretation; Lectures; Living History; Reenactments

COLLECTIONS: [Mid 19th-mid 20th c] Military artifacts or representative replicas (1850s-1880s) and civilian artifacts (1880s-1940s).

HOURS: Yr Daily 8-5

ADMISSION: $2, Children $1

FORT SAM HOUSTON

8102
Fort Sam Houston
1210 Stanley Rd, Bldg 123, 78234 [MCCS-BRL-MM, 1750 Greeley Rd, Ste 2, Bldg 4011, 78234-5002]; (p) (210) 221-1886; (f) (210) 221-1311; (c) Bexar

Federal/ 1967/ U.S. Army/ staff: 3(f); 5(p)

HISTORIC SITE: Presents the history of Fort Sam Houston.

PROGRAMS: Community Outreach; Exhibits; Guided Tours; Interpretation; Research Library/Archives

COLLECTIONS: [1845-present] Army uniforms, arms, accoutrements, equipment, documents and photos.

HOURS: Yr W-Sa 10-4

ADMISSION: No charge

8103
U.S. Army Medical Department Museum
2310 Stanley Rd, Buidling 1046, 78234 [PO Box 340244, 78234]; (p) (210) 221-6358; (f) (210) 221-6781; ameddmus@aol.com;

www.ameddgiftshop.com/museum.html; (c) Bexar

Federal/ 1955/ US Army, Department of Defense/ staff: 5(f); 1(p); 20(v)/publication: *Museum Notes*

HISTORY MUSEUM: Part of the Army Museum System. Covers the history of army medicine from 1775 to the present.

PROGRAMS: Exhibits; Film/Video; Publication; Research Library/Archives; School-Based Curriculum

COLLECTIONS: [1775-present] Uniforms, equipment, artwork, vehicles and archival material.

FORT STOCKTON

8104
Fort Stockton Historical Society

301 S Main St, 79735; (p) (915) 336-2167; (f) (915) 336-2402; txrousse@aol.com; (c) Pecos

Private non-profit/ 1955/ staff: 3(f); 5(p); 25(v)/ members: 100/publication: *The Fort Stockton Telegraph*

HISTORIC SITE; HISTORICAL SOCIETY; HISTORY MUSEUM; LIVING HISTORY/OUTDOOR MUSEUM: Operates Annie Riggs Memorial Museum operates the museum; preserves Pecos County history, Historic Fort Stockton, and Indian Wars period fort.

PROGRAMS: Annual Meeting; Community Outreach; Concerts; Exhibits; Facility Rental; Family Programs; Festivals; Guided Tours; Interpretation; Lectures; Living History; Publication

COLLECTIONS: [1867-present] Area artifacts, archaeological items, geological specimens, military relics; 7 historic structures.

HOURS: Yr M-Sa 10-5

ADMISSION: $2, Children $1, Seniors $1.50; Under 6 free

FORT WORTH

8105
Amon Carter Museum

3501 Camp Bowie Blvd, 76107-2695; (p) (817) 738-1933; (f) (817) 377-8523; ruthann.rugg@cartermuseum.org; www.cartermuseum.org; (c) Tarrant

Private non-profit/ 1961/ staff: 60(f); 19(p); 80(v)/ members: 762

ART MUSEUM; LIBRARY AND/OR ARCHIVES: Promotes history and art of Frederic Remington and Charles M. Russell; collects, preserves, and exhibits American art.

PROGRAMS: Exhibits; Guided Tours; Lectures; Publication; Research Library/Archives

COLLECTIONS: [Late 18th-early 20th c] 300,000 works of 19th and 20th c American sculpture, painting, photos.

HOURS: Yr T-Sa 10-5, Su 12-5

8106
Fort Worth Museum of Science and History

1501 Montgomery St, 76107; (p) (817) 255-9300, (888) 255-9300; (f) (817) 732-7635; webmaster@twmsh.org; www.fortworthmuseum.org; (c) Tarrant

Private non-profit/ 1941/ staff: 80(f); 150(p); 475(v)/ members: 1054/publication: *Frontiers*

HISTORY MUSEUM: Promotes science, history and technology.

PROGRAMS: Community Outreach; Exhibits; Facility Rental; Family Programs; Film/Video; Interpretation; Lectures; Publication; Research Library/Archives; School-Based Curriculum; Theatre

COLLECTIONS: Scientific instruments, taxidermy specimens, meteoritic, educational, cultural items, Pre-Columbian artifacts.

HOURS: Spring-Summer M-Sa 9-9, Su 12-9; Fall-Winter M-W 9-5, Th-Sa 9-9, Su 12-9

8107
Fort Worth Nature Center and Refuge

9601 Fossil Ridge Rd, 76135; (p) (817) 237-1111; (f) (817) 237-1168; (c) Tarrant

City/ 1964/ staff: 7(f); 3(p); 140(v)/ members: 357

LIVING HISTORY/OUTDOOR MUSEUM: Preserves and protects natural history.

PROGRAMS: Community Outreach; Exhibits; Facility Rental; Family Programs; Festivals; Guided Tours; Lectures

COLLECTIONS: 3,500 acres of native TX landscape including Crosstimbers Forest, Grand Prairie and wetlands associated with the Trinity River Basin, herbarium and reference library.

HOURS: Yr Daily 9-5

ADMISSION: No charge

8108
Fort Worth Public Library, Genealogy/Local History Collection

500 W Third St, 76102; (p) (817) 871-7740; (f) (817) 871-7734; genlhist@fortworthlibrary.org; www.fortworthlibrary.org; (c) Tarrant

City/ 1949/ staff: 5(f); 10(v)

LIBRARY AND/OR ARCHIVES: Collects local historical and genealogical materials pertaining to Fort Worth.

PROGRAMS: Exhibits; Guided Tours; Lectures; Research Library/Archives

COLLECTIONS: [1849-present] Genealogical materials of original 13 states, the midwest, south, and TX.

HOURS: Yr M-Th 9-9, F-Sa 10-6, Su 12-6

ADMISSION: No charge

8109
Historic Fort Worth, Inc.

1110 Penn St, 76102; (p) (817) 332-5875; (f) (817) 332-5877; (c) Tarrant

Private non-profit/ 1969/ staff: 4(f); 1(p)/ members: 450/publication: *Preservation Perspectives*

HISTORIC PRESERVATION AGENCY; HOUSE MUSEUM: Plans, preserves and protects Fort Worth's historic identity; maintains the Historic Eddleman-McFarland House.

PROGRAMS: Facility Rental; Guided Tours; Lectures;

8110
Log Cabin Village Historical Complex

2100 Log Cabin Village Lane, 76109; (p) (817) 926-5881; (f) (817) 922-0246; (c) Tarrant

City/ 1966/ Parks and Community Services Dept/ staff: 3(f); 13(p); 25(v)/publication: *Log Cabin Village: A History and Guide*

HISTORY MUSEUM; LIVING HISTORY/OUTDOOR MUSEUM: Preserves representative structures from TX pioneer era; provides living history museum.

PROGRAMS: Exhibits; Family Programs; Festivals; Guided Tours; Interpretation; Lectures; Living History; Publication; School-Based Curriculum

COLLECTIONS: [1840s-1890s] Documents, photo, and museum artifacts related to pioneer life in TX.

HOURS: Yr T-F 9-5, Sa 10-5, Su 1-5

ADMISSION: $2, Children $1.50, Seniors $1.50

8111
Pate Museum of Transportation

US 377 between Fort Worth & Cresson, 76101 [PO Box 711, 76101-0711]; (p) (817) 332-1161; (f) (817) 336-8441; (c) Parker

Private non-profit/ 1969/ staff: 2(f); 1(p)

HISTORY MUSEUM

PROGRAMS: Exhibits; Research Library/Archives

COLLECTIONS: [20th c]

HOURS: Yr T-Su 9-5

ADMISSION: No charge

8112
Texas and Southwestern Cattle Raisers Foundation

1301 W 7th St, 76102; (p) (817) 332-8551; (f) (817) 332-8749; clwolfe@texascattleraisers.org; www.cattleraisersmuseum.org; (c) Tarrant

Private non-profit/ 1980/ staff: 3(f); 1(p); 20(v)

HISTORY MUSEUM; RESEARCH CENTER: Preserves the heritage of ranch life. Owns and operates the Cattle Raisers Museum, an 8,000 square foot exhibit facility; the W.T. Waggoner Memorial Library, a research library devoted to the cattle and livestock industries; and The Cattleman magazine historic photograph collection.

PROGRAMS: Community Outreach; Exhibits; Guided Tours; Interpretation; Lectures; Living History; Reenactments; Research Library/Archives; School-Based Curriculum

COLLECTIONS: [Early 19th c-present] Saddles, branding irons and spurs; 3,000 volumes; Cattleman magazine photo collection; 25,000 images documenting 20th c ranch life in TX and southwest.

HOURS: Yr M-Sa 10-5, Su 1-5

ADMISSION: $3, Student $2, Children $1, Seniors $2; Under 4 free; Group rates

8113
Thistle Hill

1509 Pennsylvania Ave, 76104; (p) (817) 336-1212; (f) (817) 335-5338

FREDERICKSBURG

8114
Admiral Nimitz Museum and State Historical Center and National Museum of the Pacific War

340 E Main, 78624 [PO Box 777, 78624]; (p) (830) 997-4379; (f) (830) 997-8220;

nimitzm@ktc.com; www.nimitx-museum.org; (c) Gillespie

State/ 1969/ Texas Parks and Wildlife Dept/ staff: 12(f); 3(p); 40(v)/ members: 1500/publication: *NimitzNews*

HISTORY MUSEUM: Preserves WWII history.

PROGRAMS: Annual Meeting; Community Outreach; Concerts; Exhibits; Guided Tours; Interpretation; Lectures; Living History; Publication; Reenactments; Research Library/ Archives; School-Based Curriculum

COLLECTIONS: [World War II-Pacific Theatre (1941-1945)] POW material; VAL Japanese dive-bomber; Japanese mini submarine; Pearl Harbor memorabilia.

HOURS: Yr Daily 8-5

ADMISSION: $3, Student $1.50

FREDERICKSBURG

8115
Gillespie County Historical Society
312 W San Antonio St, 78624; (p) (830) 997-2835; (f) (830) 997-3891; gchs@ktc.com; www.ktc.nct/gchs; (c) Gillespie

Private non-profit/ 1935/ staff: 3(f); 7(p); 10(v)/ members: 250/publication: *Gillespie County: A View of Its Past*

HISTORICAL SOCIETY: Preserves County history. Maintains Pioneer Museum Complex site with 11 structures.

PROGRAMS: Annual Meeting; Community Outreach; Exhibits; Facility Rental; Festivals; Garden Tours; Guided Tours; Interpretation; Lectures; Publication; Theatre

COLLECTIONS: [1846-1945] 14 historic structures, 600 newspapers, 3,500 photos, 100 works of art, 150 textiles, 1,500 pieces of furniture, approximately 1,000 farm and industrial tools; wagons and buggies.

HOURS: Yr

FRITCH

8116
Lake Meredith Aquatic and Wildlife Museum
103 N Robey, 79036 [PO Box 758, 79036-0758]; (p) (806) 857-2458; (f) (806) 857-3229; lmmuseum@infinitytx.net

City/ 1976/ staff: 1(f); 2(p); 30(v)/ members: 50

HISTORY MUSEUM: Promotes preservation of wildlife, TX panhandle environment and ecology.

PROGRAMS: Community Outreach; Exhibits; Family Programs; Festivals; Interpretation

COLLECTIONS: Lake Meredith fish species; Native American artifacts.

HOURS: Yr M-Sa 10-5, Su 2-5

ADMISSION: Donations accepted

GAINESVILLE

8117
Cooke County Heritage Society, Inc.
210 S Dixon, 76241 [PO Box 150, 76241]; (p) (940) 668-8900; (c) Cooke

Private non-profit/ 1966/ staff: 2(f); 1(p); 14(v)/ members: 250

HISTORIC SITE; HISTORY MUSEUM

PROGRAMS: Annual Meeting; Community Outreach; Exhibits; Guided Tours; Lectures; Living History; Research Library/Archives

COLLECTIONS: [1840s-present]

HOURS: Yr T-F 10-5, Sa 12-5

ADMISSION: No charge

GALVESTON

8118
Ashton Villa
2328 Broadway, 77550; (p) (409) 762-3933; (f) (409) 762-1904; www.galvestonhistory.org; (c) Galveston

Private non-profit/ 1954/ Galveston Historical Foundation/ staff: 3(f); 6(p); 25(v)/ members: 4500/publication: *Membership Update*

HISTORICAL SOCIETY; HOUSE MUSEUM: Home to James Moreau Brown, an early Galveston community leader.

PROGRAMS: Exhibits; Facility Rental; Festivals; Guided Tours; Interpretation; Publication

COLLECTIONS: [1860-1915] Victorian furnishings, paintings, art objects, textiles, and archaeological material.

HOURS: Yr M-Sa 10-4, Su 12-4

ADMISSION: $5

8119
Bishop's Palace
14th and Broadway, 77550-4998; (p) (409) 762-2475; www.utmb.edu/galveston/homes/bishop palace.html

8120
Galveston County Historical Museum
2219 Market, 77550-1503; (p) (409) 766-2340; (f) (409) 795-2157; (c) Galveston

County; Private non-profit/ 1976/ Galveston County/Galveston Historical Foundation/ staff: 2(f); 3(p); 20(v)

HISTORY MUSEUM

PROGRAMS: Elder's Programs; Exhibits; Guided Tours; Lectures

COLLECTIONS: [1860-present] Local artifacts, photos.

HOURS: Yr M-Sa 10-4, Su 12-4

ADMISSION: No charge

8121
Garten Verein Pavilion
2704 Ave O, 77550 [2328 Broadway, 77550]; (p) (409) 762-3933; (f) (409) 762-1904; www.galvestonhistory.org; (c) Galveston

City; Private non-profit/ 1954/ City of Galveston/Galveston Historical Foundation/ staff: 3(f); 1(p)/ members: 4500

HISTORIC PRESERVATION AGENCY; HISTORICAL SOCIETY: Restores and preserves 1880 dance hall.

PROGRAMS: Facility Rental

COLLECTIONS: [1880]

HOURS: By rental only

8122
Michel B. Menard Home
1605 33rd St, 77550 [2016 Strand Ave, 77550]; (p) (409) 762-3933; (f) (409) 765-7857

1838/ Galveston Historical Foundation/ staff: 2(f); 1(p); 21(v)

COLLECTIONS: [Early-mid 19th c] Period furnishings and art.

HOURS: Yr F-Su 12-4 and by appt

8123
Moody Mansion
2618 Broadway, 77550 [PO Box 1300, 77553]; (p) (409) 762-7668; (f) (409) 762-7055

1893/ Mary Moody Northern Endowment/ staff: 6(f); 12(p)

COLLECTIONS: [Early 20th c] Robert Mitchell furnishing, textiles, clothing.

HOURS: Yr M-Sa 10-4, Su 1-4:30; closed M, Jan-Mar

8124
Powhatan House
35th & Ave O, 77550 [3427 Ave O, 77550]; (p) (409) 763-0077; (f) (409) 744-1456

1846/ Galveston Garden Club

COLLECTIONS: [1840-1890s] Furnishing; travel correspondence; Battle of Shiloh artifacts; literature, deeds; photos; Sydnor's will.

HOURS: Sa 1-3:30 by appt

ADMISSION: $2, Children $1, Seniors $1

8125
Saint Joseph's Church
2202 Ave K, 77550 [2328 Broadway, 77550]; (p) (409) 762-3933; (f) (409) 762-1904; www.galvestonhistory.org; (c) Galveston

Private non-profit/ 1954/ Galveston Historical Foundation/ staff: 2(f); 1(p); 25(v)/ members: 4500

HISTORICAL SOCIETY; HOUSE MUSEUM: Preserves Saint Joseph's Catholic Church history.

PROGRAMS: Concerts; Elder's Programs; Exhibits; Facility Rental; Guided Tours; Interpretation

COLLECTIONS: [1859-1968] Vernacular religious structure.

HOURS: Yr by appt

ADMISSION: $1

8126
Samuel May Williams Home
3601 Ave P, 77550 [2328 Broadway, 77550]; (p) (409) 762-3933; (f) (409) 762-1904; www.galvestonhistory.org; (c) Galveston

Private non-profit/ 1954/ Galveston Historical Foundation/ staff: 2(f); 1(p); 30(v)/ members: 4500/publication: *The Samuel May Williams Home*

HISTORICAL SOCIETY; HOUSE MUSEUM: Preserves history and home of Samuel May Williams.

PROGRAMS: Elder's Programs; Exhibits; Festivals; Film/Video; Guided Tours; Interpretation; Publication

COLLECTIONS: [1840-1855] Early Victorian furnishings.

HOURS: Yr Sa-Su 12-4

ADMISSION: $3, Children $2

8127
Texas Aviation Hall of Fame/Lone Star Flight Museum
2002 Terminal Dr, 77552 [PO Box 3099, 77552-0099]; (p) (409) 740-7722; (f) (409) 740-7612; (c) Galveston

Private non-profit/ 1986/ staff: 14(f); 2(p); 150(v)/ members: 1300/publication: *Aviation in the Classroom: A Teacher's Curriculum Guide; A Legend of Wings*

AVIATION MUSEUM; HISTORY MUSEUM: Acquires, restores and preserves aircraft representing the evolution of aircraft design; depicts development of aviation.

PROGRAMS: Community Outreach; Exhibits; Facility Rental; Family Programs; Guided Tours; Interpretation; Lectures; Living History; Publication; Research Library/Archives; School-Based Curriculum

COLLECTIONS: [1903-present] 35 aircrafts from early 1930s to 1970s; aviation related artifacts, education facility, research library and archives.

HOURS: Yr Daily 10-5

ADMISSION: $6, Student $5, Children $4, Seniors $4.50; Under 4 free; Group rates

8128
Texas Seaport Museum
Pier 21, No 8, 77550; (p) (409) 763-1877; (f) (409) 763-3037; tsm@phoenix.net; (c) Galveston

Private non-profit/ 1991/ Galveston Historical Foundation/ staff: 7(f); 14(p); 200(v)

HISTORY MUSEUM; LIVING HISTORY/OUTDOOR MUSEUM: Promotes maritime history.

PROGRAMS: Community Outreach; Concerts; Elder's Programs; Exhibits; Facility Rental; Family Programs; Festivals; Film/Video; Guided Tours; Interpretation; Lectures; Living History; Research Library/Archives

COLLECTIONS: [1875-1925] Artifacts, paintings and archives.

HOURS: Yr Daily 10-5

GARLAND

8129
Garland Landmark Society
200 Museum Plaza, 75046 [PO Box 469002, 75046-9002]; (p) (972) 205-2000; (c) Dallas

Private non-profit/ 1973/ staff: 10(v)/ members: 15

HISTORIC SITE; HISTORICAL SOCIETY: Collects, preserves, and interprets history of Garland.

PROGRAMS: Annual Meeting; Exhibits

COLLECTIONS: [1920s-1940s]

HOURS: Jan-Sept, Nov-Dec 1st and 3rd W 9-2, 2nd and 4th Sa 10-4

ADMISSION: No charge

GATESVILLE

8130
Coryell County Genealogical Society
811 Main St, 76528; (p) (254) 865-5367; (f) (254) 248-0986; bwross@htcomp.net; www.rootsweb.com/~txcoryl/; (c) Coryell

Private non-profit/ staff: 10(v)/ members: 90/publication: *Coryell Kin*

GENEALOGICAL SOCIETY

PROGRAMS: Annual Meeting; Publication

GEORGE WEST

8131
Grace Armantrout Museum
Hwy 281 S, 78022 [PO Box 248, 78022]; (p) (361) 449-3325; (f) (361) 449-3295; marnie@bcni.net; (c) Live Oak

Private non-profit/ 1990/ Cactus Park Museum Trust/ staff: 1(p); 70(v)/ members: 100

HISTORIC PRESERVATION AGENCY; HISTORY MUSEUM: Preserves the artifacts and history of the people and the county.

PROGRAMS: Annual Meeting; Exhibits; Lectures; Research Library/Archives

COLLECTIONS: [Early 20th c] Furniture, houseware, tools, eyeglasses, seashells, rocks, art and books from home of Miss Armantrout as well as similar items donated by local citizens.

HOURS: Yr W-Sa 1-5

ADMISSION: No charge

GIDDINGS

8132
Texas Wendish Heritage Society and Museum
1049 County Rd 212, 78942 [Route 2, Box 155, 78942-9769]; (p) (409) 366-2441; (f) (409) 366-2805; (c) Lee

Private non-profit/ 1971/ staff: 2(p); 25(v)/ members: 500

HISTORICAL SOCIETY; HISTORY MUSEUM: Preserves history of the Wends (also known as Sorbs and Lusatians).

PROGRAMS: Exhibits; Festivals; Guided Tours; Interpretation; Lectures

COLLECTIONS: [1854-present] Early TX furnishings, farm equipment, rare books, certificates, newspapers, documents, manuscripts, photos, artifacts.

HOURS: Yr T-Su 1-5

ADMISSION: $1; Children/Members free

GILMER

8133
Historic Upshur Museum
119 Simpson St, 75644-2231; (p) (903) 843-5483; (f) (903) 843-5483; (c) Upshur

Private non-profit/ 1993/ Board of Directors/ staff: 2(p); 60(v)/ members: 80

HISTORIC SITE; HISTORY MUSEUM: Preserves history of Upshur County.

PROGRAMS: Annual Meeting; Community Outreach; Exhibits; Family Programs; Guided Tours; Interpretation

HOURS: Yr M-Sa 10:30-5

ADMISSION: Donations accepted

GREENVILLE

8134
American Cotton Museum
600 I-H 30E, 75403 [PO Box 347, 75403]; (p) (903) 450-4502; (f) (903) 454-1990; cottonmuseum@cottonmuseum.com; www.cottonmuseum.com; (c) Hunt

Private non-profit/ 1987/ Board of Directors/ staff: 2(f); 2(p); 25(v)/ members: 561

HISTORIC PRESERVATION AGENCY; HISTORY MUSEUM; HOUSE MUSEUM: Preserves history of the American cotton industry, history of Hunt County.

PROGRAMS: Community Outreach; Exhibits; Facility Rental; Festivals; Guided Tours; Interpretation; Lectures; Living History; Research Library/Archives; School-Based Curriculum

COLLECTIONS: [1850-present] Cotton, local history, and general artifacts.

HOURS: Yr T, Th, Sa 10-5

ADMISSION: $2, Student $1, Children $1, Seniors $1

8135
Ende-Gaillard House
600 Interstate 30 E, 75403 [PO Box 347, 75403]; (p) (903) 454-1990, (903) 450-4502; www.cottonmuseum.com/ende.htm

HOUSE MUSEUM

8136
W. Walworth Harrison Public Library, Genealogy/Texana Room
1 Lou Finney Lane, 75401; (p) (903) 457-2992; (f) (903) 457-2961; ctaylor@ci.greenville.tx.us; www.ci.greenville.tx.us/library.htm; (c) Hunt

City/ 1953/ staff: 1(f); 5(v)

GENEALOGICAL SOCIETY: Promotes history of northeast TX.

PROGRAMS: Community Outreach; Research Library/Archives

COLLECTIONS: [1840s-present] TX census, Greenville newspapers from 1898, manuscripts of Hunt County history and rare books.

HOURS: Yr M-Th 9:30-8:30, F-Sa 9:30-5:30

ADMISSION: No charge

HALE CENTER

8137
Hale County Farm and Ranch Historical Museum
.5 mi S of Hale Center, W service gt I-27, 79041 [PO Box 834, 79041]; (p) (806) 839-2556; (c) Hale

County/ 1981/ Board of Directors/ staff: 2(f); 150(v)/ members: 100

HISTORIC SITE; HOUSE MUSEUM: Preserves heritage of early settlers.

PROGRAMS: Community Outreach; Exhibits; Festivals; Guided Tours

COLLECTIONS: [Late 19th c-present] Farm equipment, steam engine, hot ball engine, tractors, milk and cream separators.

HOURS: Yr Daily 1-5

ADMISSION: Donations accepted

HALLETTSVILLE

8138
Lavaca Historical Museum
413 N Main, 77964; (p) (361) 798-4113; (f) (361) 798-4113; (c) Lavaca

Private non-profit/ 1990/ Board of Directors/ staff: 1(p); 100(v)

Preserves local history.

COLLECTIONS: [Late 19th c-present] South central TX Old-timers Baseball Hall of Fame; medical artifacts.

HOURS: Yr T, Th, F 1-5

ADMISSION: Donations accepted

HARLINGEN

8139
Rio Grande Valley Museum
Boxwood at Raintree, 78550; (p) (956) 430-8500; (f) (956) 430-8502; rgvmuse@hiline.net; (c) Cameron

City/ staff: 3(f); 3(p)

HISTORY MUSEUM; HOUSE MUSEUM: Promotes history and natural history.

PROGRAMS: Exhibits; Facility Rental; Family Programs; Film/Video; Guided Tours; Theatre

COLLECTIONS: [Prehistory-present] TX and Rio Grande Valley artifacts, period furnishing.

HOURS: Yr W-Sa 10-4, Su 1-4

ADMISSION: $2, Children $1, Seniors $1

HENDERSON

8140
Depot Museum Complex
514 N High St, 75652; (p) (903) 657-4303; (f) (903) 657-2679; depot514@ballistic.com; www.depotmuseum.com; (c) Rusk

County/ 1978/ staff: 1(f); 5(p); 30(v)/ members: 109/publication: *East Texas Folk Life Guide*

HISTORY MUSEUM: Preserves and interprets history and culture of Rusk County.

PROGRAMS: Community Outreach; Exhibits; Festivals; Film/Video; Interpretation; Publication; School-Based Curriculum

COLLECTIONS: [1600-1946] 9 buildings with period tools and furniture.

HOURS: Yr M-Sa 9-5, Sa 9-1

ADMISSION: $2, Children $1

8141
Howard-Dickinson House
501 S Main St, 75652; (p) (903) 657-6925

1855/ Rusk County Heritage Association

COLLECTIONS: [Turn of the c] Sam Houston trunk, original furnishing.

HOURS: M-F pm by appt

HENRIETTA

8142
Clay County 1890 Jail Museum and Heritage Center
116 N Graham St, 76365 [PO Box 483, 76365]; (p) (940) 538-5655, (940) 524-3465; ccmuseum@wf.quik.com; www.pctutor.org/ccmuseum. html; (c) Clay

Private non-profit/ 1981/ Clay County Historical Society, Inc./ staff: 30(v)/ members: 300

HISTORICAL SOCIETY; HISTORY MUSEUM

PROGRAMS: Annual Meeting; Community Outreach; Exhibits; Guided Tours; Interpretation; Living History

COLLECTIONS: [1890-1950] Furniture, clothing, tools, household, farming and ranching gadgets; artifacts, documents, photos; 1890 jail building with sheriff's residence.

HOURS: Yr Th-F 10-2, Sa 1-4

ADMISSION: $2, Students $1

HEREFORD

8143
Deaf Smith County Historical Museum
400 Sampson St, 79045 [PO Box 1007, 79045]; (p) (806) 363-7070; (c) Deaf Smith

County/ 1967/ staff: 2(f); 25(v)/ members: 250

HISTORIC SITE; HISTORICAL SOCIETY; HISTORY MUSEUM: Preserves Pioneer heritage.

PROGRAMS: Annual Meeting; Exhibits; Guided Tours

COLLECTIONS: [Late 19th-early 20th c] Pioneer furniture and artifacts, clothing, photos, Native American artifacts, western saddles, hand-carved three-ring circus, Santa Fe caboose, windmill and farm implements.

HOURS: Yr M-Sa 10-5

ADMISSION: Donations accepted

HILLSBORO

8144
Harold B. Simpson History Complex
112 Lamar Dr, Hill College, 76645 [PO Box 619, 76645]; (p) (254) 582-2555; patterson@hill-college.cc.tx.us; www.hill-college.cc.tx.us; (c) Hill

State/ 1963/ Hill College/ staff: 5(f); 3(p)

HISTORY MUSEUM; LIBRARY AND/OR ARCHIVES: Promotes TX military history.

PROGRAMS: Exhibits; Film/Video; Lectures; Publication; Research Library/Archives

COLLECTIONS: [1860s-1940s] Library, archival materials, and artifacts reflective of TX military history.

HOURS: Yr M-Sa 9-4

ADMISSION: $4

HITCHCOCK

8145
Hitchcock Heritage Society, Inc.
8005 Barry Ave, 77563; (p) (409) 986-7814; (f) (409) 986-6353; kbrooks@hals.lib.tx.us; (c) Galveston

Private non-profit/ 1985/ staff: 8(v)/ members: 40/publication: *Recipes and Recollection of Hitchcock*

HISTORICAL SOCIETY; HOUSE MUSEUM: Collects, preserves and interprets Hitchcock's past; maintains house museum.

PROGRAMS: Community Outreach; Elder's Programs; Exhibits; Family Programs; Festivals; Interpretation; Living History; Publication

COLLECTIONS: [19th-20th c] Photos, furniture and clothing.

HOURS: Yr 2nd W, 4th Sa 10-1

ADMISSION: Donations accepted

HOUSTON

8146
Heritage Society, The
1100 Bagby, 77002; (p) (713) 655-1912; (f) (713) 655-7527; jcab@heritagesociety.org; www.heritagesociety.org; (c) Harris

Private non-profit/ 1954/ Board of Trustees/ staff: 12(f); 6(p); 600(v)/ members: 1500/publication: *Panorama*

HISTORICAL SOCIETY; HISTORY MUSEUM; HOUSE MUSEUM: Preserves Houston history.

PROGRAMS: Community Outreach; Exhibits; Facility Rental; Family Programs; Guided Tours; Lectures; Publication; School-Based Curriculum

COLLECTIONS: [1836-present] Decorative arts, toys, textiles, fire equipment and furniture.

HOURS: Yr M-Sa 10-4, Su 1-4

ADMISSION: $6, Student $4, Children $2, Seniors $4

8147
Houston Fire Museum
2403 Milam St, 77006; (p) (713) 524-2526; www.houstonfiremuseum.org; (c) Harris

Private non-profit/ 1982/ Board of Trustees/ staff: 3(f); 1(p); 20(v)/ members: 2300/publication: *Leather Bucket*

HISTORIC SITE; HISTORY MUSEUM: Promotes history of fire service.

PROGRAMS: Annual Meeting; Exhibits; Facility Rental; Guided Tours; Publication

COLLECTIONS: [20th c] Local artifacts, uniforms, caps, badges, fire equipment, photos and ephemera.

HOURS: Yr T-Sa 10-4

ADMISSION: $2, Student $1, Children $1, Seniors $1, Under 3 free

8148
Museum of Fine Arts, Houston
1001 Bissonnet, 77265 [PO Box 6826, 77265-6826]; (p) (713) 639-7300; (f) (713) 639-7398; www.mfah.org; (c) Harris

Private non-profit/ 1900/ Board of Trustees/ staff: 300(f); 200(p); 2400(v)/ members: 35000

ART MUSEUM; LIBRARY AND/OR ARCHIVES: Collects, exhibits and interprets art and art history.

PROGRAMS: Community Outreach; Elder's Programs; Exhibits; Facility Rental; Family Programs; Film/Video; Garden Tours; Guided Tours; Lectures; Publication; Research Library/Archives

COLLECTIONS: 6,000 years of art history.

HOURS: Yr

ADMISSION: $3, Student $1.50, Children $1.50, Seniors $1.50; Under 6 free

8149
Museum of Health and Medical Science

1515 Hermann Dr, John P McGovern Bldg, 77004-7126; (p) (713) 942-7054; (f) (713) 526-1434; info@mhms.org; www.mhms.org; (c) Harris

Private non-profit/ 1968/ staff: 26(f); 15(p); 200(v)/ members: 650

HISTORY MUSEUM: Promotes science history.

PROGRAMS: Community Outreach; Exhibits; Facility Rental; Family Programs; Lectures; School-Based Curriculum

HOURS: Yr T-Sa 9-5, Su12-5

ADMISSION: $4, Children $3

8150
Pioneer Memorial Log House Museum

1513 N MacGregor Dr, 77030 [1510 N MacGregor, 77030]; (p) (713) 522-0396, (713) 861-7426; (f) (713) 522-0396; pwl.netcom.com/~jdv3dgel/loghouse.html

1936/ Daughters of the Republic of TX/ staff: 30(v)

COLLECTIONS: [1836-1846] Flags; Run Away Scrape artifacts.

HOURS: Yr

HUMBLE

8151
Jesse H. Jones Park and Nature Center

20634 Kenswick Dr, 77338; (p) (281) 446-8588; (f) (281) 446-8832; Dconley@cp4.hctx.net; www.jjpv.org; (c) Harris

County/ 1982/ Harris County Precinct 4/ staff: 9(f); 1(p); 50(v)/publication: Parkscape

GARDEN; HISTORIC SITE; LIVING HISTORY/OUTDOOR MUSEUM: Preserves natural history.

PROGRAMS: Community Outreach; Concerts; Elder's Programs; Exhibits; Family Programs; Festivals; Garden Tours; Guided Tours; Interpretation; Lectures; Living History; Publication; Reenactments; School-Based Curriculum

COLLECTIONS: [19th-20th c] Live animals, displays and dioramas, log cabin, smokehouse, root cellar, garden, chicken house, barn, corn crib, woodshop, blacksmith shop, Akokisa Indian Village.

HOURS: Dec-Jan Daily 8-5; Nov, Feb Daily 8-6; Mar-Oct Daily 8-7

ADMISSION: No charge

HUNTSVILLE

8152
Sam Houston Memorial Museum

1836 Sam Houston Ave, 77341 [Box 2057, Sam Houston State University, 77341]; (p) (936) 294-1832; (f) (936) 294-3670; SMM_PBN@shsu.edu; www.shsu.edu/~smm_www; (c) Walker

State/ 1936/ Sam Houston State Univ/ staff: 12(f); 2(p); 60(v)/ members: 165/publication: Sam Houston

HISTORIC SITE; HISTORY MUSEUM; HOUSE MUSEUM; LIVING HISTORY/OUTDOOR MUSEUM: Preserves three original homes and buildings built by General Sam Houston.

PROGRAMS: Community Outreach; Concerts; Elder's Programs; Exhibits; Facility Rental; Family Programs; Festivals; Film/Video; Guided Tours; Interpretation; Lectures; Living History; Publication; Reenactments; Research Library/Archives; School-Based Curriculum

COLLECTIONS: [1832-1863] Manuscripts, family papers, buildings, furniture, decorative arts, agricultural equipment, military hardware, clothing, photos, portraits, and paintings.

HOURS: Yr T-Su 9-4:30

ADMISSION: No charge

8153
Walker County Historical Commission

1228 11th St, 77342 [PO Box 210, 77342-0210]; (p) (936) 295-2914, (936) 291-3581; (f) (936) 436-4928; (c) Walker

County/ 1963/ members: 25

HISTORIC PRESERVATION AGENCY; HISTORIC SITE; HOUSE MUSEUM: Promotes and preserves County history.

PROGRAMS: Exhibits; Guided Tours; Lectures; Research Library/Archives

COLLECTIONS: [1840-1915] Furniture, books, newspapers, and documents.

HOURS: Yr by appt only

ADMISSION: $3

JEFFERSON

8154
Jefferson Historical Society and Museum

223 W Austin, 75657; (p) (903) 665-2775; (c) Marion

Private non-profit/ 1948/ staff: 2(p); 30(v)/ members: 182

GENEALOGICAL SOCIETY; HISTORIC SITE; HISTORICAL SOCIETY; HISTORY MUSEUM; RESEARCH CENTER

PROGRAMS: Annual Meeting; Exhibits; Guided Tours; Research Library/Archives

COLLECTIONS: [19th c] Native American artifacts; art, genealogy, dolls, guns, farm tools, bottles, looms, doctors instruments, and Civil War artifacts.

HOURS: Yr Daily 9:30-5

ADMISSION: $3, Children $1

JOHNSON CITY

8155
Lyndon B. Johnson National Historic Park

100 Ladybird Lane, 78636 [PO Box 329, 78636]; (p) (830) 868-7128; (f) (830) 868-7863; www.nps.gov/lyjo; (c) Blanco

Federal/ 1969/ National Park Service/ staff: 50(f); 12(p); 16(v)

PRESIDENTIAL SITE: Researches, preserves, and interprets the life and heritage of the 36th president Lyndon B. Johnson.

PROGRAMS: Community Outreach; Concerts; Exhibits; Family Programs; Film/Video; Guided Tours; Interpretation; Lectures; Research Library/Archives; School-Based Curriculum

COLLECTIONS: [1867-1973] Original furnishings, farm, and ranch equipment, LBJ memorabilia, automobiles, photos, oral histories, and park history.

HOURS: Yr Daily 8:45-5

KERRVILLE

8156
Cowboy Artists of America Museum

1550 Bandera Hwy, 07029 [PO Box 294300, 7029-4300]; (p) (830) 896-2553; (f) (830) 896-2556; caam@ktc.com; www.caamuseum.com; (c) Kerr

Private non-profit/ 1983/ Board of Directors/ staff: 7(f); 6(p); 97(v)/ members: 1570/publication: Visions West

ART MUSEUM: Promotes cowboy/western history.

PROGRAMS: Community Outreach; Exhibits; Facility Rental; Guided Tours; Publication; Research Library/Archives; School-Based Curriculum

COLLECTIONS: [19th c-present] Cowboy artists paintings, US Western development, ranching.

HOURS: Yr M-Sa 9-5, Su 1-5

ADMISSION: $5, Children $1, Seniors $3.50; Under 6

8157
Schreiner Mansion Museum

226 Earl Garrett St, 78028 [PO Box 107, 78028]; (p) (830) 896-8633

HOUSE MUSEUM

KILGORE

8158
East Texas Oil Museum at Kilgore College

Hwy 259 at Ross St, 75662; (p) (903) 983-8294, (903) 983-8295; (f) (903) 983-8600; white.j@kilgore.cc.tx.us; www.easttexasoilmuseum.com; (c) Gregg

1980/ Kilgore College/ staff: 3(f); 3(p); 40(v)

HISTORY MUSEUM

PROGRAMS: Community Outreach; Exhibits; Facility Rental; Film/Video; Guided Tours; Interpretation; Lectures; School-Based Curriculum

COLLECTIONS: [1920s-1940s] Boomtown diorama with life-size livery and blacksmith, general store, barber shop, gas station, newspaper office, drugstore, theater and gristmill.

HOURS: Yr Su 2-5; Apr-Sept T-Sa 9-5; Oct-Mar T-Sa 9-4

ADMISSION: $4, Children $2

KINGSVILLE

8159
James E. Conner Museum, Texas A&M University
905 W Santa Gertrudis, 78363 [Station 1, Box 2172, 78363]; (p) (361) 593-2810; (f) (361) 593-2112; www.tamok.edu/museum/index.html; (c) Kleberg

State/ 1976/ staff: 4(f); 7(p); 75(v)/ members: 250

HISTORY MUSEUM: Collects, preserves and interprets the natural history, prehistory, history and culture of southern TX and related areas.

PROGRAMS: Community Outreach; Exhibits; Family Programs; Festivals; Guided Tours; Interpretation; Lectures

COLLECTIONS: [1790s-present] 15,000 museum artifacts.

HOURS: Yr M-Sa 9-5

ADMISSION: No charge

8160
King Ranch, Inc.
405 N Sixth St, 78364 [PO Box 1090, 78364-1090]; (p) (361) 595-1881, (361) 592-0408; (f) (361) 592-3247; krmuseum@interconnect.net; www.king-ranch.com; (c) Kleberg

Private for-profit/ 1853/ King Ranch, Inc./ staff: 5(f); 2(p)

HISTORY MUSEUM: Collects, preserves, and interprets ranching community.

PROGRAMS: Exhibits; Facility Rental; Film/Video; Lectures

COLLECTIONS: [1853-present] Photos, slides, negatives, film, oral histories, manuscripts, maps, paintings, guns, antique carriages, vintage cars.

HOURS: Museum: M-Sa 10-4, Su 1-5; Archives: M-F 8-5 by appt

ADMISSION: $4, Children $2.50; Under 5 free

KLEIN

8161
Klein, Texas Historical Foundation
18218 Theiss Mail Rd, 77379 [7200 Spring-Cypress Rd, 77379]; (p) (281) 376-4180; gserverance@compuserve.com; www.klein.texas.schools.esc4.net; (c) Harris

Private non-profit/ 1988/ Board of Trustees/ staff: 1(p); 35(v)/ members: 50/publication: *Deep Roots, Strong Branches*

HISTORIC PRESERVATION AGENCY; HISTORIC SITE; HISTORY MUSEUM; HOUSE MUSEUM: Preserves history and culture of the people, traditions and folk lore of Klein.

PROGRAMS: Community Outreach; Exhibits; Festivals; Guided Tours; Interpretation; Publication; School-Based Curriculum

COLLECTIONS: [1890-1940] Peter Wunderlich farm and outbuildings, Maria Wunderlich Home (1870), Kohrville School (1920), 1,000 photos, 1,000 museum artifacts, 200 farm tools and 180 books.

HOURS: Jan-Apr, June-Oct last Sa 11-3

ADMISSION: No charge

KOUNTZE

8162
Kirby-Hill House Museum
210 Main St, 77625; (p) (409) 246-5184; (f) (409) 246-3208

HOUSE MUSEUM

KYLE

8163
Claiborne Kyle Log House
Old Stage Coach Rd, 78640 [PO Box 367, 78640]; (p) (512) 268-2531

1850/ County

HOURS: Apr-Sept

LA GRANGE

8164
Fayette Heritage Museum and Archives
855 S Jefferson, 78945; (p) (409) 968-6418; (f) (409) 968-5357; library@fais.net; www.lagrange.fais.net/museum; (c) Fayette

City/ 1978/ staff: 2(f); 1(p)

HISTORY MUSEUM: Interprets the history of Fayette County.

PROGRAMS: Exhibits; Guided Tours; Interpretation; Research Library/Archives

COLLECTIONS: [1820s-present] Local newspapers, census records, photos, books, maps, families, towns, communities, schools, cemeteries, churches, organizations, and individuals.

HOURS: Yr T-Th 10-6, F 10-5, Sa 10-1, Su 1-5

ADMISSION: No charge

8165
Monument Hill and Kreische Brewery State Historical Parks
414 Spur 92, 78945 [414 State Loop 92, 78945]; (p) (409) 968-5658; (f) (409) 968-5659; mhkb-statepark@fais.net; www.tpwd.state.tx.us/monument/monument; (c) Fayette

State/ 1933/ Texas Parks and Wildlife Dept/ staff: 3(f); 1(p); 43(v)/publication: *The Dawson and Mier Expeditions and Their Place in Texas History*

HISTORIC PRESERVATION AGENCY; HISTORIC SITE; HISTORY MUSEUM; HOUSE MUSEUM; STATE PARK: Monument Hill burial site (Dawson Massacre 1842 and Black Bean Incident 1843). German immigrant H.L. Kriesche's brewery (1860-1884). Educates the public about the sites while managing and conserving the cultural and natural resources for the use and enjoyment of present and future generations.

PROGRAMS: Community Outreach; Elder's Programs; Exhibits; Facility Rental; Family Programs; Guided Tours; Interpretation; Lectures; Publication; School-Based Curriculum

COLLECTIONS: [1870s-1920s] Furnishings of the Kreische family; brewery implements; cooking vessels.

HOURS: Yr Daily 8-5

ADMISSION: $2; Under 13/TX Seniors free

8166
Nathaniel W. Faison Home and Museum
822 S Jefferson, 78945 [155 S Lynnwood, 78945]; (p) (409) 968-6667

HOUSE MUSEUM

LA PORTE

8167
Battleship Texas, The
3527 Battleground Rd, 77571; (p) (713) 479-4414; (f) (281) 479-4197; (c) Harris

State/ 1948/ Texas Parks and Wildlife Dept/ staff: 14(f); 60(v)/publication: *The Dreadnaught*

HISTORIC SITE; HISTORY MUSEUM: Preserves and interprets The Battleship Texas and the San Jacinto Battlefield.

PROGRAMS: Exhibits; Guided Tours; Interpretation; Living History; Publication; Reenactments; Research Library/Archives

COLLECTIONS: [WWII] Battleship Texas artifacts, ephemera.

HOURS: Yr Daily

8168
San Jacinto Museum of History Association
One Monument Circle, 77571; (p) (281) 479-2421; (f) (281) 479-2428; (c) Harris

Private non-profit/ 1938/ staff: 23(f); 3(p)

HISTORIC SITE; HISTORY MUSEUM

PROGRAMS: Exhibits; Interpretation; Reenactments; School-Based Curriculum; Theatre

COLLECTIONS: [18th-19th c]

HOURS: Yr Daily 9-6

ADMISSION: No charge

LAREDO

8169
Webb County Heritage Foundation
500 Flores Ave, 78042 [PO Box 446, 78042-0446]; (p) (956) 727-0977; (f) (956) 727-0577; heritage@surfus.net; (c) Webb

Private non-profit/ 1980/ staff: 4(f); 3(p); 1(v)/ members: 250/publication: *Laredo Legacies*

HISTORIC PRESERVATION AGENCY; HISTORICAL SOCIETY; HOUSE MUSEUM: Preserves the history and heritage of Laredo, the Tex-Mex border region and Webb County in south TX.

PROGRAMS: Annual Meeting; Community Outreach; Exhibits; Guided Tours; Lectures; Publication; Research Library/Archives

COLLECTIONS: [Late 19th-early 20th c] Maps, documents, artifacts, photos and oral histories.

HOURS: Museum: Yr T-Sa 9-4, Su 1-4; WCHF office: Yr M-F 8:30-5

ADMISSION: Donations requested

LEAGUE CITY

8170
West Bay Common School Children's Museum
210 N Kansas, 77573; (p) (281) 554-2994; (c) Galveston

Private non-profit/ 1993/ League City Historical Society, Inc./ staff: 5(p); 25(v)/ members: 58

HISTORIC SITE; HISTORICAL SOCIETY; HISTORY MUSEUM; LIVING HISTORY/OUTDOOR MUSEUM: Protects, preserves and beautifies the old historic area of League City.

PROGRAMS: Annual Meeting; Community Outreach; Exhibits; Facility Rental; Festivals; Guided Tours; Living History; School-Based Curriculum

COLLECTIONS: [19th-20th c] One room Texas schoolhouse museum from 1898 with state and local artifacts in education; 1920s icehouse and barber shop museum and a 1930's fire station/bus barn with local artifacts and memorabilia.

HOURS: Yr M-F 9-2 or by appt

ADMISSION: No charge

LIBERTY

8171
Sam Houston Regional Library and Research Center
FM 1011, 77575 [PO Box 310, 77575-0310]; (p) (436) 336-8821; samhoustoncenter@tsl.state.tx.us; www.tsl.state.tx; (c) Liberty

State/ 1977/ TX State Library and Archives Commission/ staff: 5(f); 1(p); 4(v)

HISTORY MUSEUM; HOUSE MUSEUM; RESEARCH CENTER: Serves Southeast TX with three historical houses; special collections include General Sam Houston, Martin Dies, Price Daniel, Jean Laffite and Champ d'Asile.

PROGRAMS: Annual Meeting; Exhibits; Guided Tours; Lectures; Research Library/Archives

COLLECTIONS: [1820s-present] Documents, artifacts, photos, maps, books.

HOURS: Yr M-F 8-5, Sa 9-4

ADMISSION: No charge

LIPSCOMB

8172
Wolf Creek Heritage Museum
300 Main Ave, 79056 [PO Box 69, 79056]; (p) (806) 862-4131; (f) (806) 862-2603; (c) Lipscomb

County/ 1982/ Lipscomb County Historical Commission/ staff: 6(v)

ART MUSEUM; HISTORY MUSEUM: Preserves the history of Lipscomb County.

PROGRAMS: Community Outreach; Exhibits; Festivals; Guided Tours; Research Library/Archives

COLLECTIONS: [1878-present] Prehistoric and Native American artifacts; farm implements, photos, military, ranching, lifestyle.

HOURS: Yr M, W, F 10-4, Su 2-4

ADMISSION: Donations accepted

LONGVIEW

8173
Gregg County Historical Museum
214 N Fredonia, 75606 [PO Box 3342, 75606]; (p) (903) 753-5840; (f) (903) 753-5854; (c) Gregg

Private non-profit/ 1984/ Gregg County Historical Foundation/ staff: 3(f); 42(v)/ members: 350

HISTORY MUSEUM

PROGRAMS: Community Outreach; Exhibits; Facility Rental; Family Programs; Festivals; Guided Tours; Lectures; Living History; Reenactments; Research Library/Archives; School-Based Curriculum

COLLECTIONS: [1870-1970s] Artifacts, descriptive labels, historic photos, military items, printing exhibit, the Dalton Gang bank robbery, architecture.

HOURS: Yr T-Sa 10-4

ADMISSION: $2, Student $1, Seniors $1

8174
R.G. LeTourneau Museum
2100 S Mobberley, 75607 [PO Box 7001, 75607]; (p) (903) 233-3648; (f) (903) 233-3618; gibbsb@letu.edu; www.letu.edu; (c) Gregg

Private non-profit/ 1975/ LeTourneau Univ

HISTORY MUSEUM: Promotes life of R.G. LeTourneau University founder, entrepreneur, inventor, and philanthropist.

PROGRAMS: Exhibits; Guided Tours

COLLECTIONS: [20th c] R.G. LeTourneau artifacts.

HOURS: Yr

LUBBOCK

8175
American Wind Power Center/National Windmill Project
1501 Canyon Lake Dr, 79409; (p) (806) 747-8734; (f) (806) 740-0668; charris@windmill.com; windmill.com; (c) Lubbock

Private non-profit/ 1993/ Board of Directors/ staff: 3(f); 15(v)/ members: 220

HISTORY MUSEUM; LIVING HISTORY/OUTDOOR MUSEUM

PROGRAMS: Community Outreach; Exhibits; Facility Rental; Guided Tours; Interpretation; Living History; School-Based Curriculum

COLLECTIONS: [1850-present] 81 wooden and metal mills.

HOURS: Yr T-Sa 10-5

ADMISSION: Donation

8176
National Ranching Heritage Center
3121 4th St, 79409 [PO Box 43200, 79409-3200]; (p) (806) 742-0498; (f) (806) 742-0616; ranchhc@ttu.edu; www.ttu.edu/ranchingheritagecenter; (c) Lubbock

Joint/ 1976/ State of TX/TX Tech Univ/ staff: 6(f); 4(p); 150(v)/ members: 625/publication: *Ranch Record*

HISTORY MUSEUM; HOUSE MUSEUM; LIVING HISTORY/OUTDOOR MUSEUM: Preserves and interprets the history of ranching in North America.

PROGRAMS: Annual Meeting; Community Outreach; Concerts; Exhibits; Facility Rental; Family Programs; Festivals; Guided Tours; Interpretation; Lectures; Living History; Publication; Reenactments; School-Based Curriculum

COLLECTIONS: [18th-20th c] Ranching artifacts.

HOURS: Yr M-Sa 10-5, Su 1-5

ADMISSION: No charge

8177
West Texas Historical Association
SWC, Texas Tech University, 79409; (p) (806) 742-9076; (f) (806) 742-0496; wthayb@ttacs.ttu.edu; www.lib.ttu.edu/swc/westtexas; (c) Lubbock

Private non-profit/ 1923/ staff: 1(p); 8(v)/ members: 410/publication: *West Texas Historical Association Yearbook*

HISTORICAL SOCIETY: Collects and preserves the history and culture of West TX.

PROGRAMS: Annual Meeting; Community Outreach; Family Programs; Interpretation; Lectures; Publication; Research Library/Archives

LUFKIN

8178
Museum of East Texas
503 N Second St, 75901; (p) (409) 639-4434; (f) (409) 639-4435; (c) Angelina

Private non-profit/ 1976/ staff: 5(f); 2(p); 2(v)/ members: 521

ART MUSEUM; HISTORY MUSEUM: Promotes history of East TX.

PROGRAMS: Exhibits; Facility Rental; Family Programs; Guided Tours; Lectures

COLLECTIONS: [19th-20th c] Local history items, fine arts and archaeological artifacts.

HOURS: Yr T-F

8179
Texas Forestry Museum
1905 Atkinson Dr, 75902 [PO Box 1488, 75902-1488]; (p) (409) 632-9535; (f) (409) 632-9543; info@txforestrymuseum.org; www.txforestrymuseum.org; (c) Angelina

Private non-profit/ 1972/ staff: 3(f); 2(p); 50(v)/ members: 250/publication: *Crosscut*

HISTORY MUSEUM; NATURAL HISTORY MUSEUM; RESEARCH CENTER: Preserves and interprets the rich personal and industrial culture of the East TX Pinewoods.

PROGRAMS: Community Outreach; Elder's Programs; Exhibits; Family Programs; Festivals; Guided Tours; Interpretation; Lectures; Publication; Research Library/Archives; School-Based Curriculum; Theatre

COLLECTIONS: [1880s-present] Books, photos and archival materials.

HOURS: Yr M-Sa 10-5, Su 1-5

ADMISSION: Donations

MARSHALL

8180
Harrison County Historical Commission
200 W Houston, Rm 402, 75670; (p) (903) 935-4812; (f) (903) 935-4813; agnor@internetwork.net; (c) Harrison

County; State/ Texas Historical Commission/Harrison County Commissioners' Court/ staff: 43(v)

HISTORIC PRESERVATION AGENCY: Preserves county and local history; maintains cemeteries.

PROGRAMS: Community Outreach; Research Library/Archives

COLLECTIONS: [Early-mid 19th c] Research papers on TX historical markers for Harrison County.

HOURS: Jan-Nov 2nd Th 12-1 or by appt

8181
Harrison County Historical Museum
707 N Washington, 75670; (p) (903) 938-2680; (f) (903) 927-2534; museum@prysm.net; www.eets.sfasu.edu/Harrison; (c) Harrison

City; County/ 1968/ staff: 1(f); 2(p); 20(v)/ members: 302

GENEALOGICAL SOCIETY; HISTORIC SITE; HISTORY MUSEUM: Historic museum in an old hotel built in 1846. Exhibits with pioneer, military, Caddo Indian and Civil War artifacts, including distinguished citizens such as Lady Bird Johnson, George Foreman, Robert Newhouse and Bill Moyers.

PROGRAMS: Annual Meeting; Community Outreach; Exhibits; Festivals; Lectures; Research Library/Archives

COLLECTIONS: [19th c]

HOURS: Yr T-Sa

8182
Starr Family State Historical Park
407 W Travis, 75670; (p) (903) 935-3044; (f) (903) 938-6039; www.tpwd.state.tx.us

State, Parks and Works/ staff: 1(f); 2(p); 1(v)

Home of James H. and James F. Starr.

COLLECTIONS: Victorian furnishings; textiles; photos and diaries of TX and Civil War.

HOURS: Yr

MASON

8183
Mason County Museum
Moody St, 76856 [PO Box 303, 76856]; (p) (915) 347-6411, (915) 347-5725; (c) Mason

Private non-profit/ 1963/ Mason Historical Society/ staff: 12(v)

ART MUSEUM; HISTORIC SITE; HISTORICAL SOCIETY; HISTORY MUSEUM; LIBRARY AND/OR ARCHIVES: Preserves county history.

PROGRAMS: Annual Meeting; Community Outreach; Exhibits; Film/Video; Guided Tours; Publication; Reenactments; Research Library/Archives; School-Based Curriculum

COLLECTIONS: [19th-early 20th c] Textiles, musical instruments, China, farm tools, books, pictures, and toys.

HOURS: Museum: Yr M-F 9-3; Fort: Yr Daily sunrise-sunset

ADMISSION: Donations accepted

MCDADE

8184
McDade Historical Society
557 Old Hwy 20, Ste A, 78650 [PO Box 621, 78650]; (p) (512) 273-2372; (c) Bastrop

1963/ members: 25

HISTORICAL SOCIETY; HISTORY MUSEUM: Promotes local history.

PROGRAMS: Exhibits

HOURS: Yr by appt

ADMISSION: Donations accepted

MCKINNEY

8185
Collin County Farm Museum
4 mi NW of town, 75070-9804 [RR 4, 75070-9804]; (p) (214) 424-1460; www.lone-star.net/mall/txtrails/mckinney.htm

8186
Heard Natural Science Museum and Wildlife Sanctuary
1 Nature Pl, 75069-8840; (p) (972) 562-5566; (f) (972) 548-9119; heardmuseum@texoma.net; www.heardmuseum.org

Private non-profit/ 1967/ Board of Directors/ staff: 20(f); 4(p); 358(v)/ members: 1347

GARDEN; NATURAL HISTORY MUSEUM: Preserves local and natural history.

PROGRAMS: Community Outreach; Exhibits; Facility Rental; Family Programs; Festivals; Garden Tours; Guided Tours; Interpretation; Lectures; School-Based Curriculum

COLLECTIONS: [Mid 19th-20th c] Zoological, natural, cultural, botanical interpretive areas.

HOURS: Yr M-Sa 9-5, Su 1-5

ADMISSION: $3, Children $2

MIDLAND

8187
Midland County Historical Museum
301 W Missouri, 79701 [2102 Community Lane, 79701]; (p) (915) 688-8947, (915) 682-2931; (c) Midland

County; Private non-profit/ 1932/ Midland County Historical Society/ staff: 6(v)/ members: 125

HISTORY MUSEUM; HOUSE MUSEUM: Collects and exhibits Midland County history.

PROGRAMS: Exhibits; Family Programs; Guided Tours

COLLECTIONS: [1880-present] Photos, obituaries.

HOURS: Yr M, W, F-Sa 2-5 and by appt

ADMISSION: No charge

8188
Permian Basin Petroleum Museum, Library and Hall of Fame
1500 Interstate 20 West, 79701; (p) (915) 683-4403; (f) (915) 683-4509; twhite@petrolemmuseum.org; www.petroleummuseum.org; (c) Midland

Private non-profit/ 1975/ staff: 11(f); 3(p); 200(v)/ members: 476

ART MUSEUM; RESEARCH CENTER: Promotes and preserves history of Permian Basin.

PROGRAMS: Community Outreach; Elder's Programs; Exhibits; Facility Rental; Family Programs; Guided Tours; Research Library/Archives; School-Based Curriculum

COLLECTIONS: [1920s-present] Oilfield equipment; Tom Lovell paintings.

HOURS: Yr M-Sa 9-5, Su 2-5

ADMISSION: $5, Student $4, Children $3, Seniors $4

8189
Z. Taylor Brown-Sarah Dorsey Medallion Home
213 N Weatherfor, 79701 [2102 Community Lane, 79701]; (p) (915) 682-2931; (c) Midland

Private non-profit/ 1976/ Midland Historical Society/ staff: 6(v)/ members: 125

HOUSE MUSEUM: Owns, restores, and maintains museum home.

PROGRAMS: Facility Rental; Guided Tours

COLLECTIONS: [20th c] Period furnishings, interpretive rooms.

HOURS: Yr by appt

ADMISSION: Donations accepted

MONT BELVIEU

8190
Barbers Hill/Mont Belvieu Museum
[PO Box 1048, 77580]; (p) (281) 385-1706; (f) (281) 385-2194; bhmbmuseum@imsday.com; (c) Chambers

City/ 1992/ staff: 1(p); 12(v)

HISTORY MUSEUM

PROGRAMS: Exhibits

COLLECTIONS: [1830-present] Artifacts, photos, and settlement history.

HOURS: Yr T,Th, 2nd Sa 10-2

MOUNT VERNON

8191
Franklin County Historical Association
701 S Kaufman, 75457 [PO Box 289, 75457]; (p) (903) 537-4760; cbrewer@mt-vernon.com; www.mt-vernon.com/~cbrewer/welcome.htm; (c) Franklin

Private non-profit/ 1989/ staff: 1(p); 25(v)/ members: 450/publication: *Early Days in Franklin County*

HISTORICAL SOCIETY; HISTORY MUSEUM; HOUSE MUSEUM: Promotes historical preservation.

PROGRAMS: Annual Meeting; Community Outreach; Concerts; Exhibits; Facility Rental; Festivals; Guided Tours; Publication; Reenactments; Research Library/Archives; School-Based Curriculum

COLLECTIONS: [20th c] Natural history, Native American artifacts; tools; woodcarvings.

HOURS: Yr T,Th 1-4, Sa 9:30-3

ADMISSION: No charge

NACOGDOCHES

8192
Sterne-Hoya Museum
211 S Lanana, 75961; (p) (409) 560-5426; (c) Nacogdoches

City/ 1958/ City of Nacogdoches/ staff: 1(f); 1(p);

HISTORIC SITE; HISTORY MUSEUM; HOUSE MUSEUM: Collects, preserves, researches and exhibits history of Nacogdoches.

PROGRAMS: Community Outreach; Exhibits; Facility Rental; Guided Tours

COLLECTIONS: [1830-1930] Early TX furnishings and artifacts.

HOURS: Yr M-Sa 9-12/2-5

ADMISSION: No charge

8193
Stone Fort Museum
Cor of Alumni & Griffith Blvd, SFASU campus, 75962 [PO Box 6075, Stephen F Austin State University, 75962]; (p) (409) 468-2408; (f) (409) 468-7084; cspears@sfasu.edu; (c) Nacogdoches

State/ 1936/ staff: 1(f); 5(p); 2(v)

HISTORY MUSEUM: Collects, preserves and interprets the prehistory and history of East TX.

PROGRAMS: Community Outreach; Elder's Programs; Exhibits; Guided Tours; Interpretation; Lectures

COLLECTIONS: [1689-1900] 6,000 artifacts of East TX material culture: agricultural, woodworking, household tools, printing, furniture, glassware, armaments, textiles, numismatics and personal artifacts.

HOURS: Yr T-Sa 9-5, Su 1-5

ADMISSION: No charge

NEW BRAUNFELS

8194
Children's Museum in New Braunfels, The
651 Business I35N, Ste 530, 78130; (p) (830) 620-0939; (f) (830) 606-5724; jbswift@watteam.org; www.watteam.org/museum.html; (c) Comal

Private non-profit/ 1986/ staff: 3(f); 6(p); 50(v)/ members: 525/publication: Handprint

ART MUSEUM; HISTORY MUSEUM: Promotes fine arts, culture, history and science for children.

PROGRAMS: Community Outreach; Concerts; Exhibits; Facility Rental; Family Programs; Publication

HOURS: Yr M-Sa 9-5, Su 12-5

ADMISSION: $3; Members free; Group rates

8195
Lindehieman House
309 E San Antonio, 78130; (p) (830) 609-6971, (830) 625-4816; (f) (830) 625-1343

1850/ New Braunfels Cons/ staff: 24(v)

COLLECTIONS: [1833-Present] Period furnishing.

HOURS: Yr

8196
Museum of Handmade Texas Furniture/Breustedt-Dillen Haus and Heritage Society of New Braunfels, Inc.
1370 Church Hill Dr, 78130; (p) (830) 629-6504

1858/ Heritage Society of New Braunfels, Inc./ staff: 2(f); 1(p); 45(v)

Preserves home of Andreas Breustedt, a pioneer settler; preserves history of handmade TX furniture.

COLLECTIONS: [1845-1870] 19th c handmade furnishings; household artifacts; documents, photos.

HOURS: Jan-Nov

8197
New Braunfels Conservation Society
1300 Church Hill, 78131 [PO Box 310933, 78131]; (p) (830) 629-2943; (c) Comal

Private non-profit/ 1964/ staff: 1(f); 75(v)/ members: 250

HISTORICAL SOCIETY: Preserves historical buildings, objects, and history of New Braunfels.

PROGRAMS: Facility Rental; Garden Tours; Guided Tours

HOURS: Yr T-F 10-2:30, Sa-Su 2-5

ADMISSION: $2.50, Children $0.50

8198
Sophienburg Museum and Archives
401 W Coll St, 78130; (p) (830) 629-1572; (f) (830) 629-3906; sophienburg@sat.net; www.nbtx.com/sophienburg; (c) Comal

Private non-profit/ 1926/ staff: 2(f); 4(p); 100(v)/publication: Pictorial History of New Braunfels

HISTORIC SITE; HISTORY MUSEUM; RESEARCH CENTER: Promotes history of German immigrants to TX.

PROGRAMS: Community Outreach; Elder's Programs; Exhibits; Festivals; Guided Tours; Lectures; Publication; Research Library/ Archives

COLLECTIONS: [1845-present] Artifacts, maps, documents.

HOURS: Yr M-Sa 10-5, Su 1-5

ADMISSION: $1.50

ODESSA

8199
Parker House Ranching Museum
1118 Maple, 79761; (p) (915) 335-9918; (c) Ector

Private non-profit/ 1996/ Heritage of Odessa Foundation & Museum Board of Directors/ staff: 1(f); 1(p); 5(v)/ members: 80

ART MUSEUM; GARDEN; HISTORIC PRESERVATION AGENCY; HISTORIC SITE; HISTORY MUSEUM; HOUSE MUSEUM

PROGRAMS: Annual Meeting; Community Outreach; Exhibits; Family Programs; Guided Tours; Interpretation

COLLECTIONS: [Late 19th-mid 20th c] Artwork, photos, books, maps, furniture, clothing, appliances, dishes, ranching and historical artifacts.

HOURS: Yr W, Th, Sa 10-3

ADMISSION: No charge

8200
White-Pool House Museum
112 E Murphy St, 79760 [PO Box 7363, 79760]; (p) (915) 333-4072; (f) (915) 332-9417; (c) Ector

County/ 1984/ staff: 1(f); 1(p); 8(v)/ members: 35

HISTORIC SITE; HISTORY MUSEUM; HOUSE MUSEUM: Collects, preserves, displays and makes available materials related to the White-Pool House and its owners. Interprets ranching and oil-boom era.

PROGRAMS: Exhibits; Festivals; Guided Tours

COLLECTIONS: [1887-1940] Two-story red brick house with household items and furnishings.

HOURS: Yr T-Sa 10-3

ADMISSION: No charge

ORANGE

8201
Heritage House of Orange County Association, Inc.
905 W Division, 77630; (p) (409) 886-5385; (f) (409) 886-0917; crose@exp.net; (c) Orange

Private non-profit/ 1977/ staff: 1(f); 50(v)/ members: 200/publication: Gateway to Texas

HISTORY MUSEUM; HOUSE MUSEUM: Promotes history of Orange County.

PROGRAMS: Annual Meeting; Community Outreach; Exhibits; Festivals; Guided Tours; Lectures; Publication; Research Library/ Archives; School-Based Curriculum

COLLECTIONS: [Early 19th-mid 20th c] Furniture, photos, medical items, articles from timber, shipbuilding and chemical plants.

HOURS: Yr T-F 10-4

ADMISSION: $1

8202
W.H. Stark House
610 Main St, 77631 [PO Drawer 909, 77631-0909]; (p) (409) 883-0871; (c) Orange

Private non-profit/ 1976/ Nelda C. and H.J. Lutcher Stark Foundation/ staff: 3(f); 15(p)

HOUSE MUSEUM

COLLECTIONS: [1890-1920] Original furniture, rugs, family portraits, lace curtains, silver, ceramics, glass, woodwork, and lighting.

HOURS: Yr T-Sa 10-3 by appt

ADMISSION: $2

PALACIOS

8203
Palacios Area Historical Association
401 Commence, 77465 [PO Box 11, 77465]; (p) (361) 972-1148; (f) (361) 972-3960; (c) Matagorda

Private non-profit/ 1982/ Board of Trustees/ staff: 10(v)/ members: 60

HISTORY MUSEUM: Collects, preserves and displays local history.

PROGRAMS: Annual Meeting; Community Outreach; Exhibits; Lectures; Living History; Reenactments

COLLECTIONS: [20th c] Carancahua Indian artifacts, 1685 LaSalle expedition and recent excavation information, early maps, family history and photos. Artifacts from historic ranching, maritime and fishing fleet history, local business, education and Camp Hulen history. Halfmoon Reef Lighthouse logs, Railroad Town Site information and photos.

HOURS: Yr F-Su 12-5

ADMISSION: No charge

8204
Palacios Library, Inc.
326 Main, 77465; (p) (361) 972-3234; (f) (361) 972-2142; vikijane@hotmail.com; (c) Matagorda

Private non-profit/ 1910/ Board of Directors/ staff: 2(f); 3(p); 3(v)

LIBRARY AND/OR ARCHIVES

PALESTINE

8205
Howard House Museum
1011 N Perry, 75801 [123 N Church St, 75801]; (p) (903) 729-5094

1848/ City

Preserves period home.

COLLECTIONS: [1870]

PAMPA

8206
White Deer Land Museum
112-116 S Cuyler, 79066 [PO Box 1556, 79066-1556]; (p) (806) 669-8041; (f) (806) 669-8030; museum@pan-tex.net; (c) Gray

County/ 1970/ staff: 2(f); 1(p)

HISTORIC SITE; HISTORY MUSEUM: Preserves history of White Deer Land Company.

PROGRAMS: Community Outreach; Exhibits; Facility Rental; Guided Tours; Lectures; School-Based Curriculum

COLLECTIONS: [1900-1950] 32 interpretive rooms of exhibits depicting settlers' lives.

HOURS: Spring-Summer T-Su 10-4; Fall-Winter T-Su 1-4

ADMISSION: No charge

PARIS

8207
Sam Bell Maxey House State Historic Site
812 S Church St, 75460; (p) (903) 785-5716; (f) (903) 739-2924; (c) Lamar

State/ 1976/ Texas Parks and Wildlife Department/ staff: 1(f); 1(p); 22(v)/ members: 150

HISTORIC SITE; HOUSE MUSEUM: Preserves, protects, and interprets home built by Civil War General Sam Bell Maxey.

PROGRAMS: Annual Meeting; Community Outreach; Exhibits; Facility Rental; Family Programs; Garden Tours; Guided Tours; Interpretation; Lectures; Living History; Reenactments

COLLECTIONS: [1868-1950s] Artifacts: furniture, paintings, china, silver, books, letters, theatre programs, postcards and clothing.

HOURS: Yr F, Su

PERRYTON

8208
Museum of the Plains
1200 N Main, 79070; (p) (806) 435-6400; (f) (806) 435-5732; (c) Olhiltree

Private non-profit/ 1975/ Board of Trustees/ staff: 1(f); 5(v)

HISTORY MUSEUM: Promotes history of Great Plains settlement and agricultural development.

PROGRAMS: Concerts; Exhibits; Facility Rental; Festivals; Guided Tours; Interpretation; Lectures

COLLECTIONS: [20th c] Regional pioneer artifacts, farm machinery, area archaeology and paleontology.

HOURS: Yr M-F 9-5, Sa-Su 1-5

ADMISSION: No charge

PITTSBURG

8209
Northeast Texas Rural Heritage Center and Museum
120 Quitman St, 75686 [PO Box 157, 75686-0157]; (p) (903) 856-1200; (f) (903) 856-1200; www.pittsburgtxmuseum.com; (c) Camp

Private non-profit/ 1990/ Pittsburg/Camp Co. Museum Assn/ staff: 4(p); 94(v)/ members: 350/publication: *Museum Needs*

HISTORY MUSEUM; LIVING HISTORY/OUTDOOR MUSEUM: Promotes local history.

PROGRAMS: Annual Meeting; Community Outreach; Exhibits; Facility Rental; Family Programs; Festivals; Guided Tours; Interpretation; Lectures; Living History; Publication; Research Library/Archives; School-Based Curriculum

COLLECTIONS: [1840-1950] Ephemera, maps, books, photographs, artifacts related to history and development of NE TX.

HOURS: Yr Th-Sa 10-4

ADMISSION: $3, Student $1, Senior $2

PLANO

8210
Heritage Farmstead Museum
1900 W 15th St, 75075; (p) (972) 881-0140, (972) 424-7874; (f) (972) 422-6481; museum@airmail.net; www.heritagefarmstead.org; (c) Collin

Private non-profit/ 1986/ Heritage Farmstead Association/ staff: 4(f); 2(p); 408(v)/ members: 1390

HOUSE MUSEUM: Preserves and maintains interpretive history museum.

PROGRAMS: Annual Meeting; Community Outreach; Exhibits; Facility Rental; Family Programs; Festivals; Garden Tours; Guided Tours; Interpretation; Lectures; Living History; Reenactments; Research Library/Archives; School-Based Curriculum; Theatre

COLLECTIONS: [1890-1925] 14 room Victorian farmhouse; windmill, cisterns, barns, blacksmith shop, hen house.

HOURS: Yr Daily 9-5

ADMISSION: $3.50, Children $2.50, Seniors $2.50

PORT ARTHUR

8211
Museum of the Gulf Coast
700 Proctor St, 77640; (p) (409) 982-7000; (f) (409) 982-9614; (c) Jefferson

Private non-profit/ 1994/ staff: 4(f); 5(p); 100(v)/ members: 500

HISTORY MUSEUM: Promotes regional history of southeast TX and southwest LA.

PROGRAMS: Annual Meeting; Community Outreach; Exhibits; Guided Tours; Interpretation; Lectures; Living History; Research Library/Archives; School-Based Curriculum

COLLECTIONS: [19th-20th c] Cultural, historical, natural history artifacts.

HOURS: Yr M-Sa 9-5, Su 1-5

ADMISSION: $3.50, Student $1.50, Children $1.50, Seniors $3

8212
Pompeiian Villa
1953 Lakeshore Dr, 77640; (p) (409) 983-5977

HISTORIC SITE

8213
Port Arthur Public Library
4615 9th Ave, 77642; (p) (409) 982-7257; (f) (409) 985-5969; rcline@hpl.lib.tx.us; (c) Jefferson

City/ 1918/ City of Port Arthur/ staff: 14(f); 2(p); 20(v)

LIBRARY AND/OR ARCHIVES

COLLECTIONS: [1890-present] 10,000 historic photos.

HOURS: Yr M-Th 10-9, F 10-6; June-Aug Sa 10-5, Su 2-5

ADMISSION: No charge

8214
White Haven
2545 Lakeshore Dr, 77640 [PO Box 310, 77641]; (p) (409) 985-7822, (409) 984-6101; (f) (409) 984-6032

PORT ISABEL

8215
Port Isabel Historical Museum
317 E Railroad Ave, 78578; (p) (956) 943-7602; (f) (956) 943-4346; epmeza@juno.com; (c) Cameron

City/ staff: 2(f); 12(v)/ members: 85

HISTORIC SITE; HISTORY MUSEUM

PROGRAMS: Annual Meeting; Community Outreach; Elder's Programs; Exhibits; Family Programs; Festivals; Film/Video; Guided Tours; Interpretation; Lectures; Research Library/Archives; School-Based Curriculum; Theatre

COLLECTIONS: [16th-20th c] Utilitarian and decorative objects, US-Mexican War and maritime items, photos, letters, advertisements, newspapers and Spanish shipwreck artifacts.

HOURS: Yr W-Sa 10-4, Su 1-4

ADMISSION: $3, Student $1, Children $0.50, Seniors $2

POST

8216
Garza County Historical Museum
119 N Ave N, 79356; (p) (806) 495-2207; www.garzamuseum.door.net; (c) Garza

Private non-profit/ 1972/ Caprock Cultural Association/ staff: 1(f); 1(p); 12(v)/publication: *Post City, Texas*

ALLIANCE OF HISTORICAL AGENCIES; ART MUSEUM; GARDEN; HISTORIC SITE; HISTORICAL SOCIETY; HISTORY MUSEUM; RESEARCH CENTER: Preserves historic buildings and collections.

PROGRAMS: Annual Meeting; Community Outreach; Concerts; Elder's Programs; Exhibits; Festivals; Garden Tours; Guided Tours; Interpretation; Lectures; Living History; Publication; Research Library/Archives; School-Based Curriculum

COLLECTIONS: [Prehistory-present day] Artifacts related to Post Company, pioneers, oil, ranching, farming, political, law, medical, and military.

HOURS: Yr T-Sa 10-12/1-5

ADMISSION: No charge

8217
OS Ranch Foundation Museum
201 E Main St, 79356 [PO Box 790, 79356]; (p) (806) 495-3570; (f) (806) 495-2288; (c) Garza

Private non-profit/ 1991/ staff: 2(f); 2(p); 1(v)

ART MUSEUM

PROGRAMS: Exhibits; Guided Tours

COLLECTIONS: [1850s-present]

HOURS: Yr M-Sa 10-12/1-5

ADMISSION: No charge

PRESIDIO

8218
Fort Leaton State Historic Park
3 mi E Hwy FM 170, 79845 [PO Box 2489, 79845]; (p) (915) 229-3613; (f) (915) 229-4814; bigbendranchsp@brooksdata.net

State/ 1968/ Texas Parks and Wildlife Dept/ staff: 2(f); 7(p); 5(v)

HISTORIC SITE; LIVING HISTORY/OUTDOOR MUSEUM: Restores and preserves 1848 adobe structure; portrays U.S-Mexican border period of the Chihuahua Trail.

PROGRAMS: Community Outreach; Exhibits; Facility Rental; Family Programs; Festivals; Guided Tours; Interpretation; Lectures; Living History; Reenactments

COLLECTIONS: [1848-1926] Reproductions and graphics.

HOURS: Yr Daily 8-4:30

ADMISSION: $2, Children $1

QUITMAN

8219
Governor Jim Hogg City Park and Governor Hogg Shrine State Historic Park
Hwy 37, 75783 [101 Governor Hogg Pkwy, 75783]; (p) (903) 763-2701; (f) (903) 763-5530; (c) Wood

Joint/ 1951/ City;TX Parks and Wildlife/ staff: 1(f); 3(v)

HISTORIC SITE; HISTORY MUSEUM; HOUSE MUSEUM

PROGRAMS: Exhibits; Facility Rental; Festivals; Guided Tours; Living History

COLLECTIONS: [19th c] Furniture, ceramics.

HOURS: Yr M 8-12, F-Sa 9-4, Su 1-5

ADMISSION: $3, Student $1

RAYMONDVILLE

8220
Raymondville Historical and Community Center
427 S 7th St, 78580; (p) (956) 689-6604, (956) 689-3171; estacas@vsta.com; (c) Willacy

Private non-profit/ 1967/ Board of Directors/ staff: 24(v)

HISTORIC SITE; HISTORICAL SOCIETY; HISTORY MUSEUM

PROGRAMS: Exhibits; Facility Rental; Family Programs; Guided Tours; Lectures

COLLECTIONS: [Mid 19th c-present] Farm and ranch equipment, firearms, early doctor's office, county historical documents and items from the Kennedy Ranch House.

HOURS: Yr by appt; Sept-May W 2-4:30, F 9:30-11:30

ADMISSION: $1

RICHARDSON

8221
National Museum of Communications
6305 N O'Connor Rd, 75081 [2001 Plymouth Rock, 75081]; (p) (972) 889-9872; (f) (972) 889-2329; bill@yesterdayusa.com; www.yesterdayusa.com; (c) Dallas

Private non-profit/ 1979/ staff: 5(f); 4(p); 10(v)

HISTORY MUSEUM: Preserves the history of communication, focusing on radio and television broadcasting.

PROGRAMS: Community Outreach; Exhibits; Facility Rental; Family Programs; Festivals; Film/Video; Guided Tours; Interpretation; Living History

COLLECTIONS: [1879-present] Broadcast and communications artifacts.

HOURS: Yr Daily 10-4

ADMISSION: $9.95, Children $4.95

RICHMOND

8222
Fort Bend Museum
500 Houston St, 77406 [PO Drawer 460, 77406]; (p) (281) 342-6478; (f) (281) 342-2439; mmoore@georgeranch.org; www.fortbendmuseum.org; (c) Fort Bend

Private non-profit/ 1972/ Fort Bend Museum Association/ staff: 4(f); 7(p); 200(v)/ members: 500/publication: *Heritage*

HISTORY MUSEUM; HOUSE MUSEUM: Preserves and interprets county history, with emphasis on Austin's colonial period; manages five historic properties.

PROGRAMS: Annual Meeting; Community Outreach; Exhibits; Facility Rental; Family Programs; Festivals; Guided Tours; Interpretation; Lectures; Publication

COLLECTIONS: [1821-1945] 25,000 archival and photographic materials; furnishing.

HOURS: Yr T-F 9-5, Sa 10-5, Su 1-5

ADMISSION: $3, Children $2, Seniors $2.50

8223
George Ranch Historical Park
10215 FM 762, 77469; (p) (281) 545-9212; (f) (281) 343-9316; www.georgeranch.org

Ft. Bend Museum Assoc

HOURS: Yr 9-5

ROANOKE

8224
Railroad Station Historical Society
1312 Woods Dr, 76262-8905; (p) (817) 431-8435

State/ 1968/ State of Nebraska/ staff: 2(v)/ members: 311/publication: *The Bulletin*

HISTORICAL SOCIETY: Promotes preservation of railroad stations/depots history.

PROGRAMS: Publication

ROCKPORT

8225
Fulton Mansion State Historical Site
317 Fulton Beach Rd, 78382 [PO Box 1859, Fulton, 78358]; (p) (512) 729-0386; (f) (512) 729-6581; mansion@dbstech.com; www.tpwd.state.tx.us/park/fulton/fulton.htm; (c) Arkansas

State/ 1874/ TX Parks and Wildlife Dept/ staff: 4(f); 3(p); 32(v)/ members: 87

HOUSE MUSEUM: Preserves, collects, exhibits and interprets the architecture and collections of the George and Harriet Fulton family and home.

PROGRAMS: Annual Meeting; Community Outreach; Concerts; Exhibits; Facility Rental; Family Programs; Festivals; Garden Tours; Guided Tours; Interpretation; Research Library/Archives; School-Based Curriculum

COLLECTIONS: [1874-1884] Decorative arts and textiles.

HOURS: Yr W-Su 9-3

ADMISSION: $4, Student $2

8226
Texas Maritime Museum
1202 Navigation Circle, 78382; (p) (361) 729-1271; (f) (361) 729-9938; tmm@2fords.net; www.texasmaritimemuseum.org; (c) Arkansas

Private non-profit/ 1980/ Texas Maritime Museum Association, Inc./ staff: 4(f); 1(p); 70(v)/ members: 1000/publication: *Logline*

HISTORY MUSEUM: Collects, preserves and interprets TX maritime history.

PROGRAMS: Community Outreach; Elder's Programs; Exhibits; Facility Rental; Family Programs; Festivals; Guided Tours; Interpretation; Lectures; Living History; Publication; Research Library/Archives; School-Based Curriculum

COLLECTIONS: [19th-20th c] Artifacts, archival materials, photos, prints, watercolor paintings, books, documents, full-sized vessels, charts, maps, scale models of ships and boats, tools and equipment from offshore industry.

HOURS: Yr T-Sa 10-4, Su 1-4

ADMISSION: $4, Children $2; Under 4 free

ROSENBERG

8227
Rosenberg Railroad Museum, Inc.
1879 Ave F, 77471 [PO Box 607, 77471-0607]; (p) (281) 342-4664; (f) (281) 232-0894; meiling@aol.com; (c) Fort Bend

Private non-profit/ 1993/ staff: 30(v)/ members: 116

HISTORY MUSEUM

PROGRAMS: Annual Meeting; Exhibits; Festivals

COLLECTIONS: [19th-20th c] Fort Bend County

ROUND ROCK

8228
Palm House
212 E Main St, 78664; (p) (512) 255-5805

1873/ Palm House Museum

Built by Swedish immigrants on land purchased from the Swedish Immigration Agency.

COLLECTIONS: [1873]

HOURS: Yr

SAN ANGELO

8229
Fort Concho Historic Site and Museum
630 S Oakes St, 76903; (p) (915) 491-2646; (f) (915) 657-4540; www.fortconcho.com; (c) Tom Green

City/ 1928/ staff: 13(f); 1(p); 200(v)/ members: 700/publication: Fort Concho Guidon

HISTORIC SITE; HISTORY MUSEUM; LIVING HISTORY/OUTDOOR MUSEUM: Preserves and restores historic site and buildings.

PROGRAMS: Community Outreach; Concerts; Exhibits; Facility Rental; Family Programs; Festivals; Guided Tours; Interpretation; Lectures; Living History; Publication; Reenactments; Research Library/Archives; School-Based Curriculum

COLLECTIONS: [1865-1900] Military and pioneer clothing, archaeological remains, tools, equipment, furniture, local and military history objects.

HOURS: Yr T-Sa 10-5, Su 1-5

ADMISSION: $2, Children $1.25, Seniors $1.50

SAN ANTONIO

8230
Alamo Battlefield Association
[PO Box 1963, 78297]; (p) (830) 931-3682

Private non-profit/ 1993/ staff: 7(v)/ members: 300/publication: Journal of the Alamo Battlefield Association

HISTORICAL SOCIETY: Promotes the study, interpretation, and preservation of the Alamo, the Alamo battlefield, and the Texas War for Independence.

PROGRAMS: Annual Meeting; Lectures; Publication

COLLECTIONS: [1718-present]

8231
Alamo, The
300 Alamo Plaza, 78299 [PO Box 2599, 78299]; (p) (210) 225-1391; (f) (210) 229-1343; curator@swbell.net; www.thealamo.org/; (c) Bexar

Joint/ 1905/ State of TX and The Daughters of the Republic of TX/ staff: 76(f); 7(p)/ members: 6400

GARDEN; HISTORIC SITE; HISTORY MUSEUM; RESEARCH CENTER: Preserves history of the Alamo.

PROGRAMS: Community Outreach; Exhibits; Facility Rental; Festivals; Interpretation; Lectures; Research Library/Archives; School-Based Curriculum

COLLECTIONS: Artifacts: The Alamo, TX history, 1836 battle.

HOURS: Yr M-Sa 9-5:30, Su 10-5:30

8232
Casa Navarro State Historical Park
228 S Laredo St, 78207; (p) (210) 226-4801; (f) (210) 226-4801; navarro@txdirect.net; (c) Bexar

State/ 1964/ staff: 1(f); 1(p); 5(v)

GENEALOGICAL SOCIETY; HISTORIC SITE; LIVING HISTORY/OUTDOOR MUSEUM; RESEARCH CENTER: Interprets TX's Mexican history and heritage through the life of Jose Antonio Navarro.

PROGRAMS: Elder's Programs; Exhibits; Facility Rental; Festivals; Guided Tours; Interpretation; Lectures; Living History

COLLECTIONS: [1832-1871] House hotel with period furnishing.

HOURS: Yr W-Su 10-4

ADMISSION: $2, Children $1

8233
Daughters of the Republic of Texas Library at the Alamo
300 Alamo Plaza, 78295 [PO Box 1401, 78295-1401]; (p) (210) 225-1071; (f) (210) 212-8514; drtl@drtl.org; www.drtl.org; (c) Bexar

Private non-profit/ 1945/ Daughters of the Republic of Texas, Inc./ staff: 8(f)

LIBRARY AND/OR ARCHIVES: Preserves TX history, especially 1835 Revolution and TX Republic.

PROGRAMS: Lectures; Research Library/Archives

COLLECTIONS: [19th-mid 20th c] Books, manuscripts, documents, clipping files, microfilm, photographic images, maps, periodicals, sheet music titles and assorted early newspapers.

HOURS: Yr M-Sa 9-5

ADMISSION: No charge

8234
Hertzberg Circus Museum
210 W Market St, 78205; (p) (210) 207-7819; (f) (210) 207-4468; roconnor@ci.sat.tx.us; (c) Bexar

City/ 1940/ City of San Antonio/Public Library/ staff: 5(f); 3(p); 10(v)

HISTORY MUSEUM: Collects, preserves, exhibits and interprets the American circus and popular entertainment during the 19th and early 20th c.

PROGRAMS: Exhibits; Facility Rental; Family Programs; Film/Video; Guided Tours; Interpretation; Lectures; Research Library/Archives; School-Based Curriculum; Theatre

COLLECTIONS: [1790-1940] 27,000 items such as posters, handbills, prints, photographs, memorabilia, recordings, sheet music, paintings, magazines, books and other printed material.

HOURS: Yr M-Sa 10-5; June-Aug Su 1-5

ADMISSION: $2.50, Children $1, Seniors $2

8235
Institute of Texan Cultures, The
801 S Bowie St, 78205; (p) (210) 458-2244, (210) 458-2300; (f) (210) 458-2380; pburrus@utsa.edu; www.texancultures.utsa.edu; (c) Bexar

State/ 1968/ University of TX at San Antonio/ staff: 100(f); 450(v)/ members: 550

HISTORY MUSEUM; LIVING HISTORY/OUTDOOR MUSEUM; RESEARCH CENTER: Promotes history and diverse cultures of TX.

PROGRAMS: Community Outreach; Concerts; Exhibits; Facility Rental; Family Programs; Festivals; Guided Tours; Interpretation; Living History; Publication; Research Library/Archives; School-Based Curriculum; Theatre

COLLECTIONS: [20th c] 3.5 million photographic images.

HOURS: Yr T-Su 9-5

ADMISSION: $4, Children $2, Seniors $2; Under 3 free

8236
San Antonio Conservation Society
107 King William, 78204-1399; (p) (210) 224-6163; (f) (210) 224-6168; conserve@saconservation.org; www.saconservation.org; (c) Bexar

Private non-profit/ 1924/ staff: 14(f); 6(p); 2800(v)/ members: 2800

HISTORIC PRESERVATION AGENCY; HOUSE MUSEUM; RESEARCH CENTER

PROGRAMS: Guided Tours

COLLECTIONS: [Late 19th c]

HOURS: Yr Daily 10-4

ADMISSION: $3; Under 12 free

8237
San Antonio Museum of Art
200 W Jones Ave, 78219; (p) (210) 978-8100; (f) (210) 978-8118; saart@express-news.net; www.samuseum.org; (c) Bexar

Private non-profit/ 1981/ Board of Trustees/ staff: 37(f); 20(p); 100(v)/ members: 2400

ART MUSEUM; HISTORIC SITE

PROGRAMS: Community Outreach; Concerts; Exhibits; Facility Rental; Family Programs; Festivals; Film/Video; Guided Tours; Lectures; Research Library/Archives; School-Based Curriculum

COLLECTIONS: [Ancient-present] Art objects from Latin America, Western antiquities (Greek, Roman, Egyptian), Asian art, European and American decorative and fine art.

HOURS: Yr T 10-9, W-Sa 10-5, Su 12-5

ADMISSION: $4, Student $2, Children $1.75, Seniors $2; Under 4 free

8238
Spanish Governor's Palace
105 Plaza de Armas, 78205; (p) (210) 224-0601; (f) (210) 207-7946; (c) Bexar

City/ 1749/ Parks and Rec/ staff: 2(f); 1(p)/publication: *Spanish Governor's Palace*

HISTORIC SITE; HOUSE MUSEUM: Interprets the Spanish colonial period in TX.

PROGRAMS: Exhibits; Facility Rental; Living History; Publication

COLLECTIONS: [16th-18th c] 17th c Rosewood bed, charcoal braziers, brass stirrups, a baptismal records chest and a spice cabinet.

HOURS: Yr M-Sa 9-5, Su 10-5

ADMISSION: $1.50, Children $0.75, Under 14 Free

8239
Steves Homestead
509 King William St, 78204; (p) (210) 225-5924, (210) 227-9160; (f) (210) 224-6168; conserve @saconservation.org; www.saconservation.org

1876/ San Antonio Conservation Society/ staff: 3(f); 3(p); 31(v)

COLLECTIONS: [1910-1912] Pietra-Dura mosaic table; decorative painting.

HOURS: Yr

8240
Texana/Genealogy Department, San Antonio Public Library
600 Soledad St, 78205-1208; (p) (210) 207-2500; (f) (210) 207-2558; jmyler@ci.sat.tx.us; www.sat.lib.tx.us; (c) Bexar

City/ 1903/ staff: 6(f); 18(v)/publication: *The Explorer*

LIBRARY AND/OR ARCHIVES

PROGRAMS: Community Outreach; Exhibits; Lectures; Publication

COLLECTIONS: [18th c-present] City and county artifacts.

HOURS: Yr M-Th 9-9, F-Sa 9-5, Su 11-5

ADMISSION: No charge

8241
Texas Highway Patrol Museum
811 S Alamo St, 78205 [8906 Wall St, #407, Austin, 78754]; (p) (210) 231-6030; (f) (210) 231-6020; toddr@thpa.org; www.thpa.org

Private non-profit/ 1993/ Mark Lockridge, Chair/ staff: 1(f); 1(p)/publication: *Texas Highway Patrol Magazine*

HISTORY MUSEUM: Promotes and preserves history of TX highway patrol officers.

PROGRAMS: Exhibits; Lectures; Publication; Research Library/Archives

COLLECTIONS: [1930-1980] Log books, uniforms, handcuffs, radar detectors and videos.

HOURS: Yr

8242
Texas Transportation Museum
11731 Wetmore Rd, 78247-3606; (p) (210) 490-3554; jared@stic.net; (c) Bexar

Private non-profit/ 1964/ Board of Directors/ staff: 1(f); 17(v)/ members: 250

HISTORY MUSEUM: Preserves transportation history.

PROGRAMS: Annual Meeting; Facility Rental; Guided Tours

COLLECTIONS: [Late 19th-early 20th c] 1897 horse-drawn fire truck; automobiles; Studebaker carriage; steam and diesel locomotives, cabooses; passenger and motor cars.

HOURS: Yr Th, Sa-Su 9-4

ADMISSION: $4, Children $2

8243
Witte Museum
3801 Broadway, 78209-6396; (p) (210) 357-1900; (f) (210) 357-1882; www.wittemuseum.org; (c) Bexar

Private non-profit/ 1926/ staff: 27(f); 74(p); 400(v)/ members: 3000/publication: *World of Witte*

HISTORY MUSEUM: Promotes and interprets history, science, natural history and regional art.

PROGRAMS: Community Outreach; Concerts; Exhibits; Facility Rental; Family Programs; Interpretation; Lectures; Publication; School-Based Curriculum; Theatre

COLLECTIONS: [Prehistory; 19th c-present] Archaeological and ethnographic artifacts, textiles, historic objects, documents and archives, natural history specimens, photos, art.

HOURS: Yr M, W-Sa 10-5, T 10-9, Su 12-5

ADMISSION: $5.95, Children $3.95, Seniors $4.95

SAN AUGUSTINE

8244
Cullen House, Ezekiel Cullen Chapter Daughters of the Republic of Texas
205 S Congress, 75972-0402 [PO Box 402, 75972-0402]; (p) (409) 275-5110

1847/ Daughters of the Republic of TX/ staff: 11(p); 1(v)

COLLECTIONS: [Early-mid 1800s] Furniture; tools; S. Seymour Thomas paintings.

HOURS: T-Sa 1-3

SAN MARCOS

8245
Aquarena Center
601 University, 78666; (p) (512) 245-7539; (f) (512) 245-7543; rc13@swt.edu; (c) Hays

Southwest Texas State University/ staff: 1(f); 2(p)

HISTORIC SITE; HOUSE MUSEUM

PROGRAMS: Community Outreach; Exhibits; Facility Rental; Garden Tours; Guided Tours; Interpretation; Lectures; School-Based Curriculum; Theatre

COLLECTIONS: [1800s-present] Archaeological, Native American artifacts; interpretive sites: Eli Merriman Cabin; Kyle City Jail; Grist Mill; Spanish Mission bell tower; blacksmith shop.

HOURS: Yr Daily 9:30-5

8246
Southwestern Writers Collection/Wittliff Gallery of Southwestern and Mexican Photography
Alkek Library SWT, 7th Floor, 78666-4613; (p) (512) 245-2313; (f) (512) 245-7431; cto3@swt.edu; www.library.swt.edu/swwc; (c) Hays

State/ 1986/ SWT, TX/ staff: 9(f); 2(p)/ members: 750

ART MUSEUM; RESEARCH CENTER: Collects and preserves cultural history of Southwest and TX.

PROGRAMS: Community Outreach; Exhibits; Film/Video; Guided Tours; Lectures; Research Library/Archives

COLLECTIONS: [20th c] Literature, drama, film, music and photography.

HOURS: Yr M-F 8-5, T 8-9, Sa 9-5, Su 2-6

ADMISSION: No charge

SEGUIN

8247
Sebastopol House State Historic Site
704 Zorn, 78155 [PO Box 900, 78156]; (p) (830) 379-4833; (f) (830) 401-0583

1854/ TX Parks and Wildlife Dept/ staff: 1(f); 1(p)

COLLECTIONS: [1890-1900] Furnishings, toys, archaeological artifacts.

HOURS: Yr F-M 9-4 and by appt

SHERMAN

8248
Red River Historical Museum in Sherman
301 S Walnut, 75090; (p) (903) 893-7623; (f) (903) 892-4303; rrhms@texoma.net; www.texoma.net/rrhms; (c) Grayson

Private non-profit/ 1976/ Board of Directors/ staff: 2(f); 2(p); 6(v)/ members: 133/publication: *The Sentinel*

HISTORY MUSEUM: Collects, preserves and interprets history of Grayson County and the greater North TX region.

PROGRAMS: Community Outreach; Exhibits; Facility Rental; Family Programs; Festivals; Guided Tours; Lectures; Publication; Research Library/Archives; School-Based Curriculum

COLLECTIONS: [1848-1948] Grayson County artifacts.

HOURS: Yr T-F 9-4:30, Sa 2-5

ADMISSION: $2, Children $1, Seniors $1

SMITHVILLE

8249
Smithville Heritage Society
602 Main, 78957 [PO Box 332, 78957]; (p) (512) 237-4545; (c) Bastrop

Private non-profit/ 1976/ staff: 9(v)/ members: 71/publication: *Smithville Then and Now: A Reference and Pictorial Guide to the Businesses on or near North Main Street*

HISTORIC SITE; HISTORICAL SOCIETY; HOUSE MUSEUM; RESEARCH CENTER: Collects and exhibits local history.

PROGRAMS: Community Outreach; Exhibits; Facility Rental; Family Programs; Festivals; Guided Tours; Lectures; Publication; Research Library/Archives

COLLECTIONS: [Late 19th c-present] Local newspapers, family histories, household and

SNYDER

8250
Scurry County Museum Association
6200 College Ave, 79549; (p) (915) 573-6107; (f) (915) 573-9321; (c) Scurry

Private non-profit/ 1971/ staff: 2(f); 1(p); 43(v)/ members: 140

HISTORY MUSEUM: Preserves regional history.

PROGRAMS: Community Outreach; Exhibits; Facility Rental; Family Programs; Festivals; Film/Video; Guided Tours; Interpretation; Lectures; Research Library/Archives; School-Based Curriculum

COLLECTIONS: [1850-present] Farming, ranching, oil and domestic life on the West TX Plains.

HOURS: Yr M-F 8-4

ADMISSION: No charge

STANTON

8251
Martin County Convent, Inc.
500 Carpenter St, 79782 [PO Box 1435, 79782-1435]; (p) (915) 756-3301; (f) (915) 756-2083; (c) Martin

Private non-profit/ 1988/ staff: 12(v)

HISTORIC SITE; HISTORY MUSEUM: Maintains 1884 adobe Carmelite Monastery and grounds; preserves history of Our Lady of Mercy Academy.

PROGRAMS: Annual Meeting; Exhibits; Guided Tours; Interpretation; Research Library/ Archives

COLLECTIONS: [1884-1938] Photos; materials related to Carmelites and the Sisters of Mercy.

HOURS: Yr by appt

STEPHENVILLE

8252
Stephenville Historical House Museum
525 E Washington, 76401 [385 S Washington, 76401]; (p) (254) 965-5880; (c) Erath

Joint/ 1961/ City of Stephenville/Board of Directors/ staff: 3(p); 200(v)

HISTORIC PRESERVATION AGENCY; HISTORIC SITE; HOUSE MUSEUM: Promotes Western heritage.

PROGRAMS: Annual Meeting; Community Outreach; Exhibits; Facility Rental; Family Programs; Festivals; Guided Tours; Lectures

COLLECTIONS: [1880-1940] Early farm tools, blacksmith shop, log cabins, corn crib, two-room schoolhouse, chapel, carriage house, well house and Tarleton House.

HOURS: Yr F-Su 2-5 by appt

ADMISSION: Donations

STRATFORD

8253
Sherman County Depot Museum
17 N Main, 79084 [PO Box 1248, 79084]; (p) (806) 396-2582; (f) (806) 366-2717; (c) Sherman

Private non-profit/ 1974/ Depot Museum Board/ staff: 1(p); 30(v)

HISTORICAL SOCIETY: Preserves and displays historic material.

PROGRAMS: Concerts; Festivals; Guided Tours

COLLECTIONS: [1890-1950]

HOURS: Yr M-F 12-5

ADMISSION: Donations accepted

SUGAR LAND

8254
Museum of Southern History, The
14070 SW Fwy, 77487 [PO Box 2190, 77487-2190]; (p) (281) 269-7171; (f) (281) 269-7179; snoddys@snbtx.com; (c) Fort Bend

Private non-profit/ 1978/ Board of Directors/ staff: 1(f); 4(v)

HISTORY MUSEUM: Preserves local history.

PROGRAMS: Annual Meeting; Community Outreach; Exhibits; Guided Tours; Interpretation; Lectures; Living History; Reenactments; Research Library/Archives; School-Based Curriculum

COLLECTIONS: [1860s] Furnishings, quilts, clothing, guns, medical supplies, authentic uniforms, battle displays, relics, Civil War artifacts; sharecropper's cabin.

HOURS: Yr T-F 10-4, Sa-Su 1-4

ADMISSION: $3, Children $2, Seniors $2

TEMPLE

8255
Railroad and Pioneer Museum/Archives
710 Jack Baskin; 620 E Central, 76505 [PO Box 5126, 76505]; (p) (254) 298-5172, (254) 298-5190; (f) (254) 298-5171; mirving@ci.temple.tx.us; www.ci.temple.tx.us; (c) Bell

City/ 1973/ staff: 3(f); 3(p); 75(v)/ members: 102

RESEARCH CENTER: Preserves, exhibits and educates public on railroad expansion and its influence on pioneer westward expansion.

PROGRAMS: Community Outreach; Concerts; Elder's Programs; Exhibits; Facility Rental; Family Programs; Festivals; Guided Tours; Interpretation; Lectures; Living History; Reenactments; Research Library/Archives; School-Based Curriculum

COLLECTIONS: [1881-present] Railroad and pioneer artifacts.

HOURS: Museum:Yr M-Sa 10-4, Su 12-4; Archives: Yr M-F

TEXARKANA

8256
Ace of Clubs House
420 Pine St, 75504 [PO Box 2343, 75504]; (p) (903) 793-4831; (f) (903) 793-7108; gcvanderpool@cableone.net; Texarkanamuseums.org; (c) Bowie

Private non-profit/ 1988/ Texarkana Museums System/ staff: 7(f); 2(p); 50(v)/ members: 500/publication: *Artifacts*

HOUSE MUSEUM

PROGRAMS: Annual Meeting; Community Outreach; Exhibits; Facility Rental; Guided Tours; Interpretation; Lectures; Living History; Publication; Reenactments; School-Based Curriculum

COLLECTIONS: [1880-1940] American furniture styles and decorative arts; 500 pairs Neiman Marcus shoes; letters, photos, scrapbooks, textiles.

HOURS: Yr T-Sa

8257
Discovery Place Children's Museum
215 Pine St, 75504 [PO Box 2343, 75504]; (p) (903) 793-4831; (f) (903) 793-7108; gcvanderpool@cableone.net; www.texarkanamuseums.org; (c) Bowie

Private non-profit/ 1971/ Texarkana Museums System/ staff: 7(f); 4(p); 50(v)/ members: 500/publication: *Artifacts*

HISTORY MUSEUM; NATURAL HISTORY MUSEUM: Promotes natural history and history for children.

PROGRAMS: Annual Meeting; Community Outreach; Exhibits; Facility Rental; Family Programs; Festivals; Guided Tours; Lectures; Publication; School-Based Curriculum; Theatre

HOURS: Yr T-Sa 10-4

ADMISSION: Children $4, Under 5 Free

8258
Texarkana Historical Museum, Texarkana Museums System
219 N State Line Ave, 75504 [PO Box 2343, 75504-2343]; (p) (903) 793-4831; (f) (903) 793-7108; gcvanderpool@cableone.net; www.texarkanamuseums.org; (c) Bowie

Private non-profit/ Texarkana Museums System/ staff: 7(f); 9(p); 50(v)/ members: 500/publication: *Artifacts*

HISTORIC SITE; HISTORICAL SOCIETY; HISTORY MUSEUM; RESEARCH CENTER: Houses regional history exhibits

PROGRAMS: Annual Meeting; Community Outreach; Exhibits; Family Programs; Festivals; Interpretation; Lectures; Publication; Research Library/Archives; School-Based Curriculum

COLLECTIONS: [Prehistory-present] Texarkana artifacts.

HOURS: Yr T-Sa 10-4

ADMISSION: $2

8259
Texarkana Museums System
219 N State Line Ave, 75504 [PO Box 2343, 75504-2343]; (p) (903) 793-4831; (f) (903) 793-7108; gcvanderpool@cableone.net; www.texarkanamuseums.org; (c) Bowie

Private non-profit/ 1971/ Board of Trustees/ staff: 6(f); 3(p); 37(v)/ members: 455/publication: *Artifacts*

HISTORICAL SOCIETY; HISTORY MUSEUM; HOUSE MUSEUM: Enhances the educational and cultural opportunities and the quality of life of the citizens of Texarkana, Bowie and Miller Counties and the Four States Region.

PROGRAMS: Annual Meeting; Community Outreach; Exhibits; Facility Rental; Family Programs; Festivals; Guided Tours; Lectures; Living History; Publication; Research Library/Archives; School-Based Curriculum

COLLECTIONS: [Mid-late 19th c] Over 10,000 photographs; research materials, family histories, including related documents, manuscripts; historic clothing, furnishings and personal belongings of the Henry Moore, Sr. family; Caddo pottery.

HOURS: Yr T-Sa 10-4

ADMISSION: Varies

TOMBALL

8260
Spring Creek County Historical Association
510 N Pine St, 77377 [PO Box 457, 77377-0457]; (p) (281) 255-2148; (c) Harris

Private non-profit/ 1969/ staff: 1(p); 10(v)/ members: 198

HISTORIC PRESERVATION AGENCY; HISTORICAL SOCIETY; HISTORY MUSEUM; HOUSE MUSEUM: Preserves local historical items.

PROGRAMS: Annual Meeting; Community Outreach; Exhibits; Facility Rental; Guided Tours; Research Library/Archives

COLLECTIONS: [1880-1920] Interpretive sites: doctor's office, the Trinity Evangelical Lutheran Church, fellowship hall, gazebo, farm museum, smokehouse, log buildings, the Theiss House (1889), one-room schoolhouse, outhouse and original Humble Oil camp house.

HOURS: Yr Th 10-2, Su 2-4

ADMISSION: No charge

TULIA

8261
Swisher County Archives and Museum Association
127 SW 2nd, 79088 [PO Box 445, 79088]; (p) (806) 995-2819; (c) Swisher

Private non-profit/ 1963/ staff: 1(f); 4(p); 4(v)/ members: 360

GENEALOGICAL SOCIETY; HISTORIC SITE; HISTORY MUSEUM; HOUSE MUSEUM; LIVING HISTORY/OUTDOOR MUSEUM; RESEARCH CENTER: Preserves records of Swisher County.

PROGRAMS: Annual Meeting; Community Outreach; Elder's Programs; Exhibits; Family Programs; Festivals; Guided Tours; Interpretation; Living History; Reenactments

COLLECTIONS: [Early 20th c] Documents of Swisher County.

HOURS: Yr M-F

ADMISSION: No charge

TYLER

8262
Goodman Museum, The
624 N Broadway Ave, 75702 [PO Box 2039, 75710]; (p) (903) 531-1370, (903) 531-1286; (f) (903) 531-1372

City/ 1859/ staff: 1(f)

COLLECTIONS: [1860-1900] Dinnerware, medical equipment, furnishing, clothing, furs, instruments, books, scrapbooks, diaries.

HOURS: Yr by appt

8263
Smith County Historical Society
125 S College Ave, 75702; (p) (903) 592-5993; (f) (903) 592-5993; schs@tyler.net; www.tyler.net/schs; (c) Smith

Private non-profit/ 1959/ staff: 1(f); 20(v)/ members: 450/publication: *Chronicles of Smith County, Texas*

HISTORIC PRESERVATION AGENCY; HISTORIC SITE; HISTORICAL SOCIETY; HISTORY MUSEUM: Interprets county history.

PROGRAMS: Community Outreach; Exhibits; Facility Rental; Family Programs; Guided Tours; Interpretation; Lectures; Living History; Publication; Research Library/Archives

COLLECTIONS: [Prehistory-20th c] Rare books, papers, photos, letters, newspapers, maps.

HOURS: Yr T-Sa 10-4

ADMISSION: No charge

UVALDE

8264
John Nance Garner Museum
333 N Park, 78801; (p) (830) 278-5018; (c) Uvalde

City/ 1952/ Univ of TX, Austin/ staff: 2(f)

HISTORIC SITE; PRESIDENTIAL SITE: Promotes history of John Nance Garner's political career.

PROGRAMS: Exhibits; Guided Tours; Interpretation

COLLECTIONS: [1932-1940] Garner's gavels, photos, furniture.

HOURS: Yr M-Sa 9-5

ADMISSION: $1, Children $0.50; No charge

VICTORIA

8265
McNamara House Museum
502 N Liberty, 77901; (p) (912) 575-8227; (f) (912) 575-8228; vrma@viptx.net; www.viptx.net/museum

1876/ Victoria Regional Museum Association/ staff: 2(f); 1(p)

COLLECTIONS: [1876-1920] Furniture, letterhead, memos, invoices, ledgers.

HOURS: Yr T-Su 1-5

WACO

8266
Earle-Harrison House, The
1901 N Fifth St, 76708; (p) (254) 753-2032; (f) (254) 756-3820; earleharrison@texnet.net

1858/ The G. H. Pape Foundation/ staff: 4(f); 3(p)

COLLECTIONS: [1850-1900] Decorative arts.

HOURS: M-F 9-4:30

8267
Earle-Napier-Kinnard House Museum, Historic Waco Foundation
814 S Fourth St, 76706; (p) (254) 756-0057

1858

COLLECTIONS: [1870s-1880s] Victorian and Empire furniture, books, family artifacts.

8268
East Terrace House Museum, Historic Waco Foundation
100 Mill St, 76704; (p) (254) 756-4104

1872

COLLECTIONS: [1870-1890s] High-style Victorian and Eastlake furniture.

8269
Fort House Museum, Historic Waco Foundation
503 S Fourth St, 76706; (p) (254) 756-4161

1868

COLLECTIONS: Victorian and Empire furniture; maps.

8270
Governor Bill and Vara Daniel Historic Village
S Trinity Parks Dr, 76798 [PO Box 97154, 76798-7154]; (p) (254) 710-1160; (f) (254) 710-1095; melinda_herzog@baylor.edu; www.baylor.edu; (c) McLennan

1986/ Baylor Univ/ staff: 3(f); 4(p); 30(v)/ members: 380

LIVING HISTORY/OUTDOOR MUSEUM: Interprets TX rural life in 1890 farming community.

PROGRAMS: Annual Meeting; Exhibits; Family Programs; Festivals; Guided Tours; Interpretation; Living History; School-Based Curriculum

COLLECTIONS: [Late 19th c]
HOURS: Yr M-Th 10-4, Sa 12-4
ADMISSION: $3, Children $1, Seniors $2

8271
Historic Waco Foundation
810 S Fourth St, 76706; (p) (254) 753-5166;
hwf@Hot.RR.com; www.wacocvb.com; (c)
McLennan

Private non-profit/ 1967/ Board of Directors/
staff: 3(f); 1(p); 200(v)/ members: 1000/publi-
cation: *Waco Heritage and History*

HOUSE MUSEUM: Maintains and operates
four historic house museums.

PROGRAMS: Annual Meeting; Exhibits; Facility Rental; Festivals; Guided Tours; Interpretation; Lectures; Publication

COLLECTIONS: [1850s-1900] Decorative and
fine arts, textiles.

HOURS: Yr T-F 11-3, Sa-Su 2-5
ADMISSION: $2, Student $1

8272
**McCulloch House Museum, Historic
Waco Foundation**
407 Columbus Ave, 76701; (p) (254) 756-
2828

1866

COLLECTIONS: [19th c] High-style Empire
and 19th c English furniture.

WASHINGTON

8273
Barrington Living History Farm
FM 1155 & Park Road 12, 77880 [PO Box
305, 77880]; (p) (409) 878-2214; (f) (409)
878-2810; William.Irwin@tpwd.state.tx.us;
www.tpwd.state.tx.us/park/washingt/washingt;
(c) Washington

State/ 1936/ TX Parks and Wildlife Dept/ staff:
5(f); 1(p); 25(v)/ members: 300

HISTORIC SITE; HOUSE MUSEUM; LIVING
HISTORY/OUTDOOR MUSEUM; PRESIDEN-
TIAL SITE: Operates as 1850s working farm.

PROGRAMS: Community Outreach; Con-
certs; Exhibits; Facility Rental; Festivals; Guided Tours; Interpretation; Living History; Reenactments; School-Based Curriculum; Theatre

COLLECTIONS: [1821-1860] Furnishings,
farm equipment, and items relating to Dr.
Anson Jones and his family.

HOURS: Yr Daily 8-sunset
ADMISSION: No charge

8274
Star of the Republic Museum
Washington-on-the-Brazos State Historical
Park, 77880 [PO Box 317, 77880]; (p) (936)
878-2461; (f) (936) 878-2462;
star@acmail.blinncol.edu; (c) Washington

1970/ Blinn College/ staff: 10(f); 4(p);
15(v)/publication: *Star of the Republic Museum Notes*

HISTORY MUSEUM: Interprets the history of
the Republic of TX.

PROGRAMS: Community Outreach; Exhibits;
Family Programs; Festivals; Guided Tours; Interpretation; Publication; Research Library/

Archives; School-Based Curriculum
COLLECTIONS: [1836-1846] Cultural arti-
facts.
HOURS: Yr Daily 10-5
ADMISSION: $4, Student $2; Group rates

8275
**Washington-on-the-Brazos State
Historical Park**
FM 1155 & Park Rd 12, 77880 [PO Box 305,
77880]; (p) (409) 878-2214; (f) (409) 878-2810;
wilburt.scaggs@tpwd.state.tx.us;
www.tpwd.state.tx.us/park/washingt/washingt;
(c) Washington

State/ 1916/ TX Parks and Wildlife Dept/ staff:
7(f); 3(p); 25(v)/ members: 300

HISTORIC SITE; HOUSE MUSEUM; LIVING
HISTORY/OUTDOOR MUSEUM; PRESIDEN-
TIAL SITE: Site of the signing of TX Declara-
tion of Independence.

PROGRAMS: Community Outreach; Concerts; Elder's Programs; Exhibits; Facility
Rental; Family Programs; Festivals; Guided
Tours; Interpretation; Living History; Reenactments; School-Based Curriculum; Theatre

COLLECTIONS: [1821-1860] Convention of
1836 artifacts; adoption of the Texas Declaration of Independence and Texas's first Constitution; Dr. Anson Jones artifacts.

HOURS: Yr Daily 8-sundown
ADMISSION: No charge

WESLACO

8276
Weslaco Bicultural Museum
515 S Kansas, 78599 [PO Box 8062, 78599]; (p)
(956) 968-9142; (f) (956) 447-0955; (c) Hidalgo

Private non-profit/ 1971/ Weslaco Bicultural
Museum Society, Inc/ staff: 1(f); 1(p); 25(v)/
members: 100

HISTORY MUSEUM: Collects, preserves, exhibits and presents programs ton local and
south TX history, with emphasis on agriculture.

PROGRAMS: Annual Meeting; Exhibits; Family Programs; Guided Tours; Lectures

COLLECTIONS: [1890-1960] Vintage clothing
and accessories, household furnishings, farm
implements, military, medical, business machines, Mexican pottery, natural history, toys,
photos.

HOURS: Sept-July W-F 10-12/1-4, Sa 10-4
ADMISSION: No charge

WEST COLLEGE STATION

8277
George Bush Library
1000 George Bush Dr, 77843; (p) (409) 260-
9554; (f) (409) 260-9557; library@bush.nara.
gov; www.nara.gov; (c) Brazos

WEST COLUMBIA

8278
**Varner-Hogg Plantation State
Historical Park**
1702 N 13th St, 77486 [PO Box 696, 77486];
(p) (409) 345-4656; (f) (409) 345-4412;
Varnger-Hogg@computron.net; (c) Brazoria

State/ 1958/ staff: 7(f); 1(p); 20(v)/ members:
20/publication: *History Overview (Brochure)*

ART MUSEUM; GARDEN; HISTORIC SITE;
HISTORY MUSEUM; HOUSE MUSEUM: Preserves history of plantation life.

PROGRAMS: Annual Meeting; Community
Outreach; Exhibits; Facility Rental; Family Pro-
grams; Festivals; Garden Tours; Guided Tours;
Interpretation; Lectures; Living History; Publi-
cation; Research Library/Archives; School-
Based Curriculum

COLLECTIONS: [1830-1850] Decorative arts.
HOURS: Yr W-Sa 9-4, Su 1-4
ADMISSION: $4, Student $2

WHARTON

8279
**Wharton County Museum
Association**
3615 N Richmond Rd, 77488 [PO Box 349,
77488]; (p) (409) 532-2600; (f) (409) 532-0871;
sylvia.ellis@gte.net; www.moses@wcnet.net;
(c) Wharton

County/ 1979/ Board of Trustees/ staff: 1(f);
2(p); 36(v)/ members: 215

HISTORY MUSEUM; HOUSE MUSEUM; RE-
SEARCH CENTER: Collects, preserves, and
interprets local history for present and future
generations.

PROGRAMS: Community Outreach; Exhibits;
Facility Rental; Family Programs; Guided
Tours; Lectures; Living History; Reenactments;
Research Library/Archives

COLLECTIONS: [19th-20th c] Photos of Wharton County, land grants, and maps, sulphur
mine and Shanghai Pierce Ranch exhibits,
sports memorabilia.

HOURS: Yr T-F 9:30-4:30, Sa 1-4
ADMISSION: $2, Children $0.50, Seniors $1

WHITE SETTLEMENT

8280
White Settlement Historical Museum
8320 Hanon Dr, 76108; (p) (817) 246-9719; nor-
risc@concentric.net; www.wsmuseum.tripod
.com/; (c) Tarrant

City/ 1975/ White Settlement Historical Soci-
ety/ staff: 6(v)/ members: 65/publication: *Short
History of White Settlement*

HISTORIC PRESERVATION AGENCY; HIS-
TORICAL SOCIETY; HISTORY MUSEUM:
Promotes history of white settlement.

PROGRAMS: Annual Meeting; Exhibits; Guided Tours; Publication; Research Library/
Archives

COLLECTIONS: [19th-20th c] Farm implements, blacksmith shop, windmill, Native
American utensils, kitchen equipment, log
cabin, photos, histories, and publications.

HOURS: Yr Su 1-4 and by appt
ADMISSION: No charge

WICHITA FALLS

8281
Kell House
900 Bluff St, 76301; (p) (940) 723-0623; (f) (940) 757-5424; www.scottdallas.com/heritage

1909/ Wichita County Heritage Society/ staff: 3(f); 50(v)

COLLECTIONS: [1909-1950] Family furniture, objects, china, crystal, silver, linens, and costumes.

HOURS: T, W, Su 2-4

8282
Wichita County Heritage Society
900 Bluff St, 76301; (p) (940) 723-0623; (f) (940) 767-5424; (c) Wichita

Private non-profit/ 1974/ staff: 3(f); 1(p); 300(v)/ members: 550

HISTORIC PRESERVATION AGENCY; HISTORICAL SOCIETY: Promotes, preserves, and restores landmarks of Wichita County.

PROGRAMS: Annual Meeting; Exhibits; Family Programs; Festivals; Guided Tours; Lectures

WINTERS

8283
Z.I. Hale Museum, Inc.
242 W Dale, 79567 [PO Box 211, 79567]; (p) (915) 754-2036; (c) Runnels

Private non-profit/ 1978/ staff: 50(v)/ members: 200

HISTORIC SITE; HISTORY MUSEUM: Preserves Winters area heritage.

PROGRAMS: Annual Meeting; Community Outreach; Concerts; Elder's Programs; Exhibits; Facility Rental; Family Programs; Festivals; Lectures

COLLECTIONS: [Early 20th c] Sporting, veterans, agricultural artifacts; clothing

HOURS: Yr Th-Sa 1:30-3:30

ADMISSION: Donations accepted

WOODVILLE

8284
Allan Shivers Museum
302 N Charlton, 75979; (p) (409) 283-3709; (f) (409) 283-5258

8285
Heritage Village Museum
Hwy 190 W, 75979 [PO Box 888, 75979]; (p) (409) 283-2272; (f) (409) 283-2194; (c) Tyler

Private non-profit/ 1987/ Tyler County Heritage Society/ staff: 5(f); 12(p); 300(v)/ members: 275

A replica of the pioneer days of East Texas.

PROGRAMS: Annual Meeting; Concerts; Exhibits; Facility Rental; Family Programs; Festivals; Guided Tours; Living History; Reenactments; Research Library/Archives; Theatre

COLLECTIONS: [1840-1920]

HOURS: Yr Daily 9-5

ADMISSION: $4, Children $2

YORKTOWN

8286
Yorktown Historical Society, Inc.
138 W Main St, 78164 [PO Box 1284, 78164]; (c) DeWitt

Private non-profit/ 1978/ Board of Directors/ staff: 4(p); 55(v)/ members: 80/publication: *Yorktown, Texas, 150 Anniversary*

HISTORIC SITE; HISTORICAL SOCIETY: Preserves many items of the past for the present and future.

PROGRAMS: Community Outreach; Exhibits; Family Programs; Film/Video; Guided Tours; Living History; Publication; Reenactments

COLLECTIONS: [1848-present] Communication, transportation, and recreational artifacts; tools and equipment for farming, woodworking, photography, medicine, education, homemaking.

HOURS: Yr Th, Su 2:30-4:30

ADMISSION: Donations accepted

UTAH

ALTA

8287
Alta Historical Society
Hwy 210, 84092 [PO Box 8016, 84092-8016]; (p) (801) 742-3522; (f) (801) 742-7006; (c) Salt Lake

Private non-profit/ 1995/ staff: 6(v)

HISTORICAL SOCIETY: Collect items related to Alta's history.

PROGRAMS: Exhibits; Research Library/Archives

COLLECTIONS: [1870-present] Mining tools and household items; wooden skis; photos; history videos; printed materials; and oral histories.

HOURS: May-Oct by appt; Nov-Apr M, W, F 6-9

BLANDING

8288
Edge of the Cedars State Park Museum
660 W 400 N, 84511; (p) (435) 678-2238; (f) (435) 678-3348; (c) San Juan

State/ 1978/ staff: 5(f); 6(p); 12(v)

STATE PARK: Serves as regional repository for archaeological collections excavated from public land.

PROGRAMS: Annual Meeting; Community Outreach; Concerts; Exhibits; Festivals; Interpretation; Lectures; Living History

COLLECTIONS: [850-1250] 250,000 prehistoric artifacts; Anasazi: pottery, baskets, and artifacts.

HOURS: Yr Daily

ADMISSION: $2

8289
Huck's Museum and Trading Post
1387 S Hwy 191 (79-1), 84511-3203; (p) (435) 678-2329; (c) San Juan

1975/ Hugh Acton, Betty Gordon/ staff: 1(f)

HISTORY MUSEUM

PROGRAMS: Guided Tours

COLLECTIONS: [200 BC-present] Indian Artifacts; baskets, pottery, blankets, rugs, silverwork, beadwork, paintings, and tools.

HOURS: Yr Daily 8-6

ADMISSION: $3, Children $1.50

BOULDER

8290
Anasazi State Park
460 N Hwy 12, 84716 [PO Box 1429, 84716]; (p) (435) 335-7308; (f) (435) 335-7352; nrdpr.ansp@state.ut.us; nr.state.ut.us/parks/www1/anas.htm; (c) Garfield

State/ 1970/ staff: 3(f); 1(p); 2(v)

LIVING HISTORY/OUTDOOR MUSEUM; RESEARCH CENTER: Preserves and interprets the ruins and artifacts at the Coombs Site.

PROGRAMS: Community Outreach; Concerts; Exhibits; Facility Rental; Guided Tours; Interpretation; Lectures; Research Library/Archives

COLLECTIONS: [AD 1050-1200 (Pueblo II-III)] 200,000 prehistoric artifacts, 200 volumes on Anasazi archaeology, 500 photographs, and 4 journals.

HOURS: Yr Daily

BRIGHAM CITY

8291
Brigham City Museum/Gallery
24 N 300 W, 84302 [PO Box 583, 84302]; (p) (435) 723-6769; (f) (435) 723-6769; (c) Box Elder

City/ 1970/ Brigham City Corporation/ staff: 1(f); 2(p)/publication: *Brigham City Historic Tour; Mayors of Brigham City*

ART MUSEUM; HISTORY MUSEUM: Sponsors eleven rotating art exhibits of regional and national interest; researches city history and architecture.

PROGRAMS: Exhibits; Guided Tours; Publication

COLLECTIONS: [Brigham City History 1850-1900]

HOURS: Yr T-F 11-6, Sa 1-5

ADMISSION: No charge

CASTLE DALE

8292
Museum of the San Rafael
64 N 100 East, 84523 [PO Box 1088, 84523]; (p) (435) 381-5252; (f) (435) 384-2653; jan.msr@etv.net; (c) Emery

County/ Janet J. Petersen/ staff: 4(p); 3(v)/ members: 150

NATURAL HISTORY MUSEUM: Depicts regional attributes of archeology, paleontology, Native American artifacts, mountains, deserts and natural history.

PROGRAMS: Annual Meeting; Community Outreach; Concerts; Elder's Programs; Exhibits; Facility Rental; Family Programs; Festivals; Film/Video; Guided Tours; Interpretation; Lectures; Living History; School-Based Curriculum; Theatre

COLLECTIONS: [Prehistory] Native American artifacts, natural history exhibits.

HOURS: Yr M-F 10-4, Sa 12-4

ADMISSION: Donations accepted

CEDAR CITY

8293
Iron Mission State Park and Museum & Miles Goodyear Cabin
635 N Main, 84720; (p) (433) 558-6929; (f) (435) 865-6830; nrdpr.ironmiss@state.ut.us; (c) Iron

State/ 1973/ UT Parks and Recreation/ staff: 3(f); 1(p); 15(v)

HISTORY MUSEUM: Collects, preserves, and interprets the cultural history of the Iron County region.

PROGRAMS: Community Outreach; Exhibits; Family Programs; Guided Tours; Interpretation; Lectures

COLLECTIONS: [1850-1920] Iron production and horse-drawn transportation.

HOURS: Yr Vary

ADMISSION: $3; No change

8294
Special Collection and Archives, Gerald R. Sherrattt Library, Southern UT Univ
351 W Center St, 84720; (p) (435) 586-7945; (f) (435) 865-8152; seegmiller@suu.edu; www.li.suu.edu; (c) Iron

Joint/ Southern UT Univ/ staff: 2(f); 1(p)

LIBRARY AND/OR ARCHIVES: Preserves history of southern UT 19th century settlers, southern Paiute Indians.

PROGRAMS: Exhibits; Publication

COLLECTIONS: [1851-present] Utah settlement, national parks in Utah, photos, Native American basketry, beadwork, pottery, tools and weapons.

HOURS: Yr

CENTERVILLE

8295
Historic Whitaker Home-Museum/ Centerville Historical Society
168 N Main, 84014 [511 E 400 S, 84014]; (p) (801) 295-8358; (c) Davis

Joint/ 1983/ Centerville City Corp/ staff: 2(f); 14(v)

HISTORIC PRESERVATION AGENCY; HISTORIC SITE; HISTORICAL SOCIETY; HISTORY MUSEUM; HOUSE MUSEUM

PROGRAMS: Annual Meeting; Community Outreach; Exhibits; Facility Rental; Family Programs; Festivals; Film/Video; Lectures

COLLECTIONS: [1800-present] Household items, clothing, carpenter tools, furniture, china, pictures, school desks, charts, books, police equipment, uniforms, farm equipment, pioneer wagon, farm tools.

HOURS: By appt

ADMISSION: No charge

DELTA

8296
Great Basin Historical, Inc.
328 W 100 N, 84624 [PO Box 550, 84624]; (p) (435) 864-5013; slamb@greatbasin.net; (c) Millard

Private non-profit/ 1989/ Great Basin Museum and Historical Society/ staff: 1(p); 10(v)/ members: 60

HISTORY MUSEUM

PROGRAMS: Annual Meeting; Lectures; Research Library/Archives

COLLECTIONS: [1900-present] Memorabilia; early pioneers artifacts.

HOURS: Yr

EUREKA

8297
Tintic Historical Society
241 W Main, 84628 [PO Box 218, 84628]; (p) (435) 433-6842; (f) (435) 433-6891; (c) Juab

Private non-profit/ 1973/ Board of Directors/ staff: 5(v)/ members: 50

HISTORIC SITE; HISTORICAL SOCIETY; HISTORY MUSEUM: Preserves history of mining district.

PROGRAMS: Exhibits; Guided Tours; Lectures; Research Library/Archives

COLLECTIONS: [1869-1950] Mining artifacts; tools, minerals, home life, commercial, social.

HOURS: May-Sept Daily 10-4

ADMISSION: No charge

FAIRVIEW

8298
Fairview Museum of History and Art
85 N 100 E, 84629 [Box 157, 84629]; (p) (435) 427-9216; (c) Sanpete

Private non-profit/ 1965/ Fairview Museum Corp/ staff: 10(p); 30(v)/ members: 200

ART MUSEUM; HISTORY MUSEUM: Preserves pioneer history and culture.

PROGRAMS: Annual Meeting; Concerts; Elder's Programs; Exhibits; Festivals; Guided Tours; Interpretation; Research Library/ Archives

COLLECTIONS: [1860-present] Mormon colonization, Colombian Mammoth, Indian artifacts, Avard Fairbanks sculptures, family histories archives, folk art.

HOURS: Yr Daily

ADMISSION: No charge/Donation

FARMINGTON

8299
Lagoon Corporation/Pioneer Village
375 N Lagoon Dr, 84025 [PO Box 696, 84025]; (p) (801) 451-8000; (f) (801) 451-8016; tami@lagoonpark.com; www.lagoonpark.com; (c) Davis

GARDEN; HISTORY MUSEUM; LIVING HISTORY/OUTDOOR MUSEUM

PROGRAMS: Exhibits

COLLECTIONS: [1847-1900s] Artifacts, gun collection, carriage collection, silver and coin collection, toy museum, pioneer and Victorian houses, church, co-op, clocks, dentist, military, china.

HOURS: June-Aug Daily; May, Sept, Oct Sa-Su

FILLMORE

8300
Territorial Statehouse State Park and Museum
50 W Capitol Ave, 84631; (p) (435) 743-5316; (f) (435) 743-4723; tesp@nrdomain.nrd. state.ut.us; www.nr.state.ut.us/parks; (c) Millard

State/ 1930/ Parks and Recreation/ staff: 3(f); 3(p); 5(v)

HISTORIC SITE; HISTORY MUSEUM: Preserves local history.

PROGRAMS: Community Outreach; Exhibits; Facility Rental; Family Programs; Festivals; Interpretation; Living History; Research Library/Archives; School-Based Curriculum

COLLECTIONS: [1847-1865] Pioneer artifacts, art, photos, portraits.

HOURS: Yr Summer Daily 8-8; Winter 9-6

ADMISSION: $2

FORT DOUGLAS

8301
Fort Douglas Military Museum
32 Potter St, 84113; (p) (801) 581-1251, (801) 581-1710; (f) (801) 581-9846; (c) Salt Lake

1976/ Utah National Guard/ staff: 2(f); 3(p); 10(v)/ members: 210

HISTORIC SITE; HISTORY MUSEUM: Promotes history of Fort Douglas, the militia and Utah National Guard.

PROGRAMS: Annual Meeting; Community Outreach; Exhibits; Guided Tours; Publication; Research Library/Archives

COLLECTIONS: [American Indian Wars-present] Military weapons, uniforms, equipment, and books/documents.

HOURS: Feb-Dec T-Sa 12-4

ADMISSION: No charge/Donations only

GRANTSVILLE

8302
Donner Reed Memorial Museum/ Grantsville City Corporation
90 N Cooley, 84029 [429 E Main, 84029]; (p) (435) 884-3411; (f) (435) 884-0426; wendy@ei.grantsville.ut.us; (c) Tooele

City/ 1867/ staff: 4(v)

HISTORIC PRESERVATION AGENCY; HISTORY MUSEUM: The museum is a compilation of artifacts from the Donner/Reed Party that camped in Grantsville (Twenty Wells); artifacts were recovered from the salt flat between Grantsville and Wendover.

PROGRAMS: Guided Tours

COLLECTIONS: Pioneer artifacts from the ill fated Donner /Reed Party.

HOURS: Yr Daily by appt

ADMISSION: No charge

GREEN RIVER

8303
John Wesley Powell River History Museum
855 E Main St, 84525 [Box 620, 84525]; (p) (435) 564-3427; (f) (435) 564-8407; (c) Grand

City/ 1990/ staff: 1(f); 4(p); 20(v)

HISTORY MUSEUM: Promotes history of John Wesley Powell.

PROGRAMS: Annual Meeting; Exhibits; Film/Video

HOURS: Yr Apr-Oct Daily 8-8; Nov-Apr Daily 8-5

ADMISSION: $2, Family $5, Student $1; Group rates

HURRICANE

8304
Hurricane Valley Heritage Park Foundation
35 W State St, 84737 [PO Box 91, 84737]; (c) Washington

Private non-profit/ 1988/ H.V. Heritage Park Foundation/ staff: 2(f); 4(p); 8(v)/publication: *Pioneer Homes Walking Tour*

Acquires, preserves, and promotes local pioneer and Indian history.

COLLECTIONS: [1906-1950] Artifacts, written histories, photos, interpretive plagues, artifacts, early farm machinery.

HOURS: Yr M, Th, Sa 10-6

ADMISSION: No charge

JORDON

8305
Gardner Village
1100 W 7800 S, 84088; (p) (801) 566-8903; (f) (801) 566-5390; www.gardnervillege.com

Private non-profit/ 1979/ Gardner Museum/ staff: 2(p)

HISTORIC SITE; HISTORY MUSEUM: Flour Mill built in 1877 by Archibald Gardner.

PROGRAMS: Festivals

COLLECTIONS: [1800s] Memorabilia of the life and times of Archibald Gardner, a polygamist who had 11 wives and 48 children; a mill builder who built the flour mill.

HOURS: May-Sept M-Sa 12-4, Sept-May hours vary

ADMISSION: Donations

LAYTON

8306
Heritage Museum of Layton
403 N Wasatch, 84041; (p) (801) 546-3524; (f) (801) 546-8519; (c) Davis

City/ 1980/ Layton/ staff: 1(f)

ART MUSEUM; HISTORY MUSEUM: Collects and displays historical artifacts of northern Davis County.

PROGRAMS: Community Outreach; Concerts; Exhibits; Lectures; Research Library/ Archives

COLLECTIONS: [1850-present] 1,403 historic artifacts, 1,481 historic documents, 800 photos, 74 maps, and 48 portraits and paintings.

HOURS: Yr T-F 11-6, Sa 11-6

ADMISSION: No charge

LEEDS

8307
Leeds Area Historical Society
140 N Main, 84746 [PO Box 460-819, 84746-0819]; (p) (435) 879-2050; (f) (435) 879-6905; unvrno@redrock.net; (c) Washington

City/ 1989/ staff: 10(v)/ members: 10/publication: *Leeds Area Historical Sites*

HISTORIC PRESERVATION AGENCY; HISTORIC SITE; HISTORICAL SOCIETY: Preserves history of Leeds, Silver Reef, and Harrisburg, Utah.

PROGRAMS: Community Outreach; Guided Tours

8308
Silver Reef Historical Society
1903 Wells Fargo Rd, 84746 [PO 460700, 84746]; (p) (435) 879-2254; (f) (435) 879-2866; fawn@infowest.com; (c) Washington

1886/ staff: 4(p)

HISTORIC SITE; HISTORICAL SOCIETY; HOUSE MUSEUM

PROGRAMS: Exhibits

COLLECTIONS: [1886-1950] Old Wells Fargo strong box, guns, safe, mining tools, display of area ghost town.

HOURS: Yr M-Sa 9-5

ADMISSION: No charge

LEHI

8309
North American Museum of Ancient Life
2929 N Thanksgiving Way, 84340; (p) (801) 766-5000; (f) (800) 801-5050; mail@Dinosaurpoint.com; www.Dinosaurpoint.com

Private non-profit/ 2000/ Board of Directors/ staff: 12(f); 35(p)

RESEARCH CENTER: Collects, preserves, and re-creates ancient life from the Pre-Cambrian to the Age of Mammals..

PROGRAMS: Community Outreach; Exhibits; Facility Rental; Film/Video; Guided Tours; Lectures; School-Based Curriculum; Theatre

COLLECTIONS: [Pre-Cambrian-Quaternary] Over 50 dinosaur skeletal displays; Paleozoic and Pre-Paleozoic specimens; supersaurus, brachiosaurua vertebrae.

HOURS: Yr June-Sept M-Sa 10-8; Oct-May M-Sa 12-8

ADMISSION: $14, Children $6, Seniors $12; Group rates

LOGAN

8310
Cache Valley Historical Society
196 S 100 West, 84321; (p) (435) 752-5797; (f) (435) 752-4730; (c) Cache

County, non-profit/ 1970/ staff: 12(v)/ members: 80

HISTORICAL SOCIETY: Promotes and preserves the history of Cache County, Utah.

PROGRAMS: Annual Meeting; Community Outreach; Guided Tours; Lectures

COLLECTIONS: [1820s-present]

MIDVALE

8311
Midvale Historical Society
655 W Center St, 84047; (p) (801) 561-1418; (f) (801) 567-0518; (c) Salt Lake

Private non-profit/ 1979/ Board of Directors/ staff: 23(v)/ members: 75

HISTORIC PRESERVATION AGENCY; HISTORICAL SOCIETY; HISTORY MUSEUM: Collects, preserves, and displays local history.

PROGRAMS: Annual Meeting; Community Outreach; Exhibits; Guided Tours

COLLECTIONS: Pioneer artifacts, mining, astronaut, dolls, photos.

HOURS: Yr 12-4

ADMISSION: No charge

MOAB

8312
Dan O'Lanrio Canyon County Museum
118 E Center, 84532; (p) (435) 259-7985; (c) Grand

County/ 1958/ staff: 10(v)/ members: 226/publication: *Canyon Legacy*

HISTORY MUSEUM

PROGRAMS: Annual Meeting; Lectures; Publication; Research Library/Archives

HOURS: Yr Summer 1-8; Winter M-Th 3-7, F-Sa 1-7

ADMISSION: No charge

8313
Hollywood Stuntmen's Hall of Fame, Inc.
81 W Kane Creek Blvd #12, 84532; (p) (435) 259-7027; (f) (435) 259-7027; (c) Grand

Private non-profit/ 1973/ staff: 2(f); 4(v)/ members: 75/publication: *Hall of Fame*

HISTORY MUSEUM; RESEARCH CENTER: Preserves

PROGRAMS: Annual Meeting; Exhibits; Film/Video; Lectures; Publication; Reenactments; Research Library/Archives; Theatre

COLLECTIONS: Movie artifacts, memorabilia, and ephemera primary focusing on stunt people and stars.

ADMISSION: $5.50, Student $3.50

MORGAN

8314
Morgan County Historical Society
50 W 100 N, 84050 [PO Box 727, 84050]; (p) (801) 829-6713; (f) (801) 845-6084; lsmith@state.lib.ut.us; www.morgan.lib.ut.us/

Joint/ 1979/ Morgan County Council; Private non profit/ staff: 1(f); 9(v)/publication: *Morgan County School Buildings*

HISTORIC PRESERVATION AGENCY; HISTORICAL SOCIETY; HISTORY MUSEUM; HOUSE MUSEUM; RESEARCH CENTER: Collects and preserves historical information of Morgan County.

PROGRAMS: Annual Meeting; Community Outreach; Exhibits; Family Programs; Guided Tours; Lectures; Publication; Research Library/Archives

COLLECTIONS: [1855-present] Books, microfilm, local newspapers, city and county meeting minutes, photo library, oral histories, business histories.

HOURS: Yr

OGDEN

8315
Ogden Union Station Railroad Museum
2501 Wall Ave, 84401; (p) (801) 629-8444; (f) (801) 629-8555; bobg@cu.ogden.ut.us; (c) Weber

City/ 1978/ staff: 6(f); 2(p); 80(v)/ members: 100

HISTORIC PRESERVATION AGENCY; HISTORIC SITE; HISTORY MUSEUM

PROGRAMS: Community Outreach; Concerts; Exhibits; Facility Rental; Family Programs; Festivals; Guided Tours; Interpretation; Lectures; Research Library/Archives; Theatre

COLLECTIONS: Photos, classic cars, gem and minerals, rolling railroad stock, model railroad, art.

HOURS: Yr M-Sa 10-5

ADMISSION: $3, Children $1, Seniors $2

8316
Weber County Daughters of Utah Pioneers Museum
2148 Grant Ave, 84403 [4046 S 895 East, 84403-2416]; (p) (801) 621-4891; (c) Weber

Private non-profit/ 1912/ WC DUP Museum Board/ staff: 240(p); 240(v)/ members: 1116

HISTORIC PRESERVATION AGENCY; HISTORIC SITE; HISTORY MUSEUM: Preserves history of northern UT.

PROGRAMS: Community Outreach; Exhibits; Film/Video; Guided Tours; Lectures

COLLECTIONS: [1845-1900] Artistry, toys, furniture, implements, personal history records, books and newspapers.

HOURS: Mid May-mid Sept M-Sa 9-5 and by appt

ADMISSION: No charge

OREM

8317
Orem Heritage Museum at SCERA
745 S State, 84058; (p) (801) 225-2569; (f) (801) 275-2507

Private non-profit/ 1979/ SCERA/ staff: 5(f); 40(v)

HISTORY MUSEUM: Provides, supports, and manages museum.

PROGRAMS: Exhibits; Guided Tours; Interpretation; School-Based Curriculum

COLLECTIONS: [1869-1940] Local history, pioneer exhibits, veterans, blacksmith shop, Indian, church, railroads.

HOURS: Yr May-Sept M-Sa 12:30-4:30; Sept-May by appt

PARK CITY

8318
Park City Historical Society and Museum
528 Main St, 84060 [PO Box 555, 84060]; (p) (435) 649-7457; (f) (435) 649-7384; mail@parkcityhistory.org; www.parkcityhistory.org; (c) Summit

Private non-profit/ 1984/ Park City Historical Society and Museum Board of Trustees/ staff: 3(p); 30(v)/ members: 200/publication: *Photography of Pop Jenks*

HISTORICAL SOCIETY; HISTORY MUSEUM; RESEARCH CENTER: Preserves, protects, and promotes the history of Park City, encourage preservation of Park City's historic sites, promotes public awareness of the importance of our history, operation includes museum.

PROGRAMS: Annual Meeting; Community Outreach; Exhibits; Facility Rental; Family Programs; Film/Video; Guided Tours; Interpretation; Lectures; Living History; Publication; Research Library/Archives; School-Based Curriculum

COLLECTIONS: [1870-present] Photos, artifacts, silver mining, early skiing, research notes, school; architectural preservation.

HOURS: Yr Daily M-Sa 10-7, Su 12-6

ADMISSION: No charge

PAYSON

8319
Peteetneet Culture Arts Center and Museum
10 S Peteetneet Blvd (600 E), 84651 [PO Box 603, 84651]; (p) (801) 465-9427; (c) Utah

City; Private non-profit/ 1988/ staff: 2(p); 54(v)/ members: 58

ART MUSEUM; GARDEN; HISTORIC SITE; HISTORICAL SOCIETY; HISTORY MUSEUM; LIVING HISTORY/OUTDOOR MUSEUM

PROGRAMS: Annual Meeting; Concerts; Exhibits; Family Programs; Festivals; Film/Video; Guided Tours; Lectures; Living History; Theatre

COLLECTIONS: [Victorian] Art, photos, clothing, western, pioneer artifacts.

HOURS: Yr M-Sa 10-4 and by appt

ADMISSION: No charge

PRICE

8320
College of Eastern Utah Prehistoric Museum
155 E Main, 84501 [451 E 4000 N, 84501]; (p) (800) 817-9949; (f) (435) 637-2514; pmillerceu.edu; (c) Carbon

State/ 1960/ Board of Regents/ staff: 2(f); 15(p); 40(v)/ members: 215/publication: *Al's Archives*

NATURAL HISTORY MUSEUM: Collects and maintains exhibits fossils, minerals, and Native American artifacts from eastern UT.

PROGRAMS: Community Outreach; Exhibits; Interpretation; Lectures; Publication; Research Library/Archives; School-Based Curriculum

COLLECTIONS: [Pre-history] Jurassic and Cretaceous dinosaurs; prehistoric Indian artifacts; ethnographic Ute materials.

HOURS: Yr Apr 1-Sept 30 Daily 9-6; Oct 1-Mar 5 9-5

ADMISSION: Donations accepted

PROMONTORY

8321
Golden Spike National Historical Site
, 84307 [PO Box 897, Brigham City, 84302]; (p) (453) 471-2209; (f) (453) 471-2341; GOSP_Superintendent@nps.gov; www.nps.gov/gosp/

Federal/ 1957/ National Park Service/ staff: 9(f); 8(p); 300(v)

HISTORIC SITE: Preserves history of transcontinental railroad and its construction.

PROGRAMS: Community Outreach; Exhibits; Family Programs; Festivals; Film/Video; Guided Tours; Interpretation; Lectures; Living History; Publication; Reenactments; Research Library/Archives; School-Based Curriculum

COLLECTIONS: [1865-1869] Railroad artifacts.

HOURS: Fall-Winter Daily 8-4:30; Spring-Summer Daily

PROVO

8322
McCurdy Historical Doll Museum
246 N 100 E, 84606; (p) (801) 377-9935; (f) (801) 377-5311

Private non-profit/ 1979/ staff: 2(f); 5(p)

HISTORIC PRESERVATION AGENCY; HISTORIC SITE

PROGRAMS: Concerts; Exhibits; Family Programs; Festivals; Guided Tours; Lectures

HOURS: Yr T-Sa 1-5 and by appt

ADMISSION: $2, Children $1

8323
Museum of People and Cultures
700 N 100 E, 84602 [105 Allen Hall BYU, 84602-3600]; (p) (801) 378-6112; (f) (801) 378-7123; fhss.byu-edu/authro/mopc/main.htm; (c) Utah

Private non-profit/ 1980/ Brigham Young Univ/ staff: 1(f); 2(p); 6(v)

HISTORY MUSEUM: Promotes local and cultural history; trains students in museum practices.

PROGRAMS: Community Outreach; Exhibits; Family Programs; Guided Tours; Lectures; Publication; Research Library/Archives; School-Based Curriculum

COLLECTIONS: [Prehistoric-present] Pre-historic and Native American object, Pre-Columbian artifacts, modern ethnography.

HOURS: Yr M-F 9-5 and by appt.

RANDOLPH

8324
Randolph Camp of the Daughters of Utah Pioneers
55 S 1st East, 84064 [PO Box 337, 84064]; (p) (435) 793-3435; (c) Rich

Private non-profit/ 1972/ Intl Daughters of UT Pioneers/ members: 35

HISTORICAL SOCIETY; HISTORY MUSEUM: Preserves the lives of the pioneers.

COLLECTIONS: [1847-1940] Artifacts from local residents.

HOURS: By appt

RICHMOND

8325
Utah Daughters of Pioneers
29 S State, 84333 [215 S 300 East, 84333]; (p) (435) 258-5277; (c) Cache

Private non-profit/ 1910/ staff: 2(p); 2(v)/ members: 35

GENEALOGICAL SOCIETY; HISTORIC PRESERVATION AGENCY; HISTORIC SITE; HISTORICAL SOCIETY; HISTORY MUSEUM: Preserves history of pioneers.

PROGRAMS: Community Outreach; Exhibits; Facility Rental; Guided Tours; Lectures; Living History; Publication; Research Library/ Archives; School-Based Curriculum

COLLECTIONS: [1800-present] Early settlement materials.

HOURS: Yr Th 10-3 and by appt

ADMISSION: No charge

RIVERTON

8326
River City Historical Society
1640 W 13200 S, 84065; (p) (801) 253-3020; (f) (801) 254-1810; (c) Salt Lake

City/ 1984/ staff: 2(p)

HISTORICAL SOCIETY: Collect and preserves written and oral histories.

PROGRAMS: Annual Meeting; Concerts; Elder's Programs; Exhibits; Facility Rental; Family Programs; Festivals; Garden Tours; Guided Tours; Lectures; School-Based Curriculum

COLLECTIONS: Photos of early Mormon settlements, early architecture, art.

HOURS: Yr M, W, F, Sa 1-5

ADMISSION: No charge

ROY

8327
Roy Historical Foundation
5550 S 1700 W, 84067 [PO Box 614, 84067]; (p) (801) 776-3626; (c) Weber

Private non-profit/ 1987/ Roy Historical Foundation/ staff: 27(p); 27(v)/ members: 88/publication: Volunteers' Voice

HISTORIC PRESERVATION AGENCY; HISTORICAL SOCIETY; HISTORY MUSEUM: Preserves history of early pioneers and settlers.

PROGRAMS: Annual Meeting; Community Outreach; Exhibits; Festivals; Guided Tours; Publication

COLLECTIONS: [1873-1969] Early people, houses, and business; early tools, household appliances, guns, coins, 1913 piano, 1869 pump organ, 1898 one-horse buggy, 1900 one-horse sleigh, shoes from famous people.

HOURS: Mar-Dec T-Sa 10-4:30; Su 12:30-4:30

ADMISSION: No charge

SALT LAKE CITY

8328
Alf Engen Ski Museum Foundation
515 E 100 S, Ste 200, 84102; (p) (801) 328-0389; (f) (801) 322-3890; david@fundgroup.com; engenmuseum.org; (c) Salt Lake

Private non-profit/ 1989/ staff: 1(f); 12(v)

HISTORY MUSEUM

PROGRAMS: Community Outreach; Exhibits; Facility Rental; Interpretation; Lectures; Research Library/Archives

COLLECTIONS: [1930-present] ski equipment, trophies, medals, photos, and memorabilia; and 2002 Olympic Winter Games gallery.

HOURS: Yr W-Su 10-5

ADMISSION: $6, Children $4

8329
American Research Bureau
2386 E Heritage Way, 84109; (p) (801) 484-8585; (f) (801) 484-4440; info@arb.com; www.arb.com; (c) Salt Lake

Private for-profit/ 1935/ staff: 25(f); 5(p)

LIBRARY AND/OR ARCHIVES: Collects, preserves, and maintains city directories and other local history sources.

COLLECTIONS: [20th c] 60,000 volumes of city directories and phone directories, reference tools.

8330
Beehive House
67 E S Temple, 84111 [67 E S Temple, 84111]; (p) (801) 240-2681

1854/ staff: 1(f); 5(p); 240(v)

COLLECTIONS: [1854-1877] Furniture, artifacts.

HOURS: Yr; M-F 9-4:30, Su 10-1

8331
Church of Jesus Christ of Latter-day Saints Historical Dept/ Church Library-Archives
East Wing, 84150 [50 E N Temple St, 84150-3800]; (p) (801) 240-2745; (f) (801) 240-1845; (c) Salt Lake

Private non-profit/ 1830/ staff: 41(f); 36(v)

LIBRARY AND/OR ARCHIVES

COLLECTIONS: [1830-present] Publications, manuscripts, records: 190,000 books, pamphlets, bound periodical volumes; 290,000 minute books and other handwritten volumes; 150,000 reels of microfilm, 70,000 microfiche; 12,000 transcriptions and tapes; 3,000 videotapes; 8,000 manuscripts histories; 1 million manuscripts.

HOURS: Yr M-F 8-4

ADMISSION: No charge

8332
Family History Library
35 N W Temple St, 84150-3400; (p) (801) 240-2331; (f) (801) 240-5551; fhl@ldschurch.org; www.familysearch.org; (c) Salt Lake

Private non-profit/ 1894/ The Church of Jesus Christ of Latter-day Saints/ staff: 200(f); 400(v)

GENEALOGICAL SOCIETY; RESEARCH CENTER

PROGRAMS: Community Outreach; Lectures; Research Library/Archives

COLLECTIONS: 3,500 family history centers worldwide; 278,000 volumes; 3,000 bound periodical; 2 million reels of microfilm, 711,000 microfiche; Ancestral file containing 35.6 million lineage-linked names; and the International Genealogical Index with 600 million names.

HOURS: Yr M 7:30-5, T-Sa 7:30-10pm

8333
Hellenic Cultural Association
279 S 300 West, 84108; (p) (801) 484-9708, (801) 277-9237; (c) Salt Lake

Private non-profit/ 1986/ staff: 15(v)/ members: 200

HISTORICAL SOCIETY; HISTORY MUSEUM: Preserves history and culture of Greek immigrants who settled in Salt Lake and Utah after 1900.

PROGRAMS: Annual Meeting; Community Outreach; Exhibits; Festivals; Film/Video; Guided Tours; Interpretation; Lectures; Living History; Research Library/Archives; School-Based Curriculum

COLLECTIONS: [1880-present] Photos, artifacts, dolls, Greek Native dress, mining tools, religious items.

HOURS: Yr W 9-12, Su 12-1

ADMISSION: No charge

8334
International Society Daughters of Utah Pioneers
300 N Main St, 84103-1632; (p) (801) 538-1050; (f) (801) 538-1119; dupmuseum@juno.com; (c) Salty Lake

Private non-profit/ 1901/ Mary A. Johnson, Pres/ staff: 1(f); 50(p); 32(v)/ members: 18500/publication: Pioneer Women of Faith and Fortitude; Pioneer Pathways

HISTORIC PRESERVATION AGENCY; HISTORICAL SOCIETY; HISTORY MUSEUM; HOUSE MUSEUM: Promotes pioneer history.

PROGRAMS: Annual Meeting; Community Outreach; Exhibits; Facility Rental; Family Programs; Film/Video; Guided Tours; Lectures; Publication; Research Library/Archives; School-Based Curriculum

COLLECTIONS: [1847-1900] Furniture, clothing, dishes, guns and swords, histories, photos, machinery, moving vehicles, Native American artifacts, dolls, trunks, handicraft items, fire engine, quilts, medical equipment, Civil War memorabilia, blacksmith shop.

HOURS: Yr M-Sa 9-5

ADMISSION: No charge/Donations accepted

8335
LDS Church Historical Department
50 E N Temple St, 84150-3800; (p) (801) 240-2745; (f) (801) 240-1845; (c) Salt Lake

Private non-profit/ 1830/ staff: 101(f); 1(p); 200(v)

ART MUSEUM; HISTORY MUSEUM

PROGRAMS: Community Outreach; Exhibits; Guided Tours; Lectures; Research Library/ Archives

COLLECTIONS: [1830-present] Printed and published materials, journals, diaries, photos, manuscript materials, Church records, art and artifacts.

HOURS: Yr Library & Archives: M-F 8:30-4:30; Museum: M-F 9-9; Holidays 10-7

ADMISSION: No

8336
Museum of Church History and Art
45 N W Temple St, 84150-3810; (p) (801) 240-4615; (f) (801) 240-5342; (c) Salt Lake

Private non-profit/ 1869/ The Church of Jesus Christ of Latter-day Saints/ staff: 25(f); 2(p); 250(v)

ART MUSEUM; HISTORIC SITE; HISTORY MUSEUM: Interprets the history of the Church of Jesus Christ of Latter-day Saints.

PROGRAMS: Community Outreach; Exhibits; Film/Video; Guided Tours; Interpretation; Research Library/Archives; School-Based Curriculum

COLLECTIONS: [1820-present] Artifacts and art.

HOURS: Yr Daily M-F 9-9, Sa-Su 10-7

ADMISSION: No charge

8337
This Is The Place Heritage Park
2601 Sunnyside Ave, 84108; (p) (801) 584-8391; (f) (801) 584-8325; (c) Salt Lake

Private non-profit/ 1975/ This Is The Place Foundation/ staff: 12(f); 25(p)

HISTORY MUSEUM; LIVING HISTORY/OUTDOOR MUSEUM

PROGRAMS: Exhibits; Facility Rental; Family Programs; Film/Video; Guided Tours; Interpretation; Living History; School-Based Curriculum; Theatre

COLLECTIONS: [1847-1869] Pioneer artifacts.

HOURS: May-Sept M-Sa 11-5; Visitors Center and Monument: Yr M-Sa 9-5

ADMISSION: $6, Family $20

8338
Utah Historic Trails Consortium
300 Rio Grande, 84101; (p) (801) 533-3538; (c) Salt Lake

Private non-profit/ 1994/ staff: 14(v)

ALLIANCE OF HISTORICAL AGENCIES: Identifies, preserves, marks and promotes historic trails in UT.

PROGRAMS: Community Outreach; Lectures

8339
Utah Museum of Natural History
1390 E Presidents Circle, 84112; (p) (801) 581-6928; (f) (801) 585-3684; umnhwebmaster@ raven.umnh.utah.edu; www.umnh.utah.edu; (c) Salt Lake

State/ 1969/ staff: 60(f); 25(p); 155(v)/ members: 1000

HISTORY MUSEUM; RESEARCH CENTER: Acquires, maintains and disseminates knowledge about natural history and culture.

PROGRAMS: Community Outreach; Exhibits; Facility Rental; Family Programs; Guided Tours; Interpretation; Lectures; Publication

COLLECTIONS: Natural science, geology, biology, and anthropology, botany and malacology.

HOURS: Yr M-Sa 9:30-5:30, Su 12-5

ADMISSION: $4

8340
Utah State Archives
Capitol Hill, Archive Bldg, 84114 [PO Box 141021, 84114]; (p) (801) 538-3012; (f) (801) 538-3354; research@state.ut.us; www.archives.state.ut.us; (c) Salt Lake

State/ 1951/ staff: 34(f); 1(v)

LIBRARY AND/OR ARCHIVES

PROGRAMS: Exhibits; Lectures; Research Library/Archives

COLLECTIONS: [1847-present] State and local government agency records.

HOURS: Yr M-F

8341
Utah State Historical Society
300 Rio Grande St, 84101; (p) (801) 533-3500; (f) (801) 533-3503; ushs@history.state.ut.us; www.utah.history.org; (c) Salt Lake

State/ 1897/ Board of State History/ staff: 37(f); 12(p); 40(v)/ members: 2950/publication: *Utah Historical Quarterly, Beehive History, Utah Preservation*

HISTORICAL SOCIETY; HISTORY MUSEUM; RESEARCH CENTER: Collects, preserves, and researches local history.

PROGRAMS: Annual Meeting; Community Outreach; Exhibits; Family Programs; Interpretation; Lectures; Publication; Research Library/Archives

COLLECTIONS: 1 million items: Utah, western and Mormon history.

8342
Wheeler Historic Farm Museum
6351 S 900 East, 84121; (p) (801) 264-2241; (f) (801) 264-2213; (c) Salt Lake

County/ 1976/ staff: 4(f); 30(p)/publication: *Farm Facts*

HISTORIC SITE; HISTORY MUSEUM; HOUSE MUSEUM; LIVING HISTORY/OUTDOOR MUSEUM: Preserves farming and rural life history in UT.

PROGRAMS: Concerts; Exhibits; Facility Rental; Family Programs; Festivals; Guided Tours; Interpretation; Living History; Publication

COLLECTIONS: [1890-1920] Farming and rural life: objects, structures, documents, and photos.

SANDY

8343
Sandy Museum
Historic Center St, 84070 [8744 S 150 E Center St, 84070]; (p) (801) 566-0878; (c) Salt Lake

City/ 1987/ Board of Trustees/ staff: 15(v)/ members: 40

HISTORIC PRESERVATION AGENCY; HISTORIC SITE; HISTORY MUSEUM

PROGRAMS: Annual Meeting; Community Outreach; Exhibits; Facility Rental; Family Programs; Festivals; Guided Tours; Lectures; Living History; Research Library/Archives; School-Based Curriculum

COLLECTIONS: [1850-present] Photos, artifacts, displays, furniture, clothing, local history, farm equipment.

HOURS: Yr T, Th 1-5, Sa 1-4

ADMISSION: No charge/Donations appreciated

SANTAQUIN

8344
Santaquin City Chieftain Museum
100 S & 100 W, 84655 [45 W 100 S, 84655]; (p) (801) 754-3910, (801) 754-3958

City, non-profit/ 1990/ staff: 4(f); 30(p); 4(v)/ members: 100

HISTORY MUSEUM: Preserves history of pioneer settlers.

PROGRAMS: Exhibits; Family Programs; Guided Tours

COLLECTIONS: [19th-20th c] Furniture, mining equipment, harvesting equipment, diaries, genealogy, military, pioneer photography, wagon, ore bins, historic persons, labor history, transportation.

HOURS: June-Aug F-Sa 1-4

ADMISSION: No charge

SEVIER

8345
Fremont Indian St. Park/Museum
11550 W Clear Creek Can Rd, 84766; (p) (435) 527-4631; (f) (435) 527-4735; (c) Sevier

State/ 1987/ staff: 4(f); 2(p); 10(v)

HISTORIC SITE: Interprets Fremont culture.

PROGRAMS: Community Outreach; Exhibits; Film/Video; Guided Tours; Interpretation; Lectures

COLLECTIONS: [650 AD-1350 AD] Fremont and Anasazi artifacts.

HOURS: Yr Daily Winter 9-5; Summer 9-6

SMITHFIELD

8346
Smithfield Historical Society
Central Park, 84335 [238 W 100 N, 84335]; (p) (435) 563-6226; glent@cc.usu.edu; (c) Cache

City/ 1971/ staff: 14(v)

HISTORICAL SOCIETY; HISTORY MUSEUM: Preserves historical heritage, artifacts, and cultural sites.

PROGRAMS: Annual Meeting; Community Outreach; Exhibits; Family Programs; Guided Tours; Reenactments; School-Based Curriculum

COLLECTIONS: [1860-present] Pioneer

SOUTH MAGNA

8347
Kennecott Utah Copper Bingham Canyon Mine Visitors Center

Bingham Canyon Mine, 84044 [8315 W 3595, 84044]; (c) Salt Lake

Private non-profit/ 1992/ Kennecott Charitable Foundation/ staff: 1(f); 4(p)

HISTORIC SITE: Preserves open pit copper mine.

PROGRAMS: Exhibits; Film/Video; Guided Tours

COLLECTIONS: [1903-present] Geology, mining, history, mining and mineral extraction, environmental science, and reclamation, revegatation, air and water quality, copper.

HOURS: April-Oct Daily 8-8

ADMISSION: $3

SPRINGDALE

8348
Zion National Park Museum

1 mi N of Springdale on SR 9, 84767 [Rt 9, 84767-1099]; (p) (435) 772-3256; (f) (435) 772-3426; (c) Washington

Federal/ 1909/ staff: 1(f)

HISTORIC PRESERVATION AGENCY; HISTORIC SITE; HISTORY MUSEUM; LIBRARY AND/OR ARCHIVES; LIVING HISTORY/OUTDOOR MUSEUM: Promotes history and natural history of park and environs.

PROGRAMS: Exhibits; Interpretation

COLLECTIONS: [1850-1965] Archival material.

HOURS: Yr Daily 9-4

ADMISSION: $10/vehicle

STANSBURY PARK

8349
Benson Gristmill Historic Site

325 Highway 138, 84074; (p) (435) 882-7678; mshields@trilobyte.net; (c) Tooele

County/ staff: 1(f); 9(p); 50(v)/publication: *Mill Memories*

HISTORIC SITE; LIVING HISTORY/OUTDOOR MUSEUM: Manage historic site.

PROGRAMS: Exhibits; Facility Rental; Festivals; Guided Tours; Lectures; Living History; Publication; Reenactments; School-Based Curriculum

COLLECTIONS: [1854-1900] Mill machinery, farm equipment, wagons, and pioneer artifacts.

8350
Tooele County Historical Society

51 Mill Pond, 84074; (p) (801) 882-3397; (c) Tooele

State/ 1973/ Utah State History Society/ staff: 4(v)/ members: 22

HISTORICAL SOCIETY

PROGRAMS: Film/Video; Guided Tours; Lectures

VERNAL

8351
Uintah County Library Regional History Center

155 E Main, 84078; (p) (435) 789-0091; (f) (435) 789-6822; dburton@uintah.lib.ut.us; www.uintah.lib.ut.us; (c) Uintah

County/ 1979/ staff: 1(f); 2(p); 1(v)/publication: *The Outlaw Trail Journal: Pages from the Past*

LIBRARY AND/OR ARCHIVES: Collects, preserves and disseminates local and regional history.

PROGRAMS: Community Outreach; Lectures; Publication; Research Library/Archives

COLLECTIONS: [1800s-1900s] Books, microfilm, photos, maps, artifacts, newspapers, oral history files, yearbooks.

HOURS: Yr M-Th 9-8, F-Sa 10-6

ADMISSION: No charge

8352
Utah Field House of Natural History Museum

235 E Main St, 84078; (p) (435) 789-3799; (f) (435) 789-4883; ufsp@state.ut.us; (c) Uintah

State/ 1948/ Division of Parks and Recreation/ staff: 4(f); 6(p); 10(v)

HISTORY MUSEUM: Preserves natural and cultural history.

PROGRAMS: Community Outreach; Elder's Programs; Exhibits; Festivals; Garden Tours; Interpretation; Lectures; Living History; School-Based Curriculum

COLLECTIONS: [Prehistory] Regional geologic, paleontology, archaeology, ethnological and natural artifacts of the Uinta Mountains and Basin of Northeastern UT.

HOURS: Yr Daily May 30-Sept 7 8am-9pm, Sept-May Daily 9-5

VERMONT

ADDISON

8353
Addison Town Historical Society

7099 VT Rt 22A, 05491-8919; (c) Addison

Private non-profit/ 1988/ members: 35

HISTORICAL SOCIETY

PROGRAMS: Exhibits; Lectures

8354
John Strong DAR Mansion

Rte 17, 05491 [c/o Mrs. Perry Manning, 82 Tremont St, Barre, 05641]; (p) (802) 759-2309, (802) 476-7846

1795/ staff: 2(p); 5(v)

COLLECTIONS: [Revolutionary War era] Federal and Victorian furnishings; samplers, hair wreath, clocks, Vermont-made furniture.

HOURS: May 15-Oct 15, F-M 9-5

ARLINGTON

8355
Russell Vermontiana Collection

E Arlington Rd, 05250 [Martha Canfield Library, 05250]; (p) (802) 375-6153

Private non-profit/ 1955/ staff: 10(v)

LIBRARY AND/OR ARCHIVES

COLLECTIONS: [18th-20th c]

HOURS: Yr T 9-5

BARNET

8356
Barnet Historical Society, Inc.

24 Goodwillie Rd, 05821; (p) (802) 633-2611; (c) Caledonia

Private non-profit/ 1968/ staff: 12(v)/ members: 52

COLLECTIONS: [19th c] Documents, clothing, dolls, quilts, paintings and a pump organ.

HOURS: June-Oct M-Sa 10-4

ADMISSION: Donations requested

BARTON

8357
Crystal Lake Falls Historical Association

Water St, 05822 [PO Box 253, 05822]; (c) Orleans

Private non-profit/ 1984/ staff: 10(v)/ members: 175

HISTORICAL SOCIETY; HISTORY MUSEUM; LIVING HISTORY/OUTDOOR MUSEUM: Preserves and interprets educational and industrial history of Barton.

PROGRAMS: Annual Meeting; Community Outreach; Elder's Programs; Exhibits; Family Programs; Film/Video; Guided Tours; Interpretation; Lectures; Research Library/Archives; School-Based Curriculum

COLLECTIONS: [19th-present] Artifacts, photos, memorabilia.

HOURS: June-Sept

ADMISSION: No charge

BELLOWS FALLS

8358
Rockingham Free Public Library and Museum

65 Westminster St, 05101; (p) (802) 463-4270; rockingham@dol.state.vt.us; (c) Windham

City, non-profit/ Town of Rockingham/ staff: 4(f); 6(p); 6(v)

HISTORY MUSEUM: Interprets local history.

PROGRAMS: Community Outreach; Exhibits; Family Programs; Guided Tours; Interpretation; Research Library/Archives

COLLECTIONS: [1750-present]

HOURS: May-Oct M 1-8, T 9-8, Th 1-8, F 9-5, Sa 9-12

ADMISSION: No charge

BELMONT

8359
Community Historical Museum of Mount Holly
Tarbellville Rd, 05730 [PO Box 17, 05730]; (c) Rutland

Private non-profit/ 1968/ Board of Directors/ staff: 18(v)/ members: 200

HISTORY MUSEUM: Collects, preserves and interprets local history.

PROGRAMS: Annual Meeting; Community Outreach; Exhibits; Family Programs; Interpretation; Lectures; Research Library/Archives

COLLECTIONS: [1834-present] Farm tools, period clothing, quilts, photos, post office, blacksmith equipment, agriculture, and early settlers.

HOURS: July-Aug Sa-Su 2-4 and by appt

ADMISSION: Donations accepted

BENNINGTON

8360
Bennington Museum, The
West Main St, 05201; (p) (802) 447-1571; (f) (802) 442-8305; bennmuse@sover.net; www.benningtonmuseum.com; (c) Bennington

Private non-profit/ 1928/ Board of Trustees/ staff: 12(f); 5(p); 80(v)/ members: 875/publication: *Museum Notes*

ART MUSEUM; HISTORIC SITE; HISTORICAL SOCIETY; HISTORY MUSEUM

PROGRAMS: Community Outreach; Exhibits; Facility Rental; Festivals; Guided Tours; Interpretation; Lectures; Living History; Publication; Research Library/Archives; School-Based Curriculum

COLLECTIONS: [Late 18th-mid 20th c] Documents, artifacts, pottery, military history, Vermont furniture, tools, dolls, textiles, photos, glass, paintings, sculpture, Grandma Moses schoolhouse and paintings.

HOURS: Nov-May Daily 9-5; June-Oct Daily 9-6

ADMISSION: $6, Student $5, Seniors $5; Under 13 free

BERLIN

8361
Berlin Historical Society, Inc.
1821 Scott Hill Rd, 05602; (p) (802) 223-1203; norbert925@aol.com; (c) Washington

1980/ staff: 10(v)/ members: 35

HISTORICAL SOCIETY

PROGRAMS: Annual Meeting; Exhibits; Research Library/Archives

BRADFORD

8362
Bradford Historical Society
Bradford Academy, Main St, 05033 [PO Box 301, 05033]; (p) (802) 222-9026; L_C_Coffin@Kingcon.com; (c) Orange

Private non-profit/ staff: 6(v)/ members: 70

GENEALOGICAL SOCIETY; HISTORICAL SOCIETY; HISTORY MUSEUM

PROGRAMS: Annual Meeting; Community Outreach; Concerts; Exhibits; Guided Tours

COLLECTIONS: [Mid 19th c-present] Documents, costumes, photos, school books, farm tools, and souvenirs of local business.

HOURS: Yr by appt

BRANDON

8363
Brandon Historical Society, Inc.
3600 New Rd, 05733 [PO Box 147, 05733]; (c) Rutland

Private non-profit/ 1968/ Board of Directors/ members: 39/publication: *Brandon 1761-1961*

HISTORICAL SOCIETY

PROGRAMS: Annual Meeting; Lectures; Publication

COLLECTIONS: [19th c] Iron stoves, iron weigh scales, wood toys, local newspapers, written records and photos.

BRATTLEBORO

8364
Brattleboro Historical Society, Inc.
230 Main St, 05302 [PO Box 6392, 05302]; (p) (802) 258-4957; (c) Windham

1983/ staff: 12(v)/ members: 300

HISTORICAL SOCIETY: Collects and disseminates information on local history.

PROGRAMS: Annual Meeting; Exhibits; Festivals; Guided Tours; Lectures; Publication; Research Library/Archives

COLLECTIONS: [Late 19th-early 20th c] Photos, ephemera, textiles, postcards and ceramics.

HOURS: Yr Th 1-8, Sa 9-12

BRIDPORT

8365
Bridport Historical Society
Route 22A, 05734 [3177 Crown Point Rd, 05734]; (p) (802) 758-2624; (c) Addison

Private non-profit/ 1974/ staff: 1(v)/ members: 50/publication: *There's Only One Bridport, USA*

HISTORICAL SOCIETY; HISTORY MUSEUM: Preserves history of Bridport.

PROGRAMS: Annual Meeting; Community Outreach; Exhibits; Publication

COLLECTIONS: [1800-present] Artifacts, manuscripts, clothing and photos.

HOURS: Yr by appt

ADMISSION: Donations accepted

BRISTOL

8366
Bristol Historical Society
19 W St, 05443 [PO Box 388, 05443]; (p) (802) 453-6029; (c) Addison

Private non-profit/ 1977/ staff: 4(v)/ members: 140/publication: *The Munsill Papers*

HISTORIC PRESERVATION AGENCY; HISTORIC SITE; HISTORICAL SOCIETY; HISTORY MUSEUM

PROGRAMS: Annual Meeting; Exhibits; Garden Tours; Lectures; Living History; Monthly Meeting; Publication; Research Library/Archives

COLLECTIONS: [19th-20th c] Photos, diaries, scrapbooks, yearbooks, rare and semi-rare books and papers, audio and visual tape recordings, newspaper.

HOURS: July-Sept M-F 10-4

BROOKFIELD

8367
Brookfield Historical Society
Ridge Road, 05036 [PO Box 447, 05036]; (c) Orange

Private non-profit/ 1937/ Board of Trustees/ staff: 15(v)/ members: 140

HISTORICAL SOCIETY; HOUSE MUSEUM

PROGRAMS: Annual Meeting; Exhibits; Festivals; Interpretation; Lectures

COLLECTIONS: [1850-1900] Furnishings, costumes, textiles, tools, farm equipment, books, maps, archives, photos, audio tapes.:

BROWNINGTON

8368
Orleans County Historical Society Inc.
Old Stone House Museum, 05860 [28 Old Stone House Rd, 05860]; (p) (802) 754-2022; (f) (802) 754-2022; osh@together.net; www.homepages.together.net/~nosh; (c) Orleans

Private non-profit/ 1853/ staff: 1(f); 3(p); 100(v)/ members: 900

HISTORICAL SOCIETY: Collects, preserves and interprets history of Orleans County and the Northeast Kingdom.

PROGRAMS: Annual Meeting; Community Outreach; Exhibits; Family Programs; Festivals; Guided Tours; Interpretation; Publication; Research Library/Archives; School-Based Curriculum

COLLECTIONS: [19th c] 3,000 artifacts: farm tools, furnishing, fine arts, folk art, decorative arts, textiles, household items, toys.

HOURS: May-June F-Tu; July-Aug Daily; Sept-Oct F-Tu 11-5

BROWNSVILLE

8369
West Windsor Historical Society
Route 44, 05037 [PO Box 12, 05037]; (p) (802) 484-7474; (c) Windsor

Private non-profit/ 1973/ staff: 25(v)/ members: 400/publication: *West Windsor Historical Society Newsletter*

HISTORICAL SOCIETY

PROGRAMS: Annual Meeting; Exhibits; Lectures; Reenactments; Research Library/Archives

COLLECTIONS: [1848-present] Genealogies, ledger books, land records, diaries, cemetery records, 2,000 photos, 200 museum artifacts.

HOURS: Yr W-Th 9-11:30; July Sa 4-7

ADMISSION: No charge

BURLINGTON

8370
Ethan Allen Homestead Trust
1 Ethan Allen Homestead Ste 2, 05401; (p) (802) 865-4556; (f) (802) 865-0661; eallen@together.net; www.ethanallen.earthlink.com; (c) Chittenden

Private non-profit/ 1986/ staff: 1(f); 3(p); 100(v)/ members: 450

HISTORIC SITE; HISTORY MUSEUM; HOUSE MUSEUM; LIVING HISTORY/OUTDOOR MUSEUM: Interprets early Vermont and Ethan Allen history.

PROGRAMS: Community Outreach; Elder's Programs; Exhibits; Facility Rental; Family Programs; Festivals; Garden Tours; Guided Tours; Interpretation; Lectures; Living History; Publication; Reenactments; School-Based Curriculum; Theatre

COLLECTIONS: [1609-1800] 1785 frame house, period furnishing, 10,000 archaeological artifacts.

HOURS: Yr Daily 10-5

ADMISSION: $5, Children $2.50

CALAIS

8371
Calais Historical Society
8197 County Rd, 05648; (p) (802) 223-5738; (c) Washington

Private non-profit/ staff: 6(v)/ members: 52/publication: *History of Calais*

HISTORICAL SOCIETY

PROGRAMS: Annual Meeting; Exhibits; Lectures; Living History; Publication; Research Library/Archives

HOURS: Yr by appt

CASTLETON

8372
Castleton Historical Society
Main St, 05735 [PO Box 219, 05735]; (c) Rutland

Private non-profit/ 1947/ Board of Trustees/ staff: 25(v)/ members: 80/publication: *CHS Newsletter*

HISTORIC SITE; HISTORICAL SOCIETY: Collects and preserves local history.

PROGRAMS: Annual Meeting; Community Outreach; Exhibits; Family Programs; Guided Tours; Publication

COLLECTIONS: [1800-1900] Agricultural tools and exhibits.

HOURS: June-Oct Su 1-4

ADMISSION: $2

CAVENDISH

8373
Cavendish Historical Society
Main St, 05142 [PO Box 472, 05142]; (c) Windsor

Private non-profit/ staff: 20(v)/ members: 60

HISTORIC SITE: Preserves Cavendish history.

PROGRAMS: Annual Meeting; Community Outreach; Exhibits; Facility Rental; Family Programs; Lectures

COLLECTIONS: [1800-present] Photos, farming, household tools, textiles, ledgers, diaries, ephemera.

HOURS: June-Oct Su 2-4

CHESTER

8374
Chester Historical Society
Main St, 05143 [PO Box 118, 05143]; (c) Windsor

Private non-profit/ 1966/ staff: 15(v)

HISTORICAL SOCIETY; HISTORY MUSEUM: Preserves local history.

PROGRAMS: Annual Meeting; Exhibits; Lectures

COLLECTIONS: Ephemera, school artifacts.

HOURS: June-Oct Sa-Su 2-4

ADMISSION: Donations accepted

COLCHESTER

8375
Saint Michael's College Archives
Library, 05439 [One Winooski Park, 05439]; (p) (802) 654-2408; (f) (802) 654-2630; www.smcvt.edu/library; (c) Chittenden

Private non-profit/ 1904/ staff: 1(f); 2(p); 1(v)

LIBRARY AND/OR ARCHIVES. Preserves official records of Saint Michael's College and Society of Saint Edmund.

PROGRAMS: Exhibits; Research Library/Archives

COLLECTIONS: [1903-present] Official records, college publications, administrative papers, video and audio recordings, microfilm, photos.

HOURS: Yr M-F 8-4:30

ADMISSION: No charge

CRAFTSBURY

8376
Craftsbury Historical Society
Back Common St, 05827; (p) (802) 888-5165; (c) Orleans

Private non-profit/ 1977/ members: 40/publication: *Craftsbury Chronicles*

HISTORICAL SOCIETY: Preserves local history.

PROGRAMS: Annual Meeting; Community Outreach; Exhibits; Lectures; Publication

COLLECTIONS: [19th-20th c] Maps, letters, diaries, photos, films.

HOURS: June-Aug

DANBY

8377
Mt. Tabor-Danby Historical Society
1599 Raymond Rd, 05739; (c) Rutland

Private non-profit/ 1983/ members: 8

HISTORICAL SOCIETY: Preserves local heritage.

DERBY

8378
Derby Historical Society
Main St, 05829 [PO Box 357, 05829]; (p) (802) 766-5324; (f) (802) 334-1237; gardyne@together.net; (c) Orleans

Private non-profit; State/ 1980/ Vermont Historical Society/ staff: 5(v)/ members: 50

HISTORICAL SOCIETY; HISTORY MUSEUM: Preserves local history.

PROGRAMS: Annual Meeting; Exhibits; Facility Rental; Festivals; Guided Tours; Lectures; Living History

COLLECTIONS: [1795-1950] Photos, artifacts, Derby Academy archives.

HOURS: June-Aug Su 1-4 and by appt

ADMISSION: No charge

DERBY LINE

8379
Alnobak Nebesakiak
968 Herrick Rd, 05830 [PO Box 483, 05830]; (p) (802) 766-5375; (c) Orleans

Private non-profit/ 1995/publication: *N'agizi, Nebesak News*

LIVING HISTORY/OUTDOOR MUSEUM; RESEARCH CENTER; TRIBAL MUSEUM: Promotes reclamation/maintenance of cultural heritage and to raise public awareness for and about Abenaki presence.

PROGRAMS: Community Outreach; Exhibits; Lectures; Living History; Publication; Research Library/Archives; School-Based Curriculum

COLLECTIONS: [1800s-present] Projectile points, ash splint and sweetgrass baskets, regalia, tools and utensils.

8380
Holland Historical Society
Tice Road, 05830 [RR1, 05830]; (p) (802) 895-4440; (c) Orleans

Private non-profit/ 1974/ members: 60

HISTORICAL SOCIETY; HISTORY MUSEUM: Preserves town history; maintains town church.

PROGRAMS: Annual Meeting; Exhibits; Facility Rental

COLLECTIONS: [1800-1930] Photos, clothing, church artifacts, farm tools.

HOURS: By appt

ADMISSION: Donations accepted

EAST DOVER

8381
Dover Historical Society, Inc.
105 Rte 100, 05341 [PO Box 53, 05341]; (p) (802) 464-7351; www.state.vt.us/vhs/lhs/windham.html; (c) Windham

Private non-profit/ 1975/ Board of Trustees/ staff: 12(v)/ members: 60/publication: *History of Dover, Vermont*

HISTORICAL SOCIETY: Collects and preserves local history.

PROGRAMS: Annual Meeting; Exhibits; Family Programs; Guided Tours; Lectures; Publication

COLLECTIONS: [1779-present] Local history artifacts.

HOURS: May-Oct W 10-12/2-4

ADMISSION: $5, Children $2

EDEN

8382
Eden History Association
[PO Box 33, 05652]; (p) (802) 635-2941; (c) Lamoille

Private non-profit/ 1994/ staff: 5(v)/ members: 25/publication: *A Walk in the Garden of Eden*

HISTORIC PRESERVATION AGENCY; HISTORIC SITE; HISTORICAL SOCIETY; LIVING HISTORY/OUTDOOR MUSEUM: Preserves local history.

PROGRAMS: Annual Meeting; Community Outreach; Publication; Research Library/ Archives

COLLECTIONS: Local artifacts, archives, ephemera.

FAIRFAX

8383
Fairfax Historical Society
1181 Main St, 05454 [PO Box 145, 05454]; (p) (802) 849-6638; (c) Franklin

Private non-profit/ 1963/ staff: 20(v)/ members: 25

GENEALOGICAL SOCIETY; HISTORIC SITE; HISTORICAL SOCIETY; HISTORY MUSEUM; HOUSE MUSEUM; RESEARCH CENTER: Protects and preserves history of Fairfax.

PROGRAMS: Annual Meeting; Community Outreach; Facility Rental; Festivals; Guided Tours; Living History; Research Library/ Archives; School-Based Curriculum

COLLECTIONS: [1800-present] Photos, scrapbooks, household, tradesman items.

HOURS: July-Oct Su 2-4 and by appt

ADMISSION: No charge

FAIRFIELD

8384
President Chester A. Arthur State Historic Site
Chester Arthur Rd, 05455 [National Life Bldg, Drawer 20, Montpelier, 05620-0501]; (p) (802) 828-3051; (f) (802) 828-3206; jdumville@ dca.state.vt.us; www.state.vt.us/dca/historic/ hp_sites.htm; (c) Franklin

State/ 1952/ Division for Historic Preservation/ staff: 1(f); 2(p)

HISTORIC SITE; PRESIDENTIAL SITE: Promotes Vermont history.

PROGRAMS: Exhibits; Interpretation; Publication

COLLECTIONS: [1829-1886] Arthur Family memorabilia housed in reconstructed Arthur home.

HOURS: May-Oct W-Su 11-5

ADMISSION: No charge

FAIRLEE

8385
Fairlee Historical Society
Fairlee Town Hall, 05048 [PO Box 95, 05048]; (p) (802) 333-9729; (f) (802) 333-9214; hest@together.net; (c) Orange

City, non-profit/ 1976/ staff: 2(v)/ members: 30

HISTORIC PRESERVATION AGENCY; HISTORICAL SOCIETY: Preserves local history.

PROGRAMS: Exhibits

FERRISBURGH

8386
Ferrisburgh Historical Society
, [c/o Karl DeVine, 3378 Monkton Rd, Vergennes, 05491]; (p) (802) 877-6681; (c) Addison

Private non-profit/ 1976/ members: 33/publication: *Ferrisburgh's Memories*

HISTORICAL SOCIETY; LIVING HISTORY/ OUTDOOR MUSEUM: Promotes and preserves local history.

PROGRAMS: Annual Meeting; Exhibits; Living History; Publication

COLLECTIONS: Native American books, local artifacts and local newspaper archives.

8387
Rokeby Museum
4334 Route 7, 05456; (p) (802) 877-3406; rokeby@globalnetisp.net; (c) Addison

Private non-profit/ 1961/ Board of Trustees/ staff: 3(p); 10(v)/ members: 220

HISTORIC SITE

PROGRAMS: Annual Meeting; Exhibits; Family Programs; Festivals; Guided Tours; Interpretation; Lectures; Research Library/Archives; School-Based Curriculum

COLLECTIONS: [19th c]

HOURS: May-Oct Th-Su

ADMISSION: $6

FRANKLIN

8388
Franklin Historical Society
Hannah Road, 05457 [1787 Riley Road, 05457]; (p) (802) 285-2186; (c) Franklin

Private non-profit/ 1958/ staff: 8(f)/ members: 40

HISTORICAL SOCIETY; HISTORY MUSEUM: Promotes local history.

PROGRAMS: Annual Meeting; Community Outreach; Concerts; Exhibits; Facility Rental; Guided Tours; Interpretation; Lectures; Research Library/Archives

COLLECTIONS: [1840-1900] Period

GEORGIA

8389
Georgia Historical Society
Rte 7, 05468 [PO Box 2072, 05468]; (p) (802) 524-4539; (c) Franklin

Private non-profit/ 1975/ staff: 40(v)/ members: 40

HISTORICAL SOCIETY; HISTORY MUSEUM: Collects, organizes, and preserves local history.

PROGRAMS: Annual Meeting; Community Outreach; Exhibits; Family Programs; Guided Tours; Lectures; Publication; Research Library/Archives; School-Based Curriculum

COLLECTIONS: [1788-present] 5,000 photos, 30 genealogy family files, archives, local artifacts.

HOURS: July-Aug M, W, Sa

GRAFTON

8390
Grafton Historical Society
Main St, 05146 [PO Box 202, 05146]; (p) (802) 843-2584; (c) Windham

Private non-profit/ 1962/ Board of Directors/ staff: 10(v)/ members: 300/publication: *5 Dollars and a Jug of Rum, A History of Grafton, VT, 1754-1900*

HISTORICAL SOCIETY; HISTORY MUSEUM: Collects, preserves, and promotes history of Grafton.

PROGRAMS: Annual Meeting; Exhibits; Interpretation; Lectures; Publication

COLLECTIONS: [19th-20th c] Farm, household tools, costumes, textiles, photos, dolls, toys, soapstone, ephemera, Civil War artifacts, and town records.

HOURS: May-Oct Sa-Su 10-12 / 2-4 and by appt

ADMISSION: $3

GREENSBORO

8391
Greensboro Historical Society
[PO Box 151, 05841]; (c) Orleans

Private non-profit/ 1976/ staff: 15(v)/ members: 350

HISTORICAL SOCIETY; HISTORY MUSEUM: Collects, preserves and interprets Greensboro's history.

PROGRAMS: Annual Meeting; Community Outreach; Exhibits; Festivals; Guided Tours; Lectures; Publication; Research Library/ Archives

COLLECTIONS: Photos, articles, books, maps, artifacts, videos, tapes.

HOURS: July-Sept

ADMISSION: No charge

GUILFORD

8392
Guilford Historical Society
Guilford Center Road, 05301 [236 School Rd, 05301]; ww.oldstonehousemuseum.org; (c) Windham

Private non-profit/ 1971/ Board of Trustees/ staff: 20(v)/ members: 300/publication: *Official History of Guilford Vermont, 1678-1961*

HISTORICAL SOCIETY; HISTORY MUSEUM: Collects, preserves, interprets local history and historic sites.

PROGRAMS: Annual Meeting; Exhibits; Interpretation; Lectures; Publication; School-Based Curriculum

COLLECTIONS: [1790-present] Period furnishing, weaving, toys, photos, textiles, authors' scrapbooks, slate industry, mineral springs, cemeteries, agriculture.

HOURS: June-Sept T 10-2, Sa 10-12

ADMISSION: Donations accepted

HARTFORD

8393
Hartford Historical Society
1461 Maple St, 05047 [PO Box 547, 05047]; (p) (802) 296-3132; (c) Windsor

Private non-profit/ 1987/ Board of Directors/ staff: 12(v)/ members: 200

HISTORICAL SOCIETY; HISTORY MUSEUM: Collects, preserves and displays local history.

PROGRAMS: Annual Meeting; Community Outreach; Exhibits; Facility Rental; Festivals; Lectures

COLLECTIONS: Photos, manuscripts, maps, periodicals, artifacts.

HOURS: Feb-Dec 1st Tu 6-8, 1st Sa 1:30-4

ADMISSION: Donations accepted

HARTLAND

8394
Hartland Historical Society
Damon Hall, 05048 [PO Box 297, 05048]; (p) (802) 436-3383; (f) (802) 436-3383; (c) Windsor

Private non-profit/ 1916/ staff: 4(v)/ members: 50

HISTORICAL SOCIETY: Collects papers and artifacts related to Hartland's past.

PROGRAMS: Annual Meeting; Community Outreach; School-Based Curriculum

COLLECTIONS: [1763-present] Town histories, photos, artifacts from first settlers, early house survey, genealogies.

HOURS: Yr M 1-4

ADMISSION: No charge

HEALDVILLE

8395
Crowley Cheese, Inc.
Healdville Rd, 05758; (p) (802) 259-2340; (f) (802) 259-2347; (c) Rutland

Private for-profit/ 1882/ staff: 6(f); 1(p)

HISTORIC SITE

PROGRAMS: Guided Tours

COLLECTIONS: [1885-present] Cheese molds and presses.

HOURS: Yr M-F 8-4

ISLAND POND

8396
Island Pond Historical Society
Railroad St, 05846 [PO Box 402, 05846]; (p) (802) 723-4715; (c) Essex

Private non-profit/ 1967/ Board of Directors/ staff: 6(v)/ members: 347/publication: Island Pond Historical Newsletter

ALLIANCE OF HISTORICAL AGENCIES; ART MUSEUM; HISTORIC PRESERVATION AGENCY; HISTORIC SITE; HISTORICAL SO-CIETY; HISTORY MUSEUM: Collects history of Brighton and Village of Island Pond.

PROGRAMS: Annual Meeting; Exhibits; Festivals; Lectures; Publication

COLLECTIONS: Railroading equipment, logging, agriculture, photos, archives, period furnishings.

HOURS: June-Sept

ADMISSION: Donations

JACKSONVILLE

8397
Whitingham Historical Society
Stimpson Hill Rd, 05342 [PO Box 125, 05342]

Private non-profit/ 1976/ staff: 20(v)/ members: 100

HISTORICAL SOCIETY; HISTORY MUSEUM: Preserves local history.

PROGRAMS: Annual Meeting; Lectures

COLLECTIONS: [18th-20th c] Period clothing, farm tools, clothing, furnishing, school records, toys, books, photos, kitchen and telephone equipment.

HOURS: May-Oct Su

JERICHO

8398
Jericho Historical Society
Vt Route 15, 05465 [PO Box 35, 05465]; (p) (802) 899-3225; (c) Ch Henden

Private non-profit/ 1973/ Jericho Historical Society/ staff: 45(v)/ members: 200

ART MUSEUM; HISTORIC PRESERVATION AGENCY; HISTORIC SITE; HISTORICAL SO-CIETY: Preserves local history through operation of Old Mill, Gothic house and barn.

PROGRAMS: Annual Meeting; Exhibits; Facility Rental; Lectures; Living History; Research Library/Archives

COLLECTIONS: [18th-20th c] Photos, negatives, Bentleys.

HOURS: Apr-Dec Daily 10-5

ADMISSION: No charge

LINCOLN

8399
Lincoln Historical Society
Quaker St, 05443; (p) (802) 453-2980; (c) Addison

Private non-profit/ staff: 1(p)/ members: 104

HISTORICAL SOCIETY; HISTORY MUSEUM; HOUSE MUSEUM: Collects, preserves and interprets local history.

PROGRAMS: Annual Meeting; Exhibits; Family Programs

COLLECTIONS: Maps, newspapers, local artifacts, photos.

HOURS: June-Sept Su 1-4

ADMISSION: Donations accepted

LUDLOW

8400
Black River Historical Society
14 High St, 05149 [PO Box 73, 05149]; (p) (802) 228-5050; (c) Windsor

Private non-profit/ 1972/ staff: 2(p); 13(v)/ members: 150/publication: Black River Academy

HISTORIC SITE; HISTORICAL SOCIETY; HISTORY MUSEUM; RESEARCH CENTER

PROGRAMS: Annual Meeting; Community Outreach; Concerts; Exhibits; Facility Rental; Festivals; Guided Tours; Interpretation; Lectures; Living History; Publication; Research Library/Archives; School-Based Curriculum

COLLECTIONS: [1883-1938]

HOURS: May-Columbus Day M-F 12-4

ADMISSION: Donations accepted

MANCHESTER

8401
American Museum of Fly Fishing
3657 Main St, 05254 [PO Box 42, 05254]; (p) (802) 362-3300; (f) (802) 362-3308; amff@toge; www.amff.com; (c) Bennington

Private non-profit/ 1968/ Board of Trustees/ staff: 5(f); 3(p); 20(v)/ members: 1636/publication: The American Fly Fisher

HISTORY MUSEUM; RESEARCH CENTER: Preserves fly fishing heritage.

PROGRAMS: Annual Meeting; Community Outreach; Exhibits; Festivals; Interpretation; Lectures; Publication; Research Library/ Archives

COLLECTIONS: [1600-present] Reels, rods, flies and other ephemera; library

8402
Friends of Hildene, Inc.
Route 7A S, 05254 [PO Box 377, 05254]; (p) (802) 362-1788; (f) (802) 362-1564; info@hildene.org; www.hildene.org; (c) Bennington

Private non-profit/ 1976/ Board of Trustees/ staff: 7(f); 8(p); 340(v)/ members: 1700/publication: News from Historic Hildene

HISTORICAL SOCIETY: Maintains and operates 412 acre estate of Abraham Lincoln's son Robert.

PROGRAMS: Community Outreach; Concerts; Exhibits; Facility Rental; Festivals; Garden Tours; Guided Tours; Lectures; Publication

COLLECTIONS: [20th c] Original furnishings, fittings, and personal family effects.

HOURS: May-Oct Daily 9:30-5:30

ADMISSION: $8

8403
Manchester Historical Society
Mark Skinner Library, 05254 [PO Box 363, 05254]; (p) (802) 752-2733; (c) Bennington

Private non-profit/ 1897/ staff: 5(v)/ members: 250

HISTORICAL SOCIETY; HISTORY MUSEUM: Preserves local history.

PROGRAMS: Community Outreach; Exhibits; Family Programs; Guided Tours; Interpretation; Lectures; Research Library/Archives; School-Based Curriculum

COLLECTIONS: [18th-20th c] Manuscripts, newspapers, ephemera, 7,000 glass negatives, 5,000 photos, museum artifacts.

HOURS: By appt.

MIDDLEBURY

8404
Henry Sheldon Museum of Vermont History
1 Park St, 05753; (p) (802) 388-2117; (f) (802) 388-2940; shel-mus@panther.middlebury.edu; www.middlebury.edu/~shel-mus; (c) Addison

Private non-profit/ 1882/ Sheldon Art Museum, Archaeological and Historical Society/ staff: 1(f); 8(p); 150(v)/ members: 400/publication: *Walking History of Middlebury, Treasures Gathered Here*

HISTORY MUSEUM; RESEARCH CENTER: Promotes, collects and exhibits local history.

PROGRAMS: Annual Meeting; Community Outreach; Concerts; Exhibits; Facility Rental; Family Programs; Festivals; Guided Tours; Interpretation; Lectures; Publication; Research Library/Archives; School-Based Curriculum

COLLECTIONS: [1700-present] Regional Vermont furnishing, decorative arts, portraits, household and industrial tools, letters, photos, local newspapers, books, pamphlets, manuscripts, maps, ephemera.

HOURS: Yr M-Sa 10-5

ADMISSION: $4, Student $3.50, Children $1.50, Seniors $3.50

MIDDLETOWN SPRINGS

8405
Middletown Springs Historical Society Inc.
On the Green, 05757 [PO Box 1126, 05757]; (p) (802) 235-2376; montvert@sovert.net; (c) Rutland

Private non-profit/ 1969/ Board of Trustees/ staff: 20(v)/ members: 250/publication: *History of Middletown Vermont*

HISTORICAL SOCIETY: Preserves local history.

PROGRAMS: Annual Meeting; Community Outreach; Exhibits; Facility Rental; Family Programs; Festivals; Interpretation; Lectures; Publication; School-Based Curriculum

COLLECTIONS: [1750-1970] Artifacts related to A.W. Gray Co, Montvert Hotel Resort, Mineral Springs Park.

HOURS: May-Oct Su 2-4 or by appt

ADMISSION: No charge

MONTGOMERY

8406
Montgomery Historical Society
Route 118, 05470 [PO Box 47, 05470]; (p) (802) 326-4404; (f) (802) 326-4039; (c) Franklin

Private non-profit/ staff: 12(v)/ members: 150/publication: *Montgomery Vermont: The History of a Town*

HISTORICAL SOCIETY: Promotes historical preservation.

PROGRAMS: Annual Meeting; Concerts; Exhibits; Facility Rental; Festivals; Guided Tours; Publication

COLLECTIONS: Period clothing, books, photos, maps.

HOURS: July-Sept Sa-Su 1-4

ADMISSION: No charge

MONTPELIER

8407
Bennington Battle Monument State Historic Site, Vermont Division for Historic Preservation
15 Monument Circle, 05602 [National Life Bldg, Drawer 20, 05602-0501]; (p) (802) 828-3051; (f) (802) 828-3206; jdumville@dca.state.vt.us; www.cit.state.vt.us/dca/historic/hp_sites.htm; (c) Bennington

State/ 1891/ Division for Historic Preservation/ staff: 1(f); 8(p); 2(v)/publication: *Bennington Battle Monument*

HISTORIC SITE: Preserves and promotes Vermont's historic sites.

PROGRAMS: Community Outreach; Exhibits; Festivals; Interpretation; Publication; Reenactments; School-Based Curriculum

COLLECTIONS: [1777-1891] Commemorates the Revolutionary War Battle of August 16, 1777.

HOURS: Mid Apr-Oct Daily

8408
Chimney Point State Historic Site
7305 VT Route 125, 05602 [National Life Bldg, Drawer 20, 05602-0501]; (p) (802) 828-3051; (f) (802) 828-3206; jdumville@dca.state.vt.us; www.cit.state.vt.us/dca/historic/hp_sites.htm; (c) Addison

State/ 1969/ Division for Historic Preservation/ staff: 1(f); 3(p); 3(v)

HISTORIC PRESERVATION AGENCY; HISTORIC SITE; HISTORY MUSEUM: Promotes local history.

PROGRAMS: Community Outreach; Exhibits; Family Programs; Festivals; Interpretation; Lectures; Publication; School-Based Curriculum

COLLECTIONS: Native American, early French settlement, housed in 18th century lake tavern constructed around remains of early settlement.

HOURS: May-Oct W-Su 9:30-5:30

8409
Friends of the Vermont State House
The State House, 05633 [133 State St, 05633-7101]; (p) (802) 828-5657; (f) (802) 828-3533; dschutz@state.vt.us; (c) Washington

Private non-profit/ 1981/ staff: 3(p); 115(v)/ members: 300/publication: *Vermont State House*

HISTORIC PRESERVATION AGENCY; HISTORIC SITE: Preserves local history.

PROGRAMS: Annual Meeting; Concerts; Exhibits; Guided Tours; Interpretation; Lectures; Publication; School-Based Curriculum

COLLECTIONS: [19th c] Portraits, period furnishing.

HOURS: Yr Daily

8410
Hyde Log Cabin
US Route 2, 05602 [National Life Bldg Drawer 20, 05602-0501]; (p) (802) 828-3051; (f) (802) 828-3206; jdumville@dca.state.vt.us; www.cit.state.vt.us/dca/historic/hp_sites.htm; (c) Grand Isle

State/ 1956/ Division for Historic Preservation/ staff: 1(p)

HISTORIC PRESERVATION AGENCY; HISTORIC SITE; HOUSE MUSEUM: Promotes history of pioneer settlement.

PROGRAMS: Exhibits; Publication

COLLECTIONS: [1783-present] Grand Isle artifacts housed in restored pioneer log cabin.

HOURS: July 4-Sept Th-M

8411
Montpelier Heritage Group Inc.
[PO Box 67, 05601-0671]; (p) (802) 229-5200; (f) (802) 229-5930; aotis@together.net; (c) Washington

Private non-profit/ 1973/ members: 200

HISTORICAL SOCIETY: Promotes historical, architectural, and economic value of Montpelier.

PROGRAMS: Annual Meeting; Guided Tours;

8412
Mount Independence State Historic Site
Mt Independence Rd, 05602 [National Life Bldg, Drawer 20, 05602-0501]; (p) (802) 828-3051; (f) (802) 828-3206; jdumville@dca.state.vt.us; www.cit.state.vt.us/dca/historic/hp_sites.htm; (c) Addison

State/ 1968/ Division for Historic Preservation/ staff: 1(f); 4(p); 10(v)/publication: *Mount Independence*

HISTORIC PRESERVATION AGENCY; HISTORIC SITE; HISTORY MUSEUM: 400 acre Revolutionary War site.

PROGRAMS: Annual Meeting; Community Outreach; Exhibits; Festivals; Film/Video; Guided Tours; Interpretation; Living History; Publication; Reenactments; School-Based Curriculum

COLLECTIONS: [1776-1777] Revolutionary War artifacts.

HOURS: May-Oct Daily 9:30-5:30

8413
Old Construction House State Historic Site
US Route 5, 05602 [National Life Building, Drawer 20, 05602-0501]; (p) (802) 828-3051; (f) (802) 828-3206; jdumville@dca.state.vt.us; www.cit.state.vt.us/dca/historic/hp_sites.htm; (c) Windsor

State/ 1914/ Division for Historic Preservation/ staff: 1(f); 2(p)

HISTORIC SITE: Promotes local history; interprets Vermont's constitution.

PROGRAMS: Exhibits

8414
Vermont Historical Society
109 State St, 05609; (p) (802) 828-2291; (f) (802) 828-3638; vhs@vhs.state.vt.us; www.state.vt.us/vhs; (c) Washington

Private non-profit/ 1838/ Vermont Historical Society/ staff: 10(f); 9(p); 25(v)/ members: 2400/publication: *Vermont History; Incontext*

HISTORICAL SOCIETY: Promotes Vermont history through public programs, research library, publications and operation of museum.

PROGRAMS: Annual Meeting; Community Outreach; Concerts; Elder's Programs; Exhibits; Family Programs; Film/Video; Guided Tours; Interpretation; Lectures; Publication; Research Library/Archives; School-Based Curriculum

COLLECTIONS: 20,000 artifacts, 42,000 catalogued books/serial titles, 1,200 linear feet of manuscripts, 30,000 photographs, 1,000 maps, 8,700 broadsides, New England genealogy/history.

HOURS: Yr T-F 9-4:30, Sa 9-4, Su 12-4

ADMISSION: $3, Student $2, Seniors $2; $5 Library Research fee

MORRISVILLE

8415
Noyes House Museum
122 Main St, 05661 [PO Box 1299, 05661]; (p) (802) 888-7617; (c) Lamoille

Private non-profit/ 1952/ Morristown Historical Society/ staff: 2(p); 25(v)/ members: 200

HISTORICAL SOCIETY; HISTORY MUSEUM; HOUSE MUSEUM: Preserves historic Noyes House.

PROGRAMS: Annual Meeting; Concerts; Exhibits; Family Programs; Guided Tours; Lectures; Research Library/Archives

COLLECTIONS: [19th c] Local and regional history, costumes, furnishings, toys, dolls, household and farm tools, souvenir pitchers, military artifacts, photos, maps and documents.

HOURS: June-Sept W-Sa 1-5 and by appt

ADMISSION: Donations

NEWFANE

8416
Historical Society of Windham County
RT 30, 05345 [PO Box 246, 05345]; (p) (802) 365-4148; (c) Windham

Private non-profit/ 1926/ staff: 1(p)/ members: 220

HISTORICAL SOCIETY; HISTORY MUSEUM

COLLECTIONS: [1700-1900] Period furnishing, paintings, textiles, manuscripts, photos, Civil War artifacts.

HOURS: May-Oct W-Su 12-5

ADMISSION: No charge

NORTH BENNINGTON

8417
Park-McCullough Historic House
Park & W St, 05257 [PO Box 388, 05257]; (p) (802) 442-5441; (f) (802) 442-5442; thehouse@sover.net; www.parkmccullough.org; (c) Bennington

Private non-profit/ 1968/ Park-McCullough House Association, Inc./ staff: 2(f); 5(p); 55(v)/ members: 280

HISTORIC SITE; HOUSE MUSEUM

PROGRAMS: Annual Meeting; Concerts; Exhibits; Facility Rental; Guided Tours; Research Library/Archives

COLLECTIONS: [1865-1900] 37,000 archival items, 19th century furnishing, costumes and textiles, rugs, carriages, personal items belonging to family members.

HOURS: May-late Oct Daily 10-4

ADMISSION: $6, Student $3.50, Children $4, Seniors $5; Under 12 free; Group rates

NORTH BRATTLEBORO

8418
Dummerston Historical Society
Dummerton Center, 05304 [PO Box 8064, 05304]; (c) Windham

Private non-profit/ 1977/ members: 209

HISTORICAL SOCIETY: Promotes history of the town of Dummerston.

NORTH CONCORD

8419
Concord Historical Society
Main St Town Hall, 05858 [1124 Victory Rd, 05858-7801]; (p) (802) 695-2288; (c) Essex

Private non-profit/ 1978/ Board of Directors/ staff: 6(v)/ members: 230

HISTORICAL SOCIETY; HISTORY MUSEUM; RESEARCH CENTER: Collects and preserves local history.

PROGRAMS: Annual Meeting; Community Outreach; Exhibits; Film/Video; Guided Tours; Lectures; Research Library/Archives

COLLECTIONS: Restored period rooms, hand-forged tools.

HOURS: By appt

ADMISSION: No charge

NORWICH

8420
Norwich Historical Society
37 Church St, 05055 [PO Box 1680, 05055]; (p) (802) 649-0124; (c) Windsor

Private non-profit/ 1951/ staff: 15(v)/ members: 286

HISTORICAL SOCIETY: Collects, preserves and interprets history of Norwich.

PROGRAMS: Annual Meeting; Exhibits; Living History

COLLECTIONS: Furnishings, textiles, ceramics, books, journals, scrapbooks, ephemera, artifacts, maps.

HOURS: W 2:30-4:30

ADMISSION: No charge

ORWELL

8421
Orwell Historical Society
Main St, 05760; (c) Addison

Private non-profit/ 1978/ staff: 10(v)/ members: 12

HISTORICAL SOCIETY; HISTORY MUSEUM: Promotes local history.

COLLECTIONS: [1763-present] Toys, agricultural items, school, period furnishing and clothing.

HOURS: May-Oct T, F 12-4, Sa 10-12

ADMISSION: No charge

PAWLETT

8422
Pawlett Historical Society
Rte 30, 05761 [404 Robinson Hill Rd 404 Robinson Hill Rd, 05761]; (p) (802) 325-3013; (c) Rutland

Private non-profit/ 1973/ Pawlett Historical Society/ staff: 15(v)/ members: 100/publication: *Pawlett Scrapbook*

HISTORICAL SOCIETY: Preserves local history.

PROGRAMS: Annual Meeting; Exhibits; Lectures; Publication

COLLECTIONS: [19th-20th c] Photos, documents, clothing, artifacts.

HOURS: Yr

ADMISSION: Donations

PEACHAM

8423
Peacham Historical Association
Church St, 05862 [104 Thaddeus Stevens Rd, 05862]; (p) (802) 592-3571; senturia@connriver.net; (c) Caledonia

Private non-profit/ 1920/ staff: 4(v)/ members: 117

HISTORICAL SOCIETY; HISTORY MUSEUM: Collects and preserves items related to Peacham's history.

PROGRAMS: Annual Meeting; Community Outreach; Exhibits; Festivals; Garden Tours; Guided Tours; Interpretation; Lectures; Publication; Reenactments; Research Library/Archives

COLLECTIONS: [18th-20th c] Manuscripts, photos, archives, sugaring and lumbering artifacts, quilts, clothing, tools.

HOURS: June-Oct Su-M 2-4

ADMISSION: No charge

PERU

8424
Historical Society of Peru
[PO Box 134, 05152]; (p) (802) 824-6495; (c) Bennington

Private non-profit/ 1992/ staff: 4(v)/ members: 40/publication: *More Tall Tales from Peru, Vermont*

HISTORIC PRESERVATION AGENCY; HISTORICAL SOCIETY: Preserves local history.

PROGRAMS: Annual Meeting; Guided Tours; Lectures; Publication

COLLECTIONS: [1850-present] Photos and artifacts.

ADMISSION: No charge

PITTSFORD

8425
Pittsford Historical Society, Inc.
Main St, 05763 [PO Box 423, 05763]; (p)
(802) 483-2040; www.pittsfordhistorical.org;
(c) Rutland

Private non-profit/ 1960/ members: 200/publi-
cation: *Second Century*

HISTORICAL SOCIETY: Preserves local history
through maintenance of genealogical library.

PROGRAMS: Annual Meeting; Exhibits;
Film/Video

COLLECTIONS: [19th-20th c] Household furnishings, farm implements, costumes, books,
paintings, genealogical records, local history
videos, sports exhibit.

HOURS: Mar-June, Sept-Dec Tu 9-4; July-Aug
Tu, Sa 9-4

ADMISSION: Donations accepted

PLYMOUTH

8426
Calvin Coolidge Memorial Foundation, The
Messer Hill Rd, 05056 [PO Box 97, 05056]; (p)
(802) 672-3389; (f) (802) 672-3389; info@calvin-
coolidge.org; www.calvin-coolidge.org; (c)
Windsor

Private non-profit/ 1960/ Board of Trustees/
staff: 2(f); 20(v)/ members: 800/publication:
The Real Calvin Coolidge

LIBRARY AND/OR ARCHIVES: Interprets life
of Calvin Coolidge.

PROGRAMS: Annual Meeting; Community
Outreach; Concerts; Exhibits; Lectures; Publi-
cation; Reenactments; Research Library/
Archives

COLLECTIONS: [1872-1957] Photos, papers.

HOURS: Yr Daily 9:30-5

ADMISSION: $5; Under 13 free, group rates

8427
Plymouth Vermont Historical Society
Rte 100 and Town Offler Rd, 05056; (c)
Windsor

Private non-profit/ staff: 3(p)

HISTORICAL SOCIETY; HISTORY MUSEUM:
Preserves and interprets local history.

PROGRAMS: Annual Meeting; Community
Outreach; Exhibits

COLLECTIONS: [1779-present] Calvin
Coolidge memorabilia and local artifacts.

ADMISSION: No charge

PLYMOUTH NOTCH

8428
President Calvin Coolidge State Historic Site
Plymouth Notch Historic District, 05056
[National Life Building, Montpelier, 05602-
0501]; (p) (802) 828-3051; (f) (802) 828-3206;
jdumville@dca.state.vt.us; www.state.vt.us/
dca/historic/hp_sites.htm

State/ 1948/ Division for Historic Preservation/
staff: 1(f); 30(p); 3(v)

HISTORIC PRESERVATION AGENCY; HIS-
TORIC SITE; HOUSE MUSEUM; PRESIDEN-
TIAL SITE: Promotes local history through
stewardship and interpretation of historic site.

PROGRAMS: Annual Meeting; Community Out-
reach; Concerts; Exhibits; Facility Rental; Family
Programs; Festivals; Garden Tours; Guided
Tours; Interpretation; Lectures; Publication;
Reenactments; School-Based Curriculum

COLLECTIONS: [1872-1933] Calvin Coolidge
artifacts; site is birthplace and burial ground for
30th president.

HOURS: May-Oct Daily 9:30-5:30

ADMISSION: $5

POULTNEY

8429
Poultney Historical Society
E Poultney Green, 05764 [c/o Ruth Czar, 148
Upper Road, 05764]; (p) (802) 287-5268; (c)
Rutland

Private non-profit/ 1950/ staff: 30(v)/ members:
150

HISTORIC SITE; HISTORICAL SOCIETY;
HISTORY MUSEUM: Manages three sites:
Union Academy, Melodeon Factory, and East
Poultney Schoolhouse.

PROGRAMS: Annual Meeting; Community
Outreach; Exhibits

COLLECTIONS: [1791-present] Farm equipment, clothing, local artifacts.

HOURS: June-Aug Su 1-4

ADMISSION: No charge

POWNAL

8430
Pownal Historical Society Inc.
[PO Box 313, 05261]; (p) (802) 823-4007; (c)
Bennington

Private non-profit/ 1994/ Board of Directors/
members: 80

HISTORICAL SOCIETY: Collects, preserves
and interprets local history.

PROGRAMS: Annual Meeting; Community
Outreach; Exhibits; Lectures

COLLECTIONS: [1750-present] Books, photos and archives.

PROCTOR

8431
Proctor Historical Society
Proctor Free Library, 05765 [4 Main St,
05765]; (p) (802) 459-3539; proctor_free@
dol.state.vt.us; (c) Rutland

Private non-profit/ 1973/ staff: 4(p); 4(v)

HISTORICAL SOCIETY: Promotes history of
Proctor and Vermont Marble Company.

PROGRAMS: Annual Meeting; Community
Outreach; Exhibits; Lectures; Living History

COLLECTIONS: [1850-1950] Photos, documents, maps, Vermont Marble Company
records, items belonging to US Senator Red-
field Proctor and family.

HOURS: Yr M-F 9-11/2-8; Sa 9-12

8432
Wilson Castle
W Proctor Rd, 05765 [PO Box 290, Center
Rutland, 05736]; (p) (802) 773-3284

PUTNEY

8433
Putney Historical Society
127 Main St, 05346 [PO Box 233, 05346]; (c)
Windham

Private non-profit/ 1959/ staff: 11(v)/ members: 80

HISTORICAL SOCIETY; HISTORY MUSEUM;
RESEARCH CENTER: Collects and preserves local history.

PROGRAMS: Annual Meeting; Exhibits; Family Programs; Lectures; Research Library/
Archives

COLLECTIONS: [Prehistory-present] Native
American artifacts, documents,

RANDOLPH

8434
Braintree Historical Society
RFD 1, Thayer Brook Rd, 05060; (p) (802)
728-9291; (c) Orange

Private non-profit/ 1960/ staff: 20(v)/ members:
75

HISTORIC PRESERVATION AGENCY; HIS-
TORIC SITE; HISTORICAL SOCIETY; HISTO-
RY MUSEUM

PROGRAMS: Annual Meeting; Community
Outreach; Concerts; Exhibits

COLLECTIONS: [1850-1950] Clothing, guns,
household items, farming tools, machinery
and photos.

HOURS: By appt

ADMISSION: No charge

RANDOLPH CENTER

8435
Randolph Historical Society
Salisbury St, 05061 [PO Box 15, 05061]; (p)
(802) 728-5398; (c) Orange

Private non-profit/ 1960/ staff: 6(v)/ members:
100

HISTORICAL SOCIETY: Preserves local history
through conservation and restoration efforts.

PROGRAMS: Annual Meeting; Exhibits;
Film/Video; Guided Tours; Lectures; Living
History; Publication

COLLECTIONS: [20th c] Period kitchen, parlor, barbershop, drugstore and artifacts.

HOURS: June-Oct 1st Su 1-5 and by appt

ADMISSION: No charge, donations welcome

READSBORO

8436
Readsboro Historical Society
7009 Main St, 05350 [PO Box 158, 05350-
0158]; (c) Bennington

1966/ staff: 15(v)/ members: 50/publication:
Down Through the Years, 1786-1936

HISTORIC SITE; HISTORICAL SOCIETY:
Preserves historic buildings.

PROGRAMS: Annual Meeting; Elder's Programs; Exhibits; Facility Rental; Family Programs; Publication; School-Based Curriculum

COLLECTIONS: Photos from glass plates.

HOURS: May-Oct Su 2-4

ADMISSION: Donations accepted

RICHFORD

8437
Richford Historical Society
[PO Box 606, 05476]; (p) (802) 933-6622; (c) Franklin

1980/ Board of Directors/ staff: 15(v)/ members: 25

HISTORICAL SOCIETY: Preserves local history and restores historical sites.

PROGRAMS: Annual Meeting; Exhibits

COLLECTIONS: [1800-1900] Photos, old newspapers, books, ephemera.

HOURS: July 1-Mid Oct Sa 10-4 and by appt

RICHMOND

8438
Richmond Historical Society
Bridge St, 05477 [PO Box 453, 05477]; (c) Chittenden

Joint/ 1973/ Executive Board; State/ staff: 40(v)/ members: 125

HISTORICAL SOCIETY: Promotes and preserves history of Richmond; maintains c. 1813 Old Round Church.

PROGRAMS: Guided Tours; Publication

COLLECTIONS: [1800-present]

HOURS: June-Aug Daily 10-4; Sept Sa-Su; Last week of Sept-1st week of Oct Daily

ROCKINGHAM

8439
Rockingham Meeting House Association
Rockingham Meeting House, 05101 [29 Oak Hill Terrace, Bellows Falls, 05101]; (p) (802) 463-3941; (f) (802) 463-1583; john.a.leppman@dartmouth.edu; (c) Windham

Private non-profit/ 1911/ members: 30

HISTORIC SITE; HISTORICAL SOCIETY: Supporting organization for Rockingham Meeting House, a 1787 New England meeting house.

PROGRAMS: Annual Meeting

COLLECTIONS: [18th-19th c] Preserved 1787 building, related artifacts.

HOURS: June-Oct Daily 10-5

ADMISSION: $0.50

ROXBURY

8440
Roxbury Historical Society
Route 12A, 05669; mjennings@summitvt.com; (c) Washington

1974/ Roxbury Historical Society/ staff: 5(v)

HISTORICAL SOCIETY

PROGRAMS: Exhibits; Festivals

COLLECTIONS: [1781-present] Memorabilia, town documents.

HOURS: By appt

ADMISSION: Donations accepted

ROYALTON

8441
Royalton Historical Society
Royalton Village, 05068 [4184 Route 14, 05068]; (p) (802) 763-8567; jdumville@dca.state.vt.us; (c) Windsor

Private non-profit/ 1911/ Royalton Historical Society/ staff: 3(p); 3(v)/publication: *Royalton Vermont*

HISTORICAL SOCIETY; RESEARCH CENTER: Collects and interprets local history; maintains Royalton Town House, Center Schoolhouse, St. Paul's Church.

PROGRAMS: Community Outreach; Exhibits; Guided Tours; Publication

COLLECTIONS: [1780-present] Photos, manuscripts.

HOURS: Yr by appt.

RUTLAND

8442
New England Maple Museum
US Route 7, 05701 [PO Box 1615, 05701]; (p) (802) 483-9414; (c) Rutland

Private for-profit/ 1977/ staff: 4(f); 8(p)

HISTORY MUSEUM: Collects and preserves maple sugaring industry history.

PROGRAMS: Exhibits; Film/Video

COLLECTIONS: [1800-present] Maple sugaring artifacts, tools.

HOURS: May 15-20, Nov 1-Dec 23 Daily 10-4; May 21-Oct 31 Daily 8:30-5:30

ADMISSION: $2.50

8443
Rutland Historical Society Inc.
96 Center St, 05701-4023; (p) (802) 775-2006; (c) Rutland

Private non-profit/ 1969/ Rutland Historical Society, Inc./ staff: 25(v)/ members: 500/publication: *Early Families of Rutland, History of Rutland, Vermont, 1761-1861.*

HISTORICAL SOCIETY: Preserves catalogues, exhibits and records.

PROGRAMS: Annual Meeting; Community Outreach; Elder's Programs; Exhibits; Guided Tours; Lectures; Publication; Research Library/Archives

COLLECTIONS: [1770-present] Books, photos, paintings, documents, manuscripts, artifacts.

HOURS: Yr M 6-9, Sa 1-4

ADMISSION: No charge

RYEGATE

8444
Ryegate Historical Society
54 Papermill Rd, 05042 [PO Box 366, 05042]; (p) (802) 584-3520; dwight.white@connriver.net; (c) Caledonia

Private non-profit/ 1986/ Board of Directors/ staff: 6(v)/ members: 75

HISTORIC PRESERVATION AGENCY; HISTORICAL SOCIETY: Promotes local history.

PROGRAMS: Annual Meeting; Facility Rental; Lectures; Publication

HOURS: By appt

SAINT ALBANS

8445
St. Albans Historical Museum
9 Church St, 05478 [PO Box 722, 05478]; (p) (802) 527-7933; (c) Franklin

Private non-profit/ 1970/ Board of Trustees/ staff: 2(p); 30(v)/ members: 225

HISTORY MUSEUM: Preserves and interprets local history.

PROGRAMS: Annual Meeting; Community Outreach; Exhibits; Festivals; Interpretation; Lectures; Living History; Research Library/Archives; School-Based Curriculum

COLLECTIONS: [1800-present] Exhibits, scrapbooks, diaries, photos, railway, local history, medicine, diorama.

HOURS: Mid June-Oct 1 M-F 1-4 and by appt

ADMISSION: $3; Children 14 and under free

SAINT JOHNSBURY

8446
Fairbanks Museum and Planetarium
1302 Main St, 05819-2224; (p) (802) 748-2372; (f) (802) 748-1893; fairbanks.museum@connriver.net; www.fairbanksmuseum.org; (c) Caledonia

Private non-profit/ 1890/ staff: 10(f); 10(p); 150(v)/ members: 750

NATURAL HISTORY MUSEUM

PROGRAMS: Annual Meeting; Community Outreach; Concerts; Exhibits; Family Programs; Festivals; Guided Tours; Interpretation; Lectures; Living History; Research Library/Archives; School-Based Curriculum

COLLECTIONS: [1870-present] Natural science, ethnology..

HOURS: Yr M-Sa 9-6, Su 1-5

ADMISSION: $5, Family $12, Children $3, Seniors $4

SHAFTSBURY

8447
Shaftsbury Historical Society
Route 7A, 05262 [PO Box 401, 05262]; (p) (802) 447-7488; (c) Bennington

Private non-profit/ 1967/ Board of Directors/ staff: 1(p); 20(v)/ members: 325

HISTORICAL SOCIETY; HISTORY MUSEUM: Preserves Shaftsbury history and genealogy.

PROGRAMS: Annual Meeting; Exhibits; Guided Tours; Research Library/Archives

COLLECTIONS: [1820-1890] Tools, Victoriana, religious artifacts; exhibits on creation theory.

HOURS: June-Oct T-Su 2-4

ADMISSION: Donations

SHARON

8448
Sharon Historical Society
Old Town Hall, 05065 [PO Box 176, 05065];
(c) Windsor

Private non-profit/ 1990/ staff: 20(v)/ members:
105

HISTORIC SITE; HISTORICAL SOCIETY;
HISTORY MUSEUM: Collects and preserves
local history.

PROGRAMS: Annual Meeting; Exhibits; Family Programs; Lectures; Publication

COLLECTIONS: [1860] Photos, crafts, oral
histories, family genealogy.

HOURS: July-Aug Su 1-3

ADMISSION: No charge

SHEFFIELD

8449
Sheffield Historical Society
Dane Road, 05866 [PO Box 52, 05866]; (p)
(802) 626-5735; (c) Caledonia

Private non-profit/ 1990/ staff: 6(f); 4(v)/ members: 25/publication: *Greetings from Sheffield:
A Pictorial History*

Preserves local history.

PROGRAMS: Annual Meeting; Community
Outreach; Exhibits; Family Programs; Festivals; Guided Tours; Interpretation; Lectures;
Living History; Publication; Research Library/Archives; School-Based Curriculum

COLLECTIONS: [1800-1900] Photos, medical
implements, advertising signs, woolen wagon
blankets.

HOURS: Monthly, 3rd Thursdays

ADMISSION: No charge

SHELBURNE

8450
National Museum of the Morgan Horse
3 Bostwick Rd, 05482 [PO Box 519, 05482]; (p)
(802) 985-8665; (f) (802) 985-5242;
national_museum@hotmail.com; www.
members.tripod.com/~nmmh; (c) Chittenden

1988/publication: *Donald; Morgan Horses*

COLLECTIONS: [19th-20th c] Museum artifacts, photos, manuscripts, periodicals, paintings, show memorabilia.

HOURS: Yr M-F 9-4, Sa 10-2

ADMISSION: $1

8451
Shelburne Museum
Rte 7, 05482 [PO Box 10, 05482]; (p) (802)
985-3346; (f) (802) 985-2331; museinfo@
together.net; www.shelburnemuseum.org; (c)
Chittenden

Private non-profit/ 1947/ staff: 80(f); 200(p);
75(v)/ members: 2700/publication: *Ticonderoga: Lake Champlain Steamboat*

HISTORY MUSEUM: Preserves and interprets
museum's collection of early American arts
and architecture.

PROGRAMS: Community Outreach; Concerts; Elder's Programs; Exhibits; Facility
Rental; Family Programs; Festivals; Garden
Tours; Guided Tours; Interpretation; Lectures;
Publication; Research Library/Archives;
School-Based Curriculum; Theatre

COLLECTIONS: [18th-19th c] American art,
artifacts, architecture, horse drawn vehicles,
quilts, decoys, circus memorabilia, dolls, toys,
decorative art.

HOURS: May-Oct Daily 10-5

ADMISSION: $17.50, Children $7

SOUTH LONDONDERRY

8452
Londonderry Historical Society Inc.
Custer Sharp House, Middletown Road,
05155 [PO Box 114, 05155]; (p) (802) 824-
4406; (c) Windham

Private non-profit/ 1971/ members: 150

HISTORICAL SOCIETY: Preserves historic
material; publishes local history.

PROGRAMS: Annual Meeting; Concerts; Exhibits; Facility Rental; Family Programs; Garden Tours; Lectures

COLLECTIONS: [19th-20th c] Photos, period
clothing, tools, farm implements, dolls,
ephemera.

HOURS: June-Sept Sa 10-1

ADMISSION: No charge

STRAFFORD

8453
Strafford Historical Society, Inc.
[PO Box 67, 05072]; (p) (802) 765-4321; (c)
Orange

Private non-profit/ 1955/ Board of Directors/
staff: 13(v)/ members: 190

HISTORY MUSEUM: Preserves local history
of small rural Vt town.

PROGRAMS: Annual Meeting; Exhibits; Guided Tours; Lectures

COLLECTIONS: [1761-present] Photos and
genealogical records; former copper mine.

HOURS: By appt

SWANTON

8454
Swanton Historical Society
Grand Ave & First St, 05488 [1 First St,
05488]; (c) Franklin

Private non-profit/ 1984/ Swanton Historical
Society, Inc./ staff: 14(f); 4(v)/ members:
130/publication: *History of Swanton; Swanton
Heritage*

HISTORICAL SOCIETY; HISTORY MUSEUM:
Promotes local history.

PROGRAMS: Annual Meeting; Community
Outreach; Exhibits; Family Programs; Film/
Video; Guided Tours; Lectures; Research Library/Archives

COLLECTIONS: [1800-1950] Local memorabilia.

HOURS: Yr F 2-5

ADMISSION: No charge

THETFORD

8455
Thetford Historical Society
[PO Box 33, 05074]; (c) Orange

Private non-profit/ staff: 12(v)/ members: 100

HISTORICAL SOCIETY; HISTORY MUSEUM

PROGRAMS: Annual Meeting; Exhibits; Lectures

COLLECTIONS: [19th c] Books, manuscripts,
agriculture, and period furnishing, local crafts.

HOURS: Yr M 2-4, T 10-12, Th 2-4, Su 2-5
(Open Su in Aug only)

ADMISSION: No charge

TINMOUTH

8456
Tinmouth Historical Society
5 Mtn View Rd, 05773 [515 N End Rd,
05773]; (p) (802) 446-2498; (c) Rutland

Private non-profit/ 1974/ staff: 3(v)

HISTORICAL SOCIETY: Preserves local history.

PROGRAMS: Exhibits

COLLECTIONS: Photos, town archives and
ephemera.

HOURS: Yr M-Th 8-12/1-4

WAITSFIELD

8457
Waitsfield Historical Society
Rt 100, 05673 [PO Box 816, 05673]; (p) (802)
496-2027; (c) Washington

Private non-profit/ 1970/ members: 100

HISTORICAL SOCIETY: Promotes local history.

PROGRAMS: Annual Meeting; Exhibits; Guided Tours; Interpretation; Lectures; Living History; Reenactments; Research Library/Archives

COLLECTIONS: [1800-1900] 600 glass negatives, farming life, military artifacts, decorative arts.

HOURS: Yr

ADMISSION: No charge

WATERBURY

8458
Waterbury Historical Society
28 N Main St, 05676; (p) (802) 244-7036; (f)
(802) 244-7646; empstoewst@aol.com; (c)
Washington

Private non-profit/ 1957/ staff: 10(v)/ members: 75

HISTORIC SITE; HISTORICAL SOCIETY;
HISTORY MUSEUM; HOUSE MUSEUM: Preserves local history.

PROGRAMS: Annual Meeting; Community
Outreach; Exhibits; Guided Tours; Research
Library/Archives

COLLECTIONS: Civil War memorabilia, early
VT artifacts, military, agriculture.

HOURS: By appt

ADMISSION: No charge

WEATHERSFIELD

8459
Reverend Dan Foster House, The
Weathersfield Center Rd, 05156; (p) (802) 263-5230

1775

COLLECTIONS: Geneology files on Weathersfield families; photos; documents; diaries.

WEST DANVILLE

8460
Walden Historical Committee
[PO Box 54, 05873]; (p) (802) 563-2472; walden@together.net; (c) Caledonia

Private non-profit/ 1984

GENEALOGICAL SOCIETY; HISTORIC PRESERVATION AGENCY: Preserves town history.

PROGRAMS: Community Outreach; Exhibits; Festivals; Guided Tours; Living History; Publication; Research Library/Archives

COLLECTIONS: [1700-present] Photos and archives.

HOURS: By appt only

WEST FAIRLEE

8461
West Fairlee Historical Society, Inc.
[PO Box 163, 05083]; (p) (802) 333-9594; (f) (802) 333-4497; (c) Orange

State/ 1986/ staff: 12(v)/ members: 38

HISTORICAL SOCIETY: Collects and preserves local artifacts.

PROGRAMS: Annual Meeting; Exhibits; Lectures; Research Library/Archives

COLLECTIONS: [1850-present] Oral history audio and video tapes, folklore, artifacts, photos.

HOURS: Apr-Oct M-W-F 10-4

ADMISSION: No charge

WESTMINSTER

8462
Westminster Historical Society, Inc.
Route 5, 05158 [PO Box 2, 05158]; (c) Windham

Private non-profit/ members: 100

Preserves local history.

COLLECTIONS: Artifacts

HOURS: July-Sept Su 2-4

ADMISSION: Donations accepted

WESTON

8463
Farrar Mansur
Main St, on the Green, 05161 [P O Box 247, 05161]

1795/ staff: 1(p)

COLLECTIONS: [1795-1880] Portraits; locally-made furniture; genealogy; scrapbooks; albums.

HOURS: July-Aug

8464
Weston Historical Society
On the Green, 05161 [PO Box 247, 05161]; (f) (802) 824-5225; (c) Windsor

Private non-profit/ staff: 12(v)/ members: 150

HISTORICAL SOCIETY; HISTORY MUSEUM; HOUSE MUSEUM: Collects and preserves local history; provides curatorial care of Farrar-Mansur House and Old Mill Museum.

PROGRAMS: Annual Meeting; Community Outreach; Concerts; Exhibits; Family Programs; Guided Tours; Lectures; Research Library/Archives

COLLECTIONS: [19th c] Portraits, murals, brass, copper, silver, tinware, furnishing, preindustrial cooking artifacts, wagons, tinsmithing, woodworking and farm tools.

HOURS: July-Aug

WILLIAMSTOWN

8465
Williamstown Historical Society
Main St, 2476 VT Rt 14, 05679 [PO Box 338, 05679]; (p) (802) 433-1283; www.pages.prodigy.com; (c) Orange

Private non-profit/ 1949/ Officers/Trustees/ staff: 3(v)/ members: 30

HISTORICAL SOCIETY; HISTORY MUSEUM: Collects, preserves and interprets local history.

PROGRAMS: Annual Meeting; Concerts; Exhibits; Film/Video; Interpretation; Lectures; Living History; Publication; Reenactments; Research Library/Archives; School-Based Curriculum

COLLECTIONS: Tools, clothing, photos, furnishing, books, archives, paintings, household items, memorabilia.

HOURS: May-Oct by appt

ADMISSION: No charge

WILLISTON

8466
Williston Historical Society
[PO Box 995, 05495]; (c) Chittenden

1961/ members: 100/publication: *Thomas Chittenden's Town*

HISTORICAL SOCIETY

PROGRAMS: Annual Meeting; Lectures; Publication; Research Library/Archives

COLLECTIONS: [1750-1950] Local artifacts.

HOURS: Yr

ADMISSION: Donations accepted

WILMINGTON

8467
Historical Society of Wilmington Vermont
W Main St, 05369 [PO Box 833, 05369]; (p) (802) 464-0153; (c) Windham

Private non-profit/ 1975/ staff: 3(p); 25(v)/ members: 40

HISTORICAL SOCIETY: Preserves local history.

PROGRAMS: Exhibits

COLLECTIONS: Town artifacts.

HOURS: Mar-Oct

ADMISSION: No charge

WOODSTOCK

8468
Billings Farm and Museum
River Rd, 05091 [PO Box 489, 05091]; (p) (802) 457-2355; (f) (802) 457-4663; billings.farm@valley.net; www.billingsfarm.org; (c) Windsor

Private non-profit/ 1983/ Woodstock Foundation/ staff: 17(f); 37(p); 35(v)/ members: 772

HISTORY MUSEUM; HOUSE MUSEUM; LIVING HISTORY/OUTDOOR MUSEUM: Promotes rural life through historic site and museum of agriculture.

PROGRAMS: Exhibits; Guided Tours; Interpretation; Lectures; Research Library/Archives; School-Based Curriculum

COLLECTIONS: [Late 19th c] 16,000 objects relating to agriculture and folklife in late 19th century VT and a 7,500 volume library including archives, photos and microfilms.

HOURS: May-Oct Daily 10-5; Nov-Dec Sa-Su 10-4

8469
Woodstock Historical Society
26 Elm St, 05091; (p) (802) 457-1822; (f) (802) 457-2811; whs@sover.net; (c) Windsor

Private non-profit/ 1943/ staff: 2(f); 14(p); 35(v)/ members: 398

HISTORIC SITE; HISTORICAL SOCIETY; HOUSE MUSEUM: Promotes local history through its research library, archives, meeting room and historic house.

PROGRAMS: Community Outreach; Exhibits; Facility Rental; Guided Tours; Interpretation; Publication; Reenactments; Research Library/Archives; School-Based Curriculum

COLLECTIONS: [1800-present] Decorative arts, paintings, sculpture, toys, costumes, agricultural tools, library, archives, manuscripts, books, photos, glass plates, ephemera, maps, drawings, ledgers, journals, oral histories.

HOURS: May-Oct M-Sa 10-5, Su 12-4

VIRGINIA

ABINGDON

8470
Fields-Penn 1860 House
208 W Main St, 24212 [PO Box 2256, 24212]; (p) (540) 676-0216, (800) 435-3440; (f) (540) 628-3922; Info@wkrac.org; www.wkrac.org; (c) Washington

Joint/ 1979/ Town; Board of Trustees/ staff: 3(p); 80(v)

Interprets 19th c life in Abingdon.

COLLECTIONS: [19th c]

HOURS: Yr W-Sa 1-4

ADMISSION: No charge/Donations accepted

8471

Historical Society of Washington County, Inc.

Court & Main St, County Courthouse, 24212 [PO Box 484, 24212-0484]; www.eva.org/historic/historic.htm; (c) Washington

Private non-profit/ 1936/ Board of Directors/ staff: 1(p); 45(v)/ members: 720

HISTORICAL SOCIETY: Maintains history and genealogy resources and promotes history in local schools and the community.

PROGRAMS: Annual Meeting; Community Outreach; Exhibits; Guided Tours; Lectures; Living History; Research Library/Archives; School-Based Curriculum

COLLECTIONS: [18th-19th c] Focuses on family, local, regional, and state history with emphasis on genealogical research. Artifacts, maps, manuscripts, microfilm, photographs, serials, and volumes.

HOURS: Jan-Nov M-F 10-4

ALEXANDRIA

8472

Alexandria Black History Resource Center, The

Corner of N Alfred St & Wythe St, 22314 [638 N Alfred St, 22314]; (p) (703) 838-4356; (f) (703) 706-3999

City/ staff: 2(f); 2(p); 40(v)/publication: *ABHRC Newsletter*

GENEALOGICAL SOCIETY; HISTORICAL SOCIETY; HISTORY MUSEUM; RESEARCH CENTER

PROGRAMS: Annual Meeting; Community Outreach; Exhibits; Facility Rental; Festivals; Lectures; Publication; Research Library/ Archives

COLLECTIONS: [Colonial period-present]

HOURS: Yr T-Sa 10-4

8473

Alexandria Library, Special Collections Division

717 Queen St, 22314; (p) (703) 838-4577; (f) (703) 706-3912; www.alexandria.lib.va.us

City/ 1794/ Board of Trustees/ staff: 2(f); 4(p); 1(v)/publication: *The Doorway*

LIBRARY AND/OR ARCHIVES: Alexandria history, Virginia history, Civil War

8474

Callingwood Library and Museum on Americanism

8301 E Boulevard Dr, 22308; (p) (703) 765-1652; (f) (703) 765-8390; clma1@erols.com; (c) Fairfax

Private non-profit/ 1976/ staff: 3(f); 1(p); 12(v)

HISTORIC SITE; HISTORY MUSEUM; RESEARCH CENTER: Collects, preserves and exhibits artifacts and written materials that portray patriotic themes.

PROGRAMS: Community Outreach; Concerts; Exhibits; Facility Rental; Film/Video; Guided Tours; Interpretation; Research Library/Archives

COLLECTIONS: [18th c-present] Microfiche and volumes on American civilization; artifacts; Revolutionary War interpretive room.

HOURS: Yr T-Su

8475

Carlyle House Historic Park

121 N Fairfax St, 22314; (p) (703) 549-2997; (f) (703) 549-5738

Joint/ 1976/ Northern VA Regional Park Authority; City/ staff: 3(f); 8(p); 60(v)/ members: 250/publication: *John Carlyle, Gent.*

GARDEN; HISTORIC SITE: Collects, preserves, and interprets the life and home of John Carlyle, an 18th c merchant and founder of Alexandria.

PROGRAMS: Exhibits; Facility Rental; Family Programs; Garden Tours; Guided Tours; Interpretation; Lectures; Living History; Publication; Reenactments

COLLECTIONS: [1750-1780] American and English decorative arts, archaeological objects found at Carlyle House.

HOURS: Yr Apr 1-Oct 31 T-Sa 10-4:30, Su 12-4:30; Nov 14-Mar 31 T-Sa 12-4

ADMISSION: $4; Under 11 free

8476

Fort Ward Museum and Historic Site

4301 W Braddock Rd, 22304; (p) (703) 838-4848; (f) (703) 671-7350; fortward@aol.com; ci.alexandria.va.us/oha/fortward.html; (c) Alexandria

City/ 1964/ staff: 2(f); 7(p); 10(v)/ members: 250/publication: *Fort Ward Dispatch*

HISTORIC SITE; HISTORY MUSEUM: Collects, preserves and interprets the history of the Civil War, the Defense of Washington, Fort Ward and the city of Alexandria.

PROGRAMS: Exhibits; Family Programs; Film/Video; Guided Tours; Interpretation; Lectures; Living History; Publication; Reenactments; Research Library/Archives; School-Based Curriculum

COLLECTIONS: [1860s] Civil War era objects: arms, military and medical equipment, documents, musical instruments, uniforms and artwork.

8477

Gadsby's Tavern Museum

134 S Royal St, 22314; (p) (703) 838-4242; (f) (703) 838-4270; gadsbys.tavern@alexandria.va.us; ci.alexandria.va.us/oha/gadsbystavern.html; (c) Alexandria

City/ 1976/ Office of Historic Alexandria/ staff: 2(f); 14(p); 90(v)

HISTORIC SITE; HISTORY MUSEUM; HOUSE MUSEUM: Preserves and interprets the 1770 and 1792 tavern buildings and collections.

PROGRAMS: Community Outreach; Concerts; Exhibits; Facility Rental; Family Programs; Guided Tours; Interpretation; Lectures; Living History; Research Library/Archives; School-Based Curriculum

COLLECTIONS: [1770-1810] Tavern furnishings and decorative arts, newspaper articles, photos, book and research files.

HOURS: Apr-Sept T-Sa 10-5, Su 1-5; Oct-Mar T-Sa 11-4, Su 1-4

ADMISSION: $4, Student $2; Under 11 free; Group rates

8478

George Washington Masonic National Memorial

101 Callahan Dr, 22301; (p) (703) 683-2007; (f) (703) 519-9270; www.gwmemorial.org; (c) City of Alexandria

Private non-profit/ 1910/ staff: 5(f); 28(p); 3(v)

HISTORIC SITE; HISTORY MUSEUM; LIBRARY AND/OR ARCHIVES: Constructed by the Freemasons of America to honor George Washington.

PROGRAMS: Annual Meeting; Guided Tours; Publication; Research Library/Archives

COLLECTIONS: [18th c] Seven exhibit rooms with relics and portraits of George Washington, murals, artifacts.

HOURS: Yr Daily 9-5

ADMISSION: Donations accepted

8479

Lee-Fendall House Museum

614 Oronoco St, 22314; (p) (703) 548-1789; (f) (703) 548-0931

Private non-profit/ 1974/ Virginia Trust for Historic Preservation/ staff: 1(f); 3(p); 15(v)

HOUSE MUSEUM: Interprets history of Lee Family.

PROGRAMS: Exhibits; Facility Rental; Guided Tours; Interpretation

COLLECTIONS: [1850-1870] Restored early Victorian home; Lee Family artifacts. Greene Steam factory furniture, Wilcox sewing machine and an early can opener. Antique dolls and dolls' houses.

HOURS: Feb-mid Dec

8480

Lyceum, Alexandria's History Museum, The

201 S Washington St, 22314; (p) (703) 838-4994; (f) (703) 838-4997; lyceum@ci.alexandria.va.us; www.ci.alexandria.va.us/oha/lyceum; (c) Alexandria

City/ 1985/ staff: 3(f); 3(p); 40(v)/ members: 175/publication: *The Alexandria Observer; Historic Alexandria Quarterly*

HISTORIC SITE; HISTORY MUSEUM: Introduces local history to the public.

PROGRAMS: Community Outreach; Concerts; Exhibits; Facility Rental; Family Programs; Guided Tours; Interpretation; Lectures; Living History; Publication; Reenactments; Research Library/Archives; Theatre

COLLECTIONS: [18th c-present] Silver, stoneware, furniture, textiles and documents.

HOURS: Yr M-Sa 10-5, Su 1-5

ADMISSION: No charge

8481

National Preservation Institute

[PO Box 1702, 22313]; (p) (703) 765-0100; (f) (703) 768-9350; info@npi.org; www.npi.org; (c) Alexandria

Private non-profit/ 1980/ Board of Directors/ staff: 1(f); 20(p); 22(v)

PROFESSIONAL ORGANIZATION: Provides professional training for the management, development and preservation of historic, cultural and environmental resources.

PROGRAMS: School-Based Curriculum

8482
Northern Virginia Fine Arts Association

The Athenaeum, 201 Prince St, 22314; (p) (703) 548-0035; (f) (703) 768-7471

Private non-profit/ 1961/ staff: 1(f); 3(p); 83(v)/ members: 1350

HISTORIC SITE: Exhibits fine arts at the Athenaeum.

PROGRAMS: Annual Meeting; Community Outreach; Concerts; Exhibits; Facility Rental; Family Programs; Festivals; Garden Tours; Guided Tours; Lectures

HOURS: Yr M-F

8483
Office of Historic Alexandria

405 Cameron St, 3rd Floor, 22313 [PO Box 178, City Hall, 22313]; (p) (703) 838-4554; (f) (703) 838-6451; citymail@ci.alexandria. va.us/oha; www.ci.alexandria.va.us/oha; (c) Alexandria

City/ 1982/ staff: 21(f); 70(p); 150(v)/publication: *Historic Alexandria Quarterly*

ALLIANCE OF HISTORICAL AGENCIES; HISTORIC PRESERVATION AGENCY; HISTORIC SITE; HISTORY MUSEUM; HOUSE MUSEUM; LIVING HISTORY/OUTDOOR MUSEUM: Comprised of seven historic and cultural sites: Black History Resource Center, Fort Ward Museum and Historic Site, Gadsby's Tavern Museum, The Lyceum, Alexandria Archaeology, Archives and Records Center, and Friendship Firehouse.

PROGRAMS: Community Outreach; Concerts; Exhibits; Facility Rental; Family Programs; Festivals; Film/Video; Guided Tours; Interpretation; Lectures; Living History; Publication; Research Library/Archives; School-Based Curriculum

COLLECTIONS: [18th-19th c]

HOURS: Yr Daily

ADMISSION: Prices vary

8484
Space Business Archives

1403 King St, 22314; (p) (703) 535-8090; (f) (703) 535-8093; info@spacearchive.org; www.spacearchive.org; (c) Fairfax

Private non-profit/ 1992/ staff: 2(f)/publication: *Contact*

LIBRARY AND/OR ARCHIVES: Collects, preserves and makes accessible documents and other material that traces the development of the international commercial space industry.

PROGRAMS: Publication; Research Library/ Archives

COLLECTIONS: [1940s-present] Transportation (launch vehicles, rockets, etc.), remote sensing/satellites, microgravity research, and financial/legal documents.

HOURS: Yr M-F 9-5

ADMISSION: No charge

ALTAVISTA

8485
Avoca Museum and Historical Society

1514 Main St, 24517; (p) (804) 369-1076; (f) (804) 369-1076; (c) Campbell

Joint/ 1981/ staff: 1(f); 1(p); 80(v)/ members: 237

HISTORIC SITE; HOUSE MUSEUM: Collects, preserves, and interprets artifacts and memorabilia related to the area's past.

PROGRAMS: Community Outreach; Concerts; Exhibits; Facility Rental; Guided Tours; Interpretation; Lectures; Living History; School-Based Curriculum

COLLECTIONS: [Native American and Victorian] Native American artifacts recovered in archaeological excavation and gathered in the Staunton River area and Victorian material culture objects.

HOURS: Mid Apr-Oct Th-Sa 11-3, Su 1:30-4:30

ADMISSION: $5, Children $2, Seniors $4; Under 7 free

AMELIA

8486
Amelia Historical Society

Jackson Bldg, 23002 [PO Box 113, 23002]; (p) (804) 561-3180; (c) Amelia

Private non-profit/ staff: 2(p)

HOURS: Yr

AMHERST

8487
Amherst County Museum and Historical Society

154 S Main St, 24521 [PO Box 741, 24521]; (p) (804) 946-9068; achmuseum@aol.com; members.aol.com/achmuseum/; (c) Amherst

Private non-profit/ 1976/ ACMHS Executive Board/ staff: 1(f); 1(p); 10(v)/ members: 350/publication: *Muse*

GENEALOGICAL SOCIETY; HISTORICAL SOCIETY; HISTORY MUSEUM; LIBRARY AND/OR ARCHIVES: Preserves history of Amherst County and the surrounding area.

PROGRAMS: Annual Meeting; Community Outreach; Exhibits; Interpretation; Publication; Research Library/Archives

COLLECTIONS: [Colonial-present] Tools, farming equipment, clothing, dishes, military items, and county documents.

HOURS: Yr T-Sa 9-4:30

ADMISSION: Donations accepted

APPOMATTOX

8488
Appomattox County Historical Museum

Courthouse Square, 24522 [Route 3, Box 100, 24522]; (p) (804) 352-8106; (c) Appomattox

Private non-profit/ 1976/ Appomattox County Historical Society/ staff: 2(p)/ members: 44

HISTORICAL SOCIETY: Preserves the history of Appomattox County; collects materials that establish or illustrate that history.

PROGRAMS: Exhibits

COLLECTIONS: [20th c] Historic site: County jail with interpretive rooms: school room, doctor's office, kitchen, general store, and jail

cells; Joe Sweeney collection; farm implements.

HOURS: Yr M-F 9-3

ADMISSION: $2, Children $1

8489
Appomattox Court House National Historical Park

Virginia Route 243, mi NE of Appomattox, 24522 [PO Box 218, 24522]; (p) (804) 352-8987; (f) (804) 352-8330; www.nps..gov/apco; (c) Appomattox

Federal/ 1935/ U.S. Dept. of Interior, National Park Service/ staff: 13(f); 8(p); 7(v)/publication: *Appomattox Park Handbook*

HISTORIC PRESERVATION AGENCY; HISTORIC SITE; HISTORY MUSEUM; HOUSE MUSEUM; LIVING HISTORY/OUTDOOR MUSEUM: Preserved historic village where General Robert E. Lee surrendered the Army of Northern Virginia to General Ulysses S. Grant bringing an end to the Civil War and the reunification of the nation.

PROGRAMS: Exhibits; Guided Tours; Interpretation; Living History; Publication

COLLECTIONS: [1850-1970] Approximately 11,000 artifacts consisting of military items, furnishings, archaeology, and architectural fragments.

HOURS: Yr Daily 8:30-5

ADMISSION: $4

ARLINGTON

8490
Arlington County Public Library Virginia Room

1015 N Quincy St, 22205; (p) (703) 228-5966; (f) (703) 228-7720; www.co.arlington.va.us/lib/; (c) Arlington

County/ staff: 3(f); 2(p); 7(v)

LIBRARY AND/OR ARCHIVES: Serves as repository for Arlington historical resources.

PROGRAMS: Community Outreach; Exhibits; Research Library/Archives

COLLECTIONS: Virginia Room: books, rare books, newsletters, photographs, maps, vertical files, oral history tapes, video tapes, personal paper, and records of organizations; county and state-generated publications.

HOURS: Yr M, T ,Th, Sa 10-5, W 1-9

8491
Arlington Historical Society, Inc.

1805 S Arlington Ridge Rd, 22210 [PO Box 402, 22210]; (p) (703) 892-4204; (c) Arlington

Private non-profit/ 1956/ staff: 100(v)/ members: 400

HISTORIC SITE; HISTORICAL SOCIETY; HISTORY MUSEUM; HOUSE MUSEUM: Photos and artifacts reflecting the history of Arlington County displayed in the Colonial Ban/Sellers House and the Victorian Hume School.

PROGRAMS: Annual Meeting; Community Outreach; Exhibits; Facility Rental; Guided Tours; Lectures; Publication; School-Based Curriculum

COLLECTIONS: [Civil War-present] Toys, dolls, photos, and local political memorabilia.

HOURS: Yr F-Sa 11-3, Su 2-5

8492
Federation of State Humanities Councils
1600 Wilson Boulevard #902, 22209; (p) (703) 908-9700; (f) (703) 908-9706; gleftwich@erols.com

Private non-profit/ 1977/ staff: 4(f)/ members: 56

ALLIANCE OF HISTORICAL AGENCIES: Provides support for state humanities councils.

8493
Newseum
1101 Wilson Blvd, 22209; (p) (703) 284-3700; www.newseum.org; (c) Arlington

Private non-profit/ 1997/ staff: 74(f); 110(v)/publication: *The Newseum Guidebook*

HISTORY MUSEUM: Promotes history and evolution of news and journalism.

PROGRAMS: Community Outreach; Exhibits; Facility Rental; Family Programs; Film/Video; Guided Tours; Lectures; Publication; School-Based Curriculum

COLLECTIONS: [18th-20th c] Newspapers, documents, photographs and artifacts.

HOURS: Yr M-F 9-4

ADMISSION: No charge

BASTIAN

8494
Wolf Creek Indian Village and Museum
Route 1, Box 1530, 24314; (p) (540) 688-3438; (f) (540) 688-2496; indianvillage@naxs.net; www.indianvillage.org; (c) Bland

Private non-profit/ 1996/ Bland County Historical Society/ staff: 3(f); 7(p); 3(v)/ members: 22

HISTORY MUSEUM; LIVING HISTORY/OUTDOOR MUSEUM

PROGRAMS: Exhibits; Guided Tours; Interpretation; Living History; School-Based Curriculum

COLLECTIONS: [Pre-European] Several local ground-find collections, two archaeological displays from Bland County, and maps.

BEDFORD

8495
Bedford City/County Museum
201 E Main St, 24523; (p) (540) 586-4520; (c) Bedford

Private non-profit/ 1932/ Board of Directors/ staff: 4(p); 52(v)/ members: 75

HISTORY MUSEUM; LIBRARY AND/OR ARCHIVES: Preserves and displays Bedford history for the education of our citizens and visitors.

PROGRAMS: Community Outreach; Exhibits; Facility Rental; Guided Tours; Research Library/Archives

COLLECTIONS: [5000 B.C.- 20th c] Projectile points, industrial artifacts, farm tools, and furniture.

BERRYVILLE

8496
Clarke County Historical Association
104 N Church St, N Wing, 22611 [PO Box 306, 22611]; (p) (540) 955-2600; (f) (540) 955-0285; ccha@visuallink.com; www.visuallink.net/ccha; (c) Clarke

Private non-profit/ 1939/ Board of Directors/ staff: 2(p); 20(v)/ members: 250/publication: *Proceedings*

HISTORIC SITE; HISTORICAL SOCIETY; HISTORY MUSEUM; LIVING HISTORY/OUTDOOR MUSEUM: Preserves local and regional history; owns and operates 1790s wooden-geared grist mill.

PROGRAMS: Annual Meeting; Community Outreach; Exhibits; Facility Rental; Guided Tours; Interpretation; Living History; Publication; Research Library/Archives

COLLECTIONS: [18th-20th c] Manuscripts, photographs, portraits, Civil War objects, along with local tax, census and newspaper records on microfilm.

HOURS: Museum/Archives: W-F 10:30-3:30; Mill: Th-Sa 10-5, Su 12-5

ADMISSION: $3, Children $1; Prices for Mill; Museum/Archives free

BIG STONE GAP

8497
Harry Meador Coal Museum
East Third St & Shawnee, 24219 [505 E 5th St S, 24219]; (p) (540) 523-9209; (f) (540) 523-5625; (c) Wise

Private non-profit/ Town of Big Stone Gap/ staff: 1(f)

HISTORY MUSEUM: Preserves and presents the history of the mining era.

PROGRAMS: Exhibits; Guided Tours

HOURS: Yr W-Sa 10-5, Su 1-5

ADMISSION: No charge

8498
John Fox Jr. Museum
117 Shawnee East, 24219 [106 E Gilley Ave East, 24219]; (p) (540) 523-2747, (540) 523-1795; (c) Wise

Private non-profit/ 1971/ Lonesome Pine Arts and Crafts/ staff: 20(v)

HOUSE MUSEUM

PROGRAMS: Guided Tours

COLLECTIONS: [Late 19th c] Family furniture, silver, china and crystal.

HOURS: May-Labor Day W-Su 2-5

ADMISSION: $3, Children $1, Seniors $2

8499
June Tolliver House
Clinton Ave, 24219 [PO Box 1976, 24219]; (p) (540) 523-4707, (5140) 523-1235

8500
Southwest Virginia Museum/Historical Park
10 W First St, N, 24219 [PO Box 742, 24219]; (p) (540) 523-1322; (f) (540) 523-6616; (c) Wise

State/ 1948/ Commonwealth of VA/ staff: 3(f); 9(p); 7(v)

HISTORY MUSEUM; STATE PARK: Depicts life in Southwest VA during the 1890s coal boom and pioneer period.

PROGRAMS: Community Outreach; Concerts; Elder's Programs; Exhibits; Facility Rental; Family Programs; Festivals; Guided Tours; Interpretation; Lectures; Living History; Research Library/Archives; School-Based Curriculum

COLLECTIONS: [1890s] Photos, books, paintings, furniture, decorative arts, early tools, Native American and pioneer items.

HOURS: May-Sept M-Th 10-4, F 9-4, Sa 10-5, Su 1-5; March-May, Sept-DecTu-Su

BLACKSBURG

8501
Smithfield Plantation
1000 Smithfield Plantation Rd, 24060; (p) (540) 231-3947; (f) (540) 231-3006; smithfield.plantation@vt.edu; www.mfrl.org/compages/smithfield; (c) Montgomery

Private non-profit/ 1964/ Assoc for the Preservation of VA Antiquities/ staff: 1(p); 65(v)/ members: 57

GARDEN; HISTORIC SITE; HOUSE MUSEUM; LIVING HISTORY/OUTDOOR MUSEUM: Preserves history of Preston Family; exhibits Native American artifacts.

PROGRAMS: Exhibits; Facility Rental; Family Programs; Garden Tours; Guided Tours; Interpretation; Lectures; Living History; School-Based Curriculum

COLLECTIONS: [1770-1830] Artifacts: Preston Family, Native American artifacts, tools and weaving instruments.

HOURS: Apr-early Dec Th-Su 1-5

ADMISSION: $4

BRIDGEWATER

8502
Reuel B. Pritchett Museum
East College St, lower level of Cole Hall, 22812 [Box 147, Bridgewater College, 22812]; (p) (540) 828-5462, (540) 828-5414; (f) (540) 828-5482; tbarkley@bridgewater.edu; www.bridgewater.edu; (c) Rockingham

Private non-profit/ 1954/ Bridgewater College/ staff: 2(p)

Preserves and presents items donated by the Reverend Reuel B. Prichett, a minister of the Church of the Brethren and TN farmer.

COLLECTIONS: [18th-20th c] Artifacts related to Civil War, Native Americans and pioneers such as coins, guns, glass, pottery, fossils, tools and books. Missionary memorabilia from China, India, Nigeria, the Middle East, Philippines, Nepal and the Caribbean.

HOURS: Yr M-F 1-5, Sa-Su by appt

ADMISSION: No charge

BROOKNEAL

8503
Patrick Henry Memorial Foundation
Red Hill, 24528 [1250 Red Hill Rd, 24528]; (p) (804) 376-2044; (f) (804) 376-2647; www.redhill.org; (c) Charlotte/Campbell

Private non-profit/ 1944/ Board of Trustees/ staff: 4(f); 3(p); 30(v)

HISTORIC SITE; HISTORY MUSEUM: Promotes the life of Patrick Henry; maintains and interprets Red Hill, Patrick Henry's last home and burial place.

PROGRAMS: Exhibits; Guided Tours; Interpretation; Living History; Reenactments; Research Library/Archives

COLLECTIONS: [1736-1900] Personal artifacts, letters, portraits, research archives, and genealogical information related to Patrick Henry.

8504
Willie Hodge Booth Museum
Lynchburg Ave, 24528 [PO Box 300, 24528]; (p) (804) 376-2264; (c) Campbell

Private non-profit/ 1995/ Stanton River Historical Society/ staff: 2(v)/ members: 30

HISTORICAL SOCIETY: Maintains museum and preserves history of the Stanton River area.

PROGRAMS: Annual Meeting; Community Outreach; Exhibits; School-Based Curriculum

COLLECTIONS: [1736-present] Artifacts of early white settlers and Native Americans on the Stanton River. Items on the economic development of Brookneal, the tobacco industry and Patrick Henry.

HOURS: Yr by appt

ADMISSION: No charge

BUCKINGHAM

8505
Historic Buckingham, Inc.
US Hwy 60, 23921 [PO Box 152, 23921]; (p) (804) 969-4304; (f) (804) 969-2060; (c) Buckingham

Private non-profit/ 1974/ Board of Directors/ staff: 1(p); 95(v)/ members: 400

GENEALOGICAL SOCIETY; HISTORICAL SOCIETY; HISTORY MUSEUM; HOUSE MUSEUM; RESEARCH CENTER: Promotes the restoration and preservation of Buckingham County.

PROGRAMS: Annual Meeting; Community Outreach; Exhibits; Guided Tours; Research Library/Archives

COLLECTIONS: [18th-20th c] Research library, genealogy files, photographs, and furniture.

HOURS: Apr-Nov W, Sa 1-4

ADMISSION: No charge

CAPE CHARLES

8506
Cape Charles Historical Society
814 Randolph Ave, 23310 [PO Box 11, 23310]; (p) (757) 331-1008; (c) Northampton

Private non-profit/ 1986/ staff: 1(p); 4(v)/ members: 120/publication: *A Walking Tour of Historic Cape Charles*

HISTORICAL SOCIETY; HISTORY MUSEUM

PROGRAMS: Annual Meeting; Exhibits; Lectures; Publication

COLLECTIONS: [1880-1960] Photos, monographs on local history.

HOURS: Late April-Mid Nov

CHANTILLY

8507
Sully Historic Site
3601 Sully Rd, 20151; (p) (703) 437-1794; (f) (703) 787-3314; www.fairfaxcounty.resource-management.com; (c) Fairfax

County/ 1972/ Fairfax County Park Authority, Resource Management Division/ staff: 6(f); 5(p); 105(v)/publication: *Parktakes, Calendar of Events*

GARDEN; HISTORIC SITE; HOUSE MUSEUM; LIVING HISTORY/OUTDOOR MUSEUM: Provides historic interpretive programs.

PROGRAMS: Community Outreach; Exhibits; Family Programs; Festivals; Garden Tours; Guided Tours; Interpretation; Living History; Publication; Reenactments; School-Based Curriculum

COLLECTIONS: [19th c] Original Lee family pieces, Federal period antiques, and reproductions.

HOURS: Yr W-M 11-4

ADMISSION: $5, Student $4, Children $3, Seniors $3

CHARLES CITY

8508
Berkeley Plantation
Rte 5, halfway bet Richmond & Williamsburg, 23030 [12602 Harrison Landing Rd, 23030]; (p) (804) 829-6018; (f) (804) 829-6757

1726/ Private/ staff: 2(f); 10(p)

COLLECTIONS: [Colonial to Civil War] Civil War, Native American and Colonial artifacts.

HOURS: Yr

8509
Charles City County Center for Local History
10600 Courthouse Rd, 23030 [PO Box 128, 23030]; (p) (804) 829-5609; (c) Charles City

County/ 1997/ Advisory Commission/ staff: 7(v)

HISTORY MUSEUM: Collects, preserves and promotes the history of Charles City.

PROGRAMS: Research Library/Archives

COLLECTIONS: [18th-20th c] Books, periodicals, manuscripts, microfilm, microfiche, photographs, video tapes and maps.

HOURS: Yr M-F 10-4

ADMISSION: No charge

8510
Charles City County Historical Society
16530 The Glebe Lane, 23030; (c) Charles City

Private non-profit/ 1994/ Board of Directors/ members: 200

HISTORICAL SOCIETY: Promotes and preserves local and oral histories.

PROGRAMS: Annual Meeting; Lectures

COLLECTIONS: [18th-20th c]

8511
Evelynton Plantation
6701 John Tyler Hwy, 23030; (p) (804) 829-5075; (f) (804) 829-6903; evelynton@aol.com; www.evelyntonplantation.com; (c) Charles City

Private for-profit/ 1986/ staff: 8(f); 15(p)

GARDEN; HISTORIC SITE

PROGRAMS: Facility Rental; Guided Tours; Interpretation; Reenactments; School-Based Curriculum

COLLECTIONS: [18th-19th c] Period furnishing.

HOURS: Yr Daily 9-5

ADMISSION: $8.50, Student $5.50, Seniors $7.50; $7.50 military; Under 6 free

8512
Sherwood Forest Plantation
14501 John Tyler Hwy, 23030 [PO Box 8, 23030]; (p) (804) 829-5377; (f) (804) 829-2947; info@sherwoodforest.org; www.sherwoodforest.org; (c) Charles City

Private for-profit/ 1975/ Historic Sherwood Forest Corp/ staff: 5(f); 15(p)

GARDEN; HISTORIC SITE; HOUSE MUSEUM; PRESIDENTIAL SITE: Interprets the life of President Tyler, his family and the community.

PROGRAMS: Elder's Programs; Exhibits; Facility Rental; Garden Tours; Guided Tours; Interpretation; Living History; Publication; Reenactments; School-Based Curriculum

COLLECTIONS: [17th-20th c] Porcelain, silver, portraits, paintings, furnishings and artifacts owned by President Tyler and his family.

HOURS: Yr Daily 9-5

ADMISSION: $9.50

8513
Shirley Plantation
501 Shirley Plantation Rd, 23030; (p) (804) 829-8121; (f) (804) 829-6322; information@shirleyplantation.com; www.shirleyplantation.com; (c) Charles City

Private for-profit/ 1613/ staff: 6(f); 9(p)

GARDEN; HISTORIC SITE; HISTORY MUSEUM; HOUSE MUSEUM: Preserves VA's oldest plantation.

PROGRAMS: Facility Rental; Festivals; Garden Tours; Guided Tours; Interpretation; Living History; Reenactments; School-Based Curriculum

COLLECTIONS: [18th-20th c] Furniture, silver, portraits, books, porcelain, brick outbuildings, documents, letters, journals and pictures.

HOURS: Yr Daily 9-5

ADMISSION: $10, Student $7, Seniors $9

CHARLOTTESVILLE

8514
Albemarle County Historical Society
200 Second St, NE, 22902; (p) (804) 296-1492; (f) (804) 296-4576; acohs@sctone.net; avenue.org/achs; (c) Albemarle

Private non-profit/ 1940/ staff: 2(f); 2(p); 200(v)/ members: 615

HISTORICAL SOCIETY: Promotes local history.

PROGRAMS: Annual Meeting; Exhibits; Facility Rental; Guided Tours; Interpretation; Lectures; Living History; Publication; Research Library/Archives; School-Based Curriculum

COLLECTIONS: [1744-present] 1500 artifacts related to history of Charlottesville and Albemarle County; maps, photos, manuscripts, books, serials, pamphlets, and newspapers.

HOURS: Yr M-F 9-5, Sa 10-1

8515
Ashlawn-Highland
1000 James Monroe Pkwy, 22902; (p) (804) 293-9539; (f) (804) 293-8000; ashlawnjm@aol.com; avenue.org/ashlawn; (c) Albemarle

State/ 1931/ The College of William and Mary/ staff: 5(f); 70(p)/ members: 1700

HISTORIC SITE; HOUSE MUSEUM; PRESIDENTIAL SITE: Preserves working plantation.

PROGRAMS: Concerts; Exhibits; Facility Rental; Festivals; Garden Tours; Guided Tours; Interpretation; Lectures; Living History; Reenactments; Theatre

COLLECTIONS: [Early 19th c] Original and reconstructed buildings in historic farm setting, furniture, fine and decorative arts, clothing, jewelry, and weaponry.

HOURS: Yr Nov-Mar Daily 10-5; Apr-Oct Daily 9-6

ADMISSION: $8, Children $5, Seniors $7.50

8516
International Center for Jefferson Studies
Thomas Jefferson Pkwy, Rte 53, 22902 [Monticello, PO Box 316, 22902]; (p) (804) 984-9864; (f) (804) 296-1992; icjs@monticello.org; www.monticello.org/icjs; (c) Albemarle

Private non-profit/ 1994/ Thomas Jefferson Foundation, Inc./University of Virginia/ staff: 20(f)

RESEARCH CENTER: Fosters Jefferson scholarship.

PROGRAMS: Community Outreach; Lectures; Research Library/Archives

COLLECTIONS: [18th c]

HOURS: By appt

8517
Michie Tavern ca. 1784
Route 53, Monticello Mountain, 22902 [683 Thomas Jefferson Pkwy, 22902]; (p) (804) 977-1234; (f) (804) 296-7203; info@michietavern.com; www.michietavern.com; (c) Albemarle

Private for-profit/ 1784/ staff: 25(f); 40(p)

HISTORIC SITE; HISTORY MUSEUM; HOUSE MUSEUM: Owns and operates the Sowell House, the "Ordinary" dining room, gift shop, and Meadow Run Grist Mill and General Store.

PROGRAMS: Community Outreach; Exhibits; Facility Rental; Family Programs; Guided Tours; Interpretation; Living History; School-Based Curriculum

COLLECTIONS: [18th-early 20th c] Furnishing.

HOURS: (Museum/Gift Shop) Yr Daily 9-5; (Dining) Yr Daily 11:30-3

ADMISSION: $6, Children $2; Under 6 free

8518
Thomas Jefferson Foundation (Monticello)
[PO Box 316, 22902]; (p) (434) 984-9822; (f) (434) 977-7757; pablicaffairs@monticello.org; www.monticello.org; (c) Albemarle

Private non-profit/ 1923/ Board of Trustees

HISTORY MUSEUM; HOUSE MUSEUM: Owns and operates Monticello, home of Thomas Jefferson.

PROGRAMS: Elder's Programs; Exhibits; Family Programs; Film/Video; Garden Tours; Guided Tours; Lectures; Research Library/Archives

COLLECTIONS: [1770-1826] 4,000 artifacts and works of art connected directly to Jefferson or Monticello.

HOURS: Mar-Oct Daily 8-5; Nov-Feb Daily 9-4:30

ADMISSION: $11, Children $6

CHASE CITY

8519
MacCallum More Museum and Gardens
603 Hudgins St, 23924 [PO Box 104, 23924]; (p) (804) 372-0502; (f) (804) 372-3483; mmmg@meckcom.net; (c) Mecklenburg

Private non-profit/ 1991/ Board of Directors/ staff: 1(f); 2(p); 1(v)/ members: 385

ART MUSEUM; GARDEN; HISTORY MUSEUM:

PROGRAMS: Concerts; Exhibits; Facility Rental; Family Programs; Garden Tours; Guided Tours; School-Based Curriculum

COLLECTIONS: [9500 BC-1600 AD] Native American pottery, pipes, tools, and weapons.

HOURS: Museum: M-F 10-5; Gardens Yr Daily 9-5

ADMISSION: $3.50, Children $2.50, Seniors $3

CHATHAM

8520
Pittsylvania Historical Society
[PO Box 1148, 24531]; (p) (804) 432-2172, (804) 836-3252; (c) Pittsylvania

Private non-profit/ 1976/ members: 500/publication: The Pittsylvania Packet

CHESAPEAKE

8521
Norfolk County Historical Society of Chesapeake
Chesapeake Public Library, 298 Cedar Rd, 23322; (p) (757) 547-7719

Private non-profit/ 1963/ Board of Directors/ staff: 30(v)/ members: 290

HISTORICAL SOCIETY: Collects and makes available to the public information about local history.

PROGRAMS: Annual Meeting; Community Outreach; Exhibits; Festivals; Lectures; Living History; Reenactments

COLLECTIONS: [19th-20th c]

HOURS: Yr M-Th 9-9, F-Su 9-5

ADMISSION: No charge

CHESTERFIELD

8522
Chesterfield Historical Society of Virginia
10201 Ironbridge Rd, 23832 [PO Box 40, 23832]; (p) (804) 777-9663; (f) (804) 777-9643; (c) Chesterfield

Private non-profit/ 1981/ staff: 2(f); 2(p); 50(v)/ members: 800

GENEALOGICAL SOCIETY; HISTORIC SITE; HISTORICAL SOCIETY; HISTORY MUSEUM; HOUSE MUSEUM: Collects, preserves, and interprets county history.

PROGRAMS: Community Outreach; Concerts; Exhibits; Facility Rental; Garden Tours; Guided Tours; Interpretation; Lectures; Living History; Reenactments; Research Library/Archives; School-Based Curriculum

COLLECTIONS: [19th c]

HOURS: Yr M-F 10-4, Su 1-5

8523
Henricus Foundation, The
Coxendale & Old Stage Rd, 23832 [PO Box 523, 23832]; (p) (804) 706-1340; (f) (804) 796-2677; henricus98@aol.com; (c) Chesterfield

Private non-profit/ 1985/ staff: 3(f); 4(p); 12(v)/ members: 60/publication: Henricus Revisited; Sir Thomas Dale

HISTORIC SITE; LIVING HISTORY/OUTDOOR MUSEUM: Preserves Henricus as English settlement and home of Pocahontas.

PROGRAMS: Community Outreach; Concerts; Elder's Programs; Exhibits; Facility Rental; Family Programs; Festivals; Guided Tours; Interpretation; Lectures; Living History; Publication; Reenactments; Research Library/Archives; School-Based Curriculum

COLLECTIONS: [Early 17th c] Archaeological artifacts.

HOURS: Dec-Mar T-Su 10-4; Apr-Nov T-Su 10-5

CHINCOTEAGUE

8524
Oyster and Maritime Museum
7125 Maddox Blvd, 23336 [PO Box 352, 23336]; (p) (757) 336-6117; (c) Accomac

Private non-profit/ 1968/ Board of Directors/ staff: 1(f); 1(p); 1(v)/ members: 125

HISTORIC PRESERVATION AGENCY: Preserves local history.

PROGRAMS: Elder's Programs; Exhibits

COLLECTIONS: [20th c] Shells, fossils, model boats, photos, oyster tools, diorama, aquarium, library, maps and First Order Fresnel Lens.

HOURS: Spring/Fall Sa 10-5, Su 12-4; June-Aug M-Sa 10-5, Su 12-4

ADMISSION: $3, Children $1.50

CHRISTIANSBURG

8525
Montgomery Museum and Lewis Miller Regional Art Center
300 S Pepper St, 24073; (p) (540) 382-5644; (c) Montgomery

County; Private non-profit/ 1983/ Board of Directors/ staff: 3(p)/ 16(v)/ members: 200

ART MUSEUM; GARDEN; HISTORIC SITE; HISTORY MUSEUM; HOUSE MUSEUM: Preserves and protects artifacts, photos and records of the New River Area.

PROGRAMS: Annual Meeting; Exhibits; Family Programs; Film/Video; Garden Tours; Guided Tours; Lectures; Living History; Reenactments; Research Library/Archives

COLLECTIONS: [1850s-1930s] Artifacts, photographs, records, furniture, baskets and dolls.

HOURS: Yr M-Sa 10:30-4:30, Su 1:30-4:30

CLARKSVILLE

8526
Prestwould Foundation

429 Prestwould Dr, 23927 [PO Box 872, 23927]; (p) (804) 374-8672; (c) Mecklenburg

1963/ Board of Trustees/ staff: 1(f); 50(v)/ members: 1500

GARDEN; HOUSE MUSEUM

PROGRAMS: Annual Meeting; Facility Rental; Garden Tours; Interpretation

COLLECTIONS: [1790-1830] Sites: office, loom house, smokehouses, plantation store and two-family slave house.

HOURS: Mid Apr-Oct M-Sa 12:30-3:30, Su 1:30-3:30

ADMISSION: $8, Children $3, Seniors $6; Group rates

CLIFTON FORGE

8527
Chesapeake and Ohio Historical Society, Inc.

312 E Ridgeway St, 24422 [PO Box 79, 24422]; (p) (540) 862-2210; (f) (540) 863-9159; cohs@cfw.com; www.cohs.org; (c) Alleghany

Private non-profit/ 1969/ Board of Directors/ staff: 4(f)/ members: 2500/publication: Chesapeake and Ohio Historical Magazine

HISTORICAL SOCIETY; RESEARCH CENTER: Preserves historical data, artifacts, equipment and rolling stock of the Chesapeake and Ohio Railway.

PROGRAMS: Exhibits; Interpretation; Publication; Research Library/Archives

COLLECTIONS: [Mid 19th c-present] Engineering and mechanical drawings, volumes, serials, manuscripts, photographs, artifacts, corporate records and pieces of rolling stock.

HOURS: Yr M-Sa

COURTLAND

8528
Rochelle-Prince House

22371 Main St, 23837 [PO Box 112, 23837]; (p) (757) 654-6785; amaze.net/~cliff/index.htm

1817

COLLECTIONS: [1814-1835] Furnishings; piano; cupboard; china press; local history files.

HOURS: Apr-Nov

CRITZ

8529
Reynolds Homestead

413 Homestead Lane, 24082; (p) (540) 694-7181; (f) (540) 694-7183; (c) Patrick

State/ Virginia Polytechnic Institute and State Univ/ staff: 3(f); 2(p); 30(v)

HISTORIC SITE: Preserves home of Hardin William and Nancy Cox Reynolds.

PROGRAMS: Community Outreach; Concerts; Exhibits; Facility Rental; Family Programs; Festivals; Guided Tours

COLLECTIONS: [19th c] Original furnishings include 1840s rosewood grand piano, Victorian love seats, chairs and buffet etagere; Empire sideboard and dressing table, mahogany bed, photos, painting, silver and a trunk.

HOURS: May-Oct T-Su 11-3

ADMISSION: $2, Student $1

CULPEPER

8530
Culp Cavalry Museum/Museum of Culpeper History

803 S Main St, 22701 [PO Box 951, 22701]; (p) (540) 829-1749; (f) (540) 829-9698; www.culpepermuseum.com; (c) Culpeper

Private non-profit/ 1975/ Board of Trustees/ staff: 2(f); 1(p); 25(v)/ members: 300/publication: The Culpeper Crier

HISTORY MUSEUM

PROGRAMS: Community Outreach; Exhibits; Festivals; Guided Tours; Living History; Publication; School-Based Curriculum

COLLECTIONS: [Prehistory-20th c] 210 million year old dinosaur tracts; military artifacts: Revolutionary and Civil Wars; education, commerce, and local history photos; Native American artifacts.

HOURS: Yr

8531
Memorial Foundation of the Germanna Colonies in Virginia, Inc.

[PO Box 693, 22701-0693]; (p) (540) 825-1496; (f) (540) 825-6572; office@germanna.org; www.germanna.org; (c) Culpeper

Private non-profit/ 1956/ staff: 1(f)/ members: 2000/publication: Germanna Records Series 1-15

GENEALOGICAL SOCIETY; HISTORIC SITE; HISTORICAL SOCIETY; HISTORY MUSEUM; LIVING HISTORY/OUTDOOR MUSEUM; RESEARCH CENTER: Preserves history of the Germanna Colonies, Alexander Spotswood.

PROGRAMS: Annual Meeting; Concerts; Exhibits; Family Programs; Festivals; Guided Tours; Lectures; Publication; Research Library/Archives

COLLECTIONS: [18th-19th c] Family histories, photos, maps, manuscripts and books on genealogy, history and Germanna.

DANVILLE

8532
Danville Historical Society

[PO Box 6, 24543]; (p) (804) 792-2215; ewailer@gamewood.net; (c) Pittsylvania

Joint/ 1973/ City of Danville: Private non-profit/ staff: 25(v)/ members: 120

HISTORIC PRESERVATION AGENCY; HISTORICAL SOCIETY: Preserves historical buildings, cultural history and renewal of inner city neighborhoods.

PROGRAMS: Annual Meeting; Community Outreach; Exhibits; Lectures

COLLECTIONS: [Late 19th c] Photos, architecture and historical data.

ADMISSION: No charge

8533
Danville Museum of Fine Arts and History

975 Main St, 24541; (p) (804) 793-5644; (f) (804) 799-6145; (c) Pittsylvania

Private non-profit/ 1971/ Board of Trustees/ staff: 3(f); 7(p); 90(v)/ members: 550

ART MUSEUM; HISTORIC SITE

PROGRAMS: Community Outreach; Exhibits; Facility Rental; Family Programs; Festivals; Guided Tours; Interpretation; Lectures; Reenactments; Research Library/Archives; School-Based Curriculum

COLLECTIONS: [1858-1911] Local and regional art; Victorian era decorative arts and furniture; Civil War artifacts, letters and papers; photos of Danville.

HOURS: Yr T-F 10-5, Sa-Su 2-5

ADMISSION: Donations

8534
Langhorne House

117 Broad St, 24543 [PO Box 3518, 24543]; (p) (804) 793-5422

Private non-profit/ 1988/ Board of Directors

ART MUSEUM; HISTORY MUSEUM; HOUSE MUSEUM: Preserves childhood home of Irene Langhorne Gibson and birthplace of Nancy Langhorne Astor.

PROGRAMS: Community Outreach; Exhibits; Facility Rental; Guided Tours; Interpretation

COLLECTIONS: [1870s-early 1920s] Bedroom, photographs, Charles Dana Gibson prints, Nancy Astor memorabilia (personal letters, dress, books), Langhorne memorabilia such as Civil War sword, sideboard and writing desk.

HOURS: Yr Sa-Su

ADMISSION: Donations accepted

8535
Virginia-North Carolina Piedmont Genealogy Society

2nd fl, Danville Library, 511 Patton St, 24541 [PO Box 2272, 24541]; (p) (434) 799-5195; (c) Danville

Private non-profit/ 1978/ Board of Directors/ staff: 25(v)/ members: 665/publication: Piedmont Lineages

GENEALOGICAL SOCIETY: Focuses on genealogy for VA's Pittsylvania, Halifax, Henry, and Franklin Counties and NC's Caswell, Rockingham and Person Counties.

PROGRAMS: Lectures; Monthly Meeting; Publication

COLLECTIONS: [18th-19th c] Books, microfilm census, newspapers, and computer research.

HOURS: Yr T 2-5, Th 6-9, F 10-5, Sa 10-1

ADMISSION: No charge

DAYTON

8536
Fort Harrison, Inc.
Old Route 42, Main St, 22821 [PO Box 366, 22821]; (p) (540) 879-2280; (c) Rockingham

1749/ staff: 1(f); 1(p); 40(v)/ members: 150

HISTORIC SITE; HOUSE MUSEUM: Preserves home of Daniel Harrison.

PROGRAMS: Film/Video; Guided Tours

COLLECTIONS: [18th c] Period furniture.

HOURS: Late May-Oct Sa-Su 1-4

ADMISSION: Donations accepted

8537
Harrisonburg-Rockingham Historical Society, Inc.
Bowman Rd & High St, 22821 [PO Box 716, 22821]; (p) (540) 879-2616; (f) (540) 879-2616; heritag1@shentel.net; www.heritage center.com; (c) Rockingham

Private non-profit/ 1898/ staff: 2(f); 2(p); 40(v)/ members: 1150

HISTORICAL SOCIETY; LIBRARY AND/OR ARCHIVES

PROGRAMS: Annual Meeting; Exhibits; Guided Tours; Research Library/Archives

COLLECTIONS: [19th c] Artifacts: Shenandoah Valley folk art, Civil War, General Thomas "Stonewall" Jackson's 1862 Valley Campaign.

8538
Shenandoah Valley Folk Art and Heritage Center
382 High St, 22821 [PO Box 716, 22821]; (p) (540) 879-2681, (540) 879-2616; (f) (540) 879-2616; heritag1@shentel.net; www.heritagecenter.com; (c) Rockingham

Private non-profit/ 1898/ Harrisonburg-Rockingham Historical Society/ staff: 1(f); 2(p); 40(v)/ members: 750/publication: *Rockingham Recorder*

HISTORICAL SOCIETY: Reflects the ethnic and religious backgrounds of original local settlers, German and Scots-Irish descent.

PROGRAMS: Annual Meeting; Exhibits; Interpretation; Lectures; Publication; Research Library/Archives; School-Based Curriculum

COLLECTIONS: [18th-19th c] Textiles, ceramics, painted surfaces, wood and metals; Civil War.

HOURS: (Museum) Yr M, W-Sa 10-4, Su 1-4; (Library) Yr M, W-Sa 10-4

ADMISSION: $4, Children $2, Seniors $3; Museum; Library $5/Mbrs free

DELAPLANE

8539
Sky Meadows State Park
11012 Edmonds Ln, 20144; (p) (540) 592-3556; (f) (540) 592-3617; Skymeadows@ dcr.state.va.us; (c) Fauquier

State/ 1983/ Comm of Virginia, Dept of Conservation and Recreation, State Parks Division/ staff: 3(f); 10(p); 24(v)

HOUSE MUSEUM; LIVING HISTORY/OUTDOOR MUSEUM: Protects and preserves VA's natural, cultural, scenic and historical resources. Interprets natural and mid-19th c history.

PROGRAMS: Exhibits; Family Programs; Festivals; Guided Tours; Interpretation; Living History

COLLECTIONS: [1857-1865] Furnishings reflects the lifestyle and culture of middle class farm families of northern Fauquier County.

DUMFRIES

8540
Historic Dumfries, Virginia, Inc.
3944 Cameron St, 22026 [PO Box 26, 22026]; (p) (703) 221-2218; (f) (703) 221-2218; (c) Prince William

Private non-profit/ 1974/ staff: 2(f); 3(p); 80(v)/ members: 100/publication: *Ye Olde Town Crier*

HISTORIC SITE; HISTORICAL SOCIETY; HOUSE MUSEUM: Collects, preserves, and interprets the history of the Prince William/ Dumfries regional area.

PROGRAMS: Annual Meeting; Community Outreach; Concerts; Exhibits; Festivals; Guided Tours; Lectures; Living History; Publication; Reenactments; Research Library/Archives

COLLECTIONS: [18th-20th c] Furniture and artifacts; local history and genealogy files on the area's founding families.

HOURS: Yr T-Sa 10-4

ADMISSION: $3, Children $2, Seniors $2; Under 6 free

EDINBURG

8541
Shenandoah County Historical Society, Inc.
508 Piccadilly St, Rm 104, 22824 [300 Stoney Creek Blvd, 22824]; (p) (540) 984-8200; (f) (540) 984-8207; scl@shentel.net; (c) Shenandoah

County/ 1986/ members: 100/publication: *Fairfax Line; History of Shenandoah County.*

GENEALOGICAL SOCIETY; HISTORIC PRESERVATION AGENCY; HISTORICAL SOCIETY: Collects, preserves, researches and utilizes historical and archival materials.

PROGRAMS: Annual Meeting; Community Outreach; Exhibits; Guided Tours; Lectures; Publication; Research Library/Archives

COLLECTIONS: [1750-present] Family papers and books.

HOURS: Yr by appt

EMORY

8542
Emory and Henry College
1 Garnand Dr, 24327 [PO Box 947, 24327]; (p) (540) 944-6133; (f) (540) 944-6935; ehadmiss@ ehc.edu; www.ehc.edu; (c) Washington

Private non-profit/ 1836/ Board of Trustees/ staff: 211(f); 53(p); 1(v)

HISTORIC SITE

PROGRAMS: Community Outreach; Concerts; Exhibits; Facility Rental; Guided Tours; Lectures; School-Based Curriculum; Theatre

HOURS: Yr M-F 8-4

EMPORIA

8543
Village View 1790s Mansion
221 Briggs St, 23847; (p) (804) 634-2475;

EWING

8544
Wilderness Road State Park
Route 2, Box 115, 24248; (p) (540) 445-3065; (f) (540) 445-3066; (c) Lee

State/ 1993/ staff: 3(f); 10(p); 16(v)

HISTORIC SITE; LIVING HISTORY/OUTDOOR MUSEUM

PROGRAMS: Community Outreach; Facility Rental; Family Programs; Festivals; Guided Tours; Interpretation; Lectures; Living History; School-Based Curriculum

COLLECTIONS: [1775-1877]

HOURS: Yr Daily 8-dusk

FAIRFAX

8545
Fairfax County Public Library, Virginia Room
3915 Chain Bridge Rd, 22030; (p) (703) 246-2123; (f) (703) 385-1911; va_room@co.fairfax.va.us; www.co.fairfax.va.us/library; (c) Fairfax

County/ 1939/ County of Fairfax Library Board/ staff: 3(f); 2(p); 10(v)

LIBRARY AND/OR ARCHIVES

PROGRAMS: Community Outreach; Exhibits; Guided Tours; Research Library/Archives

COLLECTIONS: [19th-20th c]

HOURS: Yr M-Th 10-9, F 10-6, Sa 10-5, Su 12-5

ADMISSION: No charge

8546
Fairfax Museum and Visitor Center
10209 Main St, 22030; (p) (703) 385-8415, (703) 385-8414; (f) (703) 385-8692; (c) Fairfax

City/ 1983/ Offices of Historic Resources/ staff: 1(f); 40(v)/ members: 150

HISTORIC SITE; HISTORY MUSEUM: Collects, preserves, and interprets the history of Fairfax City and the surrounding Northern VA area.

PROGRAMS: Community Outreach; Exhibits; Family Programs; Festivals; Interpretation; Living History; School-Based Curriculum

COLLECTIONS: [18th c-present] Artifacts: Native American, colonial Fairfax family, Civil War.

HOURS: Yr Daily 9-5

ADMISSION: No charge

8547
Historical Society of Fairfax County
[PO Box 415, 22030]; (p) (703) 246-2123; (c) Fairfax

Private non-profit/ 1950/ members: 300/publication: *Fairfax County Historical Society Yearbook*

Promotes preservation of historic sites.

8548
Living History Society, The
[PO Box 77, 22030]; (p) (703) 758-5838; (f) (703) 758-5838; gnzh23c@prodigy.com; www.livinghistoryonline.com; (c) Fairfax

Private for-profit/ 1998/ Great Oak, Inc./ staff: 4(f); 12(p)/ members: 3000/publication: *Quarterly Living History Magazine; Living History Ezine*

HISTORICAL SOCIETY: Promotes living history.

PROGRAMS: Publication

8549
National Firearms Museum
11250 Waples Mill Rd, 22030; (p) (703) 267-1600; (f) (703) 267-3913; nfmstaff@nra.org; www.nra.org/museum; (c) Fairfax

Private non-profit/ 1937/ National Rifle Association/ staff: 4(f); 2(p); 15(v)

HISTORY MUSEUM; RESEARCH CENTER: Collects, preserves, and exhibits firearms and related materials.

PROGRAMS: Exhibits; Facility Rental; Film/Video; Guided Tours; Interpretation; Lectures; Living History; Research Library/Archives; Theatre

COLLECTIONS: [1350-present] Firearms, presidential arms.

HOURS: Yr Daily 10-4

ADMISSION: No charge

8550
Ratcliffe-Allison House
10386 Main St, 22030 [10209 Main St, 22030]; (p) (703) 352-9740

1997/ Fairfax City, Inc/ staff: 1(f); 2(p); 15(v)

HISTORIC SITE: Interprets settlement, growth and development of historic Fairfax Courthouse and Fairfax.

PROGRAMS: Exhibits; Guided Tours

COLLECTIONS: [18th-19th c] American-made furnishings and decorative arts.

HOURS: By appt

ADMISSION: No charge

8551
Resource Management Division, Fairfax County Park Authority
12055 Government Center Pkwy, Ste 927, 22035; (p) (703) 324-8664; (f) (703) 324-3996; lstephenson@co.fairfax.va.us; www.co.fairfax.va.us/parks; (c) Fairfax

County/ 1950/ Fairfax County Park Authority/ staff: 189(f); 94(p); 700(v)

ARCHAEOLOGICAL SITE/MUSEUM; GARDEN; HISTORIC PRESERVATION AGENCY; HISTORIC SITE; HOUSE MUSEUM; LIVING HISTORY/OUTDOOR MUSEUM: Manages the stewardship of natural and cultural resources within the FCPA inventory.

PROGRAMS: Community Outreach; Concerts; Exhibits; Facility Rental; Family Programs; Festivals; Garden Tours; Guided Tours; Interpretation; Lectures; Living History; Reenactments; School-Based Curriculum

COLLECTIONS: [Mid 18th-early 20th c] Furniture, tools, costumes, personal accessories, toys, agricultural and milling equipment, fine and decorative arts, books, documents, textiles and commercial items.

HOURS: (Historic Sites and Nature Centers) W-M; hours vary by site

ADMISSION: Varies

FAIRFAX STATION

8552
Friends of the Fairfax Station, Inc.
1120 Fairfax Station Rd, 22039 [PO Box 7, 22039]; (p) (703) 425-9225, (703) 278-8833; fxstn@fairfax-station.org; www.fairfax-station.org; (c) Fairfax

Private non-profit/ 1977/ Board of Directors/ staff: 90(v)/ members: 180/publication: *Fairfax Station: All Aboard!*

HISTORIC SITE; HISTORICAL SOCIETY; HISTORY MUSEUM; LIVING HISTORY/OUTDOOR MUSEUM: Interprets local, railroad and Civil War history in a reconstructed Southern Railway depot.

PROGRAMS: Annual Meeting; Community Outreach; Exhibits; Facility Rental; Festivals; Guided Tours; Interpretation; Lectures; Living History; Publication; Reenactments; Research Library/Archives; School-Based Curriculum

COLLECTIONS: [Mid 19th c-present] Southern Railway and other railroad artifacts, local photographs, documents, Clara Barton/Red Cross collectibles, research books and magazines.

HOURS: Yr Su 1-4, Labor Day 12-5

ADMISSION: $2, Children $1

FANCY GAP

8553
Sidna Allen Home
Rt 2, Box 269, 24328; (p) (540) 728-2594

FERRUM

8554
Blue Ridge Institute and Museum
Ferrum College, Rt 40 W, 24088 [Ferrum College, PO Box 1000, 24088]; (p) (540) 365-4416; (f) (640) 365-4419; bri@ferrum.edu; www.blueridgeinstitute.org; (c) Franklin

Private non-profit/ 1972/ Ferrum College/ staff: 4(f); 9(p); 25(v)

LIVING HISTORY/OUTDOOR MUSEUM; RESEARCH CENTER: Documents, preserves, and interprets the regional folklife of VA.

PROGRAMS: Community Outreach; Concerts; Exhibits; Festivals; Guided Tours; Interpretation; Living History; Research Library/Archives; School-Based Curriculum

COLLECTIONS: [1800-present] Museum artifacts: furniture, textiles, folk art, folk crafts, tools, farm vehicles; archival holdings: photographic images, audio recordings, video recordings, books, manuscripts, and documents.

HOURS: Yr Galleries: M-Sa 10-4:30; Farm Museum: May-Aug Sa-Su 10-4:30

FOREST

8555
Corporation for Jefferson's Poplar Forest
Poplar Forest Dr & Foxhall Dr, 24551 [PO Box 419, 24551-0419]; (p) (804) 525-1806; (f) (804) 525-7252; www.poplarforest.org; (c) Bedford

Private non-profit/ 1983/ staff: 23(f); 4(p); 125(v)

HISTORIC SITE; HOUSE MUSEUM: Preserves and restores Poplar Forest, the 1806 octagonal retreat home and plantation of Thomas Jefferson.

PROGRAMS: Community Outreach; Concerts; Exhibits; Facility Rental; Family Programs; Festivals; Guided Tours; Lectures; Living History; Research Library/Archives; School-Based Curriculum

COLLECTIONS: [1773-1826] Archaeological and architectural artifacts, photographs, manuscripts, journals, newspapers and maps.

HOURS: Apr-Nov Daily 10-4

ADMISSION: $7, Children $1

FORT EUSTIS

8556
Matthew Jones House
Taylor Ave & Harris Rd, 23604 [PO Box 4468, 23604]; (p) (757) 878-5381, (757) 898-5090

Joint/ 1680/ Federal; Fort Eustis Historical and Archaeological Assoc/ staff: 5(v)

COLLECTIONS: [1680-present] Indian artifacts; early life artifacts; Mulberry Island families.

8557
U.S. Army Transportation Museum
Bldg 300, Besson Hall, 23604-5260; (p) (757) 878-1115; (f) (757) 878-5656; bowerb@eustis.army.mil; www.eustis.army.mil/dptmsec/museum.htm; (c) City of Newport News

Federal/ 1959/ US Army/ staff: 4(f); 1(p); 3(v)

HISTORY MUSEUM: Collects, preserves, exhibits and provides information on the history of United States Army transportation from colonial days to present.

PROGRAMS: Research Library/Archives

COLLECTIONS: [1860s-present] 108 full-sized vehicles, boats, aircraft and rail rolling stock. Photos, publications, vertical and reprint files.

HOURS: Yr T-Su 9-4:30

ADMISSION: No charge

FORT LEE

8558
U.S. Army Quartermaster Museum
OQMG USA Quartermaster Center, Bldg 5218, A Av, 23801 [OQMG USA Quartermaster Center, Building 5218, A Ave, 23801-1601]; (p) (804) 734-4203; (f) (804) 734-4359; www.qmmuseum-lee.army mil

Federal/ 1957/ US Army/ staff: 4(f); 2(v)

HISTORIC SITE; HISTORY MUSEUM; RESEARCH CENTER: Collects, preserves, exhibits, and interprets the history of the QM Corps, the Army's oldest logistic branch.

PROGRAMS: Community Outreach; Exhibits; Guided Tours; Research Library/Archives; School-Based Curriculum

COLLECTIONS: [1775-present] Uniforms, flags, and insignia.

HOURS: Yr T-F 10-5, Sa-Su 11-5

FORT MONROE

8559

Casemate Museum, The
CM #20 Bernard Rd, 23651; (p) (757) 727-3391; (f) (757) 727-3886; mroczkod@monroe.army.mil

Federal/ 1951/ US Government/ staff: 5(f); 2(p); 30(v)/publication: *Tales of Old Fort Monroe and The Casemate Papers*

HISTORY MUSEUM: Collects, preserves and exhibits artifacts, documents and photographs relating to the history of Old Point Comfort, Fort Monroe and the Coast Artillery Corps.

PROGRAMS: Community Outreach; Guided Tours; Lectures; Publication; Research Library/Archives

COLLECTIONS: [1819-present] Artifacts, books, documents and photos.

HOURS: Yr Daily 10:30-4:30

ADMISSION: No charge

FORT MYER

8560

Council on America's Military Past, USA
[PO Box 1151, 22211]; (p) (703) 912-6124, (800) 398-4693; (f) (703) 912-5666; camphartl@aol.com; (c) Arlington

Private non-profit/ 1966/ Board of Directors/ staff: 20(v)/ members: 1200/publication: *Journal of America's Military Past; Heliogram*

PROFESSIONAL ORGANIZATION: Preserves the history of military sites.

PROGRAMS: Annual Meeting; Publication

8561

Old Guard Museum, The
Commander, 3d US Infantry Attn: ANOG-OGM, 204 Le, 22211 [Commander, 3d US Infantry Attn: ANOG-OG M, 204 Lee Ave, 22211-1199]; (p) (703) 696-6670; (f) (703) 696-4256; BoganA@fmmc.army.mil; www.mdw.army.mil/oldguard

Federal/ 1962/ 3d US Infantry (The Old Guard)/ staff: 3(f)

HISTORY MUSEUM: Represents history of the US Army's oldest active infantry unit.

PROGRAMS: Exhibits; Film/Video; Research Library/Archives

COLLECTIONS: [1784-present] Military equipment, weapons, photos, artwork, archival material, and films.

HOURS: Yr M-Sa 9-4, Su 1-4

ADMISSION: No charge

FORT VALLEY

8562

Fort Valley Museum, Inc.
Route 678, 22652 [c/o Ann A Hunter, PO Box 95, 22652]; (p) (540) 933-6185; (c) Shenandoah

Private non-profit/ 1973

HOUSE MUSEUM: Preserves history of early rural VA.

PROGRAMS: Exhibits

HOURS: Mem-Labor Day Weekend Sa 1-4, Su 2-5

ADMISSION: Donations accepted

FREDERICKSBURG

8563

APVA Mary Washington Branch
1200 & 1300 Charles St; 1304 Caroline St, 22401 [1200 Charles St, 22401]; (p) (540) 373-1569, (540) 371-1494; (f) (540) 372-6587; www.apva.org

Private non-profit/ 1889/ Assoc for the Preservation of Virginia Antiquities/ staff: 40(p); 40(v)/ members: 225

GARDEN; HISTORIC SITE; HOUSE MUSEUM; LIVING HISTORY/OUTDOOR MUSEUM: Preserves Mary Washington's last home, Rising Sun Tavern; Hugh Mercer's Apothecary Shop; and St. James' House, an 18th century gentleman's home built around 1760.

PROGRAMS: Garden Tours; Guided Tours; Living History; Reenactments

COLLECTIONS: [Mid-late 18th c] Period furnishings of an 18th c tavern and gentleman's cottage; Washington/Ball memorabilia; apothecary shop/doctor's office equipment and bottles; Rising Sun Tavern.

HOURS: Mar-Nov Daily 9-5; Dec-Feb Daily 10-4; St James' House: Apr-Oct and by appt

ADMISSION: $4, Children $1.50; Group rates

8564

Belmont, The Gari Melchers Estate and Memorial Gallery
224 Washington St, 22405; (p) (540) 654-1015; (f) (540) 654-1785; (c) Stafford

State/ 1975/ Mary Washington College/ staff: 4(f); 24(p)/ members: 400

ART MUSEUM; GARDEN; HOUSE MUSEUM: Interprets life of Gari Melchers.

PROGRAMS: Community Outreach; Concerts; Exhibits; Facility Rental; Garden Tours; Guided Tours; Interpretation; Lectures; School-Based Curriculum

COLLECTIONS: [1870-1955]

HOURS: Yr M-Sa 10-5, Su 12-5

ADMISSION: $4, Student $1

8565

Fredericksburg & Spotsylvania National Military Park
120 Chatham Lane, 22405-2508; (p) (540) 371-0802, (540) 373-6122; (f) (540) 371-1907; frsp_info@nps.gov

1927/ National Parks Services

BATTLEFIELD; HISTORIC SITE; HISTORY MUSEUM; NATIONAL PARK: In 1927 the U.S. Congress established Fredericksburg and Spotsylvania County Memorial National Military Park to commemorate the heroic deeds of the men engaged at the four major battles fought in the vicinity (Fredericksburg, Chancellorsville, Wilderness, and Spotsylvania Court House). Today the park also includes the historic structures of Chatham, Ellwood, Salem Church, and the "Stonewall" Jackson Shrine.

PROGRAMS: Exhibits; Guided Tours; Interpretation; Lectures

COLLECTIONS: [Civil War Era] Artifacts, memorabilia, manuscripts, documents.

HOURS: Park grounds: daily sunrise-sunset; Fredericksburg Battlefield Visitor Center, Chancellorsville Visitor Center 9-5; Chatham Manor: 9-5

8566

Fredericksburg Area Museum and Cultural Center, Inc.
907 Princess Anne St, 22401 [PO Box 922, 22404]; (p) (540) 371-3037; (f) (540) 373-6569; famcc@fls.infi.net; www.famcc.org; (c) Independent City

Private non-profit/ 1988/ Board of Directors/ staff: 4(f); 7(p); 40(v)/ members: 807

HISTORIC SITE; HISTORY MUSEUM: Collects, interprets, and exhibits the history and culture of the Fredericksburg area.

PROGRAMS: Community Outreach; Exhibits; Facility Rental; Family Programs; Guided Tours; Lectures; Living History

COLLECTIONS: [18th-20th c] Books, clothing, photos, decorative arts; documents and artifacts on the Civil War, black history, Native Americans, industry, and the railroad.

HOURS: Mar-Nov M-Sa 10-5, Su 1-5; Dec-Feb M-Sa 10-4, Su 1-4

8567

Hugh Mercer Apothecary Shop
1020 Caroline St, 22401; (p) (540) 373-3362; (c) Fredericksburg

Private non-profit/ APVA Mary Washington Branch/ staff: 10(p)

HISTORIC SITE

PROGRAMS: Community Outreach; Exhibits; Guided Tours; Interpretation

COLLECTIONS: [18th-20th c] Pharmacy bottles, apothecary equipment, period and reproduction medical and surgical tools, medical books and documents.

HOURS: Mar-Nov Daily 9-5; Dec-Feb Daily 10-4

ADMISSION: $4, Student $1.50; Group rates

8568

James Monroe Museum and Memorial Library
908 Charles St, 22401-5810; (p) (540) 654-1043, (540) 654-2110; (f) (540) 654-1106; dvoelkel@mwc.edu; jamesmonroemuseum@mwc.edu

State/ 1927/ Comm of Virginia, Mary Washington College/ staff: 2(f); 16(p); 2(v)/ members: 375

HISTORY MUSEUM; PRESIDENTIAL SITE: Dedicated to the study, interpretation, and presentation of the life and times of the fifth president of the US.

PROGRAMS: Annual Meeting; Exhibits; Facility Rental; Festivals; Guided Tours; Lectures; Research Library/Archives

COLLECTIONS: [1760-1830] Fine and decorative arts, social history artifacts, costumes, textiles, books, papers, and documents relating to President James Monroe and his family.

HOURS: Yr Daily 10-5

8569
Mary Washington College, Center for Historic Preservation
Trinkle Hall, Room B-32, 22401 [1301 College Ave, 22401-5358]; (p) (540) 654-1356; (f) (540) 654-1068; dsanford@mwc.edu; www.mwc.edu/~dsanford/center/center.htm; (c) Fredericksburg

State/ 1980/publication: *Historic Preservation at Mary Washington College*

HISTORIC PRESERVATION AGENCY: Supports historic preservation activities; administers two sites: James Monroe Museum and Memorial Library and the Enchanted Castle Site at Germanna.

PROGRAMS: Lectures; Publication

FRONT ROYAL

8570
Warren Heritage Society
101 Chester St, 22630; (p) (540) 636-1446; (c) Warren

Private non-profit/ 1971/ Board of Directors/ staff: 1(p)/ 50(v)/ members: 288

HISTORIC PRESERVATION AGENCY; HISTORICAL SOCIETY: Displays town and county history.

PROGRAMS: Annual Meeting; Festivals; Guided Tours; Lectures; Research Library/ Archives

COLLECTIONS: [1836-present] Furniture, clothing, pictures and articles from Warren County, especially the local manufacturing plants.

HOURS: Apr-Dec M-T, Th-F 10-3

ADMISSION: $2

8571
Warren Rifles Confederate Memorial Museum, Inc.
95 Chester St, 22630 [PO Box 1304, 22630]; silwood@rma.edu; (c) Warren

Private non-profit/ 1956/ Board of Trustees/ staff: 3(p); 10(v)

HISTORY MUSEUM

PROGRAMS: Exhibits

COLLECTIONS: [1860s] Confederate era artifacts: weapons, uniforms, letters, documents, clothing and furniture.

HOURS: Apr-Oct M-Sa 9-4, Su 12-4

ADMISSION: $2; Students free

GALAX

8572
Galax-Carroll Regional Library
608 W Stuart Dr, 24333; (p) (540) 236-2042; (f) (540) 236-5153

City/ 1982/ Board of Trustees/ staff: 10(f); 10(p); 6(v)

LIBRARY AND/OR ARCHIVES: Maintains local history and genealogy.

HOURS: Yr M, W, F 9-5, T, Th 9-8, Sa 10-4, Su 2-5

ADMISSION: No charge

8573
Jeff Matthews Memorial Museum
606 W Stuart Dr, 24333; (p) (540) 236-7874; (c) Grayson

City/ 1974/ staff: 2(p)

HISTORY MUSEUM; HOUSE MUSEUM

PROGRAMS: Exhibits; School-Based Curriculum

COLLECTIONS: [18th c-present] Pictures, guns, personal items and equipment.

HOURS: Yr Sa 11-4, Su 1-4; Fall/Winter W-F 12-4; Spring/Summer W-F 1-5

ADMISSION: Donations accepted

GLOUCESTER

8574
APVA Joseph Bryan Branch
[PO Box 335, 23061]; (p) (804) 693-3663; zanoni@ccsinc.com; www.apva.org; (c) Gloucester

Private non-profit/ Assoc for the Preservation of VA Antiquities/ staff: 10(v)/ members: 200

HISTORIC PRESERVATION AGENCY; HISTORIC SITE: Preserves Warner Hall colonial graveyard and birthplace of Dr. Walter Reed.

PROGRAMS: Annual Meeting; Guided Tours

HOURS: Apr-Sept and by appt

ADMISSION: Donations accepted

8575
Gloucester Historical Society
[PO Box 1812, 23061]; (p) (804) 693-1234; (c) Gloucester

Private non-profit/ 1977/ Board of Directors/ staff: 6(v)/ members: 106

HISTORIC PRESERVATION AGENCY; HISTORICAL SOCIETY

PROGRAMS: Exhibits; Family Programs; Lectures

COLLECTIONS: [18th-20th c] Deeds, transcripts, maps, book, and genealogy records.

HOURS: Yr by appt; Apr-Oct Sa-Su 2-5

ADMISSION: Donations

8576
Gloucester Museum of History
Court Green on Main St, 23061 [PO Box 1176, 23061]; (p) (804) 693-1234, (804) 693-2659; (c) Gloucester

County/ 1990/ Board of Supervisors/Gloucester Historical Committee/ staff: 1(p); 25(v)/ members: 40

HISTORY MUSEUM: Acquires, preserves and exhibits items pertaining to county history.

PROGRAMS: Exhibits; Guided Tours

COLLECTIONS: [18th-20th c] Permanent "Old Country Store" exhibit: African American history, archaeology, schools, the military and Christmas.

HOURS: Yr W-F 10-2, Sa 12-4

8577
Walter Reed's Birthplace
Cor of Bellroi & Hickory Park Rds, 23061 [c/o PO Box 335, 23061]; (p) (804) 693-3663

HISTORY MUSEUM; HOUSE MUSEUM

COLLECTIONS: [1850s] Coin silver spoons, Walter Reed's christening gown.

HOURS: App; Special day; Special days & appt

GOOCHLAND

8578
Goochland County Historical Society
2875 River Rd W, Rte 6, 23063 [PO Box 602, 23063]; (p) (804) 556-3966; gchs1admin@earthlink.net; www.goochlandhistory.org; (c) Goochland

Private non-profit/ 1968/ Board of Directors/ staff: 1(p); 40(v)/ members: 440/publication: *Goochland County Historical Magazine*

HISTORICAL SOCIETY; HISTORY MUSEUM; RESEARCH CENTER: Preserves, presents, and interprets county history.

PROGRAMS: Annual Meeting; Exhibits; Facility Rental; Interpretation; Lectures; Publication

COLLECTIONS: [1727-present] Library with documents, maps, photographs, and artifacts.

HOURS: Apr-Nov T-F 10-3; Dec-Mar W-F 10-3

GORDONSVILLE

8579
Exchange Hotel Civil War Museum
400 S Main St, 22942 [PO Box 542, 22942]; (p) (540) 832-2944; sturkhntr@aol.com; www.gemlink.com/~exchange-hotel/home.htm; (c) Orange

Private non-profit/ 1983/ Historic Gordonsville, Inc./ staff: 4(p); 6(v)/ members: 325/publication: *The Exchange*

HISTORIC SITE; HISTORY MUSEUM: Preserves and exhibits Civil War medical history in former Confederate Gordonsville Receiving Hospital.

PROGRAMS: Annual Meeting; Exhibits; Guided Tours; Living History; Publication; Reenactments; Research Library/Archives

COLLECTIONS: [1861-1865] Civil War medical artifacts, hospital ward and surgery; Union and Confederate uniforms and equipment; period clothing and furniture.

HOURS: Mid Mar-mid Dec T-Sa 10-4

ADMISSION: $4, Children $1, Seniors $3

GREAT FALLS

8580
Colvin Run Mill Historic Site
10017 Colvin Run Rd, 22066; (p) (703) 759-2771; (f) (703) 759-7490; ann.korzeniewski@co.fairfax.va.us; www.colvinrunmill.org; (c) Fairfax

County/ 1972/ Fairfax County Park Authority/ staff: 4(f); 4(p); 40(v)/ members: 62/publication: *Almost 100 Recipes Using Cornmeal*

HISTORIC SITE: Interprets and restores water-powered gristmill.

PROGRAMS: Community Outreach; Concerts; Exhibits; Family Programs; Guided Tours; Interpretation; Lectures; Living History; Publication; Reenactments; School-Based Curriculum

COLLECTIONS: [19th-20th c] Merchant

milling artifacts: tools, receipts, milling magazines, flour; Millard family portraits, photos, clothing, and Bible.

HOURS: Yr Mar-Dec W-M 11-5; Jan-Feb W-M 11-4

ADMISSION: $4, Student $3, Children $2, Seniors $2

GUM SPRINGS

8581
Gum Springs Historical Society, Inc.
8100 Fordson Rd, 22306-3128; (p) (703) 799-1198; gshs@bellatlantic.net; www.lke-com ply.com/femn/htm/gshs/gshs.htm; (c) Fairfax

Private non-profit/ 1984/ members: 200/publication: History in Motion

GENEALOGICAL SOCIETY; HISTORIC SITE; HISTORICAL SOCIETY; HISTORY MUSEUM; LIVING HISTORY/OUTDOOR MUSEUM; RESEARCH CENTER

PROGRAMS: Annual Meeting; Community Outreach; Concerts; Exhibits; Facility Rental; Family Programs; Festivals; Film/Video; Guided Tours; Interpretation; Lectures; Living History; Publication; Research Library/Archives; School-Based Curriculum

COLLECTIONS: [Late 1700s-1960s]

HOURS: Yr T, Th 3-8, Sa 1-5

ADMISSION: $4, Children $2

HAMPTON

8582
City of Hampton Historical Collection and Fort Wool Historic Site
Hampton Arts Commission, 4205 Victoria Blvd, 23669; (p) (757) 727-1051; (f) (757) 727-1152; (c) Elizabeth City

City/ 1952/ staff: 1(f); 4(p); 5(v)

HISTORIC SITE; HISTORY MUSEUM; RESEARCH CENTER

PROGRAMS: Exhibits; Interpretation; Lectures; Living History

COLLECTIONS: [Prehistory-present] Manuscripts, photographs, archaeological objects and maps related to the City of Hampton.

HOURS: May-Sept Daily 9-5

ADMISSION: $10

8583
Hampton University Museum
Huntington Building, Hampton University, 23668; (p) (757) 727-5308; (f) (757) 727-5170; www.hamptonu.edu

Private non-profit/ 1868/ Hampton Univ/ staff: 10(f); 2(p)/ members: 956/publication: International Review of African American Art

ART MUSEUM; HISTORY MUSEUM: Preserves African, Native American, Asian, and Pacific Island art, fine arts and objects relating to the University's history.

PROGRAMS: Community Outreach; Concerts; Elder's Programs; Exhibits; Facility Rental; Family Programs; Guided Tours; Lectures; Publication; Research Library/Archives

COLLECTIONS: [Mid 19th c] African and Native American objects.

HOURS: Yr M-F 8-5, Sa 12-4

ADMISSION: Donations accepted

8584
Virginia Air and Space Center/Hampton Roads History Center
600 Settlers Landing Rd, 23669-4033; (p) (757) 727-0900; (f) (757) 727-0898; www.vasc.org

Private non-profit/ 1992/ staff: 30(f); 45(p); 300(v)/ members: 3000/publication: Center-Line

HISTORY MUSEUM: Preserves and interprets national achievements in air and space exploration and development.

PROGRAMS: Community Outreach; Elder's Programs; Exhibits; Facility Rental; Family Programs; Festivals; Film/Video; Guided Tours; Interpretation; Lectures; Publication; Research Library/Archives; School-Based Curriculum

COLLECTIONS: [20th c] Artifacts related to Hampton Roads history; two dozen air and spacecraft; NASA artifacts including Apollo XII Command Module, Lunar Excursion Module Simulator and moon rocks; aeronautics-related archival material, and library.

HOURS: Yr Daily 10-5

ADMISSION: $6.50, Children $4.50, Seniors $5.50

HANOVER

8585
Hanover County Historical Society, Inc.
Hanover Courthouse Rd/Route 301, Historic District, 23069 [PO Box 91, 23069]; (p) (804) 537-6262; (c) Hanover

Private non-profit/ 1967/ Board/ staff: 15(v)/publication: Semi-Annual Bulletin

HISTORIC SITE; HISTORICAL SOCIETY

PROGRAMS: Annual Meeting; Community Outreach; Exhibits; Family Programs; Guided Tours; Lectures; Publication; School-Based Curriculum

HOURS: Yr by appt

ADMISSION: No charge

8586
Hanover Tavern Foundation
13181 Hanover Courthouse Rd, 23069 [PO Box 487, 23069]; (p) (804) 537-5050; (f) (804) 537-5823; info@hanovertavern.org; www.hanovertavern.org; (c) Hanover

Private non-profit/ 1990/ Board of Directors/ staff: 1(f); 2(p); 40(v)

HISTORIC SITE; HISTORICAL SOCIETY: Promotes historical and cultural programming in former home of Patrick Henry.

PROGRAMS: Facility Rental; Guided Tours; Interpretation; Lectures; Living History; Reenactments; School-Based Curriculum; Theatre

COLLECTIONS: [Late 18th-20th c]

HOURS: By appt

HARDY

8587
Booker T. Washington National Monument
VA State Rt 122 between Rocky Mt & Bedford, 24101 [12130 Booker T Washington Hwy, 24101]; (p) (540) 721-2094; (f) (540) 721-5128; www.nps.gov/bowa; (c) Franklin

Federal/ 1956/ Dept of the Interior/ staff: 12(f); 6(v)

HISTORIC SITE: Preserves and protects the birth site and childhood home of Booker T. Washington.

PROGRAMS: Exhibits; Garden Tours; Guided Tours; Interpretation; Living History; School-Based Curriculum

COLLECTIONS: [1856-1865] Books, papers.

HOURS: Yr Daily

HARRISONBURG

8588
Menno Simons Historical Library
1200 Park Rd, 22802 [Eastern Mennonite University, 22802-2462]; (p) (540) 432-4178; (f) (540) 432-4977; bowmanlb@emu.edu; www.emu.edu/library/lib.htm; (c) Rockingham

Private non-profit/ 1955/ Eastern Mennonite Univ/ staff: 1(f); 1(p); 5(v)

RESEARCH CENTER: Specialized research facility in the Hartzler Library.

PROGRAMS: Research Library/Archives

COLLECTIONS: [16th c-present] Anabaptist and Mennonite history, thought and culture in Europe and America; Shenandoah Valley history and culture with emphasis on Germanic groups.

HOURS: Yr M-F 8-12/1-5

ADMISSION: Donations accepted

8589
Shenandoah Valley Mennonite Historians
1 Village Square, 22802; (p) (540) 433-7477; (f) (540) 432-4448; shenks@emu.edu; (c) Rockingham

Private non-profit/ 1993/ Executive Committee/ staff: 10(v)/ members: 250/publication: Shenandoah Mennonite Historian

HISTORICAL SOCIETY: Promotes the study, preservation and communication of the Mennonite heritage in the Shenandoah Valley of Virginia.

PROGRAMS: Annual Meeting; Exhibits; Guided Tours; Lectures; Publication

COLLECTIONS: [19th c] Dismantled two-story log house from the early 1800s.

HEATHSVILLE

8590
Northumberland County Historical Society
86 Back St, 22473 [PO Box 221, 22473]; (p) (804) 580-8581; (c) Northumberland

Private non-profit/ 1962/ staff: 1(p)/ members: 700

GENEALOGICAL SOCIETY; HISTORIC SITE;

HISTORICAL SOCIETY; HISTORY MUSEUM; RESEARCH CENTER

PROGRAMS: Annual Meeting; Exhibits; Facility Rental; Family Programs; Festivals; Guided Tours; Lectures; Publication; Research Library/ Archives; School-Based Curriculum

COLLECTIONS: [17th-19th c] Native American artifacts, arrowheads, and pipes. Civil War items, medical supplies, and antique furniture.

HOURS: Yr T-Th 9-4

ADMISSION: Donations accepted

HERNDON

8591
Historical Society of Herndon
713 Lynn St, 20172 [PO Box 99, 20172]; (c) Fairfax

Private non-profit/ 1976/ members: 70

Preserves local history.

HOURS: Apr-June, Sept-Oct Su 1-4

ADMISSION: Donations accepted

HILLSVILLE

8592
Carroll County Historical Society
305 N Main St, 24343 [PO Box 937, 24343]; (p) (540) 728-4113; (c) Carroll

Private non-profit/ 1982/ staff: 1(f)/ members: 236/publication: Chronicles

HISTORIC PRESERVATION AGENCY; HISTORICAL SOCIETY; HISTORY MUSEUM; HOUSE MUSEUM; LIVING HISTORY/OUTDOOR MUSEUM: Preserves and presents Carroll County's history.

PROGRAMS: Annual Meeting; Community Outreach; Exhibits; Facility Rental; Family Programs; Festivals; Film/Video; Guided Tours; Lectures; Living History; Publication; Research Library/Archives

COLLECTIONS: [1850s-present] Exhibits on county history.

HOURS: Yr T-F 10:30-4, Sa 10-2

ADMISSION: No charge

HOPEWELL

8593
Flowerdew Hundred Foundation
1617 Flowerdew Hundred Rd, 23860 [PO Box 1624, 23860]; (p) (804) 541-8897; (f) (804) 458-7738; flowerdew@new-quest.net; www.flowerdew.org; (c) Prince George

Private non-profit/ 1977/ staff: 2(f); 4(p)/ members: 100

ARCHAEOLOGICAL SITE/MUSEUM; HISTORY MUSEUM: Promotes historical research and educational programs.

PROGRAMS: Exhibits; Festivals; Guided Tours; Interpretation

COLLECTIONS: [Prehistory-early 20th c] Archaeological artifacts from excavations.

HOURS: Apr-mid Dec T-Sa 10-4, Su 1-4

ADMISSION: $6, Children $3, Seniors $4

8594
Historic Hopewell Foundation, Inc.
Saint Denis Chapel; Weston Manor, 23860 [PO Box 851, 23860]; (p) (804) 458-2564, (804) 458-4682; (f) (804) 458-4682; (c) Independent City

Private non-profit/ 1972/ staff: 1(f); 3(p); 50(v)/ members: 400/publication: Manorisms

GARDEN; HISTORIC PRESERVATION AGENCY; HISTORIC SITE; HISTORICAL SOCIETY; HISTORY MUSEUM; HOUSE MUSEUM: Owns three historic properties: Weston Manor, Saint Denis Chapel, and the Dr. Peter Eppes House.

PROGRAMS: Annual Meeting; Community Outreach; Concerts; Exhibits; Facility Rental; Festivals; Garden Tours; Guided Tours; Interpretation; Lectures; Publication; Reenactments; School-Based Curriculum

COLLECTIONS: [4000 BC-mid 20th c] Artifacts from two archaeological digs at Kippax and Cawsons.

HOURS: Apr-Oct M-Sa 10-4:30, Su 1-4:30

ADMISSION: $4, Seniors $3.50; $3.50 Military

INDEPENDENCE

8595
Grayson County Historical Society
116 N Independence Ave, 24348 [PO Box 529, 24348]; (c) Grayson

staff: 1(v)/ members: 350

GENEALOGICAL SOCIETY; HISTORICAL SOCIETY: Collects and preserves county history.

PROGRAMS: Research Library/Archives

COLLECTIONS: [1773-present] Books and family histories.

HOURS: Mem-Labor Day Th 10-4

ADMISSION: No charge

IRVINGTON

8596
Steamboat Era Museum, Inc.
156 King Carter Dr, 22578 [PO Box 132, 22578]; (p) (804) 438-6888; stmbteramus@riunet.net; (c) Lancaster

Private non-profit/ 2000/ staff: 1(f); 23(v)/ members: 107

HISTORY MUSEUM: Collects, preserves and interprets Chesapeake Bay steamboat history.

COLLECTIONS: 1827-1937

LEESBURG

8597
George C. Marshall International Center
217 Edwards Ferry Rd NE, 20176 [212 E Market St, 20176]; (p) (703) 777-1880; (f) (703) 777-2889

8598
Loudoun Museum, Inc., The
14-16 Loudoun St SW, 20175; (p) (703) 777-7427, (703) 777-8331; (f) (703) 737-3861; (c) Loudoun

Private non-profit/ 1967/ staff: 1(f); 11(p); 100(v)/ members: 225

HISTORY MUSEUM: Collects, cares for and interprets materials that illustrate the history of the county and its inhabitants.

PROGRAMS: Annual Meeting; Community Outreach; Exhibits; Guided Tours; Interpretation; Lectures; Living History; School-Based Curriculum

COLLECTIONS: [18th-20th c] Objects made or used in Loudoun, such as quilts, furniture, documents, maps, clothing and Civil War related items.

HOURS: Mid Jan-Dec M-Sa 10-5, Su 1-5

ADMISSION: $1, Children $0.50

8599
Morven Park
Old Waterford Rd, 20176 [PO Box 6228, 20176]; (p) (703) 777-2414; (f) (703) 771-9211; www.morvenpark.com; (c) Loudoun

Private non-profit/ 1967/ staff: 10(f); 10(p)

GARDEN; HISTORIC SITE; HOUSE MUSEUM: Interprets history of hunting.

PROGRAMS: Elder's Programs; Exhibits; Facility Rental; Family Programs; Guided Tours; Interpretation; School-Based Curriculum

8600
Oatlands, Inc.
20850 Oatlands Plantation Ln, 20175; (p) (703) 777-3174; (f) (703) 777-4427; oatlands@erols.com; www.oatlands.org; (c) Loudoun

Private non-profit/ 1965/ staff: 10(f); 22(p); 40(v)/publication: The Oatlands Column

GARDEN; HISTORIC SITE; HISTORY MUSEUM; HOUSE MUSEUM; LIVING HISTORY/ OUTDOOR MUSEUM; RESEARCH CENTER: Preserves and interprets a 19th-20th c plantation, community and country estate.

PROGRAMS: Community Outreach; Elder's Programs; Exhibits; Facility Rental; Family Programs; Festivals; Garden Tours; Guided Tours; Interpretation; Lectures; Living History; Publication; Research Library/Archives; School-Based Curriculum; Theatre

COLLECTIONS: [19th c] 2,000 museum artifacts; Sites: smokehouse, bank barn, dairy, ice house, laundry, schoolhouse and greenhouse

HOURS: Apr-Dec M-Sa 10-4:30, Su 1-4:30

ADMISSION: $8, Children $1, Seniors $7

8601
Thomas Balch Library
208 W Market St, 20176; (p) (703) 779-1328; (f) (703) 779-7363; janetbl@erols.com; www.leesburgva.com; (c) Loudoun

City/ 1922/ staff: 3(f); 4(p); 18(v)/publication: Thomas Balch Chronicle

LIBRARY AND/OR ARCHIVES: Focuses on local and family history in northern VA.

PROGRAMS: Community Outreach; Exhibits; Facility Rental; Lectures; Publication; Research Library/Archives

COLLECTIONS: [1750-1900] Books, microfilm, newspapers, photographs and manuscripts.

HOURS: Yr M 10-5, T 10-8, W 2-8, Th-F 11-5, Sa 11-4

ADMISSION: No charge

LEXINGTON

8602
George C. Marshall Foundation

VMI Parade, 24450 [PO Box 1600, 24450];
(p) (540) 463-7103; (f) (540) 464-5229; (c)
Rockbridge

Private non-profit/ 1953/ staff: 16(f); 12(p);
4(v)/ members: 1200

HISTORY MUSEUM; RESEARCH CENTER:
Interprets history of General George C. Marshall.

PROGRAMS: Exhibits; Lectures; Research Library/Archives; School-Based Curriculum

COLLECTIONS: [20th c] Artifacts, books, manuscripts, film and oral history related to 20th century military and diplomatic history.

HOURS: Yr Daily 9-5

ADMISSION: $3, Children $2

8603
Lee Chapel and Museum

Washington and Lee University, 24450-0303;
(p) (540) 463-8768; (f) (540) 463-8741;
phobbs@wlu.edu; www.wlu.edu; (c)
Rockbridge

Private non-profit/ 1867/ Washington and Lee University/ staff: 1(f); 12(p)

HISTORIC SITE; HISTORY MUSEUM: Collects, preserves and interprets the history of Washington and Lee University and the heritage of George Washington and Robert E. Lee.

PROGRAMS: Concerts; Exhibits; Guided Tours; Interpretation; Lectures

COLLECTIONS: [Late 18th-19th c] Artifacts relating to the history of Washington and Lee University, Robert E. Lee and his family; the Washington-Custis-Lee portrait collection; Edward Valentine's recumbent statue of Lee.

HOURS: Spring-Fall M-Sa 9-5, Su 2-5; Winter M-Sa 9-4, Su 2-5

8604
Rockbridge Historical Society

101 E Washington, 24450 [PO Box 514,
24450]; (p) (540) 464-1058; (c) Rockbridge

Private non-profit/ 1939/ staff: 1(p); 25(v)/
members: 600/publication: Streets of Lexington; Roads of Rockbridge.

HISTORICAL SOCIETY

PROGRAMS: Annual Meeting; Community Outreach; Concerts; Exhibits; Facility Rental; Garden Tours; Guided Tours; Interpretation; Publication; Research Library/Archives

COLLECTIONS: [1735-present] Furniture and tools are kept at the Campbell House. Papers and photos housed at Washington and Lee Library.

HOURS: Fall-Winter T-Sa 10-1; Spring-Summer T-Sa 10-3

ADMISSION: No charge

8605
Stonewall Jackson House

8 E Washington St, 24450; (p) (540) 463-
2552; (f) (540) 463-4088; sjh1@rockbridge.
net; www.stonewalljackson.org; (c)
Rockbridge

Private non-profit/ 1954/ Stonewall Jackson

Foundation/ staff: 6(f); 12(p); 50(v)

GARDEN; HISTORIC SITE; HOUSE MUSEUM: Restored home and garden of the famous Confederate general, Thomas Jonathan "Stonewall" Jackson.

PROGRAMS: Community Outreach; Exhibits; Family Programs; Guided Tours; Interpretation; Lectures; Research Library/Archives; School-Based Curriculum

COLLECTIONS: [1851-1861] Library, household furnishings, personal effects, photographs, works of art, tools and equipment.

HOURS: Yr M-Sa 9-5, Su 1-5; June-Aug M-Sa 9-6, Su 1-6

ADMISSION: $5, Student $2.50; Under 6 free; Group rates

8606
Virginia Military Institute Museum

Jackson Memorial Hall, Letcher Ave, 24450;
(p) (540) 464-7334; (f) (540) 464-7112;
gibsonke@vmi.edu; www.vmi.edu/museum

State/ 1856/ Comm of Virginia/Board of Visitors/ staff: 3(f); 3(p); 2(v)

LIBRARY AND/OR ARCHIVES

PROGRAMS: Exhibits; Lectures

COLLECTIONS: [1839-present]

HOURS: Yr Daily 9-5

ADMISSION: Donations accepted

LORTON

8607
Pohick Episcopal Church

9301 Richmond Hwy, 22079; (p) (703) 339-
6572, (703) 550-9449; (f) (703) 339-9884;
troknya@pohick.org; www.pohick.org; (c)
Fairfax

1730/ Episcopal Diocese of VA/ staff: 2(f); 3(p);
200(v)/publication: Minutes of the Vestry,
1732-1785; Families of Pohick Church, Truro
Parish

HISTORIC SITE: Parish church of Washington and Mason.

PROGRAMS: Annual Meeting; Community Outreach; Concerts; Family Programs; Festivals; Guided Tours; Lectures; Publication

COLLECTIONS: [1769-1865] Relics and artifacts include a bible/prayer book imported from England by Washington. Colonial church, Georgian architecture and late Saxon/early Norman baptismal font that was originally used as a mortar.

HOURS: Yr Daily 9-4:30

LOUISA

8608
Louisa County Historical Society

Courthouse Square, 23093 [PO Box 1172,
23093]; (c) Louisa

Private non-profit/ Board of Directors/ members: 444/publication: Louisa County Historical Society Magazine

HISTORICAL SOCIETY; HISTORY MUSEUM; HOUSE MUSEUM

PROGRAMS: Annual Meeting; Community Outreach; Exhibits; Family Programs; Festi-

vals; Film/Video; Lectures; Publication; Research Library/Archives

COLLECTIONS: [18th-20th c]

ADMISSION: No charge

LURAY

8609
Car and Carriage Caravan Museum

Luray Caverns Corp, PO Box 748, 22835; (p)
(540) 743-6551; (f) (540) 743-7088;
www.LurayCaverns.com; (c) Page

Private for-profit/ 1957/ Luray Caverns Corporation/ staff: 3(f); 4(p)

HISTORY MUSEUM: Promotes the restoration, preservation, and education of the history of transportation.

PROGRAMS: Exhibits; Festivals

COLLECTIONS: [1727-1941] Early horse-drawn vehicle, 1892 Vis-a-Vis Benz, 68 vehicles.

HOURS: Yr Mar 15-June 14 Daily 9-6; June 15-Sept 9-7; Sept-Oct 31 9-6; Nov 1-Mar 14 M-F 9-4, Sa-Su 9-5

8610
Luray Valley Farm Museum

629 W Main St, 22835; (p) (540) 743-1297

LYNCHBURG

8611
George M. Jones Memorial Library

2311 Memorial Ave, 24501; (p) (804) 846-
0501; wrhodes@jmlibrary.org;
www.jmlibrary.org

Private non-profit/ 1905/ George M. Jones Library Association/ staff: 2(f); 3(p); 8(v)/publication: JML Report

LIBRARY AND/OR ARCHIVES: Promotes genealogy and local history.

PROGRAMS: Community Outreach; Exhibits; Lectures; Publication; Research Library/Archives

COLLECTIONS: [18th-20th c] Manuscripts, maps, serials, volumes, photographs and newspapers.

HOURS: Yr T Th 1-9, W F 1-5, Sa 9-5

ADMISSION: No charge

8612
Lynchburg Museum System

901 Court St, 24505 [PO Box 60, 24505]; (p)
(434) 847-1459; (f) (804) 528-0162;
lynchburgmuseum@ci.lynchburg.va.us;
www.lynchburgmuseum.org; (c) City of
Lynchburg

City/ 1976/ staff: 3(f); 7(p); 55(v)

HISTORY MUSEUM; LIVING HISTORY/OUTDOOR MUSEUM: Operates Lynchburg Museum at the Old Court House, built in Classical Revival-style in 1855; and Point of Honor, restored 1815 Federal-style home of Dr. George Cabell.

PROGRAMS: Exhibits; Facility Rental; Family Programs; Festivals; Guided Tours; Interpretation; Living History; Research Library/Archives; School-Based Curriculum

COLLECTIONS: [Prehistoric-present] Furniture, costumes, art, photographs, machinery, decorative arts, archives; Civil War-era, business, and transportation artifacts.

HOURS: Yr Daily 10-4

ADMISSION: $1; Under 12 free

8613
Point of Honor, Inc.

112 Cabell St, 24505 [PO Box 60, 24505]; (p) (434) 847-1459; (f) (804) 528-0162; museum@ci.lynchburg.va.us; www.pointofhonor.org; (c) Lynchburg

Private non-profit/ 1978/ staff: 3(f); 7(p); 55(v)

GARDEN; HOUSE MUSEUM; LIVING HISTORY/OUTDOOR MUSEUM: Restored 1815 Federal-style mansion.

PROGRAMS: Exhibits; Facility Rental; Festivals; Guided Tours; Interpretation; Lectures; Living History; School-Based Curriculum

COLLECTIONS: [Early 19th c] Furniture, costumes, art, decorative arts, and archives.

HOURS: Yr Daily 10-4

ADMISSION: $5, Children $1, Seniors $4.50

8614
Southern Memorial Association

401 Taylor St, 24501; (p) (804) 847-1465; occ@gravegarden.org; www.gravegarden.org

Private non-profit/ 1866/ Board of Community Advisors/ staff: 1(f); 1(p); 50(v)

GARDEN; HISTORIC SITE; HISTORY MUSEUM; LIBRARY AND/OR ARCHIVES; LIVING HISTORY/OUTDOOR MUSEUM; RESEARCH CENTER: Directs educational, historical and horticultural activities of 200 year-old 26-acre Old City Cemetery, Civil War era Pest House Medical Museum, 19th c Mourning Museum, Hearse House, and Caretaker's Museum, and 1898 Station House.

PROGRAMS: Annual Meeting; Community Outreach; Exhibits; Festivals; Garden Tours; Guided Tours; Interpretation; Lectures; Research Library/Archives

COLLECTIONS: [19th c-present] Gravemarkers from 1808, Civil War-era medical instruments, traveling embalming kit, mourning jewelry and clothing, cooling coffin, cast-iron casket, showboxes of beeswax flowers and hairworks, WWI-era artifacts, burial records, photos.

HOURS: Yr Daily dawn-dusk

ADMISSION: No charge

MADISON HEIGHTS

8615
Monacan Indian Nation

2009 Kenmore Rd, 24572 [PO Box 1136, 24572]; (p) (804) 946-0389, (804) 946-5391; (f) (804) 946-0390; mnation538@aol.com; members.tripod.com/monacannation; (c) Amherst

Private non-profit/ staff: 2(f); 2(p)

RESEARCH CENTER; TRIBAL MUSEUM: Preserves Monacan culture.

PROGRAMS: Community Outreach; Festivals; Lectures; School-Based Curriculum

COLLECTIONS: Monacan pottery, baskets, ancestral pictures, artifacts and jewelry.

HOURS: Yr T-Sa 10-4

ADMISSION: Donations accepted

MANASSAS

8616
Manassas Museum System

9101 Prince William St, 20108 [PO Box 560, 20108]; (p) (703) 368-1873; (f) (703) 257-8406; (c) Independent City

City/ 1974/ staff: 6(f); 2(p); 60(v)/ members: 550/publication: *Words From the Junction*

HISTORIC SITE; HISTORY MUSEUM; HOUSE MUSEUM; LIVING HISTORY/OUTDOOR MUSEUM: Protects, preserves and promotes the historic and cultural resources of Manassas and the Northern VA Piedmont.

PROGRAMS: Annual Meeting; Community Outreach; Concerts; Exhibits; Family Programs; Guided Tours; Interpretation; Lectures; Living History; Publication; Research Library/Archives; School-Based Curriculum

COLLECTIONS: [18th-20th c] Artifacts, photographs, negatives, architectural drawings, archaeological items, maps, books and manuscripts.

HOURS: Yr T-Su 10-5

ADMISSION: $3, Student $2, Children $2, Seniors $2; Under 6 free; Group rates

8617
Manassas National Battlefield Park

12521 Lee Highway, 20109-2005; (p) (703) 361-1339, (703) 361-1339; (f) (703) 754-1107; MANA_Superintendent@nps.gov; www.nps.gov/mana/pphtml/contacts.html

1940/ National Park Service

BATTLEFIELD; HISTORIC SITE; HISTORY MUSEUM; NATIONAL PARK: Preserves history of two major Civil War battles.

COLLECTIONS: [Civil War Era] Museum, artifacts, memorabilia.

HOURS: Yr 8:30-5

8618
Prince William County Genealogical Society

Local library, 20108 [PO Box 2019, 20108-0812]; prbobpwcgs@aol.com; www.rootsweb.com/~vapwcgs/pwcgs.htm; (c) Prince William

Private non-profit/ 1980/ staff: 24(v)/ members: 150/publication: *Genealogical Cookbook; Cemetery Guide*

GENEALOGICAL SOCIETY: Provides a forum for genealogical research, education and library facilities to the general public and society members.

PROGRAMS: Annual Meeting; Community Outreach; Exhibits; Family Programs; Festivals; Lectures; Publication; Reenactments; Research Library/Archives

COLLECTIONS: [1731-present] Family histories, biographies, pedigree charts, county and state histories and other assorted genealogical publications.

HOURS: Jan-Nov T, Th 9-3

MARION

8619
Smyth County Historical and Museum Society, Inc.

109 W Strother St, 24354 [PO Box 710, 24354]; (p) (540) 783-7067; (c) Smyth

Private non-profit/ 1961/ staff: 1(p); 1(v)/ members: 135/publication: *Smyth County History, Vol. II*

HISTORICAL SOCIETY: Preserves and promotes county history, presents public programs, operates museum, historic house, law office and satellite sites.

PROGRAMS: Annual Meeting; Community Outreach; Concerts; Exhibits; Lectures; Publication; Research Library/Archives

COLLECTIONS: [1820-1920] Agricultural artifacts, period clothing, Civil War, military and mental health items, photographs, papers, books and genealogy material.

HOURS: Yr W-Th 10-3

ADMISSION: No charge

MASON NECK

8620
Gunston Hall Plantation

10709 Gunston Rd, 22079; (p) (703) 550-9220; (f) (703) 550-9480; historic@gunstonhall.org; www.gunstonhall.org; (c) Fairfax

Private non-profit; State/ 1932/ Board of Regents/Comm of VA/ staff: 20(f); 30(p); 70(v)/ members: 4000

HISTORIC SITE; HOUSE MUSEUM: Restored 18th c home of George Mason, author of the VA Declaration of Rights.

PROGRAMS: Community Outreach; Exhibits; Facility Rental; Family Programs; Film/Video; Garden Tours; Guided Tours; Interpretation; Lectures; Living History; Reenactments; Research Library/Archives; School-Based Curriculum

COLLECTIONS: [18th-19th c] Museum objects, books, manuscripts, and research files relating to George Mason and his family.

HOURS: Yr Daily 9:30-5

ADMISSION: $7, Children $3, Seniors $6, Under 6 free

MATHEWS

8621
Mathews County Historical Society, Inc.

Tompkins Cottage, Brickbat Rd, 23109 [PO Box 855, 23109-0855]; (p) (804) 725-2614; (c) Mathews

Private non-profit/ 1970/ Board of Directors/ staff: 30(v)/ members: 198/publication: *Mathews County Panorama; History and Progress of Mathews County; Tombstones of Nathews County*

HISTORIC PRESERVATION AGENCY; HISTORIC SITE; HOUSE MUSEUM; LIBRARY AND/OR ARCHIVES

PROGRAMS: Annual Meeting; Exhibits; Guided Tours; Publication; Research Library/Archives; School-Based Curriculum

COLLECTIONS: [Early 19th c] Period artifacts, household items, furniture, and clothing.

HOURS: Mar-Oct F-Sa 10-1

ADMISSION: No charge

MCDOWELL

8622
Highland Historical Society
Route 616 N, 24458 [PO Box 63, 24458]; (p) (540) 396-6169; (f) (540) 396-3568; dianpaul@cfw.com; (c) Highland

Private non-profit/ 1984/ Board of Directors/ staff: 12(v)/ members: 190

HISTORIC PRESERVATION AGENCY; HISTORIC SITE; HISTORICAL SOCIETY; HISTORY MUSEUM; LIVING HISTORY/OUTDOOR MUSEUM; RESEARCH CENTER: Restores and preserves historic documents and artifacts.

PROGRAMS: Annual Meeting; Community Outreach; Exhibits; Facility Rental; Family Programs; Festivals; Guided Tours; Interpretation; Lectures; Living History; Publication; Reenactments; Research Library/Archives

COLLECTIONS: [1860s] Maps, genealogical records and documents, Civil War and local history items.

HOURS: Yr M-F 9-5

ADMISSION: No charge

MCLEAN

8623
Arlington House, The Robert E. Lee Memorial
Within Arlington National Cemetery, 22101 [George Washington Memorial Pkwy., Turkey Run Park, 22101]; (p) (703) 557-0613; (f) (703) 557-0613; www.nps.gov/gwmp

Federal/ 1929/ staff: 11(f); 8(p); 15(v)

HISTORIC SITE; HOUSE MUSEUM: Preserves Arlington House, the residence of General Robert E. Lee prior to the Civil War.

PROGRAMS: Community Outreach; Guided Tours; Interpretation; Research Library/Archives

COLLECTIONS: [1802-1861] Original and period furnishings reflect the lifestyle of the occupants of Arlington House and its slave quarters.

HOURS: Yr Daily 9:30-4:30

8624
Claude Moore Colonial Farm at Turkey Run
Colonial Farm Rd, 22101 [6310 Georgetown Pike, 22101]; (p) (703) 442-7557; (f) (703) 442-0714; (c) Fairfax

Private non-profit/ 1973/ Friends of the Claude Moore Colonial Farm at Turkey Run/ staff: 7(f); 400(v)/ members: 700

LIVING HISTORY/OUTDOOR MUSEUM: Portrays family life on a small tenant farm in northern VA during the late colonial period.

PROGRAMS: Exhibits; Facility Rental; Family Programs; Festivals; Interpretation; Living History; Reenactments; School-Based Curriculum

COLLECTIONS: [1770s] Reproduction log farm house and tobacco house; reproduction agricultural and domestic tools.

HOURS: Apr-mid Dec W-Su 10-4:30

ADMISSION: $2, Seniors $1

8625
Virginia Canals and Navigations Society
6826 Rosemont Dr, 22101; (p) (703) 356-4027; organizations.rockbridge.net/canal/

Private non-profit/ 1977/ Board of Directors/ staff: 20(v)/ members: 381/publication: *The Tiller; Historic Virginia River Atlas Series*

PROFESSIONAL ORGANIZATION: Promotes historic canal and river research, exploration, preservation, and parks.

PROGRAMS: Annual Meeting; Exhibits; Festivals; Guided Tours; Publication

COLLECTIONS: [18th-19th c] Canal and river books, photos, research notes.

MECHANICSVILLE

8626
King William County Historical Society, Inc.
4192 Mechanicsville Turnpike, 23111; (p) (804) 779-3666; (c) King William

1973/ Executive Board/ staff: 9(v)/ members: 160/publication: *Bulletin*

HISTORIC SITE; HISTORICAL SOCIETY

PROGRAMS: Publication

COLLECTIONS: [19th-mid 20th c]

MIDDLETOWN

8627
Belle Grove Plantation
336 Belle Grove Rd, 22645 [PO Box 137, 22645]; (p) (540) 869-2028; (f) (540) 869-9638; bellgro@shentel.net; www.bellegrove.org; (c) Frederick

Private non-profit/ 1967/ Belle Grove, Inc/ staff: 5(f); 5(p); 75(v)/ members: 650/publication: *A Guide to the Hite Family Cemetery at Long Meadow; Visitor's Guide to Belle Grove Plantation and others*

HOUSE MUSEUM: Provides the public with guided tours, school programs, special events, self-guided tours, living history interpretive programs, exhibitions, a demonstration garden, public lectures, and a heritage apple orchard.

PROGRAMS: Annual Meeting; Community Outreach; Exhibits; Facility Rental; Festivals; Garden Tours; Guided Tours; Interpretation; Lectures; Living History; Publication; Reenactments; Research Library/Archives; School-Based Curriculum

COLLECTIONS: [Federal period]

HOURS: Apr-Oct M-Sa 10-4, Su 1-5; Nov Sa 10-4, Su 1-5

ADMISSION: $7, Children $3, Seniors $6; Under 7 free

MILLWOOD

8628
Burwell-Morgan Mill
Ste 15 Tannery Ln, 22646 [PO Box 306, Berryville, 22611]; (p) (540) 837-1799; (f) (540) 955-0285; ccha@visuallink.com; www.visuallink.net/ccha; (c) Clarke

Private non-profit/ 1964/ Clarke County Historical Assoc/ staff: 1(p); 6(v)

HISTORIC SITE; HISTORY MUSEUM; LIVING HISTORY/OUTDOOR MUSEUM: Operates 18th c merchant grist mill museum.

PROGRAMS: Community Outreach; Exhibits; Facility Rental; Guided Tours; Interpretation; Living History; Publication; School-Based Curriculum

COLLECTIONS: [18th-20th c] Working wooden-geared 1785 merchant mill with inside waterwheel.

HOURS: Apr-Oct Th-Su 10-5

ADMISSION: $3

8629
Historic Long Branch
830 Long Branch Lane, 22646 [PO Box 241, 22646]; (p) (540) 837-1856; (f) (540) 837-2289; lbranch@mnsinc.com; www. historiclongbranch.com; (c) Clarke

Private non-profit/ 1990/ The Harry Z. Issacs Foundation, Inc./ staff: 5(f); 1(p); 50(v)/publication: *Long Branch, A Plantation House in Clarke County, Virginia*

GARDEN; HISTORIC SITE; HOUSE MUSEUM: Protects the buildings, collections and property as a cultural resource; interprets the history, architecture, decorative arts and gardens.

PROGRAMS: Community Outreach; Exhibits; Facility Rental; Family Programs; Festivals; Film/Video; Garden Tours; Guided Tours; Interpretation; Lectures; Living History; Publication; Reenactments

COLLECTIONS: [18th-19th c] Period furnishing.

HOURS: (Groups) Yr by appt; Apr-Oct Sa-Su 12-4

ADMISSION: $6

MONTEREY

8630
Highland County Chamber of Commerce
S Spruce St, 24465 [Highland Center, 24465]; (p) (540) 468-2550; (f) (540) 468-2551; (c) Highland

Private non-profit/ 1956/ staff: 1(p); 2(v)/ members: 125

HISTORY MUSEUM: Operates local history museum.

PROGRAMS: Guided Tours; Interpretation

COLLECTIONS: [17th c-present] Maple production, Native American artifacts.

HOURS: Yr Daily sunrise-sunset

ADMISSION: Donations accepted

8631
Highland Maple Museum
US 220 S, 24465 [c/o TE Billingsley, PO Box 160, Monterey, 24465]; (c) Highland

Private non-profit/ 1983/ Highland County Chamber of Commerce/ staff: 5(v)

HISTORY MUSEUM: Interprets history of sugar and maple production.

PROGRAMS: Exhibits; Interpretation

COLLECTIONS: [17th c-present] Artifacts of

maple syrup and sugar production.

HOURS: Yr Daily sunrise-sunset

ADMISSION: No charge

MONTPELIER STATION

8632
Montpelier (James Madison's)
11407 Constitution Hwy, 22957 [PO Box 67, 22957]; (p) (540) 672-2728; (f) (540) 672-0411; education@montpelier.org; www. montpelier.org; (c) Orange

Private non-profit/ 1986/ The Montpelier Foundation/ staff: 30(f); 35(p); 100(v)/ members: 2000

HISTORIC SITE; PRESIDENTIAL SITE: Serves as memorial to President James Madison and his wife Dolly.

PROGRAMS: Community Outreach; Exhibits; Facility Rental; Family Programs; Festivals; Garden Tours; Guided Tours; Interpretation; Lectures; School-Based Curriculum

COLLECTIONS: [18th-20th c] Madison artifacts, documents, and archaeological items; Du Pont artifacts and documents.

HOURS: Yr Daily 9:30-5:30

ADMISSION: $9, Seniors $6.50

MONTROSS

8633
Northern Neck of Virginia Historical Society
Courthouse Square, 22524 [PO Box 716, 22524]; (p) (804) 493-8440; (c) Westmoreland

Private non-profit/ 1951/ staff: 3(v)/publication: *Northern Neck of Virginia Historical Magazine*

GENEALOGICAL SOCIETY; HISTORIC PRESERVATION AGENCY; HISTORICAL SOCIETY: Collects, preserves and interprets the history and documents of the local area.

PROGRAMS: Annual Meeting; Publication; Research Library/Archives

COLLECTIONS: [18th-19th c]

HOURS: Yr M-Sa 9-4:30

ADMISSION: No charge

8634
Westmoreland County Museum and Library
24 Courthouse Square, 22520 [PO Box 247, 22520]; (p) (804) 493-8440; (c) Westmoreland

County/ 1941/ Westmoreland County/ staff: 1(f); 1(p)/ members: 200

HISTORY MUSEUM: Library holds genealogy materials.

PROGRAMS: Concerts; Exhibits; Lectures

COLLECTIONS: [Late 19th-early 20th c] Fine arts, textiles, tools, papers and prehistoric to modern artifacts; C.W. Peale painting.

HOURS: Nov-Mar M-Sa 10-4; Apr-Oct M-Sa 10-5

ADMISSION: No charge

MOUNT VERNON

8635
Frank Lloyd Wright's Pope-Leighey House
9000 Richmond Hwy, 22121 [PO Box 37, 22121]; (p) (703) 780-4000; (f) (703) 780-8509; woodlawn@nthp.org; (c) Fairfax

1966/ National Trust for Historic Preservation/ staff: 9(f); 15(p); 10(v)/ members: 225

HOUSE MUSEUM: Preserves Wright-designed home.

PROGRAMS: Exhibits; Facility Rental; Festivals; Guided Tours; Interpretation; Lectures

COLLECTIONS: [Early 1940s] Historic house, Wright-designed furnishing.

HOURS: Mar-Dec Daily 10-4

ADMISSION: $6, Student $5, Children $5, Seniors $5

8636
Mount Vernon Ladies' Association
S end of the George Washington Memorial Hwy, 22121 [PO Box 110, 22121]; (p) (703) 780-2000; (f) (703) 799-8698; www.mountvernon. org; (c) Fairfax

Private non-profit/ 1853/ staff: 134(f); 154(p); 430(v)

HISTORIC SITE; HOUSE MUSEUM; LIVING HISTORY/OUTDOOR MUSEUM; PRESIDENTIAL SITE: Owns and maintains the home of George Washington, Mount Vernon.

PROGRAMS: Community Outreach; Concerts; Elder's Programs; Exhibits; Family Programs; Festivals; Garden Tours; Guided Tours; Interpretation; Lectures; Reenactments; Research Library/Archives; School-Based Curriculum

COLLECTIONS: [18th c] Decorative arts, manuscripts, and books relating to George Washington and his times.

HOURS: Yr Apr-Aug Daily 8-5; Mar, Sept, Oct Daily 9-5; Nov-Feb Daily 9-4

ADMISSION: $9, Children $4.50, Seniors $8.50

8637
Woodlawn
9000 Richmond Hwy, 22121 [PO Box 37, 22121]; (p) (703) 780-4000; (f) (703) 780-8509; woodlawn@nthp.org; (c) Fairfax

Private non-profit/ 1949/ National Trust for Historic Preservation/ staff: 9(f); 60(p); 40(v)/ members: 225

HISTORIC SITE; HOUSE MUSEUM: Preserves former home of Eleanor "Nelly" Custis, granddaughter and ward of Martha and George Washington.

PROGRAMS: Exhibits; Facility Rental; Festivals; Garden Tours; Guided Tours; Interpretation; Lectures; Research Library/Archives

COLLECTIONS: [Early 19th c] Original artifacts, needlework and period textiles.

HOURS: Mar-Dec Daily 10-4

ADMISSION: $6, Student $5, Children $5, Seniors $5

NELSON COUNTY

8638
Oak Ridge Estate
2300 Oak Ridge Rd, 22980; (p) (804) 263-4168; (f) (804) 263-4168

NEW CASTLE

8639
Craig County Historical Society
Main St, 24127 [PO Box 206, 24127]; (c) Craig

Private non-profit/ 1983/ staff: 15(v)/ members: 210/publication: *Our Proud Heritage*

GENEALOGICAL SOCIETY; HISTORICAL SOCIETY; HISTORY MUSEUM; HOUSE MUSEUM: Preserves and restores county history.

PROGRAMS: Annual Meeting; Exhibits; Festivals; Guided Tours; Publication

COLLECTIONS: [19th-20th c] Furniture, vintage clothing, linens, quilts, toys, books, glassware and pictures; items from the Civil War, World Wars I and II.

HOURS: Apr-Nov F 1-4 and by appt

ADMISSION: Donations accepted

NEW MARKET

8640
New Market Battlefield State Historical Park
8895 Collins Dr, 22844 [PO Box 1864, 22844]; (p) (540) 740-3101; (f) (540) 740-3033; nmbshp@shent; www.vmi.edu/museum/ nm; (c) Shenandoah

Private non-profit; State/ 1966/ Virginia Military Institute/ staff: 6(f); 4(p); 6(v)

HISTORIC SITE; HISTORY MUSEUM; HOUSE MUSEUM; LIVING HISTORY/OUTDOOR MUSEUM: Preserves and interprets the military and social history of the Shenandoah Valley.

PROGRAMS: Community Outreach; Exhibits; Facility Rental; Family Programs; Film/Video; Guided Tours; Interpretation; Lectures; Living History; Reenactments; Theatre

COLLECTIONS: [19th c]

HOURS: Yr Daily 9-5

ADMISSION: $5, Student $2, Children $2; Under 6 free

NEWBERN

8641
New River Historical Society/ Wilderness Road Regional Museum
5240 Wilderness Rd, 24126 [PO Box 373, 24126]; (p) (540) 674-4835, (540) 674-0598; (f) (540) 674-1266; wrrm@usit.net; (c) Pulaski

Private non-profit/ 1968/ Board of Directors/ staff: 5(p); 20(v)/ members: 450/publication: *The Journal*

HISTORIC SITE; HISTORICAL SOCIETY: Protects and preserves artifacts, sites and buildings.

PROGRAMS: Annual Meeting; Exhibits; Film/Video; Lectures; Living History; Publication; Research Library/Archives

COLLECTIONS: [1865-1935] Books, magazines and artifacts.

HOURS: Yr M-Sa 10:30-4:30, Su 1:30-4:30

NEWPORT NEWS

8642
Endview Plantation
362 Yorktown Rd, 23603; (p) (757) 887-1862; (f) (757) 888-3369; endview@ci.newport-news.va.us; (c) Independent City

City/ 1996/ staff: 2(f); 25(v)

HISTORIC SITE; LIVING HISTORY/OUTDOOR MUSEUM

PROGRAMS: Elder's Programs; Family Programs; Festivals; Guided Tours; Interpretation; Lectures; Living History; Reenactments; School-Based Curriculum

HOURS: Yr M-Sa 10-4

8643
Lee Hall Mansion
163 Yorktown Rd, 23603; (p) (757) 888-3371; (f) (757) 888-3373; www.leehall.org; (c) Independent City

City/ 1996/ staff: 4(f); 1(p); 20(v)/ members: 325

HISTORIC SITE; HOUSE MUSEUM: Collects, preserves and interprets the history of the house and its role as a Confederate headquarters during the 1862 Peninsula Campaign.

PROGRAMS: Elder's Programs; Exhibits; Facility Rental; Family Programs; Guided Tours; Interpretation; Lectures; Living History; Reenactments; School-Based Curriculum

COLLECTIONS: [1840-1865] Civil War artifacts, antebellum furnishings and decorative arts in a historic house.

HOURS: Yr M-Sa 10-4, Su 1-5

ADMISSION: $5, Children $3, Seniors $4

8644
Mariners' Museum, The
100 Museum Dr, 23606; (p) (757) 596-2222; (f) (757) 591-7320; info@mariner.org; www.mariner.org; (c) Newport News

Private non-profit/ 1930/ staff: 79(f); 46(p); 174(v)/ members: 2500/publication: *Taking the Stars: Celestial Navigation from Argonauts to Astronauts; Titanic: Fortune and Fate;* others

MARITIME MUSEUM: Preserves and interprets maritime history.

PROGRAMS: Community Outreach; Exhibits; Facility Rental; Family Programs; Film/Video; Guided Tours; Lectures; Publication; Research Library/Archives; School-Based Curriculum

COLLECTIONS: [18th-20th c] Paintings, ship models, boats, scrimshaw, figureheads; books, photos.

HOURS: Yr Daily 10-5

ADMISSION: $6, Student $4; Under 5 free

8645
Newsome House Museum and Cultural Center
2803 Oak Ave, 23607; (p) (757) 247-2360; (f) (757) 928-6754; mkayasel@ci.newport-news.va.us; www.newsomehouse.org

City/ 1991/ staff: 1(f); 3(p); 3(v)/ members:

60/publication: *A Life in Newport News: An Oral History of Inettie Banks Edwards*

ART MUSEUM; HISTORIC SITE; HISTORY MUSEUM; HOUSE MUSEUM; RESEARCH CENTER: Preserves former home of Joseph Thomas Newsome family, prominent black attorney and journalist.

PROGRAMS: Annual Meeting; Community Outreach; Elder's Programs; Exhibits; Facility Rental; Family Programs; Guided Tours; Interpretation; Lectures; Living History; Publication; Research Library/Archives; School-Based Curriculum

COLLECTIONS: [1869-1942] Personal effects, archival items and rare books pertaining to local black history.

HOURS: Yr M-Sa 10-4

ADMISSION: No charge

8646
Peninsula Jewish Historical Society
2700 Spring Rd, 23601 [25 Stratford Rd, 23601]; (p) (804) 435-0737; rena@crosslink.net

Private non-profit/ 1986/ staff: 10(v)/ members: 75

HISTORIC PRESERVATION AGENCY; HISTORICAL SOCIETY: Preserves and documents the Jewish history of the VA Peninsula.

PROGRAMS: Annual Meeting; Exhibits; Lectures

COLLECTIONS: [Late 19th c-present] Photos, newspaper clippings, artifacts, books, minutes of meetings and histories of conventions.

HOURS: Yr M-F 9-4

ADMISSION: No charge

NEWSOMS

8647
Southampton County Historical Society
33335 Statesville Rd, 23874; (p) (757) 654-6785; www.fastrus.com/~cliff/; (c) Southampton

Private non-profit/ 1964/ members: 300

HISTORIC SITE; HISTORICAL SOCIETY; HOUSE MUSEUM: Preserves local history, maintains 1835 Rochelle-Prince House and Southampton Agriculture and Forestry Museum.

PROGRAMS: Exhibits; Family Programs; Festivals; Guided Tours; Interpretation; Lectures; Reenactments; Research Library/Archives; School-Based Curriculum

COLLECTIONS: [18th-20th c] Agricultural and local history artifacts.

HOURS: Rochelle-Prince House: Mar-Nov 1st and 3rd Su 2-4; Agricultural and Forestry Museum: Mar-Nov W, Sa-Su 1-5

ADMISSION: $1; Price is for Museum; House free

NORFOLK

8648
Adam Thoroughgood House
1636 Parish Rd, 23510 [245 W. Olney Rd., 23510]; (p) (757) 664-6283; (f) (757) 460-9415; www.chrysler.org

Private non-profit/ Chrysler Museum of Art/ staff: 3(f); 10(p); 5(v)/ members: 250

HOUSE MUSEUM

PROGRAMS: Community Outreach; Garden Tours; Guided Tours; Interpretation; Lectures; Living History; School-Based Curriculum

COLLECTIONS: [17th-18thc] English furniture.

HOURS: Yr Sa 10-5, Su 1-5

ADMISSION: $4, Seniors $2.50

8649
Hampton Roads Museum
1 Waterside Dr, Ste 248, 23510; (p) (757) 322-2987; (f) (757) 322-1867; bapoulliot@nsn.cmar.navy.mil; www.hrnm.navy.mil

Federal/ 1979/ US Navy, Federal/ staff: 20(f); 10(p); 130(v)/publication: *The Daybook*

HISTORY MUSEUM: Displays two centuries of naval activities in and around the harbor of Hampton Roads from the Battle off the Capes to the present Navy. Home of the battleship "Wisconsin".

PROGRAMS: Annual Meeting; Community Outreach; Elder's Programs; Exhibits; Film/Video; Guided Tours; Interpretation; Lectures; Living History; Publication; Reenactments; Research Library/Archives; School-Based Curriculum

COLLECTIONS: [19th-20th c] Naval artifacts and artworks; ship and aircraft models, weaponry; underwater archaeological artifacts; naval uniforms; historic battles 'Wisconsin" with accompanying exhibit; audio-visual displays; photographs.

HOURS: Yr Sept-May T-Sa 10-5, Su 12-5; May Sept Daily 10-6

ADMISSION: No charge

8650
Hermitage Foundation Museum
7637 N Shore Rd, 23505 [7637 N Shore Road, 23505]; (p) (757) 423-2052; (f) (757) 423-1604

1908/ Private non-profit/ staff: 3(f); 14(p)

HOURS: Yr

8651
Hunter House Victorian Museum
240 W Freemason Ct, 23510; (p) (757) 623-9814; (f) (757) 623-0097

Private non-profit/ 1988/ Hunter Foundation/ staff: 1(f); 30(v)

HOUSE MUSEUM: Interprets Victorian lifestyle based upon the 1894 Richardsonian Romanesque home of James Wilson Hunter.

PROGRAMS: Exhibits; Family Programs; Guided Tours; Interpretation; Lectures; Living History; Reenactments; School-Based Curriculum; Theatre

COLLECTIONS: [Early 20th c] Victorian architecture, furnishings, decorative arts and medical memorabilia.

HOURS: Apr-Dec W-Sa 10-3:30, Su 12:30-3:30

ADMISSION: $3, Children $1, Seniors $2

8652
MacArthur Memorial
Bank St & City Hall Ave, 23510 [MacArthur Square, 23510]; (p) (757) 441-2965; (f) (757) 441-5389; macmen@norfolk.infi.net; www.whro.org/cl/mac; (c) Independent City

City/ 1964/ General Douglas MacArthur Foundation/ staff: 11(f); 7(p); 25(v)/ members: 750/publication: *MacArthur Report*

HISTORIC SITE; HISTORY MUSEUM; RESEARCH CENTER: Collects, preserves and interprets the life and times of General Douglas MacArthur.

PROGRAMS: Community Outreach; Elder's Programs; Exhibits; Film/Video; Guided Tours; Lectures; Publication; Research Library/Archives; School-Based Curriculum

COLLECTIONS: [1861-1964] World, US and military history from Civil War to Korean War time period. Books, photos, correspondence items, reports, messages, flags, weapons and Asian art objects.

HOURS: Yr M-Sa 10-5, Su 11-5

ADMISSION: No charge

8653
Nauticus, The National Maritime Center
1 Waterside Dr, 23510; (p) (800) 664-1080; (f) (757) 623-1287; rconti@city.norfolk.va.us; www.nauticus.org

City/ 1994/ staff: 30(f); 40(p); 60(v)/ members: 1000/publication: *Signals*

HISTORIC SITE; MARITIME MUSEUM: Science center with a maritime theme.

PROGRAMS: Community Outreach; Concerts; Elder's Programs; Exhibits; Facility Rental; Family Programs; Film/Video; Interpretation; Lectures; Publication; School-Based Curriculum; Theatre

HOURS: Mem-Labor Day Daily 10-5; Labor-Mem Day T-Sa 10-5, Su 12-5

ADMISSION: $7.50, Children $5

8654
Norfolk Historical Society
810 Front St, 23508 [PO Box 6367, 23508]; (p) (757) 625-1720

Private non-profit/ 1965/ members: 410/publication: *Fort Norfolk Courier*

HISTORIC SITE; HISTORICAL SOCIETY; LIVING HISTORY/OUTDOOR MUSEUM

PROGRAMS: Annual Meeting; Community Outreach; Concerts; Exhibits; Facility Rental; Family Programs; Festivals; Interpretation; Lectures; Living History; Publication; Reenactments; Research Library/Archives; School-Based Curriculum

COLLECTIONS: [18th-early 20th c]

HOURS: Apr-Oct by appt

ADMISSION: $2, Family $5; Group rates

8655
Ohef Sholom Temple Archives
530 Raleigh Ave, 23507; (p) (757) 625-4295; (f) (757) 625-3762; ohef2@exis.net; www.shamash.org/reform/uahc/congsluu/uaoo3

Private non-profit/ 1844/ Ohef Sholom Temple, Archives Committee/ staff: 1(p); 6(v)

LIBRARY AND/OR ARCHIVES: Provides research information on the history of Norfolk Jewry.

PROGRAMS: Community Outreach; Exhibits; Guided Tours; Lectures; Research Library/Archives

COLLECTIONS: [1850s-present] Rare books, photographs, documents and textiles.

HOURS: Yr M-F 9-5

8656
Willoughby-Baylor House and Moses Myers House
331 Bank St, 23510 [245 W Olney Rd, 23510]; (p) (757) 664-6283, (757) 664-6195; (f) (757) 441-2329; www.chrysler.org

Private non-profit/ Chrysler Museum of Art/ staff: 3(f); 10(p); 5(v)/ members: 250

HOUSE MUSEUM: Interprets historic site and collections.

PROGRAMS: Community Outreach; Family Programs; Garden Tours; Guided Tours; Interpretation; Lectures; Living History; School-Based Curriculum

COLLECTIONS: [1792-1820] Paintings by Thomas Sully, Gilbert Stuart and John Wesley Jarvis; original glass, silver and furniture; 900 pieces of early 19th century music; Federal furnishings and restored garden.

HOURS: Yr T-Sa 10-5, Su 1-5

ADMISSION: $4, Student $2, Seniors $2

OCCOQUAN

8657
Occoquan Mill House Museum
413 Mill St, 22125; (p) (703) 491-7525

ONANCOCK

8658
Kerr Place, Historic House Museum
69 Market St, 23417 [PO Box 193, 23417]; (p) (757) 787-8012; (f) (757) 787-3309; kerr@esva.net; (c) Accomack

Private non-profit/ 1957/ Eastern Shore of VA Historical Society/ staff: 3(f); 3(p); 31(v)/ members: 1000

GARDEN; HISTORIC SITE; HISTORICAL SOCIETY; HISTORY MUSEUM; HOUSE MUSEUM: Encourages and promotes the study of local history;. Interprets VA history with emphasis on eastern shore.

PROGRAMS: Annual Meeting; Community Outreach; Elder's Programs; Exhibits; Facility Rental; Family Programs; Festivals; Garden Tours; Guided Tours; Interpretation; Lectures; Reenactments; Research Library/Archives

COLLECTIONS: [18th c-present] Furnishings, decorative arts, books, letters, Bibles, photographs, and architectural objects. Maritime collection includes 45 foot log canoe and tools used in local fishing industry.

HOURS: Mar-Dec T-Sa 10-4

ADMISSION: $4; Children free

ORANGE

8659
James Madison Museum
129 Caroline St, 22960; (p) (540) 672-1776; (f) (540) 672-5366; jmmuseum@ns.gemlink.com; www.gemlink.com/~jmmuseum/; (c) Orange

Private non-profit/ 1976/ staff: 1(f); 25(v)/ members: 250

HISTORY MUSEUM: Collects and preserves artifacts and cultural heritage of 18th to 19th century Virginia; interprets life of James Madison.

PROGRAMS: Annual Meeting; Exhibits

COLLECTIONS: [18th-20th c] Books, documents, textiles, clothing, furniture, tools, dishes, houseware, agricultural items and two-story 1733 patent house.

HOURS: Yr M-F 9-4; Mar-Nov Sa 9-1, Su 1-4; Dec-Feb closed Sa-Su

ADMISSION: $4, Children $1, Seniors $3

PALMYRA

8660
Fluvanna County Historical Society
Court Square, 22963 [PO Box 8, 22963]; (p) (804) 589-1111; (f) (804) 589-1780; (c) Fluvanna

Private non-profit/ 1964/ Executive Board/ staff: 1(p); 25(v)/ members: 700/publication: *The Bulletin*

HISTORICAL SOCIETY; HISTORY MUSEUM; RESEARCH CENTER: Collects, preserves and exhibits county memorabilia.

PROGRAMS: Annual Meeting; Community Outreach; Exhibits; Film/Video; Guided Tours; Publication; Research Library/Archives

COLLECTIONS: [19th-20th c] County memorabilia, military artifacts, early agricultural implements, clothing, documents, photographs, journals and ledgers.

HOURS: June-Sept Sa-Su 1-5

8661
Old Stone Jail Museum
Court Square, 22963 [Rt 2, Box 1035, 22963]; (p) (804) 842-3378; (f) (804) 842-3374; bmiyagawa@compuserve.com; (c) Fluvanna

Private non-profit/ 1963/ Fluvanna County Historical Society/ staff: 1(p); 8(v)/ members: 607/publication: *The Bulletin*

HISTORICAL SOCIETY; HISTORY MUSEUM; RESEARCH CENTER

PROGRAMS: Annual Meeting; Exhibits; Guided Tours; Interpretation; Lectures; Publication; Research Library/Archives

COLLECTIONS: [1860-1920] Farm implements, county and military artifacts.

HOURS: June-Sept Sa 1-5, Su 2-5

ADMISSION: Donations accepted

PEARLSBURG

8662
Giles County Historical Society
208 N Main St, 24134 [PO Box 404, 24134]; (p) (540) 921-1050; gileschs@i-t.net; (c) Giles

Private non-profit/ 1980/ staff: 4(p); 20(v)/ members: 130

GENEALOGICAL SOCIETY; HISTORIC PRESERVATION AGENCY; HISTORIC SITE; HISTORICAL SOCIETY; HISTORY MUSEUM; HOUSE MUSEUM; RESEARCH CENTER: Promotes the appreciation of American heritage through the 1829 Andrew Johnson House, the Giles County Historical Museum and Research Center.

PROGRAMS: Annual Meeting; Community Outreach; Exhibits; Guided Tours; Interpretation; Publication; Research Library/Archives

COLLECTIONS: [1830-1930] Original furniture, 1850s doctors office, doll collection of period costumes, local history artifacts, Meissen China.

HOURS: Yr W-F 12-5, Sa-Su 2-5

ADMISSION: No charge

PETERSBURG

8663
Historic Petersburg Foundation, Inc.
420 Grove Ave, 23804 [PO Box 691, 23804-0691]; (p) (804) 732-2096; (f) (804) 733-0867; www.historicpetersburg.org

Private non-profit/ 1967/ staff: 1(f); 35(v)/ members: 450/publication: *Appomattox: River Sea Stories*

HISTORIC PRESERVATION AGENCY; HISTORICAL SOCIETY: Promotes historic and architectural preservation.

PROGRAMS: Annual Meeting; Guided Tours; Lectures; Publication

HOURS: Yr M-F 8:30-4:30

8664
Pamplin Historical Park and the National Museum of the Civil War Soldier
6125 Boydton Plank Rd, 23803; (p) (804) 861-2408; (f) (804) 861-2820; pamplinpark@mindspring.com; www.pamplinpark.org; (c) Dinwiddie

Private non-profit/ 1995/ R. B. Pamplin Foundation/ staff: 39(f); 19(p)

HISTORIC SITE; HOUSE MUSEUM; LIVING HISTORY/OUTDOOR MUSEUM: Operates the National Museum of the Civil War Soldier; preserves and interprets a Civil War battlefield, original Civil War earthworks, and an antebellum farmhouse "Tudor Hall."

PROGRAMS: Exhibits; Family Programs; Film/Video; Guided Tours; Interpretation; Lectures; Living History; Reenactments

COLLECTIONS: [Mid-late 19th c] Civil War artifacts: uniforms, arms, equipment and personal items; historic furnishings and housewares.

HOURS: Yr Daily 9-5

ADMISSION: $10, Children $5

8665
Petersburg Museums
15 W Bank St, 23803; (p) (804) 733-2402; (f) (804) 863-0837; ssavery@techcom.net; www.petersburg-va.org

City/ 1972/ staff: 7(f); 40(p)/publication: *African-American Sites in Petersburg; Walking Tours of Petersburg*

GARDEN; HISTORIC SITE; HISTORY MUSEUM; HOUSE MUSEUM: Collects, preserves and interprets the history of Petersburg and its surrounding region.

PROGRAMS: Community Outreach; Concerts; Elder's Programs; Exhibits; Facility Rental; Family Programs; Festivals; Film/Video; Guided Tours; Interpretation; Lectures; Living History; Publication; Reenactments; Research Library/Archives; School-Based Curriculum

COLLECTIONS: [18th-20th c] Artifacts, photos, books, manuscripts and Louis C. Tiffany windows.

HOURS: Yr Daily 9-4

ADMISSION: $3, Students $2, Seniors $2

8666
Petersburg National Battlefield
Hwy 36, 23803 [1539 Hickory Hill Rd, 23803]; (p) (804) 732-3531; (f) (804) 732-0835; (c) City of Petersburg

Federal/ 1926/ Dept of the Interior, National Park Service/ staff: 36(f); 20(p); 2(v)

HISTORIC SITE; HISTORY MUSEUM; LIVING HISTORY/OUTDOOR MUSEUM: Commemorates the campaign and siege of Petersburg, June 1864-April 1865.

PROGRAMS: Exhibits; Interpretation; Living History

COLLECTIONS: [1864-1865] Guns, cannons and uniforms.

HOURS: Yr Daily 8-5

ADMISSION: $5; $10/vehicle

POCAHONTAS

8667
Pocahontas Exhibition Coal Mine and Museum
Rte 659, 24635 [PO Box 128, 24635]; (p) (540) 945-2134; (f) (540) 945-9904; wvweb.com/www/pocahontas-mine; (c) Tazewell

City/ 1882/ staff: 4(f); 4(v)

HISTORIC SITE; HISTORY MUSEUM: Preserves lifestyles of early coal miners.

PROGRAMS: Annual Meeting; Exhibits; Facility Rental; Guided Tours

COLLECTIONS: [1880-1930s] Mining artifacts.

HOURS: Apr-Oct M-Sa 10-5, Su 12-5

ADMISSION: $6, Children $3.50; Group rates

PORTSMOUTH

8668
Lightship 101 Portsmouth
Water St at London Slip, 23705 [PO Box 248, 23705-0248]; (p) (757) 393-8741; (f) (757) 393-5244

City/ 1967/ staff: 3(f)

MARITIME MUSEUM: Restored 1915 Lightship.

PROGRAMS: Exhibits; Guided Tours; Interpretation

COLLECTIONS: [1915-1967]

HOURS: Yr T-Sa 10-5, Su 1-5

ADMISSION: $1

8669
Museum of Military History, Inc.
701 Court St, 23704; (p) (757) 393-2773; (f) (757) 393-2883; (c) Portsmouth

Private for-profit/ 1998/ Board of Directors/Staff/ staff: 3(f); 2(p); 3(v)/publication: *The Victory Garden*

HISTORY MUSEUM: Collects and displays US military heritage.

PROGRAMS: Annual Meeting; Community Outreach; Concerts; Exhibits; Facility Rental; Festivals; Film/Video; Guided Tours; Lectures; Living History; Publication; Reenactments

COLLECTIONS: [1770s-present] Uniforms, swords, guns, medals, photographs, personal belongings, equipment, cannons, portraits, prints, flags, models, vehicles, personal letters, and histories.

HOURS: Spring-Fall W-M 10-5; Winter Th-Sa 10-5, Su 12-5

ADMISSION: $5, Seniors $4

8670
Portsmouth Historical Association, Inc.
The Hill House, 220 N St, 23704 [221 N St, 23704]; (p) (757) 393-0241

Private non-profit/ 1955/ staff: 3(p); 25(v)/ members: 290

HOUSE MUSEUM: Preserves history of Portsmouth; operates Hill House.

PROGRAMS: Annual Meeting; Exhibits; Garden Tours; Guided Tours; Interpretation

COLLECTIONS: [1830-1960] Original furnishing, paintings, oriental rugs, china and glass.

HOURS: Apr-Dec W 12:30-4:30, Sa-Su 1-5

ADMISSION: $2; Members free

8671
Portsmouth Naval Shipyard Museum
2 High St, 23705 [PO Box 248, 23705-0248]; (p) (757) 393-8591; (f) (757) 393-5244

City/ 1949/ staff: 3(f); 100(v)/ members: 306

HISTORY MUSEUM: Preserves the history of Portsmouth and Norfolk Naval Shipyard.

PROGRAMS: Annual Meeting; Exhibits; Guided Tours; Interpretation; Research Library/Archives

COLLECTIONS: [1776-present] Model of Portsmouth in 1776, Norfolk Naval Shipyard, ship models, uniforms, ordnance, maps, photos and paintings.

HOURS: Yr T-Sa 10-5, Su 1-5

ADMISSION: $1

8672
Virginia Sports Hall of Fame and Museum
420 High St, 23705 [PO Box 370, 23705]; (p) (757) 393-8031; (f) (757) 393-5228; webbe@portsmouth.va.us

Private non-profit/ 1966/ staff: 3(f); 1(p); 30(v)/ members: 1000/publication: *The Sports Page*

HISTORY MUSEUM: Promotes sporting history.

PROGRAMS: Annual Meeting; Exhibits; Facility Rental; Publication

COLLECTIONS: [20th c] Sports memorabilia.

HOURS: Yr T-Sa 10-5, Su 1-5

ADMISSION: No charge

POWHATAN

8673
Powhatan County Historical Society
Old Jail behind Courthouse, Route 13, 23139 [PO Box 562, 23139]; (p) (804) 598-1139; (c) Powhatan

Private non-profit/ 1975/ staff: 12(v)/ members: 235

HISTORICAL SOCIETY: Preserves county history.

PROGRAMS: Annual Meeting; Community Outreach; Exhibits; Guided Tours; Lectures

COLLECTIONS: [1776-present] Local and state history books, genealogy files.

HOURS: Yr by appt

ADMISSION: No charge

QUANTICO

8674
Marine Corps Air Ground Museum
Elrod Ave, 22134 [2014 Anderson Ave, 22134-5002]; (p) (703) 784-2606, (703) 784-2607; (f) (703) 784-5856; (c) Prince William

Federal/ 1961/ US Marine Corps/ staff: 16(f)

HISTORY MUSEUM

PROGRAMS: Exhibits

COLLECTIONS: [1900-present]

HOURS: Apr-mid Nov T-Su 10-5

ADMISSION: No charge

RADFORD

8675
Appalachian Regional Studies Center
Buchanan House, Radford Univ, 24142 [PO Box 7014, Radford Univ, 24142]; (p) (540) 831-5366; (f) (540) 831-5004; gedwards@ radford.edu; www.radford.edu/~arsc; (c) Radford City

Joint/ 1994/ Radford Univ; State/ staff: 2(f); 5(p); 1(v)/publication: *ALCA-Lines; Stitches*

RESEARCH CENTER: Maintains resources of Appalachian mountain region culture.

PROGRAMS: Community Outreach; Concerts; Festivals; Lectures; Publication; Research Library/Archives

COLLECTIONS: [1920-present] Books, archived folklife interviews, video and audio tapes.

HOURS: Yr M-F 8-12/1-5

RANDOLPH

8676
Staunton River Battlefield State Park
1035 Fort Hill Trail, 23962; (p) (804) 454-4312; (f) (804) 454-4313; www.state.va.us/~dcr/; (c) Halifax/Charlotte

State/ 1995/ VA Dept of Conservation and Recreation/ staff: 2(f); 6(p); 30(v)

HISTORY MUSEUM: Preserves, protects, and interprets historical, cultural, natural, and recreational resources.

PROGRAMS: Community Outreach; Exhibits; Family Programs; Interpretation; Living History; Reenactments

COLLECTIONS: [Prehistory-late 19th c] Artifacts: Civil War and Native Americans.

HOURS: Mid Feb-Apr, Oct-mid Dec W-F 9-4, Su 1-4; May-Sept M-Sa 9-4:30, Su 1-4:30

ADMISSION: No charge

REEDVILLE

8677
Reedville Fishermen's Museum
504 Main St, 22539 [PO Box 305, 22539]; (p) (804) 453-6529; bunker@crosslink.net; www.rfmuseum.com; (c) Northumberland

Private non-profit/ 1987/ Greater Reedville Assoc, Inc./ staff: 1(f); 1(p); 150(v)/ members: 633

HISTORY MUSEUM: Preserves history and artifacts of the Lower Chesapeake Bay fishing industry.

PROGRAMS: Exhibits; Family Programs; Festivals; Guided Tours; Interpretation; Lectures; Research Library/Archives

COLLECTIONS: [1870-present] Photos, fishing artifacts; Site: Walker House-1875 fisherman's home.

HOURS: Mar-Apr Sa-Su 10:30-4:30; May-Oct Daily 10:30-4:30; Nov-Dec F-M 10:30-4:30

ADMISSION: $2; Under 13 free

RESTON

8678
Reston Historic Trust for Community Revitalization
1639 Washington Plaza, 20195 [PO Box 2803, 20195]; (p) (703) 709-7700; (f) (703) 709-6668; www.resttonmuseum.org; (c) Fairfax

Private non-profit/ 1997/ staff: 1(f); 2(p); 20(v)

HISTORIC SITE; HISTORY MUSEUM: Operates the Reston Storefront Museum; collects, researches and interprets American suburban history and promotes community revitalization.

PROGRAMS: Community Outreach; Concerts; Exhibits; Family Programs; Festivals; Guided Tours; Interpretation; Lectures; School-Based Curriculum

COLLECTIONS: [1961-present] Photos, documents, maps, advertisements, posters, architectural models, oral history transcripts and artifacts pertaining to Reston.

HOURS: Yr W-F 12-6, Sa 10-6, Su 12-6

ADMISSION: No charge

RICHMOND

8679
Agecroft Association
4305 Sulgrave Rd, 23221; (p) (804) 353-4241; (f) (804) 353-2151; www.agecrofthall.com

Private non-profit/ 1969/ staff: 9(f); 19(p); 2(v)

GARDEN; HOUSE MUSEUM: Preserves historic home.

PROGRAMS: Community Outreach; Concerts; Exhibits; Garden Tours; Guided Tours; Interpretation; Lectures; Living History; School-Based Curriculum; Theatre

COLLECTIONS: [16th-17th c] English furnishings and paintings, textiles, armor, and musical instruments.

HOURS: Yr T-Sa 10-4, Su 12:30-5

ADMISSION: $5, Student

8680
Allen E. Roberts Masonic Library and Museum, Inc. (Grand Lodge of Virginia AF&AM)
4115 Nine Mile Rd, 23223-4926; (p) (804) 222-3110; (f) (804) 222-4253; glofVa@erol.com; glva@web-span.com; (c) Henrico

Private non-profit/ 1994/ Board of Directors/ staff: 1(p); 1(v)/publication: *The Virginia Masonic Herald*

HISTORY MUSEUM; RESEARCH CENTER: Collects, preserves, and interprets the history of Freemasonry in VA.

PROGRAMS: Guided Tours; Publication; Research Library/Archives

COLLECTIONS: [1778-present] 8000 volumes, 300 serials, 100 reels of microfilm, 500 manuscripts, 235 portraits, prints, photos, and artifacts.

HOURS: Yr M W F 9-4

8681
Archeological Society of Virginia
3914 Forestford Rd, 23255 [PO Box 70395, 23255-0395]; (p) (804) 273-9291; (f) (804) 273-0885; www.archsocva.org; (c) Richmond City

Private non-profit/ 1940/ staff: 100(v)/ members: 800

HISTORICAL SOCIETY: Preserves and studies historic and prehistoric sites.

PROGRAMS: Annual Meeting; Community Outreach; Exhibits; Lectures; Publication

COLLECTIONS: [Prehistory and Colonial Virginia]

8682
Association for the Preservation of Virginia Antiquities (APVA)
204 W Franklin St, 23220; (p) (804) 648-1889; (f) (804) 775-0802; kostelny@apva.org; www.apva.org

Private non-profit/ 1889/ Board of Trustees/ staff: 18(f); 120(p); 200(v)/ members: 4000

HISTORIC PRESERVATION AGENCY: Owns and manages thirty-four historic sites in VA.

PROGRAMS: Annual Meeting; Exhibits; Facility Rental; Guided Tours; Lectures; Living History; Publication

COLLECTIONS: [17th-early 19th c] 5,000 decorative art objects and furnishings; 200,000

8683
Beth Ahabah Museum and Archives
1109 W Franklin St, 23220; (p) (804) 353-2668; (f) (804) 358-3451

Private non-profit/ Congregation Beth Ahabah Museum and Archives Trust/ staff: 3(p)

HISTORIC PRESERVATION AGENCY; HISTORY MUSEUM: Collects, preserves, interprets, and exhibits Jewish history and culture in Richmond, VA and the South.

PROGRAMS: Guided Tours; Interpretation; Lectures; Research Library/Archives

COLLECTIONS: [19th-20th c] Judaica (ritual objects, books, and textiles) and documents, photographs, objects.

HOURS: Yr Su-Th 10-3

ADMISSION: Donations accepted

8684
Black History Museum and Cultural Center of Virginia

00 Clay St, 23286 [PO Box 60152, 23286-9187]; (p) (804) 780-9093; (f) (804) 780-9107; Blackhist1@aol.com; members.spree.com/education/bhmv

Private non-profit/ 1981/ Board of Trustees/ staff: 1(f); 6(p); 100(v)/ members: 158

HISTORY MUSEUM: Collects, displays, and preserves artifacts and oral and written records of African Americans in VA.

PROGRAMS: Community Outreach; Concerts; Exhibits; Facility Rental; Festivals; Guided Tours; Lectures; Reenactments

COLLECTIONS: [Slavery-present] African and African American memorabilia.

HOURS: Yr T-Sa 11-4

ADMISSION: $2, Children $1, Students $1, Seniors $1

8685
Chippokes Farm and Forestry Museum

695 Chippokes Park Rd, 23219 [203 Governor St, 23219]; (p) (804) 786-7950; (f) (804) 371-8500; krw@dcr.state.va.us; (c) Surry

State/ 1990/ Chippokes Plantation Farm Foundation/ staff: 1(f); 6(p); 50(v)

HISTORY MUSEUM: Preserves history of rural VA.

PROGRAMS: Exhibits; Festivals; Guided Tours; Interpretation; School-Based Curriculum

COLLECTIONS: [1850-1930] Antique farm and forestry equipment, tools and housewares.

HOURS: Spring Sa-Su 10-4; Summer W-Su 10-6; Fall Sa-Su 1-4

ADMISSION: $2, Children $1; Group rates

8686
Elegba Folklore Society, Inc.

101 E Broad St, 23219; (p) (804) 644-3900; (f) (804) 644-3919; (c) Independent City

Private non-profit/ 1990/ Board of Directors/ staff: 2(f); 20(p); 50(v)/ members: 25

ART MUSEUM; CULTURAL CENTER

PROGRAMS: Community Outreach; Concerts; Exhibits; Facility Rental; Family Programs; Festivals; Guided Tours; Interpretation; School-Based Curriculum; Theatre

COLLECTIONS: African and Central American artifacts and folk art.

HOURS: Yr M-F 10-6, Sa 9-5 and by appt

ADMISSION: Donations accepted

8687
Henrico County Historical Society

1590 E Parham Rd, 23273 [PO Box 27032, 23273]; (p) (804) 501-5682; (c) Henrico

Private non-profit/ 1975/ Executive Board/ staff: 30(v)/ members: 285

HISTORICAL SOCIETY: Preserves and perpetuates county heritage.

PROGRAMS: Annual Meeting; Festivals; Guided Tours; Lectures; Publication

COLLECTIONS: [18th-20th c] Local history books.

ADMISSION: No charge

8688
Henrico Historic Preservation/Museum Services

8600 Dixon Powers Dr, 23273 [PO Box 27032, 23273]; (p) (804) 501-5124; (f) (804) 501-5284; gre@co.henrico.va.us; (c) Henrico County/ 1981/ staff: 6(f); 5(p); 30(v)

ART MUSEUM; HISTORIC PRESERVATION AGENCY; HISTORIC SITE; HISTORY MUSEUM; HOUSE MUSEUM; LIVING HISTORY/OUTDOOR MUSEUM; RESEARCH CENTER: Identifies, interprets, protects, restores and pursues historic and cultural resources in Henrico County.

PROGRAMS: Community Outreach; Concerts; Exhibits; Facility Rental; Family Programs; Festivals; Guided Tours; Interpretation; Lectures; Living History; Reenactments; Research Library/Archives; School-Based Curriculum

COLLECTIONS: [Prehistory-20th c] Furniture, prints, paintings, military uniforms, clothing, manuscripts, archaeological artifacts, agricultural tools and machinery; regional folk art and archival materials: maps, account books and correspondence.

HOURS: Mid Jan-Feb Sa-Su 12-4; Mar-Dec T-Su 12-4

ADMISSION: No charge

8689
Historic Richmond Foundation

707 A E Franklin St, 23219; (p) (804) 643-7407; (f) (804) 788-4244; hisrich@erols.com; www.historicrichmond.com; (c) Henrico

Private non-profit/ 1956/ staff: 5(f); 1(p)/ members: 1200

HISTORIC PRESERVATION AGENCY: Serves as a temporary steward of local historic properties until a permanent owner is identified.

PROGRAMS: Annual Meeting; Festivals; Garden Tours; Guided Tours; Interpretation; Lectures

COLLECTIONS: [18th-early 20th c]

HOURS: Yr Daily

ADMISSION: $16; Group rates

8690
John Marshall House Museum

818 E Marshall St, 23219; (p) (804) 648-7998; (f) (804) 775-0802; JMHAPVA@AOL.COM; www.apva.org; (c) Richmond

Private non-profit/ 1913/ Assn for the Preservation of VA Antiquities/ staff: 1(f); 2(p); 5(v)

HOUSE MUSEUM: Preserves and promotes the life and contributions of John Marshall to the formation of the new Federal government and Constitution law.

PROGRAMS: Community Outreach; Elder's Programs; Exhibits; Guided Tours; Interpretation; Lectures; Living History; Research Library/Archives

COLLECTIONS: [Late 18th-early 19 c] Marshall family furnishings and memorabilia in

America: locally made furniture, Marshall's Supreme Court robes and personal objects.

HOURS: Yr T-Sa 10-4:30

ADMISSION: $5, Students $3, Seniors $4

8691
Library of Virginia

800 E Broad St, 23219-8000; (p) (804) 692-3500; (f) (804) 692-3594; www.lva.lib.va.us/; (c) Independent City

State/ 1823/ staff: 175(f); 52(p); 26(v)/publication: Virginia Cavalcade

LIBRARY AND/OR ARCHIVES: Collects and preserves the documentary history and heritage of VA.

PROGRAMS: Elder's Programs; Exhibits; Facility Rental; Guided Tours; Lectures; Publication; Research Library/Archives

COLLECTIONS: [1607-present] Books and monographs.

HOURS: Yr M-Sa 9-5

ADMISSION: No charge

8692
Maggie L. Walker National Historic Site

110 1/2 E Leigh St, 23223 [3215 E Broad St, 23223]; (p) (804) 771-2017; (f) (804) 771-2226; mawa_interpreation@nps.gov; www.nps.gov/malw; (c) Richmond City

Federal/ 1978/ National Park Service/ staff: 4(f); 6(v)

HISTORIC SITE: Interprets the life and professional accomplishments of Maggie L. Walker.

PROGRAMS: Community Outreach; Exhibits; Film/Video; Guided Tours; Interpretation; Lectures; Living History; Research Library/Archives; School-Based Curriculum

COLLECTIONS: [1867-1934] Personal artifacts, furnishings.

HOURS: Yr W-Su 9-5

ADMISSION: No charge

8693
Maymont Foundation

1700 Hampton St, 23220; (p) (804) 358-7166; (f) (804) 358-9994; www.maymont.org

Private non-profit/ 1975/ staff: 45(f); 20(p); 200(v)/ members: 1600

GARDEN; HOUSE MUSEUM

PROGRAMS: Community Outreach; Concerts; Facility Rental; Family Programs; Festivals; Guided Tours; Interpretation; Lectures; Living History; School-Based Curriculum

COLLECTIONS: [1890-1920] Furniture, oriental rugs, European, American, and Asian porcelain, neo-classical sculpture, Tiffany and Co. objects; decorative and fine arts; 20th c vehicles.

HOURS: Yr T-Su 12-5

ADMISSION: $4, Children $2

8694
Meadow Farm Museum

3400 Mountain Rd, 23273 [PO Box 27032, 23273]; (p) (804) 501-5520; (f) (804) 501-5284; galo6@co.henrico.va.us; www.co.henrico.va.us/rec; (c) Henrico

County/ 1981/ Div of Recreation and Parks/ staff: 3(f); 2(p); 60(v)

HISTORIC SITE; HISTORY MUSEUM; HOUSE MUSEUM; LIVING HISTORY/OUTDOOR MUSEUM: Depicts 1810 lifestyle in period home of Dr John Sheppard.

PROGRAMS: Community Outreach; Exhibits; Family Programs; Festivals; Film/Video; Guided Tours; Interpretation; Living History; Reenactments; School-Based Curriculum

COLLECTIONS: [1750s-1860s] Prehistoric archaeological artifacts, agricultural tools and machinery, regional folk art and archival materials.

HOURS: Mar-Dec T-Su (Booked tours) 9:30-11:30, (Drop-in)

8695
Museum and White House of the Confederacy

1201 E Clay St, 23219-1615; (p) (804) 649-1861; (f) (804) 644-7150; info@moc.org; (c) Independent City

Private non-profit/ 1896/ Confederate Memorial Literacy Society/ staff: 20(f); 10(p); 10(v)/ members: 3500/publication: Museum Journal

HISTORIC SITE; HISTORY MUSEUM; HOUSE MUSEUM; PRESIDENTIAL SITE; RESEARCH CENTER: Collects, preserves and interprets the artifacts and history of the Civil War.

PROGRAMS: Community Outreach; Elder's Programs; Exhibits; Facility Rental; Family Programs; Festivals; Film/Video; Guided Tours; Interpretation; Lectures; Living History; Publication; Research Library/Archives; School-Based Curriculum

COLLECTIONS: [19th c] Southern Confederacy artifacts: uniforms, weaponry, equipage, furnishings, flags, photographs, manuscripts and numismatics.

HOURS: Yr M-Sa 10-5, Su 12-5

ADMISSION: $8, Children $5; Combo tickets; Under 7 free

8696
Old Dominion Chapter, National Railway Historical Society

102 Hull St, 23226 [PO Box 8583, 23226]; (p) (804) 231-4324, (804) 745-4735; (f) (804) 745-4735; www.odcnrhs.org

Private non-profit/ 1948/ staff: 75(v)/ members: 290/publication: Highball

HISTORICAL SOCIETY; HISTORY MUSEUM: Owns and operates the Old Dominion Railway Museum; preserves nation's railroading heritage.

PROGRAMS: Annual Meeting; Community Outreach; Elder's Programs; Exhibits; Festivals; Film/Video; Guided Tours; Interpretation; Lectures; Publication; Research Library/ Archives

COLLECTIONS: [1900-1950] 34 pieces of rolling stock; operational Virginia steam locomotive; railroad corporate records, photos, documents and artifacts.

HOURS: (Museum) Yr M-F by appt for groups, Sa 11-4, Su 1-4; (Passenger excursions) May-June, Oct, Dec Sa

ADMISSION: $16, Children $7; Museum donations accepted

8697
Old Stone House (Edgar Allan Poe Museum)

1914 - 16 E Main St, 23223; (p) (804) 648-5523, (888) 21-EAPOE; (f) (804) 648-8729; www.poemuseum.org

1737/ staff: 1(f); 9(p); 4(v)

HOUSE MUSEUM: Promotes life and works of Edgar Allan Poe.

COLLECTIONS: [1809-1849] Poe artifacts: furnishing, prints, first edition books, manuscripts, photos.

HOURS: Yr

8698
Richmond Forum, The

6968 Forest Hill Ave, 23225; (p) (804) 330-3993; (f) (804) 320-4650

1986/ staff: 4(f); 1(p); 100(v)/ members: 1600

PROFESSIONAL ORGANIZATION

PROGRAMS: Community Outreach; Lectures; Publication; School-Based Curriculum

HOURS: Yr M-F 9-5

8699
Richmond National Battlefield Park

3215 E Broad St, 23223; (p) (809) 226-1981; (f) (809) 771-8522; rich_interpretation@nps.gov; www.nps.gov/rich; (c) Hanover/Chesterfield/Henrico/Richmond City

Federal/ 1936/ National Park Service, Dept of Interior/ staff: 25(f); 14(p); 53(v)

HISTORIC PRESERVATION AGENCY; HISTORIC SITE; LIVING HISTORY/OUTDOOR MUSEUM: Commemorates the battlefields associated with the two major Union campaigns.

PROGRAMS: Community Outreach; Elder's Programs; Exhibits; Film/Video; Guided Tours; Interpretation; Lectures; Living History; Research Library/Archives; School-Based Curriculum

COLLECTIONS: [1860-1865] Civil War artifacts.

HOURS: Yr Daily 9-5

ADMISSION: No charge

8700
Saint John's Episcopal Church

2401 E Broad St, 23223; (p) (804) 648-5015; (c) Richmond City

Private non-profit/ 1741/ staff: 1(f); 25(p); 1(v)

HISTORIC SITE: Historic Landmark Site of the 2nd Virginia Convention (1775) that featured Patrick Henry's famous "Give me liberty or give me death!"

PROGRAMS: Annual Meeting; Community Outreach; Concerts; Elder's Programs; Exhibits; Facility Rental; Family Programs; Guided Tours; Interpretation; Living History; Reenactments; School-Based Curriculum

COLLECTIONS: [1741-1776] Vestry and cemetery records.

HOURS: Yr M-Sa 10-4, Su 1-4

ADMISSION: $3, Children $1, Seniors $2

8701
Tuckahoe Plantation

12601 River Rd, 23233; (p) (804) 784-5736; (f) (804) 784-5736; tuckahoe@erols.com; (c) Goochland

1979/ staff: 4(f); 2(p)

HISTORIC SITE: Preserves childhood home of Thomas Jefferson.

PROGRAMS: Annual Meeting; Community Outreach; Garden Tours; Guided Tours; Interpretation

COLLECTIONS: [1714-present]

HOURS: Yr M, Th, Su 9-4 by appt

ADMISSION: $7, Children $3.50; Group rates

8702
Valentine Museum, The/Richmond History Center

1015 E Clay St, 23219; (p) (804) 649-0711; (f) (804) 643-3510; info@valentinemuseum.com; www.valentinemuseum.com; (c) Richmond

Private non-profit/ 1892/ Board of Trustees/ staff: 16(f); 12(p); 85(v)/ members: 750

HISTORY MUSEUM; HOUSE MUSEUM; RESEARCH CENTER: Collects, preserves, and interprets materials relating to Richmond's history.

PROGRAMS: Community Outreach; Elder's Programs; Exhibits; Facility Rental; Family Programs; Guided Tours; Interpretation; Lectures; Living History; Research Library/Archives; School-Based Curriculum

COLLECTIONS: [18th-20th c] Costumes, textiles, books, manuscripts, decorative arts, fine arts, industrial arts and photos. Site: Wickham House c. 1812.

HOURS: Yr T-Sa 10-5, Su 12-5

ADMISSION: $5, Student $4, Children $4, Seniors $4; Under 3 free

8703
Virginia Association of Museums

2800 Grove Ave, 23221; (p) (804) 649-8261; (f) (804) 649-8262; vam@goacc.com; www.vamuseums.org

Private non-profit/ 1968/ staff: 3(f); 1(p); 5(v)/ members: 650/publication: Directory of Virginia Museums

Provides professional training, advocacy and resource sharing.

PROGRAMS: Annual Meeting; Community Outreach; Publication; Research Library/ Archives

HOURS: Yr M-F 9-5

8704
Virginia Aviation Museum

5701 Huntsman Rd, 23250; (p) (804) 236-3622; (f) (804) 236-3623; vam.smv.org; (c) Henrico

State/ 1987/ Science Museum of VA/ staff: 3(f); 4(p); 35(v)

HISTORIC SITE; HISTORY MUSEUM: Preserves VA air and space history.

PROGRAMS: Exhibits; Facility Rental; Family Programs; Film/Video; Guided Tours; Lectures; Research Library/Archives

COLLECTIONS: [1917-1966] Aircrafts.

HOURS: M-Sa 9:30-5, Su 12-5

ADMISSION: $5, Children $3, Seniors $4

8705
Virginia Baptist Historical Society

Univ of Richmond, Boatwright Library, VBHS Wing, 23173 [PO Box 34, 23173]; (p) (804) 289-8434; (f) (804) 289-8953; (c) City of Richmond

Private non-profit/ 1876/ staff: 2(f); 3(p); 5(v)/ members: 1000/publication: *Virginia Baptist Register*

HISTORICAL SOCIETY; HISTORY MUSEUM: Collects, preserves and promotes Baptist history.

PROGRAMS: Annual Meeting; Community Outreach; Exhibits; Guided Tours; Lectures; Living History; Publication; Research Library/ Archives

COLLECTIONS: [18th-20th c] Congregational records, state Baptist newspapers.

HOURS: Yr M-F 9-4:30

ADMISSION: No charge

8706
Virginia Department of Historic Resources
2801 Kensington Ave, 23221; (p) (804) 367-2323; (f) (804) 367-2391; www.dhr.state.va.us

State/ 1989/ staff: 41(f); 15(p)

HISTORIC PRESERVATION AGENCY; RESEARCH CENTER: Surveys and registers historic properties, highway markers and easements; provides grants, artifact loans and technical assistance to museums.

PROGRAMS: Community Outreach; Guided Tours; Lectures; Research Library/Archives; School-Based Curriculum

COLLECTIONS: [Prehistory-20th c] Over 5 million archaeological objects.

HOURS: Yr M-F 8:30-5

ADMISSION: No charge

8707
Virginia Fire and Police Museum
200 W Marshall St, 23220; (p) (804) 644-1849; (f) (804) 644-1850; sdelauder@msn.com; www.vafire-police.org; (c) Richmond

Private non-profit/ 1981/ staff: 1(f); 4(p); 5(v)/ members: 15

HISTORIC SITE: Preserves and interprets the history of VA firefighters and law enforcement officers.

PROGRAMS: Community Outreach; Exhibits; Facility Rental; Family Programs; Guided Tours; Research Library/Archives; School-Based Curriculum

COLLECTIONS: [1849-1922] Photographs, documents, equipment, textiles and toys.

HOURS: Yr T-F 10-4

ADMISSION: $2, Children $1, Seniors $1.50; Under 4 free

8708
Virginia Historical Society
428 N Blvd, 23221 [PO Box 7311, 23221-0311]; (p) (804) 358-4901, (804) 342-9665; (f) (804) 342-9647; www.vahistorical.org; (c) Richmond

Private non-profit/ 1831/ Board of Trustees/ staff: 50(f); 30(p); 170(v)/ members: 7000/publication: *Virginia Magazine of History and Biography; History Notes*

GARDEN; HISTORICAL SOCIETY; HISTORY MUSEUM; HOUSE MUSEUM; RESEARCH CENTER: Collects, preserves, and interprets Virginia's past.

PROGRAMS: Elder's Programs; Exhibits; Fa-

cility Rental; Family Programs; Garden Tours; Guided Tours; Interpretation; Lectures; Publication; Research Library/Archives; School-Based Curriculum

COLLECTIONS: [17th-20th c] Manuscripts, maps, newspapers, volumes, serials, sheet music, portraits, paintings, artifacts, and photos.

HOURS: Yr M-Sa 10-5, Su 1-5

ADMISSION: $4, Student $2, Children $2, Seniors $3; Members free

8709
Virginia Holocaust Museum
213 Roseneath Rd, 23221 [PO Box 14809, 23221]; (p) (804) 257-5400; (f) (804) 257-4314; info@va-holocaust.com; www.va-holocaust.com; (c) Richmond

Private non-profit/ 1997/ Board of Directors/ staff: 35(v)/ members: 700/publication: *De Maleyne*

HISTORY MUSEUM; RESEARCH CENTER: Preserves history of Holocaust survivor family's resettlement in Richmond.

PROGRAMS: Annual Meeting; Community Outreach; Elder's Programs; Exhibits; Film/Video; Guided Tours; Lectures; Publication; Research Library/Archives; School-Based Curriculum

COLLECTIONS: [1930s-1940s] Holocaust artifacts.

HOURS: Yr M-F 9-5, Sa 2-5, Su 1-5

ADMISSION: No charge

8710
Wilton House Museum
215 S Wilton Rd, 23226; (p) (804) 282-5936; (f) (804) 288-9805

Private non-profit/ 1952/ National Society of the Colonial Dames of America in the Commonwealth of Virginia/ staff: 2(f); 6(p); 60(v)/ members: 1400

HOUSE MUSEUM: Preserves period brick mansion.

PROGRAMS: Community Outreach; Concerts; Exhibits; Facility Rental; Guided Tours; Interpretation; Lectures; Living History; Reenactments; School-Based Curriculum

COLLECTIONS: [late 18th-early 19th c] Furniture, silver, crystal, textiles and metals.

HOURS: Mar-Jan T-Sa 10-4:30, Su 1:30-4:30

ADMISSION: $5, Seniors $4

ROANOKE

8711
Harrison Museum of African-American Culture
523 Harrison Ave NW, 24016; (p) (540) 345-4818; (f) (540) 345-4831

Private non-profit/ 1985/ staff: 3(f); 1(p)/publication: *A Pictorial*

ART MUSEUM; HISTORY MUSEUM: Researches, preserves and interprets African-American history.

PROGRAMS: Annual Meeting; Community Outreach; Concerts; Elder's Programs; Exhibits; Facility Rental; Family Programs; Festivals; Film/Video; Guided Tours; Interpretation; Lectures; Publication; Reenactments; Re-

search Library/Archives

COLLECTIONS: [18th-20th c] African artifacts, African-American history, photos, books, portraits and paintings.

HOURS: Yr T-F 10-5, Sa-Su 1-5

ADMISSION: No charge

8712
History Museum and Historical Society of Western Virginia
1 Market Sq, 24008 [PO Box 1904, 24008]; (p) (540) 342-5770; (f) (540) 224-1256; history@roanoke.infi.net; www.history-museum.org; (c) Roanoke

Private non-profit/ 1957/ Board of Directors/ staff: 3(f); 7(p); 115(v)/ members: 500/publication: *The Journal; Iron Horses in the Valley*

HISTORICAL SOCIETY; HISTORY MUSEUM; RESEARCH CENTER: Collects, preserves, promotes, interprets, and makes available materials relating to the history of western VA.

PROGRAMS: Community Outreach; Exhibits; Facility Rental; Guided Tours; Lectures; Publication; Research Library/Archives; School-Based Curriculum

COLLECTIONS: [Mid 18th c-present] Period clothing and accessories, domestic furnishings, agricultural implements and tools, children's clothing and toys, Native American artifacts, military uniforms, accoutrements, and photos.

HOURS: Yr T-F 10-4, Sa 10-5, Su 1-5

ADMISSION: $2, Student $1, Children $1, Seniors $1; Under 6 free

8713
Virginia Museum of Transportation, Inc.
303 Norfolk Ave SW, 24016; (p) (540) 342-5670; (f) (540) 342-6898; info@vmt.org; www.vmt.org; (c) Roanoke

Private non-profit/ 1976/ staff: 7(f); 5(p); 75(v)/ members: 500

HISTORY MUSEUM: Preserves and interprets VA's transportation heritage.

PROGRAMS: Annual Meeting; Community Outreach; Exhibits; Facility Rental; Family Programs; Festivals; Guided Tours; Interpretation; Lectures; Research Library/Archives; School-Based Curriculum

COLLECTIONS: [19th-20th c] Diesel and steam locomotives, vintage cars, carriages, trucks, trolleys, multi-level gauge train layout.

HOURS: Yr M-Sa 10-5, Su 12-5

ADMISSION: $6, Children $4, Seniors $5

8714
Virginia's Explore Park
3900 Rutrough Rd, 24014 [PO Box 8508, 24014-0508]; (p) (540) 427-1800; (f) (540) 427-1880; vrfa@roanoke.infi.net; www.explorepark.com; (c) Roanoke

Private non-profit/ 1985/ VA Recreational Facilities Authority/ staff: 25(f); 5(p); 89(v)

HISTORIC SITE; LIVING HISTORY/OUTDOOR MUSEUM: 19th c farmstead, schoolhouse, blacksmith shop, colonial life and Native American area.

PROGRAMS: Exhibits; Festivals; Film/Video; Interpretation; Living History; Reenactments;

School-Based Curriculum

COLLECTIONS: [17th-19th c] Farming artifacts.

HOURS: Apr F-Sa 10-6, Su 12-6; May-Oct M-Sa 10-6, Su 12-6

ADMISSION: $8, Children $4.50, Seniors $6, Under 6 free

ROCKY MOUNT

8715
Franklin County Historical Society, Inc.
65 E Court St, 24151; (p) (540) 483-1890; beverlym@swva.net; (c) Franklin

Private non-profit/ 1961/ staff: 1(p); 6(v)/ members: 200

HISTORICAL SOCIETY: Maintains genealogy research library and local history museum.

PROGRAMS: Annual Meeting; Exhibits; Family Programs; Interpretation; Research Library/ Archives

COLLECTIONS: [19th-20th c] Family histories, books.

HOURS: Yr M-Sa 9-12/1-4

ADMISSION: No charge

SALEM

8716
Salem Museum and Historical Society
801 E Main St, 24153; (p) (540) 389-6760; (f) (540) 389-6760; s.museum@rev.net; www.salemmuseum.org

Private non-profit/ 1971/ Salem Historical Society/ staff: 1(f); 2(p); 50(v)/ members: 375/publication: Guide to Historic Salem

HISTORIC PRESERVATION AGENCY; HISTORICAL SOCIETY; HISTORY MUSEUM; HOUSE MUSEUM: Documents and preserves local history in c. 1840 Williams-Brown House.

PROGRAMS: Community Outreach; Exhibits; Festivals; Guided Tours; Lectures; Publication; School-Based Curriculum

COLLECTIONS: [18th-20th c] Native American artifacts, Civil War items, documents; Walter Biggs art.

HOURS: Yr T-F 10-4, Sa 12-5

ADMISSION: No charge

SALTVILLE

8717
Museum of the Middle Appalachians
123 Palmer Ave, 24370 [PO Box 910, 24370]; (p) (540) 496-3633; (f) (540) 496-7033; (c) Smyth

Private non-profit/ 1992/ Saltville Foundation/ staff: 30(v)/ members: 200

HISTORY MUSEUM: Collects, preserves and interprets the region's history.

PROGRAMS: Annual Meeting; Community Outreach; Exhibits; Guided Tours; Interpretation; Lectures

COLLECTIONS: [Prehistory-20th c] Specimens: wooly mammoths, mastodons, bears, horses and giant ground sloths; Native American artifacts and photos.

HOURS: Yr M-Sa 10-4, Su 1-4

ADMISSION: Donations requested

8718
Salt Theater Corp
Palmer Springs Mill, PO Drawer Z, 24370; (p) (540) 496-4900; (f) (540) 496-3269; duncans@netva.com; (c) Smyth

Private non-profit/ 1994/ staff: 7(v)/publication: The Bucket Line

HISTORIC SITE: Promotes local cultural heritage; preserves historic Palmer Springs Grist Mill.

PROGRAMS: Community Outreach; Concerts; Elder's Programs; Exhibits; Facility Rental; Family Programs; Festivals; Guided Tours; Living History; Publication; Theatre

HOURS: Spring-Summer Th-Su 10-6

ADMISSION: $7

8719
Tourism Department, Town of Saltville
217 Palmer Ave, 24370 [PO Box 730, 24370]; (p) (540) 496-5342; (f) (540) 496-4814; saltville.tourism@netva.com; www.netva.com/smythcoc; (c) Smyth

City/ 1998/ Town of Saltville/ staff: 1(f)

HISTORIC SITE: Promotes site of oldest salt mine.

PROGRAMS: Community Outreach; Exhibits; Guided Tours; Reenactments

COLLECTIONS: [1795-1960s] Salt furnace replica, pioneer cabin, blacksmith shop and working beam salt well pump; Civil War fortifications and trenches.

HOURS: Yr Daily sunrise-sunset

ADMISSION: No charge

SALUDA

8720
Middlesex County Museum, Inc.
Rt 17 Business, 23149 [PO Box 121, 23149]; (p) (804) 758-3663; (f) (804) 758-0478; (c) Middlesex

Private non-profit/ 1935/ Board of Directors/ staff: 1(f); 34(v)

HISTORY MUSEUM

PROGRAMS: Concerts; Guided Tours; Interpretation

COLLECTIONS: [19th-20th c] Artifacts of water, timber, and farm industries; Lt. Gen. Lewis Burwell "Chesty" Puller; Presidents Lincoln and Grant.

HOURS: Yr W-Su 10-3

ADMISSION: No charge

SCOTTSVILLE

8721
Scottsville Museum
Main St, 24590 [PO Box 15, 24590]; (p) (804) 286-2247; (c) Albemarle

Private non-profit/ 1975/ Board of Trustees/ members: 125

HISTORY MUSEUM: Historic building housing local history exhibits.

PROGRAMS: Community Outreach; Concerts; Family Programs; Guided Tours

COLLECTIONS: [1770s-1900] Native American arrowheads, photos, old toys, dolls and stories of canal days.

HOURS: Apr-Oct Sa 10-5, Su 1-5

ADMISSION: No charge

SMITHFIELD

8722
Isle of Wight County Museum
103 Main St, 23430; (p) (757) 357-7459; (f) (757) 365-9112; (c) Isle of Wight

County/ 1976/ Museum Foundation, Inc./ staff: 1(f); 2(p); 40(v)/ members: 150

HISTORY MUSEUM

PROGRAMS: Exhibits; Film/Video; Interpretation; Research Library/Archives

COLLECTIONS: [18th-20th c] Prehistoric fossils, Native American artifacts, local colonial archaeology, war memorial gallery, Smithfield Ham Gallery, miniature colonial plantation house and kitchen with period furnishings, and a 1900 country store.

HOURS: Yr T-Sa 10-4, Su 1-5

ADMISSION: No charge

SOUTH BOSTON

8723
South Boston, Halifax County Museum
1540 Wilborn Ave, 24592 [PO Box 383, 24592]; (p) (804) 572-9200; (f) (804) 572-9200; sbhcm@halifax.com; www2.halifax.com/museum; (c) Halifax

Private non-profit/ 1982/ Board of Directors/ staff: 1(f); 2(p); 50(v)/ members: 625/publication: Civil War Letters; Our Patriots

ART MUSEUM; HISTORY MUSEUM

PROGRAMS: Annual Meeting; Community Outreach; Exhibits; Facility Rental; Guided Tours; Lectures; Publication; Research Library/ Archives

COLLECTIONS: [19th-20th c] Local artifacts.

HOURS: Yr W-Sa 10-4, Su 2-4:30

ADMISSION: No charge

SOUTH HILL

8724
South Hill Model Train Museum
201 N Mecklenburg Ave, 23920; (p) (804) 447-4547; (f) (804) 447-4461; shchamber@msinets.com; (c) Mecklenburg

Private non-profit/ 1987/ staff: 1(p); 2(v)

HISTORY MUSEUM: Promotes railroad history.

PROGRAMS: Guided Tours

COLLECTIONS: [1940s-1950s]

HOURS: Yr Daily 9-4

ADMISSION: $2, Children $1

8725
Tobacco Farm Life Museum of Virginia
306 W Main St, 23970 [201 N Mecklenburg Ave, 23970]; (p) (804) 447-2551; (f) (804) 447-4461; shchamber@msinets.com; msinets.com/shchamber; (c) Mecklenburg

1994/ South Hill Community Development As-
sociation/ staff: 1(p); 4(v)

HISTORY MUSEUM: Promotes history of farm
family in early 1800s.

PROGRAMS: Guided Tours

COLLECTIONS: [1900-1950]

HOURS: Yr Th-Sa 10-4

ADMISSION: Donations requested

8726
Virginia S. Evans Doll Museum
201 N Mecklenburg Ave, 23970; (p) (804)
447-4547; (f) (804) 447-4461;
shchamber@msinets.com; (c) Mecklenburg

Private non-profit/ 1989/ staff: 2(p); 2(v)

HISTORY MUSEUM

PROGRAMS: Guided Tours

COLLECTIONS: [1860s] Over 500 dolls.

HOURS: Yr Daily 9-4

ADMISSION: No charge

SPOTSYLVANIA

8727
Spotsylvania County Museum/F.L.N. Waller Research Library
Courthouse Rd, 22553 [PO Box 64, 22553];
(p) (540) 582-7167; (c) Spotsylvania

Private non-profit/ 1964/ Spotsylvania Historical Association, Inc./ staff: 4(p)/ members: 90

GENEALOGICAL SOCIETY; HISTORIC SITE;
HISTORICAL SOCIETY; HISTORY MUSEUM:
Promotes the history of Spotsylvania County;
promotes interest in preservation of historic
sites.

PROGRAMS: Exhibits; Research Library/
Archives

COLLECTIONS: [19th c] Early Americana,
Civil War and Native American artifacts, dolls,
swords, firearms and furniture.

HOURS: Mid Oct-mid May M-F 10-3; Mid May-
mid Oct M-Sa 10-4, Su 1-4

ADMISSION: No charge

8728
Museum of Valor
8915 Millwood Dr, 22553 [PO Box 1797,
22553]; (p) (540) 582-2043;
hartw@stuffnet.com; (c) Spotsylvania

Private non-profit/ 1990/ staff: 7(f); 8(p); 8(v)

HISTORY MUSEUM

PROGRAMS: Community Outreach; Exhibits;
Interpretation; Lectures

COLLECTIONS: [20th c] War uniforms, memorabilia.

HOURS: Yr by appt

ADMISSION: No charge

8729
Sergeant Kirkland's Museum and Historical Society, Inc.
8 Yakama Trail, 22553; (p) (540) 582-6296; (f)
(540) 582-8312; seagraver@kirklands.org;
www.kirklands.org

Private non-profit/ 1992/ Board of Directors/
staff: 1(p); 8(v)/ members: 348/publication:
Sergeant Kirkland's Press

HISTORICAL SOCIETY; RESEARCH CEN-
TER: Conducts historical research.

PROGRAMS: Annual Meeting; Community
Outreach; Exhibits; Lectures; Publication; Research Library/Archives; School-Based Curriculum

COLLECTIONS: [19th c]

HOURS: Yr by appt

ADMISSION: No charge

SPRING GROVE

8730
Brandon Plantation
23500 Brandon Rd, 23881; (p) (757) 866-
8486; (f) (757) 866-8602; (c) Prince George

Private for-profit/ 1619/ staff: 2(f); 2(p)

Historic James River plantation.

HOURS: Yr Daily dawn-dusk

ADMISSION: Grounds $5; House & Grounds
$10

STANARDSVILLE

8731
Greene County Historical Society
18 Willow Lane, 22973 [PO Box 185, 22973];
(p) (804) 985-8627; (f) (804) 985-2331; history@
ecojobs.com; www.ecojobs.com/greene; (c)
Greene

State/ 1977/ staff: 2(p); 15(v)/ members:
250/publication: *Greene Magazine*

HISTORIC SITE; HISTORICAL SOCIETY;
HISTORY MUSEUM; HOUSE MUSEUM: Collects genealogical and historical information.

PROGRAMS: Annual Meeting; Community
Outreach; Exhibits; Facility Rental; Family Pro-
grams; Garden Tours; Guided Tours; Lectures;
Publication; Research Library/Archives

COLLECTIONS: [1860s] Civil War artifacts.

HOURS: Yr M-F 11-5

ADMISSION: No charge

STANTON

8732
Museum of American Frontier Culture
1250 Richmond Rd, 24402 [PO Box 810,
Staunton, 24402-0810]; (p) (540) 332-7850;
(f) (540) 332-9989; www.frontiermuseum.org

8733
Woodrow Wilson Birthplace Foundation
18-24 N Coalter St, 24402 [PO Box 24,
Staunton, 24402-0024]; (p) (540) 885-0897;
(f) (540) 886-9874; woodrow@cfw.com;
www.woodrowwilson.org; (c) Augusta

Private non-profit/ 1938/ Board of Trustees/
staff: 8(f); 21(p); 131(v)/ members: 376/publi-
cation: *Woodrow Wilson Birthplace; The
Manse*

GARDEN; HISTORIC SITE; HOUSE MUSE-
UM; PRESIDENTIAL SITE; RESEARCH CEN-
TER: Interprets life of Woodrow Wilson.

PROGRAMS: Annual Meeting; Community
Outreach; Exhibits; Facility Rental; Family Pro-
grams; Film/Video; Garden Tours; Guided
Tours; Interpretation; Lectures; Living History;

Publication; Research Library/Archives;
School-Based Curriculum

COLLECTIONS: [1856-1924] Wilson artifacts.

HOURS: Mar-Oct Daily 9-5; Nov-Feb M-Sa 10-
4, Su 12-4

ADMISSION: $6.50, Student $4, Children $2,
Seniors $6; Under 6 free

STAUNTON

8734
Augusta County Historical Society
Augusta County Gov't Ctr, 24402 [PO Box
686, 24402-0686]; (p) (540) 248-4151;
klbrown@cfw.com;
www.augustacountyhs.org; (c) Augusta

Private non-profit/ 1964/ Board of Directors/
staff: 1(p); 15(v)/ members: 500/publication:
Augusta Annals

HISTORICAL SOCIETY: A local historical society for a prominent colonial Virginia frontier
county that focuses upon publications and
public programs.

PROGRAMS: Annual Meeting; Lectures; Publication; Research Library/Archives

COLLECTIONS: [1730-1950] Family histories,
local histories, Augusta County, Staunton and
Waynesboro ephemera.

HOURS: Yr by appt

8735
Frontier Culture Museum of Virginia
1250 Richmond Rd, 24402 [PO Box 810,
24402-0810]; (p) (540) 332-7850; (f) (540)
332-9989; www.frontiermuseum.org/; (c)
Augusta/Staunton City

Joint/ 1988/ Private non-profit; State/ staff:
38(f); 40(p); 50(v)/ members: 400

HISTORY MUSEUM; LIVING HISTORY/OUT-
DOOR MUSEUM

PROGRAMS: Community Outreach; Concerts; Exhibits; Facility Rental; Family Programs; Festivals; Film/Video; Guided Tours; Interpretation; Lectures; Living History;
Publication; Reenactments; Research Library/
Archives; School-Based Curriculum

COLLECTIONS: [1675-1830]

HOURS: Jan-mid Mar Daily 10-4; mid Mar-Dec
Daily 9-5

8736
Statler Brothers Museum
501 Thornrose Ave, 24402 [PO Box 2703,
24402-2703]; (p) (540) 885-7297; (f) (540)
885-5130; (c) Augusta

Private non-profit/ 1981/ staff: 6(f)

Promotes history of Statler Brothers.

COLLECTIONS: [1964-present]

HOURS: Yr M-F 10:30-3:30

ADMISSION: No charge

STEELE'S TAVERN

8737
McCormick's Farm and Workshop
McCormick Circle, 24476 [PO Box 100,
24476]; (p) (540) 377-2255; (f) (540) 377-
5850

STRASBURG

8738
Crystal Caverns at Hupp's Hill
33231 Old Valley Pike, 22657; (p) (540) 465-8660; (f) (540) 465-8157; www.visitthevalley.org; (c) Shenandoah

Private non-profit/ 1998/ Wayside Foundation of American History and Arts, Inc./ staff: 1(f); 4(p); 1(v)/ members: 50

HISTORIC PRESERVATION AGENCY

PROGRAMS: Community Outreach; Exhibits; Facility Rental; Family Programs; Guided Tours; Interpretation; Lectures; Living History; Reenactments; Research Library/Archives

COLLECTIONS: [Prehistory-early 20th c] Geology, paleontology and history exhibits.

HOURS: Yr Daily 10-5

ADMISSION: $8, Children $6, Seniors $6

8739
Museum of American Presidents
130 N Massanutten St, 22657; (p) (540) 465-5999; (f) (540) 465-8157; wayside@shentel.net; www.visitthevalley.org; (c) Shenandoah

Private non-profit/ 1995/ Wayside Foundation of American History and Arts, Inc./ staff: 1(f); 3(p); 1(v)/ members: 30

HISTORY MUSEUM: Promotes historic preservation, education, patriotism and social responsibility.

PROGRAMS: Community Outreach; Elder's Programs; Exhibits; Facility Rental; Family Programs; Guided Tours; Interpretation; Lectures; Living History; Research Library/Archives; School-Based Curriculum

COLLECTIONS: [1789-present] Presidential portraits, signatures, artifacts and memorabilia; reproduction colonial costumes.

HOURS: Yr Daily 10-5

ADMISSION: $3, Student $2, Children $2, Seniors $2; Under 6 free

8740
Stonewall Jackson Museum at Hupp's Hill
33229 Old Valley Pike, 22657; (p) (540) 465-5884; (f) (540) 465-8157; www.visitthevalley.org; (c) Shenandoah

Private non-profit/ 1997/ Wayside Foundation of American History and Arts, Inc./ staff: 1(f); 3(p); 1(v)/ members: 50/publication: *The Battle of Belle Grove or Cedar Creek*

HISTORIC SITE; HISTORY MUSEUM; LIVING HISTORY/OUTDOOR MUSEUM: Committed to historic preservation, education, patriotism and social responsibility. Provides both in-house exhibits and programs and outreach to the community.

PROGRAMS: Community Outreach; Exhibits; Facility Rental; Family Programs; Guided Tours; Interpretation; Lectures; Living History; Publication; Reenactments; Research Library/Archives

COLLECTIONS: [1860] Civil War artifacts, Jackson's 1862 Valley Campaign.

HOURS: Yr Daily 10-5

ADMISSION: $3, Student $2, Seniors $2; Under 6 free

8741
Strasburg Museum
East King St, 22657 [31501 Old Valley Pike, 22657]; (p) (540) 465-3428; (c) Shenandoah

Private non-profit/ 1970/ Strasburg, Inc./ staff: 2(p); 100(v)/ members: 187/publication: *Story of Strasburg, Virginia*

HISTORY MUSEUM: Collects, preserves and interprets local history.

PROGRAMS: Annual Meeting; Publication

COLLECTIONS: [19th c] Blacksmith, cooper and potter shop items; displays from colonial farms, homes, barns and businesses; railroad and Civil War relics; Native American artifacts.

HOURS: May-Oct Daily 10-4

ADMISSION: $2, Children $0.50

STRATFORD

8742
Robert E. Lee Memorial Association, Inc.
Stratford Hall Plantation, 22558; (p) (804) 493-8038; (f) (804) 493-0333; development@stratfordhall.org; www.stratfordhall.org; (c) Westmoreland

Private non-profit/ 1929/ Board of Directors/ staff: 34(f); 55(p); 19(v)/ members: 4250/publication: *Stratford Hall and the Lees of Virginia*

HISTORIC SITE; HOUSE MUSEUM: Owns and operates Stratford Hall; interprets plantation life of the Lee family.

PROGRAMS: Community Outreach; Concerts; Exhibits; Facility Rental; Family Programs; Film/Video; Garden Tours; Guided Tours; Interpretation; Lectures; Living History; Publication; Reenactments; Research Library/Archives; School-Based Curriculum

COLLECTIONS: [1740-1822] Fine and decorative arts, manuscripts, volumes, photos, serials and archaeological artifacts.

HOURS: Yr Daily 9-4:30

ADMISSION: $7, Children $3; Under 6 free

STUART

8743
Patrick County Historical Society
Blue Ridge St, 24171 [PO Box 1045, 24171]; (p) (540) 694-2840, (540) 694-7181; (c) Patrick

Private non-profit/ 1971/ Board of Directors/ staff: 1(p); 15(v)/ members: 150

HISTORY MUSEUM: Collects and preserves historical artifacts, documents and genealogical information; operates museum.

PROGRAMS: Annual Meeting; Family Programs; Guided Tours; Lectures; Research Library/Archives

COLLECTIONS: [1800-1960] Tools, clothes, photos, musical instruments, and genealogical materials.

HOURS: Yr T-Sa 10-2 and by appt

ADMISSION: No charge

SUFFOLK

8744
Riddick's Folly, Inc.
510 N Main St, 23439 [PO Box 1722, 23439]; (p) (757) 934-1390; (f) (757) 934-0411

Private non-profit/ 1977/ Board of Directors/ staff: 2(p)

HISTORIC SITE; HISTORICAL SOCIETY; HISTORY MUSEUM; HOUSE MUSEUM

PROGRAMS: Community Outreach; Exhibits; Facility Rental; Family Programs; Guided Tours; Interpretation; Lectures; Living History; School-Based Curriculum

COLLECTIONS: [1840-1860]

HOURS: Yr T-F 10-5, Su 1-5

ADMISSION: No charge

8745
Suffolk-Nansemond Historical Society
[PO Box 1255, 23434]

Private non-profit/ staff: 11(v)/ members: 550

GENEALOGICAL SOCIETY; HISTORIC PRESERVATION AGENCY; HISTORICAL SOCIETY: Promotes preservation and history.

PROGRAMS: Annual Meeting; Community Outreach; Exhibits; Family Programs; Festivals; Film/Video; Garden Tours; Guided Tours; Interpretation; Lectures; Reenactments; Research Library/Archives; School-Based Curriculum

COLLECTIONS: [19th-20th c] Periodicals, letters, pictures, drawings and artifacts.

SURRY

8746
Bacon's Castle Museum
465 Bacon's Castle Tr, 23883 [PO Box 364, 23883]; (p) (757) 357-5976; (c) Surry

Assoc for the Preservation of VA Antiquities/ staff: 10(p)

GARDEN; GENEALOGICAL SOCIETY; HISTORIC PRESERVATION AGENCY; HISTORIC SITE; HISTORICAL SOCIETY; HISTORY MUSEUM; HOUSE MUSEUM: Preserves and interprets 17th-19th c architecture.

PROGRAMS: Community Outreach; Exhibits; Garden Tours; Guided Tours; Interpretation; Lectures

COLLECTIONS: [17th-18th c] Period furniture and decorative objects in restored Jacobean style brick home.

HOURS: Mar-Nov Sa 10-4, Su 12-4; Apr-Oct T-Sa 10-4, Su 12-4

ADMISSION: $6, Student $3, Senior $4

8747
Chippokes Plantation State Park
695 Chippokes Park Rd, 23883-2406; (p) (757) 294-3625; (f) (757) 294-3299; cp1@dcr.state.va.us; www.state.va.us/-dcr_home.htm; (c) Surry

State/ 1960/ Dept of Conservation and Recreation/ staff: 7(f); 25(p); 50(v)/publication: *History of Chippokes*

HISTORIC SITE: Preserves and interprets the cultural landscape of 400 years of rural life along the James River.

PROGRAMS: Facility Rental; Family Programs; Festivals; Guided Tours; Interpretation; Publication

COLLECTIONS: [18th-20th c] Furnishing, oriental carpets, silverware, flatware, clocks in 26 historic sites.

HOURS: (Park) Yr Daily sunrise-sunset; (Mansion) Apr-May, Sept-Oct Sa-Su 1-5; June-Aug W-Su 1-5

ADMISSION: $3, Children $1.50

8748
Surry County Historical Society and Museums, Inc.
84 Main St, 23883 [PO Box 262, 23883]; egregory@techcom.net; www.techcom.net/ egregory/surrycoh.html; (c) Surry

Private non-profit/ 1998/ staff: 6(v)/ members: 325

HISTORICAL SOCIETY; HISTORY MUSEUM: Collects county history; operates museum.

PROGRAMS: Annual Meeting; Exhibits; Festivals; Lectures; Research Library/Archives

COLLECTIONS: [1607-present] Genealogy material on local African American and white settlers, county history books and prehistoric artifacts.

HOURS: Yr Sa-Su

ADMISSION: No charge

SWEET BRIAR

8749
Sweet Briar College Museum
Sweet Briar College, 24595; (p) (804) 381-6246, (804) 381-6131; (c) Amherst

Private non-profit/ 1980/ Sweet Briar College/ staff: 1(p); 3(v)

HISTORIC SITE; HISTORY MUSEUM: Preserves artifacts in 3 period sites: Alumnae House, a slave cabin and Tuscan Villa.

PROGRAMS: Guided Tours; Lectures

COLLECTIONS: [19th-20th c] Personal artifacts: costumes, furniture, jewelry, alumnae items and tools.

HOURS: Yr M-F 9-5

ADMISSION: No charge

TAPPAHANNOCK

8750
Essex County Historical Society
[PO Box 2566, 22560]; dwgaddy@crosslink.net; (c) Essex

Private non-profit/ 1951/ Executive Board/ staff: 6(v)/ members: 85/publication: *Essex County Historical Society Bulletin*

HISTORICAL SOCIETY: Collects information and materials on local history.

PROGRAMS: Annual Meeting; Lectures; Publication; Research Library/Archives

COLLECTIONS: [17th c-present] Books, pamphlets, documents, and photos.

HOURS: Yr M-F 9-5 by appt

ADMISSION: No charge

8751
Essex County Museum, Inc.
128 Prince St, 22560 [PO Box 404, 22560]; (p) (804) 443-4690; (c) Essex

Private non-profit/ 1956/ staff: 2(p); 43(v)/ members: 185

HISTORY MUSEUM: Promotes and educates about local history.

PROGRAMS: Annual Meeting; Community Outreach; Elder's Programs; Exhibits; Festivals; Guided Tours; Interpretation; Living History; School-Based Curriculum

COLLECTIONS: [17th c-present] Artifacts, photos, research notes, wall board and case exhibits.

HOURS: Yr F-Sa 10-3, Su 1-3

ADMISSION: No charge

TAZEWELL

8752
Higginbotham House Museum
3 mi SW of Tazewell, 26451 [PO Box 175, 26451]; (p) (540) 988-3800

1811/ staff: 4(p)

COLLECTIONS: [Pre-historic through early 20th c] Native American artifacts, objects related to local history, domestic and agricultural life, weaponry and the decorative and design arts.

HOURS: May-Nov

8753
Historic Crab Orchard Museum and Pioneer Park
US Rte 19 & 460, 24651 [Route 1, Box 194, 24651]; (p) (540) 988-6755; (f) (540) 988-9400; histcrab@netscope.net; www.netscope.net/~histcrab; (c) Tazewell

Private non-profit/ 1978/ staff: 5(f); 1(p); 90(v)/ members: 610/publication: *Pisgah Pathfinder*

HISTORIC SITE; HISTORY MUSEUM; LIVING HISTORY/OUTDOOR MUSEUM: Collects and interprets objects related to Central Appalachia cultural heritage.

PROGRAMS: Annual Meeting; Community Outreach; Exhibits; Facility Rental; Family Programs; Guided Tours; Interpretation; Lectures; Living History; Publication; Reenactments; Research Library/Archives; School-Based Curriculum

COLLECTIONS: [1800-1930] 15 historic log and stone dwellings, Paleolithic era objects, photos, documents, horse-drawn vehicles and fashion dolls.

HOURS: Fall-Spring M-Sa 9-5; Summer Daily 9-5

ADMISSION: $6

THE PLAINS

8754
Afro-American Historical Association of Fauquier County
4249 Loudoun Ave, 20198 [PO Box 340, 20198]; (p) (540) 253-7488; (f) (540) 788-1417; aaha@citizen.infi.net; (c) Fauquier

Private non-profit/ 1992/ staff: 12(v)/ members: 175/publication: *Annual AAHA Journal*

GENEALOGICAL SOCIETY; HISTORIC PRESERVATION AGENCY; HISTORY MUSE-

UM; RESEARCH CENTER: Preserves and restores historic landmarks related to the African American experience.

PROGRAMS: Community Outreach; Concerts; Exhibits; Guided Tours; Lectures; Publication; Research Library/Archives

COLLECTIONS: Diversified library, research repositories, paintings, statues, and artifacts of items related to African Americans and Native Americans.

HOURS: Yr T- F 10-3, Sa 1-5

VESUVIUS

8755
Blue Ridge Parkway
Mile Post 6 Blue Ridge Pkwy, 24483 [133 Whetstone Ridge Rd, 24483]; (p) (540) 377-2377; (f) (540) 377-6758; www.nps.gov/blri; (c) Augusta

Federal/ staff: 2(p); 12(v)

HISTORIC PRESERVATION AGENCY: Preserves natural and cultural heritage of the southern Appalachians.

PROGRAMS: Exhibits; Guided Tours; Interpretation; Lectures; Living History; Research Library/Archives; School-Based Curriculum

COLLECTIONS: [1860-1930]

HOURS: May-Oct Daily 9-5

VIENNA

8756
Freeman House
131 Church St NE, 22180-4503; (p) (703) 938-5187, (703) 255-6365

VIRGINIA BEACH

8757
First Landing State Park
2500 Shore Dr, 23451; (p) (757) 412-2300; (f) (757) 412-2315; firstlanding@dcr.state.va.ca

State/ 1936/ Dept of Conservation and Recreation/ staff: 10(f); 20(p); 125(v)

HISTORIC SITE; LIVING HISTORY/OUTDOOR MUSEUM: Protects and conserves natural resources.

PROGRAMS: Community Outreach; Exhibits; Facility Rental; Family Programs; Festivals; Guided Tours; Interpretation; Lectures; School-Based Curriculum

COLLECTIONS: [1607-present] Native American artifacts.

HOURS: Yr Daily 7-dusk

8758
Francis Land House Historic Site and Gardens
3131 Virginia Beach Blvd, 23452; (p) (757) 431-4000; (f) (757) 431-3733

City/ 1986/ staff: 3(f); 4(p); 65(v)/ members: 350

GARDEN; HISTORIC SITE; HISTORY MUSEUM; HOUSE MUSEUM: Educates visitors about the history of southeastern VA during the prehistoric, colonial and federal periods.

PROGRAMS: Concerts; Elder's Programs; Exhibits; Facility Rental; Family Programs; Garden Tours; Guided Tours; Interpretation; Lectures; School-Based Curriculum; Theatre

COLLECTIONS: [1730-1820] Furnishings, artifacts of Land family. Princess Anne County hsitory, Rose Hall Dress Shop.

HOURS: Yr T-Sa 9-5, Su 11-5

ADMISSION: $3.50, Student $2.50, Children $2, Seniors $3

8759
Lynnhaven House
4405 Wishart Rd, 23455 [4401 Wishart Rd, 23455]; (p) (757) 456-0351, (757) 460-1688; (f) (757) 456-0997; ahb@bueche.com

Private non-profit/ 1976/ A.P.V.A./Board of Directors/ staff: 1(p)/ 42(v)/ members: 160

HOUSE MUSEUM: Restores, maintains, documents and preserves historic Lynnhaven House (1725).

PROGRAMS: Annual Meeting; Community Outreach; Concerts; Facility Rental; Family Programs; Garden Tours; Guided Tours; Interpretation; Living History; Reenactments; School-Based Curriculum

COLLECTIONS: [1725-1750] Colonial period furniture, housewares, cooking, and food preparation utensils.

HOURS: May, Oct Sa-Su 12-4; June-Sept T-Su 12-4

ADMISSION: $4, Student $2.50, Children $2; Under 5 free

8760
Old Coast Guard Station, The
24th St & Atlantic Ave, 23458 [PO Box 24, 23458]; (p) (757) 422-1587; (f) (757) 491-8609; ftylervb2@aol.com; www.va-beach.com/old_coast

Private non-profit/ 1981/ VA Beach Maritime Museum Board of Directors/ staff: 3(f); 3(p); 60(v)/ members: 500/publication: *The Keeper*

MARITIME MUSEUM: Preserves history of VA coastal communities and maritime heritage.

PROGRAMS: Annual Meeting; Community Outreach; Exhibits; Facility Rental; Festivals; Guided Tours; Lectures; Publication; Research Library/Archives; School-Based Curriculum

COLLECTIONS: [1878-present] Artifacts and documents of Life-Saving Service/Coast Guard and coastal VA; shipwreck photos, documents.

HOURS: June-Sept M-F 10-5, Su 12-5; Oct-May T-F 10-5, Su 12-5

ADMISSION: $3, Children $1, Seniors $2.50; Military $2.50

8761
Princess Anne County/Virginia Beach Historical Society
2040 Potters Rd, 23454; (p) (757) 491-3490

Private non-profit/ 1961/ Board of Governors/ staff: 15(v)/ members: 150/publication: *Princess Anne County and Virginia Beach: A Pictorial History by Stephen S. Mansfield*

HISTORICAL SOCIETY: Promotes preservation of historical properties.

PROGRAMS: Annual Meeting; Community Outreach; Exhibits; Garden Tours; Guided Tours; Interpretation; Lectures; Publication

COLLECTIONS: [Mid 18th-early 19th c] Books

and maps.

HOURS: July-Aug W 12-4

ADMISSION: $3, Children $1.50

WALKERTON

8762
King and Queen County Historical Society
King & Queen Courthouse, 23177 [Route 1, Box 18, 23177]; (p) (804) 769-3959; www.iocc.com/-swright/k+qmain.html; (c) King and Queen

Private non-profit/ 1953/ staff: 2(p); 10(v)/ members: 450

HISTORICAL SOCIETY: Preserves county history.

PROGRAMS: Annual Meeting; Community Outreach; Exhibits; Lectures

COLLECTIONS: [19th-20th c] Account books, family histories.

HOURS: Yr by appt

ADMISSION: No charge

WARM SPRINGS

8763
Bath County Historical Society
Court House Hill, 24484 [PO Box 212, 24484]; (p) (540) 839-2546; (f) (540) 839-2566; bathcountyhistory@tds.net; rootsweb.com/~va.bath; (c) Bath

Private non-profit/ 1970/ Board of Directors/ staff: 2(p); 5(v)/ members: 600/publication: *Quarterly Newsletter*

HISTORICAL SOCIETY

PROGRAMS: Annual Meeting; Community Outreach; Exhibits; Guided Tours; Publication

COLLECTIONS: [19th c] Books, diaries, journals, manuscripts, newspapers, family correspondence, photographs, genealogical records, furniture, clothing, farm implements, guns, and maps.

HOURS: Yr M-Sa 8:30-4

ADMISSION: No charge

WARSAW

8764
Richmond County Museum
5874 Richmond Rd, 22572 [PO Box 884, 22572]; (p) (804) 333-3607, (804) 394-4901; (f) (804) 333-3408; (c) Richmond

1992/ Advisory Board/ staff: 1(p); 20(v)/ members: 150

HISTORIC SITE; HISTORY MUSEUM: Preserves the heritage and rural lifestyle of county.

PROGRAMS: Annual Meeting; Community Outreach; Concerts; Exhibits; Festivals; Film/Video; Guided Tours; Interpretation; Lectures; Reenactments; Research Library/Archives

COLLECTIONS: [Prehistory-present] Artifacts, photographs, decorative and domestic arts, correspondence, records, ledgers, tools, toys, videos, interviews, reference library, and fossils.

HOURS: Feb-mid Dec W-Sa 11-3

ADMISSION: No charge

WASHINGTON'S BIRTHPLACE

8765
George Washington Birthplace National Monument
1732 Popes Creek Rd, 22443; (p) (804) 224-1732; (f) (804) 224-2142; superintendent@nps.gov; www.nps.gov/gewa; (c) Westmoreland

Federal/ 1930/ National Park Service/ staff: 21(f); 9(p); 30(v)/publication: *George Washington Birthplace*

HISTORIC SITE; LIVING HISTORY/OUTDOOR MUSEUM; PRESIDENTIAL SITE: Preserves, protects and interprets the birthsite of George Washington.

PROGRAMS: Community Outreach; Concerts; Exhibits; Festivals; Film/Video; Garden Tours; Guided Tours; Interpretation; Living History; Publication; School-Based Curriculum

COLLECTIONS: [1730-1750] Archaeological objects.

HOURS: Yr Daily 9-5

ADMISSION: $2; Under 17 free

WAVERLY

8766
Miles B. Carpenter Museum Complex
Rte 460 W, near intersection with Rte 40, 23890 [201 Hunter St, 23890]; (p) (804) 834-3327, (804) 834-2151; (f) (804) 834-8869; folkart@usa.net; (c) Sussex

Private non-profit/ 1986/ Board of Trustees/ staff: 5(f); 20(p); 105(v)/publication: *Cutting the Mustard*

ART MUSEUM; HISTORIC SITE; HOUSE MUSEUM: Maintains three museums: Folk Art, First Peanut, and Wood Products.

PROGRAMS: Community Outreach; Concerts; Exhibits; Family Programs; Festivals; Guided Tours; Interpretation; Publication; Theatre

COLLECTIONS: [Mid 19th-20th c] Folk artist Miles Burkholder Carpenter's carvings, tools, and memorabilia; peanut farming machinery and equipment; Sussex County Wood Products

WAYNESBORO

8767
P. Buckley Moss Museum
One block S of I-64, exit 94, 22980 [150 P. Buckley Moss Dr, 22980]; (p) (540) 949-6473; (f) (540) 943-9756; mossmuseum@aol.com; www.p-buckley-moss.com

Private for-profit/ 1988/ staff: 6(f); 19(p)/publication: *Painting the Joy of the Soul*

ART MUSEUM: Promotes life and work of artist P. Buckley Moss.

PROGRAMS: Community Outreach; Concerts; Exhibits; Film/Video; Guided Tours; Interpretation; Lectures; Publication; Research Library/Archives

COLLECTIONS: [1950s-present] Original art by Patricia Buckley Moss.

HOURS: Yr M-Sa 10-6, Su 12:30-5:30

ADMISSION: No charge

8768
Waynesboro Heritage Foundation, Inc.
420 W Main St, 22980 [PO Box 517, 22980]; (p) (540) 943-3943; (c) Augusta

Private non-profit/ 1996/ Heritage Museum/ staff: 20(v)/ members: 125

Studies and preserves the physical and archival history and culture of Waynesboro.

COLLECTIONS: [1850-1950] Pictures, artifacts and memorabilia of schools, churches, businesses, industries, homes, families and local government; Native American arrowheads and tools.

HOURS: Yr T-Th 1-4, F-Sa 10-4

ADMISSION: Donations accepted

WEBER CITY

8769
Clinch Mountain Cultural Center
Route 224, 24290 [PO Box 203, Gate City, 24251]; (p) (540) 386-2465; (f) (540) 386-2354; (c) Scott

Private non-profit/ 1996/ The Homeplace/ staff: 2(f); 3(p); 20(v)

HISTORIC SITE; HISTORY MUSEUM; LIVING HISTORY/OUTDOOR MUSEUM; RESEARCH CENTER: Preserves middle Appalachian culture, life, history and folklore.

PROGRAMS: Concerts; Exhibits; Festivals; Guided Tours; Living History; Reenactments; School-Based Curriculum

COLLECTIONS: [1840-1890] Tools, housewares and farm implements in period log cabins.

HOURS: Apr-Dec W-Su 10-5

ADMISSION: $3, Children $2, Seniors $2

WEST POINT

8770
Historic Chelsea Plantation, Inc.
874 Chelsea Plantation Ln, 23181; (p) (804) 843-2386; (f) (804) 966-2215; webcentre.com/usr/chelsea; (c) King William

Private for-profit/ 1997/ Comm of VA/ staff: 2(p)

ART MUSEUM; GARDEN; HISTORIC SITE; HOUSE MUSEUM

PROGRAMS: Annual Meeting; Facility Rental; Garden Tours; Guided Tours; Interpretation

COLLECTIONS: [Early 18th-late 19th c] Art, oil paintings, and architecture.

HOURS: Yr Th-Su 10-4:30, M-W reserved for bus and group tours

ADMISSION: $9, Seniors $8

8771
West Point Historical Museum
721 Main St, 23181; (p) (804) 843-3244; (c) King William

Private non-profit/ 1994/ staff: 1(p)

HISTORY MUSEUM

PROGRAMS: Exhibits

COLLECTIONS: [Late 19th-early 20th c] Logging equipment, pictures and history literature of the Chesapeake Corp.

HOURS: Yr M-Sa 9-5

ADMISSION: No charge

WHITE MARSH

8772
Rosewell Foundation, Inc.
Old Rosewell Lane, 23183 [PO Box 1725, 23183]; (p) (804) 693-2585; (c) Gloucester

Private non-profit/ 1994/ Board of Directors/ staff: 1(f); 1(p); 60(v)/ members: 400/publication: Discovering Rosewell; The Four Families of Rosewell

HOUSE MUSEUM: Protects and preserves Rosewell Mansion site.

PROGRAMS: Annual Meeting; Exhibits; Guided Tours; Interpretation; Lectures; Publication; Research Library/Archives; School-Based Curriculum

COLLECTIONS: [18th-19th c] Archaeological exhibits.

HOURS: Yr T-Su 10-4

WILLIAMSBURG

8773
Colonial Williamsburg Foundation, The
134 N Henry St, 23187 [PO Box 1776, 23187-1776]; (p) (757) 229-1000; (f) (757) 565-8948; sarnold@cwf.org; www.history.org

Private non-profit/ 1926/ Board of Trustees/ staff: 1447(f); 408(p); 825(v)

ART MUSEUM; HISTORIC SITE; LIVING HISTORY/OUTDOOR MUSEUM

PROGRAMS: Community Outreach; Concerts; Elder's Programs; Exhibits; Facility Rental; Family Programs; Film/Video; Garden Tours; Guided Tours; Interpretation; Lectures; Living History; Reenactments; Research Library/Archives; School-Based Curriculum; Theatre

COLLECTIONS: [1750-1780] British and American fine, decorative and mechanical art; American folk art.

HOURS: Yr Daily

ADMISSION: $27, Children $16

8774
Earl Gregg Swem Library, College of William and Mary
[PO Box 8794, 23187-8794]; (p) (757) 253-4841, (757) 221-3050; (f) (757) 221-2635; spcoll@wm.edu; www.swem.wm.edu

State/ 1693/ staff: 6(f); 6(p); 2(v)

LIBRARY AND/OR ARCHIVES: Preserves, catalogues, exhibits, and makes its collection of manuscripts, rare books, and archival materials available; documents the history of the College of William and Mary.

PROGRAMS: Exhibits; Publication; Research Library/Archives

COLLECTIONS: [18th-20th c] Manuscripts and rare books relating to American and VA history.

HOURS: Yr M-F 10-4, Sa 9-1 academic yr; Summer Sa hours vary

ADMISSION: No charge

8775
James City County Historical Commission
101-E Mounts Bay Rd, 23187 [PO Box 8784, 23187-8783]; planning@james-city.va.us; www.james-city.va.us/about.history/history.html; (c) James City

County/ 1985/ Board of Supervisors/ staff: 2(f); 15(v)/publication: James City County: Keystone of the Commonwealth

HISTORIC PRESERVATION AGENCY: Preserves, protects and promotes county history through surveying, identifying, and documenting historical buildings and sites.

PROGRAMS: Annual Meeting; Community Outreach; Exhibits; Lectures; Publication

COLLECTIONS: [1607-present]

8776
Jamestown-Yorktown Foundation
Rte 31 & Colonial Pkwy, 23187 [PO Box 1607, 23187]; (p) (757) 253-4838; (f) (757) 253-5299; www.historyisfun.org; (c) James City

State/ 1982/ Secretary of Education/ staff: 146(f); 200(p); 773(v)/ members: 153/publication: Jamestown-Yorktown Foundation Dispatch

HISTORY MUSEUM; LIVING HISTORY/OUTDOOR MUSEUM: Operates Jamestown Settlement, a museum of 17th c VA, and the Yorktown Victory Center, a museum of the American Revolution.

PROGRAMS: Community Outreach; Exhibits; Facility Rental; Family Programs; Festivals; Film/Video; Guided Tours; Interpretation; Lectures; Living History; Publication; Reenactments; Research Library/Archives; School-Based Curriculum

COLLECTIONS: [17th-18th c] Archaeological artifacts, furnishings, household and nautical items, documents and artwork relating to Jamestown, VA's English origins, early colonial period and Native American culture of southeastern VA. Maps, books, currency, engravings, military equipment, medical implements, clothing, personal effects, and household objects from American Revolution.

HOURS: Yr Daily 9-5

ADMISSION: $16, Children $7.75

8777
John D. Rockefeller's Home
522 E Francis St, 23187; (p) (800) HISTORY; (f) (757) 565-8797

8778
Omohundro Institute of Early American History and Culture
[PO Box 8781, 23187-8781]; (p) (757) 221-1110; (f) (757) 221-1047; ieahcl@facstaff.wm.edu; www.wm.edu/oieahc

Private non-profit/ 1943/ staff: 18(f); 2(p)/publication: William and Mary Quarterly; Uncommon Sense

Promotes history and culture of early America.

COLLECTIONS: [1500-1815]

HOURS: Yr M-F 9-5

8779
Pegee of Williamsburg, Patterns From Historie
105 Dogwood Dr, 23185 [PO Box 127, 23187-0127]; (p) (757) 220-2722; (f) (757) 220-2722; (c) James City

1971

PROFESSIONAL ORGANIZATION: Researches historic garments and creates replica garments.

PROGRAMS: Exhibits; Lectures

COLLECTIONS: [17th c-present]

8780
Public Hospital of 1773
325 Francis St, 23187 [PO Box 1776, 23187-1776]; (p) (757) 220-7554; (f) (757) 565-8804; dthomas@cwf.org; www.colonialwilliamsburg.org

Private non-profit/ 1985/ Colonial Williamsburg Foundation/ staff: 12(f); 17(p); 80(v)

HISTORY MUSEUM: Promotes history of psychological medicine and treatment.

PROGRAMS: Exhibits

COLLECTIONS: [18th-19th c] Medical instruments; English and American decorative arts: furniture, metals, ceramics, glass, paintings, prints, maps, and textiles.

HOURS: Jan-mid-Mar Daily 11-5; mid Mar-Dec Daily 11-6

ADMISSION: $8, Children $4

WINCHESTER

8781
Abram's Delight Museum
1340 S Pleasant Valley Rd, 22601; (p) (540) 662-6519; (f) (540) 662-6991; wfchs@shentel.net; visitthevalley.org; (c) Frederick

Private non-profit/ 1960/ Winchester-Frederick County Historical Society/ staff: 6(p); 2(v)

COLLECTIONS: [1790-1840] Hollingsworth family pieces; Shenandoah Valley items.

HOURS: Apr-Oct M-Sa 10-4, Su 12-4

ADMISSION: $3.50, Children $1.75

8782
Community History Project of Shenandoah University
1460 University Dr, 22607; (p) (540) 665-4587; (f) (540) 665-4644; whofstras@su.edu; www.su.edu; (c) Frederick

1987/ staff: 1(p)

HISTORIC PRESERVATION AGENCY: Promotes historical research of Shenandoah Valley.

PROGRAMS: Community Outreach; Exhibits; Lectures

8783
George Washington's Office
32 W Cork St, 22601; (p) (540) 662-4412; (f) (540) 662-6991; wfchs@shentel.net; www.visitthevalley.org; (c) Frederick

Private non-profit/ 1950/ Winchester-Frederick County Historical Society/ staff: 1(f); 3(p); 1(v)

COLLECTIONS: [1755-1765] Period items dealing with the frontier including two owned by George Washington.

HOURS: Apr-Oct M-Sa 10-4, Su 12-4

ADMISSION: $3.50, Children $1.75

8784
Preservation of Historic Winchester, Inc.
Kurtz Cultural Center, 2 N Cameron St, 22601; (p) (540) 667-3577; (f) (540) 667-3583; kurtz@shentel.net; www.visitthevalley.org

Private non-profit/ 1964/ Board of Directors/ staff: 2(f); 3(p); 15(v)/ members: 600/publication: Winchester, Limestones, Sycamores and Architecture

ART MUSEUM; HISTORIC PRESERVATION AGENCY; HISTORY MUSEUM: Preserves the region's architectural and cultural heritage.

PROGRAMS: Annual Meeting; Community Outreach; Exhibits; Facility Rental; Family Programs; Guided Tours; Lectures; Publication; School-Based Curriculum

HOURS: Yr M-Sa 10-5, Su 12-5

ADMISSION: No charge

8785
Stonewall Jackson's Headquarters
415 N Braddock St, 27601; (p) (540) 667-3242; (f) (540) 662-6991; wfchs@shentel.net; www.visitthevalley.org; (c) Frederick

Private non-profit/ 1960/ Winchester-Frederick County Historical Society/ staff: 6(p); 1(v)

COLLECTIONS: [1830-1900] Artifacts of General Thomas Jonathan Jackson and staff.

HOURS: Apr-Oct M-Sa 10-4, Su 12-4; Nov-Mar F-Sa 10-4, Su 12-4

ADMISSION: $3.50, Children $1.75

8786
Winchester-Frederick County Historical Society
1340 S Pleasant Valley Rd, 22601; (p) (540) 662-6550; (f) (540) 662-6991; wfchs@shentel.net; www.visitthevalley.org; (c) Frederick

County, non-profit/ 1930/ staff: 1(f); 1(p); 10(v)/ members: 570

HISTORIC SITE; HISTORICAL SOCIETY; HOUSE MUSEUM: Promotes and studies local history; administers Abram's Delight Museum, Stonewall Jackson's Headquarters and George Washington's Office Museum.

PROGRAMS: Annual Meeting; Exhibits; Guided Tours; Lectures; Living History; Publication; Reenactments

COLLECTIONS: [18th-19th c] Local Native American artifacts, military equipment and Shenandoah Valley furniture.

HOURS: Apr-Oct M-Sa 10-4, Su 12-4

ADMISSION: $3.50, Children $1.75

WISE

8787
Wise County Historical Society
County Courthouse, Room 250, 24230 [PO Box 368, 24230]; (p) (540) 328-6451; wchs@naxs.com; (c) Wise

1992/ Board of Directors/ staff: 10(v)/ members: 1200/publication: The Appalachian Quarterly

GENEALOGICAL SOCIETY; HISTORIC PRESERVATION AGENCY; HISTORICAL SOCIETY; LIBRARY AND/OR ARCHIVES; RE-SEARCH CENTER: Educates about local and regional history of the Southern Appalachia region.

PROGRAMS: Annual Meeting; Community Outreach; Exhibits; Festivals; Lectures; Publication; Research Library/Archives; School-Based Curriculum

COLLECTIONS: [18th-20th c]

HOURS: Yr M-Th 9-4, F 9-1

ADMISSION: Donations accepted

WOODSTOCK

8788
Woodstock Museum of Shenandoah County
137 W Court, 22664 [PO Box 741, 22664]; (p) (540) 459-5112; (c) Shenandoah

Private non-profit/ 1969/ Museum Board

HISTORY MUSEUM; HOUSE MUSEUM: Maintains 18th c house; collects and displays local history artifacts.

PROGRAMS: Exhibits; Guided Tours

COLLECTIONS: [18th-20th c]

HOURS: May-Sept Th-Sa 10-4

ADMISSION: Donations accepted

YORKTOWN

8789
Watermen's Museum
309 Water St, 23690 [PO Box 531, 23690]; (p) (757) 887-2641; (f) (757) 888-2089; (c) York

Private non-profit/ 1980/ staff: 3(p); 50(v)/ members: 404

HISTORY MUSEUM: Interprets Chesapeake Bay culture and history.

PROGRAMS: Community Outreach; Elder's Programs; Exhibits; Facility Rental; Family Programs; Festivals; Film/Video; Guided Tours; Interpretation; Lectures; Living History; Research Library/Archives; School-Based Curriculum

COLLECTIONS: [20 c] Exhibits of Watermen, their tools, trade, culture, Native American, boats, artifacts relating to the Bay and Watermen, commercial Watermen's industry displayed.

HOURS: Apr-Dec T-Su 10-4

ADMISSION: $3, Student $1; Under 6 free

8790
Yorktown National Battlefield/Colonial National Historical Park
Colonial Pkwy, 23690 [PO Box 210, 23690]; (p) (757) 898-3400; (f) (757) 898-6346; colo_superintendent@nps.gov; www.nps.gov/colo; (c) James City/York

Federal/ 1930/ National Park Service/ staff: 89(f); 14(p); 75(v)

HISTORIC SITE: Preserves and interprets Jamestown, site of the first permanent English settlement in the New World and Yorktown Battlefield.

PROGRAMS: Exhibits; Family Programs; Film/Video; Guided Tours; Interpretation; Living History; Research Library/Archives;

School-Based Curriculum

COLLECTIONS: [1607-1781] Excavated artifacts, reports, photographs, maps, documents, paintings and commemorative objects.

HOURS: Yr Daily 9-5

ADMISSION: $7; Under 17 free

WASHINGTON

ABERDEEN

8791
Grays Harbor Historical Seaport Authority: S/V Lady Washington
712 Hagara, 98520 [PO Box 2019, 98520-0333]; (p) (800) 200-5239; (f) (360) 533-9384; ghhsa@techline.com; www.ladywashington.org; (c) Grays Harbor

Private non-profit/ 1987/ staff: 2(f); 1(p); 200(v)/ members: 306

LIVING HISTORY/OUTDOOR MUSEUM: Provides nautical and historical programs.

PROGRAMS: Community Outreach; Exhibits; Facility Rental; Family Programs; Guided Tours; Interpretation; Living History; Reenactments; Theatre

COLLECTIONS: [18th c] Sailing

AMBOY

8792
North Clark Historical Museum
21416 NE 399th St, 98601 [PO Box 296, 98601]; (p) (360) 263-4429; (c) Clark

Private non-profit/ 1988/ Board of Directors/ staff: 20(v)/ members: 183

HISTORIC SITE; HISTORY MUSEUM

PROGRAMS: Annual Meeting; Community Outreach; Exhibits; Interpretation; Publication; Research Library/Archives

COLLECTIONS: [Late 19th-early 20th c]

ANACORTES

8793
Anacortes Museum
1305 8th St, 98221; (p) (360) 293-1915; (f) (360) 293-1929; www.anacorteshistory museum.org; (c) Skagit

City/ 1958/ staff: 2(f); 3(p); 60(v)

HISTORY MUSEUM; MARITIME MUSEUM: Promotes cultural heritage of Fidalgo and Guemes Islands.

PROGRAMS: Community Outreach; Exhibits; Festivals; Guided Tours; Interpretation; Research Library/Archives; School-Based Curriculum

COLLECTIONS: [1890s-present] 5,000 photos, archives of cannery and local history manuscripts, and 25,000 artifacts related to Fidalgo and Guemes Islands.

HOURS: Yr Th-M 1-5 or by appt

ADMISSION: $2

8794
Samich Indian Nation
1610 Commerical Ave Stes A & B, 98221 [PO Box 217, 98221]; (p) (360) 293-6404;

(f) (360) 299-0790; samish@fidalgo.net; (c) Skagit

Tribal

TRIBAL MUSEUM: Promotes tribal history.

PROGRAMS: Research Library/Archives

COLLECTIONS: [1900s-present]

HOURS: Yr M-F 9-5

ANDERSON ISLAND

8795
Anderson Island Historical Society
9306 Otso Point Rd, 98303; (p) (253) 884-2135; (c) Pierce

1975/ members: 325

HISTORICAL SOCIETY; HISTORY MUSEUM; HOUSE MUSEUM

PROGRAMS: Annual Meeting; Exhibits; Festivals; Guided Tours

COLLECTIONS: [1896-1975] Machinery for egg processing and raising feed, local memorabilia, quilts, island history, stories by residents, school history, Native American baskets, saws, household furniture, and photos.

HOURS: Apr-Oct Sa-Su and Holidays 10-4

ADMISSION: Donations accepted

ARLINGTON

8796
Stillaguamish Valley Genealogical Society
20325 71st Ave NE, Ste B, 98223 [PO Box 34, 98223]; (p) (360) 435-4838; home1.gte.net/bhuson/stilly.html; (c) Snohomish

1985/ members: 100

GENEALOGICAL SOCIETY: Promotes family history and genealogy.

PROGRAMS: Annual Meeting; Community Outreach; Publication

COLLECTIONS: 5,000 books, microfilm, microfiche, CD-ROM.

HOURS: T 12-4, W 6pm-9pm, Th 10-4, 3rd Sa

8797
Stillaquamish Valley Pioneer Association/Museum
20722 67th Ave NE, 98223; (p) (360) 435-7289; (c) Snohomish

Private non-profit/ 1912/ staff: 75(v)/ members: 300

HISTORICAL SOCIETY: Collects, preserves, and displays materials and history of Arlington and Stillaquamish Valley.

PROGRAMS: Annual Meeting; Community Outreach; Exhibits; Facility Rental; Guided Tours; Interpretation; Lectures

COLLECTIONS: [Late 1800-present] Pioneer Hall, local history materials.

HOURS: Jan-Mid Nov W, Sa-Su 1-4

ADMISSION: $1; Donations

ASOTIN

8798
Asotin County Historical Museum
215 Filmore, 99402 [PO Box 367, 99402]; (p) (509) 243-4659; (c) Asotin

Private non-profit/ 1971/ Society Board of Directors/ staff: 1(p); 10(v)/ members: 300

HISTORICAL SOCIETY; HISTORY MUSEUM; LIVING HISTORY/OUTDOOR MUSEUM: Preserves history and historic artifacts of interest from Asotin county and WA.

PROGRAMS: Exhibits; Guided Tours; Interpretation; Publication; Research Library/Archives

COLLECTIONS: [1800s] Prehistoric/Native American through the Great Depression

HOURS: Mar-Oct

AUBURN

8799
White River Valley Museum
918 H St SE, 98002; (p) (253) 939-2590; (f) (253) 939-4523; (c) King

Joint/ 1969/ City; White River Valley Historical Society/ staff: 1(f); 3(p); 85(v)/ members: 550/publication: *White River Journal*

HISTORICAL SOCIETY; HISTORY MUSEUM: Preserves, collects and shares local history of Auburn, Kent, Aljma and Pacific.

PROGRAMS: Annual Meeting; Community Outreach; Exhibits; Family Programs; Guided Tours; Interpretation; Lectures; Publication; Research Library/Archives; School-Based Curriculum

COLLECTIONS: [1854-1950] Northern Pacific Railroading archives, photographs, newspapers, Japanese-American farming material culture and Gladding McBean terra-cotta.

HOURS: Yr M-F

ADMISSION: $2

BAINBRIDGE ISLAND

8800
Bainbridge Island Historical Society
7650 High School Rd, 98110; (p) (206) 842-2773; (c) Kitsap

Private non-profit/ 1949/ Board of Directors/ staff: 2(p); 30(v)/ members: 390

HISTORICAL SOCIETY; HISTORY MUSEUM: Preserves Bainbridge Island History through museum.

PROGRAMS: Annual Meeting; Community Outreach; Exhibits; Family Programs; Interpretation; Publication; Research Library/Archives

COLLECTIONS: [1858-1970] 4,600 photographs, charts, tools, exhibits, oral histories, Japanese Internment, local businesses, industries, and personalities.

HOURS: May 1-Sept 30 T, Th, Sa-Su 1-4; Oct 1-Apr 30 T, Th, Su 1-4

ADMISSION: Donations accepted

8801
Bloedel Reserve, The
7571 NE Dolphin Dr, 98110; (p) (206) 842-7631; (f) (206) 842-8970; Rbrown@Bloedelreserve.org; www.Bloedelreserve.org; (c) Kitsap

Private non-profit/ 1974/ The Arbor Fund/ staff: 25(f); 2(p); 55(v)/ members: 2600

GARDEN; HISTORIC SITE

PROGRAMS: Concerts; Facility Rental; Garden Tours; Guided Tours

HOURS: Yr W-Su 10-4

ADMISSION: $6, Seniors $4

BELLEVUE

8802
Bellevue Historical Society
2102 Bellevue Way SE, 98015 [PO Box 40535, 98015]; (p) (425) 450-1046; (f) (425) 450-1046; bhas18@juno.com; (c) King

Private non-profit/ 1986/ staff: 1(p); 50(v)/ members: 140/publication: *Heritage News*

HISTORICAL SOCIETY: Collects, preserves, exhibits, and interprets the history and heritage of Bellevue and environs.

PROGRAMS: Community Outreach; Exhibits; Festivals; Guided Tours; Interpretation; Lectures; Publication

COLLECTIONS: [1863-present] Bellevue history collection: documents, photographs, ephemera, small artifacts, clipping file, and resource library.

HOURS: Winter House:Yr Daily 10-4

8803
Rosalie Whyel Museum of Doll Art
1116 108th Ave NE, 98004-4321; (p) (425) 455-1116; (f) (425) 455-4793; dollart@dollart.com; www.dollart.dollart; (c) King

Private for-profit/ 1992/ staff: 12(f); 4(p); 20(v)/ members: 180

HISTORY MUSEUM: Dedicated to the exhibition and preservation of dolls as an art form.

PROGRAMS: Exhibits; Facility Rental; Family Programs; Lectures; Publication; Research Library/Archives

COLLECTIONS: [17th-20th c] German, French, English, American and other dolls, ethnic and folk costumed dolls, artwork by major doll artists, toys and miniatures, childhood memorabilia, vintage costumes

BELLINGHAM

8804
Roeder Home
2600 Sunset Dr, 98225; (p) (360) 733-6897; (f) (360) 676-9255; DDHanks@co.whatcom.wa.us; (c) Whatcom County/ 1972/ staff: 2(f); 20(p); 5(v)

ART MUSEUM; HOUSE MUSEUM

PROGRAMS: Concerts; Exhibits; Facility Rental; Family Programs; Festivals; Guided Tours; Publication

COLLECTIONS: [1908]

HOURS: Jan-Nov M-Th 9-4 and by appt

ADMISSION: No charge

8805
Washington State Archives, Northwest Region
808 25th St, 98225 [Western Washington Univ, MS 9123, 98225-9123]; (p) (360) 650-3125; (f) (360) 650-3323; State.Archives@wwu.edu;

www.secstate.wa.gov/archives/research.htm# StateGov; (c) Whatcom

1972/ staff: 3(f); 9(v)

LIBRARY AND/OR ARCHIVES: Preserves historical public records from local area government offices.

PROGRAMS: Research Library/Archives

COLLECTIONS: [1853-1996] Public records.

HOURS: Yr M-F 8:30-12 / 1:30-4:30 and by appt

8806
Whatcom County Historical Society
[PO Box 2116, 98227]; (p) (360) 966-2312; (c) Whatcom

Private non-profit/ members: 110/publication: *Saxon Story*

HISTORICAL SOCIETY: Promotes local history.

PROGRAMS: Community Outreach; Elder's Programs; Guided Tours; Lectures; Publication; School-Based Curriculum

BICKLETON

8807
Whoop-N-Holler (Ranch) Museum
East Rd, 99322 [1 Whitmore Rd, 99322]; (p) (509) 896-2344; (f) (509) 896-2120; (c) Klickitat

Private non-profit/ 1970/ staff: 2(f)

HISTORIC PRESERVATION AGENCY; HISTORY MUSEUM; HOUSE MUSEUM

PROGRAMS: Exhibits; Guided Tours

COLLECTIONS: [Late 1880s-early 1900s] Family artifacts.

HOURS: Apr 6-Sept Daily 10-4

ADMISSION: $3

BINGEN

8808
West Klickitat County Historical Society
202 E Humbolst, 98605 [PO Box 394, 98605]; (p) (509) 496-3228; (f) (509) 493-4309; (c) Klickitat

Private non-profit/ 1984/ staff: 3(p); 3(v)/ members: 60

HISTORICAL SOCIETY: Collects and preserves social, commercial, agricultural, industrial and Native American history.

PROGRAMS: Annual Meeting; Exhibits; Family Programs; Research Library/Archives

COLLECTIONS: [1890-1950] Native American artifacts; local photographs; pioneer and family histories; annal displays of local histories; events; businesses; county store; local biographies; logging and agricultural artifacts; glass and bottles.

BLACK DIAMOND

8809
Black Diamond Historical Society
32627 Railroad Ave, 98010 [PO Box 232, 98010]; (p) (360) 886-2327; (c) King

Private non-profit/ 1982/ staff: 10(v)/ members: 275/publication: *Black Diamond: Mining the Memories*

HISTORIC SITE; HISTORICAL SOCIETY; HISTORY MUSEUM: Records and preserves the history of mining, logging, and the railroad in the Black Diamond area through photographs, written documents, and artifacts.

PROGRAMS: Exhibits; Facility Rental; Guided Tours; Lectures; Living History; Publication

COLLECTIONS: [1880-1950] Historic documents, photographs, tools, equipment, appliances, and clothing.

BOTHELL

8810
Bothell Historical Museum Society
9919 NE 180th, 98041 [PO Box 313, 98041-0313]; (p) (425) 486-1889; (c) King

Private non-profit/ 1967/ staff: 30(v)/ members: 165

HISTORICAL SOCIETY; HISTORY MUSEUM; HOUSE MUSEUM: Preserves Bothell history.

PROGRAMS: Annual Meeting; Exhibits; Guided Tours

COLLECTIONS: [1870s-1940] Newspapers, photos.

HOURS: Apr-Dec Su 1-4

ADMISSION: Donations accepted

BREMERTON

8811
Kitsap County Historical Society Museum
280 4th St, 98337 [PO Box 903, 98337]; (p) (360) 479-6226; (f) (360) 415-9294; kchsm@telebyte.net; waynes.net/kchsm; (c) Kitsap

Private non-profit/ staff: 2(f); 1(p); 25(v)/ members: 330/publication: *The Kitsap Historian*

HISTORICAL SOCIETY; HISTORY MUSEUM: Operates county museum and archives; designates county historical sites and buildings.

PROGRAMS: Annual Meeting; Community Outreach; Exhibits; Family Programs; Guided Tours; Interpretation; Lectures; Publication; Reenactments; Research Library/Archives; School-Based Curriculum

COLLECTIONS: [1860s-1950s] Textiles, farm equipment, logging equipment, extensive archives with 150,000 images, boy scout, documentary artifacts, furniture, personal gear, uniforms, dishes and kitchen implements, tools, Victoriana, sheet music, musical instruments.

HOURS: Yr summer Daily, winter T-Sa 10-5

ADMISSION: by donation

8812
USS Turner Joy DD-951
300 Washington Beach Ave, 98337; (p) (360) 792-2457; (f) (360) 377-1020; dd951@sinclair.net; (c) Kitsap

Private non-profit/ 1993/ Bremerton Historic Ships Assoc/ staff: 4(f); 12(v)

HISTORIC SITE: Preserves USS Turner Joy (DD-951)a Forrest Sherman class destroyer.

PROGRAMS: Exhibits; Guided Tours

COLLECTIONS: [Vietnam War era] Forrest Sherman class US Navy destroyer.

HOURS: May-Sept Daily Th-M 10-5, Oct-Feb F-Su 10-4

ADMISSION: $7, Children $5, Seniors $6; Group rates available

BUCKLEY

8813
Foothills Historical Society
130 N River Ave, 98321 [PO Box 530, 98321]; (p) (360) 829-1291; jbhansen@tx3.com; (c) Pierce

Private non-profit/ 1982/ staff: 29(v)/ members: 70/publication: *The Vintage Voice*

HISTORICAL SOCIETY; HISTORY MUSEUM; HOUSE MUSEUM; LIVING HISTORY/ OUTDOOR MUSEUM: Conserves and interprets local history.

PROGRAMS: Annual Meeting; Community Outreach; Exhibits; Family Programs; Guided Tours; Interpretation; Lectures; Publication; Research Library/Archives

COLLECTIONS: [Late 1800s-1930s] Domestic and mercantile artifacts; agricultural, mercantile, logging/forestry and mining communities.

HOURS: Yr W, Th 12-4, Su 1-4

ADMISSION: Donations accepted

BURTON

8814
Island Landmarks
23832 Vashon Hwy SW, 98013 [PO Box 13112, 98013]; (p) (206) 463-2445; (f) (206) 463-2313; island_landmarks@hotmail.com; (c) King

County/ 1992/ Island Landmarks/ staff: 200(v)/ members: 250

GARDEN; HISTORIC PRESERVATION AGENCY; HISTORIC SITE; HISTORICAL SOCIETY; HOUSE MUSEUM; RESEARCH CENTER: Preserves historic architecture, landscape, and cultural resources on Vashon and Maury Islands.

PROGRAMS: Annual Meeting; Community Outreach; Exhibits; Family Programs; Festivals; Film/Video; Garden Tours; Guided Tours; Interpretation; Lectures; Research Library/ Archives; School-Based Curriculum

COLLECTIONS: [1860-present] Vashon and Maury islands artifacts.

HOURS: Yr M-F 9-5

CARNATION

8815
Tolt Historical Society
4610 Stephens St, 98014 [PO Box 91, 98014]; (p) (425) 333-4436; IsabelJ@Juno.com; (c) King

Private non-profit/ 1982/ staff: 5(v)/ members: 78/publication: *Tolt/Carnation A Town Remembered*

HISTORIC PRESERVATION AGENCY: Collects and maintains pioneer history.

PROGRAMS: Annual Meeting; Exhibits; Guided Tours; Publication

COLLECTIONS: [Late 1800-present] Tools, domestic artifacts; school memorabilia.

HOURS: Yr M-F 8:30-4:30

ADMISSION: No charge

CASHMERE

8816
Chelan County Historical Society Pioneer Village and Museum
600 Cotlets Wy, 98815 [PO Box 22, 98815]; (p) (509) 782-3230; (f) (509) 782-8905; cch-spvm@aol.com; (c) Chelan

Private non-profit/ Board of Trustees/ staff: 1(f); 1(p); 100(v)/ members: 700/publication: *Pioneer Messenger*

HISTORIC SITE; HISTORICAL SOCIETY; HISTORY MUSEUM; HOUSE MUSEUM; LIVING HISTORY/OUTDOOR MUSEUM: Collects and preserves natural and cultural history.

PROGRAMS: Annual Meeting; Community Outreach; Concerts; Exhibits; Facility Rental; Family Programs; Festivals; Film/Video; Guided Tours; Interpretation; Lectures; Living History; Publication; Reenactments; School-Based Curriculum

COLLECTIONS: [7,000BC-1920AD] Historic sites with Native American, pioneer artifacts.

HOURS: Mar-Oct T-Su 9:30-5

ADMISSION: $3, Family $6, Student $2, Seniors $2

CASTLE ROCK

8817
Castle Rock Exhibit Hall Society
147 Front Ave NW, 98611 [PO Box 721, 98611]; (p) (360) 274-6603; (f) (360) 274-6603; crexhibithall@kalama.com; www.mtsthelens.net; (c) Cowlitz

Private non-profit/ 1990/ staff: 1(f); 45(v)/ members: 63

HISTORIC PRESERVATION AGENCY; HISTORICAL SOCIETY; HISTORY MUSEUM: Preserves local history.

PROGRAMS: Exhibits; Festivals; Film/Video; Guided Tours; Interpretation

COLLECTIONS: Cowlitz Indian artifacts, logging canoes, a Smithsonian exhibit relating to Mt. St. Helens, working models of a sawmill and steam tractor, model railroad.

HOURS: Yr summer Daily 9-6; winter W-Sa 10-2

ADMISSION: No charge

CATHLAMET

8818
Wahkiakum County Historical Society
65 River St, 98612 [PO Box 541, 98612-9709]; (p) (360) 749-3954; (c) Wahkiakum

Private non-profit/ 1954/ staff: 1(f); 12(p)/ members: 138

HISTORICAL SOCIETY: Preserves history of local farming, fishing, and logging industries.

PROGRAMS: Annual Meeting

CENTRALIA

8819
Historic Borst Home
2500 W Bryden, 98531 [PO Box 609, 98531]; (p) (360) 330-7688; (f) (360) 330-7697; (c) Lewis

City/ staff: 1(f); 50(v)

HISTORIC SITE; HISTORY MUSEUM; HOUSE MUSEUM

PROGRAMS: Garden Tours; Guided Tours; Interpretation; Publication; Reenactments

COLLECTIONS: [1900s]

HOURS: May-Sept, Nov-Dec Sa-Su 1-4

ADMISSION: $2

CHEHALIS

8820
Lewis County Historical Museum
599 NW Front Wy, 98532; (p) (360) 748-0831; lchm@myhome.net; (c) Lewis

Private non-profit/ 1965/ staff: 2(f); 2(p); 40(v)/ members: 450/publication: *The Historian*

GENEALOGICAL SOCIETY; HISTORICAL SOCIETY; HISTORY MUSEUM: Collects and displays local artifacts.

PROGRAMS: Annual Meeting; Exhibits; Facility Rental; Family Programs; Festivals; Guided Tours; Interpretation; Lectures; Publication; Research Library/Archives

COLLECTIONS: [1850-1970] Photography, oral history in 1912 railroad depot.

HOURS: Yr Daily M-Sa 9-5, Su 1-5

ADMISSION: $2, Family $5, Children $1

CHELAN

8821
Lake Chelan Historical Society
204 E Woodin Ave, 98816 [PO Box 1948, 98816]; (p) (509) 682-5644; (c) Chelan

Private non-profit/ 1970/ staff: 1(p)/ 20(v)/ members: 150/publication: *History Notes*

HISTORICAL SOCIETY; HISTORY MUSEUM; RESEARCH CENTER: Operates museum of North Central WA and Lake Chelan area history.

PROGRAMS: Annual Meeting; Community Outreach; Elder's Programs; Exhibits; Guided Tours; Publication

COLLECTIONS: [Late 1800s-early 1900s] Memorabilia, pictorial histories, pioneer life, apple and fruit labels, resources material and photos.

HOURS: June-Oct M-Sa 10-4

ADMISSION: Donations accepted

CHEWELAH

8822
Chewelah Historical Society
N 501 3rd E, 99109 [PO Box 271, 99109]; (c) Stevens

City/ staff: 4(v)

HISTORICAL SOCIETY; HISTORY MUSEUM

PROGRAMS: Annual Meeting; Exhibits; Guided Tours

COLLECTIONS: [1850-present]

HOURS: 12-4

ADMISSION: No charge

COLFAX

8823
Perkins House
623 N Perkins Ave, 99111 [PO Box 67, 99111]; (p) (509) 332-5752

8824
Whitman County Historical Society
623 N Perkins Ave, 99111 [PO Box 67, 99111]; (p) (509) 397-2555; epgjr@wsu.edu; www.wsu.edu:8080/~kemyers/wchs; (c) Whitman

Private non-profit/ 1972/ staff: 50(v)/ members: 480/publication: *Bunchgrass Historian*

HISTORICAL SOCIETY; HOUSE MUSEUM; LIBRARY AND/OR ARCHIVES: Maintains a house museum.

PROGRAMS: Annual Meeting; Exhibits; Facility Rental; Lectures; Publication; Research Library/Archives

COLLECTIONS: [1870-present] Victorian home 1890-1910, artifacts of Witman County history, letter press printing history.

HOURS: Perkins House: May-Sept Th-Su 1-4; Archive Yr W 9-12

COLVILLE

8825
Stevens County Historical Society
700 N Wynne St, 99114 [PO Box 25, 99114-0025]; (p) (509) 684-5968; (c) Stevens

Private non-profit/ 1903/ staff: 60(p)/ members: 300/publication: *People's History of Stevens County*

GARDEN; HISTORIC PRESERVATION AGENCY; HISTORIC SITE; HISTORICAL SOCIETY; HISTORY MUSEUM; HOUSE MUSEUM; LIVING HISTORY/OUTDOOR MUSEUM; RESEARCH CENTER: Maintains Keller House museum.

PROGRAMS: Annual Meeting; Exhibits; Guided Tours; Interpretation; Publication; Research Library/Archives

COLLECTIONS: [Late 1800s-1950] Artifacts: Geology, Native Americans, fur traders, trappers, settlers, loggers, miners, military, schools, pioneer life, and agriculture.

HOURS: May-Sept M-Sa 10-4, Su 1-4; June-Aug M-Sa 10-4

COUPEVILLE

8826
Ebey's Landing National Historical Reserve
908 NW Alexander, 98239 [PO Box 774, 98239]; (p) (360) 678-6084; (f) (360) 678-2246; ebla_administration@nps.gov; www.nps.gov/ebla; (c) Island

Joint/ 1978/ Nat'l Park Service/ staff: 1(f); 1(p)

HISTORIC PRESERVATION AGENCY: Preserves and promotes history of Coupeville.

PROGRAMS: Publication

HOURS: Yr Daily dawn-dusk

ADMISSION: No charge

8827
Island County Historical Society & Museum
908 Alexander St, 98239 [PO Box 305, 98239]; (p) (360) 678-3310; (c) Island

Joint/ 1948/ Board of Trustees/ staff: 1(f); 1(p); 60(v)/ members: 400

HISTORIC PRESERVATION AGENCY; HISTORIC SITE; HISTORICAL SOCIETY; HISTORY MUSEUM; RESEARCH CENTER: Collects, preserves, and interprets local history.

PROGRAMS: Annual Meeting; Exhibits; Facility Rental; Family Programs; Guided Tours; Interpretation; Lectures; Research Library/Archives

COLLECTIONS: [Pre-Cambrian-1970s] Mastodon teeth and bones; textiles; Indian artifacts; assessors', auditors', and sheriffs' records and furnishings, clothing, uniforms; 12,000 photographs; family journals; portraits; Indian canoes; 1902 automobile; and books.

HOURS: Yr May-Oct Daily 10-5; Nov-May F-M 10-5

ADMISSION: $2, Family $5, Seniors $1.50; Miltary $1.50

DAVENPORT

8828
Lake Roosevelt National Recreation Area/Fort Spokane
44303 State Rt 25 N, 99122; (p) (509) 633-3836; (f) (509) 633-3834; (c) Lincoln

Federal/ 1960/ staff: 1(f)/publication: *Fort Spokane*

HISTORIC SITE; HISTORY MUSEUM; LIVING HISTORY/OUTDOOR MUSEUM: Preserves and interprets Native history and historic sites.

PROGRAMS: Exhibits; Family Programs; Film/Video; Guided Tours; Interpretation; Living History; Publication; Research Library/Archives; School-Based Curriculum

COLLECTIONS: [1880-1898] Oral histories, maps, and government records.

HOURS: June-Aug W-Su 1-6

ADMISSION: No Charge

8829
Lincoln County Historical Society
600 7th, 99122 [PO Box 585, 99122]; (p) (509) 725-6711; (c) Lincoln

Joint/ 1972/ County; Private non-profit/ staff: 1(p); 15(v)/ members: 60

GARDEN; HISTORIC PRESERVATION AGENCY; HISTORIC SITE; HISTORICAL SOCIETY; HISTORY MUSEUM; HOUSE MUSEUM; LIVING HISTORY/OUTDOOR MUSEUM: Preserve Lincoln County history.

PROGRAMS: Annual Meeting; Community Outreach; Elder's Programs; Exhibits; Family Programs; Festivals; Garden Tours; Guided Tours; Interpretation; Lectures; Living History; Publication; Reenacts; Research Library/Archives; School-Based Curriculum

COLLECTIONS: [1880-1940] Artifacts and photos.

HOURS: M-Sa 9-5

ADMISSION: Donations accepted

DAYTON

8830
Dayton Historical Depot Society
221 E Commercial St, 99328 [PO Box 1881, 99328]; (p) (509) 382-2026; (c) Columbia

Private non-profit/ 1975/ Board of Directors/ staff: 1(f); 10(v)/ members: 80

HISTORIC PRESERVATION AGENCY; HISTORIC SITE; HISTORICAL SOCIETY: Interpretation, education and preservation of local history and local historic buildings.

PROGRAMS: Annual Meeting; Community Outreach; Exhibits; Facility Rental; Festivals; Guided Tours; Interpretation; Living History; Research Library/Archives

COLLECTIONS: [1870-1930] Vintage photos, memorabilia.

HOURS: Yr T-Sa 9-5

ADMISSION: Donations requested

DES MOINES

8831
Des Moines Historical Society
730 S 225 St, 98198-6824 [PO Box 98055, 98198]; (p) (206) 824-5226; (c) King

County/ 1978/ Board of Directors/ staff: 10(v)/ members: 61/publication: *100 Years of the Waterland Community*

HISTORICAL SOCIETY; HISTORY MUSEUM: Collects, preserves, and interprets local history of the late 1890s and early 1900s.

PROGRAMS: Annual Meeting; Exhibits

COLLECTIONS: [Late 1890s-early 1900s] 1,600 pioneer photos, local newspapers from 1946-present, musical instruments, games, telephone switchboard, typewriters, first aid supplies, police and fire fighters memorabilia, lumbering, old furniture

DUPONT

8832
DuPont Historic Museum
207 Barksdale Ave, 98327; (p) (253) 964-3492, (253) 964-8121; (f) (253) 964-3554; l_overmyer@mindspring.com; (c) Pierce

Joint/ 1977/ DuPont Museum Steering Committee/ staff: 1(p); 15(v)

HISTORIC PRESERVATION AGENCY; HISTORIC SITE; HISTORICAL SOCIETY; HISTORY MUSEUM

PROGRAMS: Community Outreach; Concerts; Exhibits; Festivals; Guided Tours; Lectures; Reenactments

COLLECTIONS: [1830-present] Pictures, books, records, artifacts covering Hudson Bay/Ft. Nisquallys, Puget Sound Agriculture Co, Nisqually Mission, Wilkes Observatory.

HOURS: Yr Su 1-4, June-Aug W 7-9

ADMISSION: Donations accepted

DUVALL

8833
Duvall Historical Society
[PO Box 385, 98019]; (p) (425) 788-1266; (c) King

Private non-profit/ members: 15/publication: *Jist Cogitatin, Digging Duvall's Past*

HISTORICAL SOCIETY: Preserves local history, promotes historic restoration.

PROGRAMS: Community Outreach; Exhibits; Guided Tours; Publication; Research Library/Archives

COLLECTIONS: [1880-1960] Newspaper articles, photos, toys, tools, household tools, clothes, and kitchen implements.

EASTSOUND

8834
Crow Valley School Museum
2274 Orcas Rd, 98245; (p) (360) 376-4260; (f) (360) 376-6495; (c) San Juan

Private non-profit/ 1989/ staff: 2(p); 3(v)

COLLECTIONS: [1888-1918] Items related to early school days in San Juan County, WA.

HOURS: June-Sept Th-Sa 1-4, or by appt

ADMISSION: Donations requested

8835
Orcas Island Historical Society and Museum
181 N Beach Rd, 98245 [PO Box 134, 98245]; (p) (360) 376-4849; www.orcasisalnd.org; (c) San Juan

Private non-profit/ 1951/ staff: 1(f); 30(v)/ members: 550/publication: *Orcas Islander*

HISTORICAL SOCIETY; HISTORY MUSEUM; RESEARCH CENTER: Collect, preserve and interpret the record and object history of the Pacific Northwest as it relates to Orcas Island for the usage and enjoyment of local and visiting populations.

PROGRAMS: Annual Meeting; Elder's Programs; Exhibits; Facility Rental; Festivals; Guided Tours; Lectures; Publication; Research Library/Archives

COLLECTIONS: [1850-1940] 700 photographs, 1,000 negatives and over 4,000 objects of local early Native American and European-American pioneer origin.

HOURS: end of May-Sept T,W,Th,Sa,Su 1-4; F 1-8

ADMISSION: $2, Student $1, Children $0.50, Seniors $1

EATONVILLE

8836
Pioneer Farm Museum
7716 Ohop Valley Rd E, 98328; (p) (360) 832-6300; (f) (360) 832-4533; (c) Pierce

Private non-profit/ 1974/ staff: 1(f); 11(p)

HISTORY MUSEUM: "Hands On" living history guided tours. Learn how local Native Americans lived in harmony with nature.

PROGRAMS: Elder's Programs; Guided Tours; Interpretation; School-Based Curriculum

COLLECTIONS: [1887] Several pioneer cabins built in late 1800s.

HOURS: Mar 15-June 17 Sa-Su 11-4; June 17-Sept 2 Sa-Su 11-4; Mar 15-June15 M-F by appt

ADMISSION: $6.50, Student $5.50

EDMONDS

8837
Edmonds Historical Museum
118 5th Ave N, 98020 [PO Box 52, 98020]; (p) (425) 774-0900; (f) (425) 774-6507; (c) Snohomish

Private non-profit/ 1973/ Edmonds-South Snohomish Co. Historical Society/ staff: 1(p); 60(v)/ members: 250

HISTORY MUSEUM

PROGRAMS: Annual Meeting; Exhibits; Guided Tours; Lectures; Publication; Research Library/Archives; School-Based Curriculum

COLLECTIONS: Extensive photographic collection and archival facility focusing on local history.

HOURS: Yr W-Su 1-4

ADMISSION: suggested donation $2

ELLENSBURG

8838
Clymer Museum of Art, The
416 N Pearl St, 98926; (p) (509) 962-6416; (f) (509) 962-6424; clymermuseum@home.com; www.clymermuseum.com; (c) Kittitas

Private non-profit/ 1990/ staff: 1(f); 3(p); 35(v)/ members: 145

ART MUSEUM: Preserve and present the work of John F. Clymer and to offer a gallery for his present day contemporaries to show their work.

PROGRAMS: Community Outreach; Exhibits; Facility Rental; Festivals; Guided Tours; Lectures

COLLECTIONS: [1927-1989] A sample of John F. Clymer's work from his early works and illustration years to his historical and outdoor paintings.

HOURS: Yr Daily M-Th 10-5, F 10-8, Sa 10-5, Su 12-5

8839
Washington State Archives, Central Branch
215 E 14th St, 989267547 [Bedsoe & WA Archives Bldg, Central WA Univ, MS7547, 989267547]; (p) (509) 963-2136; (f) (509) 963-1753; archives@cwu.edu; www.cwu.edu/~archives; (c) Kittitas

State/ 1978/ staff: 3(f); 5(v)

LIBRARY AND/OR ARCHIVES: Public records archives for the nine counties of central Washington.

PROGRAMS: Research Library/Archives

COLLECTIONS: [1860-present] Collections come primarily from county and city governments. Records are also collected from school districts, special taxing districts, and regional state agencies.

HOURS: Yr M-F 8:30-4:30

ENUMCLAW

8840
Enumclaw Plateau Historical Society
1837 Marion St, 98022 [PO Box 1087, 98022]; (p) (360) 825-2294; (c) King

1994/ staff: 10(v)/ members: 250

COLLECTIONS: [1900-present]

HOURS: Undergoing restoration, not open to public

EPHRATA

8841
Grant County Historical Museum & Village
742 Basin St NW, 98823 [PO Box 1141, 98823]; (p) (509) 754-3334; (c) Grant

County; Joint; Private non-profit/ 1951/ staff: 4(f); 1(p); 15(v)/ members: 275/publication: *Memories of Grant County, WA*

HISTORIC PRESERVATION AGENCY; HISTORICAL SOCIETY; HISTORY MUSEUM: Preserve and promote interest in Grant Co history, to retain historical articles for future study and appreciation and to present an interpretation of history for the visitors.

PROGRAMS: Exhibits; Guided Tours; Living History; Publication; School-Based Curriculum

COLLECTIONS: [1893-present] Prehistoric petrified trees and fossils through the periods of the Indians, stockmen, homesteaders and into the start of the Columbia Basin Project and the Grand Coulee Dam.

HOURS: May-Sept M,T,Th,F,Sa 10-5, Su 1-4

ADMISSION: $3, Student $2; under 5 free

8842
Wanapum Dam Heritage Center
Wanapum Dam Hwy 243, 98823 [PO Box 878, 98823]; (p) (509) 754-0500; (f) (509) 766-2522; abuck@gcpud.org; (c) Grant

County/ 1966/ staff: 2(f); 2(p)

HISTORY MUSEUM: The center collects, preserves, and interprets the historical, archaeological, and cultural resources of the Columbia River, to educate visitors about the importance of preserving the rich cultural, historic and prehistoric resources.

PROGRAMS: Exhibits; Film/Video; Guided Tours; Interpretation

COLLECTIONS: [Prehistory-contact] 10,000 total ethnographic, archaeological, archival objects and photographs.

HOURS: Yr Daily M-F 8:30-4:30, Sa-Su 9-5

EVERETT

8843
Children's Museum in Snohomish County
3013 Colby, 98201; (p) (425) 258-1006; (f) (425) 258-5406; lindad@childs-museum.org; www.childs-museum.org; (c) Snohomish

Private non-profit/ 1993/ staff: 3(f); 2(p); 135(v)/ members: 300

HISTORY MUSEUM: Designed for children 2-10, provides hands-on educational exhibits of the county's history, art, science, and culture.

PROGRAMS: Community Outreach; Exhibits; Facility Rental; Family Programs; School-Based Curriculum

HOURS: Yr M-Sa 10-3

ADMISSION: $3

8844
Everett Public Library
2707 Hoyt, 98201; (p) (425) 257-8005; (f) (425) 257-8016; libnw@ci.everett.wa.; www.epls.org; (c) Snohomish

City/ 1895/ City of Everett/ staff: 2(f); 1(p)

LIBRARY AND/OR ARCHIVES

PROGRAMS: Exhibits; Guided Tours; Interpretation; Lectures; Publication

COLLECTIONS: [1890s-present] Photographs and manuscripts relating to Everett and Snohomish County history.

HOURS: Yr

8845
Monte Cristo Preservation Association
[PO Box 471, 98206]; (p) (360) 793-1534; (f) (360) 793-1534; (c) Snohomish

Private non-profit/ 1983/ staff: 30(v)/ members: 85/publication: newsletter & brochure

HISTORIC SITE: Preserve the history and environmental values of this 1890s mining town next to the Jackson Wilderness area in Washington's Cascade Mountains.

PROGRAMS: Annual Meeting; Community Outreach; Exhibits; Guided Tours; Interpretation; Publication

COLLECTIONS: [1889-1920] Physical remains of gold mining town, photographs, documents and artifacts are in members' private collections, as of yet there is no interpretive center.

8846
Snohomish County Museum and Historical Association
2817 Rockefeller Ave, 98206 [PO Box 5556, 98206]; (p) (425) 259-2022; (f) (425) 258-5402; www.snonet.org/snocomuseum/; (c) Snohomish

Private non-profit/ 1954/ staff: 1(p); 12(v)/ members: 175/publication: Snohomish County Museum News; Voices from Everett's First Century; Collected Memories

HISTORICAL SOCIETY; HISTORY MUSEUM: Collects, preserves, and interprets county history. Produces five changing exhibits annually. Maintains reference library and photo archives. Presents monthly programs by historians and authors.

PROGRAMS: Annual Meeting; Exhibits; Film/Video; Guided Tours; Lectures; Publication; Research Library/Archives

COLLECTIONS: [1850-1950] Photographs, archival material, and artifacts relevant to the history of Snohomish County.

HOURS: Yr W-Sa 1-4

ADMISSION: Donations accepted

8847
Machias Historical Society
9315 12th Pl SE, 98205; (p) (425) 334-3086; (c) Snohomish

Private non-profit/ 1984/ State of Washington/ staff: 8(v)/ members: 20

HISTORIC PRESERVATION AGENCY: The society has raised funds and restored historic Machias Community Church.

COLLECTIONS: [Early 1900s] Photographs of Machias.

FAIRCHILD AFB

8848
Fairchild Heritage Museum
100 E Bong St, 99011; (p) (509) 247-2100; (f) (509) 247-4110; fairchidmuseum@ fairchild.af.mil; (c) Spokane

Federal; Private non-profit/ 1980/ US A.F. 92ARW/Fairchild Heritage Museum Society/ staff: 2(f); 15(p); 12(v)/ members: 200

HISTORY MUSEUM

PROGRAMS: Exhibits; Guided Tours; Research Library/Archives; School-Based Curriculum

COLLECTIONS: [1939-1945, 1960-1975] Uniforms, weapons, aircraft, armaments, missiles, vehicles of military origin and the story of the people who used them.

HOURS: Yr M,W,F-Sa 10-2

ADMISSION: No charge

FERNDALE

8849
Hovander Homestead
5299 Neilson Rd, 98248; (p) (360) 384-3444; (f) (360) 384-3444; dconner@co.whatcom. wa.us; www.co.whatcom.wa.us; (c) Whatcom

County/ 1968/ Whatcom County Parks & Rec Dept/ staff: 2(f); 4(p); 30(v)

HISTORIC SITE: Facility is on the National Historic Register. Located on 730 acres adjacent to Nooksak River. Restored homestead farmhouse and barn built by Swedish architect Hokan Hovander.

PROGRAMS: Facility Rental; Family Programs; Festivals; Guided Tours; Interpretation

COLLECTIONS: [1900-1940] Collection of early 20th century furniture, farm equipment, and various collectibles.

HOURS: May-Sept

FORKS

8850
Forks Timber Museum
Hwy 101 S #1421, 98331 [PO Box 873, 98331]; (p) (360) 374-9663; (c) Clallam

Private non-profit/ 1981/ Board of Directors/ staff: 1(p); 20(v)/ members: 150

HISTORY MUSEUM: Collect, preserve, and interpret the artifacts and documents related to the history of Forks and the West End of the Olympic Peninsula.

PROGRAMS: Annual Meeting; Community Outreach; Interpretation; Lectures

COLLECTIONS: Photographs, ephemera, documents, papers, and artifacts from buttons to a Makah canoe and a steam donkey sled, representing over a century of the area's history.

HOURS: Mid Apr-Oct Daily 10-4

ADMISSION: Donations accepted

FORT LEWIS

8851
Fort Lewis Military Museum
Bldg 4320, 98433 [PO Box 331001, 98433-1001]; (p) (253) 967-7206; (f) (253) 967-0837; history@lewis.army.mil; (c) Pierce

Federal/ 1973/ US army/ staff: 3(f); 5(v)/ members: 175/publication: The Banner Quarterly Newsletter

HISTORY MUSEUM: Collect, preserve and interpret the history of Fort Lewis, the units which served here and the early military history of the Pacific Northwest.

PROGRAMS: Guided Tours; Lectures; Living History; Publication

COLLECTIONS: [1917-present] Uniforms, weapons, vehicles and memorabilia associated with Fort Lewis and the US army in the Pacific Northwest form

FRIDAY HARBOR

8852
San Juan Island National Historical Park
125 Spring St, 98250 [PO Box 429, 98250]; (p) (360) 378-2240; (f) (360) 378-2615; Bill_Gleason@nps.gov; www.nps.gob/sajh; (c) San Juan

Federal/ 1966/ staff: 8(f); 50(v)

HISTORIC SITE: San Juan Island NHP commemorates events on the island from 1835 to 1872 in connection with the final settlement of the Oregon Territory boundary, including the Pig War of 1859.

PROGRAMS: Community Outreach; Elder's Programs; Exhibits; Guided Tours; Interpretation; Lectures; Publication; Reenactments; School-Based Curriculum

COLLECTIONS: [Mid-19th c] US-British military history, One million archeological objects relating to the prehistoric Coast Salish habitation of the area and the subsequent historic occupation by the US Army, Royal Marines and Hudson's Bay Company.

HOURS: Yr Summer Daily 8:30-5; Winter Th-Su 8:30-4:30

ADMISSION: No charge

8853
Whale Museum, The
62 First St N, 98250 [PO Box 945, 98250]; (p) (630) 378-2790; www.whale-museum.org; (c) San Juan

Private non-profit/ 1979/ staff: 4(f); 6(p); 30(v)/ members: 2500/publication: Cetus

NATURAL HISTORY MUSEUM: The museum portrays the natural history of cetaceans with a special emphasis on orcas. Exhibits focus on evolution, anatomy, physiology, intelligence, acoustical phenomena, feeding ecology, and social activities.

PROGRAMS: Community Outreach; Exhibits; Family Programs; Guided Tours; Interpretation; Lectures; Publication; Research Library/Archives; School-Based Curriculum

COLLECTIONS: [20thbc] Cetacean skeletons and brains, and several life-size whale models, Archival collections include a large volume of photographic slides and prints, video and audio recordings, scientific reports and reprints.

HOURS: Yr Summer Daily 10-5; Winter call for hours

ADMISSION: $5, Student $2, Seniors $4; Under 5 free

GIG HARBOR

8854
Gig Harbor Peninsula Historical Society & Museum
42`18 Harborview Dr, 98332 [PO Box 744, 98332]; (p) (253) 858-6722; (f) (253) 853-4211; ghphs@harbornet.com; www.gigharbormuseum.org; (c) Pierce

Private non-profit/ 1963/ staff: 1(f); 1(p); 40(v)/ members: 250

HISTORICAL SOCIETY; HISTORY MUSEUM: Collect, preserve, and interpret the history of the Gig Harbor Peninsula from first contact to present.

PROGRAMS: Annual Meeting; Exhibits; Family Programs; Interpretation; Lectures; Publication; Research Library/Archives

COLLECTIONS: [1860s-1990s] General local history collections of artifacts, photographs, and papers.

GOLDENDALE

8855
Klickitat County Historical Society
127 W Broadway, 98620 [PO Box 86, 98620]; (p) (509) 773-4303; (c) Klickitat

Private non-profit/ 1962/ Board of Directors/ staff: 1(f); 2(p); 12(v)/ members: 290/publication: Klickitat Heritage; 1982 County History Book; and others

HISTORICAL SOCIETY; HOUSE MUSEUM: 20 Room house built in 1902, exhibits.

PROGRAMS: Annual Meeting; Exhibits; Guided Tours; Publication; Research Library/ Archives

COLLECTIONS: Coffee grinder collection, dolls, Indian artifacts, country store, homestead cabin, vintage clothing, photographs, and granny attic.

HOURS: Apr 1-Oct 31Daily 9-5

ADMISSION: $3, Children $1

8856
Maryhill Museum of Art
35 Maryhill Museum Dr, 98620; (p) (509) 773-3733; (f) (509) 773-6138; maryhill@gorge.net; maryhillmuseum.org; (c) Klickitat

Private non-profit/ 1923/ staff: 10(f); 7(p); 125(v)/ members: 800

ART MUSEUM; HISTORIC SITE: Located in Historic Register 1914 mansion, the museum collects, preserves and interprets 19th-early 20th c Old and New World art and regional history.

PROGRAMS: Annual Meeting; Community Outreach; Concerts; Elder's Programs; Exhibits; Facility Rental; Family Programs; Festivals; Guided Tours; Interpretation; Lectures; Publication; Research Library/Archives; School-Based Curriculum

COLLECTIONS: [1880-1920] Rodin sculptures, European and American paintings, chess sets, Native American artifacts, Russian icons, Queen Marie of Roumania regalia, Loie Fuller collection, historic photographs and archives, full-scale replica of Stonehenge.

HOURS: Mar 15-Nov 15 Daily 9-5

ADMISSION: $7, Children $2, Seniors $6; Under 6 free

8857
Presby House Museum
127 W Broadway, 98620 [Klickitat County Historical Society, PO Box 86, 98620]; (p) (509) 773-4303; www.ohwy.com/wa/k/klickchm.htm

GRANDVIEW

8858
Bleyhl Community Library
311 Division St, 98930; (p) (509) 882-9217; grandlib@televar.com; (c) Yakima

City/ 1914/ staff: 3(f); 2(p)

LIBRARY AND/OR ARCHIVES

PROGRAMS: Guided Tours

COLLECTIONS: [1906-1972] Agriculture, art, and Grandview history; high school annual; cemetery records.

HOURS: Yr M, W 1:30-9, T,Th 10-12/1:30-9, F-Sa 1:30-5:30

HOQUIAM

8859
Polson Museum
1611 Riverside Ave, 98550 [PO Box 432, 98550]; (p) (360) 533-5862; (f) (360) 533-5862; (c) Grays Harbor

Private non-profit/ 1976/ staff: 1(f); 15(v)/ members: 300

HISTORIC SITE; HISTORICAL SOCIETY; HISTORY MUSEUM; HOUSE MUSEUM; RESEARCH CENTER: The museum preserves and collects the material, written, and photographic history of Grays Harbor and its surrounding communities.

PROGRAMS: Annual Meeting; Exhibits; Facility Rental; Research Library/Archives

COLLECTIONS: [1880-present] Housed in the 26-room 1924 mansion of timber heir Arnold Polson, the museum holds 7,000 museum artifacts, 150 maps, 1,000 volumes, 200 paintings, 5,000 photographs, 400 newspapers.

HOURS: Sept-May Sa-Su 12-4; June-Aug W-Su 11-4

ADMISSION: $2

ILWACO

8860
Lewis and Clark Interpretive Center
Fort Canby State Park, Robert Gray Drive, 98624 [PO Box 488, 98624]; (p) (360) 642-3029; (c) Pacific

State/ 1977/ WA State Parks & Recreation Commission/ staff: 1(f)

HISTORIC SITE; HISTORY MUSEUM

PROGRAMS: Exhibits; Interpretation; School-Based Curriculum

HOURS: Yr Daily 10-5

ADMISSION: donations

INDEX

8861
Index Historical Society-Picket Museum
510 Ave A, 98256 [PO Box 252, 98256]; (p) (360) 793-1534; (f) (360) 793-1534; (c) Snohomish

Private non-profit/ 1984/ staff: 15(v)/ members: 50/publication: Index: An Historical Perspective

HISTORY MUSEUM: The Museum preserves and interprets this small town's mining, logging, quarrying, railroad, and social history with artifacts and the extensive use of early photography of Lee Pickett.

PROGRAMS: Annual Meeting; Exhibits; Family Programs; Guided Tours; Interpretation; Lectures; Publication; Research Library/Archives

COLLECTIONS: [1890-present] Photographs from the 1890s-present, maps, town documents, newspapers on microfilm, oral histories, artifacts, books, sheet music, and videos.

HOURS: June-Sept

8862
League of Snohomish County Heritage Organizations
[PO Box 865, 98256]; (p) (425) 388-3311; (f) (103) 388-3670; l.lindgre@co.snohomish.wa.us; www.snonet.org/loscho/; (c) Snohomish

Private non-profit/ 1983/ staff: 25(v)/ members: 68

ALLIANCE OF HISTORICAL AGENCIES: The league coordinates county organizations for mutual assistance through workshops and conferences, technical assistance, a quarterly newsletter, an awards program and countywide heritage projects.

PROGRAMS: Annual Meeting; Community Outreach; Exhibits; Family Programs

COLLECTIONS: [1860-1920] The league facilitates access to the collections of 13 museums

ISSAQUAH

8863
Issaquah Historical Museum
165 SE Andrews St & 50 Rainier Blvd N (Depot), 98027 [PO Box 695, 98027]; (p) (425) 392-3500; info@issaquahhistory.org; www.issaquahhistory.org; (c) King

Private non-profit/ 1972/ Issaquah Historical Society/ staff: 1(f); 1(p); 75(v)/ members: 300

HISTORIC SITE; HISTORICAL SOCIETY: Discovery, preservation, and dissemination of the history of Issaquah and its environs.

PROGRAMS: Annual Meeting; Exhibits; Facility Rental; Guided Tours; Interpretation; Research Library/Archives

COLLECTIONS: [Late 19th-early 20th C] Railroad equipment and memorabilia, tools, toys, and artifacts belonging to local pioneer families and industries, documents, and historic photographs.

HOURS: Depot: Sa-Su 11-3; Gilman Town Hall: F-Sa 11-3

KELSO

8864
Cowlitz County Historical Museum
405 Allen St, 98626; (p) (360) 577-3119; (f) (360) 423-9987; freeced@co.cowlitz.wa.us; www.cowlitzcounty.org; (c) Cowlitz

Private non-profit/ 1953/ staff: 3(f); 80(v)/ members: 657/publication: *Cowlitz Historical Quarterly*

HISTORICAL SOCIETY; HISTORY MUSEUM: Collects, preserves and interprets the history of Cowlitz County and the Lower Columbia.

PROGRAMS: Annual Meeting; Community Outreach; Exhibits; Family Programs; Guided Tours; Interpretation; Lectures; Publication; Research Library/Archives; School-Based Curriculum

COLLECTIONS: [mid 1800s-early 1900s] 32,000 artifacts, approx. 200 linear feet of documents including around 15,000 photographs and 75,000 negatives, covering Indians, exploration, fur trade, pioneers, logging and early 20th century.

HOURS: Yr T-Sa 9-5, Su 1-5

ADMISSION: donations

KENNEWICK

8865
East Benton County Historical Society & Museum
205 Keewaykin Dr, 99336 [PO Box 6964, 99336]; (p) (509) 582-7704; ebchs@gte.net; (c) Benton

Private non-profit/ 1982/ staff: 1(f); 2(p); 60(v)/ members: 3500/publication: *Benton County Place Names*

HISTORICAL SOCIETY; HISTORY MUSEUM: Perpetuates the history of East Benton County through educational and other programs and through the operation of the East Benton County Historical Museum.

PROGRAMS: Annual Meeting; Community Outreach; Exhibits; Family Programs; Guided Tours; Publication; Research Library/Archives

COLLECTIONS: [Late 1800s-1950s] Jay Perry Columbia River Gem Point collection, Joan Dix Historic Quilt collection, historical artifacts and photograph collection depicting life in East Benton County, obituaries, family and subject files.

HOURS: Yr T-Sa 12-4

ADMISSION: $2, Student $0.50, Children $0.50

8866
Franklin County Historical Society
305 N 4th Ave, 99301; (p) (509) 547-3714; (f) (509) 545-2168; (c) Franklin

Private non-profit/ 1968/ staff: 4(p); 25(v)/ members: 928/publication: *Franklin Flyer*

HISTORICAL SOCIETY; HISTORY MUSEUM: Preserves and promotes the history of Franklin Co through publications, programs and the operation of the Franklin Co Historical Museum.

PROGRAMS: Annual Meeting; Exhibits; Facility Rental; Lectures; Publication; Research Library/Archives

COLLECTIONS: [1884-1930] Over 5,000 photographs, Indian artifacts, spinning wheel, pioneer artifacts and tools, 1907 buggy, medical artifacts and railroad artifacts.

HOURS: Yr 1-5, Sa 10-5

ADMISSION: No charge

KENT

8867
Greater Kent Historical Society
855 E Smith St, 98032 [220 4th Ave S, 98032]; (p) (253) 813-3279; (f) (253) 859-0979; tibia6@aol.com

Private non-profit/ 1992/ staff: 1(p); 40(v)/ members: 360/publication: *quarterly newsletter*

HISTORIC PRESERVATION AGENCY; HISTORIC SITE; HISTORICAL SOCIETY; HISTORY MUSEUM; HOUSE MUSEUM: Houses the history of Kent, WA for the education and interest of the community.

PROGRAMS: Annual Meeting; Community Outreach; Exhibits; Facility Rental; Film/Video; Guided Tours; Lectures; Living History; Publication

COLLECTIONS: [1850-present]

HOURS: Yr Daily 11-3

ADMISSION: Donations

KETTLE FALLS

8868
Kettle Falls Historical Center
1121 St Paul's Mission Rd, 99141 [PO Box 396, 99141]; (p) (509) 739-6964; (c) Stevens

Private for-profit/ 1981/ staff: 1(f); 2(p); 33(v)/ members: 100/publication: *People of the Falls*

HISTORIC SITE; HISTORY MUSEUM: The organization interprets the cultures that lived at and utilized Kettle Falls on the Columbia River that are now under water after building the Grand Coulee Dam.

PROGRAMS: Annual Meeting; Exhibits; Facility Rental; Festivals; Film/Video; Interpretation; Lectures; Publication; Reenactments

COLLECTIONS: [Prehistory-present]

HOURS: May 15 - Sept 15 W-Su 11-5

ADMISSION: $2

KEYPORT

8869
Naval Undersea Museum
1 Garnett Wy, 98345 [610 Dowell St, 98345-7610]; (p) (360) 396-4148; (f) (360) 396-7944; num.kpt.nuwc.navy.mil; (c) Kitsap

Federal/ 1979/ U.S. Navy/ staff: 7(f); 140(v)/publication: *Undersea Quarterly*

HISTORY MUSEUM: Collects and interprets all aspects of naval undersea history, science and operations.

PROGRAMS: Concerts; Exhibits; Family Programs; Lectures; Publication; Research Library/Archives

COLLECTIONS: [1750-present] Undersea technology and equipment including naval and civilian diving suits and gear, undersea vehicles and submarines, torpedoes, sonar. 6,000-volume research library. Trieste II and Deep Quest.

HOURS: June-Sept Daily 10-4; Oct-May M,W,Th,F,Sa,Su 10-4

ADMISSION: No charge

LA CONNER

8870
Gaches Mansion
703 S 2nd St, 98257 [PO Box 1270, 98257]; (p) (360) 466-4288

8871
Skagit County Historical Society
501 S 4th St, 98257 [PO Box 818, 98257-0818]; (p) (360) 466-1611; histmuseum@co.skagit.wa.us; (c) Skagit

Private non-profit/ 1959/ staff: 1(f); 7(p); 130(v)/ members: 350

HISTORICAL SOCIETY; HISTORY MUSEUM: The museum actively engages the public in the understanding and enjoyment of Skagit County's unique cultural history. The museum presents this history through educational exhibits, programs, publications, and research services.

PROGRAMS: Annual Meeting; Elder's Programs; Exhibits; Family Programs; Guided Tours; Interpretation; Lectures; Living History; Publication; Research Library/Archives; School-Based Curriculum

COLLECTIONS: [Mid 19th c-present] Document related to Skagit County history; photographs, documents, books, oral histories, artifacts relating to local recreation, entertainment, art, domestic life, clothing, ethnicity, politics, communication, technology, commerce, and industry.

HOURS: Yr M-Su 11-5

ADMISSION: $2, Family $5, Seniors $1

LACEY

8872
Lacey Museum
829 1/2 Lacey St, 98503; (p) (360) 438-0209; (f) (360) 438-2669; (c) Thurston

City/ 1981/ staff: 2(p)

HISTORY MUSEUM: To preserve and interpret local heritage and collects, cares for, and exhibits historical photographs, objects, and documents related to Lacey history.

PROGRAMS: Community Outreach; Exhibits; Guided Tours; Interpretation; Lectures; Research Library/Archives

COLLECTIONS: [1850-present] Artifacts, documents, and photographs related to Lacey area history. Highlights include school photos, KGY radio station artifacts, area pioneers photos, and 1943 aerial map of Southern Puget Sound.

HOURS: Yr

LAKE STEVENS

8873
Lake Stevens Historical Society
1802 124th Ave NE, 98258 [PO Box 874, 98258]; (p) (425) 334-3944; (c) Snohomish

Private non-profit/ 1981/ staff: 35(v)/ members: 115

HISTORIC PRESERVATION AGENCY; HISTORICAL SOCIETY; HISTORY MUSEUM; HOUSE MUSEUM: We gather and preserve historical information and artifacts about Lake Stevens, and develop information methods to inform and educated the community.

PROGRAMS: Annual Meeting; Community Outreach; Exhibits; Guided Tours; Interpretation; School-Based Curriculum

COLLECTIONS: [20th c] Artifacts, special exhibits, videos, and photos.

HOURS: Yr F-Sa 1-4

ADMISSION: No charge

LANGLEY

8874
South Whidbey Historical Museum
312 Second St, 98260 [PO Box 612, 98260]; (c) Island

Private non-profit; State/ staff: 10(f); 1(v)/ members: 85/publication: *South Whidbey and its People*

HISTORIC PRESERVATION AGENCY; HISTORIC SITE; LIVING HISTORY/OUTDOOR MUSEUM

PROGRAMS: Annual Meeting; Community Outreach; Elder's Programs; Exhibits; Festivals; Living History; Publication; School-Based Curriculum

HOURS: Yr Sa-Su 1-4

ADMISSION: No charge

LIND

8875
Adams County Historical Society
I St & 2nd St, 99341 [PO Box 526, 99341]; (p) (509) 677-3393; galeirma@ritzcom.net; (c) Adams

Private non-profit/ 1956/ staff: 10(v)/ members: 75

HISTORICAL SOCIETY; HISTORY MUSEUM: The Adams County Historical Society preserves historical artifacts, photographs, and memorabilia pertinent to Adams County.

PROGRAMS: Annual Meeting; Community Outreach; Exhibits; Festivals; Guided Tours; Lectures; Monthly Meeting; Publication; Research Library/Archives; School-Based Curriculum

COLLECTIONS: [19th c-present] Collection of county newspapers, photographs, clothing, furniture, family histories, farm artifacts, and furniture.

HOURS: Yr

LONG BEACH

8876
World Kite Museum & Hall of Fame
112-3rd St NW, 98631 [PO Box 965, 98631]; (p) (360) 642-4020; (f) (360) 642-4020; jkite@willapabay.org

Private non-profit/ 1990/ staff: 1(p); 8(v)/ members: 320/publication: *The Flyer*

ART MUSEUM; HISTORY MUSEUM: Telling the significance of kites by preserving the past and the present plus promoting their fun, art, sport, and science worldwide through activities is our mission.

PROGRAMS: Elder's Programs; Exhibits; Festivals; Film/Video; Interpretation; Publication; Research Library/Archives

COLLECTIONS: [500 BC-present] 1,400 kites, 1,700 photographs, 200 books, histories, American Kite Fiers Association, printed archives, international kite magazines and newsletters.

HOURS: June-Aug Daily

LONGVIEW

8877
Stella Historical Society
8530 Ocean Beach, 98632 [c/o Helen Whitcomb, 781 Stella RD, 98632]; (p) (360) 423-9336, (360) 423-8663; (c) Cowlitz

Private non-profit/ 1976/ staff: 15(v)/ members: 70

HISTORIC PRESERVATION AGENCY; HISTORIC SITE; HISTORICAL SOCIETY: To maintain and preserve the old Stella blacksmith shop and post office as hands-on museums for the public during summer weekends or on request for a tour.

PROGRAMS: Exhibits; Festivals; Guided Tours; Interpretation; Lectures

COLLECTIONS: [Late 1800-early 1900] Artifacts relating to local logging camps, fishing and cannery industry, farming tools and equipment, and homesteading.

HOURS: July-Sept Sa-Su 11-4

ADMISSION: Donations requested

LOON LAKE

8878
Loon Lake Historical Society
4000 Colville Rd, 99148 [PO Box 26, 99148-0026]; (p) (509) 233-2222; lorindat@juno.com; (c) Stevens

Private non-profit/ 1990/ staff: 15(v)/ members: 100/publication: *Historical Happenings*

HISTORIC SITE; HISTORICAL SOCIETY; HISTORY MUSEUM; RESEARCH CENTER: Promote, discover, protect and preserve matters of an historical nature in the Loon Lake area.

PROGRAMS: Annual Meeting; Exhibits; Facility Rental; Festivals; Publication; Research Library/Archives

COLLECTIONS: [1850s-present] Many photographs and paper records of Southern Stevens County, artifacts of Morgan Park and personal histories of former presidents.

HOURS: Yr T 6-8, Sa 11-1 or by appt

ADMISSION: Donations accepted

LOPEZ ISLAND

8879
Lopez Island Historical Museum
28 Washburn Place, 98261 [PO Box 163, 98261]; (p) (360) 468-2049; lopezmuseum@rockisland.com; (c) San Juan

Private non-profit/ 1966/ Lopez Island Historical Society/ staff: 1(p); 25(v)/ members: 200

HISTORICAL SOCIETY; HISTORY MUSEUM: Collects and preserves regional history and cultural material of Lopez Island and San Juan Island, WA, operates regional historical museum.

PROGRAMS: Community Outreach; Exhibits; Family Programs; Interpretation; Lectures; Research Library/Archives

COLLECTIONS: [1850-present] Regional history, Native American artifacts, maritime, farming and fishing industries, genealogical information, archives and photos.

HOURS: May, June, Sept F-Su 12-4, July-Aug W-Su 12-4

ADMISSION: $1

LYNDEN

8880
Lynden Pioneer Museum
217 W Front St, 98264; (p) (360) 354-3675; info@lyndenpioneermuseum.com; Lyndenpioneermuseum.com; (c) Whatcom

Private non-profit/ 1976/ Lynden Heritage Foundation/ staff: 2(f); 4(p); 117(v)/ members: 323/publication: *Whatcom Moments and Memoirs*

HISTORIC PRESERVATION AGENCY; HISTORICAL SOCIETY; HISTORY MUSEUM; RESEARCH CENTER: Collects and preserves local heritage of communities along the Nooksack river valley for the purposes of establishing a sense of identity among local communities.

PROGRAMS: Community Outreach; Elder's Programs; Exhibits; Facility Rental; Family Programs; Festivals; Guided Tours; Interpretation; Lectures; Living History; Publication; Reenactments; Research Library/Archives; School-Based Curriculum

COLLECTIONS: [Prehistory-1955] Pioneer collection has 25,000 objects relating daily lifestyles of Native American and European cultures during the settlement of WA state. The transportation/automobilia collection has 5,000 objects relating to the development of transportation over the ages with a focus on automobiles and tractors.

HOURS: Yr M-Sa 10-4

ADMISSION: $3

MCCHORD AFB

8881
McChord Air Museum
Bldg 517 corner Ast & 18th St SW, 98438 [100 Main St (62 AW/CVM), 98438-1109]; (p) (253) 982-2485; (f) (253) 982-5113

Federal; Joint/ 1982/ USAF/ staff: 1(f); 60(v)/ members: 425

HISTORY MUSEUM: Exhibits McChord Field/Air Force Base's heritage to visitors, both military and civilian.

PROGRAMS: Community Outreach; Exhibits; Lectures; Living History

COLLECTIONS: [1938-present]

HOURS: Yr T-Su 12-4

ADMISSION: No Charge

MCCLEARY

8882
McCleary Historical Society
314 S 2nd St, 98557 [PO Box 554, 98557];
(p) (360) 495-3450; stevenl@olynet.com; (c)
Grays Harbor

Private non-profit/ 1976/ members: 100/publication: *McCleary Museum Newsletter*

HISTORICAL SOCIETY; HISTORY MUSEUM: Preserve and catalog items concerning the history of this small logging town.

PROGRAMS: Annual Meeting; Exhibits; Guided Tours; Publication; Research Library/Archives

COLLECTIONS: [20th c] Photographs, books, archives, periodicals, local artifacts and a working moonshine still.

HOURS: June-Aug Sa-Su 12-4 or by appt

ADMISSION: No charge

MINERAL

8883
Western Forest Industries Museum, Inc.
349 Mineral Creek Rd, 98355 [PO Box 861, Eatonville, 98328]; (p) (360) 832-2818; steamtrn@mashell.com; www.mrsr.com

Private non-profit/ 1980/ staff: 2(f); 5(p) 10(v)

HISTORY MUSEUM: Currently we run a live steam train excursion with logging trains.

PROGRAMS: Community Outreach; Exhibits; Facility Rental; Family Programs; Film/Video; Guided Tours; Lectures; Reenactments; School-Based Curriculum

COLLECTIONS: [1890-1950] We have logging equipment from the late 1800 through the 1950s, rare one of a kind pieces such as a Skookum locomotive and a 1914 Kelly-Springfield log truck.

HOURS: May-Sept Daily 11-5:30

ADMISSION: $10.50, Children $7.50

MONROE

8884
Monroe Historical Society
209 E Main St, 98272 [PO Box 1044, 98272];
(c) Snohomish

City; Private non-profit/ 1976/ staff: 50(v)/ members: 150/publication: *Newsletter: Heritage Herald*

HISTORIC SITE; HISTORICAL SOCIETY; HISTORY MUSEUM

PROGRAMS: Annual Meeting; Community Outreach; Exhibits; Film/Video; Lectures; Publication

COLLECTIONS: [Late 1800s-1950s] 1,350 photo collection, artifacts of logging, farming, railroad, businesses, pioneers of early Monroe days from founding to present.

HOURS: Yr Winter M 1-5; Summer M 1-5, Sa 11-3

ADMISSION: donations welcome

8885
Northwest Underground Explorations
[PO Box 386, 98272]; (p) (360) 794-2953,
(425) 481-2387; nwuemines@ compuserve.com;
nwuemines@cs.com; (c) Snohomish

Private non-profit/ 1986/ staff: 5(f); 25(v)/publication: *Discovering Washington's Historic Mines Vol I & II*

HISTORIC PRESERVATION AGENCY: Preserves state history.

PROGRAMS: Guided Tours; Lectures; Publication

COLLECTIONS: [1860s-1950s] Artifacts from early mining operations in WA state, photos, original documents, taped interviews and videos.

MONTESANO

8886
Chehalis Valley Historical Society
703 W Pioneer Ave, 98563; (p) (360) 249-4125; (c) Grays Harbor

Private non-profit/ staff: 15(v)/ members: 150/publication: *The Chehalis Valley Historian*

HISTORICAL SOCIETY; HISTORY MUSEUM: Operates a museum which highlights early-day Washington logging and farming activities, with an emphasis on the Chehalis River Valley in Grays Harbor County.

PROGRAMS: Annual Meeting; Publication

COLLECTIONS: [1860s-present] Early-day logging artifacts and photos; pioneer home-making artifacts; historical scrapbooks of newspaper articles from the Chehalis River Valley.

HOURS: Yr

ADMISSION: No charge

MORTON

8887
Cowlitz River Valley Historical Society
7th & Main - Backstrom Park, 98356 [Attn: Reynolds, Box 686, 98356-0686]; (p) (360) 496-6363; www.lewiscounty.com/morton; (c) Lewis

Private non-profit/ 1973/ staff: 10(v)/ members: 30

HISTORIC SITE; HISTORICAL SOCIETY; HISTORY MUSEUM: Gather and preserve artifacts and items, disseminate information pertaining to pioneer days in Lewis County, focusing on the logging and mining industries, and the local personal histories of pioneers.

PROGRAMS: Annual Meeting; Exhibits; Guided Tours; Publication

COLLECTIONS: [1880-1930] Logging equipment, mining gear, historical photos, Indian collection, artifacts, and tools, written histories of pioneer families; period kitchen stove, utensils, tools, postal history

MOSES LAKE

8888
House of Poverty, The
228 S Commerse, 98837 [PO Box 1444, 98837]; (p) (509) 765-6342; (c) Grant

Private non-profit/ 1960/ staff: 1(f); 2(p)

COLLECTIONS: Steam locomotive, railcar, automobiles.

HOURS: Yr Daily 8-4 by appt

ADMISSION: No charge

8889
Schiffner Military Police Museum
4840 Westshore Dr NE, 98837; (p) (509) 765-6374; (c) Grant

Private non-profit/ 1977

HISTORY MUSEUM: The purpose of the museum is preserving the history of the Washington State law enforcement and U.S. Military and Eastern Washington History, and promote and appreciation of that history.

PROGRAMS: Exhibits; Guided Tours; Research Library/Archives

COLLECTIONS: [Civil War-present] Uniforms, weapons, field equipment, pictures, paper memorabilia, over 2,000 book library, badge and patch collection.

HOURS: Mar-Oct T-Th and by appt

ADMISSION: Donations accepted

MT. VERNON

8890
Padilla Bay National Estuarine Research Reserve
10441 Bayview-Edison Rd, 98273; (p) (360) 428-1558; (f) (360) 428-1491; alex@padillabay. gov; inlet.geol.sc.edu/PDB/home.html; (c) Skagit

State/ 1980/ WA State Dept. of Ecology/ staff: 10(f); 3(p)

RESEARCH CENTER: Research in and education about estuaries (where fresh water meets the ocean).

PROGRAMS: Exhibits; Family Programs; Film/Video; Interpretation; Lectures; Research Library/Archives; School-Based Curriculum

COLLECTIONS: [Present] Natural history exhibits on watersheds and estuaries, a "hands-on" room for children, saltwater aquariums, outdoor trials.

HOURS: Yr W-Su 10-5

MUKILTEO

8891
Mukilteo Historical Society
304 Lincoln Ave, 98275; (p) (425) 513-9602; 103005.177@compuserve.com; (c) Snohomish

Private non-profit/ 1965/ staff: 40(v)/ members: 100

HISTORIC PRESERVATION AGENCY; HISTORICAL SOCIETY; HISTORY MUSEUM: Researching, preserving, and maintaining local historical buildings and artifacts.

PROGRAMS: Guided Tours

COLLECTIONS: [1900s]

HOURS: Apr-Sept holidays, Sa-Su 12-5

ADMISSION: No charge

NEAH BAY

8892
Makah Cultural & Research Center
1880 Bayview Ave, 98357 [PO Box 160, 98357]; (p) (360) 645-2711; (f) (360) 645-2656; mcrc@olypen.com; (c) Clallam

Private non-profit; Tribal/ 1979/ staff: 5(f); 12(p); 5(v)/ members: 300

RESEARCH CENTER; TRIBAL MUSEUM: The center is dedicated to preserving, protecting, and interpreting Makah culture and history. Exhibits include 500 year old artifacts from the Ozette site.

PROGRAMS: Guided Tours; Research Library/Archives

COLLECTIONS: 500 year old artifacts from the Ozette village site.

HOURS: Yr June 1-Sept 15 Daily 10-5; Sept 16 - May 31 W-Su 10-5

ADMISSION: $4, Student $3, Seniors $3

NESPELEM

8893
Confederated Tribes of the Colville Reservation
Box 150, 99155; (p) (509) 634-2200; (f) (509) 634-4116; (c) Okanogan

staff: 1600(f); 400(p)/publication: *Language Program*

HOURS: May-Sept Daily

ADMISSION: Donations accepted

NEWPORT

8894
Pend Oreille County Historical Society
402 S Washington Ave, 99156 [PO Box 1409, 99156-1409]; (p) (208) 447-5388; geau@povn.com; (c) Pend Oreille

Private non-profit/ 1967/ staff: 40(v)/ members: 275/publication: *Big Smoke*

HISTORIC SITE; HISTORICAL SOCIETY; HISTORY MUSEUM: Maintain museum, library and photo collection open to research, displays, publish annual book and others.

PROGRAMS: Annual Meeting; Community Outreach; Exhibits; Guided Tours; Publication; Research Library/Archives

COLLECTIONS: [1890-1950] Two buildings of items mostly pioneer days, caboose, settler's cabin, school house, outdoor shed full of tools and farming and logging equipment. Large photo collection.

HOURS: May-Sept Daily 10-4

ODESSA

8895
Odessa Historical Society
Corner of 4th Ave W & Elm St, 99159 [PO Box 536, 99159]; (p) (509) 982-2539; (c) Lincoln

Private non-profit/ 1971/ Board of Directors/ staff: 1(f); 6(p); 10(v)

HISTORICAL SOCIETY; HISTORY MUSEUM: Collects, preserves, interprets, and exhibits artifacts involving the settlement and development of the Odessa WA countryside, especially its German-Russian immigrants for the education and enjoyment of the present and future generations.

PROGRAMS: Annual Meeting; Community Outreach; Exhibits; Festivals; Guided Tours;

Research Library/Archives

COLLECTIONS: [1880-1940s] 100 years of the Odessa Record weekly newspaper, German language Bibles and books, photographs, artifacts, and family trees and histories.

HOURS: June-Sept, Dec Su 1-4; Jan-May, Nov by appt

ADMISSION: Donations accepted

OKANOGAN

8896
Okanogan County Historical Society
1410 2nd St, 98840 [PO Box 258, 98840]; (p) (509) 422-2825; (c) Okanogan

Private non-profit/ 1965/ staff: 1(p)/ members: 1200/publication: *Heritage*

HISTORICAL SOCIETY; HISTORY MUSEUM; LIVING HISTORY/OUTDOOR MUSEUM; RESEARCH CENTER

PROGRAMS: Annual Meeting; Exhibits; Publication; Research Library/Archives

COLLECTIONS: [1890-1950]

HOURS: May-Sept Daily 10-4

ADMISSION: $2

OLYMPIA

8897
Bigelow House Preservation Association
918 Glass Ave NE, 98507 [PO Box 1275, 98507]; (p) (360) 753-1215; (c) Thurston

Private non-profit/ 1993/ Board of Directors/ staff: 1(p); 30(v)/ members: 200/publication: *Bigelow House News*

HOUSE MUSEUM: The Bigelow House Preservation Association preserves the Bigelow House and interprets community history and folklife through the experiences of the first generation of Bigelows in Olympia from 1851 to 1926.

PROGRAMS: Annual Meeting; Community Outreach; Exhibits; Guided Tours; Interpretation; Living History; Publication; School-Based Curriculum

COLLECTIONS: [1851-1926] The structures, furniture, papers, and personal possessions of the Bigelow family.

HOURS: Yr Sa-Su 1-3, Th-F by appt.

OROVILLE

8898
Molson Historical Association, Molson Schoolhouse Museum
915 Nine Mile-Molson Rd, 98844; (p) (509) 485-3292; (c) Okanogan

County/ 1962/ Okanogan County Historical Society/ staff: 25(p); 25(v)

HISTORIC PRESERVATION AGENCY; HISTORIC SITE; HISTORICAL SOCIETY; HISTORY MUSEUM; HOUSE MUSEUM; LIVING HISTORY/OUTDOOR MUSEUM: Maintains Old Molson Museum and Molson Schoolhouse Museum.

PROGRAMS: Annual Meeting; Exhibits

COLLECTIONS: [Early 1900s] Brick schoolhouse, pioneer tools, dolls, toys, furniture, handtools, early appliances, household artifacts, business artifacts, school artifacts.

HOURS: Museum May-Sept Daily 10-5

8899
Old Molson Museum
915 Nine-Mile-Molson Rd, 98844; (p) (509) 485-3292; (c) Okanogan

1962/ Okanogan County Historical Society/ staff: 25(p); 25(v)

Promotes ghost town history and maintains museum.

COLLECTIONS: [Early 1900s] Site: 5-acre ghost town; early 1900s buildings, horse-drawn equipment and transportation; steam engine with thrasher, farming, and mining equipment, tools, cabin life display, household artifacts, business artifacts, and early 1900 material goods.

HOURS: Apr-Nov Daily

ADMISSION: Donations accepted

PAKESDALE

8900
McCoy Valley Museum
Main St, 99158 [c/o Evelyn J Hyden, PO Box 303, 99158]; (p) (509) 285-4101; (c) Whitman

Private non-profit/ 1980/ staff: 12(v)/ members: 12

HISTORY MUSEUM: Displays the history of Oakesdale, WA.

PROGRAMS: Community Outreach; Exhibits; Guided Tours

COLLECTIONS: [1890-1920] Original rooms depicted, post office, dentist office, hat shop, kitchen, bedroom, farm tools, photographs of original settlers dishes.

HOURS: Yr by appt

ADMISSION: donations only

POMEROY

8901
Garfield County Historical Association
708 Columbia, 99347 [Box 854, 99347]; (p) (509) 843-3925; (c) Garfield

Private non-profit/ 1977/ staff: 10(p)

HISTORICAL SOCIETY; HISTORY MUSEUM

PROGRAMS: Annual Meeting; Community Outreach; Exhibits; Guided Tours; Research Library/Archives

COLLECTIONS: [1880s-present] Pioneer items, clothing, household items, and farm equipment, displays arranged by room - school, chapel, store, drug store, parlor, dining room, kitchen, bed room and some Indian artifacts.

HOURS: Yr W,F 1-5; or by appt.

PORT ANGELES

8902
Arthur D. Feiro Marine Life Center
115 N Lincoln St, 98362 [c/o Peninsula College, 1502 E Lauridsen Blvd, 98362]; (p) (360) 417-6254; feirolab@olypen.com

Joint/ 1981/ staff: 1(f); 12(v)

RESEARCH CENTER: A marine science teaching laboratory and tourist facility emphasizing local, live marine exhibit specimens.

PROGRAMS: Exhibits; Interpretation; Lectures

COLLECTIONS: Pacific Northwest intertribal and subtidal marine organisms: live marine specimens are kept for teaching and display in various aquariums and wet tables in running sea water.

HOURS: Mid-June-Mid-Sept Daily 10-8

ADMISSION: $2, Children $1, Seniors $1

8903
Clallam County Historical Society

933 W 9th, 98362 [PO Box 1327, 98362]; (p) (360) 452-2662; (c) Clallam

Private non-profit/ 1958/ staff: 1(f); 40(v)/ members: 375/publication: *Strait News*

GENEALOGICAL SOCIETY; HISTORICAL SOCIETY; HISTORY MUSEUM

PROGRAMS: Annual Meeting; Community Outreach; Exhibits; Lectures; Publication; Research Library/Archives

COLLECTIONS: [1880s-1940s] Photos, archival material, textiles, and maritime, agricultural, merchandising artifacts and Native American baskets.

HOURS: Yr M-F

PORT GAMBLE

8904
Port Gamble Historic Museum

1 Rainier Ave, 98364 [PO Box 85, 98364]; (p) (360) 297-8074; (f) (360) 297-7455; ssmith@orminc.com; www.ptgamble.com

Private non-profit/ 1976/ staff: 1(f); 1(p); 5(v)/publication: *Time, Tide, and Timber*

HISTORIC SITE; RESEARCH CENTER: The museum represents efforts to conserve and protect a special chapter in the history of the Pacific Northwest and the forest products industry.

PROGRAMS: Exhibits; Facility Rental; Festivals; Guided Tours; Interpretation; Publication; Research Library/Archives

COLLECTIONS: [1849] All of Port Gamble history plus family and business history from Machias, Maine; San Francisco, and Portland, Oregon; Items: newspapers, portraits, photographs, museum artifacts, maps, and business records.

HOURS: May 1st-Oct 31; Nov 1-Apr 30 Daily M-F 10:30-5 and by appt

ADMISSION: $2, Student $1, Seniors $1

PORT TOWNSEND

8905
Heritage Group, The

Commanding Officer's House, Fort Worden State Park, 98368 [200 Battery Way, 98368]; (p) (360) 385-4730, (360) 379-9894; fortwordens.p.; (c) Jefferson

State/ 1978/ WA State Dept. of Parks & Recreation/ staff: 2(p); 30(v)

HOUSE MUSEUM: Administers all operation of the commanding officer's house at Fort Worden S.P. for the state of Washington.

PROGRAMS: Interpretation; Living History

COLLECTIONS: [1890-1910] Twelve rooms of late Victorian antiques present life as it might have been for the family of the commanding officer of a coast artillery fort in 1910.

HOURS: Mar-Oct, June-Aug Daily 10-5; Mar, Apr, May, Sept, Oct, Sa-Su 12-4

8906
Jefferson County Historical Society, Museum, & Research Library

210 Madison St, 98368; (p) (360) 385-1003; (f) (360) 385-1042; jchsmuseum@olympus.net; www.jchsmuseum.org; (c) Jefferson

Private non-profit/ 1951/ Jefferson County Historical Society Board of Trustees/ staff: 2(f); 3(p); 100(v)/ members: 450

HISTORICAL SOCIETY; HOUSE MUSEUM; LIBRARY AND/OR ARCHIVES: The society actively discovers, collects, preserves, and promotes the heritage of Jefferson County and Victorian Port Townsend for education and enjoyment of all. The museum includes extensive photo, archival, and artifact collections, and changing exhibits; sponsors educational programs, and presentations.

PROGRAMS: Annual Meeting; Community Outreach; Concerts; Exhibits; Festivals; Guided Tours; Interpretation; Lectures; Living History; Reenactments; Research Library/Archives; School-Based Curriculum; Theatre

COLLECTIONS: [1850-1950] 10,000 photographs, 5,000 artifacts, 450,000 archival documents, local newspaper microfilms (1889-present), and more than 500 reference books; housed in historic City Hall (built 1892) in Port Townsend (Washington's Victorian seaport), the core of a major National Landmark District.

HOURS: Feb-Dec Mo-Sa 11-4, Su 1-4

ADMISSION: $2, Children $1

POULSBO

8907
Poulsbo Historical Society

19050 Jensen Way NE, 98370 [PO Box 451, 98370]; (c) Kitsap

Private non-profit/ 1991/ staff: 10(v)/ members: 90

HISTORICAL SOCIETY

PROGRAMS: Annual Meeting; Exhibits; Festivals; Publication

HOURS: M and by appt 9:30-12:30

PULLMAN

8908
Whitman County Genealogical Society

115 W Main St, Gladish Bldg, Room 104, 99163 [PO Box 393, 99163-0393]; mgpeters@ prodigy.net; www.completebbs.com/simonsen/ wcgsindex.html; (c) Whitman

Private non-profit/ 1984/ staff: 13(v)/ members: 125

GENEALOGICAL SOCIETY; RESEARCH CENTER: Collects and preserves genealogical and historical records of Whitman County for the education and enjoyment of present and future generations.

PROGRAMS: Community Outreach; Guided Tours; Lectures; Publication; Research Library/Archives

COLLECTIONS: [19th-20th c] Books, newspapers, local publication indexes and transcriptions of Whitman County births, deaths, marriages, and probates.

HOURS: Yr W 9-12 or by appt

ADMISSION: No charge

PUYALLUP

8909
Ezra Meeker Historical Society

312 Spring St, 98371 [PO Box 103, 98371]; (p) (253) 848-1770; www.meekermansion.org; (c) Pierce

Private non-profit/ 1970/ staff: 2(p)/ members: 300

GARDEN; HISTORIC SITE; HISTORICAL SOCIETY; HOUSE MUSEUM: To preserve and protect the history of the Puyallup Valley and surrounding area, educate the public and students on the importance of Ezra Meeker and his 20 year pursuit of preserve the Oregon Trail.

PROGRAMS: Annual Meeting; Concerts; Exhibits; Facility Rental; Festivals; Guided Tours; Reenactments; Research Library/Archives; School-Based Curriculum

COLLECTIONS: [Mid 1800s]

HOURS: Mar-Dec W-Su 1-4

ADMISSION: $4, Student $3, Children $2, Seniors $3

REDMOND

8910
Marymoor Museum of Eastside History

6046 W Lake Sammamish Pkwy NE, 98073 [PO Box 162, 98073-0162]; (p) (425) 885-3684; (f) (425) 885-3684; marymoormuseum@juno.com; (c) King

Private non-profit/ 1965/ staff: 1(f); 3(p); 25(v)/ members: 150/publication: *Our Town Redmond*

HISTORIC SITE; HISTORY MUSEUM: The Museum enables diverse audiences to discover regional heritage through programs and displays about natives, pioneers, suburbanites, and the communities they created.

PROGRAMS: Community Outreach; Elder's Programs; Exhibits; Family Programs; Guided Tours; Lectures; Publication

COLLECTIONS: [Prehistory-present] Photographs, archives, textiles, tools, furniture, agriculture and logging equipment, and domestic artifacts.

HOURS: Yr T-Th

8911
Redmond Historical Society

16600 NE 80th Rm 106, 98052; (p) (425) 885-2919; redmondhistory@msn.com; (c) King

Private non-profit/ 1999/ Board of Directors/ staff: 14(v)/ members: 140

HISTORICAL SOCIETY: To discover, recover, record, preserve, and celebrate Redmond's history. Priorities include oral histories and documenting historic buildings and sites.

COLLECTIONS: [1871-present] Oral histories, newspaper clippings, documents, photographs, documents, personal histories, gathering material for archives.

RENTON

8912
Renton Historical Society
235 Mill Ave S, 98055-2133; (p) (425) 255-2330; (f) (425) 277-4400; rtnmuseum@aol.com; (c) King

1966/ staff: 1(f); 2(p); 50(v)/ members: 700/publication: *Renton Historical Quarterly*

HISTORICAL SOCIETY; HISTORY MUSEUM

PROGRAMS: Annual Meeting; Community Outreach; Exhibits; Interpretation; Lectures; Publication; Research Library/Archives; School-Based Curriculum

COLLECTIONS: [1890-1950] Industrial, social, political, and human history of the Renton, Washington area.

HOURS: Jan-Dec T-F 12-4, Sa 10-4

ADMISSION: $3, Children $1; Donations accepted

REPUBLIC

8913
Ferry County Historical Society
15 N Kean St, 99166 [PO Box 287, 99166]; (c) Ferry

Private non-profit/ 1958/ Board of Directors/ staff: 10(v)/ members: 100/publication: *Historic Republic Walking Tour*

HISTORIC PRESERVATION AGENCY; HISTORIC SITE; HISTORICAL SOCIETY; HOUSE MUSEUM: Preserve artifacts and document local history, emphasis placed on Native American culture, mining, homesteading, and early commercial activities.

PROGRAMS: Annual Meeting; Exhibits; Publication

COLLECTIONS: [1850-1950] Turn of the century photographs and artifacts relating to Indians, mining, lumber, agriculture, transportation and crafts, buildings include cabin and early 19th century home and library.

HOURS: May-Oct 10-4

ADMISSION: No charge

8914
Stonerose Interpretive Center and Eocene Fossil Site
15 N Kean St, 99166 [PO Box 987, 99166]; (p) (509) 775-2295; srfossil@televar.co; stonerosefossil.org; (c) Ferry

Private non-profit/ 1989/ staff: 1(f); 1(p); 106(v)

HISTORY MUSEUM: The fossil museum serves education, science, and tourism.

PROGRAMS: Exhibits; Interpretation; Publication

COLLECTIONS: [Eocene era] Fossils: birds, fish, insects.

HOURS: May-Oct T-Sa 10-5

ADMISSION: $2.50; No charge

RITZVILLE

8915
Doctor Frank R. Burroughs Historical Home
408 W Main St, 99169 [PO Box 106, 99169]; (p) (509) 659-1656, (509) 659-1636; (f) (509) 659-0274

City/ 1890/ City of Ritzville/ staff: 10(v)

HISTORIC SITE; HOUSE MUSEUM

COLLECTIONS: [1890-1925] Original family furnishings or community donations, rocking chairs, cameras, medical instruments, large collection of vintage clothing and a fully-equipped kitchen, medical record books, and original light fixtures.

HOURS: Yr Daily By Appt

ADMISSION: Donations accepted

8916
Dr. Frank R. Burroughs' Home & Depot Museum, Inc.
408 W Main, 99169 [9 Burke 902 S Jackson, 99169]; (p) (509) 659-1656; burke@ritzcom.net; (c) Adams

City/ 1962/ staff: 10(v)

HISTORIC SITE; HOUSE MUSEUM

PROGRAMS: Annual Meeting; Community Outreach; Exhibits; Guided Tours

COLLECTIONS: [1890-1925] Original Burrough's family furnishings or community donations, which include Dr. Burrough's 13 rocking chairs, his camera and medical books collection, and original light fixtures. Depot Museum houses railroad, farming, business, and school items form early 1900s-1950s.

HOURS: Depot: May-Sept M-F; Burroughs' Home: by appt

ROSLYN

8917
Roslyn Historical Museum
203 Penn Ave, 98941 [PO Box 281, 98941]; (p) (509) 649-2776; (c) Kittitas

Private non-profit/ 1970

HISTORICAL SOCIETY; HISTORY MUSEUM

PROGRAMS: Exhibits; Guided Tours; School-Based Curriculum

SEAHURST

8918
Highline Historical Society
[PO Box 317, 98062]; (p) (206) 246-6354; (f) (206) 241-5786; cyndiu@netquest.net; (c) King

Private non-profit/ 1994/ staff: 30(v)/ members: 250

HISTORICAL SOCIETY: Trustees supervise cemetery preservation program, archives, exhibits and oral history project.

PROGRAMS: Annual Meeting; Community Outreach; Exhibits; Guided Tours; Lectures; Research Library/Archives; School-Based Curriculum

COLLECTIONS: [1850-present] Two comprehensive local 3-D historical collections, the archives of the community newspaper, 50,000 negatives, 10,000 photos and thousands of slides.

HOURS: Yr, T-Th mornings by appt

SEATTLE

8919
Association of King County Historical Organizations
[PO Box 3257, 98114-3257]; (c) King

Private non-profit/ 1977/ staff: 25(v)/ members: 203/publication: *King County Heritage Directory*

Coordinates and advocates for local historical organizations for mutual assistance.

8920
Black Heritage Society of Washington State, Inc.
2300 E Yesler Way, 98122 [PO Box 22961, 98122-0961]; (p) (206) 525-3973; (f) (206) 526-0912; jack4428@aol.com; (c) King

Private non-profit/ 1977/ staff: 14(v)/ members: 108

HISTORICAL SOCIETY: A non-profit organization dedicated to the acquisition, preservation and exhibition of materials relating to the history of African Americans in the State of Washington.

PROGRAMS: Annual Meeting; Exhibits

COLLECTIONS: [1880s-present] Photographs, legal documents, biographies, obituaries, funeral programs, newspapers, personal and organizational letters, small three-dimensional items and ephemera.

8921
Center for Wooden Boats, The
1010 Valley St, 98109; (p) (206) 382-2628; (f) (206) 382-2699; cwboats@tripl.org; www.eskimo.com/~cwboats; (c) King

Private non-profit/ 1978/ Board of Trustees/ staff: 6(f); 3(p); 350(v)/ members: 2700/publication: *Coast Salish Canoes*

HISTORY MUSEUM; LIVING HISTORY/OUTDOOR MUSEUM; RESEARCH CENTER: Preserves boatbuilding history.

PROGRAMS: Annual Meeting; Community Outreach; Concerts; Elder's Programs; Exhibits; Facility Rental; Family Programs; Festivals; Guided Tours; Interpretation; Lectures; Living History; Publication; Research Library/Archives; School-Based Curriculum

COLLECTIONS: [1850-1950] 160 sail crafts; accessories: sail, oar, paddle, steam and internal combustion power, aboriginal canoes, sailing yachts.

8922
Coast Guard Museum Northwest
1519 Alaskan Wy S, 98134; (p) (206) 217-6993; (c) King

Private non-profit/ 1976/ staff: 3(p); 8(v)/ members: 50

HISTORY MUSEUM; RESEARCH CENTER: Collects and preserves coast guard, navy and nautical artifacts.

PROGRAMS: Elder's Programs; Exhibits; Guided Tours; Research Library/Archives

COLLECTIONS: [1800s-present] 15,000 maritime photos, 50 ship models, lighthouse lens, nautical artifacts, uniforms, supplies, coast guard ships; 3,000 books and periodicals.

HOURS: Yr M, W, F 9-3, Sa-Su 1-5

ADMISSION: No charge

8923
El Centro de la Raza
2524 16th Ave S, 98144; (p) (206) 329-9442; (f) (206) 329-0786; eortega@cartero.elcentro delaraza.com; www.elcentrodelaraza.com; (c) King

Private non-profit/ 1972/ staff: 28(f); 15(p); 110(v)

PROGRAMS: Community Outreach; Concerts; Elder's Programs; Exhibits; Facility Rental; Family Programs; Festivals; Guided Tours; School-Based Curriculum

COLLECTIONS: 3,000 photos, 50 paintings, and 300 posters.

8924
Historic Seattle Preservation & Development Authority
1117 Minor Ave, 98101; (p) (206) 622-6952; (f) (206) 622-1197; info@historicseattle.org; www.historicseattle.org; (c) King

Private non-profit/ 1974/ staff: 6(f); 4(p)/ members: 880

HISTORIC PRESERVATION AGENCY: Maintains and preserves historic buildings, landscapes and architectural artifacts.

PROGRAMS: Annual Meeting; Community Outreach; Guided Tours; Lectures

HOURS: 3rd Th 2-4

ADMISSION: No charge

8925
Hydroplane and Raceboat Museum
1605 S 93rd, 98105; (p) (206) 764-9453; (f) (206) 766-9620; hydros@thunderboats.org; thunderboats.org; (c) King

Private non-profit/ staff: 2(f); 200(v)/ members: 600/publication: *HydroLegend*

LIVING HISTORY/OUTDOOR MUSEUM

PROGRAMS: Annual Meeting; Community Outreach; Exhibits; Facility Rental; Family Programs; Festivals; Film/Video; Interpretation; Lectures; Living History; Publication; Reenactments; Research Library/Archives

COLLECTIONS: 23 race boats, newspapers, magazines.

HOURS: Yr T, Th, F 10-4

ADMISSION: No charge

8926
Klondike Gold Rush National Historical Park
117 S Main St, 98104; (p) (206) 553-7220; (f) (206) 553-0614; KLSE_Ranger_Activities@nps.gov; www.nps.gov/klse/home.htm; (c) King

Federal/ 1979/ National Park Service/ staff: 7(f); 6(p)

HISTORICAL SOCIETY: Preserves history of Seattle's contributions and the US' participation in the Klondike Gold Rush of 1897-98.

PROGRAMS: Exhibits; Family Programs; Film/Video; Interpretation; School-Based Curriculum

COLLECTIONS: [1889-1900]

HOURS: Yr Daily 9-5

ADMISSION: No charge

8927
Last Resort Fire Department
1433 NW 51 St, 98107; (p) (206) 783-4474; (f) (206) 784-1485; (c) King

Private non-profit/ 1969/ staff: 15(v)/ members: 15

HISTORIC PRESERVATION AGENCY: Preserves and displays Seattle Fire Dept history.

PROGRAMS: Festivals

COLLECTIONS: [1889-present] 16 fire engines, photos.

HOURS: Yr Daily by appt

ADMISSION: No charge

8928
Memory Lane Museum at Seattle Goodwill
Corner Rainier Ave S & S Dearbon St, 98144 [1400 S Lane St, 98144]; (p) (206) 329-1000; (f) (206) 726-1502; www.seattlegoodwill.org; (c) King

Private non-profit/ 1923/ staff: 1(p); 50(v)

HISTORY MUSEUM

PROGRAMS: Community Outreach; Exhibits; Family Programs

COLLECTIONS: [1850-present] Miss Bardahl champion hydroplane, a ten-foot Alaska brown bear, vintage clothing, mechanic's garage, World's Fair memorabilia, sports team memorabilia.

HOURS: Yr Daily

8929
Mountaineers Library, The
300 3rd Ave W, 98119; (p) (206) 284-6310; www.mountaineers.org

Private non-profit/ 1906/ Mountaineers Board/ staff: 1(p); 10(v)/ members: 15000/publication: *The Mountaineers*

LIBRARY AND/OR ARCHIVES

PROGRAMS: Publication; Research Library/ Archives

COLLECTIONS: 6,000 books, 20 magazine issues on northwestern mountaineering.

HOURS: Yr T-Th 5pm-9pm or by appt

ADMISSION: No charge

8930
Museum of Flight
9404 E Marginal Wy S, 98108-4097; (p) (206) 764-5700; (f) (206) 764-5707; www.museumof flight.org; (c) King

Private non-profit/ 1965/ Museum of Flight Foundation/ staff: 66(f); 44(p); 560(v)/ members: 19200/publication: *MOF News B-17 Remembered*

RESEARCH CENTER: Preserves aircrafts.

PROGRAMS: Annual Meeting; Community Outreach; Concerts; Elder's Programs; Exhibits; Facility Rental; Family Programs; Festivals; Guided Tours; Interpretation; Lectures; Publication; Research Library/Archives; School-Based Curriculum

COLLECTIONS: [1900-present] 118 aircrafts.

HOURS: Yr Daily 10-5, Th 10-9

8931
Museum of History and Industry
2700 24th Ave E, 98112; (p) (206) 324-1126; (f) (206) 324-1346; staff@seattlehistory.org; www.seattlehistory.org; (c) King

Private non-profit/ 1914/ staff: 19(f); 6(p); 100(v)/ members: 1500

HISTORY MUSEUM: Collects, preserves, interprets and shares the history of the people of Seattle, King County, and the Pacific Northwest.

PROGRAMS: Community Outreach; Concerts; Elder's Programs; Exhibits; Facility Rental; Family Programs; Film/Video; Guided Tours; Interpretation; Lectures; Research Library/Archives; School-Based Curriculum

COLLECTIONS: [1851-present] 75,000 rare artifacts, 2,000,000 photos.

HOURS: Yr Daily M-F 10-5

ADMISSION: $5.50, Student $3, Children $1, Seniors $3; Under 2 free

8932
Nordic Heritage Museum
3014 NW 67th St, 98117; (p) (206) 789-5707; (f) (206) 789-3271; nordic@intelistep.com; (c) King

Private non-profit/ 1979/ staff: 6(f); 4(p); 200(v)/ members: 2300/publication: *Nordic News*

HISTORY MUSEUM: Documents, preserves and interprets the heritage of Nordic Americans in the Northwest.

PROGRAMS: Annual Meeting; Community Outreach; Concerts; Exhibits; Facility Rental; Family Programs; Festivals; Film/Video; Guided Tours; Lectures; Publication

COLLECTIONS: [1800-1940] Historical artifacts, contemporary objects, textile collection, photos and material culture.

HOURS: Yr T-Sa 10-4, Su12-4

8933
Northwest Seaport Maritime Heritage Center
1002 Valley St, 98109-4332; (p) (206) 447-9800; (f) (206) 447-0598; (c) King

Private non-profit/ 1969/ Board of Directors/ staff: 1(f); 2(p); 150(v)/ members: 200

HISTORIC PRESERVATION AGENCY; HISTORIC SITE; LIVING HISTORY/OUTDOOR MUSEUM: Preserves and interprets the maritime heritage of the Pacific Northwest.

PROGRAMS: Concerts; Exhibits; Facility Rental; Guided Tours; Interpretation; Living History; Research Library/Archives; School-Based Curriculum

COLLECTIONS: [1880-1960] 1889 tugboat "Arthur Foss," 1897 lumber schooner "Wawona" and the 1904 lightship #83 "Swiftsure"; photos, logs, films.

HOURS: Yr W-Su summer 10-5, winter 12-4

ADMISSION: Donations accepted

8934
Pacific Science Center
200 2nd Ave N, 98109; (p) (206) 443-2001; (f) (206) 443-3631; www.pacsci.org; (c) King

Private non-profit/ 1962/ staff: 144(f); 243(p); 746(v)/ members: 37278/publication: *Centergram*

NATURAL HISTORY MUSEUM

PROGRAMS: Community Outreach; Exhibits; Facility Rental; Family Programs; Film/Video; Interpretation; Publication

COLLECTIONS: Fire buildings; 300 hands-on exhibits, two IMAX theatres, a planetarium.

HOURS: Yr M-F 10-5, Sa-Su 10-6; summer Daily 10-6

ADMISSION: $7.50, Children $5.50, Seniors $5.50; under 3 free

8935
Puget Sound Maritime Historical Society
[PO Box 9731, 98109-0731]; (p) (206) 624-3028; president@pugetmaritime.org; (c) King

Private non-profit/ 1948/ staff: 1(p); 35(v)/ members: 750/publication: *The Sea Chest*

HISTORICAL SOCIETY; HISTORY MUSEUM: Collects, preserves, and displays objects, artifacts and data of maritime interest.

PROGRAMS: Annual Meeting; Elder's Programs; Exhibits; Guided Tours; Lectures; Publication; Research Library/Archives; School-Based Curriculum

COLLECTIONS: [1790s-present] 55,000 maritime photos, 5,000 books, 100 periodicals, 2,000 articles.

HOURS: Yr Daily

ADMISSION: No charge

8936
Rainier Valley Historical Society
3515 S Alaska St, 98118 [PO Box 18143, 98118-0143]; (p) (206) 722-2838; (f) (360) 722-2838; marvbuzz@AOL.com; (c) King

Private non-profit/ 1891/ staff: 10(p); 1(v)/ members: 265/publication: *Rainier Valley Heritage News*

HISTORICAL SOCIETY: Preserves Rainier Valley history.

PROGRAMS: Annual Meeting; Community Outreach; Exhibits; Festivals; Interpretation; Publication

COLLECTIONS: [1890-present]

HOURS: W 10-1

ADMISSION: No charge

8937
Seattle-King County Military History Society, Inc.
9161 Matthews Ave NE, 98115-4831; (p) (206) 523-4831; (f) (206) 523-4831; (c) King

Private non-profit/ 1974/ staff: 4(p); 6(v)/ members: 15/publication: *Northwest Sentinel*

HISTORICAL SOCIETY: Records and documents military installations, lighthouses; maintains military museum.

PROGRAMS: Annual Meeting; Exhibits; Lectures; Publication; Research Library/Archives

COLLECTIONS: [18th c-present] Uniforms, insignia, flags, field equipment, hats and helmets, edge weapons, maps, photos, rubbings, posters, library.

HOURS: May-Sept Sa-Su 10-4

ADMISSION: Donations accepted

8938
Southwest Seattle Historical Society
3003 61 St SW, 98116; (p) (206) 938-5293; cjv@worldnet.att.net; (c) King

Private non-profit/ 1984/ staff: 1(p); 30(v)/ members: 350/publication: *West Side Story*

HISTORICAL SOCIETY; HISTORY MUSEUM: Preserves and protects the history and culture of the Duwamish Peninsula.

PROGRAMS: Annual Meeting; Community Outreach; Elder's Programs; Exhibits; Film/Video; Guided Tours; Publication; School-Based Curriculum

COLLECTIONS: [1851-present] Photographs, documents related to the culture and history of the Duwamish Peninsula.

HOURS: Yr Th 12-6, F 10-3, Sa 12-3, Su 12-3

ADMISSION: Donations

8939
Thomas Burke Memorial Washington State Museum
17th NE & NE 45th St, 98195 [University of Washington, Box 353010, 98195]; (p) (206) 543-5590; (f) (206) 685-3039; recept@u.washington.edu; www.washington.edu/burkemuseum; (c) King

State/ 1885/ staff: 37(f); 55(p); 127(v)/ members: 1700

NATURAL HISTORY MUSEUM: Preserves natural and cultural history of WA, the Pacific Northwest and the Pacific Rim.

PROGRAMS: Community Outreach; Exhibits; Facility Rental; Family Programs; Guided Tours; Lectures

COLLECTIONS: 4 million specimens and artifacts: ethnology, archaeology, birds, mammals, frozen tissues, vertebrate, and paleobotany.

HOURS: Yr Daily 10-5 (Th 10-8)

ADMISSION: $5.50, Student $2.50, Seniors $4

8940
Vintage Telephone Equipment Museum, The
7000 E Marginal Way S, 98108; (p) (206) 767-3012; (f) (206) 789-5464

1985/ staff: 20(p)

HISTORY MUSEUM; RESEARCH CENTER

PROGRAMS: Elder's Programs; Family Programs; Guided Tours

COLLECTIONS: Fiber optics, data sets, teletypes and toll fest boards simulated telephone poles and wire.

HOURS: Yr T 8:30-2:30 and by appt

ADMISSION: No charge/Donations

8941
Washington State Jewish Historical Society
Allen Library, Univ of WA, 98195 [SCMA, Box 352900, 98195]; (p) (206) 543-1895; (f) (206) 685-8049; sheva@u.washington.edu; www.oz.net/~arobbins; (c) King

Private non-profit/ 1980/ staff: 2(p); 50(v)/ members: 275

HISTORICAL SOCIETY: Preserves history of Jewish communities.

PROGRAMS: Annual Meeting; Community Outreach; Exhibits; Lectures; Living History; Research Library/Archives; School-Based Curriculum

COLLECTIONS: [1853-present] Organizational records, personal papers, memorabilia, documents, photos, and over 300 oral interviews documenting Jewish life.

HOURS: Yr M-Sa 10-5

8942
Wing Luke Asian Museum
407 7th Ave S, 98104; (p) (206) 623-5124; (f) (206) 623-4559; folks@wing.luke.org; www.wingluke.org; (c) King

Private non-profit/ 1965/ staff: 14(f); 3(p); 100(v)/ members: 800/publication: *Divided Destiny*

HISTORY MUSEUM: Promotes and preserves the history, culture, and traditions of Asian American communities.

PROGRAMS: Community Outreach; Exhibits; Family Programs; Festivals; Film/Video; Guided Tours; Lectures; Publication; Research Library/Archives; School-Based Curriculum

COLLECTIONS: [20th Century] 10,000 museum artifacts, photos, and archives representing Asian American experience in WA, and Asian heritage (China, Japan and Southeast Asia).

HOURS: Yr T-F 11-4:30, Sa-Su 12-4

ADMISSION: $2.50

SEQUIM

8943
Museum and Arts Center in the Sequim Dungeness Valley
175 W Cedar ST, 98382; (p) (360) 683-8110; (f) (360) 683-8364; www.olympus.net/community/mac/; (c) Clallam

Private non-profit/ 1976/ staff: 1(f); 3(p); 100(v)/ members: 530/publication: *Peninsula Art & History*

ART MUSEUM; HOUSE MUSEUM; RESEARCH CENTER

PROGRAMS: Annual Meeting; Exhibits; Facility Rental; Family Programs; Guided Tours; Publication; Research Library/Archives

COLLECTIONS: [1850-present] Sequim-Dungeness Valley artifacts, mastodon bones.

HOURS: Yr Nov-Mar M-Sa 9-4; Apr-Oct M-Sa 9-4, Su 1-4

ADMISSION: No charge, donations accepted

SHELTON

8944
Mason County Historical Society Museum
427 Railroad Ave, 98584 [PO Box 1366, 98584]; (p) (360) 426-1020; (c) Mason

Private non-profit/ 1976/ Mason County Historical Society/ staff: 1(f); 2(p); 20(v)/ members: 326

HISTORIC SITE; HISTORICAL SOCIETY; HISTORY MUSEUM; RESEARCH CENTER: Preserves records, photographs, and pioneer artifacts depicting life in Mason County.

PROGRAMS: Annual Meeting; Community Outreach; Exhibits; Facility Rental; Guided Tours; Interpretation; Lectures; Research Library/Archives; School-Based Curriculum

COLLECTIONS: [1850-1950] Newspapers, NW historical books, maps, photos, census reports, obituaries and cemetery, historic register, family and school histories, farming, logging, shellfish.

HOURS: Yr T-F 12-5, Sa 12-4

SHORELINE

8945
Shoreline Historical Museum
749 N 175th, 98133 [PO Box 7171, 98133]; (p) (206) 542-7111; (c) King

Private non-profit/ 1975/ staff: 1(f); 60(v)/ members: 480/publication: *Shoreline-Steamers, Stumps, and Strawberries*

HISTORIC SITE; HISTORY MUSEUM

PROGRAMS: Annual Meeting; Community Outreach; Exhibits; Facility Rental; Family Programs; Guided Tours; Interpretation; Lectures; Publication; Research Library/Archives; School-Based Curriculum

COLLECTIONS: [1890-1930]

HOURS: Yr T-Sa 10-4

ADMISSION: Donations

SKAMOKAWA

8946
Friends of Skamokawa Foundation
1394 WSR4, 98647 [PO Box 67, 98647]; (p) (360) 795-3007; (f) (360) 795-8119; (c) Wahkiakum

Private non-profit/ 1988/ Board of Directors/ staff: 1(p); 25(v)/ members: 400

HISTORIC PRESERVATION AGENCY; HISTORIC SITE

PROGRAMS: Annual Meeting; Community Outreach; Concerts; Elder's Programs; Exhibits; Facility Rental; Family Programs; Interpretation; Lectures; Living History

COLLECTIONS: [1844-1930] 1894 schoolhouse, Lewis & Clark visit in Nov. 1905

HOURS: Yr W-Sa 12-4, Su 1-4

ADMISSION: $2, Children $1; members free

SNOHOMISH

8947
Blackman House Museum
118 Ave B, 98290 [PO Box 174, 98290]; (p) (360) 568-5235; www.ohwy.com/wa/b/blackmam.htm

SOUTH BEND

8948
Pacific County Historical Society and Museum Foundation
1008 W Robert Bush Dr, 98586 [PO Box P, 98586-0039]; (p) (360) 875-5224; (c) Pacific

Private non-profit/ 1949/ staff: 1(f); 25(v)/ members: 625/publication: *The Sou'Weater*

HISTORICAL SOCIETY; HISTORY MUSEUM

PROGRAMS: Annual Meeting; Community Outreach; Exhibits; Festivals; Interpretation; Lectures; Publication; Research Library/Archives

COLLECTIONS: [1800-1990] Artifacts, photos and documents.

HOURS: Yr Daily

ADMISSION: No charge

SPANAWAY

8949
Spanaway Historical Society and Prairie House Museum
812 E 176th St, 98387 [PO Box 1238, 98387]; (p) (253) 536-6655; (c) Pierce

Private non-profit/ 1976/ staff: 5(f); 10(p); 25(v)/ members: 143

HOUSE MUSEUM

PROGRAMS: Annual Meeting; Exhibits; Festivals; Guided Tours; Interpretation; Lectures

COLLECTIONS: [1880s-present] Artifacts: schools, farm life, logging, and settlers.

HOURS: Yr W 11-3, Su 12-3

SPOKANE

8950
Campbell House
2316 W First Ave, 99204 [2316 W First Ave, 99204]; (p) (509) 456-3931; (f) (509) 456-7690

1898/ Eastern WA State Historical Society/ staff: 20(f); 100(v)

COLLECTIONS: [1910] 1898 original furnishings; lighting fixtures.; interior photos; business correspondence; financial records

8951
Eastern Washington State Historical Society
2316 W 1st Ave, 99204; (p) (509) 456-3931; (f) (509) 456-7690; cheneycowles.org; (c) Spokane

Private non-profit; State/ 1916/ staff: 30(f); 5(p); 300(v)/ members: 1500

ART MUSEUM; HISTORIC PRESERVATION AGENCY; HISTORICAL SOCIETY; HISTORY MUSEUM; HOUSE MUSEUM: Collects, preserves and interprets the history of Eastern WA, the inland NW, American Indian cultures and the visual arts.

PROGRAMS: Annual Meeting; Community Outreach; Exhibits; Facility Rental; Family Programs; Festivals; Guided Tours; Interpretation; Lectures; Living History; Research Library/Archives; School-Based Curriculum; Theatre

COLLECTIONS: Plateau Indian collection, overall American Indian collection, 34,000 artifacts, 1,501 fine art objects, 12,175 regional history artifacts, 500,000 items in research library and archives.

HOURS: Yr T, Th, Sa 10-5, W 10-9, Su 1-5

ADMISSION: $4, Family $10, Student $2.50, Children $2.50, Seniors $3

8952
Gonzaga University Special Collection
Foley Center, Gonzaga Univ, 99258; (p) (509) 323-3847; (f) (509) 323-5904; plowman@its.gonzaga.edu; www.foley.gonzaga.edu/spcoll/spcoll.html; (c) Spokane

Private non-profit/ 1889/ staff: 2(f); 1(p)

COLLECTIONS: Rare books: philosophy, theology and Northwest history; Gerard Manley Hopkins, Bing Crosby manuscripts.

8953
Jesuit Oregon Province Archives
Gonzaga University, 99258; (p) (509) 323-3814; (f) (509) 324-5904; jopa@its.gonzaga.edu; www.Foley.gonzaga.edu/spcoll/jopa.html; (c) Spokane

Private non-profit/ 1932/ Oregon Province of the Society of Jesus/ staff: 2(f); 1(p); 1(v)

LIBRARY AND/OR ARCHIVES: Preserves and provides access to documentary evidence of role of society of Jesus (Jesuits) in the history of AK, the Pacific Northwest, and Native Americans.

PROGRAMS: Exhibits; Research Library/Archives

COLLECTIONS: [1860-1950] Books (2,000 linear feet), manuscripts and photos (2,000 linear feet) and recording media (120 linear feet). Native American ethnology and languages and regional settlement, missions and ecclesiastical history.

HOURS: Yr M-F

8954
Spokane Fire Station Museum
3202 E Queen, 99207 [2511 N Lee St, 99207]; (p) (509) 625-7062; (f) (509) 625-0739; theckler@spokanecity.org; (c) Spokane

Private non-profit/ 1978/ staff: 20(v)/ members: 20

HISTORIC PRESERVATION AGENCY; HISTORIC SITE; HISTORICAL SOCIETY; HISTORY MUSEUM; LIVING HISTORY/OUTDOOR MUSEUM

PROGRAMS: Annual Meeting; Community Outreach; Exhibits; Festivals; Guided Tours; Interpretation

COLLECTIONS: [1890-present] 200 fire dept photos, 300 books and magazines, 2 fire engines, one Great Northern Railway caboose, boxcar, M & W car, Davenport locomotive, maps of Hillyard and Spokane, 100 museum artifacts.

HOURS: By appt

ADMISSION: No charge

STANWOOD

8955
Stanwood Area Historical Society
27112 102nd Ave NW, 98292 [PO Box 69, 98292]; (p) (360) 609-6110; kprasse@camano.net; (c) Snohomish and Island Counties

Private non-profit/ 1972/ staff: 20(v)/ members: 225/publication: *Stanwood Area ECHOES*

HISTORIC SITE; HISTORICAL SOCIETY; HISTORY MUSEUM; HOUSE MUSEUM: Discovers, collects, and preserves history and cultural heritage of the Stenwood area.

PROGRAMS: Community Outreach; Exhibits; Family Programs; Guided Tours; Interpretation; Publication; Research Library/Archives; School-Based Curriculum

COLLECTIONS: 5,000 museum artifacts, Model T Ford, shovel nose Indian canoe and buggy; archival materials, business records, 5,000 photographs and negatives, reference, maps, biographical materials.

HOURS: Jan-Nov W 1-4, Fri 10-2, Su 2-5

ADMISSION: Donations accepted

STEILACOOM

8956
Historic Fort Steilacoom Association
9601 Steilacoom Blvd SW, 98388 [PO Box 88447, 98388]; (p) (253) 756-3928; fort-steil@yahoo.com; home1.gte.net/swhite/Fort_Steilacoom.html; (c) Pierce

Private non-profit/ 1983/ staff: 15(v)/ members: 150/publication: *Historic Fort Steilacoom Newsletter*

HISTORIC PRESERVATION AGENCY; HISTORIC SITE; HISTORY MUSEUM; LIVING HISTORY/OUTDOOR MUSEUM: Maintains historic military site and living history museum.

PROGRAMS: Annual Meeting; Community Outreach; Exhibits; Facility Rental; Family Programs; Guided Tours; Interpretation; Lectures; Living History; Publication; Reenactments; Research Library/Archives; School-Based Curriculum

COLLECTIONS: [1849-1868] Military and related site artifacts.

HOURS: June-Sept 5, Su 1-4 or by appt

ADMISSION: No charge; Group rates

8957
Steilacoom Historical Museum Association
112 Main St, 98388 [PO Box 88016, 98388]; (p) (253) 584-4133; (f) (253) 581-7444; (c) Pierce

Private non-profit/ 1972/ staff: 75(v)/ members: 420/publication: *SHMA News; The Quarterly*

HISTORIC SITE; HISTORICAL SOCIETY; HISTORY MUSEUM; HOUSE MUSEUM; LIVING HISTORY/OUTDOOR MUSEUM: Preserves Steilacoom's heritage and culture.

PROGRAMS: Annual Meeting; Elder's Programs; Exhibits; Facility Rental; Guided Tours; Lectures; Living History; Publication; Research Library/Archives; School-Based Curriculum

COLLECTIONS: [1860-present] Artifacts from Steilacoom's history; Bair Drug and Hardware, a restaurant and living history museum. The Nathaniel Orr Pioneer Home Site.

HOURS: Mar-Oct

STEVENSON

8958
Columbia Gorge Interpretive Center
990 SW Rock Creek Dr, 98648 [PO Box 396, 98648]; (p) (800) 991-2338, (509) 427-8211; (f) (509) 427-7429; (c) Skamania

Private non-profit/ 1989/ staff: 4(f); 2(p); 25(v)/ members: 250/publication: *Exploration*

HISTORY MUSEUM: Interprets, collects and preserves the natural and cultural history of Skamania County and the Columbia River Gorge.

PROGRAMS: Annual Meeting; Community Outreach; Exhibits; Facility Rental; Family Programs; Festivals; Film/Video; Guided Tours; Lectures; Living History; Publication; School-Based Curriculum

COLLECTIONS: [Prehistory-1950s] Local Native American, local pioneer, Lewis & Clark, transportation, military, fishwheel, logging truck, Corliss steam engine, 1957 diesel locomotive, 1947 SP&S caboose, Japanese artifacts, fine arts.

HOURS: Yr Daily 10-5

ADMISSION: $6, Student $5, Children $4, Seniors $5; Under 5/Mbrs free

SULTAN

8959
Sultan-Sky Valley Historical Society
4th Main, 98294 [PO Box 1074, 98294]; (p) (360) 793-0650; (c) Snohomish

Private non-profit/ 1982/ staff: 6(v)/ members: 22

HISTORIC PRESERVATION AGENCY; HISTORICAL SOCIETY

PROGRAMS: Annual Meeting; Community Outreach; Exhibits; School-Based Curriculum

COLLECTIONS: [1800s-present] Artifacts: mining, logging, agriculture, household items, military, geological, railroad, industries.

HOURS: Every 1st and 3rd T 2-10

ADMISSION: No charge

SUMNER

8960
Sumner Ryan House Museum
1228 Main St, 98390 [PO Box 517, 98390]; (p) (253) 863-8936, (253) 863-4268; www.ohwy.com/wa/s/sumryahm.htm

SUNNYSIDE

8961
Sunnyside Historical Museum
4th & Grant, 98944 [Box 782, 98944]; (p) (509) 837-6013; (c) Yakima

Private non-profit/ 1972/ staff: 10(p); 12(v)

HISTORIC PRESERVATION AGENCY; HISTORIC SITE:

PROGRAMS: Community Outreach; Exhibits; Guided Tours; School-Based Curriculum

HOURS: Apr-Dec F-Su 1-4:30

ADMISSION: $2, Children $1; Under 12 free

SUQUAMISH

8962
Suquamish Museum
15838 Sandy Hook Rd, 98392 [PO Box 498, 98392-0498]; (p) (360) 394-5275; (f) (360) 598-6295; suqumuseum@hotmail.com; www.suquamish.nwn.us/museum; (c) Kitsap

1983/ staff: 3(f)/ members: 130

RESEARCH CENTER: Preserves and provides educational information of the Suquamish Tribe; provides historical tours of Port Madison Indian Reservation.

PROGRAMS: Elder's Programs; Exhibits; Facility Rental; Family Programs; Festivals; Film/Video; Guided Tours; Interpretation; Lectures; Living History; Publication

COLLECTIONS: [Pre contact-present] Oral histories, artifacts, photographs, written documents, newspapers.

HOURS: May 1-Sept 31 Daily 10-5; Oct 1-Apr 30 Sa-Su 11-4

ADMISSION: $4, Children $2, Seniors $3

TACOMA

8963
Fort Nisqually Living History Museum
5400 N Pearl St #11, 98407; (p) (253) 759-6184; (f) (253) 305-1005; fortnisqually@tacomaparks.org; (c) Pierce

1937/ Metropolitan Park District of Tacoma/ staff: 2(f); 10(p); 150(v)/ members: 120/publication: *Occurences; Journal of Northwest History During the Fur Trade*

HISTORIC SITE; LIVING HISTORY/OUTDOOR MUSEUM: Interpret Northwest history on Puget Sound.

PROGRAMS: Annual Meeting; Community Outreach; Exhibits; Facility Rental; Family Programs; Festivals; Guided Tours; Interpretation; Lectures; Living History; Publication; Reenactments; Research Library/Archives; School-Based Curriculum

COLLECTIONS: [1833-1869] Artifacts of mid-19th C British fur trade, archaeological material, ceramics, textiles, firearms, trade goods, and supporting archival documentation.

HOURS: Yr June-Aug Daily 11-6; Sept-May W-Su 11-5

ADMISSION: $3, Children $1, Seniors $2

8964
Scandinavian Cultural Center
122nd & S Park Ave, 98447 [Pacific Lutheran Univ, 98447]; (p) (253) 535-7532; (f) (253) 536-5132; (c) Pierce

Private non-profit/ 1989/ staff: 1(p); 100(v)/ members: 300/publication: *Scandinavian Scene*

CULTURAL CENTER: Preserves heritage and culture of the Nordic countries; to promote understanding of the immigrant experience.

PROGRAMS: Community Outreach; Concerts; Elder's Programs; Exhibits; Facility Rental; Family Programs; Festivals; Film/Video; Lectures; Publication

COLLECTIONS: Scandinavian artifacts.

HOURS: Yr June-Aug 31 Su, T, W 11-3

ADMISSION: No charge

8965
Shanamon Sports Museum of Tacoma-Pierce County
2727 E D St, 98421; (p) (253) 848-1360; mhblau@Nwrain.com; (c) Pierce

Private non-profit/ 1994/ staff: 15(v)

HISTORY MUSEUM: Preserves history of sports in Tacoma-Pierce County.

PROGRAMS: Exhibits

HOURS: Yr varies

8966
Tacoma Historical Society, The
3712 S Cedar #101, 98401 [PO Box 1865, 98401]; (p) (253) 472-3738; www.powerscourt.com/ths; (c) Pierce

Private non-profit/ 1989/ staff: 25(v)/ members: 350/publication: *City of Destiny Newsletter*

HISTORICAL SOCIETY: Preservates, promotes, interprets, and presents history of Tacoma.

PROGRAMS: Annual Meeting; Community Outreach; Exhibits; Family Programs; Guided Tours; Lectures; Publication

COLLECTIONS: Newspapers, directories, tax records, photos, and business records, artifacts related to local printing company and Tacoma Fire Dept.

HOURS: By appt only

8967
Washington State Historical Society
1911 Pacific Ave, 98402-3109; (p) (253) 272-3500; (f) (253) 272-9518; www.wshs.org; (c) Pierce

Private non-profit/ 1891/ staff: 38(f); 34(p); 120(v)/ members: 3897/publication: *The Magazine of Northwest History*

HISTORICAL SOCIETY; HISTORY MUSEUM; RESEARCH CENTER: Collects, preserves, and interprets materials and information that exemplify the history and culture of WA.

PROGRAMS: Annual Meeting; Community Outreach; Concerts; Exhibits; Facility Rental; Family Programs; Festivals; Film/Video; Interpretation; Lectures; Living History; Publication; Research Library/Archives; School-Based Curriculum

COLLECTIONS: [Prehistory-present] Pacific Northwest history paintings, furnishings, textiles, and ethnology. Special collections include rare books, manuscripts, maps, photos, and ephemera.

HOURS: Yr May-Sept Daily M-Sa 10-5, Su 11-5; Sept-May T-Sa 10-5, Su 11-5

ADMISSION: $7, Family $20, Student $5, Children $4, Seniors $6; Under 6 free, Th 5-8 free

TAHOLAH

8968
Quinault Cultural Center
807 5th Ave suite 1, 98587 [PO Box 189, 98587]; (p) (360) 276-8211; (f) (360) 276-4191; L.Jones@Quinnault.org; (c) Grays Harbor

staff: 1(f); 1(p)

CULTURAL CENTER; TRIBAL MUSEUM: Preserves and promotes cultural history; serves as site for exhibits and cultural activities.

PROGRAMS: Elder's Programs; Exhibits; Facility Rental; Family Programs; Guided Tours; Interpretation; Research Library/Archives

COLLECTIONS: [1800s] Artifacts

HOURS: Yr M-F 9-4

ADMISSION: Donations accepted

TENINO

8969
South Thurston County Historical Society
399 Park Ave W, 98589 [PO Box 339, 98589]; (p) (360) 364-4321; (c) Thurston

Private non-profit/ 1974/ staff: 10(v)/ members: 40

HISTORIC SITE; HISTORICAL SOCIETY; HISTORY MUSEUM: Preserves and protects South Thurston County history and artifacts.

PROGRAMS: Exhibits; Guided Tours

COLLECTIONS: [1800-1900] Artifacts from pioneer families, sandstone quarries, coal mining, logging, wooden money pieces, and press.

HOURS: Apr 15-Oct 15 F-Su 12-4

ADMISSION: No charge/Donations

TOPPENISH

8970
Toppenish Museum
One S Elm, 98948; (p) (509) 865-4545; (c) Yakima

City/ 1976/ staff: 2(p); 4(v)

ART MUSEUM; HISTORY MUSEUM

PROGRAMS: Community Outreach; Exhibits; Family Programs; Guided Tours; Lectures; Publication; Research Library/Archives

COLLECTIONS: [1800-1980] Pictures, letters, newspapers, books, scrapbooks, household items, clothing.

HOURS: Mar-Nov M-Th 1-4

ADMISSION: $1.50

8971
Yakima Valley Rail & Steam Museum Association
10 Asotin, 98948 [PO Box 889, 98948]; (p) (509) 865-1911; (c) Yakima

Joint/ 1989/ Board of Directors; City/ staff: 20(v)/ members: 300

HISTORIC PRESERVATION AGENCY; HISTORICAL SOCIETY; LIVING HISTORY/OUTDOOR MUSEUM: Supports historic preservation of Northern Pacific Railroad in the Yakima Valley.

PROGRAMS: Annual Meeting; Exhibits; Guided Tours; Interpretation; Lectures

COLLECTIONS: [1900-1950] Railroad artifacts-located in historic Northern Pacific Depot.

HOURS: May-Nov Sa-Su 10-5

ADMISSION: $2, Children $1, Seniors $1

TUMWATER

8972
Henderson House Museum
602 Des Chutes Way, 98501; (p) (360) 754-4163

8973
Tumwater Historical Association
[PO Box 4315, 98501]; (p) (360) 943-6951; (c) Thurston

Private non-profit/ staff: 20(v)/ members: 100/publication: *The History of Tumwater*

HISTORICAL SOCIETY

PROGRAMS: Annual Meeting; Family Programs; Lectures; Living History; Publication; Reenactments; School-Based Curriculum

UNION GAP

8974
Central Washington Agricultural Museum Association
4508 Main St, 98903 [PO Box 3008, 98903]; (p) (509) 457-8735; (c) Yakima

Private non-profit/ 1979/ Board of Directors/ staff: 25(v)/ members: 185

HISTORICAL SOCIETY: Collects, preserves and interprets cultural and agricultural history of Central WA area.

PROGRAMS: Annual Meeting; Festivals; Guided Tours; Publication

COLLECTIONS: Farm machinery, operating windmill, apple-packing line and blacksmith shop. Two log cabins, railroad exhibit, 3,000 hand tools.

HOURS: Yr Daily 9-5

ADMISSION: No charge/Donations

VANCOUVER

8975
Covington House
4201 Main St, 98663-1853; (p) (360) 695-6750

8976
Fort Vancouver National Historic Site
1501 E Evergreen Blvd, 98661 [612 E Reserve St, 98661]; (p) (360) 696-7655; (f) (360) 696-7657; www.nps.gov/fova/; (c) Clark

Federal/ 1829/ National Park Service/ staff: 21(f); 13(p); 200(v)/ members: 150

GARDEN; HISTORIC SITE; HISTORY MUSEUM; HOUSE MUSEUM; LIVING HISTORY/OUTDOOR MUSEUM

PROGRAMS: Community Outreach; Guided Tours; Interpretation; Lectures; Living History; Reenactments; Research Library/Archives; School-Based Curriculum

COLLECTIONS: [1820-1860] Over 1 million excavated items, spode china.

HOURS: Yr Daily Summer 9-5; Winter 9-4

ADMISSION: $2, Family $4

8977
George C. Marshall House
1301 Officers Row, 98661; (p) (360) 693-3103; (f) (360) 693-3192

1886/ City/ staff: 2(f); 5(p); 22(v)

COLLECTIONS: [1880]

HOURS: Yr M-F 9-5, Sa-Su 11-6

8978
Heritage Education Program, City of Vancouver
1301 Officers Row, 98661; (p) (360) 699-5288; (f) (360) 693-3192; lfloyd@pacifier.com; (c) Clark

City/ 1995/ staff: 1(f); 20(v)

Provides educational programming.

PROGRAMS: Community Outreach; Exhibits; Facility Rental; Guided Tours; Lectures

HOURS: Yr M-F 9-5

ADMISSION: No charge

WAITSBURG

8979
Waitsburg Historical Society
320 Main St, 99361 [PO Box 755, 99361]; (c) Walla Walla

Private non-profit/ 1971/ staff: 20(v)/ members: 150

HISTORICAL SOCIETY; HOUSE MUSEUM: Preserves and maintains Bruce House Museum, an 1883 fully restored Victorian home and carriage house.

PROGRAMS: Annual Meeting; Exhibits; Festivals; Guided Tours

COLLECTIONS: [1870-1900] Household items, photos, clothing, 1883 Victorian wood frame house, carriage house.

HOURS: June-Sept Su 1-4

ADMISSION: $1

WALLA WALLA

8980
Fort Walla Walla Museum/Walla Walla Valley Historical Society
755 Myra Rd, 99362; (p) (509) 525-7703; (f) (509) 525-7798;
info@fortwallawallamuseum.org;
www.fortwallawallamuseum.org; (c) Walla Walla

Private non-profit/ 1968/ Board of Directors/ staff: 6(f); 2(p); 300(v)/ members: 700

HISTORIC PRESERVATION AGENCY; HISTORIC SITE; HISTORICAL SOCIETY; HISTORY MUSEUM; LIVING HISTORY/OUTDOOR MUSEUM: Preserves and promotes history of Walla Walla Valley area.

PROGRAMS: Annual Meeting; Community Outreach; Exhibits; Family Programs; Festivals; Guided Tours; Living History; Research Library/Archives

COLLECTIONS: [1850-1920] Pioneer settlement of 14 original and replica buildings.

HOURS: Apr 1-Oct 31 T-Su 10-5

ADMISSION: $5, Student $4

8981
Kirkman House Museum
214 N Colville St, 99362; (p) (509) 529-4373; roger_trick@nps.gov; (c) Walla Walla

Private non-profit/ 1960/ Board of Directors/ staff: 1(p); 15(v)/ members: 100

HOUSE MUSEUM: Preserves the residence of the William Kirkman family.

PROGRAMS: Community Outreach; Exhibits; Guided Tours; Interpretation; School-Based Curriculum

COLLECTIONS: [1880-1910] Kirkman Family and period pieces, tea service, silver service, piano, and furniture of parlor, dining room and bedrooms.

HOURS: Mar-Dec W-Su

ADMISSION: $1

8982
Whitman Mission National Historic Site
Route 2, Box 247, 99362; (p) (509) 522-6360; (f) (509) 522-6355;
whimi_interpretation@nps.gov;
www.nps.gov/whmi; (c) Walla Walla

Federal/ 1936/ National Park Service/ staff: 10(f); 5(p); 20(v)

HISTORIC SITE; LIVING HISTORY/OUTDOOR MUSEUM: Preserves site of Marcus and Narcissa Whitman's missionary efforts to the Cayuse Indians.

PROGRAMS: Community Outreach; Exhibits; Film/Video; Interpretation; Living History; School-Based Curriculum

COLLECTIONS: [1830-1855] Artifacts: Native American, Cayuse, OR Trail pioneers.

HOURS: Yr Daily Fall-Spring 8-4:30, Summer 8-6

ADMISSION: $2, Family $4

WASHOUGAL

8983
Camas-Washougal Historical Society
1-16th St, 98607 [PO Box 204, 98671]; (p) (360) 835-8742; (c) Clark

Private non-profit/ 1978/ Board of Directors/ staff: 50(v)/ members: 300

HISTORIC PRESERVATION AGENCY; HISTORIC SITE; HISTORICAL SOCIETY; HISTORY MUSEUM; RESEARCH CENTER; TRIBAL MUSEUM

PROGRAMS: Community Outreach; Exhibits; Guided Tours; Interpretation; Lectures; Quarterly Meeting; Research Library/Archives

COLLECTIONS: [1800s-present] Indian artifacts, memorabilia, dolls, furniture, clothing, toys, glassware, and pioneer materials.

HOURS: Yr T-Sa 11-3

ADMISSION: $2, Student $0.50, Seniors $1; Members free

WATERVILLE

8984
Douglas County Museum
124 W Walnut, 98858 [Box 63, 98858]; (p) (509) 745-8435; (c) Douglas

Private non-profit/ 1959/ Douglas County Historical Society/ staff: 1(f); 1(p); 5(v)/ members: 101

HISTORICAL SOCIETY; HISTORY MUSEUM: Collects, preserves and exhibits regional artifact items essential to pioneer life.

PROGRAMS: Annual Meeting; Community Outreach; Exhibits; Facility Rental; Guided Tours; Interpretation; Lectures; Research Library/Archives

COLLECTIONS: [1890s-mid 1900s] Pioneer living items: clothing, household goods, musical instruments, books, toys, tools and furniture, 4,500 rock and mineral specimens including petrified woods and flourescents; Native American items.

HOURS: May-Oct T-Su 11-5

WENATCHEE

8985
Chelan County Public Utility District
Rocky Reach Dam Hwy 97A, 98801 [327 N Wenatchee Ave, 98801]; (p) (509) 663-8121; (f) (509) 667-3449; www.chelanpud.org; (c) Chelan

Private non-profit/ 1962/ staff: 4(f); 9(p)

HISTORY MUSEUM

PROGRAMS: Community Outreach; Elder's Programs; Exhibits; Film/Video; Guided Tours; Interpretation; School-Based Curriculum

COLLECTIONS: Power productive information, exhibit space, fish viewing room, theatre, local geology, prehistory, history, and development of electricity.

HOURS: Daily summer 8-6; winter 8-4

ADMISSION: No charge

8986
North Central Washington Museum
127 S Mission, 98801; (p) (509) 664-3340; (f) (509) 664-3354; (c) Chelan

Private non-profit/ 1939/ staff: 8(f); 6(p); 200(v)/ members: 595/publication: Confluence

ALLIANCE OF HISTORICAL AGENCIES; ART MUSEUM; GENEALOGICAL SOCIETY; HISTORIC PRESERVATION AGENCY; HISTORIC SITE; HISTORY MUSEUM

PROGRAMS: Annual Meeting; Community Outreach; Concerts; Exhibits; Facility Rental; Family Programs; Festivals; Guided Tours; Publication; Research Library/Archives; School-Based Curriculum; Theatre

HOURS: Yr M-Sa 10-4

ADMISSION: $3, Family $5, Children $1

WESTPORT

8987
Westport Maritime Museum
2201 Westhaven Dr, 98595 [PO Box 1074, 98595]; (p) (360) 268-0078; (f) (360) 268-0078; www.westportwa.com/museum; (c) Grays Harbor

Private non-profit/ 1985/ staff: 3(f); 30(v)/ members: 287/publication: The Foghorn

HISTORIC SITE; HISTORICAL SOCIETY; HISTORY MUSEUM: Preserves and interprets local area history.

PROGRAMS: Annual Meeting; Community Outreach; Exhibits; Facility Rental; Festivals; Guided Tours; Publication

COLLECTIONS: [1855-present] Objects and photos related to local history; 110 year old operating Fresnel Lens.

HOURS: Yr Sept-May W-Su 12-4; Jun-Aug 10-4

ADMISSION: $3

WILBUR

8988
Big Bend Historical Society, Inc.
505 NW Cole St, 99185 [PO Box 523, 99185]; (c) Lincoln

City/ 1954/ staff: 12(v)/ members: 126

HISTORY MUSEUM

COLLECTIONS: [Late 19th-mid-20th c] Photos, schoolroom, gem room, railroad room, radio and television room, genealogy and library room, kitchen, living room, and bedroom.

HOURS: Yr Daily by appt or Summer: Sa 1-5

WINLOCK

8989
Jackson Court
4583 Jackson Hwy, 98596; (p) (360) 864-2643; (f) (360) 864-2515

1848/ Parks and Recreation Dept.

COLLECTIONS: Furniture; Jackson's tools.

HOURS: July-Aug

WOODINVILLE

8990
Woodinville Historical Society
[PO Box 216, 98072-0216]; (p) (425) 483-8270; (c) King

1976/ members: 75

HISTORICAL SOCIETY: Collects and presents pictures and artifacts from Woodinville's past.

PROGRAMS: Community Outreach; Exhibits; Lectures

COLLECTIONS: [1900s] Photos, clothes, household, farm, tools, artifacts, and newspaper articles; trapper's cabin and sawmill.

WOODLAND

8991
Hulda Klager Lilac Gardens Historical Society
115 Perkin St, 98674 [PO Box 828, 98674]; (p) (360) 225-8996; (c) Cowlitz

Federal; State/ 1976/ Board of Directors/ staff: 3(p)/ members: 101

HISTORICAL SOCIETY; HOUSE MUSEUM

PROGRAMS: Community Outreach; Exhibits; Facility Rental; Festivals; Garden Tours

COLLECTIONS: [1890-present] Old trees, house, carriage house, water tower, potting shed.

HOURS: Yr Daily dawn-dusk

ADMISSION: $1 donation

YACOLT

8992
Pomery Living History Farm
20902 NE Lucia Falls Rd, 98675; (p) (360) 686-3537; (f) (360) 686-8111; pomeroy@pacifier.com; www.pacifier.com/~pomeroy/ (c) Clark

Private non-profit/ 1989/ staff: 5(p); 130(v)

LIVING HISTORY/OUTDOOR MUSEUM: Depicts 1920s farm life of SW WA state-utilizing living history interpretation.

PROGRAMS: Family Programs; Festivals; Interpretation; Living History; Reenactments; School-Based Curriculum

COLLECTIONS: [Early 20th c] Agriculture and domestic artifacts.

HOURS: June-Sept 1st full weekend Sa

YAKIMA

8993
H.M. Gilbert Homeplace
2109 W Yakima Ave, 98902 [2105 Tieton Drive, 98902]; (p) (509) 248-0747; (f) (509) 453-4890

1898/ staff: 15(v)

COLLECTIONS: [1898-1917] Furniture and decorative arts; family correspondence and pictures.

HOURS: April-Dec F/ 1st Su of month

8994
Yakima Valley Museum and Historical Association
2105 Tieton Dr, 98902-3766; (p) (509) 248-0747; (f) (509) 453-4890; info@yakimavalley museum.org; yakimavalleymuseum.org; (c) Yakima

Private non-profit/ 1952/ Yakima Valley Museum and Historical Association/ staff: 5(f); 14(p); 78(v)/ members: 935/publication: *Links*

HISTORY MUSEUM: Focuses on local natural history, Native American culture, early pioneer life, and development of local fruit and agricultural industries.

PROGRAMS: Annual Meeting; Concerts; Elder's Programs; Exhibits; Facility Rental; Family Programs; Festivals; Guided Tours; Interpretation; Lectures; Publication; Research Library/Archives; School-Based Curriculum

COLLECTIONS: [1875-present] Native American baskets and beadwork, horse-drawn vehicles, material on Supreme Court Justice William O. Douglas, historic neon advertising art, textiles, photos, furniture, decorative arts and toys.

HOURS: Yr M-F 10-5, Sa-Su 12-5

ADMISSION: $3, Family $7, Student $1.50

YELM

8995
Yelm Historic Preservation Commision
105 Yelm Ave W, 98597 [PO Box 479, 98597]; (p) (360) 458-8404; (f) (360) 458-4348; agnesb@yelmtel.com; (c) Thurston

City/ 1986/ staff: 1(p); 6(v)/publication: *Guide to Historic Resources*

HISTORIC PRESERVATION AGENCY: Supports recognition, enhancement, perpetuation, and continued use of the buildings, sites, and districts of historical significance.

PROGRAMS: Publication

WEST VIRGINIA

ANSTED

8996
Colonel George Imboden House
On Route 60, 25812 [HC 66 Box 94 B, Hico, 25854]; (p) (304) 658-5695

ARTHURDALE

8997
Arthurdale Heritage, Inc.
Q&A Roads, 26520 [PO Box 850, 26520]; (p) (304) 864-3959; (f) (304) 864-4602; ahi1934@aol.com; www.arthurdaleheritage.org; (c) Preston

Private non-profit/ 1985/ staff: 1(f); 10(v)/ members: 300/publication: *New Deal for America*

HISTORIC SITE; HISTORY MUSEUM; HOUSE MUSEUM; LIVING HISTORY/OUTDOOR MUSEUM; RESEARCH CENTER: Preserves the history of the nation's first New Deal Homestead.

PROGRAMS: Annual Meeting; Concerts; Exhibits; Facility Rental; Festivals; Interpretation; Living History; Publication; Research Library/Archives

COLLECTIONS: [1930] Homestead, forge, service station, administration building, furniture, crafts, forge equipment, photos, and maps.

HOURS: Yr M-F 10-2, Sa 12-5, Su 2-5

BECKLEY

8998
Beckley Exhibition Coal Mine
Ewart Ave, 25802 [PO Drawer AJ, 25802]; (p) (304) 256-1747; (f) (304) 256-1798; (c) Raleigh

City/ 1962/ staff: 4(f); 21(p)

HISTORIC SITE

PROGRAMS: Exhibits; Facility Rental; Festivals; Guided Tours; Interpretation

COLLECTIONS: [1920-1940] Mining artifacts.

HOURS: Apr-Nov Daily

ADMISSION: $8, Children $5

8999
Wildwood House Museum
Laurel Terrace, off S Kanawha St, 25802 [PO Drawer AJ, 25802]; (p) (304) 256-1747; (f) (304) 256-1798

1836/ City

COLLECTIONS: [Early 1800s] Furnishings.

HOURS: Jun-Aug

BELLE

9000
Belle Historical Restoration Society
Stubb Dr, 25015 [1616 W Riverview Dr, 25015]; (p) (304) 949-2336; (c) Kanawha

Private non-profit/ 1965/ staff: 12(v)/ members: 35

HISTORIC SITE; HISTORICAL SOCIETY; HISTORY MUSEUM

PROGRAMS: Guided Tours

HOURS: May-Oct 3rd Sa 10-2

ADMISSION: $3, Children $2

9001
Samuel Shrewsbury Mansion
310 Stubb Dr, 25015 [148 W Reynolds Ave, 25015-1536]; (p) (304) 949-2380, (304) 949-2398

1800

Preserves pioneer settler's home.

COLLECTIONS: [1800-1845] Furnishing; records and ledgers of salt drilling operations and mercantile companies.

HOURS: Apr-Oct

BERKELEY SPRINGS

9002
Berkeley Castle
9 W, 25411 [PO Box 3, 25411]; (p) (304) 258-3274

9003
Morgan County Historical and Genealogical Society
N Washington St, 25411 [PO Box 52, 25411]; (c) Morgan

Private non-profit/ 1976/ members: 200

GENEALOGICAL SOCIETY; HISTORICAL SOCIETY

PROGRAMS: Annual Meeting; Research Library/Archives

HOURS: Yr M-T, Th-F 9-6, W, Sa 9-12

ADMISSION: No charge

9004
Museum of the Berkeley Springs
Berkeley Springs State Park, 25411 [PO Box 99, 25411]; (p) (304) 258-3743; (c) Morgan

Private non-profit/ Board of Directors/ staff: 4(p)/ 6(v)/ members: 100

HISTORIC PRESERVATION AGENCY; HISTORIC SITE; HISTORY MUSEUM: Depicts and displays Morgan County history.

PROGRAMS: Community Outreach; Exhibits; Film/Video; Guided Tours; Reenactments

COLLECTIONS: [18th-19th c] Artifacts related to everyday life, industry and local Native Americans.

HOURS: Oct-May M-T 10-1, Th-F 3-6, Sa 10-4, Su 12-4

ADMISSION: No charge

BETHANY

9005
Alexander Campbell Mansion
Bethany College, 26032 [Historic Bethany, 26032]; (p) (304) 829-7285, (304) 829-4258; (f) (304) 829-7287; historic@mail.bethany-wv.edu; www.bethanywv.edu

1792/ Bethany College/ staff: 2(f); 3(p); 12(v)

COLLECTIONS: [1840] Period furnishing, books, clothes, paintings, genealogist, Upper Ohio Valley collection.

HOURS: Apr-Oct T-Sa, 10-12, 1-4; Su 2-4

BEVERLY

9006
Randolph County Historical Society
Main St, 26241 [PO Box 1164, Elkins, 26241]; (p) (304) 637-7424; (c) Randolph

Private non-profit/ 1924/ Board of Directors/ staff: 1(p)/ 10(v)/ members: 40

HISTORIC PRESERVATION AGENCY; HISTORIC SITE; HISTORICAL SOCIETY; HISTORY MUSEUM: Preserves and promotes county history.

PROGRAMS: Community Outreach; Exhibits; Guided Tours; Quarterly Meeting; Research Library/Archives; School-Based Curriculum

COLLECTIONS: [Mid 19th-20th c] Military, regional industry items, and photos.

HOURS: May, Sept-Oct Sa-Su 10-12; June-Aug T-Su 1-4

ADMISSION: $3, Student $1

9007
Rich Mountain Battlefield Foundation
Court St & Files Creek Rd, 26253 [PO Box 227, 26253]; (p) (304) 637-7424; (f) (304) 637-7424; richmt@richmountain.org; www.richmountain.org; (c) Randolph

Private non-profit/ 1991/ staff: 1(p); 20(v)/ members: 450

HISTORIC PRESERVATION AGENCY; HISTORIC SITE; LIVING HISTORY/OUTDOOR MUSEUM: Preserves and protects Rich Mountain Battlefield Civil War Site.

PROGRAMS: Annual Meeting; Community Outreach; Festivals; Guided Tours; Interpretation; Lectures; Living History; Publication; Reenactments

COLLECTIONS: [Mid-late 19th c] Archeological survey pieces: bullets, cannon balls, pottery, and glass.

HOURS: Visitor Center Fall-Winter M-F 11-4, Spring-Summer T-Su 10-4

ADMISSION: No charge

BLUEFIELD

9008
Eastern Regional Coal Archives
600 Commerce St, 24701; (p) (304) 325-3943; (f) (304) 325-3702; erca@raleigh.lib.wv.us; (c) Mercer

Joint/ 1986/ Craft Memorial Library Board of Directors/ staff: 2(p)

LIBRARY AND/OR ARCHIVES: Collects, preserves and makes available the historical records, photos, documents, memorabilia and artifacts of the central Appalachian coal fields.

PROGRAMS: Research Library/Archives

COLLECTIONS: [1880-1950] Photos, records, diaries, oral history tapes, blue prints, artifacts, newspapers, scripts, films, maps, rare books.

HOURS: Yr M-F 9:30-5, Sa by appt

ADMISSION: No charge

BUCKHANNON

9009
Upshur County Historical Society
81 W Main St, 26201 [PO Box 2082, 26201]; (p) (304) 472-2738; www.msys.net/uchs; (c) Upshur

Private non-profit/ 1926/ Executive Board/ staff: 1(p); 12(v)/ members: 200

GENEALOGICAL SOCIETY; HISTORIC PRESERVATION AGENCY; HISTORIC SITE; HISTORICAL SOCIETY; HISTORY MUSEUM; RESEARCH CENTER: Identifies, preserves and perpetuates county history through exhibits, published materials and educational programs; maintains museum and archives.

PROGRAMS: Community Outreach; Exhibits; Interpretation; Lectures; Living History; Research Library/Archives

COLLECTIONS: [1770s-present] Documents from families, communities, individuals, organizations and churches. Photos, Civil War records, official county courthouse records, WPA holdings, clothing, paintings, sculpture, furniture, glassware, historic buildings and films.

HOURS: (Museum) May-Sept Su 1-4; (Archives) Yr T 6-8

ADMISSION: Donations accepted

BUNKER HILL

9010
Morgan Cabin
Runnymead Rd, Rte 26, 25413 [Berkeley County Historic Landmarks Commission, 1, Martinsburg, 25401]; (p) (304) 267-4713; www.travelwv.com/his22.htm

BURLINGTON

9011
Mineral County Historical Society, Inc.
HC 84 Box 8, 26710; (p) (304) 289-3735, (304) 788-5129; (c) Mineral

Private non-profit/ 1970/ staff: 7(v)/ members: 75

Promotes local history; encourages preservation of historically significant buildings.

CEREDO

9012
Z.D. Ramsdell House
1108 B St, 25507 [PO Box 544, 25507]; (p) (304) 453-2482

CHARLESTON

9013
Craik-Patton House
2809 Kanawha Blvd, 25321 [PO Box 175, 25321]; (p) (304) 925-7564; (c) Kanawha

Private non-profit/ 1974/ National Society of Colonial Dames/ staff: 2(f); 1(p); 30(v)

HOUSE MUSEUM

PROGRAMS: Guided Tours

COLLECTIONS: [1834-1864] Period furniture and home.

HOURS: Apr-Oct Th-Su 1-4

ADMISSION: $3

9014
Kanawha Valley Historical and Preservation Society, Inc.
Peoples Bldg, Ste 817, 25328 [PO Box 2283, 25328]; (p) (304) 342-7676; 102036.3307@compuserve.com; (c) Kanawha

Private non-profit/ 1971/ staff: 12(v)/ members: 518

HISTORIC PRESERVATION AGENCY; HISTORICAL SOCIETY

PROGRAMS: Annual Meeting;

9015
West Virginia Division of Culture and History
1900 Kanawha Blvd, 25305; (p) (304) 558-0220; (f) (304) 558-2779; www.wvlc.wvnet.edu/culture/front.html; (c) Kanawha

State/ 1976/ staff: 78(f); 35(p)/publication: *West Virginia History Journal; Golden Seal Magazine*

ART MUSEUM; HISTORIC PRESERVATION AGENCY; HISTORY MUSEUM: Operates the West VA State Museum, Archives and Library; manages four historic sites.

PROGRAMS: Community Outreach; Concerts; Exhibits; Facility Rental; Family Programs; Festivals; Film/Video; Guided Tours; Publication; Research Library/Archives; Theatre

COLLECTIONS: [1840-1960] Official state, public and organizational records, personal papers, photos, moving images and other printed materials documenting state history, genealogy and culture.

HOURS: (Museum) Yr M-F 9-9, Sa-Su 1-5; (Archives/Library) Yr M-F 9-5, Sa 1-5

ADMISSION: No charge

CLARKSBURG

9016
Harrison County Historical Society
123 W Main St, 26302 [PO Box 2074, 26302]; (c) Harrison

Private non-profit/ 1968/ members: 165

HISTORIC PRESERVATION AGENCY; HISTORIC SITE; HISTORICAL SOCIETY; HISTORY MUSEUM; HOUSE MUSEUM: Represents local history.

PROGRAMS: Annual Meeting; Community Outreach; Exhibits; Guided Tours; Lectures; Publication

COLLECTIONS: [19th-mid 20th c] Objects representing local history and manufacturing.

HOURS: Yr by appt

ADMISSION: No charge

CLAY

9017
Clay County Historical Society, The
Old Clay County Courthouse, 25043 [PO Box 670, 25043]; (c) Clay

Private non-profit

HISTORICAL SOCIETY

PROGRAMS: Exhibits; Lectures

ELKINS

9018
Allegheny Regional Family History Society
Main St & Court St, 26241 [PO Box 1804, 26241]; (p) (304) 636-1650; jmccollam@neumedia.net; www.swcp.com/~dhickman/arfhs.html; (c) Randolph

Private non-profit/ 1992/ staff: 1(p); 2(v)/ members: 275

GENEALOGICAL SOCIETY; RESEARCH CENTER: Preserves and distributes family history and genealogy.

PROGRAMS: Publication; Research Library/Archives

COLLECTIONS: Family histories, genealogical books and records.

HOURS: Mar-Dec W 2-4, Sa 10-2

9019
Halliehurst
100 Campus Dr, 26241; (p) (304) 637-1243; (f) (304) 637-1419; www.dne.edu

1890/ Davis and Elkins College/ staff: 3(f)

COLLECTIONS: [1900s] Furnishing; West VA items.

HOURS: Yr

FAIRMONT

9020
Pricketts Fort Memorial Foundation
Route 3, Box 407, 26554; (p) (304) 363-3030, (800) 225-5982; (f) (304) 363-3857; pfort@westco.net; www.dmssoft.com/pfort; (c) Marion

Private non-profit; State/ 1972/ staff: 10(f); 2(p); 25(v)/ members: 450/publication: *The Gatepost*

HISTORIC SITE; HOUSE MUSEUM; LIVING HISTORY/OUTDOOR MUSEUM

PROGRAMS: Annual Meeting; Community Outreach; Concerts; Elder's Programs; Exhibits; Facility Rental; Family Programs; Festivals; Interpretation; Lectures; Living History; Publication; Reenactments; School-Based Curriculum; Theatre

COLLECTIONS: [Early 18th-mid 19th c] Military and farm equipment.

HOURS: Yr Daily 10-5

ADMISSION: $5, Children $2.50, Seniors $4.50; Under 7 free

FRANKLIN

9021
Pendleton County Historical Society, Inc.
Main St, 26807 [HC 71 Box 2, 26807]; (c) Pendleton

Private non-profit/ 1928/ Board of Directors/ staff: 7(v)/ members: 90/publication: *Pictorial History of Pendleton*

GENEALOGICAL SOCIETY; HISTORIC PRESERVATION AGENCY; HISTORICAL SOCIETY: Preserves area history.

PROGRAMS: Annual Meeting; Exhibits; Family Programs; Festivals; Guided Tours; Lectures; Publication; Research Library/Archives

COLLECTIONS: [Mid-late 19th c]

HOURS: Library: Yr M-F 9-5, Sa 9-12

ADMISSION: No charge

GASSAWAY

9022
Family Research Library and Archives of Braxton County
416 Elk St, 26624 [805 State St, 26624]; (p) (304) 364-5378; (c) Braxton

Private non-profit/ 1985/ Board of Directors/ staff: 10(v)/publication: *Braxton Heritage Book; County Cemetery Book and Birth Records (1853-1905)*

HISTORIC PRESERVATION AGENCY; RESEARCH CENTER: Preserves and researches local and family histories of central West VA and Braxton County.

PROGRAMS: Community Outreach; Publication; Research Library/Archives

COLLECTIONS: [1775-1900s] Family histories, area censuses, birth, death and marriage certificates.

HOURS: Yr F 6-9

ADMISSION: No charge

GLENVILLE

9023
Gilmer County Historical Society, Inc.
214 Walnut St, 26351; (p) (304) 462-5620; (c) Gilmer

Private non-profit/ 1957/ staff: 1(p); 1(v)/ members: 300

HISTORIC SITE: Collects, preserves and disseminates information about Gilmer County history.

PROGRAMS: Research Library/Archives

COLLECTIONS: [1845-present] Books, articles and newspapers relating to Gilmer County and local family histories.

HOURS: Yr M-F

GRAFTON

9024
Anna Jarvis Birthplace Museum
119/250 S of, 26354 [Rt 2, Box 352, 26354]; (p) (304) 265-5549

1854/ staff: 5(v)

Preserves Civil War site of General George B. McClellan's troops.

COLLECTIONS: [1854-1948] 1860 Steinway and Son piano; Bibles; newspapers; pictures.

HOURS: Apr-Dec

HAMLIN

9025
Lincoln County Genealogical Society
7999 Lynn Ave, 25523; (p) (304) 824-5481; (c) Lincoln

1980/ staff: 1(f); 3(v)/ members: 100/publication: *Lincoln Lineage*

GENEALOGICAL SOCIETY: Gathers local family histories and cemetery records.

PROGRAMS: Publication; Research Library/Archives

COLLECTIONS: [19th-20th c] Census records from Bonth, Logan, Lincoln, Cab and Kan Counties, family history, VA history.

HOURS: Yr M-F 8-5, T 8-8, Sa 9-2

ADMISSION: No charge

HARPERS FERRY

9026
Harpers Ferry National Historical Park
1 mi W of bridge just off US Rt 340, 25425
[PO Box 65, 25425]; (p) (304) 535-6298;
marsha_starkey@nps.gov; www.nps.gov/
hafe/home.htm

Federal/ National Park Service

BATTLEFIELD; HISTORIC SITE; HISTORY
MUSEUM; HOUSE MUSEUM

PROGRAMS: Exhibits; Guided Tours; School-
Based Curriculum

COLLECTIONS: [18th-20th c] Sites include
Lower Town Historic District, Maryland
Heights, Virginius Island.

HOURS: Yr Daily 8-5

ADMISSION: $5/vehicle/3 days or $3/person

HUNTINGTON

9027
Historic Madie/Thomas Carrol House
234 Guyan St, 25702 [PO Box 3266, 25702-
0266]; (p) (304) 522-0325, (304) 736-1655; (f)
(304) 733-0879

1810

COLLECTIONS: [1855-1875] 34-star federal
Cavalry flag; artifacts from archaeological
digs; Eastlake furniture.

HOURS: Apr-Dec

HUNTINTON

9028
Cabell-Wayne Historical Society
717 6th Ave, 25701; (p) (304) 529-3030; (f)
(304) 529-3043; (c) Cabell and Wayne

Private non-profit/ 1968/ staff: 20(v)/ members:
60

Promotes local history.

LEWISBURG

9029
Fort Savannah Museum
200 N Jefferson St, 24901 [204 N Jefferson
St, 24901]; (p) (304) 645-3055, (304) 645-
4010; (c) Greenbriar

Private non-profit/ 1964

HISTORIC SITE: Owns original Fort Savannah
built in 1770.

COLLECTIONS: Log building.

HOURS: Yr

ADMISSION: No charge

9030
Greenbrier Historical Society, Inc.
301 W Washington St, 24901; (p) (304) 645-
3398; (f) (304) 645-5201; info@greenbrier
historical.org; www.greenbrierhistorical.org;
(c) Greenbrier

Private non-profit/ 1963/ staff: 1(f); 3(p); 30(v)/
members: 850/publication: Journal of the
Greenbrier Historical Society; Appalachian
Springs

GENEALOGICAL SOCIETY; HISTORICAL
SOCIETY; HISTORY MUSEUM; HOUSE MU-
SEUM; RESEARCH CENTER: Preserves and

educates about the history of the Greenbrier
area from the mid 18th c to present.

PROGRAMS: Annual Meeting; Community
Outreach; Exhibits; Family Programs; Festivals; Guided Tours; Interpretation; Lectures;
Publication; Reenactments; Research Li-
brary/Archives; School-Based Curriculum

COLLECTIONS: [1750-1930] Textiles, furnishings, decorative arts, Revolutionary and Civil
War documents, photographs, newspapers,
and books.

HOURS: Yr M-Sa 10-4

ADMISSION: $3, Children $1, Seniors $2.50;
Members free

9031
Pearl S. Buck Birthplace Foundation
30 mi N on Hwy 219 from Hwy 164, [PO Box
126, Hillsboro, 24946]; (p) (304) 653-4430; (c)
Pocahontas

Private non-profit/ 1974/ Women's Club of
West Virginia/ staff: 2(f); 2(p)/ members: 98

HISTORIC SITE; HISTORY MUSEUM;
HOUSE MUSEUM: Promotes life of Pearl
Buck.

PROGRAMS: Annual Meeting

COLLECTIONS: [Early 20th c] Furnishings,
1857 Mason and Hamlin organ.

HOURS: May-Oct M-Sa 9-4:30

ADMISSION: $4, Student $1, Seniors $3.60

LOGAN

9032
Logan County Genealogical Society
Mudfork Rd, Southern WV Community/Tech
College, 25601 [PO Box 1959, 25601]; (c)
Logan

Private non-profit/ 1988/ members: 140/publi-
cation: Ancestree

GENEALOGICAL SOCIETY: Disseminates
genealogical materials at Southern West VA
Community and Technical College Library.

PROGRAMS: Lectures; Publication; Research
Library/Archives

COLLECTIONS: [18th-20th c] Genealogical
periodicals; census, cemetery, marriage, birth
and death records.

HOURS: Yr M-F 8-8; meetings 2nd M of month

LOST CREEK

9033
Watters Smith Memorial State Park
Rte 1 Duck Creek Rd, 26385 [PO Box 296,
26385]; (p) (304) 745-3081; (f) (304) 745-3631;
www.wvparks.com/wattersmithmemorial

LOWELL

9034
Graham House, The
Rt 3/12, [PO Box 218, Pence Springs,
24962]; (p) (304) 466-5502, (304) 466-3321

1770

COLLECTIONS: [1700-1800] Native American
artifacts.

HOURS: Jun-Aug

MADISON

9035
Boone County Genealogical Society
375 Main St, 25130 [PO Box 306, 25130]; (p)
(304) 369-2769; (c) Boone

Private non-profit/ 1978/ staff: 3(v)/ members:
215/publication: Boone County Quarterly

GENEALOGICAL SOCIETY: Seeks to preserve the history of Boone County's ancestors.

PROGRAMS: Monthly Meeting; Publication

COLLECTIONS: [19th c-present] Books and
microfilm on the families of Boone and surrounding counties.

HOURS: Yr 9-5

MANNINGTON

9036
West Augusta Historical Society
S Main St & Flaggy Meadow Rd, 26582 [PO
Box 414, 26582]; (p) (304) 986-1089; (c)
Marion

Private non-profit/ 1980/ Board of Directors/
staff: 25(v)/ members: 50

HISTORICAL SOCIETY: Collects, preserves
and interprets items from Marion County and
Mannington.

PROGRAMS: Exhibits; Guided Tours

COLLECTIONS: [Late 19th-early 20th c] History, artifacts and photos.

HOURS: May-Sept Su 1:30-4

ADMISSION: $2

MARTINSBURG

9037
Berkeley County Historical Society
126 E Race St, 25401 [PO Box 1624, 25401];
(p) (304) 267-4713; (c) Berkeley

County, non-profit/ 1927/ staff: 20(v)/ members: 600

GENEALOGICAL SOCIETY; HISTORIC
PRESERVATION AGENCY; HISTORY MUSE-
UM; HOUSE MUSEUM; RESEARCH CEN-
TER: Preserves, protects, and educates public
on Berkeley County history.

PROGRAMS: Annual Meeting; Exhibits; Festivals; Guided Tours; Interpretation; Lectures;
Living History; Publication; Research Li-
brary/Archives

COLLECTIONS: [18th c-present] Native
American culture, Revolutionary War, Civil
War, and military artifacts, and maps and sur-
veys of early Berkeley County.

HOURS: Yr

9038
**General Adam Stephen Memorial
Association, Inc.**
309 E John St, 25402 [PO Box 1496, 25402];
(p) (304) 267-4434; hammersl@martin.lib.wv.us;
www.travelwv.com/adam.htm; (c) Berkeley

Private non-profit/ 1959/ staff: 1(f); 15(v)/
members: 50

HISTORIC SITE; HISTORICAL SOCIETY;
HISTORY MUSEUM; HOUSE MUSEUM: Operates a colonial house museum; preserves

history of founder of Martinsburg, Revolutionary War General Adam Stephen.

PROGRAMS: Exhibits; Festivals; Film/Video; Guided Tours; Interpretation

COLLECTIONS: [1750-1830] Furnishings: colonial to post-Revolutionary period.

HOURS: May-Oct Sa-Su 2-5

ADMISSION: Donations accepted

MIDDLEBOURNE

9039
Tyler County Heritage and Historical Society
Dodd St, 26149 [PO Box 317, 26149]; (p) (304) 758-2100, (304) 758-4288; (c) Tyler

Private non-profit/ 1983/ staff: 20(v)/ members: 250

HISTORIC SITE; HISTORICAL SOCIETY; HISTORY MUSEUM

PROGRAMS: Annual Meeting; Exhibits; Festivals; Film/Video; Guided Tours

COLLECTIONS: [19th-mid 20th c] 16 rooms of historical artifacts; 1800 Williamson Family Log Cabin, and one-room schoolhouse.

HOURS: May-early Nov Su, T, Th 1-4 by appt

ADMISSION: Donations accepted

MILTON

9040
Blenko Glass Company
Located I-64 Exit 28, 25541 [PO Box 67, 25541-0067]; (p) (304) 743-9081; (f) (304) 743-0547; Blenko@usa.net; www.blenkoglass.com

1929/ Blenko Family

HISTORIC SITE; HISTORY MUSEUM: Presents history of Blenko Glass Company and glass making techniques.

PROGRAMS: Exhibits; Guided Tours

COLLECTIONS: [1929-present] Hand-blown glass, stained glass, glassware, and sheet glass.

HOURS: Yr M-Sa 8-4, Su 12-4

MOUNDSVILLE

9041
Marshall County Historical Society
13th St & Lockwood Ave, 26041 [PO Box 267, 26041]; hitnmiss49@hotmail.com; www.rootsweb.com/ wvmarsha/society2.hml; (c) Marshall

1994/ Board of Directors/ staff: 20(v)/ members: 90/publication: History of Marshall County, From Forest to Field; Schools, Churches, Cemeteries of Marshall County

GENEALOGICAL SOCIETY; HISTORICAL SOCIETY; HISTORY MUSEUM; RESEARCH CENTER: Conducts genealogy research.

PROGRAMS: Annual Meeting; Community Outreach; Concerts; Exhibits; Family Programs; Guided Tours; Lectures; Publication; Research Library/Archives

COLLECTIONS: [19th-20th c]

NEWELL

9042
Tri-State Genealogical and Historical Society
717 Washington St, 26050 [PO Box 454, 26050]; (p) (304) 387-2467; (c) Hancock

Private non-profit/ 1994/ staff: 6(v)/ members: 150

GENEALOGICAL SOCIETY; HISTORICAL SOCIETY: Promotes genealogical and historical research in the tri-state area of OH, PA and West VA.

PROGRAMS: Annual Meeting; Research Library/Archives

COLLECTIONS: [19th c] Census, cemetery and military records, city directories, family files, genealogies and obituaries.

HOURS: Yr

ADMISSION: No charge

PARKERSBURG

9043
Blennerhassett Mansion
Blennerhassett Island in the Ohio River, 26101 [Blennerhassett Island Historical State Park,137 , 26101]; (p) (304) 420-4800, (800) 225-5982; (f) (304) 420-4802

State/ 1984/ staff: 8(f); 9(p); 61(v)

Preserves 1800 home of Harmon and Margaret Blennerhassett, and site of 1806-07 Aaron Burr conspiracy.

COLLECTIONS: Furnishings, paintings; household accessories; interpretive 18th-century kitchen.

HOURS: May-Oct

9044
Oil, Gas and Industrial Historical Association
119 3rd St, 26101; (p) (304) 485-5446; (c) Wood

Private non-profit/ 1989/ staff: 30(v)/ members: 650/publication: Where It All Began

HISTORIC SITE; HISTORY MUSEUM; LIVING HISTORY/OUTDOOR MUSEUM: Preserves history of oil and gas industry.

PROGRAMS: Exhibits; Film/Video; Guided Tours; Publication

COLLECTIONS: [1850-1990s] Oil and gas exploration, drilling and processing with pictures and equipment, railroads, rivers, local environment, store, office, maps and videos.

HOURS: Yr Daily

ADMISSION: $2, Children $1

9045
Wood County Historical and Preservation Society
1306 16th St, 26101 [PO Box 565, 26101]; (p) (304) 295-9777; (c) Wood

Private non-profit/ 1980/ members: 75/publication: History and Preservation

HISTORIC PRESERVATION AGENCY; HISTORICAL SOCIETY: Preserves the heritage of Wood County.

PROGRAMS: Annual Meeting; Elder's Programs; Lectures; Publication; Research Library/ Archives

COLLECTIONS: [Early 20th c] Photos, postcards and local histories.

PINCH

9046
Elk-Blue Creek Historical Society
14 Maple Lane, [PO Box 649, Elkview, 25071]; (p) (304) 965-5016; (c) Kanawha

Private non-profit/ 1993/ staff: 66(p); 66(v)/publication: Elk River Communities in Kanawha County, Vol. 1-2

HISTORICAL SOCIETY: Publishes local histories of the Elk River and tributaries in Kanawha County.

PROGRAMS: Community Outreach; Exhibits; Publication

COLLECTIONS: [18th c-present] Written histories on family, business and military service.

HOURS: Yr by appt

ADMISSION: No charge

POCA

9047
Upper Vandalia Historical Society
[PO Box 517, 25159]; (p) (304) 755-4677; www.zoomnet/~tuswill/vandalia/html; (c) Putnam

Private non-profit/ 1961/ Elected Officers/ staff: 4(v)/ members: 110/publication: Vandalia Journal

HISTORIC PRESERVATION AGENCY; HISTORICAL SOCIETY; RESEARCH CENTER: Collects and preserves the county's historical heritage.

PROGRAMS: Lectures; Living History; Publication; Reenactments; Research Library/Archives

RIPLEY

9048
Jackson County Historical Society
[PO Box 22, 25271]; (p) (304) 372-5343; www.rootsweb.com/~wvjnckso/jack.htm; (c) Jackson

Joint/ 1969/ County; Private non-profit/ staff: 3(p); 15(v)/ members: 128/publication: Jackson County History

GENEALOGICAL SOCIETY; HISTORICAL SOCIETY; HISTORY MUSEUM; HOUSE MUSEUM; RESEARCH CENTER: Preserves local history; operates Lands Museum.

PROGRAMS: Annual Meeting; Community Outreach; Exhibits; Facility Rental; Family Programs; Festivals; Guided Tours; Interpretation; Lectures; Living History; Publication; Research Library/Archives; School-Based Curriculum

COLLECTIONS: [1830s-1940s] Local settlers items: books, newspapers, maps, Civil War memorabilia.

HOURS: Mem Day-Sept Su 1-5

ADMISSION: No charge

9049
West Virginia Baptist Historical Society
Parchment Valley Rd, 25271 [Route 2, Box 304, 25271]; (c) Jackson

Private non-profit/ 1941/ Board of Directors/ staff: 2(p)/ members: 106

HISTORIC PRESERVATION AGENCY; HISTORY MUSEUM; RESEARCH CENTER: Serves as repository and research center of Baptist history.

PROGRAMS: Annual Meeting; Exhibits; Film/Video; Guided Tours; Interpretation; Research Library/Archives

COLLECTIONS: [1865-present] Annuals of the West VA Baptist convention, bound annual reports from 25 Baptist associations, videos, slides, microfilm, computers and individual files.

HOURS: Yr M-Th 10-4 by appt.

SAINT MARYS

9050
Pleasants County Historical Society
[PO Box 335, 26170]; (p) (304) 684-7621; (c) Pleasants

Private non-profit/ 1972/ Board of Directors/ members: 35/publication: *History of Pleasants County, West Virginia*

HISTORIC PRESERVATION AGENCY; HISTORY MUSEUM: Collects and preserves local history items.

PROGRAMS: Annual Meeting; Community Outreach; Lectures; Publication

HOURS: Yr by appt

ADMISSION: No charge

SALEM

9051
Fort New Salem
Univ Ave off Rt 23 Exit from Rt 50, 26426 [Salem-International Univ, Box 500, 26426-0500]; (p) (304) 782-5245; (f) (304) 782-5395; fort@salemiu.edu; www.salemiu.edu; (c) Harrison

Private non-profit/ 1970/ Salem International Univ/ staff: 2(f); 6(p); 30(v)

LIVING HISTORY/OUTDOOR MUSEUM; RESEARCH CENTER: Promotes and preserves frontier settlement of 19th c north-central West VA.

PROGRAMS: Community Outreach; Concerts; Exhibits; Facility Rental; Family Programs; Festivals; Interpretation; Lectures; Living History; Research Library/Archives; School-Based Curriculum

COLLECTIONS: [1792-1901] Buildings, tools, furnishings, decorative arts, and reproductions.

HOURS: Apr-May, Nov-Dec M-F 10-5; Sept-Oct 10-5

SHEPHERDSTOWN

9052
Historic Shepherdstown Commission
129 E German St, 25443 [PO Box 1768, 25443]; (p) (304) 876-0910; (f) (304) 876-0910; hsc@intrepid.net; (c) Jefferson

Private non-profit/ 1972/ Board of Directors/ staff: 2(p); 25(v)/ members: 260

HISTORICAL SOCIETY; HOUSE MUSEUM: Operates local history museum; educates community on local history and preservation.

PROGRAMS: Annual Meeting; Community Outreach; Exhibits; Facility Rental; Guided Tours; Publication; School-Based Curriculum

COLLECTIONS: [1786-present] Interpretive rooms: Victorian, reception, hotel bedroom; furnishings, documents; Native American tools and objects.

HOURS: Apr-Oct Sa

SOUTH CHARLESTON

9053
Kanawha Valley Genealogical Society
21st & 2nd Ave, 25503 [PO Box 8555, 25503]; (c) Kanawha

Private non-profit/ 1977/ staff: 8(v)/ members: 350

GENEALOGICAL SOCIETY: Provides assistance and materials for genealogical research in West VA.

PROGRAMS: Research Library/Archives

HOURS: Yr 1st and 3rd W 10-4

ADMISSION: No charge

SUMMERSVILLE

9054
Nicholas County Historical and Genealogical Society
1/4 mi W on Rt 39 beyond Summersville, 26651 [PO Box 443, 26651]; (c) Nicholas

Private non-profit/ 1982/ Board of Directors/ staff: 10(v)/ members: 260/publication: *Nicholas County, West Virginia History; Nicholas County, West Virginia Heritage 2000*

GENEALOGICAL SOCIETY; HISTORICAL SOCIETY; HOUSE MUSEUM

PROGRAMS: Annual Meeting; Exhibits; Publication; Research Library/Archives

COLLECTIONS: [1860-1930] Farm tools, furnishing.

HOURS: June-Sept W Sa 2-4 and by appt

ADMISSION: Donations accepted

TERRA ALTA

9055
Americiana Museum
401 Aurora Ave, 26764; (p) (304) 789-2361; (c) Preston

1968/ staff: 1(f); 4(v)

HISTORY MUSEUM

COLLECTIONS: [Early American] Old store, period rooms, doctor's office.

HOURS: By appt

ADMISSION: $2, Children $1

9056
Preston County Historical Society
109 E Washington Ave, 26764 [102 Aurora Ave, 26764]; (p) (304) 789-2316; (c) Preston

County/ 1958/ staff: 4(v)/ members: 300/publication: *Now And Long Ago*

GENEALOGICAL SOCIETY; HISTORICAL PRESERVATION AGENCY; HISTORICAL SOCIETY; HISTORY MUSEUM

PROGRAMS: Exhibits; Publication

COLLECTIONS: [1840-1950] Photos, farm and logging implements, pioneer items, Native American tools, guns, railroad artifacts, furniture, clothing, newspapers and books.

HOURS: Yr Su and by appt

ADMISSION: No charge

UNION

9057
Monroe County Historical Society
Main St, 24983 [PO Box 465, 24983]; (c) Monroe

Private non-profit/ 1963/ Executive Board/ staff: 35(v)/ members: 149

HISTORIC SITE; HISTORICAL SOCIETY; HISTORY MUSEUM; HOUSE MUSEUM: Preserves county history.

PROGRAMS: Annual Meeting; Community Outreach; Concerts; Exhibits; Facility Rental; Guided Tours; Lectures; Publication; Research Library/Archives; School-Based Curriculum; Theatre

COLLECTIONS: [1800-present] Store records, family papers and genealogies.

HOURS: June-Dec M-Sa 10-4, Su 1-4

ADMISSION: Donations accepted

WELLSBURG

9058
Brooke County Historical Society
7th and Main St, 26070; (c) Brooke

County/ 1955/ staff: 1(v)/ members: 25

WEST UNION

9059
Doddridge County Historical Society
100 Chancery St, 26456; (p) (304) 873-2050, (304) 873-1553; (c) Doddridge

Private non-profit/ 1976/ Board of Directors/ staff: 8(v)/ members: 200

HISTORIC PRESERVATION AGENCY; HISTORIC SITE; HISTORICAL SOCIETY; HISTORY MUSEUM: Preserves and maintains historical artifacts, documents and buildings.

PROGRAMS: Exhibits; Guided Tours

COLLECTIONS: [19th-20th c] Exhibits and photos.

HOURS: May-Aug T 11-3, Sa 12-3

ADMISSION: Donations accepted

WESTON

9060
Jackson's Mill Historic Area
West Virginia Univ, Route 1 Box 210, 26452

WHEELING

9061
Friends of Wheeling
921 Main St, 26003 [PO Box 889, 26003]; (c) Ohio

Private non-profit/ 1970/ Board of Directors/ staff: 2(v)/ members: 160

HISTORIC PRESERVATION AGENCY: Preserves, protects and promotes local architectural heritage.

PROGRAMS: Annual Meeting; Community Outreach; Exhibits; Family Programs; Festivals; Guided Tours; Lectures; Research Library/Archives

COLLECTIONS: [18th-19th c] Architectural artifacts, publications, pictures, city directories, blueprints for buildings, monuments and local public utilities.

9062
Oglebay Institute Mansion Museum
Oglebay Park, 26003; (p) (304) 242-7272; (f) (304) 242-4203; www.oionline.com

1846/ staff: 4(f); 2(p); 70(v)

COLLECTIONS: [1790-1920] Furniture; glass; china; Oglebay family collection.; History of the Ohio Valley and its industries.

HOURS: Yr

9063
West Virginia Northern Community College Alumni Association Museum
1704 Market St, 26003; (p) (304) 233-5900; (c) Ohio

State/ 1986/ staff: 1(p); 12(v)

HISTORY MUSEUM: Preserves and collects items relevant to the history of Baltimore and Ohio Railroad, Hazel-Atlas Glass, New Martinsville Region Glass, the town of Wheeling.

PROGRAMS: Exhibits; Lectures

COLLECTIONS: [1850s-present] Baltimore and Ohio Railroad artifacts, papers and books; Hazel-Atlas glass, bottles, jars and company history, Viking and Paden City glass.

HOURS: Yr

9064
Wheeling Area Historical Society
136 N 19th St, 26003 [PO Box 283, 26003]; (p) (304) 277-2241; (c) Ohio

Private non-profit/ 1926/ Board of Directors/ staff: 6(v)/ members: 60

Provides research assistance.

ADMISSION: No charge

WISCONSIN

ALBANY

9065
Albany Historical Society
117 & 119 N Water St, 53502 [PO Box 464, 53502-9574]; (c) Green

Private non-profit/ 1992/ Albany Historical Society Board/ staff: 30(v)/ members: 100

ALLIANCE OF HISTORICAL AGENCIES; HISTORIC PRESERVATION AGENCY; HISTORICAL SOCIETY; HISTORY MUSEUM

PROGRAMS: Annual Meeting; Festivals

HOURS: May-Sept Sa 9-3

ADMISSION: No charge

ALMA

9066
Alma Historical Society
502 S 2nd St, 54610 [PO Box 473, 54610]; (c) Buffalo

Private non-profit/ 1978/ staff: 7(v)/ members: 62

HISTORIC SITE; HISTORICAL SOCIETY; HISTORY MUSEUM: Collects and preserves history.

PROGRAMS: Exhibits

COLLECTIONS: Clothing, photographs, and logging.

HOURS: May 30-Oct 15 Sa 1-3, Su 1-4

ADMISSION: Donations accepted

ANTIGO

9067
Langlade County Historical Society
404 Superior, 54409 [PO Box 219, 54409]; (p) (715) 627-4464; leedi@newnorth.net; (c) Langlade

Private non-profit/ staff: 1(p)/ members: 180

HISTORICAL SOCIETY; HISTORY MUSEUM; RESEARCH CENTER: Preserves, advances and disseminates county history.

PROGRAMS: Annual Meeting; Exhibits; Lectures; Research Library/Archives

COLLECTIONS: [Late 19th-mid 20th c] Logging, railroad and farm tools, photos, military hardware, clothing, government records, furniture, household items, tax archives, high school yearbooks, scrapbooks and newspapers.

HOURS: May-Sept M, W, F 9:30-3, Su 12-3

ADMISSION: No charge

APPLETON

9068
Hearthstone Historic House Museum
625 W Prospect Ave, 54911; (p) (920) 730-8204; (f) (920) 730-8266; fr.hearthstone@juno.com; (c) Outagamie

Private non-profit/ 1986/ Board of Directors/ staff: 2(f); 2(p); 125(v)/ members: 400/publication: Upstairs/Downstairs

HISTORIC SITE; HOUSE MUSEUM

PROGRAMS: Annual Meeting; Community Outreach; Exhibits; Family Programs; Guided Tours; Interpretation; Lectures; Publication; Research Library/Archives; School-Based Curriculum

COLLECTIONS: [19th c] Furnishings, fine and decorative arts, books, clothing, textiles, early electrical artifacts, phonographs and other Victorian related objects.

HOURS: Yr T-F 10-4, Su 1-4

ADMISSION: $4, Children $2; Under 7 free

9069
Outagamie County Historical Society
330 E College Ave, 54911-5715; (p) (920) 735-9370; (f) (920) 733-8636; ochs@foxvalleyhistory.org; www.foxvalleyhistory.org; (c) Outagamie

Private non-profit/ 1872/ Board of Directors/ staff: 10(f); 4(p); 300(v)/ members: 800

HISTORICAL SOCIETY; HISTORY MUSEUM; HOUSE MUSEUM: Preserves history of Outagamie County and lower Fox River Valley.

PROGRAMS: Annual Meeting; Community Outreach; Exhibits; Family Programs; Film/Video; Guided Tours; Interpretation; Lectures; Research Library/Archives; School-Based Curriculum; Theatre

COLLECTIONS: [1820s-present] Volumes, maps, manuscripts, reference information files, photos and artifacts.

HOURS: Yr T-Sa 10-5, Su 12-5; June-Aug M 10-5

ADMISSION: $4, Family $10, Children $2, Seniors $3.50; Members free

ASHIPPUN

9070
Honey Acres
N1557 Hwy 67, 53003 [PO Box 346, 53003]; (p) (920) 474-4411; (f) (920) 474-4018; (c) Dodge

Private for-profit/ 1852/ staff: 1(f); 2(p)

HISTORY MUSEUM: Promotes apiculture history.

PROGRAMS: Exhibits

COLLECTIONS: Pollination exhibits, beeswax; multi media show; Bee Tree exhibit.

HOURS: Yr M-F 9-3:30; mid May-Oct Sa-Su 12-4

ADMISSION: No charge

ASHLAND

9071
Ashland Historical Society
509 West Main St, 54806-1513; (p) (715) 682-4911; (c) Ashland

Joint/ 1980/ Private non-profit; City/ staff: 1(p)/ 15(v)/ members: 200/publication: Garland City Gazette

HISTORICAL SOCIETY; HISTORY MUSEUM: Preserves Ashland history.

PROGRAMS: Annual Meeting; Exhibits; Guided Tours; Lectures; Publication; Research Library/Archives

COLLECTIONS: [1854-present]

HOURS: Yr Winter M-F 10-2; Summer 1-4

ADMISSION: $3, Children $1, Seniors $2.50

9072
Mason Area Historical Society
63335 Ed Carlson Rd, 54806; (p) (715) 765-4788; (c) Bayfield

Private non-profit/ 1991/ Board of Directors/ staff: 15(v)/ members: 145

HISTORIC PRESERVATION AGENCY; HISTORICAL SOCIETY; HISTORY MUSEUM: Collects and preserves local history.

PROGRAMS: Annual Meeting; Community Outreach; Elder's Programs; Exhibits; Family Programs; Festivals; Film/Video; Garden Tours; Guided Tours; Interpretation; Research Library/Archives; School-Based Curriculum; Theatre

COLLECTIONS: [1875-present] Photographs, manuscripts, articles, and family histories.

HOURS: May-Sept Su 1-4

ADMISSION: No charge

9073
Northern Wisconsin History Center
[PO Box 347, 54806]; (p) (715) 685-2646; (f) (715) 685-2680; nnewago@win.bright.net; (c) Bayfield

Private non-profit/ 1989/ Board of Directors/ staff: 2(f); 2(p)/ members: 55/publication: *Heritage Highlights*

ALLIANCE OF HISTORICAL AGENCIES: Provides a network for historical organizations in Northern Wisconsin.

PROGRAMS: Annual Meeting; Community Outreach; Exhibits; Festivals; Film/Video; Living History; Publication

COLLECTIONS: [20th c]

HOURS: Yr Daily 9-5

BAILEYS HARBOR

9074
Bjorklunden Chapel
7603 Chapel Ln, 54202 [PO Box 10, 54202]; (p) (920) 839-2216; (f) (920) 839-2688; mark.d.breseman@lawrence.edu; (c) Door

Private non-profit/ 1939/ Bjorklunden/ staff: 1(f); 2(p); 8(v)

HISTORIC SITE

PROGRAMS: Facility Rental; Guided Tours

COLLECTIONS: [1939-1947] 41 hand-painted murals and carvings.

HOURS: June-Sept M W 1-4

ADMISSION: $3

BALSAM LAKE

9075
Polk County Historical Society
Main St, 54810 [PO Box 41, 54810]; (p) (715) 485-3292, (715) 485-9269; www.co.polk.wi.us/tourism/; (c) Polk

Joint/ 1931/ County; Private for profit/ staff: 1(p); 37(v)/ members: 150

HISTORIC SITE; HISTORICAL SOCIETY; HISTORY MUSEUM; HOUSE MUSEUM; TRIBAL MUSEUM: Operates two museums, conducts genealogy research, marks historic sites.

PROGRAMS: Annual Meeting; Community Outreach; Exhibits; Facility Rental; Family Programs; Festivals; Film/Video; Garden Tours; Guided Tours; Interpretation; Lectures; Publication; Research Library/Archives

COLLECTIONS: [1850-present] Exhibits on home, agriculture, military, Native Americans, education, commerce, toys and manufacturing.

HOURS: Mem Day-Labor Day M-F, Su 12:45-4, Sa 10:30-4

ADMISSION: $2, Family $4; Under 13 free

BARABOO

9076
Circus World Museum
550 Water St, 53913-2597; (p) (608) 356-8341, (608) 356-1800; ringmaster@circusworldmuseum.com; www.circusworldmuseum.com; (c) Sauk

Private non-profit/ 1959/ Circus World Museum Foundation/State Historical Society of Wisconsin/ staff: 29(f); 80(p); 213(v)

Promotes circus history.

COLLECTIONS: [1880-1930] Artifacts and archival materials: books, posters, photos, wagons, and buildings from the Ringling Brothers Circus Winter Quarters.

HOURS: May-Sept Daily 9-6; Sept-Apr M-Sa 10-4, Su 11-4

9077
Sauk County Historical Society
531 4th Ave, 53913 [PO Box 651, 53913]; (p) (608) 356-1001; schist@shopstop.net; www.saukcounty.com/schs; (c) Sauk

Private non-profit/ 1905/ staff: 1(f); 1(p); 5(v)/ members: 350

HISTORICAL SOCIETY; HISTORY MUSEUM; HOUSE MUSEUM: Collects, preserves and interprets county history.

PROGRAMS: Annual Meeting; Community Outreach; Exhibits; Lectures; Research Library/Archives

COLLECTIONS: [Prehistory-late 1960s] Native American, pioneer, medical, military, circus, natural history, geological, industrial and political items; photographs, textiles and toys.

HOURS: May-Sept T-Su

BAYFIELD

9078
Bayfield Heritage Association, Inc.
30 N Broad St, 54814 [PO Box 137, 54814]; (p) (715) 779-5958; (c) Bayfield

Private non-profit/ 1974/ staff: 10(v)/ members: 200

HISTORICAL SOCIETY: Preserves and interprets history of Bayfield and nearby Apostle Islands.

PROGRAMS: Annual Meeting; Exhibits; Interpretation; Lectures; Research Library/Archives

COLLECTIONS: Artifacts and archival materials relating to Bayfiled and Apostle Islands region: settlement, agriculture, logging/lumbering, tourism, transportation, and maritime history.

BEAVER DAM

9079
Dodge County Historical Society
105 Park Ave, 53916-2107; (p) (920) 887-1266; (c) Dodge

Private non-profit/ 1938/ Museum Board/ staff: 3(p); 10(v)/ members: 200/publication: *100 years of Beaver Dam History; Sesquicentennial History; People, Places and Things*

HISTORIC SITE; HISTORICAL SOCIETY; HISTORY MUSEUM: Conducts and assists with local history research.

PROGRAMS: Annual Meeting; Exhibits; Festivals; Guided Tours; Publication; Research Library/Archives; School-Based Curriculum

COLLECTIONS: [1841-present]

HOURS: Yr T 10-1, W-Sa 2-5

ADMISSION: Donations accepted

BELOIT

9080
Beloit Historical Society
845 Hackett St, 53511; (p) (608) 365-7835; (f) (608) 365-5999; beloiths@ticon.net; www.ticon.net/~beloiths; (c) Rock

Joint/ 1910/ Board of Trustees; City/ staff: 2(f); 3(p); 125(v)/ members: 500/publication: *Confluence*

HISTORICAL SOCIETY; HISTORY MUSEUM

PROGRAMS: Annual Meeting; Exhibits; Facility Rental; Festivals; Interpretation; Lectures; Publication; Research Library/Archives

COLLECTIONS: [1836-present] Greater Beloit area: military items, sports items, household items, toys, textiles, maps, and books.

HOURS: Lincoln Center/Museum: Yr M-F 8:30-4; Homestead: June-Sept W-Su 1-4

9081
Logan Museum of Anthropology/ Wright Museum of Art
700 College St, 53511; (p) (608) 363-2677; (f) (608) 363-2248; www.beloit.edu; (c) Rock

Private non-profit/ 1892/ Beloit College/ staff: 4(f); 15(p)/ members: 300

ANTHROPOLOGY MUSEUM; ART MUSEUM

PROGRAMS: Exhibits; Guided Tours; Interpretation; Lectures; School-Based Curriculum

COLLECTIONS: [Prehistory-present] Anthropology artifacts from North and South America and Oceania. American and European art work, Asian decorative arts.

HOURS: Yr Th-Su 11-4

ADMISSION: No charge

BELVIDERE

9082
Log Cabin
311 Whitney Blvd, 61008; (p) (815) 544-8391

BLACK EARTH

9083
Black Earth Historical Society
950 Mills St, 53515 [PO Box 214, 53515-0214]; (c) Dane

Private non-profit/ 1992/ Board of Directors/ staff: 13(v)/ members: 80/publication: *Depot Dispatch*

HISTORICAL SOCIETY: Preserves, advances, and disseminates history of the Village of Black Earth.

PROGRAMS: Annual Meeting; Exhibits; Guided Tours; Lectures; Publication

COLLECTIONS: [1850-present] Local historical items and documents.

HOURS: Last Su in May-Sept Su 1-4

BONDUEL

9084
Bonduel Community Archives
108 S First St, 54107 [PO Box 205, 54107]; (p) (715) 758-2687; (c) Shawano

Private non-profit/ 1991/ Board of Directors/ staff: 36(v)/ members: 240/publication: *The Hisrorian Newsletter*

LIBRARY AND/OR ARCHIVES: Interprets historical information.

PROGRAMS: Annual Meeting; Community Outreach; Concerts; Exhibits; Publication; Research Library/Archives

COLLECTIONS: [1863-1999] Church and cemetery records, obituaries, and family history books, local businesses, organizations, churches, and schools.

HOURS: Yr W, Sa 9-4

BOWLER

9085
Arvid E. Miller Memorial Library Museum
N8510 Mohheconnuck Rd, 54416; (p) (715) 793-4420; (f) (715) 793-1307; arlee_davids@yahoo.com; (c) S'hawano

Tribal/ 1974/ Stockbridge-Munsee Tribal Council/ staff: 2(f); 1(p); 4(v)

HISTORY MUSEUM; LIVING HISTORY/OUTDOOR MUSEUM; RESEARCH CENTER; TRIBAL MUSEUM: Researches and collects Mohican history.

PROGRAMS: Community Outreach; Exhibits; Publication; Research Library/Archives

COLLECTIONS: [Pre-contact-present] Rare books, microfilm of Green Bay Indian Agency, Huntington collection, maps dating from 1600, photographs, government documents, missionary journals, artifacts, furs, 1745 Bible.

HOURS: Yr M-F 8-4:30

ADMISSION: Donations accepted

BRILLION

9086
Brillion Historical Society
110 N Francis St, 54110 [PO Box 35, 54110]; (c) Calumet

1966/ Board of Directors/ staff: 12(v)/ members: 75

HISTORICAL SOCIETY; HISTORY MUSEUM; HOUSE MUSEUM: Maintains history of Brillion area.

PROGRAMS: Annual Meeting; Exhibits; Guided Tours

COLLECTIONS: [1880-1920]

HOURS: May-Sept 2nd Sa 1-4

BRODHEAD

9087
Brodhead Historical Society
Former Railroad Depot, 53520 [1108 1st Center Ave, 53520]; (p) (608) 897-4150; (c) Green

Joint/ 1976/ Private non-profit; City

HISTORICAL SOCIETY; HISTORY MUSEUM

PROGRAMS: Annual Meeting; Community Outreach; Exhibits; Lectures

COLLECTIONS: Railroading.

HOURS: May-Sept Sa-Su, W, Summer 1-4

BROWN DEER

9088
Brown Deer Historical Society, Inc./1884 Brown Deer School
4800 W Green Brook Dr, 53223 [8035 N Grandview Dr, 53223]; (p) (414) 354-4116; (c) Milwaukee

1971/ Board of Directors/ staff: 25(p); 25(v)/ members: 150/publication: Brown Deer-Then and Now; Brown Deer's Heritage Almanac

HISTORIC PRESERVATION AGENCY; HISTORIC SITE; HISTORICAL SOCIETY; HISTORY MUSEUM; HOUSE MUSEUM; LIVING HISTORY/OUTDOOR MUSEUM

PROGRAMS: Annual Meeting; Community Outreach; Exhibits; Guided Tours; Interpretation; Lectures; Living History; Publication; Reenactments; Research Library/Archives; School-Based Curriculum

COLLECTIONS: [1884-1920] Schoolroom furnishings and class materials, dairying artifacts, early laundry equipment, clothing, portraits of historical figures, historical publications, and display cases of toys, tools, eyeglasses, jewelry, shaving items, dishes, glassware old woven basket.

HOURS: April-Oct by appt

ADMISSION: Donations accepted

BURLINGTON

9089
Burlington Historical Society
232 N Perkins Blvd, 53105; (p) (414) 767-2884; (c) Racine

Private non-profit/ 1928/ Board of Directors/ staff: 12(v)/ members: 115/publication: Burlington, Wisconsin - First 150+ Years, 1835-1990

GARDEN; HISTORICAL SOCIETY; HISTORY MUSEUM: Educates, preserves, advances, and disseminates knowledge of history of Burlington and counties Racine, Kenosha, and Walworth.

PROGRAMS: Annual Meeting; Concerts; Exhibits; Garden Tours; Guided Tours; Interpretation; Lectures; Living History; Publication; Research Library/Archives

COLLECTIONS: [1835-1950] Documents, photographs, pioneer artifacts, business and industry, 1850 immigrant log cabin museum, and a one room 1840 brick school configured for teaching living history.

9090
Log Cabin Museum
Wehmhoff Park, 53105 [Burlington Historical Society Museum, 232 N Perk, 53105]; (p) (414) 767-2884

CAMBRIA

9091
Columbia County Historical Society
112 N Main St, 53923 [W 3988 Hwy 33, 53923]; (p) (920) 348-5516; (c) Columbia

Private non-profit/ 1958/ staff: 4(p)/ members: 47

HISTORIC SITE; HISTORICAL SOCIETY; HISTORY MUSEUM; HOUSE MUSEUM: Preserves the history and archives of Columbia County.

PROGRAMS: Annual Meeting; Exhibits; Festivals; Guided Tours; Interpretation; Lectures; Living History; Publication; Reenactments; Research Library/Archives; School-Based Curriculum

COLLECTIONS: [1850-1950] Native American and clothing displays, kitchen, library, bedroom; religion, music, children, military, sewing, tools and agricultural items; 1872 one-room schoolhouse.

HOURS: June-Sept T-Sa 1-4

ADMISSION: $1, Children $0.50

CAMPBELLSPORT

9092
Henry S. Reuss Ice Age Visitor Center and Ice Age National Scientific Reserve, Kettle Moraine State Forest, Northern Unit
N2875 Hwy 67, 53010 [N1765 Hwy G, 53010]; (p) (920) 533-8322; (f) (262) 626-2117; www.dnr.state.wi.us; (c) Fond du Lac

Joint/ 1981/ WI Dept of Natural Resources/National Federal Park Service/ staff: 12(f); 33(p); 100(v)

NATURAL HISTORY MUSEUM: Protects glacial features of the area including kames, eskers, kettles, interlobate moraine, outwash plains and drumlins.

PROGRAMS: Annual Meeting; Community Outreach; Concerts; Exhibits; Family Programs; Festivals; Film/Video; Interpretation; Lectures; Living History; School-Based Curriculum

COLLECTIONS: [Prehistory] Exhibits and artifacts related to WI stage of the last Ice Age.

CASSVILLE

9093
Cassville Historical Society
Cassville Library, 53806; (p) (608) 725-5891; (c) Grant

Private non-profit/ 1985/ Board of Directors/ staff: 3(v)/ members: 50

HISTORICAL SOCIETY: Preserves and promotes local history.

PROGRAMS: Annual Meeting; Exhibits; Lectures; Research Library/Archives

COLLECTIONS: [1890s-present] Memorabilia and photos.

HOURS: Yr by appt

ADMISSION: No charge

CEDARBURG

9094
Cedarburg Cultural Center
W 62 N 546 Washington Ave, 53012 [PO Box 84, 53012]; (p) (414) 375-3676; (f) (414) 375-3120; ccc@grafton.net; www.cedarburg culturalcenter.freeservers.com; (c) Ozaukee

Private non-profit/ 1985/ Cedarburg Corporation/Board of Directors/ staff: 3(f); 4(p); 100(v)/ members: 600

ART MUSEUM; HISTORY MUSEUM: Preserves the history and heritage of Southeastern WI.

PROGRAMS: Annual Meeting; Community Outreach; Facility Rental; Family Programs; Festivals; Guided Tours; Interpretation; Lectures; School-Based Curriculum; Theatre

COLLECTIONS: [1850-1960] Packaging and advertising art. Permanent collection contains 2,000 photos, documents, and artifacts.

HOURS: Galleries/offices: Yr T-Sa 10-5, Su 1-5;

9095
Cedarburg Public Library
W63 N583 Hanover Ave, 53012; (p) (414) 375-7640; (f) (414) 375-7618; (c) Ozaukee

City/ 1927/ staff: 9(f); 4(p)

LIBRARY AND/OR ARCHIVES: Collects and preserves books, videos, magazines, CD-ROMs, cassettes and vertical files.

PROGRAMS: Research Library/Archives

COLLECTIONS: [19th-20th c] Books, periodicals, CDs, microfilm, audio tapes, maps and vertical files.

HOURS: Yr M-Th 9-9, F-Sa 10-5, Su 1-5; June-Aug closed Su

ADMISSION: No charge

9096
Ozaukee County Historical Society
[PO Box 206, 53012]; (p) (414) 377-4510; (c) Ozaukee

Private non-profit/ 1962/ staff: 6(p); 75(v)/ members: 430

HISTORIC SITE; HISTORICAL SOCIETY; LIVING HISTORY/OUTDOOR MUSEUM; RESEARCH CENTER: Preserves, advances, and disseminates knowledge of the history and heritage of Ozaukee County.

PROGRAMS: Annual Meeting; Community Outreach; Exhibits; Family Programs; Guided Tours; Interpretation; Lectures; Living History; Reenactments; Research Library/Archives; School-Based Curriculum

COLLECTIONS: [19th-20th c] Twenty log, stone and frame buildings with period artifacts.

HOURS: June-Aug Sa-Su 12-5; Sept Sa-Su 12-5

ADMISSION: $4, Student $3, Children $1, Seniors $3

CHIPPEWA FALLS

9097
Chippewa County Historical Society
123 Allen St, 54729; (p) (715) 723-4399; (c) Chippewa

Private non-profit/ 1960/ staff: 25(v)/ members: 250/publication: The Eagle Speaks

GENEALOGICAL SOCIETY; HISTORIC SITE; HISTORICAL SOCIETY; HISTORY MUSEUM; HOUSE MUSEUM; RESEARCH CENTER: Collects and preserves records and artifacts from Chippewa County.

PROGRAMS: Annual Meeting; Community Outreach; Concerts; Exhibits; Facility Rental; Family Programs; Festivals; Guided Tours; Interpretation; Lectures; Living History; Publication; Research Library/Archives; School-Based Curriculum

COLLECTIONS: [18th-20th c] Native American and logging items; sites: Father Goldsmith Chapel and the Cook-Rutledge Mansion.

HOURS: Yr T 9-4 and by appt.

9098
Cook-Rutledge Mansion
505 W Grand Ave, 54729; (p) (715) 723-7181

1880

COLLECTIONS: [1880s] Piano; music boxes.

HOURS: Jun-Aug

COUDERAY

9099
Hideout, The, Al Capone's Northwoods Retreat
12101 W County Rd CC, 54828 [12101 W County Road CC, 54828]; (p) (715) 945-2746; (f) (745) 945-2373; wistravel.com/alcapone.html

1927/ Private/ staff: 25(f); 6(p)

COLLECTIONS: [1920s, early 1930s] Prohibition era, liquor, beer-related.

HOURS: May-Feb

CRANDON

9100
Forest County Historical and Genealogical Society
105 W Jackson St, 54520 [PO Box 432, 54520]; (p) (715) 478-5900; (c) Forest

Private non-profit/ 1990/ staff: 20(v)/ members: 65

GENEALOGICAL SOCIETY; HISTORICAL SOCIETY; HOUSE MUSEUM: Operates county history museum; documents family home transition from lower to middle class.

PROGRAMS: Annual Meeting; Exhibits

COLLECTIONS: [1900-1920s] 4 period rooms and one-room schoolhouse.

HOURS: June-Sept M-Sa 10-4

ADMISSION: No charge

9101
Forest County Potawatomi Historical and Cultural Center
5460 Everybody's Rd, 54520 [PO Box 340, 54520]; (p) (715) 478-7475, (715) 478-7400; (f) (715) 478-7483; mikea@fcpotawatomi.com; (c) Forest

Tribal/ 1994/ Forest County Potawatomi Tribe of WI/ staff: 4(f)

RESEARCH CENTER; TRIBAL MUSEUM

PROGRAMS: Exhibits; Research Library/Archives

COLLECTIONS: [Prehistory-present]

HOURS: Yr

CUDAHY

9102
Cudahy Historical Society
4647 S Kinnickinnic Ave, 53110 [PO Box 332, 53110]; (p) (414) 747-1892; (c) Milwaukee

Private non-profit/ 1972/ staff: 50(v)/ members: 125

HISTORIC SITE; HISTORICAL SOCIETY; HISTORY MUSEUM: Owns and maintains historic Cudahy Depot as a town history museum.

PROGRAMS: Annual Meeting; Community Outreach; Exhibits; Facility Rental; Festivals

HOURS: Apr-Oct last Sa of month

9103
Wisconsin Slovak Historical Society
8602 Lakeshore Dr, 53110 [PO Box 164, 53110]; (p) (414) 697-4038; (f) (414) 697-4039; drjhosmanek@prodigy.net; (c) Kenosha

Private non-profit/ 1980/ staff: 24(v)/ members: 780

Perpetuates Slovak culture and history.

DANBURY

9104
Folle Avoine Historical Park
8500 County Rd, 54830 [PO Box 159, 54830]; (p) (715) 866-8890; fahp@centuryinter.net; (c) Burnett

County, non-profit/ Burnett County Historical Society/ staff: 7(p); 78(v)/ members: 300/publication: Burnett County Historical Society Newsletter

HISTORIC SITE: Manages Folle Avoine Historical Park to serve Northwestern WI.

PROGRAMS: Annual Meeting; Community Outreach; Concerts; Exhibits; Facility Rental; Festivals; Guided Tours; Interpretation; Living History; Publication; Reenactments; School-Based Curriculum

COLLECTIONS: [1802-1804] Native American and Euro-American explorer artifacts; immigrant settler artifacts.

HOURS: May-Sept W-Su 9-5

ADMISSION: $4, Family $10, Children $4

DARLINGTON

9105
Lafayette County Historical Society
525 N Main St, 53530 [PO Box 75, 53530]; (c) Lafayette

Private non-profit/ 1981/ staff: 1(p); 5(v)/ members: 125

HISTORICAL SOCIETY: Preserves local history.

PROGRAMS: Annual Meeting; Exhibits; Lectures

COLLECTIONS: [Late 19th-early 20th c] Agriculture, local businesses, railroad memorabilia, medical displays, sports and the circus.

HOURS: June-Aug vary

ADMISSION: No charge

DE FOREST

9106
DeForest Area Historical Society
119 E Elm St, 53532 [PO Box 124, 53532]; (p) (608) 846-5519; (c) Dane

Private non-profit/ 1976/ staff: 15(v)/ members: 130/publication: News and Notes

HISTORICAL SOCIETY: Conserves, preserves, and educates about area history.

PROGRAMS: Exhibits; Guided Tours; Publication; Research Library/Archives

COLLECTIONS: [1860-1960] Photos, manuscripts, and artifacts documenting area history of families, businesses, transportation, communication, religion, and schools.

HOURS: June-Dec 2nd Su of month 1-4

ADMISSION: No charge

DE PERE

9107
DePere Historical Society
White Pillars Museum, 403 N Broadway, 54115; (p) (920) 336-3877; (c) Brown

Private non-profit/ 1970/ staff: 1(p)/ members: 165

HISTORICAL SOCIETY: Maintains local history artifacts housed in 1836 Greek Revival building.

PROGRAMS: Annual Meeting; Exhibits; Family Programs; Research Library/Archives

COLLECTIONS: [19th-20th c] Photos, maps, yearbooks, newspaper files, tax records and funeral cards.

HOURS: Yr M-F 12-4 and by appt

ADMISSION: Donations accepted

DELAFIELD

9108
Hawks Inn Historical Society
426 Wells St, 53018 [PO Box 180140, 53018]; (p) (262) 646-4794; www.hawksinn.org; (c) Waukesha

Private non-profit/ 1960/ staff: 18(v)/ members: 215

HISTORIC PRESERVATION AGENCY; HISTORIC SITE; HISTORICAL SOCIETY; HISTORY MUSEUM

PROGRAMS: Annual Meeting; Community Outreach; Concerts; Exhibits; Facility Rental; Family Programs; Film/Video; Garden Tours; Guided Tours; Interpretation; Lectures; Research Library/Archives; School-Based Curriculum

COLLECTIONS: [1846-1866] Greek Revival Stage Coach Inn 18 rooms restored and furnished, with Federal American Empire, and Early Victorian antiques.

DODGEVILLE

9109
Iowa County Historical Society
Hwy 23 & Leffler St, 53533 [PO Box 44, 53533-0044]; (p) (608) 935-7694; (c) Iowa

Private non-profit/ 1976/ Board of Directors/ staff: 1(p); 8(v)/ members: 260

HISTORICAL SOCIETY; HISTORY MUSEUM; LIVING HISTORY/OUTDOOR MUSEUM: Collects, preserves and interprets county history.

PROGRAMS: Annual Meeting; Exhibits; Family Programs; Festivals; Film/Video; Guided Tours; Lectures; Publication; Research Library/Archives; School-Based Curriculum

COLLECTIONS: [1830-present] Artifacts, manuscripts, newspapers, books, genealogies and Governor Henry Dodge displays.

HOURS: May-Sept M-F

DRUMMOND

9110
Drummond Historical Society
Eastern Ave, 54832 [PO Box 8, 54832]; (p) (715) 739-6288; (c) Bayfield

County/ 1976/ staff: 10(v)/ members: 20

HISTORICAL SOCIETY; HISTORY MUSEUM; LIVING HISTORY/OUTDOOR MUSEUM: Displays the logging operation of Rust Oven Lumber Company.

PROGRAMS: Annual Meeting; Exhibits

COLLECTIONS: [1882-1932] History of logging camps, lumber town lifestyle.

HOURS: Yr T 12:30-5:30, W, Sa 10-2, Th 11-6

ADMISSION: Donations accepted

DURAND

9111
Pepin County Historical Society, Old Courthouse Museum and Jail
Washington Sq, Box 74, 54736; (p) (715) 672-8673; (c) Pepin

Joint/ 1984/ PCHS Board of Directors/Pepin Co. Board of Supervisors/Jail Real Estate Office/ staff: 8(p); 50(v)/ members: 200/publication: *Durand 1881; Today is History*

HISTORIC PRESERVATION AGENCY; HISTORIC SITE; HISTORICAL SOCIETY; HISTORY MUSEUM: Preserves old courthouse and Pepin county history.

PROGRAMS: Annual Meeting; Community Outreach; Guided Tours; Interpretation; Living History; Publication

COLLECTIONS: [Mid 19th c-present] Artifacts, manuscripts, and photographs; original courtroom and 1895 jail.

HOURS: Late May-mid Oct Su 1-5 and by appt

ADMISSION: $1, Children $0.50

EAGLE

9112
Old World Wisconsin
S103 W37890 Hwy 67, 53119; (p) (262) 594-6300; (f) (262) 594-6342; owwvisit@idcnet.com; (c) Waukesha

State/ 1976/ State Historical Society of WI/ staff: 11(f); 2(p); 600(v)/ members: 1800

LIVING HISTORY/OUTDOOR MUSEUM: Preserves lifestyles, ideas, and challenges of early rural immigrants.

PROGRAMS: Exhibits; Facility Rental; Family Programs; Festivals; Film/Video; Garden Tours; Guided Tours; Interpretation; Lectures; Living History; Reenactments; Theatre

COLLECTIONS: [1840-1918] Reflects the ethnic diversity of WI and Upper Midwest.

HOURS: May-June, Sept-Oct Daily M-F 10-5, Sa-Su 10-4; July-Aug 10-5

ADMISSION: $11, Children $5.50, Seniors $9.90; Group rates

EAGLE RIVER

9113
Eagle River Historical Society
519 Sheridan St, 54521 [PO Box 2011, 54521]; (p) (715) 479-2396; (c) Vilas

Joint/ 1989/ Exec Officer/Board of Directors/ staff: 7(p); 15(v)/ members: 55

GENEALOGICAL SOCIETY; HISTORIC PRESERVATION AGENCY; HISTORIC SITE; HISTORICAL SOCIETY; HISTORY MUSEUM: Gathers, documents, preserves, and disseminates the early history of the Eagle River area.

PROGRAMS: Annual Meeting; Community Outreach; Exhibits; Guided Tours; Research Library/Archives

COLLECTIONS: [1850-present] Records, pictures, artifacts, and memorabilia related to Eagle River's history.

HOURS: May-Oct T-F

EAU CLAIRE

9114
Chippewa Valley Museum
1204 Carson Park Dr, 54702 [PO Box 1204, 54702]; (p) (715) 834-7871; (f) (715) 834-6624; info@cvmuseum.com; www.cvmuseum.com; (c) Eau Claire

Private non-profit/ 1967/ Board of Directors/ staff: 7(f); 9(p); 342(v)/ members: 1650

HISTORY MUSEUM: Discovers, collects, preserves and interprets regional history and culture.

PROGRAMS: Community Outreach; Exhibits; Facility Rental; Family Programs; Festivals; Guided Tours; Interpretation; Lectures; Research Library/Archives; School-Based Curriculum; Theatre

COLLECTIONS: [1850-present] Museum artifacts, historic images, archival and library items. Sites: Schlegelmich House, Anderson Log House, and Sunnyview School.

HOURS: Summer Daily 10-5; Labor Day-Mem Wknd T-Su

9115
Schlegelmilch House
517 S Farwell, 57401 [Chippewa Valley Museum, PO Box 1204, 54702]; (p) (715) 834-7871; info@cvmuseum.com; www.cvmuseum.com; (c) Eau Claire

1871/ staff: 8(f); 7(p); 10(v)

COLLECTIONS: [Late 19th and early 20th c] House, furnishings.

HOURS: Vary

EDGERTON

9116
Albion Academy Historical Society
507 Campus Ln, 53534 [PO Box 171, 53534]; (p) (608) 884-3940; (c) Dane

Private non-profit/ 1853/ staff: 16(v)/ members: 70/publication: *1853-1918 A History of Albion Academy*

HISTORICAL SOCIETY: Collects, preserves, and displays items pertaining to education in a one-room country school and the "academy" secondary school.

PROGRAMS: Annual Meeting; Exhibits; Guided Tours; Publication; Research Library/Archives

COLLECTIONS: [1880-1910] Furnishing; chapel furniture; 1000 books, including Academy text books; and country school furnishings.

HOURS: June-Aug Su 1-4

ADMISSION: $3, Family $7

9117
Sterling North Society, Ltd.
409 W Rollin St, 53534 [PO Box 173, 53534];
(p) (608) 884-3074, (608) 884-3870; (c) Rock

Private non-profit/ 1988/ Board of Directors/
staff: 40(v)/ members: 140

HISTORIC SITE; HISTORICAL SOCIETY;
HOUSE MUSEUM; RESEARCH CENTER:
Preserves Edgerton's heritage related to
North; provides public access to the North
Home/Museum.

PROGRAMS: Annual Meeting; Community
Outreach; Exhibits; Family Programs; Guided
Tours; Interpretation; Lectures; Research Li-
brary/Archives

COLLECTIONS: [20th c] Sterling North books,
family artifacts, correspondence, photos, newspaper articles, and household furnishings.

HOURS: Apr-Dec Su 1-5

ADMISSION: $3, Student $2; Under 6 free

ELKHORN

9118
Webster House Museum
9 E Rockwell St, 53121 [PO Box 273, 53121];
(p) (414) 723-4248; (c) Walworth

Joint/ 1890/ Walworth County Historical Soci-
ety/ staff: 2(p)/ members: 170

HISTORIC PRESERVATION AGENCY; HIS-
TORIC SITE; HISTORICAL SOCIETY; HISTO-
RY MUSEUM; HOUSE MUSEUM; RE-
SEARCH CENTER

PROGRAMS: Annual Meeting; Elder's Programs; Exhibits; Facility Rental; Family Programs; Festivals; Guided Tours; Lectures; Research Library/Archives; School-Based
Curriculum

COLLECTIONS: [Early 19th c] Joseph
Philbrick's piano, violin and cornet. Webster's
1837 home, Civil War artifacts, Waterfowl
items, Wistgate miniature estate, children's
items, 1889 Blooming Prairie Schoolhouse,
General John W. Boyd Carriage House and
Old Sharon Town Hall.

HOURS: May-Nov W-Su 1-5 and by appt

ADMISSION: $4, Children $2

ELLSWORTH

9119
Pierce County Historical Association
414 W Main St, 54011 [PO Box 148, 54011];
(p) (715) 273-6611; (c) Pierce

1941/ staff: 1(v)/ members: 250

HISTORICAL SOCIETY: Gathers, preserves
and makes available historical items that reflect county heritage.

PROGRAMS: Annual Meeting; Exhibits; Facility Rental; Family Programs

COLLECTIONS: [19th-20th c] Books, manuscripts, photos and artifacts related to history
of Pierce County.

HOURS: Yr M-F 1-4

ADMISSION: No charge

ELROY

9120
Elroy Area Historical Society, Inc.
259 Main St, 53929 [PO Box 35, 53929]; (p)
(608) 462-5191, (608) 462-2407; (c) Juneau

City/ 1991/ Board of Directors/ staff: 50(v)/
members: 100

GENEALOGICAL SOCIETY; HISTORICAL
SOCIETY; HISTORY MUSEUM: Collects and
preserves local artifacts.

PROGRAMS: Annual Meeting; Exhibits; Guided Tours

COLLECTIONS: [1870-present] Local memorabilia, with emphasis on agriculture, railroads
and bike trails.

HOURS: May-Sept Sa-Su 1-4

ADMISSION: $5, Family $10; No charge

EPHRAIM

9121
Ephraim Foundation, Inc., The
3060 Anderson Lane, 54211 [PO Box 165,
54211]; (p) (920) 854-9688; (f) (920) 854-7232;
efoundation@itol.com; www.ephraim.org; (c)
Door

Private non-profit/ 1949/ staff: 1(f); 5(p);
100(v)/ members: 402/publication: *The Door
County Letters; Horseshoe Island*

HISTORIC PRESERVATION AGENCY; HIS-
TORIC SITE; HISTORY MUSEUM; HOUSE
MUSEUM: Operates four museums concerning Ephraim history and a community center;
preserves artifacts and images.

PROGRAMS: Annual Meeting; Community
Outreach; Exhibits; Facility Rental; Family Pro-
grams; Guided Tours; Interpretation; Lectures;
Publication; Research Library/Archives

COLLECTIONS: [1853-1953] Photos, artifacts
and documents pertaining to history of
Ephraim.

HOURS: Mid June-Labor Day M-Sa 10:30-4;
Labor Day-Oct F-Su 10:30-4

ADMISSION: $2, Family $5

EVANSVILLE

9122
Evansville Grove Society, Inc.
[PO Box 234, 53536]; (c) Dane

Private non-profit/ Board of Directors/ staff:
10(v)/ members: 38

HISTORICAL SOCIETY: Preserves the history
of Evansville.

PROGRAMS: Annual Meeting; Garden Tours;
Guided Tours; Lectures

FIFIELD

9123
Price County Historical Society
W7213 Pine St, 54524 [PO Box 156, 54524];
(p) (715) 762-4571; (c) Price

Private non-profit/ 1959/ Board of Directors/
staff: 2(v)/ members: 255

HISTORIC SITE; HISTORICAL SOCIETY; HIS-
TORY MUSEUM: Collects, preserves, and exhibits county history for residents and visitors.

PROGRAMS: Annual Meeting; Community
Outreach; Exhibits

COLLECTIONS: [1876-1930s] Clothing,
household, and logging items, local historical
art and literature.

HOURS: June-Labor Day F-Su 1-5

ADMISSION: Donations

FISH CREEK

9124
Gibraltar Historical Association
4167 Hwy 42, 54212 [PO Box 323, 54212];
(p) (920) 868-2091; (c) Door

Private non-profit/ 1984/ Gibraltar Historical
Association Board/ staff: 2(p); 20(v)/ members:
145

HISTORIC PRESERVATION AGENCY; HIS-
TORICAL SOCIETY; HOUSE MUSEUM: Collects, researches and preserves objects and
archival materials reflecting local history.

PROGRAMS: Community Outreach; Exhibits;
Guided Tours; Interpretation; Lectures

COLLECTIONS: [1875-1900] Furnishings and
accessories for historic house; photos and artifacts.

HOURS: June-Oct F-Su 11-3

ADMISSION: $3

FLORENCE

9125
Florence County Historical Society
501 Lake St, 54121; (p) (715) 528-3203;
www.florence.co.florence.wi.us; (c) Florence

County/ 1982

HISTORY MUSEUM: Preserves 1889 Courthouse and Jail.

PROGRAMS: Annual Meeting; Community
Outreach; Exhibits

COLLECTIONS: [1889-present] Photos.

HOURS: May-Oct Daily 8-4

ADMISSION: No charge

FOND DU LAC

9126
**Fond du Lac County Historical
Society**
336 Old Pioneer Rd, 54935 [PO Box 1284,
54935]; (p) (920) 922-6390; (c) Fond du Lac

Private non-profit/ 1948/ staff: 5(p); 200(v)/
members: 160

HISTORIC SITE; HISTORICAL SOCIETY;
HISTORY MUSEUM; HOUSE MUSEUM; RE-
SEARCH CENTER

PROGRAMS: Annual Meeting; Exhibits; Family Programs; Festivals; Film/Video; Guided
Tours; Lectures; Reenactments; Research Li-
brary/Archives

COLLECTIONS: [Late 19th-early 20th c] 20
sites; period artifacts.

HOURS: Mem Day-Labor Day Daily 10-4; Sept
Sa-Su 10-4

ADMISSION: $5.50, Student $3, Children $3;
Under 5 free

9127
Fond du Lac Public Library
32 Sheboygan St, 54935; (p) (920) 929-7086; (f) (920) 929-7082; fpl@fond-du-lac.lib.wi.us; www.fond-du-lac.lib.wi.us; (c) Fond du Lac

City/ 1876/ Fond du Lac Public Library Board/ staff: 19(f); 27(p)

COLLECTIONS: [19th-20th c] Materials relative to the history and families of Fond du Lac County, its contiguous counties and WI.

HOURS: Sept-May M-Th 9-9, F 9-6, Sa 9-5, Su 1-4; June-Aug M-Th 9-8, F 9-6, Sa 9-12

FORT ATKINSON

9128
Fort Atkinson Historical Society/ Hoard Historical Museum
407 Merchants Ave, 53538; (p) (920) 563-7769; (f) (920) 568-3203; (c) Jefferson

Private non-profit/ 1939/ Board of Directors/ staff: 2(f); 3(p); 70(v)/ members: 400

HISTORICAL SOCIETY; HISTORY MUSEUM; HOUSE MUSEUM: Collects, preserves and interprets the history of Fort Atkinson and nearby communities through artifacts, documents, research and programs.

PROGRAMS: Annual Meeting; Exhibits; Facility Rental; Interpretation; Research Library/ Archives

COLLECTIONS: [18th-20th c] Native American artifacts, tools, local archives, beadwork, quilts, dolls, stuffed birds, costumes, period furniture, Lincoln Library and National Dairy Shrine Visitors Center.

FRANKLIN

9129
Franklin Historical Society
8048 Legend Dr, 53132 [7575 S 51st St, 53132]; (p) (414) 421-0168; (c) Milwaukee

Private non-profit/ 1968/ staff: 7(f)/ members: 45

HISTORICAL SOCIETY; HISTORY MUSEUM: Preserves four buildings from the 1850s as historical landmarks.

PROGRAMS: Annual Meeting; Community Outreach; Concerts; Exhibits; Facility Rental; Guided Tours; Interpretation; Lectures; Research Library/Archives

COLLECTIONS: [19th c] Household and farm tools, farm machinery.

HOURS: May-Aug 1st Su 2-4

ADMISSION: No charge

GENESEE DEPOT

9130
Ten Chimneys Foundation, Inc.
S42 W31610 Depot Rd, 53127 [PO Box 225, 53127]; (p) (414) 968-4161; (f) (414) 968-4267; staff@tenchimneys.org; www.techimneys.org; (c) Waukesha

Private non-profit/ 1996/ Board of Trustees/ staff: 6(f); 2(p); 209(v)/publication: *Ten Chimneys: The Lunts on Stage in Wisconsin*

GARDEN; HISTORIC SITE; HOUSE MUSEUM: Restores, preserves, and interprets the estate of Alfred Lunt and Lynn Fontanne.

PROGRAMS: Exhibits

COLLECTIONS: [Late 19th-mid 20th c] Century Furnishings from America, England and Scandinavian Countries, Decorative arts from late 18th-mid 20th century. Signed first edition books, archival materials of units and theater history, unique wall murals, English tinsel prints and personal effects of the Lunts.

GREEN BAY

9131
Ashwaubenon Historical Society, Inc.
737 Cormier Rd, 54324 [PO Box 28081, 54324]; (c) Brown

Private non-profit/ 1971/ members: 25

HISTORICAL SOCIETY

PROGRAMS: Annual Meeting; Community Outreach

COLLECTIONS: Military, industrial, and agricultural artifacts.

9132
Brown County Historical Society
1008 S Monroe Ave, 54301; (p) (920) 437-1840; (f) (920) 437-1840; www.browncohistorical soc.org; (c) Brown

Private non-profit/ 1899/ Board of Directors/ staff: 2(f); 2(p); 100(v)/ members: 650/publication: *Voyageur: Northeast Wisconsin's Historical Review; The Historical Bulletin*

GENEALOGICAL SOCIETY; HISTORIC PRESERVATION AGENCY; HISTORIC SITE; HISTORICAL SOCIETY; HISTORY MUSEUM; HOUSE MUSEUM; RESEARCH CENTER: Collects, preserves, and interprets local history; operates historic house museum.

PROGRAMS: Annual Meeting; Community Outreach; Exhibits; Facility Rental; Festivals; Guided Tours; Lectures; Living History; Monthly Meeting; Publication; Research Library/ Archives; School-Based Curriculum

COLLECTIONS: [1840-1890] Late nineteenth century furniture, artifacts, and artwork displayed in a 1837 Greek Revival homestead with emphasis on the Morgan L. Martin family and life in Northeastern Wisconsin in the mid to late 1800s.

HOURS: June-Aug M, W-F 10-2, Sa-Su 1-4; May Sa-Su 1-4

ADMISSION: $4, Children $2.50, Seniors $3.50

9133
Hazelwood Historic House Museum
1008 S Monroe Ave, 54305 [PO Box 1411, 54305-1411]; (p) (920) 437-1840; (f) (920) 455-4518; www.browncohistoricalsoc.org; (c) Brown

Private non-profit/ 1964/ Brown County Historical Society/ staff: 1(p); 40(v)

HOUSE MUSEUM: Houses original furnishings and artifacts of Morgan L. Martin and his family.

PROGRAMS: Community Outreach; Exhibits; Family Programs; Festivals; Guided Tours; Interpretation; Lectures; Reenactments

COLLECTIONS: [1890s] Home furnishings and artifacts of the Morgan L. Martin family.

HOURS: May Sa-Su 1-4; June-Aug M, W-F 10-2, Sa-Su 1-4

ADMISSION: $4, Children $2.50

9134
National Railroad Museum

Private non-profit/ 1958/ Board of Directors/ staff: 8(f); 65(v)/ members: 2100

HISTORY MUSEUM; LIVING HISTORY/OUTDOOR MUSEUM: Collects and preserves historical railroad equipment, artifacts, and materials; displays and interprets the history and significance of railroading.

PROGRAMS: Annual Meeting; Exhibits; Festivals; Film/Video; Guided Tours; Interpretation; Lectures; Research Library/Archives

COLLECTIONS: [1880s-1950s] Rolling stock, track construction, maintenance tools, general operation, management, and legal documents.

HOURS: Daily 9-5

ADMISSION: $7, Children $5, Seniors $6

9135
Neville Public Museum of Brown County
210 Museum Place, 54303; (p) (920) 448-4460; (f) (920) 448-4458; bc_museum@co.brown. wi.us; www.co.brown.wi.us/museum/index; (c) Brown

County/ 1915/ staff: 17(f); 2(p); 100(v)/ members: 780/publication: *Musepaper*

HISTORY MUSEUM

PROGRAMS: Annual Meeting; Community Outreach; Concerts; Elder's Programs; Exhibits; Facility Rental; Family Programs; Film/Video; Guided Tours; Interpretation; Lectures; Publication; Research Library/Archives; School-Based Curriculum

COLLECTIONS: [Prehistory-present] Archaeology, ethnology, history, geology, natural history, and fine arts materials; prints, negatives, and news film.

HOURS: Yr T,Th-Sa 9-4, W 9-9, Su 12-4

ADMISSION: Donations requested

GREEN LAKE

9136
Dartford Historical Society
501 Mill St, 54941 [PO Box 638, 54941]; (p) (920) 294-6194; (c) Green Lake

Private non-profit/ 1956/ Board of Directors/ staff: 30(v)/ members: 150

HISTORICAL SOCIETY: Collects, preserves, and interprets Green Lake area's history.

PROGRAMS: Annual Meeting; Community Outreach; Exhibits; Interpretation; Lectures; Research Library/Archives

COLLECTIONS: [1840-present] Photos, maps, newspapers, and museum artifacts.

HOURS: Yr F 10-4, Sa-Su 1-4

ADMISSION: No charge

GREENBUSH

9137
Wade House State Historic Site
W7747 Plank Rd, 53026 [PO Box 34, 53026];
(p) (920) 526-3271; (f) (920) 526-3626; wade
hous@mail.tcbi.com; (c) Sheboygan

State/ 1953/ State Historical Society of WI/
staff: 4(f); 35(p); 100(v)

HISTORIC SITE; LIVING HISTORY/ OUT-
DOOR MUSEUM: Interprets transportation
and innkeeping.

PROGRAMS: Exhibits; Family Programs;
Film/Video; Guided Tours; Interpretation; Liv-
ing History; Reenactments; School-Based
Curriculum; Theatre

COLLECTIONS: [1850-1920s] Furnishings,
reconstructed blacksmith shop and over 100
horse-drawn vehicles.

HOURS: May-Oct Daily 9-5

ADMISSION: $7.25, Children $3.25

GREENDALE

9138
Greendale Historical Society
5650 Parking St, 53129; (c) Milwaukee

Private non-profit/ 1975/ staff: 7(f)/ members:
109/publication: *Greendale Remembers*

HISTORICAL SOCIETY: Preserves the history
of Greendale.

PROGRAMS: Annual Meeting; Exhibits; Guided Tours; Lectures; Publication

COLLECTIONS: [1930-1950] Photos and documents of city development.

HOURS: Yr by appt

ADMISSION: No charge

HARTFORD

9139
Hartford Heritage Auto Museum
147 N Rural St, 53027; (p) (414) 673-7999;
(c) Washington

Private non-profit/ 1986/ Hartford Heritage,
Inc./ staff: 1(f); 4(p); 55(v)

AUTOMOBILE MUSEUM

PROGRAMS: Concerts; Exhibits; Facility
Rental; Festivals; Lectures; Research Library/
Archives

COLLECTIONS: [1920s-1950s] Signs, test
equipment, model cars, 90 vehicles of all
makes and models.

HOURS: Yr Daily 10-5

ADMISSION: $5, Student $4, Children $2, Se-
niors $4

HARTLAND

9140
Wisconsin Postal History Society
N95 W32259 County Line Rd, 53029; (p)
(414) 966-7096; (c) Waukesha

Private non-profit/ 1942/ staff: 10(v)/ members:
173/publication: *WPHS Badger Postal History*

HISTORICAL SOCIETY: Collects and disseminates information on WI postal history.

PROGRAMS: Annual Meeting; Publication
COLLECTIONS: [19th-20th c]

HAYWARD

9141
Sawyer County Historical Society, Inc.
15715 Hwy B, 54843 [PO Box 384, 54843];
(p) (715) 634-8053; wordwitt@win.bright.net;
www.sawyercountyhist.org; (c) Sawyer

Joint/ 1979/ County; Private non-profit/ staff:
12(v)/ members: 110

HISTORICAL SOCIETY; HISTORY MUSEUM;
RESEARCH CENTER: Preserves local history
through artifacts, photographs and documents; provides research assistance.

PROGRAMS: Annual Meeting; Community
Outreach; Concerts; Exhibits; Interpretation;
Lectures; Research Library/Archives

COLLECTIONS: [1880-1980] Artifacts, photographs, documents and furnishings pertaining
to local government, logging, Ojibwe history,
education, churches, resorts, tourism and
homesteading.

HOURS: June-Aug M-F 12-4

ADMISSION: $1

HILLSBORO

9142
Hillsboro Area Historical Society
Maple St, 54634 [PO Box 9, 54634]; (p) (608)
489-3322; (c) Vernon

City/ 1954/ staff: 45(v)/ members: 45

HISTORICAL SOCIETY; HISTORY MUSEUM:
Preserves the area's heritage.

HORICON

9143
Horicon Historical Society
322 Winter St, 53032 [PO Box 65, 53032]; (p)
(920) 485-2830, (920) 485-3200; (c) Dodge

Private non-profit/ 1972/ staff: 12(v)/ members:
96

GARDEN; HISTORIC PRESERVATION
AGENCY; HISTORICAL SOCIETY; HISTORY
MUSEUM; HOUSE MUSEUM

PROGRAMS: Concerts; Exhibits; Festivals;
Guided Tours; Reenactments; Research Li-
brary/Archives

COLLECTIONS: [1860s-1930s] House,
school, shed, Native American artifacts, furniture, clothes, books, maps, tax and cemetery
records, kitchen utensils, birth and death certificates, wooden loom, blacksmith shop and
tools.

HOURS: Yr by appt; May-Dec 2nd and 4th Su
of month.

HUDSON

9144
Saint Croix County Historical Society
1004 Third St, 54016; (p) (715) 386-2654; (c)
Saint Croix

Private non-profit/ 1948/ Board of Directors/
staff: 3(p); 40(v)/ members: 130/publication:
The Bulletin

GARDEN; GENEALOGICAL SOCIETY; HIS-
TORIC PRESERVATION AGENCY; HIS-
TORIC SITE; HISTORICAL SOCIETY; HISTO-
RY MUSEUM; HOUSE MUSEUM: Interprets
and preserves county records and artifacts.

PROGRAMS: Annual Meeting; Community
Outreach; Exhibits; Family Programs; Garden
Tours; Guided Tours; Interpretation; Lectures;
Publication

COLLECTIONS: [Mid-late 19th c] Dolls, clothing, farm equipment, furniture, photos, genealogies.

HOURS: May-Oct, Dec T-Sa 10-11:30/2-4:30,
Su 2-4:30

ADMISSION: $3, Student $1, Children $0.50

HURLEY

9145
Iron County Historical Museum
303 Iron St, 54534; (p) (715) 561-2244; (c)
Iron

Private non-profit/ 1966/ Iron County Historical
Society/ staff: 10(f); 4(p); 10(v)/ members: 81

HISTORY MUSEUM: Preserves, interprets,
and presents county history.

PROGRAMS: Annual Meeting; Exhibits; Guided Tours

COLLECTIONS: [19th-20th c] Artifacts related
to logging, mining, farming and weaving.
Clothing, home furnishings and library with
books, pictures and maps.

HOURS: Yr M, W, F-Sa 10-2

ADMISSION: Donations

HUSTISFORD

9146
Hustiford Historical Society
134 N Ridge St, 53034 [PO Box 12, 53034];
(p) (920) 349-3501; (c) Dodge

Private non-profit/ 1971/ Board of Officers and
Directors/ staff: 10(v)/ members: 20

HISTORICAL SOCIETY: Collects and displays
artifacts, pictures, and information of local historical interest.

PROGRAMS: Annual Meeting; Community
Outreach; Concerts; Exhibits; Festivals; Guided Tours; Research Library/Archives

COLLECTIONS: [1837-1960] John Hustis
House Museum, Roethke Shoe Shop, and
Bandstand.

HOURS: June-Sept 2nd and 4th Su of the
month 1-3

ADMISSION: Donations accepted

IOLA

9147
Iola Historical Society
Depot St, 54945 [205 E State St, 54945]; (p)
(715) 445-2401; (c) Waupaca

Private non-profit/ 1958/ Board of Officers and
Directors/ staff: 10(v)/ members: 33

HISTORIC SITE; HISTORICAL SOCIETY:
Studies and preserves local history.

PROGRAMS: Annual Meeting; Exhibits; Family Programs; Festivals; Guided Tours; Lec-

tures; Research Library/Archives; School-Based Curriculum

COLLECTIONS: [19th-20th c] Local railroad, churches, organizations, newspaper, rural town hall.

HOURS: Aug

ADMISSION: No charge

JANESVILLE

9148
Lincoln-Tallman Restoration/Rock County Historical Society
440 N Jackson St, 53547 [PO Box 8096, 53547]; (p) (608) 756-4509; (f) (608) 741-9596; (c) Rock

Joint/ 1855/ City of Janesville/Rock County Historical Society/ staff: 8(f); 7(p); 252(v)/ members: 983/publication: *Nellie Tallman: A Good and Caring Woman*

HISTORICAL SOCIETY: Preserves historic Lincoln-Tallman house.

PROGRAMS: Community Outreach; Concerts; Exhibits; Facility Rental; Family Programs; Festivals; Guided Tours; Interpretation; Lectures; Living History; Publication; Reenactments; School-Based Curriculum

COLLECTIONS: [1855-1900] Decorative arts, costumes, paintings, portraits, manuscripts and household items.

HOURS: Yr Sa-Su 9-4; June-Sept Daily 9-4; (Holiday Tours) Late Nov-Dec Daily 9-4

ADMISSION: $8, Children $4, Seniors $7

9149
Rock County Historical Society
426 N Jackson St, 53547 [PO Box 8096, 53547]; (p) (608) 756-4509, (608) 752-4519; (f) (608) 756-3036; (c) Rock

Private non-profit/ 1948/ Board of Trustees/ staff: 8(f); 7(p); 252(v)/ members: 983/publication: *Preservation Ordinances in Action: Rock County*

GENEALOGICAL SOCIETY; HISTORIC SITE; HISTORICAL SOCIETY; HISTORY MUSEUM; HOUSE MUSEUM; RESEARCH CENTER: Collects, preserves and interprets county history.

PROGRAMS: Annual Meeting; Community Outreach; Concerts; Elder's Programs; Exhibits; Facility Rental; Family Programs; Festivals; Guided Tours; Interpretation; Lectures; Publication; Reenactments; Research Library/Archives; School-Based Curriculum; Theatre

COLLECTIONS: [19th-20th c] Manuscripts, maps, newspapers, volumes, serials, sheet music, photographs, portraits, paintings, decorative arts, textiles and furnishings.

HOURS: Yr Daily 10-4

ADMISSION: $3.50, Children $2.50, Seniors $3

9150
Rock River Thresheree, Inc.
51 E Cox Rd, 53547 [PO Box 8243, 53547-8243]; (p) (608) 868-2814; (c) Rock

Private non-profit/ 1955/ staff: 250(v)/ members: 300

HISTORIC PRESERVATION AGENCY

PROGRAMS: Exhibits; Facility Rental; Living History; Reenactments

COLLECTIONS: [Late 19th-mid 20th c] Steam engines, tractors, threshing machines, saw mill, blacksmith shop, and small gas engines.

HOURS: Labor Day weekend F-M 8-5

ADMISSION: $5, Children $2

KAUKAUMA

9151
Charles A. Grignon Mansion, The
1313 Augustine St, 54130 [PO Box 247, 54130]; (p) (920) 766-3122; (f) (920) 766-9834; www.foxvalleyhistory.org

1837/ staff: 1(f)

COLLECTIONS: [1837-1862] Domestic material culture, documents, photos, architecture.

HOURS: June-Aug, Mon-Sa 10-5

KENOSHA

9152
Kenosha County Historical Society and Museum, Inc.
220-51st Place, 53140; (p) (414) 654-5770; (f) (414) 654-1730; kchs@acronet.net; www.kenoshahistorycenter.org; (c) Kenosha

Private non-profit/ 1878/ staff: 2(f); 5(p); 40(v)/ members: 550/publication: *Southport*

HISTORICAL SOCIETY

PROGRAMS: Annual Meeting; Community Outreach; Exhibits; Guided Tours; Lectures; Publication; Research Library/Archives; School-Based Curriculum

COLLECTIONS: [1835-present] Agricultural, military, labor and fashion history; furniture, lighthouse, domestic items, archival materials, industrial, and transportation artifacts.

HOURS: Yr T-F 10-4:30, Sa-Su 2-4:30

9153
Kenosha Public Museum
5608 10th Ave, 53140; (p) (414) 653-4140; (f) (414) 653-4143; mnancym@kenosha.org; (c) Kenosha

City/ 1936/ staff: 6(f); 13(p); 65(v)/ members: 2000

ANTHROPOLOGY MUSEUM; ART MUSEUM; NATURAL HISTORY MUSEUM: Focuses on fine and decorative arts, Native Americans, local archaeology.

PROGRAMS: Annual Meeting; Community Outreach; Elder's Programs; Exhibits; Family Programs; Festivals; Guided Tours; Interpretation; Lectures; Research Library/Archives; School-Based Curriculum

COLLECTIONS: [Prehistory-history] Archaeology and anthropology artifacts on Inuit, African, Pacific Islander and Asian people; geology, zoology, and botany exhibits.

HOURS: Yr Daily

ADMISSION: No charge

KEWASKUM

9154
Kewaskum Historical Society, Inc.
1202 Parkview Dr, 53040 [PO Box 394, 53040-0394]; (p) (414) 626-8484; (f) (414)

626-4909; (c) Washington

1975/ Village of Kewaskum/ staff: 6(p); 30(v)/ members: 45

HISTORICAL SOCIETY; HISTORY MUSEUM

PROGRAMS: Annual Meeting; Exhibits; Festivals; Guided Tours

COLLECTIONS: [Late 1800s-present]

HOURS: June-Sept

ADMISSION: No charge

KEWAUNEE

9155
Kewaunee County Historical Society
620 Juneau St, 54216 [PO Box 232, 54216]; (p) (920) 388-4410; (c) Kewaunee

Joint/ 1961/ State; Private non-profit/ staff: 506(v)

HISTORICAL SOCIETY

PROGRAMS: Annual Meeting; Exhibits; Guided Tours; Lectures

COLLECTIONS: [1861-early 1900s] Local histories of people and places through photos and written documents, military artifacts, toys, furniture, kitchen items, medical and agricultural equipment.

HOURS: May-Sept Daily 10-4

ADMISSION: Donations accepted

KOHLER

9156
Kohler Design Center
444 Highland Dr, 53044; (p) (920) 457-4441, (920) 457-3699; (f) (920) 457-9064; pete.fetterer@kohlerco.com; www.kohlerco.com; (c) Sheboygan

Private for-profit/ 1873/ Kohler Company/ staff: 2(f); 5(p)

CORPORATE ARCHIVES/MUSEUM: Depicts the evolution of the plumbingware company and the Village of Kohler.

PROGRAMS: Exhibits; Guided Tours; Research Library/Archives

COLLECTIONS: [1873-present] Kohler Family, Kohler Village artifacts;

HOURS: Yr M-F 9-5, Sa-Su 10-4

ADMISSION: No charge

9157
Waelderhaus
1100 W Riverside Dr, 53044; (p) (920) 452-4079; (f) (920) 452-1430

LA CROSSE

9158
La Crosse County Historical Society
112 S 9th St, 54602 [PO Box 1272, 54602-1272]; (p) (608) 782-1980; (c) La Crosse

Private non-profit/ 1898/ staff: 2(f); 5(p); 30(v)/ members: 380

HISTORICAL SOCIETY; HISTORY MUSEUM: Collects, preserves and interprets county history.

PROGRAMS: Annual Meeting; Community Outreach; Exhibits; Family Programs; Guided Tours; Lectures; Research Library/Archives

COLLECTIONS: [19th-20th c] Hixon family and local history items, county records, architectural drawings, maps, advertisements, local newspapers and photos.

HOURS: (Swarthout) Yr T-Su 10-5; (Hixon) Late May-early Sept Daily 1-5; (Riverside) Late May-early Sept Daily 10-5

ADMISSION: $3, Family $10, Children $1.50, Seniors $2.50; Group rates

LAC DU FLAMBEAU

9159
George W. Brown, Jr. Ojibwe Museum and Cultural Center
603 Peace Pipe Rd, 54538 [PO Box 804, 54538-0804]; (p) (715) 588-3333; (f) (715) 588-2355; museum@ojibwe.com; www.ojibwe.com; (c) Vilas

Tribal/ 1989/ Lac du Flambeau Band of Lake Superior Chippewa Indians/ staff: 2(f); 4(p); 2(v)/publication: *Reflections of Lac du Flambeau*

TRIBAL MUSEUM: Provides and facilitates knowledge regarding historic and contemporary Ojibwe life; advances Ojibwe national heritage.

PROGRAMS: Community Outreach; Exhibits; Facility Rental; Family Programs; Guided Tours; Lectures; Living History; Publication; Research Library/Archives

COLLECTIONS: [1870-present] Bark canoes, woven bags, photographs, audio/video footage and archival papers relating to local people.

HOURS: May-Oct M-Sa 10-4; Winter Nov-Apr T-Th 10-2

ADMISSION: $2, Children $1

9160
Lac du Flambeau Tribal Historic Preservation Office for the Lac du Flambeau Band of Lake Superior Chippewa Indians
Lac du Flambeau Indian Bowl, 54538 [PO Box 67, 54538]; (p) (715) 588-2139; (f) (715) 588-2419; ldfthpo@newnorth.net; (c) Vilas/Oneida/Iron

Tribal/ 1991/ Lac du Flambeau Tribal Council/ staff: 2(f); 1(v)

HISTORIC PRESERVATION AGENCY: Conducts archaeological investigations, educational programs and training programs in regional prehistory and history.

PROGRAMS: Community Outreach; Exhibits; Film/Video; Interpretation; Lectures; School-Based Curriculum

COLLECTIONS: [Prehistory-present] Artifacts, oral histories and notes from archaeological investigations.

ADMISSION: No charge

LADYSMITH

9161
Rusk County Historical Museum
Rusk County Fairgrounds, 54848 [c/o Henry Golat, N2754 Dicas Rd, 54848]; (c) Rusk

Private non-profit/ 1955/ staff: 9(f); 11(v)/ members: 120

HISTORICAL SOCIETY: Maintains museum complex.

PROGRAMS: Annual Meeting; Exhibits; Guided Tours

COLLECTIONS: [1900-1930] Military, logging, mining and railroad artifacts; clothing, machinery, blacksmith shop, rock display, post office, iron lung, government files; dentist, surveyor and farming tools.

HOURS: Yr F-Su 12:30-4:30

ADMISSION: Donations

LAKE DELTON

9162
Caddie Woodlawn County Park
[PO Box 467, 53940]; (p) (715) 235-2070, (715) 664-8690; discover-net.net/~dchs/sitecw.html

9163
Seth Peterson Cottage Conservancy, Inc.
S1994 Pickerel Slough Rd, 53940 [PO Box 334, 53940]; (p) (608) 254-6051; (f) (608) 254-6051; (c) Sauk

Private non-profit/ 1989/ Board of Directors/ staff: 35(v)/ members: 359/publication: *Restoring A Lost Masterpiece*

HOUSE MUSEUM: Restores, preserves, and maintains the 1958 Frank Lloyd Wright designed house.

PROGRAMS: Annual Meeting; Community Outreach; Facility Rental; Family Programs; Guided Tours; Lectures; Publication

COLLECTIONS: [1958-1960] Frank Lloyd Wright furnishing.

HOURS: Yr 2nd Su of month, 1st Su in June 1-4

ADMISSION: $2

LAKE GENEVA

9164
Geneva Lake Area Museum
818 Geneva St, 53147 [PO Box 522, 53147]; (p) (414) 248-6060; (c) Walworth

City/ 1983/ Geneva Lake History Buffs, Inc./ staff: 1(f); 30(v)/ members: 1998/publication: *Museum Musings*

HISTORY MUSEUM

PROGRAMS: Annual Meeting; Exhibits; Guided Tours; Lectures; Publication

COLLECTIONS: [1831-present] Local historical artifacts.

HOURS: Spring/Fall F-Su 1-5; Summer Th-M 1-5

ADMISSION: Donations accepted

LAKE TOMAHAWK

9165
Northland Historical Society
Kelly St, 54539 [PO Box 325, 54539]; (c) Oneida

Private non-profit; State/ 1957/ Board of Directors/ staff: 12(v)/ members: 80

HISTORIC PRESERVATION AGENCY; HOUSE MUSEUM

PROGRAMS: Annual Meeting; Exhibits; Lectures

COLLECTIONS: [Early 20th c] Mining, logging and local history artifacts related to Northern WI.

HOURS: Summer Sa 2-4

ADMISSION: No charge

LANCASTER

9166
Grant County Historical Society
129 E Maple St, 53813; (p) (608) 723-4825, (608) 723-2287; (c) Grant

Joint/ 1950/ County, non-profit; Private non-profit/ members: 150/publication: *Here and There*

GENEALOGICAL SOCIETY; HISTORIC PRESERVATION AGENCY; HISTORIC SITE; HISTORICAL SOCIETY; HISTORY MUSEUM; HOUSE MUSEUM; RESEARCH CENTER: Preserves and teaches county history; maintains the Cunningham Museum in Lancaster and Mitchell-Rountree Stone Cottage in Platteville.

PROGRAMS: Annual Meeting; Community Outreach; Exhibits; Family Programs; Guided Tours; Interpretation; Lectures; Living History; Publication; Reenactments; Research Library/Archives

COLLECTIONS: [19th-20th c] Eight rooms of artifacts on domestic life, African American culture, Civil War, World War II, farming and medical practices, dolls, education and people of local importance.

HOURS: Yr by appt

ADMISSION: Donations accepted

MADISON

9167
American Institute of the History of Pharmacy
425 N Charter St, 53706; (p) (608) 262-5378; aihp@macc.wisc.edu; (c) Dane

Private non-profit/ 1941/ staff: 1(f); 2(p)/ members: 1000/publication: *Pharmacy in History*

PROFESSIONAL ORGANIZATION

PROGRAMS: Annual Meeting; Publication

9168
Wisconsin State Historical Society
816 State St, 53706-1482; (p) (608) 264-6400; (f) (608) 264-6542; info@mail.shsw.wisc.edu; www.shsw.wisc.edu/; (c) Dane

State/ 1846/ Board of Curators/ staff: 174(f)/ members: 9000/publication: *Wisconsin Magazine of History*

HISTORIC PRESERVATION AGENCY; HISTORIC SITE; HISTORICAL SOCIETY; HISTORY MUSEUM; HOUSE MUSEUM; LIVING HISTORY/OUTDOOR MUSEUM; RESEARCH CENTER: Maintains archives and library dedicated to North American history; owns and operates history museum and 8 historic sites, administers state historic preservation programs, and maintains film archives in conjunction with the Univ of WI.

PROGRAMS: Annual Meeting; Community Outreach; Exhibits; Facility Rental; Family Programs; Guided Tours; Interpretation; Lectures;

Living History; Publication; Reenactments; Research Library/Archives; School-Based Curriculum

COLLECTIONS: [19th-20th c] Material culture and settlement artifacts.

HOURS: Headquarters: Yr M-Th 8-9, F-Sa 8-5; Museum: T-Sa 10-5, Su 12-5; Historic Sites: May-Oct Daily 10-4

ADMISSION: Varies

9169
Wisconsin Veterans Museum
30 W Mifflin St, 53703; (p) (608) 267-1799; (f) (608) 264-7615; badger.state.wi.us/agencies/dva/museum/wvmmain.html; (c) Dane

State/ 1901/ Dept of Veterans Affairs/ staff: 7(f); 15(p); 64(v)

HISTORY MUSEUM; RESEARCH CENTER: Collects, develops displays of artifacts and presents educational programs related to Civil War and WI.

PROGRAMS: Community Outreach; Exhibits; Guided Tours; Interpretation; Lectures; Reenactments; Research Library/Archives; School-Based Curriculum

COLLECTIONS: [Mid 19th c-present] Artifacts, photos, portraits, paintings, library, manuscripts and maps.

HOURS: Yr M-Sa 9-4:30, Apr-Sept Su 12-4

MANITOWOC

9170
Manitowoc County Historical Society
1701 Michigan Ave, 54221 [PO Box 574, 54221-0574]; (p) (920) 684-4445; (f) (920) 684-0573; (c) Manitowoc

Private non-profit/ 1906/ staff: 2(f); 3(p); 265(v)/ members: 1681

HISTORICAL SOCIETY; HISTORY MUSEUM; LIVING HISTORY/OUTDOOR MUSEUM; RESEARCH CENTER: Collects, interprets, preserves, and promotes county history and heritage.

PROGRAMS: Annual Meeting; Community Outreach; Concerts; Exhibits; Facility Rental; Family Programs; Festivals; Guided Tours; Interpretation; Research Library/Archives; School-Based Curriculum

COLLECTIONS: [1850-present] Archaeological artifacts, decorative arts, furniture, books, maps, business records, photographs, postcards, farm, school records and books, and agricultural implements.

HOURS: Heritage Center: M-F 9-4; Historical Village May 1-mid Oct Daily

9171
Natural Ovens Bakery of Manitowoc Wisconsin, Inc.
4300 Hwy CR, 54221 [PO Box 730, 54221-0730]; (p) (920) 758-2500, (800) 558-3535; (f) (920) 758-2594; www.naturalovens.com; (c) Manitowoc

Private for-profit/ 1976/ staff: 200(f); 20(p)

GARDEN; HISTORIC SITE; LIVING HISTORY/OUTDOOR MUSEUM

PROGRAMS: Garden Tours; Guided Tours; Lectures

COLLECTIONS: [Prehistory-20th c] Log house, barns, blacksmith shop and granary; 2-cylinder John Deere tractors, combines; grain harvesting and planting equipment;

HOURS: (Farm and Food Museum) May-Oct M-F 9-3; (Bakery Tours) Yr M, W-F 9-11

ADMISSION: Donations

9172
Rahr-West Art Museum
610 N 8th St, 54220; (p) (920) 683-4501; (f) (920) 683-5047; (c) Manitowoc

City/ 1941/ staff: 4(f); 4(p)/ members: 500

ART MUSEUM; HOUSE MUSEUM

PROGRAMS: Exhibits; Facility Rental; Guided Tours

COLLECTIONS: [20th c] Site: 1890s Victorian house, contemporary artwork.

HOURS: Yr M-F 10-4, W 10-8, Sa-Su 11-4

ADMISSION: No charge

9173
Wisconsin Maritime Museum
75 Maritime Dr, 54220; (p) (920) 684-0218; (f) (920) 684-0219; (c) Manitowoc

Private non-profit/ 1968/ staff: 8(f); 21(p); 100(v)/ members: 2000/publication: *Anchor News*

HISTORY MUSEUM

PROGRAMS: Annual Meeting; Community Outreach; Concerts; Elder's Programs; Exhibits; Facility Rental; Family Programs; Festivals; Guided Tours; Interpretation; Lectures; Publication; Research Library/Archives; School-Based Curriculum

COLLECTIONS: [1679-present]

HOURS: Yr Daily 9-5

ADMISSION: $5.95

MARINETTE

9174
Marinette County Historical Society
1 Stephenson Island, Hwy 41, 54143 [PO Box 262, 54143]; (p) (715) 732-0831, (715) 735-5922; (c) Marinette

Private non-profit/ 1932/ staff: 1(f); 1(p); 20(v)/ members: 500/publication: *The Historian*

HISTORY MUSEUM: Presents exhibits of an early trading post, Native American artifacts, logging camp equipment, miniature model logging camp, household displays.

PROGRAMS: Annual Meeting; Exhibits; Guided Tours; Publication

COLLECTIONS: [1820-present] Trading post, Native American artifacts, logging camp, farm supplies, antique furniture and a Civil War exhibit.

HOURS: May-Sept Daily 10-4:30

ADMISSION: $1.50, Children $0.50

MARION

9175
Marion Area Historical Society
Marion Park, 54950 [PO Box 321, 54950]; (p) (715) 754-2098; (c) Waupaca

Private non-profit/ 1988/ staff: 12(v)/ members: 118

HISTORICAL SOCIETY; HISTORY MUSEUM: Preserves log cabin and railroad depot.

PROGRAMS: Annual Meeting; Guided Tours; Lectures

COLLECTIONS: [Early-mid 20th c] Log cabin furnishings, town memorabilia, hand tools.

HOURS: June-Sept 4th Su of month

MARKESAN

9176
Markesan Historical Society, Inc./Grand River Valley Museum
214 E John St, 53946; (p) (920) 398-3554; (f) (920) 398-8189; krwesse@fdldotnet.com; www.markesan.com; (c) Green Lake

Private non-profit/ 1981/ Board of Directors/ staff: 105(v)/ members: 105

HISTORICAL SOCIETY; HISTORY MUSEUM: Collects the remnants of the Heritage of South Central WI.

PROGRAMS: Annual Meeting; Community Outreach; Elder's Programs; Festivals; Guided Tours; Theatre

COLLECTIONS: [1848-1948] 2 restored and furnished depots, six residential rooms, photos, items related to theater, churches, schools, agriculture, military, industry and transportation.

HOURS: Yr by appt; May-Sept Sa-Su 1-4

ADMISSION: Donations accepted

MARSHFIELD

9177
Upham Mansion
212 W 3rd St, 54449 [PO Box 142, 54449]; (p) (715) 387-3322; (c) Wood

Private non-profit/ 1952/ North Wood County Historical Society/ staff: 1(p); 80(v)/ members: 181/publication: *Mansion News*

GARDEN; HISTORIC SITE; HISTORICAL SOCIETY; HISTORY MUSEUM; HOUSE MUSEUM

PROGRAMS: Annual Meeting; Exhibits; Facility Rental; Festivals; Garden Tours; Guided Tours; Publication; Research Library/Archives

COLLECTIONS: [1880s-present] Pioneer artifacts and furnishings, clothing, household goods, utensils, toys, dolls, books, photos, Victorian furniture, cabinet, horse-drawn firehose cart, iron lung, scrapbooks.

HOURS: Yr W, Su 1:30-4 and by appt

ADMISSION: Donations accepted

MAUSTON

9178
Juneau County Historical Society
211 N Union St, 53948 [PO Box 321, 53948]; (p) (608) 462-5931; (c) Juneau

Private non-profit/ 1963/ staff: 1(f); 1(p); 70(v)/ members: 301

HISTORICAL SOCIETY; HOUSE MUSEUM

PROGRAMS: Annual Meeting; Guided Tours; Research Library/Archives

COLLECTIONS: [19th-20th c] Artifacts of Midwest rural life.

HOURS: June-Sept Sa-Su 1-4

ADMISSION: Donations accepted

MAYVILLE

9179
Mayville Historical Society, Inc.
Bridge & N German St, 53050 [PO Box 82, 53050-0082]; (p) (920) 387-5233; (f) (920) 387-5944; (c) Dodge

Private non-profit/ 1968/ Board of Directors/ staff: 50(v)/ members: 192/publication: *Wagon Wheels*

HISTORICAL SOCIETY; HOUSE MUSEUM: Collects and preserves the history of Mayville and surrounding areas.

PROGRAMS: Annual Meeting; Exhibits; Guided Tours; Publication

COLLECTIONS: [1885-present] 5 room house with period furniture, Wagon Shop museum, Brunke Cigar Factory with tools, furnished barber shop, radio-TV repair and sales room, farm equipment, and tools.

HOURS: May-Oct 2nd and 4th Su of month 1:30-4:30

ADMISSION: Donations accepted

MAZOMANIE

9180
Cross Plains-Berry Historical Society
2204 Brewery Rd, 53560 [9260 Far View Rd, 53560]; (p) (608) 798-2760; (c) Dane

Private non-profit/ 1970/ Board of Directors/ staff: 10(v)/ members: 26

HISTORICAL SOCIETY; HISTORY MUSEUM; RESEARCH CENTER: Collects and preserves documents and objects of historical interest to the townships of Berry and Cross Plains and the communities of Marxville and Pine Bluff.

PROGRAMS: Annual Meeting; Exhibits; Research Library/Archives

COLLECTIONS: [18th c-present] Blacksmith items, family histories, photos, school and business records.

HOURS: Mem Day-Sept Su 1-4:30

ADMISSION: No charge

9181
Mazomanie Historical Society
118 Brodhead, 53560 [PO Box 248, 53560-0248]; (p) (608) 795-4576; (f) (608) 795-4576; fewolf@blkearth.tds.net; www.mazoarea.com/ypahist.htm; (c) Dane

Private non-profit/ 1965/ Board of Directors/ staff: 1(p); 65(v)/ members: 110/publication: *Local Sheaves*

HISTORICAL SOCIETY; HISTORY MUSEUM: Operates museum, performs research, and publishes material to educate about local heritage.

PROGRAMS: Annual Meeting; Exhibits; Festivals; Guided Tours; Interpretation; Lectures; Publication; Research Library/Archives

COLLECTIONS: [1840-present] Textiles, tools, newspapers, photos, and genealogical records.

HOURS: May-Sept T-W, F-Sa 10-4, Su 1-5

ADMISSION: Donations accepted

MEDFORD

9182
Taylor County Historical Society
Hwys 13 & 64, 54451 [845 A E Broadway, 54451]; (p) (715) 748-3808; (c) Taylor

Joint/ 1966/ Private non-profit;Taylor County Board/ staff: 3(p); 60(v)/ members: 114/publication: *Log Cabin News*

HISTORICAL SOCIETY: Collects and preserves information and items related to county history.

PROGRAMS: Annual Meeting; Community Outreach; Exhibits; Festivals; Guided Tours; Living History; Publication; Reenactments; Research Library/Archives

COLLECTIONS: [Late 19th-early 20th c] Wildlife exhibits, logging, industrial, railroad, farming, military, musical and Victorian artifacts. County Schoolhouse, Log cabin.

HOURS: Yr Th-F 9-4 and by appt

ADMISSION: No charge

MENASHA

9183
Menasha Historical Society
650 Keyes St, 54952 [233 Sunset Dr, 54952]; (p) (920) 722-8969; (c) Winnebago

Private non-profit/ 1956/ staff: 1(v)/ members: 70

HISTORICAL SOCIETY; RESEARCH CENTER

PROGRAMS: Annual Meeting; Guided Tours; Research Library/Archives

COLLECTIONS: [19th-20th c] Books, pictures, newspaper clippings and local artifacts.

HOURS: Yr M 1:30-3:30

ADMISSION: No charge

MENOMINEE FALLS

9184
Menominee Falls Historical Society/Old Falls Village Museum
N96, W15791 County Line, 53051 [PO Box 91, 53051]; (p) (414) 250-5096; (f) (414) 250-5097; (c) Waukesha

Joint/ 1966/ Village of Menomonee Falls/Historical Society/ staff: 1(f); 20(v)/ members: 150

HISTORIC SITE; HISTORICAL SOCIETY; LIVING HISTORY/OUTDOOR MUSEUM: Gathers, preserves, educates, and exhibits artifacts and information about the origins and development of Menomonee Falls.

PROGRAMS: Annual Meeting; Exhibits; Facility Rental; Family Programs; Festivals; Guided Tours; Living History; Reenactments; Research Library/Archives

COLLECTIONS: [1830-1920] Local history objects, decorative arts, furniture, and farm/industrial implements.

HOURS: May-Sept Su 1-4

ADMISSION: $3

MENOMONIE

9185
Wilson Place Mansion, Ltd.
101 Wilson Circle, 54751; (p) (715) 235-2283; (f) (715) 235-8668; (c) Dunn

Private non-profit/ 1976/ staff: 8(p)

HISTORIC SITE; HOUSE MUSEUM: Educates the community and visitors about area and Wilson family history.

PROGRAMS: Exhibits; Festivals; Guided Tours

COLLECTIONS: [1846-1974] China, silver, furniture, fabrics, art pieces, regional clothing and bridal gowns. Family documents, Bibles, letters, deeds, Civil War records and photos.

HOURS: Spring-Fall Sa-Su 1-5; Mem Day-Labor Day Daily 1-5; Mid Nov-early Jan Daily 1-7

ADMISSION: $4.50, Student $3.50, Children $2, Seniors $4

MEQUON

9186
Crafts Museum
11458 N Laguna Dr, 53092-3118; (p) (262) 242-1571; (c) Ozaukee

Private for-profit/ 1969/ staff: 1(f); 1(v)/publication: *Ice Harvesting; Wooden Shoes Worldwide*

CULTURAL CENTER: Provides travelling programs on hand carving wooden shoes, ice harvesting story and vintage piano sheet music.

PROGRAMS: Community Outreach; Elder's Programs; Exhibits; Family Programs; Festivals; Film/Video; Lectures; Living History; Publication; Research Library/Archives

COLLECTIONS: [1500-1950] Tools, images, references and memorabilia regarding wooden shoe carving, ice harvesting and piano sheet music.

HOURS: Yr M-Sa

9187
Mequon Historical Society, Inc.
6100 W Mequon Rd, 53092-1951; (p) (414) 242-3290; dondorf@execpc.com; (c) Ozaukee

Private non-profit/ 1987/ Board of Directors/ staff: 5(v)/ members: 110

HISTORICAL SOCIETY: Preserves historic documents and research materials.

PROGRAMS: Annual Meeting; Community Outreach; Exhibits; Family Programs; Guided Tours; Interpretation; Research Library/Archives

COLLECTIONS: [1835-present] Census, school, obituary and cemetery records, local church histories, property assessments, family scrap books, genealogies, photos and plat maps.

HOURS: Yr Th

MERRILL

9188
Merrill Historical Society, Inc./Brickyard School Museum
804 E Third St, 54452; (p) (715) 536-5652; (c) Lincoln

Private non-profit/ 1978/ Board of Directors/ staff: 3(p); 7(v)/ members: 510/publication: *Jenny: 1847-1881; Northwoods Historian*

ART MUSEUM; HISTORICAL SOCIETY; HISTORY MUSEUM; HOUSE MUSEUM; RESEARCH CENTER: Collects, preserves, and interprets local history.

PROGRAMS: Annual Meeting; Community Outreach; Concerts; Elder's Programs; Exhibits; Family Programs; Festivals; Film/Video; Guided Tours; Interpretation; Lectures; Living History; Publication; Research Library/ Archives; School-Based Curriculum

COLLECTIONS: [1850-present] Logging artifacts, documents, maps, photographs, local newspapers, portraits, sculptures, and paintings.

HOURS: Merrill Historical Museum: Yr Daily 1-4; Brickyard School Museum: Yr by appt

ADMISSION: No charge

MIDDLETON

9189
Middleton Area Historical Society
7410 Hubbard Ave, 53562; (p) (608) 836-7614; (c) Dane

Private non-profit/ 1972/ staff: 10(v)/ members: 180

HISTORICAL SOCIETY; HOUSE MUSEUM: Operates museum located in a 1868 doctor's residence.

PROGRAMS: Guided Tours; Interpretation; Lectures

COLLECTIONS: [Mid 19th c-present] Local artifacts such as furniture, tools, photographs, depression glass patterns, egg cups and kitchenware.

HOURS: Mid Apr-mid Oct T-Sa 1-4 and by appt

ADMISSION: No charge

MILTON

9190
Milton Historical Society
18 S Janesville; 742 E Madison, 53563 [PO Box 245, 53563]; (p) (608) 868-7772; miltonhouse@ miltonhouse.org; www.miltonhouse.org; (c) Rock

Private non-profit/ 1948/ staff: 2(p); 106(v)/ members: 300

HISTORIC SITE; HISTORICAL SOCIETY; HISTORY MUSEUM: Preserves 1844 Stagecoach Inn and artifacts related to the Underground Railroad, founding of Milton, local pioneers and the first poured concrete building in the US.

PROGRAMS: Annual Meeting; Community Outreach; Elder's Programs; Exhibits; Facility Rental; Festivals; Guided Tours; Interpretation; Lectures; Research Library/Archives; School-Based Curriculum

COLLECTIONS: [1839-1860] Local history archives, newspapers on microfilm, photographs, diaries, obituaries, plat maps, library, school and cemetery records.

HOURS: Mem Day-Labor Day Daily 10-5

ADMISSION: $5

MILWAUKEE

9191
Captain Frederick Pabst Mansion, Inc.
2000 W Wisconsin, 53233; (p) (414) 931-0808; (f) (414) 931-1005; pabstman@execpc.com; www.pabstmansion.com; (c) Milwaukee

Private non-profit/ 1975/ staff: 4(f); 6(p); 150(v)/ members: 233

HISTORIC PRESERVATION AGENCY; HISTORIC SITE; HISTORY MUSEUM; HOUSE MUSEUM: Operates the Captain Frederick Pabst Mansion as a house museum.

PROGRAMS: Exhibits; Facility Rental; Guided Tours; Interpretation; Lectures

COLLECTIONS: [Late 19th c]

HOURS: Yr T-Sa 10-3:30, Su 12-3:30

ADMISSION: $7, Student $6, Children $3, Seniors $6

9192
Harley-Davidson Motor Company Archives
3700 W Juneau Ave, 53201; (p) (414) 343-4680, (414) 343-8973; (f) (414) 343-8786; bill_jackson@harley_davidson.com; www.harley-davidson.com; (c) Milwaukee

Private for-profit/ 1993/ staff: 5(f); 1(p)

CORPORATE ARCHIVES/MUSEUM: Preserves, protects, and perpetuates history of the Harley-Davidson Motor Company.

COLLECTIONS: [1903-present] Images, artifacts, vehicles, marketing pieces, videos, films, administrative and textual records.

9193
Historic Indian Agency House
Agency House Rd, 53211 [3110 East Hampshire St, 53211-3116]; (p) (414) 964-4313, (608) 742-6362; (c) Milwaukee/Columbia

Private non-profit/ 1932/ National Society of the Colonial Dames of America in the State of Wisconsin/ staff: 6(p); 12(v)/ members: 128/publication: *Wau-Ban, the Early Day in the Northwest*

HISTORIC SITE; HOUSE MUSEUM

PROGRAMS: Publication

COLLECTIONS: [1700s-1833] American furniture, stoneware, glass, English ceramics, archaeological artifacts, prehistoric lithics, Native American bead work and Civil War material.

HOURS: Mid May-mid Oct M-Sa 10-4, Su 11-4

ADMISSION: $3.50

9194
Milwaukee County Historical Society
910 N Old World Third St, 53203; (p) (414) 273-8288; (f) (414) 273-3268; www.milwaukee countyhistsoc.org; (c) Milwaukee

Private non-profit/ 1935/ Board of Directors/ staff: 9(f); 1(p); 35(v)/ members: 1000/publication: *Milwaukee History*

HISTORICAL SOCIETY; HISTORY MUSEUM; HOUSE MUSEUM: Collects, preserves, and disseminates materials pertaining to the history of the city and county of Milwaukee.

PROGRAMS: Annual Meeting; Community Outreach; Exhibits; Facility Rental; Family Programs; Guided Tours; Interpretation; Lectures; Publication; Reenactments; Research Library/Archives; School-Based Curriculum

COLLECTIONS: [1783-present] Manuscripts, photographs, maps, newspapers, periodicals, and artifacts.

9195
Milwaukee Public Museum, Inc.
800 W Wells St, 53233; (p) (414) 278-2700; (f) (414) 278-6100; smedley@mpm.edu; www.mpm.edu; (c) Milwaukee

Private non-profit/ 1882/ staff: 160(f); 70(p); 750(v)/ members: 12200/publication: *Lore; Wings*

HISTORY MUSEUM; NATURAL HISTORY MUSEUM: Teaches human and natural history.

PROGRAMS: Annual Meeting; Community Outreach; Exhibits; Facility Rental; Family Programs; Festivals; Film/Video; Guided Tours; Interpretation; Lectures; Living History; Publication; Research Library/Archives; School-Based Curriculum

COLLECTIONS: [Prehistory-present] Natural and human history objects and specimens.

HOURS: Yr Daily 9-5

ADMISSION: $5.50, Student $3.50, Seniors $4.50

9196
Mitchell Gallery of Flight, Milwaukee County Airport Division
5300 S Howell Ave, 53207-6189; (p) (414) 747-4503; (f) (414) 747-4525; info@mitchellgallery. org; www.mitchellgallery.org; (c) Milwaukee

Private non-profit/ 1985/ staff: 1(p); 10(v)/ members: 500/publication: *Milwaukee County's General Mitchell International Airport*

HISTORY MUSEUM: Locates, acquires, preserves, and displays artifacts, memorabilia, photographs, and artwork representing the contributions of aviation pioneers from Milwaukee County and WI.

PROGRAMS: Annual Meeting; Exhibits; Publication

COLLECTIONS: [1900-present] Aviation memorabilia, photographs, paintings, books, medals, educational exhibits, and scale models of aircraft.

HOURS: Yr Daily

9197
Villa Terrace Decorative Arts Museum
2220 N Terrace Ave, 53202; (p) (414) 271-3656; (f) (414) 271-3986

1923/ staff: 1(f); 4(p)

COLLECTIONS: [16th to 20th c] Wrought iron.

HOURS: W-Su 12-5

MINERAL POINT

9198
Pendarvis State Historic Site
114 Shake Rag St, 53565; (p) (608) 987-2122; (f) (608) 987-3738; shakeragf@mhtc.net; www.shsw.edu/; (c) Iowa

State/ 1971/ State Historical Society of WI/ staff: 3(f); 20(p); 10(v)/publication: *On the Shake Rag*

GARDEN; HISTORIC SITE; HOUSE MUSEUM; LIVING HISTORY/OUTDOOR MUSEUM: Restored early 1840s Cornish miners' colony of stone and log houses.

PROGRAMS: Exhibits; Facility Rental; Family Programs; Festivals; Garden Tours; Guided Tours; Interpretation; Living History; Publication

COLLECTIONS: [1830s-1950s] Household furnishings, exhibits on early coal and zinc mining.

MONROE

9199
Wisconsin State Genealogical Society, Inc.
2109 Twentieth Ave, 53566-3426; (p) (608) 325-2609; md2609@tds.net; www.rootsweb.com/~wsgs; (c) Green

Private non-profit/ 1939/ staff: 12(v)/ members: 1729

GENEALOGICAL SOCIETY: Encourages, facilitates, and improves the quality of genealogical study in WI and about WI families.

PROGRAMS: Annual Meeting

COLLECTIONS: [19th-20th c] Materials located in the library of the WI State Historical Society or the Milwaukee Public Library.

MOUNT HOREB

9200
Mount Horeb Area Historical Society
100 S Second St, 53572 [138 E Main St, 53572-2138]; (p) (608) 437-6486; mha_history@xoommail.com; www.mounthoreb.org; (c) Dane

Private non-profit/ 1975/ staff: 50(v)/ members: 200/publication: Mount Horeb Area Past Times

ART MUSEUM; HISTORICAL SOCIETY; HISTORY MUSEUM; RESEARCH CENTER: Gathers, preserves, and disseminates knowledge of Southwestern Dane County history, maintains archives, presents educational programs, and operates a museum with both permanent and rotating exhibits.

PROGRAMS: Annual Meeting; Community Outreach; Concerts; Elder's Programs; Exhibits; Family Programs; Guided Tours; Lectures; Publication; Research Library/Archives; School-Based Curriculum

COLLECTIONS: Local artifacts, school, church, and government records, photographs, plat maps, diaries, books, ephemera, textiles, and Montrose General Store.

HOURS: Yr F-Su 12-5

ADMISSION: Donations accepted

MUSKEGO

9201
Muskego Historical Society
W180, S7732, 53150 [PO Box 137, 53150]; (p) (414) 422-0564; (c) Waukesha

Private non-profit/ 1973/ staff: 32(v)/ members: 85

HISTORIC SITE; HISTORICAL SOCIETY: Promotes history, provides tours, and monthly gatherings. Strong focus on the Civil War.

PROGRAMS: Exhibits; Guided Tours; Living History; Reenactments

COLLECTIONS: [19th-20th c] 9 buildings, including a barn and one-room schoolhouse, with authentic furniture, machinery, and old farm implements.

HOURS: 3rd Su of Month May-Oct Su 2-3:30

NEENAH

9202
Doty Cabin
700 Lincoln St, 54957-0426 [PO Box 426, 54957-0426]; (p) (920) 751-4614

9203
Military Veterans Museum, Inc.
Park Plaza, S Main St, 54956 [PO Box 511, 54956]; (p) (920) 426-8615; (c) Winnebago

Private non-profit/ 1991/ Board of Directors/ staff: 40(v)/ members: 231

HISTORY MUSEUM: Educates youth and adults concerning the role of the citizen soldier in US wars. Promotes national pride, patriotism, and peace.

PROGRAMS: Annual Meeting; Exhibits; Guided Tours; Reenactments; Research Library/Archives; School-Based Curriculum

COLLECTIONS: [Civil War-present] Artifacts and memorabilia representing all periods of US military history.

HOURS: Yr Daily 12-5; Groups tours by appt

ADMISSION: Donations accepted

9204
Neenah Historical Society
336 Main St, 54957 [PO Box 343, 54957-0343]; (p) (920) 729-0244; neenahhistoricalsociety@powernetonline.com; (c) Winnebago

Private non-profit/ 1948/ staff: 1(f); 10(v)/ members: 350/publication: The Society Times

HISTORICAL SOCIETY; HOUSE MUSEUM: Collects and preserves local history materials, provides educational programs and a research library and operates the Hiram Smith Octagon House as a historic house museum.

PROGRAMS: Annual Meeting; Community Outreach; Exhibits; Guided Tours; Interpretation; Lectures; Publication; Research Library/Archives; School-Based Curriculum

COLLECTIONS: [1860-present] Local newspapers, photographs, archival materials, period clothing, furnishings, and collectibles.

HOURS: Yr T, Th-F 9-12/1-4, Su 1-4; Jan-Mar closed Su

ADMISSION: No charge

NEOSHO

9205
Neosho Historical Society
115 S Schuyler St, 53059 [PO Box 105, 53059-0105]; (p) (920) 625-3067, (920) 625-3189; (c) Dodge

Private non-profit/ 1975/ staff: 10(v)/ members: 24/publication: The Researcher

HISTORICAL SOCIETY; HISTORY MUSEUM: Promotes and preserves local history in southeastern Dodge County. Maintains the Old Village Hall Museum and Research Library.

PROGRAMS: Annual Meeting; Community Outreach; Exhibits; Interpretation; Living History; Publication; Research Library/Archives

COLLECTIONS: [1845-1950s] Local history displays on agriculture, mining, baking, war years, fire fighting, milling, drama, general store, brewery, smithing, and genealogical research.

HOURS: May-Oct 2nd and 4th Su 1-4; Nov-Apr 2nd Su 1-4

NEW BERLIN

9206
New Berlin Historical Society
19765 W National Ave, 53146 [5575 S Maberry Ln, 53146]; (p) (262) 679-1783; dcherman@.com; (c) Waukesha

Private non-profit/ 1964/ Board of Directors/ staff: 30(v)/ members: 70/publication: New Berlin Almanac

HISTORICAL SOCIETY: Records, restores, and recreates town history.

PROGRAMS: Annual Meeting; Festivals; Publication

COLLECTIONS: [19th-20th c] Restored farmhouse, log cabin, country store, and schoolhouse with artifacts.

HOURS: Yr by appt

ADMISSION: Donations accepted

NEW GLARUS

9207
Chalet of the Golden Fleece
618 2nd St, 53574 [PO Box 548, 53574]; (p) (608) 527-2614; (c) Green

1940/ Village of New Glarus/ staff: 2(f); 3(p)

HISTORY MUSEUM: Maintains museum.

PROGRAMS: Guided Tours

COLLECTIONS: [15th-20th c] Jewelry, sheet music, coins, stamps, woodcarvings, furniture, silver, paintings, prints, textiles, china, dolls.

HOURS: May-Oct Daily 10-4:30

ADMISSION: $3, Children $1

9208
Swiss Historical Village
612 7th Ave, 53574 [PO Box 745, 53574]; (p) (608) 527-2317; (f) (608) 527-2302; (c) Green

Private non-profit/ 1938/ New Glarus Historical Society/ staff: 25(v)/ members: 50

GENEALOGICAL SOCIETY; LIVING HISTORY/OUTDOOR MUSEUM

PROGRAMS: Annual Meeting; Festivals; Guided Tours; Reenactments

COLLECTIONS: [1845-present] Items documenting the Swiss settlement of New Glarus and the immigration of Swiss people to the United States.

HOURS: May, Sept, Oct Daily 10-4; June-Aug 9-4:30

ADMISSION: $6

NEW HOLSTEIN

9209
Timm House
1600 Wisconsin Ave, 53061 [New Holstein Historical Society, 2025 Randolph, 53061]; (p) (920) 898-4265

NEW RICHMOND

9210
New Richmond Preservation Society
1100 Heritage Dr, 54017; (p) (715) 246-3276, (888) 320-3276; (f) (715) 246-7215; nrpsinc@pressenter.com; www.pressenter.com/~nrpsinc/; (c) Saint Croix

Private non-profit/ 1982/ staff: 1(f); 2(p); 30(v)/ members: 326/publication: *Heritage Center-pieces*

HISTORIC SITE; HISTORICAL SOCIETY; HOUSE MUSEUM; LIVING HISTORY/OUTDOOR MUSEUM: Preserves the history of New Richmond and surrounding area; owns and operates the Heritage Center.

PROGRAMS: Annual Meeting; Community Outreach; Exhibits; Facility Rental; Family Programs; Festivals; Guided Tours; Interpretation; Lectures; Living History; Publication; Reenactments; School-Based Curriculum; Theatre

COLLECTIONS: [1850-present] Documents, photographs, furnishings, tools, and buildings.

HOURS: Yr M-F 10-4; May-Sept Sa-Su 11-4

ADMISSION: $4, Children $1; Under 5 free

OCONTO

9211
Oconto County Historical Society
917 Park Ave, 54153; (p) (920) 834-6206; (c) Oconto

State/ 1941/ State Historical Society of WI/ staff: 5(p); 20(v)/ members: 175/publication: *John and Almira Volk*

HISTORIC SITE; HISTORICAL SOCIETY; HISTORY MUSEUM: Preserves county history and provides education for the public about local history.

PROGRAMS: Annual Meeting; Community Outreach; Exhibits; Facility Rental; Guided Tours; Lectures; Publication

COLLECTIONS: [1850-1930] Fully furnished house, Oconto's main street, horse carriages, electric cars, pioneer and logging artifacts.

HOURS: June-Labor Day M-Sa 10-4, Su 12-4

OMRO

9212
Omro Area Historical Society
144 E Main, 54963 [PO Box 133, 54963]; (p) (920) 685-6123; (c) Winnebago

Private non-profit/ 1978/ City of Omro/ staff: 2(p); 4(v)/ members: 44

HISTORICAL SOCIETY; HISTORY MUSEUM: Preserves and presents local artifacts and histories.

PROGRAMS: Annual Meeting; Exhibits; Festivals; Film/Video; Guided Tours; Lectures; Living History

COLLECTIONS: [19th-early 20th c] Artifacts related to steamboating on the Fox River, W W I and WW II, Civil War, Spanish American War, the Korean and Vietnam Wars.

HOURS: May-Sept Sa 10-3 and by appt

ADMISSION: Donations accepted

ONALASKA

9213
Onalaska Area Historical Society
741 Oak Ave, 54650; (p) (608) 781-9568; (c) La Crosse

Private non-profit/ 1985/ Board of Directors/ staff: 30(v)/ members: 311

HISTORIC PRESERVATION AGENCY; HISTORICAL SOCIETY; HISTORY MUSEUM: Collects and preserves local historical items. Creates awareness of local heritage for education, enjoyment, and appreciation by present and future generations.

PROGRAMS: Annual Meeting; Exhibits; Guided Tours

COLLECTIONS: [Mid 19th-early 20th c] Documents, books, photographs, and portraits.

HOURS: Yr W-F 1-3

ADMISSION: No charge

ONEIDA

9214
Oneida Nation Museum
W892 County Trunk EE, 54155 [PO Box 365, 54155]; (p) (920) 869-2768; (f) (920) 869-2959; www.oneidanation.org; (c) Outagamie

Tribal/ 1979/ Oneida Tribe of Indians of WI/ staff: 8(f)

LIVING HISTORY/OUTDOOR MUSEUM; TRIBAL MUSEUM: Collects, preserves, and interprets Oneida and Iroquois history, culture, and art for the education and enjoyment of present and future generations.

PROGRAMS: Community Outreach; Exhibits; Festivals; Guided Tours; Interpretation; Lectures

COLLECTIONS: [19th-20th c] Photographs, contemporary art, ethnographic, and archaeological artifacts.

HOURS: Yr T-F 9-5; Spring-Summer Sa 10-5

OSCEOLA

9215
Osceola and St. Croix Valley Railway
Depot St, 54020 [PO Box 176, 54020]; (p) (651) 228-0263, (715) 755-3570; www.mtmuseum.org

1992/ Minnesota Transportation Museum/ staff: 1(p)

RAILROAD MUSEUM

PROGRAMS: Exhibits

COLLECTIONS: Numerous rail vehicles, including locomotives, passenger cars, freight cars, maintenance equipment, and cabooses.

HOURS: May-Oct Sa-Su

9216
Osceola Historical Society
408 Rider St & 114 Depot Rd, 54020 [PO Box 342, 54020]; (p) (715) 294-2480; (f) (215) 294-2480; lgordon@marcus-online.net; (c) Polk

Private non-profit/ 1990/ Board of Directors/ staff: 4(v)/ members: 30/publication: *Osceola: A Village Chronicle*

HISTORICAL SOCIETY: Preserves and shares the history of the Village of Osceola through programs, museum, and the Osceola Depot. Assists with historical research and inquiries.

PROGRAMS: Annual Meeting; Exhibits; Family Programs; Lectures; Publication; Research Library/Archives

COLLECTIONS: [1880s-present] Newspaper articles, obituaries, photographs, and three fully-restored period rooms.

ADMISSION: No charge

OSHKOSH

9217
Oshkosh Public Library
106 Washington Ave, 54901; (p) (920) 236-5205; www.oshkoshpubliclibrary.org; (c) Winnebago

1895/ City of Oshkosh

COLLECTIONS: [19th-20th c] Emphasis on city and county history. Cemetery transcriptions, vital statistics, newspapers, censuses, maps, city/county directories, monographs, and clipping files.

HOURS: Spring, Fall-Winter M-F 9-8:45, Sa 9-4:45, Su 1-5; Summer M-F 9-8:45, Sa 9-1

9218
Oshkosh Public Museum
1331 Algoma Blvd, 54901; (p) (920) 424-4731; (f) (920) 424-4738; info@publicmuseum.oshkosh.net; www.publicmuseum.oshkosh.net; (c) Winnebago

1924/ City of Oshkosh/ staff: 11(f); 5(p); 60(v)/ members: 400/publication: *MuseuMemo*

HISTORY MUSEUM: Preserves and interprets the history of the Lake Winnebago region of East-Central Oshkosh. Housed in the 1908 Edgar Sawyer home, listed on the National Register.

PROGRAMS: Community Outreach; Exhibits; Facility Rental; Family Programs; Lectures; Publication; Research Library/Archives; School-Based Curriculum

COLLECTIONS: [1840-1940] Reflects the history of the Lake Winnebago Region.

HOURS: Yr T-Sa 9-5, Su 1-5

ADMISSION: No charge

9219
Winnebago County Historical and Archaeological Society
234 Church Ave, 54901; (p) (920) 232-0260; (c) Winnebago

Private non-profit/ 1919/ Board of Directors/ staff: 40(v)/ members: 120

HISTORIC SITE; HISTORICAL SOCIETY; HOUSE MUSEUM: Represents, assists, and involves the community in preserving local history.

PROGRAMS: Annual Meeting; Exhibits; Facility Rental; Guided Tours; Lectures

COLLECTIONS: [1880-1910] Lumber mill memorabilia, state and local history books, manuscripts, Victoriana, and period furniture.

HOURS: June-Sept Su 2-4

ADMISSION: $1

9220
Winnebago Genealogical Society
Oshkosh Public Library, 106 Washington Ave, 54901; (c) Winnebago

Private non-profit/ 1994/ members: 106

GENEALOGICAL SOCIETY; RESEARCH CENTER: Members produce cemetery transcriptions, publish indexes, and research guides, and serve as volunteers for a variety of projects for the Oshkosh Public Library.

PALMYRA

9221
Palmyra Historical Society
W Main & Third St, 53156 [Box 265, 112 N Third St, 53156]; (p) (262) 495-2412; (c) Jefferson

Private non-profit/ 1976/ Board of Trustees/ staff: 10(v)/ members: 300

HISTORY MUSEUM; HOUSE MUSEUM: Collects, preserves, and displays local artifacts. Maintains the Carlin House and Turner Museum and sponsors Old Settlers' Day. Publishes a biannual newsletter and booklets on local history.

PROGRAMS: Community Outreach; Exhibits; Facility Rental; Film/Video; Guided Tours; Research Library/Archives

COLLECTIONS: [1840-1945] Carlin House furnished in late 19th c style. Turner Museum has changing display of area artifacts.

PARDEEVILLE

9222
Columbia County Lintner Spear Museum
112 N Main St, 53954 [104 S Main St, 53954]; (c) Columbia

County/ 1958/ Columbia County/ staff: 4(v)/ members: 45

HISTORIC SITE; HISTORICAL SOCIETY: Two floors and one room school furnished with one of a kind articles of the past.

PROGRAMS: Annual Meeting; Guided Tours

COLLECTIONS: [1850-1950]

HOURS: June-Sept T-Sa 1-4

ADMISSION: $1, Children $0.50

PEPIN

9223
Pepin Historical Museum
306 3rd St, 54759 [PO Box 269, 54759]; (p) (715) 442-3161; (c) Pepin

Private non-profit/ 1988/ Board of Directors/ staff: 8(p); 6(v)/ members: 557/publication: *Notes from Laura Ingalls Wilder Memorial Society*

HISTORIC SITE; HISTORICAL SOCIETY: Preserves the history of Laura Ingalls Wilder and the town of Pepin.

PROGRAMS: Annual Meeting; Community Outreach; Festivals; Publication

COLLECTIONS: [1860s-1920s] Tools, bedroom, and kitchen items.

HOURS: Mid May-mid Oct Daily

PESHTIGO

9224
Peshtigo Historical Society
400 Oconto Ave, 54157; (p) (715) 582-3244; mkw@cybrzn.com; (c) Marinette

Private non-profit/ 1963/ staff: 9(v)/ members: 40

HISTORIC SITE; HISTORICAL SOCIETY; HISTORY MUSEUM: Commemorates the Oct 1871 Peshtigo Fire, the nation's most devastating forest fire, taking over 1,200 lives and burning more than 1 million acres. Museum illustrates what life was like in an early lumbering community.

PROGRAMS: Community Outreach; Exhibits; Interpretation

COLLECTIONS: [1871-1900] Artifacts from the early lumbering community that survived the fire.

HOURS: May-Oct Daily 8-4:30

ADMISSION: Donations accepted

PEWAUKEE

9225
Pewaukee Area Historical Society
Clark House Museum, 206 E Wisconsin Ave, 53072 [PO Box 105, 53072]; (p) (414) 691-0233; (c) Waukesha

Private non-profit/ 1977/ staff: 300(v)/ members: 7500

HISTORICAL SOCIETY: Collects, preserves, researches, and exhibits objects from area history.

PROGRAMS: Annual Meeting; Community Outreach; Concerts; Exhibits; Family Programs; Garden Tours; Guided Tours; Interpretation; Research Library/Archives; School-Based Curriculum

COLLECTIONS: [1847-present] Arrowheads, furnishings, clothing, toys, photographs, family histories, and farm machinery.

HOURS: Research Yr Sa-Su; Main Exhibits May-Sept Sa-Su

PLATTEVILLE

9226
Mining Museum and Rollo Jamison Museum
405 E Main St, 53818 [PO Box 780, 53818-0780]; (p) (608) 348-3301; (f) (608) 348-6098; (c) Grant

City/ 1964/ City of Platteville/ staff: 3(f); 13(p); 7(v)

HISTORIC SITE; HISTORY MUSEUM: Traces the history of the Upper MS Valley Lead-Zinc District and the history of Grant County. Maintains the 1845 Bevans Lead Mine.

PROGRAMS: Annual Meeting; Exhibits; Guided Tours; Interpretation; School-Based Curriculum

COLLECTIONS: [19th-early 20th c] Artifacts related to mining, ore processing, transportation, agriculture, retail, home furnishings, clothing, and communication.

HOURS: May-Oct Daily 9-5; Nov-Apr M-F 9-4

ADMISSION: $6, Children $2.50, Seniors $5

PORT WASHINGTON

9227
Port Washington Historical Society
311 Johnson, 53074 [PO Box 491, 53074]; (p) (414) 284-7240; (c) Ozaukee

Private non-profit/ staff: 15(v)/ members: 170

HISTORICAL SOCIETY; HISTORY MUSEUM: Operates a local history museum, presents quarterly programs, and publishes a quarterly newsletter.

PROGRAMS: Annual Meeting; Community Outreach; Exhibits; Research Library/Archives

HOURS: May-Sept Su 1-3

PORTAGE

9228
Old Fort Winnebago Surgeon's Quarters
W8687 Hwy 33 E, 53901; (p) (608) 742-2949

1824/ staff: 1(f); 2(p)

COLLECTIONS: [1828-1845] Fort relics, early surgical books and instruments; Lifestyle of early 1800's.

HOURS: May 15 to Oct 15 Daily 10-4

POYNETTE

9229
Poynette Area Historical Society
116 N Main St, 53955 [PO Box 162, 53955]; (p) (608) 635-9849; (c) Columbia

Private non-profit/ 1972/ Board of Directors/ staff: 37(v)/ members: 66

HISTORICAL SOCIETY; HISTORY MUSEUM: Collects, preserves, and interprets the history of the villages of Poynette and Arlington and area townships.

PROGRAMS: Annual Meeting; Exhibits; Guided Tours; Interpretation

COLLECTIONS: [19th-20th c] Artifacts, photographs, manuscripts, family, and school histories, local newspapers on microfilm, state and local history books.

HOURS: Yr W 1-3, Sa 10-2

PRAIRIE DU CHIEN

9230
Villa Louis Historic Site
521 N Villa Louis Rd, 53821 [PO Box 65, 53821]; (p) (608) 326-2721; (f) (608) 326-5507; villalou@mhtc.net; www.shsw.wisc.edu/sites/villa/

1870/ staff: 2(f); 25(p); 85(v)

Mainatains historic house built in 1870.

COLLECTIONS: [1880s-1890s] Late 19th c decorative arts, documented with a huge archive of bills, receipts, and photographs. Excellent preserved example of British Arts and Crafts, William Morris.

HOURS: May-Oct 31 Daily 9-5

ADMISSION: $8.50, Children $4.50, Seniors $7.75

PRINCETON

9231
Princeton Historical Society

632 Water St, 54968 [321 Harvard St, 54968]; (p) (920) 295-6949; (c) Green Lake

Private non-profit/ 1983/ members: 58

HISTORIC PRESERVATION AGENCY; HISTORICAL SOCIETY; HOUSE MUSEUM: Collects and preserves the history of Princeton and the surrounding area.

PROGRAMS: Annual Meeting; Guided Tours; Research Library/Archives

COLLECTIONS: [1880s-1940] Native American arrowheads and replica of a 1950s dentist's office.

HOURS: May-Oct 2nd and 4th Sa 10-2:30

ADMISSION: Donations accepted

PULASKI

9232
Pulaski Area Historical Society, Inc.

129 W Pulaski St, 54162; (p) (920) 822-5856, (920) 822-5189; (c) Brown

Private non-profit/ 1972/ Officers and Board of Directors/ staff: 25(v)/ members: 230

HISTORICAL SOCIETY; RESEARCH CENTER: Houses memorabilia from the Pulaski area, with resources to aid individuals doing genealogy projects.

PROGRAMS: Annual Meeting; Exhibits

COLLECTIONS: [19th-20th c] Military, religious, and kitchen artifacts, farm tools, school memorabilia, and WI sesquicentennial exhibit.

HOURS: Yr by appt.

RACINE

9233
Case Corporation Archives

Marquette & Water St, 53408 [PO Box 85305, 53408]; (p) (414) 886-8557; (c) Racine

Private for-profit/ 1996/ Case Corporation/ staff: 1(p); 1(v)

CORPORATE ARCHIVES/MUSEUM: Repository for printed and illustrative materials relating to the history of Case Corporation.

PROGRAMS: Research Library/Archives

COLLECTIONS: [1880-1980] Sales literature, photographs, and engineering drawings pertaining to the history and development of corporate products, facilities, and people.

9234
Racine Heritage Museum

701 S Main St, 53403-1211; (p) (414) 636-3926; (f) (414) 636-3940; (c) Racine

Private non-profit/ 1870/ Racine County Historical Society and Museum, Inc./ staff: 2(f); 5(p); 155(v)/ members: 510/publication: The Sesquicentennial History of Racine, WI

HISTORICAL SOCIETY; HISTORY MUSEUM: Promotes and preserves the history of Southeastern WI's people, their diversity, inventions, productivity, and entrepreneurial spirit.

PROGRAMS: Annual Meeting; Community Outreach; Exhibits; Family Programs; Interpretation; Lectures; Living History; Publication; Research Library/Archives

COLLECTIONS: [1870s-present] Products invented and produced in Racine County. Artifacts and archival items associated with the sociocultural contexts of invention and production in Southeast WI.

HOURS: Yr M-Sa

ADMISSION: No charge

REEDSBURG

9235
Reedsburg Area Historical Society/ Pioneer Log Village & Museum

3 miles E of Reedsburg, Hwy 23 & 24, 53959 [PO Box 405, 53959]; (p) (608) 524-3419; (c) Sauk

1965/ Board of Directors/ staff: 20(v)/ members: 200

HISTORICAL SOCIETY: Preserve the heritage of the Reedsburg area. The log buildings are furnished with antiques.

PROGRAMS: Annual Meeting; Facility Rental; Guided Tours

COLLECTIONS: [1850s-1880s] 3 log homes, log church, blacksmith shop, log general store, one room school, and 3 museum buildings.

HOURS: June-Oct Sa-Su 1-4

ADMISSION: No charge/Donations

RHINELANDER

9236
Rhinelander Historical Society

9 S Pelham, 54501; (p) (715) 369-3833; (c) Oneida

Private non-profit/ 1991/ Board of Directors/ staff: 35(v)/ members: 176

HOUSE MUSEUM: Preserves and shares local history. Collects and displays writings and artifacts in a restored 1894 house.

PROGRAMS: Annual Meeting; Concerts; Exhibits; Guided Tours

COLLECTIONS: [1894-1950] Furnishings, military artifacts, and library with family histories.

HOURS: Fall-Winter T 10-4 and by appt; Spring-Summer M-F 10-4, Sa 12-4

RICHFIELD

9237
Richfield Historical Society

[PO Box 268, 53033]; (p) (262) 628-1074; (c) Washington

Private non-profit/ 1997/ staff: 130(v)/ members: 130/publication: Richfield Remembers The Past

HISTORICAL SOCIETY; HISTORY MUSEUM: Brings together people interested in Richfield Township's history. Collects material which will help establish or illustrate local history, provides for preservation of such material, and disseminates historical information.

PROGRAMS: Annual Meeting; Community Outreach; Exhibits; Interpretation; Lectures; Publication; Research Library/Archives

COLLECTIONS: [19th c] Photographs and genealogical material of local settlers. Historic information related to the community. Grist mill equipment, farming, and household artifacts.

RIPON

9238
Little White Schoolouse, Inc.

303 Blackburn St, 54971 [PO Box 305, 54971]; (p) (920) 748-6764; (f) (920) 748-6784; www.ripon-wi.com; (c) Fond du Lac

Private non-profit/ Ripon Area Chamber of Commerce/ staff: 6(p)

HISTORIC SITE; HISTORY MUSEUM: Collects, preserves, and interprets the birth of the Republican Party and the history of Ripon.

PROGRAMS: Exhibits

COLLECTIONS: [1850-1900] Schoolhouse furniture, books, equipment, and political artifacts.

HOURS: May-Sept Daily 10-4

ADMISSION: Donations accepted

SAINT NAZIANZ

9239
Saint Nazianz Area Historical Society

W Main St, 54232 [502 S 4th, PO Box 125, 54232]; (p) (920) 773-2155; (c) Manitowoc

Private non-profit/ 1988/ Board of Officers and Directors/ staff: 25(v)/ members: 35

HISTORICAL SOCIETY: Maintains original buildings founded as a communal society by a Roman Catholic priest.

PROGRAMS: Annual Meeting; Community Outreach; Festivals; Guided Tours

COLLECTIONS: [1850-1950] Log house, one-room schoolhouse with period furniture and photographs of town life.

HOURS: Yr by appt

SHAWANO

9240
Shawano County Historical Society, Inc.

524 N Franklin St, 54166 [1133 S Union St, 54166]; (p) (715) 526-3323; www.shawano.com; (c) Shawano

County/ 1940/ Shawano County/ staff: 1(f); 3(p); 20(v)/ members: 114/publication: Grandma's Footprints; Shawano-A Humming Good Town

GARDEN; HISTORICAL SOCIETY; HISTORY MUSEUM: Operates museum that consists of Heritage House, one-room school, log cabin, and railway station.

PROGRAMS: Annual Meeting; Community Outreach; Exhibits; Festivals; Film/Video; Guided Tours; Lectures; Publication; Research Library/Archives; School-Based Curriculum

COLLECTIONS: [1882-1935] Antique furniture, organ, china and crystal dishes, shoe repair tools, shoes, beadwork, toys, dolls, books, cheese-making exhibit, maple syrup, logging, hardware, medical, and Native American artifacts.

HOURS: June-Aug W, Sa-Su 1:30-4 and by appt

ADMISSION: Donations accepted

SHEBOYGAN

9241
Sheboygan County Historical Society Museum
3110 Erie Ave, 53081; (p) (920) 458-1103; (f) (920) 458-5152

staff: 1(f); 8(p); 12(v)

HOURS: Apr-Oct

SHEBOYGAN FALLS

9242
Sheboygan County Historical Research Center
518 Water St, 53085; (p) (920) 467-4667; (f) (920) 467-1395; schrc@execpc.com; www.schrc.org; (c) Sheboygan

Private non-profit/ 1983/ staff: 2(f); 1(p); 129(v)/ members: 807

GENEALOGICAL SOCIETY; HISTORIC PRESERVATION AGENCY; HISTORIC SITE; HISTORY MUSEUM; RESEARCH CENTER: Preserves county history.

PROGRAMS: Annual Meeting; Community Outreach; Family Programs; Festivals; Guided Tours; Interpretation; Lectures; Research Library/Archives; School-Based Curriculum

COLLECTIONS: [1850-present] Photos, prints, genealogies, reference volumes, government records, obituaries, maps, city directories, birth and death records.

HOURS: Yr T-Sa 9-4

ADMISSION: No charge

SHELL LAKE

9243
Washburn County Historical Society, Inc.
102 W 2nd Ave, 54871 [PO Box 366, 54871]; (p) 715-635-7996; http://www.rootsweb.com/~wiwashbu/wcgs.htm; (c) Washburn

County; Private non-profit/ 1954/ Board of Directors/ staff: 1(p); 25(v)/ members: 25/publication: *Historical Collections of Washburn County and the Surrounding Indianhead Country, Vol. 1-4; and other*

GENEALOGICAL SOCIETY; HISTORIC PRESERVATION AGENCY; HISTORIC SITE; HISTORICAL SOCIETY; HISTORY MUSEUM: Gathers, interprets, and shares artifacts and history of the county and surrounding Indianhead Country.

PROGRAMS: Annual Meeting; Exhibits; Festivals; Guided Tours; Interpretation; Publication; Research Library/Archives

COLLECTIONS: [1880-1950s] Photos, clothing, books, newspapers, audio tapes, maps, toys, music boxes, quilts, kitchen and souvenir objects, military uniforms, and equipment, school, church, and naturalization records, Native American, logging, and railroad items.

HOURS: June-Aug W-Sa 10-4; Springbrook F-Sa 11-4

ADMISSION: Donations accepted

SHULLSBURG

9244
Badger Historical Society
228 E Water St, 53586; (p) (608) 965-3474; (c) Lafayette

Private non-profit/ 1976/ members: 6

HISTORICAL SOCIETY: The Badger Historical Society participates in historical research.

SOUTH MILWAUKEE

9245
South Milwaukee Historical Museum
717 Milwaukee Ave, 53172; (p) (414) 762-8852; www.southmilwukee.org; (c) Milwaukee

1971/ South Milwaukee Historical Society Board of Directors/ members: 155/publication: *Centennial Book; South Milwaukee Then to Now*

HISTORICAL SOCIETY; HISTORY MUSEUM; HOUSE MUSEUM: Preserves cultural artifacts and local memorabilia.

PROGRAMS: Annual Meeting; Community Outreach; Exhibits; Festivals; Guided Tours; Lectures; Publication; School-Based Curriculum

COLLECTIONS: [1835-present] Books, manuscripts, memorabilia, furniture, clothing, photographs, and art.

HOURS: Summer Su 2-4 and by appt.

SPARTA

9246
Monroe County Historical Society, Inc.
[PO Box 422, 54656]; (p) (608) 269-8680; (f) (608) 269-8921; (c) Monroe

Private non-profit/ 1972/ members: 241

HISTORIC SITE; HISTORICAL SOCIETY; LIBRARY AND/OR ARCHIVES: Educates, preserves, advances, and disseminates knowledge of Monroe County's history.

PROGRAMS: Annual Meeting; Community Outreach; Concerts; Exhibits; Facility Rental; Guided Tours; Lectures; Publication; Research Library/Archives; School-Based Curriculum; Theatre

COLLECTIONS: Monroe County History, Photographs, cemeteries material, Manuscripts, vital records, civil/circuit records, family genealogies, census, genealogical research library, microfilm, newspapers, artifacts, military records.

HOURS: M-F 9-4:30

9247
Monroe County Local History Room
200 W Main St, 54656; (p) (608) 269-8680; (f) (608) 269-8921; MCLHR@centurytel.net; (c) Monroe

County/ 1977/ Monroe County/ staff: 1(f); 1(p); 25(v)

GENEALOGICAL SOCIETY; HISTORICAL SOCIETY; HISTORY MUSEUM: Maintains material relating to Monroe County residents.

PROGRAMS: Exhibits

COLLECTIONS: [1850-present] Library has microfilm of census and newspapers.

HOURS: Yr M-F 9-4:30, Th 9-9, Sa 10-4:30

ADMISSION: No charge

SPRING GREEN

9248
Taliesin
5481 County Hwy C, 53588 [PO Box 399, 53588]; (p) (608) 588-7900; (f) (608) 588-7514; http://www.taliesinpreservation.org/visitor/

1911/ staff: 3(f); 40(p)

Preserves Taliesin, Frank Lloyd Wright's estates; promotes organic architecture, education, history of estate.

COLLECTIONS: [1911-1959] Japanese and Chinese sculpture and screens; original Wright-designed furniture and sculpture.

HOURS: May-Oct

STANLEY

9249
Stanley Area Historical Society
228 Helgerson St, 54768 [PO Box 142, 54768]; (p) (715) 644-0464; (c) Chippewa

Private non-profit/ 1976/ members: 625/publication: *Our Town*

HISTORICAL SOCIETY: Collects and preserves artifacts and history of the area for the education and enjoyment of present and future generations.

PROGRAMS: Annual Meeting; Exhibits; Publication

COLLECTIONS: [1890-present] Artifacts and written history of the Stanley-Boyd area.

HOURS: June-Sept Sa-Su 1-4

ADMISSION: Donations accepted

STEVENS POINT

9250
Portage County Historical Society
Washington Ave, 54481 [PO Box 672, 54481]; (p) (715) 344-4423, (715) 344-7607; (c) Portage

County; Private non-profit/ 1952/ staff: 15(v)/ members: 368

HISTORICAL SOCIETY; HISTORY MUSEUM; HOUSE MUSEUM; LIVING HISTORY/OUTDOOR MUSEUM: Preserves county history and makes it available to the public through exhibits, lectures, programs, and publications so that they can better understand local heritage.

PROGRAMS: Annual Meeting; Community Outreach; Concerts; Exhibits; Facility Rental; Family Programs; Festivals; Film/Video; Garden Tours; Guided Tours; Interpretation; Lectures; Living History; Reenactments; Research Library/Archives; School-Based Curriculum

HOURS: Summer: Sa-Su 1-5

ADMISSION: $2

STURGEON BAY

9251
Door County Historical Museum
18 N 4th Ave, 54235; (p) (920) 743-5809; (c) Door

County/ 1939/ Door County/ staff: 4(p); 8(v)

HISTORY MUSEUM: Focuses on county history through educational exhibits.

PROGRAMS: Exhibits

COLLECTIONS: [18th-20th c] Artifacts related to early settlers, farmers, orchard groves, and tourism. One wing devoted to the Pioneer Fire Company, housing restored vehicles, and equipment. Wildlife exhibit features native species.

HOURS: May 1-Oct 31 Daily 10-4:30

ADMISSION: Donations

9252
Door County Maritime Museum, Inc.
120 N Madison Ave, 54235; (p) (920) 743-5958; (f) (920) 743-9483; dcmm@itol.com; www.dcmm.org; (c) Door

Private non-profit/ 1969/ staff: 5(f); 5(p); 235(v)/ members: 1099

HISTORY MUSEUM; MARITIME MUSEUM: Preserves the maritime history of Door County and the Great Lakes. Provides interpretative and educational opportunities for local residents and visitors.

PROGRAMS: Annual Meeting; Concerts; Exhibits; Facility Rental; Family Programs; Festivals; Film/Video; Guided Tours; Lectures; Publication; Research Library/Archives; School-Based Curriculum

COLLECTIONS: [Late 1800s-present] Photographs, maritime art, uniforms, and ship models.

HOURS: Yr Daily 10-5

ADMISSION: $6, Children $3

SUN PRAIRIE

9253
Sun Prairie Historical Library and Museum
115 E Main St, 53590 [300 E Main St, 53590]; (p) (608) 837-2915, (608) 837-2511; (f) (608) 825-6879; pklein@mailbag.com; (c) Dane

City/ 1967/ City of Sun Prairie/ staff: 2(p); 50(v)

HISTORY MUSEUM; LIBRARY AND/OR ARCHIVES: Collects, preserves, maintains, and displays collections on the city government and daily life of its citizens.

PROGRAMS: Community Outreach; Exhibits; Guided Tours; Research Library/Archives

COLLECTIONS: [1830-present] Documents, photographs, and artifacts on the people of the Sun Prairie area and the institutions they founded.

HOURS: Archives: Yr by appt; Exhibits: Mar-Dec Su-M 6:30-8:30, W, F-Sa 2-4

ADMISSION: No charge

SUPERIOR

9254
Douglas County Historical Society
1401 Tower Ave, Ste 10, 54880; (p) (715) 392-8449; (c) Douglas

Private non-profit/ 1854/ staff: 1(p); 20(v)/ members: 164/publication: *They Remembered Superior; Yesterdays; and others*

HISTORICAL SOCIETY; HOUSE MUSEUM: Preserves and shares the history of Douglas County through exhibits, archives, programs, events, and publications.

PROGRAMS: Annual Meeting; Community Outreach; Exhibits; Family Programs; Interpretation; Lectures; Publication; Reenactments; Research Library/Archives; School-Based Curriculum

COLLECTIONS: [Prehistory-present] Photographs, including David F. Barry collection, furniture, furnishings, clothing, Dakota, and Ojibwe artifacts.

HOURS: Yr Daily 9-5

9255
Fairlawn Mansion & Museum
906 E 2nd St, 54880; (p) (715) 394-5712

1890/ staff: 4(f); 4(p); 200(v)

COLLECTIONS: [1880] Victorian furniture and furnishings, David Barry photo collection, Native American artifacts; History of Douglas County; photos; books; maps; manuscripts.

HOURS: Yr Daily 9-5

THERESA

9256
Solomon Juneau Home
Main St, 53091; (p) (414) 488-3263; gbms01.uwgb.edu/~WISFRENCH/photos/junhouse.htm

9257
Theresa Historical Society
202 Milwaukee St, 53091; (c) Dodge

Private non-profit/ 1956/ staff: 5(f); 25(v)/ members: 75

HISTORIC PRESERVATION AGENCY; HISTORICAL SOCIETY: Preserves historic artifacts. Located at Solomon Juneau's last home, built in 1847. Juneau founded Milwaukee and Village of Theresa.

PROGRAMS: Annual Meeting; Concerts; Exhibits; Film/Video; Lectures

COLLECTIONS: [19th c] Articles used by early local settlers, including Solomon Juneau in 1847.

HOURS: Yr last Su of month 1-4

THREE LAKES

9258
Three Lakes Historical Society, Inc.
1798 Huron St, 54562 [PO Box 250, 54562]; (p) (715) 546-2295; www.newnorth.net/~robwack/museum/htm; (c) Oneida

Private non-profit/ 1981/ staff: 2(p); 30(v)/ members: 280

HISTORY MUSEUM; HOUSE MUSEUM: Preserves the area's written and visual history. Teaches this history through maintaining a museum, participating in local activities, and providing programs to the public and schools.

PROGRAMS: Annual Meeting; Community Outreach; Concerts; Exhibits; Festivals; Film/Video

COLLECTIONS: [1880-present] Artifacts and information on pioneer settlers, logging, reforestation operations, agriculture, education, local businesses, and individuals.

HOURS: June-Aug T-Sa 10-4

ADMISSION: Donations requested

TIGERTON

9259
Tigerton Area Historical Society
Swanke & Chestnut St, 54486 [PO Box 191, 54486]; (c) Shawano

State/ 1975/ State Historical Society of WI/ staff: 20(v)/ members: 40

HISTORICAL SOCIETY: Preserves history of Tigerton School District through three museums housing local records and artifacts.

PROGRAMS: Annual Meeting; Community Outreach; Exhibits; Film/Video; Guided Tours

COLLECTIONS: [1880-present] Agricultural, logging, and pioneer artifacts; school, living room, bedroom, laundry and kitchen settings.

HOURS: May-Sept Su

TWO RIVERS

9260
Two Rivers Historical Society
Washington House, 1622 Jefferson St, 54241; (p) (920) 793-2490, (888) 857-3529; (c) Manitowoc

Private non-profit/ 1962/ Board of Trustees/ staff: 75(v)/ members: 550

HISTORICAL SOCIETY; HISTORY MUSEUM: Collects, preserves, and presents memorabilia, papers, and photographs of Two Rivers and its environs. Maintains three museums including Washington House, an 1850s hotel; a convent museum; and a wood type museum in old factory building.

PROGRAMS: Annual Meeting; Exhibits; Facility Rental; Family Programs; Festivals

COLLECTIONS: [1835-present] Pictures, papers, clothing, toys, machinery, Boy and Girl Scout items, church items, and an old fashioned working ice cream parlor.

HOURS: Nov-Apr Daily 9-5; May-Oct Daily 9-9

VIROQUA

9261
Sherry-Butt House
795 N Main St, 54665 [410 S Center St, 54665]; (p) (608) 637-7336, (608) 637-7396

1870/ staff: 10(v)

COLLECTIONS: [1870-1890] Seven-piece Eastlake furniture set from Col. Butt; Eastlake bedroom set with teardrop pulls; Col. Butt's Civil War belongings; Several Civil War documents from Col. Butt, photographs.

HOURS: May-Sept Sa-Su 1-5

9262
Vernon County Historical Society
410 S Center St, 54665 [PO Box 444, 54665]; (p) (608) 637-7396; (c) Vernon

County; Private non-profit/ 1941/ staff: 3(p); 100(v)/ members: 300

HISTORIC SITE; HISTORICAL SOCIETY; HISTORY MUSEUM; RESEARCH CENTER: Promotes and guides the presentation of the county's historical heritage and encourages research, education, and publication of gathered data.

PROGRAMS: Annual Meeting; Community Outreach; Exhibits; Facility Rental; Family Programs; Film/Video; Guided Tours; Lectures; Publication; Research Library/Archives; School-Based Curriculum

COLLECTIONS: [1848-present] One room school, country church, Sherry-Butt House, Family Home of Civil War Col. Cyrus Butt with original furnishings.

HOURS: May 15-Sept 15 T-Su 12-4

ADMISSION: Donations requested

WASHBURN

9263
Bayfield County Historical Society
118 E Bayfield, 54891 [PO Box 272, 54891]; (p) (715) 373-5345; (c) Bayfield

Private non-profit/ 1972/ Board/ staff: 10(v)/publication: *Historical Happenings*

HISTORICAL SOCIETY: Operates as an umbrella agency for the individual chapters in Bayfield County. Collects, preserves, and disseminates information of Bayfield County.

PROGRAMS: Annual Meeting; Community Outreach; Exhibits; Publication

COLLECTIONS: Obsolete school records, W W I enrollments, and photographs of schools, industries, buildings, and communities.

HOURS: 1st M or by appt

9264
Washburn Area Historical Society
1 E Bayfield St, 54891 [PO Box 272, 54891]; (p) (715) 373-5591; (c) Bayfield

Private non-profit/ 1982/ staff: 20(v)/ members: 175

HISTORIC SITE; HISTORICAL SOCIETY; RESEARCH CENTER: Collects, preserves, and disseminates information on Washburn Area. Maintains museum on second floor of Washburn Museum and Cultural Center.

PROGRAMS: Annual Meeting; Guided Tours

COLLECTIONS: [1883-present] Dioramas of Dupont plant, logging industry and Brownstone Quarry; family histories, photographs, toys, furniture, and newspapers.

HOURS: Apr-Dec Daily 10-4

ADMISSION: Donations accepted

WASHINGTON ISLAND

9265
Washington Island Farm Museum
Jackson Harbor Rd, 54246 [Rt 1, Box 76, 54246]; (p) (920) 847-2156; (c) Door

Private non-profit/ Board of Directors/ staff: 1(p); 57(v)/ members: 462

HISTORIC PRESERVATION AGENCY; HISTORY MUSEUM; HOUSE MUSEUM: Preserves and exhibits artifacts relating to history of farming on Washington Island.

PROGRAMS: Annual Meeting; Exhibits; Family Programs; Festivals; Guided Tours; Interpretation; Lectures

COLLECTIONS: [1880-1930] Buildings, photos, tools, field machinery, and household items.

HOURS: June-late Oct Daily 10-4

ADMISSION: Donations requested

WATERLOO

9266
Waterloo Area Historical Society
130 W Polk St, 53594 [PO Box 52, 53594]; (c) Jefferson

Private non-profit; State/ 1967/ State Historical Society of WI/ staff: 7(v)/ members: 70/publication: *Timescape*

HISTORIC PRESERVATION AGENCY; HISTORIC SITE; HISTORICAL SOCIETY; HISTORY MUSEUM; HOUSE MUSEUM: Presents local history in displays and provides genealogy services through death and township records.

PROGRAMS: Annual Meeting; Community Outreach; Exhibits; Facility Rental; Family Programs; Festivals; Guided Tours; Interpretation; Lectures; Living History; Publication; Reenactments; Research Library/Archives; School-Based Curriculum

COLLECTIONS: [1890-1950] Artifacts from local businesses, schools, prominent families, the military, and railroad depot.

HOURS: May-Sept Su 1:30-4

ADMISSION: No charge

WATERTOWN

9267
Octagon House, The
919 Charles St, 53094-5001; (p) (920) 261-2796; www.watertownhistory.org; (c) Jefferson

Private non-profit/ 1854/ staff: 1(f); 13(p); 25(v)/ members: 350

HISTORIC SITE; HISTORICAL SOCIETY; HISTORY MUSEUM; HOUSE MUSEUM: Features 57 rooms on five floors with guided tours on the hour. Site of the first kindergarten in the US, started by Margarethe Schurz.

PROGRAMS: Annual Meeting; Community Outreach; Exhibits; Family Programs; Festivals; Guided Tours; Living History; Research Library/Archives

COLLECTIONS: [1800s]

HOURS: Sept-May Daily 11-3; May-Sept Daily 10-4

ADMISSION: $4.50

9268
Watertown Historical Society
919 Charles St, 53094; (p) (920) 261-2796; (c) Jefferson

Private non-profit/ staff: 1(f); 10(p); 30(v)/ members: 300

GENEALOGICAL SOCIETY; HISTORICAL SOCIETY; HISTORY MUSEUM; HOUSE MUSEUM: Preserves Octagon House, first kindergarten in the US and a pioneer barn.

PROGRAMS: Annual Meeting; Concerts; Guided Tours

COLLECTIONS: [19th c-present]

HOURS: May-Oct Daily 11-3

ADMISSION: $4.50, Seniors $4

WAUKESHA

9269
Waukesha County Historical Society
101 W Main St, 53185; (p) (262) 521-2859; (f) (262) 521-2865; (c) Waukesha

Private non-profit/ 1906/ Board of Trustees/ staff: 4(f); 1(p); 60(v)/ members: 520/publication: *Landmark; Timeline*

HISTORICAL SOCIETY: Preserves county history through collections, markers, publications, programs, events, tours, and meetings.

PROGRAMS: Annual Meeting; Exhibits; Family Programs; Festivals; Lectures; Publication

COLLECTIONS: [1834-present]

HOURS: Yr T-Sa 9-4:30

ADMISSION: No charge

9270
Waukesha Engine Historical Society
1000 W Saint Paul Ave, 53188-4999; (p) (262) 547-3311; (f) (262) 549-2929; ron_long@wed.dresser.com; (c) Waukesha

Private non-profit/ 1992/ staff: 9(v)/ members: 52

HISTORIC PRESERVATION AGENCY; HISTORICAL SOCIETY: Collects, preserves, and displays company memorabilia.

PROGRAMS: Exhibits

COLLECTIONS: [1906-present] Historical documents, photos, artifacts, products, and other material pertaining to the company known as Waukesha Motor Company, Waukesha Engine Division, Dresser Equipment Group, Inc.

HOURS: Yr M-F by appt

ADMISSION: No charge

WAUPACA

9271
Holly History-Genealogy Center/Hutchinson House Museum
321 S Main St, 54981; (p) (715) 258-5958, (715) 256-9980; (c) Waupaca

Private non-profit/ 1957/ Waupaca Historical Society/ staff: 25(v)/ members: 114

HISTORY MUSEUM; HOUSE MUSEUM; RESEARCH CENTER: Maintains and preserves local and state history.

PROGRAMS: Annual Meeting; Exhibits; Festivals; Guided Tours; Research Library/Archives

COLLECTIONS: [Mid-late 19th c] Museum has Victorian furnishings. Research Center with genealogies, pictures, local and state history books.

HOURS: Museum: May-Sept F-Su 1-4:30; Research Center: T 1-4, Th 7-9, Sa 1-4

ADMISSION: $2, Children $1

WAUSAU

9272
Forest History Association of Wisconsin, Inc.
410 McIndoe St, 54403; (p) (715) 693-2995; (c) Marathon

Private non-profit/ 1976/ staff: 10(v)/ members: 200/publication: *Chronology of "Firsts" in Wisconsin's Forest History; Directory of Wisconsin Logging Museums; and others*

HISTORICAL SOCIETY: Preserves and studies contributions made by pioneers of the forest product industries and forest management to WI's social and economic development.

PROGRAMS: Annual Meeting; Exhibits; Publication

COLLECTIONS: [19th-20th c] Artifacts related to log and lumber transportation by water, rail and road; sawmills and lumbermen, logging and forestry.

9273
Marathon County Historical Society
403 & 410 McIndoe St, 54403 [410 McIndoe St, 54403]; (p) (715) 842-5750; (f) (715) 848-0576; (c) Marathon

Private non-profit/ 1954/ staff: 1(f); 5(p); 30(v)/ members: 400

HISTORIC SITE; HISTORICAL SOCIETY; HISTORY MUSEUM; HOUSE MUSEUM: Collects, preserves, and exhibits materials related to the history of Wausau and Marathon County.

PROGRAMS: Annual Meeting; Community Outreach; Concerts; Exhibits; Facility Rental; Family Programs; Festivals; Film/Video; Guided Tours; Lectures; Living History; Reenactments; Research Library/Archives; School-Based Curriculum

COLLECTIONS: [1860-1960] Logging artifacts, vintage clothing, furniture, toys, dolls, business, and medical equipment.

HOURS: Yr T-Th 9-4:30, Sa-Su 1-4:30

WEST ALLIS

9274
West Allis Historical Society
8405 W National Ave, 53227; (p) (414) 541-6970; (c) Milwaukee

Private non-profit/ 1966/ staff: 17(v)/ members: 131/publication: *Buzz*

HISTORIC SITE; HISTORICAL SOCIETY; HISTORY MUSEUM: Collects and preserves history of West Allis and its environs. Museum housed in former school, built in 1887.

PROGRAMS: Annual Meeting; Exhibits; Guided Tours; Publication

COLLECTIONS: [1839-present] Artifacts related to local business, industry, and individuals.

HOURS: Yr T-Su

ADMISSION: No charge

WEST SALEM

9275
Hamlin Garland Homestead
357 W Garland St, 54669 [PO Box 884, 54669]; (p) (608) 786-1399, (608) 786-1675

1859/ staff: 26(v)

COLLECTIONS: [1915-1915] Furniture of Hamlin Garland; Books of Hamlin Garland and other authors of that time period.

HOURS: May-Sept M-Sa 10-5, Su 1-4

9276
Palmer-Gullickson Octagon Home
360 N Leonard St, 54669 [PO Box 884, 54669]; (p) (608) 786-1399, (608) 786-1675

1854/ staff: 30(v)

COLLECTIONS: [None] Village records and files.

HOURS: May-Sept M-Sa 10-5, Su 1-5

9277
West Salem Historical Society
357 W Garland St, 54669 [PO Box 884, 54669]; (p) (608) 786-1399; (c) La Crosse

Private non-profit/ 1974/ staff: 52(v)/ members: 749

HISTORIC SITE; HISTORICAL SOCIETY; HOUSE MUSEUM: Cares for and promotes local history.

PROGRAMS: Annual Meeting; Community Outreach; Festivals; Guided Tours

COLLECTIONS: [1890-1915]

HOURS: June-Aug M-Sa 10-5, Su 1-5

ADMISSION: $1

WESTBORO

9278
Washington County Historical Society, Inc.
320 S 5th St, 53095; (p) (414) 335-4678; (f) (414) 335-4612; (c) Washington

Private non-profit/ 1875/ Board of Directors/ staff: 3(f); 2(p); 75(v)

HISTORIC SITE; HISTORICAL SOCIETY; HISTORY MUSEUM; RESEARCH CENTER: Operates a 19th c courthouse, jail, and Catholic priest's home, Barn, and convent houses research library on Washington County.

PROGRAMS: Annual Meeting; Community Outreach; Concerts; Exhibits; Facility Rental; Family Programs; Festivals; Guided Tours; Interpretation; Lectures; Living History; Research Library/Archives; School-Based Curriculum

COLLECTIONS: [1848-present] Photographs, books, maps, manuscripts, records, military, manufacturing, and agricultural items.

WESTFIELD

9279
Cochrane-Nelson House Museum
125 Lawrence St, 53964 [PO Box 172, 53964]; (p) (608) 296-3182, (608) 296-3421

1903/ staff: 5(v)

COLLECTIONS: [Turn of the c] Old bottles, clothing, furniture, dishes, local industry, one-room schools, church relics, military; Growing file of family histories, newspapers, photos, maps, obituaries, community records, school censuses.

HOURS: W-Sa 1-4

9280
Marquette County Historical Society
125 Lawrence St, 53964 [PO Box 172, 53964]; (c) Marquette

County; Private non-profit/ 1969/ Board of Directors/ staff: 20(v)/ members: 139/publication: *Imprints on the Sands of Marquette County*

HISTORICAL SOCIETY; HISTORY MUSEUM; HOUSE MUSEUM: Maintains museum of historic county artifacts, records, and genealogical information.

PROGRAMS: Annual Meeting; Exhibits; Guided Tours; Publication; Research Library/Archives

COLLECTIONS: [19th-20th c] Artifacts pertaining to schools, W W I and II, domestic life, railroad, fire department, farming, and local businesses.

HOURS: Yr by appt;

WILD ROSE

9281
Wild Rose Historical Society
Main St, 54984 [PO Box 63, 54984]; (c) Waushara

Private non-profit/ 1964/ members: 72

HISTORIC SITE; HISTORICAL SOCIETY: Maintains museum that has seven buildings—house, blacksmith shop, barn, smokehouse, schoolhouse, carriage house and old bank. Also weaving room.

PROGRAMS: Exhibits; Guided Tours

COLLECTIONS: [1890s]

HOURS: June-Aug W, Sa 1-3

ADMISSION: $1, Children $0.50

WIND LAKE

9282
Town of Norway Historical Society
6419 Heg Park Rd, 53185; (p) (414) 895-6858; (c) Racine

Private non-profit/ 1978/ staff: 15(v)/ members: 80/publication: *Town of Norway: Then and Now*

HISTORICAL SOCIETY; HISTORY MUSEUM: Collects and preserves local artifacts and genealogies. Manages Museum, Farm Museum, log cabin and Eielsen House located in Heg County Park.

PROGRAMS: Annual Meeting; Exhibits; Festivals; Interpretation; Lectures; Publication; Reenactments; Research Library/Archives

COLLECTIONS: [1840-present] Farm machinery, Heg family items, Norwegian immigrant trunks, looms, wooden articles, and household goods.

HOURS: Yr by appt; May-Sept Sa-Su 12-4

ADMISSION: No charge

WISCONSIN DELLS

9283
Dells Country Historical Society
Corner of Bowman Park & Broadway, 53965 [PO Box 177, 53965]; (p) (608) 254-8321; (c) Columbia

Private non-profit/ 1981/ staff: 18(v)/ members: 35/publication: *Other Before You; The Dells*

HISTORIC SITE; HISTORICAL SOCIETY; HISTORY MUSEUM; HOUSE MUSEUM: Preserves and maintains the Bowman House and local memorabilia.

PROGRAMS: Exhibits; Festivals; Guided Tours; Publication

COLLECTIONS: [1860-1950] Tourism artifacts, photographs by H.H. Bennett and items belonging to Joseph Bailey including the thanks of Congress for saving the fleet on the Red River in 1863.

HOURS: June-Sept T-Th

WOODRUFF

9284
Doctor Kate Museum/Historical Society
923 2nd Ave, 54568 [PO Box 851, 54568]; (p) (715) 356-6896; mmdpbins@newnorth.net; www.minocqua.org; (c) Oneida

Private non-profit/ 1986/ Dr. Kate Historical Society/ staff: 15(v)/ members: 50

HISTORICAL SOCIETY; HISTORY MUSEUM: Maintains building, creates exhibits, raises funds, and greets the public.

PROGRAMS: Exhibits; Guided Tours

COLLECTIONS: [1888-present] Memorabilia related to Dr. Kate Pelham Newcomb, her medical practice, Million Penny Parades and local efforts to build a hospital in northern WI.

HOURS: Mid June-Sept M-F 11-4

ADMISSION: Donations accepted

WYOMING

AFTON

9285
Star Valley Historical Society
[PO Box 1212, 83110]; (c) Lincoln

County/ 1984/ Lincoln County/ staff: 4(v)/ members: 51

HISTORICAL SOCIETY: Offers monthly meetings with history presentations or summer treks to visit historical sites. Performs a historical play in the Old Rock Church every summer.

PROGRAMS: Annual Meeting; Exhibits; Festivals; Guided Tours; Lectures; Publication; Reenactments

BANNER

9286
Fort Phil Kearny State Historic Site
528 Wagon Box Rd, 82832; (p) (307) 684-7629; (f) (307) 684-7967; (c) Johnson

State/ 1988/ WY State Parks and Cultural Resources Dept/ staff: 2(f); 3(p)

HISTORIC SITE: Features Fort Phil Kearny, Fetterman Battlefield, and the Wagon Box Fight Site.

PROGRAMS: Exhibits; Guided Tours; Interpretation; Living History

COLLECTIONS: [Mid 19th c] Historic artifacts.

HOURS: May 15-Sept Daily; Sept 30-Nov 31 W-Su 12-4; Apr 1-May 14 W-Su 12-4

ADMISSION: $2

BIG HORN

9287
Big Horn City Historical Society
[PO Box 566, 82833]; (c) Sheridan

Private non-profit/ 1990/ staff: 50(v)/ members: 350

HISTORIC PRESERVATION AGENCY; HISTORIC SITE; HISTORICAL SOCIETY; HISTORY MUSEUM; TRIBAL MUSEUM

PROGRAMS: Annual Meeting; Exhibits; Festivals; Guided Tours; Living History; Publication; Reenactments; Research Library/Archives

COLLECTIONS: [1890-1945] Artifacts from the surrounding area, pioneer stories, school memorabilia, photographs.

HOURS: June-Aug Sa-Su 11-6

9288
Bradford Brinton Memorial
239 Brinton Rd, 82833 [PO Box 460, 82833]; (p) (307) 672-3173; (f) (307) 672-3258; gca@fiberpipe.net; (c) Sheridan

Private non-profit/ 1961/ The Northern Trust of Chicago/ staff: 3(f); 10(p)/ members: 200

ART MUSEUM; HISTORY MUSEUM; HOUSE MUSEUM: Dedicated to inform and educate the public about the lifestyle of a gentleman rancher of the 1920s and 1930s.

PROGRAMS: Exhibits; Guided Tours; Interpretation; Lectures

COLLECTIONS: [1920s-1930s] Collection emphasizes the study of the American West and early ranching: a fully furnished historic ranch house, art gallery, outbuildings, Western art, fine furnishings, Native American artifacts, books, and rare documents.

HOURS: Mid May-Sept Daily 9:30-5

ADMISSION: $3

BUFFALO

9289
Jim Gatchell Museum
100 Fort St, 82834 [PO Box 596, 82834]; (p) (307) 684-9331; (f) (307) 684-0354; jmuseum@trib.com; www.jimgatchell.com; (c) Johnson

County/ 1956/ Johnson County/Gatchell Museum Board of Directors/ staff: 1(f); 3(p); 27(v)/ members: 635/publication: *Sentry*

HISTORY MUSEUM; LIVING HISTORY/OUTDOOR MUSEUM: Emphasis on Bozeman Trail, Native Americans, and frontier military history; early settling of the Powder River region including the Johnson County "Cattle War."

PROGRAMS: Community Outreach; Exhibits; Guided Tours; Interpretation; Lectures; Living History; Publication; Research Library/Archives

COLLECTIONS: [1860-1930]

HOURS: May-Sept Daily 8-7; Oct-Dec M-F 9-5

ADMISSION: $4, Student $2, Children $2; Members free

9290
Johnson County Historical Society
[PO Box 103, 82834]; (c) Johnson

Private non-profit; State/ 1954/ WY State Historical Society/ members: 60

HISTORICAL SOCIETY; HOUSE MUSEUM: Preserves and protects local history, supports museum and educates the public on regional heritage.

PROGRAMS: Annual Meeting; Community Outreach; Exhibits; Family Programs; Garden Tours; Guided Tours; Interpretation; Lectures; Living History

CASPER

9291
Casper College Library, Special Collections
125 College Dr, 82601; (p) (307) 268-2269; (f) (307) 268-2682; kevinand@acad.cc.whecn.edu; www.cc.whecn.edu/library/sc.htm; (c) Natrona

State/ 1969/ State of WY/ staff: 15(f)

LIBRARY AND/OR ARCHIVES: Provides access to non-circulating collection of books, periodical, maps, photographs, and archival materials relating to local, state, and regional history.

PROGRAMS: Annual Meeting; Research Library/Archives

COLLECTIONS: [1820-present] Volumes, serials, maps, photos, newspaper clippings, and archival materials.

HOURS: Yr M-Th 7:30-4:30, F 7:30-4, Sa 9-5, Su 2-10

ADMISSION: No charge

9292
Fort Caspar Museum and Historic Site
4001 Fort Caspar Rd, 82604; (p) (307) 235-8462; (f) (307) 235-8464; (c) Natrona

City/ 1936/ City of Casper/ staff: 2(f); 3(p); 45(v)/ members: 90/publication: *Frontier Crossroads: A History of Fort Caspar and the Upper Platte Crossing*

HISTORIC SITE; HISTORY MUSEUM: Reconstructed 1865 fort listed on National Register. Site is also the location of the 1847 Mormon Ferry Crossing.

PROGRAMS: Annual Meeting; Community Outreach; Exhibits; Festivals; Interpretation; Lectures; Living History; Publication; Reenactments

COLLECTIONS: Artifacts related to the social and natural history of Central WY history.

HOURS: Spring-Summer M-Sa 8-7, Su 12-7; Fall-Winter M-F 8-5, Su 1-4

ADMISSION: No charge

CENTENNIAL

9293
Centennial Valley Historical Association
2734 Hwy 130, 82055 [PO Box 200, 82055]; (p) (307) 742-7158; (c) Albany

Private non-profit/ 1974/ staff: 50(v)/ members: 175/publication: *Centennial, the Real Centennial*

HISTORIC PRESERVATION AGENCY; HISTORIC SITE; HISTORICAL SOCIETY; HISTORY MUSEUM: Maintains museum housed at 1907 Laramie Hahn's Peak and Pacific Railroad.

PROGRAMS: Annual Meeting; Exhibits; Interpretation; Publication

COLLECTIONS: [1875-1925] Beehive Burner, caboose, farm and ranch machinery; materials on mining, railroading, ranching and lumbering; diorama of Cheyenne Indians, and replica of typical blacksmith's shop.

HOURS: Mid June-Sept F-M 1-4

ADMISSION: Donations accepted

CHEYENNE

9294
Cheyenne Frontier Days Old West Museum
4610 N Carey Ave, 82003 [PO Box 2720, 82003]; (p) (307) 778-7290; (f) (307) 778-7288; lizowm@aol.com; www.oldwestmuseum.com; (c) Laramie

Private non-profit/ 1979/ staff: 12(f); 3(p); 65(v)/ members: 700/publication: *Stageline*

ART MUSEUM; HISTORY MUSEUM: Focuses on art, history and rodeo relevant to the state and local area.

PROGRAMS: Community Outreach; Elder's Programs; Exhibits; Facility Rental; Family Programs; Festivals; Guided Tours; Interpretation; Lectures; Living History; Publication; Research Library/Archives; School-Based Curriculum

COLLECTIONS: [1860-present] Western heritage and art, horse-drawn vehicles, Native American, railroad, and rodeo items, clothing, photography, and archival materials.

9295
Cheyenne Genealogical Society
Laramie County Library, 2800 Central Ave, 82001; (p) (307) 635-1032; wyotom@aol.com; www.wyomingweb.net/genealogy; (c) Laramie

Private non-profit/ 1952/ staff: 15(v)/ members: 167

GENEALOGICAL SOCIETY: Stimulates and encourages family history research.

PROGRAMS: Annual Meeting

9296
Historic Governors' Mansion
300 E 21st St, 82001; (p) (307) 777-7878; sphs@missc.state.wy.us; commerce.state.wy.us/sphs/govern.htm; (c) Laramie

State/ 1977/ WY State Parks and Historic Sites/ staff: 1(f); 1(p); 10(v)

HISTORIC SITE; HOUSE MUSEUM: Built in 1904 as the residence of WY's First Families 1905-1976. Self-guided tours preceded by 20 minute video introduction.

PROGRAMS: Concerts; Facility Rental; Family Programs; Guided Tours; Interpretation

COLLECTIONS: [1905-1977] Original 1905 furniture, 1937 Louis XIV-style living room, furniture and 1950s den suite by furniture maker Thomas Molesworth.

HOURS: Yr

9297
Wyoming State Archives
Barrett Building, 2301 Central Ave, 82002; (p) (307) 777-7826; (f) (307) 777-7044; wyarchive@missc.state.wy.us; commerce.state.wy.us/cr/archives; (c) Laramie

State/ 1895/ State of Wyoming/ staff: 25(f); 6(v)

LIBRARY AND/OR ARCHIVES: Maintains public records from state and local government offices to document government activities and state history and collects privately donated materials pertaining to WY history.

PROGRAMS: Community Outreach; Exhibits; Interpretation; Research Library/Archives

COLLECTIONS: [1870-present] Photographs, manuscripts, microfilmed newspapers, oral histories, and Western History

9298
Wyoming State Museum
2301 Central Ave, 82002; (p) (307) 777-7022; (f) (307) 777-5375; wsm@state.wy.us; www.spacr.state.wy.us/cr/wsm/; (c) Laramie

State/ 1895/ State of Wyoming/ staff: 11(f); 117(v)/ members: 107

HISTORY MUSEUM: Tells the stories of WY's human and natural history. Highlights include a wildlife diorama and the hands-on history room.

PROGRAMS: Community Outreach; Exhibits; Festivals; Guided Tours; Lectures

COLLECTIONS: [1869-present] Textiles, firearms, household, military, and Native American artifacts.

HOURS: Yr May-Oct T-Sa 9-4:30; Nov-Apr T-F 9-4:30, Sa 10-2

ADMISSION: No charge

CODY

9299
Buffalo Bill Historical Center
720 Sheridan Ave, 82414; (p) (307) 587-4771; (f) (307) 587-5714; bbhc@wavecom.net; www.bbhc.org; (c) Park

Private non-profit/ 1917/ staff: 69(f); 130(p); 200(v)/ members: 4200/publication: *Points West*

ART MUSEUM; HISTORY MUSEUM: Maintains a museum complex and research library devoted to western heritage and to advancing knowledge of the American West.

PROGRAMS: Community Outreach; Concerts; Exhibits; Festivals; Interpretation; Lectures; Publication; School-Based Curriculum

COLLECTIONS: [19th-20th c] Western American art, Native American art and artifacts, Western American memorabilia related to Buffalo Bill, and collection of American firearms.

HOURS: Nov-Mar T-Su 10-3; Apr Daily 10-5; May Daily 8-8; June-Sept Daily 7-8

ADMISSION: $10, Student $6, Children $4; Under 6 free

9300
Old Trail Town, Inc.
1831 DeMaris Dr, 82414 [PO Box 696, 82414]; (p) (307) 587-5302; www.oldtrailtown.com; (c) Park

Private for-profit/ 1967/ staff: 1(f); 5(p)

HISTORY MUSEUM

PROGRAMS: Exhibits; Facility Rental; Guided Tours; Living History

COLLECTIONS: [1880-1900] 27 original cabins with furnishings or artifacts. Museum of the Old West contains Native American artifacts, Mountain Man memorabilia, mounted animals, period clothing, and furnishings.

HOURS: Mid May-Oct Daily 8-8

ADMISSION: $5

9301
Park County Historical Society Archives
1002 Sheridan Ave, 82414; (p) (307) 527-8530; (f) (307) 527-8515; (c) Park

County/ 1985/ Park County Museum Board/ staff: 2(p); 5(v)/ members: 135

HISTORICAL SOCIETY; RESEARCH CENTER: Preserves and presents county history.

PROGRAMS: Annual Meeting; Exhibits; Guided Tours; Interpretation; Lectures; Research Library/Archives; School-Based Curriculum

COLLECTIONS: [1900-1950] Manuscripts, photographs, documents, newspapers, periodicals, maps, oral histories, books, and county history artifacts.

HOURS: Yr M-F

ADMISSION: No charge

9302
Plains Indian Museum, Buffalo Bill Historical Center
720 Sheridan Ave, 82414; (p) (307) 587-4771; (f) (307) 578-4076; www.bbhc.org; (c) Park

Private non-profit/ 1917/ staff: 70(f); 45(p); 200(v)/ members: 4200/publication: *Powerful Images*

ART MUSEUM; HISTORY MUSEUM: Documents the cultures, histories and artistry of Native people of the Great Plains from their buffalo hunting past to the present.

PROGRAMS: Community Outreach; Concerts; Exhibits; Facility Rental; Family Programs; Film/Video; Guided Tours; Interpretation; Lectures; Publication; Research Library/Archives; School-Based Curriculum

COLLECTIONS: [1830-present] Art and ethnology objects, primarily representative of Northern Plains cultures; some items from Central and Southern Plains, Northwest Coast, Southwest, Eastern Woodlands and the Plateau. Limited archaeological artifacts.

DIAMONDVILLE

9303
Lincoln County Historical Society
400 Pine Ave, 83116 [PO Box 330, 83116-0330]; (c) Lincoln

County; Private non-profit/ 1968/ staff: 15(v)/ members: 35

GARDEN; HISTORIC PRESERVATION AGENCY; HISTORIC SITE; HISTORICAL SOCIETY; HISTORY MUSEUM; HOUSE MUSEUM; LIVING HISTORY/OUTDOOR MUSEUM: Preserves county history, buildings, and trails. Monthly treks to historic sites are taken during summer months.

PROGRAMS: Annual Meeting; Community Outreach; Elder's Programs; Exhibits; Family Programs; Festivals; Garden Tours; Guided Tours; Interpretation; Lectures; Living History; Publication; Reenactments; Research Library/Archives; School-Based Curriculum

9304
Stolen Bell Museum
22 Hwy 30/189, 83116 [PO Box 281, 83116];

(p) (307) 877-6676; (f) (307) 877-6709; (c) Lincoln

City/ 1906/ Town of Diamondville/ staff: 1(f)

HISTORY MUSEUM: Maintains museum located in a former firehouse.

COLLECTIONS: [20th c] Local history artifacts.

HOURS: May-Oct M-F

DOUGLAS

9305
Wyoming Pioneer Memorial Museum
400 W Center St, 82633 [PO Box 911, 82633]; (p) (307) 358-9288; (f) (307) 358-9293; aeklan@state.wy.us; commerce.state.wy.us/sphs/index.htm; (c) Converse

State/ 1956/ WY Dept of State Parks and Cultural Resources/ staff: 2(f); 1(p); 1(v)

HISTORY MUSEUM

PROGRAMS: Exhibits; Family Programs

COLLECTIONS: [Mid 19th-early 20th c] Memorabilia related to pioneer westward expansion, 1886 schoolhouse, original museum, and log cabin built in 1925.

HOURS: Yr M-F 8-5

ADMISSION: No charge

DUBOIS

9306
National Bighorn Sheep Interpretive Center
907 W Ramshorn, 82513 [PO Box 1435, 82513]; (p) (307) 455-3429, (888) 209-2795; (f) (307) 455-2567; info@bighorn.org; www.bighorn.org; (c) Fremont

Private non-profit/ 1993/ National Bighorn Sheep Interpretive Assn/ staff: 1(f); 5(p); 6(v)/ members: 300

NATURAL HISTORY MUSEUM: Promotes the story of wild sheep of the world and of North America, focusing on the Rocky Mountain Bighorn Sheep on nearby Whiskey Mountain through exhibits, tours, and programs.

PROGRAMS: Annual Meeting; Community Outreach; Exhibits; Family Programs; Guided Tours

COLLECTIONS: [20th c] Mounted specimens of wild sheep and animals that share their environment. Photos and art of bighorn sheep.

HOURS: Sept-mid Nov Daily 9-5

9307
Wind River Historical Center
909 W Ramshorn, 82513 [PO Box 896, 82513]; (p) (307) 455-2284; (f) (307) 455-2784; wrh@wyoming.com; (c) Fremont

County/ 1976/ Fremont County/ staff: 2(f); 2(p); 3(v)

HISTORY MUSEUM; RESEARCH CENTER: Presents archaeological artifacts from sheep-eater Indians, the Mountain Shoshone, and their high-altitude culture. Preserves items from the early timber industry, "tie hacks" and river drives, early cattle and dude ranching, along with geology of the Wind Rivers and Absorakas.

PROGRAMS: Annual Meeting; Elder's Programs; Exhibits; Festivals; Interpretation; Lectures; Research Library/Archives

COLLECTIONS: [1870s-1945] Geology room, archaeology of the Mountain Shoshone, Sheep Eater Indians, Wind River Tie-Hack Gallery, town's original schoolhouse, saddle shop, homestead, bunk house, and renovated resort lodge.

HOURS: June-Sept M-Su 9-5

ADMISSION: $1, Children $0.50

ENCAMPMENT

9308
Grand Encampment Museum, Inc.
[PO Box 43, 82325]; (p) (307) 327-5308, (307) 327-5558; www.trib.com/ENCAMPMENT/GEMuseum.html; (c) Carbon

Private non-profit/ 1966/ Board of Directors/ staff: 4(p); 50(v)/ members: 250

HISTORY MUSEUM; LIVING HISTORY/OUTDOOR MUSEUM: Interprets area history in the Upper Platte Valley between Snowy and Sierra Madre Ranges of the Rocky Mountains.

PROGRAMS: Annual Meeting; Exhibits; Interpretation; Living History

COLLECTIONS: [1875-1950] Mining, logging, and ranching exhibits; US Forest Service memorabilia.

HOURS: May-Sept M-Sa 10-5, Su 1-5

ADMISSION: Donations accepted

FORT BRIDGER

9309
Fort Bridger State Historic Site
37000 Business Loop I-80, 82933 [PO Box 35, 82933-0035]; (p) (307) 782-3842; (f) (307) 782-7181; lnewma@state.wy.us; www.fortbridger.com; (c) Uinta

State/ 1933/ State Parks and Historic Sites/ staff: 4(f); 10(p); 35(v)/ members: 40

HISTORIC SITE; STATE PARK: Collects, preserves, and interprets the history of WY and Fort Bridger from 1820 to 1920.

PROGRAMS: Exhibits; Festivals; Guided Tours; Interpretation; Lectures; Living History

COLLECTIONS: [1843-1890] State history artifacts from Native Americans, Overland Pioneers, and the military.

HOURS: May-Sept Daily 9-5; Apr, Oct Sa-Su 9-4:30

FORT WASHAKIE

9310
Shoshone Cultural Center
31 First St, 82514 [PO Box 1008, 82514]; (p) (307) 332-9106; (f) (307) 332-3055; (c) Fremont

Tribal/ 1988/ Shoshone Tribal Government/ staff: 4(f)

CULTURAL CENTER: Preserves and perpetuates the rich tribal heritage and culture of the Eastern Shoshone Tribe.

PROGRAMS: Exhibits; Guided Tours; Reenactments

COLLECTIONS: [1850s] Shoshone tribal history from the reservation treaty establishment, emphasizing tribal art, historic tribal individuals, historic research for Shoshone prehistory and contemporary times.

HOURS: Yr M-F 9-4

ADMISSION: Donations accepted

GILLETTE

9311
Campbell County Historical Society
[PO Box 976, 82717]; (p) (307) 682-9551; (c) Campbell

Private non-profit/ 1954/ members: 9/publication: *The Way It Was*

GENEALOGICAL SOCIETY; HISTORICAL SOCIETY: Organized to preserve Campbell County History.

PROGRAMS: Annual Meeting; Exhibits; Publication; Research Library/Archives

HOURS: Meet 2nd Sa

9312
Campbell County Rockpile Museum
900 W 2nd St, 82716; (p) (307) 682-5723; (f) (307) 686-8528; Rockpile@vcm.com; (c) Campbell

County/ 1974/ Campbell County/ staff: 3(f); 3(p); 40(v)

HISTORY MUSEUM: Promotes the cultural history of Campbell County.

PROGRAMS: Annual Meeting; Community Outreach; Exhibits; Festivals; Guided Tours; Lectures; Research Library/Archives

COLLECTIONS: [1860-1960] Collections focus on Western history: firearms, harnesses, and saddles; Agricultural: plows, harrows; Photographs of local history; Social history artifacts; Transportation: horse-drawn, autos.

HOURS: Yr Sept-May M-Sa 9-5; June-Aug Daily M-Sa

GLENDO

9313
Glendo Historical Museum
204 S Yellowstone, 82213; (p) (307) 735-4242; (f) (307) 735-4422; (c) Platte

Joint/ 1967/ City of Glendo; Museum Board/ staff: 2(v)

HISTORY MUSEUM

PROGRAMS: Community Outreach; Exhibits; Research Library/Archives

COLLECTIONS: [Prehistory-mid 20th c] Native American artifacts, fossils, local pioneer antiques, rocks, local history, and photographs.

HOURS: Yr M-F

GREEN RIVER

9314
Sweetwater County Historical Museum
3 E Flaming Gorge Way, 82935; (p) (307) 872-6435; (f) (307) 872-3234; swchm@sweetwater.net; www.sweetwatermuseum.org; (c) Sweetwater

County/ 1967/ Sweetwater County/ staff: 4(f); 10(v)

HISTORY MUSEUM: Preserves and presents county history.

PROGRAMS: Community Outreach; Exhibits; Family Programs; Guided Tours; Research Library/Archives; School-Based Curriculum

COLLECTIONS: [1820s-present] Items on Native Americans, fur trade, transportation, communication, scientific expeditions, cultural diversity, civic and economic development, material culture, military, law and order.

HOURS: Yr M-Sa

9315
Sweetwater County Historical Society
[PO Box 25, 82935]; (p) (307) 362-3138; (c) Sweetwater

Private non-profit/ 1956/ staff: 20(v)/ members: 68/publication: *Sweetwater Views*

Holds monthly meetings, one or more annual treks, and sponsors speakers and other activities promoting history. Offers scholarships.

GREYBULL

9316
Greybull Museum
325 Greybull Ave, 82426 [PO Box 348, 82426]; (p) (307) 765-2444; (c) Big Horn

City/ 1968/ City of Greybull/ staff: 4(p); 2(v)

HISTORY MUSEUM; NATURAL HISTORY MUSEUM: Presents exhibits on paleontology, archaeology, history, art, photography, and botany.

PROGRAMS: Exhibits; Facility Rental; Family Programs; Film/Video; Guided Tours; Interpretation; Lectures; Living History

COLLECTIONS: [Prehistory-20th c] Fossils, minerals, historical artifacts, and clothing.

HOURS: Yr M-F 1-5; June-Aug M-Sa 10-8

9317
Museum of Flight and Aerial Firefighting
South Big Horn County Airport, 82426 [PO Box 412, 82426]; (p) (307) 765-4322; (f) (307) 765-2535; flight@tctwest.net; www.tctwest.net/~flight; (c) Big Horn

Private non-profit/ 1987/ staff: 3(v)

AVIATION MUSEUM: Preserves an important part of aviation history. Educates people about the several types of aircraft and retardant systems that have evolved over the years into the aerial firefighting capabilities used today.

PROGRAMS: Guided Tours

COLLECTIONS: [20th c] Dozens of the last remaining examples of WW II's mighty bombers and transport aircraft.

HOURS: Spring-Summer Daily 8-5; Fall-Winter M-F 8-5

ADMISSION: $3, Children $1.50

GUERNSEY

9318
Guernsey State Park Museum
Guernsey State Park, 82214 [PO Box 429, 82214]; (p) (307) 836-2334, (307) 836-2900; (c) Platte

Federal; State/ 1939/ Bureau of Reclamation, WY Dept of Commerce/ staff: 2(p)

HISTORY MUSEUM; STATE PARK: Presents local history exhibits. Built in 1930s by the Civilian Conservation Corps.

PROGRAMS: Annual Meeting; Community Outreach; Exhibits; Family Programs; Film/Video; Interpretation; Research Library/Archives; School-Based Curriculum

COLLECTIONS: [19th-20th c] Original artwork and text on local history.

HOURS: May-Oct Daily 10-6

ADMISSION: No charge

HANNA

9319
Hanna-Basin Historical Society
300 Front St, 82327 [PO Box 252, 82327]; (c) Carbon

Private non-profit/ 1982/ Board of Directors/ staff: 4(p); 7(v)/ members: 7

HISTORIC SITE; HISTORICAL SOCIETY; HISTORY MUSEUM: Preserves local history.

PROGRAMS: Annual Meeting; Exhibits; Family Programs; Lectures

COLLECTIONS: [Late 19th-early 20th c] Photographs, manuscripts, newspapers and artifacts related to coal mining and life in the coal camps.

HOURS: Yr F 1-5; May-Sept F-Su 1-5

ADMISSION: No charge

JACKSON

9320
Jackson Hole Historical Society and Museum
105 Mercill Ave; 105 N Glenwood St, 83001 [PO Box 1005, 83001]; (p) (207) 733-9605; (f) (307) 739-9019; jhhsm@rmisp.com; (c) Teton

Private non-profit/ 1989/ Board of Directors/ staff: 3(f); 4(p); 80(v)/ members: 500/publication: *Jackson Hole, Crossroads of the Western Fur Trade, 1807-1840; David E. Jackson, Field Captain of the Rocky Mountain Fur Trade*

HISTORICAL SOCIETY; HISTORY MUSEUM; RESEARCH CENTER: Collects, interprets, and educates about the history of Jackson Hole and its environs.

PROGRAMS: Annual Meeting; Community Outreach; Exhibits; Family Programs; Festivals; Film/Video; Guided Tours; Interpretation; Lectures; Publication; Research Library/Archives; School-Based Curriculum

COLLECTIONS: [1900-1940] Native American material culture, fur trade, and settlement period history, including a document and photograph archive, artifacts and library of Western Americana.

HOURS: Society: Yr M-F 8-5; Museum: May-early Oct M-Sa 9:30-6, Su 10-5

ADMISSION: $3, Family $6, Student $1, Seniors $2; Group rates

KAYCEE

9321
Hoofprints of the Past Museum
344 Nolan Ave, 82639 [PO Box 114, 82639-0114]; (p) (307) 738-2381; (c) Johnson

Private non-profit/ 1990/ Board of Directors/ staff: 1(f); 2(p); 15(v)/ members: 125

HISTORIC PRESERVATION AGENCY; HISTORICAL SOCIETY; HISTORY MUSEUM; LIVING HISTORY/OUTDOOR MUSEUM: Collects, preserves, and interprets the history of southern Johnson County.

PROGRAMS: Annual Meeting; Community Outreach; Exhibits; Guided Tours; Research Library/Archives; School-Based Curriculum

COLLECTIONS: [1860-present] Artifacts, photographs, books, and oral histories.

HOURS: May-Oct Daily 9-5

ADMISSION: No charge

KEMMERER

9322
Fossil Butte National Monument
15 miles W of Kemmerer on Hwy 30, 83101 [PO Box 592, 83101]; (p) (307) 877-4455; (f) (307) 877-4457; fobu_administration@nps.gov; www.nps.gov/fobu; (c) Lincoln

Federal/ 1972/ National Park Service/ staff: 2(f); 6(p); 6(v)

NATIONAL PARK: Preserves a small portion of an Eocene lake. Visitor center displays and interprets fossils and the history of fossil collecting in the area.

PROGRAMS: Exhibits; Film/Video; Guided Tours; Interpretation; Lectures; Research Library/Archives

COLLECTIONS: [1860s-present] Specimens of fossil fish, flora and fauna; photo history of Fossil Butte since its inception; historical photos and Native American artifacts.

HOURS: Spring-Summer Daily 8-7; Fall-Winter Daily 8-4:30

9323
Fossil County Futures, Inc.
400 Pine Ave, 83101 [PO Box 854, 83101]; (p) (307) 877-6551; (f) (307) 877-6552; museum@hamsfork.net; (c) Lincoln

Private non-profit/ 1989/ staff: 2(f); 2(p); 15(v)

HISTORY MUSEUM; RESEARCH CENTER: Collects, preserves, researches, exhibits, and interprets materials related to the natural and cultural history of Southwest WY for the education and enjoyment of the public.

PROGRAMS: Annual Meeting; Concerts; Exhibits; Facility Rental; Family Programs; Festivals; Guided Tours; Research Library/Archives; Theatre

COLLECTIONS: [1897-1950] Artifacts related to the natural and cultural history of Southwest WY.

HOURS: Spring-Summer M-Sa 9-5; Fall-Winter M-Sa 10-4

ADMISSION: No charge

9324
J.C. Penney Homestead and Historical Foundation
107 JC Penney Dr, 83101 [722 JC Penney Dr, 83101]; (p) (307) 877-4501; (c) Lincoln

Private for-profit/ J.C. Penney Company/ staff: 5(p)

CORPORATE ARCHIVES/MUSEUM; HISTORIC SITE; HISTORY MUSEUM: The first store and home of J.C. Penney.

PROGRAMS: Guided Tours

COLLECTIONS: [1902-1930] House has period furniture with an original crib and christening gown used by J.C. Penney's children.

HOURS: May-Sept M-Sa 9-6, Su 1-6

ADMISSION: No charge

LANDER

9325
Fremont County Historical Society
[PO Box 167, 82520]; (p) (307) 332-5815; (c) Fremont

State/ 1953/ WY State Historical Society/ staff: 4(v)/ members: 100

HISTORICAL SOCIETY: Holds monthly meetings, one or two annual treks to historic sites and annual picnic. Participates in State awards nominations and History Day activities for children.

PROGRAMS: Guided Tours; Lectures

LARAMIE

9326
Albany County Historical Society
802 University Ave, 82072; (p) (307) 742-4906; (c) Albany

State/ 1954/ WY State Historical Society/ members: 80

HISTORICAL SOCIETY: Sponsors monthly meetings that encourage the study and discussion of topics in local and state history.

PROGRAMS: Lectures

ADMISSION: No charge

9327
Laramie Plains Museum
603 Ivinson, 82070; (p) (307) 742-4448; (c) Albany

Private non-profit/ 1973/ Board of Directors/ staff: 6(p); 100(v)/ members: 200

HOUSE MUSEUM: Located in a restored 1892 mansion with Victorian furnishings and artifacts that reflect local heritage.

PROGRAMS: Annual Meeting; Exhibits; Facility Rental; Guided Tours; Interpretation; Research Library/Archives; School-Based Curriculum

COLLECTIONS: [1866-1958] Photographs, textiles, decorative arts, books, furniture, buggies, sheep wagon, and fire vehicles.

9328
University of Wyoming American Heritage Center
Centennial Complex, 82071 [PO Box 3924, 82071]; (p) (307) 766-4114; (f) (307) 766-5511; ahcref@uwyo.edu; www.uwyo.edu/ahc; (c) Albany

State/ 1945/ Univ of WY/ staff: 24(f); 15(p); 5(v)

RESEARCH CENTER: Manuscript repository housing papers and records of individuals and organizations of the late 19th-20th c.

PROGRAMS: Exhibits; Lectures; Research Library/Archives

COLLECTIONS: [19th-20th c] Materials and artifacts on WY and western history, transportation, mining and petroleum history, performing arts, conservation and water resources, politics, and world affairs.

9329
Wyoming Territorial Prison Corporation
975 Snowy Range Rd, 82070; (p) (307) 745-3733; (f) (307) 745-8620; prison@lariat.org; www.wyoprisonpark.org; (c) Albany

Private non-profit/ 1986/ 1989/ staff: 5(f); 4(p); 100(v)/ members: 700

HISTORIC SITE: Preserves the Wyoming Territorial Prison, including the National U.S. Marshals Museum and many western historical events, activities, themes, sights, and entertainment.

PROGRAMS: Annual Meeting; Exhibits; Facility Rental; Family Programs; Festivals; Guided Tours; Interpretation; Lectures; Living History; Theatre

COLLECTIONS: [19th-20th c] Artifacts for the Prison and Marshals Museum, "Ranchland" and other western history cultures.

HOURS: May-Sept Daily 9-6

ADMISSION: Varies

LUSK

9330
Stagecoach Museum
322 S Main, 82225 [PO Box 367, 82225]; (p) (307) 334-2950; (f) (307) 334-2950; luskwy@coffey.com; www.luskwy.com; (c) Niobrara

Private non-profit/ 1970/ staff: 1(p); 1(v)/ members: 20

HISTORICAL SOCIETY: Serve as a tribute to early pioneers and promotes local history.

PROGRAMS: Annual Meeting; Exhibits; Guided Tours; Research Library/Archives; School-Based Curriculum

COLLECTIONS: [19th c] Pioneer furniture, old-time post office, store and transportation building with buggies and wagons.

HOURS: Apr-Aug M-F 10-4; Sept-Oct M-F by appt

ADMISSION: $2

MEETEETSE

9331
Meeteetse Museums and Archives, Inc.
1033 Park Ave, 82433 [PO Box 53, 82433]; (p) (307) 868-2423; (c) Park

County/ Park County

HISTORY MUSEUM; LIBRARY AND/OR ARCHIVES; RESEARCH CENTER: Focuses on local history, including ghost towns (Kirwin) and the Pitchfork Ranch.

PROGRAMS: Annual Meeting; Community Outreach; Exhibits; Guided Tours; Interpretation; Lectures; Research Library/Archives; School-Based Curriculum

COLLECTIONS: [1896-present] Charles Belden photographs, clothing, artifacts from local settlers, ranchers, and ranches.

HOURS: Bank Museum and Archives Jan-Apr M-T, Th 9-5; May-Sept M-F 9-5; Oct-Dec M-Th 9-5; Hall Museum mid May-Sept M-Sa 10-4, Su 1-4

ADMISSION: Donations accepted

MIDWEST

9332
Salt Creek Oil Museum
53 1/2 Peak St, 82643 [PO Box 253, 82643]; (p) (307) 437-6633, (307) 437-6513; (c) Natrona

Private non-profit/ 1980/ staff: 1(f); 2(v)/publication: *Salt Creek Oil Museum*

HISTORY MUSEUM: First welded pipeline (1922), first electrified oil field and first night-lighted football field (both 1924).

PROGRAMS: Community Outreach; Exhibits; Film/Video; Living History; Publication

COLLECTIONS: [1889-present] Oil field tools, bottles, 1920s doctor's office and beauty shop, 1940s barber shop, school desks, wheelchairs, miniature derrick, old cash register, books, and pictures.

HOURS: Yr M-F

MOORCROFT

9333
Texas Trail Museum
200 S Bighorn Ave, 82721 [PO Box 9300, 82721]; (p) (307) 756-9300; (c) Crook

Private non-profit/ 1989/ staff: 2(p)

HISTORICAL SOCIETY; HISTORY MUSEUM: Maintains community history.

PROGRAMS: Annual Meeting; Community Outreach; Elder's Programs; Exhibits; Guided Tours; Research Library/Archives

COLLECTIONS: [20th c]

HOURS: June-Aug M-F 10-4

ADMISSION: Donations accepted

NEWCASTLE

9334
Weston County Museum District, Anna Miller Museum and Upton's Red-Onion Museum
401 Delaware, 82701 [PO Box 698, 82701]; (p) (307) 746-4188; (f) (307) 746-4629; annamm@trib.com; (c) Weston

1966/ Board of Directors/CEO/ staff: 2(f); 2(p); 100(v)

HISTORICAL SOCIETY: Preserves and displays historical items to present the history of Weston County and surrounding area.

PROGRAMS: Community Outreach; Exhibits; Family Programs; Lectures; Living History; Research Library/Archives

COLLECTIONS: [1890-present] Represents northeastern Wyoming and the surrounding Black Hills area through paleontology, Native American artifacts, National Guard Cavalry and the ghost town of Cambria.

HOURS: Yr M-F 9-5; June-Aug Sa 9-12

ADMISSION: No charge

PINE BLUFFS

9335
Texas Trail Museum
3rd & Market, 82082 [PO Box 545, 82082]; (p) (307) 245-3713; (c) Laramie

Private non-profit/ 1989/ Museum Board/ members: 10

HISTORICAL SOCIETY; HISTORY MUSEUM

PROGRAMS: Annual Meeting; Community Outreach; Elder's Programs; Exhibits; Guided Tours; Research Library/Archives

COLLECTIONS: [Early 20th c] Items on Native Americans, Texas Trail, farm implements and tools, clothing and books.

HOURS: June-Aug M-Sa 9-5

ADMISSION: No charge

PINEDALE

9336
Museum of the Mountain Man
700 E Hennick on Fremont Lake Rd, 82941 [PO Box 909, 82941]; (p) (307) 367-4101; (f) (307) 367-6768; museummtman@wyoming.com; www.museumofthemountainman.com; (c) Sublette

Private non-profit/ 1936/ Sublette County Historical Society/ staff: 2(f); 3(p); 200(v)/ members: 300

HISTORICAL SOCIETY; HISTORY MUSEUM: Provides an understanding of people and cultures throughout history, emphasizing the era of the Mountain Man.

PROGRAMS: Annual Meeting; Community Outreach; Exhibits; Family Programs; Festivals; Interpretation; Lectures; Living History; Reenactments; Research Library/Archives

COLLECTIONS: [Early 19th c] Exhibits on fur trade, western exploration, Plains Indians and early settlement history of western Wyoming.

HOURS: May-Sept Daily 10-6; Oct-Apr by appt

ADMISSION: $4, Children $2, Seniors $3

POWELL

9337
Homesteader Museum
133 S Cark, 82435 [PO Box 54, 82435]; (p) (307) 754-9481; (c) Park

Private non-profit/ 1968/ staff: 1(f); 3(p); 5(v)/ members: 150

HISTORIC SITE; HISTORY MUSEUM; LIVING HISTORY/OUTDOOR MUSEUM: Collects and preserves local history. Celebrates regional heritage of the people and their way of life.

PROGRAMS: Exhibits; Family Programs; Guided Tours; Lectures; Research Library/ Archives; School-Based Curriculum

COLLECTIONS: [1909-1950s] Farm equipment, tools, beauty and barber shop equipment, school room, geological displays, veterans memorabilia, caboose, vintage clothing, photos, medical items, history of irrigation, and homesteader families.

HOURS: May-Sept T-F 11-5, Sa 11-3; Winter T, Th 10-5

ADMISSION: No charge

RAWLINS

9338
Carbon County Historical Society
500 W Walnut, 82301 [PO Box 639, 82301-0172]; (p) (307) 324-7931; (c) Carbon

County/ members: 37

HISTORICAL SOCIETY; HISTORY MUSEUM; RESEARCH CENTER: Brings together people interested in local history to share knowledge of the area and preserve landmarks.

PROGRAMS: Annual Meeting; Exhibits; Facility Rental; Guided Tours; Lectures; Living History; Publication; Research

9339
Carbon County Museum
904 W Walnut, 82301 [PO Box 52, 82301-0052]; (p) (307) 328-2740; (c) Carbon

County/ 1940/ Carbon County Museum Board/ staff: 5(p)

HISTORY MUSEUM: Displays local history artifacts.

PROGRAMS: Exhibits; Guided Tours; Research Library/Archives

COLLECTIONS: [Late 19th c-present] Pictures and period pieces.

HOURS: May-Sept M-F 10-12/1-5; Oct-Apr M, W, Sa 1-5

ADMISSION: Donations accepted

RIVERTON

9340
Riverton Museum
700 E Park Ave, 82501; (p) (307) 856-2665; (f) (307) 856-2665; ljost@wyoming.com; (c) Fremont

County/ 1969/ Fremont County Museums Board/Riverton Museum Association/ staff: 1(f); 8(v)/ members: 95

HISTORY MUSEUM: Collects, promotes, preserves, and interprets local history.

PROGRAMS: Community Outreach; Exhibits; Festivals; Guided Tours; Interpretation; Lectures; Research Library/Archives

COLLECTIONS: [20th c] Artifacts relevant to the commercial, agricultural, and mining development of central WY. Library has related primary and secondary sources, including photographs.

HOURS: Yr T-Sa

ROCK SPRINGS

9341
Rock Springs Historical Museum
201 B St, 82901 [212 D St, 82901]; (p) (307) 362-3138; (f) (307) 352-1516; (c) Sweetwater

City/ 1988/ City of Rock Springs/ staff: 2(f); 1(p); 30(v)

HISTORIC SITE; HISTORY MUSEUM: Focuses on the history of the local community and its mineral-based economy which was driven by boom and bust cycles.

PROGRAMS: Exhibits; Festivals; Guided Tours; Interpretation; Lectures; Research Library/Archives

COLLECTIONS: [1868-present] Coal mining implements, blue prints, maps of community and structures, photographs, general artifacts, oral histories, archives, and 1895 City Hall.

HOURS: Yr Sept-May W-Sa

SARATOGA

9342
Saratoga Historical and Cultural Association
104 Constitution Ave, 82331 [PO Box 1131, 82331]; (p) (307) 326-5511; members.xoom.com/kaikin/welcome; (c) Carbon

Private non-profit/ 1980/ staff: 1(p); 20(v)/ members: 200/publication: *Windows in Time; Casper Site: An Album of Family Histories*

HISTORICAL SOCIETY: Collects, preserves, and interprets local history for the education and enjoyment of present and future generations.

PROGRAMS: Annual Meeting; Community Outreach; Concerts; Publication; Research Library/Archives

COLLECTIONS: [1890s-1930s] Photographs, books, paintings by local artists, maps, news items, family manuscripts, sheet music, personal artifacts of loggers, ranchers and women; geology specimens, archaeology displays, and local business items.

HOURS: May-Sept Daily 1-5

ADMISSION: $2, Family $5, Children $1; Members/Seniors free

SAVERY

9343
Little Snake River Museum
[PO Box 13, 82332]; (p) (307) 383-7262; (c) Carbon

1972/ Board of Directors/ staff: 1(p); 4(v)

HISTORY MUSEUM; HOUSE MUSEUM: Preserves and presents a collection of buildings and exhibits from the 1870s.

PROGRAMS: Exhibits; Facility Rental; Guided Tours; Research Library/Archives

COLLECTIONS: [1870s] Log cabin of Mountain Man Jim Baker, one-room schoolhouse, two-story log house and 1890s log cabin.

HOURS: May-Oct W-Su 11-5

ADMISSION: Donations accepted

SHERIDAN

9344
King's Saddlery Museum
184 N Main, 82801; (p) (800) 443-8919; (f) (307) 672-5235; (c) Sheridan

Private non-profit/ 1989/ staff: 1(f); 2(p)

HISTORICAL SOCIETY: Preserves and presents a history of the West with saddles, guns, Native American artifacts, and beadwork.

PROGRAMS: Elder's Programs; Exhibits; Facility Rental; Guided Tours; Lectures; Living History; School-Based Curriculum

COLLECTIONS: [1860s-present] Artifacts on cowboy and Native American cultures.

HOURS: Yr M-Sa 8-5

ADMISSION: No charge

9345
Sheridan Heritage Center, Inc.
856 Broadway, 82801 [PO Box 6393, 82801]; (p) (307) 674-5440, (307) 674-4674; sheridaninn@cyberhighway.net; www.sheridaninn.com; (c) Sheridan

Private non-profit/ 1990/ staff: 1(p); 20(v)

HISTORIC PRESERVATION AGENCY; HISTORIC SITE; HISTORY MUSEUM; HOUSE MUSEUM; LIVING HISTORY/OUTDOOR MUSEUM: Operates, maintains, preserves, and restores the historic Sheridan Inn (a National Historic Landmark) and Ripley's Believe It or Not "House of 69 Gables."

PROGRAMS: Annual Meeting; Community Outreach; Elder's Programs; Exhibits; Facility Rental; Family Programs; Festivals; Guided Tours; Interpretation; Lectures; Living History; School-Based Curriculum; Theatre

COLLECTIONS: [1893-1930s] Historic Landmark Building, Buffalo Bill Bar, furniture, photographs, native animals, art, period artifacts and historical information on Buffalo Bill.

HOURS: Yr T-Sa 10-9:30

ADMISSION: Entry is free

9346
Trail End State Historic Site
400 Clarendon Ave, 82801; (p) (307) 674-4589; (f) (307) 672-1720; cgeorg@missc.state.wy.us; www.trailend.org; (c) Sheridan

State/ 1982/ Division of State Parks and Historic Sites/ staff: 2(f); 3(p); 16(v)/ members: 74/publication: *One Cowboy's Dream*

HOUSE MUSEUM: Preserves and interprets the historic home of former WY governor and US senator John B. Kendrick, his family, and his ranching operations from 1913-1933.

PROGRAMS: Community Outreach; Exhibits; Family Programs; Guided Tours; Interpretation; Publication; School-Based Curriculum; Theatre

COLLECTIONS: [1913-1933] The 33 room Flemish Revival mansion, built in 1913, houses original furnishings, family possessions, library of western Americana, and archives of the Kendrick Cattle Company.

HOURS: Apr-May, Sept-mid Dec Daily 1-4; June-Aug Daily 9-6

ADMISSION: $2; Under 18 free

9347
Wyoming Room, Sheridan County Fulmer Public Library
335 W Alger St, 82801; (p) (307) 674-8585; sherwyo@will.state.wy.us; (c) Sheridan

County/ 1986/ Board of Trustees/ staff: 2(f); 1(p); 7(v)

LIBRARY AND/OR ARCHIVES

HOURS: Yr M-T 9-9, F-Sa 9-5

ADMISSION: No charge

SINCLAIR

9348
Fort Fred Steele State Historic Site
9 miles E on I-80, 82334 [Seminoc Dam Rt, Box 30, 82334-9801]; (p) (307) 320-3013; (f) (307) 320-3013; dbrown@miss.state.wy.us; commence.state.wy.us/sphs/index.htm; (c) Carbon

State/ 1972/ WY State Parks and Historic Sites/ staff: 1(p)

HISTORIC SITE; STATE PARK: Provides a quality historical experience for the public.

PROGRAMS: Interpretation

COLLECTIONS: [1868-1886]

HOURS: May-mid Sept Daily 9-7

ADMISSION: No charge

9349
Parco/Sinclair Museum
300 Lincoln Ave, 82334 [PO Box 247, 82334]; (p) (307) 324-3058; (f) (307) 324-5520; (c) Carbon

City/ 1990/ Sinclair Town Council; Museum Board of Directors/publication: *Town of Parco/Sinclair*

HISTORIC SITE; HISTORY MUSEUM: Repository for historical items from the town and refinery. Listed on the National Register of Historic Places.

PROGRAMS: Elder's Programs; Exhibits; Family Programs; Festivals; Publication

COLLECTIONS: [1922-present] Items from local families and residents; listing of family names, clubs, organizations, businesses, activities and town officials.

HOURS: Yr M-F 9-12/1-4:30

SOUTH PASS CITY

9350
South Pass City State Historic Site
125 S Pass Main, 82520; (p) (307) 332-3684; (f) (307) 332-3688; (c) Fremont

State/ 1967/ WY State Parks and Historic Sites/ staff: 3(f); 3(p); 20(v)/ members: 250

HISTORIC SITE; STATE PARK: Historic gold mining town begun in 1867. Currently, there are 23 historic buildings, including saloons, hotel, store, houses, livery, jail, butcher shop, and school.

PROGRAMS: Exhibits; Festivals; Interpretation; Lectures; Research Library/Archives; School-Based Curriculum

COLLECTIONS: [1895-1905] Historic cultural and mining related items; original furniture on exhibit in hotel; items from 1870s and 1940s.

TEN SLEEP

9351
Ten Sleep Pioneer Museum
200 2nd St, 82442 [PO Box 65, 82442]; (p) (307) 366-2759; (c) Washakie

City/ 1971/ Town of Ten Sleep/ staff: 1(f); 8(v)

HISTORY MUSEUM: Collects and preserves tools, machinery, household furnishings, and clothing used by early settlers of the area.

PROGRAMS: Exhibits; Guided Tours

COLLECTIONS: [Prehistory-1885] Photographs of Native American rock art in local caves and articles used by early white settlers.

HOURS: May-Oct Daily 9:30-4

ADMISSION: Donations accepted

TORRINGTON

9352
Goshen County Chapter of the Wyoming State Historical Society
2959 Main, 82240-1931; (p) (307) 532-3776; svander@scottsbluff.net; (c) Goshen

Private non-profit/ 1951/ members: 55

Supports the state chapter's activities, awards, treks and research. Holds monthly meetings, sends delegates to state conventions and representatives to board meetings. Provides scholarships to college history students.

9353
Homesteaders Museum
Old UP Depot, 495 Main St, 82240 [PO Box 250, 82240]; (p) (307) 532-5612; (f) (307) 532-3537; legweak@netscape.net; (c) Goshen

City/ 1975/ Town of Torrington/ staff: 1(f); 1(p); 8(v)

HISTORY MUSEUM

PROGRAMS: Community Outreach; Exhibits; Family Programs; Interpretation

COLLECTIONS: [1882-1945] Period artifacts, rock-mineral collection, indoor and outdoor displays.

HOURS: Spring-Summer M-Sa 9:30-4; Su 1-4; Fall-Winter M-F 9:30-4

ADMISSION: No charge

WORLAND

9354
Washakie Museum
1115 Obie Sue, 82401; (p) (307) 347-4102; (f) (307) 347-4865; wmuseum@trib.com; w3.trib.com/~museum; (c) Washakie

Private non-profit/ 1986/ staff: 1(f); 9(p); 225(v)/ members: 347

ART MUSEUM; HISTORY MUSEUM: Presents Paleo-Indian exhibits, fossils, rocks, Sheepeater "Shoshone Lodge," rock shelter replica, wagons, sod house, Native American items, and photographs. Offers changing art, history, and earth science exhibits, plus music, drama, and other events.

PROGRAMS: Annual Meeting; Concerts; Exhibits; Facility Rental; Family Programs; Festivals; Guided Tours; Interpretation; Lectures; Research Library/Archives; Theatre

COLLECTIONS: [Prehistory-20th c] Plains Indian artifacts, rocks and fossils. Historical items, local and regional art from Worland, Washakie County, Big Horn Basin, Wyoming, and the West.

HOURS: Sept-Dec, Feb-June 3 M-Sa 10-4; June 4-Sept 4 M-Sa 9-6, Su 12-6

ADMISSION: No charge

WRIGHT

9355
Wright Centennial Museum
104 Ranch Ct, 82732 [PO Box 354, 82732-0354]; (c) Campbell

Private non-profit/ 1990/ staff: 4(p); 6(v)/ members: 8

HISTORY MUSEUM: Collects, preserves, and educates on the history of southern Campbell County.

PROGRAMS: Exhibits; Family Programs; School-Based Curriculum

COLLECTIONS: [Late 19th c-present] Artifacts from early homestead era, Native Americans, post office, oil and coal industry, and both W W I and II, buffalo hide coat, and dinosaur bones.

HOURS: Late May-mid Sept

PART II

Quick Reference Guides

National Archives and Records Administration (NARA) Offices

For current information please visit the NARA website at
www.nara.gov

NATIONAL ARCHIVES AND RECORDS ADMINISTRATION

National Archives Building
700 Pennsylvania Ave, NW
Washington, DC 20408-0001
(202) 501-5400
Web: www.nara.gov/

Research Hours: M, W 8:45-5; T, Th, F 8:45-9, Sa 8:45-4:45. Rotunda Hours: Yr Daily Winter: 10-5:30; Summer (Apr 1-Labor Day) 10-9

The National Archives Building is being renovated. The research rooms will remain open during the renovation. Before planing a visit, please check the web page for the latest information hours. The Rotunda will temporarily close during the renovation on July 5, 2001 and reopen in the Summer of 2003.

National Archives at College Park
Office of Regional Records Services
8601 Adelphi Rd
College Park, MD 20740-6001
(301) 713-7200
(800) 234-8861
Fax: (301) 713-7205
E-mail: see: www.nara.gov/nara/mail.html
Web: www.nara.gov/nara/dc/Archives2_directions.html

Research Hours: M, W 8:45-5; T, Th, F 8:45-9; Sa 8:45-4:45

Washington National Records Center
4205 Suitland Rd
Suitland, MD 20746-8001
(301) 457-7000
Fax: (301) 457-7117
E-mail: center@suitland.nara.gov
Web: www.nara.gov/records/wnrc.html

Facility hours: M-F 8-4:30

Research hours: M-F 8-4

Holdings: Records center holdings for Federal agency headquarters offices in the District of Columbia, Maryland, and Virginia; Federal agency field offices in Maryland, Virginia, and West Virginia; Federal courts in the District of Columbia; and U.S. Armed Forces worldwide.

Federal Register
Office Location:
800 North Capitol St, NW, Ste 700
Washington, DC 20001
Mailing Address:
Office of the Federal Register (NF)
National Archives and Records Administration
700 Pennsylvania Ave NW
Washington, DC 20408-0001
Email: fedreg.info@nara.gov
Web Site: www.nara.gov/fedreg/

Hours: M-F 8:45-5:15

PERSONNEL RECORDS CENTER

ST. LOUIS (TWO LOCATIONS):

NARA's National Personnel Records Center
Civilian Personnel Records
111 Winnebago St
St. Louis, MO 63118-4199
(314) 425-5722
Fax: (314) 538-5719
E-mail: center@cpr.nara.gov
Web: www.nara.gov/regional/cpr.html

Holdings: Civilian personnel records from Federal agencies nationwide; selected military dependent medical records.

NARA's National Personnel Records Center
Military Personnel Records
9700 Page Ave
St. Louis, MO 63132-5100
(314) 538-4247
Fax: (314) 538-4175
E-mail: center@stlouis.nara.gov
Web: www.nara.gov/regional/mpr.html

Holdings: Military personnel records, and military and retired military medical records from all services; selected dependent medical records, morning reports, rosters, and Philippine army and guerilla records.

REGIONAL RECORDS SERVICES FACILITIES

ALASKA

ANCHORAGE

NARA's Pacific Alaska Region
654 West Third Ave
Anchorage, AK 99501-2145
(907) 271-2443
Fax: (907) 271-2442
E-mail: archives@alaska.nara.gov
Web: www.nara.gov/regional/anchorag.html

Holdings: Archival holdings from Federal agencies and courts in Alaska. Microfilm holdings.

CALIFORNIA

LAGUNA NIGUEL

NARA's Pacific Region
24000 Avila Rd, First Floor-East Entrance
Laguna Niguel, CA 92677-3497
P. O. Box 6719
Laguna Niguel, CA 92607-6719
(949) 360-2641
Fax: (949) 360-2624
E-mail: archives@laguna.nara.gov
Web: www.nara.gov/regional/laguna.html

Holdings: Archival holdings from Federal agencies and courts in Arizona, southern California, and Clark County, Nevada. Call (949) 360-2641 for information. Records center holdings in the same states. Call (949) 360-2628 for information. Microfilm holdings. Call (949) 360-2641 for information.

SAN FRANCISCO (SAN BRUNO)

NARA's Pacific Region
1000 Commodore Dr
San Bruno, CA 94066-2350
(650) 876-9009
Fax: (650) 876-9233
E-mail: archives@sanbruno.nara.gov
Web: www.nara.gov/regional/sanfranc.html

Holdings: Archival holdings from Federal agencies and courts in northern California, Hawaii, Nevada (except Clark County), the Pacific Trust Territories, and American Samoa. Call (650) 876-9009 for information. Records center holdings from Federal agencies and courts in the same states and territories. Call (650) 876-9001 for information. Microfilm holdings. Call (650) 876-9009 for information.

COLORADO

DENVER

NARA's Rocky Mountain Region
Building 48, Denver Federal Center
West 6th Ave and Kipling St
Denver, CO 80225
P. O. Box 25307
Denver, Colorado 80225-0307
(303) 236-0804
Fax: (303) 236-9297
E-mail: archives@denver.nara.gov
Web: www.nara.gov/regional/denver.html

Holdings: Archival holdings from Federal agencies and courts in Colorado, Montana, New Mexico, North Dakota, South Dakota, Utah, and Wyoming. Call (303) 236-0817 for information. Records center holdings from Federal agencies and courts in the same states. Call (303) 236-0804 for information. Microfilm holdings. Call (303) 236-0817 for information.

GEORGIA

ATLANTA (EAST POINT)

NARA's Southeast Region
1557 St. Joseph Ave
East Point, GA 30344-2593
(404) 763-7474
Fax: (404) 763-7059
E-mail: center@atlanta.nara.gov
Web: www.nara.gov/regional/atlanta.html

Holdings: Archival holdings from Federal agencies and courts in Alabama, Florida, Georgia, Kentucky, Mississippi, North Carolina, South Carolina, and Tennessee. Call (404) 763-7383 for information. Records center holdings from Federal agencies and courts in the same states. Call (404) 763-7474 for information. Microfilm holdings. Call (404) 763-7477 for information.

ILLINOIS

CHICAGO

NARA's Great Lakes Region
7358 South Pulaski Rd
Chicago, IL 60629-5898
(773) 581-7816
Fax: (312) 353-1294
E-mail: archives@chicago.nara.gov
Web: www.nara.gov/regional/chicago.html

Holdings: Archival holdings from Federal agencies and courts in Illinois, Indiana, Michigan, Minnesota, Ohio, and Wisconsin. Records center holdings from Federal agencies in Illinois, Minnesota, and Wisconsin, and from Federal courts in Illinois, Indiana, Michigan, Minnesota, Ohio, and Wisconsin. Microfilm holdings.

MASSACHUSETTS

BOSTON (WALTHAM)

NARA's Northeast Region
380 Trapelo Rd
Waltham, MA 02452-6399
(781) 647-8104
Fax: (781) 647-8088
E-mail: archives@waltham.nara.gov
Web: www.nara.gov/regional/boston.html

Holdings: Archival holdings from Federal agencies and courts in Connecticut, Maine, Massachusetts, New Hampshire, Rhode Island, and Vermont. Call (781) 647-8100 for information. Records center holdings from Federal agencies and courts in the same states. Call (781) 647-8108 for information. Microfilm holdings. Call (781) 647-8100 for information.

PITTSFIELD

NARA's Northeast Region
10 Conte Dr
Pittsfield, MA 01201-8230
(413) 445-6885
Fax: (413) 445-7599
E-mail: archives@pittsfield.nara.gov
Web: www.nara.gov/regional/pittsfie.html

Holdings: Records center holdings from selected Federal agencies nationwide. Call (413) 445-6885, ext. 14 for information. Microfilm holdings. Call (413) 445-6885, ext. 24 for information.

MISSOURI

KANSAS CITY

NARA's Central Plains Region
2312 East Bannister Rd
Kansas City, MO 64131-3011
(816) 926-6272
Fax: (816) 926-6982
E-mail: archives@kansascity.nara.gov
Web: www.nara.gov/regional/kansas.html

Holdings: Archival holdings from Federal agencies and courts in Iowa, Kansas, Missouri and Nebraska. Records center holdings from the same states. Microfilm holdings.

LEE'S SUMMIT

NARA's Central Plains Region
200 Space Center Dr
Lee's Summit, MO 64064-1182
(816) 478-7079
Fax: (816) 478-7625
E-mail: center@kccave.nara.gov
Web: www.nara.gov/regional/leesumit.html

Holdings: Records center holdings from Federal agencies and courts in New Jersey, New York, Puerto Rico, and the U.S. Virgin Islands, and from most Department of Veterans Affairs and Immigration and Naturalization Service offices nationwide.

NEW YORK

NEW YORK CITY

NARA's Northeast Region
201 Varick St
New York, NY 10014-4811
(212) 337-1300
Fax: (212) 337-1306
E-mail: archives@newyork.nara.gov
Web: www.nara.gov/regional/newyork.html

Holdings: Archival holdings from Federal agencies and courts in New Jersey, New York, Puerto Rico, and the U.S. Virgin Islands. Microfilm holdings.

OHIO

DAYTON

NARA's Great Lakes Region
3150 Springboro Rd
Dayton, OH 45439-1883
(937) 225-2852
Fax: (937) 225-7236
E-mail: center@dayton.nara.gov
Web: www.nara.gov/regional/dayton.html

Holdings: Records center holdings from Federal agencies in Indiana, Michigan, and Ohio; Federal bankruptcy court records from Ohio since 1991/92; Defense Finance Accounting System records nationwide and from Germany and Korea; and Internal Revenue Service records from selected sites nationwide.

PENNSYLVANIA

PHILADELPHIA (CENTER CITY)

NARA's Mid Atlantic Region
900 Market St
Philadelphia, PA 19107-4292
(215) 597-3000
Fax: (215) 597-2303
E-mail: archives@philarch.nara.gov
Web: www.nara.gov/regional/philacc.html

Holdings: Archival holdings from Federal agencies and courts in Delaware, Maryland, Pennsylvania, Virginia, and West Virginia. Call (215) 597-9770 for information Microfilm holdings. Call (215) 597-9770 for information.

PHILADELPHIA (NORTHEAST)

NARA's Mid Atlantic Region
14700 Townsend Rd
Philadelphia, PA 19154-1096
(215) 671-9027
Fax: (215) 671-8001
E-mail: center@philfrc.nara.gov
Web: www.nara.gov/regional/philane.html

Holdings: Records center holdings from Federal agencies in Delaware and Pennsylvania and Federal courts in Delaware, Maryland, Pennsylvania, Virginia, and West Virginia. Call (215) 671-9027, ext. 105 for information.

TEXAS

FORT WORTH

NARA's Southwest Region
501 West Felix St, Building 1
Fort Worth, TX 76115-3405
P. O. Box 6216
Fort Worth, TX 76115-0216
(817) 334-5525
Fax: (817) 334-5621
E-mail: archives@ftworth.nara.gov
Web: www.nara.gov/regional/ftworth.html

Holdings: Archival holdings from Federal agencies and courts in Arkansas, Louisiana, Oklahoma, and Texas. Call (817) 334-5525 for information. Records center holdings from Federal agencies and courts in the same states. Call (817) 334-5515 for information. Microfilm holdings. Call (817) 334-5525 for information.

WASHINGTON

SEATTLE

NARA's Pacific Alaska Region
6125 Sand Point Way NE
Seattle, WA 98115-7999
(206) 526-6501
Fax: (206) 526-6575
E-mail: archives@seattle.nara.gov
Web: www.nara.gov/regional/seattle.html

Holdings: Archival holdings from Federal agencies and courts in Idaho, Oregon, and Washington (State). Records center holdings for Federal agencies and courts in the same states and Alaska. Microfilm holdings.

PRESIDENTIAL LIBRARIES

OFFICE OF PRESIDENTIAL LIBRARIES

National Archives at College Park
8601 Adelphi Rd
College Park, MD 20740-6001
(301) 713-6050
Fax: (301) 713-6045
Web: www.nara.gov/nara/president/address.html

LIBRARY GENERAL INFORMATION:

Library Research Room Hours: M-F 9-5 (closed all federal holidays). Grants are available to assist researchers studying Presidential Libraries holdings.

Museum Hours: Presidential Library museums are open every day except Thanksgiving, Christmas, and New Year's Day (the Johnson Library is only closed Christmas Day). See below for individual museum hours and fees. (**Note**: Fees are for museums, not libraries.)

GEORGE BUSH LIBRARY
1000 George Bush Dr West
College Station, TX 77845
(979) 260-9554
Fax: (979) 260-9557
Email: bush.library@nara.gov
Web: bushlibrary.tamu.edu
Hours: M-Sa 9:30-5, Su 12-5
Admission: $5; Student $4; Senior $3.50; Under 16 free

JIMMY CARTER LIBRARY
441 Freedom Parkway
Atlanta, GA 30307-1498
(404) 331-3942
Fax: (404) 730-2215
Email: carter.library@nara.gov
Web: www.jimmycarterlibrary.org/
Hours: M-Sa 9-4:45, Su 12-4:45
Admission: $5, Senior $4, Under 16 free

WILLIAM J. CLINTON PRESIDENTIAL MATERIALS PROJECT
1000 LaHarpe Boulevard
Little Rock, AR 72201
(501) 254-6866)
Fax: (501) 244-9764
Email: clinton.library@nara.gov
Web: www.clinton.nara.gov
Research sessions available by appt only.

DWIGHT D. EISENHOWER LIBRARY
200 SE 4th St
Abilene, KS 67410-2900
(785) 263-4751
Fax: (785) 263-4218
Email: eisenhower.library@nara.gov
Web: www.eisenhower.utexas.edu
Hours: Daily 9-5; Mem Day-Aug 15 8-6
Admission: $3, Senior $2.50, Under 16 free

GERALD R. FORD LIBRARY
1000 Beal Ave
Ann Arbor, MI 48109-2114
(734) 741-2218
Fax: (734) 741-2341
Email: ford.library@nara.gov
Web: www.ford.utexas.edu

GERALD R. FORD MUSEUM
303 Pearl St, NW
Grand Rapids, MI 49504-5353
(616) 451-9263
Fax: (616) 451-9570
Email: ford.museum@nara.gov
Web: www.ford.utexas.edu
Hours: Daily 9-5
Admission: $4, Senior $3, Under 16 free

HERBERT HOOVER LIBRARY
210 Parkside Dr
P.O. Box 488
West Branch, IA 52358-0488
(319) 643-5301
Fax: (319) 643-5825
Email: hoover.library@nara.gov
Web: www.hoover.nara.gov
Hours: Daily 9-5; July-Aug W 9-8
Admission: $2, Senior $1, Under 16 free

LYNDON B. JOHNSON LIBRARY
2313 Red River St
Austin, TX 78705-5702
(512) 916-5137
Fax: (512) 916-5171
Email: johnson.library@nara.gov
Web: www.lbjlib.utexas.edu/
Hours: Daily 9-5
Admission: Free

JOHN F. KENNEDY LIBRARY
Columbia Point
Boston, MA 02125-3398
PHONE: 617-929-4500
Fax: 617-929-4538
Email: kennedy.library@nara.gov
Web: www.jfklibrary.org
Hours: Daily 9-5
Admission: $8, Student/Senior $6, Youth $4, Under 12 free

NIXON PRESIDENTIAL MATERIALS STAFF
National Archives at College Park
8601 Adelphi Rd
College Park, MD 20740-6001
(301) 713-6950
Fax: (301) 713-6916
Email: nixon@nara.gov
Web: www.nara.gov/nixon/

RONALD REAGAN LIBRARY
40 Presidential Dr
Simi Valley, CA 93065-0600
(800) 410-8354
Fax: (805) 522-9621
Email: reagan.library@nara.gov
Web: www.reagan.utexas.edu
Hours: Daily 10-5
Admission: $5, Senior $3

FRANKLIN D. ROOSEVELT LIBRARY
4079 Albany Post Rd
Hyde Park, NY 12538-1999
(845) 229-8114
Fax: (845) 229-0872
Email: roosevelt.library@nara.gov
Web: www.fdrlibrary.marist.edu
Hours: Daily Nov-Mar 9-5; Apr-Oct 9-6
Admission: $10 (includes admission to Roosevelt Home)

HARRY S. TRUMAN LIBRARY
500 West U.S. Highway 24
Independence, MO 64050-1798
(816) 833-1400
Fax: (816) 833-4368
Email: truman.library@nara.gov
Web: www.trumanlibrary.org
Hours: M-S 9-5, Th 9-9, Su 12-5
Admission: $5, Senior $4.50, Children $3, Under 6 free

University Public History Programs

Compiled by David G. Vanderstel, Executive Director, National Council on Public History

For the most up to date information please contact individual history departments.
If your department is not listed here and should be, please send information to David G. Vanderstel at NCPH.

ARIZONA

Arizona State University
Public History Program
Department of History
Arizona State University
P.O. Box 872501
Tempe, AZ 85287-2501
Fax: (480) 965-0310
Web: www.asu.edu/clas/history

Directors: Noel J. Stowe, (480) 965-5775, noel.stowe@asu.edu; Beth E. Luey, (480) 965-5775, beth.luey@asu.edu; Jannelle Warren-Findley, (480) 965-5775, jannelle.warren-findley@asu.edu

Arizona State University's graduate program in public history was founded in 1980. About fifteen students are admitted each year. Students may enroll in either a M.A. or Ph.D. history program, with a concentration in public history. Approximately 300 students have graduated since the beginning of the program, with fifteen to twenty graduating annually. The program also offers on-campus workshops, mini-courses, and scholarships for off-campus workshops. Internship required.

Concentrations: Historic Preservation/Cultural Resource Management; Editing; Publishing; Historical Administration; Public Policy; Oral History; Local/Community History; Museum Studies; Business

Faculty: Beth E. Luey, M.A.; Noel J. Stowe, Ph.D.; Jannelle Warren-Findley, Ph.D. Faculty in history, public administration, anthropology, fine arts, geography, English, and other departments also participate in the program.

ARKANSAS

University of Arkansas at Little Rock
Graduate Program in History
History Department
University of Arkansas at Little Rock
2801 South University
Little Rock, AR 72204
Fax: (501) 569-3059
Web: www.ualr.edu/~history/pubhis.htm

Director: Stephen L. Recken, (501) 569-8395, slrecken@ualr.edu

Established in 1980, the program admits an average of six students per year. Public history is the only graduate program in the department. Approximately 30 students have graduated from the program, with an average number of two graduating each year. Internship required.

Concentrations: Archives; Historic Preservation/Cultural Resource Management; Museum Studies

Faculty: Stephen L. Recken, Ph.D., Program Coordinator; Johanna Miller Lewis, Ph.D., Assistant Program Coordinator. Other participating history faculty include: Edward M. Anson, Ph.D.; Deborah J. Baldwin, Ph.D.; Lester J. Bilsky, Ph.D.; S. Charles Bolton, Ph.D.; Gerald T. Hanson, Ph.D.; Thomas Kaiser, Ph.D.; Matthew Lenoe, Ph.D.; Marian Matrician, Ph.D.; James W. Miller, Ph.D.; Carl H. Moneyhon, Ph.D.; Frances Ross, Ph.D.; Laura Smoller, Ph.D.; Vincent A. Vinikas, Ph.D.; C. Fred Williams, Ph.D.; and Leroy T. Williams, Ph.D.

CALIFORNIA

California State University, Chico
Certificate Graduate Program in Public History
Department of History
California State University
Chico, CA 95929
Fax: (530) 898-6925

Director: Michael Magliari, (530) 898-6332, mmagliari@csuchico.edu

The certificate program in Public History was established in 1993, with the first courses being offered in 1992. Three or four students are admitted each year for a M.A. in history or history with certification or concentration in public history. The Certificate also is available to undergraduates seeking a B.A.

Concentrations: Historic Preservation/Cultural Resource Management; Historic Archaeology; Local Community History. Internship concentrations are offered in Archives; Editing and Publishing; and Museum Studies.

Faculty: Michael Magliari, Ph.D.

California State University, Sacramento
Capital Campus Public History Program
Department of History
California State University, Sacramento
Sacramento, CA 95819
Fax: (916) 278-6269
Web: www.csus.edu/hist/graduate.htm

Directors: Christopher J. Castaneda, (916) 278-5631, cjc@saclink.csus.edu; Kenneth Owens, emeritus

The Capital Campus Public History Program, founded in 1989, admits seven students in an average year. The program offers an M.A. in public history and a Ph.D. in public history jointly with the University of California, Santa Barbara. Approximately twenty students have graduated from the program, with an average of four students graduating each year. Internship required.

Concentrations: Archives; Historic Preservation/Cultural Resource Management; Public Policy; Oral History; Museum Studies; Business

Faculty: Christopher J. Castaneda, Ph.D.; Kenneth N. Owens, Ph.D.; Shirley A. Moore, Ph.D.; and adjunct faculty.

University of California, Riverside
Program in Historic Resources Management
Department of History
University of California
Riverside, CA 92521-0204
Fax: (909) 787-5299
Web: www.ucr.edu/history/phrm.html

Director: Clifford Trafzer, (909) 787-5401 ext 1437, histsk@ucracl.ucr.edu

The Program in Historical Resources Management at Riverside was established in 1973. It admits four students each year and offers a M.A. in history, with a specialization in historic preservation, archival management, or museum curatorship, and a Ph.D. in history with public history as a field. Approximately 104 students have graduated since the beginning of the program, with an average of four graduating each year. Internship required.

Concentrations: Archives; Historic Preservation/Cultural Resource Management; Museum Studies

Faculty: Larry Burgess, Ph.D.; Marion Mitchell-Wilson, B.S.; Harry Kelsey, Ph.D.; John Twilley, B.S.; Katherine Warren.

University of California, Santa Barbara
Joint Program in Public Historical Studies
Department of History
University of California
Santa Barbara, CA 93106
Fax: (805) 893-8795
Department of History
California State University
Sacramento, CA 95819
Fax: (916) 278-6269
Web: www.history.ucsb.edu

Directors: Ann M. Plane, UC Santa Barbara, (805) 893-2713, plane@humanitas.ucsb.edu; Christopher Castaneda, California State University-Sacramento, (916) 278-5631, cjc@saclink.csus.edu

Public Historical Studies was established at Santa Barbara in 1976. Students are admitted each year for study toward a M.A. or Ph.D. in public history. The Ph.D. is offered jointly with California State University-Sacramento. Internship required.

Concentrations: Archives; Historic Preservation/Cultural Resource Management; Editing; Historical Administration; Public Policy; Oral History; Local/Community History; Museum Studies; Business

Faculty: UCSB: Randolph Bergstrom, Ph.D.; Shelley Bookspan, Ph.D.; W. Elliott Brownlee, Ph.D.; Ann Plane, Ph.D. CSUS: Christopher Castaneda, Ph.D.; Kenneth Owens, Ph.D.

DISTRICT OF COLUMBIA

Howard University
Public History Program
Department of History
315 Douglass Hall
Howard University
Washington, DC 20059
Web: www.howard.edu

Director: Elizabeth Clark-Lewis, eclark-lewis@howard.edu

The Public History Program at Howard University offers a M.A. in public history and a Ph.D. in history, with a concentration in public history. The program, established in 1990, admits five students each year. Approximately twenty-one students have graduated, with three graduating each year. The program also offers on-campus workshops, mini or short courses and scholarships for off-campus workshops. Internship required.

Concentrations: Archives; Historic Preservation/Cultural Resource Management; Public Policy; Non-Print Media; Museum Studies

Faculty: Elizabeth Clark-Lewis, Ph.D.; Joseph Reidy, Ph.D.; Emory Tolbert, Ph.D. Adjunct faculty include: Thomas Battle, Ph.D.; Spencer Crew, Ph.D.; Walter Hill, Ph.D.; Donald Roe, Ph.D.

FLORIDA

Florida State University
Historical Administration & Public History
Department of History
Florida State University
Tallahassee, FL 32306-2200
Fax: (850) 644-6402
Web: www.fsu.edu/~history/haph.htm

Director: William Oldson, (850) 644-9541, woldson@garnet.aens.fsu.edu

The Florida State Historical Administration & Public History program, founded in 1975, admits five students each year. The program offers a M.A. in history with a concentration in public history. Approximately 89 students have graduated, with three graduating each year. Internship required.

Concentrations: Archives; Historic Preservation/Cultural Resource Management; Historical Administration; Oral History; Museum Studies.

Faculty: William Oldson, Ph.D.-Director, HAPH Program and Director of Institute on World War II and Human Experience; Gerald Clark, Operations Manager, Bureau of Archives; Vivian Young, Community Development Director, 1000 Friends of Florida; Susan Olson, Chief, Bureau of Historical Museums; Robin Sellers, Ph.D. Director, The Reichelt Program for Oral History.

GEORGIA

Armstrong Atlantic State University
Master of Arts in History with Concentration in Public History
Department of History
Armstrong Atlantic State University
Savannah, GA 31419-1997
Fax: (912) 921-5581
Web: www.armstrong.edu

Director: Christopher Hendricks, (912) 921-5833, hendrich@mail.armstrong.edu

The master's program in history offers a concentration in public history, which was established in 1984. Approximately ten students are admitted to the program annually, with three graduating each year.

Concentrations: Archives; Historic Preservation; Historical Archaeology; Oral History; Local/Community History; Museum Studies.

Faculty: Barbara Fertig, Ph.D.; Mark Finlay, Ph.D.; David Gleeson, Ph.D.; Christopher Hendricks, Ph.D.; June Hopkins, Ph.D.; Michael Price, Ph.D.; Howard Robinson, Ph.D.; Anne Yentsch, Ph.D.

ILLINOIS

Eastern Illinois University
M.A. in Historical Administration
History Department
Eastern Illinois University
216-C Coleman Hall
Charleston, IL 61920
Fax: (217) 581-7233
Web: www.eiu.edu/~history

Director: Terry A. Barnhart, (217) 581-5224, cftb@eiu.edu

The program at Eastern Illinois offers a M.A. in Historical Administration. Established in 1975, the program currently admits ten students each year. Approximately 220 students have graduated from the program, with ten graduating each year. Internship required.

Concentrations: Archives; Historic Preservation; Publishing; Historical Administration; Oral History; Local/Community History; Museum Studies

Faculty: Terry A. Barnhart, Ph.D.; Debra Ann Reid, Ph.D.; Nora Pat Small, Ph.D.; Patricia L. Miller; Richard V. Riccio.

Loyola University Chicago
Public History Program
History Department
6525 N. Sheridan Rd.
Chicago, IL 60626
Fax: (773) 508-2153
Web: www.luc.edu/depts/history/grad/public.html

Director: Patricia Mooney-Melvin, (773) 508-2238, pmooney@luc.edu

The Loyola Public History Program, established in 1981, offers an M.A./M.L.I.S. Program in conjunction with Dominican University. This joint degree program is particularly useful for those students interested in a career in archives. Public History may also be pursued at the M.A. and Ph.D. levels as a minor field. Six to ten students are admitted each year. Approximately thirty-nine students have graduated from the program, with three to four graduating each year. Internship required.

Concentrations: Archives; Historic Preservation/Cultural Resource Management; Oral History; Museum Studies

Faculty: Theodore J. Karamanski, Ph.D.; Patricia Mooney-Melvin, Ph.D.; Janet Nolan, Ph.D. Associate faculty include: Lewis Erenberg; Terry Fife; Susan Hirsch; Patrick Quinn.

Northern Illinois University
M.A. Option in Historical Administration
Department of History
Northern Illinois University
DeKalb, IL 60115
Fax: (815) 753-6302
Web: www.niu.edu/acad/history/graduate.html

Director: Barbara Posadas, (815) 753-6697, bposadas@niu.edu

The M.A. option in Historical Administration was established at Northern Illinois in 1987. Two to four students are admitted each year. Approximately twenty-three students have graduated, with one to two students graduating each year. Internship required.

Concentrations: Historical Administration; Public Policy; Oral History; Non-Print Media; Museum Studies.

Faculty: E. Taylor Atkins, Ph.D.; David Kyvig, Ph.D.; Barbara Posadas, Ph.D.; Tina Reithmaier; Milton Deemer; Drew Vandercreek, Ph.D.; Jeffrey Choun.

INDIANA

Indiana University Purdue University Indianapolis
Public History Program
Department of History
IUPUI
425 University Boulevard
Indianapolis, IN 46202
Fax: (317) 278-7800
Web: www.iupui.edu/~history

Director: Elizabeth Brand Monroe (317) 278-2255, emonroe@iupui.edu

The Public History Program at IUPUI was established in 1986 and offers a M.A. in Public History and a joint M.A.-M.L.S. with the Center on Philanthropic Studies. The Public History Program admits 10-12 students each year. Internship required. The program also works with the Center on Philanthropy, the Museum Studies Program, and the Center for Archaeology in the Public Interest. The department also hosts the Executive Offices of the National Council on Public History.

Concentrations: Archives; Editing; Museum Studies; Philanthropic Studies

Faculty: Elizabeth Brand Monroe, Ph.D.; Philip V. Scarpino, Ph.D.; Robert G. Barrows, Ph.D.; Todd Daniels-Howell, Ph.D.; David G. Vanderstel, Ph.D.

KANSAS

Wichita State University
Public History Program
Department of History
Wichita State University
Wichita, KS 67260-0045
Fax: (316) 978-3473
Web: history.twsu.edu

Director: Jay M. Price, (316) 978-3150, jprice@twsu.edu

The Public History Program, established in 1988, admits one to two students annually. Wichita State offers a M.A. in history, with a concentration in public history. The program also offers on-campus workshops. Approximately twenty students have graduated since the beginning of the program, graduating one to two each year. Internship required.

Concentrations: Archives; Historic Preservation/Cultural Resource Management; Museum Studies

Faculty: Jay M. Price, Ph.D.; Ben Tong, Ph.D. Adjunct faculty include: Mike Kelly, WSU Archives; Kathy Morgan, Wichita Historic Preservation Office; Robert Keckheiser, Director, Kansas State Historical Museum.

KENTUCKY

Murray State University
Forrest C. Pogue Public History Institute
Department of History
Murray State University
6B Faculty Hall
Murray, KY 42071-3341
Fax: (270) 762-6587
Web: campus.murraystate.edu/academic/faculty/
Bill.Mulligan/Index.htm

Director: William H. Mulligan, Jr., (270) 762-6571, bill.mulligan@murraystate.edu

The Murray State public history program was established in 1993 and admits four to six students each year. The program offers a M.A. in history and history with a concentration in public history. Approximately twelve students have graduated, with an average of two graduating each year.

Concentrations: Historic Preservation/Cultural Resource Management; Oral History; Museum Studies; Historical Administration

Faculty: James W. Hammack, Jr., Ph.D.; William H. Mulligan, Jr., Ph.D.

University of Louisville
Master of Arts in History
Department of History
University of Louisville
Louisville, KY 40292
Fax: (502) 852-0770
Web: www.uofl.edu/a-s/history/

Director: Tracy E. K'Meyer, (502) 852-6817, K'Meyer@Louisville.edu

The program at the University of Louisville offers a M.A. in history with a minor concentration in public or oral history.

Concentrations: Oral History; Local/Community History

Faculty: Tracy K'Meyer, Ph.D.; William Morison (Department of Archives).

MASSACHUSETTS

University of Massachusetts, Amherst
Public History Program
Department of History
University of Massachusetts, Amherst
Amherst, MA 01003-3930
Fax: (413) 545-6137
Web: www.umass.edu/history

Director: David Glassberg, (413) 545-1330, glassberg@history.umass.edu

The graduate program at University of Massachusetts, established in 1986, offers a M.A. in History, with a certification in public History and a Ph.D. in History. Approximately twenty-three students have graduated from the program, with two to three graduating each year. Internship required.

Concentrations: Archives; Historic Preservation/Cultural Resource Management; Museum Studies

Faculty: David Glassberg, Ph.D.

Northeastern University
Public History
Department of History 249 ME
Northeastern University
Boston, MA 02115
Fax: (617) 373-2661
Web: www.history.neu.edu

Directors: Anthony N. Penna, (617) 373-4439, apenna@lynx.neu.edu; Harvey Green, (617) 373-4444, harvey@waterloom.mv.com

Established in 1974, the program offers a M.A. and Ph.D. in history with concentration in public history. The program also has a non-degree certificate in public history. Approximately 350 students have graduated, with ten graduating each year. Internship required.

Concentrations: Archives; Historic Preservation/Cultural Resource Management; Editing; Historical Administration; Public Policy; Oral History; Non-Print Media; Local/Community History; Museum Studies.

Faculty: Ballard C. Campbell, Ph.D.; Harvey Green, Ph.D.; Gerald Herman, M.A.; Clay McShane, Ph.D.; Anthony N. Penna, D.A., Felix Matos-Rodriguez, Ph.D.

MICHIGAN

Wayne State University
Certificate in Archival Administration
Department of History
Wayne State University
3094 Faculty/Administration Building
Detroit, MI 48202
Fax: (313) 577-6987
Web: www.history.wayne.edu

Director: Philip P. Mason, (313) 577-2525, ab3697@wayne.edu

The program at Wayne State University offers M.A. and Ph.D. degrees in history, with certification or concentration in public history. The program also offers a graduate certificate in archival administration to be taken as a standalone certificate without a degree. Approximately 350 students have graduated, with ten graduating each year. The program offers mini or short courses.

Concentrations: Archives

Faculty: Philip P. Mason, Ph.D.; Douglas Haller; Brian Owens. Other faculty members and specialists also participate.

Western Michigan University
Public History Program
Department of History
1201 Oliver Street
Western Michigan University
Kalamazoo, MI 49008-5020
Fax: (616) 387-4651
Web: www.wmich.edu/history

Contacts: Kristin M. Szylvian, (616) 387-4639, K.istin.Szylvian@wmich.edu; Bruce Haight, Chairman, (616) 387-4650, Bruce.Haight@wmich.edu

Western Michigan established its graduate public history program in 1980 and its B.A. in public history in 1984. The program offers a M.A. and Ph.D. in history, with a concentration in public history. The program offers on-campus workshops and mini-courses for off-campus workshops. Two to four graduate students are admitted each year. Internship required.

Concentrations: Archives; Historic Preservation/Cultural Resource Management; Oral History; Local/Community History; Museum Studies

Faculty: Linda J. Borish, Ph.D. (affiliated); Sharon Carlson (adjunct); Michael J. Chiarappa, Ph.D.; Catherine J. Julien, Ph.D. (affiliated); Michael Nassancy (affiliated); Patrick Norris, Ph.D. (adjunct); Peter J. Schmitt, Ph.D.; Kristin Szylvian, Ph.D.

MINNESOTA

St. Cloud State University
Public History Program
Department of History
St. Cloud State University
720 4th Avenue South
St. Cloud, Minnesota 56301
Fax: (320) 529-1516
Web: condor.stcloudstate.edu/~bulletin/hist/
gprograms.html#public

Director: Lee Simpson, (320) 255-3165, lsimpson@stcloudstate.edu

The Public History Program at St. Cloud, established in 1988, admits approximately six students each year. The program offers a M.A. in public history and in history. Internship required.

Concentrations: Archives; Historic Preservation/Cultural Resource Management; Local/Community History; Museum Studies.

Faculty: Don L. Hofsommer, Ph.D.; Lee Simpson, Ph.D.

MISSOURI

Southeast Missouri State University
M.A. in History with an Emphasis in Historic Preservation
Department of History
Southeast Missouri State University
520 North Pacific
Cape Girardeau, MO 63701
Fax: (573) 651-5114
Web: www4.semo.edu/histpres

Directors: Bonnie Stepenoff, (573) 651-2831, bstepenoff@semovm.semo.edu; Joe Werne, (573) 651-2180

The Program at Southeast Missouri State was established in 1992 and admits four students each year. Students work towards an M.A. in history with certification or concentration in public history. The program offers mini or short courses. More than 100 students have graduated from the program, with approximately ten graduating each year.

Concentrations: Historic Preservation/Cultural Resource Management

Faculty: Eric Clements, Ph.D.; Steven Hoffman, Ph.D.; Bonnie Stepenoff, Ph.D.

NEVADA

University of Nevada Las Vegas
Master of Arts in Public History (Minor)
Department of History
University of Nevada Las Vegas
4505 Maryland Parkway
Box 5020
Las Vegas, NV 89154
Fax: (702) 895-1782
Web: www.unlv.edu/Colleges/Liberal_Arts/
History/

Director: Andrew Kirk, (702) 895-3544,
akirk@ccmail.nevada.edu

Established in 1999, the program admits
twelve students each year. The program offers
a M.A. in history with a concentration in public
history. Internship required.

Concentrations: Archives; Historic Preservation/Cultural Resource Management; Historical Archaeology; Oral History; Museum Studies

Faculty: Sue Fawn Chung, Ph.D.; Joanne L.
Goodwin, Ph.D.; Andrew J. Kirk, Ph.D.; Hal K.
Rothman, Ph.D.

NEW MEXICO

New Mexico State University
Public History Program
History Department
P.O. Box 30001
New Mexico State University
Las Cruces, NM 88003
Fax: (505) 646-8148
Web: web.nmsu.edu/~publhist

Director: Jon Hunner, (505) 646-2490, jhunner
@nmsu.edu

The Public History Program at New Mexico
State University was established in 1983. The
program offers a M.A. in history with a concentration in public history and admits between five and ten students each year. Approximately forty students have graduated
from the program. Internship required.

Concentrations: Historic Preservation/Cultural Resource Management; Oral History; Museum Studies

Faculty: Jon Hunner, Ph.D.; Ed Staski; Beth
O'Leary; Marsha Weisiger; Elizabeth Zauer.

NEW YORK

New York University
Program in Public History
Department of History
New York University
#525-19 University Place
New York, New York 10003
Web: www.nyu.edu/gsas/dept/history/public_
history

Director: Paul H. Mattingly, (212) 998-8631,
mattinglyp@juno.com

The New York University Program in Public
History, established in 1981, admits three to
four students each year. The program offers a
M.A. in history with a concentration in public

history and Ph.D. can receive public history as
a minor. The program offers a New York Regents Certificate in Public History. Over 120
students have graduated from the program
since its inception.

Concentrations: Local/Community History,
Public Policy, Non-Print Media, Oral History

Faculty: Paul H. Mattingly, Ph.D.; Rachel Bernstein, Peter Wosh, Ph.D.; Barbara Abrash.

University at Albany, SUNY
Graduate Program in Public History
Department of History
University at Albany, SUNY
Albany, NY 12222
Fax: (518) 442-3477
Web: www.albany.edu/history

Director: Ivan D. Steen, (518) 442-4811, oralhis
@csc.albany.edu

Established in 1983, the Program in Public
History admits eight to ten students each year.
Students receive an M.A. in Public History and
a Certificate of Advanced Study in Public History. Approximately forty students have graduated since the beginning of the program, with
three to four graduating each year. Internship
required.

Concentrations: Archives; Historical Administration; Public Policy; Local/Community History; Museum Studies

Faculty: Allen Ballard, Ph.D.; Tammis Groft,
M.A.; Richard F. Hamm, Ph.D.; Gretchen Sorin,
Ph.D.; Ivan D. Steen, Ph.D; Ann F. Withington,
Ph.D. Other participating faculty include: Graham Barker-Benfield, Ph.D.; Ronald Burch,
Ph.D.; Sung Bok Kim, Ph.D.; Joseph F. Meany,
Ph.D; John Scherer, M.A; Patricia West, Ph.D.;
Gerald Zahavi, Ph.D.; Julian Zelizer, Ph.D.

NORTH CAROLINA

Appalachian State University
Master of Arts in Public History
Department of History
P.O. Box 32072
Boone, NC 28608-2072
Fax: (828) 262-4976
Web: www.acs.appstate.edu/dept/history/ph.htm

Chair: Michael Wade, (828) 262-2282,
wademg@appstate.edu

Appalachian State's graduate program in public history was founded in 1989; it normally admits four students each year. The program offers a M.A. in history and public history.

Concentrations: Archives; Historic Preservation/Cultural Resource Management; Historical Administration; Oral History; Local/Community History; Museum Studies.

Faculty: Karl Campbell, Ph.D.; Lynne M. Getz,
Ph.D.; Timothy H. Silver, Ph.D.; Neva J. Specht,
Ph.D.; Michael G. Wade, Ph.D.; Charles A.
Watkins, Ph.D.; John Alexander Williams, Ph.D.

North Carolina State University
M.A. in Public History
Department of History
North Carolina State University
Box 8108
Raleigh, NC 27695
Fax: (919) 515-3836
Web: www2.ncsu.edu:80/ncsu/chass/history/
higrad.html

Director: John David Smith, (919) 515-3715,
smith-jd@unity.ncsu.edu

The North Carolina State University program
was established in 1984. The University offers
a M.A. in public history, in history, in history
with concentration in public history, as well as
a joint program in M.I.L.S. with University of
North Carolina-Chapel Hill. The program also
offers on-campus workshops. Fifteen students
are admitted each year. Approximately 106
students have graduated, with an estimated
eight graduating each year. Internship required.

Concentrations: Archives; Historic Preservation/Cultural Resource Management; Editing;
Publishing; Historical Archaeology; Historical
Administration; Oral History; Local/Community
History; Museum Studies; Manuscripts;
Records Management

Faculty: Viki Berger, Ph.D.; John David Smith,
Ph.D.; David Zonderman, Ph.D.; David S. Olson,
M.A., Winston Atkins; Dick Lankford, MPA.

The University of North Carolina at Greensboro
Historic Preservation and Museum Studies
Department of History
219 McIver
University of North Carolina at Greensboro
Greensboro, NC 27402
Fax: (336) 334-5910
Web: www.uncg.edu/hpms

Directors: Kathleen Franz, (336) 334-5992; Jo
Ramsay Leimenstoll, (336) 334-5320, Housing
and Interior Design Department, jrleimen
@uncg.edu

The University of North Carolina at Greensboro
offers a M.A. in history with concentration in
public history or an M.A. in interior design with
concentration in historic preservation or museum studies. Museum Studies is jointly offered
by History and Housing and Interior Design
Departments. Established in 1985, twelve to fifteen students are admitted each year. Internship required.

Concentrations: Historic Preservation/Cultural Resource Management; Museum Studies

Faculty: Kathleen Franz, Ph.D.; Phyllis Hunter,
Ph.D.; Jo Ramsay Leimenstoll, M. Arch.; Lisa
Tolbert, Ph.D.

The University of North Carolina at Wilmington
Public History Program
University of North Carolina at Wilmington
Department of History
601 S. College Road
Wilmington, NC 28403-3297
Fax: (910) 962-7011
Web: www.uncwil.edu/hist/public2.htm

Director: Virginia Stewart, (910) 962-3305, stewartv@uncwil.edu

The program was established in 1989 and admits eight students each year. Students receive a M.A. in history with a concentration in public history. Internship required.

Concentrations: Archives; Historical Administration; Public Policy; Oral History, Non-Print Media; Local/Community History; Museum Studies; Exhibition Design

Faculty: Virginia Stewart, Ph.D.; Otis L. Graham, Ph.D., Distinguished Visiting Professor.

OHIO

Kent State University
Public History Program
Department of History
Kent State University
Kent, OH 44242
Fax: (330) 672-2943
Web: www.kent.edu/history

Director: John R. Jameson, (330) 672-2882, jjameson@kent.edu

The Public History program was established in 1988. It offers a M.A. in public history and a Ph.D. in history with certification or concentration in public history. An average of five students are admitted to the program annually. Approximately 48 students have graduated since the program's inception. story with certification or concentration in public history. Internship required.

Concentrations: Archives; Historic Preservation/Cultural Resource Management; Editing; Publishing; Historical Administration; Museum Studies.

Faculty: John Jameson, Ph.D.; Molly Merryman, Ph.D.; Shirley Wajda, Ph.D.; Clarence Wunderlin, Ph.D.

The University of Toledo
Graduate Program in History
Department of History
The University of Toledo
2801 W. Bancroft
Toledo, OH 43606
Web: www.history.utoledo.edu/

Director: Diane F. Britton, (419) 530-4540, dbritto@uoft02.utoledo.edu

The Public History Program at the University of Toledo was established in 1986 and admits approximately 12 students each year. Both the M.A. and Ph.D. are offered in history, with the option of a concentration in public history.

Concentrations: Archives; Oral History; Local/Community History; Museum Studies.

Faculty: Diane Britton, Ph.D.

Wright State University
Public History Program
History Department
Wright State University
Dayton, OH 45435
Fax: (937) 775-3301
Web: www.cola.wright.edu/Dept/HST/public history.htm

Director: Marjorie McLellan, (937) 775-3111, marjorie.mclellan@wright.edu

Established in 1972, the public history program admits six students each year. The program offers a M.A. in history with a concentration in public history. The program also offers mini or short courses. Approximately 300 students have graduated from the program with four to five students graduating each year. Internship required.

Concentrations: Archives; Museum Studies

Faculty: Marjorie McLellan, Ph.D. Adjunct faculty include: Dawne Dewey, Special Collections and Archives, Wright State; Brian Hackett, Director, Montgomery County Historical Society; Robert H. Smith, Records & Information Manager, Montgomery County; John Sanford, Archivist, Special Collections and Archives, Wright State; Glenn Harper, Field Services Coordinator, Ohio Historic Preservation Office.

OKLAHOMA

Oklahoma State University
Applied History Program
Department of History
Oklahoma State University
Stillwater, OK 74078-3054
Web: history.okstate.edu/degreeprog/applied. html

Director: Bill Bryans, (405) 744-8179, bry4obl@okstate.edu

Established in 1986, the Applied History Graduate Program in public history offers a M.A. in history with a concentration in public history. Six students are admitted each year. Internship required.

Concentrations: Museum Studies; Historic Preservation/Cultural Resource Management

Faculty: Bill Bryans, Ph.D. Other faculty include: Donald Brown, Ph.D. (Anthropology); Lowell Caneday, Ph.D. (Recreation and Interpretation).

PENNSYLVANIA

Carnegie Mellon University
Program in History and Policy
Department of History
Carnegie Mellon University
Pittsburgh, PA 15213
Fax: (412) 268-1019
Web: www.history.cmu.edu

Director: Steven Schlossman, (412) 268-2880, sls@andrew.cmu.edu

The History and Policy Program, founded in 1975, admits three students each year. The program offers a Ph.D. in History and Policy. Approximately thirteen students have graduated since 1993, with two students graduating each year.

Concentrations: Public Policy

Faculty: Caroline Acker, Ph.D.; Edward Constant, Ph.D.; David Hounsehell, Ph.D.; Daniel Resnick, Ph.D.; Steven Schlossman, Ph.D.; Kiron Skinner, Ph.D.; Joel Tarr, Ph.D.

SOUTH CAROLINA

University of South Carolina
Public History Program
Department of History
University of South Carolina
Columbia, SC 29208
Fax: (803) 777-4494
Web: www.cla.sc.edu/hist/apphist.htm

Directors: Constance B. Schulz, (803) 777-4854 or 777-5195, schulz@sc.edu; Robert R. Weyeneth, (803) 777-6398, weyeneth@sc.edu

The public history program at the University of South Carolina was established in 1976 and admits twelve to fifteen students each year. The program offers a M.A. in public history and a Ph.D. in history. Approximately 125 students have graduated from the program, with eight to ten graduating each year since 1990. The program also offers on-campus workshops, mini-courses, and scholarships for off-campus workshops. Internship required.

Concentrations: Archives; Historic Preservation/Cultural Resource Management; Editing; Local/Community History; Museum Studies.

Faculty: David R. Chesnutt, Ph.D.; Walter B. Edgar, Ph.D.; Katherine C. Grier, Ph.D.; Constance B. Schulz, Ph.D.; Marcia G. Synnott, Ph.D.; Robert R. Weyeneth, Ph.D.

TENNESSEE

Middle Tennessee State University
Public History & Historic Preservation
Department of History
Middle Tennessee State University
Murfreesboro, TN 37132
Fax: (615) 898-5881
Web: www.mtsu.edu/~history

Director: Rebecca Conard, (615) 898-2423, rconard@mtsu.edu; Lorne McWatters, (615) 898-5805, damcwatters@mtsu.edu

The Middle Tennessee Historic Preservation Program was established in 1973 and admits fifteen students each year. The program offers a M.A. and Ph.D. in history with a concentration in public history. The program also has a D.A. or Doctor of Arts in Historic Preservation, but the possibility of changing that to a Ph.D. in History, with a specialization in Historic Preservation, is currently under review (2000-2001). Approximately 122 students have graduated, with six students graduating each year. Internship required.

Concentrations: Archives; Historic Preservation/Cultural Resource Management; Historical Administration; Museum Studies

Faculty: Rebecca Conard, Ph.D.; Lorne McWatters, Ph.D.

TEXAS

University of Houston
Graduate Program in Public History
Department of History
University of Houston
Houston, TX 77204-3785
Fax: (713) 743-3216
Web: vi.uh.edu/

Director: Martin V. Melosi, (713) 743-3090 or 3087, mmelosi@uh.edu

The Public History Program at the University of Houston offers a M.A. in public history as well as a M.A. or Ph.D. minor in public history. Established in 1984, the program admits three to six students each year. Approximately thirty students have graduated since the beginning of the program, with an average of two students graduating each year. Internship required.

Concentrations: Archives; Historic Preservation/Cultural Resource Management; Public Policy; Historical Exhibits.

Faculty: Martin V. Melosi, Ph.D.; Joseph Pratt, Ph.D.

Southwest Texas State University
Public History Program
History Department
601 University Drive
San Marcos, TX 78666
Fax: (512) 245-3043
Web: www.history.swt.edu/Department/Public History/pubhist.htm

Interim Director: Jesús F. de la Teja, (512) 245-2142

Established in the fall of 1998, the program admits six to eight students each year. An M.A. is offered in history with a certification or concentration in public history. Approximately five students have graduated, with three graduating each year. Internship required.

Concentrations: Archives; Historic Preservation/Cultural Resource Management; Oral History; Local/Community History; Museum Studies

Faculty: Numerous faculty and adjunct faculty members and specialists participate.

The University of Texas at Arlington
Public History Program
History Department
Box 19529
University of Texas at Arlington
Arlington, TX 76019
Fax: (817) 272-2852
Web: www.uta.edu/history/

Director: Stanley H. Palmer, (817) 272-2861/2869, history@uta.edu

The Public History Program at the University of Texas at Arlington, established in 1993, admits seven to ten students each year. The M.A. is offered in history with concentration in public history. On-campus workshops are offered in the curriculum. Approximately twenty students have graduated since the beginning of the program, with an average of three graduating each year. Internship required.

Concentrations: Archives; Oral History; Local/Community History

Faculty: Robert Fairbanks, Ph.D.; Richard Francaviglia, Ph.D.; Steven G. Reinhardt, Ph.D.; Gerald D. Saxon, Ph.D.

VIRGINIA

James Madison University
History Graduate Program
Department of History, MSC 2001
James Madison University
Harrisonburg, VA 22807
Fax: (540) 568-6556
Web: www.jmu.edu/history/outline.htm

Directors: David Owusu-Ansah, (540) 568-6743, owusuadx@jmu.edu; Gabrielle Lanier, (540) 568-3615, laniergm@jmu.edu

Established in 1987, the James Madison University program offers a M.A. with concentrations in local, state, and regional history. Approximately fifteen students have graduated from the program.

Faculty: Michael J. Galgano, Ph.D.; Clive R. Hallman, Ph.D.; Raymond Hyser, Ph.D.; Gabrielle M. Lanier, Ph.D.; Darryl Nash, M.A.; David Owusu-Ansah, Ph.D.; Kevin L. Borg; Stuart Downs; Clarence Geier.

WISCONSIN

University of Wisconsin-Milwaukee
Public History Specialization
Department of History
P.O. Box 413
Milwaukee, WI 53201
Fax: (414) 229-2435
Web: www.uwm.edu/Dept/PubHist/index.html

Director: Michael A. Gordon, (414) 229-4314, mgordon@uwm.edu

Established in 1977, the public history program at the University of Wisconsin-Milwaukee offers a M.A. in history with a concentration in public history. Approximately 130 students have graduated from the program, with eight to ten graduating each year. internship required.

Concentrations: Archives; Historic Preservation/Cultural Resource Management; Oral History; Museum Studies

Faculty: Michael A. Gordon, Ph.D. Associate faculty from other departments and the Milwaukee Public Museum also participate.

CANADA
ONTARIO

University of Waterloo
Public History Program
Department of History
University of Waterloo
Waterloo, ON N2L 3G1
Web: arts.uwaterloo.ca/HIST/history.html

Director: Kenneth McLaughlin, (519) 885-1211, kmclaugh@watarts.uwaterloo.ca

Established in 1983, the University of Waterloo program admits between six and eight students each year. The program offers a M.A. in history and public history and a Ph.D. in history. Approximately thirty students have graduated from the program, with six students graduating each year. Internship required.

Concentrations: Historic Preservation/Cultural Resource Management; Editing; Publishing; Historical Administration; Public Policy; Oral History; Local/Community History; Museum Studies

Faculty: John R. English, Ph.D.; Geoffrey Hayes, Ph.D.; Andrew Hunt, Ph.D.; Heather MacDougall, Ph.D.; Kenneth McLaughlin, Ph.D.; Wendy Mitchinson, Ph.D.; James W. Walker, Ph.D.

University of Western Ontario
Public History Programme
Department of History, SSC
University of Western Ontario
London, ON N6A 5C2
Fax: (519) 661-3646

Director: Benjamin Forster (519) 661-3646, bforster@julian.uwa.ca

Established in 1986, the program admits approximately 5 students each year. The department offers a M.A. in history and public history and a Ph.D. in history. Approximately fifty students have graduated from the program. Internship required.

Concentrations: Oral History; Local/Community History; Museum Studies.

Faculty: Benjamin Forster, Ph.D.; Jan Trimble, M.A.

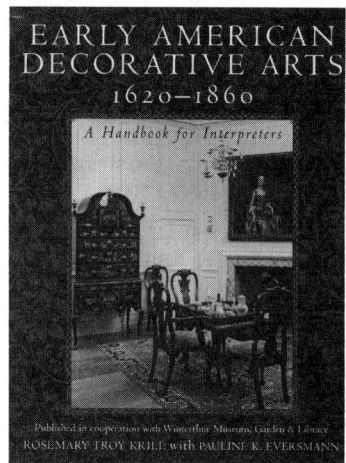

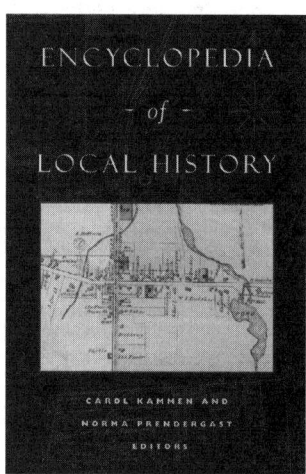

State History Offices

Alabama

Alabama Archaeological Society

13075 Moundville Archaeological Park, Moundville, AL 35474; www.gulfmart.com/org/aas.htm

Gary Mullen, President

PROGRAMS: Newsletter, magazines; annual meeting.

Alabama Department of Archives and History

624 Washington Ave., Montgomery, AL 36130; (334) 242-4435; www.archives.state.al.us/

Edwin C. Bridges, Director, State Archivist.

PROGRAMS: Archives; collecting; conservation; exhibits, library, museum; newsletters, magazines; photographic collections; public relations; records management; research; school programs; tours; adult programming such as seminars and workshops; private support organization oversight; off-site records center; outreach such as history festival and lecture series.

COMMENTS: The Alabama Department of Archives and History is the state archives, state history museum, and state records management agency.

Alabama Genealogical Society, Inc.

c/o Samford University Library, PO Box 2296, Birmingham, AL 35229

Jyl Hardy, President

PROGRAMS: Genealogy; newsletters; magazines.

Alabama Historical Association

c/o Alabama Department of Archives and History, 624 Washington Avenue, Montgomery, AL 36130; www.archives.state.al.us/aha/aha.html

Michael Thomason, President

PROGRAMS: Markers; newsletters, magazines; annual meetings and historic tours.

Alabama Historical Commission

468 South Perry Street, Montgomery, Alabama 36130; (334) 230-2668; www.preserveala.org/

Dr. Lee Warner, Executive Director, SHPO

PROGRAMS: Archaeology; AV programs; collecting; conservation; exhibits; field services; historic preservation; historic site; living history; markers; museum; newsletter, magazines; oral history; photographic collections; public relations; research; school programs; tours; planning and compliance for federal funds for historic preservation; National Register nominations; Main Street Program.

COMMENTS: Operates following state historic sites: Cahawba Historical Site; Confederate Memorial Park and Cemetery; Dr. Francis Medical and Apothecary Museum; Fendall Hall; Fort Mims; Fort Morgan; Forts Toulouse-Jackson; Gaineswood Mansion/Museum; Magnolia Grove; Belmont; John Tyler Morgan House; Joe Wheeler Plantation; State Capitol Building

Alabama Humanities Foundation

1100 Ireland Way, Suite 101, Birmingham, AL 35205; (205) 558-3980; www.ahf.net/

Robert Stewart, Executive Director

Alabama Museums Association

Box 870340, Tuscaloosa, Alabama 35487; (205) 348-7554; www.alabamamuseums.org/

Dr. John Hall, Executive Director

PROGRAMS: Newsletter, magazines; public relations; annual meetings; professional development programming.

Alabama Preservation Alliance

P.O. Box 1827, Mobile, AL 36633; (205) 438-7281.

Michael Leventhal, President.

PROGRAMS: Newsletters, magazines; annual meeting.

Alabama Public Library Service

6030 Monticello Drive, Montgomery, Alabama 36130; (334) 213-3900; www.apls.state.al.us/

Lamar Veatch, Director

PROGRAMS: AV programs; collecting; field services; library; newsletters, magazines; public relations; reference services for state government agencies and public libraries; library development to assist public libraries, guide multitype library cooperation, and help in growth of networking.

COMMENTS: Manages Division of the Blind and Physically Handicapped, which maintains and circulates material to the state's blind and physically handicapped.

Society of Alabama Archivists

c/o P.O. Box 300100, Montgomery, AL 36130; (205) 826-4465; www.duc.auburn.edu/academic/societies/soc_ala_archivists/

Tim Pennycuff, President

PROGRAMS: Newsletter, magazines; annual meetings; professional development programming.

U.S.S. Alabama Battleship Commission

Battleship Pkwy., U.S. 90, Mobile, AL 36601; (205) 433-2703.

W.J. Diffley, Executive Director

PROGRAMS: Collecting; exhibits; historic sites; library; museum; public relations; research; school programs; tours.

COMMENTS: The purpose of this commission is to maintain the U.S.S. Alabama and the state memorial park to honor the Alabamians who participated in World War II and Korea.

The White House Association

644 Washington Ave., Montgomery, AL 36130; (205) 261-4624.

Mrs. John H. Napier, III, Regent.

PROGRAMS: collecting; exhibits; historic sites; museum; tours.

COMMENTS: The purpose of this association is to manage the First White House of the Confederacy as a museum and historic site.

Alaska

Alaska and Polar Regions Department

P.O. Box 756808 Fairbanks, AK 99775-6808; Elmer E. Rasmusson Library, Univ. of Alaska-Fairbanks, Fairbanks, AK 99775; (907) 474-7261; www.uaf.edu/library/collections/apr/

Susan Grigg, Head

PROGRAMS: Archives; book publishing; collecting; oral history

Alaska Historical Commission

Dept. of Natural Resources, 3601 C. St., #1278, Anchorage, AK 99503-5921; (907) 269-8721; www.dnr.state.ak.us/parks/oha_web/ahc.htm

Lt. Gov. Fran Ulmer, Chair

Alaska Historical Society

PO Box 100299, Anchorage, AK 99510; www.alaska.net/~ahs/membership.htm

Kay Shelton, President

Alaska Humanities Forum

421 West First Avenue, Suite 300, Anchorage, AK 99501; (907) 272-5341, Fax (907) 272-3979; www.gov.state.ak.us/boards/factsheet/fact049.html

Liz Forrer, Interim Executive Director

Alaska State Archives

Dept. of Education, 141 Willoughby Ave., AK 99801; (907) 465-2275; Fax (907) 465-2465; www.archives.state.ak.us/staffhom.html

John Stewart, State Archivist

PROGRAMS: Archives; record management

Alaska State Library, Historical Collections

Dept. of Education, P.O. Box 110571, Juneau, AK 99811; (907) 465-2925; Fax (907) 465-2990; www.urova.fi/home/arktinen/polarweb/polar/lbusadsl.htm

Karen R. Crane, Director

Kathryn H. Shelton, Librarian

PROGRAMS: Library, photographs, manuscripts

Alaska State Museum

Department of Education, 395 Whittier St., Juneau, AK 99801-1718; (907) 465-2901; fax (907) 465-2976; www.museums.state.ak.us

Bruce Kato, Chief Curator

PROGRAMS: Museum

Museum Collections Advisory Committee

Dept. of Education, Alaska State Museum, 395 Whittier St., AK 99801; (907) 465-4866; touchngo.com/lglcntr/akstats/Statutes/Title14/Chapter57/Section020.htm

George Parker, Chair

PROGRAMS: Collecting; museum

Office of History and Archaeology

Alaska Division of Parks and Outdoor Recreation; 550 W. 7th Ave., Suite 1310, Anchorage, AK 99501-3565; (907) 269-8721; Fax (907) 269-8908; oha@alaska.net; www.dnr.state.ak.us/parks/oha_web/

Judith E. Bittner, Chief; SHPO

PROGRAMS: Archaeology; historic preservation

Sheldon Jackson Museum

104 College Dr., Sitka, AK 99835-7657 (907) 747-8981; Fax (907) 747-3004; www.museums.state.ak.us/

Peter Corey, Curator of Collections

PROGRAMS: Museum

UAA Archives and Manuscripts Departments

Consortium Library, 3211 Providence Dr., Anchorage, AK 99508; (907) 786-1867; www.lib.uaa.alaska.edu/archives/

Dennis F. Walle, Head

PROGRAMS: Archives

University of Alaska Museum

College of Arts and Science, Univ. of Alaska-Fairbanks, 907 Yukon Dr., Fairbanks, AK 99775; (907) 474-7505; www.uaf.edu/museum/main.html

PROGRAMS: Research, exhibits.

Arizona

Arizona Department of Library, Archives and Public Records

State Capitol, Ste., 200, 1700 W. Washington, Phoenix, AZ 85007; (602) 255-4035; Fax (602) 542-4972; services@dlapr.lib.az.us; www.dlapr.lib.az.us

Sharon G. Womack, Director

Arizona History and Archives Division

Dept. of Library, Archives and Public Records, State Capitol, Ste., 442, 1700 W. Washington, Phoenix, AZ 85007; (602) 542-4159; Fax (602) 542-4402; Archive@lib.az.us; www.dlapr.lib.az.us/archives/

Melanie Sturgeon, Division Director

Arizona Historical Society
Central Division

1300 N College, Tempe, AZ 85281; (480) 929-0292; Fax (480) 861-3537; www.tempe.gov/ahs/frames.htm

Northern Division

2340 N Fort Valley Rd, Flagstaff, AZ 86001; (520) 774-6272; Fax (520) 774-1596; www.infomagic.net/~ahsnad/

Rio Colorado Division

240 Madison Ave, Yuma, AZ 85364; (520) 782-1841; Fax (520) 783-0680; w3.arizona.edu~azhist/rio.htm

Southern Division

949 E. 2nd St., Tucson, AZ 95719; (520) 628-5774; w3.arizona.edu/~azhist/

Arizona Historical Advisory Commission

Dept. of Library, Archives and Public Records, State Capitol, Ste. 200, 1700 W. Washington, Phoenix, AZ 85007; (602) 255-4035

Sharon G. Womack, Chair

Arizona Historical Records Advisory Board

Dept. of Library, Archives and Public Records, State Capitol, Ste. 200, 1700 W. Washington, Phoenix, AZ 85007; (602) 255-4035

Sharon G. Womack, Chair

Arizona Historical Foundation

Hayden Library, 4th Fl., PO Box 871006 , Arizona State Univ. Tempe, AZ 85287; (480) 965-3283; (480) 966-1077; Azhistoricalfdn@qwest.net; www.users.qwest.net/~azhistoricalfnd

Evelyn S. Cooper, Ph.D., Director

Arizona Humanities Council

The Ellis-Shackelford House, 1242 N. Central Ave., Phoenix, AZ 85004; (602) 257-0335; Fax (602) 257-0392; www.azhumanities.org/

Dan Shilling, Executive Director

Arizona Paper and Photograph Conservation Group

c/o Library, National Park Service, P.O. Box 41058, Tucson, AZ 85717; (520) 629-6501

Arizona State Museum

1013 Univ. Blvd, Univ. of Arizona, Tucson, AZ 85721-0026; (520) 621-6281; (520) 621-2976; www.arizona.edu/~asm

George Gumerman, Director

Arizona State Parks

800 W. Washington, Ste. 415, Phoenix, AZ 85007; (602) 255-4174; www.pr.state.az.us/

Ken Travous, Executive Director

Coordinating Committee for History in Arizona

Dept. of History, Arizona State Univ., College of Liberal Arts, Tempe, AZ 85287; (480) 965-3226

Noel Stowe, President

Heritage Foundation of Arizona

402 W. Roosevelt St., Ste. C., Phoenix, AZ 85007; (602) 967-7117

Richard C. Giebner, President

State Historic Preservation Office

Arizona State Parks, 1300 W. Washington, Phoenix, AZ 85007; (602) 255-4009; www.pr.state.az.us/partnerships/shpo/shpo.html

James W. Garrison, SHPO

Museum Association of Arizona

c/o Desert Botanical Garden, 1201 N. Galvin Pkwy., Phoenix, AZ 85004; (602) 941-1217

Bob Breunig, President

Museum Division

Dept. of Library, Archives and Public Records, State Capitol, 1st Fl., 1700 W. Washington, Phoenix, AZ 85007; (602) 255-4675; Fax (602) 542-4690; http://www.dlapr.lib.az.us/museum/

Michael Carman, Division Director

Records Management Division

Dept. of Library, Archives and Public Records, 1919 W. Jefferson St., Phoenix, AZ 85009; (602) 255-3741; http://www.dlapr.lib.az.us/records/

Martin Richelsoph, C.R.M.

Arkansas

Arkansas Archeological Survey

The University of Arkansas, Fayetteville, AR 72701; (501) 575-3556; www.uark.edu/campus-resources/archinfo/index.html

Charles R. McGimsey, Director

PROGRAMS: Archaeology

Arkansas Humanities Council

10800 Financial Centre Parkway, Suite 465, Little Rock, AR 72211; (501) 221-0091; ahc@aristotle.net; www.arkhums.org/

Bob Bailey, Executive Director

Arkansas State Historic Preservation Office

Tower Building 323 Center Street, Suite 1500, Little Rock, AR 72201; (501) 324-9880; Fax (501) 324-9184; cathy@dah.state.ar.us; www.nthp.org/main/frontline/regions/states/arkansas.htm

Cathy Buford, SHPO

PROGRAMS: Historic preservation.

Arkansas Historical Association

The University of Arkansas, Dept. of History, #12 Ozark Hall, Fayetteville, AR 72701; (501) 575-5884; Fax (501) 575-2642; rhondak@comp.uark.edu

Walter L. Brown, Editor

PROGRAMS: Book publishing.

Arkansas History Commission

Parks and Tourism, #1 Capitol Mall, Little Rock, AR 72201; (501) 682-6900; www.state.ar.us/ahc/

John Ferguson, State Historian

PROGRAMS: Archives; research.

Arkansas Museum Association

6900 Cantrell Rd # M27, Little Rock, AR 72207

Allyn Lord, President

PROGRAMS: Museum.

Arkansas State Library

Dept of Education, #1 Capitol Mall, Little Rock, AR 72201; (501) 682-2053; Fax (501) 682-1529; aslref@asl.lib.ar.us; www.asl.lib.ar.us/

Jack C. Mulkey, State Librarian

PROGRAMS: Library research.

Historic Arkansas Museum

200 E. Third Street, Little Rock, AR 72201; (501) 324-9351; Fax (501) 324-9345; www.arkansashistory.com/

William B. Worthen, Director

PROGRAMS: Historic sites; museum.

Department of Arkansas Heritage

1500 Tower Building, 323 Center Street, Little Rock, AR 72201; (501) 324-9150; Fax (501) 324-9154; info@arkansasheritage.com; www.heritage.state.ar.us/visualarts/architecture/main.html

Cathie Matthews, Director

PROGRAMS: Conservation; exhibits; historic preservation; historic sites; museum.

Historic Preservation Alliance of Arkansas

910 W 2nd, Ste 200, P.O. Box 305, Little Rock, AR 72203; (501) 372-4757; Fax (501) 372-3845; thealliance@aristotle.net; www.arkansaspreservation.org/alliance

Jim Walsmith, Director

PROGRAMS: Historic preservation

Historic Resources and Museum Services

Parks and Tourism, #1 Capitol Mall, Little Rock, AR 72201; (501) 682-3603; Fax (501) 682-0081; Patricia.murphy@mail.state.ar.us; www.arkansas.com

Patty Murphy, Director

PROGRAMS: Granting source.

Old State House

Dept. of Arkansas Heritage, 300 W. Markham, Little Rock, AR 72201; (501) 371-1749; Fax (501) 324-9688; info@oldstatehouse.org; www.oldstatehouse.com/

PROGRAMS: Museum.

California

California Council for the Promotion of History

6000 J St, Sacramento, CA 95819-6059; (916) 278-4296; (916) 278-6269; ccph@csus.edu; www.csus.edu/org/ccph

PROGRAMS: Historic preservation; historic sites; newsletters, magazines; public relations.

California Council for the Humanities

San Francisco (Administrative Office)

312 Sutter Street, Suite 601, San Francisco, CA 94108; (415) 391-1474; Fax (415) 391-1312

Los Angeles

315 West Ninth Street, Suite 702, Los Angeles, CA 90015; (213) 623-5993;

San Diego

614 Fifth Avenue, Ste C, San Diego, CA 92101; (619) 232-4020;

info@calhum.org; www.calhum.org/

James Quay, Executive Director

California Heritage Preservation Commission

Office of the Secretary of State, 1020 "O" St., Sacramento, CA 95814; (916) 445-4293

Cecelia Tonsing, Chair

PROGRAMS: Archives; public relations.

California Historical Society

678 Mission Street, San Francisco CA 94105; voice (415) 357-1848; Fax (415) 357-1850; Info@calhist.org; www.calhist.org

Stephen A. Becker, Executive Director

PROGRAMS: Library; newsletters, magazines; photographic collections; research.

California Preservation Foundation

1615 Broadway, Ste. 820, Oakland, CA 94612; (510) 763-0972; (501) 763-4724 cpf_office@californiapreservation.org; www.californiapreservation.org/

John Merritt, Executive Director

PROGRAMS: Historic preservation.

California State Archives Foundation

California State Archives, 1020 "O" St., Sacramento, CA 95814; (916) 445-4293

Tom Stallard, President

PROGRAMS: Archives; public relations.

Conference of California Historical Societies

University of the Pacific, Stockton, CA 95211; (209) 946-2169; Fax (209) 946-2169; Cchs@uop.edu; www.uop.edu/organizations/CCHSBROC.html

Daryl Morrison, Executive Secretary

PROGRAMS: Archives; historic preservation; historic sites; museum; newsletters, magazines; public relations; research.

Department of Parks and Recreation

1416 9th St., P.O. Box 942896, Sacramento, CA 94296-0001; (916) 445-6477; cal-parks.ca.gov/default.asp

Rusty Areias, Director

PROGRAMS: Archaeology; collecting; conservation; exhibits; historic preservation; historic sites; living history; markers; museum; newsletters, magazines; photographic collections; public relations; research; tours.

Native American Heritage Commission

915 Capitol Mall, Rm. 364, Sacramento, CA 95814; (916) 653-4082; Fax (916) 657-5390; ceres.ca.gov/nahc/default.html

Larry Myers, Executive Secretary

PROGRAMS: Archaeology; historic sites; newsletters, magazines; public relations; relocation of human remains.

Office of Historic Preservation

Dept. of Parks and Recreation, 1416 9th St., Rm. 1442, P.O. Box 942806, Sacramento, CA 94296-0001; (916) 653-6624; Fax (916) 653-9824; calshpo@ohp.parks.ca.gov; ohp.parks.ca.gov/

Knox Mellon, SHPO

PROGRAMS: Archaeology; historic preservation; historic sites; markers; newsletters, magazines; public relations; research.

Office of Records Management

Dept. of General Services, 428 "J" St., Ste. 390, Sacramento, CA 95814; (916) 445-2294

Melodie Cato, chief

PROGRAMS: Newsletters, magazines, records management.

California State Archives

Secretary of State Complex, 1020 "O" St., Sacramento, CA 95814; (916) 653-7715; Fax (916) 653-7363; ArchivesWeb@ss.ca.gov; www.ss.ca.gov/archives/archives.htm

Walt Gray, State Archivist

PROGRAMS: Archives; collecting; conservation; exhibits; genealogy; newsletters, magazines; oral history; photographic collections; public relations; records management; research; school programs; tours.

California State Historic Records Advisory Board

California Heritage Preservation Commission, 1020 "O" St., Sacramento, CA 95814; (916) 653-7715

Walt Gray, Chair; State Archivist

PROGRAMS: Archives; conservation; oral history; photographic collections; public relations; records management; grant evaluation.

California State Library

State Library and Courts Bldg. (L&C I) 914 Capitol Mall, State Information and Reference Center, Rm. 301, (916) 654-0261; cslsirc@library.ca.go

Law Library, Rm. 305; (916) 654-0185; csllaw@library.ca.gov

Government Publications Section, Rm. 304; (916) 654-0069; cslgps@library.ca.gov; Sacramento, CA 95814; www.library.ca.gov/html/cslgen3.html

Library & Courts Building II (L&C II) 900 N Street, California Room, Rm. 200, Sacramento, CA 95814; (916) 654-0176; www.library.ca.gov/html/cslgen3.html

Sutro Library, 480 Winston Drive, San Francisco, CA 94132, (415) 731-4477; sutro@library.ca.gov; www.library.ca.gov/html/cslgen3.html

Kevin Starr, State Librarian

PROGRAMS: AV programs; collecting; conservation; exhibits; genealogy; library; newsletters, magazines; photographic collections; public relations; research; school programs; tours.

Colorado

Colorado Endowment for the Humanities

1490 Lafayette St., Suite 101, Denver, CO 80218; (303) 894-7951; (303) 864-9361; info@ceh.org; www.ceh.org/

Margaret A. Coval, Executive Director

PROGRAMS: Exhibits; newsletters, magazines; public relations, program funding.

Colorado Historical Records Advisory Board

Colorado State Archives, 1313 Sherman, Rm 1B-20, Denver, CO 80203; Voice (303) 866-2055: Fax (303) 866-2257; archives@state.co.us; www.archives.state.co.us/chrab/

Terry Ketelsen, Chair; State Archivist

PROGRAMS: Archives; field services; public relations; records management; screen and advise on NHPRC grants.

Colorado Historical Society

1300 Broadway, Denver, CO 80203; (303) 866-3682; www.coloradohistory.org/

Georgianna Contiguglia, President.

PROGRAMS: Archaeology; archives; AV programs; book publishing; collecting; conservation; exhibits; field services; genealogy; historic preservation; historic sites; library; markers; museums; newsletters, magazines; oral history; photographic collections; public relations; research; school programs; tours.

Colorado Preservation, Inc.

910 16th Street, Suite 1100, Denver, CO 80202; P.O. Box 843, Denver, CO 80201-0843; (303) 893-4260; Fax (303) 893-4333; info@coloradopreservation.org; www.colorado preservation.org

Barbara Macfarlane, President

PROGRAMS: Archaeology; field services; historic preservation; markers; newsletters, magazines; public relations; conferences; speakers bureau.

Connecticut

Connecticut Historical Commission

59 South Prospect Street, Hartford, CT 06106; (860) 566-3005; Fax (860) 566-5078; arch net@borealis.lib.uconn.edu; archnet.asu.edu/ archnet/uconn_extras/crm/conn/ctshpo.html

John W. Shannahan, SHPO

PROGRAMS: Book publishing; historic preservation; historic sites.

Connecticut Historical Society

One Elizabeth Street, Hartford, CT 06105; (860) 236-5621; Fax (860) 236-2664 ask_us@chsorg; www.chs.org

Connecticut Humanities Council

955 South Main Street, Suite E, Middletown, CT 06457; (860) 685-2260; Fax (860) 704-0429; www.cthum.org/

Bruce Fraser, Executive Director

Connecticut State Library

231 Capitol Avenue, Hartford, CT 06106; (860) 757-6565; Fax (860) 757-6503; www.cslib. org/isd.htm

Lynne Newell, Director

Connecticut State Museum and Archives

State Archives, Connecticut State Library, 231 Capitol Avenue, Hartford, CT 06106; (860) 757-6595; Fax (860) 757-6542; www.cslib. org/archives.htm

Mark H. Jones, State Archivist

Museum of Connecticut History

Connecticut State Library, 231 Capitol Avenue, Hartford, CT 06106; (860) 757-6535; Fax (860) 757-6533; www.cslib.org/museum.htm

Dean Nelson, Museum Administrator

Connecticut Trust for Historic Preservation

40 Whitney Avenue, Hamden, CT 06517-4002; (203) 562-6312; Fax (203) 773-0107; contact@cttrust.org; www.cttrust.org/

Delaware

Delaware Humanities Forum

100 West 10th Street, Ste 1009, Wilmington, DE 19801; (302) 657-0650; Fax 302-657-0655; dhfdirector@dhf.org; www.dhf.org/

Henry Hirshbiel, Executive Director

Delaware Public Archives

121 Duke of York St, Dover, DE 19901; (302) 736-95318; Fax (302) 739-2578; archives@state.de.us; www.archives.lib.de.us

Howard P. Lowell, State Archivist and Records Administrator

PROGRAMS: Archives; collecting; conservation; exhibits; genealogy; library; newsletters, magazines; photographic collections; public relations; records management; research; tours.

Delaware State Historic Preservation Office

15 The Green Dover, DE 19901-3611; (302) 739-5685; Fax: (302) 739-5660; www.state.de.us/shpo/

Joan N. Larrivee, Deputy, SHPO

PROGRAMS: Archaeology; conservation; field services; historic preservation; photographic collections; research.

Delaware State Museums

102 S. State St., Dover, DE 19901; (302) 739-5316; Fax (302) 739-6712; www.destatemuseums.org

James A. Stewart, Administrator

PROGRAMS: AV programs; collecting; conservation; exhibits, historic preservation; historic sites; living history; markers; museum; research; school programs.

Division of Historical and Cultural Affairs

Department of State, Hall of Records, 121 Duke of York St, Ste. 1, Dover, DE 19901; (302) 739-5314; Fax (302) 739-6710; www.state.de.us/sos/histcult.htm

Daniel R. Griffith, Director; SHPO

PROGRAMS: Archaeology, archives; conservation; exhibits; historic preservation; historic sites; markers; museum; newsletters, magazines; photographic collections; public relations; records management; research; school programs.

Division of Libraries

43 S. DuPont Hwy, Edgehill Shopping Center, P.O. Box 1401, Dover, DE 19903; (302) 739-4748; Fax (302) 739-6787

Louise E. Wyche, Director; State Librarian

PROGRAMS: Library; research; administers twenty-seven public libraries and two bookmobiles.

Historical Society of Delaware

505 Market St., Wilmington, DE 19801; (302) 655-7161; hsd@hsd.org; www.hsd.org/

Charles T. Lyle, Director

PROGRAMS: Archives; AV programs; book publishing; collecting; exhibits; genealogy; historic sites; library; museum; newsletters, magazines; photographic collections; public relations; research; school programs; tours.

Office of Administration, Public Information

Div. of Historical and Cultural Affairs, Dept. of State, Hall of Records, Duke of York St., P.O. Box 1401, Dover, DE 19903; (302) 736-5313

Robert F. Jacobs, Public Information Officer

PROGRAMS: Newsletters, magazines; public relations.

District of Columbia

Historic Preservation Division

District of Columbia Department of Consumer and Regulatory Affairs, 941 N. Capitol St., NE, Rm. 2500, Washington, DC 20002; (202) 442-4570; www.dchistoric.org/

Stephen J. Raiche, Chief

PROGRAMS: Archaeology, field services, historic preservation; school programs; state historic preservation office; administers DC historic landmark protection act, which is city's comprehensive law.

Historical Society of Washington, D.C., The

1307 New Hampshire Ave., NW, Washington, DC 20036-1507; 202-785-2068; www.hswdc.org/HSWMain/

Barbara Franco, Executive Director

PROGRAMS: Educational programs, exhibitions, museum, publications, research library.

Humanities Council of Washington, DC, The

925 U Street, NW, Washington, DC 20001; 202-387-8391; wdchumanities.org/

Joy F. Austin, Executive Director

Florida

Bureau of Archaeological Research

Dept. of State, Div. of Historical Resources, R. A. Gray Bldg., 500 S Bronough St., Tallahassee, FL 32399-0250; (850) 245-6444; dhr.dos.state.fl.us/bar/

James J. Miller, Bureau Chief

PROGRAMS: Archaeology; conservation; field services; historic sites; public relations; research.

Bureau of Historic Preservation

Dept. of State, Div. of Historical Resources, R. A. Gray Bldg., 500 S. Bronough St., Tallahassee, FL 32399-0250; (850) 245-6333; dhr.dos.state.fl.us/bhp/

Frederick Gaske, Bureau Chief; Deputy SHPO

PROGRAMS: Field services; historic preservation; historic sites; markers; newsletters, magazines; public relations; National Register of Historic Places, Main Street program.

Division of Historical Resources

Dept. of State, Div. of Historical Resources, R. A. Gray Bldg., 500 S. Bronough St., Tallahassee, FL 32399-0250; (850) 245-6300

Janet Matthews, Director; SHPO

PROGRAMS: Archaeology; conservation; exhibits; field services; historic preservation; historic sites; markers; museum; newsletters, magazines; public relations.

Florida History Associates

Dept. of State, Div. of Historical Resources, R. A. Gray Bldg., 500 S. Bronough St., Tallahassee, FL 32399-0250; (850) 245-6400

PROGRAMS: Archaeology; AV programs; collecting; conservation; exhibits; field services; historic preservation; historic sites; museum, newsletters, magazines; oral history; public relations; research; school programs; tours.

Florida Trust for Historic Preservation

P.O. Box 11206, Tallahassee, FL 32302; Dept. of State, Div. of Historical Resources, 500 S. Bronough Street, Room 426, Tallahassee, Florida 32399-0250; (850) 222-8128

Heather Mitchell, Executive Director

PROGRAMS: AV programs, field services; historic sites; newsletters, magazines; public relations; revolving fund.

Museum of Florida History

Dept. of State, Div. of Historical Resources, R. A. Gray Bldg., 500 S. Bronough St., Tallahassee, FL 32399-0250; (850) 245-6300

Jeana Brunson, Chief, Bureau of Historical Museums

PROGRAMS: Archaeology; AV programs; collecting; conservation; exhibits; field services; historic preservation; historic sites; museum; newsletters, magazines; oral history; public relations; research; school programs; tours.

State Historic Preservation Office

Dept. of State, Div. of Historical Resources, R. A. Gray Bldg., 500 S. Bronough St., Tallahassee, FL 32399-0250; (850) 488-1480

Janet Matthews, Director; SHPO

PROGRAMS: Archaeology; conservation; field services; historic preservation.

Georgia

Department of Archives and History

Office of Secretary of State, 330 Capitol Ave., SE, Atlanta, GA 30334; (404) 656-2358; www.sos.state.ga.us/archives/

David W. Carmicheal, Director

PROGRAMS: Archives; collecting; conservation; exhibits; field services; library; newsletters, magazines; photographic collections; public relations; records management.

Georgia Humanities Council

50 Hart Plaza, SE, Ste. 1565, Atlanta, GA 30303-2915; (404) 523-6220; www.georgiahumanities.org/

Jamol Zainaldin, President

Historic Preservation Division

156 Trinity Avenue, SW, Suite 101, Atlanta, GA 30303-3600; (404) 656-2840; www.state.ga.us/dnr/histpres/mainpage.html

W. Ray Luce, Division Director and Deputy SHPO

PROGRAMS: Archaeology; AV programs; exhibits; field services; historic preservation; library, newsletters, magazines; public relations; school programs; tours, technical assistance.

Hawaii

Archives Division

Hawaii State Archives, Kekauluohi Building, Iolani Palace Grounds Honolulu, Hawaii 96813; (808) 586-0329; www.state.hi.us/dags/archives/welcome.html

Jolyn G. Tamura, State Archives Administrator; State Archivist

PROGRAMS: Archives; collecting; exhibits; library; photographic collections; public relations; records management; references

COMMENTS: The Archives Division is made up of two branches: Historical Records and Records Management.

Hawaii Committee for the Humanities

First Hawaiian Bank Bldg., 3599 Walalae Ave., Rm. 23, Honolulu, HI 96816; (808) 732-5402; planet-hawaii.com/hch/

Edward J. Shultz, Chairman

Hawaii Historic Places Review Board

Board of Land and Natural Resources, 1151 Punchbowl St., Honolulu, HI 96813; (808) 692-8015; www.state.hi.us/dlnr/hpd/revbrd.htm

Roy K. Alameida, Chairperson Historic Preservation Division

PROGRAMS: Nominations to Hawaii and National Register of Historic Places; inventory; public relations.

Hawaii State Public Library System

Dept. of Education, 465 S. King St., Rm. B-1; Honolulu, HI 96813-5596; www.hcc.hawaii.edu/hspls/

Virginia Lowel, state librarian

PROGRAMS: AV programs; library; newsletters; magazines; photographic collections; public relations; school programs.

History and Humanities Program of State Foundation on Cultural and the Arts

Dept. of Accounting and General Services, 44 Merchant St., Honolulu, HI 96813; (808) 586-0300; www.state.hi.us/sfca/histhumanities.html

Ken Hamilton, SFCA public information officer

PROGRAMS: Book publishing; field services; historic preservation; public relations; research; public programs; administers state funding for history activities; technical services.

State Historic Preservation Division

601 Kamokila Blvd. Rm. 555, Kapolei, HI 96707; Dept. of Land and Natural Resources, (808) 692-8015; Fax (808) 692-8020; www.state.hi.us/dhr/hpd/hpgreeting.htm

Don J. Hibbard, administrator historic preservation division

PROGRAMS: Historic preservation review and compliance: archaeology; architecture; ethnography; burial sites program; oral history; library; historic sites inventory; photograph collections; public relations; research; school programs.

State Historic Preservation Office

Department of Land and Natural Resources, 1151 Punchbowl St., Honolulu, HI 96813; (808) 548-6550; www.state.hi.us/dlnr/hpd/hpgreeting.htm

Timothy E. Johns, Chair, Board of Land and Natural Resources; SHPO

PROGRAMS: Historic preservation; historic sites.

State Parks Division

Department of Land and Natural Resources, 1151 Punchbowl Street, Rm. 310, Honolulu, HI 96813; (808) 587-0300; www.state.hi.us/dlnr/Welcome.html

Ralston H. Nagata, Administrator

PROGRAMS: Preservation of historic properties; park interpretation; public curator programs; oral history; historical research.

Survey Division

Dept. of Accounting and General Services, 1151 Punchbowl St., Rm. 210, Honolulu, HI 96813.

Randal Hashimoto, State Land Surveyor and Administrator

PROGRAMS: Archives for historic land survey maps; survey records.

Idaho

Administrative Services

Idaho State Historical Society, 1109 Main Street, Suite 250, Boise, ID 83702; (208) 334-2682; www2.state.id.us/ishs/

Steve Guerber, Director

PROGRAMS: Archaeology; archives; AV programs; book publishing; collecting; conservation; exhibits; field services; genealogy; historic preservation; historic sites; library; living history; markers; museum; newsletters, magazines; public relations; records management; research; school programs; tours; fiscal management.

Historic Sites

Idaho State Historical Society, 610 N. Julia Davis Dr., Boise, ID 83702; (208) 334-2120

Ken Swanson Administrator

PROGRAMS: AV programs; collecting; conservation; exhibits; historic preservation; historic sites; museum; public relations; research; school programs; tours.

Idaho Humanities Council

217 West State Street, Boise, Idaho 83702; (208) 345-5346; www2.state.id.us/ihc/ihc.htm

Rick Ardinger, Executive Director

Historical Library & State Archives

Idaho State Historical Society, 450 North 4th Street, Boise, ID 83702; (208) 334-5335

Linda Morton-Keithley, Administrator

PROGRAMS: Archives; collecting; conservation; field services; genealogy; historic preservation; library; markers; photographic collections; public relations; records management; research.

Idaho State Historical Museum

Idaho State Historical Society, 610 N. Julia Davis Dr., Boise, ID 83702; (208) 334-2120

Kenneth J. Swanson, Administrator

PROGRAMS: AV programs; collecting; conservation; exhibits; field services; historic preservation; living history; museum; public relations; research; school programs; tours.

State Historic Preservation Office (SHPO) & Archaeological Survey

Idaho State Historical Society, 210 Main Street, Boise, ID 83702; (208) 334-3847

Ken Reid, State Archaeologist; Administrator

PROGRAMS: Archaeology; collecting; conservation; field services; historic preservation; oral history; public relations; records management; research; school programs.

Illinois

Illinois Department of Natural Resources

Lincoln Tower Plaza, 524 S. Second St., Room 500, Springfield, IL 62701; 217/782-7454; dnr.state.il.us/

Brent Manning, Director

PROGRAMS: Archaeology; collecting; conservation; exhibits; museum; newsletters, magazines; public relations; school programs; tours. Parent agency for the Illinois State Museum.

Illinois Humanities Council

203 North Wabash Avenue, Suite 2020, Chicago, Illinois 60601-2417; (312) 422-5580; www.prairie.org/

Kristina A. Valaitis, Executive Director

Illinois State Archives

Norton Building, Capitol Complex, Springfield, IL 62756; (217) 782-4682; www.sos.state.il.us/departments/archives/archives.html

John Daly, Director

PROGRAMS: Archives; collecting; conservation; exhibits; photographic collections; record management; research. Division of the Secretary of State's office; Secretary of State serves as the state archivist.

Illinois Historic Preservation Agency

500 East Madison, Springfield, Illinois 62701; Phone: (217) 785-1511; www.state.il.us/HPA/

Susan Mogerman, Director

PROGRAMS: Archaeology; book publishing; collecting; conservation; exhibits; field services; genealogy; historic preservation; historic sites; library; living history; markers; museum; newsletters, magazines; oral history; photographic collections; public relations; records management; research; school programs; tours.

Illinois State Historical Society

210 1/2 S. Sixth, Springfield, IL 62701; (217) 525-2781; www.historyillinois.org/

Rand Burnette, President

PROGRAMS: Book publishing; exhibits; markers; newsletters, magazines; public relations; tours.

Illinois State Library

300 S. 2nd Street, Springfield, IL 62701; (217) 785-5600; www.sos.state.il.us/library/sl/isl.html

Jean E. Wilkins, Director

PROGRAMS: Conservation; library; newsletters, magazines; public relations; research. Division of the Secretary of State's office; Secretary of State serves as the state librarian.

Indiana

Division of Historic Preservation and Archaeology

402 W. Washington Street, W274 , Indianapolis, Indiana 46204; (317) 232-1645; www.state.in.us/dnr/historic/

Jon Smith, Director

PROGRAMS: Archaeology; field services; historic preservation; records management; research.

Division of Indiana State Museum and Historic Sites

Dept. of Natural Resources, 202 N. Alabama, Indianapolis, IN 46204; (317) 232-1637

PROGRAMS: Collecting; exhibits; historic sites; museum; public relations; research; school programs; tours.

Division of State Parks

Dept. of Natural Resources, 100 N. Senate Ave., Rm. 616, Indianapolis, IN 46204; (317) 232-4136

William Walters, Director

PROGRAMS: Management and programming at state parks.

Historic Landmarks Foundation of Indiana, Inc.

340 West Michigan Street, Indianapolis, IN 46202; (317) 639-4534; www.historicland marks.org/

PROGRAMS: Book publishing; field services; historic preservation; historic sites; library; museum; newsletters, magazines; photographic collections; school programs; tours; information center.

Indiana Commission on Public Records

402 W. Washington St., IGCS, W472, Indianapolis, IN 46204; (317) 232-3373; www.ai.org/icpr/

F. Gerald Handfield Jr., Director; State Archivist

PROGRAMS: Archives; conservation; records management.

Indiana Historical Bureau

140 North Senate Avenue, Room 408, Indianapolis, Indiana 46204; (317) 232-2535; www.statelib.lib.in.us/www/ihb/ihb.html

PROGRAMS: Book publishing; exhibits; field services; living history; markers; newsletters, magazines; research; school programs; Governor's portraits collection.

Indiana Historical Society

450 W. Ohio St, Indianapolis,IN 46202; (317) 232-1882; www.indianahistory.org/

Sal Cilella, President

PROGRAMS: Archaeology; archives; AV programs; book publishing; collecting; conservation; exhibits; field services; genealogy; library; newsletters, magazines; photographic collections; public relations.

Indiana State Library

Indiana Library and Historical Dept., 140 N. Senate Ave., Rm. 406, Indianapolis, IN 46204; (317) 232-3675; www.statelib.lib.in.us/

C. Ray Ewick, Director; State Librarian

PROGRAMS: Collecting; field services; genealogy; library; oral history; photographic collections; research.

Indiana State Museum Society, Inc.

Indiana State Museum, 202 N. Alabama, Indianapolis, IN 46204; (317) 632-5007

Cornelius Lee Alig, President

PROGRAMS: Support organization for Indiana State Museum.

The Society of Indiana Archivists

IUPUI University Library, 755 W. Michigan St., Indianapolis, IN 46202; (317) 274-0466; caw ley.archives.nd.edu/sia/index.html

Todd J. Daniels-Howell, President

PROGRAMS: Newsletters, magazines; meetings; conferences; training; advocacy.

Iowa

Community Programs Bureau

State Historical Society of Iowa, 600 E. Locust St., Des Moines, IA 50319-0290; (515) 281-5111; www.iowahistory.org.

Lowell Soike, Deputy SHPO; Bureau Chief.

PROGRAMS: Archaeology; historic preservation; education; outreach services; histories sites.

COMMENTS: Subsumed under Historic Preservation Survey. National Register of Historic Places; Investment Tax Act Program; Certified Local Governments Program; State Historic inventories.

Library and Publications Bureau

State Historical Society of Iowa Centennial Bldg., 402 Iowa Ave., Iowa City, IA 52240-1806; (319) 335-3916; www.iowahistory.org.

Shaner Magalhaes, Bureau Chief

PROGRAMS: Book publishing; field services; newsletters; magazines; public relations; research; school programs. The development program provides liaison with a private foundation to raise funds from the private sector. Archives; collecting; conservation; genealogy; library; oral history; photographic collections; reference; manuscripts; maps; preservation.

COMMENTS: Provides liaison with a private foundation to raise funds from the private sector. Manages the membership program and grant-writing for the State Historical Society.

Museum and Museum Education

State Historical Society of Iowa, 600 E. Locust St., Des Moines, IA 50319-0290; (515) 281-5111; www.iowahistory.org.

Jerome Thompson, Bureau Chief.

PROGRAMS: Conservation; exhibits; historic sites; museum; school programs.

Archives and Records Bureau

State Historical Society of Iowa, 600 E. Locust St., Des Moines, IA 50319-0290; (515) 281-5111; www.iowahistory.org.

Gordon Hendrickson, State Archivist; Bureau Chief.

PROGRAMS: Archives; collecting; genealogy; oral history; photographic collections; reference; manuscripts; maps.

State Historical Society of Iowa

600 E. Locust St., Des Moines, IA 50319-0290; (515) 281-5111; www.iowahistory.org.

Anita Walker, Director of Department of Cultural Affairs.

PROGRAMS: Archaeology; archives; book publishing; collecting; conservation; exhibits; field service; genealogy; historic preservation; historic sites; library; markers; museum; newsletters; magazines; oral history; photographic collections; public relations; research; school programs; tours; market research; tourism.

Kansas

Kansas Anthropological Association

c/o Archeology Office, Kansas State Historical Society, 6425 SW 6th Ave., Topeka, KS 66615-1099; (785) 272-8681; www.kshs.org/resource/kaa.htm

Dick Keck, President

PROGRAMS: Archaeology; newsletters, magazines.

Kansas City Area Archivists

c/o Western Historical Manuscripts Collection, University of Missouri-Kansas City, 320 Newcomb Hall, 5100 Rockhill Road, Kansas City, MO 64110-2499; (816) 235-1543; www.umkc.edu/KCAA/

Deborah Dandridge, Co-Chair

PROGRAMS: Newsletters, magazines; professional education programs.

Kansas Humanities Council

112 SW Sixth Avenue, Suite 210, Topeka, KS 66603; phone: (785) 357-0359; fax: (785) 357-1723; email: kshumcoun@aol.com; www.ukans.edu/kansas/khc/

Marion Cott, Executive Director

Kansas State Historical Society

6425 SW 6th Ave., Topeka, KS 66615-1099; (785) 272-8681; www.kshs.org

Ramon Powers, Executive Director

PROGRAMS: Archaeology; archives; AV programs; book publishing; collecting; conservation; exhibits; genealogy; historic preservation; historic sites; library; markers; museum; newsletters, magazines; oral history; photographic collections; public relations; records management; research; school programs; tours; manuscripts.

Kansas State Library

300 S.W. Tenth Avenue, Room 343-N, Topeka, KS 66612-1593; phone: (785) 296-3296 or (800) 432-3919; fax: (785) 296-6650; www.skyways.org/KSL/

Duane Johnson, State Librarian

PROGRAMS: Library; newsletters, magazines; regional library network; services for blind and visually handicapped; legislative services.

Kentucky

Blue Grass Trust for Historic Preservation

253 Market St., Lexington, KY 40507; 606-253-0362; Fax (606) 259-9210; www.blue grasstrust.org/

Kelly Willis, Administrative Director

Kentucky Department of Parks

Capital Plaza Tower, 500 Mero Street, Suite 1100, Frankfort, KY 40601; (800) 255-7275; www.state.ky.us/agencies/parks/parkhome.htm

June Hudson, Commissioner

PROGRAMS: Historic sites; markers.

Kentucky Department of Libraries and Archives

300 Coffee Tree Rd., PO Box 537, Frankfort, KY 40602-0537; (502) 564-8300; (502) 564-5773; www.kdla.state.ky.us/

Kentucky Geological Survey

228 Mining & Mineral Resources Building, University of Kentucky, Lexington, KY 40506-0107; (859) 257-5500; Fax: 606/257-1147; www.uky.edu/KGS/home.htm

Kentucky Heritage Council

300 Washington St., Frankfort, KY, 40601; (502) 564-7005; Fax (502) 564-5820; www.state.ky.us/agencies/khc/khchome.htm

David L. Morgan, Executive Director and SHPO

PROGRAMS: Archaeology, historic preservation, and historic sites

Kentucky Historical Society

100 Broadway, Frankfurt, KY 40601; (502) 564-1792; www.state.ky.us/agencies/khs/

J. Kevin Graffagnino, Executive Director

PROGRAMS: Collecting; genealogy; historic preservation; records management.

Kentucky Humanities Council

206 East Maxwell Street, Lexington, KY 40508; (859) 257-5932; Fax: (859) 257-5933; www.kyhumanities.org/

PROGRAMS: Grants and services intended to foster greater understanding of the humanities.

Louisiana

Louisiana State Archives

3851 Essen Ln., Baton Rouge, LA 70809; (225) 922-1000

Florent Hardy, Jr., State Archivist

PROGRAMS: Archives; collecting; conservation; exhibits; field services; genealogy; historic preservation; library; newsletters, magazines; oral history; photographic collections; public relations; records management; research; school programs; tours.

Louisiana Endowment for the Humanities

938 Lafayette Street, Suite 300, New Orleans, LA 70113; (504) 523-4352; www.leh.org/

Dr. Michael Sartisky, President/Executive Director

Louisiana Office of State Parks

Louisiana Dept. of Culture, Recreation and Tourism, P.O. Box 44426, Baton Rouge, LA 70804-4426; (225) 342-8111; www.lastate parks.com

Dwight Landreneau, Assistant Secretary

PROGRAMS: AV programs; collecting; conservation; exhibits; historic sites; museum; photographic collections; records management; research; tours.

COMMENTS: Develops, operates, and maintains a system of state parks (recreation sites), state commemorative areas (historic sites), and state preservation areas (natural areas).

Louisiana State Museum

Department of Culture, Recreation and Tourism, 751 Chartres St., New Orleans, LA 70116; (504) 568-6967; lsm.crt.state.la.us/

James F. Sefcik, Director; Assistant Secretary, Dept. of Culture, Recreation and Tourism.

PROGRAMS: Archaeology; book publishing; collecting; conservation; exhibits; genealogy; historic sites; library; museum; oral history; photographic collections; public relations; research; school programs; tours.

Louisiana Office of Cultural Development

Louisiana Dept. of Culture, Recreation and Tourism, P.O. Box 44427, Baton Rouge, LA 70804; (225) 342-8200

Laurel Wyckoff, Office of Cultural Development, Assistant Secretary and SHPO

PROGRAMS: Historic preservation.

Louisiana Division Historic Preservation Office

Louisiana Dept. of Culture, Recreation and Tourism, Office of Cultural Development, P.O. Box 44247 Baton Rouge, LA 70804; (225) 342-8160

Laurel Wyckoff, Office of Cultural Development, Assistant Secretary and SHPO

PROGRAMS: Archaeology; collecting; historic preservation; markers; newsletters, magazines.

State Library of Louisiana

Louisiana Dept. of Culture, Recreation and Tourism, 701 North 4th Street, Baton Rouge, LA 70802; (225) 342-4923; www.state.lib.la.us/

Thomas F. Jaques, State Librarian

PROGRAMS: Library.

Maine

Bureau of Parks and Lands

286 Water Street, 3rd and 5th floors, Key Bank Plaza, Augusta, ME 04333; phone: (207) 287-3821; fax: (207) 287-8111; www.state.me.us/doc/parks/

Thomas A. Morrison, Director

PROGRAMS: Archaeology; book publishing; collecting; exhibits; field services; historic preservation; historic sites; museum; newsletters, magazines; public relations; research; school programs; tours.

Maine Preservation

P.O. Box 1198, Portland, ME 04104-1198; phone: (207) 775-3652; fax: (207) 775-7737; www.mainepreservation.com/home.htm

Roxanne Eflin, Executive Director

PROGRAMS: Archaeology; historic preservation; historic sites; newsletters, magazines; public relations.

Center for Maine History

485 Congress St., Portland, ME 04101; phone: (207) 774-1822; fax: (207) 775-4301; www.mainehistory.org; info@mainehistory.org

Richard D'Abate, Executive Director

PROGRAMS: Archives; book publishing; collecting; exhibits; field services, genealogy; historic preservation; historic sites; library; living history; museum; newsletters, magazines; oral history; photographic collections; public relations; records management, research; school programs; tours.

Maine Historic Preservation Commission

55 Capitol Street, State House Station 65, Augusta, Maine 04333-0065; phone: (207) 287-2132; www.state.me.us/mhpc/

Earle G. Shettleworth, Director

PROGRAMS: Archaeology; book publishing; collecting; conservation; exhibits; field services; historic preservation; historic sites; newsletters, magazines; photographic collections; public relations; records magazines; research.

Maine Humanities Council

674 Brighton Avenue, Portland, ME 04102-1012; phone: (207) 773-5051; fax: (207) 773-2416; info@mainehumanities.org; www.mainehumanities.org

Geoffrey Gratwick, Chair

Dorothy Schwartz, Executive Director

Maine Archives and Museums

60 Community Drive, Augusta, ME 04330; (207) 623-8428 ext. 296; 1-800-452-8786 ext. 296; www.mainemuseums.org

Jim Henderson, President, Maine State Archives

Maine State Archives

84 State House Station, Augusta, ME 04333-0084; phone: (207) 287-5795; fax: (207) 287-5739; www.state.me.us/sos/arc/

James S. Henderson, State Archivist

PROGRAMS: Archives; collecting; conservation; field services; genealogy; library; newsletter, magazines; public relations; records management; research.

Maine State Library

LMA Building, State House Station 64, Augusta, Maine 04333l; phone: (207) 287-5600; fax (207) 287-5615; tty: (207) 287-5622; www.state.me.us/msl/mslhome.htm

J. Gary Nichols, Maine State Librarian

PROGRAMS: AV programs; book publishing; collecting; conservation; field services; genealogy; library; newsletters, magazines; photographic collections; public relations; records management; research; tours.

Maine State Museum

3 State House Station, Augusta, ME 04333-0083; phone: (207) 287-2301; fax: (207) 287-6633; tty: (207) 287-6740; www.state.me.us/museum/homepage.asp

Joseph R. Phillips, Director

PROGRAMS: Archaeology; book publishing; collecting; conservation; exhibits; field services; library; museum; newsletters, magazines; photographic collections; public relations; records management; research; school programs; tours.

Maryland

Maryland Commission Afro-American History and Culture

Banneker-Douglass Museum of Afro-American Life and History, 84 Franklin St., Annapolis, MD 21404; (410) 974-2893

Tonya Hardy, Director

PROGRAMS: Collecting; exhibits; field services; library; museum; newsletters; oral history; photographic collections; public relations; research; school programs; tours.

Maryland Commission on Indian Affairs

c/o DHCP, 100 Community Place, Crownsville, MD 21032; (410) 514-7650

Ms. Elaine Eff, Acting Administrator

PROGRAMS: Archaeology; archives; AV programs; exhibits; field services; genealogy; historic sites; library; living history; museum; oral history; public relations; research; school programs; funding resources; cultural preservation.

Maryland Cultural Resource Management Program

580 Taylor Ave., Annapolis, MD 21401; (410) 260-8164

Ros Kimmel, Supervisor

PROGRAMS: Conservation; exhibits; historic preservation; historic sites; markers; museum; school programs; tours; publications; management of DNR's historic properties.

Maryland Association of Historic District Commissions

P.O. Box 783, Frederick, MD 21705; (410) 465-3121

Lisa Wingate, Executive Director

PROGRAMS: Field services; historic preservation; newsletters, magazines; public relations; training programs.

Maryland Historical Society

201 W. Monument St., Baltimore, MD 21201; (410) 685-3750; www.mdhs.org/

Dennis Fiori, Director

PROGRAMS: Archaeology; archives; AV programs; book publishing; collecting; exhibits; field services; genealogy; historic sites; library; living history; museum; newsletters, magazines; oral history; photographic collections; public relations; research; school programs; tours; fund raising; museum shop; editorial projects.

Maryland Historical Trust

100 Community Place, Crownsville, MD 21032; (410) 514-7600; www.marylandhistoricaltrust.net/index.html

J. Rodney Little, Director; SHPO

PROGRAMS: Archaeology; archives; AV programs; book publishing; conservation; exhibits; field services; preservation; historic sites; library; markers; newsletters, magazines; photographic collections; public relations; research; school programs; tours.

Maryland Humanities Council

Executive Plaza One, Suite 503, 11350 McCormick Road, Hunt Valley, Maryland 21031; (410) 771-0650; www.mdhc.org/

Barbara Wells Sarudy, Executive Director

PROGRAMS: Field services; historic preservation; historic sites; newsletters; public relations; membership program; fund development; administrative services to other non-profit organizations.

Maryland Records Management Division

P.O. Box 275, 7275 Waterloo Rd., Rts. 175 and U.S. 1, Jessup, MD 20794; (410) 799-1930

Paul Lamberson, Records Manager

PROGRAM: Records management.

Maryland State Archives

350 Rowe Blvd., Annapolis, MD 21401; (410) 260-6400; www.mdarchives.state.md.us/

Edward C. Papenfuse, State Archivist

PROGRAMS: Archives; book publishing; collecting; conservation; exhibits; field services; genealogy; library; photographic collections; public relations; research; school programs; tours.

State Library Resource Center

Enoch Pratt Free Library, 400 Cathedral St., Baltimore, MD 21201; (410) 396-5430

Carla Hayden, Director

PROGRAMS: Field services, library

Preservation Maryland

24 W. Saratoga St., Baltimore, MD 21201; (410) 685-2886; www.preservemd.org/

Tyler Gearhart, Executive Director

Massachusetts

Massachusetts Archives and Commonwealth Museum

220 Morrissey Blvd, Boston, MA 02125; (617) 727-2816; Fax (617) 288-8429; archives@ sec.state.ma.us; www.state.ma.us/sec/arc

Massachusetts Foundation for Humanities and Public Policy

(Main Office) 66 Bridge Street, Northampton, MA 01060; (413) 584-8440; Fax (413) 584-8440; www.mfh.org/foundation/

David Tebaldi, Executive Director

(Metro Boston Office) 125 Walnut Street, Watertown, MA 02472; (617) 923-1678; Fax (617) 923-8426;

Ellen Rothman, Associate Director

Massachusetts Historical Commission

Secretary of Commonwealth Office, 220 Morrissey Blvd., Boston, MA 02125; (617) 727-8470; Fax (617) 727-5128; mhc@sec. state.ma.us; www.state.ma.us/sec/mhc/mh cidx.htm

Judith B. McDonough, Executive Director; SHPO

PROGRAMS: Archaeology, exhibits, field services; historic preservation; historic sites, newsletters, magazines; public relations; grants; tax act review; review and compliance; National Register program.

Massachusetts Historical Society

1154 Boylston St, Boston, MA 02215; (617) 536-1608; Fax (617) 859-0074; masshist@ masshist.org; www.masshist.org

Michigan

Michigan Historical Center

717 W. Allegan, Lansing, MI 48918; (517) 373-3559; www.sos.state.mi.us/history/history.html

Sandra S. Clark, Director

PROGRAMS: Archaeology; archives; web, book and magazine publishing; collections; exhibits; 9 field museums and sites; historic preservation, historic markers; centennial farms, education; underwater archaeology.

Mackinac Island State Park Commission

Michigan Department of Natural Resources

Summer (May-September): P.O. Box 370, Mackinac Island, MI 49757; (906) 847-3328; Fax: (906) 847-3815

Winter (October-April): Knapps Centre, 4th Fl., P.O. Box 30028, Lansing, MI 48909; (517) 373-4296

mackinacparks@state.mi.us; www.mackinac parks.com/island.shtml

Carol R. Nold, director

Michigan Humanities Council

119 Pere Marquette Dr., Ste 3B, Lansing, MI 48912-1270; (517) 372-7770; Fax (517) 372-0027; mihum@voyager.net; michiganhumani ties.org/contact.html

Rick Knupfer, Director

Michigan Council for Arts and Cultural Affairs

Department of Consumer & Industry Services

525 W. Ottawa, P.O. Box 30004, Lansing, MI 48909; (517) 373-1820; artsinfo@cis.state. mi.us; www.commerce.state.mi.us/arts/home. htm

Betty Boone, Executive Director

Michigan Historic Preservation Network

P.O. Box 720, Clarkston, MI 48347-0720; (248) 625-8181; mhpn@voyager.net; www.mhpn.org

Jennifer Radcliff, President

Historical Society of Michigan

2117 Washtenaw, Ann Arbor, MI 48104; (734) 769-1828; hsm@hsofmich.org; www.hsofmich. org

Larry Wagenaar, Executive Director

Michigan Museums Association

P.O. Box 10067, 717 W. Allegan, Lansing, MI 48901-0067; (517) 482-4055; www.michigan museums.org

LuAnn Kern, Director

Minnesota

Minnesota Historical Society

345 W. Kellogg Blvd., St. Paul, MN 55102-1906; (651) 296-6126; www.mnhs.org

PROGRAMS: Archaeology; archives; AV programs; book publishing; collecting; conservation; exhibits and a travelling exhibits; field services; genealogy; historic preservation; historic sites; library; living history; photographic collections; public relations; records management; research; school programs; tours; state archives; state historic preservation office; education dept.; teacher's workshops; newspaper microfilm program; grants program; museum shops.

Minnesota Humanities Commission

987 East Ivy Avenue, St. Paul, MN 55106; (651) 774 -0105; Toll Free: (866) 268-7293; Fax (651) 774 - 0205; www.thinkmhc.org/contact.htm

PROGRAMS: Coordinates educational humanities programs.

Minnesota State Archives

345 W. Kellogg Blvd., St. Paul, MN 55102-1906; (651) 296-6126; www.mnhs.org/preserve/records/about.html

State Archaeologist

Minnesota Historical Society, 204 Research Laboratory Bldg., University of Minnesota-Duluth, Duluth, MN 55812; (218) 726-7154. Office of the State Archaeologist; Fort Snelling History Center; St. Paul, MN 55111-4061; (612) 725-2411; Fax (612) 725-2427; www.admin.state.mn.us/osa/

Mark J. Dudzik, State Archaeologist

PROGRAMS: Archaeology; collecting; conservation; field services; historic preservation; markers; newsletters; photographic collections; public relations; records management; research; school programs.

Mississippi

Archives and Library Division

Capers Building, 100 South State Street, P. O. Box 571, Jackson, MS 39205-0571; (601) 359-6876; Fax (601) 359-6964; refdesk@mdah.state.ms.us; www.mdah.state.ms.us/

Elbert R. Hillard, Director

PROGRAMS: Archaeology; archives; AV programs; book publishing; collecting; conservation; exhibits; field services; genealogy; historic preservation; historic sites; library; markers; museum; newsletters; magazines; oral history; photographic collections; public relations; records management; research, school programs; tours.

Historic Preservation Division

Department of Archives and History, GM&O Depot Building at, 618 E. Pearl St., Jackson, MS 39201; (601) 354-7326; Fax (601) 359-6955; msshpo@mdah.state.ms.us; www.mdah.state.ms.us/hpres/hprestxt.html

Ken Pool, Director; Deputy, SHPO

PROGRAMS: Archaeology; AV programs; book publishing; collecting; field services; historic preservation; markers; photographic collections; public relations; research; school programs.

Historic Properties Division

Department of Archives and History, 400 Jefferson Davis Blvd., Natchez, MS 39120; (601) 446-6502;

James F. Barnett, Jr., Director

PROGRAMS: Archaeology; AV programs; collecting; exhibits; field services; historic sites; living history; museum; public relations; research; school programs; tours.

Mississippi Historical Society

100 S. State St., Jackson, MS 39201; (601) 359-1424; www.mdah.state.ms.us/admin/mhistsoc.html

Zora A. Brown, President

PROGRAMS: Book publishing; newsletters, magazines; public relations.

Mississippi Humanities Council

3825 Ridgewood Road, Room 311, Jackson, Mississippi 39211-6463; (601) 432-6752; Fax (601) 432-6750 www.ihl.state.ms.us/mhc/index.html

Barbara Carpenter, Director

Mississippi Museums Association

111 N. Jefferson, Jackson, MS 39202; (601) 354-7303

Cathy Shropshire, President

PROGRAMS: Field services; museum; newsletters, magazines; public relations.

Records Management Division

Dept. of Archives and History, 929 High St., Jackson, MS 39202; (601) 3547688

William J. Hanna, Director; Deputy State Historical Records Coordinator

PROGRAMS: Field services; records management; microfilm service.

State Historical Museum

Dept. of Archives and History, 100 S. State St., Jackson, MS 39201; (601) 354-6222

Patti Carr Black, Director

PROGRAMS: AV programs; book publishing; collecting; conservation; exhibits; field services; museum; photographic collections; public relations; research; school programs; tours.

Missouri

Coordinating Board for Higher Education

Missouri Department of Higher Education, 3515 Amazonas Dr., Jefferson City, MO 65109-5717; 573-751-2361; Fax: 573-751-6635; boardweb@mocbhe.gov; www.cbhe.state.mo.us/taboutus.htm

Henry S. Clapper, Chairman

Missouri Humanities Council

543 Hanley Industrial Court, Suite 201, St. Louis, Missouri 63144-1905; (314) 781-9660; (800) 357-0909; Fax (314) 781-9681; mail@mohumanities.org; www.mohumani ties.org.

Christine J. Reilly, Executive Director

Missouri State Library

Missouri State Library, P.O. Box 387, Jefferson City, MO 65102-0387; Fax (573) 751-3612; libref@mail.sos.state.mo.us; mosl.sos.state.mo.us/lib-ser/libser.html

Sara Parker, State Librarian

Missouri State Museum

First Fl, Capitol Bldg Rm B2, Jefferson City, MO 65101; (573) 751-2854; (573) 526-2927; Dspjeffl@dnr.mail.state.mo.us; www.mostate parks.com/jeffersonland/museum.htm

Records Services Department

Missouri State Archives

600 W. Main, P.O. Box 1747, Jefferson City, MO 65102; (573) 751-3280; Fax (573) 526-7333; archref@sosmail.state.mo.us; mosl.sos.state.mo.us/rec-man/arch.html

Kenneth H. Winn, State Archivist

Local Records

State Information Center, P.O. Box 1747, Jefferson City, Missouri 65102; (573) 751-9047; Fax (573) 526-3867

Records Management

600 W Main St., Jefferson City, MO 65102; PO Box 778; (573)751-3319; recman@sosmail.state.mo.us; mosl.sos.state.mo.us/rec-man/sosrecma.html

Marry-Ellyn Strauser, Director

State Historical Society of Missouri

1020 Lawry St., Columbia, MO 65201-7298; (573) 882-7083; Fax (573) 884-4950; shsof mo@umsystem.edu; www.system.missouri.edu/shs/

James W. Goodrich, Executive Director

Montana

Montana Committee for the Humanities

PO Box 8036, Hellgate Station Missoula, MT 59807; (406) 243-6022; Fax (406) 243-2748; www.ihl.state.ms.us/mhc/links/states/mt.html

Margaret Kingsland, Executive Director

Montana Historical Society

PO Box 201201, 225 N. Roberts, Helena, MT 59620; (406) 444-2694; www.his.state.mt.us/

Arnold Olsen, Director

PROGRAMS: Archaeology; archives; book publishing; collecting; exhibits; field services; historic preservation; historic sites; library; museum; newsletters, magazines; oral history; photographic collections; public relations; research; school programs; tours.

Montana State Historic Preservation Program

Montana Historical Society, PO Box 201202, 225 N. Roberts, Helena, MT 59620-1202; (406) 444-7715; (406) 444-6575; www.his.state.mt.us

Mark F. Baumler, SHPO

PROGRAMS: Archaeology; certified local governments program; cultural records office; his-

toric preservation review and compliance; historic signs program; National Register of Historic Places; state preservation planning; survey and inventory; tax incentives and architectural review.

Montana State Archives

Montana Historical Society, PO Box 201201, 225 N. Roberts, Helena, MT 59620; (406) 444-2694; archives@state.mt.us; www.his.state.mt.us

Katherine Otto, State Archivist

PROGRAMS: Archives, collecting, private manuscripts and records.

Montana State Library

1515 6th Avenue, PO Box 201800, Helena, MT 59620-1800; (406) 444-3115; Fax (406) 444-5612; msl.state.mt.us/

PROGRAMS: Collecting, field services; library; national heritage program.

Museums Association of Montana

Fort Missoula Historical Museum, Missoula, MT 59801; (406) 728-3476; www.montana.edu/~mtmuse um/

Deirdre Shaw, President [Glacier National Park, West Glacier, MT 59936; (406)-888-7936, deirdre_ shaw@nps.gov]

PROGRAMS: AV programs, newsletters, magazines; public relations; annual and special meetings; Organization of Museums in Montana (private).

Records Management Section

Dept. of Administration, 1320 Bozeman St., Helena, MT 59501; (406) 444-2716

Ed Eaton, Supervisor

PROGRAMS: Records management; central microfilming.

State Museum

c/o Montana Historical Society, PO Box 201201, Helena, MT 59620; (406) 444-2694; Fax (406) 444-2696; www.montana.edu/~mt museum/

Susan Near, Museum Administrator

PROGRAMS: Collecting; exhibits; field services; museum.

Nebraska

Museum of Nebraska History

15th and P Streets, Lincoln, Nebraska, Lincoln, NE 68501-2554; PO Box 82554, Lincoln, NE 68508; (402) 471-4754; 1-800-833-6747; ednshs@inetnebr.com; www.nebraskahistory.org/sites/mnh/index.htm

Wendell Frantz, Museum Director

PROGRAMS: Archaeology; collecting; conservation; exhibits; historic sites; museum; school programs; tours.

Nebraska Committee for the Humanities

Lincoln Cr. Bldg., #422, 215 Centennial Mall South, Suite 225; Lincoln, NE 68508; (402) 474-2131; Fax (402) 474-4852; nehumanities@juno.com; www.lincolnne.com/nonprofit/nhc/

Jane R. Hood, Executive Director

Nebraska State Historical Society

PO Box 82554, 1500 R Street, Lincoln, NE 68501; (402) 471-4745; web@nebraskahistory.org ; www.nebraskahistory.org /

James A. Hanson, Director

PROGRAMS: Archaeology; archives; AV programs; book publishing; collecting; conservation; exhibits; field services; genealogy; historic preservation; historic sites; library; markers; museum; newsletters, magazines; oral history; photographic collections; public relations; records management; research; school programs; tours; Nebraska Hall of Fame.

Research Division

Nebraska State Historical Society, 1500 "R" St., Lincoln, NE 68508; (402) 471-4748

Eli R. Paul, Director

PROGRAMS: Oral history, research.

State Archives

Nebraska State Historical Society, PO Box 82554, 1500 R Street, Lincoln, NE 68501; (402) 471-4750; web@nebraskahistory.org; www.nebraskahistory.org/lib-arch/

Sherrill Daniels, Director

PROGRAMS: Archives; conservation; genealogy; library; photographic collections; records management.

State Historian

Nebraska State Historical Society, 1500 "R" St., Lincoln, NE 68508; (402) 471-4747

Sherilyn Ward, State Historian

PROGRAMS: Markers; newsletters, magazines.

State Historic Preservation Office

Nebraska State Historical Society , PO Box 82554, 1500 R Street, Lincoln, NE 68501; (402) 471-4745; www.nebraskahistory.org/histpres/

Lawrence J. Sommer, Director; SHPO

PROGRAMS: Historic preservation.

Nevada

Division of Archives and Records

100 North Stewart Street, Carson City, Nevada 89701-4285, Archives (775) 684-3310, (775) 684-3360 or 1-800-922-2880 (in-state callers only); Fax (775) 684-3330; Records Management (775) 684-3411; Micrographics and Imaging (775) 684-3414; mla.clan.lib.nv.us/docs/nsla/archives/

Guy Louis Rocha, State Archivist

PROGRAMS: Archives; exhibits, field services; genealogy; newsletters, magazines; photographic collections; public relations; records management; research; tours.

Historic Preservation Office

100 N. Stewart, Carson City, NV 89701; (775) 684-3448; Fax (775) 687-3442; dmla.clan.lib.nv.us/docs/shpo/

Ronald M. James, SHPO

Lost City Museum

721 S. Moapa Valley Blvd., PO Box 807, Overton, NV 89040; (702) 397-2193; Fax (702) 397-8987; Lostcity@comnett.net; dmla.clan.

lib.nv.us/docs/museums/lost/lostcity.htm

Kathryne Olson, Curator

Nevada State Museum

Dept. of Museums and History, 600 N. Carson St., Carson City, NV; (702) 885-4810; (775) 687-4810; www.jour.unr.edu/outpost/destinations/des.riggi.statefront.html

Nevada Historical Society

1650 N. Virginia St., Reno, NV 89503; (702) 789-0190; (775) 688-1190; dmla.clan.lib.nv.us/docs/museums/reno/his-soc.htm

Peter L. Bandurraga, Director

Nevada Humanities Committee

PO Box 8029, 1101 N. Virginia St., Reno, NV 89507; (775) 784-6587; 1-800-382-5023; Fax (775) 784-6527; www.unr.edu/nhc/

Judith Winzeler, Executive Director

Nevada State Museum and Historical Society

Dept. of Museums and History, 700 Twin Lakes Dr., Las Vegas, NV 89107; (702) 486-5205; dmla.clan.lib.nv.us/docs/museums/lv/vegas.htm

Shirl Naegle, Director

State Library and Archives

100 North Stewart Street, Carson City, NV 89701-4285; (775) 684-3360 or 1-800-922-2880 (in-state callers only); Fax (775) 684-3330; dmla.clan.lib.nv.us/docs/NSLA/

Joan G. Kerschner, State Librarian

PROGRAMS: Archives, AV programs; exhibits; field services; genealogy; library; newsletters, magazines; photographic collections; public relations; records management; research; tours.

Nevada State Railroad Museum

2180 S. Carson St., Carson City, NV 89701; (775) 687-6953; Fax (775) 687-8294; jgballwe@ clan.lib.nv.us; www.nsrm-friends.org/

John Ballweber, Curator

New Hampshire

Division of Historical Resources

Department of Cultural Resources, 19 Pillsbury Street, Box 2043, Concord, NH 03301-2043; (603)-271-3483 or (603) 271-3558; Fax (603)-271-3433; 800-735-2964; preservation@nhdhr.state.nh.us; www.state.nh.us/nhdhr/

Nancy C. Dutton, Director; SHPO

PROGRAMS: Archaeology; field services; historic preservation; historic sites; markers; research.

Joint Legislative Historical Committee

The General Court, State House, Main St., Concord, NH 03301; (603) 271-3661

James Whittemore, Chairman, Interpretations, Exhibits

New Hampshire Council for the Humanities

19 Pillsbury Street, OP Box 2228 Concord, NH 03302-2228; (603) 224-4071; Fax (603) 224-4072; www.nhhc.org/

Charles Bickford, Executive Director

New Hampshire Division of Records Management and Archives

Secretary of State, 71 S. Fruit St., Concord, NH 03301; (603) 271-2236; (603) 271-2272; Fmevers@sos.state.nh.us; www.state.nh.us/state/index.html

Frank C. Mevers, Director, State Archivist

PROGRAMS: Archives; book publishing; collecting; conservation; genealogy; photographic collections; records management; research; microfilming.

New Hampshire Historical Society

30 Park Street, Concord, NH 03301; (603) 225-3381; library@nhhistory.org; www.nhhistory.org/index.html

Frank Frisbee, Director

PROGRAMS: Archaeology; archives; book publishing; collecting; conservation; exhibits; field services; genealogy; library; living history; museum; newsletters, magazines; photographic collections; public relations; research; school programs; tours.

New Hampshire State Library

Department of Cultural Resources, 20 Park St., Concord, NH 03301; (603) 271-2144; (603) 271-2616; Fax (603) 271-6826; www.state.nh.us/nhsl/

Michael York, State Librarian

PROGRAMS: Field services; library; newsletters, magazines; genealogy.

Office of State Parks

Division of Parks and Recreation, Dept. of Resources and Economic Development, PO Box 1856, 172 Pembroke Rd., Concord, NH 03302-1856; (603) 271-3556; Nhparks@dred.state.nh.us; www.nhparks.state.nh.us

Richard McLeod, Director

PROGRAMS: Historic sites; living history; tours.

New Jersey

Archaeological Society of New Jersey
c/o Seton Hall Univ. Museum, South Orange, NJ 07079; (201) 761-9543; (201) 761-9170

Herbert C. Kraft, President

PROGRAMS: Archaeology; newsletters, magazines.

Association of New Jersey County Cultural and Heritage Agencies
c/o 841 Georges Rd., North Brunswick, NJ 08902; (201) 745-4489

Anna M. Aschkenes, President

PROGRAMS: Public relations; networking.

Bureau of Archaeology / Ethnology
New Jersey State Museum, Dept. of State, 205 W. State St., CN 530, Trenton, NJ 08625-0530; (609) 984-3895; (609) 984-3896

Lorraine Williams, Curator;State Archaeologist

PROGRAMS: Archaeology; museum; research; school programs.

Coalition for New Jersey History
c/o Patrick Clarke, Ailaire State Park, Box 394A, Allaire Rd., Farmingdale, NJ 07727; (201) 983-237;

Patrick Clarke, Chair

PROGRAMS: Public relations; lobbying.

Division of Archives and Records Management
Department of State, 225 West State St., Trenton, NJ 08625; (609) 292-6260; www.state.nj.us/state/darm/darmnews.html

Carl Niederer, Director

PROGRAMS: Archives, conservation; records management; microfilming.

Division of Parks and Forestry
Dept. of Environmental Protection, P.O. Box 404, 501 E. State St., Trenton, NJ 08625; (609) 984-6015; (800) 843-6420 or (609) 984-0370; www.state.nj.us/dep/forestry/parknj/divhome.htm

Paul Taylor, Supervising Historic Preservation Specialist, State Park Service

PROGRAMS: Historic sites.

Jerseyana and Genealogy Section
Bureau of Law and Reference, New Jersey State Library, 185 W. State St., CN 820, Trenton, NJ 08625-0520; (609) 292-8274;

Robert E. Lupp, Supervisor

PROGRAMS: Collecting; genealogy; library; photographic collections; maps; atlases, postcards; family histories; heraldry and peerages; published passenger lists; census and registers; indexes.

League of Historical Societies of New Jersey
PO Box 909, Madison, NJ 07940; www.scils.rutgers.edu/~macan/leaguelist.html

Bernard Bush, President

PROGRAMS: Public relations; lobbying; networking; public forum.

New Jersey Council for the Humanities
28 West State Street, 6th Fl., Trenton NJ 08609-1602; 1-888-FYI-NJCH or (609) 695-4838; www.njch.org/

New Jersey Committee for the Humanities
73 Easton Ave, New Brunswick, NJ 08901; (201) 932-7726

Miriam L. Murphy, Executive Director

New Jersey Documents Section
Bureau of Law and Reference, New Jersey State Library, 185 W. State St., CN 520, Trenton, NJ 08625-0520; (609) 292-6294

Robert E. Lupp, Supervisor

PROGRAMS: Collecting; library; newsletters, magazines; official depository for NJ state government publications.

New Jersey Historical Commission
Department of State, Mary Roebling Building, P.O. Box 305, 20 W. State St., Trenton, NJ 08625; (609) 292-6062

Richard Waldron, Executive Director

PROGRAMS: Book publishing; field services; newsletters, magazines; research, school programs; Afro-American program; grant program.

New Jersey Historic Trust
Department of State, PO Box 457, Trenton, NJ 08625; (609) 842-0473

Harriette Hawkins, Executive Director

PROGRAMS: Historic preservation; historic sites.

New Jersey Historical Society
52 Park Place, Newark, NJ 07102; (973) 596-8500; (973) 596-6957;

Sally Yerkovich, Executive Director

PROGRAMS: Book publishing; collecting; conservation; exhibits; genealogy; library; museum; newsletters, magazines; photographic collections; school programs; tours.

New Jersey Historic Sites Council
Department of Environmental Protection, PO Box 404, Trenton, NJ 08625; (609) 292-2023;

Mark Mutter, Chair

PROGRAMS: Historic preservation; historic sites.

New Jersey State Archives
Division of Archives and Records Management, 185 W. State St., CN 307, PO Box 307, Trenton, NJ 08625; (609) 292-6260; 292-6261 225; Fax (609) 396-2454; www.state.nj.us/state/darm/archives.html

Karl J. Neiderer, Chief Bureau of Archives and Records Preservation

PROGRAMS: Archives; library, mail reference service; publications.

New Jersey State Library
Dept. of Education, 185 W. State St., PO Box 520, CN 520; Trenton, NJ 08625-0520; (609)-292-6220; www.njstatelib.org/

Barbara F. Weaver, State Librarian

PROGRAMS: Collecting; library; newsletters, magazines; photographic collections.

New Jersey State Museum
Department of State, 205 W. State St., CN 530, PO Box 530, New Trenton, NJ 08625-0530; (609) 292-6300; (609) 292-6464; Fax (609) 599-4098; www.state.nj.us/state/museum/

Lorraine E. Williams, Acting Director

PROGRAMS: Archaeology: AV programs; book publishing; collecting; conservation; exhibits; field services; historic site; museum; newsletter; research; school programs; tours; auditorium; planetarium.

New Jersey Historic Preservation Office
Dept. of Environmental Protection, Div. of Parks & Forestry, P.O. Box 404, 501 E. State St., Trenton, NJ 08625; (609) 292-2023 or (609) 292-2028; Fax: (609) 984-0578; NJHPO@DEP.STATE.NJ.US; www.state.nj.us/dep/hpo/

Dorothy P. Guzzo, Administrator

PROGRAMS: Historic preservation, historic sites.

Preservation New Jersey
18 West Lafayette Street, Trenton, NJ 08608-2002; (609) 392-6409; Fax: (609) 392-6418; presnj@erols.com www.preservationnj.org/

Richard W. Hunter, Co-President & Treasurer

Deborah Marquis Kelly, Co-President

PROGRAMS: Historic preservation; newsletters, magazines; public relations

New Mexico

Cumbres and Toltec Scenic Railroad Commission

Box 561, Antonito, CO 81120; (719) 376-5488

Leo Schmitz, Executive Director

PROGRAMS: Conservation; historic preservation; historic sites; living history; museum; governing body for the Cumbres and Toltec Scenic Railroad.

Friends of the Cumbres and Toltec Scenic Railroad, Inc.

6005 Osuna Rd. NE,   Albuquerque, NM 87109; (505) 880-1311; Fax (505) 856-7543; www.cumbrestoltec.org/welcome.htm

William J. Lock, President

PROGRAMS: Archives; conservation; historic preservation; museum; photographic collections. A "living" museum of railroad history, operating over 64 miles of high mountain country in New Mexico and Colorado.

Historical Society of New Mexico, Inc.

Box 5819, Santa Fe, NM 87502; (505) 984-1797

Spences Wilson, President

PROGRAMS: Archives; book publishing; historic preservation; newsletters, magazines; house museum.

New Mexico Historic Preservation Division

Historic Preservation Division, Rm 320, La Villa Rivera, 228 E. Palace Ave., Santa Fe, NM 87501;(505) 827-6320; Fax (505) 827-6338; www.museums.state.nm.us/hpd/

Elmo Baca, SHPO

PROGRAMS: Archaeology; archives; book publishing; historic preservation; historic sites; markers; newsletters; records management; research; State and National Register nominations; state and federal tax credits; state permit applications; misc. information.

Museum of New Mexico

113 Lincoln Ave, Santa Fe, 87501; Box 2087, Santa Fe, NM 87504; (505) 476-5060; Fax (505) 476-5088; www.museumofnewmexico.org/home.html

Thomas Wilson, Director

PROGRAMS: Archaeology; AV programs; book publishing; collecting; conservation; exhibits; historic sites; library; museum; newsletters, magazines; photographic collections; public relations; school programs; tours; traveling exhibitions.

New Mexico Endowment for the Humanities

209 Onate Hall, Univ. of New Mexico, Albuquerque, NM 87131; (505) 277-3705; www.nmeh.org/

Craig Newbill, Executive Director

New Mexico State Library

1209 Camino Carlos Rey, Santa Fe, NM 87505; (505) 476-9700; Fax (505) 476-9701; www.stlib.state.nm.us/

Benjamin Wakashige, State Librarian

PROGRAMS: Library; collect New Mexico newspapers; maintain clipping files for current New Mexico history; produce bill indexes during legislature, New Mexico documents depository.

New Mexico State Records Center and Archives

1205 Camino Carlos Rey, Santa Fe, NM 87505; (505) 476-7900; (505) 476-7902; Fax: (505) 476-7901; asd@rain.state.nm.us; www.state.nm.us/cpr/

Elaine Olah, State Records Administrator

PROGRAMS: Archives; genealogy; markers; photographic collections; public relations; records management; research; school programs; micrographics.

New York

Division for Historic Preservation

Office of Parks, Recreation and Historic Preservation, Empire State Plaza, Albany, NY 12230; (518) 474-0468

Julia Stokes, Deputy Commissioner for Historic Preservation

PROGRAMS: Historic preservation; historic sites.

Division of Research and Collections

New York State Museum, State Education Department, Empire State Plaza, Albany, NY 12230; (518) 473-1299

Paul J. Scudiere, State Historian; Director

PROGRAMS: Archaeology; book publishing; collecting; conservation; exhibits; field services; markers; museum; photographic collections; research; responsible for chartering historical societies and history museums through the Board of Regents; responsible for biology and geology research and collections.

New York Council for the Humanities

150 Broadway, Suite 1700, New York, NY 10038; (212)233-1131; Fax: (212) 233-4607; nych@culturefront.org; www.nyhumanities.org

Jay Kaplan, Executive Director

New York State Historical Association

Lake Rd., P.O. Box 800, Cooperstown, NY 13326; (607) 547-1400; (607) 547-1404; Nysha1@aol.com; www.nysha.org

Daniel R. Porter, III, Director

PROGRAMS: Collecting; conservation; exhibits; library; living history; museum; research; tours.

Preservation League of New York State

44 Central Avenue, Albany, New York 12206-3002; (518) 462-5658; Fax 518-462-5684; info@preservenys.org; www.preservenys.org/

Scott Heyl, President

PROGRAMS: Historic preservation.

State Archives and Records Administration

State Education Department, Empire State Plaza, Albany, NY 12230; (518) 474-1195; (518) 474-8955; sarainfo@mail.nysed.gov; www.archives.nysed.gov

Larry Hackman, State Archivist

PROGRAMS: Archives; collecting; field services; genealogy; photographic collections; records management.

New York State Library

State Education Department, Empire State Plaza, Albany, NY 12230; (518) 474-5930; (518) 474-5355; nyslweb@mail.nysed.gov; www.nysl.nysed.gov/

Janet Welch, Assistant Commissioner for Libraries; State Librarian

PROGRAMS: Collecting; field services; library.

New York State Museum

Madison Ave, Rm 3140 CEC, Empire State Plaza, Albany, NY 12230; (518) 474-5812; (518) 474-5877; Fax (518) 486-3696; Csiegfri@mail.nysed.gov; www.nysm.nysed.gov/

Martin Sullivan, Assistant Commissioner

PROGRAMS: Museum.

North Carolina

North Carolina Division of Archives and History

Dept. of Cultural Resources, 109 E. Jones St., Raleigh, NC 27601; 4610 Mail Service Center, Raleigh, NC 27699-4610; (919) 733-7305; Fax (919) 733-8807; ahweb@ncmail.net; www.ah.dcr.state.nc.us/contacts/default.htm

Jeffery J. Crow, director, SHPO

PROGRAMS: Archaeology; archives; AV programs; book publishing; collecting; conservation; exhibits; field services; genealogy; historic preservation; historic sites; living history; markers; museum; newsletters, magazines; photographic collections; public relations; records management; research; school programs; tours.

North Carolina Division of State Library

109 E. Jones St., Raleigh, NC 27611; 919-733-3270; Fax 919-733-5679; statelibrary.dcr.state.nc.us/NCSLHOME.HTM

PROGRAMS: AV programs; field services; genealogy; library; research.

North Carolina Historical Commission

Dept. of Cultural Resources, 109 E. Jones St., Raleigh, NC 27611; (919) 733-7305; www.ah.dcr.state.nc.us/nc-hist-com.htm

Jerry C. Cashion, Chair

PROGRAMS: Professional oversight of the Div. of Archives and History. Advises the secretary of Dept. of Cultural Resources on the operations and needs of the state's historical agency.

North Carolina Historic Sites

532 N Wilmington St Raleigh, NC 27604; (919) 733-7862; Fax (919) 733-9515; hs@ncsl.dcr.state.nc.us; www.ah.dcr.state.nc.us/sections/hs/default.htm

North Carolina Humanities Council

200 S. Elm Street, Suite 403, Greensboro, NC 27401; (336) 334-5325; NCHC@gborocollege.edu; www.nchumanities.org

North Dakota

North Dakota Heritage Center

Archeology and Historic Preservation Division, State Historical Society of North Dakota, North Dakota Heritage Center, 612 E Boulevard Ave., Bismarck, ND 58505; (701) 328-2666; Fax (701) 328-3710; Histsoc@state.nd.us; www.DiscoverND.com/hist

Louis N. Hafermehl, Division Director; Deputy SHPO

PROGRAMS: Archaeology; historic preservation; research.

Historic Sites Division

State Historical Society of North Dakota, North Dakota Heritage Center, 612 East Boulevard Ave., Bismarck, ND 58505-0830; 58505; Fax 701-328-3710; histsoc@state.nd.us; www.state.nd.us/hist/sites.htm

Melvin Barnett, Division Director

PROGRAMS: Historic sites; markers.

Museum and Education Division

State Historical Society of North Dakota, North Dakota Heritage Center, 612 East Boulevard, Bismarck, ND 58505; (701) 328-2666; Fax (701) 328-3710; histsoc@state.nd.us; www.state.nd.us/hist/mus.htm

Chris L. Dill, Division Director

PROGRAMS: Collecting; conservation; exhibits; field services; museum; public relations; records management; research; tours.

North Dakota Humanities Council

PO Box 2191, Bismarck, ND 58502; (701) 663-1948; (70l) 255-3360; Fax (70l) 223-8724; www.ihl.state.ms.us/mhc/links/states/nd.html

Everett Albers, Executive Director

Records Management Division

Office of Management and Budget, State Capitol, Bismarck, ND 58505; (701) 328-3190; Fax (701) 328-3000; itd@state.nd.us; www.state.nd.us/itd/records/

Rick Bock, Director

PROGRAMS: Records management.

State Archives and Historical Research Library Division

State Historical Society of North Dakota, North Dakota Heritage Center, 612 Boulevard Ave, Bismarck, ND 58505; (701) 328-2668; (701)-328-2091; Fax (701) 328-3710; archives@state.nd.us; www.state.nd.us/hist/sal.htm

Gerald G. Newborg, Division Director; State Archivist

PROGRAMS: Archives; collecting; conservation; genealogy; library; oral history; photographic collections.

State Historical Society of North Dakota

State Historical Board, North Dakota Heritage Center, Bismarck, ND 58505; (701) 328-2666; (701) 328-3710; Histsoc@state.nd.us; www.state.nd.us/hist/

James E. Sperry, Superintendent; SHPO

PROGRAMS: Archaeology; archives; AV programs; book publishing; collecting; conservation; exhibits; field services; genealogy; historic preservation; historic sites; library; living history; markers; museum; newsletters, magazines; oral history; photographic collections; public relations; research; school programs; tours.

North Dakota State Library

Director of Institutions Liberty Memorial Bldg., 604 E Boulevard Ave. Dept. 250, Bismarck, ND 58505; 701-328-4622; 800-472-2104; Fax (701) 701-328-2040; ndsl.lib.state.nd.us/

Joe Linnertz, Acting State Librarian

Ohio

Ohio Historical Society

1982 Velma Ave., Columbus, OH 43211; (614) 297-2300; www.ohiohistory.org/

Programs: Archaeology; archives; AV programs; book publishing; collecting; conservation; exhibits; field services; genealogy; historic preservation; historic sites; library; living history; markers; museum; newsletters, magazines; oral history; photographic collections; public relations; records management; research; school programs; tours.

Ohio Humanities Council

471 E. Broad St., Suite 1620, Columbus, Ohio 43215; (614) 461-7802; www.ohiohumanities.org/

George Garrison, Chair

Oklahoma

Oklahoma Department of Libraries

200 NE 18th St., Oklahoma City, OK 73105-3298; (405) 521-2502; Fax: (405) 525-7804; www.odl.state.ok.us/

Susan C. McVey, Director

PROGRAMS: Archives; AV programs; book publishing; collecting; conservation; exhibits; field services; library; newsletters, magazines; oral history; photographic collections; public relations; records management; research; school programs; tours; special projects such as literacy programs.

Oklahoma Humanities Council

428 W. California, Suite 270, Oklahoma City, OK 73102; (405) 235-0280; Fax: (405) 235-0289; ohc@okhumanitiescouncil.org; www.okhumanitiescouncil.org/

Anita R. May, Ph.D, President and Executive Director

Oklahoma Historical Society

2100 N. Lincoln, Oklahoma City, OK 73105; (405) 521-2491; Fax: (405) 521-2492; www.ok-history.mus.ok.us/

Dr. Bob L. Blackburn, Executive Director; SHPO

PROGRAMS: Archives; AV programs; book publishing; collecting; conservation; exhibits; field services; genealogy; historic preservation; historic sites; library; living history; markers; museum; newsletters, magazines; oral history; photographic collections; public relations; research; school programs; tours; special projects for local groups.

Oregon

Oregon State Archives

800 Summer St. NE, Salem, OR 97310; (503) 373-0701; Fax (503) 373-0953; arcweb.sos.state.or.us

Oregon Council for the Humanities

812 SW Washington Street, Suite 225, Portland, OR 97205; (503) 241-0543; Fax (503) 241-0024; www.oregonhum.org/

Oregon Parks and Recreation Department

1115 Commercial St NE, Salem OR 97301 (503) 378-6305; www.prd.state.or.us

Michael Carrier, Director

State Historic Preservation Office

1115 Commercial St. NE Ste. 2, Salem, OR 97301-1012; (503) 378-6305; Fax (503) 378-6447; www.arcweb.sos.state.or.us/shpo/shpoabout.html

Oregon Historical Society

1200 SW Park Avenue, Portland, OR 97205-2483; phone: (503) 222-1741; Fax: (503) 221-2035; OHS information line: (503) 306-5198; orhist@ohs.org; www.ohs.org

Pennsylvania

Pennsylvania Federation of Museums and Historical Organizations

Commonwealth Keystone Building, Plaza Level, 400 North Street, Harrisburg, Pennsylvania 17120-0053; phone: (717) 787-3253; fax: (717) 772-4698; www.pamuseums.org

Robert Gingerich, President

PROGRAMS: Field services; newsletters, magazines.

Pennsylvania Historical and Museum Commission

300 North Street, Harrisburg, PA 17120; phone: (717) 787-3362; fax: (717) 783-9924; www.phmc.state.pa.us

Brent D. Glass, Executive Director; SHPO

PROGRAMS: Archaeology; archives; book publishing; collecting; conservation; exhibits; field services; genealogy; historic preservation; historic sites; living history; markers; museum; newsletters, magazines; oral history; photographic collections; public relations; research; school programs; tours; grants for museums; local history.

Pennsylvania Humanities Council

Constitution Place, 325 Chestnut St., Ste. 715, Philadelphia, PA; 19106-2607; phone: 1-800-462-0442 (in Pennsylvania only) or (215) 925-1005; fax: (215) 925-3054; phc@pahumanities.org; www.pahumanities.org

Joseph J. Kelly, Executive Director

Preservation Pennsylvania

257 North St., Harrisburg, PA 17101; phone: (717) 234-2310; fax: (717) 234-2522; e-mail: PPA@preservationpa.org; www.preservationpa.org

Patrick A. Foltz, Executive Director

PROGRAMS: Historic preservation; newsletters, magazines; revolving fund for acquisition/preservation of historic properties.

State Library of Pennsylvania

P.O. Box 1601, Harrisburg, PA 17105-1601; phone: (717) 783-5950; e-mail: ra-reference@state.pa.us; www.statelibrary.state.pa.us/libraries/site/default.asp

Gary D. Wolfe, State Librarian

Rhode Island

Rhode Island Historical Preservation Commission

Old State House, 150 Benefit Street, Providence, RI 02903; (401) 222-2678; www.rihphc.state.ri.us/main.html

Edward F. Sanderson, Director, Deputy Assistant SHPO

PROGRAMS: Archaeology; book publishing; historic preservation; historic sites; grants to museums and historical societies.

Rhode Island Historical Society

110 Benevolent St., Providence, RI 02906; (401) 331-8575; www.rihs.org/

Albert T. Klyberg, Director

PROGRAMS: Book publishing; collecting; conservation; exhibits; field services; genealogy; library; museum; newsletters, magazines; oral history; photographic collections; public relations; research; school programs; tours.

League of Rhode Island Historical Societies

Cranston Historical Society, 1351 Cranston St., Cranston, Rhode Island 02920; (401) 942-9226

Robert Drew, President

PROGRAMS: Field services; newsletters; tours; workshops.

Rhode Island Committee for the Humanities

385 Westminster Street Suite 2, Providence, RI 02903; (401) 273-2250; www.uri.edu/rich/

Charles Sullivan, Chair

Rhode Island State Archives

Secretary of State, 337 Westminster St., Providence, RI 02903; (401) 222-2353; www.state.ri.us/archives/

PROGRAMS: Archives, public records; advisory board.

Rhode Island State Library

82 Smith Street, State House Room 208, Providence, RI 02903; (401) 222-2473; www.state.ri.us/library/web.htm

Thomas Evans State Librarian

PROGRAMS: Library grants to Rhode Island Historical Society and Newport Historical Society.

South Carolina

South Carolina**Archaeological Society of South Carolina, Inc.**

c/o Institute of Archaeology and Anthropology, 1321 Pendleton St., Columbia, SC 29208-0071; phone: (803) 777-8170; fax: (803) 254-1338

Wayne D. Roberts, President

Nena Powell Rice, Contact

PROGRAMS: Archaeology; newsletter; annual meeting; journal; annual festival.

Confederate Relic Room and Museum

World War Memorial Bldg., 920 Sumter St., Columbia, SC 29201; (803) 898-8095; www.state.sc.us/crr/

Allen Roberson, Director

PROGRAMS: Collecting; exhibits; library; museum; research; school programs; tours; conservation program.

Confederation of South Carolina Local Historical Societies

c/o South Carolina Dept. of Archives and History, 8301 Parklane Rd., Columbia, SC 29223; (803) 896-6100; www.state.sc.us/scdah/histogs/historg.htm

Ray Sigmon, President

PROGRAMS: Public relations; tours; conferences; directory (produced by the Dept. of Archives and History).

Department of Parks, Recreation, and Tourism

1205 Pendleton St., Columbia, SC 29201; phone: (803) 734-0166; fax: (803) 734-1409; www.discoversouthcarolina.com

John Durst, Director

PROGRAMS: Exhibits; historic sites; research.

Governor's Mansion and Lace House Commission

800 Richland St., Columbia, SC 29201; (803) 737-1033

Joan Davis, Contact

PROGRAMS: Historic sites; museum; school programs; tours

Old Exchange Building Commission

122 E. Bay St., Charleston, SC 29401; phone: (843) 727-2165; fax: (843) 727-2163; e-mail: oldexchange@infoave.net

Frances McCarthy, Director

PROGRAMS: Exhibits; historic sites; museum; tours.

Palmetto Archives, Libraries, and Museums Council on Preservation

c/o Richie Wiggers, SC Dept. of Archives & History, 8301 Parklane Road, Columbia, SC 29223-4905; phone: (803) 896-6119; fax: (803) 896-6167; www.state.sc.us/scdah/palmcop/palmcop.html

Holly T. Herro, Chair

PROGRAMS: Conservation; newsletter; public relations; workshops; evaluations; annual meeting; preservation consultant site visits.

South Carolina Humanities Council

P.O. Box 5287, Columbia, SC 29250; phone: (803) 691-4100; fax: (803) 691-0809; www.schumanities.org

S.C. "Cal" McMeekin, Jr., Chair

Randy Akers, Executive Director

PROGRAMS: Grant program; newsletter.

South Carolina Council of Professional Archaeologists

c/o South Carolina Institute of Archaeology and Anthropology, 1321 Pendleton St., Columbia, SC 29208; phone: (803) 777-8170; fax: (803) 254-1338; diachronicresearch.com/Content/COSCAPA/

Steve Smith, President

PROGRAMS: Archaeology; conferences; publications.

South Carolina Department of Archives & History

Archives and History Center, 8301 Parklane Rd., Columbia, SC 29223; phone: (803) 896-6100; fax: (803) 896-6198; www.state.sc.us/scdah/historgs/

Rodger E. Stroup, Director; State Historic Preservation Officer

Roy H. Tryon, State Archivist and Records Administrator

PROGRAMS: Archaeology; archives; book publishing; conservation; exhibits; field services; genealogy; preservation; library; markers; newsletters, public relations; records management; research; school programs; tours; conferences; facilities rental.

South Carolina Federation of Museums

P.O. Box 100107, Columbia SC 29202-3107; phone: (803) 898-4982; fax: (803) 898-4969; scfm@museum.state.sc.us; www.southcarolinamuseums.org/scfm/

Michelle McKee Baker, President

PROGRAMS: Newsletter; magazine; conference; directory.

South Carolina Heritage Trust Program

c/o South Carolina Dept. of Natural Resources, P.O. Box 167, Columbia, SC 29202; phone: (803) 734-3893

PROGRAMS: Historic sites; cultural area land protection.

South Carolina Historical Association

c/o Rodger Stroup, SC Archives & History Center, 8301 Parklane Road, Columbia SC 29223-4905; www.usca.sc.edu/scha/

Calvin Smith, President

PROGRAMS: Newsletters; annual conference.

South Carolina Historical Society

100 Meeting St., Charleston, SC 29401; phone: (843) 723-3225; fax: (843) 723-8584; info@schistory.org; www.schistory.org/

PROGRAMS: Archives; book publishing; collecting; exhibits; field services; genealogy; library; newsletters, magazines; photographic collections; research.

South Carolina Institute of Archaeology and Anthropology

1321 Pendleton St., Columbia, SC 29208; phone: (803) 777-8170; fax: (803) 254-1338; www.cla.sc.edu/sciaa/sciaa.html

Bruce E. Rippeteau, Director, State Archaeologist

PROGRAMS: Archaeology; conservation; field opportunities; newsletter; research; journal.

South Carolina State Library

PO Box 11469, Columbia, South Carolina 29211; phone: (803) 734-8666, fax: (803) 734-8676, TDD: (803) 734-7298; www.state.sc.us/scsl/

James B. Johnson, Jr., Director

PROGRAMS: Field services; library; publications; statewide database; library for deaf and blind.

South Carolina State Museum

301 Gervais St., Columbia, SC 29201; phone: (803) 898-4921; museumservices@museum.state.sc.us; www.museum.state.sc.us/

Overton G. Ganong, Executive Director

PROGRAMS: AV programs; collecting; conservation; exhibits; field services; museum; newsletters, magazines; public relations; research; school programs; tours.

South Dakota

South Dakota Office of History

South Dakota State Historical Society, 900 Governors Dr., Pierre, SD 57501; (605) 773-3458; www.sdhistory.org/

J. R. Fisburn, Director; SHPO

PROGRAMS: AV programs; book publishing; field services; markers; newsletters, magazines; public relations; tours; administrative branch; annual meeting; awards; fund raising; membership; board and committees.

Robinson State Museum

South Dakota State Historical Society, 900 Governors Dr., Pierre, SD 57501; (605) 773-3458

David Hartley, Director

PROGRAMS: Collecting; conservation; exhibits; museum; public relations; research; school programs; tours.

Smith-Zimmerman State Museum

South Dakota State Historical Society, Dakota State University, Madison, SD 57042; (605) 256-5308

John Awald, Director

PROGRAMS: Conservation; exhibits; field services; museum; public relations; school programs; tours.

State Agricultural Heritage Museum

South Dakota State Historical Society, 925 11th Street, SDSU Box 2207C, Brookings, SD 57007, (605) 688-6226; www3.sdstate.edu/Administration/SouthDakotaStateAgricultural HeritageMuseum/

John C. Awald, Director

PROGRAMS: Collecting; conservation; exhibits; field services; museum; public relations; research; school programs; tours.

State Archaeological Research Center

South Dakota State Historical Society, P.O. Box 1257, Rapid City, SD 57709; (605) 394-1936; www.sdsmt.edu/wwwsarc/

James Haug, Acting State Archaeologist; Deputy State Archaeologist

PROGRAMS: Archaeology; collecting; conservation; exhibits; field services; historic sites; public relations; research; school programs; tours; mining permits.

State Archives

South Dakota State Historical Society, 900 Governors Dr., Pierre, SD 57501; (605) 773-3804

Marvene Riis, Acting State Archivist and Government Documents Archivist

PROGRAMS: Archives; collecting; conservation; exhibits; field services; genealogy; library; oral history; photographic collections; public relations; records management; research.

State Historical Preservation Center

State Historical Society, P.O. Box 417, Vermillion, SO 57069; (605) 677-5314

Jay D. Vogt, SHPO

PROGRAMS: AV programs; book publishing; field services; historic preservation; historic sites; public relations; research; tours; Main Street program; grants.

W.H. Over State Museum

University of South Dakota, 414 E. Clark St., Vermillion, SD 57069; (605) 677 5228; www.usd.edu/whom/

Julia Vidicka, Director

PROGRAMS: Collecting; conservation; exhibits; field services; museum; public relations; research; school programs; tours.

Tennessee

Tennessee Historical Commission

2941 Lebanon Road, Nashville, TN 37243-0442; (615) 532-1550

Herbert L. Harper, Executive Director; Deputy SHPO

PROGRAMS: Book publishing; field services; historic preservation; historic sites; markers; newsletters, magazines; grants.

Tennessee Historical Society

War Memorial Bldg., Nashville, TN 37219; (615) 741-8934

Ann Toplovich, Director

PROGRAMS: Collecting; genealogy; historic preservation; markers; newsletters, magazines; public relations; tours; quarterly journal.

Tennessee Humanities Council

1003 18th Avenue South, Nashville, TN 37212-2104; (615) 320-7001

Robert Cheatham, Executive Director

Tennessee State Library and Archives

403 7th Ave. N., Nashville, TN 37243; (615) 741- 2764; www.state.tn.us/sos/statelib/tslahome.htm

Edwin S. Gleaves, State Librarian and Archivist

PROGRAMS: Archives; conservation; field services; genealogy; historic preservation; library; photographic collections; public relations; records management; research; school programs; adult literacy; legislative recording; microfilming.

Tennessee State Museum

Fifth and Deaderick Streets, Nashville, TN 37243-1120; (615) 741-2692; www.tnmuseum.org/

Lois Riggins, Director

PROGRAMS: Archaeology; AV programs; book publishing; collecting; conservation; exhibits; historic preservation; library; living history; museum; photographic collections; public relations; research; school programs; tours.

Texas

Texas Council for the Humanities

309 South 2nd Street, Austin, TX 78704; (512) 473-8585

Ellen Temple, Chair

James Veninga, Executive Director

Texas Historical Commission

P.O. Box 12276, Austin, TX 78711; (512) 463-6100; www.thc.state.tx.us/

F. Lawerence Oaks, Executive Director; SHPO

PROGRAMS: Archaeology; archives; field services; historic preservation; historic sites; markers; museum; newsletters, magazines, oral history; photographic collections; research; Main Street program; National Register program, federal review process; heritage tourism.

Utah

Association of Utah Historians

1845 South 1800 East, Salt Lake City, UT 84108; (801) 533-7037

PROGRAMS: History advisory group.

Family and Church History Department (Church of Jesus Christ of Latter-day Saints)

50 E. North Temple, Salt Lake City, UT 84150; (801) 240-2745

PROGRAMS: Archives; AV programs; collecting; conservation; exhibits; historic sites; library; museum; oral history; photographic collections; research.

Family History Library (Church of Jesus Christ of Latter-day Saints)

35 North West Temple Street, Salt Lake City, Utah, 84150-3400; phone: (801) 240-2331 or 800-453-3860 x22331; fax: (801) 240-1584; fhl@ldschurch.org; www.familysearch.org

PROGRAMS: Collecting; conservation; genealogy; library; research.

Conference of Intermountain Archivists

P.O. Box 2048, Salt Lake City, UT 84110; phone: (801) 378-6374; www.lib.utah.edu/cima/index.html

Susan L. Corrigan, Secretary/Treasurer

John Murphy, President

PROGRAMS: Archives; collecting; conservation; oral history; photographic collections; records management.

Daughters of Utah Pioneers

300 N. Main St., Salt Lake City, Utah 84103-1699; phone: (801) 538-1050; fax: (801) 538-1119; www.daughtersofutahpioneers.com

PROGRAMS: Book publishing; collecting; exhibits; library; markers; museum; newsletters, magazines; photographic collections.

Utah State Archives and Records Service

P.O. Box 141021, State Capitol, Archives Building, Salt Lake City, UT 84114-1021; phone: (801) 538-3012, fax: (801) 538-3354; research@das.state.ut.us; www.archives.state.ut.us

Jeffrey O. Johnson, Director

PROGRAMS: Archives; conservation; exhibits; genealogy; oral history; photographic collections; records management; local government archives and record services.

Division of Parks and Recreation

1594 West North Temple Suite 116, P.O. Box 146001, Salt Lake City, UT 84114-6001; phone: (801) 538-7220; fax: (801) 538-7378; parkcomment@state.ut.us; parks.state.ut.us

Courtland Nelson, Director

PROGRAMS: Archaeology; historic sites; living history; museum.

Division of State History (Utah State Historical Society)

300 South Rio Grande St., Salt Lake City, UT 84101-1143; phone: (801) 533-3500; fax: (801) 533-3503; ushs@history.state.ut.us; www.utah.org/history/index.html

Max J. Evans, Director; SHPO

PROGRAMS: Archaeology; book publishing; collecting; conservation; exhibits; field services; genealogy; historic preservation; library; museum; newsletters, magazines; oral history; photographic collections; research; school programs; tours.

Sons of Utah Pioneers

3301 E. 2920 South, Salt Lake City, UT 84109; (801) 484-4441; www.sonsofutahpioneers.org

Dr. H. Alan Luke, President

PROGRAMS: Markers; tours.

State Library Division

250 N 1950 W Suite A, Salt Lake City, UT 84116; (801)715-6777; www.state.lib.ut.us/index.html

Amy Owen, Division Director; State Librarian

PROGRAMS: AV programs; collecting; conservation; library.

Utah Humanities Council

202 W 300 N, Salt Lake City, UT 84103; phone: (801) 359-9670; fax: (801) 531-7869; www.utahhumanities.org/

Cynthia Buckingham, Executive Director

Utah Heritage Foundation

Memorial House In Memory Grove, P. O. Box 28, Salt Lake City, Utah 84110; (801) 533-0858; www.utahheritagefoundation.com/

Lisbeth L. Henning, Executive Director

PROGRAMS: Historic preservation; public relations; school programs; tours.

Utah Statewide Archaeological Society

Division of State History, 300 Rio Grande, Salt Lake City, UT 84101; phone: (801) 533-3500; history.utah.org/Services/arusas.html

Ron Wood, Contact

PROGRAMS: Archaeology; archaeological advocacy group.

Vermont

Vermont Division for Historic Preservation

National Life Bldg., Drawer 20, Montpelier, VT 05620-0501; (802) 828-3211; www.uvm.edu/ ~vhnet/hpres/org/vdhp/vdhp1.html

Emily Wadhams, SHPO

Vermont Council on the Humanities

200 Park Street, Morrisville, Vermont 05661; phone: (802) 888-3183; fax: (802) 888-1236; info@vermonthumanities.org; www.vermon thumanities.org/

Charles R. Putney, Chair

Victor R. Swenson, Executive Director

Vermont Historical Society

109 State St., Montpelier, VT 05609-0901; phone: (802) 828-2291; fax: (802) 828-3638; vhs@vhs.state.vt.us; www.state.vt.us/vhs/

Gainor B. Davis, Ph.D., Director

PROGRAMS: Book publishing; collecting; exhibits; field services; genealogy; library; museum; newsletters, magazines; oral history; photographic collections; public records; research; school programs; tours; website.

Vermont State Archives

Redstone Building, 26 Terrace Street, Drawer 09, Montpelier, VT 05609-1101; phone: (802) 828-2363; www.vermont-archives.org

Gregory Sanford, State Archivist

Vermont Department of Libraries

109 State St., Montpelier, VT 05609-0601; phone: (802) 828-3265; fax: (802) 828-2199; dol.state.vt.us/

Sybil Brigham McShane, State Librarian

Virginia

Virginia Department of Historic Resources

2801 Kensington Ave, Richmond, VA 23221; (804) 367-2323; www.dhr.state.va.us/

H. Alexander Wise, Director

PROGRAMS: Historic resources survey, evaluation, and registration on Virginia Landmarks. Register and nomination to the National Register of Historic Places; review of state and federal projects affecting historic properties; archaeological permits on state lands and on human burials; tax credits; grants; historic highway markers; publications; archival records on historic properties; archaeological collections and conservation; archaeological research; technical assistance; exhibits; museum assistance and artifact loans; education materials and programs; regional office system.

The Library of Virginia

800 East Broad Street, Richmond, Virginia 23219, (804) 692-3500; www.lva.lib.va.us/

Nolan T. Yelich, Librarian

PROGRAMS: Archives; exhibitions; AV programs; book publishing; conservation; field services; genealogy; library; newsletters, magazines; photographic collections; map collections; public relations; records management; research; school programs; tours; public and institutional library development.

Virginia Foundation for the Humanities

145 Ednam Drive, Charlottesville, VA 22903; (434) 924-3296; www.virginia.edu/vfh/

PROGRAMS: Grants; fellowships; media productions; publications; exhibits; seminars.

Virginia Historical Society

428 North Blvd., Richmond, VA 23221 [PO Box 7311, Richmond, VA 23221-0311]; (804) 358-4901; Fax (804) 342-9647; www.vahistori cal.org

PROGRAMS: Exhibits; interpretation; lectures, publication; research lirary/archives; school programs; tours.

Charles F. Bryan, Jr., Director

Washington

Washington State Library

Joel M. Pritchard Library, 415 15th Ave SW, PO Box 42460, Olympia, WA 98504; (360) 753-5592; www.statelib.wa.gov/

Washington State Parks and Recreation Commission

7150 Cleanwater Lane, P.O. Box 42650, Olympia, WA 98504; (360) 902-8500; www.parks.wa.gov/

Washington State Historical Society

1911 Pacific Avenue, Tacoma, WA 98402; (253) 272-9747; www.wshs.org/

Eastern Washington State Historical Society/Northwest Museum of Arts & Culture

West 2316 First Ave, Spokane, WA 99204; (509) 456-3931

Office of the Secretary of State

416 14th Ave., Legislative Bldg., P.O. Box 40220, Olympia, WA 98504-0220; (360) 902-4151; www.secstate.wa.gov/

West Virginia

Archives and History Division

Dept. of Culture and History, The Cultural Center, 1900 Kanawha Boulevard, E.; Charleston, WV 25305; (304) 348-0230; www.wvculture.org/history/index.html

PROGRAMS: Archives; collecting; conservation; exhibits; field services; genealogy; historic preservation; historic sites; library; markers; museum; newsletters, magazines; photographic collections; public relations; records management; research school programs.

Camp Washington-Carver

Dept. of Culture and History, HC 35, Box 5, Clifftop WV25831; (304) 438-3005; www.wvculture.org/sites/carver.html

PROGRAMS: Field services; historic sites; public relations; school programs; tours.

Department of Culture and History

The Cultural Center, Charleston, WV 25305; (304) 558-0220; www.wvculture.org/

Director: Sheree Compton, director

PROGRAMS: Book publishing; collecting; field services; newsletters, magazines; oral history; public relations; research.

Historic Preservation Office

Dept. of Culture and History, The Cultural Center, Charleston, WV 25305; (304) 558-0220; www.wvculture.org/shpo/

Susan Pierce, Director

PROGRAMS: Archaeology; field services; historic preservation; historic sites; newsletters, magazines; public relations; research.

Library Commission

Cultural Center, 1900 Kanawha Blvd East, Charleston, WV 25305; (304) 558-2041

J.D. Waggoner, Interim Secretary

PROGRAMS: Book publishing; field services; library; newsletters, magazines; public relations; school programs.

State Museum

Dept. of Culture and History, The Cultural Center, Charleston, WV 25305; (304) 348-0230; www.wvculture.org/museum/index.html

PROGRAMS: Archaeology; collecting; conservation; exhibits; field services; historic sites; museum; public relations; research; school programs; tours.

West Virginia Independence Hall

1528 Market Street, Wheeling, WV 26003; (304)238-1300; www.wvculture.org/sites/wvih.html

PROGRAMS: Field services; historic preservation; historic sites; public relations; school programs; tours.

Wisconsin

State Historical Society of Wisconsin

816 State St., Madison, WI 53706; (608) 264-6400; www.shsw.wisc.edu/

George L. Vogt, Director

PROGRAMS: Archaeology; archives; book publishing; exhibits; field services; genealogy; historic preservation; library; markers; museum; newsletters; magazines; oral; history; photographic collections; records management; research; school programs; tours.

Wisconsin Humanities Council

222 South Bedford Street, Suite F, Madison, Wisconsin 53703; (608) 262-0706; danenet. wicip.org/whc/

Max Harris, Executive Director

Wyoming

Wyoming Department of State Parks and Cultural Resources

2301 Central Avenue, Cheyenne, WY 82002; (307) 777-6303; Cultural Resources Fax (307) 777-3543; commerce.state.wy.us

John Keck, Director

Wyoming Council for the Humanities

P.O. Box 3643, Laramie, Wyoming 82071-3643; (307) 721-9243; uwyo.edu/wch/

Robert G. Young, Executive Director

Wyoming State Archives

Barrett Building, 2301 Central Avenue, Cheyenne, WY 82002; (307) 777-7826; wyoarchives.state.wy.us/index.htm

Tony Adams, CRM, Director

PROGRAMS: The Archives provides services through three work units: Archives and Historical Research; Records Management; and Technical Services. The Archives also sponsors or participates in workshops, conferences, and various other events pertaining to Wyoming history and the preservation and management of records.

Wyoming State Archaeology

Box 3431, University of Wyoming, Laramie, WY 82071; (307) 766-5301; wyoarchaeo.state. wy.us/

Dr. Mark E. Miller, State Archaeologist

State Historic Preservation Office

Barrett Building, 2301 Central Avenue, 3rd Floor, Cheyenne, Wyoming 82002; (307) 777-7697; wyoshpo.state.wy.us/index.htm

Wyoming State Museum

Barrett Building, 2301 Central Avenue Cheyenne, WY 82002; (307) 777-7022; spacr.state.wy.us/cr/wsm/

Wyoming Historical Society

PMB #184, 1740H Dell Range Blvd., Cheyenne, WY 82009; www.wyshs.org/

PART III

Historical Organizations in Canada

ALBERTA

AIRDRIE

9356
Nose Creek Valley Museum
1701 Main St S, T4B 2B6 [Box 3351, T4B
2B6]; (p) (403) 948-6685; (f) (403) 948-6685

Private non-profit/ 1985/ staff: 1(p); 12(v)/
members: 80

HISTORY MUSEUM: Collects, preserves,
records and displays the history of the Nose
Creek Valley and surrounding areas.

PROGRAMS: Annual Meeting; Community
Outreach; Exhibits; Facility Rental; Family Programs; Guided Tours

COLLECTIONS: [Late 1800s-present] Local
history of farming, ranching, geology, native
artifacts.

HOURS: Yr Daily June-Aug 10-5; Sept-May 1-5

ADMISSION: $2; Children free

BANFF

9357
**Banff Park Museum National Historic
Site**
91 Banff Ave, T0L 0C0 [PO Box 900, T0L
0C0]; (p) (403) 762-1558; (f) (403) 762-1565;
www.worldweb.com/ParksCanadaBanff/
museum.html

Federal/ 1895/ Parks Canada/ staff: 2(f);
6(p)/publication: *A Guide to the Banff Park Museum National Historic Site*

HISTORIC SITE; NATIONAL PARK: Interprets
changing attitudes towards wildlife and the
evolution of science and museum technology.

PROGRAMS: Exhibits; Interpretation; Publication

COLLECTIONS: [Late 19th-early 20th] Mammals, birds, and insects found in Banff National Park.

HOURS: Mid May-Sept 30 Daily 10-6; Oct 1-mid May Daily 1-5

ADMISSION: $2.50, Student $1, Children $1,
Seniors $2; Under 6 free

9358
**Whyte Museum of the Canadian
Rockies**
111 Bear St, T0L 0C0 [Box 160, T0L 0C0]; (p)
(403) 762-2291; (f) (403) 762-8979;
info@whyte.org; www.whyte.org

Private non-profit/ 1958/ staff: 22(f); 10(p);
40(v)/ members: 511/publication: *The Cairn*

ART MUSEUM; HISTORIC PRESERVATION
AGENCY; HISTORY MUSEUM: Collects, preserves, and exhibits fine art and cultural materials related to the mountain culture of the
Canadian Rockies: archives.

PROGRAMS: Community Outreach; Concerts; Elder's Programs; Exhibits; Facility
Rental; Family Programs; Guided Tours; Interpretation; Lectures; Publication; Reenactments; Research Library/Archives; Theatre

COLLECTIONS: [1850-present] Art of the
Canadian Rockies, both historic and contemporary; archives and library collection; Collec-

tions: mountaineering recreation, biography,
arts and culture, environment, genealogy, national parks, tourism, business, transportation,
natural history and resources.

HOURS: Yr Summer Daily 10-6; Winter T-Su 1-5 (Th 1-9pm)

ADMISSION: $4, Student $2, Seniors $2

BEAVERLODGE

9359
South Peace Centennial Museum
2 miles W of Beaverlodge on Hwy 43, T0H
0C0 [Box 493, T0H 0C0]; (p) (780) 354-8869;
(f) (780) 354-8869

Private non-profit/ 1976/ staff: 2(f); 100(v)/
members: 100

HISTORIC SITE: Maintains 13 buildings in a
town setting.

PROGRAMS: Annual Meeting; Community
Outreach; Concerts; Facility Rental; Festivals

COLLECTIONS: [1920-1930] 13 buildings, antique tractors, steam engines and farm equipment.

HOURS: Mid May-mid Sept Daily

BOWDEN

9360
Bowden Pioneer Museum
2201-19 Ave, T0M 0K0 [PO Box 576, T0M
0K0]; (p) (403) 224-2122

Private non-profit/ 1967/ Bowden Historical
Society/ staff: 3(p)/ 40(v)/ members: 38

HISTORY MUSEUM: The Bowden Pioneer
Museum focuses on the preserving the heritage of the area's pioneers.

PROGRAMS: Annual Meeting; Concerts; Exhibits; Guided Tours; Interpretation; Research
Library/Archives

COLLECTIONS: [1900-1940] Pioneer artifacts, Robert Hoare photographic collection,
and an auto extractor invented by local pioneer, M.C. Huff.

HOURS: May-June, Sept M,W,Sa 1-4; July-Aug M-Sa 10-5

ADMISSION: Donations accepted

BROWNVALE

9361
**Brownvale North Peace Agricultural
Museum**
Junction of Hwys 2 & 737, T0H 0Z0 [PO Box
3, T0H 0Z0]; (p) (780) 597-3950; (f) (780)
597-2388

City; Private non-profit/ 1995

HISTORY MUSEUM; LIVING HISTORY/OUTDOOR MUSEUM

PROGRAMS: Interpretation; Living History;
Research Library/Archives

COLLECTIONS: Tractors, plows, horse-powered machines, construction equipment, and
homestead buildings.

ADMISSION: Donations accepted

CALGARY

9362
**Calgary Police Service Interpretive
Centre**
2nd Fl, 7th Ave SE, T2G 4Z1 [133 6th Ave
SE, T2G 4Z1]; (p) (403) 206-4565; (f) (403)
974-0508; pol7753@gov.calgary.ab.ca

Joint/ 1995/ staff: 2(f); 1(p); 75(v)

HISTORY MUSEUM: A hands-on facility designed to educate young people about crime
and its consequences.

COLLECTIONS: [1885-present] Archives,
documents, photographs, books, equipment,
uniforms, motorcycles, and vehicles that pertain to the Calgary Police Service. Also, crime
evidence and drug paraphernalia.

HOURS: Yr

ADMISSION: $2

9363
**Canadian Architectural Archives,
University of Calgary Library**
2500 University Dr NW, T2N 1N4; (p) (403) 220-7420; (f) (403) 284-2109; lmfraser@ucalgary.ca;
www.ucalgary.ca/library/CAA/Index.html

1974/ staff: 2(f); 3(p)/ members: 3

LIVING HISTORY/OUTDOOR MUSEUM: The
Canadian Architectural Archives collects, preserves, and makes available to a wide research community the work of selected twentieth century Canadian architects.

PROGRAMS: Exhibits; Guided Tours; Publication; Research Library/Archives

COLLECTIONS: [20th c] Collects documentation of the entire output of selected 20th c
Canadian architects and may include conceptual, design, presentation, and working drawings, office files, client correspondence, specifications, oral history tapes, transcripts, and
photographs.

HOURS: Yr M-F 10-4

9364
**Glenbow Museum (Glenbow-Alberta
Institute)**
130 9th Ave SE, T2G 0P3; (p) (403) 268-4100;
(f) (403) 265-9769; glenbow@glenbow.org;
www.glenbow.org

1966/ staff: 85(f); 11(p); 240(v)/ members:
4522/publication: *Glenbow*

ART MUSEUM; HISTORY MUSEUM: Focuses
on Western Canadian heritage using a multidisciplinary approach including an artifact-based, human history museum, art gallery, library, and archives.

PROGRAMS: Community Outreach; Exhibits;
Family Programs; Guided Tours; Interpretation;
Lectures; Publication; Research Library/
Archives; School-Based Curriculum

COLLECTIONS: [19th-20th c] Glenbow's geographic collecting priority is the northwest
quadrant of North America, but Glenbow also
collects material from other regions of Canada
and other regions of the world.

HOURS: Yr Daily Sa-W 9-5, Th-F 9-9

ADMISSION: $10, Family $30, Student $6,
Children $6, Seniors $7.50; Under 3 free

9365
Lord Strathcona's Horse (Royal Canadians) Museum
4520 Crowchild Trail SW, T2T 5J4; (p) (403) 242-6610; (f) (403) 974-2858; ldsL@ ncleus.com; www.nucleus.com/~rdennis

Private non-profit/ 1990/ staff: 3(f); 25(v)

HISTORY MUSEUM: Collects, preserves, and displays items from its beginning as a cavalry unit to present day operations as armored. The museum has four horses from the time and one Sherman tank.

PROGRAMS: Annual Meeting; Concerts; Exhibits; Facility Rental; Family Programs; Festivals; Film/Video; Guided Tours; Interpretation; Lectures; Research Library/Archives

COLLECTIONS: [1900-present] Form horses to tanks and all things in-between including medals and written papers to cover the history of the Regiment from 1900 to present day.

HOURS: Yr 10-4

9366
Museum of the Regiments
4520 Crowchild Trail SW, T2T 5J4; (p) (403) 974-2853; (f) (403) 974-2858; regiments@ nucleus.com; www.nucleus.com/-regiments

1990/ Board of Directors/ staff: 16(f); 208(v)/ members: 175

HISTORY MUSEUM: Collects, preserves, and interprets Canadian military history and heritage.

PROGRAMS: Concerts; Elder's Programs; Exhibits; Facility Rental; Guided Tours; Lectures; Research Library/Archives; School-Based Curriculum

COLLECTIONS: [1850-present]

HOURS: Yr Daily 10-4; Th 10-9

ADMISSION: $5, Student $2, Seniors $3;

9367
Naval Museum of Alberta, The
1820 - 24 St SW, T2T 0G6; (p) (403) 242-0002; (f) (403) 240-1966; web@navalmuseum.ab.ca; www.navalmuseum.ab.ca

Private non-profit/ 1984/ staff: 1(f); 75(v)/ members: 250

ALLIANCE OF HISTORICAL AGENCIES; ART MUSEUM; HISTORY MUSEUM: Dedicated to preserving the history of the Canadian Navy for equipment in the future.

PROGRAMS: Annual Meeting; Community Outreach; Elder's Programs; Exhibits; Facility Rental; Family Programs; Guided Tours; Lectures; Living History

COLLECTIONS: [WW I-present] Exhibits of restored naval fighter aircraft. The Seafire, Sea Ferry and Centre; exhibiting of naval artifacts from around the world.

HOURS: Yr afternoons or by appt

ADMISSION: $5, Family $12, Student $3, Children $2, Seniors $3

9368
Olympic Hall of Fame and Museum
88 Canada Olympic Rd SW, T3B 5B5; (p) (403) 247-5455; (f) (403) 286-7213; info@cada.ab.ca; www.cada.ab.ca

Private non-profit/ 1988/ staff: 3(f); 5(p); 65(v)

HISTORY MUSEUM: Maintains the park as a tribute to the achievements of Canada's Olympic athletes.

COLLECTIONS: [1988-present] 8,000 artifacts, torches, medals, sports equipment, clothing, and pins related to the Olympic area.

HOURS: Yr Daily

ADMISSION: $7

9369
Princess Patricia's Canadian Light Infantry Regimental Museum and Archives
4520 Crowchild Trail SW, T2T 5J4; (p) (403) 974-2860; (f) (403) 974-2864; www.ppcli.com/

Private non-profit/ 1954/ staff: 4(f); 30(v)

HISTORY MUSEUM: Collect, preserves, and interprets documents, photographs, records, uniforms, equipment, weapons, vehicles, medals and any other items, which have significance to the Regiment and its members.

PROGRAMS: Exhibits; Facility Rental; Film/Video; Guided Tours; Lectures; Research Library/Archives; School-Based Curriculum; Theatre

COLLECTIONS: [1914-present] 9,000 military artifacts, 4,000 photographs, 220 videos, 200 maps, 150 photo albums, 40 meters of documents, 150 original works of art.

HOURS: Yr Th-T 10-4

ADMISSION: $5, Student $2, Seniors $3; Under 13 free

CARDSTON

9370
Cardston and District Historical Society
89 3rd Ave, T0K 0K0 [PO Box 704, T0K 0K0]; (p) (403) 653-4249

City/ 1975/ staff: 4(p); 10(v)

HISTORIC SITE; HISTORICAL SOCIETY; HOUSE MUSEUM: Collects, preserves, and displays area artifacts and conducts guided tours during the summer months.

PROGRAMS: Annual Meeting; Exhibits; Guided Tours; Research Library/Archives

COLLECTIONS: [1887-present] Household articles, a small military collection, agricultural items, native items, wildlife specimens, and early communications artifacts.

HOURS: June-Aug M-Sa 10-5

ADMISSION: Donations accepted

9371
Remington-Alberta Carriage Center
623 Main St, T0K 0K0 [Box 1649, T0K 0K0]; (p) (403) 653-5139; (f) (403) 653-5160; www.remingtoncentre.com; (c) Cardston

1993/ staff: 10(f); 10(p); 50(v)/ members: 135

HISTORY MUSEUM: Maintains a museum of horse drawn transportation in North America, with a collection of over 300 vehicles, owned and operated by the Province of Alberta as part of its Historic Sites network.

PROGRAMS: Annual Meeting; Community Outreach; Exhibits; Facility Rental; Family Programs; Festivals; Film/Video; Guided Tours; Interpretation; Research Library/Archives; School-Based Curriculum; Theatre

COLLECTIONS: [1880-1920] North American horse drawn vehicles from the turn of the 18th-19th c ranging from vehicles used by the common man through elite vehicles used by the upper class. Historic structures.

HOURS: Yr May 15-Sept Daily 8-6; Sept-May 14 Daily 10-5

ADMISSION: $6.50, Family $15, Children $3, Seniors $5.50; Under 7 free

CLARESHOLM

9372
Claresholm and District Museum
Hwy #2, T0L 0T0 [Box 1000, T0L 0T0]; (p) (403) 625-3131

1967/ staff: 1(f); 6(p)

HISTORY MUSEUM: Portrays the history of Claresholm and district from prehistory to the present and is located in the old Sandstone Railway Station.

PROGRAMS: Exhibits; Research Library/Archives

COLLECTIONS: [1901-present] Artifacts covering agriculture, farming, ranching, town, and school.

HOURS: May-Sept Daily 9:30-5:30

CROWSNEST

9373
Leitch Colleries Provincial Historic Sites
Hwy #3, T0K 0E0 [Box 959 Blairmore, T0K 0E0]; (p) (403) 562-7388; (f) (403) 562-8635

Provincial/ 1983/ staff: 3(f)

HISTORIC SITE: Promotes the picturesque ruins of a powerhouse, mine manager's residence, coke ovens, washery and tipple. Interpretive displays are located on trails around the site.

PROGRAMS: Exhibits; Family Programs; Festivals; Guided Tours; Interpretation; School-Based Curriculum

COLLECTIONS: [1907-1915] The ruins of the powerhouse, mine manager's residence, coke ovens, washery, and triple.

HOURS: Yr May 15-1st M in Sept 10-6

ADMISSION: $2,

CROWSNEST PASS

9374
Frank Slide Interpretive Centre
1.5 km N of Hwy 3, T0K 0E0 [Box 959 Blairmore, T0K 0E0]; (p) (403) 562-7388; (f) (403) 562-8635; info@frankslide.com; www.frankslide.com

1985/ staff: 6(f); 6(p); 45(v)

HERITAGE AREA: Preserves and focuses on the story of the Frank Slide and the rich history of Alberta's Crowsnest Pass.

PROGRAMS: Community Outreach; Concerts; Elder's Programs; Exhibits; Family Programs; Festivals; Film/Video; Guided Tours; Interpretation; Lectures; Research Library/Archives; School-Based Curriculum; Theatre

COLLECTIONS: [1903-1957] Coal mining artifacts, 200 book library, 5,000 slides, 900 historical photographs, oral histories, resource files, archival material.

HOURS: Yr May 15-Sept 14 9-6; Sept 15-May 14 10-5

ADMISSION: $6.50, Family $15, Student $2, Seniors $5.30; Under 7 free

CZAR

9375
Prairie Panorama Museum
Shorncliffe Lake Resort, T0B 0Z0 [Box 60, T0B 0Z0]; (p) (780) 857-2155

County/ 1964/ staff: 1(p); 1(v)/ members: 1/publication: *Prairie Panorama Museum*

ART MUSEUM; GARDEN; GENEALOGICAL SOCIETY; HISTORIC PRESERVATION AGENCY; HISTORIC SITE; HISTORICAL SOCIETY; HISTORY MUSEUM; HOUSE MUSEUM; TRIBAL MUSEUM

PROGRAMS: Annual Meeting; Community Outreach; Exhibits; Guided Tours; Interpretation; Publication; School-Based Curriculum

COLLECTIONS: [1500-1997] Household items, hospital equipment, period clothing, jewelry, church artifacts, musical pieces, money, Indian materials, history books, newspapers, drilling samples, tools, machinery, transportation.

HOURS: May-Sept 10 Th 1:30-5:30, Su 2-6 and by appt

ADMISSION: Donations accepted

DONALDA

9376
Donalda and District Museum
Main St, T0B 1H0 [Box 40, T0B 1H0]; (p) (403) 883-2100; (f) (403) 883-2022; (c) Stetteler

Private non-profit/ 1980/ staff: 1(p); 30(v)/ members: 30

HISTORIC SITE; HISTORY MUSEUM: Collects, preserves, and interprets the past for education and enjoyment of present and future generations.

PROGRAMS: Annual Meeting; Community Outreach; Exhibits; Guided Tours

COLLECTIONS: 850 kerosene lamps, artifacts used by local area pioneers, coin collection, Indian artifacts.

HOURS: Yr Winter: M-F 9-4:30; Summer: M-F 9-4:30, Sa-Su 11-5

ADMISSION: $1; Under 15 free

DRAYTON VALLEY

9377
Drayton Valley District Historical Society
Box 5099, T7A 1R3; (p) (780) 542-5482; dvhist@incentre.net

Private non-profit/ 1980/ staff: 25(v)/ members: 25

HISTORICAL SOCIETY; HISTORY MUSEUM: Collects, preserves, and displays information and objects that are relevant to the people and how they made this unique area what it is today.

PROGRAMS: Annual Meeting; Community Outreach; Exhibits; Film/Video; Interpretation;

Lectures; Publication; Research Library/Archives; School-Based Curriculum

COLLECTIONS: [1900s-present] We are acquiring collection to do with the agriculture, oil industry, and logging industry, the people who worked in those areas and their personal effects.

HOURS: Yr Summer: S-W 10-5; Winter: W-Sa 10-5

DRUMHELLER

9378
Royal Tyrrell Museum of Palaeontology
6 kms NW of Drumheller, T0J 0Y0 [PO Box 7500, T0J 0Y0]; (p) (403) 823-7707; (f) (403) 823-7131; info@tyrrellmuseum.com; www.tyrrellmuseum.com

1985/ staff: 65(f); 3(p); 30(v)

HISTORIC PRESERVATION AGENCY; HISTORY MUSEUM: Maintains a museum as a research facility and a showcase for Alberta's rich prehistory. A team of scientists examine the fossil records, reconstructing Alberta during the late Cretaceous through exhibits including more than 35 complete dinosaur skeletons.

PROGRAMS: Community Outreach; Exhibits; Facility Rental; Family Programs; Guided Tours; Interpretation; Lectures; Publication; School-Based Curriculum

COLLECTIONS: [Late Cretaceous] Fossils, found primarily in Alberta, more than 110,000 catalogued specimens.

HOURS: Yr Summer Daily 9-9; Winter T-Su 10-5

ADMISSION: $6, Student $3, Seniors $5.50

EDMONTON

9379
Alberta Association of Registered Nurses
11620 - 168 St NW, T5R 3K6; (p) (780) 453-0534; (f) (780) 482-4459; lmychaj@nurses.ab.ca; www.nurses.ab.ca

1978/ Provincial Council - AARN/ staff: 1(f); 1(p)

HISTORY MUSEUM; RESEARCH CENTER: Provides research space, environment-controlled storage, and displays of major themes in nursing to support and nurture the profession in Alberta through the documentation and preservation of nursing history.

PROGRAMS: Exhibits; Interpretation; Research Library/Archives

COLLECTIONS: [1916-present] Consists of materials (textual records, minutes, registers, publications, audiovisual materials, artifacts, and rare books) of associated organizations, such as hospital schools, alumni chapters, interest groups, and military nurses.

HOURS: Yr M-F 8:30-4:30

9380
Alberta Legislature and Interpretive Centre
107 St & 98 Ave, T5K 2N6 [Visitor Services, 10820-98 Ave, T5K 2N6]; (p) (780) 427-7362; (f) (780) 427-0980

1912/ Legislative Assembly of Alberta/ staff: 6(f); 17(p); 8(v)

HOURS: Yr May 1-Oct 15 9-4; Nov-Apr 9-3

ADMISSION: No charge

9381
Edmonton Public Schools Archives and Museum
10425-99 Ave, T5K 0E5; (p) (780) 422-1970; (f) (780) 426-8192; cluck@epsb.edmonton.ab.ca; www.discoveredmonton.com/school.museum

1983/ staff: 4(f); 9(p); 10(v)/publication: *A Century and Ten: The History of Edmonton Public Schools*

HISTORIC SITE; HISTORY MUSEUM: Maintains restored legislative chamber, era classrooms, displays, curriculum-based school programs. The archives and museum are housed in historic McKay Avenue School, site of the first session of the Alberta legislature (1906).

PROGRAMS: Concerts; Exhibits; Facility Rental; Festivals; Guided Tours; Interpretation; Publication; Research Library/Archives; School-Based Curriculum

COLLECTIONS: [1881-1980] School board minutes, administrative records, personnel files, student records, classroom registers, authorized textbooks for Alberta from 1906, photographs, trophies, uniforms, furniture, curriculum material.

HOURS: Yr Winter T-F 12:30-4; Summer T-F 12:30-4, Su 1-4

ADMISSION: No charge

9382
Edmonton Telephone Historical Information Centre Foundation
10437-83 Ave, T6E 4T5 [PO Box 4459, T6E 4T5]; (p) (780) 433-1010; (f) (780) 433-4068; thc@planet.eon.net

Private non-profit/ 1985/ staff: 3(f); 25(v)/ members: 150

HISTORY MUSEUM: Collects, preserves, catalogues, and interprets artifacts and archival material pertaining to telephone technology and the history of telecommunication in Edmonton.

PROGRAMS: Annual Meeting; Community Outreach; Exhibits; Family Programs; Guided Tours

COLLECTIONS: [1885-present] Telephones, phone books, phone sets, newspaper clippings, photographs, telecommunication equipment; 2,000 artifacts in the collection from the early wooden long boxes and candlestick phones to the most recent telephones and related material.

HOURS: Yr T-F 10-4, Sa 12-4

ADMISSION: $3, Family $5, Student $2, Seniors $2

9383
Fort Edmonton Park
Fox Drive & Whitemud Dr, T5J 2R7 [PO Box 2359, T5J 2R7]; (p) (780) 496-8787; (f) (780) 496-8797; www.gov.edmonton.ab.ca/fort

City/ 1974/ staff: 25(f); 80(p); 353(v)

LIVING HISTORY/OUTDOOR MUSEUM: Maintains the park as a living history park. It depicts Edmonton's history at the 1846 Hudson's Bay fort and on the Streets of 1885,

1905 and 1920. Outdoor living history interpreters.

PROGRAMS: Community Outreach; Exhibits; Facility Rental; Family Programs; Festivals; Guided Tours; Interpretation; Living History; Publication; School-Based Curriculum

COLLECTIONS: [1846-1929] Artifacts used to furnish homes, businesses, and churches; artifacts used to present an accurate depiction of a specific era.

HOURS: 3rd week in May-Aug M-F 10-4, Sa-Su 10-6

ADMISSION: $7, Family $21, Student $5.25, Children $3.50, Seniors $5.25

9384
Loyal Edmonton Regiment Foundation, The
118 Prince of Wales Heritage Centre 10440 - 108 Ave, T5H 3Z9; (p) (780) 421-9943; (f) (780) 421-9943; lermusm@planet.eon.net

Private non-profit/ 1985/ staff: 1(f); 57(v)/ members: 189

HISTORY MUSEUM: Collects, preserves, and displays military artifacts, photographs, and archival material of northern Alberta to educate and increase the knowledge of the general public.

PROGRAMS: Community Outreach; Exhibits; Guided Tours; Interpretation; Lectures; Research Library/Archives

COLLECTIONS: [1900-present] Material on the Loyal Edmonton Regiment and its' predecessor units from 1900 to present and other military units raised in northern Alberta during this period.

HOURS: Yr T-F 10-4

ADMISSION: No charge

9385
Museums Alberta (Alberta Museums Association)
9829-103 St, T5K 0X9; (p) (780) 424-2626; (f) (780) 425-1679; info@museumsalberta.ab.ca; www.museumsalberta.ab.ca

1971/ staff: 17(f); 1(p); 50(v)/ members: 500/publication: *Alberta Museums Review*

Guides and enables Alberta's museums to ensure their meaning and relevance to society by promoting supporting excellence support through strategic initiatives and active communication programs.

HOURS: Yr M-F 8:30-4:30

9386
Provincial Museum of Alberta
12845 102nd Ave, T5N 0M6; (p) (780) 456-9102; (f) (780) 454-6629; philip.stepney@gov.ab.ca; www.pma.edmonton.ab.ca

1967/ staff: 61(f); 30(p); 200(v)/ members: 1500/publication: *Natural History & Human History Occasional Papers*

HISTORY MUSEUM; RESEARCH CENTER: Collection, preservation, and interpretation of natural and human history of Alberta and Western Canada.

PROGRAMS: Community Outreach; Concerts; Exhibits; Facility Rental; Family Programs; Festivals; Guided Tours; Interpretation; Lectures; Publication; School-Based Curriculum; Theatre

COLLECTIONS: [1850-present] 10 million plus objects pertaining to natural and human history Western Canada; ornithology, entomology, biology, mineralogy ethnology, archaeology, military; geology, ichthyology, folklife, western Canadian history, paleontology, mammalogy, electronic data base, some digital imaging, records of all known archeological and historic sites in Alberta.

HOURS: Yr Daily 9-5

ADMISSION: $6.50; Family $15; Children $3; Seniors $5.50

9387
Ukrainian Catholic Women's League of Canada Arts and Crafts Museum
10825 - 97 St, T5H 2M4; (p) (780) 466-7210

1952

HISTORY MUSEUM: Preserves and promotes Ukrainian culture in order to strengthen its identity; collects, preserves, and interprets artifacts of Ukrainian culture brought to Canada by Ukrainian settlers or made and used here, after their arrival.

PROGRAMS: Community Outreach; Exhibits; Research Library/Archives

COLLECTIONS: [1852-present] Historical, regional folk costumes, woven textiles and kilms, pottery, wood carving, Easter eggs, and household items relating to the history of the Ukrainian settlement in Western Canada. 14,000 artifacts, library and books.

HOURS: May-Aug M-F 9-4; Sept-Apr W 1-4 and by appt

ADMISSION: No charge

9388
Ukrainian Cultural Heritage Village Provincial Historic Site
25 mins E of Edmonton on Hwy 16, T6G 2P8 [8820 - 112 St, T6G 2P8]; (p) (780) 662-3640; (f) (780) 662-3273; uchv@gov.ab.ca; www.gov ab.ca/mcd/mhs/uchv/uchv.htm

1971/ staff: 25(f); 50(p); 1200(v)

LIVING HISTORY/OUTDOOR MUSEUM: Operates village as an open air museum that was built to resemble pioneer settlements in east central Alberta. Costumed interpreters lead tours that focus on the history and lifestyles of Alberta's early settlers.

PROGRAMS: Concerts; Elder's Programs; Exhibits; Facility Rental; Festivals; Film/Video; Garden Tours; Guided Tours; Interpretation; Living History; Publication; Research Library/Archives; School-Based Curriculum

COLLECTIONS: [1892-1930] Thirty-three restored historic buildings, farm machinery and implements, antique vehicles, household and commerce artifacts, textiles, product packaging, manuscript and books, photographs, and pictures.

HOURS: May 15-Sept Daily 10-6; Sept-Nov 25 Daily 10-4

ADMISSION: $6.50, Family $15, Children $3.25, Seniors $5.50; Under 7 free

9389
University of Alberta Dental Museum
Dept of Dentistry, Univ of Alberta, T6G 2N8; (p) (780) 492-5194; (f) (780) 492-1621; gsperber@ualberta.ca

1967/ staff: 1(v)

HISTORIC PRESERVATION AGENCY; HISTORY MUSEUM; HOUSE MUSEUM: Collects and preserves dental artifacts.

COLLECTIONS: [1880s-1930] Dental artifacts, instruments, Palaeoanthropological casts of hominid evolution, natural history collection of animal skulls.

HOURS: By appt

ADMISSION: No charge

9390
University of Alberta, Department of Museums and Collections Services
Univ of Alberta Campus, T6G 2E2 [Ring House # 1, T6G 2E2]; (p) (780) 492-5834; (f) (780) 492-6185; museums@gpu.srv.ualberta.ca; www.ualberta.ca/MUSEUMS/

Joint/ 1908/ staff: 9(f); 5(p); 15(v)/ members: 40/publication: *Friends*

LIBRARY AND/OR ARCHIVES: Collects material on Western Canada; natural and human history collections used in teaching and for research purposes.

PROGRAMS: Community Outreach; Exhibits; Guided Tours; Interpretation; Lectures; Publication

COLLECTIONS: 17 million objects and specimens.

HOURS: Yr M-F 8:30-4:30 and by appt

ADMISSION: No charge

9391
Victoria School Archives and Museum
10210 - 108 Ave, T5H 1A8; (p) (780) 498-8727; (f) (780) 498-8715

Private non-profit/ 1990/ staff: 1(f); 2(p); 7(v)

HISTORIC SITE: Working museum and archives situated in a school.

PROGRAMS: Annual Meeting; Exhibits; Interpretation; Lectures; Living History; Research Library/Archives; School-Based Curriculum

COLLECTIONS: [1910-present] 10,000 artifacts: photographs, textiles, books, clothing, yearbooks, and historic information pertaining to Victoria School.

HOURS: Sept-June M-F 10-2

FAIRVIEW

9392
Historic Dunvegan Provincial Park
26 km S of Fairview on Hwy #2, T0H 1L0 [Box 1330, T0H 1L0]; (p) (780) 835-7150; (f) (780) 835-5525

1805/ staff: 1(f); 8(p)/ members: 22

HISTORIC SITE: Three fully restored historic buildings, a visitor center, and campground.

PROGRAMS: Exhibits; Family Programs; Festivals; Film/Video; Guided Tours; Interpretation; Publication; School-Based Curriculum; Theatre

COLLECTIONS: [1890s] Collection related to the fur trade of Catholic Missions 1890s.

HOURS: May-Sept Daily 10-6

9393
Ramp Centennial Celebration Museum/Fairview Pioneer Museum
Box 1994, T0H 1L0; (p) (780) 835-4715

Private non-profit/ 1974/ staff: 1(f)/ members: 40

HISTORIC PRESERVATION AGENCY; HISTORY MUSEUM; LIVING HISTORY/OUTDOOR MUSEUM: Acquires, restores and catalogs articles that pertain to the history of our area.

PROGRAMS: Exhibits; Facility Rental; Guided Tours

COLLECTIONS: [Late 1880-1950s] Household, church, school, trade items, newspapers, and photographs related to regional history.

HOURS: May-Sept T-Sa

FORESTBURG

9394
Forestburg Historical Society
4707-50 St, T0B 1N0 [Box 46, T0B 1N0]; (p) (780) 582-3768; (f) (780) 582-2165; (c) Flagstaff

1976/ staff: 8(v)/ members: 35

HISTORICAL SOCIETY; HISTORY MUSEUM: Collects and displays artifacts from the local area in a museum.

PROGRAMS: Annual Meeting; Exhibits; Interpretation

COLLECTIONS: [19th-20 c] Artifacts, memorabilia, and ephemera relating to local history.

HOURS: By appt

ADMISSION: Donations accepted

FORT MACLEOD

9395
Head-Smashed-In Buffalo Jump Historic Site
18km W of Fort MacLeod on Secondary Rd 785, T0L 0Z0 [Box 1977, T0L 0Z0]; (p) (403) 553-2731; (f) (403) 553-3141; info@ head.smashed.in.com; www.head-smashed-in.com

Joint/ 1987/ staff: 7(f); 20(p)/ members: 100

HISTORIC SITE: Promotes and preserves the site and tells the story of the People of the Buffalo, and helps people understand the ingenuity of and culture of these people in using this buffalo jump for over 6,000 years.

PROGRAMS: Community Outreach; Elder's Programs; Exhibits; Interpretation

COLLECTIONS: [6000BP-1850] Archeological; replicas of bison-derived tools; clothing; photographs.

HOURS: Yr June-Sept Daily

FORT MCMURRAY

9396
Oil Sands Discovery Centre
515 Mackezie Blvd, T9H 4X3; (p) (780) 743-7167; (f) (780) 791-0710; HSS_FortMC@ ComDev_ CFHR; www.oilsandsdiscovery.com

Private non-profit/ 1985/ staff: 6(f); 2(p); 12(v)

HISTORIC SITE; HISTORY MUSEUM: Produces programs and exhibits history of the oil sands of Alberta and the technology and future of this resource. We are a science museum with special emphasis on the environment.

PROGRAMS: Community Outreach; Exhibits; Facility Rental; Family Programs; Festivals; Film/Video; Garden Tours; Guided Tours; Interpretation; Lectures; Living History; Publication; Research Library/Archives; School-Based Curriculum; Theatre

COLLECTIONS: [Mesozoic Era]

HOURS: Yr Sept 1-May 15 T-Su 10-4; May 16-Aug 31 T-Su 10-6

ADMISSION: $4

FORT SASKATCHEWAN

9397
Fort Saskatchewan Historical Society
10104-101 St, T8L 1V9; (p) (780) 998-1750; (f) (780) 998-1750; www.fortsaskinfo.com/museum

Private non-profit/ 1958/ staff: 2(f); 2(p); 12(v)/ members: 48

HISTORIC SITE; HISTORICAL SOCIETY; HISTORY MUSEUM: Dedicated to preserving and promoting the history and heritage of this district by means of operating a local museum and archives.

PROGRAMS: Annual Meeting; Exhibits; Facility Rental; Family Programs; Guided Tours; Interpretation; Lectures; Research Library/ Archives; School-Based Curriculum

COLLECTIONS: [1875-1945] Artifact, books, materials relating to the history of the North West Mounted Police and general settlement era in central Alberta.

HOURS: Summer Daily 10-6; Winter M-F 11-3

ADMISSION: $2; Under 10 free

GRANDE PRAIRIE

9398
Grande Prairie Museum
102 Area 102 St, T8V 3A8 [Box 687, T8V 3A8]; (p) (780) 532-5482; (f) (780) 831-7371; (c) Peace

Private non-profit/ 1961/ staff: 4(f); 8(p); 120(v)/ members: 300/publication: *Grande Prairie Museum News*

HISTORIC PRESERVATION AGENCY; HISTORIC SITE; HISTORICAL SOCIETY; HISTORY MUSEUM: Collects, preserves, displays, researches, and interprets the natural and material history of Grande Prairie and area.

PROGRAMS: Annual Meeting; Community Outreach; Concerts; Elder's Programs; Exhibits; Facility Rental; Family Programs; Festivals; Guided Tours; Interpretation; Lectures; Living History; Publication; Reenactments

COLLECTIONS: [1909-1959] Pioneering and farming artifacts, Native, archaeological, paleontological artifacts unique to the area.

HOURS: Yr Summer Daily 10-6; Winter Su-F 1-4

ADMISSION: $2, Children $1

GRIMSHAW

9399
Lac Cardinal Regional Pioneer Village Museum Society
[PO Box 325, T0H 1W0]; (p) (780) 332-2030

Private non-profit/ 1988/ staff: 50(v)

HISTORY MUSEUM

PROGRAMS: Annual Meeting; Guided Tours; School-Based Curriculum

COLLECTIONS: [1920s-1940s] Buildings and machinery: saw-mill, shingle mill, grain cleaning equipment, threshing-machine, blacksmith shop, pole-shed to house machinery and 1,500 artifacts.

HOURS: May-Sept F-Su 4-8

ADMISSION: Donations requested

HIGH PRAIRIE

9400
High Prairie and District Museum and Historical Society
Box 1442, T0G 1E0; (p) (780) 523-2601; (f) (780) 523-2633

Private non-profit/ 1967/ staff: 2(p); 80(v)/ members: 20

HISTORIC PRESERVATION AGENCY; HISTORICAL SOCIETY; HISTORY MUSEUM: Dedicated to the preservation of the High Prairie and Area history.

PROGRAMS: Annual Meeting; Community Outreach; Exhibits; Publication; School-Based Curriculum

COLLECTIONS: Consists of the items used by the High Prairie and area people. Includes Pioneer farming implements, fur trade tools and equipment, and armaments.

HOURS: Yr Summer T-Sa 1-5; Winter: T-Sa

HOLDEN

9401
Holden Historical Society Museum
4928 - 50 Ave, T0B 2C0 [PO Box 32, T0B 2C0]; (p) (780) 688-2465; (c) Beaver #9

Joint/ 1991/ staff: 112(v)/ members: 48/publication: *Hemstitches and Hackmores*

HISTORIC SITE; HISTORICAL SOCIETY; HISTORY MUSEUM: Publishes local area history book; collects, preserves, and displays local pioneer artifacts for present and future generations.

PROGRAMS: Annual Meeting; Exhibits; Interpretation; Publication

COLLECTIONS: [1800-1960s] 3,000 pioneer settlement period artifacts: household, tools, newspapers, retail, photographs, and personal items.

HOURS: May-Sept W, F, Su 2-4

ADMISSION: Donations accepted

ISLAY

9402
Morrison Museum Association
Box 120, T0B 2J0; (p) (780) 744-2271; (c) Vermilion River

Private non-profit/ 1962/ staff: 7(p); 7(v)/ members: 9/publication: *There'll Always Be An Islay*

HISTORIC PRESERVATION AGENCY: Operates the Morrison Museum of the Country School with its collection of furnishings typical of a country school of the 1930s and 1940s.

PROGRAMS: Annual Meeting; Exhibits; Guided Tours; Publication

COLLECTIONS: [1907-1946] Furniture and artifacts typical of a country school in the 1930s and 1940s.

HOURS: May-Oct and by appt

ADMISSION: $0.50, Children $0.25; Under 6

JASPER

9403
Jasper-Yellowhead Museum and Archives
400 Pyramid Lake Rd, T0E 1E0 [PO Box 42, T0E 1E0]; (p) (780) 852-3013; (f) (780) 852-3240; jymachin@telusplanet.net

Private non-profit/ 1977/ staff: 1(f); 3(p); 20(v)/ members: 175

HISTORICAL SOCIETY; HISTORY MUSEUM; RESEARCH CENTER

PROGRAMS: Annual Meeting; Community Outreach; Exhibits; Facility Rental; Family Programs; Film/Video; Interpretation; Research Library/Archives

COLLECTIONS: [1820-1960]

HOURS: Yr Mid May-Sept 10-9; Sept-Nov 10-5; Nov-mid May Th-Su 10-5

ADMISSION: $3, Student $2,

LETH BRIDGE

9404
Sir Alexander Galt Museum and Archives
W End of 5th Ave S on Scenic Dr, T1J 0P6 [910-4 Ave S, T1J 0P6]; (p) (403) 320-3898; (f) (403) 329-4958; museum@ city.lethbridge.ab.ca; www.schoolnet.ca/collections/prairie/prairie.htm

1888/ staff: 3(f); 6(p); 40(v)

HISTORY MUSEUM

PROGRAMS: Community Outreach; Elder's Programs; Exhibits; Facility Rental; Family Programs; Festivals; Film/Video; Guided Tours; Interpretation; Lectures; Reenactments; Research Library/Archives; School-Based Curriculum; Theatre

COLLECTIONS: [1800s-present]

HOURS: Yr Daily

ADMISSION: No charge

LETHBRIDGE

9405
Fort Whoop-up Interpretive Centre
W End of 3rd Ave S, T1J 2A4 [PO Box 1074, T1J 2A4]; (p) (403) 329-0444; (f) (403) 329-0645

1967/ staff: 2(f); 6(p); 38(v)/ members: 40/publication: Fort Hamilton Dispatch

HISTORIC SITE; LIVING HISTORY/OUTDOOR MUSEUM: Interprets trade era arising from Fort Benton Montana and Interaction between Blackfoot Confederacy, American traders and North West Mounted Police.

PROGRAMS: Annual Meeting; Exhibits; Facility Rental; Family Programs; Festivals; Film/Video; Guided Tours; Interpretation; Living History; Publication; Reenactments; School-Based Curriculum; Theatre

COLLECTIONS: [1865-1895] Era represented by buffalo robe trade; period furnishings, trade goods, furs associated with Fort Benton connection, North West Mounted Police Barracks, and display associated with police use of Fort 1875-1890.

HOURS: Yr May-Sept Daily 10-6; Oct-Apr T-F, Su 10-4

ADMISSION: $2.50, Student $1.50, Seniors $1.50; Under 6 free

LONGVIEW

9406
Bar U Ranch National Historic Site of Canada
13 km S on Longview on Hwy 22, T0L 1H0 [Box 168, T0L 1H0]; (p) (403) 395-2212, (800) 568-4996; (f) (403) 395-2331; parkscanada.pch.gc.ca

Federal/ 1995/ Parks Canada/ staff: 4(f); 65(p); 8(v)

HISTORIC SITE; LIVING HISTORY/OUTDOOR MUSEUM: Commemorates the history of ranching in Canada and the role the Bar U Ranch played.

PROGRAMS: Exhibits; Facility Rental; Family Programs; Film/Video; Guided Tours; Interpretation; Lectures; Reenactments; School-Based Curriculum

COLLECTIONS: [1882-1950] 35 existing structures.

HOURS: May-Oct Daily 10-6

ADMISSION: $7.75, Student $4.90, Seniors $6

MEDICINE HAT

9407
Friends of Medalta
703 Wood St, T1A 7E9 [Box 204, T1A 7E9]; (p) (403) 529-1070; (f) (403) 529-1070; www.medalta.org

Private non-profit/ 1986/ staff: 8(f); 3(p); 10(v)/ members: 450/publication: Know Your Medalta Stamps: The Kilns of Southeastern Alberta; and others

HISTORIC SITE; HISTORY MUSEUM: Preservation and restoration of historic pottery plants in Medicine Hat. Operates two museums, Medalta Potteries and Hycroft China.

PROGRAMS: Annual Meeting; Community Outreach; Exhibits; Guided Tours; Interpretation; Living History; Publication; Research Library/Archives

COLLECTIONS: [1912-1954] Collection of Medalta pottery, turn-of-the-century pottery manufacturing equipment in North America.

HOURS: May 15-Oct 31 Daily 9-5:30

ADMISSION: $3, Student $2, Seniors $2

9408
Medicine Hat Museum and Art Gallery
1302 Bomford Crescent SW, T1A 5E6; (p) (403) 502-8580; (f) (403) 502-8589; mhmag@city.medicine-hat.ab.ca

City/ 1954/ staff: 10(f); 4(p); 25(v)/ members: 265

ART MUSEUM; HISTORY MUSEUM: Collects, preserves, and interprets the past history of Medicine Hat and District.

COLLECTIONS: [1883-1980s] 16,000 artifacts, 350,000 photographs, manuscripts.

HOURS: Yr Daily M-F 9-5; Sa-Su 1-5, W 7pm-10pm

ADMISSION: Donations accepted

MILLET

9409
Millet and District Museum and Exhibit Room, The
5120-50 St, T0C 1Z0 [PO Box 178, T0C 1Z0]; (p) (780) 387-5558; (f) (780) 387-5548; MDHS@glink2.com; (c) Wetaskiwin

1985/ staff: 1(f); 2(p); 32(v)/ members: 50

HISTORICAL SOCIETY; HISTORY MUSEUM: Maintains and preserves Millet's cultural resources.

PROGRAMS: Annual Meeting; Exhibits; Guided Tours; Interpretation; Research Library/Archives; School-Based Curriculum

COLLECTIONS: 6,000 museum artifact, 800 photos, 18 maps, 49 architectural drawings, 15m of textual archival holdings.

HOURS: Yr May-Sept M-Sa 8:30-4:30; Sept-May T-Th 1-4:30

ADMISSION: Donations accepted

MIRROR

9410
Mirror and District Museum Association
[PO Box 246, T0B 3C0]

Private non-profit/ 1977/ staff: 1(p); 15(v)/ members: 29

HISTORIC SITE; HISTORICAL SOCIETY; HISTORY MUSEUM

PROGRAMS: Annual Meeting; Exhibits; Research Library/Archives

COLLECTIONS: [1890-present] Pioneer, early history, and railway memorabilia and artifacts.

HOURS: June-Aug T-Sa 10-6

ADMISSION: Donations accepted

OLDS

9411
Olds Historical Society / Mountain View Museum
5038 - 50 St, Z4H 1P6 [Box 3882, Z4H 1P6]; (p) (403) 556-8464; (c) Mountain View

1972/ staff: 24(v)

HISTORICAL SOCIETY; HISTORY MUSEUM; RESEARCH CENTER: Collects and preserves artifacts and printed material to illustrate local heritage.

PROGRAMS: Annual Meeting; Exhibits; Guided Tours; Interpretation

COLLECTIONS: [1895-1950] Artifacts donated by local citizens, local history, artifacts.

HOURS: Yr Jan 1-July 1and Sept 1-Dec 31 T-Th 1-5; July

PEACE RIVER

9412
Peace River Centennial Museum and Archives
10302-99 St, T8S 1K1; (p) (780) 624-4261; (f) (780) 624-4270; prcma@telusplanet.net; www.telusplanet.com/public/prcma

Private for-profit/ 1967/ staff: 2(f); 15(v)/ members: 2/publication: *A Sense of the Peace*

HISTORY MUSEUM; RESEARCH CENTER: Maintains the Northern Alberta Railway Station and history of Sir Alexander Mackenzie.

PROGRAMS: Annual Meeting; Community Outreach; Exhibits; Festivals; Film/Video; Guided Tours; Interpretation; Lectures; Living History; Publication; Reenactments; School-Based Curriculum; Theatre

COLLECTIONS: [1750-present]

HOURS: Yr May 1-Sept 1 Daily M-Th 9-5, F 9-9, Sa 10-7, Su 10-4; Sept 1-May 1 T-Sa

ADMISSION: $3, Family $6, Student $2, Seniors $2; Group rates

PINCHER CREEK

9413
Pincher Creek & District Museum/ Kootenai Brown Historical Park
1069 James Ave, T0K 1W0 [PO Box 1226, T0K 1W0]; (p) (403) 627-3684; (f) (403) 627-2916

Private non-profit/ 1966/ staff: 1(f); 2(p); 65(v)/ members: 50/publication: *Prairie Grass to Mountain Pass, Pincher Papers I*

HISTORICAL SOCIETY; HISTORY MUSEUM: Preserves and promotes local history.

PROGRAMS: Annual Meeting; Community Outreach; Exhibits; Facility Rental; Family Programs; Guided Tours; Interpretation; Lectures; Living History; Publication; Research Library/Archives; School-Based Curriculum; Theatre

COLLECTIONS: [1880-1940] 12,500 artifacts, historic sites, agricultural implements, pioneer furniture, pioneer clothing, blacksmithing tools, commerce, kitchen utensils, textbooks, archives/library, manuscripts, photos, newspapers, and publications.

HOURS: Mid May-mid Sept Daily 10-8; Mid Sept-mid May by appt

ADMISSION: $4, Student $2, Seniors $3; Under 10 free

PONOKA

9414
Fort Ostell Museum Society
5320-54 St, T4J 1L8; (p) (403) 783-5224; (c) Ponoka

Private non-profit/ 1967/ staff: 3(p); 10(v)/ members: 8

HISTORY MUSEUM: Collects, preserves, displays, and interprets the history of the Ponoka area.

PROGRAMS: Exhibits; Facility Rental; Guided Tours; Lectures; Research Library/Archives

COLLECTIONS: [1900-1950] Artifacts: agricultural, archival, photos, clothing, natural history, Native American, medicine.

HOURS: May 1-Aug 31 M-F 9-12 / 1-5, Sa-Su

RED DEER

9415
Fort Normandeau
5km W of City, 32nd St, T4N 3M4 [c/o 6300-45 Ave, T4N 3M4]; (p) (403) 347-4550; (f) (403) 347-2550; kwnc@telusplanet.net; www.city.red-deer.ab.ca/kerry

Joint/ 1986/ Private non-profit, City/ staff: 3(f); 5(p); 150(v)

HISTORIC SITE; HISTORY MUSEUM; LIVING HISTORY/OUTDOOR MUSEUM

PROGRAMS: Community Outreach; Elder's Programs; Exhibits; Facility Rental; Family Programs; Festivals; Film/Video; Guided Tours; Interpretation; Living History; Publication; Reenactments; Research Library/Archives; School-Based Curriculum; Theatre

COLLECTIONS: [1880-1895] Old fort, rocking chair, and school bell from Indian Industrial School.

HOURS: Late May-early Sept Daily 12-8

ADMISSION: Donations accepted

9416
Red Deer and District Museum
4525 47 A Ave, T4N 6Z6; (p) (403) 309-8405; (f) (403) 342-6644; museum@ museum.red-deer.ab.ca; www.museum.red-deer.ab.ca

Joint/ 1973/ City and Normandeau Cultural and Natural History Society/ staff: 6(f); 8(p); 200(v)

ART MUSEUM; HISTORY MUSEUM: Collects, preserves, studies, and interprets the cultural history of Red Deer and district.

PROGRAMS: Annual Meeting; Community Outreach; Concerts; Elder's Programs; Exhibits; Facility Rental; Family Programs; Festivals; Guided Tours; Interpretation; Lectures; Living History; Research Library/Archives; School-Based Curriculum

COLLECTIONS: [1905-present] 85,000 pieces: art, commercial, agricultural, domestic, and personal items; clothing and textile; Native American and Inuit Art.

HOURS: Yr Daily M, T, F 10-5, W, Th 10-9, Sa-Su 1-5

ADMISSION: Donations accepted

REDCLIFF

9417
Redcliff Historical Museum Society
#2, 3rd St NE, T0J 2P0 [PO Box 758, T0J 2P0]; (p) (403) 548-6260

Private non-profit/ 1981/ staff: 2(p); 13(v)/ members: 44

HISTORICAL SOCIETY; HISTORY MUSEUM: Collects, preserves and exhibits artifacts, photos and manuscripts of Redcliff and area.

PROGRAMS: Annual Meeting; Community Outreach; Exhibits; Facility Rental; Family Programs; Guided Tours; Lectures; Research Library/Archives

COLLECTIONS: [1800-1970] Photos, artifacts, Redcliff Review newspaper; recreational, commerce, industrial and domestic exhibits, Greenhouse industry and brick factory.

HOURS: May-Sept T-Su 9-4:30

ADMISSION: Donations requested

SEDGEWICK

9418
Sedgewick Historical Society
4813 47th St, T0B 4C0 [PO Box 508, T0B 4C0]; (p) (780) 384-3741

Private non-profit/ 1981/ staff: 1(p); 15(v)/ members: 128

ART MUSEUM; HISTORIC SITE; HISTORICAL SOCIETY; HISTORY MUSEUM

PROGRAMS: Annual Meeting; Exhibits; Guided Tours; Research Library/Archives

COLLECTIONS: [1919-present] Agricultural small equipment, homemaking items, jewelry, books, clothing, hats and shoes, photos, paintings, tools, oral tapes of early residents, veterinary equipment, medicine bottles, maps and documents.

HOURS: July-Aug Sa-Su

SHERWOOD PARK

9419
Strathcona County Heritage Museum
913 Ash St, T8G 2B4; (p) (780) 467-8189

Private non-profit/ 1997/ staff: 1(f); 3(p); 90(v)/ members: 109

HISTORY MUSEUM; RESEARCH CENTER: Collects, preserves, and interprets history of Strathcona County.

PROGRAMS: Annual Meeting; Community Outreach; Exhibits; Facility Rental; Family Programs; Guided Tours; Interpretation; Lectures; Research Library/Archives; School-Based Curriculum

COLLECTIONS: [1880s-1950s] Artifacts collected from Stratchcona County.

HOURS: Yr M-Sa 10-4, (Su May-Sept and long weekends)

ADMISSION: $2, Family

STONY PLAIN

9420
Multicultural Heritage Centre
5411 51 St, T7Z 1X7 [Box 2188, T7Z 1X7]; (p) (780) 963-2777; (f) (780) 963-0233

Private non-profit/ 1974/ staff: 6(f); 30(p); 100(v)/ members: 1

GARDEN; GENEALOGICAL SOCIETY; HISTORIC PRESERVATION AGENCY; HISTORIC SITE; HISTORY MUSEUM; HOUSE MUSEUM; LIVING HISTORY/OUTDOOR MUSEUM: Retains and presents the cultural heritage and history of the Stony Plain area.

PROGRAMS: Annual Meeting; Concerts; Elder's Programs; Exhibits; Facility Rental; Family Programs; Festivals; Guided Tours; Interpretation; Publication; Research Library/Archives; School-Based Curriculum; Theatre

COLLECTIONS: [1920-1950] Pioneer settlement, household objects, 2,000 photos, magazines.

HOURS: Yr Daily M-Sa 10-4, Su 10-6:30

ADMISSION: No charge

STROME

9421
Strome and District Historical Society
5029 - 50 St, T0B 4H0 [Box 151, T0B 4H0];
(p) (780) 376-3546

Private non-profit/ 1987/ staff: 1(p); 50(v)/ members: 25/publication: *Lanterns on the Prairie*

HISTORIC SITE; HISTORICAL SOCIETY; HISTORY MUSEUM; LIVING HISTORY/OUTDOOR MUSEUM: Collects, preserves, and interprets the history of Strome and area from 1900-1950.

PROGRAMS: Annual Meeting; Community Outreach; Exhibits; Guided Tours; Living History; Publication; School-Based Curriculum

COLLECTIONS: [1900-1950] 10,000 artifacts of pioneer history, 200 mounted birds and animals, 50 fossils, 40 mounted animal heads; kitchen, church, old time store.

HOURS: May-Sept T-Su 11-4

ADMISSION: $2; Under 12 free

TOFIELD

9422
Tofield Historical Society
5020-48 Ave, T0B 4J0 [Box 30, T0B 4J0]; (p) (780) 662-3944; (f) (780) 662-3929; tofield@supernet.ab.ca; www.tcnap.tofield.ab.ca

1961/ staff: 15(v)/ members: 35

HISTORY MUSEUM: Collects, preserves, researches, exhibits, and interprets history of Tofield and District.

PROGRAMS: Annual Meeting; Exhibits; Facility Rental

COLLECTIONS: [1900-1940] Artifacts, immigration material, local government records, and materials relating to school districts, industries and cultural diversity.

HOURS: Apr-Sept Daily 10-5; Oct-Mar by app

ADMISSION: No charge/Donations

VEGREVILLE

9423
Vegreville Regional Museum Society
1km E of Vegrevilleon Hwy 16A, T9C 1R3 [PO Box 328, T9C 1R3]; (p) (780) 632-7650; (f) (780) 632-6756; vrmuseum@vegnet.com; www.vegreville.com; (c) Minburn

City/ 1969/ staff: 2(f); 2(p); 30(v)/ members: 100

GARDEN; HISTORY MUSEUM; LIVING HISTORY/OUTDOOR MUSEUM: Portrays history of the founding, settlement, and development of the town of Vegreville and the surrounding areas.

PROGRAMS: Community Outreach; Elder's Programs; Exhibits; Facility Rental; Garden Tours; Guided Tours; Interpretation; Lectures; Publication; Research Library/Archives; School-Based Curriculum

COLLECTIONS: [1850-1998] Royal Canadian Mounted Police Exhibit; agricultural implements, photos, pioneer life.

HOURS: Yr May-Aug T-F 1-5; Sept-April Th 12-4, and by appt

ADMISSION: No charge/Donations

WETASKIWIN

9424
Canada's Aviation Hall of Fame
Hwy 13 W, T9A 2G1 [PO Box 6360, T9A 2G1]; (p) (780) 361-1351; (f) (780) 361-1239; cahf@telusplanet.net; www.cahf.ca

County; Joint/ 1973/ County; Private non-profit/ staff: 1(f); 1(p)/publication: *The Flyer*

HISTORY MUSEUM; RESEARCH CENTER: Promotes and preserves history of Canadian aviation.

PROGRAMS: Annual Meeting; Exhibits; Guided Tours; Publication; Research Library/ Archives

COLLECTIONS: [1909-present] Personal memorabilia; Hall of Fame.

HOURS: Yr T-Su 9-5

ADMISSION: $6.50, Family $15, Children $3, Seniors $5.50

9425
Reynolds Aviation Museum
4110 57th St, T9A 2B6; (p) (780) 352-6201; (f) (780) 352-4666; srsl@incentre.net

Joint/ 1955/ Private non-profit; City

HISTORY MUSEUM: Collects and preserves military history.

PROGRAMS: Exhibits

COLLECTIONS: [1955-present] Artifacts: military motor vehicles, amphibians, tanks, guns.

HOURS: May-Sept Daily 10-5

ADMISSION: $3.50, Children $2.50, Seniors $2.50; Under 6 free

9426
Reynolds-Alberta Museum
2 kms W of Wetaskiwin on Hwy 13, T9A 2G1 [Box 6360, T9A 2G1]; (p) (780) 361-1351; (f) (780) 361-1239; ram@gov.ab.ca; www.gov.ab.ca/mcd/mhs/ram/ram.htm; (c) Wetaskiwin

1992/ staff: 25(f); 10(p); 150(v)

HISTORY MUSEUM: Preserves and presents history of the mechanization of agriculture and the development of land and air transportation in AB.

PROGRAMS: Exhibits; Facility Rental; Guided Tours; Interpretation; Publication; Research Library/Archives

COLLECTIONS: [1890-1969] Artifacts: planes, tractors, mechanized farm implements, industrial equipment, cars, trucks, motorbikes, bicycles; trade literature, books, magazines and newspapers.

HOURS: Yr May-Sept Daily 9-7, Oct-Apr T-Su 9-5

ADMISSION: $6.50, Family $17, Children $3, Seniors $5.50

BRITISH COLUMBIA

108 MILE RANCH

9427
100 Mile and District Historical Society
Hwy 97 N, V0K 2Z0 [PO Box 225, V0K 2Z0]; (p) (250) 791-5288; (f) (250) 791-1947; trutledg@bcinternet.net

Private non-profit/ 1977/ Board of Directors/ staff: 1(f); 5(p); 10(v)/ members: 75

HISTORIC PRESERVATION AGENCY; HISTORIC SITE; HISTORICAL SOCIETY; HISTORY MUSEUM; HOUSE MUSEUM: Collects, preserves, and interprets the Gold Rush.

PROGRAMS: Exhibits; Facility Rental; Guided Tours; Research Library/Archives

COLLECTIONS: [1841-1905] Eight historic sites: 105 Ranch House, 1880 Bunk House, 1880 Post House, 1860 Box Barn 1880 Blacksmith Shop, 1880 Telegraph Building, 1882 Ice House, and the 1905 Watson Barn.

HOURS: Mid May-Mid Sept Daily 9-6

ADMISSION: Donations accepted

ABBOTSFORD

9428
Matsqui Sumas Abbotsford Museum Society
2313 Ware St, V2S 3C6; (p) (604) 853-0313; (f) (604) 853-3722; mail@msa.museum.bc.ca; www.abbotsford.net/msamuseum

Private non-profit/ 1969/ staff: 3(f); 200(v)/ members: 186/publication: *Megaphone*

HISTORIC SITE; HISTORY MUSEUM: Restored 1920s heritage home of BC timber baron, J.D. Trethewey; features fir lumber and brick industries.

PROGRAMS: Annual Meeting; Community Outreach; Exhibits; Facility Rental; Family Programs; Festivals; Guided Tours; Interpretation; Publication; Research Library/Archives; School-Based Curriculum

COLLECTIONS: [1920] Archival, photo-archival and ephemera; Trethewey family /Abbotsford Lumber Company, Clayburn Company and Sumas Reclamation Project artifacts.

HOURS: Yr Sept-June M-F 1-5; July-Aug Daily 1-5

ADMISSION: Donations requested

AGASSIZ

9429
Agassiz-Harrison Historical Society
6947 Lougheed Hwy, V0M 1A0 [PO Box 313, V0M 1A0]; (p) (604) 796-3545; (f) (604) 796-3572

Private non-profit/ 1985/ staff: 50(v)/ members: 200/publication: *Agassiz-Harrison Hisstorical Society Newsletter*

HISTORIC PRESERVATION AGENCY; HISTORICAL SOCIETY; HISTORY MUSEUM: Gathers, preserves, and displays artifacts, records, and information of historical and heritage value; maintains museum and archives.

PROGRAMS: Annual Meeting; Exhibits; Guided Tours; Publication; Research Library/Archives; School-Based Curriculum

COLLECTIONS: [1885-present] 5,000 artifacts; 5,300 photos.

HOURS: May-Sept Daily 10-4

ADMISSION: Donations accepted

ALERT BAY

9430
U'mista Cultural Centre
Front St, V0N 1A0 [PO Box 253, V0N 1A0]; (p) (250) 974-5403; (f) (250) 974-5499; umista@island.net; www.umista.org/

1974/ staff: 4(f); 4(v)/ members: 189/publication: *The Book of U'mista*

GARDEN; RESEARCH CENTER: Promotes cultural heritage of the Kwakwaka'wakw.

PROGRAMS: Annual Meeting; Exhibits; Facility Rental; Guided Tours; Publication

COLLECTIONS: [Early 19th c] 719 artifacts (repatriated masks, rattles, and other regalia), 337 audio tapes, 1,100 library books, 3,050 photos, 109 sound reels, 5,040 slides, and 789 video tapes in VHS, Beta, and DV format.

HOURS: Sept-May M-F 9-5; May-Sept Daily 9-6

ADMISSION: $5.35, Student $4.28, Children $1.07, Seniors $4.28

ATLIN

9431
Atlin Historical Society
Third St & Trainor St, V0W 1A0 [PO Box 111, V0W 1A0]; (p) (250) 651-7522; (f) (250) 651-7522

Private non-profit/ 1972/ staff: 5(v)/ members: 60/publication: *Atlin - The Story of British Columbia's Last Gold Rush*

HISTORIC PRESERVATION AGENCY; HISTORIC SITE; HISTORICAL SOCIETY; HISTORY MUSEUM: Promotes heritage preservation.

PROGRAMS: Annual Meeting; Exhibits; Facility Rental; Guided Tours; Interpretation; Publication; Research Library/Archives; Theatre

COLLECTIONS: [1898-1940] Mining, transportation, medicine, schools, households, communications, and businesses; 400 photos; manuscript and vertical files; taped interviews; movies; maps; newspapers.

HOURS: May-Sept Daily

ADMISSION: $2.50, Children $1

BARKERVILLE

9432
Barkerville Historic Town
[PO Box 19, V0K 1B0]; (p) (250) 994-3302; (f) (250) 994-3435

1958/ Ministry of Small Business, Tourism, and Culture, Heritage Branch/ staff: 19(f); 1(v)

LIVING HISTORY/OUTDOOR MUSEUM: Promotes BC history and gold mining with one hundred ten display rooms, one hundred original buildings, twenty-five reconstructions,

twenty-two businesses, street interpretation, and live theatre.

PROGRAMS: Community Outreach; Concerts; Exhibits; Facility Rental; Festivals; Guided Tours; Interpretation; Lectures; Living History; Research Library/Archives; School-Based Curriculum; Theatre

COLLECTIONS: [1860-1938]

HOURS: Yr Daily dawn-dusk

ADMISSION: $8

BARRIERE

9433
Barriere and District Heritage Society
353 Lilley Rd, V0E 1E0 [PO Box 228, V0E 1E0]; (p) (250) 672-5583

Private non-profit/ 1984/ staff: 2(p); 14(v)/ members: 16

HISTORIC PRESERVATION AGENCY; HISTORICAL SOCIETY; HISTORY MUSEUM: Preserves local history.

PROGRAMS: Annual Meeting; Exhibits; Guided Tours; Living History

COLLECTIONS: [Late 19th

BURNABY

9434
Burnaby Village Museum
6501 Deer Lake Ave, V5G 3T6; (p) (604) 293-6500; (f) (604) 293-6525

City/ 1971/ staff: 15(f); 73(p); 100(v)

HISTORY MUSEUM; LIVING HISTORY/OUTDOOR MUSEUM

PROGRAMS: Exhibits; Facility Rental; Garden Tours; Interpretation; School-Based Curriculum

COLLECTIONS: [1890-1925]

ADMISSION: $6.45, Student $4.45, Seniors $4.35

9435
Museum of Archaeology and Ethnology
Department of Archaeology Simon Fraser Univ, V5A 1S6; (p) (604) 291-3325; (f) (604) 291-5666; bwinter@sfu.ca; www.sfu.ca/archaeology/museum/

1969/ staff: 1(f); 20(v)

HISTORY MUSEUM: Collects, preserves, and exhibits archaeological, ethnological material.

PROGRAMS: Exhibits

COLLECTIONS: [5000 BP-present] Artifacts: archaeology and ethnology.

HOURS: M-F 10-12 / 1-4

ADMISSION: Donations accepted

9436
Simon Fraser University Archives and Records Management Department
8888 University Dr, V5A 1S6; (p) (604) 291-3261; (f) (604) 291-4047; archives@sfu.ca; www.sfu.ca/archives/

1968/ staff: 4(f); 1(p)

LIBRARY AND/OR ARCHIVES

PROGRAMS: Research Library/Archives

COLLECTIONS: Official University records,

documents, private papers, historical research.

HOURS: Yr M-F 9-12:30 / 1:30-4

CAMPBELL RIVER

9437
Campbell River Museum and Archives Society
470 Island Hwy, V9W 4Z9 [Box 70, Station A, V9W 4Z9]; (p) (250) 287-3103; (f) (250) 286-0109; general.inquires@crmuseum.ca; www.crmuseum.ca

City/ 1958/ Board of Trustees/ staff: 2(f); 8(p); 60(v)/ members: 850

HISTORY MUSEUM: Preserves early cultures, history, and development of Northern Vancouver Island.

PROGRAMS: Annual Meeting; Community Outreach; Exhibits; Facility Rental; Guided Tours; Interpretation; Lectures; Publication; Research Library/Archives; School-Based Curriculum

COLLECTIONS: [Pre history-early 20th c] Ethnological and archaeological material associated documentation of the area's aboriginal peoples; historic material related to area's cultural and economic development; archival material relating to area history and ethnography.

HOURS: Yr Summer: M-Sa 10-5, Su 12-5; Winter: T-Su 12-5

ADMISSION: $2.50, Seniors $2; Under 6 free

9438
Campbell River Optical Maritime Museum
Ste 102, 250 Dogwood St, V9W 2X9; (p) (250) 287-3741; (f) (250) 287-2052

Private non-profit/ 1965/ staff: 2(f); 1(p)

MARITIME MUSEUM

PROGRAMS: Guided Tours

COLLECTIONS: [1 B.C.-1998] Marine materials.

HOURS: Yr 8-11:45/1-5:30

CHASE

9439
Chase and District Museum and Archives Society
1042 Shuswap Ave, V0E 1M0 [Box 160, V0E 1M0]; (p) (250) 679-8847; cdmachin@wkpowerlink.com

County/ 1984/ staff: 1(p); 15(v)/ members: 71

HISTORICAL SOCIETY; HISTORY MUSEUM: Collects, preserves, and interprets the district's history.

PROGRAMS: Annual Meeting; Exhibits; Guided Tours; Publication; Research Library/Archives

COLLECTIONS: [1865-1950] Chase and district history, 2,000 artifacts, 1,000 photographs, 200 archival items, several maps, sheet music, and local newspapers.

HOURS: June-Sept Daily 10-4:30

COURTENAY

9440
Courtenay and District Museum and Paleontology Centre
207 - 4th St, V9N 1G7; (p) (250) 334-0686; (f) (250) 334-0619; museum@island.net; www.courtenaymuseum.bc.ca

Private non-profit/ 1961/ staff: 7(f); 3(p); 75(v)/ members: 150

HISTORICAL SOCIETY; HISTORY MUSEUM: Archives, collects, preserves, and interprets Native American, and European settlement history.

PROGRAMS: Annual Meeting; Elder's Programs; Exhibits; Family Programs; Film/Video; Guided Tours; Interpretation; Lectures; Research Library/Archives; School-Based Curriculum

COLLECTIONS: [Cretaceous-present] Paleontology specimens, 8,000 Euro- American artifacts, local newspaper archives, logging and railway artifacts.

HOURS: May-Aug Daily 10-5; Sept-April T-Sa 10-5

ADMISSION: $3, Seniors $2.50; Children free

CRANBROOK

9441
Cranbrook Archives Museum and Landmark Foundation
1 Van Horne St, V1C 4H9 [Box 400, V1C 4H9]; (p) (250) 489-3918; (f) (250) 489-5744; camal@cyberlink.bc.ca; www.crowsnest.bc.ca

Private non-profit/ 1976/ staff: 3(f); 20(p)/ members: 300/publication: Heritage Cranbrook

HISTORY MUSEUM: Preserves history of Cranbrook and the railroad.

PROGRAMS: Annual Meeting; Exhibits; Facility Rental; Guided Tours; Interpretation; Living History; Publication

COLLECTIONS: [1880-1950] Railroad.

HOURS: Yr Spring-fall Daily 8-8; Winter T-Sa 12-5

ADMISSION: $6.31

CRESTON

9442
Creston and District Historical and Museum Society
219 Devon St, V0B 1G3; (p) (250) 428-9262; (f) (250) 428-3324; crvmchin@kootenay.com

Private non-profit/ 1971/ staff: 1(f); 20(v)/ members: 57

HISTORIC SITE; HISTORICAL SOCIETY; HISTORY MUSEUM: Operates the Stone House Museum and Archives; collects, preserves, and displays the history of the Creston Valley.

PROGRAMS: Annual Meeting; Community Outreach; Exhibits; Facility Rental; Family Programs; Festivals; Guided Tours; Interpretation; Lectures; Publication; Research Library/Archives; School-Based Curriculum

COLLECTIONS: [1890-1950] 50,000 objects including photos, documents, newspapers, artifacts reflecting all aspects of society in the Creston Valley; two historic buildings; outdoor ex-

hibits of agricultural equipment and machinery.

HOURS: May-Sept Daily 10-3:30; Oct-Apr by appt

ADMISSION: $2, Student $1, Children $1

CUMBERLAND

9443
Cumberland Museum and Archives
2680 Dunsmuir Ave, V0R 1S0 [PO Box 258, V0R 1S0]; (p) (250) 336-2445; (f) (250) 336-2411; cma_chin@island.net; www.island.net/~cma_chin

1981/ staff: 1(f); 3(p); 4(v)/ members: 110

HISTORICAL SOCIETY; HISTORY MUSEUM; RESEARCH CENTER

PROGRAMS: Annual Meeting; Community Outreach; Elder's Programs; Exhibits; Family Programs; Festivals; Film/Video; Guided Tours; Research Library/Archives; School-Based Curriculum

COLLECTIONS: [1880-1980]

HOURS: Yr 9-5

ADMISSION: Donations requested

DAWSON CREEK

9444
South Peace Historical Society
900 Alaska Ave, V1G 4T6; (p) (250) 782-9595; (f) (250) 782-9538

1952/ staff: 2(f); 1(p); 10(v)/ members: 30

HISTORICAL SOCIETY: Preserves history of Dawson Creek, the Peace River country of BC and AK Highway.

PROGRAMS: Annual Meeting; Exhibits; Family Programs; Film/Video; Guided Tours; Publication; Research Library/Archives

COLLECTIONS: [1920-1960] Artifacts: railroad history, wildlife, AK highway.

HOURS:Summer Daily 8-7; Winter 10-12 / 1-4

DENMAN ISLAND

9445
Denman Seniors and Museum Society
NW Rd, Downtown, V0R 1T0 [Box 28, V0R 1T0]; (p) (250) 335-0880

Private non-profit/ 1995/ staff: 14(v)

HISTORY MUSEUM: Preserves history and artifacts of aboriginal peoples.

PROGRAMS: Annual Meeting; Exhibits; Guided Tours; Research Library/Archives

COLLECTIONS: [Late 19th-early 20th c] Aboriginal and pioneer artifacts, photographs, oral histories.

HOURS: Late June-early Sept Daily 1:30-4 and by appt

ENDERBY

9446
Enderby and District Museum Society
901 George St, Hwy 97A, U0E 1V0 [PO Box 367, V0E 1V0]; (p) (250) 838-7170; (f) (250) 838-0123

1973/ staff: 1(p); 14(v)/ members: 120

HISTORY MUSEUM: Preserves, collects, re-

searches, interprets, and exhibits representative objects and supporting archival materials relevant to the human and natural history of Enderby and the surrounding district in North Okanagan.

PROGRAMS: Annual Meeting; Community Outreach; Exhibits; Guided Tours; Lectures; Publication; Research Library/Archives

COLLECTIONS: [1880-1960] 5,500 photographs, 100 maps, 70 sound video cassettes, 18 linear meters of textual records, newspapers, 5,000 museum artifacts.

HOURS: Yr Summer M-Sa 10-5; Winter T-Sa 12-4:30

ADMISSION: Donations accepted

FORT LANGLEY

9447
British Columbia Farm Machinery and Agricultural Museum Association
9131 King St, V1M 1A0 [PO Box 279, V1M 1A0]; (p) (604) 888-2273; webit.ssimplenet.com/museum/

Private non-profit/ 1957/ staff: 31(v)/ members: 62

HISTORIC PRESERVATION AGENCY

PROGRAMS: Annual Meeting; Exhibits; Guided Tours; Interpretation; Research Library/ Archives; School-Based Curriculum

COLLECTIONS: [1900-1980] Farm mechanization.

HOURS: Apr-Oct Daily 10-4:45

ADMISSION: $4, Seniors $2

9448
Langley Centennial Museum and National Exhibition Centre
9135 King St, V1M 2S2 [PO Box 800, V1M 2S2]; (p) (604) 888-3922; (f) (604) 888-7291; museum@tol.bc.ca

City/ 1958/ staff: 4(f); 2(p); 100(v)

ART MUSEUM; HISTORY MUSEUM: .

PROGRAMS: Community Outreach; Elder's Programs; Exhibits; Family Programs; Guided Tours; Interpretation; Lectures; Publication; Research Library/Archives; School-Based Curriculum

COLLECTIONS: [1800-present] 7,500 artifacts, 127 lineal feet of non-governmental archival material, and 414 works of art.

HOURS: Yr Daily 10-5 (except M Oct 1-Apr 15)

ADMISSION: Donations accepted

FORT ST. JAMES

9449
Fort St. James National Historic Site
Box 1148, V0J 1P0; (p) (250) 996-7191; bob_ghill@pch.bc.ca; www.parkscanada.com

Federal/ 1896/ staff: 3(f); 6(p); 15(v)

HISTORIC SITE

PROGRAMS: Elder's Programs; Exhibits; Garden Tours; Interpretation; Living History; School-Based Curriculum

COLLECTIONS: [1806-1852]

HOURS: May 15-Sept 30 Daily 9-5

ADMISSION: $4

FORT ST. JOHN

9450
North Peace Historical Society
9323 - 100th St, V1J 4N4; (p) (250) 787-0430; (f) (250) 787-0405; www.schoolnet.ca/collections/north_peace

Private non-profit/ 1976/ staff: 1(f); 50(v)/ members: 145

HISTORICAL SOCIETY; HISTORY MUSEUM: Collects, preserves, and displays history of the North Peace.

PROGRAMS: Annual Meeting; Community Outreach; Exhibits; Research Library/Archives

COLLECTIONS: [1920-1940] Artifacts and materials relating to local history, archaeology, First Nations, early forts, fur trade, farming, trapping, transportation, pioneer households, early business.

HOURS: Yr Summer Daily 8-6; Winter M-Sa

FORT STEELE

9451
Fort Steele Heritage Town
9851 Highway 93/95, V0B 1N0; (p) (205) 417-6006; (f) (205) 489-2624; dwwhite@fortsteele.bc.ca; www.fortsteele.bc.ca

1963/ staff: 18(f); 4(p); 60(v)

GARDEN; HISTORIC SITE; HISTORY MUSEUM; LIVING HISTORY/OUTDOOR MUSEUM; RESEARCH CENTER: Preserves, presents, and collects the history of the Kootenay region of BC.

PROGRAMS: Community Outreach; Exhibits; Facility Rental; Family Programs; Festivals; Interpretation; Lectures; Living History; Research Library/Archives; School-Based Curriculum; Theatre

COLLECTIONS: [1880-1905] 15,000 volumes, 600 manuscripts, 4,000 maps, 45,000 photos, 50 newspaper titles, 250,000 museum artifacts.

HOURS: Yr Daily 9-8

ADMISSION: $8

GIBSONS

9452
Elphinstone Pioneer Museum
766 Winn Rd, V0N 1V0 [Box 766, V0N 1V0]; (p) (604) 886-8232; elphinstone_pioneer_museum@sunshine.net; www.gibsonslibrary.bc.ca

Private non-profit/ 1965/ staff: 2(p); 10(v)/ members: 140

GENEALOGICAL SOCIETY; HISTORIC PRESERVATION AGENCY; HISTORICAL SOCIETY; HISTORY MUSEUM: Collects, preserves, and exhibits local history and culture.

PROGRAMS: Annual Meeting; Community Outreach; Exhibits; Guided Tours; Interpretation; Publication; Research Library/Archives

COLLECTIONS: [1886-present] Pioneer history and development of the Sunshine Coast; photos.

HOURS: Yr

ADMISSION: Donations accepted

GROUNDBIRCH

9453
Bruce Groner Museum
Rd 271 Hart Hwy, V0C 1T0 [PO Box 226, V0C 1T0]; (p) (250) 780-2236; (f) (250) 780-2334

Private non-profit/ 1973/ staff: 1(f); 9(v)

HISTORIC PRESERVATION AGENCY; LIVING HISTORY/OUTDOOR MUSEUM

PROGRAMS: Annual Meeting; Festivals; Guided Tours

COLLECTIONS: [Early 19th c] Rural lifestyle.

HOURS: May-Sept Daily 9-6

ADMISSION: Donations accepted

HOPE

9454
Hope Museum
919 Water Ave, V0X 1L0 [PO Box 26, V0X 1L0]; (p) (604) 869-7322

Joint/ 1983/ staff: 2(p)/publication: *Forging A New Hope*

HISTORY MUSEUM: Preserves history and artifacts of the District municipality of Hope.

PROGRAMS: Exhibits; Publication

COLLECTIONS: [1858-1980] Artifacts: First Nations, Hudson Bay Company fur trading, Fraser River Gold Rush, CPR, CNR, Kettle Valley Railways, logging, mining, pioneer artifacts.

HOURS: May-Sept Daily 9-5

ADMISSION: Donations accepted

INVERMERE

9455
Windermere District Historical Society/Windermere Valley Museum
622-3rd St, V0A 1K0 [PO Box 2315, V0A 1K0]; (p) (250) 342-9769; wvmuseum@rockies.net;

Private non-profit/ 1958/ Board of Directors/ staff: 3(p); 30(v)/ members: 115

HISTORIC PRESERVATION AGENCY; HISTORICAL SOCIETY: Collects, preserves, and displays First Nation artifacts; compiling family histories.

PROGRAMS: Annual Meeting; Community Outreach; Elder's Programs; Exhibits; Festivals; Film/Video; Guided Tours; Research Library/Archives; School-Based Curriculum

COLLECTIONS: [1850-1950] Agriculture, transportation, mining, and logging implements, settlers effects, native tools, beadwork, photos, maps, books, manuscripts, newspapers.

HOURS: Yr July-Aug T-Sa 10-4; June-Sept M-F 1-4

ADMISSION: $2; Under 12 free

KAMLOOPS

9456
Secwepemc Museum and Heritage Park
202-355 Yellowhead Hwy, V2H 1H1; (p) (205) 828-9801; (f) (205) 372-1127; museum@secwepemc.org; www.secwepemc.org

Joint/ 1986/ Private non-profit; Tribal/ staff: 3(f); 8(p); 20(v)

TRIBAL MUSEUM: Preserves and exhibits culture and language of the Secwepemc (Shuswap) people of south-central BC.

PROGRAMS: Elder's Programs; Exhibits; Facility Rental; Guided Tours; Publication; Research Library/Archives; School-Based Curriculum; Theatre

COLLECTIONS: [Prehistoric-present] Archaeological and ethnographic material relating to the Shuswap Nation; documents; published histories, maps, photos, oral history tapes.

HOURS: Yr Sept-May M-F 8:30-4:30; June-Aug M-F 8:30-8, Sa-Su, holidays 10-6

ADMISSION: $6, Student $4, Seniors $4; Under 6 free

KASLO

9457
Kootenay Lake Historical Society
324 Front St, V0G 1M0 [Box 537, V0G 1M0]; (p) (250) 353-2525; (f) (250) 353-2525; ssmayie@pop.kin.bc.ca; www.kin.bc.ca/Archives/Mayie/MoyieHome1.html

Private non-profit/ 1958/ staff: 2(f); 10(p); 20(v)/ members: 300

HISTORIC PRESERVATION AGENCY; HISTORIC SITE; HISTORICAL SOCIETY; HISTORY MUSEUM; RESEARCH CENTER: Restores, interprets, and maintains S.S. Moyie.

PROGRAMS: Annual Meeting; Community Outreach; Concerts; Exhibits; Facility Rental; Family Programs; Festivals; Film/Video; Guided Tours; Interpretation; Living History; Publication; Reenactments; Research Library/Archives; School-Based Curriculum; Theatre

COLLECTIONS: [1895-1958] Materials and artifacts relating to steamships and Kaslo area history.

HOURS: Mid May-mid Oct Daily 9:30-5

ADMISSION: $5, Family $15, Student $4, Children $2, Seniors $4; Under 6 free

KELOWNA

9458
British Columbia Orchard Industry Museum
1304 Ellis St, V1Y 1Z8; (p) (250) 763-0433; (f) (250) 868-9272; www.kelownamuseum.com

Private non-profit/ 1989/ staff: 1(f); 50(v)/ members: 150/publication: *Orchard*

HISTORIC SITE; HISTORY MUSEUM: Preserves Okanagan history.

PROGRAMS: Annual Meeting; Community Outreach; Exhibits; Facility Rental; Festivals; Interpretation; Lectures; Publication

COLLECTIONS: [1890s-present] Artifacts: agriculture, orchard, irrigation, pest management, picking, packing, processing, transportation, and marketing.

HOURS: Yr T-Sa 10-5

ADMISSION: Donations accepted

9459
Father Pandosy Mission
Benvoulin Rd, V1Y 7V8 [PO Box 1532, V1Y 7V8]; (p) (250) 764-5386, (250) 860-8369

Private non-profit/ 1859/ staff: 1(p); 10(v)

HISTORIC SITE; HISTORICAL SOCIETY:

Maintains original Mission structures.

PROGRAMS: Exhibits; Guided Tours; Living History

COLLECTIONS: [1859-1890] Original structures from 1859 chapel, brother's dwelling, roothouse built in 1859, barn 1886, M'Doucall house 1880.

HOURS: May-Oct Daily 9am-8pm

ADMISSION: Donations accepted

9460
Kelowna Museum
470 Queensway, V1Y 6S7; (p) (250) 763-0417; (f) (250) 763-5722

Private non-profit/ 1936/ staff: 6(f); 1(p); 50(v)/ members: 150

HISTORY MUSEUM: Explores region's natural and human history; operates ethnology gallery, archives, library, BC Orchard Industry Museum, and The Wire Museum.

PROGRAMS: Annual Meeting; Community Outreach; Exhibits; Family Programs; Lectures; Research Library/Archives; School-Based Curriculum

COLLECTIONS: Natural history and human history artifacts from the Okanagan region and beyond.

HOURS: Yr T-Sa 10-5

ADMISSION: Donations accepted

9461
Wine Museum, The
1304 Ellis St, V1Y 1Z8; (p) (250) 868-0441; (f) (250) 868-9272

Private non-profit/ 1996/ staff: 1(f); 50(v)/ members: 150

HISTORIC SITE; HISTORY MUSEUM: Preserves Okanagan region wine industry history.

PROGRAMS: Annual Meeting; Community Outreach; Exhibits; Facility Rental; Family Programs; Festivals; Interpretation; Lectures

COLLECTIONS: [1920-present] Artifacts: bottles, labels, promotional material.

HOURS: Yr Daily M-Sa 10-5, Su 12-5

ADMISSION: Donations accepted

KEREMEOS

9462
South Similkameen Museum Society
604 - 6th Ave, V0X 1N0 [c/o John W Bird, RRI, Site 50, Comp 12, V0X 1N0]; (p) (205) 499-5445, (205) 499-2416

Private non-profit/ 1973/ staff: 2(p); 10(v)/ members: 25

HISTORIC SITE; HISTORY MUSEUM

PROGRAMS: Annual Meeting; Exhibits; Research Library/Archives

COLLECTIONS: [1973-1980] 1,500 artifacts, 600 photos, 75 old books, various agriculture and mining implements.

HOURS: May-Oct T-Sa 10-4:30

ADMISSION: Donations requested

KITIMAT

9463
Kitimat Centennial Museum
293 City Center, V8C 1T6; (p) (250) 632-7022; (f) (250) 632-7129; kitmuse@sno.net; www.sno.net/kitmuse

Joint/ staff: 1(f); 3(p); 2(v)/ members: 110/publication: *Birds of the Kitimat Valley; Three Towns: A History of Kitimat*

HISTORY MUSEUM: Collects, preserves, and exhibits the natural and human history of the Kitimat Valley and Haisla Nation at Kitamaat Village;

PROGRAMS: Annual Meeting; Community Outreach; Exhibits; Facility Rental; Family Programs; Guided Tours; Interpretation; Lectures; Publication; Research Library/Archives; School-Based Curriculum

COLLECTIONS: [1870-1970] Artifacts: early European settlement, First Nations, Haisla Nation at Kitamaat Village, sealife, fauna, geology, fossils, 1950s town of Kitimat.

HOURS: Yr June-Aug M-Sa 10-5; Sept-May M-F 10-5, Sa 12-5

ADMISSION: Donations accepted

LAKE COWICHAN

9464
Kaatza Historical Society
125 S Shore RD, V0R 2G0 [PO Box 135, V0R 2G0]; (p) (250) 749-6142; (f) (250) 749-3900; barbara@cow-met.com

Private non-profit/ 1975/ staff: 1(f); 1(p); 25(v)/ members: 150/publication: *Museum Musings*

HISTORICAL SOCIETY; HISTORY MUSEUM: Operates the Kaatza Station Museum and Archives; collects, catalogues, researches, preserves, and interprets the history of the Cowichan Lake area.

PROGRAMS: Annual Meeting; Exhibits; Facility Rental; Interpretation; Publication; Research Library/Archives

COLLECTIONS: [1930-1980] 400 linear meters textual records; 10 linear meters cartographic materials; 36 linear meters photos; 2 linear meters paintings and other graphics; 1 linear meter each sound and moving image recordings; 10,000 museum artifacts.

HOURS: Yr M-F 9-4, Sa-Su 1-4

ADMISSION: Donations requested

MACKENZIE

9465
Mackenzie and District Museum Society
86 Centennial, V0J 2C0 [Box 934, V0J 2C0]; (p) (250) 997-3021; chrisj@perf.bc.ca

Joint/ 1991/ staff: 1(p); 8(v)/ members: 34

HISTORY MUSEUM

PROGRAMS: Annual Meeting; Community Outreach; Exhibits; Film/Video; Guided Tours; School-Based Curriculum

COLLECTIONS: [Pre 1970] Trapping pictures, traps, re-created trapper's cabin, photos, and oral histories, fossils, maps, town's 20th Anniversary memorabilia, Alexander Mackenzie auxiliary artifacts.

MAPLE RIDGE

9466
Haney House
11612-224th St, V2X 5Z7; (p) (604) 463-1377

Private non-profit/ 1979/ staff: 2(p); 15(v)

GARDEN; HISTORIC SITE

PROGRAMS: Community Outreach; Exhibits; Facility Rental; Family Programs; Garden Tours; Guided Tours; School-Based Curriculum

COLLECTIONS: [1878-1979] Harey Family furniture, photographs, and household items.

HOURS: Yr July-Aug W-Su 1-4

ADMISSION: $2, Children $1

MERRITT

9467
Nicola Valley Museum Archives Association
2202 Jackson Ave, V1K1B8 [PO Box 1262, V1K1B8]; (p) (250) 378-4145; (f) (250) 378-4145

Joint/ 1976/ staff: 3(p); 12(v)/ members: 138/publication: *Nicola Valley Historical Quarterly*

HISTORY MUSEUM: Collects and preserves archival and museum artifacts pertinent to the area.

PROGRAMS: Annual Meeting; Exhibits; Guided Tours; Publication; Research Library/Archives

COLLECTIONS: [Late 1800s-present] 4,000 images and photos; James Teit Collection; City archival material; Merritt Herald Newspapers.

HOURS: Yr Winter M-F 10-3; Summer M-F

MISSION

9468
Mission Museum
33201 Second Ave, V2V 1J9; (p) (604) 826-1011; (f) (604) 826-1017

Private non-profit/ 1972/ staff: 1(p); 11(v)/ members: 75

HISTORICAL SOCIETY

PROGRAMS: Annual Meeting; Exhibits; Guided Tours; Interpretation; Lectures; Research Library/Archives; School-Based Curriculum

COLLECTIONS: [Early 20th c] Artifacts: Native American, early settlers; Site: former Canadian Bank of Commerce building.

HOURS: Yr Sept-June T-Th 1-4; July-Aug T-Sa 1-4

ADMISSION: Donations accepted

NANAIMO

9469
Nanaimo District Museum
100 Cameron Rd, V9R 2X1; (p) (250) 753-1821; (f) (250) 518-0125

1967/ staff: 5(f); 1(p); 45(v)/ members: 300/publication: *Nanaimo Retrospective*

HISTORY MUSEUM: Promotes local area history.

PROGRAMS: Annual Meeting; Community Outreach; Exhibits; Family Programs; Festivals; Guided Tours; Interpretation; Publication

COLLECTIONS: [2000 BC-1950] Collection focuses on mining, early European settlement, First Nations, Chinese, other local industry, maritime, costume, archival and photo collection.

HOURS: Sept-May T-Sa 9-5; June-Sept Daily 9-5

ADMISSION: $2, Student $1.75, Children $0.50, Seniors $1.75; Under 5/Mbrs free

NEW WESTMINSTER

9470
New Westminster Public Library
716-6th Ave, V3M 2B3; (p) (604) 527-4660; (f) (604) 527-4674; listener@nwpl. new-westminster.bc.ca; www.nwpl. new-westmnster.bc.ca

City/ 1865/ staff: 20(f); 45(p)/ members: 57/publication: *At the Library*

LIBRARY AND/OR ARCHIVES

PROGRAMS: Community Outreach; Concerts; Elder's Programs; Exhibits; Facility Rental; Family Programs; Film/Video; Guided Tours; Lectures; Publication; Research Library/Archives

COLLECTIONS: [1865-present] Books, historical photos, videos, compact discs, phonograph records, cassettes, CD-ROMS, magazines, newspapers, maps, pamphlets, government documents.

HOURS: Yr M-F 10-9, Sa 10-5:30, Su 1-5

ADMISSION: No charge

9471
Royal Agricultural and Industrial Society of British Columbia
204 6th St, V3L 3A1 [PO Bos 42516, 105-1003 Columbia St, V3L 3A1]; (p) (604) 522-6894; (f) (604) 522-6094

Joint/ City; Private non-profit/ staff: 1(f); 2(p); 3(v)/ members: 22

HISTORY MUSEUM

PROGRAMS: Annual Meeting; Festivals; Guided Tours

COLLECTIONS: [1890-present] Materials, artifacts, and snag boat Samson V.

HOURS: Spring Sa-Su 2-5; Summer W-Su 12-5

ADMISSION: Donations accepted

NORTH VANCOUVER

9472
Heritage Deep Cove
4360 Gallant Ave, V7G 1I2; (p) (604) 929-2607; heritagedeepcove@hotmail.com

Private non-profit/ 1985/ staff: 15(v)/ members: 20/publication: *Echoes Across the Inlet*

HISTORY MUSEUM: Collects and preserves east of the Seymour River's past.

PROGRAMS: Exhibits; Interpretation; Publication; Research Library/Archives

COLLECTIONS: [late 19th-20th c] 900 photographs, maps, manuscripts, newspapers.

HOURS: Yr Sa 12-4

ADMISSION: No charge

9473
North Vancouver Museum and Archives
209 W 4th St, V7M 1H8; (p) (604) 987-5618; (f) (604) 987-5609; nvma@northvan.museum.bc.ca; www.dnv.org/nvma

City/ 1976/ staff: 6(f); 6(p); 20(v)/ members: 75

HISTORY MUSEUM

PROGRAMS: Annual Meeting; Community Outreach; Exhibits; Family Programs; Interpretation; Lectures; Research Library/Archives; School-Based Curriculum

COLLECTIONS: [1890-1960] Materials related to community, industrial, logging, photos, shipbuilding.

HOURS: Yr T-Su 12-5

ADMISSION: Donations

OKANAGAN CENTRE

9474
Lake Country Cultural and Heritage Society
11255 Okanagan Centre Rd W, V4V 2H7; (p) (250) 766-0111; jimt@silk.net

Private non-profit/ 1984/ staff: 1(p)

COLLECTIONS: [1850-1940] Local farm, community, women's organizations.

HOURS: May-Sept W-Su 9-5

ADMISSION: Donations accepted

OLD MASSETT

9475
Old Massett Village Council Heritage Resources
162 Raven Ave, V0T 1M0 [Box 175, V0T 1M0]; (p) (250) 626-5115; (f) (250) 626-5118; heritage@island.net; www.chin.gc.ca/haida

1995/ staff: 1(f); 1(p); 4(v)

GENEALOGICAL SOCIETY; LIVING HISTORY/OUTDOOR MUSEUM; RESEARCH CENTER: Protects, preserves, and enhances cultural, social, economic, physical and spiritual well-being of the Hauda community.

PROGRAMS: Community Outreach; Elder's Programs; Exhibits; Family Programs; Film/Video; Interpretation; Living History; Research Library/Archives

COLLECTIONS: [1800s] Photos, artifacts, and people; collection of audio, video, and reel-to-reel tapes, books, museum collection and genealogy records.

HOURS: Yr M-F 8:30-4:30

OLIVER

9476
Oliver and District Heritage Society
Museum: 9728-356th Ave, Archives: 9726-350th Ave, V0H 1T0 [PO Box 847, V0H 1T0]; (p) (250) 498-4027; (f) (250) 498-4027; odhs@cablelan.nt

Private non-profit/ 1980/ staff: 1(f); 1(p); 7(v)/ members: 120/publication: *The Lamplighter*

HISTORICAL SOCIETY; HISTORY MUSEUM; RESEARCH CENTER: Collects and preserves the history of Oliver and gold mining towns of Camp McKinney and Fairview.

PROGRAMS: Annual Meeting; Exhibits; Guided Tours; Publication; Research Library/ Archives

COLLECTIONS: [1920-1990] Irrigation District records, area maps, manuscripts, community organization records, genealogical information, family papers, history of heritage buildings, local newspapers, mining and agriculture records and exhibits, oral history tapes.

HOURS: Yr Archives: M-Th 9-12/1-4; Museum: T-Th 9-12/1-4 and by appt

ADMISSION: Donations accepted

PARKSVILLE

9477
District 69 Historical Society
[PO Box 1452, V9P 2M4]; (p) (250) 248-6966; paddy@nanaimo.ark.com

Private non-profit/ 1983/ staff: 20(v)/ members: 128/publication: *A Brief History of Parksville*

HISTORICAL SOCIETY; HISTORY MUSEUM: Operates Craig Heritage Park, Museum and Archives; collects, displays, and preserves artifacts and archival material.

PROGRAMS: Annual Meeting; Community Outreach; Exhibits; Facility Rental; Festivals; Guided Tours; Interpretation; Publication; Research Library/Archives

COLLECTIONS: [Early 1800s-present] 3,000 museum artifacts, 7 heritage buildings, 10 linear meters processed archival records, 2,000 processed photographs, 25 paintings, 60 maps, 10 linear meters newspapers, information files, 15 volumes local history books.

HOURS: May-Oct Daily 9-5

ADMISSION: $2, Family $4, Children $1, Seniors $1

PENTICTON

9478
Okanagan Indian Educational Resources Society Ceniowkin Centre
Lot 43 Green Mtn Rd, V2A 6J7 [RR#2 Site 50 Comp 8, V2A 6J7]; (p) (250) 493-7181; (f) (250) 493-5302; enioukin@vip.net

Private non-profit/ 1979/ staff: 18(f); 4(p); 4(v)

ART MUSEUM; HISTORIC PRESERVATION AGENCY; RESEARCH CENTER; TRIBAL MUSEUM: Preserves aboriginal history and culture.

PROGRAMS: Annual Meeting; Community Outreach; Concerts; Elder's Programs; Exhibits; Facility Rental; Family Programs; Festivals; Film/Video; Interpretation; Lectures

COLLECTIONS: [1890-present] Artifacts and archival material relating to aboriginal history of the Okamacan Nation.

HOURS: Yr M-F 8:30-4:30

9479
Penticton 9 R.N. Atkinson Museum and Archives
785 Main St, V2A 5E3; (p) (250) 490-2451; (f) (250) 492-0440; museum@city.penticton.bc.ca; (c) Yale

City/ 1958/ staff: 2(f); 20(v)

ALLIANCE OF HISTORICAL AGENCIES;

HISTORY MUSEUM: Focuses on local and natural history.

PROGRAMS: Community Outreach; Concerts; Elder's Programs; Exhibits; Facility Rental; Family Programs; Festivals; Film/Video; Guided Tours; Interpretation; Lectures; Publication; Research Library/Archives; School-Based Curriculum

COLLECTIONS: [1860-present] Pioneer life, natural history documents, diaries, maps, books ephemera, photos, sound and moving images.

HOURS: Yr Museum: T-Sa 10-5; Ships: June-mid Sept 9-9

9480
S.S. Sicamous Restorations Society
1099 Lakeshore Dr W, V2A 1B7; (p) (250) 492-0403; (f) (250) 490-0492

Joint/ 1988/ Private non-profit; City/ staff: 2(p); 50(v)/ members: 400/publication: *The Sicamous; The Naramata*

HISTORIC SITE; HISTORICAL SOCIETY; HISTORY MUSEUM; LIVING HISTORY/OUTDOOR MUSEUM: Restores 1914 sternwheeler to its original state.

PROGRAMS: Annual Meeting; Community Outreach; Concerts; Elder's Programs; Exhibits; Facility Rental; Family Programs; Festivals; Film/Video; Garden Tours; Guided Tours; Interpretation; Lectures; Living History; Publication; Reenactments; Research Library/ archives;

COLLECTIONS: [1893-1935] Photos, artifacts, histories, ephemera, and steamboat.

HOURS: Apr-Oct M-F 9-5

ADMISSION: $3; Children free

PITT MEADOWS

9481
Pitt Meadows Heritage and Museum Society
12294 Harris Rd, V3Y 2E9; (p) (604) 465-4322; (f) (604) 465-4322

Private non-profit/ 1980/ staff: 1(p); 10(v)/ members: 26

HISTORY MUSEUM: Collects, preserves, and exhibits items relating to the pioneer and agricultural history of Pitt Meadows and area.

PROGRAMS: Annual Meeting; Community Outreach; Exhibits; Family Programs; Festivals; Guided Tours; Publication; Research Library/Archives

COLLECTIONS: [1900-1930s] Artifacts, documents, photos, and maps.

HOURS: Yr Summer W-Su 1-4; Winter Th-Su 1-4

ADMISSION: Donations accepted

PORT ALBERNI

9482
Alberni District Historical Society
4255 Wallace St, V9Y 7M7 [PO Box 284, V9Y 7M7]; (p) (250) 723-2181

Private non-profit/ 1965/ staff: 14(v)/ members: 66/publication: *Placenames of the Alberni Valley*

COLLECTIONS: [1860-present] Archives, maps, related publications covering the Alberni-Clayoquot Regional District and adjacent areas, local newspapers on microfilm, biographical information.

HOURS: Yr

ADMISSION: Donations requested

9483
McLean Mill National Historic Site
5633 Smith Rd, V9Y 7L5 [RR# Site 125 C14, V9Y 7L5]; (p) (250) 723-1376; (f) (250) 723-5910

City/ 1990/ staff: 3(f)

HISTORIC SITE: Preserves 1927 steam operated sawmill and family homes.

PROGRAMS: Exhibits; Guided Tours; Interpretation; School-Based Curriculum

COLLECTIONS: [1927-1965] Sawmilling equipment, repair facilities, logging trucks, railroad, and logging.

HOURS: Yr May 19-Sept 30 Daily 10-6

ADMISSION: Donations accepted

PORT CLEMENTS

9484
Port Clements Historical Society and Museum
45 Bayview Dr, V0T 1R0 [PO Box 417, V0T 1R0]; (p) (250) 557-4484, (250) 557-4576

Private non-profit/ 1985/ staff: 1(p); 14(v)/ members: 23

HISTORICAL SOCIETY; HISTORY MUSEUM: Preserves and displays artifacts from the logging, mining, fishing, and pioneering history of the Queen Charlotte Island.

PROGRAMS: Annual Meeting; Exhibits; Interpretation

COLLECTIONS: [1900-1980] Logging, mining, marine, and pioneering artifacts.

HOURS: Yr Summer Daily 11-4; Winter: Sa-Su 2-4

ADMISSION: $2

PORT COQUITLAM

9485
Port Coquitlam Heritage and Cultural Society, The
2571 Mary Hill Rd, V3C 1Z4; (p) (604) 927-2388; (f) (604) 446-4156

City/ 1988/ members: 55

HISTORICAL SOCIETY: Gathers local history and artifacts for Museum.

PROGRAMS: Exhibits; Festivals; Film/Video; Garden Tours; Guided Tours; Lectures; School-Based Curriculum; Theatre

COLLECTIONS: [1850-present] Pioneer family histories, artifacts, and photographs.

HOURS: W 12-4, Sa 12-4

ADMISSION: No charge

PORT HARDY

9486
Port Hardy Heritage Society/Port Hardy Museum and Archives
7110 Market St, V0N 2P0 [PO Box 2126, V0N 2P0]; (p) (250) 949-8143; (f) (250) 949-8982; museum@capescott.net

Private non-profit/ 1982/ staff: 1(f); 4(v)/ members: 80

HISTORY MUSEUM: Promotes human and natural history of the central coast and northern Vancouver Island.

PROGRAMS: Annual Meeting; Exhibits; Research Library/Archives

COLLECTIONS: [Early 20th c] Natural history specimens, fossils, whale bones, shells, and archaeological items dating back up to 8,000 years; ethnographic materials and settler materials of the early 20th century; hand logging tools.

HOURS: Yr

ADMISSION: Donations requested

PORT MOODY

9487
Port Moody Heritage Society
2734 Murray St, V3H 1J3; (p) (604) 939-1648; (f) (604) 939-1647

Private non-profit/ 1967/ staff: 1(f); 2(p); 12(v)/ members: 110

HISTORIC SITE; HISTORICAL SOCIETY; HISTORY MUSEUM: Collects and displays heritage of the Port Moody area; displays Canadian Pacific Railway history.

PROGRAMS: Annual Meeting; Lectures

COLLECTIONS: [1863-present] CPR Railway Station (1905), station items, telegraph, and local history displays.

HOURS: Yr Fall-Spring Sa-Su 10-5; Summer 10-5

ADMISSION: No charge

POUCE COUPE

9488
Pouce Coupe and District Museum and Historical Society
5006 - 49th Ave, V0C 2C0 [Box 293, V0C 2C0]; (p) (250) 786-5555; (f) (250) 786-5216

Private non-profit/ 1972/ staff: 4(p); 4(v)/ members: 12

HISTORIC PRESERVATION AGENCY; HISTORIC SITE; HISTORICAL SOCIETY; HISTORY MUSEUM; HOUSE MUSEUM

PROGRAMS: Annual Meeting; Exhibits

COLLECTIONS: [1900s] Old Railway Station, old store, farm equipment, history of the AK Highway, doctors office, school room, heritage house, old train caboose.

HOURS: May-Aug Daily 8-5

ADMISSION: Donations accepted

POWELL RIVER

9489
Powell River Historical Museum and Archives Association
4800 Marine Ave, V8A 4Z5 [PO Box 42, V8A 4Z5]; (p) (604) 485-2222; (f) (604) 485-2913; museum@aisl.bc.ca

Private non-profit/ 1967/ staff: 1(f); 2(p); 10(v)/ members: 17

HISTORY MUSEUM: Collects and provides information on the Powell River region from Jervis Inlet to Desolation Sound.

PROGRAMS: Annual Meeting; Community Outreach; Exhibits; Guided Tours; Interpretation; Research Library/Archives; School-Based Curriculum

COLLECTIONS: [1910-1960] Pulp and paper mill, artifacts and archives, First Nations, replica of hermit's cabin, Powell River artifacts.

HOURS: Yr Sept-May M-F 9-4:30; June-Aug Daily 9-5

ADMISSION: $2, Student $2, Children $1, Seniors $2; Under 5 free

PRINCE GEORGE

9490
Fraser-Fort George Regional Museum
333 Gorse St, V2L 4V7 [PO Box 1779, V2L 4V7]; (p) (250) 562-1612; (f) (250) 562-6395; info@museum.princegeorge.com; www.museum.princegeorge.com

Private non-profit/ 1958/ staff: 9(f); 8(p); 12(v)/ members: 752

HISTORIC PRESERVATION AGENCY; HISTORIC SITE; HISTORICAL SOCIETY; HISTORY MUSEUM; RESEARCH CENTER

PROGRAMS: Annual Meeting; Community Outreach; Concerts; Exhibits; Facility Rental; Family Programs; Interpretation; Lectures; Publication; Research Library/Archives; School-Based Curriculum; Theatre

COLLECTIONS: [1910-present] Forest landscape and ecosystem; cultural and scientific artifacts.

HOURS: Summer Daily 12-5; Winter 12-5

ADMISSION: $6.50, Family $10, Student $5.50, Children $4.50, Seniors $5.50

PRINCE RUPERT

9491
Museum of Northern British Columbia
100 1st Ave East, V8J 3S1 [PO Box 669, V8J 3S1]; (p) (250) 624-3207; (f) (250) 627-8009

Private non-profit/ 1929/ staff: 7(f); 20(p); 2(v)/ members: 550

ART MUSEUM; HISTORY MUSEUM; RESEARCH CENTER; TRIBAL MUSEUM: Surveys 10,000 years of Northwest Coast history.

PROGRAMS: Annual Meeting; Community Outreach; Exhibits; Facility Rental; Family Programs; Guided Tours; Interpretation; Lectures; Reenactments; Research Library/Archives

COLLECTIONS: [1924-present] First Nations historic and archeological artifacts, artwork, and settler development in regional industry.

HOURS: Yr Sept-May 9-5; June-Aug 9-8

ADMISSION: $5, Student $2, Children $1, Seniors $2

PRINCETON

9492
Princeton and District Museum and Archives Society
Vermilion Ave, V0x 1W0 [Box 281, V0x 1W0]; (p) (250) 295-7588

Private non-profit/ 1958/ staff: 10(v)/ members: 30

HISTORY MUSEUM; LIVING HISTORY/OUT-

DOOR MUSEUM

PROGRAMS: Annual Meeting; Exhibits; Guided Tours; Interpretation; Research Library/Archives

COLLECTIONS: [1900-1960] Artifacts, equipment, and material related to logging, copper, gold, and coal mining, fossils, minerals, local history.

HOURS: Summer Daily

QUATHIASKI COVE

9493
Kwagiulth Museum and Cultural Centre
#34 Weway Rd, V0P 1N0 [PO Box 8, V0P 1N0]; (p) (250) 285-3733; (f) (250) 285-3753; hmccchin@island.net; www.island.net/~kmccchin/

Private non-profit/ 1979/ staff: 2(f); 4(p)/ members: 113/publication: Prosecution or Persecution

HISTORY MUSEUM; RESEARCH CENTER: Promotes, fosters, enhances knowledge and practice of Kwakwaka'wakw culture, history, and language among the Kwakwaka'wakw people; promotes and enhances understanding and appreciation of Kwakwaka'wakw culture and history among non-native people.

PROGRAMS: Annual Meeting; Exhibits; Facility Rental; Film/Video; Guided Tours; Interpretation; Lectures; Publication; Research Library/Archives; School-Based Curriculum; Theatre

COLLECTIONS: [1920-early 1900s] Potlatch collection of K'ik'asuw artifacts.

HOURS: Yr June-Sept Daily M-Sa 10-4:30, Su 12-4:30; Oct- May M-Sa 10-4:30

ADMISSION: $3, Children $1, Seniors $2;

QUESNEL

9494
Quesnel and District Museum and Archives
705 Carson Ave, V2J 2C3 [405 Barlow Ave, V2J 2C3]; (p) (250) 992-9580; (f) (250) 992-9680; stubbs@sd28.bc.ca; www.sd28.bc.ca/museum

Private non-profit/ 1963/ staff: 1(f); 1(p); 17(v)

HISTORY MUSEUM

PROGRAMS: Community Outreach; Exhibits; Family Programs; Film/Video; Guided Tours; Interpretation; Lectures; Research Library/Archives; School-Based Curriculum

COLLECTIONS: [1880s] Artifacts: mining, farming, household, First Nations, Chinese artifacts.

HOURS: Yr

ADMISSION: $2; Under 12 free

REVELSTOKE

9495
Mount Revelstoke and Glacier National Parks
301 B 3rd St W, V0E 2S0 [Box 350, V0E 2S0]; (p) (250) 837-7500; (f) (250) 837-7536

Federal/ 1886/ staff: 1(f); 7(p)/publication: Selkirk Summit

HISTORIC SITE: Commemorates railway transportation link across Canada.

PROGRAMS: Community Outreach; Exhibits; Guided Tours; Interpretation; Publication; School-Based Curriculum; Theatre

COLLECTIONS: [1881-1917]

HOURS: Yr Daily

ADMISSION: Park fees

9496
Revelstoke and District Historical Association
315 First St W, V0E 2S0 [PO Box 1908, V0E 2S0]; (p) (250) 837-3067; (f) (205) 837-3094; rm_chin@revelstoke .net

City/ 1958/ staff: 1(f); 2(p); 5(v)/ members: 35/publication: Revelstoke-History and Heritage

HISTORICAL SOCIETY; HISTORY MUSEUM: Operates the Revelstoke Museum and Archives.

PROGRAMS: Community Outreach; Exhibits; Guided Tours; Interpretation; Lectures; Publication; Research Library/Archives

COLLECTIONS: [1890-1930]

HOURS: Yr M-Sa 10-5

ADMISSION: Donations accepted

RICHMOND

9497
Richmond Museum
180-7700 Minoru Gate, V64 1R9; (p) (604) 231-6457; (f) (604) 231-6423; museum@city.richmond.bc.ca

City/ 1968/ staff: 1(f); 2(p); 10(v)

HISTORY MUSEUM: Preserves, interprets, and collects materials related to Richmond's history.

PROGRAMS: Community Outreach; Exhibits; Family Programs; Festivals; Guided Tours; Interpretation; Lectures; School-Based Curriculum

COLLECTIONS: [1800-present] Archaeology, ethnology, textiles, furnishings, and items significant to agriculture, fishing, transportation, recreation, communications, business, technology.

HOURS: Yr M-F 9-9:30pm, Sa-Su

9498
Richmond Nature Park
11851 Westminster Hwy, V6X 1B4; (p) (604) 273-7015; (f) (604) 279-9358

Joint/ 1972/ City; Private non-profit/ staff: 2(f); 2(p); 30(v)

LIVING HISTORY/OUTDOOR MUSEUM

PROGRAMS: Community Outreach; Exhibits; Family Programs; Festivals; Guided Tours; Interpretation; Lectures; Living History; Publication; Research Library/Archives; School-Based Curriculum

COLLECTIONS: Regional plants and animals.

HOURS: Yr Nature House: Daily 9-5; Nature Park: Daily sunrise-sunset

ADMISSION: Park free; House donations requested

9499
Steveston Historical Society
3811 Moncton St, V7E 2A0; (p) (604) 271-6868; (f) (604) 271-5919

Private non-profit/ 1976/ staff: 10(v)/ members: 50

HISTORIC SITE; HISTORICAL SOCIETY; HISTORY MUSEUM: Collects, preserves, and interprets history of fishing village of Steveston.

PROGRAMS: Annual Meeting; Exhibits; Guided Tours; Interpretation; Publication; School-Based Curriculum

COLLECTIONS: Reflects multicultural social history of the commercial fishing village; small photo collection and archives.

HOURS: Yr

ROSSLAND

9500
Rossland Historical Museum and Archives
Hwy Jct 22 & 3B, VoG 1Y0 [PO Box 26, VoG 1Y0]; (p) (250) 362-7722, (888) 448-7444; (f) (250) 362-5379

City/ 1955/ staff: 1(f); 12(v)/ members: 40

HISTORIC SITE; HISTORY MUSEUM: Collects, preserves, and interprets the history of the city of Rossland; conducts guided underground mine tours into the historic Leroi Gold Mine.

PROGRAMS: Annual Meeting; Exhibits; Film/Video; Guided Tours; Research Library/Archives; School-Based Curriculum

COLLECTIONS: [1895-1927] Artifacts, textural records, maps, photographs, newspapers, rocks and minerals.

HOURS: Sa-Su 9-5

ADMISSION: $8, Family $25, Student $5, Children

SAANICHTON

9501
Heritage Acres/Saanich Historical Artifacts Society
7321 Lochside Dr, V8M 1W4; (p) (250) 652-5522; (f) (250) 652-5999; shas@ horizon.bc.ca; www.horizon.bc.ca/~shas

Private non-profit/ 1974/ staff: 50(v)/ members: 250

HISTORICAL SOCIETY; HISTORY MUSEUM: Collects, houses, restores, displays and demonstrates history of farming, country living and industry on Vancouver Island.

PROGRAMS: Annual Meeting; Exhibits; Facility Rental; Guided Tours

COLLECTIONS: [1930]

HOURS: Yr June-Sept Daily 9-4; Oct-May Daily 9-12

ADMISSION: Donations accepted

SICAMOUS

9502
Sicamous and District Museum and Historical Society
Finwayson Park, V0E 2V0 [PO Box 944, V0E 2V0]; (p) (205) 836-4654; (f) (250) 836-4666

Private non-profit/ 1981/ staff: 1(p); 15(v)/

members: 24

HISTORICAL SOCIETY: Collects and preserves information, records, and objects of historical and cultural value ; maintains a museum and archives.

PROGRAMS: Annual Meeting; Community Outreach; Exhibits; Research Library/Archives

COLLECTIONS: [1890-1960] Artifacts: logging, businesses, farming, and residences, post office.

HOURS: July-Aug T-Sa 10-4

ADMISSION: Donations

SURREY

9503
Surrey Museum and Archives
6022-176 St, V2S 4E8; (p) (604) 502-6456; (f) (604) 502-6457; BASommer@city.surrey.bc.ca; www.city.surrey.bc.ca

City/ 1958/ staff: 6(f); 6(p); 75(v)

HISTORIC SITE; HISTORY MUSEUM: Collects, preserves, interprets, exhibits local material.

PROGRAMS: Exhibits; Family Programs; Festivals; Interpretation; Research Library/Archives

COLLECTIONS: Local history, archaeological and ethnographic material; civic records, photographs, maps, community association records, historic Stewart farm.

HOURS: Yr T-Sa

TRAIL

9504
Trail Historical Society
[PO Box 405, V1R 4L7]; (p) (250) 364-1262; (f) (250) 364-0830; jdforbes@cityoftrail.com

Private non-profit/ 1953/ staff: 15(v)/ members: 30

HISTORICAL SOCIETY: Collects history of the city of Trail.

PROGRAMS: Annual Meeting; Exhibits; Interpretation; Research Library/Archives

COLLECTIONS: [1880-1940] Artifacts, memorabilia relating to the history of Trail, local sports history.

HOURS: June-Aug

ADMISSION: No charge

VANCOUVER

9505
15th Field Artillery Regiment Museum and Archives
2025 W 11th Ave, V6J 2C7; (p) (604) 666-4370; (f) (604) 666-4083

1983/ Canadian Forces-Directorate of History and Heritage/ staff: 1(p); 6(v)/ members: 60

HISTORIC SITE; HISTORY MUSEUM: Collects, preserves, and interprets the history of the 15th Field Regiment and Artillery Units.

PROGRAMS: Exhibits; Interpretation

COLLECTIONS: [1920-present] 4000 artifacts: uniforms, small arms, and artillery; 1500 photographs; and 18 linear feet of manuscripts.

HOURS: June-Aug M-F 9-3; Winter T, Th 7 pm-

9 pm, W 10-2

ADMISSION:Donations accepted

9506
Doctor Sun Yat-Sen Classical Chinese Garden
578 Carrall St, V6B 5K2; (p) (604) 662-3207; (f) (604) 682-4008; sungatsen@telvs.net; www.vancouverchinesegarden.com

Joint/ 1986/ City; Private non-profit/ staff: 7(f); 10(p); 120(v)/ members: 500/publication: Living Treasure

GARDEN: Promotes Chinese philosophy, culture, and history.

PROGRAMS: Annual Meeting; Community Outreach; Concerts; Elder's Programs; Exhibits; Facility Rental; Family Programs; Festivals; Guided Tours; Lectures; Publication; School-Based Curriculum

COLLECTIONS: Replica of Ming Dynasty (1300-1600) garden and architecture; hand carved screens, teak windows, pattern tile, hand-cut paving stones, tai hu rocks, 100 year-old bonsai trees, sculpted roof embellishments with clay roof tiles.

HOURS: Yr Daily May 1-June 14 10-6; June 15-Aug 13 9:30-7pm; Sept 1-Sept 30 10-6; Oct 1-Apr 30 1-4:30

ADMISSION: $7.50, Student $5, Seniors $6

9507
Morris and Helen Belkin Art Gallery
1825 Main Mall, V6T 1Z2 [Univ of British Columbia, V6T 1Z2]; (p) (604) 822-2759; (f) (604) 822-6689; sdwatson@unixg.ubc.ca; www.belkin-gallery.ubc.ca

1948/ staff: 4(f); 3(p); 38(v)

ART MUSEUM; RESEARCH CENTER: To research, exhibit, educate, and collect in the field of contemporary art.

PROGRAMS: Community Outreach; Exhibits; Film/Video; Guided Tours; Interpretation; Lectures; Publication; Research Library/Archives

COLLECTIONS: Contemporary visual art and archival material; research on post 1945 art.

HOURS: Yr M-F 10-5, Sa-Su 12-5

ADMISSION: Donations accepted

9508
Museum of Anthropology at the University of British Columbia
6393 NW Marine Dr, V6T 1Z2; (p) (604) 822-5087; (f) (604) 822-2974; jenwebb@ interchange.ubc.ca; www.moa.ubc.ca

Joint/ 1949/ Univ. of BC; Private non-profit/ staff: 18(f); 8(p); 65(v)/ members: 800/publication: Museum Note Series

ART MUSEUM; HISTORIC SITE; LIVING HISTORY/OUTDOOR MUSEUM; RESEARCH CENTER: Collects, preserves, researches, and displays ethnological and archaeological materials.

PROGRAMS: Community Outreach; Concerts; Elder's Programs; Exhibits; Facility Rental; Family Programs; Festivals; Film/Video; Guided Tours; Interpretation; Lectures; Living History; Publication; Research Library/Archives; School-Based Curriculum; Theatre

COLLECTIONS: 30,000 ethnographic objects and 200,000 archaeological objects (South Pacific, Asia, Africa, Europe, the Americas, and First Nations of coastal BC).

HOURS: Yr Sept 7-May 24 T 11-9, W-Su 11-5; May 25-Sept 6 Daily T 10-9, W-M 10-5

ADMISSION: $6, Student $3.50, Seniors $3.50

9509
Pacific Space Centre
1100 Chestnut St, V0J 3J9; (p) (604) 738-7827; (f) (604) 736-5665; jdickens@axionet.com; pacific-space-centre.bc.ca

1968/ staff: 23(f); 40(p); 42(v)/ members: 2200/publication: *Starry Messenger*

NATURAL HISTORY MUSEUM

PROGRAMS: Annual Meeting; Community Outreach; Concerts; Exhibits; Facility Rental; Family Programs; Lectures; Publication; School-Based Curriculum; Theatre

COLLECTIONS: [1900-present] Space and astronomy artifacts: meteorites, rocket engines, space robotics technology, space clothing and accessories.

HOURS: Yr Sept-June T-Su 10-5; July-Aug Daily 10-5

ADMISSION: $12, Family $38,

9510
Roedde House Preservation Society
1415 Barclay St, V6G 1J6; (p) (604) 684-7040; (f) (604) 681-7762; roeddehs@roeddehouse.org; www.roeddehouse.org

Private non-profit/ 1984/ staff: 1(f); 40(v)/ members: 160

GARDEN; HOUSE MUSEUM; LIVING HISTORY/OUTDOOR MUSEUM; RESEARCH CENTER

PROGRAMS: Community Outreach; Concerts; Elder's Programs; Facility Rental; Family Programs; Garden Tours; Guided Tours; Interpretation; Lectures; Living History; Publication; Research Library/Archives; School-Based Curriculum

COLLECTIONS: [1890-1910] Household and domestic furnishings, utensils, appliances, decorative and applied arts, ephemera, and archival materials relating to the Roedde family, the West End of Vancouver, and local and regional history.

HOURS: Yr T-F (Some Su) guided tour at 2pm

ADMISSION: $4, Seniors $3; Under 12 free

9511
United Church of Canada British Columbia Conference Archives, The
6000 Iona Dr, V6T 1L4; (p) (604) 822-9589; (f) (604) 822-9212; bstewart@unixg.ubc.ca; www/interchange.ubc.ca/bstewart/

Private non-profit/ 1937/ staff: 1(p); 3(v)

LIBRARY AND/OR ARCHIVES: Serves as repository for the records of The United Church and its Methodist, Presbyterian, and Congregational predecessor churches.

PROGRAMS: Publication

COLLECTIONS: [1865-1998] Records of The United Church of Canada, 1925 to the present; Methodist, Presbyterian, and Congregational records, 1860-1925.

HOURS: Yr T, Th and by appt

ADMISSION: No charge

9512
Vancouver City Archives
1150 Chestnut St, V6J 3J9; (p) (604) 736-8561; (f) (604) 736-0626; archives@city.vancouver.bc.ca; www.city.vancouver.bc.ca/City/ 1933

LIBRARY AND/OR ARCHIVES: Collects, preserves, and makes available official public records of city of Vancouver; private manuscripts, photos, maps.

PROGRAMS: Exhibits; Research Library/Archives

COLLECTIONS: [1886-present] Official records, private MSS holdings, photos relating to political, social, and economic history of the city and region.

HOURS: Yr M-F 9:30-5:30

9513
Vancouver Holocaust Education Centre
#50-950 W 41 St, V5Z 2N7; (p) (604) 264-0499; (f) (604) 264-0497; www.vhec.org

Private non-profit/ 1985/ staff: 3(f); 2(p); 100(v)/ members: 650/publication: *Zachor*

HISTORY MUSEUM

PROGRAMS: Annual Meeting; Community Outreach; Elder's Programs; Exhibits; Facility Rental; Family Programs; Film/Video; Guided Tours; Lectures; Publication; Research Library/Archives; School-Based Curriculum

COLLECTIONS: Documents, artifacts, photographs relating to the oral histories of local Holocaust survivors.

HOURS: Yr M-Th 9-5, F 9-4, some Su

ADMISSION: Donations

9514
Vancouver Maritime Museum
1905 Ogden Ave, V6J 1A3; (p) (604) 257-8300; (f) (604) 737-2621; vmm@vmm.bc.ca; www.vmm.bc.ca

City/ 1958/ staff: 6(f); 17(p); 90(v)/ members: 750/publication: *Signals*

HISTORY MUSEUM: Collects, preserves, and promotes Canada's Pacific maritime heritage.

PROGRAMS: Annual Meeting; Community Outreach; Exhibits; Facility Rental; Family Programs; Guided Tours; Lectures; Publication; Research Library/Archives

COLLECTIONS: Maps, volumes, serials, marine painting and photographs, marine artifacts.

HOURS: May-Sept Daily 10-5; Sept-May T-Sa 10-5, Su 12-5

ADMISSION: $7, Family $16, Student $4, Seniors $4

9515
Vancouver Museum
1100 Chestnut St, V6J 3S9; (p) (604) 736-4431; (f) (604) 736-5417; gruemke@vanmuseum.bc.ca; www.vanmuseum.bc.ca

City/ 1994/ staff: 11(f); 22(p); 150(v)/ members: 500

HISTORY MUSEUM: Promotes Vancouver's history.

PROGRAMS: Community Outreach; Exhibits; Facility Rental; Family Programs; Interpretation; School-Based Curriculum

COLLECTIONS: [1860-present] Artifacts.

HOURS: Yr

ADMISSION: $8, Student $5.50

9516
West Coast Railway Association
39645 Government Rd, V6B 3X2 [PO Box 2790 STN Main, V6B 3X2]; (p) (604) 898-9336; (f) (604) 898-9349; don_evans@bc.sympatico.ca; www.wcra.org

Private non-profit/ 1961/ staff: 2(f); 6(p); 400(v)/ members: 400/publication: *WCRA News*

HISTORICAL SOCIETY; RESEARCH CENTER: Collects, preserves, operates, and interprets railway heritage relative to western Canada.

PROGRAMS: Annual Meeting; Exhibits; Facility Rental; Family Programs; Festivals; Film/Video; Guided Tours; Interpretation; Living History; Publication; Research Library/Archives; School-Based Curriculum

COLLECTIONS: [1890-1960] Collection of heritage railway equipment, more than 60 locomotives and rail cars on display dating to the 1890 business car "British Columbia".

HOURS: Yr Daily 10-5

ADMISSION: $6, Family $15

VERNON

9517
Historic O'Keefe Ranch
9380 Hwy 97 N, V1T 6M8 [Box 955, V1T 6M8]; (p) (250) 542-7868; (f) (250) 542-7868; okr_chin@junction.net; www.okeeferanch.bc.ca

Private non-profit/ 1977/ staff: 3(f); 16(p); 40(v)/ members: 210

HISTORIC SITE; HISTORICAL SOCIETY; LIVING HISTORY/OUTDOOR MUSEUM: Preserves ranching and agricultural history of the North Okanagan and British Columbia Interior; contains ten pre-1900 original O'Keefe Ranch buildings and ranching museum.

PROGRAMS: Annual Meeting; Community Outreach; Concerts; Exhibits; Facility Rental; Family Programs; Festivals; Guided Tours; Interpretation; Living History; Publication; Research Library/Archives; School-Based Curriculum

COLLECTIONS: [1880-1920] O'Keefe Family buildings, artifacts (including clothing, furniture, general store items, and ranching/cowboy material), and archival records; artifacts relating to agricultural history and Victorian lifestyle.

HOURS: May-Oct Daily 9-5

ADMISSION: $6, Family $17, Children $4, Seniors $5

VICTORIA

9518
BC Heritage
5th Floor, 800 Johnson St, V8W 9W3 [PO Box 9818, V8W 9W3]; (p) (250) 356-5137; (f) (250) 356-7796; John.Adams@gems9.gov.bc.ca

Provincial/ staff: 50(f); 20(p); 200(v)

ALLIANCE OF HISTORICAL AGENCIES; HISTORIC PRESERVATION AGENCY; HISTORIC SITE: Protects and presents 30 heritage sites.

PROGRAMS: Community Outreach; Concerts; Exhibits; Facility Rental; Festivals; Garden Tours; Guided Tours; Interpretation; Lectures; Living History; Research Library/ Archives; Theatre

COLLECTIONS: [1850-1930]

HOURS: May-Sept, Dec Daily

ADMISSION: $5

9519
Canadian Scottish Regiment (Princess Mary's) Regimental Museum, The
Bay St Armoury, 715 Bay St, V8T 1R1; (p) (250) 363-8753; (f) (250) 363-3593; csr-muse@islandnet.com; www. islandnet. com/~csrmuse

Federal/ 1980/ Dept of National Defense/ staff: 12(v)

HISTORY MUSEUM: Preserves the history of the Canadian Forces regiment and its record of service.

PROGRAMS: Concerts; Exhibits; Guided Tours; Interpretation; Lectures; Research Library/Archives

COLLECTIONS: [1912-present] Maps, uniforms, medals, weapons, insignia, photographs, and personal items; 1300-volume library of military related, non-fiction books.

HOURS: Feb-May, Sept-Nov Th 8-10; June-Aug 1 T-F 9-3

ADMISSION: Donation

9520
Canadiana Costume Museum and Archives of Bristish Columbia
524 Culduthel Rd, V8Z1G17; (p) (250) 381-2206

Private non-profit/ 1974/ staff: 17(v)/ members: 46

HISTORY MUSEUM; LIBRARY AND/OR ARCHIVES: Collects, preserves, and studies evolution of Western clothing and accessories for men, women, and children.

PROGRAMS: Annual Meeting; Exhibits; Lectures; Research Library/Archives

COLLECTIONS: [1850-present] Exhibits: clothing, Canadian military uniforms.

HOURS: By appt

ADMISSION: No charge

9521
CFB Esquimalt Naval and Military Museum
Off Bldg 20 Naden; Museum Bldgs 37&39 Naden CFB, V9A 7N2 [PO Box 17000, Stn Force, V9A 7N2]; (p) (250) 363-4312, (250) 363-5655; (f) (250) 363-4252; nadenmuseum@pacificcoast.net

Federal/ 1985/ staff: 2(f); 1(p); 18(v)/publication: *The Westcoaster*

HISTORY MUSEUM: Collects, preserves, interprets, and exhibits history and heritage of the naval presence on the west coast of Canada, and the military on southern Vancouver Island.

PROGRAMS: Guided Tours; Publication; Reenactments; Research Library/Archives

COLLECTIONS: [Early 1800s-present] Artifacts and archival material representational of the Royal Canadian Navy on the west coast of

9522
City of Victoria Archives
#8 Centennial Square, V8W 1P6 [#1 Centennial Square, V8W 1P6]; (p) (250) 361-0375; archives@city.victoria.bc.ca; www.city. victoria.bc.ca/dept/archives/index.htm

City/ 1967/ staff: 3(f)

LIBRARY AND/OR ARCHIVES: Acquires, preserves, and makes accessible archival material documenting history of Victoria.

COLLECTIONS: [1862-1990s] Victoria government records (inactive), private records of Victoria, photographs, and maps.

HOURS: Yr M-F 9:30-12/1-4

ADMISSION: No charge

9523
Emily Carr House
207 Government St, V8V 2K8; (p) (205) 383-5843, (205) 361-4642; artist@emilycarr.com; www.emilcarr.com/ec_main.html

Private non-profit/ Heritage Properties

HOUSE MUSEUM: Preserves 19th c birthplace of Emily Carr, Canadian artist and author.

PROGRAMS: Exhibits; Guided Tours

COLLECTIONS: [Late-mid 19th c]

HOURS: Mid May-mid Oct 10-5 and by appt

9524
Esquimalt Municipal Archives
1149 A Esquimalt Rd, V9A 3N6; (p) (250) 414-7140; (f) (250) 414-7114; parked@mun.esquimalt.bc.ca; www.mun.esquimalt.bc.ca

City/ 1984/ staff: 1(f); 8(v)

LIBRARY AND/OR ARCHIVES: Collects, preserves, and makes available Esquimalt archival material.

PROGRAMS: Community Outreach; Exhibits; Lectures; Research Library/Archives

COLLECTIONS: [1840-present] Photos, maps, plans, manuscripts, oral history recordings, newspapers, reference files.

HOURS: Yr M-F 8:30am-12pm

ADMISSION: No charge

9525
Fort Rodd Hill and Fisgard Lighthouse National Historic Site
603 Fort Rodd Hill Rd, V9C 2W8; (p) (205) 478-5849; (f) (205) 478-8415; fort_rodd@pch.gc.ca; parkscanada.pch.gc.ca

Federal/ 1962/ staff: 9(f)

HISTORIC SITE: Preserves three coast artillery batteries and Fisgard Lighthouse.

PROGRAMS: Exhibits; Facility Rental; Interpretation

COLLECTIONS: [1860-1956] Canadian and British artillery and military artifacts relating to the coast artillery defenses of Victoria, Esquimalt, and lighthouse lenses, lighting equipment.

HOURS: Yr Mar-Oct Daily 10-6; Nov-Feb Daily 9-5:30

ADMISSION: $3, Children $1.50

9526
Friends of Hatley Park
2005 Sooke Rd, V9B 5Y2; (p) (250) 391-2551; (f) (250) 391-2500; www.royalroads.ca

Joint/ 1987/ Royal Roads Univ/Private non-profit/ staff: 3(p)/publication: *Hatley Park*

GARDEN; HISTORIC SITE; HISTORICAL SOCIETY; HOUSE MUSEUM: Collects, preserves, and interprets the Hatley Park National Historic Site.

PROGRAMS: Annual Meeting; Exhibits; Facility Rental; Festivals; Garden Tours; Guided Tours; Interpretation; Lectures; Publication

COLLECTIONS: [Edwardian] Photos, period artifacts, heritage trees and gardens.

HOURS: Yr Daily Dawn - Dusk

ADMISSION: $3; Garden free

9527
Lt.Gen E.C. Ashton Garrison Museum Ashton Armoury
724 Vanalman Ave, V8Z 3B5; (p) (250) 363-8346, (250) 477-1117; (f) (250) 363-8325

Federal/ 1994/ staff: 1(f); 2(p); 5(v)

HISTORIC PRESERVATION AGENCY; LIVING HISTORY/OUTDOOR MUSEUM; RESEARCH CENTER: Preserves and publicizes experiences of men and women of the armed forces.

PROGRAMS: Elder's Programs; Exhibits; Festivals; Guided Tours; Living History; Research Library/Archives; School-Based Curriculum

COLLECTIONS: [1850-1998] Army vehicles, weapons, uniforms, trench art, equipment, dioramas, medals, documents, papers, books; Military Museum.

HOURS: Yr T-Su

ADMISSION: Donations accepted

9528
Maltwood Art Museum and Gallery The University of Victoria
3800 Finnerty Rd, V8W 3P2 [PO Box 3025, V8W 3P2]; (p) (250) 721-8298; (f) (250) 721-8997; msegger@uvic.ca; www.maltwood.uvic.ca

1968/ staff: 5(f); 10(p)

ART MUSEUM; LIBRARY AND/OR ARCHIVES: Houses university art collection.

PROGRAMS: Exhibits; Facility Rental; Lectures; Publication; Research Library/Archives

COLLECTIONS: Arts and crafts; prints, paintings, fine, decorative, and applied arts; oriental ceramics, costumes, rugs, paintings, and sculptures; contemporary Canadian art, BC artifacts.

HOURS: Yr M-F 10-4

ADMISSION: No charge

9529
Maritime Museum of British Columbia
28 Bastion Square, V8W 1H9; (p) (250) 385-4222; (f) (250) 382-2869; info@mmbc.bc.ca; www.mmbc.bc.ca

Joint/ 1957/ Private non-profit/ staff: 2(f); 2(p); 75(v)/ members: 1000

MARITIME MUSEUM: Preserves BC maritime heritage in exploration, commerce, adventure, passenger travel.

PROGRAMS: Annual Meeting; Exhibits; Facility Rental; Family Programs; Film/Video; Interpretation; Lectures; Publication; Research Library/Archives; School-Based Curriculum

COLLECTIONS: [1890-present] 16,000 marine artifacts, 30,000 ships plans, 40,000 plus photo collection, and archives, 5,000 volume library, 1,700 local charts, 400 ship models, 1,5000 piece fine arts.

HOURS: Yr Daily 9:30-4:30

ADMISSION: $5, Family $13, Student $4, Children $2, Seniors $4

9530
Royal British Columbia Museum
675 Belleville St, V8V 1X4 [Box 9815, Prov Govt, V8V 1X4]; (p) (250) 387-3701; (f) (250) 387-5674; www.vbcml.vbcm.gov.bc.ca

1886/ staff: 112(f); 400(v)/ members: 17000

HISTORY MUSEUM: Collects and exhibits BC history.

PROGRAMS: Community Outreach; Exhibits; Facility Rental; Family Programs; Festivals; Garden Tours; Interpretation; School-Based Curriculum

COLLECTIONS: [1900-present] 10 million objects relating to modern history, ethnology and natural history.

HOURS: Daily

YALE

9531
Yale and District Historical Society
31187 Douglas St, V0K 2S0 [PO Box 74, V0K 2S0]; (p) (604) 863-2324

Private non-profit/ 1978/ staff: 10(v)/ members: 40

HISTORICAL SOCIETY; HISTORY MUSEUM

PROGRAMS: Annual Meeting; Guided Tours; Interpretation

COLLECTIONS: [1858-1890] First peoples, gold rush, Chinese, railroad era, social history.

HOURS: May-Oct Daily 9-5

MANITOBA

BOISSEVAIN

9532
Moncur Gallery
436 S Railway St, R0K 0E0 [PO Box 1241, R0K 0E0]; (p) (204) 534-6478; gmay@mail.techplus.com; town.boissevain. mb.ca/moncur/index.htm

1988/ staff: 1(p); 10(v)/publication: *Moncur Gallery*

HISTORY MUSEUM

PROGRAMS: Annual Meeting; Community Outreach; Exhibits; Film/Video; Guided Tours; Interpretation; Publication; Research Library/Archives; School-Based Curriculum

COLLECTIONS: [Ice Age-mid 1800s] Aboriginal artifacts of the Turtle Mountain area.

HOURS: Yr M-Sa 9-5

BRANDON

9533
Commonwealth Air Training Plan Museum
Hangar # 1 McGill Field, R7A 5Y5 [GRP 520, Box 3, RR # 5, R7A 5Y5]; (p) (204) 727-2444; (f) (204) 725-2334; airmuseum@mb.sympatico.ca; www.airmuseum.ca

1981/ staff: 1(f); 40(v)/ members: 1000/publication: *They Shall Grow Not Old*

HISTORY MUSEUM: Retrieves, collects, restores, displays artifacts and memorabilia associated with the British Commonwealth air training plan 1939-1943.

PROGRAMS: Annual Meeting; Community Outreach; Exhibits; Guided Tours; Publication; Research Library/Archives

COLLECTIONS: [1939-1945] Photos, uniforms, aircraft, motor vehicles, aircraft engines, books, armaments.

HOURS: Yr Daily

ADMISSION: $3.50, Student $2, Seniors $2; Under 6 free

9534
Daly House Museum
122 18th St, R7A 5A4; (p) (204) 727-1722; (f) (204) 727-1722; dalymus@mb.sympatico.ca

Private non-profit/ 1876/ staff: 1(f); 1(p); 40(v)/ members: 60

HISTORIC SITE; HOUSE MUSEUM; RESEARCH CENTER: Preserves, protects, and promotes an interest in the history and development of the City of Brandon.

PROGRAMS: Annual Meeting; Community Outreach; Exhibits; Guided Tours; Interpretation; Publication; Research Library/Archives; School-Based Curriculum

COLLECTIONS: [1882-1910] Period home built in 1882; furniture, photographs, business equipment, grocery store, medical equipment, china, textual materials, textiles, dolls.

HOURS: Yr Daily M-Sa 10-12 / 1-5, Su 12-5

ADMISSION: $2, Family $5, Children $1, Seniors $1

9535
Manitoba Agricultural Hall of Fame
Keystone Centre 1175 18th St, R7A 1L9 [1129 Queens Ave, R7A 1L9]; (p) (204) 728-3736; (f) (204) 726-6260; midwinter@ westman.wave.ca

Private non-profit/ 1976/ staff: 1(f); 12(v)/ members: 195

HISTORY MUSEUM: Induct members who meet the objective: of bettering rural living and agriculture in the province of man.

PROGRAMS: Annual Meeting

COLLECTIONS: 80 plaques of inductees life and accomplishments.

HOURS: Yr Daily 9-5

ADMISSION: No charge

DAUPHIN

9536
Fort Dauphin Museum, Inc., The
140 Jackson St, R7N 2V1 [Box 181, R7N 2V1]; (p) (204) 638-6630

Private non-profit/ 1973/ staff: 1(f); 1(p); 200(v)/ members: 30

HISTORIC PRESERVATION AGENCY; HISTORY MUSEUM; HOUSE MUSEUM; LIVING HISTORY/OUTDOOR MUSEUM

PROGRAMS: Annual Meeting; Community Outreach; Concerts; Exhibits; Facility Rental; Family Programs; Festivals; Guided Tours; Interpretation; Living History; Publication; Reenactments; Research Library/Archives; School-Based Curriculum

HOURS: Yr Oct-May M-F 9-5; May-Oct M-S 9-5

ADMISSION: $3, Family $5, Student $2

DUGALD

9537
Costume Museum of Canada
NW Junction Hwy 15 & PR 206, R0E 0K0 [PO Box 38, R0E 0K0]; (p) (204) 853-2166, (866) 853-2166; (f) (204) 853-2077; info@ costumemuseum.com;www.costumemuseum.com

Private non-profit/ 1977/ staff: 6(f); 4(p); 40(v)/ members: 450/publication: *Yearly Exhibit Guide*

ART MUSEUM; HISTORY MUSEUM: Extensive collection covering 400 years of costume history and is the Canadian repository uniquely dedicated to the collection of costume, textiles, and related accessories. Features historical costume and significant fashion treasures.

PROGRAMS: Annual Meeting; Community Outreach; Elder's Programs; Exhibits; Facility Rental; Guided Tours; Publication; Research Library/Archives; School-Based Curriculum

COLLECTIONS: [1500s-1900s] 35,000 artifacts spanning 400 years: costume, textiles, and related accessories.

HOURS: May 1-Sept 30 T-F 10-5, Sa-Su 12-5

ADMISSION: $4, Family $12, Student $3; Members free

ERIKSDALE

9538
Eriksdale Museum Inc.
Railway Ave, R0C 0W0 [Box 71, R0C 0W0]; (p) (204) 739-2621

1974/ staff: 1(p); 8(v)

HISTORY MUSEUM: Displays local history and maintains a creamery museum.

PROGRAMS: Annual Meeting; Exhibits; Guided Tours; Interpretation; Research Library/ Archives

COLLECTIONS: Local artifacts and history; agricultural materials, bottles, household items, wood stoves, furniture, trunks, sewing machine; butter making exhibits.

HOURS: May-Sept 9:30-4:30

ADMISSION: $1, Student $0.50

GARDENTON

9539
Ukrainian Museum and Village Society, Inc.
Hwy 209, R0A 0M0 [Box 88, R0A 0M0]; (p) (204) 425-3072, (204) 425-3501

Private non-profit/ 1967/ staff: 1(p); 30(v)/ members: 35

HISTORIC SITE; HISTORY MUSEUM; RE-SEARCH CENTER

PROGRAMS: Annual Meeting; Community Outreach; Concerts; Exhibits; Facility Rental; Festivals; Guided Tours

COLLECTIONS: [1886-1930] Artifacts: clothing, religious pictures, hand tools, churches, thatched roof house, one room school.

HOURS: May-Sept 9-4

ADMISSION: $2, Children $0.50

GILBERT PLAINS

9540
Wasyl Negrych Pioneer Homestead
17 km N & 3km E of Gilbert Plains, R0L 0X0 [PO Box 662, R0L 0X0]; (p) (204) 548-2477, (204) 548-2326

Private non-profit/ 1993/ staff: 2(p); 12(v)/ members: 25

HISTORIC SITE

PROGRAMS: Annual Meeting; Guided Tours

COLLECTIONS: [1920-1930] 10 log buildings built by Wasyl Negrych and family.

HOURS: July-Aug Daily 10-5

ADMISSION: $2; Under 6 free

HARTNEY

9541
Hart Cam Museum
315 E Railway St, R0M 0X0 [Box 399, R0M 0X0]; (p) (204) 858-2590; (f) (204) 858-2681

Private non-profit/ 1978/ staff: 12(v)/ members: 30

HISTORY MUSEUM: Settlement and pre-settlement artifacts, archives and genealogical records.

PROGRAMS: Annual Meeting; Exhibits; Guided Tours; Research Library/Archives

COLLECTIONS: [1860-present] Artifacts of pre and post settlement, archives of family history local history and photos.

HOURS: July-Aug Daily 11-5

ADMISSION: No charge

MORDEN

9542
Morden and District Museum, Inc.
Lower Level Morden Recreation Centre, R6M 1N9 [111 B Gilmour St, R6M 1N9]; (p) (204) 822-3406; (f) (204) 822-9414; mdmuseum@ mb.sympat.tco.ca

Private non-profit/ 1971/ staff: 12(v)

HISTORY MUSEUM: Collects, preserves, studies, exhibits, and interprets palaeontologi-cal specimens from Southern Manitoba and human artifacts.

PROGRAMS: Annual Meeting; Family Programs; Guided Tours

COLLECTIONS: [Cretaceous] Marine reptile fossils: mosasaurs, plesiosaurs, birds, fish, sharks, squid, turtles; Native and pioneer artifacts.

HOURS: June-Aug Daily 1-5; Sept-May Sa-Su 1-5

ADMISSION: $2, Student $1, Children $1; Under 5 free

PORTAGE LA PRAIRIE

9543
Fort La Reine Museum Pioneer Village and Tourist Bureau
Hwy 26 & 1 A E of Portage La Prairie, R1N3C2 [PO Box 744, R1N3C2]; (p) (204) 857-3259; (f) (204) 857-3259; (c) Portage La Prairie

1967/ staff: 1(f); 3(p); 25(v)/ members: 35/publication: *Museum News*

LIVING HISTORY/OUTDOOR MUSEUM

PROGRAMS: Concerts; Elder's Programs; Exhibits; Facility Rental; Family Programs; Festivals; Guided Tours; Publication

COLLECTIONS: [1800s-1940s] Artifacts: Native, pioneer, early explorers and fur traders.

HOURS: Daily 9-6

ADMISSION: $4; Children $2; Under 6 free

RENNIE

9544
Alfred Hole Goose Sanctuary
East of Rennie on Hwy 44, R0E 1R0 [General Delivery, R0E 1R0]; (p) (204) 369-5470; (f) (204) 369-5341

1938/ Manitoba Natural Resources/ staff: 2(p); 1(v)

LIVING HISTORY/OUTDOOR MUSEUM: Preserves Giant Canada Goose Sanctuary, and seasonal life and migratory patterns of geese.

PROGRAMS: Exhibits; Guided Tours; Interpretation

COLLECTIONS: [2000 BP, 1930-1950-present] Interpretive programs: natural resources, recent history, and cultural history of the Anishinabes.

ADMISSION: $5

ROLAND

9545
Historical Society of the R.M. of Roland, The
72nd & 3rd St, R0G 1T0 [Box 238, R0G 1T0]; (p) (204) 343-2271

Private non-profit/ 1990/ staff: 1(p); 35(v)/ members: 70

HISTORICAL SOCIETY: Gathers and preserves 4-H artifacts.

PROGRAMS: Annual Meeting; Exhibits; Guided Tours

COLLECTIONS: [1913-present] Banners, uniforms, pictures, record books, scrapbooks, newspaper clippings, metals and trophies, crafts.

HOURS: July-Aug M-Sa 1-4

ADMISSION: Donations

ROSS BURN

9546
Ross Burn Museum
Cheddar Ave, R0J 1V0 [Box 487, R0J 1V0]; (p) (204) 859-2429; (f) (204) 859-2959

City/ 1987/ staff: 1(p); 10(v)/ members: 10

HISTORY MUSEUM

PROGRAMS: Annual Meeting; Exhibits; Guided Tours

COLLECTIONS: [Late 1800] Ukrainian Pioneer village, agriculture, school room, pioneer kitchen, hospital equipment, army uniforms.

HOURS: May 1- Oct 1 Daily 9:30-6

ADMISSION: Donations accepted

SELKIRK

9547
Lower Fort Garry National Historic Site
5925 Hwy # 9, R1A 2A8 [Box 37, Group 343, RR3, R1A 2A8]; (p) (877) 534-3678, (204) 785-6075; (f) (204) 482-5887; www.parkscanada.gc.ca/garry

Federal; Joint/ 1830/ staff: 4(f); 12(p); 50(v)

HISTORIC SITE; LIVING HISTORY/OUTDOOR MUSEUM

PROGRAMS: Exhibits; Interpretation; Publication; School-Based Curriculum

COLLECTIONS: Hudson's Bay Company Collection fort artifacts.

HOURS: Mid May-1st week in Sept 9-5

ADMISSION: $5.50, Family $14, Student $3, Seniors $4; Under 6 free

9548
Marine Museum of Manitoba (Selkirk), Inc.
Corner of Queen Ave & Eveline St, R1A 2B1 [PO Box 7, R1A 2B1]; (p) (204) 482-7761; (f) (204) 785-2452; www.sirnet.mb.ca/~mbmm

Joint/ 1974/ Private non-profit

HISTORY MUSEUM; MARITIME MUSEUM

PROGRAMS: Annual Meeting; Exhibits; Facility Rental; Film/Video; Guided Tours; Interpretation; Publication; School-Based Curriculum

COLLECTIONS: [1897] Six boats, lighthouses, nautical artifacts that relate to transportation on Lake Winnipeg and the Red River.

HOURS: May-late Sept M-F 9-5, Sa-Su and holidays 10-6

ADMISSION: $3.50, Student $2, Children $2, Seniors $3; Under 6 free

SHILO

9549
Royal Canadian Artillery Museum
Bldg A-12, R0K 2A0 [PO Box 5000 Stat Main, Canadian Forces Dase Shilo, R0K 2A0]; (p) (204) 765-3000; (f) (204) 765-5031; rcamuseum@techplus.com; www.artillery.net

Federal/ 1962/ staff: 5(f); 3(p)/publication: *Gunner; Quadrant*

HISTORY MUSEUM: Preserves, collects and

interprets the history and heritage of the Canadian Artillery for the Canadian Armed Forces.

PROGRAMS: Annual Meeting; Community Outreach; Exhibits; Family Programs; Guided Tours; Interpretation; Publication; Research Library/Archives

COLLECTIONS: [1871-present] Ordinance systems, vehicles, small arm, ammunition, uniforms, personal kit, and memorabilia used by the units of the Royal Canadian Artillery; Regiment's archives and art.

HOURS: Yr Summer Daily 8-4, Sa-Su and holidays 1-4

ADMISSION: No charge

ST. ANDREWS

9550
St. Andrews Rectory National Historic Site
Corner of River Rd & St Adrews Rd, R1A 2Y1 [374 River Rd, R1A 2Y1]; (p) (204) 334-6405

Federal/ 1980/ staff: 7(p); 6(v)

HISTORIC SITE: Preserves and interprets the architecture of buildings and the religious and social aspects of the early Red River settlement from 1821-1935.

PROGRAMS: Exhibits; Family Programs; Guided Tours; Interpretation; School-Based Curriculum

COLLECTIONS: [1822-1835] Artifacts from the 1930s; education and native customs.

HOURS: May-Sept Daily 10-6

ADMISSION: Donations accepted

ST. CLAUDE

9551
Societe Historique St. Claude
31 St, R0G 1Z0 [Box 131, R0G 1Z0]; (p) (204) 379-2156; (f) (204) 379-2396; www.cpnet.net/~stclaude/hpenglish.htm

Private non-profit/ 1972/ staff: 18(v)

GENEALOGICAL SOCIETY; HISTORIC PRESERVATION AGENCY: Maintains genealogic history and local museum.

PROGRAMS: Annual Meeting; Community Outreach; Family Programs; Guided Tours; Research Library/Archives

COLLECTIONS: [1892-present] Artifacts, documents, photos, religious, agricultural machinery, dairy; materials brought by the original French settlers.

HOURS: June-Sept M-F and by appt

TAEHERNE

9552
Treherne Museum
183 Van Zile St, R0G 2V0 [Box 30, R0G 2V0]; (p) (204) 723-2583

Joint/ 1972/ Private non-profit; State/ staff: 2(p); 11(v)

HISTORY MUSEUM; HOUSE MUSEUM: Preserves and interprets history and artifacts of surrounding area.

PROGRAMS: Community Outreach; Exhibits; Guided Tours; Interpretation; School-Based Curriculum

COLLECTIONS: [1800-1900] Rural Manitoba artifacts.

HOURS: May-Sept M-F 8-5, Sa-Su 1-5

ADMISSION: Donations accepted

THOMPSON

9553
Heritage North Museum
162 Princeton Dr, R8N 2A4; (p) (204) 677-2216; (f) (204) 677-8953; hnmuseum@netra.mysterynet.mb.ca; www.netra.mysterynet.mb.ca/museum/index.htm

Private non-profit/ 1986/ staff: 1(f); 5(p)/ members: 110/publication: My Grandmother's Tipi

HISTORY MUSEUM; RESEARCH CENTER

PROGRAMS: Annual Meeting; Community Outreach; Elder's Programs; Exhibits; Facility Rental; Guided Tours; Interpretation; Lectures; Publication; Research Library/Archives

COLLECTIONS: [Prehistoric-1960] Artifacts, memorabilia, materials: First Nations, fur trade, pioneer, and natural history exhibits, mining, history, stone-carving, local crafts, furs, bead work supplies, books, jewelry.

HOURS: May-Sept Daily 10-6; Sept-Apr T-Sa 1-6

ADMISSION: $3, Student $1.50, Children $0.75, Seniors $1.50

VIRDEN

9554
Virden Pioneer Home Museum, Inc.
390 King St W, R0M 2C0 [Box 2001, R0M 2C0]; (p) (204) 748-1659; (f) (204) 748-2501

Joint/ 1970/ staff: 3(p); 11(v)/ members: 11

HOUSE MUSEUM: Maintain museum.

PROGRAMS: Annual Meeting; Community Outreach; Exhibits; Guided Tours

COLLECTIONS: [1967-1970] Victorian era home.

HOURS: June-Aug Daily 9-6

ADMISSION: Donations accepted

WASAGAMING

9555
Riding Mountain National Park
Riding Mountain National Park, R0J 2H0; (p) (800) 707-8180; (f) (204) 848-2596; RMNP_info@pch.gc.ca; parkscanada.pch.gc.ca/riding

Federal/ 1930/ staff: 50(f); 50(p)/publication: A Visitor's Guide to Riding Mountain National Park

HISTORIC SITE: Represents Southern Boreal Plains and Plateaux region of Canada.

PROGRAMS: Elder's Programs; Exhibits; Facility Rental; Family Programs; Film/Video; Garden Tours; Guided Tours; Interpretation; Publication; Research Library/Archives;

HOURS: Yr Daily

WASKADA

9556
Waskada Museum
Main St, R0M 2E0 [Box 27, R0M 2E0]; (p) (204) 673-2503; (f) (204) 673-2503

City/ 1967/ staff: 1(p); 12(v)/ members: 60

HISTORIC PRESERVATION AGENCY; HISTORY MUSEUM: Operates the museum for the village of Waskada; collects and preserves materials relating to regional history.

PROGRAMS: Annual Meeting; Community Outreach; Guided Tours

COLLECTIONS: [Late 1800-present] Farm machinery, working steam engine, old tractors, trucks, cars, a silent movie projector, whooping crane, pioneer furniture, stoves, lamps, clocks, tools, gramophones, quilts, service uniforms including a north west mounted police uniform, threshing photos, and household objects.

HOURS: June-Aug M-F 9-5; Apr, May, Sept, Oct by appt

ADMISSION: $2

WHITEMOUTH

9557
Whitemouth Municipal Museum Society
Community Growns Off Hendeson St, R0E 2G0 [PO Box 294, R0E 2G0]; (p) (204) 348-2300, (204) 348-2216

Private non-profit/ 1978/ staff: 30(v)/ members: 15

HISTORIC PRESERVATION AGENCY; HISTORIC SITE; HOUSE MUSEUM; LIVING HISTORY/OUTDOOR MUSEUM: Operates museum.

PROGRAMS: Annual Meeting; Community Outreach; Exhibits; Festivals; Guided Tours; Reenactments

COLLECTIONS: [Late 1800s-1945] Farming, railroad artifacts, medical supplies, veterinarian collection, household, school, trapping, logging, and a peat moss combine.

HOURS: June-Sept 9-5 and by appt

ADMISSION: Donations accepted

WINNEPEG

9558
Aquatic Hall of Fame and Museum of Canada
25 Poseidon Bay, R3M 3E4; (p) (204) 882-2494; (f) (204) 882-2494

Private non-profit/ 1967/ Aquatic Federation of Canada/ staff: 1(p); 7(v)

ART MUSEUM; RESEARCH CENTER

PROGRAMS: Annual Meeting; Exhibits

COLLECTIONS: Aquatic memorabilia, art.

HOURS: Yr Daily 9-10

WINNIPEG

9559
Archives des Soeurs Grises/Grey Nun Archives
151, rue Despins, R2H 0L7; (p) (204) 235-8941; (f) (204) 237-6419; cboily@sgm.mb.ca

Private non-profit/ 1976/ Grey Nuns of Manitoba/ staff: 1(f); 1(p)

LIBRARY AND/OR ARCHIVES: Acquires and preserves history of the Grey Nuns and their health care corporations in the canonical province of Saint-Boniface.

PROGRAMS: Research Library/Archives

COLLECTIONS: [1844-present] 200 linear meters of textual records, 8.6 meters of photographs, over 1000 architectural drawings, reference library with 1000 books.

HOURS: By appt

9560
Association of Manitoba Museums
206-153 Lombard Ave, R3L 0G1; (p) (204) 947-1782; (f) (204) 942-3749; amm@ escape.ca; www.escape.ca/~amm

Private non-profit/ 1972/ staff: 1(f); 2(p); 25(v)/publication: *Museums in Manitoba*

ALLIANCE OF HISTORICAL AGENCIES; HISTORIC PRESERVATION AGENCY: Preserves Manitoba's heritage by promoting and encouraging the establishment, advancement, and improvement of area museums.

PROGRAMS: Annual Meeting; Community Outreach; Exhibits; Lectures; Publication; Research Library/Archives

HOURS: Yr M-Th 8-4

9561
Centre for Mennonite Brethren Studies
169 Riverton Ave, R2L 2E5; (p) (204) 669-6575; (f) (204) 654-1865; adueck@ mbconf.ca; mbcont.ca/mb/cmhs.htm

Private non-profit/ 1969/ staff: 2(f); 4(p); 4(v)/publication: *Mennonite Historian*

HISTORIC PRESERVATION AGENCY; LIBRARY AND/OR ARCHIVES: Serves as archive and historical library of the Canadian Conference of Mennonite Brethren Churches of Canada.

PROGRAMS: Exhibits; Film/Video; Interpretation; Lectures; Publication; Research Library/Archives

COLLECTIONS: [1860-present] Official records of Canadian Mennonite Brethren Conference and agencies. Personal records of Brethren leaders, genealogical records, music, periodicals.

HOURS: Yr M-F 8:30-4:30

9562
Centre for Rupert's Land Studies
Univ of Winnipeg, 515 Portage Ave, R3B 2E9; (p) (204) 786-9003; (f) (204) 774-4134; rupert.land@uwinnipeg.ca

Private non-profit/ 1984/ staff: 2(p); 3(v)/ members: 220/publication: *Rupert's Land Newsletter; Rupert's Land Record Society*

PROFESSIONAL ORGANIZATION: Fosters communication, research, and publishing on the history and peoples of Rupert's Land.

PROGRAMS: Annual Meeting; Publication; Research Library/Archives

COLLECTIONS: [1670-present] Inventories of Rupert's Land Research Centre and Rupert's Land Record Society volumes, Colloqium papers, limited Hudson's Bay Record Society volume inventory.

HOURS: By appt

9563
Conference of Manitoba and Northwestern Ontario Archives, University of Winnipeg
Univ of Winnipeg, 515 Portage Ave, R3B 2E9; (p) (204) 783-0708; (f) (204) 786-1824; diane.haglund@uwinnipeg.ca

1925/ staff: 3(p)/publication: *Managing Your Congregation's Records*

LIBRARY AND/OR ARCHIVES

INTERPRETATION: Education; Ethnic/Religious/Cultural

PROGRAMS: Publication

COLLECTIONS: [1870-present] Archives: Methodist and Presbyterian churches 1870-1925, United Church of Canada in Manitoba 1925-present

HOURS: Yr by appt

ADMISSION: No charge

9564
Dalnavent Museum
61 Carlton St, R3C 1N7; (p) (204) 943-2835; dalnavrt@escape.ca; www.mhs.mb.ca

Private non-profit/ 1974/ staff: 2(f); 4(p); 92(v)/ members: 62

HISTORIC SITE; HOUSE MUSEUM

PROGRAMS: Exhibits; Facility Rental; Guided Tours; Interpretation; School-Based Curriculum

COLLECTIONS: [Late Victorian] Fully restored Late Victorian house; typical household furnishings, decorative arts, clothing, and accessories.

HOURS: Yr Jan-Feb Sa-Su 12-4:15; Mar-Dec Daily 10-5:15

ADMISSION: $4; Family $8; Student $2; Seniors $3

9565
Fort Garry Historical Society, Inc.
[PO Box 152, R3V 1L6]

Joint/ 1971/ Private non-profit/ staff: 4(p); 20(v)/ members: 36/publication: *FGHS Bulletin, Fort Garry Remembered, St. Norbert Revisited*

HISTORIC SITE; HISTORICAL SOCIETY; HISTORY MUSEUM; HOUSE MUSEUM: Collects, preserves, exhibits, and interprets the community's Metis and Francopone history.

PROGRAMS: Annual Meeting; Community Outreach; Exhibits; Family Programs; Guided Tours; Interpretation; Lectures; Publication

COLLECTIONS: [Late 19th c-Present] 2,200 artifacts in two restored homes, photographs, scrapbooks, oral history tapes.

HOURS: Mid May-June M-F 9-3, Su 12-5; July-Sept Th-M 10:30-5:30

ADMISSION: No charge

9566
Headquarters Museum and Air Force Heritage Park
17 Wing Winnipeg, R3J 3Y5 [1 Canadian Air Division HQ, Box 17000 Stat Force, R3J 3Y5]; (p) (204) 833-2500; (f) (204) 833-2512; pearsons@escape.ca; achq.dnd.ca

Federal/ 1993/ staff: 5(v)

HOUSE MUSEUM; LIVING HISTORY/OUT-DOOR MUSEUM: Preserves and promotes military aviation history of Canada.

PROGRAMS: Exhibits; Family Programs; Guided Tours; Lectures; Living History

COLLECTIONS: [20th c] 13 aircraft outdoors on pedestals, 3 Victoria Crosses, Battle of Britain Lace Tapestry.

HOURS: Yr Museum: M-F 8-5;

ADMISSION: No charge

9567
Historical Museum of St. James-Assiniboia
3180 Portage Ave, R3K 0Y5; (p) (204) 888-8706

City; Joint; Private non-profit/ 1971/ staff: 2(f); 4(p); 15(v)/ members: 50

HISTORY MUSEUM

PROGRAMS: Annual Meeting; Exhibits; Festivals; Guided Tours; Interpretation; School-Based Curriculum

COLLECTIONS: [1880-1930s] 2,500 objects in reserve collection, artifacts, photographs, and archival materials, decorative art, textiles, basketry, wood, ceramic, glass, leather, metal, paper, local and regional history; site: Red River Frame House.

HOURS: Yr Sept-Apr M-F 9-5; May-Aug Daily

9568
Ivan Franko Museum
200 McGregor St Main Fl, R2W 5L6 [205-200 McGregor St, R2W 5L6]; (p) (204) 589-4397

1956

HISTORY MUSEUM

9569
Le Musee de Saint-Boniface/St. Boniface Museum
494 Tache Ave, R2H 2B2; (p) (204) 237-4500; (f) (204) 986-7986

City/ 1959/ staff: 6(f); 6(p); 10(v)

HISTORIC SITE; HISTORY MUSEUM: Preserves historic building.

PROGRAMS: Community Outreach; Exhibits; Facility Rental; Guided Tours; Interpretation; Lectures; Publication; Reenactments; School-Based Curriculum

COLLECTIONS: [Late 1800-early 1900] Exhibits: French-Canadian and Metis population of Manitoba.

HOURS: Yr Nov-Feb M-F 9-5; Mar-May M-F 9-5, Su 12-4; May-Oct M-F 9-5, Sa 1-4, Su 10-8

ADMISSION: $2, Children $1.50, Seniors $1.50; Group rates

9570
Living Prairie Museum
2795 Ness Ave, R3J 3S4; (p) (204) 832-0167; (f) (204) 986-4172; prairie@mbnet.mb.ca; www.city.winnipeg.mb.ca/city/parks/enserv/interp/l

City/ 1974/ staff: 1(f); 4(p); 10(v)/ members: 60/publication: *Prairie Breeze*

HISTORIC PRESERVATION AGENCY; LIVING HISTORY/OUTDOOR MUSEUM

PROGRAMS: Annual Meeting; Community Outreach; Concerts; Elder's Programs; Exhibits; Facility Rental; Family Programs; Festivals; Garden Tours; Guided Tours; Interpretation; Lectures; Living History; Publication; Research Library/Archives; School-Based Curriculum

COLLECTIONS: [Prehistory-present] 40 acres of original prairie, artifacts, extinct animals exhibit, slide library, books, environmental education materials.

HOURS: Yr May-June Sa-Su (school hikes M-F); July-Aug Daily 10-5; Nov-Apr

9571
Manitoba Genealogical Society
Unit E, 1045 St James, R3H 1B1; (p) (204) 783-9139; (f) (204) 783-0190; mgsi@mts.net; www.mts.net/~mgsi

Private non-profit/ 1965/ staff: 64(f); 30(p); 100(v)/ members: 5800/publication: *Generations*

GENEALOGICAL SOCIETY: Promotes and encourages an interest in genealogy and family history in Manitoba.

PROGRAMS: Annual Meeting; Exhibits; Facility Rental; Lectures; Publication; Research Library/Archives

COLLECTIONS: 5,000 prints, 200 microfilm, microfiche, cemetery indexes, church registers, newspapers.

HOURS: Yr T, W, Th

9572
Manitoba Indian Cultural Education Centre, Inc.
119 Sutherland Ave, R2W 3C9; (p) (204) 942-0228; (f) (204) 947-6564; micec@mb.sympatico.ca; www.schoolmet.ca/ext/aboriginal/micec/index.html

Private non-profit/ 1975/ staff: 4(f); 5(p); 30(v)/ members: 100

CULTURAL CENTER: Promote an awareness and understanding of the Aboriginal culture to both Aboriginal and non-Aboriginal Peoples.

PROGRAMS: Community Outreach; Exhibits; Guided Tours; Interpretation; Lectures; Living History; Research Library/Archives

COLLECTIONS: 8,000 books, 300 videos, 100 educational kits, Canadian Aboriginal artifacts.

HOURS: Yr M-F 8:30-4:30

ADMISSION: No charge

9573
Manitoba Museum of Man and Nature
190 Rupert Ave, R3B 0N2; (p) (204) 956-2830; (f) (204) 942-3679; info@manitobamuseum.mb.ca; www.manitobamuseu.mb.ca

Private non-profit/ 1960/ staff: 76(f); 15(p); 250(v)

HISTORY MUSEUM: Reflects heritage of Manitoba and other regions of the world.

PROGRAMS: Annual Meeting; Community Outreach; Exhibits; Facility Rental; Family Programs; Guided Tours; Lectures; Publication; School-Based Curriculum

COLLECTIONS: Natural history collections, specimen library of plants, animals, fossils, rocks, and minerals.

HOURS: Yr May-Sept Daily 10-6; Sept-May T-F 10-4, Sa-Su 10-5

ADMISSION: $4.99, Children $3.99, Seniors $3.99

9574
Mennonite Genealogy, Inc.
790 Wellington Ave, R3C 2H6 [Box 393, R3C 2H6]; (p) (204) 772-0747; Margaret_Kroeker@Umanitoba.ca

Private non-profit/ 1967

GENEALOGICAL SOCIETY: Collects and preserves historical and family records.

PROGRAMS: Research Library/Archives

COLLECTIONS: [1700-present] 186,000 names in card files, enhanced by over 500,000 names in computer data base; published and unpublished family histories, village, church and migration records, maps, and and photos.

HOURS: Yr T-F 2-4

ADMISSION: No charge

9575
Provincial Archives of Manitoba
200 Vaughan St, R3C 1T5; (p) (204) 945-3971; (f) (204) 948-2008; pam@chc.gov.mb.ca; www.gov.mb.ca/chc/archives

State/ 1884/ staff: 45(f); 6(v)

LIBRARY AND/OR ARCHIVES: Acquires and processes records of the government, courts, and commissions; people and institutions of Manitoba; records of the Hudson's Bay Company and subsidiary companies.

PROGRAMS: Community Outreach; Research Library/Archives

COLLECTIONS: [1671-present] Hudson's Bay Company, Canadian Airways Limited; Archives of Manitoba Legal- Judicial History; political leaders, and associations.

HOURS: Sept-May T-Sa 9-4; June-Aug M-F 9-4

9576
Ross House Museum
140 Meade St N, R3C 1N7 [c/o 61 Carlton St, R3C 1N7]; (p) (204) 943-3958; dalnavrt@escape.ca; www.mhs.mb.ca

1949/ staff: 2(f); 2(p); 10(v)

HOUSE MUSEUM: Reflects the life of the Ross family within the Red River Settlement of 1854.

PROGRAMS: Exhibits; Guided Tours; Interpretation; Publication; School-Based Curriculum

COLLECTIONS: [1854] Artifacts: furnishing, 1854 family home, community post office.

HOURS: June-Aug W-Su 11-6

ADMISSION: No charge

9577
Transcona Historical Museum
141 Regent Ave West, R2C 1R1; (p) (204) 222-0423; (f) (204) 222-0208; transcon@istar.ca; members.xoom.com/Transcona

Joint/ 1967/ staff: 2(f); 5(p); 60(v)/publication: *Transcona Historical Museum Newsletter*

HISTORY MUSEUM: Collects, preserves, researches, exhibits, and interprets history of Transcona and Springfield area.

PROGRAMS: Annual Meeting; Exhibits; Family Programs; Guided Tours; Publication; Research Library/Archives; School-Based Curriculum

COLLECTIONS: [Prehistory; 20th c] 4,000 museum artifacts, 1,000 clothing and textiles artifacts, 1,000 rare books, 2,600 photographs, 40 linear feet archival documents, 250 maps and plans, 8,000 butterflies and moths, 3,500 Archaeology artifacts.

HOURS: Feb-Dec T-F 12-5, Sa 10-5

ADMISSION: No charge/Donations

9578
University of Manitoba Archives & Special Collections
331 Dafoe Library, R3T 2N2; (p) (204) 474-9986; (f) (204) 474-7577; shelley_sweeney@umanitoba.ca

1978/ staff: 4(f); 1(p)

LIBRARY AND/OR ARCHIVES: Collects, preserves, and makes available the records of the Univ of Manitoba.

PROGRAMS: Community Outreach; Exhibits; Lectures; Research Library/Archives

COLLECTIONS: [20th c] 7,000 foot textual records; 250,000 photographs and negatives; 3,000 hours audio-visual material; 38,000 books.

HOURS: Yr M-F 8:30-4:30

ADMISSION: No charge

9579
Western Canada Aviation Museum, Inc.
958 Ferry, R3H 0Y8; (p) (204) 786-5503; (f) (204) 775-4761; info@wcam.mb.ca; www.wcam.mb.ca

Private non-profit/ 1974/ staff: 6(f); 6(p); 350(v)/ members: 1200

HISTORY MUSEUM: Educates, preserves, and promotes Canada's aviation heritage.

PROGRAMS: Exhibits; Facility Rental; Family Programs; Guided Tours; Interpretation; Living History; Publication; Research Library/Archives; School-Based Curriculum

COLLECTIONS: [1930s-present] Aircraft represents aspects of Canadian aviation (home-built, commercial, military, private) engines to jet age, aviation memorabilia, photographs, artifacts, archives, air mail covers, home-built models, historical videos, simulators.

HOURS: Yr Daily M-Sa 10-4, Su 1-4

ADMISSION: $5, Family $12, Children $3; Under 3 free

NEW BRUNSWICK

AULAC

9580
Fort Beausejour National Historic Site/Lieu Historique National du Fort Beausejour
111 Fort Beausejour Rd, E4L 2W5; (p) (506) 364-5080; (f) (506) 536-4399; fort_beausjour@pch.gc.ca; (c) Westmorland

Federal/ 1926/ staff: 2(f); 5(p)/publication: *Book Shop*

HISTORIC SITE: Preserves Canada's natural and historic resources.

PROGRAMS: Elder's Programs; Exhibits; Festivals; Guided Tours; Interpretation; Lectures; Publication; Reenactments; Research Library/Archives

COLLECTIONS: [1670s-present] Photographs, maps, portraits, weapons and artillery, dishes and flatware, artifacts relevant to the French and British military occupations.

HOURS: June-Oct 15 Daily 9-5

ADMISSION: $2.50, Family $6.25, Student $1.50, Seniors $2; Group rates

BOUCTOUCHE

9581
Musee de Kent

150, ch Du Couvent, E4S 3C1; (p) (506) 743-5005; (c) Kent

Private non-profit/ 1977/ staff: 1(p); 10(v)

HISTORIC SITE; HISTORY MUSEUM; HOUSE MUSEUM: Collects, preserves, and interprets the Kent County's history.

PROGRAMS: Annual Meeting; Exhibits; Facility Rental; Guided Tours

COLLECTIONS: [1850-1960] Archival documents, photographs, Immaculate Conception Convent and religious artifacts, Acadian artifacts, furniture.

HOURS: July-Aug M-Sa 9-5:30, Su 12-6

CAMPOBELLO ISLAND

9582
Franklin D. Roosevelt Cottage

Welshpool, E0G 3H0; (p) (506) 752-2922; (f) (506) 752-6000; info@fdr.net; www.fdr.net

Federal/ 1897/ US & Canada/ staff: 14(f); 29(p)

HISTORY MUSEUM; HOUSE MUSEUM: Roosevelt Campobello International Park administered jointly by US and Canadian governments. Summer home of President Franklin D. Roosevelt at Welshpool, Campobello Island, New Brunswick, Canada.

COLLECTIONS: [1897-1950] House, furniture, books, papers, and other personal items.

DALHOUSIE

9583
Restigouche Regional Museum

George & Adelaide St, E0K 1B0 [PO Box 1717, E0K 1B0]; (p) (506) 684-7490; (f) (506) 684-7613; gurrm@nbnet.nb.ca

State/ 1967/ staff: 1(f); 3(p)/ members: 100

HISTORY MUSEUM

PROGRAMS: Annual Meeting; Community Outreach; Exhibits; Facility Rental; Family Programs; Festivals; Guided Tours; Interpretation; Lectures; Publication; Research Library/Archives

COLLECTIONS: [1850-1950] Archives: 1,600 photos, records, books.

HOURS: Yr Summer Daily M-F 9-9, Sa-Su 9-5; rest of year M-F 9-5, Sa 9-1, Su 1-5

ADMISSION: No charge

DORCHESTER

9584
Westmorland Historical Society

[PO Box 166, E0A 1M0]; (p) (506) 379-6633; (f) (506) 379-3033; (c) Westmorland

Private non-profit/ 1967/ staff: 5(p); 20(v)/ members: 200

HISTORICAL SOCIETY: Operates 3 heritage buildings as museums; provides resources for heritage and genealogical research.

PROGRAMS: Annual Meeting; Exhibits; Facility Rental; Interpretation; Reenactments

COLLECTIONS: [1840-1910] Textiles, farming equipment, carpentry tools, carriages, household collections with books, china, linens, tools.

HOURS: June -Sept 12 Daily M-Sa 10-5, Su 12-5

ADMISSION: $2

FEDERICTON

9585
Nursing History Resource Centre/Nursing Association of New Brunswick

165 Regent St, E3B 3E1; (p) (506) 459-2862; (f) (506) 459-2838; amcgee@nhnb.nb.ca; nanb@nahb.nb.ca; (c) York

Private non-profit/ staff: 1(p)

HISTORIC PRESERVATION AGENCY; HISTORY MUSEUM: Artifacts, documents, and research materials relating to nursing history.

PROGRAMS: Community Outreach; Exhibits; Guided Tours; Interpretation; Lectures

COLLECTIONS: [1790 -present] Nursing tools, uniforms, and artifacts; medical archives, oral histories written by Florence Nightingale.

HOURS: By appt

FREDERICTON

9586
Archives and Special Collections, Harriet Irving Library

Univ of New Brunswick, PO Box 7500, E3B 5H5; (p) (506) 453-4748; (f) (506) 453-4595; Mflagg@unb.ca; degaulle.hil.unb.ca/library/archives/

1931/ Univ of New Brunswick/ staff: 4(f); 4(p)

LIBRARY AND/OR ARCHIVES

PROGRAMS: Exhibits

COLLECTIONS: [19th-20th c] University archives, New Brunswick Historical and New Brunswickana.

HOURS: Yr M-F 8:30-5

9587
Department of Economic Development, Tourism and Culture-Heritage Branch

300 St Marys St, E3B 5H1 [PO Box 6000, E3B 5H1]; (p) (506) 453-2524; (f) (506) 453-2416; kim.fila@gov.nb.ca; www.gov.nb.ca/culture/heritage

HISTORIC PRESERVATION AGENCY; HISTORIC SITE; HISTORICAL SOCIETY; HISTORY MUSEUM; HOUSE MUSEUM; LIVING

HISTORY/OUTDOOR MUSEUM: Protects, develops, and commemorates provincial historic resources of significance.

PROGRAMS: Exhibits; Family Programs; Guided Tours; Living History

COLLECTIONS: [19th c]

HOURS: Daily 9-4:30

9588
New Brunswick Sports Hall of Fame

503 Queen St, E3B 5H1 [PO Box 6000, E3B 5H1]; (p) (506) 453-3747; (f) (506) 459-0481; deborah.williams@gnb.ca; www.nbsportshalloffame.nb.ca

Private non-profit/ 1970/ staff: 3(f); 5(p); 20(v)

HISTORY MUSEUM: Recognizes, collects, preserves, exhibits, and promotes New Brunswick's sporting heritage.

COLLECTIONS: [1800s-present] Artifacts and memorabilia, photographs, printed matter, equipment, uniforms, trophies, awards, and art pertaining to New Brunswick athletes, events, and sports history.

HOURS: Yr Winter M-F 12-4; Summer Daily 10-6

ADMISSION: Donations accepted

GAGETOWN

9589
Queens County Historical Society and Museum, Inc.

69 Front St or 16 Court House Rd, E0G 1V0 [PO Box 68, E0G 1V0]; (p) (506) 488-2966, (506) 488-2483; (f) (506) 488-2966; gbt@nbnet.nb.ca; (c) Queens

Private non-profit/ 1967/ staff: 1(f); 4(p); 25(v)/ members: 150/publication: Queen's County Heritage

GENEALOGICAL SOCIETY; HISTORIC SITE; HISTORICAL SOCIETY; HISTORY MUSEUM; HOUSE MUSEUM; RESEARCH CENTER: Collects, preserves, and interprets the heritage of the county.

PROGRAMS: Annual Meeting; Community Outreach; Exhibits; Facility Rental; Festivals; Guided Tours; Interpretation; Lectures; Publication; Research Library/Archives

COLLECTIONS: 3,000 museum artifacts, 2,500 photographs, 3,000 archival documents, Father of Confederation Sir Leonard Tilley artifacts, artwork.

HOURS: May-Sept, Oct-Nov Daily 10-5 and by appt

ADMISSION: $2; Under 12 free

HAMPTON

9590
Kings County Historical and Archival Society, Inc.

27 Centennial Rd, E0G 1Z0 [PO Box 5001, E0G 1Z0]; (p) (506) 832-6009; (f) (506) 832-6007; kingscm@nbnet.nb.ca; (c) Kins

Private non-profit/ 1962/ staff: 1(p); 25(v)/ members: 250/publication: Memories

HISTORIC SITE; HISTORICAL SOCIETY; HISTORY MUSEUM: Promotes local history and preserves historical sites.

PROGRAMS: Annual Meeting; Exhibits; Garden Tours; Guided Tours; Interpretation; Publication; Research Library/Archives

COLLECTIONS: [1900] Kings County artifacts.

HOURS: June 15-Sept 30 M-F

HILLSBOROUGH

9591
Heritage Hillsborough, Inc.
40 A Mill St, E0A 1X0 [PO Box 148, E0A 1X0]; (p) (506) 734-3102; (f) (506) 734-1990; (c) Albert

Private non-profit/ 1982/ staff: 1(p); 10(v)/ members: 100

HOUSE MUSEUM: Operates and maintains Steeves House Museum.

PROGRAMS: Annual Meeting; Exhibits; Facility Rental; Festivals; Guided Tours; Lectures

COLLECTIONS: [1812-1900] Colonial mansion, artifacts, furniture, textiles, and material goods.

HOURS: July 1-Sept 1 Daily 9-5

ADMISSION: $2; Family $5.50; Children $1

9592
Salem and Hillsborough Railroad, Inc.
2847 Main St, E4A 2X7; (p) (506) 734-3195, (506) 734-3733; (f) (506) 734-3711; (c) Albert

Private non-profit/ 1983/ staff: 10(p); 20(v)/ members: 70/publication: Update

HISTORIC PRESERVATION AGENCY: Tourist excursion railroad, museum, dedicated to preservation of railroad.

PROGRAMS: Exhibits; Facility Rental; Guided Tours; Publication

COLLECTIONS: [1910-1960] Railroad engines and cars, tools and equipment, publications, documents.

HOURS: July-Aug Daily 10-6

ADMISSION: $2, Children $1

KINGS LANDING

9593
Kings Landing Historical Settlement
Exit 259, Rt 2 (Trans Canada Hwy), E6K 3W3 [20 Kings Landing Service Rd, E6K 3W3]; (p) (506) 363-4999; (f) (506) 363-4989; Kings.Landing@gov.nb.ca; www.gov.nb.ca/kingslanding; (c) York

Joint/ 1974/ State/ staff: 20(f); 135(p); 55(v)/ members: 300

LIVING HISTORY/OUTDOOR MUSEUM: Depicts evolution of daily life in colonial New Brunswick and early Canada from the Loyalists to the late Victorians

PROGRAMS: Elder's Programs; Exhibits; Facility Rental; Family Programs; Festivals; Guided Tours; Interpretation; Living History; Publication; Reenacts; Research Library/Archives; School-Based Curriculum

COLLECTIONS: [Late 17th c-early 20th c] Furnishing, agricultural and horse-drawn vehicles, textiles, folk art, and tools.

HOURS: June-mid Oct Daily

ADMISSION: $10, Family $25, Student $7.25, Children $5.50, Seniors $8; Under 6 free; group rates

MENRAMCOOK

9594
Societe du Monument Lefebvre
480, rue Centrale, E4K 3S6; (p) (506) 758-9808; (f) (506) 758-9813

1988/ staff: 1(f); 1(p); 20(v)

HOURS: Daily

ADMISSION: $2, Family $5, Student $1, Seniors $1.50

MIRAMICH

9595
Saint Michael's Museum Association, Inc.
10 Howard St, E1N 3A7; (p) (506) 778-5152; (f) (506) 778-5156; mmuseum@nbnet.nb.ca; mibc.nb.ca/stmikes/default.htm; (c) Northumberland

Private non-profit/ 1975/ staff: 5(v)/ members: 18

GENEALOGICAL SOCIETY; HISTORIC PRESERVATION AGENCY; HISTORIC SITE; HISTORY MUSEUM: Preserves area history.

PROGRAMS: Exhibits; Guided Tours; Research Library/Archives

COLLECTIONS: Census and church records, tax receipt ledger, and donated local materials.

HOURS: Yr M-F 8:30-4:30

ADMISSION: No charge

MONCTON

9596
Centre d'etudes acadiennes
Univ de Moncton, E1A 3E9; (p) (506) 858-4085; (f) (506) 858-4530; basquem@umoncton.ca; www.umoncton.ca/etudeacadiennes/ea.html

1968/ staff: 6(f); 3(p)/publication: Contact-Acadie

RESEARCH CENTER: Gathers documentation on Acadia and the Acadians.

PROGRAMS: Exhibits; Guided Tours; Lectures; Publication

COLLECTIONS: [17th-20th c] Holdings: 12,300 books and pamphlets; 3,240 reels of microfilm; 3,307 feet of manuscripts; 3,435 reels of magnetic tape of Acadian folk tales and songs; 95 journals and other serials; 13 newspapers.

9597
Moncton Museum
20 Mountain Rd, E1C 2J8; (p) (506) 856-4383; (f) (506) 856-4355; (c) Westmorland

Private non-profit/ 1973/ staff: 4(f); 4(p); 6(v)

HISTORIC SITE; HISTORY MUSEUM: Collects, preserves, and interprets the history of the greater Moncton area.

PROGRAMS: Community Outreach; Exhibits; Facility Rental; Family Programs; Guided Tours; Interpretation; Lectures; Research Library/Archives; School-Based Curriculum

COLLECTIONS: [1870-1960] 20,000 artifacts, 10,000 photos, 6,000 archival documents.

HOURS: Yr M-Sa 9-4:30, Su 1-5

ADMISSION: No charge

9598
Musee Acadien (Acadian Museum)
Univ de Moncton, E1A 3E9; (p) (506) 858-4088; (f) (506) 858-4043; leblanbc@umonction.ca; www.umonction.ca/maum.html; (c) Westmorland

1886/ staff: 2(f); 5(p); 1(v)

HISTORY MUSEUM

PROGRAMS: Exhibits; Film/Video; Guided Tours; Interpretation; School-Based Curriculum

COLLECTIONS: [Late 18th-present]

HOURS: June-Sept M-F 10-5, Sa-Su 1-5; Oct-May T-F 1-4:30, Sa-Su 1-4

ADMISSION: $2, Family $5, Student $1, Seniors $1; Under 12 free

OROMOCTO

9599
CFB Gagetown Military Museum
Bldg A-5 Walnut St, E2V 4J5 [Bldg A-5 PO Box 17000 Stn Forces, E2V 4J5]; (p) (506) 422-1304; (f) (506) 422-1304; museum_gagetown@brunnet.net; www.brunnet.net/museum_gagetown

Joint/ 1973/ Canadian Forces Museum System/Organizations of Military Museums of Canada/Board of Directors/ staff: 2(f); 5(p); 1(v)

ALLIANCE OF HISTORICAL AGENCIES; HISTORIC PRESERVATION AGENCY; HISTORY MUSEUM; LIVING HISTORY/OUTDOOR MUSEUM

PROGRAMS: Community Outreach; Exhibits; Festivals; Film/Video; Guided Tours; Living History; Publication; Reenacts; Research Library/Archives

COLLECTIONS: Exhibits, artifacts, and memorabilia.

HOURS: Yr June-Aug M-F 8-4 Sa-Su 10-4; Sept-May M-F 8-4

ADMISSION: No charge/Donations

SACKVILLE

9600
Maritime Conference Archives
32 York St, E4L 4R4; (p) (506) 536-0998; (c) Westmorland

staff: 1(p)

LIBRARY AND/OR ARCHIVES: Preserves Conference, Presbytery and Pastoral Charge records of Nova Scotia, New Brunswick, Prince Edward Island, the Gaspe area of Quebec, and Bermuda.

PROGRAMS: Research Library/Archives

COLLECTIONS: [1780-present] Minutes, registers (marriage, baptism, burial), papers of prominent United Church people; denominational periodicals of the Maritimes.

HOURS: Yr T-Th 9-4

9601
Owens Art Gallery
61 York St, E4L 1E1; (p) (506) 364-2574; (f) (506) 364-2575; gkelly@mta.ca; www.mta.ca/owens/

Joint/ 1895/ staff: 4(f); 7(p)/ members: 90

ART MUSEUM: Presents exhibitions of contemporary and historical art of national and international origins.

PROGRAMS: Community Outreach; Elder's Programs; Exhibits; Family Programs; Film/Video; Guided Tours; Interpretation; Lectures; Research Library/Archives

COLLECTIONS: [18th-20th c] European and North America art.

HOURS: Yr Daily

ADMISSION: No charge

SAINT JOHN

9602
New Brunswick Historical Society
120 Union St, E2L 1A3; (p) (506) 652-3590; (c) Saint John

Private non-profit/ 1874/ staff: 1(f); 5(p); 8(v)/ members: 145/publication: *New Brunswick Historical Society Newsletter*

HISTORIC SITE; HISTORICAL SOCIETY; HISTORY MUSEUM; HOUSE MUSEUM: Preserves and promotes history of New Brunswick; operates Loyalist House Museum and small library.

PROGRAMS: Annual Meeting; Exhibits; Facility Rental; Family Programs; Guided Tours; Interpretation; Lectures; Publication; Research Library/Archives; School-Based Curriculum

COLLECTIONS: [1770-1830] Materials, artifacts, and memorabilia.

HOURS: May 18th-June 30 M-F 10-5; July 1-Sept 5 Daily 10-5; Sept 6-May 18 by appt

ADMISSION: $3, Family $7, Children $1

9603
Saint John Jewish Historical Museum
29 Wellington Row, E2L 3H4; (p) (506) 633-1833; (f) (506) 642-9926; sjjhm@nbnet.nb.ca; sjjhm.tripod.com; (c) Saint John

Private non-profit/ 1986/ staff: 1(f); 5(p); 10(v)/ members: 375

HISTORICAL SOCIETY; HISTORY MUSEUM: Preserves and displays history of Saint John Jewish community.

PROGRAMS: Annual Meeting; Community Outreach; Exhibits; Guided Tours; Interpretation; Publication; Research Library/Archives; School-Based Curriculum

COLLECTIONS: [1858-present] Documents, photographs, and recordings.

HOURS: May-Oct M-F 10-4 and July-Aug Su 1-4

ADMISSION: No charge/Donations

SHEDIAC

9604
Societe historique De La Mer Rouge
CP 1688, E0A 3G0; (p) (506) 532-5314

Private non-profit/ 1981/ staff: 15(v)/ members: 120/publication: *Sur L'Empremier*

HISTORIC PRESERVATION AGENCY; HISTORICAL SOCIETY: Promotes local history, preserves historic buildings, and sites.

PROGRAMS: Annual Meeting; Community Outreach; Concerts; Exhibits; Publication

COLLECTIONS: [19th-20th c] 2 historic buildings, society publications.

HOURS: May-Sept M-Su 10-6

ST. ANDREWS

9605
Charlotte County Archives
123 Frederick St, E0G 2X0 [PO Box 475, E0G 2X0]; (p) (506) 529-4248

Private non-profit/ 1975/ staff: 1(p); 12(v)

HISTORIC SITE; HISTORICAL SOCIETY; RESEARCH CENTER: Collects, preserves, and organizes historical documents and photos related to Charlotte County; maintains reference material and books, genealogical data for researchers.

PROGRAMS: Elder's Programs; Guided Tours; Research Library/Archives

COLLECTIONS: [1783-present] Documents, maps, photographs, reference books, indexes, microfilm, and subject files.

HOURS: Yr June-mid-Sept M-F

9606
Ross Memorial Museum
188 Montague St, E5B 1J2 [Box 603, 188 Montague St, E5B 1J2]; (p) (506) 529-5124; (f) (516) 529-5124; www.townsearch.com/rossmuseum

1980/ staff: 1(f); 1(p); 150(v)/ members: 100

HOUSE MUSEUM

PROGRAMS: Elder's Programs; Exhibits; Festivals; Interpretation; Lectures

COLLECTIONS: [Late 18th-early 20th c] Furnishing, art.

HOURS: June-Oct Summer M-Sa 10-4:30; Fall T-Sa 10-4:30

ADMISSION: Donations accepted

ST. BASILE

9607
Musee Maison Cyr and La Chapelle
321, rue Principal, E7C 1K9 [PO Box 150, E7C 1K9]; (p) (506) 263-8207; (c) Madawaska

Private non-profit/ staff: 1(p)

HISTORIC PRESERVATION AGENCY; HISTORIC SITE; HOUSE MUSEUM: Maintains Maison Cyr house museum.

PROGRAMS: Exhibits

COLLECTIONS: [1800s]

HOURS: June 20-Aug 25 Daily 10-4

ADMISSION: No charge

ST. MARTINS

9608
Quaco Historical and Library Society, Inc.
236 Main St, E0G2Z0; (p) (506) 833-4740; bar@nbnet.nb.ca

Private non-profit/ 1972/ staff: 15(v)/ members: 40

HISTORICAL SOCIETY; HISTORY MUSEUM: Preserves history and heritage of the St. Martins area.

PROGRAMS: Annual Meeting; Community Outreach; Elder's Programs; Exhibits; Facility Rental; Family Programs; Festivals; Guided Tours; Interpretation; Lectures

COLLECTIONS: Materials relating to St. Martins shipbuilding heritage and community.

HOURS: June-Sept Daily

ADMISSION: $2; Students $1; Seniors $1

ST. STEPHEN

9609
Charlotte County Museum
443 Milltown Blvd, EoG 2X0; (p) (506) 466-3295

Private non-profit/ 1980/ staff: 7(p); 40(v)/publication: *Exploring the Past - Historic*

HISTORICAL SOCIETY; HISTORY MUSEUM: Collects, preserves, and interprets the social and economic life of Charlotte County.

PROGRAMS: Annual Meeting; Community Outreach; Exhibits; Festivals; Guided Tours; Interpretation; Publication; Research Library/Archives

COLLECTIONS: [1780-1920] Social, economic, agricultural life of Charlotte County; shipbuilding and lumbering.

HOURS: June-Aug M-Su 9:30-4:30; Sept by appt

ADMISSION: Donations accepted

SUSSEX

9610
Agricultural Museum of New Brunswick
28 Perry St, E4E 2N7 [PO Box 3183, E4E 2N7]; (p) (506) 433-6799

1983/ staff: 3(p); 3(v)/ members: 85

HISTORY MUSEUM

PROGRAMS: Annual Meeting; Community Outreach; Exhibits

COLLECTIONS: [Late 1800s-early 1900s] Agricultural artifacts.

HOURS: June-Sept 15 Su 12-5, M-Sa 10-5

ADMISSION: $2, Family $5

NEWFOUNDLAND

BONAVISTA

9611
Cape Bonavista Lighthouse Provincial Historic Site
Hwy 230, A1B 4J6 [PO Box 8700, A1B 4J6]; (p) (709) 468-7444; (f) (709) 468-7300

Provincial/ Dept of Tourism, Culture, and Recreation/ staff: 3(f); 3(p)

HISTORIC SITE; HOUSE MUSEUM

INTERPRETATION: Community/State History;

PROGRAMS: Exhibits; Guided Tours; Interpretation

COLLECTIONS: [1870] Furnishing, catoptric light with six argand burners and reflectors, and a clockwork winding mechanism.

HOURS: Mid-June-Early Oct Daily

9612
Mockbeggar Plantation Provincial Historic Site
Roper St, A0C 1B0 [PO Box 8700/Dept of Tourism, Culture & Recreation, St John's, A1B 4J6]; (p) (709) 468-7300, (800) 563-6353; (f) (709) 729-0870; capebonavista@nf.aibn.com

1990/ staff: 4(f)

HISTORIC SITE; HOUSE MUSEUM

PROGRAMS: Exhibits; Guided Tours; Interpretation

COLLECTIONS: [1870-1939] Domestic furnishings, china, linens; site on early fishing plantation; Gordon Bradley historical artifacts.

HOURS: Mid June-early Oct Daily

BOYD'S COVE

9613
Boyd's Cove Beothuk Interpretation Centre
[PO Box 8700, St. John's, A1B 4J6]; (p) (709) 729-0592, (709) 656-3114; (f) (709) 729-0592; boydscove@nf.aibn.com

Provincial/ 1997/ Dept of Tourism, Culture and Recreation/ staff: 2(f); 2(p)

HISTORIC SITE: Preserves history of Beothuk people cira AD 1650-1720.

PROGRAMS: Exhibits; Guided Tours; Interpretation; Lectures

COLLECTIONS: [1650-1720] Archaeological artifacts: projectile points, adapted iron, bone, and glass.

HOURS: Mid June-Early Oct Daily 10-5:30

ADMISSION: $2.50; Group rates

CARBONEAR

9614
Baccalieu Trail Heritage Corporation
[PO Box 249, A1Y 1B6]; (p) (709) 596-1906; (f) (709) 596-2121

Private non-profit/ 1992/ staff: 1(f); 20(p); 15(v)

HISTORIC PRESERVATION AGENCY; LIVING HISTORY/OUTDOOR MUSEUM: Protects, preserves, promotes, and develops the heritage resources of the Baccalieu Trail—the Bay de Verde Peninsula.

PROGRAMS: Annual Meeting; Community Outreach; Exhibits; Interpretation; Lectures; School-Based Curriculum

COLLECTIONS: [Prehistory, 17th c-1949]

HOURS: July-Sept M-F 9-5

ADMISSION: $2

CUPIDS

9615
Cupids Historical Society, Inc.
478 Seaforest Dr, A0A 2B0 [PO Box 89, A0A 2B0]; (p) (709) 528-3467; roy.dawo@nf.sympatico.ca; www3.nfsympatico.ca/sdowe/cup.htm

1983/ staff: 15(v)/ members: 30

HISTORICAL SOCIETY: Preserves historic items of community; managest and promotes archaeological site of the John Guy 1610 plantation; operates Cupids Museum.

PROGRAMS: Annual Meeting; Exhibits; Festivals; Film/Video; Guided Tours; Interpretation; Lectures; Reenactments

COLLECTIONS: [1610-1660, 1910] Artifacts from colonial 1610-60 period, early schooling exhibit, giant Union Jack flag.

HOURS: Daily 10-5

ADMISSION: $2

GRAND BANK

9616
Southern Newfoundland Seamen's Museum
Marine Dr, A0E 1W0 [PO Box 1109, A0E 1W0]; (p) (709) 832-1484; (f) (709) 832-2053; gcrews@nf.sympatico.ca; www.delweb.com/nfmuseum

State/ staff: 2(f); 2(p)

HISTORY MUSEUM: Exhibits and interprets the regional history.

PROGRAMS: Concerts; Elder's Programs; Exhibits; Family Programs; Film/Video; Guided Tours; Interpretation; Lectures

COLLECTIONS: Artifacts, memorabilia, and material goods relating to the maritime history.

HOURS: May-Oct Su-Sa 9-5

GRAND FALLS WINDSOR

9617
Mary March Regional Museum
St. Catherine St, A2A 1W9; (p) (709) 292-4522; (f) (709) 292-4526; demasduit@thezone.net; www.delweb.com/nfmuseum

Joint/ staff: 2(f); 2(p)

HISTORY MUSEUM: Exhibits and interprets the regional history, prehistory, and natural history.

PROGRAMS: Concerts; Elder's Programs; Exhibits; Family Programs; Film/Video; Guided Tours; Interpretation; Lectures; Living History

COLLECTIONS: Historical and archaeological artifact.

HOURS: May-Oct Su-Sa 9-5

HARBOUR GRACE

9618
Conception Bay Museum
Water St, A0A 2M0 [PO Box 298, A0A 2M0]; (p) (709) 596-1309; (f) (709) 596-5465

Private non-profit/ 1969/ staff: 1(f); 7(p); 23(v)

HISTORIC SITE; HISTORY MUSEUM: Preserves, protects, collects, exhibits, and interprets the cultural human and built heritage of Harbour Grace and surrounding Conception Bay Areas.

PROGRAMS: Annual Meeting; Concerts; Elder's Programs; Exhibits; Family Programs; Guided Tours; Interpretation; Reenactments; Research Library/Archives

COLLECTIONS: [1610-1900] 1610 pirate exhibit; 1700-1800 Fisherman's room; period sitting room, aviation room, sewing area, photos, archives; Amelia Earhart exhibit.

HOURS: Summer Daily 10-1/1:30-5

ADMISSION: $2, Children $1, Seniors $1.50; Group rates

LABRADOR

9619
Labrador Straits Craft and Museum
Lanse au Amour Branch Rd, A0K 5S0 [West St. Modeste, A0K 5S0]; (p) (709) 927-5733

Private non-profit/ 1978/ staff: 1(p)/ members: 90

HISTORIC PRESERVATION AGENCY; HISTORY MUSEUM

PROGRAMS: Community Outreach; Exhibits; Living History; Research Library/Archives

COLLECTIONS: [Late 1800s-early 1900 and 6000 BC] Artifacts: Indian burial site, 6000 BC, and local inhabitants 1800s-1900s.

HOURS: June 15-Sept 15

LAMALINE

9620
Lamaline Heritage Society and Lamaline Heritage Museum
Main St, A0E 2C0 [PO Box 3, A0E 2C0]; (p) (709) 857-2864; (f) (709) 857-2021

Private non-profit/ 1993/ staff: 1(p); 10(v)

HISTORICAL SOCIETY; HISTORY MUSEUM: Preserves and protects the natural and cultural heritage.

PROGRAMS: Annual Meeting; Exhibits; Festivals; Interpretation

COLLECTIONS: [Early 1900s] Local history, artifacts, veterans' display, folklore, genealogy, 1929 tidal wave information, portraits, newspaper articles.

HOURS: May-Sept Sa-Su 10-5

ADMISSION: $2

LAWN

9621
Lawn Heritage Museum
Main St, A0E 2C0 [General Delivery, A0E 2C0]; (p) (709) 873-2319; (f) (709) 857-2021

Private non-profit/ 1989/ staff: 1(p); 10(v)

HISTORY MUSEUM: Preserves local heritage.

PROGRAMS: Annual Meeting; Exhibits; Family Programs; Festivals; Guided Tours; School-Based Curriculum

COLLECTIONS: [Early 1900s] Local history, artifacts, interpretative displays, exhibits, newspaper articles, photos.

HOURS: May-Sept

PORT AU CHOIX

9622
Port au Choix National Historic Site
Point Riche Rd, A0K 4C0 [PO Box 140, A0K 4C0]; (p) (709) 861-3522; (f) (709) 861-3827; PARKSINFO@pch.gc.ca

Federal/ 1974/ staff: 1(f); 6(p)

HISTORIC SITE: Preserves history of aboriginal occupation, European contact and early French fishery from 1713-1904.

PROGRAMS: Community Outreach; Elder's Programs; Exhibits; Family Programs; Film/Video; Guided Tours; Interpretation; Lectures

COLLECTIONS: [4000 BP-present] Prehistoric artifacts belonging to the Maritime Archaic Indian culture. Gros water and Dorset Paleoeskimo artifacts; bone, antler, stone, and ivory.

HOURS: June-Oct Daily 9:30-5

ADMISSION: $2.75, Student $1.50, Seniors $2.25; Under 6 free

PORT AU PORT

9623
Our Lady of Mercy Church and Museum
Main St, A0N 1T0 [PO Box 239, A0N 1T0]; (p) (709) 648-2632

Private non-profit/ 1991/ staff: 4(p); 6(v)

HISTORY MUSEUM: Collects, preserves, and interprets artifacts pertaining to the cultural, religious, and economic history of the Port au Port area.

PROGRAMS: Annual Meeting; Exhibits; Facility Rental; Guided Tours; Interpretation

COLLECTIONS: [1889-1960] Artifacts and archival materials pertaining to Roman Catholic religion, limestone mining, local culture, and economy.

HOURS: Apr-Dec 10-5

ADMISSION: $1, Children $0.50

SPRINGDALE

9624
H.C. Grant Heritage Museum
90 Main St, A0J 1T0 [PO Box 57, A0J 1T0]; (p) (709) 683-4313; (f) (704) 673-4969

City/ 1981/ staff: 1(f); 2(p)

HOUSE MUSEUM: Maintains museum.

PROGRAMS: Elder's Programs; Guided Tours

COLLECTIONS: [1940s-1950s] Historic Grant House, household items, artifacts, textiles, and material.

HOURS: June-Aug T-Sa 11-9

ST. ANTHONY

9625
Sir Wilfred Thomason Grenfell Historical Society, The
[PO Box 93, A0K4S0]; (p) (709) 454-4010; (f) (709) 454-4047; www3.nf.sympat.co.ca\grenfell

1976/ staff: 1(f); 1(p); 1(v)/ members: 50/publication: A Most Venturesome Course

HISTORIC SITE; HISTORICAL SOCIETY; HISTORY MUSEUM; HOUSE MUSEUM: Preserves artifacts, stories, and writings of Sir Wilfred Thomason Grenfell.

PROGRAMS: Annual Meeting; Concerts; Exhibits; Facility Rental; Family Programs; Festivals; Film/Video; Garden Tours; Guided Tours; Interpretation; Lectures; Living History; Publication; Reenactments; Research Library/Archives; Theatre

ST. JOHN'S

9626
Archives of the Roman Catholic Archdiocese
49 Bonaventure Ave, A1C 5M3 [PO Box 1363, A1C 5M3]; (p) (709) 726-3660; (f) (709) 739-6458; ldohey@seascape.com; www.del-web.com/rcec/

Private non-profit/ 1888/ staff: 2(f); 1(p); 1(v)/ members: 1

LIBRARY AND/OR ARCHIVES: Preserves history of the Catholic Church in Newfoundland, Canada.

PROGRAMS: Interpretation; Research Library/Archives

COLLECTIONS: [1784-1988] Bishops of Newfoundland papers.

HOURS: Yr M-F 9:30-4:15

9627
Cathedral of St. John the Baptist, The
Gower St, A1C 2A8 [68 Queen's Rd, A1C 2A8]; (p) (709) 726-5677; (f) (709) 726-2053; cathedral@nf.aibn.com

Private non-profit/ 1699/ staff: 4(f); 100(v)

HISTORIC SITE: Preserves cathedral on National Historic Site.

PROGRAMS: Community Outreach; Concerts; Exhibits; Guided Tours; Publication; Research Library/Archives; School-Based Curriculum

COLLECTIONS: [1100 AD-1990s] Church administration and organization; baptismal, marriage, and burial records to 1752, architectural PLANS.

HOURS: Varies

ADMISSION: No charge

9628
Centre for Newfoundland Studies
Memorial University of Newfoundland Libraries, A1B 3Y1; (p) (709) 737-7475; (f) (709) 737-2153; jritcey@mun.ca; www.mun.ca/library/cns/cns.html

1965/ staff: 15(f); 7(p)/publication: Newfoundland Periodical Article Bibliography

RESEARCH CENTER: The center collects all materials relating to Newfoundland and Labrador; past and present.

PROGRAMS: Publication; Research Library/Archives

COLLECTIONS: [Prehistory-present] The largest collection of all types of printed materials on Newfoundland and Labrador, or created in Newfoundland on Labrador.

HOURS: Yr M-Th 8:30-11, F 8:30-6, Sa 10-6, Su 1:30-10

9629
Commissariat House Provincial Historic Site
King's Bridge Rd, A1B 4J6 [Dept Tourism, Box 8700, A1B 4J6]; (p) (709) 729-6730, (800) 563-6353; (f) (709) 729-0870; commissariat@nf.aibn.com

1977/ staff: 1(f); 1(p)

HISTORIC SITE; HOUSE MUSEUM

PROGRAMS: Exhibits; Guided Tours; Interpre-

tation; Lectures; Living History; Publication

COLLECTIONS: [1830] Office and domestic furnishings.

HOURS: June-Oct Daily 10-5:30

ADMISSION: $2.50; Under 13 free

9630
Heart's Content Cable Station Provincial Historic Site
Hwy 80, A1B 4J6 [Dept. Tourism, PO Box 8700, A1B 4J6]; (p) (800) 563-6353; (f) (709) 729-0870; heartscontent@nf.aibn.com

1974

HISTORIC SITE: Preserves history of first successful transatlantic telegraph cable in 1874 cable station.

PROGRAMS: Exhibits; Film/Video; Guided Tours; Interpretation; Lectures; Living History; Publication

COLLECTIONS: [1866-1965] Telegraphic equipment.

HOURS: Mid June-early Oct Daily 10-5:30

ADMISSION: $2.50; Group rates

9631
Hiscock House Provincial Historic Site
Church Rd, A1B 4J6 [PO Box 8700, A1B 4J6]; (p) (800) 729-6353, (709) 464-2042; (f) (709) 729-0870; tourisminfo@mail.gov.nf.ca

1982/ staff: 1(f)

HISTORIC SITE; HOUSE MUSEUM

PROGRAMS: Exhibits; Guided Tours; Interpretation; Publication

COLLECTIONS: [Early 20th c] Domestic furnishings of Hiscock family.

HOURS: Mid June-early Oct Daily 10-5:30

ADMISSION: $2.50; Group rates

9632
James J. O'Mara Pharmacy Museum
488 Water St Apothecary Hall, A1E 1B3; (p) (709) 753-5877; (f) (709) 753-8615

1989/ staff: 4(p); 10(v)

HISTORIC SITE; HISTORY MUSEUM: Preserves history of pharmacy as it was practiced in Newfoundland.

PROGRAMS: Exhibits; Guided Tours; Interpretation

COLLECTIONS: [1890-1950] Site: restored drug store: oak drug store fixtures, apothecary bottles, tools.

HOURS: Mid June-early Sept Daily 10-5

ADMISSION: No charge

9633
Lillian Stevenson Nursing Archives and Museum, The
LA Miller Centre, Forest Rd, A1A 1E5; (p) (709) 737-5911; (f) (709) 737-6969

Private non-profit/ 1981/ staff: 5(v)

HISTORY MUSEUM; LIBRARY AND/OR ARCHIVES: Preserves history of General Hospital School of Nursing.

PROGRAMS: Exhibits; Guided Tours

COLLECTIONS: [1940s-1950s] Hospital and nursing equipment, instruments, beds, mannequins, uniforms, artifacts, artificial respirator, photographs of records of school of nursing and hospital.

HOURS: Yr Th

9634
M.U.N. Folklore and Language Archive
Memorial Univ of Newfoundland, A1B 3X8; (p) (709) 737-8401; (f) (709) 737-4718; MUNFLA@mun.ca

1968/ staff: 1(f); 15(p)

LIBRARY AND/OR ARCHIVES: Preserves and encourages documentation of folklore, folklife, oral history, and popular culture of Newfoundland and Labrador.

COLLECTIONS: [20th c] 30,000 audio tapes, 20,000 photographs.

HOURS: Yr M-F 10-4:30

9635
Museum Association of Newfoundland and Labrador
1 Springdale St, A1C 5X3 [PO Box 5785, A1C 5X3]; (p) (709) 722-9034; (f) (709) 722-9035; uokshevsky@mail.gov.nf.ca; www.delweb.com/manl/

Private non-profit/ 1980/ staff: 1(f); 2(p); 11(v)/ members: 280

Preserves cultural and natural heritage.

HOURS: Yr

9636
Newfoundland Historical Society
Colonial Bldg, Military Rd, A1C 2C9; (p) (709) 722-3191; (f) (709) 729-0578; nhs@thezone.net; www.infonet.st-johns.nf.ca/providers/nfldhist

1905/ staff: 1(p)/ members: 500

HISTORICAL SOCIETY: Promotes knowledge and public discussion of the history and heritage of Newfoundland and Labrador.

PROGRAMS: Annual Meeting; Community Outreach; Lectures; Publication; Research Library/Archives

COLLECTIONS: [1850-1995] Archives, donated collections, materials related to Newfoundland, books, journals.

HOURS: Yr T-Th 9:30-4:15

ADMISSION: No charge

9637
Newfoundland Museum
285 Duckworth St, A1B 4G6 [PO Box 8700, A1B 4G6]; (p) (709) 729-2329, (709) 729-6001; (f) (709) 729-2179; phoulden@mail.gov.nfca; www.delweb.com/nfmuseum

Provincial/ staff: 24(f); 4(p); 30(v)

HISTORY MUSEUM: Collects, preserves, researches, and interprets the province's history, prehistory, and natural history.

PROGRAMS: Concerts; Elder's Programs; Exhibits; Family Programs; Film/Video; Guided Tours; Interpretation; School-Based Curriculum; Theatre

COLLECTIONS: 100,000 natural history specimens, 23,000 historical artifacts; 1 million archaeological/ethnological artifacts.

HOURS: Yr T-F 9-5, Sa-Su 10-6

9638
Point Amour Lighthouse Provincial Historic Site
Off Hwy 510, L'Anse Amour Rd, Labrador, A1B 4J6 [PO Box 8700, A1B 4J6]; (p) (709) 729-0592, (709) 927-5825; (f) (709) 729-0870; lbadcock@tourism.gov.nf.ca

State/ 1858/ staff: 3(f)

HISTORIC SITE: Maintains and preserves lightkeeper's residence.

PROGRAMS: Exhibits; Guided Tours; Interpretation; Publication

COLLECTIONS: [19th c] Lighthouse, cartographic exhibits, furnishings, photos.

HOURS: Mid-June-early Oct Daily 10-5:30

ADMISSION: $2.50; Group

9639
Quidi Bidi Battery Provincial Historic Site
Cuckhold's Cove Rd, A1B 4J6 [PO Box 8700, A1B 4J6]; (p) (709) 729-2977, (709) 729-6353; (f) (709) 729-0870; info@mail.gov.vf.ca

State/ 1967/ staff: 3(f)

HISTORIC SITE: Maintains reconstructed coastal battery.

PROGRAMS: Exhibits; Guided Tours; Interpretation; Publication

COLLECTIONS: [1812] Period furnishings, equipment, muskets.

HOURS: Mid June-early Oct Daily

9640
St. Thomas' Anglican Church
8 Military Rd, A1C 2C4; (p) (709) 576-6632; (f) (709) 576-2541; st.thomas@nf.sympatico.ca

1836/ staff: 6(f)/ members: 1200/publication: *Garrison Newsletter*

HISTORY MUSEUM: Preserves church history.

PROGRAMS: Annual Meeting; Community Outreach; Concerts; Elder's Programs; Facility Rental; Family Programs; Festivals; Guided Tours; Interpretation; Lectures; Living History; Publication; Reenactments; Research Library/Archives; School-Based Curriculum; Theatre

COLLECTIONS: [1836-present] Church artifacts; birth, death, and marriage records; historical documents; pictures.

HOURS: Yr M-F 9-5, Sa on request, Su after services

ADMISSION: Donations accepted

9641
Trinity Interpretation Centre
West St, A1B 4J6 [PO Box 8700, A1B 4J6]; (p) (709) 464-2042, (800) 563-6353; (f) (709) 729-0870; info@mail.gov.nf.ca

State/ 1991/ staff: 9(f)

HISTORIC SITE: Social, cultural, and commercial archives.

PROGRAMS: Exhibits; Interpretation

COLLECTIONS: [17th-20th c] Shipwrecks artifacts.

HOURS: Mid June-early Oct Daily 10-5:30

ADMISSION: $2.50

TRINITY

9642
Lester-Garland Premises Provincial Historic Site
West St, A1B 4J6 [Dept. Tourism, Box 8700, St John's, A1B 4J6]; (p) (709) 464-2042, (709) 729-0592; (f) (709) 464-2349; lbadcock@tourism.gov.nf.ca; www.gov.nf.ca/tourism

Provincial/ 1993/ Dept Tourism, Culture, and Recreation/ staff: 1(f)

HISTORIC SITE

PROGRAMS: Guided Tours; Interpretation; Living History

COLLECTIONS: [19th-early 20th c] Furnishing; sites: mercantile building.

HOURS: June 12-Nov 23 Daily 10-5:30

ADMISSION: $2.50

TWILLINGATE

9643
Twillingate Museum Association
St Peter's Church Rd, A0G 4M0 [PO Box 369, A0G 4M0]; (p) (709) 884-2845; (f) (709) 884-2044; twa@nf.aibn.com

Private non-profit/ 1973/ staff: 2(f); 1(p); 15(v)/ members: 15

HISTORIC PRESERVATION AGENCY; HISTORY MUSEUM; HOUSE MUSEUM; LIVING HISTORY/OUTDOOR MUSEUM; RESEARCH CENTER: Promotes and preserves local history and culture.

PROGRAMS: Annual Meeting; Exhibits; Guided Tours; Interpretation; Publication; Research Library/Archives; School-Based Curriculum

COLLECTIONS: [1900] Genealogy material, Maritime Archaic Indian artifacts unearthed at Twillingate, material on Georgina Sterling, Twillingate born opera singer.

HOURS: Early May-early Oct Daily 9-9

ADMISSION: $1

WESLEYVILLE

9644
Bonavista North Regional Museum
[PO Box 257, A0G 4R0]; (p) (709) 536-2110, (709) 536-2077

1979/ staff: 3(p); 2(v)

HISTORY MUSEUM; MARITIME MUSEUM: Promotes Newfoundland and maritime history.

PROGRAMS: Exhibits; Guided Tours; Interpretation

COLLECTIONS: [Late 19th-early-20th c] Logging, domestic life, fishery, and sealing.

HOURS: June-Aug Daily 11-6 and by appt

ADMISSION: $2, Children $1

NORTHWEST TERRITORIES

IGALUIT

9645
Nunatta Sunakkutaangit Museum Society
Bldg 212, X0A 0H0 [PO Box 1900, X0A 0H0]; (p) (867) 979-5537; (f) (867) 979-4533; museum@nunanet.com

Private non-profit/ 1969/ staff: 1(p); 9(v)/ members: 55

ART MUSEUM; HISTORIC PRESERVATION AGENCY; HISTORICAL SOCIETY; HISTORY MUSEUM; TRIBAL MUSEUM

PROGRAMS: Annual Meeting; Community Outreach; Elder's Programs; Exhibits; Facility Rental; Film/Video; Guided Tours; Interpretation; Lectures; School-Based Curriculum

COLLECTIONS: [1950-1970] 300 pieces of Inuit sculpture and artwork; historical/archeological artifacts; documents and photos.

HOURS: Feb-Dec T-Su 1-5

ADMISSION: No

YELLOWKNIFE

9646
Prince of Wales Northern Heritage Centre
Ingraham Trail, X1A 2L9 [Box 1320, X1A 2L9]; (p) (876) 873-7551; (f) (867) 873-0205; www.pwnhc.learnnet.nt.ca

1979/ staff: 25(f); 2(p)

ART MUSEUM; HISTORY MUSEUM; RESEARCH CENTER: Maintains museum and archives of Northwest Territories.

PROGRAMS: Community Outreach; Exhibits; Facility Rental; Interpretation; Lectures; Research Library/Archives

COLLECTIONS: [1900] Archives: historical, legal, and financial significance to the Northwest Territories; 113,000 artifacts, 7,200 publications, 141 newspapers, 300 linear meters of government records, 130 linear meters of private records, 250,000 photos, 5,000 sound recordings.

HOURS: Yr T-Su 10:30-5

ADMISSION: Donations accepted

NOVA SCOTIA

AMHERST

9647
Cumberland County Museum
150 Church St, B4H 3C4; (p) (902) 667-2561; (f) (902) 667-0996; ccmuseum@lstar.ca; www.business.auracom.com/madhouse.ccm

Private non-profit/ 1980/ staff: 1(f); 1(p); 12(v)/ members: 120/publication: *Cumberland Reflector Newsletter*

ART MUSEUM; GARDEN; HISTORIC SITE;

HISTORICAL SOCIETY; HISTORY MUSEUM

PROGRAMS: Annual Meeting; Community Outreach; Elder's Programs; Exhibits; Facility Rental; Family Programs; Festivals; Publication; Research Library/Archives

COLLECTIONS: [1870-1910] Artifacts, oral history, maps, photographs, land grants, documents.

HOURS: Yr

ADMISSION: $1

ANNAPOLIS ROYAL

9648
Fort Anne National Historic Site
295 St George St, B0S 1A0 [PO Box 9, B0S 1A0]; (p) (902) 532-2321; (f) (902) 532-2232; atlantic_parksinfo@pch.yc.ca; parkscanada. pch.gc.ca; (c) Annapolis

Federal/ 1917/ staff: 3(f)

HISTORIC SITE: Preserves local military history.

PROGRAMS: Exhibits; Guided Tours; Interpretation

COLLECTIONS: [17th-late 18th c] Earthwork fortifications, an early 18th century gun powder magazine and 1797 British field officers' quarters.

HOURS: May 15-Oct 15 Daily 9-6

ADMISSION: $2.75, Family $7, Children $1.35, Seniors $2.25

9649
Historic Restoration Society of Annapolis County
136 St George St, B0S 1A0 [PO Box 503, B0S 1A0]; (p) (902) 532-7754, (902) 532-2041; kirbywr@ednet.ns.ca; (c) Annapolis

Private non-profit/ 1967/ staff: 1(f); 2(p)/ 40(v)/ members: 175

GENEALOGICAL SOCIETY; HISTORIC SITE; HISTORICAL SOCIETY; HISTORY MUSEUM; RESEARCH CENTER: Preserves and restores historic sites and buildings.

PROGRAMS: Annual Meeting; Community Outreach; Exhibits; Facility Rental; Family Programs; Guided Tours; Interpretation; Research Library/Archives; School-Based Curriculum

COLLECTIONS: [1850-1910] Archival/photographic, genealogical, reference library, local social historic material, costumes.

HOURS: Yr M-F, Sa

ADMISSION: No charge

9650
Port Royal National Historic Site of Canada
53 Historic Ln, B0S 1A0 [PO Box 9, B0S 1A0]; (p) (902) 532-2321; (f) (902) 532-2232; www.parkscanada.gc.ca; (c) Annapolis

Federal/ 1940/ Parks Canada, Dept. of Canada Heritage/ staff: 8(p)

HISTORIC SITE; LIVING HISTORY/OUTDOOR MUSEUM: Preserves early European settlements; maintains history of French fur traders.

PROGRAMS: Guided Tours; Interpretation; School-Based Curriculum

COLLECTIONS: [1605-1613]

HOURS: May 15-Oct 15 Daily 9-6

ADMISSION: $2.75, Family $7, Seniors

BADDECK

9651
Alexander Graham Bell National Historic Site
[PO Box 159, B0E 1B0]; (p) (902) 295-2069; (f) (902) 295-3496; agbellhs@auracom.com

Federal/ 1956/ Canadian Heritage-Parks Canada/ staff: 4(f); 3(p)

HISTORIC PRESERVATION AGENCY: Commemorates legacy of Alexander Graham Bell.

PROGRAMS: Concerts; Exhibits; Facility Rental; Guided Tours; Interpretation; Research Library/Archives

COLLECTIONS: [1847-1922] 2000 artifacts, 1900 photos, 1000 copy negatives, 500 prints; archives.

HOURS: June Daily 9-6; July 1-Aug 1 Daily 8:30-7:30; Sept 1-Oct 15 Daily 8:30-6; Oct 16-May 31 Daily 9-5

ADMISSION: $4.25, Family $10.75, Student $2.25, Seniors

BRIDGETOWN

9652
Bridgetown and Area Historical Society
12 Queen St, B0S 1C0 [PO Box 645, B0S 1C0]; (p) (902) 665-4530; lourie@fox.nstn.ca

Private non-profit/ 1979/ staff: 1(f); 25(v)/ members: 75/publication: *History of Bridgetown*

HISTORIC SITE; HISTORICAL SOCIETY; HISTORY MUSEUM: Operates the James House Museum and Tea Room; preserves local history.

PROGRAMS: Annual Meeting; Exhibits; Facility Rental; Festivals; Guided Tours; Publication; Research Library/Archives

COLLECTIONS: [1860-1900] Shipbuilding and farming

CLEMENTSPORT

9653
Old St. Edward's Loyalist Church Museum
34 Old Post Rd, B0S 1E0 [PO Box 171, B0S 1E0]; (c) Annapolis

1916/ staff: 1(p); 4(v)

HISTORIC SITE; HISTORY MUSEUM: Maintains museum in former Loyalist church.

PROGRAMS: Guided Tours; Interpretation

COLLECTIONS: [Late 18th-early 19th c] Household articles, original land grants.

HOURS: June 30-Aug 31 T-Su 10-4

ADMISSION: No charge

COLE HARBOUR

9654
Cole Harbour Rural Heritage Society
417 Poplar Dr, B2W 4L2; (p) (902) 434-0222; (f) (902) 434-0222; chrhs@hotmail.com; is.dal.ca/~stanet/databade/colehbr.html; (c) Halifax

Private non-profit/ 1973/ staff: 2(f); 8(p); 30(v)/ members: 144

GARDEN; HISTORICAL SOCIETY; HISTORY MUSEUM; HOUSE MUSEUM; LIVING HISTORY/OUTDOOR MUSEUM; RESEARCH CENTER: Collects, preserves, and interprets cultural and natural history.

PROGRAMS: Annual Meeting; Community Outreach; Concerts; Exhibits; Facility Rental; Family Programs; Festivals; Garden Tours; Guided Tours; Interpretation; Lectures; Living History; Research Library/Archives; School-Based Curriculum

COLLECTIONS: [Late 18th-mid 20th c] Farming, fishing, household and personal items; documents, photos, oral histories; heritage plants and livestock.

HOURS: May 15-Oct 15 Daily 10-4 and by appt

ADMISSION: Donations accepted

DINGWALL

9655
North Highlands Community Museum
Cape N on the Cabot Trail, B0C 1G0 [RR # 1, Cape N, B0C 1G0]; (p) (902) 383-2579; (c) Victoria

Private non-profit/ 1979/ staff: 2(f); 2(p); 30(v)/ members: 20/publication: *Cape North and Vicinity, Up Country*

GENEALOGICAL SOCIETY; HISTORIC PRESERVATION AGENCY; HISTORY MUSEUM; LIVING HISTORY/OUTDOOR MUSEUM; RESEARCH CENTER: Collects historical data, obtains and restores artifacts, maintains and operates museum buildings, and promotes interest in local history.

PROGRAMS: Annual Meeting; Community Outreach; Concerts; Exhibits; Publication; Research Library/Archives

COLLECTIONS: [1800s-mid 1900] Pioneer life and traditions; genealogy, photos; Cabot Trail, Canso Causeway, and local gypsm mining exhibits.

HOURS: June-Oct Daily 10-6

ADMISSION: Donation accepted

GLACE BAY

9656
Cape Breton Miners' Museum
42 Birkley St, B1A 5T8; (p) (902) 849-4522; (f) (902) 849-8022; cbominers@cbnet.ns.ca; www.highlander.cbnet.ns.ca/comucntr/miners/museum.html

1964/ Cape Breton Miners' Foundation/ staff: 2(f); 6(p); 25(v)

HISTORY MUSEUM: Collects, preserves, and displays artifacts, equipment, photographs, books, and documents that relate to coal mining industries and communities.

PROGRAMS: Annual Meeting; Concerts; Exhibits; Facility Rental; Festivals; Guided Tours; Interpretation; Lectures; Research Library/Archives; Theatre

COLLECTIONS: [19th c-present] Coal mining artifacts, equipment, photographs, books, and documents.

HOURS: Yr June 4-Aug 31 Daily W-M 10-6, T 10-7; Sept 4-May 31 M-F 10-4

ADMISSION: $4.50, Children $2.50

GREENWOOD

9657
Greenwood Military Aviation Museum
Ward Rd, B0P 1N0 [PO Box 786, B0P 1N0]; (p) (902) 765-1494; (f) (902) 765-5747; bnelson@ns.sympatieo.ca; gmam.ednet.ms.ca

Federal/ 1995/ staff: 1(f); 3(p); 42(v)/ members: 42

HISTORY MUSEUM: Preserves military aviation history.

PROGRAMS: Annual Meeting; Elder's Programs; Exhibits; Facility Rental; Festivals; Film/Video; Garden Tours; Guided Tours; School-Based Curriculum; Theatre

COLLECTIONS: [1942-present] Aviation artifacts, aircraft restoration: Neptune, Argus, T-33 Shooting Star, AVRO ANSON

HOURS: Yr June-Sept Daily 9-5; Sept-May T-Sa 10-4

ADMISSION: No charge

HALIFAX

9658
Halifax Citadel National Historic Site
[PO Box 9080 Station A, B3K 5M7]; (p) (902) 426-5080; (f) (902) 426-4228; www.parkscanada.gc.ca

Federal/ staff: 20(f); 80(p); 20(v)

HISTORIC SITE

PROGRAMS: Community Outreach; Exhibits; Facility Rental; Guided Tours; Interpretation; Living History; Reenactments; Research Library/Archives; School-Based Curriculum

COLLECTIONS: [1749-1900]

HOURS: Yr May-Oct

9659
Maritime Command Museum
Across from 2730 Gottinger St, B3K 5X5 [PO Box 99000 Stn Forces, B3K 5X5]; (p) (902) 427-0550; (f) (902) 427-2218; museum@marlet.hlfx.dnd.ca; www.marlant.hlfx.dnd.ca/museum; (c) Halifax

Federal/ 1974/ staff: 1(f); 15(v)/publication: *The King's Yard*

HISTORY MUSEUM: Collects, preserves, and displays history of Canada's maritime military forces.

PROGRAMS: Community Outreach; Exhibits; Facility Rental; Guided Tours; Living History; Publication

COLLECTIONS: [1910-present] Uniforms, medals, model ships, weapons, books, works of art.

HOURS: Yr M-F 9:30-3

ADMISSION: No charge

9660
Nova Scotia Sport Hall of Fame
1645 Granville St Ste 101, B2W 5C6; (p) (902) 421-1266; (f) (902) 425-1148; nsshf@ns.sympatico.ca

HISTORIC PRESERVATION AGENCY: Collects, preserves, and promotes the sport history of Nova Scotia.

PROGRAMS: Annual Meeting; Community Outreach; Exhibits; Facility Rental; Interpretation; Publication; Research Library/Archives; School-Based Curriculum

COLLECTIONS: [1880-1980] Photographs, awards, trophies, sporting equipment, uniforms.

HOURS: Yr Sept-May M-F 10-4, Sa 1:30-3; June-Aug M-F 10-4, Sa 1:30-3, Su 10:30-1:30

IONA

9661
Nova Scotia Highland Village
4119 Hwy 223, B2C 1A3; (p) (902) 725-2272; (f) (902) 725-2227; highlandvillage@gov.ns.ca; html://highlandvillage.museum.gov.ns.ca; (c) Victoria

Private non-profit/ 1959/ staff: 16(f); 50(v)/ members: 100/publication: *The Village News*

HISTORY MUSEUM; LIVING HISTORY/OUTDOOR MUSEUM; RESEARCH CENTER: Preserves history and culture of Scottish Gaels in Nova Scotia; operates genealogy and family history center.

PROGRAMS: Annual Meeting; Community Outreach; Concerts; Elder's Programs; Exhibits; Facility Rental; Family Programs; Festivals; Film/Video; Guided Tours; Interpretation; Lectures; Living History; Publication; Reenactments; Research Library/Archives; School-Based Curriculum

COLLECTIONS: [1780-1920] 3,000 objects, 10 buildings.

HOURS: May 19-July 13 and Aug 27-Oct 14 Daily 9-6; July 14-Aug 26 Daily 9-8; Rest of Yr (Visitor Center only) M-F 9-5

ADMISSION: $5, Family $10, Student $2, Seniors $4

KENTVILLE

9662
Old Kings Courthouse Museum
37 Cornwallis St, B4N 2E2; (p) (902) 678-6237; (f) (902) 679-0066; khs@khsmens.sympatico.caglinx.com; (c) Kings

Private non-profit/ 1979/ staff: 1(f); 2(p); 25(v)/ members: 400

GENEALOGICAL SOCIETY; HISTORICAL SOCIETY; HISTORY MUSEUM: Owns and operates Old Kings Courthouse Museum; preserves and promotes cultural and natural history of Kings County.

PROGRAMS: Annual Meeting; Community Outreach; Exhibits; Facility Rental; Film/Video; Interpretation; Lectures; Research Library/rchives; Theatre

COLLECTIONS: [Mid 1700s-present] 15,000 artifacts, natural history materials, genealogical archives.

HOURS: Yr Sept-Apr T-F 9:30-4:30; May-June M-F 9:30-4:30; July-Aug M-F 9:30-4:30, Sa 9-4:30

LIVERPOOL

9663
Hank Snow Country Music Centre
148 Bristol Ave, B0T 1K0 [Box 1419, B0T
1K0]; (p) (902) 354-4675; (f) (902) 354-5199;
info@hanksnow.com; www.hanksnow.com; (c)
Queens

Private non-profit/ 1997/ staff: 1(f); 4(p); 30(v)/
members: 400/publication: *Movin' On*

HISTORY MUSEUM: Promotes and preserves
classic Canadian Country music.

PROGRAMS: Annual Meeting; Community
Outreach; Concerts; Exhibits; Facility Rental;
Festivals; Guided Tours; Publication

COLLECTIONS: [1905-present] Canadian
country music costumes, artifacts, and memorabilia; railroad artifacts.

HOURS: Yr mid May-mid Oct Daily 9-5 and by
appt

ADMISSION: $3, Seniors $2

LOUISBOURG

9664
**Fortress of Louisbourg National
Historic Site**
259 Park Service Rd, B1C 2G2; (p) (902)
733-2280; (f) (902) 733-2362;
louisbourg_info@pch.gc.ca; http://fortress.
uccb.ns.ca

Federal/ Parks Canada Agency/ staff: 80(f);
150(p); 1000(v)

BATTLEFIELD; HISTORIC SITE; LIBRARY
AND/OR ARCHIVES; LIVING HISTORY/OUT-
DOOR MUSEUM; RESEARCH CENTER:
Maintains a reconstructed 18 c French Colo-
nial seaport town comprising over 50 build-
ings.

PROGRAMS: Community Outreach; Con-
certs; Exhibits; Garden Tours; Guided Tours;
Interpretation; Living History; Publication;
Reenactments; Research Library/Archives

COLLECTIONS: [1713-1758] 6,000,000 artifacts, 750,000 pages of documentation, 350
town plans, rare book collection, 14,000 reproductions and antiques, 15,000 volume library,
4,000 pieces of reproduced 18c goods.

HOURS: May-Oct 31 Daily 9:30-5; July-Aug
Fsily 9-6

ADMISSION: $11, Family $27.50, Student
$5.50, Seniors $8.25

9665
**Sydney and Louisburg Railway
Historical Society**
Main St, B0A 1M0 [PO Box 35, B0A 1M0]; (p)
(902) 733-2767; (f) (902) 733-2157; (c) Cape
Breton

Private non-profit/ 1972/ staff: 4(p); 6(v)/ members: 200

HISTORICAL SOCIETY; HISTORY MUSEUM:
Preserves history of S&L Railroad.

PROGRAMS: Annual Meeting; Community
Outreach; Concerts; Exhibits; Family Programs; Guided Tours

COLLECTIONS: [1895-present] Railroad and
local history; rolling stock.

HOURS: May-June, Sept-Oct M-F 9-5; July-

Aug Daily 8-8
ADMISSION: Donations accepted

LUNENBURG

9666
**Fisheries Museum of the
Atlantic/Lunenburg Marine Museum
Society**
68 Bluenose Dr, B0J 2C0 [PO Box 1363, B0J
2C0]; (p) (902) 634-4794; (f) (902) 634-8990;
uc.tupperja@gov.ns.ca; www.fisheries.
museum.gov.ns.ca; (c) Lunenburg

Joint/ 1965/ staff: 9(f); 32(p); 19(v)/ members:
127

LIVING HISTORY/OUTDOOR MUSEUM;
MARITIME MUSEUM: Operates museum and
aquarium.

PROGRAMS: Exhibits; Facility Rental;
Film/Video; Interpretation; Lectures; Research
Library/Archives

COLLECTIONS: [1900-present] 9,530 artifacts, 4,930 photos, 15,800 manuscripts, 280
videos, 1,800 volumes in library.

HOURS: May 5-Oct 28 Daily

NEW ROSS

9667
Ross Farm Museum
Hwy # 12, B0J 2M0 [RR # 2, B0J 2M0]; (p)
(902) 689-2210; (f) (902) 689-2264; ross-
farm@gov.ns.ca; rossfarm.museum.gov.
ns.ca; (c) Lunenburg

Private non-profit/ 1970/ Board of Directors/
staff: 7(f); 20(p); 9(v)

GARDEN; HISTORIC SITE; HISTORY MUSE-
UM; LIVING HISTORY/OUTDOOR MUSEUM

PROGRAMS: Annual Meeting; Community
Outreach; Exhibits; Family Programs; Festivals; Garden Tours; Guided Tours; Interpretation; Living History; Publication; Research Li-
brary/Archives; School-Based Curriculum

COLLECTIONS: [1700s-1950] Agricultural implements, provincial plough collection.

HOURS: Jan-Mar M-F school programs 9:30-
4:30, Sa-Su 9:30-4:30; May-Oct Daily 9:30-
5:30

ADMISSION: $5, Family $10.50, Children $1;

ORANGEDALE

9668
Orangedale Station Association
RR # 1, B0E 2K0; (p) (902) 756-3384; (f)
(902) 756-2547; (c) Inverness

Private non-profit/ 1987/ staff: 3(p); 10(v)/
members: 14

HISTORIC SITE; HISTORY MUSEUM; RE-
SEARCH CENTER: Preserves and promotes
railroad heritage on Cape Breton Island.

PROGRAMS: Annual Meeting; Concerts; Exhibits; Film/Video; Guided Tours; Interpretation

COLLECTIONS: [1890s-1980s] Rolling stock,
archival collection of railroad history, documents, pictures, railroad station.

HOURS: July-Sept W-Su 10-6

ADMISSION: Donations accepted

PORT HASTINGS

9669
Port Hastings Historical Society
9 Church St, B0E 2T0 [PO Box 115, B0E
2T0]; (p) (902) 625-1295; (c) Inverness

Private non-profit/ 1982/ staff: 4(f); 20(v)/
members: 33

GENEALOGICAL SOCIETY; HISTORICAL
SOCIETY; HISTORY MUSEUM; HOUSE MU-
SEUM: Operates Port Hastings Museum and
Archives.

PROGRAMS: Community Outreach; Concerts; Elder's Programs; Exhibits; Family Programs; Guided Tours; Publication; Research
Library/Archives

COLLECTIONS: [1850-present] Articles, artifacts, photos, books, material depicting the
founding, settlement and development.

HOURS: June, Sept, Oct M-F 9-5; July, Aug M-
F 9-6, Sa-Su 12-4

SHELBURNE

9670
J.C. Williams Dory Shop Museum
#11 Dock St, B0T 1W0 [PO Box 39, B0T
1W0]; (p) (902) 875-3141; (f) (902) 875-4141;
(c) Shelburn

City/ 1983/ staff: 1(f); 4(p); 150(v)/ members: 49

HISTORICAL SOCIETY; HISTORY MUSEUM:
Preserves history and tradition of dory making.

PROGRAMS: Exhibits; Guided Tours

COLLECTIONS: [18th-19 c] Tools, materials,
and dory equipment.

HOURS: June-Sept Daily

9671
**Ross-Thomson House and Store
Museum**
9 Charlotte Lane, B0T 1W0 [PO Box 39,
B0T 1W0]; (p) (902) 875-3141; (f) (902) 875-
4141; (c) Shelburne

City/ 1949/ staff: 1(f); 4(p); 150(v)/ members: 49

GARDEN; HISTORY MUSEUM; HOUSE MU-
SEUM: Represents Loyalist lifestyle from the
American Revolution era.

PROGRAMS: Exhibits; Garden Tours; Guided
Tours; Interpretation

COLLECTIONS: [17th-18th c] 18th c store and
chandle, military artifacts pertinent to Shelburne County, 1885 house and garden.

HOURS: May 15-Oct 15 Daily

9672
**Shelburne County Genealogical
Society**
168 Water St, B0T 1W0 [PO Box 248, B0T
1W0]; (p) (902) 875-4299; gencentre@ns.
sympatico.ca; nsgna.ednet.ns.ca/shelburne;
(c) Shelburne

Private non-profit/ 1987/ staff: 1(p); 25(v)/
members: 259

GENEALOGICAL SOCIETY; RESEARCH
CENTER: Promotes and encourages study of
family history with emphasis on Shelburne
County residents.

PROGRAMS: Annual Meeting; Community
Outreach; Elder's Programs; Family Programs;

Guided Tours; Publication; Research Library/Archives

COLLECTIONS: [1760-1999] Mayflower descendants and Loyalist primary and secondary documentation; Master ship builders and photos of their boats, fishermen records; indexed records including church, census, school reports, funeral homes, Shelburne County cemeteries and heritage homes.

HOURS: Yr M-Sa 9-5

ADMISSION: $3

9673
Shelburne County Museum
8 Maiden Lane, B0T 1W0 [PO Box 39, B0T 1W0]; (p) (902) 875-3219; (f) (902) 875-4141; (c) Shelburne

1979/ staff: 2(f); 3(p); 150(v)

GARDEN; GENEALOGICAL SOCIETY; HISTORIC SITE; HISTORICAL SOCIETY; HISTORY MUSEUM; HOUSE MUSEUM; RESEARCH CENTER: Preserves Loyalist, Black Loyalist, MicMac and shipbuilding history of Shelburne.

PROGRAMS: Exhibits; Guided Tours; Interpretation

COLLECTIONS: [17th-19th c] Local artifacts and documents.

HOURS: Oct 15-May 14 T-Sa 9:30-12/2-5; May 15-Oct 15 Daily 9:30-5:30

ADMISSION: $3

SOUTH RAWDON

9674
South Rawdon Museum Society
1761 S Rawdon Rd, B0N 1Z0 [Site 3, Box 6, RR # 1, B0N 1Z0]; (p) (902) 757-2344; hbhaley@ns.sympatico.ca; www.rawdonmuseum.com; (c) Hants

Private non-profit/ 1967/ staff: 1(f); 1(p); 3(v)/ members: 7

HISTORIC PRESERVATION AGENCY; HISTORIC SITE; HISTORY MUSEUM: Preserves historical items.

PROGRAMS: Annual Meeting; Community Outreach; Exhibits; Guided Tours; Interpretation

COLLECTIONS: [1800-1950] Artifacts: household, garden, farm, and store; school records of attendance 1891-1959; genealogies.

HOURS: June-Sept 3 M-Th 11-5, F-Su 9-5 and by appt

ADMISSION: Donations accepted

ST. PETER'S

9675
Nicolas Denys Museum
Denys, B0E 3B0 [PO Box 249, B0E 3B0]; (p) (902) 535-2137; (c) Richmond

Private non-profit/ 1967/ staff: 2(f); 10(v)

HISTORICAL SOCIETY; HISTORY MUSEUM

PROGRAMS: Annual Meeting; Exhibits; Guided Tours; Reenactments

COLLECTIONS: [1650-1900] Artifact from first settlers, library, furniture.

HOURS: June-Sept Daily 9-5

ADMISSION: $1, Children $0.50

SYDNEY

9676
Old Sydney Society
225 George St, B1P 6J4 [PO Box 912, B1P 6J4]; (p) (902) 539-1572; malthy.janet@ns.sympatics.ca; (c) Cape Breton

Private non-profit/ 1966/ staff: 1(f); 1(p); 50(v)/ members: 200/publication: *Old Sydney, Old Sydney Town; Old Sydney New Tastes*

HISTORICAL SOCIETY; HISTORY MUSEUM; HOUSE MUSEUM: Operates 4 heritage community museums.

PROGRAMS: Annual Meeting; Community Outreach; Exhibits; Facility Rental; Family Programs; Film/Video; Guided Tours; Interpretation; Lectures; Publication; Research Library/Archives; School-Based Curriculum

COLLECTIONS: [Late 18th c-present] 2,500 artifacts and 500 photos relating to Sydney and its history; Native American artifacts. steel industry. 4 sites: St. Patrick's Museum, Conit House Museum, The Lyceum, and Jost House Museum.

HOURS: Centre Yr Winter T-F 10-4, Sa 1-4; Summer M-Sa 9:30-5:30; Other museums June 1-Oct 15 M-Sa 9:30-5:30, Su 1-5:30

ADMISSION: Donations requested

SYDNEY, CAPE BRETON

9677
Beaton Institute of Cape Breton Studies
Univ College of Cape Breton, PO Box 5300, B1P 6L2; (p) (902) 563-1329; (f) (902) 532-8899; beaton@uccb.ns.ca; www.uccb.ns.ca/beaton

Federal/ 1957/ Univ College of Cape Breton/ staff: 4(f)

LIBRARY AND/OR ARCHIVES: Collects and conserves the history of Cape Breton Island.

COLLECTIONS: [19th-20th c] Social, economic, political, and cultural history of Cape Breton Island.

TUPPERVILLE

9678
Tupperville School Museum
RR 3 Bridgetown, B0S 1C0; (p) (902) 665-2427; (c) Annapolis

Private non-profit/ 1972/ staff: 20(v)/ members: 15

HISTORIC SITE; HISTORY MUSEUM: Collects and preserves artifacts pertaining to one room country school.

PROGRAMS: Annual Meeting; Exhibits; Festivals; Guided Tours; Reenactments; School-Based Curriculum

COLLECTIONS: [1870-1972] School desks, teacher's desk and chair, maps, books, portraits, scrap books, school bell, flag.

HOURS: Mid May-Sept Daily 10-6

ADMISSION: No charge

TUSKET

9679
Argyle Township Court House and Archives
8168 Hwy #3, B0W 3M0 [PO Box 101, B0W 3M0]; (p) (902) 648-2493; (f) (902) 648-0211; atcha@fox.nstn.ca; ycn.library.ns.ca/ipatcha/; (c) Yarmouth

Joint/ 1982/ Argyle Municipality History and Gen Soc & Municipality of Dist Of Argyle/ staff: 1(f); 8(p); 15(v)/ members: 436/publication: *Argus*

GENEALOGICAL SOCIETY; HISTORIC SITE; HISTORICAL SOCIETY; HISTORY MUSEUM; RESEARCH CENTER: Preserves Argyle Township Court House, Canada's oldest standing courthouse; collects and preserves archival materials.

PROGRAMS: Annual Meeting; Community Outreach; Guided Tours; Interpretation; Publication; Research Library/Archives; School-Based Curriculum

COLLECTIONS: [1805-1900] Local justice and government artifacts.

HOURS: Museum: July-Aug Daily 9-5, May-June, Sept-Oct, Nov-April; Archives: July-Aug Daily 9-5 May-June, Sept-Oct, Nov-April

ADMISSION: $2; Under 10 free

WALLACE

9680
Wallace and Area Museum
Rt 6, B0K 1Y0 [PO Box 179, B0K 1Y0]; (p) (902) 257-2191; (f) (902) 257-2191; remsheg@auracom.com; (c) Cumberland

Private non-profit/ 1984/ staff: 5(p); 15(v)/ members: 15

GARDEN; HISTORY MUSEUM; HOUSE MUSEUM; RESEARCH CENTER: Collects, exhibits, researches, preserves artifacts pertaining to Wallace history and Kennedy-Davison family.

PROGRAMS: Annual Meeting; Community Outreach; Elder's Programs; Exhibits; Facility Rental; Family Programs; Film/Video; Garden Tours; Guided Tours; Interpretation; Lectures; Research Library/Archives; School-Based Curriculum

COLLECTIONS: [Late 1800s-mid 1900] 6,000 artifacts.

HOURS: Yr Summer T-Su 9-5; Winter W-Sa 1-4

ADMISSION: No charge

WINDSOR

9681
West Hants Historical Society
281 King St, B0N 2T0 [PO Box 2335, B0N 2T0]; (p) (902) 798-4706; whhs@glinx.com

Private non-profit/ 1973/ staff: 1(f); 20(v)/ members: 120

HISTORIC PRESERVATION AGENCY: Operates museum and genealogical research library.

PROGRAMS: Annual Meeting; Concerts; Exhibits; Interpretation

COLLECTIONS: [19th c] Family histories and

genealogies.

ADMISSION: No charge

YARMOUTH

9682
Firefighter's Museum of Nova Scotia
451 Main St, B5A 4G9; (p) (902) 742-5525;
(f) (902) 742-5525; firemuse@symnpatico.ca

1973/ staff: 2(f); 4(p); 53(v)/ members: 360

HISTORY MUSEUM: Collects, preserves, and
interprets the history of firefighting in Nova
Scotia.

COLLECTIONS: Fire engines.

HOURS: June 1-Oct 15 M-Sa 9-5; July-Aug M-
Sa 9-9pm, Su 10-5; Oct 16 May 31 M-F 9-4,
Sa 1-4

ONTARIO

ALLISTON

9683
South Simcoe Pioneer Museum
Fletcher Cres, L0R 1A1 [PO Box 910, L0R
1A1]; (p) (705) 425-0167; (f) (705) 434-3006;
sspmchin@bconex.net; (c) Simcoe

City/ 1960/ staff: 1(f); 54(v)/ members: 47/pub-
lication: *South Simcoe Stagecoach*

HISTORY MUSEUM; LIVING HISTORY/OUT-
DOOR MUSEUM; RESEARCH CENTER: Presents local history of South Simcoe.

PROGRAMS: Community Outreach; Con-
certs; Elder's Programs; Exhibits; Facility
Rental; Family Programs; Festivals; Guided
Tours; Interpretation; Lectures; Living History;
Publication; Reenactments; Research Li-
brary/Archives; School-Based Curriculum

COLLECTIONS: [1840-present] Household,
agriculture, pioneer log cbin, Sir F. Banting,
Kate Atken.

HOURS: Yr Summer W-F 10-3:30, Sa-Su 11-
4:30

ADMISSION: $2; Student $1; Seniors $1

ALMONTE

9684
Mississippi Valley Textile Museum
3 Rosamond St East, K0A 1A0 [Box 784,
K0A 1A0]; (p) (613) 256-3754; (f) (613) 256-
1307; mvtm@intranet.ca

Private non-profit/ 1984/ staff: 1(f); 1(p); 25(v)/
members: 138

HISTORIC PRESERVATION AGENCY; HIS-
TORIC SITE; HISTORY MUSEUM; RE-
SEARCH CENTER: Presents history of tex-
tiles.

PROGRAMS: Annual Meeting; Community
Outreach; Exhibits; Facility Rental; Festivals;
Guided Tours; Research Library/Archives;
Theatre

COLLECTIONS: [Early 1800s] Housed in
limestone Woolen Mill; period offices, artifacts,
and machinery.

HOURS: May-Oct W-Su 11-4:30

AMELIASBURGH

9685
Ameliasburgh Historical Museum
Coleman St, K0K 1L0 [PO Box 67, K0K 1L0];
(p) (613) 968-9678; (f) (613) 962-1514; (c)
Prince Edward

County/ 1968/ staff: 1(f); 5(p); 150(v)/ members: 30

ART MUSEUM; GARDEN; HISTORY MUSE-
UM; LIVING HISTORY/OUTDOOR MUSEUM:
Interprets the history of the Bay of Quinte.

PROGRAMS: Annual Meeting; Concerts; Ex-
hibits; Facility Rental; Festivals; Living History;
Reenactments; Research Library/Archives;
School-Based Curriculum

COLLECTIONS: [1700s-present] Housewares, native artifacts, blacksmithing, carpentry tools, agricultural machinery and tools.

HOURS: May-Oct Daily 10-4

ADMISSION: $3, Student $2, Children $1, Se-
niors $2

AMHERSTBURG

9686
Fort Malden National Historic Site
100 Laird Ave, N9V 2Z2 [PO Box 38, N9V
2Z2]; (p) (519) 736-5416; (f) (519) 736-5416;
ont_fort-malden@pch.gc.ca; parkscanada.
pch.gc.ca/malden

Federal; Joint/ 1939/ staff: 7(f); 2(p); 20(v)

HISTORIC SITE: Preserves site of British de-
fensive post during the War of 1812 and the
Rebellion of 1837.

PROGRAMS: Community Outreach; Exhibits;
Guided Tours; Interpretation; Living History;
Publication; Reenactments; Research Li-
brary/Archives; School-Based Curriculum

COLLECTIONS: [1796-1860] Materials and artifacts relating to: British Military; War of 1812-
Fort Malden Garrison; Royal Navy and Provincial Marine; Indian Department; uniforms,
weapons and documents; Rebellion of 1838;
archaeological exhibits; restored barrack.

HOURS: Yr May-Oct Daily 10-5; Nov-Apr Su-F 1-5

ADMISSION: $2.75, Student $1.75, Seniors
$2.25; Group rates

9687
Marsh Collection Society
235 A Dalhousie St, N9V 1W6; (p) (519) 736-
9191; (f) (519) 736-7166; mcschin@mnsi.net;
(c) Essex

Private non-profit/ 1983/ staff: 1(f); 1(p);
4(v)/publication: *Amherstburg 1796-1996: The
New Town on the Garrison Grounds; With the
Tide; and others*

RESEARCH CENTER

PROGRAMS: Exhibits; Lectures; Research Li-
brary/Archives

COLLECTIONS: [1850-present] Photos,
books, documents, postcards, artifacts, information files, newspapers and other items relating to Amherstburg people, events, buildings and organizations, local marine history,
and genealogy.

HOURS: Yr T-F 9-4:30

ATIKOKAN

9688
John B. Ridley Research Library
Quetico Park, P0T 1C0; (p) (807) 929-2571;
(f) (807) 929-2123; andrea.allison@mnr.
gov.on.ca

State/ 1987/ staff: 1(p)

LIBRARY AND/OR ARCHIVES: Shares the
historical, scientific, interpretive, educational
and recreational interest of Quetico Park.

PROGRAMS: Family Programs; Film/Video;
Guided Tours; Interpretation; Living History;
Reenactments; Research Library/Archives

HOURS: Yr May-Sept Daily 8:30-4:30; rest of
year by appt

ADMISSION: No charge

AURORA

9689
Aurora and District Historical Society
22 Church St, L4G 1G4; (p) (905) 727-8991;
AuroraMuseum@aci.on.ca

Private non-profit/ 1963/ staff: 1(f); 20(v)/
members: 200

HISTORICAL SOCIETY; HISTORY MUSEUM;
HOUSE MUSEUM; RESEARCH CENTER:
Operates the Aurora Museum, and Hillary
House.

PROGRAMS: Community Outreach; Exhibits;
Facility Rental; Guided Tours; Interpretation;
Lectures; Research Library/Archives; School-
Based Curriculum

COLLECTIONS: [19th-20th c] Farm photos,
genealogical records.

HOURS: Yr W-Sa 10-12 / 1-5, Sun 1-5

ADMISSION: Museum: free; Hillary House: in-
quire

AYLMER

9690
Aylmer and District Museum
14 E St, N5H 3G6; (p) (519) 773-9723; (f)
(519) 773-9724

1977/ Volunteer Museum Board/ staff: 2(p);
38(v)/ members: 442

HISTORY MUSEUM: Promotes and presents
historical displays, programs, lessons, and
publications.

PROGRAMS: Annual Meeting; Community
Outreach; Concerts; Exhibits; Guided Tours;
Interpretation; Lectures; Publication; Research
Library/Archives; School-Based Curriculum

COLLECTIONS: [1880-1946] Ephemera, artifacts, and oral sources.

HOURS: Mar-Dec T,Th 9-12/1-5, W, F 1-5, Su 1-4

ADMISSION: $2, Family $5

BEAVERTON

9691
**Beaverton-Thorah-Eldon Historical
Society**
284 Simcoe St, L0K 1A0 [PO Box 314, L0K
1A0]; (p) (705) 426-9641

Private non-profit/ 1976/ staff: 1(p); 75(v)/ members: 100

HISTORICAL SOCIETY; HISTORY MUSEUM; HOUSE MUSEUM: Collects, researches, interprets, and preserves local artifacts.

PROGRAMS: Annual Meeting; Community Outreach; Exhibits; Festivals; Guided Tours; Interpretation; Lectures; Research Library/ Archives; School-Based Curriculum

COLLECTIONS: Photos, documents, maps, books, newspapers (1878-present), cemetery records, artifacts that furnish (1850) log cabin, (1900) brick house, and (1840) stone jail.

HOURS: May-June, Sept Sa-Su 1:30-4; July-Aug T-Sa 1:30-4

ADMISSION: Donations accepted

BELLEVILLE

9692
Belleville Public Library
223 Pinnacle St, K8N 3A7; (p) (613) 968-6731; (f) (613) 968-6841

City/ 1903/ Belleville Public Library Board/ staff: 16(f); 18(p)

LIBRARY AND/OR ARCHIVES

PROGRAMS: Community Outreach; Exhibits; Facility Rental; Family Programs; Guided Tours; Publication; Research Library/Archives

COLLECTIONS: Local history.

HOURS: Yr M-Th 9:30-8, F 9:30-5, Sa 9:30-5:30

9693
Glanmore National Historic Site
257 Bridge St E, K8N 1P4; (p) (613) 962-2329; (f) (613) 962-6340; glanmore@suckercreek. on.ca; www.suckercreek.on.ca/glanmore/

1973/ staff: 3(f); 2(p); 45(v)

HISTORIC SITE; HISTORY MUSEUM; HOUSE MUSEUM: Collects, preserves, researches, exhibits, and interprets loca history objects.

PROGRAMS: Community Outreach; Elder's Programs; Exhibits; Facility Rental; Family Programs; Guided Tours; Interpretation; Lectures; Research Library/Archives; School-Based Curriculum

COLLECTIONS: [1860-1900] Second Empire Mansion (1883) European and British decorative art, paintings, and furniture, Japanese and Chinese colisonne, lighting, and regional history artifacts.

HOURS: Yr July-Aug T-Su 10-4:30; Sept-May T-Su 1-4:30

ADMISSION: $3, Student $2.50, Children $1.50, Seniors $2.50

9694
O'Hara Mill Pioneer Village & Conservation Area
O'Hara Rd, 2 km W of Hwy 62, K8N 5B3 [c/o Quinte Conservation, PO Box 698, K8N 5B3]; (p) (613) 968-3434, (613) 473-2084; (f) (613) 968-8240; quinteca@bel.auracom.com; www.pec.on.ca/conservation/; (c) Hastings

Private non-profit/ 1947/ staff: 3(p)

HISTORIC SITE

PROGRAMS: Exhibits; Guided Tours; Interpre-

tation; Living History; School-Based Curriculum

COLLECTIONS: [1850] Carpenter shop, dishes, furniture, tools and farm machinery.

HOURS: July-Aug,

BRAMPTON

9695
Peel Heritage Complex
9 Wellington St East, L6W 1Y1; (p) (905) 451-9051; (f) (905) 451-4931; www.region.peel.on.ca/heritage/hcomplex.htm

County/ 1986/ staff: 6(f); 10(p); 40(v)/ members: 132

ART MUSEUM; HISTORIC SITE; HOUSE MUSEUM; RESEARCH CENTER: Collects, exhibits, and interprets the cultural heritage of Peel region.

PROGRAMS: Annual Meeting; Community Outreach; Elder's Programs; Exhibits; Facility Rental; Family Programs; Festivals; Interpretation; Lectures; Research Library/Archives; School-Based Curriculum

COLLECTIONS: [19th and 20th c] Focus on artifacts of regional significance.

HOURS: Yr Daily M-F 10-4:30, Th 6-9, Sa-Su 12-4:30

ADMISSION: $2.50, Family $7, Student $1, Seniors $1.50; Under 5/Mbrs free

BRANTFORD

9696
Bell Homestead National Historic Site
94 Tutela Heights Rd, N3T 1A1; (p) (519) 756-6220; (f) (519) 759-5975; bwood2@ city.brantford.on.ca; www.city.brantford.on.ca

City/ 1910/ staff: 2(f); 3(p); 40(v)/ members: 65

HISTORIC SITE; HOUSE MUSEUM; LIVING HISTORY/OUTDOOR MUSEUM: Collects, preserves, researches, and exhibits the historical resources of the Bell Homestead N.H.S., household of A. Melville and Eliza Bell, and invention of the telephone by A.G. Bell.

PROGRAMS: Annual Meeting; Community Outreach; Facility Rental; Guided Tours; Interpretation; Living History; School-Based Curriculum

COLLECTIONS: [1870-1881] Original and period household furnishings.

HOURS: Yr T-Su 9:30-4:30

ADMISSION: $3, Student $2.50, Seniors $2.50

9697
Woodland Cultural Centre
184 Mohawk St, N3T 5O6 [PO Box 1506, N3T 5O6]; (p) (519) 759-2650; (f) (519) 759-8912; jbedard@woodland-centre.on.ca; www.woodland-centre.on.ca; (c) Brant

Private non-profit/ 1972/ staff: 15(f); 10(p); 10(v)/ members: 40

HISTORIC PRESERVATION AGENCY; HISTORY MUSEUM; RESEARCH CENTER: Preserves and promotes the history, heritage and culture of First Nations, especially that of Eastern Woodland.

PROGRAMS: Community Outreach; Concerts; Elder's Programs; Exhibits; Facility Rental; Festivals; Film/Video; Interpretation;

Lectures; Research Library/Archives; School-Based Curriculum; Theatre

COLLECTIONS: [Pre-history-present] Archeological, historical materials, and contemporary art.

HOURS: Yr Daily M-F 9-4, Sa-Su 10-5

ADMISSION: $4; Students $3; Seniors $3

BURLINGTON

9698
Ireland House at Oakridge Farm
2168 Guelph Line, L7P 5A8; (p) (905) 332-9888; (f) (905) 332-1714; barbt@ worldchat.com

City/ 1987/ staff: 3(f); 6(p); 80(v)/ members: 125

Collects, preserves, researches, houses, exhibits and interprets the lives of the Ireland family.

COLLECTIONS: [1830-1900] Artifacts from the Ireland family.

HOURS: Yr T-F, Su 1-4, and by appt

ADMISSION: $2.75, Student $2.50, Children $1.50, Seniors $2.50

9699
Joseph Frant Museum
1240 N Shore Blvd E, L7S 1C5; (p) (906) 634-3556; (f) (905) 634-4498; jbm@ worldchat.com

Private non-profit/ 1942/ staff: 3(f); 6(p); 80(v)/ members: 125/publication: *Joseph Brant; Thayendanegea*

HISTORY MUSEUM: Collects, preserves, researches, houses, exhibits and interprets artifacts that illustrate the historical founding, settlement and development.

PROGRAMS: Community Outreach; Exhibits; Family Programs; Festivals; Guided Tours; Interpretation; Lectures; Publication; Research Library/Archives; School-Based Curriculum

COLLECTIONS: [1742-present] Materials, artifacts, Canadian costume and accessories.

HOURS: Yr T-F, Su 1-4 or by appt

ADMISSION: $2.75, Children $1.50, Seniors $2.50

9700
Spruce Lane Farm House
Bronte Creek Provincial Park, L7R 3X5 [1219 Burlock Dr, L7R 3X5]; (p) (905) 827-6911; (f) (905) 637-4120

State/ 1899/ staff: 1(f); 10(p); 25(v)

HOUSE MUSEUM: Depicts life in a rural agricultural setting.

PROGRAMS: Facility Rental; Family Programs; Festivals; Guided Tours; Interpretation; Living History; School-Based Curriculum

COLLECTIONS: [1880-1920] Late Victorian to Edwardian.

CALLANDER

9701
Callander Bay Heritage Museum
107 Lansdowne St East, P0H 1H0 [PO Box 100, P0H 1H0]; (p) (705) 752-2282; (f) (705) 752-3116

City/ 1979/ Township of North Himsworth/ staff: 3(p); 15(v)

HISTORY MUSEUM; HOUSE MUSEUM: Former home and practice of Dr. Alan Roy Dafoe.

PROGRAMS: Exhibits; Facility Rental; Festivals; School-Based Curriculum

COLLECTIONS: [Late 1800s-1950] Quintuplet's artifacts, Dr. A. R. Dafoe artifacts, artifacts: logging, lumber mills, rail systems, shipping on Lake Nipissing.

HOURS: May, June, and Sept T-Su 1-5; July-Aug 10-5

ADMISSION: Donations accepted

CARLETON PLACE

9702
Victoria School Museum
267 Edmund St, K7C 3E8; (p) (613) 253-7013; (c) Lanark

Private non-profit/ 1985/ staff: 1(p); 11(v)

HISTORY MUSEUM: Collects, preserves, researches, exhibits, and interprets local history.

PROGRAMS: Exhibits

COLLECTIONS: [1800-1960] Archives, 1,000 artifacts, school life and history of Carleton Place.

HOURS: Mid June-Sept T 1-4, W-Su 10-4

ADMISSION: Donations accepted

COBOURG

9703
Art Gallery of Northumberland
55 King St West, K9A 2M2; (p) (905) 372-0333; (f) (905) 372-1587; boukidz@eagle.ca; (c) Northumberland

Private non-profit/ 1961/ staff: 1(f); 1(p); 100(v)/ members: 385/publication: AGN

ART MUSEUM: Promotes art and art history.

PROGRAMS: Annual Meeting; Community Outreach; Concerts; Exhibits; Facility Rental; Guided Tours; Lectures; Publication; Research Library/Archives

COLLECTIONS: [1800-present] 500 pieces of historic and contemporary art.

HOURS: Yr T-F

CORNWALL

9704
Stormont, Dundas, and Glengarry Historical Society
160 Wentea St W, K6H 5T5 [PO Box 773, K6H 5T5]; (p) (613) 932-7323; (f) (313) 983-9585; (c) Stormont

Private non-profit/ 1920/ staff: 1(f); 4(p); 30(v)/ members: 150

Researches, preserves, promotes, and informs the public on history and archaeology of the counties of Stormont, Dundas, and Glengarry; operates two museums.

COLLECTIONS: [1784-present] Artifacts, documents, and related materials; Cornwall.

HOURS: Varies

ADMISSION: No charge

COSHWELL

9705
La Regional Saint Laurent, Inc.
300 Montreal Rd, K6H 6N6 [CP 1894, K6H 6N6]; (p) (613) 932-1320; (f) (613) 932-0360; sfong@cnwl.iga.net; www.cnwl.igs.net/~sfong; (c) Stormont

1987/ staff: 50(v)/ members: 205

GENEALOGICAL SOCIETY; HISTORICAL SOCIETY

PROGRAMS: Annual Meeting; Exhibits; Interpretation; Lectures; Research Library/Archives; School-Based Curriculum

COLLECTIONS: History and genealogy books, biographies, maps.

HOURS: Yr M-F

DELHI

9706
Delhi Ontario Tobacco Museum and Heritage Center
200 Talbot Rd, N4B 2A2; (p) (519) 582-0178; (f) (519) 582-0122; museum@own.delhi.on.ca

City/ 1979/ staff: 2(f); 3(p); 58(v)

HISTORY MUSEUM: Established in 1979 to model a pack barn typical of tobacco farms in the area, the museum houses agricultural, multicultural and historical exhibits related to the Township of Delhi.

PROGRAMS: Community Outreach; Elder's Programs; Exhibits; Facility Rental; Family Programs; Festivals; Guided Tours; Lectures; Research Library/Archives; School-Based Curriculum

COLLECTIONS: [1890-1960] Tobacco related machinery, artifacts, cigar store Indians, multicultural heritage, local history, and agricultural history.

HOURS: Yr May-Sept M-F 10-4:30, Su afternoons, and by appt

ADMISSION: No charge

9707
Teeterville Pioneer Museum
Teeter St, N4B 2A2 [c/o Delhi ON Tobacco Museum, 200 Talbot Rd, N4B 2A2]; (p) (519) 443-4400, (519) 582-0278; (f) (519) 582-0122; museum@town.delhi.on.ca; (c) Norfolk

Joint/ 1967/ staff: 1(p)

HISTORY MUSEUM: Maintains historic buildings and preserves regional history.

PROGRAMS: Exhibits; Family Programs; Publication; Research Library/Archives

COLLECTIONS: [1850-1970] Two historic buildings: a log smoke house and a log house built in 1849; church and drive barn; regional artifacts.

HOURS: Mid May-Sept W-Su 1-5

ADMISSION: No charge

DUNVEGAN

9708
Glengarry Pioneer Museum
Cor of Cty Rd 30 & Country Rd 24, K0C 1S0 [PO Box 45, K0C 1S0]; (p) (613) 527-1612;

kenwil@glen_net.ca; (c) Glengarry

1962/ staff: 2(p); 50(v)/ members: 100/publication: Glengarry Life

HISTORY MUSEUM: Collects, preserves, house, researches, and interprets Glengarry County and surrounding area history.

PROGRAMS: Exhibits; Facility Rental; Interpretation; Publication; Research Library/Archives

COLLECTIONS: [1850-1900] Clothing, tools, farm machinery, photos, books, maps, war memorabilia, furniture, artwork, toys, musical instruments, medical apparatus, quilts.

HOURS: May-June and Sept-Oct Sa-Su 1-5; July-Aug T-Su 1-5

ADMISSION: $2; Children free

EAR FALLS

9709
Ear Falls and District Museum
Hwy 105, P0V 1T0 [PO Box 309, 15 Spruce St, P0V 1T0]; (p) (807) 222-3624; (f) (807) 222-2384; www.cancom.net/~eflbmany/earfalls.html

City/ 1970/ staff: 1(f); 10(p)

HISTORY MUSEUM: Promotes gold mining days and transportation.

PROGRAMS: Exhibits; Guided Tours

COLLECTIONS: [350 AD-present] Native artifacts, mining, logging, and transportation equipment.

HOURS: June-Sept M-F 10-5

ADMISSION: $3, Student $1.50

ELLIOT LAKE

9710
Elliot Lake Nuclear and Mining Museum
Lester B Pearson Centre, Hwy 108, P5A 2T1; (p) (705) 848-2084; (f) (705) 848-2987

City/ 1963/ staff: 1(f); 1(p); 7(v)

HISTORY MUSEUM: Preserves mining history.

PROGRAMS: Exhibits; Festivals; Film/Video; Guided Tours; Lectures; Research Library/Archives

COLLECTIONS: Mining artifacts, equipment, materials.

HOURS: Yr Winter M-F 10-4; Summer M-F 9-8

ADMISSION: $2, Family $5, Children $1

ENGLEHART

9711
Englehart and Area Historical Museum
67 Sixth Ave, P0J 1H0 [Box 444, P0J 1H0]; (p) (705) 544-2400; (f) (705) 544-8737; noakes@ntl.sympatico.ca

1977/ staff: 1(f); 2(p); 15(v)/ members: 120

HISTORIC SITE; HISTORY MUSEUM: Collects, preserves, and interprets the founding of the town and settlement of surrounding municipalities.

PROGRAMS: Community Outreach; Exhibits; Facility Rental; Family Programs; Festivals;

Guided Tours; Interpretation; Living History; Publication; Research Library/Archives; School-Based Curriculum

COLLECTIONS: [1900-1950] Artifacts: settlers household effects, tools of trades, photographs, social history documents, homesteading records, native artifacts, art, Women's Institute Tweedsmuir histories.

HOURS: May 1- Dec 1 M-F 10-4, Sa-Su 12-4; and by appt

ADMISSION: $2, Student $1

FERGUS

9712
Wellington County Museum and Archives
County Rd 18, N1M 2W3 [RR 1, N1M 2W3]; (p) (519) 846-0916; (f) (519) 846-9630; info@wcm.on.ca; (c) Wellington

County/ 1954/ staff: 7(f); 5(p); 42(v)/ members: 382/publication: *CIRCA Newsletter*

HISTORIC SITE; HISTORY MUSEUM: Collects, interprets, and exhibits Wellington history.

PROGRAMS: Community Outreach; Concerts; Exhibits; Facility Rental; Family Programs; Festivals; Garden Tours; Guided Tours; Interpretation; Lectures; Publication; Research Library/Archives; School-Based Curriculum

COLLECTIONS: [Victorian Era] 32,000 archival records, 10,000 artifacts, 13,000 photos, 800 artworks, agricultural implements, textiles, furnishings.

HOURS: Yr Museum: Daily M-F 8:30-4:30, Sa-Su 1-5;

FONTHILL

9713
Pelham Historical Society
Pelham Public Library, L0S 1E0 [Box 903, L0S 1E0]

Private non-profit/ 1975/ staff: 5(v)/ members: 60

HISTORIC PRESERVATION AGENCY; HISTORICAL SOCIETY: Preserves material on local history researches.

PROGRAMS: Annual Meeting; Community Outreach; Publication; Research Library/ Archives

COLLECTIONS: [19th-20th c] Archives, family records, photographs, church, school records.

HOURS: By appt

FOREST

9714
Forest-Lambton Museum, Inc.
59 Broadway St, N0N 1J0 [Box 707, N0N 1J0]; (p) (519) 786-3239; (c) Lambton

Private non-profit/ 1963/ staff: 10(v)/ members: 20/publication: *Sampler Quarterly Newsletter*

HISTORY MUSEUM: Collects and preserves history of Lambton County.

PROGRAMS: Annual Meeting; Exhibits; Garden Tours; Publication; Research Library/ Archives

COLLECTIONS: [Early 1900s] Artifacts, pictures, documents, military uniforms, doll collection, flax; telephone, ectrical, railway, hand

tools. First Nations relics, fossils of Lambton County.

HOURS: June-Aug F-Su 1-5

ADMISSION: $2

FORT ERIE

9715
Mildred M. Mahoney Doll's House Gallery
657 Niagara Blvd, L2A 3H9; (p) (905) 871-5833; (f) (905) 871-2447; (c) Welland

Private non-profit/ 1983/ Board of Directors/ staff: 2(f); 1(p)/ members: 10

HISTORIC SITE: 140 fully furnished doll houses furnished in the period in which it was built (1790) also part of underground railroad.

PROGRAMS: Exhibits

COLLECTIONS: [1790-1990] Doll houses and furniture and materials.

HOURS: May 1-Dec 31 Daily 10-4

ADMISSION: $5, Children $3, Seniors $4

GANANOQUE

9716
Gananoque Museum
10 King St East, K7G 1E9 [30 King St East, K7G 1E9]; (p) (613) 382-4024; (c) Leeds and Grenville

City/ 1961/ staff: 2(p); 37(v)

HISTORY MUSEUM: Preserves heritage and culture of Gananoque.

PROGRAMS: Community Outreach; Exhibits

COLLECTIONS: [1795-1945] Local history, genealogy, industrial history.

HOURS: June-Sept Daily 10-6

ADMISSION: $1

GOLDEN LAKE

9717
Algonquin Culture and Heritage Centre
1674 Mishomis Inamo, K0J 1X0 [PO Box 100, K0J 1X0]; (p) (613) 625-2823; (f) (613) 625-2421; algen@renc.igs.net; Private non-profit/ 1950/ staff: 1(f)

HISTORY MUSEUM; TRIBAL MUSEUM: Promotes Algonquin culture.

PROGRAMS: Exhibits; Guided Tours

COLLECTIONS: Baskets, wild rice, pottery, antiques, medicine wheel teachings, food, medicinal plants, canoes, birch bark wigwam, buckskin outfits, grassdancer's regalia, mural, wood carvings, articles, and photographs.

HOURS: Feb-Oct M-F 8:30-4:30, Sa-Su 11-4

ADMISSION: Donations accepted

GORMLEY

9718
Whitchurch-Stouffville Museum
14732 Woodbine Ave, Community of Vandorf, L0H 1G0 [14732 Woodrine Ave, L0H 1G0]; (p) (905) 727-1282; (f) (905) 727-8954; wsmchin@colosseum.com

City/ 1971/ staff: 2(f); 6(p); 88(v)/ members: 98

HISTORY MUSEUM; HOUSE MUSEUM; LIVING HISTORY/OUTDOOR MUSEUM: Collects, preserves, exhibits, and interprets the natural history and historical development.

PROGRAMS: Community Outreach; Exhibits; Guided Tours; Interpretation; Lectures; Living History; Research Library/Archives; School-Based Curriculum

COLLECTIONS: [Late 1800] Household furniture, domestic implements, clothing and household textiles, fine art, photographs, documents, published works, horse-drawn vehicles, agricultural implements and tools, archaeological artifacts.

HOURS: Yr Winter M-F 1-5; Summer W-Su 10-5

ADMISSION: No charge/Donations

GRAVENHURST

9719
Bethune Memorial House National Historic Site
235 John St N, P1P 1G4; (p) (705) 687-4261; (f) (705) 687-4935; ont_bethune@pch.gc.ca; parkscanada.gc.ca/bethune; (c) Gravenhurst

Federal/ 1976/ Parks Canada/ staff: 4(f); 1(p)

HISTORIC SITE: Birthplace of Norman Bethune, a Canadian doctor.

PROGRAMS: Community Outreach; Exhibits; Festivals; Garden Tours; Guided Tours; Interpretation; School-Based Curriculum; Theatre

COLLECTIONS: [1890] Household furnishings, Bethune family artifacts.

HOURS: May-Oct Daily 10-5; Nov-Apr M-F 1-4

ADMISSION: $2.50, Student $1.25, Seniors $225; Under 5 free; group rates

GREATER NAPANEE

9720
Loyalist Cultural Centre and Museum
Adolphustown U.E. Loyalist Park, K7R 300 [Box 112, RR#1, Bath, K0H 1G0]; (p) (613) 373-2195; (f) (613) 373-0043; adolphustown@canada.com; loyal-ists. freeyellow.com

1967/ staff: 1(f); 1(p); 30(v)

HISTORIC PRESERVATION AGENCY; HISTORICAL SOCIETY; HISTORY MUSEUM; HOUSE MUSEUM; RESEARCH CENTER: Promotes history of United Empire Loyalists

PROGRAMS: Annual Meeting; Community Outreach; Exhibits; Family Programs; Guided Tours; Interpretation; Lectures; Living History; Reenactments; Research Library/Archives; School-Based Curriculum

COLLECTIONS: [1800s] Genealogical records.

HOURS: Yr May-Sept T-Sa 10-4, Su 1-5 or by appt

ADMISSION: $2, Family $5, Student $1

GUELPH

9721
McCrae House-Guelph Museums
108 Water St, N1H 4L5 [6 Dublin St S, N1H 4L5]; (p) (519) 836-1221; (f) (519) 836-5280; info@museum.guelph.on.ca; www.museum. guelphj.on.ca

City; Joint/ 1968/ staff: 6(f); 4(p); 75(v)/ members: 140

HISTORIC SITE: Exhibits, interprets, and preserves the history of John McCrae.

PROGRAMS: Community Outreach; Exhibits; Family Programs; Interpretation; Research Library/Archives; School-Based Curriculum

COLLECTIONS: [1870-1914] Artifacts related to the life of John McCrae, his family, and his participation in the Boer and First World War.

HOURS: Yr Summer Daily, Winter Su-F

ADMISSION: $4, Family $10, Student $3, Seniors $3; Under 2 free

HAMILTON

9722
Hamilton Military Museum
Dundurn Park-York Blvd, L8R 3H1; (p) (905) 546-2872; (f) (905) 546-2872; hmmchin@intellynx.net; www.city.hamilton.on.ca/cultureandcreation

City/ 1976/ staff: 3(f); 3(p); 1(v)

HISTORIC SITE; HISTORY MUSEUM: Displays Canadian military history from the War of 1812 to World War II.

PROGRAMS: Community Outreach; Concerts; Exhibits; Interpretation; Lectures; Research Library/Archives; School-Based Curriculum

COLLECTIONS: [1812-1945] Military uniforms, equipment, accessories, British Army and Navy, Canadian Army, Navy, Air Force.

HOURS: Yr Winter T-Su 1;00-5; Summer M-Su 11-5

ADMISSION: $2.25, Student

9723
Whitehern Historic House and Garden
41 Jackson St West, L8P 1L3; (p) (905) 546-2018; (f) (905) 546-4933; whchin@interlynx. net; www.city.hamilton.on ca/cultureandrecreation

City/ 1971/ staff: 2(f); 3(p); 20(v)

HISTORIC SITE; HOUSE MUSEUM: Former home of three generations of McQuestens (1848-1968), one of Hamilton's most significant families.

PROGRAMS: Elder's Programs; Exhibits; Family Programs; Garden Tours; Guided Tours; Interpretation; Lectures; School-Based Curriculum

COLLECTIONS: [1790-1968] Eight preserved rooms with original furnishings and historic finishes; fine antiques, collectibles, art works, collector's library, toys, and archives.

HOURS: Yr May-June 15 T-Su 1-4; June 15-Sept 11-4

ADMISSION: $3.50, Family $10, Student $2.50,

HARROW

9724
John R. Park Homestead & Conservation Area
915 Country Rd 50 E, N0R 1G0; (p) (579) 738-2029; (f) (579) 776-8688; jrph@erca.org; www.erca.org; (c) Essex

County/ 1978/ staff: 1(f); 8(p); 50(v)

HISTORIC SITE: Interprets the Park family and their mercantile.

PROGRAMS: Community Outreach; Elder's Programs; Exhibits; Facility Rental; Family Programs; Festivals; Guided Tours; Interpretation; Living History; Reenactments; School-Based Curriculum

COLLECTIONS: [1840-1900] 1,400 domestic and agricultural tools and furniture. 1840's house and 10 farm buildings.

HOURS: Yr vary

ADMISSION: $3, Family $10, Children $2

JORDAN

9725
Jordan Historical Museum of the Twenty
3802 Main St, L0R 1S0; (p) (905) 562-5242; (f) (905) 562-7786; jhmtchin@uaxxine.com; tourismniagara.com/jordanmuseum; (c) Lincoln

City/ 1953/ staff: 1(f); 1(p); 38(v)/ members: 173

HISTORIC SITE; HISTORY MUSEUM; LIVING HISTORY/OUTDOOR MUSEUM: Represents material culture of pioneer and Victorian/Edwardian lifestyles.

PROGRAMS: Annual Meeting; Community Outreach; Exhibits; Facility Rental; Family Programs; Festivals; Guided Tours; Interpretation; Research Library/Archives; School-Based Curriculum

COLLECTIONS: [Pioneer & Victorian/Edwardian] Features Fraktur folk art, textiles, quilts, coverlets and costumes.

HOURS: May-Sept Daily M-F 10-4, Sa-Su 1-4

ADMISSION: $3, Children $1

KEENE

9726
Lang Pioneer Village/Corporation of the County of Peterborough
470 Water, Peterborough, K9H 3M3; (p) (705) 743-0380; (f) (705) 876-1760; jplatt@cgocable. net; www.county.peterborough.on.ca

County/ 1967/ staff: 3(f); 3(p); 250(v)

LIVING HISTORY/OUTDOOR MUSEUM: Presents local history, early settlement of Peterborough County.

PROGRAMS: Concerts; Exhibits; Facility Rental; Family Programs; Festivals; Guided Tours; Interpretation; Living History; Reenactments; Research Library/Archives; School-Based Curriculum

COLLECTIONS: [1800-1900] Archives, artifacts.

HOURS: May-Sept Daily Su-F 12-5, Sa and Holidays 1-4

ADMISSION: $6, Family $15, Student $5, Children $3, Seniors $5

KINGSTON

9727
Anglican Diocese of Ontario Archives
90 Johnson St, K7L 1X7; (p) (613) 544-4774; (f) (613) 547-3745; archives@ontario. anglican.ca; www.ontario.anglican.ca

Private non-profit/ Anglican Diocese of Ontario/ staff: 1(f); 1(p); 3(v)

Acquires, preserves, temporal and spiritual memory of the Diocese.

COLLECTIONS: [1783-present] Textual records including baptism, marriage, and burial registers; photos; plans and drawings; sound and moving image; and printed material.

HOURS: Yr T-Th 1:15-4:30 or by appt

9728
Fort Henry
1 Fort Henry Dr @ Hwy 2, K7L 4V8 [PO Box 213, K7L 4V8]; (p) (613) 542-7388; (f) (613) 542-3054; ft-henry@adan.kingston-net; www.parks.on.ca

City/ 1938/ staff: 6(f); 96(p); 70(v)

HISTORIC SITE; LIVING HISTORY/OUTDOOR MUSEUM: Preserves history of Canadian confederation 1867.

PROGRAMS: Community Outreach; Concerts; Exhibits; Facility Rental; Family Programs; Festivals; Guided Tours; Interpretation; Living History; Reenactments; School-Based Curriculum

COLLECTIONS: [19th c] Fortification, artifacts related to the life of Victorian British and Canadian soldier.

HOURS: May-Sept M-Su 10-5

ADMISSION: $9.50, Children

9729
Marine Museum of the Great Lakes at Kingston
55 Ontario St, K7L 2Y2; (p) (613) 542-2261; (f) (613) 542-0043; mmuseum@stauffer. queensu.ca; www.marmus.ca

Joint; Private non-profit/ 1976/ staff: 1(f); 4(p); 162(v)/ members: 600

HISTORIC SITE; HISTORY MUSEUM; RESEARCH CENTER: Collects, educates, conserves and displays artifacts related to Great Lakes maritime commerce, labor and life; develops, operates, and maintains a marine resource center.

PROGRAMS: Annual Meeting; Elder's Programs; Exhibits; Facility Rental; Film/Video; Guided Tours; Lectures; Publication; Research Library/Archives; School-Based Curriculum

COLLECTIONS: [19th-20th c] 100,000 items composed of artifacts, records, manuscripts, photos, art, books; social history and technology of the Great Lakes.

HOURS: May 1-Oct 31 Daily 10-5

ADMISSION: $3.95, Family $8.75, Student $3.45, Seniors $3.45

9730
Museum of Health Care at Kingston, The
Ann Baillie Bldg, George St, K7L 2V7; (p) (613) 548-2419; (f) (613) 548-6042; museum@kgh.kari.net; www. museumofhealthcare.ca

Private non-profit/ 1991/ staff: 1(f); 4(p); 2(v)/ members: 250

HISTORY MUSEUM: Preserves material culture of health care in Eastern ON.

PROGRAMS: Annual Meeting; Community

Outreach; Exhibits; Lectures

COLLECTIONS: Medical surgical and laboratory instruments.

HOURS: Yr M-F 1-4 (Open weekends May-Sept 1-4)

9731
Museum Ship "Alexander Henry"
55 Ontario St, K7L 2Y2; (p) (613) 542-2261; (f) (613) 542-0043; mmuseum@stauffer. queensu.ca; www.marmus.ca

Private non-profit/ 1985/ staff: 1(f); 8(p); 30(v)/ members: 600

HISTORY MUSEUM: Preserves maritime history of Great Lakes.

PROGRAMS: Annual Meeting; Elder's Programs; Facility Rental; Family Programs; Guided Tours; Publication; Research Library/ Archives

COLLECTIONS: Ice breaker, photos, ship plans, log books, manuals, and personnel records.

HOURS: Mid May-Sept Daily 10-4

ADMISSION: $3.95, Family $8.75, Student $3.45, Seniors $3.35

9732
Pump House Steam Museum
23 Ontario St, K7L 2Y2 [55 Ontario St, K7L 2Y2]; (p) (613) 542-2261; (f) (613) 542-0043; mmuseum@stauffer.queensu.ca; www. marmus.ca

Joint; Private non-profit/ 1973/ staff: 4(p); 162(v)/ members: 600

HISTORIC SITE; HISTORY MUSEUM: Depicts importance of steam technologies of the Great Lakes Basin.

PROGRAMS: Annual Meeting; Elder's Programs; Exhibits; Family Programs; Lectures; Publication; School-Based Curriculum

COLLECTIONS: [19th -20th c] Artifacts, books, and material.

HOURS: June 1- Sept Daily 10-5

ADMISSION: $3.95, Family $8.75, Student $4.45, Seniors $4.45

9733
Royal Military College of Canada Museum
4 Passchenale Dr, K7K 7B4 [PO Box 17000 Station Forces, K7K 7B4]; (p) (613) 541-6000, (613) 541-6664; (f) (613) 542-3565; mckenzie-r@rmc.ca; www.rmc.ca/museum/

Federal; Joint/ 1962/ staff: 1(f); 5(p); 1(v)

HISTORIC SITE; HISTORY MUSEUM: Collects, preserves, and interprets material relating to the history of the Royal Military College; located in Fort Frederick 1846.

PROGRAMS: Exhibits; Publication; Research Library/Archives

COLLECTIONS: [1789-present] Materials and artifacts; Point Frederick Dockyard 1789-1852, College history from 1876, service of ex-cadets, Douglas Arms Collection, and the Leinster (silver) Plate.

HOURS: End of June-Sept Daily 10-5

ADMISSION: No charge

KIRKLAND LAKE

9734
Museum of Northern History at The Sir Harry Oakes Chateau
2 Chateau Dr, P2N 3M7 [PO Box 1148, P2N 3M7]; (p) (705) 568-8800; (f) (705) 567-6611; mnhchin@nH.sympatico.ca; www.town. kirklandlake.on.caq

City; Joint/ 1967/ staff: 2(f); 2(p); 30(v)/ members: 114

HISTORIC SITE; HISTORY MUSEUM: Provides educational and cultural programs.

PROGRAMS: Concerts; Exhibits; Facility Rental; Family Programs; Festivals; Guided Tours; Lectures; Publication

COLLECTIONS: [1900-1960] Natural specimens, artifacts, documents, books on northeastern ON.

HOURS: Yr Daily M-Sa 10-4, Su 12-4

ADMISSION: $3, Student $1.75, Seniors

KITCHENER

9735
Doon Heritage Crossroads
Homer Watson Blvd, N2G 3W5 [RR # 2, N2G 3W5]; (p) (519) 748-1914; (f) (519) 748-0009; rtom@region.waterloo.on.ca; www.region. waterloo.on.ca/doon

County/ 1957/ staff: 10(f); 30(p); 500(v)/ members: 200/publication: *Events and Exhibits*

HISTORY MUSEUM; LIVING HISTORY/OUTDOOR MUSEUM

PROGRAMS: Annual Meeting; Community Outreach; Concerts; Elder's Programs; Exhibits; Facility Rental; Family Programs; Festivals; Garden Tours; Interpretation; Lectures; Living History; Publication; Reenactments; Research Library/Archives; School-Based Curriculum

COLLECTIONS: [Prehistory-present] 26,000 catalogued objects; 15,000 uncatalogued objects. Prehistoric objects; textiles, clothing, quilts, domestic arts, furnishings, decorative and folk art; industrial, commercial, trades, transportation and communication.

HOURS: May-Sept Daily 10-4:30; Sept-Dec M-F 10-4:30

ADMISSION: $6, Family $15, Student $4, Children $3, Seniors $4

9736
Homer Watson House and Gallery
1754 Old Mill Rd, N2P 1H7; (p) (519) 748-4377; (f) (519) 748-6808; curator@ homerwatson.on.ca; www.homerwatson.on.ca

City/ 1981/ staff: 1(f); 3(p); 35(v)

ART MUSEUM; HISTORIC SITE: The house and gallery is the home of one of Canada's leading turn-of-the-century artists Homer Watson (1855-1936).

PROGRAMS: Exhibits; Family Programs; Guided Tours; Interpretation; School-Based Curriculum

COLLECTIONS: [1855-1936] Homer Watson family artifacts.

HOURS: Mid Jan-mid Dec

ADMISSION: Donations accepted

9737
Joseph Schneider Haus Museum
466 Queen St S, N2G 1W7; (p) (519) 742-7752; (f) (519) 742-0089; bususan@region. waterloo.on.ca; www.region.waterloo. on.ca/jsh

Joint/ 1979/ staff: 5(f); 10(p); 170(v)/ members: 200

GARDEN; HISTORIC SITE; HOUSE MUSEUM; LIVING HISTORY/OUTDOOR MUSEUM: Restored farm house.

PROGRAMS: Elder's Programs; Exhibits; Festivals; Garden Tours; Guided Tours; Interpretation; Lectures; Living History; Research Library/Archives; School-Based Curriculum

COLLECTIONS: [Late 18th-19th c] Artifacts of c.1850 PA German Mennonite family in ON: furniture, textiles, pottery; Canadian Germanic folk and decorative arts, Fraktur, embroidery and handweaving.

HOURS: Feb-Dec W-Sa 10-5, Su 1-5; July-Aug M-Sa 10-5, Su 1-5

ADMISSION: $2.25, Family $5, Student $1.50, Children $1.25, Seniors $1.50

9738
Woodside National Historic Site
528 Wellington St N, N2H 5L5; (p) (519) 571-5684; (f) (519) 571-5686; ont_woodside@ pch.gc.ca;ParksCanada.pch.gc.ca/parks/ Ontatio/Woodside

Federal/ 1952/ staff: 5(f); 3(p); 2(v)/publication: *Nicolson, Murray, Woodside, and the Victorian Family of John King, Ottawa: Minister of Environment*

HISTORIC SITE: Restored boyhood home of William Lyon Mackenzie King.

PROGRAMS: Community Outreach; Exhibits; Family Programs; Film/Video; Garden Tours; Guided Tours; Interpretation; Lectures; Living History; Publication; Research Library/ Archives; School-Based Curriculum

COLLECTIONS: [1886-1893] 14 furnished period rooms, artifacts.

HOURS: Mid-May-Dec 23 Daily 10-5

ADMISSION: $2.50, Family $7, Student

LITTLE CURRENT

9739
Little Current-Howland Centennial Museum
Hwy 6, P0P 1K0 [Postal Bag 2000, P0P 1K0]; (p) (705) 368-2367; (f) (705) 368-2245

Private non-profit/ 1967/ staff: 1(f); 2(p); 20(v)/ members: 120

GENEALOGICAL SOCIETY; HISTORY MUSEUM; HOUSE MUSEUM: Preserves township history.

PROGRAMS: Community Outreach; Exhibits; Facility Rental; Guided Tours; Interpretation; Publication

COLLECTIONS: [1890-1910] Farm equipment, period costumes, toys, stone-age tools

HOURS: May-Oct Daily 10-4:30 evenings by appt

ADMISSION: $3; Student $2; Children $1; Seniors $2.50

LIVELY

9740
Anderson Farm Museum
Regional Road 24, P3Y 1J3 [25 Black Lake Rd, P3Y 1J3]; (p) (705) 692-5512; (f) (705) 692-3225; anderf@isys.ca; www.town. walden.on.ca; (c) Walden

City/ 1984/ Town of Walden, Anderson Farm Museum Advisory Boar/ staff: 1(f); 12(v)/publication: *There Were No Strangers: A History of the Village of Creighton Mine*

HISTORY MUSEUM; HOUSE MUSEUM: Collects, preserves, and exhibits history of Walden.

PROGRAMS: Community Outreach; Exhibits; Facility Rental; Festivals; Guided Tours; Interpretation; Publication; Research Library/ Archives; Theatre

COLLECTIONS: [1900-1950] Agricultural/ dairy farming machinery, municipal archives, photographs, documents, Finnish immigrant artifacts, and sports trophies and equipment.

HOURS: Apr-Oct Daily 10-4

ADMISSION: $4; Children $2

LONDON

9741
London Museum of Archaelogy
1600 Attawandaron Rd, N6G 3M6; (p) (519) 473-1360; (f) (519) 473-1363; museum.of. archaelogy@julian.uwo.ca; www.uwo. ca/museum

Private non-profit/ 1933/ staff: 4(f); 5(p); 20(v)/publication: *Palisade Post*

HISTORIC SITE; RESEARCH CENTER

PROGRAMS: Community Outreach; Exhibits; Guided Tours; Interpretation; Lectures; Publication; Research Library/Archives; School-Based Curriculum; Theatre

COLLECTIONS: [1000-1650 AD] Materials on prehistory and pioneer history; Iroquois.

HOURS: Yr May-Sept, Daily 10-4:30; Sept-Dec W-Su 10-4:30; Dec-Apr, Sa-Su 1-4

ADMISSION: $3.50, Family $8, Student $2.75, Children $1.50, Seniors $2.75

9742
London Regional Children's Museum
21 Wharncliffe Rd S, N6J 4G5; (p) (519) 434-5726; (f) (519) 434-1443; (c) Middlesex

Private non-profit/ 1975/ staff: 10(f); 4(p); 150(v)/ members: 800/publication: *Thumbprint*

HISTORY MUSEUM

PROGRAMS: Community Outreach; Exhibits; Facility Rental; Family Programs; Interpretation; Publication; School-Based Curriculum

COLLECTIONS: [Late 19th-20th c] Caves, dinosaurs, Arctic, community, space, science, Victorian period, toys.

HOURS: Yr July-Aug M-Su 10-5; Sept-June T-Su 10-5

ADMISSION: $4

MARKHAM

9743
Heritage Schoolhouse
2 Valleywood Dr, L3R 8H3; (p) (905) 470-6119; (f) (905) 470-1783; hert@yrbe.edu.on.ca; www.yrbe.edu.on. ca/curricul/heritage

1993/ staff: 4(f); 1(p)

HISTORIC SITE; HISTORY MUSEUM; LIVING HISTORY/OUTDOOR MUSEUM: Collects, preserves, maintains, and exhibits archival and material culture of schools and educational institutions of York Region, ON.

PROGRAMS: Exhibits; Interpretation; Lectures; Living History; Research Library/ Archives; School-Based Curriculum

COLLECTIONS: [1850-1930]

HOURS: Yr Sept-June M-F 9-4; July-Aug M,T, W, Th 9-4

MATTAWA

9744
Samuel De Champlain Provincial Park/Voyageur Heritage Centre
Box 147, P0H 1V0; (p) (705) 744-2276; (f) (705) 744-0587

State/ 1988/ staff: 3(p)

HISTORIC SITE

PROGRAMS: Family Programs; Film/Video; Guided Tours; Interpretation; Publication; Reenactments

COLLECTIONS: [1600-1820] Amerindian, fur trade artifacts.

HOURS: June-Sept M-F 8-4, Sa-Su 1-3

ADMISSION: No charge

MIDLAND

9745
Huronia Museum and Huron-Ouendat Village
549 Little Lake Park, L4R 4P4 [PO Box 638, L4R 4P4]; (p) (705) 526-2844; (f) (705) 527-6622; hmchin@bconnex.net; www. GeorgianBayTourism.on.ca; (c) Simcoe

Private non-profit/ 1947/ staff: 6(f); 6(p); 10(v)/ members: 300

HISTORY MUSEUM: Collects, exhibits, educates, and preserves Native history in museum and recreated village.

PROGRAMS: Annual Meeting; Community Outreach; Exhibits; Facility Rental; Family Programs; Festivals; Film/Video; Guided Tours; Interpretation; Living History; Publication; Research Library/Archives; School-Based Curriculum

COLLECTIONS: [1000-1600AD] Archaeological artifacts, photos, military, genealogy.

HOURS: Yr Apr-Nov Daily 9-5; Dec-Mar M-Sa

9746
Sainte-Marie Among the Hurons
Hwy 12, across from the Martyrs' Shrine, L4R 4K8 [PO Box 160, L4R 4K8]; (p) (705) 526-7838; (f) (705) 526-9193; rvyvan@scolve.net; www.saintemarieamongthehurons.on.ca

Joint/ 1967/ staff: 15(f); 60(p); 75(v)

HISTORIC SITE; HISTORY MUSEUM; LIVING HISTORY/OUTDOOR MUSEUM: Preserves history of French Jesuit Mission to the Huron people.

PROGRAMS: Exhibits; Facility Rental; Guided Tours; Interpretation; Living History; Reenactments; School-Based Curriculum

COLLECTIONS: [17th c] Interpretive rooms, archaeological artifacts, French material culture.

HOURS: Apr-Oct Daily 10-4:45

ADMISSION; $9.75

9747
Ontario Electric Railway Historical Association
13629 Guelph Line, L9T 5A2 [PO Box 578, L9T 5A2]; (p) (519) 856-9802; (f) (519) 856-1399; streetcar@hcry.org; www.hcry.org

Private non-profit/ 1954/ staff: 75(v)/ members: 245

HISTORICAL SOCIETY: Maintains streetcar and electric railway museum.

PROGRAMS: Annual Meeting; Exhibits; Facility Rental; Family Programs; Festivals; Film/Video; Guided Tours; Interpretation; Lectures; Research Library/Archives; School-Based Curriculum

COLLECTIONS: [1860-1990] Restored operating streetcars and electric railway equipment, documents and artifacts.

HOURS: May-Oct Sa,Su and holidays10-5; July-Aug Daily; Sa-Su 10-5, M-F 10-4

ADMISSION: $7.50, Children $5.50, Seniors $6.50

MINESING

9748
Simcoe County Archives
1149 Hwy 26, L0L 1Y0 [RR 2, L0L 1Y0]; (p) (705) 726-9331; (f) (705) 725-5341; archives@bar.imag.net; www.county. simcoe.onca/

County/ 1966/ staff: 4(f)

LIBRARY AND/OR ARCHIVES: Collects and preserves Simcoe County heritage.

PROGRAMS: Community Outreach; Interpretation; Lectures; Publication; Research Library/Archives; School-Based Curriculum

COLLECTIONS: [1800-1950] 4,600 cu. Ft. of processed manuscripts, 1,000 maps, 35 newspapers, 2,000 volumes, 100,000 photos, analog and digital recording media, art and artifacts.

HOURS: Yr M-F 8:30-4:30

ADMISSION: No charge

9749
Simcoe County Museum
1151 Hwy 26, RR # 2, L0L 1Y0; (p) (705) 728-3721; (f) (705) 728-9130; museum@bar. imag.net; www.county. simcoe.on.ca

County/ 1926/ staff: 7(f); 5(p); 125(v)/ members: 210

HISTORY MUSEUM; HOUSE MUSEUM; LIVING HISTORY/OUTDOOR MUSEUM: To portray and promote the history of people of Simcoe County by the collection, preservation, interpretation, and display of natural, documentary, man-made and built heritage artifacts, pertaining to development from earliest times to a point 50 years prior to the current date.

PROGRAMS: Community Outreach; Exhibits; Facility Rental; Family Programs; Festivals; Interpretation; Lectures; Living History; Reenactments; Research Library/Archives; School-Based Curriculum

COLLECTIONS: [Prehistory-present] 14,000 pieces of applied and decorative art; 3,000 text; graphic sound; 900 from soil and water; 560 ethnological; 430 military; 300 science and technology; 160 fine art; 60 music; 5 1800s structures.

HOURS: Yr M-Sa 9-4:30, Sun 1-4:30

ADMISSION: $4, Student $3.50, Children $2.50, Seniors $3.50; Under 5 free

MISSISSAUGA

9750
Benares Historic House
1507 Clarkson Rd N, L5J 2W8; (p) (905) 822-2347; (f) (905) 822-5372; annemarie.hagan@city.mississauga.on.ca; city.mississauga.on.ca

City/ 1995/ Recreation and Parks, Community Services, City of Mississauga/ staff: 3(f); 4(p); 50(v)

GARDEN; HISTORIC SITE; HISTORY MUSEUM: Presents daily life during W W I.

PROGRAMS: Community Outreach; Concerts; Exhibits; Facility Rental; Festivals; Guided Tours; Interpretation; School-Based Curriculum; Theatre

COLLECTIONS: [1914-1919] Archaeology.

HOURS: Mar-June, Sept-Dec Su 1-4; June-July W-Su 1-4

ADMISSION: $5, Family $12, Children $1.50, Seniors $3

9751
Bradley Museum
1620 Orr Rd, L5J 4T2; (p) (905) 822-1569; (f) (905) 823-3591; annemarie.hagan@city.mississugua.on.ca; city.mississauga.on.ca

City/ 1967/ Rec and Parks, Community Services, City of Mississauga/ staff: 3(f); 4(p); 45(v)

HISTORIC SITE; HISTORY MUSEUM: Promotes daily life in 1830.

PROGRAMS: Community Outreach; Exhibits; Facility Rental; Festivals; Garden Tours; Guided Tours; Interpretation; School-Based Curriculum

COLLECTIONS: [1830s] Early domestic and agricultural life, textiles, Cherry hill site artifacts.

HOURS: Mar-June, Sept-Dec Su 1-4; July-Aug W-Su 1-4

ADMISSION: $5, Family $12,

MOORETOWN

9752
Moore Museum
94 Moore Line, N0N 1M0; (p) (519) 867-2020; lmason@twp.stclair.on.ca; (c) Lambton

1975/ Corp of the Township of St. Clair/ staff: 1(f); 2(p); 50(v)/ members: 105

HISTORY MUSEUM: Collects, preserves, re-searches, houses, exhibits, and interprets the artifacts of Moore Township.

PROGRAMS: Community Outreach; Concerts; Exhibits; Family Programs; Festivals; School-Based Curriculum

COLLECTIONS: [1800-present] Household, marine, and agricultural artifacts in interpretive log cabin and Victorian cottage; railroad, blacksmith shop.

HOURS: Mar-June W-Su 11-5; July-Aug Daily 11-5; Sept-mid Dec M-F 9-4

ADMISSION: $4, Student $3; Children $2; Seniors $3.50

MORRISBURG

9753
Upper Canada Village Parks Commission, St. Lawrence
RR # 1, K0C 1X0; (p) (613) 543-3704; (f) (613) 543-4098; www.uppercanadavillage.com/filmvil.htm State/ 1961/ staff: 6(f); 149(p)

HISTORY MUSEUM; HOUSE MUSEUM; LIVING HISTORY/OUTDOOR MUSEUM: Represents an early Ontario rural riverfront community of the 1860.

PROGRAMS: Elder's Programs; Facility Rental; Festivals; Film/Video; Garden Tours; Guided Tours; Interpretation; Lectures; Living History; Reenactments; Research Library/Archives; School-Based Curriculum

COLLECTIONS: [18th-19th c] Over 60,000 artifacts housed in historic buildings.

HOURS: May-Oct Daily

MT. BRYDGES

9754
Ska-Nah-Doht Iroquian Village and Museum
8348 Longwoods Rd Longwoods Rd Conservation Area, N0L 1W0 [8449 Irish Dr, RR # 1, N0L 1W0]; (p) (519) 264-2420; (f) (519) 264-1562; lowerthames@odyssey.on.ca; www.lowerthames-conservation.on.ca

1973/ staff: 13(f); 2(p); 24(v)

LIVING HISTORY/OUTDOOR MUSEUM: Promotes Iroquois culture.

PROGRAMS: Facility Rental; Festivals; School-Based Curriculum

COLLECTIONS: [800-1200 AD] Over 60,000 arrowheads, pottery, flora and fauna, artifacts.

HOURS: Yr Sept-June M-F 9-4:30; July 1-Sept 1 Daily 9-4:30

ADMISSION: $3, Children $2

NAPANEE

9755
Allan MacPherson House and Park
180 Elizabeth St, K7R 1B5 [PO Box 183, K7R 1B5]; (p) (613) 354-5982; (f) (613) 354-5285

Private non-profit/ 1967/ Lennox and Addington Historical Society/ staff: 80(v)/ members: 40

HISTORIC SITE

PROGRAMS: Concerts; Facility Rental; Festivals; Guided Tours

COLLECTIONS: [1826-1841] Period household artifacts.

HOURS: Mid Mar-Mid Dec W-Su and holiday & M 12-5:30

ADMISSION: $3, Family $7, Student $2, Children $1, Seniors $2

9756
Lennox and Addington County Museum and Archives
97 Thomas St East, K7R 3S9 [Postal Bag 1000, K7R 3S9]; (p) (613) 354-3027; (f) (613) 354-3112; museum@fox.nstn.ca; fox.nstn.ca/museum/; (c) Lennox & Addington County/ 1976/ staff: 3(f); 1(p); 10(v)/publication: *Bath on the Bay of Quinte; Bornon the Island*

HISTORY MUSEUM: Houses the collections of the Lennox and Addington Historical Society.

PROGRAMS: Community Outreach; Exhibits; Family Programs; Lectures; Publication; Research Library/Archives; School-Based Curriculum

COLLECTIONS: [19th-20th c] Artifacts and archives: textiles, costume, tools, technology, furniture, newspapers, photos, business and family records; 1,000 shelf feet archival collections.

HOURS: Museum: Yr May-Oct Daily 10-4:30; Nov-Mar M-F 10-4:30; Archives: T-F 10-12 / 1-4:30

ADMISSION: $3, Family $5, Student $2, Children $1, Seniors $2.50

9757
Lennox and Addington Historical Society
[PO Box 392, K79 3P5]; (p) (613) 354-3027; (c) Lennox and Addington

Private non-profit/ 1907/ staff: 160(p)/publication: *Papers and Records*

HISTORICAL SOCIETY: Collects and preserves county history; maintains Lennox and Addington County Museum, Allan Macpherson House.

PROGRAMS: Annual Meeting; Publication

COLLECTIONS: [1793-present]

9758
Old Hay Bay Church
2371 S Shore Rd, K7R 3K7 [RR #2, K7R 3K7]; (p) (613) 373-2877; (f) (613) 373-0043; staples@horizons.net

1792/ staff: 25(v)

HISTORIC SITE

PROGRAMS: Community Outreach; Exhibits; Guided Tours; Interpretation

COLLECTIONS: [1792-present] Church artifacts.

HOURS: June-Sept Daily 9-5

NEPEAN

9759
Nepean Museum, The
16 Rowley Ave, K2G 1L9; (p) (613) 723-7936; (f) (613) 723-7936; nmchin@travel-net.com; www.nepeanmuseum.on.ca/

1983/ staff: 2(f); 1(p); 35(v)/ members: 125

HISTORY MUSEUM

PROGRAMS: Annual Meeting; Community Outreach; Exhibits; Facility Rental; Family Programs; Guided Tours; Interpretation; Lectures; Publication; Research Library/Archives; School-Based Curriculum

COLLECTIONS: [1792-present] Artifacts, memorabilia.

HOURS: Yr

ADMISSION: No charge

NEWMARKET

9760
Elman W. Campbell Museum
134 Main St S, L3Y 3Y7; (p) (905) 953-5314; (f) (905) 898-2083

City/ 1982/ staff: 1(f); 2(p); 30(v)/ members: 30/publication: *Newmarket Historical Society Occasional Papers*

HISTORIC SITE; HISTORICAL SOCIETY; HISTORY MUSEUM: Collects, preserves, researches, and interprets town history.

PROGRAMS: Exhibits; Family Programs; Festivals; Guided Tours; Interpretation; Lectures; Publication; Research Library/Archives; School-Based Curriculum

COLLECTIONS: [1800-30 years BP] Tools, textiles, furniture, toys, newspapers, photos, books, manuscripts, files, maps, microfilm.

HOURS: Yr T-Sa 10-12/1-4

ADMISSION: No charge

NIAGARA FALLS

9761
Historic Fort Erie
350 Lakeshore Rd, L2E 6T2 [Niagra Parks Commission, PO Box 150, L2E 6T2]; (p) (905) 871-0540; (f) (905) 354-6041; npinfo@ niagaraparks.com; www.niagaraparks.com

1936/ staff: 12(p); 2(v)

HISTORIC SITE; HISTORY MUSEUM; LIVING HISTORY/OUTDOOR MUSEUM: Promotes 19th c fort life.

PROGRAMS: Community Outreach; Exhibits; Family Programs; Guided Tours; Interpretation; Living History; Publication; Reenactments; School-Based Curriculum

COLLECTIONS: [War of 1812] Archaeological artifacts.

HOURS: May-Nov, varies

ADMISSION: $5, Children $3

9762
Laura Secord Homestead
29 Queenston St, L2E 6T2 [PO Box 150, Niagara Parks Commission, L2E 6T2]; (p) (905) 262-4851; (f) (905) 354-6041; npinfo@niagaraparks.com; www.niagaraparks.com; (c) Niagara-on-the-Lake

Joint/ 1998/ staff: 4(p)

HISTORIC SITE: Preserves and presents Laura Secord history.

PROGRAMS: Community Outreach; Exhibits; Family Programs; Guided Tours; Interpretation; Living History; Publication; School-Based Cur-

riculum

COLLECTIONS: [1800-1835] Household furnishings, textiles, books, and artwork.

HOURS: May-Nov vary

ADMISSION: $1.75, Children $1

9763
Lundy's Lane Historical Museum
5810 Ferry St, L2G 1S9; (p) (905) 358-5082; (f) (905) 358-0920

City/ 1971/ staff: 2(f); 2(p)

HISTORIC SITE; HISTORY MUSEUM

PROGRAMS: Community Outreach; Exhibits; Research Library/Archives

COLLECTIONS: Artifacts: War of 1812, Battle of Lundy's Lane, the Battle of Queenton Heights, pioneer artifacts, Niagara Falls, textiles, Victorian.

HOURS: Yr May-Nov Daily 9-4; Dec-Apr M-F 12-4

ADMISSION: $1.60, Student $1, Seniors $1; Under 5 free

9764
McFarland House
15927 Niagara River Pkwy, L2E 6T2 [Niagara Falls Commission, PO Box 150, L2E 6T2]; (p) (905) 468-3322; (f) (905) 354-6041; npinfo@niagaraparks.com; www.niagaraparks.com; (c) Niagara-on-the-Lake

Joint/ 1959/ staff: 6(p); 12(v)

GARDEN; HISTORIC SITE; HOUSE MUSEUM; LIVING HISTORY/OUTDOOR MUSEUM: Costumed guides aid in the exploration of the fully furnished Empire period house and herb garden. Homebaked goods are produced for the tea room, and special events run year-round.

PROGRAMS: Exhibits; Family Programs; Garden Tours; Guided Tours; Interpretation

COLLECTIONS: [1800-1840] Empire period furniture, silver, art and textiles.

HOURS: May-Nov call for hours and days

ADMISSION: $1.75, Children

9765
Willoughby Township Historical Museum
9935 Niagara Pkwy, RR # 3, L2E 6S6; (p) (905) 295-4036; (f) (905) 295-4036; willomus@becon.org; niagara.becon.org/~willomus; (c) Region Niagara

City; Private non-profit/ 1968/ staff: 1(f); 4(p); 14(v)

HISTORICAL SOCIETY; HISTORY MUSEUM: Collects, preserves, interprets, and exhibits the history of Willoughby.

PROGRAMS: Community Outreach; Exhibits; Family Programs; Guided Tours; Research Library/Archives

COLLECTIONS: [Mid 1700s-1960] Pioneer settlement artifacts housed in former one-room rural schoolhouse.

HOURS: Mid May June and Sept-Oct Sa-Su 12-5; July-Aug Daily 12-5

ADMISSION: Donations accepted

NIAGARA ON THE LAKE

9766
Samuel E. Weir Collection, The
116 Queenston St, L0S 1J0 [RR # 1, L0S 1J0]

Private non-profit/ 1983/ staff: 3(f); 4(p); 8(v)

ART MUSEUM; LIBRARY AND/OR ARCHIVES

PROGRAMS: Community Outreach; Exhibits; Guided Tours; Lectures; Publication; Research Library/Archives

COLLECTIONS: [1750-1945] Canadian, American, European art; 5000 volume library.

HOURS: Mid May-mid Oct W-Sa 11-5; Su 1-5

ADMISSION: No charge

NIAGARA-ON-THE-LAKE

9767
Ghost Tours of Niagara
Fort George, L0S 1J0 [607-20 Bradmon Dr, St. Catharines, L2M 3S5]; (p) (905) 468-6621; ghosttours@hotmail.com

Private non-profit/ 1994/ Friends of Fort George/ staff: 10(p)/publication: *Niagara's Ghosts at Fort George*

HISTORICAL SOCIETY: Promotes history of Niagara, and Fort George.

PROGRAMS: Guided Tours; Lectures; Publication

COLLECTIONS: Databases of contemporary and historical accounts of Niagara region haunting.

HOURS: May-Oct Su, M, Th, vary

ADMISSION: $5, Children $2

9768
Parks Canada-Niagara National Historic Sites
Queen's Parade, L0S 1J0 [PO Box 787, L0S 1J0]; (p) (905) 468-6600, (905) 468-4257; (f) (905) 468-4638; Ron_Dale@pch.gc.ca; (c) Lincoln

Federal/ 1796/ staff: 14(f); 40(p); 60(v)

LIVING HISTORY/OUTDOOR MUSEUM: Preserves Fort George history.

PROGRAMS: Community Outreach; Exhibits; Facility Rental; Family Programs; Festivals; Guided Tours; Interpretation; Living History; Reenactments; School-Based Curriculum

COLLECTIONS: [1812] Original furnishings and artifacts, reproductions from War of 1812.

HOURS: Apr-Oct Daily 9:30-5; Nov-Mar by appt

ADMISSION: $6, Children $4, Seniors $5

NORTH BAY

9769
Buxton national historic site
100 Main St East, P1B 1A8; (p) (705) 476-2323; (f) (705) 476-9300; nbamchin@vianet.on.ca; www.city.north-bay.on.ca/museum/; (c) District of Nipissing

Private non-profit/ 1973/ staff: 2(f); 1(p); 35(v)/ members: 150

HISTORY MUSEUM: Collects, preserves, exhibits, and interprets the growth and development of North Bay.

PROGRAMS: Annual Meeting; Community Outreach; Exhibits; Guided Tours; Interpretation; School-Based Curriculum

COLLECTIONS: [1890-1945] Archives: maps, slides, photos, business records, architectural drawings, and rail memorabilia.

HOURS: Yr M-Sa 9-5

ADMISSION: $3, Student

NORTH BUXTON

9770
Buxton National Historic Site and Museum
[PO Box 53, N0P 1Y0]; (p) (519) 352-4799; (f) (519) 352-8561; jdnewby@ciacess.com; www.ciacess.com/~jdnewby/

1967/ Buxton Historical Society/ staff: 4(p); 20(v)

HISTORIC PRESERVATION AGENCY; HISTORIC SITE; HISTORICAL SOCIETY; HISTORY MUSEUM; RESEARCH CENTER: The exhibits and collection of the Buxton Museum portray the story of Elgin Settlement and the Buxton Mission, a haven for fugitive slaves. This was perhaps the most successful settlement of its kind and has been recognized as a National Historic Site.

PROGRAMS: Community Outreach; Exhibits; Festivals; Guided Tours; Reenactments; Research Library/Archives

COLLECTIONS: [1849-1900] Items that belonged to the Black pioneer families that left slavery and found freedom in Canada: household goods, agricultural equipment, papers, manuscripts, and family bibles.

HOURS: Apr-Sept W-Su 1-4:30

ADMISSION: $5

NORTH CHATHAM

9771
Chatham-Kent Museum
75 William St, N7M 4L4; (p) (519) 354-8338; (f) (519) 354-4170; cccchin@ciacess.com

City/ 1943/ staff: 2(f); 3(p); 10(v)

HISTORY MUSEUM: Preserves local history.

PROGRAMS: Exhibits; Family Programs; Guided Tours; Interpretation; Lectures; Research Library/Archives; School-Based Curriculum

COLLECTIONS: Photos.

HOURS: Yr M-Su 1-5

ADMISSION: Donations accepted

NORTH YORK

9772
Gibson House Museum, The
5172 Yonge St, M2N 5P6; (p) (416) 395-7432; (f) (416) 395-7442

City/ 1971/ staff: 2(f); 5(p); 20(v)

HOUSE MUSEUM: Restored farm home of politician, land surveyor, and farmer David Gibson and family.

PROGRAMS: Community Outreach; Elder's

Programs; Exhibits; Facility Rental; Family Programs; Guided Tours; Interpretation; Living History; School-Based Curriculum

COLLECTIONS: [1850-1860] Period furnishing, land surveying, tools.

HOURS: Jan-Aug and Oct-Dec T-F 9:30-4:40, Sa-Su and holidays 12-5

ADMISSION: $2.75, Student $2.25, Children $1.75, Seniors $2.25

OIL SPRINGS

9773
Oil Museum of Canada
2423 Kelly Rd, Box 16, N0N 1P0; (p) (519) 834-2840; (f) (519) 834-2840; omcchin@ebtech.net; (c) Lambton

County/ 1960/ staff: 1(f); 3(p); 3(v)/ members: 50/publication: *Rivers of Oil, Hard Oiler*

HISTORIC SITE; HISTORY MUSEUM; LIVING HISTORY/OUTDOOR MUSEUM

PROGRAMS: Community Outreach; Elder's Programs; Exhibits; Family Programs; Film/Video; Guided Tours; Interpretation; Lectures; Living History; Publication; Research Library/Archives; Theatre

COLLECTIONS: [1854-present] Oil industry artifacts, geological displays.

HOURS: May-Dec Daily 10-5; Jan-Apr M-F 10-5

ADMISSION: $5, Family$15; Student $4; Children $3; Seniors $4

OSHAWA

9774
Robert McLaughlin Gallery
72 Queen St Civic Centre, L1H 3Z3; (p) (950) 576-3000; (f) (905) 576-9774; communications@rmg.on.ca; www.rmg.on.ca

Private non-profit/ 1967/ staff: 8(f); 2(p); 50(v)/ members: 500

ART MUSEUM; LIBRARY AND/OR ARCHIVES: Exhibits, collects, and preserves Canadian art history.

PROGRAMS: Annual Meeting; Community Outreach; Concerts; Elder's Programs; Exhibits; Facility Rental; Family Programs; Film/Video; Guided Tours; Interpretation; Lectures; Publication; Research Library/Archives; School-Based Curriculum

COLLECTIONS: [Victorian era-present] Canadian art; paintings; historic photos; Native art.

HOURS: Yr T, W, F 10-5; Th 10-9, Sa-Su 12-4

ADMISSION: Donations accepted

OTTAWA

9775
Archives of the University of Ottawa
100 Marie-Curie, K1N 6N5 [PO Box 450, Station A, K1N 6N5]; (p) (613) 562-5750; (f) (613) 562-5198; archives@uottawa.ca; www.uottawa.ca/services/archives

Private non-profit/ 1967/ staff: 5(f); 2(p)

HISTORY MUSEUM: Preserves documents of Univ of Ottawa.

PROGRAMS: Community Outreach; Exhibits; Guided Tours; Research Library/Archives

COLLECTIONS: [1848-1998] Photos, textiles, clothing, posters, film, artifacts.

HOURS: Yr M-F 8:30-12:30/1-4

9776
Canada Agriculture Museum
Experimental Farm Dr, K1G 5A3 [PO Box 9724, Station T, K1G 5A3]; (p) (613) 991-3044; (f) (613) 947-2374; mdondoTardiff@nmstc.ca; www.agriculture.nmstc.ca

Federal/ 1983/ staff: 20(f); 3(p); 10(v)/ members: 18000

HISTORY MUSEUM: Interprets Canada's agricultural heritage.

PROGRAMS: Exhibits; Facility Rental; Festivals; Guided Tours; Interpretation; Research Library/Archives; School-Based Curriculum

COLLECTIONS: Power, tillage, harvesting, seed processing, seasonal rural industries, barn equipment, and land improvement equipment.

HOURS: Yr Daily 9-5

ADMISSION: $5, Family $12, Student $4, Children $3,

9777
Canadian Conservation Institute
1030 Innes Rd, K1A 0M5; (p) (613) 998-3721; cci-icc_services@pch.gc.ca; www.pch.gc.ca/cci-icc

Federal/ 1972/ Government of Canada/ staff: 90(f)

PROFESSIONAL ORGANIZATION: Promotes conservation and professional development workshops.

PROGRAMS: Publication; Research Library/Archives

HOURS: Yr M-F 8:30-4:30

9778
Canadian Museum of Contemporary Photography
1 Rideau Canal, K1N 9N6 [PO Box 465, Station A, K1N 9N6]; (p) (613) 990-8257; (f) (613) 990-5654; cmcp@ngc.chin.gc.ca; cmcp.gallery.ca

Federal/ 1985/ staff: 14(f); 8(p)/publication: *Exhibition Catalogues*

ART MUSEUM; LIBRARY AND/OR ARCHIVES: Collects, interprets, and disseminates contemporary Canadian photo as social documentation.

PROGRAMS: Exhibits; Facility Rental; Guided Tours; Interpretation; Publication; Research Library/Archives; School-Based Curriculum

COLLECTIONS: [1962-present] Over 160,000 photos, photo-based works, negatives and transparencies. Still photography division of the Nal Film Board of Canada, 1962-1985.

HOURS: Summer: Daily 10-6, Th 10-8;

9779
Canadian Museum of Nature
240 McCleod, K1P 6P4 [CP 3443, Station D, K1P 6P4]; (p) (613) 566-4700; (f) (613) 364-4021; www.nature.ca

1988/ Board of Trustees/ staff: 130(f); 40(p); 191(v)

HISTORY MUSEUM: Promotes natural history.

PROGRAMS: Community Outreach; Exhibits; Facility Rental; Festivals; Guided Tours; Interpretation; Lectures; Research Library/Archives; School-Based Curriculum

COLLECTIONS: [Mesozoic-present] Botany, vertebrates, invertebrates, and earth sciences.

HOURS: May 1-Oct 8 F-W 9:30-5, Th 9:30-8; Oct 9-Apr 30 T-Su 10-5, Th 10-8

ADMISSION: $6, Family $13, Student $5, Children $2.50

9780
Centre de Recherche en Civilisation Canadienne-Francaise de l'Universite d'Ottawa
Univ of Ottawa Lamoureux Hall 145 Jean-Jacques St, K1N 6N5 [145 Jean-Jacques Lussier St, PO Box 450 Stn A, K1N 6N5]; (p) (613) 562-5877; (f) (613) 562-5143; crccf@uottawa.ca; www.uottawa.ca/academic/crccf/

1958/ staff: 9(f); 1(v)/ members: 85/publication: *Bulletin du CRCCF*

LIBRARY AND/OR ARCHIVES: Supports projects in the humanities and social sciences; acquires and preserves archives.

PROGRAMS: Exhibits; Publication

COLLECTIONS: [1870-1998] 1.6 linear km of manuscripts, 1 million photos and 3,500 tapes, videocassettes, and films.

HOURS: Yr M-F 8:45-12/1-4:30 (3:30 from June-Aug)

9781
Currency Museum/Bank of Canada
245 Sparks St, K1A 0G9; (p) (613) 782-8914; (f) (613) 782-8874; museum-musee@bank-banque-canada.ca; www.bank-banque-canada.ca

Federal/ 1980/ staff: 8(f); 6(p)

HISTORY MUSEUM; RESEARCH CENTER: Promotes history of money.

PROGRAMS: Exhibits; Family Programs; Guided Tours; Interpretation; Publication; School-Based Curriculum

COLLECTIONS: [3000 BC-present] 100,000 artifacts: Canadian banknotes, pre-confederation coins and tokens; ancient, medieval and modern coins and tokens; world paper money; non-traditional forms of currency; savings banks; coinage tools; printing plates.

HOURS: Yr Sept-Apr 30 T-Su 10:30-5; May 1-Sept M-Sa 10:30-5, Su 1-5

ADMISSION: No charge

9782
National Archives of Canada
395 Wellington St, K1A 0N3; (p) (613) 995-5138; (f) (613) 995-6274; www/archives.ca

Federal/ 1872/ staff: 610(f)/publication: *The Archivist*

Preserves collective memory of the nation and government of Canada.

COLLECTIONS: [1490-present] Texts, photos, films, maps, videos, books, paintings, prints, and government files.

HOURS: Yr M-F 8:30-5

9783
National Library of Canada, Music Division/Bibliotheque
395 Wellington St, K1A 0N4; (p) (613) 996-2300; (f) (613) 952-2895; mus@nlc-bnc.ca

Federal/ 1953/ staff: 9(f); 1(p)

LIBRARY AND/OR ARCHIVES: Preserves and promotes Canadian music and musicians.

PROGRAMS: Concerts; Exhibits; Facility Rental; Lectures; Publication; Research Library/Archives

COLLECTIONS: [19th-20th c] Books, periodicals, musical scores, sheet music, concert programs, information files, commercial and non-commercial sound recordings (piano rolls, cylinders, 78-, 45-, and 33 1/3-rpm discs, cassettes, cartridges, open reel tapes, compact discs), video formats.

HOURS: Yr

9784
National Museum of Science and Technology
1867 St Laurent Blvd At Lancaster Rd, K1G 5A3 [PO Box 9724, Stn T, K1G 5A3]; (p) (613) 991-3044; (f) (613) 990-3654; scitech@nmstc.ca; www.science-tech.nmstc.ca

Federal; Joint/ 1967/ staff: 247(f); 439(v)/ members: 3332

HISTORY MUSEUM: Promotes natural history, science, and technology.

PROGRAMS: Exhibits; Facility Rental; Family Programs; Film/Video; Guided Tours; Interpretation; Lectures; Publication; Research Library/Archives; School-Based Curriculum

COLLECTIONS: [1850-present] Buggies, antique and classic cars, motorcycles, bicycles, buses, fire engines, trains, communications and space equipment, ship models, lighthouse, music boxes and telephones, clocks, household implements, computers, measurement tools, surveying tools, telescopes.

HOURS: Yr May 1- Sept Daily 9-5, F 9-9; Oct-Apr T-Su 9-5

ADMISSION: $6, Family $12, Student $5, Children $2, Seniors $5; Under 6 free

9785
Roman Catholic Archdiocesan Archives of Ottawa
1247 Kilborn Place, K1H 6K9; (p) (613) 738-5025; (f) (613) 738-0130; www.ottawa-ecclesia.org

1847/ staff: 1(f)

RESEARCH CENTER: Collects, preserves, and maintains records of the Archdiocese of Ottawa.

COLLECTIONS: Documents and correspondence.

HOURS: By appt

9786
Saint Paul University Archives
175 Main St, K1S 1C3; (p) (613) 237-0580

Private non-profit/ 1949/ staff: 1(p)

RESEARCH CENTER: Collects, preserves, and interprets Univ of Ottawa and St Paul Univ.

PROGRAMS: Research Library/Archives

COLLECTIONS: [1848-1998] 100,000 processed manuscripts, 200 registers, 2,500 volumes.

HOURS: Yr M-F 8:30-4

ADMISSION: No charge

OWEN SOUND

9787
Billy Bishop Heritage
948 3rd Ave West, N4K 4P6; (p) (519) 371-0031; (f) (519) 371-5310; info@billybishop.org; www.billybishop.org

Private non-profit/ 1979/ Board of Directors/ staff: 2(f); 3(p); 50(v)/ members: 120

HOUSE MUSEUM: Preserves the Victorian boyhood home of Canadian Ace Billy Bishop V.C.

PROGRAMS: Annual Meeting; Community Outreach; Exhibits; Festivals; Guided Tours; Interpretation; Research Library/Archives; School-Based Curriculum

COLLECTIONS: [World War I & II] Billy Bishop's bedroom filled with his memorabilia, World War I & II rooms, reference library, viewing room, hall history, parlor with original furniture, and family photos.

HOURS: Yr Jan-Apr M-F 1-4; May-Sept-Oct Daily 1-4; Jun-Aug M-Sa 10-4, Su 12-4

ADMISSION: $4, Family $10, Student $2

9788
County of Grey-Owen Sound Museum
975 6th St East, N4K 1G9; (p) (519) 376-3690, (800) 567-4739; (f) (519) 376-7970; museum@greycounty.on.ca; www.greycounty.on.ca.museum/; (c) Grey

1967/ staff: 4(f); 11(p); 250(v)

HOUSE MUSEUM; LIVING HISTORY/OUTDOOR MUSEUM: Collects and displays material culture and history.

PROGRAMS: Family Programs; Guided Tours; Living History; Publication; Research Library/Archives; School-Based Curriculum

COLLECTIONS: [1850s-1940s] First Nations artifacts, period furnishings and domestic items, spinning wheel, sawmill, garage, two steam traction engines, printing equipment, photos.

HOURS: Main building Yr; period buildings May-Oct T-F 9-5, Sa-Su 1-5

ADMISSION: $4, Student $2; Under 5 free

9789
Owen Sound Marine and Rail Museum
Former CNR Railroad Station, N4K 4K8 [1165 1st Ave West, N4K 4K8]; (p) (519) 371-3333; www.osaic.com/marinerail; (c) Grey County

Federal/ 1978/ staff: 4(v)/ members: 106

HISTORICAL SOCIETY; HISTORY MUSEUM

PROGRAMS: Annual Meeting; Exhibits; Film/Video; Guided Tours; Interpretation; Living History; Research Library/Archives; School-Based Curriculum

COLLECTIONS: [Late 19th-20th C] Maritime and rail artifacts.

HOURS: May-Oct T-Su, T-F 10-4:30, Su 1-4:30

ADMISSION: Donations accepted

PENETANGUISHENE

9790
Penetanguishene Centennial Museum
13 Burke St, L9M 1C1; (p) (705) 549-2150; (f) (705) 549-7542; pcmchin@lgs.net; www.huronet.com/penetang/2584new_site

City/ 1967/ staff: 1(f); 1(p); 40(v)/ members: 50

HISTORIC SITE; HISTORY MUSEUM: Promotes local history.

PROGRAMS: Concerts; Interpretation; Living History; Reenactments; Research Library/Archives; School-Based Curriculum

COLLECTIONS: [1875-1940] Community, lumber history.

HOURS: Yr Summer Daily 9:30-4:30; Winter 10-3

ADMISSION: $2.50, Family $5

PETERBOROUGH

9791
Canadian Canoe Museum, The
910 Monaghan Rd, K9J 7S4 [PO Box 1664, K9J 7S4]; (p) (705) 748-9153; (f) (705) 748-0616; canoemuseum@ptbo.igs.net; www.canoemuseum.net

Private non-profit/ 1975/ staff: 3(f); 6(p); 200(v)/ members: 350

HISTORIC PRESERVATION AGENCY; HISTORY MUSEUM; RESEARCH CENTER; TRIBAL MUSEUM: Preserves history of the canoe.

PROGRAMS: Exhibits; Facility Rental; Festivals; Guided Tours; Interpretation; Lectures; Living History; School-Based Curriculum

COLLECTIONS: [First peoples, European contact-present] West Coast dugouts, Arctic Kayaks, birch bark canoes.

HOURS: Yr Daily 10-4

ADMISSION: $4, Student $3, Children $2,

9792
Peterborough Historical Society
270 Brock St, K9H 2P9; (p) (705) 741-2600; (f) (705) 750-0395; history@nexicom.net; www.nexicom.net~/history/

Private non-profit/ 1896/ staff: 1(p); 50(v)/ members: 300/publication: *Peterborough Historical Society Bulletin*

HISTORICAL SOCIETY; HISTORY MUSEUM: Owned and operated by society to promote the preservation, restoration, and signage of heritage sites - maintains research and office facilities.

PROGRAMS: Annual Meeting; Community Outreach; Exhibits; Facility Rental; Guided Tours; Interpretation; Lectures; Living History; Publication; Research Library/Archives

COLLECTIONS: [1830-1870] Living interpretation of three families who lived in the house Hutchison - doctor in 1830s-1840s Sir Sandford Flenming Connal's businessman 1860s.

PETROLIN

9793
Petrolin Discovery Foundation, Inc., The
4381 Discovery Rd, N0N 1R0 [PO Box 1480, N0N 1R0]; (p) (519) 882-1897; (f) (519) 552-4209

Private non-profit/ 1980/ staff: 1(f); 4(p); 25(v)/publication: *Tales of Toil and Oil*

HISTORIC SITE; LIVING HISTORY/OUTDOOR MUSEUM: Preserves history of oil industry.

PROGRAMS: Annual Meeting; Facility Rental; Family Programs; Festivals; Film/Video; Guided Tours; Publication; Theatre

COLLECTIONS: [1866-1900] Historical oil field equipment with 20 working wells jerker line system of pumping wagons, fishing tools, derricks, Canadian drilling rig.

HOURS: May-Sept Daily 10-6; Sept-Oct 30

PORT COLBORNE

9794
Port Colborne Historical and Marine Museum
280 King St, L3K 5X8 [PO Box 572, L3K 5X8]; (p) (905) 834-7604; (f) (905) 834-6198; pcmchin@niagara.com; www.chin.qc.ca

City/ 1974/ staff: 2(f); 4(p); 100(v)/ members: 255/publication: *Museum Musings*

HISTORY MUSEUM; MARITIME MUSEUM: Promotes maritime history of Port Colborne and Welland Canal.

PROGRAMS: Community Outreach; Exhibits; Festivals; Guided Tours; Interpretation; Living History; Publication; Reenactments; Research Library/Archives; School-Based Curriculum

COLLECTIONS: 14,000 marine artifacts.

HOURS: May-Dec 12-5

ADMISSION: No charge

PORT PERRY

9795
Scugog Shores Historical Museum
16210 Island Rd, L9L 1B4; (p) (905) 985-3589; (f) (905) 985-3492; ssh-chin@durham.net; www.durham.net/~ssh-chin

Private non-profit/ 1969/ staff: 1(f); 1(p); 135(v)

LIVING HISTORY/OUTDOOR MUSEUM

PROGRAMS: Exhibits; Facility Rental; Festivals; Guided Tours; Interpretation; Living History; Research Library/Archives; School-Based Curriculum

COLLECTIONS: [1840-1940] Materials related to Lake Scugog area, Native American, Euro-Canadian cultural, and social development, history, exploration, settlement, agriculture, trade, education.

HOURS: Vary

ADMISSION: No charge

QUEENSTON

9796
Mackenzie Heritage Printery Museum
1 Queenston St, L2E 6T2 [Niagara Parks Commission, PO Box 150, Niagara Falls, L2E 6T2]; (p) (905) 262-5676; (f) (905) 354-6041; npinfo@niagaraparks.com; www. niagaraparks. com; (c) Niagara-on-the-Lake

Joint/ 1990/ staff: 4(p); 8(v)

ART MUSEUM; HISTORIC SITE; HISTORY MUSEUM; LIVING HISTORY/OUTDOOR MUSEUM: Preserves history of letterpress printing.

PROGRAMS: Community Outreach; Exhibits; Festivals; Guided Tours; Interpretation; Living History; Publication; Research Library/Archives; School-Based Curriculum

COLLECTIONS: Ppresses and typesetting machines; archives of artwork and print media.

HOURS: May-Nov vary

ADMISSION: $1.75, Children $1

RENFREW

9797
Renfrew and District Historical and Museum Society
Arthur Ave, K7V 4B1 [Box 544, K7V 4B1]; (p) (613) 432-2129

1967/ staff: 4(p); 12(v)/ members: 30

HISTORIC SITE; HISTORICAL SOCIETY: Preserves local history of Renfrew.

PROGRAMS: Exhibits; Guided Tours

COLLECTIONS: [Early 1900] Agriculture, farming tools, equipment, wedding dresses, military uniforms, dolls, toys, dishes, grist mill.

HOURS: Mid June-Sept Daily 10-4

ADMISSION: $1.75, Children $0.75

RIDGETOWN

9798
Ridge House Museum
53 Erie St S, NP 2C0 [PO Box 248, NP 2C0]; (p) (519) 674-2223; (f) (519) 674-0660

City/ 1974/ staff: 1(f); 25(v)/ members: 110

HISTORIC SITE; HOUSE MUSEUM: Depicts late 19th c lifestyle.

PROGRAMS: Annual Meeting; Community Outreach; Exhibits; Family Programs; Festivals; Guided Tours; Interpretation

COLLECTIONS: [1875] Household materials.

HOURS: Daily 10-4:30

RIDGEWAY

9799
Fort Erie Historical Museum
402 Ridge Rd, L0S 1N0 [PO Box 339, L0S 1N0]; (p) (905) 894-5322; (f) (905) 894-6851

City; Private non-profit/ 1970/ staff: 1(f); 20(v)

HISTORICAL SOCIETY; HISTORY MUSEUM; RESEARCH CENTER: Collects, preserves, researches, interprets, exhibits Fort Erie history; preserves Bertie Township Hall.

PROGRAMS: Community Outreach; Exhibits; Interpretation; Publication; School-Based Curriculum

COLLECTIONS: [Prehistory-present] 300,000 piece archaeological collection; genealogical records; photos.

HOURS: Mid June - Sept Daily 9-5

ADMISSION: $1.50, Children $0.50

9800
Ridgeway Battlefield Museum
Hwy #3 N Ridge Rd, L0S 1N0 [PO Box 339, L0S 1N0]; (p) (905) 894-3433

City/ 1983/ staff: 1(f); 20(v)

HOUSE MUSEUM: Preserve Battle of Ridgeway history.

COLLECTIONS: [1866] Historic cabin located on site of Battle of Ridgeway in 1866 (Fenian Raids); pioneer furnishings.

ADMISSION: $1, Children $0.50; No charge

ROCKTON

9801
Westfield Heritage Village
1049 Kirkwall Rd, L0R 1X0 [Westfield Heritage Village, L0R 1X0]; (p) (519) 621-8851; (f) (519) 621-6897; westfld@worldchat.com; worldchat.com/public/westfield/ westfl.htm; (c) Rockton

County/ Joint/ 1964/ staff: 4(f); 2(p); 280(v)/ members: 100

LIVING HISTORY/OUTDOOR MUSEUM

PROGRAMS: Annual Meeting; Community Outreach; Elder's Programs; Exhibits; Facility Rental; Family Programs; Film/Video; Guided Tours; Interpretation; Lectures; Living History; Reenactments; Research Library/Archives; School-Based Curriculum

COLLECTIONS: [1850s-early 1900s] 35 historical buildings, furniture, agricultural equipment, archival, books, photographs, clothing, quilts.

HOURS: Yr Mar-Dec by appt

ADMISSION: $5.50; Children $2.50; Seniors $4.50; Under 5 free

SAULT STE. MARIE

9802
Ermatinger/Clergue Heritage Site
831 Queen Ste, P6A 5X6 [PO Box 580, Sault Ste Marie, P6A 5X6]; (p) (705) 949-5733; (f) (705) 541-7023; old.stone.house@cityssm.on.ca

City/ 1970/ staff: 3(f); 3(p); 10(v)/ members: 3

HISTORIC SITE; HOUSE MUSEUM: Depicts the domestic and professional life of C.O. Ermatinger.

PROGRAMS: Community Outreach; Exhibits; Facility Rental; Family Programs; Festivals; Guided Tours; Interpretation; School-Based Curriculum

COLLECTIONS: [1800-1865] Household items, furnishings, clothing, jewelry, native artwork, painting, tools.

HOURS: Apr-May M-F 10-5; June-Sept Daily 10-5; Oct-Dec M-F 1-5, and by appt

ADMISSION: $2, Children $1.50, Seniors $1.50; Under 5 free

SIMCOE

9803
Lynnwood Arts Center
21 Lynnwood Ave, N3Y 4K8 [PO Box 67, N3Y 4K8]; (p) (519) 428-0540; (f) (519) 428-0549; lynnwood@kwic.com; (c) Norfock

Private non-profit/ 1974/ staff: 1(f); 4(p); 100(v)/ members: 300

CULTURAL CENTER: Preserves local art, culture, and heritage.

PROGRAMS: Annual Meeting; Community Outreach; Concerts; Exhibits; Facility Rental; Family Programs; Festivals; Film/Video; Publication; School-Based Curriculum

COLLECTIONS: Alex Colurir and Michael Snow art.

HOURS: Yr W 12-4, T-Th-F 12-8, Sa 10-4, Su 12-4

ADMISSION: Under 12

SIOUX LOOKOUT

9804
Sioux Lookout Museum
Wellington, P8T 1B9 [Box 1377, P8T 1B9]; (p) (807) 737-1994, (807) 737-4264

City/ staff: 2(p)

HISTORY MUSEUM: Preserves Sioux Lookout's history.

PROGRAMS: Exhibits

COLLECTIONS: [1890-1950]

HOURS: June-Sept M-F

ADMISSION: No charge

SMITH FALLS

9805
Rideau Canal Museum
34 Beckwith St, K7A 2A8; (p) (613) 284-0505; (f) (613) 283-4764; rcmc@superaie.com; (c) Lanark

Private non-profit/ 1991/ staff: 1(f); 3(p)

HISTORY MUSEUM: Preserves history of Rideau Canal.

PROGRAMS: Exhibits; Facility Rental; Guided Tours; Interpretation; School-Based Curriculum

COLLECTIONS: [1830s-1900] Tools, photos, drawings, artifacts related to the Rideau Canal story, 1826-1950.

HOURS: May-Nov Daily 10-5

ADMISSION: $2.50, Student $2, Children $1.50, Seniors $2.25

SMITHS FALLS

9806
Heritage House Museum
Old Slys Rd, K7A 4T6 [PO Box 695, K7A 4T6]; (p) (613) 283-8560; (f) (613) 283-4764; hhmchin@superaje.com; (c) Lanark

City/ 1981/ staff: 2(f); 2(p); 25(v)/ members: 100

HISTORIC SITE; HISTORY MUSEUM; HOUSE MUSEUM

PROGRAMS: Community Outreach; Exhibits; Facility Rental; Family Programs; Guided Tours; Publication; School-Based Curriculum

COLLECTIONS: 7 furnished period rooms; artifacts, textiles, Smith Falls memorabilia.

HOURS: May 1-Dec 24 Daily 10:30-4:30; Jan 2-April 30 M-F 11-4:30

ADMISSION: $3, Student $2, Children $1.50, Seniors $2.50; Under 6 free

ST. GEORGE

9807
Adelaide Hunter Hoodless Homestead
359 Blue Lake Rd, RR #1, N0E 1N0; (p) (519) 448-1130

Private non-profit/ 1957/ Federated Women's Institutes of Canada/ staff: 1(f); 10(v)/ members: 11

HISTORIC SITE: Birthplace of the founder of the Women's Institutes.

PROGRAMS: Annual Meeting; Exhibits; Facility Rental; Guided Tours; Research Library/Archives

COLLECTIONS: [1857-1910]

HOURS: Feb 20-Dec 20 M-F 10-4; Summer M-F 10-4, Su 1-5

ADMISSION: $2

ST. THOMAS

9808
Elgin County Pioneer Museum
32 Talbot St, N5P 1A3; (p) (519) 634-6537; (f) (519) 633-3884; ecpmchin@execulink.com; www.execulink.com/~ecpmchin; (c) Elgin

County/ 1957/ staff: 1(f); 1(p); 95(v)/ members: 100

HISTORY MUSEUM; HOUSE MUSEUM: Collects, displays, and preserves artifacts pertaining to the history of Elgin County, the Duncombe family, and the City of St. Thomas.

PROGRAMS: Community Outreach; Elder's Programs; Exhibits; Facility Rental; Guided Tours; Interpretation; Publication; Research Library/Archives; School-Based Curriculum

COLLECTIONS: [1800-early 1900s] Furniture, home furnishings, clothing, books, jewelry, art, medical instruments, farm implements, pottery, silver, and tools.

HOURS: Yr May-Sept T-Sa 9-12/1-5; Sept-May T-Sa 1-5

ADMISSION: $4; Children $1

9809
Elgin Military Museum, The
30 Talbot St, N5P 1A3; (p) (519) 633-7641; (f) (519) 637-0580; emmchin@execulink.com; www.execulink.com/~ecpmchin/emm.htm

Private non-profit/ 1978/ staff: 1(f); 1(p); 35(v)/publication: The Cannon Speaks

HISTORY MUSEUM: Collects identifies, preserves, and interprets items relating to Canadian military history.

PROGRAMS: Exhibits; Guided Tours; Interpretation; Publication; Research Library/Archives; School-Based Curriculum

COLLECTIONS: [1800-present] Military uniforms, equipment, weapons, models, art, photos, books, manuals, documents, and maps.

HOURS: Yr T-Su 1-6

ADMISSION: $4, Children $1

9810
St. Thomas-Elgin Public Art Centre
301 Talbot St, N5P 1B5; (p) (519) 631-4040; (f) (519) 631-4057

Private non-profit/ 1969/ staff: 1(f); 45(v)/ members: 400

ART MUSEUM; HISTORY MUSEUM: Exhibits contemporary and historical art; preserves local art history.

PROGRAMS: Annual Meeting; Exhibits; Facility Rental; Guided Tours; Lectures

COLLECTIONS: [Late 19th c-present] 600 pieces of Canadian art; William St. Thomas-Smith, F.M. Bell-Smith, Clark McDougall, Ed Zelenak, and Walter Redinger.

HOURS: Yr T-W, F 12-5, Th 12-9pm, Sa 12-4

ADMISSION: No charge

9811
Battlefield House Museum
77 King St W, L8G 5E5 [PO Box 66561, L8G 5E5]; (p) (905) 662-8458; (f) (905) 662-0529; bhmchin@binatech.on.ca; alpha.binatech. on.ca/~bhmchin

City/ 1899/ staff: 1(f); 3(p); 65(v)

HISTORIC SITE; HOUSE MUSEUM; LIVING HISTORY/OUTDOOR MUSEUM: Collects, preserves, and interprets local history.

PROGRAMS: Annual Meeting; Exhibits; Festivals; Garden Tours; Guided Tours; Interpretation; Lectures; Living History; Reenactments; Research Library/Archives; School-Based Curriculum

COLLECTIONS: [Early 19th c] Military, portraits, furniture and textiles.

HOURS: May-Sept T-Su 10-4:30

ADMISSION: $2.75, Children $1.50,

9812
Erland Lee (Museum) Home
552 Ridge Rd, K2H 8L6; (p) (905) 662-2691; (f) (905) 662-2045; erlandlh@icom.ca; www.fwio.on.ca/fwio/promo

Private non-profit/ 1972/ staff: 1(f); 1(p); 10(v)

HOUSE MUSEUM: Birthplace of Women's Institutes organization, rural educational society.

PROGRAMS: Elder's Programs; Exhibits; Facility Rental; Guided Tours; School-Based Curriculum

COLLECTIONS: [1800-1930] Furniture, farm, and household artifacts; pictorial, archival history of Women's Institutes organization.

HOURS: Apr-Dec T-Sa 10-4, Su 1-5

STRAFORD

9813
Stratford-Perth Archives
24 St Andrew St, N5A 1A3; (p) (519) 273-0399; (f) (519) 271-6265; (c) Perth

Joint/ 1972/ Municipal (public) City of Stratford and County of Perth/ staff: 4(f); 4(p); 18(v)/ members: 32

LIBRARY AND/OR ARCHIVES: Promotes, preserves, and protects the documentary heritage of Perth County.

PROGRAMS: Community Outreach; Lectures; Research Library/Archives; School-Based Curriculum

COLLECTIONS: [1830-present] Schools, newspapers, photos, maps, municipal records, census, history books, and vital statistics indexes; private manuscripts and scrapbook collections; genealogy reference library.

HOURS: Yr Stratford: M-Sa

STRATFORD

9814
Stratford-Perth Museum
270 Water St, N5A 3C9; (p) (519) 271-5311; (f) (519) 271-0191; www.cyg.net/~spmuseum

Private non-profit/ 1993/ staff: 3(f); 30(v)/ members: 400

HISTORY MUSEUM: Collects, interprets, exhibits, and conserves material culture.

PROGRAMS: Community Outreach; Exhibits; Family Programs; Guided Tours; Interpretation; School-Based Curriculum

COLLECTIONS: [19th and 20th c] 10,000 artifacts.

HOURS: Yr May-Oct Su-M 12-4, T-Sa 10-5; Nov-Apr Su 12-4, T-Sa 10-4

ADMISSION: Donation required

STRATHROY

9815
Strathroy Middlesex Museum
84 Oxford St, N7G 3A5; (p) (519) 245-0492; smmchin@execulink.com; (c) Middlesex

Private non-profit/ 1971

HISTORY MUSEUM: Preserves and interprets history of Strathroy and Middlesex County.

PROGRAMS: Community Outreach; Concerts; Exhibits; Facility Rental; Family Programs; Lectures; Research Library/Archives; School-Based Curriculum

COLLECTIONS: [1832-1960] Domestic, agricultural, industrial, textiles, archives, photographs.

HOURS: Yr T-F 10-4, Sa 1-4

ADMISSION: $1

STURGEON FALLS

9816
Musee Sturgeon River House Museum
250 Fort Rd, P0H 2G0 [Box 1390, P0H 2G0]; (p) (705) 753-4716; (f) (705) 753-5476; srhchin@onlink.net; (c) Nipissing

1967/ staff: 3(f); 20(v)

HISTORY MUSEUM; LIVING HISTORY/OUTDOOR MUSEUM: Preserves site of Hudson's Bay Company trading post and history of trapping.

PROGRAMS: Community Outreach; Exhibits; Facility Rental; Guided Tours; Interpretation

COLLECTIONS: [1850-1950] Blacksmith tools, kitchen implements, carpentry tools, farm equipment, trapping tools, traps, skinning tools and poles, logging tolls, fur press, mounted furbarers.

HOURS: Yr Mid May - Mid Oct Daily 10-5; Mid Oct-mid May M-F 10-4

SUDBURY

9817
Centre Franco-Ontarien de Folklore
38 Rue Xavier, P3C 2B9; (p) (705) 675-8986; (f) (705) 675-5809

1972/ staff: 3(f); 1(p); 10(v)/ members: 200/publication: *Les Memoires de ti-Jean, Repetoire du Patrimoine Franco-Ontarien*

HISTORY MUSEUM; RESEARCH CENTER: Promotes oral tradition and Franco-Ontarian Folklore.

PROGRAMS: Annual Meeting; Community Outreach; Exhibits; Facility Rental; Guided Tours; Interpretation; Publication; Research Library/Archives

COLLECTIONS: Audio recordings of tales, legends, and songs; manuscript; database of inventory of Franco-Ontarien heritage; 5,000 works on folklore and heritage.

HOURS: Yr M-F

THUNDER BAY

9818
Northwestern Ontario Sports Hall of Fame
219 May St S, P7E 1B5; (p) (807) 622-2852; (f) (807) 622-2736; nwosport@air.on.ca

Private non-profit/ 1978/ staff: 2(f); 1(p)/ members: 400

HISTORY MUSEUM: Preserves sports lineage of Northwestern ON.

PROGRAMS: Annual Meeting; Community Outreach; Exhibits; Research Library/Archives; School-Based Curriculum

COLLECTIONS: [Late 1800s-present] Artifacts and archives.

HOURS: Yr

9819
Old Fort William
King Rd from Broadway, P0T 2Z0 [Vickers Heights PO, P0T 2Z0]; (p) (807) 473-2312; (f) (807) 473-2344; info@oldfortwilliam.on.ca; www.oldfortwilliam.on.ca

1973/ staff: 21(f); 120(p); 200(v)

LIVING HISTORY/OUTDOOR MUSEUM: Depicts the fur trade activities of the North West Company.

PROGRAMS: Concerts; Elder's Programs; Facility Rental; Festivals; Guided Tours; Interpretation; Living History; Reenactments; Research Library/Archives; School-Based Curriculum; Theatre

COLLECTIONS: [1790s-1820s] Artifacts.

HOURS: Mid May-Mid Oct Daily 9-5

ADMISSION: $12, Family $34, Student $10, Children $9, Seniors $10; Under 5 free

9820
Paipoonge Historical Museum
Hwy 130 and Rosslyn Rd, P7C 5N5 [RR #6, P7C 5N5]; (p) (807) 939-1263; (f) (807) 939-4132; lgarrity@tbaytel.net; (c) Paipoonge

County/ 1951/ staff: 1(f); 1(p); 20(v)/ members: 100

HISTORY MUSEUM: Preserves and promotes local history.

PROGRAMS: Community Outreach; Concerts; Elder's Programs; Facility Rental; Family Programs; Guided Tours; Lectures; Research Library/Archives; School-Based Curriculum

COLLECTIONS: [1890-1960s] Collection of artifacts denoting life in a farming area.

HOURS: T-Su 1-5

ADMISSION: $2; Children free

9821
Thunder Bay Historical Museum Society, The
425 Donald St East, P7E 5V1; (p) (807) 623-0801; (f) (807) 622-6880; tbhms@tbaytel.net; www.tbaytel.net/tbhms/

Private non-profit/ 1908/ staff: 4(f); 3(p); 75(v)/ members: 1100

HISTORICAL SOCIETY; HISTORY MUSEUM: Preserves Thunder Bay history.

PROGRAMS: Annual Meeting; Exhibits; Facility Rental; Lectures; Publication; Research Library/Archives; School-Based Curriculum

COLLECTIONS: [1815-present] Papers and the records of businesses, military units, and community organizations; 150,000 images, 1,500 maps; artifacts.

HOURS: Yr June 16-Aug M-Su 11-5; Sept-June 15 T-Su 1-5

TILLSONBURG

9822
Annandale National Historic Site
30 Tillson Ave, N4G 2Z8; (p) (519) 842-2294; (f) (519) 842-9431; (c) Oxford

City/ 1973/ staff: 2(f); 65(v)/ members: 157

HISTORIC SITE: Nationally and Provincially designated historic house restored to the 1880s Aesthetic Art Style; museum.

PROGRAMS: Annual Meeting; Concerts; Exhibits; Facility Rental; Family Programs; Festivals; Guided Tours; Lectures; Publication; Research Library/Archives; School-Based Curriculum

COLLECTIONS: [1880-1940] Furnishings for the restored house; photos, textiles, clothing, bedding, Tillson family memorabilia, artifacts, business ledgers, deeds.

HOURS: Yr Sept-June M-F 9-4, Su 1-4; July-Aug M-F 9-4, Sa 12-4, Su 1-4

ADMISSION: $4, Family $10, Children $2; Group rates

TIMMINS

9823
Timmins Museum: National Exhibition Centre
70 Legion Dr, P4N 1B0 [220 Algonquin Blvd E, P4N 1B0]; (p) (705) 235-5066; (f) (705) 235-9631; tmnec@city.timmins.on.ca

City/ 1972/ staff: 3(f); 4(p); 25(v)/ members: 300/publication: Clio

HISTORY MUSEUM: Preserves, presents, and promotes the heritage, and culture of Timmins and North-Eastern Ontario.

PROGRAMS: Community Outreach; Exhibits; Facility Rental; Family Programs; Festivals; Film/Video; Guided Tours; Interpretation; Lec-

tures; Publication; Research Library/Archives; School-Based Curriculum

COLLECTIONS: [Early 20th c] 15,000 photos, art, newspapers, archival material.

HOURS: Yr M-F 9-5, Sa-Su 1-5

ADMISSION: $2, Family $4, Student $1, Seniors $1; Under 12 free

TORONTO

9824
Anglican Church of Canada, General Synod Archives
600 Jarvis St, M4Y 2J6; (p) (416) 924-9192; (f) (416) 968-7983; archives@national.anglican.ca

Private non-profit/ 1955/ Anglican Church of Canada/ staff: 2(f)

LIBRARY AND/OR ARCHIVES: Preserves Church history.

PROGRAMS: Research Library/Archives

COLLECTIONS: [1955-present] General Synod records.

HOURS: Yr M-F 9:15-4:15

9825
Anglican Diocese of Toronto Archives, The
135 Adelaide St, East, M5C 1L8; (p) (416) 363-6021; (f) (416) 363-7678; manicholls@toronto.anglican.ca; www.toronto.anglican.ca

Private non-profit/ 1839/ The Incorporated Synod of the Anglican Diocese of Toronto/ staff: 1(f); 2(v)

LIBRARY AND/OR ARCHIVES

COLLECTIONS: Collects and preserves the records of synod, its officials, clergy, parishes, andorganizations.

HOURS: Yr T-W 9-4; Summer T-W 9-3

9826
Archives of Ontario
77 Grenville St, Unit 300, M5S 1B3; (p) (416) 327-1600; (f) (416) 327-1999; reference@archives.gov.on.ca; www.gov.on.ca/MCZCR/archives

Provincial/ 1903/ Ontario Ministry of Citizenship, Culture, and Recreation/ staff: 66(f)/ members: 1

LIBRARY AND/OR ARCHIVES: Provides corporate leadership in the management and preservation of information; provides public access to ON's collective memory.

PROGRAMS: Research Library/Archives

COLLECTIONS: [1783-present] Government and private records, maps, photos, plan; 200,000 cubic feet.

HOURS: Yr M-Sa 8:30-10

9827
Archives of the Institute of the Blessed Virgin Mary
Loretto Abbey, 101 Mason Blvd, M5M 3E2; (p) (416) 487-5543; (f) (416) 485-9884; ana-ibvm@the-wire.com

Private non-profit/ 1847/ North American General Leadership - IBVM/ staff: 1(f); 3(p)

LIBRARY AND/OR ARCHIVES: Preserves

Record of the Institute of the Blessed Virgin Mary in North America.

PROGRAMS: Research Library/Archives

COLLECTIONS: [1847-present] 530 Linear feet of documents and photos.

HOURS: Yr by appt

9828
Black Creek Pioneer Village
1000 Murray Ross Pkwy, M3J 2P3; (p) (416) 736-1733; (f) (416) 661-6610

Joint/ 1960/ Toronto and Region Conservation Authority/ staff: 25(f); 40(p); 25(v)/ members: 12

LIVING HISTORY/OUTDOOR MUSEUM: Presents life in pre-confederation rural ON.

PROGRAMS: Exhibits; Facility Rental; Festivals; Garden Tours; Guided Tours; Interpretation; Living History; Reenactments; Research Library/Archives; School-Based Curriculum

COLLECTIONS: [1800-1867] Over 40 buildings, 50,000 museum artifacts, folk art, books, toys, and lighting.

HOURS: May-Dec Daily 10-5

ADMISSION: $9, Children $5, Seniors $7

9829
Canadian Association of Professional Heritage Consultants
[PO Box 1023, Station F, M4Y 2T7]; www.caphc.ca

Private non-profit/ 1987/ staff: 1(p)/ members: 200

PROFESSIONAL ORGANIZATION: Promotes heritage conservation.

PROGRAMS: Publication

9830
Canadian Lesbian and Gay Archives
56 Temperence St, Ste 201, M5W 1G2 [PO Box 639, Station A, M5W 1G2]; (p) (416) 777-2755; qveeries@clga.ca; www.clga.ca/archives/

Private non-profit/ 1973/ staff: 30(v)/ members: 350/publication: Lesbian and Gay Archivist

LIBRARY AND/OR ARCHIVES

PROGRAMS: Annual Meeting; Community Outreach; Exhibits; Facility Rental; Guided Tours; Interpretation; Lectures; Publication; Research Library/Archives

COLLECTIONS: [1960-present] 5,000 books, 6,000 periodical titles, personal and organizational records.

HOURS: Sept-July T-Th 7:30-10

ADMISSION: Donations accepted

9831
Canadian National Exhibition Archives
Exhibition Place, M6K 3C3; (p) (416) 263-3658; (f) (416) 3263-3681; Lcobon@explace.on.ca

City/ 1965/ Board of Governors of Exhibition Place/ staff: 2(f)

LIBRARY AND/OR ARCHIVES: Acquires, preserves, and makes available for research the records of the Board of Governors of Exhibition Place, the CNE Association, the Canadian International Ale Show, and the Warriors' Day Parade Council.

PROGRAMS: Community Outreach; Exhibits; Research Library/Archives

COLLECTIONS: [1879-present] Photos, film, printed material documenting the role of the CNE in promoting arts, industry, manufacturing, andagriculture in ON.

HOURS: Yr M-F 8:30-4:30

9832
Casa Loma
1 Austin Terrace, M5R 1X8; (p) (416) 923-1171; (f) (416) 923-5734; info@casaloma.org; www.casaloma.org

Private non-profit/ 1937/ staff: 21(f); 40(p)

GARDEN; HISTORIC SITE; HOUSE MUSEUM

PROGRAMS: Exhibits; Facility Rental; Family Programs; Garden Tours; Guided Tours; Interpretation; Publication; School-Based Curriculum

COLLECTIONS: [1880-1925] Furniture and decorative art in interpretive rooms.

HOURS: Yr Daily

ADMISSION: $10, Student $6, Children $6, Seniors $6

9833
City of Toronto Archives
255 Spadina Rd, M5R 2V3; (p) (416) 397-0778; (f) (416) 392-9685; archives@metrodesk.metrotor.on.ca

City/ 1998/ staff: 15(f)

LIBRARY AND/OR ARCHIVES: Preserves and provides access to records of the City.

PROGRAMS: Community Outreach; Exhibits; Facility Rental; Film/Video; Guided Tours; Research Library/Archives; School-Based Curriculum; Theatre

COLLECTIONS: 6,400 linear meters of textual records, 5,000 maps, 1.2 million photos, 110,000 architectural and engineering drawings, 3,500 sound and moving image records, 9,300 books and reports; government and non-governmental records.

HOURS: Yr M-F 10-4:30

9834
Gardiner Museum of Ceramic Art, The
S of Bloor St & Ave Rd, M5S 2C7 [111 Queen's Park, M5S 2C7]; (p) (416) 586-8080; (f) (416) 586-8085; mail@gardinermuseum.on.ca; www.gardinermuseum.on.ca

1984/ staff: 17(f); 10(p); 120(v)/ members: 800

ART MUSEUM; HISTORY MUSEUM: Promotes ceramic art and history.

PROGRAMS: Annual Meeting; Community Outreach; Concerts; Elder's Programs; Exhibits; Facility Rental; Family Programs; Festivals; Guided Tours; Interpretation; Lectures; Publication; Research Library/Archives; School-Based Curriculum

COLLECTIONS: [16th-18th c] Ancient American; Italian Renaissance majolica; English deftware; Chinese blue and white trade porcelain; large collection of early European porcelain, including Meissen, Du Paquier; French and English; Harlequin figures; contemporary ceramic art.

HOURS: Yr M,W,F 10-6, T,Th 10-8, Sa-Su 11-5

ADMISSION: $10, Family $24, Student $6, Seniors $6; Under 5 free; group rates

9835
Grange Art Gallery of Ontario, The
317 Dundas St W, M5T 1G4; (p) (416) 979-6660; (f) (416) 979-6666; Jennifer_Rieger@AGO.net; www.AGO.net

1973/ staff: 1(f); 79(v)

HISTORIC SITE: Preserves social history of Toronto.

PROGRAMS: Concerts; Elder's Programs; Family Programs; Guided Tours; Interpretation; Lectures; School-Based Curriculum

COLLECTIONS: [1835-1845] Period furniture, china, domestic artifacts.

HOURS: Yr W 12-9, Th-Su 12-4

ADMISSION: Donations requested

9836
Historic Fort York
100 Garrison Rd, M5B 1N2 [205 Yonge St, M5B 1N2]; (p) (416) 392-6907; (f) (416) 392-6917; info@torontohistory.on.ca; www.torontohistory.on.ca; (c) Tornoto

City/ 1934/ staff: 10(f); 15(p); 50(v)

HISTORIC SITE: Preserves and interprets Fort York.

PROGRAMS: Community Outreach; Exhibits; Facility Rental; Family Programs; Festivals; Guided Tours; Interpretation; Lectures; Living History; Reenactments; Research Library/Archives; School-Based Curriculum

COLLECTIONS: [1790-1930] Great Lakes region military artifacts, period room settings furnishings, officers and soldiers barracks, archaeological collections.

HOURS: Yr Daily

ADMISSION: $5

9837
HMCS Haida Historic Naval Ship
Ontario Place, M6K 3B9 [955 Lakeshore Blvd W, M6K 3B9]; (p) (416) 314-9755; (f) (416) 314-9878; hnmchin@planeteer.com; www3.sympatico.ca/hrc/haida

State/ 1943/ staff: 1(f); 9(p); 40(v)/ members: 500

HISTORIC SITE: Promotes military history in restored WW II tribal class destroyer.

PROGRAMS: Annual Meeting; Community Outreach; Facility Rental; Interpretation; Living History

COLLECTIONS: [1939-1963] Items of personal kit, naval uniforms, radio and communications equipment, cabin and mess dock furnishings, flags, drawings, photos, badges, small arms, machinery.

HOURS: May-Sept Daily

9838
Joan Baillie Archives of the Canadian
227 Front St East, M4E 1A8; (p) (416) 363-6671; (f) (416) 363-5584; birthe]@coc.ca

Private non-profit/ 1974/ staff: 1(p); 3(v)

Preserves records of opera company.

COLLECTIONS: [1950-present] Board minutes, financial records, set models, design and costume sketches, production videos and B&W photos and slides.

HOURS: Yr by appt

9839
Royal Canadian Military Institute
426 University Ave, M5X 1S9; (p) (416) 597-0286; (f) (416) 597-6919; www.tcmi.org

Private non-profit/ 1890/ staff: 1(p); 12(v)/ members: 2500

HISTORY MUSEUM: Collects military artifacts.

PROGRAMS: Concerts; Lectures; Research Library/Archives

COLLECTIONS: [1855-present] military artifacts: badges, medals, weapons.

HOURS: Yr M-Sa 9-5 by appt only

ADMISSION: No charge

9840
Royal Ontario Museum
100 Queens Park, M5S 2C6; (p) (416) 586-8000; (f) (416) 586-5863; info@rom.on.ca; www.rom.on.ca

Joint; Private non-profit; State/ 1912/ staff: 377(f); 260(p); 500(v)/ members: 3500

ART MUSEUM; HISTORY MUSEUM

PROGRAMS: Community Outreach; Concerts; Exhibits; Facility Rental; Family Programs; Film/Video; Guided Tours; Interpretation; Lectures; Publication; Research Library/Archives; School-Based Curriculum; Theatre

COLLECTIONS: [Prehistory-present] Human and natural history materials.

HOURS: Yr M-Th,Sa 10-6, F 10-9:30, Su 11-6

9841
Silverman Heritage Museum
3560 Bathurst St o/c Baycrest Centre, M6A 2E1; (p) (416) 785-2500; (f) (416) 785-4228; pdickmsm@baycrest.org; www.baycrest.org.

Private non-profit/ 1973/ staff: 1(p)

HISTORY MUSEUM: Promotes Jewish history and heritage.

PROGRAMS: Exhibits; Guided Tours; Interpretation

COLLECTIONS: [Late 19th c-1950] Jewish ceremonial objects, domestic items, religious books, photographs, documents, memorabilia related to history of Baycrest Centre.

HOURS: Yr Su-T 9-9, F

9842
Sir William Campbell Foundation
160 Queen St West, M5H 3H3; (p) (416) 597-0227; (f) (416) 975-1588; www.advsoc.on.ca

Private non-profit/ 1969/ staff: 2(f); 4(p); 40(v)

HISTORIC SITE; HOUSE MUSEUM: Preserves Campbell House, built for sixth Chief Justic of Upper Canada.

PROGRAMS: Exhibits; Facility Rental; Family Programs; Festivals; Garden Tours; Guided Tours; Interpretation; Living History; School-Based Curriculum

COLLECTIONS: [1822-1830] Georgian furniture and household items from Britain and North America.

HOURS: Yr Mid Sept-mid May M-F 9:30-4:30; Mid May-mid Sept M-F 9:30-4:30, Sa-Su 12-4:30

ADMISSION: $3.50; Student $2.50; Children $2; Seniors $2.50

9843
Textile Museum of Canada
55 Centre Ave, M5G 2H5; (p) (416) 599-5321; (f) (416) 599-2911; info@museumfortextiles.on.ca; www.museumfortextiles.on.ca

Private non-profit/ 1975/ staff: 5(f); 7(p); 150(v)/ members: 1000

HISTORY MUSEUM: Collects, exhibits, and documents textile evolution and history.

PROGRAMS: Annual Meeting; Community Outreach; Exhibits; Facility Rental; Lectures; Publication; Research Library/Archives

COLLECTIONS: 8,000 textiles:ceremonial cloths, garments, quilts, oriental rugs, coptic, pre-Columbian, Chinese, Japanese and Southeast Asian.

HOURS: Yr T, Th, F 11-5, W 11-8, Sa-Su 12-5

9844
Toronto Harbour Commission Archives
60 Harbour St, M5J 1B7; (p) (416) 863-2008; (f) (416) 863-4830; mdale@torontoport.com; www.torontoport.com

Federal/ 1911/ staff: 2(f)

LIBRARY AND/OR ARCHIVES: Operates the Port of Toronto and the Toronto City Center Airport; documents the history of Toronto waterfront development.

PROGRAMS: Research Library/Archives

COLLECTIONS: [20th c] Departmental files, photographs, engineering drawings, and publications.

HOURS: Yr M-F by appt only

9845
Town of York Historical Society, The
260 Adelaide St East, M4A 1N1; (p) (416) 865-1833; (f) (416) 865-9414; tfpo@total.net; www.townofyork.com

1983/ staff: 3(f); 2(p); 14(v)/ members: 400/publication: *Toronto 1837: A Model City*

HISTORIC SITE; HISTORICAL SOCIETY; HISTORY MUSEUM; HOUSE MUSEUM; LIVING HISTORY/OUTDOOR MUSEUM: Researches, interprets, and promotes history of early York/Toronto; operates Toronto's first Post Office.

PROGRAMS: Annual Meeting; Community Outreach; Exhibits; Family Programs; Guided Tours; Interpretation; Lectures; Living History; Publication; Research Library/Archives; School-Based Curriculum

COLLECTIONS: [1800-1870] Stampless covers, ink wells, printing equipment, correspondence of well known York/Toronto residents, archaeological finds, Post Office furnishings, desks, lap desks, portable desks.

HOURS: Yr M-F 9-4, Sa-Su 10-4

ADMISSION: No charge

9846
Trinity College Archives
6 Hoskin Ave, M5S 1H8; (p) (416) 978-2019; (f) (416) 978-2797; pilon@chass.utoronto.ca

1964/ staff: 4(p)

COLLECTIONS: [1850-present] Records of the Trinity College and related materials.

HOURS: M-W by appt

9847
York University Archives and Special Collections
Rm 305, Scott Library, M3J 1P3; (p) (416) 736-5442; (f) (416) 650-8039; archives@yorku.ca; info.library.youku.ca/depts/asc/archives.htm; (c) York

Joint/ 1970/ staff: 3(f)/publication: *Guide to Archival Holdings at York University Archives*

LIBRARY AND/OR ARCHIVES: Preserves and makes available the archives and the private archives of individuals and organizations that support research and teaching programs.

PROGRAMS: Publication; Research Library/Archives

COLLECTIONS: [19th c-present] Post-confederation Canadian studies including Canadian writers, Fine Arts, women's studies, urban reform movements.

HOURS: Yr M-F 9-4:30; Summer 10-4

UXBRIDGE

9848
Uxbridge-Scott Museum and Archives
7239 Concession 6, L9P 1N5 [Box 1301, L9P 1N5]; (p) (905) 852-5854; museum@inter-hop.net; www.uxlib.com/museum

City/ 1972/ staff: 1(f); 1(p); 20(v)

RESEARCH CENTER: Collects, preserves, and displays artifacts, photos, and documents relating to Uxbridge history.

PROGRAMS: Exhibits; Interpretation; Research Library/Archives; School-Based Curriculum

COLLECTIONS: [1800-1950] Artifacts, documents, and photos.

HOURS: May-Oct W-Su 10-5

ADMISSION: $2.50, Student $1.50

WATERLOO

9849
Brubacher House Museum
Columbia St, N2L 3G1 [Brubacher House, c/o University of Waterloo, N2L 3G1]; (p) (519) 886-3855

Joint/ 1850/ Univ of Waterloo and Conrad Grebel College/ staff: 2(p)

HISTORIC SITE; HISTORICAL SOCIETY; HISTORY MUSEUM; HOUSE MUSEUM: Offers Mennonite social history and the history of early Waterloo County.

PROGRAMS: Facility Rental; Guided Tours

COLLECTIONS: [1850-1890] 19th c Farmhouse and furnishings.

HOURS: May-Oct W-Sa 2-5 or by appt

ADMISSION: $1, Children $0.50

9850
Mennonite Archives of Ontario
200 Westmount Rd N, N2L 3G6 [Conrad Grebel College, N2L 3G6]; (p) (519) 885-0200; steiner@library.uwaterloo.ca; grebel.uwaterloo.ca/mao/

Private non-profit/ 1964/ staff: 2(p)

LIBRARY AND/OR ARCHIVES

PROGRAMS: Research Library/Archives

COLLECTIONS: [1900-1950] Archival and manuscript collections of Mennonite conferences (synods), institutions, congregations and leaders in Ontario; papers, photographs, audio/video tapes and published materials.

HOURS: Yr M-F 9-4:30

WELLAND

9851
Ball's Falls Historical Park and Conservation Area
6th Ave, RR #1, L3C 3W2 [c/o NPCA, 250 Thorold Rd. West, 3rd Floor, L3C 3W2]; (p) (905) 788-3135; (f) (905) 788-1121

1963/ Niagara Peninsula Conservation Authority/ staff: 2(f); 2(p); 30(v)

STATE PARK: Promotes planning, recreation, and heritage conservation.

PROGRAMS: Facility Rental; Festivals; Guided Tours; Interpretation

COLLECTIONS: [Early 19th c] Settlement of a small industrial complex.

HOURS: May-Sept Daily 10-4

WELLINGTON

9852
Wellington Community Historical Museum
290 Wellington Main St, K0K 3L0 [PO Box 160, K0K 3L0]; (p) (613) 399-5015

County/ 1967/ staff: 1(f); 1(p); 10(v)/ members: 1

HISTORY MUSEUM: Quaker and early pioneer history.

PROGRAMS: Exhibits; Guided Tours

COLLECTIONS: [1830-1900] Button collection, pioneer kitchen, parlor and farm.

HOURS: May 24-July 1 Sa-Su 12-4; July 1-Sept 1 M-Sa 10-4, Su 12-4

WESTPORT

9853
Rideau District Museum
Bedford St, K0G 1X0 [PO Box 305, K0G 1X0]

Private non-profit/ staff: 2(f); 1(p); 25(v)

HISTORIC SITE; HISTORICAL SOCIETY: Maintains museum.

PROGRAMS: Community Outreach; Exhibits; Guided Tours; Interpretation

COLLECTIONS: [1850-present] Original wooden blacksmith shop.

HOURS: May 30-Aug 31 M-Sa 10-4:30, Su 1-4:30; Sept Sa 10-4:30, Su 1-4:30

ADMISSION: $1

WHITBY

9854
Town of Whitby Archives
416 Centre St S, L1N 1L4 [603 Harriet St, L1N 1L4]; (p) (905) 668-5570; (f) (905) 668-1940

City/ 1968/ staff: 1(f)

LIBRARY AND/OR ARCHIVES: Archives for the Town of Whitby, Township of Whitby, Asburn, Brooklin, Myrtle, and Myrtle Station.

PROGRAMS: Research Library/Archives

COLLECTIONS: [1800-present] Genealogy files on 3,000 families; 5,000 photos; architecture; books and original documents relating to local history.

HOURS: Yr T-Th 8:30-12 / 1-4:30

ADMISSION: No charge

WILLIAMSTOWN

9855
Nor'Westers and Loyalist Museum
19651 John St, K0C 2S0 [PO Box 69, K0C 2S0]; (p) (613) 347-3547; (c) Glen Garry

Joint/ 1967/ Glen Garry Historical Society/ staff: 1(f); 12(v)

HISTORY MUSEUM: Promotes history of Sir John Johnson and his United Empire Loyalist followers; the fur trade.

PROGRAMS: Annual Meeting; Exhibits; Facility Rental; Guided Tours; Lectures; Living History; School-Based Curriculum

COLLECTIONS: [1784-1821] Early settlers farm and household tools, furniture, fabrics, Kings Royal Regiment of New York regiment uniform and land grant information. Northwest Company memorabilia, 26' birch bark canoe, large David Thompson map, felt top hats, fur press, trading post articles.

HOURS: May - Oct Daily 1:30-5:30, Sa and Holidays

WILLOWDALE

9856
Ontario Historical Society
34 Parkview Ave, M2N 3Y2; (p) (416) 226-9011; (f) (416) 226-2740

Private non-profit/ 1888/ staff: 4(f); 1(p); 120(v)/ members: 3000

HISTORICAL SOCIETY: Preserves Ontario's history.

PROGRAMS: Annual Meeting; Community Outreach; Elder's Programs; Facility Rental; Family Programs; Festivals; Interpretation; Lectures; School-Based Curriculum

HOURS: Yr M-F 9-4:30

WINDSOR

9857
Art Gallery of Windsor
3100 Howard Ave, N8X 3X8; (p) (519) 969-4494; (f) (519) 969-3732; mnsi.net/~agw

City; Private non-profit/ 1943/ staff: 19(f); 15(p)/ members: 1300

ART MUSEUM; LIBRARY AND/OR ARCHIVES: Collects, conserves, interprets, and presents Canadian art.

PROGRAMS: Annual Meeting; Community Outreach; Exhibits; Garden Tours; Guided Tours; Lectures; Research Library/Archives

COLLECTIONS: [19th and 20th c] 2500 works of art: paintings, drawings, prints, photographs, sculptures, and installations.

HOURS: Yr T-F

9858
Windsor's Community Museum
254 Pitt St West, N9A 5L5; (p) (519) 253-1812; (f) (519) 253-0919; wcmchin@mnsi.net; www.city.windsor.on.ca/wpl/museum

1958/ staff: 4(f); 2(p); 40(v)/publication: *Baby House Voices*

HISTORIC SITE; HISTORY MUSEUM; RESEARCH CENTER: Collects, preserves, researches, exhibits, and interprets objects and information relevant to the social, cultural, and industrial history of the City of Windsor.

PROGRAMS: Exhibits; Facility Rental; Family Programs; Publication; Research Library/Archives; School-Based Curriculum

COLLECTIONS: [1830-1950] Two and three dimensional objects; 13,000 artifacts, 5,000 photographs, maps, documents.

HOURS: Yr Oct 1- Apr 30 T-Sa 10-5; May 1-Sept 30 T-Sa 10-5, Su 2-5

ADMISSION:

WOODSTOCK

9859
Woodstock Museum
466 Dundas St, N4S 1C4; (p) (519) 537-8411; (f) (519) 537-7235; (c) Oxford

City/ 1947/ staff: 1(f); 2(p); 50(v)/ members: 90

HISTORIC SITE; HISTORY MUSEUM: 1853 building, Nationally designated Historic Site.

PROGRAMS: Exhibits; Facility Rental; Lectures; School-Based Curriculum

COLLECTIONS: [1830-present] Focuses on the funding on development of the city of Woodstock.

HOURS: Yr T-Sa 10-5

ADMISSION: $2, Student $1

PRINCE EDWARD ISLAND

ALBERTON

9860
Alberton Historical Preservation Foundation
Church St, C0B 1B0 [PO Box 515, C0B 1B0]; (p) (902) 853-4048

Private non-profit/ 1980/ Alberton Museum/ staff: 1(f); 2(p); 10(v)

HISTORIC PRESERVATION AGENCY; HISTORIC SITE; HISTORY MUSEUM; HOUSE MUSEUM; RESEARCH CENTER: Displays local history artifacts.

PROGRAMS: Annual Meeting; Community Outreach; Exhibits; Guided Tours; Research Library/Archives

COLLECTIONS: [18th-20th c] Industry, fishing, Native Americans, shipping, harness racing, local photos, and community life.

HOURS: June-Sept M-Sa 10-5:30, Su 1-5

ADMISSION: $3

CHARLOTTETOWN

9861
Acadian Museum, The
In Miscouche on the Lady Slipper Scenic Dr, C1A 1M6 [2 Kent St, C1A 1M6]; (p) (902) 432-2880

GENEALOGICAL SOCIETY; HISTORY MUSEUM

PROGRAMS: Exhibits; Family Programs; Festivals

COLLECTIONS: [1720-present]

HOURS: Yr

9862
Basin Head Fisheries Museum
East of Souris, Kings County, C1A 1M6 [2 Kent St, C1A 1M6]; (p) (902) 357-2966, (902) 368-6600; (c) Kings

HISTORY MUSEUM: Promotes historic inshore fishery.

PROGRAMS: Exhibits; Lectures

9863
Beaconsfield Historic House
2 Kent St, C1A 1M6; (p) (902) 368-6600

HOUSE MUSEUM

PROGRAMS: Exhibits; Festivals; Garden Tours; Guided Tours; Lectures

COLLECTIONS: [1877] Victorian home: chandeliers, furnishings, garden.

HOURS: Yr

9864
Elmira Railway Museum
East of Souris, C1A 1M6 [2 Kent St, C1A 1M6]; (p) (902) 357-2481, (902) 368-6600; (c) Kings

RAILROAD MUSEUM: Preserves Prince Edward Island's railway history.

PROGRAMS: Exhibits

COLLECTIONS: Photos, artifacts, and maps; trails; interpretive rooms.

9865
Eptek National Exhibition Centre
Summerside, C1A 1M6 [2 Kent St, C1A 1M6]; (p) (902) 888-8373

ART MUSEUM; HISTORY MUSEUM: Dedicated to history, science, and the fine arts.

PROGRAMS: Exhibits; Interpretation; Lectures

HOURS: Yr

9866
Green Park Shipbuilding Museum and Historic Yeo House
Port Hill, C1A 1M6 [2 Kent St, C1A 1M6]; (p) (902) 831-2206, (902) 368-6600; (c) Prince

HISTORY MUSEUM; HOUSE MUSEUM: Focuses on the shipbuilding industry.

9867
Parks Canada-National Historic Sites
2 Palmer's Lane, C1A 5V6; (p) (902) 566-8287; (f) (902) 566-8295

Federal/ staff: 2(f); 12(p)/ members: 6

HISTORIC SITE: Preserves historic sites: Province House and Port la Joye-Ft. Amherst

PROGRAMS: Elder's Programs; Exhibits; Festivals; Film/Video; Garden Tours; Guided Tours; Interpretation; Reenactments; School-Based Curriculum

COLLECTIONS: [1860]

HOURS: Yr

9868
Prince Edward Island Museum and Heritage Foundation
c/o Beaconsfield, 2 Kent St, C1A 1M6; (p) (902) 368-6600; (f) (902) 368-6608; peimuse@pei.sympat.co.ca; onetamedia.pe.ca/peimuseum

Provincial Crown Corporation/ staff: 12(f); 40(p); 50(v)/ members: 600/publication: *The Island Magazine*

ART MUSEUM; HISTORIC SITE; HISTORY MUSEUM; HOUSE MUSEUM; LIVING HISTORY/OUTDOOR MUSEUM; RESEARCH CENTER: Oversees seven museums.

PROGRAMS: Annual Meeting; Community Outreach; Concerts; Exhibits; Facility Rental; Festivals; Film/Video; Guided Tours; Interpretation; Living History; Publication; Research Library/Archives

HOURS: Yr

9869
Prince Edward Island Regiment Museum, The
Queen Charlotte Armoury Water St, C1A 7N1 [PO Box 1480, C1A 7N1]; (p) (902) 368-0108; (f) (902) 368-3034

Federal/ 1989/ staff: 2(p); 2(v)

HISTORY MUSEUM: Contains the military history of Prince Edward Island.

PROGRAMS: Annual Meeting; Exhibits; Guided Tours

COLLECTIONS: [1632-present] Uniforms, pictures, and badges of Canada's military.

HOURS: Yr

O'LEARY

9870
Prince Edward Island Potato Museum
1 Heritage Lane, C0B 1V0 [Box 602, C0B 1V0]; (p) (902) 859-2039; www.peipotatomuseum.com; (c) Prince

Private non-profit/ 1993/ staff: 4(p); 9(v)

HISTORY MUSEUM

PROGRAMS: Annual Meeting; Exhibits; Facility Rental; Film/Video; Guided Tours; Interpretation; Research Library/Archives

COLLECTIONS: [Late 1800s-mid 1900s] Interpretive center; machinery gallery, medical display, military display, spinning, weaving, and sewing, audio-visual equipment, photos, and early 19th c living room and bedroom artifacts.

HOURS: May 15-Oct 15 Daily M-Sa 9-5, Su 1-5

ADMISSION: $5, Family $12; Group rates

ORWELL

9871
Orwell Corner Historic Village
Vernon RR #2, C0A 2E0; (p) (902) 651-7510;

(f) (902) 368-6608; wgboyle@gov.pe.ca; (c) Queens

Joint/ 1973/ PE Museum/Orwell Corp/ staff: 5(f); 7(p); 18(v)/ members: 38/publication: *Once Upon an Island*

LIVING HISTORY/OUTDOOR MUSEUM

PROGRAMS: Annual Meeting; Community Outreach; Concerts; Exhibits; Facility Rental; Family Programs; Festivals; Guided Tours; Interpretation; Living History; Publication; School-Based Curriculum; Theatre

COLLECTIONS: [1890s] Exhibits 2,000 artifacts, 6 structures.

HOURS: Mid May-late June, Sept-Nov T-Su 9-5; late June-Sept Daily 9-5

ADMISSION: $4; Under 12/Mbrs free; group rates

SUMMERSIDE

9872
Prince Edward Island Sports Hall of Fame and Museum, Inc.
Water St, C1N 4K4 [PO Box 1523, C1N 4K4]; (p) (902) 436-0423; (f) (902) 436-9269; ktanton@pei.sympatico.ca; (c) Prince

Private non-profit/ 1968/ staff: 1(p)

HISTORY MUSEUM: Promotes sporting history.

PROGRAMS: Annual Meeting; Exhibits; Guided Tours; Publication; Research Library/Archives

COLLECTIONS: [1890-present] Sports artifacts and memorabilia, athlete profiles, and sports history.

HOURS: May-Sept M-Sa 10-9

ADMISSION: $2, Student $1

QUEBEC

ASBESTOS

9873
Musee Mineralogique d'Asbestos Inc.
104, rue Letendre, J1T 1E3; (p) (819) 879-6444, (819) 879-5308

Private non-profit/ 1974/ staff: 2(p); 7(v)

HISTORY MUSEUM: Collects, exhibits, and conserves the minerals and mining history of the Jeffrey Mine.

PROGRAMS: Exhibits; Festivals; Film/Video; Guided Tours; Interpretation; Research Library/Archives; School-Based Curriculum

COLLECTIONS: [1875-present] 2,000 mineral specimens, 4,000 photographs,1,000 maps of the Jeffrey Mine, 35 films, 1,000 documents and books, mining artifacts and surveying instruments.

HOURS: June-Aug W-Sa 11-5

ADMISSION: $1, Children $0.50

BERTHIER

9874
Musee Gilles-Villeneuve
960 ave Gilles-Villeneuve, J0K 1A0; (p) (450)

836-2714; (f) (450) 836-3067; museegv@pandore.qu.ca; www.villeneuve.com

Private non-profit/ 1988/ Comite Berthier-Villeneuve/ staff: 3(f); 3(p)/ members: 800

PROGRAMS: Exhibits; Guided Tours; Research Library/Archives

COLLECTIONS: Trophies, pictures, plaques, automobiles, collectors items, paintings all pertaining the Villeneuve family and formula one racing.

HOURS: Yr Daily 9-5, summer 9-9

ADMISSION: $6, Student $4, Seniors $5

CAUSAPSCAL

9875
Site Historique Matamajaw
53 St Jacques Sud, G0J 1J0; (p) (418) 756-5999; (f) (418) 756-3344; (c) Matapedia

Private non-profit/ 1989/ staff: 1(f); 8(p)

HISTORIC SITE: Promotes history of salmon fishing.

PROGRAMS: Exhibits; Festivals; Guided Tours; Interpretation; Living History

HOURS: June- mid Oct Daily 9:30-5:30

ADMISSION: $3.75, Family $8.45, Student $2.50, Seniors $3.25

CHATEAU-RICHER

9876
Centre d'interpretation de la cote de Beaupre
7007 Ave Royale, G0A 1N0; (p) (418) 824-3677; (f) (418) 824-5907

Private non-profit/ 1984/ staff: 2(f); 5(p)

HISTORIC SITE; HISTORY MUSEUM: Promotes cultural, geographical, historical, and patrimonial aspects of the region.

PROGRAMS: Concerts; Elder's Programs; Exhibits; Guided Tours; Interpretation

COLLECTIONS: [12th-20th c] Native Canadian, French, and English first settlers artifacts.

HOURS: June-Sept Daily 10-5

ADMISSION: $2, Children $1

CHELSEA

9877
Mackenzie King Estate
Gatineau Park, 33 Scott Rd, J9B 1R5; (p) (613) 239-5100, (800) 461-8020; dmessier@ncc-ccn.ca; www.capcan.ca

Federal/ 1984/ staff: 1(f); 8(p); 35(v)

GARDEN; HISTORIC SITE

PROGRAMS: Concerts; Elder's Programs; Family Programs; Film/Video; Garden Tours; Guided Tours; Interpretation; Lectures; Publication; School-Based Curriculum; Theatre

COLLECTIONS: [1900-1950] 2,500 objects used in country life context.

HOURS: Daily May-Oct M-F 11-5, Sa-Su 10-6

CHICOUTIMI

9878
La Pul Perie De Chicoutimi

300 Dubuc, G7J 4M1; (p) (418) 698-3100; (f) (418) 698-3058; pulperie@videotron.ca; www.reseau.qc.ca/pulperie

Private non-profit/ 1972/ staff: 10(f); 60(p)

ART MUSEUM; HISTORIC SITE; HISTORY MUSEUM; LIVING HISTORY/OUTDOOR MUSEUM

PROGRAMS: Exhibits; Family Programs; Guided Tours; Interpretation; Lectures; Living History; Publication

COLLECTIONS: [1870-1925] Museum artifacts, archaeological artifacts, art, furniture, photos.

HOURS: June, Aug, Sept M-Su 9-6; July M-Su 9-8

COTEAU-DU-LAC

9879
Coteau-du-Lac National Historic Site
308 A Chemin du Fleuve, J0P 1B0; (p) (450) 763-5631; (f) (450) 763-1654; parcscanada-que@pch.gc.ca; www.parcscanada.gc.ca/coteau

Federal/ 1972/ staff: 2(f); 7(p)

HISTORIC SITE: Coteau-Du-Lac National Historic Site contains the remains of the first lock canal built in Canada in 1779.

PROGRAMS: Guided Tours; Interpretation; Living History; School-Based Curriculum

COLLECTIONS: [1750-1815] Archaeological remains of the canal, storehouses, commandant's quarters, barracks, cookhouse, and hospital, and various metal, glass or ceramic artifacts.

HOURS: May 22-Sept 5 Daily 10-12 / 1-5; Sept 7-Oct Sa-Su 10-12 / 1-5

ADMISSION: $3, Family $6, Children $1.50, Seniors $2.25; Under 6 free

DRUMMONDVILLE

9880
Societe d'Histoire de Drummondville
545 Des Ecoles, J2B 1J6; (p) (819) 474-2318; (f) (819) 478-0399; info@histoire-drummond.qc.ca; www.histoire-drummond.qc.ca

Private non-profit/ 1957/ staff: 4(f)/ members: 60

HISTORICAL SOCIETY: Selects, and preserves documentation and archives on regional history.

PROGRAMS: Annual Meeting; Guided Tours; Interpretation; Lectures; Publication; Research Library/Archives

COLLECTIONS: [1815-present] Documents, 26,000 photos and local papers.

HOURS: Yr M-F 8:30-12 /

GASPE

9881
Grande-Grave National Historic Site/Parks Canada
Parc National Forillon, G4X 1A9 [122 Boul Gaspe, G4X 1A9]; (p) (418) 892-5553; (f) (418) 892-5951

Federal/ 1970/ staff: 8(p)

HISTORIC SITE

PROGRAMS: Exhibits; Family Programs; Film/Video; Guided Tours; Interpretation

COLLECTIONS: 26 historic buildings on the south shore of Forillon National Park.

HOURS: Mid June-Sept Daily 10-5; Sept-Oct 15 Daily 10-4

GRAND-METIS

9882
Jardins De Metis, Les (The Metis Gardens)
S Shore of St Lawrence River, G0J 1Z0 [200 Rt 132, G0J 1Z0]; (p) (418) 775-2221; (f) (418) 775-6201; reford@refordgardens.com; www.refordgardens.com; (c) La Mitis

Private non-profit/ 1926/ staff: 5(f); 24(p)/ members: 475

HOUSE MUSEUM: Historic gardens begun in 1926 by Montrealer, Elsie Reford, the gardens are among the most important in Canada. Covering more than 40 acres, the gardens are located on the south shore of the St. Lawrence River, 220 miles east of Quebec City. At the center of the property is Estevan Lodge, the historic fishing camp built by Elsie Reford's uncle, Lord Mount Stephen, founder of the Canadian Pacific Railway.

PROGRAMS: Garden Tours; Interpretation; Lectures; School-Based Curriculum

COLLECTIONS: 2,000 varieties and species of plants; 8,000 images; Reford Family objects.

HOURS: June-mid Oct 8:30-6:30

ADMISSION: $8, Student $7, Seniors $7

HOWICK

9883
Battle of the Chateauguay National Historic Site of Canada
2371 Riviere Chateauguay Nord Box 250, J0S 1G0; (p) (450) 829-2003; (f) (450) 829-3325; parcscanada-que@pch.gc.ca; parcscanada.risq.qc.ca/chateauguay

Federal/ 1978/ Parks Canada Agency/ staff: 1(f); 4(p)

HISTORIC SITE; HISTORY MUSEUM: Preserves site of Battle of Chateauguay, War of 1812.

PROGRAMS: Film/Video; Guided Tours; Interpretation; Living History; School-Based Curriculum

COLLECTIONS: [War of 1812] Scale model, movie, artifacts, and a monument.

HOURS: May 12-Sept 2 W-Su 10-5; Sept 3-Oct 7 Sa-Su 10-5

ADMISSION: $3, Family $6, Student $2.25, Children $1.50, Seniors $2.25; Under 6 free

HULL

9884
Canadian Museum of Civilization
100 Lauriek St, J8X 4H2 [CP 3100 Suce B, J8X 4H2]; (p) (819) 776-7000; (f) (819) 776-8300; www.civilization.ca

Federal/ 1989/ staff: 348(f); 142(p); 200(v)/ members: 1950/publication: *Books and CD*

Roms

ART MUSEUM; HISTORY MUSEUM; LIVING HISTORY/OUTDOOR MUSEUM: Preserves, researches, and displays Canadian prehistory, history, and culture.

PROGRAMS: Community Outreach; Concerts; Exhibits; Facility Rental; Garden Tours; Guided Tours; Interpretation; Lectures; Living History; Publication; Reenactments; Research Library/Archives; Theatre

HOURS: Oct 1-Apr 30 T-Su 9-5; May-June 30 Daily 9-6; Th 9-9; July-Oct 9 Daily Sa-W 9-6, Th-F 9-9; Oct 10-Apr 30 T-Su 9-5, Th 9-9

9885
Library and Knowledge Development Centre, Department of Canadian Heritage
15 Eddy St, Rm 2E2, K1A 0M5; (p) (819) 994-5478; (f) (819) 953-7988; pch_library@pch.gc.ca; www.pch.gc.ca

Federal/ 1993/ staff: 9(f)

LIBRARY AND/OR ARCHIVES: Preserves and promotes Canada's natural and cultural heritage.

PROGRAMS: Research Library/Archives

COLLECTIONS: 48,000 volumes (1,400 rare books), official publications, 3,000 serials, 500 video recordings, 100 CD ROMS (arts and culture), Canadian Library, and identify multiculturalism, sports, national parks, and historic sites.

HOURS: Yr M-F 8-4:30

ADMISSION: No charge

KNOWLTON

9886
Brome County Historical Society
130 Lakeside, J0E 1V0 [130 Lakeside, Box 690, J0E 1V0]; (p) (450) 243-6782

Private non-profit/ 1897/ staff: 1(f); 2(p); 25(v)/ members: 400/publication: *Yesterday of Brome County*

HISTORICAL SOCIETY; HISTORY MUSEUM

PROGRAMS: Annual Meeting; Exhibits; Facility Rental; Lectures; Publication

COLLECTIONS: [Prior to 1950] Fokker DVII, tools, equipment, dishes, furniture, textiles, jewelry, and accessories.

HOURS: Yr Daily 10-4:30

ADMISSION: $3.50, Student $1.50, Seniors $2

L'ILE AUX CAUDRES

9887
Les Moulins de l'Isle aux Caudres
247, chemin du Moulin, G0A 1X0; (p) (418) 438-2184; (f) (418) 438-2184; www.economusees.com; (c) Quebec

City/ 1982/ staff: 4(f); 6(p)

HISTORIC SITE; LIVING HISTORY/OUTDOOR MUSEUM: Maintains restored 1824 water mill and 1836 windmill; provides information on local history.

PROGRAMS: Interpretation

COLLECTIONS: [1800s-1900s] Millstone,

miller's tools, agriculture machines.

HOURS: May 15-mid Oct Daily 10-

L'ISLET-SUR-MER

9888
Musee maritime du Quebec
55, des Pionniers Est, G0R 2B0; (p) (418) 247-5001; (f) (418) 247-5002

Private non-profit/ 1968/ staff: 3(f); 15(p)/ members: 12/publication: *Transport par mer*

HISTORY MUSEUM; LIVING HISTORY/OUT-DOOR MUSEUM: Identifies, studies, preserves, develops, and displays cultural heritage of Quebec.

PROGRAMS: Exhibits; Guided Tours; Interpretation; Living History; Publication; Research Library/Archives

COLLECTIONS: [1850-1950] 3 boats; navigational aids; archival manuscripts, photos, maps, plans, drawings and posters.

HOURS: Yr May 20-June 22, Sept 4-Oct 8 Daily 10-5; June 23-Sept 3 Daily 9-6; Sept 4-May 19 T-F 10-12, 1-4

ADMISSION: Varies

LA POCATIERE

9889
Musee Francois-Pilote
100, 4e Ave, G0R 1Z0; (p) (418) 856-3145; (f) (418) 856-5611; mfprcip@globetrotter.net; www.kam.qu.ca/quoi/musees/mfranpilote/mfp 00.html

Private non-profit/ 1974/ staff: 2(f); 1(p); 3(v)/ members: 85

HISTORY MUSEUM: Illustrate the aspects of the old parish through exhibits and through patrimonial objects.

PROGRAMS: Exhibits

COLLECTIONS: [Early 20th C] Scientific objects, agricultural objects, furnishing, 400 birds and 70 mammals, tools, clothes, house accessories, dishes, horse carriage.

HOURS: Yr Daily (closed Sa in winter) 9-12, 1-5

ADMISSION: $4, Student $3, Children $2; Under 5 free; group rates

9890
Societe historique de la Cote du Sud
CP 937, G0R 1Z0; (p) (418) 856-2104; (f) (418) 856-2104; archsud@globetrotter.qc.ca

Private non-profit/ 1948/ staff: 1(f); 1(p); 8(v)/ members: 200/publication: *Le Javelier*

GENEALOGICAL SOCIETY; HISTORICAL SOCIETY: Promotes regional historic research; assists genealogical searches.

PROGRAMS: Annual Meeting; Publication; Research Library/Archives

HOURS: Yr M-F 9-5

ADMISSION: No charge

LA PRAIRIE

9891
Societe Historique De La Prairie De La Magdelen
249 Ste Marie, J5R 5H4 [CP 25005 La

Citiere, J5R 5H4]; (p) (450) 659-1393; (f) (450) 659-2857; shlm@videotron.ca; pages.infinit.net/sn

Private non-profit/ 1972/ staff: 1(f); 15(v)/ members: 150

GENEALOGICAL SOCIETY; HISTORIC SITE; HISTORICAL SOCIETY

PROGRAMS: Guided Tours; Interpretation

COLLECTIONS: 60,000 documents on history of the Prairie and region.

HOURS: Yr M-F 9-5

ADMISSION: No charge

LACHINE

9892
Fur Trade in Lachine National Historic Site, The
1255, St Joseph Blvd, H8S 2M2; (p) (514) 637-7433; (f) (514) 637-5325; llachine-mtl@pcg.gc.ca

Federal/ 1984/ staff: 3(f); 4(p)

HISTORIC SITE: Commemorates fur trade in Lachine and Montreal area.

PROGRAMS: Exhibits; Guided Tours; Interpretation; Publication; School-Based Curriculum

COLLECTIONS: 300 artifacts: pelts, trading goods, Native American artifacts, voyageur folklore, birch bark canoe.

HOURS: Apr-mid Oct Daily 10-6 closed M morning; Mid Oct-1st Su in Dec W-Su

9893
Musee de la Ville de Lachine
110, chemin de LaSalle, H8S 2X1; (p) (514) 634-3471; (f) (541) 637-6784; www.cum.qc.ca/lachine/eng/musee-e.htm

City/ 1948/ staff: 1(f); 6(p); 1(v)

ART MUSEUM; HISTORIC SITE; HISTORY MUSEUM

PROGRAMS: Exhibits; Guided Tours; Publication

COLLECTIONS: [19th-20th c] 6,000 objects: furniture, domestic tools, religious, Native American, textile, recreation, communication; 28,000 archaeological artifacts and ecofacts; 10,000 archives photos and documents.

HOURS: Apr 4-Dec 16 W-Su

MELOCHEVILLE

9894
Pointe-du-Buisson
333 Emond, J0S 1J0; (p) (450) 429-7857; (f) (450) 429-5921; (c) Beauhornois-Saloberry

City/ 1986/ staff: 1(f); 15(p); 10(v)/publication: *A Fleur de Siecles*

HISTORY MUSEUM: Promotes Native American history.

PROGRAMS: Exhibits; Family Programs; Festivals; Guided Tours; Interpretation; Living History; Publication

COLLECTIONS: [3000BC-1500AD] Archaeological artifacts: farspear, arrow heads, pottery fragments, beads, fishing instruments, bones.

HOURS: May-Sept M-F 10-5, Sa-Su

MIKAN-MANIACKI

9895
KiCigaw Libi Education Council
41 Kikinamage, J9E 3B1; (p) (819) 449-1798; (f) (819) 449-5570; gilbert.whiteduck@kza.qc.ca; www.kza.qc.ca

Private non-profit/ 1979

TRIBAL MUSEUM: Collects, preserves, and exhibits artifacts related to the Algonquin Nation.

PROGRAMS: Exhibits; Lectures; Research Library/Archives

COLLECTIONS: First Nations items.

HOURS: May-Sept M-F 8-4

ADMISSION: $1

MONTEBELLO

9896
Manoir-Papineau National Historic Site
500 Notre-Dame Box 444, J0V 1L0; (p) (819) 423-6965; (f) (819) 423-6455; parcscanada-que@pch.qc.ca; parcscanada.risq.qc.ca/papineau

Federal/ 1999/ staff: 1(f); 5(p)

GARDEN; HISTORIC SITE; HOUSE MUSEUM; LIVING HISTORY/OUTDOOR MUSEUM: Commemorates Louis-Joseph Papineau history.

PROGRAMS: Guided Tours; Interpretation; School-Based Curriculum

COLLECTIONS: [1850-1929] Manor house, granary, tea Pavilion, family museum furniture, accessories, decorative elements, clothing, posters, photos, maps, cadastres, lighting fixture, painting, carpets, curtains, mirrors, ornaments.

HOURS: May 13-Sept 3

MONTMAGUY

9897
Carrefour Mondial De L'Accordeon A Montmaguy
301, boul Tache est, CP Fl, G5V 3S3; (p) (418) 248-7927; (f) (418) 248-1596; accordeo@montmaguy; http://accordeon.montmaguy.com

Private non-profit/ 1989/ staff: 3(f); 3(p); 60(v)/ members: 50

HISTORY MUSEUM: Reflects history and design of the accordion.

PROGRAMS: Concerts; Exhibits; Festivals; Interpretation; Lectures

COLLECTIONS: Accordions, compact disc, cassettes, books, videos, sweaters, and percussion instruments.

HOURS: June-Oct Museum Daily M-F 9-5, Sa-Su 10-4

ADMISSION: $4, Children $2

MONTREAL

9898
Archives Nationales du Quebec
535 Ave Viger E, H2L 2P3; (p) (514) 873-3065; (f) (514) 873-2980;

anq.montreal@MCC.gouv.qc.ca

State/ 1971

PROGRAMS: Guided Tours; Publication; Research Library/Archives

COLLECTIONS: [1642-present] Civil state archives, civil records, records of notaries, legal records, and government records.

9899
Archives of the Diocese of Montreal
1444 Union Ave, H3A 2B8; (p) (514) 843-6577; (f) (514) 843-6344; anglicanarchives@hotmail.com

Private non-profit/ 1850/ Andrew S. Hutchison, Bishop of Montreal/ staff: 1(f); 3(v)

LIBRARY AND/OR ARCHIVES: Preserves administration records, parish records, and registers of baptism-marriage-burial.

PROGRAMS: Exhibits

COLLECTIONS: [19th-20th c] Parish register, minute books, photographs, maps and architectural plans, deeds and patent letters, and correspondence.

HOURS: Yr M-F by appt

9900
Archives Provinciales des Capucins
3650 Boulevard de la Rousseliere, H1A 2X9; (p) (514) 642-5391; (f) (514) 642-5033

Provincial/ 1977/ staff: 2(f)

LIBRARY AND/OR ARCHIVES: Collects and preserves papers of the Capuchin community.

PROGRAMS: Research Library/Archives

COLLECTIONS: [1890-present] 75 archival funds of the religious houses, missions and members; 5000 photographs; 670 maps and plans; 455 slides; 200 art reproductions; 32 video tapes.

HOURS: Yr M-F 9-3

9901
Bank of Montreal Archives and Museum
105 St Jacques St, 1st Flr, H2Y 1L6; (p) (514) 877-6810; (f) (514) 877-7341

Private non-profit/ 1960/ staff: 1(f)

LIBRARY AND/OR ARCHIVES: Preserves records of Canada's first banking institution.

PROGRAMS: Exhibits

COLLECTIONS: [1817-present] Numismatic, photos, annual reports, minute books, advertisements, branch files, and banking artifacts; records and artifacts of amalgamated banks.

HOURS: Yr Museum: M-F 10-4; Library by appt only

ADMISSION: No charge

9902
Canadian Centre for Architecture (CCA)
1920 Baile St, H3H 2S6; (p) (514) 939-7026; (f) (514) 939-7000; www.cca.qc.ca

Private non-profit/ 1979/ Board of Trustees/ staff: 160(f)

ART MUSEUM; RESEARCH CENTER: Promotes architectural history.

PROGRAMS: Concerts; Exhibits; Garden Tours; Guided Tours; Interpretation; Lectures;

Research Library/Archives

COLLECTIONS: 190,000 printed volumes, 100,00 prints and drawings, 50,000 photographs, architectural archives.

HOURS: Oct-May W F 11-6, Th 11-8, Sa-Su 11-5; June-Sept T-W, F-Su 11-6, Th 11-9

ADMISSION: $6, Student $3, Seniors $4

9903
Canadian Pacific Archives
910 Peel St, H3C 3E4 [PO Box 6042, Station Centre-Ville, H3C 3E4]; (p) (514) 395-5135; (f) (514) 395-5132; archives@cpr.ca; www.cprheritage.com

Canadian Pacific Railway

LIBRARY AND/OR ARCHIVES: Maintains images and documentation on the history of Canadian Pacific and the development of Canada.

PROGRAMS: Facility Rental

HOURS: M-F 9-4:30 by appt

9904
Centre d'histoire de Montreal
335, Place d'Youville, H2Y 3T1; (p) (514) 872-3207; (f) (514) 872-9645; chm@ville.montreal.qc.ca; www.ville.montreal.qc.ca/chm/chm.htm

City/ 1983/ staff: 4(f); 4(p)/publication: Montreal Clic

HISTORY MUSEUM: Focuses on urban history.

PROGRAMS: Exhibits; Family Programs; Guided Tours; Interpretation; Lectures; Publication; Research Library/Archives; School-Based Curriculum

COLLECTIONS: [1642-1980] Montreal memorabilia and artifacts related to interpretation.

HOURS: Jan-May T-Su 10-5; May-Sept M-Su 1-5

ADMISSION: $5, Student $3.50, Children $3.50, Seniors $3.50; Under 6 free

9905
Chateau Ramezay Museum
280 Notre Dame East, H2Y 1C5; (p) (514) 861-3708; (f) (514) 861-8317; mcrml@globetrotter.qc.ca

Private non-profit/ 1862/ staff: 6(f); 5(p); 100(v)/ members: 210

HISTORY MUSEUM

PROGRAMS: Annual Meeting; Concerts; Exhibits; Family Programs; Guided Tours; Lectures; Research Library/Archives

COLLECTIONS: [Prehistory-19th c] 20,000 objects: paintings, engravings, prints, drawings, costumes, furniture, manuscripts, and photograph.

HOURS: Yr Summer Daily 10-6; the rest of the year T-Su 10-4:30

ADMISSION: $6, Family $12, Student $4, Seniors $5

9906
Ecomusee du fier Monde
2050 Amherst St, H2L 3L8; (p) (514) 528-8444; (f) (514) 528-8686; ecomusee@globetrotter.net; www.ecomusee.qc.ca

Private non-profit/ 1980/ staff: 6(f)/ members:

65

HISTORY MUSEUM: Collects, researches, and interprets history of Montreal industries.

PROGRAMS: Exhibits; Family Programs; Guided Tours; Publication; Research Library/Archives; School-Based Curriculum

COLLECTIONS: [1850-present] Photographs, artifacts, ancient books, oral history, documentation.

HOURS: Yr W 11-8, Th-F 9-4, Sa-Su

9907
Lachine Canal National Historic Site of Canada
Guy-Favreau Complex, 200 Rene-Levesque Blvd W, W T, H2Z 1X4; (p) (514) 283-6054; (f) (514) 496-1263; Lachine-MTL@pch.gc.ca; www. Parkscanada.gc.ca/canallachine

Federal

HISTORIC SITE; HISTORY MUSEUM

PROGRAMS: Concerts; Exhibits; Festivals; Guided Tours; Interpretation; Lectures; Living History; Publication

COLLECTIONS: Historical canal and buildings, site of the first industrial park of Canada, hydraulic power.

HOURS: May-mid Oct Daily

9908
McCord Museum of Canadian History
690 Sherbrooke West, H3A 1E9; (p) (514) 398-7100; (f) (514) 398-5045; info@mccord.lan.mcgill.ca; www.musee-mccord.qc.ca

Private non-profit/ 1921/ staff: 35(f); 12(p); 80(v)/ members: 900

HISTORY MUSEUM: Conserves, studies, and presents social history and material culture of Canada, Quebec, and Montreal.

PROGRAMS: Concerts; Exhibits; Facility Rental; Guided Tours; Publication; Research Library/Archives

COLLECTIONS: [19th c] 850,000 objects: paintings, prints, and drawings; the Notman Photographic Archives, Textual Archives, the Ethnology and Archeology collection, decorative arts, and costume and textiles.

HOURS: Yr June 21-Oct 11 Daily T-F 10-6, Sa-Su 10-5, M 10-5; Oct 12-June 20 T-F 10-6, Sa-Su 10-5

ADMISSION: $7, Family $14, Student $4

9909
McGill University Archives
3459 McTavish, H3A 1Y1; (p) (514) 398-3772; (f) (514) 398-8459; www.archives.mcgill.ca

1962/ staff: 7(f); 2(p); 1(v)

CORPORATE ARCHIVES/MUSEUM: Provides records management services to university offices and faculty; manages university records retention policy.

PROGRAMS: Exhibits; Research Library/Archives

COLLECTIONS: [1821-present] Official records of the university and its department; private papers of staff and graduates; publications, scrapbooks McCrohlm, plans, film, audio.

9910
Montreal Holocaust Memorial Center/Le Centre Commemoratif De L'Holocauste S Montreal
1 Cummings Square, H3M 1M6; (p) (514) 345-2605; (f) (514) 344-2651; mhmc@total.net

Private non-profit/ 1976/ staff: 6(f); 1(p); 140(v)/ members: 2000

HISTORIC PRESERVATION AGENCY; HISTORIC SITE; HISTORY MUSEUM; RESEARCH CENTER: Collects, researches, and preserves historical, cultural, and ethnographic materials related to Jewish communities which fell under Nazi rule.

PROGRAMS: Annual Meeting; Community Outreach; Concerts; Elder's Programs; Exhibits; Family Programs; Guided Tours; Interpretation; Lectures; Theatre

COLLECTIONS: [1919-1955] Artifacts and personal memorabilia (religious and secular) in paper, leather, metal, fabric, wood, films, photographs, hand

9911
Notre Dame de Bon Secours Chapel/Marquerite Bourgeoys Museum
400 Saint Paul St East, H2Y 1H4; (p) (514) 282-8670; (f) (514) 282-8672

Private non-profit/ 1998/ Corp. de la Chapelle Notre-Dame de Bon Secours et du Musee Marquerttep-Bourgeoys/ staff: 8(f); 2(p); 20(v)

HISTORIC SITE; HISTORY MUSEUM: Presents and interprets history of site and Marquerite Bourgeoys, foundress of the Chapel and Montreal's first teacher.

PROGRAMS: Concerts; Exhibits; Guided Tours; Interpretation; Publication

COLLECTIONS: Archaeological site including Amerindian remains, vestiges of 17th c Chapel; 18th c Chapel; Museum in 19th c school house; related art and artifacts from collections of Priests of Saint Sulpice and Congregation de Notre Dame.

9912
Pointe a Calliere, Montreal Museum of Archaeology and History
350 Place Royale, H2Y 3Y5; (p) (514) 872-9150; (f) (514) 872-9151; info@musee-pointe-a-calliere.qc.ca; www.musee-pointe-a-calliere.qc.ca

Private non-profit/ 1992/ staff: 46(f); 25(p)

HISTORIC SITE; HISTORY MUSEUM; LIVING HISTORY/OUTDOOR MUSEUM

PROGRAMS: Concerts; Exhibits; Family Programs; Guided Tours; Interpretation; Publication; Reenactments

COLLECTIONS: [16th-21 c] 1 million artifacts; ethnohistory.

HOURS: Yr Sept-June T-F 10-5, Sa-Su 11-5; July-Aug T-F 10-5, Sa-Su 11-6

ADMISSION: $8.50; Group rates

9913
Universite de Montreal, Division des

Archives
2900 Boul Edouard-Montpetit, H3C 3J7 [CP 6128 Succursale Centre-Ville, H3C 3J7]; (p) (514) 343-6023; (f) (514) 343-2239; reference@archiv.umontreal.ca; www.archive.umontreal.ca/

1966/ staff: 13(f)/publication: *Guide du Chercheur and Finding Aids*

LIBRARY AND/OR ARCHIVES: Provides research materials.

PROGRAMS: Exhibits; Publication

COLLECTIONS: [1495-present] Manuscripts of history of New France to post Canadian confederation.

HOURS: May-Sept M-T 9-12/1:30-5, W 1:30-5, Th-F 9-12/1:30-5; June-Aug M-Th 9-12/1:30-5

ADMISSION: No charge

NEW RICHMOND

9914
Gaspesian British Heritage Centre
351 Perron W, G0C 2B0; (p) (418) 392-4487; (f) (418) 392-5907; (c) Bonaventure

Private non-profit/ 1984/ staff: 15(p); 40(v)/ members: 200

HISTORIC SITE: Portrays history and lifestyles of early British settlers on the Gaspe Coast from 1760-1920.

PROGRAMS: Exhibits; Interpretation

COLLECTIONS: [1760-1920] Materials related to Gaspe history, mariners maps, sheet music, music books, rare volumes of old magazines "Century", portraits, tin-types, photographs, bells greeting cards from Victorian times.

HOURS: June-Sept Daily 9-6

ADMISSION: $5, Student $3.50, Seniors $4.50; Under 6 free; group

NOTRE-DAME DE L'ILE PERROT

9915
Pointe du Moulin Historical Parc
2500 Don Quichotte Boulevard, J7V 7P2; (p) (514) 453-5936; (f) (514) 453-1473

State/ staff: 1(f); 20(p)

HISTORIC SITE: Preserves 2 historic sites: windmill (1705) and miller's house (1785).

PROGRAMS: Exhibits; Family Programs; Film/Video; Guided Tours; Interpretation; Theatre

HOURS: Mid May-Mid Oct 9-5

ADMISSION: No charge

ODANAK

9916
Musee des Abenakis d'Odabak
108 Waban-Aki, J0G 1H0; (p) (450) 568-2600; (f) (450) 568-5959; abenaki@enter-net.com

Private non-profit/ 1962/ staff: 3(f); 8(p)/ members: 55

HISTORY MUSEUM; TRIBAL MUSEUM: Maintains museum and promotes Indian culture.

PROGRAMS: Annual Meeting; Exhibits; Festivals; Guided Tours; Lectures

COLLECTIONS: Basketry and objects relating to the beginning of the colony, 1600-1715.

HOURS: Yr May-Oct Daily M-F 10-5, Sa-Su 1-5; Nov-Apr M-F 10-5, Sa-Su on reservation only

ADMISSION: $4, Student $2.60, Children $2, Seniors $3.50; Group rates

POINTE-A-LA-CROIX

9917
Battle of the Restigouche National Historic Site
Route 132, Gaspesia Peninsula, G0C 1L0 [PO Box 359, Route 132, G0C 1L0]; (p) (418) 788-5676; (f) (418) 788-5895; parcscanada-que@pch.gc.ca; www.parcscanada.gc.ca/ristigouche

Federal/ 1985/ Parks Canada Agency/ staff: 1(f); 9(p)/publication: *Battle of the Restigouche*

BATTLEFIELD: Commemorates the Restigouche Battle , the last naval battle between England and France in New France.

PROGRAMS: Exhibits; Guided Tours; Interpretation; Publication

COLLECTIONS: [1760] Artifacts and structural sections of the "Machault," French frigate excavated between 1969 and 1972 in the Restigouche River.

HOURS: June-mid Oct Daily 9-5

ADMISSION: $3.75, Family $7.50, Student $2

POINTE-AU-PERE

9918
Musee de La Mer de Pointe-au-Pere
1034 rue du Phare, G5M 1L8; (p) (418) 724-6214; (f) (418) 721-0815; museepc@globe-trotter.qc.ca; www.cnipap.qc.ca/musee-mer/html/english.htm

Private non-profit/ 1980/ staff: 1(f); 13(p); 100(v)/ members: 75

HISTORIC SITE; HISTORY MUSEUM: Interprets the history of navigational aids on the St. Lawrence River and the Shipwreck of the Empress of Ireland.

PROGRAMS: Annual Meeting; Exhibits; Film/Video; Guided Tours; Interpretation

COLLECTIONS: Artifacts that divers have recovered from the wreck of the Empress of Ireland.

HOURS: June 2-Aug 31 9-6; Sept 1-Oct 4 9-5

ADMISSION: $9.50, Student

QUEBEC

9919
Le Musee des Ursuline de Quebec
12, rue Donnacona, G1R 4T1; (p) (418) 694-0694; (f) (418) 694-2136; murq@globetrotter.net

Private non-profit/ 1964/ staff: 1(f); 3(p)

ART MUSEUM; HISTORY MUSEUM

PROGRAMS: Exhibits

COLLECTIONS: Paintings, prints, sculptures, shrines, craft items, needlework.

HOURS: May-Sept T-Sa 10-12 / 1-5; Oct-Apr T-Su 1-4:30

ADMISSION: $4, Student $2.50, Children $2

9920
Musee Bon-Pasteur
14 rue Couillard, G1R 3S9; (p) (418) 694-0243; (f) (418) 694-6233; (c) Quebec

Private non-profit/ 1992/ staff: 1(f); 1(p); 5(v)

HISTORY MUSEUM: Focuses on religious and apostolic history of Quebec.

PROGRAMS: Exhibits

COLLECTIONS: [19th c] Heritage pieces, period furniture, historical places.

HOURS: Yr T-Su 1-5

ADMISSION: $2

9921
Musee des Augustine de L'Hotel-Dieu de Quebec
32, rue Charlevoix, G1R 5C4; (p) (418) 692-2492; (f) (418) 692-2668

Private non-profit/ 1958/ staff: 2(f); 1(p); 2(v)

ART MUSEUM; HISTORIC SITE; HISTORY MUSEUM

PROGRAMS: Exhibits

COLLECTIONS: [1639-present] Medical instruments; furniture, paintings, embroideries, silver, pewter, and artifacts from everyday life. 1800 church sculptures from Thomas Baillarge. Cellars of 1695.

HOURS: Yr T-Sa 9:30-12/1:30-5, Su 1-5

ADMISSION: Donations requested

9922
Musee du Quebec
Parc Des Champs De Bataille, G1R 5H3; (p) (418) 643-2150; (f) (418) 646-3330; webmdq@mdq.org; www.mmdq.org

1933/ staff: 106(f); 41(p)/ members: 2700

ART MUSEUM

PROGRAMS: Concerts; Exhibits; Facility Rental; Family Programs; Film/Video; Guided Tours; Research Library/Archives

COLLECTIONS: [17th-20th c] Paintings, drawings, prints, photos, decorative arts.

HOURS: Yr June 1-Sept 7 Daily Th-T 1-5, W 10-9:45; Sept 8-May 31 W 11-8:45, T,Th-Su 11-5:45

ADMISSION: $5.75

9923
Musee du Royal 22e Regiment
La Citadelle, G1R 4V7 [CP 6020 Succ, Haute-ville, G1R 4V7]; (p) (418) 694-2815; (f) (418) 694-2853; reservations@lacitadelle.qc.ca; www.lacitadelle.qc.ca; (c) Quebec

Private non-profit/ 1950/ Canadian Forces/ staff: 7(f); 25(p); 4(v)/publication: La Citadelle de Quebec

Interprets Royal 22e Regiment's history, the citadel, the French Regime and the British Regime.

PROGRAMS: Exhibits; Guided Tours; Interpretation; Publication

COLLECTIONS: [1693-present] Weapons, uniforms, medals, equipment and manuscripts.

HOURS: Yr Daily Apr-Nov; Nov-Apr by reservation

ADMISSION: $6

9924
National Battlefields Commission
390 De Bernieres Ave, G1R 2L7; (p) (418) 648-3506; (f) (418) 648-3638

Federal/ 1908/ staff: 25(f); 40(p)

GARDEN; HISTORIC SITE: Acquires, preserves, and develops sites commemorating battles that were waged in Quebec City in 1759, 1760, and 1775.

PROGRAMS: Concerts; Elder's Programs; Exhibits; Family Programs; Festivals; Film/Video; Garden Tours; Guided Tours; Interpretation; Theatre

COLLECTIONS: Historic site of 108 hectares of land, fifty historical guns, 22 commemorative plaques, 20 interpretive panels, 6 monuments, 3 martello towers, 2 parks, 1 interpretation center, 1 nature trail, 1 bandstand,

RULE DES LAURENTIDES

9925
Sir Wilfrid Laurier National Historic Site
205 12 Ave, J0r 1C0 [PO Box 70, J0r 1C0]; (p) (450) 539-3702; (f) (450) 439-5721; m-syulvie_@ochette.pch.qc.ca; parcscanada.nsq.qc.ca/laurier/en/

Federal/ 1941/ staff: 1(f); 4(p)

HISTORIC SITE: Commemorates former prime minister Sir Wilfrid Laurier.

PROGRAMS: Concerts; Exhibits; Guided Tours; Interpretation

COLLECTIONS: [Mid 19th c] 600 objects and period furniture.

HOURS: May 10-June 25 M-F 9-12 / 1-5; June 26-Aug 29 W-Su 10-6

ADMISSION: $2.50, Student $1.25

SAINT-CONSTANT

9926
Canadian Railway Museum at Delson/Saint-Constant
122 A Saint-Pierre St, J5A 6G9 [120 Saint-Pierre St, J5A 6G9]; (p) (450) 638-4522; (f) (450) 638-1563; mfcd@exporail.org; www.exporail.org

Private non-profit/ 1961/ staff: 5(f); 10(p); 115(v)/ members: 1000

HISTORY MUSEUM: Promotes history and role of railways and public rail transit in Canada.

PROGRAMS: Exhibits; Family Programs; Guided Tours; Interpretation; Lectures; Publication; Research Library/Archives; School-Based Curriculum

COLLECTIONS: [1840-2000] 130 railway vehicles, 2 railway stations, a turntable, over 250,000 archives documents and 6,000 small objects.

HOURS: May-Oct Daily 9-5

ADMISSION: $6, Family $15, Student $3.50, Children $3, Seniors $5

SAINTE-FLAVIE

9927
Atlantic Salmon Interpretation Center
900 Route de la Mer, CP 59, G0J 2L0; (p) (418) 775-2969; (f) (418) 775-9466

Private non-profit/ 1985/ staff: 1(f); 14(p); 10(v)/ members: 10

HISTORY MUSEUM

PROGRAMS: Exhibits; Guided Tours; Interpretation; Theatre

COLLECTIONS: 6 aquariums, marine life.

HOURS: June-Oct Daily 9-5

ADMISSION: $7, Family $16

SHAWINIGAN

9928
Heritage Shawinigan
550 Hotel-De-Ville, G9N 8N4 [CP 22014 Succ Promenade, G9N 8N4]; (p) (819) 536-1184; (f) (819) 536-1184

Private non-profit/ 1994/ staff: 7(v)/ members: 300/publication: Shawinigan 1902-1905

HISTORICAL SOCIETY: Collects and preserves commonwealth's history.

PROGRAMS: Annual Meeting; Community Outreach; Exhibits; Lectures; Living History; Publication; Research Library/Archives

COLLECTIONS: Photos, manuscripts, newspaper titles, volumes, museum artifacts.

HOURS: Yr M-F

SHERBROOKE

9929
Musee Regimentaire Les Fusiliers de Sherbrocke
64, rue Belvedere Sud, J1H 4B4; (p) (819) 564-5940; (f) (819) 564-5641

Private non-profit/ 1985/ staff: 1(v)

HISTORY MUSEUM: Preserves and collects materials.

PROGRAMS: Exhibits; Film/Video; Lectures

COLLECTIONS: Uniforms, firearms, bombs, grenades, flags, books, documents, films and videos, photos, documents.

HOURS: Sept-Apr 7-10

9930
Societe d'Histoire de Sherbrooke, La
275 Dufferin, J1H 4M5; (p) (819) 821-5406; (f) (819) 821-5417; (c) Independent City

Private non-profit/ 1927/ Board of Trustees/ staff: 8(f); 9(p)/ members: 275

HISTORICAL SOCIETY: Preserves local and regional heritage; promotes history of Sherbrooke and the eastern townships.

PROGRAMS: Annual Meeting; Exhibits; Family Programs; Guided Tours; Interpretation; Lectures; Publication; Research Library/Archives; School-Based Curriculum

COLLECTIONS: 56 linear meters of archives, 40,000 photos, 7,500 books, 300 16mm films.

HOURS: Yr Archives: T-F 9-12 / 1-5; Exhibits: T-F 9-12 / 1-5, Sa-Su 1-5

ST-FERREOL-LES-NEIGES

9931
Corporation De Developpement Ce St Ferreol-Les-Neiges
4520 Av Royale, G0A 3R0; (p) (418) 826-3439; (f) (418) 826-1630; septchutes@car-pediem.qc.ca

Private non-profit/ 1984/ staff: 20(f); 5(p); 8(v)

HISTORIC SITE; LIVING HISTORY/OUT-DOOR MUSEUM: Promotes cultural, social, tourism, and economic development of the Cote-de-Beaupre region.

PROGRAMS: Guided Tours; Interpretation

COLLECTIONS: [1912-present] Out-of-doors technology, period photos, film, forge built in 1929, woodland footpaths and trails, hydroelectric generating stations in Quebec.

HOURS: May-Oct Daily 10-5

ADMISSION: $6, Family $17, Student $5, Children $4, Seniors

ST-PRIME

9932
Corporation de la Vieille Fromagerie Perron de Saint-Prime
148, 15ieme Ave, G8J 1L4; (p) (888) 251-4922; (f) (418) 251-1172; cheddar@destination.ca

Private non-profit/ 1990/ staff: 10(f)/ members: 35/publication: *La Fromagerie Perron de Saint-Prime*

HISTORIC SITE: Preserves history of cheese production.

PROGRAMS: Facility Rental; Family Programs; Film/Video; Guided Tours; Interpretation; Lectures; Living History; Publication

COLLECTIONS: Cheese making tools, photos, cheesemaker's house.

HOURS: May-Oct Daily 9-6

ADMISSION: $5.95, Student $3.95, Children $2.50, Seniors $4.95; Under 5 free

ST. PAUL DE L'ILE AUX NOIX

9933
Fort Lennox National Historic Site
1, 61st Ave, J0J 1G0; (p) (450) 291-5700; (f) (450) 291-4389

Federal/ staff: 15(f)/ members: 110

HISTORIC SITE

PROGRAMS: Concerts; Exhibits; Family Programs; Festivals; Guided Tours; Interpretation; Living History; Reenactments

COLLECTIONS: [1833]

HOURS: May-Sept Daily 10-6

ADMISSION: $3, Children $2.50, Seniors $4.50

STANBRIDGE EAST

9934
Missisquoi Historical Society/Missisquoi Museum
2 River St, J0J 2H0 [PO Box 186, J0J 2H0]; (p) (450) 248-3153; (f) (450) 248-0420; sochm@globetrotter.net; www.geocities.com/heartland/lake/8392; (c) Missisquoi

Private non-profit/ 1899/ staff: 1(f); 2(p); 75(v)/ members: 685/publication: *Treasure Hunt*

HISTORIC SITE; HISTORICAL SOCIETY; HISTORY MUSEUM: Collects, preserves, researches, exhibits, and publishes items pertaining to the historic past and development of Missisquoi County.

PROGRAMS: Annual Meeting; Community Outreach; Exhibits; Family Programs; Festivals; Guided Tours; Lectures; Publication; Research Library/Archives; School-Based Curriculum

COLLECTIONS: [1780-1920] 15,000 artifacts related to county history: United Empire Loyalists, Fenian Raids, settlement history, photos, manuscripts, and genealogical material.

HOURS: Historical Society M-F; Museum: June-Oct M-Su 10-5

ADMISSION: $3.50, Student $1, Children $1, Seniors $3; Group rates

STATION TERMINAL

9935
Fort No. 1 at Pointe Re Levy National Historic Site
41 Chemin Du Gobernement, G1K 7R3 [PO Box 2474, G1K 7R3]; (p) (418) 835-5182; (f) (418) 835-5443; pevcscanada-que@ph.qc.ca; pevcscanada.riq.qc.ca/fort_no1/ca/; (c) Levis

Federal/ 1865/ staff: 2(f); 5(p)/ members: 3

HISTORIC SITE: Built between 1865 and 1872, Fort No. 1 was part of a defense system composed of three forts and integrated into Quebec City's fortification.

PROGRAMS: Exhibits; Family Programs; Film/Video; Guided Tours; Interpretation

COLLECTIONS: [1860s] 1 Armstrong cannon, 3 caronades, 2 mortars, 2 cannons, costumes, 12 cannon powder barrels, tools.

HOURS: May 10-June 12 Su-F 9-4; June 13-Aug 29 M-Su 10-5; Aug 30-Oct 24 Su

9936
Grosse Ile and the Irish Memorial National Historic Site
Island in the St Lawrence River, near Montmagny, G1R 7R3 [PO Box 2474, G1R 7R3]; (p) (418) 248-9999; (f) (418) 241-5530; parcscanada-que@ph.qc.ca; www.parcscanada.ring.qc.ca/grosse_ile/; (c) Montmagny

Federal/ 1832/ staff: 6(f); 20(p)

HISTORIC SITE: Preserves former quarantine station for immigrants.

PROGRAMS: Exhibits; Film/Video; Guided Tours; Interpretation; Publication; Reenactments

COLLECTIONS: [1832-1937] 3 Cannons, 3 sterilizers, 1 ice canoe, religious artifacts, stained glass windows, ambulance, disaffection showers, statues.

HOURS: May-Oct 9-9

STE-FOY

9937
Archives Nationales du Quebec
1210 Ave du Seminaire, G1V 4N1 [PO Box 10450, G1V 4N1]; (p) (418) 643-4376; (f) (418) 646-0868; anq@mcc.gouv.qc.ca; www.anq.gouv.qc.ca

State/ 1920/ staff: 100(f); 1(p)

LIBRARY AND/OR ARCHIVES: Gathers, preserves, and disseminates collective memory.

PROGRAMS: Guided Tours; Publication; Research Library/Archives

COLLECTIONS: [17th c-present] Vital statistics, records of notaries and surveyors, records of the Provincial Government.

HOURS: Yr

TROIS RIVIERES

9938
Galerie d'art du Parc/Manoir de Tonnancour
864, rue des Ursulines CP 871, G9A 5J9; (p) (819) 374-2355; (f) (819) 374-1758; galerie_art.duparc@tr.cgocable.ca; //www.rapidus.net/gap

Private non-profit/ 1972/ staff: 1(f); 5(p); 5(v)

ART MUSEUM; HISTORIC SITE: Presents artistic and historic exhibits.

PROGRAMS: Exhibits; Interpretation

COLLECTIONS: [1712-1784-present] Artwork.

HOURS: Feb 15-Dec 15

9939
Pulp and Paper Industry Exhibition Centre
800 Parc Portuaire, CP 368, G9A 5H3; (p) (819) 372-4633; (f) (819) 374-1900; (c) Francheville

City/ 1988/ staff: 5(f)

CORPORATE ARCHIVES/MUSEUM: Preserves information and promotes knowledge of the paper and pulp industry.

PROGRAMS: Exhibits; Film/Video; Guided Tours; Interpretation

HOURS: June-Sept Daily 9-6

ADMISSION: $3, Student $1.50; Under 6 free

ULVERTON

9940
Ulverton Woolen Mills
210 Porter Rd, J0B 2B0; (p) (819) 826-3157; (f) (819) 826-6266; info@moulin.qc.ca; moulin.qc.ca

Private non-profit/ 1982/ staff: 2(f); 4(p); 9(v)/ members: 250

HISTORIC SITE: Interprets textile industry in Canada.

PROGRAMS: Exhibits; Guided Tours; Interpretation; Publication; Research Library/Archives

COLLECTIONS: Tools, machines, Celanese exhibit.

HOURS: June-Oct Daily 10-5

ADMISSION: $5, Student $4, Seniors $4

VAL-D'OR

9941
La Cite de l'Or
Bis, J9P 4P3 [90, av Perreault Box 212, J9P

4P3]; (p) (819) 825-7616; (f) (819) 825-9853; courrier@citedelor.qc.ca; www.citedelor.qc.ca

Private non-profit/ 1979/ La Corporation du Village Minier de Bourlamaque/ staff: 2(f); 28(p)/publication: *Le Journal du Mineur*

HISTORY MUSEUM: Promotes and interprets mining history.

PROGRAMS: Concerts; Exhibits; Festivals; Guided Tours; Interpretation; Publication; Research Library/Archives

COLLECTIONS: Mining exhibits, mining equipment, and material.

HOURS: Yr

VAUDREUIL-DORION

9942
Musee Regional de Vaudreuil Soulanges
431 Saint-Charles Ave, J7V 2N3; (p) (450) 455-2092; (f) (450) 455-6782

Private non-profit/ 1955/ Corp. du Musee Regional de Vaudreuil Soulanges/ staff: 3(f); 10(p)/ 20(v)/ members: 300

HISTORY MUSEUM: Conserves and exhibits Vaudreuil Soulanges region.

PROGRAMS: Concerts; Exhibits; Facility Rental; Family Programs; Festivals; Guided Tours; Lectures; Living History; Publication; Research Library/Archives

COLLECTIONS: [18th-19th c] 6,000 pieces: religious art, peasant and middle class artifacts.

HOURS: Yr M-F 9:30-4:30, T 7-4:30, Sa-Su 1-4:30

ADMISSION: $3, Family $7, Student $2,

VIEUX LEVIS

9943
Societe Historique Alphonse des Jardins
6, rue du Mont Marie, G6V 1V9; (p) (418) 835-2090; (f) (418) 835-9173; shadesjardins@videotron.ca; www.desjardins.com

Private non-profit/ 1979/ staff: 3(f); 3(p)/ members: 24

HISTORICAL SOCIETY; HOUSE MUSEUM: Conserves, preserves, researches, and publishes on Mouvement Desjardins' development and history.

PROGRAMS: Exhibits; Guided Tours; Interpretation; Publication

COLLECTIONS: [1890-present] Volumes, archives, photographs, museum artifacts, historic persons' personal belongings.

HOURS: Yr Daily M-F 10-12/1-4:30, Sa-Su 12-5

ADMISSION: No charge

SASKATCHEWAN

ARCOLA

9944
Arcola Museum

Railway Ave, S0C 0G0 [PO Box 354, S0C 0G0]; (p) (306) 455-2462

City/ 1972/ Arcola Town Council/ staff: 14(v)

HISTORY MUSEUM; HOUSE MUSEUM

PROGRAMS: Annual Meeting; Interpretation

COLLECTIONS: [1890-1950] Pioneer artifacts, tools and machinery; a furnished log house, farming machinery.

HOURS: May-Sept Fri 2-4

AVONLEA

9945
Avonlea "Heritage House" Museum
201 Main St, S0H 0C0 [PO Box 401, S0H 0C0]; (p) (306) 868-2101; (f) (306) 868-2221

City/ 1980/ staff: 2(p); 55(v)/ members: 75/publication: *Heritage House Happenings*

HISTORY MUSEUM; HOUSE MUSEUM: Collects, records, researches, preserves, and interprets local area.

PROGRAMS: Annual Meeting; Community Outreach; Exhibits; Festivals; Guided Tours; Publication; Reenactments

COLLECTIONS: [1890-present] Settlers effects and history including 4000 ranching, farming, homemaking, and business artifacts; 500 school books, maps, and story books; 100 pieces of sheet music; 100 newspapers; 200 historical papers; and 200 photos.

HOURS: June-Sept Daily 1-5

ADMISSION: $1, Student $0.50

BATTLEFORD

9946
Fort Battleford National Historic Site of Canada
[PO Box 70, S0M 0E0]; (p) (306) 937-2621; (f) (306) 937-3370; battleford.info@pchgc.ca; www.parkscanada.gc.ca/battleford

Federal/ 1923/ Parks Canada Agency/ staff: 4(f); 8(p)

HISTORIC SITE: Preserves five original buildings and historic trails, and promotes the history of the North West Mounted Police and First Nations.

PROGRAMS: Community Outreach; Family Programs; Festivals; Guided Tours; Reenactments; Research Library/Archives; School-Based Curriculum; Theatre

COLLECTIONS: [1885] Five original 1885 period buildings, barracks, commanding officers residence, officers quarters, horse stable, jail, stockade.

HOURS: May-Sept Daily 9-5

ADMISSION: $4, Student $2, Seniors

BIGGAR

9947
Biggar Museum and Gallery
105 3rd Ave W, S0K 0M0 [PO Box 1598, S0K 0M0]; (p) (306) 948-3451; (f) (306) 948-5134; bgmchin@sk.sympatico.ca; www.3.sk.sympatico.ca/beggar

Private non-profit/ 1972/ staff: 2(f); 2(p); 100(v)/publication: *Biggar: A Pictorial History*

ART MUSEUM; HISTORY MUSEUM: Promotes regional heritage and culture.

PROGRAMS: Annual Meeting; Community Outreach; Exhibits; Facility Rental; Guided Tours; Lectures; Publication

COLLECTIONS: [1909-1955] 10,000 artifacts, documents, and photos pertinent to the history of the region: small agricultural tools, railroad artifacts, household articles, toys, dolls, silent film era and Latin movie artifacts, and player piano roles.

HOURS: Sept-May M-Sa 1-5; May-Sept M-F

BRACKEN

9948
Bracken Community Museum
CPR Station, Main St, S0N 0G0 [PO Box 35, S0N 0G0]; (p) (306) 296-2054

1980/ staff: 1(f)

COLLECTIONS: Tables, chairs, sideboard lamps, dishes, stoves, saddles, harness, blacksmith tools, wrenches, bottles, 1917 school bell, books, maps, organ, scales, hay knives, and coffee grinders.

HOURS: Yr by appt

ADMISSION: Donations accepted

BRESAYLOR HAMLET

9949
Bresaylor Heritage Museum
, [PO Box 33, Paynton, S0M 2J0]; (p) (306) 895-4813

1983/ Board of Directors/ staff: 1(p); 8(v)

HISTORY MUSEUM: Preserves and presents area artifacts.

PROGRAMS: Annual Meeting; Community Outreach; Exhibits

COLLECTIONS: [1880s-1950s] Artifacts from the Bresaylor and Red River Settlements.

HOURS: July-Aug Su, W-F 1-5

ADMISSION: Donations accepted

CLIMAX

9950
Climax Community Museum, Inc.
101 1st East, S0N 0N0 [Box 59, S0N 0N0]; (p) (306) 293-2051

1982/ staff: 1(p); 3(v)/ members: 100

HISTORY MUSEUM: Collects, restores, exhibits, pioneer artifacts.

PROGRAMS: Annual Meeting; Exhibits; Guided Tours; Interpretation

COLLECTIONS: [1885-1949] Railway, Post Office, domestic, military, business, school, hospital, machinery, jails, high school artifacts.

HOURS: 1-5

ADMISSION: Donations accepted

DGEMA

9951
Deep South Pioneer Museum
Gobernment Rd, S0C 1Y0 [Box 213, S0C 1Y0]; (p) (306) 459-2431

1977/ Board of Directors/ staff: 25(v)/ members: 250

HISTORY MUSEUM: Preserves pioneer lifestyle.

PROGRAMS: Annual Meeting; Exhibits; Facility Rental; Guided Tours

COLLECTIONS: 100 tractors, 23 buildings housing artifacts: school, church, general store, drugstore, home, telephone, and farming equipment.

HOURS: Apr-Oct Su 1-5 and by appt

ADMISSION: $4, Student $2; Under 13 free

DORINTOSH

9952
Steele Narrows Historic Park/Saskatchewan Environment and Resource Management
Box 70, S0M 0T0; (p) (306) 236-7680; (f) (306) 236-7679;
Randy.Zielke.ERM@Govmail.gov.sk.ca

staff: 1(p)

HISTORIC SITE

PROGRAMS: Interpretation

HOURS: May-Sept Daily

DUCK LAKE

9953
Duck Lake Regional Interpretive Centre
5 Anderson Ave, S0K 1J0 [Box 328, S0K 1J0]; (p) (306) 467-2057; (f) (306) 467-2257;
duckmuf@sk.sympatico.ca

Private non-profit/ 1979/ staff: 2(f); 1(p); 25(v)/ members: 350

ART MUSEUM; HISTORICAL SOCIETY; HISTORY MUSEUM: Focuses on the history of the First Nation, Metis, and pioneer society, Riel Rebellion, and buffalo extinction.

PROGRAMS: Annual Meeting; Exhibits; Facility Rental; Family Programs; Festivals; Film/Video; Guided Tours; Interpretation

COLLECTIONS: [1870-1905] Native American costumes, Metis clothing, early school records and books, religious artifacts, tools used in buffalo hunts, copy of a letter written by Louis Riel, gold watch given to Gabriel Dumont by French Canadian sympathizers in New York, pioneer implements, arrowheads.

HOURS: May-Sept 10-5:30 and by appt

ADMISSION: $4, Family $10, Student $2, Seniors $3

ELBOW

9954
Elbow Museum and Historical Society
Saskatchewan Dr, S0H 1J0 [Box 207, S0H 1J0]; (p) (306) 854-2277; (f) (306) 854-2229

1968/ staff: 1(p)/ 10(v)/ members: 69

ALLIANCE OF HISTORICAL AGENCIES; HISTORIC PRESERVATION AGENCY; HISTORY MUSEUM: Promotes history and culture of this rural community.

PROGRAMS: Annual Meeting; Exhibits; Family Programs; Guided Tours

COLLECTIONS: [19th-20thc] Pioneer and Native American artifacts and materials, sod house.

HOURS: July-Sept M-Sa 1-8

ADMISSION: $2, Children $0.50

ESTERHAZY

9955
Kaposavar Historic Society
3 mi S of Esterhazy, S0A 0X0 [Box 13, S0A 0X0]; (p) (306) 745-2715

Private non-profit/ 1886/ staff: 1(p); 17(v)

HISTORIC PRESERVATION AGENCY; HISTORIC SITE; HISTORICAL SOCIETY; HISTORY MUSEUM; HOUSE MUSEUM: Maintains historic museum, church, rectory, homesteads, cemetery.

PROGRAMS: Annual Meeting; Exhibits; Guided Tours

COLLECTIONS: Homesteads, house, barn, ice house, smoke house, school with furnishings books, buggy, cutter horse-drawn, and photos.

HOURS: May 15-Sept 15 Daily 8-4 and by appt

ESTON

9956
Prairie West Historical Society, Inc.
946 2nd St SE, S0L 1A0 [Box 910, S0L 1A0]; (p) (306) 962-3772

Private non-profit/ 1977/ staff: 1(p); 40(v)/publication: *Grass to Grain*

HISTORIC PRESERVATION AGENCY; HISTORY MUSEUM; HOUSE MUSEUM: Collects, preserves, interprets and exhibits artifacts.

PROGRAMS: Annual Meeting; Community Outreach; Elder's Programs; Exhibits; Facility Rental; Family Programs; Guided Tours; Interpretation; Publication; Research Library/Archives; School-Based Curriculum

COLLECTIONS: [1905-1960] 5,000 household, personal, agricultural artifacts; documents, pictures, and clippings.

HOURS: July-Aug Su 1-5, M-Sa 9-12 / 1-5; June-Sept M-Su 1:30-4:30

ADMISSION: Donations accepted

FOAM LAKE

9957
Foam Lake Museum Association
113 Bray Ave W, S0A 1A0 [Box 1041, S0A 1A0]; (p) (306) 272-4292; (f) (306) 272-3519

City/ 1967/ staff: 1(p); 30(v)/ members: 12

HISTORY MUSEUM; HOUSE MUSEUM: Collects, preserves, and exhibits history of the founding, settlement, and development of the Foam Lake Region.

PROGRAMS: Annual Meeting; Exhibits; Guided Tours; Living History

COLLECTIONS: [19th-20 c] 5,000 cataloged artifacts displayed at two locations: the museum and Douglas House, pioneer instruments, books, and photographs.

HOURS: May-Sept F-Sa; Oct-Apr by appt

ADMISSION: No charge

HARRIS

9958
Harris Heritage Museum Society, Inc.
204 Railway Ave, S0L 1K0 [Box 187, S0L 1K0]; (p) (306) 656-2172; (f) (306) 650-2172

Private non-profit/ 1987/ staff: 1(p); 63(v)/ members: 120

HISTORY MUSEUM: Collects, preserves, researches, exhibits, and interprets local history.

PROGRAMS: Annual Meeting; Community Outreach; Exhibits; Family Programs; Festivals; Film/Video; Guided Tours; Interpretation; Living History; Reenactments; Research Library/Archives; School-Based Curriculum

COLLECTIONS: 5,537 artifacts: automotive, clothing, communication, farming, household, local business, medical, military, music, schools, sports, railway, toys, photographs, family history relating to Harris and region history.

HOURS: May-Oct T, F, Su

HUDSON BAY

9959
Hudson Bay and District Cultural Society/Hudson Bay Museum
512 Churchill St, S0E 0Y0 [Box 931, S0E 0Y0]; (p) (306) 865-2170

Private non-profit/ 1978/ staff: 3(p); 20(v)/ members: 83

HISTORIC SITE; HISTORY MUSEUM

PROGRAMS: Annual Meeting; Elder's Programs; Exhibits; Family Programs; Festivals; Film/Video; Guided Tours; Lectures; Research Library/Archives

COLLECTIONS: Pioneer, local history.

HOURS: Summer Daily

ADMISSION: Donations accepted

HUMBOLDT

9960
Humboldt & District Museum & Gallery
Corner of Main St & 6th Ave, S0K 2A0 [Box 2349, S0K 2A0]; (p) (306) 682-5226; (f) (306) 680-3144; hblt.museum@sk.sympatico.ca

City/ 1982/ staff: 2(f); 3(p); 70(v)/publication: *Humboldt on the Carlton Trail*

HISTORIC SITE; HISTORY MUSEUM: Preserves history of German, Roman Catholic settlement founded by priests of St. Peter's Abbey.

PROGRAMS: Community Outreach; Exhibits; Family Programs; Guided Tours; Publication; Research Library/Archives; School-Based Curriculum

COLLECTIONS: [1885-present] Transportation, Red River Cart on the Carlton Trail, and early telegraph history; German Catholic settlement.

HOURS: Yr T-Sa 1-5 (Summer Su 10-5)

ADMISSION: Donations accepted

KIPLING

9961
Kidling and District Historical Society
201-4th St, S0G 2S0 [Box 128, S0G 2S0]; (p)
(306) 736-2488

1974/ staff: 30(v)/publication: *Peace and Strife,
Pioneer to Progress*

HISTORICAL SOCIETY; HOUSE MUSEUM

PROGRAMS: Annual Meeting; Community
Outreach; Concerts; Elder's Programs; Exhibits; Facility Rental; Family Programs; Festivals; Film/Video; Guided Tours; Living History;
Publication

COLLECTIONS: [Late 20 c -present] Furnished pioneer home; elevator engine,
Church; dental office; service station; main
building with artifact and wall of fame.

HOURS: June 1-Oct 1 F-Su 2-5

ADMISSION: Donations accepted

LANIGAN

9962
**Lanigan and District Heritage
Association**
75 Railway Ave, S0K 2M0 [Box 4224, S0K
2M0]; (p) (306) 365-2569; (c) Lanigan

1994/ staff: 3(p); 26(v)/ members: 58

HISTORIC PRESERVATION AGENCY; HISTORY MUSEUM: Preserves early historic artifacts.

PROGRAMS: Community Outreach; Concerts; Elder's Programs; Exhibits; Facility
Rental; Film/Video; Lectures; Living History

COLLECTIONS: [1890s-1930] Agriculture,
road maintenance, railway equipment, and artifacts.

HOURS: June M-F 9-6, Sa-Su 9-5; July-Aug
M-F 8-6, Sa-Su and holidays

LUSELAND

9963
Luseland and Districts Museum
Grand Ave, S0L 2A0 [200 Hohmann St, S0L
2A0]; (p) (306) 372-4258

Joint/ 1990/ City/ staff: 14(v)

HISTORIC PRESERVATION AGENCY; HISTORICAL SOCIETY; HISTORY MUSEUM;
HOUSE MUSEUM: Collects, preserves and interprets history of the prairies and people.

PROGRAMS: Annual Meeting; Community
Outreach; Concerts; Elder's Programs; Exhibits; Facility Rental; Family Programs; Festivals; Film/Video; Lectures; Research Library/Archives; School-Based Curriculum

COLLECTIONS: [1900-1960] Artifacts: prairie
settlement-transportation, communication,
military medical, homelife, farm, archival pictures, paintings, religious, educational, crafts,
businesses.

HOURS: Sa 1-4

ADMISSION: Donations accepted

MAPLE CREEK

9964
Fort Walsh National Historic Site
55 kms SW of Maple Creek Hwy 271, S0N
1N0 [Box 278 (201 Jasper St), S0N 1N0]; (p)
(306) 662-2645, (306) 662-3590; (f) (306)
662-2711; Fort_Walsh@pch.gc.ca;
parkscanada.pch.gc.ca/parks/saskatchewan/f
ort_wals

Federal/ 1972/ staff: 2(f); 1(p); 17(v)

HISTORIC SITE; LIVING HISTORY/OUTDOOR MUSEUM: Preserves and present the
history of the Fort.

PROGRAMS: Exhibits; Guided Tours; Interpretation; Living History

COLLECTIONS: [1873-1883] American
whiskey trade, Northwest Mounted Police.

HOURS: Mid May-Oct Daily 9-5:30

ADMISSION: $6, Family $15, Children $3, Seniors $4.50; Under 6 free

9965
**South West Saskatchewan Oldtimers'
Museum**
218 Jasper St, S0N 1N0 [Box 1540, S0N
1N0]; (p) (360) 662-2474

Private non-profit/ 1926/ staff: 2(p); 30(v)/
members: 300

HISTORY MUSEUM: Preserves and interprets
Frontier Era, Saskatchewan history prior to extensive settlement.

PROGRAMS: Annual Meeting; Community
Outreach; Exhibits; Family Programs; Guided
Tours; Lectures; Publication; Research Library/Archives; School-Based Curriculum

COLLECTIONS: [1870-1910] Artifacts: Native,
Metis, fur trade, N.W.M.P., ranching, early settlement, photos, documents, and archival materials.

HOURS: May-Sept Daily 9-5:30; Oct-May T-W
9-5

ADMISSION: $3, Children $1; Uinder 5 free

MCCORD

9966
McCord and District Museum
Main St, S0H 2T0 [Box 30, S0H 2T0]; (p)
(306) 478-2522; (f) (306) 478-2403;
www.sasktourism.com; (c) Mankota

1967/ staff: 26(v)

HISTORY MUSEUM

PROGRAMS: Annual Meeting; Exhibits; Guided Tours; School-Based Curriculum

COLLECTIONS: [1929-1930] Household artifacts, small tools, items from community businesses, CPR railway artifacts, and church artifacts from McCord Community.

HOURS: May 1-Sept 30 M-Sa 8:30-12 / 1-5

ADMISSION: Donations accepted

MOOSE JAW

9967
**History of Transportation/Western
Development Museum**
50 Diefenbaker Dr, S6H 4N8 [PO Box 185,
S6H 4N8]; (p) (306) 693-5989; (f) (306) 693-
0511; swdm@sk.sympatico.ca; www.wdmuseum.sk.ca

1949/ staff: 5(f); 2(p); 156(v)

HISTORY MUSEUM

PROGRAMS: Community Outreach; Exhibits;
Facility Rental; Family Programs; Festivals;
Guided Tours; Interpretation; Living History;
Publication; School-Based Curriculum

COLLECTIONS: [1900] Air, rail, land, and watercraft collection of artifacts.

HOURS: Yr Jan-Mar T-Su 9-6; Apr-Dec Daily
9-6

ADMISSION: $6, Student $4, Children $2, Seniors $5

9968
**Sukanen Ship Pioneer Village and
Museum**
8 mi S of Moose Jaw on Hwy # 2, S6H 7T2
[Box 2071, S6H 7T2]; (p) (306) 693-7315

Private non-profit/ 1969/ staff: 5(v)/ members:
55

HISTORY MUSEUM; HOUSE MUSEUM: Operates pioneer village and museum.

PROGRAMS: Annual Meeting; Exhibits; Living
History

COLLECTIONS: [1900-1950] Pioneer town:
30 buildings, farm machinery.

HOURS: June 1-Sept 15 Daily 9-5

ADMISSION: Student $2, Seniors $3

MORSE

9969
**Morse Cultural and Heritage
Association, Inc.**
410 McKenzie St, S0H 3C0 [Box 308, S0H
3C0]; (p) (306) 629-3230; (f) (306) 629-3230

Private non-profit/ 1985/ staff: 1(f); 1(p); 12(v)

HISTORY MUSEUM: Collects and displays artifacts relevant to the development and settlement of our town and surrounding area.

PROGRAMS: Annual Meeting; Exhibits; Facility Rental; Guided Tours; School-Based Curriculum

COLLECTIONS: [1900-1950] Home, business, school, dining, farming.

HOURS: Yr 9-4:30

ADMISSION: Donations accepted

MOSSBANK

9970
Mossbank and District Museum, Inc.
3rd St N, S0H 3G0 [Box 278, S0H 3G0]; (p)
(306) 354-2889

1985/ staff: 1(p); 20(v)

HISTORIC PRESERVATION AGENCY; HISTORIC SITE; HISTORICAL SOCIETY; LIVING
HISTORY/OUTDOOR MUSEUM: Preserves
regional history and culture.

PROGRAMS: Annual Meeting; Exhibits; Festivals; Guided Tours; Interpretation; Lectures;
Research Library/Archives

COLLECTIONS: [1908-1999] Blacksmith
shop; artifacts: banking, school, and community.

HOURS: June 15-Sept 30 M-F 9-5

ADMISSION: $2

NIPAWIN

9971
Nipawin and District Living Forestry Museum
Old Hwy 35 W, S0E 1E0 [PO Box 1917, S0E 1E0]; (p) (306) 862-9299, (306) 862-3317

City/ 1967/ staff: 2(f)/ 30(v)/ members: 65

HOUSE MUSEUM; LIVING HISTORY/OUT-DOOR MUSEUM: Collects, houses, and re-stores artifacts of pioneer settlers and their families.

PROGRAMS: Elder's Programs; Exhibits; Guided Tours

COLLECTIONS: [1900-1950] Household appliances and tools, clothes of the period, cars, trucks, tractors, steam saw-mill, one room school, church, 1920 farm house, train station.

HOURS: May 15-Sept 1 Daily 1-6

ADMISSION: $2

NOKOMIS

9972
Nokomis and District Museum
Box 417, S0G 3R0; (p) (306) 528-2979; (c) Nokomis

Joint/ 1977/ City; Private non-profit/ staff: 2(p)/ 112(v)/ members: 130

HISTORY MUSEUM: Maintains museum.

PROGRAMS: Annual Meeting; Exhibits; Family Programs; School-Based Curriculum

COLLECTIONS: [1900-1998] Homesteading artifacts.

HOURS: June-Aug Daily 10-5

ADMISSION: $2, Family $5

NORTH BATTLEFORD

9973
Allen Sapp Gallery: The Gonor Collection
#1 Railway Ave, S9A 2Y6 [PO Box 460, S9A 2Y6]; (p) (306) 445-1760; (f) (306) 445-1161; sapp@sk.sympatico.ca

City/ 1989/ staff: 1(f)/ 3(p)/ 2(v)/ members: 50

ART MUSEUM: Promotes Cree, Inuit, and other Native American culture and heritage.

PROGRAMS: Exhibits; Facility Rental; Guided Tours; Interpretation; Research Library/Archives; School-Based Curriculum

COLLECTIONS: [1950-present] 300 paintings depicting life on a reservation in the 1930s and 1940s, 300 Inuit carvings and sculptures, 231 ethnic dolls, and 30 Native craft items.

HOURS: Yr June-Sept 10:30-5:30; Oct-May W-Su

9974
Heritage Farm and Village/Western Development Museum
Hwy 16 & 40, S9A 2Y1 [PO Box 183, S9A 2Y1]; (p) (306) 445-8033; (f) (306) 445-7211; wdm.nb@sk.sympatico.ca; www.wdmuseum.sk.ca

1949/ staff: 6(f)/ 6(p)/ 962(v)

HISTORY MUSEUM; LIVING HISTORY/OUT-DOOR MUSEUM: Promotes agriculture history.

PROGRAMS: Community Outreach; Exhibits; Facility Rental; Festivals; Interpretation; Living History; Publication; School-Based Curriculum

COLLECTIONS: [1900-1940] Artifacts: steam traction engines, gas tractor, and agricultural equipment; domestic and business artifacts, leisure and recreational artifacts, and transportation artifacts, farm buildings.

HOURS: Yr Oct-Apr W-Su 12:30-4:30; May-Sept Daily 9-5

ADMISSION: $6, Student $4, Children $2,

OUTLOOK

9975
Outlook and District Heritage Museum and Gallery, Inc.
100 Railway Ave East, S0L 2N0 [Box 1095, S0L 2N0]; (p) (306) 867-8285

Private non-profit/ 1984/ staff: 26(v)/ members: 22

HISTORIC PRESERVATION AGENCY; HISTORY MUSEUM: Collects, preserves, and stores pioneer history; maintains museum in former Canadian Pacific Railway Station.

PROGRAMS: Annual Meeting; Exhibits; Guided Tours; Research Library/Archives

COLLECTIONS: [1904-1930] Household items, books, newspapers, furniture, clothing, sporting equipment, lamps, and lanterns, veterinary supplies, plows, cultivators, and fire fighting equipment.

HOURS:

PELLY

9976
Fort Pelly-Livingstone Museum
305 First Ave S, S0A 2Z0 [Box 24, S0A 2Z0]; (p) (306) 595-2030

1974/ staff: 1(p)/ 20(v)/ members: 15

HISTORIC SITE; HISTORICAL SOCIETY; HISTORY MUSEUM: Preserves history of Fort Pelly and Fort Livingstone.

PROGRAMS: Annual Meeting; Community Outreach; Exhibits; Guided Tours

COLLECTIONS: [18th-19th c] Train station, box car, and caboose.

HOURS: June-Sept W-Su 11-4

ADMISSION: $1, Family $15, Children $0.50; Group rates

RAYMORE

9977
Raymore Pioneer Museum, Inc.
1st Ave, S0A 3J0 [Box 453, S0A 3J0]; (p) (306) 746-2180; (f) (306) 746-4314

1962/ staff: 10(v)

HISTORY MUSEUM: Records and displays local history.

PROGRAMS: Annual Meeting

COLLECTIONS: [Early 1900s] Pioneer household and farming equipment.

HOURS: June-Oct T-Th 2-4 and by appt

ADMISSION: Donations accepted

REGINA

9978
Museums Association of Saskatchewan
1836 Argus St, S4T 1Z4; (p) (306) 780-9279; (f) (306) 780-9463; mask@saskmuseums.org

Joint/ 1967/ staff: 6(f)/ 50(v)/ members: 280

ALLIANCE OF HISTORICAL AGENCIES: Promotes SK heritage.

PROGRAMS: Annual Meeting; Publication; Research Library/Archives

HOURS: Yr M-F

9979
Regina Plains Museum
1835 Scarth St, S4P 2G9; (p) (306) 780-9435; (f) (306) 565-2979; rp.museum@sk.sympatico.ca; www.reginaplainsmuseum.com

1960/ staff: 2(f)/ 20(v)/ members: 125

HISTORY MUSEUM: Preserves and interprets the social, cultural, economic, and political development of Regina.

PROGRAMS: Annual Meeting; Community Outreach; Exhibits; Facility Rental; Family Programs; Festivals; Interpretation; Research Library/Archives

COLLECTIONS: [Late 19th c-present] Reflects social, cultural, economic, and political development of the community.

HOURS: Yr M-F 10-4

ADMISSION: No charge

9980
Saskatchewan Archives Board-Regina
3303 Hillsdale St, S4S 0A2 [Univ of Regina, S4S 0A2]; (p) (306) 787-4068; (f) (306) 787-1197; info.regina@archives.gov.sk.ca; www.saskarchives.com

1945/publication: *Saskatchewan History*

LIBRARY AND/OR ARCHIVES: Selects, acquires, and preserves documentary evidence pertaining to the history of SK.

PROGRAMS: Community Outreach; Exhibits; Publication; Research Library/Archives

COLLECTIONS: [1870-present]

HOURS: Yr M-F 9-5

9981
Saskatchewan History and Folklore Society, Inc.
1860 Lorne St, S4P 2L7; (p) (306) 780-9204; (f) (306) 780-9489; shfs.fa@sk.sympatico.ca

Private non-profit/ 1957/ staff: 1(f)/ 1(p)/ 11(v)/ members: 553/publication: *Folklore*

HISTORICAL SOCIETY: Gathers, preserves, and promotes interest in the social history and folklore of SK.

PROGRAMS: Annual Meeting; Community Outreach; Film/Video; Publication

COLLECTIONS: [1900s] 10,000 slides, 1,200 manuscripts

HOURS: Yr M-F 8:30-12 / 1-5

9982
Saskatchewan Military Museum
1600 Elphinstone St, S4T 3N1; (p) (303) 586-

5525; (f) (306) 586-5525

Federal/ 1984/ staff: 30(v)

HISTORY MUSEUM: Collects, preserves, and displays Saskatchewan's military history.

PROGRAMS: Community Outreach; Exhibits; Guided Tours; Lectures

COLLECTIONS: [1885-present] Uniforms and accouterments, photos, film, archival material, vehicles, weapons and projectiles, paintings.

HOURS: Yr T 1-3, W-Sa 2-5

ADMISSION: Donations accepted

9983
Saskatchewan Sports Hall of Fame and Museum
2205 Victoria Ave, S4P 0S4; (p) (306) 780-9232; (f) (306) 780-9427; sshfm@dlcwest.com; www.dlcwest.com/~sshfm

Private non-profit/ 1966/ staff: 5(f); 4(p); 50(v)/ members: 1300

HISTORY MUSEUM: Preserves SK sporting history.

PROGRAMS: Annual Meeting; Community Outreach; Exhibits; Facility Rental; Family Programs; Guided Tours; Interpretation; Research Library/Archives; School-Based Curriculum

COLLECTIONS: 10,000 museum sporting artifacts, 1,000 photos, Saskatchewan Roughrider Football Club archives and artifacts, 300 inductee archive files.

HOURS: Yr May-Sept Daily 9-5, Sa-Su 1-5; Winter

ROSE VALLEY

9984
Rose Valley and District Heritage Museum, Inc.
Box 232, S0E 1M0; (p) (306) 322-2034

1985/ staff: 10(p); 20(v)/ members: 15

HISTORY MUSEUM

PROGRAMS: Annual Meeting; Community Outreach; Concerts; Guided Tours; School-Based Curriculum

COLLECTIONS: [1900-present]

HOURS: July 1- Sept 4 T-Sa 2-4

ADMISSION: No charge

ROULEAU

9985
Rouleau and District Museum
On Fair Grounds, S0G 4H0 [General Delivery, S0G 4H0]; (p) (306) 776-2519

Private non-profit/ 1988/ members: 20

HOUSE MUSEUM; LIVING HISTORY/OUTDOOR MUSEUM

PROGRAMS: Annual Meeting; Exhibits; Guided Tours

COLLECTIONS: [1910-1950] Historic structures.

HOURS: Summer Daily 12-6

ADMISSION: Donations accepted

SASKATOON

9986
Curatorial Centre/Western Development Museum
2935 Melville St, S7J 5A6 [Curatorial Centre, 2935 Melville St, S7J 5A6]; (p) (306) 934-1400; (f) (306) 934-4467; swdm@sk.sympatico.ca; www.wdmuseum.sk.ca

1949/ staff: 15(f); 5(p); 14(v)/ members: 850/publication: Sparks Off The Anvil Newsletter

HISTORY MUSEUM: Preserves history of North Battleford agriculture, Moose Jaw transportation, Saskatoon general, and Yorkton immigration.

PROGRAMS: Publication; Research Library/Archives

COLLECTIONS: [1900-1980] Agricultural artifacts, steam traction engines, gas tractors, and harvesting equipment; clothing and textiles, domestic artifacts, leisure and recreational artifacts, and transportation artifacts.

HOURS: Yr M-F

9987
Diefenbaker Canada Centre
101 Diefenbaker Place, S7N 5B8; (p) (306) 966-8384; (f) (306) 966-6207; bruce.shepard@usask.ca

1980/ staff: 4(f); 7(p)

HISTORY MUSEUM: Preserves and promotes Canadian history.

PROGRAMS: Community Outreach; Concerts; Exhibits; Facility Rental; Family Programs; Guided Tours; Interpretation; Lectures; Publication; Research Library/Archives; School-Based Curriculum

COLLECTIONS: [1895-1979] Personal Collections of Canada's 13th Prime Minister John G. Diefenbaker: 4-5,000 artifacts, 3,000,000 documents, and 8,000 photos.

HOURS: Yr Su 12:30-5, M, F 9:30-4:30, T-Th 9:30-8

ADMISSION: $2, Family $5,

9988
Fort Carlton Provincial Historic Park
26 km W of Duck Lake, S7K 2H6 [102-112 Research Dr, S7K 2H6]; (p) (306) 467-5205; (f) (306) 933-5773

1967/ staff: 1(f); 10(p)

HISTORIC SITE; HISTORY MUSEUM: Preserves reconstructed Hudson's Bay Company fur trading post.

PROGRAMS: Exhibits; Family Programs; Festivals; Guided Tours; Interpretation; School-Based Curriculum

COLLECTIONS: [1810-1885] Artifacts: fur store, buffalo robes; trade store: European trade goods, blankets, cloth, beads, knives, pots, gunpowder.

HOURS: Mid May 19-Sept 3 Daily 10-6

ADMISSION: $2.50, Family $6, Children $1

9989
Saskatchewan Archives Board-Saskatoon
Room 91 Murray Bldg, Univ of SK 3 Campus Dr, S7N 5A4; (p) (306) 933-5832; (f) (306) 933-7305; info.saskatoon@archives.gov.sk.ca; www.saskarchives.com

1945/ staff: 7(f); 1(p)/publication: Saskatchewan History

LIBRARY AND/OR ARCHIVES: Selects, acquires, and preserves documentary evidence pertaining to the history of SK Province.

PROGRAMS: Community Outreach; Exhibits; Publication; Research Library/Archives

COLLECTIONS: [1870-present] Documentary material.

HOURS: Yr M-F 9-5

9990
Saskatchewan Conference Archives
1121 College Dr, S7N 0W3; (p) (306) 966-8963

Private non-profit/ staff: 1(p); 1(v)

HISTORIC PRESERVATION AGENCY

PROGRAMS: Research Library/Archives

COLLECTIONS: Minutes of church congregations organizations, provincial, and regional governing bodies registers of baptisms, photographs of churches and representative groups.

HOURS: M-F 9-5

9991
Saskatoon Public Library-Local History Room
311-23rd St E, S7K 0J6; (p) (306) 975-7578; (f) (306) 975-7542; ruth@charly.publibsaskatoon.sk.ca; publib.saskatoon.sk.ca

City/ 1966/ staff: 3(f); 4(p)

RESEARCH CENTER: Collects, preserves, and maintains collections relating to the history of Saskatoon and area.

PROGRAMS: Exhibits; Research Library/Archives

COLLECTIONS: [1883-present] 7,467 Books, 51,000 photographs, 475 newspapers, 3,367 pamphlets, 438 manuscripts, 515 periodical titles, 6,673 microforms, 180 artifacts, and 69 scrapbooks.

HOURS: Yr call for time

ADMISSION: No charge

9992
Western Development Museum
2610 Lorne Ave S, S7J 0S6 [1910 Boomtown, 2610 Lorne Ave S, S7J 0S6]; (p) (306) 931-1910; (f) (306) 934-0525; swdm@sk.sympatico.ca; www.wdmuseum.sk.ca

1949/ staff: 8(f); 50(p); 521(v)

HISTORY MUSEUM: Depicts prarie town c. 1910

PROGRAMS: Community Outreach; Elder's Programs; Facility Rental; Family Programs; Festivals; Guided Tours; Interpretation; Living History; Publication; School-Based Curriculum

COLLECTIONS: [1900-1950] Agricultural artifacts: steam traction engines, gas tractors, and harvesting equipment; domestic and business artifacts furniture, appliance, and transportation.

HOURS: Yr Jan-MarT-Su 9-5; Apr-Dec Daily 9-5

ADMISSION: $5, Student $4.50, Children $1.75, Seniors $4.50

SHAMROCK

9993
Shamrock Museum
Box 106, S0H 3W0; (p) (306) 648-2909

staff: 2(p); 10(v)/ members: 20/publication: *Shamrock Museum*

HOUSE MUSEUM: Maintains furnished 1920 house.

PROGRAMS: Guided Tours; Living History; Publication

COLLECTIONS: Artifacts: Metis, settlement period.

HOURS: May-Sept by request

ADMISSION: No charge/Donations

SHELL LAKE

9994
Shell Lake Museum
Railway Ave, S0J 2G0 [Box 280, S0J 2G0]; (p) (360) 427-2272; (f) (306) 427-2272; rebecca.kennel@sk.sympatico.ca; www3.sk.sympatico.ca/kennr/shellake

City/ staff: 10(v)/publication: *Pages of the Past*

HISTORIC SITE; HISTORY MUSEUM

PROGRAMS: Exhibits; Festivals; Interpretation; Living History; Publication

COLLECTIONS: [1900-present] Pioneering and railroading artifacts housed in old railroad station house; historic log cabin; outdoor bread oven.

HOURS: June-Sept Sa-Su

ADMISSION: Donations accepted

STAR CITY

9995
Star City Heritage Museum
217 5th St, S0E 1P0 [PO Box 38, S0E 1P0]; (p) (306) 863-2309

19710/ staff: 1(p); 10(v)

HISTORY MUSEUM: Promotes pioneer history.

PROGRAMS: Annual Meeting; Guided Tours; School-Based Curriculum

COLLECTIONS: [1898] Articles used in the house, the school, businesses, tools made by the blacksmith, war relics, photos, machinery, threshing machine, plow, tractor, windmill, and fire engine.

HOURS: May-Sept every second W and by request 2-4

ADMISSION: $0.50, Children $0.25

WILCOX

9996
Athol Murray College of Notre Dame Archives/Museum
[PO Box 220, S0G 5E0]; (p) (306) 732-2080; (f) (306) 732-2075; nmonson@notredame.sk.ca; www.notredame.sk.ca

Private non-profit/ 1993/ Athol Murray College of Notre Dame/ staff: 1(f); 5(p); 8(v)

ART MUSEUM; HISTORY MUSEUM; RESEARCH CENTER: Collects and preserves history of Father Athol Murray and the founding of Athol Murray College of Notre Dame.

PROGRAMS: Annual Meeting; Community Outreach; Exhibits; Guided Tours; Interpretation; Research Library/Archives; School-Based Curriculum

COLLECTIONS: [1927-present] Artifacts, textual records, audio/visual tapes, and photographs and slides.

HOURS: Yr Sept-May M-F 9-12 / 1-4; June-Aug M-F 9-12 / 1-4, Sa 10-2, Su 1-4

ADMISSION: Donations

WILLOW BUNCH

9997
Willow Bunch Museum and Historical Society
8 5th St, S0H 4K0 [Box 39, S0H 4K0]; (p) (306) 473-2856; (f) (306) 473-2866; fts@sk.sympatico.ca; www.quantumlynx.com/fts/musee

Private non-profit/ 1972/ staff: 1(p); 15(v)/ members: 32

HISTORICAL SOCIETY; HISTORY MUSEUM: Preserves local history in former convent.

PROGRAMS: Annual Meeting; Community Outreach; Elder's Programs; Exhibits; Family Programs; Guided Tours; Interpretation; Research Library/Archives; School-Based Curriculum

COLLECTIONS: [1890s] Artifacts, photos, tools, technology, theater, hospital, trading post, art, religious, farming, and ranching artifacts.

HOURS:

WOOD MOUNTAIN

9998
Wood Mountain Historical Society
Wood Mountain Regional Park, S0H 4L0 [Box 53, S0H 4L0]; (p) (306) 266-4953

Private non-profit/ 1968/ staff: 3(p); 28(v)/ members: 28/publication: *They Came to Wood Mountain*

HISTORIC SITE; HISTORY MUSEUM; RESEARCH CENTER: Preserves and interprets history of the greater Wood Mountain area.

PROGRAMS: Annual Meeting; Community Outreach; Exhibits; Family Programs; Festivals; Guided Tours; Interpretation; Living History; Publication; Reenactments; Research Library/Archives; School-Based Curriculum

COLLECTIONS: [1870-1950] Artifacts related to ranch and rodeo life; photos.

HOURS: May 15-Sept 5 10-5

YORKTON

9999
Story of People/Western Development Museum
Hwy 16 A W, S3N 2V6 [PO Box 98, S3N 2V6]; (p) (306) 783-3861; (f) (306) 782-1027; wdm@sk.sympatico.ca; www.wdmuseum.sk.ca

1949/ staff: 3(f); 1(p); 146(v)

HISTORY MUSEUM: Promotes cultural diversity of pioneer immigrants to SK.

PROGRAMS: Community Outreach; Exhibits; Facility Rental; Festivals; Guided Tours; Interpretation; Living History; Publication; School-Based Curriculum

COLLECTIONS: [1900-1940] Agricultural artifacts: steam traction engines, gas tractors, and agricultural equipment; domestic and personal artifacts, leisure, and recreational artifacts.

HOURS: May-Sept Daily 9-6

ADMISSION: $6, Family $14, Student $5, Children $2, Seniors $5

YUKON

DAWSON CITY

10000
Dawson City Museum and Historical Society
5th Ave & Mission St, Y0B 1G0 [Box 303, Y0B 1G0]; (p) (867) 993-5291; (f) (867) 993-5839; dcmuseum@yknet.yk.ca; users.yknet.yk.ca/dcpages/museum.html

Private non-profit/ 1954/ staff: 2(f); 15(p); 10(v)/ members: 175

HISTORY MUSEUM: Preserves history of Klondike mining district.

PROGRAMS: Annual Meeting; Community Outreach; Exhibits; Facility Rental; Family Programs; Film/Video; Guided Tours; Interpretation; Lectures; Publication

COLLECTIONS: [1889-1976] Housed in 1901 Old Territorial Administration Building, collections include objects and photographic records of Klondike Gold Rush and industrial mining era, social and domestic artifacts, material culture of Han First Nation, narrow-gauge steam locomotives, palaeontological remains, genealogical records.

HOURS: Mid May-mid Sept gallery: Research: Yr May-Sept Daily 10-6; Sept-May M-F 9-5

ADMISSION: $5

TESLIN

10001
Teslin Historical and Museum Society
Km 1194 Alaska Hwy, Y0A 1B0 [Box 146, Y0A 1B0]; (p) (867) 390-2550; (f) (867) 390-2828; gjmuseum@yknet.yk.ca

Private non-profit/ 1979/ staff: 5(f); 10(v)

HISTORY MUSEUM: Preserves Mingit culture and heritage.

PROGRAMS: Annual Meeting; Community Outreach; Elder's Programs; Exhibits; Festivals; Film/Video; Interpretation

COLLECTIONS: [1910-1950] Mingit Artifacts.

HOURS: May-Sept Daily 9-6

ADMISSION: $3, Student $2.50, Children $1, Seniors $2.50

WHITEHORSE

10002
Heritage Branch, Department of Tourism, Government of Yukon
204 Lambert St, 3rd Floor, Y1A 2C6 [Po Box 2703, Y1A 2C6]; (p) (867) 667-5386; (f) (867) 667-8023; Jeff.Hunston@gov.yk.ca

1982/ staff: 16(f)

HISTORIC PRESERVATION AGENCY: Promotes Yukon's heritage resources, Historic Resources Act, and Land Claims Heritage Agreements.

PROGRAMS: Guided Tours; Interpretation; Publication

10003
MacBride Museum Society
1st Ave & Wood St, Y1A 3S9 [Box 4037, Y1A 3S9]; (p) (867) 667-2709; (f) (756) 633-6607

1951/ staff: 3(f); 10(p); 25(v)/ members: 155

HISTORY MUSEUM: Collects, preserves, and interprets the history of the Yukon.

PROGRAMS: Annual Meeting; Exhibits; Facility Rental; Guided Tours; Interpretation; School-Based Curriculum

COLLECTIONS: Natural history, First Nations, Mounties in the North, Gold Rush, City of Whitehorse, Alaska Highway construction. 7,000 photos, 500 First Nation artifacts, 100 Geological specimens, 200 gold samples, 10,000 historic artifacts, 2 historic buildings.

HOURS: Yr May-Sept 10-6; Winter 12-4; Sept-May Th-Sa 10-6

ADMISSION: $500, Children $3.50, Seniors $4.50

10004
Yukon Archives
400 College Dr, Y1A 2C6 [Box 2703, Y1A 2C6]; (p) (867) 667-5321; (f) (867) 393-6253; yukon.archives@gov.yk.ca; www.gov.yk.ca/depts/education/libarch/yukararch.ht

1972/ staff: 7(f); 5(p)

LIBRARY AND/OR ARCHIVES: Acquires, preserves, and makes available documentary sources related to Yukon history and cultures with particular focus on the Klondike Gold Rush, the Alaska Highway, and Yukon First Nations history.

PROGRAMS: Community Outreach; Elder's Programs; Exhibits; Film/Video; Guided Tours; Publication; Research Library/Archives

COLLECTIONS: [1898-present] 25,000 books, 11,000 pamphlets, 100 newspaper titles, 700 periodicals, 480 meters of private manuscripts and corporate records, 119,000 photographs, 12,007 maps and architectural drawings, 1647 meters of territorial, municipal, and federal government records, 2,439 sound recordings, 567 films and videos.

HOURS: Yr T-W 9-5, Th-F 1-9, Sa 10-1 / 2-6

ADMISSION: No charge

10005
Yukon Arts Centre Corporation-Gallery
300 College Dr, Y1A 5L6 [Box 5931, Y1A 5L6]; (p) (867) 667-8485; (f) (867) 393-6300; george@hypertech.yk.ca; yukonarts.yukon.net

staff: 13(f)

ART MUSEUM: Exhibits contemporary and Native American art.

PROGRAMS: Community Outreach; Concerts; Exhibits; Interpretation; Lectures; Theatre

COLLECTIONS: [20th c-present] Artwork relating to the experience of life in North-Western Canada and to first Nation's Peoples.

HOURS: Yr Daily M-F 11-5, Sa-Su 1-4

ADMISSION: Donations accepted

10006
Yukon Beringia Interpretive Centre
Alaska Hwy - Whitehorse Airport, Y1A 2C6 [Box 2703, Y1A 2C6]; (p) (867) 667-8855, (867) 667-3516; (f) (867) 667-8854; Ed.Krahn@gov.yk.ca; www.beringia.com

1997/ staff: 7(f); 2(p)

HISTORY MUSEUM; RESEARCH CENTER: Promotes history of Beringia, ice-age animals and the first peoples of North America.

PROGRAMS: Community Outreach; Concerts; Elder's Programs; Facility Rental; Family Programs; Festivals; Film/Video; Guided Tours; Interpretation; Lectures; Publication; School-Based Curriculum; Theatre

COLLECTIONS: [Ice Age] Ice Age artifacts and reproductions, dioramas, interpretive displays and exhibits.

HOURS: Mid May-mid Sept Daily; Oct-mid May Su and by appt

10007
Yukon Historical and Museum Association
3126 - 3rd Ave, Y1A 3T5 [PO Box 4357, Y1A 3T5]; (p) (867) 667-4704; (f) (867) 667-4506; yhma@yknet.yk.ca; www.yukonalaska.com

Private non-profit/ 1977/ staff: 1(f); 12(v)/ members: 166/publication: *Exploring Old Whitehorse; Edge of River; and others*

Promotes Yukon museums, historical societies, and preservation of heritage resources.

HOURS: Yr M-F 10-4

ADMISSION: $2

PART IV

Indexes

Note: All index entries use the following format: Organization Name, State, Entry ID

AFRICAN AMERICAN

AGRICULTURE

Chinqua-Penn Plantation Foundation, Inc., NC, 6417
Chippewa County Historical Society, MN, 4403
Chippewa County Historical Society, WI, 9097
Chippewa Nature Center, Inc., MI, 4190
Chippewa Valley Museum, WI, 9114
Chippokes Farm and Forestry Museum, VA, 8685
Chippokes Plantation State Park, VA, 8747
Chisago County Historical Society, MN, 4362
Chisholm Trail Museum, KS, 3072
Chisholm Trail Museum/Governor Seay Mansion, OK, 6906
Choctaw County Historical Museum, AL, 26
Christian County Historical Society Museum, IL, 2422
Churchill County Museum & Archives, NV, 5239
Cimarron Heritage Center, Inc., OK, 6849
Cincinnati Nature Center-Gorman Heritage Farm, OH, 6610
City of Bowie Museums, MD, 3602
City of Greeley Museums, CO, 1073
City of Rancho Cucamonga Historic Preservation Commission, CA, 723
Clallam County Historical Society, WA, 8903
Claresholm and District Museum, AB, 9372
Clark County Historical Society, KS, 2883
Clark County Historical Society, MO, 4764
Clark County Historical Society, SD, 7764
Clark Historical Society, NJ, 5469
Clarke County Historical Association, VA, 8496
Clarke Memorial Museum, CA, 530
Clarksville-Montgomery County Museum, TN, 7875
Claude Moore Colonial Farm at Turkey Run, VA, 8624
Clay County 1890 Jail Museum and Heritage Center, TX, 8142
Clay County Historical and Arts Council, NC, 6317
Clay County Historical Society, AL, 4
Clay County Historical Society, FL, 1439
Clay County Historical Society, IN, 2493
Clay County Historical Society, MN, 4405
Clay County Historical Society, NE, 5100
Clay County Historical Society, SD, 7854
Clay County Museum and Historical Society, MO, 4807
Clay County Museum, KS, 2897
Clear Creek History Park, CO, 1066
Clermont Historical Society, IA, 2692
Clermont State Historic Site, NY, 5918
Clewiston Museum, FL, 1397
Climax Community Museum, Inc., SK, 9950
Clinton County Historical Society, IA, 2694
Clinton County Historical Society, Inc., IN, 2532
Clinton County Historical Society, NY, 6072
Clinton County Historical Society, OH, 6818
Clinton County Historical Society, PA, 7304
Clinton Lake Historical Society, Inc., KS, 3027
Cloud County Historical Society, KS, 2904
Clover Bend Historic Preservation Association, AR, 357
Coastal Discovery Museum on Hilton Head Island, SC, 7692
Cochise County Historical Society, AZ, 213
Cochranton Heritage Society, PA, 7171
Codington County Historical Society, SD, 7857
Coffee Co/Manchester/Tullahoma Museum, Inc. Arrowheads/Aerospace Museum, TN, 7935
Coggeshall Farm Museum, RI, 7529
Cokato Museum & Akerlund Photography Studio, MN, 4296
Cole Harbour Rural Heritage Society, NS, 9654
Cole Land Transportation Museum, ME, 3404
Colleton Museum, SC, 7748
Collinsville Historical Museum, IL, 2083
Colonial Farmhouse Restoration Society of Bellerose, Inc. dba Queens County Farm Museum, NY, 5903
Colonial Pennsylvania Plantation, PA, 7313
Colonial Williamsburg Foundation, The, VA, 8773
Colorado Historical Society, CO, 1021
Colorado Springs Museum, CO, 1002
Columbia County Historical Society, NY, 5962

Columbia County Historical Society, OR, 7090
Columbia County Historical Society, WI, 9091
Columbia Gorge Discovery Center and Wasco County Historical Museum, OR, 7093
Columbia Gorge Interpretive Center, WA, 8958
Colvin Run Mill Historic Site, VA, 8580
Commerce Historical and Genealogy Society, MO, 4687
Commission of Landmarks and Museum, DE, 1312
Community Historical Museum of Mount Holly, VT, 8359
Community Historical Society, The, IA, 2794
Community History Project of Shenandoah University, VA, 8782
Community Memorial Museum of Sutter, CA, 974
Concord Township Historical Society, PA, 7174
Conejo Valley Historical Society/Stagecoach Inn Museum Complex, CA, 661
Confederate Memorial State Historic Site, MO, 4726
Connecticut Historical Society, The, CT, 1191
Conner Prairie, IN, 2524
Conrad Rice Mill, LA, 3336
Conservation Trust of Puerto Rico, The, PR, 7521
Contra Costa County Historical Society and History Center, CA, 714
Conway Historical Society, MA, 3820
Conway Historical Society, NH, 5296
Cooper County Historical Society, MO, 4856
Cooper Regional History Museum, CA, 940
Copshaholm, the Oliver Mansion, IN, 2634
Corning Painted Post Historical Society, NY, 5871
Corona Public Library-Heritage Room, CA, 502
Corporation de la Vieille Fromagerie Perron de Saint-Prime, QC, 9932
Corry Area Historical Society, PA, 7179
Cortland County Historical Society, Inc., NY, 5876
Cottonlandia Museum, MS, 4551
Cottonwood County Historical Society, MN, 4522
Cottonwood Ranch State Historic Site, KS, 3051
Council Valley Museum, ID, 1922
County of Camden, NC, 6236
County of Grey-Owen Sound Museum, ON, 9788
Courthouse Square Association, Inc., MI, 4085
Coventry Historical Society, CT, 1150
Cowley County Historical Society, KS, 3084
Cozad Historical Society—The 100th Meridian Museum, NE, 5102
Cramer-Kenyon Heritage House, Inc, SD, 7861
Cranbury Historical and Preservation Society, NJ, 5475
Craven Hall Historical Society, PA, 7485
Crazy Mountain Museum/Sweet Grass Museum Society, MT, 4974
Creston and District Historical and Museum Society, BC, 9442
Crittenden County Historical Society: Bob Wheeler Museum, KY, 3201
Crosby County Pioneer Memorial, TX, 8067
Cross Plains-Berry Historical Society, WI, 9180
Crow Wing County Historical Society, MN, 4282
Crowley Cheese, Inc., VT, 8395
Crystal Rice Plantation, LA, 3280
Culbertson Museum, MT, 4998
Cumberland County Historical Society, NJ, 5493
Cumberland County Museum, NS, 9647
Cuneo Museum and Gardens, IL, 2437
Cynthiana-Harrison County Museum, KY, 3115
D.A.R. Anna Palmer Museum, NE, 5224
Dacotah Prairie Museum, SD, 7753
Dakota City Heritage Village, MN, 4331
Dakota County Historical Society, MN, 4455
Dakota County Historical Society, NE, 5105
Dakotaland Museum, SD, 7790

Dale and Martha Hawk Foundation and Museum, ND, 6555
Dallas County Historical Museum, AR, 332
Dallas Historical Society, TX, 8073
Dancing Leaf Earth Lodge, NE, 5219
Daniel Boone Homestead, PA, 7134
Danish Immigrant Museum, The, IA, 2735
DAR Anna Palmer Museum, NE, 5225
Darien Historical Society, IL, 2095
Darlington County Historical Commission, SC, 7666
Davidson County Historical Museum, NC, 6351
Davies Manor Association, Inc., TN, 7867
Dawes County Historical Society, Inc., NE, 5095
Dawson County Historical Society, NE, 5141
Dayton Historical Depot Society, WA, 8830
DC Booth Historic National Fish Hatchery, SD, 7846
Deaf Smith County Historical Museum, TX, 8143
Dearborn Historical Museum, MI, 4100
Decatur County Historical Society, GA, 1636
Decatur County Historical Society, IN, 2542
Decatur County Museum, Inc., KS, 3016
Deep South Pioneer Museum, SK, 9951
Deer Trail Pioneer Historical Society, CO, 1014
Deerfield Area Historical Society, IL, 2101
Deerfield Historical Society, NH, 5302
DeForest Area Historical Society, WI, 9106
Del Norte County Historical Society, CA, 505
Delavan Community Historical Society, IL, 2103
Delaware Agricultural Museum and Village, DE, 1296
Delaware County Historical Association, NY, 5885
Delhi Historical Society, OH, 6612
Delhi Ontario Tobacco Museum and Heritage Center, ON, 9706
Dell Rapid Society for Historic Preservation, SD, 7773
Dells Country Historical Society, WI, 9283
Delray Beach Historical Society, Inc., FL, 1412
Delta Cultural Center, AR, 350
Delta Historical Society, AK, 153
Delta State University Archives, MS, 4537
Deming Luna Mimbres Museum, NM, 5719
Denman Seniors and Museum Society, BC, 9445
Denton County Historical Museum, Inc., TX, 8085
Denver Museum of Miniatures, Dolls, and Toys, CO, 1023
Department of Arkansas Heritage, AR, 374
Department of Economic Development, Tourism and Culture-Heritage Branch, NB, 9587
Depot Museum Complex, TX, 8140
Derby Historical Society, KS, 2909
Derby Historical Society, VT, 8378
Derry Historical Society and Museum, NH, 5304
Des Moines County Historical Society, IA, 2676
Detroit Historical Museums, MI, 4108
Deutschheim State Historic Site, MO, 4723
Deweese-Rudd Museum Group, Inc., CO, 994
Dewey County Jailhouse Museum and Annex, OK, 6972
DeWitt Historical Society of Tompkins County, The, NY, 5951
Dexter Area Historical Society and Museum, MI, 4113
Dexter Historical Society, Inc., ME, 3426
Dickey County Historical Society, ND, 6543
Dickinson County Historical Society, KS, 2873
Dickson Mounds Museum, IL, 2203
Dillard Mill State Historical Site, MO, 4690
Dillon County Historical Society, Inc., SC, 7667
Discovery Museum, CT, 1141
Discovery Museum, The, CA, 757
Dismal Swamp Canal Visitor Center, NC, 6437
District 69 Historical Society, BC, 9477
Donalda and District Museum, AB, 9376
Doon Heritage Crossroads, ON, 9735
Door County Historical Museum, WI, 9251

Dorchester Historical Society, MA, 3842
Dothan Landmarks Foundation, AL, 42
Douglas County Historical Society and Museum, SD, 7754
Douglas County Historical Society, MN, 4267
Douglas County Historical Society, OR, 7077
Douglas County Historical Society, WI, 9254
Douglas County Historical Society/Watkins Community Museum of History, KS, 2975
Douglas County Museum of History and Natural History, OR, 7078
Douglas County Museum, WA, 8984
Douglass Historical Museum and Society, KS, 2917
Dover Historical Society, IA, 2805
Dover Historical Society, OH, 6651
Downey Historical Society, CA, 518
Drayton Valley District Historical Society, AB, 9377
Dresden Historical Society, ME, 3428
Drew County Historical Museum, AR, 392
Dryden Township Historical Society, NY, 5887
Duarte Historical Society and Friends of the Library, Inc., CA, 520
Dubois County Museum, Inc., IN, 2573
Dubuque County Historical Society/Mississippi River Museum, IA, 2727
Dudley Foundation, Inc., The, CT, 1183
Duke Homestead State Historic Site and Tobacco Museum, NC, 6270
Duke University Rare Book, Manuscript and Special Collections Library, NC, 6271
Dundalk-Patapsco Neck Historical Society, MD, 3631
Dundee Township Historical Society, IL, 2453
Dunsmuir House and Gardens Historic Estate, CA, 672
DuPont Historic Museum, WA, 8832
Durham Historical Association, NH, 5308
Dutchess County Historical Society, NY, 6080
Duval Tool Museum, MD, 3736
Dysart Historical Society, IA, 2731
E. Stanley Wright Museum Foundation, Inc., NH, 5434
Eagle Historical Society and Museums, AK, 155
Eagle River Historical Society, WI, 9113
Early American Museum, IL, 2228
Early Settlers Association of the Western Reserve, The, OH, 6626
Early Works, AL, 65
East Benton County Historical Society & Museum, WA, 8865
East Carolina Village of Yesteryear, NC, 6307
East Hillsborough Historical Society, FL, 1515
East Jersey Olde Towne Village, NJ, 5568
East Tennessee Historical Society, TN, 7926
East Texas Oil Museum at Kilgore College, TX, 8158
Eastern California Museum, CA, 570
Eastern Oregon Museum, OR, 7021
Eastern Trails Museum, OK, 6980
Eastham Historical Society, MA, 3852
Eaton Florida History Room, Manatee County Central Library, FL, 1385
Ebey's Landing National Historical Reserve, WA, 8826
Edgar County Historical Society, IL, 2305
Edgecombe County Historical Society, NC, 6450
Edina Historical Society and Museum, MN, 4314
Edmond Historical Society, OK, 6878
Edwards County Historical Society, KS, 2968
Effingham Historic District Commission, NH, 5420
Eisenhower National Historic Site, PA, 7227
El Paso Museum of History, TX, 8089
Elbert County Historical Society and Museum, CO, 1082
Elbow Museum and Historical Society, SK, 9954
Eldorado Museum, IL, 2118
Elgin County Pioneer Museum, ON, 9808
Elkhorn Valley Museum and Research Center, NE, 5175
Elkton Community Museum, SD, 7776
Ella Sharp Museum, MI, 4161
Ellinwood Community Historical Society, KS, 2921
Ellis County Historical Society, KS, 2949
Ellis County Historical Society, OK, 6838
Ellwood House Museum, IL, 2102

Gallery, Inc., SK, 9975
Overland Trail Museum, CO, 1127
Overland Trail Museum, TX, 8100
Owen County Historical Society, KY, 3217
Owensboro Area Museum of Science and History, KY, 3215
Oxford Museum Association, OH, 6749
Oyster Ponds Historical Society, NY, 6052
Ozark Folk Center, The, AR, 395
P.H. Sullivan Museum; Zionsville Munce Art Center, IN, 2653
Page-Walker Arts and History Center, NC, 6240
Paine-Gillam-Scott Museum/Clinton County Historical Society, MI, 4240
Paipoonge Historical Museum, ON, 9820
Palace of the Governors Museum, NM, 5760
Palacios Area Historical Association, TX, 8203
Palacios Library, Inc., TX, 8204
Palestine Preservation Projects Society, IL, 2303
Palmyra Historical Society, WI, 9221
Panhandle-Plains Historical Museum, TX, 8045
Park County Historical Society Archives, WY, 9301
Parker House Ranching Museum, TX, 8199
Parker Museum of Clay County, IA, 2841
Parma Historical Society, ID, 1953
Pasto Agricultural Museum, PA, 7472
Patten Lumbermans Museum, ME, 3483
Patterson Homestead Museum, The, OH, 6646
Pawnee City Historical Society, NE, 5195
Peace River Centennial Museum and Archives, AB, 9412
Peacham Historical Association, VT, 8423
Pella Historical Society, IA, 2821
Pembina State Museum, ND, 6544
Pend Oreille County Historical Society, WA, 8894
Pender County Historical Society, NC, 6231
Pendleton County Historical Society, Inc., KY, 3126
Pendleton County Historical Society, Inc., WV, 9021
Pendleton District Historical, Recreational and Tourism Commission, SC, 7721
Penfield Local History Room, NY, 6068
Penn Center, Inc., SC, 7732
Pennsbury Manor/Pennsbury Society, The, PA, 7326
Pennsylvania Historical and Museum Commission, PA, 7251
Penticton 9 R.N. Atkinson Museum and Archives, BC, 9479
Perkins County Historical Society, NE, 5127
Perkins County Historical Society, SD, 7805
Perry County Historical Society, IL, 2319
Perry County Historical Society, MO, 4854
Perry Historical Society of Lake County, OH, 6755
Person County Museum of History, NC, 6420
Petaluma Museum Association, CA, 706
Peter Wentz Farmstead, PA, 7508
Petersburg Museums, VA, 8665
Pewaukee Area Historical Society, WI, 9225
Phelps County Historical Society, MO, 4877
Phelps County Historical Society, NE, 5134
Phillips County Museum, AR, 352
Phillips County Museum, MT, 5038
Philmont Museum, NM, 5713
Phoenix Museum of History, AZ, 248
Piatt Castles Company Inc., The, OH, 6813
Piatt County Museum, Inc., IL, 2255
Pickens County Museum of Art and History/Hagood Mill, SC, 7724
Pierce Historical Society Museum Complex, NE, 5197
Pierre Wibaux Museum Complex, MT, 5069
Pigua Historical Area State Memorial, OH, 6758
Pinal County Historical Society Museum, AZ, 221
Pincher Creek & District Museum/Kootenai Brown Historical Park, AB, 9413
Pine Bluff/Jefferson County Historical Museum, AR, 405
Pine County Historical Society, MN, 4271
Pine-Strawberry Archaeological and Historical Society, Inc., AZ, 251
Pioneer and Historical Society of Muskingum

County, OH, 6827
Pioneer Experience at Plainville Farms, The, NY, 6071
Pioneer Florida Museum Association, Inc., FL, 1404
Pioneer Heritage Center, LA, 3382
Pioneer Woman Museum, OK, 6952
Piper City Community Historical Society, IL, 2320
Pipestone County Historical Society, MN, 4433
Pitt Meadows Heritage and Museum Society, BC, 9481
Pittsburg Historical Society, NH, 5393
Pittsburgh History and Landmarks Foundation, PA, 7422
Pittsford Historical Society, Inc., VT, 8425
Placer County Museum, CA, 447
Plainfield Historical Society, IL, 2321
Plainfield Historical Society, NH, 5395
Plains Indians and Pioneers Museum, OK, 6985
Plantation Agriculture Museum, AR, 416
Plimoth Plantation, MA, 3961
Plumas County Museum Association, Inc., CA, 721
Plymouth County Historical Museum, IA, 2780
Plymouth Heritage Center, OH, 6760
Plymouth Meeting Historical Society, PA, 7423
Point of Honor, Inc., VA, 8613
Pointe du Moulin Historical Parc, QC, 9915
Polk County Historical Association, Inc., NC, 6451
Polk County Historical Museum, FL, 1381
Polk County Historical Society, GA, 1654
Polk County Historical Society, IA, 2720
Polk County Historical Society, MN, 4299
Polk County Historical Society, OR, 7044
Polk County Historical Society, WI, 9075
Polo Historical Society, IL, 2323
Polson Flathead Historical Museum, MT, 5046
Pomery Living History Farm, WA, 8992
Pond Spring, AL, 60
Pony Express Historical Association, Inc., MO, 4897
Pope County Historical Society, IL, 2156
Pope County Historical Society, MN, 4339
Poplar Grove Plantation, NC, 6474
Port Colborne Historical and Marine Museum, ON, 9794
Port Hudson State Historical Site, LA, 3397
Portage County Historical Society, OH, 6765
Portage County Historical Society, WI, 9250
Porter Thermometer Museum, MA, 3946
Porter-Phelps Huntington Foundation, Inc., MA, 3876
Portsmouth Historical Society, RI, 7571
Potomac Heritage Partnership, DC, 1364
Potter County Historical Society, PA, 7180
Potter Museum, NE, 5200
Pouce Coupe and District Museum and Historical Society, BC, 9488
Powder River Historical Museum, MT, 4983
Powers Museum, MO, 4670
Prairie Panorama Museum, AB, 9375
Prairie Park, MO, 4834
Prairie West Historical Society, Inc., SK, 9956
Prairieland Heritage Museum Institute, IL, 2179
Prayer Rock Museum, Inc., SD, 7759
Preble County Historical Society, OH, 6656
Preservation Association of Lincoln, NE, 5150
President Calvin Coolidge State Historic Site, VT, 8428
Preston County Historical Society, WV, 9056
Price County Historical Society, WI, 9123
Pricketts Fort Memorial Foundation, WV, 9020
Prince Edward Island Museum and Heritage Foundation, PE, 9868
Prince Edward Island Potato Museum, PE, 9870
Princeton and District Museum and Archives Society, BC, 9492
Proprietary House Association, NJ, 5597
Provincial Archives of Manitoba, MB, 9575
Provincial Museum of Alberta, AB, 9386
Putnam County Historical Society, IL, 2167
Putnam County Historical Society, Inc., MO,

4952
Putnam County Historical Society, OH, 6689
Putnam Museum of History and Natural Science, IA, 2710
Putney Historical Society, VT, 8433
Queen Anne's Museum of Eastern Shore Life, MD, 3610
Queens County Historical Society and Museum, Inc., NB, 9589
Quesnel and District Museum and Archives, BC, 9494
Quiet Valley Living Historical Farm, PA, 7461
Rabun County Historical Society, GA, 1657
Racine Heritage Museum, WI, 9234
Radcliffe Historical Society, IA, 2827
Raleigh City Museum, NC, 6411
Ralston Historical Association, NJ, 5542
Ramp Centennial Celebration Museum/Fairview Pioneer Museum, AB, 9393
Ramsey County Historical Society, MN, 4473
Ramsey Historical Association, NJ, 5612
Rancho Los Alamitos Historic Ranch and Gardens, CA, 603
Randolph Historical Society, VT, 8435
Rankin Museum of American Heritage, NC, 6281
Ransom County Historical Society, ND, 6515
Rattle & Snap Plantation, TN, 7881
Raupp Memorial Museum, IL, 2009
Raymondville Historical and Community Center, TX, 8220
Readington Township Museums, NJ, 5678
Rebecca B. Hadden Stone House Museum, PA, 7441
Rebecca Nurse Homestead, MA, 3826
Red Deer and District Museum, AB, 9416
Red River Valley Center at Moorhead, MN, 4408
Redcliff Historical Museum Society, AB, 9417
Reedley Historical Society, CA, 733
Regina Plains Museum, SK, 9979
Regional Oral History Office, CA, 463
Remick Country Doctor Museum and Farm, NH, 5424
Renfrew and District Historical and Museum Society, ON, 9797
Reno County Museum, KS, 2960
Rentschler Farm Museum, MI, 4241
Renville County Historical Society, Inc., ND, 6539
Renville County Historical Society, MN, 4412
Republic County Historical Society and Museum, KS, 2891
Resource Management Division, Fairfax County Park Authority, VA, 8551
Ressler Mill Foundation, PA, 7437
Restigouche Regional Museum, NB, 9583
Revelstoke and District Historical Association, BC, 9496
Revitalize Iva Community Improvement Association (REVIVA), SC, 7697
Reynolds Homestead, VA, 8529
Reynolds-Alberta Museum, AB, 9426
Rhode Island State Archives, RI, 7579
Rice County Historical Society, KS, 2989
Rice County Historical Society, MN, 4330
Richard B. Russell Library for Political Research and Studies, GA, 1591
Richfield Historical Society, OH, 6767
Richfield Historical Society, WI, 9237
Richmond County Museum, VA, 8764
Richmond Museum, BC, 9497
Rifle Creek Museum, CO, 1117
Riley County Historical Society and Museum, KS, 2991
Ringgold County Historical Society, IA, 2801
Ripely County Historical Society, MO, 4696
River City Historical Society, UT, 8326
River Road African American Museum and Gallery, LA, 3292
River Road Historical Society, LA, 3281
Riverdale, MD, 3698
Riverside Local History Resource Center, CA, 740
Riverside, the Farnsley-Moorman Landing, KY, 3190
Riverton Museum, WY, 9340
Robert E. Lee Memorial Association, Inc., VA, 8742
Robert S. Kerr Museum, OK, 6953
Robeson County Museum, NC, 6356
Robinson Rancheria Band of Pomo Indians,

CA, 664
Rochester Museum & Science Center, NY, 6097
Rock Island County Historical Society, IL, 2250
Rock Ledge Ranch Historic Site, CO, 1005
Rock River Thresheree, Inc., WI, 9150
Rock Springs Historical Museum, WY, 9341
Rockbridge Historical Society, VA, 8604
Rockingham Association, NJ, 5611
Rockingham County Historical Society, Inc., NC, 6460
Rocky Ford Museum, CO, 1118
Rogers Historical Museum, AR, 413
Rokeby Museum, VT, 8387
Rooks County Historical Society, Frank Walter Museum, KS, 3050
Roopville Archive and Historical Society, GA, 1765
Rose Hill Mansion, NY, 5917
Rose Hill Plantation State Historic Site, SC, 7745
Rose Valley and District Heritage Museum, Inc., SK, 9984
Rosenbach Museum and Library, PA, 7403
Roseville Historical Society, CA, 746
Roseville Historical Society, MN, 4446
Ross Farm Museum, NS, 9667
Roth Living Farm Museum, PA, 7342
Rouleau and District Museum, SK, 9985
Roxbury Historical Society, VT, 8440
Roy L. Hyatt Environmental Center, FL, 1390
Royalton Historical Society, VT, 8441
Rumford Area Historical Society, ME, 3504
Rundlet-May House, SPNEA, NH, 5405
Runestone Museum, MN, 4268
Rush County Historical Society, Inc., KS, 2970
Rusk County Historical Museum, WI, 9161
Ruth Drake Museum, SC, 7605
Rutland Historical Society, Inc., VT, 8443
Sac City Historical Museum, IA, 2830
Sacramento Archives and Museum Collection Center, CA, 764
Sacred Heart Area Historical Society, MN, 4447
Saint Francis County Museum, AR, 333
Saint Vrain Historical Society, Inc., The, CO, 1095
Sainte-Marie Among the Hurons, ON, 9746
Salem 1630: Pioneer Village, MA, 3979
Salem County Historical Society, NJ, 5623
Salida Museum, CO, 1119
Saline Area Historical Society, MI, 4242
Saline County Historical Society, NE, 5108
Salmon Brook Historical Society, Inc., CT, 1176
Sam Houston Memorial Museum, TX, 8152
Sam Rayburn House Museum, TX, 8039
San Diego Civil War Roundtable, CA, 784
San Diego Historical Society, CA, 787
San Joaquin County Historical Society and Museum, CA, 596
San Luis Obispo County Historical Society and Museum, CA, 837
San Pablo Historical Society, CA, 844
Sandown Historical Society and Museum, NH, 5418
Sandwich Historical Society, IL, 2373
Sandwich Historical Society, NH, 5286
Sandy Spring Museum, MD, 3710
Sandy Springs Historic Community Foundation, Inc., GA, 1780
Sanford Museum, FL, 1529
Sangamon County Genealogical Society, IL, 2406
Sanilac County Historical Society, MI, 4223
Santa Cruz Mission State Historic Park, CA, 874
Santa Fe Depot Museum, OK, 6960
Santa Fe Trail Museum of Gray County, Inc., KS, 2963
Santa Maria Valley Historical Society and Museum, CA, 878
Santaquin City Chieftain Museum, UT, 8344
Saratoga County Historical Society/Brookside, NY, 5807
Saratoga Heritage Preservation Commission, CA, 884
Saratoga Historical and Cultural Association, WY, 9342
Saratoga National Historical Park, NY, 6150
Saskatchewan Archives Board-Regina, SK,

AMERICAN STUDIES

Thomaston Historical Society, ME, 3526
Thornbury Historical Society, PA, 7466
Thrasher Carriage Museum, MD, 3629
Thurber House, The, OH, 6637
Tilghman Heritage Foundation, Inc., KY, 3223
Tombstone Courthouse State Historic Park, AZ, 267
Top of Oklahoma Historical Museum, OK, 6848
Torrington Historical Society, Inc., CT, 1269
Towe Auto Museum, CA, 767
Township of Ocean Historical Museum, NJ, 5583
Travel Town Museum, CA, 623
Tree Farm Archives, CT, 1250
Troy Academy and Historical Society, IA, 2850
Trustees of Reservations, MA, 4004
Tryon Palace Historic Sites and Gardens, NC, 6381
Tsongas Industrial History Center, MA, 3904
Tuckahoe Plantation, VA, 8701
Tudor Place Foundation, Inc., DC, 1369
Tuftonboro Historical Society, Inc., NH, 5368
Turn of the Century House/Mardi Gras Museum, LA, 3326
Tuskegee Institute National Historic Site, George Washington Carver Museum, AL, 125
U.S. Army Air Defense Artillery Museum, TX, 8098
U.S. Army Museum of Hawaii, HI, 1843
Ulysses S. Grant Cottage, NY, 6118
Union Cemetery Historical Society, MO, 4784
Union Township Historical Society, NJ, 5504
Union Township Historical Society, NJ, 5663
United States Army Don F. Pratt Museum, KY, 3127
United States Mint at Philadelphia, PA, 7406
Unity Archives, Unity School of Christianity, MO, 4953
University Archives and Special Collection Unit, Pollak Library, CA State Univ, Fullerton, CA, 554
University Archives of the State University of New York at Buffalo, NY, 5843
University History Institute, AR, 383
University Museum, University of Arkansas, AR, 331
University of Colorado Museum of Natural History, CO, 987
University of Iowa Hospitals and Clinics Medical Museum, IA, 2767
University of Kentucky Art Museum, KY, 3172
University of Mississippi, Music Library and Blues Archives, MS, 4611
University of North Carolina at Chapel Hill, Manuscripts Department, NC, 6243
University of Rhode Island Historic Textile and Costume Collection, RI, 7545
University of Wyoming American Heritage Center, WY, 9328
USS Alabama Battleship Memorial Park, AL, 89
USS Turner Joy DD-951, WA, 8812
Valdosta State University Archives, GA, 1829
Valentine Museum, The/Richmond History Center, VA, 8702
Valley School Historical Society, PA, 7107
Varner-Hogg Plantation State Historical Park, TX, 8278
Varnum House Museum, RI, 7539
Ventura County Maritime Museum, CA, 687
Ventura County Museum of History and Art, CA, 948
Vernon County Historical Society, MO, 4837
Vernon County Historical Society, WI, 9262
Vernon Township Historical Society, NJ, 5506
Veterinary Museum/Missouri Veterinary Medical Foundation, MO, 4760
Victoria Mansion, Inc., ME, 3495
Victorian Society in America, The, PA, 7408
Virginia Baptist Historical Society, VA, 8705
Virginia Historical Society, VA, 8708
Wachovia Historical Society, NC, 6490
Waco Historical Society, OH, 6799
Wade House State Historic Park, WI, 9137
Wadsworth Atheneum, CT, 1199
Waitsfield Historical Society, VT, 8457
Walsh County Historical Museum, ND, 6538
Walt Whitman Birthplace Association, NY, 5945
Walt Whitman House, NJ, 5457

Walter Reed's Birthplace, VA, 8577
Waltham Museum, MA, 4022
Wannamuse Institute for Arts, Culture, and Ethnic Studies, LA, 3366
Warren County Historical Society, IL, 2366
Warren County Historical Society, MO, 4961
Warren County Historical Society, OH, 6699
Warren County Historical Society, PA, 7486
Warrick County Museum, Inc., IN, 2492
Warwick Township Historical Society, PA, 7270
Washakie Museum, WY, 9354
Washington County Historical Society, GA, 1779
Washington County Historical Society, IL, 2269
Washington County Historical Society, Inc., WI, 9278
Washington County Historical Society, KS, 3071
Washington County Historical Society, MN, 4496
Washington County Historical Society, OR, 7074
Washington County Historical Society, PA, 7491
Washington Crossing Historic Park, PA, 7492
Washington's Headquarters at Valley Forge (Isaac Potts House), PA, 7478
Washington-on-the-Brazos State Historical Park, TX, 8275
Waterloo Area Historical Society, MI, 4247
Waterloo Area Historical Society, WI, 9266
Waterloo Foundation For The Arts, Inc., NJ, 5645
Waters Farm Preservation, Inc., MA, 4008
Wayne County Historical Society and Museum, OH, 6819
Wayne County Historical Society, IL, 2131
Wayne County Historical Society, MO, 4855
Wayne County Historical Society, NY, 5974
Wayne County Historical Society, PA, 7264
Wayne County Historical Society/Prairie Trails Museum, IA, 2700
Weaverville Joss House State Historic Park, CA, 958
Webb-Deane-Stevens Museum, CT, 1280
Webster House Museum, WI, 9118
Weir Farm National Historic Site, CT, 1283
Wells Fargo Historical Services, CA, 819
Wells Fargo History Museum, CA, 769
Welsh Valley Preservation Society, PA, 7276
West County Museum, CA, 888
West Georgia Museum of Tallapoosa, GA, 1815
West Texas Historical Association, TX, 8177
Western History/Genealogy Department, Denver Public Library, CO, 1033
Western Maryland Chapter, National Railway Historical Society, MD, 3630
Western Museum of Mining and Industry, CO, 1006
Western New York Documentary Heritage Program, NY, 5844
Western Reserve Historical Society, OH, 6628
Westerners International, OK, 6942
Westerville Historical Society, OH, 6815
Westville Historic Handicrafts, Inc., GA, 1726
Weymouth Historical Society, MA, 4035
Wheaton Historic Preservation Council/Wheaton History Center, IL, 2461
Wheeler Historic Farm Museum, UT, 8342
Wilderness Road State Park, VA, 8544
William A. Farnsworth Homestead, ME, 3502
William Berman Jewish Heritage Museum, The, GA, 1628
William Bull and Sarah Wells Stone House Association, NY, 5850
William Cullen Bryant Homestead, MA, 3822
William Holmes McGuffey Museum, OH, 6751
William S. Hart Museum, CA, 662
Williams College Archives and Special Collections, MA, 4037
Williamstown Historical Society, VT, 8465
Williston Historical Society, VT, 8466
Wilmington Railroad Museum Foundation, Inc., NC, 6475
Wilson County Historical Museum, KS, 2940
Wilton House Museum, VA, 8710
Winnetka Historical Society, IL, 2468
Winterthur Museum, Garden and Library, DE,

1321
Wisconsin Maritime Museum, WI, 9173
Wisconsin State Historical Society, WI, 9168
Wolf Creek Indian Village and Museum, VA, 8494
Wolfsonian-Florida International University, The, FL, 1492
Woodlawn, VA, 8637
Woodrow Wilson Birthplace Foundation, VA, 8733
Woodrow Wilson House, DC, 1377
Woodville Civic Club, Inc., MS, 4627
Wren's Nest House Museum, The, GA, 1629
Wynnewood Historical Society, OK, 6986
Wyoming Historical and Geological Society, PA, 7501
Yavapai Heritage Foundation, AZ, 253
Yolo County Historical Museum, CA, 968
York County Cultural and Heritage Commission Historical Center, SC, 7752
York County Culture and Heritage Commission, SC, 7729
York County Heritage Trust, PA, 7518
Young-Sanders Center for Study of the War Between the States, LA, 3327
Yukon Beringia Interpretive Centre, YT, 10006
Yuma Crossing State Historic Park, AZ, 295
Yuma Territorial Prison State Historic Park, AZ, 296
Zalud House, CA, 719
Zelienople Historical Society, Inc., PA, 7519
Zoar Village State Memorial, OH, 6828
Zubiwing Cultural Society, MI, 4201

ANTHROPOLOGY

A:shiwi A:wau Museum and Heritage Center, NM, 5782
Aberdeen Room Archives and Museum, MD, 3545
Agua Caliente Cultural Museum, CA, 692
Ah-Tah-Thi-Ki Museum, Seminole Tribe of Florida, FL, 1396
Aiken County Historical Museum, SC, 7596
Akta Lakota Museum and Cultural Center, SD, 7762
Akwesasne Cultural Center, Inc., aka Akwesasne Museum, NY, 5935
Alabama Historical Commission, AL, 94
Alamance County Historical Museum, Inc., NC, 6234
Alaska Historical Collection, Alaska State Library, AK, 168
Alaska State Museum, AK, 169
Alaska Support Office, National Park Service, AK, 136
Alfred P. Sloan Museum, MI, 4123
Alnobak Nebesakiak, VT, 8379
Alpine County Museum, CA, 634
Alpine Historical Society, AK, 192
Alpine Historical Society, CA, 434
AltaMira Historical Society, CA, 955
Amana Heritage Society, IA, 2659
American Indian Museum, AL, 63
American Studies Association, DC, 1327
Amerind Foundation, Inc., The, AZ, 215
Amy B.H. Greenwell Ethnobotanical Garden, HI, 1841
Anasazi Heritage Center, CO, 1035
Anasazi State Park, UT, 8290
Anchorage Museum of History and Art, AK, 138
Androscoggin Historical Society, ME, 3400
Angel Mounds State Historic Site, IN, 2517
Anniston Museum of Natural History, AL, 2
Antelope Valley Indian Museum, CA, 592
Antiquarian and Landmarks Society, CT, 1189
Appalachian Cultural Museum, The, NC, 6225
Aquarena Center, TX, 8245
Archeological Society of Virginia, VA, 8681
Archives, University of Colorado at Boulder Libraries, CO, 984
Argyle Historical Society, Inc., The, MN, 4270
Arizona Archaeological and Historical Society, AZ, 271
Arizona State Museum, AZ, 274
Arizona State University Museum of Anthropology, AZ, 264

Arkansas State University Museum, AR, 423
Associated Students for Historic Preservation (ASHP), OR, 7012
Association for Gravestone Studies, MA, 3871
Ataloa Lodge Museum, OK, 6918
Athens Historical Society, Inc., GA, 1587
Atwater Historical Society, The, OH, 6570
Auburn Avenue Research Library on African American Culture and History, GA, 1601
Augustan Society, Inc., The, CA, 509
Austin Children's Museum, TX, 8012
Aztec Museum Association, NM, 5702
Bancroft Library, The, CA, 458
Bar U Ranch National Historic Site of Canada, AB, 9406
Bay County Historical Society/Historical Museum of Bay County, MI, 4066
Bay Mills Community College Library and Heritage Center, MI, 4077
Bayou Terrebonne Waterlife Museum, LA, 3297
BC Heritage, BC, 9518
Beaufort Museum, SC, 7602
Beaverhead County Museum, MT, 5004
Belhaven Memorial Museum, NC, 6223
Bella Vista Historical Society/Museum, AR, 303
Belleville Public Library, IL, 1991
Belleville Public Library, ON, 9692
Bellevue Historical Society, WA, 8802
Berkeley Museum, SC, 7709
Berkshire Museum, The, MA, 3952
Berlin and Coos County Historical Society, NH, 5275
Berman Museum of World History, AL, 3
Bernice Pauahi Bishop Museum, HI, 1851
Bidwell Mansion State Historic Park, CA, 488
Bigheart Historical Museum, OK, 6841
Black Canyon of the Gunnison National Monument/Curecanti National Recreation Area, CO, 1074
Blackwater Draw Museum and Archaeological Site, NM, 5745
Blue Ridge Parkway, NC, 6209
Blue Ridge Parkway, VA, 8755
Bo-Cah Ama Council, CA, 540
Bowman County Historical and Genealogical Society, ND, 6502
Boyd's Cove Beothuk Interpretation Centre, NF, 9613
Brazos Valley Museum of Natural History, TX, 8043
Brevard Museum of History and Science, FL, 1398
Brick Store Museum, The, ME, 3450
Brooklyn Museum of Art, NY, 5831
Bruce Museum of Arts and Science, CT, 1177
Bryn Mawr College Libraries, PA, 7152
Buena Vista County Historical Society, IA, 2844
Buena Vista Heritage, CO, 991
Buffalo Bill Memorial Museum, CO, 1065
Buffalo Museum of Science, NY, 5840
Burnside Plantation, Inc., PA, 7127
Burpee Museum of Natural History, IL, 2350
Butte-Silver Bow Public Archives, MT, 4986
C.H. Nash Museum/Chucalissa, TN, 7939
C.M. Russell Museum, MT, 5013
Caddo Cultural Center, OK, 6847
Cahokia Mounds State Historic Site, IL, 2082
California Council for the Humanities, CA, 796
California Folklore Society, CA, 599
California Historical Resources Information System, CA, 449
California History Center and Foundation/De Anza College, CA, 507
California State Archives, CA, 751
California State Indian Museum, CA, 753
California State Parks Photographic Archives, CA, 961
Camas-Washougal Historical Society, WA, 8983
Camden County Historical Society & Museum, MO, 4811
Camden County Historical Society, NJ, 5473
Campbell County Rockpile Museum, WY, 9312
Campbell River Museum and Archives Society, BC, 9437
Canadian Canoe Museum, The, ON, 9791

ARCHAEOLOGY

9433

Barrington Preservation Society, RI, 7525
Battle of the Restigouche National Historic Site, QC, 9917
Battlefield House Museum, ON, 9811
Bay County Historical Society/Historical Museum of Bay County, MI, 4066
Bay Mills Community College Library and Heritage Center, MI, 4077
BC Heritage, BC, 9518
Beaufort Museum, SC, 7602
Beauvoir, The Jefferson Davis Home and Presidential Library, MS, 4531
Beaver Brook Farm and Transportation Museum, NH, 5372
Beaver County Historical Society, OK, 6846
Becker County Historical Society and Museum, MN, 4303
Beech Island Historical Society, SC, 7604
Behringer-Crawford Museum, KY, 3109
Belhaven Memorial Museum, NC, 6223
Bell County Museum, TX, 8037
Bellamy Mansion Museum of History and Design Arts, NC, 6467
Belle Grove Plantation, VA, 8627
Belle Meade, Queen of Tennessee Plantations, TN, 7959
Belleville Public Library, IL, 1991
Belleville Public Library, ON, 9692
Benares Historic House, ON, 9750
Bennington Museum, The, VT, 8360
Bent's Old Fort National Historic Site, CO, 1084
Berkeley County Historical Society, WV, 9037
Berkeley Museum, SC, 7709
Berkshire Museum, The, MA, 3952
Berlin and Coos County Historical Society, NH, 5275
Bernice Pauahi Bishop Museum, HI, 1851
Bethel Historical Association, Inc., OH, 6582
Beverly Historical Society and Museum, MA, 3761
Biedenharn Museum and Gardens, LA, 3323
Biggar Museum and Gallery, SK, 9947
Bigheart Historical Museum, OK, 6841
Billingsley House Museum, MD, 3734
Birmingham Historical Society, AL, 15
Black Canyon of the Gunnison National Monument/Curecanti National Recreation Area, CO, 1074
Black Hills Mining Museum, SD, 7798
Black River Historical Society, OH, 6703
Black River Historical Society, VT, 8400
Blackwater Draw Museum and Archaeological Site, NM, 5745
Bladen County Historical Society, Inc., NC, 6280
Blount Mansion Association, TN, 7922
Blount-Bridgers House/Hobson Pittman Memorial Gallery Foundation, Inc., NC, 6448
Blue Grass Trust for Historic Preservation, KY, 3160
Blue Ridge Parkway, NC, 6209
Blue Ridge Parkway, VA, 8755
Bo-Cah Ama Council, CA, 540
Bobby Davis Museum and Park, Hazard, Perry County, Kentucky, Inc., KY, 3149
Bolack Electromechanical Museum, NM, 5721
Bonneville Museum, ID, 1928
Booker T. Washington National Monument, VA, 8587
Boone County Historical Society, IA, 2671
Boone County Historical Society, IN, 2580
Boone County Historical Society, MO, 4681
Boone County Historical Society, NE, 5074
Boone's Lick State Historic Site, MO, 4649
Boonsborough Museum of History, MD, 3600
Boothbay Region Historical Society, ME, 3414
Bosque Memorial Museum, TX, 8050
Bourne Historical Society, Inc., MA, 3789
Bowman County Historical and Genealogical Society, ND, 6502
Boyd's Cove Beothuk Interpretation Centre, NF, 9613
Braddock's Field Historical Society, PA, 7141
Bradley Museum, ON, 9751
Braintree Historical Society, Inc., MA, 3792
Brazoria County Historical Museum, TX, 8009
Brazos Valley Museum of Natural History, TX, 8043

Bresaylor Heritage Museum, SK, 9949
Brevard Museum of History and Science, FL, 1398
Bridgewater Historical Society, NH, 5277
Bronx County Historical Society, NY, 5827
Brooklyn Museum of Art, NY, 5831
Brown County Historical Society, IN, 2598
Brown County Historical Society, MN, 4417
Brown County Historical Society, NE, 5071
Brown County Historical Society, OH, 6669
Brown County Historical Society, WI, 9132
Brownvale North Peace Agricultural Museum, AB, 9361
Bruce Museum of Arts and Science, CT, 1177
Brunswick Town/Fort Anderson State Historic Site, NC, 6479
Bryn Mawr College Libraries, PA, 7152
Buckeye Valley Historical and Archaeological Museum, AZ, 209
Buena Vista County Historical Society, IA, 2844
Buena Vista Heritage, CO, 991
Buffalo and Erie County Historical Society, NY, 5838
Buffalo Museum of Science, NY, 5840
Buffalo National River, AR, 346
Buffalo Trails Museum, ND, 6511
Bulloch Hall, GA, 1768
Burnside Plantation, Inc., PA, 7127
Burpee Museum of Natural History, IL, 2350
Burritt on the Mountain-A Living Museum, AL, 64
Burwell-Morgan Mill, VA, 8628
Bushy Run Battlefield, PA, 7254
Butler-Turpin Historic House, KY, 3105
Butte-Silver Bow Public Archives, MT, 4986
Byron Museum District, IL, 2011
C.H. Nash Museum/Chucalissa, TN, 7939
Cabot's Old Indian Pueblo Museum, CA, 516
Caddo Cultural Center, OK, 6847
Caddo-Pine Island Oil Museum, LA, 3364
Cahokia Courthouse State Historic Site, IL, 2012
Cahokia Mounds State Historic Site, IL, 2082
Calhoun County Museum and Cultural Center, SC, 7733
California Council for the Humanities, CA, 796
California Historical Resources Commission, CA, 748
California Historical Resources Information System, CA, 449
California History Center and Foundation/De Anza College, CA, 507
California Living Museum, CA, 450
California State Archives, CA, 751
California State Parks Photographic Archives, CA, 961
Calvert County Historical Society, Inc., MD, 3694
Camas-Washougal Historical Society, WA, 8983
Cambridge Historical Society, The, MA, 3797
Cambridge Museum, ID, 1916
Camden Archives and Museum, SC, 7615
Camp Saqawau: Environmental Education Center Forest Preserve District of Cook County, IL, 2198
Campbell County Log Cabin Museum, KY, 3087
Campbell River Museum and Archives Society, BC, 9437
Campus Martius Museum, OH, 6710
Canadian Museum of Civilization, QC, 9884
Canal Society of New Jersey, NJ, 5550
Canterbury Shaker Village, Inc., NH, 5283
Cape Charles Historical Society, VA, 8506
Cape Coral Historical Society, FL, 1391
Cape Fear Museum, NC, 6469
Carlsbad Caverns National Park, NM, 5708
Carlyle House Historic Park, VA, 8475
Carroll County Historical Society Museum, IN, 2509
Carroll County Historical Society, GA, 1650
Carroll County Historical Society, IA, 2679
Carroll County Historical Society, IL, 2261
Carroll County Historical Society, MO, 4665
Carroll County Historical Society, VA, 8592
Carroll County Wabash and Erie Canal, Inc., IN, 2510
Carroll's Hundred, MD, 3569
Carter County Museum, MT, 5005

Carver County Historical Society, MN, 4506
Cascade County Historical Museum and Archives, MT, 5014
Cascade County Historical Society, MT, 5015
Cass County Museum & Pioneer School, MN, 4508
Cassia County Historical Society, ID, 1914
Castillo de San Marcos National Monument/Fort Matanzas National Monument/ National Park Service, FL, 1522
Catalina Island Museum Society, CA, 448
Catawba Cultural Preservation Project, SC, 7728
Cavalier County Historical Society, ND, 6531
Cayuga Museum, NY, 5802
Cedar Falls Historic Village and Toy Museum, MO, 4661
Cedar Key State Museum, FL, 1393
Center City Historic Preservation Commission, MN, 4290
Center for American Archaeology, IL, 2184
Center for Anthropological Studies, NM, 5690
Center for Wooden Boats, The, WA, 8921
Center of Southwest Studies, Fort Lewis College, CO, 1036
Centerville-Washington Township Historical Society, The, OH, 6600
Central California Information Center/CA Historical Resource Information System, CA, 934
Central Coast Archaeological Information Center, CA, 858
Central Idaho Cultural Center, ID, 1942
Central Missouri State University Archives/Museum, MO, 4958
Central Nevada Historical Society/Museum, NV, 5260
Centre County Historical Society, PA, 7452
Centre d'etudes acadiennes, NB, 9596
Centre d'interpretation de la cote de Beaupre, QC, 9876
Centre for Newfoundland Studies, NF, 9628
Champlain Valley Heritage Network, NY, 5881
Charles Carroll House of Annapolis, MD, 3548
Charles City County Center for Local History, VA, 8509
Charles City County Historical Society, VA, 8510
Charles Towne Landing State Historic Site, SC, 7623
Charleston Library Society, SC, 7624
Charlotte Museum of History and Hezekina Alexander Homesite, NC, 6247
Chase and District Museum and Archives Society, BC, 9439
Chatauqua County Historical Society/ McClurg Museum, NY, 6190
Chateau Ramezay Museum, QC, 9905
Chatham Historical Society, NH, 5284
Chatham Historical Society, NJ, 5465
Chatham Historical Society, OH, 6701
Chatham Historical Society/Atwood House Musuem, MA, 3805
Chelan County Historical Society Pioneer Village and Museum, WA, 8816
Chelan County Public Utility District, WA, 8985
Chemung County Historical Society, Inc. (Chemung Valley History Museum), NY, 5899
Cheraw Lyceum, SC, 7645
Cherokee County Historical Museum, AL, 29
Cherokee County Historical Museum, NC, 6375
Cherokee Heritage Center, OK, 6971
Chester County Historical Society Museum, CA, 487
Chester Historical Society, Inc., NJ, 5468
Chesterfield Historical Society of Virginia, VA, 8522
Cheyenne County Historical Society, KS, 3038
Chicora Foundation, Inc., SC, 7650
Chief Vann House Historic Site, GA, 1655
Chieftains Museum, Inc., GA, 1761
Chimney Point State Historic Site, VT, 8408
Chimney Rock Archaeological Area, CO, 1106
Chippewa County Historical Society, MN, 4403
Chippewa County Historical Society, WI, 9097
Chippewa Nature Center, Inc., MI, 4190

Chisago County Historical Society, MN, 4362
Chisholm Trail Museum, KS, 3072
Churchill County Museum & Archives, NV, 5239
Cimarron Heritage Center, Inc., OK, 6849
Cincinnati Museum Center, OH, 6609
City of Hampton Historical Collection and Fort Wool Historic Site, VA, 8582
City of Las Vegas Museum and Rough Riders Memorial Collection, NM, 5734
City of Rocks Historical Association, ID, 1895
City of St. Augustine, Department of Historic Preservation and Heritage Tourism, FL, 1535
Clark County Historical Society, KS, 2883
Clark County Historical Society, MO, 4764
Clark County Historical Society, SD, 7764
Clark County Museum, NV, 5241
Clarke County Historical Association, VA, 8496
Clarke County Historical Society, AL, 58
Clarksville-Montgomery County Museum, TN, 7875
Clatsop County Historical Society, OR, 6990
Clausen Memorial Museum, AK, 183
Clay County Historical Society, AL, 4
Clay County Historical Society, FL, 1439
Clay County Historical Society, IN, 2493
Clay County Historical Society, MN, 4405
Clay County Historical Society, NE, 5100
Clay County Historical Society, SD, 7854
Clay County Historical Society, The, WV, 9017
Clay County Museum and Historical Society, MO, 4807
Clermont State Historic Site, NY, 5918
Cloud County Historical Society, KS, 2904
CNMI Museum of History and Culture, MP, 6556
Coastal Discovery Museum on Hilton Head Island, SC, 7692
Coastal Heritage Society, GA, 1783
Cobb County Historic Preservation Commission, GA, 1734
Cochise County Historical Society, AZ, 213
Coe Hall at Planting Fields, NY, 6060
Cohasset Historical Society, MA, 3813
College of Eastern Utah Prehistoric Museum, UT, 8320
Colleton Museum, SC, 7748
Collier County Museum, FL, 1494
Collier-Seminole State Park, FL, 1495
Colonel Davenport Historical Foundation, The, IL, 2345
Colonial Williamsburg Foundation, The, VA, 8773
Colorado Historical Society, CO, 1021
Colorado Springs Museum, CO, 1002
Columbia Gorge Discovery Center and Wasco County Historical Museum, OR, 7093
Columbia Gorge Interpretive Center, WA, 8958
Columbia State Historic Park, CA, 499
Commission for Historical and Architectural Preservation, MD, 3570
Community Historical Museum of Mount Holly, VT, 8359
Community Historical Society, The, IA, 2794
Community History Project of Shenandoah University, VA, 8782
Community Library Associaton-Regional History Dept, ID, 1934
Concord Historical Society, CA, 501
Concord Historical Society, VT, 8419
Concord Museum, MA, 3814
Conejo Valley Historical Society/Stagecoach Inn Museum Complex, CA, 661
Conner Prairie, IN, 2524
Contra Costa County Historical Society and History Center, CA, 714
Conway Historical Society, MA, 3820
Conway Historical Society, NH, 5296
Cook Inlet Historical Society, Inc., AK, 140
Cooke County Heritage Society, Inc., TX, 8117
Cooper County Historical Society, MO, 4856
Copper Valley Historical Society, AK, 150
Cornelius Low House/Middlesex County Museum, NJ, 5567
Coronado State Monument, NM, 5704
Corporation for Jefferson's Poplar Forest, VA, 8555

Grant County Historical Society, WI, 9166
Gravesend Historical Society, The, NY, 5924
Great Basin Historical, Inc., UT, 8296
Great Lakes Historical Society, The, OH, 6805
Greeley County Historical Society, KS, 3063
Greeley County Historical Society, NE, 5128
Greenbrier Historical Society, Inc., WV, 9030
Greenlawn-Centerport Historical Association, NY, 5925
Greenville Historic Preservation Commission, NC, 6308
Greenwood Museum, The, SC, 7685
Greybull Museum, WY, 9316
Grosse Ile and the Irish Memorial National Historic Site, QC, 9936
Gulf Coast Heritage Association, Inc., FL, 1500
Gulf Islands National Seashore, FL, 1440
Gulfport Historical Society, FL, 1534
Gum Springs Historical Society, Inc., VA, 8581
Gunnison County Pioneer and Historical Society, CO, 1075
Gunston Hall Plantation, VA, 8620
Gustav Jeenings Museum of Bible and Near East Studies, IN, 2476
Hackettstown Historical Society, NJ, 5495
Haffenreffer Museum of Anthropology, RI, 7531
Hamilton County Historical Society, IL, 2237
Hamilton County Historical Society, IN, 2610
Hamilton County Historical Society, Plainsman Museum, NE, 5080
Hampson Museum State Park, AR, 430
Hampton Plantation State Historic Site, SC, 7705
Hampton Roads Museum, VA, 8649
Hana Cultural Center, HI, 1844
Hancock Historical Society, NH, 5332
Hancock Shaker Village, Inc., MA, 3953
Hanover Tavern Foundation, VA, 8586
Harnett County Historical Society, NC, 6352
Harris Heritage Museum Society, Inc., SK, 9958
Harrison County Historical Museum, TX, 8181
Harrison Historical Society, ME, 3446
Harry S. Truman Birthplace State Historic Park, MO, 4796
Hart Cam Museum, MB, 9541
Hartzler-Towner Multicultural Museum at Scarritt Bennett Center, TN, 7965
Harwich Historical Society, MA, 3879
Hastings Historical Society, NY, 5929
Hastings Museum of Culture and Natural History, NE, 5132
Hattiesburg Area Historical Society and Museum, MS, 4554
Hawaii Heritage Center, HI, 1857
Hawaii State Historic Preservation Office, HI, 1878
Hayden Historical Museum Inc., IN, 2545
Head-Smashed-In Buffalo Jump Historic Site, AB, 9395
Healdsburg Museum and Historical Society, CA, 566
Heard Natural Science Museum and Wildlife Sanctuary, TX, 8186
Heart of West Texas Museum, TX, 8051
Heartland Historical Society, Inc., SD, 7791
Hebrew Union College Skirball Museum, OH, 6613
Held Poage Memorial Home and Research Library, CA, 938
Helena Library and Museum Association, AR, 351
Hells Gate State Park, ID, 1937
Henrico Historic Preservation/Museum Services, VA, 8688
Henry Sheldon Museum of Vermont History, VT, 8404
Henry Whitfield State Museum, CT, 1184
Heritage Branch, Department of Tourism, Government of Yukon, YT, 10002
Heritage Deep Cove, BC, 9472
Heritage Hill Historical Park, CA, 589
Heritage Museum Association, Inc., FL, 1567
Heritage Museum of Layton, UT, 8306
Heritage Museum, MT, 5035
Heritage North Museum, MB, 9553
Heritage Park, CA, 877
Heritage Society of Essex and Middle River,

Inc., MD, 3640
Hermitage, The, NJ, 5511
Hermitage, The, TN, 7907
Herriman State Park of Idaho, ID, 1929
Hicksville Gregory Museum, Long Island Earth Center, The, NY, 5932
Hidalgo County Historical Museum, TX, 8088
High Desert Museum, OR, 6998
High Plains Historical Society, NE, 5159
High Plains Museum, KS, 2946
High Point Historical Society, Inc., NC, 6325
Hilltop Historical Society, OH, 6631
His Lordship's Kindness, MD, 3616
Historic Annapolis Foundation, MD, 3552
Historic Arkansas Museum (Arkansas Territorial Restoration), AR, 376
Historic Bath State Historic Site, NC, 6219
Historic Bethabara Park, NC, 6482
Historic Camden Revolutionary War Site, SC, 7616
Historic Carnton Plantation, TN, 7891
Historic Charleston Foundation, SC, 7629
Historic Columbia Foundation, SC, 7652
Historic Crab Orchard Museum and Pioneer Park, VA, 8753
Historic Daniel Boone Home, MO, 4692
Historic Deerfield, Inc., MA, 3834
Historic Donaldsonville Museum, LA, 3283
Historic Dumfries, Virginia, Inc., VA, 8540
Historic Forks of the Wabash, IN, 2549
Historic Fort Erie, ON, 9761
Historic Fort Snelling, MN, 4459
Historic Halifax State Historic Site, NC, 6312
Historic Hope Foundation, Inc., NC, 6478
Historic Hopewell Foundation, Inc., VA, 8594
Historic House Trust of New York City, NY, 6010
Historic Indian Agency House, WI, 9193
Historic Kansas City Foundation, MO, 4770
Historic London Town and Gardens, MD, 3635
Historic Long Branch, VA, 8629
Historic Morven, NJ, 5608
Historic New Orleans Collection, The, LA, 3350
Historic Northampton, MA, 3941
Historic Pensacola Preservation Board, FL, 1511
Historic Preservation Alliance of Arkansas, AR, 377
Historic Rittenhouse Town Inc., PA, 7382
Historic Rosedale Plantation, NC, 6248
Historic Southern Indiana, IN, 2518
Historic Southwest Ohio, OH, 6614
Historic Springfield Foundation, Inc., MS, 4545
Historic St. Mary's City, MD, 3703
Historic Stagville, NC, 6273
Historic Upshur Museum, TX, 8133
Historic Winslow House Association, MA, 3912
Historic Yellow Springs, Inc., PA, 7167
Historical County of Rockland County, The, NY, 5990
Historical Museum at Fort Missoula, MT, 5042
Historical Museum of Southern Florida, FL, 1486
Historical Museum of the D.R. Barker Library, NY, 5911
Historical Projects of Houston County, Inc., TX, 8064
Historical Society of Douglas County, NE, 5188
Historical Society of Glastonbury, CT, 1174
Historical Society of Harford County, Inc., The, MD, 3594
Historical Society of Hopkins County, KY, 3196
Historical Society of Marshall County, IA, 2790
Historical Society of New Mexico, NM, 5756
Historical Society of Porter County, IN, 2643
Historical Society of Princeton, NJ, 5609
Historical Society of Saginaw Co., Inc./Castle Museum of Saginaw Co. History, MI, 4234
Historical Society of Seabrook, NH, 5419
Historical Society of Trappe, PA, 7172
Historical Society of Western Pennsylvania, PA, 7420
History Center, IA, 2684
History Museum and Historical Society of Western Virginia, VA, 8712

Hitchcock County Historical Society, NE, 5213
Holland Historical Trust, MI, 4152
Homesteader Museum, WY, 9337
Homesteaders Museum, WY, 9353
Homewood House Museum, MD, 3579
Homolovi Ruins State Park, AZ, 289
Hoofprints of the Past Museum, WY, 9321
Hopewell Furnace National Historic Site, PA, 7201
Hopewell Museum, KY, 3225
Hopi Cultural Preservation Office, AZ, 232
Horace Greeley Museum, KS, 3064
Horicon Historical Society, WI, 9143
Horne Creek Living Historical Farm, NC, 6390
Horry County Museum, SC, 7665
House in the Horseshoe State Historic Site, NC, 6427
Houston County Historical Commission, TX, 8065
Houston County Historical Society, MN, 4287
Houston County Visitors Center/Museum, Inc., TX, 8066
Howard County Historical Society, IA, 2705
Howard County Historical Society, IN, 2576
Howard County Historical Society, MD, 3638
Howard County Historical Society, NE, 5206
Hubbard Museum of the American West, The, NM, 5753
Huck's Museum and Trading Post, UT, 8289
Hudson Museum, University of Maine, ME, 3479
Huguenot Historical Society, NY, 5992
Humboldt & District Museum & Gallery, SK, 9960
Humboldt Museum, NV, 5263
Huronia Museum and Huron-Ouendat Village, ON, 9745
Hustiford Historical Society, WI, 9146
Hutchinson County Museum, TX, 8040
Idaho State Historical Museum, ID, 1911
Idaho State Historical Society, ID, 1912
Illinois and Michigan Canal National Heritage Corridor Commission, IL, 2218
Illinois Association of Museums, IL, 2394
Illinois State Historical Society, IL, 2397
Illinois State Museum, IL, 2399
Independence National Historical Park, PA, 7384
Indian and Colonial Research Center, Inc., CT, 1238
Indian Grinding Rock State Historic Park Chaw'se Regional Indian Museum, CA, 708
Indian Key State Historic, FL, 1443
Indian Museum of the Carolinas, Inc., NC, 6347
Indian Pueblo Cultural Center, NM, 5693
Indian Temple Mound Museum, FL, 1434
Indiana State Archives, IN, 2562
Indiana State Museum and Historic Sites, IN, 2564
Institute for Minnesota Archaeology, MN, 4460
Institute of Texan Cultures, The, TX, 8235
International Bowling Museum and Hall of Fame, MO, 4913
International Center for Jefferson Studies, VA, 8516
Inupiat Heritage Center, AK, 144
Iowa Masonic Library and Museums, IA, 2685
Iron and Steel Museum of Alabama, AL, 77
Iroquois Indian Museum, NY, 5938
Irvine Historical Society, CA, 573
Isanti County Historical Society, MN, 4288
Island County Historical Society & Museum, WA, 8827
Isle of Wight County Museum, VA, 8722
Jackson Historical Society, NH, 5343
Jackson Hole Historical Society and Museum, WY, 9320
Jackson Homestead, Newton's Museum and Historical Society, MA, 3934
Jacobsburg Historical Society, PA, 7330
James City County Historical Commission, VA, 8775
James E. Conner Museum, Texas A&M University, TX, 8159
Jamestown-Yorktown Foundation, VA, 8776
Jane Ross Reeves Octagon House Foundation, IN, 2631
Jarrot Mansion State Historic Site, IL, 2013

Jasmine Hill Gardens and Outdoors Museum, AL, 98
Jay I. Kislak Foundation, Inc., FL, 1493
Jean Lafitte National Historical Park and Preserve, LA, 3352
Jefferson Barracks Historic Site, MO, 4914
Jefferson County Historical and Genealogical Society, PA, 7145
Jefferson County Historical Society, Museum, & Research Library, WA, 8906
Jefferson National Expansion Memorial, MO, 4915
Jefferson Office of Public History, KY, 3183
Jefferson Patterson Park and Museum, MD, 3702
Jefferson Township Historical Society, PA, 7154
Jekyll Island Museum, GA, 1707
Jensen Arctic Museum, OR, 7043
Jerome County Historical Society, Inc., ID, 1931
Jesse Besser Museum, MI, 4054
Jim Gatchell Museum, WY, 9289
John B. Ridley Research Library, ON, 9688
John D. MacArthur Beach State Park, FL, 1498
John Wesley Powell Memorial Museum, Historical and Archaeological Sociey, Inc., AZ, 239
Johnson County Historical Society, IA, 2697
Johnson County Historical Society, WY, 9290
Johnson County Museum of History, IN, 2533
Jonathan Hager House and Museum, MD, 3663
Jonathan Trumbull, Junior, House Museum, CT, 1202
Joplin Historical and Mineral Museum, Inc., MO, 4762
Joseph Schneider Haus Museum, ON, 9737
Joseph Smith Historic Center, IL, 2270
Jourdan Bachman Pioneer Farm, TX, 8016
Julia A. Purnell Museum, MD, 3721
Junior Museum of Bay County, Inc., FL, 1507
Junior Museum, The, NY, 6164
Jurupa Mountains Cultural Center, CA, 738
K'Beg "Footprints" Interpretive Site, AK, 149
Kahana Valley State Park, HI, 1846
Kalamazoo Valley Museum, MI, 4165
Kalaupapa National Historical Park, HI, 1876
Kanawha Valley Historical and Preservation Society, Inc., WV, 9014
Kansas Barbed Wire Museum, KS, 2969
Kansas State Historical Society, KS, 3060
Kaua'i Museum Association, HI, 1885
Kelowna Museum, BC, 9460
Kemper County Historical Association, MS, 4544
Kenai Visitors and Cultural Center, AK, 172
Kenosha Public Museum, WI, 9153
Kenton County Historical Society, KY, 3110
Kentucky Historical Society, KY, 3134
Kentucky Museum, The, KY, 3097
Kerr Place, Historic House Museum, VA, 8658
Ketchum/Sun Valley Heritage and Ski Museum, ID, 1935
Kibbe Hancock Heritage Museum, IL, 2022
King Manor Museum, NY, 5953
Kingman County Historical Society, Inc., KS, 2967
Kings Landing Historical Settlement, NB, 9593
Kings Mountain National Military Park, SC, 7609
Kitimat Centennial Museum, BC, 9463
Kitsap County Historical Society Museum, WA, 8811
Klamath County Museums, OR, 7032
Klondike Gold Rush National Historical Park, AK, 191
Knox County Historical Sites, Inc., IL, 2191
Knox County Old Gran Cemetery Educational, Historic and Memorial Association, TN, 7930
Knox's Headquarters State Historic Site, NY, 6170
KoKe'e Natural History Museum-Huio Laka, HI, 1880
Kolomoki Mounds State Historic Park, GA, 1639
Koreshan State Historic Site, FL, 1416
Koreshan Unity Alliance, FL, 1435
Koshare Indian Museum, CO, 1085

ARCHITECTURE

Camden Archives and Museum, SC, 7615
Camden County Historical Society & Museum, MO, 4811
Camden County Historical Society, NJ, 5473
Campbell Historical Museum, CA, 480
Campus Martius Museum, OH, 6710
Camron-Stanford House Preservation Association, CA, 671
Canadian Architectural Archives, University of Calgary Library, AB, 9363
Canadian Association of Professional Heritage Consultants, ON, 9829
Canadian Centre for Architecture (CCA), QC, 9902
Canadian National Exhibition Archives, ON, 9831
Canadian Railway Museum at Delson/Saint-Constant, QC, 9926
Canal Corridor Association, IL, 2038
Canal Fulton Heritage Society, OH, 6593
Candia Historical Society, NH, 5281
Cannonsburgh Village, TN, 7954
Canterbury Shaker Village, Inc., NH, 5283
Cape Charles Historical Society, VA, 8506
Cape Fear Museum, NC, 6469
Capital Area Preservation, Inc., NC, 6394
Capitol Preservation Committee, PA, 7245
Captain Forbes House Museum, MA, 3916
Caramoor Center for Music and Arts, NY, 5960
Carlyle House Historic Park, VA, 8475
Carmel Clay Historical Society, IN, 2496
Carousel Park Commission, RI, 7540
Carpenters' Company of the City and County, The, PA, 7358
Carriage House Museum of the Queen Village Historical Society, NY, 5847
Carroll County Historical & Genealogical Society, Inc., AR, 308
Carroll County Historical Society Museum, IN, 2509
Carroll County Historical Society, GA, 1650
Carroll County Historical Society, IA, 2679
Carroll County Historical Society, IL, 2261
Carroll County Historical Society, MO, 4665
Carroll County Historical Society, VA, 8592
Carthage Historic Preservation, Inc., MO, 4667
Carver County Historical Society, MN, 4506
Casa Blanca, NY, 5793
Casa Loma, ON, 9832
Casa Navarro State Historical Park, TX, 8232
Casemate Museum, The, VA, 8559
Castillo de San Marcos National Monument/Fort Matanzas National Monument/ National Park Service, FL, 1522
Castle Tucker, SPNEA, ME, 3538
Castle, The, OH, 6711
Catalina Island Museum Society, CA, 448
Catawba County Historical Association, NC, 6382
Cathedral of Saint John the Evangelist Museum, LA, 3307
Cathedral of St. John the Baptist, The, NF, 9627
Catonsville Historical Society, Inc., The, MD, 3609
Cedar Crest, Residence of the Governor of Kansas, KS, 3055
Cedar Falls Historic Village and Toy Museum, MO, 4661
Center City Historic Preservation Commission, MN, 4290
Center for Southwest Research, NM, 5691
Center for Wooden Boats, The, WA, 8921
Center of Southwest Studies, Fort Lewis College, CO, 1036
Centerville Historical Museum, MA, 3804
Central California Information Center/CA Historical Resource Information System, CA, 934
Central City Opera House Association, CO, 1020
Central Idaho Cultural Center, ID, 1942
Central Illinois Landmarks Foundation, IL, 2312
Centralia Historical Society, Inc., MO, 4671
Centre County Historical Society, PA, 7452
Centre d'histoire de Montreal, QC, 9904
Centre d'interpretation de la cote de Beaupre, QC, 9876
Centre for Newfoundland Studies, NF, 9628
Chadds Ford Historical Society, PA, 7164

Champ Clark Honey Shuck Restoration, Inc., MO, 4652
Champaign County Historical Society, OH, 6801
Champlain Valley Heritage Network, NY, 5881
Chancellor Robert R. Livingston Masonic Library, NY, 5998
Chapel Hill Preservation Society, NC, 6241
Chapel of Rest Preservation Society, NC, 6348
Charles Carroll House of Annapolis, MD, 3548
Charles City County Center for Local History, VA, 8509
Charles City County Historical Society, VA, 8510
Charles River Museum of Industry, MA, 4018
Charles Sumner School Museum and Archives, DC, 1333
Charleston Library Society, SC, 7624
Charlotte County Museum, NB, 9609
Charlotte Hawkins Brown Historic Site, NC, 6430
Charlotte Historic District Commission, NC, 6246
Charlotte Museum of History and Hezekina Alexander Homesite, NC, 6247
Chase/Lloyd House, MD, 3549
Chatham Historical Society, NH, 5284
Chatham Historical Society, NJ, 5465
Chatham Historical Society, OH, 6701
Chatham Historical Society/Atwood House Musuem, MA, 3805
Chatillon-DeMenil House Foundation, MO, 4908
Cheekwood-Tennessee Botanical Garden & Museum of Art, TN, 7961
Chelan County Historical Society Pioneer Village and Museum, WA, 8816
Chelmsford Historical Society, MA, 3807
Chemung County Historical Society, Inc. (Chemung Valley History Museum), NY, 5899
Cheraw Lyceum, SC, 7645
Cherokee County Historical Museum, AL, 29
Cherokee County Historical Museum, NC, 6375
Cherokee Heritage Center, OK, 6971
Chesapeake and Ohio Historical Society, Inc., VA, 8527
Chester County Historical Society Museum, CA, 487
Chesterfield County Historic Preservation Commission, SC, 7646
Chestnut Hill Historical Society, PA, 7361
Chevy Chase Historical Society, MD, 3615
Chicago Architecture Foundation, IL, 2039
Chicago Athenaeum: Museum of Architecture and Design, The, IL, 2375
Chicago Historical Society, IL, 2043
Chicago Lawn Historical Society, IL, 2045
Chicago Public Library Special Collections and Preservation Division, IL, 2046
Chico Museum Association, CA, 489
Chieftains Museum, Inc., GA, 1761
Chinqua-Penn Plantation Foundation, Inc., NC, 6417
Chippewa County Historical Society, MN, 4403
Chippewa County Historical Society, WI, 9097
Church-Waddel-Brumby House Museum, GA, 1589
Cimarron Heritage Center, Inc., OK, 6849
Cincinnati Fire Museum, OH, 6608
Citadel Archives and Museum, SC, 7626
City of Bowie Museums, MD, 3602
City of Greeley Museums, CO, 1073
City of Hampton Historical Collection and Fort Wool Historic Site, VA, 8582
City of Las Vegas Museum and Rough Riders Memorial Collection, NM, 5734
City of Northfield Historic Preservation Commission, MN, 4422
City of Omaha Planning Department, NE, 5183
City of Placentia Historical Committee, CA, 709
City of St. Augustine, Department of Historic Preservation and Heritage Tourism, FL, 1535
City of Toronto Archives, ON, 9833
Civil Engineer Corps/Seabee Museum, CA, 717

Claremont Heritage, Inc., CA, 497
Clark County Museum, NV, 5241
Clark Historical Society, NJ, 5469
Clarke County Historical Association, VA, 8496
Clarke County Historical Society, AL, 58
Clarke House Museum, IL, 2047
Clarke Memorial Museum, CA, 530
Clarkston Community Historical Society, MI, 4090
Clarksville-Montgomery County Museum, TN, 7875
Clatsop County Historical Society, OR, 6990
Clay County Historical Society, AL, 4
Clay County Historical Society, FL, 1439
Clay County Historical Society, IN, 2493
Clay County Historical Society, MN, 4405
Clay County Historical Society, NE, 5100
Clay County Historical Society, SD, 7854
Clear Creek History Park, CO, 1066
Clermont Historical Society, IA, 2692
Clermont State Historic Site, NY, 5918
Cleveland Park Historical Society, DC, 1335
Clinton Birthplace Foundation, AR, 353
Cliveden of the National Trust, PA, 7364
Clover Bend Historic Preservation Association, AR, 357
Clovis Depot Model Train Museum, NM, 5717
Cobb County Historic Preservation Commission, GA, 1734
Coe Hall at Planting Fields, NY, 6060
Coffeyville Historical Society/Dalton Defenders Museum, KS, 2900
Coffin House, SPNEA, MA, 3930
Cogswell's Grant, SPNEA, MA, 3857
Cokesbury College Historical and Recreational Commission, SC, 7695
Cole Harbour Rural Heritage Society, NS, 9654
Collinsville Historical Museum, IL, 2083
Colonel Davenport Historical Foundation, The, IL, 2345
Colonial Pennsylvania Plantation, PA, 7313
Colonial Williamsburg Foundation, The, VA, 8773
Colorado Historical Society, CO, 1021
Colorado Springs Museum, CO, 1002
Colton Hall Museum, CA, 645
Columbia County Historical Society, NY, 5962
Columbia County Historical Society, OR, 7090
Columbia County Historical Society, WI, 9091
Columbia State Historic Park, CA, 499
Columbian Theatre, Museum Art Center, KS, 3069
Columbus Chapel and Boal Mansion Museum, PA, 7137
Commissariat House Provincial Historic Site, NF, 9629
Commission for Historical and Architectural Preservation, MD, 3570
Commission of Landmarks and Museum, DE, 1312
Commonwealth Air Training Plan Museum, MB, 9533
Community History Project of Shenandoah University, VA, 8782
Company of the Redwood Library and Athanaeum, The, RI, 7555
Compass Inn Museum, PA, 7290
Concord Historical Society, CA, 501
Concord Historical Society, VT, 8419
Concordia Historical Institute, MO, 4909
Conde Charlotte Museum House, AL, 80
Confederate Memorial State Historic Site, MO, 4726
Connecticut Historical Society, The, CT, 1191
Conner Prairie, IN, 2524
Conrad Mansion National Historic Site Museum, MT, 5031
Conrad/Caldwell House Museum, KY, 3180
Contemporary Museum, The, HI, 1853
Contemporary Victorian Townhouse Museum, NJ, 5655
Conway Historical Society, MA, 3820
Conway Historical Society, NH, 5296
Cooper County Historical Society, MO, 4856
Cooper Regional History Museum, CA, 940
Cooper-Hewitt National Design Museum, NY, 5999
Copshaholm, the Oliver Mansion, IN, 2634
Coral Gables Merrick House, FL, 1399
Cornish Historical Society, NH, 5298

Coronado State Monument, NM, 5704
Corporation for Jefferson's Poplar Forest, VA, 8555
Corydon Capitol State Historic Site, IN, 2500
Cottonwood Area Historical Society, MN, 4298
Cottonwood Ranch State Historic Site, KS, 3051
Courtenay and District Museum and Paleontology Centre, BC, 9440
Courthouse Square Association, Inc., MI, 4085
Coventry Historical Society, CT, 1150
Craftsman Farms Foundation, NJ, 5548
Cramer-Kenyon Heritage House, Inc, SD, 7861
Cranbrook Archives Museum and Landmark Foundation, BC, 9441
Cranbrook House and Gardens Auxiliary, MI, 4075
Craven Hall Historical Society, PA, 7485
Crawford W. Long Museum Association, GA, 1752
Creston and District Historical and Museum Society, BC, 9442
Cromwell Historical Society, CT, 1152
Crosby Arboretum, Mississippi State Univ, MS, 4600
Crowley Cheese, Inc., VT, 8395
Crystal Lake Falls Historical Association, VT, 8357
Crystal Rice Plantation, LA, 3280
Culbertson Mansion State Historic Site, IN, 2601
Cumberland County Historical Society and Hamilton Library, PA, 7157
Cumberland County Historical Society, NJ, 5493
Cumberland County Museum, NS, 9647
Cuneo Museum and Gardens, IL, 2437
Cupids Historical Society, Inc., NF, 9615
Cupola House Association, Inc., NC, 6276
Custer County Historical Society, NE, 5090
Custer County Historical Society, SD, 7767
Customs House Maritime Museum/Lowell's Boat Shop, MA, 3932
Cynthiana-Harrison County Museum, KY, 3115
D.A.R. Anna Palmer Museum, NE, 5224
Daggett House, RI, 7566
Dakota County Historical Society, MN, 4455
Dakota County Historical Society, NE, 5105
Dallas Arboretum and Botanical Society, TX, 8072
Dallas County Historical Museum, AR, 332
Dallas County Historical Society, Inc., MO, 4655
Dallas Historical Society, TX, 8073
Dalnavent Museum, MB, 9564
Daly Mansion Preservation Trust, MT, 5018
Dana-Thomas House State Historic Site, IL, 2391
Dancing Leaf Earth Lodge, NE, 5219
Daniel Boone Homestead, PA, 7134
Daniel Webster Birthplace Living History Project, NH, 5313
Danvers Historical Society, IL, 2088
Danvers Historical Society, MA, 3824
Danville Historical Society, VA, 8532
DAR Anna Palmer Museum, NE, 5225
Darien Historical Society, Inc., The, CT, 1156
Darlington County Historical Commission, SC, 7666
Darnall's Chance, MD, 3735
Daughters of the Republic of Texas Library at the Alamo, TX, 8233
David Davis Mansion State Historic Site, IL, 2003
Davidson County Historical Museum, NC, 6351
Davies Manor Association, Inc., TN, 7867
Davis Museum and Cultural Center, MA, 4026
Dayton Historical Depot Society, WA, 8830
DC Booth Historic National Fish Hatchery, SD, 7846
Decatur County Historical Society, GA, 1636
Decatur County Historical Society, IN, 2542
DeCordova Museum and Sculpture Park, MA, 3898
Deere-Wiman House, IL, 2248
Deerfield Area Historical Society, IL, 2101
Delaware Agricultural Museum and Village,

ART

COMMUNITY/STATE HISTORY

THEMES OF INTERPRETATION Community/State History 1063

Bridgton Historical Society, ME, 3415
Bridport Historical Society, VT, 8365
Brigham City Museum/Gallery, UT, 8291
Brillion Historical Society, WI, 9086
Bristol Historical Society, NH, 5278
Bristol Historical Society, VT, 8366
British Columbia Orchard Industry Museum, BC, 9458
Broad River Genealogical Society, Inc., NC, 6431
Broad Top Area Coal Miners Historical Society, Inc., PA, 7435
Brodhead Historical Society, WI, 9087
Broken Arrow Historical Society, OK, 6852
Bronx County Historical Society, NY, 5827
Brookeville Academy, MD, 3603
Brookfield Historical Society, VT, 8367
Brookfield Museum and Historical Society, Inc., CT, 1145
Brookings County Historical Society, SD, 7856
Brooklyn Historical Society, MN, 4285
Brooklyn Historical Society, OH, 6588
Brooklyn Historical Society, The, NY, 5830
Brooklyn Public Library-Brooklyn Collection, NY, 5832
Brooksville Historical Society, ME, 3416
Broome County Historical Society, NY, 5817
Broomfield Depot Museum, CO, 990
Brown County Historical Association, MO, 4947
Brown County Historical Society, IN, 2598
Brown County Historical Society, MN, 4417
Brown County Historical Society, NE, 5071
Brown County Historical Society, OH, 6669
Brown County Historical Society, WI, 9132
Brown Deer Historical Society, Inc./1884 Brown Deer School, WI, 9088
Brown-Pusey House, KY, 3120
Brownvale North Peace Agricultural Museum, AB, 9361
Brownville Historical Society, NE, 5091
Brownville/Brownville Junction Historical Society, ME, 3417
Brubacher House Museum, ON, 9849
Brucemore, Inc., IA, 2683
Brunswick Railroad Museum, MD, 3604
Brunswick Town/Fort Anderson State Historic Site, NC, 6479
Bryant Library Local History Collection, NY, 6106
Bryant Stove and Music, Inc., ME, 3527
Buena Vista County Historical Society, IA, 2844
Buena Vista Heritage, CO, 991
Buffalo and Erie County Historical Society, NY, 5838
Buffalo Bill Ranch State Historical Park, NE, 5177
Buffalo County Historical Society, NE, 5137
Buffalo Historical Society, Inc., Old Stone Church and Rectory Heritage Center, ND, 6503
Buffalo National River, AR, 346
Buffalo Trails Museum, ND, 6511
Bulloch Hall, GA, 1768
Bullock County Historical Society, AL, 126
Burbank Historical Society, CA, 473
Burgwin-Wright Museum House and Gardens, NC, 6468
Burke County Genealogical Society, NC, 6366
Burkett House Wabash County Museum, IL, 2260
Burlington County Historical Society, NJ, 5454
Burlington Historic Preservation Commission, NC, 6235
Burlington Historical Society, WI, 9089
Burnaby Village Museum, BC, 9434
Burnet County Heritage Society/Ft. Croghan Museum, TX, 8044
Burnham Tavern Museum, ME, 3459
Burnside Plantation, Inc., PA, 7127
Burrillville Historical and Preservation Society, RI, 7565
Burritt on the Mountain-A Living Museum, AL, 64
Burroughs Home, FL, 1427
Burton Historical Collection, MI, 4105
Burwell-Morgan Mill, VA, 8628
Bush House Museum, OR, 7080
Bushnell Historical Society, IL, 2010
Bushy Run Battlefield, PA, 7254
Business and Media Archvies of the Mahoning Valley, OH, 6825
Butler County Hall of Fame, IA, 2656
Butler County Historical Society, PA, 7155
Butler County Historical Society/Kansas Oil & Gas Museum, KS, 2919
Butler County Museum, IA, 2657
Butler-Turpin Historic House, KY, 3105
Butte-Silver Bow Public Archives, MT, 4986
Butterworth Center, IL, 2247
Butts County Historical Society, GA, 1703
Buxton National Historic Site and Museum, ON, 9770
buxton national historic site, ON, 9769
Bybee House and Agricultural Museum at Howell Territorial Park, OR, 7064
Byers-Evans House Museum, CO, 1019
Byron Area Historical Society, GA, 1645
Byron Museum District, IL, 2011
C.C. Graber Company, CA, 680
C.H.T.J. Southard House Museum, ME, 3498
C.M. Russell Museum, MT, 5013
Cache Valley Historical Society, UT, 8310
Caddo-Pine Island Oil Museum, LA, 3364
Cahokia Courthouse State Historic Site, IL, 2012
Calaveras County Historical Society, CA, 773
Caldwell County Historical Society Heritage Museum, NC, 6350
Caleb Pusey House and Landingford Plantation, PA, 7473
Calhoun County Historical Society, IL, 2163
Calhoun County Museum and Cultural Center, SC, 7733
California African American Museum, CA, 612
California Area Historical Society, PA, 7156
California Council for the Humanities, CA, 796
California Council for the Promotion of History, CA, 747
California Genealogical Society, CA, 669
California Heritage Council, CA, 798
California Heritage Museum, CA, 879
California Historical Resources Commission, CA, 748
California Historical Society, CA, 799
California History Center and Foundation/De Anza College, CA, 507
California History Section, California State Library, CA, 749
California State Archives, CA, 751
California State Capitol Museum, CA, 752
California State University Sacramento/Dept. of Special Collections and Univ. Archives, CA, 755
Callingwood Library and Museum on Americanism, VA, 8474
Calumet City Historical Society, IL, 2015
Calvert County Historical Society, Inc., MD, 3694
Calvin Coolidge Memorial Foundation, The, VT, 8426
Camas-Washougal Historical Society, WA, 8983
Cambria County Historical Society, PA, 7196
Cambridge Historical Commission, MA, 3796
Cambridge Historical Society, The, MA, 3797
Cambridge Museum, ID, 1916
Camden County Historical Society & Museum, MO, 4811
Camden County Historical Society, NJ, 5473
Camp Walton Schoolhouse Museum, FL, 1433
Campbell Area Genealogical and Historical Society, MO, 4660
Campbell County Rockpile Museum, WY, 9312
Campbell Historical Museum, CA, 480
Campus Martius Museum, OH, 6710
Camron-Stanford House Preservation Association, CA, 671
Canaan Historical Society, NH, 5280
Canadian Association of Professional Heritage Consultants, ON, 9829
Canadian National Exhibition Archives, ON, 9831
Canadian Railway Museum at Delson/Saint-Constant, QC, 9926
Canadian Rivers Historical Society, OK, 6889
Canadian Scottish Regiment (Princess Mary's) Regimental Museum, The, BC, 9519
Canadiana Costume Museum and Archives of Bristish Columbia, BC, 9520
Canal Corridor Association, IL, 2038
Canal Fulton Heritage Society, OH, 6593
Cannonsburgh Village, TN, 7954
Canterbury Shaker Village, Inc., NH, 5283
Canyon Life Museum, OR, 7038
Capac Community Historical Society, MI, 4081
Cape Ann Historical Association, MA, 3867
Cape Bonavista Lighthouse Provincial Historic Site, NF, 9611
Cape Breton Miners' Museum, NS, 9656
Cape Charles Historical Society, VA, 8506
Cape Coral Historical Society, FL, 1391
Cape Elizabeth Historical Preservation Society, ME, 3421
Cape Fear Museum, NC, 6469
Cape Girardeau County Genealogical Society, MO, 4748
Cape River Heritage Museum, MO, 4663
Capital Area Preservation, Inc., NC, 6394
Capitol Preservation Committee, PA, 7245
Caples House Museum, OR, 7004
Captain Forbes House Museum, MA, 3916
Captain Frederick Pabst Mansion, Inc., WI, 9191
Carbon County Historical Society, MT, 5049
Carbon County Historical Society, WY, 9338
Carbon County Museum, WY, 9339
Carillon Historical Park, Inc., OH, 6643
Carl Albert Congressional Research and Studies Center, OK, 6926
Carlisle Area Historical Society, OH, 6597
Carlsbad Caverns National Park, NM, 5708
Carlton County Historical Society, MN, 4295
Carmel Clay Historical Society, IN, 2496
Carnegie Center for Art and History, IN, 2600
Carondelet Historical Society, MO, 4907
Carpenters' Company of the City and County, The, PA, 7358
Carpinteria Valley Museum of History, CA, 485
Carriage House Museum of the Queen Village Historical Society, NY, 5847
Carroll County Historical & Genealogical Society, Inc., AR, 308
Carroll County Historical Society Museum, IN, 2509
Carroll County Historical Society, GA, 1650
Carroll County Historical Society, Gordon Browning Museum & Genealogical Library, TN, 7937
Carroll County Historical Society, IA, 2679
Carroll County Historical Society, IL, 2261
Carroll County Historical Society, MO, 4665
Carroll County Historical Society, VA, 8592
Carroll County Wabash and Erie Canal, Inc., IN, 2510
Carroll Reece Museum, TN, 7913
Carroll's Hundred, MD, 3569
Carson Valley Historical Society, NV, 5240
Carteret County Historical Society, Inc., NC, 6365
Carver County Historical Society, MN, 4506
Carver-Hill Memorial and Historical Society, Inc., FL, 1400
Cascade County Historical Museum and Archives, MT, 5014
Cascade County Historical Society, MT, 5015
Case Corporation Archives, WI, 9233
Casemate Museum, The, VA, 8559
Casper College Library, Special Collections, WY, 9291
Cass County Historical and Genealogical Societies, Inc., MO, 4719
Cass County Historical and Genealogical Society, IL, 2439
Cass County Historical Society Museum, IA, 2753
Cass County Historical Society Museum, IN, 2582
Cass County Historical Society Museum, NE, 5199
Cassia County Historical Society, ID, 1914
Cassville Historical Society, WI, 9093
Castillo de San Marcos National Monument/Fort Matanzas National Monument/ National Park Service, FL, 1522
Castle Clinton National Monument, NY, 5997
Castle Museum, ID, 1932
Castle Tucker, SPNEA, ME, 3538
Castle, The, OH, 6711
Castleton Historical Society, VT, 8372
Castro/Breen Adobe, CA, 830
Caswell County Historical Association, Inc., NC, 6491
Catalina Island Museum Society, CA, 448
Catawba County Historical Association, NC, 6382
Cathedral of Saint John the Evangelist Museum, LA, 3307
Catonsville Historical Society, Inc., The, MD, 3609
Cavalier County Historical Society, ND, 6531
Cavendish Historical Society, VT, 8373
Cayce Historical Museum, SC, 7619
Cayuga Museum, NY, 5802
Cedar Crest, Residence of the Governor of Kansas, KS, 3055
Cedar Falls Historic Village and Toy Museum, MO, 4661
Cedar Falls Historical Society, IA, 2680
Cedar Lake Historical Association, Inc., IN, 2497
Cedarburg Cultural Center, WI, 9094
Celery Flats Historical Area, MI, 4222
Centennial Hall Corp, NE, 5214
Centennial Valley Historical Association, WY, 9293
Center City Historic Preservation Commission, MN, 4290
Center for American History, The University of Texas at Austin, TX, 8013
Center for Oral History, Social Science Research, HI, 1852
Center for Southwest Research, NM, 5691
Center for Wooden Boats, The, WA, 8921
Center Harbor Historical Society, NH, 5285
Center of Southwest Studies, Fort Lewis College, CO, 1036
Centerville Historical Museum, MA, 3804
Centerville-Washington Township Historical Society, The, OH, 6600
Central California Information Center/CA Historical Resource Information System, CA, 934
Central City Opera House Association, CO, 1020
Central Idaho Cultural Center, ID, 1942
Central Kansas Flywheel, Inc., KS, 3040
Central Montana Historical Association, Inc., MT, 5034
Central Nevada Historical Society/Museum, NV, 5260
Centralia Historical Society, Inc., MO, 4671
Centre County Historical Society, PA, 7452
Centre County Library and Historical Museum, PA, 7126
Centre d'etudes acadiennes, NB, 9596
Centre d'histoire de Montreal, QC, 9904
Centre de Recherche en Civilisation Canadienne-Francaise de l'Universite d'Ottawa, ON, 9780
Centre for Mennonite Brethren Studies, MB, 9561
Centre for Newfoundland Studies, NF, 9628
CFB Gagetown Military Museum, NB, 9599
Chadds Ford Historical Society, PA, 7164
Chaffee Historical Society, Inc., MO, 4672
Chalet of the Golden Fleece, WI, 9207
Champ Clark Honey Shuck Restoration, Inc., MO, 4652
Champaign County Historical Museum, IL, 2024
Champaign County Historical Society, OH, 6801
Champlain Valley Heritage Network, NY, 5881
Chancellor Robert R. Livingston Masonic Library, NY, 5998
Chapel Hill Preservation Society, NC, 6241
Chapel of Rest Preservation Society, NC, 6348
Chapin Community Historical Society, IL, 2028
Chapman Historical Museum, NY, 5919
Chariton County Historical Society, MO, 4932
Charles Carroll House of Annapolis, MD, 3548
Charles City County Center for Local History, VA, 8509
Charles City County Historical Society, VA, 8510
Charles Mix County Historical Restoration Society, SD, 7784
Charles River Museum of Industry, MA, 4018

Charles Towne Landing State Historic Site, SC, 7623

Charleston Library Society, SC, 7624

Charleston Museum, SC, 7625

Charlotte County Museum, NB, 9609

Charlotte Hawkins Brown Historic Site, NC, 6430

Charlotte Historic District Commission, NC, 6246

Charlotte Historical Society, ME, 3422

Charlotte Museum of History and Hezekina Alexander Homesite, NC, 6247

Charlton County Historical Society, GA, 1688

Charlton Historical Society, NY, 5860

Chase and District Museum and Archives Society, BC, 9439

Chase County Historical Society, KS, 2905

Chassell Historical Organization, Inc., MI, 4086

Chataugua County Historical Society/ McClurg Museum, NY, 6190

Chatham County Historical Association, Inc., NC, 6391

Chatham Historical Society, NH, 5284

Chatham Historical Society, NJ, 5465

Chatham Historical Society, OH, 6701

Chatham Historical Society/Atwood House Musuem, MA, 3805

Chatham-Kent Historical Society, ON, 9771

Chatillon-DeMenil House Foundation, MO, 4908

Chattahoochee Valley Historical Society, AL, 128

Chattanooga African American Museum, TN, 7871

Chattanooga-Hamilton County Bicentennial Library, Local History and Genealogy Department, TN, 7872

Chattooga County Historical Society, GA, 1813

Cheekwood-Tennessee Botanical Garden & Museum of Art, TN, 7961

Chehalis Valley Historical Society, WA, 8886

Chelan County Historical Society Pioneer Village and Museum, WA, 8816

Chelan County Public Utility District, WA, 8985

Chelmsford Historical Society, MA, 3807

Chemung County Historical Society, Inc. (Chemung Valley History Museum), NY, 5899

Cheney Homestead, CT, 1206

Chenoa Historical Society, Inc., IL, 2031

Cheraw Lyceum, SC, 7645

Cherokee County Historical Museum, AL, 29

Cherokee County Historical Museum, NC, 6375

Cherokee County Kansas Genealogical/Historical Society, KS, 2903

Cherokee Heritage Center, OK, 6971

Cherokee Strip Land Rush Museum, KS, 2882

Cherokee Strip Museum Association, OK, 6833

Cherokee Strip Museum, OK, 6949

Cherry Valley Historical Association, NY, 5862

Cherryfield-Narraguagus Historical Society, ME, 3423

Chesaning Area Historical Society, MI, 4089

Chesapeake and Ohio Historical Society, Inc., VA, 8527

Chesapeake Beach Railway Museum, MD, 3612

Chesapeake Heritage Conservancy, Inc., MD, 3666

Chester County Historical Society, PA, 7500

Chester Historical Society, Inc., NJ, 5468

Chester Historical Society, VT, 8374

Chesterfield County Historic Preservation Commission, SC, 7646

Chesterfield Historical Society of Virginia, VA, 8522

Chesterfield Historical Society, Inc., NH, 5288

Chestnut Hill Historical Society, PA, 7361

Chevy Chase Historical Society, MD, 3615

Chewelah Historical Society, WA, 8822

Cheyenne County Historical Society, KS, 3038

Cheyenne Cultural Center, OK, 6868

Cheyenne Frontier Days Old West Museum, WY, 9294

Cheyenne Genealogical Society, WY, 9295

Chicago Genealogical Society, IL, 2041

Chicago Jewish Historical Society, IL, 2044

Chicago Lawn Historical Society, IL, 2045

Chicago Public Library Special Collections and Preservation Division, IL, 2046

Chichester Historical Society, NH, 5289

Chickasaw County Historical and Genealogical Society, MS, 4562

Chickasaw National Recreation Area, OK, 6968

Chico Museum Association, CA, 489

Chief Plenty Coups Museum and State Park, MT, 5048

Chief Vann House Historic Site, GA, 1655

Chieftains Museum, Inc., GA, 1761

Children's Museum of Elizabethtown, KY, 3121

Chillicothe Historical Society, IL, 2078

Chimney Point State Historic Site, VT, 8408

Chipley Historical Center, GA, 1755

Chippewa County Historical Society, MN, 4403

Chippewa County Historical Society, WI, 9097

Chippewa Nature Center, Inc., MI, 4190

Chippewa Valley Museum, WI, 9114

Chippewa-Rogues' Hollow Historical Society, OH, 6653

Chisago County Historical Society, MN, 4362

Chisholm Trail Historical Museum Society, OK, 6981

Chisholm Trail Museum/Governor Seay Mansion, OK, 6906

Choctaw County Historical Museum, AL, 26

Choctaw Nation Museum, OK, 6979

Christ Church Parish Preservation Society, SC, 7712

Christian C. Sanderson Museum, The, PA, 7165

Christian County Genealogical Society, IL, 2421

Christian County Historical Society Museum, IL, 2422

Christian County Museum and Historical Society, MO, 4849

Church of Jesus Christ of Latter-day Saints Historical Dept/Church Library-Archives, UT, 8331

Church of the Immaculate Conception, MO, 4931

Church-Waddel-Brumby House Museum, GA, 1589

Churchill County Museum & Archives, NV, 5239

CIGNA Museum and Art Collection, PA, 7362

Cimarron Heritage Center, Inc., OK, 6849

Cimarron Valley Railroad Museum, OK, 6872

Cincinnati Fire Museum, OH, 6608

Circle District Historical Society, Inc., AK, 147

Circus City Festival, Inc., IN, 2612

Citadel Archives and Museum, SC, 7626

City of Arkadelphia, AR, 298

City of Boston, Office of the City Clerk, Archives and Records Management Division, MA, 3885

City of Bowie Museums, MD, 3602

City of Greeley Museums, CO, 1073

City of Las Vegas Museum and Rough Riders Memorial Collection, NM, 5734

City of Omaha Planning Department, NE, 5183

City of Placentia Historical Committee, CA, 709

City of Rancho Cucamonga Historic Preservation Commission, CA, 723

City of Rocks Historical Association, ID, 1895

City of St. Augustine, Department of Historic Preservation and Heritage Tourism, FL, 1535

City of Toronto Archives, ON, 9833

City of Victoria Archives, BC, 9522

Civil War Preservation Trust, DC, 1334

Civil War Round Table of Western Missouri, MO, 4735

Clackamas County Historical Society, OR, 7054

Clallam County Historical Society, WA, 8903

Claremont Heritage, Inc., CA, 497

Claremont, New Hampshire Historical Society, Inc., The, NH, 5290

Clarendon County Archives, SC, 7703

Clarion County Historical Society, PA, 7168

Clark County Genealogical Library, IL, 2232

Clark County Historical Association, AR, 299

Clark County Historical Society, KS, 2883

Clark County Historical Society, MO, 4764

Clark County Historical Society, SD, 7764

Clark County Museum, NV, 5241

Clark Historical Library, MI, 4199

Clarke County Historical Association, VA, 8496

Clarke County Historical Society, AL, 58

Clarke House Museum, IL, 2047

Clarke Memorial Museum, CA, 530

Clarksville-Montgomery County Museum, TN, 7875

Clatsop County Historical Society, OR, 6990

Claude Moore Colonial Farm at Turkey Run, VA, 8624

Clawson Historical Museum, MI, 4091

Clay County 1890 Jail Museum and Heritage Center, TX, 8142

Clay County Archives and Historical Library, Inc., MO, 4806

Clay County Genealogical and Historical Society, AR, 402

Clay County Historical and Arts Council, NC, 6317

Clay County Historical Society, AL, 4

Clay County Historical Society, FL, 1439

Clay County Historical Society, IN, 2493

Clay County Historical Society, MN, 4405

Clay County Historical Society, NE, 5100

Clay County Historical Society, SD, 7854

Clay County Museum and Historical Society, MO, 4807

Clay County Museum, KS, 2897

Clay County Parks, Recreation, Historic Sites, MO, 4788

Clear Creek Canyon Historical Society of Chaffee County, Inc., CO, 1072

Clear Creek History Park, CO, 1066

Clear Creek Township Historical Society, OH, 6777

Clearwater County Historical Society, MN, 4486

Cleburne County Historical Society, AR, 347

Clermont Historical Society, IA, 2692

Clermont State Historic Site, NY, 5918

Cleveland County Historical Museum, NC, 6432

Cleveland Park Historical Society, DC, 1335

Clewiston Museum, FL, 1397

Climax Community Museum, Inc., SK, 9950

Clinch Mountain Cultural Center, VA, 8769

Clinton Birthplace Foundation, AR, 353

Clinton County Historical and Genealogy Society, Inc., MO, 4860

Clinton County Historical Society, IA, 2694

Clinton County Historical Society, Inc., IN, 2532

Clinton County Historical Society, NY, 6072

Clinton County Historical Society, OH, 6818

Clinton County Historical Society, PA, 7304

Cliveden of the National Trust, PA, 7364

Cloud County Historical Society, KS, 2904

Clover Bend Historic Preservation Association, AR, 357

Clovis Depot Model Train Museum, NM, 5717

CNMI Museum of History and Culture, MP, 6556

Coastal Discovery Museum on Hilton Head Island, SC, 7692

Coastal Georgia Historical Society, GA, 1775

Coastal Heritage Society, GA, 1783

Cobb County Historic Preservation Commission, GA, 1734

Cobb Memorial Archives, AL, 129

Cochise County Historical Society, AZ, 213

Cochranton Heritage Society, PA, 7171

Codington County Historical Society, SD, 7857

Coe Hall at Planting Fields, NY, 6060

Coffee Co/Manchester/Tullahoma Museum, Inc. Arrowheads/Aerospace Museum, TN, 7935

Coffey County Historical Society and Museum, The, KS, 2894

Coffeyville Historical Society/Dalton Defenders Museum, KS, 2900

Coffin House, SPNEA, MA, 3930

Coggeshall Farm Museum, RI, 7529

Coggon Community Historical Society, IA, 2696

Cogswell's Grant, SPNEA, MA, 3857

Cohasset Historical Society, MA, 3813

Cokesbury College Historical and Recreational Commission, SC, 7695

Cole Camp Historical Society, MO, 4680

Cole County Historical Society, MO, 4752

Cole Harbour Rural Heritage Society, NS, 9654

Colebrook Area Historical Society, NH, 5291

Coles County Genealogical Society, IL, 2029

Coles County Historical Society, IL, 2030

Colfax County Society of Art, History, and Archaeology, NM, 5749

College Football Hall of Fame, IN, 2633

College Park Aviation Museum, MD, 3619

Colleton Museum, SC, 7748

Collier County Museum, FL, 1494

Collingswood-Newton Colony Historical Society, NJ, 5472

Collinsville Historical Museum, IL, 2083

Colonel Allensworth State Historic Park, CA, 524

Colonel Davenport Historical Foundation, The, IL, 2345

Colonial Williamsburg Foundation, The, VA, 8773

Colorado Historical Society, CO, 1021

Colorado Springs Museum, CO, 1002

Colton Hall Museum, CA, 645

Columbia Archives, MD, 3624

Columbia County Cultural Museum, FL, 1468

Columbia County Historical Society, NY, 5962

Columbia County Historical Society, OR, 7090

Columbia County Historical Society, WI, 9091

Columbia County Lintner Spear Museum, WI, 9222

Columbia Gorge Discovery Center and Wasco County Historical Museum, OR, 7093

Columbia Gorge Interpretive Center, WA, 8958

Columbia State Historic Park, CA, 499

Columbian Theatre, Museum Art Center, KS, 3069

Columbus Chapel and Boal Mansion Museum, PA, 7137

Columbus Jewish Historical Society, OH, 6630

Colusa County Free Library, CA, 500

Colvin Run Mill Historic Site, VA, 8580

Comanche Crossing Historical Society, CO, 1128

Commerce Historical and Genealogy Society, MO, 4687

Commissariat House Provincial Historic Site, NF, 9629

Commission for Historical and Architectural Preservation, MD, 3570

Community Historical Museum of Mount Holly, VT, 8359

Community Historical Society, MI, 4095

Community Historical Society, The, IA, 2794

Community History Project of Shenandoah University, VA, 8782

Community Library Associaton-Regional History Dept, ID, 1934

Community Memorial Museum of Sutter, CA, 974

Company of Fifers and Drummers, The, CT, 1200

Compass Inn Museum, PA, 7290

Comstock Historic House, MN, 4406

Conception Bay Museum, NF, 9618

Concord Historical Society, CA, 501

Concord Historical Society, VT, 8419

Concord Museum, MA, 3814

Concord Township Historical Society, PA, 7174

Concordia Historical Institute, MO, 4909

Conde Charlotte Museum House, AL, 80

Conejo Valley Historical Society/Stagecoach Inn Museum Complex, CA, 661

Confederate Memorial Park at Winstead Hill, TN, 7865

Confederate Memorial Park, AL, 73

Confederate Memorial State Historic Site, MO, 4726

Conference of California Historical Societies, CA, 908

Congregation Mickve Israel, GA, 1784

Conneaut Valley Area Historical Society, PA, 7175

Connecticut Firemen's Historical Society, CT, 1207

Connecticut Historical Society, The, CT, 1191

Marland's Grand Home, OK, 6951
Marlborough Historical Society, Inc., NH, 5366
Marple Newtown Historical Society, PA, 7147
Marquette County Historical Society, Inc., MI, 4184
Marquette County Historical Society, WI, 9280
Marquette Historical Society, KS, 2994
Marquette Mission Park and Museum of Ojibwa Culture, MI, 4239
Marrett House, SPNEA, ME, 3521
Marsh Collection Society, ON, 9687
Marshall County Historical Museum, MS, 4561
Marshall County Historical Society, IL, 2192
Marshall County Historical Society, Inc., IN, 2617
Marshall County Historical Society, KS, 2997
Marshall County Historical Society, MN, 4510
Marshall County Historical Society, SD, 7758
Marshall County Historical Society, WV, 9041
Marshall Historical Society, MI, 4185
Martha's Vineyard Historical Society, MA, 3855
Martin County Convent, Inc., TX, 8251
Martin County Historical Society, MN, 4326
Martin County Historical Society, NC, 6465
Martins Ferry Area Historical Society, OH, 6715
Mary Aaron Memorial Museum, CA, 636
Maryhill Museum of Art, WA, 8856
Maryland and Pennsylvania Railroad Preservation Society, PA, 7516
Maryland Historical Society, MD, 3582
Maryland Room, C. Burr Artz Central Library, Frederick County Public Libraries, MD, 3651
Maryland State Archives, MD, 3555
Marysville Historical Commission, MI, 4186
Mascoutah Historical Society, IL, 2234
Mashantucket Pequot Museum and Research Center, CT, 1209
Mason Area Historical Society, MI, 4187
Mason Area Historical Society, WI, 9072
Mason County Historical Society Museum, WA, 8944
Mason County Historical Society/White Pine Village, MI, 4176
Mason County Museum, KY, 3203
Mason County Museum, TX, 8183
Mason Historical Society Inc., OH, 6716
Massac County Historical Society, IL, 2243
Massachusetts Archives and Commonwealth Museum, MA, 3778
Massachusetts Historical Society, MA, 3779
Massachusetts Society of Mayflower Descendants, MA, 3780
Massillon Museum, OH, 6717
Matagorda County Museum, TX, 8032
Mather Homestead Museum, Library and Memorial Park, NY, 6184
Mathias Ham House Historic Site, IA, 2729
Matsqui Sumas Abbotsford Museum Society, BC, 9428
Mattapoisett Museum and Carriage House, MA, 3913
Mattatuck Historical Society, Inc., CT, 1273
Matthew Edel Blacksmith Shop/Historical Society of Marshall County, IA, 2758
Maturango Museum of the Indian Wells Valley, CA, 735
Mauch Chunk Historical Society of Carbon County, PA, 7273
Maui Okinawa Kenjin Kai, HI, 1891
May Museum and Farmville Heritage Center, NC, 6285
Mayfield Historical Society, NY, 5981
Maynard Pioneer Museum and Park, AR, 391
Mayo House Interpretive Museum, MN, 4360
Mayville Historical Society, Inc., WI, 9179
Mazomanie Historical Society, WI, 9181
McCarter Museum of Tonkawa History, OK, 6974
McClain County Oklahoma Historical and Genealogical Society and Museum, OK, 6955
McCleary Historical Society, WA, 8882
McConaghy House, CA, 565
McCook House Civil War Museum/Carroll County Historical Society, OH, 6598
McCord and District Museum, SK, 9966
McCord Museum of Canadian History, QC, 9908

McCoy Valley Museum, WA, 8900
McCreary County Historical and Genealogical Society, Inc., KY, 3251
McCurtain County Historical Society, OK, 6899
McDade Historical Society, TX, 8184
McDowell House and Apothecary Shop, KY, 3116
McFaddin-Ward House, TX, 8035
McFarland House, ON, 9764
McFarland State Historic Park, AZ, 220
McGill University Archives, QC, 9909
McHenry County Historical Society, IL, 2431
McHenry County Illinois Genealogical Society, IL, 2087
McHenry Mansion, CA, 642
McIlhenny Company and Avery Island, Inc., Archives, The, LA, 3262
McKeesport Heritage Center, PA, 7309
McLarty Treasure Museum, FL, 1571
McLean County Museum of History, IL, 2005
McMinn County Living Heritage Museum, TN, 7863
MCP Hahnemann University Archives and Special Collections, PA, 7390
McPherson Museum, KS, 2999
Meadow Brook Hall, MI, 4226
Meadowlands Museum, NJ, 5622
Mechanicsburg Museum Association, PA, 7312
Medicine Hat Museum and Art Gallery, AB, 9408
Medina County Historical Society, OH, 6722
Meeker County Historical Society, MN, 4365
Meeteetse Museums and Archives, Inc., WY, 9331
Mellette Memorial Association, SD, 7859
Melrose Area Historical Society, MN, 4384
Memorial Foundation of the Germanna Colonies in Virginia, Inc., VA, 8531
Memory Lane Museum at Seattle Goodwill, WA, 8928
Memphis Pink Palace Museum, TN, 7947
Menasha Historical Society, WI, 9183
Menaul Historical Library of the Southwest, NM, 5694
Menczer Museum of Medicine and Dentistry, CT, 1195
Mendocino Area Parks Association, CA, 638
Mendocino County Museum, CA, 965
Mendota Museum and Historical Society, IL, 2238
Menno Simons Historical Library, VA, 8588
Mennonite Archives of Ontario, ON, 9850
Mennonite Heritage Museum, KS, 2945
Mennonite Historians of Eastern Pennsylvania, PA, 7243
Mennonite Library and Archives, KS, 3011
Menomonee Falls Historical Society/Old Falls Village Museum, WI, 9184
Mequon Historical Society, Inc., WI, 9187
Mercer County Historical Museum, OH, 6599
Mercer County Historical Society, IL, 1975
Mercer County Historical Society, PA, 7314
Merchant's House Museum, NY, 6015
Merchantville Historical Society, NJ, 5543
Meridian Historical Village, MI, 4210
Meridian Restorations Foundation, Inc., MS, 4582
Merrill Historical Society, Inc./Brickyard School Museum, WI, 9188
Merwin House, SPNEA, MA, 3999
Mesa Historical Museum, AZ, 234
Mesa Southwest Museum, AZ, 235
Metcalfe County Historical Society, KY, 3119
Metropolitan Historical Commission of Nashville and Davidson County, TN, 7968
Miami County Museum and Historical Society, IN, 2614
Miami Memorabilia Collector's Club, The, FL, 1487
Miamisburg Historical Society, The, OH, 6724
Michie Tavern ca. 1784, VA, 8517
Michigan City Historical Society, IN, 2590
Michigan Historical Center, MI, 4169
Michigan Maritime Museum, MI, 4245
Michigan Museum of Surveying, MI, 4170
Michigan Museums Association, MI, 4171
Michigan State Trust for Railway Preservation, Inc., MI, 4214
Michigan State University Archives and Historical Collections, MI, 4118
Michigan State University Museum, MI, 4119

Michigan Transit Museum, MI, 4198
Michigan Women's Historical Center and Hall of Fame, MI, 4172
Mid-America All Indian Center, Inc., KS, 3079
Mid-Atlantic Center for the Arts, NJ, 5461
Middle Border Museum of American Indian and Pioneer Life, SD, 7812
Middle Georgia Historical Society, Inc., GA, 1730
Middlebury Historical Society, NY, 6194
Middlefield Historical Society, OH, 6725
Middlesborough-Bell County Public Library, KY, 3205
Middlesex County Historical Society, CT, 1211
Middleton Area Historical Society, WI, 9189
Middleton Place, SC, 7634
Middletown Area Historical Society, PA, 7316
Middletown Springs Historical Society Inc., VT, 8405
Midgley Museum, OK, 6881
Midland County Historical Museum, TX, 8187
Midland Pioneer Museum Association, SD, 7806
Midlothian Historical Society, IL, 2245
Midvale Historical Society, UT, 8311
Midway Village and Museum Center, IL, 2355
Midwest Jesuit Archives, MO, 4917
Midwest Old Settlers and Threshers Association, IA, 2803
Milan Historical Museum, OH, 6727
Mildred M. Mahoney Doll's House Gallery, ON, 9715
Miles B. Carpenter Museum Complex, VA, 8766
Milford Historical Society and Museum, CT, 1231
Milford Historical Society and Museum, MI, 4192
Millbrook Society/Amy B. Yerkes Museum, The, PA, 7255
Millburn-Short Hills Historical Society, NJ, 5627
Mille Lacs County Historical Sociey and Depot Museum, MN, 4435
Miller County Historical Society, MO, 4951
Millet and District Museum and Exhibit Room, The, AB, 9409
Mills County Historical Society, IA, 2747
Milton Historical Society, MA, 3917
Milton Historical Society, WI, 9190
Milton-Freewater Area Historical Society/Frazier Farmstead Museum, OR, 7039
Milwaukee County Historical Society, WI, 9194
Milwaukee Public Museum, Inc., WI, 9195
Milwaukie Historical Society and Museum Inc., OR, 7040
Mine Au Breton Historical Society, Inc., MO, 4865
Minerva Area Historical Society, OH, 6728
Minidoka County Historical Society, ID, 1961
Mining Museum and Rollo Jamison Museum, WI, 9226
Minisink Valley Historical Society, NY, 6076
Minneapolis Heritage Preservation Commission, MN, 4391
Minnehaha County Historical Society, SD, 7836
Minnesota Air National Guard Historical Foundation, Inc., MN, 4466
Minnesota Archaeological Society, MN, 4467
Minnesota Chapter, Society of Architectural Historians, MN, 4394
Minnesota Historical Society Library, MN, 4469
Minnesota Historical Society, MN, 4468
Minnesota's Machinery Museum, MN, 4345
Minnetrista Cultural Center and Oakhurst Gardens, IN, 2596
Miracle of America Museum, Inc., MT, 5045
Missiles and More Museum Missiles and More Museum, NC, 6446
Mission Basilica San Diego de Alcal, CA, 781
Mission Houses Museum, HI, 1868
Mission Mill Museum/Mission Mill Musuem Association, OR, 7083
Mission Museum, BC, 9468
Mission San Francisco de Asis (Mission Dolores), CA, 808
Mission San Juan Capistrano, CA, 833
Mission San Miguel Arcangel, CA, 843

Missisquoi Historical Society/Missisquoi Museum, QC, 9934
Mississippi Baptist Historical Commission, MS, 4538
Mississippi County Historical and Genealogical Society, AR, 399
Mississippi County Historical Society, MO, 4673
Mississippi Cultural Crossroads, MS, 4602
Mississippi Department of Archives and History, MS, 4568
Mississippi Governor's Mansion, MS, 4569
Mississippi Historical Society, MS, 4570
Mississippi Valley Textile Museum, ON, 9684
Missouri Department of Natural Resources, Division of State Parks, MO, 4755
Missouri Forest Heritage Center, Inc., MO, 4756
Missouri Historical Society, MO, 4918
Missouri Masion Preservation, Inc., MO, 4757
Missouri River Frontier Museum, MO, 4852
Missouri River Outfitters, MO, 4805
Missouri State Archives, MO, 4758
Missouri State Museum, MO, 4759
Mitchell Area Historical Society, SD, 7813
Mitchell County Historical Society, IA, 2814
Mitchell County Historical Society, KS, 2892
Mitchell Museum, Floyd & Margaret, TN, 7999
Moark Regional Railroad Museum, MO, 4863
Mobile Municipal Archives, AL, 85
Mockbeggar Plantation Provincial Historic Site, NF, 9612
Modoc County Historical Society, CA, 436
Moffatt-Ladd House and Garden, NH, 5402
Mohave Museum of History and Arts, AZ, 231
Mohawk Valley Heritage Corridor, NY, 5851
Mojave River Valley Museum, CA, 454
Molly Brown House Museum, CO, 1029
Molson Historical Association, Molson Schoolhouse Museum, WA, 8898
Moncton Museum, NB, 9597
Mondak Heritage Center, MT, 5057
Monhegan Historical and Cultural Museum Association, Inc., ME, 3463
Moniteau County Historical Society, MO, 4659
Monmouth County Historical Association, NJ, 5490
Monmouth Museum, ME, 3464
Monona Historical Society, IA, 2796
Monroe County Heritage Museums, AL, 90
Monroe County Historical Association, PA, 7460
Monroe County Historical Museum, MI, 4193
Monroe County Historical Society, IL, 2443
Monroe County Historical Society, IN, 2485
Monroe County Historical Society, Inc., WI, 9246
Monroe County Historical Society, WV, 9057
Monroe County Public Library, Indiana Room, IN, 2486
Monson Historical Society, ME, 3441
Monson Museum, ME, 3465
Mont Vernon Historical Society, NH, 5373
Montana Heritage Preservation and Development Comission, MT, 5024
Montana Historical Society, MT, 5025
Montclair Historical Society, NJ, 5546
Monterey County Agricultural and Rural Life Museum, CA, 581
Monterey County Historical Society, Inc., CA, 772
Monterey State Historic Park, CA, 647
Montgomery County Department of History and Archives, NY, 5906
Montgomery County Historic Preservation Commission, MD, 3717
Montgomery County Historical Society, IA, 2828
Montgomery County Historical Society, Inc., The, MD, 3700
Montgomery County Historical Society, The, OH, 6645
Montgomery House Museum/Montour County Historical Society, PA, 7181
Montgomery Place Historic Estate, NY, 5798
Montpelier (James Madison's), VA, 8632
Montpelier Heritage Group Inc., VT, 8411
Montpelier Historical Society, Inc., IN, 2592
Montrose Historical Telephone Pioneer Museum, MI, 4196

1006
Western New Mexico University Museum, NM, 5765
Western New York Documentary Heritage Program, NY, 5844
Western North Carolina Historical Association, NC, 6215
Western Reserve Historical Society, OH, 6628
Western Rhode Island Civic Historical Society/Paine House, RI, 7535
Western Trail Historical Society and Museum of the Western Prairie, OK, 6832
Westerville Historical Society, OH, 6815
Westerville Public Library, Local History Resource Center, OH, 6816
Westfield Heritage Village, ON, 9801
Westfield Historical Society, NJ, 5673
Westminster Area Historical Society, CO, 1133
Westminster Historical Society, MA, 4031
Westmont Historical Society, IL, 2455
Westmoreland County Historical Society, PA, 7239
Westmorland Historical Society, NB, 9584
Weston County Museum District, Anna Miller Museum and Upton's Red-Onion Museum, WY, 9334
Weston Historical Museum, Inc., MO, 4969
Weston Historical Society, MA, 4033
Weston Historical Society, VT, 8464
Westport Community Association, The, ME, 3535
Westport Historical Society, CT, 1277
Westport Historical Society, MO, 4787
Westport Maritime Museum, WA, 8987
Westville Historic Handicrafts, Inc., GA, 1726
Wethersfield Historical Society, CT, 1281
Wexford County Historical Society, MI, 4079
Weymouth Historical Society, MA, 4035
Wharton County Museum Association, TX, 8279
Whatcom County Historical Society, WA, 8806
Wheat Ridge Historical Society, CO, 1134
Wheaton Historic Preservation Council/Wheaton History Center, IL, 2461
Wheeler Historic Farm Museum, UT, 8342
Whistler House Museum of Art, MA, 3905
Whitchurch-Stouffville Museum, ON, 9718
White Bear Lake Area Historical Society, MN, 4519
White County Historical Society, AR, 418
White County Historical Society, IL, 2019
White Hall Museum, AR, 429
White Hall State Historic Site, KY, 3233
White River Historical Society, CO, 1102
White River Valley Historical Society, MO, 4706
White River Valley Museum, WA, 8799
White Settlement Historical Museum, TX, 8280
White-Pool House Museum, TX, 8200
Whitehead Memorial Museum, TX, 8082
Whitehern Historic House and Garden, ON, 9723
Whitestone Hill Battlefield State Historic Site, ND, 6530
Whitewater Canal State Historic Site, IN, 2588
Whitfield-Murray Historical Society, GA, 1672
Whitingham Historical Society, VT, 8397
Whitman County Historical Society, WA, 8824
Whittier Historical Society and Museum, CA, 963
Whoop-N-Holler (Ranch) Museum, WA, 8807
Wichita Public Library, KS, 3081
Wichita-Sedgwick County Historical Museum, KS, 3082
Wicomico Historical Society, Inc., MD, 3709
Wiggins Cabin and The Old Company House, AR, 315
Wilbur Chocolate Candy Americana Museum and Store, PA, 7303
Wild Rose Historical Society, WI, 9281
Wilder Memorial Museum, Inc., IA, 2845
Wilder Ranch State Park, CA, 875
Wilderness Road State Park, VA, 8544
Wilderstein Preservation Inc., NY, 6089
Wildwood Historical Society, Inc./George F. Boyer Historical Museum, NJ, 5679
Wilkin County Historical Society, MN, 4283
Will County Historical Society, IL, 2219

Will Reed Log Home Museum, AR, 297
Willard Library, IN, 2522
William A. Farnsworth Homestead, ME, 3502
William Berman Jewish Heritage Museum, The, GA, 1628
William Bull and Sarah Wells Stone House Association, NY, 5850
William Carl Garner Visitor Center, AR, 349
William Clark Market House Museum, KY, 3224
William Cook House, AL, 100
William Hammond Mathers Museum, IN, 2489
William Henry Harrison Museum, IN, 2648
William Jennings Bryan Birthplace Museum, IL, 2372
William Otis Sawtelle Collections and Research Center, ME, 3407
William S. Hart Museum, CA, 662
William Trent House Museum, NJ, 5661
William Whitley House State Historic Site, KY, 3242
Williams College Archives and Special Collections, MA, 4037
Williamstown Historical Society, VT, 8465
Willie Hodge Booth Museum, VA, 8504
Williston Historical Society, VT, 8466
Willoughby Township Historical Museum, ON, 9765
Willoughby-Baylor House and Moses Myers House, VA, 8656
Willow Bunch Museum and Historical Society, SK, 9997
Willow Creek-China Flat Museum, CA, 966
Wilmette Historical Society and Museum, IL, 2464
Wilmington Area Historical Society, IL, 2465
Wilmington Railroad Museum Foundation, Inc., NC, 6475
Wilson County Historical Museum, KS, 2940
Wilson Czech Opera House Corporation, Foundation, KS, 3083
Wilson Historic Properties Commission, NC, 6477
Wilton Historical Society/Wilton Farm & Home Museum, ME, 3536
Wilton House Museum, VA, 8710
Wimbledon Community Museum, ND, 6554
Winchester Center Historical Assoc., CT, 1284
Winchester Historical Society, The, CT, 1290
Winchester Museum, ID, 1972
Winchester-Frederick County Historical Society, VA, 8786
Wind River Historical Center, WY, 9307
Windermere District Historical Society/Windermere Valley Museum, BC, 9455
Windham Textile and History Museum, CT, 1282
Windsor Historical Society, The, CT, 1287
Windsor's Community Museum, ON, 9858
Wine Museum, The, BC, 9461
Winfield Historical Society, IA, 2870
Wing Luke Asian Museum, WA, 8942
Winnebago Area Museum, MN, 4523
Winnebago County Historical and Archaeological Society, WI, 9219
Winnebago Genealogical Society, WI, 9220
Winnetka Historical Society, IL, 2468
Winneetoon Board Walk Back in Time, NE, 5223
Winona County Historical Society, Inc., MN, 4525
Winslow Historical Society "Old Trails Museum", AZ, 290
Winston Historical Society, MO, 4971
Winter Park Historical Association, FL, 1579
Winterthur Museum, Garden and Library, DE, 1321
Wisconsin Maritime Museum, WI, 9173
Wisconsin Postal History Society, WI, 9140
Wisconsin State Historical Society, WI, 9168
Wise County Historical Society, VA, 8787
Wishard Nursing Museum, IN, 2571
Wissahickon Valley Historical Society, PA, 7135
Witte Museum, TX, 8243
Wolcott Mill Historic Center/Huron-Clinton Metropolitan Authority, MI, 4224
Wolf Creek Heritage Museum, TX, 8172
Wolf Creek Indian Village and Museum, VA, 8494

Wolf Point Area Historical Society, MT, 5070
Wolfeboro Historical Society/Clark House, NH, 5436
Women of the West Museum, CO, 1034
Wood County Historical and Preservation Society, WV, 9045
Wood County Historical Center and Museum, OH, 6586
Wood Dale Historical Society and Yesterday's Farm Museum, IL, 2469
Woodburn Plantation, SC, 7722
Woodbury Heritage Society, MN, 4526
Woodford County Heritage Committee, KY, 3247
Woodinville Historical Society, WA, 8990
Woodrow Wilson Birthplace Foundation, VA, 8733
Woodruff Fontaine House/Memphis Chapter, APTA, TN, 7950
Woods Hole Historical Museum, MA, 4039
Woodstock Historical Society, Inc., CT, 1293
Woodstock Historical Society, VT, 8469
Woodstock Museum, ON, 9859
Woodville Civic Club, Inc., MS, 4627
Woodville Museum Inc., OR, 7076
Woolaroc Museum, OK, 6845
Worcester County Historical Society, MD, 3723
Worcester Historical Museum, MA, 4044
Workman and Temple Family Homestead Museum, CA, 496
World Museum of Mining and Hell Roarin' Gulch, The, MT, 4988
Worthington Historical Society, OH, 6820
Wrather West Kentucky Museum, KY, 3211
Wren Historical Society, OH, 6821
Wren's Nest House Museum, The, GA, 1629
Wright Air Museum, MN, 4517
Wright Centennial Museum, WY, 9355
Wright County Historical Society, MN, 4286
Wyandotte Museum, MI, 4258
Wyatt Earp Birthplace Historic House Museum, IL, 2252
Wye Grist Mill and Museum, MD, 3743
Wynnewood Historical Society, OK, 6986
Wyoming Historical and Geological Society, PA, 7501
Wyoming Pioneer Memorial Museum, WY, 9305
Wyoming State Archives, WY, 9297
Wyoming State Museum, WY, 9298
XIT Museum, TX, 8069
Yakima Valley Museum and Historical Association, WA, 8994
Yakima Valley Rail & Steam Museum Association, WA, 8971
Yale and District Historical Society, BC, 9531
Yamhill County Historical Museum, OR, 7033
Yarmouth Historical Society-Museum of Yarmouth History, ME, 3542
Yavapai Heritage Foundation, AZ, 253
Ybor City Museum Society, FL, 1561
Yell County Historical and Genealogical Association, AR, 316
Yelm Historic Preservation Commision, WA, 8995
Yeshiva University Museum, NY, 6033
Yesteryear Village at the South Florida Fairgrounds, FL, 1577
Yolo County Historical Museum, CA, 968
York County Cultural and Heritage Commission Historical Center, SC, 7752
York County Culture and Heritage Commission, SC, 7729
York County Heritage Trust, PA, 7518
Yorktown Museum, NY, 6198
Young Historical Library, KS, 2987
Young-Sanders Center for Study of the War Between the States, LA, 3327
Youngtown Historical Society, Inc., The, AZ, 291
Yukon Archives, YT, 10004
Yulee Sugar Mill Ruins State Historic Site, FL, 1403
Yuma Crossing State Historic Park, AZ, 295
Yuma Territorial Prison State Historic Park, AZ, 296
Z.I. Hale Museum, Inc., TX, 8283
Zelienople Historical Society, Inc., PA, 7519
Zion Historical Society, IL, 2474
Zippo/Case Visitors Center, PA, 7142
Zoar Village State Memorial, OH, 6828
Zubiwing Cultural Society, MI, 4201

CONSERVATION OF ARTIFACTS

1877 Peterson Station Museum, MN, 4430
1890 House and Center for the Arts, The, NY, 5875
390th Memorial Museum Foundation Inc., AZ, 270
Abbeville County Historic Preservation Commission, SC, 7594
Abbeville Cultural and Historical Alliance, LA, 3256
Aberdeen Room Archives and Museum, MD, 3545
Acadian Heritage and Culture Foundation, Inc., LA, 3285
Ackley Heritage Center, IA, 2654
Ada Historical Society, MI, 4049
Adair Cabin/John Brown Museum State Historic Site, KS, 3020
Adair County Historical Society, IA, 2749
Adair County Historical Society, MO, 4791
Adams County Historical Society, CO, 989
Adams County Historical Society, NE, 5131
Adams County Historical Society, PA, 7226
Adams County Historical Society, WA, 8875
Adams Museum, SD, 7770
Addison Historical Society, IL, 1973
Adirondack Museum, The, NY, 5820
Adler Planetarium and Astronomy Museum, IL, 2036
Admiral Nimitz Museum and State Historical Center and National Museum of the Pacific War, TX, 8114
Aerospace Education Center, AR, 364
Affton Historical Society, MO, 4901
African American Heritage Foundation of Iowa, IA, 2682
African American Museum and Library at Oakland, CA, 667
Afro-American Historical Association of Fauquier County, VA, 8754
Afton Historical Society Museum, MN, 4263
Agassiz-Harrison Historical Society, BC, 9429
Agricultural Museum of New Brunswick, NB, 9610
Air Force Enlisted Heritage Hall, AL, 91
Ak-Chin Him-Dak EcoMuseum and Archives, AZ, 233
Akta Lakota Museum and Cultural Center, SD, 7762
Alabama Civil War Roundtable, AL, 11
Alabama Department of Archives and History, AL, 92
Alabama Historical Commission, AL, 94
Alabama Historical Commission-Old Cahawba, AL, 108
Alamance Battleground State Historic Site, NC, 6232
Albany Historical Society, Inc., KS, 3037
Albany Historical Society, WI, 9065
Alberton Historical Preservation Foundation, PE, 9860
Alcatraz Island, CA, 795
Alden Kindred of America, MA, 3844
Alexander Graham Bell National Historic Site, NS, 9651
Alexander Ramsey House, MN, 4451
Alf Engen Ski Museum Foundation, UT, 8328
Alfalfa County Historical Society, OK, 6859
Algonquin Culture and Heritage Centre, ON, 9717
Alice T. Miner Colonial Collection, NY, 5861
Allagash Historical Society, ME, 3398
Allamakee County Historical Society, IA, 2862
Allegan County Historical Society and Museum, MI, 4053
Allegheny-Kiski Valley Historical Society, PA, 7465
Allen Barkley Young Historians, Inc., KY, 3220
Allen County Historical and Genealogy Society, KY, 3236
Almanzo and Laura Ingalls Wilder Association, NY, 5975
Alnobak Nebesakiak, VT, 8379
Alpine Historical Society, AK, 192
Alpine Historical Society, CA, 434
Alsi Historical and Genealogical Society, OR, 7102
Alstead Historical Society, NH, 5264
Alta District Historical Society, CA, 517
Altadena Historical Society, CA, 435

CORPORATE HISTORY

DECORATIVE ARTS

DOLLS/TOYS

Corporation, OK, 6888
Geary County Historical Society Museum, KS, 2965
Geauga County Historical Society, OH, 6589
General Daniel Bissell House Museum, MO, 4912
Geneva Historical Society, IL, 2149
Geneva Historical Society, NY, 5915
Geneva Lake Area Museum, WI, 9164
Geographical Center Historical Society and Prairie Village Museum, ND, 6545
Georgian Museum, The, OH, 6697
Germantown Historical Society, PA, 7375
Gibson House Museum, The, ON, 9772
Giles County Historical Society, TN, 7987
Giles County Historical Society, VA, 8662
Gilroy Historical Museum, CA, 556
Gilsum Historical Society, NH, 5326
Glen Ullin Museum and Association, ND, 6519
Glenbow Museum (Glenbow-Alberta Institute), AB, 9364
Glengarry Pioneer Museum, ON, 9708
Glenn H. Curtiss Museum of Local History, NY, 5928
Gloucester County Historical Society, NJ, 5680
Glove Museum, The, NY, 6007
Gold Nugget Days, Inc., CA, 697
Goleta Valley Historical Society, CA, 560
Goodhue County Historical Society, MN, 4437
Gordon County Historical Society, GA, 1646
Gore Place, MA, 4019
Governor Jim Hogg City Park and Governor Hogg Shrine State Historic Park, TX, 8219
Grace Museum, The, TX, 8003
Grafton Historical Society, VT, 8390
Graham County Historical Society Museum, AZ, 254
Graham-Ginestra House, Inc., IL, 2352
Grand Blanc Heritage Association and Museum, MI, 4132
Grand Encampment Museum, Inc., WY, 9308
Grand Meadow Heritage Commission, Inc., IA, 2859
Grand River Historical Society and Museum, MO, 4676
Grand Traverse Heritage Center, MI, 4250
Grande Prairie Museum, AB, 9398
Grant County Historical Museum & Village, WA, 8841
Grant County Historical Society and Museum, NE, 5136
Grant County Historical Society, IN, 2586
Grant County Historical Society, MN, 4315
Grant County Historical Society, SD, 7807
Grant County Historical Society, WI, 9166
Grant County Museum, KS, 3066
Graue Mill and Museum, IL, 2283
Grayslake Municipal Historical Museum, IL, 2158
Greater Harvard Area, IL, 2165
Greater Shenandoah Historical Society, IA, 2833
Greater Southwest Historical Museum, OK, 6837
Greeley County Historical Society, KS, 3063
Greeley County Historical Society, NE, 5128
Greenbelt Museum, MD, 3661
Greenbrier Historical Society, Inc., WV, 9030
Greene County Historical Society, IN, 2608
Greene County Historical Society, MO, 4942
Greene County Historical Society, NY, 5878
Greene County Historical Society, OH, 6823
Greene County Historical Society, VA, 8731
Greensboro Historical Museum, NC, 6304
Greensboro Historical Society, VT, 8391
Greenwood Museum, The, SC, 7685
Gregg County Historical Museum, TX, 8173
Grevemberg House Museum, LA, 3288
Greybull Museum, WY, 9316
Grinnell Historical Museum, IA, 2752
Grosse Ile Historical Society, MI, 4144
Grosvenor House Museum Association, MI, 4162
Grout Museum of History and Science, IA, 2860
Grundy County Museum, MO, 4949
Gulfport Historical Society, FL, 1534
Gum Springs Historical Society, Inc., VA, 8581
Gunn Memorial Library Inc., CT, 1272

Gunnison County Pioneer and Historical Society, CO, 1075
Gwinnett History Museum, GA, 1720
Hackettstown Historical Society, NJ, 5495
Hallockville, Inc., NY, 6091
Hamilton County Historical Society, Plainsman Museum, NE, 5080
Hammers House, KY, 3206
Hammond-Harwood House Association, Inc., MD, 3551
Hampton Historical Society/Tuck Museum, NH, 5330
Hampton Museum and Visitors Center, SC, 7687
Hancock County Historical Society, IA, 2674
Hancock County Historical Society, IL, 2021
Hancock County Historical Society, IN, 2540
Hancock Historical Museum, OH, 6661
Hanover Area Historical Society, PA, 7240
Hardin County Historical Museums, Inc., OH, 6693
Harn Homestead and 1889ers Museum, OK, 6933
Harold Warp Pioneer Village, NE, 5164
Harrison County Historical Museum, TX, 8181
Harrison Historical Society, ME, 3446
Hart Cam Museum, MB, 9541
Harvard Historical Society, MA, 3878
Harwich Historical Society, MA, 3879
Haskell County Historical Society, KS, 3052
Hattiesburg Area Historical Society and Museum, MS, 4554
Hayden Heritage Center, CO, 1076
Haywood County Museum, TN, 7866
Haywood Hall Museum House and Gardens, NC, 6396
Healdsburg Museum and Historical Society, CA, 566
Heart of West Texas Museum, TX, 8051
Hebron Historical and Art Society, ND, 6525
Hedge House, MA, 3956
Heflin House Museum, MS, 4604
Helena Library and Museum Association, AR, 351
Helena Township Historical Society, MI, 4052
Hellenic Cultural Association, UT, 8333
Hellenic Museum and Cultural Center, IL, 2056
Hendrick Hudson Chapter NSDAR/Robert Jenkins House, NY, 5939
Hennepin History Museum, MN, 4387
Henniker Historical Society, NH, 5336
Henrico Historic Preservation/Museum Services, VA, 8688
Henry County Historical Society Museum, IN, 2603
Henry Sheldon Museum of Vermont History, VT, 8404
Heritage Farmstead Museum, TX, 8210
Heritage Foundation of the East Grand Forks Area, Inc., The, MN, 4313
Heritage Museum Association, Inc., FL, 1567
Heritage Museum of Montgomery County, TX, 8058
Heritage Museum, MT, 5035
Heritage Museum, The, OR, 7025
Heritage Plantation of Sandwich, MA, 3983
Heritage Society of Essex and Middle River, Inc., MD, 3640
Heritage Society, The, TX, 8146
Hermitage, The, NJ, 5511
Hermitage, The, TN, 7907
Herndon Home, The, GA, 1609
Hertzberg Circus Museum, TX, 8234
Hess Heritage Museum, ID, 1959
Hewitt Historical Society, MN, 4348
Hickory County Historical Society, MO, 4724
Hidalgo County Historical Museum, TX, 8088
Hiddenite Center, Inc., NC, 6321
High Plains Historical Society, NE, 5159
High Point Historical Society, Inc., NC, 6325
Highland County Historical Society, OH, 6684
Highland Park Historical Society, IL, 2169
Highland Park Historical Society, NJ, 5507
Highspire Historical Society, PA, 7263
Hillforest Historical Foundation, Inc., IN, 2481
Historic Buckingham, Inc., VA, 8505
Historic Cabarrus, Inc., NC, 6261
Historic Carson House, NC, 6385
Historic Charlton Park Village, Museum and Recreation Area, MI, 4149
Historic Cherry Hill, NY, 5785

Historic Cold Spring Village, NJ, 5460
Historic Columbia Foundation, SC, 7652
Historic Crab Orchard Museum and Pioneer Park, VA, 8753
Historic Hamilton, Inc., OH, 6680
Historic Morrisville Society, PA, 7325
Historic Northampton, MA, 3941
Historic Palmyra, Inc., NY, 6065
Historic Pensacola Preservation Board, FL, 1511
Historic Restoration Society of Annapolis County, NS, 9649
Historic Southwest Ohio, OH, 6614
Historic Springfield Foundation, Inc., MS, 4545
Historic Whitaker Home-Museum/Centerville Historical Society, UT, 8295
Historic Winslow House Association, MA, 3912
Historical and Genealogical Society of Indiana County, PA, PA, 7268
Historical Association of Greater Cape Girardeau, MO, 4664
Historical Center for Southwest New Mexico, Inc., NM, 5751
Historical County of Rockland County, The, NY, 5990
Historical Museum at Fort Missoula, MT, 5042
Historical Museum of Anthony, Inc., KS, 2880
Historical Museum of the D.R. Barker Library, NY, 5911
Historical Projects of Houston County, Inc., TX, 8064
Historical Society of Berks County, PA, 7431
Historical Society of Carroll County, MD, 3739
Historical Society of Cheboygan County, MI, 4087
Historical Society of Delaware, DE, 1316
Historical Society of Douglas County, NE, 5188
Historical Society of Glastonbury, CT, 1174
Historical Society of Greenfield, MA, 3872
Historical Society of Haddonfield, NJ, 5496
Historical Society of Idaho Springs, CO, 1080
Historical Society of Maries County, MO, 4956
Historical Society of Marshall County, IA, 2790
Historical Society of Martin County/ The Elliot Museum, FL, 1544
Historical Society of Monterey Park, CA, 649
Historical Society of Moorestown, NJ, 5547
Historical Society of Mount Pleasant, Ohio Inc., OH, 6730
Historical Society of Newburgh Bay, NY, 6035
Historical Society of Oak Park and River Forest, IL, 2290
Historical Society of Old Newbury/Cushing House Museum, MA, 3933
Historical Society of Old Yarmouth, MA, 4047
Historical Society of Porter County, IN, 2643
Historical Society of Quincy and Adams County, IL, 2334
Historical Society of Saginaw Co., Inc./Castle Museum of Saginaw Co. History, MI, 4234
Historical Society of Scotch Plains and Fanwood, NJ, 5624
Historical Society of Western Pennsylvania, PA, 7420
History Center, IA, 2684
History Museum and Historical Society of Western Virginia, VA, 8712
History Museum for Springfield-Green County, The, MO, 4943
History San Jose, CA, 824
Hitchcock County Historical Society, NE, 5213
Ho-Chunk Historical Society, NE, 5222
Homeplace-1850, The, KY, 3143
Homesteader Museum, WY, 9337
Homesteaders Museum, WY, 9353
Hood River County Historical Museum, OR, 7024
Hooker County Historical Society, NE, 5167
Hopewell Museum, KY, 3225
Horace Greeley Museum, KS, 3064
Horicon Historical Society, WI, 9143
Hornby School Restoration Society, PA, 7340
Houghton Lake Area Historical Society, MI, 4155
Houston County Historical Commission, TX, 8065

Houston County Historical Society, MN, 4287
Houston County Visitors Center/Museum, Inc., TX, 8066
Houston Library and Museum, AL, 5
Howard County Historical Society, IA, 2705
Howard County Historical Society, IN, 2576
Howard County Historical Society, MD, 3638
Howard County Historical Society, NE, 5206
Hubbard County Historical Society, MN, 4428
Hubbard Museum of the American West, The, NM, 5753
Hudson Bay and District Cultural Society/Hudson Bay Museum, SK, 9959
Humboldt & District Museum & Gallery, SK, 9960
Humboldt Historical Museum and Society, KS, 2959
Hunterdon Historical Museum, NJ, 5471
Huntingdon County Historical Society, PA, 7266
Huntington County Historical Society, Inc., IN, 2550
Huntington Historical Society, NY, 5942
Huntsville Historical Society/Museum and Log Cabin, MO, 4731
Hustiford Historical Society, WI, 9146
Idaho State Historical Museum, ID, 1911
Illinois State Museum, IL, 2399
Imperial Calcasieu Museum, Inc., LA, 3313
Independence Historical Museum, KS, 2961
Indian Grinding Rock State Historic Park Chaw'se Regional Indian Museum, CA, 708
Indiana State Museum and Historic Sites, IN, 2564
International Society Daughters of Utah Pioneers, UT, 8334
Inupiat Heritage Center, AK, 144
Iosco County Historical Society Museum, MI, 4120
Iowa County Historical Society, IA, 2788
Iowa County Historical Society, WI, 9109
Ipswich Historical Society, MA, 3886
Ischua Valley Historical Society, Inc., NY, 5910
Island County Historical Society & Museum, WA, 8827
Island Pond Historical Society, VT, 8396
Itasca County Historical Society, MN, 4344
J.W. Parmley Historical Home Museum, SD, 7795
Jackson County Historical Society, AR, 396
Jackson County Historical Society, IA, 2786
Jackson County Historical Society, IL, 2267
Jackson County Historical Society, KS, 2956
Jackson County Historical Society, MN, 4357
Jackson County Historical Society, WV, 9048
Jackson Homestead, Newton's Museum and Historical Society, MA, 3934
James K. Polk Memorial State Historic Site, NC, 6389
James White's Fort, TN, 7929
Jamesburg Historical Association, NJ, 5517
Japanese American National Museum, CA, 618
Japanese Cultural Center of Hawaii, HI, 1866
Jarrell Plantation State Historic Site, GA, 1710
Jasper County Historical Society, IA, 2808
Jasper County Historical Society, IN, 2621
Jasper County Historical Society, SC, 7727
Jeff Matthews Memorial Museum, VA, 8573
Jefferson County Historical Society and Museum, OR, 7036
Jefferson County Historical Society, IN, 2584
Jefferson County Historical Society, MO, 4691
Jefferson County Historical Society, Museum, & Research Library, WA, 8906
Jefferson Historical Society and Museum, TX, 8154
Jefferson Valley Museum, Inc., MT, 5068
Jensen Arctic Museum, OR, 7043
Jeremiah Lee Mansion, MA, 3909
Jersey County Historical Society, IL, 2181
Jesse Besser Museum, MI, 4054
Jessie Porters Heritage House and Robert Frost Cottage, Inc., FL, 1461
John Hauck House Museum of Historic Southwest Ohio, Inc., OH, 6616
John Marshall House Museum, VA, 8690
John Paul Jones House Museum, NH, 5401
Johnson County Museum of History, IN, 2533
Johnson County Museum, KS, 3046

Inc., SK, 9969
Morton Grove Historical Museum, IL, 2259
Moulton Historical Society, IA, 2800
Mount Airy Museum of Regional History, Inc., NC, 6372
Mount Desert Island Historical Society, ME, 3466
Mount Horeb Area Historical Society, WI, 9200
Mount Lebanon Historical Society, Stagecoach Trail Museum, LA, 3291
Mount Prospect Historical Society, IL, 2262
Mount Saint Joseph Ursuline Archives, KY, 3198
Mower County Historical Society, MN, 4273
Mullan Historical Society, ID, 1949
Multicultural Heritage Centre, AB, 9420
Mulvane Historical Society, KS, 3004
Murray County Historical Society and Museum, MN, 4488
Musee de la Ville de Lachine, QC, 9893
Musee Francois-Pilote, QC, 9889
Musee Regimentaire Les Fusiliers de Sherbrocke, QC, 9929
Musee Regional de Vaudreuil Soulanges, QC, 9942
Museum and Arts Center in the Sequim Dungeness Valley, WA, 8943
Museum Association of West Louisiana, LA, 3315
Museum Management Program, National Park Service, DC, 1347
Museum of American Heritage, CA, 695
Museum of American Presidents, VA, 8739
Museum of Anthropology, CA, 491
Museum of Anthropology, KY, 3152
Museum of Appalachia, TN, 7982
Museum of Automobile History, The, NY, 6155
Museum of Beverage Containers & Advertising, TN, 7951
Museum of Childhood of Wakefield, NH, 5428
Museum of Discovery: Arkansas Museum of Science and History, AR, 379
Museum of Early Trades and Crafts, NJ, 5535
Museum of East Alabama, AL, 102
Museum of History and Art, Ontario, CA, 681
Museum of History and Industry, WA, 8931
Museum of Pioneer History, OK, 6857
Museum of Primitive Art and Culture, RI, 7570
Museum of Science and Industry, FL, 1558
Museum of Science and Industry, IL, 2065
Museum of the Albemarle, NC, 6279
Museum of the City of Lake Worth, FL, 1472
Museum of the City of New York, NY, 6023
Museum of the Fur Trade, NE, 5096
Museum of the Plains, TX, 8208
Museum of the Rockies, MT, 4982
Museum of Weapons and Early American History, FL, 1523
Museum of West Louisiana, LA, 3316
Museum Village, NY, 5985
Museums at Prophetstown, Inc., The, IN, 2482
Museums at Stony Brook, The, NY, 6151
Muskego Historical Society, WI, 9201
Mystery Castle, AZ, 247
Nantucket Maria Mitchell Association, MA, 3926
Nash County Historical Association, Inc., NC, 6419
Nashua Historical Society, The, NH, 5376
Natchez Garden Club, MS, 4587
Natchitoches Historic Foundation, LA, 3333
Nathanael Greene City County Heritage Museum, TN, 7900
National Agricultural Center and Hall of Fame, The, KS, 2893
National Automotive and Truck Museum of the United States, Inc., IN, 2480
National City Public Library, Local History Room, CA, 657
National Military Heritage Society, Inc., MO, 4895
National Motorcycle Museum and Hall of Fame, SD, 7849
National Museum of American History, Smithsonian Institution, DC, 1355
National Museum of the American Indian, Smithsonian Institution, DC, 1357
National Route 66 Museum/Old Town Complex, OK, 6879

National Society of The Colonial Dames of America, The, DC, 1359
National Society of the Colonial Dames of Louisiana Shreveport Committee, LA, 3380
Native American Museum, IN, 2640
Nauvoo Historical Society, IL, 2271
Navarre-Bethlehem Township Historical Society, OH, 6733
Neosho Historical Society, WI, 9205
Neptune Township Historical Society, NJ, 5565
Nevada County Historical Society, CA, 659
Nevada Historical Society, NV, 5255
New Almaden Quicksilver County Park Association, CA, 828
New Bern Historical Society Foundation, Inc., NC, 6379
New Bremen Historic Association, OH, 6734
New Britain Youth Museum, CT, 1220
New Brunswick Historical Society, NB, 9602
New Canaan Historical Society, The, CT, 1222
New Castle Historical Society, NY, 5859
New Hampshire Aniquarian Society, NH, 5341
New Haven Colony Historical Society, CT, 1226
New Jersey Historical Society, NJ, 5575
New London Historical Society, NH, 5378
New Providence Historical Society, NJ, 5572
New York Historical Society, The, NY, 6027
Newark Museum Association, NJ, 5576
Newell Museum, SD, 7816
Newkirk Community Historical Society, OK, 6925
Newport Historical Society, RI, 7560
Newton County Historical Society, MO, 4836
Newtown Square Historical Preservation Society, PA, 7337
Newtown-Avoca Historical Society, IA, 2667
Nezperce Historical Society, ID, 1951
Niagara County Historical Society, Inc., NY, 5973
No Man's Land Historical Society, Inc., OK, 6890
Nodaway County Historical Society/Nodaway County Heritage Collection, MO, 4821
Nokomis and District Museum, SK, 9972
Norman #1 Oil Well Museum, KS, 3006
North Andover Historical Society, MA, 3936
North Berrien Historical Society Museum, MI, 4094
North Carolina Museum of History, NC, 6405
North Dakota Heritage Center, The, ND, 6498
North Haven Historical Society, ME, 3474
North Lake Tahoe Historical Society, CA, 917
North Louisiana Folk Life, Inc., DBA Martin Homeplace, LA, 3277
Northampton County Historical and Genealogical Society, PA, 7195
Northborough Historical Society, MA, 3942
Northeastern Nevada Museum, NV, 5235
Northeastern North Dakota Heritage Assocation, ND, 6504
Northern Indiana Center for History, IN, 2636
Northern Mariposa County History Center, CA, 504
Northwest Franklin County Historical Society and Museum, OH, 6683
Norwich Historical Society, VT, 8420
Norwood Historical Society, MA, 3944
Nowata County Historical Society, OK, 6930
Noyes House Museum, VT, 8415
Nunatta Sunakkutaangit Museum Society, NT, 9645
Nutley Historical Society and Museum, NJ, 5582
O'Fallon Historical Society, IL, 2280
O'Fallon Historical Society, MT, 4972
Oak Brook Historical Society, IL, 2284
Oakland Historical Society/Nishna Heritage Museum, IA, 2809
Oakland Museum Historical Society, Inc., OR, 7052
Oakland Museum of California, CA, 673
Oberlin Historical and Improvement Organization, OH, 6747
Obion Co. Museum, The, TN, 8000
Ocean City Life-Saving Station Museum, MD, 3684
Oelwein Area Historical Society, IA, 2811
Ogle County Historical Society, IL, 2300
Ohio Historical Society, OH, 6634

Okanogan County Historical Society, WA, 8896
Okefenokee Heritage Center, GA, 1836
Oklahoma Historical Society's Museum of the Cherokee Strip, OK, 6882
Oklahoma Historical Society, OK, 6939
Old Colony Historical Society, MA, 4010
Old Courthouse Museum, CA, 854
Old Courthouse Museum, Louisiana State Museum Branch, LA, 3334
Old Davidson State Park, AR, 408
Old Economy Village, PA, 7118
Old Jail Museum, IN, 2504
Old Jail Museum, TN, 8002
Old Mill Museum, NM, 5712
Old Petersburg-Addison Historical Society, PA, 7106
Old Rugged Cross Historical Society/Museum, MI, 4225
Old Salem, NC, 6488
Old Salley School Museum, SC, 7734
Old Saybrook Historical Society, CT, 1239
Old Shawnee Town, KS, 3048
Old Sturbridge Village, MA, 4007
Old Town Museum, CO, 992
Old Town Museum, ME, 3478
Old Trails Historical Society, MO, 4815
Old World Wisconsin, WI, 9112
Old York Historical Society, ME, 3543
Olds Historical Society / Mountain View Museum, AB, 9411
Olmsted County Historical Society, MN, 4442
Onalaska Area Historical Society, WI, 9213
Onondaga Historical Association, NY, 6156
Opelousas Museum and Interpretive Center, LA, 3365
Opp Historical Society Inc., AL, 103
Orange Historical Society, Inc., CT, 1240
Orcas Island Historical Society and Museum, WA, 8835
Oregon Historical Society, OR, 7067
Oregon Trail Regional Museum, OR, 6994
Oregon-Jerusalem Historical Society, OH, 6748
Orlando R. Smith Trust (Babcock-Smith House), RI, 7591
Orleans County Historical Society Inc., VT, 8368
Oroville Chinese Temple, CA, 686
Orwell Historical Society, VT, 8421
Osage County Historical Society, KS, 2988
Osage County Historical Society, MO, 4810
Osawatomie Museum Foundation, KS, 3021
Osceola County Historical Society, McCallum Museum/Brunson Heritage Home, IA, 2834
Ossining Historical Society Museum, NY, 6054
Osterville Historical Society, MA, 3948
Oswego County Historical Society, NY, 6056
Oswego Historical Society, Inc., KS, 3025
Oswegoland Heritage Association, IL, 2301
Our Lady of Mercy Church and Museum, NF, 9623
Ouray County Historical Society, CO, 1105
Overland Historical Society, MO, 4848
Overland Trail Museum, CO, 1127
Overland Trail Museum, TX, 8100
Owen County Historical Society, KY, 3217
Owensboro Area Museum of Science and History, KY, 3215
Oxford Museum Association, OH, 6749
Oyster Ponds Historical Society, NY, 6052
P.H. Sullivan Museum; Zionsville Munce Art Center, IN, 2653
Paine-Gillam-Scott Museum/Clinton County Historical Society, MI, 4240
Paipoonge Historical Museum, ON, 9820
Palace of the Governors Museum, NM, 5760
Palestine Preservation Projects Society, IL, 2303
Palmyra Historical Society, WI, 9221
Pardee Home Museum, CA, 674
Park Ridge Historical Society, IL, 2307
Parker House Ranching Museum, TX, 8199
Parker Museum of Clay County, IA, 2841
Parsonsfield-Porter Historical Society, ME, 3487
Pascack Historical Society, NJ, 5589
Peabody Historical Society, KS, 3029
Peace River Centennial Museum and Archives, AB, 9412
Peder Engelstad Pioneer Village, MN, 4499
Peel Mansion Museum and Historic Gardens,

AR, 307
Pella Historical Society, IA, 2821
Pend Oreille County Historical Society, WA, 8894
Pendleton County Historical Society, Inc., KY, 3126
Pendleton County Historical Society, Inc., WV, 9021
Pennsylvania Historical and Museum Commission, PA, 7251
Penticton 9 R.N. Atkinson Museum and Archives, BC, 9479
People for Silver Plume, Inc., CO, 1123
Peoria Historical Society, IL, 2315
Perry County Historical Society, IL, 2319
Perry County Historical Society, MO, 4854
Perry Historical Society of Lake County, OH, 6755
Person County Museum of History, NC, 6420
Petaluma Museum Association, CA, 706
Peteetneet Culture Arts Center and Museum, UT, 8319
Peter Yegen Jr. Yellowstone County Museum, MT, 4978
Petersham Historical Society, Inc., MA, 3950
Petrified Wood Park Museum, SD, 7800
Pettaquamscutt Historical Society Inc., RI, 7544
Phelps County Historical Society, MO, 4877
Phelps County Historical Society, NE, 5134
Philadelphia Society of Numismatics, PA, 7399
Philipse Manor Hall State Historic Site, NY, 6197
Phillips County Museum, AR, 352
Phillips County Museum, MT, 5038
Piatt County Museum, Inc., IL, 2255
Pickens County Museum of Art and History/Hagood Mill, SC, 7724
Pierre Wibaux Museum Complex, MT, 5069
Pilesgrove Woodstown Historical Society, NJ, 5681
Pilgrim Monument and Provincetown Museum, MA, 3964
Pinal County Historical Society Museum, AZ, 221
Pine Bluff/Jefferson County Historical Museum, AR, 405
Pioneer and Historical Society of Muskingum County, OH, 6827
Pioneer Florida Museum Association, Inc., FL, 1404
Piper City Community Historical Society, IL, 2320
Pittock Mansion, OR, 7071
Plainfield Historical Society, IL, 2321
Plainfield Historical Society, NH, 5395
Plainville Historical Society, Inc., CT, 1241
Plumas County Museum Association, Inc., CA, 721
Plymouth Antiquarian Society, MA, 3962
Plymouth County Historical Museum, IA, 2780
Plymouth Historical Museum, MI, 4216
Pocumtuck Valley Memorial Association, MA, 3835
Polish Cultural Institute, MN, 4524
Polk County Historical Association, Inc., NC, 6451
Polk County Historical Museum, FL, 1381
Polk County Historical Society, GA, 1654
Polk County Historical Society, IA, 2720
Polk County Historical Society, MN, 4299
Polk County Historical Society, OR, 7044
Polk County Historical Society, WI, 9075
Polson Flathead Historical Museum, MT, 5046
Pony Express Historical Association, Inc., MO, 4897
Pony Express Station, NE, 5124
Pope County Historical Foundation, Inc., AR, 415
Pope County Historical Society, IL, 2156
Pope County Historical Society, MN, 4339
Port Deposit Heritage Corporation, MD, 3690
Port Isabel Historical Museum, TX, 8215
Portage County Historical Society, OH, 6765
Portage County Historical Society, WI, 9250
Porter-Phelps Huntington Foundation, Inc., MA, 3876
Portsmouth Historical Society, RI, 7571
Potter Museum, NE, 5200
Powel House, The, PA, 7401

EDUCATION

Betts House Research Center, OH, 6606
Beverly Historical Society and Museum, MA, 3761
Biblical Resource Center and Museum, TN, 7878
Bicentennial Heritage Corporation of Casey County, Kentucky, KY, 3175
Bidwell Mansion State Historic Park, CA, 488
Big Horn County Historical Society and Museum, MT, 5019
Big Ivy Historical Society, Inc., NC, 6218
Big Sioux River Valley Historical Society, IA, 2759
Bigheart Historical Museum, OK, 6841
Billingsley House Museum, MD, 3734
Billy Bishop Heritage, ON, 9787
Billy Graham Center Archives, IL, 2457
Birmingham Civil Rights Institute, AL, 14
Birmingham Historical Society, AL, 15
Birmingham Public Library, Department of Archives and Manuscripts, AL, 16
Black American West Museum and Heritage Center, CO, 1018
Black Creek Pioneer Village, ON, 9828
Black Earth Historical Society, WI, 9083
Black Heritage Museum, Inc., FL, 1483
Black Hills Mining Museum, SD, 7798
Black History Museum and Cultural Center of Virginia, VA, 8684
Black River Historical Society, OH, 6703
Black River Historical Society, VT, 8400
Black World History Wax Museum, The, MO, 4905
Blackberry Farm's Pioneer Village, IL, 1984
Blacks in Alaska History Project, Inc., AK, 139
Blackwell Library, Salisbury State University, MD, 3705
Blaine County Museum, MT, 4991
Bledsoe's Lick Historical Association, TN, 7869
Bloomington Historical Society, MN, 4278
Blue Earth County Historical Society, MN, 4378
Blue Grass Trust for Historic Preservation, KY, 3160
Blue Ridge Parkway, NC, 6209
Blue Ridge Parkway, VA, 8755
Blue Springs Historical Society, MO, 4647
Bo-Cah Ama Council, CA, 540
Boalsburg Heritage Museum, PA, 7136
Bobby Davis Museum and Park, Hazard, Perry County, Kentucky, Inc., KY, 3149
Boca Raton Historical Society, FL, 1382
Bok Tower Gardens, FL, 1470
Bonanzaville, USA, ND, 6551
Bonnet House, FL, 1421
Bonneville Museum, ID, 1928
Booker T. Washington National Monument, VA, 8587
Boone County Historical Society, IA, 2671
Boone County Historical Society, IN, 2580
Boone County Historical Society, MO, 4681
Boone County Historical Society, NE, 5074
Boone-Duden Historical Society, MO, 4842
Boot Hill Museum, Inc., KS, 2911
Boothbay Region Historical Society, ME, 3414
Border Belt Historical Society, Inc., The, NC, 6284
Bosque Memorial Museum, TX, 8050
Boston Fire Museum, MA, 3766
Boston Public Library, MA, 3768
Bostonian Society, The, MA, 3770
Bothwell Lodge State Historic Site, MO, 4934
Bottineau County Historical Society, ND, 6500
Botto House American Labor Museum, Inc., NJ, 5498
Boulder Historical Society and Museum, CO, 985
Bourne Historical Society, Inc., MA, 3789
Bowen Heritage Circle, IL, 2449
Braddock's Field Historical Society, PA, 7141
Bradford Historical Society, VT, 8362
Brandywine Battlefield Park, PA, 7162
Brandywine Conservancy, Inc., PA, 7163
Branigan Cultural Center, NM, 5730
Brazoria County Historical Museum, TX, 8009
Brazos Valley Museum of Natural History, TX, 8043
Bremer County Historical Society, IA, 2863
Brennan Historic House and Medical Office Museum, KY, 3178

Brethren in Christ Historical Society, PA, 7236
Brevard Museum of History and Science, FL, 1398
Brice's Crossroads Visitor and Interpretive Center, MS, 4528
Brick Store Museum, The, ME, 3450
Bridgeton Antiquarian League, NJ, 5451
Bridgewater Historical Society, CT, 1142
Bridgewater Historical Society, NH, 5277
Bridgton Historical Society, ME, 3415
Brillion Historical Society, WI, 9086
Bristol Historical Society, NH, 5278
Bristol Historical Society, VT, 8366
British Columbia Farm Machinery and Agricultural Museum Association, BC, 9447
Broad River Genealogical Society, Inc., NC, 6431
Broken Arrow Historical Society, OK, 6852
Bronx County Historical Society, NY, 5827
Brookeville Academy, MD, 3603
Brookfield Museum and Historical Society, Inc., CT, 1145
Brookings County Historical Society, SD, 7856
Brooklyn Historical Society, MN, 4285
Brooklyn Historical Society, OH, 6588
Brooklyn Historical Society, The, NY, 5830
Brooklyn Museum of Art, NY, 5831
Brooklyn Public Library-Brooklyn Collection, NY, 5832
Brooksville Historical Society, ME, 3416
Brown County Historical Association, MO, 4947
Brown County Historical Society, IN, 2598
Brown County Historical Society, MN, 4417
Brown County Historical Society, NE, 5071
Brown County Historical Society, OH, 6669
Brown County Historical Society, WI, 9132
Brown Deer Historical Society, Inc./1884 Brown Deer School, WI, 9088
Brownhelm Historical Association, OH, 6804
Brownvale North Peace Agricultural Museum, AB, 9361
Brownville Historical Society, NE, 5091
Brownville/Brownville Junction Historical Society, ME, 3417
Bruce Groner Museum, BC, 9453
Bruce Museum of Arts and Science, CT, 1177
Brucemore, Inc., IA, 2683
Brunswick Railroad Museum, MD, 3604
Bryant Cottage State Historic Site, IL, 1996
Buena Vista County Historical Society, IA, 2844
Buena Vista Heritage, CO, 991
Buffalo and Erie County Historical Society, NY, 5838
Buffalo and Erie County Naval and Military Park, NY, 5839
Buffalo Historical Society, Inc., Old Stone Church and Rectory Heritage Center, ND, 6503
Buffalo Museum of Science, NY, 5840
Buffalo National River, AR, 346
Buffalo Trails Museum, ND, 6511
Bulloch Hall, GA, 1768
Burbank Historical Society, CA, 473
Burkett House Wabash County Museum, IL, 2260
Burpee Museum of Natural History, IL, 2350
Burritt on the Mountain-A Living Museum, AL, 64
Bush House Museum, OR, 7080
Bushy Run Battlefield, PA, 7254
Butler County Historical Society Museum, OH, 6679
Butler County Historical Society/Kansas Oil & Gas Museum, KS, 2919
Butler County Museum, IA, 2657
Butler-Turpin Historic House, KY, 3105
Butte-Silver Bow Public Archives, MT, 4986
Butterworth Center, IL, 2247
Bybee House and Agricultural Museum at Howell Territorial Park, OR, 7064
C.H. Nash Museum/Chucalissa, TN, 7939
Cache Valley Historical Society, UT, 8310
Caddo Cultural Center, OK, 6847
Caddo-Pine Island Oil Museum, LA, 3364
Caldwell County Historical Society Heritage Museum, NC, 6350
Caldwell Kiwanis Events/Museum, ID, 1915
Calhoun County Museum and Cultural Center, SC, 7733

California Council for the Humanities, CA, 796
California Folklore Society, CA, 599
California Heritage Council, CA, 798
California Heritage Museum, CA, 879
California Historical Society, CA, 799
California Living Museum, CA, 450
California Military Museum, CA, 750
California Palace of the Legion of Honor, CA, 800
California Science Center, CA, 613
California State Archives, CA, 751
Callahan's Auto Museum, NM, 5776
Calvert County Historical Society, Inc., MD, 3694
Calvert Marine Museum, MD, 3724
Calvin Coolidge Memorial Foundation, The, VT, 8426
Camas-Washougal Historical Society, WA, 8983
Cambridge Historical Society, The, MA, 3797
Camden County Historical Society & Museum, MO, 4811
Camden County Historical Society, NJ, 5473
Camp Walton Schoolhouse Museum, FL, 1433
Campbell County Historical Society, KY, 3086
Campbell County Historical Society, WY, 9311
Campbell County Log Cabin Museum, KY, 3087
Campbell County Rockpile Museum, WY, 9312
Campbell Historical Museum, CA, 480
Campus Martius Museum, OH, 6710
Canada Agriculture Museum, ON, 9776
Canadian Association of Professional Heritage Consultants, ON, 9829
Canadian Centre for Architecture (CCA), QC, 9902
Canadian Lesbian and Gay Archives, ON, 9830
Canadian Museum of Nature, ON, 9779
Canadian Rivers Historical Society, OK, 6889
Canal Corridor Association, IL, 2038
Canal Fulton Heritage Society, OH, 6593
Canal Society of New Jersey, NJ, 5550
Cannonball House, The, GA, 1727
Cannonsburgh Village, TN, 7954
Canton Historical Society, MI, 4080
Cape Ann Historical Association, MA, 3867
Cape Breton Miners' Museum, NS, 9656
Cape Coral Historical Society, FL, 1391
Cape Fear Museum, NC, 6469
Cape Girardeau County Genealogical Society, MO, 4748
Caramoor Center for Music and Arts, NY, 5960
Carbon County Historical Society, MT, 5049
Carbon County Historical Society, WY, 9338
Carillon Historical Park, Inc., OH, 6643
Carl Albert Congressional Research and Studies Center, OK, 6926
Carlisle Area Historical Society, OH, 6597
Carlton County Historical Society, MN, 4295
Carmel Clay Historical Society, IN, 2496
Carondelet Historical Society, MO, 4907
Carriage House Museum of the Queen Village Historical Society, NY, 5847
Carroll County Farm Museum, MD, 3738
Carroll County Historical & Genealogical Society, Inc., AR, 308
Carroll County Historical Society Museum, IN, 2509
Carroll County Historical Society, GA, 1650
Carroll County Historical Society, IA, 2679
Carroll County Historical Society, IL, 2261
Carroll County Historical Society, MO, 4665
Carroll County Historical Society, VA, 8592
Carroll County Wabash and Erie Canal, Inc., IN, 2510
Carthage Historic Preservation, Inc., MO, 4667
Carver County Historical Society, MN, 4506
Carver-Hill Memorial and Historical Society, Inc., FL, 1400
Cary Cottage, OH, 6607
Cascade County Historical Museum and Archives, MT, 5014
Cascade County Historical Society, MT, 5015
Cass County Historical and Genealogical Society, IL, 2439
Cass County Historical Society Museum, IA,

2753
Cass County Historical Society Museum, IN, 2582
Cass County Historical Society Museum, NE, 5199
Cassia County Historical Society, ID, 1914
Castle Museum, ID, 1932
Castle Rock Exhibit Hall Society, WA, 8817
Castle, The, OH, 6711
Catawba County Historical Association, NC, 6382
Cathedral of Saint John the Evangelist Museum, LA, 3307
Catonsville Historical Society, Inc., The, MD, 3609
Cavalier County Historical Society, ND, 6531
Cavendish Historical Society, VT, 8373
Cedar County Historical Society, IA, 2869
Cedar County Historical Society, MO, 4945
Cedar Falls Historic Village and Toy Museum, MO, 4661
Cedar Falls Historical Society, IA, 2680
Cedar Lake Historical Association, Inc., IN, 2497
Celery Flats Historical Area, MI, 4222
Center City Historic Preservation Commission, MN, 4290
Center for American Archaeology, IL, 2184
Center for American History, The University of Texas at Austin, TX, 8013
Center for Cultural Arts, AL, 55
Center for History of Foot Care and Footwear/Temple Univ School of Podiatric Medicine, PA, 7360
Center for Southwest Research, NM, 5691
Center for Wooden Boats, The, WA, 8921
Center of Southwest Studies, Fort Lewis College, CO, 1036
Centerville-Washington Township Historical Society, The, OH, 6600
Central Kansas Flywheel, Inc., KS, 3040
Central Missouri State University Archives/Museum, MO, 4958
Central Montana Historical Association, Inc., MT, 5034
Central Ohio Fire Museum & Learning Center, OH, 6629
Centre d'etudes acadiennes, NB, 9596
Centre d'interpretation de la cote de Beaupre, QC, 9876
Centre de Recherche en Civilisation Canadienne-Francaise de l'Universite d'Ottawa, ON, 9876
Centre for Mennonite Brethren Studies, MB, 9561
Centre for Newfoundland Studies, NF, 9628
CFB Gagetown Military Museum, NB, 9599
Chadds Ford Historical Society, PA, 7164
Chambers County Museum, Inc., AL, 72
Champ Clark Honey Shuck Restoration, Inc., MO, 4652
Champaign County Historical Society, OH, 6801
Chapel Hill Preservation Society, NC, 6241
Chapin Community Historical Society, IL, 2028
Chariton County Historical Society, MO, 4932
Charles Carroll House of Annapolis, MD, 3548
Charles City County Center for Local History, VA, 8509
Charles H. Wright Museum of African American History, MI, 4106
Charles River Museum of Industry, MA, 4018
Charles Sumner School Museum and Archives, DC, 1333
Charles Towne Landing State Historic Site, SC, 7623
Charleston Chapter of National Railway Historical Society, SC, 7711
Charlotte County Museum, NB, 9609
Charlotte Hawkins Brown Historic Site, NC, 6430
Charlotte Museum of History and Hezekina Alexander Homesite, NC, 6247
Chase and District Museum and Archives Society, BC, 9439
Chase County Historical Society, KS, 2905
Chassell Historical Organization, Inc., MI, 4086
Chatauqua County Historical Society/ McClurg Museum, NY, 6190
Chatham Historical Society, NH, 5284

ETHNIC/RELIGIOUS/CULTURAL

Coffee Co/Manchester/Tullahoma Museum, Inc. Arrowheads/Aerospace Museum, TN, 7935

Cokato Museum & Akerlund Photography Studio, MN, 4296

Cole County Historical Society, MO, 4752

Colleton Museum, SC, 7748

Collinsville Historical Museum, IL, 2083

Colonel Allensworth State Historic Park, CA, 524

Colonial Williamsburg Foundation, The, VA, 8773

Colorado Historical Society, CO, 1021

Colorado Springs Museum, CO, 1002

Columbia Archives, MD, 3624

Columbia County Historical Society, NY, 5962

Columbia County Historical Society, OR, 7090

Columbia County Historical Society, WI, 9091

Columbia Gorge Discovery Center and Wasco County Historical Museum, OR, 7093

Columbia Gorge Interpretive Center, WA, 8958

Columbia State Historic Park, CA, 499

Columbus Chapel and Boal Mansion Museum, PA, 7137

Columbus Jewish Historical Society, OH, 6630

Commission for Historical and Architectural Preservation, MD, 3570

Community History Project of Shenandoah University, VA, 8782

Community Library Associaton-Regional History Dept, ID, 1934

Concordia Historical Institute, MO, 4909

Conejo Valley Historical Society/Stagecoach Inn Museum Complex, CA, 661

Confederate Memorial State Historic Site, MO, 4726

Conference of Manitoba and Northwestern Ontario Archives, University of Winnipeg, MB, 9563

Congregation Mickve Israel, GA, 1784

Congregational Christian Historical Society, MA, 3771

Congregational Library, MA, 3772

Connecticut Historical Society, The, CT, 1191

Conner Prairie, IN, 2524

Contra Costa County Historical Society and History Center, CA, 714

Cook Inlet Historical Society, Inc., AK, 140

Cooleemee Historical Association, NC, 6262

Copper Valley Historical Society, AK, 150

Coquille Indian Tribe, OR, 7050

Core Sound Waterfowl Museum, NC, 6316

Corporation De Developpement Ce St Ferreol-Les-Neiges, QC, 9931

Cortland County Historical Society, Inc., NY, 5876

Cottonwood Ranch State Historic Site, KS, 3051

Council Valley Museum, ID, 1922

Country Music Foundation, TN, 7962

Courtenay and District Museum and Paleontology Centre, BC, 9440

Cranford Historical Society, NJ, 5477

Craven Hall Historical Society, PA, 7485

Crazy Horse Memorial, SD, 7765

Croatian Ethnic Institute, IL, 2048

Crystal Lake Falls Historical Association, VT, 8357

Crystal Rice Plantation, LA, 3280

Crystal River State Archaeological Site, FL, 1402

Culbertson Museum, MT, 4998

Cumberland County Historical Society, NJ, 5493

Cumberland County Museum, NS, 9647

Cumberland Museum and Archives, BC, 9443

Cuneo Museum and Gardens, IL, 2437

Cupa Cultural Center, CA, 691

Currency Museum/Bank of Canada, ON, 9781

Custer County Historical Society, NE, 5090

Custer County Historical Society, SD, 7767

Cuyuna Heritage Preservation Society, MN, 4300

Cynthiana-Harrison County Museum, KY, 3115

Czech Heritage Preservation Society, SD, 7850

Czechoslovak Heritage Museum, IL, 2281

Dakota County Historical Society, MN, 4455

Dakotaland Museum, SD, 7790

Dallas Historical Society, TX, 8073

Dancing Leaf Earth Lodge, NE, 5219

Daniel Boone Homestead, PA, 7134

Danish Immigrant Museum, The, IA, 2735

Danish Mill Corporation, IA, 2736

Darien Historical Society, Inc., The, CT, 1156

Darnall's Chance, MD, 3735

Daughters of the Republic of Texas Library at the Alamo, TX, 8233

Davidson County Historical Museum, NC, 6351

Davis Museum and Cultural Center, MA, 4026

Dawes County Historical Society, Inc., NE, 5095

Dawson County Historical Society, NE, 5141

Deadwood Historic Preservation Commission, SD, 7771

Death Valley National Park, CA, 515

Decatur County Historical Society, GA, 1636

Decatur County Historical Society, IN, 2542

DeCordova Museum and Sculpture Park, MA, 3898

DeForest Area Historical Society, WI, 9106

Del Norte County Historical Society, CA, 505

Delaware Agricultural Museum and Village, DE, 1296

Delaware County Historical Society, OK, 6902

Delaware County Historical Society, PA, 7146

Delhi Ontario Tobacco Museum and Heritage Center, ON, 9706

Delta Cultural Center, AR, 350

Delta State University Archives, MS, 4537

Deming Luna Mimbres Museum, NM, 5719

Denton County Courthouse-on-the-Square Museum, TX, 8084

Denton County Historical Museum, Inc., TX, 8085

Denver Museum of Miniatures, Dolls, and Toys, CO, 1023

Denver Museum of Natural History, CO, 1024

Department of Arkansas Heritage, AR, 374

Department of Economic Development, Tourism and Culture-Heritage Branch, NB, 9587

Depot Museum, Inc., AL, 53

Depot Museum, MN, 4489

Derry Historical Society and Museum, NH, 5304

Des Moines County Historical Society, IA, 2676

Desert Caballeros Western Museum, AZ, 283

Detroit Historical Museums, MI, 4108

Deutschheim State Historic Site, MO, 4723

Deweese-Rudd Museum Group, Inc., CO, 994

DeWitt County Historical Museum, The, TX, 8068

DeWitt Historical Society of Tompkins County, The, NY, 5951

Dexter Historical Society, Inc., ME, 3426

Dickson Mounds Museum, IL, 2203

Dillingham Historic Preservation Commission, AK, 154

Diocesan Museum, NH, 5361

Disciples of Christ Historical Society, TN, 7963

Discovery Museum, CT, 1141

Discovery Museum, The, CA, 757

District 69 Historical Society, BC, 9477

Doctor Sun Yat-Sen Classical Chinese Garden, BC, 9506

Doll House Museum, KS, 2995

Donegal Society, The, PA, 7327

Doon Heritage Crossroads, ON, 9735

Door County Historical Museum, WI, 9251

Dorsey Chapel, MD, 3658

Douglas County Historical Society and Museum, SD, 7754

Douglas County Historical Society, MN, 4267

Douglas County Historical Society, OR, 7077

Douglas County Historical Society, WI, 9254

Douglas County Historical Society/Watkins Community Museum of History, KS, 2975

Drayton Hall, National Trust for Historic Preservation, SC, 7627

Dresden Historical Society, ME, 3428

Dubois County Museum, Inc., IN, 2573

Dubuque County-Key City Genealogical Society, IA, 2728

Duck Lake Regional Interpretive Centre, SK, 9953

Duke University Rare Book, Manuscript and Special Collections Library, NC, 6271

Duncan Cottage Museum, AK, 179

Durham Western Heritage Museum, NE, 5184

Dutchess County Historical Society, NY, 6080

Dvoracek Memorial Library, NE, 5220

Dyersville Area Historical Society, IA, 2730

Eagle Bend Historical Society/Museum, MN, 4312

Eagle River Historical Society, WI, 9113

Early American Museum, IL, 2228

Early Settlers Association of the Western Reserve, The, OH, 6626

East Chicago Room of The East Chicago Public Library, The, IN, 2514

East Jersey Olde Towne Village, NJ, 5568

East River Genealogical Forum, SD, 7860

East Tennessee Historical Society, TN, 7926

East Texas Oil Museum at Kilgore College, TX, 8158

Eastern Regional Coal Archives, WV, 9008

Eastern Trails Museum, OK, 6980

Eastern Washington State Historical Society, WA, 8951

Eaton Florida History Room, Manatee County Central Library, FL, 1385

Ecomusee du fier Monde, QC, 9906

Edge of the Cedars State Park Museum, UT, 8288

Edgefield County Historical Society, SC, 7669

Edmond Historical Society, OK, 6878

Edwards County Historical Society, IL, 1974

Eiteljorg Museum of American Indians and Western Art, IN, 2555

Eklutna Historical Park, Inc., AK, 156

El Centro de la Raza, WA, 8923

El Morro National Monument, NM, 5748

El Pueblo Museum, CO, 1110

El Rancho de las Golondrinas, NM, 5755

Elbert County Historical Society and Museum, CO, 1082

Elbow Museum and Historical Society, SK, 9954

Elegba Folklore Society, Inc., VA, 8686

Elgin Public Museum, IL, 2120

Elisabet Ney Museum, TX, 8014

Elkton Community Museum, SD, 7776

Ellis County Historical Society, KS, 2949

Ellis County Historical Society, OK, 6838

Ellsinore Pioneer Museum, MO, 4698

Elmhurst Historical Museum, IL, 2124

Elna M. Smith Foundation, AR, 320

Elphinstone Pioneer Museum, BC, 9452

Elroy Area Historical Society, Inc., WI, 9120

Elwyn B Robinson Department of Special Collections, University of North Dakota, ND, 6522

Ely Field Office, Bureau of Land Management, NV, 5237

Emmet County Historical Society, IA, 2739

EMOBA, The Museum of Black Arkansans and Performing Arts, AR, 375

Emory and Henry College, VA, 8542

Empire Mine State Historic Park, CA, 562

Enchanted World Doll Museum, SD, 7810

Enfield Shaker Museum, NH, 5312

Ephraim Foundation, Inc., The, WI, 9121

Erie County Historical Society, OH, 6772

Erie County Historical Society, PA, 7206

Ermatinger/Clergue Heritage Site, ON, 9802

Esquimalt Municipal Archives, BC, 9524

Essex County Historical Society, VA, 8750

Essex County Museum, Inc., VA, 8751

Ethnic Heritage Museum, IL, 2351

Etowah Foundation's History Center, The, GA, 1652

Eubie Blake National Jazz Institute and Cultural Center, The, MD, 3574

Eureka County Sentinel Museum, NV, 5238

Eureka Springs Historical Museum, AR, 321

Evangelical and Reformed Historical Society of the UCC, PA, 7280

Evangelical Lutheran Dept. of History and Archives, MN, 4379

Evansville Historical Foundation, MN, 4321

Fairbanks Community Museum, AK, 159

Fairbanks Museum and Planetarium, VT, 8446

Fairfax County Public Library, Virginia Room, VA, 8545

Fairfield County Historical Museum, SC, 7749

Family Research Society of Northeastern North Carolina, NC, 6278

Farmington Museum, NM, 5722

Father Marquette National Memorial and Museum, MI, 4238

Father Pandosy Mission, BC, 9459

Faust County Park/Faust Historical Village/Thornhill, MO, 4674

Favell Museum of Western Art and Indian Artifacts, OR, 7031

Fayette Heritage Museum and Archives, TX, 8164

Feinberg Library Special Collections, Plattsburgh State University, NY, 6073

Fellspoint Museum and Cultural Programs, Inc., MD, 3576

Fenton History Center—Museum and Library, NY, 5955

Field Museum, The, IL, 2050

Filipino American Historical Society of Chicago, IL, 2051

Filipino American National History Society, Santa Clara Valley Chapter, CA, 823

Fillmore Historical Museum, CA, 536

Filson Club, The, KY, 3182

Finland Minnesota Historical Society, MN, 4334

Finney County Historical Society, KS, 2943

Finnish-American Historical Society of the West, OR, 7065

First Church of Christ in Hartford, CT, 1192

First Church of Christ, Scientist, Church History Department, The, MA, 3774

First Missouri State Capitol State Historic Site, MO, 4880

First Parish Congregational Church, NH, 5310

Fishkill Historical Society, NY, 5902

Fitchburg Historical Society, MA, 3861

Fitts Museum, NH, 5282

Flathead Indian Museum, MT, 5053

Flatiron Building Heritage Center/BARC, PA, 7150

Florence Museum of Art, Science and History, SC, 7675

Florence Pioneer Museum, CO, 995

Florida History Center and Museum, FL, 1452

Florida Holocaust Museum, FL, 1527

Florida United Methodist Archives, FL, 1473

Flower Pentecostal Heritage Center, MO, 4941

Folle Avoine Historical Park, WI, 9104

Folsom Historical Society, CA, 537

Folsom Museum, NM, 5723

Fond du Lac County Historical Society, WI, 9126

Foothills Historical Society, WA, 8813

Forest History Society, NC, 6272

Forsyth County Joint Historic Properties Commission, NC, 6481

Fort Battleford National Historic Site of Canada, SK, 9946

Fort Beausejour National Historic Site/Lieu Historique National du Fort Beausejour, NB, 9580

Fort Caspar Museum and Historic Site, WY, 9292

Fort Collins Public Library, Local History Archive, CO, 1053

Fort Dauphin Museum, Inc., The, MB, 9536

Fort Edward Historical Association, Inc., NY, 5907

Fort Frederick State Park, MD, 3599

Fort Garland Museum, CO, 1056

Fort Garry Historical Society, Inc., MB, 9565

Fort Gibson Historic Site, OK, 6885

Fort Humboldt State Historic Park, CA, 531

Fort La Reine Museum Pioneer Village and Tourist Bureau, MB, 9543

Fort Leaton State Historic Park, TX, 8218

Fort McKavett State Historic Park, TX, 8101

Fort Morgan Museum, CO, 1057

Fort New Salem, WV, 9051

Fort Peck Assiniboine and Sioux, MT, 5047

Fort Point National Historic Site, CA, 802

Fort Pulaski National Monument, GA, 1788

Fort Ross State Historic Park, CA, 577

Fort Sam Houston, TX, 8102

Fort St. Joseph Museum, MI, 4206

Fort Steele Heritage Town, BC, 9451
Fort Stockton Historical Society, TX, 8104
Fort Union National Monument, NM, 5780
Fort Valley Museum, Inc., VA, 8562
Fort Walla Walla Museum/Walla Walla Valley
  Historical Society, WA, 8980
Fort Walsh National Historic Site, SK, 9964
Fort Worth Museum of Science and History,
  TX, 8106
Fortress of Louisbourg National Historic Site,
  NS, 9664
Fossil County Futures, Inc., WY, 9323
Fossil Museum, OR, 7017
Four Mile Historic Park, CO, 1025
Four Rivers Cultural Center and Museum,
  OR, 7053
Francis Land House Historic Site and
  Gardens, VA, 8758
Franco-American Center, NH, 5362
Frank Slide Interpretive Centre, AB, 9374
Frankenmuth Historical Association, MI, 4127
Fraser-Fort George Regional Museum, BC,
  9490
Freetown Village, Inc., IN, 2556
Freeborn County Historical Society, MN, 4266
Friars Point Historical Preservation Society,
  MS, 4548
Friends of Arrow Rock, Inc., MO, 4633
Friends of Historic Boonville, MO, 4650
Friends of History in Fulton, New York, Inc.,
  NY, 5912
Friends of Linden Place, RI, 7530
Friends of Old South Ferdinand, Inc., MO,
  4702
Friends of Rickwood, AL, 18
Friends of Sheldon Jackson Museum, AK,
  185
Friends of the Historical Museum, ID, 1904
Friends of the Japanese House and Garden,
  The, PA, 7372
Friends of the Wallace House and Old Dutch
  Parsonage, NJ, 5638
Frogmore Plantation and Gins, LA, 3290
Fulton County Historical Society, Inc., IN,
  2625
Fulton County Historical Society, Inc., PA,
  7308
Furniture Discovery Center, Inc., NC, 6324
Gaineswood, AL, 40
Gallaudet University Archives, DC, 1340
Gallia County Historical/Genealogical Society,
  OH, 6667
Gallup Cultural Center, NM, 5726
Galveston County Historical Museum, TX,
  8120
Gammelgarden Museum, MN, 4335
Gardiner Museum of Ceramic Art, The, ON,
  9834
Gary Historical and Cultural Society, Inc., IN,
  2534
Garza County Historical Museum, TX, 8216
GATEway to the Panhandle Museum
  Corporation, OK, 6888
Geary County Historical Society Museum,
  KS, 2965
General Commission on Archives and History
  of the United Methodist Church, NJ, 5532
General Daniel Bissell House Museum, MO,
  4912
General Sweeny's Museum, MO, 4869
Genesee Country Village and Museum, NY,
  5988
Genesee County History Department, NY,
  5808
Geneva Historical Society, IL, 2149
Geneva Historical Society, NY, 5915
Geneva Lake Area Museum, WI, 9164
Geographical Center Historical Society and
  Prairie Village Museum, ND, 6545
George M. Jones Memorial Library, VA, 8611
George W. Brown, Jr. Ojibwe Museum and
  Cultural Center, WI, 9159
Georgetown Heritage Trust, DC, 1341
Georgia Department of Archives and History,
  GA, 1605
Georgia Mountains History Museum at
  Brenau University, GA, 1694
Georgia Salzburger Society, GA, 1759
Georgia Southern University Museum, GA,
  1811
German Society of Philadelphia, The, PA,
  7374
Germans from Russia Heritage Society, ND,

6497
Germantown Historical Society, PA, 7375
Germantown Mennonite Historic Trust, PA,
  7376
Ghost Tours of Niagara, ON, 9767
Gila County Historical Museum, AZ, 227
Gilcrease Museum, OK, 6975
Glebe House Museum and Gertrude Jekyll
  Garden, CT, 1291
Glen Ridge Historical Society, NJ, 5492
Glenbow Museum (Glenbow-Alberta
  Institute), AB, 9364
Glencairn Museum, Academy of the New
  Church, PA, 7151
Glensheen Historic Estate, MN, 4307
Glocester Heritage Society, RI, 7533
Gloucester County Historical Society, NJ,
  5680
Glove Museum, The, NY, 6007
Gnadenhutten Historical Society, OH, 6673
Gold Nugget Days, Inc., CA, 697
Golden Drift Historical Society, CA, 522
Golden Drift Museum, CA, 523
Golden Spike National Historic Site, UT,
  8321
Golden State Museum, CA, 759
Gomez Mill House, NY, 5978
Goschenhoppen Historians, Inc., PA, 7237
Gothenberg Historical Society, NE, 5123
Governor Bill and Vara Daniel Historic Village,
  TX, 8270
Governor's Mansion State Historic Park, CA,
  760
Grace Museum, The, TX, 8003
Graceland University DuRose Rare Book
  Room, IA, 2779
Graceland, Elvis Presley Enterprises, TN,
  7942
Graham-Ginestra House, Inc., IL, 2352
Grand Meadow Heritage Commission, Inc.,
  IA, 2859
Grand Rapids Historical Society, MI, 4137
Grand Village of the Natchez Indians, MS,
  4584
Grande Prairie Museum, AB, 9398
Grant County Historical Society, IN, 2586
Grant County Historical Society, MN, 4315
Grant County Historical Society, SD, 7807
Grant County Historical Society, WI, 9166
Greater Fair Bluff Historical Society, NC, 6282
Greeley County Historical Society, KS, 3063
Greeley County Historical Society, NE, 5128
Greenbrier Historical Society, Inc., WV, 9030
Greensboro Historical Museum, NC, 6304
Greenwood County Historical Society, KS,
  2927
Greenwood County Historical Society, SC,
  7684
Greenwood Museum, The, SC, 7685
Grevemberg House Museum, LA, 3288
Grosse Ile and the Irish Memorial National
  Historic Site, QC, 9936
Grosse Pointe Historical Society, MI, 4145
Grout Museum of History and Science, IA,
  2860
Grover Cleveland Birthplace Memorial
  Association, NJ, 5455
Guardians of Slidell History, LA, 3386
Gum Springs Historical Society, Inc., VA,
  8581
Gwinnett History Museum, GA, 1720
Haffenreffer Museum of Anthropology, RI,
  7531
Hale Farm & Village, OH, 6577
Hallockville, Inc., NY, 6091
Hampton Museum and Visitors Center, SC,
  7687
Hampton University Museum, VA, 8583
Hancock Shaker Village, Inc., MA, 3953
Hanna-Basin Historical Society, WY, 9319
Hardin County Historical Museums, Inc., OH,
  6693
Harness Racing and Hall of Fame, NY, 5922
Harriet Beecher Stowe Slavery to Freedom
  Museum, KY, 3250
Harrison County Historical Commission, TX,
  8180
Harrison County Historical Museum, TX,
  8181
Harrison Historical Society, ME, 3446
Harrison Museum of African-American
  Culture, VA, 8711
Harrison Township Historical Society, NJ,

5564
Hartsville Museum, SC, 7688
Hartzler-Towner Multicultural Museum at
  Scarritt Bennett Center, TN, 7965
Harwich Historical Society, MA, 3879
Harwood Museum of the University of New
  Mexico, NM, 5771
Hastings Historical Society, NY, 5929
Hastings Museum of Culture and Natural
  History, NE, 5132
Hattiesburg Area Historical Society and
  Museum, MS, 4554
Hawaii Heritage Center, HI, 1857
Hawaii Okinawa Center, HI, 1892
Hawaii State Archives, HI, 1860
Hawaii's Plantation Village, HI, 1893
Hawaiian Historical Society, HI, 1861
Hawaiian Music Hall of Fame and Museum,
  HI, 1873
Hayden Historical Museum Inc., IN, 2545
Hayward Area Historical Society, CA, 564
Hebrew Union College Skirball Museum, OH,
  6613
Hellenic Cultural Association, UT, 8333
Hellenic Museum and Cultural Center, IL,
  2056
Hennepin History Museum, MN, 4387
Henry Sheldon Museum of Vermont History,
  VT, 8404
Heritage Center of Lancaster County Inc., PA,
  7281
Heritage Education Program, City of
  Vancouver, WA, 8978
Heritage Foundation of the East Grand Forks
  Area, Inc., The, MN, 4313
Heritage Foundation, Inc., GA, 1820
Heritage Hill Historical Park, CA, 589
Heritage House and Museum of Okawville,
  IL, 2296
Heritage Museum of Layton, UT, 8306
Heritage Park Foundation, ND, 6518
Herkimer County Historical Society, NY, 5931
Herndon Home, The, GA, 1609
Hertzberg Circus Museum, TX, 8234
Hess Heritage Museum, ID, 1959
Hibbing Historical Society & Museum, MN,
  4350
Hidalgo County Historical Museum, TX, 8088
Hiddenite Center, Inc., NC, 6321
High Desert Museum, OR, 6998
High Plains Heritage Center Museum, SD,
  7847
High Point Historical Society, Inc., NC, 6325
Highspire Historical Society, PA, 7263
Hillsboro Area Historical Society, WI, 9142
Hillsboro Historical Society and Museums,
  KS, 2955
Historic Allaire Village, NJ, 5437
Historic Bethabara Park, NC, 6482
Historic Bethlehem, Inc., PA, 7129
Historic Carnton Plantation, TN, 7891
Historic Charlton Park Village, Museum and
  Recreation Area, MI, 4149
Historic Cold Spring Village, NJ, 5460
Historic Columbia Foundation, SC, 7652
Historic Costume and Textiles Collection, CO,
  1054
Historic Crab Orchard Museum and Pioneer
  Park, VA, 8753
Historic Daniel Boone Home, MO, 4692
Historic Donaldsonville Museum, LA, 3283
Historic Dunvegan Provincial Park, AB, 9392
Historic Edenton State Historic Site, NC,
  6277
Historic Elmwood Cemetery, TN, 7943
Historic Fallsington, Inc., PA, 7214
Historic Fort Erie, ON, 9761
Historic Harmony Inc., PA, 7244
Historic Kansas City Foundation, MO, 4770
Historic Landmarks Foundation of Indiana,
  IN, 2557
Historic Liberty Jail, MO, 4808
Historic Mora Valley Foundation, NM, 5715
Historic Natchez Foundation, MS, 4585
Historic New Harmony, IN, 2604
Historic New Orleans Collection, The, LA,
  3350
Historic Oak View County Park, NC, 6397
Historic Oakland Foundation, Inc., GA, 1610
Historic Oakland, MD, 3625
Historic Palmyra, Inc., NY, 6065
Historic Pensacola Preservation Board, FL,
  1511

Historic Rittenhouse Town Inc., PA, 7382
Historic Rugby, Inc., TN, 7990
Historic Southern Indiana, IN, 2518
Historic Southwest Ohio, OH, 6614
Historic Springfield Foundation, Inc., MS,
  4545
Historic St. Mary's City, MD, 3703
Historic St. Marys Mission Inc., MT, 5059
Historic Stagville, NC, 6273
Historic Upshur Museum, TX, 8133
Historic Whitaker Home-Museum/Centerville
  Historical Society, UT, 8295
Historic Winslow House Association, MA,
  3912
Historical County of Rockland County, The,
  NY, 5990
Historical Genealogy Department, Allen
  County Public Library, IN, 2528
Historical Halifax Restoration Association,
  NC, 6313
Historical Museum at Fort Missoula, MT,
  5042
Historical Museum at St. Gertrude's, The, ID,
  1921
Historical Museum of Southern Florida, FL,
  1486
Historical Museum of St. James-Assiniboia,
  MB, 9567
Historical Museum of the D.R. Barker Library,
  NY, 5911
Historical Projects of Houston County, Inc.,
  TX, 8064
Historical Society of Berks County, PA, 7431
Historical Society of Carnegie, PA, 7159
Historical Society of Delaware, DE, 1316
Historical Society of Douglas County, NE,
  5188
Historical Society of Germantown, The, OH,
  6672
Historical Society of Glastonbury, CT, 1174
Historical Society of Harford County, Inc.,
  The, MD, 3594
Historical Society of Marshall County, IA,
  2790
Historical Society of Mount Pleasant, Ohio
  Inc., OH, 6730
Historical Society of New Mexico, NM, 5756
Historical Society of Ocean Grove, NJ, 5586
Historical Society of Porter County, IN, 2643
Historical Society of Princeton, NJ, 5609
Historical Society of Saginaw Co., Inc./Castle
  Museum of Saginaw Co. History, MI, 4234
Historical Society of Seabrook, NH, 5419
Historical Society of the Phoenixville Area,
  PA, 7412
Historical Society of Trappe, PA, 7172
Historical Society of Washington County, Inc.,
  VA, 8471
Historical Society of Western Pennsylvania,
  PA, 7420
Historical Society of Wilmington Vermont, VT,
  8467
History and Humanities Program of the State
  Foundation on Culture and the Arts, HI,
  1863
History Center, IA, 2684
History Museum of East Otter Trail County,
  The, MN, 4429
Hitchcock House Advisory Committee, IA,
  2781
Ho'opulapula Haraguchi Rice Mill, HI, 1845
Holden Historical Society Museum, AB, 9401
Holland Historical Trust, MI, 4152
Holocaust Documentation and Education
  Center, Inc., FL, 1497
Holocaust Memorial of Illinois, IL, 2386
Holocaust Memorial Resource and Education
  Center, Inc. of Central Florida, FL, 1478
Holy Cross History Association, IN, 2611
Homesteaders Museum, WY, 9353
Homewood House Museum, MD, 3579
Honey Creek Church Preservation Group, IA,
  2806
Honolulu Botanical Gardens, HI, 1864
Honolulu Police Department Law
  Enforcement Museum, HI, 1865
Hoofprints of the Past Museum, WY, 9321
Hoopa Tribal Museum, CA, 568
Hoover-Minthorn House Museum, The, OR,
  7047
Hopewell Furnace National Historic Site, PA,
  7201
Hopi Cultural Preservation Office, AZ, 232

THEMES OF INTERPRETATION Ethnic/Religious/Cultural 1127

Magnolia Grove Historic House Museum, AL, 57
Magnolia Mound Plantation, LA, 3271
Mahoning Valley Historical Society and The Arms Family Museum of Local History, OH, 6826
Makah Cultural & Research Center, WA, 8892
Malcolm Blue Historical Society, NC, 6200
Maltwood Art Museum and Gallery The University of Victoria, BC, 9528
Manassas Museum System, VA, 8616
Manchester Historic Association, NH, 5365
Manitowoc County Historical Society, WI, 9170
Manzanar National Historic Site, CA, 571
Marathon County Historical Society, WI, 9273
Marble Rock Historical Society, IA, 2787
Mari Sandoz Heritage Society, NE, 5098
Marianna Kistler Beach Museum of Art, KS, 2990
Marie and Eugene Callahan Museum of the American Printing House for the Blind, KY, 3186
Marin History Museum, CA, 847
Marion County Museum, SC, 7704
Maritime Conference Archives, NB, 9600
Marjorie Barrick Museum of Natural History, NV, 5246
Marlborough Historical Society, Inc., NH, 5366
Marquette County Historical Society, Inc., MI, 4184
Marquette Mission Park and Museum of Ojibwa Culture, MI, 4239
Marshall County Historical Society, IL, 2192
Marshall County Historical Society, KS, 2997
Marshall County Historical Society, MN, 4510
Marshall County Historical Society, SD, 7758
Marshall County Historical Society, WV, 9041
Martha's Vineyard Historical Society, MA, 3855
Martin and Osa Johnson Safari Museum, KS, 2895
Martin County Convent, Inc., TX, 8251
Martin Luther King, Jr. National Historic Site and Preservation District, GA, 1617
Maryhill Museum of Art, WA, 8856
Maryland Historical Society, MD, 3582
Maryland Room, C. Burr Artz Central Library, Frederick County Public Libraries, MD, 3651
Maryland State Archives, MD, 3555
Mashantucket Pequot Museum and Research Center, CT, 1209
Mason Area Historical Society, MI, 4187
Mason Area Historical Society, WI, 9072
Mason County Museum, KY, 3203
Mason County Museum, TX, 8183
Massie Heritage Interpretation Center, GA, 1795
Mattatuck Historical Society, Inc., CT, 1273
Mattye Reed African Heritage Center, North Carolina Agricultural and Technical State University, NC, 6306
Maui Historical Society, HI, 1890
Maui Okinawa Kenjin Kai, HI, 1891
Mazomanie Historical Society, WI, 9181
McCleary Historical Society, WA, 8882
McCone County Museum, MT, 4993
McCord and District Museum, SK, 9966
McFarland House, ON, 9764
McIlhenny Company and Avery Island, Inc., Archives, The, LA, 3262
McKeesport Heritage Center, PA, 7309
McKissick Museum, SC, 7654
McLean County Museum of History, IL, 2005
McMinn County Living Heritage Museum, TN, 7863
MCP Hahnemann University Archives and Special Collections, PA, 7390
Meadowcroft Museum of Rural Life, PA, 7120
Meadowlands Museum, NJ, 5622
Meeker County Historical Society, MN, 4365
Meeteetse Museums and Archives, Inc., WY, 9331
Mel Fisher Maritime Heritage Society, FL, 1464
Melrose Area Historical Society, MN, 4384
Memorial Foundation of the Germanna Colonies in Virginia, Inc., VA, 8531
Memphis Pink Palace Museum, TN, 7947
Menaul Historical Library of the Southwest, NM, 5694
Mendocino County Historical Society, Inc., CA, 939
Mendocino County Museum, CA, 965
Mendota Museum and Historical Society, IL, 2238
Menno Simons Historical Library, VA, 8588
Mennonite Archives of Ontario, ON, 9850
Mennonite Heritage Museum, KS, 2945
Mennonite Historians of Eastern Pennsylvania, PA, 7243
Mennonite Historical Society, IA, 2771
Mennonite Library and Archives, KS, 3011
Menominee County Historical Society, Inc., MI, 4188
Menominee Range Historical Foundation, MI, 4158
Mequon Historical Society, Inc., WI, 9187
Merced County Historical Society/Merced County Courthouse Museum, CA, 639
Mercer County Historical Museum, OH, 6599
Meredosia Area Historical Society, IL, 2239
Meridian Restorations Foundation, Inc., MS, 4582
Merrill Historical Society, Inc./Brickyard School Museum, WI, 9188
Mesa Historical Museum, AZ, 234
Metlakatla Tribal Rights Committee, AK, 180
Metropolitan Historical Commission of Nashville and Davidson County, TN, 7968
Michigan Iron Industry Museum, MI, 4205
Michigan Museums Association, MI, 4171
Michigan State University Museum, MI, 4119
Mid-America All Indian Center, Inc., KS, 3079
Middle Border Museum of American Indian and Pioneer Life, SD, 7812
Middlesex County Historical Society, CT, 1211
Middleton Place, SC, 7634
Midway Village and Museum Center, IL, 2355
Midwest Jesuit Archives, MO, 4917
Milan Historical Museum, OH, 6727
Milford Historical Society and Museum, CT, 1231
Milford Historical Society and Museum, MI, 4192
Mill Prong Preservation, Inc., NC, 6354
Millet and District Museum and Exhibit Room, The, AB, 9409
Millicent Rogers Museum, NM, 5774
Mills County Historical Society, IA, 2747
Milwaukee County Historical Society, WI, 9194
Milwaukee Public Museum, Inc., WI, 9195
Minerva Area Historical Society, OH, 6728
Minnesota Annual Conference Archive, MN, 4393
Minnesota Finnish American Historical Society, Chapter 38, MN, 4484
Minnesota Finnish-American Historical Society, Chapter 13 of New York Mills/ Finn Creek Museum, MN, 4420
Minnesota Historical Society Library, MN, 4469
Minnesota Historical Society, MN, 4468
Minnetrista Cultural Center and Oakhurst Gardens, IN, 2596
Miracle of America Museum, Inc., MT, 5045
Missiles and More Museum Missiles and More Museum, NC, 6446
Mission Houses Museum, HI, 1868
Mission Mill Museum/Mission Mill Musuem Association, OR, 7083
Mission San Francisco de Asis (Mission Dolores), CA, 808
Mission San Juan Capistrano, CA, 833
Mission San Luis Rey de Francia, CA, 678
Mission San Miguel Arcangel, CA, 843
Mission San Rafael Archangel, CA, 848
Missisquoi Historical Society/Missisquoi Museum, QC, 9934
Mississippi Agriculture and Forestry/National Agricultural Aviation Museum, MS, 4567
Mississippi County Historical and Genealogical Society, AR, 399
Mississippi County Historical Society, MO, 4673
Mississippi Cultural Crossroads, MS, 4602
Missouri Department of Natural Resources, Division of State Parks, MO, 4755
Missouri Historical Society, MO, 4918
Missouri State Museum, MO, 4759
Mitchell Museum of the American Indian, IL, 2129
Mizel Museum of Judaica, CO, 1028
Mobile Medical Museum, AL, 84
Mobile Municipal Archives, AL, 85
Mohawk Nation Council of Choices, NY, 6104
Mohawk Valley Heritage Corridor, NY, 5851
Molalla Area Historical Society, OR, 7042
Monacan Indian Nation, VA, 8615
Moncton Museum, NB, 9597
Monroe County Historical Museum, MI, 4193
Monson Museum, ME, 3465
Montana Heritage Preservation and Development Comission, MT, 5024
Montana Historical Society, MT, 5025
Monterey County Historical Society, Inc., CA, 772
Monterey State Historic Park, CA, 647
Montgomery County Historic Preservation Commission, MD, 3717
Montgomery County Historical Society, The, OH, 6645
Montpelier (James Madison's), VA, 8632
Montpelier Mansion, MD, 3676
Montreal Holocaust Memorial Center/Le Centre Commemoratif De L'Holocauste S Montreal, QC, 9910
Monument Hill and Kreische Brewery State Historical Parks, TX, 8165
Moody County Genealogical Organization, SD, 7780
Moose Lake Area Historical Society, MN, 4409
Moravian Historical Society, PA, 7331
Moravian Museum of Bethlehem, Inc., PA, 7131
Morikami Museum and Japanese Gardens, The, FL, 1413
Mormon Trail Center at Historic Winter Quarters, NE, 5191
Morris County Heritage Commission, NJ, 5554
Morton Grove Historical Museum, IL, 2259
Mossbank and District Museum, Inc., SK, 9970
Mounds-Midway School of Nursing Historical Society, MN, 4472
Moundville Archaeological Park, AL, 120
Mount Auburn Cemetery, MA, 3800
Mount Horeb Area Historical Society, WI, 9200
Mount Kearsarge Indian Museum, Education and Cultrural Center, NH, 5429
Mount Lebanon Historical Society, Stagecoach Trail Museum, LA, 3291
Mount Saint Joseph Ursuline Archives, KY, 3198
Mountrail County Historical Society, ND, 6546
Mower County Historical Society, MN, 4273
Mt. Zion United Methodist Church, DC, 1346
Mudock Historical Society, NE, 5168
Mullan Historical Society, ID, 1949
Multicultural Heritage Centre, AB, 9420
Mummers Museum, PA, 7393
Muscogee Genealogical Society, GA, 1659
Musee Acadien (Acadian Museum), NB, 9598
Musee de Kent, NB, 9581
Musee du Quebec, QC, 9922
Musee Francois-Pilote, QC, 9889
Musee Regimentaire Les Fusiliers de Sherbrocke, QC, 9929
Museo de las Americas, CO, 1030
Museum Association of West Louisiana, LA, 3315
Museum at Warm Springs, The, OR, 7103
Museum Center at Five Points, TN, 7876
Museum Management Program, National Park Service, DC, 1347
Museum of Anthropology at the University of British Columbia, BC, 9508
Museum of Anthropology, CA, 491
Museum of Anthropology, KY, 3152
Museum of Anthropology, Wake Forest University, NC, 6485
Museum of Appalachia, TN, 7982
Museum of Archaeology and Material Culture, NM, 5710
Museum of Art and History at the McPherson Center, CA, 872
Museum of Christian Heritage, IL, 2294
Museum of Church History and Art, UT, 8336
Museum of Discovery: Arkansas Museum of Science and History, AR, 379
Museum of Early Trades and Crafts, NJ, 5535
Museum of Fine Arts, Houston, TX, 8148
Museum of Florida History, FL, 1552
Museum of History and Industry, WA, 8931
Museum of Jewish Heritage—A Living Memorial to the Holocaust, NY, 6021
Museum of Northern Arizona, AZ, 217
Museum of Northern British Columbia, BC, 9491
Museum of Our National Heritage, MA, 3896
Museum of People and Cultures, UT, 8323
Museum of Science and History of Jacksonville, Inc., FL, 1450
Museum of the Albermarle, NC, 6279
Museum of the American Quilter's Society, KY, 3222
Museum of the City of Lake Worth, FL, 1472
Museum of the City of New York, NY, 6023
Museum of the Everglades, FL, 1418
Museum of the Great Plains, OK, 6910
Museum of the Islands Society, Inc., FL, 1540
Museum of the Native American Resource Center, NC, 6388
Museum of the New South, Inc., NC, 6249
Museum of the Plains Indian, MT, 4984
Museum of the Plains, TX, 8208
Museum of the Red River, OK, 6900
Museum of the Waxhaws and Andrew Jackson Memorial, NC, 6457
Museum of West Louisiana, LA, 3316
Museum of Western Jesuit Missions, The, MO, 4704
Museums at Prophetstown, Inc., The, IN, 2482
Musk Ox Development Corporation, AK, 182
Nanticoke Indian Museum, DE, 1305
Napa Valley Museum, CA, 972
Nashville City Cemetery Association, TN, 7969
Nathanael Greene City County Heritage Museum, TN, 7900
Natick Historical Society, MA, 3993
National Association for Cemetery Preservation, CO, 1125
National Buffalo Museum, ND, 6528
National Civil Rights Museum, TN, 7948
National Czech and Slovak Museum and Library, IA, 2686
National Hall of Fame for Famous American Indians, OK, 6835
National Japanese American Historical Society, CA, 810
National Mining Hall of Fame and Museum, The, CO, 1091
National Museum of American History, Smithsonian Institution, DC, 1355
National Museum of American Jewish History, PA, 7394
National Museum of American Jewish Military History, DC, 1356
National Museum of Roller Skating, NE, 5144
National Museum of the American Indian Cultural Resources Center, MD, 3728
National Museum of the American Indian, Smithsonian Institution, DC, 1357
National Shrine of St. Elizabeth Ann Seton, MD, 3639
National Society of The Colonial Dames of America, The, DC, 1359
National Wild Turkey Federation, SC, 7670
National Yiddish Book Center, MA, 3751
Native American Museum, IN, 2640
Nauvoo Restoration Inc., IL, 2272
Navajo Nation Museum, AZ, 288
Navarre-Anderson Trading Post, MI, 4194
Nay'dini'aa Na Tribal Cultural Center, AK, 148
Nebraska City Historical Society, NE, 5170
Nebraska Humanities Council, NE, 5146
Nebraska Jewish Historical Society, NE, 5192
Nebraska State Historical Society, NE, 5148
Neptune Township Historical Society, NJ, 5565
Nevada County Historical Society, CA, 659
Nevada Historical Society, NV, 5255
Neville Public Museum of Brown County, WI, 9135
New Almaden Quicksilver County Park Association, CA, 828
New Bedford Whaling Museum, MA, 3928
New Britain Youth Museum, CT, 1220
New Brunswick Historical Society, NB, 9602
New Castle Historical Society, NY, 5859
New England Historic Genealogical Society, MA, 3781
New Hampshire Aniquarian Society, NH,

FOLKLORE/FOLKLIFE

THEMES OF INTERPRETATION Folklore/Folklife 1135

Marquette County Historical Society, Inc., MI, 4184
Marquette Mission Park and Museum of Ojibwa Culture, MI, 4239
Martha's Vineyard Historical Society, MA, 3855
Maryhill Museum of Art, WA, 8856
Maryland Historical Society, MD, 3582
Maryland Room, C. Burr Artz Central Library, Frederick County Public Libraries, MD, 3651
Mason Area Historical Society, MI, 4187
Mason Area Historical Society, WI, 9072
Mason County Historical Society/White Pine Village, MI, 4176
Mason County Museum, KY, 3203
Mason County Museum, TX, 8183
Mason Historical Society Inc., OH, 6716
Massillon Museum, OH, 6717
Mathias Ham House Historic Site, IA, 2729
Matson Museum of Anthropology, PA, 7471
Maui Historical Society, HI, 1890
Maui Okinawa Kenjin Kai, HI, 1891
Mayo House Interpretive Society, MN, 4360
McCarter Museum of Tonkawa History, OK, 6974
McCone County Museum, MT, 4993
McCook House Civil War Museum/Carroll County Historical Society, OH, 6598
McCord Museum of Canadian History, QC, 9908
McCormick County Historical Commission, SC, 7708
McCreary County Historical and Genealogical Society, Inc., KY, 3251
McCurdy Historical Doll Museum, UT, 8322
McIlhenny Company and Avery Island, Inc., Archives, The, LA, 3262
McKissick Museum, SC, 7654
McMinn County Living Heritage Museum, TN, 7863
Meadow Garden, GA, 1634
Mechanicsburg Museum Association, PA, 7312
Melrose Area Historical Society, MN, 4384
Mendocino County Historical Society, Inc., CA, 939
Mendocino County Museum, CA, 965
Mennonite Historians of Eastern Pennsylvania, PA, 7243
Meredosia Area Historical Society, IL, 2239
Merrill Historical Society, Inc./Brickyard School Museum, WI, 9188
Merry Go Round Museum Inc., OH, 6774
Metcalfe County Historical Society, KY, 3119
Michie Tavern ca. 1784, VA, 8517
Michigan Museums Association, MI, 4171
Michigan State University Museum, MI, 4119
Mid-America All Indian Center, Inc., KS, 3079
Midwest Old Settlers and Threshers Association, IA, 2803
Milan Historical Museum, OH, 6727
Miles B. Carpenter Museum Complex, VA, 8766
Milford Historical Society and Museum, CT, 1231
Milford Historical Society and Museum, MI, 4192
Mille Lacs County Historical Sociey and Depot Museum, MN, 4435
Millet and District Museum and Exhibit Room, The, AB, 9409
Milne Special Collections and Archives, University of New Hampshire Library, NH, 5309
Milwaukee County Historical Society, WI, 9194
Milwaukee Public Museum, Inc., WI, 9195
Minerva Area Historical Society, OH, 6728
Mining and Town Museum, NM, 5740
Minnesota Finnish American Historical Society, Chapter 38, MN, 4484
Minnesota Historical Society Library, MN, 4469
Minnesota Historical Society, MN, 4468
Miracle of America Museum, Inc., MT, 5045
Mission Houses Museum, HI, 1868
Mission Mill Museum/Mission Mill Musuem Association, OR, 7083
Mission San Juan Capistrano, CA, 833
Missisquoi Historical Society/Missisquoi Museum, QC, 9934
Mississippi County Historical Society, MO, 4673
Mississippi Cultural Crossroads, MS, 4602
Mississippi Valley Educational Programs, AR, 311
Missouri Historical Society, MO, 4918
Missouri State Museum, MO, 4759
Mitchell County Historical Society, IA, 2814
Mitchell County Historical Society, KS, 2892
Moark Regional Railroad Museum, MO, 4863
Mobile Medical Museum, AL, 83
Mohawk Nation Council of Choices, NY, 6104
Mohawk Valley Heritage Corridor, NY, 5851
Molalla Area Historical Society, OR, 7042
Molson Historical Association, Molson Schoolhouse Museum, WA, 8898
Moniteau County Historical Society, MO, 4659
Monroe County Heritage Museums, AL, 90
Monroe County Historical Association, PA, 7460
Monson Historical Society, ME, 3441
Montana Heritage Preservation and Development Comission, MT, 5024
Monterey County Historical Society, Inc., CA, 772
Montpelier (James Madison's), VA, 8632
Montreal Holocaust Memorial Center/Le Centre Commemoratif De L'Holocauste S Montreal, QC, 9910
Montrose Historical Telephone Pioneer Museum, MI, 4196
Moose Lake Area Historical Society, MN, 4409
Moosehead Historical Society, ME, 3444
Mossbank and District Museum, Inc., SK, 9970
Mount Desert Island Historical Society, ME, 3466
Mount Horeb Area Historical Society, WI, 9200
Mount Saint Joseph Ursuline Archives, KY, 3198
Mountain Gateway Museum, NC, 6386
Mountain Heritage Center, NC, 6265
Mower County Historical Society, MN, 4273
Mt. Holly Historical Society, NJ, 5562
Mummers Museum, PA, 7393
Musee Francois-Pilote, QC, 9889
Musee Regional de Vaudreuil Soulanges, QC, 9942
Museo de las Americas, CO, 1030
Museum Association of West Louisiana, LA, 3315
Museum Management Program, National Park Service, DC, 1347
Museum of Anthropology at the University of British Columbia, BC, 9508
Museum of Anthropology, CA, 491
Museum of Anthropology, KY, 3152
Museum of Appalachia, TN, 7982
Museum of Art & Archaeology, University of Missouri, MO, 4685
Museum of Childhood of Wakefield, NH, 5428
Museum of Discovery: Arkansas Museum of Science and History, AR, 379
Museum of Early Southern Decorative Arts, NC, 6486
Museum of Early Trades and Crafts, NJ, 5535
Museum of Florida History, FL, 1552
Museum of Mobile, AL, 86
Museum of Northern Arizona, AZ, 217
Museum of Northern British Columbia, BC, 9491
Museum of People and Cultures, UT, 8323
Museum of Prehistory and History, AR, 414
Museum of the Albermarle, NC, 6279
Museum of the American Quilter's Society, KY, 3222
Museum of the City of Lake Worth, FL, 1472
Museum of the City of New York, NY, 6023
Museum of the Everglades, FL, 1418
Museum of the Great Plains, OK, 6910
Museum of the Native American Resource Center, NC, 6388
Museum of the New South, Inc., NC, 6249
Museum of the Plains, TX, 8208
Museum of the Waxhaws and Andrew Jackson Memorial, NC, 6457
Museum Village, NY, 5985
Museum-Lepanto USA, AR, 362
Museums at Stony Brook, The, NY, 6151
Muster Field Farm/Harvey Homestead, Inc., NH, 5387
Mystery Castle, AZ, 247
Nanticoke Indian Museum, DE, 1305
Naples Historical Society, ME, 3467
Natchitoches Historic Foundation, LA, 3333
National Cowboy Hall of Fame and Western Heritage Center, OK, 6937
National Czech and Slovak Museum and Library, IA, 2686
National Japanese American Historical Society, CA, 810
National Library of Canada, Music Division/Bibliotheque, ON, 9783
National Museum of the American Indian Cultural Resources Center, MD, 3728
National Museum of the American Indian, Smithsonian Institution, DC, 1357
National Route 66 Museum/Old Town Complex, OK, 6879
National Society of the Colonial Dames of Louisiana Shreveport Committee, LA, 3380
National Wild Turkey Federation, SC, 7670
Native American Heritage Museum, KS, 2953
Nauvoo Historical Society, IL, 2271
Navajo Nation Museum, AZ, 288
Navarre-Anderson Trading Post, MI, 4194
Nebraska Humanities Council, NE, 5146
Nebraska Jewish Historical Society, NE, 5192
Nebraska State Historical Society, NE, 5148
Neosho Historical Society, WI, 9205
New Bern Historical Society Foundation, Inc., NC, 6379
New Bremen Historic Association, OH, 6734
New Britain Youth Museum, CT, 1220
New Castle Historical Society, NY, 5859
New England Maple Museum, VT, 8442
New Hampshire Aniquarian Society, NH, 5341
New Haven Colony Historical Society, CT, 1226
New Jersey Historical Commission, NJ, 5657
New Jersey Historical Society, NJ, 5575
New Jersey Museum of Agriculture, NJ, 5578
New Mexico Farm and Ranch Heritage Museum, NM, 5732
New Mexico State Records Center and Archives, NM, 5759
New Orleans Notarial Archives, LA, 3360
New Richmond Preservation Society, WI, 9210
New Windsor Cantonment State Historic Site, NY, 6171
New York State Museum, NY, 5787
New York Transit Museum, NY, 5834
Newipswich Historical Society, NH, 5384
Newsome House Museum and Cultural Center, VA, 8645
Newton County Historical Society, MO, 4836
Newton County Historical Society/Bradley House Museum, AR, 359
Newtown-Avoca Historical Society, IA, 2667
Nicollet County Historical Society, MN, 4476
Nokomis Learning Center, MI, 4211
Nordic Heritage Museum, WA, 8932
Norfolk County Historical Society of Chesapeake, VA, 8521
North American Baptist Heritage Commission, SD, 7838
North Augusta Historical Society, SC, 7718
North Berrien Historical Society Museum, MI, 4094
North Carolina Division of Parks and Recreation, NC, 6401
North Carolina Historic Sites, NC, 6403
North Carolina Maritime Museum, NC, 6222
North Carolina Museum of History, NC, 6405
North Carolina Society of Historians, Inc., NC, 6433
North Carolina State Historic Preservation Office, Division of Archives and History, NC, 6408
North Custer Historical Society, ID, 1919
North Dakota Heritage Center, The, ND, 6498
North Highlands Community Museum, NS, 9655
North Lincoln County Historical Museum, OR, 7035
North Louisiana Folk Life, Inc., DBA Martin Homeplace, LA, 3277
North Platte Valley Historical Association, Inc., NE, 5120
Northeast Texas Rural Heritage Center and Museum, TX, 8209
Northeastern Montana Threshers and Antique Association, MT, 4999
Northeastern Nevada Museum, NV, 5235
Northern Arizona University Cline Library Special Collections and Archives Department, AZ, 218
Northern Kentucky African American Heritage Task Force, Inc., KY, 3113
Northern Wisconsin History Center, WI, 9073
Northfield Historical Society, MN, 4423
Northwest Franklin County Historical Society and Museum, OH, 6683
Northwest Montana Historical Society, Central School Museum, MT, 5032
Norwich Historical Society, VT, 8420
Nova Scotia Highland Village, NS, 9661
Nunatta Sunakkutaangit Museum Society, NT, 9645
Nursing History Resource Centre/Nursing Association of New Brunswick, NB, 9585
Oakland Museum of California, CA, 673
Ocean Spray Cranberry World, MA, 3958
Ocmulgee National Monument, GA, 1731
Odessa Historical Society, WA, 8895
Ohio Historical Society, OH, 6634
Ohr-O'Keefe Museum of Art, MS, 4532
Okefenokee Heritage Center, GA, 1836
Old Cahawba Archaeological State Park, AL, 110
Old Capitol Museum of Mississippi History, MS, 4575
Old Courthouse Museum, CA, 854
Old Courthouse Museum, Louisiana State Museum Branch, LA, 3334
Old Davidson State Park, AR, 408
Old Dillard Museum, FL, 1424
Old Fort Genealogical Society of Southeastern Kansas, Inc., KS, 2939
Old Fort Niagara Association, NY, 6199
Old Greer County Museum, OK, 6914
Old Island Restoration Foundation, FL, 1465
Old Mines Area Historical Society, MO, 4845
Old Mulkey Meetinghouse State Historic Site, KY, 3244
Old Salem, NC, 6488
Old Salley School Museum, SC, 7734
Old State Bank, AL, 38
Old Town Brunswick Preservation Association, GA, 1643
Old Trails Historical Society, MO, 4815
Old Wall Historical Society, NJ, 5664
Old Wilkes, Inc., NC, 6461
Old World Wisconsin, WI, 9112
Old York Historical Society, ME, 3543
Olmsted County Historical Society, MN, 4442
Oneida Community Mansion House, NY, 6048
Oneida Nation Museum, WI, 9214
Onondaga Historical Association, NY, 6156
Ontario Historical Society, ON, 9856
Oolagah Historical Society, OK, 6944
Opelousas Museum and Interpretive Center, LA, 3365
Opp Historical Society Inc., AL, 103
Orange County Historical Commission, CA, 855
Oregon Historical Society, OR, 7067
Oregon Trail Regional Museum, OR, 6994
Oregon-Jerusalem Historical Society, OH, 6748
Orleans County Historical Society Inc., VT, 8368
Oroville Chinese Temple, CA, 686
Orwell Corner Historic Village, PE, 9871
Orwell Historical Society, VT, 8421
Osage Village State Historic Park, MO, 4957
Ostfriesen Heritage Society, IA, 2755
Oswego County Historical Society, NY, 6056
Ouachita African American Historical Society, LA, 3325
Outer Bank Group, Cape Hatteras National Seashore, NC, 6357
Overland Trail Museum, CO, 1127
Overland Trail Museum, TX, 8100
Owen County Historical Society, KY, 3217
Owensboro Area Museum of Science and History, KY, 3215
Owensboro Museum of Fine Art, KY, 3216
Oxford Museum Association, OH, 6749
Oyster Bay Historical Society, NY, 6062
Ozark Folk Center, The, AR, 395
Pacific Asia Museum, CA, 959
Pacific County Historical Society and Museum Foundation, WA, 8948
Page-Walker Arts and History Center, NC,

FUR TRADE

GARDENS

Wylie House Museum, IN, 2490
Yamhill County Historical Museum, OR, 7033
Ybor City Museum Society, FL, 1561
Yesteryear Village at the South Florida Fairgrounds, FL, 1577
Yolo County Historical Museum, CA, 968
York County Cultural and Heritage Commission Historical Center, SC, 7752
Yukon Beringia Interpretive Centre, YT, 10006
Zalud House, CA, 719
Zoar Village State Memorial, OH, 6828

GENEALOGY

1736 Josiah Dennis Manse Museum, MA, 3841
1877 Peterson Station Museum, MN, 4430
Abbeville Cultural and Historical Alliance, LA, 3256
Aberdeen Room Archives and Museum, MD, 3545
Acadian Heritage and Culture Foundation, Inc., LA, 3285
Acadian Memorial, LA, 3375
Acadian Museum, The, PE, 9861
Acadian Village, LA, 3305
Ackley Heritage Center, IA, 2654
Adair County Historical Society, IA, 2749
Adair County Historical Society, MO, 4791
Adams County Historical Museum, IN, 2508
Adams County Historical Society, CO, 989
Adams County Historical Society, NE, 5131
Adams County Historical Society, PA, 7226
Adams County Historical Society, WA, 8875
Adams Museum, SD, 7770
Addison Historical Society, IL, 1973
Adena State Memorial: The Home of Thomas Worthington, OH, 6602
African American Heritage Center, Inc., KY, 3139
African American Museum and Library at Oakland, CA, 667
Afro-American Historical Association of Fauquier County, VA, 8754
Afton Historical Society Museum, MN, 4263
Agassiz-Harrison Historical Society, BC, 9429
Aiken-Barnwell Genealogical Society, SC, 7597
Ak-Chin Him-Dak EcoMuseum and Archives, AZ, 233
Alabama Civil War Roundtable, AL, 11
Alabama Department of Archives and History, AL, 92
Alabama Historical Commission-Old Cahawba, AL, 108
Alamance Battleground State Historic Site, NC, 6232
Alamance County Genealogical Society, NC, 6233
Alamance County Historical Museum, Inc., NC, 6234
Alaska Historical Collection, Alaska State Library, AK, 168
Albemarle County Historical Society, VA, 8514
Albemarle Genealogical Society, NC, 6258
Alberton Historical Preservation Foundation, PE, 9860
Alden Kindred of America, MA, 3844
Alexandria Black History Resource Center, The, VA, 8472
Alfalfa County Historical Society, OK, 6859
Alfred P. Sloan Museum, MI, 4123
Allagash Historical Society, ME, 3398
Allegany County Historical Society, MD, 3627
Allegany County Historical Society, NY, 5814
Allegany County Museum, NY, 5815
Allegheny Cemetery Historical Association, PA, 7414
Allegheny Regional Family History Society, WV, 9018
Allen Barkley Young Historians, Inc., KY, 3220
Allen County Historical and Genealogy Society, KY, 3236
Allen E. Roberts Masonic Library and Museum, Inc. (Grand Lodge of Virginia AF&AM), VA, 8680
Allison-Antrim Museum, Inc., PA, 7238
Almanzo and Laura Ingalls Wilder Association, NY, 5975
Alnobak Nebesakiak, VT, 8379

Alpharetta Historical Society, Inc., GA, 1583
Alpine County Museum, CA, 634
Alsi Historical and Genealogical Society, OR, 7102
Alstead Historical Society, NH, 5264
Alta District Historical Society, CA, 517
Alton Area Historical Society, IL, 1976
Amador County Archives, CA, 574
Amana Heritage Society, IA, 2659
Amelia Earhart Birthplace Museum, KS, 2884
Amelia Island Museum of History, FL, 1419
American Antiquarian Society, MA, 4040
American Catholic Historical Society, PA, 7350
American Cotton Museum, TX, 8134
American Fluorite Museum, The, IL, 2367
American Historical Society of Germans from Russia, NE, 5143
American Independence Museum, NH, 5314
American Jewish Historical Society, MA, 4016
American Manse/Whitney-Halsey House, The, NY, 5816
American Research Bureau, UT, 8329
American Swedish Historical Museum, PA, 7352
American Swedish Institute, The, MN, 4386
American-Canadian Genealogical Society, NH, 5360
American-Italian Renaissance Foundation, LA, 3340
Ames Plantation, TN, 7897
Amherst History Museum at the Strong House, MA, 3748
Amherst Museum, NY, 5796
Ancestral Trails Historical Society, Inc., KY, 3249
Ancient and Honorable Artillery Company of Massachusetts, MA, 3764
Anderson County Historical Society, KS, 2947
Anderson Township Historical Society, OH, 6605
Anderson Valley Historical Museum, CA, 470
Andover Historical Society, IL, 1979
Andover Historical Society, MA, 3753
Andover Historical Society, NH, 5267
Andrew College Archives, GA, 1666
Andrew County Museum and Historical Society, MO, 4933
Androscoggin Historical Society, ME, 3400
Anoka County Historical Society, MN, 4269
Antelope County Historical Society, NE, 5172
Apex Historical Society, NC, 6204
Appalachian Archive at Southeast Community College, The, KY, 3114
Appalachian Cultural Museum, The, NC, 6225
Appling County Heritage Center, GA, 1637
Archival Center, Archdiocese of Los Angeles, CA, 640
Archives and Regional History Collections, Western Michigan University, MI, 4163
Archives and Special Collections of DePauw University and Indiana United Methodism, IN, 2539
Archives and Special Collections, Ohio University Libraries, OH, 6568
Archives des Soeurs Grises/Grey Nun Archives, MB, 9559
Archives Nationales du Quebec, QC, 9898
Archives Nationales du Quebec, QC, 9937
Archives of Ontario, ON, 9826
Archives of the Diocese of Montreal, QC, 9899
Archives of the Evangelical Lutheran Church in America, IL, 2037
Archives of the Institute of the Blessed Virgin Mary, ON, 9827
Archives of the Roman Catholic Archdiocese, NF, 9626
Archives, University of Colorado at Boulder Libraries, CO, 984
Archivists for Congregations of Women Religious (ACWR), DC, 1331
Arenac County Historical Society, MI, 4062
Argyle Historical Society, Inc., The, MN, 4270
Argyle Township Court House and Archives, NS, 9679
Arizona Historical Society - Rio Colorado Division, AZ, 292
Arizona Jewish Historical Society, AZ, 244
Arizona State Genealogical Society, AZ, 273
Arkansas Genealogical Society, AR, 355
Arkansas History Commission, AR, 366

Arlington County Public Library Virginia Room, VA, 8490
Arlington Heights Historical Society and Museum, IL, 1981
Arlington Historical Society, The, MA, 3756
Armstrong County Historical Society, TX, 8048
Artesia Historical Museum and Art Center, NM, 5701
Arthur and Elizabeth Schlesinger Library on the History of Women in America, The, MA, 3795
Ashland Historical Society, MA, 3758
Ashland Historical Society, NH, 5268
Ashland Historical Society, WI, 9071
Ashland, the Henry Clay Estate, KY, 3159
Ashtabula Plantation, SC, 7720
Association for Gravestone Studies, MA, 3871
Association for Great Lakes Maritime History, OH, 6585
Association for the Preservation of Virginia Antiquities (APVA), VA, 8682
Association of Historical Societies of New Hampshire, NH, 5269
Association of the Descendants of Nancy Ward, Beloved Woman of the Cherokee, OK, 6851
Athens County Historical Society and Museum, OH, 6569
Athens Historical Society, Inc., GA, 1587
Athens Historical Society, ME, 3399
Athens-Clarke County Library Heritage Room, GA, 1588
Atlanta Historical Society, GA, 1598
Atlanta Historical Society, ID, 1899
Atlanta History Center, GA, 1599
Atlantic County Historical Society, The, NJ, 5629
Atwater Historical Society, The, OH, 6570
Auburn Avenue Research Library on African American Culture and History, GA, 1601
Auburn University Montgomery Library, AL, 95
Audrain County Historical Society, MO, 4826
Audubon State Commemorative Area, LA, 3371
August Schell Brewing Company Museum of Brewing, MN, 4416
Augusta Historical Society, Inc., KS, 2887
Augustan Society, Inc., The, CA, 509
Aurora County Historical Society, SD, 7826
Aurora Historical Society, NY, 5888
Aurora Historical Society, OH, 6571
Autauga County Heritage Association, AL, 105
Autauga Genealogical Society, AL, 106
Avery Memorial Association, CT, 1179
Avon Historical Society, IL, 1987
Avon Historical Society, Inc., The, CT, 1137
Avon Historical Society, OH, 6573
Aylmer and District Museum, ON, 9690
Aztec Museum Association, NM, 5702
Babcock Smith House, RI, 7590
Bacon's Castle Museum, VA, 8746
Badger Historical Society, WI, 9244
Bainbridge Island Historical Society, WA, 8800
Baker University Archives, KS, 2888
Baldwin County Genealogical Society, AL, 51
Ballwin Historical Society, MO, 4637
Baltimore County Historical Society, Inc., MD, 3618
Banner County Historical Society, NE, 5129
Barkerville Historic Town, BC, 9432
Barnes County Historical Society, ND, 6548
Barnes Museum, CT, 1256
Barnwell County Museum and Historical Board, SC, 7600
Barriere and District Heritage Society, BC, 9433
Barrington Area Historical Society, Inc., IL, 1988
Barrington New Hampshire Historical Society, NH, 5272
Barrington Preservation Society, RI, 7525
Bartholomew County Historical Society, IL, 2084
Bartlesville Area History Museum, OK, 6842
Barton County Historical Society, MO, 4795
Bates County Museum of Pioneer History, MO, 4657

Bath County Historical Society, VA, 8763
Battle of Lexington State Historic Site, MO, 4803
Battle of the Chateauguay National Historic Site of Canada, QC, 9883
Bay Area Historical Society, MN, 4487
Bay County Historical Society/Historical Museum of Bay County, MI, 4066
Bay Village Historical Society, OH, 6578
Beaton Institute of Cape Breton Studies, NS, 9677
Beaufort County Genealogical Society, NC, 6456
Beauvoir, The Jefferson Davis Home and Presidential Library, MS, 4531
Beaver County Historical Society, OK, 6846
Beaver Falls Historical Society Museum, PA, 7122
Beaver Island Historical Society, MI, 4068
Beaverhead County Museum, MT, 5004
Beaverton-Thorah-Eldon Historical Society, ON, 9691
Becker County Historical Society and Museum, MN, 4303
Bedford City/County Museum, VA, 8495
Bedford Historical Society, NH, 5273
Beech Island Historical Society, SC, 7604
Beersheba Springs Historical Society, TN, 7864
Belchertown Historical Association, MA, 3760
Bell County Historical Society and Museum, KY, 3204
Bell County Museum, TX, 8037
Bella Vista Historical Society/Museum, AR, 303
Belle Grove Plantation, VA, 8627
Belleville Area Museum, MI, 4070
Belleville Public Library, IL, 1991
Belleville Public Library, ON, 9692
Bellevue Historical Society, Inc., ID, 1900
Bellevue Historical Society, WA, 8802
Bellflower Genealogical and Historical Society, IL, 1995
Ben-Hur Museum/General Lew Wallace Study, IN, 2502
Benicia Historical Society, CA, 456
Bennett Place State Historic Site, NC, 6269
Bennington Museum, The, VT, 8360
Benson Gristmill Historic Site, UT, 8349
Benton County Historical Society, IA, 2852
Benton County Historical Society, MN, 4482
Benton County Historical Society, MO, 4962
Benton County Historical Society, OR, 7061
Benton County Historical Society, IN, 2531
Berkeley County Historical Society, WV, 9037
Berlin Historical Society, Inc., VT, 8361
Bernard Historical Society and Museum, MI, 4103
Bernice Historical Society, Inc., LA, 3274
Bernice Pauahi Bishop Museum, HI, 1851
Berrien County Historical Association, MI, 4073
Berwyn Historical Society, IL, 1999
Besancon Historical Society, IN, 2607
Bethel Historical Association, Inc., OH, 6582
Bethel Historical Society, The, ME, 3411
Beverly Historical Society and Museum, MA, 3761
Bicentennial Heritage Corporation of Casey County, Kentucky, KY, 3175
Big Bend Historical Society, Inc., WA, 8988
Big Ivy Historical Society, Inc., NC, 6218
Big Sioux River Valley Historical Society, IA, 2759
Big Springs Historical Society and Museum, NY, 5846
Bigheart Historical Museum, OK, 6841
Billings County Historical Society, ND, 6533
Biltmore Estate, NC, 6206
Birmingham Public Library, Department of Archives and Manuscripts, AL, 16
Birmingham Public Library, Linn-Henley Research Library, Tutwiler Collection of Southern History, AL, 17
Bishop Hill Heritage Association, IL, 2000
Bishop Hill State Historic Site, IL, 2001
Black Hills Mining Museum, SD, 7798
Black River Historical Society, OH, 6703
Black River Historical Society, VT, 8400
Blackberry Farm's Pioneer Village, IL, 1984
Blackburn Historical Society, MO, 4646
Blackford County Historical Society, IN, 2544
Blackhawk Genealogical Society of Rock

Civil War Library and Museum, PA, 7363
Clairborne County Historical Society, TN, 7997
Clallam County Historical Society, WA, 8903
Clarendon County Archives, SC, 7703
Clarion County Historical Society, PA, 7168
Clark County Genealogical Library, IL, 2232
Clark County Historical Association, AR, 299
Clark County Historical Society, KS, 2883
Clark County Historical Society, MO, 4764
Clark County Historical Society, SD, 7764
Clark Historical Library, MI, 4199
Clarke County Historical Association, VA, 8496
Clarkston Community Historical Society, MI, 4090
Clay County 1890 Jail Museum and Heritage Center, TX, 8142
Clay County Archives and Historical Library, Inc., MO, 4806
Clay County Genealogical and Historical Society, AR, 402
Clay County Genealogical Society, IL, 2224
Clay County Historical and Arts Council, NC, 6317
Clay County Historical Society, AL, 4
Clay County Historical Society, FL, 1439
Clay County Historical Society, IN, 2493
Clay County Historical Society, MN, 4405
Clay County Historical Society, NE, 5100
Clay County Historical Society, SD, 7854
Clay County Historical Society, The, WV, 9017
Clay County Museum, KS, 2897
Cleburne County Historical Society, AR, 347
Clermont State Historic Site, NY, 5918
Cleveland County Historical Museum, NC, 6432
Clifton Community Historical Society, KS, 2898
Clinton Birthplace Foundation, AR, 353
Clinton County Historical and Genealogy Society, Inc., MO, 4860
Clinton County Historical Society, IA, 2694
Clinton County Historical Society, Inc., IN, 2532
Clinton County Historical Society, NY, 6072
Clinton County Historical Society, OH, 6818
Clinton County Historical Society, PA, 7304
Cloud County Historical Society, KS, 2904
Clover Bend Historic Preservation Association, AR, 357
Coal County Historical and Mining Museum, Inc., OK, 6870
Coal Miners Museum, MO, 4843
Coastal Genealogical Society, NC, 6447
Cobb County Genealogical Society, Inc., GA, 1733
Cobb Memorial Archives, AL, 129
Coe Hall at Planting Fields, NY, 6060
Coffey County Historical Society and Museum, The, KS, 2894
Cohasset Historical Society, MA, 3813
Cokato Museum & Akerlund Photography Studio, MN, 4296
Cole Camp Historical Society, MO, 4680
Cole County Historical Society, MO, 4752
Cole Harbour Rural Heritage Society, NS, 9654
Coles County Genealogical Society, IL, 2029
Collinsville Historical Museum, IL, 2083
Colonel Davenport Historical Foundation, The, IL, 2345
Colorado Springs Museum, CO, 1002
Columbia County Historical Museum, FL, 1468
Columbia County Historical Society, NY, 5962
Columbia County Historical Society, OR, 7090
Columbia County Historical Society, WI, 9091
Columbia Gorge Discovery Center and Wasco County Historical Museum, OR, 7093
Columbus Chapel and Boal Mansion Museum, PA, 7137
Columbus Jewish Historical Society, OH, 6630
Colusa County Free Library, CA, 500
Commerce Historical and Genealogy Society, MO, 4687
Community Historical Museum of Mount Holly, VT, 8359
Community Historical Society, MI, 4095
Concord Historical Society, CA, 501
Concord Historical Society, VT, 8419
Concord Township Historical Society, PA, 7174
Concordia Historical Institute, MO, 4909
Conejo Valley Historical Society/Stagecoach Inn Museum Complex, CA, 661
Confederate Memorial Park at Winstead Hill, TN, 7865
Confederate Memorial State Historic Site, MO, 4726
Congregational Christian Historical Society, MA, 3771
Congregational Library, MA, 3772
Conneaut Valley Area Historical Society, PA, 7175
Connecticut Valley Historical Museum, MA, 3995
Connellsville Area Historical Society, PA, 7177
Conshohocken Historical Society, PA, 7178
Contra Costa County Historical Society and History Center, CA, 714
Cooke County Heritage Society, Inc., TX, 8117
Cooleemee Historical Association, NC, 6262
Cooper County Historical Society, MO, 4856
Coquille Indian Tribe, OR, 7050
Corona Public Library-Heritage Room, CA, 502
Corry Area Historical Society, PA, 7179
Cortland County Historical Society, Inc., NY, 5876
Coryell County Genealogical Society, TX, 8130
Council Valley Museum, ID, 1922
County of Camden, NC, 6236
County of Grey-Owen Sound Museum, ON, 9788
Courtenay and District Museum and Paleontology Centre, BC, 9440
Courthouse Square Association, Inc., MI, 4085
Coventry Historical Society, CT, 1150
Cowley County Genealogical Society, KS, 3085
Cowley County Historical Society, KS, 3084
Cowlitz County Historical Museum, WA, 8864
Craig County Historical Society, VA, 8639
Craik-Patton House, WV, 9013
Cranbury Historical and Preservation Society, NJ, 5475
Cranford Historical Society, NJ, 5477
Craven Hall Historical Society, PA, 7485
Crawford County Historical and Genealogical Society, Inc., IN, 2579
Crawford County Historical Society, GA, 1760
Crawford County Historical Society, IA, 2716
Crawford County Historical Society, IL, 2341
Crawford County Historical Society/Baldwin-Reynolds House Museum, PA, 7310
Crawford W. Long Museum Association, GA, 1752
Crazy Mountain Museum/Sweet Grass Museum Society, MT, 4974
Creston and District Historical and Museum Society, BC, 9442
Crittenden County Genealogical Society, Inc., KY, 3200
Crittenden County Historical Society: Bob Wheeler Museum, KY, 3201
Croatian Ethnic Institute, IL, 2048
Cromwell Historical Society, CT, 1152
Crow Wing County Genealogical Society, MN, 4281
Croydon Historical Society, NH, 5300
Culbertson Mansion State Historic Site, IN, 2601
Cumberland County Historical Society and Hamilton Library, PA, 7157
Cumberland County Historical Society, NJ, 5493
Cumberland County Museum, NS, 9647
Cumberland County Public Library and Information Center, Local and State History Room, NC, 6286
Cumberland Museum and Archives, BC, 9443
Cummington Historical Commission, MA, 3821
Cupa Cultural Center, CA, 691
Custer County Historical Society, NE, 5090
Custer County Historical Society, SD, 7767
Cuttyhunk Historical Society, MA, 3823
Cynthiana-Harrison County Museum, KY, 3115
Czechoslovak Heritage Museum, IL, 2281
Daggett House, RI, 7566
Dakota County Historical Society, MN, 4455
Dakota County Historical Society, NE, 5105
Dakotaland Museum, SD, 7790
Dallas County Historical Museum, AR, 332
Dallas County Historical Society, Inc., MO, 4655
Dallas Historical Society, TX, 8073
Daniel Boone and Frontier Families Research Association, MO, 4722
Daniel Boone Homestead, PA, 7134
Danish Immigrant Museum, The, IA, 2735
Danvers Historical Society, IL, 2088
Danvers Historical Society, MA, 3824
Danville Public Library-Archives, IL, 2090
Darien Historical Society, Inc., The, CT, 1156
Darke County Historical Society, OH, 6677
Darlington County Historical Commission, SC, 7666
Darnall's Chance, MD, 3735
Dartford Historical Society, WI, 9136
Daughters of the American Revolution Museum, DC, 1336
Daughters of the Republic of Texas Library at the Alamo, TX, 8233
Daughters of Union Veterans of the Civil War, 1861-1865, IL, 2392
Davidson County Historical Museum, NC, 6351
Davie County Historical and Genealogical Society, NE, 5166
Dawes County Historical Society, Inc., NE, 5095
Dawson City Museum and Historical Society, YT, 10000
Dawson County Historical Society, NE, 5141
Dead River Area Historical Society, ME, 3524
Dearborn County Historical Society, IN, 2578
Dearborn Historical Museum, MI, 4100
Decatur County Museum, Inc., KS, 3016
Decatur Genealogical Society Inc., IL, 2096
Dedham Historical Society, MA, 3827
Deer Isle Historical Society, ME, 3425
Deere-Wiman House, IL, 2248
Deerfield Historical Society, NH, 5302
Defiance Public Library, OH, 6648
DeForest Area Historical Society, WI, 9106
DeKalb County Historical Genealogical Society, IL, 2418
DeKalb County Historical Society, IN, 2479
DeKalb County Historical Society, MO, 4823
Del Norte County Historical Society, CA, 505
Delavan Community Historical Society, IL, 2103
Delaware County Historical Alliance, IN, 2595
Delaware County Historical Association, NY, 5885
Delaware County Historical Society, Inc., OH, 6649
Delaware County Historical Society, OK, 6902
Delaware County Historical Society, PA, 7146
Delhi Historical Society, OH, 6612
Delhi Ontario Tobacco Museum and Heritage Center, ON, 9706
Delta County Historical Society, CO, 1016
Delta Genealogical Society, GA, 1766
Delta State University Archives, MS, 4537
Denison Advocates, PA, 7220
Denison Homestead Museum, CT, 1214
Denton Community Historical Society, NE, 5106
Denton County Courthouse-on-the-Square Museum, TX, 8084
Denton County Historical Museum, Inc., TX, 8085
DePere Historical Society, WI, 9107
Depot Museum, MN, 4489
Derby Historical Society, CT, 1136
Derby Historical Society, KS, 2909
Derby Historical Society, VT, 8378
Derry Historical Society and Museum, NH, 5304
Derry Township Historical Society, PA, 7260
Des Moines County Genealogical Society, IA, 2675
Des Moines County Historical Society, IA, 2676
Deschutes County Historical Society, OR, 6996
Detroit Historical Museums, MI, 4108
Deutschheim State Historic Site, MO, 4723
Dewey County Jailhouse Museum and Annex, OK, 6972
DeWitt County Historical Museum, The, TX, 8068
Dewitt Historical Society, NE, 5107
Dexter Area Historical Society and Museum, MI, 4113
Dexter Historical Society, Inc., ME, 3426
Dey Mansion/Washington's Headquarters Museum, NJ, 5667
Dickey County Historical Society, ND, 6543
Dickinson County Historical Society, KS, 2873
Dinsmore Homestead Foundation, KY, 3101
Diocesan Museum, NH, 5361
District 69 Historical Society, BC, 9477
Dobson Museum, OK, 6917
Doctor C.S. Best Home and Medical Exhibit, NY, 5983
Doddridge County Historical Society, WV, 9059
Dodge County Genealogical Society, MN, 4304
Dodge County Historical Society, MN, 4381
Dodge County Historical Society, WI, 9079
Donegal Society, The, PA, 7327
Dorothy Whitfield Historic Society, CT, 1182
Douglas County Historical and Genealogical Society, Inc., MO, 4636
Douglas County Historical Society, MN, 4267
Douglas County Historical Society, OR, 7077
Douglas County Historical Society, WI, 9254
Douglas County Historical Society/Watkins Community Museum of History, KS, 2975
Douglas County Museum of History and Natural History, OR, 7078
Douglas County Museum, WA, 8984
Dover Historical Society, IA, 2805
Dover Historical Society, OH, 6651
Downer's Grove Museum, The, IL, 2110
Downingtown Historical Society, PA, 7187
Dracut Historical Society, MA, 3843
Drayton Hall, National Trust for Historic Preservation, SC, 7627
Dresden Historical Society, ME, 3428
Drew County Historical Museum, AR, 392
Drumright Historical Society, OK, 6874
Dryden Township Historical Society, NY, 5887
Duarte Historical Society and Friends of the Library, Inc., CA, 520
Dublin Historical Society, NH, 5307
Dubuque County-Key City Genealogical Society, IA, 2728
Dudley Foundation, Inc., The, CT, 1183
Duke University Rare Book, Manuscript and Special Collections Library, NC, 6271
Duncan Cultural Center, KY, 3144
Dundalk-Patapsco Neck Historical Society, MD, 3631
Dundee Township Historical Society, IL, 2453
DuPage County Genealogical Society, IL, 2220
Durham Historical Association, NH, 5308
Dutchess County Historical Society, NY, 6080
Duxbury Rural and Historical Society, MA, 3846
Dvoracek Memorial Library, NE, 5220
Dyer Memorial Library, MA, 3744
Eagle River Historical Society, WI, 9113
Earl Gregg Swem Library, College of William and Mary, VA, 8774
Early Settlers Association of the Western Reserve, The, OH, 6626
East Benton County Historical Society & Museum, WA, 8865
East Berlin Historical Preservation Society, PA, 7192
East Chicago Room of The East Chicago Public Library, The, IN, 2514
East Hillsborough Historical Society, FL, 1515
East Providence Historical Society, RI, 7541
East River Genealogical Forum, SD, 7860
East Rochester Local History, NY, 5897
East Tennessee Historical Society, TN, 7926
Eastchester Historical Society, The, NY, 5898
Eastern Kentucky Genealogical Society, Inc., KY, 3089
Eastern Oregon Museum, OR, 7021
Eastern Trails Museum, OK, 6980
Eastham Historical Society, MA, 3852
Eatonton-Putnam County Historical Society, Inc.orporation, GA, 1683

Windsor Historical Society, The, CT, 1287
Windsor's Community Museum, ON, 9858
Winnebago and Boone Counties
  Genealogical Society, IL, 2360
Winnebago Area Museum, MN, 4523
Winnebago Genealogical Society, WI, 9220
Winnetoon Board Walk Back in Time, NE,
  5223
Winona County Historical Society, Inc., MN,
  4525
Winters Heritage House Museum, PA, 7200
Winterthur Museum, Garden and Library, DE,
  1321
Wisconsin Maritime Museum, WI, 9173
Wisconsin State Genealogical Society, Inc.,
  WI, 9199
Wisconsin State Historical Society, WI, 9168
Wise County Historical Society, Inc., TX,
  8081
Wise County Historical Society, VA, 8787
Wolfeboro Historical Society/Clark House,
  NH, 5436
Woodbury Heritage Society, MN, 4526
Woodford County Historical Society, KY, 3248
Woodlawn, VA, 8637
Woodrow Wilson Birthplace Foundation, VA,
  8733
Woodside National Historic Site, ON, 9738
Woodstock Historical Society, Inc., CT, 1293
Woodstock Historical Society, VT, 8469
Worcester County Historical Society, MD,
  3723
World Methodist Museum, NC, 6345
Worthington Historical Society, OH, 6820
Wrangell Museum, AK, 203
Wren's Nest House Museum, The, GA, 1629
Wright County Historical and Genealogical
  Society, MO, 4720
Wright County Historical Society, MN, 4286
Wyanet Historical Society, IL, 2471
Wyatt Earp Birthplace Historic House
  Museum, IL, 2252
Wynnewood Historical Society, OK, 6986
Wyoming Historical and Geological Society,
  PA, 7501
Wyoming Room, Sheridan County Fulmer
  Public Library, WY, 9347
Wyoming State Archives, WY, 9297
Yamhill County Historical Museum, OR, 7033
Yell County Historical and Genealogical
  Association, AR, 316
York County Cultural and Heritage
  Commission Historical Center, SC, 7752
York County Culture and Heritage
  Commission, SC, 7729
York County Heritage Trust, PA, 7518
Yorktown Museum, NY, 6198
Young Historical Library, KS, 2987
Young-Sanders Center for Study of the War
  Between the States, LA, 3327
Ypsilanti Historical Museum, MI, 4259
Yukon Archives, YT, 10004
Z. Taylor Brown-Sarah Dorsey Medallion
  Home, TX, 8189
Zelienople Historical Society, Inc., PA, 7519
Zion Genealogical Society, IL, 2473
Zubiwing Cultural Society, MI, 4201

HEALTH SCIENCES

1932 and 1980 Lake Placid Winter Olympic
  Museum, The, NY, 5965
Aberdeen Room Archives and Museum, MD,
  3545
Alaska Historical Collection, Alaska State
  Library, AK, 168
Alberta Association of Registered Nurses,
  AB, 9379
Alfred P. Sloan Museum, MI, 4123
American Museum of Nursing, AZ, 224
American Red Cross Museum, DC, 1326
Archives and Special Collections, MCP
  Hahnemann University, PA, 7354
Archives and Special Collections, Ohio
  University Libraries, OH, 6568
Archives des Soeurs Grises/Grey Nun
  Archives, MB, 9559
Archives of Labor and Urban Affairs, MI, 4104
Archives, University of Colorado at Boulder
  Libraries, CO, 984
Arkansas Country Doctor Museum, AR, 363

Arthur and Elizabeth Schlesinger Library on
  the History of Women in America, The, MA,
  3795
Athens Historical Society, Inc., GA, 1587
Baker-Cederberg Museum and Archives, NY,
  6093
Barnes County Historical Society, ND, 6548
Bartlesville Area History Museum, OK, 6842
BC Heritage, BC, 9518
Belleville Public Library, IL, 1991
Belleville Public Library, ON, 9692
Berkshire County Historical Society, The, MA,
  3951
Birmingham Historical Society, AL, 15
Birmingham Public Library, Department of
  Archives and Manuscripts, AL, 16
Boone County Historical Society, IA, 2671
Boone County Historical Society, IN, 2580
Boone County Historical Society, MO, 4681
Boone County Historical Society, NE, 5074
Burritt on the Mountain-A Living Museum, AL,
  64
Bushnell Historical Society, IL, 2010
California Science Center, CA, 613
California State Archives, CA, 751
Canadian Lesbian and Gay Archives, ON,
  9830
Carroll County Historical & Genealogical
  Society, Inc., AR, 308
Carter-Coile Museum, GA, 1839
Cavalier County Historical Society, ND, 6531
Center for American History, The University of
  Texas at Austin, TX, 8013
Centre for Newfoundland Studies, NF, 9628
Chewelah Historical Society, WA, 8822
Children's Museum in New Braunfels, The,
  TX, 8194
Clara Barton National Historic Site, MD, 3657
Clark County Historical Society, KS, 2883
Clark County Historical Society, MO, 4764
Clark County Historical Society, SD, 7764
Clark Historical Society, NJ, 5469
Clarksville-Montgomery County Museum, TN,
  7875
Colorado Springs Museum, CO, 1002
Conner Prairie, IN, 2524
Country Doctor Museum Foundation, NC,
  6217
Crawford W. Long Museum Association, GA,
  1752
Cumberland Museum and Archives, BC,
  9443
Denver Museum of Natural History, CO, 1024
DeWitt Stetten, Jr. Museum of Medical
  Research, MD, 3598
Discovery Place Children's Museum, TX,
  8257
Doctor Samuel D. Harris National Museum of
  Dentistry, MD, 3572
Donald Kirk Piper, MD, Memorial Medical
  Museum/Saint Joseph Health Center, MO,
  4767
Dorothy Carpenter Medical Archives, NC,
  6480
Douglas County Historical Society, OR, 7077
Douglas County Historical Society, WI, 9254
Duncan Cottage Museum, AK, 179
Elgin County Pioneer Museum, ON, 9808
Emory and Henry College, VA, 8542
Fairfield County Historical Museum, SC, 7749
Fort Point National Historic Site, CA, 802
Fort Worth Museum of Science and History,
  TX, 8106
Fulton County Historical Society, Inc., IN,
  2625
Fulton County Historical Society, Inc., PA,
  7308
Garden of the Rockies Museum, MT, 5051
Garza County Historical Museum, TX, 8216
Glore Psychiatric Museum, MO, 4879
Grant County Historical Society and Museum,
  NE, 5136
Greenwood Museum, The, SC. 7685
Gretna Historical Society, LA, 3294
Grosse Ile and the Irish Memorial National
  Historic Site, QC, 9936
Grundy County Museum, MO, 4949
Harbor Branch Oceanographic Institution,
  Inc., FL, 1430
Harwich Historical Society, MA, 3879
Haskell County Historical Society, KS, 3052
Hattiesburg Area Historical Society and
  Museum, MS, 4554

Henry County Historical Society Museum, IN,
  2603
Heritage Foundation, Inc., GA, 1820
Historic Fort Snelling, MN, 4459
Historic Southwest Ohio, OH, 6614
Historical Society of Western Pennsylvania,
  PA, 7420
Homesteader Museum, WY, 9337
Indiana State Archives, IN, 2562
International Congress of Distinguished
  Awards, PA, 7386
Isanti County Historical Society, MN, 4288
James J. O'Mara Pharmacy Museum, NF,
  9632
Jeff Matthews Memorial Museum, VA, 8573
Jewish Historical Society of Metrowest, NJ,
  5675
Julia A. Purnell Museum, MD, 3721
Junior Museum of Bay County, Inc., FL, 1507
Kalaupapa National Historical Park, HI, 1876
Karpeles Manuscript Library Museum, CA,
  861
Karpeles Manuscript Library Museum, SC,
  7631
Kellogg's Cereal City, USA, MI, 4064
Kewaskum Historical Society, Inc., WI, 9154
Kirkpatrick Science and Air Space Museum
  at Omniplex, OK, 6936
Kline Creek Farm, IL, 2466
Latrobe Area Historical Society, PA, 7289
Liberty Hall Historic Site, KY, 3136
Lincoln County Historical Society, CO, 1079
Lincoln County Historical Society, KS, 2985
Lincoln County Historical Society, WA, 8829
Lincoln County Historical Society, WY, 9303
Living Prairie Museum, MB, 9570
Livingston County Historical Society, IL, 2326
Livingston County Historical Society, NY,
  5914
London Regional Children's Museum, ON,
  9742
Lyon County Historical Museum, KS, 2926
Lyon County Historical Society Museum, MN,
  4383
Macaulay Museum of Dental History/Waring
  Historical Library, SC, 7632
Marked Tree Delta Area Museum, AR, 390
Martin County Historical Society, MN, 4326
Martin County Historical Society, NC, 6465
Mason County Museum, KY, 3203
Mason County Museum, TX, 8183
McDowell House and Apothecary Shop, KY,
  3116
McGill University Archives, QC, 9909
McKeesport Heritage Center, PA, 7309
MCP Hahnemann University Archives and
  Special Collections, PA, 7390
Medical History Society of New Jersey, NJ,
  5528
Memphis Pink Palace Museum, TN, 7947
Menczer Museum of Medicine and Dentistry,
  CT, 1195
Mennonite Library and Archives, KS, 3011
Metropolitan Life Insurance Company, NY,
  6016
Michigan Museums Association, MI, 4171
Michigan State University Archives and
  Historical Collections, MI, 4118
Milton J. Rubenstein Museum of Science and
  Technology, NY, 6153
Missouri Historical Society, MO, 4918
Mobile Medical Museum, AL, 83
Monona Historical Society, IA, 2796
Morrison Historical Society, IL, 2257
Mounds-Midway School of Nursing Historical
  Society, MN, 4472
Mount Horeb Area Historical Society, WI,
  9200
Mount Sinai Archives, NY, 6018
Mount Vernon Museum of Incandescent
  Lighting, MD, 3585
Musee des Augustine de L'Hotel-Dieu de
  Quebec, QC, 9921
Musee Francois-Pilote, QC, 9889
Museum Management Program, National
  Park Service, DC, 1347
Museum of Discovery: Arkansas Museum of
  Science and History, AR, 379
Museum of Health and Medical Science, TX,
  8149
Museum of Health Care at Kingston, The,
  ON, 9730
Museum of Questionable Medical Devices,

MN, 4341
Museum of Science and History of
  Jacksonville, Inc., FL, 1450
Museum of Science and Industry, FL, 1558
Museum of Science and Industry, IL, 2065
Museum of the Native American Resource
  Center, NC, 6388
Museum of the New South, Inc., NC, 6249
Muskegon County Museum, MI, 4203
National Atomic Museum, NM, 5695
National Museum of American History,
  Smithsonian Institution, DC, 1355
National Museum of Civil War Medicine, MD,
  3648
Nevada Test Site Historical Foundation, NV,
  5248
Neville Public Museum of Brown County, WI,
  9135
New England Historic Genealogical Society,
  MA, 3781
New Hampshire Aniquarian Society, NH,
  5341
New Jersey Museum of Agriculture, NJ, 5578
New Orleans Pharmacy Museum, LA, 3361
North Carolina Museum of History, NC, 6405
Oak Park Conservatory, The, IL, 2291
Olmsted County Historical Society, MN, 4442
Opelousas Museum and Interpretive Center,
  LA, 3365
Oregon State Library, OR, 7084
Owensboro Area Museum of Science and
  History, KY, 3215
Pacific Space Centre, BC, 9509
Palacios Library, Inc., TX, 8204
Palmer Foundation for Chiropractic History,
  IA, 2709
Peace River Centennial Museum and
  Archives, AB, 9412
Pearson Museum Dept of Medical
  Humanities, IL, 2405
Penfield Local History Room, NY, 6068
Pennsbury Manor/Pennsbury Society, The,
  PA, 7326
Philadelphia Society for the Preservation of
  Landmarks, PA, 7398
Port Washington Public Library, NY, 6077
Porter Thermometer Museum, MA, 3946
Princeton Historical Society, WI, 9231
Public Health Museum in New England, MA,
  4011
Regional Oral History Office, CA, 463
Remick Country Doctor Museum and Farm,
  NH, 5424
Revelstoke and District Historical Association,
  BC, 9496
Rhode Island State Archives, RI, 7579
Ringgold County Historical Society, IA, 2801
Riverton Museum, WY, 9340
Robert B. Greenblatt, MD Library, Special
  Collections, GA, 1635
Robeson County Museum, NC, 6356
Rockbridge Historical Society, VA, 8604
Rocky Mountain Jewish Historical Society
  and Beck Archives, CO, 1031
Sacramento Archives and Museum Collection
  Center, CA, 764
Saint Francis County Museum, AR, 333
San Diego Civil War Roundtable, CA, 784
San Diego Historical Society, CA, 787
Saskatchewan Archives Board-Regina, SK,
  9980
Saskatchewan Archives Board-Saskatoon,
  SK, 9989
Scott-Ford Historic Site, Farish St Historic
  District, MS, 4576
Seneca-Iroquois National Museum, NY, 6114
Seville Historical Society, OH, 6779
Siloam Springs Museum, AR, 419
Sioux Empire Medical Museum, SD, 7840
Skagit County Historical Society, WA, 8871
South Carolina State Museum, SC, 7662
Southwest Museum of Science and
  Technology/The Science Place, TX, 8079
Special Collections, Atkins Library, University
  of North Carolina at Charlotte, NC, 6252
Special Collections, Robert W. Woodruff
  Library, Emory University, GA, 1626
Stansbury Home Preservation Association,
  CA, 492
State Museum of Pennsylvania, The, PA,
  7252
Steele County Historical Society, MN, 4427
Steele County Historical Society, ND, 6527

Stone Fort Museum, TX, 8193
Texarkana Historical Museum, Texarkana Museums System, TX, 8258
Texarkana Museums System, TX, 8259
Texas Medical Association, TX, 8026
Tuskegee Institute National Historic Site, George Washington Carver Museum, AL, 125
Twillingate Museum Association, NF, 9643
U.S. Army Medical Department Museum, TX, 8103
Universite de Montreal, Division des Archives, QC, 9913
University History Institute, AR, 383
University of Alabama at Birmingham Historical Collections, AL, 23
University of Alberta Dental Museum, AB, 9389
University of Colorado Museum of Natural History, CO, 987
University of Iowa Hospitals and Clinics Medical Museum, IA, 2767
University of Nebraska State Museum, NE, 5154
University of Wyoming American Heritage Center, WY, 9328
University South Caroliniana Society, SC, 7663
Utah State Archives, UT, 8340
Valdosta State University Archives, GA, 1829
Veterinary Museum/Missouri Veterinary Medical Foundation, MO, 4760
Victoria School Archives and Museum, AB, 9391
Wampum Area Historical Society, Inc., PA, 7484
Wannamuse Institute for Arts, Culture, and Ethnic Studies, LA, 3366
Watonwan County Historical Society, MN, 4377
Webb-Deane-Stevens Museum, CT, 1280
West Augusta Historical Society, WV, 9036
Western New York Documentary Heritage Program, NY, 5844
Whitchurch-Stouffville Museum, ON, 9718
Whitemouth Municipal Museum Society, MB, 9557
Wilson County Historical Museum, KS, 2940
Wilson Czech Opera House Corporation, Foundation, KS, 3083
Wimbledon Community Museum, ND, 6554
Wishard Nursing Museum, IN, 2571
York County Cultural and Heritage Commission Historical Center, SC, 7752

HISTORIC PERSONS

1711 Solomon Goffe House, CT, 1210
1736 Josiah Dennis Manse Museum, MA, 3841
1812 Homestead Educational Foundation, NY, 6193
1890 House and Center for the Arts, The, NY, 5875
1932 and 1980 Lake Placid Winter Olympic Museum, The, NY, 5965
A.H. Stephens State Historic Park, GA, 1663
A.W. Perry Homestead Museum, TX, 8046
Abbeville County Historic Preservation Commission, SC, 7594
Aberdeen Room Archives and Museum, MD, 3545
Abigail Adams Historical Society, Inc., The, MA, 4034
Abraham Lincoln Association, IL, 2390
Abraham Lincoln Birthplace National Historic Site, KY, 3155
Abraham Lincoln Library and Museum, TN, 7903
Abraham Lincoln Tourism Bureau of Logan County, IL, 2207
Acadian Heritage and Culture Foundation, Inc., LA, 3285
Adair Cabin/John Brown Museum State Historic Site, KS, 3020
Adair County Historical Society, IA, 2749
Adair County Historical Society, MO, 4791
Adams County Historical Society, CO, 989
Adams County Historical Society, NE, 5131
Adams County Historical Society, PA, 7226
Adams County Historical Society, WA, 8875

Adams Museum, SD, 7770
Adelaide Hunter Hoodless Homestead, ON, 9807
Adena State Memorial: The Home of Thomas Worthington, OH, 6602
Adirondack Museum, The, NY, 5820
Adsmore Museum, KY, 3231
Affton Historical Society, MO, 4901
African American Museum in Philadelphia, The, PA, 7349
Afro-American Historical Association of Fauquier County, VA, 8754
Afton Historical Society Museum, MN, 4263
Agate Fossil Beds National Monument, NE, 5130
Aiken County Historical Museum, SC, 7596
Air Force Enlisted Heritage Hall, AL, 91
Aircraft Carrier Hornet Foundation, CA, 431
Aitkin County Historical Society, MN, 4264
Ak-Chin Him-Dak EcoMuseum and Archives, AZ, 233
Alabama Civil War Roundtable, AL, 11
Alabama Historic Ironworks Commission, AL, 76
Alabama Historical Commission-Old Cahawba, AL, 108
Alachua County Historic Trust; Matheson Museum, Inc., FL, 1436
Alamance Battleground State Historic Site, NC, 6232
Alamance County Historical Museum, Inc., NC, 6234
Alamo Battlefield Association, TX, 8230
Alaska Historical Collection, Alaska State Library, AK, 168
Albany County Historical Society, WY, 9326
Albany Historical Society, WI, 9065
Albany Institute of History and Art, NY, 5783
Albuquerque Museum of Art and History, NM, 5689
Alcatraz Island, CA, 795
Alden Kindred of America, MA, 3844
Alexander and Baldwin Sugar Museum, HI, 1887
Alexander Faribault House, MN, 4328
Alexander Graham Bell National Historic Site, NS, 9651
Alexander Ramsey House, MN, 4451
Alexandria Black History Resource Center, The, VA, 8472
Alfalfa County Historical Society, OK, 6859
Alfred P. Sloan Museum, MI, 4123
Algonquin Culture and Heritage Centre, ON, 9717
Alice Austen House Museum, NY, 6143
Alice T. Miner Colonial Collection, NY, 5861
Aliceville Museum, AL, 1
Allan MacPherson House and Park, ON, 9755
Allegany County Historical Society, MD, 3627
Allegany County Historical Society, NY, 5814
Allegheny Cemetery Historical Association, PA, 7414
Allegheny-Kiski Valley Historical Society, PA, 7465
Allen Barkley Young Historians, Inc., KY, 3220
Allen County Historical and Genealogy Society, KY, 3236
Allen County-Ft. Wayne Historical Society, IN, 2525
Allen E. Roberts Masonic Library and Museum, Inc. (Grand Lodge of Virginia AF&AM), VA, 8680
Allen-Lambe House Foundation, KS, 3075
Almanzo and Laura Ingalls Wilder Association, NY, 5975
Alpine County Museum, CA, 634
Alpine Historical Society, AK, 192
Alpine Historical Society, CA, 434
Alsi Historical and Genealogical Society, OR, 7102
Alta District Historical Society, CA, 517
Altadena Historical Society, CA, 435
Alton Historical Society, Inc., NH, 5265
Alvin C. York State Historic Site, TN, 7983
Amador County Archives, CA, 574
Amalthea Historical Society, OH, 6814
Amelia Island Museum of History, FL, 1419
American Airlines C.R. Smith Museum, TX, 8080
American Antiquarian Society, MA, 4040
American Catholic Historical Society, PA, 7350

American Cotton Museum, TX, 8134
American Flag House and Betsy Ross Memorial, PA, 7351
American Fluorite Museum, The, IL, 2367
American Helicopter Museum and Education Center, PA, 7498
American Independence Museum, NH, 5314
American Indian Museum, AL, 63
American Jewish Historical Society, MA, 4016
American Manse/Whitney-Halsey House, The, NY, 5816
American Museum of Fly Fishing, VT, 8401
American Museum of Nursing, AZ, 224
American Museum of the Miniature Arts, TX, 8071
American Museum of the Moving Image, NY, 5801
American Red Cross Museum, DC, 1326
American Swedish Historical Museum, PA, 7352
American Swedish Institute, The, MN, 4386
American-Italian Renaissance Foundation, LA, 3340
Ames Heritage Association, IA, 2660
Anacortes Museum, WA, 8793
Anchorage Museum of History and Art, AK, 138
Ancient and Honorable Artillery Company of Massachusetts, MA, 3764
Anderson County Historical Society, KS, 2947
Anderson Valley Historical Museum, CA, 470
Andover Historical Society, IL, 1979
Andover Historical Society, MA, 3753
Andover Historical Society, NH, 5267
Andrew County Museum and Historical Society, MO, 4933
Andrew Jackson State Park, SC, 7701
Andrew Johnson National Historic Site and Homestead, TN, 7899
Androscoggin Historical Society, ME, 3400
Annandale National Historic Site, ON, 9822
Anoka County Historical Society, MN, 4269
Antietam National Battlefield, MD, 3714
Antiquarian and Landmarks Society, CT, 1189
Antique Auto Museum of Massachusetts, MA, 3793
Antique Wireless Association Museum of Electronic Communication, NY, 5934
Apalachicola Maritime Museum, Inc., FL, 1379
Apex Historical Society, NC, 6204
Appalachian Cultural Museum, The, NC, 6225
Appling County Heritage Center, GA, 1637
Appomattox Court House National Historical Park, VA, 8489
APVA Joseph Bryan Branch, VA, 8574
APVA Mary Washington Branch, VA, 8563
Arboretum of Los Angeles County, CA, 440
Archival Center, Archdiocese of Los Angeles, CA, 640
Archives and Special Collections, Harriet Irving Library, NB, 9586
Archives and Special Collections, MCP Hahnemann University, PA, 7354
Archives des Soeurs Grises/Grey Nun Archives, MB, 9559
Archives Nationales du Quebec, QC, 9898
Archives Nationales du Quebec, QC, 9937
Archives of Labor and Urban Affairs, MI, 4104
Archives of the Peabody Institute of The Johns Hopkins University, MD, 3558
Archives, University of Colorado at Boulder Libraries, CO, 984
Archivists for Congregations of Women Religious (ACWR), DC, 1331
Argyle Township Court House and Archives, NS, 9679
Arizona Archaeological and Historical Society, AZ, 271
Arizona Department of Library, Archives, and Public Records, AZ, 241
Arizona Hall of Fame Museum, AZ, 242
Arizona Historical Society - Northern Division, AZ, 216
Arizona Historical Society - Rio Colorado Division, AZ, 292
Arizona Historical Society - Southern Division, AZ, 272
Arizona Historical Society Museum, Arizona Historical Society - Central Division, AZ, 263
Arizona History and Archives Division,

Arizona Department of Library, Archives, and Public Records, AZ, 243
Arizona Jewish Historical Society, AZ, 244
Arizona State Capitol Museum, AZ, 245
Arkansas Country Doctor Museum, AR, 363
Arkansas Historic Wine Museum, AR, 400
Arkansas History Commission, AR, 366
Arlington County Public Library Virginia Room, VA, 8490
Arlington Historical Society, Inc., VA, 8491
Arlington Historical Society, The, MA, 3756
Armed Forces Museum, MS, 4535
Armstrong County Museum, Inc., TX, 8048
Arrow Rock State Historic Site, MO, 4631
Artesia Historical Museum and Art Center, NM, 5701
Arthur and Elizabeth Schlesinger Library on the History of Women in America, The, MA, 3795
Arthur Bowring Sandhills Ranch, NE, 5163
Arvid E. Miller Memorial Library Museum, WI, 9085
Ashland County Historical Society, OH, 6564
Ashland Historical Society, MA, 3758
Ashland Historical Society, NH, 5268
Ashland Historical Society, WI, 9071
Ashland University Archives, OH, 6565
Ashland, the Henry Clay Estate, KY, 3159
Ashlawn-Highland, VA, 8515
Ashtabula Plantation, SC, 7720
Ashton Villa, TX, 8118
Ashville Area Heritage Society, OH, 6566
Asotin County Historical Museum, WA, 8798
Aspen Historical Society, CO, 981
Association for Living History, Farm and Agricultural Museums, OH, 6732
Association for the Preservation of Historic Coles County, IL, 2236
Association for the Preservation of Historic Natchitoches, LA, 3329
Association for the Preservation of Tennessee Antiquities (APTA), TN, 7958
Association for the Preservation of Virginia Antiquities (APVA), VA, 8682
Astor House Museum, CO, 1064
Astronaut Hall of Fame, FL, 1565
Ataloa Lodge Museum, OK, 6918
Atchison County, Kansas Historical Society, KS, 2885
Athenaeum Rectory, The, TN, 7879
Athens County Historical Society and Museum, OH, 6569
Athens Historical Society, Inc., GA, 1587
Athol Murray College of Notre Dame Archives/Museum, SK, 9996
Atlanta Cyclorama, GA, 1597
Atlanta Historical Society, GA, 1598
Atlanta Historical Society, ID, 1899
Atlanta History Center, GA, 1599
Atlantic County Historical Society, The, NJ, 5629
Atwater Historical Society, The, OH, 6570
Auburn Avenue Research Library on African American Culture and History, GA, 1601
Audubon House and Tropical Gardens, FL, 1456
Audubon State Commemorative Area, LA, 3371
Auglaize County Historical Society, OH, 6786
Augusta Museum of History, GA, 1630
Aurelia Heritage Society, IA, 2666
Aurora Colony Historical Society, OR, 6992
Aurora County Historical Society, SD, 7826
Aurora Historical Society, NY, 5888
Aurora Historical Society, OH, 6571
Autauga County Heritage Association, AL, 105
Automotive Hall of Fame, MI, 4099
Autry Museum of Western Heritage, CA, 611
Avery Research Center for African American History and Culture, College of Charleston, SC, 7621
Aviation Historical Museum of Louisiana, LA, 3322
Avoca Museum and Historical Society, VA, 8485
Avon Historical Society, IL, 1987
Avon Historical Society, OH, 6573
Awbury Arboretum Association, PA, 7355
Aylmer and District Museum, ON, 9690
B&O Railroad Museum, MD, 3559
Babcock Smith House, RI, 7590
Babe Ruth Birthplace Museum, MD, 3560

Fremont County Historical Society, WY, 9325
Fremont Historical Society, NH, 5324
French Prairie Historical Society and Settlemier House, OR, 7104
Fresno Metropolitan Museum, CA, 550
Friars Point Historical Preservation Society, MS, 4548
Frick Art and Historical Center, The, PA, 7418
Friend Family Assocation Heritage Museum and Genealogical Library, MD, 3652
Friends of 'Iolani Palace, The, HI, 1855
Friends of Arrow Rock, Inc., MO, 4633
Friends of Carrillo Ranch, Inc., CA, 481
Friends of Fabyan, IL, 2148
Friends of Hatley Park, BC, 9526
Friends of Hildene, Inc., VT, 8402
Friends of History in Fulton, New York, Inc., NY, 5912
Friends of Hyde Hall, Inc., NY, 5867
Friends of John Hay National Wildlife Refuge, NH, 5380
Friends of Linden Place, RI, 7530
Friends of Medalta, AB, 9407
Friends of Monmouth Battlefield, Inc., NJ, 5649
Friends of Old South Ferdinand, Inc., MO, 4702
Friends of Raynham Hall, NY, 6061
Friends of Rickwood, AL, 18
Friends of Rock Castle, TN, 7904
Friends of Sheldon Jackson Museum, AK, 185
Friends of the Cabildo, Inc., LA, 3345
Friends of the Dr. Richard Eells House, IL, 2332
Friends of the Fairfax Station, Inc., VA, 8552
Friends of the Governor's Mansion, TX, 8015
Friends of the Historical Museum, ID, 1904
Friends of the Mansion at Smithville, NJ, 5560
Friends of the Ocean City Historical Museum, Inc., NJ, 5584
Friends of the Vermont State House, VT, 8409
Friends of the Wallace House and Old Dutch Parsonage, NJ, 5638
Friends of Thomas Leiper House, Inc., PA, 7482
Friendship Hill National Historic Site, PA, 7216
Frogmore Plantation and Gins, LA, 3290
Frontier Army Museum, KS, 2933
Frontier Culture Museum of Virginia, VA, 8735
Frontier Gateway Museum and Foundation, MT, 5011
Frontier Historical Society Museum, CO, 1063
Frontier Times Museum, TX, 8031
Fruitlands Museum, MA, 3877
Fulton County Genealogical Society, KS, 2941
Fulton Mansion State Historical Site, TX, 8225
Funk Prairie Home and Funk Gem and Mineral Museum, IL, 2384
Gadsby's Tavern Museum, VA, 8477
Gage County Historical Society, NE, 5084
Galena/Jo Daviess County Historical Society and Museum, IL, 2140
Galerie d'art du Parc/Manoir de Tonnancour, QC, 9938
Gallatin County Historical Society and Pioneer Museum, MT, 4980
Gallia County Historical/Genealogical Society, OH, 6667
Galva Historical Society, IL, 2146
Gann Museum of Saline County, Inc., AR, 304
Garden Grove Historical Society, CA, 555
Gardiner Museum of Ceramic Art, The, ON, 9834
Gardner House Museum, MI, 4051
Gardner Mansion and Museum, OK, 6853
Gardner Village, UT, 8305
Garfield County Historical Association, WA, 8901
Garretson Area Historical Society and Garretson Heritage Museum, ND, 6517
Gary Historical and Cultural Society, Inc., IN, 2534
Garza County Historical Museum, TX, 8216
Gaslamp Quarter Historical Floundation, CA, 778
Gaspesian British Heritage Centre, QC, 9914

Gastineau Channel Historical Society, AK, 170
Gates County Historical Society, NC, 6298
GATEway to the Panhandle Museum Corporation, OK, 6888
Geary County Historical Society Museum, KS, 2965
Geauga County Historical Society, OH, 6589
Geddes Historical Restoration Society, SD, 7785
Gemantown Historical Society, The, MD, 3655
Genealogical Society of Pennsylvania, The, PA, 7373
General Adam Stephen Memorial Association, Inc., WV, 9038
General Commission on Archives and History of the United Methodist Church, NJ, 5532
General Daniel Bissell House Museum, MO, 4912
General Grant National Monument, NY, 6005
General John A. Logan Museum, IL, 2266
General John J. Pershing Boyhood Home, MO, 4794
General Phineas Banning Residence Museum, CA, 967
Genesee County History Department, NY, 5808
Geneva Historical Society, IL, 2149
Geneva Historical Society, NY, 5915
Geneva Lake Area Museum, WI, 9164
George C. Marshall Foundation, VA, 8602
George M. Jones Memorial Library, VA, 8611
George W. Brown, Jr. Ojibwe Museum and Cultural Center, WI, 9159
George Washington Birthplace National Monument, VA, 8765
George Washington Carver Birthplace Association, MO, 4695
George Washington Masonic National Memorial, VA, 8478
Georgetown Heritage Trust, DC, 1341
Georgia Department of Archives and History, GA, 1605
Georgia Mountains History Museum at Brenau University, GA, 1694
Georgia O'Keeffe Foundation, The, NM, 5683
Georgia Salzburger Society, GA, 1759
Georgia Sports Hall of Fame, GA, 1728
Georgia Trust for Historic Preservation, The, GA, 1607
Georgian Museum, The, OH, 6697
Gerald R. Ford Conservation Center, NE, 5187
German Society of Philadelphia, The, PA, 7374
Germantown Historical Society, PA, 7375
Germantown Historical Society, The, MD, 3656
Gettysburg National Military Park, PA, 7229
Ghost Tours of Niagara, ON, 9767
Gibson County Historical Society, Inc., IN, 2620
Gibson House Museum, The, ON, 9772
Gila County Historical Museum, AZ, 227
Giles County Historical Society, TN, 7987
Giles County Historical Society, VA, 8662
Gilliam County Historical Society, OR, 7006
Gilsum Historical Society, NH, 5326
Glen Ellyn Historical Society-Stacy's Tavern, IL, 2151
Glen Foerd on the Delaware, PA, 7377
Glen Ridge Historical Society, NJ, 5492
Glendo Historical Museum, WY, 9313
Glengarry Pioneer Museum, ON, 9708
Glenn H. Curtiss Museum of Local History, NY, 5928
Glensheen Historic Estate, MN, 4307
Glessner House Museum, IL, 2055
Gloucester County Historical Society, NJ, 5680
Gloucester Historical Society, VA, 8575
Glove Museum, The, NY, 6007
Gold Nugget Days, Inc., CA, 697
Golden Ball Tavern Museum, MA, 4032
Golden Drift Historical Society, CA, 522
Golden Drift Museum, CA, 523
Golden Pioneer Museum, CO, 1068
Golden Spike National Historical Site, UT, 8321
Golden State Museum, CA, 759
Goleta Valley Historical Society, CA, 560
Gomez Mill House, NY, 5978
Goochland County Historical Society, VA,

8578
Goodhue County Historical Society, MN, 4437
Gordon County Historical Society, GA, 1646
Gore Place, MA, 4019
Gorgas House, AL, 118
Gorham Historical Society, ME, 3443
Gorham Historical Society, NH, 5327
Goshen Historical Society, CT, 1175
Goshen Historical Society, IN, 2538
Goshen Township Historical Society, OH, 6674
Goshen, New Hampshire Historical Society, Inc., NH, 5382
Governor Bent Museum, NM, 5769
Governor Charles B. Aycock Birthplace State Historic Site, NC, 6295
Governor Jim Hogg City Park and Governor Hogg Shrine State Historic Park, TX, 8219
Governor Richard Oglesby Mansion, IL, 2097
Governor Warner Mansion, MI, 4122
Governor's Mansion State Historic Park, CA, 760
Grace Hudson Museum and Sun House, CA, 937
Grace Museum, The, TX, 8003
Graceland, Elvis Presley Enterprises, TN, 7942
Grady County Historical Society, OK, 6863
Graeme Park, PA, 7265
Graham County Historical Society Museum, AZ, 254
Graham-Ginestra House, Inc., IL, 2352
Grand Army of Republic Civil War Museum and Library, PA, 7378
Grand Blanc Heritage Association and Museum, MI, 4132
Grand Ledge Area Historical Society Museum, MI, 4134
Grand Prairie Historical Society, AR, 318
Grand Rapids Historical Society, MI, 4137
Grand Traverse Heritage Center, MI, 4250
Grand Village of the Natchez Indians, MS, 4584
Grande Prairie Museum, AB, 9398
Grange Art Gallery of Ontario, The, ON, 9835
Granger Homestead Association, Inc., NY, 5852
Grant County Historical Society and Museum, NE, 5136
Grant County Historical Society, IN, 2586
Grant County Historical Society, Inc., KY, 3202
Grant County Historical Society, MN, 4315
Grant County Historical Society, SD, 7807
Grant County Historical Society, WI, 9166
Grantham Historical Society, Inc., NH, 5328
Graue Mill and Museum, IL, 2283
Gravesend Historical Society, The, NY, 5924
Gravette Historical Museum, AR, 342
Grays Harbor Historical Seaport Authority: S/V Lady Washington, WA, 8791
Grayslake Municipal Historical Museum, IL, 2158
Graystone Society, Inc., PA, 7170
Great Harbor Martitine Museum, ME, 3475
Great Lakes Lighthouse Museum, MI, 4179
Great Lakes Shipwreck Historical Society, MI, 4243
Greater Southwest Historical Museum, OK, 6837
Greeley County Historical Society, KS, 3063
Greeley County Historical Society, NE, 5128
Greenbelt Museum, MD, 3661
Greenbrier Historical Society, Inc., WV, 9030
Greenbrier Historical Society, TN, 7898
Greene County Historical Society, IN, 2608
Greene County Historical Society, MO, 4942
Greene County Historical Society, NY, 5878
Greene County Historical Society, OH, 6823
Greene County Historical Society, VA, 8731
Greenlawn-Centerport Historical Association, NY, 5925
Greensboro Historical Museum, NC, 6304
Greensboro Historical Society, VT, 8391
Greenville County Library, SC, 7683
Greenwood County Historical Society, KS, 2927
Greenwood County Historical Society, SC, 7684
Greenwood Military Aviation Museum, NS, 9657
Gregg County Historical Museum, TX, 8173

Gresham Historical Society, OR, 7020
Gretna Historical Society, LA, 3294
Grevemberg House Museum, LA, 3288
Grey Towers National Historic Landmark, PA, 7318
Greybull Museum, WY, 9316
Griffith Morgan Committee, Inc., NJ, 5594
Grissom Air Museum State Historic Site, IN, 2613
Gropius House, SPNEA, MA, 3899
Grosse Ile and the Irish Memorial National Historic Site, QC, 9936
Grosse Pointe Historical Society, MI, 4145
Grosvenor House Museum Association, MI, 4162
Groton Historical Society, MA, 3875
Groton Historical Society, NH, 5413
Grout Museum of History and Science, IA, 2860
Grove Heritage Association, IL, 2153
Grover Cleveland Birthplace Memorial Association, NJ, 5455
Grundy County Museum, MO, 4949
Guernsey County Historical Society, OH, 6591
Guilford Township Historical Collection of the Plainfield-Guilford Public Library, IN, 2615
Gulfport Historical Society, FL, 1534
Gunn Memorial Library Inc., CT, 1272
Gunnison County Pioneer and Historical Society, CO, 1075
Gunston Hall Plantation, VA, 8620
Guy Park Manor, NY, 5797
Gwinnett History Museum, GA, 1720
H. Earl Clark Museum, MT, 5021
H.C. Grant Heritage Museum, NF, 9624
Hackley and Hume Historic Site, MI, 4202
Haeger Pottery Collectors of America, CA, 439
Haffenreffer Museum of Anthropology, RI, 7531
Hagley Museum and Library, DE, 1315
Halifax Historical Museum, FL, 1406
Hallmark Visitors Center, The, MO, 4768
Hamilton County Historical Society, IL, 2237
Hamilton County Historical Society, IN, 2610
Hamilton County Historical Society, Plainsman Museum, NE, 5080
Hamilton Grange National Memorial, NY, 6009
Hammond Castle Museum, MA, 3869
Hammond-Harwood House Association, Inc., MD, 3551
Hampton Museum and Visitors Center, SC, 7687
Hampton Plantation State Historic Site, SC, 7705
Hampton Roads Museum, VA, 8649
Hampton University Museum, VA, 8583
Hancock County Historical Society, IA, 2674
Hancock County Historical Society, IL, 2021
Hancock County Historical Society, IN, 2540
Hancock County Museum, KY, 3148
Hancock Historical Society, NH, 5332
Hancock Shaker Village, Inc., MA, 3953
Hank Snow Country Music Centre, NS, 9663
Hanna-Basin Historical Society, WY, 9319
Hanover County Historical Society, Inc., VA, 8585
Hanover Historical Society, NH, 5333
Hanover Tavern Foundation, VA, 8586
Hanover-Horton Area Historical Society, MI, 4147
Haralson County Historical Society, GA, 1644
Hardin County Historical Society, IA, 2733
Hardin County Historical Society, KY, 3122
Harding Township Historical Society, NJ, 5573
Harlow Old Fort House, MA, 3955
Harness Racing and Hall of Fame, NY, 5922
Harnett County Historical Society, NC, 6352
Harpers Ferry National Historical Park, WV, 9026
Harriet Beecher Stowe Center, CT, 1193
Harriet Beecher Stowe Slavery to Freedom Museum, KY, 3250
Harriet Taylor Upton Association, OH, 6807
Harriet Tubman Organization, MD, 3605
Harris Heritage Museum Society, Inc., SK, 9958
Harrison County Genealogical Society, MO, 4643
Harrison County Historical Commission, TX, 8180

Harrison County Historical Museum, TX, 8181
Harrison County Historical Society, IA, 2782
Harrison County Historical Society, MO, 4644
Harrison County Historical Society, WV, 9016
Harrison Historical Society, ME, 3446
Harrison Museum of African-American Culture, VA, 8711
Harriton Association, PA, 7153
Harry Meador Coal Museum, VA, 8497
Harry S. Truman Birthplace State Historic Park, MO, 4796
Harry S. Truman Courtroom and Office, MO, 4737
Harry S. Truman Library, MO, 4738
Harry S. Truman Little White House Museum, FL, 1460
Harry S. Truman National Historic Site, MO, 4739
Hart County Historical Society, KY, 3208
Hartsville Museum, SC, 7688
Hartwick Pines State Park Logging Museum, MI, 4143
Harvard Historical Society, MA, 3878
Harwich Historical Society, MA, 3879
Haskell County Historical Society, KS, 3052
Hastings Historical Society, NY, 5929
Hattie Weber Museum of Davis, The, CA, 513
Hattiesburg Area Historical Society and Museum, MS, 4554
Haverhill Historic Society, NH, 5335
Hawaii State Archives, HI, 1860
Hawaiian Music Hall of Fame and Museum, HI, 1873
Hayden Heritage Center, CO, 1076
Hayden Historical Museum Inc., IN, 2545
Hays House Museum, MD, 3593
Hayward Area Historical Society, CA, 564
Haywood County Museum, TN, 7866
Hazelwood Historic House Museum, WI, 9133
Healy House and Dexter Cabin Museum, CO, 1088
Hearst Castle-Hearst San Simeon State Historical Monument, CA, 849
Heart of West Texas Museum, TX, 8051
Heart's Content Cable Station Provincial Historic Site, NF, 9630
Heddon Museum, MI, 4115
Hedge House, MA, 3956
Heflin House Museum, MS, 4604
Helena Library and Museum Association, AR, 351
Hellenic Cultural Association, UT, 8333
Hells Gate State Park, ID, 1937
Hemingway-Pfeiffer Museum and Educational Center, AR, 403
Henderson County Historical Society, IL, 2338
Hennepin History Museum, MN, 4387
Henney History Room-Conway Public Library, NH, 5297
Henniker Historical Society, NH, 5336
Henrico Historic Preservation/Museum Services, VA, 8688
Henricus Foundation, The, VA, 8523
Henry A. Wallace Country Life Center, IA, 2750
Henry County Historical Society Museum, IN, 2603
Henry Ford Estate-Fair Lane, The, MI, 4101
Henry Ford Museum and Greenfield Village, MI, 4102
Henry George Birthplace, PA, 7379
Henry Meade Williams Local History Department, Harrison Memorial Library, CA, 482
Henry Morrison Flagler Museum, FL, 1502
Henry Sheldon Museum of Vermont History, VT, 8404
Henry Whitfield State Museum, CT, 1184
Herbert Hoover National Historic Site, IA, 2866
Herbert S. Ford Memorial Museum, LA, 3296
Heritage Deep Cove, BC, 9472
Heritage Hill Historical Park, CA, 589
Heritage Hillsborough, Inc., NB, 9591
Heritage House of Orange County Association, Inc., TX, 8201
Heritage Museum of Montgomery County, TX, 8058
Heritage Museum of Roberts County, SD, 7844
Heritage Museum, MT, 5035
Heritage Museum, The, OR, 7025
Heritage Orange County, Inc., CA, 853
Heritage Shawinigan, QC, 9928
Herkimer County Historical Society, NY, 5931
Herman Miller, Inc. Corporate Archives and Records Services, MI, 4260
Hermitage, The, NJ, 5511
Hermitage, The, TN, 7907
Herndon Home, The, GA, 1609
Herriman State Park of Idaho, ID, 1929
Hershey Community Archives, PA, 7261
Hershey Museum, PA, 7262
Hibbing Historical Society & Museum, MN, 4350
Hickory Landmarks Society, NC, 6320
Hicks-Stearns Family Museum, CT, 1267
Hidalgo County Historical Museum, TX, 8088
Hiddenite Center, Inc., NC, 6321
Higgins Museum, The, IA, 2812
High Plains Heritage Center Museum, SD, 7847
High Point Historical Society, Inc., NC, 6325
High Point Museum and Historical Park, NC, 6326
Highland Park Historical Society, IL, 2169
Highland Park Historical Society, NJ, 5507
Highlands Hammock State Park, FL, 1532
Highlands Historical Society, The, PA, 7217
Highline Historical Society, WA, 8918
Highspire Historical Society, PA, 7263
Hill Historical Society, NH, 5337
Hill-Stead Museum, CT, 1170
Hillforest Historical Foundation, Inc., IN, 2481
Hilltop Historical Society, OH, 6631
Hillwood Museum and Gardens, DC, 1342
Hinckley Fire Museum, Inc., MN, 4351
His Lordship's Kindness, MD, 3616
Historic Allaire Village, NJ, 5437
Historic Annapolis Foundation, MD, 3552
Historic Bath State Historic Site, NC, 6219
Historic Beaufort Foundation, SC, 7603
Historic Bethabara Park, NC, 6482
Historic Borst Home, WA, 8819
Historic Boulder, Inc., CO, 986
Historic Cabarrus, Inc., NC, 6261
Historic Camden Revolutionary War Site, SC, 7616
Historic Carnton Plantation, TN, 7891
Historic Carson House, NC, 6385
Historic Charleston Foundation, SC, 7629
Historic Chelsea Plantation, Inc., VA, 8770
Historic Cold Spring Village, NJ, 5460
Historic Columbia Foundation, SC, 7652
Historic Columbus Foundation Inc., GA, 1658
Historic Crab Orchard Museum and Pioneer Park, VA, 8753
Historic Cragfont Inc., TN, 7870
Historic Daniel Boone Home, MO, 4692
Historic Deerfield, Inc., MA, 3834
Historic Donaldsonville Museum, LA, 3283
Historic Dumfries, Virginia, Inc., VA, 8540
Historic Edenton State Historic Site, NC, 6277
Historic Elmwood Cemetery, TN, 7943
Historic Fallsington, Inc., PA, 7214
Historic Forks of the Wabash, IN, 2549
Historic Fort Snelling, MN, 4459
Historic Fort York, ON, 9836
Historic General Dodge House, IA, 2701
Historic Governors' Mansion, WY, 9296
Historic Grange Estate, PA, 7259
Historic Halifax State Historic Site, NC, 6312
Historic Harmony Inc., PA, 7244
Historic Hillsborough Commission, NC, 6329
Historic Hope Foundation, Inc., NC, 6478
Historic Hopewell Foundation, Inc., VA, 8594
Historic House Trust of New York City, NY, 6010
Historic Hudson Valley, NY, 6158
Historic Jamestown Society, NC, 6335
Historic Landmarks Commission/City of Santa Barbara, CA, 859
Historic Liberty Jail, MO, 4808
Historic Long Branch, VA, 8629
Historic Madison, Inc., IN, 2583
Historic Madison, MO, 4708
Historic Mansker's Station Frontier, TN, 7896
Historic Mobile Preservation Society, AL, 81
Historic Morrisville Society, PA, 7325
Historic Morven, NJ, 5608
Historic New Harmony, IN, 2604
Historic New Orleans Collection, The, LA, 3350
Historic Northampton, MA, 3941
Historic Oak View County Park, NC, 6397
Historic Oakland Foundation, Inc., GA, 1610
Historic Palmyra, Inc., NY, 6065
Historic Pensacola Preservation Board, FL, 1511
Historic Philadelphia, Inc., PA, 7381
Historic Preservation Society of Social Circle, GA, 1807
Historic Pullman Foundation, IL, 2057
Historic Restoration Society of Annapolis County, NS, 9649
Historic Richmond Foundation, VA, 8689
Historic Rittenhouse Town Inc., PA, 7382
Historic Rock Ford Plantation, PA, 7282
Historic Rugby, Inc., TN, 7990
Historic Sahuaro Ranch, AZ, 225
Historic Ship Nautilus and Submarine Force Museum, CT, 1180
Historic Southwest Ohio, OH, 6614
Historic Springfield Foundation, Inc., MS, 4545
Historic St. Mary's City, MD, 3703
Historic St. Marys Mission Inc., MT, 5059
Historic Thomas Center, The, FL, 1437
Historic Upshur Museum, TX, 8133
Historic Waynesborough, PA, 7344
Historic Whitaker Home-Museum/Centerville Historical Society, UT, 8295
Historic Winslow House Association, MA, 3912
Historical Association of Princeville, IL, 2330
Historical Center for Southwest New Mexico, Inc., NM, 5751
Historical County of Rockland County, The, NY, 5990
Historical Museum at Fort Missoula, MT, 5042
Historical Museum at St. Gertrude's, The, ID, 1921
Historical Museum of Southern Florida, FL, 1486
Historical Museum of the D.R. Barker Library, NY, 5911
Historical Projects of Houston County, Inc., TX, 8064
Historical Shrine Foundation of San Diego County, The, CA, 779
Historical Society of Amherst, NH, 5266
Historical Society of Berks County, PA, 7431
Historical Society of Carnegie, PA, 7159
Historical Society of Delaware, DE, 1316
Historical Society of Douglas County, NE, 5188
Historical Society of Forest Park, IL, 2133
Historical Society of Forsyth County, Inc., GA, 1665
Historical Society of Fort Washington, PA, 7218
Historical Society of Germantown, The, OH, 6672
Historical Society of Glastonbury, CT, 1174
Historical Society of Greenfield, MA, 3872
Historical Society of Haddonfield, NJ, 5496
Historical Society of Hamilton Township, NJ, 5499
Historical Society of Harford County, Inc., The, MD, 3594
Historical Society of Hopkins County, KY, 3196
Historical Society of Kent County, MD, 3614
Historical Society of Marshall County, IA, 2790
Historical Society of Martin County/ The Elliot Museum, FL, 1544
Historical Society of Mount Pleasant, Ohio Inc., OH, 6730
Historical Society of New Mexico, NM, 5756
Historical Society of Oak Park and River Forest, IL, 2290
Historical Society of Old Newbury/Cushing House Museum, MA, 3933
Historical Society of Old Yarmouth, MA, 4047
Historical Society of Oregon County, MO, 4793
Historical Society of Polk County, MO, 4648
Historical Society of Porter County, IN, 2643
Historical Society of Pottawattamie County, IA, 2702
Historical Society of Quaker Hill and Pawling, NY, 6066
Historical Society of Quincy and Adams County, IL, 2334
Historical Society of Riverton, NJ, 5618
Historical Society of Scotch Plains and Fanwood, NJ, 5624
Historical Society of Talbot County, MD, 3634
Historical Society of the City of Baldwin Park, The, CA, 452
Historical Society of the Phoenixville Area, PA, 7412
Historical Society of the Town of Bolton, NY, 5821
Historical Society of the Town of Hancock, The, ME, 3445
Historical Society of Trappe, PA, 7172
Historical Society of University City, The, MO, 4954
Historical Society of Washington County, Inc., VA, 8471
Historical Society of Washington DC, DC, 1343
Historical Society of Watertown, MA, 4024
Historical Society of Western Pennsylvania, PA, 7420
Historical Society of Wilmington Vermont, VT, 8467
History and Heritage Committee/ American Society of Civil Engineers, CA, 474
History Center, IA, 2684
History Committee of the Montecito Association, The, CA, 860
History Museum for Springfield-Green County, The, MO, 4943
Hitchcock House Advisory Committee, IA, 2781
Hiwan Homestead Museum, CO, 1047
HMCS Haida Historic Naval Ship, ON, 9837
Hofstra University & Nassau County Museum: Long Island Studies Institute, NY, 5930
Holderness Historical Society, NH, 5339
Holland Historical Trust, MI, 4152
Holland Land Office Museum and Holland Purchase Historical Society, NY, 5809
Hollenberg Station State Historic Site, KS, 2948
Holley-Williams House Museum and The Salisbury Cannon Museum, CT, 1245
Hollis Historical Society, NH, 5340
Holocaust Documentation and Education Center, Inc., FL, 1497
Holocaust Memorial of Illinois, IL, 2386
Holy Cross History Association, IN, 2611
Homeplace-1850, The, KY, 3143
Homer Watson House and Gallery, ON, 9736
Homestead National Monument of America, NE, 5085
Homesteader Museum, WY, 9337
Homesteaders Museum, WY, 9353
Homewood House Museum, MD, 3579
Honolulu Botanical Gardens, HI, 1864
Honolulu Police Department Law Enforcement Museum, HI, 1865
Hoofprints of the Past Museum, WY, 9321
Hoover Historical Center, OH, 6744
Hoover-Minthorn House Museum, The, OR, 7047
Hope Lodge/Mather Mill, PA, 7219
Hopewell Museum, KY, 3225
Hopkins Historical Society, MN, 4352
Hopkins Historical Society, MO, 4729
Hopsewee Plantation, SC, 7680
Horace Greeley Museum, KS, 3064
Horicon Historical Society, WI, 9143
Horseshoe Bend National Military Park, AL, 36
Hotel de Paris Museum, CO, 1062
Houghton Lake Area Historical Society, MI, 4155
Houlka Historical Society, MS, 4563
House in the Horseshoe State Historic Site, NC, 6427
House of the Seven Gables Historic Site, MA, 3975
Houston County Historical Commission, TX, 8065
Houston County Historical Society, MN, 4287
Houston County Visitors Center/Museum, Inc., TX, 8066
Houston Library and Museum, AL, 5
Howard County Historical Society, IA, 2705
Howard County Historical Society, IN, 2576
Howard County Historical Society, MD, 3638

1166 Historic Persons THEMES OF INTERPRETATION

9280
Marsh Collection Society, ON, 9687
Marshall County Historical Society, IL, 2192
Marshall County Historical Society, Inc., IN, 2617
Marshall County Historical Society, KS, 2997
Marshall County Historical Society, MN, 4510
Marshall County Historical Society, SD, 7758
Marshall County Historical Society, WV, 9041
Marshall Gold Discovery State Histioric Park, CA, 498
Marshall Historical Society, MI, 4185
Martha A. Parsons Memorial Trust, CT, 1165
Martha Dickinson Bianchi Trust, MA, 3750
Martha's Vineyard Historical Society, MA, 3855
Martin and Osa Johnson Safari Museum, KS, 2895
Martin County Historical Society, MN, 4326
Martin County Historical Society, NC, 6465
Martin Luther King, Jr. National Historic Site and Preservation District, GA, 1617
Martin Van Buren National Historic Site, NY, 5963
Mary Aaron Memorial Museum, CA, 636
Maryland Historical Society, MD, 3582
Maryland Room, C. Burr Artz Central Library, Frederick County Public Libraries, MD, 3651
Maryland State Archives, MD, 3555
Marymoor Museum of Eastside History, WA, 8910
Marysville Historical Commission, MI, 4186
Marytown, IL, 2206
Mason County Historical Society Museum, WA, 8944
Mason County Museum, KY, 3203
Mason County Museum, TX, 8183
Mason Historical Society Inc., OH, 6716
Massac County Historical Society, IL, 2243
Massachusetts Archives and Commonwealth Museum, MA, 3778
Massachusetts Historical Society, MA, 3779
Massasoit Historical Association, RI, 7587
Massie Heritage Interpretation Center, GA, 1795
Matagorda County Museum, TX, 8032
Matchless Mine Museum, CO, 1090
Mathias Ham House Historic Site, IA, 2729
Mattapoisett Museum and Carriage House, MA, 3913
Maturango Museum of the Indian Wells Valley, CA, 735
Maui Historical Society, HI, 1890
Mayo House Interpretive Society, MN, 4360
Mazomanie Historical Society, WI, 9181
McClain County Oklahoma Historical and Genealogical Society and Museum, OK, 6955
McConaghy House, CA, 565
McCook House Civil War Museum/Carroll County Historical Society, OH, 6598
McCord Museum of Canadian History, QC, 9908
McCrae House-Guelph Museums, ON, 9721
McCurtain County Historical Society, OK, 6899
McDowell House and Apothecary Shop, KY, 3116
McFaddin-Ward House, TX, 8035
McFarland House, ON, 9764
McFarland State Historic Park, AZ, 220
McIlhenny Company and Avery Island, Inc., Archives, The, LA, 3262
McKeesport Heritage Center, PA, 7309
McKinley Memorial Library and Museum, OH, 6742
McLaughlin House National Historic Site/McLoughlin Memorial Association, OR, 7056
McLean County Museum of History, IL, 2005
McMinn County Living Heritage Museum, TN, 7863
MCP Hahnemann University Archives and Special Collections, PA, 7390
McPherson County Historical Society, Inc., KS, 2998
Meadow Brook Hall, MI, 4226
Meadow Garden, GA, 1634
Meeker County Historical Society, MN, 4365
Meeteetse Museums and Archives, Inc., WY, 9331
Mellette Memorial Association, SD, 7859
Melrose Area Historical Society, MN, 4384
Memorial Foundation of the Germanna Colonies in Virginia, Inc., VA, 8531
Memphis Pink Palace Museum, TN, 7947
Menaul Historical Library of the Southwest, NM, 5694
Mendocino Area Parks Association, CA, 638
Mendota Museum and Historical Society, IL, 2238
Mennonite Historians of Eastern Pennsylvania, PA, 7243
Menominee Range Historical Foundation, MI, 4158
Mequon Historical Society, Inc., WI, 9187
Mercer County Historical Museum, OH, 6599
Merchant's House Museum, NY, 6015
Meredosia Area Historical Society, IL, 2239
Meridian Restorations Foundation, Inc., MS, 4582
Merrick Auto Museum, NE, 5075
Merrill Historical Society, Inc./Brickyard School Museum, WI, 9188
Mesa Historical Museum, AZ, 234
Metropolitan Historical Commission of Nashville and Davidson County, TN, 7968
Miami County Museum and Historical Society, IN, 2614
Miami Design Preservation League, FL, 1491
Miami Memorabilia Collector's Club, The, FL, 1487
Miamisburg Historical Society, The, OH, 6724
Michigan City Historical Society, IN, 2590
Michigan Historical Center, MI, 4169
Michigan Maritime Museum, MI, 4245
Michigan Museum of Surveying, MI, 4170
Michigan Museums Association, MI, 4171
Michigan State University Archives and Historical Collections, MI, 4118
Michigan Transit Museum, MI, 4198
Michigan Women's Historical Center and Hall of Fame, MI, 4172
Mid-Atlantic Center for the Arts, NJ, 5461
Middle Georgia Historical Society, Inc., GA, 1730
Middlesex County Historical Society, CT, 1211
Middleton Place, SC, 7634
Middletown Springs Historical Society Inc., VT, 8405
Midland County Historical Museum, TX, 8187
Midland Pioneer Museum Association, SD, 7806
Midlothian Historical Society, IL, 2245
Midway Village and Museum Center, IL, 2355
Midwest Afro-American Genealogical Interest Coalition, MO, 4779
Midwest Jesuit Archives, MO, 4917
Mighty Eighth Air Force Heritage Museum, The, GA, 1796
Milan Historical Museum, OH, 6727
Milford Historical Society and Museum, CT, 1231
Milford Historical Society and Museum, MI, 4192
Military Museum of Southern New England, CT, 1154
Millburn-Short Hills Historical Society, NJ, 5627
Mille Lacs County Historical Sociey and Depot Museum, MN, 4435
Millet and District Museum and Exhibit Room, The, AB, 9409
Milne Special Collections and Archives, University of New Hampshire Library, NH, 5309
Milton Historical Society, MA, 3917
Milton Historical Society, WI, 9190
Milwaukee Public Museum, Inc., WI, 9195
Milwaukie Historical Society and Museum Inc., OR, 7040
Mineral County Museum and Historical Society, MT, 5060
Minerva Area Historical Society, OH, 6728
Mining and Town Museum, NM, 5740
Minnehaha County Historical Society, SD, 7836
Minnesota Air National Guard Historical Foundation, Inc., MN, 4466
Minnesota Finnish American Historical Society, Chapter 38, MN, 4484
Minnesota Historical Society Library, MN, 4469
Minnesota Historical Society, MN, 4468
Minnetonka Historical Society, MN, 4402
Missiles and More Museum Missiles and More Museum, NC, 6446
Mission Houses Museum, HI, 1868
Mission Mill Museum/Mission Mill Musuem Association, OR, 7083
Mission San Juan Capistrano, CA, 833
Missisquoi Historical Society/Missisquoi Museum, QC, 9934
Mississippi Baptist Historical Commission, MS, 4538
Mississippi County Historical and Genealogical Society, AR, 399
Mississippi Governor's Mansion, MS, 4569
Mississippi Sports Hall of Fame and Museum, MS, 4571
Mississippi Valley Educational Programs, AR, 311
Mississippi Valley Textile Museum, ON, 9684
Missouri Department of Natural Resources, Division of State Parks, MO, 4755
Missouri Historical Society, MO, 4918
Missouri Masion Preservation, Inc., MO, 4757
Missouri River Frontier Museum, MO, 4852
Missouri River Outfitters, MO, 4805
Missouri State Archives, MO, 4758
Missouri State Museum, MO, 4759
Mitchell Area Historical Society, SD, 7813
Mitchell County Historical Society, IA, 2814
Mitchell County Historical Society, KS, 2892
Mitchell Gallery of Flight, Milwaukee County Airport Division, WI, 9196
Mizel Museum of Judaica, CO, 1028
Moark Regional Railroad Museum, MO, 4863
Mobile Medical Museum, AL, 83
Mobile Medical Museum, AL, 84
Mobile Municipal Archives, AL, 85
Mockbeggar Plantation Provincial Historic Site, NF, 9612
Moffatt-Ladd House and Garden, NH, 5402
Mohawk Nation Council of Choices, NY, 6104
Mohawk Valley Heritage Corridor, NY, 5851
Mojave River Valley Museum, CA, 454
Molly Brown House Museum, CO, 1029
Molson Historical Association, Molson Schoolhouse Museum, WA, 8898
Monocacy National Battlefield, MD, 3647
Monona Historical Society, IA, 2796
Monroe County Historical Association, PA, 7460
Monroe County Historical Museum, MI, 4193
Monroe County Historical Society, IL, 2443
Monroe County Historical Society, IN, 2485
Monroe County Historical Society, Inc., WI, 9246
Monroe County Historical Society, WV, 9057
Monroe County Public Library, Indiana Room, IN, 2486
Monroe Historical Society, WA, 8884
Monroe-Union Historic Properties Commission, NC, 6363
Monson Historical Society, ME, 3441
Mont Vernon Historical Society, NH, 5373
Montana Heritage Commission/Virginia and Nevada City Project, MT, 5065
Montana Heritage Preservation and Development Comission, MT, 5024
Montana Historical Society, MT, 5025
Montauk, IA, 2693
Montclair Historical Society, NJ, 5546
Monte Cristo Cottage Museum, CT, 1229
Monterey County Historical Society, Inc., CA, 772
Monterey State Historic Park, CA, 647
Montgomery County Genealogical Society, KS, 2901
Montgomery County Historical Society, The, OH, 6645
Montgomery Historical Society, VT, 8406
Montgomery Place Historic Estate, NY, 5798
Montpelier (James Madison's), VA, 8632
Montpelier Mansion, MD, 3676
Montpelier-General Henry Knox Museum, ME, 3525
Montreal Holocaust Memorial Center/Le Centre Commemoratif De L'Holocauste S Montreal, QC, 9910
Monument Hill and Kreische Brewery State Historical Parks, TX, 8165
Moody County Genealogical Organization, SD, 7780
Moores Creek National Battlefield, NC, 6266
Moose Lake Area Historical Society, MN, 4409
Moosehead Historical Society, ME, 3444
Moravian Historical Society, PA, 7331
Moravian Museum of Bethlehem, Inc., PA, 7131
Moreland Hills Historical Society, The, OH, 6729
Morgan County Archives, AL, 37
Morgan County Historical Society, IL, 2178
Morgan County Historical Society, OH, 6720
Morgan County Historical Society, UT, 8314
Morgan Hill Historical Society, CA, 651
Morris County Historical Society, KS, 2907
Morris County Historical Society, NJ, 5555
Morris-Jumel Mansion, Inc., NY, 6017
Morrison County Historical Society, MN, 4370
Morrison Historical Society, IL, 2257
Morristown Chapter DAR/Schuyler-Hamilton House, NJ, 5556
Morton County Historical Society Museum, KS, 2920
Morven Park, VA, 8599
Mossbank and District Museum, Inc., SK, 9970
Mother Seton House Paca St, Inc., MD, 3583
Motorcycle Hall of Fame Museum, OH, 6756
Mounds-Midway School of Nursing Historical Society, MN, 4472
Mount Auburn Cemetery, MA, 3800
Mount Clare Museum House, MD, 3584
Mount Gulian Historic Site, NY, 5811
Mount Horeb Area Historical Society, WI, 9200
Mount Independence State Historic Site, VT, 8412
Mount Revelstoke and Glacier National Parks, BC, 9495
Mount Saint Joseph Ursuline Archives, KY, 3198
Mount Sopris Historical Society, CO, 997
Mount Vernon Ladies' Association, VA, 8636
Mountain View Historical Association, CA, 654
Movie Museum, The, MI, 4215
Moyer House, OR, 7001
Mt. Holly Historical Society, NJ, 5562
Mt. Pulaski Courthouse State Historic Site, IL, 2211
Mt. Pulaski Township Historical Society, IL, 2264
Mud Lake Historical Society, ID, 1967
Muheim Heritage House, AZ, 208
Multi-Lakes Association for Civil War Studies, Inc., MI, 4255
Multicultural Heritage Centre, AB, 9420
Muncy Historical Society and Museum of History, PA, 7328
Muriel L. MacGregor Charitable Trust, CO, 1045
Murray County Historical Society and Museum, MN, 4488
Murray Farmhouse at Poricy Park, NJ, 5544
Muscogee Genealogical Society, GA, 1659
Musee Acadien (Acadian Museum), NB, 9598
Musee Bon-Pasteur, QC, 9920
Musee de Kent, NB, 9581
Musee des Augustine de L'Hotel-Dieu de Quebec, QC, 9921
Musee du Royal 22e Regiment, QC, 9923
Musee Francois-Pilote, QC, 9889
Musee Regimentaire Les Fusiliers de Sherbrocke, QC, 9929
Musee Regional de Vaudreuil Soulanges, QC, 9942
Museo de las Americas, CO, 1030
Museum and White House of the Confederacy, VA, 8695
Museum Association of West Louisiana, LA, 3315
Museum at Warm Springs, The, OR, 7103
Museum Center at Five Points, TN, 7876
Museum Management Program, National Park Service, DC, 1347
Museum of Alaska Transportation & Industry, AK, 199
Museum of American Financial History, NY, 6020
Museum of American Heritage, CA, 695
Museum of American Political Life, University of Hartford, CT, 1275
Museum of American Presidents, VA, 8739
Museum of Anthropology, CA, 491
Museum of Anthropology, KY, 3152
Museum of Appalachia, TN, 7982

1184 Historic Preservation THEMES OF INTERPRETATION

McPherson County Historical Society, Inc., KS, 2998
McPherson Museum, KS, 2999
Meade County Historical Museum, KS, 3001
Meadow Brook Hall, MI, 4226
Meadow Garden, GA, 1634
Meadowcroft Museum of Rural Life, PA, 7120
Mechanicsburg Museum Association, PA, 7312
Meeker County Historical Society, MN, 4365
Meeteetse Museums and Archives, Inc., WY, 9331
Mel Fisher Maritime Heritage Society, FL, 1464
Melrose Area Historical Society, MN, 4384
Memorial Foundation of the Germanna Colonies in Virginia, Inc., VA, 8531
Menaul Historical Library of the Southwest, NM, 5694
Mendocino County Historical Society, Inc., CA, 939
Mendota Museum and Historical Society, IL, 2238
Mennonite Archives of Ontario, ON, 9850
Mennonite Historical Society, IA, 2771
Menominee County Historical Society, Inc., MI, 4188
Menominee Range Historical Foundation, MI, 4158
Mequon Historical Society, Inc., WI, 9187
Merced County Historical Society/Merced County Courthouse Museum, CA, 639
Mercer County Genealogical and Historical Society, Inc., MO, 4866
Mercer County Historical Museum, OH, 6599
Mercer County Historical Society, IL, 1975
Mercer County Historical Society, PA, 7314
Mercer Historical Society, ME, 3462
Merchant's House Museum, NY, 6015
Merchantville Historical Society, NJ, 5543
Meredosia Area Historical Society, IL, 2239
Meridian Restorations Foundation, Inc., MS, 4582
Merrick Auto Museum, NE, 5075
Merrill Historical Society, Inc./Brickyard School Museum, WI, 9188
Merry Go Round Museum Inc., OH, 6774
Merwin House, SPNEA, MA, 3999
Mesa Historical Museum, AZ, 234
Metlakatla Tribal Rights Committee, AK, 180
Metropolitan Historical Commission of Nashville and Davidson County, TN, 7968
Miami County Museum and Historical Society, IN, 2614
Miami Design Preservation League, FL, 1491
Miami Memorabilia Collector's Club, The, FL, 1487
Michie Tavern ca. 1784, VA, 8517
Michigan City Historical Society, IN, 2590
Michigan Historical Center, MI, 4169
Michigan Maritime Museum, MI, 4245
Michigan Museums Association, MI, 4171
Michigan State Trust for Railway Preservation, Inc., MI, 4214
Michigan State University Museum, MI, 4119
Michigan Transit Museum, MI, 4198
Mid-Atlantic Center for the Arts, NJ, 5461
Middle Border Museum of American Indian and Pioneer Life, SD, 7812
Middle Georgia Historical Society, Inc., GA, 1730
Middlefield Historical Society, OH, 6725
Middlesex County Museum, Inc., VA, 8720
Middleton Place, SC, 7634
Middletown Area Historical Society, PA, 7316
Middletown Historical Society Inc., RI, 7550
Middletown Springs Historical Society Inc., VT, 8405
Midland County Historical Museum, TX, 8187
Midland Pioneer Museum Association, SD, 7806
Midlothian Historical Society, IL, 2245
Midvale Historical Society, UT, 8311
Midway Museum, GA, 1739
Midway Village and Museum Center, IL, 2355
Midwest Afro-American Genealogical Interest Coalition, MO, 4779
Midwest Jesuit Archives, MO, 4917
Mifflinburg Buggy Museum, PA, 7317
Milan Historical Museum, OH, 6727
Miles B. Carpenter Museum Complex, VA, 8766
Milford Historical Society and Museum, CT, 1231
Milford Historical Society and Museum, MI, 4192
Military Museum of Southern New England, CT, 1154
Mill Prong Preservation, Inc., NC, 6354
Millbrook Society/Amy B. Yerkes Museum, The, PA, 7255
Millburn-Short Hills Historical Society, NJ, 5627
Mille Lacs County Historical Sociey and Depot Museum, MN, 4435
Miller County Historical Society, MO, 4951
Mills County Historical Society, IA, 2747
Mills Mansion State Historic Site, NY, 6142
Milton-Freewater Area Historical Society/Frazier Farmstead Museum, OR, 7039
Milwaukie Historical Society and Museum Inc., OR, 7040
Mine Au Breton Historical Society, Inc., MO, 4865
Mineral County Museum and Historical Society, MT, 5060
Minerva Area Historical Society, OH, 6728
Minidoka County Historical Society, ID, 1961
Minisink Valley Historical Society, NY, 6076
Minneapolis Heritage Preservation Commission, MN, 4391
Minnehaha County Historical Society, SD, 7836
Minnesota Air & Space Museum, MN, 4465
Minnesota Air National Guard Historical Foundation, Inc., MN, 4466
Minnesota Archaeological Society, MN, 4467
Minnesota Finnish American Historical Society, Chapter 38, MN, 4484
Minnesota Historical Society Library, MN, 4469
Minnesota Historical Society, MN, 4468
Minnesota Museum of Mining, MN, 4294
Minnesota Transportation Museum, MN, 4470
Minnetonka Historical Society, MN, 4402
Minnewaukan Historical Society, ND, 6536
Miracle of America Museum, Inc., MT, 5045
Mirror and District Museum Association, AB, 9410
Missiles and More Museum Missiles and More Museum, NC, 6446
Mission Houses Museum, HI, 1868
Mission Mill Museum/Mission Mill Museum Association, OR, 7083
Mission Museum, BC, 9468
Mission San Carlos Borromeo, CA, 483
Mission San Francisco de Asis (Mission Dolores), CA, 808
Mission San Juan Capistrano, CA, 833
Mission San Luis Rey de Francia, CA, 678
Mission San Miguel Arcangel, CA, 843
Mississippi Baptist Historical Commission, MS, 4538
Mississippi County Historical and Genealogical Society, AR, 399
Mississippi County Historical Society, MO, 4673
Mississippi Cultural Crossroads, MS, 4602
Mississippi Governor's Mansion, MS, 4569
Mississippi Valley Textile Museum, ON, 9684
Missouri Alliance For Historic Preservation, MO, 4684
Missouri Department of Natural Resources, Division of State Parks, MO, 4755
Missouri Forest Heritage Center, Inc., MO, 4756
Missouri Historical Society, MO, 4918
Missouri Masion Preservation, Inc., MO, 4757
Missouri River Frontier Museum, MO, 4852
Missouri River Outfitters, MO, 4805
Missouri State Archives, MO, 4758
Missouri Town 1855, MO, 4801
Mitchell Area Historical Society, SD, 7813
Mitchell County Historical Society, IA, 2814
Mitchell County Historical Society, KS, 2892
Mitchell Museum, Floyd & Margaret, TN, 7999
Mitchell Prehistoric Indian Village Museum and Archedome, SD, 7814
Moark Regional Railroad Museum, MO, 4863
Mobile Historic Development Commission, AL, 82
Mobile Medical Museum, AL, 83
Mobile Medical Museum, AL, 84
Mockbeggar Plantation Provincial Historic Site, NF, 9612
Modoc County Historical Society, CA, 436
Moffatt-Ladd House and Garden, NH, 5402
Mohawk Nation Council of Choices, NY, 6104
Mohawk Valley Heritage Corridor, NY, 5851
Mojave River Valley Museum, CA, 454
Molly Brown House Museum, CO, 1029
Molson Historical Association, Molson Schoolhouse Museum, WA, 8898
Moncton Museum, NB, 9597
Monhegan Historical and Cultural Museum Association, Inc., ME, 3463
Moniteau County Historical Society, MO, 4659
Monmouth Museum, ME, 3464
Monocacy National Battlefield, MD, 3647
Monona Historical Society, IA, 2796
Monroe County Heritage Museums, AL, 90
Monroe County Historical Society, IL, 2443
Monroe County Historical Society, IN, 2485
Monroe County Historical Society, WV, 9057
Monroe County Local History Room, WI, 9247
Monroe-Union Historic Properties Commission, NC, 6363
Monson Historical Society, ME, 3441
Mont Vernon Historical Society, NH, 5373
Montague Association for Restoration of Community History (MARCH), NJ, 5545
Montana Heritage Commission/Virginia and Nevada City Project, MT, 5065
Montana Historical Society, MT, 5025
Montana Preservation Alliance, MT, 4981
Montclair Historical Society, NJ, 5546
Monte Cristo Cottage Museum, CT, 1229
Monte Cristo Preservation Association, WA, 8845
Monterey County Historical Society, Inc., CA, 772
Monterey State Historic Park, CA, 647
Montgomery County Department of History and Archives, NY, 5906
Montgomery County Genealogical Society, KS, 2901
Montgomery County Historic Preservation Commission, MD, 3717
Montgomery County Historical Society, Inc., IN, 2503
Montgomery County Historical Society, Inc., MO, 4830
Montgomery County Historical Society, The, OH, 6645
Montgomery House Museum/Montour County Historical Society, PA, 7181
Montgomery Museum and Lewis Miller Regional Art Center, VA, 8525
Montgomery Place Historic Estate, NY, 5798
Montpelier (James Madison's), VA, 8632
Montpelier-General Henry Knox Museum, ME, 3525
Montrose Historical Telephone Pioneer Museum, MI, 4196
Montrose Township Historical Society, IA, 2798
Monument Hill and Kreische Brewery State Historical Parks, TX, 8165
Moore County Historical Association, Inc., NC, 6438
Moore County Historical Museum, TX, 8087
Moore Methodist Museum and Library, GA, 1810
Moores Creek National Battlefield, NC, 6266
Moose Lake Area Historical Society, MN, 4409
Moosehead Historical Society, ME, 3444
Moravia Area Historical Society, IA, 2799
Moravian Museum of Bethlehem, Inc., PA, 7131
Moravian Music Foundation, Inc., NC, 6484
Moreland Hills Historical Society, The, OH, 6729
Morgan County Archives, AL, 37
Morgan County Historical Society, IL, 2178
Morgan County Historical Society, Inc., The, GA, 1732
Morgan County Historical Society, OH, 6720
Morgan County Historical Society, UT, 8314
Morgan Hill Historical Society, CA, 651
Mormon Trail Center at Historic Winter Quarters, NE, 5191
Morris County Heritage Commission, NJ, 5554
Morris County Historical Society, KS, 2907
Morris County Historical Society, NJ, 5555
Morris County Library, New Jersey Collection, NJ, 5676
Morris-Butler House, IN, 2568
Morrison County Historical Society, MN, 4370
Morrison Historical Society, IL, 2257
Morton County Historical Society Museum, KS, 2920
Morven Park, VA, 8599
Moses-Kent House Museum, The, NH, 5318
Mossbank and District Museum, Inc., SK, 9970
Mother Seton House Paca St, Inc., MD, 3583
Mounds-Midway School of Nursing Historical Society, MN, 4472
Mount Airy Museum of Regional History, Inc., NC, 6372
Mount Auburn Cemetery, MA, 3800
Mount Clare Museum House, MD, 3584
Mount Desert Island Historical Society, ME, 3466
Mount Horeb Area Historical Society, WI, 9200
Mount Independence State Historic Site, VT, 8412
Mount Kearsarge Indian Museum, Education and Cultrural Center, NH, 5429
Mount Lebanon Historical Society, Stagecoach Trail Museum, LA, 3291
Mount Morris Historical Society/ The Mills, NY, 5987
Mount Revelstoke and Glacier National Parks, BC, 9495
Mount Saint Joseph Ursuline Archives, KY, 3198
Mount Sopris Historical Society, CO, 997
Mount Vernon Ladies' Association, VA, 8636
Movie Museum, The, MI, 4215
Mower County Historical Society, MN, 4273
Moyer House, OR, 7001
Mt. Holly Historical Society, NJ, 5562
Mt. Pulaski Township Historical Society, IL, 2264
Mt. Tabor-Danby Historical Society, VT, 8377
Mt. Zion United Methodist Church, DC, 1346
Mud Lake Historical Society, ID, 1967
Muheim Heritage House, AZ, 208
Mukilteo Historical Society, WA, 8891
Mullan Historical Society, ID, 1949
Multi-Lakes Association for Civil War Studies, Inc., MI, 4255
Multicultural Heritage Centre, AB, 9420
Muncy Historical Society and Museum of History, PA, 7328
Munroe Falls Historical Society, OH, 6731
Muriel L. MacGregor Charitable Trust, CO, 1045
Murray Farmhouse at Poricy Park, NJ, 5544
Murrell Home Site, OK, 6945
Muscogee Genealogical Society, GA, 1659
Musee Francois-Pilote, QC, 9889
Musee Regimentaire Les Fusiliers de Sherbrocke, QC, 9929
Museum and Arts Center in the Sequim Dungeness Valley, WA, 8943
Museum and White House of the Confederacy, VA, 8695
Museum Association of West Louisiana, LA, 3315
Museum Management Program, National Park Service, DC, 1347
Museum of American Heritage, CA, 695
Museum of American Political Life, University of Hartford, CT, 1275
Museum of Anthropology, CA, 491
Museum of Anthropology, KY, 3152
Museum of Appalachia, TN, 7982
Museum of Archaeology and Material Culture, NM, 5710
Museum of Art and History at the McPherson Center, CA, 872
Museum of Automobile History, The, NY, 6155
Museum of Beverage Containers & Advertising, TN, 7951
Museum of Childhood of Wakefield, NH, 5428
Museum of Christian Heritage, IL, 2294
Museum of Church History and Art, UT, 8336
Museum of Early Southern Decorative Arts, NC, 6486
Museum of Early Trades and Crafts, NJ, 5535
Museum of Flight, WA, 8930
Museum of History and Industry, WA, 8931

Museum of North Idaho, ID, 1920
Museum of Northern British Columbia, BC, 9491
Museum of Northern History at The Sir Harry Oakes Chateau, ON, 9734
Museum of Our Industrial Heritage, Inc., MA, 3873
Museum of Pioneer History, OK, 6857
Museum of Science and History of Jacksonville, Inc., FL, 1450
Museum of Southern History, The, FL, 1451
Museum of Southern History, The, TX, 8254
Museum of the Berkeley Springs, WV, 9004
Museum of the Cape Fear Historical Complex, NC, 6288
Museum of the Cherokee Indian, NC, 6254
Museum of the City of Lake Worth, FL, 1472
Museum of the Everglades, FL, 1418
Museum of the Great Plains, OK, 6910
Museum of the Islands Society, Inc., FL, 1540
Museum of the Middle Appalachians, VA, 8717
Museum of the Mountain Man, WY, 9336
Museum of the Plains, TX, 8208
Museum of the Red River, OK, 6900
Museum of the San Rafael, UT, 8292
Museum of the Southern Jewish Experience, MS, 4572
Museum of the Waxhaws and Andrew Jackson Memorial, NC, 6457
Museum of Transportation, MO, 4920
Museum of Vintage Fashion, Inc., CA, 587
Museum of West Louisiana, LA, 3316
Museum of Western Jesuit Missions, The, MO, 4704
Museum-Lepanto USA, AR, 362
Museums Association of Saskatchewan, SK, 9978
Museums at Prophetstown, Inc., The, IN, 2482
Museums at Stony Brook, The, NY, 6151
Musk Ox Development Corporation, AK, 182
Muskego Historical Society, WI, 9201
Muskegon County Museum, MI, 4203
Musselshell Valley History Museum, MT, 5052
Muster Field Farm/Harvey Homestead, Inc., NH, 5387
Mynelle Gardens, MS, 4573
Mystery Castle, AZ, 247
Mystic Seaport Museum, Inc., CT, 1216
Nanticoke Indian Museum, DE, 1305
Nantucket Historical Association, MA, 3925
Nantucket Maria Mitchell Association, MA, 3926
Napa County Historical Society, CA, 655
Napa Valley Museum, CA, 972
Naper Settlement, IL, 2268
Narragansett Indian Tribal Historic Preservation Office, RI, 7593
Nash County Historical Association, Inc., NC, 6419
Nashua Historical Society, The, NH, 5376
Nashville City Cemetery Association, TN, 7969
Natchez Garden Club, MS, 4587
Natchez Historical Society, MS, 4588
Natchitoches Historic Foundation, LA, 3333
Nathanael Greene City County Heritage Museum, TN, 7900
National Alliance of Preservation Commissions, GA, 1590
National Archives and Records Administration, MD, 3620
National Association for Cemetery Preservation, CO, 1125
National Automotive and Truck Museum of the United States, Inc., IN, 2480
National Battlefields Commission, QC, 9924
National Buffalo Museum, ND, 6528
National Building Museum, DC, 1349
National City Historical Society, CA, 656
National College of Chiropractic Heritage Museum, IL, 2222
National Firearms Museum, VA, 8549
National Historic Seaport of Baltimore, MD, 3586
National Japanese American Historical Society, CA, 810
National Maritime Museum Association, CA, 811
National Military Heritage Society, Inc., MO, 4895
National Model Aviation Museum, IN, 2597

National Museum of American History, Smithsonian Institution, DC, 1355
National Museum of Civil War Medicine, MD, 3648
National Museum of Communications, TX, 8221
National Museum of Naval Aviation, FL, 1512
National Museum of the American Indian Cultural Resources Center, MD, 3728
National New York Central Railroad Museum, IN, 2515
National Ornamental Metal Museum, TN, 7949
National Preservation Institute, VA, 8481
National Railroad Museum, WI, 9134
National Ranching Heritage Center, TX, 8176
National Register of Historic Places, National Park Service, DC, 1358
National Route 66 Museum/Old Town Complex, OK, 6879
National Scouting Museum of the Boy Scouts of America, Inc., TX, 8197
National Shrine of St. Elizabeth Ann Seton, MD, 3639
National Society of the Colonial Dames of America in California, The, CA, 812
National Society of The Colonial Dames of America, The, DC, 1359
National Society of the Colonial Dames of Louisiana Shreveport Committee, LA, 3380
National Society Sons of the American Revolution, The, KY, 3187
National Temple Hill Association, NY, 6167
National Trust for Historic Preservation, DC, 1360
National Trust for Historic Preservation, Southern Office, SC, 7636
National Wild Turkey Federation, SC, 7670
National Woman's Relief Corps Auxiliary to the Grand Army of the Republic, Inc., IL, 2403
Native Sons of Kansas City, MO, 4780
Natural Ovens Bakery of Manitowoc Wisconsin, Inc., WI, 9171
Nauvoo Historical Society, IL, 2271
Nauvoo Restoration Inc., IL, 2272
Navajo Nation Historic Preservation Department, AZ, 287
Navajo Nation Museum, AZ, 288
Naval Museum of Alberta, The, AB, 9367
Navarre-Anderson Trading Post, MI, 4194
Navarre-Bethlehem Township Historical Society, OH, 6733
Nebraska City Historical Society, NE, 5170
Nebraska Game and Parks Commission, NE, 5145
Nebraska Humanities Council, NE, 5146
Nebraska Jewish Historical Society, NE, 5192
Nebraska State Capitol D.A.S. Building Division, NE, 5147
Nebraska State Historical Society, NE, 5148
Neosho Historical Society, WI, 9205
Nethercutt Collection, The, CA, 916
Nevada County Historical Society, CA, 659
Nevada Historical Society, NV, 5255
Nevada State Railroad Museum, NV, 5231
Nevada Test Site Historical Foundation, NV, 5248
New Almaden Quicksilver County Park Association, CA, 828
New Berlin Historical Society, WI, 9206
New Bern Fireman's Museum, NC, 6377
New Bern Historic Preservation Commission, NC, 6378
New Bern Historical Society Foundation, Inc., NC, 6379
New Bern Preservation Foundation, Inc., NC, 6380
New Braunfels Conservation Society, TX, 8197
New Bremen Historic Association, OH, 6734
New Britain Industrial Museum, CT, 1219
New Brunswick Historical Society, NB, 9602
New Castle Historical Society, Inc., CO, 1104
New Castle Historical Society, NY, 5859
New England Air Museum, CT, 1288
New England Antiquities Research Association, MA, 4042
New England Carousel Museum, The, CT, 1144
New England Civil War Museum, CT, 1271
New England Electric Railway Historical Society /Seashore Trolley Museum, ME,

3453
New England Heritage Center at Bentley College, MA, 4021
New Hampshire Aniquarian Society, NH, 5341
New Hampshire Antique and Classic Boat Museum, NH, 5349
New Hampshire Farm Museum, NH, 5370
New Harmony State Historic Site, IN, 2605
New Haven Colony Historical Society, CT, 1226
New Hope Historical Society/Parry Mansion Museum, PA, 7334
New Jersey Historical Society, NJ, 5575
New Jersey Museum of Agriculture, NJ, 5578
New Jersey Postal History Society, NJ, 5557
New Lebanon Preservation Society, MO, 4839
New London Area Historical Society, OH, 6735
New London Historical Society, NH, 5378
New Madrid Historical Museum, MO, 4841
New Market Battlefield State Historical Park, VA, 8640
New Mexico Historic Preservation Division, NM, 5757
New Mexico State Monuments, NM, 5758
New Mexico State Records Center and Archives, NM, 5759
New Orleans Notarial Archives, LA, 3360
New Providence Historical Society, NJ, 5572
New Richmond Preservation Society, WI, 9210
New River Historical Society/Wilderness Road Regional Museum, VA, 8641
New Windsor Cantonment State Historic Site, NY, 6171
New York Museum of Transportation, NY, 6185
New York State Bureau of Historic Sites, NY, 6178
New York State Commission on the Restoration of the Capitol, NY, 5786
New York State Covered Bridge Society, NY, 6102
New York Transit Museum, NY, 5834
Newark Museum Association, NJ, 5576
Newark Preservation and Landmarks Committee, NJ, 5577
Newark Valley Historical Society, NY, 6034
Newbold-White House Historic Site, NC, 6318
Newell Historical Society, IA, 2807
Newipswich Historical Society, NH, 5384
Newkirk Community Historical Society, OK, 6925
Newnan-Coweta Historical Society, Male Academy Museum, GA, 1750
Newport Historical Society, RI, 7560
Newsome House Museum and Cultural Center, VA, 8645
Newton County Historical Society, MO, 4836
Newton County Historical Society/Bradley House Museum, AR, 359
Newton, New Hampshire Historical Society, NH, 5385
Newtown Historic Association, PA, 7336
Newtown Square Historical Preservation Society, PA, 7337
Newtown-Avoca Historical Society, IA, 2667
Newville Historical Society, PA, 7338
Nez Perce National Historic Park, ID, 1964
Nezperce Historical Society, ID, 1951
Nickels-Sortwell House, SPNEA, ME, 3541
Nicola Valley Museum Archives Association, BC, 9467
Nicolas Denys Museum, NS, 9675
Nicollet County Historical Society, MN, 4476
Niles Historical Society, OH, 6743
Ninety Six National Historic Site, SC, 7717
Niobrara Historical Society, NE, 5174
No Man's Land Historical Society, Inc., OK, 6890
Nobleboro Historical Society, ME, 3472
Nobles County Historical Society, Inc., MN, 4527
Noel Memorial Library, Archives, and Special Collections, LA, 3381
Nokomis and District Museum, SK, 9972
Norfolk County Historical Society of Chesapeake, VA, 8521
Norman #1 Oil Well Museum, KS, 3006
North Andover Historical Society, MA, 3936

North Berrien Historical Society Museum, MI, 4094
North Caldwell Historical Society, NJ, 5579
North Carolina Division of Archives and History, NC, 6400
North Carolina Genealogical Society, Inc., NC, 6402
North Carolina Historic Sites, NC, 6403
North Carolina Society of Historians, Inc., NC, 6433
North Carolina State Capitol, NC, 6407
North Carolina State Historic Preservation Office, Division of Archives and History, NC, 6408
North Castle Historical Society, The, NY, 5800
North Central Washington Museum, WA, 8986
North Custer Historical Society, ID, 1919
North Dakota Heritage Center, The, ND, 6498
North Hampton Historical Society, NH, 5386
North Haven Historical Society, ME, 3474
North Highlands Community Museum, NS, 9655
North Lake Tahoe Historical Society, CA, 917
North Louisiana Folk Life, Inc., DBA Martin Homeplace, LA, 3277
North Slope Borough Commission on Inupiat History, Language and Culture, AK, 145
Northborough Historical Society, MA, 3942
Northeast Minnesota Historical Center, MN, 4310
Northeast Texas Rural Heritage Center and Museum, TX, 8209
Northeastern Montana Threshers and Antique Association, MT, 4999
Northeastern Nevada Museum, NV, 5235
Northeastern North Dakota Heritage Assocation, ND, 6504
Northern Gila County Historical Society, Inc., AZ, 240
Northern Indiana Center for History, IN, 2636
Northern Kentucky African American Heritage Task Force, Inc., KY, 3113
Northern Mariposa County History Center, CA, 504
Northern Neck of Virginia Historical Society, VA, 8633
Northern Pacific Depot Museum, ID, 1969
Northern Wisconsin History Center, WI, 9073
Northfield Historical Society, MN, 4423
Northport Historical Society, NY, 6043
Northville Historical Society/Mill Race Village, MI, 4208
Northwest Information Center of the California Historical Resources Information System, CA, 744
Northwest Montana Historical Society, Central School Museum, MT, 5032
Northwest Seaport Maritime Heritage Center, WA, 8933
Northwest Underground Explorations, WA, 8885
Norwalk Historical Society, Inc., Ct, 1235
Norwegian Center Inc./Norsk Museum, IL, 2279
Norwood Historical Society, MA, 3944
Norwood Park Historical Society, IL, 2068
Notre Dame de Bon Secours Chapel/Marguerite Bourgeoys Museum, QC, 9911
Nova Scotia Sport Hall of Fame, NS, 9660
Nowata County Historical Society, OK, 6930
Nunatta Sunakkutaangit Museum Society, NT, 9645
Nutley Historical Society and Museum, NJ, 5582
Nyssa Historical Society, OR, 7051
O'Brien County Historical Society, IA, 2824
O'Fallon Historical Society, IL, 2280
O'Fallon Historical Society, MT, 4972
O'Hara Mill Pioneer Village & Conservation Area, ON, 9694
O. Henry Museum, TX, 8019
Oak Brook Historical Society, IL, 2284
Oak Hill and the Martha Berry Museum, GA, 1748
Oakland County Genealogical Society, MI, 4074
Oaklands Historic House Museum, TN, 7955
Oakley Park Museum, SC, 7671
Oakley Valley Historical Association, ID, 1952
Oakside Bloomfield Cultural Center, NJ, 5448

LABOR HISTORY

LEGAL STUDIES

LIGHTHOUSES

Mercer County Historical Museum, OH, 6599
Miami Memorabilia Collector's Club, The, FL, 1487
Michigan City Historical Society, IN, 2590
Michigan Maritime Museum, MI, 4245
Michigan Museums Association, MI, 4171
Mid-Atlantic Center for the Arts, NJ, 5461
Minnesota Historical Society Library, MN, 4469
Minnesota Historical Society, MN, 4468
Monhegan Historical and Cultural Museum Association, Inc., ME, 3463
Moore Museum, ON, 9752
Mount Vernon Museum of Incandescent Lighting, MD, 3585
Mukilteo Historical Society, WA, 8891
Musee de La Mer de Pointe-au-Pere, QC, 9918
Museum and Arts Center in the Sequim Dungeness Valley, WA, 8943
Museum Management Program, National Park Service, DC, 1347
Museum of Northern British Columbia, BC, 9491
Museum of the City of Lake Worth, FL, 1472
National Archives and Records Administration, MD, 3620
National Historic Seaport of Baltimore, MD, 3586
New Haven Colony Historical Society, CT, 1226
New Orleans Notarial Archives, LA, 3360
New York State Bureau of Historic Sites, NY, 6178
Newport Historical Society, RI, 7560
North Carolina Maritime Museum, NC, 6222
North Carolina State Historic Preservation Office, Division of Archives and History, NC, 6408
North Highlands Community Museum, NS, 9655
Northeast Minnesota Historical Center, MN, 4310
Northern Wisconsin History Center, WI, 9073
Northwest Seaport Maritime Heritage Center, WA, 8933
Ocean County Library, NJ, 5654
Ocracoke Preservation Society, Inc., NC, 6384
Old Fort Niagara Association, NY, 6199
Ontonagon County Historical Society, MI, 4212
Oregon Coast History Center, OR, 7048
Oregon Historical Society, OR, 7067
Outer Bank Group, Cape Hatteras National Seashore, NC, 6357
Outer Banks Conservationists, Inc., NC, 6358
Owen Sound Marine and Rail Museum, ON, 9789
Oyster and Maritime Museum, VA, 8524
Pacific County Historical Society and Museum Foundation, WA, 8948
Palacios Area Historical Association, TX, 8203
Palacios Library, Inc., TX, 8204
Parris Island Museum, SC, 7719
Pass Christian Historical Society, MS, 4599
Pensacola Historical Society, FL, 1513
Pilgrim Monument and Provincetown Museum, MA, 3964
Point Amour Lighthouse Provincial Historic Site, NF, 9638
Point Lookout State Park, MD, 3711
Point Pinos Lighthouse, CA, 688
Ponce de Leon Inlet Lighthouse Preservation Association, Inc., FL, 1518
Port Austin Area Historical Society, MI, 4219
Port Colborne Historical and Marine Museum, ON, 9794
Port Huron Museum, MI, 4220
Port Isabel Historical Museum, TX, 8215
Port Washington Historical Society, WI, 9227
Portland Harbor Museum, ME, 3519
Preservation New Jersey, Inc., NJ, 5660
Presque Isle County Historical Museum, MI, 4231
Puget Sound Maritime Historical Society, WA, 8935
Quaco Historical and Library Society, Inc., NB, 9608
Racine Heritage Museum, WI, 9234
Rhode Island State Archives, RI, 7579
Roanoke Island Festival Park, NC, 6359

Rock Hall Waterman's Museum, MD, 3699
Roebling Chapter, Society for Industrial Archaeology, NJ, 5558
Sacramento Archives and Museum Collection Center, CA, 764
Saint Croix Historical Society, ME, 3420
Salem Maritime National Historic Site, MA, 3980
San Luis Obispo County Historical Society and Museum, CA, 837
Santa Barbara Historical Society, CA, 863
Santa Barbara Maritime Museum, CA, 864
Scow Schooner Project, The, TX, 8030
Seacoast Science Center, NH, 5415
Seattle-King County Military History Society, Inc., WA, 8937
Shelburne County Museum, NS, 9673
Shelburne Museum, VT, 8451
Sheldon Museum and Cultural Center, Inc., AK, 165
Simcoe County Archives, ON, 9748
Sitka Historical Society/Isabel Miller Museum, AK, 188
Skagit County Historical Society, WA, 8871
Sodus Bay Historical Society, NY, 6139
South Street Seaport Museum, NY, 6030
Southeast Lighthouse Foundation, RI, 7527
Split Rock Lighthouse Rd, MN, 4503
St. Augustine Lighthouse and Museum, Inc., FL, 1538
St. Clement's Island-Potomac River Museum, MD, 3622
Steamship Historical Society of America, Inc., The, RI, 7581
Stony Point Battlefield State Historic Site, NY, 6152
Tahoe Heritage Foundation, CA, 902
Texas Maritime Museum, TX, 8226
Texas Seaport Museum, TX, 8128
Tongass Historical Museum, AK, 174
Tremont Historical Society, ME, 3408
Tri-Cities Historical Museum, MI, 4133
Trustees of Reservations, MA, 4004
Twin Light Historical Society, NJ, 5508
Village Museum, The, SC, 7707
Vinalhaven Historical Society, ME, 3530
Warwick Historical Society, RI, 7588
Watermen's Museum, VA, 8789
Western Lake Erie Historical Society, OH, 6795
Western New York Documentary Heritage Program, NY, 5844
Westport Maritime Museum, WA, 8987
Wildwood Historical Society, Inc./George F. Boyer Historical Museum, NJ, 5679
Wisconsin Maritime Museum, WI, 9173
Woods Hole Historical Museum, MA, 4039

LITERATURE

Aberdeen Room Archives and Museum, MD, 3545
Adair County Historical Society, IA, 2749
Adair County Historical Society, MO, 4791
Adirondack Museum, The, NY, 5820
African American Museum and Library at Oakland, CA, 667
African Art Museum of Maryland, MD, 3623
Afton Historical Society Museum, MN, 4263
Algonquin Culture and Heritage Centre, ON, 9717
Alice T. Miner Colonial Collection, NY, 5861
Allegany County Historical Society, MD, 3627
Allegany County Historical Society, NY, 5814
Allen Barkley Young Historians, Inc., KY, 3220
Allen County Historical and Genealogy Society, KY, 3236
Allen E. Roberts Masonic Library and Museum, Inc. (Grand Lodge of Virginia AF&AM), VA, 8680
Allison-Antrim Museum, Inc., PA, 7238
Almanzo and Laura Ingalls Wilder Association, NY, 5975
Alstead Historical Society, NH, 5264
AltaMira Historical Society, CA, 955
American Antiquarian Society, MA, 4040
American Cotton Museum, TX, 8134
American Fluorite Museum, The, IL, 2367
American Helicopter Museum and Education Center, PA, 7498
American Jewish Historical Society, MA, 4016

American Studies Association, DC, 1327
American Swedish Historical Museum, PA, 7352
American Swedish Institute, The, MN, 4386
American-Italian Renaissance Foundation, LA, 3340
Amistad Research Center, The, LA, 3341
Anderson Valley Historical Museum, CA, 470
Andrew County Museum and Historical Society, MO, 4933
Anna Maria Island Historical Society Inc., FL, 1378
Antelope County Historical Society, NE, 5172
Anthenaeum of Philadelphia, The, PA, 7353
Appalachian Consortium, Inc., NC, 6224
Archives and Manuscripts Department, Auburn University, AL, 9
Archives and Special Collections, Harriet Irving Library, NB, 9586
Archives and Special Collections, MCP Hahnemann University, PA, 7354
Archives and Special Collections, Ohio University Libraries, OH, 6568
Archives Nationales du Quebec, QC, 9898
Archives Nationales du Quebec, QC, 9937
Archives of the Institute of the Blessed Virgin Mary, ON, 9827
Arizona Jewish Historical Society, AZ, 244
Arthur and Elizabeth Schlesinger Library on the History of Women in America, The, MA, 3795
Ashtabula Plantation, SC, 7720
Asotin County Historical Museum, WA, 8798
Association for the Preservation of Historic Natchitoches, LA, 3329
Athens Historical Society, Inc., GA, 1587
Atwater Historical Society, The, OH, 6570
Auburn Avenue Research Library on African American Culture and History, GA, 1601
Auburn University Montgomery Library, AL, 95
Augustan Society, Inc., The, CA, 509
Badger Clark Memorial, SD, 7766
Bainbridge Island Historical Society, WA, 8800
Bancroft Library, The, CA, 458
Bank of Montreal Archives and Museum, QC, 9901
Barnwell County Museum and Historical Board, SC, 7600
Barriere and District Heritage Society, BC, 9433
Bartholomew County Historical Society, IL, 2084
Bartlesville Area History Museum, OK, 6842
Bay Village Historical Society, OH, 6578
Bear Lake County Rails and Trails Museum, ID, 1943
Beauregard-Keyes House, LA, 3342
Becky Thatcher Book Shop, MO, 4716
Beinecke Rare Book and Manuscript Library, CT, 1223
Bella Vista Historical Society/Museum, AR, 303
Belleville Public Library, IL, 1991
Belleville Public Library, ON, 9692
Bellport-Brookhaven Historical Society, NY, 5813
Ben-Hur Museum/General Lew Wallace Study, IN, 2502
Benares Historic House, ON, 9750
Benton County Historical Society, IA, 2852
Benton County Historical Society, MN, 4482
Benton County Historical Society, MO, 4962
Benton County Historical Society, OR, 7061
Berkeley Historical Society, CA, 460
Berkshire County Historical Society, The, MA, 3951
Berkshire Museum, The, MA, 3952
Berlin and Coos County Historical Society, NH, 5275
Berlin Historical Society, Inc., VT, 8361
Bess Streeter Aldrich House and Museum, NE, 5111
Beverly Historical Society and Museum, MA, 3761
Bidwell Mansion State Historic Park, CA, 488
Billy Bishop Heritage, ON, 9787
Birmingham Public Library, Department of Archives and Manuscripts, AL, 16
Birmingham Public Library, Linn-Henley Research Library, Tutwiler Collection of

Southern History, AL, 17
Bishop Museum and Historical Society, CA, 467
Bloomington Historical Society, MN, 4278
Blue Springs Historical Society, MO, 4647
Bonanzaville, USA, ND, 6551
Boston Athenaeum, The, MA, 3765
Boston Public Library, MA, 3768
Bowden Pioneer Museum, AB, 9360
Bracken County Historical Society, KY, 3100
Braddock's Field Historical Society, PA, 7141
Brandywine Conservancy, Inc., PA, 7163
Brennan Historic House and Medical Office Museum, KY, 3178
Bristol Historical Society, NH, 5278
Bristol Historical Society, VT, 8366
Brome County Historical Society, QC, 9886
Bronx County Historical Society, NY, 5827
Brooksville Historical Society, ME, 3416
Bryant Library Local History Collection, NY, 6106
Bryn Mawr College Libraries, PA, 7152
Buechel Memorial Lakota Museum, SD, 7832
Buffalo Historical Society, Inc., Old Stone Church and Rectory Heritage Center, ND, 6503
Buffalo Trails Museum, ND, 6511
Cabarrus Genealogy Society, NC, 6260
Caddo Cultural Center, OK, 6847
Caddo-Pine Island Oil Museum, LA, 3364
Calais Historical Society, VT, 8371
California Council for the Humanities, CA, 796
California History Section, California State Library, CA, 749
California Military Museum, CA, 750
Callingwood Library and Museum on Americanism, VA, 8474
Camas-Washougal Historical Society, WA, 8983
Cambridge Historical Society, The, MA, 3797
Camden County Historical Society & Museum, MO, 4811
Camden County Historical Society, NJ, 5473
Campus Martius Museum, OH, 6710
Canadian Rivers Historical Society, OK, 6889
Cape Ann Historical Association, MA, 3867
Cape Coral Historical Society, FL, 1391
Carroll County Historical & Genealogical Society, Inc., AR, 308
Carver-Hill Memorial and Historical Society, Inc., FL, 1400
Cascade County Historical Museum and Archives, MT, 5014
Center for American History, The University of Texas at Austin, TX, 8013
Center for History of Foot Care and Footwear/Temple Univ School of Podiatric Medicine, PA, 7360
Center for Southwest Research, NM, 5691
Center for Western Studies, SD, 7835
Center of Southwest Studies, Fort Lewis College, CO, 1036
Central Nevada Historical Society/Museum, NV, 5260
Centre for Newfoundland Studies, NF, 9628
Centre d'etudes acadiennes, NB, 9596
Centre de Recherche en Civilisation Canadienne-Francaise de l'Universite d'Ottawa, ON, 9780
CFB Gagetown Military Museum, NB, 9599
Chambers County Museum, Inc., AL, 72
Chapin Community Historical Society, IL, 2028
Charles Carroll House of Annapolis, MD, 3548
Charleston Library Society, SC, 7624
Chemung County Historical Society, Inc. (Chemung Valley History Museum), NY, 5899
Cherokee Heritage Center, OK, 6971
Chester Gould-Dick Tracy Museum, IL, 2470
Chicago Historical Society, IL, 2043
Chicago Lawn Historical Society, IL, 2045
Chicago Public Library Special Collections and Preservation Division, IL, 2046
Children's Museum of Elizabethtown, KY, 3121
Chippewa County Historical Society, MN, 4403
Chippewa County Historical Society, WI, 9097
Cimarron Valley Railroad Museum, OK, 6872
Circle District Historical Society, Inc., AK, 147

Claremont, New Hampshire Historical Society, Inc., The, NH, 5290

Clifton Community Historical Society, KS, 2898

Clinton County Historical and Genealogy Society, Inc., MO, 4860

Cloud County Historical Society, KS, 2904

Clover Bend Historic Preservation Association, AR, 357

Colorado Springs Museum, CO, 1002

Columbus Jewish Historical Society, OH, 6630

Commission for Historical and Architectural Preservation, MD, 3570

Committee for the Preservation of the Robert Penn Warren Birthplace in Todd County, Inc., KY, 3145

Commonwealth Air Training Plan Museum, MB, 9533

Community Library Associaton-Regional History Dept, ID, 1934

Company of the Redwood Library and Athanaeum, The, RI, 7555

Concord Historical Society, CA, 501

Concord Historical Society, VT, 8419

Concord Museum, MA, 3814

Connecticut Historical Society, The, CT, 1191

Conner Prairie, IN, 2524

Constitution Island Association, NY, 6186

Cooper County Historical Society, MO, 4856

Cornish Historical Society, NH, 5298

Craig County Historical Society, VA, 8639

Creston and District Historical and Museum Society, BC, 9442

Croatian Ethnic Institute, IL, 2048

Cromwell Historical Society, CT, 1152

Crystal Lake Falls Historical Association, VT, 8357

Czechoslovak Heritage Museum, IL, 2281

Dakotaland Museum, SD, 7790

Dallas County Historical Society, Inc., MO, 4655

Danville Historical Society, VA, 8532

Dawes County Historical Society, Inc., NE, 5095

Dawson County Historical Society, NE, 5141

Dickinson Homestead, MA, 3749

Doctor Samuel D. Harris National Museum of Dentistry, MD, 3572

Doctor Sun Yat-Sen Classical Chinese Garden, BC, 9506

Doll House Museum, KS, 2995

Douglas County Historical Society, MN, 4267

Douglas County Historical Society, OR, 7077

Douglas County Historical Society, WI, 9254

Douglas County Historical Society/Watkins Community Museum of History, KS, 2975

Douglas County Museum of History and Natural History, OR, 7078

Duke University Rare Book, Manuscript and Special Collections Library, NC, 6271

Duncan Cottage Museum, AK, 179

Duncan Cultural Center, KY, 3144

East Providence Historical Society, RI, 7541

East Rochester Local History, NY, 5897

East Tennessee Historical Society, TN, 7926

Eastern Trails Museum, OK, 6980

Echo Historical Museum, OR, 7011

Edgar Allan Poe National Historic Site, PA, 7368

Edith Wharton Restoration at the Mount, MA, 3892

Edward Bellamy Memorial Association, MA, 3810

Egan Institute of Maritime Studies, MA, 3920

Eisenhower Birthplace State Historical Park, TX, 8083

Eisenhower Center for American Studies, The, LA, 3344

Elkhorn Valley Museum and Research Center, NE, 5175

Elverhoj Museum of History and Art, CA, 898

Elwyn B Robinson Department of Special Collections, University of North Dakota, ND, 6522

Emily Carr House, BC, 9523

Emory and Henry College, VA, 8542

Empire State Aerosciences Museum, NY, 5920

Enos Mills Cabin, CO, 1042

Erie County Historical Society, OH, 6772

Erie County Historical Society, PA, 7206

Ermatinger/Clergue Heritage Site, ON, 9802

Ernest Hemingway Foundation of Oak Park, The, IL, 2288

Ernest Hemingway Home and Museum, FL, 1458

Ernie Pyle State Historic Site, IN, 2505

Essex County Museum, Inc., VA, 8751

Eugene Field House and St. Louis Toy Museum, MO, 4911

F. Scott and Zelda Fitzgerald Museum, AL, 96

Fairbanks Community Museum, AK, 159

Fairfax Historical Society, VT, 8383

Family Research Society of Northeastern North Carolina, NC, 6278

Federation of Orange County Historical Organization/Historical Commission, CA, 852

Feinberg Library Special Collections, Plattsburgh State University, NY, 6073

Filipino American Historical Society of Chicago, IL, 2051

Filipino American National History Society, Santa Clara Valley Chapter, CA, 823

Fillmore Historical Museum, CA, 536

Filson Club, The, KY, 3182

Fireman's Hall Museum, PA, 7370

First Church of Christ in Hartford, CT, 1192

Flamingo Gardens, FL, 1405

Flannery O'Connor Home Foundation, GA, 1787

Folsom Museum, NM, 5723

Fond du Lac County Historical Society, WI, 9126

Forbes Mill Regional History Museum and Los Gatos Museum of Art and Natural History, CA, 627

Forest History Society, NC, 6272

Fort Gibson Historic Site, OK, 6885

Fort Kearney State Historical Park, NE, 5138

Fort Walla Walla Museum/Walla Valley Historical Society, WA, 8980

Foxborough Historical Commission, MA, 3862

Framingham Historical Society, MA, 3864

Franco-American Center, NH, 5362

Franklin County Historical Association, TX, 8191

Franklin County Historical Society, Inc., VA, 8715

Friend Family Assocation Heritage Museum and Genealogical Library, MD, 3652

Friends of Old South Ferdinand, Inc., MO, 4702

Friends of Sheldon Jackson Museum, AK, 185

Friends of the Ocean City Historical Museum, Inc., NJ, 5584

Fruitlands Museum, MA, 3877

Gallaudet University Archives, DC, 1340

Gallia County Historical/Genealogical Society, OH, 6667

Garden of the Rockies Museum, MT, 5051

Garza County Historical Museum, TX, 8216

GATEway to the Panhandle Museum Corporation, OK, 6888

General Sweeny's Museum, MO, 4869

George M. Jones Memorial Library, VA, 8611

George W. Brown, Jr. Ojibwe Museum and Cultural Center, WI, 9159

German Society of Philadelphia, The, PA, 7374

Gilliam County Historical Society, OR, 7006

Glengarry Pioneer Museum, ON, 9708

Glessner House Museum, IL, 2055

Glove Museum, The, NY, 6007

Goshen, New Hampshire Historical Society, Inc., NH, 5382

Governor's Mansion, GA, 1608

Grand River Historical Society and Museum, MO, 4676

Grande Prairie Museum, AB, 9398

Greensboro Historical Society, VT, 8391

Greenwood Military Aviation Museum, NS, 9657

Gulfport Historical Society, FL, 1534

Haeger Pottery Collectors of America, CA, 439

Hanover Area Historical Society, PA, 7240

Hanover County Historical Society, Inc., VA, 8585

Harriet Beecher Stowe Center, CT, 1193

Harriet Tubman Organization, MD, 3605

Harrison County Historical Museum, TX, 8181

Harry Meador Coal Museum, VA, 8497

Hattiesburg Area Historical Society and Museum, MS, 4554

Haverford College Library, Special Collections, PA, 7257

Hawaii Heritage Center, HI, 1857

Hayden Historical Museum Inc., IN, 2545

Helena Library and Museum Association, AR, 351

Hemingway-Pfeiffer Museum and Educational Center, AR, 403

Henney History Room-Conway Public Library, NH, 5297

Henry County Historical Society Museum, IN, 2603

Henry George Birthplace, PA, 7379

Henry Meade Williams Local History Department, Harrison Memorial Library, CA, 482

Heritage Foundation, Inc., GA, 1820

Heritage Museum, MT, 5035

Heritage Museum, The, OR, 7025

Heritage Shawinigan, QC, 9928

Hess Heritage Museum, ID, 1959

Highspire Historical Society, PA, 7263

Hinckley Fire Museum, Inc., MN, 4351

Historic Aiken Foundation, SC, 7598

Historic Allaire Village, NJ, 5437

Historic Cabarrus, Inc., NC, 6261

Historic Cold Spring Village, NJ, 5460

Historic Crab Orchard Museum and Pioneer Park, VA, 8753

Historic Deerfield, Inc., MA, 3834

Historic Fort Worth, Inc., TX, 8109

Historic New Orleans Collection, The, LA, 3350

Historic Oak View County Park, NC, 6397

Historic Oakland, MD, 3625

Historic Rugby, Inc., TN, 7990

Historic Ship Nautilus and Submarine Force Museum, CT, 1180

Historic Southwest Ohio, OH, 6614

Historic Springfield Foundation, Inc., MS, 4545

Historical Museum of the D.R. Barker Library, NY, 5911

Historical Society of Douglas County, NE, 5188

Historical Society of Haddonfield, NJ, 5496

Historical Society of Harford County, Inc., The, MD, 3594

Historical Society of New Mexico, NM, 5756

Historical Society of Oak Park and River Forest, IL, 2290

Historical Society of Palm Beach County, FL, 1575

Historical Society of the Town of Greenwich, The, CT, 1149

Historical Society of the Town of Hancock, The, ME, 3445

Historical Society of Wilmington Vermont, VT, 8467

History and Humanities Program of the State Foundation on Culture and the Arts, HI, 1863

Ho'oikaika, HI, 1882

Holden Historical Society Museum, AB, 9401

Holocaust Documentation and Education Center, Inc., FL, 1497

Honey Creek Church Preservation Group, IA, 2806

Hotel de Paris Museum, CO, 1062

Houghton Lake Area Historical Society, MI, 4155

House of the Seven Gables Historic Site, MA, 3975

Houston County Historical Commission, TX, 8065

Hudson Bay and District Cultural Society/Hudson Bay Museum, SK, 9959

Hugh Thomas Miller Rare Book Room, Bulter University Libraries, IN, 2558

Huguenot Heritage, NY, 6011

Hunter House Victorian Museum, VA, 8651

Huntington Library, Art Collections, and Botanical Gardens, The, CA, 839

Illinois State Historical Society, IL, 2397

Imlay City Historical Museum, MI, 4156

Immigration History Research Center, University of Minnesota, MN, 4390

Ina Dillard Russel Library Special Collections, GA, 1741

Institute of Texan Cultures, The, TX, 8235

International Congress of Distinguished Awards, PA, 7386

International Game Fish Assn., Fishing Hall of Fame and Museum, FL, 1423

International Society Daughters of Utah Pioneers, UT, 8334

Iowa County Historical Society, IA, 2788

Iowa County Historical Society, WI, 9109

Irish American Heritage Museum, NY, 5891

Island Institute, ME, 3499

J.C. Penney Museum and Boyhood Home, MO, 4715

Jack London State Historic Park, CA, 557

Jackson County Historical Society, AR, 396

Jackson County Historical Society, IA, 2786

Jackson County Historical Society, IL, 2267

Jackson County Historical Society, KS, 2956

Jackson County Historical Society, MN, 4357

Jackson County Historical Society, WV, 9048

James A. Michener Art Museum, PA, 7190

James Fenimore Cooper Society, NY, 5868

James S. Copley Library, The, CA, 584

James Whitcomb Riley Museum Home, IN, 2567

Japanese American National Museum, CA, 618

Jasper County Historical Society, IA, 2808

Jasper County Historical Society, IN, 2621

Jasper County Historical Society, SC, 7727

Jay County Historical Society, IN, 2619

Jeff Matthews Memorial Museum, VA, 8573

Jefferson County Historical Society and Museum, OR, 7036

Jersey County Historical Society, IL, 2181

John Burroughs Association, Inc., The, NY, 6013

John G. Neihardt Center, NE, 5081

Johnson-Erickson Museum, IA, 2853

Johnston County Heritage Center, NC, 6435

Kanesville Tabernacle Visitor Center, IA, 2703

Karpeles Manuscript Library Museum, CA, 861

Karpeles Manuscript Library Museum, SC, 7631

Kate Chopin Home/Bayou Folk Museum, LA, 3332

Kaua'i Museum Association, HI, 1885

Kemerer Museum of Decorative Arts, PA, 7130

Kendall County Historical Society, IL, 2472

Key West Art and Historical Society, Inc., FL, 1462

King and Queen County Historical Society, VA, 8762

Kirkwood Historical Society, The, MO, 4792

Kitimat Centennial Museum, BC, 9463

Kona Historical Society, HI, 1879

Koreshan State Historic Site, FL, 1416

Lackawanna Historical Society, PA, 7445

Lafayette Natural History Museum and Planetarium, LA, 3309

Lake County Historical Museum, FL, 1564

Lake County Historical Society Collection, IL, 2194

Lake Region Heritage Center, Inc., ND, 6507

Lake View Iowa Historical Society, IA, 2778

Lamaline Heritage Society and Lamaline Heritage Museum, NF, 9620

Lambert Historical Society, MT, 5033

Lancaster Mennonite Historical Society, PA, 7285

Laura Ingalls Wilder Museum & Tourist Center, Inc., MN, 4509

Laura Ingalls Wilder/Rose Wilder Lane Home & Museum, MO, 4816

Lawn Heritage Museum, NF, 9621

Lawrence Historical Society, NJ, 5527

Lebanon Historical Society, IL, 2197

Lebanon Historical Society, NH, 5351

Lee County Genealogical Historical Society, Inc., NC, 6428

Leech Lake Tribal College Library, MN, 4289

Lenox Historical Society, MA, 3893

Les Cheneaux Historical Association, MI, 4084

Library Company of Philadelphia, The, PA, 7388

Limberlost State Historic Site, IN, 2536

Limerick Township Historical Society, PA, 7299

Linam Ranch Museum, NM, 5729

Lincoln Historical Society, VT, 8399

Lincoln State Monument, NM, 5736

Little House on the Prairie, KS, 2962

Stone Fort Museum, TX, 8193
Strong Museum, NY, 6099
Stuhr Museum of the Prarie Pioneer, NE, 5126
Suffolk-Nansemond Historical Society, VA, 8745
Sultan-Sky Valley Historical Society, WA, 8959
Sun Valley Center for the Arts, ID, 1966
Superior Historical Society, Inc., AZ, 262
Suquamish Museum, WA, 8962
Surface Creek Valley Historical Society, CO, 998
Swink Historical Preservation Association, OK, 6970
Talkeetna Historical Society, AK, 193
Taylors Falls Historical Society, The, MN, 4497
Tehama County Museum Foundation, Inc., CA, 921
Telephone Pioneer Museum of New Mexico, NM, 5698
Tennessee Historical Society, TN, 7977
Tennessee State Library and Archives, TN, 7978
Terrebonne Historical and Cultural Society, LA, 3299
Texas Seaport Museum, TX, 8128
Thomas Paine National Historic Association, NY, 5995
Thomas Wolfe Memorial State Historic Site, NC, 6214
Thomaston Historical Society, ME, 3526
Thorton W. Burgess Society, MA, 3849
Thurber House, The, OH, 6637
Tippecanoe County Historical Association, IN, 2577
Tri State Old Time Cowboys Museum, NE, 5122
Tri-County Historical & Museum Society of King City, MO, Inc., MO, 4790
Tri-County Historical Society and Museum, Inc., KS, 2952
Truckee-Donner Historical Society, CA, 930
Trustees of Reservations, MA, 4004
Tupperville School Museum, NS, 9678
Tuskegee Institute National Historic Site, George Washington Carver Museum, AL, 125
Twentynine Palms Historical Society, CA, 936
U'mista Cultural Centre, BC, 9430
Union County Historical Society and Heritage Museum, MS, 4591
Union County Historical Society, GA, 1638
Union County Historical Society, IA, 2706
Union County Historical Society, PA, 7296
Union County Historical Society, SD, 7775
Union Township Historical Society, NJ, 5504
Union Township Historical Society, NJ, 5663
United Society of Shakers, ME, 3469
Universite de Montreal, Division des Archives, QC, 9913
University Archives and Special Collection Unit, Pollak Library, CA State Univ, Fullerton, CA, 554
University Archives of the State University of New York at Buffalo, NY, 5843
University of Manitoba Archives & Special Collections, the Libraries, MB, 9578
University of North Carolina at Chapel Hill, Manuscripts Department, NC, 6243
University of Wyoming American Heritage Center, WY, 9328
University South Caroliniana Society, SC, 7663
Upper Vandalia Historical Society, WV, 9047
Valdosta State University Archives, GA, 1829
Valley Community Historical Society, NE, 5216
Valley Falls Historical Society, KS, 3067
Varner-Hogg Plantation State Historical Park, TX, 8278
Vegreville Regional Museum Society, AB, 9423
Victorian Society in America, The, PA, 7408
Village of Hanover Park Historic Commission, IL, 2162
Virginia Historical Society, VA, 8708
Wadsworth Area Historical Society, OH, 6806
Wallace and Area Museum, NS, 9680
Walt Whitman Birthplace Association, NY, 5945
Walt Whitman House, NJ, 5457

Wanda Gag House Assn., Inc., MN, 4419
War Eagles Air Museum, NM, 5762
Warren County Historical Society, IL, 2366
Warren County Historical Society, MO, 4961
Warren County Historical Society, OH, 6699
Warren County Historical Society, PA, 7486
Washburn County Historical Society, Inc., WI, 9243
Waukesha Engine Historical Society, WI, 9270
Wayne County Historical Society and Museum, OH, 6819
Wayne County Historical Society, IL, 2131
Wayne County Historical Society, MO, 4855
Wayne County Historical Society, NY, 5974
Wayne County Historical Society, PA, 7264
West Overton Museums and Village, PA, 7444
West Pasco Historical Society, FL, 1496
West Salem Historical Society, WI, 9277
West Texas Historical Association, TX, 8177
Western Illinois University Archives and Special Collections, IL, 2227
Western New York Documentary Heritage Program, NY, 5844
Westport Historical Society, CT, 1277
Westport Historical Society, MO, 4787
Wexford County Historical Society, MI, 4079
Wheat Ridge Historical Society, CO, 1134
Willard Library, IN, 2522
William Bull and Sarah Wells Stone House Association, NY, 5850
William Cullen Bryant Homestead, MA, 3822
William S. Hart Museum, CA, 662
Williamstown Historical Society, VT, 8465
Williston Historical Society, VT, 8466
Willoughby Township Historical Museum, ON, 9765
Wilson Czech Opera House Corporation, Foundation, KS, 3083
Wimbledon Community Museum, ND, 6554
Windermere District Historical Society/Windermere Valley Museum, BC, 9455
Wing of History, CA, 841
Winnebago County Historical and Archaeological Society, WI, 9219
Wisconsin Maritime Museum, WI, 9173
Wood Mountain Historical Society, SK, 9998
Woodside National Historic Site, ON, 9738
World Methodist Museum, NC, 6345
Wren's Nest House Museum, The, GA, 1629
Wyman Historical Museum, CO, 1009
York University Archives and Special Collections, ON, 9847

LIVING HISTORY

1711 Solomon Goffe House, CT, 1210
1736 Josiah Dennis Manse Museum, MA, 3841
1743 Palatine House/Schoharie Colonial Heritage Association, NY, 6123
1812 Homestead Educational Foundation, NY, 6193
1852 Herr Family Homestead, PA, 7287
1890 House and Center for the Arts, The, NY, 5875
Aberdeen Room Archives and Museum, MD, 3545
Acadian Heritage and Culture Foundation, Inc., LA, 3285
Acadian Memorial, LA, 3375
Acadian Village, LA, 3305
Accokeek Foundation, MD, 3547
Ace of Clubs House, TX, 8256
Adair County Historical Society, IA, 2749
Adair County Historical Society, MO, 4791
Adam Thoroughgood House, VA, 8648
Adirondack Museum, The, NY, 5820
Admiral Nimitz Museum and State Historical Center and National Museum of the Pacific War, TX, 8114
Adsmore Museum, KY, 3231
Affton Historical Society, MO, 4901
Agecroft Association, VA, 8679
Ah-Tah-Thi-Ki Museum, Seminole Tribe of Florida, FL, 1396
Aircraft Carrier Hornet Foundation, CA, 431
Ak-Chin Him-Dak EcoMuseum and Archives, AZ, 233

Alabama Civil War Roundtable, AL, 11
Alabama Constitution Hall Village, AL, 62
Alabama Historic Ironworks Commission, AL, 76
Alabama Historical Commission, AL, 94
Alabama Music Hall of Fame, AL, 122
Alamance Battleground State Historic Site, NC, 6232
Alamance County Historical Museum, Inc., NC, 6234
Alamo, The, TX, 8231
Albany Heritage Society, Inc., MN, 4265
Albany Historical Society, Inc., KS, 3037
Alden Kindred of America, MA, 3844
Alfalfa County Historical Society, OK, 6859
Allegany County Historical Society, MD, 3627
Allegany County Historical Society, NY, 5814
Allegheny Cemetery Historical Association, PA, 7414
Allen County-Ft. Wayne Historical Society, IN, 2525
Alliance for Historic Hillsborough, The, NC, 6327
Alnobak Nebesakiak, VT, 8379
Alta District Historical Society, CA, 517
Alton Area Historical Society, IL, 1976
Amalthea Historical Society, OH, 6814
Ameliasburgh Historical Museum, ON, 9685
American Cotton Museum, TX, 8134
American Helicopter Museum and Education Center, PA, 7498
American Wind Power Center/National Windmill Project, TX, 8175
American-Italian Renaissance Foundation, LA, 3340
Amherst History Museum at the Strong House, MA, 3748
Amherst Museum, NY, 5796
Andersonville National Historic Site, GA, 1584
Andersonville Oldtime Farm Area and Museum, GA, 1585
Andrew County Museum and Historical Society, MO, 4933
Andrew Jackson State Park, SC, 7701
Anna Maria Island Historical Society Inc., FL, 1378
Anniston Museum of Natural History, AL, 2
Anoka County Historical Society, MN, 4269
Antiquarian and Landmarks Society, CT, 1189
Antique Airplane Association, Inc., IA, 2817
Antique Gas and Steam Engine Museum, Inc., CA, 951
Antoine Le Claire House Historical Interpretive Center, IA, 2708
Apollo Area Historical Society, PA, 7119
Appalachian Cultural Museum, The, NC, 6225
Appling County Heritage Center, GA, 1637
Appomattox Court House National Historical Park, VA, 8489
APVA Mary Washington Branch, VA, 8563
Arbor Lodge State Historical Park, NE, 5169
Archibald Smith Plantation Home Preservationists, Inc., GA, 1767
Archives of the Institute of the Blessed Virgin Mary, ON, 9827
Arizona Historical Society - Northern Division, AZ, 216
Arizona Historical Society - Rio Colorado Division, AZ, 292
Arizona Historical Society - Southern Division, AZ, 272
Arkansas Museum of Natural Resources, AR, 420
Arkansas State University Museum, AR, 423
Arlington Heights Historical Society and Museum, IL, 1981
Arnold Expedition Historical Society, ME, 3486
Arthur Bowring Sandhills Ranch, NE, 5163
Arthurdale Heritage, Inc., WV, 8997
Arvid E. Miller Memorial Library Museum, WI, 9085
Ashland, the Henry Clay Estate, KY, 3159
Ashlawn-Highland, VA, 8515
Aspen Historical Society, CO, 981
Association for Living History, Farm and Agricultural Museums, OH, 6732
Association for the Preservation of Tennessee Antiquities (APTA), TN, 7958
Association for the Preservation of Virginia Antiquities (APVA), VA, 8682

Association of Historical Societies of New Hampshire, NH, 5269
Astor House Museum, CO, 1064
Athol Murray College of Notre Dame Archives/Museum, SK, 9996
Atlanta Cyclorama, GA, 1597
Atlanta Historical Society, GA, 1598
Atlanta Historical Society, ID, 1899
Atlanta History Center, GA, 1599
Atoka County Historical Society, OK, 6840
Atwater Historical Society, The, OH, 6570
Audubon County Historical Society, IA, 2665
Audubon State Commemorative Area, LA, 3371
August Schell Brewing Company Museum of Brewing, MN, 4416
Aurora Colony Historical Society, OR, 6992
Aurora County Historical Society, SD, 7826
Aurora Historical Society, NY, 5888
Aurora Historical Society, OH, 6571
Austin Children's Museum, TX, 8012
Austintown Historical Society, OH, 6572
Avoca Museum and Historical Society, VA, 8485
Aztec Museum Association, NM, 5702
B&O Railroad Museum, MD, 3559
Babcock Smith House, RI, 7590
Babe Ruth Birthplace Museum, MD, 3560
Baccalieu Trail Heritage Corporation, NF, 9614
Badlands Natural History Association, SD, 7794
Bagg Bonanza Historical Farm, ND, 6540
Balfour House, MS, 4614
Ballestone Preservation Society, MD, 3562
Ballwin Historical Society, MO, 4637
Baltimore Conservatory and Botanical Gardens, MD, 3563
Baltimore County Historical Society, Inc., MD, 3618
Baltimore Maritime Museum, MD, 3564
Bancroft Library, The, CA, 458
Bank of Montreal Archives and Museum, QC, 9901
Bar U Ranch National Historic Site of Canada, AB, 9406
Barkerville Historic Town, BC, 9432
Barnwell County Museum and Historical Board, SC, 7600
Barrington Living History Farm, TX, 8273
Batsto Village, NJ, 5502
Battle of Carthage, MO, 4666
Battle of Lexington State Historic Site, MO, 4803
Battlefield House Museum, ON, 9811
Battleship NORTH CAROLINA, NC, 6466
Bay Area Heritage Society/Baytown Historical Museum, TX, 8033
Bay County Historical Society/Historical Museum of Bay County, MI, 4066
Bay Village Historical Society, OH, 6578
BC Heritage, BC, 9518
Beaufort Historical Association, NC, 6221
Beaufort Museum, SC, 7602
Beaver Brook Farm and Transportation Museum, NH, 5372
Beaver Island Historical Society, MI, 4068
Beavercreek Historical Society, OH, 6580
Beck Cultural Exchange Center, TN, 7921
Becker County Historical Society and Museum, MN, 4303
Beersheba Springs Historical Society, TN, 7864
Belknap Mill Society, NH, 5348
Bell Homestead National Historic Site, ON, 9696
Bella Vista Historical Society/Museum, AR, 303
Belle Grove Plantation, VA, 8627
Belleville Public Library, IL, 1991
Belleville Public Library, ON, 9692
Bellport-Brookhaven Historical Society, NY, 5813
Ben-Hur Museum/General Lew Wallace Study, IN, 2502
Bennett Place State Historic Site, NC, 6269
Bennington Museum, The, VT, 8360
Bensenville Historical Society, IL, 1997
Bent's Old Fort National Historic Site, CO, 1084
Benton County Historical Society, IA, 2852
Benton County Historical Society, MN, 4482
Benton County Historical Society, MO, 4962

LOGGING

MARITIME

MEDICINE

LA, 3365
Oral History Research Center, Indiana
University, IN, 2487
Oregon Historical Society, OR, 7067
Oregon State Library, OR, 7084
Oregon Trail Regional Museum, OR, 6994
Orleans County Historical Society Inc., VT,
8368
Oswego Historical Society, Inc., KS, 3025
Ouray County Historical Society, CO, 1105
Owensboro Area Museum of Science and
History, KY, 3215
Paine-Gillam-Scott Museum/Clinton County
Historical Society, MI, 4240
Palmyra Historical Society, WI, 9221
Pardee Home Museum, CA, 674
Paris-Henry County Heritage Center, TN,
7984
Parker Museum of Clay County, IA, 2841
Pawnee County Historical Society and
Museum, OK, 6948
Pea Ridge National Military Park, AR, 401
Peace River Centennial Museum and
Archives, AB, 9412
Peacham Historical Association, VT, 8423
Pearson Museum Dept of Medical
Humanities, IL, 2405
Peder Engelstad Pioneer Village, MN, 4499
Pejepscot Historical Society, ME, 3419
Pend Oreille County Historical Society, WA,
8894
Pendleton County Historical Society, Inc., KY,
3126
Pendleton County Historical Society, Inc., WV,
9021
Pennsbury Manor/Pennsbury Society, The,
PA, 7326
Penticton 9 R.N. Atkinson Museum and
Archives, BC, 9479
Person County Museum of History, NC, 6420
Peter Yegen Jr. Yellowstone County Museum,
MT, 4978
Phelps County Historical Society, MO, 4877
Phelps County Historical Society, NE, 5134
Philadelphia Society for the Preservation of
Landmarks, PA, 7398
Phillips County Museum, AR, 352
Phillips County Museum, MT, 5038
Pickens County Museum of Art and
History/Hagood Mill, SC, 7724
Pierce Historical Society Museum Complex,
NE, 5197
Pioneer Florida Museum Association, Inc.,
FL, 1404
Pioneer Heritage Center, LA, 3382
Plimoth Plantation, MA, 3961
Plumas County Museum Association, Inc.,
CA, 721
Plymouth County Historical Museum, IA,
2780
Polk County Historical Society, GA, 1654
Polk County Historical Society, IA, 2720
Polk County Historical Society, MN, 4299
Polk County Historical Society, OR, 7044
Polk County Historical Society, WI, 9075
Port Hudson State Historical Site, LA, 3397
Port Washington Public Library, NY, 6077
Portage County Historical Society, OH, 6765
Portage County Historical Society, WI, 9250
Porter Thermometer Museum, MA, 3946
Porter-Phelps Huntington Foundation, Inc.,
MA, 3876
Portsmouth Historical Society, RI, 7571
Powers Museum, MO, 4670
Prairie Panorama Museum, AB, 9375
Prairie Park, MO, 4834
Preble County Historical Society, OH, 6656
Prince Edward Island Potato Museum, PE,
9870
Princeton and District Museum and Archives
Society, BC, 9492
Princeton Historical Society, WI, 9231
Pro Football Hall of Fame, OH, 6595
Project Liberty Ship, Baltimore, Inc., MD,
3587
Provincial Museum of Alberta, AB, 9386
Public Health Museum in New England, MA,
4011
Public Hospital of 1773, VA, 8780
Pueblo County Historical Society Museum
and Edward Broadhead Library, CO, 1112
Putnam County Historical Society, IL, 2167
Putnam County Historical Society, OH, 6689

Putnam Museum of History and Natural
Science, IA, 2710
Queen's Historical Room, The, HI, 1870
Quesnel and District Museum and Archives,
BC, 9494
Raleigh City Museum, NC, 6411
Randolph County Historical Society and
Museum, IN, 2651
Randolph County Historical Society, IL, 2035
Randolph County Historical Society, MO,
4829
Randolph County Historical Society, WV,
9006
Rankin Museum of American Heritage, NC,
6281
Ransom County Historical Society, ND, 6515
Raymondville Historical and Community
Center, TX, 8220
Rebecca B. Hadden Stone House Museum,
PA, 7441
Regional Oral History Office, CA, 463
Remick Country Doctor Museum and Farm,
NH, 5424
Reno County Museum, KS, 2960
Renton Historical Society, WA, 8912
Renville County Historical Society, Inc., ND,
6539
Renville County Historical Society, MN, 4412
Republic County Historical Society and
Museum, KS, 2891
Rhode Island State Archives, RI, 7579
Rice County Historical Society, KS, 2989
Rice County Historical Society, MN, 4330
Richmond National Battlefield Park, VA, 8699
River Road African American Museum and
Gallery, LA, 3292
Robert B. Greenblatt, MD Library, Special
Collections, GA, 1635
Robeson County Museum, NC, 6356
Rochester Hills Museum at Van Hoosen
Farm, MI, 4229
Rochester Museum & Science Center, NY,
6097
Rock County Historical Society, MN, 4375
Rock County Historical Society, WI, 9149
Rock Island County Historical Society, IL,
2250
Rock Springs Historical Museum, WY, 9341
Rockbridge Historical Society, VA, 8604
Rocky Mountain Jewish Historical Society
and Beck Archives, CO, 1031
Rogers Historical Museum, AR, 413
Rome Area History Museum, GA, 1763
Roseau County Historical Society, MN, 4445
Rosenbach Museum and Library, PA, 7403
Rumford Area Historical Society, ME, 3504
Rusk County Historical Museum, WI, 9161
Ruthmere, IN, 2516
Sac City Historical Museum, IA, 2830
Sacramento Archives and Museum Collection
Center, CA, 764
Sacred Heart Area Historical Society, MN,
4447
Saint Croix Historical Society, ME, 3420
Saint Francis County Museum, AR, 333
Salida Museum, CO, 1119
San Diego Civil War Roundtable, CA, 784
San Diego Historical Society, CA, 787
San Pedro Arts and Historical Society, AZ,
206
Sandy Spring Museum, MD, 3710
Sanilac County Historical Society, MI, 4223
Santa Fe Depot Museum, OK, 6960
Santaquin City Chieftain Museum, UT, 8344
Saratoga Historical and Cultural Association,
WY, 9342
Saratoga National Historical Park, NY, 6150
Saskatchewan Archives Board-Regina, SK,
9980
Saskatchewan Archives Board-Saskatoon,
SK, 9989
Saskatoon Public Library-Local History
Room, SK, 9991
Sauk County Historical Society, WI, 9077
Sellors/Barton Museum, NE, 5073
Seneca-Iroquois National Museum, NY, 6114
Seville Historical Society, OH, 6779
Shasta College Museum and Research
Center, CA, 726
Shawano County Historical Society, Inc., WI,
9240
Shelburne Museum, VT, 8451
Shelby County Historical Society/Museum, IL,

2382
Shelby County Historical Society/Museum,
TX, 8047
Sherborn Historical Society, MA, 3990
Shiloh Museum of Ozark History, AR, 422
Shirley Centennial and Historical Society, IN,
2632
Shoal Creek Living History Museum, MO,
4781
Shoreline Historical Museum, WA, 8945
Siloam Springs Museum, AR, 419
Silverton Country Historical Society, OR,
7087
Simcoe County Archives, ON, 9748
Sioux Empire Medical Museum, SD, 7840
Siskiyou County Museum, CA, 973
Ska-Nah-Doht Iroquian Village and Museum,
ON, 9754
Skagit County Historical Society, WA, 8871
Smithville Heritage Society, TX, 8249
Smoky Hill Museum, KS, 3041
Smyth County Historical and Museum
Society, Inc., VA, 8619
Society of the Cincinnati Museum at
Anderson House, The, DC, 1367
Sons and Daughters of the Cherokee Strip
Pioneers, OK, 6884
South Bannock County Historical Center
Museum, ID, 1936
South Boston, Halifax County Museum, VA,
8723
South Carolina State Museum, SC, 7662
South Central Kentucky Cultural Center, KY,
3141
South Park City Museum, CO, 1048
South Simcoe Pioneer Museum, ON, 9683
South Similkameen Museum Society, BC,
9462
Southeast Louisiana Historical Association,
LA, 3295
Southern Memorial Association, VA, 8614
Southwest Museum of Science and
Technology/The Science Place, TX, 8079
Southwest Virginia Museum/Historical Park,
VA, 8500
Space Center, The, NM, 5685
Special Collections and Archives,
Transylvania University Library, KY, 3171
Special Collections, Atkins Library, University
of North Carolina at Charlotte, NC, 6252
Special Collections, Robert W. Woodruff
Library, Emory University, GA, 1626
Spirit of Newtown Committee, Inc./Costen
House, MD, 3689
Spring Mill State Park, IN, 2591
St. Albans Historical Museum, VT, 8445
St. Clair Historical Society, MO, 4886
Stafford County Historical Society, KS, 3049
Stansbury Home Preservation Association,
CA, 492
Star of the Republic Museum, TX, 8274
State Historical Society of Iowa, Iowa
Historical Building, IA, 2722
State Museum of Pennsylvania, The, PA,
7252
Steele County Historical Society, MN, 4427
Steele County Historical Society, ND, 6527
Steppingstone Museum Association, Inc.,
MD, 3669
Sterling Rock Falls Historical Society
Museum, IL, 2413
Stillaquamish Valley Pioneer
Association/Museum, WA, 8797
Stillwater Historical Society, MT, 4995
Stone Fort Museum, TX, 8193
Strathroy Middlesex Museum, ON, 9815
Strong Museum, NY, 6099
Stuhr Museum of the Prairie Pioneer, NE,
5126
Sturdevant-McKee Foundation Inc., NE, 5079
Sully Historic Site, VA, 8507
Sultan-Sky Valley Historical Society, WA,
8959
Summerville-Dorchester Museum, SC, 7740
Sumner County Museum, TN, 7893
Suquamish Museum, WA, 8962
Swisher County Archives and Museum
Association, TX, 8261
Swiss Heritage Society, IN, 2483
Taylor County Historical Society, IA, 2668
Taylor County Historical Society, WI, 9182
Tehama County Museum Foundation, Inc.,
CA, 921

Telluride Historical Museum, CO, 1129
Texarkana Historical Museum, Texarkana
Museums System, TX, 8258
Texarkana Museums System, TX, 8259
Texas Medical Association, TX, 8026
Texas Wendish Heritage Society and
Museum, TX, 8132
This Is The Place Heritage Park, UT, 8337
Thomas County Historical Society, GA, 1824
Thomas County Historical Society, NE, 5212
Three Rivers Museum of Muskogee, Inc., OK,
6923
Tigerton Area Historical Society, WI, 9259
Tobacco Farm Life Museum of Virginia, VA,
8725
Tofield Historical Society, AB, 9422
Top of Oklahoma Historical Museum, OK,
6848
Toppenish Museum, WA, 8970
Town of Orchard Park Historical Museum &
Society, NY, 6051
Tremont Museum and Historical Society, IL,
2427
Tri-Cities Historical Museum, MI, 4133
Tri-County Historical & Museum Society of
King City, MO, Inc., MO, 4790
Trinidad Historical Museum of the Colorado
Historical Society, CO, 1131
Tularosa Basin Historical Society Museum,
NM, 5688
Tuskegee Institute National Historic Site,
George Washington Carver Museum, AL,
125
Twillingate Museum Association, NF, 9643
Tyler County Heritage and Historical Society,
WV, 9039
U.S. Army Medical Department Museum, TX,
8103
Union County Historical Society and Heritage
Museum, MS, 4591
Union County Historical Society, GA, 1638
Union County Historical Society, IA, 2706
Union County Historical Society, PA, 7296
Union County Historical Society, SD, 7775
Union Historical Society, ME, 3528
United Society of Shakers, ME, 3469
Universite de Montreal, Division des Archives,
QC, 9913
University Archives of the State University of
New York at Buffalo, NY, 5843
University History Institute, AR, 383
University Museum, Southern Illinois
University, IL, 2017
University of Alabama at Birmingham
Historical Collections, AL, 23
University of Alberta, Department of
Museums and Collections Services, AB,
9390
University of Colorado Museum of Natural
History, CO, 987
University of Iowa Hospitals and Clinics
Medical Museum, IA, 2767
University of Wyoming American Heritage
Center, WY, 9328
University South Caroliniana Society, SC,
7663
Valley County Pioneer Museum, MT, 5010
Valley Forge Historical Society, PA, 7476
Vermilion County Museum Society, IL, 2094
Verndale Historical Society, MN, 4504
Vernon County Historical Society, MO, 4837
Vernon County Historical Society, WI, 9262
Veterinary Museum/Missouri Veterinary
Medical Foundation, MO, 4760
Vicksburg Foundation for Historic
Preservation, MS, 4621
Victorian Society in America, The, PA, 7408
Village Museum, The, SC, 7707
Wabaunsee County Historical Society, KS,
2879
Wadena County Historical Society &
Museum, MN, 4507
Wadsworth Area Historical Society, OH, 6806
Wakarusa Historical Museums, IN, 2649
Wake Forest College Birthplace Society, Inc.,
NC, 6454
Wallace District Mining Museum, ID, 1971
Waltham Museum, MA, 4022
Wannamuse Institute for Arts, Culture, and
Ethnic Studies, LA, 3366
Wapello County Historical Society, IA, 2818
Warren County Historical Society, IL, 2366
Warren County Historical Society, MO, 4961

MILITARY

MINING

MUSEUM STUDIES

NATURAL HISTORY

Kaposavar Historic Society, SK, 9955
Karpeles Manuscript Library Museum, CA, 861
Karpeles Manuscript Library Museum, SC, 7631
Kaua'i Museum Association, HI, 1885
Kearney County Historical Society, NE, 5165
Kearny County Museum, KS, 2971
Kelowna Museum, BC, 9460
Kemper County Historical Association, MS, 4544
Kenai Visitors and Cultural Center, AK, 172
Kendall County Historical Society, IL, 2472
Kenosha Public Museum, WI, 9153
Kibbe Hancock Heritage Museum, IL, 2022
Kings Mountain State Park, Living History Farm, SC, 7610
Kitimat Centennial Museum, BC, 9463
Kitsap County Historical Society Museum, WA, 8811
Klamath County Museums, OR, 7032
Kline Creek Farm, IL, 2466
Klondike Gold Rush National Historical Park, AK, 191
Knight Museum, NE, 5076
KoKe'e Natural History Museum-Huio Laka, HI, 1880
Kootenay Lake Historical Society, BC, 9457
L.C. Bates Museum, ME, 3448
La Crosse County Historical Society, WI, 9158
La Pul Perie De Chicoutimi, QC, 9878
Lafayette Natural History Museum and Planetarium, LA, 3309
Lake Chicot State Park, AR, 361
Lake County Historical Museum, FL, 1564
Lake County Museum, CA, 590
Lake Erie Islands Historical Society, OH, 6764
Lake Leatherwood City Park, AR, 325
Lake Meredith Aquatic and Wildlife Museum, TX, 8116
Lake Pontchartrain Basin Maritime Musem, Inc., LA, 3318
Lake Region Heritage Center, Inc., ND, 6507
Lake View Iowa Historical Society, IA, 2778
Lake Waccamaw Depot Museum, Inc., NC, 6346
Lakes Region Historical Society, IL, 1980
Lamaline Heritage Society and Lamaline Heritage Museum, NF, 9620
Lancaster Mennonite Historical Society, PA, 7285
Las Cruces Museum of Natural History, NM, 5731
Lava Beds National Monuments, CA, 933
Lawn Heritage Museum, NF, 9621
Lawrence Historical Society, NJ, 5527
Lee County Historical Society, IL, 2107
Lehigh County Historical Society, PA, 7109
Lenni Lenape Historical Society/Museum of Indian Culture, PA, 7111
Les Cheneaux Historical Association, MI, 4084
Lewis and Clark Center, MO, 4881
Lewis and Clark National Historical Trail and Interpretive Center, MT, 5016
Lewis County Museum of Local and Natural History, TN, 7909
Libby Museum, NH, 5435
Liberty County Museum Association, MT, 4990
Library Company of Philadelphia, The, PA, 7388
Lidgerwood Community Museum, ND, 6532
Lightner Museum, The, FL, 1536
Lignumvitae State Botanical Site, FL, 1444
Limberlost State Historic Site, IN, 2536
Lincoln County Historical Society, CO, 1079
Lincoln County Historical Society, KS, 2985
Lincoln County Historical Society, WA, 8829
Lincoln County Historical Society, WY, 9303
Lincoln County Museum of History, NC, 6353
Lincoln Historical Society, VT, 8399
Lincoln State Monument, NM, 5736
Linn County Historical Museum, OR, 7000
Liriodendron, MD, 3595
Little Red Schoolhouse Nature Center, IL, 2463
Littleton Area Historical Society, NH, 5356
Living Prairie Museum, MB, 9570
Log Cabin Heritage Museum, CO, 1083
London Regional Children's Museum, ON,

9742
Long Beach Island Historical Association, NJ, 5444
Long Island Division Queens Borough Public Library, NY, 5954
Los Tubaquenos, AZ, 268
Lost City Museum, NV, 5251
Louisiana Historical Association, LA, 3310
Louisiana Office of State Parks, LA, 3267
Love County Historical Society, Inc., OK, 6915
Loveland Museum and Gallery, CO, 1097
Lower Altamaha Historical Society, GA, 1673
Lucas County Historical Society, IA, 2688
Luseland and Districts Museum, SK, 9963
Lutherville Historical Colored School #24 Museum, MD, 3681
Lyman House Memorial Museum, HI, 1847
Lyndon B. Johnson National Historic Park, TX, 8155
Lyon County Historical Museum, KS, 2926
Lyon County Museum, NY, 6195
MacBride Museum Society, YT, 10003
MacCallum More Museum and Gardens, VA, 8519
Mackinac State Historic Parks-Mackinac Island, MI, 4177
Mackinac State Historic Parks-Mackinaw City, MI, 4180
Madeira Historical Society, The, OH, 6617
Madison County Historical Society Museum, NE, 5157
Madison County Historical Society Museum, OH, 6702
Magnolia Plantation and Gardens, SC, 7633
Maidu Interpretive Center, CA, 745
Makoshika State Park, MT, 5012
Malabar Farm, OH, 6705
Malakoff Diggins State Historic Park, CA, 658
Mammoth Site of Hot Springs, SD, SD, 7788
Mammoth Spring State Park, AR, 389
Manitoba Museum of Man and Nature, MB, 9573
Manzanar National Historic Site, CA, 571
Marble Springs State Historic Farmstead, TN, 7931
Mari Sandoz Heritage Society, NE, 5098
Marion County Historical Society, The, OH, 6713
Marion County Museum of History, FL, 1533
Marion County Museum, SC, 7704
Marjorie Barrick Museum of Natural History, NV, 5246
Martha's Vineyard Historical Society, MA, 3855
Martin and Osa Johnson Safari Museum, KS, 2895
Mary March Regional Museum, NF, 9617
Marymoor Museum of Eastside History, WA, 8910
Mashantucket Pequot Museum and Research Center, CT, 1209
Mastodon State Historic Site, MO, 4732
Maturango Museum of the Indian Wells Valley, CA, 735
McCook House Civil War Museum/Carroll County Historical Society, OH, 6598
McGill University Archives, QC, 9909
McIlhenny Company and Avery Island, Inc., Archives, The, LA, 3262
McKissick Museum, SC, 7654
McMinn County Living Heritage Museum, TN, 7863
McPherson Museum, KS, 2999
Memorial Foundation of the Germanna Colonies in Virginia, Inc., VA, 8531
Memory Lane Museum at Seattle Goodwill, WA, 8928
Memphis Pink Palace Museum, TN, 7947
Mendocino Area Parks Association, CA, 638
Mesa Southwest Museum, AZ, 235
Metlakatla Tribal Rights Committee, AK, 180
Michigan Museums Association, MI, 4171
Michigan State University Museum, MI, 4119
Middleton Place, SC, 7634
Midgley Museum, OK, 6881
Milan Historical Museum, OH, 6727
Milton J. Rubenstein Museum of Science and Technology, NY, 6153
Milwaukee Public Museum, Inc., WI, 9195
Minnehaha County Historical Society, SD, 7836
Minnesota Finnish American Historical

Society, Chapter 38, MN, 4484
Minnesota Historical Society Library, MN, 4469
Minnesota Historical Society, MN, 4468
Minnetrista Cultural Center and Oakhurst Gardens, IN, 2596
Miracle of America Museum, Inc., MT, 5045
Missiles and More Museum Missiles and More Museum, NC, 6446
Mission San Luis Archaeological and Historic Site, FL, 1551
Mississippi Petrified Forest, MS, 4546
Missouri Department of Natural Resources, Division of State Parks, MO, 4755
Missouri Forest Heritage Center, Inc., MO, 4756
Missouri Mines Museum Society, MO, 4850
Missouri River Frontier Museum, MO, 4852
Missouri State Museum, MO, 4759
Mitchell County Historical Society, IA, 2814
Mitchell County Historical Society, KS, 2892
Mohawk Nation Council of Choices, NY, 6104
Mojave River Valley Museum, CA, 454
Monhegan Historical and Cultural Museum Association, Inc., ME, 3463
Moniteau County Historical Society, MO, 4659
Monocacy National Battlefield, MD, 3647
Monson Historical Society, ME, 3441
Monson Museum, ME, 3465
Monterey County Agricultural and Rural Life Museum, CA, 581
Montgomery County Historical Society, Inc., IN, 2503
Montgomery County Historical Society, Inc., MO, 4830
Monument Hill and Kreische Brewery State Historical Parks, TX, 8165
Moore County Historical Museum, TX, 8087
Moose Lake Area Historical Society, MN, 4409
Moosehead Historical Society, ME, 3444
Morden and District Museum, Inc., MB, 9542
Morrow County Museum, OR, 7022
Mound Key State Archaeological Site, FL, 1417
Moundville Archaeological Park, AL, 120
Mount Airy Museum of Regional History, Inc., NC, 6372
Mount Auburn Cemetery, MA, 3800
Mount Horeb Area Historical Society, WI, 9200
Mount Kearsarge Indian Museum, Education and Cultrural Center, NH, 5429
Mountain Heritage Center, NC, 6265
Mountaineers Library, The, WA, 8929
Mower County Historical Society, MN, 4273
Musee Francois-Pilote, QC, 9889
Musee Regional de Vaudreuil Soulanges, QC, 9942
Musee Sturgeon River House Museum, ON, 9816
Museum and Arts Center in the Sequim Dungeness Valley, WA, 8943
Museum Association of West Louisiana, LA, 3315
Museum at Warm Springs, The, OR, 7103
Museum Management Program, National Park Service, The, 1347
Museum of Coastal Carolina, NC, 6383
Museum of Cultural and Natural History, MI, 4200
Museum of Discovery: Arkansas Museum of Science and History, AR, 379
Museum of History and Art, Ontario, CA, 681
Museum of Natural History, Morro Bay State Park, CA, 652
Museum of Northern Arizona, AZ, 217
Museum of Northern British Columbia, BC, 9491
Museum of Science and History of Jacksonville, Inc., FL, 1450
Museum of Science and Industry, FL, 1558
Museum of Science and Industry, IL, 2065
Museum of the Big Bend, TX, 8005
Museum of the Great Plains, OK, 6910
Museum of the Gulf Coast, TX, 8211
Museum of the Islands Society, Inc., FL, 1540
Museum of the Middle Appalachians, VA, 8717
Museum of the Mountain Man, WY, 9336
Museum of the Plains, TX, 8208
Museum of the Rockies, MT, 4982

Museum of the San Rafael, UT, 8292
Museum Services Division Department of Recreation and Parks County of Nassau, NY, 5895
Museum Village, NY, 5985
Museums at Prophetstown, Inc., The, IN, 2482
Musk Ox Development Corporation, AK, 182
Nantucket Maria Mitchell Association, MA, 3926
Napa Valley Museum, CA, 972
Narragansett Indian Tribal Historic Preservation Office, RI, 7593
Nathanael Greene City County Heritage Museum, TN, 7900
Natick Historical Society, MA, 3993
National Agricultural Center and Hall of Fame, The, KS, 2893
National Archives and Records Administration, MD, 3620
National Battlefields Commission, QC, 9924
National Bighorn Sheep Interpretive Center, WY, 9306
National Historic Oregon Trail Interpretive Center, OR, 6993
National Museum of the American Indian Cultural Resources Center, MD, 3728
Native American Museum, IN, 2640
Natural History Museum, Division of Entomology, Snow Collection, KS, 2976
Navajo Nation Museum, AZ, 288
Nebraska Game and Parks Commission, NE, 5145
Nemaha County Historical Society, KS, 3044
Neptune Township Historical Society, NJ, 5565
Nevada State Museum and Historical Society, NV, 5247
Neville Public Museum of Brown County, WI, 9135
New Almaden Quicksilver County Park Association, CA, 828
New Hampshire Aniquarian Society, NH, 5341
New Harmony State Historic Site, IN, 2605
New Harmony Workingmen's Institute, IN, 2606
New Jersey State Museum, NJ, 5658
New Market Battlefield State Historical Park, VA, 8640
New Mexico Farm and Ranch Heritage Museum, NM, 5732
New York State Museum, NY, 5787
Newark Museum Association, NJ, 5576
Newfoundland Museum, NF, 9637
Newton County Historical Society/Bradley House Museum, AR, 359
Nicolet County Historical Society, MN, 4476
Ninepipes Museum of Early Montana, MT, 4989
Ninety Six National Historic Site, SC, 7717
No Man's Land Historical Society, Inc., OK, 6890
Nokomis and District Museum, SK, 9972
North American Museum of Ancient Life, UT, 8309
North Carolina Division of Parks and Recreation, NC, 6401
North Carolina Historic Sites, NC, 6403
North Carolina Maritime Museum, NC, 6222
North Custer Historical Society, ID, 1919
North Dakota Heritage Center, The, ND, 6498
North Slope Borough Commission on Inupiat History, Language and Culture, AK, 145
North West Company Fur Post, MN, 4431
Northeastern Nevada Museum, NV, 5235
Northeastern North Dakota Heritage Assocation, ND, 6504
Northern Arizona University Cline Library Special Collections and Archives Department, AZ, 218
Northern Indiana Historical Society, IN, 2637
Northwest Montana Historical Society and Central School Museum, MI, 4166
Nunatta Sunakkutaangit Museum Society, NT, 9645
O'Hara Mill Pioneer Village & Conservation Area, ON, 9694
Oak Park Conservatory, The, IL, 2291
Oakland Museum of California, CA, 673
Octagon House, The, WI, 9267
Ogden Union Station Railroad Museum, UT, 8315

NATURAL RESOURCES

NUMISMATICS

ORAL HISTORY

PHOTOGRAPHY

PIONEER

Association, WA, 8994
Yamhill County Historical Museum, OR, 7033
Yesteryear Village at the South Florida Fairgrounds, FL, 1577
York County Culture and Heritage Commission, SC, 7729
York County Heritage Trust, PA, 7518
Yorktown Historical Society, Inc., TX, 8286
Yukon Archives, YT, 10004
Z. Taylor Brown-Sarah Dorsey Medallion Home, TX, 8189
Zion National Park Museum, UT, 8348

POLITICS/GOVERNMENT

A.H. Stephens State Historic Park, GA, 1663
Aberdeen Room Archives and Museum, MD, 3545
Abraham Lincoln Association, IL, 2390
Abraham Lincoln Library and Museum, TN, 7903
Adams County Historical Society, CO, 989
Adams County Historical Society, NE, 5131
Adams County Historical Society, PA, 7226
Adams County Historical Society, WA, 8875
Adams Museum, SD, 7770
Adena State Memorial: The Home of Thomas Worthington, OH, 6602
Adsmore Museum, KY, 3231
African American Museum and Library at Oakland, CA, 667
African American Museum in Philadelphia, The, PA, 7349
Afton Historic Preservation Commission, MN, 4262
Agassiz-Harrison Historical Society, BC, 9429
Aiken County Historical Museum, SC, 7596
Aircraft Carrier Hornet Foundation, CA, 431
Ak-Chin Him-Dak EcoMuseum and Archives, AZ, 233
Akutan Traditional Council, AK, 132
Alabama Civil War Roundtable, AL, 11
Alabama Department of Archives and History, AL, 92
Alabama Historical Commission-Old Cahawba, AL, 108
Alamance Battleground State Historic Site, NC, 6232
Alaska Historical Collection, Alaska State Library, AK, 168
Alaska State Museum, AK, 169
Albany County Historical Society, WY, 9326
Alberta Association of Registered Nurses, AB, 9379
Alexander Ramsey House, MN, 4451
Algonquin Culture and Heritage Centre, ON, 9717
Allegany County Historical Society, MD, 3627
Allegany County Historical Society, NY, 5814
Allen Barkley Young Historians, Inc., KY, 3220
Allen County Historical and Genealogy Society, KY, 3236
Alpine County Museum, CA, 634
Amador County Archives, CA, 574
Amador Livermore Valley Museum, CA, 715
American Antiquarian Society, MA, 4040
American Cotton Museum, TX, 8134
American Independence Museum, NH, 5314
American Police Hall of Fame, FL, 1481
American Studies Association, DC, 1327
American Swedish Historical Museum, PA, 7352
Amherst Museum, NY, 5796
Ancient and Honorable Artillery Company of Massachusetts, MA, 3764
Andover Historical Society, IL, 1979
Andover Historical Society, MA, 3753
Andover Historical Society, NH, 5267
Andrew County Museum and Historical Society, MO, 4933
Andrew Johnson National Historic Site and Homestead, TN, 7899
Anna Maria Island Historical Society Inc., FL, 1378
Apex Historical Society, NC, 6204
Archives and Manuscripts Department, Auburn University, AL, 9
Archives and Regional History Collections, Western Michigan University, MI, 4163
Archives Nationales du Quebec, QC, 9898
Archives Nationales du Quebec, QC, 9937
Archives of Labor and Urban Affairs, MI, 4104
Archives of Ontario, ON, 9826
Archives, University of Colorado at Boulder Libraries, CO, 984
Argyle Township Court House and Archives, NS, 9679
Arizona Department of Library, Archives, and Public Records, AZ, 241
Arizona Hall of Fame Museum, AZ, 242
Arizona Historical Society - Northern Division, AZ, 216
Arizona Historical Society - Southern Division, AZ, 272
Arizona History and Archives Division, Arizona Department of Library, Archives, and Public Records, AZ, 243
Arizona State Capitol Museum, AZ, 245
Arkansas History Commission, AR, 366
Arlington Historical Society, Inc., VA, 8491
Arrow Rock State Historic Site, MO, 4631
Artesia Historical Museum and Art Center, NM, 5701
Arthur and Elizabeth Schlesinger Library on the History of Women in America, The, MA, 3795
Arthur Bowring Sandhills Ranch, NE, 5163
Ashland University Archives, OH, 6565
Ashland, the Henry Clay Estate, KY, 3159
Ashlawn-Highland, VA, 8515
Associated Students for Historic Preservation (ASHP), OR, 7012
Association for Living History, Farm and Agricultural Museums, OH, 6732
Astor House Museum, CO, 1064
Athens County Historical Society and Museum, OH, 6569
Athens-Clarke County Library Heritage Room, GA, 1588
Atlanta Cyclorama, GA, 1597
Atlanta History Center, GA, 1599
Atlantic County Historical Society, The, NJ, 5629
Atwater Historical Society, The, OH, 6570
Auburn Avenue Research Library on African American Culture and History, GA, 1601
Autauga County Heritage Association, AL, 105
Bainbridge Island Historical Society, WA, 8800
Baltimore County Historical Society, Inc., MD, 3618
Bancroft Library, The, CA, 458
Bannack State Park, MT, 5003
Banner County Historical Society, NE, 5129
Barkerville Historic Town, BC, 9432
Barnes County Historical Society, ND, 6548
Barnwell County Museum and Historical Board, SC, 7600
Barrington Living History Farm, TX, 8273
Barrington Preservation Society, RI, 7525
Bartholomew County Historical Society, IL, 2084
Bartlesville Area History Museum, OK, 6842
Bay County Historical Society/Historical Museum of Bay County, MI, 4066
BC Heritage, BC, 9518
Beardstown Museum, Inc., IL, 1990
Beaton Institute of Cape Breton Studies, NS, 9677
Beaufort Museum, SC, 7602
Beauvoir, The Jefferson Davis Home and Presidential Library, MS, 4531
Beinecke Rare Book and Manuscript Library, CT, 1223
Bella Vista Historical Society/Museum, AR, 303
Belle Grove Plantation, VA, 8627
Belleville Public Library, IL, 1991
Belleville Public Library, ON, 9692
Bellevue Historical Society, Inc., ID, 1900
Bellevue/LaGrange Woman's Club Charitable Trust, GA, 1715
Ben-Hur Museum/General Lew Wallace Study, IN, 2502
Bennington Battle Monument State Historic Site, Vermont Division for Historic Preservation, VT, 8407
Bergen County Division of Cultural and Historic Affairs, NJ, 5494
Berkeley Historical Society, CA, 460
Berkshire County Historical Society, The, MA, 3951
Berkshire Museum, The, MA, 3952
Berman Museum of World History, AL, 3
Berrien County Historical Association, MI, 4073
Berwyn Historical Society, IL, 1999
Beverly Historical Society and Museum, MA, 3761
Biddeford Historical Society, ME, 3412
Bidwell Mansion State Historic Park, CA, 488
Big Sioux River Valley Historical Society, IA, 2759
Bigelow House Preservation Association, WA, 8897
Billings County Historical Society, ND, 6533
Birmingham Civil Rights Institute, AL, 14
Birmingham Public Library, Department of Archives and Manuscripts, AL, 16
Bishop Hill Heritage Association, IL, 2000
Black River Historical Society, OH, 6703
Black River Historical Society, VT, 8400
Black World History Wax Museum, The, MO, 4905
Blount Mansion Association, TN, 7922
Blue Ridge Parkway, NC, 6209
Blue Ridge Parkway, VA, 8755
Bobby Davis Museum and Park, Hazard, Perry County, Kentucky, Inc., KY, 3149
Boone County Historical Society, IA, 2671
Boone County Historical Society, IN, 2580
Boone County Historical Society, MO, 4681
Boone County Historical Society, NE, 5074
Boonsborough Museum of History, MD, 3600
Bostonian Society, The, MA, 3770
Boulder City/Hoover Dam Museum, NV, 5227
Bourne Historical Society, Inc., MA, 3789
Brazoria County Historical Museum, TX, 8009
Bremer County Historical Society, IA, 2863
Bridgeport Public Library Historical Collections, CT, 1140
Bristol Historical Society, NH, 5278
Bristol Historical Society, VT, 8366
Bronx County Historical Society, NY, 5827
Brooklyn Historical Society, MN, 4285
Brooklyn Historical Society, OH, 6588
Brooklyn Historical Society, The, NY, 5830
Brownville Historical Society, NE, 5091
Bryn Mawr College Libraries, PA, 7152
Buckeye Valley Historical and Archaeological Museum, AZ, 209
Burnside Plantation, Inc., PA, 7127
Burton Historical Collection, MI, 4105
Bush House Museum, OR, 7080
Bushnell Historical Society, IL, 2010
Business and Media Archvies of the Mahoning Valley, OH, 6825
Butler-Turpin Historic House, KY, 3105
Butte-Silver Bow Public Archives, MT, 4986
Caddo Cultural Center, OK, 6847
Cahokia Courthouse State Historic Site, IL, 2012
California Council for the Humanities, CA, 796
California History Center and Foundation/De Anza College, CA, 507
California History Section, California State Library, CA, 749
California State Archives, CA, 751
California State Capitol Museum, CA, 752
California State Parks Photographic Archives, CA, 961
California State University Sacramento/Dept. of Special Collections and Univ. Archives, CA, 755
Calvert County Historical Society, Inc., MD, 3694
Calvin Coolidge Memorial Foundation, The, VT, 8426
Cambridge Historical Society, The, MA, 3797
Camden County Historical Society & Museum, MO, 4811
Camden County Historical Society, NJ, 5473
Campbell County Rockpile Museum, WY, 9312
Campbell Historical Museum, CA, 480
Candia Historical Society, NH, 5281
Cape Fear Museum, NC, 6469
Capitol Preservation Committee, PA, 7245
Carl Albert Congressional Research and Studies Center, OK, 6926
Carlsbad Caverns National Park, NM, 5708
Carpenters' Company of the City and County, The, PA, 7358
Carroll County Historical & Genealogical Society, Inc., AR, 308
Carroll County Historical Society Museum, IN, 2509
Carver County Historical Society, MN, 4506
Carver-Hill Memorial and Historical Society, Inc., FL, 1400
Cascade County Historical Museum and Archives, MT, 5014
Cass County Historical Society Museum, IA, 2753
Cass County Historical Society Museum, IN, 2582
Cass County Historical Society Museum, NE, 5199
Castle Clinton National Monument, NY, 5997
Catawba County Historical Association, NC, 6382
Cavalier County Historical Society, ND, 6531
Cedar Crest, Residence of the Governor of Kansas, KS, 3055
Center City Historic Preservation Commission, MN, 4290
Center for American History, The University of Texas at Austin, TX, 8013
Center for Southwest Research, NM, 5691
Center of Southwest Studies, Fort Lewis College, CO, 1036
Central Nevada Historical Society/Museum, NV, 5260
Centre d'etudes acadiennes, NB, 9596
Centre for Newfoundland Studies, NF, 9628
Champ Clark Honey Shuck Restoration, Inc., MO, 4652
Champaign County Historical Society, OH, 6801
Charles Carroll House of Annapolis, MD, 3548
Charles City County Center for Local History, VA, 8509
Charles H. Wright Museum of African American History, MI, 4106
Charles Sumner School Museum and Archives, DC, 1333
Charlotte Hawkins Brown Historic Site, NC, 6430
Charlotte Museum of History and Hezekina Alexander Homesite, NC, 6247
Chemung County Historical Society, Inc. (Chemung Valley History Museum), NY, 5899
Cherokee Strip Museum, OK, 6949
Chester County Archives and Records Services, PA, 7499
Chester County Historical Society Museum, CA, 487
Chesterfield County Historic Preservation Commission, SC, 7646
Chestnut Hill Historical Society, PA, 7361
Chicago Historical Society, IL, 2043
Chicago Lawn Historical Society, IL, 2045
Chicago Public Library Special Collections and Preservation Division, IL, 2046
Chief Vann House Historic Site, GA, 1655
Chimney Point State Historic Site, VT, 8408
Chippewa County Historical Society, MN, 4403
Chippewa County Historical Society, WI, 9097
Choctaw County Historical Museum, AL, 26
Citadel Archives and Museum, SC, 7626
City of Arkadelphia, AR, 298
City of Boston, Office of the City Clerk, Archives and Records Management Division, MA, 3885
City of Greeley Museums, CO, 1073
City of Northfield Historic Preservation Commission, MN, 4422
City of Toronto Archives, ON, 9833
Civil War Naval Museum, LA, 3261
Clark County Genealogical Library, IL, 2232
Clark County Historical Society, KS, 2883
Clark County Historical Society, MO, 4764
Clark County Historical Society, SD, 7764
Clark County Museum, NV, 5241
Clarke House Museum, IL, 2047
Clarksville-Montgomery County Museum, TN, 7875
Clay County Historical Society, AL, 4
Clay County Historical Society, FL, 1439
Clay County Historical Society, IN, 2493
Clay County Historical Society, MN, 4405
Clay County Historical Society, NE, 5100
Clay County Historical Society, SD, 7854
Clermont Historical Society, IA, 2692
Clermont State Historic Site, NY, 5918

Renton Historical Society, WA, 8912
Renville County Historical Society, MN, 4412
Republic County Historical Society and
   Museum, KS, 2891
Research Center for Beaver County, PA,
   7123
Restigouche Regional Museum, NB, 9583
Reston Historic Trust for Community
   Revitalization, VA, 8678
Reverend James Caldwell Chapter NSDAR,
   IL, 2180
Rhode Island Historical Society, RI, 7577
Rhode Island State Archives, RI, 7579
Rice County Historical Society, KS, 2989
Rice County Historical Society, MN, 4330
Richard B. Russell Library for Political
   Research and Studies, GA, 1591
Richard Nixon Presidential Library and
   Birthplace, CA, 971
Richmond Forum, The, VA, 8698
Riddick's Folly, Inc., VA, 8744
River Road African American Museum and
   Gallery, LA, 3292
Riverdale Historical Society, IL, 2340
Robert E. Lee Memorial Association, Inc., VA,
   8742
Robert Green Ingersoll Birthplace Museum,
   NY, 5886
Robeson County Museum, NC, 6356
Rochester Museum & Science Center, NY,
   6097
Rock House Shrine Sparta Rock House
   Chapter DAR, TN, 7996
Rock Island County Historical Society, IL,
   2250
Rockbridge Historical Society, VA, 8604
Rockingham Association, NJ, 5611
Roger Williams National Monument, RI, 7580
Rogers Historical Museum, AR, 413
Roman Catholic Archdiocesan Archives of
   Ottawa, ON, 9785
Romeoville Area Historical Society, IL, 2364
Roosevelt County Historical Museum, NM,
   5747
Rose City Area Historical Society, Inc., The,
   MI, 4233
Rose Hill Plantation State Historic Site, SC,
   7745
Rosenbach Museum and Library, PA, 7403
Roseville Historical Society, CA, 746
Roseville Historical Society, MN, 4446
Ross County Historical Society, OH, 6603
Rotch-Jones-Duff House and Garden
   Museum, Inc., MA, 3929
Royal British Columbia Museum, BC, 9530
Rumford Area Historical Society, ME, 3504
Rutherford B. Hayes Presidential Center, OH,
   6665
Sacramento Archives and Museum Collection
   Center, CA, 764
Sacramento Room, Sacramento Public
   Library, CA, 765
Sacred Heart Area Historical Society, MN,
   4447
Sagamore Hill National Historic Site, NY,
   6063
Saint Augustine Historical Society, FL, 1526
Saint John's Episcopal Church, VA, 8700
Saint Martinville Main Street, LA, 3377
Salem Museum and Historical Society, VA,
   8716
Salisbury Association History Room, CT,
   1246
Sam Bell Maxey House State Historic Site,
   TX, 8207
Sam Houston Memorial Museum, TX, 8152
Sam Rayburn House Museum, TX, 8039
Samuel F. B. Morse Historic Site, NY, 6081
San Bernardino County Archives, CA, 774
San Diego Civil War Roundtable, CA, 784
San Diego Historical Society, CA, 787
San Jacinto Museum of History Association,
   TX, 8168
Sanford Museum, FL, 1529
Sangamon County Genealogical Society, IL,
   2406
Santa Barbara Historical Society, CA, 863
Santa Maria Valley Historical Society and
   Museum, CA, 878
Saratoga National Historical Park, NY, 6150
Saskatchewan Archives Board-Regina, SK,
   9980
Saskatchewan Archives Board-Saskatoon,

SK, 9989
Saskatoon Public Library-Local History
   Room, SK, 9991
Sauk County Historical Society, WI, 9077
Sawyer County Historical Society, Inc., WI,
   9141
Schiller Park Historical Commission, IL, 2378
Schoharie County Historical Society, NY,
   6125
School of Nations Museum, The, MO, 4923
Seaside Museum and Historical Society, OR,
   7086
Senate House State Historic Site, NY, 5964
Senator George Norris State Historic Site,
   NE, 5161
Seneca-Iroquois National Museum, NY, 6114
Sequoyah's Cabin, OK, 6957
Sergeant Kirkland's Museum and Historical
   Society, Inc., VA, 8729
Seton Hall University Department of Archives,
   NJ, 5641
Seville Historical Society, OH, 6779
Shasta College Museum and Research
   Center, CA, 726
Shasta State Historic Park, CA, 891
Sheboygan County Historical Research
   Center, WI, 9242
Sheffield Historical Society, IL, 2381
Sheffield Historical Society, MA, 3989
Sheffield Historical Society, VT, 8449
Shelby County Historical Society, AL, 31
Shelby County Historical Society, OH, 6783
Sherwood Forest Plantation, VA, 8512
Shiloh Museum of Ozark History, AR, 422
Shirley Plantation, VA, 8513
Shoal Creek Living History Museum, MO,
   4781
Shrewsbury Historical Society, NJ, 5628
Sierra County Museum of Downieville, CA,
   519
Simcoe County Archives, ON, 9748
Simcoe County Museum, ON, 9749
Sioux City Public Museum, IA, 2838
Sir William Campbell Foundation, ON, 9842
Sisseton-Wahpeton Tribal Archives, SD, 7845
Sixth Floor Museum at Dealey Plaza, TX,
   8078
Skagit County Historical Society, WA, 8871
Slifer House Museum, PA, 7295
Smith-Zimmermann Heritage Museum, SD,
   7802
Smithsonian Institution Traveling Exhibition,
   DC, 1366
Smithville Heritage Society, TX, 8249
Smoky Hill Museum, KS, 3041
Smyth County Historical and Museum
   Society, Inc., VA, 8619
Society for the Preservation of New England
   Antiquities (SPNEA), MA, 3787
Society of American Archivists, IL, 2073
Society of Historic Sharonville, OH, 6782
Somerset County Historical Society, MD,
   3695
Somerset County Historical Society, NJ, 5452
Sons and Daughters of the Cherokee Strip
   Pioneers, OK, 6884
Sophienburg Museum and Archives, TX,
   8198
South Boston, Halifax County Museum, VA,
   8723
South Carolina Archives and History Center,
   SC, 7656
South Carolina State Museum, SC, 7662
South Dakota National Guard Museum, SD,
   7822
South Dakota State Archives, SD, 7823
South Dakota State Historical Society, SD,
   7824
South Milwaukee Historical Museum, WI,
   9245
South San Francisco History Room, CA, 904
South Suburban Heritage Association, IL,
   2174
Southeast Louisiana Historical Association,
   LA, 3295
Southeastern Railway Museum, GA, 1681
Southern Highland Handicraft Guild, NC,
   6213
Southern Ute Cultural Center Museum, CO,
   1081
Southington Historical Society, Ct, 1257
Southwest Virginia Museum/Historical Park,
   VA, 8500

Southwestern Archives and Manuscripts
   Collections, University of Southwestern
   Louisiana, LA, 3311
Southwestern Michigan College Museum, MI,
   4116
Southwestern Oklahoma Historical Society,
   OK, 6911
Space Business Archives, VA, 8484
Sparks Heritage Museum, NV, 5259
Spartanburg County Historical Association,
   SC, 7736
Special Collection and Archives, Leonard H.
   Axe Library, Pittsburg State University, KS,
   3031
Special Collections and Archives, W.E.B. Du
   Bois Library, University of Massachusetts,
   MA, 3752
Special Collections Department, Pullen
   Library, Georgia State University, GA, 1625
Special Collections Department, USM
   Libraries, University of Southern Mississippi,
   MS, 4557
Special Collections Library,
   Albuquerque/Bernalillo County Library
   System, NM, 5697
Special Collections, Atkins Library, University
   of North Carolina at Charlotte, NC, 6252
Special Collections, LSU Libraries, Louisiana
   State University, LA, 3273
Special Collections, Robert W. Woodruff
   Library, Emory University, GA, 1626
Spring Hope Historical Museum, NC, 6442
St. Lawrence County Historical Association,
   NY, 5856
St. Louis Park Historical Society, MN, 4450
St. Paul Police History Museum, MN, 4474
St. Petersburg Historical Society/St.
   Petersburg Museum of History, FL, 1541
Stamford Historical Society, CT, 1259
Stanly County Historic Preservation
   Commission, NC, 6203
Star of the Republic Museum, TX, 8274
State Historical Society of Iowa, Centennial
   Building, IA, 2766
State Historical Society of Iowa, Iowa
   Historical Building, IA, 2722
State Historical Society of North Dakota, ND,
   6499
State Museum of Pennsylvania, The, PA,
   7252
State Preservation Board, TX, 8020
Steele County Historical Society, MN, 4427
Steele County Historical Society, ND, 6527
Steele Narrows Historic Park/Saskatchewan
   Environment and Resource Management,
   SK, 9952
Stephens African American Museum, LA,
   3385
Sterling Rock Falls Historical Society
   Museum, IL, 2413
Stockbridge Library Association Historical
   Collection, MA, 4003
Stone Fort Museum, TX, 8193
Stones River National Battlefield, TN, 7956
Stonewall Jackson Museum at Hupp's Hill,
   VA, 8740
Storrowton Village Museum, MA, 4030
Strathroy Middlesex Museum, ON, 9815
Summit Historical Society Carter House
   Museum, NJ, 5648
Sun Prairie Historical Library and Museum,
   WI, 9253
Superior Historical Society, Inc., AZ, 262
Suquamish Museum, WA, 8962
Surratt House Museum, MD, 3617
Susan B. Anthony House, Inc., NY, 6100
Sutter's Fort State Historic Park, CA, 766
Swarthmore College Peace Collection, PA,
   7464
Sweetwater County Historical Museum, WY,
   9314
Sycamore Shoals State Historic Area, TN,
   7887
Tacoma Historical Society, The, WA, 8966
Taylors Falls Historical Society, The, MN,
   4497
Tehama County Museum Foundation, Inc.,
   CA, 921
Tempe Historical Museum, AZ, 266
Tennessee Historical Society, TN, 7977
Tennessee State Library and Archives, TN,
   7978
Tennessee State Museum, TN, 7979

Terrace Mill Foundation, MN, 4498
Terrebonne Historical and Cultural Society,
   LA, 3299
Territorial Statehouse State Park and
   Museum, UT, 8300
Tewksbury Historical Society, Inc., NJ, 5563
Texana/Genealogy Department, San Antonio
   Public Library, TX, 8240
Texarkana Museums System, TX, 8259
Thaddeus Kosciuszko National Memorial, PA,
   7405
Theodore Roosevelt Birthplace National
   Historic Site, NY, 6032
Theodore Roosevelt Inaugural National
   Historic Site, NY, 5842
This Is The Place Heritage Park, UT, 8337
Thomas J. Dodd Research Center, CT, 1261
Thomas Jefferson Foundation (Monticello),
   VA, 8518
Thomas Paine National Historic Association,
   NY, 5995
Thornbury Historical Society, PA, 7466
Three Affiliated Tribes Museum, Inc., ND,
   6542
Three Rivers Museum of Muskogee, Inc., OK,
   6923
Thunder Bay Historical Museum Society, The,
   ON, 9821
Tigerton Area Historical Society, WI, 9259
Toledo-Lucas County Public Library/ Local
   History and Genealogy Department, OH,
   6793
Tombstone Courthouse State Historic Park,
   AZ, 267
Town of DeKalb Historical Association, NY,
   5884
Town of Whitby Archives, ON, 9854
Town of York Historical Society, The, ON,
   9845
Township of Hamilton Historical Society, NJ,
   5540
Trail End State Historic Site, WY, 9346
Tread of Pioneers Museum, CO, 1126
Tri-County Historical Society and Museum,
   Inc., KS, 2952
Trinidad Historical Museum of the Colorado
   Historical Society, CO, 1131
Trinity County Historical Society, CA, 957
Trustees of Reservations, MA, 4004
Tryon Palace Historic Sites and Gardens, NC,
   6381
Tubac Presidio State Historic Park, AZ, 269
Tuskegee Institute National Historic Site,
   George Washington Carver Museum, AL,
   125
TVA Historic Collections Program, TN, 7933
U.S. Army Museum of Hawaii, HI, 1843
U.S. Border Patrol Museum and Memorial
   Library, TX, 8092
Ulysses S. Grant Cottage, NY, 6118
Ulysses S. Grant Homestead, OH, 6671
United States Capitol Historic Society, DC,
   1372
United States Mint at Philadelphia, PA, 7406
University Archives and Special Collection
   Unit, Pollak Library, CA State Univ.,
   Fullerton, CA, 554
University Archives of the State University of
   New York at Buffalo, NY, 5843
University History Institute, AR, 383
University of Central Arkansas Archives and
   Special Collections, AR, 314
University of Colorado Museum of Natural
   History, CO, 987
University of Iowa Hospitals and Clinics
   Medical Museum, IA, 2767
University of North Carolina at Chapel Hill,
   Manuscripts Department, NC, 6243
University of Rhode Island Special
   Collections, RI, 7546
University of Texas at Arlington, University
   Libraries, Special Collections Division, TX,
   8011
University of Wyoming American Heritage
   Center, WY, 9328
University South Caroliniana Society, SC,
   7663
USDA Forest Service, CA, 943
Utah State Archives, UT, 8340
Vacaville Museum, CA, 941
Valdosta State University Archives, GA, 1829
Vallejo Naval and Historical Museum, CA,
   944

RAILROADING

Bushnell Historical Society, IL, 2010
Butte-Silver Bow Public Archives, MT, 4986
Byron Museum District, IL, 2011
C.H.T.J. Southard House Museum, ME, 3498
Caldwell County Historical Society Heritage Museum, NC, 6350
Califon Historical Society, The, NJ, 5456
California History Section, California State Library, CA, 749
California State Archives, CA, 751
California State Parks Photographic Archives, CA, 961
California State Railroad Museum, CA, 754
Callander Bay Heritage Museum, ON, 9701
Calvert County Historical Society, Inc., MD, 3694
Cambria County Historical Society, PA, 7196
Cambridge Historical Society, The, MA, 3797
Cambridge Museum, ID, 1916
Camden County Historical Society & Museum, MO, 4811
Camden County Historical Society, NJ, 5473
Camp Hancock State Historic Site, ND, 6495
Campbell County Rockpile Museum, WY, 9312
Campus Martius Museum, OH, 6710
Canadian Association of Professional Heritage Consultants, ON, 9829
Canadian Museum of Civilization, QC, 9884
Canadian Pacific Archives, QC, 9903
Canadian Railway Museum at Delson/Saint-Constant, QC, 9926
Canadian Rivers Historical Society, OK, 6889
Cannonsburgh Village, TN, 7954
Canyon Life Museum, OR, 7038
Cape Charles Historical Society, VA, 8506
Cape Fear Museum, NC, 6469
Cape River Heritage Museum, MO, 4663
Carbon County Historical Society, MT, 5049
Carbon County Historical Society, WY, 9338
Carbon County Museum, WY, 9339
Carillon Historical Park, Inc., OH, 6643
Carlisle Area Historical Society, OH, 6597
Carlton County Historical Society, MN, 4295
Carmel Clay Historical Society, IN, 2496
Carpinteria Valley Museum of History, CA, 485
Carriage House Museum of the Queen Village Historical Society, NY, 5847
Carroll County Historical & Genealogical Society, Inc., AR, 308
Carroll County Historical Society, GA, 1650
Carroll County Historical Society, IA, 2679
Carroll County Historical Society, IL, 2261
Carroll County Historical Society, MO, 4665
Carroll County Historical Society, VA, 8592
Carroll Reece Museum, TN, 7913
Carson Valley Historical Society, NV, 5240
Cascade County Historical Museum and Archives, MT, 5014
Cascade County Historical Society, MT, 5015
Casey Jones Railroad Museum State Park, MS, 4613
Cass County Historical Society Museum, IA, 2753
Cass County Historical Society Museum, IN, 2582
Cass County Historical Society Museum, NE, 5199
Cass County Museum & Pioneer School, MN, 4508
Castle Museum, ID, 1932
Castle Rock Exhibit Hall Society, WA, 8817
Catawba County Historical Association, NC, 6382
Cavalier County Historical Society, ND, 6531
Cavendish Historical Society, VT, 8373
Cayce Historical Museum, SC, 7619
Cedar Falls Historical Society, IA, 2680
Cedar Key State Museum, FL, 1393
Centennial Valley Historical Association, WY, 9293
Center City Historic Preservation Commission, MN, 4290
Center for American History, The University of Texas at Austin, TX, 8013
Center for Cultural Arts, AL, 55
Center of Southwest Studies, Fort Lewis College, CO, 1036
Central California Information Center/CA Historical Resource Information System, CA, 934
Central Idaho Cultural Center, ID, 1942

Central Nevada Historical Society/Museum, NV, 5260
Centre d'etudes acadiennes, NB, 9596
Centre for Newfoundland Studies, NF, 9628
Chaffee Historical Society, Inc., MO, 4672
Chambers County Museum, Inc., AL, 72
Champaign County Historical Society, OH, 6801
Champlain Valley Heritage Network, NY, 5881
Charles River Museum of Industry, MA, 4018
Charleston Chapter of National Railway Historical Society, SC, 7711
Charleston Library Society, SC, 7624
Charlotte Museum of History and Hezekina Alexander Homesite, NC, 6247
Chase and District Museum and Archives Society, BC, 9439
Chassell Historical Organization, Inc., MI, 4086
Chatham Historical Society, NH, 5284
Chatham Historical Society, NJ, 5465
Chatham Historical Society, OH, 6701
Chatham Historical Society/Atwood House Museum, MA, 3805
Chattooga County Historical Society, GA, 1813
Chelan County Historical Society Pioneer Village and Museum, WA, 8816
Chelan County Public Utility District, WA, 8985
Chemung County Historical Society, Inc. (Chemung Valley History Museum), NY, 5899
Cherokee Strip Museum, OK, 6949
Cherryville History Association, NC, 6256
Chesaning Area Historical Society, MI, 4089
Chesapeake and Ohio Historical Society, Inc., VA, 8527
Chesapeake Beach Railway Museum, MD, 3612
Chester County Historical Society Museum, CA, 487
Chester Historical Society, Inc., NJ, 5468
Chestnut Hill Historical Society, PA, 7361
Chevy Chase Historical Society, MD, 3615
Cheyenne Frontier Days Old West Museum, WY, 9294
Chicago and Eastern Illinois Railroad Historical Society, IL, 2244
Chicago Genealogical Society, IL, 2041
Chicago Historical Society, IL, 2043
Chicago Lawn Historical Society, IL, 2045
Chillicothe Historical Society, IL, 2078
Chinese House Railroad Museum, OR, 7010
Chippewa County Historical Society, MN, 4403
Chippewa County Historical Society, WI, 9097
Chisago County Historical Society, MN, 4362
Chisholm Trail Historical Museum Society, OK, 6981
Chisholm Trail Museum, KS, 3072
Choctaw County Historical Museum, AL, 26
Choctaw Historical Society and Caboose Museum, OK, 6864
Christian County Historical Society Museum, IL, 2422
Cimarron Valley Railroad Museum, OK, 6872
City of Bowie Museums, MD, 3602
City of Las Vegas Museum and Rough Riders Memorial Collection, NM, 5734
Clackamas County Historical Society, OR, 7054
Clallam County Historical Society, WA, 8903
Clarendon County Archives, SC, 7703
Claresholm and District Museum, AB, 9372
Clarion County Historical Society, PA, 7168
Clark County Historical Society, KS, 2883
Clark County Historical Society, MO, 4764
Clark County Historical Society, SD, 7764
Clark County Museum, NV, 5241
Clark Historical Library, MI, 4199
Clarksville-Montgomery County Museum, TN, 7875
Clay County Historical Society, AL, 4
Clay County Historical Society, FL, 1439
Clay County Historical Society, IN, 2493
Clay County Historical Society, MN, 4405
Clay County Historical Society, NE, 5100
Clay County Historical Society, SD, 7854
Clay County Museum, KS, 2897
Clear Creek History Park, CO, 1066
Clear Creek Township Historical Society, OH, 6777

Clearwater County Historical Society, MN, 4486
Cleburne County Historical Society, AR, 347
Clermont Historical Society, IA, 2692
Climax Community Museum, Inc., SK, 9950
Clinton County Historical Society, Inc., IN, 2532
Clinton County Historical Society, NY, 6072
Clinton County Historical Society, PA, 7304
Cloud County Historical Society, KS, 2904
Clovis Depot Model Train Museum, NM, 5717
Coastal Heritage Society, GA, 1783
Cobb County Historic Preservation Commission, GA, 1734
Cochranton Heritage Society, PA, 7171
Codington County Historical Society, SD, 7857
Coe Hall at Planting Fields, NY, 6060
Coffee Co/Manchester/Tullahoma Museum, Inc. Arrowheads/Aerospace Museum, TN, 7935
Cole Land Transportation Museum, ME, 3404
Colfax County Society of Art, History, and Archaeology, NM, 5749
Collier County Museum, FL, 1494
Collingswood-Newton Colony Historical Society, NJ, 5472
Collinsville Historical Museum, IL, 2083
Colonel Davenport Historical Foundation, The, IL, 2345
Colorado Historical Society, CO, 1021
Colorado Railroad Museum, CO, 1067
Colorado Springs Museum, CO, 1002
Columbia County Historical Society, NY, 5962
Columbia County Historical Society, OR, 7090
Columbia County Historical Society, WI, 9091
Columbia Gorge Discovery Center and Wasco County Historical Museum, OR, 7093
Columbia Gorge Interpretive Center, WA, 8958
Comanche Crossing Historical Society, CO, 1128
Community Historical Society, The, IA, 2794
Community Library Associaton-Regional History Dept, ID, 1934
Concord Historical Society, CA, 501
Concord Historical Society, VT, 8419
Conneaut Chapter-National Railway Historical Society, OH, 6638
Conneaut Valley Area Historical Society, PA, 7175
Constitution Convention State Museum, FL, 1519
Contra Costa County Historical Society and History Center, CA, 714
Conway Historical Society, MA, 3820
Conway Historical Society, NH, 5296
Cooke County Heritage Society, Inc., TX, 8117
Cookeville Depot Museum, TN, 7883
Cooper County Historical Society, MO, 4856
Coopersville Area Historical Society, MI, 4097
Copper Valley Historical Society, AK, 150
Cordova Historical Society and Museum, AK, 152
Corry Area Historical Society, PA, 7179
Council Valley Museum, ID, 1922
Courtenay and District Museum and Paleontology Centre, BC, 9440
Cowlitz River Valley Historical Society, WA, 8887
Cozad Historical Society—The 100th Meridian Museum, NE, 5102
Cranbrook Archives Museum and Landmark Foundation, BC, 9441
Crawford County Historical Museum, KS, 3030
Crawford County Historical Society, GA, 1760
Crawford County Historical Society, IA, 2716
Crawford County Historical Society, IL, 2341
Crawford County Historical Society/Baldwin-Reynolds House Museum, PA, 7310
Creston and District Historical and Museum Society, BC, 9442
Cripple Creek and Victor Narrow Gauge Railroad, CO, 1010
Cripple Creek District Museum, CO, 1011
Cristfield Heritage Foundaiton, MD, 3626
Crossroads Village and Huckleberry Railroad, MI, 4124
Crow Wing County Historical Society, MN,

4282
Culbertson Museum, MT, 4998
Cumberland County Museum, NS, 9647
Cumberland Museum and Archives, BC, 9443
Cumbres and Toltec Scenic Railroad Commission, CO, 980
Custer County Historical Society, NE, 5090
Custer County Historical Society, SD, 7767
Cuyuna Range Historical Society, MN, 4301
Cynthiana-Harrison County Museum, KY, 3115
Dacotah Prairie Museum, SD, 7753
Dakota County Historical Society, MN, 4455
Dallas County Historical Museum, AR, 332
Dallas County Historical Society, Inc., MO, 4655
Danville Historical Society, VA, 8532
Danville Junction Chapter, NRHS, IL, 2089
Darlington County Historical Commission, SC, 7666
Dartford Historical Society, WI, 9136
Daughters of the Republic of Texas Library at the Alamo, TX, 8233
Davidson County Historical Museum, NC, 6351
Dawes County Historical Society, Inc., NE, 5095
Dawson City Museum and Historical Society, YT, 10000
Dawson County Historical Society, NE, 5141
Dayton Historical Depot Society, WA, 8830
DC Booth Historic National Fish Hatchery, SD, 7846
Deadwood Historic Preservation Commission, SD, 7771
Death Valley National Park, CA, 515
Deer Trail Pioneer Historical Society, CO, 1014
Del Norte County Historical Society, CA, 505
Dells Country Historical Society, WI, 9283
Delray Beach Historical Society, Inc., FL, 1412
Dennison Railroad Depot Museum, The, OH, 6650
Denver Museum of Miniatures, Dolls, and Toys, CO, 1023
Department of Arkansas Heritage, AR, 374
Depot Museum Complex, TX, 8140
Depot Museum, Inc., AL, 53
Depot Museum, MN, 4489
Derry Historical Society and Museum, NH, 5304
Des Moines County Historical Society, IA, 2676
Deschutes County Historical Society, OR, 6996
Detroit Historical Museums, MI, 4108
DeWitt Historical Society of Tompkins County, The, NY, 5951
Dexter Historical Society, Inc., ME, 3426
Dickey County Historical Society, ND, 6543
Dickson Mounds Museum, IL, 2203
Dillon County Historical Society, Inc., SC, 7667
Discovery Museum, CT, 1141
Discovery Museum, The, CA, 757
Dobson Museum, OK, 6917
Doddridge County Historical Society, WV, 9059
Donalda and District Museum, AB, 9376
Doniphan County Historical Society, KS, 3065
Donner Memorial State Park and Emigrant Trail Museum, CA, 929
Doon Heritage Crossroads, ON, 9735
Dorothy Page Museum, AK, 197
Douglas County Historical Society, MN, 4267
Douglas County Historical Society, OR, 7077
Douglas County Historical Society, WI, 9254
Douglas County Museum of History and Natural History, OR, 7078
Douglas County Museum, WA, 8984
Downey Historical Society, CA, 518
Driftwood Family Resort Museum and Golf (Norske Course), The, MN, 4432
Drumright Historical Society, OK, 6874
Duncan Cultural Center, KY, 3144
Durango and Silverton Narrow Gauge Railroad and Museum, CO, 1037
Durham Western Heritage Museum, NE, 5184
Dutchess County Historical Society, NY, 6080
Dyer Historical Society, Inc., IN, 2513

Wishard Nursing Museum, IN, 2571
Witte Museum, TX, 8243
Wolcott Mill Historic Center/Huron-Clinton Metropolitan Authority, MI, 4224
Woods Hole Historical Museum, MA, 4039
Woodside National Historic Site, ON, 9738
World Kite Museum & Hall of Fame, WA, 8876
Wright Brothers National Memorial, NC, 6341
Wyandotte Museum, MI, 4258
Yates Mill Associates, Inc., NC, 6416
York County Culture and Heritage Commission, SC, 7729
Yukon Beringia Interpretive Centre, YT, 10006

SOCIAL HISTORY

1812 Homestead Educational Foundation, NY, 6193
1932 and 1980 Lake Placid Winter Olympic Museum, The, NY, 5965
AAA-California State Automobile Association Archives, CA, 794
Aberdeen Room Archives and Museum, MD, 3545
Abigail Adams Historical Society, Inc., The, MA, 4034
Abraham Lincoln Tourism Bureau of Logan County, IL, 2207
Accokeek Foundation, MD, 3547
Adam Thoroughgood House, VA, 8648
Adams County Historical Society, CO, 989
Adams County Historical Society, NE, 5131
Adams County Historical Society, PA, 7226
Adams County Historical Society, WA, 8875
Adams Museum, SD, 7770
Adena State Memorial: The Home of Thomas Worthington, OH, 6602
Adirondack Museum, The, NY, 5820
Adsmore Museum, KY, 3231
Affton Historical Society, MO, 4901
African American Museum and Library at Oakland, CA, 667
African American Museum in Philadelphia, The, PA, 7349
Afro-American Cultural Center, NC, 6244
Afro-American Historical Association of Fauquier County, VA, 8754
Afton Historical Society Museum, MN, 4263
Age of Steam Railroad Museum, The, TX, 8070
Air Force Enlisted Heritage Hall, AL, 91
Airmen Memorial Museum, MD, 3727
Alabama Historical Commission-Old Cahawba, AL, 108
Alachua County Historic Trust; Matheson Museum, Inc., FL, 1436
Alamance Battleground State Historic Site, NC, 6232
Alamance County Historical Museum, Inc., NC, 6234
Alaska Historical Collection, Alaska State Library, AK, 168
Albany County Historical Society, WY, 9326
Albany Heritage Society, Inc., MN, 4265
Albany Institute of History and Art, NY, 5783
Alberta Association of Registered Nurses, AB, 9379
Alberton Historical Preservation Foundation, PE, 9860
Alexander and Baldwin Sugar Museum, HI, 1887
Alexander Ramsey House, MN, 4451
Alexandria Black History Resource Center, The, VA, 8472
Alfalfa County Historical Society, OK, 6859
Alfred P. Sloan Museum, MI, 4123
Algonquin Culture and Heritage Centre, ON, 9717
Alice T. Miner Colonial Collection, NY, 5861
Aliceville Museum, AL, 1
Allegany County Historical Society, MD, 3627
Allegany County Historical Society, NY, 5814
Allegheny Cemetery Historical Association, PA, 7414
Allen Barkley Young Historians, Inc., KY, 3220
Allen County-Ft. Wayne Historical Society, IN, 2525
Alliance for Historic Hillsborough, The, NC, 6327
Allison-Antrim Museum, Inc., PA, 7238

Alnobak Nebesakiak, VT, 8379
Alpharetta Historical Society, Inc., GA, 1583
Alton Area Historical Society, IL, 1976
Alton Historical Society, Inc., NH, 5265
Alvin Museum Society, TX, 8006
Amador County Archives, CA, 574
Amador Livermore Valley Museum, CA, 715
Amalthea Historical Society, OH, 6814
Amana Heritage Society, IA, 2659
Amelia Island Museum of History, FL, 1419
American Airlines C.R. Smith Museum, TX, 8080
American Antiquarian Society, MA, 4040
American Clock and Watch Museum, CT, 1143
American Cotton Museum, TX, 8134
American Helicopter Museum and Education Center, PA, 7498
American Jewish Historical Society, MA, 4016
American Museum of Fly Fishing, VT, 8401
American Red Cross Museum, DC, 1326
American Studies Association, DC, 1327
American Swedish Historical Museum, PA, 7352
American Swedish Institute, The, MN, 4386
American Textile History Museum, MA, 3902
American-Italian Renaissance Foundation, LA, 3340
Amherst History Museum at the Strong House, MA, 3748
Amherst Museum, NY, 5796
Anacortes Museum, WA, 8793
Ancient and Honorable Artillery Company of Massachusetts, MA, 3764
Anderson Farm Museum, ON, 9740
Anderson Valley Historical Museum, CA, 470
Andover Historical Society, IL, 1979
Andover Historical Society, MA, 3753
Andover Historical Society, NH, 5267
Andrew College Archives, GA, 1666
Andrew County Museum and Historical Society, MO, 4933
Androscoggin Historical Society, ME, 3400
Anna Maria Island Historical Society Inc., FL, 1378
Annandale National Historic Site, ON, 9822
Antelope County Historical Society, NE, 5172
Anthenaeum of Philadelphia, The, PA, 7353
Antiquarian and Landmarks Society, CT, 1189
Antique Auto Museum of Massachusetts, MA, 3793
Apalachicola Maritime Museum, Inc., FL, 1379
Apex Historical Society, NC, 6204
Appalachian Archive at Southeast Community College, The, KY, 3114
Appalachian Cultural Museum, The, NC, 6225
APVA Joseph Bryan Branch, VA, 8574
Arboretum of Los Angeles County, CA, 440
Archives and Manuscripts Department, Auburn University, AL, 9
Archives and Regional History Collections, Western Michigan University, MI, 4163
Archives and Special Collections, MCP Hahnemann University, PA, 7354
Archives and Special Collections, Ohio University Libraries, OH, 6568
Archives of Labor and Urban Affairs, MI, 4104
Archives of the Episcopal Diocese of North Carolina, NC, 6393
Archives of the Evangelical Lutheran Church in America, IL, 2037
Archives of the Peabody Institute of The Johns Hopkins University, MD, 3558
Archives of the University of Ottawa, ON, 9775
Archives, Diocese of Cleveland, OH, 6623
Archives, University of Colorado at Boulder Libraries, CO, 984
Archivists for Congregations of Women Religious (ACWR), DC, 1331
Argyle Township Court House and Archives, NS, 9679
Arizona Department of Library, Archives, and Public Records, AZ, 241
Arizona Historical Society - Northern Division, AZ, 216
Arizona Historical Society - Southern Division, AZ, 272
Arizona History and Archives Division, Arizona Department of Library, Archives, and Public Records, AZ, 243

Arkansas Historic Wine Museum, AR, 400
Arkansas History Commission, AR, 366
Arlington Heights Historical Society and Museum, IL, 1981
Arlington Historical Society, Inc., VA, 8491
Arlington Historical Society, The, MA, 3756
Arlington House, The Robert E. Lee Memorial, VA, 8623
Armstrong County Museum, Inc., TX, 8048
Arrow Rock State Historic Site, MO, 4631
Art Gallery of Northumberland, ON, 9703
Arthur and Elizabeth Schlesinger Library on the History of Women in America, The, MA, 3795
Ashlawn-Highland, VA, 8515
Ashtabula Plantation, SC, 7720
Ashton Villa, TX, 8118
Aspen Historical Society, CO, 981
Associated Students for Historic Preservation (ASHP), OR, 7012
Association for Gravestone Studies, MA, 3871
Association for Living History, Farm and Agricultural Museums, OH, 6732
Association for the Preservation of Tennessee Antiquities (APTA), TN, 7958
Astor House Museum, CO, 1064
Astronaut Hall of Fame, FL, 1565
Athenaeum Rectory, The, TN, 7879
Athens County Historical Society and Museum, OH, 6569
Athens-Clarke County Library Heritage Room, GA, 1588
Atlanta Chapter, National Railway Historical Society, GA, 1680
Atlanta Historical Society, GA, 1598
Atlanta Historical Society, ID, 1899
Atlanta History Center, GA, 1599
Atlantic County Historical Society, The, NJ, 5629
Atwater Historical Society, The, OH, 6570
Auburn Avenue Research Library on African American Culture and History, GA, 1601
Auburn University Montgomery Library, AL, 95
Audubon State Commemorative Area, LA, 3371
Augusta Museum of History, GA, 1630
Aurora Colony Historical Society, OR, 6992
Aurora Historical Society, NY, 5888
Aurora Historical Society, OH, 6571
Autauga County Heritage Association, AL, 105
Autry Museum of Western Heritage, CA, 611
Avoca Museum and Historical Society, VA, 8485
Avonlea "Heritage House" Museum, SK, 9945
Aylmer and District Museum, ON, 9690
B&O Railroad Museum, MD, 3559
Baccalieu Trail Heritage Corporation, NF, 9614
Bacon's Castle Museum, VA, 8746
Bainbridge Island Historical Society, WA, 8800
Baker University Archives, KS, 2888
Baker-Cederberg Museum and Archives, NY, 6093
Ballantine House, The, NJ, 5574
Baltimore County Historical Society, Inc., MD, 3618
Baltimore Public Works Museum, The, MD, 3565
Bancroft Library, The, CA, 458
Bank of Montreal Archives and Museum, QC, 9901
Banner County Historical Society, NE, 5129
Bar U Ranch National Historic Site of Canada, AB, 9406
Barkerville Historic Town, BC, 9432
Barlow House Museum, KY, 3095
Barnes County Historical Society, ND, 6548
Barrett House, SPNEA, NH, 5377
Barrington Living History Farm, TX, 8273
Barrington Preservation Society, RI, 7525
Bartlesville Area Historical Museum, OK, 6842
Bates County Museum of Pioneer History, MO, 4657
Battlefield House Museum, ON, 9811
Bay County Historical Society/Historical Museum of Bay County, MI, 4066
Bay Mills Community College Library and Heritage Center, MI, 4077
Bayou Terrebonne Waterlife Museum, LA,

3297
BC Heritage, BC, 9518
Beaton Institute of Cape Breton Studies, NS, 9677
Beaufort Museum, SC, 7602
Beauport, SPNEA, MA, 3866
Beaverhead County Museum, MT, 5004
Becker County Historical Society and Museum, MN, 4303
Beersheba Springs Historical Society, TN, 7864
Beinecke Rare Book and Manuscript Library, CT, 1223
Belchertown Historical Association, MA, 3760
Belknap Mill Society, NH, 5348
Bell County Museum, TX, 8037
Bell Homestead National Historic Site, ON, 9696
Bella Vista Historical Society/Museum, AR, 303
Bellamy Mansion Museum of History and Design Arts, NC, 6467
Belle Grove Plantation, VA, 8627
Belleville Public Library, IL, 1991
Belleville Public Library, ON, 9692
Bellevue Historical Society, Inc., ID, 1900
Bellevue/LaGrange Woman's Club Charitable Trust, GA, 1715
Bellport-Brookhaven Historical Society, NY, 5813
Belmont County Historical Society, OH, 6575
Belvedere-Tiburon Landmarks Society, CA, 924
Benares Historic House, ON, 9750
Benicia Historical Museum and Cultural Foundation, CA, 455
Bennett Place State Historic Site, NC, 6269
Bennington Museum, The, VT, 8360
Bent's Old Fort National Historic Site, CO, 1084
Bergen County Division of Cultural and Historic Affairs, NJ, 5494
Berkeley County Historical Society, WV, 9037
Berkeley Historical Society, CA, 460
Berkeley Museum, SC, 7709
Berkshire County Historical Society, The, MA, 3951
Berkshire Museum, The, MA, 3952
Berlin and Coos County Historical Society, NH, 5275
Berman Museum of World History, AL, 3
Bernhard Museum Complex, CA, 444
Bernice Historical Society, Inc., LA, 3274
Bernice Pauahi Bishop Museum, HI, 1851
Berrien County Historical Association, MI, 4073
Bethel Historical Association, Inc., OH, 6582
Bethel Historical Society, The, ME, 3411
Betts House Research Center, OH, 6606
Beverly Historical Society and Museum, MA, 3761
Biddeford Historical Society, ME, 3412
Bidwell House, The, MA, 3918
Big Ivy Historical Society, Inc., NC, 6218
Big Sioux River Valley Historical Society, IA, 2759
Biggar Museum and Gallery, SK, 9947
Billings County Historical Society, ND, 6533
Billings Farm and Museum, VT, 8468
Billy Graham Center Archives, IL, 2457
Billy Graham Center Museum, IL, 2458
Biltmore Estate, NC, 6206
Birmingham Civil Rights Institute, AL, 14
Birmingham Historical Society, AL, 15
Birmingham Public Library, Department of Archives and Manuscripts, AL, 16
Bisbee Mining and Historical Museum, AZ, 207
Bishop Hill Heritage Association, IL, 2000
Black Creek Pioneer Village, ON, 9828
Black Earth Historical Society, WI, 9083
Black Hawk State Historic Site/Hauberg Indian Museum, IL, 2343
Black Hills Mining Museum, SD, 7798
Black River Historical Society, OH, 6703
Black River Historical Society, VT, 8400
Black World History Wax Museum, The, MO, 4905
Blackberry Farm's Pioneer Village, IL, 1984
Blackburn Historical Society, MO, 4646
Blackhawk Automotive Museum, CA, 511
Blue Ridge Parkway, NC, 6209
Blue Ridge Parkway, VA, 8755

Clay County Historical Society, FL, 1439
Clay County Historical Society, IN, 2493
Clay County Historical Society, MN, 4405
Clay County Historical Society, NE, 5100
Clay County Historical Society, SD, 7854
Clear Creek History Park, CO, 1066
Clermont State Historic Site, NY, 5918
Clifton Community Historical Society, KS, 2898
Clinton Birthplace Foundation, AR, 353
Clinton County Historical Society, Inc., IN, 2532
Clinton County Historical Society, NY, 6072
Clinton County Historical Society, PA, 7304
CNMI Museum of History and Culture, MP, 6556
Coastal Discovery Museum on Hilton Head Island, SC, 7692
Coastal Georgia Historical Society, GA, 1775
Cobb County Historic Preservation Commission, GA, 1734
Coe Hall at Planting Fields, NY, 6060
Coffin House, SPNEA, MA, 3930
Coggeshall Farm Museum, RI, 7529
Cogswell's Grant, SPNEA, MA, 3857
Cole County Historical Society, MO, 4752
Cole Harbour Rural Heritage Society, NS, 9654
Collier County Museum, FL, 1494
Collingswood-Newton Colony Historical Society, NJ, 5472
Collinsville Historical Museum, IL, 2083
Colonel Allensworth State Historic Park, CA, 524
Colonial Williamsburg Foundation, The, VA, 8773
Colorado Historical Society, CO, 1021
Colorado Ski Museum Hall of Fame, CO, 1132
Colorado Springs Museum, CO, 1002
Columbia Archives, MD, 3624
Columbia Gorge Discovery Center and Wasco County Historical Museum, OR, 7093
Columbia State Historic Park, CA, 499
Columbian Theatre, Museum Art Center, KS, 3069
Columbus Chapel and Boal Mansion Museum, PA, 7137
Colvin Run Mill Historic Site, VA, 8580
Commissariat House Provincial Historic Site, NF, 9629
Community Historical Museum of Mount Holly, VT, 8359
Community History Project of Shenandoah University, VA, 8782
Company of Fifers and Drummers, The, CT, 1200
Compass Inn Museum, PA, 7290
Concord Museum, MA, 3814
Concordia Historical Institute, MO, 4909
Conejo Valley Historical Society/Stagecoach Inn Museum Complex, CA, 661
Confederate Memorial Park, AL, 73
Confederate Memorial State Historic Site, MO, 4726
Congregational Christian Historical Society, MA, 3771
Congregational Library, MA, 3772
Connecticut Historical Society, The, CT, 1191
Connecticut Valley Historical Museum, MA, 3995
Conner Prairie, IN, 2524
Conrad/Caldwell House Museum, KY, 3180
Conservation Corps State Museum Southern California Affiliate, CA, 776
Conservation Trust of Puerto Rico, The, PR, 7521
Contemporary Victorian Townhouse Museum, NJ, 5655
Conway Historical Society, MA, 3820
Conway Historical Society, NH, 5296
Cooke County Heritage Society, Inc., TX, 8117
Cooleemee Historical Association, NC, 6262
Cooper Regional History Museum, CA, 940
Core Sound Waterfowl Museum, NC, 6316
Cornelius Low House/Middlesex County Museum, NJ, 5567
Cornish Historical Society, NH, 5298
Corporation for Jefferson's Poplar Forest, VA, 8555
Costume Museum of Canada, MB, 9537

Council Valley Museum, ID, 1922
Courtenay and District Museum and Paleontology Centre, BC, 9440
Courthouse Square Association, Inc., MI, 4085
Coventry Historical Society, CT, 1150
Cowboy Artists of America Museum, TX, 8156
Cowley County Historical Society, KS, 3084
Cowlitz County Historical Museum, WA, 8864
Cranford Historical Society, NJ, 5477
Creston and District Historical and Museum Society, BC, 9442
Croatian Ethnic Institute, IL, 2048
Crook County Historical Society, OR, 7075
Crystal Caverns at Hupp's Hill, VA, 8738
Crystal Lake Falls Historical Association, VT, 8357
Culbertson Mansion State Historic Site, IN, 2601
Culbertson Museum, MT, 4998
Culp Cavalry Museum/Museum of Culpeper History, VA, 8530
Cumberland County Historical Society, NJ, 5493
Cumberland County Museum, NS, 9647
Cumberland Museum and Archives, BC, 9443
Currency Museum/Bank of Canada, ON, 9781
Czechoslovak Heritage Museum, IL, 2281
Dakota City Heritage Village, MN, 4331
Dakota County Historical Society, MN, 4455
Dakotaland Museum, SD, 7790
Dallas County Historical Museum, AR, 332
Dallas Historical Society, TX, 8073
Dallas Memorial Center for Holocaust Studies, TX, 8074
Dalnavent Museum, MB, 9564
Daly House Museum, MB, 9534
Dana-Thomas House State Historic Site, IL, 2391
Daniel Boone and Frontier Families Research Association, MO, 4722
Daniel Boone Homestead, PA, 7134
Daniel Webster Birthplace Living History Project, NH, 5313
Danish Immigrant Museum, The, IA, 2735
Danvers Historical Society, IL, 2088
Danvers Historical Society, MA, 3824
Danville Historical Society, VA, 8532
Darien Historical Society, Inc., The, CT, 1156
Darnall's Chance, MD, 3735
Daughters of Hawaii, HI, 1854
Daughters of the American Revolution Museum, DC, 1336
David Davis Mansion State Historic Site, IL, 2003
Davidson County Historical Museum, NC, 6351
Dawes County Historical Society, Inc., NE, 5095
Dawson City Museum and Historical Society, YT, 10000
Dawson County Historical Society, NE, 5141
Dayton Historical Depot Society, WA, 8830
Dead River Area Historical Society, ME, 3524
Deadwood Historic Preservation Commission, SD, 7771
Dearborn Historical Museum, MI, 4100
Death Valley National Park, CA, 515
Decatur County Historical Society, GA, 1636
Decatur County Historical Society, IN, 2542
Decatur House, DC, 1337
DeCordova Museum and Sculpture Park, MA, 3898
Deer Isle Historical Society, ME, 3425
Deere-Wiman House, IL, 2248
Deerfield Area Historical Society, IL, 2101
Delaware Agricultural Museum and Village, DE, 1296
Delaware County Historical Association, NY, 5885
Delaware Heritage Foundation, DE, 1313
Delaware State Museums, DE, 1298
Delhi Ontario Tobacco Museum and Heritage Center, ON, 9706
Delta Blues Museum, MS, 4536
Delta Genealogical Society, GA, 1766
Delta State University Archives, MS, 4537
Denison Advocates, PA, 7220
Denison Homestead Museum, CT, 1214
Denman Seniors and Museum Society, BC, 9445
Denton Community Historical Society, NE, 5106
Denton County Courthouse-on-the-Square Museum, TX, 8084
Denton County Historical Museum, Inc., TX, 8085
Denver Museum of Miniatures, Dolls, and Toys, CO, 1023
Department of Arkansas Heritage, AR, 374
Derby Historical Society, CT, 1136
Derry Historical Society and Museum, NH, 5304
Derry Township Historical Society, PA, 7260
Deschutes County Historical Society, OR, 6996
Deschutes Historical Center, OR, 6997
Destroyer Escort Historical Foundation, NY, 5784
Detroit Historical Museums, MI, 4108
Deutschheim State Historic Site, MO, 4723
DeWitt Historical Society of Tompkins County, The, NY, 5951
Dexter Area Historical Society and Museum, MI, 4113
Dexter Historical Society, Inc., ME, 3426
Dickey County Historical Society, ND, 6543
Dickinson County Historical Society, KS, 2873
Diefenbaker Canada Centre, SK, 9987
Dillingham Historic Preservation Commission, AK, 154
Dillon County Historical Society, Inc., SC, 7667
Dinsmore Homestead Foundation, KY, 3101
Discovery Museum, CT, 1141
Discovery Museum, The, CA, 757
District 69 Historical Society, BC, 9477
Doak House Museum/President Andrew Johnson Museum & Library, TN, 7902
Dodge City Area Arts Council/Carnegie Center for the Arts, KS, 2912
Dodge County Historical Society, MN, 4381
Dodge County Historical Society, WI, 9079
Doll House Museum, KS, 2995
Doon Heritage Crossroads, ON, 9735
Dorchester Historical Society, MA, 3842
Dorothy Whitfield Historic Society, CT, 1182
Dorsey Chapel, MD, 3658
Douglas County Historical and Genealogical Society, Inc., MO, 4636
Douglas County Historical Society, MN, 4267
Douglas County Historical Society, OR, 7077
Douglas County Historical Society, WI, 9254
Douglas County Historical Society/Watkins Community Museum of History, KS, 2975
Dover Historical Society, Inc., VT, 8381
Downer's Grove Museum, The, IL, 2110
Drayton Hall, National Trust for Historic Preservation, SC, 7627
Drayton Valley District Historical Society, AB, 9377
Dresden Historical Society, ME, 3428
Dudley Foundation, Inc., The, CT, 1183
Duke University Rare Book, Manuscript and Special Collections Library, NC, 6271
Duncan Cottage Museum, AK, 179
Dundalk-Patapsco Neck Historical Society, MD, 3631
Dundee Township Historical Society, IL, 2453
Durham Historical Association, NH, 5308
Durham Western Heritage Museum, NE, 5184
Dyer Historical Society, Inc., IN, 2513
E. Stanley Wright Museum Foundation, Inc., NH, 5434
Eagle Historical Society and Museums, AK, 155
Eagle River Historical Society, WI, 9113
Earl Gregg Swem Library, College of William and Mary, VA, 8774
Early American Museum, IL, 2228
Early Settlers Association of the Western Reserve, The, OH, 6626
East Benton County Historical Society & Museum, WA, 8865
East Carolina Village of Yesteryear, NC, 6307
East Jersey Olde Towne Village, NJ, 5568
East Providence Historical Society, RI, 7541
East River Genealogical Forum, SD, 7860
East Rochester Local History, NY, 5897
East Tennessee Historical Society, TN, 7926
East Texas Oil Museum at Kilgore College, TX, 8158

Eastern Regional Coal Archives, WV, 9008
Eastern Trails Museum, OK, 6980
Eastern Washington State Historical Society, WA, 8951
Eaton Florida History Room, Manatee County Central Library, FL, 1385
Ebenezer Maxwell Mansion, Inc., PA, 7367
Ecomusee du fier Monde, QC, 9906
Edgecombe County Cultural Arts Council, Inc., NC, 6449
Edgecombe County Historical Society, NC, 6450
Edgefield County Historical Society, SC, 7669
Edina Historical Society and Museum, MN, 4314
Edmond Historical Society, OK, 6878
Edmondston-Alston House, SC, 7628
Edward Bellamy Memorial Association, MA, 3810
Edward H. Nabb Research Center for Delmarva History and Culture at Salisbury State University, MD, 3706
Edwards County Historical Society, IL, 1974
Effingham Historic District Commission, NH, 5420
Eisenhower Center for American Studies, The, LA, 3344
Eisenhower National Historic Site, PA, 7227
El Paso Museum of History, TX, 8089
El Pueblo de Los Angeles Historical Monument, CA, 616
El Pueblo Museum, CO, 1110
Elbow Museum and Historical Society, SK, 9954
Elegba Folklore Society, Inc., VA, 8686
Elfreth's Alley Association, PA, 7369
Elgin County Pioneer Museum, ON, 9808
Elgin Military Museum, The, ON, 9809
Elk County Historical Society, PA, 7434
Elk-Blue Creek Historical Society, WV, 9046
Elkhorn Valley Museum and Research Center, NE, 5175
Ellicott City B&O Railroad Station Museum, The, MD, 3637
Ellinwood Community Historical Society, KS, 2921
Elliot Lake Nuclear and Mining Museum, ON, 9710
Ellsinore Pioneer Museum, MO, 4698
Elman W. Campbell Museum, ON, 9760
Elmhurst Historical Museum, IL, 2124
Elphinstone Pioneer Museum, BC, 9452
Elverhoj Museum of History and Art, CA, 898
Elwyn B Robinson Department of Special Collections, University of North Dakota, ND, 6522
Ely Field Office, Bureau of Land Management, NV, 5237
Empire Mine State Historic Park, CA, 562
Enderby and District Museum Society, BC, 9446
Englehart and Area Historical Museum, ON, 9711
Englewood Historical Society, NJ, 5484
Enos Mills Cabin, CO, 1042
Ephrata Cloister, PA, 7204
Epiphany Chapel and Church House, MD, 3685
Erie Canal Museum, NY, 6154
Erie County Historical Society, OH, 6772
Erie County Historical Society, PA, 7206
Erie Historical Museum and Planetarium, PA, 7207
Ernest Hemingway Foundation of Oak Park, The, IL, 2288
Escondido Historical Society and Heritage Walk Museum, CA, 529
Esquimalt Municipal Archives, BC, 9524
Essex County Historical Society, VA, 8750
Essex County Museum, Inc., VA, 8751
Ethan Allen Homestead Trust, VT, 8370
Etowah Foundation's History Center, The, GA, 1652
Eufaula Heritage Association, AL, 46
Eugene V. Debs Foundation, IN, 2639
Eureka County Sentinel Museum, NV, 5238
Eureka Springs Historical Museum, AR, 321
Evanston Historical Society, IL, 2128
Excelsior Heritage Preservation Commission, MN, 4322
Exeter Public Library, NH, 5316
F. Scott and Zelda Fitzgerald Museum, AL, 96
Fairbanks House, MA, 3828

SPORTS

American Jewish Historical Society, MA, 4016
American Museum of Fly Fishing, VT, 8401
American Studies Association, DC, 1327
American Water Ski Educational Foundation, FL, 1517
American-Italian Renaissance Foundation, LA, 3340
Anderson Farm Museum, ON, 9740
Andrew County Museum and Historical Society, MO, 4933
Androscoggin Historical Society, ME, 3400
Anna Maria Island Historical Society Inc., FL, 1378
Appalachian Cultural Museum, The, NC, 6225
Aquatic Hall of Fame and Museum of Canada, MB, 9558
Archives and Manuscripts Department, Auburn University, AL, 9
Archives and Regional History Collections, Western Michigan University, MI, 4163
Archives Nationales du Quebec, QC, 9898
Archives Nationales du Quebec, QC, 9937
Archives, University of Colorado at Boulder Libraries, CO, 984
Argyle Township Court House and Archives, NS, 9679
Artesia Historical Museum and Art Center, NM, 5701
Arthur and Elizabeth Schlesinger Library on the History of Women in America, The, MA, 3795
Ashland University Archives, OH, 6565
Ashville Area Heritage Society, OH, 6566
Association for Living History, Farm and Agricultural Museums, OH, 6732
Ataloa Lodge Museum, OK, 6918
Athens County Historical Society and Museum, OH, 6569
Atlanta Historical Society, GA, 1598
Atlanta Historical Society, ID, 1899
Auburn Avenue Research Library on African American Culture and History, GA, 1601
Augusta Museum of History, GA, 1630
Avonlea "Heritage House" Museum, SK, 9945
Babe Ruth Birthplace Museum, MD, 3560
Baker University Archives, KS, 2888
Bancroft Library, The, CA, 458
Barkerville Historic Town, BC, 9432
Barnes County Historical Society, ND, 6548
Bartlesville Area History Museum, OK, 6842
Bay Area Heritage Society/Baytown Historical Museum, TX, 8033
Beaton Institute of Cape Breton Studies, NS, 9677
Beaver Falls Historical Society Museum, PA, 7122
Beaverhead County Museum, MT, 5004
Belle Meade, Queen of Tennessee Plantations, TN, 7959
Belleville Public Library, IL, 1991
Belleville Public Library, ON, 9692
Benicia Historical Society, CA, 456
Berkshire County Historical Society, The, MA, 3951
Berlin and Coos County Historical Society, NH, 5275
Bernice Pauahi Bishop Museum, HI, 1851
Berrien County Historical Association, MI, 4073
Bertha Historical Society, Inc., MN, 4277
Berwyn Historical Society, IL, 1999
Big Sioux River Valley Historical Society, IA, 2759
Biggar Museum and Gallery, SK, 9947
Birmingham Public Library, Department of Archives and Manuscripts, AL, 16
Black River Historical Society, OH, 6703
Black River Historical Society, VT, 8400
Boston Public Library, MA, 3768
Bottineau County Historical Society, ND, 6500
Bresaylor Heritage Museum, SK, 9949
Bristol Historical Society, NH, 5278
Bristol Historical Society, VT, 8366
Bronx County Historical Society, NY, 5827
Brooklyn Historical Society, The, NY, 5830
Brooklyn Public Library-Brooklyn Collection, NY, 5832
Brunswick Railroad Museum, MD, 3604
Burton Historical Collection, MI, 4105
Bushnell Historical Society, IL, 2010
Butte-Silver Bow Public Archives, MT, 4986
C.H. Nash Museum/Chucalissa, TN, 7939

California African American Museum, CA, 612
California Historical Society, CA, 799
California History Section, California State Library, CA, 749
California State Archives, CA, 751
Cambridge Historical Society, The, MA, 3797
Camden County Historical Society & Museum, MO, 4811
Camden County Historical Society, NJ, 5473
Canadian Canoe Museum, The, ON, 9791
Canadian Rivers Historical Society, OK, 6889
Cape Breton Miners' Museum, NS, 9656
Cape Fear Museum, NC, 6469
Cardston and District Historical Society, AB, 9370
Carl Hubbell Museum, OK, 6916
Carlisle Area Historical Society, OH, 6597
Carriage House Museum of the Queen Village Historical Society, NY, 5847
Carteret County Historical Society, Inc., NC, 6365
Carver County Historical Society, MN, 4506
Carver-Hill Memorial and Historical Society, Inc., FL, 1400
Cass County Historical Society Museum, IA, 2753
Cass County Historical Society Museum, IN, 2582
Cass County Historical Society Museum, NE, 5199
Catalina Island Museum Society, CA, 448
Catawba County Historical Association, NC, 6382
Cavalier County Historical Society, ND, 6531
Cavendish Historical Society, VT, 8373
Cedar Crest, Residence of the Governor of Kansas, KS, 3055
Center for American History, The University of Texas at Austin, TX, 8013
Center for Wooden Boats, The, WA, 8921
Central Missouri State University Archives/Museum, MO, 4958
Centre for Newfoundland Studies, NF, 9628
CFB Gagetown Military Museum, NB, 9599
Chambers County Museum, Inc., AL, 72
Chapin Community Historical Society, IL, 2028
Charles H. Wright Museum of African American History, MI, 4106
Charlotte County Museum, NB, 9609
Charlotte Hawkins Brown Historic Site, NC, 6430
Chase and District Museum and Archives Society, BC, 9439
Chemung County Historical Society, Inc. (Chemung Valley History Museum), NY, 5899
Cherryville History Association, NC, 6256
Chevy Chase Historical Society, MD, 3615
Chicago Historical Society, IL, 2043
Chicago Lawn Historical Society, IL, 2045
Chief Vann House Historic Site, GA, 1655
Chippewa County Historical Society, MN, 4403
Chippewa County Historical Society, WI, 9097
Chisholm Trail Museum, KS, 3072
Choctaw County Historical Museum, AL, 26
Citadel Archives and Museum, SC, 7626
Claresholm and District Museum, AB, 9372
Clark County Historical Society, KS, 2883
Clark County Historical Society, MO, 4764
Clark County Historical Society, SD, 7764
Clarksville-Montgomery County Museum, TN, 7875
Clay County Historical Society, AL, 4
Clay County Historical Society, FL, 1439
Clay County Historical Society, IN, 2493
Clay County Historical Society, MN, 4405
Clay County Historical Society, NE, 5100
Clay County Historical Society, SD, 7854
Clermont Historical Society, IA, 2692
Climax Community Museum, Inc., SK, 9950
Cloud County Historical Society, KS, 2904
Clover Bend Historic Preservation Association, AR, 357
Coffee Co/Manchester/Tullahoma Museum, Inc. Arrowheads/Aerospace Museum, TN, 7935
Cokesbury College Historical and Recreational Commission, SC, 7695
College Football Hall of Fame, IN, 2633
Collingswood-Newton Colony Historical

Society, NJ, 5472
Collinsville Historical Museum, IL, 2083
Colorado Historical Society, CO, 1021
Colorado Ski Museum Hall of Fame, CO, 1132
Colorado Springs Museum, CO, 1002
Commission of Landmarks and Museum, DE, 1312
Community Historical Society, The, IA, 2794
Community History Project of Shenandoah University, VA, 8782
Community Library Associaton-Regional History Dept, ID, 1934
Conner Prairie, IN, 2524
Corry Area Historical Society, PA, 7179
Cortland County Historical Society, Inc., NY, 5876
County of Grey-Owen Sound Museum, ON, 9788
Cozad Historical Society—The 100th Meridian Museum, NE, 5102
Crittenden County Historical Society: Bob Wheeler Museum, KY, 3201
Croatian Ethnic Institute, IL, 2048
Crow Wing County Historical Society, MN, 4282
Crystal Lake Falls Historical Association, VT, 8357
Culp Cavalry Museum/Museum of Culpeper History, VA, 8530
Cumberland Museum and Archives, BC, 9443
Cuyuna Range Historical Society, MN, 4301
Cynthiana-Harrison County Museum, KY, 3115
Dakota County Historical Society, MN, 4455
Dakotaland Museum, SD, 7790
Dallas County Historical Society, AR, 332
Dawson County Historical Society, NE, 5141
Decatur County Historical Society, GA, 1636
Decatur County Historical Society, IN, 2542
Dell Rapid Society for Historic Preservation, SD, 7773
Derry Township Historical Society, PA, 7260
Detroit Historical Museums, MI, 4108
Dexter Historical Society, Inc., ME, 3426
Dodge County Historical Society, MN, 4381
Dodge County Historical Society, WI, 9079
Douglas County Historical Society, MN, 4267
Douglas County Historical Society, OR, 7077
Douglas County Historical Society, WI, 9254
Douglas County Historical Society/Watkins Community Museum of History, KS, 2975
Dover Historical Society, IA, 2805
Dover Historical Society, OH, 6651
Dundalk-Patapsco Neck Historical Society, MD, 3631
Dyer Historical Society, Inc., IN, 2513
E. Stanley Wright Museum Foundation, Inc., NH, 5434
E.P. "Tom" Sawyer State Park, KY, 3194
Eagle Bend Historical Society/Museum, MN, 4312
Eagle River Historical Society, WI, 9113
East Rochester Local History, NY, 5897
East Tennessee Historical Society, TN, 7926
Eastern Trails Museum, OK, 6980
Edmond Historical Society, OK, 6878
El Paso Museum of History, TX, 8089
Elgin County Pioneer Museum, ON, 9808
Elk County Historical Society, PA, 7434
Elwyn B Robinson Department of Special Collections, University of North Dakota, ND, 6522
Emmet County Historical Society, IA, 2739
Emory and Henry College, VA, 8542
Esquimalt Municipal Archives, BC, 9524
Etowah Foundation's History Center, The, GA, 1652
Farmington Museum, NM, 5722
Fenton History Center—Museum and Library, NY, 5955
Filipino American Historical Society of Chicago, IL, 2051
Filson Club, The, KY, 3182
Florida Sports Hall of Fame and Museum of Florida Sports History, FL, 1469
Foothills Historical Society, WA, 8813
Forbes Mill Regional History Museum and Los Gatos Museum of Art and Natural History, CA, 627
Forestburg Historical Society, AB, 9394
Fort Collins Museum, CO, 1052

Fort Dauphin Museum, Inc., The, MB, 9536
Fort La Reine Museum Pioneer Village and Tourist Bureau, MB, 9543
Fort Myers Historical Museum, FL, 1426
Fort Smith Museum of History, AR, 337
Fort Wallace Museum, KS, 3068
Fossil County Futures, Inc., WY, 9323
Fremont Historical Society, NH, 5324
Friends of Rickwood, AL, 18
Frontier Historical Society Museum, CO, 1063
Fulton County Historical Society, Inc., IN, 2625
Fulton County Historical Society, Inc., PA, 7308
Gage County Historical Society, NE, 5084
Gallia County Historical/Genealogical Society, OH, 6667
Garza County Historical Museum, TX, 8216
Genesee County History Department, NY, 5808
Georgetown and Scott County Museum, KY, 3140
Georgia Mountains History Museum at Brenau University, GA, 1694
Georgia Sports Hall of Fame, GA, 1728
Gloucester County Historical Society, NJ, 5680
Golden State Museum, CA, 759
Goodhue County Historical Society, MN, 4437
Goose Lake Prairie State Natural Area, IL, 2256
Goshen Township Historical Society, OH, 6674
Grand County Historical Association, CO, 1077
Grand Rapids Historical Society, MI, 4137
Grande Prairie Museum, AB, 9398
Grayslake Municipal Historical Museum, IL, 2158
Great Harbor Martitine Museum, ME, 3475
Greater Southwest Historical Museum, OK, 6837
Greensboro Historical Society, VT, 8391
Grout Museum of History and Science, IA, 2860
Gunnison County Pioneer and Historical Society, CO, 1075
Hardin County Historical Museums, Inc., OH, 6693
Harness Racing and Hall of Fame, NY, 5922
Harnett County Historical Society, NC, 6352
Hartsville Museum, SC, 7688
Harwich Historical Society, MA, 3879
Hattiesburg Area Historical Society and Museum, MS, 4554
Hayden Historical Museum Inc., IN, 2545
Hellenic Cultural Association, UT, 8333
Hellenic Museum and Cultural Center, IL, 2056
Henniker Historical Society, NH, 5336
Henry Sheldon Museum of Vermont History, VT, 8404
Heritage House of Orange County Association, Inc., TX, 8201
Heritage Museum, MT, 5035
Heritage Shawinigan, QC, 9928
Hidalgo County Historical Museum, TX, 8088
Hiddenite Center, Inc., NC, 6323
High Point Historical Society, Inc., NC, 6325
Highspire Historical Society, PA, 7263
Historic Pensacola Preservation Board, FL, 1511
Historic Southwest Ohio, OH, 6614
Historical Museum at Fort Missoula, MT, 5042
Historical Museum of the D.R. Barker Library, NY, 5911
Historical Projects of Houston County, Inc., TX, 8064
Historical Society of Carnegie, PA, 7159
Historical Society of Glastonbury, CT, 1174
Historical Society of Marshall County, IA, 2790
Historical Society of Palm Beach County, FL, 1575
Historical Society of the Tonawandas, NY, 6162
Historical Society of Western Pennsylvania, PA, 7420
History Museum of East Otter Trail County, The, MN, 4429
Holland Historical Trust, MI, 4152

TEXTILES

TRANSPORTATION/ INDUSTRY/ TECHNOLOGY

George M. Verity Riverboat Museum
Commission, IA, 2773
Georgetown Energy Museum, CO, 1059
Georgia Mountains History Museum at
Brenau University, GA, 1694
Germantown Historical Society, PA, 7375
Gig Harbor Peninsula Historical Society &
Museum, WA, 8854
Gilmore-Classic Car Club of America
Museum, MI, 4150
Glenn H. Curtiss Museum of Local History,
NY, 5928
Glensheen Historic Estate, MN, 4307
Gloucester County Historical Society, NJ,
5680
Glove Museum, The, NY, 6007
Golden Drift Historical Society, CA, 522
Golden Drift Museum, CA, 523
Golden Spike National Historical Site, UT,
8321
Golden State Museum, CA, 759
Good Old Days Vintage Motorcar Museum,
Inc., AR, 344
Goodhue County Historical Society, MN,
4437
Gorham Historical Society, ME, 3443
Gorham Historical Society, NH, 5327
Governor's Mansion State Historic Park, CA,
760
Grace Museum, The, TX, 8003
Graham-Ginestra House, Inc., IL, 2352
Grand County Historical Association, CO,
1077
Grand Encampment Museum, Inc., WY, 9308
Grand Ledge Area Historical Society
Museum, MI, 4134
Grand Traverse Heritage Center, MI, 4250
Grand Traverse Lighthouse Foundation, MI,
4207
Grande Prairie Museum, AB, 9398
Granger Homestead Association, Inc., NY,
5852
Grant County Historical Society, IN, 2586
Grant County Historical Society, MN, 4315
Grant County Historical Society, SD, 7807
Grant County Historical Society, WI, 9166
Graue Mill and Museum, IL, 2283
Grayslake Municipal Historical Museum, IL,
2158
Graystone Society, Inc., PA, 7170
Great Harbor Martitine Museum, ME, 3475
Great Lakes Historical Society, The, OH,
6805
Great Lakes Lighthouse Museum, MI, 4179
Greater Southwest Historical Museum, OK,
6837
Greenbrier Historical Society, TN, 7898
Greene County Historical Society, IN, 2608
Greene County Historical Society, MO, 4942
Greene County Historical Society, NY, 5878
Greene County Historical Society, OH, 6823
Greene County Historical Society, VA, 8731
Greensboro Historical Museum, NC, 6304
Greenwood Museum, The, SC, 7685
Greyhound Bus Origin Museum, MN, 4349
Grissom Air Museum State Historic Site, IN,
2613
Grosse Ile and the Irish Memorial National
Historic Site, QC, 9936
Grosse Ile Historical Society, MI, 4144
Grosse Pointe Historical Society, MI, 4145
Grout Museum of History and Science, IA,
2860
Grundy County Museum, MO, 4949
Guardians of Slidell History, LA, 3386
Gulf Islands National Seashore, FL, 1440
Gunnison County Pioneer and Historical
Society, CO, 1075
Guy Park Manor, NY, 5797
H.B. Fuller Company Corporate Archives,
MN, 4457
Hagerman Roundhouse Museum, Inc., MD,
3662
Hagley Museum and Library, DE, 1315
Hallmark Visitors Center, The, MO, 4768
Hamilton County Historical Society,
Plainsman Museum, NE, 5080
Hampton Historical Society/Tuck Museum,
NH, 5330
Hancock Shaker Village, Inc., MA, 3953
Hanford Mills Museum, NY, 5896
Hanna-Basin Historical Society, WY, 9319
Hanover Tavern Foundation, VA, 8586

Hapeville Depot Museum, GA, 1699
Harbor Branch Oceanographic Institution,
Inc., FL, 1430
Hardin County Historical Museums, Inc., OH,
6693
Harley-Davidson Motor Company Archives,
WI, 9192
Harnett County Historical Society, NC, 6352
Harpers Ferry National Historical Park, WV,
9026
Harrison County Historical Museum, TX,
8181
Hart County Historical Society and Museum,
GA, 1700
Hartford Heritage Auto Museum, WI, 9139
Hartsville Museum, SC, 7688
Hartwick Pines State Park Logging Museum,
MI, 4143
Harwich Historical Society, MA, 3879
Hastings Historical Society, NY, 5929
Hastings Museum of Culture and Natural
History, NE, 5132
Hattiesburg Area Historical Society and
Museum, MS, 4554
Hayden Historical Museum Inc., IN, 2545
Hayward Area Historical Society, CA, 564
Heart's Content Cable Station Provincial
Historic Site, NF, 9630
Hearthstone Historic House Museum, WI,
9068
Heartland Museum of Military Vehicles, The,
NE, 5142
Henry B. Plant Museum, FL, 1556
Henry County Historical Society Museum, IN,
2603
Henry Ford Estate-Fair Lane, The, MI, 4101
Henry Ford Museum and Greenfield Village,
MI, 4102
Henry Sheldon Museum of Vermont History,
VT, 8404
Heritage Acres/Saanich Historical Artifacts
Society, BC, 9501
Heritage Farm and Village/Western
Development Museum, SK, 9974
Heritage Museum Association, Inc., FL, 1567
Heritage Museum of Montgomery County,
TX, 8058
Heritage Museum, MT, 5035
Heritage Museum, The, OR, 7025
Heritage Plantation of Sandwich, MA, 3983
Herman Miller, Inc. Corporate Archives and
Records Services, MI, 4260
Hermitage, The, NJ, 5511
Hermitage, The, TN, 7907
Hershey Community Archives, PA, 7261
Hershey Museum, PA, 7262
Hess Heritage Museum, ID, 1959
Hidalgo County Historical Museum, TX, 8088
High Plains Heritage Center Museum, SD,
7847
High Point Historical Society, Inc., NC, 6325
High Point Museum and Historical Park, NC,
6326
Highland Park Historical Society, IL, 2169
Highland Park Historical Society, NJ, 5507
Highspire Historical Society, PA, 7263
Hightstown-East Windsor Historical Society,
NJ, 5509
Hinckley Fire Museum, Inc., MN, 4351
Hirschell Carrousel Factory Museum, NY,
6041
Historic Allaire Village, NJ, 5437
Historic Charlton Park Village, Museum and
Recreation Area, MI, 4149
Historic Cotton Exchange Welcome Center
and Museum, GA, 1632
Historic Edenton State Historic Site, NC,
6277
Historic Fort Erie, ON, 9761
Historic Fort Snelling, MN, 4459
Historic Georgetown, CO, 1061
Historic Huntsville Depot, AL, 66
Historic Landmarks Foundation of Indiana,
IN, 2557
Historic Madison, Inc., IN, 2583
Historic New Orleans Collection, The, LA,
3350
Historic Pensacola Preservation Board, FL,
1511
Historic Richmond Foundation, VA, 8689
Historic Ship Nautilus and Submarine Force
Museum, CT, 1180
Historic Southern Indiana, IN, 2518

Historic Southwest Ohio, OH, 6614
Historic Springfield Foundation, Inc., MS,
4545
Historic Takoma, Inc., MD, 3730
Historic Whitaker Home-Museum/Centerville
Historical Society, UT, 8295
Historic Winslow House Association, MA,
3912
Historical County of Rockland County, The,
NY, 5990
Historical Electronics Museum, MD, 3679
Historical Museum at Fort Missoula, MT,
5042
Historical Museum at St. Gertrude's, The, ID,
1921
Historical Museum of Southern Florida, FL,
1486
Historical Museum of the D.R. Barker Library,
NY, 5911
Historical Projects of Houston County, Inc.,
TX, 8064
Historical Society of Berks County, PA, 7431
Historical Society of Carroll County, MD, 3739
Historical Society of Chatham Township, NJ,
5466
Historical Society of Cheshire County, NH,
5345
Historical Society of Delaware, DE, 1316
Historical Society of Douglas County, NE,
5188
Historical Society of Fort Washington, PA,
7218
Historical Society of Germantown, The, OH,
6672
Historical Society of Glastonbury, CT, 1174
Historical Society of Harford County, Inc.,
The, MD, 3594
Historical Society of Marshall County, IA,
2790
Historical Society of Martin County/ The Elliot
Museum, FL, 1544
Historical Society of New Mexico, NM, 5756
Historical Society of Newburgh Bay, NY, 6035
Historical Society of Porter County, IN, 2643
Historical Society of Pottawattamie County,
IA, 2702
Historical Society of Saginaw Co., Inc./Castle
Museum of Saginaw Co. History, MI, 4234
Historical Society of the Tonawandas, NY,
6162
Historical Society of the Town of Greenwich,
The, CT, 1149
Historical Society of Washington DC, DC,
1343
Historical Society of Western Pennsylvania,
PA, 7420
History and Heritage Committee/ American
Society of Civil Engineers, CA, 474
History Center, IA, 2684
History of Transportation/Western
Development Museum, SK, 9967
HMCS Haida Historic Naval Ship, ON, 9837
Holden Historical Society Museum, AB, 9401
Holland Historical Trust, MI, 4152
Holley-Williams House Museum and The
Salisbury Cannon Museum, CT, 1245
Homestead National Monument of America,
NE, 5085
Hopewell Furnace National Historic Site, PA,
7201
Hopewell Museum, KY, 3225
Hopkins Historical Society, MN, 4352
Hopkins Historical Society, MO, 4729
Hormel Foods Corporation, MN, 4272
Houghton County Historical Society, MI, 4167
Houston County Historical Commission, TX,
8065
Houston County Historical Society, MN, 4287
Houston County Visitors Center/Museum,
Inc., TX, 8066
Howard County Historical Society, IA, 2705
Howard County Historical Society, IN, 2576
Howard County Historical Society, MD, 3638
Howard County Historical Society, NE, 5206
Howard Steamboat Museum/Clark County
Historical Society, Inc., IN, 2574
Howard W. Cannon Aviation Museum/Office
and Collections Clark County Museum, NV,
5244
Hubbard Museum of the American West, The,
NM, 5753
Huddleston Farmhouse Inn Museum, IN,
2495

Hudson Bay and District Cultural
Society/Hudson Bay Museum, SK, 9959
Hugh Moore Historical Park and Museums,
Inc./National Canal Museum, PA, 7194
Huguenot Heritage, NY, 6011
Hunterdon Historical Museum, NJ, 5471
Hutchinson County Museum, TX, 8040
Hydroplane and Raceboat Museum, WA,
8925
ical Society, AL, 45
Idaho State Historical Museum, ID, 1911
Illinois and Michigan Canal National Heritage
Corridor Commission, IL, 2218
Illinois Association of Museums, IL, 2394
Illinois Railway Museum Inc., IL, 2430
Illinois State Historical Society, IL, 2397
Illinois State Military Museum, IL, 2398
Imperial Calcasieu Museum, Inc., LA, 3313
Independence Seaport Museum, PA, 7385
Indiana Historical Society, IN, 2560
Indiana State Archives, IN, 2562
Intel Museum, CA, 870
International Congress of Distinguished
Awards, PA, 7386
Iosco County Historical Society Museum, MI,
4120
Iowa Aviation Museum, IA, 2751
Iowa Railroad Historical Society, IA, 2672
Iron County Historical and Museum Society,
MI, 4082
Iron Man Museum, The, CA, 912
Iron Mission State Park and Museum & Miles
Goodyear Cabin, UT, 8293
Iron Mountain/Iron Mine, MI, 4157
Iron Range Research Center, MN, 4293
Isanti County Historical Society, MN, 4288
Island County Historical Society & Museum,
WA, 8827
Island Institute, ME, 3499
Island Pond Historical Society, VT, 8396
Issaquah Historical Museum, WA, 8863
Itasca County Historical Society, MN, 4344
J and R Vintage Auto Museum and
Bookstore, NM, 5750
J.E. Reeves Victorian Home and Carriage
House Museum, OH, 6652
Jackson County Historical Society, AR, 396
Jackson County Historical Society, IA, 2786
Jackson County Historical Society, IL, 2267
Jackson County Historical Society, KS, 2956
Jackson County Historical Society, MN, 4357
Jackson County Historical Society, WV, 9048
Jacksonport State Park, AR, 397
Jacksonville Maritime Museum, FL, 1447
James E. Conner Museum, Texas A&M
University, TX, 8159
James J. Hill House, MN, 4462
James J. Hill Reference Library, Manuscripts
Division, MN, 4463
Jamesville Community Museum, NY, 5956
Japanese American National Museum, CA,
618
Jarrell Plantation State Historic Site, GA,
1710
Jefferson Barracks Historic Site, MO, 4914
Jefferson County Chapter, Ohio Genealogical
Society, OH, 6787
Jefferson County Historical Society, Museum,
& Research Library, WA, 8906
Jefferson County Historical Society, NY, 6181
Jefferson Landing State Historic Site, MO,
4753
Jefferson National Expansion Memorial, MO,
4915
Jersey City Museum, NJ, 5519
Jewish Historical Society of Metrowest, NJ,
5675
John Rivers Communications Museum, SC,
7630
John Wornall House Museum, MO, 4773
Johnson County Museum, KS, 3046
Johnston County Heritage Center, NC, 6435
Johnstown Area Heritage Association, PA,
7274
Jonesborough-Washington County History
Museum, TN, 7916
Joplin Historical and Mineral Museum, Inc.,
MO, 4762
Joseph Frant Museum, ON, 9699
Julia A. Purnell Museum, MD, 3721
Julian Historical Society, CA, 578
Julian Pioneer Museum, CA, 579
Junior Museum, The, NY, 6164

U.S. LEGAL HISTORY

VICTORIANA

WOMEN'S STUDIES

Alphabetical Index

Drake Well Museum, PA, 7467
Drayton Hall, National Trust for Historic Preservation, SC, 7627
Drayton Valley District Historical Society, AB, 9377
Dresden Historical Society, ME, 3428
Drew County Historical Museum, AR, 392
Driftwood Family Resort Museum and Golf (Norske Course), The, MN, 4432
Drummond Historical Society, WI, 9110
Drummond House, OK, 6898
Drumright Historical Society, OK, 6874
Drumthwacket, NJ, 5607
Dryden Township Historical Society, NY, 5887
Duarte Historical Society and Friends of the Library, Inc., CA, 520
Dublin Historical Preservation Association, CA, 521
Dublin Historical Society, NH, 5307
Dubois County Historical Society, Inc., IN, 2572
Dubois County Museum, Inc., IN, 2573
Dubuque County Historical Society/Mississippi River Museum, IA, 2727
Dubuque County-Key City Genealogical Society, IA, 2728
Duck Lake Regional Interpretive Centre, SK, 9953
Dudley Foundation, Inc., The, CT, 1183
Dugger Coal Museum, IN, 2511
Duke Homestead State Historic Site and Tobacco Museum, NC, 6270
Duke University Rare Book, Manuscript and Special Collections Library, NC, 6271
Duluth Heritage Preservation Commission, MN, 4305
Duluth Preservation Alliance, MN, 4306
Dummerston Historical Society, VT, 8418
Duncan Cottage Museum, AK, 179
Duncan Cultural Center, KY, 3144
Dundalk-Patapsco Neck Historical Society, MD, 3631
Dundee Township Historical Society, IL, 2453
Dunsmuir House and Gardens Historic Estate, CA, 672
DuPage County Genealogical Society, IL, 2220
DuPage County Historical Museum, IL, 2459
DuPont Historic Museum, WA, 8832
Durango and Silverton Narrow Gauge Railroad and Museum, CO, 1037
Durham Historical Association, NH, 5308
Durham Western Heritage Museum, NE, 5184
DuSable Museum of African American History, IL, 2049
Dutch Parsonage, NJ, 5637
Dutchess County Historical Society, NY, 6080
Duval Tool Museum, MD, 3736
Duvall Historical Society, WA, 8833
Duxbury Rural and Historical Society, MA, 3846
Dvoracek Memorial Library, NE, 5220
Dwight D. Eisenhower Library & Museum, The, KS, 2874
Dwight House, Historic Deerfield, MA, 3831
Dyckman Farm House Museum, The, NY, 6000
Dyer Dowell Victorian House, IA, 2804
Dyer Historical Society, Inc., IN, 2513
Dyer Memorial Library, MA, 3744
Dyersville Area Historical Society, IA, 2730
Dysart Historical Society, IA, 2731

E

E Clampus Vitus, CA, 758
E. St. Julien Cox House, MN, 4475
E. Stanley Wright Museum Foundation, Inc., NH, 5434
E.P. "Tom" Sawyer State Park, KY, 3194
Eagle Bend Historical Society/Museum, MN, 4312
Eagle County Historical Society, Inc., CO, 1040
Eagle Historical Society and Museums, AK, 155
Eagle River Historical Society, WI, 9113
Ear Falls and District Museum, ON, 9709
Earl Gregg Swem Library, College of William and Mary, VA, 8774

Earle-Harrison House, The, TX, 8266
Earle-Napier-Kinnard House Museum, Historic Waco Foundation, TX, 8267
Early American Museum, IL, 2228
Early Settlers Association of the Western Reserve, The, OH, 6626
Early Works, AL, 65
Earnest and Dorthy Barrow Museum, The, TX, 8093
East Benton County Historical Society & Museum, WA, 8865
East Berlin Historical Preservation Society, PA, 7192
East Carolina Village of Yesteryear, NC, 6307
East Chicago Room of The East Chicago Public Library, The, IN, 2514
East Ely Railroad Depot Museum, NV, 5233
East Haddam Historical Society and Museum, CT, 1158
East Haven Historical Society, CT, 1162
East Hillsborough Historical Society, FL, 1515
East Jersey Olde Towne Village, NJ, 5568
East Palestine Area Historical Society, OH, 6654
East Providence Historical Society, RI, 7541
East River Genealogical Forum, SD, 7860
East Rochester Local History, NY, 5897
East Tennessee Development District (ETDD), TN, 7924
East Tennessee Discovery Center, TN, 7925
East Tennessee Historical Society, TN, 7926
East Terrace House Museum, Historic Waco Foundation, TX, 8268
East Texas Oil Museum at Kilgore College, TX, 8158
Eastchester Historical Society, The, NY, 5898
Eastern California Museum, CA, 570
Eastern Colorado Historical Society, CO, 1000
Eastern Kentucky Genealogical Society, Inc., KY, 3089
Eastern Oregon Museum, OR, 7021
Eastern Regional Coal Archives, WV, 9008
Eastern Trails Museum, OK, 6980
Eastern Washington State Historical Society, WA, 8951
Eastham Historical Society, MA, 3852
Eaton Florida History Room, Manatee County Central Library, FL, 1385
Eatonton-Putnam County Historical Society, Inc.orporation, GA, 1683
Ebenezer Maxwell Mansion, Inc., PA, 7367
Ebey's Landing National Historical Reserve, WA, 8826
Echo Historical Museum, OR, 7011
Ecomusee du fier Monde, QC, 9906
Eden History Association, VT, 8382
Edgar Allan Poe Cottage, NY, 5828
Edgar Allan Poe House and Museum, MD, 3573
Edgar Allan Poe National Historic Site, PA, 7368
Edgar County Historical Society, IL, 2305
Edgar Lee Masters Memorial Museum, IL, 2317
Edge of the Cedars State Park Museum, UT, 8288
Edgecombe County Cultural Arts Council, Inc., NC, 6449
Edgecombe County Historical Society, NC, 6450
Edgefield County Historical Society, SC, 7669
Edina Historical Society and Museum, MN, 4314
Edinboro Area Historical Society, PA, 7197
Edison Birthplace Association, Inc., OH, 6726
Edison National Historic Site, NJ, 5671
Edison-Ford Winter Estates, FL, 1428
Edith Newman Culver Memorial Museum, AL, 130
Edith Wharton Restoration at the Mount, MA, 3892
Edmond Historical Society, OK, 6878
Edmonds Historical Society, WA, 8837
Edmondston-Alston House, SC, 7628
Edmonston House, The, NY, 6168
Edmonton Public Schools Archives and Museum, AB, 9381
Edmonton Telephone Historical Information Centre Foundation, AB, 9382
Edmund D. Edelman Hollywood Bowl Museum, CA, 615
Edmund S. Muskie Archives and Special

Collections Library, ME, 3456
Edna Cuddy Memorial House and Gardens, MO, 4642
Edsel and Eleanor Ford House, MI, 4146
Edward Bellamy Memorial Association, MA, 3810
Edward H. Nabb Research Center for Delmarva History and Culture at Salisbury State University, MD, 3706
Edwards County Historical Society, IL, 1974
Edwards County Historical Society, KS, 2968
Edwards House, NJ, 5440
Edwards Place Historic Home, IL, 2393
Edwards-Franklin House, NC, 6369
Effigy Mounds National Monument, IA, 2757
Effingham County Genealogical and Historical Society, IL, 2116
Effingham Historic District Commission, NH, 5420
Egan Institute of Maritime Studies, MA, 3920
Egg Harbor City Historical Society, NJ, 5480
Egmont Key Alliance, FL, 1562
Ehrman Mansion, CA, 919
Eisenhower Birthplace State Historical Park, TX, 8083
Eisenhower Center for American Studies, The, LA, 3344
Eisenhower National Historic Site, PA, 7227
Eiteljorg Museum of American Indians and Western Art, IN, 2555
Eklutna Historical Park, Inc., AK, 156
El Cajon Historical Society, CA, 525
El Centro de la Raza, WA, 8923
El Dorado County Historical Museum, CA, 712
El Morro Fortress, PR, 7522
El Morro National Monument, NM, 5748
El Paso Museum of History, TX, 8089
El Paso Public Library/Border Heritage Center, TX, 8090
El Pueblo de Los Angeles Historical Monument, CA, 616
El Pueblo Museum, CO, 1110
El Rancho de las Golondrinas, NM, 5755
Elbert County Historical Society and Museum, CO, 1082
Elbert County Historical Society, GA, 1684
Elbert Hubbard Roycroft Museum, NY, 5889
Elbow Museum and Historical Society, SK, 9954
Elburn and Countryside Historical Society, IL, 2117
Eldorado Museum, IL, 2118
Eleanor Roosevelt National Historic Site, NY, 5948
Elegba Folklore Society, Inc., VA, 8686
Eleutherian Mills Residence, DE, 1314
Eleutheros Cooke House and Garden, OH, 6771
Eleventh Circuit Historical Society, The, GA, 1602
Elfreth's Alley Association, PA, 7369
Elgin County Pioneer Museum, ON, 9808
Elgin Genealogical Society, IL, 2119
Elgin Historical Society, NE, 5109
Elgin Military Museum, The, ON, 9809
Elgin Public Museum, IL, 2120
Elihu Benjamin Washburne House State Historic Site, The, IL, 2139
Elijah Lovejoy Memorial, IL, 1978
Elijah P. Curtis Home and Museum, IL, 2241
Eliot Historical Society, ME, 3432
Elisabet Ney Museum, TX, 8014
Elisharp Museum, MI, 4160
Elizabeth Township Historical Society, PA, 7139
Elizabethtown Historical Society, PA, 7199
Elk County Historical Society, PA, 7434
Elk-Blue Creek Historical Society, WV, 9046
Elkhart County Historical Society, Inc. and Museum, IN, 2494
Elkhorn Valley Museum and Research Center, NE, 5175
Elkton Community Museum, SD, 7776
Ella Sharp Museum, MI, 4161
Ellen Payne Odom Genealogical Library, GA, 1747
Ellicott City B&O Railroad Station Museum, The, MD, 3637
Ellinwood Community Historical Society, KS, 2921
Elliot Lake Nuclear and Mining Museum, ON, 9710

Ellis County Historical Society, KS, 2949
Ellis County Historical Society, OK, 6838
Ellison House, NY, 6169
Ellsinore Pioneer Museum, MO, 4698
Ellwood House Museum, IL, 2102
Elman W. Campbell Museum, ON, 9760
Elmhurst Historical Museum, IL, 2124
Elmira Railway Museum, PE, 9864
Elna M. Smith Foundation, AR, 320
Elphinstone Pioneer Museum, BC, 9452
Elroy Area Historical Society, Inc., WI, 9120
Elverhoj Museum of History and Art, CA, 898
Elvis Presley Birthplace, MS, 4606
Elwood Haynes Museum, IN, 2575
Elwyn B Robinson Department of Special Collections, University of North Dakota, ND, 6522
Ely Field Office, Bureau of Land Management, NV, 5237
Ely-Winton Historical Society, MN, 4319
Emanuel County Historic Preservation Society, GA, 1814
Embden Historical Society, ME, 3473
Emily Carr House, BC, 9523
Emlen Physick Estate, NJ, 5458
Emmet County Historical Society, IA, 2739
Emmett Kelly Historical Museum, KS, 3043
EMOBA, The Museum of Black Arkansans and Performing Arts, AR, 375
Emory and Henry College, VA, 8542
Empire Mine State Historic Park, CA, 562
Empire State Aerosciences Museum, NY, 5920
Enchanted World Doll Museum, SD, 7810
End of the Oregon Trail Interpretive Center, OR, 7055
End-O-Line Railroad Park and Museum, MN, 4302
Ende-Gaillard House, TX, 8135
Enderby and District Museum Society, BC, 9446
Endview Plantation, VA, 8642
Enfield Historical Society, NH, 5311
Enfield Shaker Museum, NH, 5312
Englehart and Area Historical Museum, ON, 9711
Englewood Historical Society, NJ, 5484
Englewood Textile Museum, TN, 7888
Enon Community Historical Society, OH, 6658
Enos Mills Cabin, CO, 1042
Ensor Farmsite & Museum, KS, 3018
Enumclaw Plateau Historical Society, WA, 8840
Ephraim Foundation, Inc., The, WI, 9121
Ephrata Cloister, PA, 7204
Epiphany Chapel and Church House, MD, 3685
Eptek National Exhibition Centre, PE, 9865
Equitable Life Assurance Society Archives, NY, 6001
Erie Canal Museum, NY, 6154
Erie County Historical Society, OH, 6772
Erie County Historical Society, PA, 7206
Erie Historical Museum and Planetarium, PA, 7207
Erie Maritime Museum, Homeport US Brig Niagara, PA, 7208
Erie Society for Genealogical Research, PA, 7209
Eriksdale Museum Inc., MB, 9538
Erland Lee (Museum) Home, ON, 9812
Ermatinger/Clergue Heritage Site, ON, 9802
Ernest Hemingway Foundation of Oak Park, The, IL, 2288
Ernest Hemingway Home and Museum, FL, 1458
Ernest L. Blumenschein Home, NM, 5767
Ernie Pyle Branch Library, NM, 5692
Ernie Pyle State Historic Site, IN, 2505
Erskine Caldwell Birthplace and Museum, The, GA, 1746
Escondido Historical Society and Heritage Walk Museum, CA, 529
Esquimalt Municipal Archives, BC, 9524
Essex County Historical Society, VA, 8750
Essex County Museum, Inc., VA, 8751
Essex Historical Society and Shipbuilding Museum, MA, 3858
Essex Historical Society, CT, 1166
Estes Park Area Historical Museum, CO, 1043
Ethan Allen Homestead Trust, VT, 8370

I

THE WORLD IS LISTENING